best wi~

~~~~

13th . ~~ 1990

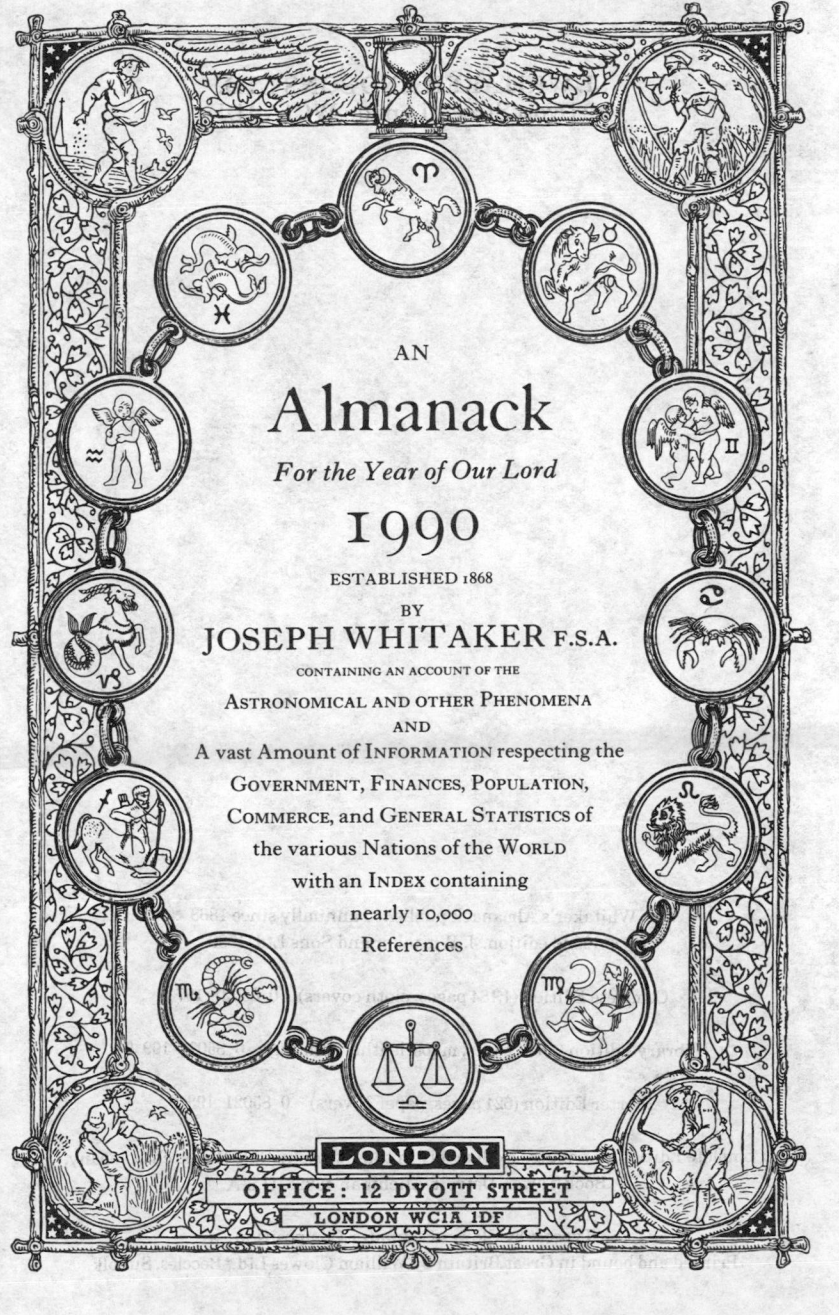

AN

Almanack

For the Year of Our Lord

1990

ESTABLISHED 1868

BY

JOSEPH WHITAKER F.S.A.

CONTAINING AN ACCOUNT OF THE

ASTRONOMICAL AND OTHER PHENOMENA

AND

A vast Amount of INFORMATION respecting the
GOVERNMENT, FINANCES, POPULATION,
COMMERCE, and GENERAL STATISTICS of
the various Nations of the WORLD
with an INDEX containing
nearly 10,000
References

LONDON

OFFICE: 12 DYOTT STREET
LONDON WC1A 1DF

J. WHITAKER AND SONS LTD.
12 Dyott Street, London WC1A 1DF

Whitaker's Almanack published annually since 1868
©122nd edition. J. Whitaker and Sons Ltd. 1989

Complete Edition (1,184 pages, cloth covers)   0 85021 197 2

Library Edition (1,184 pages, maps, leather binding)   0 85021 199 9

Shorter Edition (624 pages, paper covers)   0 85021 198 0

Complete Edition distributed exclusively in the U.S.A. by Gale Research Company,
Book Tower, Detroit, Michigan 48226, U.S.A.

Typeset by Clowes Computer Composition
Printed and bound in Great Britain by William Clowes Ltd., Beccles, Suffolk

CONTENTS

CONTENTS
(of the Complete Edition and Library Edition)
continued

PREFACE
to the 122nd Annual Volume (1990)

This 122nd edition of Whitaker's Almanack continues to provide the information which has been the staple of the Almanack since the first edition. The Almanack has expanded considerably since 1869 – this edition has three times the number of pages of the first edition – and the information is more detailed and more varied.

We seek constantly to improve and expand the information provided. In this edition the Weights and Measures section has been expanded to include SI units, and a description of the various types of nature reserves in this country has been added to the information on conservation. In addition, the information about postal and telecommunications services has been revised and a table added showing airmail zones and international dialling codes.

Other changes in this edition are a response to recent events. The full results are given of the U.K. elections to the European Parliament in June 1989. The article describing the education system in the U.K. has been rewritten to include changes introduced as a result of recent legislation, and the directory of educational bodies has been revised. A new article describes the structure of the water industry after privatization. The Government's proposals for change in the broadcasting industry, the health service and the legal profession are included in the section summarizing White Papers.

For the fifth year a quiz is included with the Almanack, a feature which has kept thousands of readers busy in recent years. This year a questionnaire is attached to the quiz form as we are interested in knowing more about readers' views of the Almanack. We hope readers will return the questionnaire even if they do not wish to enter the quiz.

As ever, thanks are due to thousands of individuals and organizations worldwide who have provided information, comments, criticism and suggestions. We are most grateful for their assistance in preparing this edition of Whitaker's Almanack.

12 Dyott Street, London WC1A 1DF
Telephone 01-836 8911
October, 1989

HILARY MARSDEN
Editor

ABBREVIATIONS

Ψ = Seaport.

A

A.—Associate of.

A.A.—Alcoholics Anonymous; Anti-Aircraft; Automobile Association.

A.A.A.—Amateur Athletic Association.

A.B.—Able-bodied seaman.

A.B.A.—Amateur Boxing Association.

abbr(ev).—abbreviation.

A.B.M.—Anti-ballistic missile defence system.

abr.—abridged.

a.c.—alternating current.

a/c.—account.

A.C.—Aircraftman; (*Ante Christum*) Before Christ; Companion, Order of Australia.

A.C.A.S.—Advisory, Conciliation and Arbitration Service.

A.C.T.—Australian Capital Territory.

A.C.T.T.—Association of Cinematograph, Television and Allied Technicians.

ad(vert)—advertisement.

A.D.—(*Anno Domini*) In the year of our Lord.

A.D.C.—Aide-de-Camp.

A.D.C. (P).—Personal A.D.C. to The Queen.

adj.—adjective.

Adjt.—Adjutant.

ad lib.—(*ad libitum*) at pleasure.

Adm.—Admiral; Admission.

adv.—adverb; advocate.

A.E.—Air Efficiency Award.

A.E.A.—Atomic Energy Authority.

A.E.M.—Air Efficiency Medal.

A.E.R.E.—Atomic Energy Research Establishment.

A.E.U.—Amalgamated Engineering Union.

A.F.C.—Air Force Cross; Association Football Club.

A.F.M.—Air Force Medal.

A.F.R.C.—Agricultural and Food Research Council.

A.F.V.—Armoured fighting vehicle.

A.G.—Adjutant-General; Attorney-General.

A.G.M.—annual general meeting; air-to-ground missile.

A.H.—(*Anno Hegirae*) In the year of the Hegira.

A.I.D.S.—Acquired Immune Deficiency Syndrome.

alt.—altitude.

a.m.—(*ante meridiem*) before noon.

A.M.—(*Anno mundi*) In the year of the world.

A.M.D.G.—(*Ad majorem Dei gloriam*) To the greater glory of God.

amp.—ampere; amplifier.

A.N.C.—African National Congress.

anon.—anonymous(ly).

A.N.Z.A.C.—Australian and New Zealand Army Corps.

A.O.—Air Officer; Officer, Order of Australia.

A.O.C.—Air Officer Commanding.

APEX—Association of Professional, Executive, Clerical and Computer Staff.

A.R.C.—Agricultural Research Council.

A.S.—Anglo-Saxon.

A.S.A.—Advertising Standards Authority; Amateur Swimming Association.

A.S.B.—*Alternative Service Book.*

A.S.E.A.N.—Association of South East Asian Nations.

A.S.H.—Action on Smoking and Health.

A.S.L.E.F.—Associated Society of Locomotive Engineers and Firemen.

A.S.L.I.B.—Association for Information Management.

A.S.T.M.S.—Association of Scientific, Technical and Managerial Staffs.

A.T.C.—Air Training Corps.

A.U.C.—(*ab urbe condita*) In the year from the foundation of Rome; (*anno urbis conditae*) In the year of the founding of the city.

A.U.T.—Association of University Teachers.

A.V.—Audio-visual; Authorized Version.

A.V.R.—Army Volunteer Reserve.

A.W.O.L.—Absent without leave.

B

b.—born; bowled.

B.A.—Bachelor of Arts.

B.A.A.—British Airports Authority; British Astronomical Association.

B.A.F.T.A.—British Academy of Film and Television Arts.

B.A.O.R.—British Army of the Rhine.

B.A.S.—Bachelor in Agricultural Science; British Antarctic Survey.

B.B.—Boys' Brigade.

B.B.C.—British Broadcasting Corporation.

B.C.—Before Christ; British Columbia.

B. Ch. (*or* Ch.B.)—Bachelor of Surgery.

B.C.L.—*do*, of Civil Law.

B. Com.—*do*, of Commerce.

B.D.—*do*, of Divinity.

B.D.A.—British Dental Association.

B.D.S. (*or* B.Ch.D.)—Bachelor of Dental Surgery.

B. Ed.—*do*, of Education.

B.E.M.—British Empire Medal.

B. Eng.—Bachelor of Engineering.

B.F.I.—British Film Institute.

B.F.P.O.—British Forces Post Office.

B.I.M.—British Institute of Management.

B.L.A.I.S.E.—British Library Automated Information Service.

B. Litt.—Bachelor of Literature *or* of Letters.

B.M.—*do*, of Medicine; British Museum.

B.M.A.—British Medical Association.

B. Mus.—Bachelor of Music.

B.O.T.B.—British Overseas Trade Board.

Bp.—Bishop.

B. Pharm.—Bachelor of Pharmacy.

B. Phil.—*do*, of Philosophy.

Br. (*or* Brit.)—Britain; British.

B.R.—British Rail.

B.R.C.S.—British Red Cross Society.

Brig.—Brigadier.

B.Sc.—Bachelor of Science.

B.S.C.—British Steel Corporation.

B.S.I.—British Standards Institution.

B.S.T.—British Summer Time.

Bt. (*or* Bart.)—Baronet.

B.T.E.C.—Business and Technician Education Council.

B.T.G.—British Technology Group.

B. Th.—Bachelor of Theology.

B.t.u.—British thermal unit.

B.V.M.—(*Beata Virgo Maria*) Blessed Virgin Mary.

B.V.M.S.—Bachelor of Veterinary Medicine and Surgery.

B.W.B.—British Waterways Board.

C

c.—(*circa*) about.

C.—Celsius; Centigrade.

C. (*or* Con.)—Conservative.

C.A.—Chartered Accountant (*Scotland*).

C.A.A.—Civil Aviation Authority.

C.A.B.—Citizens' Advice Bureau.

Cantab.—(of) Cambridge.

Cantuar.—of Canterbury (*Archbishop*).

C.A.P.—Common Agricultural Policy.

Capt.—Captain.

Caricom—Caribbean Community and Common Market.

Carliol.—of Carlisle (*Bishop*).

C.A.S.—Chief of Air Staff.

C.B.—Companion, Order of the Bath.
C.B.E.—Commander, Order of the British Empire.
C.B.I.—Confederation of British Industry.
C.C.—Chamber of Commerce; Companion, Order of Canada; City Council; County Council; County Court.
C.C.C.—County Cricket Club.
C. Chem.—Chartered Chemist.
C.D.—Civil Defence; Compact Disc; Corps Diplomatique.
Cdr.—Commander.
Cdre.—Commodore.
C.D.S.—Chief of the Defence Staff.
C.E.—Civil Engineer.
C.E.G.B.—Central Electricity Generating Board.
C. Eng.—Chartered Engineer.
Cento—Central Treaty Organization.
Cestr.—of Chester (*Bishop*).
C.E.T.—Common External Tariff; Central European Time.
cf.—(*confer*) compare.
C.F.—Chaplain to the Forces.
C.F.C.—Chlorofluorocarbon.
C.G.M.—Conspicuous Gallantry Medal.
C.G.S.—Chief of General Staff; Centimetre-gramme-second (*system*).
C.H.—Companion of Honour.
Ch.B./M.—Bachelor/Master of Surgery.
C.I.—The Imperial Order of the Crown of India; Channel Islands.
C.I.A.—Central Intelligence Agency.
Cicestr.—of Chichester (*Bishop*).
C.I.D.—Criminal Investigation Department.
C.I.E.—Companion, Order of the Indian Empire.
c.i.f.—cost, insurance and freight.
C.-in-C.—Commander-in-Chief.
C.I.P.F.A.—Chartered Institute of Public Finance and Accountancy.
C. Lit.—Companion of Literature.
C.L.J.—Commander, Order of St. Lazarus of Jerusalem.
C.M.—(*Chirurgiae Magister*) Master of Surgery.
C.M.G.—Companion, Order of St. Michael and St. George.
C.M.S.—Church Missionary Society.
C.N.A.A.—Council for National Academic Awards.
C.N.D.—Campaign for Nuclear Disarmament.
c/o—care of.
C.O.—Commanding Officer; conscientious objector.
C.O.D.—Cash on delivery.
C. of E.—Church of England.
C.O.H.S.E.—Confederation of Health Service Employees.
C.O.I.—Central Office of Information.
Col.—Colonel.
Comecon (*or* C.M.E.A.)—Council for Mutual Economic Assistance.
Cpl.—Corporal.
C.P.M.—Colonial Police Medal.
C.P.R.E.—Council for the Protection of Rural England.
C.P.V.E.—Certificate of Pre-Vocational Education.
C.R.E.—Council for Racial Equality.
C.S.E.—Certificate of Secondary Education.
C.S.I.—Companion, Order of the Star of India.
C.T.C.—Cyclists' Touring Club.
C.V.O.—Commander, Royal Victorian Order.

D

d.—(*denarius*) penny.
D.B.E.—Dame Commander, Order of the British Empire.
d.c.—direct current.
D.C.—District Council; District of Columbia.
D.C.B.—Dame Commander, Order of the Bath.
D. Ch.—(*Doctor Chirurgiae*) Doctor of Surgery.

D.C.L.—Doctor of Civil Law.
D.C.M.—Distinguished Conduct Medal.
D.C.M.G.—Dame Commander, Order of St. Michael and St. George.
D.C.V.O.—Dame Commander, Royal Victorian Order.
D.D.—Doctor of Divinity.
D.D.S.—*do*, of Dental Surgery.
D.D.T.—dichlorodiphenyl-trichloroethane (*insecticide*).
del.—(*delineavit*) he/she drew it.
D.E.S.—Department of Education and Science.
D.F.C.—Distinguished Flying Cross.
D.F.M.—Distinguished Flying Medal.
D.G.—(*Dei gratia*) By the grace of God; Director-General.
D.H.—Department of Health.
D.H.A.—District Health Authority.
D.H.S.S.—Department of Health and Social Security.
Dip. Ed.—Diploma in Education.
Dip. H. E.—Diploma in Higher Education.
Dip. Tech.—Diploma in Technology.
D.J.—Disc jockey.
D.L.—Deputy-Lieutenant.
D. Litt.—Doctor of Letters *or* of Literature.
D. Mus.—*do*, of Music.
D.N.A.—deoxyribonucleic acid.
D.N.B.—*Dictionary of National Biography*.
do.—(*ditto*) the same.
D.o.E.—Department of the Environment.
D.O.M.—(*Dominus Omnium Magister*) God the Master of All.
D.P.—Data processing.
D. Ph. (*or* D. Phil.)—Doctor of Philosophy.
D.P.P.—Director of Public Prosecutions.
Dr.—Doctor.
D.Sc.—Doctor of Science.
D.S.C.—Distinguished Service Cross.
D.S.M.—Distinguished Service Medal.
D.S.O.—Companion, Distinguished Service Order.
D.S.S.—Department of Social Security.
D.Th.(*or* D. Theol.)—Doctor of Theology.
D.T.I.—Department of Trade and Industry.
Dunelm.—of Durham (*Bishop*).
D.V.—(*Deo volente*) God willing.

E

E.—East.
Ebor.—of York (*Archbishop*).
E.C.—European Community.
E.C.G.—Electrocardiogram.
E.C.S.C.—European Coal and Steel Community.
E.C.U.—European Currency Unit.
E.D.—Efficiency Decoration.
E.E.C.—European Economic Community.
E.E.G.—Electroencephalogram.
E.E.T.P.U.—Electrical, Electronic, Telecommunication and Plumbing Union.
E.F.T.A.—European Free Trade Association.
e.g.—(*exempli gratia*) for the sake of example.
Elien.—of Ely (*Bishop*).
E.M.S.—European Monetary System.
E.N.E.A.—European Nuclear Energy Agency.
E.R.—Elizabetha Regina.
E.R.D.—Emergency Reserve Decoration.
E.R.N.I.E.—Electronic random number indicator ● equipment.
E.S.A.—European Space Agency.
E.S.P.—Extra-sensory perception.
E.S.R.C.—Economic and Social Research Council.
E.T.A.—Euzkadi ta Askatasuna (*Basque separatist organization*).
et al.—(*et alibi*) and elsewhere; (*et alii*) and others.
etc.—(*et cetera*) and the other things/and so forth.
et seq.—(*et sequentia*) and the following.
Euratom—European Atomic Energy Commission.

ex lib.—(*ex libris*) from the books of.

Exon.—of Exeter (*Bishop*).

F

f—(*forte*) loud.

F.—Fahrenheit; Fellow of.

F.A.—Football Association.

F.A.N.Y.—First Aid Nursing Yeomanry.

F.A.O.—Food and Agriculture Organization.

F.B.A.—Fellow, British Academy.

F.B.A.A.—*do*, British Association of Accountants and Auditors.

F.B.I.—Federal Bureau of Investigation.

F.B.I.M.—Fellow, British Institute of Management.

F.B.S.—*do*, Botanical Society.

F.C.A.—*do*, Institute of Chartered Accountants (*of England and Wales*).

F.C.C.A.—*do*,Chartered Association of Certified Accountants.

F.C.G.I.—*do*, City and Guilds of London Institute.

F.C.I.A.—*do*, Corporation of Insurance Agents.

F.C.I.Arb.—*do*, Chartered Institute of Arbitrators.

F.C.I.B.—*do*, Chartered Institute of Bankers; Corporation of Insurance Brokers.

F.C.I.B.S.E.—*do*, Chartered Institution of Building-Services Engineers.

F.C.I.I.—*do*, Chartered Insurance Institute.

F.C.I.S.—*do*, Institute of Chartered Secretaries and Administrators.

F.C.I.T.—*do*, Chartered Institute of Transport.

F.C.M.A.—*do*, Chartered Institute of Management Accountants.

F.C.O.—Foreign and Commonwealth Office.

fcp.—foolscap.

F.C.P.—Fellow, College of Preceptors.

F.D.—(*Fidei Defensor*) Defender of the Faith.

fec.—(*fecit*) made this.

F.Eng.—Fellow, Fellowship of Engineering.

ff—(*fecerunt*) made this (*pl.*); (*fortissimo*) very loud.

F.F.A.—*do*, Faculty of Actuaries (*in Scotland*); *do*. Institute of Financial Accountants.

F.F.A.S.—*do*, Faculty of Architects and Surveyors.

F.G.S.—*do*, Geological Society.

F.H.—Fire hydrant.

F.H.S.—Fellow, Heraldry Society.

F.H.S.M.—*do*, Institute of Health Service Management.

F.I.A.—*do*, Institute of Actuaries.

F.I.Biol.—*do*, Institute of Biology.

F.I.C.E.—*do*, Institution of Civil Engineers.

F.I.C.S.—*do*, Institution of Chartered Shipbrokers.

F.I.E.E.—*do*, Institution of Electrical Engineers.

F.I.E.R.E.—*do*, Institution of Electronic and Radio Engineers.

F.I.F.A.—International Association Football Federation.

F.I.M.—Fellow, Institute of Metals.

F.I.M.M.—*do*, Institution of Mining and Metallurgy.

F.Inst.F.—*do*, Institute of Fuel.

F.Inst.P.—*do*, Institute of Physics.

F.I.Q.S.—*do*, Institute of Quantity Surveyors.

F.I.S.—*do*, Institute of Statisticians.

F.J.I.—*do*, Institute of Journalists.

fl.—(*floruit*) flourished.

F.L.A.—Fellow, Library Association.

F.L.S.—*do*, Linnean Society.

F.M.—Field Marshal; frequency modulation.

fo.—folio.

F.O.—Flying Officer.

f.o.b.—free on board.

F.P.A.—Family Planning Association.

F.Ph.S.—Fellow, Philosophical Society.

F.R.A.D.—*do*, Royal Academy of Dancing.

F.R.Ae.S.—*do*, Royal Aeronautical Society.

F.R.A.I.—*do*, Royal Anthropological Institute.

F.R.A.M.—*do*, Royal Academy of Music.

F.R.A.S.—*do*, Royal Astronomical Society.

F.R.B.S.—*do*, Royal Botanical Society; *do*, Royal Society of British Sculptors.

F.R.C.G.P.—*do*, Royal College of General Practitioners.

F.R.C.M.—*do*, Royal College of Music.

F.R.C.O.—*do*, Royal College of Organists.

F.R.C.O.G.—*do*, Royal College of Obstetricians and Gynaecologists.

F.R.C.P., (Ed.), (I.)—*do*, Royal College of Physicians, of London, (of Edinburgh), (in Ireland).

F.R.C.Path.—*do*, Royal College of Pathologists.

F.R.C.Psych.—*do*, Royal College of Psychiatrists.

F.R.C.R.—*do*, Royal College of Radiologists.

F.R.C.S., (E(d).), (I.)—*do*, Royal College of Surgeons (of Edinburgh), (in Ireland).

F.R.C.S.Glas.—*do*, Royal College of Physicians and Surgeons of Glasgow.

F.R.C.V.S.—*do*, Royal College of Veterinary Surgeons.

F.R.Econ.S.—*do*, Royal Economic Society.

F.R.G.S.—*do*, Royal Geographical Society.

F.R.Hist.S.—*do*, Royal Historical Society.

F.R.H.S.—*do*, Royal Horticultural Society.

F.R.I.B.A.—*do*, Royal Institute of British Architects.

F.R.I.C.S.—*do*, Royal Institution of Chartered Surveyors.

F.R.Met.S.—*do*, Royal Meteorological Society.

F.R.M.S.—*do*, Royal Microscopical Society.

F.R.N.S.—*do*, Royal Numismatic Society.

F.R.Pharm.S.—*do*, Royal Pharmaceutical Society.

F.R.P.S.—*do*, Royal Photographic Society.

F.R.S.—*do*, Royal Society.

F.R.S.A.—*do*, Royal Society of Arts.

F.R.S.C.—*do*, Royal Society of Chemistry.

F.R.S.E.—*do*, Royal Society of Edinburgh.

F.R.S.L.—*do*, Royal Society of Literature.

F.R.T.P.I.—*do*, Royal Town Planning Institute.

F.S.A.—*do*, Society of Antiquaries.

F.S.S.—*do*, Statistical Society.

F.S.V.A.—*do*, Incorporated Society of Valuers and Auctioneers.

F.T.—*Financial Times*.

F.T.I.—Fellow, Textile Institute.

F.T.I.I.—*do*, Institute of Taxation.

F.Z.S.—*do*, Zoological Society.

G

G.A.T.T.—General Agreement on Tariffs and Trade.

G.B.E.—Dame/Knight Grand Cross, Order of the British Empire.

G.C.—George Cross.

G.C.B.—Dame/Knight Grand Cross, Order of the Bath.

G.C.E.—General Certificate of Education.

G.C.H.Q.—Government Communications Headquarters.

G.C.I.E.—Knight Grand Commander, Order of the Indian Empire.

G.C.L.J.—Knight Grand Cross, Order of St. Lazarus of Jerusalem.

G.C.M.G.—Dame/Knight Grand Cross, Order of St. Michael and St. George.

G.C.S.E.—General Certificate of Secondary Education.

G.C.S.I.—Knight Grand Commander, Order of the Star of India.

G.C.V.O.—Dame/Knight Grand Cross, Royal Victorian Order.

G.D.P.—Gross domestic product.

G.D.R.—German Democratic Republic (*E. Germany*).

Gen.—General.

G.H.Q.—General Headquarters.

Gib.—Gibraltar.

G.M.—George Medal.

G.M.B.—General, Municipal, Boilermakers and Allied Trades Union.

G.M.T.—Greenwich Mean Time.

G.N.P.—Gross national product.
G.O.C.—General Officer Commanding.
G.P.—General Practitioner.
Gp. Capt.—Group Captain.
G.S.O.—General Staff Officer.

H

H.A.C.—Honourable Artillery Company.
H.B.M.—Her/His Britannic Majesty('s).
H.C.F.—Highest common factor; Honorary Chaplain to the Forces.
H.E.—Her/His Excellency; His Eminence.
H.G.V.—Heavy Goods Vehicle.
H.H.—Her/His Highness; Her/His Honour; His Holiness.
H.I.M.—Her/His Imperial Majesty.
H.I.V.—Human Immunodeficiency Virus.
H.J.S.—(*hic jacet sepultus*) here lies buried.
H.M.—Her/His Majesty('s).
H.M.A.S.—Her/His Majesty's Australian Ship.
H.M.C.—Headmasters' Conference.
H.M.I.—Her/His Majesty's Inspector.
H.M.L.—Her/His Majesty's Lieutenant.
H.M.S.—Her/His Majesty's Ship.
H.M.S.O.—Her/His Majesty's Stationery Office.
H.N.C.—Higher National Certificate.
H.N.D.—Higher National Diploma.
H.O.L.M.E.S.—Home Office Large Major Enquiry System.
Hon.—Honorary; Honourable.
h.p.—horse power.
H.P.—Hire purchase.
H.Q.—Headquarters.
H.R.H.—Her/His Royal Highness.
H.S.E.—Health and Safety Executive; (*hic sepultus est*) here lies buried.
H.S.H.—Her/His Serene Highness.
H.T.R.—High temperature reactor.
H.W.M.—High water mark.

I

I.A.A.S.—Incorporated Association of Architects and Surveyors.
I.A.E.A.—International Atomic Energy Agency.
I.A.T.A.—International Air Transport Association.
I.B.A.—Independent Broadcasting Authority.
Ibid.—(*ibidem*) in the same place.
I.B.R.D.—International Bank for Reconstruction and Development.
I.C.A.O.—International Civil Aviation Organization.
I.C.B.M.—Inter-continental ballistic missile.
I.C.F.T.U.—International Confederation of Free Trade Unions.
I.C.J.—International Court of Justice.
I.C.R.C.—International Committee of the Red Cross.
Id.—(*idem*) the same.
I.D.A.—International Development Association.
i.e.—(*id est*) that is.
I.E.A.—International Energy Agency.
I.F.A.D.—International Fund for Agricultural Development.
I.F.C.—International Finance Corporation.
I.H.S.—(*Iesus Hominum Salvator*) Jesus the Saviour of Mankind.
I.L.E.A.—Inner London Education Authority.
I.L.O.—International Labour Office/Organization.
I.M.F.—International Monetary Fund.
I.M.O.—International Maritime Organization.
Inc.—Incorporated.
Incog.—(*incognito*) unknown, unrecognized.
I.N.F.—International Nuclear Force.
I.N.L.A.—Irish National Liberation Army.
In loc.—(*in loco*) in its place.
Inmarsat.—International Maritime Satellite Organization.

I.N.R.I.—(*Iesus Nazarenus Rex Iudaeorum*) Jesus of Nazareth, King of the Jews.
Inst.—(*instant*) current month.
Intelsat—International Telecommunications Satellite Consortium.
Interpol—International Criminal Police Commission.
I.O.M.—Isle of Man.
I.O.U.—I owe you.
I.O.W.—Isle of Wight.
I.Q.—Intelligence quotient.
I.R.A.—Irish Republican Army.
I.R.C.—International Red Cross.
I.S.B.N.—International Standard Book Number.
I.S.O.—Imperial Service Order.
I.T.U.—International Telecommunication Union.
I.T.V.—Independent Television.

J

J.—Judge (*after Judge's name*).
J.P.—Justice of the Peace.

K

K.—Köchel numeration (*of Mozart's works*).
K.A.N.U.—Kenyan African National Union.
K.B.E.—Knight Commander, Order of the British Empire.
K.C.B.—*do*, Order of the Bath.
K.C.I.E.—*do*, Order of the Indian Empire.
K.C.L.J.—*do*, Order of St. Lazarus of Jerusalem.
K.C.M.G.—*do*, Order of St. Michael and St. George.
K.C.S.I.—*do*, Order of the Star of India.
K.C.V.O.—*do*, Royal Victorian Order.
K.G.—Knight of the Garter.
K.G.B.—(*Komitet Gosudarstvennoi Besopasnosti*) Committee of State Security (USSR).
K.K.K.—Ku Klux Klan.
K.L.J.—Knight, Order of St. Lazarus of Jerusalem.
k.o.—knock out (*boxing*).
K.P.—Knight, Order of St. Patrick.
K.St.J.—Knight, Order of St. John of Jerusalem.
Kt.—Knight.
K.T.—Knight of the Thistle.
kV.—Kilovolt.
kW.—Kilowatt.
kWh.—Kilowatt hour.

L

L. (*or* Lib.)—Liberal.
Lab.—Labour.
Lat.—Latitude.
l.b.w.—leg before wicket.
l.c.—lower case (*printing*).
L.C.J.—Lord Chief Justice.
L.C.M.—Least/lowest common multiple.
L.D.S.—Licentiate in Dental Surgery.
L.E.A.—Local Education Authority.
L.H.D.—(*Literarum Humaniorum Doctor*) Doctor of Humane Letters/Literature.
Lic.—(*Licenciado*) lawyer (*Spanish*).
Lic. Med.—Licentiate in Medicine.
Lit.—Literary.
Lit. Hum.—(*Literae Humaniores*) Faculty of classics and philosophy, Oxford.
Litt. D.—Doctor of Letters.
L.J.—Lord Justice.
LL.B.—Bachelor of Laws.
LL.D.—Doctor of Laws.
LL.M.—Master of Laws.
L.M.—Licentiate in Midwifery.
L.M.S.S.A.—*do*, in Medicine and Surgery, Society of Apothecaries.
loc. cit.—(*loco citato*) in the place cited.
log.—logarithm.
Londin.—of London (*Bishop*).
Long.—Longitude.
L.S.—(*loco sigilli*) place of the seal.

L.S.A.—Licentiate of Society of Apothecaries.
L.s.d.—(*Librae, solidi, denarii*) £, shillings and pence.
L.S.E.—London School of Economics and Political Science.
L.S.O.—London Symphony Orchestra.
Lt.—Lieutenant.
L.T.A.—Lawn Tennis Association.
Ltd.—Limited (liability).
L.Th. (*or* L. Theol.)—Licentiate in Theology.
L.V.O.—Lieutenant, Royal Victorian Order.
L.W.M.—Low water mark.

M

M.—Member of; Monsieur.
M.A.—Master of Arts.
M.A.F.F.—Ministry of Agriculture, Fisheries and Food.
Maj.—Major.
max.—maximum.
M.B./D.—Bachelor/Doctor of Medicine.
M.B.E.—Member, Order of the British Empire.
M.C.—Master of Ceremonies; Military Cross.
M.C.C.—Marylebone Cricket Club.
M.Ch.(D.)—Master of (Dental) Surgery.
M.D.S.—*do*, of Dental Surgery.
M.E.—Middle English.
M.E.C.—Member of Executive Council.
M.Ed.—Master of Education.
mega—one million times.
M.E.P.—Member of the European Parliament.
M.F.H.—Master of Foxhounds.
Mgr.—Monsignor.
M.I.—Military Intelligence.
micro—one-millionth part.
milli—one-thousandth part.
min.—minimum.
M.I.R.A.S.—Mortgage Interest Relief at Source.
M.L.A.—Member of Legislative Assembly.
M.L.C.—Member of Legislative Council.
Mlle.—Mademoiselle.
M.L.R.—Minimum lending rate.
M.M.—Military Medal.
Mme.—Madame.
M.N.—Merchant Navy.
M.O.—Medical Officer/Orderly.
M.o.D.—Ministry of Defence.
M.o.T.—Ministry of Transport.
M.P.—Member of Parliament; Military Police.
m.p.h.—miles per hour.
M.R.—Master of the Rolls.
M.R.C.—Medical Research Council.
M.S.—Master of Surgery; Manuscript (*pl.* MSS).
M.Sc.—*do*, of Science.
M.S.C.—Manpower Services Commission.
M.S.F.—Manufacturing, Science and Finance Union.
M.T.B.—Motor torpedo boat.
M.Th.—Master of Theology.
Mus. B./D.—Bachelor/Doctor of Music.
M.V.—Merchant Vessel; Motor Vessel.
M.V.O.—Member, Royal Victorian Order.
M.W.—Medium Wave.

N

N.—North.
N.A.A.F.I.—Navy Army and Air Force Institutes.
N.A.L.G.O.—National and Local Government Officers' Association.
N.A.S.A.—National Aeronautics and Space Administration.
N.A.S./U.W.T.—National Association of Schoolmasters/Union of Women Teachers.
N.A.T.O.—North Atlantic Treaty Organization.
N.B.—New Brunswick; (*Nota bene*) note well.
N.C.O.—Non-commissioned officer.
N.E.B.—New English Bible.

N.E.D.C. (*or* NEDDY)—National Economic Development Council.
Nem. con.—(*Nemine contradicente*) no one contradicting.
N.E.R.C.—Natural Environment Research Council.
n.e.s.—not elsewhere specified.
N.F.T.—National Film Theatre.
N.F.U.—National Farmers' Union.
N.G.A.—National Graphical Association.
N.H.S.—National Health Service.
N.I.—National Insurance; Northern Ireland.
No.—(*numero*) number.
Non seq.—(*Non sequitur*) it does not follow.
Norvic.—of Norwich (*Bishop*).
N.P.—Notary Public.
N.R.A.—National Rifle Association.
N.S.—New Style (*calendar*); Nova Scotia.
N.S.P.C.C.—National Society for the Prevention of Cruelty to Children.
N.S.W.—New South Wales.
N.T.—National Theatre; National Trust; New Testament.
N.U.C.P.S.—National Union of Civil and Public Servants.
N.U.J.—*do*, of Journalists.
N.U.M.—*do*, of Mineworkers.
N.U.P.E.—*do*, of Public Employees.
N.U.R.—*do*, of Railwaymen.
N.U.S.—*do*, of Seamen; *do*, of Students.
N.U.T.—*do*, of Teachers.
N.V.Q.—National Vocational Qualification.
N.W.T.—Northwest Territory.
N.Y.—New York.
N.Z.—New Zealand.

O

O. and M.—Organization and method.
O.A.P.E.C.—Organization of Arab Petroleum Exporting Countries.
O.A.S.—Organization of American States.
O.A.U.—Organization of African Unity.
Ob. (*or* obit.)—died.
O.B.E.—Officer, Order of the British Empire.
O.C.—Officer Commanding.
O.E.—Old English; omissions excepted.
O.E.C.D.—Organization for Economic Co-operation and Development.
O.E.D.—*Oxford English Dictionary*.
Ofgas—Office of Gas Supply.
O.F.M.—Order of Friars Minor (*Franciscans*).
Oftel—Office of Telecommunications.
O.H.M.S.—On Her/His Majesty's Service.
O.M.—Order of Merit.
O.N.D.—Ordinary National Diploma.
O.P.—Opposite prompt side (*of theatre*); Order of Preachers (*Dominicans*); out of print (*books*).
op.—(*opus*) work.
op. cit.—(*opere citato*) in the work cited.
O.P.C.S.—Office of Population Censuses and Surveys.
O.P.E.C.—Organization of Petroleum Exporting Countries.
O.S.—Old Style (*calendar*); Ordnance Survey.
O.S.A.—Order of St. Augustine.
O.S.B.—Order of St. Benedict.
O. St. J.—Officer, Order of St. John of Jerusalem.
O.T.—Old Testament.
O.T.C.—Officer's Training Corps.
Oxon.—(of) Oxford; Oxfordshire.

P

p.—page (pp.—pages).
p.—(piano) softly.
P.A.—Personal Assistant; Press Association.
P.A.Y.E.—Pay as You Earn.
p.c. (*or* per cent)—(*per centum*) in the hundred.
P.C.—Police Constable; Privy Counsellor; Personal Computer.

P.C.A.S.—Polytechnics Central Admission System.
P.C.F.C.—Polytechnics' and Colleges' Funding Council.
P.D.S.A.—People's Dispensary for Sick Animals.
P.E.—Physical Education.
Petriburg—of Peterborough (*Bishop*).
Ph.D.—Doctor of Philosophy.
pinx(it)—he/she painted it.
pl.—plural.
P.L.A.—Port of London Authority.
P.L.C.—Public Limited Company.
P.L.O.—Palestine Liberation Organization.
p.m.—(*post meridiem*) after noon.
P.M.—Prime Minister.
P.M.R.A.F.N.S.—Princess Mary's Royal Air Force Nursing Service.
P.O.—Petty Officer; Pilot Officer; Post Office; postal order.
P.O.U.N.C.—Post Office Users' National Council.
P.O.W.—Prisoner of War.
p.p. (*or* per pro)—(*per procurationem*) by proxy.
P.P.S.—Parliamentary Private Secretary.
P.R.—Proportional Representation; Public Relations.
P.R.A.—President of the Royal Academy.
Pro tem.—(*pro tempore*) for the time being.
Prox.—(*proximo*) next month.
P.R.S.—President of the Royal Society.
P.R.S.E.—*do*, of Edinburgh.
Ps.—Psalm.
P.S.—(*Post scriptum*) postscript.
P.S.B.R.—Public sector borrowing requirement.
p.s.c.—passed Staff College.
P.S.V.—Public Service Vehicle.
Pte.—Private.
P.T.O.—Please turn over.

Q

Q.A.R.A.N.C.—Queen Alexandra's Royal Army Nursing Corps.
Q.A.R.N.N.S.—Queen Alexandra's Royal Naval Nursing Service.
Q.B.—Queen's Bench.
Q.C.—Queen's Counsel.
Q.E.D.—(*quod erat demonstrandum*) which was to be proved.
Q.G.M.—Queen's Gallantry Medal.
Q.H.C.—Queen's Honorary Chaplain.
Q.H.D.S.—Queen's Honorary Dental Surgeon.
Q.H.N.S.—Queen's Honorary Nursing Sister.
Q.H.P.—Queen's Honorary Physician.
Q.H.S.—Queen's Honorary Surgeon.
Q.M.G.—Quartermaster General.
Q.P.M.—Queen's Police Medal.
Q.S.—Quarter Sessions.
Q.S.O.—Quasi-stellar object (quasar); Queen's Service Order.
quango.—quasi-autonomous non-governmental organization.
q.v.—(*quod vide*) which see.

R

R.—(*Regina*) Queen; (*Rex*) King.
R.A.—Royal Academy/Academician; Royal Artillery.
R.A.C.—Royal Armoured Corps; Royal Automobile Club.
R.A.D.A.—Royal Academy of Dramatic Art.
R.A.D.C.—Royal Army Dental Corps.
R.A.E.—Royal Aerospace Establishment.
R.A.E.C.—Royal Army Educational Corps.
R.Ae.S.—Royal Aeronautical Society.
R.A.F.—Royal Air Force.
R.A.M.—Random-access memory (*computer*); Royal Academy of Music.

R.A.M.C.—Royal Army Medical Corps.
R.A.N.—Royal Australian Navy.
R. and D.—Research and development.
R.A.O.C.—Royal Army Ordnance Corps.
R.A.P.C.—Royal Army Pay Corps.
R.A.V.C.—Royal Army Veterinary Corps.
R.B.A.—Royal Society of British Artists.
R.B.S.—Royal Society of British Sculptors.
R.C.—Red Cross; Roman Catholic.
R.C.M.—Royal College of Music.
R.C.N.—Royal Canadian Navy.
R.C.N.C.—Royal Corps of Naval Constructors.
R.C.T.—Royal Corps of Transport.
R.D.—Refer to drawer (*banking*); Royal Naval and Royal Marine Forces Reserve Decoration; Rural Dean.
R.D.I.—Royal Designer for Industry (*Royal Society of Arts*).
R.E.—Religious Education; Royal Engineers.
R.E.M.E.—Royal Electrical and Mechanical Engineers.
Rep.—Representative; Republican.
Rev.—Reverend.
R.G.N.—Registered General Nurse.
R.G.S.—Royal Geographical Society.
R.H.A.—Regional Health Authority.
R.H.S.—Royal Horticultural Society; Royal Humane Society.
R.I.—Rhode Island; Royal Institute of Painters in Watercolours; Royal Institution.
R.I.A.—Royal Irish Academy.
R.I.B.A.—Royal Institute of British Architects.
R.I.P.—(*Requiescat in pace*) May he/she rest in peace.
R.L.—Rugby League.
R.M.—Registered Midwife; Royal Marines.
R.M.A.—Royal Military Academy.
R.M.N.—Registered Mental Nurse.
R.M.S.—Royal Mail Steamer.
R.N.—Royal Navy.
R.N.I.B.—Royal National Institute for the Blind.
R.N.I.D.—Royal National Institute for the Deaf.
R.N.L.I.—Royal National Lifeboat Institution.
R.N.R.—Royal Naval Reserve.
R.N.V.R.—Royal Naval Volunteer Reserve.
R.N.X.S.—Royal Naval Auxiliary Service.
R.N.Z.N.—Royal New Zealand Navy.
Ro.—(*Recto*) on the right-hand page.
R.O.C.—Royal Observer Corps.
Roffen.—of Rochester (*Bishop*).
R.O.I.—Royal Institute of Oil Painters.
R.O.M.—Read-only memory (*computer*).
ro-ro—roll-on, roll-off.
Ro.S.P.A.—Royal Society for the Prevention of Accidents.
R.P.—Royal Society of Portrait Painters.
r.p.m.—revolutions per minute.
R.R.C.—Lady of Royal Red Cross.
R.S.A.—Republic of South Africa; Royal Scottish Academician; Royal Society of Arts.
R.S.C.—Royal Shakespeare Company.
R.S.C.N.—Registered Sick Children's Nurse.
R.S.E.—Royal Society of Edinburgh.
R.S.M.—Regimental Sergeant Major.
R.S.P.B.—Royal Society for the Protection of Birds.
R.S.P.C.A.—Royal Society for the Prevention of Cruelty to Animals.
R.S.R.E.—Royal Signals and Radar Establishment.
R.S.V.P.—(*Répondez, s'il vous plaît*) Please reply.
R.S.W.—Royal Scottish Society of Painters in Watercolours.
R.T.P.I.—Royal Town Planning Institute.
R.U.—Rugby Union.
R.U.C.—Royal Ulster Constabulary.
R.V.—Revised Version (*of Bible*).
R.V.M.—Royal Victorian Medal.
R.W.S.—Royal Water Colour Society.
R.Y.S.—Royal Yacht Squadron.

S

s.—second; (*solidus*) shilling.
S.—South.
S.A.—Salvation Army; South Africa; South America; South Australia.
S.A.E.—Stamped addressed envelope.
Salop.—Shropshire.
Sarum.—of Salisbury (*Bishop*).
S.A.S.—Special Air Service Regiment.
S.B.S.—Special Boat Squadron.
Sc.D.—Doctor of Science.
S.C.M.—State Certified Midwife.
S.D.I.—Strategic Defence Initiative ("Star Wars").
S.D.L.P.—Social Democratic and Labour Party.
S.D.P.—Social Democratic Party.
S.E.A.Q.—Stock Exchange Automated Quotations system.
S.E.N.—State Enrolled Nurse.
S.E.R.C.—Science and Engineering Research Council.
S.E.R.P.S.—State Earnings Related Pension Scheme.
S.I.—(*Système Internationale d'Unités*) International System of Units; Statutory Instrument.
Sic.—So written.
Sig.—Signature; Signor.
S.J.—Society of Jesus (*Jesuits*).
S.L.D.—Social and Liberal Democrats.
S.M.P.—Statutory Maternity Pay.
S.N.P.—Scottish National Party.
S.O.G.A.T.—Society of Graphical and Allied Trades.
S.O.S.—Save Our Souls (*distress signal*).
s.p.—(*sine prole*) without issue.
sp.gr.—specific gravity.
S.P.Q.R.—(*Senatus Populusque Romanus*) The Senate and People of Rome.
Sqn. Ldr.—Squadron Leader.
S.R.N.—State Registered Nurse.
SS.—Saints.
S.S.—Steamship.
S.S.C.—Solicitor before Supreme Court (*Scotland*).
S.S.F.—Society of St. Francis.
S.S.P.—Statutory Sick Pay.
St.—Saint; Street.
stet.—let it stand (*printing*).
S.T.D.—(*Sacrae Theologiae Doctor)* Doctor of Sacred Theology; Subscriber trunk dialling.
s.t.p.—Standard temperature and pressure.
S.T.P.—(*Sacrae Theologiae Professor*) Professor of Sacred Theology.
Sub Lt.—Sub-Lieutenant.
S.W.A.P.O.—South West Africa People's Organization.

T

T.A.—Territorial Army.
T.B.—Tuberculosis.
T.C.C.B.—Test and County Cricket Board.
T.D.—Territorial Efficiency Decoration.
temp.—temperature; temporary employee.
T.E.S.—*Times Educational Supplement.*
T.G.W.U.—Transport and General Workers' Union.
T.L.S.—*Times Literary Supplement.*
T.N.T.—trinitrotoluene (*explosive*).
tr.—transpose (*printing*).
T.R.H.—Their Royal Highnesses.
Truron.—of Truro (*Bishop*).
T.T.—Teetotal; Tuberculin tested.
T.U.C.—Trades Union Congress.
T.V.—Television.
T.V.E.I.—Technical and Vocational Education Initiative.

U

U.A.E.—United Arab Emirates.
u.c.—upper case (*printing*).
U.C.A.T.T.—Union of Construction, Allied Trades and Technicians.

U.C.C.A.—Universities' Central Council on Admissions.
U.D.I.—Unilateral Declaration of Independence.
U.D.M.—Union of Democratic Mineworkers.
U.D.R.—Ulster Defence Regiment.
U.E.F.A.—Union of European Football Associations.
U.F.C.—Universities' Funding Council.
U.F.O.—Unidentified flying object.
U.H.F.—ultra-high frequency.
U.K.—United Kingdom.
U.K.A.E.A.—United Kingdom Atomic Energy Authority.
Ult.—(*ultimo*) in the preceding month.
U.N.—United Nations.
U.N.E.S.C.O.—United Nations Educational, Scientific and Cultural Organization.
U.N.I.C.E.F.—United Nations Children's Fund.
U.N.I.D.O.—United Nations Industrial Development Organization.
Unita.—National Union for the Total Independence of Angola.
U.P.U.—Universal Postal Union.
U.S. (*or* U.S.A.)—United States (of America).
U.S.D.A.W.—Union of Shop, Distributive and Allied Workers.
U.S.M.—Unlisted Securities Market.
U.S.S.R.—Union of Soviet Socialist Republics.

V

v.—(*versus*) against.
V.A.—Vicar Apostolic; Victoria and Albert Order.
V.A.D.—Voluntary Aid Detachment.
V.A.T.—Value added tax.
V.C.—Victoria Cross.
V.D.—Venereal disease; Volunteer Officers' Decoration.
V.D.U.—Visual display unit.
Ven.—Venerable.
Verb. sap.—(*Verbum sapienti satis est*) A word to the wise is enough.
V.H.F.—very high frequency.
V.I.P.—Very important person.
Viz.—(*videlicet*) namely.
Vo.—(*Verso*) on the left-hand page.
V.R.D.—Royal Naval Volunteer Reserve Officers' Decoration.
V.S.O.—Voluntary Service Overseas.
V.T.O.L.—Vertical take-off and landing (*aircraft*).

W

W.—West.
W.C.C.—World Council of Churches.
W.E.A.—Workers' Educational Association.
W.E.U.—Western European Union.
W.F.T.U.—World Federation of Trade Unions.
W.H.O.—World Health Organization.
W.I.—West Indies; Women's Institute.
Winton.—of Winchester (*Bishop*).
W.I.P.O.—World Intellectual Property Organization.
W.M.O.—World Meteorological Organization.
W.O.—Warrant Officer.
W.R.A.C.—Women's Royal Army Corps.
W.R.A.F.—Women's Royal Air Force.
W.R.N.S.—Women's Royal Naval Service.
W.R.V.S.—Women's Royal Voluntary Service.
W.S.—Writer to the Signet.

Y

Y.H.A.—Youth Hostels Association.
Y.M.C.A.—Young Men's Christian Association.
Y.T.S.—Youth Training Scheme.
Y.W.C.A.—Young Women's Christian Association.

Z

Z.A.N.U.—Zimbabwe African National Union.

CALENDAR FOR THE YEAR 1990

```
        January                February               March                  April
Su.  .. —  7 14 21 28     .. —  4 11 18 25    Su.  .. —  4 11 18 25     .. 1  8 15 22 29
M.   .. 1  8 15 22 29     .. —  5 12 19 26    M.   .. —  5 12 19 26     .. 2  9 16 23 30
Tu.  .. 2  9 16 23 30     .. —  6 13 20 27    Tu.  .. —  6 13 20 27     .. 3 10 17 24 —
W.   .. 3 10 17 24 31     .. —  7 14 21 28    W.   .. —  7 14 21 28     .. 4 11 18 25 —
Th.  .. 4 11 18 25 —      .. 1  8 15 22 —     Th.  .. 1  8 15 22 29     .. 5 12 19 26 —
F.   .. 5 12 19 26 —      .. 2  9 16 23 —     F.   .. 2  9 16 23 30     .. 6 13 20 27 —
S.   .. 6 13 20 27 —      .. 3 10 17 24 —     S.   .. 3 10 17 24 31     .. 7 14 21 28 —

          May                   June                 July                   August
Su.  .. —  6 13 20 27     .. —  3 10 17 24    Su.  .. 1  8 15 22 29     .. —  5 12 19 26
M.   .. —  7 14 21 28     .. —  4 11 18 25    M.   .. 2  9 16 23 30     .. —  6 13 20 27
Tu.  .. 1  8 15 22 29     .. —  5 12 19 26    Tu.  .. 3 10 17 24 31     .. —  7 14 21 28
W.   .. 2  9 16 23 30     .. —  6 13 20 27    W.   .. 4 11 18 25 —      .. 1  8 15 22 29
Th.  .. 3 10 17 24 31     .. —  7 14 21 28    Th.  .. 5 12 19 26 —      .. 2  9 16 23 30
F.   .. 4 11 18 25 —      .. 1  8 15 22 29    F.   .. 6 13 20 27 —      .. 3 10 17 24 31
S.   .. 5 12 19 26 —      .. 2  9 16 23 30    S.   .. 7 14 21 28 —      .. 4 11 18 25 —

        September               October              November               December
Su.  —  2  9 16 23 30     .. —  7 14 21 28    Su.  .. —  4 11 18 25     —  2  9 16 23 30
M.   —  3 10 17 24 —      .. 1  8 15 22 29    M.   .. —  5 12 19 26     —  3 10 17 24 31
Tu.  —  4 11 18 25 —      .. 2  9 16 23 30    Tu.  .. —  6 13 20 27     —  4 11 18 25 —
W.   —  5 12 19 26 —      .. 3 10 17 24 31    W.   .. —  7 14 21 28     —  5 12 19 26 —
Th.  —  6 13 20 27 —      .. 4 11 18 25 —     Th.  .. 1  8 15 22 29     —  6 13 20 27 —
F.   —  7 14 21 28 —      .. 5 12 19 26 —     F.   .. 2  9 16 23 30     —  7 14 21 28 —
S.   1  8 15 22 29 —      .. 6 13 20 27 —     S.   .. 3 10 17 24 —      1  8 15 22 29 —
```

CALENDAR FOR THE YEAR 1991

```
        January                February               March                  April
Su.  .. —  6 13 20 27     .. —  3 10 17 24    Su.  —  3 10 17 24 31     .. —  7 14 21 28
M.   .. —  7 14 21 28     .. —  4 11 18 25    M.   —  4 11 18 25 —      .. 1  8 15 22 29
Tu.  .. 1  8 15 22 29     .. —  5 12 19 26    Tu.  —  5 12 19 26 —      .. 2  9 16 23 30
W.   .. 2  9 16 23 30     .. —  6 13 20 27    W.   —  6 13 20 27 —      .. 3 10 17 24 —
Th.  .. 3 10 17 24 31     .. —  7 14 21 28    Th.  —  7 14 21 28 —      .. 4 11 18 25 —
F.   .. 4 11 18 25 —      .. 1  8 15 22 —     F.   1  8 15 22 29 —      .. 5 12 19 26 —
S.   .. 5 12 19 26 —      .. 2  9 16 23 —     S.   2  9 16 23 30 —      .. 6 13 20 27 —

          May                   June                 July                   August
Su.  .. —  5 12 19 26     .. 2  9 16 23 30    Su.  —  7 14 21 28        .. —  4 11 18 25
M.   .. —  6 13 20 27     .. —  3 10 17 24    M.   1  8 15 22 29        .. —  5 12 19 26
Tu.  .. —  7 14 21 28     .. —  4 11 18 25    Tu.  2  9 16 23 30        .. —  6 13 20 27
W.   .. 1  8 15 22 29     .. —  5 12 19 26    W.   3 10 17 24 31        .. —  7 14 21 28
Th.  .. 2  9 16 23 30     .. —  6 13 20 27    Th.  4 11 18 25 —         .. 1  8 15 22 29
F.   .. 3 10 17 24 31     .. —  7 14 21 28    F.   5 12 19 26 —         .. 2  9 16 23 30
S.   .. 4 11 18 25 —      .. 1  8 15 22 29    S.   6 13 20 27 —         .. 3 10 17 24 31

        September               October              November               December
Su.  .. 1  8 15 22 29     .. —  6 13 20 27    Su.  —  3 10 17 24        .. 1  8 15 22 29
M.   .. 2  9 16 23 30     .. —  7 14 21 28    M.   —  4 11 18 25        .. 2  9 16 23 30
Tu.  .. 3 10 17 24 —      .. 1  8 15 22 29    Tu.  —  5 12 19 26        .. 3 10 17 24 31
W.   .. 4 11 18 25 —      .. 2  9 16 23 30    W.   —  6 13 20 27        .. 4 11 18 25 —
Th.  .. 5 12 19 26 —      .. 3 10 17 24 31    Th.  —  7 14 21 28        .. 5 12 19 26 —
F.   .. 6 13 20 27 —      .. 4 11 18 25 —     F.   1  8 15 22 29        .. 6 13 20 27 —
S.   .. 7 14 21 28 —      .. 5 12 19 26 —     S.   2  9 16 23 30        .. 7 14 21 28 —
```

PUBLIC HOLIDAYS

	1990			1991		
	ENGLAND & WALES	SCOTLAND	N. IRELAND	ENGLAND & WALES	SCOTLAND	N. IRELAND
New Year	Jan. 1	Jan. 1, 2	Jan. 1	Jan. 1	Jan. 1, 2	Jan. 1
St. Patrick's Day	—	—	March 17	—	—	March 18
Good Friday	April 13*	April 13	April 13*	March 29*	March 29	March 29*
Easter Monday	April 16	—	April 16	April 1	—	April 1
May Day	May 7	May 28	May 7	May 6	May 27	May 6
Spring	May 28	May 7	May 28	May 27	May 6	May 27
Battle of Boyne	—	—	July 12	—	—	July 12
Summer	Aug. 27	Aug. 6	Aug. 27	Aug. 26	Aug. 5	Aug. 26
Christmas	Dec. 25*, 26	Dec. 25, 26	Dec. 25*, 26	Dec. 25*, 26	Dec. 25, 26	Dec. 25*, 26

* In England, Wales, and Northern Ireland, Christmas Day and Good Friday are common law holidays. In the CHANNEL ISLANDS Liberation Day (May 9) is a bank and public holiday.

NOTES FOR THE YEAR 1990

BEING THE SECOND YEAR AFTER
BISSEXTILE OR LEAP YEAR

Dominical Letter	G	St. George's Day	April 23
Epact	3	Coronation of H.M. The Queen (1953)	June 2
Golden Number (Lunar Cycle)	XV	Duke of Edinburgh's Birthday (1921)	June 10
Julian Period	6703	Queen's Official Birthday	June 16
Roman Indiction	13	Prince William of Wales' Birthday	
Solar Cycle	11	(1982)	June 21
Julian Day, Jan. 1 (begins at noon)	2,447,893	Princess of Wales' Birthday (1961)	July 1
		Queen Elizabeth the Queen Mother's	
New Year's Day	Jan. 1	Birthday (1900)	Aug. 4
Ancient Chinese New Year (Horse)	Jan. 27	Princess Royal's Birthday (1950)	Aug. 15
Accession of H.M. The Queen (1952)	Feb. 6	Princess Margaret's Birthday (1930)	Aug. 21
Duke of York's Birthday (1960)	Feb. 19	Prince Henry of Wales' Birthday (1984)	Sept. 15
St. David's Day	March 1	Lord Mayor's Day	Nov. 10
Prince Edward's Birthday (1964)	March 10	Remembrance Sunday	Nov. 11
Commonwealth Day	March 12	Prince of Wales' Birthday (1948)	Nov. 14
St. Patrick's Day	March 17	Wedding Day of H.M. The Queen (1947)	Nov. 20
Birthday of H.M. The Queen (1926)	April 21	St. Andrew's Day	Nov. 30

RELIGIOUS CALENDARS 1990

Epiphany	Jan. 6	Whit Sunday (Pentecost)	June 3
Ash Wednesday	Feb. 28	Trinity Sunday	June 10
Ramadân, first day	March 28	Corpus Christi	June 14
Passover, first day	April 10	Islamic New Year (1411)	July 24
Good Friday	April 13	Jewish New Year (5751)	Sept. 20
Easter Day	April 15	Day of Atonement (Yom Kippur)	Sept. 29
Greek Orthodox Easter	April 15	Feast of Tabernacles, first day	Oct. 4
Rogation Sunday	May 20	First Sunday in Advent	Dec. 2
Ascension Day	May 24	Christmas Day	Dec. 25
Feast of Weeks, first day	May 30		

SEASONS 1990

Northern Hemisphere

Spring Equinox	Sun enters Sign Aries	March 20d 21h	
Summer Solstice	„ „ „ Cancer	June 21d 16h	G.M.T.
Autumn Equinox	„ „ „ Libra	Sept. 23d 07h	
Winter Solstice	„ „ „ Capricornus	Dec. 22d 03h	

Southern Hemisphere

Autumn Equinox	Sun enters Sign Aries	March 20d 21h	
Winter Solstice	„ „ „ Cancer	June 21d 16h	G.M.T.
Spring Equinox	„ „ „ Libra	Sept. 23d 07h	
Summer Solstice	„ „ „ Capricornus	Dec. 22d 03h	

British Summer Time in 1990 begins March 25d 01h GMT and ends on October 28d 01h GMT.

LAW TERMS 1990

Hilary Term begins Jan. 11 and ends April 11
Easter Term begins April 24 and ends May 25
Trinity Term begins June 5 and ends July 31
Michaelmas Term begins Oct. 1 and ends Dec. 21

QUARTER DAYS
(England, Wales, N. Ireland)

Lady Day	March 25
Midsummer	June 24
Michaelmas	Sept. 29
Christmas	Dec. 25

TERM DAYS
(Scotland)

Candlemas	Feb. 2
Whitsunday	May 15
Lammas	Aug. 1
Martinmas	Nov. 11

(*Removal Terms* are May 28 and Nov. 28).

DAY OF			*Janus*, god of the portal, facing two ways, past and future. *Sun's Longitude* 300° ≈ 20ᵈ 08ʰ
Month	Week		

1	M.	**Naming of Jesus.** Maria Edgeworth b. 1767.
2	Tu.	Sir Michael Tippett b. 1905.
3	W.	J.R.R. Tolkien b. 1892. Edwin Muir d. 1959.
4	Th.	Louis Braille b. 1809. T.S. Eliot d. 1965.
5	F.	Sir Ernest Shackleton d. 1922. Amy Johnson d.
6	S.	**The Epiphany.** Fanny Burney d. 1840. [1941.
7	S.	**1st S. after Epiphany.** Francis Poulenc b. 1899.
8	M.	Wilkie Collins b. 1824. Paul Verlaine d. 1896.
9	Tu.	Gracie Fields b. 1898. Simone de Beauvoir b. 1908.
10	W.	Penny Post introduced 1840.
11	Th.	HILARY LAW SITTINGS BEGIN. William James b. 1842.
12	F.	Jack London b. 1876. Agatha Christie d. 1976.
13	S.	James Joyce d. 1941.
14	S.	**2nd S. after Epiphany.** Lewis Carroll d. 1898.
15	M.	Rosa Luxemburg and Karl Liebknecht d. 1919.
16	Tu.	Edward Gibbon d. 1794.
17	W.	Benjamin Franklin b. 1706. Anton Chekhov b. 1860.
18	Th.	A. A. Milne b. 1882. Cecil Beaton d. 1980.
19	F.	William Congreve d. 1729.
20	S.	John Ruskin d. 1900. Edmund Blunden d. 1974.
21	S.	**3rd S. after Epiphany.** Jack Nicklaus b. 1940.
22	M.	Francis Bacon b. 1561. Beatrice Webb b. 1858.
23	Tu.	Manet b. 1832. Charles Kingsley d. 1875.
24	W.	Sir Winston Churchill d. 1965.
25	Th.	**Conversion of St. Paul.** Robert Burns b. 1759.
26	F.	Proclamation of Republic of India, 1950.
27	S.	Mozart b. 1756. Verdi d. 1901.
28	S.	**4th S. after Epiphany.** Charlemagne d. 814.
29	M.	Thomas Paine b. 1737. Robert Frost d. 1963.
30	Tu.	Mahatma Gandhi assas. 1948.
31	W.	Franz Schubert b. 1797. Anna Pavlova b. 1885.

PHENOMENA

d h	
2 18	Neptune in conjunction with Sun.
4 17	Earth at perihelion (147 million km.).
6 21	Saturn in conjunction with Sun.
9 02	Mercury in inferior conjunction.
10 01	Jupiter in conjunction with Moon. Jupiter 4°S.
10 11	Saturn in conjunction with Mercury. Saturn 3°S.
18 23	Venus in inferior conjunction.
23 15	Mars in conjunction with Moon. Mars 4°N.
24 20	Mercury in conjunction with Moon. Mercury 5°N.
25 10	Saturn in conjunction with Moon. Saturn 3°N.
25 21	Venus in conjunction with Moon. Venus 9°N.

CONSTELLATIONS

The following constellations are near the meridian at

	d h		d h
Dec. 1	24	Dec. 16	23
Jan. 1	22	Jan. 16	21
Feb. 1	20	Feb. 15	19

Draco (below the Pole), Ursa Minor (below the Pole), Camelopardus, Perseus, Auriga, Taurus, Orion, Eridanus and Lepus.

MINIMA OF ALGOL

d	h	d	h
3	17	18	01
6	14	20	22
9	11	23	19
12	07	26	15
15	04	29	12

*Centenary

PHASES OF THE MOON

	d h m
☽ First Quarter	4 10 40
○ Full Moon	11 04 57
☾ Last Quarter	18 21 17
● New Moon	26 19 20

	d h
Perigee (366,980 kilometres)	7 19
Apogee (404,490 „)	19 16

Mean Longitude of Ascending Node on Jan. 1, 318°.

MONTHLY NOTES

Jan.   1. Bank Holiday in England, Wales, Scotland and Northern Ireland.

2. Bank Holiday, Scotland.

26. Australia Day. Republic Day, India.

27. Ancient Chinese New Year (Year of the Horse).

Day	Right Ascension	Dec. −	Equation of Time	Rise 52°	Rise 56°	Transit	Set 52°	Set 56°	Sidereal Time	Transit of First Point of Aries
	h m s	° '	m s	h m	h m	h m	h m	h m	h m s	h m s
1	18 44 50	23 03	− 3 17	8 08	8 31	12 04	15 59	15 36	6 41 33	17 15 37
2	18 49 15	22 58	− 3 46	8 08	8 31	12 04	16 00	15 37	6 45 29	17 11 41
3	18 53 39	22 52	− 4 14	8 08	8 31	12 04	16 01	15 38	6 49 26	17 07 45
4	18 58 04	22 46	− 4 41	8 08	8 30	12 05	16 02	15 40	6 53 22	17 03 49
5	19 02 27	22 40	− 5 08	8 07	8 30	12 05	16 04	15 41	6 57 19	16 59 53
6	19 06 51	22 33	− 5 35	8 07	8 29	12 06	16 05	15 43	7 01 16	16 55 58
7	19 11 14	22 26	− 6 02	8 07	8 29	12 06	16 06	15 44	7 05 12	16 52 02
8	19 15 36	22 18	− 6 27	8 06	8 28	12 07	16 07	15 46	7 09 09	16 48 06
9	19 19 58	22 10	− 6 53	8 06	8 27	12 07	16 09	15 47	7 13 05	16 44 10
10	19 24 19	22 02	− 7 17	8 05	8 26	12 07	16 10	15 49	7 17 02	16 40 14
11	19 28 40	21 53	− 7 42	8 04	8 26	12 08	16 12	15 51	7 20 58	16 36 18
12	19 33 00	21 43	− 8 05	8 04	8 25	12 08	16 13	15 52	7 24 55	16 32 22
13	19 37 20	21 34	− 8 28	8 03	8 24	12 09	16 15	15 54	7 28 51	16 28 26
14	19 41 39	21 23	− 8 51	8 02	8 23	12 09	16 16	15 56	7 32 48	16 24 30
15	19 45 57	21 13	− 9 12	8 01	8 22	12 09	16 18	15 58	7 36 45	16 20 34
16	19 50 15	21 02	− 9 33	8 01	8 20	12 10	16 19	16 00	7 40 41	16 16 38
17	19 54 32	20 50	− 9 54	8 00	8 19	12 10	16 21	16 01	7 44 38	16 12 43
18	19 58 48	20 38	−10 14	7 59	8 18	12 10	16 23	16 03	7 48 34	16 08 47
19	20 03 03	20 26	−10 33	7 58	8 17	12 11	16 24	16 05	7 52 31	16 04 51
20	20 07 18	20 14	−10 51	7 57	8 15	12 11	16 26	16 07	7 56 27	16 00 55
21	20 11 33	20 01	−11 09	7 55	8 14	12 11	16 28	16 09	8 00 24	15 56 59
22	20 15 46	19 47	−11 26	7 54	8 12	12 12	16 29	16 11	8 04 20	15 53 03
23	20 19 59	19 33	−11 42	7 53	8 11	12 12	16 31	16 13	8 08 17	15 49 07
24	20 24 11	19 19	−11 57	7 52	8 09	12 12	16 33	16 15	8 12 14	15 45 11
25	20 28 22	19 05	−12 12	7 51	8 08	12 12	16 35	16 17	8 16 10	15 41 15
26	20 32 32	18 50	−12 26	7 49	8 06	12 13	16 36	16 20	8 20 07	15 37 19
27	20 36 42	18 35	−12 39	7 48	8 04	12 13	16 38	16 22	8 24 03	15 33 23
28	20 40 51	18 19	−12 51	7 46	8 03	12 13	16 40	16 24	8 28 00	15 29 27
29	20 44 59	18 03	−13 02	7 45	8 01	12 13	16 42	16 26	8 31 56	15 25 32
30	20 49 06	17 47	−13 13	7 44	7 59	12 13	16 44	16 28	8 35 53	15 21 36
31	20 53 12	17 31	−13 22	7 42	7 57	12 13	16 46	16 30	8 39 50	15 17 40

Duration of Civil (C), Nautical (N), and Astronomical (A), Twilight (in minutes)

Lat.	Jan. 1 C	N	A	Jan. 11 C	N	A	Jan. 21 C	N	A	Jan. 31 C	N	A
°												
52	41	84	125	40	82	123	38	80	120	37	78	117
56	47	96	141	45	93	138	43	90	134	41	87	130

ASTRONOMICAL NOTES

MERCURY is unsuitably placed for observation at first, inferior conjunction occurring on the 9th. For the last ten days of the month Mercury may be glimpsed as a difficult morning object, magnitude +0·6 to 0·0, low above the south-eastern horizon at about the time of beginning of morning civil twilight. Despite the fact that it is at greatest western elongation on February 1st it is not very well placed for observation, since its declination is − 21°. The old crescent Moon will be near Mercury on the mornings of the 24th and 25th.

VENUS, magnitude −4, is a brilliant object in the south-western sky in the early evening for the first half of the month but rapidly drawing closer to the Sun. A few days after inferior conjunction, which occurs on the 18th, it becomes visible in the mornings before dawn, low above the E.S.E. horizon. Both in the evening and morning apparitions Venus exhibits a slender crescent appearance in the telescope.

MARS, magnitude +1·5, is a morning object, low above the south-eastern horizon, visible by about the time of beginning of morning nautical twilight. During the month Mars moves from Ophiuchus into Sagittarius.

JUPITER, magnitude −2·7, is only just past opposition, and therefore visible as a brilliant object for most of the night. The Moon, only 1 day before Full, passes 4°N. of the planet on the night of the 9–10th. Jupiter is in the western part of Gemini.

SATURN is in conjunction with the Sun on the 6th and thus unsuitably placed for observation.

ECLIPSE. An annular eclipse of the Sun occurs on the 26th. See page 74 for details.

THE MOON

Day	R.A.	Dec.	Hor. Par.	Semi-diam.	Sun's Co-long.	P.A. of Bright Limb	Phase	Age	Rise 52°	Rise 56°	Transit	Set 52°	Set 56°
	h m	°	'	'	°	°		d	h m	h m	h m	h m	h m
1	21 54	−11.8	57.6	15.7	321	249	15	3.9	10 22	10 30	15 42	21 18	21 12
2	22 43	− 5.9	58.0	15.8	334	247	24	4.9	10 35	10 37	16 28	22 39	22 39
3	23 32	+ 0.4	58.5	15.9	346	246	34	5.9	10 47	10 45	17 15	—	—
4	0 21	+ 6.7	58.9	16.0	358	246	45	6.9	11 01	10 53	18 04	0 02	0 08
5	1 13	+12.8	59.2	16.1	10	248	56	7.9	11 17	11 03	18 55	1 27	1 39
6	2 07	+18.3	59.5	16.2	22	252	68	8.9	11 38	11 17	19 51	2 55	3 15
7	3 06	+22.8	59.7	16.3	34	257	78	9.9	12 07	11 39	20 51	4 25	4 52
8	4 07	+26.0	59.7	16.3	46	264	87	10.9	12 50	12 16	21 53	5 50	6 23
9	5 12	+27.4	59.6	16.2	59	273	94	11.9	13 50	13 14	22 57	7 02	7 38
10	6 16	+27.0	59.3	16.2	71	284	98	12.9	15 05	14 34	23 58	7 56	8 28
11	7 19	+24.8	58.8	16.0	83	321	100	13.9	16 30	16 05	—	8 32	8 58
12	8 17	+21.1	58.2	15.9	95	95	99	14.9	17 55	17 37	0 54	8 58	9 16
13	9 11	+16.4	57.5	15.7	107	107	96	15.9	19 16	19 05	1 46	9 16	9 29
14	10 01	+11.0	56.7	15.5	119	112	91	16.9	20 34	20 28	2 33	9 30	9 37
15	10 47	+ 5.3	56.0	15.3	131	114	84	17.9	21 48	21 48	3 16	9 42	9 44
16	11 32	− 0.4	55.4	15.1	143	115	76	18.9	23 00	23 05	3 58	9 53	9 50
17	12 15	− 6.0	54.8	14.9	156	115	68	19.9	—	—	4 38	10 04	9 57
18	12 59	−11.3	54.5	14.8	168	113	59	20.9	0 11	0 21	5 19	10 16	10 04
19	13 44	−16.1	54.2	14.8	180	111	49	21.9	1 23	1 39	6 02	10 30	10 13
20	14 30	−20.3	54.2	14.8	192	107	40	22.9	2 35	2 57	6 46	10 49	10 26
21	15 19	−23.7	54.4	14.8	204	103	31	23.9	3 48	4 16	7 34	11 14	10 45
22	16 11	−26.1	54.7	14.9	216	97	22	24.9	4 57	5 30	8 24	11 48	11 14
23	17 05	−27.4	55.1	15.0	229	91	15	25.9	5 58	6 34	9 17	12 36	12 00
24	18 01	−27.2	55.6	15.2	241	84	8	26.9	6 47	7 22	10 11	13 39	13 05
25	18 58	−25.7	56.3	15.3	253	77	4	27.9	7 25	7 54	11 05	14 53	14 25
26	19 53	−22.8	56.9	15.5	265	69	1	28.9	7 52	8 14	11 58	16 15	15 54
27	20 47	−18.6	57.5	15.7	277	270	0	0.2	8 13	8 28	12 49	17 38	17 24
28	21 39	−13.4	58.0	15.8	290	249	2	1.2	8 29	8 39	13 38	19 02	18 54
29	22 30	− 7.5	58.5	15.9	302	245	6	2.2	8 42	8 47	14 26	20 25	20 23
30	23 20	− 1.1	58.8	16.0	314	243	12	3.2	8 55	8 54	15 13	21 49	21 53
31	0 10	+ 5.3	59.0	16.1	326	244	20	4.2	9 09	9 02	16 01	23 14	23 25

MERCURY ☿

Day	R.A.	Dec. −	Diam.	Phase	Transit		Day	R.A.	Dec. −	Diam.	Phase	Transit	5° high 52°	5° high 56°
	h m	°	"		h m			h m	°	"		h m	h m	h m
1	19 51	20.5	9	23	13 06		16	18 47	19.7	9	16	11 03	7 34	8 00
4	19 44	19.8	9	10	12 46	Mercury is too	19	18 42	20.0	9	27	10 47	7 21	7 48
7	19 30	19.4	10	2	12 20	close to the	22	18 42	20.4	8	37	10 37	7 13	7 41
10	19 13	19.3	10	1	11 52	Sun for	25	18 48	20.9	8	46	10 31	7 10	7 39
13	18 58	19.4	10	6	11 25	observation	28	18 56	21.2	7	54	10 28	7 10	7 40
16	18 47	19.7	9	16	11 03		31	19 08	21.4	7	60	10 28	7 12	7 43

VENUS ♀   MARS ♂

Day	R.A.	Dec. −	Diam.	Phase	Transit	5° high 52°	56°	Day	R.A.	Dec. −	Diam.	Phase	Transit	5° high 52°	56°
	h m	°	"		h m	h m	h m		h m	°	"		h m	h m	h m
1	20 33	17.0	54	10	13 49	17 38	17 17	1	16 32	21.9	4	97	9 50	6 38	7 09
6	20 27	16.0	58	6	13 23	17 19	16 59	6	16 47	22.5	4	97	9 45	6 38	7 11
11	20 18	15.2	61	3	12 53	16 54	16 35	11	17 02	22.9	4	97	9 41	6 37	7 12
16	20 05	14.7	62	1	12 21	16 27	16 07	16	17 18	23.3	4	96	9 37	6 36	7 12
21	19 52	14.3	62	1	11 49	15 55	15 37	21	17 33	23.6	4	96	9 32	6 34	7 12
26	19 41	14.2	60	3	11 18	15 24	15 07	26	17 49	23.7	4	96	9 28	6 32	7 10
31	19 32	14.3	58	6	10 49	14 56	14 38	31	18 04	23.8	4	95	9 24	6 29	7 07

SUNRISE AND SUNSET

Day	London a.m. h m	London p.m. h m	Bristol a.m. h m	Bristol p.m. h m	Birmingham a.m. h m	Birmingham p.m. h m	Manchester a.m. h m	Manchester p.m. h m	Newcastle a.m. h m	Newcastle p.m. h m	Glasgow a.m. h m	Glasgow p.m. h m	Belfast a.m. h m	Belfast p.m. h m
1	8 06	4 01	8 16	4 12	8 18	4 03	8 25	4 00	8 31	3 48	8 48	3 54	8 47	4 08
2	8 06	4 02	8 16	4 13	8 18	4 04	8 25	4 01	8 31	3 49	8 48	3 55	8 47	4 09
3	8 06	4 03	8 16	4 14	8 18	4 05	8 25	4 02	8 31	3 50	8 47	3 56	8 47	4 10
4	8 06	4 05	8 16	4 15	8 18	4 06	8 25	4 03	8 31	3 51	8 47	3 57	8 47	4 11
5	8 06	4 06	8 15	4 16	8 17	4 08	8 24	4 05	8 30	3 53	8 46	3 59	8 46	4 13
6	8 05	4 07	8 15	4 17	8 17	4 09	8 24	4 06	8 30	3 54	8 46	4 00	8 46	4 14
7	8 05	4 08	8 15	4 19	8 17	4 10	8 24	4 07	8 29	3 56	8 45	4 02	8 45	4 16
8	8 05	4 09	8 15	4 20	8 16	4 12	8 23	4 09	8 29	3 57	8 45	4 03	8 45	4 17
9	8 04	4 10	8 14	4 21	8 15	4 13	8 22	4 10	8 28	3 59	8 44	4 05	8 44	4 19
10	8 04	4 12	8 13	4 23	8 15	4 15	8 22	4 12	8 27	4 00	8 43	4 06	8 43	4 20
11	8 03	4 13	8 13	4 24	8 14	4 16	8 21	4 13	8 26	4 02	8 42	4 08	8 42	4 22
12	8 02	4 14	8 12	4 25	8 13	4 17	8 20	4 14	8 26	4 04	8 42	4 10	8 42	4 24
13	8 02	4 16	8 12	4 27	8 13	4 19	8 20	4 16	8 25	4 05	8 41	4 11	8 41	4 25
14	8 01	4 18	8 11	4 28	8 12	4 21	8 19	4 18	8 24	4 07	8 40	4 13	8 40	4 27
15	8 00	4 19	8 10	4 30	8 11	4 22	8 18	4 19	8 23	4 09	8 39	4 15	8 39	4 29
16	7 59	4 21	8 09	4 31	8 10	4 24	8 17	4 21	8 22	4 10	8 38	4 17	8 38	4 30
17	7 58	4 22	8 08	4 33	8 09	4 25	8 16	4 22	8 21	4 12	8 36	4 19	8 37	4 32
18	7 58	4 24	8 08	4 34	8 09	4 27	8 16	4 24	8 20	4 14	8 35	4 20	8 36	4 34
19	7 57	4 26	8 07	4 36	8 08	4 29	8 14	4 26	8 18	4 16	8 34	4 22	8 34	4 36
20	7 56	4 27	8 06	4 37	8 07	4 30	8 13	4 27	8 17	4 17	8 32	4 24	8 33	4 37
21	7 54	4 29	8 04	4 39	8 05	4 32	8 12	4 29	8 16	4 19	8 31	4 26	8 32	4 39
22	7 53	4 31	8 03	4 41	8 04	4 34	8 11	4 31	8 15	4 21	8 30	4 28	8 31	4 41
23	7 52	4 32	8 02	4 42	8 03	4 35	8 09	4 33	8 13	4 23	8 28	4 30	8 29	4 43
24	7 51	4 34	8 01	4 44	8 02	4 37	8 08	4 35	8 11	4 26	8 26	4 33	8 28	4 45
25	7 50	4 36	8 00	4 46	8 01	4 39	8 07	4 37	8 10	4 28	8 25	4 35	8 27	4 47
26	7 48	4 38	7 58	4 48	7 59	4 41	8 05	4 39	8 08	4 30	8 23	4 37	8 25	4 49
27	7 47	4 40	7 57	4 50	7 58	4 43	8 04	4 41	8 07	4 32	8 22	4 39	8 24	4 51
28	7 46	4 41	7 56	4 51	7 57	4 44	8 02	4 43	8 05	4 34	8 20	4 41	8 22	4 53
29	7 44	4 43	7 54	4 53	7 55	4 46	8 01	4 45	8 04	4 36	8 18	4 43	8 20	4 55
30	7 43	4 45	7 53	4 55	7 54	4 48	7 59	4 47	8 02	4 38	8 16	4 45	8 18	4 57
31	7 41	4 47	7 51	4 57	7 52	4 50	7 57	4 49	8 00	4 40	8 15	4 47	8 17	4 59

JUPITER ♃   SATURN ♄

Day	R.A. h m	Dec. + °	Transit h m	5° high 52° h m	5° high 56° h m	R.A. h m	Dec. - °	Transit h m	
1	6 23	23·2	23 27	7 13	7 31	19 08	22·2	12 24	Saturn is too
11	6 17	23·3	22 52	6 28	6 47	19 13	22·1	11 50	close to the
21	6 12	23·3	22 08	5 44	6 03	19 18	22·0	11 16	Sun for
31	6 08	23·4	21 24	5 01	5 20	19 23	21·8	10 41	observation

Equatorial diameter of Jupiter 46″; of Saturn 15″.   Diameters of Saturn's rings 34″ and 14″.

URANUS ⛢   NEPTUNE ♆

Day	R.A. h m	Dec. - ° ′	Transit h m	10° high 52° h m	10° high 56° h m	R.A. h m	Dec. - ° ′	Transit h m	10° high 52° h m	10° high 56° h m
1	18 25·1	23 35	11 42	9 42	11 04	18 51·9	22 03	12 08	9 50	10 46
11	18 27·7	23 34	11 05	9 05	10 26	18 53·6	22 01	11 31	9 12	10 08
21	18 30·2	23 32	10 28	8 28	9 48	18 55·2	21 59	10 53	8 34	9 29
31	18 32·6	23 30	9 51	7 51	9 10	18 56·7	21 57	10 15	7 56	8 51

Diameter 4″   Diameter 2″

DAY OF		
Month	Week	

Februa, Roman festival
of Purification
Sun's Longitude 330° ♓ 18ᵈ 22ʰ

1	Th.	Mary Wollstonecraft Shelley d. 1851.
2	F.	**Presentation of Christ.** Bertrand Russell d. 1970.
3	S.	Beau Nash d. 1762. Lord Salisbury b. 1830.
4	S.	**5th S. after Epiphany.** Carlyle d. 1881.
5	M.	Robert Peel b. 1788. Sir John Pritchard b. 1921.
6	Tu.	QUEEN'S ACCESSION 1952. Queen Anne b. 1665.
7	W.	Charles Dickens b. 1812. Ann Radcliffe d. 1823.
8	Th.	John Ruskin b. 1819.
9	F.	Alban Berg b. 1885. Jim Laker b. 1922.
10	S.	Boris Pasternak b. 1890*. Röntgen d. 1923.
11	S.	**9th S. before Easter.** John Buchan d. 1940.
12	M.	Darwin b. 1809. Abraham Lincoln b. 1809.
13	Tu.	Dame Christabel Pankhurst d. 1958.
14	W.	VALENTINE'S DAY. P. G. Wodehouse d. 1975.
15	Th.	Galileo b. 1564. Jeremy Bentham b. 1748.
16	F.	Sir Geraint Evans b. 1922.
17	S.	Molière d. 1673. Graham Sutherland d. 1980.
18	S.	**8th S. before Easter.** Paganini b. 1784.
19	M.	DUKE OF YORK b. 1960. Copernicus b. 1473.
20	Tu.	Spinoza d. 1677. Marie Rambert b. 1888.
21	W.	Nicolai Gogol d. 1852. W. H. Auden b. 1907.
22	Th.	George Washington b. 1732. Chopin b. 1810.
23	F.	Samuel Pepys b. 1633. Joshua Reynolds b. 1792.
24	S.	Wilhelm Grimm b. 1786.
25	S.	**7th S. before Easter.** Anthony Burgess b. 1917.
26	M.	Victor Hugo b. 1802. Sir Harry Lauder d. 1950.
27	Tu.	SHROVE TUESDAY. Labour Party founded 1900.
28	W.	**Ash Wednesday.** Stephen Spender b. 1909.

*Centenary

PHENOMENA

d h
1 01 Mercury at greatest elongation W. 25°.
3 15 Saturn in conjunction with Mercury. Saturn 0°2S.
5 01 Venus in conjunction with Mercury. Venus 7°N.
6 04 Jupiter in conjunction with Moon. Jupiter 4°S.
21 16 Mars in conjunction with Moon. Mars 2°N.
22 01 Saturn in conjunction with Moon. Saturn 2°N.
22 07 Venus in conjunction with Moon. Venus 8°N.
22 13 Venus at greatest brilliancy.
24 00 Mercury in conjunction with Moon. Mercury 2°S.
28 23 Saturn in conjunction with Mars. Saturn 1°N.

CONSTELLATIONS

The following constellations are near the meridian at

	d	h		d	h
Jan.	1	24	Jan.	16	23
Feb.	1	22	Feb.	15	21
Mar.	1	20	Mar.	16	19

Draco (below the Pole), Camelopardus, Auriga, Taurus, Gemini, Orion, Canis Minor, Monoceros, Lepus, Canis Major and Puppis.

MINIMA OF ALGOL

d	h	d	h
1	09	15	17
4	06	18	14
7	03	21	11
10	00	24	08
12	20	27	04

PHASES OF THE MOON

	d	h	m
☽ First Quarter	2	18	32
○ Full Moon	9	19	16
☾ Last Quarter	17	18	48
● New Moon	25	08	54

		d	h
Perigee (370,180 kilometres)		2	03
Apogee (404,510 ")		16	13
Perigee (365,730 ")		28	08

Mean Longitude of Ascending Node on Feb. 1, 317°

MONTHLY NOTES

Feb. 1. Pheasant and partridge shooting ends.

6. National Day, New Zealand.

28. First day of Lent

Day	Right Ascension	Dec. −	Equation of Time	THE SUN s.d. 16′·2 Rise 52°	Rise 56°	Transit	Set 52°	Set 56°	Sidereal Time	Transit of First Point of Aries
	h m s	° ′	m s	h m	h m	h m	h m	h m	h m s	h m s
1	20 57 17	17 14	− 13 31	7 40	7 55	12 14	16 47	16 32	8 43 46	15 13 44
2	21 01 22	16 57	− 13 39	7 39	7 54	12 14	16 49	16 35	8 47 43	15 09 48
3	21 05 26	16 40	− 13 47	7 37	7 52	12 14	16 51	16 37	8 51 39	15 05 52
4	21 09 29	16 22	− 13 53	7 36	7 50	12 14	16 53	16 39	8 55 36	15 01 56
5	21 13 31	16 04	− 13 59	7 34	7 48	12 14	16 55	16 41	8 59 32	14 58 00
6	21 17 32	15 46	− 14 03	7 32	7 46	12 14	16 57	16 43	9 03 29	14 54 04
7	21 21 33	15 27	− 14 07	7 30	7 44	12 14	16 59	16 46	9 07 25	14 50 08
8	21 25 32	15 09	− 14 10	7 29	7 41	12 14	17 00	16 48	9 11 22	14 46 12
9	21 29 31	14 50	− 14 13	7 27	7 39	12 14	17 02	16 50	9 15 19	14 42 17
10	21 33 29	14 30	− 14 14	7 25	7 37	12 14	17 04	16 52	9 19 15	14 38 21
11	21 37 27	14 11	− 14 15	7 23	7 35	12 14	17 06	16 54	9 23 12	14 34 25
12	21 41 23	13 51	− 14 15	7 21	7 33	12 14	17 08	16 57	9 27 08	14 30 29
13	21 45 19	13 31	− 14 14	7 20	7 31	12 14	17 10	16 59	9 31 05	14 26 33
14	21 49 14	13 11	− 14 13	7 18	7 28	12 14	17 12	17 01	9 35 01	14 22 37
15	21 53 08	12 50	− 14 10	7 16	7 26	12 14	17 13	17 03	9 38 58	14 18 41
16	21 57 02	12 30	− 14 07	7 14	7 24	12 14	17 15	17 05	9 42 54	14 14 45
17	22 00 55	12 09	− 14 04	7 12	7 21	12 14	17 17	17 08	9 46 51	14 10 49
18	22 04 47	11 48	− 13 59	7 10	7 19	12 14	17 19	17 10	9 50 48	14 06 53
19	22 08 38	11 27	− 13 54	7 08	7 17	12 14	17 21	17 12	9 54 44	14 02 57
20	22 12 29	11 05	− 13 49	7 06	7 14	12 14	17 23	17 14	9 58 41	13 59 02
21	22 16 20	10 44	− 13 42	7 04	7 12	12 14	17 25	17 16	10 02 37	13 55 06
22	22 20 09	10 22	− 13 35	7 02	7 10	12 14	17 26	17 18	10 06 34	13 51 10
23	22 23 58	10 00	− 13 28	6 59	7 07	12 13	17 28	17 21	10 10 30	13 47 14
24	22 27 46	9 38	− 13 20	6 57	7 05	12 13	17 30	17 23	10 14 27	13 43 18
25	22 31 34	9 16	− 13 11	6 55	7 02	12 13	17 32	17 25	10 18 23	13 39 22
26	22 35 21	8 54	− 13 01	6 53	7 00	12 13	17 34	17 27	10 22 20	13 35 26
27	22 39 08	8 31	− 12 51	6 51	6 57	12 13	17 36	17 29	10 26 17	13 31 30
28	22 42 54	8 09	− 12 41	6 49	6 55	12 13	17 37	17 31	10 30 13	13 27 34

Duration of Civil (C), Nautical (N), and Astronomical (A), Twilight (in minutes)

Lat. °	Feb. 1 C	N	A	Feb. 11 C	N	A	Feb. 21 C	N	A	Feb. 28 C	N	A
52	37	77	117	35	75	114	34	74	113	34	73	112
56	41	86	130	39	83	126	38	81	125	38	81	124

ASTRONOMICAL NOTES

MERCURY is unsuitably placed for observation throughout the month.

VENUS, magnitude − 4·6, is a brilliant object in the morning skies, visible in the E.S.E. before dawn. Telescopically it appears as a thin crescent waxing noticeably during the month as the area illuminated increases from 6 per cent to 30 per cent. On the morning of the 22nd the old crescent Moon passes 8°S. of the planet.

MARS continues to be visible as a morning object, magnitude + 1·3. However it is now at a declination of − 24°, and will be quite difficult to detect, low above the south-eastern horizon, about an hour before sunrise.

JUPITER continues to be visible as a brilliant object for most of the night, magnitude − 2·5. Even by the end of the month it can still be seen in the western sky after 03h. The gibbous Moon will be seen approaching the planet on the night of the 5-6th, passing 4°N. of it as the two bodies are setting in the west.

SATURN is too close to the Sun for observation during February.

ECLIPSE. A total eclipse of the Moon, visible from the British Isles, occurs on the 9th. See page 74 for details.

ZODIACAL LIGHT. The evening cone may be observed in the western sky after the end of twilight from the 11th to the 25th. This faint phenomenon is only visible under good conditions in the absence of both moonlight and artificial lighting.

THE MOON

Day	R.A.	Dec.	Hor. Par.	Semi-diam.	Sun's Co-long.	P.A. of Bright Limb	Phase	Age	Rise 52°	Rise 56°	Tran-sit	Set 52°	Set 56°
	h m	°	′	′	°	°		d	h m	h m	h m	h m	h m
1	1 01	+11·6	59·2	16·1	338	245	30	5·2	9 24	9 12	16 52	—	—
2	1 55	+17·2	59·2	16·1	350	249	41	6·2	9 43	9 24	17 46	0 42	0 59
3	2 51	+21·9	59·2	16·1	3	253	53	7·2	10 08	9 43	18 43	2 10	2 35
4	3 51	+25·4	59·1	16·1	15	259	64	8·2	10 45	10 13	19 43	3 35	4 07
5	4 53	+27·2	58·9	16·1	27	266	74	9·2	11 37	11 01	20 45	4 51	5 26
6	5 56	+27·3	58·7	16·0	39	273	84	10·2	12 45	12 11	21 45	5 49	6 24
7	6 58	+25·7	58·3	15·9	51	280	91	11·2	14 05	13 37	22 42	6 31	7 00
8	7 56	+22·6	57·9	15·8	63	286	96	12·2	15 29	15 08	23 35	7 00	7 22
9	8 51	+18·3	57·4	15·6	75	289	99	13·2	16 51	16 38	—	7 20	7 36
10	9 42	+13·1	56·9	15·5	88	124	100	14·2	18 11	18 03	0 23	7 36	7 45
11	10 30	+ 7·5	56·3	15·3	100	119	98	15·2	19 26	19 24	1 09	7 48	7 53
12	11 15	+ 1·7	55·7	15·2	112	119	95	16·2	20 40	20 43	1 51	8 00	8 00
13	11 59	− 4·0	55·2	15·0	124	118	90	17·2	21 52	22 00	2 33	8 11	8 06
14	12 43	− 9·5	54·7	14·9	136	117	83	18·2	23 05	23 18	3 14	8 22	8 13
15	13 28	−14·5	54·4	14·8	148	115	75	19·2	—	—	3 56	8 36	8 21
16	14 14	−19·0	54·2	14·8	160	111	67	20·2	0 17	0 37	4 40	8 52	8 32
17	15 02	−22·7	54·2	14·8	173	107	58	21·2	1 30	1 55	5 26	9 14	8 48
18	15 53	−25·4	54·4	14·8	185	102	48	22·2	2 40	3 12	6 14	9 44	9 12
19	16 46	−27·1	54·7	14·9	197	96	39	23·2	3 44	4 20	7 06	10 26	9 49
20	17 40	−27·5	55·2	15·0	209	90	29	24·2	4 39	5 15	7 59	11 21	10 45
21	18 36	−26·5	55·9	15·2	221	84	21	25·2	5 21	5 53	8 53	12 30	11 58
22	19 32	−24·1	56·6	15·4	234	79	13	26·2	5 52	6 18	9 46	13 48	13 24
23	20 26	−20·4	57·4	15·6	246	74	7	27·2	6 16	6 34	10 38	15 11	14 54
24	21 19	−15·5	58·2	15·8	258	73	2	28·2	6 34	6 46	11 28	16 36	16 25
25	22 11	− 9·8	58·9	16·0	270	85	0	29·2	6 49	6 56	12 17	18 01	17 57
26	23 02	− 3·4	59·4	16·2	282	230	1	0·6	7 02	7 04	13 06	19 27	19 29
27	23 54	+ 3·2	59·8	16·3	295	238	4	1·6	7 16	7 12	13 55	20 55	21 03
28	0 46	+ 9·8	59·9	16·3	307	241	9	2·6	7 31	7 21	14 46	22 24	22 39

MERCURY ☿

Day	R.A.	Dec. −	Diam.	Phase	Tran-sit		Day	R.A.	Dec. −	Diam.	Phase	Tran-sit	
	h m	°	″		h m			h m	°	″		h m	
1	19 12	21·5	—	—	10 29		16	20 33	20·1	—	—	10 51	
4	19 26	21·5	—	—	10 31	Mercury is too	19	20 51	19·2	—	—	10 57	Mercury is too
7	19 41	21·4	—	—	10 35	close to the	22	21 09	18·2	—	—	11 04	close to the
10	19 58	21·2	—	—	10 39	Sun for	25	21 28	17·0	—	—	11 11	Sun for
13	20 15	20·7	—	—	10 45	observation	28	21 47	15·5	—	—	11 18	observation
16	20 33	20·1	—	—	10 51		31	22 07	13·9	—	—	11 21	

VENUS ♀

Day	R.A.	Dec. −	Diam.	Phase	Tran-sit	5° high. 52°	5° high. 56°
	h m	°	″		h m	h m	h m
1	19 30	14·3	56	7	10 44	6 38	6 56
6	19 26	14·5	53	11	10 21	6 16	6 34
11	19 27	14·8	49	15	10 02	5 59	6 17
16	19 31	15·1	45	20	9 47	5 46	6 04
21	19 39	15·4	42	24	9 35	5 35	5 54
26	19 49	15·5	38	28	9 26	5 27	5 47
31	20 02	15·6	35	32	9 20	5 21	5 40

MARS ♂

Day	R.A.	Dec. −	Diam.	Phase	Tran-sit	5° high. 52°	5° high. 56°
	h m	°	″		h m	h m	h m
1	18 08	23·8	4	95	9 24	6 28	7 06
6	18 23	23·8	5	95	9 20	6 24	7 02
11	18 39	23·7	5	95	9 16	6 18	6 56
16	18 55	23·4	5	94	9 12	6 12	6 49
21	19 11	23·1	5	94	9 08	6 06	6 41
26	19 27	22·7	5	94	9 04	5 58	6 32
31	19 42	22·2	5	93	9 00	5 49	6 22

SUNRISE AND SUNSET

Day	London a.m. h m	London p.m. h m	Bristol a.m. h m	Bristol p.m. h m	Birmingham a.m. h m	Birmingham p.m. h m	Manchester a.m. h m	Manchester p.m. h m	Newcastle a.m. h m	Newcastle p.m. h m	Glasgow a.m. h m	Glasgow p.m. h m	Belfast a.m. h m	Belfast p.m. h m
1	7 40	4 49	7 50	4 59	7 51	4 52	7 56	4 51	7 59	4 42	8 13	4 50	8 15	5 02
2	7 39	4 52	7 48	5 00	7 49	4 54	7 54	4 53	7 57	4 44	8 11	4 52	8 13	5 04
3	7 37	4 52	7 46	5 02	7 47	4 56	7 52	4 55	7 55	4 46	8 09	4 54	8 11	5 06
4	7 36	4 54	7 45	5 04	7 46	4 58	7 51	4 57	7 53	4 48	8 07	4 56	8 10	5 08
5	7 34	4 56	7 43	5 06	7 44	5 00	7 49	4 59	7 51	4 50	8 05	4 58	8 08	5 10
6	7 32	4 58	7 42	5 08	7 42	5 02	7 47	5 01	7 49	4 52	8 03	5 00	8 06	5 12
7	7 31	4 59	7 40	5 09	7 40	5 04	7 45	5 03	7 47	4 55	8 01	5 03	8 04	5 14
8	7 29	5 01	7 38	5 11	7 38	5 06	7 43	5 05	7 45	4 57	7 59	5 05	8 02	5 16
9	7 27	5 03	7 37	5 13	7 36	5 08	7 41	5 07	7 43	4 59	7 57	5 07	8 00	5 18
10	7 25	5 04	7 35	5 14	7 34	5 09	7 39	5 08	7 41	5 01	7 55	5 09	7 58	5 20
11	7 23	5 06	7 33	5 16	7 32	5 11	7 37	5 10	7 39	5 03	7 53	5 11	7 56	5 22
12	7 22	5 08	7 32	5 18	7 31	5 13	7 36	5 12	7 37	5 05	7 51	5 13	7 54	5 24
13	7 20	5 10	7 30	5 20	7 29	5 15	7 34	5 14	7 35	5 07	7 49	5 15	7 52	5 26
14	7 18	5 12	7 28	5 22	7 27	5 17	7 32	5 16	7 33	5 09	7 47	5 17	7 50	5 28
15	7 16	5 14	7 26	5 24	7 25	5 19	7 30	5 18	7 31	5 11	7 45	5 19	7 48	5 30
16	7 14	5 15	7 24	5 25	7 23	5 20	7 28	5 20	7 28	5 13	7 42	5 21	7 46	5 32
17	7 12	5 17	7 22	5 27	7 21	5 22	7 26	5 22	7 26	5 16	7 40	5 24	7 44	5 34
18	7 10	5 19	7 20	5 29	7 19	5 24	7 24	5 24	7 24	5 18	7 38	5 26	7 42	5 36
19	7 08	5 21	7 18	5 31	7 17	5 26	7 21	5 26	7 21	5 20	7 35	5 28	7 39	5 38
20	7 06	5 23	7 16	5 33	7 15	5 28	7 19	5 28	7 19	5 22	7 33	5 30	7 37	5 40
21	7 04	5 25	7 14	5 35	7 13	5 30	7 17	5 30	7 17	5 24	7 31	5 32	7 35	5 42
22	7 02	5 27	7 12	5 37	7 11	5 32	7 15	5 32	7 15	5 26	7 28	5 35	7 32	5 45
23	7 00	5 28	7 10	5 38	7 09	5 33	7 12	5 34	7 12	5 28	7 26	5 37	7 30	5 47
24	6 58	5 30	7 08	5 40	7 07	5 35	7 10	5 36	7 10	5 30	7 23	5 39	7 27	5 49
25	6 55	5 32	7 05	5 42	7 04	5 37	7 08	5 38	7 08	5 32	7 21	5 41	7 25	5 51
26	6 53	5 34	7 03	5 44	7 02	5 39	7 06	5 40	7 05	5 34	7 18	5 43	7 23	5 53
27	6 51	5 36	7 01	5 46	7 00	5 41	7 03	5 42	7 03	5 36	7 16	5 45	7 20	5 55
28	6 49	5 37	6 59	5 47	6 58	5 43	7 01	5 44	7 00	5 38	7 13	5 47	7 18	5 57

JUPITER ♃ / SATURN ♄

Day	JUPITER R.A. h m	JUPITER Dec. + °	JUPITER Transit h m	5° high. 52° h m	5° high. 56° h m	SATURN R.A. h m	SATURN Dec. − °	SATURN Transit h m	
1	6 08	23·4	21 20	4 57	5 15	19 23	21·8	10 38	Saturn is too
11	6 05	23·4	20 38	4 15	4 34	19 28	21·7	10 03	close to the
21	6 04	23·4	19 58	3 35	3 53	19 32	21·5	9 28	Sun for
31	6 04	23·5	19 19	2 56	3 14	19 36	21·4	8 53	observation

Equatorial diameter of Jupiter 43″; of Saturn 15″. Diameters of Saturn's rings 35″ and 14″.

URANUS ♅ / NEPTUNE ♆

Day	URANUS R.A. h m	URANUS Dec. − ° ′	URANUS Transit h m	10° high. 52° h m	10° high. 56° h m	NEPTUNE R.A. h m	NEPTUNE Dec. − ° ′	NEPTUNE Transit h m	10° high. 52° h m	10° high. 56° h m
1	18 32·8	23 30	9 48	7 47	9 06	18 56·8	21 57	10 11	7 52	8 47
11	18 35·0	23 29	9 10	7 10	8 28	18 58·2	21 55	9 34	7 14	8 08
21	18 36·9	23 27	8 33	6 32	7 49	18 59·5	21 53	8 55	6 35	7 30
31	18 38·6	23 26	7 55	5 54	7 11	19 00·6	21 51	8 17	5 57	6 51

Diameter 4″   Diameter 2″

DAY OF		
Month	Week	*Mars*, Roman god of battle ♈ *Sun's Longitude* 0° ♈ 20ᵈ 21ʰ

1	Th.	ST. DAVID'S DAY. Dixie Dean d. 1980.
2	F.	Cardinal Archbishop of Westminster b. 1923.
3	S.	Alexander Graham Bell b. 1847.
4	S.	**1st S. in Lent.** Forth Railway Bridge opened
5	M.	Flora Macdonald d. 1790.* [1890.*
6	Tu.	Elizabeth Barrett Browning b. 1806.
7	W.	Sir John Frederick Herschel b. 1792.
8	Th.	Kenneth Grahame b. 1859.
9	F.	Comte de Mirabeau b. 1749.
10	S.	PRINCE EDWARD b. 1964. Dame Eva Turner b. 1892.
11	S.	**2nd S. in Lent.** Russian Revolution 1917.
12	M.	Vaslav Nijinsky b. 1890.*
13	Tu.	Joseph Priestley b. 1733.
14	W.	Albert Einstein b. 1879. Karl Marx 1883.
15	Th.	Julius Caesar assas. 44 B.C.
16	F.	Georg S. Ohm b. 1787. William Beveridge b. 1963.
17	S.	ST. PATRICK'S DAY. Margaret Bondfield b. 1873.
18	S.	**3rd S. in Lent.** Wilfred Owen b. 1893.
19	M.	St. Joseph of Nazareth. Diaghilev b. 1872.
20	Tu.	Henry IV d. 1413. Henrik Ibsen b. 1828.
21	W.	Johann Sebastian Bach b. 1685.
22	Th.	Goethe d. 1832. Stendhal d. 1842.
23	F.	Donald Campbell b. 1921.
24	S.	**The Annunciation.** William Morris b. 1834.
25	S.	**4th S. in Lent.** MOTHERING SUNDAY.
26	M.	Tennessee Williams b. 1912.
27	Tu.	James I d. 1625. Arnold Bennett d. 1931.
28	W.	Virginia Woolf d. 1941. Neil Kinnock b. 1942.
29	Th.	Swedenborg d. 1772. Vera Brittain d. 1970.
30	F.	Goya b. 1746. van Gogh b. 1853.
31	S.	John Donne d. 1631. Jesse Owens d. 1980.

*Centenary

PHENOMENA

d h
5 09 Jupiter in conjunction with Moon. Jupiter 4°S.
19 03 Mercury in superior conjunction.
20 21 Equinox.
21 15 Saturn in conjunction with Moon. Saturn 2°N.
22 18 Mars in conjunction with Moon. Mars 0°.4S.
23 08 Venus in conjunction with Moon. Venus 2°N.
27 10 Mercury in conjunction with Moon. Mercury 4°S.
30 07 Venus at greatest elongation W. 46°.

CONSTELLATIONS

The following are near the meridian at

	d h		d h
Feb.	1 24	Feb. 15	23
Mar.	1 22	Mar. 16	21
Apr.	1 20	Apr. 15	19

Cepheus (below the Pole), Camelopardus, Lynx, Gemini, Cancer, Leo, Canis Minor, Hydra, Monoceros, Canis Major and Puppis.

MINIMA OF ALGOL

d	h	d	h
2	01	19	06
4	22	22	03
7	19	25	00
10	16	27	21
13	12	30	17
16	09		

PHASES OF THE MOON

	d	h	m
☽ First Quarter	4	02	05
○ Full Moon	11	10	58
☾ Last Quarter	19	14	30
● New Moon	26	19	48

	d	h
Apogee (405,210 kilometres)	16	08
Perigee (360,560 ")	28	08

Mean Longitude of Ascending Node on March 1, 315°.

Summer Time in 1990 (*see* p. 72).—Begins: March 25ᵈ 01ʰ G.M.T.
Ends: October 28ᵈ 01ʰ G.M.T.

MONTHLY NOTES

March
12. Commonwealth Day.
17. Bank Holiday in Northern Ireland.
25. Lady Day. Quarter Day.
28. First day of Ramadân.
31. Financial year 1989–90 ends.

Day	Right Ascension	Dec.	Equation of Time	Rise 52°	Rise 56°	Transit	Set 52°	Set 56°	Sidereal Time	Transit of First Point of Aries
	h m s	° ′	m s	h m	h m	h m	h m	h m	h m s	h m s
1	22 46 39	−7 46	−12 30	6 47	6 52	12 12	17 39	17 34	10 34 10	13 23 38
2	22 50 24	−7 23	−12 18	6 44	6 50	12 12	17 41	17 36	10 38 06	13 19 42
3	22 54 09	−7 00	−12 06	6 42	6 47	12 12	17 43	17 38	10 42 03	13 15 47
4	22 57 53	−6 37	−11 54	6 40	6 45	12 12	17 45	17 40	10 45 59	13 11 51
5	23 01 36	−6 14	−11 40	6 38	6 42	12 12	17 46	17 42	10 49 56	13 07 55
6	23 05 19	−5 51	−11 27	6 35	6 40	12 11	17 48	17 44	10 53 52	13 03 59
7	23 09 02	−5 28	−11 13	6 33	6 37	12 11	17 50	17 46	10 57 49	13 00 03
8	23 12 44	−5 04	−10 58	6 31	6 34	12 11	17 52	17 48	11 01 45	12 56 07
9	23 16 26	−4 41	−10 44	6 29	6 32	12 11	17 53	17 50	11 05 42	12 52 11
10	23 20 07	−4 18	−10 29	6 26	6 29	12 10	17 55	17 52	11 09 39	12 48 15
11	23 23 48	−3 54	−10 13	6 24	6 27	12 10	17 57	17 55	11 13 35	12 44 19
12	23 27 29	−3 31	−9 57	6 22	6 24	12 10	17 59	17 57	11 17 32	12 40 23
13	23 31 09	−3 07	−9 41	6 20	6 22	12 10	18 00	17 59	11 21 28	12 36 27
14	23 34 49	−2 43	−9 25	6 17	6 19	12 09	18 02	18 01	11 25 25	12 32 32
15	23 38 29	−2 20	−9 08	6 15	6 16	12 09	18 04	18 03	11 29 21	12 28 36
16	23 42 09	−1 56	−8 51	6 13	6 14	12 09	18 06	18 05	11 33 18	12 24 40
17	23 45 48	−1 32	−8 34	6 10	6 11	12 08	18 07	18 07	11 37 14	12 20 44
18	23 49 27	−1 09	−8 16	6 08	6 08	12 08	18 09	18 09	11 41 11	12 16 48
19	23 53 07	−0 45	−7 59	6 06	6 06	12 08	18 11	18 11	11 45 08	12 12 52
20	23 56 45	−0 21	−7 41	6 03	6 03	12 08	18 13	18 13	11 49 04	12 08 56
21	0 00 24	+0 03	−7 24	6 01	6 01	12 07	18 14	18 15	11 53 01	12 05 00
22	0 04 03	+0 26	−7 06	5 59	5 58	12 07	18 16	18 17	11 56 57	12 01 04
23	0 07 42	+0 50	−6 48	5 57	5 55	12 07	18 18	18 19	12 00 54	11 57 08
24	0 11 20	+1 14	−6 30	5 54	5 53	12 06	18 20	18 21	12 04 50	11 53 12
25	0 14 59	+1 37	−6 12	5 52	5 50	12 06	18 21	18 23	12 08 47	11 49 17
26	0 18 37	+2 01	−5 54	5 50	5 47	12 06	18 23	18 25	12 12 43	11 45 21
27	0 22 15	+2 24	−5 35	5 47	5 45	12 05	18 25	18 27	12 16 40	11 41 25
28	0 25 54	+2 48	−5 17	5 45	5 42	12 05	18 26	18 29	12 20 37	11 37 29
29	0 29 32	+3 11	−4 59	5 43	5 39	12 05	18 28	18 32	12 24 33	11 33 33
30	0 33 11	+3 35	−4 41	5 40	5 37	12 05	18 30	18 34	12 28 30	11 29 37
31	0 36 49	+3 58	−4 23	5 38	5 34	12 04	18 32	18 36	12 32 26	11 25 41

THE SUN   s.d. 16′·1

Duration of Civil (C), Nautical (N), and Astronomical (A), Twilight (in minutes)

Lat. °	Mar. 1 C	N	A	Mar. 11 C	N	A	Mar. 21 C	N	A	Mar. 31 C	N	A
52	34	73	112	34	73	113	34	74	116	34	76	120
56	38	81	124	37	80	125	37	82	129	38	84	136

ASTRONOMICAL NOTES

MERCURY remains too close to the Sun for observation throughout the month, superior conjunction occurring on the 19th.

VENUS continues to be visible as a magnificent object in the morning skies, magnitude −4·5, though only visible for about an hour before sunrise, low above the E.S.E. horizon. On the morning of the 23rd the old crescent Moon passes 2°S. of the planet.

MARS, magnitude +1·1, is a very difficult morning object, even though it is moving steadily away from the Sun. The best chance of detecting it is about an hour before sunrise, when it is very low on the south-eastern horizon. During March Mars moves from Sagittarius into Capricornus.

JUPITER, magnitude −2·3, is still a brilliant object in the southern skies in the evening, visible until well after midnight even by the end of the month.

SATURN slowly becomes visible as a morning object low above the south-eastern horizon for a short while before the brightening twilight inhibits observation.

ZODIACAL LIGHT. The evening cone may be observed in the western sky after the end of twilight from the 13th to the 27th.

THE MOON

Day	R.A.	Dec.	Hor. Par.	Semi-diam.	Sun's Co-long.	P.A. of Bright Limb	Phase	Age	Rise 52°	Rise 56°	Tran-sit	Set 52°	Set 56°
	h m	°	′	′	°	°		d	h m	h m	h m	h m	h m
1	1 40	+15·8	59·9	16·3	319	244	17	3·6	7 49	7 32	15 41	23 55	—
2	2 37	+20·9	59·7	16·3	331	249	27	4·6	8 13	7 49	16 38	—	0 17
3	3 37	+24·7	59·4	16·2	343	255	38	5·6	8 46	8 15	17 38	1 23	1 52
4	4 39	+26·9	59·0	16·1	355	262	49	6·6	9 33	8 57	18 39	2 42	3 17
5	5 42	+27·4	58·5	15·9	8	269	60	7·6	10 35	10 00	19 39	3 45	4 21
6	6 43	+26·2	58·0	15·8	20	276	71	8·6	11 51	11 21	20 36	4 31	5 02
7	7 41	+23·5	57·6	15·7	32	281	80	9·6	13 12	12 49	21 29	5 03	5 27
8	8 36	+19·6	57·1	15·5	44	286	88	10·6	14 34	14 17	22 18	5 26	5 43
9	9 27	+14·7	56·6	15·4	56	288	94	11·6	15 53	15 43	23 03	5 43	5 53
10	10 15	+ 9·3	56·1	15·3	68	286	98	12·6	17 09	17 04	23 47	5 56	6 03
11	11 00	+ 3·7	55·6	15·2	81	267	100	13·6	18 22	18 23	—	6 08	6 09
12	11 45	− 2·1	55·2	15·0	93	142	100	14·6	19 35	19 41	0 28	6 19	6 16
13	12 29	− 7·6	54·8	14·9	105	126	98	15·6	20 47	20 58	1 09	6 30	6 23
14	13 13	−12·9	54·5	14·8	117	121	94	16·6	22 00	22 17	1 51	6 43	6 30
15	13 59	−17·5	54·2	14·8	129	116	88	17·6	23 13	23 35	2 34	6 58	6 40
16	14 46	−21·5	54·1	14·7	141	112	82	18·6	—		3 19	7 18	6 54
17	15 36	−24·5	54·1	14·8	153	106	74	19·6	0 24	0 53	4 07	7 44	7 15
18	16 28	−26·5	54·3	14·8	166	100	65	20·6	1 30	2 04	4 57	8 20	7 46
19	17 21	−27·3	54·7	14·9	178	94	56	21·6	2 28	3 04	5 48	9 09	8 33
20	18 16	−26·9	55·2	15·0	190	88	46	22·6	3 15	3 48	6 41	10 11	9 38
21	19 10	−25·0	55·9	15·2	202	82	37	23·6	3 50	4 18	7 33	11 24	10 56
22	20 04	−21·9	56·7	15·4	214	77	27	24·6	4 16	4 38	8 25	12 43	12 22
23	20 57	−17·6	57·6	15·7	227	74	18	25·6	4 37	4 52	9 15	14 06	13 52
24	21 49	−12·3	58·5	15·9	239	72	11	26·6	4 53	5 03	10 04	15 30	15 23
25	22 40	− 6·2	59·3	16·2	251	72	5	27·6	5 07	5 11	10 53	16 56	16 55
26	23 32	+ 0·4	60·1	16·4	263	82	1	28·6	5 21	5 20	11 43	18 24	18 29
27	0 25	+ 7·1	60·6	16·5	275	187	0	0·2	5 36	5 29	12 34	19 55	20 06
28	1 20	+13·5	60·8	16·6	288	232	2	1·2	5 53	5 40	13 29	21 28	21 47
29	2 18	+19·1	60·8	16·6	300	242	7	2·2	6 15	5 55	14 27	23 01	23 27
30	3 19	+23·5	60·4	16·5	312	250	14	3·2	6 46	6 18	15 28	—	—
31	4 22	+26·3	59·9	16·3	324	258	24	4·2	7 29	6 56	16 31	0 27	1 00

MERCURY ☿

Day	R.A.	Dec. −	Diam.	Phase	Transit		Day	R.A.	Dec. −	Diam.	Phase	Transit	
	h m	°	″		h m			h m	°	″		h m	
1	21 54	15·0	—	—	11 21		16	23 34	− 4·7	—	—	12 02	
4	22 13	13·3	—	—	11 29	Mercury is too	19	23 55	− 2·1	—	—	12 11	Mercury is too
7	22 33	11·4	—	—	11 37	close to the	22	0 16	+ 0·6	—	—	12 21	close to the
10	22 53	9·4	—	—	11 45	Sun for	25	0 38	+ 3·4	—	—	12 31	Sun for
13	23 13	7·1	—	—	11 53	observation	28	0 59	+ 6·3	—	—	12 41	observation
16	23 34	4·7	—	—	12 02		31	1 21	+ 9·0	—	—	12 50	

VENUS ♀   MARS ♂

Day	R.A.	Dec. −	Diam.	Phase	Transit	5° high. 52°	5° high. 56°	Day	R.A.	Dec. −	Diam.	Phase	Transit	5° high. 52°	5° high. 56°
	h m	°	″		h m	h m	h m		h m	°	″		h m	h m	h m
1	19 57	15·6	36	31	9 22	5 23	5 43	1	19 36	22·4	5	93	9 02	5 53	6 26
6	20 11	15·5	34	35	9 17	5 18	5 37	6	19 52	21·8	5	93	8 58	5 44	6 16
11	20 27	15·2	31	38	9 13	5 12	5 31	11	20 07	21·1	5	93	8 54	5 35	6 04
16	20 45	14·8	29	41	9 11	5 07	5 25	16	20 23	20·4	5	92	8 49	5 24	5 52
21	21 03	14·2	27	44	9 10	5 02	5 19	21	20 38	19·5	5	92	8 45	5 14	5 40
26	21 22	13·4	26	47	9 09	4 56	5 12	26	20 54	18·6	5	91	8 41	5 02	5 27
31	21 42	12·3	24	50	9 09	4 50	5 05	31	21 09	17·6	5	91	8 36	4 51	5 13

SUNRISE AND SUNSET

Day	London a.m. h m	London p.m. h m	Bristol a.m. h m	Bristol p.m. h m	Birmingham a.m. h m	Birmingham p.m. h m	Manchester a.m. h m	Manchester p.m. h m	Newcastle a.m. h m	Newcastle p.m. h m	Glasgow a.m. h m	Glasgow p.m. h m	Belfast a.m. h m	Belfast p.m. h m
1	6 47	5 39	6 57	5 49	6 56	5 45	6 59	5 46	6 58	5 40	7 11	5 49	7 16	5 59
2	6 45	5 41	6 55	5 51	6 53	5 47	6 56	5 48	6 55	5 42	7 08	5 52	7 13	6 01
3	6 43	5 43	6 52	5 53	6 51	5 48	6 54	5 49	6 53	5 44	7 06	5 54	7 11	6 02
4	6 41	5 45	6 50	5 55	6 49	5 50	6 52	5 51	6 51	5 46	7 03	5 56	7 09	6 04
5	6 39	5 46	6 48	5 56	6 46	5 52	6 49	5 53	6 48	5 48	7 01	5 58	7 06	6 06
6	6 37	5 48	6 46	5 58	6 44	5 54	6 47	5 55	6 46	5 50	6 58	6 00	7 04	6 08
7	6 34	5 50	6 44	6 00	6 41	5 56	6 44	5 57	6 43	5 52	6 56	6 02	7 01	6 10
8	6 32	5 51	6 42	6 01	6 39	5 58	6 42	5 59	6 41	5 54	6 53	6 04	6 59	6 12
9	6 30	5 53	6 40	6 03	6 37	5 59	6 40	6 00	6 38	5 56	6 50	6 06	6 56	6 14
10	6 28	5 55	6 37	6 05	6 35	6 01	6 38	6 02	6 36	5 58	6 48	6 08	6 54	6 16
11	6 25	5 56	6 35	6 06	6 32	6 03	6 35	6 04	6 33	6 01	6 45	6 11	6 51	6 19
12	6 23	5 58	6 33	6 08	6 30	6 05	6 33	6 06	6 31	6 03	6 43	6 13	6 49	6 21
13	6 21	6 00	6 31	6 10	6 28	6 07	6 31	6 08	6 28	6 05	6 40	6 15	6 46	6 23
14	6 19	6 01	6 29	6 11	6 26	6 08	6 29	6 10	6 26	6 07	6 38	6 17	6 44	6 25
15	6 16	6 03	6 26	6 13	6 23	6 10	6 26	6 11	6 23	6 08	6 35	6 19	6 41	6 26
16	6 14	6 05	6 24	6 15	6 21	6 12	6 24	6 13	6 21	6 10	6 32	6 21	6 39	6 28
17	6 12	6 07	6 22	6 17	6 19	6 14	6 21	6 15	6 18	6 12	6 30	6 23	6 36	6 30
18	6 09	6 08	6 19	6 18	6 16	6 15	6 19	6 17	6 16	6 14	6 27	6 25	6 34	6 32
19	6 07	6 10	6 17	6 20	6 14	6 17	6 16	6 19	6 13	6 16	6 24	6 27	6 31	6 34
20	6 05	6 12	6 15	6 22	6 12	6 19	6 14	6 21	6 11	6 18	6 22	6 29	6 29	6 36
21	6 02	6 14	6 12	6 24	6 09	6 21	6 11	6 23	6 08	6 20	6 19	6 31	6 26	6 38
22	6 00	6 15	6 10	6 25	6 07	6 22	6 09	6 25	6 06	6 22	6 16	6 33	6 24	6 40
23	5 58	6 17	6 08	6 27	6 05	6 24	6 06	6 27	6 03	6 24	6 14	6 35	6 21	6 42
24	5 56	6 19	6 06	6 29	6 02	6 26	6 04	6 28	6 01	6 25	6 11	6 37	6 19	6 43
25	5 53	6 20	6 03	6 30	6 00	6 27	6 01	6 30	5 58	6 27	6 09	6 39	6 16	6 45
26	5 51	6 22	6 01	6 32	5 58	6 29	5 59	6 32	5 56	6 29	6 06	6 41	6 14	6 47
27	5 49	6 24	5 59	6 34	5 55	6 31	5 56	6 34	5 53	6 31	6 03	6 43	6 11	6 49
28	5 46	6 25	5 56	6 35	5 53	6 32	5 54	6 35	5 50	6 33	6 00	6 45	6 08	6 51
29	5 44	6 27	5 54	6 37	5 51	6 34	5 52	6 37	5 48	6 35	5 58	6 47	6 06	6 53
30	5 42	6 29	5 52	6 38	5 49	6 36	5 50	6 39	5 45	6 37	5 55	6 49	6 03	6 55
31	5 40	6 30	5 50	6 40	5 46	6 37	5 47	6 40	5 43	6 39	5 53	6 51	6 01	6 57

	JUPITER ♃ R.A. h m	JUPITER ♃ Dec. + °	JUPITER ♃ Transit h m	JUPITER ♃ 5° high 52° h m	JUPITER ♃ 5° high 56° h m	SATURN ♄ R.A. h m	SATURN ♄ Dec. − °	SATURN ♄ Transit h m	SATURN ♄ 5° high 52° h m	SATURN ♄ 5° high 56° h m
Day										
1	6 04	23·5	19 26	3 04	3 22	19 35	21·4	9 00	5 44	6 14
11	6 05	23·5	18 48	2 26	2 44	19 39	21·3	8 24	5 07	5 37
21	6 08	23·5	18 12	1 49	2 08	19 42	21·1	7 48	4 30	5 00
31	6 12	23·5	17 37	1 14	1 32	19 45	21·0	7 11	3 52	4 22

Equatorial diameter of Jupiter 40″; of Saturn 15″. Diameters of Saturn's rings 36″ and 14″.

	URANUS ♅ R.A. h m	URANUS ♅ Dec. − ° ′	URANUS ♅ Transit h m	URANUS ♅ 10° high 52° h m	URANUS ♅ 10° high 56° h m	NEPTUNE ♆ R.A. h m	NEPTUNE ♆ Dec. − ° ′	NEPTUNE ♆ Transit h m	NEPTUNE ♆ 10° high 52° h m	NEPTUNE ♆ 10° high 56° h m
Day										
1	18 38·3	23 26	8 03	6 01	7 18	19 00·4	21 52	8 25	6 05	6 58
11	18 39·7	23 25	7 25	5 23	6 40	19 01·3	21 50	7 47	5 26	6 20
21	18 40·8	23 24	6 47	4 45	6 01	19 02·1	21 49	7 08	4 47	5 41
31	18 41·5	23 24	6 08	4 06	5 22	19 02·6	21 48	6 29	4 08	5 01

Diameter 4″   Diameter 2″

Month	Week	
1	S.	**5th S in Lent.** William Harvey b. 1578.
2	M.	Hans Christian Andersen b. 1805.
3	Tu.	Henry IV b. 1367. Kurt Weill d. 1950.
4	W.	Martin Luther King assas. 1968.
5	Th.	Bette Davis b. 1908. Karajan b. 1908.
6	F.	Raphael d. 1520. Albrecht Dürer d. 1528.
7	S.	William Wordsworth b. 1770.
8	S.	**Palm Sunday.** Mary Pickford b. 1893.
9	M.	Baudelaire b. 1821. Lenin b. 1870.
10	Tu.	William Hazlitt b. 1778. Antonia White d. 1980.
11	W.	HILARY LAW SITTINGS END. George Canning b. 1770.
12	Th.	**Maundy Thursday.** Imogen Holst b. 1907.
13	F.	**Good Friday.** Samuel Beckett b. 1906.
14	S.	**Easter Eve.** Sir John Gielgud b. 1904.
15	S.	**Easter Day.** Jean Paul Sartre d. 1980.
16	M.	Marie Tussaud d. 1850. J. M. Synge b. 1871.
17	Tu.	Benjamin Franklin d. 1790.*
18	W.	John Foxe d. 1587. Leopold Stokowski b. 1882.
19	Th.	Lord Byron d. 1824. Disraeli d. 1881.
20	F.	Napoleon III b. 1808. Adolf Hitler b. 1889.
21	S.	QUEEN ELIZABETH II b. 1926. Henry VII d. 1509.
22	S.	**1st S. after Easter.** Immanuel Kant b. 1724.
23	M.	ST. GEORGE'S DAY. Shakespeare b. 1564; d. 1616.
24	Tu.	EASTER LAW SITTINGS BEGIN. Trollope b. 1815.
25	W.	**St. Mark.** Oliver Cromwell b. 1599.
26	Th.	David Hume b. 1711. Daniel Defoe d. 1731.
27	F.	Dashiel Hammett b. 1894.
28	S.	Edward IV b. 1442. Benito Mussolini d. 1945.
29	S.	**2nd S. after Easter.** Hitchcock d. 1980.
30	M.	Mary II b. 1662. Franz Lehar b. 1870.

DAY OF

Aperire, to open. Earth opens to receive seed.

Sun's Longitude 30° ♉ 20ᵈ08ʰ

*Centenary

PHENOMENA

d	h	
1	18	Jupiter in conjunction with Moon. Jupiter 3°S.
13	15	Mercury at greatest elongation E.20°.
18	02	Saturn in conjunction with Moon. Saturn 2°N.
20	18	Mars in conjunction with Moon. Mars 3°S.
21	22	Venus in conjunction with Moon. Venus 3°S.
26	00	Mercury in conjunction with Moon. Mercury 3°S.
29	08	Jupiter in conjunction with Moon. Jupiter 3°S.

CONSTELLATIONS

The following constellations are near the meridian at

d	h		d	h
Mar. 1	24		Mar. 16	23
Apr. 1	22		Apr. 15	21
May 1	20		May 16	19

Cepheus (below the Pole), Cassiopeia (below the Pole), Ursa Major, Leo Minor, Leo, Sextans, Hydra and Crater.

MINIMA OF ALGOL

d	h		d	h
2	14		16	22
5	11		19	19
8	08		22	16
11	05		25	13
14	01		28	10

PHASES OF THE MOON

See note on *Summer Time*, p. 24.

		d	h	m
☽	First Quarter	2	10	24
○	Full Moon	10	03	18
☾	Last Quarter	18	07	02
●	New Moon	25	04	27

		d	h
Apogee (406,040 kilometres)		12	20
Perigee (357,500 ,,)		25	17

Mean Longitude of Ascending Node on April 1, 314°.

MONTHLY NOTES

April   5. Income tax year (1989–90) ends.

     10. First day of Passover.

     13. Bank Holiday in Scotland.

     14. Lent ends at midnight.

     15. Greek Orthodox Easter.

     16. Bank Holiday in England, Wales and Northern Ireland.

Day	Right Ascension	Dec. +	Equation of Time	Rise 52°	Rise 56°	Transit	Set 52°	Set 56°	Sidereal Time	Transit of First Point of Aries
	h m s	° ′	m s	h m	h m	h m	h m	h m	h m s	h m s
1	0 40 28	4 21	− 4 05	5 36	5 32	12 04	18 33	18 38	12 36 23	11 21 45
2	0 44 07	4 45	− 3 47	5 33	5 29	12 04	18 35	18 40	12 40 19	11 17 49
3	0 47 46	5 08	− 3 30	5 31	5 26	12 03	18 37	18 42	12 44 16	11 13 53
4	0 51 24	5 31	− 3 12	5 29	5 24	12 03	18 38	18 44	12 48 12	11 09 58
5	0 55 03	5 53	− 2 54	5 27	5 21	12 03	18 40	18 46	12 52 09	11 06 02
6	0 58 43	6 16	− 2 37	5 24	5 18	12 02	18 42	18 48	12 56 06	11 02 06
7	1 02 22	6 39	− 2 20	5 22	5 16	12 02	18 43	18 50	13 00 02	10 58 10
8	1 06 02	7 01	− 2 03	5 20	5 13	12 02	18 45	18 52	13 03 59	10 54 14
9	1 09 41	7 24	− 1 46	5 17	5 11	12 02	18 47	18 54	13 07 55	10 50 18
10	1 13 21	7 46	− 1 30	5 15	5 08	12 01	18 49	18 56	13 11 52	10 46 22
11	1 17 02	8 08	− 1 13	5 13	5 06	12 01	18 50	18 58	13 15 48	10 42 26
12	1 20 42	8 30	− 0 57	5 11	5 03	12 01	18 52	19 00	13 19 45	10 38 30
13	1 24 23	8 52	− 0 42	5 09	5 00	12 01	18 54	19 02	13 23 41	10 34 34
14	1 28 04	9 14	− 0 26	5 06	4 58	12 00	18 55	19 04	13 27 38	10 30 38
15	1 31 46	9 36	− 0 12	5 04	4 55	12 00	18 57	19 06	13 31 35	10 26 43
16	1 35 28	9 57	+ 0 03	5 02	4 53	12 00	18 59	19 08	13 35 31	10 22 47
17	1 39 10	10 18	+ 0 17	5 00	4 50	12 00	19 01	19 10	13 39 28	10 18 51
18	1 42 53	10 39	+ 0 31	4 58	4 48	11 59	19 02	19 12	13 43 24	10 14 55
19	1 46 36	11 00	+ 0 45	4 55	4 45	11 59	19 04	19 14	13 47 21	10 10 59
20	1 50 20	11 21	+ 0 58	4 53	4 43	11 59	19 06	19 16	13 51 17	10 07 03
21	1 54 03	11 42	+ 1 10	4 51	4 40	11 59	19 07	19 18	13 55 14	10 03 07
22	1 57 48	12 02	+ 1 23	4 49	4 38	11 59	19 09	19 20	13 59 10	9 59 11
23	2 01 33	12 22	+ 1 34	4 47	4 36	11 58	19 11	19 22	14 03 07	9 55 15
24	2 05 18	12 42	+ 1 46	4 45	4 33	11 58	19 12	19 25	14 07 04	9 51 19
25	2 09 04	13 02	+ 1 56	4 43	4 31	11 58	19 14	19 27	14 11 00	9 47 23
26	2 12 50	13 22	+ 2 07	4 41	4 28	11 58	19 16	19 29	14 14 57	9 43 28
27	2 16 37	13 41	+ 2 16	4 39	4 26	11 58	19 18	19 31	14 18 53	9 39 32
28	2 20 24	14 00	+ 2 26	4 37	4 24	11 57	19 19	19 33	14 22 50	9 35 36
29	2 24 12	14 19	+ 2 34	4 35	4 21	11 57	19 21	19 35	14 26 46	9 31 40
30	2 28 00	14 38	+ 2 43	4 33	4 19	11 57	19 23	19 37	14 30 43	9 27 44

THE SUN s.d. 16′·0

Duration of Civil (C), Nautical (N), and Astronomical (A), Twilight (in minutes)

Lat. °	Apr. 1 C	N	A	Apr. 11 C	N	A	Apr. 21 C	N	A	Apr. 30 C	N	A
52	34	76	121	35	79	128	37	84	138	39	89	152
56	38	85	137	40	90	148	42	96	167	44	105	200

ASTRONOMICAL NOTES

MERCURY is an evening object, magnitude −1·2 to +2·5, for all except the last week of the month. It may be seen low above the W.N.W. horizon at the time of end of evening civil twilight. For observers in the northern hemisphere this is the best evening apparition in 1990.

VENUS continues to be visible as a brilliant object in the morning skies but only visible for a short while before dawn, low above the E.S.E. horizon. The old crescent Moon will be seen close to the planet on the morning of the 22nd.

MARS is a morning object, magnitude +0·9, and by the end of the month will be seen low above the south-eastern horizon shortly before 04h.

JUPITER continues to be visible as a brilliant object in the south-western skies in the evenings, magnitude −2·1. Jupiter is in the constellation of Gemini. On the early evening of the 1st, the Moon, just before First Quarter, will be seen passing 3° above the planet.

SATURN, magnitude +0·6, is a morning object, low in the south-eastern sky. On the morning of the 18th, the Moon, at Last Quarter, will be seen near the planet. Saturn is in the constellation of Sagittarius.

THE MOON

Day	R.A.	Dec.	Hor. Par.	Semi-diam.	Sun's Co-long.	P.A. of Bright Limb	Phase	Age	Rise 52°	Rise 56°	Transit	Set 52°	Set 56°
	h m	°	′	′	°	°		d	h m	h m	h m	h m	h m
1	5 26	+27·3	59·3	16·2	337	265	34	5·2	8 28	7 53	17 33	1 38	2 13
2	6 29	+26·4	58·6	16·0	349	273	45	6·2	9 41	9 10	18 32	2 30	3 02
3	7 28	+24·1	57·9	15·8	1	279	56	7·2	11 01	10 36	19 26	3 06	3 32
4	8 24	+20·4	57·2	15·6	13	284	67	8·2	12 22	12 04	20 16	3 31	3 51
5	9 15	+15·8	56·5	15·4	25	287	76	9·2	13 41	13 29	21 02	3 50	4 03
6	10 03	+10·6	56·0	15·3	37	289	84	10·2	14 57	14 51	21 45	4 04	4 12
7	10 49	+ 5·1	55·5	15·1	50	289	91	11·2	16 10	16 09	22 26	4 16	4 19
8	11 33	− 0·6	55·0	15·0	62	286	96	12·2	17 22	17 26	23 07	4 27	4 26
9	12 17	− 6·1	54·7	14·9	74	276	99	13·2	18 34	18 43	23 48	4 39	4 33
10	13 01	−11·4	54·4	14·8	86	221	100	14·2	19 46	20 00	—	4 51	4 40
11	13 46	−16·2	54·2	14·8	98	138	99	15·2	20 58	21 19	0 31	5 06	4 50
12	14 33	−20·3	54·0	14·7	110	122	97	16·2	22 10	22 36	1 15	5 24	5 02
13	15 22	−23·6	54·0	14·7	123	113	93	17·2	23 18	23 50	2 02	5 48	5 20
14	16 13	−25·9	54·1	14·7	135	105	87	18·2	—	—	2 51	6 20	5 48
15	17 06	−27·0	54·3	14·8	147	98	80	19·2	0 19	0 54	3 42	7 04	6 29
16	17 59	−26·9	54·6	14·9	159	92	72	20·2	1 09	1 43	4 33	8 00	7 26
17	18 53	−25·5	55·1	15·0	171	85	63	21·2	1 48	2 18	5 25	9 08	8 38
18	19 46	−22·9	55·8	15·2	184	80	53	22·2	2 17	2 41	6 15	10 22	9 59
19	20 38	−19·1	56·5	15·4	196	75	43	23·2	2 39	2 57	7 05	11 41	11 25
20	21 29	−14·3	57·4	15·7	208	72	33	24·2	2 56	3 08	7 53	13 02	12 52
21	22 19	− 8·6	58·4	15·9	220	70	23	25·2	3 11	3 18	8 40	14 25	14 21
22	23 09	− 2·4	59·3	16·2	232	70	14	26·2	3 25	3 26	9 29	15 50	15 52
23	0 01	+ 4·2	60·2	16·4	245	73	7	27·2	3 39	3 35	10 19	17 19	17 26
24	0 55	+10·7	60·9	16·6	257	82	2	28·2	3 55	3 45	11 12	18 51	19 06
25	1 52	+16·7	61·3	16·7	269	131	0	29·2	4 15	3 59	12 09	20 26	20 48
26	2 53	+21·7	61·3	16·7	281	230	1	0·8	4 42	4 19	13 11	21 59	22 28
27	3 57	+25·3	61·1	16·6	294	249	5	1·8	5 21	4 50	14 15	23 19	23 54
28	5 03	+26·9	60·5	16·5	306	260	12	2·8	6 15	5 41	15 20	—	—
29	6 09	+26·7	59·8	16·3	318	269	20	3·8	7 26	6 53	16 23	0 22	0 55
30	7 11	+24·6	58·9	16·1	330	276	30	4·8	8 47	8 20	17 20	1 05	1 32

MERCURY ☿

Day	R.A.	Dec. +	Diam.	Phase	Transit	5° high 52°	5° high 56°	Day	R.A.	Dec. +	Diam.	Phase	Transit	5° high 52°	5° high 56°
	h m	°	″		h m	h m	h m		h m	°	″		h m	h m	h m
1	1 28	9·9	6	84	12 53	19 16	19 21	16	2 46	19·1	8	32	13 10	20 19	20 32
4	1 48	12·5	6	75	13 01	19 37	19 44	19	2 53	19·6	9	22	13 04	20 16	20 29
7	2 06	14·7	6	64	13 07	19 54	20 04	22	2 57	19·8	10	15	12 56	20 06	20 20
10	2 22	16·6	7	53	13 11	20 08	20 19	25	2 57	19·4	10	8	12 43	19 51	20 05
13	2 36	18·1	8	42	13 12	20 16	20 29	28	2 54	18·7	11	4	12 28	19 31	19 44
16	2 46	19·1	8	32	13 10	20 19	20 32	31	2 49	17·6	12	1	12 11	19 07	19 19

VENUS ♀

Day	R.A.	Dec. −	Diam.	Phase	Transit	5° high 52°	5° high 56°
	h m	°	″		h m	h m	h m
1	21 46	12·1	24	50	9 09	4 48	5 03
6	22 06	10·9	23	53	9 10	4 41	4 55
11	22 26	9·5	22	55	9 10	4 34	4 46
16	22 47	7·9	21	58	9 11	4 26	4 36
21	23 07	6·2	20	60	9 12	4 17	4 26
26	23 28	4·4	19	62	9 13	4 08	4 15
31	23 49	2·5	18	64	9 14	3 59	4 05

MARS ♂

Day	R.A.	Dec. −	Diam.	Phase	Transit	5° high 52°	5° high 56°
	h m	°	″		h m	h m	h m
1	21 12	17·4	5	91	8 35	4 48	5 11
6	21 27	16·4	5	90	8 30	4 36	4 57
11	21 42	15·2	6	90	8 25	4 24	4 43
16	21 56	14·0	6	90	8 20	4 11	4 29
21	22 11	12·8	6	90	8 15	3 58	4 14
26	22 25	11·5	6	89	8 10	3 45	3 59
31	22 39	10·2	6	89	8 04	3 32	3 45

SUNRISE AND SUNSET

Day	London a.m. h m	London p.m. h m	Bristol a.m. h m	Bristol p.m. h m	Birmingham a.m. h m	Birmingham p.m. h m	Manchester a.m. h m	Manchester p.m. h m	Newcastle a.m. h m	Newcastle p.m. h m	Glasgow a.m. h m	Glasgow p.m. h m	Belfast a.m. h m	Belfast p.m. h m
1	5 38	6 32	5 48	6 41	5 44	6 39	5 45	6 42	5 40	6 41	5 50	6 53	5 58	6 59
2	5 36	6 34	5 46	6 43	5 42	6 41	5 43	6 44	5 38	6 43	5 47	6 56	5 56	7 01
3	5 33	6 36	5 43	6 45	5 39	6 43	5 40	6 46	5 35	6 45	5 45	6 58	5 53	7 03
4	5 31	6 37	5 41	6 46	5 37	6 45	5 38	6 48	5 33	6 47	5 42	7 00	5 51	7 05
5	5 29	6 39	5 39	6 48	5 34	6 47	5 35	6 50	5 30	6 49	5 39	7 02	5 48	7 07
6	5 27	6 40	5 37	6 50	5 32	6 49	5 33	6 52	5 28	6 51	5 37	7 04	5 46	7 09
7	5 24	6 42	5 34	6 51	5 29	6 50	5 30	6 54	5 25	6 53	5 34	7 06	5 43	7 11
8	5 22	6 43	5 32	6 53	5 27	6 52	5 28	6 55	5 23	6 55	5 32	7 08	5 41	7 12
9	5 20	6 45	5 30	6 55	5 25	6 54	5 26	6 57	5 20	6 57	5 29	7 10	5 39	7 14
10	5 17	6 47	5 27	6 57	5 22	6 56	5 23	6 59	5 18	6 59	5 27	7 12	5 36	7 16
11	5 15	6 48	5 25	6 58	5 20	6 57	5 21	7 01	5 15	7 01	5 24	7 14	5 34	7 18
12	5 13	6 50	5 23	7 00	5 18	6 59	5 18	7 03	5 12	7 03	5 21	7 16	5 31	7 20
13	5 11	6 52	5 21	7 02	5 16	7 01	5 16	7 04	5 10	7 04	5 19	7 18	5 29	7 22
14	5 08	6 53	5 18	7 03	5 13	7 02	5 14	7 06	5 08	7 06	5 16	7 20	5 26	7 24
15	5 06	6 55	5 16	7 05	5 11	7 04	5 11	7 08	5 05	7 08	5 14	7 22	5 24	7 26
16	5 04	6 57	5 14	7 07	5 09	7 06	5 09	7 10	5 03	7 10	5 11	7 24	5 21	7 28
17	5 02	6 59	5 12	7 09	5 07	7 08	5 07	7 12	5 01	7 12	5 09	7 26	5 19	7 30
18	5 00	7 00	5 10	7 10	5 05	7 09	5 04	7 14	4 58	7 14	5 06	7 28	5 16	7 32
19	4 57	7 02	5 07	7 12	5 02	7 11	5 02	7 16	4 56	7 16	5 04	7 30	5 14	7 34
20	4 55	7 04	5 05	7 14	5 00	7 13	5 00	7 18	4 53	7 18	5 01	7 32	5 12	7 36
21	4 53	7 05	5 03	7 15	4 58	7 14	4 57	7 19	4 51	7 20	4 59	7 34	5 09	7 37
22	4 51	7 07	5 01	7 17	4 56	7 16	4 55	7 21	4 48	7 22	4 56	7 36	5 07	7 39
23	4 49	7 09	4 59	7 19	4 54	7 18	4 53	7 23	4 46	7 24	4 54	7 38	5 05	7 41
24	4 47	7 10	4 57	7 20	4 52	7 19	4 51	7 24	4 43	7 26	4 51	7 40	5 02	7 43
25	4 45	7 12	4 55	7 22	4 50	7 21	4 49	7 26	4 41	7 28	4 49	7 42	5 00	7 45
26	4 43	7 14	4 53	7 24	4 48	7 23	4 47	7 28	4 39	7 30	4 47	7 44	4 58	7 47
27	4 41	7 15	4 51	7 25	4 46	7 25	4 45	7 30	4 37	7 32	4 45	7 46	4 56	7 49
28	4 40	7 17	4 50	7 27	4 44	7 26	4 43	7 31	4 35	7 33	4 43	7 47	4 54	7 50
29	4 38	7 19	4 48	7 28	4 42	7 28	4 41	7 33	4 32	7 35	4 40	7 49	4 52	7 52
30	4 36	7 21	4 46	7 30	4 39	7 30	4 38	7 35	4 30	7 37	4 38	7 51	4 49	7 54

JUPITER ♃ / SATURN ♄

Day	Jupiter R.A. h m	Jupiter Dec. + °	Jupiter Transit h m	Jupiter 5° high. 52° h m	Jupiter 5° high. 56° h m	Saturn R.A. h m	Saturn Dec. − °	Saturn Transit h m	Saturn 5° high. 52° h m	Saturn 5° high. 56° h m
1	6 12	23·5	17 33	1 10	1 29	19 45	21·0	7 08	3 49	4 18
11	6 17	23·5	16 59	0 36	0 54	19 47	21·0	6 30	3 11	3 40
21	6 23	23·4	16 26	0 03	0 21	19 48	20·9	5 52	2 32	3 01
31	6 30	23·4	15 54	23 27	23 45	19 49	20·9	5 14	1 53	2 23

Equatorial diameter of Jupiter 36″; of Saturn 16″. Diameters of Saturn's rings 38″ and 14″.

URANUS ♅ / NEPTUNE ♆

Day	Uranus R.A. h m	Uranus Dec. − ° ′	Uranus Transit h m	Uranus 10° high. 52° h m	Uranus 10° high. 56° h m	Neptune R.A. h m	Neptune Dec. − ° ′	Neptune Transit h m	Neptune 10° high. 52° h m	Neptune 10° high. 56° h m
1	18 41·5	23 24	6 04	4 02	5 18	19 02·6	21 48	6 25	4 04	4 58
11	18 41·8	23 24	5 25	3 23	4 39	19 02·9	21 47	5 46	3 25	4 18
21	18 41·7	23 24	4 46	2 44	4 00	19 02·9	21 47	5 07	2 46	3 39
31	18 41·3	23 25	4 06	2 04	3 21	19 02·6	21 47	4 27	2 06	2 59

Diameter 4″ / Diameter 2″

DAY		

PHENOMENA

d	h	
4	00	Mercury in inferior conjunction.
7	05	Pluto at opposition.
15	08	Saturn in conjunction with Moon. Saturn 1°N.
19	16	Mars in conjunction with Moon. Mars 5°S.
21	15	Venus in conjunction with Moon. Venus 6°S.
22	22	Mercury in conjunction with Moon. Mercury 8°S.
27	02	Jupiter in conjunction with Moon. Jupiter 2°S.
31	03	Mercury at greatest elongation W.25°.

Month	Week	
1	Tu.	**SS. Philip and James.** Joseph Addison b. 1672.
2	W.	Jerome K. Jerome b. 1859. Bing Crosby b. 1904.
3	Th.	Machiavelli b. 1469. Golda Meir b. 1898.
4	F.	Joseph Whitaker b. 1820. Tito d. 1980.
5	S.	Sören Kierkegaard b. 1813.
6	S.	**3rd S. after Easter.** Sigmund Freud b. 1856.
7	M.	Brahms b. 1833. Tchaikovsky b. 1840.
8	Tu.	Gustave Flaubert d. 1880. V.E. Day 1945.
9	W.	John Brown b. 1800. James Barrie b. 1860.
10	Th.	Fred Astaire b. 1899. Joan Crawford d. 1977.
11	F.	Irving Berlin b. 1888. Salvador Dali b. 1904.
12	S.	Edward Lear b. 1812. Florence Nightingale b. 1820.
13	S.	**4th S. after Easter.** Daphne du Maurier b. 1907.
14	M.	**St. Matthias.** Robert Owen b. 1771.
15	Tu.	Pierre Curie b. 1859. James Mason b. 1909.
16	W.	Charles Perrault d. 1703. H.E. Bates b. 1905.
17	Th.	Edward Jenner b. 1749. Paganini d. 1840.
18	F.	Pope John Paul II b. 1920.
19	S.	Anne Boleyn exec. 1536. Nellie Melba b. 1861.
20	S.	**5th S. after Easter. Rogation Sunday.**
21	M.	Alexander Pope b. 1688. Elizabeth Fry b. 1780.
22	Tu.	Sir Arthur Conan Doyle b. 1859.
23	W.	Thomas Hood b. 1799. Sir Hugh Casson b. 1910.
24	Th.	**Ascension Day.** Queen Victoria b. 1819.
25	F.	EASTER LAW SITTINGS END. Lord Lytton b. 1803.
26	S.	Last public hanging in England 1868.
27	S.	**S. after Ascension (6th after Easter).**
28	M.	George I b. 1660. Ian Fleming b. 1908.
29	Tu.	Charles II b. 1630. G.K. Chesterton b. 1874.
30	W.	Christopher Marlowe d. 1593. Rubens d. 1640.
31	Th.	Walt Whitman b. 1819. Walter Sickert b. 1860.

CONSTELLATIONS

The following constellations are near the meridian at

d	h		d	h
Apr.	1	24	Apr. 15	23
May	1	22	May 16	21
June	1	20	June 15	19

Cepheus (below the Pole), Cassiopeia (below the Pole), Ursa Minor, Ursa Major, Canes Venatici, Coma Berenices, Bootes, Leo, Virgo, Crater, Corvus, and Hydra.

ALGOL

ALGOL is inconveniently situated for observation during May.

* Centenary.

PHASES OF THE MOON

	d	h	m
☽ First Quarter	1	20	18
○ Full Moon	9	19	31
☾ Last Quarter	17	19	45
● New Moon	24	11	47
☽ First Quarter	31	08	11

	d	h
Apogee (406,430 kilometres)	10	00
Perigee (357,340 „)	24	03

Mean Longitude of Ascending Node on May 1, 312°.

See note on *Summer Time*, p. 24.

MONTHLY NOTES

May 7. Bank Holiday, England, Wales, Scotland and N. Ireland.
   9. Liberation Day, Channel Islands.
   15. Whitsunday (Scotland). Scottish Term Day.
   28. Removal Day, Scotland.
   28. Bank Holiday, England, Wales, Scotland and N. Ireland.
   30. First day of Feast of Weeks.

Day	THE SUN Right Ascension	Dec. +	Equation of Time	Rise 52°	Rise 56°	Transit	Set 52°	Set 56°	Sidereal Time	Transit of First Point of Aries
	h m s	° ′	m s	h m	h m	h m	h m	h m	h m s	h m s
1	2 31 49	14 56	+ 2 51	4 31	4 17	11 57	19 24	19 39	14 34 39	9 23 48
2	2 35 38	15 14	+ 2 58	4 29	4 15	11 57	19 26	19 41	14 38 36	9 19 52
3	2 39 28	15 32	+ 3 05	4 27	4 12	11 57	19 28	19 43	14 42 33	9 15 56
4	2 43 18	15 50	+ 3 11	4 25	4 10	11 57	19 29	19 45	14 46 29	9 12 00
5	2 47 09	16 07	+ 3 17	4 23	4 08	11 57	19 31	19 47	14 50 26	9 08 04
6	2 51 00	16 24	+ 3 22	4 22	4 06	11 57	19 33	19 49	14 54 22	9 04 08
7	2 54 52	16 41	+ 3 26	4 20	4 04	11 57	19 34	19 51	14 58 19	9 00 13
8	2 58 45	16 57	+ 3 30	4 18	4 02	11 56	19 36	19 53	15 02 15	8 56 17
9	3 02 38	17 14	+ 3 34	4 16	4 00	11 56	19 38	19 55	15 06 12	8 52 21
10	3 06 32	17 30	+ 3 37	4 15	3 58	11 56	19 39	19 57	15 10 08	8 48 25
11	3 10 26	17 45	+ 3 39	4 13	3 55	11 56	19 41	19 58	15 14 05	8 44 29
12	3 14 21	18 01	+ 3 41	4 11	3 53	11 56	19 42	20 00	15 18 02	8 40 33
13	3 18 16	18 16	+ 3 42	4 10	3 52	11 56	19 44	20 02	15 21 58	8 36 37
14	3 22 12	18 31	+ 3 43	4 08	3 50	11 56	19 45	20 04	15 25 55	8 32 41
15	3 26 09	18 45	+ 3 43	4 07	3 48	11 56	19 47	20 06	15 29 51	8 28 45
16	3 30 06	18 59	+ 3 42	4 05	3 46	11 56	19 49	20 08	15 33 48	8 24 49
17	3 34 03	19 13	+ 3 41	4 04	3 44	11 56	19 50	20 10	15 37 44	8 20 53
18	3 38 02	19 27	+ 3 39	4 02	3 42	11 56	19 52	20 12	15 41 41	8 16 58
19	3 42 00	19 40	+ 3 37	4 01	3 41	11 56	19 53	20 13	15 45 37	8 13 02
20	3 46 00	19 53	+ 3 34	3 59	3 39	11 56	19 54	20 15	15 49 34	8 09 06
21	3 50 00	20 05	+ 3 31	3 58	3 37	11 57	19 56	20 17	15 53 31	8 05 10
22	3 54 00	20 17	+ 3 27	3 57	3 36	11 57	19 57	20 19	15 57 27	8 01 14
23	3 58 01	20 29	+ 3 22	3 56	3 34	11 57	19 59	20 20	16 01 24	7 57 18
24	4 02 03	20 41	+ 3 17	3 54	3 33	11 57	20 00	20 22	16 05 20	7 53 22
25	4 06 05	20 52	+ 3 11	3 53	3 31	11 57	20 01	20 24	16 09 17	7 49 26
26	4 10 08	21 03	+ 3 05	3 52	3 30	11 57	20 03	20 25	16 13 13	7 45 30
27	4 14 11	21 13	+ 2 59	3 51	3 28	11 57	20 04	20 27	16 17 10	7 41 34
28	4 18 15	21 23	+ 2 52	3 50	3 27	11 57	20 05	20 28	16 21 06	7 37 38
29	4 22 19	21 33	+ 2 44	3 49	3 26	11 57	20 06	20 30	16 25 03	7 33 42
30	4 26 23	21 42	+ 2 36	3 48	3 25	11 57	20 08	20 31	16 29 00	7 29 47
31	4 30 28	21 51	+ 2 28	3 47	3 23	11 58	20 09	20 33	16 32 56	7 25 51

THE SUN s.d. 15′·8

Duration of Civil (C), Nautical (N), and Astronomical (A), Twilight (in minutes)

Lat. °	May 1 C	N	A	May 11 C	N	A	May 21 C	N	A	May 31 C	N	A
52	39	90	154	41	97	179	44	106	T.A.N.	46	116	T.A.N.
56	45	106	209	49	121	T.A.N.	53	143	T.A.N.	57	T.A.N.	T.A.N.

ASTRONOMICAL NOTES

MERCURY is unsuitably placed for observation although it reaches greatest western elongation on the last day of the month.

VENUS is a splendid object in the morning skies, magnitude −4·1, though only visible for about half-an-hour before dawn, low above the eastern horizon.

MARS, magnitude +0·7, continues to be visible as a morning object. Mars is in Aquarius until towards the end of the month when it moves into Pisces. The planet has a reddish tint which is an aid to its identification.

JUPITER, magnitude −1·9, continues to be visible as a bright object in the south-western sky in the evenings. On the evening of the 26th the gibbous Moon will be seen approaching the planet. The four Galilean satellites are readily observable with any small telescope or even a good pair of binoculars provided that they are held rigidly. Times of eclipses and shadow transits of these satellites are given on page 73.

SATURN continues to be visible as a morning object low in the south-eastern sky. By the end of the month it is rising before midnight.

THE MOON

Day	R.A.	Dec.	Hor. Par.	Semi-diam.	Sun's Co-long.	P.A. of Bright Limb	Phase	Age	Rise 52°	Rise 56°	Transit	Set 52°	Set 56°
	h m	°	′	′	°	°		d	h m	h m	h m	h m	h m
1	8 09	+21·2	58·0	15·8	342	282	41	5·8	10 10	9 50	18 13	1 34	1 55
2	9 03	+16·8	57·2	15·6	355	287	52	6·8	11 30	11 17	19 00	1 55	2 10
3	9 52	+11·7	56·4	15·4	7	289	62	7·8	12 47	12 40	19 44	2 11	2 20
4	10 38	+ 6·2	55·7	15·2	19	291	72	8·8	14 01	13 58	20 26	2 24	2 28
5	11 22	+ 0·6	55·1	15·0	31	291	80	9·8	15 13	15 15	21 07	2 36	2 35
6	12 06	− 4·9	54·7	14·9	43	289	87	10·8	16 24	16 31	21 48	2 47	2 42
7	12 50	−10·2	54·4	14·8	56	285	93	11·8	17 35	17 48	22 29	2 59	2 50
8	13 34	−15·0	54·1	14·7	68	278	97	12·8	18 47	19 05	23 13	3 13	2 59
9	14 21	−19·3	54·0	14·7	80	260	99	13·8	19 58	20 23	23 59	3 30	3 10
10	15 09	−22·8	53·9	14·7	92	173	100	14·8	21 08	21 38	—	3 52	3 27
11	16 00	−25·3	54·0	14·7	104	121	99	15·8	22 11	22 45	0 47	4 22	3 51
12	16 52	−26·7	54·1	14·7	117	106	96	16·8	23 05	23 39	1 38	5 02	4 28
13	17 46	−26·9	54·4	14·8	129	96	91	17·8	23 47	—	2 29	5 55	5 21
14	18 39	−25·8	54·7	14·9	141	89	85	18·8	—	0 18	3 20	6 59	6 28
15	19 32	−23·4	55·2	15·0	153	82	77	19·8	0 18	0 44	4 10	8 10	7 45
16	20 23	−20·0	55·8	15·2	165	77	68	20·8	0 42	1 02	4 59	9 26	9 08
17	21 13	−15·6	56·5	15·4	178	73	59	21·8	1 00	1 14	5 46	10 44	10 32
18	22 02	−10·3	57·3	15·6	190	70	48	22·8	1 16	1 24	6 33	12 03	11 57
19	22 51	− 4·5	58·2	15·8	202	68	38	23·8	1 30	1 33	7 19	13 24	13 23
20	23 40	+ 1·8	59·1	16·1	214	68	27	24·8	1 43	1 41	8 06	14 48	14 53
21	0 31	+ 8·2	59·9	16·3	226	70	18	25·8	1 58	1 51	8 56	16 16	16 27
22	1 26	+14·3	60·7	16·5	239	75	9	26·8	2 15	2 02	9 50	17 48	18 07
23	2 25	+19·7	61·2	16·7	251	84	4	27·8	2 39	2 19	10 49	19 22	19 48
24	3 28	+23·9	61·4	16·7	263	110	1	28·8	3 11	2 44	11 53	20 51	21 23
25	4 34	+26·3	61·2	16·7	275	231	1	0·5	3 58	3 25	12 59	22 04	22 38
26	5 42	+26·9	60·8	16·6	288	259	4	1·5	5 03	4 29	14 05	22 57	23 27
27	6 47	+25·4	60·1	16·4	300	271	9	2·5	6 23	5 53	15 07	23 33	23 57
28	7 49	+22·4	59·2	16·1	312	279	17	3·5	7 48	7 26	16 04	23 58	—
29	8 45	+18·1	58·3	15·9	324	285	26	4·5	9 13	8 57	16 54	—	0 15
30	9 37	+13·0	57·3	15·6	337	289	36	5·5	10 33	10 24	17 41	0 16	0 27
31	10 25	+ 7·5	56·4	15·4	349	292	47	6·5	11 49	11 45	18 24	0 30	0 36

MERCURY ☿

Day	R.A.	Dec. +	Diam.	Phase	Transit		Day	R.A.	Dec. +	Diam.	Phase	Transit	
	h m	°	″		h m			h m	°	″		h m	
1	2 49	17·6	—	—	12 11		16	2 26	11·7	—	—	10 50	
4	2 43	16·3	—	—	11 53	Mercury is too	19	2 27	11·3	—	—	10 40	Mercury is too
7	2 36	14·9	—	—	11 35	close to the	22	2 30	11·2	—	—	10 32	close to the
10	2 31	13·6	—	—	11 18	Sun for	25	2 36	11·5	—	—	10 26	Sun for
13	2 27	12·5	—	—	11 03	observation	28	2 44	12·1	—	—	10 22	observation
16	2 26	11·7	—	—	10 50		31	2 54	12·9	—	—	10 21	

VENUS ♀

Day	R.A.	Dec.	Diam.	Phase	Transit	5° high 52°	5° high 56°
	h m	°	″		h m	h m	h m
1	23 49	− 2·5	18	64	9 14	3 59	4 05
6	0 10	− 0·5	17	66	9 16	3 50	3 54
11	0 31	+ 1·5	17	68	9 17	3 41	3 43
16	0 52	+ 3·6	16	70	9 18	3 32	3 32
21	1 14	+ 5·7	16	71	9 20	3 23	3 22
26	1 35	+ 7·8	15	73	9 22	3 15	3 11
31	1 57	+ 9·8	15	75	9 24	3 06	3 02

MARS ♂

Day	R.A.	Dec. −	Diam.	Phase	Transit	5° high 52°	5° high 56°
	h m	°	″		h m	h m	h m
1	22 39	10·2	6	89	8 04	3 32	3 45
6	22 53	8·8	6	88	7 59	3 19	3 30
11	23 07	7·5	6	88	7 53	3 05	3 15
16	23 21	6·1	6	87	7 47	2 52	3 00
21	23 35	4·7	7	87	7 41	2 38	2 45
26	23 49	3·2	7	87	7 35	2 25	2 31
31	0 02	1·8	7	86	7 29	2 11	2 16

SUNRISE AND SUNSET

Day	London a.m.	London p.m.	Bristol a.m.	Bristol p.m.	Birmingham a.m.	Birmingham p.m.	Manchester a.m.	Manchester p.m.	Newcastle a.m.	Newcastle p.m.	Glasgow a.m.	Glasgow p.m.	Belfast a.m.	Belfast p.m.
	h m	h m	h m	h m	h m	h m	h m	h m	h m	h m	h m	h m	h m	h m
1	4 34	7 22	4 44	7 31	4 37	7 32	4 36	7 37	4 28	7 39	4 36	7 53	4 47	7 56
2	4 32	7 24	4 42	7 33	4 35	7 34	4 34	7 39	4 26	7 41	4 34	7 55	4 45	7 58
3	4 30	7 25	4 40	7 34	4 33	7 35	4 32	7 41	4 23	7 43	4 31	7 57	4 43	8 00
4	4 28	7 27	4 38	7 36	4 31	7 37	4 30	7 43	4 21	7 45	4 29	7 59	4 41	8 02
5	4 26	7 28	4 36	7 38	4 29	7 39	4 28	7 44	4 19	7 47	4 27	8 01	4 39	8 03
6	4 24	7 30	4 34	7 40	4 27	7 41	4 26	7 46	4 17	7 49	4 25	8 03	4 37	8 05
7	4 23	7 31	4 33	7 41	4 26	7 42	4 24	7 48	4 15	7 51	4 23	8 05	4 35	8 07
8	4 21	7 33	4 31	7 43	4 24	7 44	4 22	7 50	4 13	7 53	4 21	8 07	4 33	8 09
9	4 19	7 34	4 29	7 44	4 22	7 45	4 20	7 51	4 11	7 54	4 18	8 09	4 30	8 11
10	4 18	7 36	4 28	7 46	4 21	7 47	4 18	7 53	4 09	7 56	4 16	8 11	4 28	8 13
11	4 16	7 38	4 26	7 48	4 19	7 49	4 17	7 55	4 07	7 58	4 14	8 13	4 27	8 15
12	4 14	7 39	4 24	7 49	4 17	7 50	4 15	7 57	4 05	8 00	4 12	8 15	4 25	8 17
13	4 12	7 41	4 22	7 51	4 15	7 52	4 13	7 58	4 03	8 02	4 10	8 17	4 23	8 18
14	4 11	7 42	4 21	7 52	4 14	7 53	4 11	8 00	4 02	8 04	4 09	8 19	4 21	8 20
15	4 09	7 44	4 19	7 54	4 12	7 55	4 09	8 02	4 00	8 06	4 07	8 21	4 19	8 22
16	4 08	7 46	4 18	7 56	4 11	7 57	4 08	8 03	3 58	8 07	4 05	8 23	4 18	8 23
17	4 06	7 47	4 16	7 57	4 09	7 58	4 06	8 05	3 56	8 09	4 03	8 24	4 16	8 25
18	4 05	7 49	4 15	7 59	4 08	8 00	4 05	8 07	3 55	8 11	4 01	8 26	4 15	8 27
19	4 03	7 50	4 14	8 00	4 06	8 01	4 03	8 08	3 53	8 12	4 00	8 28	4 13	8 28
20	4 02	7 52	4 13	8 02	4 05	8 03	4 02	8 10	3 51	8 14	3 58	8 30	4 11	8 30
21	4 01	7 53	4 11	8 03	4 04	8 04	4 01	8 11	3 50	8 16	3 56	8 32	4 10	8 32
22	3 59	7 54	4 10	8 04	4 02	8 05	3 59	8 12	3 48	8 17	3 54	8 33	4 08	8 33
23	3 58	7 56	4 09	8 06	4 01	8 07	3 58	8 14	3 47	8 19	3 53	8 35	4 07	8 35
24	3 57	7 57	4 08	8 07	4 00	8 08	3 57	8 15	3 45	8 21	3 51	8 37	4 05	8 37
25	3 56	7 58	4 07	8 08	3 59	8 10	3 56	8 17	3 44	8 22	3 50	8 38	4 04	8 38
26	3 55	8 00	4 05	8 09	3 57	8 11	3 54	8 18	3 42	8 24	3 48	8 40	4 02	8 40
27	3 54	8 01	4 04	8 11	3 56	8 13	3 53	8 20	3 41	8 26	3 47	8 42	4 01	8 42
28	3 53	8 02	4 03	8 12	3 55	8 14	3 52	8 21	3 40	8 27	3 46	8 43	4 00	8 43
29	3 52	8 04	4 02	8 13	3 54	8 15	3 51	8 22	3 39	8 28	3 44	8 45	3 59	8 44
30	3 51	8 05	4 01	8 14	3 53	8 17	3 50	8 24	3 38	8 30	3 43	8 46	3 58	8 46
31	3 50	8 06	4 00	8 15	3 51	8 18	3 48	8 25	3 36	8 31	3 42	8 48	3 56	8 47

JUPITER ♃ / SATURN ♄

Day	Jupiter R.A.	Jupiter Dec. +	Jupiter Transit	Jupiter 5° high 52°	Jupiter 5° high 56°	Saturn R.A.	Saturn Dec. −	Saturn Transit	Saturn 5° high 52°	Saturn 5° high 56°
	h m	°	h m	h m	h m	h m	°	h m	h m	h m
1	6 30	23·4	15 54	23 27	23 45	19 49	20·9	5 14	1 53	2 23
11	6 38	23·3	15 22	22 54	23 12	19 49	20·9	4 34	1 14	1 43
21	6 46	23·2	14 51	22 22	22 40	19 48	21·0	3 54	0 34	1 04
31	6 55	23·0	14 20	21 51	22 09	19 47	21·0	3 13	23 50	0 24

Equatorial diameter of Jupiter 34″; of Saturn 17″.   Diameters of Saturn's rings 40″ and 15″.

URANUS ♅ / NEPTUNE ♆

Day	Uranus R.A.	Uranus Dec. −	Uranus Transit	Uranus 10° high 52°	Uranus 10° high 56°	Neptune R.A.	Neptune Dec. −	Neptune Transit	Neptune 10° high 52°	Neptune 10° high 56°
	h m	° ′	h m	h m	h m	h m	° ″	h m	h m	h m
1	18 41·3	23 25	4 06	2 04	3 21	19 02·6	21 47	4 27	2 06	2 59
11	18 40·5	23 26	3 26	1 24	2 41	19 02·2	21 48	3 48	1 26	2 20
21	18 39·4	23 27	2 45	0 44	2 02	19 01·6	21 49	3 08	0 47	1 40
31	18 38·1	23 28	2 05	0 04	1 22	19 00·7	21 50	2 27	0 07	1 00

Diameter 4″   Diameter 2″

Day of Month	Week	

Junius, Roman *gens* (family).

Sun's Longitude 90° ♋ 21ᵈ 16ʰ

1	F.	John Masefield b. 1878. Marilyn Monroe b. 1926.
2	S.	CORONATION DAY 1953. Thomas Hardy b. 1840.

　　　d h
11 12　Saturn in conjunc-
　　　tion with Moon. Sat-
　　　urn 1°N.

3	S.	**Pentecost (Whit Sunday).** George V b. 1865.
4	M.	George III b. 1738. Casanova d. 1798.
5	Tu.	TRINITY LAW SITTINGS BEGIN. Stravinsky b. 1882.
6	W.	Pierre Corneille b. 1606. Thomas Mann b. 1875.
7	Th.	Paul Gaugin b. 1848. E. M. Forster d. 1970.
8	F.	Schumann b. 1810. George Sand d. 1876.
9	S.	Charles Dickens d. 1870. Sybil Thorndike d. 1976.

17 11　Mars in conjunction
　　　with Moon. Mars 6°S.
20 08　Venus in conjunction
　　　with Moon. Venus
　　　7°S.
21 16　Solstice.
21 21　Mercury in conjunc-
　　　tion with Moon. Mer-
　　　cury 4°S.
23 22　Jupiter in conjunc-
　　　tion with Moon. Ju-
　　　piter 2°S.
29 15　Uranus at opposition.

10	S.	**Trinity Sunday.** DUKE OF EDINBURGH b. 1921.
11	M.	**St. Barnabas.** John Constable b. 1776.
12	Tu.	Harriet Martineau b. 1802. George Bush b. 1924.
13	W.	Fanny Burney b. 1752. W. B. Yeats b. 1865.
14	Th.	CORPUS CHRISTI. Harriet Beecher Stowe b. 1811.
15	F.	The Black Prince b. 1330. Grieg b. 1843.
16	S.	Tom Graveney b. 1927. Brian Statham b. 1930.

CONSTELLATIONS

　The following constella-
tions are near the meridian
at

d h	d h
May　1 24	May 16 23
June 1 22	June 15 21
July　1 20	July 16 19

Cassiopeia (below the
Pole), Ursa Minor, Draco,
Ursa Major, Canes Venatici,
Bootes, Corona, Serpens,
Virgo and Libra.

17	S.	**2nd S. after Pentecost.** John Wesley b. 1703.
18	M.	Maxim Gorky d. 1936. Ethel Barrymore d. 1959.
19	Tu.	James I b. 1566. Blaise Pascal b. 1623.
20	W.	Offenbach b. 1819. Errol Flynn b. 1909.
21	Th.	PRINCE WILLIAM OF WALES b. 1982. Sartre b. 1905.
22	F.	Giuseppe Mazzini b. 1805. Judy Garland d. 1969.
23	S.	Edward VIII b. 1894. Jean Anouilh b. 1910.

ALGOL

ALGOL is inconveniently
situated for observation during June.

24	S.	**St. John the Baptist. 3rd S. after Pentecost.**
25	M.	George Orwell b. 1903. Korean War began 1950.
26	Tu.	George IV d. 1830. Pearl S. Buck b. 1892.
27	W.	Helen Keller b. 1880.
28	Th.	Henry VIII b. 1491. Rousseau b. 1712.
29	F.	**St. Peter.** Trades unions legalized 1871.
30	S.	Margery Allingham d. 1966. Nancy Mitford d. 1973.

*Centenary.

PHASES OF THE MOON

		d	h	m
○	Full Moon	8	11	01
☾	Last Quarter.......	16	04	48
●	New Moon.........	22	18	55
☽	First Quarter	29	22	07

	d	h
Apogee (406,180 kilometres)	6	04
Perigee (359,940　　,,　　)	21	11

Mean Longitude of Ascending
Node on June 1, 310°.

See note on *Summer Time*, p. 24.

MONTHLY NOTES

June 16. Queen's Official Birthday.

　　21. Longest day.

　　24. Midsummer Day. Quarter Day.

Day	Right Ascension	Dec. +	Equation of Time	Rise 52°	Rise 56°	Transit	Set 52°	Set 56°	Sidereal Time	Transit of First Point of Aries
	h m s	° ′	m s	h m	h m	h m	h m	h m	h m s	h m s
1	4 34 33	21 59	+ 2 19	3 46	3 22	11 58	20 10	20 34	16 36 53	7 21 55
2	4 38 39	22 08	+ 2 10	3 45	3 21	11 58	20 11	20 35	16 40 49	7 17 59
3	4 42 45	22 15	+ 2 01	3 45	3 20	11 58	20 12	20 37	16 44 46	7 14 03
4	4 46 51	22 23	+ 1 51	3 44	3 19	11 58	20 13	20 38	16 48 42	7 10 07
5	4 50 58	22 30	+ 1 41	3 43	3 18	11 58	20 14	20 39	16 52 39	7 06 11
6	4 55 05	22 36	+ 1 30	3 43	3 18	11 59	20 15	20 40	16 56 35	7 02 15
7	4 59 12	22 42	+ 1 20	3 42	3 17	11 59	20 16	20 41	17 00 32	6 58 19
8	5 03 20	22 48	+ 1 08	3 42	3 16	11 59	20 17	20 42	17 04 29	6 54 23
9	5 07 28	22 54	+ 0 57	3 41	3 16	11 59	20 18	20 43	17 08 25	6 50 27
10	5 11 36	22 59	+ 0 45	3 41	3 15	11 59	20 18	20 44	17 12 22	6 46 32
11	5 15 45	23 03	+ 0 34	3 40	3 14	12 00	20 19	20 45	17 16 18	6 42 36
12	5 19 53	23 07	+ 0 21	3 40	3 14	12 00	20 20	20 46	17 20 15	6 38 40
13	5 24 02	23 11	+ 0 09	3 40	3 14	12 00	20 20	20 47	17 24 11	6 34 44
14	5 28 11	23 14	− 0 03	3 40	3 13	12 00	20 21	20 47	17 28 08	6 30 48
15	5 32 21	23 17	− 0 16	3 39	3 13	12 00	20 22	20 48	17 32 04	6 26 52
16	5 36 30	23 20	− 0 29	3 39	3 13	12 01	20 22	20 49	17 36 01	6 22 56
17	5 40 39	23 22	− 0 42	3 39	3 13	12 01	20 23	20 49	17 39 58	6 19 00
18	5 44 49	23 24	− 0 55	3 39	3 13	12 01	20 23	20 49	17 43 54	6 15 04
19	5 48 59	23 25	− 1 08	3 39	3 13	12 01	20 23	20 50	17 47 51	6 11 08
20	5 53 08	23 26	− 1 21	3 39	3 13	12 01	20 24	20 50	17 51 47	6 07 12
21	5 57 18	23 26	− 1 34	3 40	3 13	12 02	20 24	20 50	17 55 44	6 03 16
22	6 01 28	23 27	− 1 47	3 40	3 13	12 02	20 24	20 51	17 59 40	5 59 21
23	6 05 38	23 26	− 2 01	3 40	3 13	12 02	20 24	20 51	18 03 37	5 55 25
24	6 09 47	23 25	− 2 14	3 40	3 14	12 02	20 24	20 51	18 07 34	5 51 29
25	6 13 57	23 24	− 2 27	3 41	3 14	12 03	20 24	20 51	18 11 30	5 47 33
26	6 18 06	23 23	− 2 39	3 41	3 15	12 03	20 24	20 51	18 15 27	5 43 37
27	6 22 15	23 21	− 2 52	3 42	3 15	12 03	20 24	20 50	18 19 23	5 39 41
28	6 26 24	23 18	− 3 05	3 42	3 16	12 03	20 24	20 50	18 23 20	5 35 45
29	6 30 33	23 15	− 3 17	3 43	3 17	12 03	20 24	20 50	18 27 16	5 31 49
30	6 34 42	23 12	− 3 29	3 43	3 17	12 04	20 23	20 49	18 31 13	5 27 53

THE SUN   s.d. 15′·8

Duration of Civil (C), Nautical (N), and Astronomical (A), Twilight (in minutes)

Lat. °	June 1 C	June 1 N	June 1 A	June 11 C	June 11 N	June 11 A	June 21 C	June 21 N	June 21 A	June 30 C	June 30 N	June 30 A
52	47	117	T.A.N.	48	125	T.A.N.	49	128	T.A.N.	49	125	T.A.N.
56	58	T.A.N.	T.A.N.	61	T.A.N.	T.A.N.	63	T.A.N.	T.A.N.	62	T.A.N.	T.A.N.

ASTRONOMICAL NOTES

MERCURY remains unsuitably placed for observation throughout the month.

VENUS, magnitude −4·0, is a splendid object in the early mornings, low above the eastern horizon before dawn. For observers in the latitudes of the British Isles its movement towards the Sun is more than offset by its northward motion in declination so that it is gradually visible for longer each morning throughout the month.

MARS, magnitude +0·4, is still a morning object. By the end of June it is visible low on the eastern horizon by about 01h.

JUPITER, magnitude −1·8, is now coming to the end of its period of evening visibility and is unlikely to be seen after the first two weeks of the month.

SATURN, magnitude +0·2, is now rising before midnight and visible low in the south-eastern sky until the long morning twilight inhibits observation.

URANUS is at opposition on the 29th, in the constellation of Sagittarius. Uranus is barely visible to the naked eye since its magnitude is +5·6, but it is readily located with only small optical aid.

TWILIGHT. Reference to the section just above these notes shows that astronomical twilight lasts all night for some time around the summer solstice (i.e. in June and July), even in southern England. Under these conditions the sky never gets completely dark since the Sun is always less than 18° below the horizon.

THE MOON

Day	R.A.	Dec.	Hor. Par.	Semi- diam.	Sun's Co- long.	P.A. of Bright Limb	Phase	Age	Rise 52°	Rise 56°	Tran- sit	Set 52°	Set 56°
	h m	°	′	′	°	°		d	h m	h m	h m	h m	h m
1	11 11	+ 1·8	55·7	15·2	1	292	57	7·5	13 02	13 03	19 06	0 43	0 44
2	11 55	− 3·7	55·1	15·0	13	292	66	8·5	14 14	14 20	19 47	0 54	0 51
3	12 38	− 9·1	54·6	14·9	25	291	75	9·5	15 25	15 36	20 28	1 06	0 58
4	13 23	−14·0	54·3	14·8	38	288	83	10·5	16 36	16 53	21 11	1 20	1 07
5	14 09	−18·4	54·1	14·7	50	283	89	11·5	17 48	18 11	21 56	1 36	1 18
6	14 57	−22·0	54·0	14·7	62	277	94	12·5	18 58	19 27	22 44	1 56	1 33
7	15 47	−24·8	54·0	14·7	74	267	98	13·5	20 04	20 37	23 34	2 24	1 55
8	16 39	−26·4	54·1	14·8	86	238	100	14·5	21 01	21 35	—	3 01	2 28
9	17 33	−26·9	54·4	14·8	99	124	100	15·5	21 46	22 18	0 25	3 50	3 16
10	18 26	−26·0	54·7	14·9	111	96	98	16·5	22 21	22 48	1 17	4 51	4 19
11	19 20	−24·0	55·0	15·0	123	85	94	17·5	22 47	23 08	2 08	6 01	5 35
12	20 11	−20·7	55·5	15·1	135	78	89	18·5	23 06	23 22	2 57	7 16	6 56
13	21 01	−16·5	56·0	15·3	147	73	81	19·5	23 22	23 32	3 44	8 33	8 19
14	21 50	−11·5	56·6	15·4	160	70	73	20·5	23 36	23 41	4 30	9 51	9 42
15	22 37	− 5·9	57·3	15·6	172	67	63	21·5	23 49	23 49	5 15	11 09	11 06
16	23 25	+ 0·2	58·0	15·8	184	67	52	22·5	—	23 58	6 00	12 29	12 32
17	0 14	+ 6·3	58·8	16·0	196	67	41	23·5	0 03	—	6 48	13 52	14 01
18	1 06	+12·3	59·5	16·2	209	70	30	24·5	0 18	0 08	7 38	15 19	15 34
19	2 01	+17·8	60·1	16·4	221	74	20	25·5	0 38	0 21	8 33	16 50	17 12
20	3 01	+22·4	60·6	16·5	233	80	11	26·5	1 05	0 41	9 33	18 20	18 50
21	4 05	+25·5	60·9	16·6	245	89	5	27·5	1 44	1 13	10 37	19 40	20 14
22	5 12	+26·9	60·9	16·6	258	104	1	28·5	2 39	2 05	11 43	20 43	21 16
23	6 19	+26·2	60·6	16·5	270	228	0	0·2	3 53	3 21	12 48	21 28	21 54
24	7 23	+23·8	60·0	16·3	282	273	2	1·2	5 18	4 52	13 48	21 58	22 18
25	8 23	+19·8	59·2	16·1	294	283	7	2·2	6 46	6 27	14 43	22 19	22 33
26	9 18	+14·8	58·4	15·9	307	289	14	3·2	8 11	7 59	15 33	22 35	22 43
27	10 08	+ 9·3	57·4	15·6	319	292	22	4·2	9 31	9 25	16 19	22 49	22 52
28	10 55	+ 3·5	56·6	15·4	331	294	31	5·2	10 47	10 46	17 02	23 01	23 00
29	11 41	− 2·2	55·8	15·2	343	294	41	6·2	12 00	12 05	17 43	23 13	23 07
30	12 25	− 7·7	55·1	15·0	355	293	51	7·2	13 12	13 22	18 25	23 26	23 15

MERCURY ☿

Day	R.A.	Dec. +	Diam.	Phase	Tran- sit		Day	R.A.	Dec. +	Diam.	Phase	Tran- sit	
	h m	°	″		h m			h m	°	″		h m	
1	2 58	13·2	—	—	10 21		16	4 20	19·9	—	—	10 45	
4	3 10	14·3	—	—	10 22	Mercury is too	19	4 42	21·2	—	—	10 56	Mercury is too
7	3 25	15·6	—	—	10 25	close to the	22	5 07	22·4	—	—	11 10	close to the
10	3 41	17·0	—	—	10 30	Sun for	25	5 33	23·4	—	—	11 24	Sun for
13	4 00	18·4	—	—	10 36	observation	28	6 01	24·1	—	—	11 41	observation
16	4 20	19·9	—	—	10 45		31	6 30	24·4	—	—	11 58	

VENUS ♀   MARS ♂

Day	R.A.	Dec. +	Diam.	Phase	Tran- sit	5° high. 52°	5° high. 56°	Day	R.A.	Dec.	Diam.	Phase	Tran- sit	5° high. 52°	5° high. 56°
	h m	°	″		h m	h m	h m		h m	°	″		h m	h m	h m
1	2 02	10·2	14	75	9 25	3 05	3 00	1	0 05	− 1·5	7	86	7 28	2 08	2 13
6	2 24	12·1	14	76	9 28	2 57	2 51	6	0 18	− 0·1	7	86	7 21	1 55	1 58
11	2 47	14·0	14	78	9 31	2 50	2 42	11	0 32	+ 1·3	7	86	7 15	1 41	1 43
16	3 10	15·7	13	79	9 34	2 45	2 35	16	0 45	+ 2·7	7	86	7 09	1 28	1 29
21	3 33	17·3	13	81	9 38	2 40	2 28	21	0 58	+ 4·0	7	85	7 02	1 14	1 14
26	3 58	18·7	13	82	9 43	2 36	2 23	26	1 11	+ 5·4	8	85	6 56	1 01	1 00
31	4 22	20·0	12	84	9 47	2 34	2 19	31	1 25	+ 6·7	8	85	6 49	0 48	0 45

SUNRISE AND SUNSET

Day	London a.m. h m	London p.m. h m	Bristol a.m. h m	Bristol p.m. h m	Birmingham a.m. h m	Birmingham p.m. h m	Manchester a.m. h m	Manchester p.m. h m	Newcastle a.m. h m	Newcastle p.m. h m	Glasgow a.m. h m	Glasgow p.m. h m	Belfast a.m. h m	Belfast p.m. h m
1	3 49	8 07	3 59	8 16	3 50	8 19	3 47	8 26	3 35	8 32	3 41	8 49	3 55	8 48
2	3 49	8 08	3 59	8 17	3 50	8 20	3 46	8 27	3 34	8 33	3 40	8 50	3 54	8 49
3	3 48	8 09	3 58	8 18	3 49	8 21	3 45	8 29	3 33	8 35	3 39	8 52	3 53	8 51
4	3 47	8 10	3 57	8 19	3 48	8 22	3 45	8 30	3 33	8 36	3 38	8 53	3 53	8 52
5	3 46	8 11	3 56	8 20	3 47	8 23	3 44	8 31	3 32	8 37	3 37	8 54	3 52	8 53
6	3 46	8 12	3 56	8 21	3 47	8 24	3 43	8 32	3 31	8 38	3 36	8 55	3 51	8 54
7	3 45	8 13	3 55	8 22	3 46	8 25	3 42	8 33	3 30	8 39	3 36	8 56	3 50	8 55
8	3 45	8 14	3 55	8 23	3 46	8 26	3 42	8 34	3 29	8 41	3 34	8 58	3 50	8 56
9	3 44	8 14	3 54	8 24	3 45	8 27	3 41	8 35	3 29	8 42	3 34	8 59	3 49	8 57
10	3 44	8 15	3 54	8 25	3 45	8 28	3 41	8 36	3 28	8 43	3 33	9 00	3 49	8 58
11	3 43	8 16	3 53	8 26	3 44	8 29	3 40	8 36	3 27	8 43	3 32	9 00	3 48	8 58
12	3 43	8 17	3 53	8 26	3 44	8 29	3 40	8 37	3 27	8 44	3 32	9 01	3 48	8 59
13	3 43	8 17	3 53	8 27	3 44	8 30	3 40	8 38	3 27	8 45	3 32	9 02	3 48	9 00
14	3 43	8 18	3 53	8 28	3 44	8 31	3 39	8 39	3 26	8 46	3 31	9 03	3 47	9 01
15	3 42	8 18	3 52	8 28	3 43	8 31	3 39	8 39	3 26	8 46	3 31	9 04	3 47	9 01
16	3 42	8 19	3 52	8 29	3 43	8 32	3 39	8 40	3 26	8 47	3 31	9 04	3 47	9 02
17	3 42	8 19	3 52	8 29	3 43	8 32	3 39	8 40	3 26	8 47	3 31	9 05	3 47	9 02
18	3 42	8 20	3 52	8 30	3 43	8 33	3 39	8 41	3 26	8 48	3 30	9 05	3 47	9 03
19	3 42	8 20	3 52	8 30	3 43	8 33	3 39	8 41	3 26	8 49	3 30	9 06	3 47	9 03
20	3 42	8 20	3 52	8 30	3 43	8 33	3 39	8 42	3 26	8 49	3 31	9 06	3 47	9 04
21	3 42	8 21	3 52	8 31	3 43	8 34	3 39	8 42	3 26	8 49	3 31	9 06	3 47	9 04
22	3 42	8 21	3 52	8 31	3 43	8 34	3 39	8 42	3 26	8 49	3 31	9 06	3 47	9 04
23	3 43	8 21	3 53	8 31	3 44	8 34	3 39	8 42	3 26	8 49	3 31	9 07	3 47	9 04
24	3 43	8 21	3 53	8 31	3 44	8 34	3 40	8 42	3 27	8 49	3 31	9 07	3 48	9 04
25	3 43	8 21	3 53	8 31	3 44	8 34	3 40	8 42	3 27	8 49	3 32	9 07	3 48	9 04
26	3 44	8 21	3 54	8 31	3 45	8 34	3 40	8 42	3 27	8 49	3 32	9 07	3 49	9 04
27	3 44	8 21	3 54	8 31	3 45	8 34	3 41	8 42	3 28	8 49	3 33	9 06	3 49	9 04
28	3 45	8 21	3 55	8 31	3 46	8 34	3 41	8 42	3 28	8 49	3 33	9 06	3 49	9 04
29	3 45	8 21	3 55	8 31	3 46	8 34	3 42	8 42	3 29	8 49	3 34	9 06	3 50	9 04
30	3 46	8 21	3 56	8 31	3 47	8 34	3 43	8 42	3 30	8 49	3 35	9 06	3 51	9 04

JUPITER ♃ · SATURN ♄

Day	Jupiter R.A. h m	Jupiter Dec. + °	Jupiter Transit h m	Jupiter 5° high 52° h m	Jupiter 5° high 56° h m	Saturn R.A. h m	Saturn Dec. − °	Saturn Transit h m	Saturn 5° high 52° h m	Saturn 5° high 56° h m
1	6 56	23·0	14 17	21 48	22 05	19 47	21·0	3 09	23 46	0 20
11	7 05	22·8	13 47	21 16	21 34	19 45	21·1	2 28	23 06	23 25
21	7 14	22·5	13 17	20 45	21 02	19 42	21·3	1 46	22 25	22 55
31	7 24	22·3	12 47	20 13	20 30	19 39	21·4	1 04	21 44	22 14

Equatorial diameter of Jupiter 32″; of Saturn 18″.　Diameters of Saturn's rings 41″ and 16″.

URANUS ♅ · NEPTUNE ♆

Day	Uranus R.A. h m	Uranus Dec. − ° ′	Uranus Transit h m	Uranus 10° high 52° h m	Uranus 10° high 56° h m	Neptune R.A. h m	Neptune Dec. − ° ′	Neptune Transit h m	Neptune 10° high 52° h m	Neptune 10° high 56° h m
1	18 38·0	23 29	2 01	0 00	1 18	19 00·7	21 50	2 23	0 03	0 56
11	18 36·4	23 30	1 20	23 15	0 38	19 00·0	21 51	1 43	23 19	0 17
21	18 34·7	23 32	0 39	22 35	23 54	18 58·6	21 53	1 03	22 39	23 33
31	18 32·9	23 33	23 54	21 54	23 14	18 57·5	21 54	0 22	21 58	22 53

Diameter 4″　　　　Diameter 2″

Day of Month	Week	
		Julius Caesar, formerly *Quintilis*, 5th month (from March). Sun's Longitude 120° ♌ 23ᵈ 02ʰ
1	S.	**4th S. after Pentecost.** PRINCESS OF WALES b. 1961.
2	M.	Hermann Hesse b. 1877. Tyrone Guthrie b. 1900.
3	Tu.	**St. Thomas.** Tom Stoppard b. 1937.
4	W.	INDEPENDENCE DAY, U.S.A., 1776. Hawthorne b.
5	Th.	Jean Cocteau b. 1889. N.H.S. began 1948. [1804.
6	F.	John Flaxman b. 1755. Beatrix Potter b. 1866.
7	S.	A. Conan Doyle d. 1930. Sir Allen Lane d. 1970.
8	S.	**5th S. after Pentecost.** Shelley d. 1822.
9	M.	Ottorino Respighi b. 1879. David Hockney b. 1937.
10	Tu.	John Calvin b. 1509. Marcel Proust b. 1871.
11	W.	Robert the Bruce b. 1274.
12	Th.	Julius Ceasar b. 102 B.C. Daguerre d. 1851.
13	F.	John Clare b. 1793. Sidney Webb b. 1859.
14	S.	FÊTE NATIONALE, FRANCE. Bastille stormed 1789.
15	S.	**6th S. after Pentecost.** ST. SWITHIN'S DAY.
16	M.	Joshua Reynolds b. 1723. Jean Corot b. 1796.
17	Tu.	Adam Smith d. 1790.* First issue of *Punch* 1841.
18	W.	Gilbert White b. 1720. Thackeray b. 1811.
19	Th.	Edgar Degas b. 1834.
20	F.	Petrarch b. 1304. Calouste Gulbenkian d. 1955.
21	S.	Robert Burns d. 1796. Hemingway b. 1898.
22	S.	**St. Mary Magdalen. 7th S. after Pentecost.**
23	M.	Raymond Chandler b. 1888. Olivia Manning d. 1980.
24	Tu.	Simón Bolívar b. 1783. Peter Sellers d. 1980.
25	W.	**St. James.** Samuel Taylor Coleridge d. 1834.
26	Th.	G. B. Shaw b. 1856. Aldous Huxley b. 1894.
27	F.	Hilaire Belloc b. 1870. Gertrude Stein d. 1946.
28	S.	Robespierre exec. 1794.
29	S.	**8th S. after Pentecost.** van Gogh d. 1890.*
30	M.	Diderot d. 1784. Henry Moore b. 1898.
31	Tu.	TRINITY LAW SITTINGS END. Loyola d. 1556.

* Centenary.

PHENOMENA

d	h	
2	17	Mercury in superior conjunction.
4	05	Earth at aphelion (152 million km.).
5	11	Neptune at opposition.
7	11	Jupiter in conjunction with Mercury. Jupiter 1°S.
8	15	Saturn in conjunction with Moon. Saturn 1°N.
14	18	Saturn at opposition.
15	06	Jupiter in conjunction with Sun.
16	03	Mars in conjunction with Moon. Mars 7°S.
20	03	Venus in conjunction with Moon. Venus 4°S.
21	18	Jupiter in conjunction with Moon. Jupiter 1°S.
23	17	Mercury in conjunction with Moon. Mercury 2°N.

CONSTELLATIONS

The following constellations are near the meridian at

	d	h		d	h
June 1	24		June 15	23
July 1	22		July 16	21
Aug. 1	20		Aug. 16	19

Ursa Minor, Draco, Corona, Hercules, Lyra, Serpens, Ophiuchus, Libra, Scorpius and Sagittarius.

MINIMA OF ALGOL

d	h		d	h
3	08		17	16
6	05		20	13
9	02		23	10
11	23		26	07
14	20		29	04

PHASES OF THE MOON

		d	h	m
○	Full Moon	8	01	23
☽	Last Quarter......	15	11	04
●	New Moon........	22	02	54
☽	First Quarter	29	14	01

	d	h
Apogee (405,350 kilometres)	3	16
Perigee (364,490 „)	19	11
Apogee (404,480 „)	31	08

Mean Longitude of Ascending Node on July 1, 309°

See note on *Summer Time*, p. 24.

MONTHLY NOTES

July   1. National Day, Canada.

        3. Dog Days begin (end Aug. 15).

        5. Tynwald Day, Isle of Man.

     12. Bank Holiday, Northern Ireland.

     24. Islamic New Year (A.H. 1411).

Day	Right Ascension	Dec. +	Equation of Time	Rise 52°	Rise 56°	Transit	Set 52°	Set 56°	Sidereal Time	Transit of First Point of Aries
	h m s	° '	m s	h m	h m	h m	h m	h m	h m s	h m s
1	6 38 50	23 08	−3 41	3 44	3 18	12 04	20 23	20 49	18 35 09	5 23 57
2	6 42 59	23 04	−3 53	3 45	3 19	12 04	20 23	20 49	18 39 06	5 20 01
3	6 47 06	23 00	−4 04	3 45	3 20	12 04	20 22	20 48	18 43 03	5 16 06
4	6 51 14	22 55	−4 15	3 46	3 21	12 04	20 22	20 47	18 46 59	5 12 10
5	6 55 21	22 50	−4 26	3 47	3 22	12 05	20 21	20 47	18 50 56	5 08 14
6	6 59 28	22 44	−4 36	3 48	3 23	12 05	20 21	20 46	18 54 52	5 04 18
7	7 03 35	22 38	−4 46	3 49	3 24	12 05	20 20	20 45	18 58 49	5 00 22
8	7 07 41	22 32	−4 56	3 50	3 25	12 05	20 20	20 44	19 02 45	4 56 26
9	7 11 47	22 25	−5 05	3 51	3 26	12 05	20 19	20 43	19 06 42	4 52 30
10	7 15 52	22 18	−5 14	3 52	3 27	12 05	20 18	20 42	19 10 38	4 48 34
11	7 19 57	22 10	−5 22	3 53	3 29	12 05	20 17	20 41	19 14 35	4 44 38
12	7 24 02	22 02	−5 30	3 54	3 30	12 06	20 16	20 40	19 18 32	4 40 42
13	7 28 06	21 54	−5 38	3 55	3 31	12 06	20 16	20 39	19 22 28	4 36 46
14	7 32 09	21 45	−5 45	3 56	3 33	12 06	20 15	20 38	19 26 25	4 32 51
15	7 36 13	21 36	−5 51	3 57	3 34	12 06	20 14	20 37	19 30 21	4 28 55
16	7 40 15	21 27	−5 58	3 59	3 36	12 06	20 13	20 35	19 34 18	4 24 59
17	7 44 18	21 17	−6 03	4 00	3 37	12 06	20 12	20 34	19 38 14	4 21 03
18	7 48 19	21 07	−6 08	4 01	3 39	12 06	20 10	20 32	19 42 11	4 17 07
19	7 52 21	20 56	−6 13	4 02	3 40	12 06	20 09	20 31	19 46 07	4 13 11
20	7 56 21	20 45	−6 17	4 04	3 42	12 06	20 08	20 30	19 50 04	4 09 15
21	8 00 21	20 34	−6 21	4 05	3 44	12 06	20 07	20 28	19 54 01	4 05 19
22	8 04 21	20 22	−6 24	4 06	3 45	12 06	20 05	20 26	19 57 57	4 01 23
23	8 08 20	20 10	−6 26	4 08	3 47	12 06	20 04	20 25	20 01 54	3 57 27
24	8 12 18	19 58	−6 28	4 09	3 49	12 06	20 03	20 23	20 05 50	3 53 31
25	8 16 16	19 45	−6 29	4 11	3 51	12 07	20 01	20 21	20 09 47	3 49 35
26	8 20 14	19 33	−6 30	4 12	3 52	12 07	20 00	20 20	20 13 43	3 45 40
27	8 24 10	19 19	−6 30	4 14	3 54	12 07	19 58	20 18	20 17 40	3 41 44
28	8 28 06	19 06	−6 30	4 15	3 56	12 06	19 57	20 16	20 21 36	3 37 48
29	8 32 02	18 52	−6 28	4 17	3 58	12 06	19 55	20 14	20 25 33	3 33 52
30	8 35 56	18 38	−6 27	4 18	4 00	12 06	19 54	20 12	20 29 30	3 29 56
31	8 39 50	18 23	−6 24	4 20	4 01	12 06	19 52	20 10	20 33 26	3 26 00

THE SUN   s.d. 15'·8

Duration of Civil (C), Nautical (N), and Astronomical (A), Twilight (in minutes)

Lat. °	July 1 C	N	A	July 11 C	N	A	July 21 C	N	A	July 31 C	N	A
52	48	124	T.A.N.	46	116	T.A.N.	44	107	T.A.N.	41	98	180
56	61	T.A.N.	T.A.N.	58	T.A.N.	T.A.N.	53	144	T.A.N.	49	122	T.A.N.

ASTRONOMICAL NOTES

MERCURY is too close to the Sun for observation.

VENUS continues to be visible as a splendid object in the morning skies, magnitude −3·9. By the end of the month it is visible above the E.N.E. horizon for as long as an hour and a half before sunrise. On the morning of the 20th the old crescent Moon, only 2 days before New, passes 4°N. of the planet.

MARS continues to be visible as a morning object, magnitude +0·1. It moves from Pisces to Aries during the month.

JUPITER is in conjunction with the Sun on the 15th and is therefore unsuitably placed for observation.

SATURN, magnitude +0·1, is at opposition on the 14th and thus visible throughout the hours of darkness. The Moon, near Full, is near the planet on the night of the 8th. Saturn is in Sagittarius. The rings of Saturn present a beautiful spectacle to the observer with only a small telescope. The rings are still well open.

NEPTUNE is at opposition on the 5th, in the constellation of Sagittarius. It is not visible to the naked eye since its magnitude is +7·9.

ECLIPSE. A total eclipse of the Sun occurs on the 22nd. See page 74 for details.

THE MOON

Day	R.A.	Dec.	Hor. Par.	Semi-diam.	Sun's Co-long.	P.A. of Bright Limb	Phase	Age	Rise 52°	Rise 56°	Transit	Set 52°	Set 56°
	h m	°	′	′	°	°		d	h m	h m	h m	h m	h m
1	13 10	−12·8	54·6	14·9	8	291	61	8·2	14 24	14 39	19 08	23 41	23 25
2	13 56	−17·4	54·3	14·8	20	288	70	9·2	15 36	15 57	19 52	—	23 38
3	14 43	−21·2	54·1	14·7	32	284	78	10·2	16 47	17 14	20 39	0 00	23 57
4	15 33	−24·2	54·1	14·7	44	279	85	11·2	17 55	18 27	21 28	0 25	—
5	16 24	−26·2	54·2	14·8	57	273	91	12·2	18 55	19 30	22 20	0 59	0 26
6	17 18	−26·9	54·4	14·8	69	265	96	13·2	19 45	20 18	23 12	1 44	1 09
7	18 12	−26·4	54·7	14·9	81	255	99	14·2	20 23	20 52	—	2 41	2 08
8	19 06	−24·6	55·1	15·0	93	192	100	15·2	20 51	21 14	0 03	3 50	3 21
9	19 58	−21·6	55·5	15·1	105	83	99	16·2	21 13	21 30	0 53	5 04	4 42
10	20 49	−17·5	56·0	15·3	117	74	96	17·2	21 30	21 41	1 42	6 22	6 06
11	21 38	−12·6	56·5	15·4	130	69	91	18·2	21 44	21 50	2 28	7 40	7 30
12	22 26	− 7·1	57·0	15·5	142	66	85	19·2	21 57	21 58	3 14	8 58	8 54
13	23 14	− 1·1	57·6	15·7	154	65	76	20·2	22 10	22 07	3 59	10 17	10 18
14	0 02	+ 5·0	58·1	15·8	166	65	66	21·2	22 25	22 16	4 45	11 38	11 45
15	0 52	+10·9	58·7	16·0	179	67	55	22·2	22 42	22 27	5 33	13 01	13 14
16	1 45	+16·5	59·2	16·1	191	70	44	23·2	23 05	22 44	6 25	14 29	14 48
17	2 42	+21·2	59·6	16·2	203	74	33	24·2	23 37	23 09	7 21	15 57	16 24
18	3 43	+24·7	59·9	16·3	215	80	22	25·2	—	23 50	8 21	17 19	17 52
19	4 47	+26·7	60·1	16·4	227	87	13	26·2	0 23	—	9 25	18 29	19 03
20	5 53	+26·7	60·1	16·4	240	95	6	27·2	1 28	0 54	10 29	19 20	19 50
21	6 57	+25·0	59·9	16·3	252	104	2	28·2	2 47	2 18	11 31	19 56	20 19
22	7 58	+21·6	59·5	16·2	264	131	0	29·2	4 15	3 53	12 29	20 21	20 38
23	8 55	+17·0	58·9	16·0	276	288	1	0·9	5 42	5 27	13 21	20 40	20 50
24	9 48	+11·5	58·1	15·8	289	293	5	1·9	7 05	6 57	14 09	20 54	21 00
25	10 37	+ 5·7	57·3	15·6	301	296	10	2·9	8 25	8 22	14 54	21 07	21 08
26	11 24	− 0·2	56·5	15·4	313	296	17	3·9	9 41	9 43	15 38	21 19	21 15
27	12 10	− 5·9	55·8	15·2	325	296	26	4·9	10 55	11 02	16 20	21 32	21 23
28	12 55	−11·2	55·2	15·0	338	294	35	5·9	12 08	12 21	17 03	21 47	21 32
29	13 41	−16·1	54·7	14·9	350	292	45	6·9	13 21	13 39	17 47	22 04	21 44
30	14 28	−20·2	54·4	14·8	2	288	54	7·9	14 33	14 57	18 33	22 26	22 01
31	15 17	−23·5	54·2	14·8	14	284	63	8·9	15 42	16 12	19 22	22 56	22 26

MERCURY ☿

Day	R.A.	Dec. +	Diam.	Phase	Transit		Day	R.A.	Dec. +	Diam.	Phase	Transit	
	h m	°	″		h m			h m	°	″		h m	
1	6 30	24·4	—	—	11 58		16	8 42	20·0	—	—	13 10	
4	6 59	24·2	—	—	12 14	Mercury is too	19	9 04	18·4	—	—	13 20	Mercury is too
7	7 27	23·7	—	—	12 30	close to the	22	9 25	16·6	—	—	13 28	close to the
10	7 53	22·7	—	—	12 45	Sun for	25	9 44	14·8	—	—	13 35	Sun for
13	8 19	21·5	—	—	12 59	observation	28	10 01	12·9	—	—	13 40	observation
16	8 42	20·0	—	—	13 10		31	10 17	10·9	—	—	13 44	

VENUS ♀

Day	R.A.	Dec. +	Diam.	Phase	Transit	5° high 52°	5° high 56°
	h m	°	″		h m	h m	h m
1	4 22	20·0	12	84	9 47	2 34	2 19
6	4 47	21·0	12	85	9 53	2 33	2 17
11	5 13	21·8	12	86	9 59	2 34	2 17
16	5 38	22·4	12	87	10 05	2 36	2 19
21	6 04	22·7	11	88	10 11	2 41	2 23
26	6 31	22·8	11	90	10 17	2 47	2 29
31	6 57	22·5	11	91	10 24	2 55	2 37

MARS ♂

Day	R.A.	Dec. +	Diam.	Phase	Transit	5° high 52°	5° high 56°
	h m	°	″		h m	h m	h m
1	1 25	6·7	8	85	6 49	0 48	0 45
6	1 38	7·9	8	85	6 42	0 34	0 31
11	1 50	9·2	8	85	6 36	0 21	0 17
16	2 03	10·3	8	84	6 29	0 08	0 03
21	2 16	11·4	9	84	6 22	23 53	23 47
26	2 29	12·5	9	84	6 14	23 40	23 33
31	2 41	13·5	9	84	6 07	23 28	23 20

SUNRISE AND SUNSET

Day	London a.m.	London p.m.	Bristol a.m.	Bristol p.m.	Birmingham a.m.	Birmingham p.m.	Manchester a.m.	Manchester p.m.	Newcastle a.m.	Newcastle p.m.	Glasgow a.m.	Glasgow p.m.	Belfast a.m.	Belfast p.m.
	h m	h m	h m	h m	h m	h m	h m	h m	h m	h m	h m	h m	h m	h m
1	3 46	8 21	3 56	8 30	3 47	8 33	3 43	8 41	3 30	8 48	3 35	9 05	3 51	9 03
2	3 47	8 20	3 57	8 30	3 48	8 33	3 44	8 41	3 31	8 48	3 36	9 05	3 52	9 03
3	3 48	8 20	3 58	8 29	3 49	8 32	3 45	8 40	3 32	8 47	3 37	9 04	3 53	9 02
4	3 49	8 20	3 59	8 29	3 50	8 32	3 46	8 40	3 33	8 47	3 38	9 04	3 54	9 02
5	3 49	8 20	3 59	8 29	3 50	8 32	3 47	8 39	3 34	8 46	3 39	9 03	3 55	9 01
6	3 50	8 19	4 00	8 28	3 51	8 31	3 48	8 39	3 35	8 45	3 40	9 02	3 56	9 01
7	3 51	8 18	4 01	8 27	3 52	8 30	3 49	8 38	3 36	8 45	3 41	9 02	3 57	9 00
8	3 52	8 18	4 02	8 27	3 53	8 30	3 50	8 38	3 37	8 44	3 42	9 01	3 58	9 00
9	3 53	8 17	4 03	8 26	3 54	8 29	3 51	8 37	3 38	8 43	3 43	9 00	3 59	8 59
10	3 54	8 16	4 04	8 25	3 55	8 28	3 52	8 36	3 39	8 42	3 44	8 59	4 00	8 58
11	3 55	8 16	4 05	8 25	3 56	8 28	3 53	8 35	3 41	8 41	3 46	8 58	4 01	8 57
12	3 56	8 15	4 06	8 24	3 57	8 27	3 54	8 34	3 42	8 40	3 47	8 57	4 02	8 56
13	3 57	8 14	4 07	8 23	3 58	8 26	3 55	8 33	3 43	8 39	3 48	8 56	4 03	8 55
14	3 58	8 13	4 08	8 22	3 59	8 25	3 56	8 32	3 44	8 38	3 50	8 55	4 04	8 54
15	3 59	8 12	4 10	8 22	4 01	8 24	3 58	8 31	3 46	8 37	3 51	8 53	4 06	8 53
16	4 00	8 11	4 11	8 21	4 02	8 23	3 59	8 30	3 47	8 36	3 53	8 52	4 07	8 52
17	4 01	8 10	4 12	8 20	4 03	8 22	4 00	8 29	3 48	8 35	3 54	8 51	4 08	8 51
18	4 03	8 09	4 13	8 19	4 05	8 21	4 02	8 28	3 50	8 33	3 56	8 49	4 10	8 49
19	4 04	8 08	4 15	8 18	4 06	8 19	4 03	8 26	3 51	8 32	3 57	8 48	4 11	8 48
20	4 05	8 07	4 16	8 17	4 08	8 18	4 05	8 25	3 53	8 30	3 59	8 46	4 13	8 46
21	4 06	8 05	4 17	8 15	4 09	8 17	4 06	8 24	3 55	8 29	4 01	8 45	4 15	8 45
22	4 08	8 04	4 18	8 14	4 11	8 15	4 08	8 22	3 56	8 27	4 02	8 43	4 16	8 43
23	4 09	8 03	4 20	8 13	4 12	8 14	4 09	8 21	3 58	8 26	4 04	8 42	4 18	8 42
24	4 10	8 02	4 21	8 12	4 13	8 13	4 10	8 20	4 00	8 24	4 06	8 40	4 20	8 40
25	4 12	8 00	4 22	8 10	4 15	8 11	4 12	8 18	4 01	8 23	4 07	8 38	4 21	8 39
26	4 13	7 59	4 24	8 09	4 16	8 10	4 13	8 17	4 03	8 21	4 09	8 37	4 23	8 37
27	4 14	7 57	4 25	8 07	4 17	8 08	4 14	8 15	4 04	8 19	4 11	8 35	4 24	8 35
28	4 16	7 56	4 26	8 06	4 19	8 07	4 16	8 14	4 06	8 18	4 12	8 33	4 26	8 34
29	4 18	7 54	4 28	8 04	4 21	8 05	4 18	8 12	4 08	8 16	4 14	8 31	4 28	8 32
30	4 19	7 53	4 29	8 03	4 22	8 04	4 19	8 10	4 09	8 14	4 16	8 29	4 29	8 30
31	4 21	7 51	4 31	8 01	4 24	8 02	4 21	8 09	4 11	8 12	4 18	8 27	4 31	8 29

JUPITER ♃   SATURN ♄

Day	R.A.	Dec. +	Transit		R.A.	Dec. −	Transit	5° high. 52°	5° high. 56°
	h m	°	h m		h m	°	h m	h m	h m
1	7 24	22·3	12 47	Jupiter is too	19 39	21·4	1 04	4 20	3 50
11	7 33	21·9	12 17	close to the Sun	19 36	21·5	0 22	3 37	3 06
21	7 43	21·6	11 47	for observation	19 33	21·6	23 35	2 53	2 22
31	7 52	21·2	11 17		19 30	21·8	22 53	2 10	1 39

Equatorial diameter of Jupiter 31″; of Saturn 18″.   Diameters of Saturn's rings 42″ and 16″.

URANUS ♅   NEPTUNE ♆

Day	R.A.	Dec. −	Transit	10° high. 52°	10° high. 56°	R.A.	Dec. −	Transit	10° high. 52°	10° high. 56°
	h m	° ′	h m	h m	h m	h m	° ′	h m	h m	h m
1	18 32·9	23 33	23 54	1 58	0 37	18 57·5	21 54	0 22	2 42	1 48
11	18 31·2	23 35	23 13	1 16	23 51	18 56·3	21 56	23 38	2 01	1 07
21	18 29·5	23 36	22 32	0 35	23 09	18 55·2	21 58	22 57	1 21	0 26
31	18 28·0	23 37	21 51	23 50	22 28	18 54·1	21 59	22 17	0 40	23 41

Diameter 4″   Diameter 2″

Day of		
Month	Week	Julius Caesar *Augustus*, formerly *Sextilis*, 6th month (from March). *Sun's Longitude* 150° ♍ 23ᵈ 09ʰ

Sun's Longitude 150° ♍ 23ᵈ 09ʰ

Month	Week	
1	W.	Queen Anne d. 1714. Herman Melville b. 1819.
2	Th.	Sir Arthur Bliss b. 1891.
3	F.	Rupert Brooke b. 1887. Colette d. 1954.
4	S.	QUEEN ELIZABETH THE QUEEN MOTHER b. 1900.
5	S.	**9th S. after Pentecost.** Maupassant b. 1850.
6	M.	**Transfiguration.** Hiroshima 1945.
7	Tu.	Joseph Jacquard d. 1834.
8	W.	PRINCESS BEATRICE OF YORK b. 1988.
9	Th.	John Dryden b. 1631. Philip Larkin b. 1922.
10	F.	Charles Keene b. 1823. Whistler b. 1834.
11	S.	Henry James Pye d. 1813. Charlotte Yonge b. 1823.
12	S.	**10th S. after Pentecost.** George IV b. 1762.
13	M.	John Ireland b. 1879. Basil Spence b. 1907.
14	Tu.	John Galsworthy b. 1867. Leonard Woolf d. 1969.
15	W.	PRINCESS ROYAL b. 1950. Walter Scott b. 1771.
16	Th.	Marvell d. 1678. Georgette Heyer b. 1902.
17	F.	Wilfred Scawen Blunt b. 1840.
18	S.	Lord Russell b. 1792.
19	S.	**11th S. after Pentecost.** Ogden Nash b. 1902.
20	M.	George Villiers, 1st Duke of Buckingham b. 1592.
21	Tu.	PRINCESS MARGARET b. 1930. William IV b. 1765.
22	W.	Richard III d. 1485. Debussy b. 1862.
23	Th.	Constant Lambert b. 1905. Valentino d. 1926.
24	F.	**St. Bartholomew.** Aubrey Beardsley b. 1872.
25	S.	Ivan the Terrible b. 1530.
26	S.	**12th S. after Pentecost.** Isherwood b. 1904.
27	M.	Georg Hegel b. 1770. C.S. Forester b. 1899.
28	Tu.	Goethe b. 1749. Tolstoy b. 1828.
29	W.	Lady Diana Cooper b. 1892.
30	Th.	Mary Wollstonecraft Shelley b. 1797.
31	F.	John Bunyan d. 1688. Baudelaire d. 1867.

*Centenary.

PHENOMENA

d	h	
4	18	Saturn in conjunction with Moon. Saturn 2°N.
11	20	Mercury at greatest elongation E. 27°.
13	00	Jupiter in conjunction with Venus. Jupiter 0°·04S.
13	15	Mars in conjunction with Moon. Mars 7°S.
18	13	Jupiter in conjunction with Moon. Jupiter 0°·4S.
19	00	Venus in conjunction with Moon. Venus 0°·4N.
22	11	Mercury in conjunction with Moon. Mercury 0°·1N.

CONSTELLATIONS

The following constellations are near the meridian at

d	h		d	h
July 1	24		July 16	23
Aug. 1	22		Aug. 16	21
Sept. 1	20		Sept. 15	19

Draco, Hercules, Lyra, Cygnus, Sagitta, Ophiuchus, Serpens, Aquila and Sagittarius.

MINIMA OF ALGOL

d	h		d	h
1	00		18	05
3	21		21	02
6	18		23	23
9	15		26	20
12	12		29	17
15	09			

PHASES OF THE MOON

	d	h	m
○ Full Moon	6	14	19
☾ Last Quarter	13	15	54
● New Moon	20	12	39
☽ First Quarter	28	07	34

	d	h
Perigee (369,080 kilometres)	15	10
Apogee (404,220 „)	28	03

Mean Longitude of Ascending Node on Aug. 1, 307°.

See note on *Summer Time*, p. 24.

MONTHLY NOTES

Aug. 1. Lammas. Scottish Term Day.

6. Bank Holiday, Scotland.

13. Grouse shooting begins.

27. Bank and General Holiday, England, Wales and N. Ireland.

Day	Right Ascension	Dec. +	Equation of Time	Rise 52°	Rise 56°	Transit	Set 52°	Set 56°	Sidereal Time	Transit of First Point of Aries
	h m s	° ′	m s	h m	h m	h m	h m	h m	h m s	h m s
1	8 43 44	18 08	− 6 21	4 21	4 03	12 06	19 50	20 08	20 37 23	3 22 04
2	8 47 37	17 53	− 6 18	4 23	4 05	12 06	19 49	20 06	20 41 19	3 18 08
3	8 51 29	17 38	− 6 13	4 24	4 07	12 06	19 47	20 04	20 45 16	3 14 12
4	8 55 21	17 22	− 6 08	4 26	4 09	12 06	19 45	20 02	20 49 12	3 10 16
5	8 59 12	17 06	− 6 03	4 27	4 11	12 06	19 44	20 00	20 53 09	3 06 20
6	9 03 02	16 50	− 5 57	4 29	4 13	12 06	19 42	19 58	20 57 05	3 02 25
7	9 06 52	16 33	− 5 50	4 31	4 15	12 06	19 40	19 56	21 01 02	2 58 29
8	9 10 41	16 17	− 5 43	4 32	4 17	12 06	19 38	19 53	21 04 59	2 54 33
9	9 14 30	16 00	− 5 35	4 34	4 18	12 06	19 36	19 51	21 08 55	2 50 37
10	9 18 18	15 42	− 5 26	4 35	4 20	12 05	19 34	19 49	21 12 52	2 46 41
11	9 22 06	15 25	− 5 17	4 37	4 22	12 05	19 32	19 47	21 16 48	2 42 45
12	9 25 53	15 07	− 5 08	4 39	4 24	12 05	19 30	19 44	21 20 45	2 38 49
13	9 29 39	14 49	− 4 58	4 40	4 26	12 05	19 29	19 42	21 24 41	2 34 53
14	9 33 25	14 31	− 4 47	4 42	4 28	12 05	19 27	19 40	21 28 38	2 30 57
15	9 37 10	14 12	− 4 36	4 43	4 30	12 05	19 24	19 37	21 32 34	2 27 01
16	9 40 55	13 53	− 4 24	4 45	4 32	12 04	19 22	19 35	21 36 31	2 23 05
17	9 44 40	13 34	− 4 12	4 47	4 34	12 04	19 20	19 33	21 40 28	2 19 10
18	9 48 23	13 15	− 3 59	4 48	4 36	12 04	19 18	19 30	21 44 24	2 15 14
19	9 52 07	12 56	− 3 46	4 50	4 38	12 04	19 16	19 28	21 48 21	2 11 18
20	9 55 50	12 36	− 3 32	4 52	4 40	12 03	19 14	19 26	21 52 17	2 07 22
21	9 59 32	12 16	− 3 18	4 53	4 42	12 03	19 12	19 23	21 56 14	2 03 26
22	10 03 14	11 56	− 3 04	4 55	4 44	12 03	19 10	19 21	22 00 10	1 59 30
23	10 06 55	11 36	− 2 48	4 56	4 46	12 03	19 08	19 18	22 04 07	1 55 34
24	10 10 36	11 16	− 2 33	4 58	4 48	12 02	19 06	19 16	22 08 03	1 51 38
25	10 14 17	10 55	− 2 17	5 00	4 50	12 02	19 03	19 13	22 12 00	1 47 42
26	10 17 57	10 35	− 2 00	5 01	4 52	12 02	19 01	19 11	22 15 57	1 43 46
27	10 21 37	10 14	− 1 43	5 03	4 54	12 02	18 59	19 08	22 19 53	1 39 50
28	10 25 16	9 53	− 1 26	5 05	4 56	12 01	18 57	19 06	22 23 50	1 35 55
29	10 28 55	9 32	− 1 09	5 06	4 58	12 01	18 55	19 03	22 27 46	1 31 59
30	10 32 33	9 10	− 0 51	5 08	5 00	12 01	18 52	19 00	22 31 43	1 28 03
31	10 36 12	8 49	− 0 32	5 09	5 02	12 00	18 50	18 58	22 35 39	1 24 07

THE SUN   s.d. 15′·8

Duration of Civil (C), Nautical (N), and Astronomical (A), Twilight (in minutes)

Lat. °	Aug. 1 C	Aug. 1 N	Aug. 1 A	Aug. 11 C	Aug. 11 N	Aug. 11 A	Aug. 21 C	Aug. 21 N	Aug. 21 A	Aug. 31 C	Aug. 31 N	Aug. 31 A
52	41	97	177	39	89	153	37	83	138	35	79	127
56	48	120	T.A.N.	45	106	205	42	96	166	40	89	147

ASTRONOMICAL NOTES

MERCURY, despite being at greatest eastern elongation on the 11th, is not suitably placed for observation.

VENUS, magnitude − 3·9, is still a splendid morning object, visible above the E.N.E. horizon before dawn. On the morning of the 9th Venus passes 7°S. of Pollux while it will be close to Jupiter for a few days around the 12th: Jupiter is two magnitudes fainter than Venus.

MARS, magnitude − 0·2, is a morning object, though now visible in the eastern sky before midnight. Mars is passing from Aries into Taurus and by the end of August is south of the Pleiades.

JUPITER, after the first week of the month, becomes visible as a morning object, low in the east before dawn. Jupiter, magnitude − 1·8, moves from Gemini into Cancer during the month.

SATURN is still visible in the southern skies for the greater part of the night though by the end of the month it will be too close to the south-western horizon to be seen after midnight. On the evenings of the 4th and 31st the gibbous Moon will be seen near the planet.

ECLIPSE. A partial eclipse of the Moon occurs on the 6th. See page 74 for details.

METEORS. The maximum of the famous Perseid meteor shower occurs on the night of August 12–13. The Moon, at Last Quarter, will provide some hindrance to observation.

THE MOON

Day	R.A.	Dec.	Hor. Par.	Semi-diam.	Sun's Co-long.	P.A. of Bright Limb	Phase	Age	Rise 52°	Rise 56°	Transit	Set 52°	Set 56°
	h m	°	′	′	°	°		d	h m	h m	h m	h m	h m
1	16 08	− 25·7	54·2	14·8	27	278	72	9·9	16 46	17 20	20 12	23 37	23 02
2	17 01	− 26·8	54·4	14·8	39	273	80	10·9	17 39	18 14	21 04	—	23 55
3	17 55	− 26·7	54·7	14·9	51	267	87	11·9	18 22	18 53	21 56	0 30	—
4	18 49	− 25·3	55·2	15·0	63	261	93	12·9	18 54	19 19	22 47	1 35	1 04
5	19 42	− 22·6	55·7	15·2	75	256	97	13·9	19 18	19 37	23 37	2 48	2 23
6	20 34	− 18·8	56·2	15·3	88	255	100	14·9	19 36	19 50	—	4 06	3 48
7	21 25	− 14·1	56·7	15·5	100	59	100	15·9	19 52	20 00	0 24	5 25	5 13
8	22 14	− 8·6	57·3	15·6	112	62	98	16·9	20 05	20 08	1 11	6 44	6 38
9	23 02	− 2·6	57·8	15·7	124	62	93	17·9	20 19	20 17	1 57	8 04	8 04
10	23 51	+ 3·5	58·2	15·9	136	62	87	18·9	20 33	20 25	2 43	9 25	9 31
11	0 41	+ 9·6	58·6	16·0	148	64	79	19·9	20 49	20 36	3 31	10 49	11 00
12	1 33	+ 15·3	58·9	16·0	161	66	69	20·9	21 10	20 50	4 21	12 15	12 32
13	2 28	+ 20·2	59·1	16·1	173	71	58	21·9	21 38	21 12	5 15	13 41	14 06
14	3 27	+ 24·0	59·3	16·2	185	76	46	22·9	22 18	21 46	6 13	15 05	15 36
15	4 29	+ 26·3	59·4	16·2	197	83	35	23·9	23 14	22 40	7 15	16 18	16 52
16	5 33	+ 26·9	59·4	16·2	210	89	24	24·9	—	23 55	8 17	17 14	17 46
17	6 36	+ 25·8	59·3	16·1	222	96	15	25·9	0 26	—	9 18	17 55	18 21
18	7 37	+ 22·9	59·0	16·1	234	102	8	26·9	1 49	1 24	10 16	18 23	18 43
19	8 35	+ 18·8	58·6	16·0	246	105	3	27·9	3 15	2 57	11 10	18 44	18 57
20	9 28	+ 13·7	58·1	15·8	259	98	0	28·9	4 40	4 28	12 00	19 00	19 08
21	10 19	+ 8·0	57·5	15·7	271	313	0	0·5	6 01	5 55	12 46	19 14	19 16
22	11 06	+ 2·1	56·9	15·5	283	303	3	1·5	7 19	7 18	13 30	19 26	19 24
23	11 53	− 3·8	56·2	15·3	295	301	7	2·5	8 34	8 39	14 13	19 39	19 32
24	12 39	− 9·3	55·6	15·1	307	298	13	3·5	9 49	9 59	14 57	19 53	19 41
25	13 25	− 14·4	55·0	15·0	320	296	20	4·5	11 02	11 18	15 41	20 09	19 51
26	14 12	− 18·8	54·6	14·9	332	292	29	5·5	12 15	12 37	16 26	20 29	20 06
27	15 01	− 22·4	54·4	14·8	344	288	38	6·5	13 26	13 54	17 14	20 56	20 27
28	15 51	− 25·0	54·2	14·8	356	283	47	7·5	14 32	15 05	18 03	21 32	20 59
29	16 43	− 26·5	54·3	14·8	9	277	57	8·5	15 30	16 05	18 54	22 19	21 44
30	17 37	− 26·9	54·5	14·9	21	271	66	9·5	16 17	16 50	19 46	23 19	22 46
31	18 30	− 25·9	54·9	15·0	33	265	75	10·5	16 53	17 21	20 37	—	—

MERCURY ☿

Day	R.A.	Dec. +	Diam.	Phase	Transit		Day	R.A.	Dec.	Diam.	Phase	Transit	
	h m	°	″		h m			h m	°	″		h m	
1	10 22	10·3	—	—	13 45		16	11 18	+ 1·7	—	—	13 41	
4	10 36	8·4	—	—	13 47	Mercury is too	19	11 25	+ 0·5	—	—	13 35	Mercury is too
7	10 49	6·6	—	—	13 48	close to the	22	11 29	− 0·5	—	—	13 27	close to the
10	11 00	4·8	—	—	13 47	Sun for	25	11 30	− 1·1	—	—	13 16	Sun for
13	11 10	3·2	—	—	13 45	observation	28	11 29	− 1·3	—	—	13 02	observation
16	11 18	1·7	—	—	13 41		31	11 24	− 1·0	—	—	12 45	

VENUS ♀

Day	R.A.	Dec. +	Diam.	Phase	Transit	5° high. 52°	5° high. 56°
	h m	°	″		h m	h m	h m
1	7 02	22·5	11	91	10 25	2 57	2 39
6	7 28	21·9	11	92	10 32	3 06	2 50
11	7 54	21·1	11	93	10 38	3 18	3 02
16	8 20	20·0	11	94	10 44	3 30	3 16
21	8 45	18·7	10	94	10 49	3 43	3 30
26	9 10	17·2	10	95	10 55	3 57	3 46
31	9 35	15·4	10	96	10 59	4 12	4 02

MARS ♂

Day	R.A.	Dec. +	Diam.	Phase	Transit	5° high. 52°	5° high. 56°
	h m	°	″		h m	h m	h m
1	2 43	13·7	9	84	6 06	23 25	23 17
6	2 55	14·6	9	84	5 58	23 13	23 04
11	3 07	15·5	10	84	5 50	23 00	22 50
16	3 19	16·3	10	84	5 42	22 48	22 37
21	3 30	17·1	10	85	5 34	22 35	22 24
26	3 41	17·8	11	85	5 25	22 22	22 10
31	3 52	18·4	11	85	5 16	22 10	21 57

SUNRISE AND SUNSET

Day	London a.m. h m	London p.m. h m	Bristol a.m. h m	Bristol p.m. h m	Birmingham a.m. h m	Birmingham p.m. h m	Manchester a.m. h m	Manchester p.m. h m	Newcastle a.m. h m	Newcastle p.m. h m	Glasgow a.m. h m	Glasgow p.m. h m	Belfast a.m. h m	Belfast p.m. h m
1	4 22	7 49	4 32	7 59	4 25	8 00	4 23	8 07	4 13	8 10	4 20	8 25	4 33	8 27
2	4 24	7 48	4 34	7 58	4 27	7 59	4 24	8 05	4 15	8 08	4 22	8 23	4 34	8 25
3	4 25	7 46	4 35	7 56	4 28	7 57	4 26	8 03	4 17	8 06	4 24	8 21	4 36	8 23
4	4 27	7 44	4 37	7 54	4 30	7 55	4 28	8 01	4 18	8 04	4 25	8 19	4 38	8 21
5	4 28	7 43	4 38	7 53	4 31	7 54	4 29	7 59	4 20	8 02	4 27	8 17	4 39	8 19
6	4 30	7 41	4 40	7 51	4 33	7 52	4 31	7 57	4 22	8 00	4 29	8 15	4 41	8 17
7	4 32	7 39	4 42	7 49	4 35	7 50	4 33	7 55	4 24	7 58	4 31	8 13	4 43	8 15
8	4 33	7 37	4 43	7 47	4 36	7 48	4 35	7 53	4 26	7 56	4 33	8 11	4 45	8 13
9	4 35	7 36	4 45	7 45	4 38	7 46	4 36	7 51	4 27	7 54	4 35	8 08	4 47	8 10
10	4 36	7 34	4 46	7 43	4 39	7 44	4 38	7 49	4 29	7 52	4 37	8 06	4 49	8 08
11	4 38	7 32	4 48	7 41	4 41	7 42	4 40	7 47	4 31	7 50	4 39	8 04	4 51	8 06
12	4 40	7 30	4 50	7 40	4 43	7 40	4 42	7 45	4 33	7 48	4 41	8 02	4 53	8 04
13	4 41	7 29	4 51	7 38	4 44	7 38	4 43	7 43	4 35	7 46	4 43	8 00	4 54	8 02
14	4 42	7 27	4 52	7 36	4 46	7 36	4 45	7 41	4 37	7 43	4 45	7 57	4 56	8 00
15	4 44	7 25	4 54	7 34	4 48	7 34	4 47	7 39	4 39	7 41	4 47	7 55	4 58	7 58
16	4 46	7 23	4 56	7 32	4 50	7 32	4 49	7 37	4 41	7 39	4 49	7 53	5 00	7 56
17	4 47	7 21	4 57	7 30	4 52	7 30	4 51	7 35	4 43	7 37	4 51	7 51	5 02	7 54
18	4 48	7 19	4 58	7 28	4 53	7 28	4 52	7 33	4 44	7 34	4 52	7 48	5 03	7 51
19	4 50	7 17	5 00	7 26	4 55	7 26	4 54	7 31	4 46	7 32	4 54	7 46	5 05	7 49
20	4 52	7 14	5 02	7 24	4 56	7 23	4 55	7 28	4 48	7 30	4 56	7 44	5 07	7 47
21	4 53	7 12	5 03	7 22	4 58	7 21	4 57	7 26	4 50	7 27	4 58	7 41	5 09	7 44
22	4 55	7 10	5 05	7 20	5 00	7 19	4 59	7 24	4 52	7 25	5 00	7 39	5 10	7 42
23	4 56	7 08	5 06	7 18	5 01	7 17	5 00	7 22	4 53	7 23	5 01	7 37	5 12	7 40
24	4 58	7 06	5 08	7 16	5 03	7 15	5 02	7 20	4 55	7 20	5 03	7 34	5 14	7 38
25	5 00	7 04	5 10	7 14	5 05	7 13	5 04	7 17	4 57	7 18	5 05	7 32	5 16	7 35
26	5 01	7 01	5 11	7 11	5 06	7 10	5 06	7 15	4 59	7 15	5 07	7 29	5 18	7 33
27	5 03	6 59	5 13	7 09	5 08	7 08	5 07	7 13	5 01	7 13	5 09	7 27	5 19	7 31
28	5 05	6 57	5 15	7 07	5 10	7 06	5 09	7 10	5 03	7 10	5 11	7 24	5 21	7 28
29	5 06	6 55	5 16	7 05	5 12	7 04	5 11	7 08	5 05	7 08	5 13	7 22	5 23	7 26
30	5 08	6 53	5 18	7 03	5 13	7 02	5 13	7 06	5 07	7 06	5 15	7 19	5 25	7 23
31	5 09	6 51	5 19	7 01	5 14	7 00	5 14	7 03	5 08	7 03	5 17	7 16	5 27	7 20

	JUPITER ♃					SATURN ♄				
Day	R.A.	Dec. +	Transit	5° high. 52°	5° high. 56°	R.A.	Dec.	Transit	5° high. 52°	5° high. 56°
	h m	°	h m	h m	h m	h m	°	h m	h m	h m
1	7 53	21·2	11 14	3 55	3 39	19 30	21·8	22 48	2 06	1 34
11	8 02	20·7	10 44	3 27	3 12	19 27	21·9	22 06	1 23	0 51
21	8 11	20·3	10 14	2 59	2 45	19 25	22·0	21 25	0 40	0 08
31	8 20	19·9	9 43	2 31	2 17	19 23	22·1	20 44	23 54	23 22

Equatorial diameter of Jupiter 32″; of Saturn 18″. Diameters of Saturn's rings 41″ and 17″.

	URANUS ♅					NEPTUNE ♆				
Day	R.A.	Dec. −	Transit	10° high. 52°	10° high. 56°	R.A.	Dec. −	Transit	10° high. 52°	10° high. 56°
	h m	° ′	h m	h m	h m	h m	° ′	h m	h m	h m
1	18 27·9	23 37	21 47	23 46	22 23	18 54·0	21 59	22 13	0 36	23 37
11	18 26·6	23 38	21 06	23 05	21 42	18 53·1	22 01	21 33	23 51	22 56
21	18 25·6	23 38	20 26	22 25	21 01	18 52·3	22 02	20 53	23 11	22 15
31	18 24·9	23 39	19 46	21 45	20 21	18 51·6	22 03	20 13	22 31	21 35

Diameter 4″   Diameter 2″

DAY OF		
Month	**Week**	*Septem* (seven), 7th month of Roman (pre-Julian) Calendar. *Sun's Longitude* 180° ♎ 23ᵈ 07ʰ

1	S.	Pope Adrian IV d. 1159. Edward Alleyn b. 1566.
2	S.	**13th S. after Pentecost.** Fire of London 1666.
3	M.	Britain declared war on Germany, 1939.
4	Tu.	Anton Bruckner b. 1824. Darius Milhaud b. 1892.
5	W.	Pieter Brueghel d. 1569. Douglas Bader d. 1982.
6	Th.	James II d. 1701. Elie Halévy b. 1870.
7	F.	Elizabeth I b. 1533. Catherine Parr d. 1548.
8	S.	**Blessed Virgin Mary.** Dvořák b. 1841.
9	S.	**14th S. after Pentecost.** Mallarmé d. 1898.
10	M.	Arnold Palmer b. 1929.
11	Tu.	D. H. Lawrence b. 1885. Krushchev d. 1971.
12	W.	Maurice Chevalier b. 1888. Jesse Owens b. 1913.
13	Th.	Arnold Schönberg b. 1874. J. B. Priestley b. 1894.
14	F.	Dante Alighieri d. 1321. Isadora Duncan d. 1927.
15	S.	PRINCE HENRY OF WALES b. 1984. BATTLE OF BRITAIN DAY.
16	S.	**15th S. after Pentecost.** Maria Callas d. 1977.
17	M.	Tobias Smollett d. 1771.
18	Tu.	Samuel Johnson b. 1709. Hazlitt d. 1830.
19	W.	Dr. Barnardo d. 1905. William Golding b. 1911.
20	Th.	Mungo Park b. 1771. Stevie Smith b. 1902.
21	F.	**St. Matthew.** H. G. Wells b. 1866.
22	S.	Michael Faraday b. 1791.
23	S.	**16th S. after Pentecost.** Baroness Orczy b. 1865.
24	M.	Institution of the George Cross 1940.
25	Tu.	Shostakovich b. 1906. E. M. Remarque d. 1970.
26	W.	T. S. Eliot b. 1888. James Keir Hardie d. 1915.
27	Th.	Jesuits given Papal recognition 1540.
28	F.	Georges Clemenceau b. 1841. Nasser d. 1970.
29	S.	**St. Michael and All Angels.** Zola d. 1902.
30	S.	**17th S. after Pentecost.** Lord Raglan b. 1788.

PHENOMENA

d	h	
1	00	Saturn in conjunction with Moon. Saturn 2°N.
8	04	Mercury in inferior conjunction.
10	21	Mars in conjunction with Moon. Mars 6°S.
15	06	Jupiter in conjunction with Moon. Jupiter 0°·2N.
15	09	Venus in conjunction with Mercury. Venus 3°N.
17	19	Mercury in conjunction with Moon. Mercury 2°N.
18	01	Venus in conjunction with Moon. Venus 4°N.
23	07	Equinox.
24	04	Mercury at greatest elongation W.18°.
28	08	Saturn in conjunction with Moon. Saturn 1°N.

CONSTELLATIONS

The following constellations are near the meridian at

d	h		d	h
Aug. 1	24		Aug. 16	23
Sept. 1	22		Sept. 15	21
Oct. 1	20		Oct. 16	19

Draco, Cepheus, Lyra, Cygnus, Vulpecula, Sagitta, Delphinus, Equuleus, Aquila, Aquarius and Capricornus.

MINIMA OF ALGOL

d	h		d	h
1	13		18	18
4	10		21	15
7	07		24	12
10	04		27	09
13	01		30	06
15	21			

* Centenary.

PHASES OF THE MOON

		d	h	m
○	Full Moon	5	01	46
☾	Last Quarter	11	20	53
●	New Moon	19	00	46
☽	First Quarter	27	02	06

	d	h
Perigee (368,380 kilometres)	9	11
Apogee (404,800 „)	24	22

Mean Longitude of Ascending Node on Sept. 1, 306°

See note on *Summer Time*, p. 24.

MONTHLY NOTES

Sept. 1. Partridge shooting begins.

20. Jewish New Year (A.M. 5751).

29. Jewish Day of Atonement (Yom Kippur).

29. Michaelmas. Quarter day.

Day	THE SUN								Sidereal Time	Transit of First Point of Aries
	Right Ascension	Dec.	Equation of Time	Rise		Transit	Set			
				52°	56°		52°	56°		
	h m s	° ′	m s	h m	h m	h m	h m	h m	h m s	h m s
1	10 39 49	+8 27	− 0 14	5 11	5 04	12 00	18 48	18 55	22 39 36	1 20 11
2	10 43 27	+8 05	+ 0 06	5 13	5 05	12 00	18 46	18 53	22 43 32	1 16 15
3	10 47 04	+7 44	+ 0 25	5 14	5 07	11 59	18 43	18 50	22 47 29	1 12 19
4	10 50 41	+7 22	+ 0 44	5 16	5 09	11 59	18 41	18 48	22 51 26	1 08 23
5	10 54 18	+6 59	+ 1 04	5 18	5 11	11 59	18 39	18 45	22 55 22	1 04 27
6	10 57 54	+6 37	+ 1 24	5 19	5 13	11 58	18 36	18 42	22 59 19	1 00 31
7	11 01 30	+6 15	+ 1 45	5 21	5 15	11 58	18 34	18 40	23 03 15	0 56 35
8	11 05 07	+5 52	+ 2 05	5 22	5 17	11 58	18 32	18 37	23 07 12	0 52 40
9	11 08 42	+5 30	+ 2 26	5 24	5 19	11 57	18 30	18 34	23 11 08	0 48 44
10	11 12 18	+5 07	+ 2 47	5 26	5 21	11 57	18 27	18 32	23 15 05	0 44 48
11	11 15 54	+4 44	+ 3 08	5 27	5 23	11 57	18 25	18 29	23 19 01	0 40 52
12	11 19 29	+4 22	+ 3 29	5 29	5 25	11 56	18 23	18 26	23 22 58	0 36 56
13	11 23 05	+3 59	+ 3 50	5 31	5 27	11 56	18 20	18 24	23 26 55	0 33 00
14	11 26 40	+3 36	+ 4 11	5 32	5 29	11 56	18 18	18 21	23 30 51	0 29 04
15	11 30 15	+3 13	+ 4 32	5 34	5 31	11 55	18 16	18 19	23 34 48	0 25 08
16	11 33 50	+2 50	+ 4 54	5 36	5 33	11 55	18 13	18 16	23 38 44	0 21 12
17	11 37 26	+2 26	+ 5 15	5 37	5 35	11 55	18 11	18 13	23 42 41	0 17 16
18	11 41 01	+2 03	+ 5 36	5 39	5 37	11 54	18 09	18 11	23 46 37	0 13 20
19	11 44 36	+1 40	+ 5 58	5 40	5 39	11 54	18 06	18 08	23 50 34	0 09 25
20	11 48 11	+1 17	+ 6 19	5 42	5 41	11 53	18 04	18 05	23 54 30	0 05 29
21	11 51 47	+0 53	+ 6 40	5 44	5 43	11 53	18 02	18 03	23 58 27	{ 0 01 33 / 23 57 37
22	11 55 22	+0 30	+ 7 01	5 45	5 44	11 53	17 59	18 00	0 02 24	23 53 41
23	11 58 58	+0 07	+ 7 22	5 47	5 46	11 52	17 57	17 57	0 06 20	23 49 45
24	12 02 33	−0 17	+ 7 43	5 49	5 48	11 52	17 55	17 55	0 10 17	23 45 49
25	12 06 09	−0 40	+ 8 04	5 50	5 50	11 52	17 52	17 52	0 14 13	23 41 53
26	12 09 45	−1 03	+ 8 25	5 52	5 52	11 51	17 50	17 49	0 18 10	23 37 57
27	12 13 21	−1 27	+ 8 46	5 54	5 54	11 51	17 48	17 47	0 22 06	23 34 01
28	12 16 57	−1 50	+ 9 06	5 55	5 56	11 51	17 45	17 44	0 26 03	23 30 06
29	12 20 33	−2 13	+ 9 26	5 57	5 58	11 50	17 43	17 41	0 29 59	23 26 10
30	12 24 10	−2 37	+ 9 46	5 59	6 00	11 50	17 41	17 39	0 33 56	23 22 14

Duration of Civil (C), Nautical (N), and Astronomical (A), Twilight (in minutes)

Lat. °	Sept. 1			Sept. 11			Sept. 21			Sept. 30		
	C	N	A	C	N	A	C	N	A	C	N	A
52	35	79	127	34	76	120	34	74	115	34	73	113
56	39	89	146	38	84	135	37	82	129	37	80	126

ASTRONOMICAL NOTES

MERCURY is a morning object, magnitude +1·7 to −1·0, during the second half of the month, visible low above the eastern horizon around the time of beginning of morning civil twilight. This is the most suitable morning apparition of the year for observers in the northern hemisphere. On the morning of the 17th the old crescent Moon will be seen approaching the planet.

VENUS is a splendid object in the morning skies, magnitude −3·9, visible above the eastern horizon before dawn. It is getting noticeably closer to the Sun and by the end of the month will only be seen for about 10–15 minutes before being lost in the glare of the rising Sun.

MARS, magnitude −0·6, is now becoming quite a prominent object in the sky from the late evening onwards. Late on the evening of the 10th the Moon,

at Last Quarter, passes 6°N. of the planet. Mars is in Taurus and on the morning of the 25th passes 4°N. of Aldebaran.

JUPITER, magnitude −1·9, is a bright morning object in the eastern sky, visible for several hours before dawn. On the morning of the 15th the old crescent Moon will be seen very close to the planet.

SATURN, magnitude +0·4, continues to be visible low in the southern and south-western skies in the evenings.

ZODIACAL LIGHT. The morning cone may be seen stretching up from the eastern horizon before the beginning of morning twilight from the 17th to the end of the month. This faint phenomenon is only visible under good conditions, in the absence of both moonlight and artificial lighting.

THE MOON

Day	R.A.	Dec.	Hor. Par.	Semi-diam.	Sun's Co-long.	P.A. of Bright Limb	Phase	Age	Rise 52°	Rise 56°	Tran-sit	Set 52°	Set 56°
	h m	°	′	′	°	°		d	h m	h m	h m	h m	h m
1	19 24	−23·7	55·5	15·1	45	260	83	11·5	17 20	17 42	21 27	0 28	0 01
2	20 16	−20·3	56·1	15·3	57	257	90	12·5	17 41	17 57	22 16	1 44	1 23
3	21 07	−15·8	56·8	15·5	70	255	95	13·5	17 58	18 08	23 04	3 03	2 49
4	21 57	−10·5	57·5	15·7	82	258	99	14·5	18 12	18 17	23 51	4 23	4 15
5	22 46	− 4·6	58·1	15·8	94	320	100	15·5	18 26	18 26	—	5 45	5 42
6	23 36	+ 1·6	58·7	16·0	106	49	99	16·5	18 40	18 35	0 38	7 07	7 10
7	0 26	+ 7·9	59·1	16·1	118	57	95	17·5	18 56	18 45	1 26	8 31	8 40
8	1 19	+13·8	59·4	16·2	130	62	89	18·5	19 16	18 59	2 17	9 58	10 14
9	2 15	+19·0	59·5	16·2	143	67	81	19·5	19 42	19 18	3 11	11 27	11 49
10	3 14	+23·1	59·5	16·2	155	72	71	20·5	20 18	19 48	4 08	12 53	13 22
11	4 15	+25·8	59·4	16·2	167	79	60	21·5	21 09	20 35	5 09	14 09	14 43
12	5 18	+26·8	59·2	16·1	179	86	49	22·5	22 15	21 43	6 11	15 10	15 43
13	6 21	+26·1	58·9	16·0	191	93	37	23·5	23 34	23 07	7 11	15 55	16 23
14	7 22	+23·7	58·6	16·0	204	99	27	24·5	—	—	8 09	16 26	16 48
15	8 19	+20·0	58·2	15·9	216	103	18	25·5	0 57	0 37	9 03	16 49	17 04
16	9 12	+15·3	57·7	15·7	228	106	10	26·5	2 20	2 07	9 53	17 06	17 16
17	10 03	+ 9·9	57·3	15·6	240	106	5	27·5	3 41	3 33	10 40	17 21	17 25
18	10 51	+ 4·1	56·8	15·5	253	99	1	28·5	4 59	4 56	11 24	17 33	17 33
19	11 37	− 1·7	56·2	15·3	265	29	0	29·5	6 15	6 17	12 08	17 46	17 41
20	12 23	− 7·4	55·7	15·2	277	315	1	1·0	7 29	7 37	12 51	17 59	17 50
21	13 09	−12·6	55·2	15·0	289	304	4	2·0	8 43	8 57	13 35	18 15	18 00
22	13 56	−17·3	54·8	14·9	301	298	9	3·0	9 57	10 16	14 20	18 34	18 13
23	14 44	−21·2	54·4	14·8	314	292	15	4·0	11 09	11 34	15 07	18 58	18 32
24	15 34	−24·1	54·2	14·8	326	287	23	5·0	12 18	12 48	15 56	19 30	18 59
25	16 26	−26·0	54·2	14·8	338	281	31	6·0	13 19	13 52	16 46	20 12	19 38
26	17 19	−26·7	54·3	14·8	350	275	40	7·0	14 10	14 43	17 37	21 06	20 33
27	18 12	−26·2	54·5	14·9	3	269	49	8·0	14 49	15 19	18 27	22 11	21 41
28	19 05	−24·4	55·0	15·0	15	263	59	9·0	15 20	15 44	19 17	23 23	22 59
29	19 57	−21·5	55·6	15·1	27	259	68	10·0	15 43	16 01	20 06	—	—
30	20 47	−17·5	56·3	15·3	39	255	77	11·0	16 01	16 14	20 53	0 39	0 22

MERCURY ☿

Day	R.A.	Dec.	Diam.	Phase	Tran-sit		Day	R.A.	Dec. +	Diam.	Phase	Tran-sit	5° high. 52°	5° high. 56°
	h m	°	″		h m			h m	°	″		h m	h m	h m
1	11 22	−0·8	—	—	12 39		16	10 43	6·7	9	14	11 03	5 02	4 59
4	11 14	+0·3	—	—	12 19	Mercury is too	19	10 45	7·6	8	26	10 53	4 47	4 45
7	11 04	+1·8	—	—	11 57	close to the	22	10 51	7·8	8	39	10 49	4 42	4 38
10	10 54	+3·5	—	—	11 36	Sun for	25	11 02	7·3	7	53	10 48	4 43	4 41
13	10 47	+5·3	—	—	11 17	observation	28	11 17	6·3	6	66	10 51	4 52	4 50
16	10 43	+6·7	—	—	11 03		31	11 34	4·8	6	77	10 57	5 05	5 04

VENUS ♀

Day	R.A.	Dec. +	Diam.	Phase	Tran-sit	5° high. 52°	5° high. 56°
	h m	°	″		h m	h m	h m
1	9 39	15·1	10	96	11 00	4 15	4 05
6	10 04	13·1	10	97	11 05	4 30	4 22
11	10 27	11·0	10	97	11 09	4 45	4 39
16	10 51	8·8	10	98	11 12	5 00	4 56
21	11 14	6·5	10	98	11 16	5 16	5 14
26	11 37	4·0	10	99	11 19	5 31	5 32
31	12 00	1·6	10	99	11 22	5 47	5 49

MARS ♂

Day	R.A.	Dec. +	Diam.	Phase	Tran-sit	5° high. 52°	5° high. 56°
	h m	°	″		h m	h m	h m
1	3 54	18·5	11	85	5 14	22 07	21 54
6	4 04	19·1	11	86	5 04	21 54	21 41
11	4 13	19·6	12	86	4 54	21 41	21 28
16	4 22	20·0	12	87	4 42	21 27	21 12
21	4 29	20·4	13	87	4 31	21 12	20 58
26	4 36	20·8	13	88	4 18	20 57	20 42
31	4 42	21·1	14	89	4 04	20 41	20 26

SUNRISE AND SUNSET

Day	London a.m.	London p.m.	Bristol a.m.	Bristol p.m.	Birmingham a.m.	Birmingham p.m.	Manchester a.m.	Manchester p.m.	Newcastle a.m.	Newcastle p.m.	Glasgow a.m.	Glasgow p.m.	Belfast a.m.	Belfast p.m.
	h m	h m	h m	h m	h m	h m	h m	h m	h m	h m	h m	h m	h m	h m
1	5 11	6 48	5 21	6 58	5 16	6 57	5 16	7 01	5 10	7 01	5 19	7 14	5 29	7 18
2	5 13	6 46	5 23	6 56	5 18	6 55	5 18	6 58	5 12	6 58	5 21	7 11	5 31	7 15
3	5 14	6 44	5 24	6 54	5 19	6 53	5 20	6 56	5 14	6 56	5 23	7 09	5 33	7 13
4	5 16	6 42	5 26	6 51	5 21	6 50	5 22	6 54	5 16	6 53	5 25	7 06	5 35	7 11
5	5 17	6 39	5 27	6 49	5 22	6 48	5 23	6 51	5 18	6 50	5 27	7 03	5 36	7 08
6	5 19	6 37	5 29	6 47	5 24	6 46	5 25	6 49	5 20	6 48	5 29	7 01	5 38	7 06
7	5 21	6 35	5 31	6 45	5 26	6 43	5 27	6 46	5 22	6 45	5 31	6 58	5 40	7 03
8	5 23	6 33	5 33	6 42	5 28	6 41	5 29	6 44	5 24	6 43	5 33	6 56	5 42	7 01
9	5 24	6 31	5 34	6 40	5 30	6 38	5 31	6 41	5 26	6 40	5 35	6 53	5 44	6 58
10	5 26	6 28	5 36	6 37	5 31	6 36	5 32	6 39	5 27	6 38	5 37	6 50	5 45	6 56
11	5 27	6 26	5 37	6 35	5 33	6 33	5 34	6 36	5 29	6 35	5 39	6 48	5 47	6 53
12	5 29	6 24	5 39	6 33	5 35	6 31	5 36	6 34	5 31	6 33	5 41	6 45	5 49	6 51
13	5 30	6 22	5 40	6 31	5 37	6 29	5 38	6 32	5 33	6 30	5 43	6 42	5 51	6 48
14	5 32	6 19	5 42	6 29	5 38	6 26	5 39	6 29	5 35	6 28	5 45	6 40	5 53	6 46
15	5 33	6 17	5 43	6 27	5 40	6 24	5 41	6 27	5 37	6 25	5 47	6 37	5 55	6 43
16	5 35	6 15	5 45	6 24	5 42	6 22	5 43	6 22	5 39	6 22	5 49	6 34	5 57	6 40
17	5 36	6 12	5 46	6 22	5 43	6 19	5 44	6 22	5 41	6 20	5 51	6 32	5 59	6 38
18	5 38	6 10	5 48	6 20	5 45	6 17	5 46	6 20	5 43	6 17	5 53	6 29	6 01	6 35
19	5 40	6 08	5 50	6 18	5 47	6 15	5 48	6 17	5 44	6 14	5 55	6 26	6 02	6 32
20	5 41	6 05	5 51	6 15	5 48	6 12	5 49	6 15	5 46	6 12	5 56	6 24	6 04	6 30
21	5 43	6 03	5 53	6 13	5 50	6 10	5 51	6 12	5 48	6 09	5 58	6 21	6 06	6 27
22	5 44	6 00	5 54	6 10	5 51	6 07	5 53	6 10	5 50	6 07	6 00	6 18	6 08	6 25
23	5 46	5 58	5 56	6 08	5 53	6 05	5 55	6 07	5 52	6 04	6 02	6 16	6 10	6 22
24	5 48	5 56	5 58	6 06	5 55	6 03	5 56	6 05	5 53	6 02	6 04	6 13	6 11	6 20
25	5 49	5 54	5 59	6 04	5 56	6 01	5 58	6 02	5 55	5 59	6 06	6 10	6 13	6 17
26	5 51	5 51	6 01	6 01	5 58	5 58	6 00	6 00	5 57	5 57	6 08	6 08	6 15	6 15
27	5 53	5 49	6 03	5 59	6 00	5 56	6 02	5 57	5 59	5 54	6 10	6 05	6 17	6 12
28	5 54	5 46	6 04	5 56	6 01	5 53	6 04	5 55	6 01	5 52	6 12	6 02	6 19	6 10
29	5 56	5 44	6 06	5 54	6 03	5 51	6 05	5 52	6 02	5 49	6 14	6 00	6 20	6 07
30	5 58	5 42	6 08	5 52	6 05	5 49	6 07	5 50	6 04	5 47	6 16	5 57	6 22	6 05

JUPITER ♃   SATURN ♄

Day	R.A.	Dec. +	Transit	5° high. 52°	5° high. 56°	R.A.	Dec. −	Transit	5° high. 52°	5° high. 56°
	h m	°	h m	h m	h m	h m	°	h m	h m	h m
1	8 21	19·8	9 40	2 28	2 14	19 23	22·1	20 40	23 50	23 18
11	8 29	19·4	9 09	2 00	1 46	19 22	22·1	19 59	23 09	22 37
21	8 36	19·0	8 37	1 30	1 17	19 21	22·2	19 19	22 29	21 57
31	8 43	18·6	8 04	1 00	0 48	19 21	22·2	18 40	21 50	21 18

Equatorial diameter of Jupiter 33″; of Saturn 18″. Diameters of Saturn's rings 39″ and 16″.

URANUS ♅   NEPTUNE ♆

Day	R.A.	Dec. −	Transit	10° high. 52°	10° high. 56°	R.A.	Dec. −	Transit	10° high. 52°	10° high. 56°
	h m	° ′	h m	h m	h m	h m	° ′	h m	h m	h m
1	18 24·8	23 39	19 42	21 41	20 17	18 51·6	22 03	20 09	22 27	21 31
11	18 24·5	23 39	19 02	21 01	19 38	18 51·2	22 04	19 29	21 47	20 51
21	18 24·5	23 39	18 23	20 22	18 58	18 51·0	22 05	18 49	21 07	20 11
31	18 25·0	23 38	17 44	19 43	18 20	18 51·0	22 05	18 10	20 28	19 32

Diameter 4″   Diameter 2″

DAY OF		
Month	Week	

Octo (eight), 8th month of Roman (pre-Julian) Calendar.

Sun's Longitude 210° ♏ 23ᵈ 16ʰ

1	M.	MICHAELMAS LAW SITTINGS BEGIN.
2	Tu.	Archbishop of Canterbury b. 1921.
3	W.	Francis of Assisi d. 1226. Eleonora Duse b. 1859.
4	Th.	Rembrandt d. 1669. Damon Runyon b. 1884.
5	F.	Denis Diderot b. 1713. Jacques Offenbach d. 1880.
6	S.	Tennyson d. 1892. Helen Wills-Moody b. 1905.
7	S.	**18th S. after Pentecost.** Mario Lanza d. 1959.
8	M.	Henry Fielding d. 1754. Kathleen Ferrier d. 1953.
9	Tu.	John Lennon b. 1940. André Maurois d. 1967.
10	W.	Jean Watteau b. 1684. Henry Cavendish b. 1731.
11	Th.	Huldreich Zwingli d. 1531. Cocteau d. 1963.
12	F.	Edward VI b. 1537. Vaughan Williams b. 1872.
13	S.	Henry Irving d. 1905. Margaret Thatcher b. 1925.
14	S.	**19th S. after Pentecost.** Gen. Eisenhower b. 1890.*
15	M.	DUCHESS OF YORK b. 1959. Nietzsche b. 1844.
16	Tu.	Oscar Wilde b. 1854. Günter Grass b. 1927.
17	W.	Arthur Miller b. 1915. Sir Philip Sidney d. 1586.
18	Th.	**St. Luke.** Canaletto b. 1697.
19	F.	Charles I b. 1600. Leigh Hunt b. 1784.
20	S.	Sir Richard Burton d. 1890.* Anna Neagle b. 1904.
21	S.	**20th S. after Pentecost.** Geoffrey Boycott b. 1940.
22	M.	Liszt b. 1811. Sarah Bernhardt b. 1845.
23	Tu.	Robert Bridges b. 1844. Pele b. 1940.
24	W.	Sybil Thorndike b. 1882. Christian Dior d. 1957.
25	Th.	Chaucer d. 1400. Pablo Picasso b. 1881.
26	F.	Danton b. 1759. William Hogarth d. 1764.
27	S.	Dylan Thomas b. 1914.
28	S.	**9th S. before Christmas.** Evelyn Waugh b. 1903.
29	M.	**SS. Simon and Jude.** James Boswell b. 1740.
30	Tu.	R. B. Sheridan b. 1751. Dostoevsky b. 1821.
31	W.	HALLOWMASS EVE. John Keats b. 1795.

*Centenary.

PHENOMENA

d	h	
8	18	Mars in conjunction with Moon. Mars 5°S.
12	19	Jupiter in conjunction with Moon. Jupiter 0°·9N.
16	06	Venus in conjunction with Mercury. Venus 0°·02S.
18	08	Venus in conjunction with Moon. Venus 6°N.
18	10	Mercury in conjunction with Moon. Mercury 6°N.
22	04	Mercury in superior conjunction.
25	18	Saturn in conjunction with Moon. Saturn 1°N.

CONSTELLATIONS

The following constellations are near the meridian at

	d	h		d	h
Sept.	1	24	Sept.	15	23
Oct.	1	22	Oct.	16	21
Nov.	1	20	Nov.	15	19

Ursa Major (below the Pole), Cepheus, Cassiopeia, Cygnus, Lacerta, Andromeda, Pegasus, Capricornus, Aquarius and Piscis Austrinus.

MINIMA OF ALGOL

d	h	d	h
3	02	20	07
5	23	23	04
8	20	26	01
11	17	28	22
14	14	31	19
17	10		

Summer Time in 1990 (*see* p. 72).—Ends: October 28ᵈ 01ʰ G.M.T.

PHASES OF THE MOON

	d	h	m
○ Full Moon	4	12	02
☾ Last Quarter	11	03	31
● New Moon	18	15	37
☽ First Quarter	26	20	26

	d	h
Perigee (363,240 kilometres)	6	18
Apogee (405,820 ,,)	22	16

Mean Longitude of Ascending Node on Oct. 1, 304°

MONTHLY NOTES

Oct.
1. Pheasant shooting begins.
4. First day of Feast of Tabernacles..

Day	Right Ascension h m s	Dec. — ° ′	Equation of Time m s	Rise 52° h m	Rise 56° h m	Transit h m	Set 52° h m	Set 56° h m	Sidereal Time h m s	Transit of First Point of Aries h m s
1	12 27 47	3 00	+10 06	6 00	6 02	11 50	17 38	17 36	0 37 53	23 18 18
2	12 31 24	3 23	+10 25	6 02	6 04	11 49	17 36	17 33	0 41 49	23 14 22
3	12 35 01	3 47	+10 44	6 04	6 06	11 49	17 34	17 31	0 45 46	23 10 26
4	12 38 39	4 10	+11 03	6 05	6 08	11 49	17 31	17 28	0 49 42	23 06 30
5	12 42 17	4 33	+11 22	6 07	6 10	11 48	17 29	17 26	0 53 39	23 02 34
6	12 45 56	4 56	+11 40	6 09	6 12	11 48	17 27	17 23	0 57 35	22 58 38
7	12 49 34	5 19	+11 58	6 10	6 14	11 48	17 24	17 20	1 01 32	22 54 42
8	12 53 14	5 42	+12 15	6 12	6 16	11 48	17 22	17 18	1 05 28	22 50 46
9	12 56 53	6 05	+12 32	6 14	6 18	11 47	17 20	17 15	1 09 25	22 46 51
10	13 00 33	6 28	+12 48	6 15	6 20	11 47	17 18	17 13	1 13 22	22 42 55
11	13 04 14	6 50	+13 04	6 17	6 22	11 47	17 16	17 10	1 17 18	22 38 59
12	13 07 55	7 13	+13 20	6 19	6 24	11 47	17 13	17 08	1 21 15	22 35 03
13	13 11 37	7 36	+13 35	6 21	6 26	11 46	17 11	17 05	1 25 11	22 31 07
14	13 15 19	7 58	+13 49	6 22	6 28	11 46	17 09	17 03	1 29 08	22 27 11
15	13 19 01	8 20	+14 03	6 24	6 31	11 46	17 07	17 00	1 33 04	22 23 15
16	13 22 45	8 42	+14 16	6 26	6 33	11 46	17 05	16 58	1 37 01	22 19 19
17	13 26 28	9 05	+14 29	6 28	6 35	11 45	17 02	16 55	1 40 57	22 15 23
18	13 30 13	9 27	+14 41	6 29	6 37	11 45	17 00	16 53	1 44 54	22 11 27
19	13 33 58	9 48	+14 53	6 31	6 39	11 45	16 58	16 50	1 48 50	22 07 31
20	13 37 43	10 10	+15 04	6 33	6 41	11 45	16 56	16 48	1 52 47	22 03 36
21	13 41 30	10 32	+15 14	6 35	6 43	11 45	16 54	16 45	1 56 44	21 59 40
22	13 45 16	10 53	+15 24	6 36	6 45	11 45	16 52	16 43	2 00 40	21 55 44
23	13 49 04	11 14	+15 33	6 38	6 47	11 44	16 50	16 41	2 04 37	21 51 48
24	13 52 52	11 35	+15 41	6 40	6 49	11 44	16 48	16 38	2 08 33	21 47 52
25	13 56 41	11 56	+15 49	6 42	6 51	11 44	16 46	16 36	2 12 30	21 43 56
26	14 00 31	12 17	+15 56	6 43	6 54	11 44	16 44	16 34	2 16 26	21 40 00
27	14 04 21	12 37	+16 02	6 45	6 56	11 44	16 42	16 31	2 20 23	21 36 04
28	14 08 12	12 57	+16 07	6 47	6 58	11 44	16 40	16 29	2 24 19	21 32 08
29	14 12 04	13 18	+16 12	6 49	7 00	11 44	16 38	16 27	2 28 16	21 28 12
30	14 15 56	13 37	+16 16	6 51	7 02	11 44	16 36	16 25	2 32 13	21 24 16
31	14 19 50	13 57	+16 20	6 52	7 04	11 44	16 34	16 22	2 36 09	21 20 21

THE SUN s.d. 16′·1

Duration of Civil (C), Nautical (N), and Astronomical (A), Twilight (in minutes)

Lat. °	Oct. 1 C	Oct. 1 N	Oct. 1 A	Oct. 11 C	Oct. 11 N	Oct. 11 A	Oct. 21 C	Oct. 21 N	Oct. 21 A	Oct. 31 C	Oct. 31 N	Oct. 31 A
52	34	73	113	34	73	112	34	74	113	36	75	114
56	37	80	125	37	80	124	38	81	124	40	83	126

ASTRONOMICAL NOTES

MERCURY continues to be visible as a morning object for the first week of the month, magnitude −1·0. It may be detected low on the eastern horizon around the time of beginning of morning civil twilight.

VENUS is a morning object, magnitude −3·9, but only visible for the first ten days of the month, low above the E.S.E. horizon for a few minutes before dawn. Thereafter the planet is too close to the Sun for observation.

MARS is now becoming quite a bright object in the night sky, its magnitude brightening during the month from −0·9 to −1·6, as it moves towards opposition. By the end of the month it may be seen low in the east by 19h. When the gibbous Moon rises on the evening of the 8th Mars will be seen passing 5°S. of it.

JUPITER continues to be visible as a brilliant morning object, magnitude −2·1. By the end of the month it is rising in the east well before midnight. On the night of the 12–13th observers will see the old crescent Moon rising at about the same time as Jupiter (around midnight).

SATURN is still visible low in the south-western sky in the evenings, magnitude +0·5. On the evening of the 25th the Moon passes 2°S. of the planet.

THE MOON

Day	R.A.	Dec.	Hor. Par.	Semi-diam.	Sun's Co-long.	P.A. of Bright Limb	Phase	Age	Rise 52°	Rise 56°	Tran-sit	Set 52°	Set 56°
	h m	°	′	′	°	°		d	h m	h m	h m	h m	h m
1	21 37	−12·6	57·1	15·6	51	253	85	12·0	16 17	16 25	21 40	1 58	1 47
2	22 26	−7·0	57·9	15·8	63	253	92	13·0	16 31	16 34	22 27	3 18	3 13
3	23 16	−0·9	58·8	16·0	76	257	97	14·0	16 46	16 43	23 16	4 40	4 40
4	0 07	+5·4	59·5	16·2	88	279	100	15·0	17 01	16 53	—	6 05	6 11
5	1 00	+11·6	60·0	16·3	100	32	99	16·0	17 20	17 06	0 07	7 33	7 45
6	1 56	+17·2	60·3	16·4	112	56	97	17·0	17 44	17 24	1 01	9 03	9 23
7	2 56	+21·9	60·4	16·4	124	66	91	18·0	18 18	17 50	1 59	10 33	11 00
8	3 58	+25·0	60·2	16·4	136	74	83	19·0	19 05	18 32	3 00	11 56	12 28
9	5 03	+26·5	59·9	16·3	149	82	74	20·0	20 08	19 35	4 03	13 04	13 37
10	6 07	+26·2	59·4	16·2	161	90	63	21·0	21 24	20 55	5 06	13 54	14 23
11	7 08	+24·2	58·8	16·0	173	97	52	22·0	22 46	22 24	6 05	14 29	14 52
12	8 06	+20·7	58·2	15·9	185	102	41	23·0	—	23 53	7 00	14 54	15 11
13	9 00	+16·3	57·6	15·7	197	106	30	24·0	0 08	—	7 50	15 13	15 24
14	9 50	+11·1	57·1	15·5	209	108	21	25·0	1 28	1 19	8 37	15 28	15 34
15	10 38	+5·5	56·5	15·4	222	109	13	26·0	2 46	2 41	9 22	15 41	15 42
16	11 24	−0·2	56·0	15·3	234	107	7	27·0	4 01	4 02	10 05	15 54	15 50
17	12 10	−5·8	55·6	15·1	246	101	3	28·0	5 14	5 20	10 47	16 07	15 59
18	12 55	−11·1	55·1	15·0	258	80	1	29·0	6 28	6 39	11 30	16 21	16 09
19	13 42	−15·9	54·8	14·9	271	343	0	0·3	7 41	7 58	12 15	16 39	16 21
20	14 30	−20·0	54·4	14·8	283	306	2	1·3	8 54	9 16	13 01	17 01	16 38
21	15 19	−23·2	54·2	14·8	295	294	5	2·3	10 04	10 32	13 50	17 30	17 02
22	16 10	−25·4	54·1	14·7	307	286	10	3·3	11 07	11 40	14 39	18 09	17 36
23	17 03	−26·4	54·0	14·7	319	279	17	4·3	12 02	12 35	15 30	18 58	18 25
24	17 55	−26·2	54·2	14·8	332	272	24	5·3	12 45	13 16	16 20	19 58	19 28
25	18 48	−24·9	54·4	14·8	344	266	33	6·3	13 19	13 45	17 09	21 07	20 41
26	19 39	−22·4	54·9	14·9	356	261	42	7·3	13 44	14 05	17 57	22 20	22 00
27	20 29	−18·8	55·5	15·1	8	256	52	8·3	14 04	14 19	18 44	23 35	23 21
28	21 18	−14·4	56·2	15·3	20	253	62	9·3	14 20	14 30	19 30	—	—
29	22 06	−9·2	57·1	15·6	32	251	71	10·3	14 35	14 40	20 16	0 52	0 44
30	22 55	−3·4	58·0	15·8	45	250	80	11·3	14 49	14 49	21 02	2 11	2 09
31	23 44	+2·8	59·0	16·1	57	251	88	12·3	15 04	14 59	21 52	3 33	3 36

MERCURY ☿

Day	R.A.	Dec.	Diam.	Phase	Transit	5° high 52°	5° high 56°	Day	R.A.	Dec. −	Diam.	Phase	Transit	
	h m	°	″		h m	h m	h m		h m	°	″		h m	
1	11 34	+4·8	6	77	10 57	5 05	5 04	16	13 08	5·8	—	—	11 33	
4	11 52	+2·9	6	85	11 03	5 21	5 22	19	13 27	8·0	—	—	11 40	Mercury is too close to the Sun for observation
7	12 11	+0·9	5	91	11 11	5 39	5 42	22	13 46	10·2	—	—	11 46	
10	12 30	−1·3	5	95	11 18	5 58	6 03	25	14 04	12·2	—	—	11 53	
13	12 49	−3·6	5	97	11 25	6 17	6 24	28	14 23	14·1	—	—	12 00	
16	13 08	−5·8	5	99	11 33	6 36	6 45	31	14 41	16·0	—	—	12 06	

VENUS ♀

Day	R.A.	Dec.	Diam.	Phase	Transit	
	h m	°	″		h m	
1	12 00	+1·6	—	—	11 22	
6	12 23	−0·9	—	—	11 26	
11	12 46	−3·4	—	—	11 29	Venus is too close to the Sun for observation
16	13 09	−5·9	—	—	11 32	
21	13 32	−8·3	—	—	11 36	
26	13 56	−10·7	—	—	11 40	
31	14 19	−12·9	—	—	11 44	

MARS ♂

Day	R.A.	Dec. +	Diam.	Phase	Transit	5° high 52°	5° high 56°
	h m	°	″		h m	h m	h m
1	4 42	21·1	14	89	4 04	20 41	20 26
6	4 47	21·4	14	90	3 49	20 24	20 09
11	4 50	21·7	15	91	3 33	20 06	19 50
16	4 53	21·9	15	92	3 15	19 47	19 31
21	4 53	22·2	16	93	2 56	19 27	19 10
26	4 52	22·4	16	95	2 35	19 05	18 48
31	4 50	22·5	17	96	2 13	18 41	18 24

SUNRISE AND SUNSET

Day	London a.m. h m	London p.m. h m	Bristol a.m. h m	Bristol p.m. h m	Birmingham a.m. h m	Birmingham p.m. h m	Manchester a.m. h m	Manchester p.m. h m	Newcastle a.m. h m	Newcastle p.m. h m	Glasgow a.m. h m	Glasgow p.m. h m	Belfast a.m. h m	Belfast p.m. h m
1	5 59	5 40	6 09	5 50	6 06	5 47	6 09	5 48	6 06	5 45	6 18	5 55	6 24	6 03
2	6 01	5 37	6 11	5 47	6 08	5 44	6 11	5 45	6 08	5 42	6 20	5 52	6 26	6 00
3	6 03	5 35	6 13	5 45	6 10	5 42	6 13	5 43	6 10	5 39	6 22	5 49	6 28	5 57
4	6 04	5 33	6 14	5 43	6 11	5 40	6 14	5 41	6 12	5 37	6 24	5 47	6 30	5 55
5	6 06	5 31	6 16	5 41	6 13	5 37	6 16	5 38	6 14	5 34	6 26	5 44	6 32	5 52
6	6 08	5 29	6 17	5 39	6 15	5 35	6 18	5 36	6 16	5 31	6 28	5 41	6 34	5 49
7	6 09	5 26	6 19	5 36	6 16	5 33	6 19	5 34	6 18	5 29	6 30	5 39	6 36	5 47
8	6 11	5 24	6 20	5 34	6 18	5 30	6 21	5 31	6 20	5 26	6 32	5 36	6 38	5 44
9	6 13	5 22	6 22	5 32	6 20	5 28	6 23	5 29	6 22	5 24	6 34	5 34	6 40	5 42
10	6 14	5 20	6 23	5 30	6 22	5 26	6 25	5 27	6 24	5 22	6 36	5 31	6 42	5 40
11	6 16	5 18	6 25	5 28	6 24	5 23	6 27	5 24	6 26	5 19	6 38	5 29	6 44	5 37
12	6 18	5 15	6 27	5 25	6 25	5 21	6 28	5 22	6 27	5 17	6 40	5 26	6 45	5 35
13	6 19	5 13	6 29	5 23	6 27	5 19	6 30	5 20	6 29	5 15	6 42	5 24	6 47	5 33
14	6 21	5 11	6 30	5 21	6 29	5 16	6 32	5 17	6 31	5 12	6 44	5 21	6 49	5 30
15	6 22	5 09	6 32	5 19	6 31	5 14	6 34	5 15	6 33	5 10	6 46	5 19	6 51	5 28
16	6 24	5 07	6 34	5 17	6 33	5 12	6 36	5 12	6 35	5 07	6 48	5 16	6 53	5 25
17	6 26	5 05	6 36	5 15	6 35	5 10	6 38	5 10	6 37	5 04	6 50	5 13	6 55	5 23
18	6 27	5 02	6 37	5 12	6 36	5 07	6 40	5 08	6 40	5 02	6 53	5 11	6 57	5 21
19	6 29	5 00	6 39	5 10	6 38	5 05	6 42	5 06	6 42	5 00	6 55	5 09	6 59	5 19
20	6 31	4 58	6 41	5 08	6 40	5 03	6 44	5 03	6 44	4 57	6 57	5 06	7 01	5 16
21	6 33	4 56	6 43	5 06	6 42	5 01	6 46	5 01	6 46	4 55	6 59	5 04	7 03	5 14
22	6 34	4 54	6 44	5 04	6 43	4 59	6 47	4 59	6 47	4 53	7 01	5 01	7 05	5 11
23	6 36	4 52	6 46	5 02	6 45	4 57	6 49	4 56	6 49	4 50	7 03	4 59	7 07	5 09
24	6 38	4 50	6 48	5 00	6 47	4 55	6 51	4 54	6 51	4 48	7 05	4 57	7 09	5 07
25	6 40	4 48	6 50	4 58	6 49	4 53	6 53	4 52	6 53	4 46	7 07	4 54	7 11	5 04
26	6 41	4 46	6 51	4 56	6 50	4 51	6 55	4 50	6 55	4 44	7 09	4 52	7 13	5 02
27	6 43	4 44	6 53	4 54	6 52	4 49	6 57	4 48	6 57	4 41	7 11	4 49	7 15	5 00
28	6 45	4 42	6 55	4 52	6 54	4 47	6 59	4 46	7 00	4 39	7 14	4 47	7 17	4 58
29	6 47	4 40	6 57	4 50	6 56	4 45	7 01	4 44	7 02	4 37	7 16	4 45	7 19	4 56
30	6 49	4 38	6 59	4 48	6 58	4 43	7 03	4 42	7 04	4 35	7 18	4 43	7 21	4 54
31	6 51	4 36	7 00	4 46	6 59	4 41	7 04	4 40	7 06	4 33	7 20	4 41	7 23	4 52

JUPITER ♃ / SATURN ♄

Day	JUPITER R.A. h m	JUPITER Dec. + °	JUPITER Transit h m	JUPITER 5° high. 52° h m	JUPITER 5° high. 56° h m	SATURN R.A. h m	SATURN Dec. − °	SATURN Transit h m	SATURN 5° high. 52° h m	SATURN 5° high. 56° h m
1	8 43	18·6	8 04	1 00	0 48	19 21	22·2	18 40	21 50	21 18
11	8 49	18·2	7 31	0 29	0 17	19 22	22·1	18 02	21 12	20 40
21	8 55	17·9	6 57	23 54	23 42	19 24	22·1	17 24	20 35	20 02
31	8 59	17·6	6 22	23 20	23 08	19 26	22·0	16 47	19 58	19 26

Equatorial diameter of Jupiter 36″; of Saturn 17″. Diameters of Saturn's rings 38″ and 15″.

URANUS ⛢ / NEPTUNE ♆

Day	URANUS R.A. h m	URANUS Dec. − ° ′	URANUS Transit h m	URANUS 10° high. 52° h m	URANUS 10° high. 56° h m	NEPTUNE R.A. h m	NEPTUNE Dec. − ° ′	NEPTUNE Transit h m	NEPTUNE 10° high. 52° h m	NEPTUNE 10° high. 56° h m
1	18 25·0	23 38	17 44	19 43	18 20	18 51·0	22 05	18 10	20 28	19 32
11	18 25·7	23 38	17 06	19 05	17 42	18 51·3	22 05	17 31	19 49	18 53
21	18 26·9	23 37	16 28	18 27	17 04	18 51·9	22 05	16 52	19 10	18 14
31	18 28·3	23 36	15 50	17 49	16 27	18 52·6	22 04	16 14	18 32	17 36

Diameter 4″   Diameter 2″

Month	Week	*Novem* (nine), 9th month of Roman (pre-Julian) Calendar. *Sun's Longitude* 240° ♐ 22ᵈ 14ʰ

1	Th.	**All Saints.** Edmund Blunden b. 1896.
2	F.	ALL SOULS. Edward V b. 1470.
3	S.	Vincenzo Bellini b. 1801. Matisse d. 1954.
4	S.	**8th S. before Christmas.** William III b. 1650.
5	M.	Guy Fawkes Night (1605). Lester Piggott b. 1935.
6	Tu.	Colley Cibber b. 1671. Paderewski b. 1860.
7	W.	Marie Curie b. 1867. Joan Sutherland b. 1926.
8	Th.	Arnold Bax d. 1883. César Franck d. 1890.*
9	F.	Edward VII b. 1841. Chamberlain d. 1940.
10	S.	Oliver Goldsmith b. 1728. Schiller b. 1759.
11	S.	**7th S. before Christmas.** ARMISTICE DAY 1918.
12	M.	Canute d. 1035. Alexander Borodin b. 1833.
13	Tu.	Edward III b. 1312. R. L. Stevenson b. 1850.
14	W.	PRINCE OF WALES b. 1948. Claude Monet b. 1840.
15	Th.	Johann Kepler b. 1630. Aneurin Bevan b. 1897.
16	F.	John Bright b. 1811. Clark Gable d. 1960.
17	S.	Mary I d. 1558. Eric Gill d. 1940.
18	S.	**6th S. before Christmas.** Marcel Proust d. 1922.
19	M.	Thomas Shadwell d. 1692. Indira Gandhi b. 1917.
20	Tu.	QUEEN'S WEDDING DAY 1947.
21	W.	Voltaire b. 1694. André Gide b. 1869.
22	Th.	George Eliot b. 1819. Gen. de Gaulle b. 1890.*
23	F.	Perkin Warbeck d. 1499. Thomas Tallis d. 1585.
24	S.	John Knox d. 1572. Spinoza b. 1632.
25	S.	**5th S. before Christmas.** Andrew Carnegie b. 1835.
26	M.	William Cowper b. 1731. John McAdam d. 1836.
27	Tu.	Anders Celsius b. 1701. Eugene O'Neill d. 1953.
28	W.	William Blake b. 1757. Friedrich Engels b. 1820.
29	Th.	Louisa M. Alcott b. 1832. C. S. Lewis b. 1898.
30	F.	**St. Andrew.** Jonathan Swift b. 1667.

* Centenary.

PHENOMENA

d	h	
1	15	Venus in superior conjunction.
5	02	Mars in conjunction with Moon. Mars 3°S.
9	06	Jupiter in conjunction with Moon. Jupiter 2°N.
10	09	Pluto in conjunction with Sun.
17	18	Venus in conjunction with Moon. Venus 5°N.
18	19	Mercury in conjunction with Moon. Mercury 2°N.
22	04	Saturn in conjunction with Moon. Saturn 0°·6N.
27	21	Mars at opposition.

CONSTELLATIONS

The following constellations are near the meridian at

	d	h		d	h
Oct.	1	24	Oct.	16	23
Nov.	1	22	Nov.	15	21
Dec.	1	20	Dec.	16	19

Ursa Major (below the Pole), Cepheus Cassiopeia, Andromeda, Pegasus, Pisces, Aquarius and Cetus.

MINIMA OF ALGOL

d	h	d	h
3	15	17	23
6	12	20	20
9	09	23	17
12	06	26	14
15	03	29	11

PHASES OF THE MOON

	d	h	m
○ Full Moon	2	21	48
☾ Last Quarter	9	13	02
● New Moon	17	09	05
☽ First Quarter	25	13	11

		d	h
Perigee (358,630 kilometres)		3	23
Apogee (406,530 ,,)		19	03

Mean Longitude of Ascending Node on Nov. 1, 302°.

MONTHLY NOTES

Nov. 1. Fox-hunting begins.

     10. Lord Mayor's Show.

     11. Remembrance Sunday.

     11. Martinmas. Scottish Term Day.

     28. Removal Day, Scotland.

Day	Right Ascension	Dec. −	Equation of Time	Rise 52°	Rise 56°	Transit	Set 52°	Set 56°	Sidereal Time	Transit of First Point of Aries
	h m s	° ′	m s	h m	h m	h m	h m	h m	h m s	h m s
1	14 23 44	14 17	+16 22	6 54	7 06	11 44	16 32	16 20	2 40 06	21 16 25
2	14 27 38	14 36	+16 24	6 56	7 08	11 44	16 30	16 18	2 44 02	21 12 29
3	14 31 34	14 55	+16 25	6 58	7 11	11 44	16 29	16 16	2 47 59	21 08 33
4	14 35 30	15 13	+16 25	7 00	7 13	11 44	16 27	16 14	2 51 55	21 04 37
5	14 39 28	15 32	+16 24	7 01	7 15	11 44	16 25	16 12	2 55 52	21 00 41
6	14 43 26	15 50	+16 23	7 03	7 17	11 44	16 23	16 10	2 59 48	20 56 45
7	14 47 25	16 08	+16 20	7 05	7 19	11 44	16 22	16 08	3 03 45	20 52 49
8	14 51 24	16 26	+16 17	7 07	7 21	11 44	16 20	16 06	3 07 42	20 48 53
9	14 55 25	16 43	+16 13	7 09	7 23	11 44	16 18	16 04	3 11 38	20 44 57
10	14 59 27	17 00	+16 08	7 10	7 25	11 44	16 17	16 02	3 15 35	20 41 01
11	15 03 29	17 17	+16 02	7 12	7 27	11 44	16 15	16 00	3 19 31	20 37 06
12	15 07 32	17 34	+15 56	7 14	7 30	11 44	16 14	15 58	3 23 28	20 33 10
13	15 11 36	17 50	+15 48	7 16	7 32	11 44	16 12	15 56	3 27 24	20 29 14
14	15 15 41	18 06	+15 40	7 18	7 34	11 44	16 11	15 54	3 31 21	20 25 18
15	15 19 47	18 22	+15 30	7 19	7 36	11 45	16 09	15 53	3 35 17	20 21 22
16	15 23 54	18 37	+15 20	7 21	7 38	11 45	16 08	15 51	3 39 14	20 17 26
17	15 28 01	18 52	+15 09	7 23	7 40	11 45	16 07	15 49	3 43 11	20 13 30
18	15 32 10	19 07	+14 58	7 25	7 42	11 45	16 05	15 48	3 47 07	20 09 34
19	15 36 19	19 21	+14 45	7 26	7 44	11 45	16 04	15 46	3 51 04	20 05 38
20	15 40 29	19 35	+14 31	7 28	7 46	11 46	16 03	15 45	3 55 00	20 01 42
21	15 44 40	19 48	+14 17	7 30	7 48	11 46	16 02	15 43	3 58 57	19 57 46
22	15 48 51	20 02	+14 02	7 31	7 50	11 46	16 00	15 42	4 02 53	19 53 51
23	15 53 04	20 15	+13 46	7 33	7 52	11 46	15 59	15 40	4 06 50	19 49 55
24	15 57 17	20 27	+13 30	7 35	7 54	11 47	15 58	15 39	4 10 46	19 45 59
25	16 01 31	20 39	+13 12	7 36	7 56	11 47	15 57	15 38	4 14 43	19 42 03
26	16 05 46	20 51	+12 54	7 38	7 58	11 47	15 56	15 36	4 18 40	19 38 07
27	16 10 01	21 02	+12 35	7 39	7 59	11 48	15 55	15 35	4 22 36	19 34 11
28	16 14 17	21 13	+12 16	7 41	8 01	11 48	15 55	15 34	4 26 33	19 30 15
29	16 18 34	21 24	+11 55	7 42	8 03	11 48	15 54	15 33	4 30 29	19 26 19
30	16 22 51	21 34	+11 34	7 44	8 05	11 49	15 53	15 32	4 34 26	19 22 23

Duration of Civil (C), Nautical (N), and Astronomical (A), Twilight (in minutes)

Lat. °	Nov. 1 C	N	A	Nov. 11 C	N	A	Nov. 21 C	N	A	Nov. 30 C	N	A
52	36	75	115	37	78	117	38	80	120	39	82	123
56	40	84	127	41	87	130	43	90	134	45	93	137

ASTRONOMICAL NOTES

MERCURY is unsuitably placed for observation throughout November.

VENUS is too close to the Sun for observation, superior conjunction occurring on the 1st.

MARS, magnitude −2·0, reaches opposition on the 27th and thus is visible throughout the hours of darkness. On the night of the 4–5th the gibbous Moon passes 3°N. of the planet. Mars is retrograding in Taurus and passes 6°N. of Aldebaran on the 13th. Mars has an orbit which is more eccentric than any of the other major planets except Pluto and Mercury. As a result the times of closest approach to the Earth and of opposition need not coincide. In 1990, for example, the difference in time between these two events is 7d 16h, as closest approach occurs at 20d 04h.

JUPITER, magnitude −2·2, is a brilliant morning object, rising before midnight and crossing the meridian well before dawn. On the morning of the 9th the Moon, at Last Quarter, passes 2°S. of the planet, around the time of sunrise.

SATURN, magnitude +0·6, continues to be visible as an evening object low in the south-western sky. Saturn is in Sagittarius. On the evening of the 21st the crescent Moon will be seen aproaching the planet.

THE MOON

Day	R.A.	Dec.	Hor. Par.	Semi-diam.	Sun's Co-long.	P.A. of Bright Limb	Phase	Age	Rise 52°	Rise 56°	Transit	Set 52°	Set 56°
	h m	°	′	′	°	°		d	h m	h m	h m	h m	h m
1	0 36	+ 9·0	59·8	16·3	69	256	95	13·3	15 21	15 10	22 44	4 59	5 08
2	1 31	+14·9	60·5	16·5	81	269	99	14·3	15 43	15 26	23 41	6 29	6 44
3	2 30	+20·0	61·0	16·6	93	356	100	15·3	16 13	15 49	—	8 01	8 24
4	3 33	+23·9	61·1	16·7	105	60	98	16·3	16 56	16 25	0 43	9 30	10 00
5	4 39	+26·0	61·0	16·6	118	75	93	17·3	17 54	17 22	1 48	10 48	11 21
6	5 46	+26·3	60·5	16·5	130	86	86	18·3	19 09	18 39	2 54	11 47	12 17
7	6 50	+24·7	59·9	16·3	142	94	77	19·3	20 32	20 08	3 56	12 28	12 53
8	7 51	+21·5	59·1	16·1	154	101	67	20·3	21 56	21 39	4 54	12 57	13 16
9	8 47	+17·2	58·3	15·9	166	105	56	21·3	23 18	23 07	5 47	13 18	13 31
10	9 39	+12·1	57·5	15·7	178	109	45	22·3	—	—	6 36	13 35	13 42
11	10 27	+ 6·6	56·8	15·5	190	111	35	23·3	0 36	0 31	7 21	13 48	13 51
12	11 13	+ 1·0	56·1	15·3	203	111	25	24·3	1 51	1 51	8 04	14 01	13 59
13	11 58	− 4·6	55·5	15·1	215	110	17	25·3	3 04	3 09	8 46	14 14	14 08
14	12 44	− 9·9	55·0	15·0	227	107	11	26·3	4 17	4 27	9 29	14 28	14 17
15	13 29	−14·8	54·7	14·9	239	102	5	27·3	5 29	5 44	10 12	14 45	14 29
16	14 17	−19·0	54·4	14·8	251	91	2	28·3	6 42	7 02	10 58	15 06	14 44
17	15 06	−22·4	54·1	14·8	264	57	0	29·3	7 52	8 18	11 45	15 33	15 06
18	15 56	−24·8	54·0	14·7	276	314	0	0·6	8 58	9 29	12 34	16 08	15 37
19	16 49	−26·1	53·9	14·7	288	288	2	1·6	9 55	10 28	13 25	16 54	16 13
20	17 41	−26·2	54·0	14·7	300	277	6	2·6	10 42	11 14	14 15	17 51	17 20
21	18 34	−25·1	54·1	14·7	312	269	11	3·6	11 19	11 46	15 05	18 56	18 29
22	19 25	−22·9	54·4	14·8	325	262	18	4·6	11 46	12 08	15 52	20 07	19 46
23	20 15	−19·7	54·8	14·9	337	257	26	5·6	12 07	12 24	16 39	21 20	21 04
24	21 03	−15·6	55·3	15·1	349	253	35	6·6	12 25	12 36	17 23	22 34	22 24
25	21 50	−10·7	56·0	15·3	1	250	45	7·6	12 39	12 46	18 08	23 50	23 45
26	22 37	− 5·3	56·8	15·5	13	248	55	8·6	12 53	12 55	18 52	—	—
27	23 24	+ 0·6	57·8	15·7	25	248	65	9·6	13 07	13 04	19 39	1 07	1 08
28	0 13	+ 6·6	58·7	16·0	38	249	75	10·6	13 23	13 15	20 28	2 28	2 34
29	1 06	+12·4	59·7	16·3	50	252	84	11·6	13 42	13 28	21 21	3 53	4 05
30	2 02	+17·8	60·5	16·5	62	258	92	12·6	14 07	13 47	22 20	5 23	5 42

MERCURY ☿

Day	R.A.	Dec. −	Diam.	Phase	Transit		Day	R.A.	Dec. −	Diam.	Phase	Transit	
	h m	°	″		h m			h m	°	″		h m	
1	14 48	16·5	—	—	12 09		16	16 22	23·4	—	—	12 44	
4	15 06	18·2	—	—	12 15	Mercury is too	19	16 41	24·3	—	—	12 51	Mercury is too
7	15 25	19·7	—	—	12 22	close to the	22	17 00	25·0	—	—	12 58	close to the
10	15 44	21·1	—	—	12 29	Sun for	25	17 18	25·5	—	—	13 05	Sun for
13	16 03	22·3	—	—	12 36	observation	28	17 37	25·8	—	—	13 11	observation
16	16 22	23·4	—	—	12 44		31	17 54	25·9	—	—	13 17	

VENUS ♀

Day	R.A.	Dec. −	Diam.	Phase	Transit	
	h m	°	″		h m	
1	14 24	13·4	—	—	11 45	
6	14 49	15·5	—	—	11 49	
11	15 14	17·4	—	—	11 55	Venus is too
16	15 39	19·1	—	—	12 00	close to the
21	16 05	20·6	—	—	12 07	Sun for
26	16 31	21·9	—	—	12 13	observation
31	16 58	22·9	—	—	12 21	

MARS ♂

Day	R.A.	Dec. +	Diam.	Phase	Transit	5° high 52°	5° high 56°
	h m	°	″		h m	h m	h m
1	4 49	22·5	17	96	2 08	18 36	18 19
6	4 45	22·7	17	97	1 44	18 11	17 54
11	4 39	22·8	18	98	1 19	17 45	17 28
16	4 32	22·8	18	99	0 52	17 18	17 01
21	4 24	22·8	18	100	0 25	16 51	16 33
26	4 16	22·7	18	100	23 51	16 24	16 06
31	4 07	22·6	18	100	23 24	15 57	15 40

SUNRISE AND SUNSET

Day	London a.m. h m	London p.m. h m	Bristol a.m. h m	Bristol p.m. h m	Birmingham a.m. h m	Birmingham p.m. h m	Manchester a.m. h m	Manchester p.m. h m	Newcastle a.m. h m	Newcastle p.m. h m	Glasgow a.m. h m	Glasgow p.m. h m	Belfast a.m. h m	Belfast p.m. h m
1	6 52	4 34	7 02	4 44	7 01	4 39	7 06	4 38	7 08	4 31	7 22	4 39	7 25	4 50
2	6 54	4 33	7 04	4 43	7 03	4 37	7 08	4 36	7 10	4 29	7 24	4 37	7 27	4 48
3	6 56	4 31	7 06	4 41	7 05	4 36	7 10	4 35	7 12	4 27	7 26	4 35	7 29	4 46
4	6 58	4 29	7 07	4 39	7 07	4 34	7 12	4 33	7 14	4 25	7 28	4 33	7 31	4 44
5	6 59	4 28	7 09	4 38	7 09	4 32	7 14	4 31	7 16	4 23	7 30	4 31	7 33	4 42
6	7 01	4 26	7 10	4 36	7 11	4 30	7 16	4 29	7 18	4 21	7 32	4 29	7 35	4 40
7	7 03	4 24	7 12	4 34	7 13	4 28	7 18	4 27	7 20	4 19	7 34	4 27	7 37	4 38
8	7 05	4 23	7 14	4 33	7 15	4 26	7 20	4 25	7 22	4 17	7 36	4 25	7 39	4 36
9	7 07	4 21	7 16	4 31	7 16	4 24	7 21	4 23	7 24	4 15	7 38	4 23	7 40	4 34
10	7 08	4 20	7 18	4 30	7 18	4 23	7 23	4 22	7 26	4 13	7 40	4 21	7 42	4 33
11	7 10	4 18	7 19	4 28	7 20	4 21	7 25	4 20	7 28	4 11	7 42	4 19	7 44	4 31
12	7 11	4 16	7 21	4 26	7 22	4 19	7 27	4 18	7 30	4 09	7 44	4 17	7 46	4 29
13	7 13	4 15	7 23	4 25	7 24	4 18	7 29	4 17	7 32	4 08	7 46	4 15	7 48	4 27
14	7 15	4 13	7 25	4 23	7 26	4 16	7 31	4 15	7 34	4 06	7 49	4 13	7 51	4 25
15	7 16	4 12	7 26	4 22	7 27	4 15	7 33	4 13	7 36	4 04	7 51	4 12	7 53	4 24
16	7 18	4 11	7 28	4 21	7 29	4 14	7 35	4 12	7 38	4 03	7 53	4 10	7 55	4 22
17	7 20	4 09	7 30	4 19	7 31	4 12	7 37	4 10	7 40	4 01	7 55	4 08	7 57	4 20
18	7 22	4 08	7 32	4 18	7 33	4 11	7 39	4 09	7 42	3 59	7 57	4 06	7 59	4 19
19	7 23	4 07	7 33	4 17	7 34	4 10	7 41	4 07	7 44	3 58	7 59	4 05	8 01	4 17
20	7 25	4 05	7 35	4 15	7 36	4 08	7 43	4 06	7 46	3 56	8 01	4 03	8 03	4 16
21	7 27	4 04	7 37	4 14	7 38	4 07	7 44	4 05	7 48	3 55	8 03	4 02	8 04	4 15
22	7 28	4 03	7 38	4 13	7 39	4 06	7 46	4 03	7 50	3 53	8 05	4 00	8 06	4 13
23	7 30	4 02	7 40	4 12	7 41	4 05	7 48	4 02	7 52	3 52	8 07	3 59	8 08	4 12
24	7 32	4 01	7 42	4 11	7 43	4 04	7 50	4 01	7 54	3 51	8 09	3 58	8 10	4 11
25	7 33	4 00	7 43	4 10	7 44	4 03	7 51	4 00	7 55	3 50	8 11	3 56	8 11	4 10
26	7 35	3 59	7 45	4 09	7 46	4 02	7 53	3 59	7 57	3 49	8 12	3 55	8 13	4 09
27	7 36	3 58	7 46	4 08	7 47	4 01	7 54	3 58	7 59	3 48	8 14	3 54	8 15	4 08
28	7 38	3 57	7 48	4 08	7 49	4 00	7 56	3 57	8 01	3 47	8 16	3 53	8 17	4 07
29	7 40	3 56	7 50	4 07	7 51	3 59	7 58	3 56	8 02	3 46	8 18	3 52	8 18	4 06
30	7 41	3 56	7 51	4 06	7 52	3 58	7 59	3 56	8 04	3 45	8 20	3 51	8 20	4 05

JUPITER ♃ | SATURN ♄

Day	R.A. h m	Dec. + °	Transit h m	5° high. 52° h m	5° high. 56° h m	R.A. h m	Dec. − °	Transit h m	5° high. 52° h m	5° high. 56° h m
1	8 59	17·6	6 18	23 16	23 05	19 26	22·0	16 44	19 55	19 23
11	9 02	17·4	5 42	22 41	22 29	19 29	21·9	16 07	19 19	18 47
21	9 04	17·3	5 05	22 04	21 53	19 33	21·8	15 31	18 44	18 13
31	9 05	17·3	4 26	21 25	21 14	19 37	21·7	14 56	18 10	17 39

Equatorial diameter of Jupiter 39″; of Saturn 16″.   Diameters of Saturn's rings 36″ and 14″.

URANUS ♅ | NEPTUNE ♆

Day	R.A. h m	Dec. − ° ′	Transit h m		R.A. h m	Dec. − ° ′	Transit h m	
1	18 28·5	23 36	15 46	Uranus is too close to the Sun for observation	18 52·7	22 04	16 10	Neptune is too close to the Sun for observation
11	18 30·3	23 35	15 08		18 53·7	22 03	15 32	
21	18 32·4	23 33	14 31		18 54·9	22 02	14 54	
31	18 34·6	23 31	13 54		18 56·2	22 01	14 16	

Diameter 4″   Diameter 2″

Day of Month	Week	
		Decem (ten), 10th month of Roman (pre-Julian) Calendar. *Sun's Longitude* 270° ♑ 22ᵈ 03ʰ
1	S.	Edmund Campion exec. 1581.
2	S.	**Advent Sunday.** Maria Callas b. 1923.
3	M.	Frederic Leighton b. 1830. Oswald Mosley d. 1980.
4	Tu.	Samuel Butler b. 1835. Edith Cavell b. 1865.
5	W.	Christina Rossetti b. 1830. Walt Disney b. 1901.
6	Th.	Henry VI b. 1421. Joseph Conrad b. 1857.
7	F.	Pietro Mascagni b. 1863. Joyce Cary b. 1888.
8	S.	Mary, Queen of Scots b. 1542. Sibelius b. 1865.
9	S.	**2nd S. in Advent.** John Milton b. 1608.
10	M.	Emily Dickinson b. 1830. Alfred Nobel d. 1896.
11	Tu.	Hector Berlioz b. 1803. Solzhenitsyn b. 1918.
12	W.	Gustave Flaubert b. 1821. John Osborne b. 1929.
13	Th.	Laurens van der Post b. 1906.
14	F.	George Washington d. 1799. George VI b. 1895.
15	S.	Grigori Rasputin assas. 1916.
16	S.	**3rd S. in Advent.** Noel Coward b. 1899.
17	M.	Ford Maddox Ford b. 1873.
18	Tu.	Charles Wesley b. 1707. Ben Travers d. 1980.
19	W.	Emily Brontë d. 1848. Jean Genet b. 1910.
20	Th.	John Steinbeck d. 1968. Bill Brandt d. 1983.
21	F.	Michaelmas Law Sittings End. Stalin b. 1879.
22	S.	Puccini b. 1858. Peggy Ashcroft b. 1907.
23	S.	**4th S. in Advent.** Richard Arkwright b. 1732.
24	M.	Christmas Eve. Matthew Arnold b. 1822.
25	Tu.	**Christmas Day.** Dorothy Wordsworth b. 1771.
26	W.	**St. Stephen.** Boxing Day.
27	Th.	**St. John.** Marlene Dietrich b. 1904.
28	F.	**The Holy Innocents.** Mary II d. 1694.
29	S.	Thomas Becket killed 1170.
30	S.	**1st S. after Christmas.** Kipling b. 1865.
31	M.	Charles Edward Stuart b. 1720. Matisse b. 1869.

* Centenary.

PHENOMENA

d	h	
1	22	Mars in conjunction with Moon. Mars 3°S.
6	07	Mercury at greatest elongation E.21°.
6	15	Jupiter in conjunction with Moon. Jupiter 2°N.
18	06	Venus in conjunction with Moon. Venus 1°N.
18	09	Mercury in conjunction with Moon. Mercury 2°N.
19	00	Venus in conjunction with Mercury. Venus 1°S.
19	16	Saturn in conjunction with Moon. Saturn 0°·2N.
22	03	Solstice.
24	08	Mercury in inferior conjunction.
29	00	Mars in conjunction with Moon. Mars 2°S.
31	16	Uranus in conjunction with Sun.

CONSTELLATIONS

The following constellations are near the meridian at

	d	h		d	h
Nov.	1	24	Nov.	15	23
Dec.	1	22	Dec.	16	21
Jan.	1	20	Jan.	16	19

Ursa Major (below the Pole), Ursa Minor (below the Pole), Cassiopeia, Andromeda, Perseus, Triangulum, Aries, Taurus, Cetus and Eridanus.

MINIMA OF ALGOL

d	h	d	h
2	07	19	12
5	04	22	09
8	01	25	06
10	22	28	03
13	19	31	00
16	16		

PHASES OF THE MOON

		d	h	m
○	Full Moon	2	07	50
☾	Last Quarter	9	02	04
●	New Moon	17	10	22
☽	First Quarter	25	03	16
○	Full Moon	31	18	35

		d	h
Perigee (356,530 kilometres)		2	11
Apogee (406,580 „)		16	04
Perigee (357,750 „)		31	00

Mean Longitude of Ascending Node on Dec. 1, 301°.

MONTHLY NOTES

Dec. 10. Grouse shooting ends.

       22. Shortest day.

       25. Christmas Day. Quarter Day.

       25, 26. Bank Holiday, England, Wales, Scotland and N. Ireland.

       31. Various licences expire.

	THE SUN					s.d. 16'·3			Sidereal Time	Transit of First Point of Aries
Day	Right Ascension	Dec. —	Equation of Time	Rise 52°	Rise 56°	Transit	Set 52°	Set 56°		
	h m s	° ′	m s	h m	h m	h m	h m	h m	h m s	h m s
1	16 27 10	21 44	+11 13	7 45	8 06	11 49	15 52	15 31	4 38 22	19 18 27
2	16 31 28	21 53	+10 51	7 47	8 08	11 49	15 52	15 30	4 42 19	19 14 31
3	16 35 48	22 02	+10 28	7 48	8 10	11 50	15 51	15 29	4 46 16	19 10 35
4	16 40 08	22 10	+10 04	7 49	8 11	11 50	15 51	15 29	4 50 12	19 06 40
5	16 44 29	22 18	+ 9 40	7 51	8 13	11 51	15 50	15 28	4 54 09	19 02 44
6	16 48 50	22 26	+ 9 15	7 52	8 14	11 51	15 50	15 27	4 58 05	18 58 48
7	16 53 12	22 33	+ 8 50	7 53	8 16	11 51	15 49	15 27	5 02 02	18 54 52
8	16 57 34	22 40	+ 8 24	7 54	8 17	11 52	15 49	15 26	5 05 58	18 50 56
9	17 01 57	22 46	+ 7 58	7 55	8 18	11 52	15 49	15 26	5 09 55	18 47 00
10	17 06 20	22 52	+ 7 31	7 57	8 20	11 53	15 49	15 26	5 13 51	18 43 04
11	17 10 44	22 58	+ 7 04	7 58	8 21	11 53	15 48	15 25	5 17 48	18 39 08
12	17 15 08	23 02	+ 6 37	7 59	8 22	11 54	15 48	15 25	5 21 45	18 35 12
13	17 19 33	23 07	+ 6 09	8 00	8 23	11 54	15 48	15 25	5 25 41	18 31 16
14	17 23 57	23 11	+ 5 40	8 01	8 24	11 55	15 48	15 25	5 29 38	18 27 20
15	17 28 23	23 15	+ 5 12	8 01	8 25	11 55	15 48	15 25	5 33 34	18 23 25
16	17 32 48	23 18	+ 4 43	8 02	8 26	11 56	15 49	15 25	5 37 31	18 19 29
17	17 37 14	23 20	+ 4 13	8 03	8 27	11 56	15 49	15 25	5 41 27	18 15 33
18	17 41 40	23 22	+ 3 44	8 04	8 28	11 57	15 49	15 25	5 45 24	18 11 37
19	17 46 06	23 24	+ 3 14	8 04	8 28	11 57	15 49	15 26	5 49 20	18 07 41
20	17 50 32	23 25	+ 2 45	8 05	8 29	11 57	15 50	15 26	5 53 17	18 03 45
21	17 54 59	23 26	+ 2 15	8 06	8 30	11 58	15 50	15 26	5 57 14	17 59 49
22	17 59 25	23 26	+ 1 45	8 06	8 30	11 59	15 51	15 27	6 01 10	17 55 53
23	18 03 52	23 26	+ 1 15	8 07	8 31	11 59	15 51	15 28	6 05 07	17 51 57
24	18 08 18	23 26	+ 0 45	8 07	8 31	12 00	15 52	15 28	6 09 03	17 48 01
25	18 12 45	23 25	+ 0 15	8 07	8 31	12 00	15 53	15 29	6 13 00	17 44 05
26	18 17 11	23 23	− 0 14	8 08	8 31	12 00	15 53	15 30	6 16 56	17 40 09
27	18 21 37	23 21	− 0 44	8 08	8 32	12 01	15 54	15 30	6 20 53	17 36 14
28	18 26 03	23 18	− 1 14	8 08	8 32	12 01	15 55	15 31	6 24 49	17 32 18
29	18 30 29	23 15	− 1 43	8 08	8 32	12 02	15 56	15 32	6 28 46	17 28 22
30	18 34 55	23 12	− 2 12	8 08	8 32	12 02	15 57	15 33	6 32 43	17 24 26
31	18 39 20	23 08	− 2 41	8 08	8 32	12 03	15 58	15 34	6 36 39	17 20 30

Duration of Civil (C), Nautical (N), and Astronomical (A), Twilight (in minutes)

Lat. °	Dec. 1 C	N	A	Dec. 11 C	N	A	Dec. 21 C	N	A	Dec. 31 C	N	A
52	40	82	123	41	84	125	41	85	126	41	84	125
56	45	93	138	47	96	141	47	97	142	47	96	141

ASTRONOMICAL NOTES

MERCURY, despite being at greatest eastern elongation on the 6th, is unsuitably placed for observation.

VENUS is to close to the Sun for observation at first but gradually becomes visible in the evenings for the last week of the month. It will only be seen for a very short while after sunset, low above the south-western horizon. Its magnitude is −3·9.

MARS, just past opposition, is still visible for the greater part of the night though its magnitude fades from −1·9 to −1·0 during the month. The Moon passes north of Mars on the night of December 1–2 and again on December 28–29. Mars is in Taurus moving slowly westwards between the Pleiades and the Hyades.

JUPITER continues to be visible as a brilliant object in the night sky, magnitude −2·4, and by the end of the month is visible above the eastern horizon shortly after 19h. Jupiter is in the constellation of Cancer. The gibbous Moon is near the planet on the evening of the 6th.

SATURN is approaching the end of its evening apparation and is only visible low in the south-western sky for a short while. Before the end of the year it is lost in the evening twilight. The waxing crescent Moon, only 2¼ days old, may be seen near the planet on the evening of the 19th, if conditions are good.

METEORS. The maximum of the well-known Geminid meteor shower occurs during the night of the 13th–14th. Conditions are quite favourable since the old crescent Moon does not rise until shortly before 06h.

THE MOON

Day	R.A.	Dec.	Hor. Par.	Semi-diam.	Sun's Co-long.	P.A. of Bright Limb	Phase	Age	Rise 52°	Rise 56°	Transit	Set 52°	Set 56°
	h m	°	′	′	°	°		d	h m	h m	h m	h m	h m
1	3 03	+22·2	61·1	16·7	74	268	97	13·6	14 43	14 15	23 24	6 54	7 20
2	4 08	+25·2	61·5	16·7	86	301	100	14·6	15 34	15 02	—	8 20	8 51
3	5 16	+26·3	61·4	16·7	98	67	99	15·6	16 43	16 11	0 31	9 30	10 02
4	6 24	+25·4	61·1	16·6	110	88	96	16·6	18 06	17 39	1 38	10 21	10 48
5	7 28	+22·7	60·5	16·5	123	98	90	17·6	19 34	19 14	2 41	10 56	11 17
6	8 28	+18·6	59·6	16·2	135	104	81	18·6	21 00	20 47	3 38	11 21	11 36
7	9 23	+13·5	58·7	16·0	147	109	72	19·6	22 22	22 15	4 30	11 40	11 49
8	10 13	+ 7·9	57·7	15·7	159	112	62	20·6	23 40	23 38	5 17	11 55	11 59
9	11 01	+ 2·2	56·8	15·5	171	113	51	21·6	—	—	6 02	12 08	12 08
10	11 47	− 3·5	56·0	15·3	183	113	41	22·6	0 54	0 58	6 45	12 21	12 16
11	12 32	− 8·8	55·3	15·1	195	111	31	23·6	2 07	2 16	7 27	12 35	12 25
12	13 16	−13·8	54·8	14·9	208	109	23	24·6	3 20	3 33	8 11	12 51	12 36
13	14 05	−18·1	54·4	14·8	220	105	15	25·6	4 32	4 51	8 55	13 10	12 50
14	14 53	−21·7	54·1	14·8	232	100	9	26·6	5 43	6 07	9 42	13 35	13 10
15	15 43	−24·3	54·0	14·7	244	93	4	27·6	6 50	7 19	10 31	14 08	13 38
16	16 35	−25·9	53·9	14·7	256	82	1	28·6	7 50	8 23	11 21	14 50	14 18
17	17 28	−26·3	54·0	14·7	268	36	0	29·6	8 40	9 12	12 11	15 44	15 12
18	18 21	−25·4	54·1	14·7	281	281	1	0·8	9 20	9 48	13 01	16 48	16 20
19	19 12	−23·5	54·3	14·8	293	266	3	1·8	9 50	10 13	13 50	17 57	17 34
20	20 02	−20·4	54·6	14·9	305	258	7	2·8	10 13	10 31	14 36	19 10	18 53
21	20 51	−16·5	54·9	15·0	317	253	13	3·8	10 31	10 44	15 21	20 23	20 12
22	21 38	−11·8	55·4	15·1	329	249	20	4·8	10 46	10 54	16 05	21 37	21 31
23	22 24	− 6·6	56·0	15·3	342	247	29	5·8	11 00	11 03	16 48	22 52	22 50
24	23 10	− 1·0	56·7	15·4	354	246	38	6·8	11 13	11 12	17 32	—	—
25	23 57	+ 4·8	57·5	15·7	6	246	49	7·8	11 27	11 21	18 18	0 08	0 12
26	0 46	+10·5	58·3	15·9	18	248	59	8·8	11 44	11 32	19 08	1 28	1 38
27	1 39	+15·9	59·2	16·1	30	251	70	9·8	12 05	11 47	20 02	2 52	3 08
28	2 36	+20·6	60·0	16·3	42	256	80	10·8	12 33	12 10	21 02	4 20	4 43
29	3 38	+24·1	60·7	16·5	54	262	89	11·8	13 15	12 45	22 06	5 47	6 16
30	4 44	+26·1	61·1	16·7	67	270	95	12·8	14 14	13 41	23 13	7 05	7 38
31	5 51	+26·1	61·3	16·7	79	282	99	13·8	15 30	15 01	—	8 06	8 37

MERCURY ☿

Day	R.A.	Dec. −	Diam.	Phase	Transit		Day	R.A.	Dec. −	Diam.	Phase	Transit	
	h m	°	″		h m			h m	°	″		h m	
1	17 54	25·9	—	—	13 17		16	18 43	23·5	—	—	13 03	
4	18 11	25·7	—	—	13 21	Mercury is too	19	18 36	22·6	—	—	12 43	Mercury is too
7	18 25	25·4	—	—	13 23	close to the	22	18 23	21·8	—	—	12 17	close to the
10	18 36	24·9	—	—	13 22	Sun for	25	18 06	21·0	—	—	11 48	Sun for
13	18 43	24·2	—	—	13 15	observation	28	17 49	20·5	—	—	11 20	observation
16	18 43	23·5	—	—	13 03		31	17 38	20·2	—	—	10 59	

VENUS ♀ 　　　　MARS ♂

Day	R.A.	Dec. −	Diam.	Phase	Transit	5° high. 52°	5° high. 56°	Day	R.A.	Dec. +	Diam.	Phase	Transit	5° high. 52°	5° high. 56°
	h m	°	″		h m	h m	h m		h m	°	″		h m	h m	h m
1	16 58	22·9	10	99	12 21	15 24	14 49	1	4 07	22·6	18	100	23 24	6 56	7 14
6	17 25	23·6	10	99	12 28	15 25	14 48	6	4 00	22·4	17	99	22 57	6 28	6 45
11	17 53	24·1	10	99	12 36	15 29	14 50	11	3 53	22·2	17	99	22 31	6 01	6 18
16	18 20	24·2	10	98	12 44	15 37	14 57	16	3 48	22·1	16	98	22 06	5 35	5 52
21	18 48	24·0	10	98	12 52	15 47	15 08	21	3 44	22·0	15	97	21 42	5 11	5 27
26	19 15	23·5	10	98	12 59	15 59	15 23	26	3 41	21·9	15	96	21 20	4 48	5 05
31	19 42	22·6	10	97	13 06	16 14	15 40	31	3 40	21·9	14	95	21 00	4 27	4 44

SUNRISE AND SUNSET

Day	London a.m.	London p.m.	Bristol a.m.	Bristol p.m.	Birmingham a.m.	Birmingham p.m.	Manchester a.m.	Manchester p.m.	Newcastle a.m.	Newcastle p.m.	Glasgow a.m.	Glasgow p.m.	Belfast a.m.	Belfast p.m.
	h m	h m	h m	h m	h m	h m	h m	h m	h m	h m	h m	h m	h m	h m
1	7 42	3 55	7 52	4 06	7 53	3 58	8 00	3 55	8 05	3 44	8 21	3 50	8 21	4 04
2	7 44	3 54	7 54	4 05	7 55	3 57	8 02	3 54	8 07	3 43	8 23	3 49	8 23	4 03
3	7 45	3 54	7 55	4 05	7 56	3 56	8 03	3 53	8 09	3 42	8 25	3 48	8 25	4 02
4	7 47	3 53	7 57	4 04	7 58	3 56	8 05	3 53	8 10	3 41	8 26	3 47	8 26	4 01
5	7 48	3 53	7 58	4 03	7 59	3 55	8 06	3 52	8 12	3 40	8 28	3 46	8 28	4 00
6	7 49	3 52	7 59	4 03	8 01	3 55	8 08	3 52	8 13	3 40	8 29	3 46	8 29	4 00
7	7 51	3 52	8 00	4 03	8 02	3 54	8 09	3 51	8 15	3 39	8 31	3 45	8 31	3 59
8	7 52	3 52	8 01	4 02	8 03	3 54	8 10	3 51	8 16	3 39	8 32	3 45	8 32	3 59
9	7 53	3 51	8 03	4 02	8 05	3 53	8 12	3 50	8 18	3 38	8 34	3 44	8 34	3 58
10	7 54	3 51	8 04	4 02	8 06	3 53	8 13	3 50	8 19	3 38	8 35	3 44	8 35	3 58
11	7 55	3 51	8 05	4 02	8 07	3 53	8 14	3 50	8 20	3 38	8 36	3 44	8 36	3 58
12	7 56	3 51	8 06	4 01	8 08	3 53	8 15	3 50	8 21	3 38	8 37	3 43	8 37	3 58
13	7 57	3 51	8 07	4 01	8 09	3 53	8 16	3 50	8 22	3 38	8 39	3 43	8 38	3 58
14	7 58	3 51	8 07	4 01	8 10	3 53	8 17	3 50	8 23	3 38	8 40	3 43	8 39	3 58
15	7 59	3 51	8 08	4 01	8 11	3 53	8 18	3 50	8 24	3 38	8 41	3 43	8 40	3 58
16	8 00	3 51	8 09	4 02	8 12	3 53	8 19	3 50	8 25	3 38	8 42	3 43	8 41	3 58
17	8 01	3 52	8 10	4 02	8 13	3 53	8 20	3 50	8 26	3 38	8 42	3 43	8 42	3 58
18	8 02	3 52	8 11	4 02	8 14	3 53	8 21	3 50	8 27	3 38	8 43	3 43	8 43	3 58
19	8 02	3 52	8 11	4 02	8 14	3 53	8 21	3 50	8 27	3 38	8 44	3 44	8 43	3 58
20	8 03	3 53	8 12	4 03	8 15	3 54	8 22	3 51	8 28	3 39	8 45	3 44	8 44	3 59
21	8 04	3 53	8 13	4 03	8 16	3 54	8 23	3 51	8 29	3 39	8 46	3 44	8 45	3 59
22	8 04	3 54	8 13	4 04	8 16	3 55	8 23	3 52	8 29	3 40	8 46	3 45	8 45	4 00
23	8 05	3 54	8 14	4 04	8 17	3 55	8 24	3 52	8 30	3 40	8 46	3 45	8 46	4 00
24	8 05	3 55	8 14	4 05	8 17	3 56	8 24	3 53	8 30	3 41	8 47	3 46	8 46	4 01
25	8 06	3 55	8 15	4 05	8 18	3 56	8 25	3 53	8 31	3 41	8 47	3 47	8 47	4 01
26	8 06	3 56	8 15	4 06	8 18	3 57	8 25	3 54	8 31	3 42	8 48	3 47	8 47	4 02
27	8 06	3 57	8 15	4 07	8 18	3 58	8 25	3 55	8 31	3 43	8 48	3 48	8 47	4 03
28	8 06	3 57	8 15	4 08	8 18	3 59	8 25	3 56	8 31	3 44	8 48	3 49	8 47	4 04
29	8 07	3 58	8 16	4 09	8 19	4 00	8 26	3 56	8 32	3 44	8 48	3 50	8 48	4 04
30	8 07	3 59	8 16	4 10	8 19	4 01	8 26	3 57	8 32	3 45	8 48	3 51	8 48	4 05
31	8 07	4 00	8 16	4 11	8 19	4 02	8 26	3 58	8 32	3 46	8 48	3 52	8 48	4 06

JUPITER ♃

Day	R.A.	Dec. +	Transit	5° high 52°	5° high 56°
	h m	°	h m	h m	h m
1	9 05	17·3	4 26	21 25	21 14
11	9 04	17·4	3 46	20 44	20 33
21	9 02	17·6	3 04	20 02	19 50
31	8 59	17·8	2 22	19 18	19 06

SATURN ♄

Day	R.A.	Dec. −	Transit	5° high 52°	5° high 56°
	h m	°	h m	h m	h m
1	19 37	21·7	14 56	18 10	17 39
11	19 41	21·5	14 21	17 36	17 05
21	19 45	21·4	13 46	17 03	16 33
31	19 50	21·2	13 12	16 30	16 00

Equatorial diameter of Jupiter 43″; of Saturn 15″. Diameters of Saturn's rings 35″ and 13″.

URANUS ♅

Day	R.A.	Dec. −	Transit	
	h m	° ′	h m	
1	18 34·6	23 31	13 54	Uranus is too
11	18 37·0	23 29	13 17	close to the Sun
21	18 39·6	23 27	12 40	for observation
31	18 42·2	23 24	12 04	

Diameter 4″

NEPTUNE ♆

Day	R.A.	Dec. −	Transit	
	h m	° ′	h m	
1	18 56·2	22 01	14 16	Neptune is too
11	18 57·6	21 59	13 38	close to the Sun
21	18 59·2	21 57	13 00	for observation
31	19 00·8	21 55	12 22	

Diameter 2″

NOTES ON ASTRONOMICAL SECTION

GENERAL

The astronomical data are given in a form suitable for those who practise naked-eye astronomy or use small telescopes. No attempt has been made to replace the *Astronomical Almanac* for professional astronomers. Positions of the heavenly bodies are given only to the degree of accuracy required by amateur astronomers for setting telescopes, or for plotting on celestial globes or star atlases. Where intermediate positions are required, linear interpolation may be employed.

All data are, unless otherwise stated, for 0^h Greenwich Mean Time (G.M.T.), i.e. at the midnight at the beginning of the day named.

(*See also* notes on British Summer Time, p. 72).

Definitions of the terms used cannot be given in an ephemeris of this nature. They must be sought in astronomical literature and text-books. Probably the best source for the amateur is Norton's *Star Atlas and Reference Book* (Longman, 17th edition, 1987; £12·95), which contains an excellent introduction to observational astronomy, and the finest series of star maps yet produced for showing stars visible to the naked eye. Certain more extended ephemerides are available in the British Astronomical Association Handbook, an annual popular among amateur astronomers. (Secretary: Burlington House, Piccadilly, London, W1V 0NL)

A special feature has been made of the times when the various heavenly bodies are visible in the British Isles. Since two columns, calculated for latitudes 52° and 56°, are devoted to risings and settings, the range 50° to 58° can be covered by interpolation and extrapolation. The times given in these columns are G.M.T.'s for the meridian of Greenwich. An observer west of this meridian must add his longitude (in time) and vice versa.

In accordance with the usual convention in astronomy, + and − indicate respectively north and south latitudes or declinations.

PAGE ONE OF EACH MONTH

The Zodiacal signs through which the Sun is passing during each month are illustrated. The date of transition from one sign to the next, to the nearest hour, is also given.

The **festivals and holy days** in black-letter type are those observed by the Church of England.

Under the heading PHENOMENA will be found particulars of the more important conjunctions of the Sun, Moon and planets with each other, and also the dates of eclipses and other astronomical phenomena of special interest.

The CONSTELLATIONS listed each month are those that are near the meridian at the beginning of the month at 22^h local mean time. Allowance must be made for Summer Time if necessary. The fact that any star crosses the meridian 4^m earlier each night or 2^h earlier each month may be used, in conjunction with the lists given each month, to find what constellations are favourably placed at any moment. The table preceding the list of constellations may be extended indefinitely at the rate just quoted.

Times of MINIMA OF ALGOL are approximate times of the middle of the period of diminished light.

The Principal PHASES OF THE MOON are the G.M.T.'s when the difference between the longitude of the Moon and that of the Sun is 0°, 90°, 180° or 270°. The times of perigee and apogee are those when the Moon is nearest to, and farthest from, the Earth, respectively. The nodes or points of intersection of the Moon's orbit and the ecliptic make a complete retrograde circuit of the ecliptic in about 19 years. From a knowledge of the longitude of the ascending node and the inclination, whose value does not vary much from 5°, the path of the Moon among the stars may be plotted on a celestial globe or star atlas.

The MONTHLY NOTES are self-explanatory.

PAGE TWO OF EACH MONTH

The Sun's semi-diameter, in arc, is given once a month.

The right ascension given is that of the true Sun. The right ascension of the mean Sun is obtained by applying the equation of time, with the sign given, to the right ascension of the true Sun, or, more easily, by applying 12^h to the column Sidereal Time. The direction in which the equation of time has to be applied in different problems is a frequent source of confusion and error. Apparent Solar Time is equal to the Mean Solar Time plus the Equation of Time. For example at noon on Aug. 8 the Equation of Time is $-5^m 39^s$ and thus at 12^h Mean Time on that day the Apparent Time is $12^h - 5^m 39^s = 11^h 54^m 21^s$.

The Greenwich Sidereal Time at 0^h and the Transit of the First Point of Aries (which is really the mean time when the sidereal time is 0^h) are used for converting mean time to sidereal time and vice versa.

The G.M.T. of transit of the Sun at Greenwich may also be taken as the local mean time (L.M.T.) of transit in any longitude. It is independent of latitude. The G.M.T. of transit in any longitude is obtained by adding the longitude to the time given if west, and vice versa.

The legal importance of SUNRISE and SUNSET is that the Road Vehicles Lighting Regulations 1984 (S.I. 1984 No. 812) requires lights on vehicles to be used during the hours of darkness. This is defined as the period between half an hour after sunset and half an hour before sunrise, throughout the year. However, revised Lighting Regulations are expected to come into operation by the end of 1989. These will retain the requirement defined by the 1984 Regulations for the use of headlamps on vehicles, but it is proposed to make the use of front and rear position lamps on vehicles compulsory during the period between sunset and sunrise.

In all laws and regulations "sunset" refers to the local sunset, i.e. the time at which the Sun sets at the place in question. This common-sense interpretation has been upheld by legal tribunals. Thus the necessity for providing for different latitudes and longitudes, as already described, is evident.

The times of SUNRISE and SUNSET are those when the Sun's upper limb, as affected by refraction, is on the true horizon of an observer at sea-level. Assuming the mean refraction to be 34′, and the Sun's semi-diameter to be 16′, the time given is that when the true zenith distance of the Sun's centre is 90° + 34′ + 16′ or 90° 50′, or, in other words, when the depression of the Sun's centre below the true horizon is 50′. The upper limb is then 34′ below the true horizon, but is brought there by refraction. It is true, of course, that an observer on a ship might see the Sun for a minute or so longer, because of the dip of the horizon, while another viewing the sunset over hills or mountains would record an earlier time. Nevertheless, the moment when the true zenith distance of the Sun's centre is 90° 50′ is a precise time dependent only on the latitude and longitude of the place, and independent of its altitude above sea-level, the contour of its horizon, the vagaries of refraction or the small seasonal change in the Sun's semi-diameter; this moment is suitable in every way as a definition of sunset (or sunrise) for all statutory purposes. (For further information *see* footnote.)

It is well known that light reaches us before sunrise and also continues to reach us for some time after sunset. The interval between darkness and sunrise or sunset and darkness is called twilight. Astronomically speaking, twilight is considered to begin or end when the Sun's centre is 18° below the horizon, as no light from the Sun can then reach the observer. As thus defined twilight may last several hours; in high latitudes at the summer solstice the depression of 18° is not reached, and twilight lasts from sunset to sunrise.

The need for some sub-division of twilight was met some years ago by dividing the gathering darkness into four steps.

(1) *Sunrise or Sunset,* defined as above.
(2) *Civil twilight,* which begins or ends when the Sun's centre is 6° below the horizon. This marks the time when operations requiring daylight may commence or must cease. In England it varies from about 30 to 60 minutes after sunset and the same interval before sunrise.
    "Lighting-up time" is a crude attempt to approximate to civil twilight over the British Isles.
(3) *Nautical twilight,* which begins or ends when the Sun's centre is 12° below the horizon. This marks the time when it is, to all intent and purposes, completely dark.
(4) *Astronomical twilight,* which begins or ends when the Sun's centre is 18° below the horizon. This marks theoretical perfect darkness. It is of little practical importance, especially if nautical twilight is tabulated.

To assist observers the durations of civil, nautical and astronomical twilights are given at intervals of ten days. The beginning of a particular twilight is found by subtracting the duration from the time of sunrise, while the end is found by adding the duration

to the time of sunset. Thus the beginning of astronomical twilight in latitude 52°, on the Greenwich meridian, on March 11 is found as 06ʰ 24ᵐ − 113ᵐ = 04ʰ 31ᵐ and similarly the end of civil twilight as 17ʰ 57ᵐ + 34ᵐ = 18ʰ 31ᵐ.

The letters T.A.N. (twilight all night) are printed when twilight lasts all night.

Under the heading Astronomical Notes will be found notes describing the position and visibility of all the planets and also of other phenomena; these are intended to guide naked-eye observers, or those using small telescopes.

PAGE THREE OF EACH MONTH

The Moon moves so rapidly among the stars that its position is given only to the degree of accuracy that permits linear interpolation. The right ascension and declination are geocentric, i.e. for an imaginary observer at the centre of the Earth. To an observer on the surface of the Earth the position is always different, as the altitude is always less on account of parallax which may reach 1°.

The lunar terminator is the line separating the bright from the dark part of the Moon's disk. Apart from irregularities of the lunar surface, the terminator is elliptical, because it is a circle seen in projection. It becomes the full circle forming the limb, or edge, of the Moon at New and Full Moon. The selenographic longitude of the terminator is measured from the mean centre of the visible disk, which may differ from the visible centre by as much as 8°, because of libration.

Instead of the longitude of the terminator the Sun's selenographic colongitude is tabulated. It is numerically equal to the selenographic longitude of the morning terminator, measured eastward from the mean centre of the disk. Thus its value is approximately 270° at New Moon, 360° at First Quarter, 90° at Full Moon and 180° at Last Quarter.

The Position Angle of the Bright Limb is the position angle of the midpoint of the illuminated limb, measured eastward from the north point on the disk. The column Phase shows the percentage of the area of the Moon's disk illuminated; this is also the illuminated percentage of the diameter at right angles to the line of cusps. The terminator is a semi-ellipse whose major axis is the line of cusps, and whose semi-minor axis is determined by the tabulated percentage; from New Moon to Full Moon the east limb is dark, and vice versa.

The times given as moonrise and moonset are those when the upper limb of the Moon is on the horizon of an observer at sea-level. The Sun's horizontal parallax is about 9″, and is negligible when considering sunrise and sunset, but that of the Moon averages

SUNRISE, SUNSET and MOONRISE, MOONSET

The tables have been constructed for the meridian of Greenwich, and for latitudes 52° and 56°. They give Greenwich Mean Time (G.M.T.) throughout the year. To obtain the G.M.T. of the phenomenon as seen from any other latitude and longitude in the British Isles, first interpolate or extrapolate for latitude by the usual rules of proportion. To the time thus found the longitude (expressed in time) is to be *added* if west (as it usually is in Great Britain) or *subtracted* if east. If the longitude is expressed in degrees and minutes of arc, it must be converted to time at the rate of 1° = 4ᵐ and 15′ = 1ᵐ.

A method of calculating rise and set times for other places in the world is given on pp. 70 and 71.

about 57′. Hence the computed time represents the moment when the true zenith distance of the Moon is 90° 50′ (as for the Sun) minus the horizontal parallax. The time required for the Sun or Moon to rise or set is about four minutes (except in high latitudes). (For further information, *see* footnote on p. 65.)

The G.M.T. of transit of the Moon over the meridian of Greenwich is given: these times are independent of latitude, but must be corrected for longitude. For places in the British Isles it suffices to add the longitude if west, and vice versa. For more remote places a further correction is necessary because of the rapid movement of the Moon relative to the stars. The entire correction is conveniently determined by first finding the west longitude λ of the place. If the place is in west longitude, λ is the ordinary west longitude; if the place is in east longitude λ is the complement to 24ʰ (or 360°) of the longitude and will be greater than 12ʰ (or 180°). The correction then consists of two positive portions, namely λ and the fraction λ/24 (or λ°/360) multiplied by the difference between consecutive transits. Thus for Sydney, N.S.W., the longitude is 10ʰ 05ᵐ east, so λ = 13ʰ 55ᵐ and the fraction λ/24 is 0·58. The transit on the local date 1990 September 27 is found as follows:

	d	h	m
G.M.T. of transit at Greenwich .....Sept.	26	17	37
λ		13	55
0·58 × (18ʰ 27ᵐ − 17ʰ 37ᵐ)			29
G.M.T. of transit at Sydney	27	08	01
Corr. to N.S.W. Standard Time		10	00
Local standard time of transit	27	18	01

It is evident of course, that for any given place the quantities λ and the correction to local standard time may be combined permanently, being here 23ʰ 55ᵐ.

Positions of Mercury are given for every third day, and those of Venus and Mars for every fifth day; they may be interpolated linearly. The column PHASE shows the illuminated percentage of the disk. In the case of the inner planets this approaches 100 at superior conjunction and 0 at inferior conjunction. When the phase is less than 50 the planet is crescent-shaped or horned; for greater phases it is gibbous. In

the case of the exterior planet Mars, the phase approaches 100 at conjunction and opposition, and is a minimum at the quadratures.

Since the planets cannot be seen when on the horizon, the actual times of rising and setting are not given; instead, the time when the planet has an apparent altitude of 5° has been tabulated. If the time of transit is between 00ʰ and 12ʰ the time refers to an altitude of 5° above the eastern horizon: if between 12ʰ and 24ʰ, to the western horizon. The phenomenon tabulated is the one that occurs between sunset and sunrise; unimportant exceptions to these rules may occur because changes are not made during a month, except in the case of Mercury. The times given may be interpolated for latitude and corrected for longitude as in the case of the Sun and Moon.

The G.M.T. at which the planet transits the Greenwich meridian is also given. The times of transit are to be corrected to local meridians in the usual way, as already described.

PAGE FOUR OF EACH MONTH

The G.M.T.'s of Sunrise and Sunset may be used not only for these phenomena, but also for lighting-up times, which, under the Road Vehicles Lighting Regulations, 1984, are from half an hour after sunset to half an hour before sunrise throughout the year. (*See* p. 64 for a fuller explanation and proposed changes.)

The particulars for the four outer planets resemble those for the planets on Page Three of each month, except that, under Uranus and Neptune, times when the planet is 10° high instead of 5° high are given; this is because of the inferior brightness of these planets. The polar diameter of Jupiter is about 3″ less than the equatorial diameter, while that of Saturn is about 2″ less. The diameters given for the rings of Saturn are those of the major axis (in the plane of the planet's equator) and the minor axis respectively. The former has a small seasonal change due to the slightly varying distance of the Earth from Saturn, but the latter varies from zero when the Earth passes through the ring plane every 15 years to its maximum opening half-way between these periods. The rings were open at their widest extent in 1988.

TIME

From the earliest ages, the natural division of time into recurring periods of day and night has provided the practical time scale for the everyday activities of mankind. Indeed, if any alternative means of time measurement is adopted, it must be capable of adjustment so as to remain in general agreement with the natural time scale defined by the diurnal rotation of the Earth on its axis. Ideally the rotation should be measured against a fixed frame of reference; in practice it must be measured against the background provided by the celestial bodies. If the Sun is chosen as the reference point, we obtain Apparent Solar Time, which is the time indicated by a sundial. It is not a uniform time, but is subject to variations which amount to as much as a quarter of an hour in each direction. Such wide variations cannot be tolerated in a practical time scale, and this has led to

the concept of Mean Solar Time in which all the days are exactly the same length and equal to the average length of the Apparent Solar Day.

The positions of the stars in the sky are specified in relation to a fictitious reference point in the sky known as the First Point of Aries (or the Vernal Equinox). It is therefore convenient to adopt this same reference point when considering the rotation of the Earth against the background of the stars. The time scale so obtained is known as Apparent Sidereal Time.

Greenwich Mean Time

The daily rotation of the Earth on its axis causes the Sun and the other heavenly bodies to appear to cross the sky from East to West. It is convenient to represent this relative motion as if the Sun really performed a daily circuit around a fixed Earth. Noon in Apparent Solar Time may then be defined as the time at which the Sun transits across the observer's meridian. In Mean Solar Time, noon is similarly defined by the meridian transit of a fictitious Mean Sun moving uniformly in the sky with the same average speed as the true Sun. Mean Solar Time observed on the meridian of the transit circle telescope of the Old Royal Observatory at Greenwich is called Greenwich Mean Time (G.M.T.). The mean solar day is divided into 24 hours and, for astronomical and other scientific purposes, these are numbered 0 to 23, commencing at midnight. Civil time is usually reckoned in two periods of 12 hours, designated a.m. (*ante meridiem*, i.e. before noon) and p.m. (*post meridiem*, i.e. after noon).

Universal Time

Before 1925 January 1 G.M.T. was reckoned in 24 hours commencing at noon: since that date it has been reckoned from midnight. In view of the risk of confusion in the use of the designation G.M.T. before and after 1925, the International Astronomical Union recommended in 1928 that astronomers should employ the term Universal Time, U.T. (or Weltzeit, W.Z.) to denote G.M.T. measured from Greenwich Mean Midnight.

In precision work it is necessary to take account of small variations in Universal Time. These arise from small irregularities in the rotation of the Earth. Observed astronomical time is designated U.T.0. Observed time corrected for the effects of the motion of the poles (giving rise to a "wandering" in longitude) is designated U.T.1. There is also a seasonal fluctuation in the rate of rotation of the Earth arising from meteorological causes, often called the annual fluctuation. U.T.1 corrected for this effect is designated U.T.2 and provides a time scale free from short-period fluctuations. It is still subject to small secular and irregular changes.

Apparent Solar Time

As has been mentioned on page 66, the time shown by a sundial is called Apparent Solar Time. It differs from Mean Solar Time by an amount known as the Equation of Time, which is the total effect of two causes which make the length of the apparent solar day non-uniform. One cause of variation is that the orbit of the Earth is not a circle, but an ellipse, having the Sun at one focus. As a consequence, the angular speed of the Earth in its orbit is not constant; it is greatest at the beginning of January when the Earth is nearest the Sun. The other cause is due to the obliquity of the ecliptic; the plane of the equator (which is at right-angles to the axis of rotation of the Earth) does not coincide with the ecliptic (the plane defined by the apparent annual motion of the Sun around the celestial sphere) but is inclined to it at an angle of 23° 26′. As a result, the apparent solar day is shorter than average at the equinoxes and longer at the solstices. From the combined effects of the components due to obliquity and eccentricity, the equation of time reaches its maximum values in February (−14 mins.) and early November (+16 mins.). It has a zero value on four dates during the year, and it is only on these dates (approx. April 15, June 14, Sept. 1, and Dec. 25) that a sundial shows Mean Solar Time.

Sidereal Time

A sidereal day is the duration of a complete rotation of the Earth with reference to the First Point of Aries. The term sidereal (or "star") time is perhaps a little misleading since the time scale so defined is not exactly the same as that which would be defined by successive transits of a selected star, as there is a small progressive motion between the stars and the First Point of Aries due to the precession of the Earth's axis. This makes the length of the sidereal day shorter than the true period of rotation by 0·008 seconds. Superimposed on this steady precessional motion are small oscillations called nutation, giving rise to fluctuations in apparent sidereal time amounting to as much as 1·2 seconds. It is therefore customary to employ Mean Sidereal Time, from which these fluctuations have been removed. The conversion of G.M.T. to Greenwich sidereal time (G.S.T.) may be performed by adding the value of the G.S.T. at 0^h on the day in question (Page Two of each month) to the G.M.T. converted to sidereal time using the table on p. 72.

Example. To find the G.S.T. at August $8^d\ 02^h\ 41^m\ 11^s$ G.M.T.

				h	m	s
G.S.T. at 0^h	..	..	..	21	04	59
G.M.T.	..	..	..	2	41	11
Acceleration for 2^h	..	..	..			20
,, ,, $41^m\ 11^s$	..	..				7
Sum = G.S.T. =	..	..	..	23	46	37

If the observer is not on the Greenwich meridian then his longitude, measured positively westwards from Greenwich, must be subtracted from the G.S.T. to obtain Local Sidereal Time (L.S.T.). Thus, in the above example, an observer 5^h east of Greenwich, or 19^h west, would find his L.S.T. as $4^h\ 46^m\ 37^s$.

Ephemeris Time

In the study of the motions of the Sun, Moon and planets, observations taken over an extended period are used in the preparation of tables giving the apparent position of the body each day. A table of this sort is known as an ephemeris, and may be used in the comparison of current observations with tabulated positions. A detailed examination of the observations made over the past 300 years shows that the Sun, Moon and planets appear to depart from their predicted positions by amounts proportional to their mean motions. The only satisfactory explanation is that the time scale to which the observations were referred was not uniform as had been supposed. Since the time scale was based on the rotation of the Earth, it follows that this rotation is subject to irregularities. The fact that the discrepancies between the observed and ephemeris positions were proportional to the mean motions of the bodies made it possible to secure agreement by substituting a revised time scale and recomputing the ephemeris positions. The time scale which brings the ephemeris into agreement with the observations is known as Ephemeris Time (E.T.).

The new unit of time has been defined in terms of the apparent annual motion of the Sun. Thus the second is now defined in terms of the annual motion of the Earth in its orbit around the Sun

(1/31556925·9747 of the Tropical Year for 1900 January $0^d 12^h$ E.T.) instead of in terms of the diurnal rotation of the Earth on its axis (1/86 400 of the Mean Solar Day). In many branches of scientific work other than astronomy there has been a demand for a unit of time that is invariable, and the second of Ephemeris time was adopted by the Comité International des Poids et Mésures in 1956. The length of the unit has been chosen to provide general agreement with U.T. throughout the 19th and 20th centuries. During 1990 the estimated difference E.T. − U.T. is 58 seconds. The precise determination of E.T. from astronomical observations is a lengthy process, as the accuracy with which a single observation of the Sun can be made is far less than that obtainable in, for instance, a comparison between clocks. It is therefore necessary to average the observations over an extended period. Largely on account of its faster motion, the position of the Moon may be observed with greater accuracy, and a close approximation to Ephemeris Time may be obtained by comparing observations of the moon with its ephemeris position. Even in this case, however, the requisite standard of accuracy can only be achieved by averaging over a number of years.

Atomic Time

The fundamental standards of time and frequency must be defined in terms of a periodic motion adequately uniform, enduring and susceptible of measurement. This has led in the past to the adoption of standards based on the observed motions in the Solar System. Recent progress has made it possible to consider the use of other natural standards, such as atomic or molecular oscillations. The oscillations so far employed are not in fact continuous periodic motions such as the revolution of the electrons in their orbits around the nuclei. The continuous oscillations are generated in an electrical circuit, the frequency of which is then compared or brought into coincidence with the frequency characteristic of the absorption or emission by the atoms or molecules when they change between two selected energy levels. At the National Physical Laboratory regular comparisons have been made since the middle of 1955 between quartz clocks of high stability and a frequency defined by atoms of caesium. The standard has proved of great value in the precise calibration of frequencies and time intervals: it has also been possible to build up a scale of "atomic time" by using continuously-running quartz clocks calibrated in terms of the caesium frequency standard.

Terrestrial Dynamical Time

A new time scale, known as Terrestrial Dynamical Time (T.D.T.) has recently been defined in terms of international atomic time in such a way that, for most purposes, it can be regarded as a continuation of atomic time.

Radio Time Signals

The establishment of a uniform time system by the assessment of the performance of standard clocks in terms of astronomical observations is the work of a national observatory, and standard time is then made generally available by means of radio time signals. In the United Kingdom, the Royal Greenwich Observatory controls the "6-pips" radio signals emitted by the British Broadcasting Corporation. The British Telecom Speaking Clock is corrected to the National Physical Laboratory caesium beam atomic frequency standard at the British Telecom International Radio Station at Rugby.

For survey and scientific purposes, in which the highest accuracy is required, special signals are transmitted on behalf of the National Physical Laboratory from Rugby Radio Station. The signals consist of a standard frequency carrier of 60 kHz (MSF) which switches off for half a second to denote the passing of one minute and for a tenth of a second to denote the passing of one second. Also transmitted are two binary coded decimal (BCD) time codes giving time of day and calendar information. The service is continuous except for a maintenance period from 1000–1400 UTC on the first Tuesday of each month.

The Coordinated Universal Time (UTC) system standard frequency emissions and radio time signals are broadcast on MSF, and by other national transmitters, eg. by WWV and WWVH in the U.S.A. in conformity with the International Atomic Time Scale. The time intervals between pips correspond exactly to the seconds defined as follows: "The second is the duration of 9 192 631 770 periods of the radiation corresponding to the transition between the 2 hyperfine levels of the ground state of the caesium 133 atom."

As the rate of rotation of the Earth is variable the time signals are adjusted by the introduction of a leap second when necessary in order that UTC shall not depart from UT by more than $0^s·9$. For convenience leap seconds are introduced when necessary, on the last second of a month, preferably on Dec. 31 and/or June 30. In the case of a positive leap second $23^h 59^m 60^s$ is followed one second later by $0^h 00^m 00^s$ of the first day of the month. In the case of a negative leap second (required if the Earth were to have a sudden change of rate and begin to gain relative to UTC) $23^h 59^m 58^s$ is followed one second later by $0^h 00^m 00^s$ of the first day of the month.

From 1972 Jan. 1 the six pips on the BBC have consisted of 5 short pips from second 55 to second 59 followed by one lengthened pip, the start of which indicates the exact minute.

STANDARD TIME

In the year 1880 it was enacted by statute that the word "time", when it occurred in any legal document relating to Great Britain, was to be interpreted, unless otherwise specifically stated, as the Mean Time of the Greenwich meridian. Summer Time is the "legal" time during the period in which its use is ordained. Since the year 1883 the system of Standard Time by Zones has been gradually accepted, and now almost throughout the world a Standard Time which differs from that of Greenwich by an integral number of hours, either fast or slow, is used.

The large territories of the United States and Canada are divided into zones approximately $7\frac{1}{2}°$ on either side of central meridians. The important ones are given below; there are in addition zones from 3 to 12 hours fast in the U.S.S.R.

Variations from the standard time of some countries occurs during part of the year: these are decided annually and are usually referred to as Summer Time or Daylight Saving Time. Countries in which variations may occur are indicated with an asterisk.

Fast on Greenwich Time

In the Tonga Islands the time 13 *h* fast and in Chatham Is. 12 *h* 45 *m* fast on Greenwich is used, as the Date line is to the East of them.

12 hours fast
Fiji; Kiribati; Kusaie I.; Marshall Is.; Nauru; *New Zealand; Tuvalu; *USSR (Zone 10).

11½ hours fast
Kiribati (Banaba); Norfolk I.

11 hours fast
Kiribati (Phoenix Is.); Kuril Is.; New Caledonia; Ponape I.; Sakhalin; Solomon Is.; *USSR (Zone 9); *Vanuatu.

10 hours fast
Admiralty Is.; *Australian Capital Territory; Guam; Kiribati (Kiritimati I.); Mariana Is.; *New South Wales (except Broken Hill Area); Papua New Guinea; Queensland; *Tasmania; Truk Is.; *USSR (Zone 8); *Victoria; Yap Is.

9½ hours fast
*New South Wales (Broken Hill Area); Northern Territory (Aus); *South Australia.

9 hours fast
Irian Jaya; Japan; Korea (North and South); Molucca Is; Palau Is.; *USSR (Zone 7).

8 hours fast
Bali; Brunei; *China; Hong Kong; †Kalimantan (South and East); Macao; Malaysia; *Mongolia; Philippines; Singapore; Sulawesi; *Taiwan; Timor; *USSR (Zone 6); Western Australia.

7 hours fast
Christmas I. (Indian Ocean); Java; Kalimantan (West and Middle); Kampuchea; Laos; Sumatra; Thailand; *USSR (Zone 5); Vietnam.

6½ hours fast
Burma; Cocos Keeling Is.

6 hours fast
Bangladesh; Bhutan; *USSR (Zone 4).

5¾ hours fast
Nepal.

5½ hours fast
India; Sri Lanka.

5 hours fast
Maldives; Pakistan; *USSR (Zone 3).

4½ hours fast
Afghanistan.

4 hours fast
Mauritius; Oman; Réunion; Seychelles; United Arab Emirates; *USSR (Zone 2).

3½ hours fast
Iran.

3 hours fast
Bahrain; Comoro Is.; Djibouti; Ethiopia; *Iraq; Kenya; Kuwait; Madagascar; Qatar; Saudi Arabia; Somalia; Tanzania; Uganda; *USSR (Zone 1); Yemen (North and South).

2 hours fast
Botswana; *Bulgaria; Burundi; *Crete; *Cyprus; *Egypt; *Finland; *Greece; *Israel; *Jordan, *Lebanon; Lesotho; Malawi; Mozambique; Namibia; *Romania; Rwanda; South Africa; Sudan; Swaziland; *Syria; *Turkey; Zaire (Haut-Zaire, Kasai, Kivu, Shaba); *Zambia; Zimbabwe.

1 hour fast
*Albania; Algeria; *Andorra; Angola; *Austria; *Belgium; Benin; Cameroon; Central African Republic; Chad; Congo; *Czechoslovakia; *Denmark; Equatorial Guinea; *France; Gabon; *Germany (East and West); *Gibraltar; *Greenland (Scoresby Sound); *Hungary; *Italy; *Libya; *Liechtenstein; *Luxembourg; *Malta; *Monaco; *Netherlands; Niger; Nigeria; *Norway; *Poland; *San Marino; *Spain; Svalbard; *Sweden; *Switzerland; *Tunisia; *Vatican City State; *Yugoslavia; Zaire (Kinshasa, Mbandaka).

Greenwich Time

Ascension I.; Burkina; *Canary Is.; *Channel Is.; Côte d'Ivoire; *Faroe Is.; Gambia; Ghana; Greenland (Danmarks Havn and Mesters Vig); Guinea; Guinea Bissau; Iceland; *Ireland (Republic); Liberia; *Madeira; Mali; Mauritania; *Morocco; *Portugal; St. Helena; São Tomé & Principe; Senegal; Sierra Leone; Togo; Tristan da Cunha; *U.K (*see* p. 72).

Slow on Greenwich time

1 hour slow
*Azores; Cape Verde Is.; Greenland (E. Coast N. of Angmagssalik).

2 hours slow
*Fernando de Noronha I.; South Georgia.

3 hours slow
Argentina; *Brazil (eastern); French Guiana; *Greenland (Angmagssalik and W. Coast); Guyana; *St. Pierre and Miquelon; Suriname; *Uruguay.

3½ hours slow
*Newfoundland.

4 hours slow (Atlantic time)
Anguilla; Antigua; Aruba; Barbados; *Bermuda; Bolivia; *Brazil; (western); *Chile; *Dominica; Dominican Republic; *Falkland Is.; Greenland (Thule area); Grenada; Guadeloupe; *Labrador; Martinique; Montserrat; Netherlands Antilles; *New Brunswick; *Northwest Territories (E of 68°W.); *Nova Scotia; *Quebec (E of 63°W.); *Paraguay; Puerto Rico; St. Kitts; St. Lucia; St. Vincent; Tobago; Trinidad; Venezuela; Virgin Is.

5 hours slow
*Bahamas; *Brazil (Acre territory); Cayman Is.; Colombia; *Cuba; Ecuador; *Haiti; Jamaica; *Northwest Territories (68°W. to 85°W.); *Ontario (E. of 90° W.); Panama; *Peru; *Quebec (W. of 63°W.); *Turks and Caicos Is.; *U.S.A. (eastern time).

6 hours slow
Belize; Costa Rica, Guatemala; Honduras; *Manitoba; Mexico (eastern); Nicaragua; Northwest Territories (85° W. to 102° W.); *Ontario (W. of 90° W.); *El Salvador; *Saskatchewan (E. of 106°W.); *U.S.A. (central time).

7 hours slow
*Alberta; Mexico (central); Northwest Territories (102° W. to 120° W.); *Saskatchewan (W. of 106° W.); *U.S.A. (mountain time).

8 hours slow
*Alaska (S.E. coast); *British Columbia; Mexico (western); *U.S.A. (Pacific time); *Yukon.

8½ hours slow
Pitcairn I.

9 hours slow
*Alaska (E. of 169°30′W.).

10 hours slow
Aleutian Is. (W. of 169°30′ W.); Christmas I. (Pacific Ocean); French Polynesia; *Hawaii; Society Is.; Tuamotu archipelago; Tubuai Is.

11 hours slow
Midway Is.; Niue; Samoa.

---

† The Indonesian territory on Borneo I.

RISING AND SETTING TIMES

Table 1. Hour Angle

Dec.	Latitude and Declination of Opposite Signs						0°	Latitude and Declination of Same Signs					
	50°	45°	40°	30°	20°	10°		10°	20°	30°	40°	45°	50°
°	h m	h m	h m	h m	h m	h m	h m	h m	h m	h m	h m	h m	h m
0	6 00	6 00	6 00	6 00	6 00	6 00	6 00	6 00	6 00	6 00	6 00	6 00	6 00
1	5 55	5 56	5 57	5 58	5 59	5 59	6 00	6 01	6 01	6 02	6 03	6 04	6 05
2	5 50	5 52	5 53	5 55	5 57	5 58	6 00	6 02	6 03	6 05	6 07	6 08	6 10
3	5 45	5 48	5 50	5 53	5 56	5 58	6 00	6 02	6 04	6 07	6 10	6 12	6 15
4	5 40	5 44	5 46	5 51	5 54	5 57	6 00	6 03	6 06	6 09	6 14	6 16	6 20
5	5 36	5 40	5 43	5 48	5 52	5 56	6 00	6 04	6 08	6 12	6 17	6 20	6 24
6	5 31	5 36	5 39	5 46	5 51	5 56	6 00	6 04	6 09	6 14	6 21	6 24	6 29
7	5 26	5 32	5 36	5 44	5 50	5 55	6 00	6 05	6 10	6 16	6 24	6 28	6 34
8	5 21	5 27	5 33	5 41	5 48	5 54	6 00	6 06	6 12	6 19	6 27	6 33	6 39
9	5 16	5 23	5 29	5 39	5 47	5 53	6 00	6 07	6 13	6 21	6 31	6 37	6 44
10	5 11	5 19	5 26	5 37	5 45	5 53	6 00	6 07	6 15	6 23	6 34	6 41	6 49
11	5 06	5 15	5 22	5 34	5 44	5 52	6 00	6 08	6 16	6 26	6 38	6 45	6 54
12	5 01	5 11	5 19	5 32	5 42	5 51	6 00	6 09	6 18	6 28	6 41	6 49	6 59
13	4 56	5 06	5 15	5 29	5 40	5 51	6 00	6 09	6 20	6 31	6 45	6 54	7 04
14	4 51	5 02	5 12	5 27	5 39	5 50	6 00	6 10	6 21	6 33	6 48	6 58	7 09
15	4 46	4 58	5 08	5 24	5 38	5 49	6 00	6 11	6 22	6 36	6 52	7 02	7 14
16	4 40	4 53	5 04	5 22	5 36	5 48	6 00	6 12	6 24	6 38	6 56	7 07	7 20
17	4 35	4 49	5 00	5 19	5 35	5 48	6 00	6 12	6 25	6 41	7 00	7 11	7 25
18	4 29	4 44	4 57	5 17	5 33	5 47	6 00	6 13	6 27	6 43	7 03	7 16	7 31
19	4 23	4 39	4 53	5 14	5 31	5 46	6 00	6 14	6 29	6 46	7 07	7 21	7 37
20	4 17	4 35	4 49	5 11	5 30	5 45	6 00	6 15	6 30	6 49	7 11	7 25	7 43
21	4 11	4 30	4 44	5 09	5 28	5 44	6 00	6 16	6 32	6 51	7 16	7 30	7 49
22	4 04	4 25	4 40	5 06	5 26	5 44	6 00	6 16	6 34	6 54	7 20	7 35	7 56
23	3 58	4 19	4 36	5 03	5 24	5 43	6 00	6 17	6 36	6 57	7 24	7 41	8 02
24	3 52	4 14	4 32	5 00	5 23	5 42	6 00	6 18	6 37	7 00	7 28	7 46	8 08
25	3 45	4 09	4 28	4 58	5 21	5 41	6 00	6 19	6 39	7 02	7 32	7 51	8 15
26	3 38	4 03	4 24	4 55	5 19	5 40	6 00	6 20	6 41	7 05	7 36	7 57	8 22
27	3 30	3 57	4 19	4 52	5 17	5 39	6 00	6 21	6 43	7 08	7 41	8 03	8 30
28	3 23	3 51	4 14	4 48	5 15	5 38	6 00	6 22	6 45	7 12	7 46	8 09	8 37
29	3 15	3 45	4 09	4 45	5 14	5 38	6 00	6 22	6 46	7 15	7 51	8 15	8 45

SUNRISE AND SUNSET

The local mean time of sunrise or sunset (as defined on page 64) may be found by determining the appropriate hour angle from the table above and applying it to the time of transit given in the ephemeris for each month. The hour angle is negative for sunrise and positive for sunset. A small correction to the hour angle, which always has the effect of increasing it numerically, is necessary to allow for the Sun's semi-diameter (16′) and for refraction (34′). This correction may be obtained from Table 2. The resulting local mean time may be converted into the standard time of the country by taking the difference between the longitude of the standard meridian of the country and that of the place, and adding it to the local mean time if the place is west of the standard meridian, and subtracting it if the place is east of the standard meridian.

Example.—Required the N.Z. Mean Time (12ʰ fast on G.M.T.) of sunset on May 24 at Auckland. The latitude is 36° 50′ south (or minus) and the longitude 11ʰ 39ᵐ east. Taking the declination as +20°·7, we find

	h m
Tabular entry for 30° Lat. and Dec. 20°, opposite signs	+ 5 11
Proportional part for 6° 50′ of Lat.	− 15
Proportional part for 0°·7 of Dec.	− 3
Correction (Table 2)	+ 6
Hour angle	4 59
Sun transits	11 57
Longitudinal correction	+ 21
N.Z. Mean Time	17 17

Table 2. Correction for Refraction and Semi-Diameter

Latitude	Declination			
	0°	10°	20°	29°
°	m	m	m	m
0	3	3	4	4
20	4	4	4	4
30	4	4	4	5
40	4	4	5	6
50	5	5	6	8

MOONRISE AND MOONSET

It is possible to calculate the times of moonrise and moonset using Table 1 though the method is more complicated because the apparent motion of the Moon is much more rapid and also more variable than that of the Sun.

The parallax of the Moon, about 57′, is near to the sum of the semi-diameter and refraction but has the opposite effect on these times. It is thus convenient to neglect all three quantities in the method outlined below.

Method

1. With arguments φ, δ_0 enter Table 1 on p. 70 to determine h_0 where h_0 is negative for moonrise and positive for moonset.

2. Form approximate times from
$$t_R = T_0 + \lambda + h_0$$
$$t_S = T_0 + \lambda + h_0$$

3. Determine δ_R, δ_S for times t_R, t_S respectively.

4. Re-enter Table 1 on p. 70 with—
    (a) arguments φ, δ_R to determine h_R
    (b) arguments φ, δ_S to determine h_S

5. Form $t_R = T_0 + \lambda + h_R + AX$
   $t_S = T_0 + \lambda + h_S + AX$

   where A = $(\lambda + h)$

   $X = (T_0 - T_{-1})$ if $(\lambda + h)$ is negative
   and $X = (T_1 - T_0)$ if $(\lambda + h)$ is positive

   AX is the respondent in Table 3.

Table 3. Longitude Correction

A \ X	40^m	45^m	50^m	55^m	60^m	65^m	70^m
h	m	m	m	m	m	m	m
1	2	2	2	2	3	3	3
2	3	4	4	5	5	5	6
3	5	6	6	7	8	8	9
4	7	8	8	9	10	11	12
5	8	9	10	11	13	14	15
6	10	11	13	14	15	16	18
7	12	13	15	16	18	19	20
8	13	15	17	18	20	22	23
9	15	17	19	21	23	24	26
10	17	19	21	23	25	27	29
11	18	21	23	25	28	30	32
12	20	23	25	28	30	33	35
13	22	24	27	30	33	35	38
14	23	26	29	32	35	38	41
15	25	28	31	34	38	41	44
16	27	30	33	37	40	43	47
17	28	32	35	39	43	46	50
18	30	34	38	41	45	49	53
19	32	36	40	44	48	51	55
20	33	38	42	46	50	54	58
21	35	39	44	48	53	57	61
22	37	41	46	50	55	60	64
23	38	43	48	53	58	62	67
24	40	45	50	55	60	65	70

Example.—To find the times of moonrise and moonset at Vancouver ($\varphi = +49°$, $\lambda = +8^h 12^m$) on 1990 Jan. 22. The starting data (from p. 18) are

$$
\begin{array}{ll}
 & \text{h} \quad \text{m} \\
T_{-1} = & 7 \quad 34 \\
T_0 = & 8 \quad 24 \\
T_1 = & 9 \quad 17 \\
\delta = & -26°
\end{array}
$$

1. $h_0 = \quad 3^h 43^m$
2. Approximate values
   $t_R = 22^d 08^h 24^m + 8^h 12^m + (-3^h 43^m)$
   $\quad = 22^d 12^h 53^m$
   $t_S = 22^d 08^h 24^m + 8^h 12^m + (+3^h 43^m)$
   $\quad = 22^d 20^h 19^m$
3. $\delta_R = -26°·9$
   $\delta_S = -27°·3$
4. $h_R = -3^h 36^m$
   $h_S = +3^h 33^m$
5. $t_R = 22^d 08^h 24^m + 8^h 12^m + (-3^h 36^m) + 10^m$
   $\quad = 22^d 13^h 10^m$
   $t_S = 22^d 08^h 24^m + 8^h 12^m + (+3^h 33^m) + 27^m$
   $\quad = 22^d 20^h 36^m$

To get the L.M.T. of the phenomenon the longitude is subtracted from the G.M.T. thus
Moonrise = $22^d 13^h 10^m - 8^h 12^m = 22^d 04^h 58^m$
Moonset = $22^d 20^h 36^m - 8^h 12^m = 22^d 12^h 24^m$

Notation

φ = latitude of observer
λ = longitude of observer (measured positively towards the west)
T_{-1} = time of transit of Moon on previous day
T_0 = time of transit of Moon on day in question
T_1 = time of transit of Moon on following day
δ_0 = approximate declination of Moon
δ_R = declination of Moon at moonrise
δ_S = declination of Moon at moonset
h_0 = approximate hour angle of Moon
h_R = hour angle of Moon at moonrise
h_S = hour angle of Moon at moonset
t_R = time of moonrise
t_S = time of moonset

ASTRONOMICAL CONSTANTS

Solar Parallax	8″·794
Precession for the year 1990	50″·288
„ in R.A.	3^s·074
„ in Declination	20″·044
Constant of Nutation	9″·202
Constant of Aberration	20″·496
Mean Obliquity of Ecliptic (1990)	23° 26′ 26″
Moon's Equatorial Hor. Parallax	57′02″·70
Velocity of Light in vacuo *per sec*	299792·5 km.
Solar motion *per sec*	20·0 km.
Equatorial radius of the Earth	6378·140 km.
Polar radius of the Earth	6356·755 km.

North Galactic Pole } R.A. 12^h 49^m (1950·0).
(I.A.U. *Standard*). } Dec. 27°·4 N.
Solar Apex .... R.A. 18^h 06^m Dec. +30°

Length of Year	Tropical	365·24220
(*In Mean Solar Days*)	Sidereal	365·25636
	Anomalistic	365·25964
	(*Perihelion to Perihelion*)	
	Eclipse	346·6200

		d h m s
Length of Month	New Moon to New	29 12 44 02·9
(*Mean Values*)	Sidereal	27 07 43 11·5
	Anomalistic	27 13 18 33·2
	(*Perigee to Perigee*)	

MEAN AND SIDEREAL TIME

Acceleration

h	m s	h	m s	m s	s
1	0 10	13	2 08	0 00	0
2	0 20	14	2 18	3 02	1
3	0 30	15	2 28	9 07	2
4	0 39	16	2 38	15 13	3
5	0 49	17	2 48	21 18	4
6	0 59	18	2 57	27 23	5
7	1 09	19	3 07	33 28	6
8	1 19	20	3 17	39 34	7
9	1 29	21	3 27	45 39	8
10	1 39	22	3 37	51 44	9
11	1 48	23	3 47	57 49	10
12	1 58	24	3 57	60 00	

Retardation

h	m s	h	m s	m s	s
1	0 10	13	2 08	0 00	0
2	0 20	14	2 18	3 03	1
3	0 29	15	2 27	9 09	2
4	0 39	16	2 37	15 15	3
5	0 49	17	2 47	21 21	4
6	0 59	18	2 57	27 28	5
7	1 09	19	3 07	33 34	6
8	1 19	20	3 17	39 40	7
9	1 28	21	3 26	45 46	8
10	1 38	22	3 36	51 53	9
11	1 48	23	3 46	57 59	10
12	1 58	24	3 56	60 00	

MEAN REFRACTION

Alt.	Ref.	Alt.	Ref.
° '		° '	
1 20	21	4 30	10
1 30	20	5 06	9
1 41	19	5 50	8
1 52	18	6 44	7
2 05	17	7 54	6
2 19	16	9 27	5
2 35	15	11 39	4
2 52	14	15 00	3
3 12	13	20 42	2
3 34	12	32 20	1
4 00	11	62 17	0
4 30		90 00	

The length of a sidereal day in mean time is $23^h 56^m 04^s·09$. Hence 1^h M.T. $= 1^h + 9^s·86$ S.T. and 1^h S.T. $= 1^h − 9^s·83$ M.T.

To convert an interval of mean time to the corresponding interval of sidereal time, enter the acceleration table with the given mean time (taking the hours and the minutes and seconds separately) and add the acceleration obtained to the given mean time. To convert an interval of sidereal time to the corresponding interval of mean time, take out the retardation for the given sidereal time and subtract.

The columns for the minutes and seconds of the argument are in the form known as Critical Tables. To use these tables, find in the appropriate left-hand column the two entries between which the given number of minutes and seconds lies; the quantity in the right-hand column between these two entries is the required acceleration or retardation. Thus the acceleration for 11^m26^s (which lies between the entries 9^m07^s and 15^m13^s) is 2^s. If the given number of minutes and seconds is a tabular entry, the required acceleration or retardation is the entry in the right-hand column *above* the given tabular entry; e.g. the retardation for 45^m46^s is 7^s.

Example.—Convert $14^h27^m35^s$ from S.T. to M.T.

	h	m	s
Given S.T.	14	27	35
Retardation for 14^h		2	18
Retardation for 27^m35^s			5
Corresponding M.T.	14	25	12

For further explanation, see p. 67.
The refraction table is also in the form of a critical table.

THE SUMMER TIME ACTS

In 1916 an Act ordained that during a defined period of that year the legal time for general purposes in Great Britain should be one hour in advance of Greenwich Mean Time. The *Summer Time Acts*, 1922 to 1925, defined the period during which Summer Time was to be in force, stabilizing practice until the war.

During the Second World War the duration of Summer Time was extended and in the years 1941–45 and in 1947, Double Summer Time (2 hrs. in advance of Greenwich Mean Time) was in force. After the war, Summer Time was extended in each year from 1948–1952 and 1961–1964 by Order in Council.

Central European Time, during which clocks were kept one hour ahead of Greenwich Mean Time throughout the year, was in force between Oct. 27, 1968 and Oct. 31, 1971.

The most recent legislation is the Summer Time Act, 1972, which enacted that "the period of summer time for the purposes of this Act is the period beginning at two o'clock, Greenwich mean time, in the morning of the day after the third Saturday in March or, if that day is Easter Day, the day after the second Saturday in March, and ending at two o'clock, Greenwich mean time, in the morning of the day after the fourth Saturday in October."

The duration of Summer Time can be varied by Order in Council and in recent years alterations have been made to bring the operation of Summer Time in Britain closer to similar provisions in other countries of the European Community. Subject to parliamentary approval of the Summer Time Order 1989, the duration of Summer Time in 1990 will be from March 25 to October 28. As in recent years, the hour of changeover will be 01^h Greenwich Mean Time.

The duration of Summer Time during the last few years is given in the following table.

1978 Mar. 19—Oct. 29	1984 Mar. 25—Oct. 28
1979 Mar. 18—Oct. 28	1985 Mar. 31—Oct. 27
1980 Mar. 16—Oct. 26	1986 Mar. 30—Oct. 26
1981 Mar. 29—Oct. 25	1987 Mar. 29—Oct. 25
1982 Mar. 28—Oct. 24	1988 Mar. 27—Oct. 23
1983 Mar. 27—Oct. 23	1989 Mar. 26—Oct. 29

ASTRONOMERS ROYAL

John Flamsteed, first Astronomer Royal ..1675–1719	Sir William Henry Mahoney Christie 1881–1910
Edmund Halley 1720–1742	Sir Frank Watson Dyson 1910–1933
James Bradley 1742–1762	Sir Harold Spencer Jones 1933–1955
Nathaniel Bliss 1762–1764	Sir Richard van der Riet Woolley 1955–1971
Nevil Maskelyne 1765–1811	Sir Martin Ryle 1972–1982
John Pond.............................1811–1835	Prof. Sir Francis Graham Smith 1982–
Sir George Biddell Airy 1835–1881	

PHENOMENA OF JUPITER'S SATELLITES, 1990

January

d	h	m	Sat.	Phen.
1	19	26	II	Ec.R.
5	00	22	I	Sh.I.
5	02	36	I	Sh.E.
5	18	21	III	Sh.I.
5	21	21	III	Sh.E.
5	23	56	I	Ec.R.
6	18	50	I	Sh.I.
6	21	04	I	Sh.E.
7	01	06	II	Sh.I.
7	03	47	II	Sh.E.
7	18	24	I	Ec.R.
7	19	04	IV	Sh.I.
7	20	54	IV	Sh.E.
8	22	01	II	Ec.R.
10	17	06	II	Sh.E.
12	02	16	I	Sh.I.
12	04	30	I	Sh.E.
12	22	20	III	Sh.I.
13	01	22	III	Sh.E.
13	01	51	I	Ec.R.
13	20	45	I	Sh.I.
13	22	59	I	Sh.E.
14	03	43	II	Sh.I.
14	06	24	II	Sh.E.
14	20	19	I	Ec.R.
15	17	27	I	Sh.E.
16	00	37	II	Ec.R.
16	02	18	IV	Ec.D.
16	04	18	IV	Ec.R.
17	19	43	II	Sh.E.
19	04	11	I	Sh.I.
20	02	21	III	Sh.I.
20	03	46	I	Ec.R.
20	05	23	III	Sh.E.
20	22	39	I	Sh.I.
21	00	53	I	Ec.R.
21	22	15	I	Ec.R.
22	19	22	I	Sh.E.
23	03	13	II	Ec.R.
23	19	30	III	Ec.R.
24	19	39	II	Sh.I.
24	22	20	II	Sh.E.
28	00	34	I	Sh.I.
28	02	48	I	Sh.E.
29	00	10	I	Ec.R.
29	19	03	I	Sh.I.
29	21	17	I	Sh.E.
30	18	38	I	Ec.R.
30	20	26	III	Ec.D.
30	23	31	III	Ec.R.
31	22	16	II	Sh.I.

February

d	h	m	Sat.	Phen.
1	00	57	II	Sh.E.
1	20	17	IV	Ec.D.
1	22	35	IV	Ec.R.
2	19	07	II	Ec.R.
4	02	29	I	Sh.I.
4	04	43	I	Sh.E.
5	02	05	I	Ec.R.
5	20	58	I	Sh.I.
5	23	12	I	Sh.E.
6	20	34	I	Ec.R.
7	00	26	III	Ec.D.
7	03	32	III	Ec.R.
8	00	52	II	Sh.I.
8	03	34	II	Sh.E.
9	21	44	II	Ec.R.
11	04	24	I	Sh.I.
12	04	00	I	Ec.R.
12	22	53	I	Sh.I.
13	01	07	I	Sh.E.
13	22	29	I	Ec.R.
14	19	36	I	Sh.E.
15	03	29	II	Sh.I.
17	00	20	II	Ec.R.
17	18	20	III	Sh.I.
17	21	25	III	Sh.E.
18	19	28	II	Sh.E.
20	00	48	I	Sh.I.
20	03	02	I	Sh.E.
21	00	24	I	Ec.R.
21	19	17	I	Sh.I.
21	21	31	I	Sh.E.
22	18	53	I	Ec.R.
24	02	57	II	Ec.R.
24	22	20	III	Sh.I.
25	01	26	III	Sh.E.
25	19	24	II	Sh.I.
25	22	05	II	Sh.E.
27	01	03	IV	Sh.I.
27	02	43	I	Sh.I.
28	02	19	I	Ec.R.
28	21	12	I	Sh.I.
28	23	26	I	Sh.E.

March

d	h	m	Sat.	Phen.
1	20	48	I	Ec.R.
4	02	20	III	Sh.I.
4	22	00	II	Sh.I.
5	00	42	II	Sh.E.
6	18	53	II	Ec.R.
7	19	37	III	Sh.E.
7	23	07	I	Sh.I.
8	01	21	I	Sh.E.
8	22	44	I	Ec.R.
9	19	50	I	Sh.E.
12	00	37	III	Sh.I.
13	21	31	II	Ec.R.
14	20	28	III	Ec.D.
14	23	38	III	Ec.R.
15	01	03	I	Sh.I.
15	19	04	IV	Sh.I.
15	21	52	IV	Sh.E
16	00	39	I	Ec.R.
16	19	32	I	Sh.I.
16	21	46	I	Sh.E.
17	19	08	I	Ec.R.
21	00	08	II	Ec.R.
22	00	28	III	Ec.D.
22	19	13	II	Sh.E.
23	21	27	I	Sh.I.
23	23	41	I	Sh.E.
24	21	03	I	Ec.R.
28	02	46	II	Ec.R.
29	21	49	II	Sh.E.
30	23	23	I	Sh.I.
31	01	37	I	Sh.E.
31	22	58	I	Ec.R.

April

d	h	m	Sat.	Phen.
1	20	06	I	Sh.E.
1	21	32	III	Sh.E.
5	21	43	II	Sh.I.
6	00	25	II	Sh.E.
8	22	02	I	Sh.E.
8	22	22	III	Sh.I.
9	20	26	IV	Ec.D.
9	23	34	IV	Ec.R.
14	21	20	II	Ec.R.
15	21	42	I	Sh.I.
15	23	57	I	Sh.E.
16	21	17	I	Ec.R.
22	23	38	I	Sh.I.
23	23	12	I	Ec.R.
26	20	29	III	Ec.D.
30	21	30	II	Sh.E.

May

d	h	m	Sat.	Phen.
1	22	17	I	Sh.E.
7	21	22	II	Sh.I.
8	21	58	I	Sh.I.
9	21	31	I	Ec.R.
14	21	39	III	Sh.E.
16	21	12	II	Ec.R.

November

d	h	m	Sat.	Phen.
27	23	25	III	Ec.R.

December

d	h	m	Sat.	Phen.
1	02	18	I	Ec.D.
1	23	37	I	Sh.I.
2	01	54	I	Sh.E.
4	23	50	III	Ec.R.
5	03	24	III	Ec.R.
7	02	46	II	Sh.I.
7	05	39	II	Sh.E.
7	07	02	I	Sh.I.
8	04	12	I	Ec.D.
8	21	41	II	Ec.D.
8	23	37	IV	Sh.E.
9	01	31	I	Sh.I.
9	03	47	I	Sh.E.
9	22	40	I	Ec.D.
10	22	15	I	Sh.E.
12	03	49	III	Sh.I.
12	07	24	III	Ec.R.
14	05	22	II	Sh.I.
15	06	05	I	Ec.D.
15	21	17	III	Ec.D.
16	00	14	II	Ec.D.
16	03	24	I	Sh.I.
16	05	40	I	Sh.E.
17	00	34	I	Ec.D.
17	02	43	IV	Ec.D.
17	07	25	IV	Ec.R.
17	21	33	II	Sh.E.
17	21	52	I	Sh.E.
18	00	08	I	Sh.E.
19	07	47	III	Ec.D.
22	21	43	III	Sh.I.
23	01	16	III	Sh.E.
23	02	47	II	Ec.D.
23	05	17	I	Sh.I.
23	07	33	I	Sh.E.
24	02	28	I	Ec.D.
24	21	15	II	Sh.I.
24	23	45	I	Sh.I.
25	00	09	II	Sh.E.
25	02	02	I	Sh.E.
25	20	56	I	Ec.D.
26	20	30	I	Sh.E.
30	01	40	III	Sh.I.
30	05	14	III	Sh.E.
30	05	21	II	Ec.D.
30	07	10	I	Sh.I.
31	04	22	I	Ec.D.
31	23	52	II	Sh.I.

Jupiter's satellites transit across the disk from east to west, and pass behind the disk from west to east. The shadows that they cast also transit across the disk. With the exception at times of Satellite IV, the satellites also pass through the shadow of the planet, i.e. they are eclipsed. Just before opposition the satellite disappears in the shadow to the west of the planet, and reappears from occultation on the east limb. Immediately after opposition the satellite is occulted at the west limb, and reappears from eclipse to the east of the planet. At times approximately two to four months before and after opposition, both phases of eclipses of Satellite III may be seen. When Satellite IV is eclipsed, both phases may be seen.

The list of phenomena gives most of the eclipses and shadow transits visible in the British Isles under favourable conditions.

Ec. = Eclipse		R. = Reappearance
Sh. = Shadow transit		I. = Ingress
D. = Disappearance		E. = Egress

CELESTIAL PHENOMENA FOR OBSERVATION IN 1990

ECLIPSES

There will be four eclipses during 1990, two of the Sun and two of the Moon. (Penumbral eclipses are not mentioned in this section as they are difficult to observe).

1. An annular eclipse of the Sun on January 26 is visible as a partial eclipse from South Island, New Zealand, the eastern part of the South Pacific Ocean, the Southern Ocean, Antarctica except the extreme east, South America except the north west, and the western part of the South Atlantic Ocean. The eclipse begins at $17^h\ 13^m$ and ends at $21^h\ 48^m$. The annular phase begins in Antarctica at $18^h\ 55^m$ and ends at $20^h\ 06^m$ in the South Atlantic Ocean. The maximum duration of the annular phase is $2^m\ 03^s$.

From South Island, New Zealand, only a small partial eclipse is visible, beginning around the time of sunrise.

2. A total eclipse of the Moon on February 9 is visible from north-west Alaska, the arctic regions, North Pacific Ocean, Australasia, Asia, the Indian Ocean, part of Antarctica, Africa, Europe including the British Isles, the north-east Atlantic Ocean, Iceland and Greenland. The eclipse begins at $17^h\ 30^m$ and ends at $20^h\ 54^m$. Totality lasts from $18^h\ 51^m$ to $19^h\ 33^m$.

3. A total eclipse of the Sun on July 22. The path of totality begins on the southern coast of Finland, passes along the north coast of Asia and across the extreme north-eastern part of Asia and ends in the Pacific Ocean between the Hawaiian Islands and North America. The partial phase is visible from Scandinavia except the south west, north of Greenland, north of Asia, the Arctic Regions, north-western part of North America, the Hawaiian Islands and the North Pacific Ocean. The eclipse begins at $00^h\ 40^m$ and ends at $05^h\ 24^m$, the total phase begins at $01^h\ 53^m$ and ends at $04^h\ 11^m$. The maximum duration of totality is $2^m\ 33^s$.

4. A partial eclipse of the Moon on August 6 is visible from south-west Alaska, the Pacific Ocean except the extreme east, Antarctica. Australasia, the south and eastern parts of Asia and the eastern part of the Indian Ocean. The eclipse begins at $12^h\ 43^m$ and ends at $15^h\ 39^m$. The time of maximum eclipse is $14^h\ 11^m$ when 0·68 of the Moon's diameter is obscured.

LUNAR OCCULTATIONS

No planets or bright stars are occulted by the Moon in 1990.

Observations of the times of these occultations are made by both amateur and professional astronomers. Such observations are later analysed to yield accurate positions of the Moon: this is one method of determining the difference between ephemeris time and universal time.

Many of the observations made by amateurs are obtained with the use of a stop-watch which is compared with a time signal immediately after the observation. Thus an accuracy of about one-fifth of a second is obtainable, though the observer's personal equation may amount to one-third or one-half of a second.

The list on the opposite page includes most of the occultations visible under favourable conditions in the British Isles. No occultation is included unless the star is at least 10° above the horizon and the Sun sufficiently far below the horizon to permit the star to be seen with the naked eye or in a small telescope. The altitude limit is reduced from 10° to 2° for stars and planets brighter than magnitude 2·0 and such occultations are also predicted in daylight.

The column Phase shows whether a disappearance (D) or reappearance (R) is to be observed. The column headed "El. of Moon" gives the elongation of the Moon from the Sun, in degrees. The elongation increases from 0° at New Moon to 180° at Full Moon and on to 360° (or 0°) at New Moon again. Times and position angles (P), reckoned from the north point in the direction north, east, south, west, are given for Greenwich (Lat. 51° 30′, Long. 0°) and Edinburgh (Lat. 56° 00′, Long. 3° 12′ west).

The coefficients a and b are the variations in the G.M.T. for each degree of longitude (positive to the west) and latitude (positive to the north) respectively: they enable approximate times (to within about 1^m generally) to be found for any point in the British Isles. If the point of observation is $\Delta\lambda$ degrees west and $\Delta\phi$ degrees north, the approximate time is found by adding $a.\Delta\lambda + b.\Delta\phi$ to the given G.M.T.

As an illustration the reappearance of z.c. 543 on February 3 at Liverpool will be found from both Greenwich and Edinburgh.

	Greenwich	Edinburgh
	°	°
Longitude	0·0	+3·2
Long. of Liverpool	+3·0	+3·0
$\Delta\lambda$	+3·0	−0·2
Latitude	+51·5	+56·0
Lat. of Liverpool	+53·4	+53·4
$\Delta\phi$	+1·9	−2·6
	h m	h m
G.M.T.	22 14·7	22 02·6
$a.\Delta\lambda$	−1·8	+0·2
$b.\Delta\phi$	−4·8	+4·7
	22 08·1	22 07·5

If the occultation is given for one station but not the other, the reason for the suppression is given by the following code.

N = star not occulted.

A = star's altitude less than 10° (2° for bright stars and planets).

S = Sun not sufficiently below the horizon.

G = occultation is of very short duration.

It will be noticed that in some cases the coefficients a and b are not given: this is because the occultation is so short that prediction for other places by means of these coefficients would not be reliable.

LUNAR OCCULTATIONS, 1990

Date	Z.C. No.	Mag.	Phase	El. of Moon	Greenwich				Edinburgh			
					U.T.	a	b	P	U.T.	a	b	P
				°	h m	m	m	°	h m	m	m	°
Jan. 7	552	3·0	D.D.	132	14 45·9	−0·6	0·7	130	14 49·2	−0·2	1·2	118
7	552	3·0	R.B.	132	15 14·9	0·7	2·6	195	15 27·1	0·4	2·2	208
Feb. 3	539	4·4	D.D.	105	21 53·8	−0·7	−3·1	130	21 39·8	−0·9	−2·0	113
3	538	5·6	D.D.	105	21 55·0	−1·2	0·5	44	21 55·7	−1·2	1·7	25
3	542	5·9	D.D.	105	22 8·5	−0·8	−2·1	113	21 57·7	−0·9	−1·5	99
3	543	6·5	D.D.	105	22 14·7	−0·6	−2·5	120	22 2·6	−0·8	−1·8	106
3	541	4·0	D.D.	105	N				22 15·9	..	..	157
3	548	6·7	D.D.	105	22 44·4	−0·3	−3·1	131	22 31·1	−0·6	−2·3	115
3	555	6·8	D.D.	106	23 26·8	..	..	22	N			
6	1055	5·8	D.D.	144	22 30·4	−1·4	−0·7	99	22 24·1	−1·4	−0·1	87
7	1092	5·8	D.D.	148	A				6 2·4	0·5	−1·3	107
Mar. 1	370	6·1	D.D.	61	21 39·6	−0·2	−0·8	65	21 35·3	−0·3	−0·7	54
4	833	7·1	D.D.	100	20 4·8	−1·3	−1·0	100	19 57·4	−1·3	−0·4	87
4	844	5·7	D.D.	101	22 21·5	−0·8	−1·3	88	22 13·5	−0·9	−1·1	80
4	849	6·5	D.D.	101	23 23·3	0·2	−2·8	145	23 11·6	−0·0	−2·5	137
6	1161	6·2	D.D.	127	23 59·1	−1·3	−0·9	71	23 51·5	−1·3	−0·6	65
9	1486	4·6	D.D.	160	18 40·8	..	..	54	N			
30	552	3·0	D.D.	50	9 16·8	0·0	1·4	89	9 23·5	0·1	1·5	82
30	552	3·0	R.B.	50	10 8·2	0·1	1·8	235	10 16·3	−0·0	1·8	244
Apr. 28	900	4·9	D.D.	52	20 28·4	0·5	−2·8	153	20 17·5	0·2	−2·6	145
29	1070	5·2	D.D.	65	20 49·0	−0·1	−2·1	132	20 39·0	−0·2	−2·1	128
May 2	1442	5·0	D.D.	103	21 53·0	−1·2	−1·4	93	21 43·1	−1·2	−1·3	91
2	1441	6·4	D.D.	103	21 53·4	..	..	61	21 44·8	..	..	57
10	2287	3·0	R.D.	193	23 22·1	−1·5	0·7	274	A			
13	2554	4·4	R.D.	215	0 23·5	−1·6	1·4	242	A			
Jun. 2	1800	5·4	D.D.	119	21 14·9	−1·3	−1·3	124	S			
13	3079	4·2	R.D.	232	1 39·9	−0·9	1·8	198	1 44·3	−0·9	1·5	203
20	552	3·0	D.B.	331	A				17 41·1	0·3	−1·0	78
July 18	552	3·0	D.B.	304	A				0 24·3	0·6	1·3	53
18	545	4·3	R.D.	304	0 37·4	0·4	1·3	254	0 44·4	0·4	1·3	260
18	552	3·0	R.D.	304	1 2·7	0·3	1·2	272	1 9·1	0·2	1·2	278
18	560	3·8	R.D.	305	1 35·6	0·3	1·6	240	1 43·6	0·3	1·5	247
18	561	5·2	R.D.	305	1 39·1	0·2	1·4	256	1 46·1	0·2	1·4	263
31	2287	3·0	D.D.	114	18 45·3	−2·0	0·8	63	18 42·7	−1·8	0·8	61
31	2287	3·0	R.B.	114	19 49·6	−1·4	−0·8	324	19 42·5	−1·2	−0·5	326
Aug. 16	852	5·0	R.D.	302	1 24·3	..	..	189	1 40·5	0·7	2·3	212
31	2809	4·9	D.D.	129	19 18·5	..	..	140	S			
Oct. 7	440	4·6	R.D.	215	1 14·8	−0·7	2·5	207	1 21·4	−0·9	1·7	225
7	560	3·8	R.D.	226	19 38·2	..	..	328	N			
30	3494	4·6	D.D.	139	22 41·3	−1·4	−0·6	83	22 35·9	−1·1	−0·1	68
Nov. 4	537	3·8	R.D.	199	5 16·3	0·1	−3·7	323	..			
4	552	3·0	D.B.	199	5 40·6	−0·8	−0·1	46	5 38·4	−0·9	0·4	32
4	545	4·3	R.D.	200	6 2·7	−0·2	−1·5	274	5 54·6	−0·2	−1·8	284
4	552	3·0	R.D.	200	6 24·2	0·2	−2·3	305	6 13·3	0·2	−2·9	317
5	852	5·0	D.D.	222	20 40·7	..	..	340	N			
25	3308	6·2	D.D.	94	21 19·1	−0·9	−0·9	73	21 13·7	−0·7	−0·4	57
30	440	4·6	D.D.	159	21 48·2	−1·7	−0·4	106	21 43·9	−1·3	0·4	89
Dec. 9	1623	5·4	R.D.	272	6 57·5	−1·1	−1·4	312	6 48·6	−0·9	−1·2	315
22	3269	4·3	D.D.	63	20 54·5	−0·1	0·3	31	A			
25	89	6·5	D.D.	100	21 42·3	−1·0	−1·4	89	21 34·4	−0·9	−0·8	73
27	370	6·1	D.D.	126	21 38·9	−1·2	0·6	53	21 39·7	−1·0	1·3	35
29	545	4·3	D.D.	143	3 35·2	−0·1	−0·8	61	3 31·1	−0·3	−0·7	53
29	552	3·0	D.D.	143	4 15·1	..	..	16	N			
29	552	3·0	R.B.	143	4 32·2	..	..	336	N			
29	560	3·8	D.D.	143	4 39·3	−0·0	−0·4	45	4 37·1	−0·2	−0·4	37
29	703	6·3	D.D.	153	N				21 56·0	..	..	148

MEAN PLACES OF STARS, 1990·5

NAME	Mag.	R.A.	Dec.	Spectrum
		h m	° ′	
α Andromedæ *Alpheratz*	2·1	0 07·9	+29 02	A0p
β Cassiopeiæ *Caph*	2·3	0 08·7	+59 06	F5
γ Pegasi *Algenib*	2·8	0 12·7	+15 08	B2
α Phœnicis	2·4	0 25·8	−42 21	K0
α Cassiopeiæ *Schedar*	2·2	0 40·0	+56 29	K0
β Ceti *Diphda*	2·0	0 43·1	−18 02	K0
γ Cassiopeiæ*	Var.	0 56·1	+60 40	B0p
β Andromedæ *Mirach*	2·1	1 09·2	+35 34	M0
δ Cassiopeiæ	2·7	1 25·2	+60 11	A5
α Eridani *Achernar*	0·5	1 37·4	−57 17	B5
β Arietis *Sheratan*	2·6	1 54·1	+20 46	A5
γ Andromedæ *Almak*	2·3	2 03·3	+42 17	K0
α Arietis *Hamal*	2·0	2 06·6	+23 25	K2
α Ursæ Minoris *Polaris*	2·0	2 21·7	+89 13	F8
β Persei *Algol**	Var.	3 07·5	+40 55	B8
α Persei *Mirfak*	1·8	3 23·6	+49 50	F5
η Tauri *Alcyone*	2·9	3 46·9	+24 05	B5p
α Tauri *Aldebaran*	0·9	4 35·4	+16 29	K5
β Orionis *Rigel*	0·1	5 14·1	− 8 13	B8p
α Aurigæ *Capella*	0·1	5 16·0	+45 59	G0
γ Orionis *Bellatrix*	1·6	5 24·6	+ 6 20	B2
β Tauri *Elnath*	1·7	5 25·7	+28 36	B8
δ Orionis	2·2	5 31·5	− 0 18	B0
α Leporis	2·6	5 32·3	−17 50	F0
ε Orionis	1·7	5 35·7	− 1 12	B0
ζ Orionis	1·8	5 40·2	− 1 57	B0
κ Orionis	2·1	5 47·3	− 9 40	B0
α Orionis *Betelgeuse**	Var.	5 54·7	+ 7 24	M0
β Aurigæ *Menkalinan*	1·9	5 58·8	+44 57	A0p
β Canis Majoris *Mirzam*	2·0	6 22·3	−17 57	B1
α Carinæ *Canopus*	−0·7	6 23·7	−52 41	F0
γ Geminorum *Alhena*	1·9	6 37·2	+16 24	A0
α Canis Majoris *Sirius*	−1·5	6 44·7	−16 42	A0
ε Canis Majoris	1·5	6 58·3	−28 58	B1
δ Canis Majoris	1·9	7 08·0	−26 23	F8p
α Geminorum *Castor*	1·6	7 34·0	+31 55	A0
α Canis Minoris *Procyon*	0·4	7 38·8	+ 5 15	F5
β Geminorum *Pollux*	1·1	7 44·7	+28 03	K0
ζ Puppis	2·3	8 03·2	−39 59	Od
γ Velorum	1·8	8 09·2	−47 18	Oap
ε Carinæ	1·9	8 22·3	−59 29	K0
δ Velorum	2·0	8 44·4	−54 40	A0
λ Velorum *Suhail*	2·2	9 07·6	−43 24	K5
β Carinæ	1·7	9 13·1	−69 41	A0
ι Carinæ	2·2	9 16·8	−59 14	F0
α Hydræ *Alphard*	2·0	9 27·1	− 8 37	K2
α Leonis *Regulus*	1·3	10 07·9	+12 01	B8
γ Leonis *Algeiba*	1·9	10 19·4	+19 53	K0
β Ursæ Majoris *Merak*	2·4	11 01·3	+56 26	A0
α Ursæ Majoris *Dubhe*	1·8	11 03·1	+61 48	K0

* γ Cassiopeiæ, 1989 mag. 2·5. β Persei, mag. 2·2 to 3·2.
  α Orionis, mag. 0·1 to 1·2.

The positions of heavenly bodies on the celestial sphere are defined by two co-ordinates, right ascension and declination, which are analogous to longitude and latitude on the surface of the Earth. If we imagine the plane of the terrestrial equator extended indefinitely, it will cut the celestial sphere in a great circle known as the celestial equator. Similarly the plane of the Earth's orbit, when extended, cuts in the great circle called the ecliptic. The two intersections of these circles are known as the First Point of Aries and the First Point of Libra. If from any star a perpendicular be drawn to the celestial equator, the length of this perpendicular is the star's declination. The arc, measured eastwards along the equator from the First Point of Aries to the foot of this perpendicular, is the right ascension. An alternative definition of right ascension is that it is the angle at the celestial pole (where the Earth's axis, if prolonged, would meet the sphere) between the great circles to the First Point of Aries and to the star.

The plane of the Earth's equator has a slow movement, so that our reference system for right ascension and declination is not fixed. The consequent alteration in these quantities from year to year is called precession. In right ascension it is an increase of about 3ˢ a year for equatorial stars, and larger or smaller changes in either direction for stars near the poles, depending on the right ascension of the star. In declination it varies between + 20″ and − 20″ according to the right ascension of the star.

A star or other body crosses the meridian when the sidereal time is equal to its right ascension. The altitude is then a maximum, and may be deduced by remembering that the altitude of the elevated pole is numerically equal to the latitude, while that of the equator at its intersection with the meridian is equal to the co-latitude, or complement of the latitude.

MEAN PLACES OF STARS, 1990·5

Name	Mag.	R.A.	Dec.	Spectrum
		h m	° '	
δ Leonis	2·6	11 13·6	+20 35	A3
β Leonis *Denebola*	2·1	11 48·6	+14 38	A2
γ Ursæ Majoris *Phecda*	2·4	11 53·3	+53 45	A0
γ Corvi	2·6	12 15·3	−17 29	B8
α Crucis	1·0	12 26·1	−63 03	B1
γ Crucis	1·6	12 30·6	−57 04	M3
γ Centauri	2·2	12 41·0	−48 54	A0
γ Virginis	2·7	12 41·2	− 1 24	F0
β Crucis	1·3	12 47·2	−59 38	B1
ε Ursæ Majoris *Alioth*	1·8	12 53·6	+56 01	A0*p*
α Canum Venaticorum	2·9	12 55·6	+38 22	A0*p*
ζ Ursæ Majoris *Mizar*	2·1	13 23·5	+54 58	A2*p*
α Virginis *Spica*	1·0	13 24·7	−11 07	B2
η Ursæ Majoris *Alkaid*	1·9	13 47·2	+49 22	B3
β Centauri *Hadar*	0·6	14 03·1	−60 20	B1
θ Centauri	2·1	14 06·1	−36 19	K0
α Bootis *Arcturus*	0·0	14 15·2	+19 14	K0
α Centauri *Rigil Kent*	0·1	14 39·0	−60 48	G0
ε Bootis	2·4	14 44·6	+27 07	K0
β Ursæ Minoris *Kochab*	2·1	14 50·7	+74 12	K5
α Coronæ Borealis *Alphecca* ..	2·2	15 34·3	+26 45	A0
δ Scorpii	2·3	15 59·8	−22 36	B0
β Scorpii	2·6	16 04·9	−19 47	B1
α Scorpii *Antares*	1·0	16 28·8	−26 25	M0
α Trianguli Australis	1·9	16 47·6	−69 01	K2
ε Scorpii	2·3	16 49·5	−34 17	K0
α Herculis*	Var.	17 14·2	+14 24	M3
λ Scorpii	1·6	17 33·0	−37 06	B2
α Ophiuchi *Rasalhague*	2·1	17 34·5	+12 34	A5
θ Scorpii	1·9	17 36·6	−43 00	F0
κ Scorpii	2·4	17 41·8	−39 02	B2
γ Draconis	2·2	17 56·4	+51 29	K5
ε Sagittarii *Kaus Australis* ...	1·9	18 23·5	−34 23	A0
α Lyræ *Vega*	0·0	18 36·6	+38 46	A0
σ Sagittarii	2·0	18 54·7	−26 19	B3
β Cygni *Albireo*	3·1	19 30·3	+27 56	K0
α Aquilæ *Altair*	0·8	19 50·3	+ 8 51	A5
α Capricorni	3·8	20 17·5	−12 35	G5
γ Cygni	2·2	20 21·9	+40 14	F8*p*
α Pavonis	1·9	20 24·9	−56 46	B3
α Cygni *Deneb*	1·3	20 41·1	+45 15	A2*p*
α Cephei *Alderamin*	2·4	21 18·4	+62 33	A5
ε Pegasi	2·4	21 43·7	+ 9 50	K0
δ Capricorni	2·9	21 46·5	−16 10	A5
α Gruis	1·7	22 07·6	−47 00	B5
δ Cephei*	3·7	22 28·8	+58 22	*
β Gruis	2·1	22 42·1	−46 56	M3
α Piscis Austrini *Fomalhaut* ..	1·2	22 57·1	−29 40	A3
β Pegasi *Scheat*	2·4	23 03·3	+28 02	M0
α Pegasi *Markab*	2·5	23 04·3	+15 09	A0

* α Herculis, mag. 3·1 to 3·9.

δ Cephei, mag. 3·7 to 4·4, Spectrum F5 to G0.

Thus in London (Lat. 51° 30′) the meridian altitude of *Sirius* is found as follows:

	°	′
Altitude of equator	38	30
Declination south	16	42
Difference	21	48

The altitude of *Capella* (Dec. +45° 59′) at lower transit is:

	°	′
Altitude of pole	51	30
Polar distance of star	44	01
Difference	7	29

The brightness of a heavenly body is denoted by its magnitude. Omitting the exceptionally bright stars *Sirius* and *Canopus*, the twenty brightest stars are of the first magnitude, while the faintest stars visible to the naked eye are of the sixth magnitude. The magnitude scale is a precise one, as a difference of five magnitudes represents a ratio of 100 to 1 in brightness. Typical second magnitude stars are *Polaris* and the stars in the Belt of Orion. The scale is most easily fixed in memory by comparing the stars with Norton's *Star Atlas* (see page 64). The stars *Sirius* and *Canopus* and the planets Venus and Jupiter are so bright that their magnitudes are expressed by negative numbers. A small telescope will show stars down to the ninth or tenth magnitude, while stars fainter than the twentieth magnitude may be photographed by long exposures with the largest telescopes.

Some of the astronomical information in this ALMANACK has been taken from *Astronomical Phenomena*, and is published here by arrangement with, and with the permission of, the Controller of H.M. Stationery Office.

ELEMENTS OF THE SOLAR SYSTEM

Orb	Mean Distance from Sun (Earth=1)	Mean Distance from Sun km. 10⁶	Sidereal Period	Synodic Period	Incl. of Orbit to Ecliptic	Diameter	Mass (Earth=1)	Period of Rotation on Axis
			y d	Days	° ′	km.		d h m
Sun	...	...	...	...		1,392,000	332,948	25 09
Mercury	0·39	58	88	116	7 00	4,880	0·055	59
Venus...........	0·72	108	225	584	3 24	12,100	0·815	243
Earth	1·00	150	1 0	...	...	12,756eq.	1·00	23 56
Mars............	1·52	228	1 322	780	1 51	6,790	0·107	24 37
Jupiter	5·20	778	11 315	399	1 18	142,800eq. 134,200p.	318	9 50 9 56
Saturn	9·54	1427	29 167	378	2 29	120,000eq. 108,000p.	95	10 14 10 38
Uranus..........	19·19	2870	84 6	370	0 46	52,000	14·6	16—28
Neptune.........	30·07	4497	164 288	367	1 46	48,400	17·2	18—20
Pluto	39·46	5950	247 255	367	17 09	3,000?	0·01	6 09

THE SATELLITES

Name	Star Mag.	Mean distance from Primary	Sidereal Period of Revolution	Name	Star mag.	Mean distance from Primary	Sidereal Period of Revolution
Earth		km.	d	*Saturn*		km.	d
Moon	—	384,400	27·322	Janus	14	151,000	0·695
				Epimetheus.......	15	151,000	0·694
Mars				Mimas	13	186,000	0·942
Phobos	12	9,400	0·319	Enceladus	12	238,000	1·370
Deimos	13	23,500	1·262	Tethys	10	295,000	1·888
				Telesto	19	295,000	1·888
Jupiter				Calypso	18	295,000	1·888
XVI. Metis	17	128,000	0·295	Dione	10	377,000	2·737
XV. Adrastea	19	129,000	0·298	—...............	18	377,000	2·737
V. Amalthea	14	181,000	0·498	Rhea	10	527,000	4·518
XIV. Thebe	15	222,000	0·675	Titan	8	1,222,000	15·945
I. Io	5	422,000	1·769	Hyperion	14	1,481,000	21·277
II. Europa	5	671,000	3·551	Iapetus	11	3,561,000	79·331
III. Ganymede	5	1,070,000	7·155	Phoebe	16	12,954,000	550·4
IV. Callisto	6	1,880,000	16·689				
XIII. Leda	20	11,090,000	239	*Uranus*			
VI. Himalia	15	11,480,000	251	Miranda	17	129,000	1·414
X. Lysithea	18	11,720,000	259	Ariel	14	191,000	2·520
VII. Elara	17	11,740,000	260	Umbriel	15	266,000	4·144
XII. Ananke.......	19	21,200,000	631	Titania..........	14	436,000	8·706
XI. Carme	18	22,600,000	692	Oberon	14	583,000	13·463
VIII. Pasiphae	18	23,500,000	735				
IX. Sinope	18	23,700,000	758	*Neptune*			
				Triton	14	355,000	5·877
Saturn				Nereid	19	5,510,000	360·21
Atlas.............	18	138,000	0·602				
—...............	16	139,000	0·613	*Pluto*			
—...............	16	142,000	0·629	Charon...........	17	19,700	6·387

THE EARTH

The shape of the Earth is that of an oblate spheroid or solid of revolution whose meridian sections are ellipses not differing much from circles, whilst the sections at right angles are circles. The length of the equatorial axis is about 12,756 kilometres, and that of the polar axis is 12,714 kilometres. The mean density of the Earth is 5·5 times that of water, although that of the surface layer is less. The Earth and Moon revolve about their common centre of gravity in a lunar month; this centre in turn revolves round the Sun in a plane known as the ecliptic, that passes through the Sun's centre. The Earth's equator is inclined to this plane at an angle of 23½°. This tilt is the cause of the seasons. In mid-latitudes, and when the Sun is high above the Equator, not only does the high noon altitude make the days longer, but the Sun's rays fall more directly on the Earth's surface; these effects combine to produce summer. In equatorial regions the noon altitude is large throughout the year, and there is little variation in the length of the day. In higher latitudes the noon altitude is lower, and the days in summer are appreciably longer than those in winter.

The average velocity of the Earth in its orbit is 30 kilometres a second. It makes a complete rotation on its axis in about 23ʰ 56ᵐ of mean time, which is the sidereal day. Because of its annual revolution round the Sun, the rotation with respect to the Sun, or the solar day, is more than this by about four minutes

(*see* p. 66). The extremity of the axis of rotation, or the North Pole of the Earth, is not rigidly fixed, but wanders over an area roughly 20 metres in diameter.

TERRESTRIAL MAGNETISM

A magnetic compass points along the horizontal component of a magnetic line of force. These directions converge on the "magnetic dip-poles", the places where a freely suspended magnetized needle would become vertical. Not only do the positions of these poles change with time, but their exact location is ill-defined, particularly so in the case of the north dip-pole where the lines of force, on the north side of it, instead of converging radially, tend to bunch into a channel. Although it is therefore unrealistic to attempt to specify the locations of the dip-poles exactly, the present adopted positions are 77°·0 N., 102°·4 W. and 65°·3 S., 139°·2 E. The two magnetic dip-poles are thus not antipodal, the line joining them passing the centre of the Earth at a distance of about 1,200 kilometres. The distances of the magnetic dip-poles from the north and south geographical poles are about 1,400 and 2,700 kilometres respectively.

There is also a "magnetic equator", at all points of which the vertical component of the Earth's magnetic field is zero and a magnetized needle remains horizontal. This line runs between 2° and 10° north of the geographical equator in the eastern hemisphere, turns sharply south off the West African coast, and crosses South America through Brazil, Bolivia and Peru; it recrosses the geographical equator in mid-Pacific.

Reference has already been made to secular changes in the Earth's field. The following table indicates the changes in magnetic declination (or variation of the compass). Similar, though much smaller, changes have occurred in "dip" or magnetic inclination. Secular changes differ throughout the world. Although the London observations strongly suggest a cycle with a period of several hundred years, an exact repetition is unlikely.

London			Greenwich		
1580	11° 15′	E.	1850	22° 24′	W.
1622	5 56	E.	1900	16 29	W.
1665	1 22	W.	1925	13 10	W.
1730	13 00	W.	1950	9 07	W.
1773	21 09	W.	1975	6 39	W.

In order that up-to-date information on the variation of the compass may be available, many governments publish magnetic charts on which there are lines (isogonic lines) passing through all places at which specified values of declination will be found at the date of the chart.

In the British Isles, isogonic lines now run approximately north-east to south-west. Though there are considerable local deviations due to geological causes, a rough value of magnetic declination may be obtained by assuming that at 50° N. on the meridian of Greenwich, the value in 1990 is 4° 16′ west and allowing an increase of 10′ for each degree of latitude northwards and one of 24′ for each degree of longitude westwards. For example, at 53° N., 5° W., declination will be about 4° 16′ + 30′ + 120′, i.e. 6° 46′

west. The average annual change at the present time is about 9′ decrease.

The number of magnetic observatories is about 200—widely scattered over the globe. There are three in Great Britain run by the British Geological Survey: at Hartland, North Devon, at Eskdalemuir in Dumfriesshire, Scotland, and at Lerwick, Shetland Islands. Some recent annual mean values of the magnetic elements for Hartland are given below.

The normal worldwide terrestrial magnetic field corresponds approximately to that of a very strong small bar magnet near the centre of the Earth but with appreciable smooth spatial departures. The origin and slow secular change of the normal field are not yet fully understood but are generally ascribed to electric currents associated with fluid motions in the Earth's core. Superimposed on the normal field are local and regional anomalies whose magnitudes may in places exceed that of the normal field; these are due to the influence of mineral deposits in the Earth's crust. A small proportion of the field is of external origin, mostly associated with electric currents in the ionosphere. The configuration of the external field and the ionization of the atmosphere depend on the incident particle and radiation flux. There are, therefore, short-term and non-periodic as well as diurnal, 27-day, seasonal and 11-year periodic changes in the magnetic field, dependent upon the position of the Sun and the degree of solar activity.

Year	Declina-tion West	Dip or Inclina-tion	Hori-zontal Force	Vertical Force
	° ′	° ′	oersted	oersted
1950	11 06	66 54	0·1848	0·4334
1955	10 30	66 49	0·1859	0·4340
1960	9 59	66 44	0·1871	0·4350
1965	9 30	66 34	0·1887	0·4354
1970	9 06	66 26	0·1903	0·4364
1975	8 32	66 17	0·1921	0·4373
1980	7 44	66 10	0·1933	0·4377
1985	6 56	66 08	0·1938	0·4380
1988	6 30	66 08	0·1939	0·4384

Magnetic Storms

Occasionally, sometimes with great suddenness, the Earth's magnetic field is subject for several hours to marked disturbance. In extreme cases, departures in field intensity of as much as one tenth the normal value are experienced. In many instances, such disturbances are accompanied by widespread displays of aurorae, marked changes in the incidence of cosmic rays, an increase in the reception of "noise" from the Sun at radio frequencies together with rapid changes in the ionosphere and induced electric currents within the Earth which adversely affect radio and telegraphic communications. The disturbances are generally ascribed to changes in the stream of neutral and ionized particles which emanates from the Sun and through which the Earth is continuously passing. Some of these changes are associated with visible eruptions on the Sun, usually in the region of sunspots. There is a marked tendency for disturbances to recur after intervals of about 27 days, the apparent period of rotation of the Sun on its axis, which is consistent with the sources being located on particular areas of the Sun.

ARTIFICIAL SATELLITES

Orbits

To consider the orbit of an artificial satellite it is best to imagine that one is looking at the Earth from a distant point in space. The Earth would then be seen to be rotating about its axis inside the orbit described by the rapidly revolving satellite. The inclination of a satellite orbit to the Earth's equator (which generally remains almost constant throughout the satellite's lifetime) gives at once the maximum range of latitudes over which the satellite passes. Thus a satellite whose orbit has an inclination of 53° will pass overhead all latitudes between S. 53° and N. 53°, but would never be seen in the zenith of any place nearer the poles than these latitudes. If we consider a particular place on the earth, whose latitude is less than the inclination of the satellite's orbit then the Earth's rotation carries this place first under the northbound part of the orbit and then under the southbound position of the orbit, these two occurrences being always less than 12 hours apart for satellites moving in direct orbits (i.e. to the east). (For satellites in retrograde orbits the words "northbound" and "southbound" should be interchanged in the preceding statement.) As the value of the latitude of the observer increases and approaches the value of the inclination of the orbit, so this interval gets shorter until (when the latitude is equal to the inclination) only one overhead passage occurs each day.

Observation of satellites

The regression of the orbit around the Earth causes alternate periods of visibility and invisibility, though this is of little concern to the radio or radar observer. To the visual observer the following cycle of events normally occurs (though the cycle may start in any position): invisibility, morning observations before dawn, invisibility, evening observations after dusk, invisibility, morning observations before dawn, and so on. With reasonably high satellites and for observers in high latitudes around the summer solstice the evening observations follow the morning observations without interruption as sunlight passing over the polar regions can still illuminate satellites which are passing over temperate latitudes at local midnight. At the moment all satellites rely on sunlight to make them visible though a satellite with a flashing light has been suggested for a future launching. The observer must be in darkness or twilight in order to make any useful observations and the durations of twilight and the sunrise, sunset times given on Page Two of each month will be a useful guide.

Some of the satellites are visible to the naked eye and much interest has been aroused by the spectacle of a bright satellite disappearing into the Earth's shadow. The event is even more fascinating telescopically as the disappearance occurs gradually as the satellite traverses the Earth's penumbral shadow, and during the last few seconds before the eclipse is complete the satellite may change colour (under suitable atmospheric conditions) from yellow to red. This is because the last rays of sunlight are refracted through the denser layers of our atmosphere before striking the satellite.

Some satellites rotate about one or more axes so that a periodic variation in brightness is observed. This was particularly noticeable in several of the U.S.S.R. satellites.

Satellite research has provided some interesting results. Among them may be mentioned a revised value of the Earth's oblateness, 1/298·2, and the discovery of the Van Allen radiation belts.

Launchings

Apart from their names, e.g. Cosmos 6 Rocket, the satellites are also classified according to their date of launch. Thus 1961 α refers to the first satellite launching of 1961. A number following the Greek letter indicated the relative brightness of the satellites put in orbit. From the beginning of 1963 the Greek letters were replaced by numbers and the numbers by roman letters e.g. 1963–01A. For all satellites successfully injected into orbit the table gives the designation and names of the main objects (in the order A, B, C . . . etc.), the launch date and some initial orbital data. These are the inclination to the equator (i), the nodal period of revolution (P), the eccentricity, e, and the perigee height.

Artificial Satellites Launched in 1987–88

Designation	Satellite	Launch date	i	P	e	Perigee height (km)
1987–		1987				
91	Cosmos 1894, launcher	October 28	1·3	1441·6	0·001	35833
92	Cosmos 1895, rocket, engine	November 11	70·4	89·7	0·005	228
93	Cosmos 1896, rocket	November 14	64·8	89·3	0·004	209
94	Progress 33, rocket	November 20	51·7	90·1	0·008	231
95	TV-Sat 1	November 21	0·1	1422·6	0·007	35217
96	Cosmos 1897, launcher	November 26	1·4	1435·1	0·001	35718
97	USA 28, rocket	November 29	?	?	?	?
98	Cosmos 1898, rocket	December 1	74·0	100·8	0·002	778
99	Cosmos 1899, rocket, engine	December 7	70·4	89·6	0·007	208
100	Reduga 21, launcher	December 10	1·5	1435·7	0·000	35768

Desig-nation	Satellite	Launch date	i	P	e	Perigee height (km)
1987–		1987				
101	Cosmos 1900, rocket, platform	December 12	65·0	89·8	0·001	256
102	Cosmos 1901, rocket	December 14	64·9	89·7	0·013	173
103	Cosmos 1902, rocket	December 15	65·8	92·4	0·003	368
104	Soyuz TM4, rocket	December 21	51·6	89·8	0·003	255
105	Cosmos 1903, launcher rocket, launcher, rocket	December 21	63·0	717·6	0·738	588
106	Cosmos 1904, rocket	December 23	82·9	104·9	0·003	967
107	Cosmos 1905, rocket	December 25	70·4	89·6	0·004	228
108	Cosmos 1906, rocket	December 26	82·6	89·9	0·001	257
109	Ekran 17, launcher	December 27	1·6	1431·8	0·006	35459
110	Cosmos 1907, rocket	December 29	72·8	92·3	0·004	356
1988–						
01	Cosmos 1908, rocket	January 6	82·5	97·8	0·002	635
02	Cosmos 1909–1914, rocket	January 15	82·6	114·1	0·000	1412
03	Progress 34, rocket	January 20	51·6	89·6	0·002	242
04	Cosmos 1915, rocket, engine	January 26	72·9	90·3	0·013	195
05	Meteor 2–17, rocket	January 30	82·5	104·1	0·002	938
06	DMSP 2–04	February 3	98·8	101·4	0·001	820
07	Cosmos 1916, rocket	February 3	64·9	89·8	0·014	171
08	USA 30, rocket	February 8	28·6	89·9	0·008	224
09	Cosmos 1917–1919	February 17	64·8	87·8	0·001	162
10	Cosmos 1920, rocket	February 18	82·6	88·7	0·005	179
11	Cosmos 1921, rocket, engine	February 19	70·0	90·4	0·013	206
12	Sakura 3A	February 19	0·1	1416·7	0·028	34252
13	Cosmos 1922, launcher rocket, rocket, launcher	February 26	62·9	708·9	0·735	614
14	China 22, rocket	March 7	0·5	1457·1	0·010	35784
15	Cosmos 1923, rocket, engine	March 10	72·8	89·7	0·005	227
16	Cosmos 1924–1931, rocket	March 11	74·0	115·7	0·004	1460
17	Molniya 1–71, launcher rocket, launcher, rocket	March 11	63·0	699·4	0·738	461
18	Spacenet 3R, Telecom 1C	March 11	0·1	1429·7	0·003	35555
19	Cosmos 1932, rocket, platform	March 14	65·0	89·7	0·001	252
20	Cosmos 1933, rocket	March 15	82·5	97·7	0·002	635
21	IRS–1A, rocket	March 17	82·5	97·7	0·002	634
22	Molniya 1–72, launcher rocket, launcher, rocket	March 17	62·9	735·1	0·740	644
23	Cosmos 1934, rocket	March 22	82·9	104·8	0·004	952
24	Progress 35, rocket	March 23	51·6	88·7	0·005	181
25	Cosmos 1935, rocket	March 24	67·2	89·4	0·012	167
26	San Marco 5, rocket	March 25	3·0	93·1	0·026	263
27	Cosmos 1936, rocket	March 30	64·8	89·7	0·005	229
28	Gorizont 15, launcher	March 31	1·4	1476·3	0·002	36501
29	Cosmos 1937, rocket	April 5	74·0	100·7	0·003	770
30	Cosmos 1938, rocket, engine	April 11	72·9	89·7	0·005	225
31	Foton 1, rocket, engine	April 14	62·9	90·4	0·012	216
32	Cosmos 1939, rocket	April 20	98·0	97·5	0·003	618
33	Transit 23, 24, rocket	April 26	90·3	108·7	0·019	1019
34	Cosmos 1940, launcher, stages	April 26	1·3	1436·1	0·000	35776
35	Cosmos 1941, rocket, engine	April 27	70·3	89·2	0·003	216
36	Ekran 18, launcher, stages	May 6	0·4	1435·9	0·000	35767
37	Cosmos 1942, rocket	May 12	67·1	89·8	0·015	167
38	Progress 36, rocket	May 13	51·7	90·0	0·008	223
39	Cosmos 1943, rocket	May 15	71·0	102·0	0·000	849
40	Intelsat 5A F–13, stage	May 18	7·6	636·5	0·721	475
41	Cosmos 1944, rocket	May 19	64·8	89·2	0·004	214
42	Cosmos 1945, rocket	May 19	70·4	89·2	0·003	215
43	Cosmos 1946–8, stages	May 21	64·9	675·7	0·001	19113
44	Molniya 3–32	May 26	62·8	718·1	0·738	587
45	Cosmos 1949, rocket	May 28	65·0	92·8	0·001	404

Desig-nation	Satellite	Launch date	i	P	e	Perigee height (km)
1988–		1988				
46	Cosmos 1950, rocket	May 30	73·6	116·0	0·002	1484
47	Cosmos 1951, rocket, engine	May 31	82·3	89·9	0·001	275
48	Soyuz TM5, rocket	June 7	51·6	90·7	0·004	281
49	Cosmos 1952, rocket, engine	June 11	70·0	89·7	0·004	230
50	Cosmos 1953, rocket	June 14	82·5	97·8	0·002	633
51	Meteosat P2, Oscar 13, PAS1	June 15	0·6	1429·4	0·004	35503
52	Nova 2, rocket	June 16	90·1	109·0	0·003	1155
53	Cosmos 1954, rocket	June 21	74·0	100·8	0·002	780
54	Cosmos 1955, rocket	June 22	64·8	89·8	0·014	167
55	Cosmos 1956, rocket, engine	June 23	82·4	91·6	0·003	332
56	Okean 1, rocket	July 5	82·5	97·8	0·002	635
57	Cosmos 1957, rocket, engine	July 7	82·6	89·8	0·001	254
58	Phobos 1	July 7	(space probe to Mars)			
59	Phobos 2	July 12	(space probe to Mars)			
60	Cosmos 1958, rocket	July 14	65·8	92·4	0·003	371
61	Progress 37, rocket	July 18	51·6	90·0	0·006	236
62	Cosmos 1959, rocket	July 18	82·9	104·8	0·003	958
63	Insat 1C, ECS5	July 21	0·3	1444·8	0·000	35950
64	Meteor 3–02, rocket	July 26	83·5	109·4	0·001	1186
65	Cosmos 1960, rocket	July 28	65·8	94·4	0·004	463
66	Cosmos 1961, launcher, stages	August 1	1·5	1463·0	0·002	36213
67	China 23, rocket	August 5	63·0	89·7	0·008	206
68	Cosmos 1962, rocket, engine	August 8	70·0	89·2	0·004	206
69	Molniya 1–73, launcher rocket, launcher, rocket	August 12	62·8	737·9	0·743	582
70	Cosmos 1963, rocket	August 16	64·8	89·7	0·013	173
71	Gorizont, 16, launcher, stages	August 18	1·5	1435·5	0·001	35736
72	Cosmos 1964, rocket	August 23	70·0	89·7	0·004	231
73	Cosmos 1965, rocket	August 23	82·3	89·9	0·001	260
74	Transit 25, 26, rocket	August 25	90·0	107·5	0·010	1035
75	Soyuz TM6	August 29	51·6	88·4	0·001	190
76	Cosmos 1966, launcher rocket, launcher, rocket	August 30	62·9	708·5	0·735	594
77	USA 31, rocket, ?	September 2				
78	USA 32, rocket	September 5				
79	Cosmos 1967, rocket, engine	September 6	72·9	89·6	0·004	228
80	China 24, rocket	September 6	99·1	102·9	0·001	884
81	G Star 3, SBS5	September 8	1·5	982·8	0·299	16583
82	Cosmos 1968, rocket, engine	September 9	82·3	89·9	0·001	260
83	Progress 38, rocket	September 10	51·6	88·7	0·004	185
84	Cosmos 1969, rocket	September 15	67·1	89·6	0·013	166
85	Cosmos 1970–1972, launcher, stages	September 16	64·9	675·7	0·001	19116
86	Sakura 3B, stages	September 16	30·7	89·6	0·010	197
87	Offeq 1, rocket	September 19	142·9	98·6	0·064	248
88	Cosmos 1973, rocket	September 22	72·9	92·3	0·004	356
89	NOAA 11	September 24	98·9	102·1	0·001	850
90	Molniya 3–33, launcher rocket, launcher, rocket	September 29	62·8	701·6	0·732	629

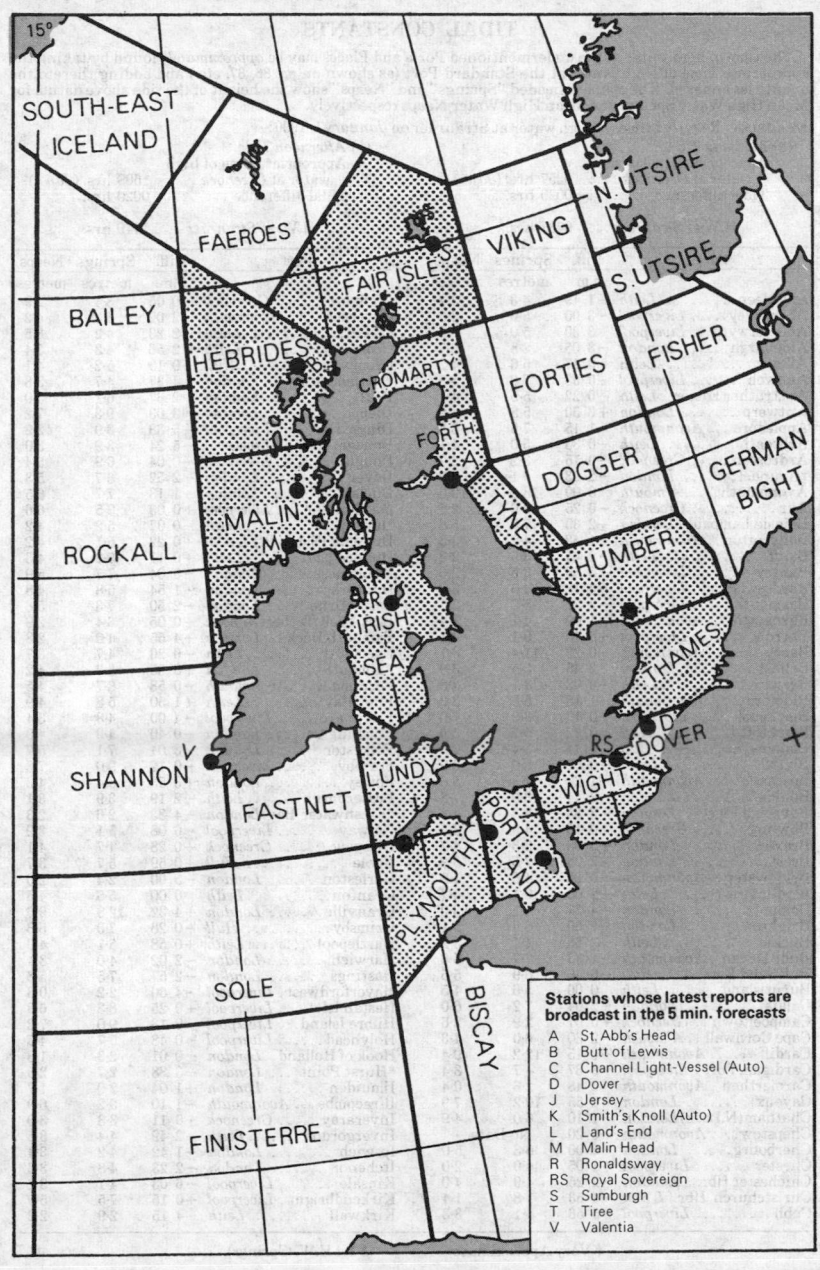

Stations whose latest reports are broadcast in the 5 min. forecasts

A   St. Abb's Head
B   Butt of Lewis
C   Channel Light-Vessel (Auto)
D   Dover
J   Jersey
K   Smith's Knoll (Auto)
L   Land's End
M   Malin Head
R   Ronaldsway
RS Royal Sovereign
S   Sumburgh
T   Tiree
V   Valentia

TIDAL CONSTANTS

The time of high water at the undermentioned Ports and Places may be *approximately* found by taking the appropriate Time of High Water at the Standard Port (as shown on pp. 86, 87, etc.) and adding thereto the quantities annexed. The columns headed "Springs" and "Neaps" show the height of the tide above datum for Mean High Water Springs and Mean High Water Neaps respectively.

EXAMPLE.—Required times of high water at Stranraer on *January* 1, 1990:—

(a) *Morning Tide.*
Appropriate time of high
water at *Greenock* .... 0257 hrs. (*Jan.* 1)
Tidal difference .... −0020 hrs.

H.W at *Stranraer* ... 0237 hrs.

(b) *Afternoon Tide.*
Appropriate time of high
water at *Greenock* .... 1509 hrs. (*Jan* 1).
Tidal difference .... −0020 hrs.

H.W. at *Stranraer* .. 1449 hrs.

Port	Diff.	Springs	Neaps	Port	Diff.	Springs	Neaps
	h.m.	metres	metres		h.m.	metres	metres
Aberdeen.........*Leith*	−1 19	4·3	3·4	Coulport .... *Greenock*	−0 05	3·4	2·9
Aberdovey..... *Liverpool*	−3 00	5·0	3·5	Coverack .... *Avonmouth*	−2 02	5·3	4·2
Aberystwyth .. *Liverpool*	−3 30	5·0	3·5	Cowes.......... *London*	−2 23	4·2	3·5
Aldeburgh...... *London*	−3 05	2·8	2·7	Cromarty........*Leith*	−2 56	4·3	3·4
Alloa............*Leith*	+0 47	5·6	4·2	Cromer.......... *Hull*	+0 19	5·2	4·1
Amlwch..... *Liverpool*	−0 33	7·3	5·8	Dartmouth ..... *London*	+4 37	4·7	3·8
Anstruther Easter . *Leith*	−0 22	5·5	4·4	Deal .... *London*	−2 37	6·1	5·0
Antwerp .... *London*	+0 50	5·8	4·2	Dieppe .... *London*	−3 03	9·3	7·2
Appledore ... *Avonmouth*	−1 15	7·5	5·2	Dingle Hbr. .... *Liverpool*	+5 38	3·9	2·9
Arbroath..........*Leith*	−0 33	5·0	4·1	Donegal Hbr. ... *Liverpool*	−5 24	3·9	3·0
Ardrossan ... *Greenock*	−0 15	3·2	2·7	Douglas ..... *Liverpool*	−0 04	6·9	5·4
†Arundel...... *London*	−2 03	3·1	2·2	Dover .... *London*	−2 52	6·7	5·3
Avonmouth ....*A'mouth*	0 00	13·2	10·0	Duclair........ *London*	−1 13	7·7	6·5
Ayr .... *Greenock*	−0 25	3·0	2·6	Duddon Bar ... *Liverpool*	+0 03	8·5	6·6
Baie de Lampaul . *London*	+2 30	7·5	5·8	Dunbar ....*Leith*	−0 07	5·2	4·2
Ballycotton.. *Avonmouth*	−1 43	4·2	3·3	Dundalk (Sldr's Pt) *L'pool*	+0 22	5·1	4·2
Banff..............*Leith*	−2 44	3·5	2·8	Dundee.............*Leith*	+0 11	5·3	4·3
Bantry .... *Liverpool*	+5 59	3·5	2·6	Dungeness...... *London*	−3 04	7·7	5·9
Bardsey Island . *Liverpool*	−3 18	4·5	3·3	Dunkirk ...... *London*	−1 54	5·8	4·8
Barmouth ..... *Liverpool*	−2 57	5·0	3·5	Eastbourne ..... *London*	−2 50	7·3	5·6
Barnstaple .. *Avonmouth*	−1 00	4·1	1·4	East Loch Tarbert *G'nock*	+0 05	3·4	2·9
Barrow ...... *Liverpool*	+0 15	9·1	7·1	Exmouth Dock .. *London*	+4 55	4·0	2·8
Barry .... *Avonmouth*	−0 22	11·4	8·7	Eyemouth ....*Leith*	−0 20	4·7	3·7
Belfast .... *London*	−2 45	3·5	3·0	Falmouth ...... *London*	+3 35	5·3	4·2
Berwick..........*Leith*	−0 02	4·7	3·8	Ferryside... *Avonmouth*	−0 58	6·7	4·5
Bideford .. *Avonmouth*	−1 15	5·9	3·6	Filey Bay ....*Leith*	+1 50	5·8	4·9
Blackpool ..... *Liverpool*	−0 10	8·9	7·0	Fishguard .... *Liverpool*	−4 00	4·8	3·4
Blacktoft .... *Hull*	+0 32	5·7	3·9	Flushing ..... *London*	−0 40	4·9	4·0
Blakeney .... *Hull*	+0 44	3·4	2·0	Folkestone ..... *London*	−3 04	7·1	5·7
Blyth ....*Leith*	+0 50	5·0	3·9	Formby ..... *Liverpool*	−0 12	9·0	7·3
Boscastle .... *Avonmouth*	−1 20	7·3	5·6	Fowey .... *London*	+3 53	5·4	4·3
Boulogne ...... *London*	−2 44	8·9	7·2	Fraserburgh ....*Leith*	−2 19	3·9	3·1
Bovisand Pier... *London*	+3 55	5·3	4·3	*Freshwater Bay *London*	−4 33	2·6	2·3
Bowling....... *Greenock*	+0 15	4·0	3·4	Galway ..... *Liverpool*	−6 08	5·1	3·9
Braye .... *London*	+5 33	6·3	4·7	Glasgow ..... *Greenock*	+0 28	4·7	4·1
Brest............ *London*	+2 28	7·5	5·9	Goole .... *Hull*	+0 59	5·7	3·7
Bridgwater .. *Avonmouth*	−0 22	4·6	1·9	Gorleston ..... *London*	−5 00	2·4	2·0
Bridlington.......*Leith*	+2 03	6·1	4·7	Granton..........*Leith*	0 00	5·6	4·5
Bridport .... *London*	+4 37	4·1	3·0	Granville........ *London*	+4 32	12·8	9·6
Brighton ...... *London*	−2 50	6·5	5·1	Grimsby .... *Hull*	−0 28	7·0	5·6
Buckie ....*Leith*	−2 56	4·1	3·2	Hartlepool ....*Leith*	+0 58	5·1	4·0
Bude Haven . *Avonmouth*	−1 33	7·7	5·8	Harwich .... *London*	−2 02	4·0	3·4
Bull Sand Fort ..... *Hull*	−0 46	6·9	5·5	Hastings .... *London*	−2 57	7·5	5·8
Burntisland ....*Leith*	0 00	5·6	4·5	Haverfordwest . *Liverpool*	−4 50	2·2	0·3
Calais.......... *London*	−2 04	7·2	6·0	Hestan Islet .. *Liverpool*	+0 25	8·3	6·3
Campbeltown . *Greenock*	+0 07	2·9	2·6	Hilbre Island... *Liverpool*	−0 13	9·0	7·2
Cape Cornwall .. *A'mouth*	−2 30	6·0	4·3	Holyhead...... *Liverpool*	−0 48	5·7	4·5
Cardiff ..... *Avonmouth*	−0 15	12·2	9·4	Hook of Holland . *London*	−0 01	2·3	1·8
Cardigan, Port . *Liverpool*	−3 37	4·7	3·4	*Hurst Point ... *London*	−3 38	2·7	2·3
Carmarthen . *Avonmouth*	−0 48	2·6	0·4	Ijmuiden .... *London*	+1 04	2·0	1·7
Cayeux........ *London*	−2 55	10·2	7·9	Ilfracombe .. *Avonmouth*	−1 10	9·2	6·9
Chatham (N.Lock) *London*	−1 10	6·0	4·9	Inveraray .... *Greenock*	+0 11	3·3	3·0
Chepstow... *Avonmouth*	+0 20	No Data		Invergordon ....*Leith*	−2 49	4·4	3·5
Cherbourg...... *London*	−6 00	6·3	5·0	Ipswich .... *London*	−1 42	4·2	3·4
Chester ..... *Liverpool*	+1 05	4·0	2·0	Itchenor .... *London*	−2 23	4·8	3·8
Chichester Hbr. . *London*	−2 25	4·9	4·0	Kinsale ...... *Liverpool*	−6 03	4·1	3·2
Christchurch Hbr. *L'don*	−4 53	1·8	1·4	Kirkcudbright . *Liverpool*	+0 15	7·5	5·9
Cobh .... *Liverpool*	−5 56	4·1	3·3	Kirkwall ....*Leith*	−4 15	2·9	2·2

† Very Approximate.   * 1st H.W. (Springs).

Port	Diff.	Springs	Neaps	Port	Diff.	Springs	Neaps
	h.m.	metres	metres		h.m.	metres	metres
Knights Town . *Liverpool*	+5 36	3.9	3.0	Ramsey (I.O.M.) *Liverpool*	+0 04	7.2	5.7
Lamlash...... *Greenock*	−0 26	3.2	2.7	Ramsgate....... *London*	−2 32	4.9	3.8
Le Havre ..... *London*	−3 55	7.8	6.5	†Rosslare .... *Liverpool*	−5 23	1.9	1.4
Lerwick.......... *Leith*	−3 49	2.2	1.6	Rosyth .... *Leith*	+0 07	5.8	4.7
Limerick Dock . *Liverpool*	−4 24	5.9	4.5	Ryde .... *London*	−2 23	4.5	3.7
Littlehampton .. *London*	−2 33	5.5	4.3	St. Helier .... *London*	+4 48	11.1	8.1
Lizard Point . *Avonmouth*	−2 17	5.3	4.2	St. Ives ...... *Avonmouth*	−1 55	6.6	4.9
Llanddwyn Island *L'pool*	−1 53	5.0	4.0	St. Malo ...... *London*	+4 27	12.1	9.1
Llanelli ..... *Avonmouth*	−0 56	7.8	5.8	St. Peter Port ... *London*	+4 54	9.0	6.7
Loch Moidart .. *Greenock*	+6 00	4.8	3.5	Salcombe ...... *London*	+4 10	5.3	4.1
Londonderry ... *London*	−5 37	2.7	2.0	Saltash.......... *London*	+4 10	5.6	4.5
Looe .... *London*	+3 55	5.4	4.2	Scarborough.......*Leith*	+1 33	5.7	4.6
Lossiemouth .... *Leith*	−3 01	4.1	3.2	Scheveningen... *London*	+0 24	2.1	1.8
Lowestoft ...... *London*	−4 25	2.4	2.1	Scrabster .... *Leith*	+6 04	5.0	3.7
Lulworth Cove.. *London*	+5 00	2.3	1.5	Seaham .... *Leith*	+0 53	5.2	4.1
Lundy Island *Avonmouth*	−1 23	8.0	5.9	Selsey Bill ..... *London*	−2 28	5.3	4.4
Lyme Regis .... *London*	+4 55	4.3	3.1	Sennen Cove . *Avonmouth*	−2 30	6.1	4.8
*Lymington .... *London*	−3 33	3.0	2.6	Sharpness Dock .*A'mouth*	+0 42	9.3	5.8
Margate........ *London*	−1 52	4.8	3.9	Sheerness ..... *London*	−1 16	5.7	4.8
Maryport...... *Liverpool*	+0 24	8.6	6.6	Shoreham ...... *London*	−2 43	6.2	5.0
Menai Bridge .. *Liverpool*	−0 28	7.4	5.9	Silloth .... *Liverpool*	+0 35	9.2	7.1
Mevagissey..... *London*	+3 53	5.4	4.3	Southampton ... *London*	−2 52	4.5	3.7
Middlesbrough.....*Leith*	+1 09	5.6	4.5	Southend ...... *London*	−1 22	5.7	4.8
Milford Haven .. *Liverpool*	−5 07	7.0	5.2	Southwold ...... *London*	−3 50	2.5	2.2
Minehead .. *Avonmouth*	−0 40	10.6	8.1	Stirling .... *Leith*	+1 13	2.9	1.6
Montrose.........*Leith*	−0 19	4.8	3.9	Stonehaven.......*Leith*	−1 09	4.5	3.6
Morecambe ... *Liverpool*	+0 01	9.5	7.6	Stornoway ... *Liverpool*	−4 15	4.8	3.7
Mostyn Quay .. *Liverpool*	−0 17	8.5	6.7	Stranraer .... *Greenock*	−0 20	3.0	2.5
Newburgh......*Leith*	+0 48	4.1	3.0	Stromness .... *Leith*	−5 34	3.6	2.7
Newcastle on Tyne . *Leith*	+0 54	5.3	4.1	Sunderland.......*Leith*	+0 51	5.2	4.2
Newhaven...... *London*	−2 48	6.6	5.2	*Swanage ...... *London*	−5 13	2.0	1.6
Newlyn ..... *Avonmouth*	−2 24	5.6	4.4	Swansea..... *Avonmouth*	−0 49	9.6	7.3
Newport(Gwent) *A'mouth*	−0 15	12.1	9.0	Tarn Point .... *Liverpool*	+0 05	8.3	6.4
Newquay ...... *London*	−1 58	7.0	5.3	Tay River (Bar) .... *Leith*	−0 21	5.2	4.2
New Quay (Card.) . *L'pool*	−3 30	4.9	3.4	Tees R. (Ent.) ...... *Leith*	+1 08	5.5	4.3
North Shields ... *Leith*	+0 51	5.0	3.9	Teignmouth .... *London*	+4 37	4.8	3.6
North Sunderland .. *Leith*	+0 05	4.8	3.7	Tenby .... *Avonmouth*	−1 05	8.4	6.3
N. Woolwich .... *London*	−0 20	7.0	5.7	Tilbury.......... *London*	−0 49	6.4	5.3
Oban .... *Greenock*	+5 45	4.0	2.9	Tobermory .... *Liverpool*	−5 12	4.4	3.3
Old Lynn Road..... *Hull*	+0 05	7.3	5.8	Torquay........ *London*	+4 40	4.9	3.7
Orfordness ..... *London*	−2 50	2.8	2.7	*Totland Bay ... *London*	−3 53	2.7	2.3
Ostend .... *London*	−1 32	5.1	4.2	Troon .... *Greenock*	−0 25	3.2	2.7
Padstow ..... *Avonmouth*	−1 45	7.3	5.6	Truro .... *London*	+3 43	5.3	4.2
Peel .... *Liverpool*	−0 02	5.3	4.2	Tyne River (Ent.).... *Leith*	+0 56	5.1	3.9
Peterhead ....*Leith*	−1 59	3.8	3.1	Walton-on-Naze. *London*	−2 10	4.2	3.4
Plymouth ...... *London*	+4 05	5.5	4.4	Waterford Hbr . *Liverpool*	−4 54	4.6	3.6
Poole (Entrance) *London*	−5 03	2.0	1.6	Weston S. Mare .*A'mouth*	−0 25	12.0	9.0
Porlock Bay . *Avonmouth*	−0 50	10.2	7.8	†Wexford Hbr.. *Liverpool*	−5 03	1.7	1.4
Porthcawl .. *Avonmouth*	−0 53	9.9	7.5	Whitby.......... *Leith*	+1 22	5.4	4.3
Portmadoc..... *Liverpool*	−2 45	5.1	3.4	Whitehaven ... *Liverpool*	+0 10	8.0	6.3
Portland ...... *London*	+5 10	2.1	1.4	Wick .... *Leith*	−3 26	3.4	2.7
Portpatrick.... *Liverpool*	+0 22	3.8	3.0	Wisbech Cut .... *Hull*	+0 01	7.0	5.1
Portsmouth.... *London*	−2 23	4.7	3.8	Workington ... *Liverpool*	+0 20	8.2	6.4
Port Talbot .. *Avonmouth*	−0 53	9.6	7.3	Worthing ...... *London*	−2 38	6.1	4.8
Preston ...... *Liverpool*	+0 10	5.3	3.3	*Yarmth.(I.O.W.) *London*	−2 53	3.1	2.5
Pwllheli .... *Liverpool*	−3 07	5.0	3.4	Youghal .... *Liverpool*	−5 50	4.2	3.3

† Very Approximate.   * 1st H.W. (Springs).

Tidal data is no longer available for a number of places which formerly appeared in the list above. These places (with the name of the substitute now recorded) are: *Air Point* (Mostyn Quay); *Alderney* (Braye); *Ardrishaig* (East Loch Tarbert); *Arisaig* (Loch Moidart); *Ayr Pt.*, I.o.M. (Peel); *Beachy Head* (Eastbourne); *Beaumaris* (Menai Bridge); *Brieile* (Scheveningen); *Broughty Ferry* (Newburgh); *Burryport* (Whiteford Lighthouse); *Caen* (Cayeux); *Caernarvon* (Llanddwyn Is.); *Devonport* (Plymouth); *Dumbarton* (Bowling); *Fareham* (Itchenor); *Fifeness* (Anstruther Easter); *Glasson Dock* (Tarn Pt.); *Gravesend* (Tilbury); *Greenwich* (R. Albert Dock); *Honfleur Harbour* (Duclair); *Hythe* (Totland Bay); *Lancaster* (Duddon Bar); *Loch Long* (Coulport); *Lynmouth* (Porlock Bay); *Nash Pt.* (Chepstow); *Neath* (Porthcawl); *Needles Pt.* (Freshwater Bay); *Nore Lt.* (Chatham); *Pembroke Dock* (Milford Haven); *Penzance* (Newlyn); *Plymouth Breakwater* (Bovisand Pier); *Port Harrington* (Hestan Islet); *Portishead* (Avonmouth); *St. Agnes* (Coverack); *St. Annes* (Blackpool); *St. Mary's* (Sennen Cove); *Spurn Head* (Bull Sand Fort); *Start Pt.* (Lulworth Cove); *Stockton* (Seaham); *Sutton Bridge* (Blacktoft); *Torbay* (Torquay); *Ushant* (Baie de Lampaul); *Valentia Harbour* (Knights Town); *Woolwich* (N. Woolwich); *Worms Head* (Ferryside); *Yarmouth Roads* (Gorleston).

Tidal predictions (pp. 86–97) for London Bridge, Liverpool, Avonmouth, Hull, Dún Laoghaire and Leith are computed by the Proudman Oceanographic Laboratory, copyright reserved. Those for Greenock have been supplied by the Hydrographer of the Navy and are crown copyright.

JANUARY, 1990

High Water at the undermentioned Places (G.M.T.*)—

Datums of Predictions:
- London Bridge — †Datum of Predictions 3·20 m. below
- Liverpool — †Datum of Predictions 4·93 m. below
- Avonmouth — †Datum of Predictions 6·50 m. below
- Hull (Albert Dock) — †Datum of Predictions 3·90 m. below
- Greenock — †Datum of Predictions 1·62 m. below
- Leith — †Datum of Predictions 2·90 m. below
- Dun Laoghaire — ‡Datum of Predictions 0·20 m. above

Day of Month	Day of Week	LB Mn.	Ht.	LB Aft.	Ht.	Liv. Mn.	Ht.	Liv. Aft.	Ht.	Avon. Mn.	Ht.	Avon. Aft.	Ht.	Hull Mn.	Ht.	Hull Aft.	Ht.	Green. Mn.	Ht.	Green. Aft.	Ht.	Leith Mn.	Ht.	Leith Aft.	Ht.	Dun L. Mn.	Ht.	Dun L. Aft.	Ht.
1	M	0413	6·9	1642	7·0	0130	8·8	1348	9·1	0943	12·6	2203	12·6	0854	7·0	2057	7·3	0257	3·3	1509	3·6	0510	5·2	1721	5·3	0154	3·7	1403	4·1
2	Tu	0448	6·8	1723	6·8	0211	8·6	1430	9·0	1024	12·5	2245	12·4	0935	6·9	2138	7·2	0340	3·3	1548	3·6	0553	5·1	1806	5·3	0240	3·7	1450	4·1
3	W	0526	6·6	1807	6·6	0256	8·4	1517	8·8	1108	12·2	2329	12·3	1019	6·8	2223	7·0	0424	3·3	1630	3·5	0642	5·0	1855	5·2	0331	3·6	1540	4·0
4	Th	0607	6·5	1856	6·5	0345	8·2	1609	8·6	1156	11·8			1108	6·5	2316	6·8	0511	3·2	1718	3·4	0733	4·8	1948	5·1	0428	3·5	1639	3·9
5	F	0657	6·3	1958	6·1	0442	8·0	1709	8·3	0019	11·2	1255	11·3			1207	6·7	0606	3·1	1818	3·3	0830	4·7	2046	4·9	0533	3·5	1746	3·8
6	Sa	0806	6·2	2112	6·2	0551	7·9	1822	8·1	0124	10·9	1411	10·9	0021	6·7	1320	6·5	0709	3·1	1933	3·2	0935	4·8	2154	5·0	0644	3·6	1901	3·7
7	Su	0927	6·2	2226	6·3	0707	7·8	1938	8·1	0247	10·7	1529	11·1	0137	6·6	1436	6·4	0818	3·2	2053	3·1	1045	4·9	2308	5·1	0750	3·6	2010	3·7
8	M	1047	6·3	2336	6·4	0819	8·1	2049	8·4	0404	11·1	1642	11·6	0254	6·6	1549	6·5	0925	3·2	2203	3·2	1153	5·1			0848	3·7	2114	3·8
9	Tu			1200	6·5	0922	8·5	2152	8·7	0513	11·6	1749	12·2	0413	6·6	1651	6·6	1025	3·5	2307	3·3	0019	5·1	1249	5·1	0941	3·9	2208	3·8
10	W	0038	6·5	1303	6·5	1019	8·9	2247	9·2	0614	12·2	1846	12·8	0519	6·8	1743	6·8	1120	3·2			0120	5·4	1349	5·3	1030	4·0	2259	3·9
11	Th	0131	6·7	1355	6·7	1108	9·3	2334	9·2	0706	12·8	1935	12·9	0612	7·0	1827	7·0			1209	3·6	0215	5·6	1439	5·5	1116	4·1	2347	3·9
12	F	0218	6·7	1443	7·0	1154	9·3			0751	12·9	2019	12·8	0700	7·1	1907	7·2	0005	3·3	1255	3·8	0304	5·6	1524	5·6			1202	4·2
13	Sa	0300	6·9	1527	7·2	0018	9·2	1236	9·5	0833	13·0	2058	13·0	0742	7·1	1945	7·4	0058	3·3	1337	3·8	0349	5·5	1607	5·6	0032	3·9	1246	4·2
14	Su	0341	7·0	1607	7·3	0059	9·1	1316	9·4	0912	12·8	2136	12·8	0820	7·1	2022	7·5	0145	3·3	1416	3·8	0431	5·3	1648	5·5	0114	3·8	1332	4·2
15	M	0419	7·0	1647	7·1	0137	9·0	1352	9·4	0949	12·6	2212	12·6	0857	6·9	2058	7·4	0227	3·3	1454	3·8	0510	5·0	1731	5·3	0159	3·7	1415	4·1
16	Tu	0455	6·8	1723	6·9	0213	8·8	1427	9·1	1023	12·3	2244	12·3	0932	6·7	2135	7·3	0305	3·2	1530	3·7	0552	4·7	1812	5·1	0242	3·6	1500	3·9
17	W	0530	6·7	1801	6·5	0250	8·6	1505	8·8	1055	12·0	2316	12·0	1007	6·6	2212	7·2	0341	3·1	1607	3·5	0633	4·4	1853	4·9	0328	3·4	1546	3·7
18	Th	0608	6·3	1841	6·0	0328	8·3	1546	8·3	1130	11·5	2353	11·9	1044	6·5	2254	6·8	0417	3·0	1646	3·3	0715	4·1	1936	4·6	0416	3·2	1636	3·5
19	F	0652	6·0	1928	5·7	0413	7·9	1634	7·9			1212	11·5	1127	6·1	2346	6·6	0455	3·0	1731	3·2	0759	3·9	2022	4·5	0508	3·1	1736	3·3
20	Sa	0748	5·7	2025	5·5	0509	7·5	1737	7·6	0041	10·2	1307	10·8			1227	5·9	0539	3·0	1827	3·0	0847	3·7	2120	4·3	0618	3·1	1848	3·3
21	Su	0854	5·5	2125	5·5	0622	7·1	1857	7·2	0147	9·7	1419	9·9	0100	5·8	1342	5·7	0633	2·9	1938	2·8	0957	3·6	2233	4·3	0725	3·2	1956	3·3
22	M	1000	5·4	2226	5·6	0741	7·1	2016	7·6	0305	9·6	1536	9·6	0223	6·4	1458	6·0	0745	2·8	2100	2·6	1108	3·6	2347	4·3	0821	3·3	2053	3·3
23	Tu	1109	5·5	2332	5·8	0846	7·5	2115	8·0	0424	10·1	1651	10·4	0341	6·7	1603	6·7	0908	2·8	2212	2·7			1214	4·4	0909	3·5	2139	3·4
24	W			1212	5·8	0936	8·2	2202	8·4	0526	10·8	1749	11·6	0441	7·1	1654	7·1	1014	2·8	2309	2·8	0047	4·6	1307	4·5	0951	3·6	2222	3·6
25	Th	0031	6·2	1303	6·2	1019	8·5	2242	8·9	0614	12·1	1835	12·2	0527	7·4	1736	7·4	1104	3·0	2357	2·9	0137	4·8	1351	4·7	1030	3·8	2259	3·7
26	F	0119	6·5	1347	6·6	1058	8·9	2320	9·2	0655	12·2	1916	13·1	0607	7·6	1814	7·6	1226	3·2			0222	5·1	1431	4·8	1106	4·0	2337	3·8
27	Sa	0204	6·8	1429	7·0	1137	9·2	2358	9·6	0734	13·1	1955	13·4	0645	7·8	1849	7·7	0041	3·1	1304	3·4	0258	5·3	1506	5·0	1144	4·1		
28	Su	0243	7·1	1510	7·4			1215	9·6	0812	13·4	2033	13·5	0720	8·0	1926	7·8	0123	3·3	1341	3·5	0334	5·5	1541	5·3	0015	3·8	1222	4·2
29	M	0321	7·0	1548	7·4	0036	9·2	1253	9·6	0850	13·4	2110	13·6	0757	7·8	2002	7·7	0204	3·3	1418	3·6	0409	5·6	1618	5·6	0051	3·9	1300	4·3
30	Tu	0357	7·3	1626	7·3	0114	9·2	1331	9·6	0929	13·6	2148	13·4	0834	7·4	2039	7·5	0243	3·3	1454	3·7	0447	5·7	1700	5·7	0132	3·9	1342	4·3
31	W	0431	7·2	1704	7·2	0152	9·1	1411	9·5	1009	13·0	2227	13·0	0912	7·3	2118	7·3	0322	3·4	1532	3·7	0527	5·6	1744	5·6	0214	3·8	1425	4·2

* All times shown are Greenwich Mean Time.   *†Difference of height in metres from Ordnance Datum (Newlyn).*   *‡Difference of height in metres from Ordnance Datum (Dublin).*

FEBRUARY, 1990

High Water at the undermentioned Places (G.M.T.*)—

Day of Month	Day of Week	LONDON BRIDGE †Datum of Predictions 3·20 m. below				LIVERPOOL †Datum of Predictions 4·93 m. below				AVONMOUTH †Datum of Predictions 6·50 m. below				HULL (Albert Dock) †Datum of Predictions 3·90 m. below				GREENOCK †Datum of Predictions 1·62 m. below				LEITH †Datum of Predictions 2·90 m. below				DUN LAOGHAIRE ‡Datum of Predictions 0·20 m. above			
		Mn. h.m.	Ht. m.	Aft. h.m.	Ht. m.	Mn. h.m.	Ht. m.	Aft. h.m.	Ht. m.	Mn. h.m.	Ht. m.	Aft. h.m.	Ht. m.	Mn. h.m.	Ht. m.	Aft. h.m.	Ht. m.	Mn. h.m.	Ht. m.	Aft. h.m.	Ht. m.	Mn. h.m.	Ht. m.	Aft. h.m.	Ht. m.	Mn. h.m.	Ht. m.	Aft. h.m.	Ht. m.
1	Th	0508	7.0	1744	6.7	0233	8.9	1453	8.8	1048	12.9	2306	12.3	0953	7.0	2202	7.4	0401	3.3	1611	3.6	0615	5.1	1831	5.4	0300	3.8	1514	4.1
2	F	0546	6.7	1828	6.3	0317	8.5	1541	8.8	1132	12.0	2349	11.4	1037	6.7	2251	7.1	0444	3.2	1656	3.4	0703	4.9	1922	5.2	0353	3.6	1610	3.9
3	Sa	0632	6.5	1924	6.1	0407	8.1	1638	8.2	—	—	1222	11.4	1132	6.3	2353	6.6	0531	3.1	1749	3.2	0758	4.7	2020	4.7	0456	3.5	1718	3.7
4	Su	0735	6.2	2036	6.0	0516	7.7	1757	7.7	0045	10.6	1337	10.3	—	—	1243	6.0	0627	3.0	1900	2.9	0906	4.6	2136	4.6	0611	3.4	1842	3.5
5	M	0901	6.0	2156	6.0	0645	7.5	1927	7.6	0215	10.1	1507	10.1	0114	6.3	1412	6.0	0735	2.9	2034	2.8	1027	4.6	2304	4.7	0729	3.4	2004	3.5
6	Tu	1031	6.0	2318	6.1	0811	8.0	2049	8.0	0345	10.3	1631	10.3	0253	6.4	1539	6.2	0857	2.9	2205	2.9	1147	4.7	—	—	0838	3.6	2115	3.6
7	W	1153	6.3	—	—	0919	8.3	2152	8.4	0504	11.0	1743	11.4	0417	6.7	1644	6.6	1013	3.1	2312	3.0	0020	5.0	1252	5.0	0937	3.7	2212	3.7
8	Th	0025	6.4	1257	6.6	1014	8.8	2241	8.8	0607	11.9	1838	12.1	0519	7.0	1732	7.0	1112	3.3	—	—	0120	5.1	1346	5.2	1028	3.9	2259	3.8
9	F	0120	6.6	1348	6.8	1101	9.2	2325	9.1	0656	12.5	1923	12.6	0607	7.2	1812	7.3	0005	3.1	1200	3.5	0212	5.3	1432	5.4	1112	4.1	2340	3.8
10	Sa	0206	6.8	1432	7.1	1140	9.4	—	—	0737	13.1	2001	13.1	0646	7.2	1849	7.7	0050	3.1	1243	3.6	0255	5.5	1511	5.6	1152	4.2	—	—
11	Su	0246	7.0	1510	7.2	0003	9.5	1218	9.4	0815	13.2	2037	13.2	0721	7.1	1924	7.7	0130	3.1	1321	3.7	0333	5.5	1548	5.6	0016	3.8	1230	4.2
12	M	0321	7.1	1545	7.2	0036	9.4	1252	9.3	0849	13.3	2110	13.3	0755	7.0	1958	7.8	0205	3.2	1357	3.7	0406	5.4	1623	5.5	0051	3.8	1308	4.2
13	Tu	0355	7.1	1619	7.1	0109	9.1	1323	9.1	0921	13.3	2141	13.3	0826	6.8	2030	7.7	0238	3.2	1431	3.6	0441	5.3	1657	5.4	0128	3.7	1346	4.1
14	W	0426	6.9	1649	6.9	0140	8.9	1354	8.9	0950	13.0	2209	13.0	0857	6.5	2104	7.4	0310	3.3	1504	3.2	0514	5.1	1734	5.1	0203	3.6	1422	3.9
15	Th	0457	6.8	1720	6.8	0211	8.5	1425	8.6	1020	12.5	2237	12.5	0928	6.2	2136	7.0	0341	3.2	1536	3.2	0549	4.8	1809	4.9	0239	3.5	1501	3.7
16	F	0530	6.6	1754	6.4	0243	8.2	1458	8.1	1120	11.8	2304	11.8	0959	5.8	2212	6.5	0412	3.0	1609	3.0	0624	4.5	1847	4.7	0318	3.4	1543	3.4
17	Sa	0608	6.2	1834	6.1	0319	8.0	1538	7.5	1158	11.1	2334	11.1	1034	5.4	2252	6.1	0445	2.9	1647	2.9	0704	4.4	1928	4.4	0354	3.2	1633	3.2
18	Su	0655	5.8	1921	5.8	0406	7.5	1631	7.3	—	—	1257	10.2	1118	5.8	2351	5.6	0525	2.6	1734	2.6	0750	4.3	2026	4.2	0504	3.1	1743	3.1
19	M	0754	5.5	2020	5.5	0513	6.8	1757	6.8	0021	9.2	1433	9.6	0021	6.5	1231	6.6	0618	2.5	1834	2.4	0854	4.2	2144	4.1	0618	3.1	1908	3.0
20	Tu	0905	5.2	2129	5.3	0649	6.8	1941	7.3	0145	9.0	1613	10.6	0135	6.4	1409	6.3	0737	2.5	1954	2.4	1019	4.3	2314	4.2	0734	3.2	2021	3.1
21	W	1024	5.3	2249	5.7	0813	7.2	2051	7.8	0338	9.6	1719	11.6	0307	6.8	1527	6.7	0937	2.6	2145	2.5	1141	4.4	—	—	0835	3.3	2116	3.3
22	Th	1146	5.7	—	—	0911	7.8	2141	8.2	0454	10.6	1808	12.0	0417	7.2	1626	6.3	1040	2.9	2251	2.8	0023	4.6	1241	4.6	0924	3.3	2159	3.5
23	F	0005	5.9	1239	6.2	0956	8.5	2221	8.9	0544	11.3	1852	13.0	0506	7.5	1711	7.6	1125	3.1	2339	3.0	0116	4.8	1328	5.0	1005	3.5	2237	3.7
24	Sa	0056	6.5	1324	6.6	1035	9.0	2259	9.5	0629	12.0	1933	13.1	0546	7.6	1750	7.8	—	—	1205	3.5	0159	5.1	1407	5.3	1043	3.8	2313	3.9
25	Su	0140	6.9	1406	7.0	1115	9.5	2336	9.6	0710	13.0	2012	13.7	0622	7.8	1825	8.0	0022	3.1	1243	3.6	0236	5.4	1443	5.6	1120	4.2	2350	4.0
26	M	0219	7.2	1446	7.4	1153	9.8	—	—	0751	13.6	2050	14.1	0657	7.9	1902	7.9	0102	3.3	1320	3.7	0309	5.6	1518	5.8	1158	4.3	—	—
27	Tu	0257	7.5	1525	7.6	0014	10.0	1231	9.8	0830	14.1	2128	14.1	0733	8.0	1938	7.7	0141	3.3	1356	3.6	0345	5.6	1555	5.9	0026	4.4	1237	4.4
28	W	0334	7.5	1603	7.5	0052	9.6	1310	9.6	0908	14.2	—	—	0809	8.1	2016	8.1	0220	3.4	1433	3.7	0423	5.6	1637	5.8	0104	4.0	1318	4.4

*All times shown are Greenwich Mean Time.   †Difference of height in metres from Ordnance Datum (Newlyn).   ‡Difference of height in metres from Ordnance Datum (Dublin).

MARCH, 1990

High Water at the undermentioned Places (G.M.T.*)—

Datum of Predictions (below/above Ordnance Datum):
London Bridge †3·20 m. below · Liverpool †4·93 m. below · Avonmouth †6·50 m. below · Hull (Albert Dock) †3·90 m. below · Greenock †1·62 m. below · Leith †2·90 m. below · Dun Laoghaire ‡0·20 m. above

Day	Wk	LB Mn	Ht	LB Aft	Ht	Liv Mn	Ht	Liv Aft	Ht	Avon Mn	Ht	Avon Aft	Ht	Hull Mn	Ht	Hull Aft	Ht	Green Mn	Ht	Green Aft	Ht	Leith Mn	Ht	Leith Aft	Ht	DunL Mn	Ht	DunL Aft	Ht
1	Th	0409	7.4	1641	7.1	0130	9.5	1349	9.7	0948	13.8	2206	13.3	0847	7.5	2057	7.9	0257	3.4	1511	3.7	0505	5.5	1722	5.7	0147	4.0	1404	4.3
2	F	0448	7.2	1722	6.7	0209	9.2	1432	9.3	1028	13.0	2244	12.3	0928	7.2	2142	7.2	0416	3.3	1551	3.5	0550	5.2	1810	5.4	0233	3.9	1454	4.1
3	Sa	0529	6.9	1805	6.3	0253	8.7	1519	8.7	1111	11.8	2325	11.3	1012	6.8	2234	7.0	0516	3.3	1635	3.3	0640	5.0	1902	5.1	0324	3.7	1552	3.8
4	Su	0618	6.5	1857	6.0	0343	8.1	1620	7.9	——	——	1200	10.7	1105	6.3	——	——	0500	3.1	1729	3.1	0736	4.7	2007	4.8	0429	3.5	1703	3.5
5	M	0724	6.1	2008	5.8	0455	7.5	1747	7.4	0021	10.2	1316	9.8	——	——	1218	6.4	0601	2.9	1839	2.7	0847	4.5	2130	4.6	0548	3.5	1834	3.3
6	Tu	0847	5.9	2129	5.8	0632	7.3	1926	7.4	0152	9.6	1450	9.6	0112	5.9	1358	6.1	0655	2.9	2040	2.6	1016	4.5	2304	4.6	0713	3.5	2003	3.4
7	W	1019	6.0	2258	6.0	0804	7.6	2046	7.8	0328	9.9	1621	10.0	0300	5.9	1528	6.5	0835	2.9	2213	2.9	1141	4.7	——	——	0828	3.7	2115	3.6
8	Th	1142	6.4	——	——	0911	8.2	2142	8.4	0452	11.3	1729	11.3	0416	6.5	1630	6.5	1005	3.0	2308	3.0	0016	4.9	1244	4.9	0928	3.7	2207	3.6
9	F	0008	6.8	1242	6.8	1000	8.8	2226	8.9	0551	12.5	1819	12.3	0509	6.9	1715	6.9	1101	3.2	2351	3.4	0112	5.1	1335	5.2	1018	3.9	2249	3.7
10	Sa	0103	7.1	1331	7.1	1042	9.1	2304	9.0	0636	12.5	1900	12.7	0550	7.0	1751	7.3	1145	3.4	——	——	0158	5.3	1415	5.4	1059	4.0	2323	3.8
11	Su	0147	7.2	1412	7.2	1119	9.3	2337	9.2	0716	12.9	1937	13.0	0624	7.0	1825	7.3	0030	3.5	1224	3.5	0236	5.4	1451	5.5	1136	4.1	2354	3.8
12	M	0225	7.1	1447	7.2	1153	9.3	——	——	0749	13.4	2011	13.3	0655	7.3	1859	7.7	0105	3.2	1300	3.5	0308	5.4	1523	5.5	——	——	1209	4.0
13	Tu	0257	7.1	1519	7.0	0008	9.2	1224	9.3	0822	13.4	2042	13.3	0726	7.3	1931	7.7	0138	3.2	1333	3.5	0338	5.3	1553	5.3	0023	3.8	1243	3.9
14	W	0327	7.0	1548	6.9	0038	9.1	1253	9.2	0851	13.4	2110	13.3	0755	7.3	2004	7.6	0209	3.2	1404	3.4	0407	5.2	1625	5.3	0053	3.8	1315	3.8
15	Th	0355	6.9	1614	6.6	0107	8.9	1321	8.9	0919	13.1	2136	12.7	0823	6.9	2036	7.3	0238	3.0	1434	3.3	0438	5.1	1658	5.1	0125	3.7	1349	3.7
16	F	0424	6.8	1642	6.6	0135	8.7	1349	8.6	0948	12.5	2202	12.0	0851	6.6	2107	6.9	0305	3.0	1504	3.1	0508	4.9	1732	4.9	0159	3.6	1424	3.6
17	Sa	0457	6.6	1713	6.3	0205	8.4	1420	8.1	1013	11.7	2224	11.1	0921	6.6	2139	6.6	0332	2.9	1535	3.0	0542	4.7	1808	4.7	0236	3.5	1503	3.4
18	Su	0533	6.3	1750	6.0	0239	8.0	1457	7.6	1040	10.9	2248	10.3	0950	6.3	2214	6.3	0401	2.7	1611	2.8	0620	4.5	1849	4.5	0318	3.5	1552	3.2
19	M	0615	6.0	1831	5.6	0319	7.5	1545	7.1	1112	9.9	2323	9.4	1028	5.9	2305	5.9	0436	2.7	1655	2.6	0706	4.3	1949	4.3	0413	3.2	1656	3.0
20	Tu	0706	5.6	1923	5.3	0421	7.1	1705	6.6	——	——	1203	8.8	1126	5.5	——	——	0522	2.6	1753	2.4	0810	4.1	2109	4.1	0521	3.1	1821	3.0
21	W	0812	5.3	2032	5.3	0556	6.8	1855	6.8	0035	8.9	1324	8.8	0045	5.4	1320	5.5	0626	2.5	1908	2.4	0932	4.1	2237	4.1	0642	3.1	1944	3.1
22	Th	0941	5.3	2207	5.7	0730	7.0	2015	7.3	0230	8.9	1519	9.3	0227	5.7	1446	5.5	0834	2.5	2111	2.5	1057	4.3	——	——	0754	3.3	2044	3.3
23	F	1108	5.7	2330	5.7	0834	7.8	2107	8.0	0406	10.0	1638	10.5	0341	6.1	1548	6.4	1005	2.8	2310	2.8	——	——	1204	4.6	0848	3.6	2130	3.6
24	Sa	——	——	1208	6.4	0922	8.5	2150	8.6	0506	11.3	1733	11.7	0434	6.7	1637	7.1	0034	3.1	1252	3.0	0042	4.8	1253	5.0	0932	4.1	2208	4.0
25	Su	0024	6.9	1256	7.3	1004	9.1	2230	9.1	0557	12.5	1821	12.7	0516	6.9	1718	7.7	0114	3.3	1331	3.3	0126	5.1	1334	5.4	1014	4.1	2244	4.0
26	M	0109	7.3	1338	7.5	1045	9.6	2309	9.5	0642	13.3	1906	13.4	0554	7.6	1757	8.0	0153	3.4	1410	3.4	0203	5.4	1412	5.7	1053	4.2	2320	4.1
27	Tu	0149	7.5	1419	7.6	1126	10.0	2349	9.7	0726	13.9	1947	13.9	0631	7.7	1835	8.1	0231	3.5	1451	3.5	0239	5.6	1449	5.9	1131	4.4	——	——
28	W	0229	7.6	1458	7.6	——	——	1207	10.1	0808	14.1	2027	14.1	0707	7.7	1914	8.1	0310	3.4	1534	3.3	0316	5.7	1530	6.0	——	——	1212	4.3
29	Th	0307	7.4	1538	7.4	0028	9.8	1248	10.0	0849	14.1	2107	13.8	0745	7.7	1957	8.1	0349	3.4	1612	3.6	0356	5.7	1615	5.9	0037	4.2	1257	4.3
30	F	0348	7.6	1619	7.1	0107	9.6	1330	9.6	0929	13.8	2146	13.3	0825	7.6	2042	7.6	0429	3.3	1653	3.5	0441	5.5	1703	5.7	0122	4.1	1346	4.2
31	Sa	0431	7.3	1702	6.8	0149	9.2	1416	9.2	1013	12.6	2228	12.1	0907	7.2	2131	7.2	0513	3.2	1738	3.4	0529	5.3	1756	5.4	0208	4.0	1439	4.0

* All times shown are Greenwich Mean Time. †Difference of height in metres from Ordnance Datum (Newlyn). ‡Difference of height in metres from Ordnance Datum (Dublin).

APRIL, 1990

High Water at the undermentioned Places (G.M.T.*)—

Day of Month	Day of Week	London Bridge †Datum of Predictions 3·20 m. below				Liverpool †Datum of Predictions 4·93 m. below				Avonmouth †Datum of Predictions 6·50 m. below				Hull (Albert Dock) †Datum of Predictions 3·90 m. below				Greenock †Datum of Predictions 1·62 m. below				Leith †Datum of Predictions 2·90 m. below				Dun Laoghaire ‡Datum of Predictions 0·20 m. above			
		Mn.	Ht.	Aft.	Ht.	Mn.	Ht.	Aft.	Ht.	Mn.	Ht.	Aft.	Ht.	Mn.	Ht.	Aft.	Ht.	Mn.	Ht.	Aft.	Ht.	Mn.	Ht.	Aft.	Ht.	Mn.	Ht.	Aft.	Ht.
		h.m.	m.	h.m.	m.	h.m.	m.	h.m.	m.	h.m.	m.	h.m.	m.	h.m.	m.	h.m.	m.	h.m.	m.	h.m.	m.	h.m.	m.	h.m.	m.	h.m.	m.	h.m.	m.
1	Su	0519	6·9	1749	6·9	0236	8·7	1508	8·5	1058	11·4	2315	11·0	0953	6·8	2227	6·7	0351	3·3	1622	3·1	0622	5·0	1853	5·0	0304	3·8	1540	3·7
2	M	0614	6·5	1842	6·5	0331	8·1	1614	7·7	1153	10·3			1049	6·3	2337	6·1	0434	3·2	1718	2·8	0722	4·7	2001	4·7	0409	3·6	1655	3·4
3	Tu	0720	6·2	1948	6·0	0447	7·6	1742	7·3	0015	10·0	1304	9·6	0116		1201	5·8	0523	2·9	2043	2·6	0835	4·5	2124	4·6	0528	3·4	1827	3·3
4	W	0834	6·0	2104	5·9	0618	7·4	1913	7·4	0135	9·6	1429	9·5	0251		1338	5·9	0624	2·9	2156	2·8	1002	4·7	2250	4·7	0656	3·6	1954	3·3
5	Th	0959	6·0	2231	6·0	0744	7·7	2025	7·8	0304	9·9	1555	10·2	0357		1505	6·1	0809	3·0	2243	2·9	1122	4·7	2356	4·9	0810	3·6	2058	3·5
6	F	1119	6·4	2344	6·4	0847	8·2	2118	8·3	0426	10·8	1701	11·2	0445	6·5	1604	6·5	0944	3·2	2324	3·0			1223	5·0	0909	3·7	2148	3·6
7	Sa			1219	6·8	0935	8·6	2200	8·6	0523	11·7	1750	12·0	0523	6·7	1648	6·8	1038	3·1			0049	5·1	1311	5·1	0958	3·9	2226	3·7
8	Su	0038	6·8	1306	7·1	1016	8·9	2235	8·8	0608	12·3	1831	12·9	0556	6·9	1726	7·3	1121	3·1			0132	5·2	1350	5·3	1037	4·0	2258	3·8
9	M	0121	7·0	1345	7·2	1051	9·1	2308	9·0	0646	12·7	1907	12·9	0625	7·1	1800	7·4	0001	3·1	1158	3·3	0207	5·3	1424	5·4	1112	4·0	2326	3·8
10	Tu	0158	7·0	1419	7·1	1123	9·1	2339	9·1	0721	12·7	1941	13·1	0655	7·2	1832	7·4	0035	3·1	1233	3·2	0238	5·3	1455	5·4	1144	3·9	2354	3·8
11	W	0230	7·0	1449	7·0	1154	9·1			0754	13·1	2012	12·9	0724	7·1	1906	7·2	0108	3·1	1306	3·1	0307	5·2	1524	5·3			1215	3·9
12	Th	0258	6·9	1514	6·9	0008	8·9	1224	8·9	0823	13·0	2040	12·9	0752	7·1	1938	7·1	0139	3·1	1336	3·1	0335	5·2	1555	5·3	0021	3·8	1246	3·8
13	F	0325	6·8	1539	6·8	0036	9·0	1253	8·9	0851	13·1	2107	12·8	0820	6·9	2011	7·0	0207	3·0	1406	2·9	0403	5·2	1628	5·2	0051	3·7	1320	3·6
14	Sa	0356	6·7	1609	6·7	0106	9·0	1323	8·8	0919	13·1	2132	11·8	0850	6·6	2043	6·6	0233	3·0	1436	2·9	0436	5·1	1704	5·1	0126	3·7	1356	3·5
15	Su	0430	6·6	1641	6·6	0137	8·8	1355	8·5	0946	11·4	2156	10·3	0921	6·3	2115	6·3	0300	2·9	1509	2·7	0510	5·0	1743	4·9	0204	3·5	1438	3·3
16	M	0508	6·4	1718	6·5	0212	8·5	1433	8·1	1014	10·6	2223	9·8	0959	5·7	2155	5·9	0330	2·9	1547	2·6	0549	4·8	1829	4·7	0249	3·3	1525	3·1
17	Tu	0549	6·2	1758	6·2	0254	8·1	1522	7·7	1048	9·5	2302	9·3	1055	5·4	2245	5·6	0405	2·7	1634	2·6	0638	4·6	1927	4·5	0332	3·3	1626	3·1
18	W	0636	5·9	1846	5·9	0352	7·7	1633	7·1	1139	9·5			0005	5·5	1227	5·4	0450	2·6	1731	2·5	0739	4·4	2037	4·2	0442	3·3	1742	3·1
19	Th	0737	5·6	1949	5·6	0513	7·1	1805	6·9	0010	9·4	1252	9·5	0144	5·6	1358	6·5	0550	2·6	1844	2·6	0853	4·4	2153	4·3	0555	3·2	1901	3·2
20	F	0900	5·6	2119	5·6	0638	7·1	1926	7·4	0141	9·5	1427	10·7	0256	6·0	1503	7·0	0725	2·6	2028	2·9	1009	4·3	2302	4·5	0706	3·4	2003	3·4
21	Sa	1024	5·9	2244	5·9	0747	7·5	2023	8·0	0317	10·5	1552	11·5	0352	6·5	1556	7·6	0917	2·8	2143	2·9	1116	4·4	2359	4·7	0806	3·6	2053	3·6
22	Su	1130	6·4	2346	6·4	0842	7·9	2112	8·6	0424	11·5	1655	12·5	0440	6·9	1642	7·9	1013	2·8	2234	3·2			1210	5·0	0857	3·8	2135	3·8
23	M			1222	6·9	0929	9·1	2157	9·1	0522	12·5	1749	13·7	0522	7·2	1727	7·9	1058	3·4	2320	3·4	0047	5·1	1257	5·1	0941	4·1	2214	4·0
24	Tu	0035	6·9	1309	6·9	1014	9·9	2240	9·7	0612	13·3	1838	13·8	0603	7·5	1811	7·6	1141	3·3			0128	5·4	1340	5·4	1023	4·2	2252	4·1
25	W	0120	7·1	1352	7·1	1059	9·9	2323	9·5	0700	13·7	1923	13·9	0643	7·6	1857	7·5	0003	3·3	1223	3·3	0208	5·6	1422	5·8	1106	4·3	2331	4·2
26	Th	0202	7·3	1433	7·4	1144	10·0			0747	13·9	2006	13·5	0724	7·6	1944	7·4	0045	3·4	1306	3·4	0248	5·7	1508	5·8	1151	4·3		
27	F	0246	7·3	1517	7·5	0007	9·8	1229	9·8	0832	13·5	2050	12·9	0808	7·4	2034	7·3	0126	3·4	1350	3·3	0333	5·6	1557	5·6	0013	4·2	1239	4·2
28	Sa	0332	7·5	1602	7·5	0050	9·6	1317	9·5	0917	13·1	2135	11·6	0853	7·4	2127	6·5	0207	3·4	1437	3·3	0422	5·5	1650	5·3	0100	4·2	1332	4·1
29	Su	0421	7·3	1648	7·3	0137	9·0	1406	9·0	1003	12·3	2220	11·0	0942	6·8	2224		0248	3·4	1525	3·0	0514	5·3	1746	5·0	0153	4·0	1428	3·9
30	M	0515	7·0	1737	7·0	0226	8·8	1501	8·4	1052	11·3	2311	11·0					0330	3·4	1616	3·0	0609	5·0	1845	5·0	0250	3·9	1532	3·6

*All times shown are Greenwich Mean Time.   †Difference of height in metres from Ordnance Datum (Newlyn).   ‡Difference of height in metres from Ordnance Datum (Dublin).

MAY, 1990

High Water at the undermentioned Places (G.M.T.*)—

Day of Month	Day of Week	London Bridge †Datum 3.20 m. below — Mn.	Ht.	Aft.	Ht.	Liverpool †Datum 4.93 m. below — Mn.	Ht.	Aft.	Ht.	Avonmouth †Datum 6.50 m. below — Mn.	Ht.	Aft.	Ht.	Hull (Albert Dock) †Datum 3.90 m. below — Mn.	Ht.	Aft.	Ht.	Greenock †Datum 1.62 m. below — Mn.	Ht.	Aft.	Ht.	Leith †Datum 2.90 m. below — Mn.	Ht.	Aft.	Ht.	Dun Laoghaire ‡Datum 0.20 m. above — Mn.	Ht.	Aft.	Ht.
1	Tu	0610	6.7	1831	6.7	0324	8.3	1606	7.8	1147	10.4	—	—	1035	6.4	2333	6.0	0414	3.4	1713	2.8	0710	4.8	1951	4.8	0354	3.7	1645	3.4
2	W	0709	6.4	1928	6.4	0433	7.9	1722	7.5	0007	10.3	1248	9.9	—	—	1140	5.8	0502	3.2	1825	2.7	0817	4.6	2102	4.6	0509	3.6	1810	3.3
3	Th	0813	6.1	2034	6.1	0550	7.7	1839	7.7	0113	10.0	1357	9.8	0100	5.8	1302	6.0	0601	3.1	2005	2.7	0932	4.6	2215	4.7	0630	3.5	1929	3.3
4	F	0928	5.9	2155	5.9	0706	7.8	1948	8.0	0226	10.2	1510	10.3	0220	5.8	1426	6.2	0729	2.9	2115	2.8	1045	4.7	2320	4.8	0741	3.6	2030	3.5
5	Sa	1045	6.3	2311	6.2	0809	8.0	2042	8.3	0341	10.7	1619	10.2	0324	6.0	1528	6.6	0904	3.0	2205	2.9	1147	4.8	—	—	0841	3.7	2116	3.6
6	Su	1147	6.5	—	—	0900	8.3	2125	8.5	0444	11.4	1712	10.7	0412	6.3	1616	6.6	1003	3.1	2248	3.0	0012	4.9	1237	5.1	0928	3.7	2155	3.6
7	M	0005	6.6	1235	6.6	0942	8.5	2203	8.6	0532	12.3	1756	11.6	0451	6.5	1657	6.7	1048	3.1	2328	3.1	0056	5.0	1312	5.1	1009	3.8	2228	3.7
8	Tu	0050	6.7	1314	6.8	1019	8.6	2237	8.7	0614	12.5	1835	12.4	0525	6.7	1734	7.0	1128	3.1	—	—	0133	5.1	1353	5.2	1046	3.8	2256	3.7
9	W	0128	6.8	1349	6.9	1054	8.7	2309	8.7	0652	12.6	1912	12.6	0557	6.9	1810	7.0	0005	3.1	1204	3.0	0205	5.1	1429	5.2	1117	3.8	2324	3.8
10	Th	0202	6.8	1418	6.8	1126	8.7	2340	8.9	0726	12.6	1944	12.6	0627	7.0	1845	7.0	0039	3.0	1239	2.9	0235	5.1	1459	5.2	1150	3.7	2354	3.8
11	F	0232	6.8	1444	6.8	1158	8.7	—	—	0758	12.4	2015	12.4	0657	7.0	1919	6.9	0111	3.0	1311	2.9	0305	5.1	1534	5.1	—	—	1222	3.6
12	Sa	0303	6.7	1512	6.8	0012	8.6	1231	8.6	0827	12.1	2043	12.1	0727	6.9	1952	6.9	0140	3.0	1344	2.8	0337	5.1	1609	5.1	0026	3.7	1257	3.5
13	Su	0335	6.7	1545	6.7	0045	8.4	1304	8.4	0858	11.7	2112	11.6	0758	6.8	2026	6.8	0209	3.0	1419	2.8	0411	5.0	1646	4.9	0103	3.7	1336	3.4
14	M	0412	6.6	1620	6.6	0119	8.3	1340	8.3	0928	11.2	2142	11.2	0830	6.6	2104	6.6	0239	3.0	1456	2.8	0449	4.9	1727	4.8	0143	3.6	1418	3.4
15	Tu	0451	6.5	1657	6.5	0157	8.0	1419	7.9	1002	10.8	2217	10.7	0905	6.4	2146	6.4	0312	3.0	1538	2.8	0532	4.7	1814	4.7	0227	3.5	1506	3.3
16	W	0532	6.3	1736	6.4	0240	7.8	1508	7.8	1041	10.3	2302	10.4	0948	6.0	2237	6.3	0351	3.0	1626	2.8	0620	4.6	1906	4.6	0315	3.5	1601	3.2
17	Th	0618	6.2	1822	6.2	0334	7.7	1609	7.8	1130	10.3	—	—	1041	5.9	2339	6.0	0436	3.0	1720	2.8	0714	4.5	2005	4.5	0410	3.5	1704	3.2
18	F	0713	6.1	1920	6.1	0440	7.7	1722	7.6	0000	10.2	1232	10.5	1150	5.9	—	—	0531	2.9	1826	2.8	0815	4.5	2109	4.5	0511	3.5	1816	3.3
19	Sa	0823	6.0	2034	6.0	0550	7.8	1834	7.8	0112	10.3	1348	10.3	—	—	1307	6.0	0646	2.9	1945	2.9	0921	4.4	2213	4.4	0620	3.5	1920	3.4
20	Su	0941	6.1	2156	6.4	0657	8.1	1938	8.1	0233	11.0	1510	10.8	0206	6.1	1415	6.2	0820	2.9	2058	2.9	1026	4.6	2313	4.6	0725	3.7	2014	3.6
21	M	1051	6.4	2305	6.4	0759	8.5	2034	9.0	0346	11.6	1619	11.5	0307	6.4	1514	6.5	0928	3.1	2155	2.9	1126	4.8	—	—	0821	3.8	2102	3.8
22	Tu	1150	6.7	—	—	0854	9.0	2127	9.5	0448	12.3	1718	12.3	0402	6.8	1610	6.9	1020	3.2	2245	2.9	0005	5.0	1220	5.3	0912	4.0	2145	3.9
23	W	0001	6.7	1242	6.7	0946	9.3	2214	9.6	0546	13.2	1812	13.1	0452	7.1	1704	7.1	1109	3.3	2332	3.0	0054	5.2	1312	5.5	0959	4.1	2226	4.0
24	Th	0053	6.9	1330	6.9	1038	9.6	2302	9.6	0639	13.2	1903	13.3	0540	7.4	1756	7.4	1158	3.3	—	—	0141	5.4	1402	5.7	1047	4.1	2309	4.1
25	F	0142	7.0	1415	7.0	1127	9.6	2350	9.6	0730	13.1	1951	13.2	0625	7.6	1848	7.5	0018	3.3	1248	3.3	0228	5.6	1454	5.6	1136	4.1	2355	4.1
26	Sa	0233	7.2	1501	7.0	1218	9.5	—	—	0819	12.8	2039	12.9	0710	7.6	1940	7.6	0103	3.4	1339	3.3	0317	5.5	1547	5.6	—	—	1226	4.2
27	Su	0324	7.3	1549	7.0	0039	9.3	1307	9.3	0908	12.7	2125	12.5	0757	7.5	2030	7.6	0148	3.5	1430	3.2	0407	5.4	1640	5.4	0046	4.2	1322	3.9
28	M	0414	7.3	1637	6.9	0127	8.9	1359	8.9	0956	12.1	2213	11.8	0842	7.4	2122	7.4	0231	3.6	1520	3.2	0501	5.4	1735	5.1	0140	4.1	1418	3.8
29	Tu	0506	7.2	1725	6.7	0218	8.6	1451	8.6	1042	11.5	2259	11.2	0929	7.2	2214	7.2	0314	3.6	1610	3.1	0555	5.3	1829	5.0	0238	4.0	1518	3.6
30	W	0557	6.9	1812	6.4	0311	8.1	1546	8.1	1130	10.9	2349	10.5	1019	6.8	2312	6.8	0358	3.5	1701	3.0	0651	5.0	1927	4.9	0338	3.9	1625	3.4
31	Th	0649	6.6	1903	6.2	0407	8.2	1647	7.7	—	—	1219	10.5	1112	6.5	—	—	0445	3.4	1757	2.9	0750	4.8	2026	4.7	0443	3.7	1738	3.3

* All times shown are Greenwich Mean Time.   †Difference of height in metres from Ordnance Datum (Newlyn).   ‡Difference of height in metres from Ordnance Datum (Dublin).

JUNE, 1990

High Water at the undermentioned Places (G.M.T.*)—

Day of Month	Day of Week	LONDON BRIDGE †Datum of Predictions 3·20 m. below				LIVERPOOL †Datum of Predictions 4·93 m. below				AVONMOUTH †Datum of Predictions 6·50 m. below				HULL (Albert Dock) †Datum of Predictions 3·90 m. below				GREENOCK †Datum of Predictions 1·62 m. below				LEITH †Datum of Predictions 2·90 m. below				DUN LAOGHAIRE ‡Datum of Predictions 0·20 m. above			
		Mn.	Ht.	Aft.	Ht.	Mn.	Ht.	Aft.	Ht.	Mn.	Ht.	Aft.	Ht.	Mn.	Ht.	Aft.	Ht.	Mn.	Ht.	Aft.	Ht.	Mn.	Ht.	Aft.	Ht.	Mn.	Ht.	Aft.	Ht.
1	F	0744	6·3	1959	6·0	0508	7·9	1751	7·5	0041	10·6	1314	10·3	0017	5·9	1215	6·3	0537	3·3	1906	2·8	0851	4·7	2130	4·6	0555	3·6	1848	3·3
2	Sa	0846	6·1	2105	5·9	0614	7·7	1856	7·5	0140	10·6	1416	10·4	0128	5·8	1328	6·2	0644	3·1	2018	2·9	0956	4·6	2231	4·6	0703	3·6	1948	3·4
3	Su	0957	6·1	2221	6·0	0719	7·7	1955	7·7	0243	10·7	1521	10·7	0233	5·9	1440	6·2	0808	3·0	2118	2·9	1058	4·7	2327	4·7	0803	3·6	2040	3·4
4	M	1104	6·2	2326	6·2	0816	8·0	2046	8·0	0349	11·0	1623	11·1	0327	6·1	1538	6·4	0918	2·9	2209	2·9	1154	4·8	----	--	0855	3·6	2121	3·5
5	Tu	1157	6·4	----	--	0905	8·2	2128	8·2	0448	11·3	1718	11·5	0413	6·3	1627	6·5	1011	2·9	2254	2·9	0014	4·8	1240	4·8	0939	3·6	2156	3·6
6	W	0017	6·3	1241	6·3	0949	8·3	2207	8·3	0539	11·6	1803	11·9	0454	6·4	1711	6·6	1056	2·9	2336	3·0	0056	4·9	1323	4·9	1018	3·6	2228	3·7
7	Th	0059	6·4	1316	6·4	1028	8·3	2244	8·4	0622	11·8	1845	12·1	0530	6·6	1751	6·6	1137	2·8	----	--	0135	5·0	1403	5·0	1053	3·6	2259	3·8
8	F	0135	6·5	1349	6·5	1105	8·5	2320	8·6	0702	11·9	1921	12·1	0604	6·7	1829	6·6	0013	2·8	1216	2·8	0211	5·0	1442	5·1	1128	3·5	2333	3·8
9	Sa	0211	6·5	1422	6·7	1140	8·5	2356	8·7	0738	11·9	1955	12·0	0636	6·8	1904	6·6	0048	3·0	1254	2·8	0246	5·0	1519	5·1	----	--	1204	3·5
10	Su	0246	6·6	1457	6·7	----	--	1215	8·5	0812	11·8	2027	11·9	0709	6·8	1940	6·6	0121	3·0	1332	2·8	0321	5·1	1556	5·1	0008	3·8	1240	3·5
11	M	0324	6·6	1534	6·7	0031	8·8	1252	8·4	0846	11·7	2101	11·7	0744	6·7	2016	6·5	0154	3·1	1412	2·9	0357	5·1	1634	5·0	0044	3·8	1318	3·5
12	Tu	0402	6·7	1610	6·7	0107	8·7	1328	8·3	0919	11·6	2136	11·6	0820	6·7	2056	6·5	0229	3·2	1453	2·9	0435	5·0	1713	5·0	0125	3·8	1401	3·5
13	W	0441	6·7	1645	6·7	0147	8·6	1409	8·2	0956	11·5	2214	11·5	0858	6·7	2136	6·4	0305	3·2	1534	3·0	0516	5·0	1757	4·8	0207	3·8	1446	3·4
14	Th	0519	6·6	1722	6·6	0229	8·5	1453	8·1	1035	11·4	2258	11·4	0939	6·6	2221	6·3	0344	3·2	1618	3·0	0601	4·9	1842	4·7	0252	3·8	1535	3·4
15	F	0601	6·5	1803	6·5	0315	8·3	1543	7·9	1119	11·2	2346	11·2	1026	6·5	2312	6·2	0427	3·2	1706	3·0	0650	4·9	1934	4·6	0342	3·8	1631	3·4
16	Sa	0649	6·3	1852	6·3	0407	8·2	1642	7·8	----	--	1211	11·0	1119	6·5	----	--	0515	3·1	1801	3·0	0742	4·8	2029	4·6	0436	3·7	1731	3·4
17	Su	0748	6·2	1954	6·1	0508	8·2	1747	7·8	0043	11·1	1313	10·9	0011	6·1	1222	6·4	0614	3·0	1904	3·0	0841	4·8	2128	4·7	0539	3·7	1837	3·5
18	M	0900	6·2	2112	6·1	0614	8·2	1856	8·0	0155	11·1	1432	11·0	0119	6·1	1333	6·5	0728	3·0	2013	3·0	0942	4·9	2231	4·8	0645	3·7	1939	3·6
19	Tu	1013	6·3	2227	6·3	0723	8·4	2002	8·3	0311	11·3	1546	11·4	0226	6·3	1440	6·7	0843	3·0	2103	3·1	1048	5·0	2331	4·9	0751	3·7	2032	3·7
20	W	1119	6·5	2336	6·5	0827	8·6	2103	8·6	0420	11·7	1652	12·1	0331	6·5	1546	6·9	0947	3·1	2213	3·1	1154	5·1	----	--	0848	3·8	2124	3·8
21	Th	----	--	1219	6·6	0928	8·9	2157	9·0	0525	12·1	1753	12·4	0431	6·8	1652	7·1	1048	3·2	2307	3·2	0029	5·1	1256	5·3	0944	3·9	2209	4·0
22	F	0038	6·6	1314	6·6	1026	9·3	2251	9·3	0625	12·5	1849	12·7	0526	7·0	1751	7·2	1143	3·2	2358	3·3	0127	5·3	1354	5·5	1036	3·9	2256	4·1
23	Sa	0134	6·7	1404	6·7	1119	9·3	2342	9·5	0721	12·9	1941	12·9	0615	7·2	1846	7·3	1239	3·2	----	--	0214	5·4	1448	5·6	1127	3·9	2345	4·2
24	Su	0227	6·9	1451	6·9	----	--	1210	9·3	0812	12·8	2029	13·0	0700	7·3	1935	7·3	0046	3·5	1333	3·2	0307	5·5	1540	5·6	----	--	1219	3·9
25	M	0317	7·2	1538	7·2	0031	9·5	1259	9·2	0858	12·7	2114	12·9	0745	7·4	2023	7·4	0133	3·7	1424	3·3	0356	5·6	1629	5·6	0035	4·2	1311	3·8
26	Tu	0404	7·3	1623	7·3	0117	9·4	1345	9·0	0942	12·5	2157	12·5	0827	7·4	2108	7·3	0217	3·7	1510	3·5	0446	5·6	1718	5·2	0128	4·2	1403	3·8
27	W	0451	7·3	1706	7·1	0202	9·2	1430	8·7	1024	12·1	2238	12·1	0910	7·3	2152	7·1	0300	3·7	1553	3·7	0535	5·3	1807	5·2	0220	4·1	1457	3·7
28	Th	0536	7·1	1747	6·9	0246	8·9	1514	8·3	1105	11·6	2319	11·7	0953	7·1	2237	7·0	0341	3·6	1635	3·7	0625	5·1	1855	4·9	0313	4·0	1552	3·6
29	F	0621	6·7	1831	6·7	0331	8·5	1602	7·9	1144	11·3	----	--	1037	6·9	2323	6·5	0424	3·6	1719	3·1	0715	5·1	1945	4·9	0410	4·0	1652	3·4
30	Sa	0706	6·4	1919	6·2	0420	8·1	1652	7·6	0001	11·3	1228	10·8	1127	6·5	----	--	0509	3·4	1809	2·9	0807	4·7	2037	4·6	0510	3·6	1756	3·3

* All times shown are Greenwich Mean Time.   † Difference of height in metres from Ordnance Datum (Newlyn).   ‡ Difference of height in metres from Ordnance Datum (Dublin).

JULY, 1990

High Water at the undermentioned Places (G.M.T.*)—

Day of Month	Day of Week	London Bridge †Datum 3·20 m. below Mn.	Ht.	Aft.	Ht.	Liverpool †Datum 4·93 m. below Mn.	Ht.	Aft.	Ht.	Avonmouth †Datum 6·50 m. below Mn.	Ht.	Aft.	Ht.	Hull (Albert Dock) †Datum 3·90 m. below Mn.	Ht.	Aft.	Ht.	Greenock †Datum 1·62 m. below Mn.	Ht.	Aft.	Ht.	Leith †Datum 2·90 m. below Mn.	Ht.	Aft.	Ht.	Dun Laoghaire ‡Datum 0·20 m. above Mn.	Ht.	Aft.	Ht.
1	Su	0758	6·1	2016	5·9	0515	7·7	1753	7·4	0049	10·9	1320	10·5	0017	5·9	1229	6·2	0601	3·1	1909	2·8	0901	4·6	2133	4·5	0616	3·5	1859	3·3
2	M	0857	5·9	2122	5·8	0618	7·4	1900	7·5	0145	10·6	1422	10·4	0120	5·8	1341	6·0	0704	2·9	2020	2·8	1010	4·5	2232	4·5	0720	3·4	1956	3·3
3	Tu	1002	5·9	2233	5·8	0728	7·3	2004	7·5	0250	10·5	1529	10·4	0226	5·8	1454	5·9	0819	2·7	2126	2·8	1105	4·5	2331	4·5	0820	3·4	2044	3·4
4	W	1106	5·9	2339	5·9	0830	7·5	2058	7·8	0359	10·6	1638	10·8	0328	6·0	1559	6·0	0929	2·7	2223	2·9	—	—	1205	4·5	0909	3·4	2126	3·5
5	Th	—	—	1201	6·1	0924	7·8	2145	8·2	0505	10·9	1734	11·2	0421	6·2	1652	6·2	1026	2·7	2310	3·0	0023	4·6	1258	4·6	0953	3·4	2203	3·6
6	F	0031	6·0	1245	6·1	1009	8·0	2226	8·5	0558	11·2	1822	11·6	0506	6·4	1737	6·3	1116	2·8	2352	3·0	0110	4·8	1348	4·8	1033	3·5	2239	3·7
7	Sa	0113	6·2	1326	6·3	1049	8·3	2304	8·5	0643	11·5	1902	11·8	0546	6·6	1817	6·5	1201	2·8	—	—	0153	4·9	1428	4·9	1109	3·5	2313	3·8
8	Su	0154	6·4	1406	6·5	1126	8·5	2342	8·9	0721	11·7	1938	12·0	0621	6·8	1852	6·6	0031	3·1	1244	2·8	0231	5·1	1508	5·1	1145	3·6	2348	3·9
9	M	0233	6·6	1446	6·7	—	—	1203	8·7	0758	11·8	2013	12·1	0655	6·8	1927	6·8	0107	3·2	1325	3·0	0307	5·2	1544	5·2	—	—	1222	3·6
10	Tu	0311	6·8	1524	6·8	0018	9·0	1238	8·7	0833	12·0	2049	12·3	0730	7·1	2004	6·9	0144	3·3	1404	3·1	0342	5·3	1618	5·3	0026	4·0	1258	3·6
11	W	0349	6·8	1559	6·9	0055	9·1	1316	8·7	0908	12·1	2125	12·5	0806	7·2	2040	6·9	0220	3·4	1443	3·2	0417	5·3	1655	5·3	0104	4·0	1339	3·7
12	Th	0427	6·9	1633	6·8	0133	9·1	1352	8·5	0945	12·4	2203	12·5	0843	7·2	2118	6·9	0256	3·4	1522	3·3	0457	5·2	1734	5·1	0144	4·0	1420	3·7
13	F	0504	6·8	1706	6·7	0211	9·0	1433	8·3	1021	12·4	2242	12·5	0922	7·2	2159	6·8	0333	3·4	1602	3·4	0539	5·2	1818	5·0	0227	4·0	1504	3·6
14	Sa	0542	6·6	1742	6·6	0251	8·8	1515	8·1	1101	12·0	2325	11·9	1003	6·9	2242	6·6	0412	3·4	1644	3·4	0625	5·2	1903	4·9	0313	4·0	1554	3·6
15	Su	0624	6·5	1824	6·4	0338	8·4	1606	7·9	1144	11·5	—	—	1049	6·8	2333	6·5	0454	3·3	1732	3·3	0713	5·0	1954	4·8	0404	3·9	1653	3·5
16	M	0714	6·2	1919	6·2	0431	8·1	1708	7·8	0014	11·0	1238	11·1	1147	6·6	—	—	0545	3·2	1826	3·3	0808	5·0	2052	4·7	0504	3·8	1759	3·5
17	Tu	0820	6·2	2036	6·1	0539	8·1	1822	8·1	0119	10·6	1355	10·7	0036	6·4	1238	6·4	0648	3·1	1929	3·0	0911	4·8	2159	4·7	0616	3·6	1908	3·6
18	W	0938	6·1	2159	6·2	0657	8·0	1940	8·3	0243	10·7	1519	10·9	0152	6·1	1418	6·4	0805	3·0	2039	3·0	1027	4·8	2311	4·8	0730	3·6	2011	3·8
19	Th	1054	6·2	2320	6·5	0813	8·2	2050	8·9	0402	11·2	1634	11·2	0310	6·3	1542	6·5	0924	3·0	2147	3·1	1145	4·9	—	—	0840	3·7	2109	3·9
20	F	—	—	1204	6·5	0922	8·9	2152	9·2	0515	11·4	1743	11·9	0420	6·3	1654	6·9	1036	3·1	2250	3·2	0018	5·1	1254	5·1	0939	3·7	2202	4·1
21	Sa	0032	6·5	1304	6·7	1021	9·2	2245	9·5	0619	12·0	1842	12·4	0518	6·9	1751	7·1	1140	3·1	2345	3·4	0119	5·3	1353	5·3	1035	3·8	2250	4·2
22	Su	0131	6·7	1355	6·9	1113	9·6	2333	9·3	0714	12·5	1931	12·9	0604	7·2	1841	7·2	1236	3·5	—	—	0212	5·5	1445	5·4	1123	3·9	2337	4·2
23	M	0222	6·9	1442	7·0	0018	9·3	1242	9·4	0801	13·0	2016	13·2	0648	7·4	1924	7·3	0034	3·5	1325	3·3	0259	5·6	1531	5·5	—	—	1211	3·9
24	Tu	0307	7·0	1524	7·3	0059	9·4	1323	9·3	0843	13·0	2057	13·2	0727	7·6	2005	7·3	0119	3·7	1409	3·4	0343	5·4	1614	5·6	0025	4·3	1256	3·9
25	W	0349	7·3	1603	7·0	0138	9·1	1359	8·9	0921	12·9	2135	13·1	0806	7·6	2043	7·2	0201	3·8	1449	3·5	0427	5·6	1655	5·6	0110	4·3	1340	3·8
26	Th	0430	7·0	1641	7·0	0215	8·7	1436	8·5	0957	12·7	2210	12·7	0844	7·6	2121	6·9	0241	3·8	1526	3·5	0510	5·2	1738	5·5	0157	4·2	1424	3·7
27	F	0508	6·7	1716	6·7	0251	8·2	1514	8·2	1033	12·2	2244	12·3	0922	7·4	2157	6·7	0319	3·6	1602	3·6	0554	5·2	1819	5·2	0243	4·1	1511	3·6
28	Sa	0546	6·3	1754	6·3	0331	7·7	1556	7·7	1105	11·7	2318	11·7	1002	7·0	2234	6·4	0356	3·4	1638	3·4	0637	5·0	1902	5·0	0331	3·9	1600	3·4
29	Su	0624	6·1	1835	6·1	0417	7·6	1649	7·6	1140	11·1	2357	11·1	1044	6·6	2316	6·1	0435	3·1	1718	3·2	0721	4·7	1946	4·7	0421	3·6	1655	3·3
30	M	0707	5·8	1927	5·8	0518	7·6	1758	7·1	—	—	1222	10·5	1134	6·1	—	—	0517	3·0	1804	3·0	0808	4·5	2035	4·4	0521	3·4	1757	3·2
31	Tu	0759	5·6	2030	5·6	0615	7·1	1850	7·1	0045	9·9	1320	10·3	0011	5·8	1245	5·7	0607	2·8	1903	2·7	0903	4·3	2134	4·3	0631	3·2	1905	3·2

*All times shown are Greenwich Mean Time.   †Difference of height in metres from Ordnance Datum (Newlyn).   ‡Difference of height in metres from Ordnance Datum (Dublin).

AUGUST, 1990

High Water at the undermentioned Places (G.M.T.*)—

Day of Month	Day of Week	London Bridge †Datum 3·20 m. below Mn. h.m.	Ht.	Aft. h.m.	Ht.	Liverpool †Datum 4·93 m. below Mn. h.m.	Ht.	Aft. h.m.	Ht.	Avonmouth †Datum 6·50 m. below Mn. h.m.	Ht.	Aft. h.m.	Ht.	Hull (Albert Dock) †Datum 3·90 m. below Mn. h.m.	Ht.	Aft. h.m.	Ht.	Greenock †Datum 1·62 m. below Mn. h.m.	Ht.	Aft. h.m.	Ht.	Leith †Datum 2·90 m. below Mn. h.m.	Ht.	Aft. h.m.	Ht.	Dun Laoghaire ‡Datum 0·20 m. above Mn. h.m.	Ht.	Aft. h.m.	Ht.
1	W	0900	5·6	2138	5·5	0638	6·9	1921	7·1	0151	9·8	1439	9·6	0121	5·7	1408	5·5	0709	2·6	2026	2·6	1015	4·3	2245	4·3	0741	3·2	2004	3·3
2	Th	1004	5·6	2257	5·5	0802	7·1	2032	7·5	0314	9·9	1604	9·9	0237	5·6	1532	5·6	0830	2·6	2151	2·7	1132	4·3	2354	4·4	0841	3·4	2054	3·5
3	F	1118	5·7	—	—	0905	7·5	2124	8·0	0437	10·1	1712	10·6	0348	6·0	1635	6·0	0959	2·6	2249	2·9	—	—	1237	4·5	0930	3·4	2137	3·6
4	Sa	0005	6·0	1219	5·8	0952	8·1	2207	8·5	0537	10·7	1800	11·3	0442	6·3	1722	6·5	1100	2·7	2334	3·0	0049	4·6	1328	4·7	1011	3·5	2215	3·8
5	Su	0052	6·3	1306	6·1	1033	8·3	2247	8·8	0621	11·3	1841	11·8	0525	6·6	1800	7·0	1147	2·9	—	—	0134	4·9	1412	4·9	1049	3·6	2252	3·9
6	M	0134	6·7	1348	6·5	1108	8·6	2322	9·0	0700	11·8	1917	12·4	0601	6·9	1835	7·0	0013	3·0	1229	3·0	0213	5·1	1452	5·1	1123	3·7	2326	4·1
7	Tu	0213	7·0	1426	6·8	1143	8·7	2358	9·2	0737	12·4	1954	12·7	0635	7·1	1907	7·2	0051	3·3	1308	3·2	0247	5·3	1523	5·2	1158	3·8	—	—
8	W	0251	7·2	1503	7·1	0035	9·5	1218	9·1	0813	12·6	2030	13·1	0710	7·4	1941	7·2	0127	3·5	1346	3·3	0321	5·5	1556	5·3	0002	4·2	1233	3·9
9	Th	0328	7·2	1538	7·2	0110	9·5	1255	9·5	0849	13·0	2107	13·3	0744	7·6	2016	7·2	0202	3·6	1424	3·4	0356	5·6	1630	5·4	0039	4·2	1310	3·9
10	F	0404	7·1	1612	7·2	0147	9·4	1330	9·5	0925	13·1	2143	13·3	0820	7·6	2053	7·2	0237	3·6	1501	3·4	0434	5·6	1709	5·4	0118	4·3	1350	3·9
11	Sa	0440	6·8	1644	7·1	0226	9·2	1408	9·2	1002	12·9	2221	12·8	0858	7·5	2131	6·7	0313	3·6	1538	3·3	0517	5·5	1751	5·3	0200	4·3	1433	3·8
12	Su	0518	6·7	1720	7·0	0310	8·8	1449	8·9	1038	12·3	2301	12·1	0938	7·3	2212	6·4	0350	3·6	1618	3·3	0602	5·3	1838	5·2	0246	4·1	1521	3·7
13	M	0557	6·4	1801	6·8	0403	8·3	1535	8·3	1118	11·6	2347	11·5	1024	6·9	2301	6·9	0431	3·4	1702	3·1	0649	5·2	1927	5·0	0339	3·7	1618	3·6
14	Tu	0645	6·1	1855	6·6	0516	7·8	1637	7·8	—	—	1205	10·7	1122	6·5	—	—	0519	3·2	1751	3·0	0746	4·9	2027	4·8	0442	3·5	1728	3·5
15	W	0748	5·9	2015	6·3	0646	7·5	1801	7·5	0050	10·3	1327	10·0	0004	6·1	1238	6·1	0620	2·9	1851	2·9	0855	4·7	2141	4·6	0559	3·5	1847	3·6
16	Th	0910	5·9	2145	6·0	0813	7·6	1931	7·6	0223	10·0	1501	10·1	0130	6·1	1416	6·3	0742	2·9	2006	2·9	1022	4·7	2306	4·7	0723	3·7	2000	3·8
17	F	1034	6·0	2313	6·0	0922	7·8	2047	7·9	0352	10·1	1627	10·8	0303	6·1	1549	6·9	0924	3·0	2132	3·0	1147	4·8	—	—	0840	3·7	2102	4·0
18	Sa	1151	6·3	—	—	1016	7·9	2146	8·2	0512	11·1	1737	11·7	0414	6·9	1655	7·0	1041	3·3	2241	3·3	0017	4·9	1253	4·9	0942	3·8	2158	4·2
19	Su	0027	6·6	1253	6·2	1101	8·4	2235	8·9	0612	12·1	1832	12·5	0506	7·3	1746	7·3	1138	3·3	2335	3·5	0115	5·2	1348	5·2	1033	3·9	2244	4·3
20	M	0123	6·8	1342	6·6	1142	9·2	2319	9·3	0700	12·7	1917	13·0	0550	7·6	1827	7·3	1226	3·6	—	—	0205	5·4	1435	5·4	1116	3·9	—	—
21	Tu	0209	7·0	1425	6·8	—	—	2357	9·7	0742	13·3	1957	13·5	0628	7·8	1904	7·4	0020	3·7	1308	3·4	0246	5·6	1515	5·6	0008	4·3	1232	3·9
22	W	0250	7·1	1503	7·0	0034	9·6	1218	9·4	0819	13·3	2033	13·1	0704	7·8	1938	7·8	0102	3·8	1346	3·7	0324	5·7	1553	5·6	0049	4·3	1310	3·9
23	Th	0328	7·2	1539	7·1	0107	9·4	1253	9·2	0854	13·1	2107	13·5	0741	7·8	2012	7·3	0140	3·8	1454	3·8	0403	5·6	1629	5·4	0129	4·1	1347	3·8
24	F	0403	7·3	1612	7·2	0140	9·1	1326	8·8	0928	13·1	2139	13·1	0817	7·4	2046	6·9	0216	3·8	1527	3·4	0440	5·3	1705	5·3	0208	4·1	1427	3·7
25	Sa	0435	7·3	1642	7·2	0212	8·7	1358	8·3	0957	12·0	2209	11·9	0851	7·4	2118	6·6	0251	3·5	1558	3·3	0519	5·3	1741	5·0	0250	3·8	1508	3·6
26	Su	0506	7·0	1716	7·1	0247	8·2	1430	8·0	1027	11·2	2238	10·9	0927	7·4	2149	6·2	0324	3·3	1631	3·2	0558	5·0	1819	4·8	0335	3·6	1556	3·4
27	M	0539	6·7	1754	6·9	0327	7·9	1507	7·7	1055	10·3	2309	10·0	1003	6·5	2224	5·8	0358	3·0	1707	3·0	0637	4·7	1857	4·5	0428	3·3	1653	3·3
28	Tu	0617	6·5	1841	6·7	0420	7·6	1555	7·4	1126	10·3	2347	9·8	1045	5·9	2306	5·5	0434	2·8	1753	2·7	0721	4·5	1942	4·3	0535	3·3	1804	3·3
29	W	0703	6·2	1938	6·0	0546	7·4	1701	7·0	—	—	1210	9·4	1146	5·4	—	—	0518	2·8	1858	2·6	0816	4·3	2041	4·2	0635	3·3	1919	3·2
30	Th	0801	5·8	2050	5·6	0733	6·9	1836	6·6	0041	9·1	1327	9·1	0019	5·4	1326	5·2	0613	2·6	2012	2·7	0932	4·2	2159	4·2	0658	3·1	2018	3·5
31	F	0912	5·5	2213	5·3	—	—	2002	6·8	0216	8·7	1529	8·7	0151	5·5	1501	5·4	0727	2·5	2108	2·7	1059	4·2	2320	4·3	0810	3·2	2108	3·5

* All times shown are Greenwich Mean Time.   †Difference of height in metres from Ordnance Datum (Newlyn).   ‡Difference of height in metres from Ordnance Datum (Dublin).

SEPTEMBER, 1990

High Water at the undermentioned Places (G.M.T.*)—

Day of Month	Day of Week	London Bridge †Datum 3.20 m. below Mn.	Ht.	Aft.	Ht.	Liverpool †Datum 4.93 m. below Mn.	Ht.	Aft.	Ht.	Avonmouth †Datum 6.50 m. below Mn.	Ht.	Aft.	Ht.	Hull (Albert Dock) †Datum 3.90 m. below Mn.	Ht.	Aft.	Ht.	Greenock †Datum 1.62 m. below Mn.	Ht.	Aft.	Ht.	Leith †Datum 2.90 m. below Mn.	Ht.	Aft.	Ht.	Dun Laoghaire ‡Datum 0.20 m. above Mn.	Ht.	Aft.	Ht.
1	Sa	1037	5.4	2334	5.6	0842	7.9	2058	7.9	0404	9.3	1641	10.1	0311	5.8	1612	5.8	0933	2.6	2223	2.9	0021		1209	4.4	0902	3.4	2107	3.7
2	Su	1151	5.8	—	—	0928	8.5	2142	8.4	0505	10.3	1729	11.1	0412	6.2	1658	6.3	1039	2.8	2308	3.2	0109	4.6	1302	4.7	0944	3.6	2146	3.9
3	M	0025	6.1	1239	6.3	1007	9.0	2220	8.9	0551	11.3	1810	12.0	0457	6.7	1734	6.7	1123	3.0	2348	3.4	0147	4.9	1346	5.0	1021	3.8	2223	4.1
4	Tu	0106	6.6	1320	6.8	1042	9.2	2255	9.2	0632	12.1	1849	12.7	0533	7.1	1808	7.1	0025	3.5	1204	3.4	0222	5.2	1422	5.3	1055	4.0	2258	4.2
5	W	0147	7.0	1359	7.1	1116	9.4	2332	9.4	0710	12.7	1928	13.2	0608	7.4	1841	7.3	0101	3.6	1242	3.4	0255	5.5	1455	5.5	1128	4.1	2334	4.4
6	Th	0225	7.3	1434	7.4	1151	9.4	—	—	0748	13.2	2006	13.6	0643	7.7	1914	7.5	0136	3.7	1320	3.4	0330	5.7	1529	5.6	—	—	1204	4.1
7	F	0301	7.4	1510	7.5	0045	9.5	1228	9.5	0826	13.6	2044	13.6	0719	7.8	1949	7.6	0212	3.7	1358	3.5	0409	5.8	1604	5.6	0011	4.4	1240	4.1
8	Sa	0338	7.3	1545	7.4	0123	9.7	1304	9.7	0903	13.6	2122	13.6	0755	7.8	2025	7.7	0249	3.7	1435	3.5	0450	5.8	1644	5.5	0051	4.4	1320	4.1
9	Su	0414	7.1	1621	7.2	0204	9.8	1342	9.7	0939	13.5	2202	13.3	0834	7.8	2103	7.8	0328	3.6	1512	3.5	0541	5.7	1728	5.3	0136	4.4	1404	4.1
10	M	0454	6.7	1702	6.9	0250	9.7	1425	9.4	1017	13.1	2242	12.9	0918	7.4	2145	7.8	0411	3.4	1551	3.5	0634	5.5	1816	5.1	0224	4.2	1454	3.9
11	Tu	0534	6.3	1749	6.5	0348	8.8	1514	8.8	1058	12.4	2332	11.9	1007	6.9	2235	7.4	0501	3.2	1634	3.4	0737	5.2	1909	4.8	0320	4.0	1553	3.7
12	W	0624	6.0	1849	6.2	0508	8.1	1620	8.1	1151	11.4	—	—	1109	6.4	2342	6.9	0604	2.9	1721	3.3	0854	4.9	2015	4.6	0428	3.7	1706	3.6
13	Th	0730	5.7	2009	5.9	0646	7.4	1753	7.7	0042	9.8	1316	9.7	0117	5.8	1235	6.4	0742	2.8	1819	3.1	1024	4.6	2136	4.5	0552	3.5	1831	3.7
14	F	0851	5.7	2136	6.0	0812	7.4	1926	7.8	0212	9.6	1450	9.9	0254	6.1	1427	6.0	0935	2.9	1939	3.1	1144	4.9	—	—	0723	3.5	1951	3.9
15	Sa	1017	5.9	2304	6.3	1000	8.4	2039	8.4	0343	10.1	1619	10.8	0400	6.6	1548	5.9	1037	3.3	2123	3.2	0104	5.2	1245	5.1	0840	3.6	2054	4.1
16	Su	1136	6.4	—	—	1041	8.9	2134	8.9	0501	11.2	1725	11.9	0449	7.0	1645	6.5	1124	3.4	2229	3.4	0149	5.5	1334	5.4	0937	3.8	2148	4.2
17	M	0012	6.8	1235	6.8	1118	9.2	2217	9.2	0556	12.2	1814	12.7	0529	7.3	1729	6.7	—	—	1205	3.6	0227	5.6	1416	5.5	1022	3.9	2232	4.3
18	Tu	0106	7.1	1323	7.1	1150	9.3	2257	9.3	0639	12.8	1855	13.2	0604	7.6	1805	7.0	0038	3.7	1242	3.4	0302	5.6	1452	5.4	1059	4.0	2310	4.3
19	W	0149	7.3	1404	7.2	0005	9.3	1221	9.3	0717	13.2	1931	13.4	0639	7.7	1838	7.3	0114	3.7	1317	3.4	0335	5.6	1525	5.5	1133	4.0	2347	4.0
20	Th	0227	7.3	1439	7.2	0036	9.5	1252	9.5	0752	13.4	2005	13.5	0714	7.6	1909	7.6	0148	3.6	1351	3.4	0408	5.6	1558	5.4	—	—	1205	4.0
21	F	0301	7.3	1511	7.2	0107	9.4	1321	9.4	0825	13.3	2037	13.5	0749	7.6	1941	7.7	0220	3.5	1422	3.3	0444	5.0	1630	5.0	0023	4.3	1236	3.9
22	Sa	0332	7.1	1541	7.0	0137	9.0	1352	9.0	0856	13.3	2107	12.5	0823	7.5	2011	7.7	0251	3.3	1452	3.3	0520	4.7	1703	4.8	0058	4.0	1310	3.8
23	Su	0400	6.9	1610	6.9	0209	8.6	1427	8.6	0925	12.5	2135	11.7	0856	7.0	2040	7.2	0322	3.0	1520	3.3	0600	4.4	1737	4.6	0135	3.8	1346	3.7
24	M	0427	6.7	1642	6.7	0246	8.2	1510	8.2	0950	11.7	2202	10.7	0928	6.3	2110	7.2	0357	2.8	1548	3.1	0645	4.1	1815	4.4	0213	3.5	1424	3.5
25	Tu	0458	6.5	1719	6.4	0335	7.6	1610	7.6	1016	11.1	2230	9.8	1004	5.8	2139	6.8	0440	2.6	1621	3.0	0741	4.2	1859	4.2	0254	3.3	1508	3.5
26	W	0533	6.3	1803	6.1	0454	7.1	1743	7.2	1041	10.2	2301	9.0	1054	5.4	2214	6.3	0534	2.7	1702	2.9	0855	4.4	2000	4.3	0343	3.2	1601	3.4
27	Th	0615	5.9	1853	5.8	0645	6.6	1916	7.2	1113	9.3	2347	8.7	—	—	2311	5.8	0646		1759	2.8	1018		2116	4.6	0446	3.1	1709	3.3
28	F	0706	5.6	1959	5.5	0802	6.7	2018	7.8	—	—	1217	8.7	0102	5.4	1238	5.4	0853		1942	2.7	1130		2234		0610	3.1	1826	3.4
29	Sa	0815	5.3	2125	5.3					0102	8.5	1419	8.7	0226	5.7	1415	5.4			2143	3.0			2340		0729	3.2	1934	3.5
30	Su	0950	5.3	2248	5.6					0307	9.3	1552	9.7			1529	5.8									0827	3.5	2028	3.7

*All times shown are Greenwich Mean Time.   †Difference of height in metres from Ordnance Datum (Newlyn).
   ‡Difference of height in metres from Ordnance Datum (Dublin).

OCTOBER, 1990

High Water at the undermentioned Places (G.M.T.*)—

Datum of Predictions (Difference of height in metres from Ordnance Datum): London Bridge 3·20 m. below; Liverpool 4·93 m. below; Avonmouth 6·50 m. below; Hull (Albert Dock) 3·90 m. below; Greenock 1·62 m. below; Leith 2·90 m. below; Dun Laoghaire 0·20 m. above.

(Mn. = morning; Aft. = afternoon; Ht. in metres.)

Day	Wk	LB Mn	LB Ht	LB Aft	Liv Mn	Liv Ht	Liv Aft	Avon Mn	Avon Ht	Avon Aft	Avon Ht	Hull Mn	Hull Ht	Hull Aft	Hull Ht	Green Mn	Green Ht	Green Aft	Green Ht	Leith Mn	Leith Ht	Leith Aft	Leith Ht	DunL Mn	DunL Ht	DunL Aft	DunL Ht
1	M	1109	5·8	2347	0851	7·9	2104	0419	10·1	1647	11·0	0329	6·2	1620	6·3	1005	3·0	2233	3·2	0030	4·9	1224	4·7	0911	3·7	2112	4·0
2	Tu	0034	6·7	1203	0931	8·5	2145	0511	11·3	1733	12·1	0419	6·7	1659	6·8	1051	3·2	2313	3·4	0112	5·3	1310	5·1	0949	3·9	2151	4·2
3	W	0116	7·1	1246	1009	9·0	2223	0557	12·3	1818	13·0	0459	7·2	1736	7·1	1132	3·4	2352	3·6	0149	5·6	1348	5·3	1023	4·1	2228	4·4
4	Th	0155	7·3	1327	1045	9·4	2301	0641	13·1	1900	13·6	0537	7·5	1810	7·4			1212	3·5	0226	5·8	1423	5·6	1058	4·2	2305	4·5
5	F	0233	7·4	1405	1123	9·7	2340	0721	13·5	1942	13·9	0615	7·8	1846	7·6	0029	3·7	1251	3·6	0304	5·9	1458	5·7	1133	4·3	2345	4·5
6	Sa	0311	7·4	1443			1201	0802	13·7	2023	13·9	0653	7·9	1923	7·6	0107	3·7	1330	3·6	0347	5·7	1537	5·7			1211	4·3
7	Su	0352	7·2	1522	0021	10·0	1241	0842	13·7	2104	13·5	0734	7·9	2001	7·5	0146	3·7	1408	3·6	0435	5·5	1620	5·6	0028	4·5	1253	4·3
8	M	0434	6·8	1604	0103	9·5	1323	0922	13·2	2148	12·6	0818	7·7	2042	7·2	0227	3·5	1448	3·7	0527	5·1	1708	5·5	0114	4·3	1340	4·0
9	Tu	0520	6·4	1652	0148	9·3	1408	1004	12·3	2234	11·6	0905	7·3	2127	6·9	0310	3·5	1528	3·6	0625	4·9	1800	5·2	0207	3·9	1435	4·0
10	W	0614	6·0	1747	0239	8·7	1503	1051	11·2	2329	10·6	0959	6·7	2220	6·4	0358	3·3	1610	3·6	0732	4·7	1858	4·7	0307	3·7	1536	3·9
11	Th	0719	5·8	1850	0342	8·0	1613	1151	10·3			1105	6·2	2326	6·1	0452	3·1	1658	3·5	0850	4·7	2006	4·6	0418	3·5	1650	3·7
12	F	0832	6·0	2002	0504	7·5	1742	0038	9·8	1307	9·9			1239	5·9	0600	2·9	1754	3·3	1013	4·9	2126	4·5	0546	3·5	1816	3·8
13	Sa	0953	6·0	2121	0635	7·5	1907	0155	9·7	1430	10·1	0057	5·9	1419	6·2	0751	2·9	1915	3·2	1124		2245	5·0	0716	3·7	1934	4·0
14	Su	1112		2242	0752	7·9	2015	0321	10·3	1555	10·9	0232	6·2	1531	6·6	0922	3·0	2102	3·3			2352	5·3	0825	3·7	2038	4·1
15	M			2350	0850	8·4	2108	0433	11·2	1658	11·9	0336	6·6	1623	6·9	1013	3·2	2206	3·5	0043	5·3	1221	5·4	0919	3·9	2128	4·2
16	Tu	0041	7·2	1211	0935	8·8	2152	0526	12·1	1746	12·6	0426	7·0	1705	7·0	1058	3·4	2253	3·6	0126	5·5	1309	5·4	1002	3·9	2212	4·2
17	W	0124	7·3	1257	1014	9·2	2230	0611	12·7	1828	13·1	0505	7·4	1739	7·2	1137	3·4	2334	3·5	0202	5·5	1349	5·3	1036	4·0	2250	4·2
18	Th	0201	7·2	1338	1049	9·2	2304	0649	13·0	1904	13·1	0540	7·5	1810	7·4			1214	3·4	0236	5·4	1424	5·2	1107	4·0	2324	4·1
19	F	0233	7·1	1413	1120	9·2	2336	0724	13·2	1938	13·2	0615	7·6	1841	7·5	0011	3·6	1249	3·4	0341	5·3	1455	4·9	1137	4·1	2358	4·0
20	Sa	0301	7·1	1444	1151	9·1	2336	0757	13·2	2009	13·1	0650	7·7	1910	7·2	0119	3·5	1322	3·4	0416	5·0	1526	4·7			1206	4·0
21	Su	0327	7·0	1512	0008	9·1	1222	0827	13·6	2039	13·2	0726	7·2	1940	6·9	0151	3·2	1352	3·3	0452	4·7	1557	4·5	0030	4·0	1237	3·9
22	M	0353	6·8	1543	0038	8·5	1252	0856	13·2	2107	12·6	0759	6·6	2008	6·3	0222	3·1	1420	3·2	0532	4·5	1629	4·4	0106	3·8	1313	3·8
23	Tu	0424	6·7	1616	0109	8·5	1324	0922	11·9	2135	12·3	0830	6·3	2036	6·1	0255	3·0	1447	3·1	0613	4·3	1704	4·5	0143	3·7	1352	3·7
24	W	0501	6·6	1654	0141	8·5	1359	0948	11·1	2203	11·4	0904	6·0	2105	5·9	0332	3·0	1516	3·0	0713	4·2	1743	5·0	0224	3·4	1436	3·6
25	Th	0540	6·4	1734	0219	7·7	1440	1013	10·3	2234	10·9	0941	5·9	2142	5·6	0417	2·9	1549	3·0	0818	4·3	1829	5·1	0311	3·2	1524	3·5
26	F	0627	6·1	1821	0305	7·3	1535	1048	9·7	2319	9·9	1028	5·6	2233	5·3	0503	2·8	1630	3·1	0931	4·5	1926		0409	3·2	1624	3·6
27	Sa	0726	5·7	1917	0412	6·9	1651	1146	9·1			1143	5·3	2357	5·3	0622	2·8	1725	3·0	1039	4·5	2033		0520	3·3	1730	3·6
28	Su	0851	5·5	2033	0542	6·9	1814	0024	9·1	1310	9·4			1320	5·7	0803	2·9	1845	2·9	1137	4·8	2143		0637	3·3	1841	3·8
29	M	1016	5·5	2156	0702	6·9	1923	0155	9·9	1451	9·9	0133	5·7	1432	6·1	0921	3·1	2045	3·1			2250		0741	3·5	1943	4·0
30	Tu	1119	5·8	2302	0801	7·8	2018	0325	10·2	1559	10·7	0239	6·1	1529	6·3	1013	3·3	2148	3·3			2345		0831	3·7	2034	4·0
31	W		6·3	2356	0849	8·5	2104	0428	11·4	1655	11·1	0334	6·6	1617	6·7	1137	3·4	2234	3·4			1226		0914	4·0	2118	4·2

*All times shown are Greenwich Mean Time. †Difference of height in metres from Ordnance Datum (Newlyn).
‡Difference of height in metres from Ordnance Datum (Dublin).

NOVEMBER, 1990

High Water at the undermentioned Places (G.M.T.*)—

Datum of Predictions: London Bridge †3·20 m. below; Liverpool †4·93 m. below; Avonmouth †6·50 m. below; Hull (Albert Dock) †3·90 m. below; Greenock †1·62 m. below; Leith †2·90 m. below; Dun Laoghaire ‡0·20 m. above.

Day of Month	Day of Week	LB Mn.	LB Ht.	LB Aft.	LB Ht.	Liv Mn.	Liv Ht.	Liv Aft.	Liv Ht.	Avon Mn.	Avon Ht.	Avon Aft.	Avon Ht.	Hull Mn.	Hull Ht.	Hull Aft.	Hull Ht.	Gk Mn.	Gk Ht.	Gk Aft.	Gk Ht.	Leith Mn.	Leith Ht.	Leith Aft.	Leith Ht.	DL Mn.	DL Ht.	DL Aft.	DL Ht.
1	Th	0043		1210	6·8	0932	9·0	2149	9·5	0522	12·4	1746	13·0	0421	7·1	1659	7·1	1057	3·4	2316	3·6	0032	5·3	1309	5·3	0952	4·1	2159	4·3
2	F	0127	7·0	1255	7·1	1014	9·0	2233	9·8	0611	13·1	1834	13·5	0506	7·4	1740	7·4	1140	3·6	2358	3·6	0115	5·6	1350	5·5	1029	4·3	2240	4·4
3	Sa	0208	7·2	1337	7·3	1057	9·7	2316	10·0	0657	13·5	1920	13·7	0550	7·6	1821	7·5			1222	3·6	0157	5·8	1430	5·7	1106	4·4	2323	4·4
4	Su	0250	7·2	1420	7·5	1140	9·9			0741	13·7	2006	13·8	0635	7·7	1902	7·6	0041	3·6	1303	3·7	0243	5·9	1514	5·7	1148	4·4		
5	M	0335	7·2	1505	7·6	0003	9·9	1224	9·7	0826	13·6	2053	13·6	0721	7·8	1944	7·5	0125	3·6	1344	3·8	0330	5·9	1601	5·7	0009	4·4	1233	4·4
6	Tu	0423	7·1	1556	7·5	0049	9·6	1310	9·6	0911	13·2	2141	12·8	0809	7·8	2027	7·3	0212	3·5	1426	3·8	0421	5·7	1652	5·5	0100	4·2	1323	4·3
7	W	0512	6·9	1648	7·5	0140	9·2	1359	9·4	0957	12·3	2230	11·7	0901	7·2	2115	6·7	0301	3·3	1509	3·8	0518	5·5	1747	5·3	0157	4·1	1420	4·2
8	Th	0605	6·6	1744	6·8	0233	8·7	1456	9·1	1048	11·5	2323	10·9	0956	6·7	2206	6·7	0352	3·3	1552	3·8	0617	5·2	1847	5·1	0259	3·9	1523	4·0
9	F	0703	6·3	1843	6·5	0335	8·1	1602	8·6	1144	10·8			1058	6·3	2306	6·3	0448	3·0	1639	3·7	0719	5·0	1952	4·9	0409	3·7	1633	3·9
10	Sa	0806	6·1	1945	6·3	0447	7·7	1715	8·0	0022	10·3	1246	10·4	0022		1221	6·2	0554	2·8	1734	3·4	0829	4·8	2101	4·8	0528	3·5	1752	3·8
11	Su	0919	6·0	2054	6·2	0604	7·6	1831	8·0	0127	10·1	1357	10·1	0151	6·2	1347	6·3	0723	2·8	1846	3·4	0942	4·8	2213	4·8	0651	3·6	2011	3·9
12	M	1038	6·0	2210	6·3	0716	7·8	1938	8·2	0239	10·4	1511	10·9	0300	6·3	1454	6·5	0843	2·9	2022	3·1	1050	4·9	2318	5·0	0758	3·8	2104	4·0
13	Tu	1140	6·3	2318	6·6	0815	8·1	2034	8·5	0350	10·7	1619	11·5	0353	6·5	1549	6·7	0939	3·2	2132	3·3	1148	5·1			0851	3·9	2149	4·0
14	W			1229	6·8	0904	8·4	2121	8·8	0449	11·1	1712	12·1	0438	6·7	1633	6·9	1026	3·3	2233	3·4	0011		1236	5·2	0935	3·9	2228	4·0
15	Th	0011	6·8	1312	6·9	0945	8·7	2202	8·9	0537	12·3	1756	12·4	0518	6·9	1709	7·0	1108	3·5	2306	3·4	0056	5·1	1317	5·3	1011	4·0	2303	4·0
16	F	0056	6·9	1348	7·0	1021	9·0	2238	8·9	0618	12·8	1836	12·6	0556	7·0	1743	7·0	1147		2345	3·5	0135	5·3	1354	5·3	1043	4·0	2336	3·9
17	Sa	0133	7·0	1420	6·9	1055	9·0	2312	9·0	0656	12·8	1913	12·7	0632	7·0	1815	6·9	0022	3·2	1223	3·4	0211	5·3	1429	5·3	1112	4·0		
18	Su	0205	6·9	1451	6·9	1127	9·0	2346	9·0	0731	12·7	1947	12·3	0707	6·9	1846	6·7	0056	3·1	1257	3·1	0246	5·3	1500	5·2	1143	4·0	1215	4·0
19	M	0233	6·9	1524	6·8	0018	8·7	1200	9·0	0804	12·7	2018	12·3	0741	6·7	1914	6·6	0130	3·1	1327	3·1	0321	5·2	1532	5·1	0009	3·8	1250	4·0
20	Tu	0300	6·8	1559	6·7	0050	8·5	1232	8·7	0833	12·3	2047	11·4	0813	6·6	1944	6·4	0204	3·0	1356	3·0	0356	5·1	1606	5·0	0043	3·7	1329	3·9
21	W	0331	6·7	1637	6·5	0124	8·2	1306	8·5	0903	11·8	2117	10·6	0849	6·4	2015	6·2	0251	3·0	1425	3·0	0433	4·9	1641	4·9	0120	3·6	1410	3·9
22	Th	0404	6·5	1716	6·4	0202	8·1	1341	8·2	0932	11·0	2149	10·2	0928	6·2	2050	6·0	0321	3·1	1457	3·1	0512	4·7	1722	4·8	0201	3·5	1456	3·8
23	F	0441	6·5	1800	6·3	0246	7·7	1422	8·0	1003	10·8	2223	10·1	1014	6·0	2128	5·8	0406	3·2	1532	3·2	0557	4·5	1806	4·7	0246	3·4	1546	3·7
24	Sa	0519	6·3	1848	6·0	0339	7·3	1510	7·9	1041	10·5	2306	10·2	1108	5·8	2216		0458	3·2	1614	3·3	0645	4·5	1856	4·6	0336	3·4	1645	3·7
25	Su	0601	6·1	1948	5·9	0445	7·4	1609	7·7	1130	10·1					1217		0559	3·1	1704	3·1	0740	4·5	1953	4·5	0436	3·4	1748	3·8
26	M	0652	5·9	2104	5·9	0558	7·8	1716	7·7	0000	10·1	1234	10·4	0029	6·0	1436	6·0	0715	3·1	1809	3·1	0841	4·6	2053	4·5	0543	3·5	1854	3·7
27	Tu	0757	5·8	2216	6·2	0706	8·3	1824	8·3	0107	10·4	1354	11·1	0142	6·2	1534	6·2	0832	3·2	1939	3·2	0945	4·7	2156	5·0	0651	3·6	1954	3·9
28	W	0919	5·9	2319	6·5	0806	8·8	1928	8·8	0232	10·5	1514	11·9	0246	6·6	1627	6·6	0932	3·3	2057	3·3	1046	5·0	2256	5·2	0750	3·8	2048	4·0
29	Th	1033	6·2			0858	9·2	2026	9·2	0346	11·3	1619	12·6	0343	6·9			1023	3·4	2154	3·3	1142	5·0	2353	5·2	0840	4·0	2135	4·2
30	F	1133	6·6			0945	9·0	2119	9·2	0448	12·1	1718								2244	3·4			1234		0924			

* All times shown are Greenwich Mean Time.   †Difference of height in metres from Ordnance Datum (Newlyn).

‡Difference of height in metres from Ordnance Datum (Dublin).

DECEMBER, 1990

High Water at the undermentioned Places (G.M.T.*)—

Places, with †/‡ Datum of Predictions:
- **London Bridge** — †Datum of Predictions 3·20 m. below
- **Liverpool** — †Datum of Predictions 4·93 m. below
- **Avonmouth** — †Datum of Predictions 6·50 m. below
- **Hull (Albert Dock)** — †Datum of Predictions 3·90 m. below
- **Greenock** — †Datum of Predictions 1·62 m. below
- **Leith** — †Datum of Predictions 2·90 m. below
- **Dun Laoghaire** — ‡Datum of Predictions 0·20 m. above

Column key: Mn. = morning h.m., Ht. = height (m.), Aft. = afternoon h.m., Ht. = height (m.)

Day of Month	Day of Week	LB Mn	LB Ht	LB Aft	LB Ht	Liv Mn	Liv Ht	Liv Aft	Liv Ht	Avon Mn	Avon Ht	Avon Aft	Avon Ht	Hull Mn	Hull Ht	Hull Aft	Hull Ht	Green Mn	Green Ht	Green Aft	Green Ht	Leith Mn	Leith Ht	Leith Aft	Leith Ht	DL Mn	DL Ht	DL Aft	DL Ht
1	Sa	0014	6·8	1228	6·9	0949	9·2	2210	9·5	0544	12·8	1812	13·1	0440	7·3	1716	7·2	1110	3·5	2333	3·5	0046	5·4	1322	5·4	1005	4·2	2222	4·2
2	Su	0103	6·9	1319	7·1	1037	9·5	2301	9·7	0638	13·2	1906	13·3	0533	7·5	1803	7·4	1156	3·7	——	—	0138	5·6	1409	5·6	1047	4·3	2309	4·2
3	M	0151	7·0	1408	7·2	1125	9·7	2351	9·7	0727	13·4	1957	13·4	0625	7·6	1848	7·5	0022	3·8	1241	3·8	0228	5·7	1458	5·7	1131	4·3	2359	4·2
4	Tu	0237	7·0	1458	7·4	——	—	1214	9·7	0816	13·4	2046	13·4	0716	7·6	1933	7·5	0105	3·9	1325	3·9	0320	5·8	1548	5·7	——	—	1221	4·4
5	W	0325	7·1	1550	7·5	0042	9·6	1303	9·6	0904	13·2	2134	13·2	0806	7·5	2018	7·3	0205	3·9	1409	3·9	0413	5·7	1640	5·6	0051	4·1	1311	4·3
6	Th	0413	7·0	1642	7·4	0133	9·3	1352	9·3	0950	12·8	2221	12·8	0856	7·2	2103	7·1	0256	3·5	1453	4·0	0506	5·6	1734	5·5	0147	4·0	1407	4·3
7	F	0502	6·9	1733	7·1	0225	8·9	1444	9·0	1038	12·2	2308	11·6	0945	6·9	2149	6·9	0346	3·4	1537	4·0	0600	5·4	1829	5·3	0246	3·8	1506	4·2
8	Sa	0550	6·7	1825	6·8	0318	8·4	1538	8·6	1126	11·6	2356	11·0	1038	6·5	2241	6·6	0436	3·2	1622	3·9	0657	5·1	1926	5·1	0349	3·6	1609	4·1
9	Su	0639	6·4	1919	6·5	0414	8·0	1637	8·2	——	—	1215	11·1	1139	6·3	2339	6·6	0529	3·2	1712	3·7	0757	4·9	2025	4·9	0457	3·5	1718	4·0
10	M	0734	6·2	2018	6·2	0516	7·7	1742	8·0	0048	10·7	1312	10·9	——	—	1252	6·4	0632	3·1	1812	3·5	0859	4·8	2128	4·8	0611	3·5	1831	3·9
11	Tu	0836	6·0	2125	6·1	0625	7·6	1849	7·8	0147	10·6	1415	10·8	0050	6·4	1401	6·1	0746	3·1	1929	3·3	1003	4·8	2233	4·8	0719	3·5	1939	3·8
12	W	0950	6·0	2235	6·2	0730	7·7	1954	7·9	0253	10·7	1524	11·0	0208	6·4	1501	6·0	0854	3·1	2048	3·2	1105	4·8	2333	4·9	0817	3·6	2035	3·7
13	Th	1102	6·2	2336	6·4	0826	7·9	2049	8·0	0402	11·1	1630	11·3	0314	6·4	1553	6·3	0950	3·2	2150	3·1	1159	4·9	——	—	0905	3·7	2126	3·7
14	F	——	—	1200	6·4	0914	8·2	2135	8·2	0459	11·5	1725	11·7	0410	6·5	1638	6·5	1039	3·3	2240	3·1	0025	4·9	1247	5·0	0945	3·7	2208	3·7
15	Sa	0025	6·5	1246	6·6	0956	8·5	2217	8·4	0550	12·0	1811	12·2	0458	6·6	1719	6·6	1123	3·3	2325	3·1	0110	5·0	1328	5·0	1021	3·8	2246	3·7
16	Su	0104	6·6	1326	6·6	1034	8·7	2255	8·5	0634	12·3	1852	12·3	0542	6·6	1756	6·6	——	—	1202	3·4	0152	5·0	1406	5·1	1053	3·9	2319	3·7
17	M	0140	6·7	1402	6·6	1111	8·9	2330	8·6	0717	12·3	1930	12·2	0619	6·7	1828	6·7	0005	3·0	1237	3·4	0232	5·1	1442	5·2	1124	3·9	2352	3·7
18	Tu	0212	6·7	1437	6·7	1144	8·9	——	—	0747	12·3	2002	12·1	0655	6·7	1857	6·7	0043	3·1	1310	3·5	0308	5·1	1515	5·2	1158	3·6	——	—
19	W	0246	6·8	1512	6·8	0004	8·6	1218	8·9	0819	12·2	2034	11·9	0727	6·7	1930	6·7	0120	3·1	1342	3·5	0343	5·2	1550	5·2	0026	3·6	1232	3·6
20	Th	0321	6·8	1549	6·8	0038	8·6	1253	8·8	0850	12·1	2105	11·7	0801	6·7	2002	6·7	0157	3·2	1414	3·5	0419	5·2	1624	5·1	0101	3·6	1308	3·6
21	F	0356	6·8	1626	6·7	0113	8·5	1328	8·8	0922	11·8	2139	11·6	0836	6·7	2039	6·7	0235	3·2	1447	3·4	0454	5·1	1702	5·1	0140	3·5	1347	3·5
22	Sa	0430	6·7	1702	6·6	0148	8·3	1406	8·5	0956	11·8	2213	11·3	0914	6·6	2117	6·3	0314	3·1	1523	3·2	0533	5·0	1742	5·0	0220	3·5	1428	3·5
23	Su	0505	6·6	1740	6·5	0226	8·1	1447	8·5	1033	11·6	2251	11·3	0955	6·6	2157	6·1	0355	3·1	1602	3·1	0616	4·8	1827	4·9	0304	3·5	1513	3·5
24	M	0540	6·4	1821	6·3	0310	8·0	1534	8·3	1113	11·4	——	—	1038	6·3	2244	6·4	0440	3·1	1645	3·2	0703	4·7	1915	4·8	0354	3·4	1603	3·5
25	Tu	0621	6·1	1912	6·1	0402	7·8	1627	8·2	0027	10·8	1206	11·1	1129	6·1	——	—	0531	3·0	1737	3·2	0755	4·6	2008	4·8	0453	3·5	1702	3·7
26	W	0713	6·0	2016	6·0	0502	7·7	1732	8·1	0141	10·6	1419	10·8	0049	6·4	1232	6·5	0631	3·1	1844	3·1	0854	4·6	2107	4·8	0600	3·7	1810	3·7
27	Th	0826	6·0	2132	6·1	0614	7·8	1849	8·4	0307	10·9	1546	11·3	0202	6·5	1344	6·6	0740	3·2	2004	3·1	0958	4·6	2214	4·9	0706	3·8	1919	3·8
28	F	0949	6·1	2244	6·3	0727	8·0	1955	8·4	0419	11·5	1654	11·9	0314	6·7	1456	6·7	0848	3·3	2116	3·1	1103	4·8	2324	5·0	0807	3·7	2023	3·8
29	Sa	1102	6·3	——	—	0832	8·4	2100	8·7	0525	11·9	1758	12·4	0424	6·9	1602	6·9	0949	3·3	2219	3·1	——	—	1207	5·0	0900	3·8	2121	4·0
30	Su	——	—	1210	6·6	0932	8·9	2159	9·1	0625	12·4	1857	12·8	0527	7·2	1701	7·2	1044	3·4	2318	3·3	0029	5·2	1305	5·2	0949	4·0	2212	4·0
31	M	0048	6·7	1310	6·8	1026	9·3	2254	9·4	0720	12·9	1951	12·9	0627	7·4	1751	7·3	1136	3·6	——	—	0128	5·4	1358	5·5	1036	4·1	2303	4·0

*All times shown are Greenwich Mean Time.   †Difference of height in metres from Ordnance Datum (Newlyn).
‡Difference of height in metres from Ordnance Datum (Dublin).

WEATHER IN THE UNITED KINGDOM, 1988–89

(1988) July.—Rainfall totals were well above normal in most areas and more than three times the normal amount was received at Carlisle (Cumbria). In the extreme south-east of England amounts were near or slightly below normal in places. It was the wettest July over England since 1936, the wettest over Wales since 1939, and the wettest over Scotland since 1869. Aspatria (Cumbria) with 30 days of rain equalled Stornoway's record of the greatest number of days with rain in a month. Rain, heavy at times, or showers, sometimes accompanied by thunder, occurred somewhere in the United Kingdom on almost every day. Most of the month's major events were disrupted, including Wimbledon which was virtually washed out on the 3rd, the Royal Agricultural Show at Stoneleigh (Warks.) where the ring was waterlogged on the 4th, and the Open Golf Championship. Thunderstorms occurred widely between the 1st and 8th mainly over England, and were again widespread over southern England on the 26th. On the 25th 62 mm (2·44 in) of rain fell at Onich (Highland). Northern areas had a stormy day on the 25th when Scotland had its strongest July winds for 50 years, bringing down trees which blocked many roads in central and southern Scotland. Gusts of 68 knots (78 mph) were recorded at Invergordon (Highland) and Leuchars (Fife) and 67 knots (77 mph) at Lossiemouth (Grampian). Many roads were blocked by falling trees in Northern Ireland, Ballymena (Co. Antrim), Lisnaskea (Co. Fermanagh) and Belfast being affected. In northern England the cross-Pennine road was closed to high-sided vehicles. There was widespread fog over hills and coasts in many western and northern areas on the 22nd and 23rd. Monthly mean temperatures were below normal nearly everywhere but were above normal in northern and eastern Scotland. Sheffield (S. Yorkshire) with 21·5°C (70·7°F) had its lowest July maximum temperature since 1965. At Hampstead (Greater London) 21·4°C (70·5°F) was the lowest maximum since 1909. The highest temperature recorded during the month was 24·7°C (76·5°F) at Margate (Kent) on the 21st and 23rd, while the lowest was −0·3°C (31·5°F) at Alwen (Clwyd) on the 6th. Sunshine totals were generally below normal except in some places in eastern Scotland and the Western Isles where they were near or just above normal. Sheffield had its lowest July sunshine total since 1980 and it was the third dullest July at North Wyke (Devon) since 1959. The highest daily total was 15·3 hours at Guernsey on the 11th: the highest monthly totals were 235·5 hours at Herne Bay (Kent) and 247·9 hours at Guernsey.

August.—Rainfall totals were above average in most of Scotland, Wales, Northern Ireland and parts of northwest and southwest England, but below average elsewhere. Rain fell on the 1st around the Firth of Forth and on north-eastern coasts of England with thunder and hail at times. Rain and thunder occurred on the 2nd in central and eastern parts of England. On the 9th and 10th there was rain in western Scotland followed by rain generally on the 11th when 76 mm (3·0 in) fell at Dingwall (Highland). On the 14th and 18th most western and northern areas were wet and 54 mm (2·1 in) of rain fell at Cassley (Highland) on the 14th and 58 mm (2·3 in) fell at Holme Moss (W. Yorkshire) on the 18th. There was further heavy rain over Cumbria on the 29th and in many places on the 30th and 31st. At Trassey Slievenaman (Co. Down) 95 mm (3·7 in) of rain fell on the 31st while 59 mm (2·3 in) fell at Princetown (Devon). Winds were strong over Scotland on the 15th and 27th but the highest gust was 65 knots (74·9 mph) recorded at Gwennap Head (Cornwall) on the

31st. Monthly mean temperatures were below normal nearly everywhere in the United Kingdom. Many areas were hot between the 5th and 10th, especially in the east. Cheltenham (Glos.) recorded a temperature of 30·2°C (86·4°F) on the 7th. Norfolk had a hot day on the 14th when temperature reached 26·0°C (78·8°F) at Cromer. It was very warm in central and eastern England on the 17th when the temperature reached 26·9°C (80·4°F) at Heathrow. On the 18th south-east England and East Anglia became hot early, when Margate (Kent) recorded a temperature of 27·7°C (81·9°F) but cooled down during the afternoon. The lowest temperature recorded during the month was 0·0°C (32·0°F) at Crannich (Highland) on the 22nd. Sunshine totals were generally above normal in England and Wales east of a line from Rhyl (Clwyd) to Southampton (Hampshire). Totals were below normal in other areas. The 6th was the sunniest day over England and Wales when many places had 14 hours of sunshine. The highest daily total was 14·9 hours at Morecambe (Lancashire) on the 7th and the highest monthly total was 243·6 hours at Folkestone (Kent).

September.—Rainfall totals were below normal nearly everywhere with less than half the normal amount in many parts of England and Wales. By contrast the Cape Wrath (Highland) area had one and a half times the normal amount. On the 1st rain spread across north-east Scotland and there were thunderstorms in eastern England from Northumberland to Sussex. It was a wet day in Northern Ireland. On the 2nd there were further thunderstorms in south and south-east England and more rain in Scotland. Gales occurred on the 1st and 2nd especially in south-west England where many places recorded gusts of more than 50 knots (57·6 mph) on the 1st. The 4th was a wet day in Northern Ireland and further rain fell in Scotland between the 5th and 7th. Overnight fog was persistent in the south west on the 6th and there was early morning fog in parts of England and Wales on the 7th and 10th. There were further widespread thunderstorms in the north and west on the 7th and 8th. On the morning of the 8th dust was deposited at several places in Wales, at Low Etherly (Co. Durham) and at Coventry (Warks.) Rain affected all areas on the 11th and showers continued on the 13th and 14th. Thunderstorms occurred in southern England on the 13th. Most places had wet periods after the 22nd with heavy rain at times and 73 mm (2·87 in) fell at Moel Cynnedd (Powys) on the 25th. The first snow of the season fell on the Grampians on the 28th and hail was widespread over some western areas on the 28th and over Scotland on the 29th. A mini tornado was reported in Cumbria on the 28th. Monthly mean temperatures were generally near normal over the United Kingdom as a whole but rather warmer in the east of the Highland Region of Scotland. The highest temperature recorded during the month was 26·9°C (80·4°F) at Northolt (Greater London) on the 7th and the lowest was −3·8°C (25·2°F) at Carnwath (Strathclyde) on the 30th. Sunshine totals were near normal everywhere but rather sunnier in the northeast. The highest daily total was 12·1 hours at Baltasound (Shetland) on the 3rd and the highest monthly total was 180 hours at Porthcawl (Mid Glamorgan).

October.—Rainfall totals were above average in most areas with parts of Tayside and the Grampian Region receiving about twice the normal amount. On the 1st a gust of 61 knots (70·2 mph) was recorded at Butt of Lewis (Western Isles). On the 5th 53 mm (2·1 in) of rain fell at Princetown (Devon) and Bastreet (Cornwall). On the 6th there were gusts of

67 knots (77·2 mph) at Gwennap Head (Cornwall), and 65 knots (74·9 mph) at Aberporth (Dyfed) and at Rhoose (South Glamorgan). Thunder occurred in many parts of England on the 6th and there was widespread hail on the 6th and 7th. A gust of 80 knots (92·1 mph) was recorded at Lowther Hill (Dumfries and Galloway) on the 7th. Thunder was again widespread on the 12th. On the 14th fog was widespread in the Midlands and eastern England, and on the 15th and 16th fog was dense in northern areas. On the 17th dust was deposited at Keyworth (Notts.) and further dust was deposited in south-east England on the 18th. Thunderstorms occurred over a wide area of England and Wales on the 18th and 19th, and lightning cut power supplies at Stoke-on-Trent on the 19th. Heavy rain on the 19th flooded parts of Liverpool and the Wirral to 2 metres (6·6 ft) deep in places causing much damage in the area. At Crosby 82 mm (3·2 in) of rain fell in the day. On the 20th and 21st there were areas of dense fog particularly in the Midlands and south-east England. Fog was widespread in eastern England on the 25th and very heavy rain fell on the Mourne Mountain area of Northern Ireland. At Trassey 97 mm (3·8 in) fell and 81 mm (3·2 in) fell at Bryansford (Co. Down). Many places across Northern Ireland had more than 20 mm (0·8 in) and there were floods, blocked roads and structural damage. On the 28th snow fell over Orkney, Shetland and the Scottish mountains to give 10 cm (3·9 in) at Cairngorm (Grampian) on the 29th. Monthly mean temperatures were generally below normal over Scotland, Northern Ireland and parts of northern England but near or slightly above elsewhere. On the 7th the temperature fell to −7°C (19·4°F) at Carnwath (Strathclyde) and the night of the 30th was the coldest in October at Sheffield for 33 years. The highest temperature of the month was 21·5°C (70·7°F) at East Malling and at Wye (Kent) on the 18th and at Faversham (Kent) on the 19th. The lowest temperature was −8·5°C (16·7°F) at St. Harmon (Powys) on the 31st. Sunshine totals were below normal north-east of a line from the Isle of Lewis to the Thames Estuary but normal or slightly above elsewhere. The highest daily total was 10·6 hours at Eastbourne and Hastings (E. Sussex) and the highest monthly total was 137·9 hours at Hayling Island (Hampshire).

November.—Rainfall totals were below normal in most areas but they were above normal in parts of north-east England. Some parts of south-west and central-southern England had less than a quarter of the normal amount. It was the driest November since 1956 over Wales and the driest in England since 1978. It was the second driest since 1957 in Northern Ireland. Only widespread heavy rain on the 29th prevented the month being exceptionally dry over England and Wales. Winds reached gale force over south-west England on the 3rd, 6th and 7th. The 11th was a stormy day in the north when a gust of 61 knots (70·2 mph) was recorded at Lerwick and at Fair Isle (Shetland). In south-west England winds approached gale force on the 11th leaving many roads blocked by fallen trees and telegraph poles. Also on the 11th there were thunderstorms in the far north of Scotland with hail in places. On the 14th fog was widespread, persisting all day in places. On the 20th snow over central Scotland moved south to affect most of northern and eastern England as far south as east Kent. Snow lay over much of England north of the Thames with from 9 to 12 cms (3·5 to 4·7 in) in some hilly places. Much of Wales and south-west England had rain. There were wintry showers on the 21st and 22nd and parts of east Kent had 15 cm (5·9 in) of level snow: 10 cm (3·9 in) was measured in parts of Yorkshire. On the 22nd fog formed overnight and persisted all day on the 23rd in the Manchester area.

On the 29th many places in Wales and south-west England had more than 30 mm (1·2 in) of rain. Nantmor (Gwynedd) had 75 mm (2·9 in) and Princetown (Devon) had 57 mm (2·2 in). Monthly mean temperatures were generally above normal in Scotland but below normal elsewhere. The 10th was a very mild day with temperatures 5°C (9°F) above normal from southern England to north-east Scotland but by contrast the 21st with ice, sleet and rain made driving conditions hazardous as temperatures fell to −3°C (26·6°F) in England and to −5°C (23·0°F) in Scotland. The highest temperature of the month was 18·0°C (64·4F) at Guernsey on the 9th and the lowest was −11·6°C (11·1°F) at Carnwath (Strathclyde) on the 22nd. Sunshine totals were above normal nearly everywhere except for some coastal parts of north-west Scotland. Glasgow had its sunniest November since 1947 and Edinburgh had its sunniest since 1939. The highest daily total was 9·3 hours at Westonbirt Arboretum (Glos.) on the 4th and the highest monthly total was 130·8 hours at Jersey. The highest mainland total was 116·6 hours at St. Mawgan (Cornwall).

December.—Rainfall totals were well below normal everywhere except western Scotland and a few places in north Wales and north-west England. The east coast of Scotland was very dry. In general most of the rainfall fell in the first five days of the month and hail was frequent in western areas during the first week. Much of the Thames Valley and the area south of it received less than 4 mm (0·2 in) of rain after the 4th. In particular Benson (Oxfordshire) had only 2·2 mm (0·09 in) and Heathrow (Greater London) only 2·8 mm (0·1 in). Exeter (Devon) had only 3·3 mm (0·13 in) after the 5th. Hampstead (Greater London) had its driest December since 1933, Lyonshall (Hereford and Worcester) its driest since 1947, and Northwood (Greater London) its driest since 1959. Snow was lying on the Scottish peaks for most of the month. On the 4th gusts of more than 50 knots (57·6 mph) with torrential rain swept through south-west England, uprooting trees and telegraph poles and blocking many roads. By dawn on the 14th fog was dense and slow to clear in parts of East Anglia. On the 21st the wind gusted to 74 knots (85·2 mph) at Butt of Lewis (Western Isles) and on the 22nd a gust of 84 knots (96·7 mph) was recorded at Lerwick (Shetland). Hail was frequent in northern Scotland on the 22nd and 23rd and there was heavy rain over northern Wales on the 24th. At Sumburgh (Shetland) a gust of 75 knots (86·4 mph) was recorded on the 24th. Monthly mean temperatures were well above normal everywhere with averages 3·7°C (6·7°F) above normal in the area of Lyncham (Wiltshire). Hampstead and Northwood (Greater London) and Lyonshall (Hereford and Worcester) had their mildest December since 1974. At Sheffield (S. Yorkshire) the mean temperature equalled that of December 1934, both being mildest since 1882. Many places had a frost-free December. The highest temperature recorded during the month was 16·5°C (61·7°F) at Castledawson Hillhead (Co. Londonderry) on the 28th and the lowest was −5·7°C (21·7°F) at Grantown-on-Spey (Highland) on the 3rd. Sunshine totals were below normal nearly everywhere except eastern areas of England and Scotland and parts of the west Highlands where they were above normal. Bradford (W. Yorkshire) had its sunniest December on record with 47 hours—the previous record of 46 hours was in 1926. The highest daily total was 7·3 hours at Folkestone (Kent) on the 12th and the highest monthly total was 71 hours at Boulmer (Northumberland).

Year (1988).—The main features of the weather of 1988 were the gales over England and Wales in

January and February and over Scotland and Northern Ireland in July, and the very wet weather of July with its disruption of most of the month's events including Wimbledon, the Royal Agricultural Show and the Open Golf Championship. January was mild, windy and generally very wet. It was the wettest in England and Wales since 1948. Heavy rain on the 2nd caused a landslip between Bideford and Torrington (Devon) and gales uprooted trees and caused power failures in north Devon. On the 4th a tanker was blown from its moorings at Milford Haven (Dyfed) and glass panels were blown out of the roof of Cardiff Central Market injuring three women. On the 5th lightning demolished the steeple of a Swansea chapel and on the 6th the Severn Bridge was closed for only the third time in its history. On the 21st and 22nd 18 cm (7·1 in) of snow fell in central England and on the 29th torrential rain caused severe flooding from Gloucestershire to Kent. February started with widespread gales on the 1st and 2nd. On the 9th trees were uprooted and traffic disrupted in Devon and Cornwall and there was much structural damage in north-west England including to the Town Hall roof at Bury (Greater Manchester). A bus was blown over at Chesterfield (Derbyshire) and rail services were delayed between London and Glasgow. On the 9th and 10th heavy snow drifts blocked roads across the Pennines and there was heavy snow in north Devon. On the 28th there was 30 cm (11·8 in) of snow in the Grampians, blocking some roads. February was very sunny in places and Bablake (Warks.) had its highest total since 1895. March was an unsettled month with sleet and snow in many places. It was the wettest March in Northern Ireland since 1903. On the 24th there were widespread thunderstorms from southern Scotland to East Anglia and lightning damaged buildings at Donnington (Lincs.). April was a changeable month, mild and rather dull with generally average rainfall. It was the fifth month in succession with temperatures above normal nearly everywhere. Arbroath (Grampian) had nearly three times its normal rainfall. May was warm and sunny everywhere except on the east coast. It was the sixth successive month with above normal temperatures. On the 1st a climber was killed by lightning near Grasmere (Cumbria) and hail at Moel-y-Crio (Clwyd) caused much damage to fruit trees and hedges. There was widespread flooding in the Thames Valley and north-west London during thunderstorms on the 8th. June was a generally dry month in most places with above average sunshine in northern areas. Over England and Wales it was the driest June since 1976 and over Scotland it was the driest this century. At Abbotsinch (Strathclyde) it was the driest June since 1868, together with 1921 and 1926 which had the same total. July was a particularly wet month in many areas and rain or showers, sometimes with thunder, occurred somewhere in the United Kingdom on almost every day. It was the wettest July in England since 1936, in Wales since 1939 and in Scotland since 1869. Northern areas had storms on the 25th when Scotland had its strongest winds for 50 years bringing down trees and blocking many roads. Roads were also blocked in Northern Ireland and roads across the Pennines were closed. August was a generally unsettled month and rain fell on almost every day in some western areas of England. There were large falls in Snowdonia and Cumbria on the 29th and in many places on the 30th. Norfolk, Suffolk and parts of the Thames Estuary stayed mostly dry. September was another mainly unsettled month but rainfall was below normal nearly everywhere. The first snow of the season fell in Scotland on the 29th. Dust was deposited in Durham, Wales and Warwickshire during the month. October was generally wet and rather dull. There was widespread hail on the 6th and 7th. On the 18th and 19th thunderstorms were

widespread over England and Wales. Lightning cut power supplies at Stoke-on-Trent, and parts of Liverpool and the Wirral were flooded to a depth of 2 metres (6·6 ft) in places. Crosby had 82 mm (3·2 in) of rain on the 19th. On the 20th and 21st there were areas of dense fog in the Midlands and south-east England and on the 25th heavy rain in Northern Ireland caused flooding, blocked roads and structural damage. November was generally very dry and sunny in most parts of England and Wales. It was one of the driest on record in many places. Scotland and Northern Ireland were also sunny but had outbreaks of heavy rain in places. The 11th was a stormy day in the far north, and in south-west England gales left many roads blocked by fallen trees and telegraph poles. On the 20th snow covered much of England north of the Thames. Glasgow had its sunniest November since 1947 and Edinburgh had its sunniest since 1939. Fog formed frequently overnight during the month. December was very mild with below average rainfall in most areas but windy with gales at times. Gusts of over 50 knots (57·6 mph) with torrential rain swept through south-west England on the 4th leaving roads blocked by fallen trees. After the 4th much of the Thames Valley and the area just south of it received less than 4 mm (0·16 in) of rain for the rest of the month. The highest temperature recorded during the year was 30·2°C (86·4°F) at Cheltenham (Glos.) on August 7th and the lowest was −11·6°C (11·1°F) at Carnwath (Strathclyde) on November 22nd. The highest sunshine totals for the year were 1,869·2 hours at St. Helier (Jersey) and 1,850·7 hours at Bognor Regis (W. Sussex).

(1989) January.—Rainfall totals were below normal over England and Wales and eastern Scotland. By contrast western Scotland had one of the wettest January's on record, with up to three times the normal amount of rainfall over the western Highlands. In Glen Shiel one gauge recorded a total of 855 mm (33·7 in) while at Insch near Aberdeen only 6 mm (0·24 in) were recorded. At Cape Wrath (Highland) it was the wettest January since 1941, while at Craibstone (Grampian) it was the driest since 1925. Bradford (W. Yorkshire) had its driest January since 1953 and Ashover (Derbyshire) its driest since 1966. The three months November to January inclusive were the driest since 1879 over England and Wales with a general total of 136 mm (5·4 in) being only 50 per cent of normal. The incidence of snow or sleet falling was well below normal everywhere. There were gales in the north on the 3rd. The 11th was a wet day over much of Scotland with falls of 57 mm (2·2 in) at Balquhidder (Central) and 52 mm (2·1 in) at Livingstone (Lothian). The 13th was a wet day practically everywhere and 57 mm (2·2 in) of rain fell at Dalwhinnie (Highland). A gust of 76 knots (87·5 mph) was recorded at Stornoway (Western Isles) on the 13th and 75 knots (86·4 mph) was recorded at Butt of Lewis on the 14th. During the 14th and 15th a total of 110 mm (4·7 in) of rain fell in the Spey catchment, causing the river to flood, and on the 14th six places between Loch Quoich and Invergarry recorded more than 100 mm (3·9 in), the greatest amount being 156·5 mm (6·2 in) at Achangart (Highland). On the 14th and 15th 122 mm (4·8 in) fell at Killin (Central). A gust of 74 knots (85·2 mph) was recorded at Lerwick (Shetland) on the 15th. There were further gales in the north on the 17th. On the 18th and 20th overnight fog, widespread at times, developed in southern areas. Gusts of 73 knots (84·1 mph) were recorded at Fair Isle (Shetland) and Kirkwall (Orkney) on the 29th and there were further fog patches in southern areas. Monthly mean temperatures were well above normal everywhere ranging from 2°C (3·6°F) above in southern England to 5°C (9·0°F) above in northern Scotland. Glasgow had its mildest January since 1868 and Braemar (Grampian) its mildest since 1856. Paisley (Strathclyde) had its warmest January since 1889 and Northern Ireland had its warmest since 1932. The highest temperature of the month was 15·5°C (59·9°F) at Torrisdale (Highland) on the 27th, and the lowest was −6·5°C (20·3°F) at Butser (Hampshire) on the 11th and Grendon Underwood (Buckinghamshire) on the 19th. Sunshine totals were above normal everywhere except in Northern Ireland and northern and western Scotland. Wick (Highland) had its sunniest January since 1946 and Bradford (W. Yorkshire) had its sunniest on record. The highest daily total was 8·9 hours at Dunkeswell (Devon) on the 29th and the highest monthly total was 93 hours at Eastbourne (E. Sussex).

February.—Rainfall totals were above normal nearly everywhere west of a line from Banff (Grampian) to Beachy Head (East Sussex) but below elsewhere. Rainfall was four and a half times the average near Fort Augustus (Highland) but less than half the average in parts of Lincolnshire. Over England and Wales the period from November to February was the second driest this century. On the 4th and 5th rainfall was prolonged and very heavy in the western Highlands causing flooding and landslides. Bridges, roads, houses and farmland were affected over a wide area and the railway bridge over the Ness at Inverness was swept away on the 7th. At Fort William 83·7 mm (3·3 in) fell on the 5th and 131·7 mm (5·2 in) fell on the 6th. At Kinlochewe 170 mm (6·7 in) of rain fell on the 5th. There were severe gales in nothern areas on the 13th with gusts of 92 knots (105·9 mph) at Butt of Lewis (Western Isles), 93 knots (107·1 mph) at Benbecula (Western Isles) and 100 knots (115·2) at Fair Isle (Shetland). At Fraserburgh (Grampian) the wind increased from 15 knots (17·3 mph) to 60 knots (69·1 mph) in 1½ hours and a gust of 123 knots (141·7 mph) was a new record for a low-level station. Traffic was disrupted and trees brought down as far south as Leicestershire and north Wales, with buses and lorries being blown over. In Dunfermline (Fife) nine people were injured when the roof of a hospital ward was blown off. On the 15th and 16th many northern areas had snow and sleet and 9 cm (3·5 in) of snow lay in the Grampians. Southern areas had snow and sleet on the 17th. On the 19th Scotland and northern England had snow, continuing in Scotland on the 20th. There was snow on the 24th, considerable across parts of Wales, the Peak District and the southern Pennines. Winds were strong in south-west England on the 25th when a gust of 81 knots (93·3 mph) was recorded at Gwennap Head (Cornwall). Snow fell in many places on the 25th and there were drifts 2 metres (6·6 ft) deep in parts of the Cotswolds. Stow-on-the-Wold and Chipping Norton were cut off for a time. On the 25th the pressure fell to below 950 millibars over southern England, the lowest pressure there since 1870. Monthly mean temperatures were above normal everywhere. Ashover (Derbyshire) had its warmest February on record. The highest temperature of the month was 15·9°C (60·6°F) at East Bergholt (Suffolk) on the 6th and the lowest was −10·6°C (12·9°F) at Carnwath (Strathclyde) on the 27th. Sunshine totals were above average nearly everywhere except the western side of Scotland. Bradford (W. Yorkshire) had its sunniest February on record. The highest daily total was 9·9 hours at Long Sutton (Hampshire) on the 23rd and the highest monthly total was 128 hours at Culterty (Grampian).

March.—Rainfall totals were above normal in most parts of the United Kingdom but some eastern coastal areas of Scotland and England were rather dry. Newcastle-upon-Tyne had less than 30 per cent

of the normal amount. In spite of the rainfall over England being above average for March, the period November to March was the fifth driest since 1910. It was the driest November to March over England and Wales since 1975–76. On the 5th a gust of 60 knots (69·1 mph) was recorded at Aberporth (Dyfed) and on the 8th 65 mm (2·56 in) of rain fell at Nantmor (Gwynedd) with a further 51 mm (2·01 in) on the 9th. On the 14th there were severe gales in the coastal areas and a gust of 76 knots (87·5 mph) was recorded at Berry Head (Devon). On the 16th there were snow and sleet showers over England and Wales and on the 17th there were snow showers over Shetland. On the 18th rain spread to all areas with snow in the north. On the 21st dust was deposited at Keyworth (Notts.) and on the 23rd 59 mm (2·32 in) of rain fell at Holme Moss (W. Yorkshire). A gust of 68 knots (78·3 mph) was recorded at Benbecula (Western Isles). On the 26th there were overnight fog patches in south-east England and on the 31st dust was deposited at Chagford (Devon). Monthly mean temperatures were generally above normal. Much of East Anglia and south east England had a very warm day on the 6th which was one of the warmest early March days of this century. The 26th was a very warm day over England and Wales and the temperature reached 19·3°C (66·7°F) at Easthampstead (Berkshire) on the 28th. The highest temperature of the month was 19·9°C (67·8°F) at East Hoathly (E. Sussex) on the 28th and at the London Weather Centre on the 31st. The lowest temperature was −8·2°C (17·2°F) at Leadhills (Strathclyde) on the 17th. Sunshine totals were generally above average in Scotland and northern England but below in southern areas. The highest daily total was 11·1 hours at Glasgow (Strathclyde) on the 17th and at Wyton (Cambridgeshire) on the 30th. The highest monthly total was 144 hours at Aberdeen (Grampian).

April.—Rainfall totals were above normal in most places in England, Wales and Northern Ireland but below normal in Scotland. On the 1st 57 mm (2·2 in) of rain fell at Trassey Slievenaman (Co. Down). Wintry showers affected eastern England and eastern Scotland on the 3rd and 4th, becoming widespread with rain, sleet and snow over much of England, north Wales and southern Scotland. Blizzard conditions existed over higher ground on the 5th. Sleet and snow fell for much of the day on the 5th with 3 to 6 cm (1·2 to 2·4 in) in southern England. Holme Moss (W. Yorkshire) had a depth of 40 cm (15·7 in). On the 7th a golfer was struck by lightning and badly burned at Southampton. The 11th was a particularly stormy day over south-west England and south Wales. A mean wind of 49 knots (56·4 mph) at Milford Haven (Dyfed) equalled the previous highest speed for April and a new record gust of 84 knots (96·7 mph) was recorded. Aberporth recorded a gust of 78 knots (89·8 mph), the highest for 50 years in that area. The strong winds brought chaos to roads and ships in the Irish Sea, blew down trees and telegraph poles and caused much structural damage throughout Wales. At Milford Haven slates were blown from the roofs of many buildings causing roads to be closed to traffic and pedestrians. Thousands of homes in Devon, Cornwall and south-west and central Wales were without power when falling trees brought down power lines. On the 13th Halstead (Essex) had a violent thunderstorm with heavy rain and hail causing local flooding. Hail lay to a depth of 5 cm (2·0 in) for a while. Snow fell in some places on the 22nd and 13 cm (5·1 in) lay at Knochan Nature Reserve near Ullapool (Highland) on the 24th. There was sleet and snow overnight on the 24th–25th with 10 cm (3·9 in) lying at Nottingham on the 25th. Monthly mean temperatures were below normal nearly everywhere except at Lerwick (Shetland) which had a mean slightly above normal. The 1st was warm in most southern and western areas when 17·6°C (63·7°F) was recorded at Little Butser (Hampshire), 17·4°C (63·3°F) at Valley (Gwynedd) and 17·0°C (62·6°F) at Poolewe (Highland). The highest temperature of the month was 18·0°C (64·4°F) at Kew (Greater London) and the lowest was −7·6°C (18·3°F) at Eskdalemuir (Dumfries and Galloway) on the 24th. Sunshine totals were below normal nearly everywhere except for parts of central southern England, south-west England, and southern and western Wales where they were slightly above. The highest daily total was 16·3 hours at Inverness (Highland) on the 1st and the highest monthly total was 211 hours at The Lizard (Cornwall).

May.—Rainfall totals were well below normal except in parts of Scotland. Some areas of eastern and southern England were particularly dry. Central London had its driest May for about 300 years and over England and Wales it was the driest since 1896 and fifth driest since 1727. Areas close to the Thames Estuary had less than 1 mm (0·04 in) of rain in the whole month. Central London had 0·9 mm (0·035 in) and Manston and Ulcombe (Kent) both had only 0·4 mm (0·16 in). Worthing (W. Sussex) had its driest May since 1902 and Colchester (Essex) had its driest since 1896. On the 4th extensive dust was reported at Winterbourne (West Midlands) and on the 9th a dust devil was seen at Hurst Green (Surrey). The night of the 9th–10th was cold with ground frost as far south as the Midlands. Northern and western areas had rain on the 11th with snow on the Scottish mountains. There were thunderstorms down the east coast from Yorkshire to Norfolk. The 19th brought thunderstorms to northern England and north Wales, and a flash flood caused extensive damage in the Halifax area of West Yorkshire. Red sand was deposited at Winterbourne (West Midlands) on the 23rd. Many places had thunderstorms on the 23rd and 24th, with very heavy rain and flooding in several areas. On the 24th lightning set fire to homes, villages were flooded and thousands of houses plunged into darkness as storms hit the Thames Valley. A further storm area was from Derby to Grantham and intense electrical activity was reported at Keyworth (Notts.) with heavy rain and local flooding. At South Farnborough (Hampshire) 50 mm (1·2 in) of rain fell in three hours. About 95 per cent of the month's rainfall fell during the storms of the 24th. Sleet was reported over Orkney and Shetland on the 29th, when the north and west were cool. Other areas enjoyed a warm, sunny Bank Holiday. Monthly mean temperatures were above normal in all areas. A mean temperature of 14·4°C (57·9°F) at Hampstead (Greater London) was the highest for May since 1909. On the 21st the temperature rose to 27·4°C (81·3°F) at Kinlochewe (Highland) and at Cape Wrath (Highland) 24·4°C (75·9°F) was the highest May temperature since 1940. On the 24th Wyton (Cambridgeshire) recorded 28·4°C (83·1°F), the highest May temperature there since records began in 1954. The highest temperature of the month was 29·4°C (84·9°F) at

Heathrow (Greater London) on the 23rd and the lowest was −2·6°C (27·3°F) at Tummel Bridge (Tayside) on the 10th. Sunshine totals were mostly well above normal with some places having record totals. Most places south of a line from south Devon to north Norfolk had in excess of 300 hours in the month; the last time such a large area had so much sunshine in May was in 1909. Oxford with 301 hours had its highest total since 1879 and at Newtown Linford (Leics.) 263 hours was the highest total ever recorded there for any month. The highest daily total was 15·9 hours at Lerwick (Shetland) on the 21st and 22nd, and the highest monthly total was 335 hours at Folkestone (Kent).

June.—Rainfall totals were below normal in the south-western third of England and Wales but above normal elsewhere, with the Liverpool area being particularly wet. Most areas had scattered showers on the 1st when central and southern England had prolonged and heavy rain locally. Showers occurred in many areas on the 2nd and 3rd. On the 5th and 6th thundery showers became widespread and prolonged in some areas, notably in a belt from Merseyside to south-east England. Gillingham (Kent) had a layer of hail several centimetres deep on the 6th. Thunderstorms were again widespread in areas away from the extreme north and extreme south on the 8th. On the 13th there were heavy thunderstorms over northern England and north-west Wales, with scattered rain in other western areas. There were isolated heavy showers on the 14th. On the 21st there were showers on the east coast and overnight on the 21st–22nd there were thunderstorms in parts of East Anglia and Kent. On the 26th rain spread into northwestern areas and crossed all areas on the 27th, bringing to an end a dry spell which had lasted 18 days in some places. Rainfall was particularly heavy and prolonged over north Wales and northern England. The Liverpool area had in excess of 40 mm (1·57 in). Many places had further rain on the 27th with thunderstorms in eastern England. Rain crossed Scotland on the 28th, to clear southern England on the 29th. Again rainfall was heavy in several areas. On the 30th yet more rain fell in a belt from north Wales and Lancashire to Humberside, Lincolnshire and Norfolk. The heaviest rain was again in the Liverpool area and 53 mm (2·09 in) fell at Crosby (Merseyside). Monthly mean temperatures were mostly above average except in Scotland, Northumberland and Cumbria where they were near, or a little below average. On the 19th the temperature reached 30°C (86°F) at Fort Augustus (Highland) and on the 20th it was a hot day almost everywhere with temperatures of more than 30°C (86°F) at several places. A temperature of 30·5°C (86·9°F) was recorded at both Finningley (S. Yorkshire) and Kew (Greater London). The lowest temperature of the month was −4·0°C (24·8°F) at Kinbrace (Highland). Sunshine totals were above normal everywhere in the United Kingdom. The highest monthly totals were 323·7 hours at St. Helier (Jersey) and 308·4 hours at Eastbourne (East Sussex).

AVERAGE AND GENERAL VALUES, 1987–1989 (June)

Month	Rainfall (mm)				Temperature (°C)				Bright Sunshine (hrs per day)			
	Aver. 1941–1970	1987	1988	1989	Aver. 1951–1980	1987	1988	1989	Aver. 1951–1980	1987	1988	1989
England and Wales												
January........	86	30	154	47	4·0	1·4	5·8	6·7	1·6	1·7	1·7	2·1
February.......	65	58	63	87	4·1	4·1	5·2	6·4	2·3	2·3	3·7	3·3
March	59	83	94	85	5·9	4·6	6·6	7·8	3·6	3·3	3·1	3·5
April..........	58	66	42	84	8·2	10·3	8·5	6·9	5·1	5·3	4·6	4·6
May	67	48	60	21	11·3	10·3	12·0	13·2	6·3	6·3	6·5	9·0
June	61	102	37	52	14·3	13·1	14·6	14·7	6·7	4·1	5·8	8·0
July	73	77	138	—	16·0	16·2	15·1	—	5·9	5·6	4·9	—
August........	90	72	92	—	15·9	16·0	15·7	—	5·5	5·1	5·8	—
September	83	67	66	—	14·0	14·2	13·8	—	4·6	5·1	4·8	—
October	83	171	92	—	11·0	10·3	11·1	—	3·3	3·4	3·3	—
November	97	81	49	—	7·1	7·2	6·2	—	2·1	1·8	3·0	—
December	90	59	44	—	5·1	6·1	7·7	—	1·5	1·7	1·3	—
YEAR	912	914	931	—	9·8	9·5	10·2	—	4·1	3·8	4·1	—
Scotland												
January........	137	70	193	200	3·5	2·0	4·2	7·3	1·3	1·2	1·4	1·3
February.......	104	95	149	255	3·4	3·5	4·5	5·1	2·4	2·2	2·2	3·1
March	92	142	159	178	5·1	3·8	5·0	5·7	3·3	3·5	3·1	3·6
April..........	90	76	85	70	7·1	8·5	7·2	6·0	5·0	4·1	4·1	4·5
May	91	77	55	56	9·9	9·3	10·5	10·7	5·7	5·7	6·5	7·0
June	92	101	33	77	12·7	11·0	13·6	12·5	5·9	4·6	6·1	6·5
July	112	120	202	—	13·9	14·3	13·7	—	4·9	3·9	4·1	—
August........	129	126	187	—	13·9	13·8	13·9	—	4·6	4·2	4·1	—
September	137	160	156	—	12·2	11·9	12·3	—	3·7	4·9	3·9	—
October	149	165	177	—	9·8	8·2	9·3	—	2·6	2·7	2·4	—
November	142	107	91	—	6·0	6·4	6·0	—	1·7	1·5	2·1	—
December	156	114	150	—	4·5	5·2	7·3	—	1·1	1·1	0·9	—
YEAR	1431	1353	1637	—	8·5	8·2	9·0	—	3·5	3·3	3·4	—

TEMPERATURE, RAINFALL AND WIND SPEED RECORDS

WORLD: The maximum air temperature recorded is 57·8°C. (136°F.) at San Louis, Mexico on August 11, 1933; the minimum air temperature recorded is −89·2°C. (−128·56°F.) at Vostok, Antarctica on July 21, 1983. The greatest rainfall recorded in one day is 1,870 mm. (73·62 in.) at Cilaos, Isle de Réunion on March 16, 1952; the greatest rainfall in one calendar month is 9,300 mm. (366·14 in.) at Cherrapunji, Assam in July 1861, the greatest annual total being 22,990 mm. (905·12 in.) also at Cherrapunji in 1861. The highest gust recorded was 201 knots (231 mph) at Mount Washington Observatory, New Hampshire, U.S.A. on April 12, 1934.

UNITED KINGDOM: The maximum air temperature recorded is 38·1°C. (100·5°F.) at Tonbridge, Kent on July 22 1868; the minimum air temperature recorded is −27·2°C. (−17°F.) at Braemar (Grampian) on February 11, 1895 and 10th January 1982. The greatest rainfall recorded in one day is 280 mm. (11 in.) at Martinstown, Dorset on July 18, 1955. The greatest annual total is 6,528 mm. (257 in.) at Sprinkling Tarn, Cumbria in 1954. The highest gust recorded was 150 knots (173 mph) at Cairngorm (Highland) on March 20, 1986. The highest low-level (below 200 m. (656 ft.)) gust was 123 knots (141·7 mph) at Fraserburgh (Grampian) on February 13, 1989. The highest mean hourly speed was 92 knots (106 mph) at Great Dun Fell (Cumbria) in December 1974. The highest low-level mean hourly speed was 72 knots (83 mph) at Shoreham-by-Sea (Sussex) on October 16, 1987.

WIND FORCE MEASURES

The **Beaufort Scale** of wind force has been accepted internationally and is used in communicating weather conditions. Devised originally by Admiral Sir Francis Beaufort in 1805, it now consists of the numbers 0–17, each representing a certain strength or velocity of wind at 10 m. (33 ft.) above ground in the open.

Scale No.	Wind Force	M.p.h.	Knots	Scale No.	Wind Force	M.p.h.	Knots
0	Calm	1	1	9	Strong gale	47–54	41–47
1	Light air	1–3	1–3	10	Whole gale	55–63	48–55
2	Slight breeze	4–7	4–6	11	Storm	64–72	56–63
3	Gentle breeze	8–12	7–10	12	Hurricane	73–82	64–71
4	Moderate breeze	13–18	11–16	13	—	83–92	72–80
5	Fresh breeze	19–24	17–21	14	—	93–103	81–89
6	Strong breeze	25–31	22–27	15	—	104–114	90–99
7	High wind	32–38	28–33	16	—	115–125	100–108
8	Gale	39–46	34–40	17	—	126–136	109–118

TEMPERATURE, RAINFALL AND SUNSHINE
IN THE UNITED KINGDOM

The following table gives mean air temperature (°C), total monthly rainfall (mm) and mean daily bright sunshine (hrs) at a representative selection of climatological reporting stations in the United Kingdom during the year July 1988 to June 1989 and the calendar year 1988. The heights (in metres) of the reporting stations above mean sea level are also given.

Station	Ht. in mtrs.	July Temp. °C	July Rain mm	July Sun hrs	August Temp. °C	August Rain mm	August Sun hrs	September Temp. °C	September Rain mm	September Sun hrs	October Temp. °C	October Rain mm	October Sun hrs
Aberdeen (Dyce) .	65	13.9	84	5.4	13.8	74	4.7	12.1	60	5.3	8.9	151	2.4
Aberporth	134	13.4	77	4.5	14.1	79	5.2	12.9	76	5.1	10.9	99	3.7
Aldergrove	68	13.9	120	4.0	14.0	112	4.1	12.3	83	3.6	9.9	98	3.1
Aspatria	61	13.9	167	4.9	14.3	93	5.8	12.1	114	4.2	9.9	83	3.4
Bala	163	13.3	134	3.6	13.3	123	4.4	11.7	140	3.7	8.9	115	2.8
Birmingham (Elmdon)	98	14.7	104	4.7	15.1	56	5.9	13.1	54	4.6	10.0	32	3.2
Boulmer	23	14.0	118	5.7	14.3	50	6.1	12.5	56	5.4	9.7	71	3.1
Bournemouth (Hurn)	10	15.2	74	6.3	15.5	70	5.7	13.9	36	5.3	11.5	119	3.8
Bradford	134	14.5	125	—	14.7	88	—	12.2	42	—	9.7	115	3.1
Braemar	339	12.3	146	3.6	12.3	96	4.5	10.7	71	4.5	6.7	130	1.9
Buxton	307	13.1	183	4.2	13.5	150	5.3	11.2	141	4.0	8.3	133	2.7
Cambridge	24	15.5	95	5.0	16.4	47	6.2	—	46	4.6	—	43	3.3
Cheltenham	65	15.5	128	—	16.1	76	5.3	14.1	57	3.8	10.9	62	3.2
Clacton-on-Sea	16	16.3	86	6.0	16.7	27	7.1	14.3	33	4.9	12.1	65	4.0
Douglas	85	13.7	129	—	13.9	116	5.2	12.5	111	4.8	10.6	108	2.8
Dumfries	49	13.5	196	3.9	13.7	123	4.9	11.9	101	4.6	9.3	145	3.0
Dundee	45	14.2	103	—	14.5	130	5.4	12.6	52	4.9	9.2	105	2.4
Durham	102	14.1	115	5.3	14.7	46	6.4	12.5	44	5.4	9.9	76	3.2
East Malling	33	15.7	95	6.2	16.5	31	7.0	14.4	41	4.7	11.9	65	3.7
Edinburgh	134	13.5	143	4.6	14.1	77	5.6	12.3	61	4.2	9.1	56	2.7
Glasgow	107	13.4	169	3.3	13.3	175	4.4	11.9	126	4.4	8.7	129	2.6
Gogerddan	31	14.3	146	3.7	14.5	134	4.4	12.9	102	4.4	10.7	108	3.5
Hastings	45	15.5	58	6.7	16.5	37	7.0	15.0	46	4.4	12.8	94	3.8
Hull	2	15.6	80	—	16.1	57	—	13.7	29	—	10.7	48	—
Inverness	4	13.7	110	3.8	13.7	123	3.5	12.3	28	4.2	8.6	81	2.3
Leeming	32	—	114	4.5	15.3	74	5.7	13.1	26	5.0	9.9	91	3.0
Lerwick	82	12.3	156	4.1	11.8	108	3.1	10.9	97	3.0	8.3	177	1.4
London (Heathrow)	25	16.1	76	5.2	17.1	61	6.3	14.8	28	4.9	12.0	56	3.6
Long Ashton	51	14.7	112	4.9	15.4	117	5.5	13.8	86	5.0	11.3	104	3.4
Lowestoft	25	16.1	71	4.8	16.7	30	5.8	14.1	22	4.1	11.3	30	2.7
Manchester (Ringway)	75	14.5	135	4.0	14.9	106	5.0	12.8	59	3.8	10.3	66	3.5
Manston	44	16.0	39	6.7	16.8	21	7.2	14.6	27	4.6	12.3	81	3.6
Melbury	143	13.6	169	4.0	14.1	140	4.6	13.1	117	4.4	—	137	3.1
Morecambe	7	14.6	157	4.4	15.2	157	5.3	13.1	97	4.6	10.8	119	3.6
Nottingham (Watnall)	117	14.6	142	5.0	15.3	48	5.7	13.1	47	4.7	10.1	58	3.2
Oxford	63	15.3	97	4.5	16.1	39	5.8	14.1	40	4.6	11.3	39	3.9
Penzance	19	14.7	117	6.0	15.1	114	6.1	14.4	42	5.7	12.5	143	3.3
Plymouth	27	14.6	98	5.9	15.1	97	5.8	14.1	45	5.8	12.3	138	3.4
Prestwick	16	13.9	119	4.0	14.2	108	4.3	12.5	119	3.6	9.9	93	3.1
Rhoose	65	14.8	144	5.3	15.3	118	5.3	13.7	96	5.3	11.2	118	3.8
St. Mawgan	103	14.2	143	5.6	15.0	113	5.8	13.9	50	5.3	11.7	159	3.5
Shawbury	72	14.3	102	5.0	14.5	67	5.6	12.9	31	4.5	9.5	49	3.0
Sheffield	131	15.1	107	5.0	15.5	79	5.8	13.1	52	5.5	10.1	89	2.4
Skegness	5	15.7	137	—	16.1	38	—	13.7	20	5.1	—	—	—
Southampton	3	15.5	60	5.8	15.9	61	6.0	14.7	30	—	12.3	84	—
Stornoway	15	12.6	165	3.4	12.7	108	3.0	11.6	129	2.7	9.1	136	2.3
Tenby	5	14.1	154	4.7	14.3	145	5.4	13.1	72	5.2	11.3	137	3.3
Tiree	9	12.9	155	5.8	13.0	183	4.2	11.9	142	3.0	10.0	135	2.7
Torbay (Torquay)	8	15.5	85	6.4	15.8	86	5.7	14.6	28	5.3	12.1	95	3.1
Trawscoed	63	14.1	149	3.2	14.1	110	4.1	12.5	131	4.2	10.5	108	3.3
Ventnor	135	14.5	50	5.9	15.9	39	6.1	14.9	43	5.4	12.9	103	3.5
Waddington	68	15.1	133	5.0	15.7	48	6.2	13.3	21	4.6	10.3	34	3.5
Weymouth	21	15.1	62	6.2	15.7	63	5.8	14.9	29	5.9	12.5	106	3.8
Whitby	41	14.5	72	5.4	15.0	49	6.7	12.9	34	5.1	10.0	87	3.0
Worthing	2	15.4	61	6.6	15.9	40	6.6	14.5	39	5.4	12.5	70	4.0
Writtle	35	15.7	81	—	16.2	45	—	—	49	—	11.1	51	—

TEMPERATURE, RAINFALL AND SUNSHINE IN THE UNITED KINGDOM—*contd.*

Mean temperature of the air (°C), rainfall (mm) and bright sunshine (as mean hours per day) at a representative selection of reporting stations during the year July 1988 to June 1989. Fuller details of the weather are given in the *Monthly Weather Report* published by the Meteorological Office.

| | 1988 | | | | | | | | | 1989 | | | | | |
| | November | | | December | | | Year | | | January | | | February | | |
Station	Temp. °C	Rain mm	Sun hrs	Temp. °C	Rain mm	Sun hrs	Temp. °C	Rain mm	Sun hrs	Temp. °C	Rain mm	Sun hrs	Temp. °C	Rain mm	Sun hrs
Aberdeen (Dyce)	5.7	67	2.6	6.7	23	1.6	8.5	900	4.1	6.6	13	2.3	4.8	38	4.5
Aberporth	6.9	37	3.3	8.3	37	0.9	9.7	898	4.3	6.7	70	2.3	6.1	72	2.8
Aldergrove	5.8	44	2.2	7.2	71	1.2	9.3	955	3.7	6.5	52	1.7	5.3	61	3.2
Aspatria	5.6	49	3.1	7.2	93	0.9	9.2	1030	4.1	7.1	87	1.4	5.8	131	2.6
Bala	4.2	62	2.4	7.4	106	0.9	8.7	359	3.3	5.9	79	1.4	5.5	154	2.6
Birmingham (Elmdon)	4.4	33	2.6	7.4	35	1.2	9.5	658	3.8	5.8	30	1.9	5.6	52	3.3
Boulmer	5.8	67	3.3	7.5	23	2.3	8.9	664	4.4	6.7	9	2.5	5.5	34	3.9
Bournemouth (Hurn)	5.7	23	3.5	7.3	23	1.6	10.2	730	4.7	6.1	35	2.3	6.2	80	3.3
Bradford	5.1	44	2.8	7.1	53	1.5	9.2	926	—	6.3	27	1.8	5.7	92	3.5
Braemar	3.7	53	1.8	5.3	40	0.7	7.0	951	3.3	5.4	68	1.0	2.5	125	2.5
Buxton	4.1	59	3.0	6.1	92	0.8	8.1	1495	3.4	5.0	67	1.7	4.3	135	2.7
Cambridge	—	31	2.7	7.3	24	1.5	—	590	3.8	6.0	26	2.4	6.1	47	3.7
Cheltenham	5.5	28	2.8	7.9	33	1.0	10.5	743	—	6.0	47	2.1	6.0	113	3.4
Clacton-on-Sea	6.2	35	3.2	6.7	28	1.8	10.3	622	4.5	5.9	37	2.7	6.1	38	3.2
Douglas	7.3	106	2.3	8.2	93	1.2	9.7	1179	—	7.4	86	1.6	6.1	123	3.0
Dumfries	4.9	51	2.4	7.1	61	1.4	8.6	1147	3.8	6.7	97	1.3	5.5	104	2.8
Dundee	5.6	68	2.6	6.5	15	—	9.1	830	—	6.9	22	1.9	5.4	48	4.0
Durham	5.5	65	2.9	7.3	28	2.0	9.2	643	4.2	6.3	7	2.1	5.3	48	3.2
East Malling	5.9	28	3.0	7.5	12	1.3	10.5	619	4.3	6.0	23	2.4	6.3	46	3.2
Edinburgh	—	43	2.6	7.0	23	1.2	—	702	—	6.9	48	1.5	—	—	—
Glasgow	5.3	78	2.7	6.9	95	1.1	—	1240	3.2	6.7	103	1.0	4.8	—	—
Gogerddan	5.7	64	2.8	8.1	64	0.7	10.0	1108	3.9	7.1	79	1.9	6.5	77	2.6
Hastings	7.7	30	3.7	7.9	19	1.3	10.9	737	4.6	7.3	25	2.9	6.9	51	2.9
Hull	5.9	41	—	7.5	18	—	10.1	568	—	6.6	21	—	6.3	30	—
Inverness	6.3	32	2.1	7.7	58	0.8	9.1	790	3.3	7.5	54	2.1	5.1	148	3.4
Leeming	4.7	66	2.7	7.5	16	1.9	—	654	4.0	6.2	9	1.9	5.9	41	3.6
Lerwick	5.7	129	0.7	5.9	129	0.2	7.5	1304	2.8	6.3	144	0.6	4.1	250	1.5
London (Heathrow)	5.9	16	3.0	7.6	9	1.2	10.9	552	4.1	6.3	26	1.9	6.4	40	3.4
Long Ashton	6.0	42	2.9	8.0	20	1.1	10.3	911	4.2	6.8	53	2.1	6.7	108	3.6
Lowestoft	6.3	32	2.8	6.5	26	1.2	10.1	572	3.8	5.5	28	1.7	5.8	39	3.4
Manchester (Ringway)	5.2	51	2.9	7.1	51	1.1	9.7	886	3.7	6.3	35	2.0	5.9	81	3.4
Manston	6.6	56	3.2	7.1	17	1.4	10.5	560	4.6	5.9	24	2.6	6.2	25	3.7
Melbury	—	68	2.8	—	79	0.5	—	1405	3.9	6.7	95	2.1	6.6	151	2.9
Morecambe	5.7	53	3.2	7.5	117	1.0	10.0	1133	4.2	6.9	45	1.6	6.3	110	3.0
Nottingham (Watnall)	5.1	32	3.3	6.9	27	1.6	9.5	711	3.9	5.6	26	2.1	5.1	51	3.1
Oxford	5.3	29	3.1	7.7	13	1.5	10.3	572	3.8	6.3	33	2.2	6.5	55	3.8
Penzance	9.5	74	3.6	9.9	62	0.8	11.3	1207	4.6	8.5	73	2.2	8.3	108	3.9
Plymouth	8.2	47	3.5	9.5	50	0.9	11.0	1017	4.7	7.7	57	2.3	7.7	130	3.3
Prestwick	6.1	64	2.9	8.0	111	0.8	9.3	1095	3.8	5.2	105	1.2	6.1	94	2.5
Rhoose	6.3	39	3.1	8.1	31	1.2	10.3	1027	4.4	6.7	57	2.6	6.3	87	3.7
St. Mawgan	8.3	71	3.9	9.1	61	0.9	10.7	1184	4.6	7.7	61	2.3	7.3	125	3.5
Shawbury	4.5	39	2.5	7.5	22	1.1	9.3	681	3.9	5.8	22	2.1	5.5	48	3.5
Sheffield	5.7	51	2.3	7.6	36	1.1	9.8	916	3.7	6.5	21	1.7	6.0	75	3.3
Skegness	5.9	28	3.8	6.7	17	2.1	—	—	—	5.7	35	2.4	5.3	19	3.8
Southampton	6.9	18	3.5	8.1	19	1.3	10.9	633	—	6.9	25	2.1	7.0	80	3.6
Stornoway	6.9	93	1.3	7.0	111	0.6	8.5	1295	2.9	7.3	228	0.9	4.7	181	2.0
Tenby	7.5	53	3.1	8.7	36	1.0	10.3	1227	4.3	7.5	77	2.1	—	—	—
Tiree	7.7	102	1.5	8.3	101	0.5	9.3	1362	3.7	7.9	154	1.0	5.7	184	2.4
Torbay (Torquay)	8.5	29	3.2	9.3	33	1.1	11.3	881	4.5	7.9	43	2.5	7.7	108	3.3
Trawscoed	5.5	69	2.6	8.0	80	0.3	9.7	1252	3.3	6.4	84	1.5	6.3	115	2.5
Ventnor	8.2	28	3.8	8.3	37	1.7	10.9	705	4.8	7.5	27	2.7	7.3	59	3.3
Waddington	5.0	41	3.4	6.9	24	1.8	9.5	615	4.1	5.7	21	2.3	5.5	26	3.9
Weymouth	7.7	36	3.3	8.7	28	1.3	11.0	729	4.7	7.8	25	2.3	7.7	73	3.4
Whitby	5.7	71	3.4	7.5	19	2.1	9.2	629	4.2	5.9	11	2.3	5.9	35	4.0
Worthing	6.9	29	3.7	8.0	28	1.4	10.7	639	4.8	6.9	27	2.6	6.7	53	3.1
Writtle	5.1	30	—	6.7	19	1.1	10.0	595	—	5.4	26	2.2	5.7	36	3.4

TEMPERATURE, RAINFALL AND SUNSHINE IN THE UNITED KINGDOM—*contd.*

Mean temperature of the air (°C), rainfall (mm.) and bright sunshine (as mean hours per day) at a representative selection of reporting stations during the year July 1988 to June 1989. Fuller details of the weather are given in the *Monthly Weather Report* published by the Meteorological Office.

| | | | | | | | | | | 1989 | | |
Station	March Temp. °C	March Rain mm	March Sun hrs	April Temp. °C	April Rain mm	April Sun hrs	May Temp. °C	May Rain mm	May Sun hrs	June Temp. °C	June Rain mm	June Sun hrs
Aberdeen (Dyce)	5·7	49	4·6	5·5	54	4·6	10·3	42	7·1	12·3	50	7·1
Aberporth	7·1	86	3·4	6·5	64	6·2	12·1	12	8·6	13·3	42	8·4
Aldergrove	6·3	77	3·6	6·1	80	4·4	11·3	30	8·0	13·7	71	7·3
Aspatria	6·4	135	3·8	6·3	48	5·5	11·7	24	8·4	13·3	55	7·5
Bala	6·5	184	3·1	5·3	112	3·9	11·3	20	7·9	12·5	75	6·9
Birmingham (Elmdon)	7·3	61	3·2	6·3	88	3·9	12·8	15	8·2	14·5	73	7·7
Boulmer............	6·1	27	5·1	5·8	31	4·9	10·3	17	7·6	12·1	58	8·5
Bournemouth (Hurn)	8·0	93	3·4	6·7	68	5·9	13·6	12	10·2	14·9	38	9·2
Bradford	6·9	79	3·1	5·8	91	3·0	12·3	24	7·1	14·1	75	6·7
Braemar	3·5	127	3·7	3·7	40	4·0	9·3	37	6·7	11·0	45	5·9
Buxton.............	5·5	146	3·1	4·5	119	4·0	11·4	40	8·3	13·1	105	7·6
Cambridge..........	8·2	40	3·2	6·9	76	4·1	13·5	6	8·7	15·3	41	7·2
Cheltenham	7·9	88	3·3	7·1	113	4·3	14·6	54	7·6	15·4	50	7·1
Clacton-on-Sea......	7·7	50	3·5	7·1	59	4·2	13·0	5	10·2	14·4	42	8·8
Douglas	6·5	117	4·1	6·5	102	5·5	11·3	15	8·8	13·0	65	7·8
Dumfries	5·9	138	3·9	5·9	69	4·4	10·9	28	7·9	12·5	38	6·6
Dundee	6·1	49	4·2	6·4	27	4·8	11·7	26	6·9	13·5	33	—
Durham	6·5	21	4·2	6·0	50	4·7	11·4	8	7·9	13·5	52	7·1
East Malling	8·5	59	3·3	7·5	85	4·3	13·9	2	10·1	15·3	40	9·1
Edinburgh..........	5·9	50	3·9	5·8	33	4·7	11·2	35	6·9	13·1	54	6·2
Glasgow	5·4	131	—	6·2	68	—	11·3	30	—	—	42	—
Gogerddan	7·3	113	2·7	6·4	96	5·8	12·3	16	8·7	13·6	85	7·6
Hastings	8·3	62	3·6	7·7	86	5·5	14·2	4	10·7	15·3	52	9·5
Hull	7·7	55	—	6·7	50	—	13·1	13	—	15·0	42	—
Inverness	6·1	79	4·1	6·3	30	4·2	11·5	48	6·6	13·3	53	5·9
Leeming............	6·9	43	3·9	6·1	51	4·0	12·3	5	8·2	14·3	78	8·1
Lerwick	4·7	146	3·3	5·5	58	4·6	8·2	67	6·7	9·9	42	6·3
London (Heathrow)	8·7	57	3·2	7·9	64	4·8	15·5	12	1·0	16·7	35	8·6
Long Ashton........	8·1	99	3·7	6·9	85	5·7	—	—	—	—	—	—
Lowestoft	7·9	43	—	6·9	58	—	12·8	9	—	14·5	70	—
Manchester (Ringway)	7·1	66	2·8	6·4	77	4·2	12·9	32	8·3	14·5	81	8·1
Manston	8·3	43	3·6	7·5	77	4·3	13·4	0	10·5	15·0ᵇ	48	9·2
Melbury............	7·5	161	2·7	6·0	93	5·3	12·7	27	8·2	13·2	47	8·7
Morecambe	7·1	121	3·6	7·3	52	5·6	12·7	22	8·9	14·7	73	7·8
Nottingham (Watnall)..........	6·9	68	3·5	5·9	115	3·9	12·7	15	8·6	14·7	54	8·0
Oxford	8·3	47	3·3	7·3	64	4·5	14·1	29	9·7	15·7	46	8·1
Penzance	9·1	129	3·4	8·1	86	6·8	13·9	6	8·5	15·1	27	9·0
Plymouth	8·7	103	3·2	7·5	82	6·2	14·4	6	10·1	15·3	21	9·2
Prestwick	6·1	121	3·0	6·3	51	5·0	11·4	25	7·9	13·0	60	7·7
Rhoose	7·7	94	3·0	6·7	60	5·8	13·9	10	9·0	14·7	61	8·3
St. Mawgan.........	8·2	99	2·9	7·3	84	6·9	14·2	23	9·3	14·7	39	9·6
Shawbury	6·9	48	3·4	5·9	80	4·3	12·5	26	8·3	14·1	43	8·0
Sheffield	—	78	4·1	6·1	115	3·6	13·3	26	9·1	15·1	54	8·5
Skegness	7·3	46	3·6	6·5	45	4·4	11·9	5	—	14·1	45	8·9
Southampton	8·5	80	3·3	7·9	74	5·3	15·2	4	10·2	16·3	37	8·9
Stornoway	5·2	163	3·5	5·7	51	4·7	9·4	48	6·2	10·8	75	5·2
Tenby	7·9	153	3·3	6·4	66	5·9	12·8	7	8·4	13·9	56	8·1
Tiree..............	6·0	172	3·6	6·0	78	5·9	9·9	30	7·9	11·5	57	7·4
Torbay (Torquay) ...	8·9	98	3·0	7·6	74	5·1	14·3	1	9·3	15·3	25	8·1
Trawscoed..........	7·3	133	2·3	5·9	99	4·6	12·1	24	6·8	13·2	80	6·2
Ventnor............	8·6	67	3·6	7·7	61	5·9	14·3	5	10·7	15·8	28	9·6
Waddington	7·2	44	3·6	6·1	82	4·1	12·9	8	9·4	14·6	75	8·0
Weymouth	8·6	90	3·1	7·5	69	6·0	13·9	2	10·4	15·3	13	8·5
Whitby.............	7·1	30	4·2	6·0	43	4·5	11·4	25	8·7	13·5	60	8·3
Worthing	8·3	58	3·5	7·5	48	5·5	14·2	3	10·3	15·5	28	9·4
Writtle.............	8·0	52	3·4	6·9	70	4·2	13·1	10	9·7	14·8	44	8·3

METEOROLOGICAL OBSERVATIONS, LONDON (HEATHROW)

Weather Record, July, 1988

Day	Max. °C	Min. °C	Wind speed knots	Rainfall mm	Sunshine hrs
1	20.1	13.2	7.5	0.8	4.1
2	19.0	12.7	7.3	2.8	10.2
3	16.5	13.4	6.7	13.5	1.9
4	17.1	13.3	7.7	5.9	0.9
5	21.4	14.1	4.9	8.2	7.6
6	19.5	13.6	8.6	1.4	8.1
7	19.4	14.4	9.3	0.0	7.9
8	20.2	15.1	7.9	0.0	9.2
9	19.9	15.4	7.8	0.0	6.3
10	18.6	16.0	11.7	2.7	0.0
11	20.7	15.1	7.5	1.5	12.8
12	20.5	15.6	6.0	5.6	3.8
13	19.5	13.2	6.4	4.0	2.7
14	17.6	14.2	7.4	0.5	1.4
15	20.5	15.0	6.5	0.0	6.6
16	18.1	14.7	5.9	10.5	3.1
17	19.9	14.0	5.9	0.2	1.9
18	22.6	16.0	7.0	0.0	9.5
19	20.7	14.7	3.5	0.2	5.7
20	21.7	16.7	4.0	0.2	3.5
21	23.0	16.2	7.8	5.5	1.8
22	21.0	16.1	8.4	8.4	0.1
23	21.7	18.4	8.7	0.1	0.5
24	20.8	15.1	10.9	0.0	11.1
25	21.0	15.0	11.2	0.4	3.5
26	21.2	14.0	7.3	0.2	8.4
27	21.0	14.9	6.4	0.2	8.4
28	17.5	14.6	9.0	0.0	0.0
29	18.9	13.8	8.9	0.7	12.7
30	19.5	13.1	8.8	1.1	6.4
31	20.3	14.8	5.4	1.6	1.6
Total	—	—	—	76.2	161.7
Mean	20.0	14.7	7.5	—	—
Temp. °F	68.0	58.5	—	—	—
Average	22.0	12.9	8.2	51.0	189.7

Weather Record, August, 1988

Max. °C	Min. °C	Wind speed knots	Rainfall mm	Sunshine hrs	Day
19.7	15.4	3.5	0.0	2.5	1
19.5	13.5	2.7	7.3	0.8	2
20.9	15.8	3.8	0.0	9.9	3
21.1	16.3	5.4	0.0	4.2	4
22.5	16.5	4.4	0.0	8.6	5
27.4	16.6	2.5	0.0	13.7	6
29.1	19.4	6.3	0.0	13.5	7
26.6	19.1	4.9	0.2	7.7	8
23.8	18.0	4.9	0.0	7.6	9
20.2	16.0	5.1	0.0	2.5	10
20.1	15.1	5.7	0.5	3.9	11
22.2	14.0	0.0	0.0	7.6	12
20.0	15.2	6.9	0.0	0.5	13
22.6	16.9	9.3	0.1	5.9	14
22.6	16.3	4.3	0.0	10.7	15
24.0	16.9	3.1	0.0	13.5	16
26.9	20.0	5.1	0.0	11.4	17
25.7	17.5	7.6	4.6	7.2	18
21.7	14.9	9.7	2.2	7.0	19
22.2	14.4	8.6	1.5	8.1	20
16.9	13.1	6.0	0.5	0.1	21
22.6	13.6	3.7	0.0	7.7	22
24.0	15.9	4.5	1.1	2.0	23
26.9	14.2	6.6	1.1	2.7	24
25.7	13.9	8.8	0.0	7.1	25
21.7	14.8	4.5	0.0	1.1	26
21.2	14.4	8.6	1.5	8.1	27
16.9	13.1	6.0	0.5	0.1	28
20.6	14.3	7.6	0.0	9.8	29
21.0	15.2	8.4	13.1	5.7	30
20.1	12.2	6.9	28.2	6.1	31
—	—	—	60.9	195.3	Total
21.7	15.7	6.0	—	—	Mean
71.1	60.3	—	—	—	Temp. °F
21.6	12.7	8.0	58.0	176.4	Average

Weather Record, September, 1988

Day	Max. °C	Min. °C	Wind speed knots	Rainfall mm	Sunshine hrs
1	18.9	14.2	11.1	4.1	2.9
2	17.2	12.3	11.4	2.7	7.4
3	19.2	12.5	6.1	0.0	7.8
4	20.0	14.1	5.7	0.5	9.9
5	22.1	15.5	4.5	0.0	6.4
6	24.1	14.2	3.0	0.0	7.7
7	26.2	18.0	5.8	0.0	11.2
8	25.7	19.4	5.6	0.0	8.6
9	22.8	16.4	4.6	0.0	9.8
10	23.0	15.5	4.2	0.0	8.0
11	19.1	12.0	4.5	0.1	4.6
12	18.6	13.0	7.3	0.4	5.2
13	14.9	10.8	5.5	0.3	2.6
14	14.7	12.0	8.1	0.0	0.1
15	16.1	12.7	5.6	0.3	4.0
16	19.6	12.6	4.5	0.0	7.5
17	18.4	14.3	4.2	0.0	0.0
18	18.3	13.1	2.5	0.0	4.0
19	17.4	11.7	2.6	0.0	5.5
20	13.4	9.7	2.2	0.0	0.0
21	17.6	12.4	2.6	0.0	0.0
22	19.6	12.2	6.2	3.6	2.3
23	17.0	11.5	11.3	0.0	8.8
24	16.5	14.1	11.1	2.0	0.0
25	20.5	15.0	9.3	0.0	1.1
26	19.1	15.5	10.4	1.7	0.1
27	17.2	15.6	9.5	9.3	0.0
28	16.7	9.9	10.7	2.8	3.2
29	15.7	9.5	4.8	0.0	9.1
30	15.0	9.1	2.4	0.0	10.0
31					
Total	—	—	—	27.8	147.8
Mean	18.8	13.3	6.2	—	—
Temp. °F	65.8	55.9	—	—	—
Average	19.2	10.6	7.9	56.0	144.7

Weather Record, October, 1988

Max. °C	Min. °C	Wind speed knots	Rainfall mm	Sunshine hrs	Day
16.0	8.3	3.6	0.0	8.6	1
17.1	9.0	2.2	0.0	9.1	2
17.6	10.5	2.1	0.0	2.1	3
16.6	13.0	6.3	2.0	0.0	4
15.9	10.4	5.5	8.0	3.3	5
15.4	9.3	12.3	3.0	4.9	6
13.3	9.0	13.2	0.0	6.5	7
13.7	9.2	9.6	20.2	0.1	8
13.7	9.8	7.3	9.6	1.1	9
13.9	7.7	5.1	0.0	9.9	10
13.3	9.8	9.7	2.9	0.8	11
15.4	9.6	6.0	2.3	2.9	12
14.5	9.4	3.6	0.0	1.1	13
17.5	11.2	5.0	0.0	2.6	14
14.6	13.3	7.2	0.0	0.0	15
15.0	13.0	7.1	0.0	0.0	16
14.8	12.8	7.7	0.3	0.0	17
19.0	14.3	7.3	0.8	0.1	18
19.3	14.4	4.7	2.1	2.0	19
16.3	9.5	3.0	0.1	3.9	20
17.0	7.1	3.1	0.1	4.9	21
17.5	12.5	5.4	0.0	6.1	22
16.3	12.4	4.6	0.5	0.5	23
16.5	12.5	3.6	4.4	2.2	24
16.5	13.7	4.5	0.0	0.1	25
15.1	13.3	8.3	0.0	0.8	26
16.8	11.7	8.6	0.0	3.2	27
15.3	9.5	4.0	0.0	7.5	28
11.1	5.1	3.1	0.0	8.2	29
10.6	3.1	2.9	0.0	8.7	30
10.7	2.4	2.1	0.0	8.8	31
—	—	—	56.3	110.0	Total
15.5	10.2	5.8	—	—	Mean
59.9	50.4	—	—	—	Temp. °F
15.2	7.6	7.8	56.0	104.4	Average

Entries of Maximum Temperature cover the day period 9–21 h.; Minimum Temperature the night period 21–9 h. entered to the day of reading; Rainfall is for the 24 hours commencing at 9 h. on the day of entry; Sunshine is for the 24 hours 0–24 h.; Mean Wind Speed is 10 metres above the ground. 100 knots = 115·1 m.p.h.; 100 mm. = 3·94 ins.; °F. = 9/5°C. + 32.
Averages are for the period 1951–1980 except for mean wind speed which is for 1961–1980.

Weather Record, November, 1988

Day	Temperature Max. °C	Temperature Min. °C	Wind speed knots	Rain-fall mm	Sun-shine hrs
1	12·2	0·3	2·2	0·0	8·1
2	11·1	3·9	3·0	0·0	3·4
3	8·9	2·9	7·4	0·0	8·3
4	7·7	0·5	5·4	0·0	8·6
5	9·8	0·9	2·0	0·0	5·3
6	9·4	0·6	1·8	0·0	0·6
7	11·7	4·0	4·3	0·0	4·2
8	9·4	5·5	6·3	1·7	0·0
9	16·0	14·2	5·9	0·0	0·2
10	16·0	13·1	7·4	0·0	0·2
11	13·1	9·0	2·1	0·3	0·4
12	12·1	5·5	2·3	0·0	1·5
13	10·8	5·1	3·5	0·0	7·6
14	11·0	3·5	2·5	0·0	4·3
15	7·1	1·4	2·0	0·0	0·1
16	12·2	5·3	3·9	0·0	5·8
17	13·8	8·9	5·2	0·2	0·0
18	11·0	6·9	6·7	0·2	0·0
19	6·5	2·6	2·0	2·2	0·0
20	5·7	0·5	6·9	0·5	2·0
21	4·0	−0·7	5·2	0·0	4·9
22	5·5	−2·5	2·7	0·1	6·4
23	6·9	−0·7	2·0	0·0	6·1
24	7·1	−2·3	2·0	0·0	1·7
25	4·0	1·2	2·0	0·0	0·0
26	6·3	1·5	2·1	0·0	0·0
27	6·1	−0·4	2·2	0·3	5·7
28	11·5	6·0	6·5	0·7	0·0
29	9·6	7·4	3·9	9·7	0·0
30	13·0	6·6	4·8	0·1	3·8
31					
Total	—	—	—	16·0	89·2
Mean	9·7	3·7	3·9	—	—
Temp. °F	49·5	38·7	—	—	—
Average	10·2	3·9	8·9	62·0	64·0

Weather Record, December, 1988

Temperature Max. °C	Temperature Min. °C	Wind speed knots	Rain-fall mm	Sun-shine hrs	Day
8·0	3·5	5·1	0·0	0·0	1
3·7	2·6	2·4	0·1	0·0	2
10·0	3·4	5·0	5·4	0·3	3
9·2	5·6	8·1	0·6	0·0	4
8·0	4·1	5·0	0·1	1·5	5
7·6	3·9	7·6	0·0	4·0	6
7·0	1·2	2·8	0·0	2·9	7
10·5	6·4	4·7	0·0	0·1	8
13·1	8·8	5·0	0·0	0·0	9
13·1	9·8	4·7	0·0	6·2	10
11·1	8·2	4·9	0·2	0·3	11
10·4	5·0	5·3	0·0	5·8	12
10·8	5·5	2·1	0·0	0·0	13
9·6	7·1	2·5	0·0	0·0	14
8·8	7·6	2·0	0·0	0·0	15
9·3	5·7	2·5	0·0	0·0	16
8·1	2·2	3·0	0·0	2·4	17
10·6	4·6	6·7	0·0	0·2	18
12·2	6·9	12·4	0·5	4·2	19
7·9	3·4	3·7	0·0	0·2	20
12·1	9·5	5·4	0·0	0·0	21
12·1	9·3	10·2	0·0	0·3	22
13·5	9·0	12·5	0·0	1·0	23
13·5	9·1	7·9	0·0	0·0	24
12·1	10·3	4·3	0·1	0·0	25
13·9	11·0	9·7	1·9	0·0	26
11·4	7·0	3·8	0·0	5·6	27
12·9	8·8	4·7	0·0	2·5	28
9·8	7·9	3·7	0·0	0·0	29
8·8	6·0	2·3	0·0	0·0	30
9·2	6·9	2·0	0·0	0·0	31
—	—	—	8·9	37·5	Total
10·3	6·5	5·2	—	—	Mean
50·5	43·7	—	—	—	Temp. °F
7·9	2·2	7·0	55·0	43·9	Average

Weather Record, January, 1989

Day	Temperature Max. °C	Temperature Min. °C	Wind speed knots	Rain-fall mm	Sun-shine hrs
1	8·3	6·3	2·5	0·0	0·0
2	8·2	3·0	4·8	0·0	0·0
3	6·2	4·8	6·6	0·4	0·0
4	11·2	5·2	8·3	0·0	3·8
5	10·4	3·0	6·8	3·7	0·0
6	10·7	7·9	3·6	0·0	4·0
7	11·7	8·5	3·0	0·0	0·0
8	10·4	8·8	4·7	0·0	0·0
9	11·4	9·4	5·3	0·2	0·0
10	8·3	2·2	2·7	0·0	5·7
11	9·0	0·4	5·9	0·2	5·6
12	9·8	2·3	6·8	5·0	0·9
13	11·7	4·1	8·0	3·8	1·1
14	10·0	5·8	10·0	0·0	7·3
15	11·0	7·6	8·0	0·0	0·0
16	10·3	7·9	6·9	1·5	1·0
17	9·8	3·8	4·3	0·3	0·7
18	7·5	−0·5	1·9	0·0	6·1
19	4·6	−2·3	2·1	0·2	0·0
20	6·8	3·0	3·2	4·4	0·0
21	10·2	4·0	6·2	2·1	2·7
22	9·3	1·2	3·5	0·0	7·5
23	11·6	6·8	4·7	0·0	1·9
24	8·0	3·5	5·9	0·0	2·9
25	5·1	3·0	5·1	0·0	0·0
26	11·1	4·8	3·1	0·0	3·6
27	11·6	6·7	7·2	0·0	0·4
28	10·1	3·6	5·1	4·0	0·0
29	7·5	−1·9	2·5	0·2	3·0
30	8·7	1·9	2·1	0·0	0·9
31	7·5	3·2	3·2	0·0	0·1
Total	—	—	—	26·0	59·2
Mean	9·3	4·1	5·0	—	—
Temp. °F	48·7	39·4	—	—	—
Average	6·7	1·1	8·6	51·0	48·8

Weather Record, February, 1989

Temperature Max. °C	Temperature Min. °C	Wind speed knots	Rain-fall mm	Sun-shine hrs	Day
4·4	2·9	2·5	0·0	0·0	1
5·5	1·0	2·4	0·0	0·5	2
10·6	1·4	6·3	0·0	4·4	3
11·2	8·1	12·0	0·5	0·1	4
12·2	8·5	6·3	0·0	1·7	5
15·0	10·0	10·7	0·0	8·3	6
12·3	7·7	7·8	0·0	5·2	7
12·1	4·4	3·5	0·0	5·0	8
12·0	3·5	5·3	0·0	6·7	9
9·6	3·9	3·7	0·0	0·5	10
11·1	0·7	5·7	0·1	5·9	11
11·2	3·9	5·7	0·0	3·5	12
10·7	5·8	8·7	2·4	0·4	13
9·7	4·9	8·5	0·0	6·1	14
11·5	3·6	9·4	1·5	0·1	15
7·8	1·8	3·2	6·1	3·2	16
11·4	3·6	5·9	5·1	0·1	17
13·5	12·2	13·0	0·2	0·0	18
13·0	9·5	10·1	0·5	0·0	19
10·4	4·1	5·5	0·0	7·5	20
10·6	3·5	2·6	0·5	8·9	21
9·7	3·8	6·2	2·4	0·4	22
8·5	2·0	7·3	1·8	8·5	23
6·2	4·2	11·3	2·5	0·0	24
6·1	3·1	8·0	9·2	0·5	25
8·3	3·2	10·5	6·3	4·3	26
9·6	2·1	7·4	1·1	3·8	27
9·5	3·1	8·8	0·0	8·6	28
					29
					30
					31
—	—	—	40·2	94·2	Total
10·1	4·5	7·1	—	—	Mean
50·2	40·1	—	—	—	Temp. °F
7·3	1·3	9·3	38·0	62·2	Average

Weather Record, March, 1989

Day	Temperature Max. °C	Temperature Min. °C	Wind speed knots	Rain-fall mm	Sun-shine hrs
1	8.8	5.5	1.6	1.1	0.4
2	12.4	5.6	6.3	5.5	2.0
3	11.0	6.6	4.0	0.3	2.4
4	13.0	7.6	4.7	0.5	0.8
5	15.7	10.9	7.4	0.0	5.9
6	17.6	11.6	6.6	0.4	4.4
7	9.6	5.8	4.2	0.0	0.1
8	10.3	3.7	5.5	0.2	5.6
9	11.4	8.9	12.0	1.0	0.0
10	11.9	9.1	7.3	2.6	0.0
11	11.5	7.0	2.9	0.0	1.9
12	10.6	5.6	7.1	0.5	0.0
13	11.8	6.9	12.7	0.0	8.5
14	10.2	6.1	9.8	0.0	8.0
15	12.1	8.4	6.3	6.2	3.7
16	6.8	2.8	7.7	10.0	0.0
17	8.3	3.4	5.4	0.0	4.9
18	9.9	4.0	8.6	0.7	0.0
19	13.4	10.3	8.7	4.0	1.1
20	11.3	4.7	7.2	11.0	6.9
21	10.7	4.3	6.1	2.8	0.1
22	13.5	4.2	12.9	0.5	2.6
23	8.4	5.4	9.6	1.3	3.7
24	14.9	7.7	14.6	0.0	2.3
25	11.7	6.5	5.3	0.0	5.0
26	16.9	10.6	6.2	0.0	8.2
27	18.8	12.7	4.4	0.0	6.9
28	18.6	9.1	5.1	0.0	3.0
29	15.1	9.0	4.8	0.0	0.5
30	18.4	9.0	3.8	0.0	10.0
31	18.8	9.1	3.4	0.0	9.1
Total	—	—	—	56.6	100.0
Mean	12.7	7.2	7.2	—	—
Temp. °F	54.9	45.0	—	—	—
Average	10.2	2.6	9.5	43.0	110.8

Weather Record, April, 1989

Temperature Max. °C	Temperature Min. °C	Wind speed knots	Rain-fall mm	Sun-shine hrs	Day
14.3	7.7	9.0	4.5	7.4	1
11.8	6.3	6.5	1.1	2.1	2
8.0	3.2	9.7	0.0	6.0	3
6.9	1.0	13.0	10.9	3.8	4
4.5	0.5	4.7	11.5	0.0	5
6.0	3.0	4.1	2.2	0.0	6
11.8	6.0	7.0	0.4	8.7	7
12.9	6.6	3.8	0.0	11.3	8
14.8	8.4	6.2	0.5	6.1	9
14.0	7.4	7.6	1.8	2.9	10
13.2	9.3	13.3	8.2	2.9	11
14.0	9.3	4.3	0.2	6.6	12
14.0	7.8	3.4	0.0	7.9	13
14.0	8.0	4.8	0.0	10.0	14
14.2	8.5	6.9	0.0	11.2	15
12.0	7.3	10.6	2.2	0.1	16
8.9	6.4	5.7	0.1	0.0	17
13.6	6.7	3.3	0.0	7.0	18
11.4	8.5	3.5	0.0	6.1	19
10.4	5.0	7.1	1.1	4.8	20
12.2	7.0	7.1	0.2	5.9	21
12.3	7.5	3.4	0.0	1.6	22
13.6	6.0	4.2	0.0	0.4	23
6.6	2.6	5.0	9.5	0.0	24
8.8	4.1	4.9	0.1	2.9	25
11.4	5.6	4.5	6.3	11.8	26
8.9	5.8	5.3	2.6	0.1	27
13.9	7.9	3.3	0.2	12.8	28
9.3	6.9	3.7	0.1	1.1	29
14.9	10.0	5.9	0.5	3.0	30
—	—	—	64.2	144.5	Total
11.4	6.3	6.1	—	—	Mean
52.5	43.3	—	—	—	Temp. °F
13.2	4.6	8.3	41.0	146.9	Average

Weather Record, May, 1989

Day	Temperature Max. °C	Temperature Min. °C	Wind speed knots	Rain-fall mm	Sun-shine hrs
1	16.3	12.0	4.9	0.0	0.1
2	20.6	13.4	3.6	0.0	11.9
3	22.9	15.0	3.8	0.0	12.6
4	23.6	14.1	4.8	0.0	12.9
5	25.0	16.6	4.2	0.0	11.3
6	16.9	11.4	5.8	0.0	13.2
7	19.1	11.3	2.7	0.0	13.8
8	21.9	14.4	3.3	0.0	12.6
9	19.6	13.5	4.5	0.0	11.8
10	18.3	12.4	4.1	0.0	10.3
11	18.1	9.2	7.0	0.4	4.3
12	14.1	9.9	10.4	1.2	6.6
13	15.9	10.2	6.3	0.0	6.5
14	17.9	13.9	4.6	0.0	1.7
15	21.0	15.0	6.3	0.0	12.5
16	20.9	15.8	4.5	0.0	11.6
17	22.0	16.8	2.4	0.0	9.9
18	24.1	18.0	3.3	0.0	7.6
19	24.5	19.1	5.7	0.0	13.0
20	25.2	15.6	7.8	0.0	11.4
21	27.0	20.2	7.1	0.0	12.4
22	25.9	19.9	7.8	0.0	10.5
23	29.4	22.0	4.6	0.0	12.6
24	28.2	17.3	3.7	10.5	3.7
25	18.5	11.7	8.8	0.0	3.0
26	19.7	11.7	8.9	0.0	12.7
27	19.2	12.9	7.4	0.0	14.4
28	21.3	14.1	4.5	0.0	14.8
29	22.6	16.5	4.1	0.0	13.9
30	16.1	10.5	7.3	0.0	8.5
31	16.2	11.6	4.7	0.0	8.0
Total	—	—	—	12.1	310.0
Mean	21.0	14.4	5.4	—	—
Temp. °F	69.8	57.9	—	—	—
Average	17.1	7.8	8.5	48.0	196.1

Weather Record, June, 1989

Temperature Max. °C	Temperature Min. °C	Wind speed knots	Rain-fall mm	Sun-shine hrs	Day
13.4	9.4	3.7	0.0	1.5	1
15.9	11.4	3.7	0.0	8.4	2
15.3	10.4	3.2	0.0	2.5	3
16.2	11.1	5.7	0.0	12.6	4
17.9	10.6	4.3	2.5	7.8	5
12.4	9.4	3.9	12.8	0.3	6
16.6	11.2	6.1	0.1	5.8	7
16.3	10.8	4.3	2.0	0.1	8
19.3	13.5	4.9	0.1	7.6	9
22.2	16.4	4.3	0.0	3.6	10
23.4	16.6	5.3	0.0	9.9	11
28.6	21.4	6.4	0.0	10.1	12
27.8	21.0	5.7	0.0	12.1	13
27.7	22.1	4.1	0.0	6.9	14
27.7	19.9	5.6	0.0	10.0	15
27.0	18.9	4.6	0.0	10.5	16
27.6	18.9	4.9	0.0	10.9	17
26.6	20.3	7.0	0.0	15.1	18
29.1	19.6	6.8	0.0	14.6	19
30.2	22.6	3.8	0.0	14.6	20
23.0	18.1	7.3	0.0	10.8	21
19.6	14.4	6.8	0.0	5.2	22
25.3	17.4	4.1	0.0	14.8	23
25.0	17.7	4.5	0.0	13.8	24
26.9	18.3	6.7	0.0	15.2	25
23.5	17.6	8.2	9.9	9.8	26
19.7	13.8	8.8	1.9	5.6	27
18.7	13.8	9.0	3.6	5.7	28
19.0	10.5	4.7	2.4	5.4	29
21.3	16.0	6.3	0.2	7.3	30
—	—	—	35.5	258.5	Total
22.1	15.8	5.5	—	—	Mean
71.8	60.4	—	—	—	Temp. °F
20.5	10.9	8.4	51.0	206.0	Average

CHRONOLOGICAL NOTES

GEOLOGICAL TIME

The earth is thought to have come into existence approximately 4,600 million years ago, but for nearly half this time, the ARCHEAN era, it was uninhabited; life is generally believed to have emerged in the succeeding PROTEROZOIC era. The Archean and the Proterozoic eras are often together referred to as the PRECAMBRIAN. Although primitive forms of life e.g. algae and bacteria, existed during the Proterozoic era, it is not until the strata of Palaeozoic rocks is reached that abundant fossilized remains appear, initially of small shellfish, followed by plants, primitive fishes and, in the Devonian period (c.400 million B.C.), land-living plants and amphibia.

Since the Precambrian, there have been three great geological eras:

PALAEOZOIC ("ancient life") c.570–c.250 million B.C.
  (i) *Cambrian.* Mainly sandstones, slate and shales; limestones in Scotland. Shelled fossils and invertebrates e.g. trilobites and brachiopods appear.
  (ii) *Ordovician.* Mainly shales and mudstones e.g. in N. Wales; limestones in Scotland.
  (iii) *Silurian.* Shales, mudstones and some limestones, found mostly in Wales and southern Scotland.
  (iv) *Devonian.* Old red sandstone, shale, limestone and slate, e.g. in S. Wales and the West Country. "The age of fishes"—proliferation of fish fossils. First traces of land-living life.
  (v) *Carboniferous.* Coal-bearing rocks, millstone grit, limestone and shale.
  (vi) *Permian.* Marls, sandstones and clays, named after the area of Russia where these strata are widespread. First large-scale appearance of reptile fossils.

There were two great phases of mountain building in the Palaeozoic area: the *Caledonian,* characterized in Britain by N.E.–S.W. lines of hills and valleys; and the later *Hercyian,* widespread in W. Germany and adjacent areas, and in Britain exemplified in E.–W. lines of hills and valleys.

The end of the Palaeozoic was marked by the extensive glaciations of the Permian period in the southern continents and the decline of amphibians; it was succeeded by an era of warm conditions.

MESOZOIC ("middle forms of life") c.250-c.65 million B.C.
  (i) *Triassic.* Mostly sandstone, e.g. in the W. Midlands.
  (ii) *Jurassic.* Mainly limestones and clays, typically displayed in the Jura Mts. and in England in a N.E.–S.W. belt from Lincolnshire and the Wash to the Severn and the Dorset coast.
  (iii) *Cretaceous.* Mainly chalk, clay and sands, e.g. in Kent and Sussex.

Giant reptiles were dominant during the Mesozoic, but it was at this time that marsupial mammals first appeared, as well as *Archaeopteryx lithographica,* the earliest known species of bird. Coniferous trees and flowering plants also developed during the era and, with the birds and the mammals, were the main species to survive into the Caenozoic (or Cenozoic) era. The giant reptiles became extinct.

CAENOZOIC ("recent life") from c.65 million B.C.
  (i) *Eocene.* The emergence of new forms of life, i.e. existing species.
  (ii) *Oligocene.* Fossils of a few still existing species.
  (iii) *Miocene.* Fossil remains show a balance of existing and extinct species.
  (iv) *Pliocene.* Fossil remains show a majority of still existing species.
  (v) *Pleistocene.* The majority of remains are those of still existing species.
  (vi) *Holocene.* The present, post-glacial period. Existing species only, except for a few exterminated by man.

In the last 25 million years, from the Miocene through the Pliocene, the Alpine-Himalayan and the circum-Pacific phases of mountain building reached their climax. During the Pleistocene period ice sheets repeatedly locked up masses of water as land ice; its weight depressed the land, but the locking-up of the water lowered the sea-level by 100–200 metres. The glaciations and interglacials of the Ice Age are extremely difficult to date and classify, but recent scientific opinion considers the Pleistocene to have begun approximately 1·7 million years ago. The last glacial retreat, merging into the Holocene period, was 10,000 years ago.

EARLY MAN

Any consideration of the history of man must start with the fact that all members of the human race belong to one species of animal, i.e. *Homo sapiens,* the definition of a species being in biological terms that all its members can interbreed. As a species of mammal it is possible to group man with other similar types, known as the primates. Amongst these is found a sub-group, the apes, which includes, in addition to man, the chimpanzees, gorillas, orang-utans and gibbons. All lack a tail, have shoulder blades at the back, and a Y-shaped chewing pattern on the surface of their molars, as well as showing the more general primate characteristics of four incisors, a thumb which is able to touch the fingers of the same hand, and finger and toe nails instead of claws. All the factors available to scientific study suggest that human beings have chimpanzees and gorillas as their nearest relatives in the animal world. However, there remains the possibility that there once lived creatures, now extinct, which were closer to modern man than the chimpanzees and gorillas. To decide whether or not this is the case it is necessary to consider the fossil evidence to see if any extinct ape-like forms shared with modern man the characteristics of having flat faces (i.e. the absence of a pronounced muzzle), being bipedal, and possessing large brains.

There are two broad groups of extinct apes recognised by specialists. First the ramapithecines, the remains of which, mainly jaw fragments, have been found in East Africa, Asia, and Turkey. They lived about 14 to 8 million years ago, and from the evidence of their teeth it seems they chewed more in the manner of modern man than the other presently living apes. The second group, the australopithecines, have left much more numerous remains amongst which sub-groups may be detected, although the geographic spread is limited to South and East Africa. Living between 5 and 1·5 million years ago, they were closer relatives of modern man to the extent that they walked upright, did not have an extensive muzzle, and had similar types of pre-molars. The first australopithecine remains were recognised at Taung in South Africa in 1924, and subsequent discoveries include those at the famous site of Olduvai Gorge in Tanzania. Perhaps the most impressive discovery was made at Hadar in Ethiopia in 1974 when about half a skeleton, known as "Lucy", was found.

Also in East Africa, between 2 million and 1·5 million years ago, lived a hominid group which not only walked upright, had a flat face, and a large brain case, but also made simple pebble and flake stone tools. On present evidence these habilines seem to have been the first people to make tools, however crude. This facility is related to the larger brain size and human beings are the only animals to make implements to be used in other processes. These early pebble tool users, because of their distinctive characteristics, have been grouped as a separate sub-species, now extinct, of the genus *Homo*, and are known as *Homo habilis*.

The use of fire, again a human characteristic, is associated with another group of extinct hominids whose remains, about a million years old, are found in South and East Africa, China, Indonesia, North Africa and Europe. No doubt the mastery of the techniques of making fire helped the colonisation of the colder northern areas and in this respect the site of Vertesszollos in Hungary is of particular importance. *Homo erectus* is the name given to this group of fossils and it now includes a number of famous individual discoveries from earlier decades, for example, Solo Man, Heidelberg Man, and especially Peking Man who lived at the cave site at Choukoutien, which has yielded evidence of fire and burnt bone.

The well known group, Neanderthal Man, or *Homo sapiens neandertalensis*, is an extinct form of modern man who lived between about 100,000 and 40,000 years ago, thus spanning the last Ice Age. Indeed, its ability to adapt to the cold climate on the edge of the ice sheets is one of its characteristic features, the remains being only found in Europe, Asia and the Middle East. Complete neanderthal skeletons were found during excavations at Tabun in Israel together with evidence of tool-making and the use of fire. Distinguished by very large brains, it seems that neanderthal man was the first to develop recognisable social customs, especially deliberate burial rites. Why the neanderthalers became extinct is not clear, but it may be connected with the climatic changes at the end of the Ice Ages which would have seriously affected their food supplies; possibly they became too specialised for their own good.

The Swanscombe skull is the only known human fossil remains found in England. Some specialists see Swanscombe Man (or, more probably, woman) as a neanderthaler. Others group these remains together with the Steinheim skull from Germany, seeing both as a separate sub-species, *Homo sapiens steinheimenses*. Unfortunately there is just too little evidence as yet on which to form a final judgment.

Modern Man, *Homo sapiens sapiens*, the surviving sub-species of *Homo sapiens*, had evolved to our present physical condition and had colonised much of the world by about 30,000 years ago. There are many previously distinguished individual specimens, for example Cromagnon Man, which may now be grouped together as *Homo sapiens sapiens*. It was modern man who spread to the New World by crossing the landbridge between Siberia and Alaska and thence moved south through North and into South America. Equally it is modern man who over the last 30,000 years has been responsible for the major developments in technology, art and civilisation generally.

One of the problems for those studying fossil man is the lack in many cases of sufficient quantities of fossil bone for analysis. It is important that theories should be tested against evidence, and not the evidence made to fit the theory. The celebrated Piltdown hoax is perhaps the best known example of "fossils" being forged to fit what was seen in some quarters as the correct theory of man's evolution.

HUMAN CULTURAL DEVELOPMENT

The Eurocentric bias of early archaeologists meant that the search for a starting point for the development and transmission of cultural ideas, especially by migration, trade and warfare, concentrated unduly on Europe and the Near East. The Three Age System, whereby pre-history was divided into a Stone Age, Bronze Age, and Iron Age, was devised by Christian Thomsen, curator of the National Museum of Denmark, in the early nineteenth century, to facilitate the classification of the Museum's collections. The descriptive adjectives referred to the materials from which the implements and weapons were made, and came to be regarded as the dominant features of the societies to which they related. The refinement of the Three Age System once dominated archaeological thought and still remains a generally accepted concept in the popular mind. However, it is now seen by archaeologists as an inadequate model for human development.

Common sense alone suggests that there were no complete breaks between one so-called "Age" and another, any more than contemporaries would have regarded 1485 as a complete break between medieval and modern English history. Nor can the Three Age System be applied universally. In some areas it is necessary to insert a Copper Age, while in Africa south of the Sahara there would seem to be no Bronze Age at all; in Australia, Old Stone Age societies survived, while in South America, New Stone Age communities existed into modern times. The civilisations in other parts of the world clearly invalidate a Eurocentric theory of human development.

The concept of the "Neolithic Revolution", associated with the domestication of plants and animals, was a development of particular importance in the human cultural pattern. It reflected change from the primitive hunter/gatherer economies to a more settled agricultural way of life and therefore, so the argument goes, made possible the development of urban civilisation. However, it can no longer be argued that this "Revolution" took place only in one area from which all development stemmed. Though it appears that the cultivation of wheat and barley was first undertaken, together with the domestication of cattle and goats/sheep in the Fertile Crescent, there is evidence that rice was first deliberately planted and pigs domesticated in South East Asia; maize first cultivated in Central America and llamas first domesticated in South America. It has been recognized increasingly in recent years that cultural changes can take place independently of each other in different parts of the world at different rates and different times. There is no need for a general diffusionist theory.

Although scholars will continue to study the particular societies which interest them, it may be possible to obtain a reliable chronological framework, in absolute terms of years, against which the cultural development of any particular area may be set. The development and refinement of radiocarbon dating and other scientific methods of producing absolute chronologies is enabling the cross-referencing of societies to be undertaken. As the techniques of dating become more rigorous in application and the number of scientifically obtained dates increases, the attainment of an absolute chronology for prehistoric societies throughout the world comes closer to being achieved.

TIME MEASUREMENT AND CALENDARS

MEASUREMENTS OF TIME

Measurements of time are based on the time taken by the earth to rotate on its axis (*day*); by the moon to revolve round the earth (*month*); and by the earth to revolve round the sun (*Year*). From these, which are not commensurable, certain average or mean intervals have been adopted for ordinary use.

The Day begins at midnight and is divided into 24 hours of 60 minutes, each of 60 seconds. The hours are counted from midnight up to 12 noon (when the sun crosses the meridian), and these hours are designated A.M. (*ante meridiem*); and again from noon up to 12 midnight, which hours are designated P.M. (*post meridiem*), except when the *twenty-four hour* reckoning is employed. The 24-hour reckoning ignores A.M. and P.M., and the hours are numbered 0 to 23 from midnight to midnight.

Colloquially the 24 hours are divided into *day* and *night*, day being the time while the sun is above the horizon (including the four stages of twilight defined on p. 65). Day is subdivided further into *morning*, the early part of daytime, ending at noon; *afternoon* from noon to 6 p.m. and *evening*, which may be said to extend from 6 p.m. until midnight. *Night*, the dark period between day and day, begins at the close of Astronomical Twilight (*see* p. 65) and extends beyond midnight to sunrise the next day.

The names of the Days—Sunday, Monday, Tuesday (Tyr or Tiw = god of war), Wednesday (Woden or Odin), Thursday (Thor), Friday (Frigga = wife of Odin, or Freyja = goddess of love), and Saturday—are derived from Old English translations or adaptions of the Roman titles (Sol, Luna, Mars, Mercurius, Jupiter, Venus and Saturnius).

The Week is a period of 7 days.

The Month in the ordinary calendar is approximately the twelfth part of a year, but the lengths of the different months vary from 28 (or 29) days to 31.

The Year.—The *Equinoctial* or *Tropical Year* is the time that the earth takes to revolve round the sun from equinox to equinox, or 365·2422 mean solar days. The *Calendar Year* consists of 365 days, but a year the date of which is divisible by 4, without remainder, is called *bissextile* (see Roman Calendar) or *Leap Year* and consists of 366 days, one day being added to the month February, so that a date "leaps over" a day of the week. The last year of a century is not a leap year unless its number is divisable by 400 (e.g. the years 1800 and 1900 had only 365 days).

The Solstice.—A Solstice is the point in the Tropical Year at which the Sun attains its greatest distance, north or south, from the Equator. In the northern hemisphere the greatest distance north of the Equator is the Summer Solstice and the greatest distance south is the Winter Solstice.

The Summer Solstice is also the *Longest Day*, measured from sunrise to sunset. At the Solstice the Sun, reaching its greatest northern declination, appears to stand still, the times of sunrise and sunset and the consequent length of the day showing no variation for several days together, before and after the longest day (June 21 or 22). For the remainder of this century the longest day will fall each year on June 21.

The date of the Solstice varies according to locality. If the Solstice falls on June 21 late in the day by Greenwich time, that day will be the longest of the year at Greenwich even though it may be by only a second of time or a fraction thereof, but it will be on June 22, local date, in Japan, and so June 22 will be

the longest day there and at places in eastern longitudes.

Leaving aside the question of locality, the date of the Solstice is also affected by the length of the Tropical Year, which is 365¼ days less about 11 minutes. If a Solstice happens late on June 21 in one year, it will be nearly six hours later in the next, i.e. early on June 22, and that will be the longest day. This delay of the Solstice is not permitted to continue because the extra day in Leap Year brings it back a day in the Calendar.

However, because of the 11 minutes above mentioned, the additional day in Leap Year brings the Solstice back too far by 44 minutes, and the time of the Solstice in the Calendar is earlier as the century progresses. (In the year 2000 the Summer Solstice reaches its earliest date for 100 years, i.e., June 21^d 02^h.) To remedy this the last year of a century is in most cases not a Leap Year, and the omission of the extra day puts the date of the Solstice later by about six hours too much, compensation for which is made by making the fourth centennial year a Leap Year.

Similar considerations apply to the day of the Winter Solstice, or the *Shortest Day* of the year. For the remainder of this century the shortest day will fall on Dec. 21 in two years of four and on Dec. 22 in the remaining two years. In the year 2000 the Winter Solstice reaches its earliest date, i.e., Dec. 21^d 13^h. The difference due to locality also prevails in the same sense as for the longest day.

At Greenwich the Sun sets at its earliest by the clock about ten days before the shortest day, which is a circumstance that may require explanation. The daily change in the time of sunset is due in the first place to the Sun's movement southwards at this time of the year, which diminishes the interval between the Sun's transit, and its setting, and, secondly, because of the daily decrease of the Equation of Time which causes the time of Apparent noon to be continuously later, day by day, and so in a measure counteracts the first effect. The rates of the change of these two quantities are not equal, nor are they uniform, but are such that their combination causes the date of earliest sunset to be Dec. 12 or 13 at Greenwich. In more southerly latitudes the effect of the movement of the Sun is less, and the change in the time of sunset depends on that of the Equation of Time to a greater degree, and the date of earliest sunset is earlier than it is at Greenwich.

The Equinox is the point at which the Sun crosses the Equator and day and night are of equal length all over the world. This occurs in March (Vernal Equinox—about March 21) and September (Autumnal Equinox—about September 21).

The Historical Year.—Before the year 1752, two Calendar systems were in use in England. The Civil or Legal Year began on March 25, while the Historical Year began on January 1. Thus the Civil or Legal date March 24 1658, was the same day as the Historical date March 24, 1659; and a date in that portion of the year is written as: March 24 165⅞, the lower figure showing the Historical year.

The New Year.—In England in the seventh century, and as late as the thirteenth, the year was reckoned from Christmas Day, but in the twelfth century the Anglican Church began the year with the Feast of The Annunciation of the Blessed Virgin (Lady Day) on March 25 and this practice was adopted generally in the fourteenth century. The Civil or Legal year in the British Dominions (exclusive of Scotland) began with "Lady Day" until 1751. But in and since 1752 the civil year has begun with Jan. 1. Certain dividends are still paid by the Bank of England on dates based on Old Style. New Year's Day in Scotland was changed from March 25 to Jan. 1 in 1600.

On the Continent of Europe Jan. 1 was adopted as the first day of the year by Venice in 1522, Germany in 1544, Spain, Portugal, and the Roman Catholic Netherlands in 1556, Prussia, Denmark and Sweden in 1559, France 1564, Lorraine 1579, Protestant Netherlands 1583, Russia 1725, and Tuscany 1751.

The Masonic Year.—Two dates are quoted in warrants, dispensations etc., issued by the United Grand Lodge of England, those for the current year being expressed as *Anno Domini* 1990—*Anno Lucis* 5990. This *Year of Light* is based on the Book of Genesis I: 3, the 4000 year difference being derived, in modified form, from *Ussher's Notation*, published in 1654, which places the Creation of the World in 4,004 B.C.

Regnal Years.—These are the years of a sovereign's reign, and each begins on the anniversary of his or her accession: e.g. Regnal year 39 of the present Queen begins on Feb. 6, 1990. The *Summer Time Act* of 1925, for example, is quoted as 15 and 16 Geo. V. c. 64, because it became law in the session which extended over part of both of these regnal years. The regnal years of Edward VII began on January 22, which was the day of Queen Victoria's death in 1901, so that Acts passed in that reign are, in general, quoted with only one year number, but year 10 of the series ended on May 6, 1910, being the day on which King Edward died, and Acts of the Parliamentary Session 1910 are headed 10 Edw. VII. and 1 Geo. V.; Acts passed in 1936 were dated 1 Edw. VIII. and 1 Geo. VI.; Acts passed in 1952 were dated 16 Geo. VI. and 1 Elizabeth II.

The system was used for dating Acts of Parliament until 1962. Since 1962 Acts of Parliament have been dated by the calendar year.

Dog Days.—The days about the heliacal rising of the Dog Star, noted from ancient times as the hottest and most unwholesome period of the year in the northern hemisphere. Their incidence has been variously calculated as depending on the Greater or Lesser Dog Star (Sirius or Procyon) and their duration has been reckoned as from 30 to 54 days. A generally accepted period is from July 3 to Aug. 15.

Metonic (Lunar, or Minor) **Cycle.**—In the year 432 B.C. Meton, an Athenian astronomer, found that 235 Lunations are very nearly, though not exactly equal in duration to 19 Solar Years, and, hence, after 19 years the Phases of the Moon recur on the same days of the month (nearly). The dates of Full Moon in a cycle of nineteen years were inscribed in figures of gold on public monuments in Athens, and the number showing the position of a year in the Cycle is called the **Golden Number** of that year.

Roman Indiction.—A period of fifteen years, instituted for fiscal purposes about A.D. 300.

Solar (or Major) **Cycle.**—A period of twenty-eight years, in any corresponding year of which the days of the week recur on the same day of the month.

Julian Period.—Proposed by Joseph Scaliger in 1582. The period is 7980 Julian years, and its first year coincides with the year 4713 B.C. 7980 is the product of the number of years in the Solar Cycle, the Metonic Cycle and the cycle of the Roman Indication ($28 \times 19 \times 15$).

Epact.—The age of the calendar Moon, diminished by one day, on January 1, in the ecclesiastical lunar calendar.

THE FOUR SEASONS

Spring, the first season of the year, is defined astronomically to begin in the northern hemisphere at the Vernal Equinox when the Sun enters the sign Aries and to terminate at the Summer Solstice. In Great Britain, Spring in popular parlance comprises the months of March, April and May. In the southern hemisphere Spring corresponds with Autumn in the northern hemisphere.

Summer, the second and warmest season, begins astronomically in the northern hemisphere at the Summer Solstice when the Sun enters the sign of Cancer, and terminates at the Autumnal Equinox. In popular parlance Summer in Great Britain includes the months of June, July and August. In the southern hemisphere Summer corresponds with Winter in the northern hemisphere.

Autumn, the third season, begins astronomically in the northern hemisphere at the Autumnal Equinox when the Sun enters the sign Libra and ends at the Winter Solstice. In Great Britain it is popularly held to include the months of September, October and November. A warm period sometimes occurs round about St. Luke's Day (Oct. 18) and is known as "St. Luke's Summer". A warm period occurring round about Martinmas (Nov. 11) is known as "St. Martin's Summer". In the southern hemisphere Autumn corresponds with Spring of the northern.

Winter, the fourth and coldest season, begins astronomically in the northern hemisphere at the Winter Solstice when the Sun enters the sign of Capricornus, and ends at the Vernal Equinox. In Great Britain the season is popularly held to comprise the months of December, January and February. In the southern hemisphere it corresponds with Summer of the northern.

THE CHRISTIAN CALENDAR

In the Christian chronological system the years are distinguished by cardinal numbers before or after the Incarnation, the period being denoted by the letters B.C. (Before Christ) or, more rarely, A.C. (*Ante Christum*), and A.D. (*Anno Domini*—In the Year of Our Lord). The correlative dates of the epoch are the 4th year of the 194th Olympiad, the 753rd year from the Foundation of Rome, A.M. 3761 (Jewish Chronology), and the 4714th year of the Julian Period.

The system was introduced into Italy in the sixth century, and though first used in France in the seventh it was not universally established there until about the eighth century. It has been said that the

system was introduced into England by St. Augustine (A.D. 596), but was probably not generally used until some centuries later. It was ordered to be used by the Bishops at the Council of Chelsea, A.D. 816. The actual date of the birth of Christ is somewhat uncertain.

The Julian Calendar.—In the Julian Calendar all the centennial years were Leap Years, and for this reason towards the close of the sixteenth century there was a difference of 10 days between the tropical and calendar years; the equinox fell on March 11 of the Calendar, whereas at the time of the Council of

Nicaea, A.D. 325, it had fallen on March 21. In 1582 Pope Gregory ordained that Oct. 5 should be called Oct. 15 and that of the end-century years only the fourth should be a Leap Year (*see* p. 112).

The Gregorian Calendar was adopted by Italy, France, Spain, and Portugal in 1582; by Prussia, the German Roman Catholic States, Switzerland, Holland, and Flanders on Jan. 1, 1583, Poland 1586, Hungary 1587, the German and Netherland Protestant States and Denmark 1700; Great Britain and her Dominions (including the North American Colonies) in 1752, by the omission of eleven days (Sept. 3 being reckoned as Sept. 14). Sweden omitted the leap day in 1700 but observed leap days in 1704 and 1708, and reverted to the Julian calendar by having two leap days in 1712; the Gregorian Calendar was adopted in 1753 by the omission of eleven days (Feb. 18 being reckoned as March 1). Japan adopted the calendar in 1872, China in 1912, Bulgaria in 1915, Turkey and Soviet Russia in 1918, Yugoslavia and Romania in 1919, and Greece in February, 1923.

In the same year that the change was made in England from the Julian to the Gregorian Calendar, the beginning of the new year was also changed from March 25 to January 1 (*see* p. 112–113).

The Orthodox Churches.—Some Orthodox Churches still use the Julian reckoning, but the majority of Greek Churches and the Romanian Orthodox Church have adopted a modified "New Calendar", observing the Gregorian Calendar for fixed feasts and the Julian for movable feasts.

The Orthodox Church year begins on September 1. There are four fast periods, and in addition to Pascha (Easter), twelve great feasts, as well as numerous commemorations of the Saints of the Old and New Testaments throughout the year.

The Dominical Letter is one of the letters A–G which are used to denote the Sundays in successive years. If the first day of the year is a Sunday the letter is A; if the second, B; the third, C; and so on. Leap year requires two letters, the first for Jan. 1—Feb. 29, the second for March 1—Dec. 31.

Epiphany.—The Feast of the Epiphany, commemorating the manifestation of Christ, later became associated with the offering of gifts by the Magi. The day was of exceptional importance from the time of the Council of Nicaea (A.D. 325) as the primate of Alexandria was charged at every Epiphany Feast with the announcement in a letter to the Churches of the date of the forthcoming Easter. The day was of considerable importance in Britain as it influenced dates, ecclesiastical and lay, e.g. **Plow Monday**, when work was resumed in the fields, falls upon the Monday in the first full week after the Epiphany.

Lent.—The Teutonic word *Lent*, which denotes the Fast preceding Easter, originally meant no more than the Spring season; but from Anglo-Saxon times, at least, it has been used as the equivalent of the more significant Latin term **Quadragesima**, meaning the "Forty Days" or, more literally, the fortieth day. As early as the fifth century some of the Fathers of the Church put forward the view that the forty days Fast is of Apostolic origin, but this is not supported or believed by modern scholars; and it appears to some that it dates from the early years of the fourth century. There is some suggestion that the Fast was kept originally for only forty hours. **Ash Wednesday** is the first day of Lent, which ends at midnight before Easter Day.

Sexagesima and Septuagesima.—It has been suggested that the unmeaning application of the names *Sexagesima* and *Septuagesima* to the second and third Sundays before Lent was made by analogy with the names *Quadragesima* and *Quinquagesima*.

Another less likely conjecture is that *Septuagesima* means the seventh day before the Octave of Easter. It is not certain whether the name *Quinquagesima* is due to the fact that the Sunday in question is the fiftieth day before Easter (reckoned inclusive) or was simply formed on the analogy of *Quadragesima* (*New English Dictionary*).

Mothering Sunday is the fourth Sunday in Lent.

Palm Sunday, the Sunday before Easter and the beginning of Holy Week, commemorates the triumphal entry of Christ into Jerusalem and is celebrated in Britain (when palm is not available) by branches of willow gathered for use in the decoration of churches on that day.

Maundy Thursday is the day before Good Friday, the name itself being a corruption of *dies mandati* (day of the mandate) when Christ washed the feet of the disciples and gave them the mandate to love one another.

Easter Day is the first Sunday after the full moon which happens upon, or next after, the 21st day of March; and if the full moon happens upon a Sunday, Easter Day is the Sunday after. This definition is contained in an Act of Parliament (24 Geo. II., cap. 23), and explanation is given in the preamble to the Act that the day of Full Moon depends on certain tables that have been prepared. These are the tables whose essential points are given in the early pages of the Book of Common Prayer. The Moon referred to is not the real Moon of the heavens, but a hypothetical Moon on whose "Full" the date of Easter depends, and the lunations of this "Calendar" Moon consist of twenty-nine and thirty days alternately with certain necessary modifications to make the date of its Full agree as nearly as possible with that of the real Moon, which is known as the **Paschal Full Moon**. As at present ordained, Easter falls on one of 35 days— (March 22–April 25).

A Fixed Easter.—On June 15, 1928, the House of Commons agreed to a motion for the third reading of the Bill that Easter Day shall, in the Calendar year next but one after the commencement of the Act and in all subsequent years, be *the first Sunday after the second Saturday in April*. Easter would thus fall between April 9 and 15, both inclusive—that is, on the second or third Sunday in April. A clause in the Bill provided that before it shall come into operation regard shall be had to any opinion expressed officially by the various Christian Churches. Efforts by the World Council of Churches to secure a unanimous choice of date for Easter by its member Churches have so far been unsuccessful.

Holy Days and Saints Days were the normal factors in early times for settling the dates of future and recurrent appointments, e.g. the **Quarter Days** in England and Wales are the Feast of the Nativity, the Feast of the Annunciation, the Feast of St. John the Baptist and the Feast of St. Michael and All Angels, while **Term Days** in Scotland are Candlemas (Feast of the Purification), Whitsunday (a fixed date), Lammas (Loaf Mass) and Martinmas (St. Martin's Day). **Law Sittings** in England and Wales commence on the Feast of St. Hilary and the term which begins on Old Michaelmas Day ends on the former feast of St. Thomas the Apostle.

Red Letter Days (*see also* p. 155) were Holy Days and Saints Days indicated in early ecclesiastical calendars by letters printed in red ink. The days to be distinguished in this way were finally approved at the Council of Nicaea, A.D. 325.

Rogation Days.—These are the Monday, Tuesday and Wednesday preceding Ascension Day (Holy Thursday) and in the fifth century were ordered by the Church to be observed as public fasts with solemn processions and supplications. The processions were discontinued as religious observances at the Reformation, but survive in the ceremony known as "Beating the Parish Bounds". **Rogation Sunday** is the Sunday before Ascension Day.

Ascension Day is forty days after Easter Day.

Ember Days.—The Ember Days at the Four Seasons are the Wednesday, Friday and Saturday (a) before the third Sunday in Advent, (b) before the second Sunday in Lent, and (c) before the Sundays nearest to the Festivals of St. Peter, and St. Michael and All Angels.

Whit Sunday or **Pentecost** is seven weeks after Easter Day. It is generally said that this name is a variant of White Sunday, and was so called from the albs or white robes of the newly baptized, but other derivations have been suggested.

Trinity Sunday is eight weeks after Easter Day, on the Sunday following Whit Sunday, and subsequent Sundays are sometimes reckoned in the Church of England as "after Trinity".

Thomas Becket (1118–1170) was consecrated Archbishop of Canterbury on the Sunday after Whit Sunday and his first act was to ordain that the day of his consecration should be held as a new festival in honour of the Holy Trinity. The observance thus originated spread from Canterbury throughout the whole of Christendom.

Advent Sunday is the Sunday nearest to St. Andrew's Day, Nov. 30, which allows three Sundays between Advent and Christmas Day in all cases.

A TABLE OF THE MOVABLE FEASTS TO THE YEAR 2025

Year	Ash Wednesday	Easter	Ascension	Whit Sunday (Pentecost)	Sundays after Pentecost	Advent Sunday
1990	Feb. 28	April 15	May 24	June 3	20	Dec. 2
1991	Feb. 13	March 31	May 9	May 19	22	Dec. 1
1992	March 4	April 19	May 28	June 7	19	Nov. 29
1993	Feb. 24	April 11	May 20	May 30	20	Nov. 28
1994	Feb. 16	April 3	May 12	May 22	21	Nov. 27
1995	March 1	April 16	May 25	June 4	20	Dec. 3
1996	Feb. 21	April 7	May 16	May 26	21	Dec. 1
1997	Feb. 12	March 30	May 8	May 18	22	Nov. 30
1998	Feb. 25	April 12	May 21	May 31	20	Nov. 29
1999	Feb. 17	April 4	May 13	May 23	21	Nov. 28
2000	March 8	April 23	June 1	June 11	19	Dec. 3
2001	Feb. 28	April 15	May 24	June 3	20	Dec. 2
2002	Feb. 13	March 31	May 9	May 19	22	Dec. 1
2003	March 5	April 20	May 29	June 8	19	Nov. 30
2004	Feb. 25	April 11	May 20	May 30	20	Nov. 28
2005	Feb. 9	March 27	May 5	May 15	22	Nov. 27
2006	March 1	April 16	May 25	June 4	20	Dec. 3
2007	Feb. 21	April 8	May 17	May 27	21	Dec. 2
2008	Feb. 6	March 23	May 1	May 11	23	Nov. 30
2009	Feb. 25	April 12	May 21	May 31	20	Nov. 29
2010	Feb. 17	April 4	May 13	May 23	21	Nov. 28
2011	March 9	April 24	June 2	June 21	18	Nov. 27
2012	Feb. 22	April 8	May 17	May 27	21	Dec. 2
2013	Feb. 13	March 31	May 9	May 19	22	Dec. 1
2014	March 5	April 20	May 29	June 8	19	Nov. 30
2015	Feb. 18	April 5	May 14	May 24	21	Nov. 29
2016	Feb. 10	March 27	May 5	May 15	22	Nov. 27
2017	March 1	April 16	May 25	June 4	20	Dec. 3
2018	Feb. 14	April 1	May 10	May 20	22	Dec. 2
2019	March 6	April 21	May 30	June 9	19	Dec. 1
2020	Feb. 26	April 12	May 21	May 31	20	Nov. 29
2021	Feb. 17	April 4	May 13	May 23	21	Nov. 28
2022	March 2	April 17	May 26	June 5	19	Nov. 27
2023	Feb. 22	April 9	May 18	May 28	21	Dec. 3
2024	Feb. 14	March 31	May 9	May 19	22	Dec. 1
2025	March 5	April 20	May 29	June 8	19	Nov. 30

NOTES CONCERNING TABLE OF MOVABLE FEASTS

Ash Wednesday (first day in Lent) can fall at earliest on February 4 and at latest on March 10.
Easter Day can fall at earliest on March 22 and at latest on April 25.
Ascension Day can fall at earliest on April 30 and at latest on June 3.
Whit Sunday (Pentecost) can fall at earliest on May 10 and at latest on June 13.
Trinity Sunday is the Sunday after *Whit Sunday.*
Corpus Christi falls on the Thursday after *Trinity Sunday.*
There are not less than 18 and not more than 23 *Sundays after Pentecost.*
Advent Sunday is the Sunday nearest to November 30.

A TABLE OF EASTER DAYS AND SUNDAY LETTERS, 1500 TO 2025

		1500—1599	1600—1699	1700—1799	1800—1899	1900—1999	2000—2025
d	Mar. 22	1573	1668	1761	1818		
e	„ 23	1505-16	1600	1788	1845-56	1913	2008
f	„ 24		1611-95	1706-99		1940	
g	„ 25	1543-54	1627-38-49	1722-33-44	1883-94	1951	
A	„ 26	1559-70-81-92	1654-65-76	1749-58-69-80	1815-26-37	1967-78-89	
b	Mar. 27	1502-13-24-97	1608-87-92	1785-96	1842-53-64	1910-21-32	2005-16
c	„ 28	1529-35-40	1619-24-30	1703-14-25	1869-75-80	1937-48	
d	„ 29	1551-62	1635-46-57	1719-30-41-52	1807-12-91	1959-64-70	
e	„ 30	1567-78-89	1651-62-73-84	1746-55-66-77	1823-34	1902-75-86-97	
f	„ 31	1510-21-32-83-94	1605-16-78-89	1700-71-82-93	1839-50-61-72	1907-18-29-91	2002-13-24
g	April 1	1526-37-48	1621-32	1711-16	1804-66-77-88	1923-34-45-56	2018
A	„ 2	1553-64	1643-48	1727-38-52(NS)	1809-20-93-99	1961-72	
b	„ 3	1575-80-86	1659-70-81	1743-63-68-74	1825-31-36	1904-83-88-94	
c	„ 4	1507-18-91	1602-13-75-86-97	1708-79-90	1847-58	1915-20-26-99	2010-21
d	„ 5	1523-34-45-56	1607-18-29-40	1702-13-24-95	1801-63-74-85-96	1931-42-53	2015
e	April 6	1539-50-61-72	1634-45-56	1729-35-40-60	1806-17-28-90	1947-58-69-80	
f	„ 7	1504-77-88	1667-72	1751-65-76	1822-33-44	1901-12-85-96	
g	„ 8	1509-15-20-99	1604-10-83-94	1705-87-92-98	1849-55-60	1917-28	2007-12
A	„ 9	1531-42	1615-26-37-99	1710-21-32	1871-82	1939-44-50	2023
b	„ 10	1547-58-69	1631-42-53-64	1726-37-48-57	1803-14-87-98	1955-66-77	
c	April 11	1501-12-63-74-85-96	1658-69-80	1762-73-84	1819-30-41-52	1909-71-82-93	2004
d	„ 12	1506-17-28	1601-12-91-96	1789	1846-57-68	1903-14-25-36-98	2009-20
e	„ 13	1533-44	1623-28	1707-18	1800-73-79-84	1941-52	
f	„ 14	1555-60-66	1639-50-61	1723-34-45-54	1805-11-16-95	1963-68-74	
g	„ 15	1571-82-93	1655-66-77-88	1750-59-70-81	1827-38	1900-06-79-90	2001
A	April 16	1503-14-25-36-87-98	1609-20-82-93	1704-75-86-97	1843-54-65-76	1911-22-33-95	2006-17
b	„ 17	1530-41-52	1625-36	1715-20	1808-70-81-92	1927-38-49-60	2022
c	„ 18	1557-68	1647-52	1731-42-56	1802-13-24-97	1954-65-76	
d	„ 19	1500-79-84-90	1663-74-85	1747-67-72-78	1829-35-40	1908-81-87-92	
e	„ 20	1511-22-95	1606-17-79-90	1701-12-83-94	1851-62	1919-24-30	2003-14-25
f	April 21	1527-38-49	1622-33-44	1717-28	1867-78-89	1935-46-57	2019
g	„ 22	1565-76	1660	1739-53-64	1810-21-32	1962-73-84	
A	„ 23	1508	1671		1848	1905-16	2000
b	„ 24	1519	1603-14-98	1709-91	1859		2011
c	„ 25	1546	1641	1736	1886	1943	

THE JEWISH CALENDAR

Origin.—The story in the Book of Genesis that the Flood began on the seventeenth day of the second month; that after the end of 150 days the waters were abated; and that on the seventeenth day of the seventh month the Ark rested on Mount Ararat, indicates a calendar of some kind and that the writers recognized 30 days as the length of a lunation. There is other mention of months by their original numbers in the Book of Genesis and in establishing the rite of the Passover Moses spoke of *Abib* as the month when the Israelites came out from Egypt and Abib was to be the first month of the year. In the first Book of Kings three months are mentioned by name, Ziv the second month, Ethanim the seventh and Bul the eighth, but these are not names now in use. After the Dispersion, Jewish communities were left in considerable doubt as to the times of Fasts and Festivals, and this led to the formation of the Jewish Calendar as used today, which, it is said, was done in A.D. 358 by Rabbi Hillel II, a descendant of Gamaliel—though some assert that it did not happen until much later. This calendar is luni-solar, and is based on the lengths of the lunation and of the tropical year as found by Hipparchus (c. 120 B.C.) which differ little from those adopted at the present day. The year A.M. 5750 (1989–90) is the 12th year of the 303rd *Metonic* (Minor or Lunar) *Cycle* of 19 years and the 10th year of the 206th *Solar* (or Major) *Cycle* of 28 years since the Era of the Creation, which the Jews hold to have occurred at the time of the Autumnal Equinox in the year known in the Christian Calendar as 3760 B.C. (954 of the Julian Period). The epoch or starting point of Jewish Chronology corresponds to Oct. 7, 3761 B.C. At the beginning of each Solar Cycle the *Tekufah* of Nisan (the vernal equinox) returns to the same day and to the same hour.

The hour is divided into 1080 *minims* and the month between one new moon and the next is reckoned as 29 days, 12 hours, 793 minims. The normal calendar year, called a Common Regular year, consists of 12 months of 30 days and 29 days alternately. Since 12 months such as these comprise only 354 days, in order that each of them shall not diverge greatly from an average place in the solar year, a thirteenth month is occasionally added after the fifth month of the Civil year (which commences on the first day of the month Tishri), or as the penultimate month of the Ecclesiastical (which commences on the first day of month Nisan), the years when this happens being called Embolismic or Leap years. Of the 19 years that form a Metonic cycle, 7 are leap years; they occur at places in the cycle indicated by the numbers 3, 6, 8, 11, 14, 17, 19, these places being chosen so that the accumulated excesses of the solar years should be as small as possible. The first of each month is called the day of New Moon, though it is not necessarily the day of astronomical New Moon, that being the day on which conjunction of Sun and Moon occurs, but there is generally a difference of a day or two. In practice, in a month which follows one of 30 days, the day preceding its first day is also observed as a day of New Moon. The dates on which the first days of the months fall depend on that of the first of Tishri, which therefore controls the dates of fasts and festivals in the Jewish year. For certain ceremonial reasons connected with these, the first of Tishri must not fall on a Sunday, Wednesday or Friday, and if this should happen as the result of the computation it is postponed to the following day. Also, if the New Moon of Tishri falls on any day of the week at noon or later than noon, then the following day is to be taken for the celebration of that New Moon and is Tishri 1, provided that it is not one of the forbidden days, in which case there is a further postponement of a day. These rules and others have been considered in detail, and finally a calendar scheme has been drawn up in which a Jewish year is of one of the following six types: Minimal Common (353 days), Regular Common (354 days), Full Common (355 days), Minimal Leap (383 days), Regular Leap (384 days), or Full Leap (385 days).

The Regular year has an alternation of 30 and 29 days. In a full year, whether Common or Leap, Marcheshvan, the second month of the Civil year, has 30 days instead of 29; in Minimal years Kislev, the third month, has 29 instead of 30. The additional month in Leap years which is called Adar I, and precedes the month called Adar in Common years and Adar II, or Ve-Adar, in Leap, always has 30 days, but neither this, nor the other variations mentioned, is allowed to change the number of days in the other months which still follow the alternation of the normal twelve. In Leap years the month intercalated precedes Adar and usurps its name, but the usual Adar festivals are kept in Ve-Adar.

These are the main features of the Jewish Calendar which must be considered permanent, because as a Jewish law it cannot be altered except by a great Sanhedrin.

The Jewish day begins between sunset and nightfall. The time used is that of the meridian of Jerusalem, which is $2h.\,21m.$ in advance of Greenwich Mean Time. Rules for the beginning of Sabbaths and Festivals were laid down for the latitude of London in the eighteenth century and hours for nightfall are now fixed annually by the Chief Rabbi.

Jewish Calendar 5750–51

Jewish Month					A.M. 5750					A.M. 5751	
Tishri	1	..	..	..	1989 September	30	..	..	1990 September	20
Marcheshvan	1	..	..	..		October	30	..	..	October	20
Kislev	1	..	..	..		November	29	..	..	November	18
Tebet	1	..	..	..		December	29	..	..	December	18
Shebat	1	..	..	..	1990 January	27	..	..	1991 January	16
*Adar	1	..	..	..		February	26	..	..	February	15
Ve-Adar	1	..	..	..							
Nisan	1	..	..	..		March	27	..	..	March	16
Iyar	1	..	..	..		April	26	..	..	April	15
Sivan	1	..	..	..		May	25	..	..	May	14
Tammuz	1	..	..	..		June	24	..	..	June	13
Ab	1	..	..	..		July	23	..	..	July	12
Elul	1	..	..	..		August	22	..	..	August	11

A.M. 5750 (750) is a Full Common Year of 12 months, 51 Sabbaths and 355 days. A.M. 5751 (751) is a Regular Common Year of 12 months, 51 Sabbaths and 354 days.

*Known as Adar Rishon in Leap Years.

Jewish Fasts and Festivals

Tishri	1–2	Rosh Hashanah (New Year).	*Tebet*	10	Fast of Tebet.
„	3	*Fast of Gedaliah.	†*Adar*	13	§Fast of Esther.
„	10	Yom Kippur (Day of Atonement).	„ „	14	Purim.
„	15–21	Succoth (Feast of Tabernacles).	„ „	15	Shushan Purim.
„	21	Hoshana Rabba.	*Nisan*	15–22	Pesach (Passover).
„	22	Shemini Atseret (Solemn Assembly).	*Sivan*	6–7	Shavuot (Feast of Weeks).
„	23	Simchat Torah (Rejoicing of the Law).	*Tammuz*	17	*Fast of Tammuz.
Kislev	25	Chanukah (Dedication of the Temple) begins.	*Ab*	9	*Fast of Ab.

NOTES.

* If these dates fall on the Sabbath the Fast is kept on the following day.

† Ve-Adar in Leap Years.

§ This fast is observed on Adar 11 (or Ve-Adar 11 in Leap Years) if Adar 13 falls on a Sabbath.

THE ROMAN CALENDAR

Roman historians adopted as an epoch the Foundation of Rome, which is believed to have happened in the year 753 B.C., and the ordinal number of the years in Roman reckoning is followed by the letters A.U.C. (*Ab Urbe Condita*), so that the year 1990 is 2743 A.U.C. (MMDCCXLIII). The Calendar that we know has developed from one established by Romulus, who is said to have used a year of 304 days divided into ten months, beginning with March, to which Numa added January and February, making the year consist of 12 months of 30 and 29 days alternately, with an additional day so that the total was 355. It is also said that Numa ordered an intercalary month of 22 or 23 days in alternate years, making 90 days in eight years, to be inserted after Feb. 23, but there is some doubt as to the origination and the details of the intercalation in the Roman Calendar, though it is certain that some scheme of this kind was inaugurated and not fully carried out, for in the year 46 B.C. Julius Cæsar, who was then Pontifex Maximus,

found that the Calendar had been allowed to fall into some confusion. He therefore sought the help of the Egyptian astronomer Sosigenes, which led to the construction and adoption (45 B.C.) of the Julian Calendar, and, by a slight alteration, to the Gregorian now in use. The year 46 B.C. was made to consist of 445 days, and is called the *Year of Confusion.* In the Roman (Julian) Calendar the days of the month were counted backwards from three fixed points, or days, and an intervening day was said to be so many days *before* the next coming point, the first *and* last being counted. These three points were (*a*) the Kalends; (*b*) the Nones; and (*c*) the Ides. Their positions in the months and the method of counting from them will be seen in the table below. The year containing 366 days was called *bissextilis annus*, as it had a doubled sixth day (*bissextus dies*) before the March Kalends on Feb. 24—*ante diem sextum Kalendas Martias*, or a.d. VI Kal. Mart.

Present Days of the Month	March, May, July, October have thirty-one days	January, August, December have thirty-one days	April, June, September, November have thirty days	February has twenty-eight days, and in Leap Year twenty-nine
1	Kalendis.	Kalendis.	Kalendis.	Kalendis.
2	VI.	IV.	IV.	IV.
3	V. ante Nonas.	III. ante Nonas.	III. ante Nonas.	III. ante Nonas.
4	IV.	pridie Nonas.	pridie Nonas.	pridie Nonas.
5	III.	Nonis.	Nonis.	Nonis.
6	pridie Nonas.	VIII.	VIII.	VIII.
7	Nonis.	VII.	VII.	VII.
8	VIII.	VI. ante Idus.	VI. ante Idus.	VI. ante Idus.
9	VII.	V.	V.	V.
10	VI. ante Idus.	IV.	IV.	IV.
11	V.	III.	III.	III.
12	IV.	pridie Idus.	pridie Idus.	pridie Idus.
13	III.	Idibus.	Idibus.	Idibus.
14	pridie Idus.	XIX.	XVIII.	XVI.
15	Idibus.	XVIII.	XVII.	XV.
16	XVII.	XVII.	XVI.	XIV.
17	XVI.	XVI.	XV.	XIII.
18	XV.	XV.	XIV.	XII.
19	XIV.	XIV.	XIII.	XI.
20	XIII.	XIII.	XII.	X.
21	XII. ante Kalendas (of the month following).	XII. ante Kalendas (of the month following).	XI. ante Kalendas (of the month following).	IX. ante Kalendas Martias.
22	XI.	XI.	X.	VIII.
23	X.	X.	IX.	VII.
24	IX.	IX.	VIII.	*VI.
25	VIII.	VIII.	VII.	V.
26	VII.	VII.	VI.	IV.
27	VI.	VI.	V.	III.
28	V.	V.	IV.	pridie Kalendas Martias.
29	IV.	IV.	III.	
30	III.	III.	pridie Kalendas	
31	pridie Kalendas (Aprilis, Iunias, Sextilis, Novembris).	pridie Kalendas (Februarias, Septembris, Ianuarias).	(Maias, Quinctilis, Octobris, Decembris).	* (repeated in Leap Year).

ROMAN NUMERALS

1	I	9	IX	17	XVII	70	LXX	600	DC
2	II	10	X	18	XVIII	80	LXXX	700	DCC
3	III	11	XI	19	XIX	90	XC	800	DCCC
4	IV	12	XII	20	XX	100	C	900	CM
5	V	13	XIII	30	XXX	200	CC	1000	M
6	VI	14	XIV	40	XL	300	CCC	1500	MD
7	VII	15	XV	50	L	400	CD	1900	MCM
8	VIII	16	XVI	60	LX	500	D	2000	MM

Other Examples: 43=XLIII; 66=LXVI; 98=XCVIII.

339=CCCXXXIX; 619=DCXIX; 988=CMLXXXVIII; 996=CMXCVI.

1674=MDCLXXIV; 1962=MCMLXII; 1990=MCMXC.

A bar placed over a numeral has the effect of multiplying the number by 1,000, e.g.:

$6,000 = \overline{VI}$; $16,000 = \overline{XVI}$; $160,000 = \overline{CLX}$; $666,000 = \overline{DCLXVI}$.

THE MUSLIM CALENDAR

The basic date of the Muslim Calendar is the *Hejira*, or Flight of Muhammad from Mecca to Medina, the corresponding date of which is A.D. 622, July 16, in the Julian Calendar. Hejira years are used principally in Iran, Turkey, Egypt, in various Arabian states, in certain parts of India and in Malaysia. The system was adopted about A.D. 632, commencing from the first day of the month preceding the Hejira. The years are purely lunar and consist of 12 months containing in alternate sequence 30 or 29 days, with the intercalation of one day at the end of the 12th month at stated intervals in each cycle of 30 years, the object of the intercalation being to reconcile the date of the first of the month with the date of the actual New Moon. Some adherents still take the date of the evening of the first visibility of the crescent as that of the first of the month. In each cycle of 30 years 19 are common and contain 354 days and 11 are intercalary (355 days), the latter being called *kabishah*.

The mean length of the Hejira year is 354 days, 8 hours, 48 minutes and the period of mean lunation is 29 days, 12 hours, 44 minutes.

To ascertain if a Hejira year is common or *kabishah* divide it by 30; the quotient gives the number of completed cycles and the remainder shows the place of the year in the current cycle. If the remainder is 2, 5, 7, 10, 13, 16, 18, 21, 24, 26 or 29 the year is *kabishah* and consists of 355 days.

Hejira year A.H. 1410 (no remainder) and A.H. 1411 (remainder one) are both common years.

Hejira Years 1410 and 1411

Name and Length of Month	A.H. 1410		A.H. 1411	
Muharram (30)	1989 Aug.	4	1990 July	24
Safar (29)	Sept.	3	Aug.	23
Rabia I (30)	Oct.	2	Sept.	21
Rabia II (29)	Nov.	1	Oct.	21
Jumāda I (30)	Nov.	30	Nov.	19
Jumāda II (29)	Dec.	30	Dec.	19
Rajab (30)	1990 Jan.	28	1991 Jan.	17
Shaabān (29)	Feb.	27	Feb.	16
Ramadān (30)	Mar.	28	Mar.	17
Shawwāl (29)	April	27	April	16
Dhū'l-Qa'da (30)	May	26	May	15
Dhū'l-Hijja (29 or 30)	June	25	June	14

OTHER EPOCHS AND CALENDARS

China.—Until the year A.D. 1911 a lunar calendar was in force in China, but with the establishment of the Republic the Government adopted the Gregorian Calendar, and the new and old systems were used simultaneously by the people for several years. Since 1930 the publication and use of the old Calendar have been banned by the Government, and an official Chinese Calendar, corresponding with the European or Western system, is compiled, but the old lunar calendar is still in use to some extent in China. The old Chinese Calendar, with a cycle of 60 years, is still in use in Tibet, Hong Kong, Singapore, Malaysia and elsewhere in South-East Asia.

Ethiopia.—In the Coptic Calendar, which is used by part of the population of Egypt and Ethiopia, the year is made up of 12 months of 30 days each, followed, in general, by 5 complementary days. Every fourth year is an Intercalary or Leap year and in these years there are 6 complementary days. The Intercalary year of the Coptic Calendar immediately precedes the Leap year of the Julian Calendar. The Era is that of Diocletian or the Martyrs, the origin of which is fixed at A.D. 284, Aug. 29 (Julian date).

Greece.—Ancient Greek chronology was reckoned in *Olympiads*, cycles of 4 years corresponding with the periodic Olympic Games held on the plain of Olympia in Elis once in 4 years, the intervening years being the first, second, etc., of the Olympiad which received the name of the victor at the Games. The first recorded Olympiad is that of Choroebus, 776 B.C.

India.—In addition to the Muslim reckoning there are six eras used in India. The principal astronomical system was the *Kaliyuga Era*, which appears to have been adopted in the fourth century A.D. It began on Feb. 18, 3102 B.C. The chronological system of Northern India, known as the *Vikrama Samvat Era*, prevalent in Western India, began on Feb. 23, 57 B.C. The year A.D. 1990 is, therefore, the year 2047 of the Vikrama Era.

The *Saka Era* of Southern India dating from A.D. 78, March 3, was declared the uniform national calendar of the Republic of India with effect from March 22, 1957, to be used concurrently with the Gregorian Calendar. As revised, the year of the new

Saka Era begins at the spring equinox, with five successive months of 31 days and seven of 30 days in ordinary years; six months of each length in leap years. The year A.D. 1990 is 1912 of the revised *Saka Era*.

In the Hills, the *Saptarshi Era* dates from the moment when the Saptarshi, or saints, were translated and became the stars of the Great Bear in 3076 B.C.

The *Buddhists* reckoned from the death of Buddha in 543 B.C. (the actual date being 487 B.C.); and the epoch of the *Jains* was the death of Vardhamana, the founder of their faith, in 527 B.C.

Iran.—The chronology of Iran is the Era of Hejira, which began on A.D. 622, July 16. The *Zoroastrian Calendar* was used in pre-Muslim days and is still employed by Zoroastrians in Iran and India (Parsees) with an era beginning A.D. 632, June 16.

Japan.—The Japanese Calendar is the Gregorian, and is essentially the same as that in use by Western nations, the years, months and weeks being of the same length and beginning on the same days as those of the Western Calendar. The numeration of the years is different, for Japanese chronology is based on a system of epochs or periods, each of which begins at the accession of an Emperor or other important occurrence, the method being not unlike the former British system of Regnal years, but differing from it in the particular that each year of a period closes on Dec. 31. The Japanese scheme begins about A.D. 650 and the three latest epochs are defined by the reigns of Emperors, whose actual names are not necessarily used:

Epoch Taishō from 1912 Aug. 1 to 1926 Dec. 25

„ Shōwa „ 1926 Dec. 26 to 1989 Jan. 7

„ Heisei „ 1989 Jan. 8

Hence the year Heisei 2 begins Jan. 1, 1990. The months are not named. They are known as First Month, Second Month, etc., first month being the equivalent to January. The days of the week are Nichiyōbi (Sun-day), Getsuyōbi (Moon-day), Kayōbi (Fire-day), Suiyōbi (Water-day), Mokuyōbi (Wood-day), Kinyōbi (Metal-day), Doyōbi (Earth-day).

To select the correct calendar for any year between 1770 and 2025, together with the dates of Easter in each of those years, consult the Index below

INDEX TO CALENDARS

Year		Year		Year		Year		Year		Year	
1770	C	1813	K	1856	F*	1899	A	1942	I	1985	E
1771	E	1814	M	1857	I	1900	C	1943	K	1986	G
1772	H*	1815	A	1858	K	1901	E	1944	N*	1987	I
1773	K	1816	D*	1859	M	1902	G	1945	C	1988	L*
1774	M	1817	G	1860	B*	1903	I	1946	E	1989	A
1775	A	1818	I	1861	E	1904	L*	1947	G	1990	C
1776	D*	1819	K	1862	G	1905	A	1948	J*	1991	E
1777	G	1820	N*	1863	I	1906	C	1949	M	1992	H*
1778	I	1821	C	1864	L*	1907	E	1950	A	1993	K
1779	K	1822	E	1865	A	1908	H*	1951	C	1994	M
1780	N*	1823	G	1866	C	1909	K	1952	F*	1995	A
1781	C	1824	J*	1867	E	1910	M	1953	I	1996	D*
1782	E	1825	M	1868	H*	1911	A	1954	K	1997	G
1783	G	1826	A	1869	K	1912	D*	1955	M	1998	I
1784	J*	1827	C	1870	M	1913	G	1956	B*	1999	K
1785	M	1828	F*	1871	A	1914	I	1957	E	2000	N*
1786	A	1829	I	1872	D*	1915	K	1958	G	2001	C
1787	C	1830	K	1873	G	1916	N*	1959	I	2002	E
1788	F*	1831	M	1874	I	1917	C	1960	L*	2003	G
1789	I	1832	B*	1875	K	1918	E	1961	A	2004	J*
1790	K	1833	E	1876	N*	1919	G	1962	C	2005	M
1791	M	1834	G	1877	C	1920	J*	1963	E	2006	A
1792	B*	1835	I	1878	E	1921	M	1964	H*	2007	C
1793	E	1836	L*	1879	G	1922	A	1965	K	2008	F*
1794	G	1837	A	1880	J*	1923	C	1966	M	2009	I
1795	I	1838	C	1881	M	1924	F*	1967	A	2010	K
1796	L*	1839	E	1882	A	1925	I	1968	D*	2011	M
1797	A	1840	H*	1883	C	1926	K	1969	G	2012	B*
1798	C	1841	K	1884	F*	1927	M	1970	I	2013	E
1799	E	1842	M	1885	I	1928	B*	1971	K	2014	G
1800	G	1843	A	1886	K	1929	E	1972	N*	2015	I
1801	I	1844	D*	1887	M	1930	G	1973	C	2016	L*
1802	K	1845	G	1888	B*	1931	I	1974	E	2017	A
1803	M	1846	I	1889	E	1932	L*	1975	G	2018	C
1804	B*	1847	K	1890	G	1933	A	1976	J*	2019	E
1805	E	1848	N*	1891	I	1934	C	1977	M	2020	H*
1806	G	1849	C	1892	L*	1935	E	1978	A	2021	K
1807	I	1850	E	1893	A	1936	H*	1979	C	2022	M
1808	L*	1851	G	1894	C	1937	K	1980	F*	2023	A
1809	A	1852	J*	1895	E	1938	M	1981	I	2024	D*
1810	C	1853	M	1896	H*	1939	A	1982	K	2025	G
1811	E	1854	A	1897	K	1940	D*	1983	M		
1812	H*	1855	C	1898	M	1941	G	1984	B*		

* Leap Year

A

```
          January              February                March
Su. ..  1  8 15 22 29        5 12 19 26            5 12 19 26
M.  ..  2  9 16 23 30        6 13 20 27            6 13 20 27
Tu. ..  3 10 17 24 31        7 14 21 28            7 14 21 28
W.  ..  4 11 18 25        1  8 15 22            1  8 15 22 29
Th. ..  5 12 19 26        2  9 16 23            2  9 16 23 30
F.  ..  6 13 20 27        3 10 17 24            3 10 17 24 31
S.  ..  7 14 21 28        4 11 18 25            4 11 18 25

           April                 May                   June
Su. ..  2  9 16 23 30        7 14 21 28            4 11 18 25
M.  ..  3 10 17 24        1  8 15 22 29            5 12 19 26
Tu. ..  4 11 18 25        2  9 16 23 30            6 13 20 27
W.  ..  5 12 19 26        3 10 17 24 31            7 14 21 28
Th. ..  6 13 20 27        4 11 18 25            1  8 15 22 29
F.  ..  7 14 21 28        5 12 19 26            2  9 16 23 30
S.  1  8 15 22 29        6 13 20 27            3 10 17 24

           July                 August              September
Su. ..  2  9 16 23 30        6 13 20 27            3 10 17 24
M.  ..  3 10 17 24 31        7 14 21 28            4 11 18 25
Tu. ..  4 11 18 25        1  8 15 22 29            5 12 19 26
W.  ..  5 12 19 26        2  9 16 23 30            6 13 20 27
Th. ..  6 13 20 27        3 10 17 24 31            7 14 21 28
F.  ..  7 14 21 28        4 11 18 25            1  8 15 22 29
S.  1  8 15 22 29        5 12 19 26            2  9 16 23 30

          October              November              December
Su. ..  1  8 15 22 29        5 12 19 26            3 10 17 24 31
M.  ..  2  9 16 23 30        6 13 20 27            4 11 18 25
Tu. ..  3 10 17 24 31        7 14 21 28            5 12 19 26
W.  ..  4 11 18 25        1  8 15 22 29            6 13 20 27
Th. ..  5 12 19 26        2  9 16 23 30            7 14 21 28
F.  ..  6 13 20 27        3 10 17 24            1  8 15 22 29
S.  ..  7 14 21 28        4 11 18 25            2  9 16 23 30
```

B (Leap year)

```
          January              February                March
Su. ..  1  8 15 22 29        5 12 19 26            4 11 18 25
M.  ..  2  9 16 23 30        6 13 20 27            5 12 19 26
Tu. ..  3 10 17 24 31        7 14 21 28            6 13 20 27
W.  ..  4 11 18 25        1  8 15 22 29            7 14 21 28
Th. ..  5 12 19 26        2  9 16 23            1  8 15 22 29
F.  ..  6 13 20 27        3 10 17 24            2  9 16 23 30
S.  ..  7 14 21 28        4 11 18 25            3 10 17 24 31

           April                 May                   June
Su. ..  1  8 15 22 29        6 13 20 27            3 10 17 24
M.  ..  2  9 16 23 30        7 14 21 28            4 11 18 25
Tu. ..  3 10 17 24        1  8 15 22 29            5 12 19 26
W.  ..  4 11 18 25        2  9 16 23 30            6 13 20 27
Th. ..  5 12 19 26        3 10 17 24 31            7 14 21 28
F.  ..  6 13 20 27        4 11 18 25            1  8 15 22 29
S.  ..  7 14 21 28        5 12 19 26            2  9 16 23 30

           July                 August              September
Su. ..  1  8 15 22 29        5 12 19 26            2  9 16 23 30
M.  ..  2  9 16 23 30        6 13 20 27            3 10 17 24
Tu. ..  3 10 17 24 31        7 14 21 28            4 11 18 25
W.  ..  4 11 18 25        1  8 15 22 29            5 12 19 26
Th. ..  5 12 19 26        2  9 16 23 30            6 13 20 27
F.  ..  6 13 20 27        3 10 17 24 31            7 14 21 28
S.  ..  7 14 21 28        4 11 18 25        1  8 15 22 29

          October              November              December
Su. ..  7 14 21 28        4 11 18 25            2  9 16 23 30
M.  ..  1  8 15 22 29        5 12 19 26            3 10 17 24 31
Tu. ..  2  9 16 23 30        6 13 20 27            4 11 18 25
W.  ..  3 10 17 24 31        7 14 21 28            5 12 19 26
Th. ..  4 11 18 25        1  8 15 22 29            6 13 20 27
F.  ..  5 12 19 26        2  9 16 23 30            7 14 21 28
S.  ..  6 13 20 27        3 10 17 24        1  8 15 22 29
```

Easter Days

March 26.	1815 1826 1837 1967 1978 1989.
April 2.	1809 1893 1899 1961.
April 9.	1871 1882 1939 1950 2023.
April 16.	1775 1786 1797 1843 1854 1865 1911
April 23.	1905. [1922 1933 1995 2006 2017.

Easter Days

April 1.	1804 1888 1956.
April 8.	1792 1860 1928 2012.
April 22.	1832 1984.

C

	January	February	March
Su.	7 14 21 28	4 11 18 25	4 11 18 25
M.	1 8 15 22 29	5 12 19 26	5 12 19 26
Tu.	2 9 16 23 30	6 13 20 27	6 13 20 27
W.	3 10 17 24 31	7 14 21 28	7 14 21 28
Th.	4 11 18 25	1 8 15 22	1 8 15 22 29
F.	5 12 19 26	2 9 16 23	2 9 16 23 30
S.	6 13 20 27	3 10 17 24	3 10 17 24 31

	April	May	June
Su.	1 8 15 22 29	6 13 20 27	3 10 17 24
M.	2 9 16 23 30	7 14 21 28	4 11 18 25
Tu.	3 10 17 24	1 8 15 22 29	5 12 19 26
W.	4 11 18 25	2 9 16 23 30	6 13 20 27
Th.	5 12 19 26	3 10 17 24 31	7 14 21 28
F.	6 13 20 27	4 11 18 25	1 8 15 22 29
S.	7 14 21 28	5 12 19 26	2 9 16 23 30

	July	August	September
Su.	1 8 15 22 29	5 12 19 26	2 9 16 23 30
M.	2 9 16 23 30	6 13 20 27	3 10 17 24
Tu.	3 10 17 24 31	7 14 21 28	4 11 18 25
W.	4 11 18 25	1 8 15 22 29	5 12 19 26
Th.	5 12 19 26	2 9 16 23 30	6 13 20 27
F.	6 13 20 27	3 10 17 24 31	7 14 21 28
S.	7 14 21 28	4 11 18 25	1 8 15 22 29

	October	November	December
Su.	7 14 21 28	4 11 18 25	2 9 16 23 30
M.	1 8 15 22 29	5 12 19 26	3 10 17 24 31
Tu.	2 9 16 23 30	6 13 20 27	4 11 18 25
W.	3 10 17 24 31	7 14 21 28	5 12 19 26
Th.	4 11 18 25	1 8 15 22 29	6 13 20 27
F.	5 12 19 26	2 9 16 23 30	7 14 21 28
S.	6 13 20 27	3 10 17 24	1 8 15 22 29

Easter Days

March 25.	1883	1894	1951.			
April 1.	1866	1877	1923	1934	1945	2018.
April 8.	1787	1798	1849	1855	1917	2007.
April 15.	1770	1781	1827	1838	1900	1906 1979
April 22.	1810	1821	1962	1973.		[1990 2001.

D (Leap year)

	January	February	March
Su.	7 14 21 28	4 11 18 25	3 10 17 24 31
M.	1 8 15 22 29	5 12 19 26	4 11 18 25
Tu.	2 9 16 23 30	6 13 20 27	5 12 19 26
W.	3 10 17 24 31	7 14 21 28	6 13 20 27
Th.	4 11 18 25	1 8 15 22	7 14 21 28
F.	5 12 19 26	2 9 16 23	1 8 15 22 29
S.	6 13 20 27	3 10 17 24	2 9 16 23 30

	April	May	June
Su.	7 14 21 28	5 12 19 26	2 9 16 23 30
M.	1 8 15 22 29	6 13 20 27	3 10 17 24
Tu.	2 9 16 23 30	7 14 21 28	4 11 18 25
W.	3 10 17 24	1 8 15 22 29	5 12 19 26
Th.	4 11 18 25	2 9 16 23 30	6 13 20 27
F.	5 12 19 26	3 10 17 24 31	7 14 21 28
S.	6 13 20 27	4 11 18 25	1 8 15 22 29

	July	August	September
Su.	7 14 21 28	4 11 18 25	1 8 15 22 29
M.	1 8 15 22 29	5 12 19 26	2 9 16 23 30
Tu.	2 9 16 23 30	6 13 20 27	3 10 17 24
W.	3 10 17 24 31	7 14 21 28	4 11 18 25
Th.	4 11 18 25	1 8 15 22 29	5 12 19 26
F.	5 12 19 26	2 9 16 23 30	6 13 20 27
S.	6 13 20 27	3 10 17 24 31	7 14 21 28

	October	November	December
Su.	6 13 20 27	3 10 17 24	1 8 15 22 29
M.	7 14 21 28	4 11 18 25	2 9 16 23 30
Tu.	1 8 15 22 29	5 12 19 26	3 10 17 24 31
W.	2 9 16 23 30	6 13 20 27	4 11 18 25
Th.	3 10 17 24 31	7 14 21 28	5 12 19 26
F.	4 11 18 25	1 8 15 22 29	6 13 20 27
S.	5 12 19 26	2 9 16 23 30	7 14 21 28

Easter Days

March 24.	1940.	
March 31.	1872	2024.
April 7.	1776	1844 1912 1996.
April 14.	1816	1968.

E

	January	February	March
Su.	6 13 20 27	3 10 17 24	3 10 17 24 31
M.	7 14 21 28	4 11 18 25	4 11 18 25
Tu.	1 8 15 22 29	5 12 19 26	5 12 19 26
W.	2 9 16 23 30	6 13 20 27	6 13 20 27
Th.	3 10 17 24 31	7 14 21 28	7 14 21 28
F.	4 11 18 25	1 8 15 22	1 8 15 22 29
S.	5 12 19 26	2 9 16 23	2 9 16 23 30

	April	May	June
Su.	7 14 21 28	5 12 19 26	2 9 16 23 30
M.	1 8 15 22 29	6 13 20 27	3 10 17 24
Tu.	2 9 16 23 30	7 14 21 28	4 11 18 25
W.	3 10 17 24	1 8 15 22 29	5 12 19 26
Th.	4 11 18 25	2 9 16 23 30	6 13 20 27
F.	5 12 19 26	3 10 17 24 31	7 14 21 28
S.	6 13 20 27	4 11 18 25	1 8 15 22 29

	July	August	September
Su.	7 14 21 28	4 11 18 25	1 8 15 22 29
M.	1 8 15 22 29	5 12 19 26	2 9 16 23 30
Tu.	2 9 16 23 30	6 13 20 27	3 10 17 24
W.	3 10 17 24 31	7 14 21 28	4 11 18 25
Th.	4 11 18 25	1 8 15 22 29	5 12 19 26
F.	5 12 19 26	2 9 16 23 30	6 13 20 27
S.	6 13 20 27	3 10 17 24 31	7 14 21 28

	October	November	December
Su.	6 13 20 27	3 10 17 24	1 8 15 22 29
M.	7 14 21 28	4 11 18 25	2 9 16 23 30
Tu.	1 8 15 22 29	5 12 19 26	3 10 17 24 31
W.	2 9 16 23 30	6 13 20 27	4 11 18 25
Th.	3 10 17 24 31	7 14 21 28	5 12 19 26
F.	4 11 18 25	1 8 15 22 29	6 13 20 27
S.	5 12 19 26	2 9 16 23 30	7 14 21 28

Easter Days

March 24.	1799.			[1918	1929	1991	2002 2013.
March 31.	1771	1782	1793	1839	1850	1861	1907
April 7.	1822	1833	1901	1985.			
April 14.	1805	1811	1895	1963	1974.		
April 21.	1867	1878	1889	1935	1946	1957	2019.

F (Leap year)

	January	February	March
Su.	6 13 20 27	3 10 17 24	2 9 16 23 30
M.	7 14 21 28	4 11 18 25	3 10 17 24 31
Tu.	1 8 15 22 29	5 12 19 26	4 11 18 25
W.	2 9 16 23 30	6 13 20 27	5 12 19 26
Th.	3 10 17 24 31	7 14 21 28	6 13 20 27
F.	4 11 18 25	1 8 15 22 29	7 14 21 28
S.	5 12 19 26	2 9 16 23	1 8 15 22 29

	April	May	June
Su.	6 13 20 27	4 11 18 25	1 8 15 22 29
M.	7 14 21 28	5 12 19 26	2 9 16 23 30
Tu.	1 8 15 22 29	6 13 20 27	3 10 17 24
W.	2 9 16 23 30	7 14 21 28	4 11 18 25
Th.	3 10 17 24	1 8 15 22 29	5 12 19 26
F.	4 11 18 25	2 9 16 23 30	6 13 20 27
S.	5 12 19 26	3 10 17 24 31	7 14 21 28

	July	August	September
Su.	6 13 20 27	3 10 17 24 31	7 14 21 28
M.	7 14 21 28	4 11 18 25	1 8 15 22 29
Tu.	1 8 15 22 29	5 12 19 26	2 9 16 23 30
W.	2 9 16 23 30	6 13 20 27	3 10 17 24
Th.	3 10 17 24 31	7 14 21 28	4 11 18 25
F.	4 11 18 25	1 8 15 22 29	5 12 19 26
S.	5 12 19 26	2 9 16 23 30	6 13 20 27

	October	November	December
Su.	5 12 19 26	2 9 16 23 30	7 14 21 28
M.	6 13 20 27	3 10 17 24	1 8 15 22 29
Tu.	7 14 21 28	4 11 18 25	2 9 16 23 30
W.	1 8 15 22 29	5 12 19 26	3 10 17 24 31
Th.	2 9 16 23 30	6 13 20 27	4 11 18 25
F.	3 10 17 24 31	7 14 21 28	5 12 19 26
S.	4 11 18 25	1 8 15 22 29	6 13 20 27

Easter Days

March 23.	1788	1856	2008.
April 6.	1828	1980.	
April 13.	1884	1952.	
April 20.	1924.		

G

	January	February	March
Su.	5 12 19 26	2 9 16 23	2 9 16 23 30
M.	6 13 20 27	3 10 17 24	3 10 17 24 31
Tu.	7 14 21 28	4 11 18 25	4 11 18 25
W.	1 8 15 22 29	5 12 19 26	5 12 19 26
Th.	2 9 16 23 30	6 13 20 27	6 13 20 27
F.	3 10 17 24 31	7 14 21 28	7 14 21 28
S.	4 11 18 25	1 8 15 22	1 8 15 22 29

	April	May	June
Su.	6 13 20 27	4 11 18 25	1 8 15 22 29
M.	7 14 21 28	5 12 19 26	2 9 16 23 30
Tu.	1 8 15 22 29	6 13 20 27	3 10 17 24
W.	2 9 16 23 30	7 14 21 28	4 11 18 25
Th.	3 10 17 24	1 8 15 22 29	5 12 19 26
F.	4 11 18 25	2 9 16 23 30	6 13 20 27
S.	5 12 19 26	3 10 17 24 31	7 14 21 28

	July	August	September
Su.	6 13 20 27	3 10 17 24 31	7 14 21 28
M.	7 14 21 28	4 11 18 25	1 8 15 22 29
Tu.	1 8 15 22 29	5 12 19 26	2 9 16 23 30
W.	2 9 16 23 30	6 13 20 27	3 10 17 24
Th.	3 10 17 24 31	7 14 21 28	4 11 18 25
F.	4 11 18 25	1 8 15 22 29	5 12 19 26
S.	5 12 19 26	2 9 16 23 30	6 13 20 27

	October	November	December
Su.	5 12 19 26	2 9 16 23 30	7 14 21 28
M.	6 13 20 27	3 10 17 24	1 8 15 22 29
Tu.	7 14 21 28	4 11 18 25	2 9 16 23 30
W.	1 8 15 22 29	5 12 19 26	3 10 17 24 31
Th.	2 9 16 23 30	6 13 20 27	4 11 18 25
F.	3 10 17 24 31	7 14 21 28	5 12 19 26
S.	4 11 18 25	1 8 15 22 29	6 13 20 27

Easter Days

March 23.	1845	1913.					
March 30.	1777	1823	1834	1902	1975	1986	1997.
April 6.	1806	1817	1890	1947	1958	1969.	
April 13.	1800	1873	1879	1941.		[2014	2025.
April 20.	1783	1794	1851	1862	1919	1930	2003

H (Leap year)

	January	February	March
Su.	5 12 19 26	2 9 16 23	1 8 15 22 29
M.	6 13 20 27	3 10 17 24	2 9 16 23 30
Tu.	7 14 21 28	4 11 18 25	3 10 17 24 31
W.	1 8 15 22 29	5 12 19 26	4 11 18 25
Th.	2 9 16 23 30	6 13 20 27	5 12 19 26
F.	3 10 17 24 31	7 14 21 28	6 13 20 27
S.	4 11 18 25	1 8 15 22 29	7 14 21 28

	April	May	June
Su.	5 12 19 26	3 10 17 24 31	7 14 21 28
M.	6 13 20 27	4 11 18 25	1 8 15 22 29
Tu.	7 14 21 28	5 12 19 26	2 9 16 23 30
W.	1 8 15 22 29	6 13 20 27	3 10 17 24
Th.	2 9 16 23 30	7 14 21 28	4 11 18 25
F.	3 10 17 24	1 8 15 22 29	5 12 19 26
S.	4 11 18 25	2 9 16 23 30	6 13 20 27

	July	August	September
Su.	5 12 19 26	2 9 16 23 30	6 13 20 27
M.	6 13 20 27	3 10 17 24 31	7 14 21 28
Tu.	7 14 21 28	4 11 18 25	1 8 15 22 29
W.	1 8 15 22 29	5 12 19 26	2 9 16 23 30
Th.	2 9 16 23 30	6 13 20 27	3 10 17 24
F.	3 10 17 24 31	7 14 21 28	4 11 18 25
S.	4 11 18 25	1 8 15 22 29	5 12 19 26

	October	November	December
Su.	4 11 18 25	1 8 15 22 29	6 13 20 27
M.	5 12 19 26	2 9 16 23 30	7 14 21 28
Tu.	6 13 20 27	3 10 17 24	1 8 15 22 29
W.	7 14 21 28	4 11 18 25	2 9 16 23 30
Th.	1 8 15 22 29	5 12 19 26	3 10 17 24 31
F.	2 9 16 23 30	6 13 20 27	4 11 18 25
S.	3 10 17 24 31	7 14 21 28	5 12 19 26

Easter Days

March 29.	1812	1964.		
April 5.	1896.			
April 12.	1868	1936	2020.	
April 19.	1772	1840	1908	1992.

I

	January	February	March
Su.	4 11 18 25	1 8 15 22	1 8 15 22 29
M.	5 12 19 26	2 9 16 23	2 9 16 23 30
Tu.	6 13 20 27	3 10 17 24	3 10 17 24 31
W.	7 14 21 28	4 11 18 25	4 11 18 25
Th.	1 8 15 22 29	5 12 19 26	5 12 19 26
F.	2 9 16 23 30	6 13 20 27	6 13 20 27
S.	3 10 17 24 31	7 14 21 28	7 14 21 28

	April	May	June
Su.	5 12 19 26	3 10 17 24 31	7 14 21 28
M.	6 13 20 27	4 11 18 25	1 8 15 22 29
Tu.	7 14 21 28	5 12 19 26	2 9 16 23 30
W.	1 8 15 22 29	6 13 20 27	3 10 17 24
Th.	2 9 16 23 30	7 14 21 28	4 11 18 25
F.	3 10 17 24	1 8 15 22 29	5 12 19 26
S.	4 11 18 25	2 9 16 23 30	6 13 20 27

	July	August	September
Su.	5 12 19 26	2 9 16 23 30	6 13 20 27
M.	6 13 20 27	3 10 17 24 31	7 14 21 28
Tu.	7 14 21 28	4 11 18 25	1 8 15 22 29
W.	1 8 15 22 29	5 12 19 26	2 9 16 23 30
Th.	2 9 16 23 30	6 13 20 27	3 10 17 24
F.	3 10 17 24 31	7 14 21 28	4 11 18 25
S.	4 11 18 25	1 8 15 22 29	5 12 19 26

	October	November	December
Su.	4 11 18 25	1 8 15 22 29	6 13 20 27
M.	5 12 19 26	2 9 16 23 30	7 14 21 28
Tu.	6 13 20 27	3 10 17 24	1 8 15 22 29
W.	7 14 21 28	4 11 18 25	2 9 16 23 30
Th.	1 8 15 22 29	5 12 19 26	3 10 17 24 31
F.	2 9 16 23 30	6 13 20 27	4 11 18 25
S.	3 10 17 24 31	7 14 21 28	5 12 19 26

Easter Days

March 22.	1818.						
March 29.	1807	1891	1959	1970.		[1953	2015.
April 5.	1795	1801	1863	1874	1885	1931	1942
April 12.	1789	1846	1857	1903	1914	1925	1998
April 19.	1778	1829	1835	1981	1987.		[2009.

J (Leap year)

	January	February	March
Su.	4 11 18 25	1 8 15 22 29	7 14 21 28
M.	5 12 19 26	2 9 16 23	1 8 15 22 29
Tu.	6 13 20 27	3 10 17 24	2 9 16 23 30
W.	7 14 21 28	4 11 18 25	3 10 17 24 31
Th.	1 8 15 22 29	5 12 19 26	4 11 18 25
F.	2 9 16 23 30	6 13 20 27	5 12 19 26
S.	3 10 17 24 31	7 14 21 28	6 13 20 27

	April	May	June
Su.	4 11 18 25	2 9 16 23 30	6 13 20 27
M.	5 12 19 26	3 10 17 24 31	7 14 21 28
Tu.	6 13 20 27	4 11 18 25	1 8 15 22 29
W.	7 14 21 28	5 12 19 26	2 9 16 23 30
Th.	1 8 15 22 29	6 13 20 27	3 10 17 24
F.	2 9 16 23 30	7 14 21 28	4 11 18 25
S.	3 10 17 24	1 8 15 22 29	5 12 19 26

	July	August	September
Su.	4 11 18 25	1 8 15 22 29	5 12 19 26
M.	5 12 19 26	2 9 16 23 30	6 13 20 27
Tu.	6 13 20 27	3 10 17 24 31	7 14 21 28
W.	7 14 21 28	4 11 18 25	1 8 15 22 29
Th.	1 8 15 22 29	5 12 19 26	2 9 16 23 30
F.	2 9 16 23 30	6 13 20 27	3 10 17 24
S.	3 10 17 24 31	7 14 21 28	4 11 18 25

	October	November	December
Su.	3 10 17 24 31	7 14 21 28	5 12 19 26
M.	4 11 18 25	1 8 15 22 29	6 13 20 27
Tu.	5 12 19 26	2 9 16 23 30	7 14 21 28
W.	6 13 20 27	3 10 17 24	1 8 15 22 29
Th.	7 14 21 28	4 11 18 25	2 9 16 23 30
F.	1 8 15 22 29	5 12 19 26	3 10 17 24 31
S.	2 9 16 23 30	6 13 20 27	4 11 18 25

Easter Days

March 28.	1880	1948.	
April 4.	1920.		
April 11.	1784	1852	2004.
April 18.	1824	1976.	

K

	January	*February*	*March*
Su.	.. 3 10 17 24 31	7 14 21 28	7 14 21 28
M.	.. 4 11 18 25	1 8 15 22	1 8 15 22 29
Tu.	.. 5 12 19 26	2 9 16 23	2 9 16 23 30
W.	.. 6 13 20 27	3 10 17 24	3 10 17 24 31
Th.	.. 7 14 21 28	4 11 18 25	4 11 18 25
F.	1 8 15 22 29	5 12 19 26	5 12 19 26
S.	2 9 16 23 30	6 13 20 27	6 13 20 27

	April	*May*	*June*
Su.	.. 4 11 18 25	2 9 16 23 30	6 13 20 27
M.	.. 5 12 19 26	3 10 17 24 31	7 14 21 28
Tu.	.. 6 13 20 27	4 11 18 25	1 8 15 22 29
W.	.. 7 14 21 28	5 12 19 26	2 9 16 23 30
Th.	.. 1 8 15 22 29	6 13 20 27	3 10 17 24
F.	.. 2 9 16 23 30	7 14 21 28	4 11 18 25
S.	.. 3 10 17 24	1 15 22 29	5 12 19 26

	July	*August*	*September*
Su.	.. 4 11 18 25	1 8 15 22 29	5 12 19 26
M.	.. 5 12 19 26	2 9 16 23 30	6 13 20 27
Tu.	.. 6 13 20 27	3 10 17 24 31	7 14 21 28
W.	.. 7 14 21 28	4 11 18 25	1 8 15 22 29
Th.	.. 1 8 15 22 29	5 12 19 26	2 9 16 23 30
F.	.. 2 9 16 23 30	6 13 20 27	3 10 17 24
S.	.. 3 10 17 24 31	7 14 21 28	4 11 18 25

	October	*November*	*December*
Su.	.. 3 10 17 24 31	7 14 21 28	5 12 19 26
M.	.. 4 11 18 25	1 8 15 22 29	6 13 20 27
Tu.	.. 5 12 19 26	2 9 16 23 30	7 14 21 28
W.	.. 6 13 20 27	3 10 17 24	1 8 15 22 29
Th.	.. 7 14 21 28	4 11 18 25	2 9 16 23 30
F.	1 8 15 22 29	5 12 19 26	3 10 17 24 31
S.	2 9 16 23 30	6 13 20 27	4 11 18 25

Easter Days

March 28.	1869	1875	1937.		[2010	2021.
April 4.	1779	1790	1847	1858 1915	1926	1999
April 11.	1773	1819	1830	1841 1909	1971	1982
April 18.	1802	1813	1897	1954 1965.		[1993.
April 25.	1886	1943.				

L (Leap year)

	January	*February*	*March*
Su.	.. 3 10 17 24 31	7 14 21 28	6 13 20 27
M.	.. 4 11 18 25	1 8 15 22 29	7 14 21 28
Tu.	.. 5 12 19 26	2 9 16 23	1 8 15 22 29
W.	.. 6 13 20 27	3 10 17 24	2 9 16 23 30
Th.	.. 7 14 21 28	4 11 18 25	3 10 17 24 31
F.	1 8 15 22 29	5 12 19 26	4 11 18 25
S.	2 9 16 23 30	6 13 20 27	5 12 19 26

	April	*May*	*June*
Su.	.. 3 10 17 24	1 8 15 22 29	5 12 19 26
M.	.. 4 11 18 25	2 9 16 23 30	6 13 20 27
Tu.	.. 5 12 19 26	3 10 17 24 31	7 14 21 28
W.	.. 6 13 20 27	4 11 18 25	1 8 15 22 29
Th.	.. 7 14 21 28	5 12 19 26	2 9 16 23 30
F.	1 8 15 22 29	6 13 20 27	3 10 17 24
S.	2 9 16 23 30	7 14 21 28	4 11 18 25

	July	*August*	*September*
Su.	.. 3 10 17 24 31	7 14 21 28	4 11 18 25
M.	.. 4 11 18 25	1 8 15 22 29	5 12 19 26
Tu.	.. 5 12 19 26	2 9 16 23 30	6 13 20 27
W.	.. 6 13 20 27	3 10 17 24 31	7 14 21 28
Th.	.. 7 14 21 28	4 11 18 25	1 8 15 22 29
F.	1 8 15 22 29	5 12 19 26	2 9 16 23 30
S.	2 9 16 23 30	6 13 20 27	3 10 17 24

	October	*November*	*December*
Su.	.. 2 9 16 23 30	6 13 20 27	4 11 18 25
M.	.. 3 10 17 24 31	7 14 21 28	5 12 19 26
Tu.	.. 4 11 18 25	1 8 15 22 29	6 13 20 27
W.	.. 5 12 19 26	2 9 16 23 30	7 14 21 28
Th.	.. 6 13 20 27	3 10 17 24	1 8 15 22 29
F.	.. 7 14 21 28	4 11 18 25	2 9 16 23 30
S.	1 8 15 22 29	5 12 19 26	3 10 17 24 31

Easter Days

March 27.	1796	1864	1932	2016.
April 3.	1836	1904	1988.	
April 17.	1808	1892	1960.	

M

	January	*February*	*March*
Su.	.. 2 9 16 23 30	6 13 20 27	6 13 20 27
M.	.. 3 10 17 24 31	7 14 21 28	7 14 21 28
Tu.	.. 4 11 18 25	1 8 15 22	1 8 15 22 29
W.	.. 5 12 19 26	2 9 16 23	2 9 16 23 30
Th.	.. 6 13 20 27	3 10 17 24	3 10 17 24 31
F.	.. 7 14 21 28	4 11 18 25	4 11 18 25
S.	1 8 15 22 29	5 12 19 26	5 12 19 26

	April	*May*	*June*
Su.	.. 3 10 17 24	1 8 15 22 29	5 12 19 26
M.	.. 4 11 18 25	2 9 16 23 30	6 13 20 27
Tu.	.. 5 12 19 26	3 10 17 24 31	7 14 21 28
W.	.. 6 13 20 27	4 11 18 25	1 8 15 22 29
Th.	.. 7 14 21 28	5 12 19 26	2 9 16 23 30
F.	.. 1 8 15 22 29	6 13 20 27	3 10 17 24
S.	.. 2 9 16 23 30	7 14 21 28	4 11 18 25

	July	*August*	*September*
Su.	.. 3 10 17 24 31	7 14 21 28	4 11 18 25
M.	.. 4 11 18 25	1 8 15 22 29	5 12 19 26
Tu.	.. 5 12 19 26	2 9 16 23 30	6 13 20 27
W.	.. 6 13 20 27	3 10 17 24 31	7 14 21 28
Th.	.. 7 14 21 28	4 11 18 25	1 8 15 22 29
F.	1 8 15 22 29	5 12 19 26	2 9 16 23 30
S.	2 9 16 23 30	6 13 20 27	3 10 17 24

	October	*November*	*December*
Su.	.. 2 9 16 23 30	6 13 20 27	4 11 18 25
M.	.. 3 10 17 24 31	7 14 21 28	5 12 19 26
Tu.	.. 4 11 18 25	1 8 15 22 29	6 13 20 27
W.	.. 5 12 19 26	2 9 16 23 30	7 14 21 28
Th.	.. 6 13 20 27	3 10 17 24	1 8 15 22 29
F.	.. 7 14 21 28	4 11 18 25	2 9 16 23 30
S.	1 8 15 22 29	5 12 19 26	3 10 17 24 31

Easter Days

March 27.	1785	1842	1853	1910 1921	2005.
April 3.	1774	1825	1831	1983 1994.	
April 10.	1803	1814	1887	1898 1955	1966 1977.
April 17.	1870	1881	1927	1938 1949	2022.
April 24.	1791	1859	2011.		

N (Leap year)

	January	*February*	*March*
Su.	.. 2 9 16 23 30	6 13 20 27	5 12 19 26
M.	.. 3 10 17 24 31	7 14 21 28	6 13 20 27
Tu.	.. 4 11 18 25	1 8 15 22	7 14 21 28
W.	.. 5 12 19 26	2 9 16 23	1 8 15 22 29
Th.	.. 6 13 20 27	3 10 17 24	2 9 16 23 30
F.	.. 7 14 21 28	4 11 18 25	3 10 17 24 31
S.	1 8 15 22 29	5 12 19 26	4 11 18 25

	April	*May*	*June*
Su.	.. 2 9 16 23 30	7 14 21 28	4 11 18 25
M.	.. 3 10 17 24	1 8 15 22 29	5 12 19 26
Tu.	.. 4 11 18 25	2 9 16 23 30	6 13 20 27
W.	.. 5 12 19 26	3 10 17 24 31	7 14 21 28
Th.	.. 6 13 20 27	4 11 18 25	1 8 15 22 29
F.	.. 7 14 21 28	5 12 19 26	2 9 16 23 30
S.	1 8 15 22 29	6 13 20 27	3 10 17 24

	July	*August*	*September*
Su.	.. 2 9 16 23 30	6 13 20 27	3 10 17 24
M.	.. 3 10 17 24 31	7 14 21 28	4 11 18 25
Tu.	.. 4 11 18 25	1 8 15 22 29	5 12 19 26
W.	.. 5 12 19 26	2 9 16 23 30	6 13 20 27
Th.	.. 6 13 20 27	3 10 17 24 31	7 14 21 28
F.	.. 7 14 21 28	4 11 18 25	1 8 15 22 29
S.	1 8 15 22 29	5 12 19 26	2 9 16 23 30

	October	*November*	*December*
Su.	.. 1 8 15 22 29	5 12 19 26	3 10 17 24 31
M.	.. 2 9 16 23 30	6 13 20 27	4 11 18 25
Tu.	.. 3 10 17 24 31	7 14 21 28	5 12 19 26
W.	.. 4 11 18 25	1 8 15 22 29	6 13 20 27
Th.	.. 5 12 19 26	2 9 16 23 30	7 14 21 28
F.	.. 6 13 20 27	3 10 17 24	1 8 15 22 29
S.	.. 7 14 21 28	4 11 18 25	2 9 16 23 30

Easter Days

March 26.	1780.		
April 2.	1820	1972.	
April 9.	1944.		
April 16.	1876.		
April 23.	1848	1916	2000.

The World

The **superficial area** of the Earth is estimated to be 196,836,000 square miles, of which 55,786,000 square miles are land and 141,050,000 square miles water. The **diameter** of the Earth at the Equator is 7,926·5 English miles, and at the Poles 7,900 English miles. The **equatorial circumference** is 24,901·8 English miles, divided into 360 *degrees of longitude*, each of 69·17 English (or 60 geographical) miles; these degrees are measured from the Meridian of Greenwich, and numbered East and West of that point to meet in the Antipodes at the 180th degree. Distance North and South of the Equator is marked by *parallels of latitude*, which proceed from zero (at the Equator) to 90° at the Poles.

The velocity of a given point of the Earth's surface at the Equator exceeds 1,000 miles an hour (24,901·8 miles in 24 hours); the Earth's velocity in its orbit round the Sun is about 66,600 miles an hour (584,000,000 miles in 365¼ days). The Earth is distant from the Sun 93,000,000 miles, on the average.

AREA AND POPULATION

The total population of the world in mid-1985, was estimated at 4,837,500,000, compared with 3,003,000,000 in 1960 and 2,070,000,000 in 1930.

Continent, etc.	Area		Estimated Population, mid-1985
	Sq. miles '000	Sq. km. '000	
Africa	11,704	30,313	555,000,000
North America[1]	8,311	21,525	264,000,000
Latin America[2]	7,933	20,547	405,000,000
Asia[3]	10,637	27,549	2,813,000,000
Europe[4]	1,915	4,961	497,000,000
U.S.S.R.	8,649	22,402	279,000,000
Oceania[5]	3,286	8,510	24,500,000
TOTAL	52,435	135,807	4,837,500,000

[1] Includes Greenland and Hawaii.

[2] Mexico and the remainder of the Americas south of the U.S.A.

[3] Includes Asiatic Turkey, excludes U.S.S.R.

[4] Includes European Turkey, excludes U.S.S.R.

[5] Includes Australia, New Zealand and the islands inhabited by Micronesian, Melanesian and Polynesian peoples.

Source: *U.N. Demographic Yearbook 1985 (pub. 1987).*

A United Nations report (*The Future Growth of World Population*) in 1958, pointed out that the population of the world had increased since the beginning of the 20th Century at an unprecedented rate: in 1850 it was estimated at 1,094,000,000 and in 1900 at 1,550,000,000, an increase of 42 per cent in 50 years. By 1925 it had risen to 1,907,000,000—23 per cent in 25 years—and by 1950 it had reached 2,500,000,000, an increase of 31 per cent in 25 years. Levels of population and the trend in distribution of the population by continents as forecast for the year 2000 were:—

	[millions]	
	2000	
Continent, etc.	Estimated Population	Per cent
Africa	517	8·2
North America	312	5·0
Latin America[†]	592	9·4
Asia (excluding U.S.S.R.)	3,870	61·8
Europe (including U.S.S.R.)	947	15·1
Oceania	29	0·5
World	6,267	100

[†] Mexico and the remainder of the Americas south of U.S.A.

THE CONTINENTS

Africa is the second largest continent. It is surrounded by sea except for the narrow isthmus of Suez in the north-east, through which is cut the Suez Canal. The Equator passes through the middle of the continent. Its extreme longitudes are 17° 20′ W. at Cape Verde, Senegal, and 51° 24′ E. at Ras Hafun, Somalia. The extreme latitudes are 37° 20′ N. at Cape Blanco, Tunisia, and 34° 50′ S. at Cape Agulhas, South Africa, about 5,000 miles apart.

North America, including Mexico, is surrounded by ocean except in the south, where the isthmian states of Central America link North America with South America. Its extreme longitudes are 55° 5′ W. at Cape Prince of Wales, Alaska, and 55° 40′ W. at Cape Charles, Newfoundland. The extreme latitudes are about 82° N. in the Arctic Ocean and 15° N. in the south of Mexico. The West Indies, about 65,000 square miles in area, extend from about 27° N. to 10° N. latitude.

South America lies mostly in the southern hemisphere: the Equator passes through the north of the continent. It is surrounded by ocean except where it is joined to Central America in the north by the narrow isthmus through which is cut the Panama Canal. Its extreme longitudes are 34° 47′ W. at Cape Branco in Brazil and 81° 20′ W. at Punta Pariña, Peru. The extreme latitudes are 12° 25′ N. at Punta Gallinas, Colombia, and 55° 59′ S. at Cape Horn, Chile.

Antarctica lies almost entirely within the Antarctic Circle (66° 33′ S.) and is too hostile an environment for unsupported human habitation. (*See also* p. 134.)

Asia is the largest continent and occupies about a third of the world's land surface. The extreme longitudes are about 26° E. on the west coast of Asia Minor and 169° 45′ W. at Mys Dežneva (East Cape), U.S.S.R., a distance of about 6,000 miles. Its extreme northern latitude is 77° 45′ N. at Cape Čeljuskin, U.S.S.R., and it extends over 5,000 miles south to about 1° 15′ N. of the Equator. The islands of Japan, the Philippines and Indonesia ring the continent to the east and south-east.

Australia is the smallest of the continents and lies in the southern hemisphere. It is entirely surrounded by ocean. Its extreme longitudes are 113° 9′ E. at Steep Point and 153° 38′ E. at Cape Byron. The extreme latitudes are 10° 40′ S. at Cape York and 39° S. at South East Point.

Europe, including European Russia, is the smallest continent in the northern hemisphere. Its extreme latitudes are 71° 11′ N. at North Cape in Norway, and 36° 23′ N. at Cape Matapan in southern Greece, a distance of about 2,400 miles. Its breadth from Cape da Roca in Portugal (9° 30′ W.) in the west to the Urals is about 3,300 miles. The division between Europe and Asia is generally regarded as being the Ural Mountains and, in the south, the valley of the Manych, which stretches from the Caspian Sea to the mouth of the Don.

Countries and Their Capitals

No complete survey of many countries has yet been achieved and consequently accurate area figures are not always available. Similarly, many countries have not recently, or have never, taken a census. The areas and populations of countries given below are derived from estimated figures published by the United Nations. The conversion factors used are: (i) to convert square miles to square km.—multiply by 2·589988; (ii) to convert square km. to square miles—multiply by 0·3861022.

Accurate and up-to-date data for the populations of capital cities are scarce, and definitions of cities' extent differ. The figures given below are the latest estimates available, and where it is known that the figure applies to an urban agglomeration this is indicated.

Where later information becomes available during printing, the new figures are given in the overseas sections of the ALMANACK.

*latest census result   u.a. urban-agglomeration   Ψ seaport

AFRICA

COUNTRY	AREA Sq. Miles	AREA Sq. Km.	POPULATION	CAPITAL	POPULATION OF CAPITAL
Algeria...............	919,595	2,381,741	22,971,558	Ψ Algiers	3,250,000
Angola...............	481,354	1,246,700	8,754,000	Ψ Luanda	1,000,000
Benin	43,484	112,622	4,444,000	Ψ Porto Novo	208,258
Botswana	224,607	581,730	1,200,000	Gaborone	110,000
Burkina..............	105,869	274,200	8,846,929	Ouagadougou	375,001
Burundi..............	10,747	27,834	4,718,000	Bujumbura	150,000
Cameroon	183,569	475,442	10,927,000	Yaoundé	522,000
Cape Verde Islands	1,557	4,033	326,000	Ψ Praia	57,748
Central African Rep. ..	240,535	622,984	2,608,000	Bangui	473,817
Chad	495,755	1,284,000	5,018,000	Ndjaména	402,000
Comoros..............	838	2,171	444,000	Moroni	17,267
Congo	132,047	342,000	1,740,000	Brazzaville	600,000
Côte d'Ivoire..........	124,503	322,463	10,056,000	Ψ Abidjan	3,000,000
Djibouti	8,494	22,000	430,000	Ψ Djibouti..........	200,000
Egypt	386,662	1,001,449	52,000,000	Cairo	14,000,000
Equatorial Guinea	10,830	28,051	392,000	Ψ Malabo	34,980
Ethiopia.............	471,778	1,221,900	43,350,000	Addis Ababa	1,464,901
Gabon................	103,347	267,667	1,151,000	Ψ Libreville	251,000
Gambia	4,361	11,295	695,886*	Ψ Banjul (u.a.)	44,536*
Ghana	92,100	238,537	13,588,000	Ψ Accra (u.a.)	1,420,066*
Guinea	94,926	245,857	6,075,000	Ψ Conakry	763,000
Guinea-Bissau	13,948	36,125	890,000	Ψ Bissau	109,486*
Kenya	224,961	582,646	20,333,000	Nairobi	1,103,554
Lesotho	11,720	30,355	1,443,853*	Maseru	288,951*
Liberia	43,000	111,369	2,300,000	Ψ Monrovia	425,000
Libya	679,362	1,759,540	3,500,000	Ψ Tripoli	1,000,000
Madagascar	226,669	587,041	11,000,000	Antananarivo	1,000,000
Malawi...............	45,747	118,484	7,982,607*	Lilongwe.........	175,000*
Mali	478,791	1,240,000	8,206,000	Bamako	600,000
Mauritania...........	397,955	1,030,700	1,888,000	Nouakchott	500,000
Mauritius	790	2,045	1,036,000	Ψ Port Louis	138,272
Mayotte	144	372	67,000	Mamoundzou.....	12,000
Morocco..............	172,414	446,550	27,000,000	Ψ Rabat............	1,123,000
Western Sahara	102,703	266,000	163,868	Laayoune	96,784
Mozambique	309,495	801,590	14,000,000	Ψ Maputo	1,000,000
Namibia..............	318,261	824,292	1,184,000	Windhoek........	110,000
Niger	489,191	1,267,080	6,317,550	Niamey	399,100
Nigeria	356,669	923,768	100,000,000	Ψ Lagos	3,000,000
Réunion..............	969	2,510	555,000	St. Denis	109,072
Rwanda	10,169	26,338	6,070,000	Kigali	156,000
St. Helena	47	122	5,564	Ψ Jamestown	1,330
Ascension I.	34	88	1,081	Ψ Georgetown	..
Tristan da Cunha ...	40	104	311	Ψ Edinburgh	..
Sao Tomé & Príncipé ..	372	964	108,000	Ψ São Tomé	25,000
Senegal	75,750	196,192	6,540,000	Ψ Dakar	1,000,000
Seychelles	108	280	65,032	Ψ Victoria	24,733
Sierra Leone	27,699	71,740	3,700,000*	Ψ Freetown	470,000*
Somalia	246,201	637,657	5,800,000	Ψ Mogadishu	1,000,000
South Africa..........	471,445	1,221,031	32,392,000	{ Pretoria (u.a.) .... Ψ Cape Town (u.a.)..	822,925 1,911,521
Sudan................	967,500	2,505,813	21,550,000	Khartoum (u.a.) ..	2,000,000
Swaziland	6,704	17,363	731,000	Mbabane	30,000
Tanzania	364,900	945,087	21,733,000	Ψ Dar es Salaam	1,096,000
Togo	21,925	56,785	3,030,000	Ψ Lomé	366,476
Tunisia	63,170	163,610	7,205,106	Ψ Tunis	1,394,749
Uganda	91,259	236,036	16,398,000	Kampala (u.a.)	631,000
Zaire	905,567	2,345,409	34,671,607*	Kinshasa	2,778,281*
Zambia	290,586	752,614	6,666,000	Lusaka (u.a.)	641,000
Zimbabwe	150,804	390,580	9,000,000	Harare...........	658,364

AMERICA

(For symbols, etc., *see* introductory note on page 125.)

COUNTRY	AREA Sq. Miles	AREA Sq. Km.	POPULATION	CAPITAL	POPULATION OF CAPITAL
North America					
Canada................	3,849,646	9,970,537	25,309,330*	Ottawa (*u.a.*)	819,263*
Greenland............	840,004	2,175,600	52,940	Ψ Godthab	..
Mexico...............	761,605	1,972,547	78,524,000	Mexico City (*u.a.*).	18,748,000
St. Pierre and Miquelon	93	242	6,500	Ψ St. Pierre	..
United States........	3,618,787	9,372,614	231,106,727	Washington, D.C. (*u.a.*)	3,646,000
Central America and the West Indies					
Anguilla	35	91	7,000	The Valley	500
Antigua and Barbuda..	170	440	81,500	Ψ St. John's	30,000
Aruba................	75	193	62,500	Ψ Oranjestad	20,000
Bahamas	5,380	13,935	237,090*	Ψ Nassau............	135,437*
Barbados	166	431	253,000	Ψ Bridgetown	7,466
Belize	8,867	22,965	166,000	Belmopan	2,935
Bermuda	20	53	56,000	Ψ Hamilton	1,669
Cayman Islands	100	259	24,900	Ψ George Town	11,000
Costa Rica............	19,575	50,700	2,816,558	San José (*u.a.*) ...	1,031,102
Cuba.................	42,804	110,861	10,356,400	Ψ Havana	2,100,000
Dominica.............	290	751	76,000	Ψ Roseau	8,346
Dominican Republic ...	18,816	48,734	6,416,000*	Ψ Santo Domingo (*u.a.*)	1,313,172*
Grenada..............	133	344	112,000	Ψ St. George's	7,500
Guadeloupe...........	687	1,779	334,000	Ψ Basse-Terre	15,778
Guatemala	42,042	108,889	7,963,000	Guatemala City ...	1,300,000
Haiti.................	10,714	27,750	6,585,000	Ψ Port au Prince ...	1,000,000
Honduras	43,277	112,088	4,372,000	Tegucigalpa	640,900
Jamaica	4,244	10,991	2,355,100	Ψ Kingston (*u.a.*) ..	696,300
Martinique	425	1,102	331,000	Ψ Fort de France....	100,576
Montserrat	38	98	11,900	Ψ Plymouth	3,000
Netherlands Antilles ..	371	961	188,000	Ψ Willemstad	50,000
Nicaragua	50,193	130,000	3,500,000	Managua.........	615,000
Panama	29,762	77,082	2,227,254	Ψ Panama City	608,890
Puerto Rico..........	3,435	8,897	3,451,000	Ψ San Juan (*u.a.*) ...	1,816,300
St. Christopher and Nevis	101	261	45,100	Ψ Basseterre	15,000
St. Lucia	238	616	138,000	Ψ Castries..........	55,000
St. Vincent and the Grenadines	150	388	104,000	Ψ Kingstown	33,694
El Salvador	8,124	21,041	5,480,000	San Salvador (*u.a.*)	2,000,000
Trinidad and Tobago ..	1,981	5,130	1,185,000	Ψ Port of Spain	59,649
Turks and Caicos Is. ...	166	430	14,000	Ψ Grand Turk	3,146
Virgin Islands:—					
British	59	153	13,000	Ψ Road Town	2,479
U.S.................	132	342	106,000	Ψ Charlotte Amalie .	11,842
South America					
Argentina............	1,068,302	2,766,889	30,564,000	Ψ Buenos Aires (*u.a.*)	3,323,000
Bolivia...............	424,165	1,098,581	6,429,000	La Paz	1,000,000
Brazil	3,286,488	8,511,965	135,564,000	Brasilia	1,576,657
Chile.................	292,258	756,945	12,074,000	Santiago	4,132,293
Colombia	439,737	1,138,914	26,525,670*	Bogotá	3,967,988*
Ecuador	109,484	283,561	9,378,000	Quito	1,003,875
Falkland Islands	4,700	12,173	1,916	Ψ Stanley	1,231
French Guiana........	35,135	91,000	86,000	Ψ Cayenne	38,135
Guyana	83,000	214,969	790,000	Ψ Georgetown	185,000
Paraguay.............	157,048	406,752	4,000,000	Asunción (*u.a.*) ...	729,307*
Peru	496,225	1,285,216	19,700,000	Lima (*u.a.*)	5,258,600
South Georgia	1,580	4,092	500	..	..
Suriname.............	63,037	163,265	410,000	Ψ Paramaribo	110,000
Uruguay	68,037	176,215	3,012,000	Ψ Montevideo	1,355,312
Venezuela	352,144	912,050	17,323,000	Caracas	1,816,901

ASIA

(For symbols, etc., *see* introductory note on page 125.)

COUNTRY	AREA Sq. Miles	AREA Sq. Km.	POPULATION	CAPITAL	POPULATION OF CAPITAL
Afghanistan	250,000	647,497	18,136,000	Kabul...........	2,000,000
Bahrain..............	240	622	457,600	Ψ Manama	121,986*
Bangladesh...........	55,598	143,998	110,000,000	Dhaka	5,000,000
Bhutan	18,147	47,000	1,417,000	Thimphu.........	15,000
Brunei	2,226	5,765	241,000	Bandar Seri Begawan.......	58,000
Burma (Myanmar)	261,218	676,552	37,153,000	Ψ Rangoon (*u.a.*)....	3,973,872
China¹	3,705,408	9,596,961	1,160,000,000	Beijing (Peking) ..	9,957,000
Taiwan	13,800	35,742	19,460,000	Taipei	2,507,620
Hong Kong	413	1,071	5,700,000	Ψ Victoria	..
India................	1,269,346	3,287,590	750,900,000	Delhi	6,222,000
Indonesia	735,358	1,904,569	165,030,000	Ψ Jakarta	6,503,449
Iran	636,296	1,648,000	52,000,000	Tehran	6,000,000
Iraq.................	167,925	434,924	16,278,316*	Baghdad	3,205,645
Israel	8,019	20,770	4,404,000	Jerusalem........	506,200
Japan	145,834	377,708	121,740,000	Tokyo (*u.a.*)	11,680,282
Jordan	37,738	97,740	2,910,000	Amman	1,100,000
Kampuchea...........	69,898	181,035	7,284,000	Ψ Phnom Penh	500,000
Korea D.P.R. (North) ..	46,540	120,538	20,385,000	Pyongyang	1,500,000
Korea Rep. of (South) ..	38,025	98,484	42,000,000	Seoul	9,991,089
Kuwait	6,880	17,818	1,695,128*	Ψ Kuwait (city).....	400,000
Laos	91,429	231,800	4,117,000	Vientiane........	120,000
Lebanon.............	4,015	10,400	2,668,000	Ψ Beirut	702,000
Macao	6	16	450,000	Ψ Macao	..
Malaysia	127,317	329,749	16,921,300*	Kuala Lumpur....	1,103,200
Maldives	115	298	200,000	Ψ Malé.............	46,334
Mongolia............	604,250	1,565,000	2,000,000	Ulan Bator	505,000
Nepal	54,342	140,747	18,000,000	Kathmandu	235,000
Oman	82,030	212,457	1,500,000	Ψ Muscat	400,000
Pakistan	307,374	746,045	96,180,000	Islamabad (*u.a.*) ...	350,000
Philippines	115,831	300,000	58,700,000	Ψ Manila	1,630,485
Qatar	4,247	11,000	380,000	Ψ Doha	220,000
Saudi Arabia	830,000	2,149,640	12,400,000	Riyadh	1,000,000
Singapore	224	581	2,612,800	..	..
Sri Lanka	25,332	65,610	15,837,000	Ψ Colombo	643,000
Syria	71,498	185,180	11,338,000	Damascus	1,168,000
Thailand	198,457	514,000	54,536,000	Ψ Bangkok	5,400,000
Turkey (in Asia)	292,261	756,953	44,485,734*	Ankara	3,196,460
U.S.S.R. (in Asia)......	6,498,486	16,831,000	63,070,000	..	..
United Arab Emirates .	32,278	83,600	1,600,000	..	..
Vietnam	127,242	329,556	64,500,000	Hanoi...........	925,000
Yemen A.R. (North) ...	75,290	195,000	9,250,000	Sana'a	427,185
Yemen P.D.R. (South) .	128,560	332,968	2,500,000	Ψ Aden	270,000

¹ Including Tibet.

THE SEVEN WONDERS OF THE WORLD

I. THE PYRAMIDS OF EGYPT.—From Gizeh (near Cairo) to a southern limit 60 miles distant. The oldest is that of Zoser, at Saqqara, built about 2,700 B.C. The Great Pyramid of Cheops covers more than 12 acres and was originally 481 ft. in height and 756 × 756 ft. at the base.

II. THE HANGING GARDENS OF BABYLON.—Adjoining Nebuchadnezzar's palace, 60 miles south of Baghdad. Terraced gardens, ranging from 75 to 300 ft. above ground level, watered from storage tanks on the highest terrace.

III. THE TOMB OF MAUSOLUS.—At Halicarnassus, in Asia Minor. Built by the widowed Queen Artemisia about 350 B.C. The memorial originated the term mausoleum.

IV. THE TEMPLE OF ARTEMIS AT EPHESUS.—Ionic temple erected about 350 B.C. in honour of the goddess and burned by the Goths in A.D. 262.

V. THE COLOSSUS OF RHODES.—A bronze statue of Apollo, set up about 280 B.C. According to legend it stood at the harbour entrance of the seaport of Rhodes.

VI. THE STATUE OF ZEUS.—At Olympia in the plain of Elis, constructed of marble inlaid with ivory and gold by the sculptor Phidias, about 430 B.C.

VII. THE PHAROS OF ALEXANDRIA.—A marble watch tower and lighthouse on the island of Pharos in the harbour of Alexandria.

EUROPE AND THE MEDITERRANEAN

(For symbols, etc., *see* introductory notes on page 125.)

COUNTRY	AREA		POPULATION	CAPITAL	POPULATION OF CAPITAL
	Sq. Miles	Sq. Km.			
Albania	11,099	28,748	3,410,000	Tirana	210,757
Andorra..............	175	453	40,000	Andorra La Vella .	16,000
Austria	32,374	83,849	7,557,000	Vienna	1,531,346
Belgium	11,781	30,513	9,858,895	Brussels (*u.a.*)	976,536
Bulgaria	42,823	110,912	8,948,388*	Sofia.............	1,114,759
Cyprus	3,572	9,251	691,700	Nicosia	166,900
Czechoslovakia	49,370	127,869	15,500,000	Prague...........	1,190,576
Denmark	16,629	43,069	5,124,794	Ψ Copenhagen (*u.a.*).	1,495,736
Faroe Is.	540	1,399	46,000	Ψ Thorshavn	..
Finland	137,851	337,032	4,954,000	Ψ Helsinki	486,626
France	211,208	547,026	55,600,000*	Paris (*u.a.*)	8,706,963*
German D.R. (East)	41,768	108,178	16,661,423	East Berlin	1,246,872
Germany, F.R. (West)[1]	95,976	248,577	61,149,000	Bonn	291,400
Gibraltar.............	2	6	30,077	Ψ Gibraltar	..
Greece	50,944	131,944	10,002,000	Athens (*u.a.*)	3,027,331*
Hungary	35,919	93,030	10,658,000	Budapest.........	2,072,000
Iceland...............	39,768	103,000	247,024	Ψ Reykjavik (*u.a.*) .	93,270
Ireland, Republic of....	27,136	70,283	3,543,000	Ψ Dublin	502,749*
Italy	116,304	301,225	57,193,708	Rome (*u.a.*)	2,821,420
Liechtenstein.........	61	157	28,181	Vaduz	4,919
Luxembourg	998	2,586	365,900	Luxembourg	77,500
Malta and Gozo	122	316	345,636	Ψ Valletta	9,239*
Monaco	0·4	1	27,063	Monaco-ville	1,234
Netherlands	15,770	40,844	14,669,000	Ψ Amsterdam (*u.a.*) .	1,031,000
Norway[2]	125,181	324,219	4,224,606	Ψ Oslo	450,808
Poland	120,725	312,677	37,203,000	Warsaw	1,644,626
Portugal[3]	35,553	92,082	10,229,000	Ψ Lisbon	807,937
Romania	91,699	237,500	22,823,500	Bucharest........	1,961,189
San Marino	23	61	22,361	San Marino	..
Spain[4]	194,897	504,782	38,818,355	Madrid (*u.a.*)	4,731,224
Sweden	173,732	449,964	8,358,139	Ψ Stockholm (*u.a.*) .	1,435,474
Switzerland	15,943	41,293	6,566,800	Berne............	135,000
Turkey (in Europe)	9,121	23,623	6,942,780*		..
UNITED KINGDOM[5]	94,227	244,046	56,972,700	Ψ London (*u.a.*)	6,775,200
England.............	50,363	130,439	47,407,000		..
Wales	8,018	20,768	2,836,000	Ψ Cardiff...........	279,500
Scotland	30,414	78,772	5,112,000	Ψ Edinburgh	438,232
Northern Ireland	5,452	14,121	1,575,200	Ψ Belfast..........	303,800
U.S.S.R. (in Europe) ...	2,150,975	5,571,000	218,607,000	Moscow..........	8,815,000
Vatican City State	0·2	0·44	1,000	Vatican City	..
Yugoslavia	98,766	255,804	23,123,000	Belgrade	1,455,000

[1] Data include West Berlin.

[2] Excludes Svalbard and Jan Mayen Is. (approx. 24,101 sq. miles (62,422 sq. km.) and 3,000 population).

[3] Includes Madeira (314 sq. miles) and the Azores (922 sq. miles).

[4] Includes Balearic Is., Canary Is., Ceuta and Melilla.

[5] Includes Isle of Man (227 sq. miles (588 sq. km.), 64,282 population), and Channel Is. (75 sq. miles (195 sq. km.), 137,196 population).

OCEANIA

(For symbols, etc., *see* introductory notes on page 125.)

COUNTRY	AREA Sq. Miles	AREA Sq. Km.	POPULATION	CAPITAL	POPULATION OF CAPITAL
Australia.............	2,967,909	7,686,848	16,676,800	Canberra.........	281,000
Norfolk Island	14	36	1,977*	Ψ Kingston.........	..
Fiji	7,055	18,274	715,373*	Ψ Suva........	75,000
French Polynesia	1,544	4,000	172,000	Ψ Papeete	22,967
Guam	212	549	127,675	Agaña	896
Kiribati	281	728	63,800*	Tarawa	24,400
Marshall Is...........	70	181	45,000	Majuro	15,000
Micronesia, Fed. States of.	271	701	100,000	Kolonia	6,000
Nauru	8	21	8,042*	Ψ Nauru	..
New Caledonia........	7,358	19,058	153,000	Ψ Noumea..........	60,112
New Zealand..........	103,736	268,676	3,307,084*	Ψ Wellington (u.a.)..	325,200
Cook Islands	91	236	17,185*	Avarua	..
Niue	100	259	2,155	Alofi.............	..
Ross Dependency*...	286,696	750,310	..	..	..
Northern Mariana Is ..	184	476	22,000	Saipan	17,000
Palau	192	497	14,000	Koror...........	8,100
Papua New Guinea	178,260	461,691	3,500,000	Ψ Port Moresby	139,300
Pitcairn Islands	1·9	5	52	..	..
Samoa, Eastern (U.S.)..	76	197	37,450	Ψ Pago Pago	3,055
Samoa, Western......	1,097	2,842	163,000	Ψ Apia	33,100*
Solomon Islands......	10,983	28,446	285,176*	Ψ Honiara.........	30,499*
Tonga	270	699	97,000	Ψ Nuku'alofa	28,899
Tuvalu..............	10	25	8,229	Ψ Funafuti	2,856
Vanuatu	4,706	12,190	140,154	Ψ Vila	14,184
Wallis and Futuna Is...	106	274	13,100	Ψ Mata-Utu	..

* Includes permanent shelf ice.

THE LARGEST CITIES OF THE WORLD*

Ψ = Seaport	Population	Ψ = Seaport	Population
MEXICO CITY, Mexico	18,748,000	Ψ Los Angeles, U.S.A.................	8,505,000
CAIRO, Egypt	14,000,000	São Paulo, Brazil	8,490,763
Ψ Shanghai, China	12,620,000	Ψ Bombay, India	8,202,000
TOKYO, Japan	11,680,282	Ψ LONDON, U.K......................	6,775,200
SEOUL, South Korea	9,991,089	Manila, Philippines..................	6,720,050
Ψ BUENOS AIRES, Argentina	9,968,000	Ψ JAKARTA, Indonesia	6,503,449
BEIJING, China	9,957,000	Karachi, Pakistan	6,500,000
Ψ Calcutta, India......................	9,166,000	DELHI, India	6,220,000
Moscow, U.S.S.R.	8,815,000	Chicago, U.S.A.	6,199,000
PARIS, France	8,706,963	TEHRAN, Iran	6,000,000
Ψ New York, U.S.A.	8,529,000		

* In most cases figures refer to urban agglomerations.

WORLD GEOGRAPHICAL STATISTICS

North America

River......Mississippi–Missouri–Red Rock	3,741 miles
Lake ......Superior	31,000 sq miles
Mountain ..McKinley	20,320 ft
Waterfall ...Yosemite, California	2,425 ft

South America

River......Amazon	4,007 miles
Lake ......Titicaca	3,205 sq miles
Mountain ..Aconcagua	22,834 ft
Waterfall ...Angel, Venezuela	3,212 ft

Africa

River......Nile	4,145 miles
Lake ......Victoria	26,800 sq miles
Mountain ..Kilimanjaro	19,340 ft
Waterfall ...Tugela, Natal	3,110 ft

Europe

River......Volga, USSR	2,293 miles
Lake ......Ladoga, USSR	6,826 sq miles
Mountain ..Elbruz, Caucasus	18,481 ft
Waterfall ...Utigard, Norway	2,625 ft

Asia

River......Yenisei, Mongolia–USSR	3,442 miles
Lake ......Aral Sea, USSR	25,500 sq miles
Mountain ..Everest	29,028 ft
Waterfall ...Gersoppa, India	830 ft

Oceania

River......Murray–Darling, Australia	2,350 miles
Lake ......Eyre, Australia	3,700 sq miles
Mountain ..Cook, New Zealand	12,349 ft
Waterfall ...Sutherland, New Zealand	1,904 ft

OCEAN AREAS AND DEPTHS

Oceans

Name	Area of Basin (sq. miles)	Greatest Depth (feet)	
Pacific	63,800,000	Mariana Trench	36,198
Atlantic.......	31,830,000	Milwaukee Deep	30,238
Indian	28,360,000	Java Trench	25,344
Arctic.........	5,500,000	....	18,050

Seas

Name	Area of Basin (sq. miles)	Greatest Depth (feet)	
South China ...	1,148,500	....	16,452
Caribbean[1] ...	1,020,000	Cayman Trench	25,216

Seas

Name	Area of Basin (sq. miles)	Greatest Depth (feet)	
Mediterranean.[2]	966,750	Ionian Basin	16,801
Bering	875,750	....	13,442
Gulf of Mexico .	590,000	Sigsbee Deep	17,070
Okhotsk	589,800	Kuril Trough	11,069
East China	482,300	Okinawa Trench	8,914
Hudson Bay ...	475,800	....	c. 1,500
Japan	389,000	....	12,276
Andaman	308,000	....	14,500
North Sea	222,125	Skaggerak	2,400
Banda Sea	180,000	Weber Basin	24,400
Black Sea (and Sea of Azov) .	178,500	....	7,257
Red Sea	169,000	....	8,984

[1] Excluding the Gulf of Mexico.
[2] Excluding the Black Sea.

PRINCIPAL LAND AREAS OF THE WORLD BELOW SEA LEVEL
(With approx. greatest depth in feet below Mean Sea Level.)

Africa: Libyan Desert Depressions:—
Qattara (440), Faiyum (150).
Wadi Ryan (140), Sittra (110),
Areg (80), Wadi Natrun (75).
Melfa (60), Siwa (55), Bahrain (50).
Eritrea: Salt Plains depression (385).
Algeria-Tunisia: Shott Melghir and El Gharsa (90)*.

America: Death Valley (275), Salton Sea (245)*.
Asia: Jordan Valley, Dead Sea (1290)*.
China: Sinkiang, Turfan Basin (980).
U.S.S.R.–Iran: Caspian Sea (85)*.
Arabia: Trucial Oman-U.A.E. (70).
Australia: Lake Eyre (40).
Europe: Netherlands coastal areas (15).

* Water surface

PRINCIPAL HEIGHTS ABOVE SEA LEVEL

	Feet		Feet
Africa: Kilimanjaro	19,340	*England:* Scafell Pike....................	3,210
North America: McKinley	20,320	*Wales:* Snowdon	3,560
South America: Aconcagua	22,834	*Scotland:* Ben Nevis	4,406
Antarctica: Vinson Massif	16,864	*Ireland:* Carrantuohill....................	3,414
Asia: Everest	29,028	*Oceania:*	
Europe: Elbruz	18,481	*Australia:* Kosciusko	7,316
Alps—Mont Blanc......................	15,771	*New Zealand:* Cook	12,349

THE LARGEST ISLANDS

Name of Island	Ocean	Area in Sq. Miles	Name of Island	Ocean	Area in Sq. Miles
Greenland	Arctic	840,004	Sulawesi (Celebes)	Indian	72,987
New Guinea	Pacific	300,000	South Island, N.Z.	Pacific	58,093
Borneo....................	Pacific	280,100	Java	Indian	48,763
Madagascar	Indian	226,658	North Island, N.Z.	Pacific	44,281
Baffin Island	Arctic	183,810	Newfoundland	Atlantic	43,359
Sumatra	Indian	182,860	Cuba	Atlantic	42,804
Honshu	Pacific	88,031	Luzon.....................	Pacific	40,420
Great Britain[1]	Atlantic	84,186	Iceland	Atlantic	39,769
Victoria Island	Arctic	81,930	Mindanao	Pacific	36,381
Ellesmere Island	Arctic	75,767	Ireland...................	Atlantic	32,595

[1] Mainland only.

THE WORLD'S LARGEST LAKES

The areas of some of these lakes are subject to seasonal variation.

Name	Locality	Length (Miles)	Area (Sq. Miles)	Name	Locality	Length (Miles)	Area (Sq. Miles)
Caspian Sea	Asia	760	143,000	Balkhash	U.S.S.R.	376	6,700
Superior	North America	383	31,800	Nettilling	Baffin Island	120	5,000
Victoria	Africa	210	26,800	Amadjuak	Baffin Island	75	4,000
Aral	U.S.S.R.	280	25,500	Bangweulu[1]	Africa	150	3,800
Huron	North America	206	23,100				(max)
Michigan	North America	321	22,300	Onega	U.S.S.R.	145	3,753
Tanganyika	Africa	430	12,700	Eyre[1]	Australia	130	3,700
Great Bear	Canada	200	12,275	Titicaca	South America	110	3,205
Baikal	U.S.S.R.	395	12,200	Nicaragua	Nicaragua	110	3,190
Malawi	Africa	363	11,430	Athabasca	Canada	208	3,120
Great Slave	Canada	300	11,030	Gairdner	Australia	100	3,000
Erie	North America	241	9,910	Turkana			
Winnipeg	Canada	264	9,465	(Rudolf)	Africa	154	2,473
Chad[1]	Africa	175	9,000	Reindeer	Canada	152	2,467
			(max)	Issyk-Kul	U.S.S.R.	115	2,445
Ontario	North America	193	7,550	Koko-Nor[1]	China	68	2,300
Ladoga	U.S.S.R.	136	6,826				(max)

[1] Area varies considerably according to season.

THE WORLD'S HIGHEST VOLCANOES

ACTIVE

Volcano	Locality	Height in Feet	Volcano	Locality	Height in Feet
Antofalla	Argentina	21,162	Nyamuragira	Zaire	10,150
Guallatiri	Chile	19,882	Mt. St. Helens	Cascade Range, U.S.A.	9,677
Cotopaxi	Ecuador	19,347	Tambora	Indonesia	9,351
Kluchevskaya	U.S.S.R.	15,913	Villarrica	Chile	9,325
Mt. Wrangell	Alaska	14,000	Ruapehu	New Zealand	9,175
Mauna Loa	Hawaii	13,680	Paricutin	Mexico	9,100
Cameroon	Cameroon	13,350	Asama	Japan	8,340
Erebus	Antarctica	12,450	Ngauruhoe	New Zealand	7,515
Nyiragongo	Zaire	11,385	Hecla	Iceland	4,747
Iliamna	Aleutian Range, U.S.A.	11,000	Vesuvius	Italy	4,198
Etna	Sicily	10,853	Kilauea	Hawaii	4,077
Chillan	Chile	10,500	Stromboli	Lipari Is., Italy	3,038

DORMANT

Volcano	Locality	Height in Feet	Volcano	Locality	Height in Feet
Llullaillaco	Chile	22,057	Haleakala	Hawaii	10,022
Cayembe	Ecuador	18,982	The Peak	Tristan da Cunha	6,760
Demavend	Iran	18,384	Tongariro	New Zealand	6,458
Popocatepetl	Mexico	17,887	Pelée	Martinique	4,800
Pico de Teide	Tenerife	12,198	Soufrière	St Vincent	4,200
Semerou	Java	12,060			

BELIEVED EXTINCT

Volcano	Locality	Height in Feet	Volcano	Locality	Height in Feet
Aconcagua	Andes	22,834	Antisana	Ecuador	18,713
Chimborazo	Ecuador	20,561	Citlaltepetl	Mexico	18,700
Kilimanjaro	Tanzania	19,340	Elbruz	Caucasus	18,481

THE WORLD'S HIGHEST MOUNTAINS

The following list contains some of the principal peaks of such ranges as the Himalayas and the Andes, and the highest mountains in other ranges.

Name	Range or Country	Height in Feet	Name	Range or Country	Height in Feet
Everest	Himalayas	29,028	Llullaillaco	Andes	22,057
K2	Karakoram	28,250	Sajama	Andes	21,463
Kanchenjunga	Himalayas	28,208	Illimani	Andes	21,200
Makalu I	Himalayas	27,824	Chimborazo	Andes	20,561
Dhaulagiri	Himalayas	26,810	McKinley	Alaska	20,320
Nanga Parbat	Himalayas	26,660	Logan	Yukon	19,850
Annapurna	Himalayas	26,504	Cotopaxi	Andes	19,347
Nanda Devi	Himalayas	25,646	Kilimanjaro	Tanzania	19,340
Kamet	Himalayas	25,446	Citlaltepetl	Sierra Madre	18,700
Namcha Barwa	China	25,445	Elbruz	Caucasus	18,481
Minya Konka	China	24,890	St. Elias	Alaska	18,008
Communism Peak	Pamirs	24,590	Popocatepetl	Mexico	17,887
Pobedy Peak	Tian Shan	24,406	Foraker	Alaska	17,395
Lenin Peak	Pamirs	23,406	Lucania	Yukon	17,150
Aconcagua	Andes	22,834	Kenya	Kenya	17,058
Ojos del Salado	Andes	22,588	Ararat	Armenia	16,945
Bonete	Andes	22,545	Vinson Massif	Antarctica	16,864
Huascaran	Andes	22,204	Mont Blanc	Alps	15,771

THE WORLD'S LARGEST WATERFALLS

Greatest in height		Total height ft.	Greatest single drop ft.
Angel	Venezuela	3,212	2,648
Tugela	S. Africa	3,110	1,350
Utigard	Norway	2,625	1,970
Mongefossen..	Norway	2,540	
Yosemite	California,		
	U.S.A......	2,425	1,430
Mardalsfoss....	Norway	2,154	974
Tyssestrengane	Norway	2,120	948
Kukenaam	Venezuela	2,000	
Sutherland ...	New Zealand ..	1,904	815
Takkakaw	Canada.......	1,650	1,200
Ribbon	California,		
	U.S.A......	1,612	1,612
King George VI	Guyana	1,600	
Wollomombi ...	Australia.....	1,580	1,100
Roraima.......	Guyana	1,500	
Gavarnie	France	1,385	

Greatest in height		Total height ft.	Greatest single drop ft.
BRITISH ISLES			
Eas Coul Aulin	Scotland	658	
Caldron Snout*	England	450	
Powerscourt ...	Ireland	350	
Pistyll Rhaeadr	Wales	300	

* Cataracts—no sheer drop.

Greatest in width		Width yd.
Khone Cataracts	Laos	11,667
Guayra..............	Brazil	5,300
Victoria	Zimbabwe-Zambia ..	1,534
Niagara	Canada–U.S.A........	1,200

THE LONGEST RIVERS

River	Outflow	Length in Miles
Nile...................	Mediterranean.....	4,145
Amazon	Atlantic...........	4,007
Mississippi-Missouri– Red Rock	Gulf of Mexico	3,741
Yenisei...............	Arctic.............	3,442
Yangtze..............	North Pacific	3,436
Ob-Irtysh............	Arctic.............	3,362
Hwang-ho (Yellow River)..............	North Pacific	3,000
Zaire (Congo)	Atlantic...........	2,920
Lena	Arctic.............	2,734
Amur	North Pacific	2,700
Mackenzie-Peace	Beaufort Sea	2,635
Mekong	China Sea	2,600
Niger	Gulf of Guinea	2,600
Rio de la Plata-Parana .	Atlantic...........	2,485
Murray-Darling.......	Southern Ocean ...	2,350
Volga	Caspian Sea	2,293
Zambezi	Indian Ocean	2,200
Madeira..............	(1)	2,100
Purus (Coxiuara)......	(1)	2,000
Yukon	Bering Sea	1,979
St. Lawrence	Gulf of St. Lawrence	1,945
Rio Grande del Norte ..	Gulf of Mexico	1,885
Ganges-Brahmaputra ..	Bay of Bengal	1,800
São Francisco........	Atlantic...........	1,800
Indus	Arabian Sea	1,790
Danube	Black Sea.........	1,770
Salween (No Chiang) ..	Gulf of Martaban .	1,750
Tigris-Euphrates	Persian Gulf	1,700
Tocantins	Pará River	1,700
Orinoco	Atlantic...........	1,700

Great Britain

Severn	Bristol Channel	220
Thames	North Sea	215

(1) Tributaries of the Amazon.

SOME FAMOUS BRIDGES

Among the outstanding *suspension bridges* of the World are the Verrazano Narrows Bridge, New York (main span, 4,260 ft.); the Golden Gate Bridge, San Francisco (4,200 ft.); Mackinac Bridge, Michigan (3,800 ft.); Bosporus, Turkey (3,523 ft.); George Washington Bridge, New York (3,500 ft.); the Ponte 25 April (Tagus Bridge), Portugal (3,323 ft.); Forth Road Bridge, Scotland (3,300 ft.); Severn Bridge, England (3,240 ft.); Tacoma Bridge, Washington, U.S.A. (2,800 ft.); Orinoco Bridge, Venezuela (2,336 ft.) and the Kanmon Bridge, Japan (2,336 ft.). Lengths shown above are all those of the main or longest span. The Humber Bridge was opened in 1981 and has the longest single central span, 4,626 ft., of any suspension bridge in the world.

The Transbay Bridge (*suspension and cantilever*), crossing San Francisco Bay from Oakland to San Francisco is 7¼ miles long, with spans of 2,310 ft. each.

Among important *steel arch* bridges are the New River Gorge Bridge, Virginia, U.S.A. (1,700 ft); the Bayonne Bridge, from New Jersey to Staten Island, U.S.A. (1,652 ft.); Sydney Harbour Bridge, Australia (1,650 ft.); the Runcorn-Widnes Bridge, England (1,082 ft.); and the Glen Canyon Bridge over the Colorado River, U.S.A. (1,028 ft.). Major *concrete trestle* bridges include the Lake Pontchartrain Causeway, U.S.A. of 2,170 spans extending 23·87 miles and the Oosterscheldebrug, Netherlands, 3·12 miles long. The Chesapeake Bay Bridge-Tunnel (17·6 miles long) has 12·5 miles of *concrete trestle* bridge. Gladesville Bridge, Sydney, Australia, is a *concrete arch* bridge of 1,000 ft. span. The Tay Bridge in Scotland is a *steel box girder* bridge supported on twin piers (42 spans), 7,365 ft long.

GREAT SHIP CANALS OF THE WORLD

Canal	Opened	Length, miles	Depth (ft.)†	Width (ft.)†
Corinth (Greece)	1893	4	26	72
Kiel (Germany)	1895	61	31	132
Manchester (England)	1894	35·5	30	120
North Sea (Netherlands)	1876	14·5	43	148
Panama	1914	50·5	39·5	500
St. Lawrence Seaway (Canada)	1959	378*	27	200
Suez (Egypt)	1869	100	42	197
Terneuzen-Ghent (Netherlands–Belgium) ...	1895	18·5	38	102

† Of largest vessels permitted.   * Includes Lake Ontario and Welland Canal.

INLAND WATERWAYS.—The British Waterways Board are the navigational authority for nearly 2,000 miles of canals and river navigations in England, Scotland and Wales. Some 340 miles are maintained and are being developed as Commercial Waterways for use by freight-carrying vessels, and another 1,200 miles, the Cruising Waterways, are being developed for boating, fishing and other leisure activities. The remaining 500 miles, the Remainder Waterways, are maintained with due regard to safety, public health and the preservation of amenities. Over a third of this remaining mileage is being, or has been, restored to navigation. The Manchester Ship Canal, Bridgewater Canal, Rochdale Canal, River Thames and Fenland Waterways are among those which are the responsibility of other authorities.

LONGEST RAILWAY TUNNELS

E.R. = Eastern Region; L.M.R. = London Midland Region;
S.R. = Southern Region; W.R. = Western Region

United Kingdom

		Miles	Yards
Severn	W.R.	4	484
Totley	E.R.	3	950
Standedge	E.R.	3	66
Sodbury	W.R.	2	924
Disley	L.M.R.	2	346
Ffestiniog	L.M.R.	2	338
Bramhope	E.R.	2	241
Cowburn	L.M.R.	2	182
Sevenoaks	S.R.	1	1693
Morley	E.R.	1	1609
Box	W.R.	1	1452
Dove Holes	L.M.R.	1	1224
Littleborough (Summit)	L.M.R.	1	1125
Anderston	S.R.	1	1010
Ponsbourne	E.R.	1	924
Bleamoor	L.M.R.	1	869
Polhill	S.R.	1	851
Queensbury	E.R.	1	741
Kilsby	L.M.R.	1	666
Lydden	S.R.	1	609
Strood	S.R.	1	569
Oxted	S.R.	1	501
Clayton	S.R.	1	499
Penge	S.R.	1	381
Merstham New (Quarry)	S.R.	1	353
Greenock	Scottish Region	1	351

		Miles	Yards
Bradway	E.R.	1	267
Sough	L.M.R.	1	255
Watford, New	L.M.R.	1	230
Llangyfelach	W.R.	1	193
Caerphilly	W.R.	1	173
Abbot's Cliff	S.R.	1	182
Halton	L.M.R.	1	176
Corby	L.M.R.	1	160
Wenvoe	W.R.	1	107
Sapperton	W.R.	1	100
Wymington	L.M.R.	1	100

The London Underground *Northern Line* between Morden and East Finchley by the City Branch serves 25 stations and uses tunnels totalling 17¼ miles in length.

The World
(Submarine tunnels are not included)

		Miles	Yards
Simplon	Switzerland–Italy	12	560
Apennine	Italy	11	880
St. Gotthard	Switzerland	9	550
Lötschberg	Switzerland	9	130
Mont Cenis	Italy	8	870
Cascade	United States	7	1410
Arlberg	Austria	6	650
Moffat	United States	6	200
Shimizu	Japan	6	70

THE ARCTIC OCEAN

The Arctic Ocean consists of a deep sea over 2,000 fathoms, on the southern margin of which there is a broad continental shelf with numerous islands. Into this deeper sea there is only one broad channel, about 700 miles, between Greenland and Scandinavia. Bering Strait is only 49 miles wide and 27 fathoms deep. The southern boundary of the Arctic Ocean is the Wyville-Thomson and Faeroe-Icelandic submarine ridge, which separates the North Atlantic from the Norwegian and Greenland Seas. The Norwegian Deep lies between Norway and Jan Mayen and Iceland; it exceeds 1,500 fathoms. The Greenland Deep, of similar depth, lies between Spitsbergen and Greenland. These two depressions are separated by a somewhat deeply submerged ridge from the east of Jan Mayen to Bear Island, south of Spitsbergen. A shallow ridge from the north-west of Spitsbergen to Greenland separates the Greenland Sea from the deep North Polar Basin. This extends from the north of Spitsbergen and Franz Josef Land to the north of the New Siberia Islands and of the North American Arctic Archipelago. Another more shallow depression is Baffin Bay, less than 1,000 fathoms. This is separated from the North Atlantic by a submarine ridge. Barent's Sea, between Spitsbergen, Norway and Novaya Zemlya, and the Kara Sea, between Novaya Zemlya and the Siberian coast, are respectively below 200 and 100 fathoms. The total area of the Arctic Sea is about 5·5 million square miles, of which 2·3 million square miles are probably covered with floating ice.

DISTANCE OF THE HORIZON

The limit of distance to which one can see varies with the height of the spectator. The greatest distance at which an object on the surface of the sea, or of a level plain, can be seen by a person whose eyes are at a height of five feet from the same level is nearly three miles. At a height of 20 feet the range is increased to nearly six miles, and an approximate rule for finding the range of vision for small heights is to increase the square root of the number of feet that the eye is above the level surface by a third of itself, the result being the distance of the horizon in miles, but is slightly in excess of that in the table below, which is computed by a more precise formula. The table may be used conversely to show the distance of an object of given height that is just visible from a point in the surface of the earth or sea. Refraction is taken into account both in the approximate rule and in the Table.

At a height of	the range is	At a height of	the range is	At a height of	the range is
5 ft.	2·9 miles	500 ft	29·5 miles	4,000 ft	83·3 miles
20 „	5·9 „	1,000 „	41·6 „	5,000 „	93·1 „
50 „	9·3 „	2,000 „	58·9 „	20,000 „	186·2 „
100 „	13·2 „	3,000 „	72·1 „		

THE ANTARCTIC

THE ANTARCTIC is generally defined as the area lying within the Antarctic Convergence—the zone where cold northward-flowing Antarctic sea water sinks below warmer southward-flowing water. This zone is at about lat. 50° S. in the Atlantic Ocean and lat. 55°–62° S. in the Pacific Ocean. The continent itself lies almost entirely within the Antarctic Circle, an area of about 5·5 million square miles, 99 per cent of which is permanently ice-covered. The average thickness of the ice is 7,100 ft. but in places exceeds 14,500 ft., submerging entire mountain ranges; some mountains protrude—the highest being Vinson Massif, 16,066 ft. The ice amounts to some 7·2 million cubic miles and represents more than 90 per cent of the world's fresh water.

Along one-third of the Antarctic coastline, land-ice flowing outwards forms extensive ice shelves, fragments of which break off to form tabular icebergs, leaving ice cliffs up to 150 ft. high. Much of the sea freezes in winter, forming fast ice which breaks up in summer and drifts north as pack ice. The presence of ice and continuous darkness in winter restrict access to the coastline by sea to the summer months.

The most conspicuous physical features of the continent are its high inland plateau (much of it over 10,000 ft.), the Transantarctic Mountains (which together with the large embayments of the Weddell Sea and Ross Sea mark the approximate boundary between Greater and Lesser Antarctica), and the mountainous Antarctic Peninsula and off-lying islands (which extend northwards towards South America). The continental shelf averages about 20 miles in width (half the global mean, and in places it is non-existent) and reaches exceptional depths (1,300–2,600 ft., which is 3–6 times the global mean).

Climate.—On land, summer temperatures range from just below freezing around the coast to −34° C. (about − 30° F.) on the plateau, and in winter − 20° C. (about − 4° F.) on the coast to − 65° C. (about − 85° F.) inland. Over a large area the maxima do not exceed − 15° C. (+5° F.).

Precipitation is scanty over the plateau but amounts to 25–76 cms. (10–30 ins.) (water equivalent) along the coast and some scientific stations are permanently buried by snow. Some rain falls over the more northerly areas in summer. Gravity winds on the plateau slopes and cyclonic storms further north can both exceed 100 m.p.h. and gusts have been known to reach 150 m.p.h. Visibility can be reduced to zero in blizzards.

Flora and Fauna.—Although a small number of flowering plants, ferns and clubmosses occur on the sub-Antarctic islands, only two (a grass and a pearlwort) extend south of 60° S. Antarctic vegetation is dominated by lichens and mosses, with a few liverworts, algae, and fungi. Most of these occur around the coast or on islands, but lichens and some mosses also occur inland.

The only land animals are tiny insects and mites with nematodes, rotifers, and tardigrades in the mosses, but large numbers of seals, penguins, and other sea-birds go ashore to breed in the summer. The emperor penguin is the only species which breeds ashore throughout the winter. In contrast, the Antarctic seas abound with life—a wide variety of invertebrates (including krill) and fish providing food for the seals, penguins, and other birds and a residual population of whales.

Exploration and Antarctic Treaty.—In the 180 years from Captain James Cook's circumnavigation of the Antarctic in 1772–75 to the mid-1950's, about half of all expeditions to the Antarctic were British and a number of these made major contributions to geographical and scientific knowledge of the area. Notable were the expeditions of Sir James Clark Ross, Captain Robert Scott, and Sir Ernest Shackleton.

Apart from four years during World War II, British Antarctic research has been continuous since 1925, and most of it is now organized and carried out by the British Antarctic Survey (a component of the Natural Environment Research Council).

The world-wide International Geophysical Year, 1957–58, gave great impetus to Antarctic research. Prior to the mid-1950's, only 17 stations were operated in the Antarctic by four nations and vast areas of the continent were still unknown. By 1957, 44 stations had been established by 12 nations. The co-operative scientific effort proved so fruitful that the 12 nations involved pledged themselves to continue to promote scientific and technical co-operation unhampered by politics (territorial claims being left in abeyance) and agreed that the continent should be used for peaceful purposes only. These aims were embodied in the Antarctic Treaty (covering the area south of lat. 60° S., excluding the high seas but including the ice shelves), which came into force in 1961. It has since been signed by a further 25 acceding nations, 7 of which are active in the Antarctic and have therefore been accorded consultative status.

Potential resources.—Increasing pressure on the world's food and mineral supplies has stimulated the search for new sources even in the extremely hostile polar environment. Minerals have been found in great variety but not in commercially exploitable concentrations in accessible localities. (For example, coal seams occur in the Theron Mountains and Horlick Mountains.)

There are indications that off-shore hydrocarbons could be present but mostly below great depths of stormy, ice-infested seas. However, the Antarctic Treaty nations and their scientific advisors are already considering the environmental implications of possible mineral exploration and exploitation.

Currently, the chief interest is in marine protein, including the shrimp-like krill already fished commercially by Japan, Poland and U.S.S.R. Basic research to ensure rational management of stocks of this key organism is being continued by international groups, but it is estimated that they could sustain a yield equal to the present total annual world fish catch.

Scientific research.—At present, five British stations are maintained in the British Antarctic Territory and at South Georgia. Two are biological stations, two geophysical observatories, and one is the centre for airborne earth sciences.

There are a number of permanently occupied stations operated by other nations including one maintained at the South Pole by the U.S.A

The staff of these stations and summer field-workers are the only people present on the continent and off-lying islands. There are no indigenous inhabitants.

(British Antarctic Survey, *see* entry on p. 349).

THE UNITED KINGDOM

The United Kingdom comprises Great Britain (England, Wales and Scotland) and Northern Ireland.

AREA

Sq. miles	England	Wales	Scotland	N. Ireland	U.K.*
Land	50,070	7,968	29,761	5,206	93,005
Inland water	293	50	653	246	1,242
Total	50,363	8,018	30,414	5,452	94,247

* Excludes the Isle of Man (221 sq. miles) and the Channel Islands (75 sq. miles)

POPULATION

CENSUS RESULTS, 1801–1981

Before 1801 there existed no official return of the population of either England or Scotland. Estimates of the population of England at various periods, calculated from the number of baptisms, burials and marriages, are: in 1570, 4,160,221; 1600, 4,811,718; 1630, 5,600,517; 1670, 5,773,646; 1700, 6,045,008; 1750, 6,517,035.

Thousands

	United Kingdom			England and Wales			Scotland			Northern Ireland†		
	Total	Male	Female	Total	Male	Female	Total	Male	Female	Total	Male	Female
1801	11,944	5,692	6,252	8,893	4,255	4,638	1,608	739	869	1,443	698	745
1811	13,368	6,368	7,000	10,165	4,874	5,291	1,806	826	980	1,397	668	729
1821	15,472	7,498	7,974	12,000	5,850	6,150	2,092	983	1,109	1,380	665	715
1831	17,835	8,647	9,188	13,897	6,771	7,126	2,364	1,114	1,250	1,574	762	812
1841	20,183	9,819	10,364	15,914	7,778	8,137	2,620	1,242	1,378	1,649	800	849
1851	22,259	10,855	11,404	17,928	8,781	9,146	2,889	1,376	1,513	1,443	698	745
1861	24,525	11,894	12,631	20,066	9,776	10,290	3,062	1,450	1,612	1,396	668	728
1871	27,431	13,309	14,122	22,712	11,059	11,653	3,360	1,603	1,757	1,359	647	712
1881	31,015	15,060	15,955	25,974	12,640	13,335	3,736	1,799	1,936	1,305	621	684
1891	34,264	16,593	17,671	29,003	14,060	14,942	4,026	1,943	2,083	1,236	590	646
1901	38,237	18,492	19,745	32,528	15,729	16,799	4,472	2,174	2,298	1,237	590	647
1911	42,082	20,357	21,725	36,070	17,446	18,625	4,761	2,309	2,452	1,251	603	648
1921	44,027	21,033	22,994	37,887	18,075	19,811	4,882	2,348	2,535	1,258	610	648
1931	46,038	22,060	23,978	39,952	19,133	20,819	4,843	2,326	2,517	1,243	601	642
1951	50,225	24,118	26,107	43,758	21,016	22,742	5,096	2,434	2,662	1,371	668	703
1961	52,709	25,481	27,228	46,105	22,304	23,801	5,179	2,483	2,697	1,425	694	731
1971	55,515	26,952	28,562	48,750	23,683	25,067	5,229	2,515	2,714	1,536	755	781
1981	55,776	27,064	28,701	49,154	23,873	25,281	5,130	2,466	2,664	1,491	725	756

NOTES.
1. Because of the War there was no Census in 1941.
2. The last official Census of Population in respect of England and Wales, Scotland, Northern Ireland, the Isle of Man and Guernsey, was taken on the night of April 5, 1981.
3. † All figures refer to the area which is now Northern Ireland. Figures for N. Ireland in 1921 and 1931 are estimates based on the Censuses held in 1926 and 1937.

ISLANDS

The figures given above do not include islands of the British Seas. Populations of these islands at census years since 1900 were:—

	ISLE OF MAN			JERSEY			GUERNSEY		
	Total	Male	Female	Total	Male	Female	Total	Male	Female
1901	54,752	25,496	29,256	52,576	23,940	28,636	43,042	21,140	21,902
1911	52,016	23,937	28,079	51,898	24,014	27,884	45,001	22,215	22,786
1921	60,284	27,329	32,955	49,701	22,438	27,263	40,529	19,303	21,226
1931	49,308	22,443	26,865	50,462	23,424	27,038	42,743	20,675	22,068
1951	55,123	25,749	29,464	57,296	27,282	30,014	45,747	22,094	23,380
1961	48,151	22,060	26,091	57,200	27,200	30,000	47,178	22,890	24,288
1971	56,289	26,461	29,828	72,532	35,423	37,109	52,708	25,382	27,326
1981	64,679	30,901	33,778	77,000	37,000	40,000	56,000	27,000	29,000

Births and Marriages (Thousands)

	Live births				Marriages			
	United Kingdom	England and Wales		Scotland	Northern Ireland	United Kingdom	England and Wales		Scotland	Northern Ireland
		Total	Wales				Total	Wales		
1981	730·8	634·5	35·8	69·1	27·3	397·8	352·0	19·8	36·2	9·6
1982	719·2	625·9	35·7	66·2	27·0	387·0	342·2	19·0	34·9	9·9
1983	721·5	629·1	35·5	65·1	27·3	389·3	344·3	19·9	35·0	10·0
1984	729·6	636·8	35·9	65·1	27·7	395·8	349·0	19·2	36·3	10·4
1985	750·7	656·4	36·8	66·7	27·6	393·1	346·4	19·1	36·4	10·3
1986	755·0	661·0	37·0	65·8	28·2	393·9	347·9	19·5	35·8	10·2
1987	755·6	681·5	37·8	66·2	27·9	397·9	351·8	19·5	35·8	10·4
1988	787·6	693·6	38·8	66·1	27·8†	—	—	—	35·6	10·0†
1988 1st quarter	197·5	173·4	9·6	16·9	7·2†	52·4	46·2	2·6	5·0	1·3†
2nd quarter	200·2	176·5	9·9	16·5	7·2†	112·0	99·1	5·5	10·1	2·9†
3rd quarter	203·1	179·1	10·2	16·8	7·1†	152·4	135·2	7·2	13·2	4·2†
4th quarter	186·8	164·6	9·1	15·9	6·3†	—	—	—	7·3	1·6†

† Provisional.

Divorce

	1981	1982	1983	1984	1985	1986	1987
England and Wales							
Decrees absolute, granted:							
Number	145,713	146,698	147,479	144,501	160,300	153,903	151,007
Rate per 1,000 married couples	*11·9*	*12·0*	*12·2*	*12·0*	*13·4*	*12·8*	*12·6†*
Scotland							
Decrees absolute, granted:							
Number	9,894	11,288	13,238	11,906	13,371	13,063	12,133
Rate per 1,000 married couples	*8·0*	*9·2*	*11·0*	*9·9*	*11·2*	*11·1*	*10·2*
Northern Ireland							
Petitions filed:							
Nullity of marriage	9	5	—	6	6	6	4
Divorce.	1,645	1,734	1,577	1,749	1,986	1,630	1,834
Judicial separation	2	2	9	5	15	17	7

† Provisional.

Deaths Registered* (Thousands)

	Total					Infants under one year				
	United Kingdom	England and Wales		Scotland	Northern Ireland	United Kingdom	England and Wales		Scotland	Northern Ireland
		Total	Wales				Total	Wales		
1981	658·0	577·9	35·0	63·8	16·3	8·16	7·02	0·45	0·78	0·36
1982	662·8	581·9	35·2	65·0	15·9	7·90	6·78	0·38	0·75	0·37
1983	659·1	579·6	35·2	63·5	16·0	7·36	6·38	0·38	0·65	0·33
1984	644·9	566·9	33·7	62·3	15·7	7·00	6·04	0·31	0·67	0·29
1985	670·6	590·7	35·5	64·0	16·0	7·03	6·14	0·36	0·62	0·27
1986	660·7	581·2	34·7	63·5	16·1	7·18	6·31	0·35	0·58	0·29
1987	644·3	567·0	33·9	62·0	15·3	7·08	6·27	0·36	0·56	0·24
1988	649·2	571·4	34·0	62·0	15·8	7·06	6·27	0·29	0·54	0·25
1988 1st quarter	180·4	159·5	9·3	16·5	4·5†	2·03	1·81	0·09	0·15	0·07†
2nd quarter	155·6	136·3	8·3	15·3	4·0†	1·72	1·52	0·07	0·13	0·07†
3rd quarter	147·1	129·3	7·6	14·2	3·5†	1·51	1·33	0·08	0·13	0·06†
4th quarter	166·1	146·3	8·7	15·9	3·8†	1·80	1·61	0·06	0·13	0·06†

* Excluding stillbirths. † Provisional.

Deaths Analysed By Cause, 1987

	England & Wales	Scotland	N. Ireland†
Total deaths	563,546	62,014	15,334
Deaths from natural causes	545,723	59,328	14,572
Infections and parasitic diseases	2,375	250	63
Cholera	—	—	—
Typhoid fever	2	—	—
Shigellosis and amoebiasis	4	—	—
Enteritis and other diarrhoeal diseases	101	7	—
Tuberculosis of respiratory system	329	29	13
Other tuberculosis, including late effects	296	47	1
Diphtheria	—	—	—
Whooping cough	5	—	—
Streptococcal sore throat and scarlatina	5	—	—
Meningococcal infection	155	17	6
Acute poliomyelitis	—	—	1
Smallpox	—	1	—
Measles	6	—	1
Louse-borne typhus and other rickettisioses	2	1	—
Malaria	7	1	—
Syphilis	35	1	—
Neoplasms	142,451	14,793	3,417
Malignant neoplasm of stomach	9,509	985	239
Malignant neoplasm of trachea, bronchus and lung	35,138	4,290	759
Malignant neoplasm of breast	13,840	1,245	312
Malignant neoplasm of uterus	3,377	327	73
Leukaemia	3,650	312	83
Benign and unspecified neoplasms	1,283	111	42
Endocrine, nutritional and metabolic diseases and immunity disorders	9,810	730	78
Diabetes mellitus	7,637	540	57
Nutritional deficiencies	74	12	1
Diseases of blood and blood-forming organs	2,323	190	27
Anaemias	1,329	89	14
Mental disorders	12,437	918	35
Diseases of nervous system and sense organs	10,953	788	174
Meningitis	260	22	4
Diseases of the circulatory system	271,061	31,057	7,602
Acute rheumatic fever	8	—	5
Chronic rheumatic heart disease	2,415	242	53
Hypertensive disease	3,760	324	69
Ischaemic heart disease	155,235	18,405	4,538
Diseases of pulmonary circulation and other forms of heart disease	21,112	2,222	796
Cerebrovascular disease	69,450	8,225	1,818
Diseases of the respiratory system	57,075	6,793	2,269
Influenza	190	36	2
Pneumonia	24,603	3,750	1,510
Bronchitis, emphysema	9,821	632	158
Asthma	1,898	159	50
Diseases of the digestive system	17,669	1,915	368
Ulcer of stomach and duodenum	4,307	422	77
Appendicitis	115	8	3
Hernia of abdominal cavity and other intestinal obstruction	1,900	166	41
Chronic liver disease and cirrhosis	2,709	401	58
Diseases of the genito-urinary system	7,696	842	237
Nephritis, nephrotic syndrome and nephrosis	4,488	514	147
Hyperplasia of prostate	530	34	9
Complications of pregnancy, childbirth etc.	46	2	1
Abortion	5	—	—
Diseases of the skin and subcutaneous tissue	734	79	28
Diseases of the musculo-skeletal system	5,192	252	46
Congenital anomalies	1,794	225	91
Certain conditions originating in the perinatal period	198	230	79
Birth trauma, hypoxia, birth asphyxia and other respiratory conditions	78	131	31
Signs, symptoms and other ill-defined conditions	3,909	264	57
Deaths from accidents and violence	17,823	2,686	762
All accidents	11,524	1,858	542
Motor vehicle accidents	4,836	582	228
Suicide and self-inflicted injury	3,986	522	86
All other external causes	2,313	306	134

† provisional.

Resident Population by Sex and Age 1987

Thousands

	All ages	0–4	5–14	15–44	45–59/64*	60/65†–74	75 or over
Males							
United Kingdom	27,736·8	1,888·7	3,627·1	12,730·8	5,995·8	2,223·8	1,270·7
England	23,115·7	1,560·3	2,981·9	10,608·5	5,016·0	1,870·5	1,078·5
Wales	1,377·1	93·3	182·0	612·6	305·5	119·1	64·7
Scotland	2,470·6	164·9	330·3	1,156·1	532·6	185·5	101·3
Northern Ireland .	773·4	70·3	132·9	353·5	141·8	48·7	26·3
Females							
United Kingdom	29,193·4	1,796·6	3,435·4	12,450·7	4,635·1	4,370·2	2,505·3
England	24,290·9	1,484·4	2,823·2	10,383·9	3,848·7	3,640·1	2,110·7
Wales	1,459·1	88·8	171·8	601·2	232·2	235·1	130·0
Scotland	2,641·5	157·3	313·2	1,126·5	437·5	393·4	213·5
Northern Ireland .	801·8	66·2	127·3	339·0	116·7	101·6	51·1

*59 for women, 64 for men.
†60 for women, 65 for men.

Birth Rates 1987

Live births per 1,000 women in age groups:

	15–19*	20–24	25–29	30–34	35–39	40–44†
United Kingdom	31	94	126	81	27	5
England	30	93	125	82	27	5
Wales	37	104	124	75	22	5
Scotland	32	90	119	72	21	3
Northern Ireland	29	118	161	113	51	11

*Includes also births to mothers under 15.
†Includes also births to mothers 45 or over.

Death Rates 1987

Deaths per 1,000 population in age groups:

	0–4	5–14	15–24	25–34	35–44	45–54	55–64	65–74	75 or over
Males									
United Kingdom	2·5	0·2	0·8	0·9	1·7	5·2	16·4	42·0	111·3
England	2·5	0·2	0·8	0·9	1·6	4·9	15·8	40·9	109·8
Wales	2·6	0·2	0·8	0·8	1·8	5·5	17·2	43·5	112·8
Scotland	2·3	0·3	0·9	1·1	2·3	6·8	20·0	48·8	121·2
Northern Ireland .	2·3	0·3	1·1	1·3	2·0	5·3	17·9	46·6	121·1
Females									
United Kingdom	2·0	0·2	0·3	0·5	1·1	3·3	9·4	23·3	83·6
England	2·0	0·2	0·3	0·5	1·1	3·2	9·1	22·6	82·8
Wales	2·0	0·2	0·3	0·4	1·2	3·5	9·7	23·9	82·6
Scotland	1·8	0·2	0·3	0·5	1·3	4·0	11·4	28·1	89·2
Northern Ireland .	1·8	0·1	0·4	0·6	1·3	3·1	9·9	26·0	89·3

MIGRATION
Acceptances for settlement by nationality

Geographical region and nationality	Number of persons		
	1985	1986	1987
Belgium	100	110	60
Denmark	150	140	110
France	580	490	420
Germany (Federal Republic)	750	550	450
Greece	250	220	240
Italy	540	400	260
Luxembourg	—	—	—
Netherlands	460	410	280
Portugal	230	200	230
Spain	440	360	370
European Community	**3,490**	**2,880**	**2,430**
Austria	120	80	100
Cyprus	420	370	380
Finland	110	110	140
Malta	180	160	120
Norway	230	170	180
Sweden	390	350	490
Switzerland	170	160	130
Turkey	480	400	460
Yugoslavia	130	130	170
Other Western Europe	**2,240**	**1,950**	**2,160**
Bulgaria	20	20	10
Czechoslovakia	20	20	40
German Democratic Republic	10	—	—
Hungary	50	40	50
Poland	370	250	270
Romania	20	20	20
U.S.S.R.	50	40	70
Eastern Europe	**540**	**380**	**470**
Europe: total	**6,270**	**5,220**	**5,060**
Argentina	50	50	40
Barbados	60	40	60
Brazil	170	160	160
Canada	1,500	1,200	1,180
Chile	70	40	40
Colombia	170	140	160
Cuba	—	—	—
Guyana	200	140	180
Jamaica	350	490	510
Mexico	70	70	80
Peru	80	50	50
Trinidad and Tobago	160	160	140
U.S.A.	4,170	3,740	3,710
Uruguay	10	—	—
Venezuela	50	40	40
West Indies Associated States	—	—	—
Americas: total	**7,130**	**6,310**	**6,350**
Algeria	70	60	80
Egypt	350	240	250
Ethiopia	30	50	60
Ghana	660	520	920
Kenya	520	340	400
Libya	170	130	100
Mauritius	410	260	300
Morocco	160	140	170

Geographical region and nationality	Number of persons		
	1985	1986	1987
Nigeria	500	560	780
Sierra Leone	70	90	100
Somalia	20	70	70
South Africa	790	730	1,020
Sudan	110	50	70
Tanzania	330	240	210
Tunisia	40	50	30
Uganda	50	80	90
Zambia	100	120	150
Zimbabwe	320	270	350
Africa: total	**4,710**	**4,000**	**5,150**
Bangladesh	5,330	4,760	3,080
India	5,500	4,140	4,610
Pakistan	6,680	5,530	3,930
Indian sub-continent	**17,510**	**14,430**	**11,620**
Iran	2,210	1,640	1,450
Iraq	550	430	450
Israel	340	320	300
Jordan	90	140	130
Kuwait	10	10	10
Lebanon	250	190	220
Saudi Arabia	30	30	30
Syria	90	80	100
Middle East	**3,580**	**2,840**	**2,690**
China	140	100	120
Indonesia	60	60	60
Japan	1,010	890	1,300
Malaysia	630	560	630
Philippines	780	990	1,240
Singapore	160	110	140
Sri Lanka	930	800	720
Thailand	340	410	470
BDTC Hong Kong*	950	860	920
Remainder of Asia	**5,000**	**4,780**	**5,600**
Asia: total	**26,090**	**22,040**	**19,920**
Australia	3,780	2,850	3,020
New Zealand	2,880	2,510	2,690
Australasia: total	**6,660**	**5,360**	**5,710**
British Overseas Citizens	2,180	1,670	1,860
Other countries not elsewhere specified	900	700	890
Stateless†	1,420	1,520	1,040
All nationalities	**55,360**	**46,820**	**45,980**
Foreign	26,840	23,270	22,160
Commonwealth	28,520	23,550	23,810
Old Commonwealth	8,160	6,560	6,900
New Commonwealth and Pakistan	27,050	22,520	20,850
Foreign excluding Pakistan	20,150	17,740	18,230

*British Dependent Territories Citizens. †Includes refugees from South-East Asia.

ENGLISH KINGS AND QUEENS A.D. 827 TO 1603

Name	DYNASTY	MARRIED	Access.	Died	Age	Rgnd. (Yrs.)
Saxons and Danes						
EGBERT	King of Wessex and all England		827	839	—	12
ETHELWULF	Son of Egbert		839	858	—	19
ETHELBALD	Son of Ethelwulf		858	860	—	2
ETHELBERT	Son of Ethelwulf		858	866	—	8
ETHELRED	Son of Ethelwulf		866	871	—	5
ALFRED THE GREAT	Son of Ethelwulf	Ealhswith of Gaini	871	899	52	28
EDWARD THE ELDER	Son of Alfred the Great	1st, Egwyn; 2nd, Elfled; 3rd, Eadgifu	899	925	55	26
ATHELSTAN	Eldest son of Edward the Elder by Egwyn		925	940	45	15
EDMUND	Third son of Edward the Elder by Eadgifu	1st, Elgifu; 2nd, Ethelfled	940	946	25	6
EDRED	Fourth son of Edward the Elder by Eadgifu		946	955	32	9
EDWY	Son of Edmund by Elgifu	1st, Ethelfled; 2nd, Elfthryth	955	959	18	3
EDGAR	Second son of Edmund by Elgifu		959	975	32	17
EDWARD THE MARTYR	Son of Edgar by Ethelfled		975	978	17	4
ETHELRED II	Younger son of Edgar by Elfthryth	1st, Elfgifu; 2nd, Emma, dau. of Richard, Duke of Normandy.	978	1016	48	37
EDMUND IRONSIDE	Eldest son of Ethelred II by Elfgifu	1st, Elfgifu of Deira; 2nd, Emma, widow of Ethelred II.	1016	1016	27	0
CANUTE THE DANE	By conquest and election		1017	1035	40	18
HAROLD I	Son of Canute by Elfgifu		1035	1040	—	5
HARDICANUTE	Son of Canute by Emma		1040	1042	24	2
EDWARD THE CONFESSOR	Son of Ethelred II (by Emma)	Edith, dau. of Earl of Godwin	1042	1066	62	24
HAROLD II	Son of Earl Godwin		1066	1066	44	0
	The House of Normandy					
WILLIAM I	Obtained the Crown by conquest	Matilda, dau. of Baldwin, Count of Flanders	1066	1087	60	21
WILLIAM II	Third son of William I	(Died unmarried)	1087	1100	43	13
HENRY I	Youngest son of William I	1st, Matilda, dau. of Malcolm Canmore, K. of Scotland; 2nd Adelicia, dau. of Godfrey, D. of Louvaine.	1100	1135	67	35
STEPHEN	Third son of Stephen, Count of Blois, by Adela, fourth dau. of William I.	Matilda, dau. of Eustace, Count of Boulogne.	1135	1154	50	19
	The House of Plantagenet					
HENRY II	Son of Geoffrey Plantagenet by Matilda, only dau. of Henry I; his grandmother, Matilda of Scotland, was a lineal descendant of Alfred and Egbert.	Eleanor, dau. of Guienne and divorced Queen of Louis VII of France.	1154	1189	56	35
RICHARD I	Eldest surviving son of Henry II	Berengaria, dau. of Sancho VI, K. of Navarre	1189	1199	42	10
JOHN	Sixth and youngest son of Henry II	1st Avisa, dau. of E. of Gloucester, divorced upon grounds of consanguinity; 2nd Isabella dau. of Aymer, Count of Angoulème.	1199	1216	50	17
HENRY III	Elder son of John	Eleanor, dau. of Raymond, Count of Provence	1216	1272	65	56
EDWARD I	Eldest surviving son of Henry III	1st Eleanor, dau. of Ferdinand III, K. of Castile; 2nd Margaret, dau. of Philip III, the Hardy, K. of France.	1272	1307	68	35
EDWARD II	Eldest surviving son of Edward I	Isabella, dau. of Philip IV, the Fair, K. of France	1307	1327	43	20

Name	DYNASTY	MARRIED	Access.	Died	Age	Rgnd. Yrs.
EDWARD III	Eldest son of Edward II	Philippa, dau. of William, Count of Holland and Hainault.	1327	1377	65	50
RICHARD II	Son of the Black Prince, eldest son of Edward III (died 1400).	1st Anne, dau. of Emp. Charles IV; 2nd Isabel, dau. of Charles VI of France.	1377	dep. 1399	34	22
The House of Lancaster						
HENRY IV	Son of John of Gaunt, 4th son of Edward III.	1st Mary de Bohun, dau. of the E. of Hereford; 2nd Joanna of Navarre, widow of John de Montfort, D. of Brittany.	1399	1413	47	13
HENRY V	Eldest surviving son of Henry IV	Katherine, dau. of Charles VI, K. of France	1413	1422	34	9
HENRY VI	Only son of Henry V (died 1471)	Margaret of Anjou, dau. of René, D. of Anjou.	1422	dep. 1461	49	39
The House of York						
EDWARD IV	Son of Richard, grandson of Edmund, fifth son of Edward III; and of Anne, great-grand-daughter of Lionel, third son of Edward III.	Elizabeth Widvile (or Woodville), dau. of Sir Richard Widvile and widow of Sir John Grey of Groby.	1461	1483	41	22
EDWARD V	Eldest son of Edward IV	(Died unmarried)	1483	1483	13	75 days
RICHARD III	Younger brother of Edward IV	Anne, dau. of the E. of Warwick, and widow of Edward, Prince of Wales, son of Henry VI.	1483	1485	32	2
The House of Tudor						
HENRY VII	Son of Edmund, eldest son of Owen Tudor, by Katherine, widow of Henry V; his mother, Margaret Beaufort, was great-grand-daughter of John of Gaunt.	Elizabeth, dau. of Edward IV	1485	1509	53	24
HENRY VIII	Only surviving son of Henry VII	1st Katherine of Aragon, widow of his elder brother Arthur, (divorced); 2nd Anne, dau. of Sir Thomas Boleyn, (beheaded); 3rd Jane, dau. of Sir John Seymour, (died in childbirth of a son, aft. Edward VI); 4th Anne, sister of William, D. of Cleves, (divorced); 5th Catherine Howard, niece of the Duke of Norfolk, (beheaded); 6th Catherine, dau. of Sir Thomas Parr and widow of Edward Nevill, Lord Latimer.	1509	1547	56	38
EDWARD VI	Son of Henry VIII by Jane Seymour	(Died unmarried)	1547	1553	16	6
JANE	Grand-daughter of Mary, younger sister of Henry VIII, (beheaded Feb. 12, 1554).	Lord Guildford Dudley	1553	1554	17	14 days
MARY I	Daughter of Henry VIII by Katherine of Aragon.	Philip II of Spain	1553	1558	43	5
ELIZABETH I	Daughter of Henry VIII by Anne Boleyn	(Died unmarried)	1558	1603	69	44

BRITISH KINGS AND QUEENS FROM 1603

Name	DYNASTY	MARRIED	Access.	Died	Age	Rgnd. Yrs.
	The House of Stuart					
JAMES I (VI OF SCOT.)	Son of Mary, Queen of Scots, grand-daughter of James IV and Margaret, daughter of Henry VII.	Anne, dau. of Frederick II of Denmark	1603	1625	59	22
CHARLES I	Only surviving son of James I	Henrietta-Maria, dau. of Henry IV of France	1625	Beh. 1649	48	24
	Commonwealth declared May 19, 1649					
	Oliver Cromwell, Lord Protector, 1653—8: Richard Cromwell, Lord Protector, 1659					
CHARLES II	Eldest son of Charles I (restored 1660)	Catharine, dau. of John IV, K. of Portugal, and sister of Alphonso VI.	1649	1685	55	36
JAMES II (VII OF SCOT.)	Second son of Charles I (died 1701) (Interregnum, Dec. 11, 1688—Feb. 13, 1689)	1st, Lady Anne Hyde, dau. of Edward, E. of Clarendon, who died before James ascended the throne; 2nd Mary Beatrice Eleanor d'Este, dau. of Alphonso, D. of Modena.	1685	dep. 1688	68	3
WILLIAM III and	Son of William, Prince of Orange and grandson of Charles I		1689	{1702 {1694	51 33	13 6
MARY II	Eldest daughter of James II					
ANNE	Second daughter of James II	Prince George of Denmark	1702	1714	49	12
	The House of Hanover					
GEORGE I	Son of Elector of Hanover, by Sophia, daughter of Elizabeth, daughter of James I.	Sophia, dau. of George William, D. of Celle.	1714	1727	67	13
GEORGE II	Only son of George I	Wilhelmina Caroline, dau. of John Frederick, Margrave of Brandenburg-Anspach.	1727	1760	77	33
GEORGE III	Grandson of George II	Charlotte Sophia, dau. of Charles Lewis Frederick, D. of Mecklenburg-Strelitz.	1760	1820	81	59
GEORGE IV	Eldest son of George III (Regent from February 5, 1811.	Caroline, dau. of Charles William Ferdinand, D. of Brunswick-Wolfenbuttel.	1820	1830	67	10
WILLIAM IV	Third son of George III	Adelaide, dau. of George Frederick Charles, D. of Saxe-Meiningen.	1830	1837	71	7
VICTORIA	Daughter of Edward, 4th son of George III	Francis Albert Augustus Charles Emmanuel, D. of Saxe, Pr. of Saxe-Coburg and Gotha.	1837	1901	81	63
	The House of Saxe-Coburg					
EDWARD VII	Eldest son of Victoria	Alexandra, dau. of Christian IX, K. of Denmark.	1901	1910	68	9
	The House of Windsor					
GEORGE V	Surviving son of Edward VII	Victoria Mary, dau. of Francis, D. of Teck	1910	1936	70	25
EDWARD VIII	Eldest son of George V (abdicated 1936)	Mrs. Wallis Warfield (after abdication)	1936	1972	77	325 days
GEORGE VI	Second son of George V	Lady Elizabeth Bowes-Lyon, dau. of 14th Earl of Strathmore and Kinghorne (H.M. QUEEN ELIZABETH THE QUEEN MOTHER).	1936	1952	56	15
ELIZABETH II	Elder daughter of George VI	Philip, son of Prince Andrew of Greece (H.R.H. THE DUKE OF EDINBURGH).	1952	WHOM GOD PRESERVE.		

SCOTTISH KINGS AND QUEENS A.D. 1057 to 1603

Name	SOVEREIGN	MARRIED	Access.	Died
MALCOLM III (CANMORE)	Son of Duncan I	1st Ingibiorg, widow of Thorfinn, Earl of Orkney; 2nd Margaret, sister of Edgar the Atheling.	1057	1093
DONALD BÁN	Brother of Malcolm Canmore.	....	1093	—
DUNCAN II	Son of Malcolm Canmore, by first marriage	....	1094	1094
DONALD BÁN	(Restored)	....	1094	1097
EDGAR	Son of Malcolm Canmore, by second marriage	(Died unmarried)	1097	1107
ALEXANDER I	Son of Malcolm Canmore	Sybilla, natural dau. of Henry I of England	1107	1124
DAVID I	Son of Malcolm Canmore	Matilda, dau. of Waltheof, Earl of Northumbria, widow of Simon, Earl of Northampton.	1124	1153
MALCOLM IV (THE MAIDEN)	Son of Henry, eldest son of David I	(Died unmarried)	1153	1165
WILLIAM I (THE LION)	Brother of Malcolm the Maiden.	Ermengarde, dau. of Richard, Viscount of Beaumont.	1165	1214
ALEXANDER II	Son of William the Lion.	1st Joanna, dau. of King John; 2nd Mary, dau. of Ingelram de Coucy (*Picard*).	1214	1249
ALEXANDER III	Son of Alexander II, by second marriage	1st Margaret, dau. of Henry III of England; 2nd Joleta, dau. of the Count de Dreux.	1249	1286
MARGARET (THE MAID OF NORWAY)	Daughter of Eric II of Norway, granddaughter of Alexander III.	(Died unmarried)	1286	1290
JOHN BALIOL	Great-grandson of 2nd daughter of David, Earl of Huntingdon, brother of William the Lion.	....	1292	1296
ROBERT I (BRUCE)	Grandson of eldest daughter of David, Earl of Huntingdon, brother of William the Lion.	1st Isabella, dau. of Donald, Earl of Mar; 2nd Elizabeth de Burgh, sister of Earl of Ulster.	1306	1329
DAVID II	Son of Robert I, by second marriage	1st Joanna, dau. of Edward II of England; 2nd Margaret, widow of Sir John Logie (divorced, 1369).	1329	1371
ROBERT II (STEWART)	Son of Marjorie, daughter of Robert I by first marriage, and Walter the Steward.	1st Elizabeth, dau. of Sir Robert Mure (or More) of Rowallan; 2nd Euphemia, dau., of Hugh, Earl of Ross, widow of John, Earl of Moray.	1371	1390
ROBERT III	(John, Earl of Carrick) son of Robert II	Annabella, dau. of Sir John Drummond of Stobhall, niece of Margaret Logie.	1390	1406
JAMES I	Son of Robert III	Jane Beaufort, dau. of John, Earl of Somerset, 4th son of John of Gaunt and grandson of Edward III of England.	1406	1437
JAMES II	Son of James I	Mary, dau. of Arnold, Duke of Gueldres.	1437	1460
JAMES III	Eldest son of James II	Margaret, dau. of Christian I of Denmark, Norway and Sweden.	1460	1488
JAMES IV	Eldest son of James III	Margaret Tudor, dau. of Henry VII	1488	1513
JAMES V	Son of James IV	1st Madeleine, dau. of Francis I of France; 2nd Mary of Lorraine, dau. of Duc de Guise, widow of Duc de Longueville.	1513	1542
MARY	Daughter of James V, by second marriage	1st Francis, Dauphin of France; 2nd Henry, Lord Darnley; 3rd James, Earl of Bothwell.	1542	1587
JAMES VI (Ascended the Throne of England 1603)	Son of Mary, by second marriage	Anne, dau. of Frederick II of Denmark	1567	1625

WELSH SOVEREIGNS AND PRINCES

WALES was ruled by Sovereign Princes from the 'earliest times' until the death of Llywelyn in 1282. The first English Prince of Wales was the son of Edward I, and was born in Caernarvon town on April 25, 1284. According to a discredited legend, he was presented to the Welsh chieftains as their Prince, in fulfilment of a promise that they should have a Prince who 'could not speak a word of English' and should be native born. This son, who afterwards became Edward II, was created 'Prince of Wales and Earl of Chester' at the famous Lincoln Parliament on February 7, 1301. The title Prince of Wales is borne after individual conferment and is not inherited at birth, though some Princes have been declared and styled Prince of Wales but never formally so created (*s.*). The title was conferred on Prince Charles by Her Majesty the Queen on July 26, 1958. He was invested at Caernarvon on July 1, 1969.

Independent Princes, A.D. 844 to 1282		English Princes, since A.D. 1301	
Rhodri the Great	844–878	Edward, b. 1284 (Edwd. II), cr. Pr. of Wales	1301
Anarawd, son of Rhodri	878–916	Edward the Black Prince, s. of Edward III	1343
Hywel Dda, the Good	916–950	Richard (Richard II), s. of the Black Prince	1376
Iago ab Idwal (or Ieuaf)	950–979	Henry of Monmouth (Henry V)	1399
Hywel ab Ieuaf, the Bad	979–985	Edward of Westminster, son of Henry VI	1454
Cadwallon, his brother	985–986	Edward of Westminster (Edward V)	1471
Maredudd ab Owain ap Hywel Dda	986–999	Edward, son of Richard III (d. 1484)	1483
Cynan ap Hywel ab Ieuaf	999–1008	Arthur Tudor, son of Henry VII	1489
Llywelyn ap Seisyll	1018–1023	Henry Tudor (Hen. VIII), s. of Henry VII	1504
Iago ab Idwal ap Meurig	1023–1039	Henry Stuart, son of James I (d. 1612)	1610
Gruffydd ap Llywelyn ap Seisyll	1039–1063	Charles Stuart (Charles I), s. of James I	1616
Bleddyn ap Cynfyn	1063–1075	Charles (Charles II), son of Charles I ... (*s.*) c. 1638	
Trahaern ap Caradog	1075–1081	James Francis Edward, "The Old Pre-	
Gruffydd ap Cynan ab Iago	1081–1137	tender" (d. 1766) ... (*s.*) 1688	
Owain Gwynedd	1137–1170	George Augustus (Geo. II), s. of George I	1714
Dafydd ab Owain Gwynedd	1170–1194	Frederick Lewis, s. of George II (d. 1751)	1729
Llywelyn Fawr, the Great	1194–1240	George William Frederick (George III)	1751
Dafydd ap Llywelyn	1240–1246	George Augustus Frederick (George IV)	1762
Llywelyn ap Gruffydd ap Llywelyn	1246–1282	Albert Edward (Edward VII)	1841
		George (George V)	1901
		Edward (Edward VIII)	1910
		Charles Philip Arthur George	1958

THE FAMILY OF QUEEN VICTORIA

QUEEN VICTORIA (Alexandrina Victoria) *was born* May 24, 1819; *succeeded* to the Throne June 20, 1837; *married* Feb. 10, 1840 (Francis) Albert Augustus Charles Emmanuel, Duke of Saxony, Prince of Saxe-Coburg and Gotha (H.R.H. ALBERT, PRINCE CONSORT *born* Aug. 26, 1819, *died* Dec. 14, 1861); *died* Jan. 22, 1901. Her Majesty had *issue*:—

1. H.R.H. Princess Victoria Adelaide Mary Louisa (*Princess Royal*) (1840–1901), *m.*, 1858, Frederic (1831–88), *German Emperor* 1888. *Issue*:—

(1) H.I.M. Wilhelm II (1859–1941), *German Emperor* 1888–1918, *m.*, 1st, 1881, Princess Augusta Victoria of Schleswig-Holstein-Sonderburg-Augustenburg (1858–1921), and 2nd, 1922, Princess Hermine of Reuss (1887–1947). *Issue*:—

(a) Prince Wilhelm (1882–1951), (*Crown Prince* 1888–1918), *m.* Duchess Cecilie of Mecklenburg-Schwerin (1884–1954); *issue*:—Prince Wilhelm (1906–40); Prince Ludwig Ferdinand (b. 1907), *m.*, 1938, Grand Duchess Kira (*see* p. 145); Prince Hubertus (1909–50); Prince Friedrich Georg (1911–66); Princess Alexandrine Irene (b. 1915); Princess Cecilie (1917–75).

(b) Prince Eitel-Friedrich (1883–1942), *m.* Duchess Sophie of Oldenburg (marriage dissolved 1926).

(c) Prince Adalbert (1884–1948), *m.* Duchess Adelheid of Saxe-Meiningen; *issue*:—Princess Victoria Marina (1917–81); Prince Wilhelm Victor (b. 1919).

(d) Prince August Wilhelm (1887–1949), *m.* Princess Alexandra of Schleswig-Holstein-Sonderburg-Glücksburg (marriage dissolved 1920); *issue*:—Prince Alexander (b. 1912).

(e) Prince Oskar (1888–1958), *m.* Countess von Ruppin; *issue*:—Prince Oskar (1915–39); Prince Burchard (b. 1917); Princess Herzeleide (b. 1918); Prince Wilhelm (b. 1922).

(f) Prince Joachim (1890–1920), *m.* Princess

Marie of Anhalt; *issue*:—Prince Karl (1916–75).

(g) Princess Viktoria Luise (1892–1980), *m.*, 1913, Ernst, Duke of Brunswick; *issue*:—Prince Ernst (1914–87); Prince Georg (b. 1915); Princess Frederika (1917–81), *m.* Paul I, King of the Hellenes (*see* p. 145); Prince Christian (1919–81); Prince Welf Heinrich (b. 1923).

(2) Princess Charlotte (1860–1919), *m.*, 1878, Bernhard, Duke of Saxe-Meiningen (1851–1914). *Issue*:—Princess Feodora (1879–1945), *m.*, 1898, Prince Heinrich XXX of Reuss.

(3) Prince Heinrich (1862–1929), *m.*, 1888, Princess Irene of Hesse. *Issue*:—

(a) Prince Waldemar (1889–1945), *m.* Princess Calixsta of Lippe.

(b) Prince Sigismund (1896–1978), *m.* Princess Charlotte of Saxe-Altenberg; *issue*:—Princess Barbe (b. 1920); Prince Alfred (b. 1924).

(4) Princess Victoria (1866–1929), *m.*, 1st, 1890, Prince Adolf of Schaumburg-Lippe, and 2nd, 1927, Alexander Zubkov.

(5) Prince Joachim Waldemar (1868–79)

(6) Princess Sophie (1870–1932), *m.*, 1889, Constantine I, *King of the Hellenes*, 1913–17, 1920–22. *Issue*:—

(a) George II (1890–1947), *King of the Hellenes* 1922–24 and 1935–47, *m.*, 1921, Princess Elisabeth of Roumania (marriage dissolved 1935).

(b) Alexander (1893–1920), *King of the Hellenes* 1917–20, *m.*, 1919, Aspasia Manos; *issue*:—Princess Alexandra (b. 1921), *m.*, 1944, King Petar II of Yugoslavia.

(c) Princess Helena (1896–1982), *m.*, 1921, King Carol of Roumania, (marriage dissolved 1928); *issue*:—Michael (*b.* 1921), *King of Roumania* 1927–30, 1940–47, *m.*, 1948, Princess Anne of Bourbon Parma, and has issue (five daughters).

(d) Paul I (1901–64), *King of the Hellenes* 1947–64, *m.*, 1938, Princess Frederika of Brunswick (*see* p. 144); *issue*:—King Constantine II (*b.* 1940), *m.*, 1964, Princess Anne-Marie of Denmark, and has issue; Princess Sophia (*b.* 1938), *m.*, 1962, Juan Carlos I, KING OF SPAIN, and has issue; Princess Irene (*b.* 1942).

(e) Princess Irene (1904–74), *m.*, 1939, 4th Duke of Aosta; *issue*:—Prince Amedeo (*b.* 1943).

(f) Princess Katherine (*Lady Katherine Brandram*) (*b.* 1913), *m.*, 1947, Major R. C. A. Brandram, M.C., T.D.; *issue*:—R. Paul G. A. Brandram (*b.* 1948).

(7) Princess Margarethe (1872–1954), *m.*, 1893, Prince Friedrich Karl of Hesse (1868–1940). *Issue*:—

(a) Prince Friedrich Wilhelm (1893–1916).

(b) Prince Maximilian (1894–1914).

(c) Prince Philipp (1896–1980), *m.*, 1925, Princess Mafalda of Italy; *issue*:—Prince Moritz (*b.* 1926); Prince Heinrich (*b.* 1927); Prince Otto (*b.* 1937); Princess Elisabeth (*b.* 1940).

(d) Prince Wolfgang (*b.* 1896), *m.*, 1st, 1924, Princess Marie Alexandra of Baden, and 2nd, 1948, Ottilie Möller.

(e) Prince Richard (1901–).

(f) Prince Christoph (1901–43), *m.*, 1930, Princess Sophie of Greece (*see* p. 146).

2. H.M. KING EDWARD VII (*see* p. 146).

3. H.R.H. Princess Alice Maud Mary (1843–78), *m.*, 1862, Prince Louis (1837–92), *Grand Duke of Hesse*, 1877–92. *Issue*:—

(1) Victoria (1863–1950), *m.*, 1884, Prince Louis of Battenberg, afterwards *Admiral of the Fleet 1st Marquess of Milford Haven. Issue*:—

(a) Alice (1885–1969), *m.*, 1903, Prince Andrew of Greece, having issue (*see* p. 146).

(b) Louise (1889–1965), *m.*, 1923, Gustaf VI Adolf, *King of Sweden* 1950–73.

(c) George, 2nd Marquess of Milford Haven (1892–1938), *m.*, 1916, Countess Nadejda, daughter of Grand Duke Michael of Russia; *issue*:—Lady Tatiana (1917–88); David Michael, 3rd Marquess (1919–70).

(d) Louis, 1st Earl Mountbatten of Burma (1900–79), *m.*, 1922, Edwina Ashley, daughter of Lord Mount Temple; *issue*:—Patricia (*b.* 1924), Pamela (*b.* 1929).

(2) Elizabeth (1864–1918), *m.*, 1884, Grand Duke Sergius of Russia.

(3) Irene (1866–1953), *m.* Prince Heinrich of Prussia (*see* p. 144).

(4) Ernst Ludwig (1868–1937), Grand Duke of Hesse 1892–1918, *m.*, 1st, 1894, Princess Victoria of Saxe-Coburg, and 2nd, 1905, Princess Eleonore of Solms-Hohensolmslich. *Issue*:—

(a) George, Grand Duke of Hesse (1906–37), *m.* Princess Cecilie of Greece and Denmark (*see* p. 146).

(b) Ludwig, Grand Duke of Hesse (1908–68), *m.*, 1937, Margaret, daughter of 1st Lord Geddes.

(5) Frederick William (1870–73).

(6) Alix (*Tsaritsa of Russia*) (1872–1918), *m.*, 1894, Nicholas II (*Tsar of All the Russias*), assassinated July 16, 1918. *Issue*:—

(a) Grand Duchess Olga (1895–1918).

(b) Grand Duchess Tatiana (1897–1918).

(c) Grand Duchess Marie (1899–1918).

(d) Grand Duchess Anastasia (1901–1918).

(e) Alexis, Tsarevitch of Russia (1904–1918).

(7) Marie (1874–1878).

4. H.R.H. Prince Alfred William Patrick Albert, *Duke of Edinburgh, Admiral of the Fleet* (1844–1900), *m.*, 1874, Grand Duchess Marie Alexandrovna of Russia (1853–1920); succeeded as *Duke of Saxe-Coburg and Gotha* Aug. 22, 1893. *Issue*:—

(1) Alfred (*Prince of Saxe-Coburg*) (1874–1899).

(2) Marie (1875–1938), *m.*, 1893, King Ferdinand of Roumania. *Issue*:—

(a) Carol II (1893–1953), *King of Roumania* 1930–40, *m.*, 1st, 1918, Joana Lambrino, 2nd, 1921, Princess Helena of Greece (*see* above), and 3rd, 1947, Mrs. Elena Tampeanu.

(b) Elisabeth (1894–1956), *m.*, 1921, King George II of the Hellenes (*see* p. 144).

(c) Marie (1900–61), *m.*, 1922, King Alexander of Yugoslavia; *issue*:—Petar (1923–70), *King of Yugoslavia* 1934–45; Prince Tomislav (*b.* 1928), *m.*, 1st, 1957, Princess Margarita of Baden (*see* p. 146), and 2nd, 1982, Linda Bonney; Prince Andrej (*b.* 1929).

(d) Prince Nicolas (*b.* 1903).

(e) Princess Ileana (*b.* 1909), *m.*, 1st, 1931, Archduke Anton of Austria, and 2nd, 1954, Dr. Stefan Issarescu; *issue*:—Archduke Stefan (*b.* 1932); Archduchess Maria Ileana (1933–59); Archduchess Alexandra (*b.* 1935); Archduke Dominic (*b.* 1937); Archduchess Maria Magdalena (*b.* 1939); Archduchess Elisabeth (*b.* 1942).

(f) Prince Mircea (1913–16).

(3) Victoria Melita (1876–1936), *m.*, 1st, 1894, Grand Duke Ernst of Hesse, and 2nd, 1905, the Grand Duke Kirill of Russia. *Issue*:—

(a) Marie Kirillovna (1907–51), *m.*, 1925, Prince Friedrich Karl of Leiningen; *issue*:—Prince Emich (*b.* 1926); Prince Karl (*b.* 1928); Princess Kira-Melita (*b.* 1930); Princess Margarita (*b.* 1932); Princess Mechtilde (*b.* 1936); Prince Friedrich (*b.* 1938).

(b) Kira Kirillovna (1909–67), *m.*, 1938, Prince Ludwig of Prussia; *issue*:—Prince Friedrich Wilhelm (*b.* 1939); Prince Michael (*b.* 1940); Princess Marie (*b.* 1942); Princess Kira (*b.* 1943); Prince Louis Ferdinand (1944–77); Prince Christian (*b.* 1946); Princess Xenia (*b.* 1949).

(c) Vladimir Kirillovitch (*b.* 1917), *m.*, 1948, Princess Leonida Bagration-Mukhransky; *issue*:—Grand Duchess Maria (*b.* 1953).

(4) Alexandra (1878–1942), *m.*, 1896, Prince (Ernst) of Hohenlohe Langenburg. *Issue*:—

(a) Gottfried (1897–1960), *m.*, Princess Margarita of Greece (*see* p. 146).

(b) Maria (1899–1967), *m.* Prince Frederick of Schleswig-Holstein-Sonderburg-Glücksburg; *issue*:—Prince Peter (1922–80); Princess Marie (*b.* 1927).

(c) Princess Alexandra (1901–63).

(d) Princess Irma (*b.* 1902).

(5) Princess Beatrice (1884–1966), *m.*, 1909, Prince Alfonso, Infante of Spain. *Issue*:—

(a) Prince Alvaro (*b.* 1910), *m.* Carla Parodi-Delfino; *issue*:—Princess Gerarda (*b.* 1939); Prince Alonso (1941–75); Princess Beatriz (*b.* 1943); Prince Alvaro (*b.* 1947).

(b) Prince Alonso (*b.* 1912).

(c) Prince Ataulfo (*b.* 1913).

5. H.R.H. Princess Helena Augusta Victoria (1846–1923), *m.*, 1866, Prince Christian of Schleswig-Holstein-Sonderburg-Augustenburg (1831–1917). *Issue*:—

(1) Prince Christian Victor (1867–1900).

(2) Prince Albert (1869–1931).

(3) Princess Helena (1870–1948).

(4) Princess Marie Louise (1872–1956), *m.*, 1891, Prince Aribert of Anhalt (marriage dissolved 1900).

(5) Prince Harold (May 12–20, 1876).

6. H.R.H. Princess Louise Caroline Alberta (1848–1939), *m.*, 1871, the Marquess of Lorne, afterwards *9th Duke of Argyll* (1845–1914); without *issue*.

7. H.R.H. Prince Arthur William Patrick Albert, *Duke of Connaught, Field Marshal* (1850–1942), *m.*,

1879, Princess Louisa of Prussia (1860–1917). *Issue:*—

(1) Princess Margaret (1882–1920), *m.*, 1905, Crown Prince Gustaf Adolf, afterwards *King of Sweden* 1950–73. *Issue:*—

(a) Gustaf Adolf, Duke of Västerbotten (1906–47), *m.*, 1932, Princess Sybil of Saxe-Coburg-Gotha; *issue:*—Princess Margaretha (*b.* 1934); Princess Birgitta (*b.* 1937); Princess Désirée (*b.* 1938); Princess Christina (*b.* 1943); Carl XVI Gustaf, KING OF SWEDEN (*b.* 1946).

(b) Count Sigvard Bernadotte (*b.* 1907); *m.*, *issue:*—Count Michael (*b.* 1944).

(c) Princess Ingrid (*Queen Mother of Denmark*) (*b.* 1910), *m.*, 1935, Frederick IX, *King of Denmark* (1899–72); *issue:*—Margrethe II, QUEEN OF DENMARK (*b.* 1940); Princess Benedikte (*b.* 1944); Princess Anne-Marie (*Queen of the Hellenes*) (*b.* 1946).

(d) Prince Bertil, Duke of Halland (*b.* 1912), *m.*, 1976, Mrs. Lilian Craig.

(e) Count Carl Bernadotte (*b.* 1916), *m.*, 1946, Mrs. Kerstin Johnson.

(2) Prince Arthur (1883–1938), *m.*, 1913, H.H. the Duchess of Fife (*see* below).

(3) Princess (Victoria) Patricia (1886–1974), *m.*, 1919, Adm. Hon. Sir Alexander Ramsay. *Issue:*—Hon. Alexander Ramsay of Mar (*b.* 1919), *m.*, 1956, Hon. Flora Fraser, LADY SALTOUN.

8. H.R.H. Prince Leopold George Duncan Albert,

Duke of Albany (1853–84), *m.*, 1882, Princess Helena of Waldeck (1861–1922). *Issue:*—

(1) Princess Alice (1883–1981), *m.*, 1904, Prince Alexander of Teck, afterwards *1st Earl of Athlone*. *Issue:*—

(a) Lady May (*b.* 1906), *m.*, 1931, Sir Henry Abel-Smith, K.C.M.G., K.C.V.O., D.S.O.; *issue:*—Anne (*b.* 1932); Richard (*b.* 1933); Elizabeth (*b.* 1936).

(b) Rupert, *Viscount Trematon* (1907–28).

(2) Charles Edward (1884–1954), *Duke of Saxe-Coburg-Gotha* 1900–18, *m.*, 1905, Princess Victoria Adelheid of Schleswig-Holstein-Sonderburg-Glücksburg. *Issue:*—Prince Johann (1906–72); Princess Sibylle (1908–); Prince Dietmar (1909–); Princess Caroline (1912–83); Prince Friedrich (*b.* 1918).

9. H.R.H. Princess Beatrice Mary Victoria Feodore (1857–1944), *m.*, 1885, Prince Henry of Battenberg (1858–96). *Issue:*—

(1) Alexander, *1st Marquess of Carisbrooke* (1886–1960), *m.*, 1917, Lady Irene Denison. *Issue:*—Lady Iris Mountbatten (1920–82).

(2) Victoria Eugénie (1887–1969), *m.*, 1906, Alfonso XIII (1886–1941) *King of Spain* 1886–1931. *Issue:*—Prince Alfonso (1907–); Prince Jaime (1908–75); Princess Beatrice (*b.* 1909); Princess Maria (*b.* 1911); Prince Juan (*b.* 1913); Prince Gonzale (1914–).

(3) Major Lord Leopold Mountbatten (1889–1922).

(4) Maurice (1891–1914), died of wounds received in action.

THE FAMILY OF KING EDWARD VII

KING EDWARD VII (Albert Edward), eldest son of Queen Victoria, *born* Nov. 9, 1841; *married* March 10, 1863, Her Royal Highness Princess Alexandra Caroline Marie Charlotte Luise Julia of Denmark (*Queen Alexandra*, *born* Dec. 1, 1844; *died* Nov. 20, 1925); *succeeded* to the Throne Jan. 22, 1901; *died* May 6, 1910. *Issue:*—

1. H.R.H. Prince Albert Victor Christian Edward, *Duke of Clarence and Avondale and Earl of Athlone* (1864–92).

2. H.M. KING GEORGE V (*see* p. 147). Assumed by Royal Proclamation (June 17, 1917) for his House and Family as well as for all descendants in the male line of Queen Victoria who are subjects of these Realms, the name of WINDSOR (*see* p. 148).

3. H.R.H. Louise Victoria Alexandra Dagmar, *Princess Royal* (1867–1931), *m.*, 1889, 1st Duke of Fife (1849–1912). *Issue:*—

(1) H.H. Princess Alexandra, Duchess of Fife (1891–1959), *m.*, 1913, H.R.H. Prince Arthur of Connaught (*see* above). *Issue:*—

(a) Alastair Arthur, Duke of Connaught (1914–43).

(2) H.H. Princess Maud (1893–1945), *m.*, 1923, 11th Earl of Southesk. *Issue:*—

(a) THE DUKE OF FIFE (*b.* 1929).

4. H.R.H. Princess Victoria Alexandra Olga Mary (1868–1935).

5. H.R.H. Princess Maud Charlotte Mary Victoria (1869–1938), *m.*, 1896, Haakon VII (1872–1957), *King of Norway* 1905–57. *Issue:*—

(1) H.M. Olav V, K.G., K.T., G.C.B., G.C.V.O., KING OF NORWAY (*b.* 1903), *m.*, 1929, H.R.H. Princess Märtha of Sweden (died 1954). *Issue:*—

(a) H.R.H. Princess Ragnhild (*b.* 1930).

(b) H.R.H. Princess Astrid (*b.* 1932).

(c) H.R.H. Prince Harald, *Crown Prince of Norway*, G.C.V.O. (*b.* 1937).

6. H.R.H. Prince Alexander John Charles Albert (April 6–7, 1871).

THE FAMILY OF PRINCE ANDREW OF GREECE

Prince Andrew of Greece (1882–1944), *m.*, 1903, Princess Alice of Battenberg (*H.R.H. Princess Andrew of Greece*), (1885–1969) (*see* p. 145); *issue:*—

(1) Princess Margarita (1905–1981), *m.*, 1931, Prince Gottfried of Hohenlohe-Langenburg (*see* p. 145); *issue:*—Prince Kraft (*b.* 1935), Princess Beatrix (*b.* 1936), Prince George (*b.* 1938), Prince Ruprecht and Prince Albrecht (*b.* 1944).

(2) Princess Theodora (1906–1969), *m.*, 1931, Prince Berthold of Baden (*d.* 1963); *issue:*—Princess Margarita (*b.* 1932, *m.*, 1957, Prince Tomislav of Yugoslavia (*see* p. 145)), Prince Max (*b.* 1933), Prince Ludwig (*b.* 1937).

(3) Princess Cecilie (1911–1937), *m.*, George, Grand

Duke of Hesse (*see* p. 145), accidentally killed with husband and two sons, 1937.

(4) Princess Sophie, *b.* 1914, *m.*, 1st, 1930, Prince Christoph of Hesse (*see* p. 145); *issue:*—Princess Christina (*b.* 1933), Princess Dorothea (*b.* 1934), Prince Charles (*b.* 1937), Prince Rainer (*b.* 1939), Princess Clarissa (*b.* 1944); *m.*, 2nd, 1946, Prince Georg of Hanover; *issue:*—Prince George (*b.* 1949); Princess Friederike (*b.* 1954).

(5) Prince Philip (H.R.H. THE PRINCE PHILIP, DUKE OF EDINBURGH), *b.* 1921 (*see* p. 148).

THE FAMILY OF KING GEORGE V

KING GEORGE V (George Frederick Ernest Albert), second son of King Edward VII, *born* June 3, 1865; *married* July 6, 1893, Her Serene Highness Princess Victoria Mary Augusta Louise Olga Pauline Claudine Agnes (*Queen Mary, born* May 26, 1867; *died* March 24, 1953); *succeeded* to the Throne May 6, 1910; *died* Jan. 20, 1936. *Issue:*—

1. H.R.H. Prince Edward Albert Christian George Andrew Patrick David, *born* June 23, 1894, *succeeded* to the Throne as KING EDWARD VIII, Jan. 20, 1936; *abdicated* Dec. 11, 1936; *created Duke of Windsor*, 1936; *married* June 3, 1937, Mrs. Wallis Warfield (Her Grace The Duchess of Windsor, *born* June 19, 1896; *died* April 24, 1986), *died* May 28, 1972.

2. H.R.H. Prince Albert Frederick Arthur George, *born* Dec. 14, 1895; *married* April 26, 1923, Lady Elizabeth Bowes-Lyon (H.M. QUEEN ELIZABETH THE QUEEN MOTHER), daughter of the 14th Earl of Strathmore and Kinghorne, *succeeded* to the Throne as KING GEORGE VI, Dec. 11, 1936; *died* Feb. 6, 1952, having had issue (*see* pp. 148 and 149).

3. H.R.H. Princess (Victoria Alexandra Alice) **Mary** (*Princess Royal*), *born* April 25, 1897, *married* Feb. 28, 1922, the 6th Earl of Harewood (*born* Sept. 9, 1882; *died* May 24, 1947), *died* Mar. 28, 1965. *Issue:*—
  (1) George Henry Hubert Lascelles, 7TH EARL OF HAREWOOD, K.B.E., *born* Feb. 7, 1923; *married* 1st, Sept. 29, 1949, Maria (Marion) Stein (marriage dissolved 1967); *issue,* (*a*) David Henry George, Viscount Lascelles, *born* Oct. 21, 1950; (*b*) James Edward, *born* Oct. 5, 1953; (*c*) Robert Jeremy Hugh, *born* Feb. 14, 1955; 2nd, July 31, 1967, Mrs. Patricia Tuckwell; *issue,* (*d*) Mark Hubert, *born* July 5, 1964.
  (2) Gerald David Lascelles, *born* Aug. 21, 1924, *married* 1st, July 15, 1952, Miss Angela Dowding (marriage dissolved, 1978); *issue,* (*a*) Henry Ulick, *born* May 19, 1953; 2nd, Nov. 17, 1978, Mrs. Elizabeth Colvin; *issue,* (*b*) Martin David, born Feb. 9, 1962.

4. H.R.H. Prince Henry William Frederick Albert, Duke of Gloucester, Earl of Ulster and Baron Culloden, *born* March 31, 1900, *married* Nov. 6, 1935, Lady Alice Christabel Montagu-Douglas-Scott, daughter of the 7th Duke of Buccleuch (H.R.H. PRINCESS ALICE, DUCHESS OF GLOUCESTER, G.C.B., C.I., G.C.V.O., G.B.E., Grand Cordon of Al Kamal, Air Marshal, Colonel-in-Chief of The Royal Hussars (Prince of Wales's Own), The King's Own Scottish Borderers, Royal Corps of Transport, Royal Australian Corps of Transport, Royal New Zealand Corps of Transport, Deputy Colonel-in-Chief, The Royal Anglian Regiment, Air Chief Commandant W.R.A.F., *born* Dec. 25, 1901); *died* June 10, 1974. *Issue:*
  (1) H.R.H. Prince WILLIAM Henry Andrew Frederick, *born* Dec. 18, 1941; *accidentally killed* Aug. 28, 1972.
  (2) H.R.H. Prince Richard Alexander Walter George (H.R.H. THE DUKE OF GLOUCESTER), G.C.V.O., Colonel-in-Chief, The Gloucestershire Regiment, Royal Pioneer Corps, Honorary Colonel Royal Monmouth-shire Royal Engineers (Militia), Grand Prior of the Order of St. John of Jerusalem. *Born* Aug. 26, 1944, *married* July 8, 1972, Birgitte Eva van Deurs (H.R.H. THE DUCHESS OF GLOUCESTER, G.C.V.O., *born* June 20), Colonel-in-Chief, Royal Army Educational Corps, Royal Irish Rangers (27th (Inniskilling) 83rd and 87th), Royal Australian Army Educational Corps, Royal New Zealand Educational Corps, and has *issue:*—
  (*a*) Alexander Patrick Gregers Richard, Earl of Ulster, *born* Oct. 24, 1974;
  (*b*) Davina Elizabeth Alice Benedikte (Lady Davina Windsor), *born* Nov. 19, 1977;
  (*c*) Rose Victoria Birgitte Louise (Lady Rose Windsor), *born* March 1, 1980.
  Residences—Kensington Palace, W8 4PU; Barnwell Manor, Peterborough.

5. H.R.H. Prince George Edward Alexander Edmund, Duke of Kent, Earl of St. Andrews and Baron Downpatrick, *born* Dec. 20, 1902, *married* Nov. 29, 1934, H.R.H. Princess Marina of Greece and Denmark (*born* Nov. 30, O.S., 1906; *died* Aug. 27, 1968); *killed on active service,* Aug. 25, 1942. *Issue:*—
  (1) H.R.H. Prince Edward George Nicholas Paul Patrick (H.R.H. THE DUKE OF KENT), K.G., G.C.M.G., G.C.V.O., Personal A.D.C. to the Queen, Major General, Hon. Air Vice-Marshal, Colonel-in-Chief The Royal Regiment of Fusiliers, The Devonshire and Dorset Regiment, The Lorne Scots Regiment (Peel, Dufferin and Hamilton Regiment), Colonel Scots Guards. *Born* Oct. 9, 1935, *married* June 8, 1961, Katharine Lucy Mary Worsley (H.R.H. THE DUCHESS OF KENT, G.C.V.O., *born* Feb. 22, 1933), Hon. Major General, Colonel-in-Chief 4th/7th Royal Dragoon Guards, The Prince of Wales's Own Regiment of Yorkshire, Army Catering Corps, Controller Commandant Women's Royal Army Corps, Hon. Colonel The Yorkshire Volunteers, daughter of Sir William Worsley, Bt., and has *issue:*—
  (*a*) George Philip Nicholas, Earl of St. Andrews, *born* June 26, 1962, *married* Jan. 9, 1988, Sylvana Tomaselli and has *issue,* Edward Edmund Maximilian George, Lord Downpatrick, *born* Dec. 2, 1988;
  (*b*) Helen Marina Lucy (Lady Helen Windsor), *born* April 28, 1964;
  (*c*) Nicholas Charles Edward Jonathan (Lord Nicholas Windsor), *born* July 25, 1970.
  Residences—York House, St. James's Palace, SW1; Anmer Hall, Norfolk.
  (2) H.R.H. Princess Alexandra Helen Elizabeth Olga Christabel (H.R.H. PRINCESS ALEXANDRA, THE HON. LADY OGILVY), G.C.V.O., Colonel-in-Chief, 17th/21st Lancers, The King's Own Royal Border Regiment, The Queen's Own Rifles of Canada, The Canadian Scottish Regiment (Princess Mary's), Deputy Colonel-in-Chief The Light Infantry, Deputy Hon. Colonel The Royal Yeomanry, Patron and Air Chief Commandant Princess Mary's Royal Air Force Nursing Service, Patron Queen Alexandra's Royal Naval Nursing Service. *Born* Dec. 25, 1936, *married* April 24, 1963, The Hon. Sir Angus Ogilvy, K.C.V.O., 2nd son of the 12th Earl of Airlie (*born* Sept. 14, 1928) and has *issue:*—
  (*a*) James Robert Bruce, *born* Feb. 29, 1964, *married* July 30, 1988, Miss Julia Rawlinson;
  (*b*) Marina Victoria Alexandra, *born* July 31, 1966.
  Residence—Thatched House Lodge, Richmond Park, Surrey. *Office*—22 Friary Court, St. James's Palace, SW1A 1BJ.
  (3) H.R.H. Prince Michael George Charles Franklin (H.R.H. PRINCE MICHAEL OF KENT), *born* July 4, 1942, *married* June 30, 1978, Baroness Marie-Christine Agnes Hedwig Ida von Reibnitz (H.R.H. PRINCESS MICHAEL OF KENT), and has *issue:*—
  (*a*) Frederick Michael George David Louis (Lord Frederick Windsor), *born* April 6, 1979;
  (*b*) Gabriella Marina Alexandra Ophelia (Lady Gabriella Windsor), *born* April 23, 1981.
  Residences—Kensington Palace, W8 4PU; Nether Lypiatt Manor, Stroud, Glos.

6. H.R.H. Prince John Charles Francis, *born* July 12, 1905; *died* Jan. 18, 1919.

THE HOUSE OF WINDSOR

Her Most Excellent Majesty **ELIZABETH THE SECOND** (Elizabeth Alexandra Mary of Windsor) by the Grace of God, of the United Kingdom of Great Britain and Northern Ireland and of Her other Realms and Territories Queen, Head of the Commonwealth, Defender of the Faith, Sovereign of the British Orders of Knighthood and Sovereign Head of the Order of St. John, Lord High Admiral of the United Kingdom, Colonel-in-Chief of The Life Guards, The Blues and Royals (Royal Horse Guards and 1st Dragoons), The Royal Scots Dragoon Guards (Carabiniers and Greys), 16th/5th The Queen's Royal Lancers, Royal Tank Regiment, Corps of Royal Engineers, Grenadier Guards, Coldstream Guards, Scots Guards, Irish Guards, Welsh Guards, The Royal Welch Fusiliers, The Queen's Lancashire Regiment, The Argyll and Sutherland Highlanders (Princess Louise's), The Royal Green Jackets, Royal Army Ordnance Corps, Corps of Royal Military Police, The Queen's Own Mercian Yeomanry, The Duke of Lancaster's Own Yeomanry, The Governor General's Horse Guards, The King's Own Calgary Regiment, Canadian Forces Military Engineers Branch, Royal 22e Regiment, Governor-General's Foot Guards, The Canadian Grenadier Guards, Le Régiment de la Chaudière, 2nd Bn. Royal New Brunswick Regiment (North Shore), The 48th Highlanders of Canada, The Argyll and Sutherland Highlanders of Canada (Princess Louise's), The Calgary Highlanders, Royal Australian Engineers, Royal Australian Infantry Corps, Royal Australian Army Ordnance Corps, Royal Australian Army Nursing Corps, The Corps of Royal New Zealand Engineers, Royal New Zealand Infantry Regiment, Royal New Zealand Army Ordnance Corps, Royal Malta Artillery, The Malawi Rifles, Captain-General of Royal Regiment of Artillery, The Honourable Artillery Company, Combined Cadet Force, Royal Regiment of Canadian Artillery, Royal Regiment of Australian Artillery, Royal Regiment of New Zealand Artillery, Royal New Zealand Armoured Corps, Air-Commodore-in-Chief, Royal Auxiliary Air Force, Royal Air Force Regiment, Royal Observer Corps, Air Reserve (of Canada), Royal Australian Air Force Reserve, Territorial Air Force (New Zealand), Commandant-in-Chief, Royal Air Force College, Cranwell, Hon. Air Commodore, R.A.F. Marham, Hon. Commissioner, Royal Canadian Mounted Police, Master of the Merchant Navy and Fishing Fleets, Head of the Civil Defence Corps.

Elder daughter of His late Majesty King George VI and of Her Majesty Queen Elizabeth the Queen Mother; *born* at 17 Bruton Street, London, W1, April 21, 1926, *succeeded* to the Throne February 6, 1952, *crowned* June 2, 1953; having *married*, November 20, 1947, in Westminster Abbey, Philip, Duke of Edinburgh, Earl of Merioneth and Baron Greenwich (H.R.H. THE PRINCE PHILIP, DUKE OF EDINBURGH, *born* June 10, 1921), K.G., K.T., O.M., G.B.E., A.C., Q.S.O., P.C., Admiral of the Fleet, Field Marshal, Marshal of the Royal Air Force, Admiral of the Fleet, Royal Australian Navy, Field Marshal, Australian Military Forces, Marshal of the Royal Australian Air Force, Admiral of the Fleet, Royal New Zealand Navy, Field Marshal New Zealand Army, Marshal of the Royal New Zealand Air Force, Captain General, Royal Marines, Colonel-in-Chief, The Queen's Royal Irish Hussars, The Duke of Edinburgh's Royal Regiment (Berkshire and Wiltshire), The Queen's Own Highlanders (Seaforth and Camerons), Corps of Royal Electrical and Mechanical Engineers, Intelligence Corps, Army Cadet Force, The Royal Canadian Regiment, The Royal Hamilton Light Infantry (Wentworth Regiment), The Cameron Highlanders of Ottawa, The Queen's Own Cameron Highlanders of Canada, The Seaforth Highlanders of Canada, The Royal Canadian Army Cadets, The Royal Australian Electrical and Mechanical Engineers, The Australian Cadet Corps, Corps of Royal New Zealand Electrical and Mechanical Engineers, Colonel of Grenadier Guards, Hon. Colonel, Edinburgh and Heriot-Watt Universities Officers' Training Corps, The Trinidad and Tobago Regiment, Admiral, Royal Canadian Sea Cadets, Air Commodore-in-Chief, Royal New Zealand Air Force, Air Training Corps, Royal Canadian Air Cadets, Hon. Air Commodore, R.A.F. Kinloss, Master of the Corporation of Trinity House, Ranger of Windsor Park, Admiral Sea Cadet Corps, Hon. Colonel Leicester and Derbyshire Yeomanry PAQ Sqn. *See* p. 146.

Official Residences—Buckingham Palace, SW1; Windsor Castle, Berks.; Palace of Holyroodhouse, Edinburgh.
Private Residences—Sandringham, Norfolk; Balmoral Castle, Aberdeenshire.

CHILDREN OF HER MAJESTY

H.R.H. THE PRINCE OF WALES (CHARLES Philip Arthur George), K.G., K.T., G.C.B., A.K., Q.S.O., P.C., A.D.C., Prince of Wales and Earl of Chester, Duke of Cornwall and Duke of Rothesay, Earl of Carrick and Baron Renfrew, Lord of the Isles and Great Steward of Scotland, Personal A.D.C. to the Queen, Great Master of the Order of the Bath, Captain Royal Navy, Group Captain Royal Air Force, Colonel-in-Chief 5th Royal Inniskilling Dragoon Guards, The Cheshire Regiment, The Royal Regiment of Wales (24th/41st Foot), The Gordon Highlanders, The Parachute Regiment, 2nd King Edward VII's Own Gurkha Rifles (The Sirmoor Rifles), The Royal Canadian Dragoons, Lord Strathcona's Horse (Royal Canadians), Royal Regiment of Canada, Royal Winnipeg Rifles, Royal Australian Armoured Corps, The Royal Pacific Islands Regiment, Colonel, Welsh Guards, Air Commodore-in-Chief Royal New Zealand Air Force, Hon. Air Commodore, R.A.F. Brawdy.

Born November 14, 1948, *married* July 29, 1981, Lady Diana Frances Spencer (H.R.H. THE PRINCESS OF WALES, *born* July 1, 1961), Colonel-in-Chief 13th/18th Royal Hussars (Queen Mary's Own), The Royal Hampshire Regiment, The Princess of Wales's Own Regiment (of Canada), Hon. Air Commodore, R.A.F. Wittering, youngest daughter of the 8th Earl Spencer and the Hon. Mrs. Shand Kydd; and has *issue*, (a) William Arthur Philip Louis (H.R.H. PRINCE WILLIAM OF WALES), *born* June 21, 1982; and (b) Henry Charles Albert David (H.R.H. PRINCE HENRY OF WALES), *born* Sept. 15, 1984.

Residences—Highgrove, Doughton, Tetbury, Glos.; Kensington Palace, W8. *Office*—St. James's Palace, SW1.

H.R.H. THE PRINCESS ROYAL (ANNE Elizabeth Alice Louise), G.C.V.O., F.R.S., Chief Commandant Women's Royal Naval Service, Colonel-in-Chief 14th/20th King's Hussars, Royal Corps of Signals, The Royal Scots (The Royal Regiment), The Worcestershire and Sherwood Foresters Regiment (29th/45th Foot), 8th Canadian Hussars (Princess Louise's), Canadian Forces Communications and Electronics Branch, Grey and Simcoe Foresters Militia, The Royal Regina Rifle Regiment, Royal Australian Corps of Signals, Royal New Zealand Corps of Signals, Royal New Zealand Nursing Corps, Hon. Colonel London University Officers' Training Corps, Hon. Air Commodore, R.A.F. Lyneham, Commandant-in-Chief, (Ambulance and Nursing Cadets) St. John Ambulance, Commandant-in-Chief, Women's Transport Service (FANY), Dame of Justice, Order of St. John.

Born August 15, 1950, *married* Nov. 14, 1973, Capt. Mark Anthony Peter Phillips, C.V.O. (*born* Sept. 22, 1948), Personal A.D.C. to the Queen; and has *issue*, (*a*) Peter Mark Andrew, *born* Nov. 15, 1977; and (*b*) Zara Anne Elizabeth, *born* May 15, 1981.

Residence—Gatcombe Park, Minchinhampton, Stroud, Glos. *Office*—Buckingham Palace, SW1.

H.R.H. THE DUKE OF YORK (ANDREW Albert Christian Edward), Duke of York, Earl of Inverness and Baron Killyleagh, C.V.O., Personal A.D.C. to the Queen, Lieutenant, Royal Navy, Colonel-in-Chief The Staffordshire Regiment (The Prince of Wales's). *Born* Feb. 19, 1960, *married* July 23, 1986, Miss Sarah Margaret Ferguson (H.R.H. THE DUCHESS OF YORK, *born* October 15, 1959), younger daughter of Major Ronald Ferguson and Mrs. Hector Barrantes; and has *issue*, Beatrice Elizabeth Mary (H.R.H. PRINCESS BEATRICE OF YORK), *born* Aug. 8, 1988.

Residence—Buckingham Palace, SW1.

H.R.H. PRINCE EDWARD ANTONY RICHARD LOUIS, C.V.O., *born* March 10, 1964.

MOTHER OF HER MAJESTY

H.M. QUEEN ELIZABETH THE QUEEN MOTHER (Elizabeth Angela Marguerite) (daughter of the 14th Earl of Strathmore and Kinghorne), Lady of the Garter, Lady of the Thistle, C.I., G.M.V.O., G.B.E., Dame, Grand Cross of the Order of St. John, Royal Victorian Chain, Colonel-in-Chief 1st The Queen's Dragoon Guards, The Queen's Own Hussars, 9th/12th Royal Lancers (Prince of Wales's) The King's Regiment, The Royal Anglian Regiment, The Light Infantry, The Black Watch (Royal Highland Regiment), Royal Army Medical Corps, The Black Watch (Royal Highland Regiment) of Canada, The Toronto Scottish Regiment, Canadian Forces Medical Services, Royal Australian Army Medical Corps, Royal New Zealand Army Medical Corps, Hon. Colonel The Royal Yeomanry, The London Scottish, Commandant-in-Chief R.A.F. Central Flying School, Women's Royal Naval Service, Women's Royal Army Corps, Women's Royal Air Force, Patron St. Andrew's Ambulance Association, Commandant-in-Chief Nursing Corps and Divisions, Commandant-in-Chief (Nursing) St. John's Ambulance, Lord Warden and Admiral of the Cinque Ports and Constable of Dover Castle. *Born* August 4, 1900, *married* April 26, 1923, Prince Albert Frederick Arthur George of Windsor, Duke of York (*see* page 147).

Residences.—Clarence House, St. James's Palace, SW1; Royal Lodge, Windsor Great Park, Berks.; Castle of Mey, Caithness, Scotland.

SISTER OF HER MAJESTY

H.R.H. THE PRINCESS MARGARET, COUNTESS OF SNOWDON (Margaret Rose), C.I., G.C.V.O., Colonel-in-Chief, 15th/19th The King's Royal Hussars, The Royal Highland Fusiliers (Princess Margaret's Own Glasgow and Ayrshire Regiment), Queen Alexandra's Royal Army Nursing Corps, The Highland Fusiliers of Canada, The Princess Louise Fusiliers, The Bermuda Regiment, Deputy Colonel-in-Chief, The Royal Anglian Regiment, Hon. Air Commodore, R.A.F. Coningsby, Grand President, St. John Ambulance Association and Brigade, Dame Grand Cross of the Order of St. John of Jerusalem, President of the Girl Guides Association.

Born Aug. 21, 1930; *married* May 6, 1960, Anthony Charles Robert Armstrong-Jones, G.C.V.O. (*born* March 7, 1930, son of the late Ronald Armstrong-Jones, Q.C. and the Countess of Rosse, *created* Earl of Snowdon, 1961, Constable of Caernarvon Castle, *marriage dissolved*, 1978); and has *issue*, (*a*) David Albert Charles, Viscount Linley, *born* Nov. 3, 1961; and (*b*) Sarah Frances Elizabeth (Lady Sarah Armstrong-Jones), *born* May 1, 1964.

Residence.—Kensington Palace, W8 4PU.

Order of Succession to the Throne

1. H.R.H. The Prince of Wales
2. H.R.H. Prince William of Wales
3. H.R.H. Prince Henry of Wales
4. H.R.H. The Duke of York
5. H.R.H. Princess Beatrice of York
6. H.R.H. Prince Edward
7. H.R.H. The Princess Royal
8. Master Peter Phillips
9. Miss Zara Phillips
10. H.R.H. Princess Margaret, Countess of Snowdon
11. Viscount Linley
12. Lady Sarah Armstrong-Jones
13. H.R.H. the Duke of Gloucester
14. Earl of Ulster
15. Lady Davina Windsor
16. Lady Rose Windsor
17. H.R.H. The Duke of Kent
18. Lord Downpatrick
19. Lord Nicholas Windsor
20. Lady Helen Windsor
21. Lord Frederick Windsor
22. Lady Gabriella Windsor
23. H.R.H. Princess Alexandra, Hon. Lady Ogilvy
24. Mr. James Ogilvy
25. Miss Marina Ogilvy.

THE QUEEN'S HOUSEHOLD

Lord Chamberlain, The Earl of Airlie, K.T., P.C., G.C.V.O.
Lord Steward, The Viscount Ridley, T.D.
Master of the Horse, The Earl of Westmorland, K.C.V.O.
Treasurer of the Household, T. Garel Jones, M.P.
Comptroller of the Household, A. Goodlad, M.P.
Vice Chamberlain, A. Durant, M.P.

Gold Stick, Maj.-Gen. Lord Michael Fitzalan Howard, G.C.V.O., C.B., C.B.E., M.C.; Gen. Sir Desmond Fitzpatrick, G.C.B., D.S.O., M.B.E., M.C.
Vice-Adm. of the United Kingdom, Adm. Sir Anthony Griffin, G.C.B.
Rear-Adm. of the United Kingdom, Adm. Sir Anthony Morton, G.B.E., K.C.B.
First and Principal Naval Aide-de-Camp, Adm. Sir Julian Oswald, G.C.B.
Flag Aide de Camp, Adm. Sir Jeremy Black, K.C.B., D.S.O., M.B.E.
Aides-de-Camp General, Gen. Sir John Chapple, G.C.B., C.B.E.; Gen. Sir Charles Huxtable, K.C.B., C.B.E.; Gen. Sir Robert Pascoe, K.C.B., M.B.E.
Air Aides-de-Camp, Air Chief Marshal Sir Peter Harding, G.C.B.; Air Chief Marshal Sir Patrick Hine, G.C.B.

Mistress of the Robes, The Duchess of Grafton, G.C.V.O.
Ladies of the Bedchamber, The Countess of Airlie, C.V.O.; The Lady Farnham.
Extra Ladies of the Bedchamber, The Marchioness of Abergavenny, D.C.V.O.; The Countess of Cromer, C.V.O.
Women of the Bedchamber, Hon. Mary Morrison, D.C.V.O.; Lady Susan Hussey, D.C.V.O.; Mrs. John Dugdale, D.C.V.O.; The Lady Elton.
Extra Women of the Bedchamber, Mrs. John Woodroffe, C.V.O.; Lady Rose Baring, D.C.V.O., Mrs. Michael Wall, D.C.V.O.; Lady Abel Smith, D.C.V.O.; Mrs Robert de Pass.
Extra Equerries, Vice-Adm. Sir Peter Ashmore, K.C.B., K.C.V.O., D.S.C.; Lt.-Col. The Lord Charteris of Amisfield, P.C., G.C.B., G.C.V.O., O.B.E., Q.S.O.; Sir Robert Fellowes, K.C.V.O., C.B.; Sir Edward Ford, K.C.B., K.C.V.O., E.R.D.; Rear-Adm. John Garnier, C.B.E., L.V.O.; Rear-Adm. Sir Paul Greening, K.C.V.O.; Brig. Sir Geoffrey Hardy-Roberts, K.C.V.O., C.B., C.B.E.; The Rt. Hon. Sir William Heseltine, G.C.V.O., K.C.B.; Rear-Adm. Sir Hugh Janion, K.C.V.O.; Lt.-Col. Sir John Johnston, G.C.V.O., M.C.; Sir Peter Miles, K.C.V.O.; Lt.-Col. Sir John Miller, G.C.V.O., D.S.O., M.C.; Air Cdre. Sir Dennis Mitchell, K.B.E., C.V.O., D.F.C., A.F.C.; The Lord Moore of Wolvercote G.C.B., G.C.V.O., C.M.G., Q.S.O.; Lt.-Col. Sir Eric Penn, G.C.V.O., O.B.E., M.C.; Lt.-Col. W. H. M. Ross, O.B.E.; Cdr. Sir Philip Row, K.C.V.O., O.B.E., R.N.; Air Vice-Marshal John Severne, L.V.O., O.B.E., A.F.C.; Group Capt. Peter Townsend, C.V.O., D.S.O., D.F.C.; Rear Adm. Sir Richard John Trowbridge, K.C.V.O.; Lt.-Col. G. West; Air Cdre. Sir Archie Little Winskill, K.C.V.O., C.B.E., D.F.C., A.E.

THE PRIVATE SECRETARY'S OFFICE
Buckingham Palace, S.W.1.

Private Secretary to The Queen, The Rt. Hon. Sir William Heseltine, G.C.V.O., K.C.B.
Deputy Private Secretary, Sir Robert Fellowes, K.C.V.O., C.B.
Assistant Private Secretary, K. Scott, C.M.G.
Press Secretary, R. Janvrin, L.V.O.
Deputy Press Secretary, J. Haslam, L.V.O.
Assistant Press Secretaries, G. Crawford; R. W. Arbiter.
Chief Clerk, Mrs. G. S. Coulson, M.V.O.
Secretary to the Private Secretary, Miss E. Pearce, M.V.O.
Head of Information and Correspondence Section, Mrs. J. Bean, M.V.O.
Clerks, Mrs. J. Atwell, M.V.O.; Mrs. C. H. Good; Miss A. Kennedy; J. Mordaunt, M.V.O.; Miss H. Spiller; Miss A. Gabett; Mrs. P. Bachelier.
Press Office, Miss K. McGrigor; Mrs. R. Murdo-Smith, L.V.O.; Mrs. A. Neal, L.V.O.
Lady in Waiting's Office, Mrs. D. Phillips; Mrs. A. Vince.

The Queen's Archives
Round Tower, Windsor Castle.

Keeper of The Queen's Archives, The Rt. Hon. Sir William Heseltine, G.C.V.O., K.C.B.
Assistant Keeper, O. Everett, L.V.O.
Registrar, Lady de Bellaigue, M.V.O.
Assistant Registrar, Miss P. Clark, L.V.O.
Curator of the Photographic Collection, Miss F. Dimond, M.V.O.

THE PRIVY PURSE AND TREASURER'S OFFICE
Buckingham Palace, S.W.1.

Keeper of the Privy Purse and Treasurer to The Queen, Maj. Sir Shane Blewitt, K.C.V.O.
Deputy Keeper of the Privy Purse and Deputy Treasurer, J. Parsons.
Chief Accountant and Paymaster, F. Mintram, L.V.O.
Personnel Officer, G. Franklin, C.V.O.
Administrative Officer, D. Waters, C.V.O.
Asst. Chief Accountant and Paymaster, D. Walker, L.V.O.
Assistant Personnel Officer, Mrs. D. Larkins.
Superintendent of Public Enterprises, E. Hewlett.
Accountants, Mrs. J. Maitland, L.V.O.; Mrs. D. Mowbray, M.V.O.; Miss R. Ward; Mrs. W. Johnson.
Clerks, Mrs. C. Auton, M.V.O.; Miss F. Juniper; Miss C. McCarthy; Miss H. Pearce; Miss G. Wickham, M.V.O.; Miss L. Buggé; Miss C. Hall.
Clerk of Stationery, W. Cotton.
Land Agent, Sandringham, J. Loyd, C.V.O.
Resident Factor, Balmoral, M. Leslie, L.V.O.

Royal Almonry

Lord High Almoner, The Rt. Rev. the Lord Bishop of St. Albans.
Hereditary Grand Almoner, The Marquess of Exeter.
Sub-Almoner, Rev. Canon A. D. Caesar, L.V.O., F.R.C.O.
Secretary, P. Wright, C.V.O.
Assistant Secretary, D. Waters, C.V.O.

THE LORD CHAMBERLAIN'S OFFICE
Buckingham Palace, S.W.1.

Comptroller, Lt.-Col. G. West, C.V.O.
Assistant Comptroller, Lt.-Col. M. Ross, O.B.E.
Secretary, J. E. P. Titman, C.V.O.
Assistant Secretary, P. D. Hartley, M.V.O.
State Invitations Assistant, Maj. J. C. Leech.
Registrar, J. Spencer.
Clerks, Miss S. Hay, M.V.O.; Miss C. Britton; Mrs. J. Marsham; Miss H. Asprey; Mrs. V. Cunningham.
Permanent Lords in Waiting, Lt. Col. The Lord Charteris of Amisfield, P.C., G.C.B., G.C.V.O., O.B.E.; The Lord Maclean, P.C., K.T., G.C.V.O., K.B.E.
Lords in Waiting, The Lord Somerleyton; The Viscount Boyne; The Viscount Long; The Viscount Ullswater; The Lord Reay; The Earl of Strathmore and Kinghorne.
Gentlemen Ushers, C. Greig, C.V.O., C.B.E.; Lt.-Col. Sir Julian Paget, Bt., C.V.O.; Air Chief Marshal Sir Neville Stack, K.C.B., C.V.O., A.F.C.; Group Capt. J. Slessor; Maj. N. Chamberlayne-Macdonald, L.V.O., O.B.E.; Air Chief Marshal Sir Roy Austen-Smith, K.B.E., C.B., D.F.C.; Vice-Adm. Sir David Loram, K.C.B., L.V.O.; Capt. M. Barrow, D.S.O., R.N.; Capt. M. Fulford-Dobson, R.N.; Lt. Gen. Sir Richard Vickers, K.C.B., L.V.O., O.B.E.
Extra Gentlemen Ushers, Capt. A. Yates, L.V.O., R.N.; Maj. T. Harvey, C.V.O., D.S.O.; Air Vice-Marshal Sir Ranald Reid, K.C.B., D.S.O., M.C.; E. Butler, C.V.O.; Maj.-Gen. Sir Cyril Colquhoun, K.C.V.O., C.B., O.B.E.; Lt.-Col. Sir John Hugo, K.C.V.O., O.B.E.; Vice-Adm. Sir Ronald Brockman, K.C.B., C.S.I., C.I.E., C.V.O., C.B.E.; Air Marshal Sir Maurice Heath, K.B.E., C.B., C.V.O.; Sir James Scholtens, K.C.V.O.; Sir Patrick O'Dea, K.C.V.O.; Brig.-Gen. S. Cooper, C.V.O., O.B.E., C.D.; Adm. Sir David Williams, G.C.B.; Capt. M. Tufnell, C.V.O., D.S.C., R.N.; H. Davis, C.V.O., C.M.; Maj.-Gen. R. Reid, C.V.O., M.C., C.D.; Lt.-Cdr. J. Holdsworth, C.V.O., O.B.E., R.N.; Capt. P. Blackman, R.A.N.; Col. G. Leigh, C.V.O., C.B.E.; Lt.-Cdr. Sir Russell Wood, K.C.V.O., V.R.D.; Col. D. Lawrence.
Gentleman Usher to the Sword of State, Gen. Sir Edward Burgess, K.C.B., O.B.E.
Gentleman Usher of the Black Rod, Air Chief Marshal Sir John Gingell, G.B.E., K.C.B.
Serjeants at Arms, F. Mintram, L.V.O.; J. E. P. Titman, C.V.O.; M. Tims, C.V.O.

Marshal of the Diplomatic Corps, Lt.-Gen. Sir John Richards, K.C.B.
Vice-Marshal, R. Hervey, C.M.G.

Constable & Governor of Windsor Castle, Adm. Sir David Hallifax, K.C.B., K.B.E.
Keeper of the Jewel House, Tower of London, Maj. Gen. C. Tyler, C.B.
Master of The Queen's Music, Malcolm Williamson, C.B.E.
Poet Laureate, Ted Hughes, O.B.E.
Bargemaster, E. Hunt.
Keeper of the Swans, F. J. Turk, M.V.O.
Superintendent of the State Apartments, St. James's Palace, T. Taylor, M.V.O., M.B.E.

ROYAL COLLECTION DEPARTMENT
St. James's Palace, S.W.1.

Director of Royal Collection and Surveyor of The Queen's Works of Art, Sir Geoffrey de Bellaigue, K.C.V.O., F.S.A.
Surveyor of The Queen's Pictures, C. Lloyd.
Librarian, The Royal Library, Windsor Castle, O. Everett, L.V.O.
Deputy Surveyor of The Queen's Works of Art, H. Roberts.

Surveyor Emeritus of The Queen's Pictures, Sir Oliver Millar, G.C.V.O., F.B.A., F.S.A.
Adviser for The Queen's Works of Art, Sir Francis Watson, K.C.V.O., F.B.A., F.S.A.
Librarian Emeritus, Sir Robin Mackworth-Young, G.C.V.O., F.S.A.
Curator of the Print Room, The Hon. Mrs. Roberts, M.V.O.
Registrar, M. Bishop, M.V.O.
Assistant to Registrar, Miss C. Hunter-Craig.
Assistants to Surveyor of The Queen's Works of Art, Mrs. J. Harland, M.V.O.; D. Rantin-Hunt.
Assistants to Surveyor of The Queen's Pictures, C. Noble, Miss C. Crichton-Stuart.
Inventory Assistant, Mrs. S. Newton.
Clerks, Miss V. Colfox; Miss C. Hunter-Craig; Miss C. Neville; Miss J. Impey; Miss M. Pullen.

ASCOT OFFICE
St. James's Palace, S.W.1.

Her Majesty's Representative at Ascot, Col. Sir Piers Bengough, K.C.V.O., O.B.E.
Secretary, Miss L. Thompson-Royd.

ECCLESIASTICAL HOUSEHOLD
The College of Chaplains.

Clerk of the Closet, Rt. Rev. Bishop of Chelmsford.
Deputy Clerk of the Closet, Rev. Canon A. D. Caesar, L.V.O., F.R.C.O.
Chaplains to The Queen, Ven. E. J. G. Ward, L.V.O.; Rev. J. R. W. Stott; Rev. A. H. H. Harbottle, L.V.O.; Ven. D. N. Griffiths, R.D.; Canon A. Glendining, L.V.O.; Canon J. G. Grimwade; Canon D. Landreth, T.D.; Canon J. V. Bean; Canon P. A. Welsby, Ph.D.; Rev. K. Huxley; Ven. R. Simpson, L.V.O.; Ven. P. Ashford; Canon G. A. Elcoat; Canon D. C. Gray, T.D.; Canon J. Treadgold; Ven. D. Scott; Canon E. James; Canon J. Hester; Rev. S. Pedley; Rev. D. Tonge; Rev. Canon C. Craston; Rev. Canon N. M. Ramm; Rev. Canon D. N. Hole; Rev. M. A. Moxon; Canon R. J. W. Bevan; Canon R. T. W. McDermid; Canon G. Murphy, L.V.O.; Canon R. H. C. Lewis; Rev. D. J. Burgess; Rev. E. R. Ayerst; Rev. R. S. Clarke; Rev. Canon C. J. Hill; Rev. J. H. Williams, L.V.O.; Ven. K. Pound; Rev. J. Haslam.
Extra Chaplains, Canon J. S. D. Mansel, K.C.V.O., F.S.A.; Preb. S. A. Williams, C.V.O.

Chapels Royal

Dean of the Chapels Royal, The Bishop of London.
Sub-Dean of Chapels Royal, Rev. Canon A. D. Caesar, L.V.O., F.R.C.O.
Priests in Ordinary, Rev. W. Booth; Rev. A. Ford; Rev. G. Watkins.
Organist, Choirmaster and Composer, R. J. Popplewell, F.R.C.O., F.R.C.M.
Domestic Chaplain—Buckingham Palace, Rev. Canon A. D. Caesar, L.V.O., F.R.C.O.
Domestic Chaplain—Windsor Castle, The Dean of Windsor.
Domestic Chaplain—Sandringham, Canon G. R. Hall.
Chaplain—Royal Chapel, Windsor Great Park, Rev. Canon J. Treadgold.
Chaplain—Hampton Court Palace, Rev. Canon M. Moore.
Chaplain—Tower of London, Rev. N. A. Hood.
Organist and Choirmaster—Hampton Court Palace, Gordon Reynolds, L.V.O., A.R.C.M.

MEDICAL HOUSEHOLD

Head of the Medical Household and Physician, A. Dawson, M.D., F.R.C.P.
Physician, R. W. Davey, M.B., B.S.

Serjeant Surgeon, W. Slack, M.CH., F.R.C.S.
Surgeon, J. Dawson, M.S., F.R.C.S.
Surgeon Oculist, P. Holmes Sellors, B.M., B.CH., F.R.C.S.
Surgeon Gynaecologist, G. D. Pinker, C.V.O., F.R.C.S.(Edin.), F.R.C.O.G.
Surgeon Dentist, N. A. Sturridge, C.V.O., L.D.S., B.D.S., D.D.S.
Orthopaedic Surgeon, D. R. Sweetnam, F.R.C.S.
Physician to the Household, R. Thompson, D.M., F.R.C.P.
Surgeon to the Household, B. Jackson, M.S., F.R.C.S.
Surgeon Oculist to the Household, T. J. ffytche, F.R.C.S., L.R.C.P.
Apothecary to The Queen and to the Household, N. R. Southward, L.V.O., M.B., B.chir., M.R.C.P.
Apothecary to the Household at Windsor, J. H. D. Briscoe, M.A., M.B., B.chir., M.R.C.G.P., D.Obst., R.C.O.G.
Apothecary to the Household at Sandringham, H. K. Ford, L.V.O., M.B., F.R.C.G.P.
Coroner of The Queen's Household, J. Burton, M.B., B.S., M.R.C.S., L.R.C.P..

CENTRAL CHANCERY
OF THE ORDERS OF KNIGHTHOOD
St. James's Palace, S.W.1.

Secretary, Maj. Gen. D. H. G. Rice, C.V.O., C.B.E.
Assistant Secretary, Sqn. Ldr. B. Sowerby, M.V.O.
Clerks, J. McGurk, M.V.O.; Miss S. Koller, M.V.O.; Miss R. Wells; Miss T. Perfect; Miss L. Dove; Miss F. Bean.

The Honorable Corps of Gentlemen at Arms
St. James's Palace, S.W.1.

Captain, The Lord Denham, P.C.; Lieutenant, Maj. D. Jamieson, V.C.; Standard Bearer, Col. A. Way, M.C.; Clerk of the Cheque & Adjutant, Maj. T. St. Aubyn; Harbinger, Lt.-Col. R. Steele, M.B.E.

Gentlemen of the Corps

Brigadier, A. N. Breitmeyer.
Colonels, T. Hall, O.B.E.; Sir Piers Bengough, K.C.V.O., O.B.E.; Hon. N. Crossley, T.D.; T. Wilson; D. Fanshawe, O.B.E.; J. Baker.
Lieutenant-Colonels, P. Hodgson; W. S. P. Lithgow; Sir James Scott, Bt.; R. Mayfield, D.S.O.; B. Lockhart; Hon. P. H. Lewis.
Majors, The Lord Suffield, M.C.; Sir Torquhil Matheson of Matheson, Bt.; F. J. H. Matheson; A. A. J. Nunn; Sir Philip Duncombe, Bt.; I. B. Ramsden, M.B.E.; M. J. Drummond-Brady; A. Arkwright; G. M. B. Colenso-Jones; T. Gooch, M.B.E.; J. B. B. Cockcroft; C. J. H. Gurney; J. R. E. Nelson.
Captain, The Lord Monteagle of Brandon.

The Queen's Bodyguard of the Yeoman of the Guard
St. James's Palace, S.W.1.

Captain, The Viscount Davidson; Lieutenant, Col. A. B. Pemberton, C.V.O., M.B.E.; Clerk of the Cheque and Adjutant, Col. G. W. Tufnell; Ensign, Lt.-Col. S. Longsdon; Exons., Maj. C. Marriott; Maj. C. Enderby.

MASTER OF THE HOUSEHOLD'S
DEPARTMENT
Board of Green Cloth
Buckingham Palace, S.W.1.

Master of the Household, Rear-Adm. Sir Paul Greening, K.C.V.O.
Deputy Master of the Household, Lt.-Col. B. A. Stewart-Wilson, C.V.O.
Assistants to the Master of the Household, M. D. Tims, C.V.O.; M. Parker, M.V.O.
Chief Clerk, M. Jephson, M.V.O.
Deputy to Assistant, M. Bovaird.

Senior Clerk, S. Stacey.
Clerks, Miss S. Derry, M.V.O.; Miss S. Fergus, M.V.O.; Miss S. Crossley.
Superintendent, Windsor Castle, Maj. B. Eastwood, M.B.E.
Assistant to Superintendent, Capt. R. McClosky, M.V.O..
Palace Steward, C. S. Dickman, M.V.O., R.V.M.
Chief Housekeeper, Miss H. Colebrook.

ROYAL MEWS DEPARTMENT
Buckingham Palace, S.W.1.

Crown Equerry, Lt.-Col. S. Gilbart-Denham.
Equerries, Lt.-Col. B. A. Stewart-Wilson, C.V.O.; Cdr. T. Laurence; Capt. the Hon. Richard Margesson (temp.).
Veterinary Surgeon, P. S. Dunn, L.V.O., M.R.C.V.S.
Supt. Royal Mews, Buckingham Palace, Maj. A. Smith, M.B.E.
Comptroller of Stores, Maj. L. Marsham, M.V.O..
Chief Clerk, P. Almond.
Deputy Chief Clerk, A. Marshall.
Office Keeper, P. M. Goodman, M.V.O.

HER MAJESTY'S HOUSEHOLD
IN SCOTLAND

Hereditary Lord High Constable, The Earl of Erroll.
Hereditary Master of the Household, The Duke of Argyll.
Lord Lyon King of Arms, Malcolm R. Innes of Edineight, C.V.O., W.S.
Hereditary Bearer of the Royal Banner of Scotland, The Earl of Dundee.
Hereditary Bearer of the Scottish National Flag, The Earl of Lauderdale.
Hereditary Keepers:—
  Holyrood, The Duke of Hamilton and Brandon.
  Falkland, N. J. Crichton-Stuart.
  Stirling, The Earl of Mar and Kellie.
  Dunstaffnage, The Duke of Argyll.
Hereditary Carver, Sir Ralph Anstruther, K.C.V.O., M.C.
Keeper of Dumbarton Castle, Brig. A. S. Pearson, C.B., D.S.O., O.B.E., M.C., T.D.
Governor of Edinburgh Castle, Lt.-Gen. Sir John MacMillan, K.C.B.
Dean of the Order of the Thistle, The Very Rev. G. I. Macmillan.
Dean of the Chapel Royal, Very Rev. Prof. R. A. S. Barbour, M.C., D.D.
Chaplains in Ordinary, Very Rev. R. A. S. Barbour, M.C., D.D.; Rev. W. J. Morris, D.D., LL.D., Ph.D.; Rev. H. W. M. Cant; Rev. K. MacVicar, M.B.E., D.F.C., T.D.; Rev. A. J. C. Macfarlane; Rev. J. McLeod; Very Rev. G. I. Macmillan; Very Rev. W. B. Johnston, D.D.; Rev. M. D. Craig; Rev. W. B. R. Macmillan.
Extra Chaplains, Very Rev. the Lord MacLeod of Fuinary, M.C., D.D.; Very Rev. Prof. J. S. Stewart, D.D.; Rev. Prof. E. P. Dickie, M.C., D.D.; Very Rev. R. L. Small, C.B.E., D.D.; Very Rev. W. R. Sanderson, D.D.; Very Rev. R. W. V. Selby Wright, C.V.O., T.D., D.D., F.R.S.E., F.S.A.(scot.); Rev. T. J. T. Nicol, M.V.O., M.B.E., M.C., T.D.; Very Rev. G. T. H. Reid, M.C., D.D.; Very Rev. Prof. J. McIntyre, C.V.O., D.D., F.R.S.E.; Rev. C. Forrester-Paton.
Domestic Chaplain, Balmoral, Rev. J. A. K. Angus, T.D.
Historiographer, Prof. G. Donaldson, C.B.E., F.B.A., F.R.S.E.
Botanist, Prof. D. Henderson, C.B.E., F.R.S.E.
Painter and Limner, D. A. Donaldson, R.S.A., R.P.
Sculptor in Ordinary, Prof. Sir Eduardo Paolozzi.
Astronomer, Prof. M. S. Longair, Ph.D.

Physicians in Scotland, P. Brunt, M.D., F.R.C.P.; A. L. Muir, M.D., F.R.C.P.

Surgeons in Scotland, I. B. Macleod, M.B., ch.B., F.R.C.S.; J. Engeset, Ch.M., F.R.C.S.

Extra Surgeons in Scotland, Prof. Sir Charles Illingworth, C.B.E., M.D., F.R.C.S.Ed.; Prof. Sir Donald Douglas, M.B.E., Ch.M., M.S., D.Sc., F.R.C.S.

Apothecary to the Household at Balmoral, D. J. A. Glass, M.B., Ch.B.

Apothecary to the Household at the Palace of Holyroodhouse, Dr. H. Gebbie, M.B., M.R.C.G.P.

Heralds and Pursuivants of Arms, see page 297.

THE QUEEN'S BODY GUARD FOR SCOTLAND

Royal Company of Archers.
Archers' Hall, Edinburgh.

Captain-General and Gold Stick for Scotland, Col. The Lord Clydesmuir, K.T., C.B., M.B.E., T.D.

Captains, Maj. The Lord Home of the Hirsel, K.T.; The Duke of Buccleuch and Queensberry, K.T., V.R.D.; Lt.-Col. Sir John Gilmour, Bt., D.S.O., T.D.; Maj. Sir Hew Hamilton-Dalrymple, Bt., K.C.V.O.

Lieutenants, Maj. The Earl of Wemyss and March, K.T.; The Earl of Airlie, K.T., G.C.V.O.; The Earl of Dalhousie, K.T., G.C.V.O., G.B.E., M.C.; Capt. Sir Iain Tennant, K.T.

Ensigns, Maj.-Gen. The Earl Cathcart, C.B., D.S.O., M.C.; Capt. N. E. F. Dalrymple-Hamilton, C.V.O., M.B.E., D.S.C., R.N.; The Marquess of Lothian, K.C.V.O.; Cdre. Sir John Clerk of Penicuik, Bt., C.B.E., V.R.D.

Brigadiers, The Earl of Elgin and Kincardine, K.T.; Col. G. R. Simpson, D.S.O., L.V.O., T.D.; Maj. D. H. Butter, M.C.; The Earl of Minto, O.B.E.; Maj.-Gen. Sir John Swinton, K.C.V.O., O.B.E.; Gen. Sir Michael Gow, G.C.B.; The Hon. Lord Elliott, M.C.; Maj. The Hon. L. H. C. Maclean; The Rt. Hon. George Younger, T.D., M.P.; Capt. G. Burnet, L.V.O.; The Marquess of Graham; Lt.-Gen. Sir Norman Arthur, K.C.B.; The Hon. Sir William Macpherson of Cluny, T.D.

Adjutant, Maj. The Hon. L. H. C. Maclean.

Surgeon, Dr. P. A. P. Mackenzie, T.D.

Chaplain, Very Rev. R. Selby Wright, C.V.O., T.D., D.D., F.R.S.E.

President of the Council and Silver Stick for Scotland, Maj. Sir Hew Hamilton-Dalrymple, Bt., K.C.V.O.

Vice-President, The Earl of Dalhousie, K.T., G.C.V.O., G.B.E., M.C.

Secretary, Col. H. F. O. Bewsher, O.B.E..

Treasurer, R. A. G. Douglas-Miller.

HOUSEHOLD OF THE PRINCE PHILIP, DUKE OF EDINBURGH

Private Secretary and Treasurer, B. H. McGrath, C.V.O.

Assistant Private Secretary, Brig. C. Robertson.

Equerry, Maj. Sir Guy Acland, Bt.

Extra Equerries, J. B. V. Orr, C.V.O.; Sir Richard Davies, K.C.V.O., C.B.E.; Lord Buxton of Alsa.

Temporary Equerries, Capt. A. J. Fraser; Capt. A. Rogers.

Chief Clerk and Accountant, V. G. Jewell, M.V.O.

HOUSEHOLD OF QUEEN ELIZABETH THE QUEEN MOTHER

Lord Chamberlain, Maj. the Earl of Dalhousie, K.T., G.C.V.O., G.B.E., M.C.

Comptroller and Extra Equerry, Capt. Sir Alastair Aird, K.C.V.O.

Private Secretary and Equerry, Lt.-Col. Sir Martin Gilliat, G.C.V.O., M.B.E.

Treasurer and Equerry, Maj. Sir Ralph Anstruther, Bt., K.C.V.O., M.C.

Equerry, Maj. R. Seymour, L.V.O.

Press Secretary and Extra Equerry, Maj. A. J. S. Griffin, C.V.O.

Extra Equerry, The Lord Sinclair, L.V.O.

Equerry (Temp.), Capt. G. A. C. Bassett.

Apothecary to the Household, Dr. N. Southward, L.V.O., M.B., B.Chir., M.R.C.P.

Surgeon-Apothecary to the Household (Royal Lodge, Windsor), Dr. J. Briscoe, M.R.C.G.P., D.Obst., R.C.O.G.

Mistress of the Robes, The Dowager Duchess of Abercorn, G.C.V.O.

Ladies of the Bedchamber, The Dowager Viscountess Hambleden, D.C.V.O.; The Lady Grimthorpe, C.V.O.

Women of the Bedchamber, Ruth, Lady Fermoy, D.C.V.O., O.B.E.; Mrs Patrick Campbell-Preston, C.V.O.; Lady Elizabeth Basset, D.C.V.O.; Lady Angela Oswald.

Extra Women of the Bedchamber, Lady Victoria Wemyss, C.V.O.; Lady Jean Rankin, D.C.V.O.; Miss Jane Walker-Okeover.

Clerk Comptroller, M. Blanch, L.V.O.

Clerk Accountant, J. P. Kyle, L.V.O.

Clerks, Mrs. R. Murphy, L.V.O.; Miss F. Fletcher, M.V.O.

HOUSEHOLD OF THE PRINCE AND PRINCESS OF WALES

Private Secretary and Treasurer to The Prince and Princess of Wales, Sir John Riddell, Bt.

Deputy Private Secretary, D. Wright.

Assistant Private Secretary and Comptroller to The Prince and Princess of Wales, Cdr. R. J. Aylard, R.N.

Assistant Private Secretary to The Prince of Wales, G. Salter.

Secretary to the Duchy of Cornwall and Keeper of the Records, D. W. N. Landale.

Equerry to The Prince of Wales, Cdr. A. F. L. Watson.

Extra Equerries to The Prince of Wales, The Hon. Edward Adeane, C.V.O.; Sqn. Ldr. Sir David Checketts, K.C.V.O.; G. J. Ward; Col. J. Q. Winter.

Lady in Waiting and Assistant Private Secretary to The Princess of Wales, Miss Anne Beckwith-Smith.

Equerry to The Princess of Wales, Lt. Cdr. P. D. C. J. Jephson, R.N.

Extra Ladies in Waiting, Mrs. George West; Viscountess Campden; Mrs. Max Pike; Miss Alexandra Loyd; The Hon. Mrs. Vivian Baring; Mrs. James Lonsdale.

HOUSEHOLD OF THE DUKE AND DUCHESS OF YORK

Private Secretary and Equerry to The Duke and Duchess of York, Lt.-Col. S. O'Dwyer.

Equerry, Capt. G. W. McLean.

Ladies in Waiting, Mrs. John Spooner; Mrs. John Floyd; Miss Lucy Manners; Mrs. Harry Cotterell.

HOUSEHOLD OF THE PRINCE EDWARD

Private Secretary and Equerry to the Prince Edward, Lt.-Col. S. O'Dwyer.

HOUSEHOLD OF THE PRINCESS ROYAL

Private Secretary, Lt.-Col. P. Gibbs, L.V.O.

Assistant Private Secretary, The Hon. Mrs. Louloudis.

Ladies in Waiting, Mrs. Richard Carew Pole, L.V.O.; The Hon. Mrs. Legge-Bourke, L.V.O.; Mrs. Malcolm Wallace; Mrs. Timothy Holderness-Roddam; Mrs. Charles Ritchie.

Extra Ladies in Waiting, Mrs. Andrew Feilden, L.V.O.; Miss Victoria Legge-Bourke, L.V.O.; Mrs. Malcolm Innes, L.V.O.; The Countess of Lichfield.

HOUSEHOLD OF THE PRINCESS MARGARET, COUNTESS OF SNOWDON

Private Secretary and Comptroller, The Lord Napier and Ettrick, C.V.O.
Personal Secretary, Miss M. Murray Brown, C.V.O.
Extra Ladies in Waiting, Lady Elizabeth Cavendish, L.V.O.; Mrs. Alastair Aird, L.V.O.; Mrs. Robin Benson, L.V.O.; Lady Juliet Townsend, L.V.O.; Mrs. Jane Stevens; The Hon. Mrs. Wills, L.V.O.; The Lady Glenconner; The Hon. Mrs. Whitehead, L.V.O.; The Countess Alexander of Tunis; Mrs. Charles Vyvyan.

HOUSEHOLD OF THE DUKE AND DUCHESS OF GLOUCESTER

Comptroller, Private Secretary and Equerry, Maj. N. Barne.
Assistant Private Secretary to The Duchess of Gloucester, Miss Suzanne Marland.
Extra Equerry, Lt.-Col. Sir Simon Bland, K.C.V.O.
Ladies in Waiting, Mrs. Michael Wigley, L.V.O.; Mrs. Euan McCorquodale; Mrs. Howard Page.
Extra Lady in Waiting, Miss Jennifer Thomson.

HOUSEHOLD OF PRINCESS ALICE, DUCHESS OF GLOUCESTER

Comptroller, Private Secretary and Equerry, Maj. N. Barne.
Extra Equerry, Lt.-Col. Sir Simon Bland, K.C.V.O.
Ladies in Waiting, Dame Jean Maxwell-Scott, D.C.V.O.; Mrs. Michael Harvey.
Extra Ladies in Waiting, Miss Dorothy Meynell, C.V.O.; Miss Diana Harrison; The Hon. Jane Walsh, L.V.O.; Miss Jane Egerton Warburton, L.V.O.

HOUSEHOLD OF THE DUKE AND DUCHESS OF KENT

Private Secretary, A. Palmer, C.M.G., C.V.O.
Extra Equerry, Cmdr. Sir Richard Buckley, K.C.V.O.
Ladies in Waiting, Mrs. Alan Henderson, C.V.O.; Mrs. David Napier, L.V.O.; Miss Sarah Partridge.
Extra Lady in Waiting, Mrs. Peter Wilmot-Sitwell.

HOUSEHOLD OF PRINCESS ALEXANDRA

Private Secretary and Extra Lady in Waiting, Miss Mona Mitchell, C.V.O.
Lady in Waiting, Lady Mary Mumford, C.V.O.
Extra Equerry, Maj. P. C. Clarke, C.V.O.
Extra Lady in Waiting, Mrs. Peter Afia.

HOUSEHOLD OF PRINCE AND PRINCESS MICHAEL OF KENT

Equerry, Lt.-Col. Sir Christopher Thompson, Bt.
Ladies in Waiting, The Hon. Mrs. Leatham; Miss Anne Frost.

THE QUEEN'S BIRTHDAY, 1990

The date for the observance of the Queen's Birthday in 1990 both at home and abroad will be Saturday, June 16.

ROYAL SALUTES

On the Anniversaries of the Birth, Accession and Coronation of the Sovereign and on the Anniversaries of the birth of H.M. the Queen Mother and H.R.H. the Duke of Edinburgh a salute of 62 guns is fired on the wharf at the Tower of London.

On extraordinary and triumphal occasions, such as on the occasion of the Sovereign opening, proroguing or dissolving Parliament in Person, or when passing through London in procession, except when otherwise ordered, 41 guns only are fired.

On the occasion of the birth of a Royal infant a salute of 41 guns is fired from the two Saluting Stations in London, i.e. Hyde Park and the Tower of London.

Constable of the Royal Palace and Fortress of London, Field Marshal Sir Roland Gibbs, G.C.B., C.B.E., D.S.O., M.C.
Lieutenant of the Tower of London, Lt.-Gen. Sir Derek Boorman, K.C.B.
Resident Governor and Keeper of the Jewel House, Maj.-Gen. C. Tyler, C.B.
Master Gunner of St. James's Park, Gen. Sir Martin Farndale, K.C.B.
Master Gunner within the Tower, Col. M. Ring.

THE ROYAL ARMS

QUARTERLY.—1st and 4th *gules*, three lions passant guardant in pale *or* (*England*); 2nd *or*, a lion rampant within a double tressure flory counterflory *gules* (*Scotland*); 3rd *azure*, a harp *or*, stringed *argent* (*Ireland*); the whole encircled with the Garter.
SUPPORTERS.—*Dexter*: a lion rampant guardant *or*, imperially crowned. *Sinister*: a unicorn *argent*, armed crined and unguled *or*, gorged with a coronet composed of crosses patées and fleurs de lis, a chain affixed passing between the forelegs and reflexed over the back.
BADGES.—The red and white rose united (*England*), a thistle (*Scotland*); a harp *or*, the strings *argent*, with a shamrock leaf *vert* (*Ireland*); upon a mount *vert*, a dragon passant wings elevated *gules* (*Wales*).

THE UNION FLAG

The national flag of the United Kingdom is the Union Flag, generally known as the Union Jack, the name deriving from the use of the Union Flag on the jack-staff of naval vessels. It is a combination of the cross of the patron saint of England, St. George (*cross gules in a field argent*), the cross of the patron saint of Scotland, St. Andrew (*saltire argent in a field azure*) and a cross similar to that of St. Patrick, patron saint of Ireland (*saltire gules in a field argent*). The Union Flag was first introduced in 1606 after the union of England and Scotland, the cross of St. Patrick being added in 1801.

ANNUITIES TO THE ROYAL FAMILY

The annuity payable to Her Majesty is known as the Civil List, and is payable out of the Consolidated Fund under the authority of a Civil List Act following the recommendation of a Parliamentary Select Committee.

The allocation for the calendar year 1989 was as follows:—

The Queen	£4,658,000
Queen Elizabeth The Queen Mother	404,000
The Duke of Edinburgh	225,300
Duke of York	155,400
Prince Edward	20,000
The Princess Royal	140,400
The Princess Margaret	136,700
Princess Alice, Duchess of Gloucester	55,400
*Duke of Gloucester	110,000
*Duke of Kent	148,500
*Princess Alexandra	141,600
	6,195,300
*Refunded by The Queen	400,100
Total	5,795,200

The land revenues of the Crown in England and Wales have been collected on the public account since 1760, when George III surrendered them and received a fixed annual payment or Civil List. For details of income from the Crown Estate, *see* page 307.

THE FLYING OF FLAGS

Days for hoisting the Union Flag on Government Buildings (from 8 a.m. to sunset).

February 6 (1952).—Her Majesty's Accession.
February 19 (1960).—Birthday of The Duke of York.
March 1.—St. David's Day (in Wales only).
March 10 (1964).—Birthday of The Prince Edward.
March 12.—Commonwealth Day 1990.
April 21 (1926).—Birthday of Her Majesty The Queen.
April 23.—St. George's Day (in England only). Where a building has two or more flagstaffs the Cross of St. George may be flown in addition to the Union Jack but not in a superior position.
June 2 (1953).—Coronation Day.
June 10 (1921).—Birthday of The Duke of Edinburgh.
June 16.—Queen's Official Birthday, 1990.
July 1 (1961).—Birthday of The Princess of Wales.
Aug. 4 (1900).—Birthday of Her Majesty Queen Elizabeth the Queen Mother.
Aug. 15 (1950).—Birthday of The Princess Royal.
Aug. 21 (1930).—Birthday of The Princess Margaret.
Nov. 11.—Remembrance Sunday, 1990.
Nov. 14 (1948).—Birthday of The Prince of Wales.
Nov. 20 (1947).—Her Majesty's Wedding Day.
Nov. 30.—St. Andrew's Day (in Scotland only).
And on the occasion of the opening and closing of Parliament by the Queen, flags should be flown on Government buildings in the Greater London area, whether or not Her Majesty performs the ceremony in person.

The only additions to the above list will be those notified to the Department of the Environment by Her Majesty's command and communicated by the Ministry to the other Departments. The list applies to all Government Buildings in London and elsewhere in the United Kingdom. In cases where it has been the practice to fly the Union Flag daily, e.g. on some Custom Houses, that practice may continue.

Flags will be flown at half-mast on the following occasions:

(a) From the announcement of the death up to the funeral of the Sovereign, except on Proclamation Day, when they are hoisted right up from 11 A.M. to sunset.

(b) The funerals of members of the Royal Family, subject to special commands from Her Majesty in each case.

(c) The funerals of Foreign Rulers, subject to special commands from Her Majesty in each case.

(d) The funerals of Prime Ministers and ex-Prime Ministers of the United Kingdom.

(e) Other occasions by special command of Her Majesty.

On occasions when days for flying flags coincide with days for flying flags at half mast the following rules will be observed. Flags will be flown: (a) although a member of the Royal Family, or a near relative of the Royal Family, may be lying dead, unless special commands be received from Her Majesty to the contrary, and (b) although it may be the day of the funeral of a Foreign Ruler. If the body of a very distinguished subject is lying at a Government Office the flag may fly at half mast on that office until the body has left (provided it is a day on which the flag would fly) and then the flag is to be hoisted right up. On all other Government Buildings the flag will fly as usual.

The *Royal Standard* is only to be hoisted when the Queen is actually present in the building, and never when Her Majesty is passing in procession.

RED-LETTER DAYS

Scarlet Robes are worn by the Judges of the Queen's Bench Division on *Red-Letter Days*.

RED-LETTER DAYS AND STATE OCCASIONS, 1990.

Jan.	25. Conversion of St. Paul.	*May*	24. Ascension Day.	*July*	25. St. James.
Feb.	2. Purification.	*June*	2. Coronation Day.	*Aug.*	4. Birthday of Queen Elizabeth the Queen Mother.
,,	6. Queen's Accession.	,,	10. Birthday of The Duke of Edinburgh.		
,,	28. Ash Wednesday.			*Oct.*	18. St. Luke.
Mar.	1. St. David.	,,	11. St. Barnabas.	,,	28. St. Simon and St. Jude.
,,	25. Annunciation.	,,	16. Queen's Official Birthday (1990).	*Nov.*	1. All Saints.
Apr.	21. Queen's Birthday.	,,	24. St. John the Baptist.	,,	10. Lord Mayor's Day.
,,	25. St. Mark.	,,	29. St. Peter.	,,	14. Birthday of The Prince of Wales.
May	1. St. Philip and St. James.	*July*	3. St. Thomas.	,,	30. St. Andrew.
,,	14. St. Matthias.				

THE MILITARY KNIGHTS OF WINDSOR

Founded in 1348 after the Wars in France to assist English Knights, who, having been prisoners in the hands of the French, had become impoverished by the payments of heavy ransoms. They received a pension and quarters in Windsor Castle. Edward III founded the Order of the Garter later in the same year, incorporating the Knights of Windsor and the College of St. George into its foundation and raising the number of Knights to 26 to correspond with the number of the Knights of the Garter. Known later as the Alms Knights or Poor Knights of Windsor, their establishment was reduced under the will of King Henry VIII to 13 and Statutes were drawn up by Queen Elizabeth I.

In 1833 King William IV changed their designation to The Military Knights and granted them their present uniform which consists of a scarlet tail-coat with white cross sword-belt, crimson sash and cocked hat with plume. The badges are the Shield of St. George and the Star of the Order of the Garter. The Knights receive a small stipend in addition to their Army pensions and quarters in Windsor Castle. They take part in all ceremonies of the Noble Order of the Garter and attend Sunday morning service in St. George's Chapel as representatives of the Knights of the Garter.

Applications for appointment should be made to The Military Secretary, Ministry of Defence, Army Dept.
Governor, Maj.-Gen. Peter Downward, C.B., D.S.O., D.F.C.
Military Knights, Maj. H. Smith, M.B.E., R.V.M.; Maj. A. E. Wollaston, M.V.O.; Brig. A. L. Atkinson, O.B.E.; Brig. J. F. Lindner, O.B.E., M.C.; Brig. A. C. Tyler, C.B.E., M.C.; Maj. W. L. Thompson, M.V.O., M.B.E., D.C.M.; Maj. L. W. Dickerson; Maj. J. C. Cowley, D.C.M.; Lt.-Col. N. L. West; Maj. G. R. Mitchell; M.B.E., B.E.M.; Lt.-Col. R. L. C. Tamplin.
Supernumerary, Lt.-Col. A. R. Clark, M.C.

THE PEERAGE

The rules which govern the creation and succession of Peerages are extremely complicated. There are, technically, five separate Peerages, the Peerage of England, of Scotland, of Ireland, of Great Britain, and of the United Kingdom. The Peerage of Great Britain dates from 1707 when an Act of Union combined the two Kingdoms of England and Scotland and separate Peerages were discontinued; and the Peerage of the United Kingdom from 1801 when Great Britain and Ireland were combined under an Act of Union. Some Scottish Peers have received additional Peerages of Great Britain or of the United Kingdom since 1707, and some Irish Peers additional Peerages of the United Kingdom since 1801. The Peerage of Ireland was not entirely discontinued from 1801 but holders of Irish Peerages, whether pre-dating or created subsequent to the Union of 1801, are not entitled to sit in the House of Lords if they have no additional English, Scottish, Great Britain or United Kingdom Peerage. (However, they are eligible for election to the House of Commons and to vote in Parliamentary elections, which other Peers are not.) An Irish Peer holding a Peerage of a lower grade which enables him to sit in the House of Lords is introduced there by the title which enables him to sit, though for all other purposes he is known by his higher title. In the Peerage of Scotland there is no rank of Baron; the equivalent rank is Lord of Parliament, abbreviated to 'Lord' (the female equivalent is 'Lady'). All Peers of England, Scotland, Great Britain or the United Kingdom who are of full age (21 years) and of British nationality are entitled to sit in the House of Lords. Most hereditary peerages pass on death to the nearest male heir; but certain ancient Peerages pass on death to the nearest heir, male or female, and several are held by women (*see also* pp. 176–7). Since the Peerage Act, 1963, women Peers in their own Right have been entitled to sit in the House of Lords, subject to the same qualifications as men.

Non-hereditary or Life Peerages, in the degree of Baron or Baroness, have been conferred by the Crown since 1876 on eminent judges, the Lords of Appeal or Law Lords, to enable them to carry out the judicial functions of the House of Lords, and since 1958 on men and women of distinction in public life, giving them seats in the House of Lords. Life Peers are addressed identically as an hereditary Peer, and their children have the same courtesy style as the children of an hereditary Peer.

No fees for Dignities have been payable since 1937. The House of Lords surrendered the ancient right of Peers to be tried for treason or felony by their peers in 1948.

Peerages Extinct Since the Last Issue

DUKEDOMS.—Newcastle (*cr.* 1756).
BARONIES.—Ailwyn (*cr.* 1921).
LIFE PEERAGES.—*See* p. 182.

Disclaimer of Peerages

The Peerage Act, 1963, enables Peers to disclaim their Peerages for life. Peers alive in 1963 could disclaim within 12 months after the passing of the Act (July 31, 1963; a person subsequently succeeding to a Peerage may disclaim within 12 months (one month if an M.P.) after the date of succession, or of attaining his or her majority, if later. The disclaimer is irrevocable but does not affect the descent of the Peerage after the disclaimant's death, and children of a disclaimed Peer may, if they wish, retain their precedence and any courtesy titles and styles borne as children of a Peer.

EARLS: Durham (1970); Home (1963); Sandwich (1964).
VISCOUNTS: Hailsham (1963); Stansgate (1963).
BARONS: Altrincham (1963); Archibald (1975); Merthyr (1977); Reith (1972); Sanderson of Ayot (1971); Silkin (1972); Southampton (1964).

Peers Who Are Minors

VISCOUNTS: Dillon (*b.* 1973).
BARONS: Gretton (*b.* 1975).

COMPOSITION OF THE HOUSE OF LORDS (At Aug. 31, 1989)

Archbishops and Bishops	26	
Peers by Succession	763	(20 women)
Hereditary Peers of first creation (including the Prince of Wales)	21	
Life Peers under the Appellate Jurisdiction Act 1876	21	
Life Peers under the Life Peerages Act 1958	353	(45 women)
TOTAL	1184	
Of whom:		
Peers without Writs of Summons	95	
Peers on Leave of Absence from the House	152	

Contractions and Symbols.—S. or I. appended to the date of creation denotes a *Scottish* or *Irish* title, the further addition of a * implies that the Peer in question holds also an *Imperial* title, which is specified (after the name) by its more definite description as *Engl., Brit.,* or *U.K.* When both titles are alike, as in the case of Argyll, this star is appended to the conjoined date below, and it then denotes that such date is that of the imperial creation. The mark ° signifies that there is no 'of' in the Marquessate or Earldom so designated; *b.* signifies born; *s.,* succeeded; *m.,* married; *w.,* widower or widow; *M.,* minor; † Information on *Eldest Son or Heir* not ascertained at time of going to press.

ROYAL DUKES

Style, His Royal Highness The Duke of ——.
Addressed as, Sir, or more formally, May it please your Royal Highness.

1947 *Edinburgh,* The Prince Philip, Duke of Edinburgh, K.G., K.T., O.M., G.B.E., P.C., *b.* 1921, *m.* (*see* p. 148).
1337 *Cornwall,* Charles, Prince of Wales, Duke of Cornwall (*Scottish Duke, Rothesay,* 1398). K.G., K.T., G.C.B., P.C., *b.* 1948, *m.* (*see* p. 148).
1986 *York,* The Prince Andrew, Duke of York, C.V.O., *b.* 1960, *m.* (*see* p. 149).
1928 *Gloucester* (2nd), Richard, Duke of Gloucester, G.C.V.O., *b.* 1944, *s.* 1974, *m.* (*see* p. 147).
1934 *Kent* (2nd), Edward, Duke of Kent, K.G., G.C.M.G., G.C.V.O., *b.* 1935, *s.* 1942, *m.* (*see* p. 147).

ARCHBISHOPS

Style, The Most Rev. His Grace The Lord Archbishop of——.
Addressed as, My Lord Archbishop; or, Your Grace.

*Introd. to House
of Lords*

1973   *Canterbury* (102nd), Robert Alexander Kennedy Runcie, M.C., P.C.,
     b. 1921, *m. Consecrated Bishop of St. Albans,* 1970, *trans.* 1980.

1973   *York* (95th), John Stapylton Habgood, P.C., PH.D., *b.* 1927, *m.
Consecrated Bishop of Durham,* 1973, *trans.* 1983.

DUKES

Style, His Grace The Duke of——.
Addressed as, My Lord Duke; or, Your Grace.
The eldest sons of Dukes and Marquesses take, by courtesy, their father's second title.
The other sons and the daughters are styled Lord Edward, Lady Caroline. etc.

Created.	*Title, Order of Succession, Name, etc.*	*Eldest Son or Heir.*
1868 I.*	*Abercorn* (5th), James Hamilton (6th *Brit. Marq.,* 1790, and 14th *Scott. Earl,* 1606 both *Abercorn*), *b.* 1934, *s.* 1979, *m.*	Marquess of Hamilton, *b.* 1969.
1701 S. ⎫ 1892* ⎭	*Argyll,* Ian Campbell (12th *Scottish* and 5th *U.K.* Duke, *Argyll*), *b.* 1937, *s.* 1973, *m.*	Marquess of Lorne, *b.* 1968.
1703 S.	*Atholl* (10th), George Iain Murray, *b.* 1931, *s.* 1957.	Godfrey P. *M.*, D.S.O., *b.* 1901.
1682	*Beaufort* (11th), David Robert Somerset, *b.* 1928, *s.* 1984, *m.*	Marquess of Worcester, *b.* 1952.
1694	*Bedford* (13th), John Robert Russell, *b.* 1917, *s.* 1953, *m.*	Marquess of Tavistock, *b.* 1940.
1663 S.*	*Buccleuch* (9th) & (11th) *Queensberry* (1684), Walter Francis John Montagu Douglas Scott, K.T., V.R.D. (8th *Engl. Earl, Doncaster,* 1662), *b.* 1923, *s.* 1973, *m.*	Earl of Dalkeith, *b.* 1954.
1694	*Devonshire* (11th), Andrew Robert Buxton Cavendish, M.C., P.C., *b.* 1920, *s.* 1950, *m.*	Marquess of Hartington, *b.* 1944.
1900	*Fife* (3rd), James George Alexander Bannerman Carnegie, *b.* 1929, *s.* 1959. (*see* p. 146).	Earl of Macduff, *b.* 1961.
1675	*Grafton* (11th), Hugh Denis Charles FitzRoy, K.G., *b.* 1919, *s.* 1970, *m.*	Earl of Euston, *b.* 1947.
1643 S.*	*Hamilton* (15th) & *Brandon* (12th) (*Brit.* 1711), Angus Alan Douglas Douglas-Hamilton (*Premier Peer of Scotland*), *b.* 1938, *s.* 1973, *m.*	Marquess of Douglas and Clydesdale, *b.* 1978.
1766 I.*	*Leinster* (8th), Gerald FitzGerald (*Premier Duke, Marquess and Earl of Ireland*; 8th *Brit. Visct., Leinster,* 1747) *b.* 1914, *s.* 1976, *m.*	Marquess of Kildare, *b.* 1948.
1719	*Manchester* (12th), Angus Charles Drogo Montagu, *b.* 1938, *s.* 1985, *m.*	Viscount Mandeville, *b.* 1962.
1702	*Marlborough* (11th), John George Vanderbilt Henry Spencer-Churchill, *b.* 1926, *s.* 1972, *m.*	Marquess of Blandford, *b.* 1955.
1707 S.*	*Montrose* (7th), James Angus Graham (5th *Brit. Earl, Graham,* 1722), *b.* 1907, *s.* 1954, *m.*	Marquess of Graham, *b.* 1935.
1756	*Newcastle* (10th), Edward Charles Pelham-Clinton, *b.* 1920, *s.* Nov. 1988, *died* Dec. 1988.	None to Dukedom. To Earldom of Lincoln, Edward H. Fiennes-Clinton. *b. 1913*
1483	*Norfolk* (17th), Miles Francis Stapleton Fitzalan-Howard, K.G., G.C.V.O., C.B., C.B.E., M.C. (*Premier Duke and Earl*; 12th *Eng. Baron Beaumont,* 1309, *s.* 1971; 4th *U.K. Baron Howard of Glossop,* 1869, *s.* 1972), *b.* 1915, *s.* 1975, *m.* (*Earl Marshal*).	Earl of Arundel and Surrey, *b.* 1956.
1766	*Northumberland* (11th), Henry Alan Walter Richard Percy, *b.* 1953, *s.* 1988.	Lord Ralph G.A.*P.*, *b.* 1956.
1716	*Portland* (9th), Victor Frederick William Cavendish-Bentinck, C.M.G. *b.* 1897, *s.* 1980, *m.*	None to Dukedom. To Earldom of Portland, Henry N. *B.*, *b.* 1919.
1675	*Richmond* (9th) & *Gordon* (4th) (*U.K.* 1876), Frederick Charles Gordon Lennox (9th *Scott. Duke, Lennox,* 1675), *b.* 1904, *s.* 1935, *m.*	Earl of March and Kinrara, *b.* 1929.
1707 S.*	*Roxburghe* (10th), Guy David Innes-Ker (5th *U.K. Earl, Innes,* 1837), *b.* 1954, *s.* 1974, *m.* (*Premier Baronet of Scotland*).	Marquess of Bowmont and Cessford, *b.* 1981.
1703	*Rutland* (10th), Charles John Robert Manners, C.B.E., *b.* 1919, *s.* 1940, *m.*	Marquess of Granby, *b.* 1959.
1684	*St. Albans* (14th), Murray de Vere Beauclerk, *b.* 1939, *s.* 1988, *m.*	Earl of Burford, *b.* 1965.
1547	*Somerset* (19th), John Michael Edward Seymour, *b.* 1952, *s.* 1984, *m.*	Lord Seymour, *b.* 1982.
1833	*Sutherland* (6th), John Sutherland Egerton, T.D. (5th *U.K. Earl Ellesmere,* 1846), *b.* 1915, *s.* 1963, *m.*	Cyril R. *E.*, *b.* 1905.
1814	*Wellington* (8th), Arthur Valerian Wellesley, L.V.O., O.B.E., M.C. (9th *Irish Earl, Mornington,* 1760), *b.* 1915, *s.* 1972, *m.*	Marquess of Douro, *b.* 1945.
1874	*Westminster* (6th), Gerald Cavendish Grosvenor, *b.* 1951, *s.* 1979, *m.*	None to Dukedom. To Marquessate of Westminster, Earl of Wilton, *b.* 1921 (*see* p. 163).

MARQUESSES

Style, The Most Hon. The Marquess of——. *Addressed as,* My Lord Marquess.
In titles marked ° the 'of' is *not* used. For the style of Marquesses' sons and daughters,
see under DUKES, above.

Created.	Title, Order of Succession, Name, etc.	Eldest Son or Heir.
1916	*Aberdeen and Temair* (6th), Alastair Ninian John Gordon (12th *Scott. Earl, Aberdeen,* 1682), *b.* 1920, *s.* 1984, *m.*	Earl of Haddo, *b.* 1955.
1876	*Abergavenny* (5th), John Henry Guy Nevill, K.G., O.B.E., *b.* 1914, *s.* 1954, *m.*	Guy R. G. *N., b.* 1945.
1821	*Ailesbury* (8th), Michael Sidney Cedric Brudenell-Bruce, *b.* 1926, *s.* 1974, *m.*	Earl of Cardigan, *b.* 1952.
1831	*Ailsa* (7th), Archibald David Kennedy, O.B.E., (19th *Scott. Earl, Cassillis,* 1509), *b.* 1925, *s.* 1957, *m.*	Earl of Cassillis, *b.* 1956.
1815	*Anglesey* (7th), George Charles Henry Victor Paget, *b.* 1922, *s.* 1947, *m.*	Earl of Uxbridge, *b.* 1950.
1789	*Bath* (6th), Henry Frederick Thynne, *b.* 1905, *s.* 1946, *m.*	Viscount Weymouth, *b.* 1932.
1826	*Bristol* (7th), Frederick William John Augustus Hervey, *b.* 1954, *s.* 1985.	Lord Frederick W. C. N. W. *H., b.* 1961.
1796	*Bute* (6th), John Crichton-Stuart (11th *Scott. Earl, Dumfries,* 1633), *b.* 1933, *s.* 1956, *m.*	Earl of Dumfries, *b.* 1958.
1812	°*Camden* (6th), David George Edward Henry Pratt, *b.* 1930, *s.* 1983.	Earl of Brecknock, *b.* 1965.
1815	*Cholmondeley* (6th), George Hugh Cholmondeley, G.C.V.O., M.C. (10th *Irish Viscount, Cholmondeley,* 1661), *b.* 1919, *s.* 1968, *m.* (*Lord Great Chamberlain*).	Earl of Rocksavage, *b.* 1960.
1816 I.*	°*Conyngham* (7th), Frederick William Henry Francis Conyngham (7th *U.K. Baron, Minster, U.K.* 1821), *b.* 1924, *s.* 1974, *m.*	Earl of Mount Charles, *b.* 1951.
1791 I.*	*Donegall* (7th), Dermot Richard Claud Chichester, L.V.O. (7th *Brit. Baron, Fisherwick,* 1790, 6th *Brit. Baron, Templemore,* 1831), *b.* 1916, *s.* to Marquessate, 1975: to Templemore Barony, 1953, *m.*	Earl of Belfast, *b.* 1952.
1789 I.*	*Downshire* (8th), (Arthur) Robin Ian Hill (8th *Brit. Earl, Hillsborough,* 1772), *b.* 1929, *s.* 1989.	Earl of Hillsborough, *b.* 1959.
1801 I.*	*Ely* (8th) Charles John Tottenham (8th *U.K. Baron, Loftus,* 1801), *b.* 1913, *s.* 1969, *m.*	Viscount Loftus, *b.* 1943.
1801	*Exeter* (8th), (William) Michael Anthony Cecil, *b.* 1935, *s.* 1988, *m.*	Lord Burghley, *b.* 1970.
1800 I.*	*Headfort* (6th), Thomas Geoffrey Charles Michael Taylour (4th *U.K. Baron, Kenlis,* 1831), *b.* 1932, *s.* 1960, *m.*	Earl of Bective, *b.* 1959.
1793	*Hertford* (8th), Hugh Edward Conway Seymour (9th *Irish Baron, Conway,* 1712), *b.* 1930, *s.* 1940, *m.*	Earl of Yarmouth, *b.* 1958.
1599 S.*	*Huntly* (13th), Granville Charles Gomer Gordon (*Premier Marquess of Scotland*) (5th *U.K. Baron, Meldrum,* 1815), *b.* 1944, *s.* 1987, *m.*	Earl of Aboyne, *b.* 1973.
1784	*Lansdowne* (8th), George John Charles Mercer Nairne Petty-Fitzmaurice, P.C. (8th *Irish Earl. Kerry,* 1723), *b.* 1912, *s.* 1944, *w.*	Earl of Shelburne, *b.* 1941.
1902	*Linlithgow* (4th), Adrian John Charles Hope (10th *Scott. Earl, Hopetoun* 1703), *b.* 1946, *s.* 1987, *m.*	Earl of Hopetoun, *b.* 1969.
1816 I.*	*Londonderry* (9th), Alexander Charles Robert Vane-Tempest-Stewart (6th *U.K. Earl, Vane,* 1823), *b.* 1937, *s.* 1955, *m.*	Viscount Castlereagh, *b.* 1972.
1701 S.*	*Lothian* (12th), Peter Francis Walter Kerr, K.C.V.O. (6th *U.K. Baron, Kerr,* 1821), *b.* 1922, *s.* 1940, *m.*	Earl of Ancram, *b.* 1945.
1917	*Milford Haven* (4th), George Ivar Louis Mountbatten, *b.* 1961, *s.* 1970, *m.*	Lord Ivar A. M. *M., b.* 1963.
1838	*Normanby* (4th), Oswald Constantine John Phipps, K.G., C.B.E. (8th *Irish Baron, Mulgrave,* 1767), *b.* 1912, *s.* 1932, *m.*	Earl of Mulgrave, *b.* 1954.
1812	*Northampton* (7th), Spencer Douglas David Compton, *b.* 1946, *s.* 1978.	Earl Compton, *b.* 1973.
1825 I.*	*Ormonde* (7th), James Hubert Theobald Charles Butler, M.B.E. (7th *U.K. Baron, Ormonde,* 1821), *b.* 1899, *s.* 1971, *w.*	None to Marquessate. To Earldoms of Ormonde and Ossory, Viscount Mountgarret, *b.* 1936 (*see,* p. 165).
1682 S.	*Queensberry* (12th), David Harrington Angus Douglas, *b.* 1929, *s.* 1954.	Viscount Drumlanrig, *b.* 1967.
1926	*Reading* (4th), Simon Charles Henry Rufus Isaacs, *b.* 1942, *s.* 1980, *m.*	Viscount Erleigh, *b.* 1986.
1789	*Salisbury* (6th), Robert Edward Peter Cecil, *b.* 1916, *s.* 1972, *m.*	Viscount Cranborne, *b.* 1946.
1800 I.*	*Sligo* (10th), Denis Edward Browne (10th *U.K. Baron, Monteagle,* 1806), *b.* 1908, *s.* 1952, *m.*	Earl of Altamont, *b.* 1939.
1787	°*Townshend* (7th), George John Patrick Dominic Townshend, *b.* 1916, *s.* 1921, *w.*	Viscount Raynham, *b.* 1945.
1694 S.*	*Tweeddale* (13th), Edward Douglas John Hay (4th *U.K. Baron, Tweeddale,* 1881), *b.* 1947, *s.* 1979.	Lord Charles D. M. *H., b.* 1947.
1789 I.*	*Waterford* (8th), John Hubert de la Poer Beresford (8th *Brit. Baron, Tyrone,* 1786), *b.* 1933, *s.* 1934, *m.*	Earl of Tyrone, *b.* 1958.
1551	*Winchester* (18th), Nigel George Paulet (*Premier Marquess of England*), *b.* 1941, *s.* 1968, *m.*	Earl of Wiltshire, *b.* 1969.
1892	*Zetland* (3rd), Lawrence Aldred Mervyn Dundas (5th *U.K. Earl of Zetland,* 1838, 6th *Brit. Baron Dundas,* 1794), *b.* 1908, *s.* 1961, *m.*	Earl of Ronaldshay, *b.* 1937.

EARLS

Style, The Right Hon. The Earl of ——. (See also note, p. 187). Addressed as, My Lord. Where marked ° the 'of' is not used. The eldest sons of Earls take, by courtesy, their father's second title, the younger sons being styled the Hon., e.g. the Hon. John ——, but the daughters Lady Elizabeth ——, etc.

Created.	Title, Order of Succession, Name, etc.	Eldest Son or Heir.
1639 s.	*Airlie* (13th), David George Coke Patrick Ogilvy, K.T., G.C.V.O., P.C., b. 1926, s. 1968, m. (*Lord Chamberlain*).	Lord Ogilvy, b. 1958.
1696	*Albemarle* (10th), Rufus Arnold Alexis Keppel, b. 1965, s. 1979.	Crispian W. J. K., b. 1948.
1952	°*Alexander of Tunis* (2nd), Shane William Desmond Alexander, b. 1935, s. 1969, m.	Hon. Brian J. A., b. 1939.
1826	°*Amherst* (5th), Jeffery John Archer Amherst, M.C., b. 1896, s. 1927.	(None.)
1662 s.	*Annandale and Hartfell* (11th), Patrick Andrew Wentworth Hope Johnstone, b. 1941, *claim established* 1985, m.	Lord Johnstone, b. 1971.
1789 I.	°*Annesley* (10th), Patrick Annesley, b. 1924, s. 1979, m.	Hon. Philip H.A., b. 1927.
1785 I.	*Antrim* (9th), Alexander Randal Mark McDonnell, b. 1935, s. 1977, m. (*Viscount Dunluce*).	Hon. Randal A. St. J. M., b. 1967.
1762 I.*	*Arran* (9th), Arthur Desmond Colquhoun Gore (5th *U.K. Baron Sudley,* 1884), b. 1938, s. 1983, m.	Paul A. G., C.M.G., C.V.O., b. 1921.
1955	°*Attlee* (2nd), Martin Richard Attlee, b. 1927, s. 1967, m.	Viscount Prestwood, b. 1956.
1714	*Aylesford* (11th), Charles Ian Finch-Knightley, b. 1918, s. 1958, m.	Lord Guernsey, b. 1947.
1937	°*Baldwin of Bewdley* (4th), Edward Alfred Alexander Baldwin, b. 1938, s. 1976, m.	Viscount Corvedale, b. 1973.
1922	*Balfour* (4th), Gerald Arthur James Balfour, b. 1925, s. 1968, m.	Eustace A. G. B., b. 1921.
1772	°*Bathurst* (8th), Henry Allen John Bathurst, b. 1927, s. 1943, m.	Lord Apsley, b. 1961.
1919	°*Beatty* (3rd), David Beatty, b. 1946, s. 1972.	Viscount Borodale, b. 1973.
1797 I.	*Belmore* (8th), John Armar Lowry-Corry, b. 1951, s. 1960, m.	Viscount Corry, b. 1985.
1739 I.* } 1937 }	*Bessborough,* Frederick Edward Neuflize Ponsonby (10th *Irish* and 2nd *U.K. Earl Bessborough*), b. 1913, s. 1956, m.	Arthur M. L. P., b. 1912 (to Irish Earldom only).
1815	*Bradford* (7th), Richard Thomas Orlando Bridgeman, b. 1947, s. 1981, m.	Viscount Newport, b.1980.
1677 s.	*Breadalbane and Holland* (10th), John Romer Boreland Campbell, b. 1919, s. 1959.	(None.)
1469 s.*	*Buchan* (17th), Malcolm Harry Erskine, (8th *U.K. Baron Erskine* 1806), b. 1930, s. 1984, m.	Lord Cardross, b. 1960.
1746	*Buckinghamshire* (10th), (George) Miles Hobart-Hampden, b. 1944, s. 1983, m.	Lt.-Cdr. Sir Robert Hobart, Bt., b. 1915.
1800	°*Cadogan* (7th), William Gerald Charles Cadogan, M.C., b. 1914, s. 1933, m.	Viscount Chelsea, b. 1937.
1878	°*Cairns* (6th), Simon Dallas Cairns, b. 1939, s. 1989, m.	Viscount Garmoyle, b. 1965.
1455 s.	*Caithness* (20th), Malcolm Ian Sinclair, b. 1948, s. 1965, m.	Lord Berriedale, b. 1981.
1800 I.	*Caledon* (7th), Nicholas James Alexander, b. 1955, s. 1980.	Earl Alexander of Tunis (*see* above).
1661	*Carlisle* (12th), Charles James Ruthven Howard, M.C. (12th *Scott. Baron, Ruthven of Freeland*, 1651), b. 1923, s. 1963, m.	Viscount Morpeth, b. 1949.
1793	*Carnarvon* (7th), Henry George Reginald Molyneux Herbert, K.C.V.O., K.B.E., b. 1924, s. 1987, m.	Lord Porchester, b. 1956.
1748 I.*	*Carrick* (9th), Brian Stuart Theobald Somerset Caher Butler (3rd *U.K. Baron, Butler,* 1912), b. 1931, s. 1957, m.	Viscount Ikerrin, b. 1953.
1800 I.	°*Castle Stewart* (8th), Arthur Patrick Avondale Stuart, b. 1928, s. 1961, m.	Viscount Stuart, b. 1953.
1814	°*Cathcart* (6th), Alan Cathcart, C.B., D.S.O., M.C. (15th *Scott. Baron, Cathcart*, 1447), b. 1919, s. 1927, m.	Lord Greenock, b. 1952.
1647 I.	*Cavan* (13th), Roger Cavan Lambart, b. 1944, s. 1988.	Arthur O.R.L., b. 1909.
1827	°*Cawdor* (6th), Hugh John Vaughan Campbell, b. 1932, s. 1970, m.	Viscount Emlyn, b. 1962.
1801	*Chichester* (9th), John Nicholas Pelham, b. 1944, s. 1944, m.	Richard A. H. P., b. 1952.
1803 I.*	*Clancarty* (8th), William Francis Brinsley Le Poer Trench (7th *U.K. Visct. Clancarty,* 1823), b. 1911, s. 1975, m.	Nicholas P. R. *Le P. T.,* b. 1952.
1776 I.*	*Clanwilliam* (7th), John Herbert Meade (5th *U.K. Baron Clanwilliam,* 1828), b. 1919, s. 1989, m.	Lord Gillford, b. 1960.
1776	*Clarendon* (7th), George Frederick Laurence Hyde Villiers, b. 1933, s. 1955, m.	Lord Hyde, b. 1976.
1620 I.*	*Cork* (13th) & *Orrery* (13th)(I. 1660), Patrick Reginald Boyle (9th *Brit. Baron, Boyle of Marston*, 1711), b. 1910, s. 1967, m.	Hon. John W. B., D.S.C., b. 1916.
1850	*Cottenham* (8th), Kenelm Charles Everard Digby Pepys, b. 1948, s. 1968, m.	Viscount Crowhurst, b. 1983.
1762 I.*	*Courtown* (9th), James Patrick Montagu Burgoyne Winthrop Stopford (8th *Brit. Baron, Saltersford*, 1796), b. 1954, s. 1975, m.	Viscount Stopford, b. 1988.
1697	*Coventry* (11th), George William Coventry, b. 1934, s. 1940, m.	Viscount Deerhurst, b. 1957.
1857	°*Cowley* (7th), Garret Graham Wellesley, b. 1934, s. 1975, m.	Viscount Dangan, b. 1965.
1892	*Cranbrook* (5th), Gathorne Gathorne-Hardy, b. 1933, s. 1978, m.	Lord Medway, b. 1968.
1801	*Craven* (8th), Simon George Craven, b. 1961, s. 1983.	Rupert J. E. C., b. 1926.
1398 s.*	*Crawford* (29th) & *Balcarres* (12th) (s. 1651), Robert Alexander Lindsay, P.C., (*Premier Earl on Union Roll,* 5th *U.K. Baron, Wigan,* 1826, and *Baron Balniel* (Life Peer)), b. 1927, s. 1975, m.	Lord Balniel, b. 1958.

Created.	Title, Order of Succession, Name, etc.	Eldest Son or Heir.
1861	*Cromartie* (4th), Roderick Grant Francis Mackenzie, M.C., T.D., *b.* 1904, *s.* 1962, *m.*	Viscount Tarbat, *b.* 1948.
1901	*Cromer* (3rd), George Rowland Stanley Baring, K.G., G.C.M.G., M.B.E., P.C., *b.* 1918, *s.* 1953, *m.*	Viscount Errington, *b.* 1946.
1633 s.*	*Dalhousie* (16th), Simon Ramsay, K.T., G.C.V.O., G.B.E., M.C. (4th *U.K. Baron, Ramsay, 1875*), *b.* 1914, *s.* 1950, *m.*	Lord Ramsay, *b.* 1948.
1725 I.*	*Darnley* (11th), Adam Ivo Stuart Bligh (20th *English Baron, Clifton of Leighton Bromswold,* 1608), *b.* 1941, *s.* 1980, *m.*	Lord Clifton, *b.* 1968.
1711	*Dartmouth* (9th), Gerald Humphry Legge, *b.* 1924, *s.* 1962, *m.*	Viscount Lewisham, *b.* 1949.
1761	°*De La Warr* (11th), William Herbrand Sackville, *b.* 1948, *s.* 1988, *m.*	Lord Buckhurst, *b.* 1979.
1622	*Denbigh* (11th) & *Desmond* (10th) (I. 1622), William Rudolph Michael Feilding, *b.* 1943, *s.* 1966, *m.*	Viscount Feilding, *b.* 1970.
1485	*Derby* (18th), Edward John Stanley, M.C., *b.* 1918, *s.* 1948, *m.*	Edward R. W. S., *b.* 1962.
1553	*Devon* (17th), Charles Christopher Courtenay, *b.* 1916, *s.* 1935, *m.*	Lord Courtenay, *b.* 1942.
1800 I.*	*Donoughmore* (8th), Richard Michael John Hely-Hutchinson (8th *U.K. Visct., Hutchinson,* 1821), *b.* 1927, *s.* 1981, *m.*	Viscount Suirdale, *b.* 1952.
1661 I.*	*Drogheda* (11th), Charles Garrett Ponsonby Moore, K.G., K.B.E. (2nd *U.K. Baron. Moore,* 1954), *b.* 1910, *s.* 1957, *m.*	Viscount Moore, *b.* 1937.
1837	*Ducie* (6th), Basil Howard Moreton, *b.* 1917, *s.* 1952, *m.*	Lord Moreton, *b.* 1951.
1860	*Dudley* (4th), William Humble David Ward, *b.* 1920, *s.* 1969, *m.*	Viscount Ednam, *b.* 1947.
1660 s.*	*Dundee* (12th), Alexander Henry Scrymgeour, (2nd *U.K. Baron, Glassary,* 1954), *b.* 1949, *s.* 1983, *m.*	Lord Scrymgeour, *b.* 1982.
1669 s.	*Dundonald* (15th), Iain Alexander Douglas Blair Cochrane, *b.* 1961, *s.* 1986, *m.*	Baron Cochrane of Cults, *b.* 1922 (*see,* p. 169).
1686 s.	*Dunmore* (11th), Kenneth Randolph Murray, *b.* 1913, *s.* 1981, *w.*	Viscount Fincastle, *b.* 1946.
1822 I.	*Dunraven and Mount-Earl* (7th), Thady Windham Thomas Wyndham-Quin, *b.* 1939, *s.* 1965, *m.*	(None).
1833	*Durham.* Disclaimed for life 1970.	
1837	*Effingham* (6th), Mowbray Henry Gordon Howard (16th *E. Baron, Howard of Effingham,* 1554), *b.* 1905, *s.* 1946, *m.*	Lt.-Cdr. David P. M. A. H., *b.* 1939.
1507 s. 1859*	} *Eglinton* (18th) & (9th) *Winton* (1600), Archibald George Montgomerie (16th *U.K. Earl Winton,* 1859), *b.* 1939, *s.* 1966, *m.*	Lord Montgomerie, *b.* 1966.
1733 I.*	*Egmont* (11th), Frederick George Moore Perceval (9th *Brit. Baron, Lovel & Holland,* 1762), *b.* 1914, *s.* 1932, *m.*	Viscount Perceval, *b.* 1934.
1821	*Eldon* (5th), John Joseph Nicholas Scott, *b.* 1937, *s.* 1976, *m.*	Viscount Encombe, *b.* 1962.
1633 s.*	*Elgin* (11th), & *Kincardine* (15th) (s. 1647), Andrew Douglas Alexander Thomas Bruce, (4th *U.K. Baron, Elgin,* 1849), K.T., *b.* 1924, *s.* 1968, *m.*	Lord Bruce, *b.* 1961.
1789 I.*	*Enniskillen* (7th), Andrew John Galbraith Cole (5th *U.K. Baron, Grinstead,* 1815) *b.* 1942, *s.* 1989, *m.*	Arthur G.C., *b.* 1920.
1789 I.*	*Erne* (6th), Henry George Victor John Crichton (3rd *U.K. Baron, Fermanagh,* 1876), *b.* 1937, *s.* 1940, *m.*	Viscount Crichton, *b.* 1971.
1452 s.	*Erroll* (24th), Merlin Sereld Victor Gilbert Hay (*Hereditary Lord High Constable and Knight Marischal of Scotland*), *b.* 1948, *s.* 1978, *m.*	Lord Hay, *b.* 1984.
1661	*Essex* (10th), Robert Edward de Vere Capell, *b.* 1920, *s.* 1981, *m.*	Viscount Malden, *b.* 1944.
1711	°*Ferrers* (13th), Robert Washington Shirley, P.C., *b.* 1929, *s.* 1954, *m.*	Viscount Tamworth, *b.* 1952.
1789	°*Fortescue* (7th), Richard Archibald Fortescue, *b.* 1922, *s.* 1977, *m.*	Viscount Ebrington, *b.* 1951.
1841	*Gainsborough* (5th), Anthony Gerard Edward Noel, *b.* 1923, *s.* 1927, *m.*	Viscount Campden, *b.* 1950.
1623 s.*	*Galloway* (13th), Randolph Keith Reginald Stewart (6th *Brit. Baron, Stewart of Garlies,* 1796), *b.* 1928, *s.* 1978, *m.*	Andrew C. S., *b.* 1949.
1703 s.*	*Glasgow* (10th), Patrick Robin Archibald Boyle (4th *U.K. Baron, Fairlie,* 1897), *b.* 1939, *s.* 1984, *m.*	Viscount of Kelburn, *b.* 1978.
1806 I.*	*Gosford* (7th), Charles David Nicholas Alexander John Sparrow Acheson (5th *U.K. Baron, Worlingham,* 1835), *b.* 1942, *s.* 1966, *m.*	Hon. Patrick B. V. M. A., *b.* 1915.
1945	*Gowrie* (2nd), Alexander Patric Greysteil Hore-Ruthven, P.C. (3rd *U.K. Baron, Ruthven of Gowrie,* 1919), *b.* 1939, *s.* 1955, *m.*	Viscount Ruthven of Canberra, *b.* 1964.
1684 I.*	*Granard* (9th), Arthur Patrick Hastings Forbes, A.F.C. (4th *U.K. Baron, Granard,* 1806), *b.* 1915, *s.* 1948, *m.*	Peter A. E. H. F., *b.* 1957.
1833	°*Granville* (5th), Granville James Leveson-Gower, M.C., *b.* 1918, *s.* 1953, *m.*	Lord Leveson, *b.* 1959.
1806	°*Grey* (6th), Richard Fleming George Charles Grey, *b.* 1939, *s.* 1963, *m.*	Philip K. G., *b.* 1940.
1752	*Guilford* (9th), Edward Francis North, *b.* 1933, *s.* 1949, *m.*	Lord North, *b.* 1971.
1619 s.	*Haddington* (13th), John George Baillie-Hamilton, *b.* 1941, *s.* 1986, *m.*	Lord Binning, *b.* 1985.
1919	°*Haig* (2nd), George Alexander Eugene Douglas Haig, O.B.E., *b.* 1918, *s.* 1928, *m.*	Viscount Dawick, *b.* 1961.
1944	*Halifax* (3rd), Charles Edward Peter Neil Wood (5th *U.K. Viscount, Halifax,* 1866), *b.* 1944, *s.* 1980, *m.*	Lord Irwin, *b.* 1977.
1898	*Halsbury* (3rd), John Anthony Hardinge Giffard, F.R.S., *b.* 1908, *s.* 1943, *w.*	Adam E. G., *b.* 1934.
1754	*Hardwicke* (10th), Joseph Philip Sebastian Yorke, *b.* 1971, *s.* 1974.	Richard C. J. Y., *b.* 1916.
1812	*Harewood* (7th), George Henry Hubert Lascelles, K.B.E., *b.* 1923, *s.* 1947, *m.* (*See also* p. 147).	Viscount Lascelles, *b.* 1950.

Created.	Title, Order of Succession, Name, etc.	Eldest Son or Heir.
1742	*Harrington* (11th), William Henry Leicester Stanhope (8th *Brit. Viscount, Stanhope of Mahon,* 1717), *b.* 1922, *s.* 1929, *m.*	Viscount Petersham, *b.* 1945.
1809	*Harrowby* (7th), Dudley Danvers Granville Coutts Ryder, T.D., *b.* 1922, *s.* 1987, *m.*	Viscount Sandon, *b.* 1951.
1605 s.	*Home. Disclaimed for life* 1963.	
1821	°*Howe* (7th), Frederick Richard Penn Curzon, *b.* 1951, *s.* 1984, *m.*	Charles M. P. *C.*, *b.* 1967.
1529	*Huntingdon* (15th), Francis John Clarence Westenra Plantagenet Hastings, *b.* 1901, *s.* 1939, *m.*	Lt.-Col. Robin H. W. S. *H.*, D.S.O., O.B.E., M.C., *b.* 1917.
1885	*Iddesleigh* (4th), Stafford Henry Northcote, *b.* 1932, *s.* 1970, *m.*	Viscount St. Cyres, *b.* 1957.
1756	*Ilchester* (9th), Maurice Vivian de Touffreville Fox-Strangways, *b.* 1920, *s.* 1970, *m.*	Hon. Raymond G. *F.-S.*, *b.* 1921.
1929	*Inchcape* (3rd), Kenneth James William Mackay, *b.* 1917, *s.* 1939, *m.*	Viscount Glenapp, *b.* 1943.
1919	*Iveagh* (3rd), Arthur Francis Benjamin Guinness, *b.* 1937, *s.* 1967.	Viscount Elveden, *b.* 1969.
1925	°*Jellicoe* (2nd), George Patrick John Rushworth Jellicoe, K.B.E., D.S.O., M.C., P.C., *b.* 1918, *s.* 1935, *m.*	Viscount Brocas, *b.* 1950.
1697	*Jersey* (9th), George Francis Child-Villiers (12th *Irish Visct., Grandison,* 1620), *b.* 1910, *s.* 1923, *m.*	Viscount Villiers, *b.* 1948.
1822 I.	*Kilmorey* (6th), Richard Francis Needham, M.P., *b.* 1942, *s.* 1977, *m.*	Viscount Newry and Morne, *b.* 1966.
1866	*Kimberley* (4th), John Wodehouse, *b.* 1924, *s.* 1941, *m.*	Lord Wodehouse, *b.* 1951.
1768 I.	*Kingston* (11th), Barclay Robert Edwin King-Tenison, *b.* 1943, *s.* 1948.	Viscount Kingsborough, *b.* 1969.
1633 s.*	*Kinnoull* (15th), Arthur William George Patrick Hay (9th *Brit. Baron, Hay of Pedwardine,* 1711), *b.* 1935, *s.* 1938, *m.*	Viscount Dupplin, *b.* 1962.
1677 s.*	*Kintore* (12th), (James) Ian Keith (2nd *U.K. Visct., Stonehaven,* 1938), *b.* 1908, *s.* to Viscountcy, 1941, to Earldom, 1974, *m.*	Lord Inverurie, *b.* 1939.
1914	°*Kitchener of Khartoum* (3rd), Henry Herbert Kitchener, T.D., *b.* 1919, *s.* 1937.	(None.)
1756 I.	*Lanesborough* (9th), Denis Anthony Brian Butler, T.D., *b.* 1918, *s.* 1950.	Henry A. B. C. *B.*, *b.* 1909.
1624 s.	*Lauderdale* (17th), Patrick Francis Maitland, *b.* 1911, *s.* 1968, *m.*	Viscount Maitland, *b.* 1937.
1837	*Leicester* (6th), Anthony Louis Lovel Coke, *b.* 1909, *s.* 1976, *m.*	Viscount Coke, *b.* 1936.
1641 s.	*Leven* (14th) *& Melville* (13th) (s. 1690), Alexander Robert Leslie Melville, *b.* 1924, *s.* 1947, *m.*	Lord Balgonie, *b.* 1954.
1831	*Lichfield* (5th), Thomas Patrick John Anson, *b.* 1939, *s.* 1960.	Viscount Anson, *b.* 1978.
1803 I.*	*Limerick* (6th), Patrick Edmund Pery, K.B.E. (6th *U.K. Baron, Foxford,* 1815), *b.* 1930, *s.* 1967, *m.*	Viscount Glentworth, *b.* 1963.
1572	*Lincoln* (18th), Edward Horace Fiennes-Clinton, *b.* 1913, *s.* 1988, *m.*	Edward D. *F.-C.*, *b.* 1943.
1633 s.	*Lindsay* (16th), James Randolph Lindesay-Bethune, *b.* 1955, *s.* 1989, *m.*	Hon. John M. *L.-B.*, *b.* 1929.
1626	*Lindsey* (14th) *and Abingdon* (9th) (1682), Richard Henry Rupert Bertie, *b.* 1931, *s.* 1963, *m.*	Lord Norreys, *b.* 1958.
1776 I.	*Lisburne* (8th), John David Malet Vaughan, *b.* 1918, *s.* 1965, *m.*	Viscount Vaughan, *b.* 1945.
1822 I.*	*Listowel* (5th), William Francis Hare, G.C.M.G., P.C., (3rd *U.K. Baron, Hare,* 1869), *b.* 1906, *s.* 1931, *m.*	Viscount Ennismore, *b.* 1964.
1905	*Liverpool* (5th), Edward Peter Bertram Savile Foljambe, *b.* 1944, *s.* 1969, *m.*	Viscount Hawkesbury, *b.* 1972.
1945	°*Lloyd George of Dwyfor* (3rd), Owen Lloyd George, *b.* 1924, *s.* 1968, *m.*	Viscount Gwynedd, *b.* 1951.
1785 I.*	*Longford* (7th), Francis Aungier Pakenham, K.G., P.C. (6th *U.K. Baron, Silchester,* 1821; 1st *U.K. Baron, Pakenham,* 1945), *b.* 1905, *s.* 1961, *m.*	Thomas F. D. *P.*, *b.* 1933.
1807	*Lonsdale* (7th), James Hugh William Lowther, *b.* 1922, *s.* 1953, *m.*	Viscount Lowther, *b.* 1949.
1838	*Lovelace* (5th), Peter Axel William Locke King (12th *British Baron, King,* 1725), *b.* 1951, *s.* 1964, *m.*	(None.)
1795 I.*	*Lucan* (7th), Richard John Bingham (3rd *U.K. Baron, Bingham,* 1934), *b.* 1934, *s.* 1964, *m.*	Lord Bingham, *b.* 1967.
1880	*Lytton* (5th), John Peter Michael Scawen Lytton (18th *English Baron, Wentworth,* 1529), *b.* 1950, *s.* 1985, *m.*	Viscount Knebworth, *b.* 1989.
1721	*Macclesfield* (8th), George Roger Alexander Thomas Parker, *b.* 1914, *s.* 1975, *m.*	Viscount Parker, *b.* 1943.
1800	*Malmesbury* (6th), William James Harris, T.D., *b.* 1907, *s.* 1950, *m.*	Viscount FitzHarris, *b.* 1946.
1776 & 1792	*Mansfield and Mansfield* (8th), William David Mungo James Murray (14th *Scott. Visct., Stormont,* 1621), *b.* 1930, *s.* 1971, *m.*	Viscount Stormont, *b.* 1956.
1565 s.	*Mar* (13th) *& Kellie* (15th) (s. 1616), John Francis Hervey Erskine, *b.* 1921, *s.* 1955, *m.*	Lord Erskine, *b.* 1949.
1785 I.	*Mayo* (10th), Terence Patrick Bourke, *b.* 1929, *s.* 1962, *m.*	Lord Naas, *b.* 1953.
1627 I.*	*Meath* (14th), Anthony Windham Normand Brabazon (5th *U.K. Baron, Chaworth,* 1831), *b.* 1910, *s.* 1949, *m.*	Lord Ardee, *b.* 1941.
1766 I.	*Mexborough* (8th), John Christopher George Savile, *b.* 1931, *s.* 1980, *m.*	Viscount Pollington, *b.* 1959.
1813	*Minto* (6th), Gilbert Edward George Lariston Elliot-Murray-Kynynmound, O.B.E., *b.* 1928, *s.* 1975, *w.*	Viscount Melgund, *b.* 1953.
1562 s.*	*Moray* (20th), Douglas John Moray Stuart (12th *Brit. Baron, Stuart of Castle Stuart,* 1796), *b.* 1928, *s.* 1974, *m.*	Lord Doune, *b.* 1966.
1815	*Morley* (6th), John St. Aubyn Parker, *b.* 1923, *s.* 1962, *m.*	Viscount Boringdon, *b.* 1956.

Created.	Title, Order of Succession, Name, etc.	Eldest Son or Heir.
1458 s.	*Morton* (22nd), John Charles Sholto Douglas, *b.* 1927, *s.* 1976, *m.*	Lord Aberdour, *b.* 1952.
1789	*Mount Edgcumbe* (8th), Robert Charles Edgcumbe, *b.* 1939, *s.* 1982, *m.*	Piers V. E., *b.* 1946.
1831	*Munster* (7th), Anthony Charles FitzClarence, *b.* 1926, *s.* 1983, *m.*	(None).
1805	°*Nelson* (9th), Peter John Horatio Nelson, *b.* 1941, *s.* 1981, *m.*	Viscount Merton, *b.* 1971.
1660 s.	*Newburgh* (12th), Prince Filippo Giambattista Francesco Aldo Maria Rospigliosi, *b.* 1942, *s.* 1986, *m.*	Princess Benedetta F. M. R., *b.* 1974.
1827 I.	*Norbury* (6th), Noel Terence Graham-Toler, *b.* 1939, *s.* 1955, *m.*	Viscount Glandine, *b.* 1967.
1806 I.*	*Normanton* (6th), Shaun James Christian Welbore Ellis Agar (9th *Brit. Baron, Mendip*, 1791) (4th *U.K. Baron, Somerton*, 1873), *b.* 1945, *s.* 1967, *m.*	Viscount Somerton, *b.* 1982.
1647 s.	*Northesk* (13th), Robert Andrew Carnegie, *b.* 1926, *s.* 1975, *w.*	Lord Rosehill, *b.* 1954.
1801	*Onslow* (7th), Michael William Coplestone Dillon Onslow, *b.* 1938, *s.* 1971, *m.*	Viscount Cranley, *b.* 1967.
1696 s.	*Orkney* (8th), Cecil O'Bryen Fitz-Maurice, *b.* 1919, *s.* 1951, *m.*	O. Peter *St. John*, *b.* 1938.
1925	*Oxford and Asquith* (2nd), Julian Edward George Asquith, K.C.M.G., *b.* 1916, *s.* 1928, *m.*	Viscount Asquith, *b.* 1952.
1929	°*Peel* (3rd), William James Robert Peel (4th *U.K. Viscount Peel*, 1895), *b.* 1947, *s.* 1969, *m.*	Viscount Clanfield, *b.* 1976.
1551	*Pembroke* (17th) & *Montgomery* (14th) (1605), Henry George Charles Alexander Herbert, *b.* 1939, *s.* 1969.	Lord Herbert, *b.* 1978.
1605 s.	*Perth* (17th), John David Drummond, P.C., *b.* 1907, *s.* 1951, *m.*	Viscount Strathallan, *b.* 1935.
1905	*Plymouth* (3rd), Other Robert Ivor Windsor-Clive (15th *English Baron, Windsor*, 1529), *b.* 1923, *s.* 1943, *m.*	Viscount Windsor, *b.* 1951.
1785 I.	*Portarlington* (7th), George Lionel Yuill Seymour Dawson-Damer, *b.* 1938, *s.* 1959, *m.*	Viscount Carlow, *b.* 1965.
1743	*Portsmouth* (10th), Quentin Gerard Carew Wallop, *b.* 1954, *s.* 1984.	Viscount Lymington, *b.* 1981.
1804	*Powis* (7th), George William Herbert (8th *Irish Baron, Clive*, 1762), *b.* 1925, *s.* 1988, *m.*	Viscount Clive, *b.* 1952.
1765	*Radnor* (8th), Jacob Pleydell-Bouverie, *b.* 1927, *s.* 1968, *m.*	Viscount Folkestone, *b.* 1955.
1831 I.*	*Ranfurly* (7th), Gerald Françoys Needham Knox (8th *U.K. Baron, Ranfurly*, 1826), *b.* 1929, *s.* 1988, *m.*	Viscount Northland, *b.* 1957.
1771 I.	*Roden* (9th), Robert William Jocelyn, *b.* 1909, *s.* 1956, *m.*	Viscount Jocelyn, *b.* 1938.
1801	*Romney* (7th), Michael Henry Marsham, *b.* 1910, *s.* 1975, *m.*	Julian C. M., *b.* 1948.
1703 s.*	*Rosebery* (7th), Neil Archibald Primrose (3rd *U.K. Earl, Midlothian*, 1911), *b.* 1929, *s.* 1974, *m.*	Lord Dalmeny, *b.* 1967.
1806 I.	*Rosse* (7th), William Brendan Parsons, *b.* 1936, *s.* 1979, *m.*	Lord Oxmantown, *b.* 1969.
1801	*Rosslyn* (7th), Peter St. Clair-Erskine, *b.* 1958, *s.* 1977, *m.*	Lord Loughborough, *b.* 1986.
1457 s.	*Rothes* (21st), Ian Lionel Malcolm Leslie, *b.* 1932, *s.* 1975, *m.*	Lord Leslie, *b.* 1958.
1861	°*Russell* (5th), Conrad Sebastian Robert Russell, *b.* 1937, *s.* 1987, *m.*	Viscount Amberley, *b.* 1968.
1915	°*St. Aldwyn* (2nd), Michael John Hicks Beach, G.B.E., T.D., P.C., *b.* 1912, *s.* 1916, *m.*	Viscount Quenington, *b.* 1950.
1815	*St. Germans* (10th), Peregrine Nicholas Eliot, *b.* 1941, *s.* 1988, *m.*	Lord Eliot, *b.* 1966.
1660	*Sandwich. Disclaimed for life* 1964.	
1690	*Scarbrough* (12th), Richard Aldred Lumley (13th *Irish Visct., Lumley*, 1628), *b.* 1932, *s.* 1969, *m.*	Viscount Lumley, *b.* 1973.
1701 s.	*Seafield* (13th), Ian Derek Francis Ogilvie-Grant, *b.* 1939, *s.* 1969, *m.*	Viscount Reidhaven, *b.* 1963.
1882	*Selborne* (4th), John Roundell Palmer, K.B.E., *b.* 1940, *s.* 1971, *m.*	Viscount Wolmer, *b.* 1971.
1646 s.	*Selkirk* (10th), (George) Nigel Douglas-Hamilton, K.T., G.C.M.G., G.B.E., A.F.C., A.E.P.C., Q.C., *b.* 1906, *s.* 1940, *m.*	The Master of Selkirk, *b.* 1939.
1672	*Shaftesbury* (10th), Anthony Ashley-Cooper, *b.* 1938, *s.* 1961, *m.*	Lord Ashley, *b.* 1977.
1756 I.*	*Shannon* (9th), Richard Bentinck Boyle (8th *Brit. Bn., Carleton* 1786), *b.* 1924, *s.* 1963.	Viscount Boyle, *b.* 1960.
1442	*Shrewsbury & Waterford* (22nd) (I. 1446), Charles Henry John Benedict Crofton Chetwynd Chetwynd-Talbot (*Premier Earl of England and Ireland; Earl Talbot*, 1784), *b.* 1952, *s.* 1980, *m.*	Viscount Ingestre, *b.* 1978.
1961	*Snowdon* (1st), Antony Charles Robert Armstrong-Jones, G.C.V.O., *b.* 1930, *m.* (*See also* p. 149).	Viscount Linley, *b.* 1961 (*see also* p. 149).
1880	°*Sondes* (5th), Henry George Herbert Milles-Lade, *b.* 1940, *s.* 1970.	(None.)
1633 s.*	*Southesk* (11th), Charles Alexander Carnegie, K.C.V.O. (3rd *U.K. Baron, Balinhard*, 1869), *b.* 1893, *s.* 1941, *m.*	The Duke of Fife, *b.* 1929 (*see* pp. 146 and 157).
1765	°*Spencer* (8th), Edward John Spencer, L.V.O., *b.* 1924, *s.* 1975, *m.*	Viscount Althorp, *b.* 1964.
1703 s.*	*Stair* (13th), John Aymer Dalrymple, K.C.V.O., M.B.E (6th *U.K. Baron, Oxenfoord*, 1841), *b.* 1906, *s.* 1961, *m.*	Viscount Dalrymple, *b.* 1961.
1984	*Stockton* (2nd), Alexander Daniel Alan Macmillan, *b.* 1943, *s.* 1986, *m.*	Viscount Macmillan of Ovenden, *b.* 1974.
1821	*Stradbroke* (6th), Robert Keith Rous, *b.* 1937, *s.* 1983, *m.*	Viscount Dunwich, *b.* 1961.
1847	*Strafford* (8th), Thomas Edmund Byng, *b.* 1936, *s.* 1984, *m.*	Viscount Enfield, *b.* 1964.
1606 s.*	*Strathmore and Kinghorne* (18th), Michael Fergus Bowes Lyon (16th *Scottish Earl, Strathmore*, 1677, & 18th *Kinghorne*, 1606; 5th *U.K. Earl, Strathmore & Kinghorne*, 1937), *b.* 1957, *s.* 1987, *m.*	Lord Glamis, *b.* 1986.
1603	*Suffolk* (21st) & *Berkshire* (14th) (1626), Michael John James George Robert Howard, *b.* 1935, *s.* 1941, *m.*	Viscount Andover, *b.* 1974.

Created.	Title, Order of Succession, Name, etc.	Eldest Son or Heir.
1955	*Swinton* (2nd), David Yarburgh Cunliffe-Lister, *b.* 1937, *s.* 1972, *m.*	Hon. Nicholas J. C.-L., *b.* 1939.
1714	*Tankerville* (10th), Peter Grey Bennet, *b.* 1956, *s.* 1980.	Rev. the Hon. George A. G. B., *b.* 1925.
1822	°*Temple of Stowe* (8th), (Walter) Grenville Algernon Temple-Gore-Langton, *b.* 1924, *s.* 1988, *m.*	Hon. James G. T.-G.-L., *b.* 1955.
1815	*Verulam* (7th), John Duncan Grimston (11th *Irish Visct., Grimston,* 1719; 16th *Scott. Baron, Forrester of Corstorphine,* 1633), *b.* 1951, *s.* 1973, *m.*	Viscount Grimston, *b.* 1978.
1729	°*Waldegrave* (12th), Geoffrey Noel Waldegrave, K.G., G.C.V.O., T.D., *b.* 1905, *s.* 1936, *m.*	Viscount Chewton, *b.* 1940.
1759	*Warwick* & °*Brooke* (8th) (*Brit.* 1746), David Robin Francis Guy Greville (8th *Earl Brooke* and 8th *Earl of Warwick*), *b.* 1934, *s.* 1984.	Lord Brooke, *b.* 1957.
1633 s.*	*Wemyss* (12th) & *March* (8th) (s. 1697), Francis David Charteris, K.T. (5th *U.K. Baron, Wemyss,* 1821), *b.* 1912, *s.* 1937, *w.*	Lord Neidpath, *b.* 1948.
1621 I.	*Westmeath* (13th), William Anthony Nugent, *b.* 1928, *s.* 1971, *m.*	Hon. Sean C. W. N., *b.* 1965.
1624	*Westmorland* (15th), David Anthony Thomas Fane, K.C.V.O., *b.* 1924, *s.* 1948, *m.* (*Master of the Horse*).	Lord Burghersh, *b.* 1951.
1876	*Wharncliffe* (5th), Richard Alan Montagu Scott Wortley, *b.* 1953, *s.* 1987, *m.*	Viscount Carlton, *b.* 1980.
1801	*Wilton* (7th), Seymour William Arthur John Egerton, *b.* 1921, *s.* 1927, *m.*	Baron Ebury, *b.* 1934 (*see* p. 170).
1628	*Winchilsea* (16th) & *Nottingham* (11th) (1675), Christopher Denys Stormont Finch Hatton, *b.* 1936, *s.* 1950, *m.*	Viscount Maidstone, *b.* 1967.
1766 I.	°*Winterton* (7th), Robert Chad Turnour, *b.* 1915, *s.* 1962, *m.*	N. Cecil T., D.F.M., C.D., *b.* 1919.
1956	*Woolton* (3rd), Simon Frederick Marquis, *b.* 1958, *s.* 1969, *m.*	(None.)
1837	*Yarborough* (7th), John Edward Pelham, *b.* 1920, *s.* 1966, *m.*	Lord Worsley, *b.* 1963.

VISCOUNTS

Style, The Right Hon. The Viscount ——. (*See also* note, p. 187), *Addressed as,* My Lord. The eldest sons of Viscounts and Barons have no distinctive title; they, as well as their brothers and sisters, are styled the Hon. Robert, Hon. Mary, etc.

Created.	Title, Order of Succession, Name, etc.	Eldest Son or Heir.
1945	*Addison* (3rd), Michael Addison, *b.* 1914, *s.* 1976, *m.*	Hon. William M. W. A., *b.* 1945.
1946	*Alanbrooke* (3rd), Alan Victor Harold Brooke, *b.* 1932, *s.* 1972.	(None).
1919	*Allenby* (3rd), Lt.-Col. Michael Jaffray Hynman Allenby, *b.* 1931, *s.* 1984, *m.*	Hon. Henry J. H. A., *b.* 1968.
1911	*Allendale* (3rd), Wentworth Hubert Charles Beaumont, *b.* 1922, *s.* 1956, *m.*	Hon. Wentworth P. I. B., *b.* 1948.
1642 s.	*of Arbuthnott* (16th), John Campbell Arbuthnott, C.B.E., D.S.C., *b.* 1924, *s.* 1966, *m.*	Master of Arbuthnott, *b.* 1950.
1751 I.	*Ashbrook* (10th), Desmond Llowarch Edward Flower, K.C.V.O., M.B.E., *b.* 1905. *s.* 1936, *m.*	Hon. Michael L. W. F., *b.* 1935.
1917	*Astor* (4th), William Waldorf Astor, *b.* 1951, *s.* 1966, *m.*	Hon. William W. A., *b.* 1979.
1781 I.	*Bangor* (7th), Edward Henry Harold Ward, *b.* 1905, *s.* 1950, *m.*	Hon. William M. D. W., *b.* 1948.
1720 I.*	*Barrington* (11th), Patrick William Daines Barrington (5th *U.K. Baron Shute,* 1880), *b.* 1908, *s.* 1960.	(None.)
1925	*Bearsted* (4th), Peter Montefiore Samuel, M.C., T.D., *b.* 1911, *s.* 1986, *m.*	Hon. Nicholas A. S., *b.* 1950.
1963	*Blakenham* (2nd), Michael John Hare, *b.* 1938, *s.* 1982, *m.*	Hon. Caspar J. H., *b.* 1972.
1935	*Bledisloe* (3rd), Christopher Hiley Ludlow Bathurst, Q.C., *b.* 1934, *s.* 1979, *m.*	Hon. Rupert E. L. B., *b.* 1964.
1712	*Bolingbroke* (7th) & *St. John* (8th) (1716), Kenneth Oliver Musgrave St. John, *b.* 1927, *s.* 1974, *m.*	Hon. Henry F. St. J., *b.* 1957.
1960	*Boyd of Merton* (2nd), Simon Donald Rupert Neville Lennox-Boyd, *b.* 1939, *s.* 1983, *m.*	Hon. Benjamin A. L.-B., *b.* 1964.
1717 I.*	*Boyne* (10th), Gustavus Michael George Hamilton-Russell (4th *U.K. Baron, Brancepeth,* 1866), *b.* 1931, *s.* 1942, *m.*	Hon. Gustavus M. S. H.-R., *b.* 1965.
1929	*Brentford* (4th), Crispin William Joynson-Hicks, *b.* 1933, *s.* 1983, *m.*	Hon. Paul W. J.-H., *b.* 1971.
1929	*Bridgeman* (3rd), Robin John Orlando Bridgeman, *b.* 1930, *s.* 1982, *m.*	Hon. William O. C. B., *b.* 1968.
1868	*Bridport* (4th), Alexander Nelson Hood (7th *Duke of Brontë in Sicily,* 1799, *and* 6th *Irish Baron, Bridport* 1794), *b.* 1948, *s.* 1969, *m.*	Hon. Peregrine A. N. H., *b.* 1974.
1952	*Brookeborough* (3rd), Alan Henry Brooke, *b.* 1952, *s.* 1987, *m.*	Hon. Christopher A. B., *b.* 1954.
1933	*Buckmaster* (3rd), Martin Stanley Buckmaster, O.B.E., *b.* 1921, *s.* 1974.	Hon. Colin J. B., *b.* 1923.
1939	*Caldecote* (2nd), Robert Andrew Inskip, K.B.E., D.S.C., *b.* 1917, *s.* 1947, *m.*	Hon. Piers J. H. I., *b.* 1947.
1941	*Camrose* (2nd), (John) Seymour Berry, T.D., *b.* 1909, *s.* 1954, *m.*	Baron Hartwell, M.B.E., T.D., *b.* 1911 (*see* p. 179).
1954	*Chandos* (3rd), Thomas Orlando Lyttelton, *b.* 1953, *s.* 1980, *m.*	Hon. Oliver A. L., *b.* 1986.

Created.	Title, Order of Succession, Name, etc.	Eldest Son or Heir.
1665 I.	Charlemont (14th), John Day Caulfeild (18th *Irish Baron, Caulfeild of Charlemont*, 1620), *b.* 1934, *s.* 1985, *m.*	Hon. John D. C., *b.* 1966.
1921	Chelmsford (3rd), Frederic Jan Thesiger, *b.* 1931, *s.* 1970, *m.*	Hon. Frederic C. P. *T.*, *b.* 1962.
1717 I.	Chetwynd (10th), Adam Richard John Casson Chetwynd, *b.* 1935, *s.* 1965, *m.*	Hon. Adam D. *C.*, *b.* 1969.
1911	Chilston (4th), Alastair George Akers-Douglas, *b.* 1946, *s.* 1982, *m.*	Hon. Oliver I. *A.-D.*, *b.* 1973.
1902	Churchill (3rd), Victor George Spencer (5th *U.K. Baron Churchill*, 1815), *b.* 1934, *s.* 1973.	None to Viscountcy. To Barony, R. Harry R. *S.*, *b.* 1926.
1718	Cobham (11th), John William Leonard Lyttelton (8th *Irish Baron, Westcote*, 1776), *b.* 1943, *s.* 1977, *m.*	Hon. Christopher C. *L.*, *b.* 1947.
1902	Colville of Culross (4th), John Mark Alexander Colville, Q.C. (13th *Scott. Baron, Colville of Culross*, 1604), *b.* 1933, *s.* 1945, *m.*	Master of Colville, *b.* 1959.
1826	Combermere (5th), Michael Wellington Stapleton-Cotton, *b.* 1929, *s.* 1969, *m.*	Hon. Thomas R. W. *S.-C.*, *b.* 1969.
1917	Cowdray (3rd), Weetman John Churchill Pearson, T.D. (3rd *U.K. Baron, Cowdray*, 1910), *b.* 1910, *s.* 1933, *m.*	Hon. Michael O. W. *P.*, *b.* 1944.
1927	Craigavon (3rd), Janric Fraser Craig, *b.* 1944, *s.* 1974.	(None).
1886	Cross (3rd), Assheton Henry Cross, *b.* 1920, *s.* 1932.	(None).
1943	Daventry (3rd), Francis Humphrey Maurice FitzRoy Newdegate, *b.* 1921, *s.* 1986, *m.*	Hon. James E. *F.N.*, *b.* 1960.
1937	Davidson (2nd), John Andrew Davidson, *b.* 1928, *s.* 1970, *m.*	Hon. Malcolm W. M. *D.*, *b.* 1934.
1956	De L'Isle (1st), William Philip Sidney, V.C., K.G., G.C.M.G., G.C.V.O., P.C., (6th *Baron De L'Isle and Dudley*, 1835), *b.* 1909, *s.* to Barony 1945, *m.*	Maj. Hon. Philip J. A. *S.*, M.B.E., *b.* 1945.
1776 I.	De Vesci (7th), Thomas Eustace Vesey (8th *Irish Baron, Knapton*, 1750), *b.* 1955, *s.* 1983, *m.*	Nicholas I. *V.*, *b.* 1954.
1917	Devonport (3rd), Terence Kearley, *b.* 1944, *s.* 1973.	Chester D. H. *K.*, *b.* 1932.
1964	Dilhorne (2nd), John Mervyn Manningham-Buller, *b.* 1932, *s.* 1980, *m.*	Hon. James E.*M.-B.*, *b.* 1956.
1622 I.	Dillon (22nd), Henry Benedict Charles Dillon, *b.* 1973, *s.* 1982, *M.*	Hon. Richard A. L. *D.*, *b.* 1948.
1785 I.	Doneraile (10th), Richard Allen St. Leger, *b.* 1946, *s.* 1983, *m.*	Hon. Nathaniel W. R. St. J. *St. L.*, *b.* 1971.
1680 I.*	Downe (11th), John Christian George Dawnay (4th *U.K. Baron, Dawnay*, 1897), *b.* 1935, *s.* 1965, *m.*	Hon. Richard H. *D.*, *b.* 1967.
1959	Dunrossil (2nd), John William Morrison, C.M.G., *b.* 1926, *s.* 1961, *m.*	Hon. Andrew W. R. *M.*, *b.* 1953.
1964	Eccles (1st), David McAdam Eccles, C.H., K.C.V.O., P.C., *b.* 1904, *m.*	Hon. John D. *E.*, C.B.E., *b.* 1931.
1897	Esher (4th), Lionel Gordon Baliol Brett, C.B.E., *b.* 1913. *s.* 1963, *m.*	Hon. Christopher L. B. *B.*, *b.* 1936.
1816	Exmouth (10th), Paul Edward Pellew, *b.* 1940, *s.* 1970, *m.*	Hon. Edward F. *P.*, *b.* 1978.
1620 S.	Falkland (15th), Lucius Edward William Plantagenet Cary (*Premier Scottish Viscount on the Roll*), *b.* 1935, *s.* 1984, *m.*	Master of Falkland, *b.* 1963.
1720	Falmouth (9th), George Hugh Boscawen (26th *Eng. Baron, Le Despencer*, 1264), *b.* 1919, *s.* 1962.	Hon. Evelyn A. H. *B.*, *b.* 1955.
1918	Furness (2nd), William Anthony Furness, *b.* 1929, *s.* 1940.	(None).
1720 I.*	Gage (7th), George John St. Clere Gage, (6th *Brit. Baron, Gage*, 1790), *b.* 1932, *s.* 1982.	Hon. Henry N. *G.*, *b.* 1934.
1727 I.	Galway (12th), George Rupert Monckton-Arundell, *b.* 1922, *s.* 1980, *m.*	Hon. John P. *M.*, *b.* 1952.
1478 I.*	Gormanston (17th), Jenico Nicholas Dudley Preston (*Premier Viscount of Ireland*; 5th *U.K. Baron, Gormanston*, 1868), *b.* 1939, *s.* 1940, *w.*	Hon. Jenico F. T. *P.*, *b.* 1974.
1816 I.	Gort (8th), Colin Leopold Prendergast Vereker, *b.* 1916, *s.* 1975, *m.*	Hon. Foley R.S.P.*V.*, *b.* 1951.
1900	Goschen (4th), Giles John Harry Goschen, *b.* 1965, *s.* 1977.	(None.)
1849	Gough (5th), Shane Hugh Maryon Gough, *b.* 1941, *s.* 1951.	(None.)
1937	Greenwood (2nd), David Henry Hamar Greenwood, *b.* 1914, *s.* 1948.	Hon. Michael G. H. *G.*, *b.* 1923.
1929	Hailsham. Disclaimed for life 1963.	
1891	Hambleden (4th), William Herbert Smith, *b.* 1930, *s.* 1948, *m.*	Hon. William H. B. *S.*, *b.* 1955.
1884	Hampden (6th), Anthony David Brand, *b.* 1937, *s.* 1975, *m.*	Hon. Francis A. *B.*, *b.* 1970.
1936	Hanworth (2nd), David Bertram Pollock, *b.* 1916, *s.* 1936, *m.*	Hon. David S. G. *P.*, *b.* 1946.
1791 I.	Harberton (10th), Thomas de Vautort Pomeroy, *b.* 1910, *s.* 1980, *m.*	Hon. Robert W. *P.*, *b.* 1916.
1846	Hardinge (6th), Charles Henry Nicholas Hardinge, *b.* 1956, *s.* 1984, *m.*	Hon. Andrew H. *H.*, *b.* 1960.
1791 I.	Hawarden (8th), Robert Leslie Eustace Maude, *b.* 1926, *s.* 1958, *m.*	Hon. Robert C. W. L. *M.*, *b.* 1961.
1960	Head (2nd), Richard Antony Head, *b.* 1937, *s.* 1983, *m.*	Hon. Henry J. *H.*, *b.* 1980.
1550	Hereford (18th), Robert Milo Leicester Devereux (*Premier Viscount of England*), *b.* 1932, *s.* 1952.	Hon. Charles R. de B. *D.*, *b.* 1975.
1842	Hill (8th), Antony Rowland Clegg-Hill, *b.* 1931, *s.* 1974.	Peter D. R. C. *C.-H.*, *b.* 1945.
1796	Hood (7th), Alexander Lambert Hood (7th *Irish Baron, Hood*, 1782), *b.* 1914, *s.* 1981, *m.*	Hon. Henry L. A. *H.*, *b.* 1958.
1956	Ingleby (2nd), Martin Raymond Peake, *b.* 1926, *s.* 1966, *m.*	(None.)

Created.	*Title, Order of Succession, Name, etc.*	*Eldest Son or Heir.*
1945	*Kemsley* (2nd), (Geoffrey) Lionel Berry, *b.* 1909, *s.* 1968, *m.*	Richard G. *B.*, *b.* 1951.
1911	*Knollys* (3rd), David Francis Dudley Knollys, *b.* 1931, *s.* 1966, *m.*	Hon. Patrick N. M. *K.*, *b.* 1962.
1895	*Knutsford* (6th), Michael Holland-Hibbert, *b.* 1926, *s.* 1986, *m.*	Hon. Henry T. *H.-H.*, *b.* 1959.
1945	*Lambert* (3rd), Michael John Lambert, *b.* 1912, *s.* 1989, *m.*	(None.)
1954	*Leathers* (2nd), Frederick Alan Leathers, *b.* 1908, *s.* 1965, *m.*	Hon. Christopher G. *L.*, *b.* 1941.
1922	*Leverhulme* (3rd), Philip William Bryce Lever, K.G., T.D., *b.* 1915, *s.* 1949, *w.*	(None.)
1781 I.	*Lifford* (9th), (Edward) James Wingfield Hewitt, *b.* 1949, *s.* 1987, *m.*	Hon. James T. W. *H.*, *b.* 1979.
1921	*Long* (4th), Richard Gerard Long, *b.* 1929, *s.* 1967, *m.*	Hon. James R. *L.*, *b.* 1960.
1957	*Mackintosh of Halifax* (3rd), (John) Clive Mackintosh, *b.* 1958, *s.* 1980, *m.*	Hon. Thomas H. G. *M.*, *b.* 1985.
1955	*Malvern* (3rd), Ashley Kevin Godfrey Huggins, *b.* 1949, *s.* 1978.	Hon. M. James *H.*, *b.* 1928.
1945	*Marchwood* (3rd), David George Staveley Penny, *b.* 1936, *s.* 1979, *m.*	Hon. Peter G. W. *P.*, *b.* 1965.
1942	*Margesson* (2nd), Francis Vere Hampden Margesson, *b.* 1922, *s.* 1965, *m.*	Capt. Hon. Richard F. D. *M.*, *b.* 1960.
1660 I.*	*Massereene* (13th) & (6th) *Ferrard* (1797), John Clotworthy Talbot Foster Whyte-Melville Skeffington (6th *U.K. Baron, Oriel,* 1821), *b.* 1914, *s.* 1956, *m.*	Hon. John D. C. W.-M. F. *S.*, *b.* 1940.
1802	*Melville* (9th), Robert David Ross Dundas, *b.* 1937, *s.* 1971, *m.*	Hon. Robert H. K. *D.*, *b.* 1984.
1916	*Mersey* (4th), Richard Maurice Clive Bigham, *b.* 1934, *s.* 1979, *m.*	Hon. Edward J. H. *B.*, *b.* 1966.
1717 I.*	*Midleton* (12th), Alan Henry Brodrick (9th *Brit. Baron, Brodrick of Peper Harow,* 1796), *b.* 1949, *s.* 1988, *m.*	Hon. Ashley, R. *B.*, *b.* 1980.
1962	*Mills* (3rd), Christopher Philip Roger Mills, *b.* 1956, *s.* 1988, *m.*	(None.)
1716 I.	*Molesworth* (11th), Richard Gosset Molesworth, *b.* 1907, *s.* 1961, *w.*	Hon. Robert B. K. *M.*, *b.* 1959.
1801 I.*	*Monck* (7th), Charles Stanley Monck (4th *U.K. Baron, Monck,* 1866), *b.* 1953, *s.* 1982.	Hon. George S. *M.*, *b.* 1957.
1957	*Monckton of Brenchley* (2nd), Gilbert Walter Riversdale Monckton, C.B., O.B.E., M.C., *b.* 1915, *s.* 1965, *m.*	Hon Christopher W. *M.*, *b.* 1952.
1935	*Monsell* (2nd), Henry Bolton Graham Eyres Monsell, *b.* 1905, *s.* 1969.	(None.)
1946	*Montgomery of Alamein* (2nd), David Bernard Montgomery, C.B.E, *b.* 1928, *s.* 1976, *m.*	Hon. Henry D. *M.*, *b.* 1954.
1550 I.*	*Mountgarret* (17th), Richard Henry Piers Butler (4th *U.K. Baron, Mountgarret,* 1911), *b.* 1936, *s.* 1966, *m.*	Hon. Piers J. R. *B.*, *b.* 1961.
1964	*Muirshiel* (1st), John Scott Maclay, K.T., C.H., C.M.G., P.C., *b.* 1905, *w.*	(None.)
1952	*Norwich* (2nd), John Julius Cooper, *b.* 1929, *s.* 1954, *m.*	Hon. Jason C. D. B. *C.*, *b.* 1959.
1651 S.	*of Oxfuird* (13th), George Hubbard Makgill, *b.* 1934, *s.* 1986, *m.*	Master of Oxfuird, *b.* 1969.
1873	*Portman*, (9th), Edward Henry Berkeley Portman, *b.* 1934, *s.* 1967, *m.*	Hon. Christopher E. B. *P.*, *b.* 1958.
1743 I.*	*Powerscourt* (10th), Mervyn Niall Wingfield (4th *U.K. Baron, Powerscourt,* 1885), *b.* 1935, *s.* 1973, *m.*	Hon. Mervyn A. *W.*, *b.* 1963.
1900	*Ridley* (4th), Matthew White Ridley, T.D., *b.* 1925, *s.* 1964, *m.* (*Lord Steward*).	Hon. Matthew W. *R.*, *b.* 1958.
1960	*Rochdale* (1st), John Durival Kemp, O.B.E., T.D. (2nd *U.K. Baron, Rochdale,* 1913), *b.* 1906, *s.* to Barony 1945, *m.*	Hon. St. John D. *K.*, *b.* 1938.
1919	*Rothermere* (3rd), Vere Harold Esmond Harmsworth, *b.* 1925, *s.* 1978, *m.*	Hon. Harold J. E. V. *H.*, *b.* 1967.
1937	*Runciman of Doxford* (2nd), Walter Leslie Runciman, O.B.E., A.F.C., A.E. (3rd *U.K. Baron, Runciman,* 1933), *b.* 1900, *s.* 1949, *m.*	Hon. W. G. (Garry) *R.*, C.B.E., F.B.A., *b.* 1934.
1918	*St. Davids* (2nd), Jestyn Reginald Austen Plantagenet Philipps (19th *English Baron, Strange of Knokin* 1299, 7th *English Baron, Hungerford,* 1426 *and De Moleyns,* 1445), *b.* 1917, *s.* to Viscountcy 1938, to Baronies 1974, *m.*	Hon. Colwyn J. J. *P.*, *b.* 1939.
1801	*St. Vincent* (7th), Ronald George James Jervis, *b.* 1905, *s.* 1940, *m.*	Hon. Edward R. J. *J.*, *b.* 1951.
1937	*Samuel* (3rd), David Herbert Samuel, PH.D., *b.* 1922, *s.* 1978, *m.*	Hon. Dan J. *S.*, *b.* 1925.
1911	*Scarsdale* (3rd), Francis John Nathaniel Curzon (7th *Brit. Baron, Scarsdale,* 1761), *b.* 1924, *s.* 1977, *m.*	Hon. Peter G. N. *C.*, *b.* 1949.
1905	*Selby* (4th), Michael Guy John Gully, *b.* 1942, *s.* 1959, *m.*	Hon. Edward T. W. *G.*, *b.* 1967.
1805	*Sidmouth* (7th), John Tonge Anthony Pellew Addington, *b.* 1914, *s.* 1976, *w.*	Hon. Jeremy F. *A.*, *b.* 1947.
1940	*Simon* (2nd), John Gilbert Simon, C.M.G., *b.* 1902, *s.* 1954, *m.*	Hon. Jan D. *S.*, *b.* 1940.
1960	*Slim* (2nd), John Douglas Slim, O.B.E., *b.* 1927, *s.* 1970, *m.*	Hon. Mark W. R. *S.*, *b.* 1960.
1954	*Soulbury* (2nd), James Herwald Ramsbotham, *b.* 1915, *s.* 1971, *w.*	Hon. Sir Peter E. *R.*, G.C.M.G., G.C.V.O., *b.* 1919.
1776 I.	*Southwell* (7th), Pyers Anthony Joseph Southwell, *b.* 1930, *s.* 1960, *m.*	Hon. Richard A. P. *S.*, *b.* 1956.
1942	*Stansgate. Disclaimed for life* 1963.	

Created.	Title, Order of Succession, Name, etc.	Eldest Son or Heir.
1959	*Stuart of Findhorn* (2nd), David Randolph Moray Stuart, *b.* 1924, *s.* 1971, *m.*	Hon. James D. S., *b.* 1948.
1957	*Tenby* (3rd), William Lloyd George, *b.* 1927, *s.* 1983, *m.*	Hon. Timothy H. G. *L. G., b.* 1962.
1952	*Thurso* (2nd), Robin Macdonald Sinclair, *b.* 1922, *s.* 1970, *m.*	Hon. John A. S., *b.* 1953.
1983	*Tonypandy* (1st), (Thomas) George Thomas, P.C., *b.* 1909.	(None).
1721	*Torrington* (11th), Timothy Howard St. George Byng, *b.* 1943, *s.* 1961, *m.*	John L. *B.*, M.C., *b.* 1919.
1936	*Trenchard* (3rd), Hugh Trenchard, *b.* 1951, *s.* 1987, *m.*	Hon. Alexander T. *T.*, *b.* 1978.
1921	*Ullswater* (2nd), Nicholas James Christopher Lowther, *b.* 1942, *s.* 1949, *m.*	Hon. Benjamin J. *L.*, *b.* 1975.
1621 I.	*Valentia* (15th), Richard John Dighton Annesley, *b.* 1929, *s.* 1983, *m.*	Hon. Francis W. D. *A., b.* 1959.
1964	*Watkinson* (1st), Harold Arthur Watkinson, C.H., P.C., *b.* 1910, *m.*	(None.)
1952	*Waverley* (2nd), David Alastair Pearson Anderson, *b.* 1911, *s.* 1958, *m.*	Hon. John D. F. *A.*, *b.* 1949.
1938	*Weir* (3rd), William Kenneth James Weir, *b.* 1933, *s.* 1975, *m.*	Hon. James W. H. *W.*, *b.* 1965.
1983	*Whitelaw* (1st), William Stephen Ian Whitelaw, C.H., M.C., P.C., *b.* 1918, *m.*	(None).
1918	*Wimborne* (3rd), Ivor Fox-Strangways Guest (4th *U.K. Baron, Wimborne,* 1880), *b.* 1939, *s.* 1967, *m.*	Hon. Ivor M.V.*G.*, *b.* 1968.
1923	*Younger of Leckie* (3rd), Edward George Younger, O.B.E., T.D., *b.* 1906, *s.* 1946, *w.*	Rt. Hon. George K. H. *Y.*, T.D., M.P., *b.* 1931.

BISHOPS

Style, The Right Rev. The Lord Bishop of ——. *Addressed as,* My Lord.

The Bishops of London, Durham and Winchester always have seats in the House of Lords: the other 21 seats are filled by the remaining diocesan Bishops in order of seniority. The Bishop of Sodor and Man and the Bishop of Gibraltar are not eligible to sit in the House of Lords.

Introd. to House of Lords		Election as Diocesan Bp. confirmed	Trans. to present See
1977	*London* (130th), Graham Douglas Leonard, P.C., *b.* 1921, *cons.* 1964, *m.*	1973	1981
1984	*Durham* (92nd), David Edward Jenkins, *b.* 1925, *cons.* 1984, *m.*	1984	—
1982	*Winchester* (95th), Colin Clement Walter James, *b.* 1926, *cons.* 1973, *m.*	1977	1985
1976	*Southwark* (7th), Ronald Oliver Bowlby, *b.* 1926, *cons.* 1973, *m.*	1973	1980
1979	*Hereford* (102nd), John Richard Gordon Eastaugh, *b.* 1920, *cons.* 1974, *m.*	1974	
1979	*Chichester* (102nd), Eric Waldram Kemp, D.D., *b.* 1915, *cons.* 1974, *m.*	1974	
1980	*Liverpool* (6th), David Stuart Sheppard, *b.* 1929, *cons.* 1969, *m.*	1975	
1981	*Gloucester* (37th), John Yates, *b.* 1925, *cons.* 1972, *m.*	1975	
1984	*Ripon* (11th), David Nigel de Lorentz Young, *b.* 1931, *cons.* 1977, *m.*	1977	
1984	**Ely* (66th), Peter Knight Walker, *b.* 1919, *cons.* 1972, *m.*	1977	
1985	*Chelmsford* (7th), John Waine, *b.* 1930, *cons.* 1975, *m.*	1978	1986
1985	*Manchester* (9th), Stanley Eric Francis Booth-Clibborn, *b.* 1924, *cons.* 1979, *m.*	1979	
1985	*Leicester* (4th), Cecil Richard Rutt, C.B.E., *b.* 1925, *cons,* 1966, *m.*	1979	
1985	*Sheffield* (5th), David Ramsay Lunn, *b.* 1930, *cons.* 1980.	1980	
1985	*St. Albans* (8th), John Bernard Taylor, *b.* 1929, *cons.* 1980, *m.*	1980	
1985	*Newcastle* (10th), Andrew Alexander Kenny Graham, *b.* 1929, *cons.* 1977.	1981	
1985	**Truro* (12th), Peter Mumford, *b.* 1922, *cons.* 1974, *m.*	1981	
1986	*Salisbury* (76th), John Austin Baker, *b.* 1928, *cons.* 1982, *m.*	1982	
1987	*Worcester* (111th), Philip Harold Ernest Goodrich, *b.* 1929, *cons.* 1973, *m.*	1982	
1987	*Chester* (39th), Michael Alfred Baughen, *b.* 1930, *cons.* 1982, *m.*	1982	
1988	*Guildford* (7th), Michael Edgar Adie, *b.* 1929, *cons.* 1983, *m.*	1983	
1988	*Bradford* (7th), Robert Kerr Williamson, *b.* 1932, *cons.* 1984, *m.*	1984	
1988	*Lichfield* (97th), Keith Norman Sutton, *b.* 1934, *cons.* 1978, *m.*	1984	

Bishops awaiting seats, in order of seniority

Peterborough (36th), William John Westwood, *b.* 1925, *cons.* 1975, *m.*	1984	
Portsmouth (7th), Timothy John Bavin, *b.* 1935, *cons.* 1974.	1985	
Exeter (69th), (Geoffrey) Hewlett Thompson, *b.* 1929, *cons.* 1974, *m.*	1985	
Bristol (54th), Barry Rogerson, *b.* 1936, *cons.* 1979, *m.*	1985	
Wakefield (10th), David Michael Hope, D.Phil., *b.* 1940, *cons.* 1985.	1985	
Coventry (7th), Simon Barrington-Ward, *b.* 1930, *cons.* 1985, *m.*	1985	
Norwich (70th), Peter John Nott, *b.* 1933, *cons.* 1977, *m.*	1985	
St. Edmundsbury and Ipswich (8th), John Dennis, *b.* 1931, *cons.* 1979, *m.*	1986	
Lincoln (70th), Robert Maynard Hardy, *b.* 1936, *cons.* 1980, *m.*	1986	

	Election as Diocesan Bp. confirmed	Trans. to present See
Oxford (41st), Richard Douglas Harries, *b.* 1936, *cons.* 1987, *m.*	1987	
Birmingham (7th), Mark Santer, *b.* 1936, *cons.* 1981, *m.*	1987	
Bath and Wells (75th), George Leonard Carey, PH.D., *b.* 1935, *cons.* 1988, *m.*	1987	
Derby (5th), Peter Spencer Dawes, *b.* 1928, *cons.* 1988, *m.*	1988	
Southwell (9th), Patrick Burnet Harris, *b.* 1934, *cons.* 1988, *m.*	1988	
Rochester (105th), (Anthony) Michael (Arnold) Turnbull, *b.* 1935, *cons.* 1988, *m.*	1988	
Blackburn (7th), Alan David Chesters, *b.* 1937, *cons.* 1989, *m.*	1989	
Carlisle, confirmation of appointment awaited.		

* The Bishop of Ely retires in Dec. 1989. The Bishop of Truro retires in Nov. 1989.

BARONS

Style, The Right Hon. The Lord ——. (*See also* note, p. 187).
Addressed as, My Lord.

Created.	Title, Order of Succession, Name, etc.	Eldest Son or Heir.
1911	*Aberconway* (3rd), Charles Melville McLaren, *b.* 1913, *s.* 1953, *m.*	Hon. Henry C. *M.*, *b.* 1948.
1873	*Aberdare* (4th), Morys George Lyndhurst Bruce, K.B.E., P.C., *b.* 1919, *s.* 1957, *m.*	Hon. Alastair J. L. *B.*, *b.* 1947.
1835	*Abinger* (8th), James Richard Scarlett, *b.* 1914, *s.* 1943, *m.*	Hon. James H. *S.*, *b.* 1959.
1869	*Acton* (4th), Richard Gerald Lyon-Dalberg-Acton, *b.* 1941, *s.* 1989, *m.*	Hon. John C. F. H. *L.-D.-A.*, *b.* 1966.
1887	*Addington* (6th), Dominic Bryce Hubbard, *b.* 1963, *s.* 1982.	Hon. Michael W. L. *H.*, *b.* 1965.
1955	*Adrian* (2nd), Richard Hume Adrian, F.R.S., *b.* 1927, *s.* 1977, *m.*	(None.)
1907	*Airedale* (4th), Oliver James Vandeleur Kitson, *b.* 1915, *s.* 1958.	(None.)
1896	*Aldenham* (6th), and (4th) *Hunsdon of Hunsdon* (1923), Vicary Tyser Gibbs, *b.* 1948, *s.* 1986, *m.*	Son, *b.* 1989.
1962	*Aldington* (1st), Toby Austin Richard William Low, K.C.M.G., C.B.E., D.S.O., T.D., P.C., *b.* 1914, *m.*	Hon Charles H. S. *L.*, *b.* 1948.
1902	*Allerton* (3rd), George William Lawies Jackson, *b.* 1903, *s.* 1925, *w.*	(None.)
1945	*Altrincham. Disclaimed for life* 1963.	
1929	*Alvingham* (2nd), Maj.-Gen. Robert Guy Eardley Yerburgh, C.B.E., *b.* 1926, *s.* 1955, *m.*	Capt. Hon. Robert R. G. *Y.*, *b.* 1956.
1892	*Amherst of Hackney* (4th), William Hugh Amherst Cecil, *b.* 1940, *s.* 1980, *m.*	Hon. Hugh W. A. *C.*, *b.* 1968.
1881	*Ampthill* (4th), Geoffrey Denis Erskine Russell, C.B.E., *b.* 1921, *s.* 1973.	Hon. David W. E. *R.*, *b.* 1947.
1947	*Amwell* (2nd), Frederick Norman Montague, *b.* 1912, *s.* 1966, *m.*	Hon. Keith N. *M.*, *b.* 1943.
1863	*Annaly* (5th), Luke Robert White, *b.* 1927, *s.* 1970, *m.*	Hon. Luke R. *W.*, *b.* 1954.
1949	*Archibald. Disclaimed for life* 1975.	
1885	*Ashbourne* (4th), Edward Barry Greynville Gibson, *b.* 1933, *s.* 1983, *m.*	Hon. Edward C. d'O. *G.*, *b.* 1967.
1835	*Ashburton* (6th), Alexander Francis St. Vincent Baring, K.G., K.C.V.O., *b.* 1898, *s.* 1938, *w.*	Hon. Sir John F. H. *B.*, C.V.O., *b.* 1928.
1892	*Ashcombe* (4th), Henry Edward Cubitt, *b.* 1924, *s.* 1962, *m.*	M. Robin *C.*, *b.* 1936.
1911	*Ashton of Hyde* (3rd), Thomas John Ashton, T.D., *b.* 1926, *s.* 1983, *m.*	Hon. Thomas H. *A.*, *b.* 1958.
1800 I.	*Ashtown* (6th), Christopher Oliver Trench, *b.* 1931, *s.* 1979.	Sir Nigel C. C. *T.*, K.C.M.G., *b.* 1916.
1956	*Astor of Hever* (3rd), John Jacob Astor, *b.* 1946, *s.* 1984, *m.*	Hon. Philip D. P. *A.*, *b.* 1959.
1789 I. 1793* }	*Auckland* (9th), Ian George Eden (9th *Brit. Baron, Auckland*), *b.* 1926, *s.* 1957, *m.*	Hon. Robert I. B. *E.*, *b.* 1962.
1313	*Audley* (25th), Richard Michael Thomas Souter, *b.* 1914, *s.* 1973, *m.*	Three co-heiresses.
1900	*Avebury* (4th), Eric Reginald Lubbock, *b.* 1928, *s.* 1971, *m.*	Hon. Lyulph A. J. *L.*, *b.* 1954.
1718 I.	*Aylmer* (13th), Michael Anthony Aylmer, *b.* 1923, *s.* 1982, *m.*	Hon. A. Julian *A.*, *b.* 1951.
1929	*Baden-Powell* (3rd), Robert Crause Baden-Powell, *b.* 1936, *s.* 1962, *m.*	Hon. David M. *B.-P.*, *b.* 1940.
1780	*Bagot* (9th), Heneage Charles Bagot, *b.* 1914, *s.* 1979, *m.*	Hon. Charles H. S. *B.*, *b.* 1944.
1953	*Baillieu* (3rd), James William Latham Baillieu, *b.* 1950, *s.* 1973, *m.*	Hon. Robert L. *B.*, *b.* 1979.
1607 s.	*Balfour of Burleigh* (8th), Robert Bruce, *b.* 1927, *s.* 1967, *m.*	Hon. Victoria *B.*, *b.* 1973.
1945	*Balfour of Inchrye* (2nd), Ian Balfour, *b.* 1924, *s.* 1988, *m.*	(None.)
1924	*Banbury of Southam* (3rd), Charles William Banbury, *b.* 1953, *s.* 1981, *m.*	(None.)
1698	*Barnard* (11th), Harry John Neville Vane, T.D., *b.* 1923, *s.* 1964, *m.*	Hon. Henry F. C. *V.*, *b.* 1959.
1887	*Basing* (5th), Neil Lutley Sclater-Booth, *b.* 1939, *s.* 1983, *m.*	Hon. Stuart W. S.-*B.*, *b.* 1969.
1917	*Beaverbrook* (3rd), Maxwell William Humphrey Aitken, *b.* 1951, *s.* 1985, *m.*	Hon. Maxwell F. *A*, *b.* 1977.
1647 s.	*Belhaven and Stenton* (13th), Robert Anthony Carmichael Hamilton, *b.* 1927, *s.* 1961, *m.*	Master of Belhaven, *b.* 1953.
1848 I.	*Bellew* (7th), James Bryan Bellew, *b.* 1920, *s.* 1981, *m.*	Hon. Bryan E. *B.*, *b.* 1943.
1856	*Belper* (4th), (Alexander) Ronald George Strutt, *b.* 1912, *s.* 1956.	Hon. Richard H. *S.*, *b.* 1941.
1938	*Belstead* (2nd), John Julian Ganzoni, P.C., *b.* 1932, *s.* 1958.	(None.)
1922	*Bethell* (4th), Nicholas William Bethell, *b.* 1938, *s.* 1967.	Hon. James N. *B.*, *b.* 1967.

Created.	Title, Order of Succession, Name, etc.	Eldest Son or Heir.
1938	*Bicester* (3rd), Angus Edward Vivian Smith, *b.* 1932, *s.* 1968.	Hugh C. V. *S., b.* 1934.
1903	*Biddulph* (5th), (Anthony) Nicholas Colin Maitland Biddulph, *b.* 1959, *s.* 1988.	Hon. William I. R. *M.B., b.* 1963.
1938	*Birdwood* (3rd), Mark William Ogilvie Birdwood, *b.* 1938, *s.* 1962, *m.*	(None.)
1958	*Birkett* (2nd), Michael Birkett, *b.* 1929, *s.* 1962, *m.*	Hon. Thomas *B., b.* 1982.
1907	*Blyth* (4th), Anthony Audley Rupert Blyth, *b.* 1931, *s.* 1977, *m.*	Hon. Riley A. J. *B., b.* 1955.
1797	*Bolton* (7th), Richard William Algar Orde-Powlett, *b.* 1929, *s.* 1963, *m.*	Hon. Harry A. N. *O.-P., b.* 1954.
1452 s.	*Borthwick* (23rd), John Henry Stuart Borthwick, T.D., *b.* 1905, *claim succeeded* 1986, *w.*	Master of Borthwick, *b.* 1940.
1922	*Borwick* (4th), James Hugh Myles Borwick, M.C., *b.* 1917, *s.* 1961, *m.*	Hon. George S. *B., b.* 1922.
1761	*Boston* (10th), Timothy George Frank Boteler Irby, *b.* 1939, *s.* 1978, *m.*	Hon. George W. E. B. *I., b.* 1971.
1942	*Brabazon of Tara* (3rd), Ivon Anthony Moore-Brabazon, *b.* 1946, *s.* 1974, *m.*	Hon. Benjamin R. *M.-B., b.* 1983.
1880	*Brabourne* (7th), John Ulick Knatchbull, *b.* 1924, *s.* 1943, *m.*	Lord Romsey, *b.* 1947, *see* p. 176.
1925	*Bradbury* (2nd), John Bradbury, *b.* 1914, *s.* 1950, *m.*	Hon. John *B., b.* 1940.
1962	*Brain* (2nd), Christopher Langdon Brain, *b.* 1926, *s.* 1966, *m.*	Hon. Michael C. *B.,* D.M., *b.* 1928.
1938	*Brassey of Apethorpe* (3rd), David Henry Brassey, *b.* 1932, *s.* 1967, *m.*	Hon. Edward *B., b.* 1964.
1788	*Braybrooke* (9th), Henry Seymour Neville, *b.* 1897, *s.* 1943, *w.*	Hon. Robin H. C. *N., b.* 1932.
1957	*Bridges* (2nd), Thomas Edward Bridges, G.C.M.G., *b.* 1927, *s.* 1969, *m.*	Hon. Mark T. *B., b.* 1954.
1945	*Broadbridge* (3rd), Peter Hewett Broadbridge, *b.* 1938, *s.* 1972, *m.*	Martin H. *B., b.* 1929.
1933	*Brocket* (3rd), Charles Ronald George Nall-Cain, *b.* 1952, *s.* 1967, *m.*	Hon. Alexander C. C. *N.C., b.* 1984.
1860	*Brougham and Vaux* (5th), Michael John Brougham, *b.* 1938, *s.* 1967.	Hon. Charles W. *B., b.* 1971.
1945	*Broughshane* (2nd), Patrick Owen Alexander Davison, *b.* 1903, *s.* 1953, *m.*	Hon. W. Kensington *D.,* D.S.O., D.F.C., *b.* 1914.
1776	*Brownlow* (7th), Edward John Peregrine Cust, *b.* 1936, *s.* 1978, *m.*	Hon. Peregrine E. Q. *C., b.* 1974.
1942	*Bruntisfield* (1st), Victor Alexander George Anthony Warrender, M.C., T.D., *b.* 1899, *m.*	Col. Hon. John R. *W.,* O.B.E., M.C., T.D., *b.* 1921.
1950	*Burden* (2nd), Philip William Burden, *b.* 1916, *s.* 1970, *m.*	Hon. Andrew P. *B., b.* 1959.
1529	*Burgh* (7th), Alexander Peter Willoughby Leith, *b.* 1935, *s.* 1959, *m.*	Hon. Alexander G. D. *L., b.* 1958.
1903	*Burnham* (5th), William Edward Harry Lawson, *b.* 1920, *s.* 1963, *m.*	Hon. Hugh J. F. *L., b.* 1931.
1897	*Burton* (3rd), Michael Evan Victor Baillie, *b.* 1924, *s.* 1962, *m.*	Hon. Evan M. R. *B., b.* 1949.
1643	*Byron* (13th), Robert James Byron, *b.* 1950, *s.* 1989, *m.*	†
1937	*Cadman* (3rd), John Anthony Cadman, *b.* 1938, *s.* 1966, *m.*	Hon. Nicholas A. J. *C., b.* 1977.
1796	*Calthorpe* (10th), Peter Waldo Somerset Gough-Calthorpe, *b.* 1927, *s.* 1945, *m.*	(None.)
1945	*Calverley* (3rd), Charles Rodney Muff, *b.* 1946, *s.* 1971, *m.*	Hon. Jonathan E. *M., b.* 1975.
1383	*Camoys* (7th), (Ralph) Thomas Campion George Sherman Stonor, *b.* 1940, *s.* 1976, *m.*	Hon. R. William R. T. *S., b.* 1974.
1715 I.	*Carbery* (11th), Peter Ralfe Harrington Evans-Freke, *b.* 1920, *s.* 1970, *m.*	Hon. Michael P. *E.-F., b.* 1942.
1834 I. 1838* }	*Carew* (6th), William Francis Conolly-Carew, C.B.E. (6th *U.K. Baron, Carew,* 1838), *b.* 1905, *s.* 1927, *m.*	Hon. Patrick T. *C.-C., b.* 1938.
1916	*Carnock* (4th), David Henry Arthur Nicolson, *b.* 1920, *s.* 1982.	Nigel *N.,* M.B.E., *b.* 1917.
1796 I. 1797* }	*Carrington* (6th), Peter Alexander Rupert Carington, K.G., G.C.M.G., C.H., M.C., P.C., (6th *Brit. Baron, Carrington,* 1797), *b.* 1919, *s.* 1938, *m.*	Hon. Rupert F. J. *C., b.* 1948.
1812 I.	*Castlemaine* (8th), Roland Thomas John Handcock, M.B.E., *b.* 1943, *s.* 1973.	Terence R. *H., b.* 1902.
1936	*Catto* (2nd), Stephen Gordon Catto, *b.* 1923, *s.* 1959, *m.*	Hon. Innes G. *C., b.* 1950.
1918	*Cawley* (3rd), Frederick Lee Cawley, *b.* 1913, *s.* 1954, *m.*	Hon. John F. *C., b.* 1946.
1937	*Chatfield* (2nd), Ernle David Lewis Chatfield, *b.* 1917, *s.* 1967, *m.*	(None.)
1858	*Chesham* (5th), John Charles Compton Cavendish, P.C., *b.* 1916, *s.* 1952, *m.*	Hon. Nicholas C. *C., b.* 1941.
1945	*Chetwode* (2nd), Philip Chetwode, *b.* 1937, *s.* 1950.	Hon. Roger *C., b.* 1968.
1945	*Chorley* (2nd), Roger Richard Edward Chorley, *b.* 1930, *s.* 1978, *m.*	Hon. Nicholas R. D. *C., b.* 1966.
1858	*Churston* (4th), Richard Francis Roger Yarde-Buller, V.R.D., *b.* 1910, *s.* 1930, *m.*	Hon. John F. *Y.-B., b.* 1934.
1946	*Citrine* (2nd), Norman Arthur Citrine, *b.* 1914, *s.* 1983, *m.*	Hon. Ronald E. *C., b.* 1919.
1800 I.	*Clanmorris* (8th), Simon John Ward Bingham, *b.* 1937, *s.* 1988, *m.*	John T. *B., b.* 1923.
1672	*Clifford of Chudleigh* (14th), Thomas Hugh Clifford, *b.* 1948, *s.* 1988, *m.*	Hon. Alexander T. H. *C., b.* 1985.
1299	*Clinton* (22nd), Gerard Nevile Mark Fane Trefusis, *b.* 1934, *title called out of abeyance* 1965, *m.*	Hon. Charles P. R. F. *T., b.* 1962.
1955	*Clitheroe* (2nd), Ralph John Assheton, *b.* 1929, *s.* 1984, *m.*	Hon. Ralph C. *A., b.* 1962.
1919	*Clwyd* (3rd), (John) Anthony Roberts, *b.* 1935, *s.* 1987, *m.*	Hon. John M. *R., b.* 1971.
1948	*Clydesmuir* (2nd), Ronald John Bilsland Colville, K.T., C.B., M.B.E., T.D., *b.* 1917, *s.* 1954, *m.*	Hon. David R. *C., b.* 1949.

Created.	*Title, Order of Succession, Name, etc.*	*Eldest Son or Heir.*
1960	*Cobbold* (2nd), David Antony Fromanteel Lytton Cobbold, *b.* 1937, *s.* 1987, *m.*	Hon. Henry F. L. C., *b.* 1962.
1919	*Cochrane of Cults* (3rd), Thomas Charles Anthony Cochrane, *b.* 1922, *s.* 1968.	Hon. R. H. Vere C., *b.* 1926.
1954	*Coleraine* (2nd), (James) Martin (Bonar) Law, *b.* 1931, *s.* 1980, *m.*	Hon. James P. B. L., *b.* 1975.
1873	*Coleridge* (5th), William Duke Coleridge, *b.* 1937, *s.* 1984, *m.*	Hon. James D. C., *b.* 1967.
1946	*Colgrain* (3rd), David Colin Campbell, *b.* 1920, *s.* 1973, *m.*	Hon. Alastair C. L. C., *b.* 1951.
1917	*Colwyn* (3rd), (Ian) Anthony Hamilton-Smith, C.B.E., *b.* 1942, *s.* 1966, *m.*	Hon. Craig P. H.-S., *b.* 1968.
1956	*Colyton* (1st), Henry Lennox d'Aubigné Hopkinson, C.M.G., P.C., *b.* 1902, *m.*	Hon. Nicholas H. E. H., *b.* 1932.
1841	*Congleton* (8th), Christopher Patrick Parnell, *b.* 1930, *s.* 1967, *m.*	Hon. John P. C. P., *b.* 1959.
1927	*Cornwallis* (3rd), Fiennes Neil Wykeham Cornwallis, O.B.E., *b.* 1921, *s.* 1982, *m.*	Hon. F. W. Jeremy C., *b.* 1946.
1874	*Cottesloe* (4th), John Walgrave Halford Fremantle, G.B.E., T.D., *b.* 1900, *s.* 1956, *m.*	Hon. John T. F., *b.* 1927.
1929	*Craigmyle* (3rd), Thomas Donald Mackay Shaw, *b.* 1923, *s.* 1944, *m.*	Hon. Thomas C. S., *b.* 1960.
1899	*Cranworth* (3rd), Philip Bertram Gurdon, *b.* 1940, *s.* 1964, *m.*	Hon. Sacha W. R. G., *b.* 1970.
1959	*Crathorne* (2nd), Charles James Dugdale, *b.* 1939, *s.* 1977, *m.*	Hon. Thomas A. J. D., *b.* 1977.
1892	*Crawshaw* (4th), William Michael Clifton Brooks, *b.* 1933, *s.* 1946.	Hon. David G. B., *b.* 1934.
1940	*Croft* (2nd), Michael Henry Glendower Page Croft, *b.* 1916, *s.* 1947, *w.*	Hon. Bernard W. H. P. C., *b.* 1949.
1797 I.	*Crofton* (7th), Guy Patrick Gilbert Crofton, *b.* 1951, *s.* 1989, *m.*	Hon. Arthur B. A. C., *b.* 1957.
1375	*Cromwell* (7th), Godfrey John Bewicke-Copley, *b.* 1960, *s.* 1982.	Hon. Thomas D. B.-C., *b.* 1964.
1947	*Crook* (2nd), Douglas Edwin Crook, *b.* 1926, *s* 1989, *m.*	Hon. Robert D. E. C., *b.* 1955.
1920	*Cullen of Ashbourne* (2nd), Charles Borlase Marsham Cokayne, M.B.E., *b.* 1912, *s.* 1932, *m.*	Hon. Edmund W. M. C., *b.* 1916.
1914	*Cunliffe* (3rd), Roger Cunliffe, *b.* 1932, *s.* 1963, *m.*	Hon. Henry C., *b.* 1962.
1927	*Daresbury* (2nd), Edward Greenall, *b.* 1902, *s.* 1938, *w.*	Hon. Edward G. G., *b.* 1928.
1924	*Darling* (2nd), Robert Charles Henry Darling, *b.* 1919, *s.* 1936, *m.*	Hon. Robert J. H. D., *b.* 1944.
1946	*Darwen* (3rd), Roger Michael Davies, *b.* 1938, *s.* 1988, *m.*	Hon. Paul, D., *b.* 1962.
1923	*Daryngton* (2nd), Jocelyn Arthur Pike Pease, *b.* 1908, *s.* 1949.	(None.)
1932	*Davies* (3rd), David Davies, *b.* 1940, *s.* 1944, *m.*	Hon. David D. D., *b.* 1975.
1812 I.	*Decies* (6th), Arthur George Marcus Douglas de la Poer Beresford, *b.* 1915, *s.* 1944, *m.*	Hon. Marcus H. T. *de la P.B.*, *b.* 1948.
1299	*de Clifford* (27th), John Edward Southwell Russell, *b.* 1928, *s.* 1982, *m.*	Hon. William S. R., *b.* 1930.
1851	*De Freyne* (7th), Francis Arthur John French, *b.* 1927, *s.* 1935, *m.*	Hon. Fulke C. A. J. F., *b.* 1957.
1821	*Delamere* (5th), Hugh George Cholmondeley, *b.* 1934, *s.* 1979, *m.*	Hon. Thomas P. G. C., *b.* 1968.
1838	*de Mauley* (6th), Gerald John Ponsonby, *b.* 1921, *s.* 1962, *m.*	Col. Hon. Thomas M. P., T.D., *b.* 1930.
1937	*Denham* (2nd), Bertram Stanley Mitford Bowyer, P.C., *b.* 1927, *s.* 1948, *m.*	Hon. Richard G. G. B., *b.* 1959.
1834	*Denman* (5th), Charles Spencer Denman, C.B.E., M.C., T.D., *b.* 1916, *s.* 1971, *w.*	Hon. Richard T. S. D., *b.* 1946.
1885	*Deramore* (6th), Richard Arthur de Yarburgh-Bateson, *b.* 1911, *s.* 1964, *m.*	(None.)
1887	*De Ramsey* (3rd), Ailwyn Edward Fellowes, K.B.E., T.D., *b.* 1910, *s.* 1925, *w.*	Hon. John A. F., *b.* 1942.
1264	*de Ros* (28th), Peter Trevor Maxwell, *b.* 1958, *s.* 1983, *m. (Premier Baron of England).*	Hon. Diana E. M., *b.* 1957.
1881	*Derwent* (5th), Robin Evelyn Leo Vanden-Bempde-Johnstone, L.V.O., *b.* 1930, *s.* 1986, *m.*	Hon. Francis P. H. V.-B.-J., *b.* 1965.
1831	*De Saumarez* (6th), James Victor Broke Saumarez, *b.* 1924, *s.* 1969, *m.*	Hon. Eric D. S., *b.* 1956.
1910	*de Villiers* (3rd), Arthur Percy de Villiers, *b.* 1911, *s.* 1934.	Hon. Alexander C. *de V.*, *b.* 1940.
1930	*Dickinson* (2nd), Richard Clavering Hyett Dickinson, *b.* 1926, *s.* 1943, *m.*	Hon. Martin H. D., *b.* 1961.
1620 I. 1765* }	*Digby* (12th), Edward Henry Kenelm Digby, (6th *Brit. Baron, Digby*), *b.* 1924, *s.* 1964, *m.*	Hon. Henry N. K. D., *b.* 1954.
1615	*Dormer* (16th), Joseph Spencer Philip Dormer, *b.* 1914, *s.* 1975.	Geoffrey H. D., *b.* 1920.
1943	*Dowding* (2nd), Derek Hugh Tremenheere Dowding, *b.* 1919, *s.* 1970, *m.*	Hon. Piers H. T. D., *b.* 1948.
1800 I.	*Dufferin and Clandeboye* (10th), Francis George Blackwood, *b.* 1916, *s.* 1988, *m.*	Hon. John F. B., *b.* 1944.
1929	*Dulverton* (2nd), (Frederick) Anthony Hamilton Wills, C.B.E., T.D., *b.* 1915, *s.* 1956, *m.*	Hon. G. Michael H. W., *b.* 1944.
1800 I.	*Dunalley* (6th), Henry Desmond Graham Prittie, *b.* 1912, *s.* 1948, *m.*	Hon. Henry F. C. P., *b.* 1948.
1324 I.	*Dunboyne* (28th), Patrick Theobald Tower Butler, V.R.D., *b.* 1917, *s.* 1945, *m.*	Hon. John F. B., *b.* 1951.
1802	*Dunleath* (4th), Charles Edward Henry John Mulholland, T.D., *b.* 1933, *s.* 1956, *m.*	Sir Michael H. M., Bt., *b.* 1915.

Created.	*Title, Order of Succession, Name, etc.*	*Eldest Son or Heir.*
1439 I.	*Dunsany* (19th), Randal Arthur Henry Plunkett (20th *Irish, Baron, Killeen,* 1449), *b.* 1906, *s.* 1957, *m.*	Hon. Edward J. C. P., *b.* 1939.
1780	*Dynevor* (9th), Richard Charles Uryan Rhys, *b.* 1935, *s.* 1962.	Hon. Hugo G. U. R., *b.* 1966.
1928	*Ebbisham* (2nd), Rowland Roberts Blades, T.D., *b.* 1912, *s.* 1953, *m.*	(None.)
1857	*Ebury* (6th), Francis Egerton Grosvenor, *b.* 1934, *s.* 1957, *m.*	Hon. Julian F. M. G., *b.* 1959.
1963	*Egremont* (2nd), *& Leconfield* (7th) (1859), John Max Henry Scawen Wyndham, *b.* 1948, *s.* 1972, *m.*	Hon. George R. V. W., *b.* 1983.
1643	*Elibank* (14th), Alan D'Ardis Erskine-Murray, *b.* 1923, *s.* 1973, *m.*	Master of Elibank, *b.* 1964.
1802	*Ellenborough* (8th), Richard Edward Cecil Law, *b.* 1926, *s.* 1945, *w.*	Maj. Hon. Rupert E. H. L., *b.* 1955.
1509 s.*	*Elphinstone* (18th), James Alexander Elphinstone (4th *U.K. Baron Elphinstone,* 1885), *b.* 1953, *s.* 1975, *m.*	Master of Elphinstone, *b.* 1980.
1934	*Elton* (2nd), Rodney Elton, T.D., *b.* 1930, *s.* 1973, *m.*	Hon. Edward P. E., *b.* 1966.
1964	*Erroll of Hale* (1st), Frederick James Erroll, T.D., P.C., *b.* 1914, *m.*	(None.)
1964	*Erskine of Rerrick* (2nd), Iain Maxwell Erskine, *b.* 1926, *s.* 1980, *m.*	(None.)
1627 s.	*Fairfax of Cameron* (14th), Nicholas John Albert Fairfax, *b.* 1956, *s.* 1964, *m.*	Hon. Edward N. T. F., *b.* 1984.
1961	*Fairhaven* (3rd), Ailwyn Henry George Broughton, *b.* 1936, *s.* 1973, *m.*	Hon. James H. A. B., *b.* 1963.
1916	*Faringdon* (3rd), Charles Michael Henderson, *b.* 1937, *s.* 1977, *m.*	Hon. James H. H., *b.* 1961.
1756 I.	*Farnham* (12th), Barry Owen Somerset Maxwell, *b.* 1931, *s.* 1957, *m.*	Hon. Simon K. M., *b.* 1933.
1856 I.	*Fermoy* (6th), Patrick Maurice Burke Roche, *b.* 1967, *s.* 1984.	Hon. E. Hugh B. R., *b.* 1972.
1826	*Feversham* (6th), Charles Antony Peter Duncombe, *b.* 1945, *s.* 1963, *m.*	Hon. Jasper O. S. D., *b.* 1968.
1798 I.	*ffrench* (8th), Robuck John Peter Charles Mario ffrench, *b.* 1956, *s.* 1986.	Hon. John C. M. J. F. *ff.*, *b.* 1928.
1909	*Fisher* (3rd), John Vavasseur Fisher, D.S.C., *b.* 1921, *s.* 1955, *m.*	Hon. Patrick V. F., *b.* 1953.
1295	*Fitzwalter* (21st), (Fitzwalter) Brook Plumptre, *b.* 1914, *called out of abeyance,* 1953, *m.*	Hon. Julian B. P., *b.* 1952.
1776	*Foley* (8th), Adrian Gerald Foley, *b.* 1923, *s.* 1927, *m.*	Hon. Thomas H. F., *b.* 1961.
1445 s.	*Forbes* (22nd), Nigel Ivan Forbes, K.B.E. (*Premier Baron of Scotland*), *b.* 1918, *s.* 1953, *m.*	Master of Forbes, *b.* 1946.
1821	*Forester* (8th), (George Cecil) Brooke Weld-Forester, *b.* 1938, *s.* 1977, *m.*	Hon. Charles R. G. W.-F., *b.* 1975.
1922	*Forres* (4th), Alastair Stephen Grant Williamson, *b.* 1946, *s.* 1978, *m.*	Hon. George A. M. W., *b.* 1972.
1917	*Forteviot* (3rd), Henry Evelyn Alexander Dewar, M.B.E., *b.* 1906, *s.* 1947, *w.*	Hon. John J. E. D., *b.* 1938.
1951	*Freyberg* (2nd), Paul Richard Freyberg, O.B.E., M.C., *b.* 1923, *s.* 1963, *m.*	Hon. Valerian B. F., *b.* 1970.
1917	*Gainford* (3rd), Joseph Edward Pease, *b.* 1921, *s.* 1971, *m.*	Hon. George P., *b.* 1926.
1818 I.	*Garvagh* (5th), (Alexander Leopold Ivor) George Canning, *b.* 1920, *s.* 1956, *m.*	Hon. Spencer G. S. de R. C., *b.* 1953.
1942	*Geddes* (3rd), Euan Michael Ross Geddes, *b.* 1937, *s.* 1975, *m.*	Hon. James G. N. G., *b.* 1969.
1876	*Gerard* (4th), Robert William Frederick Alwyn Gerard, *b.* 1918, *s.* 1953.	Anthony R. H. G., *b.* 1949.
1824	*Gifford* (6th), Anthony Maurice Gifford, Q.C., *b.* 1940, *s.* 1961, *m.*	Hon. Thomas A. G., *b.* 1967.
1917	*Gisborough* (3rd), Thomas Richard John Long Chaloner, *b.* 1927, *s.* 1951, *m.*	Hon. Thomas P. L. C., *b.* 1961.
1960	*Gladwyn* (1st), (Hubert Miles) Gladwyn Jebb, G.C.M.G., G.C.V.O., C.B., *b.* 1900, *m.*	Hon. Miles A. G. J., *b.* 1930.
1899	*Glanusk* (4th), David Russell Bailey, *b.* 1917, *s.* 1948, *m.*	Hon. Christopher R. B., *b.* 1942.
1918	*Glenarthur* (4th), Simon Mark Arthur, *b.* 1944, *s.* 1976, *m.*	Hon. Edward A. A., *b.* 1973.
1911	*Glenconner* (3rd), Colin Christopher Paget Tennant, *b.* 1926, *s.* 1983, *m.*	Hon. Charles E. P. T., *b.* 1957.
1964	*Glendevon* (1st), John Adrian Hope, P.C., *b.* 1912, *m.*	Hon. Julian J. S. H., *b.* 1950.
1922	*Glendyne* (3rd), Robert Nivison, *b.* 1926, *s.* 1967, *m.*	Hon. John N., *b.* 1960.
1939	*Glentoran* (2nd), Daniel Stewart Thomas Bingham Dixon, K.B.E., P.C. (N.I.), *b.* 1912, *s.* 1950, *w.*	Hon. Thomas R. V. D., M.B.E., *b.* 1935.
1909	*Gorell* (4th), Timothy John Radcliffe Barnes, *b.* 1927, *s.* 1963, *m.*	Hon. Ronald A. H. B., *b.* 1931.
1953	*Grantchester* (2nd), Kenneth Bent Suenson-Taylor, C.B.E., Q.C., *b.* 1921, *s.* 1976, *m.*	Hon. Christopher J. S.-T., *b.* 1951.
1782	*Grantley* (7th), John Richard Brinsley Norton, M.C., *b.* 1923, *s.* 1954, *m.*	Hon. Richard W. B. N., *b.* 1956.
1794 I.	*Graves* (8th), Peter George Wellesley Graves, *b.* 1911, *s.* 1963, *m.*	Evelyn P. G., *b.* 1926.
1445 s.	*Gray* (22nd), Angus Diarmid Ian Campbell-Gray, *b.* 1931, *s.* 1946, *w.*	Master of Gray, *b.* 1964.
1950	*Greenhill* (2nd), Stanley Ernest Greenhill, M.D., *b.* 1917, *s.* 1967, *m.*	Hon. Malcolm G., *b.* 1924.
1927	*Greenway* (4th), Ambrose Charles Drexel Greenway, *b.* 1941, *s.* 1975, *m.*	Hon. Mervyn S. K. G., *b.* 1942.
1902	*Grenfell* (3rd), Julian Pascoe Francis St. Leger Grenfell, *b.* 1935, *s.* 1976, *m.*	Francis P. J. G., *b.* 1938.
1944	*Gretton* (4th), John Lysander Gretton, *b.* 1975, *s.* 1989, M.	(None.)
1955	*Gridley* (2nd), Arnold Hudson Gridley, *b.* 1906, *s.* 1965, *m.*	Hon. Richard D. A. G., *b.* 1956.
1964	*Grimston of Westbury* (2nd), Robert Walter Sigismund Grimston, *b.* 1925, *s.* 1979, *m.*	Hon. Robert J. S. G., *b.* 1951.
1886	*Grimthorpe* (4th), Christopher John Beckett, O.B.E., *b.* 1915, *s.* 1963, *m.*	Hon. Edward J. B., *b.* 1954.

Created.	Title, Order of Succession, Name, etc.	Eldest Son or Heir.
1945	*Hacking* (3rd), Douglas David Hacking, *b.* 1938, *s.* 1971, *m.*	Hon. Douglas F. *H.*, *b.* 1968.
1950	*Haden-Guest* (4th), Peter Haden Haden-Guest, *b.* 1913, *s.* 1987, *m.*	Hon. Christopher *H.-G.*, *b.* 1948.
1886	*Hamilton of Dalzell* (3rd), John d'Henin Hamilton, G.C.V.O., M.C., *b.* 1911, *s.* 1952, *m.*	Hon. James L. *H.*, *b.* 1938.
1874	*Hampton* (6th), Richard Humphrey Russell Pakington, *b.* 1925, *s.* 1974, *m.*	Hon. John H. A. *P.*, *b.* 1964.
1939	*Hankey* (2nd), Robert Maurice Alers Hankey, K.C.M.G., K.C.V.O., *b.* 1905, *s.* 1963, *m.*	Hon. Donald R. A. *H.*, *b.* 1938.
1958	*Harding of Petherton* (2nd), John Charles Harding, *b.* 1928, *s.* 1989, *m.*	Hon. William A. J. *H.*, *b.* 1969.
1910	*Hardinge of Penshurst* (3rd), George Edward Charles Hardinge, *b.* 1921, *s.* 1960, *m.*	Hon. Julian A. *H.*, *b.* 1945.
1876	*Harlech* (6th), Francis David Ormsby-Gore, *b.* 1954, *s.* 1985, *m.*	Hon. Jasset D. C. *O.-G.*, *b.* 1986.
1939	*Harmsworth* (2nd), Cecil Desmond Bernard Harmsworth, *b.* 1903, *s.* 1948, *m.*	Hon. Thomas H. R. *H.*, *b.* 1939.
1815	*Harris* (6th), George Robert John Harris, *b.* 1920, *s.* 1984.	Derek M. *H.*, *b.* 1916.
1954	*Harvey of Tasburgh* (2nd), Peter Charles Oliver Harvey, *b.* 1921, *s.* 1968, *m.*	Hon. John W. *H.*, *b.* 1923.
1295	*Hastings* (22nd), Edward Delaval Henry Astley, *b.* 1912, *s.* 1956, *m.*	Hon. Delaval T. H. *A.*, *b.* 1960.
1835	*Hatherton* (8th), Edward Charles Littleton, *b.* 1950, *s.* 1985, *m.*	Hon. Thomas E. *L.*, *b.* 1977.
1776	*Hawke* (10th), (Julian Stanhope) Theodore Hawke, *b.* 1904, *s.* 1985, *m.*	Hon. Edward G. *H.*, *b.* 1950.
1927	*Hayter* (3rd), George Charles Hayter Chubb, K.C.V.O., C.B.E., *b.* 1911, *s.* 1967, *m.*	Hon. G. William M. *C.*, *b.* 1943.
1945	*Hazlerigg* (2nd), Arthur Grey Hazlerigg, M.C., T.D., *b.* 1910, *s.* 1949, *w.*	Hon. Arthur G. *H.*, *b.* 1951.
1797 I.	*Headley* (7th), Charles Rowland Allanson-Winn, *b.* 1902, *s.* 1969, *m.*	Hon. John R. *A.-W.*, *b.* 1934.
1943	*Hemingford* (3rd), (Dennis) Nicholas Herbert, *b.* 1934, *s.* 1982, *m.*	Hon. Christopher D. C. *H.*, *b.* 1973.
1906	*Hemphill* (5th), Peter Patrick Fitzroy Martyn Martyn-Hemphill, *b.* 1928, *s.* 1957, *m.*	Hon. Charles A. M. *M.-H.*, *b.* 1954.
1799 I.*	*Henley* (8th), Oliver Michael Robert Eden (6th *U.K. Baron, Northington*, 1885), *b.* 1953, *s.* 1977, *m.*	Hon. John W. O. *E.*, *b.* 1988.
1800 I.*	*Henniker* (8th), John Patrick Edward Chandos Henniker-Major, K.C.M.G., C.V.O., M.C. (4th *U.K. Baron, Hartismere*, 1866), *b.* 1916, *s.* 1980, *m.*	Hon. Mark I. P. C. *H.-M.*, *b.* 1947.
1886	*Herschell* (3rd), Rognvald Richard Farrer Herschell, *b.* 1923, *s.* 1929, *m.*	(None.)
1935	*Hesketh* (3rd), Thomas Alexander Fermor-Hesketh, *b.* 1950, *s.* 1955, *m.*	Hon. Robert *F.-H.*, *b.* 1951.
1828	*Heytesbury* (6th), Francis William Holmes à Court, *b.* 1931, *s.* 1971, *m.*	Hon. James W. H. *à C.*, *b.* 1967.
1886	*Hindlip* (5th), Henry Richard Allsopp, *b.* 1912, *s.* 1966, *m.*	Hon. Charles H. *A.*, *b.* 1940.
1950	*Hives* (2nd), John Warwick Hives, C.B.E., *b.* 1913, *s.* 1965, *m.*	Matthew P. *H.*, *b.* 1971.
1912	*Hollenden* (3rd), Gordon Hope Hope-Morley, *b.* 1914, *s.* 1977, *m.*	Hon. Ian H. H.-*M.*, *b.* 1946.
1897	*HolmPatrick* (3rd), James Hans Hamilton, *b.* 1928, *s.* 1942, *m.*	Hon. Hans J. D. *H.*, *b.* 1955.
1933	*Horder* (2nd), Thomas Mervyn Horder, *b.* 1910, *s.* 1955.	(None.)
1797 I.	*Hotham* (8th), Henry Durand Hotham, *b.* 1940, *s.* 1967, *m.*	Hon. William B. *H.*, *b.* 1972.
1881	*Hothfield* (5th), George William Anthony Tufton, T.D., *b.* 1904, *s.* 1986, *w.*	Hon. Anthony C. S. *T.*, *b.* 1939.
1597	*Howard de Walden* (9th), John Osmael Scott-Ellis, T.D. (5th *U.K. Baron, Seaford*, 1826), *b.* 1912, *s.* 1946, *m.*	To Barony of Howard de Walden, four co-heiresses. To Barony of Seaford, Colin H. F. *Ellis*, *b.* 1946.
1930	*Howard of Penrith* (2nd), Francis Philip Howard, *b.* 1905, *s.* 1939, *m.*	Hon. Philip E. *H.*, *b.* 1945.
1960	*Howick of Glendale* (2nd), Charles Evelyn Baring, *b.* 1937, *s.* 1973, *m.*	Hon. David E. C. *B.*, *b.* 1975.
1796 I.	*Huntingfield* (6th), Gerard Charles Arcedeckne Vanneck, *b.* 1915, *s.* 1969, *m.*	Hon. Joshua C. *V.*, *b.* 1954.
1866	*Hylton* (5th), Raymond Hervey Jolliffe, *b.* 1932, *s.* 1967, *m.*	Hon. William H. M. *J.*, *b.* 1967.
1933	*Iliffe* (2nd), Edward Langton Iliffe, *b.* 1908, *s.* 1960, *m.*	Robert P. R. *I.*, *b.* 1944.
1543 I.	*Inchiquin* (18th), Conor Myles John O'Brien, *b.* 1943, *s.* 1982.	Murrough R. *O'B.*, *b.* 1910.
1962	*Inchyra* (1st), Frederick Robert Hoyer Millar, G.C.M.G., C.V.O., *b.* 1900, *m.*	Hon. Robert C. R. H. *M.*, *b.* 1935.
1964	*Inglewood* (2nd), (William) Richard Fletcher-Vane, *b.* 1951, *s.* 1989, *m.*	Hon. Christopher J. *F.-V.*, *b.* 1953.
1919	*Inverforth* (4th), Andrew Peter Weir, *b.* 1966, *s.* 1982.	Hon. John V. *W.*, *b.* 1935.
1941	*Ironside* (2nd), Edmund Oslac Ironside, *b.* 1924, *s.* 1959, *m.*	Hon. Charles E. G. *I.*, *b.* 1956.
1952	*Jeffreys* (3rd), Christopher Henry Mark Jeffreys, *b.* 1957, *s.* 1986, *m.*	Hon. Alexander C. D. *J.*, *b.* 1959.
1924	*Jessel* (2nd), Edward Herbert Jessel, C.B.E., *b.* 1904, *s.* 1950, *m.*	(None.)
1906	*Joicey* (4th), Michael Edward Joicey, *b.* 1925, *s.* 1966, *m.*	Hon. James M. *J.*, *b.* 1953.
1937	*Kenilworth* (4th), (John) Randle Siddeley, *b.* 1954, *s.* 1981, *m.*	(None).
1935	*Kennet* (2nd), Wayland Hilton Young, *b.* 1923, *s.* 1960, *m.*	Hon. William A. T. *Y.*, *b.* 1957.

Created.	Title, Order of Succession, Name, etc.	Eldest Son or Heir.
1776 I. ⎤ 1886* ⎦	*Kensington* (8th), Hugh Ivor Edwardes (5th *U.K. Baron, Kensington*), *b.* 1933, *s.* 1981, *m.*	Hon. William O. A. *E.*, *b.* 1964.
1951	*Kenswood* (2nd), John Michael Howard Whitfield, *b.* 1930, *s.* 1963, *m.*	Hon. Michael C. *W.*, *b.* 1955.
1788	*Kenyon* (5th), Lloyd Tyrell-Kenyon, C.B.E., *b.* 1917, *s.* 1927, *m.*	Hon. Lloyd *T.-K.*, *b.* 1947.
1947	*Kershaw* (4th), Edward John Kershaw, *b.* 1936, *s.* 1962, *m.*	Hon. John C. E. *K.*, *b.* 1971.
1943	*Keyes* (2nd), Roger George Bowlby Keyes, *b.* 1919, *s.* 1945, *m.*	Hon. Charles W. P. *K.*, *b.* 1951.
1909	*Kilbracken* (3rd), John Raymond Godley, D.S.C., *b.* 1920, *s.* 1950, *m.*	Hon. Christopher J. *G.*, *b.* 1945.
1900	*Killanin* (3rd), Michael Morris, M.B.E., T.D., *b.* 1914, *s.* 1927, *m.*	Hon. G. Redmond F. *M.*, *b.* 1947.
1943	*Killearn* (2nd), Graham Curtis Lampson, *b.* 1919, *s.* 1964, *m.*	Hon. Victor M. G. A. *L.*, *b.* 1941.
1789 I.	*Kilmaine* (7th), John David Henry Browne, *b.* 1948, *s.* 1978, *m.*	Hon. John F. S. *B.*, *b.* 1983.
1831	*Kilmarnock* (7th), Alastair Ivor Gilbert Boyd, *b.* 1927, *s.* 1975, *m.*	Hon. Robin J. *B.*, *b.* 1941.
1941	*Kindersley* (3rd), Robert Hugh Molesworth Kindersley, *b.* 1929, *s.* 1976.	Hon. Rupert J. M. *K.*, *b.* 1955.
1223 I.	*Kingsale* (35th), John de Courcy (*Premier Baron of Ireland*), *b.* 1941. *s.* 1969.	Nevinson R. *de C.*, *b.* 1920.
1682 S. ⎤ 1860* ⎦	*Kinnaird* (13th), Graham Charles Kinnaird (5th *U.K. Baron, Kinnaird*), *b.* 1912, *s.* 1972, *m.*	(None.)
1902	*Kinross* (5th), Christopher Patrick Balfour, *b.* 1949, *s.* 1985, *m.*	Hon. Alan I. *B.*, *b.* 1978.
1951	*Kirkwood* (3rd), David Harvie Kirkwood, PH.D., *b.* 1931, *s.* 1970, *m.*	Hon. James S. *K.*, *b.* 1937.
1800 I	*Langford* (9th), Geoffrey Alexander Rowley-Conwy, O.B.E., *b.* 1912, *s.* 1953, *m.*	Hon. Owain G. *R.-C.*, *b.* 1958.
1942	*Latham* (2nd), Dominic Charles Latham, *b.* 1954, *s.* 1970.	Anthony M. *L.*, *b.* 1954.
1431	*Latymer* (8th), Hugo Nevill Money-Coutts, *b.* 1926, *s.* 1987, *m.*	Hon. Crispin J. A. N. *M.-C.*, *b.* 1955.
1869	*Lawrence* (5th), David John Downer Lawrence, *b.* 1937, *s.* 1968.	(None.)
1947	*Layton* (3rd), Geoffrey Michael Layton, *b.* 1947, *s.* 1989.	Hon. David *L.*, M.B.E., *b.* 1914.
1839	*Leigh* (5th), John Piers Leigh, *b.* 1935, *s.* 1979, *m.*	Hon. Christopher D. P. *L.*, *b.* 1960.
1962	*Leighton of St. Mellons* (2nd), (John) Leighton Seager, *b.* 1922, *s.* 1963, *m.*	Hon. Robert W. H. L. *S.*, *b.* 1955.
1797	*Lilford* (7th), George Vernon Powys, *b.* 1931, *s.* 1949, *m.*	Hon. Mark V. *P.*, *b.*, 1975.
1945	*Lindsay of Birker* (2nd), Michael Francis Morris Lindsay, *b.* 1909, *s.* 1952, *m.*	Hon. James F. *L.*, *b.* 1945.
1758 I.	*Lisle* (7th), John Nicholas Horace Lysaght, *b.* 1903, *s.* 1919, *m.*	Patrick J. *L.*, *b.* 1931.
1895	*Loch* (4th), Spencer Douglas Loch, M.C., *b.* 1920, *s.* 1982, *m.*	(None.)
1850	*Londesborough* (9th), Richard John Denison, *b.* 1959, *s.* 1968, *m.*	(None.)
1541 I.	*Louth* (16th), Otway Michael James Oliver Plunkett, *b.* 1929, *s.* 1950, *m.*	Hon. Jonathan O. *P.*, *b.* 1952.
1458 S. ⎤ 1837* ⎦	*Lovat* (15th), Simon Christopher Joseph Fraser, D.S.O., M.C., T.D. (4th *U.K. Baron, Lovat*), *b.* 1911, *s.* 1933, *m.*	Master of Lovat, *b.* 1939.
1946	*Lucas of Chilworth* (2nd), Michael William George Lucas, *b.* 1926, *s.* 1967, *m.*	Hon. Simon W. *L.*, *b.* 1957.
1929	*Luke* (2nd), Ian St. John Lawson-Johnston, K.C.V.O., T.D., *b.* 1905, *s.* 1943, *m.*	Hon. Arthur C. St. J. *L.-J.*, *b.* 1933.
1839	*Lurgan* (5th), John Desmond Cavendish Brownlow, O.B.E., *b.* 1911, *s.* 1984.	(None.)
1914	*Lyell* (3rd), Charles Lyell, *b.* 1939, *s.* 1943.	(None.)
1859	*Lyveden* (6th), Ronald Cecil Vernon, *b.* 1915, *s.* 1973, *m.*	Hon. Jack L. *V.*, *b.* 1938.
1959	*MacAndrew* (3rd), Christopher Anthony Colin MacAndrew, *b.* 1945, *s.* 1989, *m.*	Son, *b.* 1983.
1776 I.	*Macdonald* (8th), Godfrey James Macdonald of Macdonald, *b.* 1947, *s.* 1970, *m.*	Hon. Godfrey E. H. T. *M.*, *b.* 1982.
1949	*Macdonald of Gwaenysgor* (2nd), Gordon Ramsay Macdonald, *b.* 1915, *s.* 1966, *m.*	Hon. Kenneth L. *M.*, *b.* 1921.
1937	*McGowan* (3rd), Harry Duncan Cory McGowan, *b.* 1938, *s.* 1966, *m.*	Hon. Harry J. C. *M.*, *b.* 1971.
1922	*Maclay* (3rd), Joseph Paton Maclay, *b.* 1942, *s.* 1969, *m.*	Hon. Joseph P. *M.*, *b.* 1977.
1955	*McNair* (3rd), Duncan James McNair, *b.* 1947, *s.* 1989.	Hon. William S. A. *M.*, *b.* 1958.
1951	*Macpherson of Drumochter* (2nd), (James) Gordon Macpherson, *b.* 1924, *s.* 1965, *m.*	Hon. James A. *M.*, *b.* 1979.
1937	*Mancroft* (3rd), Benjamin Lloyd Stormont Mancroft, *b.* 1957, *s.* 1987.	(None.)
1807	*Manners* (5th), John Robert Cecil Manners, *b.* 1923, *s.* 1972, *m.*	Hon. John H. R. *M.*, *b.* 1956.
1922	*Manton* (3rd), Joseph Rupert Eric Robert Watson, *b.* 1924, *s.* 1968, *m.*	Capt. Hon. Miles R. M. *W.*, *b.* 1958.
1908	*Marchamley* (3rd), John William Tattersall Whiteley, *b.* 1922, *s.* 1949, *m.*	Hon. William F. *W.*, *b.* 1968.
1964	*Margadale* (1st), John Granville Morrison, T.D., *b.* 1906, *w.*	Hon. James I. *M.*, T.D., *b.* 1930.
1961	*Marks of Broughton* (2nd), Michael Marks, *b.* 1920, *s.* 1964.	Hon. Simon R. *M.*, *b.* 1950.
1930	*Marley* (2nd), Godfrey Pelham Leigh Aman, *b.* 1913, *s.* 1952, *m.*	(None.)
1964	*Martonmere* (2nd), John Stephen Robinson, *b.* 1963, *s.* 1989.	David A. *R.*, *b.* 1965.

Created.	*Title, Order of Succession, Name, etc.*	*Eldest Son or Heir.*

1776 I. *Massy* (9th), Hugh Hamon John Somerset Massy, *b.* 1921, *s.* 1958, *m.*
    Hon. David H. S. *M.*, *b.* 1947.

1935 *May* (3rd), Michael St. John May, *b.* 1931, *s.* 1950, *m.*
    Hon. Jasper B. St. J. *M.*, *b.* 1965.

1928 *Melchett* (4th), Peter Robert Henry Mond, *b.* 1948, *s.* 1973.
    (None.)

1925 *Merrivale* (3rd), Jack Henry Edmond Duke, *b.* 1917, *s.* 1951, *m.*
    Hon. Derek J. P. *D.*, *b.* 1948.

1911 *Merthyr. Disclaimed for life* 1977.

1919 *Meston* (3rd), James Meston, *b.* 1950, *s.* 1984, *m.*
    Hon. Thomas J. D. *M.*, *b.* 1977.

1838 *Methuen* (6th), Anthony John Methuen, *b.* 1925, *s.* 1975.
    Hon. Robert A. H. *M.*, *b.* 1931.

1711 *Middleton* (12th), (Digby) Michael Godfrey John Willoughby, M.C., *b.* 1921, *s.* 1970, *m.*
    Hon. Michael C. J. *W.*, *b.* 1948.

1939 *Milford* (2nd), Wogan Philipps, *b.* 1902, *s.* 1962, *m.*
    Hon. Hugo J. L. *P.*, *b.* 1929.

1933 *Milne* (2nd), George Douglass Milne, T.D., *b.* 1909, *s.* 1948, *m.*
    Hon. George A. *M.*, *b.* 1941.

1951 *Milner of Leeds* (2nd), Arthur James Michael Milner, A.E., *b.* 1923, *s.* 1967, *m.*
    Hon. Richard J. *M.*, *b.* 1959.

1947 *Milverton* (2nd), Rev. Fraser Arthur Richard Richards, *b.* 1930, *s.* 1978, *m.*
    Hon. Michael H. *R.*, *b.* 1936.

1873 *Moncreiff* (5th), Harry Robert Wellwood Moncreiff, *b.* 1915, *s.* 1942, *w.*
    Hon. Rhoderick H. W. *M.*, *b.* 1954.

1884 *Monk Bretton* (3rd), John Charles Dodson, *b.* 1924, *s.* 1933, *m.*
    Hon. Christopher M. *D.*, *b.* 1958.

1885 *Monkswell* (5th), Gerard Collier, *b.* 1947, *s.* 1984, *m.*
    Hon. James A. *C.*, *b.* 1977.

1728 *Monson* (11th), John Monson, *b.* 1932, *s.* 1958, *m.*
    Hon. Nicholas J. *M.*, *b.* 1955.

1885 *Montagu of Beaulieu* (3rd), Edward John Barrington Douglas-Scott-Montagu, *b.* 1926, *s.* 1929, *m.*
    Hon. Ralph *D.-S.-M.*, *b.* 1961.

1839 *Monteagle of Brandon* (6th), Gerald Spring Rice, *b.* 1926, *s.* 1946, *m.*
    Hon. Charles J. S. *R.*, *b.* 1953.

1943 *Moran* (2nd), (Richard) John (McMoran) Wilson, K.C.M.G., *b.* 1924, *s.* 1977, *m.*
    Hon. James M. *W.*, *b.* 1952.

1918 *Morris* (3rd), Michael David Morris, *b.* 1937, *s.* 1975, *m.*
    Hon. Thomas A. S. *M.*, *b.* 1982.

1950 *Morris of Kenwood* (2nd), Philip Geoffrey Morris, *b.* 1928, *s.* 1954, *m.*
    Hon. Jonathan D. *M.*, *b.* 1968.

1945 *Morrison* (2nd), Dennis Morrison, *b.* 1914, *s.* 1953.
    (None.)

1831 *Mostyn* (5th), Roger Edward Lloyd Lloyd-Mostyn, M.C., *b.* 1920, *s.* 1965, *m.*
    Hon. Llewellyn R. L. *L.-M.*, *b.* 1948.

1933 *Mottistone* (4th), David Peter Seely, C.B.E., *b.* 1920, *s.* 1966, *m.*
    Hon. Peter J. P. *S.*, *b.* 1949.

1945 *Mountevans* (3rd), Edward Patrick Broke Evans, *b.* 1943, *s.* 1974, *m.*
    Hon. Jeffrey de C. R. *E.*, *b.* 1948.

1283 *Mowbray* (26th), *Segrave* (27th) (1283), & *Stourton* (23rd) (1448), Charles Edward Stourton, C.B.E., *b.* 1923, *s.* 1965, *m.*
    Hon. Edward W. S. *S.*, *b.* 1953.

1932 *Moyne* (2nd), Bryan Walter Guinness, *b.* 1905, *s.* 1944, *m.*
    Hon. Jonathan B. *G.*, *b.* 1930.

1929 *Moynihan* (3rd), Antony Patrick Andrew Cairnes Berkeley Moynihan, *b.* 1936, *s.* 1965, *m.*
    Hon. Andrew B. *M.*, *b.* 1989.

1781 I. *Muskerry* (8th), Hastings Fitzmaurice Tilson Deane, *b.* 1907, *s.* 1966, *m.*
    Hon. Robert F. *D.*, *b.* 1948.

1627 s. *Napier* (14th) & *Ettrick* (5th) (*U.K.* 1872), Francis Nigel Napier, C.V.O., *b.* 1930, *s.* 1954, *m.*
    Master of Napier, *b.* 1962.

1868 *Napier of Magdala* (6th), Robert Alan Napier, *b.* 1940, *s.* 1987, *m.*
    Hon. James R. *N.*, *b.* 1966.

1940 *Nathan* (2nd), Roger Carol Michael Nathan, *b.* 1922, *s.* 1963, *m.*
    Hon. Rupert H. B. *N.*, *b.* 1957.

1960 *Nelson of Stafford* (2nd), Henry George Nelson, *b.* 1917, *s.* 1962, *m.*
    Hon. Henry R. G. *N.*, *b.* 1943.

1959 *Netherthorpe* (3rd), James Frederick Turner, *b.* 1964, *s.* 1982.
    Hon. Patrick A. *T.*, *b.* 1971.

1946 *Newall* (2nd), Francis Storer Eaton Newall, *b.* 1930, *s.* 1963, *m.*
    Hon. Richard H. E. *N.*, *b.* 1961.

1776 I. *Newborough* (7th), Robert Charles Michael Vaughan Wynn, D.S.C., *b.* 1917, *s.* 1965, *m.*
    Hon. Robert V. *W.*, *b.* 1949.

1892 *Newton* (4th), Peter Richard Legh, *b.* 1915, *s.* 1960, *m.*
    Hon. Richard T. *L.*, *b.* 1950.

1930 *Noel-Buxton* (3rd), Martin Connal Noel-Buxton, *b.* 1940, *s.* 1980, *m.*
    Hon. Charles C. *N.-B.*, *b.* 1975.

1957 *Norrie* (2nd), (George) Willoughby Moke Norrie, *b.* 1936, *s.* 1977, *m.*
    Hon. Mark W. J. *N.*, *b.* 1972.

1884 *Northbourne* (5th), Christopher George Walter James, *b.* 1926, *s.* 1982, *m.*
    Hon. Charles W. H. *J.*, *b.* 1960.

1866 *Northbrook* (5th), Francis John Baring, *b.* 1915, *s.* 1947, *m.*
    Hon. Francis T. *B.*, *b.* 1954.

1878 *Norton* (7th), John Arden Adderley, O.B.E., *b.* 1915, *s.* 1961, *m.*
    Hon. James N. A. *A.*, *b.* 1947.

1906 *Nunburnholme* (4th), Ben Charles Wilson, *b.* 1928, *s.* 1974, *m.*
    Hon. Charles T. *W.*, *b.* 1935.

1950 *Ogmore* (2nd), Gwilym Rees Rees-Williams, *b.* 1931, *s.* 1976, *m.*
    Hon. Morgan *R.-W.*, *b.* 1937.

1870 *O'Hagan* (4th), Charles Towneley Strachey, *b.* 1945, *s.* 1961, *m.*
    Hon. Richard T. *S.*, *b.* 1950.

1868 *O'Neill* (4th), Raymond Arthur Clanaboy O'Neill, T.D., *b.* 1933, *s.* 1944, *m.*
    Hon. Shane S. C. *O'N.*, *b.* 1965.

1836 I.* *Oranmore and Browne* (4th), Dominick Geoffrey Edward Browne (2nd *U.K. Baron Mereworth*, 1926), *b.* 1901, *s.* 1927, *m.*
    Hon. Dominick G. T. *B.*, *b.* 1929.

1933 *Palmer* (3rd), Raymond Cecil Palmer, O.B.E., *b.* 1916, *s.* 1950, *m.*
    Adrian B. N. *P.*, *b.* 1951.

1914 *Parmoor* (4th), (Frederick Alfred) Milo Cripps, *b.* 1929, *s.* 1977.
    M. Anthony L. *C.*, C.B.E., D.S.O., T.D., Q.C., *b.* 1913.

1937 *Pender* (3rd), John Willoughby Denison-Pender, *b.* 1933, *s.* 1965, *m.*
    Hon. Henry J. R. *D.-P.*, *b.* 1968.

Created.	Title, Order of Succession, Name, etc.	Eldest Son or Heir.
1866	*Penrhyn* (6th), Malcolm Frank Douglas-Pennant, D.S.O., M.B.E., *b.* 1908, *s.* 1967, *m.*	Hon. Nigel *D.-P.*, *b.* 1909.
1603	*Petre* (18th), John Patrick Lionel Petre, *b.* 1942, *s.* 1989, *m.*	Hon. Dominic W. *P.*, *b.* 1966.
1918	*Phillimore* (3rd), Robert Godfrey Phillimore, *b.* 1939, *s.* 1947, *m.*	Hon. Claud S. *P.*, *b.* 1911.
1945	*Piercy* (3rd), James William Piercy, *b.* 1946, *s.* 1981.	Hon. Mark E. P. *P.*, *b.* 1953.
1827	*Plunket* (8th), Robin Rathmore Plunket, *b.* 1925, *s.* 1975, *m.*	Hon. Shaun A. F. S. *P.*, *b.* 1931.
1831	*Poltimore* (7th), Mark Coplestone Bampfylde, *b.* 1957, *s.* 1978, *m.*	Hon. Henry A. W. *B.*, *b.* 1985.
1690 s.	*Polwarth* (10th), Henry Alexander Hepburne-Scott, T.D., *b.* 1916, *s.* 1944, *m.*	Master of Polwarth, *b.* 1947.
1930	*Ponsonby of Shulbrede* (3rd), Thomas Arthur Ponsonby, *b.* 1930, *s.* 1976, *m.*	Hon. Frederick M. T. *P.*, *b.* 1958.
1958	*Poole* (1st), Oliver Brian Sanderson Poole, C.B.E., T.D., P.C., *b.* 1911, *m.*	Hon. David C. *P.*, *b.* 1945.
1852	*Raglan* (5th), FitzRoy John Somerset, *b.* 1927, *s.* 1964.	Hon. Geoffrey *S.*, *b.* 1932.
1932	*Rankeillour* (4th), Peter St. Thomas More Henry Hope, *b.* 1935, *s.* 1967.	Michael R. *H.*, *b.* 1940.
1953	*Rathcavan* (2nd), Phelim Robert Hugh O'Neill, P.C. (N.I.), *b.* 1909, *s.* 1982, *m.*	Hon. Hugh D. T. *O'N.*, *b.* 1939.
1916	*Rathcreedan* (2nd), Charles Patrick Norton, T.D., *b.* 1905, *s.* 1930, *m.*	Hon. Christopher J. *N.*, *b.* 1949.
1868 I.	*Rathdonnell* (5th), Thomas Benjamin McClintock–Bunbury, *b.* 1938, *s.* 1959, *m.*	Hon. William L. *M.-B.*, *b.* 1966.
1911	*Ravensdale* (3rd), Nicholas Mosley, M.C., *b.* 1923, *s.* 1966, *m.*	Hon. Shaun N. *M.*, *b.* 1949.
1821	*Ravensworth* (8th), Arthur Waller Liddell, *b.* 1924, *s.* 1950, *m.*	Hon. Thomas A. H. *L.*, *b.* 1954.
1821	*Rayleigh* (6th), John Gerald Strutt, *b.* 1960, *s.* 1988.	Hon. Hedley V. *S.*, *b.* 1915.
1937	*Rea* (3rd), John Nicolas Rea, M.D., *b.* 1928, *s.* 1981, *m.*	Hon. Matthew J. *R.*, *b.* 1956.
1628 s.	*Reay* (14th), Hugh William Mackay, *b.* 1937, *s.* 1963, *m.*	Master of Reay, *b.* 1965.
1902	*Redesdale* (5th), Clement Napier Bertram Mitford, *b.* 1932, *s.* 1963, *m.*	Hon. Rupert B. *M.*, *b.* 1967.
1940	*Reith. Disclaimed for life* 1972.	
1928	*Remnant* (3rd), James Wogan Remnant, C.V.O., *b.* 1930, *s.* 1967, *m.*	Hon. Philip J. *R.*, *b.* 1954.
1806 I.	*Rendlesham* (8th), Charles Anthony Hugh Thellusson, *b.* 1915, *s.* 1943, *w.*	Hon. Charles W. B. *T.*, *b.* 1954.
1933	*Rennell* (3rd), (John Adrian) Tremayne Rodd, *b.* 1935, *s.* 1978, *m.*	Hon. James R. D. T. *R.*, *b.* 1978.
1964	*Renwick* (2nd), Harry Andrew Renwick, *b.* 1935, *s.* 1973, *m.*	Hon. Robert J. *R.*, *b.* 1966.
1885	*Revelstoke* (4th), Rupert Baring, *b.* 1911, *s.* 1934.	Hon. John *B.*, *b.* 1934.
1905	*Ritchie of Dundee* (5th), (Harold) Malcolm Ritchie, *b.* 1919, *s.* 1978, *m.*	Hon. Charles R. R. *R.*, *b.* 1958.
1935	*Riverdale* (2nd), Robert Arthur Balfour, *b.* 1901, *s.* 1957, *m.*	Hon. Mark R. *B.*, *b.* 1927.
1961	*Robertson of Oakridge* (2nd), William Ronald Robertson, *b.* 1930, *s.* 1974, *m.*	Hon. William B. E. *R.*, *b.* 1975.
1938	*Roborough* (2nd), Massey Henry Edgcumbe Lopes, *b.* 1903, *s.* 1938, *m.*	Hon. Henry M. *L.*, *b.* 1940.
1931	*Rochester* (2nd), Foster Charles Lowry Lamb, *b.* 1916, *s.* 1955, *m.*	Hon. David C. *L.*, *b.* 1944.
1934	*Rockley* (3rd), James Hugh Cecil, *b.* 1934, *s.* 1976, *m.*	Hon. Anthony R. *C.*, *b.* 1961.
1782	*Rodney* (9th), John Francis Rodney, *b.* 1920, *s.* 1973, *m.*	Hon. George B. *R.*, *b.* 1953.
1651 s.*	*Rollo* (13th), Eric John Stapylton Rollo (4th *U.K. Baron, Dunning,* 1869), *b.* 1915, *s.* 1947, *m.*	Master of Rollo, *b.* 1943.
1959	*Rootes* (2nd), William Geoffrey Rootes, *b.* 1917, *s.* 1964, *m.*	Hon. Nicholas G. *R.*, *b.* 1951.
1796 I. 1838*	*Rossmore* (7th), William Warner Westenra (6th *U.K. Baron, Ross-more*), *b.* 1931, *s.* 1958, *m.*	Hon. Benedict W. *W.*, *b.* 1983.
1939	*Rotherwick* (2nd), (Herbert) Robin Cayzer, *b.* 1912, *s.* 1958, *w.*	Hon. H. Robin *C.*, *b.* 1954.
1885	*Rothschild* (3rd), Nathaniel Mayer Victor Rothschild, G.B.E., G.M., F.R.S., *b.* 1910, *s.* 1937, *m.*	Hon. N. C. Jacob *R.*, *b.* 1936.
1911	*Rowallan* (3rd), Arthur Cameron Corbett, *b.* 1919, *s.* 1977.	Hon. John P. C. *C.*, *b.* 1947.
1947	*Rugby* (2nd), Alan Loader Maffey, *b.* 1913, *s.* 1969, *m.*	Hon. Robert C. *M.*, *b.* 1951.
1919	*Russell of Liverpool* (3rd), Simon Gordon Jared Russell, *b.* 1952, *s.* 1981, *m.*	Hon. Edward C. S. *R.*, *b.* 1985.
1876	*Sackville* (6th), Lionel Bertrand Sackville-West, *b.* 1913, *s.* 1965, *m.*	Hugh R. I. *S.-W.*, M.C., *b.* 1919.
1964	*St. Helens* (2nd), Richard Francis Hughes-Young, *b.* 1945, *s.* 1980, *m.*	Hon. Henry T. *H.-Y.*, *b.* 1986.
1559	*St. John of Bletso* (21st), Anthony Tudor St. John, *b.* 1957, *s.* 1978.	Edmund O. *St. J.*, *b.* 1927.
1887	*St. Levan* (4th), John Francis Arthur St. Aubyn, D.S.C., *b.* 1919, *s.* 1978, *m.*	Hon. O. Piers *St. A.*, M.C., *b.* 1920.
1885	*St. Oswald* (5th), Derek Edward Anthony Winn, *b.* 1919, *s.* 1984, *m.*	Hon. Charles R. A. *W.*, *b.* 1959.
1960	*Sanderson of Ayot. Disclaimed for life* 1971.	
1945	*Sandford* (2nd), Rev. John Cyril Edmondson, D.S.C., *b.* 1920, *s.* 1959, *m.*	Hon. James J. M. *E.*, *b.* 1949.
1871	*Sandhurst* (5th), (John Edward) Terence Mansfield, D.F.C., *b.* 1920, *s.* 1964, *m.*	Hon. Guy R. J. *M.*, *b.* 1949.
1802	*Sandys* (7th), Richard Michael Oliver Hill, *b.* 1931, *s.* 1961, *m.*	Marcus T. *H.*, *b.* 1931.
1888	*Savile* (3rd), George Halifax Lumley-Savile, *b.* 1919, *s.* 1931.	Hon. Henry L. T. *L.-S.*, *b.* 1923.
1447	*Saye and Sele* (21st), Nathaniel Thomas Allen Fiennes, *b.* 1920, *s.* 1968, *m.*	Hon. Richard I. *F.*, *b.* 1959.
1932	*Selsdon* (3rd), Malcolm McEacharn Mitchell-Thomson, *b.* 1937, *s.* 1963, *m.*	Hon. Callum M. M. *M.-T.*, *b.* 1969.
1916	*Shaughnessy* (3rd), William Graham Shaughnessy, *b.* 1922, *s.* 1938, *m.*	Hon. Michael J. *S.*, *b.* 1946.

Created.	Title, Order of Succession, Name, etc.	Eldest Son or Heir.
1946	*Shepherd* (2nd), Malcolm Newton Shepherd, P.C., *b.* 1918, *s.* 1954, *m.*	Hon. Graeme G. S., *b.* 1949.
1964	*Sherfield* (1st), Roger Mellor Makins, G.C.B., G.C.M.G., F.R.S., *b.* 1904, *w.*	Hon. Christopher J. M., *b.* 1942.
1902	*Shuttleworth* (5th), Charles Geoffrey Nicholas Kay-Shuttleworth, *b.* 1948, *s.* 1975, *m.*	Hon. Thomas E. K.-S., *b.* 1976.
1950	*Silkin. Disclaimed for life* 1972.	
1963	*Silsoe* (2nd), David Malcolm Trustram Eve, Q.C., *b.* 1930, *s.* 1976, *m.*	Hon. Simon R. T. E., *b.* 1966.
1947	*Simon of Wythenshawe* (2nd), Roger Simon, *b.* 1913, *s.* 1960, *m.*	Hon. Matthew S., *b.* 1955.
1449 s.	*Sinclair* (17th), Charles Murray Kennedy St. Clair, L.V.O., *b.* 1914, *s.* 1957, *m.*	Master of Sinclair, *b.* 1968.
1957	*Sinclair of Cleeve* (3rd), John Lawrence Robert Sinclair, *b.* 1953, *s.* 1985.	(None.)
1919	*Sinha* (3rd), Sudhindro Prosanno Sinha, *b.* 1920, *s.* 1967, *m.*	Hon. Sushanto S., *b.* 1953.
1828	*Skelmersdale* (7th), Roger Bootle-Wilbraham, *b.* 1945, *s.* 1973, *m.*	Hon. Andrew B.-W., *b.* 1977.
1916	*Somerleyton* (3rd), Savile William Francis Crossley, *b.* 1928, *s.* 1959, *m.*	Hon. Hugh F. S. C., *b.* 1971.
1784	*Somers* (8th), John Patrick Somers Cocks, *b.* 1907, *s.* 1953, *m.*	Philip S. S. C., *b.* 1948.
1780	*Southampton. Disclaimed for life* 1964.	
1917	*Southborough* (4th), Francis Michael Hopwood, *b.* 1922, *s.* 1982, *w.*	(None.)
1959	*Spens* (3rd), Patrick Michael Rex Spens, *b.* 1942, *s.* 1984, *m.*	Hon. Patrick N. G. S., *b.* 1968.
1640	*Stafford* (15th), Francis Melfort William Fitzherbert, *b.* 1954, *s.* 1986, *m.*	Hon. Benjamin J. B. F., *b.* 1983.
1938	*Stamp* (4th), Trevor Charles Bosworth Stamp, M.D., F.R.C.P., *b.* 1935, *s.* 1987, *m.*	Hon. Nicholas C. T. S., *b.* 1978.
1839	*Stanley of Alderley* (8th) & *Sheffield* (8th) (1738 I.), Thomas Henry Oliver Stanley (7th *U.K. Baron Eddisbury*, 1848), *b.* 1927, *s.* 1971, *m.*	Hon. Richard O. S., *b.* 1956.
1318	*Strabolgi* (11th), David Montague de Burgh Kenworthy, *b.* 1914, *s.* 1953, *m.*	Rev. Hon. Jonathan M. A. K., *b.* 1916.
1954	*Strang* (2nd), Colin Strang, *b.* 1922, *s.* 1978, *m.*	(None.)
1955	*Strathalmond* (3rd), William Roberton Fraser, *b.* 1947, *s.* 1976, *m.*	Hon. William G. F., *b.* 1976.
1936	*Strathcarron* (2nd), David William Anthony Blyth Macpherson, *b.* 1924, *s.* 1937, *m.*	Hon. Ian D. P. M., *b.* 1949.
1955	*Strathclyde* (2nd), Thomas Galloway Dunlop du Roy de Blicquy Galbraith, *b.* 1960, *s.* 1985.	Hon. Charles W. du R. de B. G., *b.* 1962.
1900	*Strathcona and Mount Royal* (4th), Donald Euan Palmer Howard, *b.* 1923, *s.* 1959, *m.*	Hon. Donald A. S. H., *b.* 1961.
1836	*Stratheden & Campbell* (1841) (6th), Donald Campbell, *b.* 1934, *s.* 1988, *m.*	Hon. David A. C., *b.* 1963.
1884	*Strathspey* (5th), Donald Patrick Trevor Grant of Grant, *b.* 1912, *s.* 1948, *m.*	Hon. James P. G., *b.* 1943.
1838	*Sudeley* (7th), Merlin Charles Sainthill Hanbury-Tracy, *b.* 1939, *s.* 1941, *m.*	Desmond A. J. H-T., *b.* 1928.
1786	*Suffield* (11th), Anthony Philip Harbord-Hamond, M.C., *b.* 1922, *s.* 1951, *m.*	Hon. Charles A. A. H.-H., *b.* 1953.
1893	*Swansea* (4th), John Hussey Hamilton Vivian, *b.* 1925, *s.* 1934, *m.*	Hon. Richard A. H. V., *b.* 1957.
1907	*Swaythling* (3rd), Stuart Albert Samuel Montagu, O.B.E., *b.* 1898, *s.* 1927, *m.*	Hon. David C. S. M., *b.* 1928.
1919	*Swinfen* (3rd), Roger Mynors Swinfen Eady, *b.* 1938, *s.* 1977, *m.*	Hon. Charles R. P. S. E., *b.* 1971.
1935	*Sysonby* (3rd), John Frederick Ponsonby, *b.* 1945, *s.* 1956.	(None.)
1831 I.	*Talbot of Malahide* (10th), Reginald John Richard Arundell, *b.* 1931, *s.* 1987, *m.*	Hon. Richard J. T. A., *b.* 1957.
1946	*Tedder* (2nd), John Michael Tedder, SC.D., PH.D., D.SC., *b.* 1926, *s.* 1967, *m.*	Hon. Robin J. T., *b.* 1955.
1884	*Tennyson* (4th), Harold Christopher Tennyson, *b.* 1919, *s.* 1951.	Hon. Mark A. T., D.S.C., *b.* 1920.
1918	*Terrington* (4th), (James Allen) David Woodhouse, *b.* 1915, *s.* 1961, *m.*	Hon. C. Montague W., D.S.O., O.B.E., *b.* 1917.
1940	*Teviot* (2nd), Charles John Kerr, *b.* 1934, *s.* 1968, *m.*	Hon. Charles R. K., *b.* 1971.
1616	*Teynham* (20th), John Christopher Ingham Roper-Curzon, *b.* 1928, *s.* 1972, *m.*	Hon. David J. H. I. R.-C., *b.* 1965.
1964	*Thomson of Fleet* (2nd), Kenneth Roy Thomson, *b.* 1923, *s.* 1976, *m.*	Hon. David K. R. T., *b.* 1957.
1792	*Thurlow* (8th), Francis Edward Hovell-Thurlow-Cumming-Bruce, K.C.M.G., *b.* 1912, *s.* 1971, *m.*	Hon. Roualeyn R. H.-T.-C.-B., *b.* 1952.
1876	*Tollemache* (5th), Timothy John Edward Tollemache, *b.* 1939, *s.* 1975, *m.*	Hon. Edward J. H. T., *b.* 1976.
1564 s.	*Torphichen* (15th), James Andrew Douglas Sandilands, *b.* 1946, *s.* 1975, *m.*	Douglas R. A. S., *b.* 1926.
1947	*Trefgarne* (2nd), David Garro Trefgarne, P.C., *b.* 1941, *s.* 1960, *m.*	Hon. George G. T., *b.* 1970.
1921	*Trevethin* (4th), *and Oaksey* (2nd), John Geoffrey Tristram Lawrence, O.B.E. (2nd *U.K. Baron, Oaksey*, 1947), *b.* 1929, *s.* 1971, *m.*	Hon. Patrick J. T. L., *b.* 1960.
1880	*Trevor* (4th), Charles Edwin Hill-Trevor, *b.* 1928, *s.* 1950, *m.*	Hon. Marke C. H.-T., *b.* 1970.
1461 I.	*Trimlestown* (19th), Charles Aloysius Barnewall, *b.* 1899, *s.* 1937, *w.*	Hon. Anthony E. B., *b.* 1928.
1940	*Tryon* (3rd), Anthony George Merrik Tryon, *b.* 1940, *s.* 1976, *m.*	Hon. Charles G. B. T., *b.* 1976.
1935	*Tweedsmuir* (2nd), John Norman Stuart Buchan, C.B.E., C.D., *b.* 1911, *s.* 1940, *m.*	Hon. William B., *b.* 1916.

Created.	Title, Order of Succession, Name, etc.	Eldest Son or Heir.
1523	*Vaux of Harrowden* (10th), John Hugh Philip Gilbey, *b.* 1915, *s.* 1977, *m.*	Hon. Anthony W. *G.*, *b.* 1940.
1800 I.	*Ventry* (8th), Andrew Wesley Daubeny de Moleyns, *b.* 1943, *s.* 1987, *m.*	Hon. Francis W. *D. de M.*, *b.* 1965.
1762	*Vernon* (10th), John Lawrance Vernon, *b.* 1923, *s.* 1963, *m.*	Robert *Vernon-Harcourt*, *b.* 1918.
1922	*Vestey* (3rd), Samuel George Armstrong Vestey, *b.* 1941, *s.* 1954, *m.*	Hon. William G. *V.*, *b.* 1983.
1841	*Vivian* (5th), Anthony Crespigny Claude Vivian, *b.* 1906, *s.* 1940, *w.*	Hon. Nicholas C. L. *V.*, *b.* 1935.
1934	*Wakehurst* (3rd), (John) Christopher Loder, *b.* 1925, *s.* 1970, *m.*	Hon. Timothy W. *L.*, *b.* 1958.
1723	*Walpole* (10th), Robert Horatio Walpole, *b.* 1938, *s.* 1989, *m.* (*8th Brit. Baron Walpole of Wolterton*, 1756).	Hon. Jonathan R. H. *W.*, *b.* 1967.
1780	*Walsingham* (9th), John de Grey, M.C., *b.* 1925, *s.* 1965, *m.*	Hon. Robert *de G.*, *b.* 1969.
1936	*Wardington* (2nd), Christopher Henry Beaumont Pease, *b.* 1924, *s.* 1950, *m.*	Hon. William S. *P.*, *b.* 1925.
1792 I.	*Waterpark* (7th), Frederick Caryll Philip Cavendish, *b.* 1926, *s.* 1948, *m.*	Hon. Roderick A. *C.*, *b.* 1959.
1942	*Wedgwood* (4th), Piers Anthony Weymouth Wedgwood, *b.* 1954, *s.* 1970, *m.*	John *W.*, C.B.E., M.D., *b.* 1919.
1861	*Westbury* (5th), David Alan Bethell, M.C., *b.* 1922, *s.* 1961, *m.*	Hon. Richard N. *B.*, M.B.E., *b.* 1950.
1944	*Westwood* (2nd), William Westwood, *b.* 1907, *s.* 1953, *m.*	Hon. William G. *W.*, *b.* 1944.
1935	*Wigram* (2nd), (George) Neville (Clive) Wigram, M.C., *b.* 1915, *s.* 1960, *w.*	Maj. Hon. Andrew F. C. *W.*, M.V.O., *b.* 1949.
1491	*Willoughby de Broke* (21st), Leopold David Verney, *b.* 1938, *s.* 1986, *m.*	Hon. Rupert G. *V.*, *b.* 1966.
1946	*Wilson* (2nd), Patrick Maitland Wilson, *b.* 1915, *s.* 1964, *m.*	(None.)
1937	*Windlesham* (3rd), David James George Hennessy, C.V.O., P.C., *b.* 1932, *s.* 1962, *w.*	Hon. James *H.*, *b.* 1968.
1951	*Wise* (2nd), John Clayton Wise, *b.* 1923, *s.* 1968, *m.*	Hon. Christopher J. C. *W.*, Ph.D., *b.* 1949.
1869	*Wolverton* (7th), Christopher Richard Glynn, *b.* 1938, *s.* 1988, *m.*	Hon. Andrew J. *G.*, *b.* 1943.
1928	*Wraxall* (2nd), George Richard Lawley Gibbs, *b.* 1928, *s.* 1931.	Hon. Sir Eustace H. B. *G.*, K.C.V.O., C.M.G., *b.* 1929.
1915	*Wrenbury* (3rd), John Burton Buckley, *b.* 1927, *s.* 1940, *m.*	Hon. William E. *B.*, *b.* 1966.
1838	*Wrottesley* (6th), Clifton Hugh Lancelot de Verdon Wrottesley, *b.* 1968, *s.* 1977.	Hon. Mark *W.*, *b.* 1951.
1919	*Wyfold* (3rd), Hermon Robert Fleming Hermon-Hodge, *b.* 1915, *s.* 1942.	(None.)
1829	*Wynford* (8th), Robert Samuel Best, M.B.E., *b.* 1917, *s.* 1943, *m.*	Hon. John P. *B.*, *b.* 1950.
1308	*Zouche* (18th), James Assheton Frankland, *b.* 1943, *s.* 1965, *m.*	Hon. William T. A. *F.*, *b.* 1984.

WOMEN PEERS IN THEIR OWN RIGHT

Peerages falling under this heading are the result of regular inheritance in lines which are open to females in default of males. A Peeress in her Own Right retains her title after marriage, and if her husband's rank is the superior she is designated by the two titles jointly, the inferior one last: her hereditary claim still holds good in spite of any marriage whether higher or lower. No rank held by a woman can confer any title or even precedence upon her husband but the rank of a woman Peer in her Own Right is inherited by her eldest son (or perhaps daughter), to whomsoever she may have been married.
Where marked ° the 'of' is not used.

COUNTESSES IN THEIR OWN RIGHT

Style, The Countess of —— *Addressed as,* My Lady.

Created.	Title, Name, etc.	Eldest Son or Heir.
1643 s.	*Dysart* (11th in line), Rosamund Agnes Greaves, *b.* 1914, *s.* 1975.	Lady Katherine *Grant of Rothiemurchus*, *b.* 1918.
1633 s.	*Loudoun* (13th in line), Barbara Huddleston Abney-Hastings, *b.* 1919, *s.* 1960, *m.*	Lord Mauchline, *b.* 1942.
c. 1115 s.	*Mar* (31st in line), Margaret of Mar (*Premier Earldom of Scotland*), *b.* 1940, *s.* 1975, *m.*	Mistress of Mar, *b.* 1963.
1947	°*Mountbatten of Burma* (2nd in line), Patricia Edwina Victoria Knatchbull, *b.* 1924, *s.* 1979, *m.*	Lord Romsey, *b.* 1947 (*see also* p. 168).
c. 1235 s.	*Sutherland* (24th in line), Elizabeth Millicent Sutherland, *b.* 1921, *s.* 1963, *m.*	Lord Strathnaver, *b.* 1947.

BARONESSES IN THEIR OWN RIGHT

Style, The Baroness —— *Addressed as,* My Lady.

Created.	Title, Name, etc.	Eldest Son or Heir.
1421	*Berkeley* (17th in line), Mary Lalle Foley-Berkeley, *b.* 1905, *title called out of abeyance,* 1967.	Hon. Cynthia E. *Gueterbock*, *b.* 1909.

Created.	Title, Name, etc.	Eldest Son or Heir.
1455	*Berners* (15th in line), Vera Ruby Williams, *b.* 1901, *s.* 1950, *m.*	Two co-heiresses.
1529	*Braye* (8th in line), Mary Penelope Aubrey–Fletcher, *b.* 1941, *s.* 1985, *m.*	Hon. Ambrose J. Verney-Cave, *b.* 1906.
1321	*Dacre* (27th in line), Rachel Leila Douglas-Home, *b.* 1929, *title called out of abeyance*, 1970, *m.*	Hon. James T. A. *D.-H.*, *b.* 1952.
1332	*Darcy de Knayth* (18th in line), Davina Marcia Ingrams, *b.* 1938, *s.* 1943, *w.*	Hon. Caspar D. *I.*, *b.* 1962.
1439	*Dudley* (14th in line), Barbara Amy Felicity Hamilton, *b.* 1907, *s.* 1972, *m.*	Hon. Jim. A. H. *Wallace*, *b.* 1930.
1490 s.	*Herries of Terregles* (14th in line), Anne Elizabeth Fitzalan-Howard, *b.* 1938, *s.* 1975, *m.*	Lady Mary K. *Mumford*, C.V.O., *b.* 1940.
1602 s.	*Kinloss* (12th in line), Beatrice Mary Grenville Freeman-Grenville, *b.* 1922, *s.* 1944, *m.*	Master of Kinloss, *b.* 1953.
1663	*Lucas of Crudwell* (10th in line) & *Dingwall* (13th in line) (Scottish Lordship 1609), Anne Rosemary Palmer, *b.* 1919, *s.* 1958, *m.*	Hon. Ralph M. *P.*, *b.* 1951.
1681 s.	*Nairne* (12th in line), Katherine Evelyn Constance Bigham (*Katherine, Viscountess Mersey*), *b.* 1912, *s.* 1944, *w.*	Viscount Mersey, *b.* 1934 (*see* p. 165).
1945	*Portal of Hungerford* (2nd in line), Rosemary Ann Portal, *b.* 1923, *s.* 1971.	(None).
1445 s.	*Saltoun* (20th in line), Flora Marjory Fraser, *b.* 1930, *s.* 1979, *m.*	Hon. Katharine I. M. I. *F.*, *b.* 1957.
1489 s.	*Sempill* (20th in line), Ann Moira Sempill, *b.* 1920, *s.* 1965, *m.*	Master of Sempill, *b.* 1949.
1628	*Strange* (16th in line), Jean Cherry Drummond, *b.* 1928, *title called out of abeyance*, 1986, *m.*	Hon. Adam H. *D.*, *b.* 1953.
1313	*Willoughby de Eresby* (27th in line), Nancy Jane Marie Heathcote-Drummond-Willoughby, *b.* 1934, *s.* 1983.	Two co-heiresses.

LIFE PEERS

Created under the Appellate Jurisdiction Act, 1876 (as amended)

BARONS

Created		
1986	*Ackner*, Desmond James Conrad Ackner, P.C., *b.* 1920, *m.*	Lord of Appeal in Ordinary.
1981	*Brandon of Oakbrook*, Henry Vivian Brandon, M.C., P.C., *b.* 1920, *m.*	Lord of Appeal in Ordinary.
1980	*Bridge of Harwich*, Nigel Cyprian Bridge, P.C., *b.* 1917, *m.*	Lord of Appeal in Ordinary.
1982	*Brightman*, John Anson Brightman, P.C., *b.* 1911, *m.*	Lord of Appeal (retired).
1957	*Denning*, Alfred Thompson Denning, P.C., *b.* 1899, *m.*	Lord of Appeal (retired).
1961	*Devlin*, Patrick Arthur Devlin, P.C., F.B.A., *b.* 1905, *m.*	Lord of Appeal (retired).
1974	*Edmund-Davies*, (Herbert) Edmund Edmund-Davies, P.C., *b.* 1906, *m.*	Lord of Appeal (retired).
1986	*Goff of Chieveley*, Robert Lionel Archibald Goff, P.C., *b.* 1926, *m.*	Lord of Appeal in Ordinary.
1985	*Griffiths*, (William) Hugh Griffiths, M.C., P.C., *b.* 1923, *m.*	Lord of Appeal in Ordinary.
1987	*Jauncey of Tullichettle*, Charles Eliot Jauncey, P.C., *b.* 1925, *m.*	Lord of Appeal in Ordinary.
1977	*Keith of Kinkel*, Henry Shanks Keith, P.C., *b.* 1922, *m.*	Lord of Appeal in Ordinary.
1971	*Kilbrandon*, Charles James Dalrymple Shaw, P.C., *b.* 1906, *m.*	Lord of Appeal (retired).
1979	*Lane*, Geoffrey Dawson Lane, A.F.C., P.C., *b.* 1918, *m.*	Lord of Appeal (Lord Chief Justice).
1986	*Oliver of Aylmerton*, Peter Raymond Oliver, P.C., *b.* 1921, *m.*	Lord of Appeal in Ordinary.
1962	*Pearce*, Edward Holroyd Pearce, P.C., *b.* 1901, *w.*	Lord of Appeal (retired).
1980	*Roskill*, Eustace Wentworth Roskill, P.C., *b.* 1911, *m.*	Lord of Appeal (retired).
1972	*Salmon*, Cyril Barnet Salmon, P.C., *b.* 1903, *m.*	Lord of Appeal (retired).
1977	*Scarman*, Leslie George Scarman, O.B.E., P.C., *b.* 1911, *m.*	Lord of Appeal (retired).
1982	*Templeman*, Sydney William Templeman, M.B.E., P.C., *b.* 1920, *w.*	Lord of Appeal in Ordinary.
1964	*Wilberforce*, Richard Orme Wilberforce, C.M.G., O.B.E., P.C., *b.* 1907, *m.*	Lord of Appeal (retired).

Created under Life Peerages Act, 1958

Life Peerages were conferred on the following: in the New Years Honours List 1989, Rt. Hon. Sally Oppenheim-Barnes, Prof. Sir Jack Lewis, Sir John Sainsbury; in the Queen's Birthday Honours List 1989, Prof. Ian McColl, Sir Eric Sharp, Sir John Walton.

BARONS

Created.		
1974	*Alexander of Potterhill*, William Picken Alexander, PH.D., *b.* 1905, *m.*	
1988	*Alexander of Weedon*, Robert Scott Alexander, Q.C., *b.* 1936, *m.*	
1976	*Allen of Abbeydale*, Philip Allen, G.C.B., *b.* 1912, *m.*	
1961	*Alport*, Cuthbert James McCall Alport, T.D., P.C., *b.* 1912, *w.*	
1965	*Annan*, Noel Gilroy Annan, O.B.E., *b.* 1916, *m.*	
1970	*Ardwick*, John Cowburn Beavan, *b.* 1910, *m.*	
1988	*Armstrong of Ilminster*, Robert Temple Armstrong, G.C.B., C.V.O., *b.* 1927, *m.*	

Created.
1973 *Ashby,* Eric Ashby, D.SC., F.R.S., *b.* 1904, *m.*
1967 *Aylestone,* Herbert William Bowden, C.H., C.B.E., P.C., *b.* 1905, *m.*
1982 *Bancroft,* Ian Powell Bancroft, G.C.B., *b.* 1922, *m.*
1974 *Banks,* Desmond Anderson Harvie Banks, C.B.E., *b.* 1918, *m.*
1974 *Barber,* Anthony Perrinott Lysberg Barber, T.D., P.C., *b.* 1920, *w.*
1983 *Barnett,* Joel Barnett, P.C., *b.* 1923, *m.*
1982 *Bauer,* Prof. Peter Thomas Bauer, D.SC., *b.* 1915.
1967 *Beaumont of Whitley,* Rev. Timothy Wentworth Beaumont, *b.* 1928, *m.*
1979 *Bellwin,* Irwin Norman Bellow, *b.* 1923, *m.*
1981 *Beloff,* Max Beloff, *b.* 1913, *m.*
1981 *Benson,* Henry Alexander Benson, G.B.E., *b.* 1909, *m.*
1969 *Bernstein,* Sidney Lewis Bernstein, *b.* 1899, *m.*
1971 *Blake,* Robert Norman William Blake, F.B.A., *b.* 1916, *m.*
1983 *Blanch,* Rt. Rev. Stuart Yarworth Blanch, P.C., *b.* 1918, *m.*
1978 *Blease,* William John Blease, *b.* 1914, *m.*
1980 *Boardman,* Thomas Gray Boardman, M.C., T.D., *b.* 1919, *m.*
1986 *Bonham-Carter,* Mark Raymond Bonham Carter, *b.* 1922, *m.*
1976 *Boston of Faversham,* Terence George Boston, Q.C.,*b.* 1930, *m.*
1984 *Bottomley,* Arthur George Bottomley, O.B.E., P.C., *b.* 1907, *m.*
1972 *Boyd-Carpenter,* John Archibald Boyd-Carpenter, P.C., *b.* 1908, *m.*
1987 *Bramall,* Edwin Noel Westby Bramall, G.C.B., O.B.E., M.C., *Field Marshal, b.* 1923, *m.*
1976 *Briggs,* Asa Briggs, *b.* 1921, *m.*
1974 *Briginshaw,* Richard William Briginshaw, *m.*
1976 *Brimelow,* Thomas Brimelow, G.C.M.G., O.B.E., *b.* 1915, *m.*
1975 *Brookes,* Raymond Percival Brookes, *b.* 1909, *m.*
1979 *Brooks of Tremorfa,* John Edward Brooks, *b.* 1927, *m.*
1983 *Broxbourne,* Derek Colclough Walker-Smith, T.D., Q.C., P.C., *b.* 1910, *m.*
1974 *Bruce of Donington,* Donald William Trevor Bruce, *b.* 1912, *m.*
1983 *Bruce-Gardyne,* John (Jock) Bruce-Gardyne, *b.* 1930, *m.*
1976 *Bullock,* Alan Louis Charles Bullock, F.B.A., *b.* 1914, *m.*
1988 *Butterfield,* (William) John (Hughes) Butterfield, O.B.E., D.M., *b.* 1920, *m.*
1985 *Butterworth,* John Blackstock Butterworth, C.B.E., *b.* 1918, *m.*
1978 *Buxton of Alsa,* Aubrey Leland Oakes Buxton, M.C., *b.* 1918, *m.*
1965 *Caccia,* Harold Anthony Caccia, G.C.M.G., G.C.V.O., *b.* 1905, *m.*
1987 *Callaghan of Cardiff,* (Leonard) James Callaghan, K.G., P.C., *b.* 1912, *m.*
1984 *Cameron of Lochbroom,* Kenneth John Cameron, P.C., *b.* 1931, *m.*
1981 *Campbell of Alloway,* Alan Robertson Campbell, Q.C., *b.* 1917, *m.*
1974 *Campbell of Croy,* Gordon Thomas Calthrop Campbell, M.C., P.C., *b.* 1921, *m.*
1966 *Campbell of Eskan,* John (Jock) Middleton Campbell, *b.* 1912, *w.*
1964 *Caradon,* Hugh Mackintosh Foot, G.C.M.G., K.C.V.O., O.B.E., P.C., *b.* 1907, *w.*
1987 *Carlisle of Bucklow,* Mark Carlisle, Q.C., P.C., *b.* 1929, *m.*
1983 *Carmichael of Kelvingrove,* Neil George Carmichael, *b.* 1921.
1975 *Carr of Hadley,* (Leonard) Robert Carr, P.C., *b.* 1916, *m.*
1987 *Carter,* Denis Victor Carter, *b.* 1932, *m.*
1977 *Carver,* (Richard) Michael (Power) Carver, G.C.B., C.B.E., D.S.O., M.C., *Field Marshal, b.* 1915, *m.*
1982 *Cayzer,* (William) Nicholas Cayzer, *b.* 1910, *m.*
1964 *Chalfont,* (Alun) Arthur Gwynne Jones, O.B.E., M.C., P.C., *b.* 1919, *m.*
1985 *Chapple,* Frank Joseph Chapple, *b.* 1921, *m.*
1978 *Charteris of Amisfield,* Martin Michael Charles Charteris, G.C.B., G.C.V.O., O.B.E., P.C., *b.* 1913, *m.*
1963 *Chelmer,* Eric Cyril Boyd Edwards, M.C., T.D., *b.* 1914, *m.*
1987 *Chilver,* (Amos) Henry Chilver, F.R.S., *b.* 1926, *m.*
1977 *Chitnis,* Pratap Chidamber Chitnis, *b.* 1936, *m.*
1979 *Cledwyn of Penrhos,* Cledwyn Hughes, C.H., P.C., *b.* 1916, *m.*
1978 *Cockfield,* (Francis) Arthur Cockfield, P.C., *b.* 1916, *m.*
1987 *Cocks of Hartcliffe,* Michael Francis Lovell Cocks, P.C., *b.* 1929, *m.*
1980 *Coggan,* Rt. Rev. (Frederick) Donald Coggan, P.C., Royal Victorian Chain, *b.* 1909, *m.*
1964 *Collison,* Harold Francis Collison, C.B.E., *b.* 1909, *m.*
1987 *Colnbrook,* Humphrey Edward Gregory Atkins, K.C.M.G., P.C., *b.* 1922, *m.*
1981 *Constantine of Stanmore,* Theodore Constantine, C.B.E., A.E., *b.* 1910, *m.*
1959 *Craigton,* Jack Nixon Browne, C.B.E., P.C., *b.* 1904, *m.*
1987 *Crickhowell,* (Roger) Nicholas Edwards, P.C., *b.* 1934, *m.*
1978 *Croham,* Douglas Albert Vivian Allen, G.C.B., *b.* 1917, *m.*
1974 *Cudlipp,* Hugh Cudlipp, O.B.E., *b.* 1913, *m.*
1979 *Dacre of Glanton,* Hugh Redwald Trevor-Roper, *b.* 1914, *m.*
1986 *Dainton,* Frederick Sydney Dainton, PH.D., SC.D., F.R.S., *b.* 1914, *m.*
1974 *Davies of Penrhys,* Gwilym Elfed Davies, *b.* 1913, *m.*
1983 *Dean of Beswick,* Joseph Jabez Dean, *b.* 1922.
1986 *Deedes,* William Francis Deedes, M.C., P.C., *b.* 1913, *m.*
1976 *Delfont,* Bernard Delfont, *b.* 1909, *m.*
1970 *Diamond,* John Diamond, P.C., *b.* 1907, *m.*
1967 *Donaldson of Kingsbridge,* John George Stuart Donaldson, O.B.E., *b.* 1907, *m.*
1988 *Donaldson of Lymington,* John Francis Donaldson, P.C., *b.* 1920, *m.* (*Master of the Rolls*).
1985 *Donoughue,* Bernard Donoughue, D.PHIL., *b.* 1934, *m.*
1987 *Dormand of Easington,* John Donkin Dormand, *b.* 1919, *m.*
1983 *Eden of Winton,* John Benedict Eden, P.C., *b.* 1925, *m.*
1985 *Elliott of Morpeth,* Robert William Elliott, *b.* 1920, *m.*

Created.

1972 *Elworthy,* (Samuel) Charles Elworthy, K.G., G.C.B., C.B.E., D.S.O., L.V.O., D.F.C., A.F.C., *Marshal of the Royal Air Force, b.* 1911, *w.*

1974 *Elwyn-Jones,* Frederick Elwyn-Jones, C.H., P.C., *b.* 1909, *m.*

1981 *Elystan-Morgan,* Dafydd Elystan Elystan-Morgan, *b.* 1932, *m.*

1980 *Emslie,* George Carlyle Emslie, M.B.E., P.C., *b.* 1919, *m.* (*Lord Justice-General of Scotland*).

1983 *Ennals,* David Hedley Ennals, P.C., *b.* 1922, *m.*

1978 *Evans of Claughton,* (David Thomas) Gruffydd Evans, *b.* 1928, *m.*

1983 *Ezra,* Derek Ezra, M.B.E., *b.* 1919, *m.*

1983 *Fanshawe of Richmond,* Anthony Henry Fanshawe Royle, K.C.M.G., *b.,* 1927, *m.*

1958 *Ferrier,* Victor Ferrier Noel-Paton, E.D., *b.* 1900, *w.*

1983 *Fitt,* Gerard Fitt, *b.* 1926, *m.*

1970 *Fletcher,* Eric George Molyneux Fletcher, P.C., Ll.D., *b.* 1903, *m.*

1979 *Flowers,* Brian Hilton Flowers, F.R.S., *b.* 1924, *m.*

1967 *Foot,* John Mackintosh Foot, *b.* 1909, *m.*

1982 *Forte,* Charles Forte, *b.* 1908, *m.*

1962 *Franks,* Oliver Shewell Franks, O.M., G.C.M.G., K.C.B., K.C.V.O., C.B.E., P.C., F.B.A., *b.* 1905, *w.*

1989 *Fraser of Carmyllie,* Peter Lovat Fraser, Q.C., P.C., *b.* 1945, *m.*

1974 *Fraser of Kilmorack,* (Richard) Michael Fraser, C.B.E., *b.* 1915, *m.*

1982 *Gallacher,* John Gallacher, *b.* 1920, *m.*

1979 *Galpern,* Myer Galpern, *b.* 1903.

1963 *Gardiner,* Gerald Austin Gardiner, C.H., P.C., *b.* 1900, *m.*

1975 *Gibson,* (Richard) Patrick (Tallentyre) Gibson, *b.* 1916, *m.*

1979 *Gibson-Watt,* (James) David Gibson-Watt, M.C., P.C., *b.* 1918, *m.*

1977 *Glenamara,* Edward Watson Short, C.H., P.C., *b.* 1912, *m.*

1965 *Goodman,* Arnold Abraham Goodman, C.H., *b.* 1913.

1987 *Goold,* James Duncan Goold, *b.* 1934, *m.*

1982 *Gormley,* Joseph Gormley, O.B.E., *b.* 1917, *m.*

1976 *Grade,* Lew Grade, *b.* 1906, *m.*

1983 *Graham of Edmonton,* (Thomas) Edward Graham, *b.*1925, *m.*

1967 *Granville of Eye,* Edgar Louis Granville, *b.* 1899, *m.*

1983 *Gray of Contin,* James (Hamish) Hector Northey Gray, P.C., *b.* 1927, *m.*

1974 *Greene of Harrow Weald,* Sidney Francis Greene, C.B.E., *b.* 1910, *m.*

1974 *Greenhill of Harrow,* Denis Arthur Greenhill, G.C.M.G., O.B.E., *b.* 1913, *m.*

1975 *Gregson,* John Gregson, *b.* 1924.

1968 *Grey of Naunton,* Ralph Francis Alnwick Grey, G.C.M.G., G.C.V.O., O.B.E., *b.* 1910, *m.*

1983 *Grimond,* Joseph Grimond, T.D., P.C., *b.* 1913, *m.*

1970 *Hailsham of St. Marylebone,* Quintin McGarel Hogg, K.G., C.H., P.C., *b.* 1907, *m.*

1983 *Hanson,* James Edward Hanson, *b.* 1922, *m.*

1974 *Harmar-Nicholls,* Harmar Harmar-Nicholls, *b.* 1912, *m.*

1974 *Harris of Greenwich,* John Henry Harris, *b.* 1930, *m.*

1979 *Harris of High Cross,* Ralph Harris, *b.* 1924, *m.*

1968 *Hartwell,* (William) Michael Berry, M.B.E., T.D., *b.* 1911, *w.*

1971 *Harvey of Prestbury,* Arthur Vere Harvey, C.B.E., *b.* 1906, *m.*

1974 *Harvington,* Robert Grant Grant-Ferris, A.E., P.C., *b.* 1907, *m.*

1978 *Hatch of Lusby,* John Charles Hatch, *b.* 1917.

1987 *Havers,* (Robert) Michael (Oldfield) Havers, P.C., *b.* 1923, *m.*

1984 *Henderson of Brompton,* Peter Gordon Henderson, K.C.B., *b.* 1922, *m.*

1967 *Heycock,* Llewellyn Heycock, C.B.E., *b.* 1905, *m.*

1979 *Hill-Norton,* Peter John Hill-Norton, G.C.B., *Admiral of the Fleet, b.* 1915, *m.*

1967 *Hirshfield,* Desmond Barel Hirshfield, *b.* 1913, *m.*

1979 *Holderness,* Richard Frederick Wood, P.C., *b.* 1920, *m.*

1974 *Home of the Hirsel,* Alexander Frederick Douglas-Home, K.T., P.C., *b.* 1903, *m.*

1979 *Hooson,* (Hugh) Emlyn Hooson, Q.C., *b.* 1925, *m.*

1974 *Houghton of Sowerby,* (Arthur Leslie Noel) Douglas Houghton, C.H., P.C., *b.* 1898, *m.*

1978 *Howie of Troon,* William Howie, *b.* 1924, *m.*

1961 *Hughes,* William Hughes, C.B.E., P.C., *b.* 1911, *m.*

1966 *Hunt,* (Henry Cecil) John Hunt, K.G., C.B.E., D.S.O., *b.* 1910, *m.*

1980 *Hunt of Tanworth,* John Joseph Benedict Hunt, G.C.B., *b.* 1919, *m.*

1978 *Hunter of Newington,* Robert Brockie Hunter, M.B.E., F.R.C.P., *b.* 1915, *m.*

1978 *Hutchinson of Lullington,* Jeremy Nicolas Hutchinson, Q.C., *b.* 1915, *m.*

1982 *Ingrow,* John Aked Taylor, O.B.E., T.D., *b.* 1917, *m.*

1987 *Irvine of Lairg,* Alexander Andrew Mackay Irvine, Q.C., *b.* 1940, *m.*

1979 *Irving of Dartford,* Sydney Irving, P.C., *b.* 1918, *m.*

1968 *Jacques,* John Henry Jacques, *b.* 1905, *m.*

1988 *Jakobovits,* Immanuel Jakobovits, *b.* 1921, *m.*

1959 *James of Rusholme,* Eric John Francis James, *b.* 1909, *m.*

1987 *Jay,* Douglas Patrick Thomas Jay, P.C., *b.* 1907, *m.*

1987 *Jenkin of Roding,* (Charles) Patrick (Fleeming) Jenkin, P.C., *b.* 1926, *m.*

1987 *Jenkins of Hillhead,* Roy Harris Jenkins, P.C., *b.* 1920, *m.*

1981 *Jenkins of Putney,* Hugh Gater Jenkins, *b.* 1908, *m.*

1981 *John-Mackie,* John John-Mackie, *b.* 1909, *m.*

1987 *Johnston of Rockport,* Charles Collier Johnston, T.D., *b.* 1915, *m.*

1987 *Joseph,* Keith Sinjohn Joseph, C.H., P.C., *b.* 1918.

1983 *Kaberry of Adel,* Donald Kaberry, T.D., *b.* 1907, *m.*

1981 *Kadoorie,* Lawrence Kadoorie, C.B.E., *b.* 1899, *m.*

1976 *Kagan,* Joseph Kagan, *b.* 1915, *m.*

Created.

1970 *Kearton,* (Christopher) Frank Kearton, O.B.E., F.R.S., *b.* 1911, *m.*
1980 *Keith of Castleacre,* Kenneth Alexander Keith, *b.* 1916, *m.*
1985 *Kimball,* Marcus Richard Kimball, *b.* 1928, *m.*
1983 *King of Wartnaby,* John Leonard King, *b.* 1918, *m.*
1965 *Kings Norton,* Harold Roxbee Cox, PH.D., *b.* 1902, *m.*
1975 *Kirkhill,* John Farquharson Smith, *b.* 1930, *m.*
1974 *Kissin,* Harry Kissin, *b.* 1912, *m.*
1987 *Knights,* Philip Douglas Knights, C.B.E., Q.P.M., *b.* 1920, *m.*
1964 *Leatherland,* Charles Edward Leatherland, O.B.E., *b.* 1898, *w.*
1979 *Lever of Manchester,* Harold Lever, P.C., *b.* 1914, *m.*
1982 *Lewin,* Terence Thornton Lewin, K.G., G.C.B., L.V.O., D.S.C., *Admiral of the Fleet, b.* 1920, *m.*
1989 *Lewis of Newnham,* Jack Lewis, F.R.S., *b.* 1928, *m.*
1965 *Lloyd of Hampstead,* Dennis Lloyd, Q.C., LL.D., *b.* 1915, *m.*
1973 *Lloyd of Kilgerran,* Rhys Gerran Lloyd, C.B.E., Q.C., *b.* 1907, *m.*
1974 *Lovell-Davis,* Peter Lovell Lovell-Davis, *b.* 1924, *m.*
1979 *Lowry,* Robert Lynd Erskine Lowry, P.C., P.C.(N.I.), *b.* 1919, *w.* (*Lord of Appeal in Ordinary*).
1980 *McAlpine of Moffat,* (Robert) Edwin McAlpine, *b.* 1907, *m.*
1984 *McAlpine of West Green,* (Robert) Alistair McAlpine, *b.* 1942, *m.*
1988 *Macaulay of Bragar,* Donald Macaulay, Q.C., *b.* 1933.
1975 *McCarthy,* William Edward John McCarthy, *b.* 1925, *m.*
1976 *McCluskey,* John Herbert McCluskey, *b.* 1929, *m.*
1989 *McColl of Dulwich,* Ian McColl, F.R.C.S., F.R.C.S.E., *b.* 1933, *m.*
1966 *McFadzean,* William Hunter McFadzean, K.T., *b.* 1903, *m.*
1980 *McFadzean of Kelvinside,* Francis Scott McFadzean, *b.* 1915, *w.*
1978 *McGregor of Durris,* Oliver Ross McGregor, *b.* 1921, *m.*
1982 *McIntosh of Haringey,* Andrew Robert McIntosh, *b.* 1933, *m.*
1979 *Mackay of Clashfern,* James Peter Hymers Mackay, P.C., *b.* 1927, *m.* (*Lord High Chancellor*).
1988 *Mackenzie-Stuart,* Alexander John Mackenzie Stuart, *b.* 1924, *m.*
1974 *Mackie of Benshie,* George Yull Mackie, C.B.E., D.S.O., D.F.C., *b.* 1919, *w.*
1971 *Maclean,* Charles Hector Fitzroy Maclean, K.T., G.C.V.O., K.B.E., Royal Victorian Chain, P.C., *b.* 1916, *m.*
1982 *MacLehose of Beoch,* (Crawford) Murray MacLehose, K.T., G.B.E., K.C.M.G., K.C.V.O., *b.* 1917, *m.*
1967 *MacLeod of Fuinary,* Very Rev. George Fielden MacLeod, M.C., D.D., *b.* 1895, *w.*
1967 *Mais,* Alan Raymond Mais, G.B.E., T.D., E.R.D., *b.* 1911, *m.*
1981 *Marsh,* Richard William Marsh, P.C., *b.* 1928, *m.*
1985 *Marshall of Goring,* Walter Charles Marshall, C.B.E., F.R.S., *b.* 1932, *m.*
1980 *Marshall of Leeds,* Frank Shaw Marshall, *b.* 1915, *m.*
1987 *Mason of Barnsley,* Roy Mason, P.C., *b.* 1924, *m.*
1980 *Matthews,* Victor Collin Matthews, *b.* 1919, *m.*
1983 *Maude of Stratford-upon-Avon,* Angus Edmund Upton Maude, T.D., P.C., *b.* 1912, *m.*
1981 *Mayhew,* Christopher Paget Mayhew, *b.* 1915, *m.*
1985 *Mellish,* Robert Joseph Mellish, P.C., *b.* 1913, *m.*
1979 *Miles,* Bernard James Miles, C.B.E., *b.* 1907, *m.*
1978 *Mishcon,* Victor Mishcon, *b.* 1915, *m.*
1981 *Molloy,* William John Molloy, *b.* 1918, *m.*
1961 *Molson,* (Arthur) Hugh (Elsdale) Molson, P.C., *b.* 1903, *m.*
1986 *Moore of Wolvercote,* Philip Brian Cecil Moore, G.C.B., G.C.V.O., C.M.G., P.C., *b.* 1921, *m.*
1967 *Morris of Grasmere,* Charles Richard Morris, K.C.M.G., *b.* 1898, *w.*
1985 *Morton of Shuna,* Hugh Drennan Baird Morton, *b.* 1930, *m.*
1971 *Moyola,* James Dawson Chichester-Clark, P.C. (N.I.), *b.* 1923, *m.*
1984 *Mulley,* Frederick William Mulley, P.C., *b.* 1918, *m.*
1985 *Murray of Epping Forest,* Lionel Murray, O.B.E., P.C., *b.* 1922, *m.*
1964 *Murray of Newhaven,* Keith Anderson Hope Murray, K.C.B., PH.D., *b.* 1903.
1979 *Murton of Lindisfarne,* (Henry) Oscar Murton, O.B.E., T.D., P.C., *b.* 1914, *m.*
1975 *Northfield,* (William) Donald Chapman, *b.* 1923.
1966 *Nugent of Guildford,* (George) Richard (Hodges) Nugent, P.C., *b.* 1907, *m.*
1973 *O'Brien of Lothbury,* Leslie Kenneth O'Brien, G.B.E., P.C., *b.* 1908, *m.*
1970 *O'Neill of the Maine,* Terence Marne O'Neill, P.C. (N.I.), *b.* 1914, *m.*
1976 *Oram,* Albert Edward Oram, *b.* 1913, *m.*
1971 *Orr-Ewing,* (Charles) Ian Orr-Ewing, O.B.E., *b.* 1912, *m.*
1974 *Paget of Northampton,* Reginald Thomas Paget, Q.C., *b.* 1908, *m.*
1975 *Parry,* Gordon Samuel David Parry, *b.* 1925, *m.*
1967 *Penney,* William George Penney, O.M., K.B.E., PH.D., D.S.C., F.R.S., *b.* 1909, *m.*
1982 *Pennock,* Raymond William Pennock, *b.* 1920, *m.*
1979 *Perry of Walton,* Walter Laing Macdonald Perry, O.B.E., F.R.S., F.R.S.E., *b.* 1921, *m.*
1987 *Peston,* Maurice Harry Peston, *b.* 1931, *m.*
1983 *Peyton of Yeovil,* John Wynne William Peyton, P.C., *b.* 1919, *m.*
1975 *Pitt of Hampstead,* David Thomas Pitt, *b.* 1913, *m.*
1959 *Plowden,* Edwin Noel Plowden, G.B.E., K.C.B., *b.* 1907, *m.*
1987 *Plumb,* Charles Henry Plumb, *b.* 1925, *m.*
1981 *Plummer of St. Marylebone,* (Arthur) Desmond (Herne) Plummer, T.D., *b.* 1914, *m.*
1973 *Porritt,* Arthur Espie Porritt, G.C.M.G., G.C.V.O., C.B.E., *b.* 1900, *m.*
1987 *Prior,* James Michael Leathes Prior, P.C., *b.* 1927, *m.*
1975 *Pritchard,* Derek Wilbraham Pritchard, *b.* 1910, *m.*
1982 *Prys-Davies,* Gwilym Prys Prys-Davies, *b.* 1923, *m.*
1987 *Pym,* Francis Leslie Pym, M.C., P.C., *b.* 1922, *m.*
1982 *Quinton,* Anthony Meredith Quinton, *b.* 1925, *m.*

Created.

1978   *Rawlinson of Ewell*, Peter Anthony Grayson Rawlinson, P.C., Q.C., b. 1919, m.
1976   *Rayne*, Max Rayne, b. 1918, m.
1983   *Rayner*, Derek George Rayner, b. 1926.
1987   *Rees*, Peter Wynford Innes Rees, P.C., Q.C., b. 1926, m.
1988   *Rees-Mogg*, William Rees-Mogg, b. 1928, m.
1970   *Reigate*, John Kenyon Vaughan-Morgan, P.C., b. 1905, m.
1978   *Reilly*, Paul Reilly, b. 1912, m.
1979   *Renton*, David Lockhart-Mure Renton, K.B.E., T.D., P.C., Q.C., b. 1908, w.
1979   *Richardson*, John Samuel Richardson, L.V.O., M.D., F.R.C.P., b. 1910, m.
1983   *Richardson of Duntisbourne*, Gordon William Humphreys Richardson, K.G., M.B.E., T.D, P.C., b. 1915, m.
1987   *Rippon of Hexham*, (Aubrey) Geoffrey (Frederick) Rippon, P.C., Q.C., b. 1924, m.
1961   *Robens of Woldingham*, Alfred Robens, P.C., b. 1910, m.
1977   *Roll of Ipsden*, Eric Roll, K.C.M.G., C.B., b. 1907, m.
1987   *Ross of Newport*, Stephen Sherlock Ross, b. 1926, m.
1975   *Ryder of Eaton Hastings*, Sydney Thomas Franklin (Don) Ryder, b. 1916, m.
1962   *Sainsbury*, Alan John Sainsbury, b. 1902, m.
1989   *Sainsbury of Preston Candover*, John Davan Sainsbury, b. 1927, m.
1977   *Saint Brides*, John Morrice Cairns James, G.C.M.G., C.V.O., M.B.E., P.C., b. 1916, m.
1987   *St. John of Fawsley*, Norman Antony Francis St. John-Stevas, P.C., b. 1929.
1985   *Sanderson of Bowden*, Charles Russell Sanderson, b. 1933, m.
1979   *Scanlon*, Hugh Parr Scanlon, b. 1913, m.
1976   *Schon*, Frank Schon, b. 1912, m.
1972   *Seebohm*, Frederic Seebohm, T.D., b. 1909, m.
1978   *Sefton of Garston*, William Henry Sefton, b. 1915, m.
1958   *Shackleton*, Edward Arthur Alexander Shackleton, K.G., O.B.E., P.C., b. 1911, m.
1989   *Sharp of Grimsdyke*, Eric Sharp, C.B.E., b. 1916, m.
1959   *Shawcross*, Hartley William Shawcross, G.B.E., P.C., Q.C., b. 1902, w.
1980   *Sieff of Brimpton*, Marcus Joseph Sieff, O.B.E., b. 1913, m.
1971   *Simon of Glaisdale*, Jocelyn Edward Salis Simon, P.C., b. 1911, m. (*Lord of Appeal, retired*).
1978   *Smith*, Rodney Smith, K.B.E., F.R.C.S., b. 1914, m.
1965   *Soper*, Rev. Donald Oliver Soper, PH.D., b. 1903, m.
1983   *Stallard*, Albert William Stallard, b. 1921, m.
1987   *Stevens of Ludgate*, David Robert Stevens, b. 1936, w.
1979   *Stewart of Fulham*, Robert Michael Maitland Stewart, C.H., P.C., b. 1906, w.
1981   *Stodart of Leaston*, James Anthony Stodart, P.C., b. 1916, m.
1983   *Stoddart of Swindon*, David Leonard Stoddart, b. 1926, m.
1969   *Stokes*, Donald Gresham Stokes, T.D., b. 1914, m.
1979   *Strauss*, George Russell Strauss, P.C., b. 1901, m.
1981   *Swann*, Michael Meredith Swann, PH.D., F.R.S., b. 1920, m.
1971   *Tanlaw*, Simon Brooke Mackay, b. 1934, m.
1978   *Taylor of Blackburn*, Thomas Taylor, C.B.E., b. 1929, m.
1968   *Taylor of Gryfe*, Thomas Johnston Taylor, b. 1912, m.
1982   *Taylor of Hadfield*, Francis Taylor, b. 1905, m.
1966   *Taylor of Mansfield*, Harry Bernard Taylor, C.B.E., b. 1895, w.
1987   *Thomas of Gwydir*, Peter John Mitchell Thomas, P.C., Q.C., b. 1920, w.
1981   *Thomas of Swynnerton*, Hugh Swynnerton Thomas, b. 1931, m.
1977   *Thomson of Monifieth*, George Morgan Thomson, K.T., P.C., b. 1921, m.
1967   *Thorneycroft*, (George Edward) Peter Thorneycroft, C.H., P.C., b. 1909, m.
1962   *Todd*, Alexander Robertus Todd, O.M., D.SC., D.Phil., F.R.S., b. 1907, w.
1981   *Tordoff*, Geoffrey Johnson Tordoff, b. 1928, m.
1987   *Trafford*, Joseph Anthony Porteous Trafford, b. 1932, m.
1974   *Tranmire*, Robert Hugh Turton, K.B.E, M.C., P.C., b. 1903, m.
1979   *Underhill*, (Henry) Reginall Underhill, C.B.E., b. 1914, m.
1985   *Vinson*, Nigel Vinson, L.V.O., b. 1931, m.
1974   *Wallace of Campsie*, George Wallace, b. 1915, m.
1974   *Wallace of Coslany*, George Douglas Wallace, b. 1906, m.
1961   *Walston*, Henry David Leonard George Walston, C.V.O., b. 1912, m.
1989   *Walton of Detchant*, John Nicholas Walton, T.D., F.R.C.P., b. 1922, m.
1972   *Watkins*, Tudor Elwyn Watkins, b. 1903, m.
1977   *Wedderburn of Charlton*, Kenneth William Wedderburn, b. 1927, m.
1976   *Weidenfeld*, (Arthur) George Weidenfeld, b. 1919.
1980   *Weinstock*, Arnold Weinstock, b. 1924, m.
1965   *Wells-Pestell*, Reginald Alfred Wells-Pestell, C.B.E., b. 1910, m.
1978   *Whaddon*, (John) Derek Page, b. 1927, m.
1974   *Wigoder*, Basil Thomas Wigoder, Q.C., b. 1921, m.
1985   *Williams of Elvel*, Charles Cuthbert Powell Williams, C.B.E., b. 1933, m.
1963   *Willis*, Edward Henry Willis, b. 1918, m.
1969   *Wilson of Langside*, Henry Stephen Wilson, P.C., Q.C., b. 1916, m.
1983   *Wilson of Rievaulx*, (James) Harold Wilson, K.G., O.B.E., P.C., F.R.S., b. 1916, m.
1975   *Winstanley*, Michael Platt Winstanley, b. 1918, m.
1965   *Winterbottom*, Ian Winterbottom, b. 1913, m.
1985   *Wolfson*, Leonard Gordon Wolfson, b. 1927, m.
1987   *Wyatt of Weeford*, Woodrow Lyle Wyatt, b. 1918, m.
1978   *Young of Dartington*, Michael Young, PH.D., b. 1915, m.
1984   *Young of Graffham*, David Ivor Young, P.C., b. 1932, m.
1971   *Zuckerman*, Solly Zuckerman, O.M., K.C.B., F.R.S., M.D., D.SC., b. 1904, m.

BARONESSES

Created.

1979 *Airey of Abingdon*, Diana Josceline Barbara Neave Airey, *b.* 1919, *w.*
1970 *Bacon*, Alice Martha Bacon, C.B.E., P.C., *b.* 1911.
1967 *Birk*, Alma Birk, *b.* 1921, *m.*
1987 *Blackstone*, Tessa Ann Vosper Blackstone, PH.D., *b.* 1942.
1987 *Blatch*, Emily May Blatch, C.B.E., *b.* 1937, *m.*
1964 *Brooke of Ystradfellte*, Barbara Muriel Brooke, D.B.E., *b.* 1908, *w.*
1962 *Burton of Coventry*, Elaine Frances Burton, *b.* 1904.
1982 *Carnegy of Lour*, Elizabeth Patricia Carnegy of Lour, *b.* 1925.
1982 *Cox*, Caroline Anne Cox, *b.* 1937, *m.*
1978 *David*, Nora Ratcliff David, *b.* 1913, *m.*
1974 *Delacourt-Smith of Alteryn*, Margaret Rosalind Delacourt-Smith, *b.* 1916, *m.*
1978 *Denington*, Evelyn Joyce Denington, D.B.E., *b.* 1907, *m.*
1972 *Elles*, Diana Louie Elles, *b.* 1921, *m.*
1958 *Elliot of Harwood*, Katharine Elliot, D.B.E., *b.* 1903, *w.*
1981 *Ewart-Biggs*, (Felicity) Jane Ewart-Biggs, *b.* 1929, *w.*
1975 *Faithfull*, Lucy Faithfull, O.B.E., *b.* 1910.
1974 *Falkender*, Marcia Matilda Falkender, C.B.E., *b.* 1932.
1974 *Fisher of Rednal*, Doris Mary Gertrude Fisher, *b.* 1919, *w.*
1981 *Gardner of Parkes*, (Rachel) Trixie (Anne) Gardner, *b.* 1927, *m.*
1988 *Hart of South Lanark*, Judith Constance Mary Hart, D.B.E., P.C., *b.* 1924, *m.*
1985 *Hooper*, Gloria Dorothy Hooper, *b.* 1939.
1965 *Hylton-Foster*, Audrey Pellew Hylton-Foster, *b.* 1908, *w.*
1979 *Jeger*, Lena May Jeger, *b.* 1915, *w.*
1967 *Llewelyn-Davies of Hastoe*, (Annie) Patricia Llewelyn-Davies, P.C., *b.* 1915, *w.*
1978 *Lockwood*, Betty Lockwood, *b.* 1924, *w.*
1979 *McFarlane of Llandaff*, Jean Kennedy McFarlane, *b.* 1926.
1971 *Macleod of Borve*, Evelyn Hester Macleod, *b.* 1915, *w.*
1970 *Masham of Ilton*, Susan Lilian Primrose Cunliffe-Lister, *b.* 1935, *m.* (*Countess of Swinton*).
1982 *Nicol*, Olive Mary Wendy Nicol, *b.* 1923, *m.*
1989 *Oppenheim-Barnes*, Sally Oppenheim-Barnes, P.C., *b.* 1930, *m.*
1964 *Phillips*, Norah Phillips, *b.* 1910, *w.*
1974 *Pike*, (Irene) Mervyn (Parnicott) Pike, D.B.E., *b.* 1918.
1981 *Platt of Writtle*, Beryl Catherine Platt, C.B.E., *b.* 1923, *m.*
1974 *Robson of Kiddington*, Inga-Stina Robson, *b.* 1919, *w.*
1979 *Ryder of Warsaw*, (Margaret) Susan Cheshire, C.M.G., O.B.E., *b.* 1924, *m.*
1971 *Seear*, (Beatrice) Nancy Seear, P.C., *b.* 1913.
1967 *Serota*, Beatrice Serota, *b.* 1919, *m.*
1973 *Sharples*, Pamela Sharples, *b.* 1923, *m.*
1974 *Stedman*, Phyllis Stedman, O.B.E., *b.* 1916, *m.*
1980 *Trumpington*, Jean Alys Barker, *b.* 1922, *w.*
1985 *Turner of Camden*, Muriel Winifred Turner, *b.* 1927, *m.*
1974 *Vickers*, Joan Helen Vickers, D.B.E., *b.* 1907.
1985 *Warnock*, Helen Mary Warnock, D.B.E., *b.* 1924, *m.*
1970 *White*, Eirene Lloyd White, *b.* 1909, *w.*
1971 *Young*, Janet Mary Young, P.C., *b.* 1926, *m.*

LIFE PEERAGES EXTINCT SINCE LAST ISSUE.—Cooper of Stockton Heath (*cr.* 1966); Roberthall (*cr.* 1969); Wade (*cr.* 1964); Lee of Asheridge (*cr.* 1970); Basnett (*cr.* 1987); Fraser of Tullybelton (*cr.* 1975); Chelwood (*cr.* 1974); Kahn (*cr.* 1965); Gaitskill (*cr.* 1963); Olivier (*cr.* 1970); Bowden (*cr.* 1963); Cross of Chelsea (*cr.* 1971); Hill of Luton (*cr.* 1963).

COURTESY TITLES

Holders of Courtesy Titles are addressed in the same manner as holders of substantive titles.

From this list it will be seen that, for example, the Marquess of Blandford is heir to the Dukedom of Marlborough, and Viscount Althorp to the Earldom of Spencer. Titles of second heirs are also given, and the Courtesy Title of the father of a second heir is indicated by *; e.g., Earl of Burlington, eldest son of *Marquess of Hartington.

Marquesses

Blandford—*Marlborough, D.*
Bowmont—*Roxburghe, D.*
Douglas and Clydesdale—*Hamilton, D.*
*Douro—*Wellington, D.*
*Graham—*Montrose, D.*
Granby—*Rutland, D.*
Hamilton—*Abercorn, D.*
*Hartington—*Devonshire, D.*
*Kildare—*Leinster, D.*
Lorne—*Argyll, D.*
*Tavistock—*Bedford, D.*
Worcester—*Beaufort, D.*

Earls

*Aboyne—*Huntly, M.*
Altamont—*Sligo, M.*
Ancram—*Lothian, M.*
Arundel and Surrey—*Norfolk, D.*
Bective—*Headfort, M.*
Belfast—*Donegall, M.*
*Brecknock—*Camden, M.*
Burford—*St. Albans, D.*
Burlington—*Hartington, M.*
Cardigan—*Ailesbury, M.*
Cassillis—*Ailsa, M.*
Compton—*Northampton, M.*
Dalkeith—*Buccleuch, D.*
Dumfries—*Bute, M.*
*Euston—*Grafton, D.*
Haddo—*Aberdeen and Temair, M.*
Hillsborough—*Downshire, M.*
*Hopetoun—*Linlithgow, M.*
Macduff—*Fife, D.*
*March and Kinrara—*Richmond, D.*
*Mount Charles—*Conyngham, M.*
Mornington—*Douro, M.*
Mulgrave—*Normanby, M.*
Offaly—*Kildare, M.*
Rocksavage—*Cholmondeley, M.*
*Ronaldshay—*Zetland, M.*
*St. Andrews—*Kent, D.*
*Shelburne—*Lansdowne, M.*
Tyrone—*Waterford, M.*
Ulster—*Gloucester, D.*
Uxbridge—*Anglesey, M.*
Wiltshire—*Winchester, M.*
Yarmouth—*Hertford, M.*

Viscounts

Althorp—*Spencer, E.*

Amberley—*Russell, E.*
Andover—*Suffolk and Berkshire, E.*
Anson—*Lichfield, E.*
Asquith—*Oxford & Asquith, E.*
Boringdon—*Morley, E.*
Borodale—*Beatty, E.*
Boyle—*Shannon, E.*
Brocas—*Jellicoe, E.*
Calne and Calstone—*Shelburne, E.*
Campden—*Gainsborough, E.*
Carlow—*Portarlington, E.*
Carlton—*Wharncliffe, E.*
Castlereagh—*Londonderry, M.*
Chelsea—*Cadogan, E.*
Chewton—*Waldegrave, E.*
Clanfield—*Peel, E.*
Clive—*Powis, E.*
Coke—*Leicester, E.*
Corry—*Belmore, E.*
Corvedale—*Baldwin of Bewdley, E.*
Cranborne—*Salisbury, M.*
Cranley—*Onslow, E.*
Crichton—*Erne, E.*
Crowhurst—*Cottenham, E.*
Dalrymple—*Stair, E.*
Dangan—*Cowley, E.*
Dawick—*Haig, E.*
Deerhurst—*Coventry, E.*
Drumlanrig—*Queensberry, M.*
Dunwich—*Stradbroke, E.*
Dupplin—*Kinnoull, E.*
Ebrington—*Fortescue, E.*
Ednam—*Dudley, E.*
Elveden—*Iveagh, E.*
Emlyn—*Cawdor, E.*
Encombe—*Eldon, E.*
Ennismore—*Listowel, E.*
Enfield—*Strafford, E.*
Erleigh—*Reading, M.*
Errington—*Cromer, E.*
Feilding—*Denbigh, E.*
Fincastle—*Dunmore, E.*
FitzHarris—*Malmesbury, E.*
Folkestone—*Radnor, E.*
Garmoyle—*Cairns, E.*
Glandine—*Norbury, E.*
Glenapp—*Inchcape, E.*
Glentworth—*Limerick, E.*
Grimstone—*Verulam, E.*
Gwynedd—*Lloyd George of Dwyfor, E.*
Hawkesbury—*Liverpool, E.*
Ikerrin—*Carrick, E.*
Ingestre—*Shrewsbury, E.*
Ipswich—*Euston, E.*
Jocelyn—*Roden, E.*
Kelburn—*Glasgow, E.*

Kingsborough—*Kingston, E.*
Knebworth—*Lytton, E.*
Lascelles—*Harewood, E.*
Lewisham—*Dartmouth, E.*
Linley—*Snowdon, E.*
Loftus—*Ely, M.*
Lowther—*Lonsdale, E.*
Lumley—*Scarbrough, E.*
Lymington—*Portsmouth, E.*
Macmillan of Ovenden—*Stockton, E.*
Maidstone — *Winchilsea and Nottingham, E.*
Maitland—*Lauderdale, E.*
Malden—*Essex, E.*
Mandeville—*Manchester, D.*
Melgund—*Minto, E.*
Merton—*Nelson, E.*
Moore—*Drogheda, E.*
Morpeth—*Carlisle, E.*
Newport—*Bradford, E.*
Newry and Mourne—*Kilmorey, E.*
Northland—*Ranfurly, E.*
Parker—*Macclesfield, E.*
Perceval—*Egmont, E.*
Petersham—*Harrington, E.*
Pollington—*Mexborough, E.*
Prestwood—*Attlee, E.*
Quenington—*St. Aldwyn, E.*
Raynham—*Townshend, M.*
Reidhaven—*Seafield, E.*
Ruthven of Canberra—*Gowrie, E.*
St. Cyres—*Iddesleigh, E.*
Sandon—*Harrowby, E.*
Slane—*Mount Charles, E.*
Somerton—*Normanton, E.*
Stopford—*Courtown, E.*
Stormont—*Mansfield, E.*
Strathallan—*Perth, E.*
Stuart—*Castle Stewart, E.*
Suirdale—*Donoughmore, E.*
Tamworth—*Ferrers, E.*
Tarbat—*Cromartie, E.*
Tiverton—*Halsbury, E.*
Vaughan—*Lisburne, E.*
Villiers—*Jersey, E.*
Weymouth—*Bath, M.*
Windsor—*Plymouth, E.*
Wolmer—*Selborne, E.*

Barons (Lord—)

Aberdour—*Morton, E.*
Apsley—*Bathurst, E.*
Ardee—*Meath, E.*
Ashley—*Shaftesbury, E.*

Balgonie—*Leven & Melville, E.*
Balniel—*Crawford and Balcarres, E.*
Berriedale—*Caithness, E.*
Bingham—*Lucan, E.*
Binning—*Haddington, E.*
Brooke—*Warwick, E.*
Bruce—*Elgin, E.*
Buckhurst—*De La Warr, E.*
Burghersh—*Westmorland, E.*
Burghley—*Exeter, M.*
Cardross—*Buchan, E.*
Clifton—*Darnley, E.*
Courtenay—*Devon, E.*
Dalmeny—*Rosebery, E.*
Doune—*Moray, E.*
Downpatrick—*St. Andrews, E.*
Dundas—*Ronaldshay, E.*
Eliot—*St. Germans, E.*
Erskine—*Mar & Kellie, E.*
Fintrie—*Graham, M.*
Gillford—*Clanwilliam, E.*
Glamis—*Strathmore, E.*
Greenock—*Cathcart, E.*
Guernsey—*Aylesford, E.*
Hay—*Erroll, E.*
Herbert—*Pembroke, E.*
Howland—*Tavistock, M.*
Hyde—*Clarendon, E.*
Inverurie—*Kintore, E.*
Irwin—*Halifax, E.*
Johnstone—*Annandale and Hartfell, E.*
Leslie—*Rothes, E.*
Leveson—*Granville, E.*
Loughborough—*Rosslyn, E.*
Mauchline—*Loudoun, C.*
Medway—*Cranbrook, E.*
Montgomerie—*Eglinton and Winton, E.*
Moreton—*Ducie, E.*
Naas—*Mayo, E.*
Neidpath—*Wemyss & March, E.*
Norreys—*Lindsey & Abingdon, E.*
North—*Guilford, E.*
Ogilvy—*Airlie, E.*
Oxmantown—*Rosse, E.*
Porchester—*Carnarvon, E.*
Ramsay—*Dalhousie, E.*
Romsey—*Mountbatten of Burma, C.*
Rosehill—*Northesk, E.*
Scrymgeour—*Dundee, E.*
Settrington—*March and Kinrara, E.*
Seymour—*Somerset, D.*
Strathnaver—*Sutherland, C.*
Wodehouse—*Kimberley, E.*
Worsley—*Yarborough, E.*

Surnames of Peers differing from their Titles

The following symbols indicate the rank of the peer holding each title: C. Countess; D. Duke; E. Earl; M. Marquess; V. Viscount; *Life Peer/Peeress. Where no designation is given, the title is that of an hereditary Baron or Baroness.

Abney-Hastings—
 Loudoun, C.
Acheson—Gosford, E.
Adderley—Norton
Addington—Sidmouth,
 V.
Agar—Normanton, E.
Airey—A. of Abingdon*
Aitken—Beaverbrook
Akers-Douglas—
 Chilston, V.
Alexander—A. of
 Potterhill*
Alexander—A. of Tunis,
 E.
Alexander—A. of
 Weedon*
Alexander—Caledon, E.
Allen—A. of Abbeydale*
Allen—Croham*
Allanson-Winn—Headley
Allsopp—Hindlip
Aman—Marley
Anderson—Waverley, V.
Annesley—Valentia, V.
Anson—Lichfield, E.
Armstrong—A. of
 Ilminster*
Armstrong-Jones—
 Snowdon, E.
Arthur—Glenarthur
Arundell—Talbot of
 Malahide
Ashley-Cooper—
 Shaftesbury, E.
Ashton—A. of Hyde
Asquith—Oxford &
 Asquith, E.
Assheton—Clitheroe
Astley—Hastings
Astor—A. of Hever
Atkins—Colnbrook*
Aubrey-Fletcher—Braye
Bailey—Glanusk
Baillie—Burton
Baillie Hamilton—
 Haddington, E.
Baldwin—B. of Bewdley,
 E.
Balfour—B. of Inchrye
Balfour—Kinross
Balfour—Riverdale
Bampfylde—Poltimore
Banbury—B. of Southam
Baring—Ashburton
Baring—Cromer, E.
Baring—Howick of
 Glendale
Baring—Northbrook
Baring—Revelstoke
Barker—Trumpington*
Barnes—Gorell
Barnewall—Trimlestown
Bathurst—Bledisloe, V.
Beauclerk—St. Albans,
 D.
Beaumont—Allendale, V.
Beaumont—B. of
 Whitley*
Beavan—Ardwick*
Beckett—Grimthorpe

Bellow—Bellwin*
Bennet—Tankerville, E.
Beresford—Decies
Beresford—Waterford, M.
Berry—Camrose, V.
Berry—Hartwell*
Berry—Kemsley, V.
Bertie—Lindsey, E.
Best—Wynford
Bethell—Westbury
Bevan—Lee of Asheridge*
Bewicke-Copley—
 Cromwell
Bigham—Mersey, V.
Bigham—Nairne
Bingham—Clanmorris
Bingham—Lucan, E.
Blackwood—Dufferin &
 Clandeboye
Blades—Ebbisham
Bligh—Darnley, E.
Bootle-Wilbraham—
 Skelmersdale
Boscawen—Falmouth, V.
Boston—Boston of
 Faversham*
Bourke—Mayo, E.
Bowden—Aylestone*
Bowes Lyon—Strathmore,
 E.
Bowyer—Denham
Boyd—Kilmarnock
Boyle—Cork & Orrery, E.
Boyle—Glasgow, E.
Boyle—Shannon, E.
Brabazon—Meath, E.
Brand—Hampden, V.
Brandon—B. of
 Oakbrook*
Brassey—B. of Apethorpe
Brett—Esher, V.
Bridge—B. of Harwich*
Bridgeman—Bradford, E.
Brodrick—Midleton, V.
Brooke—Alanbrooke, V.
Brooke—Brookeborough,
 V.
Brooke—B. of
 Ystradfellte*
Brooks—B. of Tremorfa*
Brooks—Crawshaw
Brougham—Brougham
 and Vaux
Broughton—Fairhaven
Browne—Craigton*
Browne—Kilmaine
Browne—Oranmore and
 Browne
Browne—Sligo, M.
Brownlow—Lurgan
Bruce—Aberdare
Bruce—Balfour of
 Burleigh
Bruce—B. of Donington*
Bruce—Elgin and
 Kincardine, E.
Brudenell-Bruce—
 Ailesbury, M.
Buchan—Tweedsmuir
Buckley—Wrenbury
Burton—B. of Coventry*

Butler—Carrick, E.
Butler—Dunboyne
Butler—Lanesborough, E.
Butler—Mountgarret, V.
Butler—Ormonde, M.
Buxton—B. of Alsa*
Byng—Strafford, E.
Byng—Torrington, V.
Callaghan—C. of Cardiff*
Cameron—C. of
 Lochbroom*
Campbell—Argyll, D.
Campbell—Breadalbane
 and Holland, E.
Campbell—C. of Alloway*
Campbell—C. of Croy*
Campbell—C. of Eskan*
Campbell—Cawdor, E.
Campbell—Colgrain
Campbell—Stratheden
 and Campbell
Campbell-Gray—Gray
Canning—Garvagh
Capell—Essex, E.
Carington—Carrington
Carlisle—C. of Bucklow*
Carmichael—C. of
 Kelvingrove*
Carnegie—Fife, D.
Carnegie—Northesk, E.
Carnegie—Southesk, E.
Carr—C. of Hadley*
Cary—Falkland, V.
Caulfeild—Charlemont,
 V.
Cavendish—Chesham
Cavendish—Devonshire,
 D.
Cavendish—Waterpark
Cavendish-Bentinck—
 Portland, D.
Cayzer—Rotherwick
Cecil—Amherst of
 Hackney
Cecil—Exeter, M.
Cecil—Rockley
Cecil—Salisbury, M.
Chaloner—Gisborough
Chapman—Northfield*
Charteris—C. of
 Amisfield*
Charteris—Wemyss and
 March, E.
Cheshire—Ryder of
 Warsaw*
Chetwynd-Talbot—
 Shrewsbury, E.
Chichester—Donegall, M.
Chichester-Clark—
 Moyola*
Child-Villiers—Jersey, E.
Cholmondeley—Delamere
Chubb—Hayter
Clegg-Hill—Hill, V.
Clifford—Clifford of
 Chudleigh
Cochrane—C. of Cults
Cochrane—Dundonald,
 E.
Cocks—C. of Hartcliffe*
Cocks—Somers

Cokayne—Cullen of
 Ashbourne
Coke—Leicester, E.
Cole—Enniskillen, E.
Collier—Monkswell
Colville—Clydesmuir
Colville—C. of Culross, V.
Compton—Northampton,
 M.
Conolly-Carew—Carew
Constantine—C. of
 Stanmore*
Cooper—Norwich, V.
Corbett—Rowallan
Courtenay—Devon, E.
Cox—Kings Norton*
Craig—Craigavon, V.
Crichton—Erne, E.
Crichton-Stuart—Bute,
 M.
Cripps—Parmoor
Crossley—Somerleyton
Cubitt—Ashcombe
Cunliffe-Lister—
 Masham of Ilton*
Cunliffe-Lister—
 Swinton, E.
Curzon—Howe, E.
Curzon—Scarsdale, V.
Cust—Brownlow
Dalrymple—Stair, E.
Daubeny de Moleyns—
 Ventry
Davies—Darwen
Davies—D. of Penrhys*
Davison—Broughshane
Dawnay—Downe, V.
Dawson-Damer—
 Portarlington, E.
Dean—D. of Beswick*
Deane—Muskerry
de Courcy—Kingsale
de Grey—Walsingham
Delacourt-Smith—
 Delacourt Smith of
 Alteryn*
Denison—Londesborough
Denison-Pender—Pender
Devereux—Hereford, V.
Dewar—Forteviot
De Yarburgh-Bateson—
 Deramore
Dixon—Glentoran
Dodson—Monk Bretton
Donaldson—D. of
 Kingsbridge*
Donaldson—D. of
 Lymington*
Dormand—D. of
 Easington*
Douglas—Morton, E.
Douglas—Queensberry,
 M.
Douglas-Hamilton—
 Hamilton, D.
Douglas-Hamilton—
 Selkirk, E.
Douglas-Home—Dacre
Douglas-Home—Home of
 the Hirsel*

Douglas–Pennant—
  Penrhyn
Douglas–Scott–
  Montagu—*Montagu of*
  Beaulieu
Drummond—*Perth, E.*
Drummond—*Strange*
Dugdale—*Crathorne*
Duke—*Merrivale*
Duncombe—*Feversham*
Dundas—*Melville, V.*
Dundas—*Zetland, M.*
Eady—*Swinfen*
Eden—*Auckland*
Eden—*E. of Winton**
Eden—*Henley*
Edgcumbe—*Mount*
  Edgcumbe, E.
Edmondson—*Sandford*
Edwardes—*Kensington*
Edwards—*Chelmer**
Edwards—*Crickhowell**
Egerton—*Sutherland, D.*
Egerton—*Wilton, E.*
Eliot—*St. Germans, E.*
Elliot—*E. of Harwood**
Elliot-Murray-
  Kynynmound—*Minto,*
  E.
Elliott—*E. of Morpeth**
Erroll—*E. of Hale*
Erskine—*Buchan, E.*
Erskine—*E. of Rerrick*
Erskine—*Mar & Kellie,*
  E.
Erskine-Murray—
  Elibank
Evans—*E. of Claughton**
Evans—*Mountevans*
Evans-Freke—*Carbery*
Eve—*Silsoe*
Eyres Monsell—*Monsell,*
  V.
Fairfax—*F. of Cameron*
Fane—*Westmorland, E.*
Feilding—*Denbigh, E.*
Fellowes—*De Ramsey*
Fermor-Hesketh—
  Hesketh
Fiennes—*Saye & Sele*
Fiennes-Clinton—
  Lincoln, E.
Finch Hatton—
  Winchilsea, E.
Finch-Knightley—
  Aylesford, E.
Fisher—*F. of Rednal**
Fitzalan–Howard—
  Herries of Terregles
Fitzalan–Howard—
  Norfolk, D.
FitzClarence—*Munster,*
  E.
FitzGerald—*Leinster, D.*
Fitzherbert—*Stafford*
Fitz–Maurice—*Orkney,*
  E.
FitzRoy—*Grafton, D.*
FitzRoy Newdegate—
  Daventry, V.
Fletcher-Vane—
  Inglewood
Flower—*Ashbrook, V.*
Foley-Berkeley—
  Berkeley

Foljambe—*Liverpool, E.*
Foot—*Caradon**
Forbes—*Granard, E.*
Fox-Strangways—
  Ilchester, E.
Frankland—*Zouche*
Fraser—*F. of Carmyllie**
Fraser—*F. of Kilmorack**
Fraser—*Lovat*
Fraser—*Saltoun*
Fraser—*Strathalmond*
Freeman-Grenville—
  Kinloss
Fremantle—*Cottesloe*
French—*De Freyne*
Galbraith—*Strathclyde*
Ganzoni—*Belstead*
Gardner—*G. of Parkes**
Gathorne-Hardy—
  Cranbrook, E.
Gibbs—*Aldenham*
Gibbs—*Wraxall*
Gibson—*Ashbourne*
Giffard—*Halsbury, E.*
Gilbey—*Vaux of*
  Harrowden
Glyn—*Wolverton*
Godley—*Kilbracken*
Goff—*G. of Chieveley**
Gordon—*Aberdeen, M.*
Gordon—*Huntly, M.*
Gordon Lennox—
  Richmond, D.
Gore—*Arran, E.*
Gough-Calthorpe—
  Calthorpe
Graham—*G. of*
  Edmonton*
Graham—*Montrose, D.*
Graham-Toler—*Norbury,*
  E.
Grant of Grant—
  Strathspey
Grant-Ferris—
  Harvington*
Granville—*G. of Eye**
Gray—*G. of Contin**
Greaves—*Dysart, C.*
Greenall—*Daresbury*
Greene—*G. of Harrow*
  Weald*
Greenhill—*G. of Harrow**
Greville—*Warwick, E.*
Grey—*G. of Naunton**
Grimston—*G. of Westbury*
Grimston—*Verulam, E.*
Grosvenor—*Ebury*
Grosvenor—*Westminster,*
  D.
Guest—*Wimborne, E.*
Guinness—*Iveagh, E.*
Guinness—*Moyne*
Gully—*Selby, V.*
Gurdon—*Cranworth*
Gwynne Jones—
  Chalfont*
Hamilton—*Abercorn, D.*
Hamilton—*Belhaven and*
  Stenton
Hamilton—*Dudley*
Hamilton—*H. of Dalzell*
Hamilton—*Holm Patrick*
Hamilton-Russell—
  Boyne, V.

Hamilton-Smith—
  Colwyn
Hanbury-Tracy—
  Sudeley
Handcock—*Castlemaine*
Harbord-Hamond—
  Suffield
Harding—*H. of Petherton*
Hardinge—*H. of*
  Penshurst
Hare—*Blakenham, V.*
Hare—*Listowel, E.*
Harmsworth—
  Rothermere, V.
Harris—*H. of Greenwich**
Harris—*H. of High Cross**
Harris—*Malmesbury, E.*
Hart—*H. of South*
  Lanark*
Harvey—*H. of Prestbury**
Harvey—*H. of Tasburgh*
Hastings—*Huntingdon,*
  E.
Hatch—*H. of Lusby**
Hay—*Erroll, E.*
Hay—*Kinnoull, E.*
Hay—*Tweeddale, M.*
Heathcote-Drummond-
  Willoughby—
  Willoughby de Eresby
Hely-Hutchinson—
  Donoughmore, E.
Henderson—*Faringdon*
Henderson—*H. of*
  Brompton*
Hennessy—*Windlesham*
Henniker-Major—
  Henniker
Hepburne-Scott—
  Polwarth
Herbert—*Carnarvon, E.*
Herbert—*Hemingford*
Herbert—*Pembroke, E.*
Herbert—*Powis, E.*
Hermon-Hodge—*Wyfold*
Hervey—*Bristol, M.*
Hewitt—*Lifford, V.*
Hicks Beach—*St.*
  Aldwyn, E.
Hill—*Downshire, M.*
Hill—*Sandys*
Hill-Trevor—*Trevor*
Hobart-Hampden—
  Buckinghamshire, E.
Hogg—*Hailsham of St.*
  Marylebone*
Holland-Hibbert—
  Knutsford, V.
Holmes à Court—
  Heytesbury
Hood—*Bridport, V.*
Hope—*Glendevon*
Hope—*Linlithgow, M.*
Hope—*Rankeillour*
Hope Johnstone—
  Annandale and
  Hartfell, E.
Hope-Morley—*Hollenden*
Hopkinson—*Colyton*
Hopwood—*Southborough*
Hore Ruthven—*Gowrie,*
  E.
Houghton—*H. of*
  Sowerby*

Hovell-Thurlow-
  Cumming-Bruce—
  Thurlow
Howard—*Carlisle, E.*
Howard—*Effingham, E.*
Howard—*H. of Penrith*
Howard—*Strathcona*
Howard—*Suffolk and*
  Berkshire, E.
Howie—*H. of Troon**
Hubbard—*Addington*
Huggins—*Malvern, V.*
Hughes—*Cledwyn of*
  Penrhos*
Hughes-Young—*St.*
  Helens
Hunt—*H. of Tanworth**
Hunter—*H. of*
  Newington*
Hutchinson—*H. of*
  Lullington*
Ingrams—*Darcy de*
  Knayth
Innes-Ker—*Roxburghe,*
  D.
Inskip—*Caldecote, V.*
Irby—*Boston*
Irvine—*I. of Lairg**
Irving—*I. of Dartford**
Isaacs—*Reading, M.*
Jackson—*Allerton*
James—*J. of Rusholme**
James—*Northbourne*
James—*Saint Brides**
Jauncey—*J. of*
  Tullichettle*
Jebb—*Gladwyn*
Jenkin—*J. of Roding**
Jenkins—*J. of Hillhead**
Jenkins—*J. of Putney**
Jervis—*St. Vincent, V.*
Jocelyn—*Roden, E.*
Johnston—*J. of*
  Rockport*
Jolliffe—*Hylton*
Joynson-Hicks—
  Brentford, V.
Kaberry—*K. of Adel**
Kay-Shuttleworth—
  Shuttleworth
Kearley—*Devonport, V.*
Keith—*K. of Castleacre**
Keith—*K. of Kinkel**
Keith—*Kintore, E.*
Kemp—*Rochdale, V.*
Kennedy—*Ailsa, M.*
Kenworthy—*Strabolgi*
Keppel—*Albemarle, E.*
Kerr—*Lothian, M.*
Kerr—*Teviot*
King—*Lovelace, E.*
King—*K. of Wartnaby**
King-Tenison—*Kingston,*
  E.
Kitchener—*K. of*
  Khartoum, E.
Kitson—*Airedale*
Knatchbull—*Brabourne*
Knatchbull-
  Mountbatten of Burma,
  C.
Knox—*Ranfurly, E.*
Lamb—*Rochester*
Lambart—*Cavan, E.*
Lampson—*Killearn*

Lascelles—Harewood, E.
Law—Coleraine
Law—Ellenborough
Lawrence—Trevethin and Oaksey
Lawson—Burnham
Lawson-Johnston—Luke
Legge—Dartmouth, E.
Legh—Newton
Leith—Burgh
Lennox-Boyd—Boyd of Merton; V.
Le Poer Trench—Clancarty, E.
Leslie—Rothes, E.
Leslie Melville—Leven and Melville, E.
Lever—Leverhulme, V.
Lever—L. of Manchester*
Leveson-Gower—Granville, E.
Lewis—L. of Newnham*
Liddell—Ravensworth
Lindesay-Bethune—Lindsay, E.
Lindsay—Crawford, E.
Lindsay—L. of Birker
Littleton—Hatherton
Llewelyn-Davies—Llewelyn-Davies of Hastoe*
Lloyd—L. of Hampstead*
Lloyd—L. of Kilgerran*
Lloyd George—Lloyd George of Dwyfor, E.
Lloyd George—Tenby, V.
Lloyd-Mostyn—Mostyn
Loder—Wakehurst
Lopes—Roborough
Low—Aldington
Lowry-Corry—Belmore, E.
Lowther—Lonsdale, E.
Lowther—Ullswater, V.
Lubbock—Avebury
Lucas—L. of Chilworth
Lumley—Scarbrough, E.
Lumley-Savile—Savile
Lyon-Dalberg-Acton—Acton
Lysaght—Lisle
Lyttelton—Chandos, V.
Lyttelton—Cobham, V.
Lytton Cobbold—Cobbold
McAlpine—M. of Moffat*
McAlpine—M. of West Green*
Macaulay—M. of Bragar*
McClintock-Bunbury—Rathdonnell
McColl—M. of Dulwich*
Macdonald—M. of Gwaenysgor
Macdonald of Macdonald—Macdonald
McDonnell—Antrim, E.
McFadzean—M. of Kelvinside*
McFarlane—M. of Llandaff*
McGregor—M. of Durris*
McIntosh—M. of Haringey*

Mackay—Inchcape, E.
Mackay—M. of Clashfern*
Mackay—Reay
Mackay—Tanlaw*
Mackenzie—Cromartie, E.
Mackie—John-Mackie*
Mackie—M. of Benshie*
Mackintosh—M. of Halifax, V.
McLaren—Aberconway
Maclay—Muirshiel, V.
MacLehose—M. of Beoch*
Macleod—M. of Borve*
MacLeod—M. of Fuinary*
Macmillan—Stockton, E.
Macpherson—M. of Drumochter
Macpherson—Strathcarron
Maffey—Rugby
Maitland—Lauderdale, E.
Makgill—Oxfuird, V.
Makins—Sherfield
Manners—Rutland, D.
Manningham-Buller—Dilhorne, V.
Mansfield—Sandhurst
Marks—M. of Broughton
Marquis—Woolton, E.
Marshall—M. of Goring*
Marshall—M. of Leeds*
Marsham—Romney, E.
Martyn-Hemphill—Hemphill
Mason—M. of Barnsley*
Maude—Hawarden, V.
Maude—M. of Stratford-upon-Avon*
Maxwell—de Ros
Maxwell—Farnham
Meade—Clanwilliam, E.
Mercer Nairne Petty-Fitzmaurice—Lansdowne, M.
Millar—Inchyra
Milles-Lade—Sondes, E.
Milner—M. of Leeds
Mitchell-Thomson—Selsdon
Mitford—Redesdale
Monckton—M. of Brenchley, V.
Monckton-Arundell—Galway, V.
Mond—Melchett
Money-Coutts—Latymer
Montagu—Manchester, D.
Montagu—Swaythling
Montagu Douglas Scott—Buccleuch, D.
Montagu Stuart Wortley—Wharncliffe, E.
Montague—Amwell
Montgomerie—Eglinton, E.
Montgomery—M. of Alamein, V.
Moore—Drogheda, E.
Moore—M. of Wolvercote*

Moore-Brabazon—Brabazon of Tara
Moreton—Ducie, E.
Morris—Killanin
Morris—M. of Grasmere*
Morris—M. of Kenwood
Morrison—Dunrossil, V.
Morrison—Margadale
Morton—M. of Shuna*
Mosley—Ravensdale
Mountbatten—Milford Haven, M.
Muff—Calverley
Mulholland—Dunleath
Murray—Atholl, D.
Murray—Dunmore, E.
Murray—Mansfield and Mansfield, E.
Murray—M. of Epping Forest*
Murray—M. of Newhaven*
Murton—M. of Lindisfarne*
Nall-Cain—Brocket
Napier—Napier and Ettrick
Napier—N. of Magdala
Needham—Kilmorey, E.
Nelson—N. of Stafford
Nevill—Abergavenny, M.
Neville—Braybrooke
Nicolson—Carnock
Nivison—Glendyne
Noel—Gainsborough, E.
Noel-Paton—Ferrier*
North—Guilford, E.
Northcote—Iddesleigh, E.
Norton—Grantley
Norton—Rathcreedan
Nugent—N. of Guildford*
Nugent—Westmeath, E.
O'Brien—Inchiquin
O'Brien—O'Brien of Lothbury*
Ogilvie-Grant—Seafield, E.
Ogilvy—Airlie, E.
Oliver—O. of Aylmerton*
O'Neill—O'Neill of the Maine*
O'Neill—Rathcavan
Orde-Powlett—Bolton
Ormsby-Gore—Harlech
Page—Whaddon*
Paget—Anglesey, M.
Paget—P. of Northampton*
Pakenham—Longford, E.
Pakington—Hampton
Palmer—Lucas of Crudwell
Palmer—Selborne, E.
Parker—Macclesfield, E.
Parker—Morley, E.
Parnell—Congleton
Parsons—Rosse, E.
Paulet—Winchester, M.
Peake—Ingleby, V.
Pearson—Cowdray, V.
Pease—Daryngton
Pease—Gainford
Pease—Wardington
Pelham—Chichester, E.
Pelham—Yarborough, E.

Pellew—Exmouth, V.
Penny—Marchwood, V.
Pepys—Cottenham, E.
Perceval—Egmont, E.
Percy—Northumberland, D.
Perry—P. of Walton*
Pery—Limerick, E.
Peyton—P. of Yeovil*
Philipps—Milford
Philipps—St. Davids, V.
Phipps—Normanby, M.
Pitt—P. of Hampstead*
Platt—P. of Writtle*
Pleydell-Bouverie—Radnor, E.
Plummer—P. of St. Marylebone*
Plumptre—Fitzwalter
Plunkett—Dunsany
Plunkett—Louth
Pollock—Hanworth, V.
Pomeroy—Harberton, V.
Ponsonby—Bessborough, E.
Ponsonby—de Mauley
Ponsonby—P. of Shulbrede
Ponsonby—Sysonby
Portal—P. of Hungerford
Powys—Lilford
Pratt—Camden, M.
Preston—Gormanston, V.
Primrose—Rosebery, E.
Prittie—Dunalley
Ramsay—Dalhousie, E.
Ramsbotham—Soulbury, V.
Rawlinson—R. of Ewell*
Rees-Williams—Ogmore
Rhys—Dynevor
Richards—Milverton
Richardson—R. of Duntisbourne*
Rippon—R. of Hexham*
Ritchie—R. of Dundee
Robens—R. of Woldingham*
Roberts—Clwyd
Robertson—R. of Oakridge
Robinson—Martonmere
Robson—R. of Kiddington*
Roche—Fermoy
Rodd—Rennell
Roll—R. of Ipsden*
Roper-Curzon—Teynham
Rospigliosi—Newburgh, E.
Ross—R. of Newport*
Rous—Stradbroke, E.
Rowley-Conwy—Langford
Royle—Fanshawe of Richmond*
Runciman—R. of Doxford, V.
Russell—Ampthill
Russell—Bedford, D.
Russell—de Clifford
Russell—R. of Liverpool
Ryder—Harrowby, E.
Ryder—R. of Eaton Hastings*

C. Countess; D. Duke; E. Earl; M. Marquess; V. Viscount; * Life Peer.

Sackville—*De La Warr,* E.
Sackville-West—Sackville
Sainsbury—S. of Preston Candover*
St. Aubyn—St. Levan
St. Clair—Sinclair
St. Clair-Erskine—Rosslyn, E.
St. John—Bolingbroke and St. John, V.
St. John—St. John of Blesto
St. John-Stevas—St. John of Fawsley*
St. Leger—Doneraile, V.
Samuel—Bearsted, V.
Sanderson—S. of Bowden*
Sandilands—Torphichen
Saumarez—De Saumarez
Savile—Mexborough, E.
Scarlett—Abinger
Sclater-Booth—Basing
Scott—Eldon, E.
Scott-Ellis—Howard de Walden
Scrymgeour—Dundee, E.
Seager—Leighton of St. Mellons
Seely—Mottistone
Sefton—S. of Garston*
Seymour—Hertford, M.
Seymour—Somerset, D.
Sharp—S. of Grimsdyke*
Shaw—Craigmyle
Shaw—Kilbrandon*
Shirley—Ferrers, E.
Short—Glenamara*
Siddeley—Kenilworth
Sidney—De L'Isle, V.
Sieff—S. of Brimpton*
Simon—S. of Glaisdale*
Simon—S. of Wythenshawe
Sinclair—Caithness, E.

Sinclair—S. of Cleeve
Sinclair—Thurso, V.
Skeffington—Massereene, V.
Smith—Bicester
Smith—Hambleden, V.
Smith—Kirkhill*
Somerset—Beaufort, D.
Somerset—Raglan
Souter—Audley
Spencer—Churchill, V.
Spencer-Churchill—Marlborough, D.
Spring Rice—Monteagle of Brandon
Stanhope—Harrington, E.
Stanley—Derby, E.
Stanley—Stanley of Alderley & Sheffield
Stapleton-Cotton—Combermere, V.
Stevens—S. of Ludgate*
Stewart—Galloway, E.
Stewart—S. of Fulham*
Stodart—S. of Leaston*
Stoddart—S. of Swindon*
Stonor—Camoys
Stopford—Courtown, E.
Stourton—Mowbray
Strachey—O'Hagan
Strutt—Belper
Strutt—Rayleigh
Stuart—Castle Stewart, E.
Stuart—Moray, E.
Stuart—S. of Findhorn, V.
Suenson-Taylor—Grantchester
Taylor—Ingrow*
Taylor—T. of Blackburn*
Taylor—T. of Gryfe*
Taylor—T. of Hadfield*
Taylor—T. of Mansfield*
Taylour—Headfort, M.
Temple-Gore-Langton—Temple of Stowe, E.

Tennant—Glenconner
Thellusson—Rendlesham
Thesiger—Chelmsford, V.
Thomas—T. of Gwydir*
Thomas—T. of Swynnerton*
Thomas—Tonypandy, V.
Thomson—T. of Fleet
Thomson—T. of Monifieth*
Thynne—Bath, M.
Tottenham—Ely, M.
Trefusis—Clinton
Trench—Ashtown
Trevor-Roper—Dacre of Glanton*
Tufton—Hothfield
Turner—Netherthorpe
Turner—T. of Camden*
Turnour—Winterton, E.
Turton—Tranmire*
Tyrell-Kenyon—Kenyon
Vanden-Bempde-Johnstone—Derwent
Vane—Barnard
Vane-Tempest-Stewart—Londonderry, M.
Vanneck—Huntingfield
Vaughan—Lisburne, E.
Vaughan-Morgan—Reigate*
Vereker—Gort, V.
Verney—Willoughby de Broke
Vernon—Lyveden
Vesey—De Vesci, V.
Villiers—Clarendon, E.
Vivian—Swansea
Walker-Smith—Broxbourne*
Wallace—W. of Campsie*
Wallace—W. of Coslany*
Wallop—Portsmouth, E.
Walton—W. of Detchant*
Ward—Bangor, V.
Ward—Dudley, E.

Warrender—Bruntisfield
Watson—Manton
Wedderburn—W. of Charlton*
Weir—Inverforth
Weld-Forester—Forester
Wellesley—Cowley, E.
Wellesley—Wellington, D.
Westenra—Rossmore
White—Annaly
Whiteley—Marchamley
Whitfield—Kenswood
Williams—Berners
Williams—W. of Elvel*
Williamson—Forres
Willoughby—Middleton
Wills—Dulverton
Wilson—Moran
Wilson—Nunburnholme
Wilson—W. of Langside*
Wilson—W. of Rievaulx*
Windsor—Gloucester, D.
Windsor—Kent, D.
Windsor-Clive—Plymouth, E.
Wingfield—Powerscourt, V.
Winn—St. Oswald
Wodehouse—Kimberley, E.
Wood—Halifax, E.
Wood—Holderness*
Woodhouse—Terrington
Wyatt—W. of Weeford*
Wyndham—Egremont & Leconfield
Wyndham-Quin—Dunraven, E.
Wynn—Newborough
Yarde-Buller—Churston
Yerburgh—Alvingham
Yorke—Hardwicke, E.
Young—Kennet
Young—Y. of Dartington*
Young—Y. of Graffham*
Younger—Y. of Leckie, V.

C. Countess; D. Duke; E. Earl; M. Marquess; V. Viscount; * Life Peer.

THE PREFIX RIGHT HONOURABLE

By established custom, members of the Privy Council are entitled to the style 'The Right Honourable', usually abbreviated to The Right (or Rt.) Hon. All Cabinet Ministers must be members of the Privy Council. The Archbishops of Canterbury and York, the Bishop of London, the Lord Chancellor and the Lords Justices of Appeal are admitted to the Privy Council upon their appointment to office.

In the case of Privy Counsellors who are peers the prefix The Right Honourable may be absorbed in the prefix of a higher dignity (e.g. His Royal Highness, His Grace, or Most Honourable). The style of peers below the rank of Marquess is 'Right Honourable' whether or not they are Privy Counsellors. Because it is not apparent from the use of a prefix whether a peer is a Privy Counsellor, it is common practice to add the initials P.C. after their name. In any other circumstances it is incorrect to use the initials P.C. after a person's name. (If used, the letters P.C. follow all honours and decorations awarded by the Crown.)

188						[1990

ORDERS OF CHIVALRY

The Most Noble Order of the Garter (1348)—K.G.

Ribbon, Garter Blue. *Motto*, Honi soit qui mal y pense (*Shame on him who thinks evil of it*).
The number of Knights Companions is limited to 24.

SOVEREIGN OF THE ORDER—THE QUEEN

Lady of the Garter—H.M. QUEEN ELIZABETH THE QUEEN MOTHER, 1936.

Royal Knights

H.R.H. The Duke of Edinburgh, 1947.
H.R.H. The Prince of Wales, 1958.
H.R.H. The Duke of Kent, 1985.

Extra Knights Companions and Ladies

Princess Juliana of the Netherlands, 1958.
H.M. The King of Norway, 1959.
H.M. The King of The Belgians, 1963.
H.R.H. The Grand Duke of Luxemburg, 1972.
H.M. The Queen of Denmark, 1979.
H.M. The King of Sweden, 1983
H.M. The King of Spain, 1988.

H.M. The Queen of the Netherlands, 1989.

Knights Companions

The Viscount De L'Isle, 1968.
The Lord Ashburton, 1969.
Sir Cennydd Traherne, 1970.
The Earl Waldegrave, 1971.
The Earl of Longford, 1971.
The Earl of Drogheda, 1972.
The Lord Shackleton, 1974.
The Marquess of Abergavenny, 1974.
The Lord Wilson of Rievaulx, 1976.
The Duke of Grafton, 1976.
The Earl of Cromer, 1977.
The Lord Elworthy, 1977.
The Lord Hunt, 1979.
Sir Paul Hasluck, 1979.
Sir Richard Hull, 1980

The Duke of Norfolk, 1983
The Lord Lewin, 1983
The Lord Richardson of Duntisbourne, 1983
The Marquess of Normanby, 1985
The Lord Carrington, 1985
The Lord Callaghan of Cardiff, 1987.
The Viscount Leverhulme, 1988.
The Lord Hailsham of St. Marylebone, 1988.
Prelate, The Bishop of Winchester.
Chancellor, The Marquess of Abergavenny, K.G., O.B.E.
Register, The Dean of Windsor.
Garter King of Arms, Lt.-Col. Sir Colin Cole, K.C.V.O., T.D.
Gentleman Usher of the Black Rod, Air Chief Marshal Sir John Gingell, G.B.E., K.C.B.
Secretary, D. H. B. Chesshyre, L.V.O.

The Most Ancient and Most Noble Order of the Thistle—K.T.

Ribbon, Green. *Motto*, Nemo me impune lacessit (*No one provokes me with impunity*).
The number of Knights is limited to 16.

SOVEREIGN OF THE ORDER—THE QUEEN

Lady of the Thistle—H.M. QUEEN ELIZABETH THE QUEEN MOTHER, 1937

Royal Knights

H.R.H. The Duke of Edinburgh, 1952.
H.R.H. The Prince of Wales (*Duke of Rothesay*), 1977.

Extra Knight

H.M. The King of Norway, 1962.

Knights

The Lord Home of the Hirsel, 1962.
The Earl of Wemyss and March, 1966.
The Lord Maclean, 1969.

The Earl of Dalhousie, 1971.
The Lord Clydesmuir, 1972.
The Viscount Muirshiel, 1973.
Sir Donald Cameron of Lochiel, 1973.
The Earl of Selkirk, 1976.
The Lord McFadzean, 1976.
The Hon. Lord Cameron, 1978.
The Duke of Buccleuch and Queensberry, 1978.
The Earl of Elgin and Kincardine, 1981.
The Lord Thomson of Monifieth, 1981.

The Lord MacLehose of Beoch, 1983.
The Earl of Airlie, 1985.
Capt. Sir Iain Tennant, 1986.
Chancellor, The Lord Home of the Hirsel.
Dean, The Very Rev. G. I. Macmillan.
Secretary and Lord Lyon King of Arms, Malcolm R. Innes of Edingight, C.V.O., W.S.
Usher of the Green Rod, Rear-Admiral D.A. Dunbar-Nasmith, C.B., D.S.C.

The Most Honourable Order of the Bath (1725)

Ribbon, Crimson. *Motto*, Tria juncta in uno (*Three joined in one*). (Remodelled 1815, and enlarged many times since. The Order is divided into civil and military divisions.)

G.C.B. Mil.		G.C.B. Civ.		K.C.B. Mil.		K.C.B. Civ.		C.B. Mil.

THE SOVEREIGN; *Great Master and First or Principal Knight Grand Cross*, H.R.H. The Prince of Wales, K.G., K.T., G.C.B.; *Dean of the Order*, The Dean of Westminster; *Bath King of Arms*, Air Chief Marshal Sir David Evans, G.C.B., C.B.E.; *Registrar and Secretary*, Air Marshal Sir Denis Crowley-Milling, K.C.B., C.B.E., D.S.O., D.F.C.; *Genealogist*, Dr. C. Swan, C.V.O., PH.D.; *Gentleman Usher of the Scarlet Rod*, Rear-Admiral D. E. Macey, C.B.; *Deputy Secretary*, Maj.-Gen. D. H. G. Rice, C.V.O., C.B.E.; *Chancery*, Central Chancery of the Orders of Knighthood, St. James's Palace, SW1A 1BH.—G.C.B., Knight (or Dame) Grand Cross; K.C.B., Knight Commander; D.C.B., Dame Commander; C.B., Companion. Women became eligible for the Order from Jan. 1, 1971.

O.M.Mil.

The Order of Merit (1902)—O.M.
Ribbon, Blue and Crimson.

O.M.Civ.

This Order is designed as a special distinction for eminent men and women without conferring a knighthood upon them. The Order is limited in numbers to 24, with the addition of foreign honorary members. Membership is of two kinds, Military and Civil, the badge of the former having crossed swords, and the latter oak leaves. Membership is denoted by the suffix O.M., which follows the first class of the Order of the Bath and precedes the letters designating membership of the inferior classes of the Bath and all classes of the lesser Orders of Knighthood.

THE SOVEREIGN
H.R.H. THE DUKE OF EDINBURGH (1968)

Dorothy Hodgkin, 1965.
The Lord Zuckerman, 1968.
The Lord Penney, 1969.
Dame Veronica Wedgwood, 1969.
Sir Isaiah Berlin, 1971.
Sir George Edwards, 1971.
Sir Alan Hodgkin, 1973.
Sir Ronald Syme, 1976.
The Lord Todd, 1977.

The Lord Franks, 1977.
Gp. Capt. Leonard Cheshire, V.C., 1981.
Sir Andrew Huxley, 1983.
Sir Sidney Nolan, 1983.
Sir Michael Tippett, 1983.
Rev. Prof. Owen Chadwick, K.B.E., 1983.
Graham Greene, 1986.

Frederick Sanger, 1986.
Air Commodore Sir Frank Whittle, 1986.
Sir Yehudi Menuhin, 1987.
Prof. Sir Ernst Gombrich, 1988.
Dr. Max Perutz, 1988.
Honorary Member, Mother Teresa, 1983.

Secretary and Registrar, Sir Edward Ford, K.C.B., K.C.V.O.
Chancery, Central Chancery of the Orders of Knighthood, St. James's Palace, SW1A 1BH.

G.C.S.I.

The Most Exalted Order of the Star of India (1861)

Ribbon, Light Blue, with White Edges. *Motto*, Heaven's Light our Guide.
THE SOVEREIGN; *Registrar*, Maj.-Gen. D. H. G. Rice, C.V.O., C.B.E.; G.C.S.I. Knight Grand Commander; K.C.S.I., Knight Commander; C.S.I., Companion. No conferments since 1947.

G.C.I.E.

The Most Distinguished Order of St. Michael and St. George (1818)

Ribbon, Saxon Blue, with Scarlet centre. *Motto*, Auspicium melioris aevi (Token of a better age)
THE SOVEREIGN; *Grand Master*, H.R.H. The Duke of Kent, K.G., G.C.M.G., G.C.V.O., A.D.C.; *Prelate*, The Rt. Rev. the Bishop of Coventry; *Chancellor*, The Lord Carrington, K.G., G.C.M.G., C.H., M.C., P.C.; *Secretary*, Sir Patrick Wright, G.C.M.G.; *Registrar*, Sir John Graham, Bt., G.C.M.G.; *King of Arms*, Sir Oliver Wright, G.C.M.G., G.C.V.O., D.S.C.; *Gentleman Usher of the Blue Rod*, Sir John Moreton, K.C.M.G., K.C.V.O., M.C.; *Dean*, The Dean of St. Paul's; *Deputy Secretary*, Maj.-Gen. D. H. G. Rice, C.V.O., C.B.E. *Chancery*, Central Chancery of the Orders of Knighthood, St. James's Palace, SW1A 1BH.—G.C.M.G., Knight (or Dame) Grand Cross; K.C.M.G., Knight Commander; D.C.M.G., Dame Commander; C.M.G., Companion.

G.C.I.E.

The Most Eminent Order of the Indian Empire (1868)

Ribbon, Imperial Purple. *Motto*, Imperatricis auspiciis (*Under the auspices of the Empress*).
THE SOVEREIGN; *Registrar*, Maj.-Gen. D. H. G. Rice, C.V.O., C.B.E.; G.C.I.E., Knight Grand Commander; K.C.I.E., Knight Commander; C.I.E., Companion. No conferments since 1947.

The Imperial Order of the Crown of India (for Ladies)—C.I.

Instituted Dec. 31, 1877. Badge, the royal cipher in jewels within an oval, surmounted by an Heraldic Crown and attached to a bow of light blue watered ribbon, edged white. The honour does not confer any rank or title upon the recipient. No conferments have been made since 1947.

H.M. THE QUEEN, 1947.
H.M. Queen Elizabeth the Queen Mother, 1931.

H.R.H. The Princess Margaret, Countess of Snowdon, 1947.

H.R.H. The Princess Alice, Duchess of Gloucester, 1937.
H.H. Maharani of Travancore, 1929.

The Royal Victorian Order (1896)

Ribbon, Blue, with Red and White Edges. *Motto*, Victoria.
THE SOVEREIGN; *Grand Master*, H.M. Queen Elizabeth The Queen Mother; *Chancellor*, The Lord Chamberlain; *Secretary*, The Keeper of the Privy Purse; *Registrar*, The Secretary of the Central Chancery of the Orders of Knighthood; *Chaplain*, The Rev. J. Robson. *Hon. Genealogist*, D. H. B. Chesshyre, L.V.O.; G.C.V.O., Knight or Dame Grand Cross; K.C.V.O., Knight Commander; D.C.V.O., Dame Commander; C.V.O., Commander; L.V.O., Lieutenant; M.V.O., Member.

The Most Excellent Order of the British Empire (1917)

Ribbon, Rose pink edged with pearl grey with vertical pearl stripe in centre (Military Division); without vertical pearl stripe (Civil Division). *Motto*, For God and the Empire.

G.B.E.   K.B.E.

THE SOVEREIGN: *Grand Master*, H.R.H. The Prince Philip, Duke of Edinburgh, K.G., P.C., K.T., O.M., G.B.E., F.R.S.; *Prelate*, The Bishop of London; *King of Arms*, Admiral Sir Anthony Morton, G.B.E., K.C.B.; *Registrar*, Maj.-Gen. D. H. G. Rice, C.V.O., C.B.E.; *Secretary*, Sir Robin Butler, K.C.B., C.V.O.; *Dean*, The Dean of St. Paul's; *Gentleman Usher of the Purple Rod*, Sir Robin Gillett, Bt., G.B.E.; *Chancery*, Central Chancery of the Orders of Knighthood, St. James's Palace, SW1A 1BH. G.B.E., Knight or Dame Grand Cross; K.B.E. Knight Commander; D.B.E., Dame Commander; C.B.E., Commander; O.B.E., Officer; M.B.E., Member. The Order was divided into *Military* and *Civil* divisions in Dec. 1918.

Order of the Companions of Honour (1917)—C.H.

Ribbon, Carmine, with Gold Edges.

This Order consists of one Class only and carries with it no title. It ranks after the 1st Class of the Order of the British Empire, i.e., Knights and Dames Grand Cross (Mil. and Civ. Div.). The number of awards is limited to 65 (excluding honorary members) and the Order is open to both sexes. *Secretary and Registrar*, The Secretary of the Central Chancery of the Orders of Knighthood.

Anthony, Rt. Hon. John, 1982.
Ashley, Rt. Hon. Jack, 1975.
Aylestone, The Lord, 1975.
Brenner, Sydney, 1987.
Carrington, The Lord, 1983.
Casson, Sir Hugh, 1985.
Cledwyn of Penrhos, The Lord, 1977.
de Valois, Dame Ninette, 1982.
Eccles, The Viscount, 1984.
Elwyn-Jones, The Lord, 1976.
Fraser, Rt. Hon. Malcolm, 1977.
Freud, Lucian, 1983.
Gardiner, The Lord, 1975.
Gielgud, Sir John, 1977.
Glenamara, The Lord, 1976.
Goodman, The Lord, 1972.
Gorton, Rt. Hon. Sir John, 1971.

Greene, Graham, 1966.
Hailsham of St. Marylebone, The Lord, 1974.
Hawking, Prof. Stephen, 1989.
von Hayek, Prof. Friedrich, 1984.
Healey, Rt. Hon. Denis, 1979.
Houghton of Sowerby, The Lord, 1967.
Jones, James, 1978.
Joseph, The Lord, 1986.
Muirshiel, The Viscount, 1962.
Muldoon, Rt. Hon. Sir Robert, 1977.
Pasmore, Victor, 1981.
Perutz, Prof. Max Ferdinand, 1975.
Piper, John, 1972.
Popper, Prof. Sir Karl, 1982.
Powell, Anthony, 1987.
Powell, Sir Philip, 1984.

Rahman, Tunku Abdul, 1960.
Runciman, Hon. Sir Steven, 1984.
Rylands, George, 1987.
Sanger, Frederick, 1981.
Smith, Arnold Cantwell, 1975.
Somare, Rt. Hon. Michael, 1978.
Stewart of Fulham, The Lord, 1969.
Summerson, Sir John, 1987.
Talboys, Rt. Hon. Brian, 1981.
Tebbit, Rt. Hon. Norman, 1987.
Thorneycroft, The Lord, 1980
Tippett, Sir Michael, 1979.
Trudeau, Rt. Hon. Pierre, 1984.
Watkinson, The Viscount, 1962.
Whitelaw, The Viscount, 1974.
Honorary Members, Lee Kuan Yew, 1970; Dr. Joseph Luns, 1971.

The Distinguished Service Order (1886)—D.S.O.

Ribbon, Red, with Blue Edges.

Bestowed in recognition of especial services in action of commissioned officers in the Navy, Army and Royal Air Force and (since 1942) Mercantile Marine. The members are Companions only and rank immediately before the 4th Class of the Royal Victorian Order. A Bar may be awarded for any additional act of service.

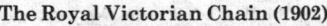

The Imperial Service Order (1902)—I.S.O.

Ribbon, Crimson, with Blue Centre.

Appointment of Companion of this Order shall be open to those members of the Civil Services whose eligibility shall be determined by the grade held by such persons. The Order consists of THE SOVEREIGN and Companions (not exclusively male) to a number not exceeding 1,700 of whom 1,100 may belong to the Home Civil Services and 600 to Overseas Civil Services. *Secretary*, Sir Robin Butler, K.C.B., C.V.O. *Registrar*, Maj.-Gen. D. H. G. Rice, C.V.O., C.B.E., St. James's Palace, SW1A 1BH.

The Royal Victorian Chain (1902)

Founded by King Edward VII, in 1902. It confers no precedence on its holders.

H.M. THE QUEEN
H.M. QUEEN ELIZABETH THE QUEEN MOTHER, 1937.

Princess Juliana of the Netherlands, 1950.
H.M. The King of Norway, 1955.
H.M. The King of Thailand, 1960.
H.I.H. The Crown Prince of Ethiopia, 1965.
H.M. The King of Jordan, 1966.
H.M. King Zahir Shah of Afghanistan, 1971.

Rt. Hon. Roland Michener, 1973.
H.M. The Queen of Denmark, 1974.
H.M. The King of Nepal, 1975.
H.M. The King of Sweden, 1975.
The Right Rev. The Lord Coggan, 1980.
Ratu Sir George Cakobau, 1982.

H.M. The Queen of the Netherlands, 1982.
The Lord Maclean, 1984.
General Antonio Eanes, 1985.
H.M. The King of Spain, 1986.
H.M. The King of Saudi Arabia, 1987.

BARONETS, KNIGHTS GRAND CROSS, KNIGHTS GRAND COMMANDERS, KNIGHTS COMMANDERS AND KNIGHTS BACHELOR

Badge of Baronets
of England, Great Britain, U.K.,
(and Ireland marked I.).

Badge of Baronets
of Scotland or Nova Scotia
(marked S. or N.S.).

NOTES CONCERNING BARONETS

Clause II of the Royal Warrant of February 8, 1910, ordains as follows:—'That no person whose name is not entered upon the Official Roll shall be received as a Baronet, or shall be addressed or mentioned by that title in any Civil or Military Commission, Letters Patent or other official document.'

Baronets are addressed as Sir (with Christian name) and in writing as Sir Robert *A*—, Bt. Baronet's wives are addressed (formally) as Your Ladyship and Lady *A*—, without any Christian name unless a daughter of a Duke, Marquess or Earl, in which case The Lady Mary *A*—; if daughter of a Viscount or Baron The Hon. Lady *A*—.

NOTES CONCERNING KNIGHTS GRAND CROSS, ETC.

Knights Grand Cross, Knights Grand Commanders and Knights Commanders are addressed in the same manner as Baronets (*q.v.*), but in writing the appropriate initials (G.C.B., K.C.B., etc.) are appended to surname after Bt. if they are also baronets or in place of 'Bt.' if they are not. Knights Bachelor are addressed as Sir —— — (first or Christian name) and in writing as Sir —— B——. The wife of a Knight Grand Cross, Knight Grand Commander, Knight Commander or Knight Bachelor is addressed as stated for the wife of a Baronet.

NOTES CONCERNING KNIGHTS BACHELOR

The Knights Bachelor do not constitute a Royal Order, but comprise the surviving representation of the ancient State Orders of Knighthood. The Register of Knights Bachelor, instituted by James I in the 17th century, lapsed, and in 1908 a voluntary Association under the title of The Society of Knights (now The Imperial Society of Knights Bachelor by Royal command) was formed with the primary object of continuing the various registers dating from 1257 and obtaining the uniform registration of every created Knight Bachelor. In 1926 a design for a badge to be worn by Knights Bachelor was approved and adopted, a miniature reproduction being shown above; in 1974 a neck badge and miniature were added. The Officers of the Society are:—*Knight Principal*, Sir Colin Cole, K.C.V.O., T.D.; *Chairman of Council*, Sir David Napley; *Prelate*, Rt. Rev. and Rt. Hon. The Bishop of London; *Hon. Registrar*, Sir Roger Falk, O.B.E.; *Hon. Treasurer*, Sir Peter Lane; *Clerk to the Council*, R. M. Esden; *Deputy Clerk*, Lt. Col. G. H. H. Coles; *Office*, 21 Old Buildings, Lincoln's Inn, WC2A 3UJ.

BARONETAGE AND KNIGHTAGE
(Revised to Aug. 31, 1989)
Peers are not included in this list

When an obelisk (†) precedes a name it indicates that, at the time of going to press, the Baronet concerned has not been registered on the Official Roll of the Baronetage. The date of creation of the Baronetcy is given in parenthesis ( ).

A full entry in italic type indicates that the recipient of a Knighthood died during the year in which the honour was conferred. The name is included for purposes of record.

Aarvold, *Hon.* Sir Carl Douglas, Kt., O.B.E., T.D.

Abal, Sir Tei, Kt., C.B.E.

Abbott, Sir Albert Francis, Kt., C.B.E.

Abdy, Sir Valentine Robert Duff, Bt. (1850).

Abel, Sir Seselo (Cecil) Charles Geoffrey, Kt., O.B.E.

Abeles, Sir (Emil Herbert) Peter, Kt.

Abell, Sir Anthony Foster, K.C.M.G.

Abercromby, Sir Ian George, Bt. (s. 1636).

Abraham, Sir Edward Penley, Kt., C.B.E., F.R.S.

Acheson, *Prof.* Sir (Ernest) Donald, K.B.E.

Ackers, Sir James George, Kt.

Ackroyd, Sir John Robert Whyte, Bt. (1956).

Acland, Sir Antony Arthur, G.C.M.G., K.C.V.O.

Acland, *Maj.* Sir (Christopher) Guy (Dyke), Bt. (1890).

Acland, *Maj.-Gen.* Sir John Hugh Bevil, K.C.B., C.B.E.

Acland, Sir Richard Thomas Dyke, Bt. (1644).

Acton, Sir Harold Mario Mitchell, Kt., C.B.E.

Adam, Sir Christopher Eric Forbes, Bt. (1917).

Adams, Sir Philip George Doyne, K.C.M.G.

Adams-Schneider, *Rt. Hon.* Sir Lancelot Raymond, K.C.M.G.

Adamson, Sir (William Owen) Campbell, Kt.

Adcock, Sir Robert Henry, Kt., C.B.E.

Addison, Sir William Wilkinson, Kt.

Ademola, *Rt. Hon.* Sir Adetokunbo Adegboyega, K.B.E.

Adrien, *Hon.* Sir Maurice Latour-, Kt.

Agnew, Sir Crispin Hamlyn, Bt. (s. 1629).

Agnew, Sir (John) Anthony Stuart, Bt. (1895).

Agnew, *Cdr.* Sir Peter Garnett, Bt. (1957).

Agnew, Sir (William) Godfrey, K.C.V.O., C.B.

Ah-Chuen, Sir Moi Lin Jean Etienne, Kt.

Aiken, *Air Chief Marshal* Sir John Alexander Carlisle, K.C.B.

Ainley, Sir (Alfred) John, Kt., M.C.

Ainsworth, Sir (Thomas) David, Bt. (1916).

Aird, *Capt.* Sir Alastair Sturgis, K.C.V.O.

Aird, Sir (George) John, Bt. (1901).

Airey, Sir Lawrence, K.C.B.

Airy, *Maj. Gen.* Sir Christopher John, K.C.V.O., C.B.E.

Aisher, Sir Owen Arthur, Kt.

Aitchison, Sir Charles Walter de Lancey, Bt. (1938).

Aitken, Sir Robert Stevenson, Kt., M.D., D.Phil.

Akehurst, *Gen.* Sir John Bryan, K.C.B., C.B.E.

Akers-Jones, Sir David, K.B.E., C.M.G.

Albert, Sir Alexis François, Kt., C.M.G., V.R.D.

Albu, Sir George, Bt. (1912).

Aldington, Sir Geoffrey William, K.B.E., C.M.G.

Aldous, *Hon.* Sir William, Kt.

Alexander, Sir Alexander Sandor, Kt.

Alexander, Sir Charles Gundry, Bt. (1945).

Alexander, Sir Claud Hagart-, Bt. (1886).

Alexander, *Hon.* Sir Darnley Arthur Raymond, Kt., C.B.E.

Alexander, Sir Douglas, Bt. (1921).

Alexander, Sir (John) Lindsay, Kt.

Alexander, *Prof.* Sir Kenneth John Wilson, Kt.

Alexander, Sir Michael O'Donal Bjarne, K.C.M.G.

Alexander, Sir Norman Stanley, Kt., C.B.E.

†Alexander, Sir Patrick Desmond William Cable-, Bt. (1809).

Allan, Sir Anthony James Allan Havelock-, Bt. (1858).

Allan, Sir Colin Hamilton, K.C.M.G., O.B.E.

Allard, Sir Gordon Laidlaw, Kt.

Allen, *Prof.* Sir Geoffrey, Kt., Ph.D., F.R.S.

Allen, Sir George Oswald Browning, Kt., C.B.E., T.D.

Allen, *Hon.* Sir Peter Austin Philip Jermyn, Kt.

Allen, Sir Peter Christopher, Kt.

Allen, Sir Richard Hugh Sedley, K.C.M.G.

Allen, Sir William Guilford, Kt.

Allen, Sir (William) Kenneth (Gwynne), Kt.

Alleyne, *Rev.* Sir John Olpherts Campbell, Bt., (1769).

Alliance, Sir David, Kt., C.B.E.

Allinson, Sir (Walter) Leonard, K.C.V.O., C.M.G.

Alliott, *Hon.* Sir John Downes, Kt.

Alment, Sir (Edward) Anthony John, Kt.

Althaus, Sir Nigel Frederick, Kt.

Alun-Jones, Sir (John) Derek, Kt.

Ambo, *Rt. Rev.* George, K.B.E.

Amies, Sir (Edwin) Hardy, K.C.V.O.

Anderson, *Prof.* Sir (James) Norman (Dalrymple), Kt., O.B.E., Q.C., F.B.A.

Anderson, *Maj.-Gen.* Sir John Evelyn, K.B.E.

Anderson, Sir John Muir, Kt., C.M.G.

Anderson, Sir Kenneth, K.B.E., C.B.

Anderson, *Hon.* Sir Kevin Victor, Kt.

Anderson, *Vice-Adm.* Sir Neil Dudley, K.B.E., C.B.

Anderson, *Prof.* Sir (William) Ferguson, Kt., O.B.E.

Andrew, Sir Robert John, K.C.B.

Andrews, *Hon.* Sir Dormer George, Kt.

Ansell, *Col.* Sir Michael Picton, Kt., C.B.E., D.S.O.

Anson, *Vice-Adm.* Sir Edward Rosebery, K.C.B.

Anson, *Rear-Adm.* Sir Peter, Bt., C.B. (1831).

Anstey, *Brig.* Sir John, Kt., C.B.E., T.D.

Anstruther, Sir Ralph Hugo, Bt. K.C.V.O., M.C. (s. 1694).

Anthony, Sir (Michael) Mobolaji Bank-, K.B.E.

Antico, Sir Tristan Venus, Kt.

Antrobus, Sir Philip Coutts, Bt. (1815).

Appleyard, Sir Raymond Kenelm, K.B.E.

Arbuthnot, Sir John Sinclair-Wemyss, Bt., M.B.E., T.D. (1964).

Arbuthnot, Sir Keith Robert Charles, Bt. (1823).

Archdale, *Cdr.* Sir Edward Folmer, Bt., D.S.C., R.N. (1928).

Archer, *Gen.* Sir (Arthur) John, K.C.B., O.B.E.

Archer, Sir Clyde Vernon Harcourt, Kt.

Arculus, Sir Ronald, K.C.M.G., K.C.V.O.

Armitage, *Air Chief Marshal* Sir Michael John, K.C.B., C.B.E.

Armitage, Sir Robert Perceval, K.C.M.G., M.B.E.

Armstrong, Sir Andrew Clarence Francis, Bt., C.M.G. (1841).

Armstrong, Sir Thomas Henry Wait, Kt., D.MUS.

Armytage, Sir John Martin, Bt. (1738).

Arnold, *Rt. Hon.* Sir John Lewis, Kt.

Arnott, Sir Alexander John Maxwell, Bt. (1896).

Arnott, *Prof.* Sir (William) Melville, Kt., T.D., M.D.

Arrindell, Sir Clement Athelston, G.C.M.G., G.C.V.O.

Arrowsmith, Sir Edwin Porter, K.C.M.G.

Arthur, *Lt.-Gen.* Sir (John) Norman Stewart, K.C.B.

Arthur, Sir Stephen John, Bt. (1841).

Ashburnham, Sir Denny Reginald, Bt. (1661).

Ashe, Sir Derick Rosslyn, K.C.M.G.

Ashley, Sir Bernard Albert, Kt.

Ashmore, *Admiral of the Fleet* Sir Edward Beckwith, G.C.B., D.S.C.

Ashmore, *Vice-Adm.* Sir Peter William Beckwith, K.C.B., K.C.V.O., D.S.C.

Ashworth, Sir Herbert, Kt.

Aske, *Rev.* Sir Conan, Bt. (1922).

Askew, Sir Bryan, Kt.

Astley, Sir Francis Jacob Dugdale, Bt. (1821).

Aston, Sir Harold George, Kt., C.B.E.

Aston, *Hon.* Sir William John, K.C.M.G.

Astor, *Hon.* Sir John Jacob, Kt., M.B.E.

Astwood, *Hon.* Sir James Rufus, Kt.

Astwood, *Lt.-Col.* Sir Jeffrey Carlton, Kt., C.B.E., E.D.

Atcherley, Sir Harold Winter, Kt.

Atiyah, Sir Michael Francis, Kt., Ph.D., F.R.S.

Atkinson, *Air Marshal* Sir David William, K.B.E.

Atkinson, Sir Frederick John, K.C.B.

Atkinson, Sir John Alexander, K.C.B., D.F.C.

Atkinson, *Maj.-Gen.* Sir Leonard Henry, K.C.B.

Atkinson, Sir Robert, Kt., D.S.C.

Attenborough, Sir David Frederick, Kt., C.B.E., F.R.S.

Attenborough, Sir Richard Samuel, Kt., C.B.E.

Atwell, Sir John William, Kt., C.B.E., F.R.S.E.

Atwill, Sir (Milton) John (Napier), Kt.

Audland, Sir Christopher John, K.C.M.G.

Audley, Sir George Bernard, Kt.

Auld, *Hon.* Sir Robin Ernest, Kt.

†Austin, Sir Michael Trescawen, Bt. (1894).

Austin, *Vice-Adm.* Sir Peter Murray, K.C.B.

Aykroyd, Sir Cecil William, Bt. (1929).

Aykroyd, Sir William Miles, Bt., M.C. (1920).

†Aylmer, Sir Richard John, Bt. (I 1622).

Backhouse, Sir Jonathan Roger, Bt. (1901).

Bacon, Sir Nicholas Hickman Ponsonby, Bt. *Premier Baronet of England* (1611 and 1627).

Bacon, Sir Sidney Charles, Kt., C.B.

Baddeley, Sir John Wolsey Beresford, Bt. (1922).

Baddiley, *Prof.* Sir James, Kt., Ph.D., D.SC., F.R.S., F.R.S.E.

Badenoch, Sir John, Kt., D.M., F.R.C.P.

Badger, Sir Geoffrey Malcolm, Kt.

Bagge, Sir John Alfred Picton, Bt. (1867).

Bagnall, *Field Marshal* Sir Nigel Thomas, G.C.B., C.V.O., M.C.

Bailey, Sir Alan Marshall, K.C.B.

Bailey, Sir Brian Harry, Kt., O.B.E.

Bailey, Sir Derrick Thomas Louis, Bt., D.F.C. (1919).

Bailey, *Prof.* Sir Harold Walter, Kt., D.PHIL., F.B.A.

Bailey, Sir John Bilsland, K.C.B.

Bailey, Sir Richard John, Kt., C.B.E.

Bailey, Sir Stanley Ernest, Kt., C.B.E., Q.P.M.

Baillie, Sir Gawaine George Hope, Bt. (1823).

Baines, *Prof.* Sir George Grenfell-, Kt., O.B.E.

Baird, Sir David Charles, Bt. (1809).

Baird, *Lt.-Gen.* Sir James Parlane, K.B.E., M.D.

Baird, Sir James Richard Gardiner, Bt., M.C. (s. 1695).

Baird, *Vice-Adm.* Sir Thomas Henry Eustace, K.C.B.

Bairsto, *Air Marshal* Sir Peter Edward, K.B.E., C.B.

Baker, Sir (Allan) Ivor, Kt., C.B.E.

Baker, Sir Humphrey Dodington Benedict Sherston-, Bt. (1796).

Baker, *Hon.* Sir (Thomas) Scott (Gillespie), Kt.

Balcombe, *Rt. Hon.* Sir (Alfred) John, Kt.

Balderstone, Sir James Schofield, Kt.

Baldwin, Sir Peter Robert, K.C.B.

Balfour, *Gen.* Sir (Robert George) Victor FitzGeorge-, K.C.B., C.B.E., D.S.O., M.C.

Ball, *Air Marshal* Sir Alfred Henry Wynne, K.C.B., D.S.O., D.F.C.

Ball, Sir Charles Irwin, Bt. (1911).

Ball, Sir Christopher John Elinger, Kt.

Ball, *Prof.* Sir Robert James, Kt., Ph.D.

Balmer, Sir Joseph Reginald, Kt.

Banks, Sir Maurice Alfred Lister, Kt.

Banner, Sir George Knowles Harmood-, Bt. (1924).

Bannerman, *Lt.-Col.* Sir Donald Arthur Gordon, Bt. (s. 1682).

Bannister, Sir Roger Gilbert, Kt., C.B.E., D.M., F.R.C.P.

Barber, Sir Derek Coates, Kt.

Barber, *Hon.* Sir (Edward Hamilton) Esler, Kt.

Barber, Sir William Francis, Bt., T.D. (1960).

Barclay, Sir Colville Herbert Sanford, Bt. (s. 1668).

Barclay, Sir Roderick Edward, G.C.V.O., K.C.M.G.

Barford, Sir Leonard, Kt.

Baring, Sir Charles Christian, Bt. (1911).

Baring, *Hon.* Sir John Francis Harcourt, Kt., C.V.O.

Barker, Sir Alwyn Bowman, Kt., C.M.G.

Barker, Sir Harry Heaton, Kt., K.B.E.

Barker, Sir William, K.C.M.G., O.B.E.

Barlow, Sir Christopher Hilaro, Bt. (1803).

Barlow, Sir (George) William, Kt.

Barlow, Sir John Kemp, Bt. (1907).

Barlow, Sir Thomas Erasmus, Bt., D.S.C. (1902).

Barnard, Sir (Arthur) Thomas, Kt., C.B., O.B.E.

Barnard, *Capt.* Sir George Edward, Kt.

Barnard, Sir Joseph Brian, Kt.

Barnes, Sir Denis Charles, K.C.B.

Barnes, Sir (Ernest) John (Ward), K.C.M.G., M.B.E.

Barnes, Sir James George, Kt., M.B.E.

Barnes, Sir Kenneth, K.C.B.

Barnett, *Air Chief Marshal* Sir Denis Hensley Fulton, G.C.B., C.B.E., D.F.C.

Barnett, Sir Oliver Charles, Kt., C.B.E., Q.C.

Barnewall, Sir Reginald Robert, Bt. (I. 1623).

Barraclough, *Air Chief Marshal* Sir John, K.C.B., C.B.E., D.F.C., A.F.C.

Barraclough, Sir Kenneth James Priestley, Kt., C.B.E., T.D.

Barran, Sir David Haven, Kt.

Barran, Sir John Napoleon Ruthven, Bt. (1895).

Barratt, Sir Lawrence Arthur, Kt.

Barratt, Sir Richard Stanley, Kt., C.B.E., Q.P.M.

Barrett, *Lt.-Gen.* Sir David William Scott-, K.B.E., M.C.

Barrett, *Lt.-Col.* Sir Dennis Charles Titchener, Kt., T.D.

Barrington, Sir Alexander (Fitzwilliam Croker), Bt. (1831).

Barritt, Sir David Thurlow, Kt.

Barron, Sir Donald James, Kt.

Barrow, *Capt.* Sir Richard John Uniacke, Bt. (1835).

Barrowclough, Sir Anthony Richard, Kt., Q.C.

Barry, Sir (Lawrence) Edward (Anthony Tress), Bt. (1899).

Barry, Sir (Philip) Stuart Milner-, K.C.V.O., C.B., O.B.E.

Bartlett, Sir Henry David Hardington, Bt., M.B.E. (1913).

Barton, *Prof.* Sir Derek Harold Richard, Kt., F.R.S., F.R.S.E.

Barttelot, *Lt.-Col.* Sir Brian Walter de Stopham, Bt., O.B.E. (1875).

Barwick, *Rt. Hon.* Sir Garfield Edward John, G.C.M.G.

Basten, Sir Henry Bolton, Kt., C.M.G.

Batchelor, Sir Ivor Ralph Campbell, Kt., C.B.E.

Bate, Sir David Lindsay, K.B.E.

Bate, Sir (Walter) Edwin, Kt., O.B.E.

Bateman, Sir Cecil Joseph, K.B.E.

Bateman, Sir Geoffrey Hirst, Kt., F.R.C.S.

Bateman, Sir Ralph Melton, K.B.E.

Bates, *Prof.* Sir David Robert, Kt., D.Sc., F.R.S.

Bates, *Maj.-Gen.* Sir (Edward) John (Hunter), K.B.E., C.B., M.C.

Bates, Sir Geoffrey Voltelin, Bt., M.C. (1880).

Bates, Sir John David, Kt., C.B.E., V.R.D.

Bates, Sir (John) Dawson, Bt., M.C. (1937).

Batho, Sir Maurice Benjamin, Bt. (1928).

Bathurst, *Adm.* Sir (David) Benjamin, K.C.B.

Bathurst, Sir Frederick Peter Methuen Hervey-, Bt. (1818).

Bathurst, Sir Maurice Edward, Kt., C.M.G., C.B.E., Q.C.

Batsford, Sir Brian Caldwell Cook, Kt.

Batten, Sir John Charles, K.C.V.O.

Battishill, Sir Anthony Michael William, K.C.B.

Batty, Sir William Bradshaw, Kt., T.D.

Baxendell, Sir Peter Brian, Kt., C.B.E.

Baxter, *Prof.* Sir (John) Philip, K.B.E., C.M.G.

Bayliss, *Prof.* Sir Noel Stanley, Kt., C.B.E.

Bayliss, Sir Richard Ian Samuel, K.C.V.O., M.D., F.R.C.P.

Bayly, *Vice-Adm.* Sir Patrick Uniacke, K.B.E., C.B., D.S.C.

Baynes, Sir John Christopher Malcolm, Bt. (1801).

Bazley, Sir Thomas Stafford, Bt. (1869).

Beach, *Gen.* Sir (William Gerald) Hugh, G.B.E., K.C.B., M.C.

Beale, Sir William Francis, Kt., O.B.E.

Beament, Sir James William Longman, Kt., Sc.D., F.R.S.

Beattie, *Hon.* Sir Alexander Craig, Kt.

Beattie, *Hon.* Sir David Stuart, G.C.M.G., G.C.V.O.

Beauchamp, Sir Christopher Radstock Proctor-, Bt. (1745).

Beaumont, Sir George (Howland Francis), Bt. (1661).

Beaumont, Sir Richard Ashton, K.C.M.G., O.B.E.

Beavis, *Air Chief Marshal* Sir Michael Gordon, K.C.B., C.B.E., A.F.C.

Becher, Sir William Fane Wrixon, Bt., M.C. (1831).

Beck, Sir Edgar Charles, Kt., C.B.E.

Beck, Sir Edgar Philip, Kt.

Beckett, *Capt.* Sir (Martyn) Gervase, Bt., M.C. (1921).

Beckett, Sir Terence Norman, K.B.E.

Bedbrook, Sir George Montario, Kt., O.B.E.

Bedingfeld, *Capt.* Sir Edmund George Felix Paston-, Bt. (1661).

Beecham, John Stratford Roland, Bt. (1914).

Beeley, Sir Harold, K.C.M.G., C.B.E.

Beetham, *Marshal of the Royal Air Force* Sir Michael James, G.C.B., C.B.E., D.F.C., A.F.C.

Beevor, Sir Thomas Agnew, Bt. (1784).

Begg, Sir Neil Colquhoun, K.B.E.

Begg, *Admiral of the Fleet* Sir Varyl Cargill, G.C.B., D.S.O., D.S.C.

Beit, Sir Alfred Lane, Bt. (1924).

Beith, Sir John Greville Stanley, K.C.M.G.

Beldam, *Hon.* Sir (Alexander) Roy (Asplan), Kt.

Bell, Sir Gawain Westray, K.C.M.G., C.B.E.

Bell, Sir (George) Raymond, K.C.M.G., C.B.

Bell, Sir John Lowthian, Bt. (1885).

Bell, Sir (William) Ewart, K.C.B.

Bell, Sir William Hollin Dayrell Morrison-, Bt. (1905).

Bellew, *Hon.* Sir George Rothe, K.C.B., K.C.V.O., F.S.A.

Bellew, Sir Henry Charles Gratton-, Bt. (1838).

Bellinger, Sir Robert Ian, G.B.E.

Bellingham, Sir Noel Peter Roger, Bt. (1796).

Bengough, *Col.* Sir Piers, K.C.V.O., O.B.E.

Benn, Sir James Jonathan, Bt. (1914).

Benn, *Capt.* Sir (Patrick Ion) Hamilton, Bt. (1920).

Bennett, *Rt. Hon.* Sir Charles Moihi Te Arawaka, Kt., D.S.O.

Bennett, *Rt. Hon.* Sir Frederic Mackarness, Kt.

Bennett, Sir Hubert, Kt.

Bennett, Sir John Mokonuiarangi, Kt.

Bennett, *Lt.-Gen.* Sir Phillip Harvey, K.B.E.

Bennett, Sir Reginald Frederick Brittain, Kt., V.R.D.

Bennett, Sir Ronald Wilfrid Murdoch, Bt. (1929).

Benson, Sir Christopher John, Kt.

Benson, Sir (William) Jeffrey, Kt.

Benthall, Sir (Arthur) Paul, K.B.E.

Bentley, Sir William, K.C.M.G.

Berger, *Vice-Adm.* Sir Peter Egerton Capel, K.C.B., M.V.O., D.S.C.

Berghuser, *Hon.* Sir Eric, Kt., M.B.E.

Berkeley, Sir Lennox Randal Francis, Kt., C.B.E.

Berlin, Sir Isaiah, Kt., O.M., C.B.E.

Bernard, Sir Dallas Edmund, Bt. (1954).

Berney, Sir Julian Reedham Stuart, Bt. (1620).

Berrill, Sir Kenneth Ernest, G.B.E., K.C.B.

Berthon, *Vice-Adm.* Sir Stephen Ferrier, K.C.B.

Berthoud, Sir Martin Seymour, K.C.V.O., C.M.G.

Bethune, Sir Alexander Maitland Sharp, Bt. (s. 1683).

Bethune, *Hon.* Sir (Walter) Angus, Kt.

Bevan, Sir Martyn Evan Evans, Bt. (1958).

Bevan, Sir Timothy Hugh, Kt.

Beynon, *Prof.* Sir (William John) Granville, Kt., C.B.E., PH.D., D.SC., F.R.S.

Bibby, Sir Derek James, Bt., M.C. (1959).

Bickersteth, *Rt. Rev.* John Monier, K.C.V.O.

Biddulph, Sir Ian D'Olier, Bt. (1664).

Bide, Sir Austin Ernest, Kt.

Biggs, Sir Norman Paris, Kt.

Billiere, *Lt. Gen.* Sir Peter Edgar de la Cour de la, K.C.B., C.B.E., D.S.O., M.C.

Bing, Sir Rudolf Franz Josef, K.B.E.

Bingham, *Hon.* Sir Eardley Max, Kt., Q.C.

Bingham, *Rt. Hon.* Sir Thomas Henry, Kt.

Bird, *Col.* Sir Richard Dawnay Martin-, Kt., C.B.E., T.D.

Bird, Sir Richard Geoffrey Chapman, Bt. (1922).

Birkin, Sir John Christian William, Bt. (1905).

Birkmyre, Sir Henry, Bt. (1921).

Birley, Sir Derek Sydney, Kt.

Birtwistle, Sir Harrison, Kt.

Bishop, Sir Frederick Arthur, Kt., C.B., C.V.O.

Bishop, Sir George Sidney, Kt., C.B., O.B.E.

Bishop, *Instructor Rear-Adm.* Sir William, K.B.E., C.B.

Bjelke-Petersen, *Hon.* Sir Johannes, K.C.M.G.

Black, Sir Cyril Wilson, Kt.

Black, *Prof.* Sir Douglas Andrew Kilgour, Kt., M.D., F.R.C.P.

Black, Sir Hermann David, Kt.

Black, Sir James Whyte, Kt., F.R.C.P., F.R.S..

Black, *Adm.* Sir John Jeremy, K.C.B., D.S.O., M.B.E.

Black, Sir Robert Brown, G.C.M.G., O.B.E.

Black, Sir Robert David, Bt. (1922).

Blacker, *Gen.* Sir Cecil Hugh, G.C.B., O.B.E., M.C.

Blackett, Sir George William, Bt. (1673).

Blackman, Sir Frank Milton, K.C.V.O., O.B.E.

Blackwell, Sir Basil Davenport, Kt.

Blair, Sir Alastair Campbell, K.C.V.O., T.D., W.S.

Blair, *Lt.-Gen.* Sir Chandos, K.C.V.O., O.B.E., M.C.

Blair, Sir Edward Thomas Hunter, Bt. (1786).

Blair-Kerr, *Hon.* Sir Alastair, Kt.

Blake, Sir Alfred Lapthorn, K.C.V.O., M.C.

Blake, Sir Francis Michael, Bt. (1907).

Blake, Sir (Thomas) Richard (Valentine), Bt. (I. 1622).

Blaker, Sir John, Bt. (1919).

Blaker, *Rt. Hon.* Sir Peter Allan Renshaw, K.C.M.G., M.P.

Blakiston, Sir Ferguson Arthur James, Bt. (1763).

Bland, Sir Henry Armand, Kt., C.B.E.

Bland, *Lt.-Col.* Sir Simon Claud Michael, K.C.V.O.

Blaxter, Sir Kenneth Lyon, Kt., F.R.S., F.R.S.E.

Blelloch, Sir John Nial Henderson, K.C.B.

Blennerhassett, Sir (Marmaduke) Adrian Francis William, Bt. (1809).

Blewitt, *Maj.* Sir Shane Gabriel Basil, K.C.V.O.

Blois, Sir Charles Nicholas Gervase, Bt. (1686).

Blomefield, Sir Thomas Charles Peregrine, Bt. (1807).

Bloomfield, *Hon.* Sir John Stoughton, Kt., Q.C.

Bloomfield, Sir Kenneth Percy, K.C.B.

Blosse, *Capt.* Sir Richard Hely Lynch-, Bt. (1622).

Blount, Sir Walter Edward Alpin, Bt., D.S.C. (1642).

Blundell, Sir Michael, K.B.E.

Blunden, Sir George, Kt.

Blunden, Sir Philip Overington, Bt. (I. 1766).

Blunt, Sir David Richard Reginald Harvey, Bt. (1720).

Blyth, Sir James, Kt.

Boardman, *Prof.* Sir John, Kt., F.S.A., F.B.A.

Boardman, Sir Kenneth Ormrod, Kt.

Bodily, *Hon.* Sir Jocelyn, Kt., V.R.D.

Bodmer, Sir Walter Fred, Kt., PH.D., F.R.S.

Body, Sir Richard Bernard Frank Stewart, Kt., M.P.

Boevey, Sir Thomas Michael Blake Crawley-, Bt. (1784).

Boileau, Sir Guy (Francis), Bt. (1838).

Boles, Sir Jeremy John Fortescue, Bt. (1922).

Boles, Sir John Dennis, Kt., M.B.E.

Bolland, Sir Edwin, K.C.M.G.

Bollers, *Hon.* Sir Harold Brodie Smith, Kt.

Bolte, *Hon.* Sir Henry Edward, G.C.M.G.

Bolton, Sir Frederic Bernard, Kt., M.C.

Bonallack, Sir Richard Frank, Kt., C.B.E.

Bonar, Sir Herbert Vernon, Kt., C.B.E.

Bond, Sir Kenneth Raymond Boyden, Kt.

Bondi, *Prof.* Sir Hermann, K.C.B., F.R.S.

Bonham, *Maj.* Sir Antony Lionel Thomas, Bt. (1852).

Bonsall, Sir Arthur Wilfred, K.C.M.G., C.B.E.

Bonsor, Sir Nicholas Cosmo, Bt., M.P. (1925).

Boolell, Sir Satcam, Kt.

Boon, Sir Peter Coleman, Kt.

Boord, Sir Nicolas John Charles, Bt. (1896).

Boorman, *Lt.-Gen.* Sir Derek, K.C.B.

Booth, Sir Angus Josslyn Gore-, Bt. (I. 1760).

Booth, Sir Christopher Charles, Kt., M.D., F.R.C.P.

Booth, Sir Douglas Allen, Bt. (1916).

Booth, Sir Gordon, K.C.M.G., C.V.O.

Booth, Sir Robert Camm, Kt., C.B.E., T.D.

Boothby, Sir Brooke Charles, Bt. (1660).

Boreel, Sir Francis David, Bt. (1645).

Boreham, Sir (Arthur) John, K.C.B.

Boreham, *Hon.* Sir Leslie Kenneth Edward, Kt.

Bornu, The Waziri of, K.C.M.G., C.B.E.

Borrie, Sir Gordon Johnson, Kt., Q.C.

Borthwick, Sir John Thomas, Bt. M.B.E. (1908).

Bossom, *Hon.* Sir Clive, Bt. (1953).

Boswall, Sir (Thomas) Alford Houstoun-, Bt. (1836).

Boswell, *Lt.-Gen.* Sir Alexander Crawford Simpson, K.C.B., C.B.E.

Bosworth, Sir Neville Bruce Alfred, Kt., C.B.E.

Bottomley, Sir James Reginald Alfred, K.C.M.G.

Boughey, Sir John George Fletcher, Bt. (1798).

Boulton, Sir (Harold Hugh) Christian, Bt. (1905).

Boulton, Sir William Whytehead, Bt., C.B.E., T.D. (1944).

Bourne, Sir (John) Wilfrid, K.C.B.

Bovell, *Hon.* Sir (William) Stewart, Kt.

Bowater, Sir Euan David Vansittart, Bt. (1939).

Bowater, Sir (John) Vansittart, Bt. (1914).

Bowden, Sir Frank, Bt. (1915).

Bowen, Sir Geoffrey Fraser, Kt.

†Bowen, Sir Mark Edward Mortimer, Bt. (1921).

Bowen, *Hon.* Sir Nigel Hubert, K.B.E.

Bower, *Air Marshal* Sir Leslie William Clement, K.C.B., D.S.O., D.F.C.

Bower, *Lt.-Gen.* Sir Roger Herbert, K.C.B., K.B.E.

Bowlby, Sir Anthony Hugh Mostyn, Bt. (1923).

Bowman, Sir George, Bt. (1961).

Bowman, Sir John Paget, Bt. (1884).

Bowman-Shaw, Sir (George) Neville, Kt.

Bowmar, Sir Charles Erskine, Kt.

Bowness, Sir Alan, Kt., C.B.E.

Bowness, Sir Peter Spencer, Kt., C.B.E.

Boxer, *Air Vice-Marshal* Sir Alan Hunter Cachemaille, K.C.V.O., C.B., D.S.O., D.F.C.

Boyce, Sir Robert Charles Leslie, Bt. (1952).

Boyd, Sir Alexander Walter, Bt. (1916).

Boyd, *Prof.* Sir Robert Lewis Fullarton, Kt., C.B.E., D.SC., F.R.S.

Boyes, Sir Brian Gerald Barratt-, K.B.E.

Boyle, *Marshal of the Royal Air Force* Sir Dermot Alexander, G.C.B., K.C.V.O., K.B.E., A.F.C.

Boyle, Sir Lawrence, Kt., PH.D.

Boyle, Sir Stephen Gurney, Bt. (1904).

Boyne, Sir Henry Brian, Kt., C.B.E.

Boynton, Sir John Keyworth, Kt., M.C.

Boyson, *Rt. Hon.* Sir Rhodes, Kt., M.P.

Brabham, Sir John Arthur, Kt., O.B.E.

Bradbeer, Sir John Derek Richardson, Kt., O.B.E., T.D.

Bradbury, *Surgeon Vice-Adm.* Sir Eric Blackburn, K.B.E., C.B.

Bradford, Sir Edward Alexander Slade, Bt. (1902).

Bradlaw, *Prof.* Sir Robert Vivian, Kt., C.B.E.

Bradman, Sir Donald George, Kt.

Bradshaw, Sir Kenneth Anthony, K.C.B.

Bradshaw, *Lt.-Gen.* Sir Richard Phillip, K.B.E.

Brain, Sir (Henry) Norman, K.B.E., C.M.G.

Braine, *Rt. Hon.* Sir Bernard Richard, Kt., M.P.

Braithwaite, Sir (Joseph) Franklin Madders, Kt.

Braithwaite, Sir Rodric Quentin, K.C.M.G.

Bramall, Sir (Ernest) Ashley, Kt.

Bramley, *Prof.* Sir Paul Anthony, Kt.

Branch, Sir William Allan Patrick, Kt.

Brancker, Sir (John Eustace) Theodore, Kt., Q.C.

Branigan, Sir Patrick Francis, Kt., Q.C.

Brassey, *Col.* Sir Hugh Trefusis, K.C.V.O., O.B.E., M.C.

Bray, Sir Theodor Charles, Kt., C.B.E.

Braynen, Sir Alvin Rudolph, Kt.

Brearley, Sir Norman, Kt., C.B.E., D.S.O., M.C., A.F.C.

Bremridge, Sir John Henry, K.B.E.

Brennan, *Hon.* Sir (Francis) Gerard, K.B.E.

Brett, Sir Lionel, Kt.

Brickwood, Sir Basil Greame, Bt. (1927).

Bridges, *Hon.* Sir Phillip Rodney, Kt., C.M.G.

Brierley, Sir Ronald Alfred, Kt.

Brierley, Sir Zachry, Kt., C.B.E.

Briggs, *Hon.* Sir Geoffrey Gould, Kt.

Bright, Sir Keith, Kt.

Brinckman, Sir Theodore George Roderick, Bt. (1831).

Brisco, Sir Donald Gilfrid, Bt. (1782).

Briscoe, Sir John Leigh Charlton, Bt., D.F.C. (1910).

Brise, Sir John Archibald Ruggles-, Bt., C.B., O.B.E., T.D. (1935).

Bristow, *Hon.* Sir Peter Henry Rowley, Kt.

Brittan, *Rt. Hon.* Sir Leon, Kt., Q.C.

Britton, Sir Edward Louis, Kt., C.B.E.

Broackes, Sir Nigel, Kt.

Broadbent, Sir Ewen, K.C.B., C.M.G.

Broadbent, Sir George Walter, Bt. (1893).

Broadhurst, *Air Chief Marshal* Sir Harry, G.C.B., K.B.E., D.S.O., D.F.C., A.F.C.

Brockhoff, Sir Jack Stuart, Kt.

Brocklebank, Sir Aubrey Thomas, Bt. (1885).

Brockman, *Vice-Adm.* Sir Ronald Vernon, K.C.B., C.V.O., C.S.I., C.I.E., C.B.E.

Brockman, *Hon.* Sir Thomas Charles Drake-, Kt., D.F.C.

Brodie, Sir Benjamin David Ross, Bt. (1834).

Brogan, *Lt.-Gen.* Sir Mervyn Francis, K.B.E., C.B.

Bromhead, Sir John Desmond Gonville, Bt. (1806).

Bromley, Sir Rupert Charles, Bt. (1757).

Bromley, Sir Thomas Eardley, K.C.M.G.

Brook, Sir Robin, Kt., C.M.G., O.B.E.

†Brooke, Sir Alistair Weston, Bt. (1919).

Brooke, Sir Francis George Windham, Bt. (1903).

Brooke, *Hon.* Sir Henry, Kt.

Brooke, Sir (Norman) Richard (Rowley), Kt., C.B.E.

Brooke, Sir Richard Neville, Bt. (1662).

Brookes, Sir Wilfred Deakin, Kt., C.B.E., D.S.O.

Brooksbank, Sir (Edward) Nicholas, Bt. (1919).

Broom, *Air Marshal* Sir Ivor Gordon, K.C.B., C.B.E., D.S.O., D.F.C., A.F.C.

Broughton, *Air Marshal* Sir Charles, K.B.E., C.B.

Broughton, Sir Evelyn Delves, Bt. (1661).

Broun, Sir Lionel John Law, Bt. (s. 1686).

Brown, Sir Allen Stanley, Kt., C.B.E.

Brown, Sir (Arthur James) Stephen, K.B.E.

Brown, *Adm.* Sir Brian Thomas, K.C.B., C.B.E.

Brown, *Lt.-Col.* Sir Charles Frederick Richmond, Bt. (1863).

Brown, Sir (Cyril) Maxwell Palmer, K.C.B., C.M.G.

Brown, Sir David, Kt.

Brown, *Vice-Adm.* Sir David Worthington, K.C.B.

Brown, Sir Derrick Holden-, Kt.

Brown, Sir Douglas Denison, Kt.

Brown, *Hon.* Sir Douglas Dunlop, Kt.

Brown, Sir Edward Joseph, Kt., M.B.E.

Brown, *Prof.* Sir (Ernest) Henry Phelps, Kt., M.B.E., F.B.A.

Brown, Sir (Frederick Herbert) Stanley, Kt., C.B.E.

Brown, *Prof.* Sir (George) Malcolm, Kt., F.R.S

Brown, Sir John Douglas Keith, Kt.

Brown, Sir John Gilbert Newton, Kt., C.B.E.

Brown, Sir Mervyn, K.C.M.G., O.B.E..

Brown, *Hon.* Sir Ralph Kilner, Kt., O.B.E., T.D.

Brown, Sir Raymond Frederick, Kt., O.B.E.

Brown, Sir Robert Crichton-, K.C.M.G., C.B.E., T.D.

Brown, *Hon.* Sir Simon Denis, Kt.

Brown, *Rt. Hon.* Sir Stephen, Kt.

Brown, Sir Thomas, Kt.

Brown, Sir William Brian Piggott-, Bt. (1903).

Browne, *Rt. Hon.* Sir Patrick Reginald Evelyn, Kt., O.B.E., T.D.

Brownrigg, Sir Nicholas (Gawen), Bt. (1816).

Bruce, Sir Arthur Atkinson, K.B.E., M.C.

Bruce, Sir (Francis) Michael Ian, Bt. (s. 1628).

Bruce, Sir Hervey James Hugh, Bt. (1804).

Bruce, *Rt. Hon.* Sir (James) Roualeyn Hovell-Thurlow-Cumming-, Kt.

Brunner, Sir John Henry Kilian, Bt. (1895).

Brunton, Sir (Edward Francis) Lauder, Bt. (1908).

Brunton, Sir Gordon Charles, Kt.

Bryan, Sir Arthur, Kt.

Bryan, Sir Paul Elmore Oliver, Kt., D.S.O., M.C.

Bryce, *Hon.* Sir (William) Gordon, Kt., C.B.E.

Bryson, *Vice-Adm.* Sir Lindsay Sutherland, K.C.B.

Buchan, Sir John, Kt., C.M.G.

Buchanan, Sir Andrew George, Bt. (1878).

Buchanan, Sir Charles Alexander James Leith-, Bt. (1775).

Buchanan, *Prof.* Sir Colin Douglas, Kt., C.B.E.

Buchanan, *Vice-Adm.* Sir Peter William, K.B.E.

Buck, Sir (Philip) Antony (Fyson), Kt., Q.C., M.P.

Buckley, *Rt. Hon.* Sir Denys Burton, Kt., M.B.E.

Buckley, Sir John William, Kt.

Buckley, *Rear-Adm.* Sir Kenneth Robertson, K.B.E.

Buckley, *Lt.-Cdr.* Sir (Peter) Richard, K.C.V.O.

Buckley, *Hon.* Sir Roger John, Kt.

Bulkeley, Sir Richard Harry David Williams-, Bt., T.D. (1661).

Bull, Sir Simeon George, Bt. (1922).

Bull, Sir Walter Edward Avenon, K.C.V.O.

Bullard, Sir Giles Lionel, K.C.V.O., G.M.G.

Bullard, Sir Julian Leonard, G.C.M.G.

Bullus, Sir Eric Edward, Kt.

Bulmer, Sir William Peter, Kt.

Bultin, Sir Bato, Kt., M.B.E.

Bunbury, Sir Michael William, Bt. (1681).

Bunbury, Sir (Richard David) Michael Richardson-, Bt. (I. 1787).

Bunch, Sir Austin Wyeth, Kt., C.B.E.

Bunting, Sir (Edward) John, K.B.E.

Burbidge, Sir Herbert Dudley, Bt. (1916).

Burbury, *Hon.* Sir Stanley Charles, K.C.M.G., K.C.V.O., K.B.E.

Burdett, Sir Savile Aylmer, Bt. (1665).

Burgen, Sir Arnold Stanley Vincent, Kt., F.R.S.

Burgess, *Gen.* Sir Edward Arthur, K.C.B., O.B.E.

Burgh, Sir John Charles, K.C.M.G., C.B.

†Burke, Sir James Stanley Gilbert, Bt. (I. 1797).

Burke, *Prof.* Sir Joseph Terence, K.B.E.

Burley, Sir Victor George, Kt., C.B.E.

Burman, Sir (John) Charles, Kt.

Burman, Sir Stephen France, Kt., C.B.E.

Burnet, Sir James William Alexander (Sir Alastair Burnet), Kt.

Burnett, *Air Chief Marshal* Sir Brian Kenyon, G.C.B., D.F.C., A.F.C.

Burnett, Sir David Humphery, Bt., M.B.E., T.D. (1913).

Burnett, Sir John Harrison, Kt.

Burnett, Sir Walter John, Kt.

Burney, Sir Cecil Denniston, Bt. (1921).

Burns, Sir Charles Ritchie, K.B.E., M.D.

Burns, Sir John Crawford, Kt.

Burns, Sir Terence, Kt.

Burns, *Maj.-Gen.* Sir (Walter Arthur) George, K.C.V.O., C.B., D.S.O., O.B.E., M.C.

Burrell, Sir John Raymond, Bt. (1774).

Burrenchobay, Sir Dayendranath, K.B.E., C.M.G., C.V.O.

Burrows, Sir Bernard Alexander Brocas, G.C.M.G.

Burston, Sir Samuel Gerald Wood, Kt., O.B.E.

Burt, *Hon.* Sir Francis Theodore Page, K.C.M.G.

Burton, Sir Carlisle Archibald, Kt., O.B.E.

Burton, Sir George Vernon Kennedy, Kt., C.B.E.

Burton, *Air Marshal* Sir Harry, K.C.B., C.B.E., D.S.O.

Burton-Chadwick, Sir Joshua Kenneth, Bt. (1935).

Busby, Sir Matthew, Kt., C.B.E.

Bush, *Adm.* Sir John Fitzroy Duyland, G.C.B., D.S.C.

Busk, Sir Douglas Laird, K.C.M.G.

Butler, *Rt. Hon.* Sir Adam Courtauld, Kt.

Butler, Sir Clifford Charles, Kt., Ph.D., F.R.S.

Butler, Sir (Frederick) (Edward) Robin, K.C.B., C.V.O.

Butler, Sir Michael Dacres, G.C.M.G.

Butler, Sir (Reginald) Michael (Thomas), Bt. (1922).

Butler, *Hon.* Sir Richard Clive, Kt.

Butler, *Col.* Sir Thomas Pierce, Bt., C.V.O., D.S.O., O.B.E. (1628).

Butt, Sir (Alfred) Kenneth Dudley, Bt. (1929).

Butterworth, Sir (George) Neville, Kt.

Buxton, Sir Thomas Fowell Victor, Bt. (1840).

Buzzard, Sir Anthony Farquhar, Bt. (1929).

Byatt, Sir Hugh Campbell, K.C.V.O., C.M.G.

Byers, Sir Maurice Hearne, Kt., C.B.E., Q.C.

Byford, Sir Lawrence, Kt., C.B.E., Q.P.M.

Byrne, Sir Clarence Askew, Kt., O.B.E., D.S.C.

Cable, Sir James Eric, K.C.V.O., C.M.G.

Cadbury, Sir (George) Adrian (Hayhurst), Kt.

Cadell, *Vice-Adm.* Sir John Frederick, K.B.E.

Cadwallader, Sir John, Kt.

Caffyn, *Brig.* Sir Edward Roy, K.B.E., C.B., T.D.

Cahn, Sir Albert Jonas, Bt. (1934).

Cain, Sir Edward Thomas, Kt., C.B.E.

Cain, Sir Henry Edney Conrad, Kt.

Caine, Sir Michael Harris, Kt.

Caine, Sir Sydney, K.C.M.G.

Cairncross, Sir Alexander Kirkland, K.C.M.G.

Cakobau, *Ratu* Sir George, G.C.M.G., G.C.V.O., O.B.E., Royal Victorian Chain.

Caldwell, *Surgeon Vice-Adm.* Sir (Eric) Dick, K.B.E., C.B.

Callaghan, Sir Allan Robert, Kt., C.M.G.

Callaghan, Sir Bede Bertrand, Kt., C.B.E.

Callard, Sir Eric John, Kt.

Callaway, *Prof.* Sir Frank Adams, Kt., C.M.G., O.B.E.

Calley, Sir Henry Algernon, Kt., D.S.O., D.F.C.

Callinan, Sir Bernard James, Kt., C.B.E., D.S.O., M.C.

Calne, *Prof.* Sir Roy Yorke, Kt., F.R.S.

Calthorpe, Sir Euan Hamilton Anstruther-Gough-, Bt. (1929).

Cameron of Lochiel, Sir Donald Hamish, K.T., C.V.O., T.D.

Cameron, Sir (Eustace) John, Kt., C.B.E.

Cameron, Sir James Clark, Kt., C.B.E., T.D.

Cameron, *Hon.* Sir John, Kt., D.S.C., Q.C. (Lord Cameron).

Cameron, Sir John Watson, Kt., O.B.E.

Camilleri, *His Hon.* Sir Luigi Antonio, Kt, Ll.D.

Campbell, Sir Alan Hugh, G.C.M.G.

Campbell, Sir Clifford Clarence, G.C.M.G., G.C.V.O.

Campbell, Sir Colin Moffat, Bt., M.C. (s. 1668).

Campbell, *Col.* Sir Guy Theophilus Halswell, Bt., O.B.E., M.C. (1815).

Campbell, *Maj.-Gen.* Sir Hamish Manus, K.B.E., C.B.

Campbell, *Cdr.* Sir Ian Tofts, C.B.E., V.R.D.

Campbell, Sir Ilay Mark, Bt. (1808).

Campbell, Sir Matthew, K.B.E., C.B., F.R.S.E.

Campbell, Sir Niall Alexander Hamilton, Bt. (1831).

Campbell, Sir Ralph Abercromby, Kt.

Campbell, Sir Robin Auchinbreck, Bt. (s. 1628).

Campbell, Sir Thomas Cockburn-, Bt. (1821).

Campbell, *Hon.* Sir Walter Benjamin, Kt.

Campbell, *Hon.* Sir William Anthony, Kt.

Campion, Sir Harry, Kt., C.B., C.B.E.

Cantley, *Hon.* Sir Joseph Donaldson, Kt., O.B.E.

Carden, *Lt.-Col.* Sir Henry Christopher, Bt., O.B.E. (1887).

Carden, Sir John Craven, Bt. (I. 1787).

Carew, Sir Rivers Verain, Bt. (1661).

Carey, Sir Peter Willoughby, G.C.B.

Carlill, *Vice-Adm.* Sir Stephen Hope, K.B.E., C.B., D.S.O.

Carlisle, Sir John Michael, Kt.

Carmichael, Sir David Peter William Gibson-Craig-, Bt. (s. 1702 and 1831).

Carmichael, Sir John, K.B.E.

Carnac, *Rev. Canon* Sir (Thomas) Nicholas Rivett-, Bt. (1836).

Carnegie, *Lt.-Gen.* Sir Robin Macdonald, K.C.B., O.B.E.

Carnegie, Sir Roderick Howard, Kt.

Carnwath, Sir Andrew Hunter, K.C.V.O.

Caro, Sir Anthony Alfred, Kt., C.B.E.

Carpenter, *Very Rev.* Edward Frederick, K.C.V.O.

Carr, Sir (Albert) Raymond (Maillard), Kt.

Carr, *Air Marshal* Sir John Darcy Baker-, K.B.E., C.B., A.F.C.

Carreras, *Lt.-Col.* Sir James, K.C.V.O., M.B.E.

Carrick, *Hon.* Sir John Leslie, K.C.M.G.

Carsberg, *Prof.* Sir Bryan Victor, Kt.

Carswell, *Hon.* Sir Robert Douglas, Kt.

Carter, Sir Charles Frederick, Kt., F.B.A.

Carter, Sir Derrick Hunton, Kt., T.D.

Carter, Sir John, Kt., Q.C.

Carter, Sir John Alexander, Kt.

Carter, Sir William Oscar, Kt.

Cartland, Sir George Barrington, Kt., C.M.G.

Cartledge, Sir Bryan George, K.C.M.G.

Cary, Sir Roger Hugh, Bt. (1955).

Cash, Sir Gerald Christopher, G.C.M.G., G.C.V.O., O.B.E.

Cass, Sir John Patrick, Kt., O.B.E.

Cassel, Sir Harold Felix, Bt., T.D., Q.C. (1920).

Cassels, *Field Marshal* Sir (Archibald) James Halkett, G.C.B., K.B.E., D.S.O.

Cassels, Sir John Seton, Kt., C.B.

Cassels, *Adm.* Sir Simon Alastair Cassillis, K.C.B., C.B.E.

Cassidi, *Adm.* Sir (Arthur) Desmond, G.C.B.

Casson, Sir Hugh Maxwell, C.H., K.C.V.O., P.P.R.A., F.R.I.B.A.

Cater, Sir Jack, K.B.E.

Cater, Sir John Robert, Kt.

Catherwood, Sir (Henry) Frederick (Ross), Kt.

Catling, Sir Richard Charles, Kt., C.M.G., O.B.E.

Cato, *Hon.* Sir Arnott Samuel, K.C.M.G.

Caughey, Sir Thomas Harcourt Clarke, K.B.E.

Caulfield, *Hon.* Sir Bernard, Kt.

Cave, Sir Charles Edward Coleridge, Bt. (1896).

Cave, Sir (Charles) Philip Haddon-, K.B.E., C.M.G.

Cave, Sir Robert Cave-Browne-, Bt. (1641).

Cawley, Sir Charles Mills, Kt., C.B.E., Ph.D.

Cayley, Sir Digby William David, Bt. (1661).

Cayzer, Sir James Arthur, Bt. (1904).

Cazalet, *Hon.* Sir Edward Stephen, Kt.

Cazalet, Sir Peter Grenville, Kt.

Cecil, *Rear-Adm.* Sir (Oswald) Nigel Amherst, K.B.E., C.B.

Chacksfield, *Air Vice-Marshal* Sir Bernard Albert, K.B.E., C.B.

Chadwick, *Rev. Prof.* Henry, K.B.E.

Chadwick, *Rev. Prof.* (William) Owen, O.M., K.B.E., F.B.A.

Chalk, *Hon.* Sir Gordon William Wesley, K.B.E.

Chamberlain, *Hon.* Sir Reginald Roderic St. Clair, Kt.

Chan, *Rt. Hon.* Sir Julius, K.B.E.

Chance, Sir (George) Jeremy ffolliott, Bt. (1900).

Chancellor, Sir Christopher John, Kt., C.M.G.

Chandler, Sir Colin Michael, Kt.

Chandler, Sir Geoffrey, Kt., C.B.E.

Chaney, *Hon.* Sir Frederick Charles, K.B.E., A.F.C.

Chapman, Sir David Robert Macgowan, Bt. (1958).

Chapman, Sir George Alan, Kt.

Chapman, *Hon.* Sir Stephen, Kt.

Chapple, *Gen.* Sir John Lyon, G.C.B., C.B.E.

Charles, Sir Joseph Quentin, Kt.

Charnley, Sir (William) John, Kt., C.B.

Chau, *Hon.* Sir Sik-Nin, Kt., C.B.E.

Chaytor, Sir George Reginald, Bt. (1831).

Cheadle, Sir Eric Wallers, Kt., C.B.E.

Cheeketts, *Sqn. Ldr.* Sir David John, K.C.V.O.

Cheetham, Sir Nicolas John Alexander, K.C.M.G.

Chesterman, Sir (Dudley) Ross, Kt., Ph.D.

Chesterton, Sir Oliver Sidney, Kt., M.C.

Chetwood, Sir Clifford Jack, Kt.

Chetwynd, Sir Arthur Ralph Talbot, Bt. (1795).

Cheung, Sir Oswald Victor, Kt., C.B.E.

Cheyne, Sir Joseph Lister Watson, Bt., O.B.E. (1908).

Chichester, Sir (Edward) John, Bt. (1641).

Child, Sir (Coles John) Jeremy, Bt. (1919).

Chilton, *Air Marshal* Sir (Charles) Edward, K.B.E., C.B.

Chilton, *Brig.* Sir Frederick Oliver, Kt., C.B.E., D.S.O.

Chitty, Sir Thomas Willes, Bt. (1924).

Cholmeley, Sir Montague John, Bt. (1806).

Christie, Sir George William Langham, Kt.

Christie, *Hon.* Sir Vernon Howard Colville, Kt.

Christie, Sir William, Kt., M.B.E.

Christison, *Gen.* Sir (Alexander Frank) Philip, Bt., G.B.E., C.B., D.S.O., M.C. (1871).

Christofas, Sir Kenneth Cavendish, K.C.M.G., M.B.E.

Christopherson, Sir Derman Guy, Kt., O.B.E., D.Phil., F.R.S.

Chung, Sir Sze-yuen, Kt., G.B.E.

Clapham, Sir Michael John Sinclair, K.B.E.

Claringbull, Sir (Gordon) Frank, Kt., Ph.D.

Clark, Sir George Anthony, Bt. (1917).

Clark, Sir John Allen, Kt.

Clark, Sir John Douglas, Bt. (1886).

Clark, Sir John Stewart-, Bt. (1918).

Clark, Sir Robert Anthony, Kt., D.S.C.

Clark, Sir Robin Chichester-, Kt.

Clark, Sir Thomas Edwin, Kt.

Clark, Sir William Gibson, Kt., M.P.

Clarke, Sir (Charles Mansfield) Tobias, Bt. (1831).

Clarke, *Prof.* Sir Cyril Astley, K.B.E., M.D., SC.D., F.R.S., F.R.C.P.

Clarke, Sir Ellis Emmanuel Innocent, G.C.M.G.

Clarke, Sir (Henry) Ashley, G.C.M.G., G.C.V.O.

Clarke, Sir Jonathan Dennis, Kt.

Clarke, Sir Rupert William John, Bt., M.B.E. (1882).

Clay, Sir Richard Henry, Bt. (1841).

Clayson, Sir Eric Maurice, Kt.

Clayton, Sir David Robert, Bt., (1732).

Clayton, *Air Marshal* Sir Gareth Thomas Butler, K.C.B., D.F.C.

Clayton, Sir Robert James, Kt., C.B.E.

Cleary, Sir Joseph Jackson, Kt.

Clegg, Sir Walter, Kt.

Cleminson, Sir James Arnold Stacey, Kt., M.C.

Clerk, Sir John Dutton, Bt., C.B.E., V.R.D. (s. 1679).

Clerke, Sir John Edward Longueville, Bt. (1660).

Clifford, Sir Roger Joseph, Bt. (1887).

Clothier, Sir Cecil Montacute, K.C.B., Q.C.

Clowes, *Col.* Sir Henry Nelson, K.C.V.O., D.S.O., O.B.E.

Clucas, Sir Kenneth Henry, K.C.B.

Clutterbuck, *Vice-Adm.* Sir David Granville, K.B.E., C.B.

Coates, Sir Ernest William, Kt., C.M.G.

Coates, Sir Frederick Gregory Lindsay, Bt. (1921).

Coats, Sir Alastair Francis Stuart, Bt. (1905).

Coats, Sir William David, Kt.

Cobban, Sir James Macdonald, Kt., C.B.E., T.D.

Cochrane, Sir (Henry) Marc (Sursock), Bt. (1903).

Cockburn, Sir John Elliot, Bt. (s. 1671).

Cockburn, Sir Robert, K.B.E., C.B., Ph.D.

Cockcroft, Sir Wilfred Halliday, Kt., D.Phil.

Cockerell, Sir Christopher Sydney, Kt., C.B.E., F.R.S.

Cockram, Sir John, Kt.

Codrington, Sir Simon Francis Bethell, Bt. (1876).

Codrington, Sir William Alexander, Bt. (1721).

Coghill, Sir Egerton James Nevill Tobias, Bt. (1778).

Cohen, Sir Bernard Nathaniel Waley-, Bt. (1961).

Cohen, Sir Edward, Kt.

Coldstream, Sir George Phillips, K.C.B., K.C.V.O., Q.C.

Cole, Sir (Alexander) Colin, K.C.V.O., T.D.

Cole, Sir David Lee, K.C.M.G., M.C.

Cole, Sir (Robert) William, Kt.

Coles, Sir (Arthur) John, K.C.M.G.

Coles, Sir Norman Cameron, Kt.

Colfox, Sir (William) John, Bt. (1939).

Collett, Sir Christopher, G.B.E.

Collett, Sir Ian Seymour, Bt. (1934).

Collins, Sir Arthur James Robert, K.C.V.O.

Collins, *Vice-Adm.* Sir John Augustine, K.B.E., C.B.

Collyear, Sir John Gowen, Kt.

Colman, Sir Michael Jeremiah, Bt. (1907).

Colquhoun, *Maj.-Gen.* Sir Cyril Harry, K.C.V.O., C.B., O.B.E.

Colquhoun of Luss, Sir Ivar Iain, Bt. (1786).

Colt, Sir Edward William Dutton Bt. (1694).

Colthurst, Sir Richard La Touche, Bt. (1744).

Combs, Sir Willis Ide, K.C.V.O., C.M.G.

Compston, *Vice-Adm.* Sir Peter Maxwell, K.C.B.

Compton, Sir Edmund Gerald, G.C.B., K.B.E.

Compton Miller, Sir John (Francis), Kt., M.B.E., T.D.

Comyn, *Hon.* Sir James, Kt.

Conant, Sir John Ernest Michael, Bt. (1954).

Conran, Sir Terence Orby, Kt.

Constable, Sir Robert Frederick Strickland-, Bt. (1641).

Constantine, *Air Chief Marshal* Sir Hugh Alex, K.B.E., C.B., D.S.O.

Cook, *Prof.* Sir Alan Hugh, Kt.

Cook, Sir Christopher Wymondham Rayner Herbert, Bt. (1886).

Cook, Sir (Philip) Halford, Kt., O.B.E.

Cooke, Sir Charles Fletcher-, Kt., Q.C.

Cooke, *Lt.-Col.* Sir David William Perceval, Bt. (1661).

Cooke, *Rt. Hon.* Sir Robin Brunskill, K.B.E.

Cooley, Sir Alan Sydenham, Kt., C.B.E.

Coop, Sir Maurice Fletcher, Kt.

Cooper, *Rt. Hon.* Sir Frank, G.C.B., C.M.G.

Cooper, *Gen.* Sir George Leslie Conroy, G.C.B., M.C.

Cooper, Sir Patrick Graham Astley, Bt. (1821).

Cooper, Sir Richard Powell, Bt. (1905).

Cooper, Sir William Daniel Charles, Bt. (1863).

Cooper, Sir William Henry, Kt., C.B.E.

Cooper, *Prof.* Sir (William) Mansfield, Kt.

Coote, Sir Christopher John, Bt., *Premier Baronet of Ireland* (I. 1621).

Copas, *Most Rev.* Virgil, K.B.E., D.D.

Copisarow, Sir Alcon Charles, Kt.

Corbet, Sir John Vincent, Bt., M.B.E. (1808).

Corby, Sir (Frederick) Brian, Kt.

Corfield, *Rt. Hon.* Sir Frederick Vernon, Kt., Q.C.

Corfield, Sir Kenneth George, Kt.

Cork, Sir Kenneth Russell, G.B.E.

Corley, Sir Kenneth Sholl Ferrand, Kt.

Cormack, Sir Magnus Cameron, K.B.E.

Corness, Sir Colin Ross, Kt.

Cornford, Sir (Edward) Clifford, K.C.B.

Cornforth, Sir John Warcup, Kt., C.B.E., D.Phil., F.R.S.

Corry, Sir William James, Bt. (1885).

Cortazzi, Sir (Henry Arthur) Hugh, G.C.M.G.

Cory, Sir Clinton James Donald, Bt. (1919).

Costar, Sir Norman Edgar, K.C.M.G.

Cotter, *Lt.-Col.* Sir Delaval James Alfred, Bt., D.S.O. (I. 1763).

Cotterell, Sir John Henry Geers, Bt. (1805).

Cotton, Sir John Richard, K.C.M.G., O.B.E.

Cotton, *Hon.* Sir Robert Carrington, K.C.M.G.

Cottrell, Sir Alan Howard, Kt., Ph.D., F.R.S.

Cotts, Sir (Robert) Crichton Mitchell, Bt. (1921).

Coulson, Sir John Eltringham, K.C.M.G.

Couper, Sir (Robert) Nicholas (Oliver), Bt. (1841).

Court, *Hon.* Sir Charles Walter Michael, K.C.M.G., O.B.E.

Couzens, Sir Kenneth Edward, K.C.B.

Covacevich, Sir (Anthony) Thomas, Kt., D.F.C.

Cowan, Sir Robert, Kt.

Cowen, *Rt. Hon. Prof.* Sir Zelman, G.C.M.G., G.C.V.O., Q.C.

Cowley, *Lt.-Gen.* Sir John Guise, K.B.E., C.B.

Cowperthwaite, Sir John James, K.B.E., C.M.G.

Cox, Sir Anthony Wakefield, Kt., C.B.E., F.R.I.B.A.

Cox, *Prof.* Sir David Roxbee, Kt., F.R.S.

Cox, Sir (Ernest) Gordon, K.B.E., T.D., D.S.C., F.R.S.

Cox, Sir Geoffrey Sandford, Kt., C.B.E.

Cox, Sir (George) Trenchard, Kt., C.B.E., F.S.A.

Cox, *Vice-Adm.* Sir John Michael Holland, K.C.B.

Cox, Sir John William, Kt., C.B.E.

Cox, Sir Mencea Ethereal, Kt.,

Cradock, Sir Percy, G.C.M.G.

Craig, Sir (Albert) James (Macqueen), G.C.M.G.

Craig, *Marshal of the R.A.F.* Sir David Brownrigg, G.C.B., O.B.E.

Cramer, *Hon.* Sir John Oscar, Kt.

Crane, Sir James William Donald, Kt., C.B.E.

Craufurd, Sir Robert James, Bt. (1781).

Craven, *Air Marshal* Sir Robert Edward, K.B.E., C.B., D.F.C.

Crawford, *Prof.* Sir Frederick William, Kt.

Crawford, *Hon.* Sir George Hunter, Kt.

Crawford, Sir (Robert) Stewart, G.C.M.G., C.V.O

Crawford, *Prof.* Sir Theodore, Kt.

Crawford, *Vice-Adm.* Sir William Godfrey, K.B.E., C.B., D.S.C.

Crawshaw, *Hon.* Sir (Edward) Daniel (Weston), Kt.

Crawshay, *Col.* Sir William Robert, Kt., D.S.O., E.R.D., T.D.

Creagh, *Maj.-Gen.* Sir (Kilner) Rupert Brazier-, K.B.E., C.B., D.S.O.

Crichton, Sir Andrew James Maitland-Makgill-, Kt.

Crill, Sir Peter Leslie, Kt., C.B.E.

Cripps, Sir Cyril Humphrey, Kt.

Cripps, Sir John Stafford, Kt., C.B.E.

Crisp, Sir (John) Peter, Bt. (1913).

Critchett, Sir Ian (George Lorraine), Bt. (1908).

Croft, Sir John Archibald Radcliffe, Bt. (1818).

Croft, Sir Owen Glendower, Bt. (1671).

†Crofton, Sir Hugh Denis, Bt. (1801).

Crofton, *Prof.* Sir John Wenman, Kt.

Crofton, Sir Malby Sturges, Bt. (1838).

Croker, Sir Walter Russell, K.B.E.

Crookenden, *Lt.-Gen.* Sir Napier, K.C.B., D.S.O., O.B.E.

Croom-Johnson, *Rt. Hon.* Sir David Powell, Kt., D.S.C., V.R.D.

Cross, Sir Barry Albert, Kt., C.B.E., F.R.S.

Cross, *Air Chief Marshal* Sir Kenneth Brian Boyd, K.C.B., C.B.E., D.S.O., D.F.C.

Crossland, Sir Leonard, Kt.

Crossley, Sir Nicholas John, Bt. (1909).

Crouch, Sir David Lance, Kt.

Cruthers, Sir James Winter, Kt.

Cubbon, Sir Brian Crossland, G.C.B.

Cubitt, Sir Hugh Guy, Kt., C.B.E.

Cuckney, Sir John Graham, Kt.

Cumber, Sir John Alfred, Kt., C.M.G., M.B.E., T.D.

Cumming, Sir William Gordon Gordon-, Bt. (1804).

Cuninghame, Sir John Christopher Foggo Montgomery-, Bt. (N.S. 1672).

†Cuninghame, Sir William Henry Fairlie-, Bt., (s. 1630).

Cunliffe, Sir David Ellis, Bt. (1759).

Cunningham, Sir Charles Craik, G.C.B., K.B.E., C.V.O.

Cunningham, *Lt.-Gen.* Sir Hugh Patrick, K.B.E.

Cunynghame, Sir Andrew David Francis, Bt. (s. 1702).

Cunynghame, Sir James Ogilvy Blair-, Kt., O.B.E.

Curle, Sir John Noel Ormiston, K.C.V.O., C.M.G.

Curran, Sir Samuel Crowe, Kt., D.S.C., Ph.D., F.R.S., F.R.S.E.

Currie, *Prof.* Sir Alastair Robert, Kt., F.R.C.P., F.R.C.P.E., F.R.S.E.

†Currie, Sir Donald Scott, Bt. (1847).

Currie, Sir Neil Smith, Kt., C.B.E.

Curtis, Sir (Edward) Leo, Kt.

Curtis, Sir William Peter, Bt. (1802).

Curtiss, *Air Marshal* Sir John Bagot, K.C.B., K.B.E.

Curwen, Sir Christopher Keith, K.C.M.G.

Cuthbertson, Sir Harold Alexander, Kt.

Cutler, Sir (Arthur) Roden, V.C., K.C.M.G., K.C.V.O., C.B.E.

Cutler, Sir Charles Benjamin, K.B.E., E.D

Cutler, Sir Horace Walter, Kt., O.B.E.

Dacie, *Prof.* Sir John Vivian, Kt., M.D., F.R.S.

Dalais, Sir Adrien Pierre, Kt.

Dale, Sir William Leonard, K.C.M.G.

Dalrymple, *Maj.* Sir Hew Fleetwood Hamilton-, Bt., K.C.V.O. (s. 1697).

Dalton, Sir Alan Nugent Goring, Kt., C.B.E.

Dalton, *Vice-Adm.* Sir Geoffrey Thomas James Oliver, K.C.B.

Dalton, *Vice-Adm.* Sir Norman Eric, K.C.B., O.B.E.

Daly, *Lt.-Gen.* Sir Thomas Joseph, K.B.E., C.B., D.S.O.

Dalyell, Sir Tam, Bt., M.P. (N.S. 1685).

Daniel, Sir Goronwy Hopkin, K.C.V.O., C.B., D.Phil.

Daniell, Sir Peter Averell, Kt., T.D.

Danks, Sir Alan John, K.B.E.

Darby, *Prof.* Sir Henry Clifford, Kt., C.B.E.

Darby, Sir Peter Howard, Kt., C.B.E., Q.F.S.M.

Darell, Sir Jeffrey Lionel, Bt., M.C. (1795).

Dargie, Sir William Alexander, Kt., C.B.E.

Darling, Sir Clifford, Kt.

Darling, Sir James Ralph, Kt., C.M.G., O.B.E.

Darling, *Gen.* Sir Kenneth Thomas, G.B.E., K.C.B., D.S.O.

Darlington, *Rear-Adm.* Sir Charles Roy, K.B.E.

Darvall, Sir (Charles) Roger, Kt., C.B.E.

Dashwood, Sir Francis John Vernon Hereward, Bt., *Premier Baronet of Great Britain* (1707).

Dashwood, Sir Richard James, Bt. (1684).

Daunt, Sir Timothy Lewis Achilles, K.C.M.G.

Davenport, *Lt.-Col.* Sir Walter Henry Bromley-, Kt., T.D.

David, Sir Jean Marc, Kt., C.B.E., Q.C.

Davidson, Sir Robert James, Kt.

Davie, Sir Antony Francis Ferguson-, Bt. (1847).

Davie, Sir Paul Christopher, Kt.

Davies, *Air Marshal* Sir Alan Cyril, K.C.B., C.B.E.

Davies, *Hon.* Sir (Alfred William) Michael, Kt.

Davies, Sir Alun Talfan, Kt., Q.C.

Davies, Sir (David) Arthur, K.B.E.

Davies, Sir David Henry, Kt.

Davies, *Hon.* Sir (David Herbert) Mervyn, Kt., M.C., T.D.

Davies, Sir David Joseph, Kt.

Davies, *Vice-Adm.* Sir Lancelot Richard Bell, K.B.E.

Davies, Sir Oswald, Kt., C.B.E.

Davies, Sir Peter Maxwell, Kt., C.B.E.

Davies, Sir Richard Harries, K.C.V.O., C.B.E.

Davies, Sir Victor Caddy, Kt., O.B.E.

Davis, Sir Charles Sigmund, Kt., C.B.

Davis, Sir Colin Rex, Kt., C.B.E.

Davis, *Hon.* Sir (Dermot) Renn, Kt., O.B.E.

Davis, Sir (Ernest) Howard, Kt., C.M.G., O.B.E.

Davis, Sir John Gilbert, Bt. (1946).

Davis, Sir John Henry Harris, Kt.

Davis, Sir Maurice Herbert, Kt., O.B.E.

Davis, Sir Rupert Charles Hart-, Kt.

Davis, *Hon.* Sir Thomas Robert Alexander Harries, K.B.E.

Davis, Sir (William) Allan, G.B.E.

Davison, *Rt. Hon.* Sir Ronald Keith, G.B.E., C.M.G.

Dawbarn, Sir Simon Yelverton, K.C.V.O., C.M.G.

Dawson, *Hon.* Sir Daryl Michael, K.B.E., C.B.

Dawson, Sir Hugh Michael Trevor, Bt. (1920).

Dawson, *Air Chief Marshal* Sir Walter Lloyd, K.C.B., C.B.E., D.S.O.

Dawtry, Sir Alan (Graham), C.B.E., T.D.

Day, Sir Derek Malcolm, K.C.M.G.

Day, Sir (Judson) Graham, Kt.

Day, Sir Robin, Kt.

Deakin, Sir (Frederick) William (Dampier), Kt., D.S.O.

Dean, Sir (Arthur) Paul, Kt., M.P.

Dean, Sir Patrick Henry, G.C.M.G.

Deane, *Hon.* Sir William Patrick, K.B.E.

Dearing, Sir Ronald Ernest, Kt., C.B.

de Bellaigue, Sir Geoffrey, K.C.V.O.

Debenham, Sir Gilbert Ridley, Bt. (1931).

De Bunsen, Sir Bernard, Kt., C.M.G.

Deer, Sir (Arthur) Frederick, Kt., C.M.G.

de Hoghton, Sir (Richard) Bernard (Cuthbert), Bt. (1611).

De la Bère, Sir Cameron, Bt. (1953).

Delacombe, *Maj.-Gen.* Sir Rohan, K.C.M.G., K.C.V.O., K.B.E., C.B., D.S.O.

de la Mare, Sir Arthur James, K.C.M.G., K.C.V.O.

de la Rue, Sir Eric Vincent, Bt. (1898).

de Lotbinière, *Lt.-Col.* Sir Edmond Joly, Kt.

Delve, Sir Frederick William, Kt., C.B.E.

de Montmorency, Sir Arnold Geoffroy, Bt. (I 1631).

Denholm, Sir John Ferguson (Ian), Kt., C.B.E.

Denman, Sir (George) Roy, K.C.B., C.M.G.

Denning, *Lt.-Gen.* Sir Reginald Francis Stewart, K.C.V.O., K.B.E., C.B.

Denny, Sir Alistair Maurice Archibald, Bt. (1913).

Denny, Sir Anthony Coningham de Waltham, Bt. (I 1782).

Dent, Sir John, Kt., C.B.E.

Denton, *Prof.* Sir Eric James, Kt., C.B.E., F.R.S.

Derbyshire, Sir Andrew George, Kt.

Derham, Sir Peter John, Kt.

de Trafford, Sir Dermot Humphrey, Bt. (1841).

Deverell, Sir Colville Montgomery, G.B.E., K.C.M.G., K.C.V.O.

Devesi, Sir Baddeley, G.C.M.G., G.C.V.O.

Devitt, Sir Thomas Gordon, Bt. (1916).

de Waal, Sir (Constant Henrik) Henry, K.C.B., Q.C.

Dewey, Sir Anthony Hugh, Bt. (1917).

Dewhurst, *Prof.* Sir (Christopher) John, Kt.

†d'Eyncourt, Sir Mark Gervais Tennyson-, Bt. (1930).

Dhenin, *Air Marshal* Sir Geoffrey Howard, K.B.E., A.F.C., G.M., M.D.

Dhrangadhra, H.H. the Maharaja Raj Saheb of, K.C.I.E.

Dibela, *Hon.* Sir Kingsford, G.C.M.G.

Dick, Sir John Alexander, M.C.

Dickinson, Sir Harold Herbert, Kt.

Dickinson, Sir Samuel Benson, Kt.

Dilbertson, Sir Geoffrey, C.B.E.

Dilke, Sir John Fisher Wentworth, Bt. (1862).

Dill, Sir Nicholas Bayard, Kt., C.B.E.

Dillon, *Rt. Hon.* Sir (George) Brian (Hugh), Kt.

Dillon, Sir John Vincent, Kt., C.M.G.

Dillon, Sir Max, Kt.

Diver, *Hon.* Sir Leslie Charles, Kt.

Dixon, Sir John George, Bt. (1919).

Dobson, Sir Denis William, K.C.B., O.B.E., Q.C.

Dobson, *Gen.* Sir Patrick John Howard-, G.C.B.

Dobson, Sir Richard Portway, Kt.

Dodds, Sir Ralph Jordan, Bt. (1964).

Dodson, Sir Derek Sherborne Lindsell, K.C.M.G., M.C.

Dodsworth, Sir John Christopher Smith-, Bt. (1784).

Doll, *Prof.* Sir (William) Richard (Shaboe), Kt., O.B.E., F.R.S., D.M., M.D., D.SC.

Dollery, Sir Colin Terence, Kt.

Donald, Sir Alan Ewen, K.C.M.G.

Donald, *Air Marshal* Sir John George, K.B.E.

Donaldson, Sir Dawson, K.C.M.G.

Donne, *Hon.* Sir Gaven John, K.B.E.

Donne, Sir John Christopher, Kt.

Dookun, Sir Dewoonarain, Kt.

Dorman, *Lt.-Col.* Sir Charles Geoffrey, Bt., M.C. (1923).

Dorman, Sir Maurice Henry, G.C.M.G., G.C.V.O.

Dos Santos, Sir Errol Lionel, Kt., C.B.E.

Dougherty, *Maj.-Gen.* Sir Ivan Noel, Kt., C.B.E., D.S.O., E.D.

Douglas, *Prof.* Sir Donald Macleod, Kt., M.B.E.

Douglas, Sir (Edward) Sholto, Kt.

Douglas, Sir Robert McCallum, Kt., O.B.E.

Douglas, *Rt. Hon.* Sir William Randolph, K.C.M.G.

Dover, *Prof.* Sir Kenneth James, Kt., D.Litt., F.B.A., F.R.S.E.

Down, Sir Alastair Frederick, Kt., O.B.E., M.C., T.D.

Downey, Sir Gordon Stanley, K.C.B.

Downs, Sir Diarmuid, Kt., C.B.E.

Downward, Sir William Atkinson, Kt.

Dowson, Sir Philip Manning, Kt., C.B.E., A.R.A.

Doyle, Sir Reginald Derek Henry, Kt., C.B.E.

†D'Oyly, Sir Nigel Hadley Miller, Bt. (1663).

Drake, Sir (Arthur) Eric (Courtney), Kt., C.B.E.

Drake, *Hon.* Sir (Frederick) Maurice, Kt., D.F.C.

Drew, Sir Arthur Charles Walter, K.C.B.

Drew, *Lt.-Gen.* Sir (William) Robert (Macfarlane), K.C.B., C.B.E., F.R.C.P.

Dreyer, *Adm.* Sir Desmond Parry, G.C.B., C.B.E., D.S.C.

Dring, *Lt.-Col.* Sir Arthur John, K.B.E., C.I.E.

Drinkwater, Sir John Muir, Kt., Q.C.

Driver, Sir Antony Victor, Kt.

Driver, Sir Arthur John, Kt.

Driver, Sir Eric William, Kt.

Drury, Sir (Victor William) Michael, Kt., O.B.E.

Dryden, Sir John Stephen Gyles, Bt. (1733 and 1795).

du Cann, *Rt. Hon.* Sir Edward Dillon Lott, K.B.E.

Duckmanton, Sir Talbot Sydney, Kt., C.B.E.

Duckworth, *Maj.* Sir Richard Dyce, Bt. (1909).

du Cros, Sir Claude Philip Arthur Mallet, Bt. (1916).

Duff, *Rt. Hon.* Sir (Arthur) Antony, G.C.M.G., C.V.O., D.S.O., D.S.C.

Duffus, *Hon.* Sir William Algernon Holwell, Kt.

Dugdale, Sir William Stratford, Bt., M.C. (1936).

Duke, *Maj.-Gen.* Sir Gerald William, K.B.E., C.B., D.S.O.

Dunbar, Sir Archibald Ranulph, Bt. (s. 1700).

Dunbar, Sir David Hope-, Bt. (s. 1664).

Dunbar, Sir Drummond Cospatrick Ninian, Bt., M.C. (s. 1698).

Dunbar, Sir Jean Ivor, Bt. (s. 1694).

Dunbar of Hempriggs, Dame Maureen Daisy Helen, Btss. (s. 1706).

Duncan, Sir James Blair, Kt.

Duncombe, Sir Philip Digby Pauncefort-, Bt. (1859).

Dundas, Sir Hugh Spencer Lisle, Kt., C.B.E., D.S.O., D.F.C.

Dunham, Sir Kingsley Charles, Kt., Ph.D., F.R.S., F.R.S.E.

Dunlop, Sir (Ernest) Edward, Kt., C.M.G., O.B.E.

Dunlop, Sir Thomas, Bt. (1916).

Dunlop, Sir William Norman Gough, Kt.

Dunn, *Air Marshal* Sir Eric Clive, K.B.E., C.B., B.E.M.

Dunn, *Lt.-Col.* Sir (Francis) Vivian, K.C.V.O., O.B.E.

Dunn, *Air Marshal* Sir Patrick Hunter, K.B.E., C.B., D.F.C.

Dunn, *Rt. Hon.* Sir Robin Horace Walford, Kt., M.C.

Dunnett, Sir (Ludovic) James, G.C.B., C.M.G.

Dunning, Sir Simon William Patrick, Bt. (1930).

Dunphie, *Maj.-Gen.* Sir Charles Anderson Lane, Kt., C.B., C.B.E., D.S.O.

Dunstan, *Lt.-Gen.* Sir Donald Beaumont, K.B.E., C.B.

†Duntze, Sir Daniel Evans, Bt. (1774).

Dupree, Sir Peter, Bt. (1921).

Dupuch, Sir (Alfred) Etienne (Jerome), Kt., O.B.E.

Durand, *Rev.* Sir (Henry Mortimer) Dickon, Bt. (1892).

Durham, Sir Kenneth, Kt.

Durie, Sir Alexander Charles, Kt., C.B.E.

Durkin, *Air Marshal* Sir Herbert, K.B.E., C.B.

Durrant, Sir William Henry Estridge, Bt. (1784).

Duthie, *Prof.* Sir Herbert Livingston, Kt.

Duthie, Sir Robert Grieve (Robin), Kt., C.B.E.

Duval, Sir (Charles) Gaetan, Kt.

Duxbury, *Air Marshal* Sir (John) Barry, K.C.B., C.B.E.

Dyer, *Prof.* Sir (Henry) Peter (Francis) Swinnerton-, Bt., K.B.E., F.R.S. (1678).

Dyke, Sir David William Hart, Bt. (1677).

Earle, *Air Chief Marshal* Sir Alfred, G.B.E., C.B.

Earle, Sir (Hardman) George (Algernon), Bt. (1869).

East, Sir (Lewis) Ronald, Kt., C.B.E.

Eastham, *Hon.* Sir (Thomas) Michael, Kt.

Eastick, *Brig.* Sir Thomas Charles, Kt., C.M.G., D.S.O., E.D.

Easton, *Air Cdre.* Sir James Alfred, K.C.M.G., C.B., C.B.E.

Eastwood, Sir John Bealby, Kt.

Eberle, *Adm.* Sir James Henry Fuller, G.C.B.

Ebrahim, Sir (Mahomed) Currimbhoy, Bt. (1910).

Eburne, Sir Sidney Alfred William, Kt., M.C.

Eccles, Sir John Carew, Kt., D.Phil., F.R.S.

Echlin, Sir Norman David Fenton, Bt. (I. 1721).

Eckersley, Sir Donald Payze, Kt., O.B.E.

Edden, *Vice-Adm.* Sir (William) Kaye, K.B.E., C.B.

†Edge, Sir William, Bt. (1937).

Edmenson, Sir Walter Alexander, Kt., C.B.E.

Edmonstone, Sir Archibald Bruce Charles, Bt. (1774).

Edwardes, Sir Michael Owen, Kt.

Edwards, Sir Christopher John Churchill, Bt. (1866).

Edwards, Sir George Robert, Kt., O.M., C.B.E., F.R.S.

Edwards, Sir (John) Clive (Leighton), Bt. (1921).

Edwards, Sir Llewellyn Roy, Kt.

Edwards, *Prof.* Sir Samuel Frederick, Kt., F.R.S.

Egan, Sir John Leopold, Kt.

Egerton, Sir John Alfred Roy, Kt.

Egerton, Sir (Philip) John (Caledon) Grey-, Bt. (1617).

Egerton, Sir Seymour John Louis, G.C.V.O.

Egerton, Sir Stephen Loftus, K.C.M.G.

Eggleston, *Hon.* Sir Richard Moulton, Kt.

Eichelbaum, *Rt. Hon.* Sir Thomas, G.B.E.

Eley, Sir Geoffrey Cecil Ryves, Kt., C.B.E.

†Eliott of Stobs, Sir Charles Joseph Alexander, Bt. (s 1666).

Elliot, Sir Gerald Henry, Kt.

Elliott, Sir Hugh Francis Ivo, Bt., O.B.E. (1917).

Elliott, Sir Norman Randall, Kt., C.B.E.

Elliott, Sir Randal Forbes, K.B.E.

Elliott, *Prof.* Sir Roger James, Kt., F.R.S.

Elliott, Sir Ronald Stuart, Kt.

Ellis, Sir John Rogers, Kt., M.B.E., M.D., F.R.C.P.

Ellis, Sir Ronald, Kt.

Ellison, *Rt. Rev.* and *Rt. Hon.* Gerald Alexander, K.C.V.O.

Ellison, *Col.* Sir Ralph Harry Carr-, Kt., T.D.

Ellwood, *Air Marshal* Sir Aubrey Beauclerk, K.C.B., D.S.C.

Elphinstone, Sir John, Bt. (s 1701).

Elphinstone, Sir (Maurice) Douglas (Warburton), Bt., T.D. (1816).

Elton, Sir Arnold, Kt., C.B.E.

Elton, Sir Charles Abraham Grierson, Bt. (1717).

Elton, *Prof.* Sir Geoffrey Rudolph, Kt., F.B.A.

Elworthy, Sir Peter Herbert, Kt.

Elyan, Sir (Isadore) Victor, Kt.

Emery, Sir Peter Frank Hannibal, Kt., M.P.

Empson, *Adm.* Sir (Leslie) Derek, G.B.E., K.C.B.

Emson, *Air Marshal* Sir Reginald Herbert, K.B.E., C.B., A.F.C.

Engholm, Sir Basil Charles, K.C.B.

Engineer, Sir Noshirwan Phirozshah, Kt.

Engle, Sir George Lawrence Jose, K.C.B., Q.C.

English, Sir Cyril Rupert, Kt.

English, Sir David, Kt.

Entwistle, Sir (John Nuttall) Maxwell, Kt.

Ereaut, Sir (Herbert) Frank Cobbold, Kt.

Errington, *Col.* Sir Geoffrey Frederick, Bt. (1963).

Errington, Sir Lancelot, K.C.B.

Erskine, Sir (Thomas) David, Bt. (1821).

Esmonde, Sir Thomas Francis Grattan, Bt. (I. 1629).

Espie, Sir Frank Fletcher, Kt., O.B.E.

†Esplen, Sir John Graham, Bt. (1921).

Eustace, Sir Joseph Lambert, G.C.M.G., G.C.V.O.

Evans, Sir Anthony Adney, Bt. (1920).

Evans, *Hon.* Sir Anthony Howell Meurig, Kt., R.D.

Evans, Sir Athol Donald, K.B.E.

Evans, *Air Chief Marshal* Sir David George, G.C.B., C.B.E.

Evans, Sir Francis Loring Gwynne-, Bt. (1913).

Evans, Sir Geraint Llewellyn, Kt., C.B.E.

Evans, Sir Richard Mark, K.C.M.G., K.C.V.O.

Evans, Sir (Robert) Charles, Kt.

Evans, Sir (William) Vincent (John), G.C.M.G., M.B.E., Q.C.

Eveleigh, *Rt. Hon.* Sir Edward Walter, Kt., E.R.D.

Everard, *Maj.-Gen.* Sir Christopher Earle Welby-, K.B.E., C.B.

Everard, Sir Robin Charles, Bt. (1911).

Everson, Sir Frederick Charles, K.C.M.G.

†Every, Sir Henry John Michael, Bt. (1641).

Ewans, Sir Martin Kenneth, K.C.M.G.

Ewart, Sir (William) Ivan (Cecil), Bt., D.S.C. (1887).

Ewbank, *Hon.* Sir Anthony Bruce, Kt.

Ewin, Sir (David) Ernest Thomas Floyd, Kt., O.B.E., M.V.O.

Ewing, *Vice-Adm.* Sir (Robert) Alastair, K.B.E., C.B., D.S.C.

Ewing, Sir Ronald Archibald Orr-, Bt. (1886).

Eyre, Sir Graham Newman, Kt., Q.C.

Eyre, *Maj.-Gen.* Sir James Ainsworth Campden Gabriel, K.C.V.O., C.B.E.

Eyre, Sir Reginald Edwin, Kt.

Faber, Sir Richard Stanley, K.C.V.O., C.M.G.

Fadahunsi, Sir Joseph Odeleye, K.C.M.G.

Fagge, Sir John William Frederick, Bt. (1660).

Fairbairn, *Hon.* Sir David Eric, K.B.E., D.F.C.

Fairbairn, Sir (James) Brooke, Bt. (1869).

Fairbairn, Sir Nicholas Hardwick, Kt., Q.C., M.P.

Fairfax, Sir Vincent Charles, Kt., C.M.G.

Fairgrieve, Sir (Thomas) Russell, Kt., C.B.E., T.D.

Fairhall, *Hon.* Sir Allen, K.B.E.

Falconer, *Hon.* Sir Douglas William, Kt., M.B.E.

Falk, Sir Roger Salis, Kt., O.B.E.

Falkiner, Sir Edmond Charles, Bt. (I. 1778).

Falkner, Sir (Donald) Keith, Kt.

Falle, Sir Samuel, K.C.M.G., K.C.V.O., D.S.C.

Falvey, *Hon.* Sir John Neil, K.B.E., Q.C.

Faridkot, *Col.* H.H. the Raja of, K.C.S.I.

Farmer, Sir (Lovedin) George Thomas, Kt.

Farndale, *Gen.* Sir Martin Baker, K.C.B.

Farquhar, Sir Michael Fitzroy Henry, Bt. (1796).

Farquharson, *Rt. Hon.* Sir Donald Henry, Kt.

Farquharson, Sir James Robbie, K.B.E.

Farr, Sir John Arnold, Kt., M.P.

Farrar-Hockley, *Gen.* Sir Anthony Heritage, G.B.E., K.C.B., D.S.O., M.C.

Farrer, Sir Charles Matthew, K.C.V.O.

Farrington, Sir Henry Francis Colden, Bt. (1818).

Faulkner, Sir Eric Odin, Kt., M.B.E.

Faulkner, Sir Percy, K.B.E., C.B.

Fawcus, Sir (Robert) Peter, K.B.E., C.M.G.

Fawkes, Sir Randol Francis, Kt.

Fawcett, Sir James Edmund Sandford, Kt., D.S.C., Q.C.

Fayrer, Sir John Lang Macpherson, Bt., (1896).

Feilden, Sir Bernard Melchior, Kt., C.B.E.

Feilden, Sir Henry Wemyss, Bt., (1846).

Feldman, Sir Basil Samuel, Kt.

Fell, Sir Anthony, Kt.

Fellowes, Sir Robert, K.C.V.O., C.B.

Fenn, Sir Nicholas Maxted, K.C.M.G.

Fennessy, Sir Edward, Kt., C.B.E.

Ferens, Sir Thomas Robinson, Kt., C.B.E.

Ferguson, *Lt.-Col.* Sir Neil Edward Johnson-, Bt., T.D. (1906).

Fergusson of Kilkerran, Sir Charles, Bt. (s. 1703).

Fergusson, Sir Ewan Alastair John, K.C.M.G.

Fergusson, Sir James Herbert Hamilton Colyer-, Bt. (1866).

Feroze, Sir Rustam Moolan, Kt., F.R.C.S.

ffolkes, Sir Robert Francis Alexander, Bt. (1774)

Fieldhouse, Sir Harold, K.B.E., C.B.

Fieldhouse, *Admiral of the Fleet* Sir John David Elliott, G.C.B., G.B.E.

Fielding, Sir Colin Cunningham, Kt., C.B.

Fielding, Sir Leslie, K.C.M.G.

Fiennes, Sir John Saye Wingfield Twisleton-Wykeham-, K.C.B., Q.C.

Fiennes, Sir Maurice Alberic Twisleton-Wykeham-, Kt.

Fiennes, Sir Ranulph Twisleton-Wykeham-, Bt. (1916).

Figg, Sir Leonard Clifford William, K.C.M.G.

Figgess, Sir John George, K.B.E., C.M.G.

Figgures, Sir Frank Edward, K.C.B., C.M.G.

Figures, Sir Colin Frederick, K.C.M.G., O.B.E.

Fingland, Sir Stanley James Gunn, K.C.M.G.

Finlay, Sir David Ronald James Bell, Bt. (1964).

Finley, Sir Peter Hamilton, Kt., O.B.E., D.F.C.

Finniston, Sir (Harold) Montague Kt., Ph.D., F.R.S.

Finsberg, Sir Geoffrey, Kt., M.B.E., M.P.

Firth, *Prof.* Sir Raymond William, Kt., Ph.D., F.B.A.

Fish, Sir Hugh, Kt., C.B.E.

Fisher, Sir George Read, Kt., C.M.G.

Fisher, *Hon.* Sir Henry Arthur Pears, Kt.

Fisher, Sir Nigel Thomas Loveridge, Kt., M.C.

Fison, Sir (Richard) Guy, Bt., D.S.C. (1905).

Fitch, *Adm.* Sir Richard George Alison, K.C.B.

Fitzgerald, *Rev.* (Sir) Edward Thomas, Bt. (1903).

FitzGerald, Sir George Peter Maurice, Bt., M.C., *The Knight of Kerry* (1880).

†FitzHerbert, Sir Richard Ranulph, Bt. (1784).

Fitzmaurice, *Lt.-Col.* Sir Desmond FitzJohn, Kt., C.I.E.

Fitzpatrick, *Gen.* Sir (Geoffrey Richard) Desmond, G.C.B., D.S.O., M.B.E., M.C.

Fitzpatrick, *Air Marshal* Sir John Bernard, K.B.E., C.B.

Flanagan, Sir James Bernard, Kt., C.B.E.

Flavelle, Sir (Joseph) David Ellsworth, Bt. (1917).

Fleming, *Instructor Rear-Adm.* Sir John, K.B.E., D.S.C.

Fleming, *Rt. Rev.* (William) Launcelot Scott, K.C.V.O., D.D.

Fletcher, *Hon.* Sir Alan Roy, Kt.

Fletcher, Sir Alexander MacPherson, Kt.

Fletcher, Sir James Muir Cameron, Kt.

Fletcher, Sir John Henry Lancelot Aubrey-, Bt. (1782).

Fletcher, Sir Leslie, Kt., D.S.C.

Fletcher, Sir Norman Seymour, Kt.

Fletcher, *Air Chief Marshal* Sir Peter Carteret, K.C.B., O.B.E., D.F.C., A.F.C.

Floyd, Sir Giles Henry Charles, Bt. (1816).

Foley, Sir (Thomas John) Noel, Kt., C.B.E.

Foot, Sir Geoffrey James, Kt.

Foots, Sir James William, Kt.

Forbes, *Hon.* Sir Alastair Granville, Kt.

Forbes of Pitsligo, Sir Charles Edward Stuart-, Bt. (s. 1626).

Forbes of Brux, *Hon.* Sir Ewan, Bt. (s. 1630).

Forbes, *Maj.* Sir Hamish Stewart, Bt., M.B.E., M.C. (1823).

Forbes, *Vice-Adm.* Sir John Morrison, K.C.B.

Ford, *Capt.* Sir Aubrey St. Clair-, Bt., D.S.O., R.N. (1793).

Ford, Sir David Robert, K.B.E., L.V.O., O.B.E.

Ford, *Maj.* Sir Edward William Spencer, K.C.B., K.C.V.O.

Ford, *Air Marshal* Sir Geoffrey Harold, K.B.E., C.B.

Ford, Sir Henry Russell, Bt. (1929).

Ford, *Prof.* Sir Hugh, Kt., F.R.S.

Ford, Sir John Archibald, K.C.M.G., M.C.

Ford, Sir Richard Brinsley, Kt., C.B.E.

Ford, *Gen.* Sir Robert Cyril, G.C.B., C.B.E.

Foreman, Sir Philip Frank, Kt., C.B.E.

Forman, Sir John Denis, Kt., O.B.E.

Forrest, *Prof.* Sir (Andrew) Patrick (McEwen), Kt.

Forrest, Sir James Alexander, Kt.

Forrest, *Rear-Adm.* Sir Ronald Stephen, K.C.V.O.

Forster, Sir Archibald William, Kt.

Forster, Sir Oliver Grantham, K.C.M.G., M.V.O.

Forwood, Sir Dudley Richard, Bt. (1895).

Foster, *Prof.* Sir Christopher David, Kt.

Foster, Sir John Gregory, Bt. (1930).

Foster, Sir Robert Sidney, G.C.M.G., K.C.V.O.

Foulis, Sir Ian Primrose Liston-, Bt. (s. 1634).

Foulkes, Sir Nigel Gordon, Kt.

Fowden, Sir Leslie, Kt., F.R.S.

†Fowke, Sir David Frederick Gustavus, Bt. (1814).

Fowler, Sir (Edward) Michael Coulson, Kt.

Fox, Sir (Henry) Murray, G.B.E.

Fox, Sir (John) Marcus, Kt., M.B.E., M.P.

Fox, *Rt. Hon.* Sir Michael John, Kt.

Frame, Sir Alistair Gilchrist, Kt.

France, Sir Arnold William, G.C.B.

France, Sir Christopher Walter, K.C.B.

Francis, Sir Horace William Alexander, Kt., C.B.E.

Francis, Sir Richard Trevor Langford, K.C.M.G.

Frank, Sir Douglas George Horace, Kt., Q.C.

Frank, Sir (Frederick) Charles, Kt., O.B.E., F.R.S.

Frank, Sir Robert Andrew, Bt. (1920).

Frankel, Sir Otto Herzberg, Kt., D.SC., F.R.S.

Franklin, Sir Eric Alexander, Kt., C.B.E.

Franklin, Sir Michael David Milroy, K.C.B., C.M.G.

Franks, Sir Arthur Temple, K.C.M.G.

Fraser, Sir Angus McKay, K.C.B., T.D.

Fraser, Sir Basil Malcolm, Bt. (1921).

Fraser, Sir Bruce Donald, K.C.B.

Fraser, Sir Charles Annand, K.C.V.O.

Fraser, *Gen.* Sir David William, G.C.B., O.B.E.

Fraser, Sir Douglas Were, Kt., I.S.O.

Fraser, *Air Marshal Rev.* Sir (Henry) Paterson, K.B.E., C.B., A.F.C.

Fraser, Sir Ian, Kt., D.S.O., O.B.E.

Fraser, Sir Ian James, Kt., C.B.E., M.C.

Fraser, Sir (James) Campbell, Kt.

Fraser, *Prof.* Sir James David, Bt. (1943).

Fraser, Sir William Kerr, G.C.B.

Frederick, Sir Charles Boscawen, Bt. (1723).

Freeland, Sir John Redvers, K.C.M.G.

Freeman, *His Eminence Cardinal* James Darcy, K.B.E.

Freeman, Sir James Robin, Bt. (1945).

Freeman, Sir Ralph, Kt., C.V.O., C.B.E.

Freer, *Air Chief Marshal* Sir Robert William George, G.B.E., K.C.B.

Freeth, *Hon.* Sir Gordon, K.B.E.

French, *Hon.* Sir Christopher James Saunders, Kt.

Fretwell, Sir George Herbert, K.B.E., C.B.

Fretwell, Sir (Major) John (Emsley), G.C.M.G.

Freud, Sir Clement Raphael, Kt.

Froggatt, Sir Leslie Trevor, Kt.

Froggatt, Sir Peter, Kt.

Frossard, Sir Charles Keith, Kt.

Frost, *Hon.* Sir (Thomas) Sydney, Kt.

Fry, *Hon.* Sir William Gordon, Kt.

Fryberg, Sir Abraham, Kt., M.B.E.

Fuchs, Sir Vivian Ernest, Kt., PH.D.

Fuller, *Hon.* Sir John Bryan Munro, Kt.

Fuller, Sir John William Fleetwood, Bt. (1910).

Fung, *Hon.* Sir Kenneth Ping-Fan, Kt., C.B.E.

Furness, Sir Stephen Roberts, Bt. (1913).

Gadsden, Sir Peter Drury Haggerston, G.B.E.

Gage, Sir Berkeley Everard Foley, K.C.M.G.

Gairy, *Rt. Hon.* Sir Eric Matthew, Kt.

Gaius, *Rt. Rev.* Saimon, K.B.E.

Gallwey, Sir Philip Frankland Payne-, Bt. (1812).

Galsworthy, Sir John Edgar, K.C.V.O., C.M.G.

Gamble, Sir David Hugh Norman, Bt. (1897).

Gandell, Sir Alan Thomas, Kt., C.B.E.

Ganilau, *Ratu* Sir Penaia Kanatabatu, G.C.M.G., K.C.V.O., K.B.E., D.S.O.

Gardner, Sir Douglas Bruce Bruce-, Bt. (1945).

Gardner, Sir Edward Lucas, Kt., Q.C.

Gardner-Thorpe, *Col.* Sir Ronald, G.B.E., T.D.

Garland, *Hon.* Sir Patrick Neville, Kt.

Garland, *Hon.* Sir Ransley Victor, K.B.E.

Garlick, Sir John, K.C.B.

Garner, Sir Anthony Stuart, Kt.

Garran, Sir (Isham) Peter, K.C.M.G.

Garrett, *Hon.* Sir Raymond William, Kt., A.F.C.

Garrioch, Sir (William) Henry, Kt.

Garrod, *Lt. Gen.* Sir John Martin Carruthers, K.C.B., O.B.E.

Garthwaite, Sir William Francis Cuthbert, Bt., D.S.C. (1919).

Garvey, Sir Ronald Herbert, K.C.M.G., K.C.V.O., M.B.E.

Gascoigne, *Maj.-Gen.* Sir Julian Alvery, K.C.M.G., K.C.V.O., C.B., D.S.O.

Gaskell, Sir Richard Kennedy Harvey, Kt.

Gatehouse, *Hon.* Sir Robert Alexander, Kt.

Geddes, Sir (Anthony) Reay (Mackay), K.B.E.

Gentry, *Maj.-Gen.* Sir William George, K.B.E., C.B., D.S.O.

George, Sir Arthur Thomas, Kt.

Gerken, *Vice-Adm.* Sir Robert William Frank, K.C.B., C.B.E.

Gethin, Sir Richard Joseph St. Lawrence, Bt. (1 1665).

Ghurburrun, Sir Rabindrah, Kt.

Gibb, Sir Francis Ross (Frank), Kt., C.B.E.

Gibbings, Sir Peter Walter, Kt.

Gibbon, *Gen.* Sir John Houghton, G.C.B., O.B.E.

Gibbons, Sir (John) David, K.B.E.

Gibbons, Sir William Edward Doran, Bt. (1752).

Gibbs, *Hon.* Sir Eustace Hubert Beilby, K.C.V.O., C.M.G.

Gibbs, *Air Marshal* Sir Gerald Ernest, K.B.E., C.I.E., M.C.

Gibbs, *Rt. Hon.* Sir Harry Talbot, G.C.M.G., K.B.E.

Gibbs, *Rt. Hon.* Sir Humphrey Vicary, G.C.V.O., K.C.M.G., O.B.E.

Gibbs, *Field Marshal* Sir Roland Christopher, G.C.B., C.B.E., D.S.O., M.C.

Gibson, Sir Alexander Drummond, Kt., C.B.E.

Gibson, Sir Christopher Herbert, Bt. (1931).

Gibson, *Rev.* Sir David, Bt. (1926).

Gibson, *Vice-Adm.* Sir Donald Cameron Ernest Forbes, K.C.B., D.S.C.

Gibson, Sir Donald Evelyn Edward, Kt., C.B.E.

Gibson, *Hon.* Sir Peter Leslie, Kt.

Gibson, *Rt. Hon.* Sir Ralph Brian, Kt.

Giddings, *Air Marshal* Sir (Kenneth Charles) Michael, K.C.B., O.B.E., D.F.C., A.F.C.

Gielgud, Sir (Arthur) John, Kt., C.H.

Giffard, Sir (Charles) Sydney (Rycroft), K.C.M.G.

Gilbert, *Brig.* Sir Herbert Ellery, K.B.E., D.S.O.

Gilbert, *Air Chief Marshal* Sir Joseph Alfred, K.C.B., C.B.E.

Gilbertson, Sir Geoffrey, Kt., C.B.E.

Gilbey, Sir (Walter) Derek, Bt. (1893).

Gilchrist, Sir Andrew Graham, K.C.M.G.

Gilkison, Sir Alan Fleming, Kt., C.B.E.

Gillett, Sir Robin Danvers Penrose, Bt., G.B.E., R.D. (1959).

Gilliat, *Lt.-Col.* Sir Martin John, G.C.V.O., M.B.E.

Gilmour, *Rt. Hon.* Sir Ian Hedworth John Little, Bt., M.P. (1926).

Gilmour, Sir John Edward, Bt., D.S.O., T.D. (1897).

Gingell, *Air Chief Marshal* Sir John, G.B.E., K.C.B.

Girolami, Sir Paul, Kt.

Gladstone, Sir (Erskine) William, Bt. (1846).

Glasspole, Sir Florizel Augustus, G.C.M.G, G.C.V.O.

Glen, Sir Alexander Richard, K.B.E., D.S.C.

Glenn, Sir (Joseph Robert) Archibald, Kt., O.B.E.

Glidewell, *Rt. Hon.* Sir Iain Derek Laing, Kt.

Glock, Sir William Frederick, Kt., C.B.E.

Glover, *Gen.* Sir James Malcolm, K.C.B., M.B.E.

Glover, Sir Victor Joseph Patrick, Kt.

Glyn, Sir Anthony Geoffrey Leo Simon, Bt. (1927).

Glyn, Sir Richard Lindsay, Bt., (1759 and 1800).

Goad, Sir (Edward) Colin (Viner), K.C.M.G.

Godber, Sir George Edward, G.C.B., D.M.

Goff, Sir Robert (William) Davis-, Bt. (1905).

Gohel, Sir Jayvantsinhji Kayaji, Kt., C.B.E.

Gold, Sir Arthur Abraham, Kt., C.B.E.

Gold, Sir Joseph, Kt.

Goldberg, *Prof.* Sir Abraham, Kt., M.D., D.SC., F.R.C.P.

Golding, Sir John Simon Rawson, Kt., O.B.E.

Golding, Sir William Gerald, Kt., C.B.E.

Goldman, Sir Samuel, K.C.B.

Goldsmith, Sir James Michael, Kt.

Gombrich, *Prof.* Sir Ernst Hans Josef, Kt., C.B.E., Ph.D., F.B.A., F.S.A.

Gooch, Sir (Richard) John Sherlock, Bt. (1746).

Gooch, Sir Robert Douglas, Bt. (1866).

Goodall, Sir (Arthur) David Saunders, K.C.M.G.

Goodall, Sir Reginald, Kt., C.B.E.

Goodenough, Sir Richard Edmund, Bt. (1943).

Goodhart, Sir Philip Carter, Kt., M.P.

Goodhart, Sir Robert Anthony Gordon, Bt. (1911).

Goodhart, Sir William Howard, Kt., Q.C.

Goodhew, Sir Victor Henry, Kt.

Goodison, Sir Alan Clowes, K.C.M.G.

Goodison, Sir Nicholas Proctor, Kt.

Goodson, Sir Mark Weston Lassam, Bt. (1922).

Goodwin, Sir Matthew Dean, Kt., C.B.E.

Goody, *Most Rev.* Launcelot John, K.B.E.

Goold, Sir George Leonard, Bt. (1801).

Goold, Sir James Duncan, Kt.

Gordon, Sir Alexander John, Kt., C.B.E.

Gordon, Sir Andrew Cosmo Lewis Duff-, Bt. (1813).

Gordon, Sir Charles Addison Somerville Snowden, K.C.B.

Gordon, Sir Keith Lyndell, Kt., C.M.G.

Gordon, Sir (Lionel) Eldred (Peter) Smith-, Bt. (1838).

Gordon, Sir Robert James, Bt. (s. 1706).

Gordon, Sir Sidney Samuel, Kt., C.B.E.

Gordon Lennox, Lord Nicholas Charles, K.C.M.G., K.C.V.O.

Gore, Sir Richard Ralph St. George, Bt. (I. 1622).

Goring, Sir William Burton Nigel, Bt. (1627).

Gorton, *Rt. Hon.* Sir John Grey, G.C.M.G., C.H.

Goschen, Sir Edward Christian, Bt., D.S.O. (1916).

Gosling, Sir (Frederick) Donald, Kt.

Goulding, Sir (Ernest) Irvine, Kt.

Goulding, Sir (William) Lingard Walter, Bt. (1904).

Gourlay, *Gen.* Sir (Basil) Ian (Spencer), K.C.B., O.B.E., M.C., R.M.

Gourlay, Sir Simon Alexander, Kt.

Govan, Sir Lawrence Herbert, Kt.

Gow, *Gen.* Sir (James) Michael, G.C.B.

Gowans, Sir James Learmonth, Kt., C.B.E., F.R.C.P., F.R.S.

Gowans, *Hon.* Sir (Urban) Gregory, Kt.

Gowing, *Prof.* Sir Lawrence Burnett, Kt., C.B.E.

Graaff, Sir de Villiers, Bt., M.B.E. (1911).

Grabham, Sir Anthony Henry, Kt.

Graesser, *Col.* Sir Alastair Stewart Durward, Kt., D.S.O., O.B.E., M.C., T.D.

Graham, Sir Charles Spencer Richard, Bt. (1783).

Graham, Sir James Bellingham, Bt. (1662).

Graham, Sir John Alexander Noble, Bt., K.G.M.G. (1906).

Graham, Sir John Moodie, Bt. (1964).

Graham, Sir (John) Patrick, Kt.

Graham, Sir Norman William, Kt., C.B.

Graham, Sir Peter Alfred, Kt., O.B.E.

Graham, Sir Ralph Wolfe, Bt. (1629).

Graham, *Hon.* Sir Samuel Horatio, Kt., C.M.G., O.B.E.

Grandy, *Marshal of the Royal Air Force* Sir John, G.C.B., G.C.V.O., K.B.E., D.S.O.

Grant, Sir Archibald, Bt. (s. 1705).

Grant, Sir Clifford, Kt.

Grant, Sir (John) Anthony, Kt., M.P.

Grant, Sir Kenneth Lindsay, Kt., O.B.E.

Grant, Sir Patrick Alexander Benedict, Bt. (s. 1688).

Grantham, *Adm.* Sir Guy, G.C.B., C.B.E., D.S.O.

Granville, Sir Keith, Kt., C.B.E.

Gray, Sir (Francis) Anthony, K.C.V.O.

Gray, Sir John Archibald Browne, Kt., SC.D., F.R.S.

Gray, *Vice-Adm.* Sir John Michael Dudgeon, K.B.E., C.B.

Gray, *Lt.-Gen.* Sir Michael Stuart, K.C.B., O.B.E.

Gray, Sir William Hume, Bt. (1917).

Gray, Sir William Stevenson, Kt.

Graydon, *Air Marshal* Sir Michael James, K.C.B., C.B.E.

Grayson, Sir Rupert Stanley Harrington, Bt. (1922).

Green, Sir (Edward) Stephen (Lycett), Bt., C.B.E. (1886).

Green, Sir George Ernest, Kt.

Green, *Hon.* Sir Guy Stephen Montague, K.B.E.

Green, Sir Kenneth, Kt.

Green, Sir Owen Whitley, Kt.

Green, Sir Peter James Frederick, Kt.

Greenaway, Sir Derek Burdick, Bt., C.B.E. (1933).

Greenborough, Sir John, K.B.E.

Greene, Sir (John) Brian Massy-, Kt.

Greengross, Sir Alan David, Kt.

Greening, *Rear-Adm.* Sir Paul Woollven, K.C.V.O.

Greenwell, Sir Edward Bernard, Bt. (1906).

Greeves, *Maj.-Gen.* Sir Stuart, K.B.E., C.B., D.S.O., M.C.

Gregson, Sir Peter Lewis, K.C.B.

Grenside, Sir John Peter, Kt., C.B.E.

Gretton, *Vice-Adm.* Sir Peter William, K.C.B., D.S.O., O.B.E., D.S.C.

Grey, Sir Anthony Dysart, Bt. (1814).

Grey, Sir Paul Francis, K.C.M.G.

†Grierson, Sir Michael John Bewes, Bt. (s. 1685).

Grieve, *Prof.* Sir Robert, Kt.

Griffin, *Adm.* Sir Anthony Templer Frederick Griffith, G.C.B.

Griffin, Sir (Charles) David, Kt., C.B.E.

Griffin, Sir John Bowes, Kt., Q.C.

Griffiths, Sir Eldon Wylie, Kt., M.P.

Griffiths, Sir (Ernest) Roy, Kt.

Griffiths, Sir John Norton-, Bt. (1922).

Griffiths, Sir Percival Joseph, K.B.E., C.I.E.

Griffiths, Sir Reginald Ernest, Kt., C.B.E.

Grimwade, Sir Andrew Sheppard, Kt., C.B.E.

Grindrod, *Most Rev.* John Basil Rowland, K.B.E.

Grinstead, Sir Stanley Gordon, Kt.

Groom, *Air Marshal* Sir Victor Emmanuel, K.C.V.O., K.B.E., C.B., D.F.C.

Grose, *Vice-Adm.* Sir Alan, K.B.E.

Grotrian, Sir Philip Christian Brent, Bt. (1934).

Grove, Sir Charles Gerald, Bt. (1874).

Grove, Sir Edmund Frank, K.C.V.O.

Groves, Sir Charles Barnard, Kt., C.B.E.

Grugeon, Sir John Drury, Kt.

Guinness, Sir Alec, Kt., C.B.E.

Guinness, Sir Howard Christian Sheldon, Kt., V.R.D.

Guinness, Sir Kenelm Ernest Lee, Bt. (1867).

Guise, Sir John, G.C.M.G., K.B.E.

Guise, Sir John Grant, Bt. (1783).

Gujadhur, Sir Radhamohun, Kt., C.M.G.

†Gull, Sir Rupert William Cameron, Bt. (1872).

Gunn, *Prof.* Sir John Currie, Kt., C.B.E.

Gunn, Sir William Archer, K.B.E., C.M.G.

Hay, Sir Hamish Grenfell, Kt.

Hay, Sir James Brian Dalrymple-, Bt. (1798).

†Hay, Sir Ronald Nelson, Bt. (s. 1703).

Hayday, Sir Frederick, Kt., C.B.E.

Haydon, Sir Walter Robert, K.C.M.G.

Hayes, Sir Brian David, G.C.B.

Hayes, Sir Claude James, K.C.M.G.

Hayes, *Vice-Adm.* Sir John Osier Chattock, K.C.B., O.B.E.

Hayhoe, *Rt. Hon.* Sir Bernard John (Barney), Kt., M.P.

Hayman, Sir Peter Telford, K.C.M.G., C.V.O., M.B.E.

Hayr, *Air Marshal* Sir Kenneth William, K.C.B., C.B.E., A.F.C.

Hayter, Sir William Goodenough, K.C.M.G.

Hayward, Sir Anthony William Byrd, Kt.

Hayward, Sir Jack Arnold, Kt., O.B.E.

Hayward, Sir Richard Arthur, Kt., C.B.E.

Haywood, Sir Harold, K.C.V.O., O.B.E.

Head, Sir Francis David Somerville, Bt. (1838).

Healey, Sir Charles Edward Chadwyck-, Bt. (1919).

Heap, Sir Desmond, Kt.

Heath, Sir Mark Evelyn, K.C.V.O., C.M.G.

Heath, *Air Marshal* Sir Maurice Lionel, K.B.E., C.B., C.V.O.

Heathcoat Amory, Sir Ian, Bt. (1874).

Heathcote, *Brig.* Sir Gilbert Simon, Bt., C.B.E. (1733).

Heathcote, Sir Michael Perryman, Bt. (1733).

Heaton, Sir Yvo Robert Henniker-, Bt. (1912).

Heiser, Sir Terence Michael, K.C.B.

Hele, Sir Ivor Thomas Henry, Kt., C.B.E.

Hellaby, Sir (Frederick Reed) Alan, Kt.

Hellings, *Gen.* Sir Peter William Cradock, K.C.B., D.S.C., M.C., R.M.

Henderson, Sir Denys Hartley, Kt.

Henderson, Sir James Thyne, K.B.E., C.M.G.

Henderson, Sir (John) Nicholas, G.C.M.G.

Henderson, *Adm.* Sir Nigel Stuart, G.B.E., K.C.B.

Henderson, Sir William MacGregor, Kt., D.SC., F.R.S.

Henley, Sir Douglas Owen, K.C.B.

Henley, *Rear-Adm.* Sir Joseph Charles Cameron, K.C.V.O., C.B.

Hennessy, Sir James Patrick Ivan, K.B.E., C.M.G.

Hennessy, Sir John Wyndham Pope-, Kt., C.B.E., F.B.A., F.S.A.

Henniker, *Brig.* Sir Mark Chandos Auberon, Bt., C.B.E., D.S.O., M.C. (1813).

Henry, Sir Denis Aynsley, Kt., O.B.E., Q.C.

Henry, *Hon.* Denis Robert Maurice, Kt.

Henry, Sir James Holmes, Bt., C.M.G., M.C., T.D., Q.C. (1923).

Henry, *Hon.* Sir Trevor Ernest, Kt.

Hepburn, Sir Ninian Buchan Archibald John Buchan-, Bt. (1815).

Herbecq, Sir John Edward, K.C.B.

Herbert, *Adm.* Sir Peter Geoffrey Marshall, K.C.B., O.B.E.

Hermon, Sir John Charles, Kt., O.B.E., Q.P.M.

Heron, Sir Conrad Frederick, K.C.B., O.B.E.

Herries, Sir Michael Alexander Robert Young-, Kt., O.B.E., M.C.

Heseltine, *Rt. Hon.* Sir William Frederick Payne, G.C.V.O., K.C.B.

Hetherington, Sir Arthur Ford, Kt., D.S.C.

Hetherington, Sir Thomas Chalmers, K.C.B., C.B.E., T.D., Q.C.

Heward, *Air Chief Marshal* Sir Anthony Wilkinson, K.C.B., C.B.E., D.F.C., A.F.C.

Hewetson, Sir Christopher Raynor, Kt., T.D.

Hewetson, *Gen.* Sir Reginald Hackett, G.C.B., C.B.E., D.S.O.

Hewett, Sir John George, Bt., M.C. (1813).

Hewitt, Sir (Cyrus) Lenox (Simson), Kt., O.B.E.

Hewitt, Sir Nicholas Charles Joseph, Bt. (1921).

Heygate, Sir George Lloyd, Bt. (1831).

Heyman, Sir Horace William, Kt.

Heywood, Sir Oliver Kerr, Bt. (1838).

Hezlet, *Vice-Adm.* Sir Arthur Richard, K.B.E., C.B., D.S.O., D.S.C.

Hibbert, Sir Reginald Alfred, G.C.M.G.

Hickey, Sir Justin, Kt.

Hickman, Sir (Richard) Glenn, Bt. (1903).

Hielscher, Sir Leo Arthur, Kt.

Higgins, Sir Christopher Thomas, Kt.

Higgins, *Hon.* John Patrick Basil, Kt.

Higgs, Sir (John) Michael (Clifford), Kt.

Hildreth, *Maj.-Gen.* Sir (Harold) John (Crossley), K.B.E.

Hildyard, Sir David Henry Thoroton, K.C.M.G., D.F.C.

Hiley, *Hon.* Sir Thomas Alfred, K.B.E.

Hilgendorf, Sir Charles, Kt., C.M.G.

†Hill, Sir Alexander Rodger Erskine-, Bt. (1945).

Hill, Sir Arthur Alfred, Kt., C.B.E.

Hill, *Prof.* Sir Austin Bradford, Kt., C.B.E., Ph.D., D.SC., F.R.S.

Hill, Sir Brian John, Kt.

Hill, Sir James Frederick, Bt. (1917).

Hill, Sir John McGregor, Kt., Ph.D.

Hill, Sir John Maxwell, Kt., C.B.E., D.F.C.

Hill, Sir Richard George Rowley, Bt., M.B.E. (I. 1779).

Hillary, Sir Edmund, K.B.E.

Hills, Sir Graham John, Kt.

Himsworth, Sir Harold Percival, K.C.B., M.D., F.R.S.

Hine, *Air Chief Marshal* Sir Patrick Bardon, G.C.B.

Hines, Sir Colin Joseph, Kt., O.B.E.

Hinsley, *Prof.* Sir Francis Harry, Kt., O.B.E., F.B.A.

Hirsch, *Prof.* Sir Peter Bernhard, Kt., Ph.D., F.R.S.

Hirst, *Hon.* Sir David Cozens-Hardy, Kt.

Hoare, Sir Peter Richard David, Bt. (1786).

Hoare, Sir Timothy Edward Charles, Bt. (I. 1784).

Hobart, Sir John Vere, Bt. (1914).

Hobday, Sir Gordon Ivan, Kt.

Hobhouse, Sir Charles Chisholm, Bt., T.D. (1812).

Hobhouse, *Hon.* Sir John Stewart, Kt.

Hobson, Sir Harold, Kt., C.B.E.

Hockaday, Sir Arthur Patrick, K.C.B., C.M.G.

Hodge, Sir John Rowland, Bt., M.B.E. (1921).

Hodge, Sir Julian Stephen Alfred, Kt.

Hodges, *Air Chief Marshal* Sir Lewis MacDonald, K.C.B., C.B.E., D.S.O., D.F.C.

Hodgkin, *Prof.* Sir Alan Lloyd, O.M., K.B.E., F.R.S., SC.D.

Hodgkinson, *Air Chief Marshal* Sir (William) Derek, K.C.B., C.B.E., D.F.C., A.F.C.

Hodgson, Sir Maurice Arthur Eric, Kt.

Hodgson, *Hon.* Sir (Walter) Derek (Thornley), Kt.

Hodson, Sir Michael Robin Adderley, Bt. (I. 1789).

Hoffenberg, *Prof.* Sir Raymond, K.B.E.

Hoffman, *Hon.* Sir Leonard Hubert, Kt.

Hogg, *Maj.* Sir Arthur Ramsay, Bt., M.B.E. (1846).

Hogg, Sir Christopher Anthony, Kt.

†Hogg, Sir Edward William Lindsay-, Bt. (1905).

Hogg, *Vice-Adm.* Sir Ian Leslie Trower, K.C.B., D.S.C.

Hogg, Sir John Nicholson, Kt., T.D.

Holcroft, Sir Peter George Culcheth, Bt. (1921).

Holden, Sir David Charles Beresford, K.B.E., C.B., E.R.D.

Holden, Sir Edward, Bt. (1893).

Holden, Sir John David, Bt. (1919).

Holder, Sir John Henry, Bt. (1898).

Holder, *Air Marshal* Sir Paul Davie, K.B.E., C.B., D.S.O., D.F.C., Ph.D.

Holderness, Sir Richard William, Bt. (1920).

Holdsworth, Sir (George) Trevor, Kt.

Holland, Sir Clifton Vaughan, Kt.

Holland, Sir Geoffrey, K.C.B.

Holland, Sir Guy (Hope), Bt. (1917).

Holland, Sir Kenneth Lawrence, Kt., C.B.E., Q.F.S.M.

Holland, Sir Philip Welsby, Kt.

Hollings, *Hon.* Sir (Alfred) Kenneth, Kt., M.C.

Hollis, *Hon.* Sir Anthony Barnard, Kt.

Hollom, Sir Jasper Quintus, K.B.E.

Holloway, *Hon.* Sir Barry Blyth, K.B.E.

Holm, Sir Carl Henry, Kt., O.B.E.

Holmes, *Prof.* Sir Frank Wakefield, Kt.

Holmes, Sir Maurice Andrew, Kt.

Holmes, Sir Peter Fenwick, Kt., M.C.

Holroyd, *Air Marshal* Sir Frank Martyn, K.B.E., C.B.

Holt, Sir James Richard, K.B.E.

Holt, Sir John Anthony Langford-, Kt.

Home, Sir David George, Bt. (s. 1671).

Hone, *Maj.-Gen.* Sir (Herbert) Ralph, K.C.M.G., K.B.E., M.C., T.D., Q.C.

Honywood, Sir Filmer Courtenay William, Bt. (1660).

Hood, Sir Alexander William Fuller-Acland-, Bt. (1806).

Hood, Sir Harold Joseph, Bts., T.D. (1922).

Hookway, Sir Harry Thurston, Kt.

Hoole, Sir Arthur Hugh, Kt.

Hooper, Sir Leonard James, K.C.M.G., C.B.E.

Hope, Sir (Charles) Peter, K.C.M.G., T.D.

Hope, Sir John Carl Alexander, Bt. (s 1628).

Hope, Sir Robert Holms-Kerr, Bt. (1932)

Hopkin, Sir David Armand, Kt.

Hopkin, Sir (William Aylsham) Bryan, Kt., C.B.E.

Hopkins, *Adm.* Sir Frank Henry Edward, K.C.B., D.S.O., D.S.C.

Hopkins, Sir James Sidney Rawdon Scott-, Kt.

Hopkinson, Sir (Henry) Thomas, Kt., C.B.E.

Hordern, Sir Michael Murray, Kt., C.B.E.

Hordern, Sir Peter Maudslay, Kt., M.P.

Horlick, *Vice-Adm.* Sir Edwin John, K.B.E.

Horlick, Sir John James Macdonald, Bt. (1914).

Hornby, Sir Simon Michael, Kt.

Horne, Sir Alan Gray Antony, Bt. (1929).

Horsfall, Sir John Musgrave, Bt., M.C., T.D. (1909).

Horsley, *Air Marshal* Sir (Beresford) Peter (Torrington), K.C.B., C.B.E., M.V.O., A.F.C.

Hort, Sir James Fenton, Bt. (1767).

Hoskyns, Sir Benedict Leigh, Bt. (1676).

Hoskyns, Sir John Austin Hungerford Leigh, Kt.

Houldsworth, Sir (Harold) Basil, Bt. (1956).

†Houldsworth, Sir Richard Thomas Reginald, Bt. (1887).

Hounsfield, Sir Godfrey Newbold, Kt., C.B.E.

House, *Lt.-Gen.* Sir David George, G.C.B., K.C.V.O., C.B.E., M.C.

Houssemayne du Boulay, Sir Roger William, K.C.V.O., C.M.G.

How, Sir Friston Charles, Kt., C.B.

Howard, Sir (Hamilton) Edward de Coucey, Bt., G.B.E. (1955).

Howard, *Prof.* Sir Michael Eliot, Kt., C.B.E., M.C.

Howard, *Maj.-Gen.* Lord Michael Fitzalan-, G.C.V.O., C.B., C.B.E., M.C.

Howard, Sir Walter Stewart, Kt., M.B.E.

Howe, *Rt. Hon.* Sir (Richard Edward) Geoffrey, Kt., Q.C., M.P.

Howie, Sir James William, Kt., M.D.

Howlett, *Gen.* Sir Geoffrey Hugh Whitby, K.B.E., M.C.

Hoyle, *Prof.* Sir Fred, Kt., F.R.S.

Hoyos, *Hon.* Sir Fabriciano Alexander, Kt.

Huckle, Sir (Henry) George, Kt., O.B.E.

Huddie, Sir David Patrick, Kt.

Hudleston, *Air Chief Marshal* Sir Edmund Cuthbert, G.C.B., C.B.E.

Hudson, Sir Havelock Henry Trevor, Kt.

Hudson, *Lt.-Gen.* Sir Peter, K.C.B., C.B.E.

Huggins, *Hon.* Sir Alan Armstrong, Kt.

Hugh-Jones, Sir Wynn Normington, Kt., M.V.O.

Hughes, Sir David Collingwood, Bt. (1773).

Hughes, *Prof.* Sir Edward Stuart Reginald, Kt., C.B.E.

Hughes, Sir Jack William, Kt.

Hughes, *Air Marshal* Sir (Sidney Weetman) Rochford, K.C.B., C.B.E., A.F.C.

Hughes, Sir Trevor Denby Lloyd-, Kt.

Hughes, Sir Trevor Poulton, K.C.B.

Hugo, *Lt.-Col.* Sir John Mandeville, K.C.V.O., O.B.E.

Hull, *Field Marshal* Sir Richard Amyatt, K.G., G.C.B., D.S.O.

Hulme, *Hon.* Sir Alan Shallcross, K.B.E.

Hulse, Sir (Hamilton) Westrow, Bt. (1739).

Hulton, Sir Geoffrey Alan, Bt. (1905).

Hume, Sir Alan Blyth, Kt., C.B.

Humphreys, Sir Olliver William, Kt., C.B.E.

Humphreys, Sir (Raymond Evelyn) Myles, Kt.

Hunn, Sir Jack Kent, Kt., C.M.G.

Hunt, Sir David Wathen Stather, K.C.M.G., O.B.E.

Hunt, Sir John Leonard, Kt., M.P.

Hunt, *Adm.* Sir Nicholas John Streynsham, G.C.B., L.V.O.

Hunt, Sir Rex Masterman, Kt., C.M.G.

Hunt, Sir Robert Frederick, Kt., C.B.E.

Hunter, *Hon.* Sir Alexander Albert, K.B.E.

Hunter, Sir Ian Bruce Hope, Kt., M.B.E.

Hurley, Sir John Garling, Kt., C.B.E.

Hurrell, Sir Anthony Gerald, K.C.V.O., C.M.G.

Hutchinson, *Hon.* Sir Ross, Kt., D.F.C.

Hutchison, *Lt.-Cdr.* Sir (George) Ian Clark, Kt., R.N.

Hutchison, *Hon.* Sir Michael, Kt.

Hutchison, Sir Peter, Bt. (1939).

Hutchison, Sir Peter Craft, Bt. (1956).

Hutchison, Sir (William) Kenneth, Kt., C.B.E., F.R.S.

Hutson, Sir Francis Challenor, Kt., C.B.E.

Hutton, *Rt. Hon.* Sir (James) Brian Edward, Kt.

Hutton, Sir Leonard, Kt.

Huxley, *Prof.* Sir Andrew Fielding, Kt., O.M., F.R.S.

Huxtable, *Gen.* Sir Charles Richard, K.C.B., C.B.E.

Hyatali, *Hon.* Sir Isaac Emanuel, Kt.

Ibbs, Sir (John) Robin, Kt., K.B.E.

Ihaka, *Ven.* Sir Kingi Matutaera, Kt., M.B.E.

Illingworth, *Prof.* Sir Charles Frederick William, Kt., C.B.E.

Imbert, Sir Peter Michael, Kt., Q.P.M.

Inch, Sir John Ritchie, Kt., C.V.O., C.B.E.

Inge, *Lt. Gen.* Sir Peter Anthony, K.C.B.

Ingilby, Sir Thomas Colvin William, Bt. (1866).

Inglefield, Sir Gilbert Samuel, G.B.E., T.D.

Inglis, Sir Brian Scott, Kt.

Inglis of Glencorse, Sir Roderick John, Bt. (s. 1703).

Ingram, Sir James Herbert Charles, Bt. (1893).

Innes, Sir Charles Kenneth Gordon, Bt. (N.S. 1686).

Innes, Sir Peter Alexander Berowald, Bt. (s. 1628).

Inniss, *Hon.* Sir Clifford de Lisle, Kt.

Irish, Sir Ronald Arthur, Kt., O.B.E.

Irvine, *Rt. Hon.* Sir Bryant Godman, Kt.

Irvine, *Dr.* Sir Robin Orlando Hamilton, Kt.

Irving, *Rear-Adm.* Sir Edmund George, K.B.E., C.B.

Irwin, Sir James Campbell, Kt., O.B.E., E.D.

Isham, Sir Ian Vere Gyles, Bt. (1627).

Jack, *Hon.* Sir Alieu Sulayman, Kt.

Jackman, *Air Marshal* Sir (Harold) Douglas, K.B.E., C.B.

Jackson, *Air Marshal* Sir Brendan James, K.C.B.

Jackson, Sir (John) Edward, K.C.M.G.

Jackson, *Hon.* Sir Lawrence Walter, K.C.M.G.

Jackson, Sir Michael Roland, Bt. (1902).

Jackson, Sir Nicholas Fane St. George, Bt. (1913).

Jackson, *Air Vice-Marshal* Sir Ralph Coburn, K.B.E., C.B.

Jackson, Sir Robert, Bt. (1815).

Jackson, *Cdr.* Sir Robert Gillman Allen, K.C.V.O., C.M.G., O.B.E.

Jackson, *Gen.* Sir William Godfrey Fothergill, G.B.E., K.C.B., M.C.

Jackson, Sir William Thomas, Bt. (1869)

Jacob, *Lt.-Gen.* Sir (Edward) Ian (Claud), G.B.E., C.B.

Jacob, Sir Isaac Hai, Kt., Q.C.

Jacobi, *Dr.* Sir James Edward, Kt., O.B.E.

Jacobs, Sir David Anthony, Kt.

Jacobs, *Hon.* Sir Kenneth Sydney, K.B.E.

Jacobs, Sir Piers, K.B.E.

Jacobs, Sir Wilfred Ebenezer, G.C.M.G., G.C.V.O., O.B.E., Q.C.

Jacomb, Sir Martin Wakefield, Kt.

Jaffray, Sir William Otho, Bt. (1892).

Jagatsingh, *Hon.* Sir Kher, Kt.

Jakeway, Sir (Francis) Derek, K.C.M.G., O.B.E.

James, Sir Cynlais Morgan, K.C.M.G.

James, Sir Gerard Bowes Kingston, Bt. (1823).

Jamieson, *Air Marshal* Sir David Ewan, K.B.E., C.B.

Janion, *Rear-Adm.* Sir Hugh Penderel, K.C.V.O.

Jansen, Sir Ross Malcolm, K.B.E.

Janvrin, *Vice-Adm.* Sir (Hugh) Richard Benest, K.C.B., D.S.C.

Jardine, Sir Andrew Colin Douglas, Bt. (1916).

Jardine, *Maj.* Sir (Andrew) Rupert (John) Buchanan-, Bt., M.C. (1885).

Jardine of Applegirth, Sir Alexander Maule, Bt. (s. 1672).

Jarratt, Sir Alexander Anthony, Kt., C.B.

Jarrett, Sir Clifford George, K.B.E., C.B.

Jawara, *Hon.* Sir Dawda Kairaba, Kt.

Jay, Sir Antony Rupert, Kt.

Jeewoolall, Sir Ramesh, Kt.

Jeffcoate, Sir (Thomas) Norman (Arthur), Kt., M.D., F.R.C.S.

Jefferson, Sir George Rowland, Kt., C.B.E.

Jefferson, Sir Mervyn Stewart Dunnington-, Bt. (1958).

Jehangir, Sir Hirji, Bt. (1908).

Jejeebhoy, Sir Rustom, Bt. (1857).

Jellicoe, Sir Geoffrey Alan, Kt., C.B.E., F.R.I.B.A.

Jenkins, Sir Owain Trevor, Kt.

†Jenkinson, Sir John Banks, Bt. (1661).

Jenks, Sir Richard Atherley, Bt. (1932).

Jennings, Sir Albert Victor, Kt.

Jennings, Sir Raymond Winter, Kt., Q.C.

Jennings, *Prof.* Sir Robert Yewdall, Kt., Q.C.

Jenour, Sir (Arthur) Maynard (Chesterfield), Kt., T.D.

Jephcott, *Hon.* Sir Bruce Reginald, Kt., C.B.E.

Jephcott, Sir (John) Anthony, Bt. (1962).

Jessel, Sir Charles John, Bt. (1883).

Joel, *Hon.* Sir Asher Alexander, K.B.E.

John, Sir Rupert Godfrey, Kt.

Johnson, Sir John Rodney, K.C.M.G.

Johnson, Sir Peter Colpoys Paley, Bt. (1755).

Johnson, *Hon.* Sir Robert Lionel, Kt.

†Johnson, Sir Robin Eliot, Bt. (1818).

Johnson, Sir Ronald Ernest Charles, Kt., C.B.

Johnson Smith, Sir Geoffrey, Kt., M.P.

Johnston, Sir Alexander, G.C.B., K.B.E.

Johnston, Sir Charles Collier, Kt., T.D.

Johnston, Sir (David) Russell, Kt., M.P.

Johnston, Sir Edward Alexander, K.B.E., C.B.

Johnston, Sir John Baines, G.C.M.G., K.C.V.O.

Johnston, *Lt.-Col.* Sir John Frederick Dame, G.C.V.O., M.C.

Johnston, *Lt.-Gen.* Sir Maurice Robert, K.C.B., O.B.E.

Johnston, Sir Thomas Alexander, Bt. (s. 1626).

Johnstone, Sir Frederic Allan George, Bt. (s. 1700).

Jolliffe, Sir Anthony Stuart, G.B.E.

Jones, *Lt.-Gen.* Sir (Charles) Edward Webb, K.C.B., C.B.E.

Jones, Sir Christopher Lawrence-, Bt. (1831).

Jones, *Air Marshal* Sir Edward Gordon, K.C.B., C.B.E., D.S.O., D.F.C.

Jones, Sir (Edward) Martin Furnival, Kt., C.B.E.

Jones, *Rt. Hon.* Sir Edward Warburton, Kt.

Jones, Sir Ewart Ray Herbert, Kt., D.S.C., Ph.D., F.R.S.

Jones, Sir Francis Avery, Kt., C.B.E., F.R.C.P.

Jones, *Air Marshal* Sir George, K.B.E., C.B., D.F.C.

Jones, Sir Glyn Smallwood, G.C.M.G., M.B.E.

Jones, Sir Harry Ernest, Kt., C.B.E.

Jones, Sir James Duncan, K.C.B.

Jones, Sir (John) Kenneth (Trevor), Kt., C.B.E., Q.C.

Jones, Sir John Lewis, K.C.B., C.M.G.

Jones, Sir John Prichard-, Bt. (1910).

Jones, Sir Keith Stephen, Kt.

Jones, *Hon.* Sir Kenneth George Illtyd, Kt.

Jones, *Air Marshal* Sir Laurence Alfred, K.C.B., C.B., A.F.C.

Jones, Sir (Owen) Trevor, Kt.

Jones, Sir Robert Edward, Kt.

Jones, Sir Simon Warley Frederick Benton, Bt. (1919).

Jones, Sir (Thomas) Philip, Kt., C.B.

Jones, Sir (William) Emrys, Kt.

Jordan, *Air Marshal* Sir Richard Bowen, K.C.B., D.F.C.

Joseph, *Maj.* Sir (Herbert) Leslie, Kt.

Jowitt, *Hon.* Sir Edwin Frank, Kt.

Judge, *Hon.* Sir Igor, Kt.

Jugnauth, *Rt. Hon.* Sir Anerood, K.C.M.G., Q.C.

Jungius, *Vice-Adm.*, Sir James George, K.B.E.

Junor, Sir John Donald Brown, Kt.

Jupp, *Hon.* Sir Kenneth Graham, Kt., M.C.

Kalo, Sir Kwamala, Kt., M.B.E.

Kan Yuet-Keung, Sir, G.B.E.

Kapi, *Hon.* Sir Mari, Kt., C.B.E.

Karimjee, Sir Tayabali Hassanali Alibhoy, Kt.

Katsina, The Emir of, K.B.E., C.M.G.

Katz, Sir Bernard, Kt., F.R.S.

Kavali, Sir Thomas, Kt., O.B.E.

Kawharu, *Prof.* Sir Ian Hugh, Kt.

Kay, *Prof.* Sir Andrew Watt, Kt.

Kaye, Sir David Alexander Gordon, Bt. (1923).

Kaye, Sir Emmanuel, Kt., C.B.E.

Kaye, Sir John Phillip Lister Lister-, Bt. (1812).

Keane, Sir Richard Michael, Bt. (1801).

Keatinge, Sir Edgar Mayne, Kt., C.B.E.

Keeble, Sir (Herbert Ben) Curtis, G.C.M.G.

Keith, *Prof.* Sir James, K.B.E.

Kellett, Sir Brian Smith, Kt.

Kellett, Sir Stanley Charles, Bt. (1801).

Kelliher, Sir Henry Joseph, Kt.

Kelly, *Rt. Hon.* Sir (John William) Basil, Kt.

Kelly, Sir William Theodore, Kt., O.B.E.

Kemsley, *Col.* Sir Alfred Newcombe, K.B.E., C.M.G., E.D.

Kendrew, Sir John Cowdery, Kt., C.B.E., SC.D., F.R.S.

Kenilorea, *Rt. Hon.* Sir Peter, K.B.E.

Kennard, *Lt.-Col.* Sir George Arnold Ford, Bt. (1891).

Kennaway, Sir John Lawrence, Bt. (1791).

Kennedy, Sir Albert Henry, Kt.

Kennedy, Sir Clyde David Allen, Kt.

Kennedy, Sir Francis, K.C.M.G., C.B.E.

Kennedy, *Hon.* Sir Ian Alexander, Kt.

Kennedy, Sir Michael Edward, Bt., (1836).

Kennedy, *Hon.* Sir Paul Joseph Morrow, Kt.

Kennedy, *Air Chief Marshal* Sir Thomas Lawrie, G.C.B., A.F.C.

Kennedy-Good, Sir John, K.B.E.

Kennon, *Vice-Adm.* Sir James Edward Campbell, K.C.B., C.B.E.

Kenny, *Gen.* Sir Brian Leslie Graham, K.C.B., C.B.E.

Kent, Sir Harold Simcox, G.C.B., Q.C.

Kenyon, Sir George Henry, Kt.

Kermode, Sir Ronald Graham Quale, K.B.E.

Kerr, *Vice-Adm.* Sir John Beverley, K.C.B.

Kerr, *Rt. Hon.* Sir (John) Robert, G.C.M.G., G.C.V.O.

Kerr, *Rt. Hon.* Sir Michael Robert Emanuel, Kt.

Kerruish, Sir (Henry) Charles, Kt., O.B.E.

Kerry, Sir Michael James, K.C.B., Q.C.

Kershaw, Sir (John) Anthony, Kt., M.C.

Keswick, Sir William Johnston, Kt.

Keville, Sir (William) Errington, Kt., C.B.E.

Kidd, Sir Robert Hill, K.B.E., C.B.

Kidu, *Hon.* Sir Buri (William), Kt.

Kikau, *Ratu* Sir Jone Latianara, K.B.E.

Kiki, *Hon.* Sir (Albert) Maori, K.B.E.

Kilage, *Dr.* Sir Ignatius, G.C.M.G.

Killen, *Hon.* Denis James, K.C.M.G.

Killick, Sir John Edward, G.C.M.G.

Kilpatrick, *Prof.* Sir Robert, Kt., C.B.E.

Kilpatrick, Sir William John, K.B.E.

Kimber, Sir Charles Dixon, Bt. (1904).

Kinahan, Sir Robert George Caldwell, Kt., E.R.D.

King, Sir Albert, Kt., O.B.E.

King, *Gen.* Sir Frank Douglas, G.C.B., M.B.E.

King, Sir James Granville Le Neve, Bt., T.D. (1888).

King, *Vice-Adm.* Sir Norman Ross Dutton, K.B.E.

King, Sir Richard Brian Meredith, K.C.B., M.C.

King, Sir Sydney Percy, Kt., O.B.E.

King, Sir Wayne Alexander, Bt. (1815).

Kingman, *Prof.* Sir John Frank Charles, Kt., F.R.S.

Kingsland, Sir Richard, Kt., C.B.E., D.F.C.

Kingsley, Sir Patrick Graham Toler, K.C.V.O.

Kinloch, Sir David, Bt. (s. 1686).

Kinloch, Sir John, Bt. (1873).

Kirby, *Hon.* Sir Richard Clarence, Kt.

Kirkpatrick, Sir Ivone Elliott, Bt. (s. 1685).

Kirwan, Sir (Archibald) Laurence Patrick, K.C.M.G., T.D.

Kitson, *Gen.* Sir Frank Edward, G.B.E., K.C.B., M.C.

Kitson, Sir Timothy Peter Geoffrey, Kt.

Kitto, *Rt. Hon.* Sir Frank Walters, K.B.E.

Kleinwort, Sir Kenneth Drake, Bt. (1909).

Klug, Sir Aaron, Kt.

Knight, Sir Allan Walton, Kt., C.M.G.

Knight, Sir Arthur William, Kt.

Knight, Sir Harold Murray, K.B.E., D.S.C.

Knight, *Air Chief Marshal* Sir Michael William Patrick, K.C.B., A.F.C.

Knill, Sir John Kenelm Stuart, Bt. (1893).

Knipe, Sir Leslie Francis, Kt., M.B.E.

Knott, Sir John Laurence, Kt., C.B.E.

Knowles, Sir Charles Francis, Bt. (1765).

Knowles, Sir Leonard Joseph, Kt., C.B.E.

Knowles, Sir Richard Marchant, Kt.

Knox, *Hon.* Sir John Leonard, Kt.

Knox, *Hon.* Sir William Edward, Kt.

Kornberg, *Prof.* Sir Hans Leo, Kt., D.SC., SC.D., PH.D., F.R.S.

Krusin, Sir Stanley Marks, Kt., C.B.

Kurongku, *Most. Rev.* Peter, K.B.E.

Labouchere, Sir George Peter, G.B.E., K.C.M.G.

Lacon, Sir Edmund Vere, Bt. (1818).

Lacy, Sir Hugh Maurice Pierce, Bt. (1921).

Lagesen, *Air Marshal* Sir Philip Jacobus, K.C.B., D.F.C., A.F.C.

Laidlaw, Sir Christophor Charles Fraser, Kt.

Laing, Sir Hector, Kt.

Laing, Sir (John) Maurice, Kt.

Laing, Sir (William) Kirby, Kt.

Lake, Sir (Atwell) Graham, Bt. (1711).

Laker, Sir Frederick Alfred, Kt.

Lakin, Sir Michael, Bt. (1909).

Laking, Sir George Robert, K.C.M.G.

Lamb, Sir Albert (Larry), Kt.

Lamb, Sir Albert Thomas, K.B.E., C.M.G., D.F.C.

Lamb, Sir Lionel Henry, K.C.M.G., O.B.E.

Lambert, Sir Anthony Edward, K.C.M.G.

Lambert, Sir Edward Thomas, K.B.E., C.V.O.

Lambert, Sir John Henry, K.C.V.O., C.M.G.

†Lambert, Sir Peter John Biddulph, Bt. (1711).

Lancaster, *Vice-Adm.* Sir John Strike, K.B.E., C.B.

Landau, Sir Dennis Marcus, Kt.

Lane, Sir David William Stennis Stuart, Kt.

Lane, Sir Peter Stewart, Kt.

Lang, *Lt.-Gen.* Sir Derek Boileau, K.C.B., D.S.O., M.C.

Langham, Sir James Michael, Bt. (1660).

Langley, *Maj.-Gen.* Sir Henry Desmond Allen, K.C.V.O., M.B.E.

Langrishe, Sir Hercules Ralph Hume, Bt. (I. 1777).

Lapsley, *Air Marshal* Sir John Hugh, K.B.E., C.B., D.F.C., A.F.C.

Lapun, *Hon.* Sir Paul, Kt.

Larcom, Sir (Charles) Christopher Royde, Bt. (1868).

Larmour, Sir Edward Noel, K.C.M.G.

Lartigue, Sir Louis Cools-, Kt., C.M.G.

Lasdun, Sir Denys Louis, Kt., C.B.E., F.R.I.B.A.

Latey, *Rt. Hon.* Sir John Brinsmead, Kt., M.B.E.

Latham, Sir Richard Thomas Paul, Bt. (1919).

Latimer, Sir (Courtenay) Robert, Kt., C.B.E.

Latimer, Sir Graham Stanley, K.B.E.

Laucke, *Hon.* Sir Condor Louis, K.C.M.G.

Lauder, Sir Piers Robert Dick-, Bt. (s. 1690).

Laughton, Sir Anthony Seymour, Kt.

Laurantus, Sir Nicholas, Kt., M.B.E.

Laurence, Sir Peter Harold, K.C.M.G., M.C.

Laurie, Sir Robert Bayley Emilius, Bt. (1834).

Lavan, *Hon.* Sir John Martin, Kt.

Law, *Adm.* Sir Horace Rochfort, G.C.B., O.B.E., D.S.C.

Lawes, Sir (John) Michael Bennet, Bt. (1882).

Lawler, Sir Peter James, Kt., O.B.E.

Lawrence, Sir David Roland Walter, Bt. (1906).

Lawrence, Sir Guy Kempton, Kt., D.S.O., O.B.E., D.F.C.

Lawrence, Sir John Patrick Grosvenor, Kt., C.B.E.

Lawrence, Sir John Waldemar, Bt., O.B.E. (1858).

Lawrence, Sir William Fettiplace, Bt. (1867).

Lawson, Sir Christopher Donald, Kt.

Lawson, *Col.* Sir John Charles Arthur Digby, Bt., D.S.O., M.C. (1900).

Lawson, *Hon.* Sir Neil, Kt.

Lawson, *Gen.* Sir Richard George, K.C.B., D.S.O., O.B.E.

Lawson, Sir William Howard, Bt. (1841).

Lawton, *Prof.* Sir Frank Ewart, Kt.

Lawton, *Rt. Hon.* Sir Frederick Horace, Kt.

Layden, Sir John (Jack), Kt.

Layfield, Sir Frank Henry Burland Willoughby, Kt., Q.C.

Lazarus, Sir Peter Esmond, K.C.B.

Lea, *Lt.-Gen.* Sir George Harris, K.C.B., D.S.O., M.B.E.

Lea, *Vice-Adm.*, Sir John Stuart Crosbie, K.B.E.

Lea, Sir (Thomas) Julian, Bt. (1892).

Leach, *Admiral of the Fleet* Sir Henry Conyers, G.C.B.

Leach, Sir Ronald George, G.B.E.

Leahy, Sir John Henry Gladstone, K.C.M.G.

Lean, Sir David, Kt., C.B.E.

Learmont, *Lt.-Gen.* Sir John Hartley, K.C.B., C.B.E.

Leask, *Lt.-Gen.* Sir Henry Lowther Ewart Clark, K.C.B., D.S.O., O.B.E.

Leather, Sir Edwin Hartley Cameron, K.C.M.G., K.C.V.O.

Leaver, Sir Christopher, G.B.E.

Le Bailly, *Vice-Adm.* Sir Louis Edward Stewart Holland, K.B.E., C.B.

Le Cheminant, *Air Chief Marshal* Sir Peter de Lacey, G.B.E., K.C.B., D.F.C.

Lechmere, Sir Berwick Hungerford, Bt. (1818).

Ledger, Sir Frank, (Joseph Francis), Kt.

Ledwidge, Sir (William) Bernard (John), K.C.M.G.

Lee, Sir Arthur James, K.B.E., M.C.

Lee, *Air Chief Marshal* Sir David John Pryer, G.B.E., C.B.

Lee, Sir (Henry) Desmond (Pritchard), Kt.

Lee, *Brig.* Sir Leonard Henry, Kt., C.B.E.

Lee, Sir Quo-wei, Kt., C.B.E.

Lee, *Col.* Sir William Allison, Kt., O.B.E., T.D.

Leeds, Sir Christopher Anthony, Bt. (1812).

Lees, *Air Marshal* Sir Ronald Beresford, K.C.B., C.B.E., D.F.C.

Lees, Sir Thomas Edward, Bt. (1897).

Lees, Sir Thomas Harcourt Ivor, Bt. (1804).

Lees, Sir (William) Antony Clare, Bt. (1937).

Leese, Sir John Henry Vernon, Bt. (1908).

Le Fanu, *Maj.* Sir (George) Victor (Sheridan), K.C.V.O.

le Fleming, Sir William Kelland, Bt. (1705).

Legard, Sir Charles Thomas, Bt. (1660).

Leggatt, *Hon.* Sir Andrew Peter, Kt.

Leggatt, Sir Hugh Frank John, Kt.

Leggett, Sir Clarence Arthur Campbell, Kt., M.B.E.

Leigh, Sir John, Bt. (1918).

Leigh, Sir Neville Egerton, K.C.V.O.

Leighton, Sir Michael John Bryan, Bt. (1693).

Leitch, Sir George, K.C.B., O.B.E.

Leith, Sir Andrew George Forbes-, Bt. (1923).

Le Marchant, Sir Francis Arthur, Bt. (1841).

Le Masurier, Sir Robert Hugh, Kt., D.S.C.

Lemon, Sir (Richard) Dawnay, Kt., C.B.E.

Leng, *Gen.* Sir Peter John Hall, K.C.B., M.B.E., M.C.

Lennard, *Rev.* Sir Hugh Dacre Barrett-, Bt. (1801).

Leon, Sir John Ronald, Bt. (1911).

Leonard, *Hon.* Sir (Hamilton) John, Kt.

Lepping, Sir George Geria Dennis, G.C.M.G., M.B.E.

Le Quesne, Sir (Charles) Martin, K.C.M.G.

Le Quesne, Sir (John) Godfray, Kt., Q.C.

Leslie, Sir Colin Alan Bettridge, Kt.

Leslie, Sir John Norman Ide, Bt. (1876).

†Leslie, Sir (Percy) Theodore, Bt. (s. 1625).

Lethbridge, Sir Thomas Periam Hector Noel, Bt. (1804).

Leuchars, Sir William Douglas, K.B.E.

Leupena, Sir Tupua, G.C.M.G., M.B.E.

Levene, Sir Peter Keith, K.B.E.

Lever, Sir (Tresham) Christopher Arthur Lindsay, Bt. (1911).

Levey, Sir Michael Vincent, Kt., M.V.O.

Levine, Sir Montague Bernard, Kt.

Levinge, Sir Richard George Robin, Bt. (I. 1704).

Levy, Sir Ewart Maurice, Bt. (1913).

Lewando, Sir Jan Alfred, Kt., C.B.E.

Lewis, Sir Allen Montgomery, G.C.M.G., G.C.V.O., Q.C.

Lewis, *Adm.* Sir Andrew Mackenzie, K.C.B.

Lewis, Sir Ian Malcolm, Kt.

Lewis, Sir Kenneth, Kt.

Lewis, Sir Terence Murray, Kt., O.B.E., Q.P.M.

Lewis, Sir William Arthur, Kt.

Lewthwaite, Sir William Anthony, Bt. (1927).

Ley, Sir Francis Douglas, Bt., M.B.E., T.D. (1905).

Leyland, Sir Philip Vyvyan Naylor-, Bt. (1895).

Lickley, Sir Robert Lang, Kt., C.B.E.

Lidbury, Sir John Towersey, Kt.

Lidderdale, Sir David William Shuckburgh, K.C.B.

Liddle, Sir Donald Ross, Kt.

Liggins, Sir Edmund Naylor, Kt., T.D.

Lighthill, Sir (Michael) James, Kt., F.R.S.

Lighton, Sir Christopher Robert, Bt., M.B.E. (I. 1791).

Lim, Sir Han-Hoe, Kt., C.B.E.

Linacre, Sir (John) Gordon (Seymour), Kt., C.B.E., A.F.C., D.F.M.

Lincoln, Sir Anthony Handley, K.C.M.G., C.V.O.

Lincoln, *Hon.* Sir Anthony Leslie Julian, Kt.

Lindley, Sir Arnold Lewis George, Kt.

Lindop, Sir Norman, Kt.

Lindsay, Sir James Harvey Kincaid Stewart, Kt.

Lindsay, Sir Ronald Alexander, Bt., (1962).

Lintott, Sir Henry John Bevis, K.C.M.G.

Lithgow, Sir William James, Bt. (1925).

Little, *Hon.* Sir Douglas Macfarlan, Kt.

Little, *Most Rev.* Thomas Francis, K.B.E.

Littler, Sir (James) Geoffrey, K.C.B.

Livermore, Sir Harry, Kt.

Livesay, *Vice-Adm.* Sir Michael Howard, K.C.B.

Llewellyn, Sir David Treharne, Kt.

Llewellyn, Sir Henry Morton, Bt., C.B.E. (1922).

Llewellyn, *Lt.-Col.* Sir Michael Rowland Godfrey, Bt. (1959).

Llewelyn, Sir John Michael Dillwyn-Venables-, Bt. (1890).

Lloyd, *Rt. Hon.* Sir Anthony John Leslie, Kt.

Lloyd, Sir Ian Stewart, Kt., M.P.

Lloyd, Sir (John) Peter (Daniel), Kt.

Lloyd, Sir Richard Ernest Butler, Bt., (1960).

Lloyd-Jones, Sir (Peter) Hugh (Jefferd), Kt.

Lloyd Jones, Sir Richard Anthony, K.C.B.

Loader, Sir Leslie Thomas, Kt., C.B.E.

Loane, *Most Rev.* Marcus Lawrence, K.B.E.

Lobo, Sir Rogerio Hyndman, Kt., K.B.E.

Lock, *Cdr.* Sir (John) Duncan, Kt.

Lockhart, Sir Simon John Edward Francis Sinclair-, Bt. (s. 1636).

Lockspeiser, Sir Ben, K.C.B., F.R.S.

Lockwood, Sir Joseph Flawith, Kt.

Loder, Sir Giles Rolls, Bt. (1887).

Lodge, Sir Thomas, Kt.

Loehnis, Sir Clive, K.C.M.G.

Logan, Sir Donald Arthur, K.C.M.G.

Logan, Sir Raymond Douglas, Kt.

Lokoloko, Sir Tore, G.C.M.G., G.C.V.O., O.B.E.

Longden, Sir Gilbert James Morley, Kt., M.B.E.

Longland, Sir David Walter, Kt., C.M.G.

Longland, Sir John Laurence, Kt.

Longley, Sir Norman, Kt., C.B.E.

Looker, Sir Cecil Thomas, Kt.

Loram, *Vice-Adm.* Sir David Anning, K.C.B., M.V.O.

Lorimer, Sir (Thomas) Desmond, Kt.

Lousada, Sir Anthony Baruh, Kt.

Love, Sir Makere Rangiatea Ralph, Kt.

Lovell, Sir (Alfred Charles) Bernard, Kt., O.B.E., F.R.S.

Lovelock, Sir Douglas Arthur, K.C.B.

Loveridge, Sir John Henry, Kt., C.B.E.

Loveridge, Sir John Warren, Kt.

Lovill, Sir John Roger, Kt., C.B.E.

Low, Sir Alan Roberts, Kt.

Low, Sir James Richard Morrison-, Bt. (1908).

Lowe, *Air Chief Marshal* Sir Douglas Charles, G.C.B., D.F.C., A.F.C.

Lowe, *Air Vice-Marshal* Sir Edgar Noel, K.B.E., C.B.

Lowe, Sir Thomas William Gordon, Bt. (1918).

Lowry, Sir John Patrick, Kt., C.B.E.

Lowson, Sir Ian Patrick, Bt. (1951).

Lowther, *Maj.* Sir Charles Douglas, Bt. (1824).

Loyd, Sir Francis Alfred, K.C.M.G., O.B.E.

Lu, Sir Tseng Chi, Kt.

Lubbock, Sir Alan, Kt., F.S.A.

Lucas, Sir Cyril Edward, Kt., C.M.G., F.R.S.

Lucas, Sir Thomas Edward, Bt. (1887).

Luckhoo, *Hon.* Sir Joseph Alexander, Kt.

Luckhoo, Sir Lionel Alfred, K.C.M.G., C.B.E., Q.C.

Lucy, Sir Edmund John William Hugh Cameron-Ramsay-Fairfax-, Bt. (1836).

Luddington, Sir Donald Collin Cumyn, K.B.E., C.M.G., C.V.O.

Luke, *Hon.* Sir Emile Fashole, K.B.E.

Lumsden, Sir David James, Kt.

Lus, *Hon.* Sir Pita, Kt., O.B.E.

Lush, *Hon.* Sir George Hermann, Kt.

Lushington, Sir John Richard Castleman, Bt. (1791).

Lusty, Sir Robert Frith, Kt.

Luyt, Sir Richard Edmonds, G.C.M.G., K.C.V.O., D.C.M.

Lyell, Sir Nicholas Walter, Kt., Q.C., M.P.

Lygo, *Adm.* Sir Raymond Derek, K.C.B.

Lyle, Sir Gavin Archibald, Bt. (1929).

Lyons, Sir Edward Houghton, Kt.

Lyons, Sir (Isidore) Jack, Kt., C.B.E.

Lyons, Sir James Reginald, Kt.

Lyons, Sir John, Kt.

Lyons, *His Hon.* Sir Rudolph, Kt., Q.C.

McAdam, Sir Ian William James, Kt., O.B.E.

Macadam, Sir Peter, Kt.

McAlpine, Sir Robin, Kt., C.B.E.

Macara, Sir (Charles) Douglas, Bt. (1911).

Macartney, Sir John Barrington, Bt. (I. 1799).

McAvoy, Sir (Francis) Joseph, Kt., C.B.E.

McCaffrey, Sir Thomas Daniel, Kt.

McCall, Sir (Charles) Patrick Home, Kt., M.B.E., T.D.

McCallum, Sir Donald Murdo, Kt., C.B.E.

McCamley, Sir Graham Edward, Kt., M.B.E.

McCarthy, *Rt. Hon.* Sir Thaddeus Pearcey, K.B.E.

McCaw, *Hon.* Sir Kenneth Malcolm, Kt., Q.C.

McClellan, *Col.* Sir Herbert Gerard Thomas, Kt., C.B.E., T.D.

McClintock, Sir Eric Paul, Kt.

McCollum, *Hon.* Sir William, Kt.

McConnell, *Cdr.* Sir Robert Melville Terence, Bt., V.R.D. (1900).

McCowan, *Hon.* Sir Anthony James Denys, Kt.

McCowan, Sir Hew Cargill, Bt. (1934).

McCrea, *Prof.* Sir William Hunter, Kt., F.R.S.

McCullough, *Hon.* Sir (Iain) Charles (Robert), Kt.

McCusker, Sir James Alexander, Kt.

MacDermott, *Rt. Hon.* Sir John Clarke, Kt.

McDermott, Sir (Lawrence) Emmet, K.B.E.

MacDonald, *Gen.* Sir Arthur Leslie, K.B.E., C.B.

McDonald, *Air Chief Marshal* Sir Arthur William Baynes, K.C.B., A.F.C.

McDonald, Sir Duncan, Kt., C.B.E.

Macdonald, Sir Herbert George deLorme, K.B.E.

Macdonald of Sleat, Sir Ian Godfrey Bosville, Bt. (s. 1625).

Macdonald, *Vice-Adm.* Sir Roderick Douglas, K.B.E.

McDonald, *Hon.* Sir William John Farquhar, Kt.

MacDougall, Sir (George) Donald (Alastair), Kt., C.B.E., F.B.A.

McDowell, Sir Henry McLorinan, K.B.E.

McEvoy, *Air Chief Marshal* Sir Theodore Newman, K.C.B., C.B.E.

McEwen, Sir John Roderick Hugh, Bt. (1953).

McEwin, *Hon.* Sir (Alexander) Lyell, K.B.E.

McFarland, Sir John Talbot, Bt. (1914).

Macfarlane, Sir (David) Neil, Kt., M.P.

Macfarlane, Sir George Gray, Kt., C.B.

McFarlane, Sir Ian, Kt.

Macfarlane, Sir James Wright, Kt.

Macfarlane, Sir Norman Somerville, Kt.

McGeoch, *Vice-Adm.* Sir Ian Lachlan Mackay, K.C.B., D.S.O., D.S.C.

Macgregor, Sir Edwin Robert, Bt. (1828).

MacGregor of MacGregor, Sir Gregor, Bt. (1795).

McGregor, Sir Ian Alexander, Kt., C.B.E., F.R.S.

MacGregor, Sir Ian Kinloch, Kt.

McGrigor, *Capt.* Sir Charles Edward, Bt. (1831).

McInerney, *Hon.* Sir Murray Vincent, Kt.

McIntosh, *Vice-Adm.* Sir Ian Stewart, K.B.E., C.B., D.S.O., D.S.C.

Macintosh, Sir Robert Reynolds, Kt., M.D.

McIntosh, Sir Ronald Robert Duncan, K.C.B.

McKaig, *Adm.* Sir (John) Rae, K.C.B., C.B.E.

McKay, *Hon.* Sir Donald Norman, K.C.M.G.

Mackay, Sir (George Patrick) Gordon, Kt., C.B.E.

McKay, Sir James Wilson, Kt.

McKay, Sir John Andrew, Kt., C.B.E.

Mackay, Sir William Calder, Kt., O.B.E., M.C.

McKee, *Maj.* Sir (William) Cecil, Kt., E.R.D.

MacKenna, Sir Bernard Joseph Maxwell, Kt.

McKenzie, Sir Alexander, K.B.E.

Mackenzie, Sir Alexander Alwyne Henry Charles Brinton Muir-, Bt. (1805).

Mackenzie, Sir (Alexander George Anthony) Allan, Bt. (1890).

Mackenzie, *Vice-Adm.* Sir Hugh Stirling, K.C.B., D.S.O., D.S.C.

Mackenzie, Sir Robert Evelyn, Bt. (s. 1673).

†Mackenzie, Sir Roderick McQuhae, Bt. (s. 1703).

McKenzie, Sir Roy Allan, K.B.E.

Mackeson, Sir Rupert Henry, Bt. (1954).

Mackie, Sir Maitland, Kt., C.B.E.

MacKinlay, Sir Bruce, Kt., C.B.E.

McKinnon, *Hon.* Sir Stuart Neil, Kt.

McKissock, Sir Wylie, Kt., O.B.E., F.R.C.S.

Macklin, Sir Bruce Roy, Kt., O.B.E.

Mackworth, *Cdr.* Sir David Arthur Geoffrey, Bt. (1776).

Maclaren, Sir Hamish Duncan, K.B.E., C.B., D.F.C.

MacLaurin, Sir Ian Charter, Kt.

Maclean, Sir Donald Og Grant, Kt.

Maclean, Sir Fitzroy Hew, Bt., C.B.E. (1957).

McLean, Sir Francis Charles, Kt., C.B.E.

MacLean, *Vice-Adm.* Sir Hector Charles Donald, K.B.E., C.B., D.S.C.

Maclean, Sir Robert Alexander, K.B.E.

MacLellan, Sir (George) Robin (Perronet), Kt., C.B.E.

McLennan, Sir Ian Munro, K.C.M.G., K.B.E.

McLeod, Sir Charles Henry, Bt. (1925).

MacLeod, Sir (Hugh) Roderick, Kt.

McLeod, Sir Ian George, Kt.

McLintock, Sir Michael William, Bt. (1934).

Maclure, Sir John Robert Spencer, Bt. (1898).

McMahon, Sir Brian Patrick, Bt. (1817).

McMahon, Sir Christopher William, Kt.

McMichael, Sir John, Kt., M.D., F.R.S., F.R.C.P.

Macmillan, Sir Alexander McGregor Graham, Kt.

Macmillan, Sir (James) Wilson, K.B.E.

MacMillan, *Lt. Gen.* Sir John Richard Alexander, K.C.B., C.B.E.

MacMillan, Sir Kenneth, Kt.

McMullin, *Rt. Hon.* Sir Duncan Wallace, Kt.

Macnab, *Brig.* Sir Geoffrey Alex Colin, K.C.M.G., C.B.

Macnaghten, Sir Patrick Alexander, Bt. (1836).

McNair-Wilson, Sir Patrick Michael Ernest David, Kt., M.P.

McNair-Wilson, Sir (Robert) Michael Conal, Kt., M.P.

McNamara, *Air Chief Marshal* Sir Neville Patrick, K.B.E.

Macnaughton, *Prof.* Sir Malcolm Campbell, Kt.

McNee, Sir David Blackstock, Kt., Q.P.M.

McNeice, Sir (Thomas) Percy (Fergus), Kt., C.M.G., O.B.E.

McNeill, *Hon.* Sir David Bruce, Kt.

McPetrie, Sir James Carnegie, K.C.M.G., O.B.E.

MacPherson, Sir Keith Duncan, Kt.

Macpherson of Cluny, *Hon.* Sir William Alan, Kt., T.D.

McQuarrie, Sir Albert, Kt.

Macready, Sir Nevil John Wilfrid, Bt. (1923).

Macrory, Sir Patrick Arthur, Kt.

McShine, *Hon.* Sir Arthur Hugh, Kt.

Mactaggart, Sir John Auld, Bt. (1938).

McTiernan, *Rt. Hon.* Sir Edward Aloysius, K.B.E.

Madden, *Adm.* Sir Charles Edward, Bt., G.C.B. (1919).

Maddocks, Sir Kenneth Phipson, K.C.M.G., K.C.V.O.

Maddox, Sir (John) Kempson, Kt., V.R.D., M.D.

Madigan, Sir Russel Tullie, Kt., O.B.E.

Magarey, Sir James Rupert, Kt.

†Magnus, Sir Laurence Henry Philip, Bt. (1917).

Maguire, *Air Marshal* Sir Harold John, K.C.B., D.S.O., O.B.E.

Mahon, Sir (John) Denis, Kt., C.B.E.

Mahon, Sir William Walter, Bt. (1819).

Main, Sir Peter Tester, Kt., E.R.D.

Maini, Sir Amar Nath, Kt., C.B.E.

Mais, *Hon.* Sir (Robert) Hugh, Kt.

Maitland, Sir Donald James Dundas, G.C.M.G., O.B.E.

Maitland, Sir Richard John, Bt. (1818).

Makins, Sir Paul Vivian, Bt. (1903).

Malcolm, Sir David Peter Michael, Bt. (s. 1665).

Malet, *Col.* Sir Edward William St. Lo, Bt., O.B.E. (1791).

Mallaby, Sir Christopher Leslie George, K.C.M.G.

†Mallinson, Sir William John, Bt. (1935).

Malone, *Hon.* Sir Denis Eustace Gilbert, Kt.

Mamo, Sir Anthony Joseph, Kt., O.B.E.

Manchester, Sir William Maxwell, K.B.E.

Mander, Sir Charles Marcus, Bt. (1911).

Manduell, Sir John, Kt., C.B.E.

Mann, *Rt. Hon.* Sir Michael, Kt.

Mann, *Rt. Rev.* Michael Ashley, K.C.V.O.

Mann, Sir Rupert Edward, Bt. (1905).

Mansel, *Rev. Canon* James Seymour Denis, K.C.V.O.

Mansel, Sir Philip, Bt. (1622).

Mansergh, *Vice-Adm.* Sir (Cecil) Aubrey (Lawson), K.B.E., C.B., D.S.C.

Mansfield, *Vice-Adm.* Sir (Edward) Gerard (Napier), K.C.V.O.

Mansfield, Sir Philip (Robert Aked), K.C.M.G.

Mant, Sir Cecil George, Kt., C.B.E.

Manzie, Sir (Andrew) Gordon, K.C.B.

Mara, *Rt. Hon. Ratu* Sir Kamisese Kapaiwai Tuimacilai, G.C.M.G., K.B.E.

March, Sir Derek Maxwell, K.B.E.

Marchant, Sir Herbert Stanley, K.C.M.G., O.B.E.

Margetson, Sir John William Denys, K.C.M.G.

Marjoribanks, Sir James Alexander Milne, K.C.M.G.

Mark, Sir Robert, G.B.E.

Markham, Sir Charles John, Bt. (1911).

Marking, Sir Henry Ernest, K.C.V.O., C.B.E., M.C.

Marling, Sir Charles William Somerset, Bt., (1882).

Marr, Sir Leslie Lynn, Bt. (1919).

Marre, Sir Alan Samuel, K.C.B.

Marriner, Sir Neville, Kt., C.B.E.

Marriott, Sir Hugh Cavendish Smith-, Bt. (1774).

Marsack, Sir Charles Croft, K.B.E.

Marsden, Sir Nigel John Denton, Bt., (1924).

Marshall, Sir Arthur Gregory George, Kt., O.B.E.

Marshall, Sir Colin Marsh, Kt.

Marshall, Sir Denis Alfred, Kt.

Marshall, *Prof.* Sir (Oshley) Roy, Kt., C.B.E.

Marshall, Sir Peter Harold Reginald, K.C.M.G.

Marshall, Sir Robert Braithwaite, K.C.B., M.B.E.

Mars-Jones, *Hon.* Sir William Lloyd, Kt., M.B.E.

Martell, *Vice-Adm.* Sir Hugh Colenso, K.B.E., C.B.

Martin, *Vice-Adm.* Sir John Edward Ludgate, K.C.B., D.S.C.

Martin, *Prof.* Sir (John) Leslie, Kt., Ph.D.

Martin, Sir John Miller, K.C.M.G., C.B., C.V.O.

Martin, *Col.* Sir Robert Andrew St. George, K.C.V.O., O.B.E.

Martin, Sir Sidney Launcelot, Kt.

Marwick, Sir Brian Allan, K.B.E., C.M.G.

Marychurch, Sir Peter Harvey, K.C.M.G.

Masefield, Sir Peter Gordon, Kt.

Mason, *Hon.* Sir Anthony Frank, K.B.E.

Mason, Sir (Basil) John, Kt., C.B., D.S.C., F.R.S.

Mason, Sir Frederick Cecil, K.C.V.O., C.M.G.

Mason, Sir John Charles Moir, K.C.M.G.

Mason, *Prof.* Sir Ronald, K.C.B., F.R.S.

Matane, Sir Paulias Nguna, Kt., C.M.G., O.B.E.

Mather, Sir (David) Carol (Macdonell), Kt., M.C.

Mather, *Prof.* Sir Kenneth, C.B.E., D.S.C., F.R.S.

Mather, Sir William Loris, Kt., C.V.O., O.B.E., M.C., T.D.

Mathers, Sir Robert William, Kt.

Matheson, Sir (James Adam) Louis, K.B.E., C.M.G.

Matheson of Matheson, Sir Torquhil Alexander, Bt. (1882).

Mathias, Sir Richard Hughes, Bt. (1917).

Matthews, Sir Peter Alec, Kt.

Matthews, Sir Peter Jack, Kt., C.V.O., O.B.E., Q.P.M.

Matthews, Sir Stanley, Kt., C.B.E.

Mavor, *Air Marshal* Sir Leslie Deane, K.C.B., A.F.C.

†Maxwell, Sir Michael Eustace George, Bt. (s. 1681).

Maxwell, Sir Nigel Mellor Heron-, Bt. (s. 1683).

Maxwell, Sir Robert Hugh, K.B.E.

May, *Rt. Hon.* Sir John Douglas, Kt.

May, Sir Kenneth Spencer, Kt., C.B.E.

Mayall, Sir (Alexander) Lees, K.C.V.O., C.M.G.

Mayhew, *Rt. Hon.* Sir Patrick Barnabas Burke, Kt., Q.C., M.P.

Mayhew-Sanders, Sir John Reynolds, Kt.

Maynard, *Hon.* Sir Clement Travelyan, Kt.

Maynard, *Air Chief Marshal* Sir Nigel Martin, K.C.B., C.B.E., D.F.C., A.F.C.

Meade, Sir (Richard) Geoffrey (Austin), K.B.E., C.M.G., C.V.O.

Meaney, Sir Patrick Michael, Kt.

Medlycott, Sir Mervyn Tregonwell, Bt. (1808).

Megarry, *Rt. Hon.* Sir Robert Edgar, Kt., F.B.A.

Megaw, *Rt. Hon.* Sir John, Kt., C.B.E., T.D.

Meinertzhagen, Sir Peter, Kt., C.M.G.

Mellon, Sir James, K.C.M.G.

Mellor, Sir John Francis, Bt. (1924).

Melville, Sir Harry Work, K.C.B., Ph.D., D.SC., F.R.S.

Melville, Sir Leslie Galfreid, K.B.E.

Melville, Sir Ronald Henry, K.C.B.

Mensforth, Sir Eric, Kt., C.B.E., F.Eng.

Menter, Sir James Woodham, Kt., Ph.D., SC.D., F.R.S.

Menteth, Sir James Wallace Stuart-, Bt. (1838).

Menuhin, Sir Yehudi, O.M., K.B.E.

Menzies, Sir Peter Thomson, Kt.

Messervy, Sir (Roney) Godfrey (Collumbell), Kt.

Meyer, Sir Anthony John Charles, Bt., M.P. (1910).

Meyjes, Sir Richard Anthony, Kt.

Meyrick, Sir David John Charlton, Bt. (1880).

Meyrick, Sir George Christopher Cadafael Tapps-Gervis-, Bt., (1791).

Miakwe, *Hon.* Sir Akepa, K.B.E.

Michael, Sir Peter Colin, Kt., C.B.E.

Micklethwait, Sir Robert Gore, Kt., Q.C.

Middleton, Sir George Humphrey, K.C.M.G.

Middleton, Sir Peter Edward, G.C.B.

Middleton, Sir Stephen Hugh, Bt. (1662).

Miers, Sir (Henry) David Alastair Capel, K.B.E., C.M.G.

Milbank, Sir Anthony Frederick, Bt. (1882).

Milburn, Sir Anthony Rupert, Bt. (1905).

Miles, Sir Peter Tremayne, K.C.V.O.

Miles, Sir William Napier Maurice, Bt. (1859).

Millais, Sir Ralph Regnault, Bt. (1885).

Millar, Sir Oliver Nicholas, G.C.V.O., F.B.A.

Millar, Sir Ronald Graeme, Kt.

Millard, Sir Guy Elwin, K.C.M.G., C.V.O.

Miller, Sir Douglas Sinclair, K.C.V.O., C.B.E.

Miller, Sir Hilary Duppa (Hal), Kt., M.P.

Miller, Sir (Ian) Douglas, Kt.

Miller, Sir John Holmes, Bt. (1705).

Miller, *Lt.-Col.* Sir John Mansel, G.C.V.O., D.S.O., M.C.

Miller, Sir (Joseph) Holmes, Kt., O.B.E.

Miller, Sir (Oswald) Bernard, Kt.

Miller, Sir Peter North, Kt.

Miller, Sir Stephen James Hamilton, K.C.V.O., M.D., F.R.C.S.

Miller of Glenlee, Sir (Frederick William) Macdonald, Bt. (1788).

Millett, *Hon.* Sir Peter Julian, Kt.

Milling, *Air Marshal* Sir Denis Crowley-, K.C.B., C.B.E., D.S.O., D.F.C.

Mills, *Vice-Adm.* Sir Charles Piercy, K.C.B., C.B.E., D.S.C.

Mills, Sir Frank, K.C.V.O., C.M.G.

Mills, Sir John Lewis Ernest Watts, Kt., C.B.E.

Mills, Sir Peter Frederick Leighton, Bt. (1921).

Mills, Sir Peter McLay, Kt.

Milman, Sir Dermot Lionel Kennedy, Bt. (1800).

Milne, Sir John Drummond, Kt.

Milner, Sir (George Edward) Mordaunt, Bt. (1717).

Milnes Coates, Sir Anthony Robert, Bt. (1911).

Milton-Thompson, *Surgeon Vice-Adm.* Sir Godfrey James, K.B.E.

Minhinnick, Sir Gordon Edward George, K.B.E.

Minogue, *Hon.* Sir John Patrick, Kt., Q.C.

Miskin, *Hon.* Sir James William, Kt., Q.C.

Mitchell, *Air Cdre.* Sir (Arthur) Dennis, K.B.E., C.V.O., D.F.C., A.F.C.

Mitchell, Sir David Bower, Kt., M.P.

Mitchell, Sir Derek Jack, K.C.B., C.V.O.

Mitchell, Sir Hamilton, K.B.E.

Mitchell, Sir (Seton) Steuart Crichton, K.B.E., C.B.

Mobbs, Sir (Gerald) Nigel, Kt.

Moberly, Sir John Campbell, K.B.E., C.M.G.

Moberly, Sir Patrick Hamilton, K.C.M.G.

Mocatta, Sir Alan Abraham, Kt., O.B.E.

Moffat, *Lt.-Gen.* Sir (William) Cameron, K.B.E.

Mogg, *Gen.* Sir (Herbert) John, G.C.B., C.B.E., D.S.O.

Moir, Sir Ernest Ian Royds, Bt. (1916).

Moller, *Hon.* Sir Lester Francis, Kt.

†Molony, Sir Thomas Desmond, Bt. (1925).

Monro, Sir Hector Seymour Peter, Kt., M.P.

Monson, Sir (William Bonnar) Leslie, K.C.M.G., C.B.

Montgomery, Sir (Basil Henry) David, Bt. (1801).

Montgomery, Sir (William) Fergus, Kt., M.P.

Mookerjee, Sir Birendra Nath, Kt.

Moollan, Sir Abdool Hamid Adam, Kt.

Moollan, *Hon.* Sir Cassam (Ismael), Kt.

Moon, Sir Peter James Scott, K.C.V.O., C.M.G.

Moon, Sir Peter Wilfred Giles Graham-, Bt. (1855).

†Moon, Sir Roger, Bt. (1887).

Moore, Sir Edward Stanton, Bt., O.B.E. (1923).

Moore, Sir Francis Thomas, Kt.

Moore, Sir Henry Roderick, Kt., C.B.E.

Moore, *Hon.* Sir John Cochrane, Kt.

Moore, *Maj.-Gen.* Sir (John) Jeremy, K.C.B., O.B.E., M.C.

Moore, Sir John Michael, K.C.V.O., C.B., D.S.C.

Moore, *Prof.* Sir Norman Winfrid, Bt. (1919).

Moore, Sir William Roger Clotworthy, Bt., T.D. (1932).

Moores, Sir John, Kt., C.B.E.

Mootham, Sir Orby Howell, Kt.

Mordaunt, Sir Richard Nigel Charles, Bt. (1611).

Moreton, Sir John Oscar, K.C.M.G., K.C.V.O., M.C.

Morgan, *Maj.-Gen.* Sir David John Hughes-, Bt., C.B., C.B.E. (1925).

Morgan, Sir Ernest Dunstan, K.B.E.

Morgan, Sir John Albert Leigh, K.C.M.G.

Morgan-Giles, *Rear-Adm.* Sir Morgan Charles, Kt., D.S.O., O.B.E., G.M.

Morland, *Hon.* Sir Michael, Kt.

Morpeth, Sir Douglas Spottiswoode, Kt., T.D.

Morris, *Air Marshal* Sir Arnold Alec, K.B.E., C.B.

Morris, *Air Marshal* Sir Douglas Griffith, K.C.B., C.B.E., D.S.O., D.F.C.

Morris, Sir Robert Byng, Bt. (1806).

Morrison, *Hon.* Sir Charles Andrew, Kt., M.P.

Morritt, *Hon.* Sir (Robert) Andrew, Kt., C.V.O.

Morrow, Sir Ian Thomas, Kt.

Morse, Sir Christopher Jeremy, K.C.M.G.

Morton, *Adm.* Sir Anthony Storrs, G.B.E., K.C.B.

Morton, Sir Brian, Kt.

Moseley, Sir George Walker, K.C.B.

Moser, *Prof.* Sir Claus Adolf, K.C.B., C.B.E., F.B.A.

†Moss, Sir David John Edwards-, Bt. (1868).

Mostyn, *Gen.* Sir (Joseph) David Frederick, K.C.B., C.B.E.

†Mostyn, Sir William Basil John, Bt. (1670).

Mott, Sir John Harmer, Bt. (1930).

Mott, Sir Nevill Francis, Kt., F.R.S.

Mount, Sir James William Spencer, Kt., C.B.E., B.E.M.

Mount, Sir William Malcolm, Bt. (1921).

Mountain, Sir Denis Mortimer, Bt. (1922).

Mowbray, Sir John, Kt.

Mowbray, Sir John Robert, Bt. (1880).

Moynihan, Sir Noel Henry, Kt.

Muir, Sir John Harling, Bt. (1892).

Muir, Sir Laurence Macdonald, Kt.

Muir Wood, Sir Alan Marshall, Kt., F.R.S.

Muirhead, Sir David Francis, K.C.M.G., C.V.O.

Muldoon, *Rt. Hon.* Sir Robert David, G.C.M.G., C.H.

Mulholland, Sir Michael Henry, Bt. (1945).

Mullens, *Lt,-Gen.* Sir Anthony Richard Guy, K.C.B., O.B.E.

Munn, Sir James, Kt., O.B.E.

Munro, Sir Alasdair Thomas Ian, Bt. (1825).

Munro, Sir Ian Talbot, Bt. (s. 1634).

Munro, *Hon.* Sir Robert Lindsay, Kt., C.B.E.

Munro, Sir Sydney Douglas Gun-, G.C.M.G., M.B.E.

Murley, Sir Reginald Sydney, K.B.E., T.D., F.R.C.S.

Murphy, Sir Leslie Frederick, Kt.

Murray, *Rear-Adm.* Sir Brian Stewart, K.C.M.G.

Murray, *Hon.* Sir Donald Bruce, Kt.

Murray, Sir Donald Frederick, K.C.V.O., C.M.G.

Murray, Sir James, K.C.M.G.

Murray, Sir John Antony Jerningham, Kt., C.B.E.

Murray, Sir Nigel Andrew Digby, Bt. (s. 1628).

Murray, Sir Patrick Ian Keith, Bt. (s. 1673).

Murray, Sir Rowland William Patrick, Bt. (s. 1630).

Murrie, Sir William Stuart, G.C.B., K.B.E.

Mursell, Sir Peter, Kt., M.B.E.

Musgrave, Sir Christopher Patrick Charles, Bt. (1611).

Musgrave, Sir Richard James, Bt. (I. 1782).

Musker, Sir John, Kt.

Musson, *Gen.* Sir Geoffrey Randolph Dixon, G.C.B., C.B.E., D.S.O.

Mustill, *Rt. Hon.* Sir Michael John, Kt.

Myers, Sir Kenneth Ben, Kt., M.B.E.

Myers, Sir Philip Alan, Kt., O.B.E., Q.P.M.

Myers, *Prof.* Sir Rupert Horace, K.B.E.

†Mynors, Sir Richard Baskerville, Bt. (1964).

Mynors, *Prof.* Sir Roger Aubrey Baskerville, Kt., F.B.A.

Nabarro, Sir John David Nunes, Kt., M.D., F.R.C.P.

Nairn, Sir Michael, Bt. (1904).

Nairn, Sir Robert Arnold Spencer-, Bt. (1933).

Nairne, *Rt. Hon.* Sir Patrick Dalmahoy, G.C.B., M.C.

Nalder, *Hon.* Sir Crawford David, Kt.

Nall, Sir Michael Joseph, Bt., R.N. (1954).

Napier, Sir Oliver John, Kt.

Napier, Sir Robin Surtees, Bt. (1867).

Napier, Sir William Archibald, Bt. (s 1627).

Napley, Sir David, Kt.

Narain, Sir Sathi, K.B.E.

Neal, Sir Eric James, Kt.

Neal, Sir Leonard Francis, Kt., C.B.E.

Neale, Sir Alan Derrett, K.C.B., M.B.E.

Neave, Sir Arundell Thomas Clifton, Bt. (1795).

Nedd, *Hon.* Sir Robert Archibald, Kt.

Neill, *Rt. Hon.* Sir Brian Thomas, Kt.

Neill, Sir Francis Patrick, Kt., Q.C.

Neill, *Rt. Hon.* Sir Ivan, Kt.

Nelson, *Maj.-Gen.* Sir (Eustace) John (Blois), K.C.V.O., C.B., D.S.O., O.B.E., M.C.

Nelson, *Air Marshal* Sir (Sidney) Richard (Carlyle), K.C.B., O.B.E., M.D.

Nelson, *Maj.* Sir William Vernon Hope, Bt. (1912).

Nepean, *Lt.-Col.* Sir Evan Yorke, Bt. (1802).

Ness, *Air Marshal* Sir Charles Ernest, K.C.B., C.B.E.

Neville, Sir Richard Lionel John Baines, Bt. (1927).

Newbold, Sir Charles Demorée, K.B.E., C.M.G., Q.C.

Newman, Sir Francis Hugh Cecil, Bt. (1912).

Newman, Sir Geoffrey Robert, Bt. (1836).

Newman, Sir Jack, Kt., C.B.E.

Newman, Sir Kenneth Leslie, Kt., G.B.E.

Newns, Sir (Alfred) Foley (Francis Polden), K.C.M.G., C.V.O.

Newsam, Sir Peter Anthony, Kt.

Newton, Sir (Harry) Michael (Rex), Bt. (1900).

Newton, Sir Kenneth Garnar, Bt., O.B.E., T.D. (1924).

Newton, Sir (Leslie) Gordon, Kt.

Ngata, Sir Henare Kohere, K.B.E.

Niall, Sir Horace Lionel Richard, Kt., C.B.E.

Nicholas, Sir David, Kt., C.B.E.

Nicholas, Sir Herbert Richard, Kt., O.B.E.

Nicholas, Sir John William, K.C.V.O., C.M.G.

Nicholls, *Rt. Hon.* Sir Donald James, Kt.

Nicholls, *Air Marshal* Sir John Moreton, K.C.B., C.B.E., D.F.C., A.F.C.

Nichols, Sir Edward Henry, Kt., T.D.

Nicholson, Sir Bryan Hubert, Kt.

Nicholson, *Hon.* Sir David Eric, Kt.

Nicholson, Sir Godfrey, Bt. (1958).

Nicholson, Sir John Norris, Bt., K.B.E., C.I.E. (1912).

Nicholson, *Hon.* Sir Michael, Kt.

Nicholson, Sir Robin Buchanan, Kt., Ph.D., F.R.S.

Nickerson, Sir Joseph, Kt.

Nickson, Sir David Wigley, K.B.E.

Nicolson, Sir David Lancaster, Kt.

Nield, Sir Basil Edward, Kt., C.B.E., Q.C.

Nield, Sir William Alan, G.C.M.G., K.C.B.

Nightingale, Sir Charles Manners Gamaliel, Bt. (1628).

Nightingale, Sir John Cyprian, Kt., C.B.E., B.E.M., Q.P.M.

Nimmo, *Hon.* Sir John Angus, Kt., C.B.E.

Niven, Sir (Cecil) Rex, Kt., C.M.G., M.C.

Nixon, Sir Edwin Ronald, Kt., C.B.E.

Nixon, *Rev.* Sir Kenneth Michael John Basil, Bt. (1906).

Noad, Sir Kenneth Beeson, Kt., M.D.

Noble, Sir Iain Andrew, Bt., O.B.E. (1923).

Noble, Sir Marc Brunel, Bt. (1902).

Noble, Sir (Thomas Alexander) Fraser, Kt., M.B.E.

Nock, Sir Norman Lindfield, Kt.

Nolan, *Hon.* Sir Michael Patrick, Kt.

Nolan, Sir Sidney Robert, Kt., O.M., C.B.E.

Nombri, Sir Joseph Karl, Kt., I.S.O., B.E.M.

Norman, Sir Arthur Gordon, K.B.E., D.F.C.

Norman, *Vice-Adm.* Sir (Horace) Geoffrey, K.C.V.O., C.B., C.B.E.

Norman, Sir Mark Annesley, Bt. (1915).

Norman, *Prof.* Sir Richard Oswald Chandler, K.B.E., F.R.S.

Norman, Sir Robert Henry, Kt., O.B.E.

Norman, Sir Robert Wentworth, Kt.

Normanton, Sir Tom, Kt., T.D.

Norris, *Vice-Adm.* Sir Charles Fred Wivell, K.B.E., C.B., D.S.O.

Norris, *Air Chief Marshal* Sir Christopher Neil Foxley-, G.C.B., D.S.O., O.B.E.

Norris, Sir Eric George, K.C.M.G.

Norris, *Hon.* Sir John Gerald, Kt., E.D.

North, Sir Thomas Lindsay, Kt.

North, Sir (William) Jonathan (Frederick), Bt. (1920).

Norton, Sir Clifford John, K.C.M.G., C.V.O.

Norwood, Sir Walter Neville, Kt.

Nossal, Sir Gustav Joseph Victor, Kt., C.B.E.

Nosworthy, Sir John Reeve, Kt., C.B.E.

Nott, *Rt. Hon.* Sir John William Frederic, K.C.B.

Nourse, *Rt. Hon.* Sir Martin Charles, Kt.

Nugent, Sir John Edwin Lavallin, Bt. (I. 1795).

Nugent, *Maj.* Sir Peter Walter James, Bt. (1831).

Nugent, Sir Robin George Colborne, Bt. (1806).

Nuttall, Sir Nicholas Keith Lillington, Bt. (1922).

Nutting, *Rt. Hon.* Sir (Harold) Anthony, Bt. (1903).

Oakeley, Sir John Digby Atholl, Bt. (1790).

Oakes, Sir Christopher, Bt. (1939).

Oakshott, *Hon.* Sir Anthony Hendrie, Bt. (1959).

Oates, Sir Thomas, Kt., C.M.G., O.B.E.

Oatley, Sir Charles William, Kt., O.B.E., F.R.S.

Obolensky, *Prof.* Sir Dimitri, Kt.

O'Brien, Sir Frederick William Fitzgerald, Kt.

O'Brien, Sir Richard, Kt., D.S.O., M.C.

O'Brien, Sir Timothy John, Bt. (1849).

O'Brien, *Adm.* Sir William Donough, K.C.B., D.S.C.

†O'Connell, Sir Maurice James Donagh MacCarthy, Bt. (1869).

O'Connor, *Rt. Hon.* Sir Patrick McCarthy, Kt.

O'Dea, Sir Patrick Jerad, K.C.V.O.

Odell, Sir Stanley John, Kt.

Ogden, Sir (Edward) Michael, Kt., Q.C.

Ogilvie, Sir Alec Drummond, Kt.

Ogilvy, *Hon.* Sir Angus James Bruce, K.C.V.O.

Ogilvy, Sir David John Wilfrid, Bt. (s. 1626).

Ognall, *Hon.* Sir Harry Henry, Kt.

O'Halloran, Sir Charles Ernest, Kt.

Ohlson, Sir Brian Eric Christopher, Bt. (1920).

Okeover, *Capt.* Sir Peter Ralph Leopold Walker-, Bt. (1886).

Olewale, *Hon.* Sir Niwia Ebia, Kt.

Oliphant, Sir Mark (Marcus Laurence Elwin), K.B.E., F.R.S.

Oliver, Sir (Frederick) Ernest, Kt., C.B.E., T.D.

O'Loghlen, Sir Colman Michael, Bt. (1838).

Olver, Sir Stephen John Linley, K.B.E., C.M.G.

O'Neil, *Hon.* Sir Desmond Henry, Kt.

Ongley, *Hon.* Sir Joseph Augustine, Kt.

Onslow, Sir John Roger Wilmot, Bt. (1797).

Oppenheim, Sir Alexander, Kt., O.B.E., D.SC., F.R.S.E.

Oppenheim, Sir Duncan Morris, Kt.

Oppenheim, Sir Michael Bernard Grenville, Bt. (1921).

Oppenheimer, Sir Philip Jack, Kt.

Opperman, *Hon.* Sir Hubert Ferdinand, Kt., O.B.E.

Orde, Sir John Alexander Campbell-, Bt. (1790).

O'Regan, *Hon.* Sir John Barry, Kt.

Ormond, Sir John Davies Wilder, Kt., B.E.M.

Ormrod, *Rt. Hon.* Sir Roger Fray Greenwood, Kt.

Orr, *Rt. Hon.* Sir Alan Stewart, Kt., O.B.E.

Orr, Sir David Alexander, Kt., M.C.

Orr, Sir John Henry, Kt., O.B.E., Q.P.M.

Osborn, Sir John Holbrook, Kt.

Osborn, Sir Richard Henry Danvers, Bt. (1662).

Osborne, Sir Peter George, Bt. (I. 1629).

Osifelo, Sir Frederick Aubarua, Kt., M.B.E.

Osman, Sir (Abdool) Raman Mahomed, G.C.M.G., C.B.E.

Osmond, Sir Douglas, Kt., C.B.E.

Osmond, Sir (Stanley) Paul, Kt., C.B.

Oswald, *Adm.* Sir John Julian Robertson, G.C.B.

Otton, Sir Geoffrey John, K.C.B.

Otton, *Hon.* Sir Philip Howard, Kt.

Oulton, Sir Antony Derek Maxwell, G.C.B., Q.C.

Outram, Sir Alan James, Bt. (1858).

Overall, Sir John Wallace, Kt., C.B.E., M.C.

Overton, Sir Hugh Thomas Arnold, K.C.M.G.

Owen, Sir Geoffrey, Kt.

Owen, Sir Hugh Bernard Pilkington, Bt. (1813).

†Owen, Sir Hugo Dudley Cunliffe-, Bt. (1920).

Owen, *Hon.* Sir John Arthur Dalziel, Kt.

Owo, The Olowo of, Kt.

Oxford, Sir Kenneth Gordon, Kt., C.B.E., Q.P.M.

Packard, *Lieut.-Gen.* Sir (Charles) Douglas, K.B.E., C.B., D.S.O.

Padmore, Sir Thomas, G.C.B.

Page, Sir Alexander Warren, Kt., M.B.E.

Page, Sir (Arthur) John, Kt.

Page, Sir Frederick William, Kt., C.B.E.

Page, Sir John Joseph Joffre, Kt., O.B.E.

Paget, Sir John Starr, Bt. (1886).

Paget, Sir Julian Tolver, Bt., C.V.O. (1871).

Pain, *Lt.-Gen.* Sir (Horace) Rollo (Squarey), K.C.B., M.C.

Pain, *Hon.* Sir Peter Richard, Kt.

Palin, *Air Marshal* Sir Roger Hewlett, K.C.B., O.B.E.

Palliser, *Rt. Hon.* Sir (Arthur) Michael, G.C.M.G.

Palmer, Sir Derek James, Kt.

Palmer, Sir (Charles) Mark, Bt. (1886).

Palmer, *Gen.* Sir (Charles) Patrick (Ralph), K.B.E.

Palmer, Sir Geoffrey Christopher John, Bt. (1660).

Palmer, Col. Hon. Sir Gordon William Nottage, K.C.V.O., O.B.E., T.D.

Palmer, Sir John Chance, Kt.

Palmer, Sir John Edward Somerset, Bt. (1791).

Palmer, *Maj.-Gen.* Sir (Joseph) Michael, K.C.V.O.

Panckridge, *Surgeon Vice-Adm.* Sir (William) Robert (Silvester), K.B.E., C.B.

Pao, Sir Yue-Kong, Kt., C.B.E.

Paolozzi, Sir Eduardo Luigi, Kt., C.B.E., R.A.

Pape, *Hon.* Sir George Augustus, Kt.

Pararajasingam, Sir Sangarapillai, Kt.

Parbo, Sir Arvi Hillar, Kt.

Parham, *Adm.* Sir Frederick Robertson, G.B.E., K.C.B., D.S.O.

Parish, Sir David Elmer Woodbine, Kt., C.B.E.

Park, *Hon.* Sir Hugh Eames, Kt.

Parker, Sir (Arthur) Douglas Dodds-, Kt.

Parker, Sir Douglas William Leigh, Kt., O.B.E.

Parker, Sir Karl Theodore, Kt., C.B.E., Ph.D., F.B.A.

Parker, Sir Peter, Kt., L.V.O.

Parker, Sir Richard (William) Hyde, Bt. (1681).

Parker, *Rt. Hon.* Sir Roger Jocelyn, Kt.

Parker, *Vice-Adm.* Sir (Wilfred) John, K.B.E., C.B., D.S.C.

Parker, Sir (William) Alan, Bt. (1844).

Parkes, Sir Alan Sterling, Kt., C.B.E., Ph.D., D.SC., SC.D., F.R.S.

Parkes, Sir Basil Arthur, Kt., O.B.E.

Parkes, Sir Edward Walter, Kt.

Parkinson, Sir Nicholas Fancourt, Kt.

Parry, Sir Ernest Jones-, Kt.

Parry, Sir (Frank) Hugh (Nigel), Kt., C.B.E.

Parry-Evans, *Air Chief Marshal* Sir David, K.C.B., C.B.E.

Parsons, Sir Anthony Derrick, G.C.M.G., M.V.O., M.C.

Parsons, Sir (John) Michael, Kt.

Parsons, Sir Richard Edmund (Clement Fownes), K.C.M.G.

Part, Sir Antony Alexander, Kt., G.C.B., M.B.E.

Pascoe, *Gen.* Sir Robert Alan, K.C.B., M.B.E.

Pasley, Sir John Malcolm Sabine, Bt. (1794).

Paterson, Sir Dennis Craig, Kt.

Paterson, Sir George Mutlow, Kt., O.B.E., Q.C.

Paterson, Sir John Valentine Jardine, Kt.

Paton, Sir (Thomas) Angus (Lyall), Kt., C.M.G., F.R.S.

Paton, *Prof.* Sir William Drummond Macdonald, Kt., C.B.E., D.M., F.R.S., F.R.C.P.

Pattie, *Rt. Hon.* Sir Geoffrey Edwin, Kt., M.P.

Pattinson, *Hon.* Sir Baden, K.B.E.

Paul, Sir John Warburton, G.C.M.G., O.B.E., M.C.

Payne, Sir Norman John, Kt., C.B.E.

Peach, Sir Leonard Harry, Kt.

Peacock, *Prof.* Sir Alan Turner, Kt., D.S.C.

Peacock, Sir Geoffrey Arden, Kt., C.V.O.

Pearce, Sir Austin William, Kt., C.B.E., Ph.D.

Pearce, Sir Eric Herbert, Kt., O.B.E.

Peard, *Rear-Adm.* Sir Kenyon Harry Terrell, K.B.E.

Pearman, *Hon.* Sir James Eugene, Kt., C.B.E.

Pearson, Sir Francis Fenwick, Bt., M.B.E. (1964).

Pearson, Sir (James) Denning, Kt.

Pearson, *Gen.* Sir Thomas Cecil Hook, K.C.B., C.B.E., D.S.O.

Peart, *Prof.* Sir William Stanley, Kt., M.D., F.R.S.

Pease, Sir (Alfred) Vincent, Bt. (1882).

Pease, Sir Richard Thorn, Bt. (1920).

Peat, Sir Gerrard Charles, K.C.V.O.

Peat, Sir Henry, K.C.V.O., D.F.C.

Peck, Sir Edward Heywood, G.C.M.G.

Peck, Sir John Howard, K.C.M.G.

Pedder, *Vice-Adm.* Sir Arthur Reid, K.B.E., C.B.

Pedder, *Air Marshal* Sir Ian Maurice, K.C.B., O.B.E., D.F.C.

Pedler, Sir Frederick Johnson, Kt.

Peek, Sir Francis Henry Grenville, Bt. (1874).

Peek, *Vice-Adm.* Sir Richard Innes, K.B.E., C.B., D.S.C.

Peel, Sir John Harold, K.C.V.O.

Peel, Sir (William) John, Kt.

Peierls, Sir Rudolf Ernst, Kt., C.B.E., D.SC., D.Phil., F.R.S.

Peirse, Sir Henry Grant de la Poer Beresford-, Bt. (1814).

Peirse, *Air Vice-Marshal* Sir Richard Charles Fairfax, K.C.V.O., C.B.

Pelly, Sir John Alwyne, Bt. (1840).

Pemberton, Sir Francis Wingate William, Kt., C.B.E.

Penn, *Lt.-Col.* Sir Eric Charles William Mackenzie, G.C.V.O., O.B.E., M.C.

Percival, Sir Anthony Edward, Kt., C.B.

Percival, *Rt. Hon.* Sir (Walter) Ian, Kt., Q.C.

Pereira, Sir (Herbert) Charles, Kt., D.SC., F.R.S.

Perkins, *Surgeon Vice-Adm.* Sir Derek Duncombe Steele-, K.C.B., K.C.V.O.

Perring, Sir Ralph Edgar, Bt. (1963).

Perris, Sir David (Arthur), Kt., M.B.E.

Perry, Sir David Howard, K.C.B.

Perry, Sir (David) Norman, Kt., M.B.E.

Pestell, Sir John Richard, K.C.V.O.

Peterkin, Sir Neville, Kt.

Petersen, Sir Jeffrey Charles, K.C.M.G.

Petit, Sir Dinshaw Manockjee, Bt. (1890).

Peto, Sir Henry George Morton, Bt. (1855).

Peto, Sir Michael Henry Basil, Bt. (1927).

Petrie, Sir Peter Charles, Bt., C.M.G. (1918).

Pettigrew, Sir Russell Hilton, Kt.

Pettit, Sir Daniel Eric Arthur, Kt.

Philips, *Prof.* Sir Cyril Henry, Kt.

Philipson, Sir Robert James, (Sir Robin Philipson), Kt., R.A.

Phillips, *Prof.* Sir David Chilton, Kt., K.B.E., Ph.D., F.R.S.

Phillips, Sir Fred Albert, Kt., C.V.O.

Phillips, Sir Henry Ellis Isidore, Kt., C.M.G., M.B.E.

Phillips, Sir Horace, K.C.M.G.

Phillips, *Hon.* Sir Nicholas Addison, Kt.

Phillips, Sir Robin Francis, Bt. (1912).

Phipps, *Vice-Adm.* Sir Peter, K.B.E., D.S.C., V.R.D.

Pickard, Sir Cyril Stanley, K.C.M.G.

Pickering, Sir Edward Davies, Kt.

Pickthorn, Sir Charles William Richards, Bt. (1959).

Pidgeon, Sir John Allan Stewart, Kt.

Piers, Sir Charles Robert Fitzmaurice, Bt. (I. 1661).

Pigot, Sir George Hugh, Bt. (1764).

Pigott, Sir Berkeley Henry Sebastian, Bt. (1808).

Pike, Sir Philip Ernest Housden, Kt., Q.C.

Pike, *Lt.-Gen.* Sir William Gregory Huddleston, K.C.B., C.B.E., D.S.O.

Pilcher, Sir (Charlie) Dennis, Kt., C.B.E.

Pilcher, Sir John Arthur, G.C.M.G.

Pilditch, Sir Richard Edward, Bt. (1929).

Pile, Sir Frederick Devereux, Bt. M.C. (1900).

Pile, Sir William Dennis, G.C.B., M.B.E.

Pilkington, Sir Lionel Alexander Bethune, (Sir Alastair), Kt., F.R.S.

Pilkington, Sir Thomas Henry Milborne-Swinnerton-, Bt. (s. 1635).

Pill, *Hon.* Sir Malcolm Thomas, Kt.

Pillar, *Adm.* Sir William Thomas, G.B.E, K.C.B.

Pindling, *Rt. Hon.* Sir Lynden Oscar, K.C.M.G.

Pinsent, Sir Christopher Roy, Bt. (1938).

Piper, Sir David Towry, Kt., C.B.E.

Pippard, *Prof.* Sir (Alfred) Brian, Kt., F.R.S.

Pirbhai, Sir Eboo, Kt., O.B.E.

Pirie, *Gp. Capt.* Sir Gordon Hamish, Kt., C.V.O., C.B.E.

Pitblado, Sir David Bruce, K.C.B., C.V.O.

Pitoi, Sir Sere, Kt., C.B.E.

Pitt, Sir Harry Raymond, Kt., Ph.D., F.R.S.

Pitts, Sir Cyril Alfred, Kt.

Pixley, Sir Neville Drake, Kt., M.B.E., V.R.D.

Pizey, *Adm.* Sir (Charles Thomas) Mark, G.B.E., C.B., D.S.O.

Plaister, Sir Sydney, Kt., C.B.E.

Plastow, Sir David Arnold Stuart, Kt.

†Platt, Sir (Frank) Lindsey, Bt. (1958).

Platt, *Prof.* Hon. Sir Peter, Bt. (1959).

Playfair, Sir Edward Wilder, K.C.B.

Pliatzky, Sir Leo, K.C.B.

Plimmer, Sir Clifford Ulric, K.B.E.

Plowman, Sir (John) Anthony, Kt.

Plowman, *Hon.* Sir John Robin, Kt., C.B.E.

Plumb, *Prof.* Sir John Harold, Kt.

Pochin, Sir Edward Eric, Kt., C.B.E., M.D., F.R.C.P.

Poett, *Gen.* Sir (Joseph Howard) Nigel, K.C.B., D.S.O.

Pole, *Col.* Sir John Gawen Carew, Bt., D.S.O., T.D. (1628).

Pole, Sir Peter Van Notten, Bt. (1791).

Pollard, Sir (Charles) Herbert, Kt., C.B.E.

Pollen, Sir John Michael Hungerford, Bt. (1795).

Pollock, Sir George, Kt., Q.C.

Pollock, Sir George Frederick, Bt. (1866).

Pollock, Sir Giles Hampden Montagu-, Bt. (1872).

Pollock, *Admiral of the Fleet* Sir Michael Patrick, G.C.B., M.V.O., D.S.C.

Pollock, Sir William Horace Montagu-, K.C.M.G.

Ponsonby, Sir Ashley Charles Gibbs, Bt., M.C. (1956).

Pontin, Sir Frederick William, Kt.

Poore, Sir Herbert Edward, Bt. (1795).

Pope, *Vice-Adm.* Sir (John) Ernle, K.C.B.

Pope, Sir Joseph Albert, Kt., D.SC., Ph.D.

Popper, *Prof.* Sir Karl Raimund, Kt., C.H., Ph.D., F.R.S.

Popplewell, *Hon.* Sir Oliver Bury, Kt.

Portal, Sir Jonathan Francis, Bt. (1901).

Porter, *Prof.* Sir George, Kt., F.R.S., Ph.D., SC.D.

Porter, Sir John Simon Horsbrugh-, Bt. (1902).

Porter, Sir Leslie, Kt.

Porter, *Air Marshal* Sir (Melvin) Kenneth (Drowley), K.C.B., C.B.E.

Porter, *Hon.* Sir Murray Victor, Kt.

Porter, *Rt. Hon.* Sir Robert Wilson, Kt., Q.C.

Posnett, Sir Richard Neil, K.B.E., C.M.G.

Potter, Sir (Joseph) Raymond (Lynden), Kt.

Potter, *Hon.* Sir Mark Howard, Kt.

Potter, *Maj.-Gen.* Sir (Wilfrid) John, K.B.E., C.B.

Potter, Sir (William) Ian, Kt.

Potts, *Hon.* Sir Francis Humphrey, Kt.

Pound, Sir John David, Bt. (1905).

Pountain, Sir Eric John, Kt.

Powell, Sir (Arnold Joseph) Philip, Kt., C.H., O.B.E., R.A., F.R.I.B.A.

Powell, Sir Nicholas Folliott Douglas, Bt. (1897).

Powell, Sir Richard Royle, G.C.B., K.B.E., C.M.G.

Power, Sir Alastair John Cecil, Bt. (1924).

Powles, Sir Guy Richardson, K.B.E., C.M.G., E.D.

Poynton, Sir (Arthur) Hilton, G.C.M.G.

Prain, Sir Ronald Lindsay, Kt., O.B.E.

Prendergast, Sir John Vincent, K.B.E., C.M.G., G.M.

Prentice, *Rt. Hon.* Sir Reginald Ernest, Kt.

Prentice, *Hon.* Sir William Thomas, Kt., M.B.E.

Prescott, Sir Mark, Bt. (1938).

Preston, Sir Kenneth Huson, Kt.

Preston, Sir Peter Sansome, K.C.B.

Preston, Sir Ronald Douglas Hildebrand, Bt. (1815).

Prevost, Sir Christopher Gerald, Bt. (1805).

Price, Sir Charles Keith Napier Rugge-, Bt. (1804).

Price, Sir David Ernest Campbell, Kt., M.P.

Price, Sir Francis Caradoc Rose, Bt. (1815).

Price, Sir Frank Leslie, Kt.

Price, Sir (James) Robert, K.B.E.

Price, Sir Leslie Victor, Kt., O.B.E.

Price, Sir Norman Charles, K.C.B.

Price, Sir Robert John Green-, Bt. (1874).

Prichard, Sir Montague Illtyd, Kt., C.B.E., M.C.

Prickett, *Air Chief Marshal* Sir Thomas Other, K.C.B., D.S.O., D.F.C.

Prideaux, Sir Humphrey Povah Treverbian, Kt., O.B.E.

Prideaux, Sir John Francis, Kt., O.B.E.

Primrose, Sir Alasdair Neil, Bt. (1903).

Pringle, *Air Marshal* Sir Charles Norman Seton, K.B.E.

Pringle, *Lt.-Gen.* Sir Steuart (Robert), Bt., K.C.B., R.M. (s. 1683).

Pritchard, Sir Asa Hubert, Kt.

Pritchard, Sir John Michael, Kt., C.B.E.

Pritchard, Sir Neil, K.C.M.G.

Pritchett, Sir Victor Sawdon, Kt., C.B.E.

Proby, Sir Peter, Bt. (1952).

Proctor, Sir Roderick Consett, Kt., M.B.E.

Proud, Sir John Seymour, Kt.

Pryke, Sir David Dudley, Bt. (1926).

Pugh, Sir Idwal Vaughan, K.C.B.

Pugsley, *Prof.* Sir Alfred Grenvile, Kt., O.B.E., D.SC., F.R.S.

Pullen, Sir William Reginald James, K.C.V.O.

Pullinger, Sir (Francis) Alan, Kt., C.B.E.

Pumphrey, Sir (John) Laurence, K.C.M.G.

Purchas, *Rt. Hon.* Sir Francis Brooks, Kt.

Quayle, Sir (John) Anthony, Kt., C.B.E.

Quicke, Sir John Godolphin, Kt., C.B.E.

Quilliam, *Hon.* Sir (James) Peter, Kt.

Quilter, Sir Anthony Raymond Leopold Cuthbert, Bt. (1897).

Quinlan, Sir Michael Edward, K.C.B.

Quirk, *Prof.* Sir (Charles) Randolph, C.B.E., F.B.A.

Rabukawaqa, Sir Josua Rasilau, K.B.E., M.V.O.

Raby, Sir Victor Harry, K.B.E., C.B., M.C.

Radcliffe, Sir Sebastian Everard, Bt. (1813).

Radclyffe, Sir Charles Edward Mott-, Kt.

Radford, Sir Ronald Walter, K.C.B., M.B.E.

Radzinowicz, *Prof.* Sir Leon, Kt., Ll.D.

Rae, *Hon.* Sir Wallace Alexander Ramsay, Kt.

Raeburn, Sir Michael Edward Norman, Bt. (1923).

Raeburn, *Maj.-Gen.* Sir (William) Digby (Manifold), K.C.V.O., C.B., D.S.O., M.B.E.

Raffray, Sir Piat Joseph Raymond Andre, Kt.

Raikes, *Vice-Adm.* Sir Iwan Geoffrey, K.C.B., C.B.E., D.S.C.

Ralli, Sir Godfrey Victor, Bt., T.D. (1912).

Ramphal, Sir Shridath Surendranath, Kt., C.M.G.

Ramphul, Sir Baalkhristna, Kt.

Rampton, Sir Jack Leslie, K.C.B.

Ramsay, Sir Alexander William Burnett, Bt. (1806).

Ramsay, Sir Thomas Meek, Kt., C.M.G.

Ramsbotham, *Lt.-Gen.* Sir David John, K.C.B., C.B.E.

Ramsbotham, *Hon.* Sir Peter Edward, G.C.M.G., G.C.V.O.

Ramsden, Sir Geoffrey Charles Frescheville, Kt., C.I.E.

Ramsden, Sir John Charles Josslyn, Bt. (1689).

Ramsey, Sir Alfred Ernest, Kt.

Randle, *Prof.* Sir Philip John, Kt.

Ranger, Sir Douglas, Kt., F.R.C.S.

Rank, Sir Benjamin Keith, Kt., C.M.G.

†Rankin, Sir Ian Niall, Bt. (1898).

Raper, *Vice-Adm.* Sir (Robert) George, K.C.B.

Rasch, *Maj.* Sir Richard Guy Carne, Bt. (1903).

Rashleigh, Sir Richard Harry, Bt. (1831).

Rattee, *Hon.* Sir Donald Keith, Kt.

Rault, Sir Louis Joseph Maurice, Kt.

Rawlins, *Surgeon Vice-Adm.* Sir John Stuart Pepys, K.B.E.

Rawlinson, Sir Anthony Henry John, Bt. (1891).

Rayne, Sir Edward, Kt., C.V.O.

Read, *Air Marshal* Sir Charles Frederick, K.B.E., C.B., D.F.C., A.F.C.

Read, *Gen.* Sir (John) Antony (Jervis), G.C.B., C.B.E., D.S.O., M.C.

Read, Sir John Emms, Kt.

Reade, Sir Clyde Nixon, Bt. (1661).

Reay, *Lt.-Gen.* Sir (Hubert) Alan John, K.B.E.

Redgrave, *Maj.-Gen.* Sir Roy Michael Frederick, K.B.E., M.C.

Redmayne, Sir Nicholas, Bt. (1964).

Redmond, Sir James, Kt.

Redwood, Sir Peter Boverton, Bt. (1911).

Reece, Sir Charles Hugh, Kt.

Reece, Sir James Gordon, Kt.

Reed, *Hon.* Sir Nigel Vernon, Kt., C.B.E.

Rees, Sir (Charles William) Stanley, Kt., T.D.

Reeve, *Hon.* Sir (Charles) Trevor, Kt.

Reeves, *Most Rev.* Paul Alfred, G.C.M.G., G.C.V.O.

Reffell, *Adm.* Sir Derek Roy, K.C.B.

Refshauge, *Maj-Gen.* Sir William Dudley, K.B.E., C.B.E.

Reid, Sir Alexander James, Bt. (1897).

Reid, *Hon.* Sir George Oswald, Kt., Q.C.

Reid, *Air Vice-Marshal* Sir (George) Ranald Macfarlane, K.C.B., D.S.O., M.C.

Reid, Sir (Harold) Martin (Smith), K.B.E., C.M.G.

Reid, Sir Hugh, Bt. (1922).

Reid, Sir John James Andrew, K.C.M.G., C.B., T.D.

Reid, Sir Norman Robert, Kt.

Reid, Sir Robert Basil, Kt., C.B.E.

Reilly, Sir (D'Arcy) Patrick, G.C.M.G., O.B.E.

Reilly, *Lt.-Gen.* Sir Jeremy Calcott, K.C.B., D.S.O.

Reiss, Sir John Anthony Ewart, Kt., B.E.M.

Renals, Sir Stanley, Bt. (1895).

Rendell, Sir William, Kt.

Rennie, Sir John Shaw, G.C.M.G., O.B.E.

Renouf, Sir Clement William Bailey, Kt.

Renouf, Sir Francis Henry, Kt.

Renshaw, Sir (Charles) Maurice Bine, Bt. (1903).

Renwick, Sir Richard Eustace, Bt. (1921).

Renwick, Sir Robin William, K.C.M.G.

Reporter, Sir Shapoor Ardeshirji, K.B.E.

Rex, *Hon.* Sir Robert Richmond, K.B.E., C.M.G.

Reynolds, Sir David James, Bt. (1923).

Reynolds, Sir Peter William John, Kt., C.B.E.

Rhodes, Sir Basil Edward, Kt., C.B.E., T.D.

Rhodes, Sir John Christopher Douglas, Bt. (1919).

Rhodes, Sir Peregrine Alexander, K.C.M.G.

Richards, *Hon.* Sir Edward Trenton, Kt., C.B.E.

Richards, Sir (Francis) Brooks, K.C.M.G., D.S.C.

Richards, Sir James Maude, Kt., C.B.E.

Richards, *Lt.-Gen.* Sir John Charles Chisholm, K.C.B., R.M.

Richards, Sir Rex Edward, Kt., D.SC., F.R.S.

Richardson, Sir Anthony Lewis, Bt. (1924).

Richardson, *Gen.* Sir Charles Leslie, G.C.B., C.B.E., D.S.O.

Richardson, *Air Marshal* Sir (David) William, K.B.E.

Richardson, Sir Egerton Rudolf, Kt., C.M.G.

Richardson, Sir (Horace) Frank, Kt.

Richardson, *Rt. Hon.* Sir Ivor Lloyd Morgan, Kt.

Richardson, Sir (John) Eric, Kt., C.B.E.

Richardson, Sir (Lionel) Earl George, Kt.

Richardson, *Lt.-Gen.* Sir Robert Francis, K.C.B., C.V.O., C.B.E.

Richardson, Sir Simon Alaisdair Stewart-, Bt. (s. 1630).

Riches, Sir Derek Martin Hurry, K.C.M.G.

Riches, *Gen.* Sir Ian Hurry, K.C.B., D.S.O.

Richmond, Sir Alan James, Kt.

Richmond, *Rt. Hon.* Sir Clifford Parris, K.B.E.

Richmond, Sir John Christopher Blake, K.C.M.G.

Richmond, Sir John Frederick, Bt. (1929).

Richmond, *Prof.* Sir Mark Henry, Kt., F.R.S.

Rickett, Sir Denis Hubert Fletcher, K.C.M.G., C.B.

Ricketts, Sir Robert Cornwallis Gerald St. Leger, Bt. (1828).

Ricks, Sir John Plowman, Kt.

Riddell, Sir John Charles Buchanan, Bt. (s. 1628).

Ridley, Sir Adam (Nicholas), Kt.

Ridley, Sir Sidney, Kt.

Ridsdale, Sir Julian Errington, Kt., C.B.E., M.P.

Rigby, *Lt.-Col.* Sir (Hugh) John (Macbeth), Bt. (1929).

Riley, Sir Ralph, Kt., F.R.S.

Ring, Sir Lindsay Roberts, G.B.E.

Ringadoo, *Hon.* Sir Veerasamy, G.C.M.G.

Ripley, Sir Hugh, Bt. (1880).

Risk, Sir Thomas Neilson, Kt.

Risson, *Maj.-Gen.* Sir Robert Joseph Henry, Kt., C.B., C.B.E., D.S.O., E.D.

Ritchie, Sir James Edward Thomson, Bt., T.D. (1918).

Rix, Sir Brian Norman Roger, Kt., C.B.E.

Rix, Sir John, Kt., M.B.E.

Roberts, Sir Bryan Clieve, K.C.M.G., Q.C.

Roberts, *Hon.* Sir Denys Tudor Emil, K.B.E., Q.C.

Roberts, Sir (Edward Fergus) Sidney, Kt., C.B.E.

Roberts, Sir Frank Kenyon, G.C.M.G., G.C.V.O.

Roberts, Sir Geoffrey Newland, Kt., C.B.E., A.F.C.

Roberts, *Brig.* Sir Geoffrey Paul Hardy-, K.C.V.O., C.B., C.B.E.

Roberts, Sir Gilbert Howland Rookehurst, Bt. (1809).

Roberts, Sir Gordon James, Kt., C.B.E.

Roberts, Sir Samuel, Bt. (1919).

Roberts, Sir Stephen James Leake, Kt.

Roberts, Sir William James Denby, Bt. (1909).

Robertson, *Prof.* Sir Alexander, Kt., C.B.E.

Robertson, Sir James Anderson, Kt., C.B.E.

Robertson, *Prof.* Sir Rutherford Ness, Kt., C.M.G.

Robins, Sir Ralph Harry, Kt.

Robinson, Sir Albert Edward Phineas, Kt.

Robinson, *Prof.* Sir (Edward) Austin (Gossage), Kt., C.M.G., O.B.E., F.B.A.

Robinson, Sir John Beverley, Bt. (1854).

Robinson, Sir John James Michael Laud, Bt. (1660).

Robinson, *Rt. Hon.* Sir Kenneth, Kt.

Robinson, Sir Niall Bryan Lynch-, Bt., D.S.C. (1920).

Robinson, Sir Wilfred Henry Frederick, Bt. (1908).

Robotham, *Hon.* Sir Lascelles Lister, Kt.

Robson, *Prof.* Sir James Gordon, Kt., C.B.E.

Robson, Sir Thomas Buston, Kt., M.B.E.

Robson, *Vice-Adm.* Sir (William) Geoffrey (Arthur), K.B.E., C.B., D.S.O., D.S.C.

Roch, *Hon.* Sir John Ormond, Kt.

Roche, Sir David O'Grady, Bt. (1838).

Rodger, Sir William Glendinning, Kt., O.B.E.

Rodgers, Sir John Charles, Bt. (1964).

Rodrigues, Sir Alberto Maria, Kt., C.B.E., E.D.

Roe, *Air Chief Marshal* Sir Rex David, G.C.B., A.F.C.

Rogers, Sir Frank Jarvis, Kt.

Rogers, *Air Chief Marshal* Sir John Robson, K.C.B., C.B.E.

Rogers, Sir Philip, G.C.B., C.M.G.

Rogers, Sir Philip James, Kt., C.B.E.

Roll, *Rev.* Sir James William Cecil, Bt. (1921).

Rooke, Sir Denis Eric, Kt., C.B.E.

Roper, *Hon.* Sir Clinton Marcus, Kt.

Ropner, Sir John Bruce Woollacott, Bt. (1952).

Ropner, Sir Robert Douglas, Bt. (1904).

Roscoe, Sir Robert Bell, K.B.E.

Rose, Sir Alec Richard, Kt.

Rose, *Hon.* Sir Christopher Dudley Roger, Kt.

Rose, Sir Clive Martin, G.C.M.G.

Rose, Sir David Lancaster, Bt. (1874).

Rose, Sir Julian Day, Bt. (1872 and 1909).

Rosier, *Air Chief Marshal* Sir Frederick Ernest, G.C.B., C.B.E., D.S.O.

Roskill, Sir Ashton Wentworth, Kt., Q.C.

Ross, Sir Alexander, Kt.

Ross, Sir Archibald David Manisty, K.C.M.G.

Ross, Sir (James) Keith, Bt., R.D., F.R.C.S. (1960).

Ross, Sir Lewis Nathan, Kt., C.M.G.

Rosser, Sir Melvyn Wynne, Kt.

Rossi, Sir Hugh Alexis Louis, Kt., M.P.

Rostron, Sir Frank, Kt., M.B.E.

Roth, *Prof.* Sir Martin, Kt., M.D., F.R.C.P.

Rothenstein, Sir John Knewstub Maurice, Kt., C.B.E., Ph.D.

Rothnie, Sir Alan Keir, K.C.V.O., C.M.G.

Rothschild, Sir Evelyn Robert Adrian de, Kt.

Rougier, *Hon.* Sir Richard George, Kt.

Rous, *Hon.* Sir Anthony Gerald Roderick, K.C.M.G., O.B.E.

Row, *Hon.* Sir John Alfred, Kt.

Row, *Cdr.*, Sir Philip John, K.C.V.O., O.B.E., R.N.

Rowe, Sir Henry Peter, K.C.B., Q.C.

Rowe-Ham, Sir David Kenneth, G.B.E.

Rowell, Sir John Joseph, Kt., C.B.E.

Rowland, *Air Marshal* Sir James Anthony, K.B.E., D.F.C., A.F.C.

Rowlands, *Air Marshal* Sir John Samuel, K.B.E., G.C.

Rowley, Sir Charles Robert, Bt. (1836).

Rowley, Sir Joshua Francis, Bt. (1786).

Rowling, *Rt. Hon.* Sir Wallace Edward, K.C.M.G.

Rowntree, Sir Norman Andrew Forster, Kt.

Roxburgh, *Vice-Adm.* Sir John Charles Young, K.C.B., C.B.E., D.S.O., D.S.C.

Royden, Sir Christopher John, Bt. (1905).

Rucker, Sir Arthur Nevil, K.C.M.G., C.B., C.B.E.

Rumbold, Sir Henry John Sebastian, Bt. (1779).

Rumbold, Sir (Horace) Algernon (Fraser), K.C.M.G., C.I.E.

Rumbold, Sir Jack Seddon, Kt.

Runciman, *Hon.* Sir Steven (James Cochran Stevenson), Kt., C.H.

Rusby, *Vice-Adm.* Sir Cameron, K.C.B., M.V.O.

Russell, Sir Archibald Edward, Kt., C.B.E., F.R.S.

Russell, Sir Charles Ian, Bt. (1916).

Russell, Sir Evelyn Charles Sackville, Kt.

Russell, Sir George Michael, Bt. (1812).

Russell, Sir (Robert) Mark, K.C.M.G.

Russell, Sir Spencer Thomas, Kt.

Russell, *Rt. Hon.* Sir (Thomas) Patrick, Kt.

Russo, Sir Peter George, Kt., C.B.E.

Rutter, Sir Frank William Eden, K.B.E.

Ryan, Sir Derek Gerald, Bt. (1919).

Rycroft, Sir Richard Newton, Bt. (1784).

Ryrie, Sir William Sinclair, K.C.B.

Sainsbury, Sir Robert James, Kt.

St. Aubyn, Sir (John) Arscott Molesworth-, Bt. (1689).

St. George, Sir Denis Howard, Bt. (I. 1766).

St. Johnston, Sir Kerry, Kt.

Sainty, Sir John Christopher, K.C.B.

Sakzewski, Sir Albert, Kt.

Salt, Sir Anthony Houlton, Bt. (1869).

Salt, Sir (Thomas) Michael John, Bt. (1899).

Samuel, Sir Jon Michael Glen, Bt. (1898).

Samuelson, Sir (Bernard) Michael (Francis), Bt. (1884).

Sandberg, Sir Michael Graham Ruddock, Kt., C.B.E.

Sanders, Sir Robert Tait, K.B.E., C.M.G.

Sanderson, Sir (Frank Philip) Bryan, Bt. (1920).

Sandilands, Sir Francis Edwin Prescott, Kt., C.B.E.

Sarei, Sir Alexis Holyweek, Kt., C.B.E.

Sarell, Sir Roderick Francis Gisbert, K.C.M.G., K.C.V.O.

Sargant, Sir (Henry) Edmund, Kt.

Saunders, *Hon.* Sir John Anthony Holt, Kt., C.B.E., D.S.O., M.C.

Saunders, Sir Owen Alfred, Kt., D.S.C., F.R.S.

Saunders, Sir Peter, Kt.

Sauzier, Sir (André) Guy, Kt., C.B.E., E.D.

Savage, Sir Ernest Walter, Kt.

Saville, *Hon.* Sir Mark Oliver, Kt.

Savory, Sir Reginald Charles Frank, Kt., C.B.E.

Say, *Rt. Rev.* Richard David, K.C.V.O.

Schiemann, *Hon.* Sir Konrad Hermann Theodor, Kt.

Scholey, Sir David Gerald, Kt., C.B.E.

Scholey, Sir Robert, Kt., C.B.E.

Scholtens, Sir James Henry, K.C.V.O.

Schubert, Sir Sydney, Kt.

Schultz, Sir (Joseph) Leopold, Kt., O.B.E.

Schuster, Sir (Felix) James Moncrieff, Bt., O.B.E. (1906).

Scipio, Sir Hudson Rupert, Kt.

Scoon, Sir Paul, G.C.M.G., G.C.V.O., O.B.E.

Scoones, *Maj.-Gen.* Sir Reginald Laurence, K.B.E., C.B., D.S.O.

Scopes, Sir Leonard Arthur, K.C.V.O., C.M.G., O.B.E.

Scott, Sir Anthony Percy, Bt. (1913).

Scott, Sir (Charles) Hilary, Kt.

Scott, Sir (Charles) Peter, K.B.E., C.M.G.

Scott, Sir David Aubrey, G.C.M.G.

Scott, Sir George Edward, Kt., C.B.E.

Scott, Sir Ian Dixon, K.C.M.G., K.C.V.O., C.I.E.

Scott, Sir James Walter, Bt. (1962).

Scott, Sir Michael, K.C.V.O., C.M.G.

Scott, Sir Michael Fergus Maxwell, Bt. (1642).

Scott, Sir Oliver Christopher Anderson, Bt. (1909).

Scott, *Prof.* Sir Philip John, K.B.E.

Scott, *Hon.* Sir Richard Rashleigh Folliott, Kt.

Scott, Sir Terence Charles Stuart Morrison-, Kt., D.S.C., D.SC.

Scott, Sir Walter, Bt. (1907).

Scott, *Rear-Adm.* Sir (William) David (Stewart), K.B.E., C.B.

Scowen, Sir Eric Frank, Kt., M.D., D.SC., LL.D., F.R.C.P., F.R.C.S.

Scrivenor, Sir Thomas Vaisey, Kt., C.M.G.

Seale, Sir John Henry, Bt. (1838).

Seaman, Sir Keith Douglas, K.C.V.O., O.B.E.

Sebright, Sir Peter Giles Vivian, Bt. (1626).

Seccombe, Sir (William) Vernon Stephen, Kt.

Secombe, Sir Harry Donald, Kt., C.B.E.

Seconde, Sir Reginald Louis, K.C.M.G., C.V.O.

Seely, Sir Nigel Edward, Bt. (1896).

Seeto, Sir Ling James, Kt., M.B.E.

Seeyave, Sir Rene Sow Choung, Kt., C.B.E.

Selby, Sir Kenneth, Kt.

Seligman, Sir Peter Wendel, Kt., C.B.E.

Sells, Sir David Perronet, Kt.

Senior, Sir Edward Walters, Kt., C.M.G.

Sergeant, Sir Patrick, Kt.

Series, Sir (Joseph Michel) Emile, Kt., C.B.E.

Serpell, Sir David Radford, K.C.B., C.M.G., O.B.E.

Seton, Sir Iain Bruce, Bt. (s. 1663).

Seton, Sir Robert James, Bt. (s. 1683).

Severne, *Air Vice-Marshal* Sir John de Milt, K.C.V.O., O.B.E., A.F.C.

Sewell, Sir (John) Allan, Kt., I.S.O.

Seymour, *Cdr.* Sir Michael Culme-, Bt., R.N. (1809).

Shakerley, Sir Geoffrey Adam, Bt. (1838).

Shakespeare, Sir William Geoffrey, Bt. (1942).

Shapland, Sir William Arthur, Kt.

Sharp, Sir Adrian, Bt. (1922).

Sharp, Sir George, Kt., O.B.E.

Sharp, Sir Kenneth Johnston, Kt., T.D.

Sharp, Sir Milton Reginald, Bt. (1920).

Sharp, Sir Richard Lyall, K.C.V.O., C.B.

Sharp, Sir (William Harold) Angus, K.B.E., Q.P.M.

Sharpe, Sir Frank Victor, Kt., C.M.G., O.B.E., E.D.

Sharpe, *Hon.* Sir John Henry, Kt., C.B.E.

Sharpe, Sir Reginald Taaffe, Kt., Q.C.

Shattock, Sir Gordon, Kt.

Shaw, Sir Brian Piers, Kt.

Shaw, Sir (Charles) Barry, Kt., C.B., Q.C.

Shaw, Sir (John) Giles (Dunkerley), Kt., M.P.

Shaw, Sir John Michael Robert Best-, Bt. (1665).

Shaw, Sir Michael Norman, Kt., M.P.

Shaw, Sir Robert, Bt. (1821).

Shaw, Sir Roy, Kt.

Shaw, Sir Run Run, Kt., C.B.E.

Sheen, *Hon.* Sir Barry Cross, Kt.

Sheffield, Sir Reginald Adrian Berkeley, Bt. (1755).

Shehadie, Sir Nicholas Michael, Kt., O.B.E.

Shelbourne, Sir Philip, Kt.

Sheldon, *Hon.* Sir (John) Gervase (Kensington), Kt.

Shelley, Sir John Richard, Bt. (1611).

Shelton, Sir William Jeremy Masefield, Kt., M.P.

Shepheard, Sir Peter Faulkner, Kt., C.B.E.

Shepheard, Sir Victor George, K.C.B.

Shepherd, Sir Peter Malcolm, Kt., C.B.E.

Shepperd, Sir Alfred Joseph, Kt.

Sherlock, Sir Philip Manderson, K.B.E.

Sherman, Sir Alfred, Kt.

Sherman, Sir Louis, Kt., O.B.E.

Shields, Sir Neil Stanley, Kt., M.C.

Shiffner, Sir Henry David, Bt. (1818).

Shillington, Sir (Robert Edward) Graham, Kt., C.B.E.

Shock, Sir Maurice, Kt.

Sholl, *Hon.* Sir Reginald Richard, Kt.

Shone, Sir Robert Minshull, Kt., C.B.E.

Short, *Brig.* Sir Noel Edward Vivian, Kt., M.B.E., M.C.

Shuckburgh, Sir (Charles Arthur) Evelyn, G.C.M.G., C.B.

Shuckburgh, Sir Rupert Charles Gerald, Bt. (1660).

Sich, Sir Rupert Leigh, Kt., C.B.

Siddall, Sir Norman, Kt., C.B.E.

Sidey, *Air Marshal* Sir Ernest Shaw, K.B.E., C.B., M.D.

Sie, Sir Banja Tejan-, G.C.M.G.

Simeon, Sir John Edmund Barrington, Bt. (1815).

Simmons, *Air Marshal* Sir Michael George, K.C.B., A.F.C.

Simonet, Sir Louis Marcel Pierre, Kt., C.B.E.

Simpson, *Hon.* Sir Alfred Henry, Kt.

Simpson, Sir Joseph Trevor, K.B.E.

Simpson, Sir William James, Kt.

Sinclair, Sir Clive Marles, Kt.

Sinclair, Sir George Evelyn, Kt., F.R.S.

Sinclair, Sir Ian McTaggart, K.C.M.G., Q.C.

Sinclair, Sir John Rollo Norman Blair, Bt. (s. 1704).

Sinclair, *Prof.* Sir Keith, Kt., C.B.E.

Sinclair, *Air Vice-Marshal* Sir Laurence Frank, G.C., K.C.B., C.B.E., D.S.O.

Sinclair, Sir Ronald Ormiston, K.B.E.

Singh, *Hon.* Sir Vijay Raghubir, Kt.

Singhania, Sir Padampat, Kt.

Singleton, Sir Edward Henry Sibbald, Kt.

Sinnamon, Sir Hercules, Kt., O.B.E.

Sisson, Sir Roy, Kt.

Sitwell, Sir (Sacheverell) Reresby, Bt. (1808).

Skeet, Sir Trevor Herbert Harry, Kt., M.P.

Skeggs, Sir Clifford George, Kt.

Skellerup, Sir Valdemar Reid, Kt., C.B.E.

Skingsley, *Air Chief Marshal* Sir Anthony Gerald, K.C.B.

Skinner, Sir Thomas Edward, K.B.E.

Skinner, Sir (Thomas) Keith (Hewitt), Bt. (1912).

Skipwith, Sir Patrick Alexander d'Estoteville, Bt. (1622).

Skyrme, Sir (William) Thomas (Charles), K.C.V.O., C.B., C.B.E.,T.D.

Slade, Sir Benjamin Julian Alfred, Bt. (1831).

Slade, *Rt. Hon.* Sir Christopher John, Kt.

Slaney, *Prof.* Sir Geoffrey, K.B.E.

Slater, *Vice-Adm.* Sir John Cunningham Kirkwood, K.C.B., L.V.O.

Slattery, *Rear-Adm.* Sir Matthew Sausse, K.B.E., C.B.

Sleight, Sir John Frederick, Bt. (1920).

Slimmings, Sir William Kenneth MacLeod, Kt., C.B.E.

Sloman, Sir Albert Edward, Kt., C.B.E.

Slynn, *Hon.* Sir Gordon, Kt.

Smallpeice, Sir Basil, K.C.V.O.

Smallwood, *Air Chief Marshal* Sir Denis Graham, G.B.E., K.C.B., D.S.O., D.F.C.

Smart, *Prof.* Sir George Algernon, Kt., M.D., F.R.C.P.

Smart, Sir Jack, Kt., C.B.E.

Smedley, Sir Harold, K.C.M.G., M.B.E.

Smeeton, *Vice-Adm.* Sir Richard Michael, K.C.B., M.B.E.

Smiley, Sir Hugh Houston, Bt. (1903).

Smirk, Sir (Frederick) Horace, K.B.E., M.D.

Smith, Sir Alan, Kt., C.B.E., D.F.C.

Smith, Sir Alexander Mair, Kt., Ph.D.

Smith, Sir Arthur Henry, Kt.

Smith, Sir Charles Bracewell-, Bt. (1947).

Smith, Sir Christopher Sydney Winwood, Bt. (1809).

Smith, Sir Cyril, Kt., M.B.E., M.P.

Smith, *Prof.* Sir David Cecil, Kt., F.R.S.

Smith, Sir Dudley (Gordon), Kt., M.P.

Smith, *Maj.-Gen.* Sir (Francis) Brian Wyldbore-, Kt., C.B., D.S.O., O.B.E.

Smith, *Prof.* Sir (Francis) Graham, Kt., F.R.S.

Smith, Sir (Frank) Ewart, Kt.

Smith, *Col.* Sir Henry Abel, K.C.M.G., K.C.V.O., D.S.O.

Smith, Sir Howard Frank Trayton, G.C.M.G.

Smith, *Hon.* Sir James Alfred, Kt., C.B.E., T.D.

Smith, Sir (James) Eric, Kt., C.B.E., SC.D., F.R.S.

Smith, Sir John Hamilton-Spencer-, Bt. (1804).

Smith, Sir John Kenneth Newson-, Bt. (1944).

Smith, Sir John Lindsay Eric., Kt., C.B.E.

Smith, Sir Leonard Herbert, Kt., C.B.E.

Smith, Sir Leslie Edward George, Kt.

Smith, Sir Raymond Horace, K.B.E.

Smith, Sir Reginald Beaumont, Kt.

Smith, Sir Richard Rathbone Vassar-, Bt., T.D. (1917).

Smith, Sir (Richard) Robert Law-, Kt., C.B.E., A.F.C.

Smith, Sir Robert Courtney, Kt., C.B.E.

Smith, Sir Robert Hill, Bt., (1945).

Smith, *Air Marshal* Sir Roy David Austen-, K.B.E., C.B., D.F.C.

Smith, Sir (Thomas) Gilbert, Bt. (1897).

Smith, *Adm.* Sir Victor Alfred Trumper, K.B.E., C.B., D.S.C.

Smith, Sir William Reardon Rear don-, Bt. (1920).

Smith, Sir (William) Reginald Verdon, Kt.

Smith, Sir (William) Richard Prince-, Bt. (1911).

Smith-Ryland, Sir Charles Mortimer Tollemache, Bt. (1897).

Smithers, *Prof.* Sir David Waldron, Kt., M.D.

Smithers, Sir Peter Henry Berry Otway, Kt., V.R.D., D.Phil.

Smithers, *Hon.* Sir Reginald Allfree, Kt.

Smyth, Sir Thomas Weyland Bowyer-, Bt., (1661).

Smyth, Sir Timothy John, Bt. (1955).

Snelling, Sir Arthur Wendell, K.C.M.G., K.C.V.O.

Snelson, Sir Edward Alec Abbott, K.B.E.

Soame, Sir Charles John Buckworth-Herne-, Bt. (1697).

Sobell, Sir Michael, Kt.

Sobers, Sir Garfield St. Auburn, Kt.

Solomon, Sir David Arnold, Kt., M.B.E.

Solomons, *Hon.* Sir (Louis) Adrian, Kt.

Solti, Sir Georg, K.B.E.

Somers, *Rt. Hon.* Sir Edward Jonathan, Kt.

Somerset, Sir Henry Beaufort, Kt., C.B.E.

Somerville, *Brig.* Sir John Nicholas, Kt., C.B.E.

Somerville, Sir Robert, K.C.V.O.

Sopwith, Sir Charles Ronald, Kt.

Soutar, *Air Marshal* Sir Charles John Williamson, K.B.E.

South, Sir Arthur, Kt.

Southby, Sir John Richard Bilbe, Bt. (1937).

Southern, Sir Richard William, Kt., F.B.A.

Southern, Sir Robert, Kt., C.B.E.

Southey, Sir Robert John, Kt., C.M.G.

Southward, Sir Leonard Bingley, Kt., O.B.E.

Southward, Sir Ralph, K.C.V.O., F.R.C.P.

Southwood, *Prof.* Sir (Thomas) Richard (Edmund), Kt., F.R.S.

Southworth, Sir Frederick, Kt., Q.C.

Souyave, *Hon.* Sir (Louis) Georges, Kt.

Sowrey, *Air Marshal* Sir Frederick Beresford, K.C.B., C.B.E., A.F.C.

Soysa, Sir Warusahennedige Abraham Bastian, Kt., C.B.E.

Sparkes, Sir Robert Lyndley, Kt.

Sparrow, Sir John, Kt.

Spearman, Sir Alexander Young Richard Mainwaring, Bt. (1840).

Speed, Sir Robert William Arney, Kt., C.B., Q.C.

Speelman, Sir Cornelis Jacob, Bt. (1686).

Speight, *Hon.* Sir Graham Davies, Kt.

Speir, Sir Rupert Malise, Kt.

Spencer, Sir Kelvin Tallent, Kt., C.B.E., M.C.

Spender, *Prof.* Sir Stephen Harold, Kt., C.B.E.

Spicer, Sir James Wilton, Kt., M.P.

Spicer, Sir Peter James, Bt. (1906).

Spooner, Sir James Douglas, Kt.

Spotswood, *Marshal of the Royal Air Force* Sir Denis Frank, G.C.B., C.B.E., D.S.O., D.F.C.

Spratt, *Col.* Sir Greville Douglas, G.B.E., T.D.

Springer, Sir Hugh Worrell, G.C.M.G., G.C.V.O., C.B.E.

Spry, *Brig.* Sir Charles Chambers Fowell, Kt., C.B.E., D.S.O.

Spry, *Hon.* Sir John Farley, Kt.

Stabb, *Hon.* Sir William Walter, Kt., Q.C.

Stack, *Air Chief Marshal* Sir (Thomas) Neville, K.C.B., C.V.O., C.B.E., A.F.C.

Stainton, Sir (John) Ross, Kt., C.B.E.

Stakis, Sir Reo Argiros, Kt.

Stallard, Sir Peter Hyla Gawne, K.C.M.G., C.V.O., M.B.E.

Stallworthy, Sir John Arthur, Kt., F.R.C.S.

Stamer, Sir (Lovelace) Anthony, Bt. (1809).

Stanbridge, *Air Vice-Marshal* Sir Brian Gerald Tivy, K.C.V.O., C.B.E., A.F.C.

Stanford, *Adm.* Sir Peter Maxwell, G.C.B., L.V.O.

Stanier, *Brig.* Sir Alexander Beville Gibbons, Bt., D.S.O., M.C. (1917).

Stanier, *Field Marshal* Sir John Wilfred, G.C.B., M.B.E.

Stanley, *Rt. Hon.* Sir John Paul, Kt., M.P.

†Staples, Sir Thomas, Bt. (I. 1628).

Stapleton, Sir (Henry) Alfred, Bt. (1679).

Stark, Sir Andrew Alexander Steel, K.C.M.G., C.V.O.

Starke, *Hon.* Sir John Erskine, Kt.

Starkey, Sir John Philip, Bt. (1935).

Starrit, Sir James, K.C.V.O.

Statham, Sir Norman, K.C.M.G., C.V.O.

Staughton, *Rt. Hon.* Sir Christopher Stephen Thomas Jonathan Thayer, Kt.

Staveley, Sir John Malfroy, K.B.E., M.C.

Staveley, *Admiral of the Fleet* Sir William Doveton Minet, G.C.B.

Steedman, *Air Chief Marshal* Sir Alasdair (Alexander McKay Sinclair), G.C.B., C.B.E., D.F.C.

Steel, Sir David Edward Charles, Kt., D.S.O., M.C., T.D.

Steel, *Maj.* Sir (Fiennes) William Strang, Bt. (1938).

Steel, Sir James, Kt., C.B.E.

Steele, Sir (Philip John) Rupert, Kt.

Steere, Sir Ernest Henry Lee-, K.B.E.

Stenhouse, Sir Nicol, Kt.

Stening, *Col.* Sir George Grafton Lees, Kt., E.D.

Stephen, *Rt. Hon.* Sir Ninian Martin, G.C.M.G., G.C.V.O., K.B.E.

Stephens, Sir David, K.C.B., C.V.O.

Stephenson, Sir Henry Upton, Bt. (1936).

Stephenson, *Rt. Hon.* Sir John Frederick Eustace, Kt.

Sterling, Sir Jeffrey Maurice, Kt., C.B.E.

Sternberg, Sir Sigmund, Kt.

Stevens, *Vice-Adm.* Sir John Felgate, K.B.E., C.B.

Stevens, Sir Laurence Houghton, Kt., C.B.E.

Stevenson, *Vice-Adm.* Sir (Hugh) David, K.B.E.

Stevenson, Sir Simpson, Kt.

Stewart, Sir Alan, K.B.E.

Stewart, Sir Alan d'Arcy, Bt. (I. 1623).

Stewart, Sir David Brodribb, Bt., T.D. (1960).

Stewart, Sir David James Henderson-, Bt. (1957).

Stewart, Sir Edward Jackson, Kt.

Stewart, *Prof.* Sir Frederick Henry, Kt., Ph.D., F.R.S., F.R.S.E.

Stewart, Sir Houston Mark Shaw-, Bt., M.C., T.D. (s. 1667)

Stewart, Sir Hugh Charlie Godfray, Bt. (1803).

Stewart, Sir James Douglas, Kt.

Stewart, Sir John Keith Watson, Bt. (1920).

Stewart, Sir Michael Norman Francis, K.C.M.G., O.B.E.

Stewart, Sir Robertson Huntly, Kt., C.B.E.

Stewart, Sir Ronald Compton, Bt. (1937).

Steyn, *Hon.* Sir Johan Van Zyl, Kt.

Stibbon, *Gen.* Sir John James, K.C.B., O.B.E.

Stinson, Sir Charles Alexander, K.B.E.

Stirling, Sir Alexander John Dickson, K.B.E., C.M.G.

Stockdale, Sir Arthur Noel, Kt.

Stockdale, Sir Thomas Minshull, Bt. (1960).

Stocker, *Rt. Hon.* Sir John Dexter, Kt., M.C., T.D.

Stoddart, *Wg. Cdr.* Sir Kenneth Maxwell, K.C.V.O., A.E.

Stoker, *Prof.* Sir Michael George Parke, Kt., C.B.E., F.R.C.P., F.R.S., F.R.S.E.

Stokes, Sir John Heydon Romaine, Kt., M.P.

Stone, *Prof.* Sir (John) Richard (Nicholas), KT., C.B.E.

Stonhouse, Sir Philip Allan, Bt. (1628).

Stonor, *Air Marshal* Sir Thomas Henry, K.C.B.

Storey, *Hon.* Sir Richard, Bt. (1960).

Stormonth Darling, Sir James Carlisle, Kt., C.B.E., M.C., T.D.

Stott, Sir Adrian George Ellingham, Bt. (1920).

Stow, Sir Christopher Philipson-, Bt., D.F.C. (1907).

Stow, Sir John Montague, G.C.M.G., K.C.V.O.

Stowe, Sir Kenneth Ronald, G.C.B., C.V.O.

Stracey, Sir John Simon, Bt. (1818).

Strachey, Sir Charles, Bt. (1801).

Stradling Thomas, Sir John, Kt., M.P.

Straker, Sir Michael Ian Bowstead, Kt., C.B.E.

Stratton, *Lt.-Gen.* Sir William Henry, K.C.B., C.V.O., C.B.E., D.S.O.

Strawson, *Prof.* Sir Peter Frederick, Kt., F.B.A.

Street, *Hon.* Sir Laurence Whistler, K.C.M.G.

Streeton, Sir Terence George, K.B.E., C.M.G.

Strong, Sir Roy Colin, Kt., Ph.D., F.S.A.

Stronge, Sir James Anselan Maxwell, Bt. (1803).

Stroud, *Prof.* Sir (Charles) Eric, Kt., F.R.C.P.

Strutt, Sir Nigel Edward, Kt., T.D.

Stuart, Sir James Keith, Kt.

Stuart, Sir Kenneth Lamonte, Kt.

†Stuart, Sir Phillip Luttrell, Bt. (1660).

Stuart-Smith, *Rt. Hon.* Sir Murray, Kt.

Stubblefield, Sir (Cyril) James, Kt., D.SC., F.R.S.

Stubbs, Sir James Wilfrid, K.C.V.O., T.D.

Stucley, *Lt.* Sir Hugh George Coplestone Bampfylde, Bt. (1859).

Studd, Sir Edward Fairfax, Bt. (1929).

Studd, Sir Peter Malden, G.B.E., K.C.V.O.

Studholme, Sir Paul Henry William, Bt. (1956).

Style, *Lt. Cdr.* Sir Godfrey William, Kt., C.B.E., D.S.C., R.N.

†Style, Sir William Frederick, Bt. (1627).

Suffield, Sir (Henry John) Lester, Kt.

Sugden, Sir Arthur, Kt.

Sullivan, Sir Desmond John, Kt.

Sullivan, Sir Richard Arthur, Bt. (1804).

Summerfield, *Hon.* Sir John Crampton, Kt., C.B.E.

Summers, Sir Felix Roland Brattan, Bt. (1952).

Summerson, Sir John Newenham, Kt., C.H., C.B.E., F.B.A., F.S.A.

Sunderland, *Prof.* Sir Sydney, Kt., C.M.G.

Surridge, Sir (Ernest) Rex (Edward), Kt., C.M.G.

Sutherland, Sir John Brewer, Bt. (1921).

Sutherland, Sir Maurice, Kt.

Sutherland, Sir William George MacKenzie, Kt.

Suttie, Sir (George) Philip Grant-, Bt. (s. 1702).

Sutton, Sir Frederick Walter, Kt., O.B.E.

Sutton, *Air Marshal* Sir John Matthias Dobson, K.C.B.

Sutton, Sir Richard Lexington, Bt. (1772).

Sutton, Sir Stafford William Powell Foster-, K.B.E., C.M.G., Q.C.

Swaffield, Sir James Chesebrough, Kt., C.B.E., R.D.

Swallow, Sir William, Kt.

Swan, *Lt. Col.* Sir William Bertram, K.C.V.O., C.B.E., T.D.

Swann, Sir Anthony Charles Christopher, Bt., C.M.G., O.B.E., (1906).

Swanwick, Sir Graham Russell, Kt., M.B.E.

Swartz, *Hon.* Sir Reginald William Colin, K.B.E., E.D.

Swayne, Sir Ronald Oliver Carless, Kt., M.C.

Swinson, Sir John Henry Alan, Kt., O.B.E.

Swinton, *Maj.-Gen.* Sir John, K.C.V.O., O.B.E.

Swire, Sir Adrian Christopher, Kt.

Swiss, Sir Rodney Geoffrey, Kt., O.B.E.

Swynnerton, Sir Roger John Massy, Kt., C.M.G., O.B.E., M.C.

Sykes, Sir Francis Godfrey, Bt. (1781).

Sykes, Sir John Charles Anthony le Gallais, Bt. (1921).

Sykes, Sir Tatton Christopher Mark, Bt. (1783).

Syme, Sir Ronald, Kt., O.M., F.B.A.

Symington, *Prof.* Sir Thomas, Kt., M.D., F.R.S.E.

Symons, *Vice-Adm.* Sir Patrick Jeremy, K.B.E.

Synge, Sir Robert Carson, Bt. (1801).

Tait, *Adm.* Sir (Allan) Gordon, K.C.B., D.S.C.

Tait, Sir James Sharp, Kt., D.SC., LlD., Ph.D.

Tait, Sir Peter, K.B.E.

Talbot, *Vice-Adm.* Sir (Arthur Allison) FitzRoy, K.B.E., C.B., D.S.O.

Talbot, *Hon.* Sir Hilary Gwynne, Kt.

Tancred, Sir Henry Lawson-, Bt. (1662).

Tangaroa, *Hon.* Sir Tangoroa, M.B.E.

Tange, Sir Arthur Harold, Kt., C.B.E.

Tansley, Sir Eric Crawford, Kt., C.M.G.

Tapp, *Maj.-Gen.* Sir Nigel Prior Hanson, K.B.E., C.B., D.S.O.

Tapsell, Sir Peter Hannay Bailey, Kt., M.P.

Tate, *Lt.-Col.* Sir Henry, Bt. (1898).

Taukala, Sir David Dawea, Kt., M.B.E.

Tavaiqia, *Ratu* Sir Josaia, K.B.E.

Tavare, Sir John, Kt., C.B.E.

Taylor, *Lt.-Gen.* Sir Allan Macnab, K.B.E., M.C.

Taylor, Sir Alvin Burton, Kt.

Taylor, Sir (Arthur) Godfrey, Kt.

Taylor, Sir Cyril Julian Hebden, Kt.

Taylor, Sir George, Kt., D.SC., F.R.S., F.R.S.E.

Taylor, Sir Henry Milton, Kt.

Taylor, Sir James, Kt., M.B.E., D.SC.

Taylor, Sir John Lang, K.C.M.G.

Taylor, Sir Michael Goodiff, Kt., C.B.E.

Taylor, Sir Nicholas Richard Stuart, Bt. (1917).

Taylor, *Rt. Hon.* Sir Peter Murray, Kt.

Tebbit, Sir Donald Claude, G.C.M.G.

Te Heuheu, Sir Hepi Hoani, K.B.E.

Telford, Sir Robert, Kt., C.B.E.

Temple, Sir Ernest Sanderson, Kt., M.B.E., Q.C.

Temple, Sir John Meredith, Kt.

Temple, Sir Rawden John Afamado, Kt. C.B.E., Q.C.

Temple, *Maj.* Sir Richard Anthony Purbeck, Bt., M.C. (1876).

Templeton, Sir John Marks, Kt.

Tennant, *Capt.* Sir Iain Mark, Kt.

Tennant, Sir Mark Dalcour, K.C.M.G., C.B.

Tennant, Sir Peter Frank Dalrymple, Kt., C.M.G., O.B.E.

Teo, Sir Fiatau Penitala, G.C.M.G., G.C.V.O., I.S.O., M.B.E.

Terry, Sir George Walter Roberts, Kt., C.B.E., Q.P.M.

Terry, Sir John Elliott, Kt.

Terry, Sir Michael Edward Stanley Imbert-, Bt. (1917).

Terry, *Air Chief Marshal* Sir Peter David George, G.C.B., A.F.C.

Tetley, Sir Herbert, K.B.E., C.B.

Tett, Sir Hugh Charles, Kt.

Thiess, Sir Leslie Charles, Kt., C.B.E.

Thomas, Sir Derek Morison David, K.C.M.G.

Thomas, Sir Frederick William, Kt.

Thomas, Sir (Godfrey) Michael (David) Bt. (1694).

Thomas, Sir Jeremy Cashel, K.C.M.G.

Thomas, Sir John Maldwyn, Kt.

Thomas, Sir Keith Vivian, Kt.

Thomas, Sir Patrick Muirhead, Kt., D.S.O., T.D.

Thomas, Sir Robert Evan, Kt.

Thomas, *Hon.* Sir Swinton Barclay, Kt.

Thomas, Sir William James Cooper, Bt., T.D. (1919).

Thomas, Sir (William) Michael (Marsh), Bt. (1918).

Thomas, *Adm.* Sir (William) Richard Scott, K.C.B., O.B.E.

Thompson, Sir Christopher Peile, Bt. (1890).

Thompson, Sir Edward Hugh Dudley, Kt., M.B.E., T.D.

Thompson, Sir Edward Walter, Kt.

Thompson, *Vice-Adm.* Sir Hugh Leslie Owen, K.B.E.

Thompson, Sir (Humphrey) Simon Meysey-, Bt. (1874).

Thompson, *Hon.* Sir John, Kt.

Thompson, Sir Paul Anthony, Bt. (1963).

Thompson, Sir Peter Anthony, Kt.

Thompson, Sir Ralph Patrick, Kt.

Thompson, Sir Richard Hilton Marler, Bt. (1963).

Thompson, Sir Robert Grainger Ker, K.B.E., C.M.G., D.S.O., M.C.

Thompson, Sir (Thomas) Lionel Tennyson, Bt. (1806).

Thomson, Sir Adam, Kt., C.B.E.

Thomson, Sir Evan Rees Whitaker, Kt.

Thomson, Sir (Frederick Douglas) David, Bt. (1929).

Thomson, Sir Ivo Wilfrid Home, Bt. (1925).

Thomson, Sir John, K.B.E., T.D.

Thomson, Sir John Adam, G.C.M.G.

Thomson, Sir John (Ian) Sutherland, K.B.E., C.M.G.

Thorn, Sir John Samuel, Kt., O.B.E.

Thorne, *Maj.-Gen.* Sir David Calthrop, K.B.E.

Thorne, Sir Peter Francis, K.C.V.O., C.B.E.

Thornton, *Lt.-Gen.* Sir Leonard Whitmore, K.C.B., C.B.E.

Thornton, Sir Peter Eustace, K.C.B.

Thorold, Sir Anthony Henry, Bt., O.B.E., D.S.C. (1642).

Thorpe, *Hon.* Sir Mathew Alexander, Kt.

Thouron, Sir John Rupert Hunt, K.B.E.

Throckmorton, Sir Robert George Maxwell, Bt. (1642).

Thwaites, Sir Bryan, Kt., Ph.D.

Thwin, Sir U, Kt.

Tibbits, *Capt.* Sir David Stanley, Kt., D.S.C.

Tickell, Sir Crispin Charles Cervantes, G.C.M.G., K.C.V.O.

Tidbury, Sir Charles Henderson, Kt.

Tikaram, Sir Moti, K.B.E.

Tilney, Sir John Dudley Robert Tarleton, Kt., T.D.

Tippet, *Vice-Adm.* Sir Anthony Sanders, K.C.B.

Tippett, Sir Michael Kemp, Kt., O.M., C.H., C.B.E.

Tirvengadum, Sir Harry Krishnan, Kt.

Titterton, *Prof.* Sir Ernest William, Kt., C.M.G.

Tizard, Sir John Peter Mills, Kt.

Tod, *Air Marshal* Sir John Hunter Hunter-, K.B.E., C.B.

Todd, Sir Ian Pelham, K.B.E., F.R.C.S.

Todd, *Hon.* Sir (Reginald Stephen) Garfield, Kt.

Tollemache, *Maj.-Gen.* Sir Humphry Thomas, Bt., C.B., C.B.E., R.M. (1793).

Tololo, Sir Alkan, K.B.E.

Tombs, Sir Francis Leonard, Kt.

Tomkins, Sir Alfred George, Kt., C.B.E.

Tomkins, Sir Edward Emile, G.C.M.G., C.V.O.

Tomlinson, *Prof.* Sir Bernard Evans, Kt., C.B.E.

Tomlinson, Sir (Frank) Stanley, K.C.M.G.

Tooley, Sir John, Kt.

Tooth, Sir (Hugh) John Lucas-, Bt. (1920).

Tooth, *Hon.* Sir (Seymour) Douglas, Kt.

ToRobert, Sir Henry Thomas, K.B.E.

Tory, Sir Geofroy William, K.C.M.G.

Touche, Sir Anthony George, Bt. (1920).

Touche, Sir Rodney Gordon, Bt. (1962).

Tovey, Sir Brian John Maynard, K.C.M.G.

ToVue, Sir Ronald, Kt., O.B.E.

Townley, Sir John Barton, Kt.

Townsend, *Rear-Adm.* Sir Leslie William, K.C.V.O., C.B.E.

Townsing, Sir Kenneth Joseph, Kt., C.M.G.

Trafford, Sir (Joseph) Anthony Porteous, Kt.

Traherne, Sir Cennydd George, K.G., T.D.

Traill, Sir Alan Towers, G.B.E.

Trant, *Gen.* Sir Richard Brooking, K.C.B.

Travancore, *Maj.-Gen.* H.H. the Maharajah of, G.C.S.I., G.C.I.E.

Travers, Sir Thomas à'Beckett, Kt.

Treacher, *Adm.* Sir John Devereux, K.C.B.

Trehane, Sir (Walter) Richard, Kt.

Trelawny, Sir John Barry Salusbury-, Bt. (1628).

Trench, Sir Nigel Clive Cosby, K.C.M.G.

Trench, Sir Peter Edward, Kt., C.B.E., T.D.

Trescowthick, Sir Donald Henry, K.B.E.

Trethowan, Sir (James) Ian (Raley), Kt.

Trethowan, *Prof.* Sir William Henry, Kt. C.B.E., F.R.C.P.

Trevaskis, Sir (Gerald) Kennedy (Nicholas), K.C.M.G., O.B.E.

Trevelyan, Sir George Lowthian, Bt. (1874).

Trevelyan, Sir Norman Irving, Bt. (1662).

Trewby, *Vice-Adm.* Sir (George Francis) Allan, K.C.B.

Trinder, Sir (Arnold) Charles, G.B.E.

Tritton, Sir Anthony John Ernest, Bt. (1905).

†Trollope, Sir Anthony Simon, Bt. (1642).

Trotman-Dickenson, Sir Aubrey Fiennes, Kt.

Trotter, Sir Ronald Ramsay, Kt.

Troubridge, Sir Thomas Richard, Bt. (1799).

Troughton, Sir Charles Hugh Willis, Kt., C.B.E., M.C., T.D.

Troup, *Vice-Adm.* Sir (John) Anthony (Rose), K.C.B., D.S.C.

Trowbridge, *Rear-Adm.* Sir Richard John, K.C.V.O.

Truscott, Sir George James Irving, Bt. (1909).

Tuck, Sir Bruce Adolph Reginald, Bt. (1910).

Tucker, *Hon.* Sir Richard Howard, Kt.

Tudor, *Hon.* Sir James Cameron, K.C.M.G.

Tudor Evans, *Hon.* Sir Haydn, Kt.

Tuite, Sir Christopher Hugh, Bt., Ph.D. (1622).

Tuivaga, Sir Timoci Uluiburotu, Kt.

Tuke, Sir Anthony Favill, Kt.

Tupper, Sir Charles Hibbert, Bt. (1888).

Turbott, Sir Ian Graham, Kt., C.M.G., C.V.O.

Turing, Sir John Dermot, Bt. (s 1638).

Turnbull, *Prof.* Sir Alexander Cuthbert, Kt., C.B.E.

Turnbull, Sir Richard Gordon, G.C.M.G.

Turner, *Rt. Hon.* Sir Alexander Kingcome, K.B.E.

Turner, *Adm.* Sir (Arthur) Francis, K.C.B., D.S.C.

Turner, *Hon.* Sir Michael John, Kt.

Tuti, *Rev.* Dudley, K.B.E.

Tuzo, *Gen.* Sir Harry Craufurd, G.C.B., O.B.E., M.C.

Twiss, *Adm.* Sir Frank Roddam, K.C.B., K.C.V.O., D.S.C.

Tyler, *Maj.-Gen.* Sir Leslie Norman, K.B.E., C.B.

Tyree, Sir (Alfred) William, Kt., O.B.E.

Tyrrell, Sir Murray Louis, K.C.V.O., C.B.E.

Tyrwhitt, Sir Reginald Thomas Newman, Bt. (1919).

Udoma, *Hon.* Sir (Egbert) Udo, Kt.

Unsworth, Hon. Sir Edgar Ignatius Godfrey, Kt., C.M.G.

Unwin, Sir Keith, K.B.E., C.M.G.

Ure, Sir John Burns, K.C.M.G., L.V.O.

Urquhart, Sir Brian Edward, K.C.M.G., M.B.E.

Urwick, Sir Alan Bedford, K.C.V.O., C.M.G.

Usher, Sir Leonard Gray, K.B.E.

Usher, Sir Peter Lionel, Bt. (1899).

Vallat, Sir Francis Aimé, G.B.E., K.C.M.G., Q.C.

Vallings, *Vice-Adm.* Sir George Montague Francis, K.C.B.

Vanderfelt, Sir Robin Victor, K.B.E.

van der Post, Sir Laurens Jan, Kt., C.B.E.

Vane, Sir John Robert, Kt., D.Phil., D.SC., F.R.S

Vangeke, *Most Rev.* Louis, K.B.E.

Vanneck, *Air Cdre.* Hon. Sir Peter Beckford Rutgers, G.B.E., C.B., A.F.C.

van Straubenzee, Sir William Radcliffe, Kt., M.B.E.

Vasquez, Sir Alfred Joseph, Kt., C.B.E., Q.C.

Vaughan, Sir (George) Edgar, K.B.E.

Vaughan, Sir Gerard Folliott, Kt., M.P., F.R.C.P.

Vavasour, *Cdr.* Sir Geoffrey William, Bt., D.S.C., R.N. (1828).

Veale, Sir Alan John Ralph, Kt.

Veira, Sir Philip Henry, K.B.E.

Verco, Sir Walter John George, K.C.V.O.

Verney, Sir John, Bt., M.C., T.D. (1946).

Verney, Sir Ralph Bruce, Bt., K.B.E. (1818).

Vernon, Sir James, Kt., C.B.E.

Vernon, Sir Nigel John Douglas, Bt. (1914).

Vesey, Sir (Nathaniel) Henry (Peniston), Kt., C.B.E.

Vestey, Sir (John) Derek, Bt. (1921).

Vial, Sir Kenneth Harold, Kt., C.B.E.

Vick, Sir (Francis) Arthur, Kt., O.B.E., Ph.D.

Vickers, *Lt.-Gen.* Sir Richard Maurice Hilton, K.C.B., M.V.O., O.B.E.

Victoria, Sir (Joseph Aloysius) Donatus, Kt., C.B.E.

Villiers, Sir Charles Hyde, Kt., M.C.

Villiers, *Vice-Adm.* Sir (John) Michael, K.C.B., O.B.E.

Vincent, *Gen.* Sir Richard Frederick, K.C.B., D.S.O.

Vincent, Sir William Percy Maxwell, Bt. (1936).

Vinelott, *Hon.* Sir John Evelyn, Kt.

Vines, Sir William Joshua, Kt., C.M.G.

Vyse, *Lt.-Gen.* Sir Edward Dacre Howard-, K.B.E., C.B., M.C.

Vyvyan, Sir John Stanley, Bt. (1645).

Waddell, Sir Alexander Nicol Anton, K.C.M.G., D.S.C.

Waddell, Sir James Henderson, Kt., C.B.

Wade, *Prof.* Sir Henry William Rawson, Kt., Q.C., F.B.A.

Wade, *Air Chief Marshal* Sir Ruthven Lowry, K.C.B., D.F.C.

Wade, Sir (William) Oulton, Kt.

Wade-Gery, Sir Robert Lucian, K.C.M.G., K.C.V.O.

Waechter, Sir (Harry Leonard) d'Arcy, Bt. (1911).

Wagner, Sir Anthony Richard, K.C.B., K.C.V.O.

Waite, *Hon.* Sir John Douglas, Kt.

Wake, Sir Hereward, Bt., M.C., (1621).

Wakefield, Sir (Edward) Humphry (Tyrell), Bt. (1962).

Wakefield, Sir Norman Edward, Kt.

Wakefield, Sir Peter George Arthur, K.B.E., C.M.G.

Wakeford, *Air Marshal* Sir Richard Gordon, K.C.B., O.B.E., M.V.O., A.F.C.

Wakeley, Sir John Cecil Nicholson, Bt., F.R.C.S. (1952).

Wakeman, Sir (Offley) David, Bt. (1828).

Walker, *Rev.* Alan Edgar, Kt., O.B.E.

Walker, Sir Allan Grierson, Kt., Q.C.

Walker, *Lt.-Gen.* Sir Antony Kenneth Frederick, K.C.B.

Walker, Sir Baldwin Patrick, Bt. (1856).

Walker, Sir (Charles) Michael, G.C.M.G.

Walker, *Vice-Adm.* Sir (Charles) Peter (Graham), K.B.E., C.B., D.S.C.

Walker, Sir Edward Ronald, Kt., C.B.E.

Walker, Sir Gervas George, Kt.

Walker, *Maj.* Sir Hugh Ronald, Bt. (1906).

Walker, Sir James Graham, Kt., M.B.E.

Walker, Sir James Heron, Bt. (1868).

Walker, Sir Michael Leolin Forestier-, Bt. (1835).

Walker, *Gen.* Sir Walter Colyear, K.C.B., C.B.E., D.S.O.

Wall, *Dr. Hon.* Sir Gerard Aloysius, Kt.

Wall, Sir Patrick Henry Bligh, Kt., M.C., V.R.D.

Wall, Sir Robert William, Kt., O.B.E.

Wallace, Sir Ian James, Kt., C.B.E.

Waller, *Hon.* Sir (George) Mark, Kt.

Waller, *Rt. Hon.* Sir George Stanley, Kt., O.B.E.

Waller, Sir (John) Keith, Kt., C.B.E.

Waller, Sir John Stainer, Bt. (1815).

Waller, Sir Robert William, Bt. (1 1780).

Walley, Sir John, K.B.E., C.B.

Walsh, Sir Alan, Kt., D.SC., F.R.S.

Walsh, Sir David Philip, K.B.E., C.B.

Walsh, Prof. Sir John Patrick, K.B.E.

Walsham, *Rear-Adm.* Sir John Scarlett Warren, Bt., C.B., O.B.E. (1831).

Walter, Sir Harold Edward, Kt.

Walters, *Prof.* Sir Alan Arthur, Kt.

Walters, Sir Dennis Murray, Kt., M.B.E., M.P.

Walters, Sir Frederick Donald, Kt.

Walters, Sir Peter Ingram, Kt.

Walters, Sir Roger Talbot, K.B.E., F.R.I.B.A.

Walton, Sir John Robert, Kt.

Wan, Sir Wamp, Kt., M.B.E.

Wanstall, *Hon.* Sir Charles Gray, Kt.

Ward, *Hon.* Sir Alan Hylton, Kt.

Ward, Sir Arthur Hugh, K.B.E.

Ward, *Gen.* Sir Dudley, G.C.B., K.B.E., D.S.O.

Ward, Sir John Guthrie, G.C.M.G.

Ward, Sir Joseph James Laffey, Bt. (1911).

Ward, *Maj.-Gen.* Sir Philip John Newling, K.C.V.O., C.B.E.

Ward, Sir Terence George, Kt., C.B.E.

Wardale, Sir Geoffrey Charles, K.C.B.

Wardlaw, Sir Henry (John), Bt. (s 1631).

Wardle, Sir Thomas Edward Jewell, Kt.

Ware, Sir Henry Gabriel, K.C.B.

Waring, Sir (Alfred) Holburt, Bt. (1935).

Warmington, *Lt.-Cdr.* Sir Marshall George Clitheroe, Bt., R.N. (1908).

Warner, Sir (Edward Courtenay) Henry, Bt. (1910).

Warner, Sir Edward Redston, K.C.M.G., O.B.E.

Warner, Sir Frederick Archibald, G.C.V.O., K.C.M.G.

Warner, Sir Frederick Edward, Kt., F.R.S.

Warner, *Hon.* Sir Jean-Pierre Frank Eugene, Kt.

Warnock, Sir Geoffrey James, Kt.

Warren, Sir Alfred Henry, Kt., C.B.E.

Warren, Sir Brian Charles Pennefather, Bt. (1784).

Warren, Sir Frederick Miles, K.B.E.

Warren, Sir (Harold) Brian (Seymour), Kt.

Wass, Sir Douglas William Gretton, G.C.B.

Waterhouse, *Hon.* Sir Ronald Gough, Kt.

Waterlow, Sir Christopher Rupert, Bt. (1873).

Waterlow, Sir (James) Gerard, Bt. (1930).

Waters, *Lt. Gen.* Sir Charles John, K.C.B., C.B.E.

Wates, Sir Christopher Stephen, Kt.

Watkins, *Rt. Hon.* Sir Tasker, Kt., V.C.

Watson, Sir Bruce Dunstan, Kt.

Watson, Sir Francis John Bagott, K.C.V.O., F.B.A., F.S.A.

Watson, Sir (James) Andrew, Bt. (1866).

Watson, Sir John Forbes Inglefield-, Bt. (1895).

Watson, Sir Michael Milne-, Bt., C.B.E. (1937).

Watson, Sir (Noel) Duncan, K.C.M.G.

Watson, *Vice-Adm.* Sir Philip Alexander, K.B.E., M.V.O.

Watt, Sir George Steven Harvie-, Bt., T.D., Q.C. (1945).

Watt, *Surgeon Vice-Adm.* Sir James, K.B.E., F.R.C.S.

Watts, Sir Arthur Desmond, K.C.M.G.

Watts, *Lt. Gen.* Sir John Peter Barry Condliffe, K.B.E., C.B., M.C.

Wauchope, Sir Patrick George Don-, Bt. (s. 1667).

Way, Sir Richard George Kitchener, K.C.B., C.B.E.

Wayne, *Prof.* Sir Edward Johnson, Kt., M.D., Ph.D.

Weatherall, *Prof.* Sir David John, Kt., F.R.S.

Weatherall, *Vice-Adm.* Sir James Lamb, K.B.E.

Weaver, Sir Tobias Rushton, Kt., C.B.

Webb, *Lt.-Gen.* Sir Richard James Holden, K.B.E., C.B.

Webb, Sir Thomas Langley, Kt.

Webster, *Very Rev.* Alan Brunskill, K.C.V.O.

Webster, *Vice-Adm.* Sir John Morrison, K.C.B.

Webster, *Hon.* Sir Peter Edlin, Kt.

Wedderburn, Sir Andrew John Alexander Ogilvy-, Bt. (1803).

Wedgwood, Sir John Hamilton, Bt., T.D. (1942).

Weeks, Sir Hugh Thomas, Kt., C.M.G.

Weinberg, Sir Mark Aubrey, Kt.

Weipers, *Prof.* Sir William Lee, Kt.

Weir, Sir Michael Scott, K.C.M.G.

Weir, Sir Roderick Bignell, Kt.

Weiss, Sir Eric, Kt.

Welby, Sir (Richard) Bruno Gregory, Bt. (1801).

Welch, Sir John Reader, Bt. (1957).

Weld, *Col.* Sir Joseph William, Kt., O.B.E., T.D.

Weldon, Sir Anthony William, Bt. (I. 1723).

Welensky, *Rt. Hon.* Sir Roy, (Roland), K.C.M.G.

Wellings, Sir Jack Alfred, Kt., C.B.E.

Wells, Sir Charles Maltby, Bt., T.D. (1944).

Wells, Sir John Julius, Kt.

West-Russell, *Hon.* Sir David Sturrock, Kt.

Westbrook, Sir Neil Gowanloch, Kt., C.B.E.

Westerman, Sir (Wilfred) Alan, Kt., C.B.E.

Wheatley, Sir (George) Andrew, Kt., C.B.E.

Wheeler, Sir Ernest Richard, K.C.V.O., M.B.E.

Wheeler, Sir Frederick Henry, Kt., C.B.E.

Wheeler, Sir Harry Anthony, Kt., O.B.E.

Wheeler, *Air Chief Marshal* Sir (Henry) Neil (George), G.C.B., C.B.E., D.S.O., D.F.C., A.F.C.

Wheeler, Sir John Hieron, Bt. (1920).

Wheeler, *Hon.* Sir Kenneth Henry, Kt.

Wheler, Sir Edward Woodford, Bt. (1660).

Whishaw, Sir Charles Percival Law, Kt.

Whitaker, *Maj.* Sir James Herbert Ingham, Bt. (1936).

White, Sir Christopher Robert Meadows, Bt. (1937).

White, Sir Dick Goldsmith, K.C.M.G., K.B.E.

White, Sir Frederick William George, K.B.E., Ph.D., F.R.S.

White, Sir George Stanley James, Bt. (1904).

White, Sir Harold Leslie, Kt., C.B.E.

White, *Wg.-Cdr.* Sir Henry Arthur Dalrymple-, Bt., D.F.C. (1926).

White, *Hon.* Sir John Charles, Kt., M.B.E.

White, Sir John Woolmer, Bt. (1922).

White, Sir Lynton Stuart, Kt., M.B.E., T.D.

White, *Adm.* Sir Peter, G.B.E.

White, Sir Thomas Astley Woollaston, Bt. (1802).

White, Sir (Vincent) Gordon (Lindsay), K.B.E.

Whitehead, Sir John Stainton, K.C.M.G., C.V.O.

Whitehead, Sir Rowland John Rathbone, Bt. (1889).

Whiteley, Sir Hugo Baldwin Huntington-, Bt. (1918).

Whiteley, *Gen.* Sir Peter John Frederick, K.B.E., O.B.E., R.M.

Whitfield, Sir Cecil Vincent Wallace, Kt.

Whitford, *Hon.* Sir John Norman Keates, Kt.

Whitley, *Air Marshal* Sir John René, K.B.E., C.B., D.S.O., A.F.C.

Whitmore, Sir Clive Anthony, G.C.B., C.V.O.

Whitmore, Sir John Henry Douglas, Bt. (1954).

Whitteridge, Sir Gordon Coligny, K.C.M.G., O.B.E.

Whittle, *Air Cdre.* Sir Frank, O.M., K.B.E., C.B., F.R.S.

Whyte, Sir William Erskine Hamilton, K.C.M.G.

Wickerson, Sir John Michael, Kt.

Wicks, Sir James Albert, Kt.

Wigan, Sir Alan Lewis, Bt. (1898).

Wiggin, Sir John Henry, Bt., M.C. (1892).

Wigglesworth, Sir Vincent Brian, Kt., C.B.E., M.D., F.R.S.

Wigram, *Rev. Canon* Sir Clifford Woolmore, Bt. (1805).

Wilbraham, Sir Richard Baker, Bt. (1776).

Wilford, Sir (Kenneth) Michael, G.C.M.G.

Wilkins, Sir Graham John, Kt.

Wilkins, *Lt.-Gen.* Sir Michael Compton Lockwood, K.C.B., O.B.E.

Wilkinson, Sir (David) Graham (Brook) Bt. (1941).

Wilkinson, *Prof.* Sir Denys Haigh, Kt., F.R.S.

Wilkinson, *Prof.* Sir Geoffrey, Kt., F.R.S.

Wilkinson, *Rt. Hon.* Sir Nicolas Christopher Henry Browne-, Kt.

Wilkinson, Sir Peter Allix, K.C.M.G., D.S.O., O.B.E.

Wilkinson, Sir Philip William, Kt.

Wilkinson, Sir (Robert Francis) Martin, Kt.

Wilkinson, Sir William Henry Nairn, Kt.

Willatt, Sir (Robert) Hugh, Kt.

Willcocks, Sir David Valentine, Kt., C.B.E., M.C.

Williams, Sir Alastair Edgcumbe James Dudley-, Bt. (1964).

Williams, Sir Alwyn, Kt., PH.D., F.R.S.

Williams, Sir Anthony James, K.C.M.G.

Williams, Sir (Arthur) Gareth Ludovic Emrys Rhys, Bt. (1918).

Williams, *Prof.* Sir Bruce Rodda, K.B.E.

Williams, *Adm.* Sir David, G.C.B.

Williams, Sir David Innes, Kt.

Williams, *Hon.* Sir Denys Ambrose, Kt.

Williams, Sir Donald Mark, Bt. (1866).

Williams, Sir Edgar Trevor, Kt., C.B., C.B.E., D.S.O.

Williams, *Hon.* Sir Edward Stratten, K.C.M.G., K.B.E.

Williams, Sir Francis John Watkin, Bt., Q.C. (1798).

Williams, Sir Henry Sydney, Kt., O.B.E.

Williams, Sir (John) Leslie, Kt., C.B.E.

Williams, Sir John Robert, K.C.M.G.

Williams, Sir Leonard, K.B.E., C.B.

Williams, Sir Osmond, Bt., M.C. (1909).

Williams, Sir Peter Watkin, Kt.

Williams, *Prof.* Sir Robert Evan Owen, Kt., M.D., F.R.C.P.

Williams, Sir (Robert) Philip Nathaniel, Bt. (1915).

Williams, Sir Robin Philip, Bt. (1953).

Williams, Sir (William) Maxwell (Harries), Kt.

Williamson, *Marshal of the Royal Air Force* Sir Keith Alec, G.C.B., A.F.C.

Williamson, Sir (Nicholas Frederick) Hedworth, Bt. (1642).

Willink, Sir Charles William, Bt. (1957).

Willis, *Hon.* Sir Eric Archibald, K.B.E., C.M.G.

Willis, *Vice-Adm.* Sir (Guido) James, K.B.E.

Willison, *Lt.-Gen.* Sir David John, K.C.B., O.B.E., M.C.

Willison, Sir John Alexander, Kt., O.B.E.

Willoughby, *Maj.-Gen.* Sir John Edward Francis, K.B.E., C.B.

Wills, Sir David Seton, Bt. (1904).

Wills, Sir (Hugh) David Hamilton, Kt., C.B.E., T.D.

Wills, Sir John Spencer, Kt.

Wills, Sir John Vernon, Bt., T.D. (1923).

Wilmot, Sir Henry Robert, Bt. (1759).

Wilmot, *Cdr.* Sir John Assheton Eardley-, Bt., M.V.O., D.S.C., R.N. (1821).

Wilson, Sir Alan Herries, Kt., F.R.S.

Wilson, *Lt.-Gen.* Sir (Alexander) James, K.B.E., M.C.

Wilson, Sir Angus Frank Johnstone, Kt., C.B.E.

Wilson, Sir Anthony, Kt.

Wilson, Sir Austin George, Kt., O.B.E.

Wilson, Sir Charles Haynes, Kt.

Wilson, Sir David, Bt. (1920).

Wilson, Sir David Clive, K.C.M.G.

Wilson, Sir David Mackenzie, Kt.

Wilson, Sir Geoffrey Masterman, K.C.B., C.M.G.

Wilson, Sir James William Douglas, Bt. (1906).

Wilson, Sir John Foster, Kt., C.B.E.

Wilson, Sir John Gardiner, Kt., C.B.E.

Wilson, Sir John Martindale, K.C.B.

Wilson, Sir (Mathew) Martin, Bt. (1874).

Wilson, Sir Reginald Holmes, Kt.

Wilson, Sir Robert, Kt., C.B.E.

Wilson, Sir Robert Donald, Kt.

Wilson, *Rt. Rev.* Roger Plumpton, K.C.V.O., D.D.

Wilson, Sir Roland, K.B.E.

Wilson, *Hon.* Sir Ronald Darling, K.B.E., C.M.G.

Wilton, Sir (Arthur) John, K.C.M.G., K.C.V.O., M.C.

Wiltshire, Sir Frederick Munro, Kt., C.B.E.

Windeyer, Sir Brian Wellingham, Kt.

Wingate, *Capt.* Sir Miles Buckley, K.C.V.O.

Winnifrith, Sir (Alfred) John (Digby), K.C.B.

Winnington, Sir Francis Salwey William, Bt. (1755).

Winskill, *Air Cdre.* Sir Archibald Little, K.C.V.O., C.B.E., D.F.C.

Winterbottom, Sir Walter, Kt., C.B.E.

Wiseman, Sir John William, Bt. (1628).

Wolfson, Sir David, Kt.

Wolfson, Sir Isaac, Bt., F.R.S. (1962).

Wolseley, Sir Charles Garnet Richard Mark, Bt. (1628).

Wolseley, Sir Garnet, Bt. (1 1745).

Wolstenholme, Sir Gordon Ethelbert Ward, Kt., O.B.E.

Wombwell, Sir George Philip Frederick, Bt. (1778).

Womersley, Sir Peter John Walter, Bt. (1945).

Wontner, Sir Hugh Walter Kingwell, G.B.E., C.V.O.

Wood, Sir Anthony John Page, Bt. (1837).

Wood, Sir David Basil Hill-, Bt. (1921).

Wood, Sir Frederick Ambrose Stuart, Kt.

Wood, Sir Henry Peart, Kt., C.B.E.

Wood, *Prof.* Sir John Crossley, Kt., C.B.E.

Wood, *Hon.* Sir John Kember, Kt., M.C.

Wood, Sir Martin Francis, Kt., O.B.E.

Wood, Sir Russell Dillon, K.C.V.O., V.R.D.

Wood, Sir William Alan, K.C.V.O., C.B.

Woodcock, Sir John, Kt., C.B.E., Q.P.M.

Woodfield, Sir Philip John, K.C.B., C.B.E.

Woodhouse, *Rt. Hon.* Sir (Arthur) Owen, K.B.E., D.S.C.

Woodroffe, *Most Rev.* George Cuthbert Manning, K.B.E.

Woodroofe, Sir Ernest George, Kt., PH.D.

Woodruff, *Prof.* Sir Michael Francis Addison, Kt., D.S.C., F.R.S., F.R.C.S.

Woods, Sir Colin Philip Joseph, K.C.V.O., C.B.E.

Woods, *Most Rev.* Frank, K.B.E., D.D.

Woods, *Rt. Rev.* Robert Wilmer, K.C.M.G., K.C.V.O.

Woodward, *Hon.* Sir (Albert) Edward, Kt., O.B.E.

Woodward, *Adm.* Sir John Forster, G.B.E., K.C.B.

Woolf, *Rt. Hon.* Sir Harry Kenneth, Kt.

Woolf, Sir John, Kt.

Woollaston, Sir (Mountford) Tosswill, Kt.

Wordie, Sir John Stewart, Kt., C.B.E., V.R.D.

Worsley, *Gen.* Sir Richard Edward, G.C.B., O.B.E.

Worsley, Sir (William) Marcus (John), Bt. (1838).

Worthington, *Air Vice Marshal* Sir Geoffrey Luis, K.B.E., C.B.

Wraight, Sir John Richard, K.B.E., C.M.G.

Wraxall, Sir Charles Frederick Lascelles, Bt. (1813).

Wrey, Sir (Castel Richard) Bourchier, Bt. (1628).

Wright, Sir Allan Frederick, K.B.E.

Wright, Sir Denis Arthur Hepworth, G.C.M.G.

Wright, Sir Edward Maitland, Kt., D.Phil.,Ll.D., D.SC., F.R.S.E.

Wright, Sir (John) Oliver, G.C.M.G., G.C.V.O., D.S.C.

Wright, Sir Patrick Richard Henry, G.C.M.G.

Wright, Sir Paul Hervé Giraud, K.C.M.G., O.B.E.

Wright, *Hon.* Sir Reginald Charles, Kt.

Wright, Sir Richard Michael Cory-, Bt. (1903).

Wright, Sir Rowland Sydney, Kt., C.B.E.

Wrightson, Sir Charles Mark Garmondsway, Bt. (1900).

Wykeham, *Air Marshal* Sir Peter Guy, K.C.B., D.S.O., O.B.E., D.F.C., A.F.C.

Wylie, Sir Campbell, Kt., E.D., Q.C.

Wynn, Sir David Watkin Williams-, Bt. (1688).

Wynter, Sir Luther Reginald, Kt., C.B.E.

Yang, *Hon.* Ti Liang, Kt.

Yapp, Sir Stanley Graham, Kt.

Yarrow, Sir Eric Grant, Bt., M.B.E. (1916).

Yeend, Sir Geoffrey John, Kt., C.B.E.

Yellowlees, Sir Henry, K.C.B.

Yocklunn, Sir John (Soong Chung), K.C.V.O.

Youens, Sir Peter William, Kt., C.M.G., O.B.E.

Young, Sir Brian Walter Mark, Kt.

Young, *Lt.-Gen.* Sir David Tod, K.B.E., C.B., D.F.C.

Young, Sir George Samuel Knatchbull, Bt., M.P. (1813).

Young, *Hon.* Sir Harold William, K.C.M.G.

Young, Sir John Kenyon Roe, Bt. (1821).

Young, *Hon.* Sir John McIntosh, K.C.M.G.

Young, Sir Leslie Clarence, Kt., C.B.E.

Young, Sir Norman Smith, Kt.

Young, Sir Richard Dilworth, Kt.

Young, Sir Robert Christopher Mackworth-, G.C.V.O.

Young, Sir Roger William, Kt.

Young, Sir Stephen Stewart Templeton, Bt. (1945).

Young, Sir William Neil, Bt. (1769).

Younger, *Maj.-Gen.* Sir John William, Bt., C.B.E. (1911).

Younger, Sir William McEwan, Bt., D.S.O. (1964).

Zeidler, Sir David Ronald, Kt. C.B.E.

Zoleveke, Sir Gideon Pitabose, K.B.E.

Zunz, Sir Gerhard Jacob (Jack), Kt.

Zurenuo, *Rt. Rev.* Zurewe Kamong, Kt., O.B.E.

Baronetcies Extinct (Since last issue).—Readhead (U.K., 1922); Cunard (U.K., 1859).

Dames Grand Cross and Dames Commanders of the Order of the Bath, the Order of St. Michael and St. George, the Royal Victorian Order and the Order of the British Empire

NOTE.—Dames Grand Cross (G.C.B., G.C.M.G., G.C.V.O. or G.B.E.) and Dames Commanders (D.C.B., D.C.M.G., D.C.V.O. or D.B.E.) are addressed in a manner similar to that of Knights Grand Cross or Knights Commanders, e.g. Miss Florence Smith after receiving the honour would be addressed as Dame Florence, and in writing as Dame Florence Smith, G. (or D.) C.B., G. (or D.) C.M.G., G. (or D.) C.V.O., OR G. (or D.) B.E. Where such award is made to a lady already in enjoyment of a higher title the appropriate letters are appended to her name, e.g. The Countess of —— G.C.V.O. Women Peers in their own right, and Life Peers, are not included in this list. Dames Grand Cross rank after wives of Baronets and before wives of Knights Grand Cross. Dames Commanders rank after the wives of Knights Grand Cross and before the wives of Knights Commanders.

DAMES GRAND CROSS AND DAMES COMMANDERS

H.M. Queen Elizabeth The Queen Mother, K.G., K.T., C.I., G.M.V.O.

H.R.H. The Princess Royal, G.C.V.O.

H.R.H. The Princess Margaret, Countess of Snowdon, C.I., G.C.V.O.

H.R.H. The Duchess of Gloucester, G.C.V.O.

H.R.H. The Princess Alice, Duchess of Gloucester, G.C.B., C.I., G.C.V.O., G.B.E.

H.R.H. The Duchess of Kent, G.C.V.O.

H.R.H. The Princess Alexandra of Kent, G.C.V.O.

Abel Smith, Lady, D.C.V.O.

Abercorn, Mary, Duchess of, G.C.V.O.

Abergavenny, The Marchioness of, D.C.V.O.

Albemarle, The Countess of, D.B.E.

Anderson, Dame Judith, D.B.E.

Anderson, *Brig.* Hon. Dame Mary Mackenzie (Mrs. Pihl), D.B.E.

Anglesey, The Marchioness of, D.B.E.

Ashcroft, Dame Peggy, D.B.E.

Baker, Dame Janet Abbott (Mrs. Shelley), D.B.E.

Baring, Lady Rose Gwendolen Louisa, D.C.V.O.

Barnes, Dame (Alice) Josephine (Mary Taylor), D.B.E., F.R.C.P., F.R.C.S.

Basset, Lady Elizabeth, D.C.V.O.

Beaurepaire, Dame Beryl Edith, D.B.E.

Berry, Dame Alice Miriam, D.B.E.

Bishop, Dame (Margaret) Joyce, D.B.E.

Blaxland, Dame Helen Frances, D.B.E.

Booth, *Hon.* Dame Margaret Myfanwy Wood, D.B.E.

Bottomley, Dame Bessie Ellen, D.B.E.

Boyd, Dame Vivienne Myra, D.B.E.

Brazill, Dame Josephine (Sister Mary Philippa), D.B.E.

Breen, Dame Marie Freda, D.B.E.

Bridges, Dame Mary Patricia, D.B.E.

Brown, Dame Beryl Paston, D.B.E.

Brown, Dame Gillian Gerda, D.C.V.O., C.M.G.

Browne, Lady Moyra Blanche Madeleine, D.B.E.

Bryans, Dame Anne Margaret, D.B.E.

Bryce, Dame Isabel Graham, D.B.E.

Burnside, Dame Edith, D.B.E.

Butler-Sloss, *Rt. Hon.* Dame (Ann) Elizabeth (Oldfield), D.B.E.

Buttfield, Dame Nancy Eileen, D.B.E.

Bynoe, Dame Hilda Louisa, D.B.E.

Cartwright, Dame Mary Lucy, D.B.E., SC.D., D.Phil., F.R.S.

Cartwright, Dame Silvia Rose, D.B.E.

Cayford, Dame Florence Evelyn, D.B.E.

Chesterton, Dame Elizabeth Ursula, D.B.E.

Clay, Dame Marie Mildred, D.B.E.

Clayton, Dame Barbara Evelyn (Mrs. Klyne), D.B.E.

Cleland, Dame Rachel, D.B.E.

Clode, Dame (Emma) Frances (Heather), D.B.E.

Coles, Dame Mabel Irene, D.B.E.

Conan Doyle, *Air Cmdt.* Dame Jean Lena Annette (Lady Bromet), D.B.E.

Cooper, Dame Whina, D.B.E.

Coulshed, Dame (Mary) Frances, D.B.E., T.D.

Cozens, *Brig.* Dame (Florence) Barbara, D.B.E., R.R.C.

Crowe, Dame Sylvia, D.B.E.

Daws, Dame Joyce Margaretta, D.B.E.

De La Warr, Sylvia, Countess, D.B.E.

Dell, Dame Miriam Patricia, D.B.E.

Dench, Dame Judith Olivia (Mrs. Williams), D.B.E.

de Valois, Dame Ninette, C.H., D.B.E.

Dickson, Dame Violet Penelope, D.B.E.

Donaldson, Dame (Dorothy) Mary, G.B.E.

Dugdale, Kathryn Edith Helen (Mrs. John Dugdale), D.C.V.O.

Dunn, Dame Lydia, D.B.E.

Durack, Dame Mary (Mrs. H. C. Miller), D.B.E.

Emerton, Dame Audrey Caroline, D.B.E.

Evans, Lady Olwen Elizabeth Carey, D.B.E.

Fenner, Dame Peggy Edith, D.B.E., M.P.

Fermoy, Ruth Sylvia, Lady, D.C.V.O., O.B.E.

Fitton, Dame Doris Alice (Mrs. Mason), D.B.E.

Fonteyn, Dame Margot, D.B.E.

Fookes, Dame Janet Evelyn, D.B.E., M.P.

Fraser, Dame Dorothy Rita, D.B.E.

Friend, Dame Phyllis Muriel, D.B.E.

Frink, Dame Elisabeth, D.B.E., R.A.

Frost, Dame Phyllis Irene, D.B.E.

Fry, Dame Margaret Louise, D.B.E.

Gallagher, Dame Monica Josephine, D.B.E.

Gardiner, Dame Helen Louisa, D.B.E., M.V.O.

Gibbs, Dame Molly Peel, D.B.E.

Giles, *Air Cmdt.* Dame Pauline (Mrs. Parsons), D.B.E., R.R.C.

Godwin, Dame (Beatrice) Anne, D.B.E.

Golding, Dame (Cecilie) Monica, D.B.E.

Goodman, Dame Barbara, D.B.E.

Gordon, Dame Minita Elmira, G.C.M.G., G.C.V.O.

Grafton, The Duchess of, G.C.V.O.

Green, Dame Mary Georgina, D.B.E.

Grey, Dame Beryl Elizabeth (Mrs. Svenson), D.B.E.

Guilfoyle, Dame Margaret Georgina Constance, D.B.E.

Hall, Dame Catherine Mary, D.B.E.

Hambleden, Patricia, Viscountess, D.C.V.O.

Hammond, Dame Joan Hood, D.B.E.

Hedley-Miller, Dame Mary Elizabeth, D.C.V.O., C.B.

Heilbron, *Hon.* Dame Rose, D.B.E.

Henrison, Dame Anne Elizabeth Rosina, D.B.E.

Herbison, Dame Jean Marjory, D.B.E., C.M.G.

Hercus, *Hon.* Dame (Margaret) Ann, D.C.M.G.

Hill, Dame Elizabeth Mary, D.B.E.

Hill, *Air Cdre.* Dame Felicity Barbara, D.B.E.

Hiller, Dame Wendy (Mrs. Gow), D.B.E.

Holland-Martin, Rosamund Mary, Lady, D.B.E.

Horsman, Dame Dorothea Jean, D.B.E.

Howard, Dame Rosemary Christian, D.B.E.

Hunter, Dame Pamela, D.B.E.

Hurley, *Prof.* Dame Rosalinde (Mrs. Gortvai), D.B.E.

Hussey, Lady Susan Katharine, D.C.V.O.

Isaacs, Dame Albertha Madeline, D.B.E.

James, Dame Naomi Christine, D.B.E.

Jenkins, Dame (Mary) Jennifer (Lady Jenkins of Hillhead), D.B.E.

Jessel, Dame Penelope, D.B.E.

Jones, Dame Gwyneth (Mrs. Haberfeld-Jones), D.B.E.

Kekedo, Dame Mary, D.B.E., B.E.M.

Kelleher, Dame Joan, D.B.E.

Kellett-Bowman, Dame (Mary) Elaine, D.B.E., M.P.

Kettlewell, *Cmdt.* Dame Marion Mildred, D.B.E.

Kilroy, Dame Alix Hester Marie (Lady Meynell), D.B.E.

Kirk, Dame (Lucy) Ruth, D.B.E.

Knight, Dame (Joan Christabel) Jill, D.B.E., M.P.

Kramer, *Prof.* Dame Leonie Judith, D.B.E.

Lancaster, Dame Jean, D.B.E.

Lister, Dame Unity Viola, D.B.E.

Litchfield, Dame Ruby Beatrice, D.B.E.

Lloyd, Dame Hilda Nora, D.B.E.

Lowrey, *Air Cmdt.* Dame Alice, D.B.E., R.R.C.

Lynn, Dame Vera (Mrs. Lewis), D.B.E.

Mackinnon, Dame (Una) Patricia, D.B.E.

Macknight, Dame Ella Annie Noble, D.B.E., M.D.

Macmillan of Ovenden, Katharine, Viscountess, D.B.E.

Maconchy, Dame Elizabeth Violet (Mrs. Le Fanu), D.B.E.

Mann, Dame Ida Caroline, D.B.E., D.SC., F.R.C.S.

Markova, Dame Alicia, D.B.E.

Maxwell-Scott, Dame Jean Mary Monica, D.C.V.O.

Menzies, Dame Pattie Maie, G.B.E.

Metge, Dr. Dame (Alice) Joan, D.B.E.

Miles, Dame Margaret, D.B.E.

Miller, Dame Mabel Flora Hobart, D.B.E.

Mitchell, *Hon.* Dame Roma Flinders, D.B.E.

Morrison, *Hon.* Dame Mary Anne, D.C.V.O.

Mueller, Dame Anne Elisabeth, D.C.B.

Munro, Dame Alison, D.B.E.

Murdoch, Dame Elisabeth Joy, D.B.E.

Murdoch, Dame (Jean) Iris (Mrs. Bayley), D.B.E.

Murray, Dame (Alice) Rosemary, D.B.E., D.Phil.

Niccol, Dame Kathleen Agnes, D.B.E.

Norris, Dame Ada May, D.B.E., C.M.G.

Ollerenshaw, Dame Kathleen Mary, D.B.E., D.Phil.

Park, Dame Merle Florence (Mrs. Bloch), D.B.E.

Parker, Dame Marjorie Alice Collett, D.B.E.

Paterson, Dame Betty Fraser Ross, D.B.E.

Pepys, Lady (Mary) Rachel, D.C.V.O.

Pickerill, Dame Cecily Mary Wise, D.B.E.

Plowden, The Lady, D.B.E.

Prendergast, Dame Simone Ruth, D.B.E.

Prentice, Dame Winifred Eva, D.B.E.

Purves, Dame Daphne Helen, D.B.E.

Pyke, Lady, D.B.E.

Quinn, Dame Sheila Margaret Imelda, D.B.E.

Railton, *Brig.* Dame Mary, D.B.E.

Railton, Dame Ruth (Mrs. King), D.B.E.

Rankin, Lady Jean Margaret Florence, D.C.V.O.

Raven, Dame Kathleen Annie (Mrs. Ingram), D.B.E.

Reader, Dame Audrey Tattie Hinchcliff, D.B.E.

Reader-Harris, Dame (Muriel) Diana, D.B.E.

Riddelsdell, Dame Mildred, D.C.B., C.B.E.

Ridley, Dame (Mildred) Betty, D.B.E.

Rivett-Drake, *Brig.* Dame Jean Elizabeth Rivett, D.B.E.

Roberts, Dame Joan Howard, D.B.E.

Roberts, Dame Shelagh Marjorie, D.B.E.

Robertson, *Cmdt.* Dame Nancy Margaret, D.B.E.

Roe, Dame Raigh Edith, D.B.E.

Rue, Dame (Elsie) Rosemary, D.B.E.

Salas, Dame Margaret Laurence, D.B.E.

Saunders, Dame Cicely Mary Strode, D.B.E., F.R.C.P.
Scott, Dame Catherine Campbell, D.B.E.
Scott, Dame Margaret, (Dame Catherine Margaret Mary Denton), D.B.E.
Seccombe, Dame Joan Anna Dalziel, D.B.E.
Shenfield, Dame Barbara Estelle, D.B.E.
Shepherd, Dame Margaret Alice, D.B.E.
Sherlock, *Prof.* Dame Sheila Patricia Violet, D.B.E., M.D., F.R.C.P.
Smieton, Dame Mary Guillan, D.B.E.
Smith, Dame Margot, D.B.E.
Snagge, Dame Nancy Marion, D.B.E.
Soames, Mary, Lady, D.B.E.
Stark, Dame Freya (Mrs. Perowne), D.B.E.
Stephens, *Air Cmdt.* Dame Anne, D.B.E.

Stewart, Dame Muriel Acadia, D.B.E.
Sutherland, Dame Joan (Mrs. Bonynge), D.B.E.
Taylor, Dame Jean Elizabeth, D.C.V.O.
Te Atairangikaahu, Arikinui, D.B.E.
Te Kanawa, Dame Kiri Janette (Mrs. Park), D.B.E.
Tilney, Dame Guinevere (Lady Tilney), D.B.E.
Tizard, Dame Catherine Anne, D.B.E.
Tokiel, Dame Rosa, D.B.E.
Turner, Dame Eva, D.B.E.
Turner, *Brig.* Dame Margot, D.B.E., R.R.C.
Tyrwhitt, *Brig.* Dame Mary Joan Caroline, D.B.E., T.D.
Uatioa, Dame Mere, D.B.E.
Uvarov, Dame Olga, D.B.E.
Van Praagh, Dame Peggy, D.B.E.

Varley, Dame Joan Fleetwood, D.B.E.
Vaughan, Dame Janet Maria (Mrs. Gourlay), D.B.E., F.R.S.
Wakehurst, Margaret, Lady, D.B.E.
Walker, Dame Susan Armour, D.B.E.
Wall, (Alice) Anne, (Mrs. Michael Wall), D.C.V.O.
Warburton, Dame Anne Marion, D.C.V.O., C.M.G.
Wedega, Dame Alice, D.B.E.
Wedgwood, Dame (Cicely) Veronica, O.M., D.B.E.
Weston, Dame Margaret Kate, D.B.E.
Williamson, Dame (Elsie) Marjorie, D.B.E., Ph.D.
Wormald, Dame Ethel May, D.B.E.
Yarwood, Dame Elizabeth Ann, D.B.E.
Yonge, Dame (Ida) Felicity (Ann), D.B.E.

THE VICTORIA CROSS, V.C.
FOR CONSPICUOUS BRAVERY

The ribbon *is Crimson* for all Services (until 1918 it was *Blue* for Royal Navy).

Instituted on January 29, 1856, the Victoria Cross was awarded retrospectively to 1854, the first being held by Lt. C. D. Lucas, R.N. for bravery in the Baltic Sea on June 21, 1854 (gazetted Feb. 24, 1857). The first 62 Crosses were presented by Queen Victoria in Hyde Park, London, on June 26, 1857.

The V.C. is worn before all other decorations, on the left breast, and consists of a cross-pattée of bronze, 1¼ inches in diameter, with the Royal Crown surmounted by a lion in the centre, and beneath there is the inscription 'For Valour'. Holders of the V.C. receive a tax-free annuity of £100, irrespective of need or other conditions. In 1911, the right to receive the Cross was extended to Indian soldiers, and in 1920 a Royal Warrant extended the right to Matrons, Sisters and Nurses, and the staff of the Nursing Services and other services pertaining to hospitals and nursing, and to civilians of either sex regularly or temporarily under the orders, direction or supervision of the Naval, Military, or Air Forces of the Crown.

Surviving Recipients of the Victoria Cross
(as at Aug. 31, 1989)

Agansing Rai, *Havildar* (Gurkha Rifles), *World War* 1944
Ali Haidar, *Jemadar* (Frontier Force Rifles), *World War* 1945
Annand, *Capt.* R. W. (Durham L.I.), *World War* 1940
Bhanbhagta Gurung, *Capt.* (2nd Gurkha Rifles), *World War* 1945
Bhandari Ram, *Capt.* (Baluch R.), *World War* . . 1944
Burton, *Cpl.* R. H. (Duke of Wellington's R.), *World War* 1944
Campbell, *Brig.* L. M., D.S.O., O.B.E., T.D. (A. & S. Highrs.), *World War* 1943
Chapman, *Sgt.* E. T., B.E.M. (Monmouthshire R.), *World War* 1945
Cheshire, *Group Capt.* G. L., O.M., D.S.O., D.F.C. (R.A.F.), *World War* 1944
Cruickshank, *Fl. Lt.* J. A. (R.A.F.V.R.), *World War* 1944
Cutler, Sir A. R., K.C.M.G., K.C.V.O., C.B.E. (Australia), *World War* 1941
De L'Isle, *Maj.* The Viscount, K.G., P.C., G.C.M.G., G.C.V.O. (*Hon.* W. P. Sidney) (Gren. Gds.), *World War* 1944

Eardley, *Sgt.* G. H., M.M. (K.S.L.I.), *World War* 1944
Elliott, *Lt.* the Rev. K. (N.Z.M.F.), *World War* . . 1942
Ervine-Andrews, *Lt.-Col.* H. M. (E. Lancs. R.), *World War* 1940
Foote, *Maj.-Gen.* H. R. B., C.B., D.S.O. (R. Tank R.), *World War* 1942
Fraser, *Cdr.* I. E., D.S.C. (R.N.R.), *World War* 1945
Ganju Lama, *Jemadar*, M.M. (Gurkha Rifles), *World War* 1944
Gardner, *Capt.* P. J., M.C. (R.T.R.), *World War* . . 1941
Ghale, *Subedar* Gaje (Gurkha Rifles), *World War* 1943
Gian Singh, *Jemadar* (Punjab R.), *World War* . . 1945
Gould, *Lt.* T. W. (R.N.), *World War* 1942
Hinton, *Sgt.* J. D. (N.Z.M.F.), *World War* 1941
Jackson, *W.O.* N. C. (R.A.F.V.R.), *World War* 1944
Jamieson, *Maj.* D. A. (R. Norfolk R.), *World War* 1944
Kenna, *Pte.* E. (Australian M.F.), *World War* . . . 1945
Kenneally, *C.-Q.-M.-S.* J. P. (Irish Gds.), *World War* 1943
Lachiman Gurung, *Rifleman* (Gurkha Rifles), *World War* 1945

Learoyd, *Wing-Cmdr.* R. A. B. (R.A.F.), *World War*..1940
Mahony, *Lt.-Col.* J. K., C.D. (Westminster R., Canada), *World War*......................1944
Merritt, *Lt.-Col.* C. C. I., C.D. (S. Saskatchewan R.), *World War*..........................1942
Norton, *Capt.* G. R., M.M. (S.A.M.F.), *World War*..................................1944
Parkash Singh, *Maj.* (Punjab R.), *World War*...1943
Payne, *W.O.* K. (Australian Army), *Vietnam*...1969
Place, *Rear-Adm.* B. C. G., C.B., D.S.C. (R.N.), *World War*..................................1943
Porteous, *Col.* P. A. (R.A.), *World War*.........1942
Rambahadur Limbu, *Lt.* M.V.O. (Gurkha Rifles), *Sarawak* 1965
Reid, *Fl.-Lt.* W. (R.A.F.V.R.), *World War*.......1943
Smith, *Sgt.* E. A., C.D. (Seaforth Highrs. of Canada), *World War*......................1944

Smythe, *Capt.* Q. G. M. (S.A.M.F.), *World War*..1942
Speakman, *Sgt.* W. (Black Watch), *Korea* 1951
Starcevich, *Pte.* L. T. (Australia), *World War*..1945
Tilston, *Maj.* F. A. (Essex Scottish, Canada), *World War* 1945
Tulbahadur Pun, *W.O. I.* (Gurkha Rifles), *World War* 1944
Umrao Singh, *Sub-Major* (I.A.), *World War* 1944
Upham, *Capt.* C. H. (and Bar, 1942), (N.Z.M.F.), *World War* 1941
Watkins, *Maj. Rt. Hon.* Sir Tasker (Welch R.), *World War* 1944
Wilson, *Lt.-Col.* E. C. T. (E. Surrey R.), *World War*....................................1940
Wright, *C.S.M.* P. H. (Coldstream Gds.), *World War*......................................1943

THE GEORGE CROSS, G.C. (1940)

FOR GALLANTRY

The ribbon is *Dark Blue* threaded through a bar adorned with laurel leaves.

INSTITUTED September, 24th, 1940 (with amendments, November 3rd, 1942).

The George Cross is worn before all other decorations (except the V.C.) on the left breast § and consists of a plain silver cross with four equal limbs, the cross having in the centre a circular medallion bearing a design showing St. George and the Dragon. The inscription 'For Gallantry' appears round the medallion and in the angle of each limb of the cross is the Royal cypher 'G VI' forming a circle concentric with the medallion. The reverse is plain and bears the name of the recipient and the date of the award. The cross is suspended by a ring from a bar adorned with laurel leaves on dark blue ribbon 1½ inches wide.

The cross is intended primarily for civilians and awards to the fighting services are confined to actions for which purely military honours are not normally granted. It is awarded only for acts of the greatest heroism or of the most conspicuous courage in circumstances of extreme danger. From April 1, 1965, holders of the Cross have received a tax-free annuity of £100.

§ When worn by a woman it may be worn on the left shoulder from a ribbon of the same width and colour fashioned into a bow.

Empire Gallantry Medal.—The Royal Warrant which ordained that the grant of the Empire Gallantry Medal should cease authorized holders of that medal to return it to the Central Chancery of the Orders of Knighthood and to receive in exchange the George Cross. A similar provision applied to posthumous awards of the Empire Gallantry Medal made after the outbreak of war in 1939.

In October 1971 all surviving holders of the Albert Medal and the Edward Medal exchanged those decorations for the George Cross.

THE ORDER OF ST. JOHN

The Most Venerable Order of the Hospital of St. John of Jerusalem

St. John's Gate, Clerkenwell, EC1M 4DA

Grand Prior, H.R.H. The Duke of Gloucester, G.C.V.O.

Lord Prior, The Lord Grey of Naunton, G.C.M.G., G.C.V.O., O.B.E.
Chancellor, The Lord Vestey.

PRINCIPAL DECORATIONS AND MEDALS (in order of Precedence)

Victoria Cross. (V.C.)—1856.

George Cross. (G.C.)—1940.

British Orders of Knighthood, Etc. (for order in which worn, *see* pp. 188–90).

Baronet's Badge

Knight Bachelor's Badge

Decorations

Royal Red Cross. (Class I—R.R.C.)—1883.—For ladies.

Distinguished Service Cross. (D.S.C.)—1914.—For officers of R.N. below the rank of Captain, and Warrant Officers.

Military Cross. (M.C.)—Dec. 1914.—Awarded to Captains, Lieutenants, and Warrant Officers (CI I. and II.) in the Army and Indian and Colonial Forces.

Distinguished Flying Cross. (D.F.C.)—1918.—For officers and Warrant Officers in the R.A.F. (and Fleet Air Arm from April 9, 1941) for acts of gallantry when flying in active operations against the enemy.

Air Force Cross. (A.F.C.)—1918.—Instituted as preceding but for acts of courage or devotion to duty when flying, although not in active operations against the enemy (extended to Fleet Air Arm since April 9, 1941).

Royal Red Cross (Class II—A.R.R.C.).

Order of British India.

Kaisar-i-Hind Medal.

Order of St. John.

Medals for Gallantry and Distinguished Conduct

Union of South Africa Queen's Medal for Bravery, in Gold.

Distinguished Conduct Medal. (D.C.M.)—1854.—Awarded to warrant officers, non-commissioned officers and men of the Army and R.A.F.

Conspicuous Gallantry Medal. (C.G.M.)—1874.—Is bestowed upon warrant officers and men of the R.N. and since 1942 of Mercantile Marine and R.A.F.

The George Medal. (G.M.)—1940.

Queen's Police Medal for Gallantry.

Queen's Fire Service Medal for Gallantry.

Royal West African Frontier Force Distinguished Conduct Medal.

King's African Rifles Distinguished Conduct Medal.

Indian Distinguished Service Medal.

Union of South Africa Queen's Medal for Bravery, in Silver.

Distinguished Service Medal. (D.S.M.)—1914.—For chief petty officers, petty officers and men, of all branches of the Royal Navy, and since 1942 of Mercantile Marine; non-commissioned officers and men of the Royal Marines; all other persons holding corresponding positions in Her Majesty's Service afloat.

Military Medal. (M.M.)—1916.—For warrant and non-commissioned officers and men and serving women.

Distinguished Flying Medal. (D.F.M.)—1918.—and the Air Force Medal. (A.F.M.)—For warrant and non-commissioned officers and men for equivalent services as for D.F.C. and A.F.C. (extended to Fleet Air Arm, 1941).

Constabulary Medal (Ireland).

Medal for Saving Life at Sea.

Indian Order of Merit (Civil).

Indian Police Medal for Gallantry.

Ceylon Police Medal for Gallantry.

Sierra Leone Police Medal for Gallantry.

Sierra Leone Fire Brigades Medal for Gallantry.

Colonial Police Medal for Gallantry. (C.P.M.)

Queen's Gallantry Medal.—1974.

Royal Victorian Medal. (R.V.M.)—(Gold, Silver and Bronze).

British Empire Medal. (B.E.M.)—(formerly the Medal of the Order of the British Empire, for Meritorious Service; also includes the Medal of the Order awarded before Dec. 29, 1922).

Queen's Police (Q.P.M.) and Fire Services Medals for Distinguished Service, (Q.F.S.M.).

Queen's Medal for Chiefs.

War Medals and Stars (in order of date).

Polar Medals (in order of date).

Imperial Service Medal.

Police Medals for Valuable Service.

Badge of Honour.

Jubilee, Coronation and Durbar Medals.

King George V, King George VI and Queen Elizabeth II Long and Faithful Service Medals.

Efficiency and Long Service Decorations and Medals.

Medal for Meritorious Service.

Long Service and Good Conduct Medal—(Military).

Naval Long Service and Good Conduct Medal.

Royal Marine Meritorious Service Medal.

Royal Air Force Meritorious Service Medal.

Royal Air Force Long Service and Good Conduct Medal.

Medal for Long Service and Good Conduct (Ulster Defence Regiment).

Police and Fire Brigade Long Service and Good Conduct Medal.

Colonial Police and Fire Brigades Long Service Medal.

Colonial Prison Service Medal.

Army Emergency Reserve Decoration. (E.R.D.)—1952.

Volunteer Officer's Decoration. (V.D.)

Volunteer Long Service Medal.

Volunteer Officer's Decoration (for India and the Colonies).

Volunteer Long Service Medal (for India and the Colonies).

Colonial Auxiliary Forces Officer's Decoration.

Colonial Auxiliary Forces Long Service Medal.

Medal for Good Shooting (Naval).

Militia Long Service Medal.

Imperial Yeomanry Long Service Medal.

Territorial Decoration. (T.D.)—1908.

Efficiency Decoration. (E.D.).

Territorial Efficiency Medal.

Efficiency Medal.

Special Reserve Long Service and Good Conduct Medal.

Decoration for Officers, Royal Navy Reserve. (R.D.)—1910.

Decoration for Officers, R.N.V.R. (V.R.D.)

Royal Naval Reserve Long Service and Good Conduct Medal.

R.N.V.R. Long Service and Good Conduct Medal.

Royal Naval Auxiliary Sick Berth Reserve Long Service and Good Conduct Medal.

Royal Fleet Reserve Long Service and Good Conduct Medal.

Royal Naval Wireless Auxiliary Reserve Long Service and Good Conduct Medal.

Air Efficiency Award. (A.E.)—1942.

Ulster Defence Regiment Medal.

The Queen's Medal.—(For champion shots in the R.N., R.M., R.N.Z.N., Army, R.A.F.).

Cadet Forces Medal.—1950.

Coast Life Saving Corps Long Service Medal.—1911.

Special Constabulary Long Service Medal.

Royal Observer Corps Medal.

Civil Defence Long Service Medal.

Royal Ulster Constabulary Service Medal.

Service Medal of the Order of St. John.

Badge of the Order of the League of Mercy.

Voluntary Medical Service Medal.—1932.

Women's Royal Voluntary Service Medal.

Colonial Special Constabulary Medal.

Foreign Orders, Decorations and Medals (in order of date).

THE PRIVY COUNCIL

Apart from Cabinet Ministers, who must be Privy Counsellors and are sworn in on first assuming office, membership of the Council (retained for life) is accorded by the Sovereign on the recommendation of the Prime Minister to eminent people in independent monarchical countries of the Commonwealth.

THE UNITED KINGDOM CONSTITUTION

The United Kingdom constitution is not contained in any single document but has evolved in the course of time, formed partly by statute, partly by common law and partly by convention. A constitutional monarchy, the United Kingdom is governed by Ministers of the Crown in the name of the Sovereign, who is head both of the state and the government.

The organs of government are the *legislature* (Parliament), the *executive* and the *judiciary*. The executive consists of Her Majesty's Government (Cabinet and other Ministers), government departments (*see* pp. 293–375), local authorities (*see* Index), and public corporations operating nationalized industries or social or cultural services (*see* pp. 293–375). The judiciary, i.e. judges, pronounce on the law, both written and unwritten, interpret statutes and are responsible for the enforcement of the law; the judiciary is independent of both the legislature and the executive (*see* Law Courts and Offices).

THE MONARCHY

The Sovereign personifies the state and is, in law, an integral part of the legislature, head of the executive, head of the judiciary, the Commander-in-Chief of all armed forces of the Crown and the 'Supreme Governor' of the Church of England. The seat of the monarchy is in the United Kingdom. In the Channel Islands and the Isle of Man, which are Crown dependencies, the Sovereign is represented by a Lieutenant-Governor; in the member states of the Commonwealth of which the Sovereign is head of state, her representative is a Governor-General (*see also* p. 625); in United Kingdom dependencies the Sovereign is usually represented by a Governor, who is responsible to the British Government.

Although the powers of the monarchy are now very limited, restricted mainly to the advisory and ceremonial, there are important acts of government which require the participation of the Sovereign. These include summoning, proroguing and dissolving Parliament, giving Royal Assent to Bills passed by Parliament, appointing important office-holders, e.g. government ministers, judges, bishops, and governors, conferring peerages, knighthoods and other honours, and granting pardon to a person wrongly convicted of a crime. An important function is appointing a Prime Minister, by convention the leader of the political party which enjoys, or can secure, a majority of votes in the House of Commons. In international affairs the Sovereign as head of State has the power to declare war and make peace, to recognize foreign states and governments, to conclude treaties and to annex or cede territory. However, as the Sovereign entrusts executive power to Ministers of the Crown and acts on the advice of her Ministers, which she cannot ignore, in practice royal prerogative powers are exercised by Ministers, who are responsible to Parliament.

Ministerial responsibility does not diminish the Sovereign's importance to the smooth working of government. She holds meetings of the Privy Council, gives audiences to her Ministers and other officials at home and overseas, receives accounts of Cabinet decisions, reads dispatches and signs state papers; she must be informed and consulted on every aspect of national life; and she must show complete impartiality.

In the event of the Sovereign's absence abroad, it is necessary to appoint *Counsellors of State* under Letters Patent to carry out the chief functions of the Monarch, including the holding of Privy Councils and giving Royal Assent to Acts passed by Parliament. The normal procedure is to appoint as Counsellors three or four members of the Royal Family among those remaining in the United Kingdom. In the event of the Sovereign on accession being under the age of eighteen years, or at any time unavailable or incapacitated by infirmity of mind or body for the performance of the royal functions, provision is made for a Regency.

THE PRIVY COUNCIL

The Sovereign in Council, or Privy Council, was the chief source of executive power until the system of Cabinet government developed. Now its main function is to advise the Sovereign to approve Orders in Council and to advise on the issue of royal proclamations. The Council's own statutory responsibilities (independent of the powers of the Sovereign in Council) include powers of supervision over the registering bodies for the medical and allied professions. A full Council is summoned only on the death of the Sovereign or when the Sovereign announces his or her intention to marry (for full list of Counsellors, *see* pp. 229–30).

There are a number of advisory Privy Council committees, whose meetings the Sovereign does not attend. Some are prerogative committees, such as those dealing with legislative matters submitted by the legislatures of the Channel Islands and the Isle of Man or with applications for charters of incorporation; and some are provided for by statute, e.g. those for the universities of Oxford and Cambridge and the Scottish universities.

The Judicial Committee of the Privy Council is the final court of appeal from courts of the United Kingdom dependencies, courts of independent Commonwealth countries which have retained the right of appeal, courts of the Channel Islands and the Isle of Man, some professional and disciplinary committees, and church sources. The Committee is composed of all Privy Counsellors who hold, or have held, high judicial office, although usually only three or five hear each case.

Administrative work is carried out by the Privy Council Office under the direction of the Lord President of the Council, a Cabinet Minister.

PARLIAMENT

Parliament is the supreme law-making authority and can legislate for the United Kingdom as a whole or for any parts of it separately (the Channel Islands and the Isle of Man are Crown dependencies and not part of the United Kingdom). The main functions of Parliament are to pass laws, to provide (by voting taxation) the means of carrying on the work of government and to scrutinize government policy and administration, particularly proposals for expenditure. International treaties and agreements are by custom presented to Parliament before ratification.

Parliament emerged during the late thirteenth and early fourteenth centuries. The nucleus of early Parliaments were the officers of the King's household and the King's judges, joined by such ecclesiastical and lay magnates as the King might summon to form a prototype "House of Lords", and occasionally by the knights of the shires, burgesses and proctors of the lower clergy. By the end of Edward III's reign a "House of Commons" was beginning to appear: the first known Speaker was elected in 1377.

Parliamentary procedure is based on custom and precedent, partly formulated in the Standing Orders of both Houses (*see* p. 237), and each House has the right to control its own internal proceedings and to commit for contempt. The system of debate in the two Houses is similar; when a motion has been moved, the Speaker proposes the question as the subject of a debate. Members speak from wherever they have been sitting. Questions are decided by a vote on a simple majority. Draft legislation is introduced, in either House, as a Bill. Bills can be introduced by a Government Minister or a private Member, but in practice the majority of Bills which become law are introduced by the Government. To become law, a Bill must be passed by each House (for parliamentary stages, see **Bill**, p. 235) and then sent to the Sovereign for the Royal Assent, after which it becomes an Act of Parliament.

Proceedings of both Houses are public, except on extremely rare occasions. The minutes (called Votes and Proceedings in the Commons, and Minutes of Proceedings in the Lords) and the speeches (The Official Report of Parliamentary Debates, *Hansard*) are published daily. Proceedings are also recorded for sound transmission on radio and television and preserved by the Parliamentary Sound Archive. Since January 1985, the House of Lords has allowed television cameras into its debates and Select Committees: the House of Commons is considering an experiment in televising its proceedings.

By the Parliament Act of 1911, the maximum duration of a Parliament is five years, if not previously dissolved, the term being reckoned from the date given on the writs for the new Parliament. The maximum life has been prolonged by legislation in such rare circumstances as the two world wars (Jan. 31, 1911–Nov. 25, 1918; Nov. 26, 1935–June 15, 1945). Dissolution and writs for a general election are ordered by the Queen on the advice of the Prime Minister. The life of a Parliament is divided into *sessions*, usually of one year in length, beginning and ending most often in October or November.

THE HOUSE OF LORDS

The House of Lords consists of the Lords Spiritual and Temporal. The Lords Spiritual are the Archbishops of Canterbury and York, the Bishops of London, Durham and Winchester, and the 21 senior diocesan Bishops of the Church of England. The Lords Temporal consist of all hereditary Peers and Peeresses of England, Scotland, Great Britain and the United Kingdom who have not disclaimed their Peerages, Life Peers and Peeresses created under the Life Peerages Act 1958, and those Lords of Appeal in

Ordinary created Life Peers under the Appellate Jurisdiction Act 1876, as amended (Law Lords). Disclaimants of an hereditary Peerage lose their right to sit in the House of Lords but gain the right to vote at Parliamentary elections and to offer themselves for election to the House of Commons. (*See also* p. 156). Peers who do not wish to attend sittings of the House of Lords may apply for leave of absence for the duration of a Parliament.

Until the beginning of this century the House of Lords had considerable power, being able to veto any Bill submitted to it by the House of Commons, but those powers were greatly reduced by the Parliament Act of 1911 and subsequently by the Parliament Act of 1949 (*see* **Parliament Acts 1911 and 1949**, p. 236).

Combined with its legislative role, the House of Lords has judicial powers as the ultimate Court of Appeal for Courts in Great Britain and Northern Ireland, except for criminal cases in Scotland. These powers are exercised by the Lord Chancellor and the Law Lords.

Members of the House of Lords are unpaid. However, they are entitled to reimbursement of travelling expenses on parliamentary business within the U.K. and certain other expenses incurred for the purpose of attendance at sittings of the House, within a maximum for each day of £60·00 for overnight subsistence, £23·00 for day subsistence and incidental travel, and £23·00 for secretarial costs, postage and certain additional expenses.

The House is presided over by the Lord Chancellor, who is *ex officio* Speaker of the House. A panel of deputy Speakers is appointed by Royal Commission. The first deputy Speaker is the Chairman of Committees, appointed at the beginning of each session, a salaried officer of the House who takes the chair in Committee of the whole House and in some Select Committees. He is assisted by a panel of Deputy Chairmen, headed by the salaried Principal Deputy Chairman of Committees, who is also Chairman of the European Communities Committee of the House. The permanent officers include the Clerk of the Parliaments, who is in charge of the administrative staff collectively known as the Parliament Office; the Gentleman Usher of the Black Rod, who is also Serjeant-at-Arms in attendance upon the Lord Chancellor and is responsible for security and for accommodation and services in the House of Lords; and the Yeoman Usher who is Deputy Serjeant-at-Arms and assists Black Rod in his duties.

OFFICERS OF THE HOUSE OF LORDS

Speaker, The Rt. Hon. the Lord Mackay of Clashfern £12,810
  Private Secretary, J. P. Stockton.
Chairman of Committees, The Rt. Hon. the Lord Aberdare, K.B.E. £37,047
Principal Deputy Chairman of Committees, The Baroness Serota £33,537

Clerk of the Parliaments, Sir John Sainty, K.C.B. £72,000
Clerk Assistant and Clerk of the Journals, M. A. J. Wheeler-Booth .... £48,100–£59,800
Reading Clerk and Principal Clerk, Public Bills, J. M. Davies .... £39,600–£49,600
Counsel to Chairman of Committees, D. Rippengal, C.B., Q.C. .... £48,100–£59,800
Second Counsel, Mrs. E. Denza, C.M.G. £39,600–£49,600
Assistant Counsel, N. J. Adamson, C.B., Q.C. £32,175–£35,845
Principal Clerks, J. A. Vallance White (*Judicial Office and Fourth Clerk at the Table*); M. G. Pownall (*Private Bill and Overseas Offices*); P. D. G. Hayter (*Committees*) .... £35,845–£49,600

Chief Clerks, C. A. J. Mitchell; B. P. Keith; R. H. Walters, D.Phil.; D. R. Beamish; Mrs. F. M. Martin .... £29,920–£38,536
Senior Clerks, D. F. Slater (*Seconded as Secretary to the Leader of the House and Chief Whip*); Dr. F. P. Tudor; E. C. Ollard; Miss M. E. De Groose; A. Makower .... £19,110–£28,708
Clerk of the Records, H. S. Cobb, F.S.A. £29,920–£38,536
Deputy Clerk of the Records, D. J. Johnson, F.S.A. .... £23,383–£34,576
Assistant Clerks of the Records, J. C. Morgan (*Sound Archives*); S. K. Ellison £19,110–£28,708
Accountant, C. Preece............. £19,110–£34,576

Assistant Accountant, Miss J. M.
  Lansdown .... £16,299–£20,323
Judicial Taxing Clerk, C. G. Osborne
                                £16,299–£20,323
Librarian, R. H. V. C. Morgan ..... £29,920–£38,536
Deputy Librarian, D. L. Jones. ..... £23,383–£34,576
Library Clerks, P. G. Davis, ph.d.; Miss I. L.
  Victory, ph.d. .... £19,110–£28,708
Examiners of Petitions for Private Bills,
  M. G. Pownall; R. J. Willoughby.
Gentleman Usher of the Black Rod and
  Serjeant-at-Arms, Air Chief Marshal Sir
  John Gingell, g.b.e., k.c.b. .... £39,600–£49,600
Yeoman Usher of the Black Rod and Deputy
  Serjeant-at-Arms, Air Cdre. A. C. Curry,
  o.b.e............................ £19,110–£28,708
Staff Superintendent, Maj. F. P. Horsfall, m.b.e.
Shorthand Writer, Mrs. E. M. C. Holland ...... *fees*
Editor, Official Report (Hansard), Mrs.
  M. E. Villiers .... £28,230–£36,329
Deputy do., G. R. Goodbarne .... £21,220–£31,293

THE HOUSE OF COMMONS

The Members of the House of Commons are elected by universal adult suffrage. For electoral purposes, the United Kingdom is divided into constituencies, each of which returns one Member to the House of Commons, the Member being the candidate who obtains the largest number of votes cast in the constituency. To ensure equitable representation the four Boundary Commissions keep constituency boundaries under review and recommend any redistribution of seats which may seem necessary due to population movements, etc. The number of seats was raised to 640 in 1945, then reduced to 625 in 1948, and subsequently rose to 630 in 1955, 635 in 1970 and 650 in 1983. Of the present 650 seats there are 523 for England, 38 for Wales, 72 for Scotland and 17 for Northern Ireland. Elections are by secret ballot, each elector casting one vote: voting is not compulsory. When a seat becomes vacant between General Elections, a by-election is held.

British subjects and citizens of the Irish Republic can stand for election as Members of Parliament (M.P.s) provided they are 21 or over and not subject to disqualification. Those disqualified from sitting in the House include undischarged bankrupts, people sentenced to more than one year's imprisonment, clergy of the Church of England, Church of Scotland, Church of Ireland and Roman Catholic Church, peers, and holders of certain offices listed in the House of Commons Disqualification Act 1975 (e.g. members of the judiciary, Civil Service, regular armed forces, police forces, some local government officers and some members of public corporations and government commissions). A candidate does not require any party backing but his or her nomination for election must be supported by the signatures of ten people registered in the constituency. A candidate must also deposit with the returning officer £500, which is forfeit if the candidate does not receive more than 5 per cent of the votes cast. All election expenses, except the candidate's personal expenses, are subject to a statutory limit of £3,648, plus 3·1 pence for each elector in a borough constituency or 4·1 pence for each elector in a county constituency. (*See* pp. 241–248 for an alphabetical list of M.P.s, pp. 249–276 for the results of the last General Election and subsequent by-elections).

The week's business of the House is outlined each Thursday by the Leader of the House, after consultation between the Chief Government Whip and the Chief Opposition Whip. A quarter to a third of the time will be taken up by the Government's legislative programme, and the rest by other business, e.g. question time. As a rule Bills likely to raise political controversy are introduced in the Commons before going on to the Lords, and the Commons claims exclusive control in respect of national taxation and expenditure. Bills such as the Finance Bill, which imposes taxation, and the Consolidated Fund Bills, which authorize expenditure, must begin in the Commons. A Bill of which the financial provisions are subsidiary may begin in the Lords; and the Commons may waive their rights in regard to Lords' amendments affecting finance.

The Commons has a public register of M.P.s' financial, and certain other, interests. Members must also disclose any relevant financial interest or benefit in a matter before the House when taking part in a debate, in certain other proceedings of the House or in consultations with other Members, with Ministers or civil servants.

Since 1911 Members of the House of Commons have received salary payments; facilities for free travel were introduced in 1924. Members are entitled to claim income tax relief on expenses incurred in the course of their Parliamentary duties. Salary rates since 1911 as follows:

	p.a.		p.a.
1911.........	£400	1978 June	£6,897
1931.........	360	1979 June	9,450
1934.........	380	1980 June	11,750
1935.........	400	1981 June	13,950
1937.........	600	1982 June	14,510
1946.........	1,000	1983 June	15,308
1954.........	1,250	1984 Jan......	16,106
1957.........	1,750	1985 Jan......	16,904
1964.........	3,250	1986 Jan......	17,702
1972 Jan.....	4,500	1987 Jan......	18,500
1975 June	5,750	1988 Jan......	22,548
1976 June	6,062	1989 Jan......	24,107
1977 July	6,270		

In October 1969 Members were granted an allowance for secretarial and research expenses. In 1987 this became known as the Office Costs Allowance, and in April 1988 rose to £22,588 a year.

Also, since January 1972, Members can claim reimbursement for the additional cost of staying overnight away from their main residence while on Parliamentary business. In August 1988 this was set at £9,298 a year. Since 1984 this has been non-taxable.

From March 1980 provision was made enabling each Member in receipt of Secretarial and Research Allowance to contribute sums to an approved pension scheme for the provision of a pension, or other benefits, for or in respect of persons whose salary is met by him, from the Office Costs Allowance. For the year from April 1, 1989, this sum is £24,903 a year.

The cost of travel allowances for 1988–89 was stated in June 1989 to be £5,707,783 (car mileage claims £3,954,898, rail travel £632,051 and air travel £448,976, spouse/children travel £395,451, extended travel within U.K. £72,949, and secretarial travel £203,458).

The Ministerial Salaries and Members' Pensions Act 1965 established a contributory pension fund providing pensions for former Members of Parliament and for dependents of deceased former Members. The Fund was reconstituted and the scheme restructured to bring it into line with pension schemes in the public sector by the Parliamentary and Other Pensions Acts 1972: further Acts modifying the arrangements for Members, Ministers and certain office-holders were passed in 1976, 1978, 1981, 1984 and 1987. The Parliamentary and Other Pensions Act 1987 is an enabling measure which provides that the detailed provisions may be contained in subordinate legislation. The arrangements now provide a pension of one-fiftieth of salary for each year of pensionable service with a maximum of two-thirds of salary at age 65. Pension is normally payable at age 65, for men and women, or on later retirement. Pensions may be paid earlier e.g. on ill-health retirement. The widow/widower of a former Member receives a pension of one-half of the late Member's pension. Pensions are index-linked. Members contribute 9 per cent of salary to the pension fund: there is an Exchequer contribution, currently slightly less than half the amount contributed by Members.

The House of Commons Members' Fund provides for annual or lump sum grants to ex-Members, their widows or widowers, and children whose incomes are below certain limits. Alternatively, payments of £1,578 per annum to ex-Members with at least ten years service and who left the House of Commons before October 1964 and £789 per annum to their widows or widowers are made as of right. Members contribute £24 per annum and the Exchequer £115,000 per annum to the Fund. The income of the Fund in 1987–88 was £220,922 and estimated expend-

iture on grants and payments was £141,056. The net assets of the Fund as at September 30, 1987 amounted to £1,490,633.

The House of Commons is presided over by the Speaker, who has considerable powers to maintain order in the House. His deputy, the Chairman of Ways and Means, and two Deputy Chairmen may preside over sittings of the House of Commons; they are elected by the House, and, like the Speaker, neither speak nor vote other than in their official capacity. The staff of the House are employed by a Commission chaired by the Speaker. The Heads of House of Commons Departments (*see* below) are permanent officers of the House, not M.P.s. The Clerk of the House is the principal adviser to the Speaker on the privileges and procedures of the House, the conduct of the business of the House, and Committees. The Serjeant-at-Arms is responsible for security, ceremonial, and for accommodation in the Commons part of the Palace of Westminster.

OFFICERS AND OFFICIALS OF THE HOUSE OF COMMONS

Speaker, The Rt. Hon. Bernard Weatherill, M.P. for Croydon North East £54,357
Chairman of Ways and Means, The Rt. Hon. Harold Walker, M.P. for Doncaster Central £42,357
First Deputy Chairman of Ways and Means, Sir Paul Dean, M.P. for Woodspring £39,347
Second Deputy Chairman of Ways and Means, Miss Betty Boothroyd, M.P. for West Bromwich West .. £39,347

Offices of the Speaker and Chairman of Ways and Means

Speaker's Secretary, P. J. Kitcatt, C.B.
£29,920–£33,352
Speaker's Counsel, H. Knorpel, C.B., Q.C.;
G. E. Gammie, C.B., Q.C. .... £37,600–£40,900
Chaplain to the Speaker, The Rev. Canon D. Gray, T.D.
Secretary to the Chairman of Ways and Means, R. I. S Phillips

Department of the Clerk of the House

Clerk of the House of Commons, C. J. Boulton, C.B. £72,000
Clerk Asst., J. F. Sweetman, T.D. .... £48,100–£50,400
Clerk of Committees, D. W. Limon .. £48,100–£50,400
Principal Clerks—
  Public Bills, H. M. Barclay
  Journal Office, W. R. McKay
  Table Office, C. B. Winnifrith
  Overseas Office, R. B. Sands
  Select Committees, G. Cubie
  Second Clerk of Select Committees,
    A. J. Hastings
  Private Bills, R. J. Willoughby
  Standing Committees, J. R. Rose
Financial Committees, D. G. Millar. £35,845–£40,900
Deputy Principal Clerks, S. A. L. Panton;
  M. R. Jack, PH.D.; Mrs. J. Sharpe; Ms. A. Milner-Barry; R. W. G. Wilson; W. A. Proctor; F. A. Cranmer; R. J. Rogers; C. R. M. Ward, PH.D.; Ms. H. E. Irwin; D. W. N. Doig; A. Sandall; D. L. Natzler; E. P. Silk; D. F. Harrison .... £29,920–£33,352
Senior Clerks, Mrs. S. A. de Ste. Croix; A. R. Kennon; D. W. Robson; L. C. Laurence-Smyth; S. J. Patrick; D. J. Gerhold; C. J. Poyser; S. J. Priestley; A. H. Doherty; P. A. Evans; R. I. S. Phillips; R. G. James; Miss E. J. Baker; Miss P. A. Helme; D. R Lloyd; R. A. Lambert; J. B. Ingram (*acting*); I. C. Gilbert (*acting*); J. Darling (*acting*); J. M. Hope (*acting*) .... £19,110–£24,356

Clerk of Services Sub-Committees, K. J. Brown .... £18,242–£23,226
Examiners of Petitions for Private Bills, R. J. Willoughby; M. G. Pownall.
Registrar of Members' Interests, A. J. Hastings
Taxing Officer, R. J. Willoughby.

Department of the Serjeant-at-Arms

Serjeant-at-Arms, Sir Alan Urwick, K.C.V.O., C.M.G. .... £37,600–£40,900
Deputy Serjeant-at-Arms, P. N. W. Jennings..................... £29,920–£33,352
Assistant Serjeant-at-Arms, M. J. A. Cummins .... £22,301–£28,512
Deputy Assistant Serjeants-at-Arms, P. A. J. Wright; J. F. Collins .... £19,110–£24,356

Department of the Library

Librarian, D. Menhennet, D.Phil ... £37,600–£40,900
Deputy Librarian, D. J. T. Englefield
£35,845–£37,165

Library and Information Service

Assistant Librarians, G. F. Lock; Miss J. B. Tanfield .... £29,920–£33,352
Deputy Assistant Librarians, S. Z. Young; Mrs. H. R. Coates; Miss P. J. Baines; K. G. Cuninghame; Mrs. J. M. Wainwright; C. C. Pond, PH.D.; Mrs. C. B. Andrews; R. C. Clements; Mrs. J. M. Lourie .. £23,383–£29,920
Senior Library Clerks, Ms. F. Poole; Mrs. J. M. Fiddick; C. R. Barclay; Mrs. C. M. Gillie; R. J. Ware, D.Phil; Ms. D. Gore, PH.D; R. J. Twigger; B. K. Winetrobe; T. N. Edmonds; R. J. Cracknell; Miss O. M. Gay; Miss E. M. McInnes; Mrs. G. L. Allen; Miss M. Baber .... £19,110–£24,356

Vote Office

Deliverer of the Vote, G. R. Russell . £23,383–£29,920
Deputy Deliverer of the Vote, H. C. Foster
£19,110–£24,356

Administration Department

Head of Administration Department, G. A.
Roberts .... £37,600–£40,900
Accountant, J. L. G. Dobson .... £35,845–£37,165
Deputy Accountant, A. J. Lewis .... £29,920–£33,352
Senior Assistant Accountant, A. R. Marskell
£23,383–£29,920
Assistant Accountants, M. J. Barram; Miss
M. M. McColl; M. Fletcher ..... £19,110–£24,356
Head of Establishments Office, B. A. Wilson
£29,920–£33,352
Deputy Head of Establishments Office, J. A.
Robb .... £23,383–£29,920
Computer Officer, R. S. Morgan .... £29,920–£33,352
Internal Auditor, A. A. Cameron... £19,110–£24,356
Staff Inspector, R. C. Collins .... £19,110–£24,356

Department of the Official Report

Editor, I. D. Church .... £35,845–£37,165
Deputy Editor, P. Walker .... £23,383–£29,920
Principal Assistant Editors, R. V. Hadlow;
J. Gourley; J. Withers; W. G. Garland
£21,869–£27,948
Assistant Editors, Miss. V. Grainger; J.
Ledgerwood; Miss V. A. A. Clarke; Miss H.
Hales; Miss G. L. Sutherland .... £19,705–£25,131

Refreshment Department

General Manager, W. J. J. Smillie .. £23,383–£29,920
Deputy General Manager, E. J. Nash
£19,110–£24,356
Catering Accountant, D. R. W. Wood
£19,110–£24,356

PARLIAMENTARY INFORMATION

The following is a short glossary of aspects of work of Parliament:

(*Unless otherwise stated, references are to* House of Commons *procedures.*)

Adjournment Debate.—Usually a half-hour debate introduced by a backbencher at the end of business for the day. The subjects raised are often local or personal issues.

Bill.—Proposed legislation is termed a *Bill.* The stages of a Public Bill (for Private Bills, *see* below) in the House of Commons are as follows:

First Reading: There is no debate at this stage, which nowadays merely constitutes an order to have the Bill printed.

Second Reading: The debate on the principles of the Bill.

Committee Stage: The detailed examination of a Bill, clause by clause. In most cases this takes place in a *Standing Committee,* or the whole House may act as a Committee. A *Special Standing Committee* may take evidence before embarking on detailed scrutiny of the Bill. Very rarely, a Bill may be examined by a *Select Committee* (*see* below).

Report Stage: Detailed review of a Bill as amended in Committee.

Third Reading: Final debate on a Bill.

Public Bills go through the same stages in the House of Lords, except that in almost all cases the Committee Stage is taken in the Committee of the Whole House.

A Bill may start in either House, and has to pass through both Houses to become law.

Both Houses have to agree the same text of a Bill, so that the *Amendments* made by the second House are then considered in the originating House and if not agreed, sent back or themselves amended, until agreement is reached.

Chiltern Hundreds.—A legal fiction, a nominal office of profit under the Crown, the acceptance of which requires a Member to vacate his seat. The Manor of Northstead is similar. These are the only means by which an M.P. may resign.

Closure & Guillotine.—To prevent deliberate waste of time of either House, a motion may be made that the question be now put. In the House of Commons, if the Speaker decides that the rights of a minority are not being prejudiced and 100 members support the closure motion in a division, if carried, the original motion is put to the House, without further debate. The *Guillotine* represents a more rigorous and systematic application of the Closure. Under this system, a Bill proceeds in accordance with a rigid timetable and discussion is limited to the time allotted to each group of clauses. The Closure is hardly ever used in the Lords, and there is no procedure for a guillotine. The completion of business in the Lords is traditionally ensured by agreement from all sides of the House.

Consolidated Fund Bill.—A Bill to authorize issue of money to maintain Government services. The Bill is dealt with without debate, but afterwards members may raise topics of public or local importance.

Delegated Legislation.—Many Statutes empower Ministers to make delegated legislation, with little or no reference back to Parliament, usually by means of Statutory Instruments. These fall into four broad categories:—(i) Affirmative Instruments, which are subject to approval by resolutions of both Houses before they can come into or remain in force; (ii) Negative Instruments, which are subject to annulment by resolution of either House; (iii) General Instruments, which include those not required to be laid before Parliament and those which are required to be so laid but are not subject to approval or annulment; (iv) Special Procedure Orders, against which parties outside Parliament may lodge petitions.

Dissolution.—Parliament comes to an end either by Dissolution by the Sovereign, on the advice of the Prime Minister, or the expiration of the term of five years for which the House of Commons was elected. Dissolution is normally effected by a Royal Proclamation.

Early Day Motion.—A motion put on the Notice Paper by an M.P. without in general the real prospect of its being debated. Such motions are expressions of backbench opinion.

Emergency Debate.—In the Commons a method of obtaining prompt discussion of a matter of urgency is by moving the adjournment under Standing Order No. 20 for the purpose of discussing a specific and important matter that should have urgent consideration. A member may ask leave to make this motion by giving written notice to the Speaker, usually before 12 noon, and if the Speaker considers the matter of sufficient importance and it obtains the support of 40 members, it is discussed usually at 7 p.m. on the following day.

Father of the House.—The Member whose continuous service in the House of Commons, is the longest. The present Father of the House is the Rt. Hon. Sir Bernard Braine, elected first in 1950.

General Synod Measure.—A measure passed by the national assembly of the Church of England under the Church of England Assembly (Powers) Act 1919. These measures are considered by the Joint Ecclesiastical Committee, who make a report. They are then considered by both Houses, and if approved, sent for the Royal Assent.

Hansard.—The official report of debates in both Houses (and in Standing Committees) published by H.M.S.O., normally on the day after the sitting concerned.

Hours of Meeting.—The House of Commons meets on Monday, Tuesday, Wednesday and Thursday at 2.30 p.m., and on Friday at 9.30 a.m. The House of Lords normally meets at 2.30 p.m. on Monday, Tuesday and Wednesday and at 3 p.m. on Thursday. In the latter part of the Session, the House of Lords sometimes sits on Fridays at 11 a.m.

Hybridity.—A Public Bill which is considered to affect specific private or local interests, as distinct from *all* such interests of a single category, is called a Hybrid Bill and is subject to a special form of scrutiny.

Leader of the Opposition.—In 1937 the office of Leader of the Opposition was recognized and a salary of £2,000 per annum was assigned to the post, thus following a practice which had prevailed in the Dominion of Canada since 1906. In June 1989 the salary was £49,707. The present Leader of the Opposition is the Rt. Hon. Neil Kinnock.

The Lord Chancellor.—The Lord High Chancellor of Great Britain is (*ex officio*) the Speaker of the House of Lords. Unlike the Speaker of the House of Commons, he is a member of the Government, takes part in debates and votes in divisions. He has none of the powers to maintain order that the Speaker in the Commons has, these powers being exercised in the Lords by the House as a whole. The Lord Chancellor sits in the Lords on one of the *Woolsacks*, couches covered with red cloth and stuffed with wool. If he wishes to address the House in any way except formally as Speaker, he leaves the Woolsack and steps towards his place as a peer.

Naming.—When a member has been named by the Speaker for a breach of order, i.e. contrary to the practice of the House called by surname and not addressed as the "Hon. Member for ... (her/his constituency)", the Leader of the House moves that the offender "be suspended from the service of the House" for (in the case of a first offence) a period of five sitting days. Should the member offend again, the period of suspension is increased.

Opposition Day.—A day on which the topic for debate is chosen by the Opposition. There are 20 such days in a normal session. On 17 days, subjects are chosen by the Leader of the Opposition; on the remaining three days by the leader of the next largest opposition party.

Parliament Acts 1911 and 1949.—Under these Acts Bills may become law without the consent of the Lords.

Since at least the 18th century the Commons have had the privilege of having bills concerned with supply (i.e. taxation and money matters) passed without amendment by the Lords; though until 1911 the Lords retained the right to reject such bills outright.

By the Parliament Act 1911 a Bill which has been endorsed by the Speaker of the House of Commons as a Money Bill, and has been passed by the Commons and sent up to the Lords at least one month before the end of a session, can become law without the consent of the Lords if it is not passed by them without amendment within a month.

Under the Parliament Acts 1911 and 1949, if the Lords reject any other Public Bill (except one to prolong the life of a Parliament) which has been passed by the Commons in two successive sessions then that Bill shall (unless the Commons direct to the contrary) become law without the consent of the Lords. The Lords have power, therefore, to delay a Public Bill for thirteen months from its first Second Reading in the House of Commons.

Prime Minister's Questions.—The Prime Minister answers questions from 3.15 to 3.30 pm on Tuesdays and Thursdays. Nowadays the "open question" predominates. Members tend to ask the Prime Minister what are her or his official engagements for the day: a supplementary question on virtually any topic can then be put.

Private Bill.—A Bill promoted by a body or an individual to give powers additional to, or in conflict with, the general law, and to which a separate procedure applies.

Private Members' Bill.—A Public Bill promoted by a Member who is not a member of H.M. Government.

Private Notice Question.—A question adjudged of urgent importance on submission to the Speaker (in the Lords, the Leader of the House), answered at the end of oral questions—usually at 3.30 p.m.

Privilege.—The following are covered by the privilege of Parliament: (i) freedom from interference in going to, attending at, and going from, Parliament; (ii) freedom of speech in Parliamentary proceedings; (iii) the printing and publishing of anything relating to the proceedings of the two Houses is subject to privilege; (iv) each House is the guardian of its dignity and may punish any insult to the House as a whole.

Prorogation.—The bringing to an end, by the Sovereign on the advice of the Government, of a Session of Parliament. Public Bills which have not completed all their stages lapse on Prorogation.

Queen's Speech.—The Speech delivered by H.M. The Queen at the State Opening of Parliament, in which the Government's programme for the session is set forth. The Speech is, in fact, drafted for and approved by the Cabinet.

Question Time.—Oral questions are answered by Ministers in the Commons from 2.30 to 3.30 pm every day except Friday. They are also taken at the start of the Lords sittings, with a daily limit of four oral questions.

Royal Assent.—The Royal Assent is signified by Letters Patent to such Bills and Measures as have passed both Houses of Parliament (or Bills which have been passed under the Parliament Acts 1911 and 1949). The Sovereign has not given Royal Assent in person since 1854. On occasion, for instance in the Prorogation of Parliament, Royal Assent may be pronounced to the two Houses by Lords Commissioners; but more usually Royal Assent is notified to each House sitting separately in accordance with the Royal Assent Act 1967. The Norman formulae for Royal Assent are then endorsed on the Acts by the Clerk of the Parliaments.

The power to withhold assent resides with the Sovereign, but has not been exercised in the United Kingdom since 1707, in the reign of Queen Anne.

Select Committees consisting usually of 10–15 members of all parties are a means used by both Houses in order to investigate certain matters.

Most Select Committees in the House of Commons are now tied to Departments—each Committee investigates subjects within a Government Department's remit. These are: Agriculture, Defence,

Education, Science and Arts, Employment, Energy, Environment, Foreign Affairs, Home Affairs, Social Services, Trade and Industry, Transport, Treasury and Civil Service, Welsh Affairs. The Scottish Affairs Committee is in temporary abeyance.

There are other House of Commons Select Committees dealing with Public Accounts (i.e. the spending by H.M. Government of money voted by Parliament) and European Legislation, and also domestic committees dealing, for example, with Privilege and Services. Major Select Committees usually take evidence in public: their evidence and reports are published by H.M.S.O.

The principal Select Committee in the House of Lords is that on the European Communities, which has, at present, six sub-committees dealing with all areas of Community policy. The House of Lords also has a Select Committee on Science and Technology, which appoints sub-committees to deal with specific subjects. In addition, *ad hoc* Select Committees have been set up from time to time to investigate specific subjects, e.g. overseas trade, murder and life imprisonment. There are also some Joint Committees of the two Houses, e.g. the Joint Committee on Statutory Instruments.

The Speaker.—The Speaker of the House of Commons is the spokesman and president of the Chamber. He is elected by the House at the beginning of each Parliament or when the previous Speaker retires or dies. He neither speaks in debates nor votes in divisions except when the voting is equal.

Standing Orders.—Rules which have from time to time been agreed by each House of Parliament to regulate the conduct of its business. These orders are not irrevocable, may be revised, amended or repealed, and are from time to time suspended or dispensed with.

State Opening.—This marks the start of each new session of Parliament. Parliament is normally opened, in the presence of both Houses, by the Queen in person, who makes the Speech from the Throne which outlines the Government's policies for the coming session (*see* **Queen's Speech**). In the absence of the Queen, Parliament is opened by Royal Commission, and the Queen's Speech is read by one of the Lords Commissioners specially appointed by Letters Patent for the occasion.

Strangers.—Anyone who is not a Member or Officer of the House is a *stranger*. Visitors are generally admitted to debates of both Houses but may be excluded if the House so decides. In practice this happens only in time of war.

Ten Minute Rule.—A colloquial term for Standing Order No. 19, under which backbenchers have an opportunity on Tuesdays and Wednesdays to state for about ten minutes why a Bill on a certain subject should be introduced. Time is also available for a short opposing speech.

Vacant Seats.—When a vacancy occurs in the House of Commons during a session of Parliament, the Writ for the by-election is moved by a Whip of the party to which the member whose seat has been vacated belonged. If the House is in recess, the Speaker can issue a warrant for a writ, should two members certify to him that a seat is vacant.

Whips.—In order to secure the attendance of Members of a particular party in Parliament on all occasions, and particularly on the occasion of an important vote, Whips (originally known as "Whippers-in") are appointed. The written appeal or circular letter issued by them is also known as a "whip", its urgency being denoted by the number of times it is underlined. Failure to respond to a three-line whip, headed "Most important", is tantamount in the Commons to secession (at any rate temporarily) from the party. Whips are officially recognized by Parliament and are provided with office accommodation in both Houses. In both Houses, Government and some Opposition Whips receive salaries from public funds.

PUBLIC INFORMATION SERVICE.—Enquiries from the general public and organizations of all kinds about the work, practices, composition and history of the House of Commons are answered by the Public Information Office, House of Commons, SW1A 0AA (01-219 4272). This office also edits the House of Commons Weekly Information Bulletin (published by H.M.S.O.). A series of factsheets on the work and processes of the House is available. The Journal and Information Office, House of Lords, SW1A 0PW (01-219 3107) answers queries relating to the procedure and practice of the Lords.

HER MAJESTY'S GOVERNMENT

Her Majesty's Government is the body of Ministers responsible for the administration of national affairs, determining policy and introducing into Parliament any legislation necessary to give effect to government policy. The majority of Ministers are members of the House of Commons but members of the House of Lords may also hold Ministerial responsibility. The Lord Chancellor is always a member of the House of Lords. The Prime Minister is, by recent convention, always a member of the House of Commons.

THE PRIME MINISTER

The office of Prime Minister, which had been in existence for nearly 200 years, was officially recognised in 1905 and its holder was granted a place in the Table of Precedence. The Prime Minister, by tradition also First Lord of the Treasury and Minister for the Civil Service, is appointed by the Sovereign and is usually the leader of the party which enjoys, or can secure, a majority in the House of Commons. Other Ministers are appointed by the Sovereign on

the recommendation of the Prime Minister, who also allocates functions amongst Ministers and has the power to obtain their resignation or dismissal individually.

The Prime Minister informs the Sovereign of state and political matters, advises on the dissolution of Parliament, and makes recommendations for important Crown appointments, the award of honours, etc.

As the chairman of Cabinet meetings and leader of a political party, the Prime Minister is responsible for translating party policy into government activity: and as leader of the Government the Prime Minister is responsible to Parliament and to the electorate for the policies and their implementation.

The Prime Minister also represents the nation in international affairs, e.g. summit conferences.

THE CABINET

The Cabinet developed during the 18th century as an inner committee of the Privy Council, which was the chief source of executive power until that time. It is composed of about 20 Ministers chosen by the Prime Minister, usually the heads of government departments (generally known as Secretaries of State unless they have a special title, e.g. Chancellor of the Exchequer) and the holders of various traditional offices.

The Cabinet's functions are the final determination of policy, control of government and co-ordination of government departments. The exercise of its functions is dependent upon enjoying majority support in the House of Commons. Cabinet meetings are held in private, taking place once or twice a week during parliamentary sittings and less often during a recess. Proceedings are confidential, the members being bound by their oath as Privy Counsellors not to disclose information about the proceedings.

The convention of collective responsibility means that the Cabinet acts unanimously even when Cabinet Ministers do not all agree on a subject. The policies of departmental Ministers must be consistent with the policies of the Government as a whole, and once the Government's policy has been decided, each Minister is expected to support it or resign.

The convention of Ministerial responsibility holds a Minister, as the political head of his or her department, accountable to Parliament for the department's work. Departmental Ministers usually decide all matters within their responsibility, although on matters of political importance they normally consult their colleagues collectively. A decision by a departmental Minister is binding on the Government as a whole.

HER MAJESTY'S GOVERNMENT

THE CABINET

Prime Minister, First Lord of the Treasury and Minister for the Civil Service, THE RT. HON. MARGARET HILDA THATCHER, M.P., *born* Oct. 13, 1925.

Lord President of the Council and Leader of the House of Commons, The Rt. Hon. Sir (Richard Edward) Geoffrey Howe, Q.C., M.P., *born* Dec. 20, 1926.

Chancellor of the Exchequer, The Rt. Hon. Nigel Lawson, M.P., *born* March 11, 1932.

Lord High Chancellor, The Rt. Hon. the Lord Mackay of Clashfern, *born* July 2, 1927.

Secretary of State for the Home Department, The Rt. Hon. Douglas Richard Hurd, C.B.E., M.P., *born* March 8, 1930.

Secretary of State for Foreign and Commonwealth Affairs, The Rt. Hon. John Major, M.P., *born* March 29, 1943.

Secretary of State for Wales, The Rt. Hon. Peter Edward Walker, M.B.E., M.P., *born* March 25, 1932.

Secretary of State for Employment, The Rt. Hon. (Peter) Norman Fowler, M.P., *born* Feb. 2, 1938.

Secretary of State for Defence, The Rt. Hon. Thomas Jeremy King, M.P., *born* June 13, 1933.

Secretary of State for Trade and Industry, The Rt. Hon. Nicholas Ridley, M.P., *born* Feb. 17, 1929.

Chancellor of the Duchy of Lancaster, The Rt. Hon. Kenneth Wilfred Baker, M.P., *born* Nov. 3, 1934.

Secretary of State for Health, The Rt. Hon. Kenneth Henry Clarke, Q.C., M.P., *born* July 2, 1940.

Secretary of State for Education and Science, The Rt. Hon. John Roddick Russell MacGregor, O.B.E., M.P., *born* Feb. 14, 1937.

Secretary of State for Scotland, The Rt. Hon. Malcolm Leslie Rifkind, Q.C., M.P., *born* June 21, 1946.

Secretary of State for Transport, The Rt. Hon. Cecil Edward Parkinson, M.P., *born* Sept. 1, 1931.

Secretary of State for Energy, The Rt. Hon. John Wakeham, M.P., *born* June 22, 1932.

Lord Privy Seal and Leader of the House of Lords, The Rt. Hon. The Lord Belstead, *born* Sept. 30, 1932.

Secretary of State for Social Security, The Rt. Hon. Antony Harold Newton, O.B.E.., M.P., *born* Aug. 29, 1937.

Secretary of State for the Environment, The Rt. Hon. Christopher Francis Patten, M.P., *born* May 12, 1944.

Secretary of State for Northern Ireland, The Rt. Hon. Peter Leonard Brooke, M.P., *born* March 3, 1934.

Minister of Agriculture, Fisheries and Food, The Rt. Hon. John Selwyn Gummer, M.P., *born* Nov. 26, 1939.

Chief Secretary to the Treasury, The Rt. Hon. Norman Stewart Hughson Lamont, M.P., *born* May 8, 1942.

LAW OFFICERS

Attorney-General, The Rt. Hon. Sir Patrick Barnabas Burke Mayhew, Q.C., M.P.

Lord Advocate, The Rt. Hon. The Lord Fraser of Carmyllie, Q.C.

Solicitor-General, Sir Nicholas Walter Lyell, Q.C., M.P.

Solicitor-General for Scotland, Alan Ferguson Rodger, Q.C.*

(* not a member of the House of Commons)

OTHER MINISTERS

Parliamentary Secretary to the Treasury, The Rt. Hon. David Waddington, Q.C., M.P.

Paymaster General, The Earl of Caithness.

Financial Secretary to the Treasury, Peter Lilley, M.P.

MINISTERS OF STATE

Agriculture, Fisheries and Food, (no appointment made).

Defence, The Hon. Archibald Hamilton, M.P. (*Armed Forces*); The Hon. Alan Clark, M.P. (*Defence Procurement*).

Education and Science, Mrs. Angela Rumbold, C.B.E., M.P.

Employment, Timothy Eggar, M.P.

Energy, The Rt. Hon. Peter Morrison, M.P.

Environment, Michael Howard, Q.C., M.P. (*Housing, Planning*); David Hunt, M.P. (*Local Government, Inner Cities*); David Trippier, R.D., M.P. (*Environment and Countryside*).

Foreign and Commonwealth Affairs, The Rt Hon. Lynda Chalker, M.P. (*Minister for Overseas Development*); Hon. William Waldegrave, M.P.; Hon. Francis Maude, M.P.; The Lord Brabazon of Tara.

Health, David Mellor, Q.C., M.P.; The Lord Trafford.

Home Office, The Earl Ferrers, P.C.; John Patten, M.P.; Timothy Renton, M.P.

Northern Ireland, The Rt. Hon. John Cope, M.P.

Privy Council Office, The Rt. Hon. Richard Luce, M.P. (*Minister for the Arts*).

Scottish Office, Ian Lang, M.P.; The Lord Sanderson of Bowden.
Social Security, Rt. Hon. Nicholas Scott, M.B.E., M.P.
Trade and Industry, The Hon. Douglas Hogg, M.P.; The Lord Trefgarne, P.C.
Transport, Michael Portillo, M.P. (*Public Transport*).
Treasury, Richard Ryder, O.B.E., M.P. (*Economic Secretary*).
Welsh Office, Wyn Roberts, M.P.

UNDER-SECRETARIES OF STATE

Agriculture, Fisheries and Food, The Baroness Trumpington; David Maclean, M.P.; David Curry, M.P.
Defence, Michael Neubert, M.P. (*Armed Forces*); The Earl of Arran (*Defence Procurement*).
Education and Science, Robert Jackson, M.P.; Alan Howarth. C.B.E., M.P.
Employment, Patrick Nicholls, M.P.; The Lord Strathclyde.
Energy, Michael Spicer, M.P.

Environment, Christopher Chope, O.B.E., M.P.; The Hon. Colin Moynihan, M.P. (*Minister for Sport*); Mrs. Virginia Bottomley, M.P.; The Lord Hesketh.
Foreign and Commonwealth Affairs, The Hon. Timothy Sainsbury, M.P.
Health, Roger Freeman, M.P.
Home Office, Peter Lloyd, M.P.
Northern Ireland Office, Dr. Brian Mawhinney, M.P.; Richard Needham, M.P.; Peter Bottomley, M.P.; The Lord Skelmersdale.
Scottish Office, Michael Forsyth, M.P.; Lord James Douglas-Hamilton, M.P.
Social Security, The Lord Henley; Mrs. Gillian Shephard, M.P.
Trade and Industry, Eric Forth, M.P.; John Redwood, M.P.
Transport, Robert Atkins, M.P.; Patrick McLoughlin, M.P.
Treasury, The Lords Commissioners (*see* Government Whips).
Welsh Office, Ian Grist, M.P.

GOVERNMENT WHIPS

HOUSE OF LORDS

Captain of the Honourable Corps of Gentlemen-at-Arms (Chief Whip), The Rt. Hon. The Lord Denham.
Captain of the Queen's Bodyguard of the Yeoman of the Guard (Deputy Chief Whip), The Viscount Davidson.
Lords in Waiting, The Viscount Long; The Viscount Ullswater; The Lord Reay; The Earl of Strathmore and Kinghorne.

HOUSE OF COMMONS

Parliamentary Secretary to the Treasury (Chief Whip), The Rt. Hon. David Waddington, Q.C., M.P.

Treasurer of the H.M. Household (Deputy Chief Whip), Tristan Garel-Jones, M.P.
Comptroller of H.M. Household, Alastair Goodlad, M.P.
Vice-Chamberlain of H.M. Household, Anthony Durant, M.P.
Lords Commissioners, Kenneth Carlisle, M.P.; David Lightbown, M.P.; Stephen Dorrell, M.P.; John Taylor, M.P.; David Heathcoat-Amory, M.P.
Assistant Whips, Michael Fallon, M.P.; The Hon. Thomas Sackville, M.P.; Sydney Chapman, M.P.; Gregory Knight, M.P.; Irvine Patrick, O.B.E., M.P.

GOVERNMENT BY PARTY

Before the reign of William and Mary the principal Officers of State were chosen by and were responsible to the Sovereign alone and not to Parliament or the nation at large. Such officers acted sometimes in concert with one another, but more often independently, and the fall of one did not, of necessity, involve that of others, although all were liable to be dismissed at any moment.

In 1693 the Earl of Sunderland recommended to William III the advisability of selecting a Ministry from the political party which enjoyed a majority in the House of Commons and the first united Ministry was drawn in 1696 from the Whigs, to which party the King owed his throne, the principal members being Russell (the Admiral), Somers (the Advocate), Lord Wharton and Charles Montague (afterwards Chancellor of the Exchequer). This group became known as the *Junto* and was regarded with suspicion as a novelty in the political life of the nation, being a small section meeting in secret apart from the main body of Ministers. It may be regarded as the forerunner of the *Cabinet* and in course of time it led to the establishment of the principle of joint responsibility of Ministers, so that internal disagreement caused a change of personnel or resignation of the whole body of Ministers.

The accession of George I, who was unfamiliar with the English language, led to a disinclination on the part of the Sovereign to preside at meetings of his Ministers and caused the appearance of a *Prime Minister*, a position first acquired by Robert Walpole in 1721 and retained without interruption for 20 years and 326 days.

In 1828 the old party of the Whigs became known as *Liberals*, a name originally given to it by its opponents to imply laxity of principles, but gradually accepted by the party to indicate its claim to be pioneers and champions of political reform and progressive legislation. In 1861 a Liberal Registration Association was founded and Liberal Associations became widespread. In 1877 a National Liberal Federation was formed, with headquarters in London. The Liberal Party was in power for long periods during the second half of the nineteenth century and for several years during the first quarter of the twentieth century, but after a split in the party the numbers elected were small from 1931. In March 1988, the Liberals and the Social Democratic Party merged under the title *Social and Liberal Democrats* (*see* below).

Soon after the change from Whig to Liberal the Tory Party became known as *Conservative*, a name traditionally believed to have been invented by John Wilson Croker in 1830 and to have been generally adopted about the time of the passing of the Reform Act of 1832 to indicate that the preservation of national institutions was the leading principle of the party. After the Home Rule crisis of 1886 the dissentient Liberals entered into a compact with the Conservatives, under which the latter undertook not to contest their seats, but a separate *Liberal Unionist* organization was maintained until 1912, when it was united with the Conservatives.

The Labour Party.—Labour candidates for Parliament made their first appearance at the General Election of 1892, when there were 27 standing as "Labour" or "Liberal-Labour."

In 1900 the *Labour Representation Committee* was

set up in order to establish a distinct Labour Group in Parliament, with its own whips, its own policy, and a readiness to co-operate with any party which might be engaged in promoting legislation in the direct interest of labour. In 1906 the L.R.C. became known as *The Labour Party.*

Social Democratic Party.—The Council for Social Democracy was announced by four former Labour Cabinet Ministers on Jan. 25, 1981. Subsequently a number of sitting Labour Members of Parliament, together with one Conservative, joined the new group, and on March 26, 1981 the Social Democratic Party was launched. Later in the year the S.D.P. and the Liberal Party formed an electoral *Alliance*. In 1988 a majority of the S.D.P. agreed on a merger with the Liberal Party but a minority continue as a separate party under the S.D.P. title.

The government of the day is formed by the party which wins the largest number of seats in the House of Commons at a General Election, or which has the support of a majority of members in the House of Commons. By tradition, the leader of the majority party is asked by the Sovereign to form a government, while the largest minority party becomes the official Opposition with its own leader and own "Shadow Cabinet". Leaders of the Government and Opposition sit on the front benches of the Commons with their supporters (the back-benchers) sitting behind them.

When a party is in Opposition and its leadership becomes vacant, it makes its free choice among the various personalities available; but if the party is in office, the Sovereign's choice may anticipate, and in a certain sense forestall, the decision of the party.

POLITICAL PARTIES

CONSERVATIVE AND UNIONIST PARTY, Central Office, 32 Smith Square, SW1P 3HH. (Tel: 01-222 9000).— *Party Chairman*, The Rt. Hon. K. Baker, M.P.; *Deputy Chairman*, The Rt. Hon. the Lord Young of Graffham; *Vice Chairmen*, T. Arnold, M.P.; Dame Joan Seccombe, O.B.E.; Sir James Spicer, M.P.; *Hon. Treasurers*, Lord McAlpine of West Green; Sir Oulton Wade; Sir Hector Laing.

SCOTTISH CONSERVATIVE PARTY, Central Office, 3 Chester Street, Edinburgh EH3 7RF. (Tel: 031-226 4426).—*Chairman*, M. B. Forsyth, M.P.; *Deputy Chairman*, W. Hughes; *Hon. Treasurer*, Sir Matthew Goodwin, C.B.E.; *Chief Exec.*, J. J. MacKay.

LABOUR PARTY, 150 Walworth Road, SE17 1JT. (Tel: 01-703 0833).—*Chair*, The Rt. Hon. N. Kinnock, M.P.; *Vice Chair*, D. Skinner, M.P.; *Treasurer*, S. McCluskie; *Gen. Sec.*, L. Whitty; *Parliamentary Party Leader*, The Rt. Hon. N. Kinnock, M.P.; *Deputy Leader*, The Rt. Hon. R. Hattersley, M.P.; *Leader of the Labour Peers*, Lord Cledwyn of Penrhos, C.H.

SHADOW CABINET, 1988–89.—Rt. Hon. N. Kinnock, M.P. (*Leader*); Rt. Hon. R. Hattersley, M.P. (*Deputy Leader; Shadow Home Secretary*); D. Foster, M.P. (*Chief Whip*); Rt. Hon. S. Orme, M.P. (*Chair, Parliamentary Party*); G. Brown, M.P. (*Chief Secretary to the Treasury*); Rt. Hon. J. Smith, M.P. (*Shadow Chancellor*); Rt. Hon. G. Kaufman, M.P. (*Shadow Foreign Secretary*); Dr. D. Clark, M.P. (*Agriculture and Rural Affairs*); R. Cook, M.P. (*Health and Social Security*); D. Dewar, M.P. (*Scotland*); F. Dobson, M.P. (*Leader of the House*); B. Gould, M.P. (*Trade and Industry*); A. Blair, M.P. (*Energy*); M. Meacher, M.P. (*Employment*); J. Straw, M.P. (*Education*); B. Jones, M.P. (*Wales*); J. Prescott, M.P. (*Transport*); Dr J. Cunningham, M.P. (*Environment*); Ms. J. Richardson, M.P. (*Women's Rights*); Rt. Hon. Lord Cledwyn of Penrhos, C.H. (*Leader of the Labour Peers*); Lord Ponsonby of Shulbrede (*Chief Whip, Lords*); Lord Dean of Beswick.

Labour Chief Whip in the House of Lords is Lord Ponsonby of Shulbrede. Labour Chief Whip in the House of Commons is D. Foster, M.P.

PLAID CYMRU, 51 Cathedral Road, Cardiff CF1 9HD. (Tel: 0222-31944).—*Chairman*, D. Huws; *Deputy Chairman*, I. W. Jones, M.P.; *Hon. Treasurer*, D. Watkins; *Sec.*, D. Williams; *Party President*, D. E. Thomas, M.P.; *Vice-President*, D. Iwan.

SCOTTISH NATIONAL PARTY, 6 North Charlotte Street, Edinburgh EH2 4JH. (Tel: 031-226 3661).— *National Convenor*, G. Wilson; *Deputy Vice Convenor*, A. Salmond, M.P.; *National Treasurer*, A. Morgan; *National Sec.*, J. Swinney; *Parliamentary Party Leader*, Mrs. M. Ewing, M.P.; *Chief Whip*, A. Welsh, M.P.

SOCIAL AND LIBERAL DEMOCRATS, 4 Cowley Street, SW1P 3NB. (Tel: 01-222 7999).—*President*, I. W. Wrigglesworth; *Deputy Chair*, T. Clement Jones; *Hon. Treasurer*, T. Razzell; *Chief Executive*, A. Ellis, O.B.E.; *Leader of the Party*, The Rt. Hon. Paddy Ashdown, M.P.; *Leader of the S.L.D. Peers*, The Rt. Hon. the Lord Jenkins of Hillhead.

SCOTTISH SOCIAL AND LIBERAL DEMOCRATS, 4 Clifton Terrace, Edinburgh EH12 5DR. (Tel: 031-337 2314).—*Chairman*, J. Bannerman; *Hon. Treasurer*, K. Smith; *Party President*, Sir Russell Johnston, M.P.; *Party Leader*, M. G. Bruce, M.P.

WELSH SOCIAL AND LIBERAL DEMOCRATS, 91 St. Mary Street, Cardiff CF1 1DW. (Tel: 0222-382210).— *Chairman*, Ms. J. Randerson; *Treasurer*, Dr. G. Morrison; *Party President*, T. Ellis; *Party Leader*, R. Livsey, M.P.

S.L.D. Whips in the House of Lords are: *Chief Whip*, Lord Tordoff; *Deputy Whips*, Viscount Falkland, Lord McNair. S.L.D. Whips in the House of Commons are: *Chief Whip*, J. R. Wallace, M.P.; *Deputy Whips*, A. Kirkwood, M.P.; M. Taylor, M.P.

SOCIAL DEMOCRATIC PARTY, 25–28 Buckingham Gate, SW1E 6LD. (Tel: 01-828 3979).—*President*, J. Cartwright, M.P.; *National Sec.*, Ms. F. Wilson; *Parliamentary Leader*, The Rt. Hon. Dr. D. Owen, M.P.; *Leader of the S.D.P. Peers*, Baroness Stedman.

The S.D.P. Whip in the House of Lords is Lord Walston. The S.D.P. Whip in the House of Commons is J. Cartwright, M.P.

NORTHERN IRELAND

SOCIAL DEMOCRATIC AND LABOUR PARTY, 38 University Street, Belfast BT7 1FZ. (Tel: 0232-323428).— *Chairman*, A. Maginness; *Deputy Chairmen*, M. Durkan, S.J. Murphy; *Hon. Treasurer*, P. Brannigan; *Gen. Sec.*, P. McGlone; *Parliamentary Party Leader*, J. Hume, M.P.; *Deputy Leader*, S. Mallon, M.P.; *Chief Whip*, E. McGrady, M.P.

ULSTER DEMOCRATIC UNIONIST PARTY, 296 Albertbridge Road, Belfast BT5 4GX. (Tel: 0232-458557).— *Chairman*, J. McClure; *Deputy Chairman*, S. Gibson; *Hon. Treasurer*, D. Herron; *Sec.*, A. Kane; *Parliamentary Party Leader*, Dr. I. Paisley, M.P.; *Deputy Leader*, P. Robinson, M.P.

ULSTER UNIONIST COUNCIL, 3 Glengall Street, Belfast BT12 5AE. (Tel: 0232-324601).—*Chairman*, J. Allen; *Vice Chairman*, A. J. Wilson; *Hon. Treasurer*, J. Cunningham; *Party Sec.*, J. Wilson; *Party Leader*, The Rt. Hon. J. H. Molyneaux, M.P.

ALPHABETICAL LIST OF MEMBERS OF THE HOUSE OF COMMONS

(as at end July 1989)

S.L.D. = Social and Liberal Democrat. For other abbreviations, *see* page 249

	Maj.
Abbott, Ms. Diane J. (*b.* 1953), *Lab., Hackney, N. and Stoke Newington*	7,678
*Adams, Allen S. (*b.* 1946), *Lab., Paisley, N.*	14,442
*Adams, Gerard (*b.* 1948), *S.F., Belfast, W.* .	2,221
*Adley, Robert J. (*b.* 1935), *C., Christchurch*	22,374
*Aitken, Jonathan W. P. (*b.* 1942), *C., Thanet, S.*	13,683
*Alexander, Richard T. (*b.* 1934), *C., Newark*	13,543
*Alison, Rt. Hon. Michael J. H. (*b.* 1926), *C., Selby*	13,779
Allason, Rupert W. S. (*b.* 1951), *C., Torbay*	8,820
Allen, Graham W. (*b.* 1953), *Lab., Nottingham, N.*	1,665
*Alton, David P. P.(*b.* 1951), *S.L.D., Liverpool, Mossley Hill*	2,226
*Amery, Rt. Hon. H. Julian (*b.* 1919), *C., Brighton, Pavilion*	9,142
*Amess, David A. A. (*b.* 1952), *C., Basildon*	2,649
Amos, Alan T. (*b.* 1952), *C., Hexham*	8,066
*Anderson, Donald (*b.* 1939), *Lab., Swansea, E.*	19,338
Arbuthnot, James N. (*b.* 1952), *C., Wanstead and Woodford*	16,412
*Archer, Rt. Hon. Peter K., Q.C. (*b.* 1926), *Lab., Warley, W.*	5,393
Armstrong, Ms. Hilary J. (*b.* 1945), *Lab., Durham, N.W.*	10,162
Arnold, Jacques A. (*b.* 1947), *C., Gravesham*	8,792
*Arnold, Thomas R. (*b.* 1947), *C., Hazel Grove*	1,840
*Ashby, David G. (*b.* 1940), *C., Leicestershire, N.W.*	7,828
*Ashdown, Rt. Hon. J. J. D. (Paddy) (*b.* 1941), *S.L.D., Yeovil*	5,700
*Ashley, Rt. Hon. Jack, C. H. (*b.* 1922), *Lab., Stoke-on-Trent, S.*	5,053
*Ashton, Joseph W. (*b.* 1933), *Lab., Bassetlaw*	5,613
*Aspinwall, Jack H. (*b.* 1933), *C., Wansdyke*	16,144
*Atkins, Robert J. (*b.* 1946), *C., S. Ribble* .	8,430
*Atkinson, David A. (*b.* 1940), *C., Bournemouth, E.*	14,683
*Baker, Rt. Hon. Kenneth W. (*b.* 1934), *C., Mole Valley*	16,076
*Baker, Nicholas B. (*b.* 1938), *C., Dorset, N.*	11,907
*Baldry, Antony B. (*b.* 1950), *C., Banbury* .	17,330
*Banks, Robert G. (*b.* 1937), *C., Harrogate* .	11,902
*Banks, Tony L. (*b.* 1943), *Lab., Newham, N. W.*	8,496
Barnes, Harold (*b.* 1936), *Lab., Derbyshire, N.E.*	3,720
*Barnes, Mrs. Rosemary S. (*b.* 1946), *S.D.P., Greenwich*	2,141
*Barron, Kevin J. (*b.* 1946), *Lab., Rother Valley*	15,790
*Batiste, Spencer L. (*b.* 1945), *C., Elmet*	5,356
Battle, John D. (*b.* 1951), *Lab., Leeds, W.* .	4,692
*Beaumont-Dark, Anthony M. (*b.* 1932), *C., Birmingham, Selly Oak*	2,584
*Beckett, Mrs. Margaret M. (*b.* 1943), *Lab., Derby, S.*	1,516
*Beggs, J. Roy (*b.* 1936), *O.U.P., Antrim, E.*	15,360
*Beith, Alan J. (*b.* 1943), *S.L.D., Berwick-upon-Tweed*	9,503
*Bell, Stuart (*b.* 1938), *Lab., Middlesbrough*	14,958
*Bellingham, Henry C. (*b.* 1955), *C., Norfolk, N.W.*	10,825
*Bendall, Vivian W. H. (*b.* 1938), *C., Ilford, N.*	12,090
*Benn, Rt. Hon. Anthony N. W. (*b.* 1925), *Lab., Chesterfield*	8,577

	Maj.
*Bennett, Andrew F. (*b.* 1939), *Lab., Denton and Reddish*	8,250
Bennett, Nicholas J. (*b.* 1949), *C., Pembroke*	5,700
*Benyon, William R. (*b.* 1930), *C., Milton Keynes*	13,701
*Bermingham, Gerald E. (*b.* 1940), *Lab., St. Helens, S.*	13,801
*Bevan, A. David G. (*b.* 1928), *C., Birmingham, Yardley*	2,522
*Bidwell, Sydney J. (*b.* 1917), *Lab., Ealing, Southall*	7,977
*Biffen, Rt. Hon. W. John (*b.* 1930), *C., Shropshire, N.*	14,415
*Blackburn, John G. (*b.* 1933), *C., Dudley, W.*	10,244
*Blair, Anthony C. L. (*b.* 1953), *Lab., Sedgefield*	13,058
*Blaker, Rt. Hon. Sir Peter K.C.M.G. (*b.* 1922), *C., Blackpool, S.*	6,744
Blunkett, David (*b.* 1947), *Lab., Sheffield, Brightside*	24,191
Boateng, Paul Y. (*b.* 1951), *Lab., Brent, S.*	7,931
*Body, Sir Richard (*b.* 1927), *C., Holland with Boston*	17,595
*Bonsor, Sir Nicholas, Bt. (*b.* 1942), *C., Upminster*	16,857
*Boothroyd, Miss Betty (*b.* 1929), *Lab., West Bromwich, W.*	5,253
*Boscawen, Hon. Robert T., M.C. (*b.* 1923), *C., Somerton and Frome*	9,538
Boswell, Timothy E. (*b.* 1942), *C., Daventry*	19,690
*Bottomley, Peter J. (*b.* 1944), *C., Eltham* ..	6,460
*Bottomley, Mrs. Virginia H. B. M. (*b.* 1948), *C., Surrey, S. W.*	14,343
*Bowden, Andrew, M.B.E. (*b.* 1930), *C., Brighton, Kemptown*	9,260
*Bowden, Gerald F., T.D. (*b.* 1935), *C., Dulwich*	180
Bowis, John C. (*b.* 1945), *C., Battersea*	857
*Boyes, Roland (*b.* 1937), *Lab., Houghton and Washington*	20,193
*Boyson, Rt. Hon. Sir Rhodes (*b.* 1925), *C., Brent, N.*	15,720
Bradley, Keith J. C. (*b.* 1950), *Lab., Manchester, Withington*	3,391
*Braine, Rt. Hon. Sir Bernard (*b.* 1914), *C., Castle Point*	19,248
*Brandon-Bravo, Martin M. (*b.* 1932), *C., Nottingham, S.*	2,234
*Bray, Dr. Jeremy W. (*b.* 1930), *Lab., Motherwell, S.*	16,930
Brazier, Julian W. H. (*b.* 1953), *C., Canterbury*	14,891
*Bright, Graham F. J. (*b.* 1942), *C., Luton, S.*	5,115
*Brooke, Rt. Hon. Peter L. (*b.* 1934), *C., City of London and Westminster, S.*	12,042
*Brown, Dr. J. Gordon (*b.* 1951), *Lab., Dunfermline, E.*	19,589
*Brown, Michael R. (*b.* 1951), *C., Brigg and Cleethorpes*	12,248
*Brown, Nicholas H. (*b.* 1950), *Lab., Newcastle upon Tyne, E.*	12,500
*Brown, Ronald D. M. (*b.* 1940), *Lab., Edinburgh, Leith*	11,327
*Browne, John E. D. D. (*b.* 1938), *C., Winchester*	7,479
Bruce, Ian C. (*b.* 1947), *C., Dorset, S.*	15,067
*Bruce, Malcolm G. (*b.* 1944), *S.L.D., Gordon*	9,519

SMALL MAJORITIES

The following Members were returned in June 1987 with majorities of fewer than 1,000 votes.

WOMEN MEMBERS

The number of women M.P.s returned in June 1987 (41) was the highest ever.

Ms. Diane Abbott (*Lab.*, *Hackney N. and Stoke Newington*); Ms. Hilary Armstrong (*Lab.*, *Durham N.W.*); *Mrs. Rosemary Barnes (*SDP*/*All.*, *Greenwich*); *Mrs. Margaret Beckett (*Lab.*, *Derby S.*); *Miss Betty Boothroyd (*Lab.*, *West Bromwich W.*); *Mrs. Virginia Bottomley (*C.*, *Surrey S.W.*); *Mrs. Lynda Chalker (*C.*, *Wallasey*); *Mrs. Ann Clwyd (*Lab.*, *Cynon Valley*); *Mrs. Edwina Currie (*C.*, *Derbyshire S.*); *Hon. Mrs. Gwyneth Dunwoody (*Lab.*, *Crewe and Nantwich*); Mrs. Margaret Ewing (*S.N.P.*, *Moray*); *Dame Peggy Fenner (*C.*, *Medway*); *Miss Janet Fookes (*C.*, *Plymouth Drake*); Mrs. Maria Fyfe (*Lab.*, *Glasgow Maryhill*); *Mrs. Llinos Golding (*Lab.*, *Newcastle-under-Lyme*); Mrs. Mildred Gordon (*Lab.*, *Bow and Poplar*); Mrs. Theresa Gorman (*C.*, *Billericay*); *Ms. Harriet Harman (*Lab.*, *Peckham*); Mrs. Maureen Hicks (*C.*, *Wolverhampton N.E.*); *Mrs. Elaine Kellett-Bowman (*C.*, *Lancaster*); *Dame Jill Knight (*C.*, *Birmingham Edgbaston*).

Miss Joan Lestor (*Lab.*, *Eccles*); Mrs. Alice Mahon (*Lab.*, *Halifax*); Mrs. Ray Michie (*L.*/*All.*, *Argyll and Bute*); Dr. Marjorie Mowlam (*Lab.*, *Redcar*); Miss Emma Nicholson (*C.*, *Devon W. and Torridge*); *Mrs. Elizabeth Peacock (*C.*, *Batley and Spen*); Ms. Dawn Primarolo (*Lab.*, *Bristol S.*); Miss Joyce Quin (*Lab.*, *Gateshead E.*); *Ms. Jo Richardson (*Lab.*, *Barking*); *Mrs. Marion Roe (*C.*, *Broxbourne*); Ms. Joan Ruddock (*Lab.*, *Lewisham Deptford*); *Mrs. Angela Rumbold (*C.*, *Mitcham and Morden*); Mrs. Gillian Shephard (*C.*, *Norfolk S.W.*); *Ms. Clare Short (*Lab.*, *Birmingham Ladywood*); Mrs. Ann Taylor (*Lab.*, *Dewsbury*); *Rt. Hon. Mrs. Margaret Thatcher (*C.*, *Finchley*); Ms. Joan Walley (*Lab.*, *Stoke-on-Trent*); Miss Ann Widdecombe (*C.*, *Maidstone*); *Mrs. Ann Winterton (*C.*, *Congleton*); Mrs. Audrey Wise (*Lab.*, *Preston*).

The number of women M.P.s rose to 42 in June 1989 with the election of Kate Hoey.

THE HOUSE OF COMMONS BY CONSTITUENCIES, JUNE 1987

The figures following the name of each Constituency denote the total number of *Electors* in the Parliamentary Division at the General Election of June 11, 1987.

An asterisk * denotes membership of the last House. The majority in the 1983 General Election (and in any subsequent by-election) is shown below the 1987 result. For **by-elections** since the 1987 General Election, *see* p. 275–6.

Abbreviations — *C.* = Conservative; *D.U.P.* = Democratic Unionist Party; *Ind.* = Independent; *L./All., S.D.P./All.* = Liberal and Social Democratic Alliance; *Lab.* = Labour; *O.U.P.* = Official Unionist Party; *P.C.* = Plaid Cymru; *S.D.L.P.* = Social Democratic and Labour Party; *S.F.* = Sinn Fein; *S.N.P.* = Scottish National Party; *U.P.U.P* = Ulster Popular Unionist Party.

All. = Alliance Party (N.I.); *B.N.* = British Nationalist; *Bread* = Creek Road Fresh Bread Party; *B.T.* = Blancmange Thrower; *C.D.* = Christian Democrat; *C.M.N.H.Y.* = Common Market No, Hanging Yes; *Comm.* = Communist Party; *C.P.R.P.* = Capital Punishment Referendum Party; *C.P.W.S.M.L.* = Capital Punishment Will Save More Lives; *C.S.* = Christian Socialist Opposing Secret Masonic Government; *D.C.* = Democratic Commonwealth Party; *Dem.* = Independent Democrat; *Ecol.* = Ecology (N.I.); *Ex. Lab. Mod.* = Ex Labour Moderate; *Falk.* = Right of Falkland Islands to elect Westminster M.P.; *F.D.P.* = Fancy Dress Party; *Fell.* = Fellowship Party; *F.P.* = Feudal Party; *Gait. Lab.* = Gaitskell Labour; *Gold* = Gold Party; *Grem.* = Gremloid; *Grn.* = Green Party; *H.P.* = Human Party; *I.C.C.* = Independent Community Campaigner, East Oxford People; *I.C.N.* = Independent Christian Nationalist; *L.A.O.* = Law and Order; *L.A.P.P.* = Let's Have Another Party Party; *L.M.* = Loony Official Monster Raving Party; *M.L.* = Moderate Labour Party; *N.F.F.G.* = National Front Flag Group; *N.P.R.* = National People's Rally; *O.F.P.* = Official Fidgeyitous Party; *O.O.B.P.C.* = Only Official Best Party Candidate; *O.S.M.* = Orkney and Shetland Movement; *P.I.P.* = Public Independent Plaintiff; *Prot. U.* = Protestant Unionist; *P.R.P.* = Protestant Reformation Party; *R.A.B.I.E.S.* = Rainbow Alliance Brixton Insane Extremist Section; *R.C.P.* = Return Capital Punishment; *Real U.* = Real Unionist; *R.F.* = Red Front; *Ret.* = Retired; *R.R.P.R.C.* = Revolutionary Reform Party Representative of Christ; *S.E.* = Spare the Earth; *S.L.D.* = Social and Liberal Democrat; *S.P.G.B.* = Socialist Party of Great Britain; *W.P.* = Workers' Party (N.I.); *W.R.P.* = Workers' Revolutionary Party.

ENGLAND

Aldershot (Hants)
E. 80,797

*J. M. G. Critchley, C.		35,272
R. A. Hargreaves, *L./All.*		17,488
I. H. Pearson, *Lab.*		7,061
C. maj.		17,784
(June '83, C. maj. 12,218)		

Aldridge-Brownhills
(W. Midlands)
E. 62,129

*R. C. S. Shepherd, C.		26,434
C. Duncan, *Lab.*		14,038
G. Betteridge, *S.D.P./All.*		9,084
C. maj.		12,396
(June '83, C. maj. 12,284)		

Altrincham and Sale
(Gtr. Manchester)
E. 67,611

*Sir F. Montgomery, C.		27,746
J. Mulholland, *L./All.*		13,518
D. Hinder, *Lab.*		10,617
C. Maj.		14,228
(June '83, C. maj. 10,911)		

Amber Valley (Derbys)
E. 68,478

*P. A. C. L. Oppenheim, C.		28,603
D. M. Bookbinder, *Lab.*		19,103
S. Reynolds, *L./All.*		7,904
C. maj.		9,500
(June '83, C. maj. 3,318)		

Arundel (W. Sussex)
E. 78,683

*R. M. Marshall, C.		34,356
Dr. J. M. M. Walsh, *L./All.*		15,476
P. Slowe, *Lab.*		6,177
C. maj.		18,880
(June '83, C. maj. 15,705)		

Ashfield (Notts)
E. 70,937

*D. F. Haynes, Lab.		22,812
B. G. Coleman, *C.*		18,412
Mrs. F. B. Stein, *L./All.*		13,542
Lab. maj.		4,400
(June '83, Lab. maj. 6,087)		

Ashford (Kent)
E. 70,052

*H. K. Speed, C.		29,978
N. N. Macmillan, *S.D.P./All.*		14,490
M. J. Wiggins, *Lab.*		7,775
Dr. C. A. Porter, *Grn.*		778
C. maj.		15,488
(June '83, C. maj. 13,911)		

Ashton-under-Lyne
(Gtr. Manchester)
E. 58,440

*Rt. Hon. R. E. Sheldon, Lab.		22,389
H. L. Cadman, *C.*		13,103
M. J. Hunter, *L./All.*		7,760
Lab. maj.		9,286
(June '83, Lab. maj. 7,697)		

Aylesbury (Bucks)
E. 76,919

*Rt. Hon. T. H. F. Raison, C.		32,970
M. A. Soole, *S.D.P./All.*		16,412
Ms. J. Larner, *Lab.*		7,936
C. maj.		16,558
(June '83, C. maj. 14,920)		

Banbury (Oxon)
E. 69,455

*A. B. Baldry, C.		29,716
D. C. Rowland, *S.D.P./All.*		12,386
J. A. Honeybone, *Lab.*		10,789
C. maj.		17,330
(June '83, C. maj. 13,025)		

Barking (Gtr. London)
E. 51,639

*Ms. J. Richardson, Lab.		15,307
W. K. Sharp, *C.*		11,898
J. K. Gibb, *L./All.*		7,336
Lab. maj.		3,409
(June '83, Lab. maj. 4,026)		

Barnsley (S. Yorks)

CENTRAL *E.* 55,902

E. E. Illsley, *Lab.*		26,139
Mrs. V. Prais, *C.*		7,088
Mrs. S. A. M. Holland, *L./All.*		5,928
Lab. maj.		19,051
(June '83, Lab. maj. 14,173)		

EAST *E.* 53,505

*T. Patchett, Lab.		28,948
W. J. Clappison, *C.*		5,437
G. J. Griffiths, *L./All.*		4,482
Lab. maj.		23,511
(June '83, Lab. maj. 17,492)		

WEST AND PENISTONE *E.* 61,091

*A. McKay, Lab.		26,498
A. J. C. Duncan, *C.*		12,307
R. Hall, *S.D.P./All.*		7,409
Lab. maj.		14,191
(June '83, Lab. maj. 10,342)		

Barrow and Furness (Cumbria)
E. 69,288

*C. S. Franks, C.		25,431
P. Phizacklea, *Lab.*		21,504
R. W. Phelps, *S.D.P./All.*		7,799
C. maj.		3,927
(June '83, C. maj. 4,577)		

Basildon (Essex)
E. 68,500

*D. A. A. Amess, C.		21,858
J. G. H. Fulbrook, *Lab.*		19,209
R. M. Auvray, *L./All.*		9,139
C. maj.		2,649
(June '83, C. maj. 1,379)		

Basingstoke (Hants)
E. 78,003

*A. R. F. Hunter, C.		33,657
D. Bennett, *S.D.P./All.*		15,764
P. Daden, *Lab.*		10,632
C. maj.		17,893
(June '83, C. maj. 12,450)		

Bassetlaw (Notts)
E. 68,043

*J. W. Ashton, *Lab.*		25,385
D. R. J. Selves, *C.*		19,772
W. G. Smith, *S.D.P./All.*		7,616
Lab. maj.		5,613
(June '83, Lab. maj. 3,831)		

Bath (Avon)
E. 65,246

*C. F. Patten, *C.*		23,515
J. M. Dean, *S.D.P./All.*		22,103
Mrs. J. Smith, *Lab.*		5,507
D. N. Wall, *Grn.*		687
C. maj.		1,412
(June '83, C. maj. 5,304)		

Batley and Spen (W. Yorks)
E. 74,347

*Mrs. E. J. Peacock, *C.*		25,512
K. J. Woolmer, *Lab.*		24,150
K. Burke, *S.D.P./All.*		8,372
A. Harrison, *M.L.*		689
C. maj.		1,362
(June '83, C. maj. 870)		

Battersea (Gtr. London)
E. 66,979

J. C. Bowis, *C.*		20,945
*A. Dubs, *Lab.*		20,088
D. I. Harries, *S.D.P./All.*		5,634
Ms. S. G. Willington, *Grn.*		559
A. B. Bell, *W.R.P.*		116
C. maj.		857
(June '83, Lab. maj. 3,276)		

Beaconsfield (Bucks)
E. 67,713

*T. J. Smith, *C.*		33,324
D. H. Ive, *L./All.*		11,985
K. J. Harper, *Lab.*		5,203
C. maj.		21,339
(June '83, C. maj. 18,300)		

Beckenham (Gtr. London)
E. 60,110

*Sir P. C. Goodhart, *C.*		24,903
C. G. Darracott, *L./All.*		11,439
K. G. Ritchie, *Lab.*		7,888
C. maj.		13,464
(June '83, C. maj. 12,670)		

Bedfordshire

MID E. 80,673

*N. W. Lyell, *Q.C.*, *C.*		37,411
N. C. Hills, *S.D.P./All.*		14,560
J. Heywood, *Lab.*		11,463
C. maj.		22,851
(June '83, C. maj. 17,381)		

NORTH E. 73,536

*Sir T. H. H. Skeet, *C.*		29,845
Mrs. J. V. Lennon, *L./All.*		13,340
C. B. Henderson, *Lab.*		13,140
C. D. Slee, *O.O.B.P.C.*		435
C. maj.		16,505
(June '83, C. maj. 13,849)		

SOUTH WEST E. 78,956

*W. D. Madel, *C.*		36,140
J. R. Burrow, *S.D.P./All.*		13,835
P. H. Dimoldenberg, *Lab.*		11,352
P. J. Rollings, *Grn.*		822
C. maj.		22,305
(June '83, C. maj. 15,731)		

Berkshire East
E. 87,820

*A. J. MacKay, *C.*		39,094
Mrs. L. A. Murray, *S.D.P./All.*		16,468
R. J. E. Evans, *Lab.*		9,287
C. maj.		22,626
(June '83, C. maj. 16,099)		

Berwick-upon-Tweed (Nthmb)
E. 54,378

*A. J. Beith, *L./All.*		21,903
T. Middleton, *C.*		12,400
S. Lambert, *Lab.*		7,360
N. Pamphilion, *Grn.*		379
L./All. maj.		9,503
(June '83, L./All. maj. 8,215)		

Bethnal Green and Stepney
(Gtr. London)
E. 55,769

*Rt. Hon. P. D. Shore, *Lab.*		15,490
J. A. Shaw, *L./All.*		10,206
Lady O. H. Maitland, *C.*		6,176
Ms. S. Gasquoine, *Comm.*		232
Lab. maj.		5,284
(June '83, Lab. maj. 6,358)		

Beverley (Humberside)
E. 78,923

J. D. Cran, *C.*		31,459
J. Bryant, *L./All.*		18,864
M. Shaw, *Lab.*		9,901
C. maj.		12,595
(June '83, C. maj. 13,869)		

Bexhill and Battle
(E. Sussex)
E. 65,288

*C. F. Wardle, *C.*		33,570
R. Kiernan, *S.D.P./All.*		13,051
D. K. Watts, *Lab.*		3,903
C. maj.		20,519
(June '83, C. maj. 19,746)		

Bexleyheath
(Gtr. London)
E. 59,448

*C. D. Townsend, *C.*		24,866
B. C. Standen, *L./All.*		13,179
J. F. Little, *Lab.*		8,218
C. maj.		11,687
(June '83, C. maj. 10,258)		

Billericay (Essex)
E. 79,535

*Mrs. T. E. Gorman, *C.*		33,741
M. Birch, *S.D.P./All.*		15,755
R. Howitt, *Lab.*		11,942
C. maj.		17,986
(June '83, C. maj. 14,615)		

Birkenhead (Merseyside)
E. 65,662

*F. Field, *Lab.*		27,883
K. J. Costa, *C.*		12,511
R. Kemp, *L./All.*		7,095
Lab. maj.		15,372
(June '83, Lab. maj. 9,714)		

Birmingham (W. Midlands)

EDGBASTON E. 54,416

*Dame J. C. J. Knight, D.B.E., *C.*		18,595
J. Wilton, *Lab.*		10,014
J. C. Binns, *S.D.P./All.*		7,843
P. Simpson, *Grn.*		559
S. T. Hardwick, *Ind. C.*		307
C. maj.		8,581
(June '83, C. maj. 11,418)		

ERDINGTON E. 54,179

*R. Corbett, *Lab.*		17,037
P. J. Johnston, *C.*		14,570
N. Biddlestone, *S.D.P./All.*		5,530
Lab. maj.		2,467
(June '83, Lab. maj. 231)		

HALL GREEN E. 61,148

A. R. Hargreaves, *C.*		20,478
Mrs. E. Brook, *Lab.*		12,857
M. Wilkes, *S.D.P./All.*		12,323
C. maj.		7,621
(June '83, C. maj. 9,373)		

HODGE HILL E. 59,296

*T. A. G. Davis, *Lab.*		19,872
S. Eyre, *C.*		15,083
K. G. Hardeman, *L./All.*		5,868
Lab. maj.		4,789
(June '83, Lab. maj. 5,092)		

LADYWOOD E. 58,761

*Ms. C. Short, *Lab.*		21,971
S. T. Lee, *C.*		11,943
G. S. Sangha, *S.D.P./All.*		3,532
Ms. J. Millington, *Grn.*		650
Lab. maj.		10,028
(June '83, Lab. maj. 9,030)		

NORTHFIELD E. 73,319

*R. D. King, *C.*		24,024
J. F. Spellar, *Lab.*		20,889
J. Gordon, *S.D.P./All.*		8,319
C. maj.		3,135
(June '83, C. maj. 2,760)		

PERRY BARR E. 73,767

*J. W. Rooker, *Lab.*		25,894
J. D. B. Taylor, *C.*		18,961
D. D. Webb, *L./All.*		6,514
Lab. maj.		6,933
(June '83, Lab. maj. 7,402)		

SELLY OAK E. 72,213

*A. M. Beaumont-Dark, *C.*		23,305
A. Bore, *Lab.*		20,721
Mrs. C. Cane, *L./All.*		8,128
Ms. M. Hackett, *Grn*		611
C. maj.		2,584
(June '83, C. maj. 5,396)		

SMALL HEATH   E. 56,722
*Rt. Hon. D. H. Howell,
  Lab. 22,787
P. Nischal, C. 7,266
J. A. M. Hemming, S.D.P./All. 3,600
A. Clawley, Grn. 559
P. R. Sheppard, Comm. ... 154
  Lab. maj. 15,521
  (June '83, Lab. maj. 15,252)

SPARKBROOK   E. 53,093
*Rt. Hon. R. S. G. Hattersley,
  Lab. 20,513
N. A. Khan, C. 8,654
R. Dimmick, S.D.P./All. ... 3,803
R. Ambler, Grn. 526
P. Khan, R.F. 229
  Lab. maj. 11,859
  (June '83, Lab. maj. 10,548)

YARDLEY   E. 56,957
*A. D. G. Bevan, C. 17,931
G. Edge, Lab. 15,409
L. Smith, L./All. 8,734
  C. maj. 2,522
  (June '83, C. maj. 2,865)

Bishop Auckland (Durham)
E. 72,147

*D. Foster, Lab. 25,648
R. Wight, C. 18,613
G. Irwin, L./All. 9,195
  Lab. maj. 7,035
  (June '83, Lab. maj. 4,306)

Blaby (Leics)
E. 77,094

*Rt. Hon. N. Lawson, C. ... 37,732
R. E. Lustig, L./All. 15,556
J. M. Roberts, Lab. 9,046
  C. maj. 22,176
  (June '83, C. maj. 17,116)

Blackburn (Lancs)
E. 74,801

*J. W. Straw, Lab. 27,965
Mrs. A. C. Cheetham, C. ... 22,468
M. A. Ali, S.D.P./All. 5,602
  Lab. maj. 5,497
  (June '83, Lab. maj. 3,055)

Blackpool (Lancs)

NORTH   E. 58,893
*N. A. Miscampbell, Q.C., C. 20,680
E. Kirton, Lab. 13,359
C. J. Heyworth, L./All. ... 9,032
  C. maj. 7,321
  (June '83, C. maj. 10,152)

SOUTH   E. 57,567
*Rt. Hon. Sir P. A. R. Blaker,
  K.C.M.G., C. 20,312
Mrs. S. Baugh, Lab. 13,568
J. Allitt, S.D.P./All. 8,405
  C. maj. 6,744
  (June '83, C. maj. 10,138)

Blaydon (Tyne & Wear)
E. 66,301

*J. D. McWilliam, Lab. ... 25,277
V. P. Nunn, S.D.P./All. ... 12,789
P. R. Pescod, C. 12,147
  Lab. maj. 12,488
  (June '83, Lab. maj. 7,222)

Blyth Valley (Nthmb)
E. 59,104

R. Campbell, Lab. 19,604
Miss R. M. Brownlow,
  S.D.P./All. 18,751
Dr. R. Kinghorn, C. 7,823
  Lab. maj. 853
  (June '83, Lab. maj. 3,243)

Bolsover (Derbys)
E. 65,452

*D. E. Skinner, Lab. 28,453
M. R. Lingens, C. 14,333
M. H. Fowler, S.D.P./All. . 7,836
  Lab. maj. 14,120
  (June '83, Lab. maj. 13,848)

Bolton (Gtr. Manchester)

NORTH EAST   E. 59,382
*P. G. Thurnham, C. 20,742
F. R. White, Lab. 19,929
J. H. Alcock, S.D.P./All. .. 6,060
  C. maj. 813
  (June '83, C. maj. 2,443)

SOUTH EAST   E. 65,932
*D. W. Young, Lab. 26,791
S. Windle, C. 15,410
F. Harasiwka, L./All. 7,161
  Lab. maj. 11,381
  (June ' 83, Lab. maj. 8,753)

WEST   E. 69,843
*T. G. Sackville, C. 24,779
G. J. Harkin, Lab. 20,186
D. T. Eccles, S.D.P./All. .. 10,936
  C. maj. 4,593
  (June '83, C. maj. 7,152)

Boothferry (Humberside)
E. 75,176

D. M. Davis, C. 31,716
Mrs. J. D. Davies, L./All. . 12,746
R. Donson, Lab. 12,498
  C. maj. 18,970
  (June '83, C. maj. 17,420)

Bootle (Merseyside)
E. 71,765

*A. Roberts, Lab. 34,975
P. R. Papworth, C. 10,498
P. Denham, S.D.P./All. ... 6,820
  Lab. maj. 24,477
  (June '83, Lab. maj. 15,139)

Bosworth (Leics)
E. 77,186

D. A. S. Tredinnick, C. ... 34,145
D. C. Bill, L./All. 17,129
R. S. Hall, Lab. 10,787
Mrs. D. Freer, Grn 660
  C. maj. 17,016
  (June '83, C. maj. 17,294)

Bournemouth (Dorset)

EAST   E. 75,232
*D. A. Atkinson, C. 30,925
Dr. J. Millward, L./All. ... 16,242
I. A. Taylor, Lab. 5,885
  C. maj. 14,683
  (June '83, C. maj. 11,416)

WEST   E. 74,444
*J. V. Butterfill, C. 30,117
P. G. M. Craven, S.D.P./
  All. 17,466
R. W. Jones, Lab. 7,018
  C. maj. 12,651
  (June '83, C. maj. 13,331)

Bow and Poplar (Gtr. London)
E. 59,178

Ms. M. Gordon, Lab. 15,746
E. Flounders, L./All. 11,115
D. C. Hughes, C. 6,810
P. S. Chappell, W.R.P. 274
  Lab. maj. 4,631
  (June '83, Lab. maj. 5,861)

Bradford (W. Yorks)

NORTH   E. 67,430
C. P. Wall, Lab. 21,009
*G. J. Lawler, C. 19,376
A. M. Berkeley, S.D.P./All. 8,656
  Lab. maj. 1,633
  (June '83, C. maj. 1,602)

SOUTH   E. 69,588
G. R. Cryer, Lab. 21,230
G. T. Hall, C. 20,921
T. Lindley, S.D.P./All. ... 9,109
  Lab. maj. 309
  (June '83, Lab. maj. 110)

WEST   E. 70,763
*M. F. Madden, Lab. 25,775
I. Duncan-Smith, C. 18,224
M. Moghal, S.D.P./All. ... 5,657
  Lab. maj. 7,551
  (June '83, Lab. maj. 3,337)

Braintree (Essex)
E. 76,994

*A. H. Newton, O.B.E., C. ... 32,978
I. G. Bing, S.D.P./All. 16,121
B. Stapleton, Lab. 11,764
  C. maj. 16,857
  (June '83, C. maj. 13,441)

Brent (Gtr. London)

EAST   E. 61,020
K. R. Livingstone, Lab. ... 16,772
Miss H. S. Crawley, C. 15,119
D. W. Finkelstein, S.D.P./
  All. 5,710
R. Q. Dooley, Ind. Lab. ... 1,035
M. Litvinoff, Grn. 716
  Lab. maj. 1,653
  (June '83, Lab. maj. 4,834)

NORTH   E. 63,081
*Dr. R. Boyson, C. 26,823
P. Patel, Lab. 11,103
C. Mularczyk, S.D.P./All. . 6,868
  C. maj. 15,720
  (June '83, C. maj. 14,651)

SOUTH   E. 62,772
*P. Y. Boateng, Lab. 21,140
A. J. Paterson, C. 13,209
M. T. Harskin, L./All. 6,375
  Lab. maj. 7,931
  (June '83, Lab. maj. 10,519)

Brentford and Isleworth
(Gtr. London)
E. 71,715

*Rt. Hon. Sir B. J. Hayhoe,		
C.		26,230
Ms. A. Keen, *Lab.*		18,277
Dr. D. M. W. Wilks, *S.D.P./*		
All.		9,626
T. Cooper, *Grn.*		849
C. maj.		7,953

(June '83, C. maj. 9,387)

Brentwood and Ongar (Essex)
E. 67,521

*R. A. McCrindle, C.		32,258
N. R. Amor, *L./All.*		13,337
J. W. Orpe, *Lab.*		7,042
Mrs. M. E. Willis, *Grn.*		686
C. maj.		18,921

(June '83, C. maj. 14,202)

Bridgwater (Somerset)
E. 67,480

*Rt. Hon. T. J. King, C.		27,177
C. Clarke, *S.D.P./All.*		15,982
J. Turner, *Lab.*		9,594
C. maj.		11,195

(June '83, C. maj. 10,697)

Bridlington (Humberside)
E. 80,126

*J. E. Townend, C.		32,351
E. I. Marshall, *S.D.P./All.*		15,030
L. M. Bird, *Lab.*		10,653
R. D. Myerscough, *Grn.*		983
C. maj.		17,321

(June '83, C. maj. 16,609)

Brigg and Cleethorpes
(Humberside)
E. 80,096

*M. R. Brown, C.		29,723
I. Powney, *L./All.*		17,475
T. Geraghty, *Lab.*		13,876
C. maj.		12,248

(June '83, C. maj. 12,189)

Brighton (E. Sussex)
KEMPTOWN *E.* 60,271

*A. Bowden, M.B.E., *C.*		24,031
J. S. Bassam, *Lab.*		14,771
C. Berry, *L./All.*		6,080
C. maj.		9,260

(June '83, C. maj. 9,378)

PAVILION *E.* 58,910

*Rt. Hon. H. J. Amery, C.		22,056
D. S. Hill, *Lab.*		12,914
K. F. Carey, *S.D.P/All.*		8,459
C. maj.		9,142

(June '83, C. maj. 11,132)

Bristol (Avon)
EAST *E.* 63,840

*J. Sayeed, C.		21,906
R. R. Thomas, *Lab.*		17,783
D. M. E. Foster, *L./All.*		10,247
P. M. Kingston, *N.F.F.G.*		286
C. maj.		4,123

(June '83, C. maj. 1,789)

NORTH WEST *E.* 72,876

*M. C. Stern, C.		26,953
T. W. Walker, *Lab.*		20,001
J. M. G. Kirkaldy, *S.D.P./*		
All.		10,885
C. maj.		6,952

(June '83, C. maj. 6,327)

SOUTH *E.* 68,733

Ms. D. Primarolo, Lab.		20,798
P. S. Cutcher, *C.*		19,394
Mrs. H. S. Long, *S.D.P./All.*		9,952
G. R. Vowles, *Grn.*		600
Ms. C. M. Meghji, *R.F.*		149
Lab. maj.		1,404

(June '83, Lab. maj. 4,419)

WEST *E.* 72,357

*Hon. W. A. Waldegrave, C.		24,695
G. R. P. Ferguson, *L./All.*		16,992
Mrs. M. C. Georghiou, *Lab.*		11,337
Mrs. G. A. Dorey, *Grn.*		1,096
Ms. V. Ralph, *Comm.*		134
C. maj.		7,703

(June '83, C. maj. 10,178)

Bromsgrove (H & W)
E. 69,494

*H. D. Miller, C.		29,051
J. D. Ward, *Lab.*		12,366
D. L. Cropp, *S.D.P./All.*		11,663
C. maj.		16,685

(June '83, C. maj. 17,175)

Broxbourne (Herts)
E. 70,631

*Mrs. M. A. Roe, C.		33,567
Mrs. E. Yates, *L./All.*		10,572
P. Parry, *Lab.*		8,984
C. maj.		22,995

(June '83, C. maj. 17,466)

Broxtowe (Notts)
E. 71,780

*J. T. Lester, C.		30,462
K. Fleet, *Lab.*		13,811
K. M. Melton, *L./All.*		12,562
C. maj.		16,651

(June '83, C. maj. 15,078)

Buckingham
E. 70,036

*G. G. H. Walden, C.M.G.,		
C.		32,162
C. M. Burke, *L./All.*		13,636
M. Groucutt, *Lab.*		9,053
C. maj.		18,526

(June '83, C. maj. 13,968)

Burnley (Lancs)
E. 65,956

*P. L. Pike, Lab.		25,140
H. Elletson, *C.*		17,583
R. H. Baker, *S.D.P./All.*		9,241
Lab. maj.		7,557

(June '83, Lab. maj. 770)

Burton (Staffs)
E. 73,252

*I. J. Lawrence, Q.C., *C.*		29,160
D. Heptonstall, *Lab.*		19,330
K. A. Hemsley, *L./All.*		9,046
C. maj.		9,830

(June '83, C. maj. 11,647)

Bury (Gtr. Manchester)
NORTH *E.* 67,961

*A. J. H. Burt, C.		28,097
D. Crausby, *Lab.*		21,186
D. Vasmer, *L./All.*		6,804
C. maj.		6,911

(June '83, C. maj. 2,792)

SOUTH *E.* 65,039

*D. A. G. Sumberg, C.		23,878
D. Boden, *Lab.*		21,199
D. A. Eyre, *S.D.P./All.*		6,772
C. maj.		2,679

(June '83, C. maj. 3,720)

Bury St. Edmunds (Suffolk)
E. 76,619

*Sir E. W. Griffiths, C.		33,672
Sir R. Harland, *S.D.P./All.*		12,214
C. L. Greene, *Lab.*		9,841
Ms. I. M. J. Wakelam, *Grn.*		1,057
C. maj.		21,458

(June '83, C. maj. 16,122)

Calder Valley (W. Yorks)
E. 73,398

*D. Thompson, C.		25,892
D. M. Chaytor, *Lab.*		19,847
D. T. Shutt, *L./All.*		13,761
C. maj.		6,045

(June '83, C. maj. 7,999)

Cambridge
E. 69,336

*R. V. Rhodes James, C.		21,624
Mrs. S. V. T. B. Williams,		
S.D.P./All.		16,564
C. J. Howard, *Lab.*		15,319
Ms. M. E. Wright, *Grn.*		597
C. maj.		5,060

(June '83, C. maj. 5,968)

Cambridgeshire
NORTH EAST *E.* 74,231

M. D. Moss, C.		26,983
*C. R. Freud, L./All.		25,555
R. J. Harris, *Lab.*		4,891
C. maj.		1,428

(June '83, L./All. maj. 5,195)

SOUTH EAST *E.* 73,216

J. E. T. Paice, C.		32,901
P. C. Lee, *S.D.P./All.*		15,399
T. G. Ling, *Lab.*		7,694
C. maj.		17,502

(June '83, C. maj. 13,764)

SOUTH WEST *E.* 81,658

*Sir J. A. Grant, C.		36,622
D. C. Nicholls, *L./All.*		18,371
Ms. J. Billing, *Lab.*		8,434
C. maj.		18,251

(June '83, C. maj. 13,867)

Cannock and Burntwood (Staffs)
E. 68,137

*J. G. D. Howarth, C.		24,186
G. E. Roberts, *Lab.*		21,497
N. Stanley, *L./All.*		8,698
C. maj.		2,689

(June '83, C. maj. 2,045)

Canterbury (Kent)
E. 76,062

J. W. H. Brazier, *C.*	......	30,273
J. Purchese, *L./All.*	......	15,382
Ms. L. A. Keen, *Lab.*	.....	9,494
S. Dawe, *Grn.*	....	947
Miss J. M. White, *I.C.N.*	..	157
C. maj.	....	14,891

(June '83, C. maj. 15,742)

Carlisle (Cumbria)
E. 55,053

E. A. Martlew, *Lab.*	......	18,311
W. G. Hodgson, *C.*	....	17,395
R. S. Hunt, *S.D.P./All*	....	7,655
Lab. maj.	....	916

(June '83, Lab. maj. 71)

Carshalton and Wallington
(Gtr. London)
E. 69,120

*F. N. Forman, *C.*	....	27,984
J. D. Grant, *S.D.P./All.*	..	13,575
Mrs. J. G. Baker, *Lab.*	....	9,440
R. W. Steel, *Grn.*	....	843
C. maj.	....	14,409

(June '83, C. maj. 10,755)

Castle Point (Essex)
E. 65,992

*Rt. Hon. Sir B. R. Braine, *C.*	....	29,681
Miss A. P. Bastow, *S.D.P./ All.*	....	10,433
W. A. Deal, *Lab.*	....	9,422
C. maj.	....	19,248

(June '83, C. maj. 15,417)

Cheadle
(Gtr. Manchester)
E. 68,332

S. R. Day, *C.*	....	30,484
A. B. Leah, *L./All.*	....	19,853
Ms. A. Coffey, *Lab.*	......	5,037
C. maj.	....	10,631

(June '83, C. maj. 9,380)

Chelmsford (Essex)
E. 82,564

S. H. M. Burns, *C.*	....	35,231
S. G. Mole, *L./All.*	....	27,470
C. E. Playford, *Lab.*	......	4,642
A. C. Slade, *Grn.*	....	486
C. maj.	....	7,761

(June '83, C. maj. 378)

Chelsea
(Gtr. London)
E. 49,534

*N. P. Scott, M.B.E., *C.*	.....	18,443
Mrs. J. M. Ware, *L./All.*	..	5,124
D. J. Ward, *Lab.*	....	4,406
Ms. N. Kortvelyessy, *Grn.*		587
C. maj.	....	13,319

(June '83, C. maj. 12,021)

Cheltenham (Glos)
E. 79,234

*C. G. Irving, *C.*	....	31,371
R. G. Holme, *L./All.*	......	26,475
M. Luker, *Lab.*	....	4,701
C. maj.	....	4,896

(June '83, C. maj. 5,518)

Chertsey and Walton (Surrey)
E. 71,448

*G. E. Pattie, *C.*	....	32,119
Mrs. S. K. Stapely, *S.D.P./ All.*	....	14,650
H. G. Trace, *Lab.*	....	7,185
C. maj.	....	17,469

(June '83, C. maj. 15,699)

Chesham and Amersham
(Bucks)
E. 71,751

*Rt. Hon. Sir I. H. J. L. Gilmour, Bt., *C.*	....	34,504
A. T. Ketteringham, *L./All.*		15,064
P. A. Goulding, *Lab.*	......	5,170
Mrs. A. G. Darnbrough, *Grn.*	....	760
C. maj.	....	19,440

(June '83, C. maj. 15,879)

Chester, City of
E. 65,845

*Hon. P. H. Morrison, *C.*	..	23,582
D. Robinson, *Lab.*	....	18,727
R. A. Stunell, *L./All.*	.....	10,262
C. maj.	....	4,855

(June '83, C. maj. 9,099)

Chesterfield (Derbys)
E. 70,357

*Rt. Hon. A. N. W. Benn, *Lab.*	....	24,532
A. H. Rogers, *L./All.*	.....	15,955
R. P Grant, *C.*	....	13,472
Lab. maj.	....	8,577

(June '83, Lab. maj. 7,763)
(March '84, Lab. maj. 6,264)

Chichester (W. Sussex)
E. 81,019

*R. A. Nelson, *C.*	....	37,274
P. F. Weston, *L./All.*	.....	17,097
D. Morrison, *Lab.*	....	4,751
I. F. N. Bagnall, *Grn.*	.....	1,196
C. maj.	....	20,177

(June '83, C. maj. 20,117)

Chingford (Gtr. London)
E. 56,797

*Rt. Hon. N. B. Tebbit, *C.*	..	27,110
J. G. Williams, *L./All.*	.....	9,155
Ms. M. I. Cosin, *Lab.*	.....	6,650
Ms. E. Newton, *Grn.*	.....	634
C. maj.	....	17,955

(June '83, C. maj. 12,414)

Chipping Barnet (Gtr. London)
E. 60,876

*S. B. Chapman, *C.*	....	24,686
J. Skinner, *L./All.*	....	9,815
D. Perkin, *Lab.*	....	8,115
C. maj.	....	14,871

(June '83, C. maj. 12,393)

Chislehurst (Gtr. London)
E. 55,535

*R. E. Sims, *C.*	....	24,165
R. A. Younger-Ross, *L./All.*		9,658
S. H. Ward, *Lab.*	....	8,115
C. maj.	....	14,507

(June '83, C. maj. 12,061)

Chorley (Lancs)
E. 78,541

*D. R. Dover, *C.*	....	29,015
A. J. Watmough, *Lab.*	....	20,958
I. A. Simpson, *L./All.*	.....	9,706
A. S. Holgate, *Grn.*	....	714
C. maj.	....	8,057

(June '83, C. maj. 10,275)

Christchurch (Dorset)
E. 70,964

*R. J. Adley, *C.*	....	35,656
Miss H. J. McKenzie, *S.D.P./All.*	....	13,282
Ms. C. E. Longhurst, *Lab.*		5,174
C. maj.	....	22,374

(June '83, C. maj. 19,738)

Cirencester and Tewkesbury
(Glos)
E. 84,071

*Rt. Hon. N. Ridley, *C.*	....	36,272
P. T. Beckerlegge, *L./All.*	.	23,610
J. D. Naysmith, *Lab.*	.....	5,342
M. A. Curtis, *Male O.A.P.*	..	283
C. maj.	....	12,662

(June '83, C. maj. 13,827)

The City of London and
Westminster South
E. 57,428

*Hon. P. L. Brooke, *C.*	.....	19,333
Ms. J. C. G. Smithard, *S.D.P./All*	....	7,291
Ms. R. E. Bush, *Lab.*	.....	6,821
C. maj.	....	12,042

(June '83, C. maj. 13,387)

Colchester (Essex)

NORTH E. 82,420

*Sir P. A. F. Buck, Q.C., *C.*	.	32,747
A. Hayman, *S.D.P./All.*	.	19,124
R. A. Green, *Lab.*	....	10,768
C. maj.	....	13,623

(June '83, C. maj. 15,048)

SOUTH, AND MALDON E. 84,392

*Rt. Hon. J. Wakeham, *C.*		34,894
J. W. Stevens, *S.D.P./All.*		19,411
Ms. S. Bigwood, *Lab.*	......	9,229
C. maj.	....	15,483

(June '83, C. maj. 12,165)

Colne Valley (W. Yorks)
E. 70,199

G. E. G. Riddick, *C.*	......	20,457
N. J. Priestley, *L./All.*	....	18,780
J. A. Harman, *Lab.*	......	16,353
M. R. Mullany, *Grn.*	.....	614
C. maj.	....	1,677

(June '83, L./All. maj. 3,146)

Congleton (Cheshire)
E. 68,172

*Mrs. J. A. Winterton, *C.*	..	26,513
I. M. Brodie-Browne, *L./ All.*	....	18,544
M. Knowles, *Lab.*	....	9,810
C. maj.	....	7,969

(June '83, C. maj. 8,459)

Copeland (Cumbria)
E. 54,695

*Dr. J. A. Cunningham,
Lab. 20,999
A. R. M. Toft, C. 19,105
E. T. Colgan, S.D.P./All. . 4,052
R. A. Gibson, Grn. 319
Lab. maj. 1,894
(June '83, Lab. maj. 1,837)

Corby (Northants)
E. 66,119

*W. R. Powell, C. 23,323
H. A. Feather, Lab. 21,518
T. G. Whittington, L./
All. 7,805
C. maj. 1,805
(June '83, C. maj. 3,168)

Cornwall

NORTH E. 72,375
*G. A. Neale, C. 29,862
M. N. Mitchell, L./All. ... 24,180
Ms. C. Herries, Lab. 3,719
C. maj. 5,682
(June '83, C. maj. 5,059)

SOUTH EAST E. 70,248
*R. A. Hicks, C. 28,818
I. P. Tunbridge, L./All. ... 22,211
P. A. Clark, Lab. 4,847
C. maj. 6,607
(June '83, C. maj. 8,354)

Coventry (W. Midlands)

NORTH EAST E. 67,479
J. Hughes, Lab. 25,832
C. Prior, C. 13,965
S. Wood, L./All. 7,502
A. McNally, Comm. 310
Lab. maj. 11,867
(June '83, Lab. maj. 8,775)

NORTH WEST E. 53,090
*G. Robinson, Lab. 19,450
J. Powell, C. 13,787
T. Jones, S.D.P./All. 6,455
Lab. maj. 5,663
(June '83, Lab. maj. 3,038)

SOUTH EAST E. 51,880
*D. J. Nellist, Lab. 17,969
A. Grant, C. 11,316
F. Devine, S.D.P./All. 8,095
N. Hutchinson, Grn. 479
Lab. maj. 6,653
(June '83, Lab. maj. 2,682)

SOUTH WEST E. 65,567
*J. P. Butcher, C. 22,318
R. E. G. Slater, Lab. 19,108
R. Wheway, L./All. 10,166
C. maj. 3,210
(June '83, C. maj. 6,447)

Crawley (W. Sussex)
E. 72,076

*Hon. A. N. W. Soames, C. . 29,259
P. J. Leo, Lab. 17,121
D. N. Simmons, S.D.P./All. 12,674
C. maj. 12,138
(June '83, C. maj. 11,814)

Crewe and Nantwich (Cheshire)
E. 72,961

*Hon. Mrs. G. P. Dunwoody,
Lab. 25,457
Mrs. A. F. Browning, C. .. 24,365
Dr. K. N. Roberts, S.D.P./
All. 8,022
Lab. maj. 1,092
(June '83, Lab. maj. 290)

Crosby (Merseyside)
E. 83,914

*G. M. Thornton, C. 30,836
A. F. S. Donovan, S.D.P./
All. 23,989
C. W. Cheetham, Lab. 11,992
C. maj. 6,847
(June '83, C. maj. 3,401)

Croydon (Gtr. London)

CENTRAL E. 55,410
*Rt. Hon. J. E. M. Moore, C. 22,133
Ms. B. T. Prentice, Lab. .. 9,516
T. Burgess, S.D.P./All. ... 7,435
C. maj. 12,617
(June '83, C. maj. 11,821)

NORTH EAST E. 63,129
*Rt. Hon. B. B. Weatherill,
(The Speaker) 24,188
Miss C. Patrick, Lab. 11,669
J. D. Goldie, S.D.P./All. .. 8,128
The Speaker maj. 12,519
(June '83, C. maj. 11,627)

NORTH WEST E. 57,369
*H. J. Malins, C. 18,665
M. H. Wicks, Lab. 14,677
L. A. Rowe, L./All. 6,363
C. maj. 3,988
(June '83, C. maj. 4,092)

SOUTH E. 65,085
*Sir W. G. Clark, C. 30,732
I. Morrison, L./All. 11,669
G. R. Davies, Lab. 4,679
P. C. Baldwin, Grn. 900
C. maj. 19,063
(June '83, C. maj. 17,440)

Dagenham (Gtr. London)
E. 61,714

*B. C. Gould, Lab. 18,454
R. J. M. Neill, C. 15,985
J. Carter, S.D.P./All 7,088
Lab. maj. 2,469
(June '83, Lab. maj. 2,997)

Darlington (Durham)
E. 65,940

*M. Fallon, C. 24,831
O. O'Brien, Lab. 22,170
A. Collinge, L./All. 6,289
C. maj. 2,661
(June '83, C. maj. 3,438)

Dartford (Kent)
E. 72,632

*R. J. Dunn, C. 30,685
B. J. Clarke, Lab. 15,756
M. G. Bruce, S.D.P./All. .. 10,439
K. J. Davenport, F.D.P. ... 491
C. maj. 14,929
(June '83, C. maj. 13,563)

Daventry (Northants)
E. 69,241

T. E. Boswell, C. 31,353
I. R. Miller, L./All. 11,663
Mrs. L. M. A. W. Koumi,
Lab. 11,097
C. maj. 19,690
(June '83, C. maj. 13,136)

Davyhulme (Gtr. Manchester)
E. 65,558

*W. S. Churchill, C. 23,633
J. Nicholson, Lab. 15,434
D. I. Wrigley, L./All. 11,637
C. maj. 8,199
(June '83, C. maj. 9,014)

Denton and Reddish
(Gtr. Manchester)
E. 69,533

*A. F. Bennett, Lab. 26,023
P. Slater, C. 17,773
T. I. Huffer, S.D.P./All. .. 8,697
Lab. maj. 8,250
(June '83, Lab. maj. 5,125)

Derby

NORTH E. 71,738
*G. Knight, C. 26,561
P. Whitehead, Lab. 20,236
S. F. Connolly, L./All. 7,268
E. Wall, Grn. 291
C. maj. 6,325
(June '83, C. maj. 3,506)

SOUTH E. 68,825
*Mrs. M. M. Beckett, Lab. . 21,003
P. F. Leighton, C. 19,487
Ms. P. N. Mellor, S.D.P./
All. 7,608
Lab. maj. 1,516
(June '83, Lab. maj. 421)

Derbyshire

NORTH EAST E. 70,314
H. Barnes, Lab. 24,747
J. H. Hayes, C. 21,027
S. P. Hardy, S.D.P./All. .. 9,985
Lab. maj. 3,720
(June '83, Lab. maj. 2,006)

SOUTH E. 80,045
*Mrs. E. Currie, C. 31,927
J. D. Whitby, Lab. 21,616
J. Edgar, S.D.P./All. 11,509
C. maj. 10,311
(June '83, C. maj. 8,613)

WEST E. 70,782
*P. A. McLoughlin, C. 31,224
C. R. Walmsley, L./All. ... 20,697
W. Moore, Lab. 6,875
C. maj. 10,527
(June '83, C. maj. 15,325)
(May '86, C. maj. 100)

Devizes (Wilts)
E. 86,047

*Hon. C. A. Morrison, C. .. 36,372
Mrs. L. E. Siegle, L./All. .. 18,542
R. W. Buxton, Lab. 11,487
C. maj. 17,830
(June '83, C. maj. 15,624)

Devon

NORTH   *E.* 67,474

*A. Speller, C	28,071
M. A. Pinney, *L./All.*	23,602
Ms. A. Marjoram, *Lab.*	3,467
C. maj.	4,469
(June '83, C. maj. 8,727)	

WEST AND TORRIDGE   *E.* 74,550

Miss E. H. Nicholson, C.	29,484
J. P. A. Burnett, *L./All.*	23,016
D. G. Brenton, *Lab.*	4,990
F. Williamson, *Grn.*	1,168
C. maj.	6,468
(June '83, C. maj. 12,351)	

Dewsbury (W. Yorks)
E. 70,836

Mrs. W. A. Taylor, Lab.	23,668
*J. Whitfield, C.	23,223
A. Mills, *S.D.P./All.*	8,907
Lab. maj.	445
(June '83, C. maj. 2,086)	

Doncaster (S. Yorks)

CENTRAL   *E.* 69,699

*Rt. Hon. H. Walker, Lab.	26,266
Miss P. E. Rawlings, *C.*	18,070
J. A. Gore-Browne, *S.D.P./*	
All.	7,004
Lab. maj.	8,196
(June '83, Lab. maj. 2,508)	

NORTH   *E.* 72,986

*M. C. Welsh, Lab.	32,950
R. J. Shepherd, *C.*	13,015
P. Norwood, *S.D.P./All.*	7,394
Lab. maj.	19,935
(June '83, Lab. maj. 12,711)	

Don Valley (S. Yorks)
E. 74,500

*M. Redmond, Lab.	29,200
C. H. Gallagher, *C.*	17,733
W. K. Whitaker, *L./All.*	8,027
Lab. maj.	11,467
(June '83, Lab. maj. 6,466)	

Dorset

NORTH   *E.* 72,844

*N. B. Baker, C.	32,854
Dr. G. W. Tapper, *L./All.*	20,947
J. Hanley, *Lab.*	3,819
C. maj.	11,907
(June '83, C. maj. 11,380)	

SOUTH   *E.* 72,855

I. C. Bruce, *C.*	30,184
B. Ellis, *L./All.*	15,117
Ms. B. Dench, *Lab.*	9,494
A. Hayler, *Ind.*	244
C. maj.	15,067
(June '83, C. maj. 15,098)	

WEST   *E.* 64,360

*J. W. Spicer, C.	28,305
T. Jones, *L./All.*	15,941
D. Watson, *Lab.*	6,123
C. maj.	12,364
(June '83, C. maj. 13,952)	

Dover (Kent)
E. 68,997

D. L. Shaw, *C.*	25,343
S. S. E. W. Love, *Lab.*	18,802
G. Nice, *S.D.P./All.*	10,942
C. maj.	6,541
(June '83, C. maj. 9,220)	

Dudley (W. Midlands)

EAST   *E.* 75,206

*Rt. Hon. Dr. J. W. Gilbert,	
Lab.	24,942
Mrs. E. Jones, *C.*	21,469
K. Monks, *S.D.P./All.*	7,965
Lab. maj.	3,473
(June '83, Lab. maj. 5,816)	

WEST   *E.* 81,789

*J. G. Blackburn, C.	32,224
G. Titley, *Lab.*	21,980
G. P. T. Lewis, *L./All.*	10,477
C. maj.	10,244
(June '83, C. maj. 8,723)	

Dulwich (Gtr. London)
E. 56,355

*G. F. Bowden, C.	16,563
Miss C. L. Hoey, *Lab.*	16,383
Dr. A. N. G. Harris, *S.D.P./*	
All.	5,664
A. Goldie, *Grn.*	432
C. maj.	180
(June '83, C. maj. 1,859)	

Durham

CITY OF   *E.* 66,567

G. N. Steinberg, *Lab.*	23,382
D. Stoker, *S.D.P./All.*	17,257
C. M. Colquhoun, *C.*	11,408
Lab. maj.	6,125
(June '83, Lab. maj. 1,973)	

NORTH   *E.* 72,115

*G. H. Radice, Lab.	30,798
Dr. D. Jeary, *S.D.P./All.*	12,365
N. C. Gibbon, *C.*	11,602
Lab. maj.	18,433
(June '83, Lab. maj. 13,437)	

NORTH WEST   *E.* 61,302

Ms. H. J. Armstrong, *Lab.*	22,947
D. Iceton, *C.*	12,785
C. Foote Wood, *L./All.*	9,349
Lab. maj.	10,162
(June '83, Lab. maj. 6,356)	

Ealing (Gtr. London)

ACTON   *E.* 67,176

*Sir G. S. K. Young, Bt., C.	25,499
P. J. Portwood, *Lab.*	13,256
S. R. D. Brooks, *S.D.P./All.*	8,973
C. maj.	12,243
(June '83, C. maj. 10,092)	

NORTH   *E.* 71,634

*H. Greenway, C.	30,100
H. J. Benn, *Lab.*	14,947
A. H. J. Miller, *L./All.*	8,149
Mrs. K. Fitzherbert, *Grn.*	577
C. maj.	15,153
(June '83, C. maj. 6,291)	

SOUTHALL   *E.* 74,843

*S. J. Bidwell, Lab.	26,480
M. A. Truman, *C.*	18,503
Mrs. M. Howes, *L./All.*	6,947
R. F. Lugg, *W.R.P.*	256
Lab. maj.	7,977
(June '83, Lab. maj. 11,116)	

Easington (Durham)
E. 64,863

J. S. Cummings, *Lab.*	32,396
W. J. Perry, *C.*	7,757
G. Morpeth, *L./All.*	7,447
Lab. maj.	24,639
(June '83, Lab. maj. 14,792)	

Eastbourne (E. Sussex)
E. 74,144

*I. Gow, T.D., C.	33,587
P. G. Driver, *L./All.*	16,664
A. Patel, *Lab.*	4,928
Ms. R. Addison, *Grn.*	867
C. maj.	16,923
(June '83, C. maj. 13,486)	

Eastleigh (Hants)
E. 87,552

*Sir D. E. C. Price, C.	35,584
M. J. Kyrle, *L./All.*	22,229
D. J. C. Bull, *Lab.*	11,599
C. maj.	13,355
(June '83, C. maj. 13,008)	

Eccles (Gtr. Manchester)
E. 66,961

Miss J. Lestor, *Lab.*	25,346
Mrs. M. E. J. Packalow, *C.*	15,647
P. C. W. Beatty, *S.D.P./All.*	8,924
Lab. maj.	9,699
(June '83, Lab. maj. 6,005)	

Eddisbury (Cheshire)
E. 73,894

*A. R. Goodlad, C.	29,474
R. I. Fletcher, *L./All.*	13,639
Mrs. C. Grigg, *Lab.*	13,574
A. Basden, *Grn.*	976
C. maj.	15,835
(June '83, C. maj. 14,846)	

Edmonton (Gtr. London)
E. 66,080

*Dr. I. D. Twinn, C.	24,556
B. G. Grayston, *Lab.*	17,270
M. Lawson, *S.D.P./All.*	6,115
C. maj.	7,286
(June '83, C. maj. 1,193)	

Ellesmere Port and Neston
(Cheshire)
E. 71,344

*M. Woodcock, C.	25,664
Miss H. M. Jones, *Lab.*	23,811
S. A. Holbrook, *S.D.P./All.*	8,143
D. J. E. Carson, *P.R.P.*	185
C. maj.	1,853
(June '83, C. maj. 7,087)	

Elmet (W. Yorks)
E. 69,024

*S. L. Batiste, C.	....	25,658
C. Burgon, Lab.	....	20,302
J. D. Macarthur, S.D.P./		
All.	....	8,755
C. maj.	....	5,356
(June '83, C. maj. 7,856)		

Eltham (Gtr. London)
E. 54,063

*P. J. Bottomley, C.	....	19,752
D. Vaughan, Lab.	....	13,292
E. J. Randall, L./All.	.....	8,542
C. maj.	....	6,460
(June '83, C. maj. 7,592)		

Enfield (Gtr. London)

NORTH E. 69,488

*T. J. C. Eggar, C.	....	28,758
M. Upham, Lab.	....	14,743
Ms. H. Leighter, S.D.P./		
All.	....	7,633
M. Chantler, Grn.	......	644
C. maj.	....	14,015
(June '83, C. maj. 11,716)		

SOUTHGATE E. 66,600

*M. D. X. Portillo, C.	......	28,445
N. Harvey, L./All.	......	10,100
R. Course, Lab.	....	9,114
S. Rooney, Grn.	....	696
C. maj.	....	18,345
(June '83, C. maj. 15,819)		
(Dec. '84, C. maj. 4,711)		

Epping Forest (Essex)
E. 67,804

*Sir J. A. Biggs-Davison, C.		31,536
A. Humphris, S.D.P./All.	...	10,023
S. Murray, Lab.	....	9,499
R. Denhard, Grn.	....	695
C. maj.	....	21,513
(June '83, C. maj. 15,378)		
(see also p. 276)		

Epsom and Ewell (Surrey)
E. 70,683

*Hon. A. G. Hamilton, C.	..	33,145
Mrs. M. J. Joachim, L./All.		12,384
Mrs. D. B. Follett, Lab.	...	7,751
C. maj.	....	20,761
(June '83, C. maj. 17,195)		

Erewash (Derbys)
E. 76,545

*P. L. Rost, C.	....	28,775
R. W. Jones, Lab.	....	19,021
Ms. C. P. Moss, S.D.P./All.		11,442
C. maj.	....	9,754
(June '83, C. maj. 11,319)		

Erith and Crayford
(Gtr. London)
E. 59,292

*D. A. Evennett, C.	....	20,203
C. F. Hargrave, Lab.	......	13,209
*A. J. Wellbeloved, S.D.P./		
All.	....	11,300
C. maj.	....	6,994
(June '83, C. maj. 920)		

Esher (Surrey)
E. 62,117

I. C. Taylor, M.B.E., C.	....	31,334
A. J. Barnett, L./All.	.....	12,266
N. J. V. Lucas, Lab.	......	4,197
C. maj.	....	19,068
(June '83, C. maj. 15,912)		

Exeter (Devon)
E. 75,208

*J. G. Hannam, C.	....	26,922
M. S. Thomas, S.D.P./All.		19,266
J. A. Vincent, Lab.	......	13,643
R. J. Vail, Grn.	....	597
N. D. Byles, L.A.P.P.	....	209
C. maj.	....	7,656
(June '83, C. maj. 9,880)		

Falmouth and Camborne
(Cornwall)
E. 68,612

*W. D. Mudd, C.	....	23,725
J. C. Marks, S.D.P./All.	..	18,686
J. Cosgrove, Lab.	....	11,271
F. Zapp, L.M.	....	373
C. maj.	....	5,039
(June '83, C. maj. 11,025)		

Fareham (Hants)
E. 76,974

*P. R. C. Lloyd, C.	....	36,781
T. Slack, L./All.	....	17,986
M. Merritt, Lab.	....	5,451
C. maj.	....	18,795
(June '83, C. maj. 16,316)		

Faversham (Kent)
E. 79,039

*R. D. Moate, C.	....	31,074
E. M. Goyder, S.D.P./All.	..	17,096
P. Dangerfield, Lab.	.....	12,616
C. maj.	....	13,978
(June '83, C. maj. 14,597)		

Feltham and Heston
(Gtr. London)
E. 81,062

*R. P. Ground, Q.C., C.	....	27,755
C. Hinds, Lab.	....	22,325
J. Daly, S.D.P./All.	......	9,623
C. maj.	....	5,430
(June '83, C. maj. 2,148)		

Finchley (Gtr. London)
E. 57,727

*Rt. Hon. Mrs. M. H. Thatcher, C.	....	21,603
J. Davies, Lab.	....	12,690
D. Howarth, L./All.	......	5,580
Lord Buckethead, Grem.	.	131
Miss M. St. Vincent, Gold		59
C. maj.	....	8,913
(June '83, C. maj. 9,314)		

Folkestone and Hythe (Kent)
E. 64,406

*M. Howard, Q.C., C.	....	27,915
J. R. MacDonald, L./All.	..	18,789
V. S. Anand, Lab.	....	3,720
C. maj.	....	9,126
(June '83, C. maj. 11,670)		

Fulham (Gtr. London)
E. 54,498

M. H. M. Carrington, C.	..	21,752
*W. R. N. Raynsford, Lab.	.	15,430
P. A. C. Marshall, S.D.P./		
All.	....	4,365
Ms. J. Grimes, Grn.	......	465
C. maj.	....	6,322
(June '83, C. maj. 4,789)		
(April '86, Lab. maj. 3,503)		

Fylde (Lancs)
E. 63,246

J. M. Jack, C.	....	29,559
Mrs. E. A. Smith, L./All.	...	11,787
G. Smith, Lab.	....	6,955
H. Fowler, R.C.P.	....	405
C. maj.	....	17,772
(June '83, C. maj. 17,102)		

Gainsborough and Horncastle
(Lincs)
E. 69,760

*E. J. E. Leigh, C.	....	28,621
D. A. Grace, L./All.	......	18,898
R. Naylor, Lab.	....	6,156
C. maj.	....	9,723
(June '83, C. maj. 5,067)		

Gateshead East (Tyne & Wear)
E. 67,953

Miss J. G. Quin, Lab.	...	28,895
F. W. Rogers, C.	....	11,667
N. G. Rippeth, S.D.P./All.		8,231
Lab. maj.	....	17,228
(June '83, Lab. maj. 10,322)		

Gedling (Notts)
E. 68,398

A. J. B. Mitchell, C.	......	29,492
V. R. Coaker, Lab.	....	12,953
D. Morton, S.D.P./All.	....	11,684
C. maj.	....	16,539
(June '83, C. maj. 14,664)		

Gillingham (Kent)
E. 71,847

*J. R. Couchman, C.	......	28,711
L. R. Andrews, L./All.	.....	16,162
D. J. Bishop, Lab.	....	9,230
C. maj.	....	12,549
(June '83, C. maj. 10,843)		

Glanford and Scunthorpe
(Humberside)
E. 72,816

E. A. Morley, Lab.	....	24,733
*R. S. Hickmet, C.	....	24,221
C. Nottingham, S.D.P./All.		7,762
K. S. Trivedi, Ind.	....	104
Lab. maj.	....	512
(June '83, C. maj. 637)		

Gloucester
E. 76,910

D. C. French, C.	....	29,826
D. Hulme, Lab.	....	17,791
J. Hilton, L./All.	....	12,417
C. maj.	....	12,035
(June '83, C. maj. 12,537)		

Gloucestershire West
E. 77,994

*P. Marland, C.	....	29,257
P. E. S. Nielson, Lab.	.....	17,578
J. T. Watkinson, S.D.P./		
All.	....	16,440
C. maj.	....	11,679
(June '83, C. maj. 9,652)		

Gosport (Hants)
E. 68,113

*P. J. Viggers, C.	....	29,804
P. J. Chegwyn, L./All.	.....	16,081
A. Lloyd, Lab.	....	5,053
C. maj.	....	13,723
(June '83, C. maj. 14,451)		

Grantham (Lincs)
E. 79,434

*Hon. D. M. Hogg, C.	......	33,988
J. P. Heppell, L./All.	.....	12,685
M. B. Gent, Lab.	....	12,197
Mrs. P. A. Hewis, Grn.	...	700
C. maj.	....	21,303
(June '83, C. maj. 18,911)		

Gravesham (Kent)
E. 72,759

J. A. Arnold, C.	....	28,891
M. A. Coleman, Lab.	.....	20,099
R. I. Crawford, L./All.	....	8,724
C. maj.	....	8,792
(June '83, C. maj. 8,463)		

Great Grimsby (Humberside)
E. 68,501

*A. V. Mitchell, Lab.	......	23,463
C. F. Robinson, C.	......	14,679
P. W. Genney, S.D.P./All.		13,457
Lab. maj.	....	8,784
(June '83, Lab. maj. 731)		

Great Yarmouth
(Norfolk)
E. 65,770

*M. R. H. Carttiss, C.	.....	25,336
J. Cannell, Lab.	....	15,253
S. D. Maxwell, S.D.P./All.		8,387
C. maj.	....	10,083
(June '83, C. maj. 11,200)		

Greenwich (Gtr. London)
E. 50,830

*Mrs. R. S. Barnes, S.D.P./		
All.	....	15,149
Mrs. D. F. M. Wood, Lab.	.	13,008
J. G. C. Antcliffe, C.	.....	8,695
Ms. J. Thomas, Grn.	.....	346
R. Mallone, Fell.	....	59
Ms. P. Clinton, Comm.	...	58
S.D.P./All. maj.	....	2,141
(June '83, Lab. maj. 1,211)		
(Feb. '87, S.D.P./All. maj. 6,611)		

Guildford (Surrey)
E. 77,872

*Rt. Hon. D. A. R. Howell, C.		32,504
Mrs. M. L. Sharp, S.D.P./		
All.	....	19,897
R. J. Wolverson, Lab.	....	6,216
C. maj.	....	12,607
(June '83, C. maj. 11,824)		

Hackney (Gtr. London)
NORTH AND STOKE NEWINGTON
E. 66,771

Ms. D. J. Abbott, Lab.	....	18,912
O. Letwin, C.	....	11,234
S. H. Taylor, S.D.P./All.	..	7,446
D. J. Fitzpatrick, Grn.	...	997
Ms. Y. T. Anwar, R.F.	....	228
Lab. maj.	....	7,678
(June '83, Lab. maj. 8,545)		

SOUTH AND SHOREDITCH E. 70,873

*B. C. J. Sedgemore, Lab.	..	18,799
M. C. Northcroft-Brown, C.		11,277
J. D. Roberts, L./All.	.....	8,812
D. Green, Comm.	....	403
Lab. maj.	....	7,522
(June '83, Lab. maj. 7,691)		

Halesowen and Stourbridge
(W. Midlands)
E. 78,017

*J. H. R. Stokes, C.	......	31,037
T. J. Sunter, Lab.	....	17,229
D. C. A. Simon, S.D.P./All.		13,658
C. maj.	....	13,808
(June '83, C. maj. 13,316)		

Halifax (W. Yorks)
E. 73,392

Mrs. A. Mahon, Lab.	.....	24,741
*R. Galley, C.	....	23,529
F. L. Cockcroft, S.D.P./All.		8,758
Lab. maj.	....	1,212
(June '83, C. maj. 1,869)		

Halton (Cheshire)
E. 73,848

*Rt. Hon. G. J. Oakes, Lab.	.	32,065
J. Hardman, C.	....	17,487
Ms. H. Clucas, S.D.P./All.		8,272
Lab. maj.	....	14,578
(June '83, Lab. maj. 6,829)		

Hammersmith (Gtr. London)
E. 48,285

*C. S. Soley, Lab.	....	15,811
N. J. A. Deva, C.	....	13,396
S. H. J. A. Knott, L./All.	...	5,241
D. P. Kirk, Grn.	....	453
P. J. F. Fitzpatrick, R.F.	...	125
Miss M. M. A. Carrick,		
Humanist	....	98
Lab. maj.	....	2,415
(June '83, Lab. maj. 1,954)		

Hampshire
EAST E. 86,363

*M. J. Mates, C.	....	43,093
R. Booker, L./All.	....	19,307
C. Lloyd, Lab.	....	4,443
C. maj.	....	23,786
(June '83, C. maj. 18,327)		

NORTH WEST E. 69,965

*D. B. Mitchell, C.	....	31,470
I. H. Wills, L./All.	....	18,033
Ms. A. Burnage, Lab.	....	4,980
C. maj.	....	13,437
(June '83, C. maj. 12,122)		

Hampstead and Highgate
(Gtr. London)
E. 63,301

*Sir G. Finsberg, M.B.E., C.	.	19,236
P. J. Turner, Lab.	....	17,015
Mrs. A. Sofer, S.D.P./All.		8,744
G. Weiss, Rainbow	....	137
Ms. S. Ellis, Humanist	....	134
C. maj.	....	2,221
(June '83, C. maj. 3,370)		

Harborough (Leics)
E. 74,700

*Sir J. A. Farr, C.	....	35,216
T. J. Swift, L./All.	....	16,406
P. Harley, Lab.	....	7,646
C. maj.	....	18,810
(June '83, C. maj. 18,485)		

Harlow (Essex)
E. 70,286

*J. J. J. Hayes, C.	....	26,017
A. S. Newens, Lab.	......	20,140
Mrs. M. C. Eden-Green,		
S.D.P./All.	....	8,915
C. maj.	....	5,877
(June '83, C. maj. 3,674)		

Harrogate (N. Yorks)
E. 75,761

*R. G. Banks, C.	....	31,167
J. R. Leach, S.D.P./All.	.	19,265
A. J. Wright, Lab.	....	5,671
C. maj.	....	11,902
(June '83, C. maj. 15,888)		

Harrow (Gtr. London)
EAST E. 81,124

*H. J. M. Dykes, C.	....	32,302
D. J. Brough, Lab.	......	14,029
Mrs. Z. Gifford, L./All.	...	13,251
C. maj.	....	18,273
(June '83, C. maj. 12,668)		

WEST E. 74,041

R. G. Hughes, C.	....	30,456
S. P. Bayliss, S.D.P./All.	..	15,012
C. Bastin, Lab.	....	9,665
C. maj.	....	15,444
(June '83, C. maj. 11,021)		

Hartlepool (Cleveland)
E. 68,686

*E. Leadbitter, Lab.	.....	24,296
P. C. Catchpole, C.	......	17,007
A. Preece, L./All.	....	7,047
I. J. Cameron, Ind.	......	1,786
Lab. maj.	....	7,289
(June '83, Lab. maj. 3,090)		

Harwich (Essex)
E. 77,149

*Sir J. E. Ridsdale, C.B.E., C.		29,344
Miss E. Lynne, L./All.	....	17,262
R. Knight, Lab.	....	9,920
C. A. Humphrey, O.F.P.	...	161
C. maj.	....	12,082
(June '83, C. maj. 12,502)		

Hastings and Rye (E. Sussex)
E. 72,758

*K. R. Warren, *C.*		26,163
D. J. Amies, *L./All.*		18,816
Ms. J. Hurcombe, *Lab.*		6,825
D. Howell, *L.M.*		242
S. P. Davies, *N.P.R.*		194
C. maj.		7,347
(June '83, C. maj. 10,980)		

Havant (Hants)
E. 76,344

*Sir I. S. Lloyd, *C.*		32,527
Mrs. E. E. Cleaver, *S.D.P./ All.*		16,017
J. A. Phillips, *Lab.*		8,030
G. W. Fuller, *Bread*		373
C. maj.		16,510
(June '83, C. maj. 11,956)		

Hayes and Harlington
(Gtr. London)
E. 58,240

*T. P. Dicks, *C.*		21,355
P. F. Fagan, *Lab.*		15,390
Ms. S. Slipman, *S.D.P./All.*		6,641
C. maj.		5,965
(June '83, C. maj. 4,234)		

Hazel Grove (Gtr. Manchester)
E. 65,717

*T. R. Arnold, *C.*		24,396
A. M. Vos, *L./All.*		22,556
J. G. Ford, *Lab.*		6,354
Ms. F. K. Chapman, *Grn.*		346
C. maj.		1,840
(June '83, C. maj. 2,022)		

Hemsworth (W. Yorks)
E. 54,951

G. J. Buckley, *Lab.*		27,859
E. H. Garnier, *C.*		7,159
J. D. Wooffindin, *L./All.*		6,568
Lab. maj.		20,700
(June '83, Lab. maj. 14,190)		

Hendon (Gtr. London)

NORTH E. 55,095

*J. M. Gorst, *C.*		20,155
Ms. J. Manson, *Lab.*		9,223
Ms. E. Davies, *S.D.P./All.*		6,859
C. maj.		10,932
(June '83, C. maj. 9,025)		

SOUTH E. 54,560

J. L. Marshall, *C.*		19,341
M. O. Palmer, *L./All.*		8,217
Miss L. Christian, *Lab.*		7,261
C. maj.		11,124
(June '83, C. maj. 6,433)		

Henley (Oxon)
E. 65,443

*Rt. Hon. M. R. D. Heseltine, *C.*		29,978
J. Madeley, *L./All.*		12,896
M. B. Barber, *Lab.*		6,173
C. maj.		17,082
(June '83, C. maj. 13,781)		

Hereford
E. 67,075

*C. R. Shepherd, *C.*		24,865
C. F. Green, *L./All.*		23,452
V. S. Woodell, *Lab.*		4,031
C. maj.		1,413
(June '83, C. maj. 2,277)		

Hertford and Stortford
E. 75,508

*B. Wells, *C.*		33,763
R. E. Wotherspoon, *S.D.P./ All.*		16,623
Mrs. P. R. E. Sumner, *Lab.*		7,494
G. C. Cole, *Grn.*		814
C. maj.		17,140
(June '83, C. maj. 12,929)		

Hertfordshire

NORTH E. 78,694

*B. H. I. H. Stewart, R.D., *C.*		31,750
G. W. Binney, *L./All.*		20,308
A. Gorst, *Lab.*		11,782
C. maj.		11,442
(June '83, C. maj. 9,943)		

SOUTH WEST E. 75,643

*R. L. Page, *C.*		32,791
I. M. Blair, *L./All.*		17,007
I. Willmore, *Lab.*		8,966
C. maj.		15,784
(June '83, C. maj. 12,194)		

WEST E. 78,966

*R. B. Jones, *C.*		31,760
N. A. Hollinghurst, *S.D.P./ All.*		16,836
A. McBrearty, *Lab.*		15,317
C. maj.		14,924
(June '83, C. maj. 9,576)		

Hertsmere (Herts)
E. 73,367

*Rt. Hon. C. E. Parkinson, *C.*		31,278
L. S. Brass, *L./All.*		13,172
F. Ward, *Lab.*		10,835
C. maj.		18,106
(June '83, C. maj. 14,870)		

Hexham (Nthmb)
E. 56,360

A. T. Amos, *C.*		22,370
E. M. Robson, *L./All.*		14,304
M. R. Wood, *Lab.*		8,103
Mrs. S. M. Wood, *Grn.*		336
C. maj.		8,066
(June '83, C. maj. 8,308)		

Heywood and Middleton
(Gtr. Manchester)
E. 59,487

*J. Callaghan, *Lab.*		21,900
R. E. Walker, *C.*		15,052
I. Greenhalgh, *S.D.P./All.*		6,953
Lab. maj.		6,848
(June '83, Lab. maj. 3,974)		

High Peak (Derbys)
E. 69,926

*C. J. Hawkins, *C.*		25,715
Mrs. J. McCrindle, *Lab.*		16,199
Dr. J. Oldham, *S.D.P./All.*		14,389
C. maj.		9,516
(June '83, C. maj. 9,940)		

Holborn and St. Pancras
(Gtr. London)
E. 70,589

*F. G. Dobson, *Lab.*		22,966
P. J. Luff, *C.*		14,113
S. McGrath, *L./All.*		7,994
M. J. Gavan, *R.F.*		300
Lab. maj.		8,853
(June '83, Lab. maj. 7,259)		

Holland with Boston (Lincs)
E. 65,539

*Sir R. B. F. S. Body, *C.*		27,412
Mrs. C. Le Brun, *L./All.*		9,817
J. D. Hough, *Lab.*		9,734
D. James, *Local Voice*		405
C. maj.		17,595
(June '83, C. maj. 11,736)		

Honiton (Devon)
E. 77,259

*Sir P. F. H. Emery, *C.*		34,931
G. Tatton-Brown, *S.D.P./ All.*		18,369
S. Pollentine, *Lab.*		4,988
S. Hughes, *L.M.*		747
C. maj.		16,562
(June '83, C. maj. 14,769)		

Hornchurch (Gtr. London)
E. 62,397

*R. C. Squire, *C.*		24,039
A. R. Williams, *Lab.*		13,345
M. L. C. Long, *L./All.*		9,609
C. maj.		10,694
(June '83, C. maj. 9,184)		

Hornsey and Wood Green
(Gtr. London)
E. 80,594

*Sir H. A. L. Rossi, *C.*		25,397
Mrs. B. M. R. Roche, *Lab.*		23,618
D. Eden, *S.D.P./All.*		8,928
Ms. E. Crosbie, *Grn.*		1,154
C. maj.		1,779
(June '83, C. maj. 3,899)		

Horsham (W. Sussex)
E. 86,135

*Sir P. M. Hordern, *C.*		39,775
Mrs. J. Pearce, *S.D.P./All.*		15,868
M. Shrimpton, *Lab.*		5,435
T. Metheringham, *Grn.*		1,383
C. maj.		23,907
(June '83, C. maj. 21,785)		

Houghton and Washington
(Tyne & Wear)
E. 77,906

*R. Boyes, *Lab.*		32,805
J. M. Callanan, *C.*		12,612
R. F. Kenyon, *S.D.P./All.*		10,090
Lab. maj.		20,193
(June '83, Lab. maj. 13,821)		

Hove (E. Sussex)
E. 72,626

*Hon. T. A. D. Sainsbury, C.	28,952
Mrs. M. E. Collins, S.D.P./	
All.	10,734
D. K. Turner, Lab.	9,010
T. A. Layton, S.E.	522
C. maj.	18,218
(June '83, C. maj. 17,219)	

Huddersfield (W. Yorks)
E. 66,413

*B. J. Sheerman, Lab.	23,019
N. J. Hawkins, C.	15,741
J. Smithson, L./All.	10,773
N. A. L. Harvey, Grn.	638
Lab. maj.	7,278
(June '83, Lab. maj. 3,955)	

Huntingdon (Cambs)
E. 86,186

*Rt. Hon. J. Major, C.	40,530
A. J. Nicholson, S.D.P./All.	13,486
D. M. Brown, Lab.	8,883
B. Lavin, Grn.	874
C. maj.	27,044
(June '83, C. maj. 20,348)	

Hyndburn (Lancs)
E. 60,529

*J. K. Hargreaves, C.	21,606
K. Coombes, Lab.	19,386
J. Strak, S.D.P./All.	7,423
F. Smith, Grn.	297
C. maj.	2,220
(June '83, C. maj. 21)	

Ilford (Gtr. London)

NORTH E. 60,433

*V. W. H. Bendall, C.	24,110
P. Jeater, Lab.	12,020
G. Tobbell, S.D.P./All.	7,757
C. maj.	12,090
(June '83, C. maj. 11,201)	

SOUTH E. 58,572

*N. G. Thorne, O.B.E., T.D., C.	20,351
K. Jones, Lab.	15,779
R. J. Scott, L./All.	5,928
C. maj.	4,572
(June '83, C. maj. 4,566)	

Ipswich (Suffolk)
E. 68,165

M. F. Irvine, C.	23,328
*K. T. Weetch, Lab.	22,454
H. P. Nicholson, S.D.P./All.	6,596
D. T. Lettice, W.R.P.	174
C. maj.	874
(June '83, Lab. maj. 1,077)	

Isle of Wight
E. 98,694

B. J. A. Field, C.	40,175
M. Young, L./All.	33,733
K. Pearson, Lab.	4,626
C. maj.	6,442
(June '83, L./All. maj. 3,503)	

Islington (Gtr. London)

NORTH E. 58,917

*J. B. Corbyn, Lab.	19,577
E. G. Noad, C.	9,920
A. Whelan, S.D.P./All.	8,560
C. Ashby, Grn.	1,131
Lab. maj.	9,657
(June '83, Lab. maj. 5,607)	

SOUTH AND FINSBURY E. 57,910

*C. R. Smith, Lab.	16,511
G. Cunningham, S.D.P./	
All.	15,706
A. Mitchell, C.	8,482
P. Powell, Grn.	382
S. Dowsett, S.P.G.B.	81
Ms. J. Early, H.P.	56
Lab. maj.	805
(June '83, Lab. maj. 363)	

Jarrow (Tyne & Wear)
E. 62,845

*D. Dixon, Lab.	29,651
P. Yeoman, C.	10,856
P. Freitag, L./All.	6,230
Lab. maj.	18,795
(June '83, Lab. maj. 13,877)	

Keighley (W. Yorks)
E. 65,831

*G. P. A. Waller, C.	23,903
A. Rye, Lab.	18,297
J. H. Wells, L./All.	10,041
C. maj.	5,606
(June '83, C. maj. 2,774)	

Kensington (Gtr. London)
E. 48,212

*Sir B. M. Rhys Williams,	
Bt., C.	14,818
B. T. Bousquet, Lab.	10,371
W. H. Goodhart, S.D.P./	
All.	5,379
R. E. Shorter, Grn.	528
Miss L. Carrick, Humanist	65
Mrs. M. Hughes, P.I.P.	30
C. maj.	4,447
(June '83, C. maj. 5,101)	
(see also p. 275)	

Kent Mid
E. 72,456

*A. J. B. Rowe, C.	28,719
G. D. Colley, L./All.	13,951
J. A. Hazelgrove, Lab.	9,420
C. maj.	14,768
(June '83, C. maj. 12,543)	

Kettering (Northants)
E. 65,965

*R. N. Freeman, C.	26,532
Mrs. C. M. Goodhart,	
S.D.P./All.	15,205
A. M. Minto, Lab.	10,229
C. maj.	11,327
(June '83, C. maj. 8,586)	

Kingston-upon-Hull

EAST E. 68,657

*J. L. Prescott, Lab.	27,287
P. Jackson, C.	12,598
T. Wright, L./All.	8,572
Lab. maj.	14,689
(June '83, Lab. maj. 10,074)	

NORTH E. 73,288

*J. K. McNamara, Lab.	26,123
Miss A. O'Brien, C.	13,954
S. W. Unwin, S.D.P./All.	10,962
Lab. maj.	12,169
(June '83, Lab. maj. 6,028)	

WEST E. 55,636

*S. J. Randall, Lab.	19,527
M. R. C. Humphrys, C.	11,397
M. Bond, S.D.P./All.	6,669
Lab. maj.	8,130
(June '83, Lab. maj. 3,654)	

Kingston upon Thames
(Gtr. London)
E. 54,839

*Rt. Hon. N. S. H. Lamont,	
C.	24,198
R. M. Hayes, L./All.	13,012
R. Markless, Lab.	5,676
J. Baker, C.P.W.S.M.L.	175
C. maj.	11,186
(June '83, C. maj. 8,872)	

Kingswood (Avon)
E. 73,089

*R. A. Hayward, C.	26,300
R. L. Berry, Lab.	21,907
Mrs. P. Whittle, S.D.P./All.	10,382
C. maj.	4,393
(June '83, C. maj. 1,797)	

Knowsley (Merseyside)

NORTH E. 52,960

*G. E. Howarth, Lab.	27,454
Ms. R. Cooper, L./All.	6,356
R. C. A. Brown, C.	4,922
D. Hallsworth, R.F.	538
Lab. maj.	21,098
(June '83, Lab. maj. 17,191)	
(Nov. '86, Lab. maj. 6,724)	

SOUTH E. 65,643

*S. F. Hughes, Lab.	31,378
A. J. Hall, C.	10,532
Mrs. R. Watmough, S.D.P./	
All.	6,760
Lab. maj.	20,846
(June '83, Lab. maj. 11,769)	

Lancashire West
E. 76,094

*K. H. Hind, C.	26,500
C. Pickthall, Lab.	25,147
R. Jermyn, S.D.P./All.	8,972
C. maj.	1,353
(June '83, C. maj. 6,858)	

Lancaster (Lancs)
E. 57,229

*Mrs. M. E. Kellett-Bow-	
man, C.	21,142
J. Gallacher, Lab.	14,689
Mrs. K. C. Brooks, L./All.	9,003
P. F. F. Jones, Grn.	473
C. maj.	6,453
(June '83, C. maj. 10,636)	

Langbaurgh (Cleveland)
E. 79,193

*J. R. Holt, C.		26,047
P. Harford, Lab.		23,959
R. A. J. Ashby, L./All.		12,405
C. maj.		2,088
(June '83, C. maj. 6,024)		

Leeds (W. Yorks)

CENTRAL E.59,019

*D. J. Fatchett, Lab.		21,270
D. Schofield, C.		9,765
Dr. Karen Lee, S.D.P./All.		6,853
W. Innis, Comm.		355
Lab. maj.		11,505
(June '83, Lab. maj. 8,222)		

EAST E. 61,178

*Rt. Hon. D. W. Healey, C.H.,		
M.B.E., Lab.		20,932
J. S. W. Sheard, C.		11,406
Miss M. G. Clay, L./All.		10,630
Lab. maj.		9,526
(June '83, Lab. maj. 6,095)		

NORTH EAST E. 64,631

T. J. R. Kirkhope, C.		22,196
P. M. Crystal, S.D.P./All.		13,777
O. B. Glover, Lab.		12,292
Ms. C. D. Nash, Grn.		416
C. maj.		8,419
(June '83, C. maj. 8,995)		

NORTH WEST E. 68,227

*Dr. K. Hampson, C.		22,480
B. Peters, L./All.		17,279
Ms. J. Thomas, Lab.		11,210
A. Stevens, Grn.		663
C. maj.		5,201
(June '83, C. maj. 8,537)		

SOUTH AND MORLEY E. 60,726

*Rt. Hon. M. Rees, Lab.		21,551
Mrs. T. C. Holdroyd, C.		14,840
E. J. V. Dawson, S.D.P./		
All.		7,099
Lab. maj.		6,711
(June '83, Lab. maj. 5,854)		

WEST E. 66,344

J. D. Battle, Lab.		21,032
*M. J. Meadowcroft, L./All.		16,340
P. D. Allott, C.		11,276
Lab. maj.		4,692
(June '83, L./All. maj. 2,048)		

Leicester

EAST E. 66,372

N. K. A. S. Vaz, Lab.		24,074
*P. N. E. Bruinvels, C.		22,150
Mrs. A. M. Ayres, S.D.P./		
All.		5,935
Lab. maj.		1,924
(June '83, C. maj. 933)		

SOUTH E. 73,236

J. Marshall, Lab.		24,901
*D. H. Spencer, Q.C., C.		23,024
R. Pritchard, L./All.		7,773
B. Fewster, Grn.		390
M. M. Mayat, Ind. Lab.		192
Ms. R. F. Manners, W.R.P.		96
Lab. maj.		1,877
(June '83, C. maj. 7)		

WEST E. 67,829

*G. E. Janner, Q.C., Lab.		22,156
J. S. W. Cooper, C.		20,955
W. Edgar, S.D.P./All.		6,708
Lab. maj.		1,201
(June '83, Lab. maj. 1,712)		

Leicestershire North West
E. 70,633

*D. G. Ashby, C.		27,872
Mrs. S. A. Waddington,		
Lab.		20,044
D. S. Emmerson, L./All.		10,034
Miss H. T. Michetschlager,		
Grn.		570
C. maj.		7,828
(June '83, C. maj. 6,662)		

Leigh (Gtr. Manchester)
E. 69,155

*L. F. Cunliffe, Lab.		30,064
L. B. A. Browne, C.		13,458
S. D. Jones, S.D.P./All.		7,743
Lab. maj.		16,606
(June '83, Lab. maj. 12,314)		

Leominster (H & W)
E. 69,977

*P. Temple-Morris, C.		31,396
S. C. Morris, L./All.		17,321
A. C. R. Chappell, Lab.		4,444
Mrs. F. M. Norman, Grn.		1,102
C. maj.		14,075
(June '83, C. maj. 9,786)		

Lewes (E. Sussex)
E. 73,181

*J. R. Rathbone, C.		32,016
D. F. Bellotti, L./All.		18,396
R. P. Taylor, Lab.		4,973
A. G. P. Sherwood, Grn.		970
C. maj.		13,620
(June '83, C. maj. 13,904)		

Lewisham (Gtr. London)

DEPTFORD E.58,151

Ms. J. M. Ruddock, Lab.		18,724
M. C. Punyer, C.		11,953
Ms. A. M. E. Braun, S.D.P./		
All.		6,513
P. K. Makepeace, Grn.		568
Lab. maj.		6,771
(June '83, Lab. maj. 6,032)		

EAST E. 59,627

*Hon. C. B. Moynihan, C.		19,873
M. R. Profitt, Lab.		15,059
Mrs. V. W. Stone, S.D.P./		
All.		9,118
C. maj.		4,814
(June '83, C. maj. 1,909)		

WEST E. 62,923

*J. C. Maples, C.		20,995
J. P. Dowd, Lab.		17,223
Ms. S. C. Titley, L./All.		7,247
C. maj.		3,772
(June '83, C. maj. 2,506)		

Leyton (Gtr. London)
E. 57,662

*H. M. Cohen, Lab.		16,536
S. Banks, L./All.		11,895
D. N. Gilmartin, C.		11,692
Lab. maj.		4,641
(June '83, Lab. maj. 4,516)		

Lincoln
E. 77,049

*K. M. Carlisle, C.		27,097
N. J. Butler, Lab.		19,614
P. Zentner, S.D.P./All.		11,319
T. B. Kyle, R.R.P.R.C.		232
C. maj.		7,483
(June '83, C. maj. 10,286)		

Lindsey East (Lincs)
E. 74,027

*Sir P. H. B. Tapsell, C.		29,048
J. C. L. Sellick, L./All.		20,432
K. Stevenson, Lab.		6,206
C. maj.		8,616
(June '83, C. maj. 7,517)		

Littleborough and Saddleworth
(Gtr. Manchester)
E. 66,074

*G. K. Dickens, C.		22,027
C. Davies, L./All.		15,825
P. Stonier, Lab.		13,299
C. maj.		6,202
(June '83, C. maj. 5,650)		

Liverpool

BROADGREEN E. 63,091

*T. Fields, Lab.		23,262
R. Pine, L./All.		17,215
M. R. G. Seddon, C.		7,413
Lab. maj.		6,047
(June '83, Lab. maj. 3,800)		

GARSTON E. 61,280

*E. Loyden, Lab.		24,848
P. B. Feather, C.		11,071
R. Isaacson, S.D.P./All.		10,370
K. Timlin, W.R.P.		98
Lab. maj.		13,777
(June '83, Lab. maj. 4,002)		

MOSSLEY HILL E. 60,954

*D. P. P. Alton, L./All.		20,012
J. A. Devaney, Lab.		17,786
W. M. Lightfoot, C.		8,005
L./All. maj.		2,226
(June '83, L./All. maj. 4,195)		

RIVERSIDE E. 53,328

*R. Parry, Lab.		25,505
S. Fitzsimmons, C.		4,816
B. S. Chahal, S.D.P./All.		3,912
Ms. C. A. Gardner, Comm.		601
Lab. maj.		20,689
(June '83, Lab. maj. 17,378)		

WALTON E. 73,118

*E. S. Heffer, Lab.		34,661
P. R. Clark, L./All.		11,408
I. A. Mays, C.		7,738
Lab. maj.		23,253
(June '83, Lab. maj. 14,115)		

WEST DERBY *E.* 60,522
*R. N. Wareing, Lab. 29,021
J. E. Backhouse, *C.* 8,525
M. Ferguson, *S.D.P./All.* .. 6,897
   Lab. maj. 20,496
   (June '83, Lab. maj. 11,843)

Loughborough (Leics)
E. 73,660

*S. J. Dorrell, C. 31,931
C. J. Wrigley, *Lab.* 14,283
R. G. Fox, *S.D.P./All.* 11,499
R. Gupta, *Grn.* 656
   C. maj. 17,648
   (June '83, C. maj. 16,180)

Ludlow (Salop)
E. 66,187

C. J. F. Gill, R.D., *C.* 27,499
D. Phillips, *L./All.* 15,800
K. Harrison, *Lab.* 7,724
   C. maj. 11,699
   (June '83, C. maj. 11,303)

Luton (Beds)

NORTH *E.* 74,235
*J. R. Carlisle, C. 30,997
M. Wright, *Lab.* 15,424
J. D. Stephen, *S.D.P./All.* .. 11,166
   C. maj. 15,573
   (June '83, C. maj. 11,981)

SOUTH *E.* 71,231
*G. F. J. Bright, C. 24,762
W. D. McKenzie, *Lab.* 19,647
P. Chapman, *L./All.* 9,146
   C. maj. 5,115
   (June '83, C. maj. 4,621)

Macclesfield (Cheshire)
E. 76,093

*N. R. Winterton, C. 33,208
A. B. Haldane, *L./All.* 14,116
Ms. C. Pinder, *Lab.* 11,563
   C. maj. 19,092
   (June '83, C. maj. 20,679)

Maidstone (Kent)
E. 72,987

Miss A. N. Widdecombe, *C.* 29,100
C. J. Sutton-Mattocks, *L./*
   All. 18,736
K. P. Brooks, *Lab.* 6,935
Mrs. P. A. Kemp, *Grn.* 717
   C. maj. 10,364
   (June '83, C. maj. 7,226)

Makerfield (Gtr. Manchester)
E. 70,819

I. McCartney, *Lab.* 30,190
L. A. Robertson, *C.* 14,632
B. Hewer, *L./All.* 8,838
   Lab. maj. 15,558
   (June '83, Lab. maj. 10,876)

Manchester

BLACKLEY *E.* 58,814
*K. Eastham, Lab. 22,476
K. Nath, *C.* 12,354
H. Showman, *S.D.P./All.* .. 8,041
   Lab. maj. 10,122
   (June '83, Lab. maj. 6,456)

CENTRAL *E.* 62,928
*R. K. Litherland, Lab. ... 27,428
M. R. W. Banks, *C.* 7,561
B. W. McColgan, *S.D.P./*
   All. 5,250
   Lab. maj. 19,867
   (June '83, Lab. maj. 18,485)

GORTON *E.* 64,243
*Rt. Hon. G. B. Kaufman,
   Lab. 24,615
J. Kershaw, *C.* 10,550
K. A. Whitmore, *L./All.* ... 9,830
Ms. P. Lawrence, *R.F.* 253
   Lab. maj. 14,065
   (June '83, Lab. maj. 9,965)

WITHINGTON *E.* 65,343
K. J. C. Bradley, Lab. 21,650
*F. J. Silvester, C. 18,259
Mrs. A. Jones, *L./All.* 9,978
M. T. Abberton, *Grn.* 524
   Lab. maj. 3,391
   (June '83, C. maj. 2,373)

WYTHENSHAWE *E.* 58,287
*Rt. Hon. A. Morris, Lab. .. 23,881
D. G. Sparrow, *C.* 12,026
Ms. J. Butterworth,
   S.D.P./All. 5,921
Ms. S. Connelly, *R.F.* 216
   Lab. maj. 11,855
   (June '83, Lab. maj. 10,684)

Mansfield (Notts)
E. 66,764

J. A. Meale, *Lab.* 19,610
C. Hendry, *C.* 19,554
B. Answer, *S.D.P./All.* 11,604
B. Marshall, *M.L.* 1,580
   Lab. maj. 56
   (June '83, Lab. maj. 2,216)

Medway (Kent)
E. 64,103

*Dame P. Fenner, D.B.E., C. 23,889
V. Hull, *Lab.* 13,960
Mrs. J. Horne-Roberts,
   S.D.P./All. 8,450
Ms. J. V. Rosser, *Grn.* 504
   C. maj. 9,929
   (June '83, C. maj. 8,656)

Meriden (W. Midlands)
E. 78,444

*I. C. Mills, C. 31,935
R. H. Burden, *Lab.* 15,115
Ms. C. E. Parkinson,
   S.D.P./All. 10,896
   C. maj. 16,820
   (June '83, C. maj. 15,018)

Middlesbrough (Cleveland)
E. 60,789

*S. Bell, Lab. 25,747
R. J. Orr-Ewing, *C.* 10,789
P. A. Hawley, *L./All.* 6,594
   Lab. maj. 14,958
   (June '83, Lab. maj. 9,669)

Milton Keynes (Bucks)
E. 97,041

*W. R. Benyon, C. 35,396
W. T. Rodgers, *S.D.P./All.* 21,695
Ms. Y. V. A. Brownfield-
   Pope, *Lab.* 16,111
A. H. Francis, *Grn.* 810
   C. maj. 13,701
   (June '83, C. maj. 11,522)

Mitcham and Morden
(Gtr. London)
E. 63,089

*Mrs. A. C. R. Rumbold,
   C.B.E., C. 23,002
Ms. S. McDonagh, *Lab.* ... 16,819
B. L. H. Douglas-Mann,
   S.D.P./All. 7,930
   C. maj. 6,183
   (June '83, C. maj. 6,451)

Mole Valley (Surrey)
E. 67,715

*Rt. Hon. K. W. Baker, C. .. 31,689
Mrs. S. P. Thomas, *L./All.* 15,613
C. M. B. King, *Lab.* 4,846
   C. maj. 16,076
   (June '83, C. maj. 14,718)

Morecambe and Lunesdale
(Lancs)
E. 55,718

*Hon. M. A. Lennox-Boyd,
   C. 22,327
Mrs. J. Greenwell, *S.D.P./*
   All. 10,542
D. Smith, *Lab.* 9,535
   C. maj. 11,785
   (June '83, C. maj. 12,194)

Newark (Notts)
E. 67,555

*R. T. Alexander, C. 28,070
D. Barton, *Lab.* 14,527
G. A. Emerson, *S.D.P./All.* 9,833
   C. maj. 13,543
   (June '83, C. maj. 14,283)

Newbury (Berks)
E. 75,187

*R. M. C. McNair-Wilson, C. 35,266
D. D. Rendel, *L./All.* 18,608
R. C. Stapley, *Lab.* 4,765
   C. maj. 16,658
   (June '83, C. maj. 13,038)

Newcastle-under-Lyme (Staffs)
E. 66,053

*Mrs. L. Golding, Lab. 21,618
A. L. Thomas, *L./All.* 16,486
P. C. J. Ridgway, *C.* 14,863
M. J. Nicklin, *Ex Lab.*
   Mod. 397
   Lab. maj. 5,132
   (June '83, Lab. maj. 2,804)
   (July '86, Lab. maj. 799)

Newcastle upon Tyne

CENTRAL *E.* 63,682
J. M. Cousins, *Lab.* 20,416
*P. R. G. Merchant, C. 17,933
Dr. N. Martin, *S.D.P./All.* 7,304
R. J. Bird, *Grn.* 418
K. Williams, *R.F.* 111
   Lab. maj. 2,483
   (June '83, C. maj. 2,228)

EAST *E.* 59,369
*N. H. Brown, Lab. 23,677
Miss J. G. A. Riley, *C.* 11,177
P. J. Arnold, *L./All.* 6,728
J. Keith, *Comm.* 362
Lab. maj. 12,500
(June '83, Lab. maj. 7,492)

NORTH *E.* 69,178
D. J. Henderson, *Lab.* ... 22,424
J. W. Shipley, *L./All.* 17,181
J. W. Tweddle, *C.* 12,915
Lab. maj. 5,243
(June '83, Lab. maj. 2,556)

New Forest (Hants)
E. 75,083
*P. M. E. D. McNair-Wilson,
C. 37,188
R. Karn, *L./All.* 15,456
J. I. Hampton, *Lab.* 4,856
C. maj. 21,732
(June '83, C. maj. 20,925)

Newham (Gtr. London)
NORTH EAST *E.* 60,787
*R. Leighton, Lab. 20,220
P. Davis, *C.* 11,984
Ms. H. Steele, *L./All.* 6,772
Lab. maj. 8,236
(June '83, Lab. maj. 8,509)

NORTH WEST *E.* 47,568
*T. L. Banks, Lab. 15,677
J. C. Wylie, *C.* 7,181
R. H. Redden, *S.D.P./All.* . 4,920
Ms. A. V. Degrandis-
Harrison, *Grn.* 497
Lab. maj. 8,496
(June '83, Lab. maj. 6,918)

SOUTH *E.* 50,244
*N. J. Spearing, Lab. 12,935
J. Fairrie, *C.* 10,169
A. J. Kellaway, *S.D.P./All.* . 6,607
Lab. maj. 2,766
(June '83, Lab. maj. 7,311)

Norfolk
MID *E.* 73,893
*R. A. Ryder, O.B.E., C. .. 32,758
G. J. E. Graham, *S.D.P./*
All. 14,750
K. Luckey, *Lab.* 10,272
C. maj. 18,008
(June '83, C. maj. 15,515)

NORTH *E.* 69,790
*R. F. Howell, C. 28,822
N. R. Anthony, *S.D.P./All.* 13,512
A. Earle, *Lab.* 10,765
M. G. Filgate, *Grn.* 960
C. maj. 15,310
(June '83, C. maj. 13,223)

NORTH WEST *E.* 73,739
*H. C. Bellingham, C. 29,393
C. Brocklebank-Fowler,
S.D.P./All. 18,568
F. Dignan, *Lab.* 10,184
C. maj. 10,825
(June '83, C. maj. 3,147)

SOUTH *E.* 78,372
*Rt. Hon. J. R. R. Mac-
Gregor, O.B.E., *C.* 33,912
R. A. P. Carden, *L./All.* ... 21,494
L. Addison, *Lab.* 8,047
C. maj. 12,418
(June '83, C. maj. 12,135)

SOUTH WEST *E.* 74,240
Mrs. G. P. Shephard, *C.* .. 32,519
M. Scott, *L./All.* 12,083
Ms. M. Page, *Lab.* 11,844
C. maj. 20,436
(June '83, C. maj. 14,910)

Normanton (W. Yorks)
E. 62,899
*W. O'Brien, Lab. 23,303
M. D. M. Smith, *C.* 16,016
R. J. Macey, *S.D.P./All.* ... 7,717
Lab. maj. 7,287
(June '83, Lab. maj. 4,183)

Northampton
NORTH *E.* 69,294
*A. R. Marlow, C. 24,816
O. J. Granfield, *Lab.* 15,560
A. S. Rounthwaite, *L./All.* 10,690
M. Green, *Grn.* 471
S. Colling, *W.R.P.* 156
C. maj. 9,256
(June '83, C. maj. 9,860)

SOUTH *E.* 76,071
*M. W. L. Morris, C. 31,864
J. Dickie, *Lab.* 14,061
G. Hopkins, *S.D.P./All.* ... 10,639
Mrs. M. Hamilton, *Grn.* .. 647
C. maj. 17,803
(June '83, C. maj. 15,126)

Northavon (Avon)
E. 78,483
*J. A. Cope, C. 34,224
Mrs. C. Willmore, *L./All.* . 19,954
D. Norris, *Lab.* 8,762
C. maj. 14,270
(June '83, C. maj. 12,983)

Norwich (Norfolk)
NORTH *E.* 62,725
*H. P. Thompson, C. 22,772
Miss M. H. R. Honeyball,
Lab. 14,996
T. P. Nicholls, *L./All.* 11,922
C. maj. 7,776
(June '83, C. maj. 5,879)

SOUTH *E.* 64,421
J. L. Garrett, *Lab.* 19,666
*J. A. Powley, C. 19,330
C. J. M. Hardie, *S.D.P./All.* 12,896
Lab. maj. 336
(June '83, C. maj. 1,712)

Norwood (Gtr. London)
E. 56,602
*J. D. Fraser, Lab. 18,359
D. C. R. Grieve, *C.* 13,636
M. M. Noble, *S.D.P./All.* .. 12,579
F. M. Jackson, *R.A.B.I.E.S.* 171
R. J. Hammond, *C.D.* 151
Lab. maj. 4,723
(June '83, Lab. maj. 2,883)

Nottingham
EAST *E.* 68,266
*M. Knowles, C. 20,162
M. Aslam, *Lab.* 19,706
S. Parkhouse, *L./All.* 6,887
K. Malik, *R.F.* 212
C. maj. 456
(June '83, C. maj. 1,464)

NORTH *E.* 69,620
G. W. Allen, *Lab.* 22,713
*R. G. J. Ottaway, C. 21,048
S. C. Fernando, *S.D.P./All.* 5,912
J. H. Peck, *Comm.* 879
Lab. maj. 1,665
(June '83, C. maj. 362)

SOUTH *E.* 72,807
*M. M. Brandon-Bravo, C. . 23,921
A. Simpson, *Lab.* 21,687
L. V. Williams, *S.D.P./All.* 7,517
C. maj. 2,234
(June '83, C. maj. 5,715)

Nuneaton (Warwicks)
E. 68,287
*L. D. Stevens, M.B.E., C. .. 24,630
Mrs. V. A. Veness, *Lab.* .. 18,975
A. Trembath, *S.D.P./All.* .. 10,550
Dr. J. Morrissey, *Grn.* 719
C. maj. 5,655
(June '83, C. maj. 5,061)

Old Bexley and Sidcup
(Gtr. London)
E. 50,831
*Rt. Hon. E. R. G. Heath,
M.B.E., *C.* 24,350
T. H. Pearce, *L./All.* 8,076
H. J. A. Stoate, *Lab.* 6,762
C. maj. 16,274
(June '83, C. maj. 12,718)

Oldham (Gtr. Manchester)
CENTRAL AND ROYTON
E. 65,277
*J. A. Lamond, Lab. 21,759
J. A. Farquhar, *C.* 15,480
Mrs. A. Dunn, *S.D.P./All.* 7,956
Lab. maj. 6,279
(June '83, Lab. maj. 3,312)

WEST *E.* 57,178
*M. H. Meacher, Lab. 20,291
Mrs. J. M. Jacobs, *C.* 14,324
Miss M. R. Mason, *L./All.* 6,478
Lab. maj. 5,967
(June '83, Lab. maj. 3,180)

Orpington (Gtr. London)
E. 59,608
*I. R. Stanbrook, C. 27,261
J. H. Fryer, *L./All.* 14,529
S. J. Cowan, *Lab.* 5,020
C. maj. 12,732
(June '83, C. maj. 10,151)

Oxford
EAST *E.* 62,145
A. D. Smith, *Lab.* 21,103
*S. J. Norris, C. 19,815
Mrs. M. Godden, *L./All.* .. 7,648
D. Dalton, *Grn.* 441
P. S. Mylvaganam, *I.C.C.* . 60
Lab. maj. 1,288
(June '83, C. maj. 1,267)

WEST AND ABINGDON E. 69,193
*J. H. C. Patten, C. 25,171
C. M. P. Huhne, S.D.P./All. 20,293
J. G. Power, Lab. 8,108
D. Smith, Grn. 695
   C. maj. 4,878
(June '83, C. maj. 7,151)

Peckham (Gtr. London)
E. 59,261

*Ms. H. Harman, Lab. 17,965
Mrs. L. K. F. Ingram, C. .. 8,476
R. H. Shearman, L./All. .. 5,878
Miss D. Robinson, Grn. ... 628
   Lab. maj. 9,489
(June '83, Lab. maj. 8,824)

Pendle (Lancs)
E. 63,588

*J. R. L. Lee, C. 21,009
Mrs. S. Renilson, Lab. 18,370
A. G. Lishman, L./All. ... 12,662
   C. maj. 2,639
(June '83, C. maj. 6,135)

Penrith and the Border
(Cumbria)
E. 70,994

*D. J. Maclean, C. 33,148
D. J. Ivison, L./All. 15,782
J. M. P. Hutton, Lab. 6,075
   C. maj. 17,366
(June '83, C. maj. 15,421)
(July '83, C. maj. 552)

Peterborough (Cambs)
E. 84,284

*Dr. B. S. Mawhinney, C. .. 30,624
A. MacKinlay, Lab. 20,840
D. W. Green, L./All. 9,984
N. A. Callaghan, Grn. 506
   C. maj. 9,784
(June '83, C. maj. 10,439)

Plymouth (Devon)

DEVONPORT E. 64,741
*Rt. Hon. Dr. D. A. L. Owen,
   S.D.P./All. 21,039
T. Jones, C. 14,569
I. Flintoff, Lab. 14,166
   S.D.P./All. maj. 6,470
(June '83, S.D.P./All. maj. 4,936)

DRAKE E. 51,186
*Miss J. E. Fookes, C. 16,195
D. Astor, S.D.P./All. 13,070
D. Jamieson, Lab. 9,451
Ms. P. Barber, Grn. 493
   C. maj. 3,125
(June '83, C. maj. 8,585)

SUTTON E. 64,120
*Hon. A. K. M. Clark, C. .. 23,187
B. Tidy, L./All. 19,174
R. D. Maddern, Lab. 8,310
   C. maj. 4,013
(June '83, C. maj. 11,687)

Pontefract and Castleford
(W. Yorks)
E. 64,414

*G. Lofthouse, Lab. 31,656
J. H. Mallins, C. 10,030
M. F. Taylor, L./All. 5,334
D. M. Lees, R.F. 295
   Lab. maj. 21,626
(June '83, Lab. maj. 13,691)

Poole (Dorset)
E. 76,673

*J. D. Ward, C.B.E., C. 34,159
R. J. Whitley, S.D.P./All. .. 19,351
M. Shutler, Lab. 5,901
   C. maj. 14,808
(June '83, C. maj. 14,429)

Portsmouth (Hants)

NORTH E. 80,501
*P. H. S. Griffiths, C. 33,297
Mrs. E. Mitchell, S.D.P./
   All. 14,896
D. Miles, Lab. 12,016
   C. maj. 18,401
(June '83, C. maj. 17,999)

SOUTH E. 76,292
   D. Martin, C. 23,534
*M. T. Hancock, S.D.P./All. 23,329
K. Gardiner, Lab. 7,047
R. Hughes, 657 Party 455
   C. maj. 205
(June '83, C. maj. 12,335)
(June '84, S.D.P./All. maj. 1,341)

Preston (Lancs)
E. 64,459

Mrs. A. Wise, Lab. 23,341
Dr. R. T. Chandran, C. ... 12,696
J. P. Wright, L./All. 8,452
   Lab. maj. 10,645
(June '83, Lab. maj. 6,978)

Pudsey (W. Yorks)
E. 71,681

*J. G. D. Shaw, C. 25,457
J. P. F. Cummins, L./All. . 19,021
N. Taggart, Lab. 11,461
   C. maj. 6,436
(June '83, C. maj. 5,314)

Putney (Gtr. London)
E. 63,108

*D. J. Mellor, C. 24,197
P. G. Hain, Lab. 17,290
Ms. S. Harlow, L./All. 5,934
S. Desorgher, Grn. 508
   C. maj. 6,907
(June '83, C. maj. 5,019)

Ravensbourne (Gtr. London)
E. 59,365

*J. L. Hunt, C. 28,295
G. Campbell, S.D.P./All. .. 11,376
M. D'Arcy, Lab. 5,087
A. Waide, B.N. 184
   C. maj. 16,919
(June '83, C. maj. 15,512)

Reading (Berks)

EAST E. 72,311
*Sir G. Vaughan, C. 28,515
Mrs. S. M. Baring, S.D.P./
   All. 12,298
M. J. Salter, Lab. 11,371
P. J. Unsworth, Grn. 667
A. B. Shone, C.S. 125
   C. maj. 16,217
(June '83, C. maj. 11,508)

WEST E. 70,391
*R. A. B. Durant, C. 28,122
K. H. Lock, L./All. 11,369
M. E. Orton, Lab. 10,819
E. P. Wilson, Grn. 542
   C. maj. 16,753
(June '83, C. maj. 11,399)

Redcar (Cleveland)
E. 63,393

Dr. Marjorie Mowlam, Lab. 22,824
P. J. Bassett, C. 15,089
G. Nightingale, S.D.P./All. 10,298
   Lab. maj. 7,735
(June '83, Lab. maj. 3,104)

Reigate (Surrey)
E. 71,940

*G. A. Gardiner, C. 30,925
Mrs. E. A. Pamplin, S.D.P./
   All. 12,752
R. P. Spencer, Lab. 7,460
G. Brand, Grn. 1,026
   C. maj. 18,173
(June '83, C. maj. 16,307)

Ribble Valley (Lancs)
E. 62,644

*Rt. Hon. D. C. Waddington,
   Q.C., C. 30,136
M. Carr, S.D.P./All. 10,608
G. Pope, Lab. 8,781
   C. maj. 19,528
(June '83, C. maj. 18,591)

Richmond and Barnes
(Gtr. London)
E. 54,700

*J. J. Hanley, C. 21,729
A. J. Watson, L./All. 19,963
M. D. Gold, Lab. 3,227
Miss C. M. Matthews, Grn. 610
   C. maj. 1,766
(June '83, C. maj. 74)

Richmond (N. Yorks)
E. 79,277

*Rt. Hon. L. Brittan, Q.C.,
   C. 34,995
D. Lloyd-Williams, L./All. 15,419
F. Robson, Lab. 6,737
   C. maj. 19,576
(June '83, C. maj. 18,066)
(see also p. 276)

Rochdale (Gtr. Manchester)
E. 68,703

*C. Smith, M.B.E., L./All. .. 22,245
D. Williams, Lab. 19,466
C. Condie, C. 9,561
   L./All. maj. 2,779
(June '83, L./All. maj. 7,587)

Rochford (Essex)
E. 76,048

*Dr. M. Clark, C.	....	35,872
P. Young, L./All.	....	16,178
D. Weir, Lab.	....	7,308
C. maj.	....	19,694
(June '83, C. maj. 13,102)		

Romford (Gtr. London)
E. 55,668

*M. J. Neubert, C.	....	22,745
N. J. M. Smith, Lab.	......	9,274
J. H. Bates, L./All.	......	8,195
F. J. Gibson, Grn.	....	385
C. maj.	....	13,471
(June '83, C. maj. 10,574)		

Romsey and Waterside (Hants)
E. 79,136

*M. K. B. Colvin, C.	....	35,303
A. T. Bloss, S.D.P./All.	...	20,031
S. J. Roberts, Lab.	....	7,213
C. maj.	....	15,272
(June '83, C. maj. 13,690)		

Rossendale and Darwen (Lancs)
E. 75,038

*D. A. Trippier, C.	....	28,056
Mrs. J. Anderson, Lab.	...	23,074
P. J. Hulse, L./All.	....	9,097
C. maj.	....	4,982
(June '83, C. maj. 8,821)		

Rotherham (S. Yorks)
E. 61,521

*J. S. Crowther, Lab.	......	25,422
J. C. C. Stevens, C.	......	9,410
P. J. Bowler, L./All.	......	7,766
Lab. maj.	....	16,012
(June '83, Lab. maj. 11,709)		

Rother Valley (S. Yorks)
E. 66,416

*K. J. Barron, Lab.	....	28,292
P. R. Rayner, C.	....	12,502
J. R. Boddy, S.D.P./All.	..	9,240
M. R. Driver, W.R.P.	.....	145
Lab. maj.	....	15,790
(June '83, Lab. maj. 8,625)		

Rugby and Kenilworth (Warwicks)
E. 76,654

*J. F. Pawsey, C.	....	31,485
J. Airey, Lab.	....	15,221
D. R. Owen-Jones, L./All.	..	14,343
C. maj.	....	16,264
(June '83, C. maj. 14,241)		

Ruislip-Northwood (Gtr. London)
E. 56,365

*J. A. D. Wilkinson, C.	....	27,418
Mrs. D. Darby, L./All.	....	10,447
Ms. H. A. Smith, Lab.	.....	5,913
C. maj.	....	16,971
(June '83, C. maj. 12,982)		

Rushcliffe (Notts)
E. 72,797

*Rt. Hon. K. H. Clarke, Q.C.,		
C.	....	34,214
L. George, S.D.P./All.	....	13,375
P. Tipping, Lab.	....	9,631
Ms. H. Wright, Grn.	.....	991
C. maj.	....	20,839
(June '83, C. maj. 20,220)		

Rutland and Melton (Leics)
E. 77,846

*M. A. Latham, C.	....	37,073
R. C. Renold, L./All.	.....	14,051
L. C. Burke, Lab.	....	8,680
C. maj.	....	23,022
(June '83, C. maj. 18,353)		

Ryedale (N. Yorks)
E. 83,205

J. R. Greenway, C.	....	35,149
*Mrs. E. L. Shields, L./All.	.	25,409
J. Beighton, Lab.	....	5,340
C. maj.	....	9,740
(June '83, C. maj. 16,142)		
(May '86, L./All. maj. 4,940)		

Saffron Walden (Essex)
E. 73,185

*A. G. B. Haselhurst, C.	...	33,354
M. P. Hayes, L./All.	......	16,752
R. Gifford, Lab.	....	6,674
G. B. Hannah, Grn.	......	816
W. O. Smedley, C.M.N.H.Y.		217
C. maj.	....	16,602
(June '83, C. maj. 15,363)		

St. Albans (Herts)
E. 75,281

*P. B. Lilley, C.	....	31,726
A. S. B. Walkington, L./All.	20,845
A. McWalter, Lab.	....	6,922
Ms. E. V. Field, Grn.	.....	788
W. H. Pass, C.P.R.P.	.....	110
C. maj.	....	10,881
(June '83, C. maj. 8,561)		

St. Helens (Merseyside)

NORTH   E. 70,836

*J. Evans, Lab.	....	28,989
Miss M. J. Libby, C.	.....	14,729
N. P. Derbyshire, L./All.	..	10,300
Lab. maj.	....	14,260
(June '83, Lab. maj. 9,259)		

SOUTH   E. 69,449

*G. E. Bermingham, Lab.	..	27,027
A. J. Brown, C.	....	13,226
P. J. Briers, S.D.P./All.	..	9,252
Lab. maj.	....	13,801
(June '83, Lab. maj. 9,662)		

St. Ives (Cornwall)
E. 67,448

*D. A. Harris, C.	....	25,174
H. H. J. Carter, S.D.P./All.	17,619
I. Hope, Lab.	....	9,275
C. maj.	....	7,555
(June '83, C. maj. 7,859)		

Salford East (Gtr. Manchester)
E. 58,087

*Rt. Hon. S. Orme, Lab.	...	22,555
C. W. H. McFall, C.	......	10,499
P. Keaveney, S.D.P./All.	.	5,105
S. G. Murray, W.R.P.	....	201
Lab. maj.	....	12,056
(June '83, Lab. maj. 9,541)		

Salisbury (Wilts)
E. 76,221

*S. R. Key, C.	....	31,612
P. A. Mitchell, S.D.P./All.	.	20,169
Ms. T. E. Seabourne, Lab.		5,455
S. W. Fletcher, Ind.	......	372
C. maj.	....	11,443
(June '83, C. maj. 7,174)		

Scarborough (N. Yorks)
E. 74,612

*Sir M. N. Shaw, C.	......	27,672
Mrs. H. Callan, S.D.P./All.	.	14,046
M. Wolstenholme, Lab.	..	12,913
C. maj.	....	13,626
(June '83, C. maj. 13,929)		

Sedgefield (Durham)
E. 60,866

*A. C. L. Blair, Lab.	......	25,965
N. B. S. Hawkins, C.	.....	12,907
R. I. Andrew, S.D.P./All.	.	7,477
Lab. maj.	....	13,058
(June '83, Lab. maj. 8,281)		

Selby (N. Yorks)
E. 71,378

*Rt. Hon. M. J. H. Alison,		
C.	....	28,611
J. T. Grogan, Lab.	....	14,832
J. E. F. Longman, L./All.	.	12,010
C. maj.	....	13,779
(June '83, C. maj. 15,965)		

Sevenoaks (Kent)
E. 73,179

*G. M. Wolfson, C.	....	32,945
S. R. Jakobi, L./All.	......	15,600
G. A. Green, Lab.	....	7,379
C. maj.	....	17,345
(June '83, C. maj. 15,706)		

Sheffield (S. Yorks)

ATTERCLIFFE   E. 67,051

*A. E. P. Duffy, Lab.	......	28,266
G. J. Perry, C.	....	11,075
Ms. H. E. Woolley, S.D.P./All.		9,549
Lab. maj.	....	17,191
(June '83, Lab. maj. 11,612)		

BRIGHTSIDE   E. 64,982

D. Blunkett, Lab.	....	31,208
Miss M. C. Glyn, C.	......	7,017
J. A. Leeman, L./All.	.....	6,434
Lab. maj.	....	24,191
(June '83, Lab. maj. 15,209)		

CENTRAL *E.* 61,156
*R. G. Caborn, *Lab.* 25,872
B. Oxley, *C.* 6,530
Ms. F. C. Hornby, *S.D.P./*
All. 5,314
C. T. Dingle, *R.F.* 278
K. E. Petts, *Comm.* 203
Lab. maj. 19,342
(June '83, Lab. maj. 16,790)

HALLAM *E.* 74,158
C. I. Patnick, *C.* 25,649
P. J. Gold, *L./All.* 18,012
M. C. Savani, *Lab.* 11,290
Ms. L. M. Spencer, *Grn.* .. 459
C. maj. 7,637
(June '83, C. maj. 11,774)

HEELEY *E.* 73,931
*W. Michie, *Lab.* 28,425
N. P. Mearing-Smith, *C.* .. 13,985
P. Moore, *S.D.P./All.* 10,811
Lab. maj. 14,440
(June '83, Lab. maj. 8,368)

HILLSBOROUGH *E.* 76,312
*M. H. Flannery, *Lab.* 26,208
D. Chadwick, *L./All.* 22,922
J. D. Sykes, *C.* 10,396
Lab. maj. 3,286
(June '83, Lab. maj. 1,546)

Sherwood (Notts)
E. 71,378
*A. S. Stewart, *C.* 26,816
W. S. G. Bach, *Lab.* 22,321
S. R. Thompstone, *S.D.P./*
All. 9,343
C. maj. 4,495
(June '83, C. maj. 658)

Shipley (W. Yorks)
E. 68,705
*Sir J. M. Fox, M.B.E., *C.* ... 26,941
W. J. L. Wallace, *L./All.* .. 14,311
C. R. B. Butler, *Lab.* 12,669
C. M. Harris, *Grn.* 507
C. maj. 12,630
(June '83, C. maj. 11,445)

Shoreham (W. Sussex)
E. 71,318
*Rt. Hon. R. N. Luce, *C.* .. 33,660
J. A. Ingram, *L./All.* 16,590
P. Godwin, *Lab.* 5,053
C. maj. 17,070
(June '83, C. maj. 15,766)

Shrewsbury and Atcham (Salop)
E. 70,689
*D. L. Conway, *C.* 26,027
R. Hutchison, *L./All.* 16,963
Mrs. E. M. Owen, *Lab.* ... 10,797
G. Hardy, *Grn.* 660
C. maj. 9,064
(June '83, C. maj. 8,624)

Shropshire North
E. 77,122
*Rt. Hon. W. J. Biffen, *C.* .. 30,385
G. Smith, *L./All.* 15,970
R. Hawkins, *Lab.* 11,866
C. maj. 14,415
(June '83, C. maj. 11,667)

Skipton and Ripon
(N. Yorks)
E. 72,199

D. M. Curry, *C.* 33,128
S. J. Cooksey, *L./All.* 15,954
T. L. Whitfield, *Lab.* 6,264
Ms. L. S. Williams, *Grn.* .. 825
C. maj. 17,174
(June '83, C. maj. 15,046)

Slough (Berks)
E. 73,424

*J. A. Watts, *C.* 26,166
E. Lopez, *Lab.* 22,076
M. Goldstone, *S.D.P./All* .. 7,490
C. maj. 4,090
(June '83, C. maj. 3,106)

Solihull (W. Midlands)
E. 78,123

*J. M. Taylor, *C.* 35,844
G. E. Gadie, *L./All.* 14,058
Mrs. S. E. Knowles, *Lab.* .. 8,791
C. maj. 21,786
(June '83, C. maj. 17,394)

Somerton and Frome
(Somerset)
E. 68,773

*Hon. R. T. Boscawen, M.C.,
C. 29,351
R. G. Morgan, *L./All.* 19,813
I. S. Kelly, *Lab.* 5,461
C. maj. 9,538
(June '83, C. maj. 9,227)

Southampton (Hants)

ITCHEN *E.* 72,687
*C. R. Chope, O.B.E., *C.* ... 24,419
J. Y. Denham, *Lab.* 17,703
R. C. Mitchell, *S.D.P./All.* 13,006
C. maj. 6,716
(June '83, C. maj. 5,290)

TEST *E.* 73,918
*S. J. A. Hill, *C.* 25,722
A. P. V. Whitehead, *Lab.* .. 18,768
Mrs. V. Rayner, *L./All.* ... 11,950
C. maj. 6,954
(June '83, C. maj. 9,346)

Southend (Essex)

EAST *E.* 59,073
*E. M. Taylor, *C.* 23,753
H. J. Berkeley, *S.D.P./All.* 9,906
D. R. Scully, *Lab.* 7,296
C. maj. 13,847
(June '83, C. maj. 10,691)

WEST *E.* 68,415
*Rt. Hon. H. P. G. Channon,
C. 28,003
G. Grant, *L./All.* 19,603
Mrs. A. Smith, *Lab.* 3,899
C. maj. 8,400
(June '83, C. maj. 8,033)

South Hams (Devon)
E. 78,583

*A. D. Steen, *C.* 34,218
R. F. Chave, *L./All.* 21,072
*W. W. Hamilton, *Lab.* 5,060
C. G. Titmuss, *Grn.* 1,178
T. C. Langsford, *L.M.* 277
C. maj. 13,146
(June '83, C. maj. 12,401)

Southport (Merseyside)
E. 71,443

R. C. Fearn, *L./All.* 26,110
N. M. Thomas, *C.* 24,261
Mrs. A. Moore, *Lab.* 3,483
J. R. G. Walker, *Grn.* 653
L./All. maj. 1,849
(June '83, C. maj. 5,039)

South Ribble (Lancs)
E. 72,177

*R. J. Atkins, *C.* 28,133
D. F. Roebuck, *Lab.* 19,703
J. A. Holleran, *L./All.* 11,746
C. maj. 8,430
(June '83, C. maj. 12,659)

South Shields (Tyne & Wear)
E. 60,754

*Dr. D. G. Clark, *Lab.* 24,882
M. L. D. Fabricant, *C.* 11,031
Ms. M. Meling, *S.D.P./All.* 6,654
E. G. Dunn, *Dem.* 408
Lab. maj. 13,851
(June '83, Lab. maj. 6,402)

Southwark and Bermondsey
(Gtr. London)
E. 55,438

*S. H. W. Hughes, *L./All.* .. 17,072
J. Bryan, *Lab.* 14,293
O. Heald, *C.* 4,522
P. N. Power, *Comm.* 108
L./All. maj. 2,779
(June '83, L./All. maj. 5,164)

Spelthorne (Surrey)
E. 72,967

D. Wilshire, *C.* 32,440
Mrs. M. Cunningham,
S.D.P./All. 12,390
D. F. J. Welfare, *Lab.* 9,227
C. maj. 20,050
(June '83, C. maj. 13,506)

Stafford
E. 72,431

*W. N. P. Cash, *C.* 29,541
C. B. Phipps, *S.D.P./All.* .. 15,834
Ms. N. Hafeez, *Lab.* 12,177
C. maj. 13,707
(June '83, C. maj. 14,277)
(May '84, C. maj. 3,980)

Staffordshire

MID *E.* 71,252
*B. J. Heddle, *C.* 28,644
C. R. St. Hill, *Lab.* 13,990
T. A. Jones, *L./All.* 13,114
J. G. Bazeley, *Ind. C.* 836
C. maj. 14,654
(June '83, C. maj. 13,880)

MOORLANDS E. 74,302
*D. L. Knox, C. 31,613
Mrs. V. Ivers, Lab. 17,186
J. P. Corbett, S.D.P./All. .. 10,950
   C. maj. 14,427
   (June '83, C. maj. 16,566)

SOUTH E. 79,261
*P. T. Cormack, C. 37,708
Mrs. F. Oborski, L./All. ... 12,440
P. Bateman, Lab. 11,805
   C. maj. 25,268
   (June '83, C. maj. 19,760)

SOUTH EAST E. 66,176
*D. L. Lightbown, C. 25,115
Miss E. Gluck, S.D.P./All. .. 14,230
D. Spilsbury, Lab. 13,874
   C. maj. 10,885
   (June '83, C. maj. 10,898)

Stalybridge and Hyde
(Gtr. Manchester)
E. 67,983

*T. Pendry, Lab. 24,401
R. N. Greenwood, C. 18,738
P. J. Ashenden, S.D.P./All. . 7,311
   Lab. maj. 5,663
   (June '83, Lab. maj. 4,362)

Stamford and Spalding (Lincs)
E. 70,560

J. Q. Davies, C. 31,000
Miss R. Bryan, L./All. 17,009
P. E. Lowe, Lab. 6,882
   C. maj. 13,991
   (June '83, C. maj. 11,756)

Stevenage (Herts)
E. 69,525

*T. J. R. Wood, C. 23,541
B. R. M. Stoneham, S.D.P./
   All. 18,201
M. R. C. Withers, Lab. ... 14,229
   C. maj. 5,340
   (June '83, C. maj. 1,755)

Stockport (Gtr. Manchester)
E. 60,059

*A. R. Favell, C. 19,410
Mrs. S. Haines, Lab. 16,557
J. L. Begg, S.D.P./All. 10,365
M. Shipley, Grn. 573
   C. maj. 2,853
   (June '83, C. maj. 5,786)

Stockton (Cleveland)

NORTH E. 70,329
*F. Cook, Lab. 26,043
D. J. C. Faber, C. 17,242
N. F. G. Bosanquet, S.D.P./
   All. 9,712
   Lab. maj. 8,801
   (June '83, Lab. maj. 1,870)

SOUTH E. 75,279
T. R. Devlin, C. 20,833
*I. W. Wrigglesworth,
   S.D.P./All. 20,059
J. M. Scott, Lab. 18,600
   C. maj. 774
   (June '83, S.D.P./All. maj. 102)

Stoke-on-Trent (Staffs)

CENTRAL E. 65,987
*M. Fisher, Lab. 23,842
D. Stone, C. 14,072
I. Cundy, S.D.P./All. 7,462
   Lab. maj. 9,770
   (June '83, Lab. maj. 8,250)

NORTH E. 74,184
Ms. J. L. Walley, Lab. 25,459
R. Davies, C. 16,946
S. J. Simmonds, S.D.P./All. 11,665
   Lab. maj. 8,513
   (June '83, Lab. maj. 8,203)

SOUTH E. 70,806
*Rt. Hon. J. Ashley, C.H.,
   Lab. 24,794
D. Hartshorne, C. 19,741
P. Wild, L./All. 7,669
   Lab. maj. 5,053
   (June '83, Lab. maj. 7,105)

Stratford-upon-Avon (Warwicks)
E. 81,263

*A. T. Howarth, C.B.E., C. .. 38,483
D. G. Cowcher, L./All. 17,318
R. H. Rhodes, Lab. 6,335
   C. maj. 21,165
   (June '83, C. maj. 17,917)

Streatham (Gtr. London)
E. 60,519

*W. J. M. Shelton, C. 18,916
Ms. A. Tapsall, Lab. 16,509
M. Tuffrey, L./All. 6,663
   C. maj. 2,407
   (June '83, C. maj. 5,902)

Stretford (Gtr. Manchester)
E. 57,568

*A. J. Lloyd, Lab. 22,831
D. Dougherty, C. 13,429
D. Lee, S.D.P./All. 5,125
   Lab. maj. 9,402
   (June '83, Lab. maj. 4,342)

Stroud (Glos)
E. 81,275

R. M. Knapman, C. 32,883
A. A. Walker-Smith, L./
   All. 20,508
T. Levitt, Lab. 12,145
   C. maj. 12,375
   (June '83, C. maj. 11,714)

Suffolk

CENTRAL E. 79,199
*M. N. Lord, C. 32,422
T. Dale, L./All. 16,132
M. Walker, Lab. 11,817
   C. maj. 16,290
   (June '83, C. maj. 14,731)

COASTAL E. 75,684
*Rt. Hon. J. S. Gummer, C. 32,834
Mrs. J. M. Miller, S.D.P./
   All. 17,554
Mrs. S. A. Reeves, Lab. ... 7,534
J. W. Holloway, Grn. 1,049
   C. maj. 15,280
   (June '83, C. maj. 15,622)

SOUTH E. 81,954
*T. S. K. Yeo, C. 33,972
C. M. N. Bradford, L./All. . 17,729
A. C. Bavington, Lab. 11,876
   C. maj. 16,243
   (June '83, C. maj. 11,269)

Sunderland
(Tyne & Wear)

NORTH E. 75,674
*R. A. Clay, Lab. 29,767
I. S. Picton, C. 15,095
T. Jenkinson, L./All. 8,518
   Lab. maj. 14,672
   (June '83, Lab. maj. 7,196)

SOUTH E. 74,947
C. J. Mullin, Lab. 28,823
G. E. Howe, C. 16,210
K. Hudson, S.D.P./All. 7,768
D. N. Jacques, Grn. 516
   Lab. maj. 12,613
   (June '83, Lab. maj. 5,548)

Surbiton (Gtr. London)
E. 45,428

*R. P. Tracey, C. 19,861
D. T. Burke, S.D.P./All. ... 10,120
A. McGowan, Lab. 5,111
Ms. J. Vidler, Grn. 465
   C. maj. 9,741
   (June '83, C. maj. 8,749)

Surrey

EAST E. 59,528
*Rt. Hon. Sir R. E. G. Howe,
   Q.C., C. 29,126
M. A. J. Anderson, L./All. . 11,000
M. Davis, Lab. 4,779
D. Newell, Grn. 1,044
   C. maj. 18,126
   (June '83, C. maj. 15,436)

NORTH WEST E. 83,083
*W. M. J. Grylls, C. 38,535
C. Brodie, L./All. 14,960
J. Cooper, Lab. 6,751
   C. maj. 23,575
   (June '83, C. maj. 21,018)

SOUTH WEST E. 73,018
*Mrs. V. H. B. M. Bottomley,
   C. 34,024
G. D. Scott, L./All. 19,681
J. K. P. Evers, Lab. 3,224
M. J. Green, Ind. C. 299
   C. maj. 14,343
   (June '83, C. maj. 14,351)
   (May '84, C. maj. 2,599)

Sussex Mid
E. 80,147

*R. T. Renton, C. 37,781
N. S. E. Westbrook, L./All. 19,489
R. Hughes, Lab. 4,573
   C. maj. 18,292
   (June '83, C. maj. 16,744)

Sutton and Cheam
(Gtr. London)
E. 63,850

*D. N. Macfarlane, C. 29,710
R. D. Grieg, L./All. 13,992
Ms. L. Monk, Lab. 5,202
   C. maj. 15,718
   (June '83, C. maj. 10,264)

Sutton Coldfield (W. Midlands)
E. 72,329

*Rt. Hon. P. N. Fowler, C. .	34,475
T. Bick, L./All.	13,292
P. McLoughlin, Lab.	6,104
C. maj.	21,183
(June '83, C. maj. 18,984)	

Swindon (Wilts)
E. 86,150

*S. C. Coombs, C.	29,385
Ms. G. Johnston, Lab.	24,528
D. J. Scott, S.D.P./All. ...	13,114
C. maj.	4,857
(June '83, C. maj. 1,395)	

Tatton (Cheshire)
E. 71,904

*M. N. Hamilton, C.	30,128
Ms. B. Gaskin, S.D.P./All.	13,034
Ms. H. A. Blears, Lab.	11,760
M. G. Gibson, F.P.	263
C. maj.	17,094
(June '83, C. maj. 13,960)	

Taunton (Somerset)
E. 74,145

D. J. Nicholson, C.	30,248
M. A. K. Cocks, S.D.P./All.	19,868
Dr. G. Reynolds, Lab.	8,754
C. maj.	10,380
(June '83, C. maj. 12,567)	

Teignbridge (Devon)
E. 71,872

*P. C. M. Nicholls, C.	30,693
R. D. Ryder, L./All.	20,268
J. Greenwood, Lab.	6,413
A. Hope, L.M.	312
C. maj.	10,425
(June '83, C. maj. 8,218)	

Thanet (Kent)

NORTH   E.69,723

*R. J. Gale, C.	29,225
N. R. M. Cranston, S.D.P./ All.	11,745
A. M. Bretman, Lab.	8,395
D. R. Condor, Grn.	996
C. maj.	17,480
(June '83, C. maj. 14,545)	

SOUTH   E.62,761

*J. W. P. Aitken, C.	25,135
W. H. Pitt, L./All.	11,452
C. Wright, Lab.	9,673
C. maj.	13,683
(June '83, C. maj. 14,051)	

Thurrock (Essex)
E. 67,594

T. S. Janman, C.	20,527
*Dr. O. A. McDonald, Lab.	19,837
D. S. Benson, S.D.P./All. .	7,970
C. maj.	690
(June '83, Lab. maj. 1,722)	

Tiverton (Devon)
E. 68,210

*R. J. Maxwell-Hyslop, C. .	29,875
D. J. Morrish, L./All.	20,663
Mrs. J. A. Northam, Lab. .	3,400
W. J. Jones, L.A.O.	434
C. maj.	9,212
(June '83, C. maj. 7,886)	

Tonbridge and Malling (Kent)
E. 76,797

*Rt. Hon. J. P. Stanley, C. .	33,990
M. J. Ward, S.D.P./All. ..	17,561
D. G. Still, Lab.	7,803
M. D. S. Easter, B.N.	369
C. maj.	16,429
(June '83, C. maj. 13,520)	

Tooting (Gtr. London)
E. 68,116

*T. M. Cox, Lab.	21,457
M. A. Winter, C.	20,016
J. N. Ambache, S.D.P./All.	6,423
Ms. M. Vickery, Grn.	621
Lab. maj.	1,441
(June '83, Lab. maj. 2,659)	

Torbay (Devon)
E. 70,435

R. W. S. Allason, C.	29,029
N. D. Bye, L./All.	20,209
G. R. Taylor, Lab.	4,538
C. maj.	8,820
(June '83, C. maj. 6,555)	

Tottenham (Gtr. London)
E. 76,092

B. A. L. Grant, Lab.	21,921
P. L. Murphy, C.	17,780
S. Etherington, L./All. ...	8,983
D. Nicholls, Grn.	744
P. Nealon, Gsoll. Lab.	638
Ms. C. L. Dixon, W.R.P. ..	205
Lab. maj.	4,141
(June '83, Lab. maj. 9,396)	

Truro (Cornwall)
E. 72,432

*M. O. J. Taylor, L./All. ...	28,368
N. F. St. Aubyn, C.	23,615
J. R. King, Lab.	5,882
L./All. maj.	4,753
(June '83, L./All. maj. 10,480)	
(March '87, L./All. maj. 14,617)	

Tunbridge Wells (Kent)
E. 76,291

*Sir P. B. B. Mayhew, Q.C., C.	33,111
Mrs. D. A. Buckrell, L./All.	16,989
P. L. Sloman, Lab.	6,555
C. maj.	16,122
(June '83, C. maj. 15,126)	

Twickenham (Gtr. London)
E. 64,661

*T. F. H. Jessel, C.	27,331
J. Waller, L./All.	20,204
Ms. V. C. M. Vaz, Lab.	4,415
D. S. Batchelor, Grn.	746
C. maj.	7,127
(June '83, C. maj. 4,792)	

Tyne Bridge
(Tyne & Wear)
E. 58,152

*D. G. Clelland, Lab.	23,131
M. W. Bates, C.	7,558
J. C. Mansfield, S.D.P./All.	6,005
Lab. maj.	15,573
(June '83, Lab. maj. 11,693)	
(Dec '85, Lab. maj. 6,575)	

Tynemouth
(Tyne & Wear)
E. 74,407

*N. G. Trotter, C.	25,113
P. Cosgrove, Lab.	22,530
D. F. Mayhew, L./All.	10,446
C. maj.	2,583
(June '83, C. maj. 9,609)	

Upminster (Gtr. London)
E. 66,613

*Sir N. C. Bonsor, Bt., C. ..	27,946
J. Martin, S.D.P./All.	11,089
D. R. O'Flynn, Lab.	11,069
C. maj.	16,857
(June '83, C. maj. 12,814)	

Uxbridge (Gtr. London)
E. 63,157

*J. M. Shersby, C.	27,292
D. Keys, Lab.	11,322
A. Goodman, S.D.P./All. .	9,164
I. Flindall, Grn.	549
C. maj.	15,970
(June '83, C. maj. 12,837)	

Vauxhall (Gtr. London)
E. 66,538

*S. K. Holland, Lab.	21,364
D. R. Lidington, C.	12,345
S. H. V. Acland, S.D.P./All.	7,764
Ms. J. Owens, Grn.	770
D. J. S. Cook, Comm.	223
K. Oluremi, R.F.	117
Lab. maj.	9,019
(June '83, Lab. maj. 7,780)	
(see also p. 276)	

Wakefield (W. Yorks)
E. 69,580

D. M. Hinchliffe, Lab.	24,509
N. J. Hazell, C.	21,720
Dr. L. Kamal, S.D.P./All .	6,350
Lab. maj.	2,789
(June '83, Lab. maj. 360)	

Wallasey (Merseyside)
E. 67,216

*Mrs. L. Chalker, C.	22,791
L. Duffy, Lab.	22,512
J. K. Richardson, S.D.P./ All.	8,363
C. maj.	279
(June '83, C. maj. 6,708)	

Wallsend (Tyne & Wear)
E. 76,688

*W. E. Garrett, Lab.	32,709
D. Milburn, C.	13,325
Mrs. J. Phylactou, S.D.P./ All.	11,508
Lab. maj.	19,384
(June '83, Lab. maj. 12,514)	

Walsall (W. Midlands)

NORTH   E. 68,331

*D. J. Winnick, *Lab.*		21,458
Mrs. L. Hertz, *C.*		19,668
I. Shires, *L./All.*		9,285
Lab. maj.		1,790
(June '83, Lab. maj. 2,824)		

SOUTH   E. 66,746

*B. T. George, *Lab.*		22,629
G. E. Postles, *C.*		21,513
L. A. King, *L./All.*		6,241
Lab. maj.		1,116
(June '83, Lab. maj. 702)		

Walthamstow (Gtr. London)
E. 48,691

H. H. F. Summerson, *C.*		13,748
*E. P. Deakins, *Lab.*		12,236
P. L. Leighton, *S.D.P./All.*		8,852
Dr. Z. I. Malik, *D.C.*		396
C. maj.		1,512
(June '83, Lab. maj. 1,305)		

Wansbeck (Nthmb)
E. 62,639

*J. Thompson, *Lab.*		28,080
Mrs. S. Mitchell, *L./All.*		11,291
D. Walton, *C.*		9,490
Lab. maj.		16,789
(June '83, Lab. maj. 7,831)		

Wansdyke (Avon)
E. 75,239

*J. H. Aspinwall, *C.*		31,537
R. B. Blackmore, *L./All.*		15,393
I. White, *Lab.*		14,231
C. maj.		16,144
(June '83, C. maj. 13,066)		

Wanstead and Woodford
(Gtr. London)
E. 57,921

J. N. Arbuthnot, *C.*		25,701
J. R. Bastick *L./All.*		9,289
Mrs. L. Hilton, *Lab.*		6,958
C. maj.		16,412
(June '83, C. maj. 14,354)		

Wantage (Oxon)
E. 66,499

*R. V. Jackson, *C.*		27,951
Mrs. W. Tumin, *S.D.P./All.*		15,795
S. Ladyman, *Lab.*		8,055
C. maj.		12,156
(June '83, C. maj. 10,125)		

Warley (W. Midlands)

EAST   E. 55,706

*A. M. W. Faulds, *Lab.*		19,428
A. Antoniou, *C.*		13,843
J. J. Jordan, *S.D.P./All.*		5,396
Lab. maj.		5,585
(June '83, Lab. maj. 3,391)		

WEST   E. 57,526

*Rt. Hon. P. K. Archer, *Q.C.*, *Lab.*		19,825
W. Williams, *C.*		14,432
Miss E. Todd, *L./All.*		6,027
Lab. maj.		5,393
(June '83, Lab. maj. 5,268)		

Warrington (Cheshire)

NORTH   E. 75,627

*E. D. H. Hoyle, *Lab.*		27,422
L. Jones, *C.*		19,409
C. Bithel, *S.D.P./All.*		10,046
Lab. maj.		8,013
(June '83, Lab. maj. 5,277)		

SOUTH   E. 76,219

C. J. Butler, *C.*		24,809
A. Booth, *Lab.*		21,200
I. Marks, *L./All.*		13,112
C. maj.		3,609
(June '83, C. maj. 6,465)		

Warwick and Leamington
E. 72,763

*Sir D. G. Smith, *C.*		27,530
K. P. O'Sullivan, *S.D.P./All.*		13,548
Ms. A. Christina, *Lab.*		13,019
Ms. J. A. Alty, *Grn.*		1,214
C. maj.		13,982
(June '83, C. maj. 13,032)		

Warwickshire

NORTH   E. 70,687

*Hon. F. A. A. Maude, *C.*		25,453
M. O'Brien, *Lab.*		22,624
Mrs. S. J. Neale, *S.D.P./All.*		8,382
C. maj.		2,829
(June '83, C. maj. 2,585)		

Watford (Herts)
E. 73,540

*W. A. T. T. Garel-Jones, *C.*		27,912
M. J. Jackson, *Lab.*		16,176
Mrs. F. M. Beckett, *S.D.P./All.*		13,202
C. maj.		11,736
(June '83, C. maj. 12,006)		

Waveney (Suffolk)
E. 81,889

D. J. Porter, *C.*		31,067
J. A. Lark, *Lab.*		19,284
D. Beaven, *S.D.P./All.*		13,845
C. maj.		11,783
(June '83, C. maj. 14,298)		

Wealden (E. Sussex)
E. 73,057

*Sir G. J. Johnson Smith, *C.*		35,154
D. Sinclair, *S.D.P./All.*		15,044
C. Ward, *Lab.*		4,563
C. maj.		20,110
(June '83, C. maj. 17,185)		

Wellingborough (Northants)
E. 70,450

*P. D. Fry, *C.*		29,038
J. Currie, *Lab.*		14,968
L. E. Stringer, *L./All.*		11,047
C. maj.		14,070
(June '83, C. maj. 12,056)		

Wells (Somerset)
E. 67,195

*D. P. Heathcoat-Amory, *C.*		28,624
A. A. S. Butt Philip, *L./All.*		20,083
P. James, *Lab.*		4,637
J. S. Fish, *Falk.*		134
C. maj.		8,541
(June '83, C. maj. 6,575)		

Welwyn Hatfield (Herts)
E. 73,607

D. J. Evans, *C.*		27,164
Miss L. P. Granshaw, *S.D.P./All.*		16,261
C. R. Pond, *Lab.*		15,699
B. I. Dyson, *Ind. C.*		401
C. maj.		10,903
(June '83, C. maj. 12,246)		

Wentworth (S. Yorks)
E. 63,886

*P. Hardy, *Lab.*		30,205
W. J. Hague, *C.*		10,113
D. M. Eglin, *S.D.P./All.*		6,031
Lab. maj.		20,092
(June '83, Lab. maj. 15,935)		

West Bromwich (W. Midlands)

EAST   E. 58,239

*P. C. Snape, *Lab.*		18,162
R. F. Woodhouse, *C.*		17,179
M. G. Smith, *L./All.*		7,268
Lab. maj.		983
(June '83, Lab. maj. 298)		

WEST   E. 58,944

*Miss B. Boothroyd, *Lab.*		19,925
F. A. Betteridge, *C.*		14,672
A. Collingbourne, *S.D.P./All.*		4,877
Lab. maj.		5,253
(June '83, Lab. maj. 6,639)		

Westbury (Wilts)
E. 84,860

*D. M. Walters, *M.B.E.*, *C.*		34,256
D. J. Hughes, *L./All.*		24,159
H. W. Thomas, *Lab.*		7,982
C. maj.		10,097
(June '83, C. maj. 8,506)		

Westminster North
(Gtr. London)
E. 59,263

*J. D. Wheeler, *C.*		19,941
Ms. J. F. Edwards, *Lab.*		16,631
R. J. De Ste Croix, *S.D.P./All.*		5,116
D. Stutchfield, *Grn.*		450
C. maj.		3,310
(June '83, C. maj. 1,710)		

Westmorland and Lonsdale
(Cumbria)
E. 70,237

*Rt. Hon. T. M. Jopling, *C.*		30,259
S. Collins, *L./All.*		15,339
C. Halfpenny, *Lab.*		6,968
C. maj.		14,920
(June '83, C. maj. 16,587)		

Weston-super-Mare (Avon)
E. 76,341

*A. W. Wiggin, T.D., C.	....	28,547
J. R. Crockford-Hawley,		
S.D.P./All.	....	20,549
P. J. Loach, Lab.	.....	6,584
Dr. R. H. Lawson, Grn.	...	2,067
C. maj.	....	7,998
(June '83, C. maj. 9,491)		

Wigan (Gtr. Manchester)
E. 72,064

*R. Stott, C.B.E., Lab.	......	33,955
K. R. Wade, C.	.....	13,493
K. J. White, L./All.	.....	7,732
Lab. maj.	....	20,462
(June '83, Lab. maj. 17,305)		

Wiltshire North
E. 80,712

*R. F. Needham, C.	....	35,309
C. S. M. Graham, L./All.	..	24,370
Mrs. C. Reid, Lab.	....	4,443
C. maj.	....	10,939
(June '83, C. maj. 7,232)		

Wimbledon (Gtr. London)
E. 63,353

Dr. C. Goodson-Wickes, C.		24,538
A. C. Slade, L./All.	....	13,237
Ms. C. M. Bickerstaff, Lab.		10,428
C. maj.	....	11,301
(June '83, C. maj. 11,546)		

Winchester (Hants)
E. 76,507

*J. E. D. D. Browne, C.	....	32,195
J. L. MacDonald, S.D.P./		
All.	....	24,716
F. C. Inglis, Lab.	....	4,028
Ms. J. P. Walker, Grn.	....	565
C. maj.	....	7,479
(June '83, C. maj. 13,047)		

Windsor and Maidenhead
(Berks)
E. 79,319

*Dr. A. Glyn, E.R.D., C.	....	33,980
S. J. Jackson, L./All.	......	16,144
Ms. H. B. De Lyon, Lab.	...	6,678
W. O. Board, Ind. C.	.....	1,938
P. Gordon, Grn.	......	711
Ms. P. H. Stephenson, B.T.		328
C. maj.	....	17,836
(June '83, C. maj. 18,203)		

Wirral (Merseyside)

SOUTH   E. 62,251

*G. B. Porter, C.	....	24,821
J. S. Swarbrooke, Lab.	...	13,858
P. N. Gilchrist, L./All.	...	10,779
C. maj.	....	10,963
(June '83, C. maj. 13,838)		

WEST   E. 63,597

*D. J. F. Hunt, M.B.E., C.	...	25,736
A. H. Dunn, Lab.	....	13,013
A. J. Brame, L./All.	......	10,015
D. Burton, Grn.	....	806
C. maj.	....	12,723
(June '83, C. maj. 15,151)		

Witney (Oxon)
E. 75,284

*Rt. Hon. D. R. Hurd, C.B.E.,		
C.	....	33,458
Miss M. E. Burton, L./All.		14,994
Ms. C. Collette, Lab.	.....	9,733
C. maj.	....	18,464
(June '83, C. maj. 12,712)		

Woking (Surrey)
E. 82,476

*C. G. D. Onslow, C.	......	35,990
P. Goldenberg, L./All.	....	19,446
Miss A. J. Pollack, Lab.	..	6,537
C. maj.	....	16,544
(June '83, C. maj. 16,237)		

Wokingham (Berks)
E. 85,474

J. A. Redwood, C.	....	39,808
J. C. Leston, L./All.	.....	19,421
P. J. Morgan, Lab.	....	5,622
C. maj.	....	20,387
(June '83, C. maj. 15,698)		

Wolverhampton (W. Midlands)

NORTH EAST   E. 63,464

Mrs. M. P. Hicks, C.	......	19,857
K. Purchase, Lab.	....	19,653
M. Pearson, L./All.	......	7,623
C. maj.	....	204
(June '83, Lab. maj. 214)		

SOUTH EAST   E. 55,710

D. Turner, Lab.	....	19,760
J. P. Mellor, C.	....	13,362
R. F. Whitehouse, L./All.	.	7,258
Lab. maj.	....	6,398
(June '83, Lab. maj. 5,012)		

SOUTH WEST   E. 68,586

*N. W. Budgen, C.	......	26,235
R. Lawrence, Lab.	....	15,917
B. Lamb, S.D.P./All.	.....	9,616
C. maj.	....	10,318
(June '83, C. maj. 11,520)		

Woodspring (Avon)
E. 76,289

*Sir P. Dean, C.	....	34,134
Mrs. C. R. Coleman, L./All.		16,282
D. L. T. Chapple, Lab.	....	8,717
Dr. B. R. Keeble, Grn.	....	1,208
C. maj.	....	17,852
(June '83, C. maj. 15,132)		

Woolwich (Gtr. London)
E. 58,071

*J. C. Cartwright, S.D.P./		
All.	....	17,137
J. Austin Walker, Lab.	...	15,200
A. Salter, C.	....	8,723
S.D.P./All.maj.	....	1,937
(June '83, S.D.P./All. maj. 2,725)		

Worcester
E. 68,980

*Rt. Hon. P. E. Walker,		
M.B.E., C.	....	25,504
M. J, Webb, Lab.	....	15,051
J. J. Caiger, S.D.P./All.	..	12,386
C. maj.	....	10,453
(June '83, C. maj. 10,871)		

Worcestershire

MID   E. 80,591

*M. E. Forth, C.	....	31,854
P. Pinfield, Lab.	....	16,943
E. Harwood, S.D.P./All.	..	12,954
C. maj.	....	14,911
(June '83, C. maj. 14,205)		

SOUTH   E. 77,237

*W. M. H. Spicer, C.	.....	32,277
P. J. Chandler, L./All.	....	18,632
R. J. Garnett, Lab.	....	6,374
G. M. H. Woodford, Grn.	.	1,089
C. maj.	....	13,645
(June '83, C. maj. 11,389)		

Workington (Cumbria)
E. 56,911

*D. N. Campbell-Savours,		
Lab.	....	24,019
Miss A. C. B. McIntosh, C.		17,000
G. W. Badger, L./All.	.....	4,853
Lab. maj.	....	7,019
(June '83, Lab. maj. 7,128)		

Worsley (Gtr. Manchester)
E. 73,208

*T. Lewis, Lab.	....	27,157
Mrs. V. Horman, C.	......	19,820
D. Cowpe, L./All.	....	9,507
Lab. maj.	....	7,337
(June '83, Lab. maj. 4,139)		

Worthing (W. Sussex)
E. 77,000

*Rt. Hon. T. L. Higgins, C.		34,573
B. A. Clare, L./All.	....	16,072
J. Deen, Lab.	....	5,387
C. maj.	....	18,501
(June '83, C. maj. 15,253)		

The Wrekin (Salop)
E. 82,520

B. J. Grocott, Lab.	....	27,681
*P. W. Hawksley, C.	......	26,225
G. Cook, S.D.P./All.	.....	10,737
Lab. maj.	....	1,456
(June '83, C. maj. 1,331)		

Wycombe (Bucks)
E. 71,918

*R. W. Whitney, O.B.E., C.	..	28,209
T. E. G. Hayhoe, S.D.P./		
All.	....	14,390
J. R. W. Huddart, Lab.	...	9,773
C. maj.	....	13,819
(June '83, C. maj. 13,197)		

Wyre (Lancs)
E. 67,066

K. D. R. Mans, C.	....	26,800
I. C. Murdoch, S.D.P./All.		12,139
P. Ainscough, Lab.	......	10,725
R. Brown, Grn.	....	874
C. maj.	....	14,661
(June '83, C. maj. 14,811)		

Wyre Forest (H & W)
E. 70,784

A. M. V. Coombs, C.	.....	25,877
A. J. Batchelor, L./All.	...	18,653
N. Knowles, Lab.	....	10,365
C. maj.	....	7,224
(June '83, C. maj. 8,177)		

Yeovil (Somerset)
E. 70,390

*J. J. D. Ashdown, L./All. .	28,841
G. D. S. Sandeman, C.	23,141
J. Fitzmaurice, Lab.	4,099
L./All. maj.	5,700
(June '83, L./All. maj. 3,406)	

York (N. Yorks)
E. 79,297

*C. R. Gregory, C.	25,880
H. Bayley, Lab.	25,733
J. V. Cable, S.D.P./All. ..	9,898
A. D. Dunnett, Grn.	637
C. maj.	147
(June '83, C. maj. 3,647)	

WALES

Aberavon (W. Glam)
E. 52,280

*Rt. Hon. J. Morris, Q.C., Lab.	27,126
Mrs. M. Harris, L./All. ...	6,517
P. Warrick, C.	5,861
Miss A. Howells, P.C.	1,124
Lab. maj.	20,609
(June '83, Lab. maj. 15,539)	

Alyn and Deeside (Clwyd)
E. 58,674

*S. B. Jones, Lab.	22,916
N. J. Twilley, C.	16,500
E. C. H. Owen, S.D.P./All.	7,273
J. D. Rogers, P.C.	478
Lab. maj.	6,416
(June '83, Lab. maj. 1,368)	

Blaenau Gwent
E. 56,011

*Rt.Hon. M. M. Foot, Lab. ..	32,820
A. R. Taylor, C.	4,959
D. I. McBride, L./All.	3,847
S. Morgan, P.C.	1,621
Lab. maj.	27,861
(June '83, Lab. maj. 23,705)	

Brecon and Radnor (Powys)
E. 49,394

*R. A. L. Livsey, L./All. ...	14,509
J. P. Evans, C.	14,453
F. R. Willey, Lab.	12,180
J. H. Davies, P.C.	535
L./All. maj.	56
(June '83, C. maj. 8,784)	
(July '84, L./All. maj. 559)	

Bridgend (Mid Glam)
E. 57,389

W. J. Griffiths, Lab.	21,893
*P. C. Hubbard-Miles, C. ..	17,513
R. Smart, S.D.P./All.	5,590
Miss L. McAllister, P.C. ..	1,065
Lab. maj.	4,380
(June '83, C. maj. 1,327)	

Caernarfon (Gwynedd)
E. 45,661

*D. W. Wigley, P.C.	20,338
F. F. E. Aubel, C.	7,536
D. Rhys Williams, Lab. ...	5,632
J. H. Parsons, L./All.	2,103
P.C. maj.	12,802
(June '83, P.C. maj. 10,989)	

Caerphilly (Mid Glam)
E. 64,154

*R. Davies, Lab.	28,698
M. E. Powell, C.	9,531
M. G. Butlin, L./All.	6,923
L. G. Whittle, P.C.	3,955
Lab. maj.	19,167
(June '83, Lab. maj. 11,553)	

Cardiff (S. Glam)

CENTRAL E. 52,980

*I. Grist, C.	15,241
J. O. Jones, Lab.	13,255
M. J. German, L./All.	12,062
Ms. S. M. Caiach, P.C.	535
C. maj.	1,986
(June '83, C. maj. 3,452)	

NORTH E. 54,704

*G. H. Jones, C.	20,061
S. H. Tarbet, Lab.	11,827
A. W. Jeremy, S.D.P./All.	11,725
Ms. E. M. Bush, P.C.	692
C. maj.	8,234
(June '83, C. maj. 6,848)	

SOUTH AND PENARTH E. 58,714

A. E. Michael, Lab.	20,956
G. J. J. Neale, C.	16,382
Mrs. J. E. Randerson, L./All.	6,900
Ms. S. A. Edwards, P.C. ..	599
Lab. maj.	4,574
(June '83, Lab. maj. 2,276)	

WEST E. 57,363

H. R. Morgan, Lab.	20,329
*S. Terlezki, C.	16,284
R. G. Drake, S.D.P./All. ..	7,300
P. J. Keelan, P.C.	736
Lab. maj.	4,045
(June '83, C. maj. 1,774)	

Carmarthen (Dyfed)
E. 65,252

A. W. Williams, Lab.	19,128
R. Richards, C.	14,811
H. T. Edwards, P.C.	12,457
G. G. Jones, S.D.P./All. ..	7,203
G. E. Oubridge, Grn.	481
Lab. maj.	4,317
(June '83, Lab. maj. 1,154)	

Ceredigion and Pembroke North
(Dyfed)
E. 63,141

*G. W. Howells, L./All.	17,683
O. J. Williams, C.	12,983
J. R. Davies, Lab.	8,965
C. G. Davis, P.C.	7,848
Mrs. M. A. Wakefield, Grn.	821
L./All. maj.	4,700
(June '83, L./All. maj. 5,639)	

Clwyd

NORTH WEST E. 66,118

*Sir A. J. C. Meyer, Bt., C. .	24,116
K. L. Thomas, Lab.	12,335
O. G. Griffiths, L./All.	11,279
R. K. Davies, P.C.	1,966
C. maj.	11,781
(June '83, C. maj. 9,989)	

SOUTH WEST E. 58,158

M. D. Jones, Lab.	16,701
*R. L. Harvey, C.	15,673
R. T. Ellis, S.D.P./All. ...	10,778
E. L. Jones, P.C.	3,987
Lab. maj.	1,028
(June '83, C. maj. 1,551)	

Conwy (Gwynedd)
E. 52,862

*I. W. P. Roberts, C.	15,730
J. R. Roberts, L./All.	12,706
Ms. E. Williams, Lab.	9,049
R. Davies, P.C.	3,177
C. maj.	3,024
(June '83, C. maj. 4,268)	

Cynon Valley (Mid Glam)
E. 49,621

*Mrs. A. Clwyd, Lab.	26,222
K. D. Butler, S.D.P./All. ..	4,651
M. A. Bishop, C.	4,638
Mrs. D. L. Richards, P.C. .	2,549
Lab. maj.	21,571
(June '83, Lab. maj. 13,074)	
(May '84, Lab. maj. 12,835)	

Delyn (Clwyd)
E. 63,541

*K. W. T. Raffan, C.	21,728
D. G. Hanson, Lab.	20,504
D. J. Evans, L./All.	8,913
D. J. Owen, P.C.	1,329
C. maj.	1,224
(June '83, C. maj. 5,944)	

Gower (W. Glam)
E. 58,871

*G. L. Wardell, Lab.	22,138
G. A. L. Price, C.	16,374
D. H. O. Elliott, S.D.P./All.	7,645
J. G. M. Edwards, P.C. ...	1,341
Lab. maj.	5,764
(June '83, Lab. maj. 1,205)	

Islwyn (Gwent)
E. 50,414

*Rt. Hon. N. G. Kinnock, Lab.	28,901
J. Twitchen, C.	5,954
Ms. J. Gasson, S.D.P./All.	3,746
A. Richards, P.C.	1,932
Lab. maj.	22,947
(June '83, Lab. maj. 14,380)	

Llanelli (Dyfed)
E. 63,845

*Rt. Hon. D. J. D. Davies, Lab.	29,506
P. J. Circus, C.	8,571
M. J. Shrewsbury, L./All. .	6,714
A. Price, P.C.	5,088
Lab. maj.	20,935
(June '83, Lab. maj. 13,606)	

Meirionnydd Nant Conwy
(Gwynedd)
E. 31,632

*D. E. Thomas, P.C.	10,392
D. T. Jones, C.	7,366
H. G. Roberts, Lab.	4,397
D. L. Roberts, S.D.P./All.	3,847
P.C. maj.	3,026

(June '83, P.C. maj. 2,643)

Merthyr Tydfil and Rhymney
(Mid Glam)
E. 58,285

*E. Rowlands, Lab.	33,400
N. M. Walters, C.	5,270
P. Verma, L./All.	3,573
Mrs. J. Davies, P.C.	2,085
Lab. maj.	28,130

(June '83, Lab. maj. 22,730)

Monmouth (Gwent)
E. 58,468

*Sir J. Stradling Thomas, C.	22,387
Ms. K. Gass, Lab.	13,037
C. Lindley, S.D.P./All.	11,313
Mrs. S. Meredudd, P.C.	363
C. maj.	9,350

(June '83, C. maj. 9,343)

Montgomery (Powys)
E. 39,808

*A. C. Carlile, Q.C. L./All.	14,729
D.M. Evans, C.	12,171
E. D. W. Llewellyn Jones, Lab.	3,304
C. Clowes, P.C.	1,412
L./All. maj.	2,558

(June '83, L./All. maj. 668)

Neath (W. Glam)
E. 55,261

*D. R. Coleman, Lab.	27,612
M. R. T. Howe, C.	7,034
J. Warman, S.D.P./All.	6,132
H. John, P.C.	2,792
Lab. maj.	20,578

(June '83, Lab. maj. 13,604)

Newport (Gwent)

EAST E. 52,199

*R. J. Hughes, Lab.	20,518
G. R. Webster-Gardiner, C.	13,454
Mrs. F. A. David, S.D.P./All.	7,383
G. Butler, P.C.	458
Lab. maj.	7,064

(June '83, Lab. maj. 2,630)

WEST E. 55,455

P. P. Flynn, Lab.	20,887
*M. N. F. Robinson, C.	18,179
G. W. Roddick, L./All.	5,903
D. J. Bevan, P.C.	377
Lab. maj.	2,708

(June '83, C. maj. 581)

Ogmore (Mid Glam)
E. 51,255

*R. Powell, Lab.	28,462
M. F. Barratt, C.	6,170
Ms. M. James, S.D.P./All.	3,954
J. G. Jones, P.C.	1,791
T. H. Spence, Ind. Lab.	652
Lab. maj.	22,292

(June '83, Lab. maj. 17,364)

Pembroke (Dyfed)
E. 70,360

N. J. Bennett, C.	23,314
B. J. Rayner, Lab.	17,614
P. E. C. Jones, L./All.	14,832
O. Osmond, P.C.	1,119
C. maj.	5,700

(June '83, C. maj. 9,356)

Pontypridd (Mid Glam)
E. 61,255

*B. T. John, Lab.	26,422
D. Swayne, C.	9,145
P. G. Sain-Ley-Berry, S.D.P./All.	8,865
D. L. Bowen, P.C.	2,498
Lab. maj.	17,277

(June '83, Lab. maj. 8,744)
(see also p. 276)

Rhondda (Mid Glam)
E. 60,931

*A. R. Rogers, Lab.	35,015
G. R. Davies, P.C.	4,261
J. R. YorkWilliams, S.D.P./All.	3,930
S. H. Reid, C.	3,611
A. True, Comm.	869
Lab. maj.	30,754

(June '83, Lab. maj. 21,370)

Swansea (W. Glam)

EAST E. 57,200

*D. Anderson, Lab.	27,478
R. D. Lewis, C.	8,140
Rev. D. W. Thomas, L./All.	6,380
C. Reid, P.C.	1,145
Lab. maj.	19,338

(June '83, Lab. maj. 13,535)

WEST E. 59,836

*Rt. Hon. A. J. Williams, Lab.	22,089
N. M. Evans, C.	15,027
M. Ford, L./All.	7,019
N. Williams, P.C.	902
Mrs. J. V. Harman, Grn.	469
Lab. maj.	7,062

(June '83, Lab. maj. 2,350)

Torfaen (Gwent)
E. 59,896

P. P. Murphy, Lab.	26,577
G. R. Blackburn, L./All.	9,027
R. Gordon, C.	8,632
J. Evans, P.C.	577
M. Witherden, Grn.	450
Lab. maj.	17,550

(June '83, Lab. maj. 8,285)

Vale of Glamorgan (S. Glam)
E. 65,310

*Sir H. R. Gower, C.	24,229
J. W. P. Smith, Lab.	17,978
D. K. Davies, S.D.P./All.	8,633
P. G. Williams, P.C.	946
C. maj.	6,251

(June '83, C. maj. 10,393)
(see also p. 276)

Wrexham (Clwyd)
E. 62,401

*Dr. J. C. Marek, Lab.	22,144
R. H. W. Graham-Palmer, C.	17,992
M. Thomas, L./All.	9,808
D. Watkins, P.C.	539
Lab. maj.	4,152

(June '83, Lab. maj. 424)

Ynys Môn/Anglesey
(Gwynedd)
E. 52,633

I. W. Jones, P.C.	18,580
R. Evans, C.	14,282
C. Parry, Lab.	7,252
I. L. Evans, S.D.P./All.	2,863
P.C. maj.	4,298

(June '83, C. maj. 1,684)

SCOTLAND

Aberdeen (Grampian)

NORTH E. 63,214

*R. Hughes, Lab.	24,145
R. Smith, S.D.P./All.	7,867
Mrs. G. E. C. Scanlan, C.	6,330
P. Greenhorn, S.N.P.	5,827
Lab. maj.	16,278

(June '83, Lab. maj. 9,144)

SOUTH E. 62,943

F. Doran, Lab.	15,917
*G. P. Malone, C.	14,719
I. G. Philip, S.D.P./All.	8,844
M. F. Weir, S.N.P.	2,776
Lab. maj.	1,198

(June '83, C. maj. 3,581)

Angus East (Tayside)
E. 61,060

A. Welsh, S.N.P.	19,536
*P. L. Fraser, Q.C., C.	17,992
R. Mennie, Lab.	4,971
I. Mortimer, S.D.P./All.	3,592
S.N.P. maj.	1,544

(June '83, C. maj. 3,527)

Argyll and Bute (S'clyde)
E. 48,700

Mrs. J. R. Michie, L./All.	13,726
*J. J. MacKay, C.	12,332
R. Shaw, S.N.P.	6,297
D. Tierney, Lab.	4,437
L./All. maj.	1,394

(June '83, C. maj. 3,844)

Ayr (S'clyde)
E. 66,450

*Rt. Hon. G. K. H. Younger, T.D., C.	20,942
K. MacDonald, Lab.	20,760
K. M. Moody, L./All.	7,859
C. Weir, S.N.P.	3,548
C. maj.	182

(June '83, C. maj. 7,987)

Banff and Buchan (Grampian)
E. 62,149

A. E. A. Salmond, S.N.P.	.	19,462
A. McQuarrie, C.	....	17,021
G. M. Burness, *S.D.P./All.*		4,211
J. Livie, *Lab.*	....	3,281
S.N.P. maj.	....	2,441
(June '83, C. maj. 937)		

Caithness and Sutherland
(H'land)
E. 31,279

R. A. R. Maclennan,		
S.D.P./All.	....	12,338
R. L. Hamilton, *C.*	......	3,844
A. Byron, *Lab.*	....	3,437
K. MacGregor, *S.N.P.*	.....	2,371
W. A. Mowat, *Ind. L.*	....	686
B. Planterose, *Grn.*	......	333
S.D.P./All. maj.		8,494
(June '83, S.D.P./All. maj. 6,843)		

**Carrick, Cumnock and Doon
Valley** (S'clyde)
E. 56,360

G. Foulkes, Lab.	....	25,669
S. Stevenson, *C.*	....	8,867
Mrs. M. Ali, *S.D.P./All.*	..	4,106
C. D. Calman, *S.N.P.*	.....	4,094
Lab. maj.	....	16,802
(June '83, Lab. maj. 11,370)		

Clackmannan (Central)
E. 49,083

M. J. O'Neill, Lab.	....	20,317
Dr. A. Macartney, *S.N.P.*	.	7,916
J. Parker, *C.*	....	5,620
Mrs. A. Watters, *S.D.P./*		
All.	....	3,961
Lab. maj.	....	12,401
(June '83, Lab. maj. 9,639)		

Clydebank and Milngavie
(S'clyde)
E. 50,152

A. Worthington, *Lab.*	....	22,528
K. Hirstwood, *C.*	......	6,224
R. Ackland, *S.D.P./All.*	....	5,891
S. Fisher, *S.N.P.*	....	4,935
Lab. maj.	....	16,304
(June '83, Lab. maj. 7,715)		

Clydesdale (S'clyde)
E. 61,620

J. Hood, *Lab.*	....	21,826
R. Robertson, *C.*	....	11,324
J. Boyle, *S.D.P./All.*	.....	7,909
M. Russell, *S.N.P.*	......	7,125
Lab. maj.	....	10,502
(June '83, Lab. maj. 4,866)		

Cumbernauld and Kilsyth
(S'clyde)
E. 45,427

N. Hogg, Lab.	....	21,385
T. Johnston, *S.N.P.*	......	6,982
C. S. Deans, *S.D.P./All.*	...	4,059
Mrs. A. E. Thomson, *C.*	...	3,227
Lab. maj.	....	14,403
(June '83, Lab. maj. 9,928)		

Cunninghame (S'clyde)

NORTH   *E.* 54,817

B. D. H. Wilson, *Lab.*	....	19,061
J. A. Corrie, C.	....	14,594
D. J. Herbison, *S.D.P./All.*		5,185
M. Brown, *S.N.P.*	....	4,076
Lab. maj.	....	4,467
(June '83, C. maj. 1,637)		

SOUTH   *E.* 49,842

D. Lambie, Lab.	....	22,728
E. R. Gibson, *C.*	....	6,095
J. A. Boss, *L./All.*	....	4,426
Mrs. K. Ullrich, *S.N.P.*	....	4,115
Lab. maj.	....	16,633
(June '83, Lab. maj. 11,768)		

Dumbarton (S'clyde)
E. 58,968

J. McFall, *Lab.*	....	19,778
R. F. Graham, *C.*	....	14,556
R. Mowbray, *S.D.P./All.*	..	6,060
Ms. J. Herriot, *S.N.P.*	....	5,564
Lab. maj.	....	5,222
(June '83, Lab. maj. 2,115)		

Dumfries (D & G)
E. 59,347

Sir H. S. P. Monro, C.	....	18,785
Ms. C. W. Phillips, *Lab.*	..	11,292
J. R. McCall, *S.D.P./All.*	..	8,064
T. McAlpine, *S.N.P.*	.....	6,391
P. M. Thomas, *Grn.*	......	349
C. maj.	....	7,493
(June '83, C. maj. 8,694)		

Dundee (Tayside)

EAST   *E.* 60,805

J. McAllion, *Lab.*	....	19,539
R. G. Wilson, S.N.P.	.....	18,524
P. Cook, *C.*	....	5,938
Mrs. M. von Romberg, *L./*		
All.	....	2,143
Lab. maj.	....	1,015
(June '83, S.N.P. maj. 5,016)		

WEST   *E.* 61,926

E. Ross, Lab.	....	24,916
J. A. Donnelly, *C.*	....	8,390
A. N. Morgan, *S.N.P.*	.....	7,164
Ms. R. Lonie, *S.D.P./All.*	.	5,922
S. R. Mathewson, *Comm.*	.	308
Lab. maj.	....	16,526
(June '83, Lab. maj. 10,150)		

Dunfermline (Fife)

EAST   *E.* 51,175

Dr. J. G. Brown, Lab.	....	25,381
C. Shenton, *C.*	....	5,792
Ms. E. Harris, *L./All.*	.....	4,122
Mrs. A. McGarny, *S.N.P.*	.	3,901
Lab. maj.	....	19,589
(June '83, Lab. maj. 11,301)		

WEST   *E.* 51,063

R. G. Douglas, Lab.	.....	18,493
P. R. Gallie, *C.*	....	9,091
F. A. Moyes, *S.D.P./All.*	..	8,288
G. Hughes, *S.N.P.*	....	3,435
Lab. maj.	....	9,402
(June '83, Lab. maj. 2,474)		

East Kilbride (S'clyde)
E. 63,097

A. P. Ingram, Lab.	....	24,491
D. R. E. Sullivan, *S.D.P./*		
All.	....	11,867
P. M. Walker, *C.*	....	7,344
J. H. Taggart, *S.N.P.*	.....	6,275
Lab. maj.	....	12,624
(June '83, Lab. maj. 4,336)		

East Lothian
E. 65,046

J. D. Home Robertson,		
Lab.	....	24,583
S. M. Langdon, *C.*	....	14,478
A. Robinson, *L./All.*	......	7,929
A. Burgon-Lyon, *S.N.P.*	..	3,727
A. Marland, *Grn.*	....	451
Lab. maj.	....	10,105
(June '83, Lab. maj. 6,241)		

Eastwood (S'clyde)
E. 61,872

J. A. Stewart, C.	....	19,388
R. Leishman, *S.D.P./All.*	.	13,374
P. A. Grant-Hutchison,		
Lab.	....	12,305
J. Findlay, *S.N.P.*	....	4,033
C. maj.	....	6,014
(June '83, C. maj. 8,595)		

Edinburgh (Lothian)

CENTRAL   *E.* 59,529

A. M. Darling, Lab.	......	16,502
Sir A. Fletcher, C.	....	14,240
A. Myles, *L./All.*	....	7,333
B. Shaw, *S.N.P.*	....	2,559
Mrs. L. M. Hendry, *Grn.*	..	438
Lab. maj.	....	2,262
(June '83, C. maj. 2,566)		

EAST   *E.* 48,895

G. S. Strang, Lab.	....	18,257
J. F. Renz, *C.*	....	8,962
Mrs. J. Aitken, *L./All.*	....	5,592
M. Bovey, *S.N.P.*	....	3,434
Lab. maj.	....	9,295
(June '83, Lab. maj. 5,866)		

LEITH   *E.* 60,359

R. D. M. Brown, Lab.	....	21,104
D. A. Y. Menzies, *C.*	.....	9,777
Mrs. S. Wells, *S.D.P./All.*	.	7,843
W. Morrison, *S.N.P.*	.....	4,045
Lab. maj.	....	11,327
(June '83, Lab. maj. 4,973)		

PENTLANDS   *E.* 58,125

Rt. Hon. M. L. Rifkind, Q.C.,		
C.	....	17,278
M. Lazarowicz, *Lab.*	.....	13,533
K. A. Smith, *S.D.P./All.*	..	11,072
D. N. MacCormick, *S.N.P.*		3,264
C. maj.	....	3,745
(June '83, C. maj. 4,309)		

SOUTH   *E.* 63,842

N. Griffiths, Lab.	....	18,211
*M. A. F. J. K. Ancram (Earl		
of Ancram), C.*	....	16,352
D. A. Graham, *S.D.P./All.*		10,900
Mrs. R. Moore, *S.N.P.*	....	2,455
Mrs. R. Clark, *Grn.*	......	440
Lab. maj.	....	1,859
(June '83, C. maj. 3,655)		

WEST *E.* 62,214
*Lord James Douglas-Hamilton, C. 18,450
D. G. King, *L./All.* 17,216
M. McGregor, *Lab.* 10,957
N. Irons, *S.N.P.* 2,774
C. maj. 1,234
(June '83, C. maj. 498)

Falkirk (Central)

EAST *E.* 52,564
*H. Ewing, Lab. 21,379
K. H. Brookes, *C.* 7,356
R. N. F. Halliday, *S.N.P.* . 6,056
Mrs. E. G. Dick, *S.D.P./All.* 4,624
Lab. maj. 14,023
(June '83, Lab. maj. 10,061)

WEST *E.* 50,222
*D. A. Canavan, Lab. 20,256
D. R. D. Thomas, *C.* 6,704
I. R. Goldie, *S.N.P.* 6,696
M. J. Harris, *L./All.* 4,841
Lab. maj. 13,552
(June '83, Lab. maj. 8,978)

Fife

CENTRAL *E.* 56,090
H. B. McLeish, *Lab.* 22,827
R. E. Aird, *C.* 7,118
Mrs. T. M. Little, *L./All.* .. 6,487
D. Hood, *S.N.P.* 6,296
Lab. maj. 15,709
(June '83, Lab. maj. 7,794)

NORTH EAST *E.* 52,266
W. M. Campbell, C.B.E. Q.C., *L./All.* 17,868
*J. S. B. Henderson, C. 16,421
A. M. E. Gannon, *Lab.* 2,947
F. D. Roche, *S.N.P.* 2,616
L./All. maj. 1,447
(June '83, C. maj. 2,185)

Galloway and Upper Nithsdale (D & G)
E. 53,429

*I. B. Lang, C. 16,592
S. F. Norris, *S.N.P.* 12,919
J. McKercher, *L./All.* 6,001
J. Gray, *Lab.* 5,298
D. Kenny, *Ret.* 230
C. maj. 3,673
(June '83, C. maj. 5,461)

Glasgow (S'clyde)

CATHCART *E.* 49,307
*J. A. Maxton, Lab. 19,623
W. A. Harvey, *C.* 8,420
Miss M. Craig, *S.D.P./All.* 5,722
W. A. Steven, *S.N.P.* 3,883
Lab. maj. 11,203
(June '83, Lab. maj. 4,230)

CENTRAL *E.* 51,137
*R. McTaggart, Lab. 21,619
B. Jenkin, *C.* 4,366
Dr. J. Bryden, *L./All.* 3,528
A. Wilson, *S.N.P.* 3,339
A. Brooks, *Grn.* 290
J. P. McGoldrick, *Comm.* . 265
D. Owen, *R.F.* 126
Lab. maj. 17,253
(June '83, Lab. maj. 10,962)
(see also p. 276)

GARSCADDEN *E.* 47,958
*D. C. Dewar, Lab. 23,178
A. Brophy, *S.N.P.* 4,201
T. N. A. Begg, *C.* 3,660
S. Callison, *S.D.P./All.* ... 3,211
Lab. maj. 18,977
(June '83, Lab. maj. 13,474)

GOVAN *E.* 50,616
*Rt. Hon. B. Millan, Lab. .. 24,071
A. Ferguson, *S.D.P./All.* . 4,562
Mrs. J. R. Girsman, *C.* ... 4,411
F. McCabe, *S.N.P.* 3,851
D. Chalmers, *Comm.* 237
Lab. maj. 19,509
(June '83, Lab. maj. 13,057)
(see also p. 276)

HILLHEAD *E.* 57,836
G. Galloway, *Lab.* 17,958
*Rt Hon. R. H. Jenkins, S.D.P./All. 14,707
B. D. Cooklin, *C.* 6,048
W. Kidd, *S.N.P.* 2,713
A. Whitelaw, *Grn.* 443
Lab. maj. 3,251
(June '83, S.D.P./All. maj. 1,164)

MARYHILL *E.* 52,371
Mrs. M. Fyfe, *Lab.* 23,482
Miss E. M. A. Attwooll, *L./All.* 4,118
G. Roberts, *S.N.P.* 3,895
S. R. R. Kirk, *C.* 3,307
D. Spaven, *Grn.* 539
Lab. maj. 19,364
(June '83, Lab. maj. 11,203)

POLLOK *E.* 51,396
J. Dunnachie, *Lab.* 23,239
Mrs. G. French, *C.* 5,256
J. Shearer, *L./All.* 4,445
A. Doig, *S.N.P.* 3,528
D. Fogg, *Grn.* 362
Lab. maj. 17,983
(June '83, Lab. maj. 11,532)

PROVAN *E.* 43,744
J. Wray, *Lab.* 22,032
W. Ramsay, *S.N.P.* 3,660
Miss A. Strutt, *C.* 2,336
J. Morrison, *S.D.P./All.* .. 2,189
Lab. maj. 18,372
(June '83, Lab. maj. 15,385)

RUTHERGLEN *E.* 57,313
T. McAvoy, *Lab.* 24,790
R. E. Brown, *L./All.* 10,795
G. Hamilton, *C.* 5,088
J. Higgins, *S.N.P.* 3,584
Lab. maj. 13,995
(June '83, Lab. maj. 9,126)

SHETTLESTON *E.* 53,604
*D. Marshall, Lab. 23,991
J. M. S. Fisher, *C.* 5,010
J. MacVicar, *S.N.P.* 4,807
Miss P. Clarke, *L./All.* ... 3,942
Lab. maj. 18,981
(June '83, Lab. maj. 12,416)

SPRINGBURN *E.* 51,563
*M. J. Martin, Lab. 25,617
B. O'Hara, *S.N.P.* 3,554
M. Call, *C.* 2,870
D. Rennie, *L./All.* 2,746
Lab. maj. 22,063
(June '83, Lab. maj. 17,599)

Gordon (Grampian)
E. 73,479

*M. G. Bruce, L./All. 26,770
P. R. Leckie, *C.* 17,251
Mrs. M. C. Morrell, *Lab.* .. 6,228
G. E. Wright, *S.N.P.* 3,876
L./All. maj. 9,519
(June '83, L./All. maj. 850)

Greenock and Port Glasgow (S'clyde)
E. 57,756

*Dr. N. A. Godman, Lab. ... 27,848
J. H. Moody, *L./All.* 7,793
T. J. D. Pearson, *C.* 4,199
T. Lenehan, *S.N.P.* 3,721
Lab. maj. 20,055
(June '83, Lab. maj. 4,625)

Hamilton (S'clyde)
E. 62,205

*G. I. M. Robertson, Lab. .. 28,563
G. S. Mond, *C.* 6,901
T. Mackay, *L./All.* 6,302
C. Crossley, *S.N.P.* 6,093
Lab. maj. 21,662
(June '83, Lab. maj. 15,019)

Inverness, Nairn and Lochaber (H'land)
E. 66,743

*Sir D. R. Johnston, L./All. 17,422
D. Stewart, *Lab.* 11,991
Mrs. A. T. Keswick, *C.* ... 10,901
N. P. Johnson, *S.N.P.* 7,001
L./All. maj. 5,431
(June '83, L./All. maj. 7,298)

Kilmarnock and Loudoun (Grampian)
E. 62,648

*W. McKelvey, Lab. 23,713
Mrs. A. K. Bates, *C.* 9,586
G. Leslie, *S.N.P.* 8,881
P. Kerr, *S.D.P./All.* 6,698
Lab. maj. 14,127
(June '83, Lab. maj. 8,800)

Kincardine and Deeside (Grampian)
E. 63,587

*Rt. Hon. A. L. Buchanan-Smith, C. 19,438
N. R. Stephen, *L./All.* 17,375
J. K. Thomaneck, *Lab.* 7,624
Mrs. F. E. Duncan, *S.N.P.* . 3,082
Mrs. L. M. Perica, *Grn.* ... 299
C. maj. 2,063
(June '83, C. maj. 7,796)

Kirkcaldy (Fife)
E. 53,439

Dr. L. G. Moonie, *Lab.* ... 20,281
I. G. Mitchell, *C.* 8,711
D. Stewart, *S.D.P./All.* ... 7,118
W. A. R. Mullin, *S.N.P.* .. 4,794
Lab. maj. 11,570
(June '83, Lab. maj. 5,331)

Linlithgow (Lothian)
E. 59,542

*T. Dalyell, *Lab.* 21,869
J. Sillars, *S.N.P.* 11,496
T. R. Armstrong Wilson, *C.* 6,828
Mrs. H. McDade, *S.D.P./
All.* 5,840
J. Glassford, *Comm.* 154
Lab. maj. 10,373
(June '83, Lab. maj. 11,361)

Livingston (Lothian)
E. 56,583

*R. F. Cook, *Lab.* 19,110
R. McCreadie, *L./All.* 8,005
Dr. M. N. A. Mayall, *C.* ... 7,860
K. MacAskill, *S.N.P.* 6,969
Lab. maj. 11,105
(June '83, Lab. maj. 4,951)

Midlothian
E. 60,549

*A. Eadie, B.E.M., *Lab.* 22,553
A. R. Dewar, *S.D.P./All.* ... 10,300
Dr. F. Riddell, *C.* 8,527
I. Chisholm, *S.N.P.* 4,947
I. Smith, *Grn.* 412
Lab. maj. 12,253
(June '83, Lab. maj. 6,156)

Monklands (S'clyde)
EAST E. 49,644

*Rt. Hon. J. Smith, Q.C., *Lab.* 22,649
J. Love, *C.* 6,260
K. Gibson, *S.N.P.* 4,790
Mrs. S. Grieve, *L./All.* 3,442
Lab. maj. 16,389
(June '83, Lab. maj. 9,799)

WEST E. 50,874

*T. Clarke, C.B.E., *Lab.* ... 24,499
G. Lind, *C.* 6,166
Ms. A. McQueen, *S.D.P./
All.* 4,408
K. Bovey, *S.N.P.* 4,260
Lab. maj. 18,333
(June '83, Lab. maj. 12,264)

Moray (Grampian)
E. 62,201

Mrs. M. Ewing, *S.N.P.* ... 19,510
*A. Pollock, *C.* 15,825
C. R. C. Smith, *Lab.* 5,118
D. G. M. Skene, *L./All.* ... 4,724
S.N.P. maj. 3,685
(June '83, C. maj. 1,713)

Motherwell (S'clyde)
NORTH E. 57,632

Dr. J. Reid, *Lab.* 29,825
A. Currie, *S.N.P.* 6,230
R. Hargrave, *C.* 4,939
G. Swift, *L./All.* 3,558
Lab. maj. 23,595
(June '83, Lab. maj. 17,894)

SOUTH E. 52,127

*Dr. J. W. Bray, *Lab.* 22,957
J. Wright, *S.N.P.* 6,027
J. S. Bercow, *C.* 5,702
W. R. MacGregor, *S.D.P./
All.* 4,463
R. Somerville, *Comm.* 223
Lab. maj. 16,930
(June '83, Lab. maj. 12,349)

Orkney and Shetland (Islands)
E. 31,047

*J. R. Wallace, *L./All.* 8,881
R. W. A. Jenkins, *C.* 4,959
J. H. Aberdein, *Lab.* 3,995
J. Goodlad, *O.S.M.* 3,095
G. K. Collister, *Grn.* 389
L./All. maj. 3,922
(June '83, L./All. maj. 4,150)

Paisley (S'clyde)
NORTH E. 49,487

*A. S. Adams, *Lab.* 20,193
Mrs. E. F. Laing, *C.* 5,751
Miss E. P. McCartin,
S.D.P./All. 5,741
I. Taylor, *S.N.P.* 4,696
Lab. maj. 14,442
(June '83, Lab. maj. 7,587)

SOUTH E. 51,127

*N. F. Buchan, *Lab.* 21,611
A. M. Carmichael, *L./All* . 5,826
Miss D. A. Williamson, *C.* 5,644
J. R. Mitchell, *S.N.P.* 5,398
Lab. maj. 15,785
(June '83, Lab. maj. 6,529)

Perth and Kinross (Tayside)
E. 63,443

*N. H. Fairbairn, Q.C., *C.* .. 18,716
J. M. Fairlie, *S.N.P.* 13,040
S. Donaldson, *L./All.* 7,969
J. W. McConnell, *Lab.* ... 7,490
C. maj. 5,676
(June '83, C. maj. 6,733)

Renfrew West and Inverclyde
(S'clyde)
E. 56,189

T. Graham, *Lab.* 17,525
*Mrs. A. A. McCurley, *C.* .. 13,472
Dr. J. D. Mabon, *S.D.P./
All.* 9,669
C. Campbell, *S.N.P.* 4,578
Lab. maj. 4,053
(June '83, C. maj. 1,322)

Ross, Cromarty and Skye
(H'land)
E. 52,369

*C. P. Kennedy, *S.D.P./All.* 18,809
F. Spencer Nairn, *C.* 7,490
M. M. MacMillan, *Lab.* ... 7,287
R. M. Gibson, *S.N.P* 4,492
S.D.P./All. maj. 11,319
(June '83, S.D.P./All. maj. 1,704)

Roxburgh and Berwickshire
(Borders)
E. 43,140

*A. J. Kirkwood, *L./All.* ... 16,388
Dr. L. Fox, *C.* 12,380
T. Luckhurst, *Lab.* 2,944
M. Douglas, *S.N.P.* 1,586
L./All. maj. 4,008
(June '83, L./All. maj. 3,396)

Stirling (Central)
E. 57,836

*M. B. Forsyth, *C.* 17,591
M. Connarty, *Lab.* 16,643
I. McFarlane, *L./All.* 6,804
I. M. Lawson, *S.N.P.* 4,897
C. maj. 948
(June '83, C. maj. 5,133)

Strathkelvin and Bearsden
(S'clyde)
E. 62,676

S. L. Galbraith, *Lab.* 19,639
*M. W. Hirst, *C.* 17,187
J. Bannerman, *L./All.* 11,034
G. Paterson, *S.N.P.* 3,654
Lab. maj. 2,452
(June '83, C. maj. 3,700)

Tayside North
E. 53,985

*W. C. Walker, *C.* 18,307
K. J. N. Guild, *S.N.P.* 13,291
P. F. Regent, *L./All.* 5,201
J. Whytock, *Lab.* 3,550
C. maj. 5,016
(June '83, C. maj. 10,099)

**Tweeddale, Ettrick and Lauder-
dale** (Borders)
E. 37,875

*Rt. Hon. D. M. S. Steel, *L./
All.* 14,599
Mrs. S. Finlay-Maxwell, *C.* 8,657
N. Glen, *Lab.* 3,320
A. Lumsden, *S.N.P.* 2,660
L./All. maj. 5,942
(June '83, L./All. maj. 8,539)

Western Isles (Islands)
E. 23,507

C. A. MacDonald, *Lab.* ... 7,041
I. Smith, *S.N.P.* 4,701
K. MacIver, *S.D.P./All.* ... 3,419
M. Morrison, *C.* 1,336
Lab. maj. 2,340
(June '83, S.N.P. maj. 3,712)

NORTHERN IRELAND

Antrim
EAST E. 60,587

*J. R. Beggs, *O.U.P.* 23,942
S. Neeson, *All.* 8,582
A. Kelly, *W.P.* 936
O.U.P. maj. 15,360
(June '83, OUP. maj. 367)
(Jan. '86, O.U.P. maj. 24,981)

NORTH E. 65,733

*Rev. I. R. K. Paisley,
D.U.P.* 28,383
S. Farren, *S.D.L.P.* 5,149
G. Williams, *All.* 5,140
S. Reagan, *S.F.* 2,633
D.U.P. maj. 23,234
(June '83, D.U.P. maj. 13,173)
(Jan. '86, D.U.P. maj. 33,024)

SOUTH *E.* 61,649
*C. Forsythe, O.U.P. 25,395
G. Mawhinney, *All.* 5,808
D. McClelland, *S.D.L.P.* .. 3,611
H. Cushinan, *S.F.* 1,592
    O.U.P. maj. 19,587
    (June '83, O.U.P. maj. 6,792)
    (Jan. '86, O.U.P. maj. 28,217)

Belfast

EAST *E.* 54,628
*P. D. Robinson, D.U.P. ... 20,372
Dr. J. Alderdice, *All.* 10,574
F. Cullen, *W.P.* 1,314
J. O'Donnell, *S.F.* 649
    D.U.P. maj. 9,798
    (June '83, D.U.P. maj. 7,989)
    (Jan. '86, D.U.P. maj. 21,690)

NORTH *E.* 59,124
*A. C. Walker, O.U.P. 14,355
A. Maginness, *S.D.L.P.* ... 5,795
G. Seawright, *Prot. U.* ... 5,671
P. McManus, *S.F.* 5,062
S. Lynch, *W.P.* 3,062
T. Campbell, *All.* 2,871
    O.U.P. maj. 8,560
    (June '83, O.U.P. maj. 7,079)
    (Jan. '86, O.U.P. maj. 16,577)

SOUTH *E.* 54,208
*Rev. W. M. Smyth, O.U.P. 18,917
D. Cook, *All.* 6,963
Dr. A. McDonnell, *S.D.L.P.* 4,268
G. Carr, *W.P.* 1,528
S. McKnight, *S.F.* 1,030
    O.U.P. maj. 11,954
    (June '83, O.U.P. maj. 9,724)
    (Jan. '86, O.U.P. maj. 14,136)

WEST *E.* 59,324
*G. Adams, S.F. 16,862
Dr. J. G. Hendron, *S.D.L.P.* 14,641
F. Miller, *O.U.P.* 7,646
Mrs. M. McMahon, *W.P.* . 1,819
    S.F. maj. 2,221
    (June '83, S.F. maj. 5,445)

Down

NORTH *E.* 65,018
*J. A. Kilfedder, U.P.U.P. . 18,420
R. McCartney, *Real U.* ... 14,467
J. Cushnahan, *All.* 7,932
    U.P.U.P. maj. 3,953
    (June '83, U.P.U.P. maj. 13,846)
    (Jan. '86, U.P.U.P. maj. 22,727)

SOUTH *E.* 71,235
E. K. McGrady, *S.D.L.P.* . 26,579
*Rt. Hon. J. E. Powell, M.B.E.,
    O.U.P. 25,848
Ms. G. Ritchie, *S.F.* 2,363
Miss S. E. Laird, *All.* 1,069
D. O'Hagan, *W.P.* 675
    S.D.L.P. maj. 731
    (June '83, O.U.P. maj. 548)
    (Jan. '86, O.U.P. maj. 1,842)

Fermanagh and South Tyrone
E. 68,979

*K. Maginnis, O.U.P. 27,446
P. Corrigan, *S.F.* 14,623
Mrs. R. Flanagan, *S.D.L.P.* 10,581
D. Kettyles, *W.P.* 1,784
J. Haslett, *All.* 941
    O.U.P. maj. 12,823
    (June '83, O.U.P. maj. 7,676)
    (Jan. '86, O.U.P. maj. 12,579)

Foyle
E. 70,519

*J. Hume, S.D.L.P. 23,743
G. Campbell, *D.U.P.* 13,883
M. McGuiness, *S.F.* 8,707
Mrs. E. Zammitt, *All.* 1,276
E. Melaugh, *W.P.* 1,022
    S.D.L.P. maj. 9,860
    (June '83, S.D.L.P. maj. 8,148)

Lagan Valley
E. 64,873

*Rt. Hon. J. H. Molyneaux,
    O.U.P. 29,101
S. A. Close, *All.* 5,728
B. McDonnell, *S.D.L.P.* ... 2,888
P. J. Rice, *S.F.* 2,656
J. T. Lowry, *W.P.* 1,215
    O.U.P. maj. 23,373
    (June '83, O.U.P. maj. 17,216)
    (Jan. '86, O.U.P. maj. 29,186)

Londonderry East
E. 71,031

*W. Ross, O.U.P. 29,532
A. Doherty, *S.D.L.P.* 9,375
J. Davey, *S.F.* 5,464
P. McGowan, *All.* 3,237
F. Donnelly, *W.P.* 935
M. H. Samuel, *Ecol.* 281
    O.U.P. maj. 20,157
    (June '83, O.U.P. maj. 7,262)
    (Jan. '86, O.U.P. maj. 28,921)

Newry and Armagh
E. 66,027

*S. Mallon, S.D.L.P. 25,137
J. F. Nicholson, *O.U.P.* ... 19,812
J. McAllister, *S.F.* 6,173
W. H. Jeffrey, *All.* 664
J. O'Hanion, *W.P.* 482
    S.D.L.P. maj. 5,325
    (June '83, O.U.P. maj. 1,554)
    (Jan. '86, S.D.L.P. maj. 2,583)

Strangford
E. 64,429

*Rt. Hon. J. D. Taylor,
    O.U.P. 28,199
A. J. Morrow, *All.* 7,553
Miss I. E. Hynds, *W.P.* ... 1,385
    O.U.P. maj. 20,646
    (June '83, O.U.P. maj. 7,370)
    (Jan. '86, O.U.P. maj. 30,634)

Ulster, Mid-
E. 67,256

*Rev. R. T. W. McCrea,
    D.U.P. 23,004
P. D. Haughey, *S.D.L.P.* .. 13,644
S. Begley, *S.F.* 12,449
P. Bogan, *All.* 1,846
P. J. McClean, *W.P.* 1,133
    D.U.P. maj. 9,360
    (June '83, D.U.P. maj. 78)
    (Jan. '86, D.U.P. maj. 9,697)

Upper Bann
E. 64,540

*J. H. McCusker, O.U.P. ... 26,037
Mrs. B. Rodgers, *S.D.L.P.* 8,676
B. P. Curran, *S.F.* 3,126
Mrs. M. F. A. Cook, *All.* .. 2,487
T. French, *W.P.* 2,004
    O.U.P. maj. 17,361
    (June '83, O.U.P. maj. 17,081)
    (Jan. '86, O.U.P. maj. 22,333)

BY-ELECTIONS (Since 1987 General Election)

Kensington (Gtr. London)
(July 14, 1988)

J. D. Fishburn, *C.* 9,829
Mrs. A. Holmes, *Lab.* 9,014
W. Goodhart, *S.L.D.* 2,546
J. Martin, *S.D.P.* 1,190
P. Hobson, *Grn Party* 572
Mrs. C. Payne, *Rainbow Alliance Payne and Pleasure Party* 193
'Lord' Sutch, *Monster Raving Loony Rock Music Party* 61
J. Duignan, *London Class War* 60
B. Goodier, *Anti Left Wing Fascist* 31
B. McDermott, *Free Trade Liberal Party—Europe Out* 31
R. Edey, *Fair Wealth Distribution Fair Housing Provision* 30
W. Scola, *The Leveller Party* 27
J. Crowley, *Anti-Yuppie Revolutionary Crowleyist Vegetarian Visionary* .. 24
J. Connell, *Peace—Stop ITN Manipulation* 20
Dr. K. Trivedi, *Independent Janata Party* 5
    C. maj. 815

Glasgow Govan (S'clyde)
(Nov. 10, 1988)

J. Sillars, S.N.P.		14,677
R. Gillespie, Lab.		11,123
G. Hamilton, C.		2,207
B. Ponsonby, S.L.D.		1,246
G. Campbell, Grn.		345
D. Chalmers, Comm.		281
'Lord' Sutch, Monster Raving Loony Party		174
F. Clark, Rainbow Zippy Alliance		51
S.N.P. maj		3,554

Epping Forest (Essex)
(Dec. 15, 1988)

S. J. Norris, C.		13,183
A. J. Thompson, S.L.D.		8,679
S. W. Murray, Lab.		6,261
M. G. Pettman, S.D.P.		4,077
A. M. Simms, Grn.		672
Ms. T. Wingfield, Independent National Front		286
'Lord' Sutch, Monster Raving Loony Liberal Christmas		208
J. Moore, Rainbow Alliance Change the World		33
B. G. Goodier, Vote No Belsen for South Africans		16
C. maj.		4,504

Pontypridd (Mid Glam)
(Feb. 23, 1989)

Dr. K. Howells, Lab.		20,549
S. Morgan, P.C.		9,755
N. Evans, C.		5,212
T. Ellis, S.L.D.		1,500
T. Thomas, S.D.P.		1,199
D. Richards, Comm.		239
D. Black, Ind.		57
Lab. maj.		10,794

Richmond (N. Yorks.)
(Feb. 23, 1989)

W. Hague, C.		19,543
M. Potter, S.D.P.		16,909
Mrs. B. Pearce, S.L.D.		11,589
F. Robson, Lab.		2,591
Dr. R. Upsall, Grn.		1,473
'Lord' Sutch, Monster Raving Loony Party		167
A. Mills, University Information Officer		113
Miss L. St. Claire, Corrective Party		106
N. Watkins, Official Liberal		70
C. maj.		2,634

Vale of Glamorgan (S. Glam)
(May 4, 1989)

J. Smith, Lab.		23,342
R. Richards, C.		17,314
F. Leavers, S.L.D.		2,017
J. Dixon, P.C.		1,672
K. Davies, S.D.P.		1,098
Miss M. Wakefield, Grn.		971
C. Tiarks, Protect the N.H.S.		847
'Lord' Sutch, Monster Raving Loony Party		266
E. Roberts, Welsh Independence		148
Miss L. St. Claire, Corrective Party		39
D. Black, Ind.		32
Lab. maj.		6,028

Glasgow Central (S'clyde)
(June 15, 1989)

M. Watson , Lab.		14,480
A. Neil, S.N.P.		8,018
A. Hogarth, C.		2,028
Ms. I. Brandt, Grn.		1,019
R. McCreadie, S.L.D.		411
P. Kerr, S.D.P.		253
Ms. L. Murdoch, Revolutionary Communist		141
W. Kidd, Scottish Socialist .		137
D. Lettice, Workers Revolutionary		48
Lab. maj.		6,462

Vauxhall (Gtr. London)
(June 15, 1989)

Ms. K. Hoey, Lab.		15,191
M. Keegan, C.		5,425
M. Tuffrey, S.L.D.		5,043
H. Bewley, Grn.		1,767
H. Andrew, People's Candidate		302
D. Allen, The Greens		264
R. Narayan, Barrister, Civil Liberties Activist in Brixton		179
D. Milligan, Revolutionary Communist		177
P. Harrington, Official National Front		127
'Lord' Sutch, Monster Raving Loony Mad Hatters ..		106
D. Black, Christian Alliance		86
E. Budden, National Front		83
G. Rolth, Fellowship		21
W. Scola, Leveller		21
Lab. maj.		9,766

PARLIAMENTARY ASSOCIATIONS

COMMONWEALTH PARLIAMENTARY ASSOCIATION (1911)

The Commonwealth Parliamentary Association consists of 114 branches in the national, state, provincial or territorial parliaments in the countries of the Commonwealth. Commonwealth Parliamentary conferences and general assemblies are held every year in different countries of the Commonwealth.

President (1988–89), Hon. Lawson A. Weekes, M.P., Speaker of the House of Assembly (*Barbados*).

Vice President (1988–89), Hon. D. N. E. Mutasa, M.P., Speaker of the House of Assembly (*Zimbabwe*).

Secretary-General, Dr. the Hon. David Tonkin, 7 Old Palace Yard, SW1P 3JY.

Secretary, United Kingdom Branch, P. Cobb, O.B.E., Westminster Hall, Houses of Parliament, SW1.

THE INTER-PARLIAMENTARY UNION (1889)

To facilitate personal contact between Members of all Parliaments in the promotion of representative institutions, peace and international co-operation.
Secretary General, P. Cornillon, Place du Petit-Saconnex, B.P. 99, 1211 Geneva 19, Switzerland.

British Group

Palace of Westminster, SW1A 0AA

Hon. Presidents, The Lord Chancellor; Mr. Speaker.
President, The Rt. Hon. Margaret Thatcher, M.P.
Chairman, M. Marshall, M.P.
Secretary, Capt. P. J. Shaw, R.N.

EUROPEAN PARLIAMENT—U.K. MEMBERS

(as at end June 1989)
An asterisk* denotes membership of the previous Parliament.

UNITED KINGDOM ELECTIONS TO EUROPEAN PARLIAMENT (June 15, 1989)

(*Corr.* = Corrective Party: *Hum.* = Humanist Party; *I.C.P.* = International Communist Party; *Lab. R.G.* = Labour for Regional Government; *M.K.* = Mebyon Kernow; *W. Reg.* = Wessex Regionalists; for other abbreviations, *see* p. 249)

Bedfordshire South
E. 569,506

*P. G. Beazley, C.	73,406
T. McWalter, Lab.	70,429
D. Everett, Grn.	34,508
W. M. Johnston, S.L.D. ..	8,748
R. Muller, S.D.P.	3,067
C. maj.	*2,977*
(June '84, C. maj. 14,982)	

Birmingham East
E. 531,081

Mrs. C. M. Crawley, Lab.	96,588
M. J. C. Harbour, C.	49,640
P. M. Simpson, Grn.	22,589
J. C. Binns. S.D.P.	5,424
J. M. E. C. Roodhouse, S.L.D.	4,010
M. Wingfield, N.F.	1,471
Lab. maj.	*46,948*
(June '84, Lab maj. 21,383)	

Birmingham West
E. 515,817

J. E. Tomlinson, Lab.	86,545
C. F. Robinson, C.	55,685
J. D. Bentley, Grn.	21,384
S. Reynolds, S.L.D.	7,673
Lab. maj.	*30,860*
(June '84, Lab. maj. 6,244)	

Bristol
E. 562,277

I. White, Lab.	87,753
*R. J. Cottrell, C.	77,771
D. N. Wall, Grn.	39,436
C. Boney, S.L.D.	16,309
G. McEwen, W. Reg.	1,017
Lab. maj.	*9,982*
(June '84, C. maj. 17,644)	

Cambridge and Bedfordshire North
E. 562,539

*Sir F. Catherwood, C. ...	84,044
M. Strube, Lab.	51,723
Ms. M. E. Wright, Grn. ..	37,956
A. N. Duff, S.L.D.	15,052
C. maj.	*32,321*
(June '84, C. maj. 47,216)	

Cheshire East
E. 518,311

B. Simpson, Lab.	74,721
*Sir T. Normanton, C.	72,857
C. C. White, Grn.	21,456
Mrs. B. Fraenkel, S.L.D. .	12,344
Lab. maj.	*1,864*
(June '84, C. maj. 18,376)	

Cheshire West
E. 543,256

L. Harrison, Lab.	102,962
*A. Pearce, C.	79,761
G. L. Nicholls, Grn.	25,933
J. Rankin, S.L.D.	9,333
Lab. maj.	*23,201*
(June '84, C. maj. 9,692)	

Cleveland and Yorkshire North
E. 571,254

D. Bowe, Lab.	94,953
*Sir P. Vanneck, C.	70,861
O. Dumpleton, Grn.	17,225
T. M. Mawston, S.L.D. ..	8,470
R. I. Andrew, S.D.P	7,970
Lab. maj.	*24,092*
(June '84, C. maj. 2,625)	

Cornwall and Plymouth
E. 542,527

*C. J. P. Beazley, C.	88,376
P. A. Tyler, S.L.D.	68,559
Ms D. Kirk, Lab.	41,466
H. Hoptrough, Grn.	24,581
C. Lawry, M.K.	4,224
C. maj.	*19,817*
(June '84, C. maj. 17,751)	

The Cotswolds
E. 558,115

*Lord Plumb of Coleshill, C.	94,852
Mrs. S. Limb, Grn........	49,174
T. Levitt, Lab.	48,180
L. A. Rowe, S.L.D.	18,196
C. maj.	*45,678*
(June '84, C. maj. 48,942)	

Cumbria and Lancashire North
E. 561,263

W. R. Fletcher Vane, C. ..	84,035
J. M. P. Hutton, Lab......	81,644
Mrs. C. E. Smith, Grn. ...	21,262
E. E. Hill, S.L.D.	12,590
J. Bates, S.D.P.	4,206
C. maj.	*2,391*
(June '84, C. maj. 23,795)	

Derbyshire
E. 564,429

*G. W. Hoon, Lab.	105,018
P. Jenkinson, C.	72,630
S. Molloy, S.L.D.	46,132
E. Wall, Grn.	20,781
Mrs. A. M. Ayres, S.D.P. .	3,858
Lab. maj.	*33,388*
(June '84, Lab maj. 6,853)	

Devon
E. 596,671

*Lord O'Hagan, C.	110,518
P. S. Christie, Grn.	53,220
W. J. Cairns, Lab.	40,675
M. Edmunds, S.L.D.	23,306
R. Edwards, S.D.P.	7,806
S. B. F. Hughes, L.M.	2,241
Lady Rous, W. Reg.	385
C. maj.	*57,298*
(June '84, C. maj. 56,610)	

Dorset East and Hampshire West
E. 608,895

*B. M. D. Cassidy, C.	111,469
Ms. K. I. Bradbury, Grn. .	49,695
H. R. White, Lab.	38,011
H. R. Legg, S.L.D.	21,809
C. maj.	*61,774*
(June '84, C. maj. 59,891)	

Durham
E. 530,137

*S. S. Hughes, Lab........	124,448
R. Hull, C.	37,600
Ms. H. I. Lennox, Grn. ...	18,770
P. Freitag, S.L.D.	8,369
Lab. maj.	*86,848*
(June '84, Lab. maj. 61,227)	

Essex North East
E. 598,542

Miss A. C. B. McIntosh, C.	92,758
Ms. H. J. Bryan, Lab.	53,360
C. R. Keene, Grn.	45,163
Miss D. P. Wallis, S.L.D. .	16,939
C. maj.	*39,398*
(June '84, C. maj. 54,302)	

Essex South West
E. 569,011

Miss P. E. Rawlings, C. ..	77,408
J. W. Orpe, Lab.	68,005
Mrs. M. E. Willis, Grn. ...	32,242
T. P. Allen, S.L.D.	10,618
C. maj.	*9,403*
(June '84, C. maj. 16,021)	

Glasgow
E. 487,199

*Mrs. J. O. Buchan, Lab. .	107,818
A. Brophy, S.N.P.	48,586
Mrs. A. K. Bates, C.	20,761
D. L. Spaven, Grn.	12,229
J. Morrison, S.L.D.......	3,887
D. Chalmers, Comm.	1,164
J. Simons, I.C.P.	193
Lab. maj.	*59,232*
(June '84, Lab. maj. 65,733)	

Greater Manchester Central
E. 481,023

*E. Newman, Lab.	86,914
Miss C. E. Gillan, C.	48,047
B. Candeland, Grn.	19,742
J. H. Mulholland, S.L.D. .	9,437
S. M. Millson, S.D.P.	2,769
S. Knight, Hum.	1,045
Lab. maj.	*38,867*
(June '84, Lab. maj. 28,077)	

Greater Manchester East
E. 506,930

*J. G. Ford, Lab.	93,294
R. N. Greenwood, C......	58,793
M. J. Shipley, Grn.	19,090
A. B. Leah, S.L.D.	16,645
Lab. maj.	*34,501*
(June '84, Lab. maj. 8,651)	

Greater Manchester West
E. 522,476

G. Titley, Lab.	109,228
P. H. Twyman, C.	59,093
D. W. Milne, Grn.	22,778
A. H. Cruden, S.L.D.	6,940
Mrs. B. Archer, S.D.P....	4,526
Lab. maj.	*50,135*
(June '84, Lab. maj. 37,698)	

Hampshire Central
E. 546,630

*E. T. Kellett-Bowman, C..		78,651
Ms. A. Mawle, Lab......		50,977
Mrs. S.J. Penton, Grn. ...		33,186
D. W. G. Chidgey, S.L.D..		18,418
C. maj...............		27,674

(June '84, C. maj. 44,821)
(see p. 281 for by-election result)

Hereford and Worcester
E. 595,504

*Sir J. Scott-Hopkins, C..		87,898
C. A. Short, Lab........		62,233
Ms. F. M. Norman, Grn...		49,296
Mrs. J. D. Davies, S.L.D..		13,569
C. maj...............		25,665

(June '84, C. maj. 39,934)

Hertfordshire
E. 517,137

*D. N. Prag, C.		86,898
V. S. Anand, Lab.		43,556
M. F. Ames, Grn.........		37,277
M. D. Phelan, S.L.D.		13,456
Mrs. C. Treves Brown, S.D.P.		5,048
C. maj...............		43,342

(June '84, C. maj. 45,932)

Highlands and Islands
E. 313,877

*Mrs. W. M. Ewing, S.N.P.		66,297
Sir A. McQuarrie, C.....		21,602
N. MacAskill, Lab.......		17,848
M. Gregson, Grn.		12,199
N. Michison, S.L.D.		10,644
S.N.P. maj............		44,695

(June '84, S.N.P. maj. 16,277)

Humberside
E. 504,219

P. D. Crampton Lab.		74,163
*R. C. Battersby, C.		57,835
Mrs. J. C. Clark, Grn.....		23,835
F. L. Parker, S.L.D.		3,989
S. W. Unwin, S.D.P.		3,419
Lab. maj..............		16,328

(June '84, C. maj. 8,015)

Kent East
E. 575,789

*C. M. Jackson, C.		85,667
G. N. J. Perry, Lab.......		56,706
Ms. P. A. Kemp, Grn.....		36,931
A. F. C. Morris, S.L.D. ...		15,470
C. maj...............		28,961

(June '84, C. maj. 48,867)

Kent West
E. 569,725

*G. B. Patterson, C.		82,519
P. L. Sloman, Lab........		58,469
J. Tidy, Grn.............		33,202
J. B. Doherty, S.L.D......		16,087
C. maj...............		24,050

(June '84, C. maj. 34,630)

Lancashire Central
E. 537,610

*M. J. Welsh, C...........		81,125
G. W. T. Smith, Lab.......		75,437
Mrs. H. Ingham, Grn.....		28,777
Ms. J. Ross-Mills, S.L.D. ..		7,378
C. maj...............		5,688

(June '84, C. maj. 26,195)

Lancashire East
E. 529,740

*M. J. Hindley, Lab.......		96,926
R. W. Sturdy, C.		57,778
S. Barker, Grn.		20,728
M. Hambley, S.L.D.		12,661
Lab. maj..............		39,148

(June '84, Lab. maj. 7,905)

Leeds
E. 519,631

*M. McGowan, Lab.......		97,385
J. W. Tweddle, C.		54,867
C. R. Lord, Grn.		22,558
Mrs. J. Ewens, S.L.D.		11,720
Lab. maj..............		42,518

(June '84, Lab. maj. 10,357)

Leicester
E. 579,050

Ms. I. M. Read, Lab......		90,798
*F. A. Tuckman, C........		75,476
C. J. Davis, Grn.		33,081
A. G. Barrett, Ind. C.		6,996
G. W. Childs, S.L.D.		6,791
Lab. maj..............		15,322

(June '84, C. maj. 2,892)

Lincolnshire
E. 586,156

*W. F. Newton Dunn, C. ..		92,043
S. Taggart, Lab.		71,393
Ms. J. Steranka, Grn....		24,908
J. P. Heppell, S.L.D.		14,341
C. maj...............		20,650

(June '84, C. maj. 45,445)

London Central
E. 486,558

*A. S. Newens, Lab. Co-op.		78,561
Ms. H. S. Crawley, C.		67,019
Ms. N. Kortvelyessy, Grn.		28,087
Miss S. A. Ludford, S.L.D.		7,864
W. D. E. Mallinson, S.D.P.		2,957
'Lord' D. E. Sutch, L.M. .		841
Ms. L. St-Claire, Corr. ...		707
J. S. Swinden, Hum......		304
Lab. Co-op maj.		11,542

(June '84, Lab. maj. 13,297)

London East
E. 530,548

*Miss C. Tongue, Lab.		92,803
A. R. Tyrrell, C..........		65,418
Ms. E. L. Crosbie, Grn. ...		21,388
J. K. Gibb, S.L.D.		7,341
D. A. O'Sullivan, I.C.P. ..		717
Lab. maj..............		27,385

(June '84, Lab. maj. 12,159)

London North
E. 573,043

Ms. P. Green, Lab. Co-op.		85,536
R. M. Lacey, C.		79,699
S. Clark, Grn...........		30,807
Ms. H. F. Leighter, S.L.D.		8,917
P. Burns, Ind.		2,016
Ms. L. Reith, Comm......		850
Lab. Co-op. maj.		5,837

(June '84, C. maj. 4,853)

London North East
E. 510,138

*A. Lomas, C.		76,085
M. Trend, C.............		28,318
Mrs. J. D. Lambert, Grn...		25,949
S. Banks, S.L.D.		9,575
Ms. N. C. Temple, Comm..		1,129
Lab. maj..............		47,767

(June '84, Lab. maj. 52,665)

London North West
E. 506,707

*Lord Bethell, C.........		74,900
A. K. Toms, Lab.		67,500
I. E. Flindall, Grn.......		28,275
C. D. Noyce, S.L.D.......		10,553
C. maj...............		7,400

(June '84, C. maj. 7,422)

London South and Surrey East
E. 495,942

*C. J. O. Moorhouse, C. ...		78,256
R. J. E. Evans, Lab.......		47,440
G. F. Brand, Grn.		31,854
P. H. Billenness, S.L.D. ..		14,967
C. maj...............		30,816

(June '84, C. maj. 44,657)

London, South East
E. 558,815

*P. N. Price, C.		80,619
D. J. Earnshaw, Lab.		73,029
Dr. E. C. McPhee, Grn....		37,576
A. A. Kinch, S.D.P.		10,196
Mrs. M. C. Williams, S.L.D.		9,052
W. E. Turner, Ind.		456
C. maj		7,590

(June '84, C. maj. 20,015)

London, South Inner
E. 528,188

*R. A. Balfe, Lab Co-op ...		90,378
R. J. Wheatley, C........		45,360
Ms. P. A. Shepherd, Grn...		26,230
M. J. Pindar, S.L.D.		10,277
P. N. Power, Comm.		1,277
Ms. D. Weppler, Comm. League..................		323
Lab. Co-op maj		45,018

(June '84, Lab. maj. 31,481)

London South West
E. 486,412

Ms A. J. Pollack, Lab. ...		74,298
*Dame S. M. Roberts, C. ..		73,780
Ms. M. A. Elson, Grn.....		35,476
J. C. Field, S.L.D.		10,400
Lab. maj..............		518

(June '84, C. maj. 6,867)

London West
E. 515,581

*M. N. Elliott, Lab........		92,959
B. Donnelly, C.		78,151
J. R. Hywell-Davies, Grn.		32,686
J. G. Parry, S.L.D.......		9,309
J. Rogers-Davies, S.D.P. .		2,877
Lab. maj..............		14,808

(June '84, Lab. maj. 5,229)

Lothians
E. 523,506

*D. W. Martin, Lab.	......	90,840
Mrs. C. M. Blight, C.	.....	52,014
J. Smith, S.N.P.	....	44,935
R. C. M. Harper, Grn	.....	22,983
K. Leadbetter, S.L.D.	....	9,222
Lab. maj.	....	*38,826*

(June '84, Lab. maj. 25,924)

Merseyside East
E. 519,514

T. Wynn, Lab.	......	107,288
E. N. Farthing, C.	....	30,421
R. L. Georgeson, Grn.	....	20,018
R. M. Clayton, S.L.D.	....	5,658
Lab. maj.	....	*76,867*

(June '84, Lab. maj. 49,039)

Merseyside West
E. 508,722

*K. A. Stewart, Lab.	......	93,717
M. D. Byrne, C.	....	43,900
L. Brown, Grn.	....	23,052
Mrs. H. F. Clucas, S.L.D.	..	16,327
D. J. E. Carson, P.R.P.	....	1,747
Lab. maj.	....	*49,817*

(June '84, Lab. maj. 13,197)

Midlands Central
E. 539,211

Ms. C. M. Oddy, Lab.	....	76,736
*J. de Courcy Ling, C.	....	71,643
Ms. J. A. Alty, Grn.	.....	42,622
I. Cundy, S.L.D.	....	8,450
Lab. maj.	....	*5,093*

(June '84, C. maj. 12,729)

Midlands West
E. 529,505

*J. A. W. Bird, Lab.-Co-op.		105,529
M. J. Whitby, C.	....	63,165
J. Raven, Grn.	....	21,787
Mrs. F. M. Oborski, S.L.D.		6,974
Lab. Co-op maj.	....	*42,364*

(June '84, Lab. maj. 19,685)

Norfolk
E. 577,576

*P. F. Howell, C.	....	92,385
Ms. M. Page, Lab.	......	71,478
M. Macartney-Filgate, Grn.	40,575
R. A. Lawes, S.L.D.	.....	8,902
S. D. Maxwell, S.D.P.	....	4,934
C. maj.	....	*20,907*

(June '84, C. maj. 36,857)

Northamptonshire
E. 587,733

*A. M. H. Simpson, C.	....	86,695
M. Coyne, Lab.	......	66,248
Ms. A. T. Bryant, Grn.	...	43,071
R. Church, S.L.D.	.....	11,619
C. maj.	....	*20,447*

(June '84, C. maj. 39,859)

Northumbria
E. 514,083

*G. J. Adam, Lab.	....	110,688
P. Yeoman, C.	......	50,648
Ms. A. Lipman, Grn.	.....	24,882
Viscount Morpeth, S.L.D.		10,983
Lab. maj.	....	*60,040*

(June '84, Lab. maj. 15,700)

Nottingham
E. 565,354

K. Coates, Lab.	....	92,261
*M. L. Kilby, C.	....	77,748
Mrs. S. E. Blount, Grn.	...	34,097
A. Swift, S.L.D.	....	6,693
Lab. maj.	....	*14,513*

(June '84, C. maj. 16,126)

Oxford and Buckinghamshire
E. 560,730

*J. E. M. Elles, C.	....	92,483
R. Gifford, Lab.	......	44,965
T. H. Andrewes, Grn.	....	42,058
R. Johnston, S.L.D.	.....	14,405
R. C. Turner, Ind.	....	3,696
C. maj.	....	*47,518*

(June '84, C. maj. 49,081)

Scotland Mid and Fife
E. 534,638

*A. Falconer, Lab.	......	102,246
K. W. MacAskill, S.N.P.	.	50,089
A. Christie, C.	....	46,505
G. Moreton, Grn.	......	14,165
M. Black, S.L.D.	....	8,857
Lab. maj.	....	*52,157*

(June '84, Lab. maj. 27,166)

Scotland North East
E. 554,408

H. McGubbin, Lab.	......	65,348
Dr. A. Macartney, S.N.P.		62,735
*J. L. C. Provan, C.	....	56,835
M. Hill, Grn.	......	15,584
S. Horner, S.L.D.	....	12,704
Lab. maj.	....	*2,613*

(June '84, C. maj. 9,171)

Scotland South
E. 491,865

A. Smith, Lab.	....	81,366
*A. H. Hutton, C.	....	65,673
M. Brown, S.N.P.	....	35,155
J. Button, Grn.	....	11,658
J. E. McKercher, S.L.D.	.	10,368
Lab. maj.	....	*15,693*

(June '84, Lab. maj. 3,137)

Sheffield
E. 564,409

R. Barton, Lab.	....	109,677
T. S. R. Mort, C.	....	40,401
P. L. Scott, Grn.	....	26,844
A. H. Rogers, S.L.D.	....	10,910
D. E. Hyland, I.C.P.	.....	657
Lab. maj.	....	*69,276*

(June '84, Lab. maj. 46,283)

Shropshire and Stafford
E. 597,554

*C. J. Prout, C.	....	85,896
D. J. A. Hallam, Lab.	....	83,352
R. T. C. Saunders, Grn.	..	29,637
C. Hards, S.L.D.	....	10,568
C. maj.	....	*2,544*

(June '84, C. maj. 24,932)

Somerset and Dorset West
E. 582,098

*Mrs. M. E. Daly, C.	......	106,716
Dr. R. H. Lawson, Grn.	..	54,496
Ms. D. M. Organ, Lab.	...	46,210
M. Mactaggart, S.L.D.	...	28,662
A. P. B. Mockler, W. Reg.		930
C. maj.	....	*52,220*

(June '84, C. maj. 40,251)

Staffordshire East
E. 581,127

*G. W. Stevenson, Lab.	...	94,873
M. F. Spungin, C.	....	63,104
S. Parker, Grn.	....	23,415
R. C. Dodson, S.L.D.	.....	7,046
Lab. maj.	....	*31,769*

(June '84, Lab. maj. 7,867)

Strathclyde East
E. 494,274

*K. D. Collins, Lab.	......	109,170
G. A. Leslie, S.N.P.	.....	48,853
M. Dutt, C.	....	22,233
A. Whitelaw, Grn.	......	9,749
G. Lait, S.L.D.	....	4,276
Lab. maj.	....	*60,317*

(June '84, Lab. maj. 63,462)

Strathclyde West
E. 493,067

*H. R. McMahon, Lab.	...	89,627
C. M. Campbell, S.N.P.	...	50,036
S. J. Robin, C.	....	45,872
G. Campbell, Grn.	......	16,461
D. J. Herbison, S.L.D.	....	8,098
Lab. maj.	....	*39,591*

(June '84, Lab. maj. 23,038)

Suffolk
E. 550,131

*A. E. Turner, C.	....	82,481
M. D. Cornish, Lab.	.....	56,788
A. C. Slade, Grn.	....	37,305
P. R. Odell, S.L.D.	......	12,660
C. maj.	....	*25,693*

(June '84, C. maj. 47,098)

Surrey West
E. 515,881

T. N. B. Spencer, C.	.....	89,674
E. Haywood, Grn.	......	40,332
H. G. Trace, Lab.	....	28,313
A. Davies, S.L.D.	....	18,042
B. M. Collignon, S.D.P.	..	3,676
C. maj.	....	*49,342*

(June '84, C. maj. 52,588)

Sussex East
E. 553,536

*Sir J. Stewart-Clark, Bt.,		
C.	......	96,388
Ms. G. Roles, Lab.	....	43,094
Ms. R. Addison, Grn	.....	42,316
Mrs. D. Venables, S.L.D.	.	16,810
D. Howells,. L.M.	....	1,181
C. maj.	....	*53,294*

(June '84, C. maj. 65,621)

Sussex West
E. 554,664

*R. M. Seligman, C.	......	95,821
I. F. M. Bagnall, Grn.	....	49,588
M. Shrimpton, Lab.	.....	32,006
Dr. J. M. M. Walsh, S.L.D.	24,855
C. maj.	....	*46,233*

(June '84, C. maj. 57,502)

Thames Valley
E. 542,855

J. C. C. Stevens, C.	......	73,070
Ms. H. B. de Lyon, Lab.	...	46,579
P. Gordon, Grn.	....	36,865
D. B. Griffiths, S.L.D.	....	14,603
C. maj.	....	*26,491*

(June '84, C. maj. 38,805)

Tyne and Wear
E. 530,953

A. J. Donnelly, *Lab.*		126,682
N. C. Gibbon, *C.*		30,902
R. Stather, *Grn.*		18,107
P. J. Arnold, *S.L.D.*		6,101
T. P. Kilgallon, *S.P.G.B.*		919
Lab. maj.		*95,780*
(June '84, Lab. maj. 49,414)		

Wales Mid and West
E. 547,740

*Rev. D. R. Morris, *Lab.*		105,670
O. J. Williams, *C.*		53,758
Ms. B. I. McPake, *Grn.*		29,852
Dr. P. J. S. Williams, *P.C.*		26,063
G. A. Sinclair, *S.L.D.*		10,031
Lab. maj.		*51,912*
(June '84, Lab. maj. 36,452)		

Wales North
E. 540,230

J. Wilson, *Lab.*		83,638
*Miss B. A. Brookes, *C.*		79,178
Dr. D. E. Thomas, *P.C.*		64,120
P. H. W. Adams, *Grn.*		15,832
R. K. Marshall, *S.L.D.*		10,056
Lab. maj.		*4,460*
(June '84, C. maj. 12,278)		

Wales South
E. 520,911

W. David, *Lab.*		108,550
A. R. Taylor, *C.*		45,993
G. P. Jones, *Grn.*		25,993
P. J. Keelan, *P.C.*		10,727
P. K. Verma, *S.L.D.*		4,037
D. A. T. Thomas, *S.D.P.*		3,513
Lab. maj.		*62,557*
(June '84, Lab. maj. 44,258)		

Wales South East
E. 561,068

*L. T. Smith, *Lab.*		138,872
R. J. Young, *C.*		30,384
M. J. Witherden, *Grn.*		27,869
Ms. J. Evans, *P.C.*		14,152
P. Nicholls-Jones, *S.L.D.*		4,661
Lab. maj.		*108,488*
(June '84, Lab. maj. 95,557)		

Wight and Hampshire East
E. 574,332

*R. J. Simmonds, *C.*		90,658
Dr. A. D. Burnett, *Lab.*		51,228
S. L. Rackett, *Grn.*		40,664
Ms. V. A. Rayner, *S.L.D.*		19,569
C. maj.		*39,430*
(June '84, C. maj. 42,928)		

Wiltshire
E. 568,875

*Mrs. C. F. Jackson, *C.*		93,200
G. A. Harris, *Lab.*		46,887
J. V. Hughes, *Grn.*		46,735
P. N. Crossley, *S.L.D.*		18,302
J. A. Cade, *Ind.*		4,809
C. maj.		*46,313*
(June '84, C. maj. 26,469)		

York
E. 542,998

*E. H. C. McMillan-Scott, *C.*		81,453
J. T. Grogan, *Lab.*		66,351
R. Bell, *Grn.*		27,525
A. Collinge, *S.L.D.*		12,542
C. maj.		*15,102*
(June '84, C. maj. 36,402)		

Yorkshire South
E. 518,995

*N. West, *Lab.*		121,060
W. J. Clappison, *C.*		29,276
A. Grace, *Grn.*		19,063
B. Boulton, *S.L.D.*		5,039
Lab. maj.		*91,784*
(June '84, Lab. maj. 67,749)		

Yorkshire South West
E. 523,322

*T. Megahy, *Lab.*		108,444
G. T. Horton, *C.*		42,543
Mrs. S. Leyland, *Grn.*		25,677
J. A. D. Ridgway, *S.L.D.*		10,352
Lab. maj.		*65,901*
(June '84, Lab. maj. 44,173)		

Yorkshire West
E. 564,001

*B. H. Seal, *Lab.*		108,644
G. T. Hall, *C.*		70,717
N. Parrott, *Grn.*		28,308
P. Wrigley, *S.L.D.*		9,765
Lab. maj.		*37,927*
(June '84, Lab. maj. 20,854)		

Northern Ireland
E. 1,105,551

Rev. I. R. K. Paisley, M.P., D.U.P.		160,110
J. Hume, M.P., S.D.L.P.		136,335
J. F. Nicholson, *O.U.P.*		118,785
D. Morrison, *S.F.*		48,914
J. T. Alderdice, *All.*		27,905
A. Kennedy, *C.*		25,789
M. H. Samuel, *Ecol.*		6,569
S. Lynch, *W.P.*		5,590
M. Langhammer, *Lab. R.G.*		3,540
B. Caul, *Lab. 87*		1,274

Rev. I. R. K. Paisley, J. Hume and J. F. Nicholson were elected by the single transferable voting system.

BY-ELECTION (since last edition)

Hampshire Central
(December 15, 1988)

Edward Kellett-Bowman, C.		38,039
John Arnold, *Lab.*		16,597
David Chidgey, *S.L.D.*		13,392
Lord Attlee, *S.D.P.*		5,952
Sally Penton, *Grn.*		3,603
C. maj.		*21,442*

PARLIAMENTARY SUMMARY 1989–90

The House of Lords re-assembled after the summer recess on October 10 and the House of Commons on October 20.

On October 20 the Home Secretary (Douglas Hurd) made a statement confirming that the Government was to ban the broadcasting of interviews with members and supporters of terrorist organizations in Northern Ireland. On November 2 Mr. Hurd moved a motion to impose the ban which, after heated debate, was carried by 243 votes to 179.

In the House of Lords on October 24 an Opposition amendment to the Housing Bill to give tenants greater protection from harrassment was defeated by 100 votes to 89.

On October 25, during Prime Minister's questions, the Leader of the Opposition, Neil Kinnock, called Mrs Thatcher a 'cheat' during exchanges on the freezing of child benefit. Mr. Kinnock was forced by the Speaker to withdraw the remark.

On October 31 the Rate Support Grants Bill passed its second reading by 252 votes to 198. The Firearms (Amendment) Bill was given a third, unopposed, reading in the House of Lords and was passed back to the Commons for consideration of the Lords' amendments.

FINANCIAL STATEMENT

On November 8 the Chancellor of the Exchequer (Nigel Lawson) presented his autumn financial statement, and announced increased spending on a number of Government programmes. Mr. Lawson told the Commons that public expenditure was likely to remain at the forecast £167,000 million and that only £250 million of the £3,500 million reserve was likely to be used. He said, 'The main reasons for this shortfall were the extra £1 billion in privatization proceeds and the reduction of social security spending of almost £1 billion as a direct result of the sharper-than-expected fall in unemployment and a saving of some £750 million, largely due to extra housing receipts under the right-to-buy programme.

'Taken together with the strong growth in the economy this year and the containment of debt interest now that the Budget is in surplus, this means that total public spending this year, even excluding privatization proceeds, will be less than 40 per cent of national income, the first time this has happened for over twenty years.

'Looking ahead, the Cabinet agreed in July that public spending over the next three years should keep as close as possible to the existing planning totals and should continue to fall as a share of national income. The plans I am about to announce meet both those objectives.'

PUBLIC EXPENDITURE

'For 1989–90, the planning total published in the last public expenditure White Paper was £167 billion. It will remain at £167 billion.

'For 1990–91, however, the planning total has been set at £179.5 billion, some £3.25 billion more than the previously published figure. For 1991–92, the planning total has been set at £191.5 billion.

'These totals include the same level of reserves as in last year's plans, that is to say, £3.5 billion in the first year, £7 billion in the second year and £10.5 billion in the third.

'They also incorporate an unchanged estimate of privatization proceeds of £5 billion a year.

'Over the three survey years as a whole, the real growth in spending on programmes will be over 3 per cent a year.

'Overall public spending, excluding privatization proceeds, will rise by less than 2 per cent a year, well within the prospective growth of the economy as a whole. In other words, total public spending, excluding privatization proceeds, will continue to decline as a proportion of national income.

'But, at the same time, substantial additional funds have been made available for the Government's most important public expenditure priorities.'

SPENDING PROGRAMMES

The Chancellor then gave details of increased expenditure on the National Health Service and on roads. He continued: 'Gross provision for public sector housing investment is being increased by around £440 million in 1989–90 and £340 million the following year. But thanks to the success of the Government's right-to-buy policy, this is more than financed by extra receipts.

'Defence spending is to be increased by £150 million in 1989–90 and £600 million in 1990–91. These significant increases are designed to provide a firm framework for the next three years within which our defence programme can be planned with confidence.

'The new plans imply an overall increase of £2.25 billion in public sector capital spending in 1989–90. This includes extra investment in hospitals, housing, prisons and roads. There is provision for higher investment by the nationalized industries, including further anti-pollution investment by the water authorities.'

Turning to National Insurance, the Chancellor said: 'The lower earnings limit will be increased next April to £43 a week, in line with the single person's pension, and the upper earnings limit will be raised to £325 a week. The upper limits for the 5 per cent and 7 per cent reduced rate bands will also be increased, to £75 a week and £115 a week respectively. The upper limit for the 9 per cent rate for employers will be raised to £165 a week.

'Over recent years, we have steadily reduced the Treasury supplement, the taxpayers' contribution to the National Insurance Fund. From 18 per cent in 1979, it now stands at 5 per cent. We now propose to carry this policy to its logical conclusion and to abolish the supplement altogether. The necessary legislation will be introduced early in the new session.'

Mr Lawson concluded, 'In short, after two years of unexpectedly rapid expansion, growth next year is forecast to return to a sustainable level, and one which compares well with the economic performance of the 1970s; while inflation will resume its downward path.

'The public finances are in substantial surplus and will remain so, with public spending on priority programmes continuing to increase, while overall public spending continues to fall as a share of G.D.P., to a level in 1991–92 not seen for a quarter of a century.'

End of Session

On November 7 the Government published a Broadcasting White Paper and Mr. Hurd made a statement outlining his proposals. The chief Labour spokesman on home affairs (Roy Hattersley) said that the proposals were a retreat from the concept of public sector broadcasting and would result in less diversity and lower standards.

The Education Secretary (Kenneth Baker) outlined the proposals contained in the Education White Paper on November 9. The proposals included a student loans scheme. The Opposition Education spokesman, Jack Straw, accused Mr. Baker of betraying the nation's future and Simon Hughes of the S.L.D. said that the proposals were 'the biggest disincentive to students from very poor and working families to go on to higher education that has been announced since the last war'.

On November 10, following the publication of the report on the King's Cross Underground fire, the Transport Secretary (Paul Channon) detailed a series of measures to improve safety. Following several hours of debate on Lord's amendments to the Housing Bill, a Government motion to adjourn further consideration of the Bill was accepted by 149 votes to 46. On November 11 the Bill was passed to the House of Lords.

On November 11 the Parliamentary session ended, the fourth longest in history, having begun in June 1987.

THE QUEEN'S SPEECH

The Queen opened the new session of Parliament on November 22 and in her speech, which outlined the Government's legislative programme, said:

'I look forward with much pleasure to a visit by her Majesty Queen Beatrix of The Netherlands as part of the celebrations of the William and Mary Tercentenary.

'I also look forward to visiting Barbados next March to mark the 350th anniversary of the House of Assembly there and to being present next autumn on the occasion of the Commonwealth heads of government meeting in Malaysia.

'My Government will strive for balanced and verifiable measures of arms control and for a world-wide ban on chemical weapons. They strongly support the Unted States' proposals for 50 per cent reductions in American and Soviet strategic nuclear weapons. They will work for the elimination of disparities in conventional forces in Europe with the aim of achieving a stable balance at lower levels.

'My Government will continue to strive to break down the barriers between East and West and to ensure that the Vienna Review Conference on Security and Co-operation in Europe leads to further progress on human rights. They look forward to building further on the improved relationship with the Soviet Union and to a visit to this country by the Soviet leader, President Gorbachev.

'My Government look forward to the completion of the Soviet troop withdrawal from Afghanistan and will continue to work for the restoration of that country's independence and non-aligned status. They will continue to play a full part in the work of the United Nations and to work for peaceful solutions to regional conflicts.

'My Government will continue to work with our European Community partners to complete the single market, to reinforce budgetary discipline and further to reform the common agricultural policy. They will play a full part in multilateral negotiations designed to liberalize international trade and agriculture.

'My Government will honour their commitments to the people of the Falkland Islands while continuing to seek more normal relations with Argentina. They will continue to discharge their responsibilities towards Hong Kong and its people and will work closely with the Chinese Government to implement the Sino-British joint declaration.

'My Lords and members of the House of Commons, my Government will continue to pursue firm financial policies designed to bear down on inflation. They will continue to promote enterprise and to foster the conditions necessary for the sustained growth of output and employment.

'A Bill will be brought forward to reform the law on local government capital and housing finance, on home improvement grants, and on the conduct of local authority business.

'My Government will continue to attach very great importance to protecting our environment, both nationally and internationally.

'A Bill will be introduced for England and Wales to establish a National Rivers Authority and to provide for the sale of the utility functions of the water authorities.

'Legislation will be introduced to restructure and to provide for the sale of the electricity supply industry in Great Britain.

'A Bill will be introduced to remove unnecessary obstacles to employment, particularly in relation to women and young people, and to alter training arrangements.

'My Government will vigorously pursue their policies for reducing crime. A Bill will be introduced to replace the Prevention of Terrorism (Temporary Provisions) Act. Legislation will be brought forward to provide for a national membership scheme to control admission to football matches.

'A Bill will be introduced to replace Section 2 of the Official Secrets Act, 1911, with provisions prohibiting only disclosures of information which would be harmful to the public interest.

'A Bill will be introduced to put the Security Service on a statutory basis under the authority of the Secretary of State.

'A Bill will be introduced to improve and rationalize the law governing the care and protection of children.

'My Government will continue to take action to raise standards throughout education.

'My Government are committed to strengthening the National Health Service and to ensuring that it is developed and improved in an efficient way that offers choice to patients.

'For Scotland, legislation will be brought forward to enable parents to choose that their children's schools should be managed outside the control of local authorities. A Bill will be introduced to transfer the Scottish Bus Group to the private sector.

'In Northern Ireland, my Government will continue their efforts to eradicate terrorism, to give elected representatives greater involvement in the affairs of the province, and to maintain close co-operation with the Republic of Ireland. A Bill will be laid before you to strengthen the law of Northern Ireland on fair employment. Legislation will be introduced to extend the franchise for local elections and to require from candidates a declaration against terrorism.

'A Bill will be brought forward to amend the law on social security.

'Legislation will be introduced to reform company law and the law on mergers.

'A Bill will be brought forward to modify the driver licensing system and to provide for new systems of route guidance for drivers.

'Other measures will be laid before you.'

Debate on the Queen's Speech

Mr. Kinnock attacked the Government's record on the environment and said that the Queen's Speech contained only the vacuous statement that 'the Government will continue to attach very great importance to protecting our environment both nationally and internationally'. The S.L.D. leader, Paddy Ashdown, deplored the leaking of large parts of the Speech to the press and accused the Government of treating Parliament with contempt.

On November 23 the S.D.P. leader (David Owen) criticized the Government's record on basic freedoms. The Home Secretary (Douglas Hurd) outlined his proposals for putting the Security Services on a statutory basis and was attacked by his Labour counterpart, Roy Hattersley, who felt that the proposed new Official Secrets Act would be more authoritarian than the existing one. On November 24 the Social Security Secretary, John Moore, announced benefit increases for about 2.6 million of the less well off and the disabled, to be implemented in October 1989.

Sir Geoffrey Howe, the Foreign Secretary, opened the fourth day of debate on the Queen's Speech by calling on the Soviet Union to improve its human rights record. He emphasized the Government's reluctance to attend an international conference on human rights intended to take place in Moscow in 1991 unless there was an improvement in the Soviet Union's record. On November 28 the Environment Secretary (Nicholas Ridley) pledged to introduce two Bills, the first introducing an integrated system of pollution control and the second reforming waste disposal law.

On December 5 the Elected Authorities (Northern Ireland) Bill, which provides that any person standing for election in Northern Ireland must declare that they do not support terrorist organizations, received a second reading in the House of Commons.

Salmonella Crisis

The Health Secretary (Kenneth Clarke) made a statement concerning salmonella contamination of eggs. During the debate that followed there was criticism of the Under Secretary for Health, Mrs. Edwina Currie, following her remark the previous weekend about there being a high level of salmonella in eggs. On December 19 the Minister of Agriculture, Fisheries and Food (John MacGregor) outlined a £19 million package to help stabilize the egg market, which had experienced a marked drop in sales following Mrs. Currie's remarks. Protests from egg producers had caused Mrs. Currie to resign her post on December 16. Dr. David Clark (Labour) accused Mr. MacGregor of complacency and of not tackling the main issue of the extent of salmonella in eggs and poultry.

During two days of debate on the privatization of the water industry beginning on December 7, Dr. John Cunningham, the Labour spokesman on the environment, said that his party would not allow private monopolies in water to exist. A Labour government, he said, would take them back into public ownership. On December 8 the Water Bill passed its second reading by 301 votes to 241.

On December 12, following the Clapham Junction train disaster, Mr. Channon announced a public inquiry into the tragedy. Members from all parties praised the emergency services and expressed sympathy for the bereaved and injured.

The Defence Secretary (George Younger) told the House of Commons on December 20 that the Ministry of Defence had decided to fund a demonstration phase of the Challenger Mark II tank by Vickers Defence Systems. The all-night sitting of the House of Commons was suspended for seven minutes after Labour member Tam Dalyell refused to break off an attack on the fitness of Leon Brittan to become a European Commissioner. When the sitting resumed Mr. Dalyell left the chamber.

Secrets and Security

On December 21, during debate on the Official Secrets Bill, the Labour spokesman on home affairs, Roy Hattersley, said that the Bill had been described as designed to increase the amount of official information available to the public, but in fact was intended to provide a new method by which availability of information was reduced and obstructed. The Home Secretary, Mr. Hurd, moving the Bill, said that the Bill came from a Government that had freed more information than any of its recent predecessors. The Bill was given a second reading by 298 votes to 221.

On January 10 Labour M.P.s strongly criticized the Transport Secretary, Paul Channon, for his failure to tell airlines and airport authorities about a bomb warning received shortly before the Lockerbie air disaster. John Prescott (Labour) said that the Lockerbie tragedy revealed 'muddles of procedure and excessive secrecy'.

During the committee stage debate on the Security Services Bill on January 16, Tory back-benchers said that independent scrutiny for MI5 would eventually be accepted, despite Government resistance to the idea. On the second day of the debate, Mr. Hurd, defining the purposes of the Bill, said that 'the narrow party-political interests of the government of the day have no part under this Bill'. On January 25 John Patten, Minister of State at the Home Office, confirmed that innocent people could face prosecution under the Bill if they sought certain information from M.P.s.

In a debate on January 24 on the failure of the Ministry of Agriculture to give proper protection to consumers, Dr. David Clark (Labour) said 'many of our citizens have died as a result of the Government's failure to protect our food adequately'. Richard Ryder, Under Secretary for Agriculture, rejected the allegations and said that the Government was preparing the biggest food Bill since 1938. A Government amendment commending the work of the Ministry of Agriculture was carried by 313 votes to 206 and the amended motion was carried by 280 votes to 211.

Health

The Health Secretary (Kenneth Clarke) introduced a Health Service White Paper on January 31. The Labour spokesman on health, Robin Cook, called the White Paper 'a prescription for a National Health Service run by accountants for civil servants, written by people who will always put a healthy balance before healthy patients.'

On February 2 the Football Spectators Bill was given a second reading in the House of Lords. The Right of Reply Bill, intended to give people a form of quick redress against factual inaccuracies printed about them in newspapers and periodicals, was given an unopposed second reading in the House of Commons on February 3.

In a debate on February 6 on the Government's proposal to guillotine the Water Bill, the Opposition spokesman on the environment, Dr. John Cunningham, criticized the Government and said that privatization would cause huge increases in costs to consumers. The Government motion to guillotine was carried by 272 votes to 199.

The Minister for the Arts (Richard Luce) announced on February 8 that the Government had decided not to proceed with a proposal to allow local authorities to launch premium library-lending services, and to charge for them. The Government's plans for the future of broadcasting, set out in the Broadcasting White Paper, were endorsed by 275 votes to 203.

During Commons questions on food contamination on February 16, Opposition members called for the resignation of the Minister of Agriculture, and the Government was accused of a cover-up.

In the House of Lords on February 20, an amendment to allow for the football membership identity scheme to be phased in division by division was carried by 124 votes to 121. The Government had wished all 92 league clubs to introduce the scheme by 1992.

Iran

On February 21 the Foreign Secretary (Sir Geoffrey Howe) announced that all Britain's diplomats had been withdrawn from Iran following the death threats to the author Salman Rushdie. The Opposition gave full support to the withdrawal. On March 8 Sir Geoffrey Howe announced that, for security reasons, some Iranians living in Britian were being asked to leave. Again he received full support from the Opposition.

During debate on the Official Secrets Bill, Dr. David Owen (S.D.P.) said that the Bill would prevent former ministers from publishing their memoirs. Julian Amery (Conservative) said that the Bill as it stood would at some time cause discomfort to the Government and for that reason he would abstain. The Bill was given a third reading by 320 votes to 195 and passed to the House of Lords.

On March 6 the Transport Secretary (Paul Channon) announced an independent public inquiry into the Purley rail crash. The Government's record of investment in British Rail was criticized by the Labour Transport spokesman, John Prescott.

On March 10 a Labour M.P., Harry Barnes, said that he would rather go to prison than pay the community charge. He was accused by the Home Office Minister, John Patten, of 'inciting people to break the law'.

THE BUDGET

On March 14, prior to the Budget speech, the Scottish Nationalist Party member, Jim Sillars, was ordered to leave the Chamber by the Speaker and was then suspended from the Chamber for five days. Mr. Sillars had persisted in raising a point of order at the time that the Leader of the Opposition, Mr. Kinnock, was standing at the Dispatch Box to ask the Chancellor for his Budget speech. Finally, the Chancellor, Mr. Lawson, presented his sixth budget 15 minutes later than scheduled. In his statement the Chancellor said that the background to the 1989 Budget was the unprecedented strength of the British economy, coupled with the continuing and overriding need to combat inflation.

The Chancellor began with an account of the performance of the economy in 1988 and the prospects for 1989, set in the context of the past 10 years. He said that the Government came to office with two central objectives—to defeat inflation, and to breathe new life into a moribund economy—and a clear idea of how to achieve those objectives.

'The first and most urgent task we faced was to damp down the inflationary fires that had raged in the 1970s and wrought so much economic and social havoc. And we succeeded. Between 1974 and 1979 inflation had averaged more than 15 per cent. Over the past six years it has averaged 5 per cent—still not good enough, but a massive improvement.

'For the economy as a whole our productivity growth has been second only to that of Japan among all the major nations during the 1980s. And our productivity growth in manufacturing has exceeded even that of Japan.

'But it is not just our economic performance that has been transformed: so have our prospects for the future. Over the past seven years, investment has grown more than twice as fast as consumption, creating the increased capacity necessary to meet future demand. Total business investment is now a higher proportion of national income than ever before. And its quality had improved immeasurably, too; as has the quality of British management. We have seen a dramatic and long-overdue improvement in company profits. And a remarkable growth in the total number of businesses, last year at the rate of more than a thousand a week.

'We had in 1988 a second successive year of growth at 4.8 per cent, with unemployment falling by over half a million, to well below the European average.

'Manufacturing output grew particularly rapidly, by more than 7 per cent, to a level well above the previous peak.'

INFLATION

'But total spending also grew by getting on for 7 per cent, mainly because of the boom in industrial investment, in itself a welcome event, but also because of continued strong growth in consumer spending. This last was financed to an unprecedented degree by borrowing, overwhelmingly mortgage borrowing.

'Inevitably the rapid growth of total spending led to renewed inflationary pressure. To some extent this was diverted into a sharp rise in imports, and hence into the deficit on the current account of the balance of payments.

'The real threat is posed by the increase in inflation itself. Excluding the distorting effect of mortgage interest payments, the RPI rose by 4.5 per cent last year, much the same as the average over the previous five years. But this underlying rate increased significantly through the year and now stands at 5.5 per cent.

'The outlook for 1989 is for inflation to rise a little further over the next few months, from 7.5 per cent including mortgage interest payments to about 8 per cent, before falling back in the second half of the year to 5.5 per cent in the fourth quarter and perhaps 4.5 per cent in the second quarter of 1990.

'Some slowdown in real growth is inevitable as we get inflation back on to a downward path—indeed, it has almost certainly already begun to happen. Overall growth is forecast to fall from the 4.5 per cent recorded last year to 2.5 per cent this year, with growth through the year at 2 per cent.

'But the question of just how 'soft' or 'hard' the so-called landing will be is not in the hands of Government alone. The Government's task is to reduce inflation by acting, through monetary policy, to bring down the growth of national income in money terms. The task of business and industry is to control their pay and other costs. The more successfully they do so, the less costly in terms of output and employment the necessary adjustment will be.'

MONETARY POLICY

The Chancellor went on to deal with monetary policy.

'For 1989–90, the target range for M0 will be 1–5 per cent, at envisaged in last year's MTFS. Although it will start the year above the top of that range, its very low growth over the past six months–below 3 per cent at an annualized rate–suggests that it will fairly soon come back within the range.

'As in the past two years, there is no target for the growth of broad money, or liquidity, but I will continue to take it into account in assessing monetary conditions.

'Short-term interest rates remain the essential instrument of monetary policy. I repeat what I have stated clearly on a number of previous occasions: interest rates will stay as high as is needed for as long as is needed. For there will be no letting up in our determination to get on top of inflation.'

PUBLIC SECTOR FINANCE

The Chancellor turned to fiscal policy, saying that when the Government first took office the public sector borrowing requirement was over 5 per cent of G.D.P.

'This we steadily reduced over the years as a deliberate act of policy until, by 1987–88, the PSBR (Public Sector Borrowing Rate) had been eliminated altogether and we started to repay the public debt.

'Accordingly, last year I budgeted for a further Public Sector Debt Repayment, or PSDR, of some £3 billion. In the event, it looks like turning out between four and five times as large, at £14 billion, or 3 per cent of G.D.P. Even if there had been no privatization proceeds at all, the public finances would still be in surplus, to the tune of some £7 billion.

'Government debt as a proportion of G.D.P. is now lower than at any time since the First World War.

'Meanwhile, I am today adding one more entry to the long list of financial controls which we have swept away during our term of office. The last surviving relic of the post-war apparatus for the direction of capital by the State is the Control of Borrowing Order, which since 1946 has involved first the Treasury and then the Bank of England in giving consents for equity and bond issues in the capital markets. As from today it will no longer be necessary for companies wishing to make capital market issues to obtain the Bank of England's consent to the timing of such issues.

'I reaffirm the principle of the balanced budget. However, given the substantial surplus we now have, the path of prudence and caution must be to return to balance not overnight, but gradually, over a period of years. Thus we can expect further years of debt repayment ahead of us.

'Moreover, given the particular uncertainties there are at the present time, I believe it would be right to budget for 1989–90 for a surplus similar to that secured in the year now ending; in other words, a further public sector debt repayment, or PSDR, of some £14 billion. This means that, in the space of three years, we shall have repaid roughly a sixth of the public debt that has accumulated over two centuries. But it also means that it will not be possible in this year's Budget to reduce the burden of taxation; that is to say, to reduce taxation as a share of national income.

'I am sure the whole House will agree that it is essential for taxpayer confidentiality to be properly protected. I therefore propose to introduce provisions in this year's Finance Bill to ensure that it will continue to be a criminal offence for officials or former officials of either of the Revenue Departments to reveal information about the private affairs of a specific taxpayer.'

TAXATION ON BUSINESS

Turning to taxation on business the Chancellor said, 'I propose to keep the small companies' rate in line with the basic rate of income tax for 1989–90 and to leave the main corporation tax rate unchanged. But I propose to increase the small companies' rate band substantially, by 50 per cent.

'Thus the small companies' rate will apply to companies with profits of under £150,000 and the 35 per cent rate will only be reached at profits of £750,000. These changes will reduce the corporation tax burden for more than half of all those companies that do not already enjoy the benefit of the small companies' rate.

'I propose to increase the value-added tax (VAT) threshold to £23,600, the maximum permitted under European Community law.

'I also have to set the scales for the private use of company cars. This remains far and away the most widespread benefit in kind. When I doubled the car scales in last year's Budget, I made it clear that this still left this benefit significantly undertaxed.

'Accordingly, I propose to increase the car scales by one third for 1989–90. The yield from this will be £160 million in 1989–90 and £200 million in 1990–91. There will be no change in the fuel scales.

'One of the many undesirable features of an income tax system with several higher rates was that since taxpayer's marginal rate could well be very different in different years, the question of which year income related to made a great deal of difference. This was true of Schedule E, where the strict rule is that income is taxed in the year to which it relates, on an accruals basis.

'I therefore propose that income tax under Schedule E should in future be assessed on a receipts basis, with a simple principle that you pay the tax when you receive the income. This will have a transitional cost of £80 million in 1989–90 and £60 million in 1990–91, but in the long term it will yield both extra revenue and a significant saving in both taxpayer's time and Inland Revenue staff.'

TAXATION OF SAVINGS

Turning to the taxation of savings, Mr. Lawson said that the role of tax reform is to encourage enterprise and improve economic performance in the medium term. He continued, 'It is wholly inappropriate as a response to short-term or cyclical phenomena. So for the taxation of savings, the Government's policy is clear. It is to strengthen and deepen popular capitalism in Britain by encouraging in particular wider share ownership.

'Personal equity plans, or P.E.P.s, were first announced in my 1986 Budget, and started up in January 1987. As the House knows, those who invest in these plans pay no further tax at all, either on the dividends they receive or on any capital gains they may make—indeed, there is no need for them to get involved with the Inland Revenue at all.

'Firstly, I propose to raise the annual limit on the overall amount that can be invested in a P.E.P. from £3,000 to £4,800.

'Second, within that, I propose to raise substantially the amount that can be invested in unit trusts or investment trusts.

'At present, P.E.P. investors are limited to £540 a year, or a quarter of their P.E.P., whichever is the greater, in unit or investment trusts. I propose to increase this limit very substantially, to £2,400 a year; and the whole of a P.E.P. will be able to be invested in unit or investment trusts, up to this limit. To qualify for tax relief, the unit or investment trusts will be required to invest wholly or mainly in UK equities.

'Third, at present, only cash may be paid into a P.E.P. I propose that investors should also be permitted to place directly into a P.E.P. shares obtained by subscribing to new equity issues, including privatization issues.

'Finally, I propose to make a number of important simplifications to the P.E.P. rules so as to make the scheme more flexible, better directed to the needs of small and new investors, and cheaper to administer.'

EMPLOYEES' SHARES

'I also have a number of improvements to announce specifically designed to encourage employee share ownership.

'At present the annual limits on the value of shares which can be given under all-employee profit-sharing schemes are £1,250 or 10 per cent of salary up to a ceiling of £5,000. I propose to raise these cash limits to £2,000 and £6,000 respectively.

'Second, I propose to increase the monthly limit on contributions to all-employee save-as-you-earn share option schemes from £100 to £150, and at the same time to double the maximum discount from market value at which options may be granted from 10 per cent to 20 per cent.

'Third, a number of Conservative M.P.s have been concerned that current tax law may be inhibiting the development of employee share ownership plans, otherwise known as Esops. These are distinguished from ordinary approved employee share schemes by the fact that they use a wider variety of finance, acquire more shares and tend to operate on a longer timescale.

'I propose to make it clear that companies' contributions to Esops qualify for corporation tax relief, provided they meet certain requirements designed to ensure that the employees acquire direct ownership of the shares within a reasonable time. I hope that this will encourage more British companies, particularly in the unquoted sector, to consider setting up Esops.'

The Chancellor also proposed changes to profit-related pay schemes.

'First, as I have previously announced, I propose to abolish the restriction that, to qualify for the tax relief, prospective profit-related pay must equal at least 5 per cent of total pay. Second, I propose to raise the limit on the annual amount of profit-related pay which can attract relief from £3,000 to £4,000.

'Third, I propose to enable employers to set up schemes for headquarters and other central units using the profits of the whole company or group for their profit calculations. And fourth, to help share schemes and Esops as well as profit-related pay, I propose to change the so-called material interest rules which at present may unnecessarily exclude employees from schemes where they can already benefit from a trust set up for employees.'

TAXATION OF LIFE ASSURANCE

Mr. Lawson had a number of important changes to the taxation of life assurance to propose.

'First, many life offices write pension business as well as life assurance, and they are not required to keep the two businesses entirely separate for tax purposes. This enables them to set the unrelieved expenses of the pensions business against the income and gains of their life business, thus giving their life profits unduly favourable tax treatment. The life offices themselves have accepted that this treatment is anomalous and I propose to end it.

'This change will come into force on January 1, 1990. Together with some related measures to put the taxation of life offices' pension business onto a proper footing, it will yield some £150 million in 1990–91.

'I propose that the expenses incurred by life offices in attracting new business should continue to be fully deductible for tax purposes from the income and gains of life funds, but should in future be spread over a period of seven years. To give the industry time to adjust, this change will be phased in gradually over the next four years, starting on January 1, 1990.

'I can say here and now that I propose, as from January 1, 1990, to abolish Life Assurance Policy Duty. And I also propose, from the same date, that the rate of tax payable on the policyholders' share of income and gains of life offices, which at present stands at 35 per cent on unfranked investment income and 30 per cent on realized capital gains, should be reduced to the basic rate of income tax.

'The net effect of all these changes to the taxation of life assurance will be a cost of £20 million in 1989–90 and a yield of £45 million in 1990–91, rising somewhat in subsequent years.

'Later this year, U.K. unit trusts will be able to compete freely in Europe and will face competition from analogous Community investment schemes here. At present, trusts investing in gilt-edged securities or other bonds face a tax disadvantage. They pay corporation tax at 35 per cent on their income but can pass on a credit of only the basic rate to their investor. So I propose that from January 1, 1990, as for life assurance companies, the corporation tax rate on unit trusts that come within the new European Community rules will be equal to the basic rate of income tax. Their investors will then get full credit for all the U.K. tax the trusts pay.'

PENSION SCHEMES

'The tax treatment accorded to pension schemes is particularly favourable; and the extent of this privilege has to be circumscribed by Inland Revenue rules. So pension schemes only qualify for tax relief if they meet certain conditions, notably that the pension paid may not exceed two thirds of final salary: and if they fall foul of any of these rules, they lose all relief.

'I propose to make it possible for employers to provide whatever pensions package they believe necessary to recruit and reward their employees.

'However, while it is clearly right that employers should be free to provide whatever pension they see fit, it would not be right to make the present generous tax treatment open ended. I therefore propose to set a limit on the pensions which may be paid from tax-approved occupational schemes, based on a final salary of £60,000 a year.

'I have deliberately set the ceiling at a level which will leave the vast majority of employees unaffected, and it will be subject to annual uprating in line with inflation.

'The introduction of this ceiling on tax relief also enables me to simplify and improve the rules for the majority of pension scheme members, in particular to ease the conditions under which people can take early retirement.

'I also propose to simplify very substantially the rules concerning additional voluntary contributions to pension schemes, or A.V.C.s. In particular, the present requirements for freestanding A.V.C.s place a heavy administrative burden on employers. These requirements will be greatly reduced.

'Furthermore, if A.V.C. investments perform very well, occupational pensions may at present have to be reduced to keep total benefits within the permitted limits. I propose that in future any surplus A.V.C. funds should be returned to employees, subject to a special tax charge.

'I have two proposals today to make personal pensions still more attractive.

'First, I propose to make it easier for people in personal pension schemes to manage their own investments.

'Second, I propose to increase substantially the annual limits, as a percentage of earnings, on contributions to personal pensions for those over the age of 35.'

TAXES ON SPENDING

Mr. Lawson went on to inform the House about changes to V.A.T. 'Her Majesty's Government are obliged to implement the European Court's judgement that certain of our zero rates of V.A.T. on supplies to business, notably on non-residential construction, but also on fuel and power and on water, are not lawful.

'This derives from the court's interpretation of the Community's sixth V.A.T. directive to which the U.K. agreed in 1977. The necessary changes will be introduced in this year's Finance Bill, and draft clauses have already been published.

'From April 1, V.A.T. will be payable in respect of all non-residential construction unless carried out under agreements entered into before the court ruling. And from August 1 landlords will have the option to tax rents, which means that in most cases no extra V.A.T. will be paid at all.

'So far as water for industry and fuel and power for business use are concerned, V.A.T. will not be payable until July 1990. V.A.T. on fuel and power will apply to business users above a specified threshold. Private households will remain zero rated.

'I have been particularly concerned about the impact of the European Court's ruling on charities.

'Unfortunately, charities' business activities cannot lawfully be shielded from the effects of the ruling, but I have been able to retain zero-rates for construction, water, fuel and power for all charities' non-business activities, for churches, and for most residential accommodation such as hospices, students' hostels and old people's homes.

'I have considered whether there is anything further I can sensibly do to assist charities with their V.A.T. bills in these special circumstances. I propose to relieve charities from V.A.T. on fund-raising events, on sterilizing equipment for medical use, and on classified advertising.

'I also propose to relieve from car tax cars leased to the disabled.

'But in general, I continue to believe that the best way of helping charitable causes through the tax system is through directly encouraging the act of charitable giving.

'The Payroll Giving Scheme, which I introduced in my 1986 Budget, has been growing steadily. Some 3,400 schemes have now been set up, and over 100,000 employees are already participating, quite a few of them giving the full £240 annual limit for tax relief. I now propose to double that limit to £480, or £40 a month.'

EXCISE DUTIES

Turning to excise duties Mr. Lawson said that he proposed to assist the Government's commitment to phasing out leaded petrol by increasing further the tax differential in favour of unleaded petrol. This will now be 4 pence a gallon cheaper. He also proposed to raise the tax on two and three-star petrol. This is intended to encourage garages to phase out two-star petrol and to encourage remaining two-star users to switch to unleaded fuel.

The Chancellor said that these changes would lead to a loss of revenue of some £40 million in 1989–90. He proposed to recoup this from Vehicle Excise Duty.

'At the present time, a bus or a coach has to have 66 seats before it pays as much in Vehicle Excise Duty as a family car. I propose to rectify this anomaly by increasing the tax rates of this group of vehicles so that they cover their track costs. I also propose to increase the rates of duty for the heaviest non-articulated lorries, to put them on a more equal footing with articulated lorries. At the same time I propose to simplify the system, greatly reducing the number of separate rates of Vehicle Excise Duty.'

TAXES ON CAPITAL

Mr. Lawson said that he had no further changes to propose this year in the rates of excise duty, nor to either the basic or higher rate of income tax. He continued, 'Since I aligned the rates of income and capital gains tax in last year's Budget, it follows that I also propose no change this year in the capital gains tax rates. However, I do have a few announcements to make concerning capital gains tax.

'With the advent of independent taxation from April 1990, married women will acquire their own capital gains tax threshold, so that a married couple will enjoy two such exemptions. In the light of this,

I propose to maintain the capital gains tax threshold at £5,000 for 1989–90.

'Second, I propose to abolish the general holdover relief for gifts.

'But while the general holdover relief will go, I propose to retain it for gifts of business, farm and heritage assets. And of course gifts between husband and wife will continue to be exempt.

'Moreover I propose to extend the existing relief for all gifts to charities to gifts of land and buildings to housing associations. Where instead of being given away the land is sold at less than market value, any capital gains tax will be based on the actual proceeds rather than, as now, on the market value. I also propose that such gifts and concessionary sales be normally exempt from inheritance tax.

'In the case of gifts of personal belongings, these benefit from chattels relief, under which any items worth less than £3,000 on disposal are entirely exempt from capital gains tax. I propose to double the chattels exemption limit to £6,000.

'Third, I propose to change the tax treatment of certain bonds so as to simplify the tax rules and prevent a loss of yield by the use of indexation to create losses and the conversion of income into capital gains.'

TAXES ON INCOME

'To return to income tax, I propose to raise all the main income tax thresholds and allowances by the statutory indexation factor of 6.8 per cent, rounded up. Thus the single person's allowance will rise by £180 to £2,785, and the married man's allowance will rise by £280 to £4,375. The basic rate limit will rise by £1,400 to £20,700.

'The single age allowance will rise by £220 to £3,400, and the married age allowance by £350 to £5,385. The higher level of age allowance will rise by £230 to £3,540 for a single person, and by £360 to £5,565 for a married couple.

I have a number of measures to help the elderly. In 1987 I introduced a new and more generous age allowance for those aged 80 and over. I now propose to extend it to include all those aged 75 and over.

'The income limit for the age allowance will rise by £800 to £11,400, again in line with indexation. However, I propose to reduce the rate at which the age allowance is withdrawn above this income limit. I propose that in future it should be withdrawn at the rate of £1 of allowance for each £2 of income above the limit, instead of the present rate of £2 in every £3. This means that the marginal tax rate for those in the withdrawal band will be reduced to well below 40 per cent.

'The Finance Bill will also include the provisions to establish the new tax relief for the over-60s health insurance premiums, which I announced to the House in January, and which will take effect from April next year, at a cost of £40 million in 1990–91.

'I have one further change to make to help pensioners. Under the earnings rule, any pensioner who decides to continue to work after reaching the statutory retirement age sees his or her pension docked at a rate of 50 per cent on every £1 earned between £75 and £79 a week, rising to 100 per cent for every £1 earned over £79 a week. This rule applies until he or she has reached five years beyond the state pension age.

'The Secretary of State for Social Security and I have agreed that the pensioners' earnings rule should be abolished from the beginning of October, the earliest practicable date. The necessary legislation will be included in the Social Security Bill currently before the House.

'The cost to public expenditure will be £190 million in 1989–90, which will be entirely met from the reserve. But the net cost of this measure will be significantly reduced by the income tax payable on the increased pensions.

'Those who wished to defer taking their pension will remain entirely free to do so, and will continue to earn a higher pension in return.'

NATIONAL INSURANCE

Mr. Lawson had one further measure to propose.

'It has long been a feature of the National Insurance system that, once people earn more than the lower earnings limit, which in 1989–90 will be £43, they have to pay National Insurance contributions at the same rate on the whole of their earnings up to the upper earnings limit. There are currently three different rates—5 per cent and 7 per cent for those on lower pay, and the standard rate of 9 per cent.

'The two reduced rates, which I introduced for both employers and employees in my 1985 Budget, cut ... the burden of National Insurance contributions on the low paid. But the highly desirable reduction in the steep step at the lower earnings limit was achieved at the expense of creating two small steps further up the earnings scale.

'This is not a real problem so far as employers' contributions are concerned. But it is for employees. For it inevitably means that, at certain points on the income scale, people can still be worse off if they earn more. Their extra earnings take them from a lower rate band to a higher one, and they therefore lose more in National Insurance contributions than they gain in extra pay.

'In agreement with the Secretary of State for Social Security, I now propose to build on my 1985 reform. For pretty well everyone who pays employee National Insurance contributions, I propose to reduce to only 2 per cent the rate of contributions on their earnings up to and including the lower earnings limit. On their earnings above that limit, there will be a single rate of 9 per cent, up to the upper earnings limit, which has already been set for 1989–90 at £325 a week.

'This will abolish altogether the steps which at present exist at earnings, for 1989–90, of £75 and £115 a week.

'There will be no change in the contributions payable by employers.

'The new system will take effect from the beginning of October, the earliest practicable date. The cost will be £1 billion in 1989–90 and £2.8 billion in 1990–91. The necessary legislation will be included in the Social Security Bill currently before the House.

'The total additional cost of all the measures in this Budget, on an indexed basis, is under £2 billion in 1989–90 and £3.5 billion in 1990–91.'

The Chancellor concluded, 'In this Budget I have reaffirmed the Government's commitment to the defeat of inflation through the maintenance of prudent monetary and fiscal policies. I have budgeted for a debt repayment of £14 billion—the largest ever. I have announced a major reform of, and reduction in, employees' National Insurance contributions; and I have honoured our pledge to abolish the earnings rule for pensioners.'

Debate on the Budget

Mr. Kinnock, the Leader of the Opposition, in his response to the Budget, said 'this is not a budget for low-paid workers. It is another con job from a low-down Chancellor'. Dr. David Owen said that the Chancellor had certainly chosen caution in this Budget. Following four days of debate the Budget motion was carried by 341 votes to 222 and the procedure resolution on future taxation was carried by 337 votes to 221.

On March 21 the Transport Secretary, Mr. Channon, disavowed reports that he had told journalists that the police knew the identities and whereabouts of the terrorists who had blown up PanAm flight 103 over Lockerbie in December 1988. During a heated debate Peter Snape (Labour) was ordered by the Speaker to withdraw an accusation that Mr. Channon was a liar.

On March 22 the Northern Ireland Secretary (Tom King) announced to the House of Commons that he had given provisional agreement for the sale of the Harland and Wolff shipyard in Belfast to a management-employee buyout team.

Energy

Peter Bottomley, Under Secretary of State for Transport, told the House of Commons on March 23 that regulations requiring lorries carrying explosives to display hazard warning labels would be brought before Parliament within a month. This followed the explosion in Peterborough the previous day of an unmarked van carrying explosives: a fireman died in the explosion.

On April 5, the first day of the report stage of the Electricity Bill, the Energy Secretary (Cecil Parkinson) said that the privatization of electricity would not lead to increased use of nuclear power. This followed a claim by Malcolm Bruce (S.D.P.) that the Bill gave nuclear power a privileged and distorted position. On April 10 the Bill was given a third reading by 251 votes to 193.

During an Opposition-led debate on pensions and other benefits on April 11, the Social Security Secretary (John Moore) accused the Labour spokesman, Robin Cook, of abusing Parliamentary procedures by repeatedly intervening to question the Government's record. Mr. Cook said that pensioners had been 'cheated by the Government'. The Opposition motion deploring the Government's pension record was defeated by 308 votes to 220.

Following the Hillsborough Stadium tragedy on April 15, the Home Secretary (Douglas Hurd) announced that Lord Justice Taylor would carry out a full and independent inquiry. The Government rejected requests to postpone further consideration of the Bill introducing a national membership scheme for Football League clubs.

On April 25 the Finance Bill implementing the Budget proposals passed its second reading by 271 votes to 186. In the House of Lords the Electricity Bill was given a second reading.

On April 27 the Security Service Bill completed its passage through Parliament. It was given Royal Assent within thirty minutes of completing its passage.

On May 2 a Labour motion calling for changes to the National Health Service to be delayed until the electorate could vote on them was defeated by 279 votes to 181. During a debate on teacher shortages and low morale in the profession the Education Secretary (Kenneth Baker) announced that the Government would toughen the criteria governing teacher-training courses.

Water

In the House of Lords on May 4 a Conservative back-bench amendment to the Water Bill was defeated by 208 votes to 112. The amendment aimed to turn the ten regional water authorities into statutory water companies rather than public limited companies. On May 8 a cross-party amendment aimed at imposing a special duty on the privatized industry to protect the environment and promote recreation was defeated by 108 votes to 92.

The Government was castigated on May 10 by Labour M.P.s over the leaflet about the community charge which it had prepared for distribution nation-wide. Distribution was prevented by a High Court injunction on May 9 because of inaccuracies in the leaflet. Labour's environment spokesman, Dr. John Cunningham, said 'Mr. Ridley [the Environment Secretary] prevaricated, obfuscated and delayed for six hours before ensuring that the Court's decision was put into practice'. Peter Pike (Labour) called on Mr. Ridley to resign. In the absence of Mr. Ridley from the House the Labour charges were answered by John Gummer, Minister of State for Local Government. On May 11 Labour members continued the attack and during Prime Minister's questions waved copies of the leaflet, which they said were still being delivered. The Leader of the Opposition, Neil Kinnock, had received one.

Following the violent end of the pro-democracy demonstrations in China, the Foreign Secretary, Sir Geoffrey Howe, said on June 7 that there could be no question of Britain continuing normal business with the Chinese authorities and that the visit to Britain of the Chinese Minister of Justice had been cancelled. He said that the Government understood the concern felt by the people of Hong Kong. During Prime Minister's questions Mrs. Thatcher made it clear that the Government did not believe that it could resolve Hong Kong's crisis of confidence in the Chinese government by giving Hong Kong residents right of abode in the United Kingdom.

On June 13 Mr Kenneth Clarke announced to the House of Commons that the Government was advising the public not to eat any brand of hazelnut yoghurt following an outbreak of botulism in north-west England and in Wales.

Football Bill

In the House of Lords on June 16, the Government survived attempts to shelve its legislation introducing a compulsory football membership scheme until after the judicial inquiry into the Hillsborough disaster had published its findings. An Opposition amendment was defeated by 96 votes to 83 and the Football Spectators Bill received its third reading. During the second reading of the Football Spectators Bill in the House of Commons, several Conservative back-bench M.P.s joined with Labour in expressing reservations about the Bill. However, the Bill was given a second reading on June 27 by 330 votes to 252.

In the House of Lords on July 3 the Archbishop of Canterbury (Dr. Robert Runcie) urged the House to permit the ending of the absolute bar on divorcees becoming priests. The Earl of Lauderdale opposed any change and protested that the priesthood was being tampered with. On July 18 the House of Commons rejected the proposal by 51 votes to 45.

On July 4 the Antarctic Minerals Bill was given a second reading in the House of Commons and on July 17 the Bill passed its third reading by 171 votes to 65. The Water Bill completed its passage through Parliament on July 4 when the House of Lords passed it. Royal Assent was granted, paving the way for privatization in November 1989.

Labour members accused the Government of a climbdown when Lord Young in the Lords and Mr. Tony Newton in the Commons announced the Government's response to the Monopolies and Mergers Commission inquiry into the supply of beer. The proposed changes would enable a 'major freeing of the market' without obliging brewers to dispose of large numbers of pubs and clubs. Brian Gould, Labour spokesman on Trade and Industry, said that the Government had succumbed to the lobbying power of the big brewers.

On July 24 the Energy Secretary, Cecil Parkinson, announced that Britain's nine Magnox nuclear power stations would not be privatized as had been planned.

The House of Lords rose for the summer recess on July 27, and the House of Commons rose on July 28.

PUBLIC ACTS OF PARLIAMENT 1988–89

This list of Public Acts commences with one Public Act which received the Royal Assent before September 1988 and which was mentioned briefly in the last summary. Those Public Acts which follow received the Royal Assent after August 1988. The date stated after each Act is the date on which it came into operation.

Local Government (Finance) Act 1988, c. 41 (various dates) creates community charges (popularly known as the poll tax) in favour of certain authorities, creates a new rating system, and makes other necessary provisions in connection with the imposition of the new tax and its collection and the financing of local authorities. It also amends the Scottish law on the community charge.

Housing (Scotland) Act 1988, c. 43 (various dates) establishes a body known as Scottish Homes with functions relating to housing; makes provision for houses let on tenancies in Scotland; gives the right to acquire certain houses occupied by secure tenants from public sector landlords to Scottish Homes and approved persons; provides as to the limit on discount on the price of houses purchased by secure tenants and for local authority grants to help local authority tenants obtain alternative accommodation to local authority housing; and makes provision for various other matters connected with housing in Scotland.

Foreign Marriage (Amendment) Act 1988, c. 44 (day to be appointed) amends the Act of 1892 and repeals certain obsolete enactments relating to the validation of marriages of British subjects solemnized outside the U.K.

Firearms (Amendment) Act 1988, c. 45 (various dates, some to be appointed) amends the 1968 Act and makes further provision for the regulation of the possession of, and transactions relating to, firearms and ammunition.

European Communities (Finance) Act 1988, c. 46 (Nov. 15, 1988) amends the definition of 'the Treaties' and 'the Community Treaties' in the European Communities Act 1972, s. 1(2) in order to include the decision of the Council of the Communities made on June 24, 1988 on the Communities' system of resources and the undertaking by the representatives of the E.C. governments to make payments to finance the E.C. general budget for the financial year 1988 (as confirmed at their meeting within the Council on June 24, 1988 in Luxembourg).

School Boards (Scotland) Act 1988, c. 47 (various dates, some to be appointed) makes new provision for the government of public schools in Scotland.

Copyright, Designs and Patents Act 1988, c. 48 (various dates, some to be appointed) restates and amends the law relating to copyright; makes new provisions concerning the rights of performers; confers a design right in original designs and amends the Registered Designs Act 1949; makes provisions relating to patent agents and trade mark agents and confers patents and designs jurisdiction on certain county courts; amends the law of patents by, for example, making provision for devices designed to circumvent copy-protection of works in electronic form, and new provision penalizing the fraudulent reception of transmissions. The Act also continues the copyright of J. M. Barrie's *Peter Pan* in favour of The Hospital for Sick Children, Great Ormond Street, London, and makes other provision with respect to financial provision and to trade mark protection.

Health and Medicines Act 1988, c. 49 (various dates, some to be appointed) provides for sight testing and instruction in health and welfare in relation to the N.H.S.; amends the Medicines Acts 1968 and 1971; and empowers the Secretary of State to make regulations about H.I.V. testing kits and services.

Housing Act 1988, c. 50 (various dates, some to be appointed) makes further provision for houses let on tenancies or occupied under licences; amends the Rent Act 1977 and the Rent (Agriculture) Act 1976; and establishes a body, Housing for Wales, with functions relating to housing associations. The Act makes various other provisions connected with housing including conferring on approved persons the right to acquire from public sector landlords certain houses occupied by secure tenants.

Rate Support Grants Act 1988, c. 51 (Nov. 15, 1988) makes further provision as to rate support grants.

Road Traffic Act 1988, c. 52 (May 15, 1989) consolidates certain enactments relating to road traffic, and makes amendments to give effect to recommendations of the Law Commission and the Scottish Law Commission.

Road Traffic Offenders Act 1988, c. 53 (most provisions on May 15, 1989) consolidates certain enactments relating to the prosecution and punishment (including the punishment without conviction) of road traffic offenders with amendments to give effect to recommendations of the Law Commission and the Scottish Law Commission.

Road Traffic (Consequential Provisions) Act 1988, c. 54 (all provisions except parts of Schedule 2 on May 15, 1989) makes provision for repeals, consequential amendments, transitional and transitory matters, and savings in connection with the consolidation in the Road Traffic Act 1988 and the Road Traffic Offenders Act 1988.

Consolidated Fund (No. 2) Act 1988, c. 55 (Dec. 20, 1988) applies certain sums out of the Consolidated Fund to the service of the years ending on March 31, 1989 and 1990.

Petroleum Royalties (Relief) and Continental Shelf Act 1988, c. 1 (Feb. 7, 1989) confers on holders of certain petroleum licences an exemption from royalties (including royalties in kind) in respect of petroleum from certain onshore and offshore fields, and confers power to amend the Continental Shelf (Designation of Additional Areas) Order 1974 to give effect to an Agreement made between the U.K. and the Republic of Ireland relating to their respective rights in relation to the continental shelf.

Consolidated Fund Act 1989, c. 2 (March 15, 1989) applies certain sums out of the Consolidated Fund to the service of the years ending on March 31, 1988 and 1989.

Elected Authorities (Northern Ireland) Act 1989, c. 3 (various dates, some to be appointed) amends the law relating to the franchise at elections to district councils in Northern Ireland; provides for a declaration against terrorism to be made by candidates at district councils and the Northern Ireland Assembly and by persons co-opted as members of district councils; amends Local Government Act (Northern Ireland) 1972, ss. 3, 4.

Prevention of Terrorism (Temporary Provisions) Act 1989, c. 4 (various dates, some to be appointed) makes provision in place of the 1984 Act; makes further provision in relation to powers of search under, and persons convicted of scheduled offences within, the meaning of the Northern Ireland (Emergency Provisions) Act 1978; and enables the Secretary of State to prevent the establishment of new explosives factories, magazines and stores in Northern Ireland.

Security Service Act 1989, c. 5 (days to be appointed) places the Security Service on a statutory basis; enables certain actions to be taken on the authority of warrants issued by the Home Secretary, with provision for the issue of such warrants to be kept under review by a commissioner; provides for the investigation of complaints about the service by a tribunal or by the commissioner.

Official Secrets Act 1989, c. 6 (day to be appointed) replaces section 2 of the 1911 Act with provisions protecting more limited classes of official information.

Atomic Energy Act 1989, c. 7 (day or days to be appointed) increases the financial limit imposed by section 2(1) of the Nuclear Industry (Finance) Act 1977 in relation to British Nuclear Fuels P.L.C. to £2,000 million; makes provision for the recovery of certain expenses by the Health and Safety Executive; amends sections 18 and 19 of the Nuclear Installations Act 1965 and makes provision in connection with the Convention on Assistance in the Case of Nuclear Accident or Radiological Emergency.

National Maritime Museum Act 1989, c. 8 (day or days to be appointed) transfers land to the trustees of the National Maritime Museum and provides for the functions of the trustees and for connected purposes.

Civil Aviation (Air Navigation Charges) Act 1989, c. 9 (May 25, 1989) enables charges imposed under section 73(1)(a) of the Civil Aviation Act 1982 to be prescribed in units of account defined by reference to more than one currency.

Disabled Persons (Northern Ireland) Act 1989, c. 10 (day or days to be appointed) makes provision equivalent to the Disabled Persons (Services, Consultation and Representation) Act 1986 for Northern Ireland.

Police Officers (Central Service) Act 1989, c. 11 (July 3, 1989) amends section 43 of the Police Act 1964 and section 38 of the Police (Scotland) Act 1967 and makes a number of repeals relating to central service.

Hearing Aid Council (Amendment) Act 1989, c. 12 (part on Sept. 3, 1989 and the rest on Jan. 1, 1990) amends the 1968 Act relating to dispensing hearing aids, the composition of the Council and connected matters.

Dock Work Act 1989, c. 13 (all except s. 7(2) and Schedule 1, Part II, on July 3, 1989, the rest on the dissolution date of the Board) abolishes the Dock

Workers Employment Scheme 1967; repeals the Dock Workers (Regulation of Employment) Act 1946 and dissolves the National Dock Labour Board.

Control of Pollution (Amendment) Act 1989, c. 14 (day or days to be appointed) provides for the registration of carriers of controlled waste and makes further provision with respect to powers exercisable in relation to vehicles used for illegal waste disposal.

Water Act 1989, c. 15 (various dates) makes arrangements for the privatization of the water industry in England and Wales; introduces major changes to the existing structure of water pollution in Great Britain; *inter alia* amends the law relating to water supply; creates the National Rivers Authority to take over the regulatory functions of existing water authorities; and for various other matters connected with water, sewerage, flood defence and fisheries.

Parking Act 1989, c. 16 (day to be appointed) amends the Road Traffic Regulations Act 1984 in relation to parking.

Control of Smoke Pollution Act 1989, c. 17 (Sept. 21, 1989) amends the Clean Air Acts 1956 and 1968 and the Public Health Act 1936.

Common Land (Rectification of Registers) Act 1989, c. 18 (July 21, 1989) provides for the removal of land on which there is and has been since August 5, 1945 a dwellinghouse, or land ancillary thereto, from registers maintained under the Commons Registration Act 1965.

International Parliamentary Organizations (Registration) Act 1989, c. 19 (July 21, 1989) sets up a register of publicly-financed international parliamentary organizations which receive an annual grant-in-aid to fund both British and International Secretariats and whose members are from both Houses of Parliament.

Licensing (Amendment) Act 1989, c. 20 (Sept. 21, 1989) amends section 62 of the 1964 Act by increasing the permitted licensing hours in clubs from five to six.

Antarctic Minerals Act 1989, c. 21 (day to be appointed) provides for exploitation and exploration of mineral resources in Antarctica; it also enables proceedings under the law of the British Antarctic Territory to be brought in England and Wales.

Road Traffic (Driver Licensing and Information System) Act 1989, c. 22 (day or days to be appointed) amends the law relating to driving licences, including abolishing special licences for H.G.V.s and P.S.V.s; regulates the operation of systems providing drivers of motor vehicles with guidance and information from automatically processed data.

Transport (Scotland) Act 1989, c. 23 (Sept. 21, 1989) provides for the transfer to the private sector of the operations of the Scottish Transport Group, other than its shipping operations.

Social Security Act 1989, c. 24 (various dates, some to be appointed) amends the law relating to social security and occupational and personal pension schemes. It also provides for certain employment-related benefit schemes.

Appropriation Act 1989, c. 25 (July 27, 1989) applies a sum out of the Consolidated Fund to the service of the year ending on March 31, 1990; appropriates the supplies granted in the parliamentary session and repeals certain Consolidated Fund and Appropriation Acts.

Finance Act 1989, c. 26 (July 27, 1989) grants certain duties, alters others and amends the law relating to the National Debt and the Public Revenue. For example, it enacts provisions dealing with the E.C. requirements for V.A.T. on commercial property, abolishes the capital gains tax hold over relief on gifts, imposes a slightly different basis for some employees for P.A.Y.E., repeals the close company provisions and brings in a number of anti-avoidance provisions regarding foreign and non-resident companies and trusts.

Pesticides (Fees and Enforcement) Act 1989, c. 27 (Sept. 27, 1989) amends sections 18 (concerned with approval of pesticides) and 19 (enforcement powers) of the Food and Environment Protection Act 1985.

Representation of the People Act 1989, c. 28 (day or days to be appointed) amends the law relating to overseas British citizens wishing to vote at Parliamentary and European Parliamentary elections, and the expenses of candidates at parliamentary by-elections.

Electricity Act 1989, c. 29 (various dates, some to be appointed) provides for the privatization of the electricity industry; provides for the appointment and functions of a Director General of Electricity Supply and of consumers' committees for the electricity supply industry; and for various other connected matters.

Dangerous Dogs Act 1989, c. 30 (Aug. 27, 1989) extends the powers available to a court on a complaint under section 2 of the Dogs Act 1871, together with additional rights of appeal and enhanced penalties.

Human Organ Transplants Act 1989, c. 31 (part on July 27 and 28, 1989, the rest on a day or days to be appointed) prohibits commercial dealings in human organs intended for transplanting and restricts the transplanting of human organs between people who are not genetically related.

Fair Employment (Northern Ireland) Act, c. 32 (day or days to be appointed) establishes a Fair Employment Tribunal for Northern Ireland, offices of President and Vice President of the Industrial Tribunals and the Fair Employment Tribunal; amends the Act of 1976; provides for promotion of equality of opportunity in employments and occupations in Northern Ireland between persons of different religious beliefs.

Extradition Act 1989, c. 33 (part on July 27 and the rest on Sept. 27, 1989) consolidates, with amendments, enactments relating to extradition under the Criminal Justice Act 1988, the Fugitive Offenders Act 1967 and the Extradition Acts 1870 to 1935.

Law of Property (Miscellaneous Provisions) Act 1989, c. 34 (Ss. 1 and 4 on a day to be appointed, the rest on Sept. 27, 1989) abolishes the rule in *Bain* v. *Fothergill* and makes new provision with respect to deeds and their execution and contracts for the sale or other disposition of interests in land.

Continental Shelf Act 1989, c. 35 (July 27, 1989) amends section 3 of the Petroleum Royalties (Relief) and Continental Shelf Act 1989.

GOVERNMENT AND PUBLIC OFFICES

SALARIES 1989-90

Ministerial Salaries
(as at Jan. 1, 1989)

Prime Minister	£34,479*
Secretary of State	£34,479
Minister of State (Lords)	£37,047
Minister of State (Commons)	£24,209
Parliamentary Under Secretary	£18,219

* The Prime Minister's salary is £46,109 but since July 1980 she has drawn the same salary as a Cabinet Minister.

(Ministers who are Members of the House of Commons receive a (reduced) Parliamentary salary (£18,148 in 1989) in addition to this ministerial salary.)

Civil Service (Basic) Salaries
(from April 1, 1989)

+Secretary to the Cabinet and Head of the Home Civil Service	£89,500
+Permanent Secretary to the Treasury	£83,750
+Head of the Diplomatic Service	£83,750
+Grade 1	£72,000
+Grade 1A	£66,000
+Grade 2	£48,100-£50,450
+Grade 3	£37,600-£42,900
Grade 4	£34,095-£35,415
Grade 5	£28,170-£31,602
Grade 6	£21,633-£28,170
Grade 7	£17,360-£22,606
Senior Executive Officer	£13,318-£17,149
Higher Executive Officer (D)	£12,064-£15,179
Higher Executive Officer	£10,851-£13,996
Executive Officer	£6,379-£11,185
Administration Trainee	£9,516-£11,232

+These grades do not attract London Weighting.
London Weighting, since July 1, 1988, is:

Inner zone	£1,750 a year
Intermediate zone	£1,000 a year
Outer zone	£725 a year

The Home Civil Service's unified pay and grading structure for senior personnel represents the following:

Grade	Title
1	Permanent Secretary.
1A	Second Permanent Secretary.
2	Deputy Secretary.
3	Under Secretary.
4	Chief Scientific Officer B, Professional and Technology Directing A.
5	Assistant Secretary, Deputy Chief Scientific Officer, Professional and Technology Directing B.
6	Senior Principal, Senior Principal Scientific Officer, Professional and Technology Superintending Grade.
7	Principal.

ADVISORY, CONCILIATION AND ARBITRATION SERVICE
27 Wilton Street, SW1X 7AX
[01-210 3000]

The Advisory, Conciliation and Arbitration Service (ACAS) is an independent organization set up under the Employment Protection Act, 1975, under the management of a Council appointed by the Secretary of State for Employment. The functions of the Service are to provide facilities for conciliation, mediation and arbitration as a means of avoiding and resolving industrial disputes; and to provide advisory services to industry on industrial relations and matters affecting the quality of working life.

ACAS also has offices in Aldershot, Birmingham, Bristol, Cardiff, Glasgow, Leeds, Liverpool, Manchester, Newcastle upon Tyne and Nottingham.
Chairman, D. B. Smith, C.B.
Chief Conciliation Officer (G4), D. G. Boyd, C.B.E.
Director of Resources and General Policy Branch (G5), E. Norcross.

MINISTRY OF AGRICULTURE, FISHERIES AND FOOD
Whitehall Place, SW1A 2HH†
[01-270 3000]

The Ministry of Agriculture, Fisheries and Food is responsible for administering government policy for agriculture, horticulture, fisheries and food in England and for many food matters in the United Kingdom as a whole. Some of the Ministry's responsibilities for animal health extend to Great Britain. The Agricultural Development and Advisory Service (ADAS) is part of the Ministry. In association with the other Agricultural Departments in the U.K. and the Intervention Board for Agricultural Produce, the Ministry is responsible for the administration of the E.C. common agricultural and fisheries policies and for various national support schemes. It administers arrangements for the control and eradication of animal and plant diseases and for assistance to capital investment in farm and horticultural businesses and flood defence; it exercises responsibilities relating to environmental and rural issues and applied research and development.

The Ministry encourages the development of efficient and competitive food and drink manufacturing industries and, the food and drink importing, distributive and catering trades. It is concerned with the supply and quality of food, food compositional standards, and the labelling and advertising of food and has certain responsibilities for ensuring public health standards in the manufacture, preparation and distribution of basic foods, and planning to safeguard essential food supplies in times of emergency.

Minister, THE RT. HON. JOHN GUMMER, M.P.
  Principal Private Secretary (G7), A. J. Lebrecht.
  Asst. Private Secretary, S. D. Lambert.
  Parliamentary Private Secretary, J. M. Jack, M.P.
  Special Adviser, R. Gueterbock.
Parliamentary Secretary (Lords), THE BARONESS TRUMPINGTON (*Horticulture, Pesticides, Research*).
  Private Secretary, L. D. Harris.
Parliamentary Secretary (Commons), DAVID CURRY, M.P. (*Farming*).
  Private Secretary, Mrs. L. Reay.
Parliamentary Secretary (Commons), DAVID MACLEAN, M.P. (*Food, Countryside*).
  Private Secretary, M. H. P. Hill.
Parliamentary Clerk, R. L. Alderton.
Permanent Secretary (G1), D. H. Andrews, C.B., C.B.E.
  Private Secretary, Miss P. R. Phillips.

ESTABLISHMENT DEPARTMENT
Director of Establishments (G3), J. W. Hepburn.

Manpower Division
Victory House, 30-34 Kingsway, WC2B 6TU
[01-405 4310]
Head of Division (G5), M. T. Haddon.

---

†Unless otherwise stated, this is the main address of Divisions of the Ministry.

Establishments (General) Division
Victory House, 30–34 Kingsway, WC2B 6TU
[01–405 4310]
Head of Division (G5), Mrs. A. M. Pickering.

Staff Training Branch*
Principal (G7), G. F. Buxton, O.B.E.

Welfare Branch
Victory House, 30–34 Kingsway, WC2B 6TU
[01–405 4310]
Chief Welfare Officer (S.E.O.), D. J. Jones.

Personnel Division
Victory House, 30–34 Kingsway, WC2B 6TU
[01–405 4310]
Head of Division (G5), Mrs. K. J. A. Brown.

FINANCE DEPARTMENT

Principal Finance Officer (G3), B. H. B. Dickinson.

Financial Planning Division*
Head of Division (G5), H. B. Brown.

Financial Guidance Division*
Head of Division (G5), R. C. McIvor.

Financial Management Division*
Head of Division (G5), C. J. Lawson.

Audit Division*
Director of Audit (G5), D. V. Fisher.
Deputy Directors of Audit (G6), F. W. Martin; D. J. Littler.

Purchasing and Supply Unit
Director (G5), vacant.

LEGAL DEPARTMENT
55 Whitehall, SW1A 2EY
[01–270 3000]

Legal Adviser and Solicitor (G2), G. J. Jenkins, Q.C.
Principal Assistant Solicitors (G3), A. E. Munir; B. T. Atwood.

Legal Division A1
Assistant Solicitor (G5), P. D. Davis.

Legal Division A2
Assistant Solicitor (G5), A. Yavash.

Legal Division A3
Assistant Solicitor (G5), J. H. Jordan.

Legal Division A4
Assistant Solicitor (G5), Miss E. A. Stephens.

Legal Division A5
Assistant Solicitor (G5), J. E. G. Vaux.

Legal Division B1
Assistant Solicitor (G5), J. F. McCleary.

Legal Division B2
Assistant Solicitor (G5), D. J. Pearson.

Legal Division B3
Assistant Solicitor (G5), R. W. Dyer.

Legal Division B4
Assistant Solicitor (G5), M. C. P. Thomas.

Investigation Unit
Chief Investigation Officer (SEO), A. F. N. Maloney.

MANAGEMENT SERVICES

Under Secretary (G3), M. Madden.

*At Nobel/Ergon House, 17 Smith Square, SW1P 3JR [01-238 3000].

Information Technology Directorate
Government Buildings, Epsom Road,
Guildford, Surrey GU1 2LD
[0483-68121]

Director (G4), D. Selwood.
Assistant Directors (G5), R. J. Wheeler; D. V. Orchard; (G6), A. G. Matthews; R. F. Syrett.

Building Projects Unit
Rivers House, 30–34 Albert
Embankment, SE1 7TL
[01-238 3000]
Head of Division (G5), J. S. Buchanan.

Office Services Division*
Head of Division (G6), J. E. Nunn, D.F.C.

Management Services Division
Rivers House, 30–34 Albert
Embankment, SE1 7TL
[01-238 3000]
Head of Division (G5), P. A. Cocking.

Information Division
Chief Information Officer (G5), J. Coe.
Chief Press Officer, S. Dugdale.
Principal Librarian (G7), T. C. J. Norton.

CHIEF SCIENTIST'S GROUP

Chief Scientist (Fisheries and Food) (G3), M. E. Knowles, Ph.D.*
Chief Scientist (Agriculture and Horticulture) (G3), D. W. F. Shannon, Ph.D.*

RESEARCH AND DEVELOPMENT REQUIREMENTS DIVISION*

Head of Division (G5), C. J. A. Barnes.

FOOD SCIENCE DIVISION I*

Deputy Chief Scientific Officer (G5), vacant.

FOOD SCIENCE DIVISION II*

Head of Division (G5), W. H. B. Denner, Ph.D.

AGRICULTURAL COMMODITIES

Deputy Secretary (G2), R. J. Packer.

EUROPEAN COMMUNITY AND EXTERNAL TRADE POLICY

Under Secretary (G3), R. J. D. Carden.

European Community Division I
Head of Division (G5), C. I. Llewelyn.

European Community Division II
Head of Division (G6), D. Maskell.

External Trade Policy Division
Head of Division (G5), D. P. Hunter.

ARABLE CROPS, PIGS AND POULTRY

Under Secretary (G3), Miss V. K. Timms.

Cereals, Set-Aside and Extensification Division
Head of Division (G5), R. E. Melville.

Sugar, Oils and Fats Division
Head of Division (G5), R. S. Thomas.

Pigs, Eggs and Poultry Division
Head of Division (G5), M. Ring.

MEAT

Under Secretary (G3), S. Wentworth.

Beef Division
Head of Division (G5), J. R. Cowan.

Sheep Division
Head of Division (G5), A. T. Cahn.

Livestock Subsidies Division
Head of Division (G6), G. Belchamber.

MILK

Under Secretary (G3), P. W. Murphy.

Milk (European Communities)
Head of Division (G5), P. Elliott.

Milk Marketing and Potatoes
Head of Division (G5), I. C. Redfern.

FISHERIES AND FOOD

Deputy Secretary (G2), C. W. Capstick, C.M.G.

FISHERIES DEPARTMENT*

Fisheries Secretary (G3), C. R. Cann.

Marine Environmental Protection Division
Head of Division (G5), P. M. Boyling.

Fisheries Division I
Head of Division (G5), G. W. Noble.

Fisheries Division II
Head of Division (G5), A. R. Burne.

Fisheries Division III
Head of Division (G5), Mrs. A. M. Blackburn.

Sea Fisheries Inspectorate
Chief Inspector (G6), M. G. Jennings.

Fisheries Research
Director of Fisheries Research and Development for Great Britain (G4), D. J. Garrod, Ph.D.
Deputy Directors of Fisheries Research (G5), Dr. J. G. Shepherd; Dr. R. J. Pentreath.

Fisheries Laboratory
Pakefield Road, Lowestoft, Suffolk NR33 0HT
[0502–62244]

Fisheries Laboratory
Remembrance Avenue, Burnham-on-Crouch,
Essex CM0 8HA
[0621–782658]

Fisheries Experiment Station
Benarth Road, Conwy, Gwynedd LL32 8UB
[049–263 3883]

Fish Diseases Laboratory
The Nothe, Weymouth, Dorset DT4 8UB
[03057–72137]
Officer-in-Charge (Principal Scientific Officer) (G7),
B. J. Hill, Ph.D.

Torry Research Station
P.O. Box 31, 135 Abbey Road,
Aberdeen AB9 8DG
[0224–877071]
Director (G5), G. Hobbs, Ph.D.

FOOD, DRINK AND MARKETING POLICY

Under Secretary (G3), D. H. Griffiths.

*At Nobel/Ergon House, 17 Smith Square, SW1P 3JR [01–238 3000].

Food Industry, Marketing and Competition Policy Division
Head of Division (G5), J. D. Garnett.

Alcoholic Drinks Division
Head of Division (G5), C. R. Bodrell.

External Relations and Trade Promotion Division
Head of Division (G5), A. H. Abbott.

Tropical Foods*
Head of Division (G5), R. J. Dalton.

EMERGENCIES, FOOD PROTECTION SAFETY AND STANDARDS*

Under Secretary (G3), Mrs. E. A. J. Attridge.

Food Safety, Fertilizers and Feedstuffs Standards Division*
Head of Division (G5), R. C. McKinley.

Food Standards Division*
Head of Division (G5), C. A. Cockbill.

Emergencies and Food Protection Division
Head of Division (G5), G. F. Meekings.

Pesticides Safety*
Head of Division (G5), G. A. Hollis.

Food Legislation*
Head of Division (G5), Miss L. J. Neville-Rolfe.

LAND AND RESOURCES

Deputy Secretary (G2), B. J. G. Hilton.

LANDS AND ENVIRONMENTAL AFFAIRS

Under Secretary (G3), J. A. Anderson.*

Rural Structures and Grants Division*
Head of Division (G5), Miss S. E. Brown.

Land Use and Tenure Division*
Head of Division (G5), G. P. McLachlan.

Environmental Protection Division*
Head of Division (G5), P. P. Nash.

Conservation Policy Division*
Head of Division (G5), Mrs. E. Buttle.

ANIMAL HEALTH

Under Secretary (G3), A. R. Cruickshank.

Veterinary Medicines Directorate
New Haw, Weybridge, Surrey KT15 3NB
[0932-336911]
Director (G4), J. M. Rutter, Ph.D.
Deputy Directors (G5), F. J. H. Scollen; A. R. M. Kidd.

Animal Health Division
Government Buildings, Hook Rise South,
Tolworth, Surbiton, Surrey KT6 7NF
[01–337 6611]
Head of Division (G5), R. C. Lowson.

Animal Welfare Division
Government Buildings, Hook Rise South,
Tolworth, Surbiton, Surrey KT6 7NF
[01–337 6611]
Head of Division (G5), A. J. Perrins.

Meat Hygiene Division
Tolworth Tower, Surbiton, Surrey KT6 7DX
[01–399 5191]
Head of Division (G5), M. J. Griffiths.

HORTICULTURE, SEEDS, PLANT HEALTH AND FLOOD PROTECTION
Under Secretary (G3), G. P. Jupe.

Horticulture Division*
Head of Division (G5), Miss V. A. Smith.

Plant Variety, Rights Office and Seeds
White House Lane, Huntingdon Road,
Cambridge CB3 0LF
[0223–277151]
Head of Division (G5), J. Harvey.

Plant Health Division*
Head of Division (G5), J. C. Edwards.

Flood Defence Division*
Rivers House, 30–34 Albert
Embankment, SE1 7TL
[01-238 3000]
Head of Division (G5), J. R. Park, Ph.D.

ECONOMICS AND STATISTICS
Under Secretary (G3), R. E. Mordue.

Economics (Farm Business) Division
Senior Economic Adviser (G5), Mrs. S. M. Dickinson.

Economics (International) Division
Senior Economic Adviser (G5), R. W. Irving.

Economics (Resource Use) Division
Senior Economic Adviser (G5), A. P. Power, Ph.D.

Statistics (Agricultural Commodities) Division*
Chief Statistician (G5), P. J. Lund, Ph.D.

Statistics (Census and Prices) Division
Government Buildings, Epsom Road,
Guildford GU1 2LD
[0483–68121]
Chief Statistician (G5), D. E. Bradbury.

Economics and Statistics (Food)
Senior Economic Adviser (G5), J. M. Slater, Ph.D.

Agricultural Resources Policy Division
Head of Division (G5), H. R. Neilson.

AGRICULTURAL DEVELOPMENT AND ADVISORY SERVICE (A.D.A.S.) AND REGIONAL ORGANIZATION
Director General of A.D.A.S. and Regional Organization/Chief Scientific Adviser (G2), Prof. R. L. Bell, C.B., Ph.D.

ADAS AND REGIONAL ADMINISTRATION
Director of Regional Administration (G3), D. J. Coates.

Eastern, Block C, Government Buildings, Brooklands Avenue, Cambridge CB2 2DR (0223–358911).—*Regional Director (G4),* G. K. Bruce.

Northern, Block 2, Government Buildings, Lawnswood, Leeds LS16 5PY (0532–611223).—*Regional Director (G4),* A. F. Baines.

---

*At Nobel/Ergon House, 17 Smith Square, SW1P 3JR [01-238 3000].

South Eastern, Block A, Government Offices, Coley Park, Reading RG1 6DT (0734–581222).—*Regional Director (G4),* G. M. Trevelyan.

South Western, Block 3, Government Bldgs., Burghill Road, Westbury-on-Trym, Bristol BS10 6NJ (0272–500000).—*Regional Director (G4),* B. F. Shorney.

Midlands and Western, Woodthorne, Wolverhampton WV6 8TQ (0902–754190).—*Regional Director (G4),* A. D. Bailey.

Wales, Plas Crug, Aberystwyth SY23 1PQ.—*Chief A.D.A.S. Officer (G5),* T. M. K. Evans.

A.D.A.S. and Regional Management Division
Head of Division (G5), B. J. Harding.*

FARM AND COUNTRYSIDE SERVICE

Director of F.C.S. (G3), P. Needham.*
Head of Product Services (G4), J. B. Finney.
Staff Officer (G5), I. M. Tring.

A.D.A.S. Marketing Unit
Head of Unit (G5), D. E. Bawcutt.*

A.D.A.S. Information Services Unit
Rivershill House, St. Georges Road
Cheltenham
Head of Unit (G5), R. W. Swain.

RESEARCH AND DEVELOPMENT SERVICE

Director of R.D.S. (G3), P. J. Bunyan, D.Sc., Ph.D.*
Director of Field Research and Development (G4), A. D. Hughes.*
Director A.D.A.S. Central Science Laboratory (G4), P. I. Stanley, Ph.D.
Staff Officer (G6), W. J. Stubbs.*

A.D.A.S. Central Science Laboratory Slough
London Road, Slough, Berks. SL3 7HJ
[0753–34626]

A.D.A.S. Central Science Laboratory Harpenden
Hatching Green, Harpenden, Herts. AL5 2BD
[0582–75241]
Director of Harpenden Laboratory (G5), H. J. Gould.

STATE VETERINARY SERVICE
Government Buildings, Hook Rise South,
Tolworth, Surbiton, Surrey KT15 3NB
[01–337 6611]

Chief Veterinary Officer (G3A), K. C. Meldrum.
Director of Veterinary Field Services (G3), I. Crawford.
Director of Veterinary Laboratories (G3), W. A. Watson, C.B., Ph.D.
Staff Officer (G5), W. A. Edwards.

Central Veterinary Laboratory,
New Haw, Weybridge, Surrey KT15 3NB
[09323–41111]

Lasswade Veterinary Laboratory,
East of Scotland College of Agriculture,
The Bush Estate, Penicuik,
Midlothian EH26 09N
[031–445 4811]

Cattle Breeding Centre,
Shinfield, Reading, Berks. RG2 9BZ
[0734–883157]

AGRICULTURAL AND FOOD RESEARCH COUNCIL
Central Office, Wiltshire Court,
Farnsby Street, Swindon SN1 5AT
[0793-514242]

The Agricultural and Food Research Council (A.F.R.C.) is an independent body established by Royal Charter. It is funded from the Science Budget of the Department of Education and Science, receives commissions from the Ministry of Agriculture, Fisheries and Food, and does research for industry and other bodies.

The Council is responsible for research done in its institutes and in U.K. university departments funded through its research grants scheme. It advises the Department of Agriculture and Fisheries for Scotland (D.A.F.S.) on research in the Scottish Agricultural Research Institutes.

The institutes funded through A.F.R.C. and D.A.F.S., and the university groups supported, form the Agricultural and Food Research Service.

Chairman, The Earl of Selborne, K.B.E.
Deputy Chairman and Secretary, Prof. W. D. P. Stewart, F.R.S.E., F.R.S.
Members, Prof. R. L. Bell, C.B.; Prof. T. L. Blundell, F.R.S.; T. E. Boswell; Prof. D. Boulter; J. E. Cross; R. N. Crossett; Prof. J. M. M. Cunningham, C.B.E., F.R.S.E.; Prof. A. W. Cuthbert, F.R.S.; D. F. Goodwin; A. C. Green; L. P. Hamilton, C.B.; Prof. J. L. Harper, F.R.S.; Prof. W. F. H. Jarrett; Prof. J. R. Krebs; M. Mackie; Prof. A. Nienow; J. A. Parry, C.B.E.; G. T. Pryce; B. C. Read, C.B.E.; Dr. D. W. F. Shannon; Prof. R. Whittenbury.
Assessors, Prof. E. C. Cocking, F.R.S.; Dr. R. F. Coleman, F.R.S.E.; J. I. Davies, M.B.E.; K. Meldrum; Dr. C. McMurray.
Deputy Secretary (G2), Prof. J. Hearn.
Director of Central Office (G3), B. G. Jamieson, Ph.D.
Heads of Divisions (G5), R. Prideaux (*Finance*); J. Dickens (*Personnel*); Dr. J. V. Lake (*Research*); vacant (*Policy*).
Commercial Policy Section (G7), S. M. Lawrie.
Principal Information Officer (G7), M. A. Winstanley.
For institutes and units of the Agricultural and Food Research Service, *see* Index.

COLLEGE OF ARMS OR HERALDS COLLEGE
Queen Victoria Street, EC4V 4BT
[01-248 2762]

The College is the official repository of the Arms and pedigrees of English, Northern Irish, and Commonwealth families and their descendants, and its records include official copies of the records of Ulster King of Arms, the originals of which remain in Dublin. The 13 officers of the College specialize in genealogical and heraldic work for their respective clients.

Arms have been and still are granted by Letters Patent from the Kings of Arms under Authority delegated to them by the Sovereign, such authority having been expressly conferred on them since at least the fifteenth century. A right to Arms can only be established by the registration in the official records of the College of Arms of a pedigree showing direct male line descent from an ancestor already appearing therein as being entitled to Arms, or by making application through the College of Arms for a Grant of Arms.

The College of Arms is open Mon.–Fri. 10–4, when an Officer of Arms is in attendance to deal with enquiries by the public, though such enquiries may also be directed to any of the Officers of Arms, either personally or by letter.

Earl Marshal, His Grace the Duke of Norfolk, K.G., G.C.V.O., C.B., C.B.E., M.C.

Kings of Arms

Garter, Sir Colin Cole, K.C.V.O., T.D., F.S.A.
Clarenceux, Sir Anthony Wagner, K.C.B., K.C.V.O., F.S.A.
Norroy and Ulster, J. P. B. Brooke-Little, C.V.O., F.S.A.

Heralds

York (and Registrar), C. M. J. F. Swan, C.V.O., Ph.D., F.S.A.
Chester, D. H. B. Chesshyre, F.S.A.
Windsor, T. D. Mathew.
Lancaster, P. L. Gwynn-Jones.
Somerset, T. Woodcock.
Richmond, P. L. Dickinson.

Earl Marshal's Secretary, Sir Walter Verco, K.C.V.O., Surrey Herald Extraordinary.

Pursuivants

Portcullis, P. B. Spurrier.
Bluemantle, T. D. McCarthy.
Rouge Croix, H. E. Paston-Bedingfeld.
Rouge Dragon, T. H. S. Duke.

COURT OF THE LORD LYON
H.M. New Register House, Edinburgh EH1 3YT
[031–556 7255]

The Court of the Lord Lyon is the Scottish Court of Chivalry, (including the genealogical jurisdiction of the *Ri-Sennachie* of Scotland's Celtic Kings) and adjudicates rights to arms and administration of The Scottish Public Register of All Arms and Bearings and Public Register of All Genealogies. The Lord Lyon presides and judicially establishes rights to existing arms or succession to Chiefship, or for cadets with scientific "differences" showing position in clan or family. Pedigrees are also established by decrees of Lyon Court, and by Letters Patent. As Royal Commissioner in Armory, he grants Patents of Arms (which constitute the grantee and heirs noble in the Noblesse of Scotland) to "virtuous and well-deserving" Scotsmen, and petitioners (personal or corporate) in Her Majesty's overseas realms of Scottish connection, and issues birthbrieves.

Lord Lyon King of Arms, Malcolm Rognvald Innes of Edingight, C.V.O., W.S., F.S.A. *scot.*

Heralds

Albany, J. A. Spens, R.D., W.S.
Rothesay, Sir Crispin Agnew of Lochnaw, Bt.
Ross, C. J. Burnett, F.S.A. *scot.*

Pursuivants

Kintyre, J. C. G. George, F.S.A. *scot.*
Unicorn, Alastair Campbell of Airds, younger, F.S.A. *scot.*

Lyon Clerk and Keeper of Records, Mrs. C. G. W. Roads, F.S.A. *scot.*
Procurator-Fiscal, I. R. Guild, C.B.E., W.S.
Herald Painter, Mrs. J. Phillips.
Macer, T. C. Gray.

ART GALLERIES, ETC.

OFFICE OF ARTS AND LIBRARIES
Horse Guards Road, SW1P 3AL
[01–270 3000]

The Office of Arts and Libraries, formerly part of the Department of Education and Science, became a separate department in 1983. It has general responsibilities for arts policy and its broad objectives are to assist the provision and development of the performing and visual arts, to maintain and enhance the collections of national museums and art galleries, to help preserve the national heritage and to sustain and develop national collections of literary and archive material. It directly funds some 20 bodies including the Arts Council, the eleven national museums and galleries, the British Library and its St. Pancras project. The Office of Arts and Libraries also has policy responsibilities towards the public library and local museum services. The Government Art Collection, which is responsible for the acquisition, maintenance and display of works of art in major government buildings in this country and abroad, forms part of the Office of Arts and Libraries.

Minister for the Arts, THE RT. HON. RICHARD LUCE, M.P.
  Private Secretary, M. Le Jeune.
  Parliamentary Private Secretary, J. Hanley, M.P.
Head of the Office of Arts and Libraries (Deputy Secretary), C. E. Henderson.

Arts and Heritage
Assistant Secretary, R. H. Stone.
Principals, P. J. Fallon; Miss M. J. Lamont; S. J. Alcock; Miss C. R. Morrison.

Museums, Galleries,Finance and Establishments
Assistant Secretary, Mrs. S. D. Brown.
Principals, I. D. Baxter; D. M. Mainwood; E. A. Yeo.

Libraries and Information Services
Assistant Secretary, C. C. Leamy.
Principal, A. Poulter.
Library Advisers, P. J. Beauchamp; Miss C. R. Lutyens.

British Library Project St. Pancras
Project Director, J. R. W. Pardey.
Principal, E. T. James.

Government Art Collection
Curator, Dr. W. Baron.

ARTS COUNCIL OF GREAT BRITAIN
105 Piccadilly, W1V 0AU
[01-629 9495]

The Arts Council, an independent body established by Royal Charter in 1946, is Great Britain's principal channel for public financial support of the arts. It funds the major arts organizations in England, the Regional Arts Associations and the Scottish and Welsh Arts Councils. It also provides a service of advice, information and help to artists, arts organizations and the general public.

Its aims are to develop and improve the understanding and practice of the arts and to increase their accessibility to the public.

The Council receives a grant-in-aid from the Government, and for the year 1989–90 the amount is £155 million.
Chairman, P. Palumbo.
Secretary-General, L. Rittner.

ROYAL FINE ART COMMISSION
7 St. James's Square, SW1Y 4JU
[01–839 6537]

Appointed in May, 1924, the Commission is required to advise Departments of State on, and call their attention to, any project or development which might affect national or public amenities.
Chairman, The Lord St. John of Fawsley, P.C.
Commissioners, R. D. Carter, C.B.E.; Dame Elizabeth Chesterton, D.B.E.; Sir Philip Dowson, C.B.E.; M. Girouard, PH.D.; Sir Alexander Gordon, C.B.E.; The Duke of Grafton, K.G., F.S.A.; M. J. Hopkins; R. MacCormac; P. Nuttgens, C.B.E., PH.D.; Mrs. J. Nutting; D. Hamilton Fraser, R.A.; Sir Philip Powell, C.H., O.B.E., R.A.; J. Sutherland; Miss W. Taylor, C.B.E.; W. Whitfield, C.B.E.; J. Winter, M.B.E.; H. T. Moggridge, O.B.E.; S. A. Lipton.
Secretary (G6), S. Cantacuzino, C.B.E.

ROYAL FINE ART COMMISSION FOR SCOTLAND
9 Atholl Crescent,
Edinburgh EH3 8HA
[031–229 1109]

Chairman, Prof. A. J. Youngson, C.B.E.
Commissioners, Miss K. Borland; J. Boys, F.R.I.B.A.; W. D. Campbell; B. Gasson, O.B.E.; Dr. Deborah Howard, PH.D., F.S.A.; W. K. Mackay; A. S. Matheson, F.R.I.B.A.; Prof. I. Metzstein; G. Ogilvie-Laing; R. R. Steedman, R.S.A.; Mrs. F. M. E. Walker.
Secretary, C. Prosser.

NATIONAL GALLERY
Trafalgar Square, WC2N 5DN
[01–839 3321]

Hours of opening.—Weekdays 10–6, Sun. 2–6. Closed on Good Friday, Christmas Eve, Christmas Day, Boxing Day, New Year's Day and May Day Bank Holiday.

The National Gallery was founded in 1824, following a Parliamentary grant of £60,000 for the purchase and exhibition of the Angerstein collection of pictures. The present site was first occupied in 1838 and enlarged and improved at various times throughout the years. A substantial extension to the north of the building with a public entrance in Orange Street was opened in 1975, and a new wing, the Sainsbury wing, is under construction. Expenses for 1989–90 are estimated at £12,425,000.

Board of Trustees
Chairman, Hon. J. Rothschild.
Trustees, H.R.H. The Prince of Wales, K.G., K.T., G.C.B., P.C.; Mrs. C. Hubbard; M. Cowdy; Lord Alexander of Weedon, Q.C.; F. St. J. Gore, C.B.E.; B. Gascoigne; M. Andrews; P. Troughton; Sir Rex Richards, F.R.S.; The Countess of Airlie, C.V.O.; Sir Derek Oulton, K.C.B., Q.C.

Officers
Salaries

Director	£45,100
Grade 5	£33,352–£34,576
Grade 6	£29,920–£31,030

Director, R. N. MacGregor.
Keepers (G5), Dr. A. J. W. Braham; A. J. W. Smith.
Deputy Keepers (G6), Dr. C. P. H. Brown; M. J. Wilson.
Chief Restorer (G5), M. H. Wyld.
Scientific Adviser (G5), Dr. J. S. Mills.
Bursar (G5), Ms. C. E. Macready.
Head of Building, Mrs. J. Evans.

NATIONAL PORTRAIT GALLERY
St. Martin's Place, WC2H 0HE
[01–930 1552]

Open Mon.–Fri. 10–5. Sat. 10–6. Sun. 2–6.

A grant was made in 1856 to form a gallery of the portraits of the most eminent persons in British history. The present building was opened in 1896, £80,000 being contributed to its cost by Mr. W. H. Alexander; an extension erected at the expense of Lord Duveen was opened in 1933. An outstation was opened at Bodelwyddan Castle in 1988.

Chairman, The Rev. Prof. W. O Chadwick, O.M., K.B.E., F.B.A.

Trustees, The Lord President of the Council (*ex officio*); The President of the Royal Academy of Arts (*ex officio*); The Duke of Grafton, K.G., F.S.A.; Sir Oliver Millar, G.C.V.O., F.B.A., F.S.A.; J. Roberts, D.PHIL.; Prof. B. R. Morris, D.PHIL.; Mrs. S. Crosland; Prof. M. Gowing, C.B.E., F.B.A.; The Marquess of Anglesey, F.S.A; H. Keswick; Prof. N. Lynton; The Lord Sieff of Brimpton, O.B.E.; The Lord Weidenfeld; Sir Eduardo Paolozzi; J. Tusa.

Director, J. T. Hayes, C.B.E., PH.D., F.S.A. £34,769
Keeper and Deputy Director, M. Rogers, D.Phil.
£33,352

TATE GALLERY
Millbank, SW1P 4RG
[01–821 1313]

Hours of opening.—Weekdays 10–5.50. Sun. 2–5.50. Closed on New Year's Day, Good Friday, May Day Holiday, Christmas Eve, Christmas Day and Boxing Day.

The Tate Gallery comprises the National Collections of British painting and 20th century painting and sculpture. Works are displayed at the Gallery as two collections: The British Collection and the Modern Collection. The Gallery was opened in 1897, the cost of erection (£80,000) being defrayed by Sir Henry Tate, who also contributed the nucleus of the present collection. The Turner Wing, built at the expense of Sir Joseph Duveen was opened in 1920. Lord Duveen defrayed the cost of galleries to contain the collection of modern foreign painting, completed in 1926, and a new sculpture hall, completed in 1937. The latest extension to the Tate Gallery, the Clore Gallery for the Turner Collection, was opened by H.M. The Queen on April 1, 1987. The Tate Gallery Liverpool, sited in the Albert Dock opened in May 1988. Total government funding for 1989–90 is £12,447,000.

Board of Trustees

Chairman, D. Stevenson.
Trustees, The Countess of Airlie, C.V.O.; Sir Anthony Caro, C.B.E.; G. de Botton; J. Golding; D. Puttnam, C.B.E.; Sir Mark Weinberg; Mrs. C. Hubbard; W. Govett; Mrs. P. Ridley; M. Craig-Martin.

Officers
Salaries

Director £45,400	
Grade 5 . . . . £28,170–£31,602	
Grade 6 . . . . £21,633–£28,170	

Director, N. Serota.
Keeper of the British Collection (G5), vacant.
Keeper of the Modern Collection (G5), R. Morphet
Keeper of Conservation (G5), The Viscount Dunluce
Curator of the Turner Collection (G6), A. Wilton
Deputy Keepers (G6), L. A. Parris; Miss R. Rattenbury; R. Perry.

Secretary and Head of Administration (G6), R. Aylward.

Tate Gallery Liverpool
Albert Dock, Liverpool L3 4BB
[051–709 3223]

Open Tues.–Sun., 11–7. Admission free.
Curator (G6), R. Francis.

WALLACE COLLECTION
Hertford House, Manchester Square, W1M 6BN
[01–935 0687]

Admission free. Open on weekdays 10–5: Sun. 2–5. Closed on Good Friday, December 24–26, January 1 and May Day.

The Wallace Collection was bequeathed to the nation by the widow of Sir Richard Wallace, Bt., on her death in 1897, and Hertford House was subsequently acquired by the Government. The collection includes pictures, drawings and miniatures, French furniture, sculpture, bronzes, porcelain, armour and miscellaneous *objets d'art.* The total net expenses for 1989–90 were estimated at £1,626,000.
Director, J. A. S. Ingamells.
Assistants to Director, P. Hughes; Miss R. J. Savill.
Head of Administration, A. W. Houldershaw.

NATIONAL GALLERIES OF SCOTLAND
The Mound, Edinburgh EH2 2EL
[031–556 8921]

Chairman of the Trustees, A. M. Grossart.
Trustees, The Countess of Rosebery; J. Packer, O.B.E.; A. R. Cole-Hamilton; Mrs. L. W. Gibbs; Sir Norman Macfarlane; J. D. Richards, C.B.E.; R. W. Begg; Dr. T. Johnston; Prof. A. A. Tait.

Salaries 1989

Director . . . . £30,344–£31,844	
Keeper . . . . £18,786–£25,335	
Assistant Keeper/Curator . . . . £12,024–£20,292	

Director, T. Clifford.
Keeper of Conservation, J. P. Dick.
Keeper of Information (Asst. Keeper), R. Dalrymple.
Secretary (Asst. Keeper), W. J. Sinclair.

Comprising:

National Gallery of Scotland
The Mound, Edinburgh
[031–556 8921]

Open: Mon.–Sat. 10–5; Sun. 2–5; Closed December 25, 26, 31; January 1, 2, 3.
Keeper, M. Clarke.
Assistant Keepers, Miss L. M. Errington, PH.D.; Ms. J. Lloyd Williams.
Keeper of Prints and Drawings, H. Macandrew.

Scottish National Portrait Gallery
1 Queen Street, Edinburgh
[031–556 8921]

Hours—as for National Gallery of Scotland.
Keeper, D. Thomson, PH.D.
Assistant Keepers, Miss R. K. Marshall, PH.D.; J. E. Holloway.
Curator of Photography, Miss S. F. Stevenson.

Scottish National Gallery of Modern Art
Belford Road, Edinburgh EH4 3DR
[031–556 8921]

Hours—as for National Gallery of Scotland.

Keeper, R. Calvocoressi.
Assistant Keeper, K. S. Hartley.

(For other British Art Galleries, *see* Index.)

UNITED KINGDOM ATOMIC ENERGY AUTHORITY
11 Charles II Street, SW1Y 4QP
[01–930 5454]

Established by the Atomic Energy Authority Act, 1954, the Authority is responsible for providing research and development support for the U.K. nuclear power programme. It also undertakes work on other civil applications of nuclear energy and on various projects outside the nuclear field on repayment. Since April 1986 the UKAEA has been required by the Government to operate on a quasi-commercial footing. The UKAEA has eight laboratories and a London headquarters employing some 12,000 people.
Chairman, J. G. Collier £75,000
Members (full-time), Dr. G. G. E. Low, C.B.E.; C. C. S. Chapman; Dr. B. L. Eyre.
Members (part-time) Prof. Sir Peter Hirsch, F.R.S.; J. Bullock; R. Sanderson, O.B.E.; J. N. Maltby, C.B.E.; Prof. Sir Roger Elliott, F.R.S; J. A. Gardiner (*each* £6,400).
Secretary, M. A. W. Baker.

THE AUDIT COMMISSION FOR LOCAL AUTHORITIES IN ENGLAND AND WALES
1 Vincent Square, SW1P 2PN
[01–828 1212]

The Audit Commission was set up in 1983. Its main responsibility is for appointing external auditors for local authorities and certain other public bodies in England and Wales. The auditors may be from the District Audit Service or from a private firm of accountants. The Commission also tries to ensure that local authorities are getting, and giving, value for money through special studies of their services. More recently, the Government has extended the Audit Commission's powers to carry out the external audit of the National Health Service.

The Commission has 15–17 members appointed by the Secretary of State for the Environment in consultation with the Secretary of State for Wales. Though appointed by the Secretary of State the Commissioners are responsible to Parliament.
Chairman, D. J. S. Cooksey.
Deputy Chairman, H. S. Axton.
Controller of Audit, H. J. Davies.
Deputy Controller, J. C. Nicholson, C.B.E.

THE COMMISSION FOR LOCAL AUTHORITY ACCOUNTS IN SCOTLAND
18 George Street, Edinburgh EH2 2QU
[031–226 7346]

The Commission was set up in 1975. It is responsible for securing the audit of the accounts of Scottish local authorities and certain joint boards and joint committees. Amongst its duties the Commission is required to deal with reports made by the Controller of Audit on items of account contrary to law; incorrect accounting; and losses due to misconduct, negligence and failure to carry out statutory duties.

Members are appointed by the Secretary of State for Scotland.
Chairman, Prof. J. R. Small.
Controller of Audit, J. Broadfoot.
Secretary, K. Ferguson.

THE BANK OF ENGLAND
Threadneedle Street, EC2R 8AH

The Bank of England was incorporated in 1694 under Royal Charter. It is the banker of the Government on whose behalf it manages the Note Issue and the National Debt. As central reserve bank of the country, the Bank keeps the accounts of British banks, who maintain with it a proportion of their cash resources, and of most overseas central banks.
Governor, Rt. Hon. Robin Leigh-Pemberton.
Deputy Governor, Sir George Blunden.
Directors, Dr. D. V. Atterton, C.B.E.; Hon. Sir John Baring, C.V.O.; Sir Adrian Cadbury; F. B. Corby; Sir Colin Corness; A. D. Crockett; J. S. Fleming; R. D. Galpin; E. A. J. George; Sir Robert Haslam; Sir Martin Jacomb; Sir Hector Laing; G. H. Laird; B. Quinn; Sir David Scholey, C.B.E.; D. A. Walker; Sir Leslie Young, C.B.E.
Associate Directors, P. H. Kent; H. C. E. Harris.
Advisers to the Governor, J. P. Charkham; A. L. Coleby; Sir Peter Petrie.
Assistant Directors, I. Plenderleith; R. A. Barnes.
Chief of Banking Department (*Chief Cashier*), G. M. Gill.
Chief Registrar, J. G. Drake.
General Manager, Printing Works, A. W. Jarvis.
Secretary, G. A. Croughton.
Head of Information Division, J. R. E. Footman.
The Auditor, J. Bartlett.

BOUNDARY COMMISSIONS

The Commissions are constituted under the Parliamentary Constituencies Act, 1986. The Speaker of the House of Commons is ex-officio chairman of all four Commissions in the United Kingdom. Each of the four Commissions is required by law to keep the parliamentary constituencies in their part of the United Kingdom under review. Each of the three Commissions in Great Britain is required by law to keep the European Parliamentary constituencies in their part of Great Britain under review.

England
St. Catherines House, 10 Kingsway, WC2B 6JP
[01–242 0262]

Deputy Chairman, The Hon. Mr. Justice Knox.
Joint Secretaries, R. McLeod; Mrs. M. E. Moxon.

Wales
St. Catherines House, 10 Kingsway, WC2B 6JP
[01–242 0262]

Deputy Chairman, The Hon. Mr. Justice Anthony Evans.
Joint Secretaries, R. McLeod; Mrs. M. E. Moxon.

Scotland
St. Andrew's House, Edinburgh EH1 3DE
[031–244 2196-8]

Deputy Chairman, The Hon. Lord Davidson.
Secretary, A. Simmen, O.B.E.

Northern Ireland
c/o Northern Ireland Office,
Whitehall, SW1A 2AZ
[01–210 6569]

Deputy Chairman, Mr. Justice Higgins.
Secretary, J. R. Fisher.

BRITISH BROADCASTING CORPORATION
Broadcasting House, W1A 1AA
[01–580 4468]

The B.B.C. was incorporated under Royal Charter as successor to the British Broadcasting Company, Ltd., whose licence expired Dec. 31, 1926. Its present Charter came into force Aug. 1, 1981, for 15 years. The Chairman, Vice-Chairman and other Governors are appointed by the Queen in Council. The B.B.C. is financed by revenue from receiving licences for the Home services and by grant-in-aid from Parliament for the External services. The total number of receiving licences in the U.K. at March 31, 1989 was 19,395,963, of which 1,926,805 were for monochrome receivers and 17,469,158 for colour receivers. Annual television fees are: monochrome £22; colour £66. Television licence fees became index-linked from April 1, 1988.

Board of Governors
(as at Aug. 1, 1989)

Chairman, M. Hussey. £37,360
Vice-Chairman, The Lord Barnett, P.C. £9,605
Governors, J. Kincade, PH.D. *(N. Ireland);* J. Parry *(Wales);* Sir Graham Hills, PH.D., D.SC., F.R.S.E. *(Scotland)* . . . . *(each)*£9,605
Sir Curtis Keeble; Dr. J. Roberts; W. B. Jordan; J. K. Oates; Miss P. D. James, O.B.E. . . . *(each)* £4,790

Board of Management
(as at Aug. 1, 1989)

Director-General, M. Checkland.
Deputy Director-General, J. Birt.
Managing Directors, P. Fox *(Network Television);* D. Hatch *(Network Radio);* J. Tusa *(External Broadcasting);* R. Neil *(Regional Broadcasting).*
Directors, W. Dennay *(Engineering);* H. James *(Corporate Affairs);* I. Phillips *(Finance);* R. Chase *(Personnel).*

Other Senior Staff

Director, News and Current Affairs, I. Hargreaves.
Director, Resources, Radio, D. Thomas.
Director, Resources, Television, C. Taylor.
Deputy Managing Director, External Broadcasting, D. Witherow.
Deputy Director of Engineering, C. Sandbank.
Head of Policy and Planning Unit, Ms. P. Hodgson.
Controller, BBC-1, J. Powell.
Controller BBC-2, A. Yentob.
Assistant Managing Director, Network Television, W. Wyatt.
Controller Radio 1, J. Beerling.
Controller Radio 2, B. Marriott.
Controller Radio 3, J. Drummond.
Controller Radio 4, M. Green.
Controller, Scotland, P. Chalmers.
Controller, Wales, G. Price.
Controller, N. Ireland, Rev. Dr. C. Morris.
Chief Political Adviser, Ms. M. Douglas.
Controller, Editorial Policy, J. Wilson.
Controller Information Services, M. Bunce.
The Secretary, J. McCormick.
Legal Adviser, vacant.
Chief Executive, B.B.C. Enterprises, J.Arnold-Baker.

BRITISH COAL CORPORATION
Hobart House, Grosvenor Place, SW1X 7AE
[01–235 2020]

The British Coal Corporation (formerly the National Coal Board) was constituted in 1946 and took over the mines on January 1, 1947.

Chairman, Sir Robert Haslam.
Deputy Chairman and Operations Director, J. H. Northard, C.B.E.
Deputy Chairman, D. W. Kendall.
Executive Members, M. J. Edwards, C.B.E. *(Commercial Director);* M. H. Butler *(Finance Director);* K. Moses, C.B.E. *(Technical Director).*
*Non-Executive Members,*C. Barker; Dr. D. V. Atterton, C.B.E.; Dr. T. J. Parker; Sir Ronald Dearing, C.B.; D. B. Walker; J. P. Erbé.
Secretary, M. S. Shelton.
Industrial Relations Director, K. Hunt.
Director, Group Operations, A. Wheeler.

THE BRITISH COUNCIL
10 Spring Gardens, SW1A 2BN
[01–930 8466]

The British Council was established in 1934 and incorporated by Royal Charter in 1940.

It is an independent, non-political organization which promotes Britain abroad. It provides access to British ideas, talents and experience in education and training, books and periodicals, the English language, the arts, the sciences and technology.

The Council is represented in more than eighty countries and runs 138 offices, 116 libraries and 52 English language schools around the world.

The Council's annual turnover in 1989–90 is estimated at £312 million, including grants from the Foreign and Commonwealth Office and the Overseas Development Administration. The Council's own earnings now exceed £72 million.

Chairman, Sir David Orr, M.C.
Director-General, Sir Richard Francis, K.C.M.G.
£62,750

BRITISH RAILWAYS BOARD
Euston House, 24 Eversholt Street,
P.O. Box 100, NW1 1DZ
[01–928 5151]

The British Railways Board came into being on Jan. 1, 1963 under the terms of the Transport Act, 1962. The Board became responsible for the provision of railway services in Great Britain and for catering and other services formerly carried on by the British Transport Commission.

Chairman, Sir Robert Reid, C.B.E. £92,691
Vice-Chairmen, D. Fowler, C.B.E.; D. D. Kirby, C.B.E.
Members, H. G. DeVille, C.B.E.*; S. D. Jenkins*; D. P. Hornby*; A. J. G. Sheppard*; R. W. Tookey, C.B.E.*; Ms. A. Biss*; Miss K. T. Kantor*; D. L. Davies; J. B. Cameron; J. K. Welsby, D. E. Rayner; J. J. O'Brien.

* Part-time members, paid *pro rata.*

B.S.I. (BRITISH STANDARDS INSTITUTION)
2 Park Street, W1A 2BS
[Enquiry Section: B.S.I., Linford Wood, Milton Keynes, MK14 6LE. Tel. 0908–221166]

B.S.I. (the British Standards Institution) is the recognized authority in the U.K. for the preparation and publication of national standards for industrial and consumer products. In consultation with the interests concerned, B.S.I. prepares standards relating to nearly every sector of the nation's industry and trade.

British Standards are issued for voluntary adoption, though in a number of cases compliance with a British Standard is required by legislation. B.S.I. operates certification schemes under which industrial and consumer products are certified as complying with the relevant British Standard and manufacturers satisfying the requirements of such schemes may use the Institution's certification trade marks, known as the 'Kitemark' and the 'Safety Mark'.

B.S.I. is financed by voluntary subscriptions, an annual Government grant, the sale of its publications, and fees for testing and certification. There are more than 20,000 subscribing members of B.S.I.

Director General, Dr. I. Dunstan.

BRITISH TECHNOLOGY GROUP
101 Newington Causeway, SE1 6BU
[01–403 6666]

British Technology Group (B.T.G.) is a self-financing technology transfer organization. It is appointed by the Government to license new scientific and engineering products to industry and provides finance for the development of new technology. B.T.G. promotes the development of commercial use of new technology arising from research at U.K. universities, polytechnics, research councils and Government research establishments. B.T.G. provides finance where further development is needed before inventions can be licensed to industry. B.T.G. can also offer finance to companies that want to develop new products and processes based on their own technology.

Chairman, C. Barker.
Chief Executive, I. A. Harvey.

BRITISH TOURIST AUTHORITY
Thames Tower, Black's Road, W6 9EL
[01–846 9000]

The British Tourist Authority has specific responsibility for promoting tourism to Great Britain from overseas. It also has a general responsibility for the promotion and development of tourism and tourist facilities within Great Britain as a whole. With the agreement of the corresponding bodies in Northern Ireland, the Channel Islands and the Isle of Man, the Authority may also carry out promotion overseas on behalf of those territories.

Chairman, D. R. Y. Bluck, O.B.E. (*part-time*).
Chief Executive, M. G. Medlicott.

English Tourist Board
Thames Tower, Black's Road, W6 9EL
[01–846 9000]

Scottish Tourist Board
23 Ravelston Terrace, Edinburgh EH4 3EU
[031–332 2433]

Wales Tourist Board
Brunel House, 2 Fitzalan Road, Cardiff CF2 1UY
[0222–499909]

The English Tourist Board, the Scottish Tourist Board and the Wales Tourist Board are responsible for developing and marketing the tourist industry in their respective countries. The Boards' main objectives are to promote holidays and to encourage the provision and improvement of tourist amenities.

BRITISH WATERWAYS BOARD
Melbury House, Melbury Terrace, NW1 6JX
[01–262 6711]

Chairman, D. C. Ingman (*part-time*).
Vice-Chairman, Sir Peter Hutchison, Bt. (*part-time*).
Members (*all part-time*), J. Gordon; Dr. B. Goodman; M. Golder; D. H. R. Yorke.
Chief Executive, B. C. Dice.
Secretary and Parliamentary Adviser, T. T. Luckcuck.

BROADCASTING STANDARDS COUNCIL
5–8 The Sanctuary, SW1P 3JS
[01–233 0544]

The Council was set up in 1988 to develop a code on the portrayal of sex and of violence and standards of taste and decency in all forms of broadcasting and video work in consultation with producers and the public; and to commission relevant research. Members of the Council are appointed by the Home Secretary. (The appointments are part-time.)

Chairman, The Lord Rees-Mogg £30,000
Deputy Chairman, Miss J. Barrow, O.B.E.

          £15,000–£22,000
Members, R. Barker, O.B.E., R.D.; The Bishop of Peterborough; A. Dubs; Dr. R. Brinley Jones; Dr. Jean Curtis-Raleigh; Rev. C. Robertson ... £9,000
Director, C. Shaw.
Deputy Director, D. Houghton.

THE BROADS AUTHORITY
Thomas Harvey House, 18 Colegate,
Norwich NR3 1BQ
[0603–610734]

The Broads Authority is a special statutory authority set up under the Norfolk and Suffolk Broads Act 1988, with powers and responsibilities similar to those of National Park Authorities. The functions of the Authority, as set out in the Act, are: to conserve and enhance the natural beauty of the Broads; to promote the enjoyment of the Broads by the public; and to protect the interests of navigation.

The Authority comprises 35 members, appointed by Norfolk County Council (4); Suffolk County Council (2); Broadland District Council (2); Great Yarmouth Borough Council (2); North Norfolk District Council (2); Norwich City Council (2); South Norfolk District Council (2); Waveney District Council (2); the Countryside Commission (2); the Nature Conservancy Council (1); the Great Yarmouth Port and Haven Commissioners (2); Anglian Water (1); the Secretary of State for the Environment (9); and two from amongst members of the Authority's statutory Navigation Committee who are not already members of the Authority.

Chairman, J. S. Peel, M.C.
Chief Executive, M. A. Clark.

CABINET OFFICE

The Cabinet Office comprises the Secretariat, who support Ministers collectively in the conduct of Cabinet business; and the Office of the Minister for the Civil Service (O.M.C.S.) which is responsible for the management and organization of the Civil Service and recruitment into it, efficiency, and senior appointments. Other functions are from time to time laid on the Office, some ephemerally and some permanently. Non-departmental Ministers may be attached to the Office.

The functions of the Cabinet Office (O.M.C.S.) are in support of the Prime Minister in her capacity as Minister for the Civil Service, with responsibility for day-to-day supervision delegated to the Minister of State, Privy Council Office.

(For **Salaries,** *see* page 293)

PRIME MINISTER'S OFFICE

Prime Minister and Minister for the Civil Service, THE RT. HON. MARGARET THATCHER, M.P.
Principal Private Secretary to the Prime Minister, (*G3*), A. Turnbull.
Private Secretaries to the Prime Minister, C. D. Powell (*Overseas Affairs*); P. R. C. Gray (*Economic Affairs*);

D. Morris (*Parliamentary Affairs*); Miss C. A. Slocock (*Home Affairs*).
Personal Assistant to the Prime Minister, Mrs. T. Gaisman.
Secretary for Appointments (G5), Mrs. A. Ponsonby.
Foreign Affairs Adviser, Sir Percy Cradock, G.C.M.G.
Political Secretary, J. Whittingdale.
Policy Unit, G. Guise; Miss C. Sinclair; J. Mills; G. D. Bourne; Prof. B. Griffiths; A. Dunlop; I. K. Whitehead; H. Harris-Hughes; Sir Alan Walters.
Chief Press Secretary, B. Ingham.
Deputy Chief Press Secretary, T. J. Perks.
Assistant Private Secretaries to Prime Minister, Miss J. Drever; Miss J. L. Wilkinson.
Parliamentary Private Secretary, Hon. M. Lennox-Boyd, M.P.
Adviser on Efficiency, Sir Angus Fraser, K.C.B., T.D.

Efficiency Unit
70 Whitehall, SW1A 2AS

Head of Unit (G3), D. Brereton.
Assistant Secretaries (G5), Mrs. S. Hughes; J. M. Cunningham.

Secretary to the Cabinet and Head of Home Civil Service, Sir Robin Butler, K.C.B., C.V.O.

Ceremonial Branch
Ceremonial Officer (G5), J. H. Thompson, C.B.

SECRETARIAT
70 Whitehall, SW1A 2AS
[01–270 3000]

Deputy Secretaries (G2), Sir Christopher Curwen, K.C.M.G.; D. Hadley; P. J. Weston, C.M.G.; R. T. J. Wilson.
Chief Scientific Adviser, J. W. Fairclough.
Under Secretaries (G3), G. W. Monger; H. V. B. Brown; P. J. C. Mawer; A. C. D. Macrae; J. F. Mogg; W. D. Reeves.
Assistant Secretaries (G5), G. Barrassi; Brig. J. A. J. Budd; H. Burke, C.B.E.; R. E. Escritt; F. M. Merifield; M. Nicholson; A. L. C. Quigley; R. P. Short; L. Parker; Mrs. G. Craig; D. G. Manning; P. I. Bailey; J. Dilling; Dr. C. C. Bradley.
Senior Principals (G6), A. R. Bell; C. K. Davies; P. C. F. Gilbert; P. F. Tero; Dr. J. N. Wingfield; I. Dixon; P. D. Finch.

ESTABLISHMENT OFFICER'S GROUP
Principal Establishment and Finance Officer, (G3), S. R. Davie.

Information Services
Chief Press Officer (G6), J. P. Lawson.

Establishment Division
Deputy Establishment Officer (G5), A. Phillips.

Finance Division
Senior Finance Officer (G6), Miss J. M. E. Buchan.

Internal Audit
Principal (G7), I. C. R. Boulton.

Historical Section
Hepburn House, Marsham Street, SW1P 4HW
[01–217 6032]

Departmental Records Adviser (G6), Miss. P. Andrews.

OFFICE OF THE MINISTER FOR THE CIVIL SERVICE
Horse Guards Road, SW1P 3AL
[01–270 3000]

Second Permanent Secretary (G1A), E. P. Kemp, C.B.
Director of Management Development and Training (G2), B. T. Gilmore.
Security Adviser, Air Commodore P. V. Mayall, C.B.E

Personnel Management and Development Group
Under Secretary (G3), Mrs. P. A. Denham.
Assistant Secretaries (G5), Mrs. S. Collins; Ms. C. M. Bentley; R. D. J. Wright.

Senior Staff and Europe Division
Under Secretary and Director, Public Appointments Unit (G3), G. T. Morgan.
Assistant Secretary (G5), G. H. Wollen.

Machinery of Government
Assistant Secretary (G5), Dr. J. P. Spencer.

Security Division
Assistant Secretary (G5), H. H. Taylor.

Information Officers Management Unit
Assistant Secretary (G5), Ms. A. Nash.

Occupational Health Service
Tilbury House, Petty France, SW1H 9EU

Medical Adviser and Acting Director of Occupational Health Service, Dr. G. S. Sorrie.
Principal Medical Officers, Dr. P. J. Constable (*Deputy Medical Adviser*); Dr. A. N. Hepburn.

Civil Service Commission
Alencon Link, Basingstoke, Hants. RG21 1JB
[0256–29222]

First Commissioner (G2), J. H. Holroyd.
Commissioners (G3), B. Walmsley; (*G4*), J. K. Moore (*Director, Civil Service Selection Board*).
Commissioners (part-time), D. P. Hornby; G. L. Dennis; Miss D. Whittingham.
Assistant Secretary (G5), C. J. Parry.
Senior Principals (G6), A. S. Halford; R. B. M. Payne; G. S. Royston; P. J. Wiggett.

Civil Service Selection Board
24 Whitehall, SW1A 2ED

Director (G4), J. K. Moore.
Deputy Director (G6), Mrs. D. C. Miller.
Chief Psychologist (G6), F. D. Bedford.

Top Management Programme
Director (G2), B. T. Gilmore.
Deputy Directors (G5), Miss V. M. Dews; W. D. Harding.

Civil Service College
Sunningdale Park, Ascot, Berks. SL5 0QE
[0990–23444]
London: 11 Belgrave Road, SW1V 1RB
[01–834 6644]

Principal (G3), R. Jackling.
College Policy Planning Manager (G5), Mrs. E. A. Shaw.
Directors (G5), J. Allen; A. A. Carter; Dr. R. J. Smith; Mrs. V. H. Stamler; D. P. Laughein.
College Secretary (G6), P. Cook.

CABLE AUTHORITY
Gillingham House, 38–44 Gillingham Street,
SW1V 1HU
[01–821 6161]

The Cable Authority is the statutory body established by the Cable and Broadcasting Act 1984 to grant franchises for the operation of new cable systems and to licence the provision of and regulate the content of cable programme services, including those satellite television channels which are carried on cable networks.
Chairman, R. Burton.
Deputy Chairman, Prof. J. Ring, C.B.E.
Members, Mrs. A. Ballard; P. Johnson; Mrs. E. MacDonald-Brown; P. Paine, C.B.E., D.F.C; P. Darwin.
Director-General, J. Davey.
Secretary, A. Hewitt.

CENTRAL STATISTICAL OFFICE
Great George Street, SW1P 3AQ
[01–270 3000]

With effect from July 31, 1989, the Central Statistical Office (formerly part of the Cabinet Office), the Business Statistics Office and certain other parts of the Department of Trade and Industry, together with some parts of the Department of Employment, were combined to form a separate government department responsible to the Chancellor of the Exchequer. It retains the name Central Statistical Office. Its work encompasses data collection from businesses and the preparation of macro-economic statistics; statistics relating to institutional sectors and financial statistics; the retail prices index and the family expenditure survey; liaison with international statistical bodies and central management of the Government Statistical Services (G.S.S.).
Director and Head of the Government Statistical Service (G1A), J. Hibbert.
Private Secretary, I. Cope.
Deputy Director (G3+), M. J. Erritt.
Principal Establishment Officer (G5), F. Martin.
Head of Information (G5), J. B. Wright.
National Accounts Quality Control (G5), R. J. Scott.

Directorate A

Deputy Director of the CSO (G3), M. J. Erritt.
Heads of Branches (G5):
  International and social statistics, T. J. Griffin.
  G.S.S. management and policy, P. P. Altobell.
  Methodology, survey control and classifications, P. B. Kenny.

Directorate B
The Business Statistics Office,
Cardiff Road, Newport, Gwent NP9 1XG
[0633–815696]

Director (G3), N. Harvey.
Heads of Branches (G5):
  Short term production and products, D. R. Lewis.
  Censuses, stocks, capital expenditure, C. J. Spiller.
  Distribution and services; prices; purchases, R. M. Norton.
  Registers, legal, statistical computing, Dr. R. L. Butchart.
  Newport computing, C. C. Maskall.

Directorate C

Assistant Director (G3), R. G. Ward.
Heads of Branches (G5):
  National accounts co-ordination, Miss S. P. Carter.
  Total domestic expenditure, K. Mansell.

GDP(O), IOP and industrial statistics, D. C. K. Stirling.

Directorate D

Assistant Director (G3), J. E. Kidgell.
Heads of Branches (G5):
  Balance of payments current account, G. Jenkinson.
  Financial accounts, B. J. Buckingham.
  Private sector accounts, Dr. G. A. Keenay.
  Overseas transactions; research and development statistics, P. H. Richardson.

Directorate E

Assistant Director (G3), P. D. Dworkin.
Heads of Branches (G5):
  Information systems and strategy, Dr. J. H. Ludley.
  Retail prices, expenditure, taxes and benefits, D. J. Sellwood.
  Press, publications, publicity, J. B. Wright.

CERTIFICATION OFFICE FOR TRADE UNIONS AND EMPLOYERS' ASSOCIATIONS
27 Wilton Street, SW1X 7AZ
[01–210 3733/4]

The Certification Officer is an independent statutory authority appointed by the Secretary of State for Employment. He is responsible for receiving and scrutinizing annual returns from trade union and employers' associations; for reimbursing certain costs of trade unions' postal ballots; for dealing with complaints concerning trade union elections; for ensuring observance of statutory requirements governing political funds and trade union mergers; and for certifying the independence of trade unions.
Certification Officer, M. Wake.
Assistant Certification Officer, G. S. Osborne.

Scotland
58 Frederick Street, Edinburgh EH2 1LN
[031–226 3224]

Assistant Certification Officer for Scotland, J. L. J. Craig.

CHARITY COMMISSION
St. Alban's House, 57–60 Haymarket, SW1Y 4QX
[01–210 3000]

Northern Office:
Graeme House, Derby Square, Liverpool L2 7SB
[051–227 3191]

The Charity Commissioners are appointed under the Charities Act, 1960, principally to further the work of charities in England and Wales by giving advice and information, and by investigating and checking abuses. The Commissioners maintain a register of charities; give consent to land transactions; help to modernize the purposes and administrative machinery of charities; and, in the name of one of their staff, the Official Custodian for Charities, hold investments for charities.

Salaries

Commissioners	£34,095–£47,600
Grade 5	£28,170–£41,225
Grade 6	£21,633–£35,415
Grade 7	£17,360–£26,958

Chief Commissioner, R. I. L Guthrie.
Commissioners, J. Farquharson; R. M. C. Venables.
Commissioners (part-time), M. Webber; Mrs. D. H. Yeo.

Deputy Commissioners (G5), J. A. Dutton; J. F. Claricoat; Mrs. J. F. Quint; G. S. Goodchild; K. M. Dibble.
Asst. Commissioners (G6), Mrs. H. M. Phillips; Miss D. F. Taylor; S. K. Sen; P. P. White; N. M. Mackenzie; D. C. Raikes; Miss V. A. Nuttall; S. Slack; M. J. Harbottle; I. M. Davies; P. W. Somerfield.
Secretary and Asst. Commissioner (G5), D. Forrest.
Director of Operations and Asst. Commissioner (G5), J. H. Vining.
Asst. Commissioners (G7), R. E. Hatton; A. O. Polak; Miss S. M. St. C. Smith; M. C. T. Seymour; Miss C. F. Byrne; K. M. Dickin; M. J. McManus; R. E. Edwards; G. B. Ward.
Official Custodian for Charities (G6), R. J. Crick.
Deputy Official Custodian (G7), Mrs. S. E. Gillingham.
Establishment Officer (G6), J. M. Samuels.

OFFICE OF THE
CHIEF ADJUDICATION OFFICER
Cumberland House,
15–17 Cumberland Place, Southampton SO9 2DD
[0703–330066]

The Chief Adjudication Officer is an independent authority under the Social Security Act, 1975 (as amended) appointed by the Secretary of State for Social Services to give advice to adjudication officers (who make decisions of first instance on all claims for Social Security cash benefits), to keep under review the operation of the system of adjudication and to report annually to the Secretary of State on adjudication standards. The Office also enters written observations on all appeals made to the Social Security Commissioners.
Chief Adjudication Officer, M. E. H. Platt.

CHURCH COMMISSIONERS

1 Millbank, SW1P 3JZ
[01–222 7010]

The Church Commissioners were established on April 1, 1948, by the amalgamation of *Queen Anne's Bounty* (established 1704) and the *Ecclesiastical Commissioners* (established 1836).

The Commissioners' main task is to improve the stipends and housing of the Church of England clergy and to provide them and their widows with adequate pensions and assistance with housing in retirement. They also carry out administrative duties in connection with pastoral reorganization and redundant churches, and have been designated by the General Synod as the Central Stipends Authority of the Church of England.

The Commissioners' income for the year ended Dec. 31, 1988, was derived from the following sources:—

	£ million
Stock exchange investments	54·8
Land and property	53·5
Mortgages, loans, etc.	15·3
Trust income, and diocesan/parish contributions for stipends	59·6
	£183·5

This income was applied as follows:—

Clergy stipends	100·1
Clergy and widows' pensions	44·7
Clergy houses	22·7
Episcopal administration and payments to Chapters	6·8
Church buildings	4·5

Administrative expenses of the Commissioners and related bodies	10·1
Carried forward	5·6
	£189·1

Constitution

The 2 Archbishops, the 41 diocesan Bishops, 5 deans or provosts, 10 other clergy and 10 laymen appointed by the General Synod; 4 laymen nominated by the Queen; 4 persons nominated by the Archbishop of Canterbury; The Lord Chancellor; The Lord President of the Council; the First Lord of the Treasury; The Chancellor of the Exchequer; The Secretary of State for the Home Department; The Speaker of the House of Commons; The Lord Chief Justice; The Master of the Rolls; The Attorney-General; The Solicitor-General; The Lord Mayor and two Aldermen of the City of London; The Lord Mayor of York and one representative from each of the Universities of Oxford and Cambridge.

Church Estates Commissioners

First, Sir Douglas Lovelock, K.C.B.
Second, Rt. Hon. Michael Alison, M.P.
Third, Mrs. M. H. Laird.

Officers

Secretary, J. E. Shelley.
Deputy Secretary, P. Locke.
Under Secretary (Pastoral), D. J. Day.
Assistant Secretaries, D. I. Archer (*Chief Accountant*); P. H. P. Shaw, L.V.O. (*Estates*); R. M. Hutchings (*Commercial Property*); W. R. Herbert (*Establishment Officer*); J. M. Davies (*Redundant Churches*); D. N. Goodwin (*Pastoral*); R. S. Hopgood (*Stipends and Allocations*); J. W. Ferguson (*Computer*); D. J. B. Long (*Houses*); C. P. Canton (*Bishoprics*); P. G. Brealey (*Investments*).
Deputy Accountant and Trust Officer, G. C. Baines.
Press & Information Officer, M. D. Elengorn.
Principals, A. W. Atkins; P. D. Chadwick; M. G. S. Farrell; Miss A. M. Mackie; E. G. Peacock; G. Wills; J. A. W. Elloy; C. R. Bullen; N. M. Waring; J. M. Shirley.

Legal Department

Official Solicitor, E. W. Wills.
Deputy Solicitor, J. P. Guy.
Solicitors (G6), Miss J. M. Bland; J. D. Carter; Miss S. M. S. Jones; R. D. C. Murray.
Senior Legal Assistant, Mrs. S. E. Prosser.

Main Agents

Messrs. Cluttons, 5 Great College Street, SW1.
Messrs. Smiths Gore, The King's Lodgings, Minster Precincts, Peterborough.
Messrs. Chesterton, Lalonde, 54 Brooke Street, W1.

CIVIL AVIATION AUTHORITY
C.A.A. House, 45–59 Kingsway, WC2B 6TE
[01–379 7311]

The C.A.A. is responsible for the economic regulation of U.K. airlines by licensing air routes, air travel organizers and approving fares; for the safety regulation of U.K. civil aviation by the certification of airlines and aircraft, and by licensing aerodromes, flight crew and aircraft engineers; and, through the National Air Traffic Services, for the provision of air traffic control and telecommunications services.

Chairman, C. Tugendhat (*part-time*) £60,000
Managing Director, T. Murphy.
Secretary, Miss G. M. E. White.

COMMONWEALTH DEVELOPMENT CORPORATION
1 Bessborough Gardens, SW1V 2JQ
[01–828 4488]

The Corporation's area of operations covers British dependent territories and, with Ministerial approval, any Commonwealth or other developing country. At present, the Corporation is authorized to operate in 36 Commonwealth and 16 non-Commonwealth countries in addition to the British dependent territories. The Corporation is authorized to borrow up to £750,000,000.

Chairman (*part-time*), P. Leslie.
Deputy Chairman (*part-time*), Sir Michael Caine.
Members (*part-time*), Mrs. A. Wright; V. Robertson, O.B.E.; M. D. Nightingale, O.B.E.; Prof. M. Faber; M. Robinson.
General Manager, J. D. Eccles, C.B.E.

COMMONWEALTH SECRETARIAT
(*see* p. 626)

COMMONWEALTH WAR GRAVES COMMISSION
2 Marlow Road, Maidenhead, Berkshire SL6 7DX
[0628–34221]

The Commonwealth War Graves Commission (formerly Imperial War Graves Commission) was founded by Royal Charter in 1917. It is responsible for the commemoration of 1,695,000 members of the forces of the Commonwealth who fell in the two world wars. More than one million graves are maintained in 23,104 burial grounds throughout the world. Over three-quarters of a million men and women who have no known grave or who were cremated are commemorated by name on memorials built by the Commission.

The funds of the Commission are derived from the six Governments participating in its work—the U.K., Australia, Canada, India, New Zealand and South Africa.

President, H.R.H. The Duke of Kent, K.G., G.C.M.G., G.C.V.O.
Chairman, The Secretary of State for Defence in the U.K.
Vice-Chairman, Gen. Sir Robert Ford, G.C.B., C.B.E.
Members, The Secretary of State for the Environment in the U.K.; The High Commissioners for Australia, Canada, India, and New Zealand; the Ambassador for the Republic of South Africa; Air Chief Marshal Sir John Gingell, G.B.E., K.C.B.; Capt. Sir Miles Wingate, K.C.V.O.; Maj.-Gen. D. Smith, C.B.E., D.S.O.; The Rt. Hon. J. D. Concannon; Dame Janet Fookes, D.B.E., M.P.; Sir Derek Day, K.C.M.G.; Sir Nigel Mobbs; Adm. Sir Nicholas Hunt, G.C.B, L.V.O.
Director-General, J. Saynor.
Deputy Director-Generals, D. Kennedy (*Administration*); N. B. Osborn, O.B.E. (*Operations*).
Directors, R. Wilson (*Finance*); A. Coombe (*Works*); P. J. Noakes (*Horticulture*); H. Mackay (*Management Services*); T. F. Penfold (*Personnel*); J. P. D. Gee (*Information and Secretariat*).
Legal Adviser and Solicitor, G. C. Reddie.
Hon. Botanical Adviser, Prof. G. T. Prance, D.PHIL., F.L.S.
Hon. Artistic Adviser, Prof. Sir Peter Shepheard, C.B.E.

Imperial War Graves Endowment Fund
Trustees, Gen. Sir Robert Ford, G.C.B., C.B.E.; H. U. A. Lambert; The Lord Remnant, C.V.O.
Hon. Secretary to the Trustees, R. D. Wilson.

COUNTRYSIDE COMMISSION
John Dower House, Crescent Place,
Cheltenham, Glos. GL50 3RA
[0242–521381]

The Countryside Commission is an independent agency set up in 1968 to promote the conservation and enhancement of landscape beauty in England and Wales, to encourage the provision and improvement of facilities in the countryside for enjoyment, including the need to secure access for open air recreation. Since April 1982 the Commission has been funded by annual grant from the Department of the Environment. Members of the Commission are appointed by the Secretary of State for the Environment and the Secretary of State for Wales acting jointly.

Chairman, Sir Derek Barber.
Director General (G3), A. A. C. Phillips.
Directors (G5), R. Clarke (*Policy*); M. J. Kirby (*Regions*); M. Taylor (*Resources*).
National Heritage Adviser, Mrs. M. D. Laverack.
Head of Corporate Planning (G7), T. Robinson.
Head of Conservation Branch (G7), R. Roberts.
Head of Recreation & Access Branch (G7), J. W. B. Worth.
Head of Communications Branch (G7), C. Pugsley.
Head of Finance and Establishments (G7), V. Ellis.
Head of National Parks and Planning Branch (G7), R. Lloyd.
Head of Training and Voluntary Action Branch (G7), K. Turner.
Regional Officers (G7), G. Taylor (*Newcastle*); K. Buchanan (*Cambridge*); Dr. S. A. Bucknall (*Leeds*); E. Holdaway (*Bristol*); R. T. Thomas (*Manchester*); D. E. Coleman (*London*); F. S. Walmsley (*Birmingham*); Ms. H. MacIlwaine (*Task Force Trees*).

Office for Wales
Ladywell House, Newtown, Powys, SY16 1RD
[0686–626799]

Chairman, R. E. M. Rees.
Principal Officer (G7), A. M. H. Fitton.

COUNTRYSIDE COMMISSION FOR SCOTLAND
Battleby, Redgorton, Perth, PH1 3EW
[0738–27921]

Established under the Countryside (Scotland) Act, 1967, with functions for the provision, development and improvement of facilities for the enjoyment of the Scottish countryside, and for the conservation and enhancement of its natural beauty and amenity.

Chairman, J. R. Carr (*part-time*).
Commissioners, J. M. S. Arnott (*Vice-Chairman*); Dr. D. J. Bennet; Prof. C. H. Gimingham; Prof. J. I. Cunningham; Q. Brown; D. Grainger; R. D. Cramond, C.B.E.; Mrs. S. Harvey; A. W. Henry; I. Miller; Dr. W. E. S. Mutch; W. M. Turnbull.
Director, D. Campbell.
Asst. Directors, J. M. Fladmark (*Research and Development*); J. R. Turner (*Planning*); M. A. Payne (*Communications and Training*); W. T. Band (*Finance and Administration*).

COVENT GARDEN MARKET AUTHORITY
Covent House, New Covent Garden Market,
SW8 5NX
[01–720 2211]

The Covent Garden Market Authority is constituted under the Covent Garden Market Acts, 1961 to 1966, the members being appointed by the Minister of Agriculture, Fisheries and Food. The Authority owns and operates the 60-acre New Covent Garden Markets (fruit, vegetable, flowers) which have been trading since 1974.

Chairman, W. P. Bowman, O.B.E. *(part-time).*
Members (part-time), P. J. Hunt; E. I. Kingston; J. A. Harvey; R. Smith, O.B.E.
General Manager, Dr. P. M. Liggins.
Secretary, vacant.

CRIMINAL INJURIES COMPENSATION BOARD
Blythswood House, 200 West Regent Street, Glasgow G2 4SW
[041–221 0945]

LONDON OFFICE: Whittington House, 19 Alfred Place, WC1E 7LG
[01–636 9501 and 01–636 2812]

The Board was constituted in 1964 to administer the Government scheme for *ex gratia* payments of compensation to victims of crimes of violence.

Chairman, The Lord Carlisle of Bucklow, P.C., Q.C. £53,400
Members, J. F. A. Archer, Q.C.; Sir Derek Bradbeer; M. S. R. Bruce, Q.C.; D. Calcutt, Q.C.; H. Carlisle, Q.C.; B. W. Chedlow, Q.C.; Miss B. Cooper, Q.C.; Miss D. Cotton, Q.C.; J. D. Crowley, Q.C.; T. Dawson, Q.C.; C. Fawcett, Q.C.; W. Gage, Q.C.; B. Green, Q.C.; G. M. Hamilton, Q.C.; Sir Arthur Hoole; J. Law, Q.C.; M. E. Lewer, Q.C.; J. Leighton Williams, Q.C.; C. Lindsay, Q.C.; Lord Macaulay of Bragar, Q.C.; D. Mackay, Q.C.; Sir Denis Marshall; Mrs. B. Mills, Q.C.; Sir Michael Morland, Q.C.; Sir John Palmer; I. M. S. Park, C.B.E.; Miss S. Ritchie, Q.C.; D. B. Robertson, Q.C.; C. Seagroatt, Q.C.; Mrs. J. Smith, Q.C.; R. Smith, Q.C.; L. Stuart Shields, Q.C.; D. M. Thomas, O.B.E., Q.C.; D. O. Thomas, Q.C.; P. Weitzman, Q.C.; C. H. Whitby, Q.C.
Secretary and Solicitor, D. M. North.
Deputy Secretary, D. J. White.

CROFTERS COMMISSION
4–6 Castle Wynd, Inverness IV2 3EQ
[0463–237231]

Chairman (part-time), H. Maclean.
Members (part-time), A. I. Macarthur; B. T. Hunter; D. A. Morrison; P. Morrison; I. G. Munro; D. Macdonald.
Secretary (G6), A. Johnston.

CROWN AGENTS FOR OVERSEA GOVERNMENTS AND ADMINISTRATIONS
St. Nicholas House, St. Nicholas Road, Sutton, Surrey, SM1 1EL
[01–643 3311]

The Crown Agents act on behalf of governments and public authorities in the developing world Incorporated by Act of Parliament, they provide commercial, financial and professional services to public sector authorities and the major international development agencies. They do not act for individuals or for commercial concerns in the private sector.
Chairman, Sir Peter Graham, O.B.E.
Managing Director, P. F. Berry.

CROWN ESTATE COMMISSIONERS
13–16 Carlton House Terrace, SW1Y 5AH
[01–210 3000]

The Land Revenues of the Crown in England and Wales have been collected on the public account since

1760, when George III surrendered them and received a fixed annual payment or Civil List. At the time of the surrender the gross revenues amounted to about £89,000 and the net return to about £11,000.

In the year ended March 31, 1989, the gross income from the Crown Estate totalled £81,500,000. The total expenditure was £22,000,000. The sum of £41,000,000 was paid to the Exchequer in 1988–89 as Surplus Revenue.

The Land Revenues in Ireland have been carried to the Consolidated Fund since 1820; from April 1, 1923, as regards Southern Ireland, they have been collected and administered by the Irish Government. The Land Revenues in Scotland were transferred to the Commissioners in 1833.

First Commissioner and Chairman (part-time), The Earl of Mansfield and Mansfield.
Second Commissioner (and Secretary)(G2), C. Howes.
Commissioners (part-time), R. B. Caws, C.B.E.; P. Sober; O. H. Colburn; G. D. Lillingston, C.B.E.; Capt. Sir Iain Tennant, K.T.; J. N. C. James.
Deputy Chief Executive, H. B. Clarke £53,550
Business Manager, Agricultural Estates (G5), R. J. Mulholland.
Crown Estate Surveyor (G6), C. F. Hynes.
Corporate Services Manager (G6), M. Beckwith.
Principals (G6), F. G. Parrish; *(G7),* J. Stumbke; J. S. Ellingford; J. E. Ford.
Organization and Establishments Officer (G7), R. Blake.
Accountant and Receiver-General (G5), D. E. G. Griffiths.
Legal Adviser, M. L. Davies ...... £32,219–£33,819
Senior Principals (G6), H. Turnsek; J. B. Postgate.
Principals (G7), R. T. Hayward; P. Horner.
Senior Legal Assistant, M. A. J. Cordingley.

Scotland
10 Charlotte Square, Edinburgh

Crown Estate Receiver for Scotland (G6), M. J. Gravestock.
Solicitor, Scotland, D. F. Stewart.

Windsor Estate

Surveyor and Deputy Ranger, A. R. Wiseman, M.V.O. £36,786
Crown Estate Forestry Officer and Chief Forester, Windsor *(G7),* J. J. Taylor.

BOARD OF CUSTOMS AND EXCISE
New King's Beam House, 22 Upper Ground, SE1 9PJ
[01–620 1313]

Commissioners of Customs were first appointed in 1671 and housed by the King in London. The present 'Long Room' in the Custom House, Lower Thames Street, EC3, replaced that built by Charles II and was rebuilt after destruction by fire in 1718 and 1814. The Excise Department was formerly under the Inland Revenue Department and was amalgamated with the Customs Department on April 1, 1909.

H.M. Customs and Excise is responsible for collecting and administering customs and excise duties and value added tax and advises the Chancellor of the Exchequer on any matters connected with them. The Department is also responsible for preventing and detecting the evasion of revenue laws and for enforcing a range of prohibitions and restrictions on the importation of certain classes of goods. In addition, the Department undertakes certain agency work on behalf of other departments, including the

compilation of U.K. overseas trade statistics from customs import and export documents.
(For **Salaries,** *see* page 293).

The Board

Chairman (G1), J. B. Unwin, C.B.
  Private Secretaries, Miss J. E. Andrews; Miss J. H. Daniels.
Deputy Chairmen (G2), Mrs. V. P. M. Strachan; P. Jefferson Smith.
Commissioners (G3), R. Craggs; D. J. Howard; P. Nash; A. W. Russell; Ms. D. J. Seammen; P. G. Wilmott.

Headquarters Office

Assistant Secretaries (G5), I. D. Savins; P. R. H. Allen; J. Vaughan; P. Kent; D. A. Walton; D. F. O. Battle; B. J. Cockerell; J. W. Tracey; D. E. Barratt; J. C. Stevenson; Mrs. F. R. Boardman; D. Gaw; M. R. Brown; N. Hodson; R. Shepherd; I. Walton; A. Killikelly; M. J. Eland; A. C. Sawyer; M. Peach; C. Arnott; R. L. H. Lawrence; K. M. Romansk; Ms. D. Barrett.
Head of Press and Information Division (G7), G. G. Hammond.

V.A.T. Central Unit

Controller (G5), M. J. Wardle.
Deputy Controller (G6), B. Smith.

Solicitor's Office

Solicitor (G2), P. V. H. Smith C.B.
Principal Assistant Solicitors (G3), G. F. Butt; D. E. J. Nissen.
Assistant Solicitors (G5), P. Breuer; P. J. C. Ellis; M. Michael; R. D. S. Wylie; M. A. Cooper; G. W. M. McFarlane; D. E. T. S. Keefe; M. C. K. Gasper; Miss A. E. Bolt; G. Fotherby; D. Pratt; Miss S. G. Linton.

Accountant and Comptroller-General's Office

Accountant and Comptroller-General (G5), P. A. Blomfield.
Deputy Accountants-General (G6), J. E. Ebery; L. J. Haugh.

Statistical Office

Controller (G5), M. E. Pratt.

Investigation Division

Chief Investigation Officer (G5), F. D. Tweddle.

Collectors of Customs and Excise (G5)
England and Wales

Birmingham: M. W. Summers.
Dover: R. Crossley.
East Anglia: R. N. Lewis.
East Midlands: C. J. Packman.
Leeds: W. J. G. Prollins.
Liverpool: C. Roberts.
London Airports: J. Bugge.
London City and South: F. A. D. Rush.
London Port: A. C. Morrow.
London North and West: C. A. Bray.
Manchester: D. Smith.
Northampton: P. E. St. Quentin.
Northern England: J. McKenzie.
Reading: J. H. Tee.
Southampton: R. I. Bolt.
South Wales and the Borders: A. Ferguson.
South West England: M. W. G. Lloyd.

Scotland

Edinburgh: W. F. Coghill.
Glasgow & Clyde: T. F. Jessop.

Northern Ireland

Belfast: B. E. Barclay, C.B.E.

OFFICE OF THE DATA PROTECTION REGISTRAR
Springfield House, Water Lane, Wilmslow, Cheshire SK9 5AX
[Admin.: 0625–535711; Enquiries: 0625–535777]

The Office of the Data Protection Registrar was created by the Data Protection Act, 1984. It is the Registrar's duty to compile and maintain the Register of Data Users and Computer Bureaux and provide facilities for members of the public to examine the Register; promote observance of the data protection principles; consider complaints made by data subjects; disseminate information about the Act; encourage the production of codes of practice by trade associations and other bodies, to guide data users in complying with the data protection principles; co-operate with other parties to the Council of Europe Convention and act as U.K. authority for the purposes of Article 13 of the Convention; report annually to Parliament on the performance of his functions under the Act.
Registrar, E. J. Howe.

MINISTRY OF DEFENCE
See **Armed Forces Section**

DESIGN COUNCIL
28 Haymarket, SW1Y 4SU
[01–839 8000]

The Design Council's aim is to improve the design of British products by: advising companies on up-to-date practice in engineering and industrial design; the annual British Design Awards; publishing information to help manufacturers, designers, and others professionally involved in design; and promoting improvements in design education at all levels. There is a Design Centre in London and offices in Glasgow, Cardiff, Belfast, Wolverhampton and Manchester. The Design Council is funded partly by a Government grant-in-aid and partly by earned revenues.
Chairman, Sir Simon Hornby.
Director, I. Owen.

THE DUCHY OF CORNWALL
10 Buckingham Gate, SW1E 6LA
[01–834 7346]

The Duchy of Cornwall was instituted by Edward III in 1337 for the support of his eldest son, Edward, the Black Prince, and since 1503 the eldest surviving son of the Sovereign has, as heir apparent, succeeded to the Dukedom by inheritance. As the oldest of the English Duchies, it has enjoyed a long association with the Crown. Before elevation to a dukedom, it was an earldom from 1227, when Richard, King of the Romans and younger brother of Henry III, was created Earl of Cornwall.

The Prince's Council

H.R.H. The Prince of Wales, K.G., K.T., G.C.B; Sir Nicholas Henderson, G.C.M.G. (*Lord Warden of the Stannaries*); Hon. Sir John Baring, C.V.O. (*Receiver General*); R. J. A. Carnwath, Q.C. (*Attorney-General to the Prince of Wales*); D. W. N. Landale (*Secretary and Keeper of the Records*); Sir John Riddell, Bt.; J. E. Pugsley; J. N. C. James; A. M. J. Galsworthy.

Other Officers of the Duchy of Cornwall

Auditors, J. H. Bowman; P. L. Ainger; H. Hughes.
Solicitor, M. H. Boyd-Carpenter.

Assistant Secretary, K. J. S. Knott.
Sheriff (1989–90), G. E. M. Trinick, O.B.E.

THE DUCHY OF LANCASTER
Lancaster Place, Strand, WC2E 7ED
[01–836 8277]

The estates and jurisdiction known as the Duchy and County Palatine of Lancaster have been attached to the Crown since 1399, when John of Gaunt's son came to the throne as Henry IV. As the Lancaster inheritance it goes back to 1265. Edward III erected Lancashire into a County Palatine in 1351.
Chancellor of the Duchy of Lancaster, THE RT. HON. KENNETH BAKER, M.P.
    Private Secretary, J. Alty.
Attorney-General and Attorney and Serjeant within the County Palatine of Lancaster, J. F. Parker, Q.C.
Receiver-General, Maj. Sir Shane Blewitt, K.C.V.O.
Vice-Chancellor, The Hon. Mr. Justice Scott.
Clerk of the Council and Keeper of Records, M. K. Ridley.
Solicitor, W. O. Farrer.
Asst. Solicitor, I. J. Dicker.
Chief Clerk, P. C. Clarke, C.V.O.

ECONOMIC AND SOCIAL RESEARCH COUNCIL
Cherry Orchard East, Kembrey Park,
Swindon SN2 6UQ
[0793–513838]

The E.S.R.C. was set up by Royal Charter in 1965 for the promotion of social science research. The Council carries out its role by awarding research grants, by initiating research and research contracts, by funding designated research centres, and by awarding postgraduate studentships and bursaries. In addition, the Council provides advice and disseminates knowledge on the social sciences.
Chairman, Prof. H. Newby.
Secretary, D. Stafford.

DEPARTMENT OF EDUCATION AND SCIENCE
Elizabeth House, York Road, SE1 7PH
[01–934 9000]

The Government Department of Education was, until the establishment of a separate office, a Committee of the Privy Council appointed in 1839 to supervise the distribution of certain grants which had been made by Parliament since 1834. The Act of 1899 established the Board of Education, with a President and Parliamentary Secretary, and created a Consultative Committee. The Education Act of 1944 established the Ministry of Education. In April 1964 the office of the Minister of Science was combined with the Ministry to form the Department of Education and Science. The cost of administration for the financial year 1989–90 was estimated at £73,477,000. (For **Salaries**, *see* page 293.)

Secretary of State for Education and Science, THE RT. HON. JOHN MACGREGOR, O.B.E., M.P.
    Private Sec., S. T. Crowne.
    Parliamentary Private Secretary, A. Stewart, M.P.
Minister of State, MRS. ANGELA RUMBOLD, C.B.E., M.P.
    Private Secretary, Mrs. L. J. Chapman.
    Parliamentary Private Secretary, Q. Davies, M.P.
Parliamentary Under Secretaries of State, ROBERT JACKSON, M.P.; ALAN HOWARTH, C.B.E., M.P.
Permanent Secretary (*G1*), J. Caines, C.B.
    Private Secretary, C. Barnham.
Deputy Secretaries (*G2*), R. H. Bird, C.B. (*H.E. Adviser*); E. J. Bolton, C.B.E. (*S.C.I.*); N. W. Stuart; J. M. M. Vereker; A. J. Wiggins.

Under Secretaries (*G3*), P. Benwell, (*Chief Architect*); M. M. Capey (*Director of Establishments*); A. E. D. Chamier; C. A. Clark; J. E. Coleman (*Legal Adviser*); D. M. Forester; J. C. Hedger; R. D. Horne; D. G. Libby; B. M. Norbury; N. J. Sanders (*Accountant General*); C. H. Saville; F. M. Scott; P. A. Shaw; N. Summers; W. B. Wakefield (*Director of Statistics*); J. Wilde; D. A. Wilkinson.

Schools Branch 1

Assistant Secretaries (*G5*), Mrs. H. K. Douglas; R. J. Green; Miss C. E. Hodkinson; M. J. Richardson.
Principals (*G7*), D. H. Griffiths; M. H. Sharpe; D. K. Timms; Mrs. S. J. Trundle; A. Wilshaw; P. Chorley; A. D. Adamson; Miss S. Phippard; Miss C. Bienkowska; B. C. Willett.

Schools Branch 2

Assistant Secretaries (*G5*), Miss D. C. Fordham; Ms. J. F. Cramphorn; A. J. Shaw.
Senior Principal (*G6*), P. S. Lewis.
H.M. Inspectors (*G6*), S. J. Rogers; S. Robson; Mrs. P. Gibbon.
Principals (*G7*), D. Barwick; Mrs. G. W. Dishart; C. Dowe; I. A. Loveless; Mrs. P. A. Masters; Mrs. J. D. Nisbet; J. F. Bird; N. Cornwell; C. Dee; D. Noble; A. Sevier.

Schools Branch 3

Assistant Secretaries (*G5*), Mrs. H. M. Williams; Miss A. J. Benham; M. D. Phipps; A. J. Wye.
Staff Inspector (*G5*), A. Clegg.
Principals (*G7*), C. De Grouchy; Mrs. S. G. Evans; Miss K. J. Fleay; M. P. Howarth; S. N. Jardine; Mrs. S. Jetha; W. A. Smyth; A. B. Thompson; L. B. Webb; Miss J. D. Worsfold.

Schools Branch 4

Assistant Secretaries (*G5*), Miss A. Stewart; Miss J. Partington; A. G. B. Woollard; Miss P. Laidlaw; C. P. Marshall (*Staff Inspector*).
H.M. Inspector (*G6*), A. Callender.
Principals (*G7*), N. Flint; S. Kershaw; Miss N. Bartman; Ms. S. Gane; D. Foster; S. Hillier; M. F. Neale; N. Roberts (*Accountant*); R. Troedson.

Architects and Building Branch

Chief Architect (*G3*), P. Benwell.
Deputy Chief Architect, A. J. Branton.
Superintending Architects, M. S. Hacker; G. J. Parker; A. C. Thompson; J. J. Wilson.
Superintending Engineer (*Mechanical and Electrical*), (vacant).
Chief Quantity Surveyor, B. G. Whitehouse.
Principals (*G7*), K. L. R. English; A. G. Myatt.
Principal Architects, R. W. U. Alcock; E. C. Bissell; Mrs. D. Holt; Miss E. J. Lloyd-Jones; P. Lenssen; D. S. Nightingale; Miss B. M. T. Sanders; D. F. Wicks.
Principal Quantity Surveyors, A. A. Jones; J. L. S. Sinclair; M. E. H. Sturt.
Principal Engineer, M. J. Patel.
Principal Furniture Designer, N. J. Carter.
S.P.T.O. Architects, S. Aswat; A. J. Benson-Wilson; J. R. C. Brooke; G. E. Hughes; Miss L. Watson; T. J. Williamson.
S.P.T.O. Quantity Surveyors, T. W. A. Carden; G. Wonnacott.
S.P.T.O. Engineers, R. Heard; R. L. Daniels.

Further and Higher Education Branch 1

Assistant Secretaries (*G5*), A. N. Brown; E. R. Morgan; D. M. Williams.
Senior Principal (*G6*), Dr. E. J. Herbert.
Principals (*G7*), K. Baxter; Ms G. Beauchamp; A. Clarke; Miss L. M. Clarke; M. F. Hipkins; P. J. Hodgman; W. A. Irvine; M. F. Neale.

Further and Higher Education Branch 2

Assistant Secretaries (G5), Mrs. C. M. Chattaway; R. D. Hull; Mrs. J. Ledger.
Principals (G7), J. K. Bushnell; A. J. Coles; K. Davey; G. H. N. Evans; P. W. Fulford-Jones; A. G. Short; Miss C. E. Treen; M. J. P. Vann; Mrs. D. T. Wood.

Further and Higher Education Branch 3

Assistant Secretaries (G5), M. B. Baker; Miss M. d'Armenia; T. B. Jeffery; M. J. G. Smith.
Senior Principal (G6), D. I. B. Hardy.
Principals (G7), Miss A. Barlow; M. J. Jubb; M. L. Lyons; S. Lee; R. J. Wood.

Science Branch

Assistant Secretaries (G5), G. J. Mungeam; R. P. Ritzema; P. J. Thorpe.
Principals (G7), A. Callaghan; K. C. Humphrey; L. J. R. Dando; K. D. J. Root; A. Smyth.

Information Branch

Assistant Secretary (G5), P. A. Shaw.
Chief Information Officers (G7), A. P. Duncan; C. R. Stephens.

Teachers Pay and General Branch

Assistant Secretaries (G5), R. W. Chattaway; B. D. Cullen (*Senior Economic Adviser*); H. W. B. Davies.
Senior Principal Scientific Officer (G6), R. B. Ladley.
Principals (G7), M. Barker; T. P. Franklin; A. J. Sargent.

Pensions Branch
Mowden Hall, Staindrop Road,
Darlington, Co. Durham DL3 9BG
[0325–460155]

Assistant Secretary (G5), J. Wilde.
Principals (G7), D. G. Halladay; K. M. Miles.

Teachers Supply, Training and International Relations Branch

Assistant Secretaries (G5), B. Bekhradnia; S. R. C. Jones; J. W. Whitaker.
Principals (G7), B. D. Glickman; Mrs. M. J. Lawrence; J. C. Sheridan; Ms. E. Slater; M. Wardle; M. Williams.

Information Technology Branch

Assistant Secretary (G5), F. M. Scott.
Senior Principals (G6), A. Cowan; A. H. Tyler.
Principals (G7), A. Allison; A. M. Cooper; B. Lillburn; Mrs. N. A. T. Malt; Mrs. J. D. Nisbet.

Statistics Branch

Chief Statisticians (G5), J. W. Gardner; H. M. Dale.
Data Administrator (G6), P. G. Gott.
Statisticians (G7), A. Barnett; A. J. Barnett; Miss A. C. Brown; R. E. Dew; R. M. Ellison; D. J. Hodges; R. K. Jain; Mrs. S. Keith; S. N. Kew; Mrs. A. E. Mellor; J. Pascoe; N. D. Rudoe.

Legal Branch

Assistant Legal Advisers (G5), D. J. Aries; F. L. Croft; M. Harris.
Assistant Solicitor (G6), A. D. Preston.
Senior Legal Assistant (G6), N. P. Beach.

Library

Chief Librarian, D. N. Allum.

Finance Branch

Assistant Secretaries (G5), R. L. Smith; P. Smith; M. C. Stark.
Senior Principal (G6), W. Gamble (*Assistant Accountant General*).
Principals (G7), E. A. Alcock; P. J. Edwards; P. L.

Jones; Ms. R. M. King; D. R. Pollard; G. D. S. Sandeman; B. G. Townsend; C. Walker; J. J. Watson.

H.M. Inspectorate (England)

Senior Chief Inspector (G2), E. J. Bolton, c.b.
Chief Inspectors (G4), B. C. Arthur, c.b.e.; J. A. Everson; A. R. Marshall; T. P. Melia; Miss A. C. Millett; A. J. Rose; B. D. Short; M. J. Tomlinson.
Divisional Inspectors (G5), B. A. Chaplin; Miss V. J. Evans; B. W. Howes; L. Jackson; E. Scott; K. W. Thomas; D. E. Walker.
Staff Inspectors (G5), T. H. Bennetts; R. G. Booth; P. L. Bradbury; R. J. Brake; P. Brown; D. G. Buckland; R. A. Callender; B. J. Chopping; P. R. Clarke; M. J. Convey; D. A. Cormican; A. T. Cox; L. S. Crickmore; D. A. Denegri; B. Denton; Mrs. G. M. Dolden; Mrs. V. E. Emmett; Mrs. G. Everson; J. H. Fairhurst; D. Fraser; G. R. Frater; A. Gibson; G. Goldstein; J. G. Goulding; V. Green; R. A. S. Hennessey; G. A. Hicks; P. Highfield; M. W. Himsworth; D. Hollingsworth; D. G. Labon; Miss B. J. Lewis; D. J. Marjoram; P. F. Marlow; C. P. Marshall; J. H. Mayhew; R. W. Mycock; G. T. Peaker; P. J. Pearson; C. M. Richards; C. H. Selby; P. Singh; Mrs. M. M. Smart; D. E. Soulsby; Mrs. B. Staniland; D. W. Taylor; D. R. Trainor; A. F. Turberfield; A. D. J. Turner; Mrs. S. P. Twite; J. R. Ungoed-Thomas; D. L. West; C. C. B. Wightwick; J. B. Willcock; T. Wylie; R. E. Young.
H.M. Inspectors (G6), Mrs. C. A. Agambar; W. Agnew; D. W. Airey; Mrs. G. M. V. Alexander; K. J. Anglesey; P. L. Armitage; A. Ashworth; D. Baillie; W. G. Bakehouse; Mrs. C. A. Baker; Mrs. E. M. Baker; C. Banks; Miss D. M. L. Barlow; J. H. Barnes; Mrs. J. M. Barnes; G. Barratt; R. E. Barrett; Ms. E. P. Baxell; Mrs. I. M. B. Beckett; P. E. B. Belshaw; J. F. Bennett; S. G. L. Bignell; D. B. F. Billimore; Miss. V. Blackburn; Ms. S. B. Blatton; A. J. Boddington; Mrs. C. M. Bond; Mrs. E. J. Boucher; Miss E. Bourne; Mrs. M. T. Boyd-Clarke; D. J. Bradbury; M. H. Bradley; Miss P. A. Brain; T. E. Brand; Mrs. H. S. Bridge; E. F. H. Brittain; J. Broadbent; F. Brook; Mrs. J. M. Brookes; Miss C. M. Brooks; A. W. Brown; Mrs. M. A. Buckingham; M. J. Buckley; Miss K. Bull; J. M. Burgess; Mrs. G. M. Burke; Ms. M. E. Caistor; M. J. Campbell; P. Candlish; N. Carr; Mrs. J. Carswell; M. J. Caton; B. Chandler; Ms. J. A. Cheong; Miss D. H. Chorley; Mrs. M. S. Christie; D. Clare; P. Clarke; G. Clay; R. S. W. Clements; D. G. Close; D. A. Coe; J. E. M. Cohn; B. Colbeck; M. J. Collier; Mrs. P. M. Collins; Mrs. M. A. Cooke; P. Cradock; G. Cranmer; Mrs. G. K. Crawford; J. Creedy; Miss K. Cross; Ms. B. J. Cusdin; D. K. Dana; Mrs. J. Darroch; C. M. Davies; J. Dawson; J. Devlin; T. Dickinson; T. Dillon; A. Dobson; Ms. C. R. Donoughue; J. A. S. Dossett; P. W. Dougill; M. A. Dowling; R. G. Dyke; K. H. Dyson; Mrs. M. E. Eade; P. D. Edwards; Mrs. C. Elliott; D. L. Elliott; J. A. Elliott; L. J. Ellis; M. A. Emery; Mrs. J. E. Ensing; C. B. L. Evans; K. J. Evans; Ms. C. Farrell; Mrs. B. E. Fawcett; Ms. F. D. Finlay; B. P. Fitzgerald; J. Fitzpatrick; I. G. Forrest; D. H. M. Foster; E. F. Foster; Ms. M. C. Fraser; P. S. Friend; Mrs. C. Frisby; B. Frost; C. C. Frost; D. J. Frost; R. C. Frost; B. S. Furness; P. Gannon; D. A. Gardiner; P. H. W. Garwood; I. Gera; Mrs. P. M. Gibbon; Mrs. J. E. A. Gifford; G. A. Gill; C. R. Gillings; C. Goodhead; Mrs E. M. Goodwin; Mrs. K. N. Gosling; C. D. Gould; C. Goulding; Miss S. Gracey; D. I. Grant; J. D. Green; B. Gregson-Allcott; N. Grenyer; P. Griffiths; R. H. Griffiths; Mrs. F. Hadley; Mrs. C. E. Hague; E. E. J. Haidon; D. S. Hale; D. J. Halligan; N. J. Hallmark; J. A. Hamer; P. G. Hancock; J. N. Hardwick; J. S. Hardwick; R. A. Hargreaves; B. R. Harris; D. J. Hart; R. Hartley; A. Harvey; R. C.

Harvey; Mrs. G. M. Hayes; G. M. Hearnshaw; Miss L. M. Hencher; M. L. Hening; J. F. Herbert; Mrs. J. S. Herbert; J. A. Hertrich; P. M. Hesketh; D. Hibbert; J. M. Hibbs; J. F. H. Hilbourne; W. J. Hill; Mrs. G. A. Hindhaugh; D. G. Holford; T. Holland; Ms. M. H. Hollingsworth; J. R. Holmes; C. Hooper; F. X. Horan; J. E. Hosegood; D. J. House; M. J. Howarth; B. A. F. Hubbard; B. R. Hudson; V. C. Hughes; J. E. Hunt; P. J. Hunt; J. B. Huskins; J. N. Hutchinson; Mrs. M. A. V. Huxley; J. S. Ingleson; P. F. J. Irvine; A. R. Ivatts; M. J. Ive; H. A. James; R. K. James; T. M. Jardine; B. D. Jelly; Miss S. H. Johns; P. W. R. Johnson; H. B. Joicey; B. Jones; Mrs. M. E. Jones; M. G. Jones; P. R. Jones; R. Kapadia; W. D. Kaye; Mrs. A. C. Keelan-Towner; M. Kerrigan; M. A. Khan; B. L. King; D. P. King; K. King; A. V. Kirwan; D. Knighton; J. B. Knox; A. J. Lacey; G. N. E. Lageard; Miss E. J. M. Layson; J. W. F. Learmonth; J. P. Leigh; D. Lewis; D. F. Lewis; D. J. Lewis; Mrs. J. M. Lingard; E. R. B. Little; G. R. Little; A. W. Littlewood; W. G. K. Lloyd; Miss B. M. Lockwood; A. B. Lomax; R. Long; J. A. Low; T. L. Lusty; J. A. Mabey; B. McCafferty; C. McCall; Mrs. H. M. Macdonald; D. G. McEnhill; D. C. McIntosh; M. McLaughlin; Mrs. P. R. Maclay; Mrs. J. McLean; I. A. McNally; M. E. Madden; Mrs. J. P. Maddick; J. R. Marriott; G. D. Marrow; J. G. Marshall; E. S. Martin; Mrs. M. M. Martin; W. P. Massam; Miss E. M. Matthews; J. E. Mattick; M. R. E. Mealing; B. R. Meech; Miss B. E. Megson; G. Merlane; B. E. Merton; K. Miller; H. Millington; D. Mills; P. Milton; Miss H. A. Moffat; Ms. J. L. Mokades; A. R. H. Monk; D. Moon; D. L. Moore; P. R. Moore; S. H. Morris; Miss F. A. Munday; P. Muschamp; H. Myers; C. Needham; Ms. S. M. Nicholls; A. J. Nisbett; P. M. Nixon; M. Norman; Mrs. G. I. Oldham; P. I. Orr; B. C. O'Sullivan; Mrs. S. O'Sullivan; W. E. Owen; H. M. Page; R. L. Page-Jones; A. C. Parfitt; K. Parker; D. J. Parks; J. M. Parsons; Miss E. L. Passmore; I. M. Paterson; Mrs. D. M. Penn; Miss J. M. Phillips; P. Piddock; K. Pinder; M. W. A. Pitts; E. A. Pollard; M. R. Potter; C. Potts; C. P. Power; Mrs. B. F. Pratley; A. E. Price; Mrs. M. P. Pryce; M. E. Pullee; P. C. Purdy; W. J. Rea; C. J. Redman; J. C. Richardson; P. H. Roberts; A. S. Robertson; C. Robinson; G. Robson; I. A. Rodger; S. J. A. Rogers; A. C. Rowe; C. Rowe; D. H. Rutt; M. J. Ryder; W. H. Salaman; Mrs. J. Sartain; Mrs. K. J. Saunders; B. Sayer; Ms. M. Sayer; J. C. Schenk; D. J. Scott; P. L. Seaborne; G. W. Searle; Mrs. P. J. Selwood; R. V. L. Shannon; D. T. V. Sharman; D. I. Shelton; A. R. Shirley; Mrs. V. M. Sida; P. J. Silvester; Mrs. D. E. Simmonds; Mrs. P. A. Simpson; D. Singleton; G. Sleightholme; B. J. Smeaton; B. J. Smith; P. J. C. Smith; P. R. Smith; Ms. S. P. Soul; Mrs. M. F. Spence; J. D. Stannard; Ms. O. M. Stannard; J. Stanyer; J. W. Steel, O.B.E.; J. M. Steels; J. B. Stevenson; Mrs. M. T. Stiles; R. W. Stockdale, O.B.E.; M. M. Stone; C. F. Stoneman; Mrs. J. E. Storrie; R. Storrs; Ms. M. E. Stride; R. Summersby; D. P. Swain; A. Sykes; D. W. Sylvester; F. Taylor; J. A. Taylor; R. S. Taylor; A. F. Thomas; D. L. Thorburn; R. M. Thorpe; J. Tierney; M. J. Todd; P. N. Toft; B. D. Tomkins; J. V. Townshend; J. E. Trickey; Ms. L. J. Tumman; G. C. Turner; Mrs. J. W. Turner; E. A. Vallis; B. C. L. Walker; Mrs. C. V. Wall; A. Walmsley; Miss P. Walters; M. Wardlow; Mrs. A. P. Warren; R. K. Warren; N. G. Warwick; J. M. Watson; M. R. Webb; Mrs. J. M. Webberley; R. R. Weir; D. J. Wells; P. E. Weston; K. J. Wheeldon; R. Whitburn; Miss F. White; J. White; F. Whiteman; D. G. Whittaker; Ms. S. M. Wiles; D. G. Williams; J. R. Williams; K. G. Williams; Mrs. S. A. Williams; G. R. Wilson; J. D. Woodhouse; Mrs. S. A. Woodroffe; J. A. Woodrow; J. I. Wragg; Miss B. M. Wright; D.

Wynne; Miss A. P. Yeomans; F. P. Young; A. J. Youngs.

H.M. Inspectorate Support Services

Principals (G7), C. Boxall; G. A. Holley.

H.M. Inspectorate (Wales)

(See Welsh Office)

Establishments and Organization Branch

Assistant Secretaries (G5), E. B. Granshaw; Miss J. Gilbey.
Senior Principal (G6), H. H. Barrick.
Principals (G7), C. Bramley; Miss A. F. Brown; R. S. Daruwalla; K. R. Fitzgerald; K. M. Miles; D. A. Robins.

OFFICE OF ELECTRICITY REGULATION
Hagley House, Hagley Road,
Birmingham B16 8QG

The Office of Electricity Regulation (Offer) is a regulatory body set up under the Electricity Act 1989. It is headed by the Director General of Electricity Supply, who is independent of Ministerial control.
Director General, Prof. S. C. Littlechild.
Deputy Director General, Ms. P. A. Boys.

CENTRAL ELECTRICITY GENERATING BOARD
Sudbury House, 15 Newgate Street, EC1A 7AU
[01–634 5111]

Under the Electricity Act 1989, which received Royal Assent in August 1989, the Central Electricity Generating Board has been split into three successor companies. The companies will be vested on January 1, 1990, and will be wholly owned by the Secretary of State for Energy. Flotation on the stock market will follow in 1990.

The three successor companies are:
NATIONAL POWER, Sudbury House, EC1A 7AU.
POWERGEN, 53 New Broad Street, EC2M 1JJ.
NATIONAL GRID, Bankside House, Sumner Street, SE1 9JU.

ELECTRICITY SUPPLY COMPANIES

Under the Electricity Act 1989, the Electricity Boards are to be replaced by private companies wholly owned by the Government in Jan. 1990. Flotation on the stock market will follow in 1990.

England and Wales

London, Templar House, 81–87 High Holborn, WC1V 6NU.
South Eastern, Grand Avenue, Hove, East Sussex BN3 2LS.
Southern, Southern Electricity House, Littlewick Green, Maidenhead, Berks.
South Western, Electricity House, Colston Avenue, Bristol BS1 4TS.
Eastern, P.O. Box 40, Wherstead, Ipswich, Suffolk IP9 2AQ.
East Midlands, P.O. Box 4, North P.D.O., 398 Coppice Road, Arnold, Nottingham NG5 7HX.
Midlands, P. O. Box 8 Mucklow Hill, Halesowen, West Midlands B62 8BP.
South Wales, St. Mellons, Cardiff CF3 9XW.
Merseyside and North Wales, Sealand Road, Chester.
Yorkshire, Wetherby Road, Scarcroft, Leeds LS14 3HS.
North Eastern, Carliol House, Newcastle upon Tyne NE99 1SE.
North Western, Talbot Road, Manchester M16 0HQ.

Scotland

North of Scotland Hydro-Electric Board, 16 Rothesay Terrace, Edinburgh EH3 7SE. (031–225 1361)
South of Scotland Electricity Board, Spean Street, Glasgow G44 4BE. (041–637 7177)

DEPARTMENT OF EMPLOYMENT
Caxton House, Tothill Street, SW1H 9NF
[01–273 3000]

The Department of Employment is responsible for the Government policy of promoting a competitive and efficient labour market conducive to the growth of employment and the reduction of unemployment. Its main tasks are to help people acquire and improve their skills and competence for work, to help unemployed people, to promote the creation and growth of small firms and self-employment, to encourage industries to train their workforce, and to develop tourism.

Many of the executive functions carried out in the Department's area of policy interest are exercised by separate public agencies reporting to the Secretary of State for Employment. These include the Health and Safety Commission and A. C. A. S. and, within the Department, the Employment Service and the Training Agency.
(For **Salaries**, *see* page 293).

Secretary of State for Employment, THE RT. HON. NORMAN FOWLER, M.P.
 Principal Private Secretary (G5), C. M. Norris.
 Parliamentary Private Secretary, P. Thurham, M.P.
Minister of State, TIMOTHY EGGAR, M.P.
 Private Secretary, S. Bainbridge.
Under Secretaries of State, PATRICK NICHOLLS, M.P.; THE LORD STRATHCLYDE.
 Private Secretaries, Ms. E. Norman; Ms. C. Rainey.
 Parliamentary Clerk, S. J. Loach.
Permanent Secretary (G1), Sir Geoffrey Holland, K.C.B.
 Private Secretary, Ms. M. Niven.
Deputy Secretaries (G2), I. Manley, C.B.; G. Reid.
Legal Adviser (G3), H. R. L. Purse.
Special Advisers, W. Lightfoot; Miss C. Stratton.

The Employment Service

Chief Executive (G3+), M. E. G. Fogden.
Deputy Chief Executive (G3), J. Turner.
Director of Field Operations (G4), J. W. Cooper.
Director of Personnel and Business Services (G4), D. B. Price.
Director of Programmes (G4), M. Emmott.

The Training Agency
See entry on page 368

Industrial Relations

Grade 3, R. S. Allison; E. G. Whybrew.
Grade 5, D. W. Brown; A. G. Johnson; P. A. L. Parker; D. A. Roberts; M. C. Davey.
Chief Wages Inspector (G6), J. A. Dyble.
Secretary of Wages Councils, G. Knorpel.

International and Tourism Division

Grade 3, R. A. David.
Grade 5, Mrs. R. Le Guen; P. Brannen; Mrs. J. Whitaker; Mrs. J. Peretz.

Economic Research and Briefing

Chief Economic Adviser (G3), D. Stanton.
Grade 5, Ms. H. Canter; Ms. P. Meadows; Mrs. Z. Hornstein; D. Bower.

Employment and Training Policy Division

Grade 3, C. F. Tucker.
Grade 5, M. J. Brimmer; I. Fair; Miss M. C. Fahey; Dr. P. Buley (*Small Firms*); J. W. Dewsbury (*Careers Service*).

Personnel and Business Services Division

Director of Personnel (G3), A. W. Brown.
Head of Business Services (G4), M. H. Davies.
Head of Group Personnel Unit (G5), R. K. Harrison.
Director of Computing (G5), vacant.
Head of Personnel Services Branch (G5), D. Lifton.

Information Division

Head of Information (G5), B. Sutlieff.
Deputy Head of Information (G6), M. Helm.

Finance and Resource Management Division

Director and Principal Finance Officer (G3), D. G. Talintyre.
Grade 5, K. J. Jordan; Mrs. A. V. Wheatcroft; P. Robson; Miss W. A. C. Harris.

Solicitor's Office

Legal Adviser (G3), H. R. L. Purse.

Statistics Division

Director of Statistics (G3), P. J. Stibbard.
Chief Statisticians (G5), M. J. N. Hughes; D. J. Sellwood; D. Fenwick; Ms. M. Rout.

DEPARTMENT OF ENERGY
1 Palace Street, SW1E 5HE
[01–238 3000]

The Department of Energy is responsible within the Government for the development of policies in relation to all forms of energy. It also discharges governmental functions connected with the publicly-owned coal and electricity industries. It is responsible for the Atomic Energy Authority; is the sponsoring Department for the nuclear power industry and is responsible for the development of oil and gas resources on the British sector of the Continental Shelf. It is the sponsoring Department for the oil industry and is responsible for international aspects of energy problems, including relations and co-operation with oil producing countries. The Department is the co-ordinating body for energy efficiency policy and for encouraging the development of new sources of energy.
(For **Salaries**, *see* page 293).

Secretary of State for Energy, THE RT. HON. JOHN WAKEHAM, M.P.
 Principal Private Secretary, S. H. Haddrill.
 Parliamentary Private Secretary, T. Baldry, M.P.
Minister of State for Energy, THE RT. HON. PETER MORRISON, M.P.
 Private Secretary, A. Mitchell.
 Parliamentary Private Secretary, Dr. I. Twinn, M.P.
Parliamentary Under-Secretary of State, MICHAEL SPICER, M.P.
Permanent Under Secretary of State (G1), G. H. Chipperfield, C.B.
 Private Secretary, C. P. Nichols.
Deputy Secretary (G2), J. R. S. Guinness.
Chief Scientific Adviser, Sir Sam Edwards, F.R.S.
Parliamentary Clerk, T. Collingridge.

Establishment and Finance Division

Principal Establishment and Finance Officer (G3), M. S. Buckley.
Director of Resource Management (G4), C. C. Wilcock.
Assistant Secretaries (G5), R. Beasley; J. Morris; P. D. Atkinson; Ms. P. Boys; Dr. D. P. Hauser.

Electricity Division

Under Secretary (G3), W. I. Macintyre.
Assistant Secretaries (G5), G. W. Thynne; Dr. A. Eggington; W. J. Rickett; G. S. Dart.

Chief Electrical Engineering Inspector (G7), D. C. Gore.

Coal Division

Under Secretary (G3), R. Heathcote.
Assistant Secretaries (G5), M. H. Atkinson; E. Pash.

Atomic Energy Division

Under Secretary (G3), Dr. T. Walker.
Assistant Secretaries (G5), P. H. Agrell; B. Hampton; Dr. J. G. Wright; A. J. T. Steele.

Energy Technology Division

Chief Scientist (G3), Dr. J. Rae.
Deputy Chief Scientific Officers (G5), Dr. R. G. S. Skipper; G. Bevan.
Assistant Secretary (G5), Dr. W. D. Evans.
Senior Principal Scientific Officers (G6), H. F. Ferguson; R. A. Meir; Dr. S. E. R. Hiscocks; G. S. Dearnley; W. Macpherson; Dr. D. Fairmaner.

International Unit

Assistant Secretary (G5), S. W. Freemantle.

Energy Efficiency Office

Director General (G3), Dr. E. G. Finer.
Directors (G5), P. G. P. D. Fullerton; M. Keay; J. E. P. Miles.
Director (G6), Dr. D. Hauser.

Economics and Statistics Division

Under Secretary (G3), E. H. M. Price.
Chief Statistician (G5), T. S. Simmons.
Senior Economic Advisers (G5), S. A. Price; S. F. D. Powell; G. R. Horton.

Oil and Gas Division

Under Secretary (G3), D. R. Davis.
Assistant Secretaries (G5), W. C. F. Butler; Ms. A. Beaton; N. A. C. Hirst; J. R. Wakely.

Gas and Oil Measurement Branch
Government Buildings, Saffron Road, Wigston,
Leicester
[0533–785354]

Director (G5), J. Plant.
Senior Chief Examiner (G6), G. A. Paul-Clark.

Petroleum Engineering Division

Director of P.E.D. (G3), P. T. Harding.
Reservoir Evaluation Specialist I, I. W. G. Hughes.
Reservoir Evaluation Specialists II, J. R. V. Brooks; D. W. Mann.
Reservoir Evaluation Specialist I, J. R. Petrie.
Petroleum Specialists II, R. Giles; D. R. Clementson; B. B. Moore; N. G. Marguerie.
Senior Principal Scientific Officer (G6), J. N. Mansfield.
Assistant Director Engineer (G6), G. N. Marriott.

Offshore Supplies Office
Alhambra House, 45 Waterloo Street,
Glasgow G2 6AS
[041–221 8777]

Director General (G3), J. E. d'Ancona.
Director Industry (G5), W. E. Allison.
Director Policy and Administration (G5), A. E. Maule.
Director Research and Development (G5), C. P. Carter.
Director China Unit (G6), Dr. K. P. Forrest.
Senior Principal Business Development (G6), H. Holden.
Senior Principal Scientific Officer (G6), Dr. K. Tregonning.
Assistant Director Engineers (G6), H. M. Whiteside; P. R. Taylor.

Information Division

Head of Information (G5), Ms. A. MacLean.
Deputy Head of Information (G6), Mrs. A. Wadsworth.
Chief Press Officer (G7), N. Hayes.

DEPARTMENT OF THE ENVIRONMENT
2 Marsham Street, SW1P 3EB
[01–276 3000]

The Department of the Environment is responsible for planning and land use; local government; housing, construction; inner city areas; new towns; environmental protection; conservation areas and countryside affairs; royal parks and palaces; historic buildings and ancient monuments; sport and recreation. The Property Services Agency is responsible for all construction activities, supplies and transport at home and abroad for all Government departments including the Ministry of Defence and some repayment clients including British Telecom.
(For **Salaries**, *see* page 293)

Secretary of State for the Environment, THE RT. HON. CHRISTOPHER PATTEN, M.P.
Private Secretary, R. F. M. Bright.
Special Adviser, P. R. J. Rock.
Parliamentary Private Secretary, R. Key, M.P.
Minister for Housing and Planning, MICHAEL HOWARD, Q.C., M.P.
Private Secretary, A. G. Riddell.
Parliamentary Private Secretary, R. King, M.P.
Minister for Local Government and Inner Cities, DAVID HUNT, M.B.E., M.P.
Private Secretary, T. F. Beattie.
Minister for Environment and Countryside, DAVID TRIPPIER, R.D., M.P.
Private Secretary, Mrs. S. Bishop.
Parliamentary Under Secretaries of State:—
THE HON. COLIN MOYNIHAN, M.P. (*also Minister for Sport*); CHRISTOPHER CHOPE, O.B.E., M.P.; MRS. VIRGINIA BOTTOMLEY, M.P.; THE LORD HESKETH.
Private Secretaries, P. Stamp (*to Hon. C. Moynihan*); D. Mottershead (*to Mr. Chope*); P. E. Grice (*to Mrs. Bottomley*); S. Stringer (*to Lord Hesketh*).
Lord in Waiting, vacant.
Parliamentary Clerk, Ms. K. Jennings.
Permanent Secretary (G1), Sir Terence Heiser, K.C.B.
Private Secretary, M. J. Bailey.
Second Permanent Secretary and Chief Executive, P.S.A. (G1A), Sir Gordon Manzie, K.C.B.
Private Secretary, J. A. Hammond.

Information

Director (G4), Miss J. Caines.
Grade 5, J. Gee; Ms. P. Alexander.

PLANNING, INNER CITIES, REGIONAL DEVELOPMENT, LAND AND PROPERTY

Deputy Secretary (G2), J. Delafons, C.B.

Inner Cities

Under Secretary (G3), A. J. Butler.
Head of Divisions (G5), W. B. Solesbury; C. P. Evans; A. C. B. Ramsay; Mrs. L. A. C. Simcock.

Land and Property

Director (G4), C. K. Howes.
Grade 6, J. C. White.

Planning and Development Control

Under Secretary (G3), C. J. S. Brearley.
Grade 5, D. N. Donaldson; A. H. Corner; R. S. Horsman.

Planning Services

Director (G4), J. B. Wilson.
Grade 5, R. C. Mabey; J. A. Zetter; A. F. Richardson.
Grade 6, D. C. Stroud.
Grade 7, P. Morgan.

MERSEYSIDE TASK FORCE

Under Secretary (G3), D. R. Bradley.
Controllers (G5), D. J. Morrison; S. P. Sage.

CHIEF ARCHITECTURAL ADVISER ON THE BUILT ENVIRONMENT

Grade 2, J. B. Jefferson, c.b., c.b.e.
Grade 5, J. E. Turner.

HOUSING AND CONSTRUCTION

Deputy Secretary (G2), P. F. Owen, c.b.

Housing Associations and Private Rented Sector

Director (G3), R. U. Young.
Heads of Divisions (G5), P. J. J. Britton; R. J. Gibson; M. J. C. Faulkner; J. F. Stoker.
Grade 6, J. S. Gill.

Housing Monitoring and Analysis

Under Secretary (G3), D. C. L. Wroe.
Grade 5, J. E. Turner; A. E. Holmans, c.b.e.; W. H. Stott; R. F. Sellwood; D. T. I. G. Davies; N. Dorling; Mrs. J. Littlewood.

Public Housing Management and Resources

Under Secretary (G3), A. G. Watson.
Heads of Divisions (G5), J. Stevens; D. V. Teasdale; I. H. Nicol; J. Jacobs; P. F. Everall; G. L. Laufer.
Grade 6, J. D. Harvey.

Construction Industry

Director (G3), D. A. McDonald.
Heads of Divisions (G5), A. D. Fagin; G. I. Fuller; I. C. Macpherson; F. D. Sando.

Sports and Recreation Directorate

Director (G3), D. A. McDonald.
Head of Division (G5), N. A. J. Kinghan.

Building Research Establishment

Director (G3), R. G. Courtney.
Deputy Director (G4), J. M. Baker.
Heads of Departments and Stations (G5), Dr. J. B. Menzies; N. O. Milbank; B. O. Hall; Dr. W. D. Woolley.
Heads of Services/Research (G6), A. J. M. Harrison; Mrs. J. Lemessany; Dr. J. K. Eaton; Dr. J. F. A. Moore; Dr. A. B. Birtles; R. E. Baldwin; Dr. V. A. C. Crisp; Dr. L. H. Everett; B. B. Pigott; Dr. J. M. W. Morgan; C. R. Durham; Dr. M. J. McCall; P. A. MacDermott; H. W. Harrison; J. R. Britten; R. M. C. Driscoll; W. G. B. Phillips; Dr. N. J. Cook; Dr. P. J. Nixon; Dr. J. R. F. Burdett.
Heads of Laboratories and Services (G7), P. W. Staff; A. J. Butler; Dr. J. P. Cornish; J. Hartup; T. W. Payne; A. J. Newman.

FINANCE AND LOCAL GOVERNMENT

Deputy Secretary, Principal Finance Officer (G2), F. A. Osborn.

Local Government Finance Policy

Under Secretary (G3), N. W. Summerton.
Deputy Director (G4), Mrs. D. S. Phillips.
Heads of Divisions (G5), D. L. H. Roberts; P. J. J. Britton; J. E. Roberts; R. Jones; J. S. Parker; P. Rowsell; Mrs. C. Wells.

Housing, Water and Central Finance

Under Secretary (G3), P. J. Fletcher.
Heads of Divisions (G5), G. Adams; B. Redfern; D. A. C. Heigham; (G6), G. Knowles.
Head of Internal Audit (G6), M. R. Haselip.

Local Government

Under Secretary (G3), R. J. A. Sharp.
Heads of Divisions (G5), R. D. Compton; A. J. C. Simcock; H. C. T. Fawcett; (G6), P. G. Iredale.

Economics

Chief Economic Adviser (G3), Dr. J. H. Rickard.

LEGAL

Solicitor and Legal Adviser (G2), M. J. Ware, c.b.
Deputy Solicitors (G3), J. G. Medcalf; J. G. Roscoe.
Assistant Solicitors (G5), Ms. S. D. Unerman; J. L. Comber; Mrs. J. L. Weinberg; J. A. Catlin; P. J. Szell; D. J. Serjeant; I. D. Day; Miss A. Brett-Holt; C. M. Vine; Mrs. S. Headley.

CHIEF ENVIRONMENTAL SCIENTIST

Chief Scientist (G3), Dr. D. J. Fisk.
Head of Division (G5), C. L. Robson.

ENVIRONMENT PROTECTION

Deputy Secretary (G2), D. J. Burr.

Directorate of Rural Affairs

Under Secretary (G3), R. J. Green.
Grade 5, A. Flexman; R. Bunce; D. R. Lewis.
Grade 6, C. Folland.

H.M. Inspectorate of Pollution

Director (G3), B. D. Ponsford.
Deputy Director (G4), Dr. F. S. Feates
Chief Inspectors (G5), J. M. Thayer; M. F. Tunnicliffe; Dr. A. J. Duncan; A. Windsor.
Superintending Inspectors (G6), Dr. M. Jones; I. Handyside; L. N. Stuffins; A. S. Pearce; Dr. G. Rae; Dr. S. R. A. Brown.
District Inspectors, G. G. Jones; M. R. Walters; J. Downs; Dr. L. A. Hales; J. E. Hooper; B. T. Head; Dr. K. Speakman; E. F. Tomlinson; A. H. Brown; Dr. E. Hutton; D. D. B. H. Munns; Dr. J. K. Allen; J. L. Barnett.

Air, Noise and Wastes Directorate

Under Secretary (G3), Dr. D. J. Fisk.
Grade 5, N. Sanders; F. C. Argent.
Grade 6, Dr. A. J. Apling; D. L. Pounder; J. Bentley.

Central Directorate of Environmental Protection

Under Secretary (G3), J. Hobson.
Grade 5, Miss F. McConnell; Dr. N. J. King; P. S. MacCormack; G. N. Bendon.
Grade 6, Dr. P. J. Corcoran; Dr. D. J. Bryce.

Water Group

Deputy Secretary (G2), A. P. Brown.

Water Directorate

Director (G3), Miss D. A. Nichols.
Heads of Divisions (G5), M. G. Healey; C. R. Hook; J. W. Smith; J. P. Henry; D. L. H. Roberts.

Water Privatization Directorate

Director (G3), J. A. L. Gunn.
Head of Division (G5), A. D. Whetnall; R. J. Dorrington; Mrs. J. Williams; P. G. Waller; L. B. Hicks; C. Bolt.

PROPERTY SERVICES AGENCY

Chief Executive (G1A), Sir Gordon Manzie, K.C.B..
Private Secretary, J. Hammond.

DEPUTY CHIEF EXECUTIVE 1

Deputy Chief Executive (G2), A. R. Atherton.

Home Regional Services

Director (G3), P. J. M. Butter.
Assistant Directors (G5), J. W. Deane; R. Kent; E. R. Turtle.
Head of Works Division (G6), M. J. Riley.

Scottish Services

Director (G3), A. G. Gosling.
Assistant Directors (G5), D. R. Smith; J. S. Wilson; B. A. Taylor.

Central Office for Wales

Director (G4), J. H. Clemits.
Deputy Director (G5), A. N. Towers.
Admin. Officer (G6), A. L. S. Richard.

Regions (Home)

London Region:
Director (G3), G. Hopkinson.
Assistant Directors (G5), Mrs. M. Clare; P. M. Livesey; W. J. Purdie; R. E. Kendrick; J. Mutch; D. Addison.
Eastern Region:
Director (G4), A. J. B. Staveley.
Deputy Director (G5), F. Rowson.
Admin. Officer (G6), M. Williams.
Midland Region:
Director (G4), R. M. Jordan.
Deputy Director (G5), D. G. P. Iszatt.
Admin. Officer (G6), J. Knott.
North East Region:
Director (G4), G. Flanagan.
Deputy Director (G5), G. H. Sowden.
Admin. Officer (G6), W. M. McAndrew.
North West Region:
Director (G4), M. M. Harrison.
Deputy Director (G5), D. A. R. Reeson.
Admin. Officer (G6), F. Smith.
South East Region:
Director (G4), S. P. Todd.
Deputy Director (G5), P. M. Pryke.
Admin. Officer (G6), R. G. S. Leeson.
South West Region:
Director (G4), M. Baggott.
Deputy Director (G5), J. Mitchell.
Admin. Officer (G6), E. A. Reid.
Southern Region:
Director (G4), M. R. Newey.
Deputy Director (G5), F. Rymill.
Admin. Officer (G6), G. R. Byers.

Property Management

Director (G4), D. O. McCreadie.
Grade 4, M. Nelson.
Grade 5, D. J. Philips.

Professional Estate Surveying

Chief Estate Surveyor (G4), vacant.
Head of Divisions (G6), M. S. Jennet; J. D. Turfitt; A. J. Butler; L. G. Collett.

DEPUTY CHIEF EXECUTIVE 2

Deputy Chief Executive (G2), J. P. G. Rowcliffe.

Civil Projects

Director (G3), R. Gray.
Grade 5, B. H. Brown; W. H. M. Clarke; R. Holland; M. R. Sutton; J. G. Dilliway.
Grade 6, R. M. Hosangady.

Defence Services I

Director (G3), R. G. S. Johnston.
Grade 5, H. L. Froome-Lewis; M. Clayton; R. G. Jones; M. Latham.
Grade 6, R. K. Houghton.
Germany:
Director (G4), R. B. Perry.
Regional Works Officer (G5), P. W. Berrington.
Regional Admin. Officer (G6), C. G. W. Wilkes.

Defence Services II

Director (G3), S. G. D. Duguid.
Grade 5, M. B. Chammings; J. G. Chisnell; A. K. W. Morgan; A. J. Hazeldine; A. Porteous.
Grade 6, K. A. Holme.

Defence Estates Services Division

Grade 5, M. D. Clarke.

DIRECTOR GENERAL OF DESIGN SERVICES

Director General (G2), J. B. Jefferson, C.B., C.B.E.

Directorate of Architectural Services

Director (G4), J. E. Jeavons.
Directors (G5), C. A. P. Crooke; M. G. Stuart.

Building and Quantity Surveying Services

Director (G4), K. A. Miles.
Assistant Directors (G5), M. Barnes; M. G. Stuart.

Civil Engineering Services

Director (G4), H. P. Webber.
Assistant Directors (G5), D. A. Woodward; J. K. Chatterjee.

Mechanical and Electrical Engineering Services

Director (G4), R. C. Cracknell.
Assistant Director (G5), J. Fisher.

Works Contracts Policy

Director (G4), vacant.
Deputy Director (G5), M. J. Wanstall.

PSA ESTABLISHMENTS

Principal Establishment Officer (G3), P. S. Draper.
Grade 5, R. A. Stead; D. S. Ashworth; Dr. M. S. Barratt; L. B. Hicks.

Information Technology, Management and Office Systems

Grade 4, D. Evans.

Computing Division:
Grade 5, A. J. Spires.
Grade 6, B. Edgill; T. Gibson.

PSA FINANCE

Principal Finance Officer (G3), R. A. Gomme.
Public Expenditure (G5), I. G. Urquhart.
Controller of Accounts (G5), J. A. Pearson.
Head of Internal Audit (G5), M. Reece.
Grade 6, N. Halliwell.

BUSINESS DEVELOPMENT DIRECTORATE

Director (G3), R. A. Munday.
Grade 4, P. Leonard.
Grade 5, G. D. Miles; J. Bridgeman; Ms. D. S. Kahn.
Grade 6, A. L. Cole.

THE CROWN SUPPLIERS

Controller (G3), D. T. Routh.
Financial Controller (G5), J. Cousins.
Assistant Controllers (G5), E. L. Pinfold; A. H. Pollington; B. G. Rosser.
Grade 6, R. Thrower; A. F. M. Munro.

ORGANIZATION, ESTABLISHMENTS AND HERITAGE
2 Marsham Street, SW1P 3EB
[01–276 3000]

Director General (G2), P. C. McQuail.

Personnel

Director (G3), K. E. C. Sorensen.
Grade 5, H. D. Hallett; Mrs. A. Heath; R. Bayly.
Chief Librarian (G6), P. Kirwan.
Chief Welfare Officer (G7), R. J. Lintern.

Administrative Resources

Director (G3), Mrs M. McDonald.
Grade 4, P. Leonard.
Grade 5, Miss L. F. Bell; D. A. R. Peel; L. Packer; B. Rosser.
Grade 6, R. H. Cheeseman; D. Tridgell; R. Bendall.

Heritage and Royal Estate

Director (G3), Ms. E. C. Turton.
Grade 5, J. J. Randall; T. E. Radice.

Historic Royal Palaces Agency
The Birdwood Annexe, Hampton Court Palace,
East Molesey, Surrey KT8 9AU

(An Executive Agency within the Department of the Environment.)
Chief Executive (G3), D. C. Beeton.
Director of Finance and Resources (G5), Ms. S. A. Booth.
Marketing Director, (vacant).
Administrator, Hampton Court Palace (G5), J. Yarnall (*acting*).
Resident Governor, H.M. Tower of London (G5), Maj.-Gen. C. Tyler (retd.).
Curator, Kensington Palace State Apartments and Court Dress Collection (G7), N. J. Arch.
Manager, Banqueting House (HEO), Miss L. M. Kennedy.

PLANNING INSPECTORATE

Chief Planning Inspector (G3), H. S. Crow.
Deputy Chief Planning Inspector (G4), J. R. Mossop.
Director of Operations (G4), A. J. M. Morgan.
Assistant Chief Planning Inspectors (G5), Miss G. M. Pain; G. Lidbury; J. G. Greenfield; J. T. Graham.
Head of Administration (G5), D. A. C. Marshall.

REGIONAL OFFICES

West Midlands, Birmingham.—*Regional Director (G3)*, D. R. Ritchie. *Regional Controllers (G5)*, J. E. Northover; D. L. Saunders; Mrs. P. M. Holland.
Yorkshire and Humberside, Leeds.—*Regional Director (G3)*, J. F. Ballard. *Regional Controllers (G5)*, I. H. Crowther; J. A. M. Hastings.
North West, Manchester.—*Regional Director (G3)*, D. C. Renshaw. *Regional Controllers (G5)*, B. C. Isherwood; P. Styche; (*G6*), J. N. Atkinson.
Northern, Newcastle upon Tyne.—*Regional Director (G3)*, J. A. Owen. *Regional Controllers (G5)*, Ms. D. Caudle; R. G. Bell.
South West, Bristol.—*Regional Director (G3)*, G. M. Wedd, C.B. *Regional Controller (G5)*, S. McQuillin.
East Midlands, Nottingham.—*Regional Director (G4)*, P. M. Hewitt, O.B.E. *Regional Controller (G6)*, G. Meynell, M.B.E.; R. J. Smith.
South East, London W14.—*Regional Director (G3)*, D. Gruffydd Jones. *Regional Controllers (G5)*, A. F. Richardson; R. Williams; J. A. Colley; (*G6*), E. G. Everett.
Eastern, Bedford.—*Regional Director (G3)*, A. Whitfield. *Regional Controllers (G5)*, A. Z. Levy; R. A. Bird.

LONDON REGIONAL OFFICE

Under Secretary (G3), A. A. Pelling.
Grade 5, J. G. Grevatt; A. Buchanan; B. Strong; (vacant).

ROYAL COMMISSION ON ENVIRONMENTAL POLLUTION
Church House, Great Smith Street, SW1P 3BL
[01–276 2080]

Set up on Feb. 20, 1970, 'to advise on matters, both national and international, concerning the pollution of the environment; on the adequacy of research in this field; and the future possibilities of danger to the environment.'
Chairman, The Lord Lewis of Newnham, F.R.S.
Members, Prof. Dame Barbara Clayton, D.B.E.; Prof. G. R. Conway; The Earl of Cranbrook; J. W. Edmonds; The Lord Nathan; Prof. D. E. Newland; J. J. R. Pope, O.B.E.; Dr. C. W. Suckling, C.B.E., F.R.S.; Prof. M. P. Vessey; Prof. H. Charnock, F.R.S.; L. C. G. Gilling, O.B.E.; Prof. E. M. Rothschild; Prof. Z. A. Silberston, O.B.E.; Prof. W. D. P. Stewart, F.R.S.
Secretary, B. Glicksman.

EQUAL OPPORTUNITIES COMMISSION
Overseas House, Quay Street, Manchester M3 3HN
[061–833 9244]

PRESS OFFICE: 1 Bedford Street, WC2 (01–379 6323)

REGIONAL OFFICES: St. Andrew House, 141 West Nile Street, Glasgow G1 2RN (041–332 8018)
Caerwys House, Windsor Place, Cardiff (0222–43552)

The Commission was set up by Parliament in 1975 as a result of the passing of the Sex Discrimination Act. It works towards the elimination of discrimination by virtue of sex or marital status and to promote equality of opportunity between men and women generally.
Chair, Mrs. J. Foster...................... £41,790
Deputy Chair, Mrs. J. O'Dell.............. £17,540
Members, Mrs. K. Boardman; D. Guereca; Prof. G. Powell; A. Simpkin; Mrs. P. Turner; Mrs. E. Walker; Miss M. Monk; Mrs. M. Prosser; Lady Brittan; Mrs. A. Hasan; N. Cowan; Ms. B. Hillon.
Chief Executive, Miss V. Amos.

EXCHEQUER AND AUDIT DEPARTMENT
See **National Audit Office**

**EXPORT CREDITS GUARANTEE
DEPARTMENT**
P.O. Box 272, Export House,
50 Ludgate Hill, EC4M 7AJ
[01–382 7000]
Crown Building, Cathays Park,
Cardiff CF1 3NH
[0222–824000]

The Export Credits Guarantee Department (ECGD), the official export credit insurer, is a separate government department responsible to the Secretary of State for Trade and Industry and functions under the Export Guarantees and Overseas Investment Act 1978. This enables ECGD to encourage U.K. exports by making available export credit insurance to British firms engaged in selling overseas and to guarantee repayment to banks in Britain providing finance for export credit for goods sold on credit terms of two years or more. Guarantees under Section 1 of the Act are given after consultation with an Advisory Council of bankers and businessmen.

The Act also empowers ECGD to insure British private investment overseas against political risks, such as war, expropriation and restrictions on remittances.

Chief Executive, M. G. Stephens.
Directors (G3), G. E. J. Breach; R. G. Codd; C. Foxall; M. T. Hawtin; D. H. Twyford.
Heads of Divisions (G5), C. M. Bossom; A. J. Bray; G. Bromley; J. G. M. Cochrane; D. R. Coombe; D. C. Cooper; R. I. Fear; A. P. Fowell; T. M. Jaffray; R. F. Lethbridge; K. G. Lockwood; M. J. Long; V. P. Lunn Rockliffe; R. W. MacGregor; M. D. Pentecost; Mrs. V. A. Randall; R. A. Ranson; J. K. Sedman; Dr. R. Van Slooten; J. R. Weiss; R. Wild.
Senior Principals (G6), G. C. Bird; D. Q. Bryars; P. J. Callaghan; J. D. Cameron; D. Collins; D. A. Green; K. Dixey; A. P. G. Hare; L. S. W. Montgomery; B. Southwell; D. L. Townley; Miss J. West.
Principals (G7), Miss J. Albutt; J. S. Astruc; J. E. Atkinson; D. D. Baird; D. I. Calvert; A. L. Childs; Mrs. H. V. Cieslik; Mrs. A. C. Cowie; D. M. Cox; A. B. Coyne; M. J. Crane; R. P. D. Crick; J. C. W. Croall; L. Easterbrook; J. B. Eilbeck; D. Elliott; R. X. Fear; G. C. Fisher; J. M. Foster; Mrs. J. A. Fulwood; P. C. Gaudoin; N. F. George; R. Gotts; R. T. Griffiths; P. Hambleton; R. Hardy; G. H. Hill; R. Holloway; B. S. Hooper; P. Jackson; P. F. Jennings; Miss S. J. Johnson; C. D. Jones; G. G. Jones; K. Jones; R. Jones; N. A. Lambert; Mrs. F. M. Lewis; I. Mackay; J. S. McKibbin; Mrs. M. Maddox; S. Merchack; D. W. Miller; D. J. Morris; A. J. E. Muckersie; P. L. Neal; G. A. Newhouse; R. C. Parry; R. J. Pomeroy; S. C. Pond; A. B. Redmayne; S. Rosenthal; M. Russell; M. Scales; R. Scott; B. M. Sidwell, T.D.; K. R. Smith; R. G. Smith; J. S. Snowdon; I. J. Summers; R. S. Summers; J. Sweeney; Ms. P. K. Terry; C. M. Thorogood; D. A. H. Tickner; J. A. Tyler; E. J. Walsby; A. R. Watt; R. A. Watt; T. West; F. Whitehead; J. M. Willis; D. L. Wyatt; J. A. Youd; G. A. Young.
Principal Information Officer, G. Hicks.

Regional Offices

Belfast: Windsor House, 9–15 Bedford Street, BT2 7EG (0232–231743); *Birmingham:* Colmore Centre, 115 Colmore Row, B3 3SB (021–233 1771); *Bristol:* Robinson Building, 1 Redcliffe Street, BS1 6NP (0272–299971); *Cambridge:* Three Crowns House, 72–80 Hills Road, CB2 1NJ (0223–68801); *City of London:*

Export House, 50 Ludgate Hill, EC4M 7AY (01–726 4050); *Croydon:* Sunley House, Bedford Park, Croydon, CR9 4HL (01–680 5030); *Glasgow:* Berkeley House, 285 Bath Street, G2 4JL (041–332 8707); *Leeds:* West Riding House, 67 Albion Street, LS1 5AA (0532–450631); *Manchester:* Townbury House, Blackfriars Street, Salford M3 5AL (061–834 8181).

Export Guarantees Advisory Council

Chairman, P. E. Leslie.
Deputy Chairman, T. W. B. Sallitt.
Other Members, E. L. Brooks; The Hon. D. Douglas-Home; D. Eustace; R. H. George, C.B.E.; A. G. Gormly; S. M. F. Harris; M. Riding; Dr. K. Scholes.

OFFICE OF FAIR TRADING
Field House, Bream's Buildings, EC4A 1PR
[01–242 2858]

The Office of Fair Trading is a government department responsible for the administration of the Fair Trading Act, 1973, the Consumer Credit Act, 1974, the Restrictive Trade Practices Act, 1976, the Estate Agents Act, 1979, the Competition Act, 1980, and the Control of Misleading Advertisements Regulations, 1988. Under the supervision of the Director General of Fair Trading the office keeps under review commercial activities in the U.K. and aims to protect the consumer against unfair practices and is divided between five main areas: consumer affairs, consumer credit, monopolies and mergers, restrictive trade practices and anti-competitive practices.
Director General, Sir Gordon Borrie, Q.C.
Deputy Director General (G2), A. J. Lane.

Consumer Affairs Division

Director (G3), R. J. Thomas.
Assistant Directors (G5), H. J. Charman; S. G. Linstead, D. W. Lightfoot.

Competition Policy Division

Director (G3), Dr. M. Howe.
Assistant Directors (G5), Dr. A. Marshall; P. Mason; A. J. White; A. G. Atkinson.

Legal Division

Director (G3), R. Woolman.
Assistant Directors (G5), M. A. Khan; P. T. Rostron.

Senior Economic Adviser (G5), D. Elliot.
Establishment and Finance Officer (G5), Miss C. Banks.
Chief Information Officer (G6), J. E. Perry.

**FOREIGN AND COMMONWEALTH
OFFICE**
Downing Street, SW1A 2AL
[01-270 3000]

The Foreign and Commonwealth Office provides, mainly through diplomatic missions, the means of communication between the British Government and other governments and international governmental organizations for the discussion and negotiation of all matters falling within the field of international relations. It is responsible for alerting the British Government to the implications of developments overseas; for protecting British interests overseas; for protecting British citizens abroad; for explaining British policies to, and cultivating friendly relations with, Governments overseas and for the discharge of British responsibilities to the dependent territories.

Salaries

For Ministerial salaries, *see* page 293.

Diplomatic Service
(since April 1, 1989)

Permanent Under Secretary and Head of the Diplomatic Service	£83,750
Senior Grade Salary Point 1 (SP1)	£72,000
Deputy to the Permanent Under Secretary	£66,000
Senior Grade Salary Point 2 (SP2)	£59,800
Senior Grade Salary Point 3 (SP3)	£48,100–£50,400
Senior Grade Salary Point 4 (SP4)	£45,400
Senior Grade Salary Point 5 (SP5)	£37,600–£40,900
Diplomatic Service Grade 4 (DS4)	£28,170–£31,602
Diplomatic Service Grade 5 (DS5)	£17,360–£22,606

Secretary of State, THE RT. HON. JOHN MAJOR, M.P.
Private Secretary, J. S. Wall, L.V.O.
Assistant Private Secretaries, R. H. T. Gozney; R. N. Peirce.
Social Secretary, Mrs. L. McBride.
Parliamentary Private Secretary, A. Favell, M.P.
Ministers of State for Foreign and Commonwealth Affairs, THE HON. WILLIAM WALDEGRAVE, M.P.; THE HON. FRANCIS MAUDE, M.P.; THE LORD BRABAZON OF TARA.
Private Secretaries, M. J. Lyall Grant; R. V. Court; S. J. Fraser.
Parliamentary Private Secretaries:
To Mr. Waldegrave, A. Mitchell, M.P.
To Mr. Maude, D. Davis, M.P.
Minister of State for Foreign and Commonwealth Affairs (Minister for Overseas Development), THE RT. HON. LYNDA CHALKER, M.P.
Private Secretary, M. A. Wickstead.
Parliamentary Private Secretary, D. French, M.P.
Parliamentary Under Secretary of State, THE HON. TIMOTHY SAINSBURY, M.P.
Private Secretary, M. A. Hatfull.
Parliamentary Relations Unit, J. D. F. Holt (*Head*); C. A. Hamilton (*Deputy Head and Parliamentary Clerk*).
Permanent Under Secretary of State and Head of the Diplomatic Service, Sir Patrick Wright, G.C.M.G.
Private Secretary, G. D. Adams.
Deputy to the Permanent Under Secretary and Political Director, Sir John Fretwell, G.C.M.G.
Deputy Under Secretaries (SP2), Sir Mark Russell, K.C.M.G. (*Chief Clerk*); D. H. Gillmore, C.M.G.; W. R. Tomkys, C.M.G.; N. P. Bayne, C.M.G.; J. D. I. Boyd, C.M.G.
H.M. Vice-Marshal of the Diplomatic Corps, R. Hervey, C.M.G.
Assistant Under Secretaries (SP5), P. R. Fearn, C.M.G.; P. J. Goulden, C.M.G.; D. J. Moss, C.M.G.(*Deputy Chief Clerk*); D. E. S. Blatherwick, O.B.E. (*Principal Finance Officer and Chief Inspector*); R. J. Carrick, C.M.G., L.V.O.; The Hon. D. Gore-Booth; D. J. E. Ratford, C.M.G., C.V.O.; P. S. Fairweather, C.M.G.; J. O. Kerr, C.M.G.; D. Slater, C.M.G.; R. J. T. McLaren, C.M.G.; I. S. Winchester C.M.G. (*Director of Communications & Technical Services*); Miss R. J. Spence.
Legal Adviser, Sir Arthur Watts, K.C.M.G., Q.C.
Second Legal Adviser, H. G. Darwin, C.M.G.
Deputy Legal Advisers, D. H. Anderson, C.M.G.; F. D. Berman, C.M.G.
Legal Counsellors, M. C. Wood; A. I. Aust; I. D.

Hendry; K. J. Chamberlain; D. M. Edwards; Mrs. A. Glover.
International Labour Adviser, A. E. Smith.
Overseas Police Adviser (DS4), J. W. Kelland, L.V.O., Q.P.M.

Signals Department (Government Communications Headquarters)
Priors Road, Cheltenham, Glos. GL52 5AJ
[0242–221491]

Director (G2), J. Adye.
Principal Establishment Officer (G3), G. Wynn.

Heads of Departments (DS4) and Assistant Heads of Department (DS5)

Aid Policy Dept., C. Raleigh; *Asst.*, T. J. David.
Arms Control and Disarmament Dept., P. D. R. Davies; *Asst.*, Dr. R. Pullen.
Central African Dept., C. A. K. Cullimore; *Asst.*, C. Gray.
Claims Dept., J. Thomas.
Commercial Management and Exports Dept., R. Reeve; *Asst.*, Miss P. M. Kelly, M.B.E.
Commonwealth Co-ordination Dept., T. C. S. Stitt.
Communications Administration Dept., P. M. Piddington; *Assts.*, R. J. Saltwell; J. Bambrough.
Communications Engineering Dept., R. Castle-Smith, M.B.E.
Communications Operations Dept., D. A. Wright, O.B.E..
Communications Planning Staff, D. J. Briggs.
Conference on Security and Co-operation in Europe Unit, P. W. Summerscale.
Consular Dept., J. Harrison, L.V.O.; *Asst.*, J. W. MacDonald.
Cultural Relations Dept., J. N. Elam; *Assts.*, I. Rawlinson, O.B.E.; S. F. Howarth.
Defence Dept., P. Yarnold; *Asst.*, J. Noakes.
East African Dept., R. Edis; *Asst.*, M. R. Crompton.
Eastern European Dept., C. Hulse, O.B.E.; *Asst.*, Miss A. W. Lewis.
Economic Advisers, S. H. Broadbent; *Deputy Head*, J. M. C. Rollo.
Economic Relations Dept., T. L. Richardson; *Asst.*, J. White.
European Community Dept. (External), Miss R. J. Spencer; *Asst.*, P. S. Collecott.
European Community Dept. (Internal), M. Arthur; *Asst.*, N. Sheinwald.
Falkland Islands Dept., D. E. Tatham; *Asst.*, J. Dew.
Far Eastern Dept., A. N. R. Millington; *Asst.*, B. McCleary.
Finance Dept., C. D. Crabbie; *Deputy Head of Dept.*, G. F. Griffiths; *Assts.*, I. Knight Smith; F. Calleghan.
Hong Kong Dept., A. R. Paul; *Asst.*, Miss R. Marsden.
Information Dept., R. J. S. Muir; *Assts.* S. D. R. Brown; K. Passmore.
Information Technology Dept., K. R. Willis; *Asst.*, N. O. Rampton.
Internal Audit Unit, (vacant).
Library and Records Dept., Miss P. M. Barnes; *Assts.*, R. L. E. Foreman; Miss M. Clay, O.B.E.
Management Review Staff, A. F. Smith; *Deputy Head*, J. Anning.
Maritime, Aviation and Environment Dept., R. C. Beetham, L.V.O.; *Asst.*, J. Hughes.
Medical and Staff Welfare Unit, C. Edgerton, O.B.E.; *Deputy Head*, F. Scutt.

---

* Joint Foreign and Commonwealth Office/Overseas Development Administration Dept.

Mexico and Central America Dept., A. L. S. Coltman; *Asst.*, D. F. C. Ridgway.

Middle East Dept., J. R. Young; *Asst.*, S. Lamport.

Migration and Visa Dept., D. M. Harrison, O.B.E.; *Asst.*, J. Smith-Laittan.

Narcotics Control and Aids Dept., D. Fall.

Nationality and Treaty Dept., P. V. Rollitt; *Asst.*, A. Harrington.

Near East and North Africa Dept., A. F. Goulty; *Asst.*, J. S. Laing.

News Dept., R. A. Burns.

North America Dept., D. A. Burns.

Office Services and Transport Dept., I. McCluney; *Asst.*, P. McDermott, M.V.O.

Overseas Estate Dept., M. H. R. Bertram; *Deputy Head*, M. E. Cook.

Overseas Inspectorate, D. E. S. Blatherwick, O.B.E. (*Chief Inspector and Principal Finance Officer*); *Inspectors*, R. Chase; Miss M. I. Rothwell; G. M. Gowlland, L.V.O.; R. Bedford.

Permanent Under Secretary's Dept., C. C. R. Battiscombe; *Deputy Head*, P. J. Torry.

Personnel Operations Dept., E. Clay; *Deputy Head*, H. J. S. Pearce; *Assts.*, P. A. Heald, M.B.E.; J. R. Cowling; E. Chaplin, O.B.E.

Personnel Policy Dept., A. M. Goodenough; *Asst.*, T. Phillips.

Personnel Services Dept., A. P. F. Bache; *Assts.*, G. Edmonds-Brown; G. C. Fedrick.

Policy Planning Staff, R. Cooper, M.V.O.; *Asst.*, J. Powell.

Protocol Dept., D. MacLeod; *Assts.*, T. C. Almond, O.B.E.; S. W. F. Martin, L.V.O. (*First Assistant Marshal of the Diplomatic Corps*).

Republic of Ireland Dept., T. J. B. George.

Research Dept., Director, A. St. J. Figgis; *Regional Directors*, C. J. S. Rundle, O.B.E. (*Africa & Middle East*); K. C. Walker (*Asia*); Miss S. Morphet (*Atlantic*); J. R. Banks (*Soviet Union & E. Europe*).

Science, Energy and Nuclear Dept., P. Wetton; *Deputy Head*, R. Smith.

Security Dept., A. Ford; *Asst.*, M. Hickson, L.V.O.

Security Co-ordination Dept., A. Green; *Asst.*, N. Armour.

Security Policy Dept., P. Lever; *Asst.*, W. G. Ehrman.

South America Dept., C. R. L. de Chassiron; *Asst.*, J. M. Cresswell.

South Asian Dept., F. N. Richards; *Asst.*, W. B. Sinton.

South-East Asian Dept., D. H. Colvin; *Asst.*, P. K. C. Thomas.

Southern African Dept., R. Dales; *Asst.*, G. Berg.

Southern European Dept., M. C. S. Weston, C.V.O.

South Pacific Dept., R. Thomas; *Asst.*, M. J. Peart, L.V.O.

Soviet Dept., S. N. P. Hemans, C.V.O.; *Asst.*, D. Gowan.

Technical Security Dept., M. J. B. Smith; *Assts.*, R. Read; J. Gould.

Training Dept., T. T. Macan; *Director of Language Centre*, J. Moore.

United Nations Dept., A. Brenton; *Asst.*, N. A. Thorne.

West African Dept., Miss M. G. Fort; *Asst.*, F. X. Gallagher, O.B.E.

West Indian and Atlantic Dept., R. S. Gorham; *Asst.*, P. A. Penfold, O.B.E.

Western European Dept., H. N. H. Synnott; *Assts.*, J. C. J. Ramsden; J. W. Guy, O.B.E.

CORPS OF QUEEN'S MESSENGERS
Foreign and Commonwealth Office, SW1A 2AH

Superintendent of the Corps of Queen's Messengers, Maj. I. G. M. Bamber.

Queen's Messengers, Maj. J. E. A. Andre; Cdr. R. D. D. Bamford; Cdr. D. H. Barraclough; Maj. G. M. Benson; Lt.-Cdr. B. R. Bezance; Lt. Cdr. K. E. Brown; Lt.-Col. W. P. A. Bush; Lt.-Col. M. B. de S. Clayton; Lt.-Col. J. B. B. Clee; Capt. G. Courtauld; Maj. F. C. W. Courtenay-Thompson; Col. J. M. Deans; Maj. P. T. Dunn; Lt.-Col. J. W. A. Fleming, O.B.E.; Capt. N. C. E. Gardner; Cdr. P. G. Gregson; J. W. Hannah, M.B.E.; J. O. Hollis; Wg. Cdr. J. O. Jewiss; Lt.-Col. P. S. Kerr-Smiley; Lt.-Col. J. M. C. Kimmins; Lt.-Col. R. C. Letchworth; G. F. Miller; Lt.-Col. A. R. Murray; Maj. D. R. Nevile; Maj. K. J. Rowbottom; Maj. M. R. Senior; Lt.-Col. H. M. L. Smith; Maj. P. M. O. Springfield; Maj. J. S. Steele; Col. D. W. F. Taylor.

FOREIGN COMPENSATION COMMISSION
Alexandra House, Kingsway, WC2B 6TT
[01–438 7045]

The Commission was set up by the Foreign Compensation Act 1950 primarily to distribute under Orders in Council funds received from other governments in accordance with agreements to pay compensation for expropriated British property and other losses sustained by British nationals.

The Commission has the further duty of registering claims for British-owned property in contemplation of agreements with other countries, and it has done so in seven instances since 1950.

Chairman, A. W. E. Wheeler, C.B.E. £48,100
Commissioners, J. A. S. Hall, D.F.C., Q.C.; Sir Alan Leslie; I. M. P. Evans.
Secretary and Chief Examiner, D. H. Wright.

FORESTRY COMMISSION
231 Corstorphine Road, Edinburgh EH12 7AT
[031–334 0303]

The Forestry Commission has the legal status of, and functions as a Government department. It reports directly to Forestry Ministers (i.e. the Minister of Agriculture, Fisheries and Food, the Secretary of State for Scotland, and the Secretary of State for Wales), to whom it is responsible for advice on forestry policy and for the implementation of that policy in Great Britain. There is a statutorily-appointed Chairman and Board of Commissioners (four full-time and six part-time) with prescribed duties and powers. The full-time Commissioners form the Executive Board.

As the Forestry Authority for Great Britain, the Commission is also responsible for carrying out certain regulatory functions in connection with plant health and felling licensing, for conducting forestry research, and administering grant-aid schemes for private woodlands. As the Forestry Enterprise, the Commission has a primary responsibility to provide timber for industry. In discharging their functions, the Forestry Commissioners are charged with endeavouring to achieve a reasonable balance between the needs of forestry and conservation.

Chairman, J. R. Johnstone, C.B.E. (*part-time*)
£27,116
Director-General and Deputy Chairman, G. J. Francis £50,400
Commissioner for Private Forestry and Development, R. T. Bradley £40,900

Commissioner for Administration and Finance,
D. T. J. Rutherford £40,900
Commissioner for Operations, D. L. Foot £40,900
Secretary to the Commissioners, P. J. Clarke . £34,095

REGISTRY OF FRIENDLY SOCIETIES
15 Great Marlborough Street, W1V 2AX
[01-437 9992]

The Registry of Friendly Societies is a Government department serving two statutory bodies, the Building Societies Commission, and the Central Office of the Registry of Friendly Societies, together with the Assistant Registrar of Friendly Societies for Scotland.

The Building Societies Commission was established by the Building Societies Act, 1986. The Commission is responsible for the supervision of building societies, and administers the system of regulation. It also advises the Treasury and other Government departments on matters relating to building societies.

The Central Office of the Registry of Friendly Societies provides a public registry for mutual organizations registered under the Building Societies Act, 1986, Friendly Societies Act, 1974, and the Industrial and Provident Societies Act, 1965. It is responsible for the supervision of friendly societies and credit unions, and advises the Government on issues affecting those societies. The Chief Registrar has certain powers to arbitrate in disputes between members and registered societies. He also acts as the Industrial Assurance Commissioner.
(For **Salaries,** see page 293)

Building Societies Commission

Chairman, J. M. Bridgeman, C.B..
Deputy Chairman, Mrs. R. E. J. Gilmore.
Commissioners, D. Hobson; T. F. Mathews; S. Proctor, C.B.E.; G. Sammons; H. R. C. Walden, C.B.E.

Central Office

Chief Registrar, J. M. Bridgeman, C.B.
Assistant Registrars, A. Wilson; A. J. Perrett; R. N. Williams.

The Registry

First Commissioner and Chief Registrar (G2), J. M. Bridgeman, C.B.

Staff serving the Building Societies Commission:
Grade 5, Mrs. R. E. J. Gilmore.
Grade 5, T. F. Mathews; Mrs. P. Diggle; Mrs. A. M. Halsey; J. M. Palmer.
Grade 7, A. G. Tebbutt; N. F. Digance; Mrs. S. A. Russell; D. A. W. Stevens; E. Engstrom; M. E. Duff; D. W. Lee; K. McGuinness; S. M. Uttley; D. S. Bobker.

Staff serving the Central Office:
Assistant Registrar (G4), A. Wilson.
Grade 7, F. da Rocha; N. J. F. Fawcett; C. T. Martyn.

Central Services

Assistant Registrar (G5), A. J. Perrett.
Legal Staff (G6), Mrs. V. Edwards; P. G. Ashcroft.
Establishment and Finance Officer (G6), M. L. Battenti.

Registry of Friendly Societies, Scotland
58 Frederick Street, Edinburgh, EH2 1NB
[031-226 3224]

Assistant Registrar (G5), J. L. J. Craig, w.s.

GAMING BOARD FOR GREAT BRITAIN
Berkshire House, 168–173 High Holborn,
WC1V 7AA
[01-240 0821]

Established on October 25, 1968, to maintain a broad oversight of developments in gaming in Great Britain, to check prospective gaming licensees management and staff, and to advise the Home Secretary on making regulations which may be needed for the further control of gaming.
Chairman, N. A. Ward Jones, V.R.D. (part-time)
£25,075
Members, P. B. Kavanagh, C.B.E., Q.P.M.; Lady Ibbs; W. N. Hunter Smart; M. H. Hogan (part-time)
£10,055
Secretary, P. R. Burleigh.

OFFICE OF GAS SUPPLY
Southside, 105 Victoria Street, SW1E 6QT
[01-828 0898]

The Office of Gas Supply (Ofgas) is a regulatory body set up under the Gas Act 1986. It is headed by the Director General of Gas Supply who is independent of Ministerial control.

The principal function of Ofgas is to monitor British Gas' activities as a public gas supplier and, where necessary, enforce the conditions of that company's authorization to act as a public gas supplier. Other functions are to grant authorizations to other suppliers of gas through pipes; to investigate complaints on matters where enforcement powers may be exercisable; to fix and publish maximum charges for reselling gas; to publish information and advice for the benefit of tariff customers; to keep under review developments concerning the gas supply industry; to settle the terms on which other suppliers have access to British Gas' pipelines in the event of disagreement.
Director General, J. McKinnon.
Deputy Director General, M. R. Keay.
Legal Adviser, D. R. M. Long.
Business Adviser, R. E. T. Long.
Public Affairs Adviser, I. Cooke.
Consumer Affairs Adviser, W. Macleod.
Administration Manager, P. Schrapel.

THE GOVERNMENT ACTUARY
22 Kingsway, WC2B 6LE
[01-242 6828]

The Government Actuary provides a consulting service to Government departments, nationalized industries and Commonwealth Governments. His actuaries advise on social security schemes and superannuation arrangements within the public sector at home and abroad, on population and other statistical studies, and on Government supervision of insurance companies and friendly societies.
Government Actuary, C. D. Daykin.
Directing Actuaries, D. H. Loades; G. G. Newton; M. A. Pickford.
Chief Actuaries, D. G. Ballantine; J. L. Field; R. T. Foster; T. W. Hewitson; P. H. Hinton; A. G. Young.
Senior Actuaries, E. I. Battersby; P. L. Burt; B. J. Coode; A. P. Gallop; C. A. Harris; F. A. Honeysett; A. I. Johnston; Mrs. I. W. Lane; J. M. MacLeod; P. Merricks; A. P. Pavelin; D. F. Renn.

GOVERNMENT HOSPITALITY FUND
8 Cleveland Row, SW1A 1DH
[01–210 3000]

Instituted in 1908 for the purpose of organizing official hospitality on a regular basis, with a view to the promotion of international goodwill.
Minister in Charge, The Lord Brabazon of Tara.
Secretary, Brig. A. Cowan, M.B.E.

DEPARTMENT OF HEALTH
Richmond House, 79 Whitehall, SW1A 2NS
[01–210 3000]

The Department of Health was formed in July 1988 by the division of the Department of Health and Social Security into two separate departments.

The Department is responsible for the administration of the National Health Service in England and for the personal social services run by local authorities in England for children, the elderly, infirm, handicapped and other persons in need. It has functions relating to food hygiene and welfare foods. The Department is also concerned with the medical treatment of war pensioners, and is responsible for the ambulance and first aid services in emergency, under the Civil Defence Act, 1948. The Department represents the U.K. on the World Health Organization. Responsibility for the administration of the Health Services in Wales was transferred to the Welsh Office on April 1, 1969.
(For **Salaries**, *see* page 293.)
Secretary of State for Health, THE RT. HON. KENNETH CLARKE, Q.C., M.P.
Private Secretary, A. J. McKean.
Special Adviser to the Secretary of State, Mrs. T. Keswick.
Ministers of State, DAVID MELLOR, Q.C., M.P.; THE LORD TRAFFORD.
Private Secretary, A. Davey.
Parliamentary Under Secretary of State, ROGER FREEMAN, M.P.
Private Secretary, Mrs. M. Kirk.
Permanent Secretary (G1), Sir Christopher France, K.C.B.
Private Secretary (G7), Miss H. Gwyan.
Chief Medical Officer (G1A), Prof. Sir Donald Acheson, K.B.E.
Chief Scientist, Prof. F. W. O'Grady, C.B.E., T.D.

NATIONAL HEALTH SERVICE POLICY BOARD
Chairman, The Secretary of State.
Deputy Chairman, Sir Roy Griffiths.
Members, Sir Donald Acheson, K.B.E. (*Chief Medical Officer*); Sir James Ackers; Prof. C. Chantler; Mrs. J. Cumberledge, C.B.E.; Sir Graham Day; Sir Kenneth Durham; Sir Christopher France, K.C.B. (*Permanent Secretary*); R. Freeman, M.P. (*Parliamentary Under Secretary*); D. Mellor, Q.C., M.P. (*Minister of State*); D. Nichol, C.B.E.; Sir Robert Scholey, C.B.E.

NATIONAL HEALTH SERVICE MANAGEMENT EXECUTIVE
Chief Executive, D. Nichol, C.B.E.
Deputy Chief Executive and Director of Operations, G. A. Hart, C.B.
Director of Planning & Information, M. J. Fairey.
Director of Personnel, P. J. Wormald.
Director of Financial Management, Ms. S. Masters.

Medical Adviser, Dr. R. Oliver, C.B.
Director, Family Practitioner Services, B. Rayner, C.B.
Deputy Chief Nursing Officer, Miss S. P. C. Wright-Warren, C.B.E.
Property Adviser, D. N. I. Pearce, C.B.E.

HEALTH AND PERSONAL SOCIAL SERVICES GROUP
Deputy Secretary (G2), T. S. Heppell, C.B.

Health Service Division
Under Secretary (G3), Miss R. O. B. Pease.
Assistant Secretaries (G5), Miss P. M. C. Winterton; J. C. Dobson; J. A. Parker.
Senior Principal (G6), J. C. Stopes-Roe.

Hotel and Dietetic Services Branch
Chief Officer, D. G. Thomson.
Deputy Chief Officer, Hotel and Dietetic Services (G7), B. Frost.
Deputy Chief Officer, Domestic Services (G7), Miss I. D. Oliver.

Priority Care Division
Under Secretary (G3), C. Graham.
Assistant Secretaries (G5), A. D. Bacon; K. Jacobsen.

Community/Childrens Services Division
Under Secretary (G3), J. Halliday.
Assistant Secretaries (G5), C. E. Stone; N. Boyd; R. P. S. Hughes; Mrs. L. Fosh.

Child Health, Maternity and Prevention Division and Aids Unit
Under Secretary (G3), N. M. Hale.
Assistant Secretaries (G5), J. C. Middleton; W. Burroughs; R. Cunningham; A. Barton.

International Relations (Health)
Assistant Secretary (G5), G. C. M. Lupton.

FAMILY PRACTITIONERS SERVICES AND MEDICINES
Deputy Secretary (G2), B. R. Rayner.

Division FPS1
Under Secretary (G3), J. F. Shaw.
Assistant Secretaries (G5), D. Walden; J. Sharpe; D. Wild; B. A. R. Smith; G. J. F. Podger.

Division FPS2
Under Secretary (G3), B. Bridges.
Assistant Secretaries (G5), Miss J. Nisbet; K. J. Guinness; B. A. Harrison.

Medicines Control Agency
Director (G3), Dr. K. H. Jones.
Assistant Secretaries (G5), D. O. Hagger; W. Robertson.

N.H.S. MANAGEMENT BOARD OPERATIONS GROUP
Director of Operations (G2), G. A. Hart, C.B.

Regional Liaison Division
Under Secretary (G3), A. Merifield.
Assistant Secretaries (G5), A. J. Davies; N. Glass; Mrs. K. Caines.

HEALTH BUILDING DIRECTORATE

Director of Health Building (G3), M. A. Meager.

HBD1—NHS Building Procurement

Assistant Director (G5) and Chief Surveyor, D. A. Butler.
Superintending Architect (G6), B. Hitchcox.
Superintending Engineer (G6), R. S. Body.
Superintending Surveyor (G6), R. W. Davis.

HBD2—NHS Building Procurement

Assistant Director (G5), G. G. Mayers.
Superintending Architects (G6), A. J. Noakes; W. R. Hyslop.
Superintending Engineer (G6), G. D. Fisher.

HBD3—Nucleus Development

Assistant Director (G5) and Chief Architect, P. L. Ward.
Superintending Architect (G6), L. Bartholomew.
Superintending Engineer (G6), J. M. Singh.
Superintending Surveyors (G6), D. A. Eastwood; K. J. I. McSweeney.

HBD4—Technology and Safety

Assistant Director (G5) and Chief Engineer, L. W. H. Arrowsmith.
Superintending Engineer (G6), B. C. Oliver.
Superintending Surveyor (G6), D. W. Luscombe.

HBD5—Administrative Support

Assistant Secretary (G5), P. R. Gant.
Superintending Engineer (G6), R. J. Tuthill.

ESTATE AND PROPERTY MANAGEMENT DIRECTORATE

Property Adviser to the NHS Management Board (G2), D. N. I. Pearce.

Policy Branch

Assistant Secretary (G5), T. Whiteley.
Superintending Estate Surveyor (G6), J. C. Ellis.
Superintending Engineer (G6), T. Wagstaff.

Performance Branch

Assistant Director (G5), C. Davies.
Superintending Estate Surveyor (G6), M. Bridgford.

N.H.S. PROCUREMENT DIRECTORATE

Director of Procurement and Distribution (G3), T. Critchley.
Assistant Directors (G5), Miss M. N. Duncan; Dr. D. C. Potter; E. H. W. Luxton; B. J. Love; E. M. Sutherland.
Product Group Heads (G6), C. Bray; R. W. B. Allen; A. D. C. Shipley; Dr. N. A. Slark; Dr. R. G. Mellish.
Commercial Executives (G6), F. G. Doyle; A. Doveston; T. Bird; R. Buchanan; K. Gill; J. Smith; R. G. Hill.

N.H.S. MANAGEMENT BOARD PERSONNEL GROUP

Director of Operations (Personnel) (G2), P. J. Wormald.

Division HAP

Under Secretary (G3), N. B. J. Gurney.
Assistant Secretaries (G4), R. M. Drury; (G5), J. M. Rogers; R. M. Orton; I. Jewesbury.

Information Technology and Planning Division

Director of Planning and Information Technology (G2), M. J. Fairey, C.B.
Assistant Secretaries (G5), C. M. O'Rourke; R. T. Rogers.
Senior Principals (G6), M. A. O'Flynn; Mrs. L. Masterman.

Research Management Division

Chief Scientist (G2), Prof. F. W. O'Grady, C.B.E., T.D.
Deputy Chief Scientist, Director of Research Management (G3), J. Barnes.
Assistant Secretary (G5), D. M. Woolley.
Senior Medical Officers (G5), Dr. M. B. Dastgir; Dr. E. Wilson; Dr. M. Cuthbert.
Senior Principal Research Officers (G6), P. J. Hennessy; Ms. H. Canter.

Social Services Inspectorate

Chief Inspector (G2), W. B. Utting.
Deputy Chief Inspectors (G4), J. H. Barnes; Miss C. Hey.
Assistant Chief Inspectors (HQ), Miss J. Baraclough; Mrs. P. K. Hall; S. Mitchell; J. G. Smith; Mrs. W. Rose.
Assistant Chief Inspectors (Regions), S. Allard; P. Brearley; J. K. Corcoran; J. Cypher; D. Gilroy; B. D. Harrison; D. G. Lambert; Miss S. Markham; B. E. Stimpson; Miss A. Taylor.

MEDICAL DIVISIONS (HEALTH AND PERSONAL SOCIAL SERVICES)

Chief Medical Officer (G1A), Sir Donald Acheson, K.B.E.
Deputy Chief Medical Officers (G2), Dr. M. E. Abrams; Dr. R. M. Oliver, C.B.; Dr. E. L. Harris, C.B.

MEDICAL DIVISIONS UNDER DR. ABRAMS
Division CDPNM

Senior Principal Medical Officer (G3), Dr. P. R. Greenfield.
Principal Medical Officer (G4), Dr. J. M. Graham.
Senior Medical Officers (G5), Dr. E. Cloake; Dr. D. Ernaelsteen; Dr. P. Clarke; Dr. L. B. Hunt; Dr. W. J. Modle; Dr. S. Munday; Dr. A. Rawson; Dr. I. A. F. Lister Cheese.
Medical Officer (G6), Dr. J. G. Ablett.
Principal Research Officer (G7), R. Wenlock.

Division E

Senior Medical Officer (G4), Dr. R. Young.
Medical Officer (G6), vacant.

Division MHI

Senior Principal Medical Officer (G3), Dr. J. L. Reed.
Principal Medical Officers (G4), Dr. J. Shanks; Dr. R. Jenkins.
Senior Medical Officers (G5), Dr. D. F. M. Black; Dr. P. G. Mason; Dr. D. J. Brooksbank; Dr. D. Jenes.

Division PCR

Senior Principal Medical Officer (G3), Dr. G. C. Rivett.
Principal Medical Officer (G4), Dr. J. D. F. Bellamy.
Senior Medical Officers (G5), Dr. W. G. Griffiths; Dr. W. Miller; Dr. V. R. Press.

Toxicology and Environmental Health

Senior Principal Medical Officer (G3), Dr. J. Steadman.
Principal Medical Officers (G4), Dr. G. Matthew; Dr. G. Diggle.

MEDICAL DIVISIONS UNDER DR. OLIVER
Division HPS

Senior Principal Medical Officer (G3), Dr. N. P. Halliday.
Senior Medical Officers (G5), Dr. M. Prophet; Dr. N. Melia; Dr. P. Bourdillon; Dr. D. Rothman; Dr. R. Hangartner.
Principal Scientific Officer (G7), M. R. Godfrey.

Division MPO

Senior Principal Medical Officer (G4), Dr. G. Winyard.
Senior Medical Officers (G5), Dr. J. P. Doyle; Dr. L.J. Martin; Dr. W. Thorne; Dr. G. N. Brown; Dr. D. Holt; Dr. J. Lloyd.
Medical Officer (G6), Dr. D. Macpherson.

Division MME

Senior Principal Medical Officer (G3), Dr. A. J. Isaacs.
Senior Medical Officers (G5), Dr. D. P. Mason; Dr. J. R. Lissamore; Dr. M. Smith; Dr. B. Ely.
Assistant Secretary (G5), N. F. Duncan.
Principals (G7), Mrs. V. Keating; P. W. D. Lawrence; J. Gooderham.

MEDICAL DIVISIONS UNDER DR. HARRIS
Division MCA

Director (G3), Dr. K. H. Jones.
Principal Medical Officers (G4), Dr. D. Jefferys; Dr. P. N. Adams; Dr. S. M. Wood.
Senior Medical Officers (G5), Dr. G. L. Ben; Dr. E. G. Brown; Dr. B. Davies; Dr. J. Dunne; Dr. S. M. Eisen; Dr. K. Fowler; Dr. J. Hilton; Dr. D. Looi; Dr. A. Nath; Dr. J. A. Nicholson; Dr. J. M. Raine; Dr. F. Rotblat; Dr. A. Scott; Dr. R. Shah; Dr. P. Tsintis; Dr. K. A. Winship.

Division IMCD

Senior Principal Medical Officer (G3), Dr. D. Walford.
Principal Medical Officer (G4), (vacant).
Senior Medical Officers (G5), Dr. J. Barnes; Dr. A. Fenton Lewis; Dr. P. A. Hyzler; Dr. H. Murrell; Dr. R. G. Penn; Dr. P. Exon; Dr. J. Berrie; Dr. G. Greenberg; Dr. D. M. Salisbury; Dr. H. Williams.
Medical Officers (G6), Dr. A. Dawson; Dr. H. Nicholas.
Environmental Health Officers, M. Jacob; E. W. Kingcott.

Division SEB

Senior Principal Medical Officer (G3), Dr. J. Metters.
Chief Scientific Officer, Dr. F. P. Woodford.
Principal Medical Officer (G4), Dr. H. Pickles.
Senior Medical Officers (G5), Dr. P. R. Dendy; Dr. P. M. Furnell; Dr. S. P. Vahl; Dr. H. Sutton; Dr. A. Resman.
Medical Officer (G6), Dr. J. Chodera.

Dental Division

Chief Dental Officer, Dr. M. C. Downer.
Senior Dental Officers, R. B. Mouatt; C. Howard; J. M. G. Hunt.

Nursing Division

Chief Nursing Officer, Mrs. A. A. B. Poole.
Deputy Chief Nursing Officer, Miss S. P. C. Wright-Warren, C.B.E.
Principal Nursing Officers, M. A. Clark; Mrs. D. A. Patey; J. Tait; Mrs. A. Dawar; Miss C. Clifford.

Pharmaceutical Division

Chief Pharmaceutical Officer, Dr. B. A. Wills.
Deputy Chief Pharmaceutical Officers (G5), B. H. Hartley; Dr. P. R. Noyce; Dr. A. R. Rogers; A. G. Stewart.
Superintending Pharmaceutical Officers (G6), K. J. Ayling; A. C. Cartwright; Miss D. Hepburn; Dr. R. C. Hutton; Dr. B. R. Matthews; J. R. V. Merrills; Dr. J. Purves; Miss M. L. Rabouhans; S. L. Turner.

Information Division

Director of Information (G4), Miss R. Christopherson.
Deputy Directors (G6), C. P. Wilson (*news*); G. Meredith (*publicity*).

NATIONAL HEALTH SERVICE
Regional Health Authorities

The Chairmen, and members of Regional Health Authorities are appointed by the Secretary of State for Social Services.

Northern, Benfield Road, Walker Gate, Newcastle upon Tyne. *Chairman*, Prof. Sir Bernard Tomlinson, C.B.E., M.D. *Regional General Manager*, D. Hague.
Yorkshire, Park Parade, Harrogate. *Chairman*, Sir Brian Askew. *Regional General Manager*, A. Foster.
Trent, Fulwood House, Old Fulwood Road, Sheffield. *Chairman*, Sir Michael Carlisle. *Regional General Manager*, B. Edwards, C.B.E.
East Anglia, Union Lane, Chesterton, Cambridge. *Chairman*, C. Walker. *Regional General Manager*, A. Liddell.
North East Thames, 40 Eastbourne Terrace, W2. *Chairman*, D. Berriman. *Regional General Manager*, T. Hunt.
North West Thames, 40 Eastbourne Terrace, W2. *Chairman*, W. Doughty. *Regional General Manager*, D. J. Kenny.
South East Thames, Thrift House, Collington Avenue, Bexhill-on-Sea, E. Sussex. *Chairman*, Sir Peter Baldwin, K.C.B. *Regional General Manager*, P. A. Griffiths.
South West Thames, 40 Eastbourne Terrace, W2. *Chairman*, Mrs. J. Cumberlege, C.B.E. *Regional General Manager*, A. J. Kember.
Wessex, Highcroft, Romsey Road, Winchester, Hants. *Chairman*, Prof. Sir Bryan Thwaites, PH.D. *Regional General Manager*, J. Hoare.
Oxford, Old Road, Headington, Oxford. *Chairman*, Sir Gordon Roberts, C.B.E. *Regional General Manager*, R. M. Nicolls.
South Western, King Square House, 26–27 King Square, Bristol. *Chairman*, Sir Vernon Seccombe. *Regional General Manager*, Miss C. E. Hawkins.
West Midlands, Arthur Thompson House, 146–150 Hagley Road, Birmingham. *Chairman*, Sir James Ackers. *Regional General Manager*, K. F. Bales.
Mersey, Hamilton House, 24 Pall Mall, Liverpool. *Chairman*, Sir Donald Wilson. *Regional General Manager*, D. Nichol, C.B.E.
North Western, Gateway House, Piccadilly South, Manchester. *Chairman*, Sir John Page, O.B.E. *Regional General Manager*, D. Allison.

Special Health Authorities

Health Education Authority, Hamilton House,

Mabledon Place, WC1H 9TX. *Chairman,* Sir Donald Maitland, G.C.M.G., O.B.E.; *Chief Executive,* Dr. Spencer Hagard.

Disablement Services Authority, 14 Russell Square, WC1. *Chairman,* Lord Holderness, P.C.; *Chief Executive,* M. G. Jeremiah.

Special Hospitals Service Authority
Charles House, Kennington High Street, W14

The Special Hospitals Service is provided by four hospitals: Rampton; Broadmoor; Moss Side; and Park Lane.
Chairman, Dr. D. E. Edmond.
Chief Executive, C. Kaye.

SCOTTISH HOME AND HEALTH DEPARTMENT
and
NATIONAL HEALTH SERVICE, SCOTLAND
See **Scottish Office**

DEPARTMENTS OF HEALTH AND SOCIAL SECURITY—COMMON SERVICES ADMINISTRATION AND FINANCE GROUP
Principal Establishments and Finance Officer (G2), J. F. Mayne, C.B.

FINANCE GROUP
Finance Division A
Under Secretary (Health) (G3), J. H. James.
Assistant Secretaries (G5), M. Harris; P. Garland.

Finance Division B
Under Secretary (Health) (G4), Ms. M. E. Stuart.
Assistant Secretaries (G5), Mrs. R. Grimshaw; H. Jones; P. F. Slade; Miss A. Mithani.

Financial Management Directorate
Director of Financial Management (G2), Ms. S. V. Master.
Deputy Directors (G3), R. Jefferies; R. J. Kerr; R. J. Peters; T. Scott.

Finance Division D
Under Secretary (Social Security) (G3), Mrs. E. A. Woods.
Assistant Secretaries (G5), J. T. Hughes; J. R. Simpson; C. N. Leivers; Mrs. J. Clayton.

N.H.S. Superannuation Branch
Executive Director (Personnel) (G4), R. M. Drury.
Senior Principal (G6), D. Napier.

Statistics and Management Information Division (SMI)
Director of Statistics and Information Management (G3), Dr. R. Gibbs.
Chief Statisticians (G5), Miss P. W. Annesley; J. N. Lithgow; R. Willmer; T. Orchard; G. J. O. Phillpotts.

Economic Adviser's Office (Health)
Chief Economic Adviser (G3), C. H. Smee.
Senior Economic Advisers (G5), G. C. Fiegehen; J. W. Hurst; M. A. Parsonage.

Operational Research Service (Health)
Under Secretary (G3), C. H. Smee.
Director (G4), Dr. A. A. Holt.
Branch Heads (G6), F. M. Gayton; Dr. G. H. D. Royston; Dr. D. J. Hughes.

Central Management Support
Assistant Secretary (G5), R. W. D. Venning.
Senior Principals (G6), D. E. Matthews; J. Parker.

Departmental Personnel Management
Principal Establishment Officer (G3), N. L. J. Montagu.
Assistant Secretaries (G5), R. J. Tilney; P. E. Turner; I. Magee; B. K. Gilbert.

Solicitor's Office
Solicitor (G2), P. K. J. Thompson.
Principal Assistant Solicitors (G3), Mrs. M. A. Morgan; A. O. Roberts.
Proceedings Operational Director (G4), G. E. Beaven.

HEALTH AND SAFETY COMMISSION
Baynards House, 1 Chepstow Place,
Westbourne Grove, W2 4TF
[01–243 6000]

The Health and Safety Commission is made up of eight representatives of trade unions, employers and local authorities and a full-time chairman appointed by the Secretary of State for Employment. Its primary functions are: to secure the health, safety and welfare of people at work; to protect the public from risks arising from work activities; to control the storage and use of explosives, highly flammable or other dangerous substances.
Chairman, Dr. E. J. Cullen.
Members, D. Mason; Dr. M. C. Shannon; Dr. C. M. Thomas; R. Eberlie; P. Jacques; Dr. A. H. Raper, C.B.E.; Miss A. Maddocks; A. Tuffin.
Secretary, M. F. Downing.

HEALTH AND SAFETY EXECUTIVE
Broad Lane, Sheffield S3 7HQ
[0742–752539]
Stanley Precinct, Trinity Road,
Bootle, Merseyside L20 3QY
[051–951 4381]
Baynards House, 1 Chepstow Place,
Westbourne Grove, W2 4TF
[01–221 0870]

The Health and Safety Executive is a statutory body consisting of a director general and two other people appointed by the Commission. It advises the Commission, and its staff are the primary instrument for carrying out the Commission's policies.

Through a network of 20 area offices, H.S.E. inspectors visit and review work activities, giving expert advice and guidance and, where necessary, issuing enforcement notices and initiating prosecutions. The Employment Medical Advisory Services, the operational arm of the Medical Division, is also based on the area offices. Other inspectorates within H.S.E. monitor or enforce standards and give advice and guidance in specific sectors of industry or employment.
Director General (G2), J. D. Rimington.*
Deputy Director General (G2), D. C. T. Eves.*
Member of the Executive, D. J. Hodgkins.

H.M. Factory Inspectorate
H.M. Chief Inspector of Factories (G3), A. J. Linehan.†

H.M. Agricultural Inspectorate
H.M. Chief Agricultural Inspector (G3), C. Boswell.†

H.M. Mines and Quarries Inspectorate
H.M. Chief Inspector of Mines and Quarries (G3), Dr. M. D. Jones.†

H.M. Nuclear Installations Inspectorate
H.M. Chief Inspector of Nuclear Installations (G3), E.
A. Ryder.*

Safety Policy Division
Director (G3), D. J. Hodgkins.*

Hazardous Substances Division
Director (G3), C. D. Burgess, C.B.*

Technology Division
(includes H.M. Explosives Inspectorate and Major
Hazards Unit).
Director (G3), A. C. Barrell.†

Research and Laboratory Services Division
Director (G3), Dr. J. McQuaid.§

Medical Division
(includes the Employment Medical Advisory Service).
Director of Medical Services (G3), Dr. J. T. Carter.*

Solicitor's Office
Solicitor (G4), A. D. Osborne.*

Resources and Planning Division
(including the Accident Prevention Advisory Unit).
Director (G3), A. W. Brown.*

HIGHLANDS AND ISLANDS DEVELOPMENT BOARD
Bridge House, 20 Bridge Street,
Inverness IV1 1QR
[0463–234171]

The Board, a grant-aided body, responsible to the
Secretary of State for Scotland, has two broad
objectives. These are (1) to assist the people of the
Highlands and Islands to improve their economic and
social conditions; (2) to enable the Highlands and
Islands to play a more effective part in the economic
and social development of the nation. To this end the
Board will concert, promote, assist or undertake
measures for economic and social development.
Chairman, Sir Robert Cowan.
Secretary, J. A. MacAskill.

HISTORIC BUILDINGS AND MONUMENTS COMMISSION FOR ENGLAND (ENGLISH HERITAGE)
Fortress House,
23 Savile Row, W1X 2HE
[01–734 6010]

Under the National Heritage Act, 1983, the duties
of the Commission are: (i) to secure the preservation
of ancient monuments and historic buildings; (ii) to
promote the preservation and enhancement of conservation areas; (iii) to promote the public's enjoyment of, and advance their knowledge of, ancient
monuments and historic buildings and their preservation. The Commission has advisory committees on
historic buildings, ancient monuments, historic
areas, and London.
Chairman, The Lord Montagu of Beaulieu.
Deputy Chairman, S. D. Jenkins.
Commissioners, H.R.H. The Duke of Gloucester; Prof.
B. Cunliffe; A. H. Emery; D. W. Insall; Sir George
Moseley; J. Newman; The Earl of Shelburne; Dr.
P. Hollis; D. Somerset; Sir Hugh Cubitt.
Chief Executive, Miss J. A. Page.

§ Based in Sheffield.
† Based in Bootle.
* Based in London.

WELSH HISTORIC MONUMENTS (CADW)
Brunel House, 2 Fitzalan Road,
Cardiff CF2 1UY
[0222–465511]

Chairman, The Marquess of Anglesey, F.S.A., F.R.S.
Members, W. Lindsay Evans; Prof. J. Eynon, F.R.I.B.A.,
F.S.A.; The Earl Lloyd George of Dwyfor; T. Lloyd;
Prof. G. Williams, C.B.E., D.Litt., F.S.A.; R. Haslam.
Secretary, R. W. Hughes.

HISTORIC BUILDINGS COUNCIL FOR SCOTLAND
20 Brandon Street, Edinburgh EH3 5RA
[031–556 8400]

Chairman, Sir Nicholas Fairbairn, Q.C., M.P.
Members, R. Clow; Prof. J. D. Dunbar-Nasmith, C.B.E.,
F.R.I.B.A.; M. Ellington; I. Hutchison, O.B.E.; The
Lord Jauncey, P.C.; K. Martin; J. A. M. Mitchell,
C.B., C.V.O., M.C.; Rev. K. Nugent, S.J.; Mrs. M.
Richards; Prof. A. J. Rowan; H. F. Smith, M.B.E.
Secretary, I. G. Dewar.

ROYAL COMMISSION ON THE HISTORICAL MONUMENTS OF ENGLAND
Fortress House, 23 Savile Row, W1X 2JQ
[01–734 6010]

The Royal Commission on the Historical Monu-
ments of England was established in 1908. The Royal
Commission is the national body charged with the
recording and analysing of ancient and historical
monuments and buildings. It compiles, preserves and
makes publicly available the national archive of such
material, which is housed in the National Monuments
Record.
Chairman, Miss D. Park, C.M.G., O.B.E.
Commissioners, Prof. M. W. Beresford, F.B.A.; Prof.
R. Bradley, F.S.A.; R. A. Buchanan, Ph.D.; Prof. J.
D. Evans, Ph.D., Litt.D, F.B.A., F.S.A.; D. J. Keene,
Ph.D.; Prof. G. H. Martin, C.B.E., D.Phil., F.S.A.; Prof.
G. I. Meirion-Jones, Ph.D., F.S.A.; Prof. J. K. Downes,
Ph.D., F.S.A.; Prof. A. C. Thomas, D.Litt., F.S.A.; Prof.
M. Biddle, F.B.A., F.S.A.; Prof. P. E. Lasko, C.B.E.,
F.B.A., F.S.A.; Prof. M. Todd, F.S.A.; Mrs. B. K.
Cherry, F.S.A.; R. D. H. Gem, Ph.D., F.S.A; T. R. M.
Longman.
Secretary, T. G. Hassall, F.S.A.

ROYAL COMMISSION ON ANCIENT AND HISTORICAL MONUMENTS IN WALES
Edleston House, Queens Road,
Aberystwyth SY23 2HP
[0970–624381]

The Commission was appointed in 1908 to make an
inventory of the ancient and historical monuments
in Wales and Monmouthshire. The Commission also
includes the National Monuments Record for Wales.
Chairman, Prof. G. Williams C.B.E., F.B.A., F.S.A.
Commissioners, Prof. L. Alcock, F.S.A.; M. R. Apted,
Ph.D., F.S.A.; G. C. Boon, F.S.A.; R. W. Brunskill,
Ph.D.; Prof. D. Ellis Evans, D.Phil., F.B.A.; R. M.
Haslam, F.S.A.; J. G. Jenkins, D.SC., F.S.A.; J. B.
Smith; G. J. Wainwright, Ph.D., F.S.A.; Prof. J. G.
Williams.
Secretary, P. Smith, F.S.A.

ROYAL COMMISSION ON ANCIENT AND HISTORICAL MONUMENTS OF SCOTLAND
54 Melville Street, Edinburgh EH3 7HF
[031–225 5994]

The Commission was appointed in 1908 to make an
inventory of the ancient and historical monuments

of Scotland and to specify those that seem most worthy of preservation. The Commission also includes the National Monuments Record of Scotland.
Chairman, The Earl of Crawford and Balcarres, P.C.
Commissioners, Prof. A. A. M. Duncan, F.B.A., F.R.S.E.; Prof. J. D. Dunbar-Nasmith, C.B.E., F.R.I.B.A.; Prof. Rosemary Cramp, C.B.E., F.S.A.; H. M. Colvin, C.V.O., C.B.E., F.B.A.; Prof. L. Alcock, F.S.A., F.R.S.E.; Prof. G. Jobey, D.S.O., F.S.A; Mrs. P. E. Durham; Prof. T. C. Smout, Ph.D.; The Hon. Lord Cullen.
Secretary, J. G. Dunbar, F.S.A.

ANCIENT MONUMENTS BOARD FOR WALES
Brunel House, 2 Fitzalan Road, Cardiff CF2 1UY
[0222–465511]

Chairman, Prof. G. Williams, C.B.E., F.B.A., F.S.A.
Members, G. C. Boon, F.S.A.; R. B. Heaton, F.R.I.B.A.; Prof. R. R. Davies, D.Phil.; R. G. Keen; Mrs. F. Lynch-Llewellyn, F.S.A.; D. Moore, R.D., F.S.A.; P. Smith, F.S.A.
Secretary, I. Gibson.

ANCIENT MONUMENTS BOARD FOR SCOTLAND
20 Brandon Street, Edinburgh EH3 5RA
[031–244 3076]

Chairman, Prof. E. C. Fernie, F.S.A., F.S.A.Scot.
Members, J. G. Dunbar, F.S.A., F.S.A.Scot.; A. Fenton, C.B.E., F.R.S.E., F.S.A., F.S.A.Scot.; The Lady Grimond; Prof. L. Alcock, F.S.A., F.R.S.E., F.S.A.Scot.; J. Simpson, F.S.A.Scot.; Sir Jamie Stormonth Darling, C.B.E., M.C., T.D., W.S.; Prof. J. J. Wilkes, Ph.D., F.S.A., F.S.A.Scot.; Mrs. E. V. W. Proudfoot, F.S.A., F.S.A.Scot.; Mrs. K. Dalyell; R. J. Mercer.
Secretary, J. C. Judson.

HOME-GROWN CEREALS AUTHORITY
Hamlyn House, Highgate Hill, N19 5PR
[01–263 3391]

Constituted under the Cereals Marketing Act, 1965, the Authority consists of 9 members representing U.K. cereal growers, 9 representing dealers in, or processors of, grain and 3 independent members. The purpose of the Authority is to improve the production and marketing of U.K. grain. The Authority also provides certain agency services to the Intervention Board for Agricultural Produce in connection with the application of the Common Agricultural Policy in the U.K.
Chairman, G. B. Nelson.
General Manager, C. J. Ames.

British Cereal Exports
Chairman, R. J. Cherrington.
Manager, J. B. Rose.

HOME OFFICE
50 Queen Anne's Gate, SW1H 9AT
[01–273 3000]

The Home Office deals with those internal affairs in England and Wales which have not been assigned to other Government Departments. The Home Secretary is particularly concerned with the administration of justice; criminal law; the treatment of offenders including probation and the prison service; the police; immigration and nationality; passport policy matters; community relations; certain public safety matters; fire and civil defence services and also with broad questions of national broadcasting policy. He personally is the link between The Queen

and the public and exercises certain powers on her behalf including that of the Royal Pardon.

Other subjects dealt with include electoral arrangements; addresses and petitions to The Queen; ceremonial and formal business connected with honours; requests for extradition of criminals; scrutiny of local authority byelaws; grant of licences for scientific experiments on animals; cremations, burials and exhumations; firearms; dangerous drugs and poisons, general policy on laws relating to shops, liquor licensing, gaming and lotteries, charitable collections and marriage; theatre and cinema licensing; coordination of government action in relation to the voluntary social services; and sex discrimination and race relations policy.

The Home Secretary is also the link between the U.K. Government and the governments of the Channel Islands and the Isle of Man.

(For **Salaries,** *see* page 293)

Secretary of State for the Home Department, THE RT. HON. DOUGLAS HURD, C.B.E., M.P.
Principal Private Secretary (G5), C. J. Walters.
Private Secretaries, Miss C. Bannister; P. R. C. Storr.
Parliamentary Private Secretary, T. Yeo, M.P.
Ministers of State, THE EARL FERRERS, P.C.; TIMOTHY RENTON, M.P.; JOHN PATTEN, M.P.
Parliamentary Under Secretary of State, PETER LLOYD, M.P.
Parliamentary Private Secretaries:
To Mr. Patten, H. Malins, M.P.
To Mr. Renton, M. Brandon-Bravo, M.P.
Parliamentary Clerk, J. Gilbert.
Permanent Under Secretary of State (G1), Sir Clive Whitmore, G.C.B., C.V.O.
Private Secretary, R. G. Yates.
Chief Medical Officer (at Department of Health), Prof. Sir Donald Acheson, K.B.E.

Legal Adviser's Branch
Legal Adviser (G2), A. H. Hammond.
Principal Assistant Legal Advisers (G3), D. J. Bentley; Miss P. A. Edwards.
Assistant Legal Advisers, R. J. Clayton; Mrs. S. A. Evans; A. M. C. Inglese; D. Seymour; A. W. D. Wilson.
Senior Principal Legal Assistants, Mrs. J. M. Jones; J. O'Meara; C. M. L. Osborne; Mrs. C. Price.

CRIMINAL AND STATISTICS DEPARTMENTS
Deputy Under Secretary (G2), D. E. R. Faulkner, C.B.

Criminal Policy Department
Assistant Under Secretary of State (G3), G. L. Angel.
Heads of Divisions (G5), R. J. Baxter; A. Cogbill; P. C. Edwards; Mrs. E. France; Miss J. M. Goose.
Principals (G7), D. M. Ackland; N. Benger; T. K. Cobley; F. E. Cook; F. H. Eggleston; L. D. Hay; Mrs. C. Lehman; K. MacKenzie; Mrs. R. M. Mitev; T. C. Morris; A. Pickersgill; Miss J. B. Rumble; G. Sutton; G. L. Thomas; R. J. Weatherill; Mrs. V. M. Wilsdon; R. B. Woodland.
Chief Inspector, Drugs Branch (G6), P. G. Spurgeon.

Research and Planning Unit
Head of Unit (G5), Mrs. M. Tuck, C.B.E.
Grade 6, P. J. Jordan; R. Tarling; G. R. Walmsley.
Principals (G7), J. A. Ditchfield; Dr. P. J. Ekblom; Dr. S. Field; Dr. P. Grove; Mrs. K. E. Howard; Mrs. P. Mayhew; Ms. P. M. Morgan; Miss J. W. Mott; Dr. G. I. U. Mair; J. F. Mcleod; A. D. Moxon; W. E. Saulsbury; Dr. L. J. F. Smith; F. P. E. Southgate; Ms. J. Vennard.

Statistical Department

Assistant Under Secretary of State (G3), C. P. Nuttall.
Chief Statisticians (G5), C. G. Lewis; J. L. Walker; P. W. Ward.
Statisticians (G7), Ms. A. Barber; G. G. Barclay; T. Benn; Dr. A. V. Bishop; L. Davidoff; Mrs. P. Dowdeswell; P. F. Collier; Miss V. Gray; Miss G. Goddard; Mrs. R. Passmore; Z. J. Frosztega; K. M. Jackson; Ms. C. D. Morgan; R. Pape; Mrs. P. A. Penneck; P. E. Ramell; Ms. K. Shaw; R. M. Taylor.

Criminal Justice and Constitutional Department

Assistant Under Secretary of State (G3), M. E. Head.
Heads of Divisions (G5), S. S. Bampton; E. A. Grant; Miss P. C. Drew; A. Harding.
Principals (G7), Miss M. V. A. Allibone; R. M. Bradley; N. M. Clowes; M. P. Cook; J. L. Gilhespy; M. J. Gillespie; Miss G. M. Griffith; H. D. Hillier; J. M. Hough; A. J. Lewis; A. D. MacFarlane; D. Massey; Miss S. R. Muir; Mrs. E. A. Sandars; K. W. Smalldon; C. P. Stevens; J. Wake; Mrs. J. S. Waters.
Chief Inspector of Probation (G4), C. H. Thomas, O.B.E.
Deputy Chief Inspector of Probation (G6), D. F. Duchemin, T.D.

Animals (Scientific Procedure) Inspectorate

Chief Inspector, Dr. R. M. Watt.
Superintending Inspectors, C. B. Hart; Dr. W. D. Tavernor.

POLICE DEPARTMENT

Deputy Under Secretary (G2), J. A. Chilcot.

Police Department

Assistant Under Secretaries of State (G3), S. W. Boys Smith; S. G. Norris; G. J. Wasserman.
Heads of Divisions (G5), M. J. Addison; Mrs. P. G. W. Catto; J. W. Cane; J. L. Goddard; K. H. Heal; J. Le Vay; J. M. Lyons; E. Soden; C. B. J. Sutton; F. J. Warne.
Senior Principals (G6), D. R. Birleson; Dr. H. Goldman.
Principals (G7), C. E. Birt; Mrs. F. Clarkson; D. W. A. Cole; T. P. R. Crompton; P. R. Curwen; C. M. Dolphin; C. C. R. Hudson; L. T. Hughes; Dr. G. K. Laycock; K. Mackenzie; M. R. Matthews; Miss E. B. Moody; J. F. Nicholson; A. Norbury; J. M. Potts; P. W. Pugh; Miss P. Ransford; R. P. Rhodes; S. J. Rimmer; A. C. Sinfield; R. E. Smith; K. D. Sutton; A. Townsend; Mrs. A. Underhill; P. F. Vallance; S. C. Wells; A. Wolfenden; Miss M. S. Wooldridge; R. C. Yeates.

Scientific Research and Development Branch
Horseferry House,
Dean Ryle Street, SW1
[01–217 3000]

Director (G5), (vacant).
Deputy Directors (G6), T. R. Mann; Dr. D. M. S. Peace; Dr. J. R. Stealey; Dr. G. Turnbull; Dr. P. A. Young.
Principal Scientific Officers (G7), C. J. Aldridge; A. C. F. Barton; Dr. B. J. Blain; R. J. Brett; E. C. Brown; Dr. G. A. Carr-Hill; R. H. Doney; R. J. Harry; Dr. J. A. Harwood; T. Kent; Dr. S. R. Lewis; D. J. Meakin; Mrs. M. B. Manolias; D. D. O'Brien; R. Oliver; C. D. Payne; Dr. F. Preston; Dr. G. E. Scott; R. C. Stephen; R. Walker; Dr. I. P. Williamson.

Headquarters Forensic Science Service
Horseferry House
Dean Ryle Street, SW1
[01–217 3000]

Director General (G4), Dr. J. Thompson.

Head of Administration (G6), J. P. Emery.
Principals (G7), R. J. M. Anderson; J. Glaze; D. S. Loxley.

Police National Computer Organization
Horseferry House,
Dean Ryle Street, SW1
[01–217 3000]

Technical Development Director (G5), A. Holt.
Deputy Assistant Commissioner, J. F. Newing, Q.P.M.
Senior Principals (G6), G. M. Cole; D. W. Punshon.
Principals (G7), E. L. Brannan; Mrs. P. Cocks; G. T. Coulthard; D. H. Faulks; J. A. Henderson; P. D. Hill-Jones; A. F. G. Hitchman; D. C. Moulton; D. A. Quarmby; R. J. Reason; B. G. Stocking; R. H. Watt.

Directorate of Telecommunications
Horseferry House,
Dean Ryle Street, S.W.1
[01–217 3000]

Director of Telecommunications (G5), A. J. Pearson.
Deputy Directors (G6), I. Aitken; N. K. Finlayson; R. Ginman; D. A. Hendon; R. M. Hughes.
Head of Purchasing Supply and Contract Unit, M. P. Gore.
Principals (G7), C. J. Barron; R. W. G. Dyce; R. C. Eaton; R. Harry; W. Hogg; A. Hulme; A. N. Kent; J. Leary; J. L. Mumford; K. O'Sullivan; M. A. Parker; T. R. Peters; M. J. Phillips; D. A. Pooley; A. A. Sipson; K. Staves; D. C. J. Theobald; P. M. Tomlinson.

H.M. Inspectorate of Constabulary

H.M. Chief Inspector of Constabulary, Sir Richard Barratt, C.B.E., Q.P.M. £56,297
H.M. Inspectors, J. H. Brownlow, C.B.E., Q.P.M.; D. Elliott, Q.P.M.; C. McLachlan, C.B.E., Q.P.M.; Sir Philip Myers, O.B.E., Q.P.M.; C. Sampson, C.B.E., Q.P.M.; Sir John Woodcock, C.B.E., Q.P.M. . . £50,901

Police Staff College
Bramshill House, Basingstoke, Hampshire
RG27 0JW
[025 126–2931]

Commandant, R. S. Bunyard, C.B.E., Q.P.M.
Deputy Commandant and Director of Courses, D. P. Griffiths.
Secretary (G7), K. J. Sheehan.

BROADCASTING, EQUAL OPPORTUNITIES, IMMIGRATION AND NATIONALITY DEPARTMENTS

Deputy Under Secretary (G2), A. J. Langdon.

Broadcasting and Miscellaneous Department

Assistant Under Secretary of State (G3), C. L. Scoble.
Heads of Divisions (G5), S. B. Hickson; N. M. Johnson; L. P. Wright.
Principals (G7), D. A. L. Cooke; R. Eagle; N. M. McLean; G. H. Marriage; J. Sibson; R. B. Snow.

Equal Opportunities and General Department

Assistant Under Secretary of State (G3), R. J. Fries.
Heads of Divisions (G5), Mrs. P. A. Lee, C.B.E.; G. P. Pratt.
Principals (G7), J. P. Casey; Mrs. D. Grice; C. Harnett; M. J. I. Hill; P. J. Honour; Mrs. G. Moody; Mrs. M. E. Moxon; D. J. Rigby.

Voluntary Services Unit

Assistant Secretary (G5), Mrs. B. H. Fair.
Principals (G7), A. C. Crook; Miss C. Dale; A. V. H. Stainer; Ms. J. Thorpe.

Immigration and Nationality Department
Lunar House, 40 Wellesley Road, Croydon, Surrey,
CR9 2BY
[01–760 plus ext.]

Assistant Under Secretaries of State (G3), R. M.
Morris; T. C. Platt.
Heads of Divisions (G5), J. I. Chisholm; Miss V. R.
Dews; R. A. Harrington; T. J. Kavanagh; N. C.
Sanderson; N. R. Varney.
Senior Principal (G6), D. M. McQueen; C. J. Saunders.
Principals (G7), Mrs. H. Bayne; B. D. Bishop; M.
Boyle; W. F. Bryant; J. G. Burgess; J. G. Daley;
Mrs. C. Kellas; C. R. Miller; J. S. Page; Mrs. E. C.
L. Pallett; Ms. C. Pelham; D. A. Peters; R. P.
Ritchie; S. Spence; P. A. Stanton; R. S. Weekes; P.
N. Wrench.

Immigration Service

Chief Inspector (G4), P. Tompkins.
Deputy Chief Inspectors (G6), G. Boiling; Miss K.
Collins; T. Farrage; D. J. McDonough.
Assistant Chief Inspectors (G7), J. M. Durose; G.
Maguire; V. Hogg; K. Rogers.

Passport Department
Clive House, Petty France, SW1H 9HD
[01–271 3000]

Heads of Divisions (G5), J. E. Hayzelden; E. B.
Nicholls.
Deputy Head of Division (G6), C. B. Manchip.
Principals (G7), Mrs P. A. Almond; R. I. Henderson;
T. Lonsdale.

PRISON SERVICE
Cleland House, Page Street, SW1P 4LN
[01–217 3000]

Non-Civil Service grade salaries

H. M. Chief Inspector of Prisons	£48,100
Prison Service Grade 1 (PSI)	£33,079
Prison Service Grade 2 (PSII)	£33,004
Prison Service Grade 3 (PSIII)	£28,440
Prison Service Grade 4 (PSIV)	£22,636–£24,377

Director-General of the Prison Service (G2), C. J.
Train, C.B.
Deputy Director-General of the Prison Service (G3),
B. A. Emes.

Prisons Department

Assistant Under Secretaries of State (Directors) (G3),
J. G. Pilling *(Personnel and Finance);* W. J. A.
Innes *(Operational Policy);* Miss M. A. Clayton
(Directorate of Services); Dr. R. J. Wool *(Medical
Services).*
Non-Executive Members, Miss P. Downs; (vacant).
Heads of Divisions (G5), B. O. Bubbear; B. M.
Caffarey; D. R. Dewick; W. R. Fittall; P. R. A.
Fulton; G. E. Guy; Mrs. V. V. R. Harris; J. A.
Ingman; W. A. Jeffrey; J. Lynch; Miss C. J.
Stewart; R. R. Tilt.
Deputy Director of Prison Medical Services (G4), Dr.
P. J. Hynes.
Principal Medical Officers (G4), Dr. P. Arrowsmith;
Dr. J. M. Sinclair.
Senior Principals (G6), T. K. Cobley; P. Cook; R. E.
Corrigan; C. F. Drewitt; G. E. Dunkley; M. Ireson;
M. J. A. Prowse; D. F. Scagell; Miss A. Smith.
Governors (PSI), D. A. Brown; R. Jacques; J. E.
Simmons.
Principals (G7), D. Aldridge; C. Allison; Miss M. E.
Bowden; P. Broadhurst; M. J. Brown; A. D.
Burgess; B. G. Chaplin; B. Charlson; Ms. R. Collins-
Rice; A. D. Cory; H. M. C. Crudge; M. J. Davies; P.
Dawson; J. Derry; P. Done; J. Duke-Evans; Miss
L. F. Gill; Ms. V. Gray; S. Hadjipavlon; Mrs. M. G.

Hollocks; N. F. M. Home; M. W. Jarvis; F. N.
Jasper; B. Johnson; Miss B. Latimer; Miss D.
Loudon; M. J. Murphy; Mrs. S. Murray; K. R.
North; J. S. Nottingham; P. G. V. Pike; M. J. A.
Prowse; Miss G. Romney; J. Simpson; P. Sleighth-
olme; R. E. Smith; G. H. Thomas; A. G. Thomson;
P. Ward; Miss S. Weinel; W. F. Whiting; A. T.
Williams; T. J. Wilson; D. I. M. Wright; E. Wright;
P. Wright; R. A. Wright.
Governors (PSII), W. J. Abbott; B. G. Chaplin; D.
Curtis; M. R. J. Gander; P. J. Leonard; B.
McLuckie; J. Marriott; M. Mogg; M. Newell; S. C.
A. Pryor.
Prison Service Chaplaincy (G6), Ven. K. S. Pound.
Director of Psychological Services, P. H. Shapland.
Chief Education Officer, I. G. Benson.
Chief Physical Education Officer (G6), M. W. Denton.
Governors (PSIII), R. B. Clark; R. Daly; Miss M.
Gorman; Miss U. M. B. McCollum; W. R. Quirie;
R. J. Talbot; J. Uzzell; C. P. Welsh.

Directorate of Works
Abell House, John Islip Street, SW1P 4LH
[01–217 3000]

Chief Architect and Director of Works (G4), W. L.
Sparks.
Superintending Architects (G6), J. H. Cooper; A. W.
Gillman; R. W. T. Haines; S. Mahraj.
Principal Professional and Technology Officers (G7),
O. P. Astaniotis; P. J. Attwater; J. K. Chamberlain;
J. A. Doohan; C. F. Drewitt; M. C. Hayes; G. E.
Hickey; J. V. R. Hillyer; R. T. Lewis; A. A.
Newman; C. A. G. Poole; R. S. Putland; K. T.
Stannard; B. A. Stickley; M. Sweeny.
Principals (G7), D. Mannings; P. Luscombe.

Prison Service Industries and Farms
Lunar House, Wellesley Road, Croydon,
Surrey CR9 2BY
[01–686 0688/686 3441]

Director (G5), Miss J. MacNaughton.
Group Managers (G6), J. D. Cleary; M. Codd; G. C.
Robertson; J. H. Smith; J. Weller.
Principals (G7), J. A. Byrd; B. D. Feist; R. Fisher; A.
Gillcrist; W. Heppolette; N. F. Montgomery-Pott;
D. E. Neville; T. Senior; A. Sweeney; J. A. Ward;
A. S. Wilson.

Supply and Transport Branch
Crown House, 52 Elizabeth Street,
Corby, Northants.
[Corby 202101]

Director (G6), D. J. Hardwick.
Principals (G7), R. C. Brett; D. J. Brown; M.
Fitzgerald; J. Harvey; S. Sirikanda; A. S. Thomp-
son.

Prison Service Regional Offices

Midland, Birmingham:
Regional Director (G5), J. R. Sandy.
Deputy Regional Director, (vacant).
Assistant Regional Directors (G7), W. L. Mowbray
(Administration); (PSII), J. O'Neill *(Young Of-
fenders); (PSII)* J. R. Wilkinson *(Operations).*

South West, Bristol:
Regional Director (G5), I. M. Dunbar.
Deputy Regional Director, A. H. Rayfield.
Assistant Regional Directors (G7), S. E. Bass *(Admin-
istration); (G7),* J. W. Plumb *(Young Offenders);
(PSII),* R. D. Dixon *(Adult Offenders).*

North, Manchester:
Regional Director (G5), A. W. Driscoll, Q.G.M..
Deputy Regional Director, A. Papps.
Assistant Regional Directors (PSII), F. V. Weigh
(Operation I Division); (PSII), A. Stapleton *(Oper-
ation II Division); (G7),* P. J. Rudgard *(Management*

Support II Division); (*PSII*), R. Halward (*Regimes I Division*).

South East, Woking:
Regional Director (*G5*), G. Dadds.
Deputy Regional Director, D. M. Brook.
Assistant Regional Directors (*PSII*), J. L. Harrison; J. Thomas-Ferrand (*Operations*); K. M. Brewer (*Young Offenders*); Mrs. M. M. Donnelly (*Women*).
Assistant Regional Director (*G7*), (vacant) (*Administration*).

PRISONS
Governors

Acklington, Northumberland, C. Harder.
Albany, I.o.W., P. J. Kitteridge.
Aldington, Kent, J. Hone.
Ashwell, Leics., R. Curtis.
Askham Grange, Yorks., R. Smith.
Bedford, C. Scott.
Birmingham, P. Buxton.
Blantyre House, J. Semple.
Blundeston, Suffolk, Miss J. M. Fowler.
Bristol, R. Smith.
Brixton, SW2., R. E. Withers.
Camp Hill, I.o.W., D. M. Morrison.
Canterbury, D. Twiner.
Cardiff, A. K. Rawson.
Channings Wood, Devon, J. C. Mullens.
Chelmsford, D. B. Sinclair.
Coldingley, Surrey, R. Clarke.
Cookham Wood, P. J. Meakings.
Dartmoor, R. J. May.
Dorchester, B. Coatsworth.
Downview, Surrey, D. Aram.
Drake Hall, Stafford, R. J. Crouch.
Durham, H. D. Jones.
East Sutton Park, G. Gibson.
Erlestoke Park, R. S. Brandon.
Exeter, D. Alderson.
Featherstone, Wolverhampton, L. M. Wiltshire.
Ford, Sussex, Maj. B. Smith.
Frankland, Durham, (vacant).
Full Sutton, B. V. Smith.
Garth, T. A. Bone.
Gartree, Leics., R. S. Duncan.
Gloucester, J. Alldridge.
Grendon and Spring Hill, Bucks., M. F. G. Selby.
Haverigg, Cumbria, D. I. Lockwood.
Highpoint, Newmarket, J. Hunter.
Hindley, Lancs., J. H. M. Anderson.
Holloway, N7, T. M. O'Sullivan.
Hull, P. M. Wheatley.
Kingston, Portsmouth, Miss M. R. Allen.
Kirkham, Lancs., Maj. R. B. Coombs.
Lancaster, W. J. Ginn.
Leeds, C. J. Jones.
Leicester, C. J. Williams.
Lewes, T. M Turner.
Leyhill, Glos., N. W. A. Wall.
Lincoln, W. J. MacGowan.
Lindholme, Doncaster, D. J. Thompson.
Littlehey, S. J. Twinn.
Liverpool, A. N. Joseph.
Long Lartin, Worcs., J. Whitty.
Maidstone, G. Gregory-Smith.
Manchester, F. B. O'Friel.
Morton Hall, Lincoln, (vacant).
New Hall, H. G. Owen.
Northeye, Sussex, L. R. Merricks.
North Sea Camp, M. L. Knight.
Norwich, A. J. Barclay.
Nottingham, H. Reid.
Oxford, (vacant).
Parkhurst, I.o.W., J. Blakey.
Pentonville N7, R. J. Kendrick.
Preston, B. A. Wilson.

Ranby, F. Abbott.
Reading, D. Myers.
Rochester, D. Wilson.
Rudgate, W. Yorks., D. Whitehead.
Send, Surrey, A. C. Smith.
Shepton Mallet, C. T. Nellins.
Shrewsbury, G. Ross.
Stafford, D. Shaw.
Standford Hill, W. J. Cooper.
Stocken, R. P. Feeney.
Styal, Cheshire, G. Walker.
Sudbury Fosten, Derbys., L. Stones.
Swaleside, Kent, B. W. Sutton.
Swansea, C. T. Erickson.
Thorp Arch, W. Yorks, G. Barnard.
The Verne, Dorset, D. G. Longley.
Wakefield, T. J. Gadd.
Wakefield Service College, J. W. Staples.
Wandsworth, SW18., C. G. Clarke.
Wayland, T. C. H. Newth.
Winchester, J. C. Newell.
Wormwood Scrubs, W12., D. M. Brooke.
Wymott, Preston, C. B. Scott.

YOUNG OFFENDER INSTITUTIONS
Governors

Aylesbury, J. W. Dring.
Buckley Hall, Lancs., C. R. Griffiths.
Bullwood Hall, Essex, Miss U. M. B. McCollam.
Campsfield House, Oxford, T. E. Moss.
Castington, R. Mitchell.
Deerbolt, P. A. Whitehouse.
Dover, T. G. Murtagh.
Drake Hall, R. J. Crouch.
East Sutton Park, Kent, G. Gibson.
Eastwood Park, Glos., M. A. Cook.
Everthorpe, Humberside, T. Davies.
Feltham, A. M. E. de Frisching.
Glen Parva, Leics., J. H. Rumball.
Grendon/Spring Hill, M. F. G. Selby.
Guys Marsh, Dorset, G. Brunskill.
Haslar, Hants., J. J. O'Neill.
Hatfield, Yorks., W. J. Clark.
Hewell Grange, Worcs., D. Bamber.
Hollesley Bay Colony, Suffolk, Miss S. F. McCormick.
Huntercombe and Finnamore Wood, Oxon., Miss A. W. Hair.
Kirklevington, Cleveland, B. Smith.
Lowdham Grange, Notts., R. S. Radcliffe.
The Mount, I. Ward.
New Hall, H. G. Owen.
Northallerton, J. N. Brooke.
Onley, Warwicks., R. Doughty.
Portland, Dorset, M. Langdon.
Rochester, D. Wilson.
Stoke Heath, Salop, A. Cruikshank.
Styal, Cheshire, G. Walker.
Swinfen Hall, Staffs., (vacant).
Thorn Cross, D. Hall.
Usk and Prescoed, Gwent, D. T. Williams.
Wellingborough, P. Atherton.
Werrington, Staffs., P. E. Salter.
Wetherby, Yorks., A. Holman.
Whatton, Notts., M. A. Lewis.

REMAND CENTRES
Governors

Ashford, Middx., P. J. Earnshaw.
Brockhill, Worcs., P. T. Hanglin.
Cardiff, A. K. Rawson.
Feltham, A. M. E. de Frisching.
Glen Parva, J. H. Rumball.
Latchmere House, Surrey, P. B. Wailen.
Low Newton, Co. Durham, K. Forster.
Pucklechurch, Bristol, D. C. Leach.
Risley, Cheshire, I. Boon.

Inspectorate of Prisons

H.M. Chief Inspector of Prisons, His Hon. Judge Tumim.
H.M. Deputy Chief Inspector of Prisons (G5), M. D. Jenkins.
H.M. Inspectors (Gov. I), C. Allen; Miss J. Kinsley, O.B.E.; D. J. Jarvis; *(Gov. IV),* A. Lucas; *(G7),* J. J. Courtney; B. J. Wells.
Principal (G7), S. C. Handley.

ESTABLISHMENT, FINANCE AND MANPOWER, FIRE AND EMERGENCY PLANNING DEPARTMENTS

Deputy Under Secretary (G2), M. J. Moriarty, C.B..

Establishment Department

Assistant Under Secretary of State (G3), A. R. Rawsthorne *(Personnel, Organization and Management Services).*
Heads of Divisions (G5), B. W. Buck; P. Canovan; Mrs. C. Crawford; T. J. Flesher; Mrs. E. J. Grimsey; J. S. Smedley.
Senior Principals (G6), D. J. Grant; F. R. Hayhurst; M. H. Rumble.
Principals (G7), K. Aylen; W. Black; D. J. Blackwood; J. W. Bradley; G. Brown; M. Carr; R. C. Case; G. J. Edwards; B. Elliott; A. Fishwick; D. H. Gannon; J. A. Greenland; R. A. Hemmings; B. J. Jordan; Miss D. London; Mrs. S. Mann; Mrs. J. Morgan; Mrs. E. C. L. Pallett; R. Ritchie; K. E. R. Rogers; D. G. Ross; J. S. Sarjantson; A. Silver; S. E. Wharton.

Home Office Unit at Civil Service Selection Board
Kirkland House, 24 Whitehall, SW1A 2ED
[01–210 plus extension]

Assistant Secretary (G5), R. J. Miles.
Principal Psychologist, F. D. Bedford.

Public Relations Branch

Director of Information Services (G4), B. L. Mower.
Deputy Director, J. Haslam.
Principal Information Officers (G7), C. R. Seabrook; R. Windsor.

Finance and Manpower Department

Assistant Under Secretary of State (Principal Finance Officer) (G3), M. C. Malone Lee.
Heads of Divisions (G5), M. P. Bolt; N. A. Nagler; G. K. Sandiford.
Senior Principals (G6), T. A. S. Devon; D. W. Diamond; A. K. Holman.
Principals (G7), I. J. Acton; R. Braganza; G. Brindle; A. D. Chadwick; R. Creedon; S. W. Davidson; C. I. Dickinson; P. Durbin; G. B. Fox; B. R. Gange; F. Gorton; P. W. Jones; J. W. Maloney; D. J. Moon; D. Mullarky; G. L. Thomas.

Fire and Emergency Planning Department

Assistant Under Secretary of State (G3), A. H. Turney.
Heads of Divisions (G5), P. E. Bolton; R. R. G. Watts; R. M. Whalley.
Grade 6, B. S. Luetchford.
Principals (G7), F. J. Archer; B. R. Barrett; D. H. Evans; R. Kornick; B. Lockett; D. J. Moss; D. J. Mould; Miss S. E. Paul; T. E. Russell; G. Underwood; A. Walmsley; Mrs. S. M. K. Willmington.

H.M. Fire Service Inspectorate

H.M. Chief Inspector, Sir Reginald Doyle, C.B.E.
H.M. Inspectors , D. A. Buswell; S. D. Christian; B. T. A. Collins; T. Greenwood; A. F. Kilford; P. A. Kilshaw; D. N. McCallum, O.B.E.; W. C. Perry, M.B.E.; H. V. Reed; N. F. Roundell, C.B.E., Q.F.S.M.; C. H. Sanders; G. J. Tinley.
Senior Engineering Inspector, R. M. Simpson, O.B.E.

Fire Service College
Moreton-in-Marsh, Gloucestershire GL56 0RH
[0608–50831]

Commandant, G. Clarke, C.B.E.
Deputy Commandant, F. N. David.
Secretary (G7), J. A. Gundersen.

Civil Defence College
The Hawkhills, Easingwold, Yorks. YO6 3EG
[0347–21406]

Head of College (G5), J. B. Bettridge, C.B.E.
Vice-Principal, J. D. Shallow, M.C.

Home Office H.Q. U.K. Warning and Monitoring Organization
James Wolfe Road, Cowley, Oxford OX4 2PT
[0865–776005]

Director (G6), R. F. Cooke.
Deputy Director I (G7), W. P. Lawrie.
Deputy Director II (G7), D. L. Warden.

Women's Royal Voluntary Service
234–244 Stockwell Road, SW9 9SP
[01–733 3388]

National Chairman, Hon. Mrs. Mary Corsar.

HORSERACE TOTALISATOR BOARD
74 Upper Richmond Road, SW15 2SU
[01–874 6411]

Established by the Betting, Gaming and Lotteries Act, 1963, as successor in title to the Racecourse Betting Control Board established by the Racecourse Betting Act, 1928.

Its function is to operate totalisators on approved racecourses in Great Britain, and it also provides on- and off-course cash and credit offices. Under the Horserace Totalisator and Betting Levy Board Act, 1972, it is further empowered to offer bets at starting price (or other bets at fixed odds) on any sporting event.

Chairman, Lord Wyatt of Weeford £64,000
Members, The Lord Chapple; Mrs. P. Hastings; Hon. D. Montagu; P. S. Winfield; J. F. Sanderson; H.R.H. Prince Michael of Kent.

HOUSING CORPORATION
149 Tottenham Court Road, W1P 0BN
[01–387 9466]

Established by Parliament in 1964, the Housing Corporation registers, promotes, funds and supervises housing associations. There are over 2,400 registered associations in England providing more than half a million homes. Housing associations are non-profit making bodies run by voluntary committees.

The Corporation's duties have been extended under the provisions of the Housing Act 1988 to cover responsibilities for the payments of capital and revenue grants to housing associations, for helping tenants interested in Tenants' Choice, and the approval and revocation of potential new landlords under this policy.

Chairman, Sir Hugh Cubitt, C.B.E.

INDEPENDENT BROADCASTING AUTHORITY
70 Brompton Road, SW3
[01–584 7011]

The Independent Television Authority was created by Act of Parliament in 1954 to provide an additional television broadcasting service to that provided by the British Broadcasting Corporation. In 1972 it was renamed the Independent Broadcasting Authority and its functions were extended to cover the provision of independent local radio.

The main functions of the Authority are to appoint the ILR and ITV programme companies; to own and operate transmitters; to supervise the programmes provided by contractors and the Channel Four Television Company and their scheduling; and to control advertising. The programme companies pay the Authority a rental to enable it to carry out its duties.

Fifteen ITV programme companies provide programmes in 14 regions (two companies operate in London, one at the weekends, the other during the week). By June, 1989, 62 Independent Local Radio areas were broadcasting in the U.K. (in London, there are two companies, one providing a news and information service, and the second general entertainment and information). Both ITV and ILR are financed mainly by the sale of advertising time.

The Authority consists of a Chairman and eleven members appointed by the Home Secretary and a permanent staff under the Director General.

Chairman, G. Russell, C.B.E.

Deputy Chairman, The Lord Chalfont, O.B.E., M.C., P.C.

Members, Prof. J. F. Fulton (*Northern Ireland*); J. R. Purvis (*Scotland*); G. R. Peregrine (*Wales*); Sir Michael Caine; R. A. Grantham; Prof. A. Cullen, O.B.E., F.R.S., Lady Popplewell; R. Sondhi; Mrs. P. Mathias.

Acting Director General, Lady Littler.
Director of Television, D. Glencross.
Director of Radio, P. A. C. Baldwin.
Director of Engineering, Dr. J. Forrest.
Director of Finance, P. Rogers.
Controller of Advertising, F. Willis.
Controller of Public Affairs, Miss S. Thane.
Secretary, K. Blyth.
Regional Officers, M. J. Fay (*Yorkshire*); E. Lewis (*Wales and West of England*); A. D. Fleck (*Northern Ireland*); S. Perkins (*East of England*); D. Lee (*North-West England*); B. Marjoribanks (*Scotland*); J. Dougray (*North-East England and the Borders*); N. J. Reedy (*East and West Midlands*); J. B. Scott (*South of England and Channel Islands*).

INDUSTRIAL INJURIES ADVISORY COUNCIL
Friars House, 157–168 Blackfriars Road, SE1 8EU
[01–972 3316/7]

The Industrial Injuries Advisory Council is a statutory body under the Social Security Act, 1975, which considers and advises the Secretary of State for Social Services on Regulations and other questions relating to industrial injuries benefits or their administration.

Chairman, Prof. J. M. Harrington.
Members, G. Applebey; Miss J. C. Brown; Prof. M. J. Cinnamond; Dr. D. Coggon; Dr. R. J. Donaldson, O.B.E.; Dr. G. A. Hard; P. R. A. Jacques; Dr. C. P. Juniper; G. Lloyd, C.B.E.; T. W. Mawer; Dr. A. J. Newman Taylor; Mrs. M. Prosser; Dr. E. Roman; Dr. A. Sinclair; Miss B. Swiadkowska; G. M. Thompson.
Secretary, A. L. Perl.

CENTRAL OFFICE OF INFORMATION
Hercules Road, SE1 7DU
[01–928 2345]

The Central Office of Information is a common service department which produces information and publicity material, and supplies publicity services, for other Government departments on a repayment basis. In the U.K. it conducts Government display press, television, radio and poster advertising, produces and distributes booklets, leaflets, films, television and radio material, exhibitions, photographs and other visual material; and distributes departmental press notices. For the overseas departments it supplies British Information posts overseas with press, radio and television material, booklets, magazines, reference services, films, exhibitions, photographs, display and reading room material; arranges tours in the U.K. for official visitors from overseas. Administrative responsibility for the Central Office of Information rests with H.M. Treasury Ministers, while the ministers whose departments it serves are responsible for the policy expressed in its work.

(For **Salaries**, *see* page 293)

Director-General (G4), G. M. Devereau.
  Private Secretary, Ms. T. E. Sharp.
Deputy Director-General (G5), J. Bolitho.

CENTRAL SERVICES GROUP
Client Services
Director (G6), Miss J. Luke.

Communications Services
Director (G6), J. A. Leys.

OVERSEAS PUBLICITY GROUP
Group Director (G5), P. T. Brazier.

Overseas Press Services
Director (G6), G. L. Stickland.

Overseas Publications & Foreign Languages
Director (G6), R. Smith.

Overseas Visitors & Information Studies
Director (G6), D. A. Smith.

VISUAL MEDIA AND RADIO GROUP
Group Director (G5), R. N. Hooper.

Films & Television
Director (G6), C. E. Skinner.

Exhibitions and Photographs
Director (G6), vacant.

HOME PUBLICITY GROUP
Group Director (G5), D. A. Low.

Advertising
Director (G6), K. C. Belben.

Home Publications
Director (G6), M. Jacobson.

Research
Director (G6), M. C. Warren.

ADMINISTRATION SERVICES GROUP
Principal Establishment and Finance Officer (G5), D. A. Truman.
Personnel and Office Services Director (G6), W. J. Colwill.
Finance and Management Services Director (G6), K. E. Williamson.

REGIONAL OFFICES
North Eastern, Wellbar House, Gallowgate, Newcastle upon Tyne.—*Regional Director (G7)*, R. P. Haslam.

Yorkshire and Humberside, City House, New Station Street, Leeds.—*Regional Director (G6),* A. S. Poole, L.V.O.

Eastern, Three Crowns House, 72–80 Hills Road, Cambridge.—*Regional Director (G7),* D. Dowle.

London and South Eastern, Hercules Road, SE1 7DU.—*Regional Director (G6),* vacant.

South Western, The Pithay, Bristol.—*Regional Director (G7),* P. D. Yorke.

Midlands, Five Ways Tower, Frederick Road, Edgbaston, Birmingham.—*Regional Director (G6),* P. J. Woodford.

North Western, Sunley Building, Piccadilly Plaza, Manchester.—*Regional Director (G6),* O. J. B. Prince-White.

BOARD OF INLAND REVENUE
Somerset House, WC2R 1LB
[01–438 6622]

The Board of Inland Revenue was constituted under the Inland Revenue Board Act, 1849, by the consolidation of the Board of Excise and the Board of Stamps and Taxes. In 1909 the administration of excise duties was transferred to the Board of Customs. The Board of Inland Revenue administers and collects direct taxes—mainly income tax, corporation tax, capital gains tax, inheritance tax, stamp duty, development land tax and petroleum revenue tax—and advises the Chancellor of the Exchequer on policy questions involving them. The Head Office is in London and there are Inspectors of Taxes offices and Collection offices throughout the United Kingdom. The Department's Valuation Office is responsible for valuing property for tax purposes, for compensation and for compulsory purchase and (in England and Wales) for local rating purposes. In 1986–87 Inland Revenue collected over £57,000 million tax.

(For **Salaries,** *see* page 293)

The Board

Chairman (G1), Sir Anthony Battishill, K.C.B.
  Private Secretary, R. F. S. Evers.
Deputy Chairmen (G2), A. J. G. Isaac, C.B.; T. J. Painter.
  Private Secretary, Miss J. M. Goold.
Directors General (G2), D. B. Rogers, C.B.; J. H. Beighton.
Commissioner: Chief Valuer (G2), R. R. B. Shutler.

Subject Divisions

Directors (G3), P. Lewis; C. W. Corlett; B. T. Houghton; E. McGivern; D. Y. Pitts; M. A. Johns; K. V. Deacon; J. H. Roberts.
Senior Principal Inspector of Taxes (G4), J. C. Campbell; K. A. Skinner, C.B.E.; R. E. Creed; J. Moule; M. D. E. Newstead; E. K. Pearson; G. F. Hamilton; W. Northend; J. M. L. Davenport; J. K. Duxbury; D. W. Hugo; I. N. Hunter; B. Sadler; J. F. Hall; J. M. Phalp; A. J. O'Brien.
Grade 5, B. A. Mace; M. Prescott; J. D. Farmer; D. L. Shaw; H. B. Thompson; M. F. Cayley; J. H. Reed; M. J. G. Elliott; J. P. B. Bryce; P. W. Fawcett; J. B. Shepherd; Miss M. A. Hill; B. O'Connor; L. E. Jaundoo; M. A. Keith; C. Stewart; A. W. Kuczys; C. R. Massingham; A. G. Nield; C. D. Sullivan.
Principal Inspectors of Taxes (G5), R. C. Mountain; M. L. Gordon; J. W. Calder; J. Potter; T. R. Evans; J. F. Leverington; I. S. Gerrie; A. J. Wardrop; A. Cummins; A. Beauchamp; R. E. Haigh; A. Harrison; D. F. Parratt; D. A. Smith; J. T. Cawdron; A. C. Williams.
Controller of Oil Taxation Office (G4), M. Templeman.

Central Division

Grade 3, G. H. Bush.
Grade 5, S. J. McManus; R. B. Willis.
Senior Economic Adviser (G5), R. Weeden.

Management Divisions

Director of Personnel (G3), P. B. G. Jones.
Assistant Directors (G4), G. Findley; G. F. Hamilton; (G5) R. Neilson; N. C. Munro; Mrs. C. Hubbard; R. A. Hutton, J. T. Tudor; M. K. Robins.
Director of Manpower and Support Services (G3), J. M. Crawley.
Assistant Directors (G5); D. Ward; R. R. Martin; A. W. Bryant.
Head of Operational Research (G5), R. P. R. Tilley.
Director of Information Technology (G3), S. C. T. Matheson.
Deputy Director of Information Technology (G4), J. A. Pinder.
Assistant Directors (G5), A. M. Paterson; R. A. Hamilton; I. P. Crump; E. Wilson; C. J. Thompson; B. T. Glassberg; R. Assirati.
Director of Operations (G3), C. Cherry.
Deputy Director of Operations (G4), D. W. Muir.
Assistant Directors (G4), E. J. Gribbon; (G5) J. H. Keelty; J. C. Jones; Miss M. James; J. M. Thomas; M. Hodgson; R. S. Hurcombe; F. J. Brannigan; D. J. Timmons.
BROCS Project Office (G5), J. E. Yard.
Controller, Enforcement Office (G5), R. F. Bruford.
Head of Communications Group (G5), P. C. Tharby.
Press Secretary (G7), Miss F. A. McFarlane.

Finance Division

Principal Finance Officer (G3), J. M. Crawley.
Assistant Secretaries (G5), I. R. Spence; R. Warden.
Controller, Central Accounting Office (G6), J. Gray.
Chief Internal Auditor (G6), N. Buckley.

Statistics Division

Director (G3), J. R. Calder.
Chief Statisticians (G5), J. B. Dearman; R. J. Eason; F. A. Fitzpatrick; I. Stewart.
Computing (G6), R. James.

Office of the Controller of Stamps
South-West Wing, Bush House, Strand, WC2B 4QN
and Barrington Road, Worthing, W. Sussex
BN12 4XH

Controller (G6), D. E. Pipe, O.B.E.

Capital Taxes Office
Minford House, Rockley Road, W14 0DF

Controller (G4), G. A. Spencer.
Deputy Controllers (G5), B. D. Kent; R. J. Draper.
Asst. Controllers (G6), M. Swann; D. J. Ferley; C. A. Oldridge; H. V. Capon; R. T. Kablean; J. Blagden; T. J. Plumb; R. Shanks; N. Tant.
Boards Actuarial Adviser (G6), D. R. Erasmus.
Senior Principal (G6), P. Twiddy.

Solicitor of Inland Revenue
Somerset House, WC2R 1LB

Solicitor (G2), R. K. Miller, C.B.
Principal Assistant Solicitors (G3), B. E. Cleave; J. D. H. Johnston; P. L. Ridd.
Assistant Solicitors (G5), R. J. Alderman; C. J. C. Baron; J. C. H. Bates; S. Bousher; K. Brown; K. O. Butterfield; A. J. Gunz; J. F. W. Hinson; N. R. Phillips; A. K. S. Shaw; R. W. Thornhill; R. Waterson; Miss A. E. Wyman.

Superannuation Funds Office
Lynwood Road, Thames Ditton, Surrey KT7 0DP

Controller (G5), R. G. Lusk.

Assistant Controllers (G6), I. A. Young; R. C. Full-brook.

Inspector of Foreign Dividends Office
Lynwood Road, Thames Ditton, Surrey KT7 0DP
Inspector of Foreign Dividends (G6), J. Steele.

Office of the Chief Valuer
New Court, Carey Street, WC2A 2JE

Chief Valuer (G2), R. R. B. Shutler.
Deputy Chief Valuers (G3), A. J. Langford; R. J. Pawley.
Assistant Chief Valuers (G4), R. A. Dales; P. Upton.
Superintending Valuers (G5), G. I. Coe; W. A. M. Jones, C.B.E.; M. J. Loveridge; O. T. Morgan; W. J. Reed; A. B. Prior.
Assistant Directors (G5), J. H. Ebdon; R. F. Moore; D. K. Park; T. R. Peckham.

INLAND REVENUE (SCOTLAND)
80 Lauriston Place, Edinburgh EH3 9SL

Controller (G4), W. S. Linkie, C.B.E.
Group Controllers (G5), J. Brown; G. M. McGregor; G. Watson; R. I. Ford.

Controller (Stamps)
16 Picardy Place, Edinburgh EH1 3NF
Controller, D. G. Hunter.

Capital Taxes Office
16 Picardy Place, Edinburgh EH1 3NF

Registrar (G5), P. G. Bruce, M.B.E.
Deputy Registrar (G6), vacant.
Chief Examiners (G7), G. Mackie; Mrs. J. A. Templeton; W. Young; J. Telford; T. E. Naysmith; C. G. Hogg; Miss A. Forbes.

Solicitor's Office
80 Lauriston Place, Edinburgh EH3 9SL

Solicitor, T. H. Scott.
Senior Principals (Legal) (G6), I. K. Laing; D. S. Wishart.
Principal (Legal), H. M. Milne.

Office of the Chief Valuer, Scotland
15 Drumsheugh Gardens, Edinburgh EH3 7UN

Chief Valuer (G4), J. A. Sutherland.
Assistant Chief Valuer (G5), M. A. Newbury.

INTERVENTION BOARD FOR AGRICULTURAL PRODUCE
Fountain House, Queen's Walk,
Reading RG1 7QW
[0734–583626]

The Intervention Board for Agricultural Produce was formed as a Government Department on November 22, 1972, and became operational on Feb. 1, 1973. The Board is responsible for the implementation of European Community regulations covering the market support arrangements of the Common Agricultural Policy. Members of the Board are appointed by and are responsible to the Agricultural Ministers of the U.K.
(For **Salaries**, *see* page 293)

Chairman, A. J. Ellis, C.B.E.
Chief Executive (G3), G. Stapleton.
Finance Officer and Director General of Corporate Services (G4), D. J. Coates.

Heads of Divisions
Finance Division (G5), J. Diserens.
External Trade Division (G5), G. N. Dixon.
Crops Division (G5), H. MacKinnon.
Livestock Products Division (G5), R. A. Saunderson.

Establishments Services (G6), R. J. Lovell.
Computer Services (G6), E. M. Abbott.

U.K. Seeds Executive
Chairman, Prof. J. C. Murdoch, O.B.E., Ph.D.
Members, T. M. Clucas; J. Harvey; Prof. J. D. Hayes, Ph.D.; P. R. Hayward, O.B.E.; I. C. Henderson; D. R. Thomas; W. P. Watt; I. M. Whitelaw.

LAND AUTHORITY FOR WALES
The Custom House, Custom House Street,
Cardiff CF1 5AP
[0222–223444]

The Authority is responsible for acquiring and disposing of land needed for private development in Wales.
Chairman, G. D. Inkin, O.B.E. (*part-time*) £23,688
Chief Executive, B. Ryan.

LAND REGISTRIES

H.M. LAND REGISTRY
Lincoln's Inn Fields, WC2A 3PH
[01-405 3488]

The registration of title to land was first introduced in England and Wales by the Land Registry Act, 1862: H.M. Land Registry operates today under the Land Registration Acts, 1925 to 1986. The object of registering title to land is to create and maintain a register of land owners whose title is guaranteed by the State and so to simplify the transfer, mortgage and other dealings with real property. In certain areas of the country registration of title is compulsory on sale: voluntary registration in the non-compulsory areas has been common and it is still possible to register building estates, upon certain conditions, in any part of England or Wales. However, under the Land Registration Act, 1966, the voluntary first registration of land in non-compulsory areas was curtailed to accelerate the extension of the compulsory system to all built-up areas of the country. The intention is that registration of title shall ultimately be universal throughout England and Wales.

H.M. Land Registry is administered under the Lord Chancellor by the Chief Land Registrar and the work is decentralized to a number of regional offices. The Chief Land Registrar is also responsible for the Land Charges Department and the Agricultural Credits Department.
(For **Salaries**, *see* page 293)

Headquarters Office
Chief Land Registrar (G2), E. J. Pryer.
Chief Executive (G3), J. J. Manthorpe.
Senior Land Registrar (G5), Mrs. J. G. Totty.
Principal Establishment Officer (G5), E. G. Beardsall.
Controller (Registration) (G5), G. N. French.
Controller (Management Services) (G5), R. J. Fenn.
Land Registrar (G5), G. R. Tooke.

Birkenhead District Land Registry
Old Market House, Hamilton Street,
Birkenhead L41 5JW
[051–647 2377]
District Land Registrar (G5), M. G. Garwood.
Area Manager (G6), J. Eccles.

Coventry District Land Registry
Greyfriars Business Centre,
2 Eaton Road, Coventry CV1 2SD
[0203–632442]
District Land Registrar (G5), S. P. Kelway.
Area Manager (G6), J. C. Lillistone.

Croydon District Land Registry
Sunley House, Bedford Park, Croydon CR9 3LE
[01–686 8833]

District Land Registrar (G5), D. M. J. Moss.
Area Manager (G6), G. Hix.

Durham District Land Registry
Southfield House, Southfield Way,
Durham DH1 5TR
[091–3866151]

District Land Registrar (G5), P. H. Curnow.
Area Manager (G6), D. J. Long.

Gloucester District Land Registry
Twyver House, Bruton Way,
Gloucester GL1 1DQ
[0452–28666]

District Land Registrar (G5), W. W. Budden.
Area Manager (G6), M. H. Spooner.

Harrow District Land Registry
Lyon House, Lyon Road, Harrow,
Middx. HA1 2EU
[01–427 8811]

District Land Registrar (G5), M. L. Wood.
Area Manager (G6), D. I. Whyte.

Kingston upon Hull District Land Registry
Earle House, Portland Street, Hull HU2 8JN
[0482–223244]

District Land Registrar (G5), S. R. G. Coveney.
Area Manager (G7), E. Howard.

**Land Charges and Agricultural Credits
Department**
Burrington Way, Plymouth PL6 3LP
[0752–779831]

Superintendent of Land Charges (G7), H. Myers.

Leicester District Land Registry
Thames Tower, 99 Burleys Way,
Leicester LE1 3UB
[0533–510010]

Assistant Land Registrar, M. Jeffrey.
Area Manager (G7), B. Warriner.

Lytham District Land Registry
Birkenhead House, Lytham St. Annes,
Lancs. FY8 5AB
[0253–736999]

District Land Registrar (G5), J. G. Cooper.
Area Manager (G6), E. J. Stringer.

Nottingham District Land Registry
Chalfont Drive, Nottingham NG8 3RN
[0602–291166]

District Land Registrar (G5), P. J. Timothy.
Area Manager, (G6), W. Whitaker.

Peterborough District Land Registry
Touthill Close, City Road,
Peterborough PE1 1XN
[0733–555666]

District Land Registrar (G5), M. Avens.
Area Manager (G6), B. J. Andrews.

Plymouth District Land Registry
Plumer House, Tailyour Road,
Crownhill, Plymouth PL6 5HY
[0752–701234]

District Land Registrar (G5), A. J. Pain.
Area Manager(G6), K. Robinson.

Stevenage District Land Registry
Brickdale House, Danestrete, Stevenage,
Herts. SG1 1XG
[0438–313003]

District Land Registrar (G5), D. M. T. Mullett.
Area Manager (G6), A. Gould.

Swansea District Land Registry
Tybryn Glas High Street,
Swansea SA1 1PW
[0792–458877]

District Land Registrar (G5), G. A. Hughes.
Area Manager (G6), B. E. G. Martin.

Telford District Land Registry
Stafford Park 15, Telford,
Shropshire TF3 3BB
[0952–290355]

District Land Registrar (G5), M. A. Roche.
Area Manager (G6), R. D. Moseley.

Tunbridge Wells District Land Registry
Curtis House, Hawkenbury, Tunbridge Wells,
Kent TN2 5AQ
[0892–510015]

District Land Registrar (G5), C. J. West.
Area Manager (G6), B. E. Kitching.

Weymouth District Land Registry
1 Cumberland Drive, Weymouth,
Dorset DT4 9TT
[03057–776161]

District Land Registrar (G5), Mrs. P. M. Reeson.
Area Manager (G6), R. R. C. Green.

Computer Services Division
Burrington Way,
Plymouth PL5 3LP
[0752–779831]

Head of Division (G6), A. A. Restorick.

DEPARTMENT OF THE REGISTERS OF SCOTLAND
Meadowbank House, 153 London Road,
Edinburgh EH8 7AU
[031–659 6111]

The Registers of Scotland consist of:—
(1) General Register of Sasines and Land Register
of Scotland; (2) Register of Deeds in the Books of
Council and Session; (3) Register of Protests; (4)
Register of English and Irish Judgments; (5) Register
of Service of Heirs; (6) Register of the Great Seal; (7)
Register of the Quarter Seal; (8) Register of the
Prince's Seal; (9) Register of Crown Grants; (10)
Register of Sheriffs' Commissions; (11) Register of
the Cachet Seal; (12) Register of Inhibitions and
Adjudications; (13) Register of Entails; (14) Register
of Hornings.
The General Register of Sasines and the Land
Register of Scotland form the chief security in
Scotland of the rights of land and other heritable (or
real) property.
Keeper of the Registers of Scotland (G4), J. Robertson.
Deputy Keeper (G5), R. C. Brown.
Senior Assistant Keepers (G6), A. G. Rennie; A. A.
Snowdon; G. C. Warrender.
Assistant Keepers (G7), J. Anderson; R. C. Clark; J.
Cogle; B. J. Corr; A. M. Falconer; A. B. Farmer; R.
C. Fulton; J. Knox; H. Hosken; D. Lorimer; D.
McCallum; Mrs. A. McDonald; D. Manson; A. G.

T. New; D. L. Nicoll; A. W. Ramage; J. Rynn; I. M. Tainsh.

LAW COMMISSION
England and Wales
Conquest House, 37–38 John Street,
Theobalds Road, WC1N 2BQ
[01–242 0861]

Set up on June 16, 1965, under the Law Commissions Act, 1965, to make proposals to the Government for the examination of the law and for its revision where it is unsuited for modern requirements, obscure, or otherwise unsatisfactory. It recommends to the Lord Chancellor programmes for the examination of different branches of the law and suggests whether the examination should be carried out by the Commission itself or by some other body. The Commission is also responsible for the preparation of Consolidation and Statute Law (Repeals) Bills.

Chairman, The Hon. Mr. Justice Beldam.
Members, T. M. Aldridge; J. Beatson; R. Buxton, Q.C.; Prof. B. M. Hoggett, Q.C.
Secretary, M. H. Collon.

Scottish Law Commission
140 Causewayside, Edinburgh EH9 1PR
[031-668 2131]

Chairman, The Hon. Lord Davidson.
Commissioners, Dr. E. M. Clive; C. G. B. Nicholson, Q.C. *(full-time)*; Prof. P. N. Love, C.B.E.; W. Nimmo Smith, Q.C. *(part-time)*.
Secretary, K. S. Barclay.

LAW OFFICERS' DEPARTMENTS
Attorney-General's Chambers,
Royal Courts of Justice, WC2A 2LL
[01–936 6602]
Attorney General's Chambers,
Royal Courts of Justice, Belfast BT1 3JY
[0232–235111]

The Law Officers of the Crown for England and Wales are the Attorney General and the Solicitor General. The Attorney General is the Minister responsible for the work of the Law Officers' Departments: the Treasury Solicitor's Department, the Crown Prosecution Service, the Serious Fraud Office, and the Legal Secretariat to the Law Officers. The Director of Public Prosecutions (who is head of the Crown Prosecution Service), the Director of Public Prosecutions for Northern Ireland, and the Director of the Serious Fraud Office are responsible to the Attorney General for the performance of their duties.

The Attorney General is the Government's principal legal adviser, dealing with questions of law arising on Bills, issues of legal policy, and major international and domestic litigation involving the Government. The Solicitor General is responsible for such matters as the Attorney General delegates to him.

Attorney General, THE RT. HON. SIR PATRICK MAYHEW, Q.C., M.P. .... £36,679†
Parliamentary Private Secretary, D. A. Sumberg, M.P.
Solicitor General, SIR NICHOLAS LYELL, Q.C., M.P. £29,959†
Parliamentary Private Secretary, P. Ground, Q.C., M.P.
Legal Secretary (G3), Miss J. L. Wheldon.
Asst. Legal Secretary (G4), M. L. Carpenter.
† Excluding reduced Parliamentary salary of £18,148.

THE LAY OBSERVER'S OFFICE
Royal Courts of Justice, Strand, WC2A 2LL
[01–936 6695]

The Lay Observer's Office was established in 1975 and is funded by the Lord Chancellor's Department. The function of the Lay Observer is to monitor the Solicitor's Complaints Bureau's handling of complaints made to it about the conduct of solicitors or solicitors' employees. The Lay Observer is independent and is appointed by the Lord Chancellor.
Lay Observer (G5), L. Lightman.
Clerk, J. S. Twist.

Solicitors Complaints Bureau
Portland House, Stag Place, SW1E 5BL
[01–834 2288]

Director, J. P. S. Thompson.

LEGAL AID BOARD
5th Floor, Newspaper House,
8–16 Great New Street, EC4A 3BN
[01–353 7411]

The Legal Aid Board has the general function of ensuring that advice, assistance and representation are available, in accordance with the Legal Aid Act 1988. It took over from the Law Society on April 1, 1989 responsibility for administering legal aid. The Board is a non-departmental government body whose members are appointed by the Lord Chancellor.
Chairman, J. Pitts.
Members, M. Acland; Ms. D. Beale; A. Blake; Ms. H. Bradley; L. Devonald; K. Farrow; Ms. S. Harold; G. Hibbert; D. Sinker; J. Smith; P. Soar.
Chief Executive, S. Orchard.

SCOTTISH LEGAL AID BOARD
44 Drumsheugh Gardens,
Edinburgh EH3 7SW
[031–226 7061]

The Scottish Legal Aid Board was set up under the Legal Aid (Scotland) Act 1986. It is responsible for ensuring that advice, assistance and representation are available, in accordance with the Act. The Board is a non-departmental government body whose members are appointed by the Secretary of State for Scotland.
Chairman, D. B. Grant, C.B.E., T.D.
Members, G. Barrie; A. R. Brownlie, O.B.E.; Prof. T. F. Carbery, O.B.E.; B. G. Donald; A. Gilchrist; B. Gill, Q.C.; R. J. Livingstone; R. N. M. MacLean, Q.C.; P. C. Rendle; G. H. Speirs; Mrs. A. B. Ward; J. A. C. Weir.
Chief Executive, A. M. Douglas.

LIBRARIES

OFFICE OF ARTS AND LIBRARIES
(*see* entry on page 298)

THE BRITISH LIBRARY
2 Sheraton Street, W1V 4BH
[01–636 1544]

The British Library is the U.K.'s national library and occupies the central position in the library and information network. The Library aims to serve scholarship, research, industry, commerce and all other major users of information. Its services are based on collections which include over 18 million volumes (books, manuscripts, maps, newspapers and other serials, stamps and music), 1 million discs, 55,000 hours of tape recordings, in more than 20 buildings in London and one complex in West

Yorkshire, amounting to over 328 miles of shelving growing at the rate of 8 miles every year.

The British Library was established on July 1, 1973 under the British Library Act, 1972. It brought together the library departments of the British Museum, the National Central Library, the National Lending Library for Science and Technology, the British National Bibliography Ltd and, in 1974, the functions of the Office for Scientific and Technical Information. Subsequently the Library took responsibility for other organizations: the India Office Library and Records and the H.M.S.O. Binderies in 1982; and the National Sound Archive in 1983. Since 1985 they have all been regrouped into three service areas, a Research and Development Department plus a corporate administrative centre.

Access to the Humanities and Social Sciences reading rooms in Great Russell Street is limited to holders of a British Library Reader's Pass, and information about eligibility (basically, academic researchers and investigative professionals) is available from the Reader Admissions Office. The Aldwych and Holborn reading rooms of the Science Reference and Information Service are open to the general public without charge or formality.

The Library's exhibition galleries are housed in the British Museum building in Great Russell Street. On permanent display are famous items from the national written archive including the Magna Carta, the Lindisfarne Gospels and Shakespeare's First Folio.

The British Library will be moving to purpose-built accommodation at St. Pancras, London NW1 in 1991 (open to the public in 1993).

Board Members

Chairman, The Lord Quinton.
Chief Executive and Deputy Chairman, K. R. Cooper.
Directors General, J. M. Smethurst; D. Russon.
Part-time Members, The Lord Adrian, M.D., F.R.S.; The Lord Windlesham, C.V.O., P.C.; Prof. A. S. Forty, Ph.D., D.SC.; Prof. B. Morris; D. Owen; Sir Robin Mackworth-Young, K.C.V.O., F.S.A.; R. E. Utiger, C.B.E.; T. J. Rix; Dame Anne Warburton, D.C.V.O., C.M.G.; H. Heaney.

HUMANITIES AND SOCIAL SCIENCES

Director General, J. M. Smethurst.

Preservation Service

Great Russell Street WC1B 3DG
[01-323 7619]

Director, Dr. D. W. Clements.

Collection Development

Director, B. C. Bloomfield.

Oriental Collections
Store Street WC1E 7DG
[01-323 7642]

India Office Library and Records
197 Blackfriars Road SE1 8NG
[01-928 9531]

English Language, Western, Eastern European Printed Books
Great Russell Street WC1B 3DG
[01-323 7676]

Special Collections

Director, Mrs. S. J. Tyacke.

Western Manuscripts, Maps, Manuscript and Printed Music, Stamps
Great Russell Street WC1B 3DG
[01-323 7513]

Public Services, Planning and Administration

Director, A. Phillips.

Reading rooms for Great Russell Street collections, Official Publications
Great Russell Street WC1B 3DG
[01-323 7676]

Information Sciences Service
7 Ridgmount Street WC1E 7AE
[01-323 7688]

The National Sound Archive
29 Exhibition Road SW7 2AS
[01-589 6603]

Newspaper Library
Colindale Avenue, NW9 5HE
[01-323 7357]

SCIENCE, TECHNOLOGY AND INDUSTRY

Director General, D. Russon.

Document Supply Centre

Boston Spa, Wetherby, W. Yorks. LS23 7BQ
[0937-843434]

Director, D. Bradbury.

Science Reference and Information Service

25 Southampton Buildings, Chancery Lane
WC2A 1AW
[01-323 7494]
and 9 Kean Street WC2B 4AT
[01-323 7288]

Director, A. Gomersall.

Acquisitions Processing and Cataloguing

2 Sheraton Street W1V 4BH
[01-323 7077]

Director, Mrs. J. Butcher.

Computing and Telecommunications

2 Sheraton Street, W1V 4BH
[01-323 7077]

Director, J. Mahoney.

National Bibliographic Service

2 Sheraton Street, W1V 4BH
[01-323 7077]

Director, S. Ede.

RESEARCH AND DEVELOPMENT DEPARTMENT

2 Sheraton Street W1V 4BH
[01-323 7060]

Director, B. J. Perry.

CENTRAL ADMINISTRATION

2 Sheraton Street, WC1V 4BH
[01-323 7132]

Director, L. Bell.

NATIONAL LIBRARY OF SCOTLAND

George IV Bridge, Edinburgh EH1 1EW
[031-226 4531]

Open free. Reading Room, weekdays, 9.30–8.30; Sat. 9.30–1. Map Room, weekdays, 9.30–5; Sat. 9.30–1. Exhibition, weekdays, 9.30–5; Sat. 9.30–1; Sun. 2–5 (closed on Sun. Oct.–April).

The Library, which was founded as the Advocates' Library in 1682, became the National Library of Scotland by Act of Parliament in 1925. It continues to share the rights conferred by successive Copyright Acts since 1710. Its collections of printed books and MSS., augmented by purchase and gift, are very large and it has an unrivalled Scottish collection. The present building was opened by H.M. the Queen in 1956.

The Reading Room is for reference and research which cannot conveniently be pursued elsewhere. Admission is by ticket issued to an approved applicant.

Salaries

Librarian .... £34,095–£39,688
Keeper .... £21,633–£32,826
Curator Grade C .... £17,360–£26,958
Chairman of the Trustees, M. F. Strachan, C.B.E. F.R.S.E.
Librarian and Secretary to the Trustees, Prof. E. F. D. Roberts, C.B.E., Ph.D., F.R.S.E.
Secretary of the Library, I. D. McGowan.
Curators Grade C, M. C. Graham; J. E. McIntyre.
Keepers of Printed Books, A. M. Marchbank, Ph.D.; Ms. A. Matheson, Ph.D.
Curators Grade C, T. A. Cherry; R. Duce; Ms. A. E. Harvey Wood; B. P. Hillyard, D.Phil.; S. Holland; Ms. R. I. Hope; W. A. Kelly; J. M. Morris; Ms. J. M. Wilkes.
Keeper of Manuscripts, P. M. Cadell.
Curators Grade C, I. G. Brown, Ph.D., F.S.A.; I. C. Cunningham; I. F. Maciver; S. M. Simpson; Ms. E. D. Yeo.
Director of Computer Services and Research (Keeper), B. Gallivan.
Curator Grade C, R. F. Guy.
Director of Scottish Science Library (Keeper), Ms. A. J. Bunch.

THE NATIONAL LIBRARY OF WALES
Llyfrgell Genedlaethol Cymru
Aberystwyth, Dyfed SY23 3BU
[0970–623816]

Readers' room open on weekdays, 9.30 a.m. to 6 p.m. (Saturdays, 5 p.m.); closed on Sundays and Bank Holidays. Admission by Reader's Ticket.

Founded by Royal Charter, 1907, and maintained by annual grant from the Treasury. One of the six libraries entitled to privileges under Copyright Act. Contains about 15,000,000 printed books, 40,000 manuscripts, 4,000,000 deeds and documents, and numerous maps, prints and drawings, and audiovisual collection. Specializes in manuscripts and books relating to Wales and the Celtic peoples. Repository for pre-1858 Welsh probate records. Approved by the Master of the Rolls as a repository for manorial records and tithe documents, and by the Lord Chancellor for certain legal records. Bureau of the Regional Libraries Scheme for Wales.
Librarian, B. F. Roberts, Ph.D., F.S.A.
Secretary, D. B. Lloyd.
Heads of Departments, D. Huws (*Manuscripts and Records*); J. L. Madden (*Printed Books*); D. H. Owen (*Pictures and Maps*).

LIGHTHOUSE AUTHORITIES

CORPORATION OF TRINITY HOUSE
Trinity House, Tower Hill, EC3N 4DH
[01–480 6601]

Trinity House, the first General Lighthouse and Pilotage Authority in the Kingdom, was a body of importance when Henry VIII granted the institution its first charter in 1514. The Corporation is the General Lighthouse Authority for England, Wales and the Channel Islands, with certain statutory jurisdiction over aids to navigation maintained by local harbour authorities. It is also responsible for dealing with wrecks dangerous to navigation, except those occurring within port limits or wrecks of H.M. ships. The Trinity House Lighthouse Service is maintained out of the General Lighthouse Fund which is provided from light dues levied on ships at ports of the U.K. and Republic of Ireland. The Corporation's former responsibilities for pilotage were transferred to harbour authorities with effect from Oct. 1, 1988.

The affairs of the Corporation are controlled by a board of Elder Brethren, who are master mariners with long experience of command in the Royal and Merchant Navy together with figures from the world of commerce, and the Secretary. A separate Board, which comprises Elder Brethren, senior staff and outside representatives currently controls the Lighthouse Service. The Board is assisted by administrative and technical staff. The Elder Brethren also act as nautical assessors in marine cases in the Admiralty Division of the High Court of Justice.

Elder Brethren

Master, H.R.H. the Duke of Edinburgh, K.G.
Deputy Master, Capt. P. M. Edge.
Elder Brethren, Capt. I. R. C. Saunders; Capt. P. F. Mason, C.B.E.; H.R.H. the Prince of Wales, K.G.; Capt. Sir George Barnard; Capt. R. N. Mayo, C.B.E.; Capt. Sir David Tibbits, D.S.C., R.N.; Capt. D. A. G. Dickens; Capt. J. E. Bury; Capt. J. A. N. Bezant, D.S.C., R.D., R.N.R. (*ret.*); Capt. Sir Miles Wingate, K.C.V.O.; Capt. D. J. Cloke; The Lord Wilson of Rievaulx, K.G., O.B.E., F.R.S.; Rt. Hon. Edward Heath, M.B.E., M.P.; The Viscount Runciman of Doxford, O.B.E., A.F.C.; Capt. T. Woodfield, O.B.E.; Sir Arthur Drake, C.B.E.; The Lord Simon of Glaisdale, P.C.; Admiral of the Fleet the Lord Lewin, K.G., G.C.B., M.V.O., D.S.C.; Capt. D. T. Smith, R.N.; Commander Sir Robin Gillett, G.B.E., R.D., R.N.R.; The Lord Shackleton, K.G., O.B.E., P.C.; Sir John Cuckney; Capt. D. J. Orr; The Lord Carrington, K.G., C.H., K.C.M.G., M.C., P.C.

Officers

Secretary, J. B. Fuller.
Deputy Secretary, M. J. Faulkner.
Director of Engineering, D. A. S. Vennings.
Director of Finance, K. W. Clark.
Personnel Manager, Mrs. B. C. Heesom.
Navigation Manager, N. J. Cutmore.
Legal and Information Manager, D. I. Brewer.
Chief Superintendent, Capt. J. H. Barnes.
Depot Manager, Harwich, S. J. W. Dunning.
Engineering Manager, F. E. J. Holden.
Surveyor of Shipping, J. K. Rankin.
Manager, Corporate Department, R. Dobb.
Information Officer, Mrs. L. A. Dennison.

CLYDE PORT AUTHORITY
16 Robertson Street, Glasgow G2 8DS
[041-221 8733]

The Authority is a self-governing statutory body established by individual Act of Parliament and provides sea port facilities within a 450 sq. mile area of jurisdiction which encompasses the River Clyde, its estuary and sea lochs.
Chairman, R. W. S. Easton, C.B.E.
Managing Director, J. Mather.
Director and Secretary, G. P. Johnston.
Director and Marine Operations, Capt. D. B. McMurray.

COMMISSIONERS OF NORTHERN LIGHTHOUSES
84 George Street, Edinburgh EH2 3DA.
[031-226 7051]

The Commissioners of Northern Lighthouses are the General Lighthouse Authority for Scotland and the Isle of Man. The present Board owes its origin to an Act of Parliament passed in 1786. At present the Commissioners operate under the Merchant Shipping Act, 1894 and are 19 in number.

The Commissioners control 29 major manned lighthouses, 55 major automatic lighthouses, 112 minor lights and many lighted and unlighted buoys. They have a fleet of 2 motor vessels.

Commissioners
The Lord Advocate, the Solicitor General for Scotland, the Lord Provosts of Edinburgh, Glasgow and Aberdeen; the Provost of Inverness; the Chairman of Argyll & Bute District Council; the Sheriffs-Principal of North Strathclyde, Tayside, Central & Fife, Grampian, Highlands & Islands, South Strathclyde, Dumfries & Galloway, Lothians & Borders, and Glasgow & Strathkelvin; W. D. H. Gregson, C.B.E.; T. Macgill; Capt. J. A. MacLeod; Capt. A. F. Dickson, O.B.E.; Capt. W. B. Kinley; A. J. Struthers.

Officers
General Manager, Cdr. J. M. Mackay, M.B.E.
Secretary, I. A. Dickson.
Engineer-in-Chief, W. Paterson.

LOCAL COMMISSIONERS

COMMISSION FOR LOCAL ADMINISTRATION IN ENGLAND
21 Queen Anne's Gate, SW1H 9BU
[01-222 5622]

Local Commissioners (Local Ombudsmen) are responsible for investigating complaints from members of the public against local authorities (but not town and parish councils); water authorities; police authorities; the Commission for New Towns and new town development corporations (housing functions); and urban development corporations (town and country planning functions). The Commissioners are appointed by the Crown on the recommendation of the Secretary of State for the Environment.

Certain types of action are excluded from investigation, particularly personnel matters and commercial transactions unless they relate to the purchase or sale of land. Complaints can be sent direct to the Local Ombudsman or through a councillor, although the Local Ombudsman will not consider a complaint unless the Council has had an opportunity to investigate and reply to a complainant.

A free booklet *Complaint about the Council? How to Complain to your Local Ombudsman* is available from the Commission's office.
Chairman of the Commission and Local Commissioner, D. C. M. Yardley, D.Phil. £72,000
Vice Chairman and Local Commissioner, F. G. Laws
£51,400
Local Commissioner, Mrs. P. A. Thomas £50,400
Member, The Parliamentary Commissioner for Administration
Secretary, G. D. Adams £33,075

COMMISSION FOR LOCAL ADMINISTRATION IN WALES
Derwen House, Court Road, Bridgend CF31 1BN
[0656-61325/6]

The Local Commissioner for Wales has similar powers to the Local Commissioners in England. The Commissioner is appointed by the Crown on the recommendation of the Secretary of State for Wales. A free booklet *Your Local Ombudsman in Wales* is available from the Commission's office.
Local Commissioner, H. F. Jones.
Secretary, D. Bowen.

COMMISSIONER FOR LOCAL ADMINISTRATION IN SCOTLAND
5 Shandwick Place, Edinburgh EH2 4RG
[031-229 4472]

The Local Commissioner for Scotland has similar powers to the Local Commissioners in England, and is appointed by the Crown on the recommendation of the Secretary of State for Scotland.
Local Commissioner, R. G. E. Peggie, C.B.E.
Secretary, K. Bratton

LONDON REGIONAL TRANSPORT
55 Broadway, SW1H 0BD
[01-222 5600]

Subject to the financial objectives and principles approved by the Secretary of State for Transport, London Regional Transport has a general duty to provide or secure the provision of public transport services for Greater London.
Chairman, C. W. Newton £80,000
Members, J. Telford Beasley; M. Marsh £60,000

LORD ADVOCATE'S DEPARTMENT
Fielden House, 10 Great College Street,
SW1P 3SL
[01-276 3000]

The Law Officers for Scotland are the Lord Advocate and the Solicitor-General for Scotland. The Lord Advocate's Department is responsible for drafting Scottish legislation, for providing legal advice to other departments on Scottish questions and for assistance to the Law Officers for Scotland in certain of their legal duties.
Lord Advocate, THE LORD FRASER OF CARMYLLIE, P.C., Q.C. £42,067
Solicitor-General for Scotland, ALAN F. RODGER, Q.C.
£36,515
Legal Secretary and First Parliamentary Draftsman, N. J. Adamson, C.B., Q.C. £50,600
Senior Asst. Legal Secs. and Parliamentary Draftsmen, G. M. Clark; D. J. S. Duncan; G. Kowalski; P. J. Layden, T.D.; J. C. McCluskie .. £37,600–£40,900
Asst. Legal Secs. and Deputy Parliamentary Draftsmen, J. D. Harkness; D. C. Macrae; C. A. M. Wilson
£30,425–£34,095

LORD CHANCELLOR'S DEPARTMENT
House of Lords, SW1A 0PW
[01-219 3000]

The Lord Chancellor is responsible for promoting general reforms in the civil law, for the procedure of the civil courts and for the administration of the Supreme Court (Court of Appeal, High Court and Crown Court) and county courts in England and Wales, and for legal aid schemes. He is responsible for advising the Crown on the appointment of judges and certain other officers and is himself responsible for the appointment of Masters and Registrars of the

High Court and District and County Court Registrars and magistrates. He is responsible for ensuring that letters patent and other formal documents are passed in the proper form under the Great Seal of the Realm, of which he is the custodian. The work in connection with this is carried out under his direction in the Office of the Clerk of the Crown in Chancery.
(For **Salaries**, *see* page 293)

Lord Chancellor, THE LORD MACKAY OF CLASHFERN,
  P.C. £91,500
  Private Secretary, J. P. Stockton.
Permanent Secretary (*G1*), T. S. Legg, C.B.
  Private Secretary, Mrs. E. Hutcheson.

Crown Office

Clerk of the Crown in Chancery (*G1*), T. S. Legg, C.B.
Deputy Clerk of the Crown in Chancery (*G2*), R. Potter.
Clerk of the Chamber, Miss J. L. Waine.

COURT SERVICE POLICY AND LEGAL SERVICES
Trevelyan House, 30 Great Peter Street,
SW1P 2BY
[01–210 8872]

Deputy Secretary (*G2*), R. Potter.

Court Service Management Group

Head of Group (*G4*), J. F. Brindley.
Heads of Divisions (*G5*), D. E. Staff; R. A. Vincent; R. J. Clark.

Policy and Legal Services Group

Head of Group (*G3*), J. G. H. Gasson.
Heads of Divisions (*G5*), W. Arnold; M. Kron; R. H. H. White; C. W. V. Everett.

JUDICIAL APPOINTMENTS AND LEGISLATION
House of Lords, SW1A 0PW
[01–219 4311]

Deputy Secretary (*G2*), M. D. Huebner.

Judicial Appointments Group
House of Lords, SW1A 0PW
[01–219 3000]

Head of Group (*G3*), J. L. Heritage.
Heads of Divisions (*G5*), R. C. Stoate; M. Sayers.

26–28 Old Queen Street, SW1H 2HP
[01–210 3537]
Grade 5, R. V. Gobler; G. Norman.

Legislation Group
26–28 Old Queen Street, SW1H 2HP
[01–210 3508]

Head of Group (*G3*), L. Oates.
Heads of Divisions (*G5*), P. Graham Harris; M. H. Collon; M. C. L. Carpenter.

Establishment and Finance Group
Trevelyan House, 30 Great Peter Street, SW1P 2BY
[01–210 8512]

Principal Establishment and Finance Officer (*G3*), B. Cousins, C.B.E.
Heads of Divisions (*G5*), Miss J. E. Court; D. S. Mortimer; D. Nooney; Mrs. N. A. Oppenheimer.
Principal Information Officer (*G7*), Miss J. Morley.

Public Trust Office
Stewart House, 24 Kingsway, WC2B 6JX
[01–405 4300]

Public Trustee and Accountant General (*G3*), J. Boland.

Asst. Public Trustee and Deputy Accountant General (*G5*), P. J. Farmer.
Asst. Public Trustee (*G5*), R. C. Annis.

22 Kingsway, WC2B 6LE
[01–936 6000]

Head of Courts Funds Office (*G7*), I. J. MacBean.

Ecclesiastical Patronage
10 Downing Street, S.W.1
[01–233 3000]

Secretary for Ecclesiastical Patronage, J. R. Catford.
Assistant Secretary for Ecclesiastical Patronage (*G7*), N. Wheeler.

See also **Law Courts and Offices**

LORD GREAT CHAMBERLAIN'S OFFICE
House of Lords, SW1A 0PW
[01–219 3100]

The Lord Great Chamberlain is a Great Officer of State, the office being hereditary since the grant of Henry I to the family of De Vere, Earls of Oxford.
Lord Great Chamberlain, The Marquess of Cholmondeley, G.C.V.O., M.C.
Secretary to the Lord Great Chamberlain, Air Chief Marshal Sir John Gingell, G.B.E., K.C.B.
Clerk to the Lord Great Chamberlain, Miss J. M. Drewett.

LORD PRIVY SEAL'S OFFICE
Privy Council Office,
Whitehall, SW1A 2AT

As leader of the House of Lords, the Lord Privy Seal is responsible to the Prime Minister for the arrangement of government business in the House. He also has a responsibility to the House itself to advise it on procedural matters and other difficulties which arise.
Lord Privy Seal, and Leader of the House of Lords, THE LORD BELSTEAD, P.C.
Private Secretary, N. F. J. Gibbons.
Assistant Private Secretary, R. Appleton.

OFFICE OF MANPOWER ECONOMICS
22 Kingsway, WC2B 6JY
[01–405 5944]

The Office of Manpower Economics was set up in 1971. It is an independent non-statutory organization which is responsible for servicing independent review bodies which advise on the pay of various public service groups (*see* entries under "Review Bodies"), the Pharmacists Review Panel, the Police Negotiating Board and the Civil Service Arbitration Tribunal. The Office is also responsible for servicing *ad hoc* bodies of inquiry and for undertaking research into pay and associated matters as requested by Government.
Director, N. Covington.
Assistant Secretaries (*G5*), D. W. R. Lewis; K. R. Perry; P. J. H. Edwards.

MEDICAL RESEARCH COUNCIL
20 Park Crescent, W1N 4AL
[01–636 5422]

The Medical Research Council is the main Government agency for the promotion of medical and related biological research. The Council employs its own research staff and also provides grants for other institutions and for individuals who are not members of its own staff, thus complementing the research resources of the universities and hospitals.
Chairman, The Earl Jellicoe, K.B.E., D.S.O., M.C., P.C.

Deputy Chairman and Secretary, D. A. Rees, PH.D., D.SC., F.R.S.

Members, Sir Donald Acheson, K.B.E., D.M., F.R.C.P.; Belinda Banham, C.B.E.; Sir Austin Bide; S. Brenner, D.PHIL., F.R.C.P., F.R.S.; J. T. Carter; D. L. Crouch, M.P.; M. J. Crumpton, PH.D., F.R.S.; Prof. C. J. Dickinson, D.M., F.R.C.P.; I. S. Macdonald, M.D.; Prof. P. J. Morris, PH.D., F.R.C.S.; Prof. J. M. Newsom-Davis, M.D., F.R.C.P.; Prof. F. W. O'Grady, C.B.E.; Prof. J. K. Wing, M.D., PH.D.

Administrative Secretary, Ms. N. Morris.

Neurobiology and Mental Health Board

Chairman, A. D. Baddeley, PH.D.

Cell Biology and Disorders Board

Chairman, Prof. G. Radda.

Physiological Systems and Disorders Board

Chairman, Prof. D. K. Peters, F.R.C.P.

Tropical Medicine Research Board

Chairman, Dr. J. W. B. Smith.

Health Services Research Committee

Chairman, Prof. J. K. Wing, M.D., PH.D.

HEADQUARTERS OFFICE

Second Secretary, D. Evered, D.SC., M.D., F.R.C.P.

Medical Division

Heads of Division, D. James, PH.D.; J. Alwen, PH.D.

Administrative Division

Administrative Secretary, Ms. N. Morris.
Assistant Secretaries, B. C. Dodd; J. E. A. Hay; D. Smith, PH.D.

Secretariat

Assistant Secretary, N. H. Winterton.

National Institute for Medical Research
Mill Hill, N.W.7
[01–959 3666]

Director, J. Stehel, PH.D., F.R.S.

Clinical Research Centre
Watford Road, Harrow, Middlesex
[01–864 5311]

Director, Dr. K. E. Kirkham.

Research Units

Anatomical Neuropharmacology Unit, Dept. of Pharmacology, University of Oxford, South Park Road, Oxford OX1 3QT. *Director*, Prof. A. D. Smith, D.PHIL.

Applied Psychology Unit, 15 Chaucer Road, Cambridge CB2 2EF. *Director*, A. D. Baddeley, PH.D.

Biostatistics Unit, 5 Shaftesbury Road, Cambridge CB2 2BW. *Director*, N. E. Day, PH.D.

Blood Group Unit, University College, London, Wolfson House, 4 Stephenson Way, NW1 2EH. *Director*, Patricia Tippett, PH.D.

Blood Pressure Unit, Western Infirmary, Glasgow G11 6NT. *Director*, A. F. Lever, F.R.C.P., F.R.S.E.

Brain Metabolism Unit, University Dept. of Pharmacology, 1 George Square, Edinburgh EH8 9JZ. *Director*, G. Fink, M.D., D.PHIL.

Cell Biophysics Unit, Dept. of Biophysics, King's College, 26–29 Drury Lane, WC2. *Director*, Prof. B. B. Boycott, F.R.S.

Cell Mutation Unit, University of Sussex, Falmer, Brighton BN1 9RR. *Director*, Prof. B. A. Bridges, PH.D.

Cellular Immunology Unit, Sir William Dunn School of Pathology, Oxford OX1 3RE. *Director*, Dr. A. F. Williams, PH.D.

Child Psychiatry Unit, Institute of Psychiatry, De Crespigny Park, Denmark Hill, SE5 8AF. *Director*, Prof. M. Rutter, C.B.E., M.D., F.R.C.P.

Clinical Oncology and Radiotherapeutics Unit, M.R.C. Centre, Hills Road, Cambridge CB2 2QH. *Hon. Director*, Prof. N. M. Bleehen, F.R.C.P., F.R.C.R.

Clinical Pharmacology Unit, University Department of Clinical Pharmacology, Radcliffe Infirmary, Woodstock Road, Oxford OX2 6HE. *Hon. Director*, Prof. D. G. Grahame-Smith, PH.D., F.R.C.P.

Cognitive Development Unit, 17 Gordon Street, WC1. *Director*, Prof. J. Morton, PH.D.

Cyclotron Unit, Hammersmith Hospital, Ducane Road, W12. *Director*, K. I. Gibson, PH.D.

Dental Research Unit, London Hospital Medical College, 30/32 Newark Street, E1 2AA. *Director*, Prof. N. W. Johnson, PH.D.

Unit on the Development and Integration of Behaviour, Subdept. of Animal Behaviour, Madingley, Cambridge CB3 8AA. *Hon. Director*, Prof. R. A. Hinde, D.PHIL., SC.D., F.R.S

Dunn Nutrition Unit, Downhams Lane, Milton Road, Cambridge. *Director*, R. G. Whitehead, PH.D.

Environmental Epidemiology Unit, Southampton General Hospital, Southampton SO9 4XY. *Director*, Prof. D. J. P. Barker, M.D., PH.D., F.R.C.P.

Epidemiology and Medical Care Unit, Northwick Park Hospital, Watford Road, Harrow, Middx. *Director*, T. W. Meade, D.M., F.R.C.P.

Epidemiology Unit (South Wales), 4 Richmond Road, Cardiff. *Director*, P. C. Elwood, M.D., F.R.C.P.

Unit for Epidemiological Studies in Psychiatry, University Dept. of Psychiatry, Royal Edinburgh Hospital, Morningside Park, Edinburgh EH10 5HF. *Director*, N. B. Kreitman, M.D.

Experimental Embryology and Teratology Unit, St. George's Hospital Medical School, Cranmer Terrace, SW17 0RE. *Director*, D. G. Whittingham, D.SC.

Human Biochemical Genetics Unit, Galton Laboratory, University College London, Wolfson House, 4 Stephenson Way, NW1. *Hon. Director*, D. A. Hopkinson, M.D.

Human Genetics Unit, Western General Hospital, Crewe Road, Edinburgh EH4 2XU. *Director*, Prof. H. J. Evans, PH.D., F.R.S.E.

M.R.C. Human Movement and Balance Unit, Institute of Neurology, National Hospital, Queens Square, WC1. *Director*, J. D. Hood, PH.D., D.SC.

Immunochemistry Unit, University Department of Biochemistry, South Parks Road, Oxford OX1 3QU. *Director*, K. B. M. Reid, PH.D.

Institute of Hearing Research, University of Nottingham, Nottingham NG7 2RD. *Director*, M. P. Haggard, PH.D.

M.R.C. Laboratories, Carshalton, Woodmansterne Road, Carshalton, Surrey, SM5 4EF. *Laboratory Manager*, T. B. Pendry.

M.R.C. Laboratories, The Gambia, Fajara, near Banjul, The Gambia, W. Africa. *Director*, B. M. Greenwood, M.D., F.R.C.P.

M.R.C. Laboratories, Jamaica, University of the West Indies, Mona, Kingston, Jamaica. *Director*, Prof. G. R. Serjeant, C.M.G., M.D., F.R.C.P.

Leukaemia Unit, Royal Postgraduate Medical School, Ducane Road, W12 0HS. *Hon. Director*, Prof. L. Luzzatto, M.D., F.R.C.P.

Mammalian Development Unit, University College London, Wolfson House, 4 Stephenson Way, NW1. *Director*, Anne McLaren, D.PHIL., F.R.S.

Medical Sociology Unit, 6, Lilybank Gardens, Glasgow, G12 8QQ. *Director*, Sally Macintyre, PH.D.

Laboratory of Molecular Biology, Hills Road, Cambridge CB2 2QH. *Director*, Sir Aaron Klug, PH.D., F.R.S.

Molecular Genetics Unit, M.R.C. Centre, Hills Road, Cambridge CB2 2QH. *Director*, S. Brenner, D.PHIL., D.SC., F.R.C.P., F.R.S.

Molecular Haematology Unit, John Radcliffe Hospital,

Headington, Oxford OX3 9DU. *Director*, Prof. D. J. Weatherall, M.D., F.R.C.P., F.R.S.

M.R.C. Molecular Immunopathology Unit, University Medical School, Hills Road, Cambridge CB2 2QH. *Director*, Prof. P. J. Lachmann, SC.D., F.R.C.P., F.R.S.

Molecular Neurobiology Unit, University Medical School, Hills Road, Cambridge CB2 2QH. *Director*, Prof. E. A. Barnard.

Neurochemical Pathology Unit, Newcastle General Hospital, Westgate Road, Newcastle upon Tyne NE4 6BE. *Director*, Prof. J. A. Edwardson, Ph.D.

Neurological Prostheses Unit, Institute of Psychiatry, De Crespigny Park, Denmark Hill, SE5. *Hon. Director*, Prof. G. S. Brindley, M.D., F.R.C.P., F.R.S.

Neuro-Otology Unit, The Institute of Neurology, National Hospital, Queen Square, WC1N 3BG. *Director*, J. D. Hood.

A.F.R.C./M.R.C. Neuropathogenesis Unit, Ogston Building, West Mains Road, Edinburgh. *Director*, (vacant).

Radiobiology Unit, Chilton, Didcot, Oxon. OX11 0RD *Director*, Prof. G. E. Adams, Ph.D., D.SC.

Reproductive Biology Unit, Centre for Reproductive Biology, 37 Chalmers St., Edinburgh EH3 9EW. *Director*, D. W. Lincoln, D.SC.

Social and Applied Psychology Unit, Dept. of Psychology, University of Sheffield S10 2TN. *Director*, P. B. Warr, Ph.D.

Social Psychiatry Unit, Institute of Psychiatry, De Crespigny Park, Denmark Hill, SE5. *Director*, Prof. J. K. Wing, M.D., Ph.D.

Toxicology Unit, M.R.C. Laboratories, Woodmansterne Road, Carshalton, Surrey SM5 4EF. *Director*, T. A. Connors, D.SC., Ph.D.

Tuberculosis and Related Infections Unit, Hammersmith Hospital, Du Cane Road, W12 0HS. *Director*, Dr. J. Ivanyi, M.D., Ph.D.

Virology Unit, Institute of Virology, Church Street, Glasgow G11 5JR. *Hon. Director*, Prof. J. H. Subak-Sharpe, Ph.D., F.R.S.E.

MONOPOLIES AND MERGERS COMMISSION
New Court, 48 Carey Street, WC2A 2JT
[01–324 1467]

The Commission was established in 1948 as the Monopolies and Restrictive Practices Commission and was reconstituted on subsequent occasions. It became the Monopolies and Mergers Commission in 1973. The Commission has the duty of investigating and reporting on questions referred to it with respect to (a) the existence or possible existence of monopolies not registrable under the Restrictive Trade Practices Act, 1976, and relating to the supply of goods or services in the U.K. or part of the U.K. or to the supply of goods for export; (b) the transfer of a newspaper or newspaper's assets; (c) the creation or possible creation of a merger qualifying for investigation within the meaning of the Fair Trading Act, 1973.

References may be made to the Commission on the general effect on the public interest of specified monopoly or other uncompetitive practices and of restrictive labour practices.

The Competition Act, 1980, provides for the reference to the Commission of particular anti-competitive practices and of questions of efficiency, costs, service provided and possible abuse of monopolies in the public sector. In respect of recently-privatized industries, references to the Commission may be made in certain circumstances, with regard to their respective industries, by the Director General of Telecommunications, the Civil Aviation Authority, the Director General of Gas Supply, the Director General

of Water Services and the Director General of Electricity Supply.

Chairman, M. S. Lipworth £72,000
Deputy Chairmen, H. H. Hunt, C.B.E. (£25,210); H. H. Liesner, C.B. (£25,210); D. G. Richards, C.B.E. (£28,995).
Members, Sir James Ackers; A. G. Armstrong; C. C. Baillieu; Prof. M. E. Beesley, C.B.E.; F. E. Bonner, C.B.E.; L. Britz; K. S. Carmichael, C.B.E.; R. Davies; P. H. Dean; J. Evans; A. Ferry, M.B.E.; P. S. G. Flint; D. G. Goyder; M. R. Hoffman; J. D. Keir, Q.C.; Miss P. K. R. Mann; G. C. S. Mather; L. A. Mills; J. D. Montgomery; B. C. Owens; D. P. Thomson; C. A. Unwin, M.B.E.; S. Wainwright, C.B.E.; Prof. G. Whittington; R. Young.
each £10,149
Secretary, S. N. Burbridge.

MUSEUMS

MUSEUMS AND GALLERIES COMMISSION
7 St. James's Square, SW1Y 4JU
[01–839 9341]

Established in February 1931 as the Standing Commission on Museums and Galleries, the Commission was re-named and took up new functions in September 1981. Its sponsor department is the Office of Arts and Libraries. The Commission advises the Government, including the Department of Education for Northern Ireland, the Scottish Education Department and Welsh Office, on museum affairs. There are 15 Commissioners, appointed by the Prime Minister.

The Commission's executive functions include the services of the National Museums Security Adviser; allocation of grants to the seven Area Museum Councils in England; funding and monitoring of the work of the Museum Documentation Association; directly administering a capital grant scheme for non-national museums, and various other grant schemes. The Commission administers the arrangements for government indemnities and the acceptance of works of art in lieu of Inheritance Tax, and it has responsibility for the two Purchase Grant Funds for local museums managed on its behalf by the Victoria and Albert and Science Museums. The Commission's Conservation Unit advises on conservation and operates grants schemes for conservators. The Travelling Exhibitions Unit promotes and encourages travelling exhibitions. A registration scheme for museums in the U.K. is being implemented with the assistance of the Commission.

Chairman, Prof. B. Morris, D.Phil.
Members, The Marchioness of Anglesey, D.B.E.; F. Atkinson, O.B.E.; R. Begg, C.B.E.; L. Brandes, C.B.; The Lord Dainton, F.R.S.; F. Dunning, O.B.E.; Prof. Sir John Hale, F.B.A.; T. W. I. Hodgkinson, C.B.E.; J. Last, C.B.E.; Sir Hugh Leggatt; The Lord O'Neill, T.D.; The Lord Rees, P.C., Q.C.; R. H. Smith; Dame Margaret Weston, D.B.E.; Adm. Sir David Williams, G.C.B.
Secretary, P. Longman.

THE BRITISH MUSEUM
Great Russell Street, WC1B 3DG
[01–636 1555]

Antiquities collections, coins and medals, prints and drawings. Open weekdays (including Bank Holidays) 10–5 and Sun. 2.30–6. Closed on Good Friday, Christmas Eve, Christmas Day, Boxing Day, New Year's Day and the first Monday in May. The ethnographical collections are displayed in The Museum of Mankind at 6 Burlington Gardens, W1. Opening times as above.

The British Museum may be said to date from 1753, when Parliament granted funds to purchase the collections of Sir Hans Sloane and the Harleian manuscripts, and for their proper housing and maintenance. The building (Montagu House) was opened in 1759. The present buildings were erected between 1823 and the present day, and the original collection has increased to its present dimensions by gifts and purchases. The administrative expenses, including work and building in progress, were estimated at £24,643,000 in 1989–90.

Board of Trustees

Appointed by the Sovereign: H.R.H. The Duke of Gloucester, G.C.V.O. *Appointed by the Prime Minister:* The Lord Windlesham, C.V.O., P.C. (*Chairman*); Sir Matthew Farrer, K.C.V.O.; G. C. Greene, C.B.E.; Prof. E. T. Hall, D.Phil., F.S.A., F.B.A.; C. E. A. Hambro; Sir Peter Harrop, K.C.B.; S. Keswick; Hon. Mrs. Marten, O.B.E.; Mrs. M. Moore; Prof. G. H. Treitel, D.C.L., F.B.A., Q.C.; S. Towneley, PH.D.; Sir Ian Trethowan; The Lord Weinstock; Prof. W. Whitfield, C.B.E.; Sir Oliver Wright, G.C.M.G., G.C.V.O., D.S.C.

Nominated by the learned Societies: The Lord Adrian, M.D., F.R.S. (*Royal Society*); Dame Elisabeth Frink, D.B.E., R.A. (*Royal Academy*); Sir Claus Moser, K.C.B., C.B.E. (*British Academy*); Prof. W. Watson, C.B.E., F.S.A., F.B.A. (*Society of Antiquaries*)

Appointed by the Trustees of the British Museum: Sir David Attenborough, C.B.E., F.R.S.; Prof. Rosemary Cramp, C.B.E., F.S.A.; Prof. Sir John Hale, F.S.A., F.B.A.; Prof. P. Lasko, C.B.E., F.S.A., F.B.A.

Salaries

Grade 2	£50,400
Grade 4	£34,095–£35,415
Grade 5	£28,170–£31,602
Grade 6	£21,633–£28,170
Grade 7	£17,360–£22,606
Head of Press and P.R.	£13,999–£17,032
Press and P.R. Officer	£10,994–£13,999

Officers

Director (G2), Sir David Wilson.
Deputy Director (G4), Ms. J. M. Rankine.
Secretary (G6), G. B. Morris.
Assistant to the Director (G7), Ms. M. L. Caygill.
Head of Public Services (G6), G. A. L. House.
Head of Design (G6), Margaret Hall, O.B.E.
Head of Education (G7), J. F. Reeve.
Head of Press and Public Relations, A. E. Hamilton.
Press and Public Relations Officer, Miss A. F. Dunkels.
Head of Administration (G6), C. E. I. Jones.
Head of Building and Security Services (G6), P. E. Youngs.
Head of Architectural and Building Services (G7), C. J. Walker.
Head of Finance (G7), G. E. Cooper.
Head of Personnel and Office Services (G7), Miss B. A. Hughes.
Head of Management Services (G7), D. E. Williams.
Keeper of Prints and Drawings (G5), J. K. Rowlands.
Deputy Keeper (G6), A. V. Griffiths.
Assistant Keepers (G7), Ms. F. A. Carey; N. J. L. Turner; Ms. L. Stainton; M. B. Royalton-Kisch.
Keeper of Coins and Medals (G5), J. P. C. Kent.
Deputy Keeper (G6), M. J. Price.
Assistant Keepers (G7), M. G. Powell-Jones; Ms. M. M. Archibald; A. M. Burnett; B. J. Cook.
Keeper of Egyptian Antiquities (G5), W. V. Davies.
Assistant Keepers (G7), M. L. Bierbrier; A. J. Spencer.
Keeper of Western Asiatic Antiquities (G5), J. E. Curtis.
Assistant Keepers (G7), C. B. F. Walker; I. L. Finkel.

Keeper of Greek and Roman Antiquities (G5), B. F. Cook.
Deputy Keeper (G6), vacant.
Assistant Keepers (G7), Ms. S. E. C. Walker; Ms. V. Tatton-Brown; D. J. R. Williams.
Keeper of Medieval and Later Antiquities (G5), N. M. Stratford.
Deputy Keepers (G6), G. H. Tait; J. Cherry; Ms. L. E. Webster.
Assistant Keepers (G7), D. Kidd; D. Buckton; T. H. Wilson.
Keeper of Prehistoric and Romano-British Antiquities (G5), I. H. Longworth.
Deputy Keepers (G6), I. M. Stead; T. W. Potter.
Assistant Keepers (G7), I. A. Kinnes; Ms. J. M. Cook.
Keeper of Japanese Antiquities (G5), L. R. H. Smith.
Keeper of Oriental Antiquities (G5), Ms. J. M. Rawson.
Deputy Keeper (G6), J. M. Rogers.
Assistant Keepers (G7), W. Zwalf; Ms. A. S. L. Farrer; J. R. Knox.
Keeper of Ethnography (G5), M. D. McLeod.
Deputy Keeper (G6), B. Durrans.
Assistant Keepers (G7), Ms. E. M. Carmichael; Ms. S. G. Weir; Ms. D. Starzecka; J. C. H. King; J. B. Mack; N. F. Barley.
Keeper of Scientific Research (G5), M. Tite.
Principal Scientific Officers (G7), P. T. Craddock; M. J. Hughes; I. C. Freestone; Ms. S. G. E. Bowman; E. J. Neville.
Keeper of Conservation (G5), W. A. Oddy.
Principal Scientific Officer (G7), V. D. Daniels.
Principal Conservator (G7), Ms. H. P. Lane.

THE BRITISH MUSEUM (NATURAL HISTORY)
Cromwell Road, SW7 5BD
[01–938 9123]

Open Mon.–Sat. (except New Year's Day, Good Friday, May Day, Christmas Eve, Christmas Day and Boxing Day) 10–6, Sun. 1–6. Admission, £2·50.

The Natural History Museum originates from the natural history departments of the British Museum. During the 19th century the natural history collections grew extensively and in 1881 they were moved to South Kensington. In 1963, the Natural History Museum became completely independent with its own body of Trustees. The Zoological Museum, Tring, bequeathed by the second Lord Rothschild, has formed part of the Museum since 1938. The Geological Museum merged with the Natural History Museum in 1985 (opening times are as given above). Research workers are admitted to the libraries and study collections by Student's Ticket, applications for which should be made in writing to the Director.

The administrative expenses were estimated at £21,732,000 in 1988–89.

(For **Salaries,** *see* page 293).

Board of Trustees

Chairman, Sir Walter Bodmer, F.R.S.
Appointed by the Prime Minister: Sir Owen Green; Prof. J. M. Thomas, F.R.S.; G. M. Ronson; E. N. K. Clarkson, F.R.S.E; Mrs. J. M. D'Abo; D. H. Henderson; Prof. R. May, F.R.S.
Nominated by the Royal Society: Prof. Sir Andrew Huxley, O.M., F.R.S.
Appointed by the Trustees of the British Museum (Natural History): Prof. H. B. Whittington, F.R.S.; R. J. Carter; Prof. B. K. Follett, F.R.S.
Director (G3), N. R. Chalmers, PH.D.
Associate Director (Scientific Development) (G5), J. F. Peake.
Secretary (G5), C. J. E. Legg.
Assistant to the Director (G7), vacant.

Marketing and Development Department

Head (G6), A. P. Harvey.
Deputy Head and Corporate Communications Manager (G7), C. E. Metcalf.
Marketing Manager (G7), Mrs. J. A. Nadolski.

Department of Zoology

Keeper (G5), C. R. Curds, D.SC.
Deputy Keepers (G6), R. J. Lincoln, Ph.D.; I. R. Bishop, O.B.E. (*acting*).
Grade 6 , J. D. Taylor, Ph.D.
Grade 7, E. N. Arnold, Ph.D.; G. A. Boxhall, Ph.D.; R. A. Bray, Ph.D.; P. F. S. Cornelius, Ph.D.; A. A. Fincham; J. D. George, Ph.D.; D. I. Gibson, Ph.D.; R. W. Ingle, Ph.D.; Mrs. J. Jewell, Ph.D.; N. R. Merrett; C. B. Moncrieff; P. B. Mordan, Ph.D.; H. M. Platt, Ph.D.; D. M. Roberts, Ph.D.; D. Rollinson, Ph.D.; V. R. Southgate, Ph.D.

Bird Section
Park Street, Tring, Herts.
[044 282-4181]

Grade 6, I. R. Bishop, O.B.E.

Department of Entomology

Keeper (G5), L. A. Mound, D.SC.
Deputy Keepers (G6), D. R. Ragge, Ph.D.; R. I. Vane-Wright.
Grade 6, R. L. Blackman, Ph.D.; R. W. Crosskey, D.SC.
Grade 7, P. C. Barnard, Ph.D.; B. Bolton; Mrs. J. M. Cox, Ph.D.; M. G. Fitton, Ph.D.; I. D. Gauld, Ph.D.; P. M. Hammond; D. Hollis; W. J. Knight, Ph.D.; G. S. Robinson, Ph.D.; K. S. O. Sattler, Ph.D.; A. J. Shelley, Ph.D.; N. E. Stork, Ph.D.; R. T. Thompson; W. G. Tremewan.

Department of Botany

Keeper (G5), J. F. M. Cannon.
Keeper designate (G6), S. Blackmore, Ph.D.
Deputy Keeper (G6), P. W. James.
Grade 7, A. O. Chater; A. Eddy; D. J. Galloway, Ph.D.; C. J. Humphries, Ph.D.; A. C. Jermy; D. M. John, Ph.D.; R. J. Pankhurst; J. H. Price; I. Tittley.

Department of Palaeontology

Keeper (G5), L. R. M. Cocks, D.SC.
Deputy Keepers (G6), M. K. Howarth, Ph.D.; H. G. Owen, Ph.D.
Grade 6, C. Patterson, Ph.D.; R. A. Fortey, SC.D; P. J. Andrews, Ph.D.
Grade 7, C. H. C. Brunton, Ph.D.; P. L. Forey, Ph.D.; A. W. Gentry, D.Phil.; R. P. S. Jefferies, Ph.D.; Miss T. I. Molleson; N. J. Morris, D.Phil.; C. P. Nuttall; J. B. Richardson, Ph.D.; B. R. Rosen, Ph.D.; A. B. Smith, Ph.D.; C. B. Stringer, Ph.D.; P. D. Taylor, Ph.D.; J. E. P. Whittaker, Ph.D.

Department of Mineralogy

Keeper (G5), P. Henderson, D.Phil.
Deputy Keeper (G6), vacant.
Grade 6, R. Hutchison, Ph.D.
Grade 7, A. M. Clark, Ph.D.; G. Cressey, Ph.D.; A. J. Criddle; A. L. Graham, Ph.D.; R. R. Harding, D.Phil.; R. F. Symes, Ph.D.; A. R. Woolley, Ph.D.

Department of Administrative Services

Head and Finance and Establishment Officer (G5), C. J. E. Legg.
Building Manager (G6), R. H. Essex.
Personnel Officer (G7), Mrs. P. H. I. Orchard.
Finance and Organization (G7), E. G. Hartman.
Publications Officer (G6), C. A. P. Reynard.
Grade 7, B. S. Martin.

Department of Library Services

Head (G6), R. E. R. Banks.
Deputy Head (G7), Miss P. Gilbert.

Department of Public Services

Head (G5), R. S. Miles, D.SC.
Deputy Head (G6), G. C. S. Clarke, Ph.D.
Operations Manager (G6), M. B. McBratney.
Contracts and Production Manager (G7), R. G. Nash.
Technical Services Manager (G7), J. Furlong.

Geological Museum
Exhibition Road, South Kensington, SW7 2DE
[01-938 8932]

The Museum's three public galleries have major displays of gems and basic earth science.

MUSEUM OF LONDON
London Wall, EC2Y 5HN
[01-600 3699]

The Museum of London opened in 1976. It is based on the amalgamation of the former Guildhall Museum and London Museum. The Museum is controlled by a Board of Governors, appointed (nine each) by the Government and the Corporation of London. The exhibition illustrates the history of London from prehistoric times to the present day.
Chairman of Board of Governors, R. M. Robbins, C.B.E., F.S.A.
Director, M. G. Hebditch, F.S.A.

THE SCIENCE MUSEUM
South Kensington, SW7 2DD
[01-938 8000]

Open on Mon.–Sat. 10–6; Sun. 11–6. Closed on New Year's Day, Good Friday, May Day Bank Holiday, Christmas Eve, Christmas Day and Boxing Day. Admission charge.

The Science Museum, part of the National Museum of Science & Industry, houses the national collections of science, technology, industry and medicine. The Museum began as the Science Collection of the South Kensington Museum and first opened in 1857. In 1883, it acquired the collections of the Patent Museum and in 1909 the Science Collections were transferred to the new Science Museum, leaving the Art Collections with the Victoria and Albert Museum.

Some of the Museum's commercial aircraft, agricultural machinery, and road and rail transport collections are at Wroughton, near Swindon, Wilts., and are open for public viewing on selected weekends during the summer.

The Museum is responsible for the Concorde Exhibition at the Fleet Air Arm Museum, Yeovilton.

The running expenses, including building costs, of the Museum, the Science Museum Library, the National Railway Museum and the National Museum of Photography, Film and Television are estimated at £17,709,000 for 1989–90.

(For **Salaries**, see page 293.)

Director, Dr. N. Cossons, O.B.E.

RESOURCE MANAGEMENT DIVISION

Assistant Director (G5), J. J. Defries.
Head of Personnel and Training (G7), C. Gosling.
Finance Officer (G7), vacant.
Buildings Manager (G7), I. Brown.
Curator C (G7), J. C. Robinson.

COLLECTIONS MANAGEMENT DIVISION

Assistant Director (G5), Dr. T. Wright.

Department of Physical Sciences

Keeper (G5), Dr. D. A. Robinson.
Curators (G7), Dr. D. Vaughan; Dr. A. Q. Morton; Dr. A. K. Newmark; Dr. J. Darius; C. N. Brown.

Department of Medical Sciences

Keeper (G5), Dr. B. Bracegirdle.
Curator (G7), Dr. G. M. Lawrence.

Department of Engineering

Keeper (G5), Dr. E. J. S. Becklake.
Curators (G7), Dr. B. P. Bowers; A. E. Butcher; P. D. Stephens; D. D. Swade.

Department of Transport

Acting Keeper (G6), Dr. R. F. Bud.
Curator (G7), P. R. Mann.

MARKETING DIVISION

Assistant Director (G5), C. M. Pemberton.
Marketing Executive (G7), Ms. K. Booth.

PUBLIC SERVICES DIVISION

Assistant Director (G5), T. Suthers.
Head of Operations and House Management (G6), I. M. Ball.
Head of Education (G7), Dr. A. W. Wilson.

RESEARCH AND INFORMATION SERVICES DIVISION
[01–938 8234]

A national library of science, specializing in the history of science and technology. Bibliographies supplied. Photocopying and microfilm service. Open Mon.–Sat. 10–5.30. Closed on Sundays and Bank Holiday weekends.
Assistant Director (G5), Prof. J. R. Durant.
Head of Library and Information Service (G6), Dr. L. D. Will.

NATIONAL RAILWAY MUSEUM
Leeman Road, York YO2 4XJ
[0904–621261]

The Museum, opened in 1975, houses the national rail transport collection. Locomotives, rolling stock and carriages are displayed to illustrate the technical, social and economic story of the development of railways in Britain. Open Mon.–Sat. 10–6, Sun. 11–6.
Head of Museum (G5), Dr. J. A. Coiley.
Deputy Head (G7), R. Shorland-Ball.

NATIONAL MUSEUM OF PHOTOGRAPHY, FILM AND TELEVISION
Prince's View, Bradford BD5 0TR
[0274–727488]

The Museum, opened in 1983, collects, conserves and displays photography, film and television materials and equipment. The Museum has the only IMAX cinema in the U.K. Open Tues.–Sun. 11–6, with special exhibition galleries open to 7.30.
Head of Museum (G5), C. J. Ford.
Head of Development (G7), Miss M. Benton.

THE VICTORIA AND ALBERT MUSEUM
South Kensington, SW7 2RL
[01–938 8500]

Open Mon.–Sat. 10–5.50, Sun. 2.30–5.50. Closed Christmas Eve, Christmas Day, Boxing Day, New Year's Day and May Day. The National Art Library is open Tues.–Sat. 10–5 (closed 1–2 Sat.) and the Print Room Tues.–Fri. 10–5, Sat. 10–1, 2–4.30. Donations are invited.

A museum of all branches of fine and applied art, the Victoria and Albert Museum descends directly from the Museum of Manufactures, which opened in Marlborough House in 1852 after the Great Exhibition of 1851. The Museum was moved in 1857 to become part of the collective South Kensington Museum. It was renamed the Victoria and Albert Museum in 1899. The branch museum at Bethnal Green was opened in 1872 and the building is the most important surviving example of the type of glass and iron construction used by Paxton for the Great Exhibition. The Victoria and Albert Museum also administers the Wellington Museum (Apsley House), Ham House, Osterley Park, and the Theatre Museum.
Director and Secretary (G3), Mrs. E. A. L. Esteve-Coll.
Assistant Director of Collections (G5), J. D. W. Murdoch.

Department of Ceramics

Keeper (G5), D. M. Archer (*acting*).
Assistant Keeper (G7), Dr. O. Watson.

Department of Conservation

Keeper (G5), Dr. J. Ashley-Smith.

Far Eastern Department

Keeper (G6), Miss R. Kerr (*acting*).
Assistant Keeper (G7), A. C. Clunas.

Department of Furniture and Interior Design

Keeper (G6), S. S. Jervis (*acting*).

Indian Department

Keeper (G6), Dr. D. Swallow (*acting*).
Assistant Keeper (G7), J. S. Guy.

National Art Library

Keeper (G5), J. F. van den Wateren.
Assistant Keeper (G7), Dr. R. Watson.

Metalwork Department

Keeper (G6), Mrs. P. Glanville (*acting*).
Assistant Keepers (G7), Miss M. Campbell; E. R. Edgecumbe.

Prints, Drawings, Photographs and Paintings Department

Keeper (G6), Miss S. B. Lambert (*acting*).
Assistant Keepers (G7), L. S. Lambourne; M. Haworth-Booth; M. Snodin.

Department of Sculpture

Keeper (G6), P. E. D. Williamson (*acting*).
Assistant Keeper (G7), M. Baker.

Department of Textiles and Dress

Keeper (G6), Miss N. K. A. Rothstein (*acting*).
Assistant Keepers (G7), Mrs. M. Ginsburg; Mrs. V. D. Mendes; Miss W. Hefford.

Administration

Assistant Director, Administration (G5), J. Close.

Department of Public Services

Keeper (G5), J. Earle.

BETHNAL GREEN MUSEUM OF CHILDHOOD
Cambridge Heath Road, Bethnal Green, E2 9PA
[01–980 3204]

Open Mon.–Thurs. and on Sat. 10–6, Sun. 2.30–6.
Closed every Friday, May Day, Christmas Eve,
Christmas Day, Boxing Day and New Year's Day.
Keeper (G6), A. P. Burton.

THEATRE MUSEUM
1E Tavistock Street, WC2E 7PA
[01–836 7891]

Open Tues.–Sun. 11–7. Closed Mon. except Bank
Holidays. Admission £2.25, concessions £1.25.
Keeper (G6), Dr. J. Fowler (*acting*).

THE COMMONWEALTH INSTITUTE
Kensington High Street, W8 6NQ
[01–603 4535]

The Commonwealth Institute is a centre for
information about the Commonwealth. It is funded
by the British Government with contributions from
other Commonwealth Governments. The Institute
is controlled by a Board of Governors which includes
the High Commissioners of all Commonwealth countries represented in London. The Institute has
permanent exhibitions on all Commonwealth nations, plus educational resource, information and
conference centres.

Open Mon.–Sat. 10–5, Sun. 2–5. Admission free.
Closed Good Friday, May Day, Christmas Eve,
Christmas Day, Boxing Day and New Year's Day.
Director General, J. F. Porter.
Director of Education, G. Brandt.
Chief Administrative Officer, P. Kennedy.
Head of Media and Resources, R. Varney.

IMPERIAL WAR MUSEUM
Lambeth Road, SE1 6HZ
[01–735 8922]

Open daily 10–6. Closed Christmas Eve, Christmas
Day, Boxing Day and New Year's Day. Admission,
£2·50; concessions, £1·25; free day on Fridays. The
Reference departments are open Mon.–Sat. 10–5, Sat.
by appointment only.

The Museum, founded in 1917, illustrates and
records all aspects of the two world wars and other
military operations involving Britain and the Commonwealth since 1914. It was opened in its present
home, formerly Bethlem Hospital or Bedlam, in 1936.
The Museum also administers H.M.S. *Belfast* in the
Pool of London, Duxford Airfield near Cambridge
and The Cabinet War Rooms in Westminster.

Expenses for 1989–90 are estimated at £11,307,000.
(For **Salaries,** *see* page 293.)

Director General (G4), A. C. N. Borg, Ph.D., F.S.A.
*Deputy Director General and Head of the Research
  and Information Office (G5),* R. W. K. Crawford.
Secretary (G6), J. J. Chadwick.
Special Assistant to the Director (G7), Mrs. S. R.
  Burgess.
Establishment Officer (G7), G. A. Kelly.
Finance Officer (G7), Mrs. P. A. Whitfield.
Museum Superintendent (G7), D. A. Needham.
*Senior Keeper and Keeper of Audio-Visual Records
  (G5),* G. T. C. Coultass.
Director of Duxford Airfield (G5), E. O. Inman.
Director of H.M.S. Belfast (G5), Capt. F. A. Collins,
  R.N.
Keeper of the Department of Museum Services (G6), C.
  Dowling, D.Phil.
Keeper of the Department of Documents (G6), R. W. A.
  Suddaby.
*Keeper of the Department of Exhibits and Firearms
  (G6),* D. J. Penn.

Keeper of the Department of Printed Books (G6), G.
  M. Bayliss, Ph.D.
Keeper of the Department of Art (G6), Miss A. H.
  Weight.
Keeper of the Department of Film (G6), Miss A. E.
  Fleming.
*Keeper of the Department of Information Retrieval
  (G6),* R. B. N. Smither.
Keeper of the Department of Photographs (G6), Miss
  K. J. Carmichael.
Keeper of the Department of Sound Records (G6), Mrs.
  M. A. Brooks.
Curator of the Cabinet War Rooms (G7), E. J. Wenzel.

NATIONAL MARITIME MUSEUM
Greenwich, SE10 9NF
[01–858 4422]

Open Mon.–Sat., 10–6 (10–5 in winter); Sun. 2–6 (2–
5 in winter). Closed Jan. 1, Good Friday, May Day
Bank Holiday and Dec. 24–26. Admission charge.

Reading Room open Mon.–Fri., 10–5; readers'
tickets available on written application to Reader
Services Section.

Established by Act of Parliament in 1934, the
National Maritime Museum illustrates the maritime
history of Great Britain in the widest sense, underlin-
ing the importance of the sea and its influence on the
nation's power, wealth, culture, technology and
institutions. The Museum is in two groups of
buildings in Greenwich Park—the main buildings
centred around the Queen's House (built by Inigo
Jones, 1616–35) and the Old Royal Observatory
(including Wren's Flamsteed House) to the south.
The collections include paintings, actual craft and
ship models, ships' lines, prints and drawings, atlases
and charts, navigational and astronomical instruments, uniforms and relics, books and MSS.
Director, R. L. Ormond.

NATIONAL ARMY MUSEUM
Royal Hospital Road, SW3 4HT
[01–730 0717]

Established by Royal Charter (1960). History of
five centuries of the British Army : includes the story
of the Indian Army up to Independence in 1947.
Open, Mon.–Sat., 10–5.30; Sun. 2–5.30. The Indian
Army room at R.M.A. Sandhurst, Camberley, Surrey
may be viewed by appointment.
Director, I. G. Robertson.
Personal Assistant to the Director, Miss E. Christie.
Assistant Directors, D. K. Smurthwaite; A. J. Guy.
Museum Secretary, Maj. P. R. Bateman.

ROYAL AIR FORCE MUSEUM
Grahame Park Way,
Hendon, NW9 5LL
[01–205 2266]

Situated on the former airfield at Hendon, the
Museum illustrates the development of aviation from
before the Wright brothers to the present-day R.A.F.
Over 60 historic aircraft are on display from the
Museum's collection. The complex includes Battle of
Britain and Bomber Command halls.
Open daily, 10–6. Closed Dec. 24, 25, 26, Jan. 1,
Admission charge.
Director, M. A. Fopp.
Keepers, D. C. R. Elliott; P. G. Murton; R. Simpson;
  A. C. Harold; J. Freeborn; M. C. Nutt.

**THE NATIONAL MUSEUMS AND
GALLERIES ON MERSEYSIDE**
William Brown Street, Liverpool L3 8EN
[051–207 0001]

The Board of Trustees of the National Museums

and Galleries on Merseyside was established in 1986 to take over responsibility for the museums and galleries previously administered by Merseyside County Council. Various stores ancillary to the collections are also the responsibility of the body. It is grant-aided by the Minister for Arts.

All properties, except the Large Objects Collection, are open all year except Jan. 1, Dec. 24–26 and Good Friday. Opening times for all properties (except the Maritime Museum and the Large Objects Collection) are Mon.–Sat. 10–5, Sun. 2–5. Opening times for the Merseyside Maritime Museum are daily 10.30–5.30. Admission charge. Opening times for the Large Objects Collection are Easter–Sept., daily 10–5.

Chairman of the Board of Trustees, Sir Leslie Young, C.B.E.
Director, R. Foster.
Head of Central Services, P. Sudbury, PH.D.
Keeper of Art Galleries, J. Treuherz.
Keeper of Conservation, J. France.

Liverpool Museum
William Brown Street, Liverpool

Keeper, E. Greenwood.

Merseyside Maritime Museum
Albert Dock, Liverpool
[051–709 1551]

Keeper, M. Stammers.

Large Objects Collection
Princes Dock, Liverpool

Museum of Labour History
County Sessions House, Islington, Liverpool

Walker Art Gallery
William Brown Street, Liverpool

Lady Lever Art Gallery
Port Sunlight Village, Bebington, Wirral
[051–645 3623]

Sudley Art Gallery
Mossley Hill Road, Liverpool

(For other Museums in England, *see* Index)

THE NATIONAL MUSEUM OF WALES
Amgueddfa Genedlaethol Cymru
Cardiff CF1 3NP
[0222–397951]

Open Tues.–Sat., 10–5. Sun. 2.30–5. Closed on Mondays, Christmas Eve, Christmas Day, Boxing Day, New Year's Day and Good Friday. Admission charge.

President, Hon. J. Davies.
Vice-President, C. R. T. Edwards.
Director, D. W. Dykes, PH.D., F.S.A.
Chief Executive, A. Wilson.
Keepers, M. G. Bassett, PH.D. (*Geology*); B. A. Thomas, PH.D. (*Botany*); P. M. Morgan (*Zoology*); H. S. Green, PH.D. (*Archaeology*); T. J. Stevens (*Art*).

Welsh Folk Museum
Amgueddfa Werin Cymru
St. Fagans, Nr. Cardiff

Open April–Oct., daily 10–5; Nov.–March, Mon.–Sat. 10–5. Admission charge. Closed on Christmas Eve, Christmas Day, Boxing Day, New Year's Day and Good Friday.
Curator, J. G. Jenkins, PH.D.
Keepers, E. Scourfield, PH.D.; E. William, PH.D.; D. R. Saer.

Roman Legionary Museum, Caerleon
Caerleon, Gwent.

Contains material found on the site of the Roman fortress of Isca and its suburbs. Open Mon.–Sat. 10–6, Sun. 2–6 (closes 4.30 p.m. mid–Oct. to mid-March.) Closed Dec. 24–26, Jan. 1 and Good Friday. Admission charge.

Turner House Art Gallery
Plymouth Road, Penarth, Nr. Cardiff

Open Tues.–Sat. 11–12.45 and 2–5, Sun. 2–5. Closed Mondays, except Bank Holidays, and on Christmas Eve, Christmas Day, Boxing Day, New Year's Day, Good Friday, and May Day.

Museum of the North
Llanberis, Gwynedd

A multi-media presentation of the history of Wales, and about the electricity supply industry. Open June to mid-Sept. 9.30–6; mid-Sept.–May, 10–5. Closed Dec. 24–26, Jan. 1 and Good Friday. Admission charge.

Welsh Slate Museum
Llanberis, Gwynedd

Open Easter–Sept. daily 9.30–5.30. Admission charge.

Segontium Roman Fort Museum
Beddgelert Road, Caernarfon, Gwynedd

Open weekdays at 9.30, Sundays at 2. Closes at 6 from May to September, at 5.30 in March, April and October, at 4 from November to February. Closed Christmas Eve, Christmas Day, Boxing Day, New Year's Day and Good Friday. On the site of the fort, the museum is in the guardianship of the Welsh Office. Contains mostly material excavated there.

Museum of the Welsh Woollen Industry
Dre-fach Felindre, nr. Llandysul, Dyfed

It occupies part of a working mill. Open April–Sept., Mon.–Sat. 10–5; Oct.–March, Mon.–Fri. 10–5. Admission charge.

Welsh Industrial and Maritime Museum
Bute Street, Cardiff

Open Tues.–Sat. 10–5; Sun. 2.30–5. Closed Mondays, Christmas Eve, Christmas Day, Boxing Day, New Year's Day and Good Friday. Admission charge.
Keeper, S. Owen-Jones, PH.D.

Yr Hen Gapel
Tre'r-ddôl, nr. Aberystwyth, Dyfed

The museum portrays 19th century religious life in Wales. Open 9.30–5 Monday–Saturday from April–September. Admission free.

NATIONAL MUSEUMS OF SCOTLAND
Chambers Street, Edinburgh EH1 1JF
[031–225 7534]

Open, Mon.–Sat., 10–5 and Sun., 2–5.
The National Museums of Scotland have one Director and one Board of Trustees, and include, the Royal Museum of Scotland, Chambers Street, and the Royal Museum of Scotland, Queen Street in Edinburgh, as well as the Scottish United Services Museum, the Scottish Agricultural Museum at Ingliston, the Museum of Flight at East Fortune, Shambellie House Museum of Costume near Dumfries, Leith Custom House Gallery and Biggar Gasworks Museum.

Director, R. G. W. Anderson, D.Phil. £35,415
Keeper, Department of History & Applied Art (G5), Miss D. Idiens.
Keeper, Department of Geology (G5), W. D. I. Rolfe PH.D.

Keeper, Department of Natural History (G5), M. Shaw, D.Phil.
Keeper, Department of Science, Technology and Working Life (G5), D. Bryden.
Deputy Keepers (G6), Sheila Brock, PH.D.; S. C. Wood; D. V. Clarke, PH.D.; Ms C. V. Glenn.

NATIONAL AUDIT OFFICE
157–197 Buckingham Palace Road, SW1W 9SP
[01–798 7000]

The National Audit Office came into existence under the National Audit Act 1983, to replace and continue the work of the former Exchequer and Audit Department. The Act reinforced the Office's total financial and operational independence from the Government and brought its head, the Comptroller and Auditor General, into a closer relationship with Parliament as an Officer of the House of Commons.

The National Audit Office provides independent information, advice and assurance to Parliament and the public about all aspects of the financial operations of government departments and many other bodies receiving public funds. This it does by examining and certifying the accounts of these organizations; and by regularly publishing reports to Parliament on the results of its value for money investigations of the economy, efficiency and effectiveness with which public resources have been used. The National Audit Office is also the auditor by agreement of the accounts of certain international and other organizations. In addition, the office authorizes the issue of public funds to Government departments.

Comptroller and Auditor General, J. B. Bourn, C.B.
    Private Secretary, T. J. Bristow.
Deputy Comptroller and Auditor General, H. D. Myland, C.B.
Assistant Auditor Generals, D. A. Dewar; M. J. Goodson; J. A. Higgins; R. N. Le Marechal.
Directors, P. J. C. Keemer; M. R. J. Paul; P. J. Beck; J. A. Davies; I. R. W. Hargest; R. W. Locke; T. Dobson; P. O'Keefe; A. G. Brown; T. J. Lovett; G. J. S. Frith; C. L. Press; B. D. Baker; C. K. Beauchamp; L. H. Hughes; M. C. Pfleger; R. M. Bennett; B. Hogg; R. J. McCourt; J. Marshall; A. R. Murray; J. Parsons; J. M. Pearce; R. A. Skeen; R. E. Spurgeon.
Deputy Directors, A. W. Bird; E. J. Weeks; C. J. Day; D. C. Page; J. E. Smith; W. L. Ewing; G. J. McKeown; M. V. Pettet; A. G. Roberts; A. Cunningham; G. G. Jones; K. Maclean; M. L. Daynes; D. R. Corsby; R. W. Tycer; J. J. Jones; D. J. Woodward; J. B. Cavanagh; J. Darling; P. R. Duncombe; R. J. Eales; D. A. Ferguson; Mrs. H. Jackson; Miss J. Lawler; J. S. McEwen; Miss C. Mawhood; A. Parker; R. A. Pocock; J. O. A. Thompson; P. G. Woodward.

NATIONAL CONSUMER COUNCIL
20 Grosvenor Gardens, SW1W 0DH
[01–730 3469]

The National Consumer Council was set up by the Government in 1975 and is funded by a grant-in-aid from the Department of Trade and Industry. The Council safeguards and furthers the interests of consumers and speaks up for them to public utilities, business, industry, the professions, and Government, both central and local.
Chairman, The Baroness Oppenheim-Barnes, P.C.
Director, M. Healy.

NATIONAL DEBT OFFICE
see **National Investment and Loans Office**.

NATIONAL ECONOMIC DEVELOPMENT OFFICE
Millbank Tower, Millbank, SW1P 4QX
[01–217 4000]

The National Economic Development Council brings together Government, management and unions to tackle issues vital to jobs and economic growth, by identifying obstacles to economic development and promoting change.

Council
Government Members, The Chancellor of the Exchequer (*Chairman*); the Secretaries of State for Education and Science, Employment, Energy, Environment, and Trade and Industry.
Management Members, J. M. M. Banham; Sir Trevor Holdsworth; Adm. Sir Raymond Lygo, K.C.B.; D. A. G. Monk; T. J. O'Connor; Sir Thomas Risk.
Trade Union Members, R. Bickerstaffe; Miss B. Dean; J. Edmonds; W. Jordan, R. Todd; N. Willis.
Independent Members, Sir James Ackers; E. A. Hammond, O.B.E.; The Rt. Hon. Robin Leigh-Pemberton; Sir Bryan Nicholson; Mrs. R. E. Waterhouse, C.B.E; G. B. Wolfson.
Director-General, W. A. Eltis.
Secretary to the Council, M. Couchman.
Industrial Director, D. Fraser.
Economic Director, K. Mayhew.

NATIONAL GALLERIES
See **Art Galleries**

NATIONAL HERITAGE MEMORIAL FUND
10 St James's Street, SW1A 1EF
[01–930 0963]

The National Heritage Memorial Fund was established in 1980 as an independent body, and is intended as a memorial to those who have died for the U.K. The Fund is empowered, by the National Heritage Act 1980, to give financial assistance towards the cost of acquiring, maintaining or preserving land, buildings, works of art and other objects of outstanding interest which are also of importance to the national heritage. The Fund is administered by up to eleven Trustees, appointed by the Prime Minister.

The Fund's major sources of money are the Department of the Environment and the Office of Arts and Libraries, each of which gives annual grants. In its first nine years, the Fund spent £100 million in carrying out its responsibilities.

Trustees
The Lord Charteris of Amisfield (*Chairman*); The Marquess of Anglesey; Sir Nicholas Goodison; Prof. F. G. T. Holliday; Sir Martin Jacomb; C. Kinahan; Sir Oliver Millar; Prof. B. R. Morris; Sir Norman Macfarlane; M. McCrum; Cdr. L. M. M. Saunders Watson.
Director, Ms. G. Naylor.

NATIONAL INSURANCE JOINT AUTHORITY
151 Great Titchfield Street, W1P 8AD
[01–636 1696]

The Authority's function is to co-ordinate the operation of social security legislation in Great Britain and Northern Ireland, including the necessary financial adjustments between the two National Insurance Funds.
Members, The Secretary of State for Social Security;

the Head of the Department of Health and Social Services for Northern Ireland.
Secretary, Mrs. D. W. Joannou.

NATIONAL INVESTMENT AND LOANS OFFICE
Royex House, Aldermanbury Square, EC2V 7LR
[01–606 7321]

The National Investment and Loans Office was set up on April 1, 1980 by merging the staffs of the National Debt Office and the Public Works Loan Board. The Department provides staff and services for the National Debt Commissioners and the Public Works Loan Commissioners.
Director, I. H. Peattie.
Establishment Officer, A. G. Ladd.

National Debt Office
Comptroller General, I. H. Peattie.

Public Works Loan Board
Chairman, J. E. A. R. Guinness, C.B.E.
Deputy Chairman, R. J. Dent.
Other Commissioners, Miss F. M. Cook; Miss V. J. Di Palma, O.B.E.; G. Ross Russell; P. Brackfield; D. H. Adams; R. A. Chapman; R. Emmott; B. Fieldhouse; A. Morton; I. C. Wilson.
Secretary, I. H. Peattie.
Assistant Secretary, D. L. Hammond.

NATIONAL RADIOLOGICAL PROTECTION BOARD
Chilton, Didcot, Oxon. OX11 0RQ
[0235–831600]

The National Radiological Protection Board is an independent statutory body created by the Radiological Protection Act 1970. The Government's purpose was to establish a national point of authoritative reference in radiological protection.
Chairman, Sir Richard Southwood, F.R.S.
Director, Dr. R. H. Clarke.

NATIONAL RIVERS AUTHORITY
Rivers House, 30–34 Albert Embankment, SE1 7TL
[01–820 0101]

The National Rivers Authority (N.R.A.) is an independent body set up under the Water Act 1989 to take over the regulatory and other river functions of the former water authorities in England and Wales. Its responsibilities include monitoring the quality of water and controlling pollution, and the management of water resources, flood defence and fisheries.
The N.R.A. has a board of 15 members, two of whom are appointed by the Minister of Agriculture, Fisheries and Food, one by the Secretary of State for Wales, and the rest by the Secretary of State for the Environment.
Chairman, The Lord Crickhowell, P.C.
Chief Executive, Dr. J. Bowman, C.B.E.
Chief Scientist, Dr. J. Pentreath.
Technical Director, Dr. C. Swinnerton.
Finance Director, P. Partridge.
Personnel Director, P. Humphreys.
External Affairs Director, Ms. M. Evans.

DEPARTMENT FOR NATIONAL SAVINGS
Charles House, 375 Kensington High Street,
W14 8SD
[01–605 9300]

The Department for National Savings was established as a Government Department in 1969. The Department is responsible for the administration of a wide range of schemes for personal savers. (For details of schemes, *see* National Savings section). (For Salaries, *see* page 293)

Director of Savings (G2), J. A. Patterson, C.B.
Deputy Director (G3), C. D. Butler.
Establishment Officer (G5), D. S. Speedie.
Finance Officer (G5), C. Ward.
Controllers (G5), Mrs. S. Cullum (*Marketing & Information*); R. S. Watts; J. Stamp; E. B. Senior; P. N. S. Hickman Robertson.
Senior Principals (G6), D. W. Kellaway; I. T. Standen; R. H. Lee; I. Forsyth; A. S. McGill; D. H. Monaghan; M. A. Nicholls.
Principals (G7), A. G. Muir; W. J. Herd; D. K. Paterson; A. J. V. Cummings; Dr. A. Fort; W. J. Ferrier; H. Johnson; J. W. Davison; D. Newton; A. B. Wood; P. Finnie; C. E. Funk; I. Jordinson; A. Brown; K. R. Tyerman; T. Threlfall; B. Paley; A. T. Stevenson; H. Webster; J. Wheatley; T. J. F. McMahon; C. McVey; R. A. Nichol; N. Thistlethwaite; J. B. Dunphy; J. C. Foreman; D. Wilson; P. B. Robinson; G. V. Wise; A. S. Lamond; D. Jeffrey; R. H. Mitchell; J. Bolam; R. W. Day.

NATIONAL THEATRE BOARD
South Bank, SE1 9PX
[01–928 2033]

Chairman, The Lady Soames, D.B.E.
Members, R. Baird; The Lord Chorley; R. Clutton; M. Codron; Dame Judi Dench, D.B.E.; J. Hannam, M.P.; Sara Hogg; S. Lipton; Sonia Melchett; R. M. Mills; The Lord Mishcon; Sir Derek Mitchell, K.C.B., C.V.O.; Sir Michael Palliser, G.C.M.G.; Lois Sieff; J. Whitney; Sir Peter Parker, L.V.O.
Secretary, D. Gosling.

NATIONAL TRAINING TASK FORCE
214 Gray's Inn Road, WC1X 8HL
[01–278 0363]

The National Training Task Force was established by the Government to advise the Secretary of State for Employment and to assist him in carrying out his training responsibilities throughout Great Britain.
Chairman, Brian Wolfson.
Members, R. Dawe; Sir Peter Bowness; L. Spencer; Sir Eric Pountain; Sir Melvyn Rosser; Sir Peter Thompson; T. Cleaver; Mrs. P. Leith; M. Rowarth; Ms. S. Mirman; Sir David Nickson; Sir James Ackers; W. Jordan; A. Sheppard.

NATURAL ENVIRONMENT RESEARCH COUNCIL
Polaris House, North Star Avenue,
Swindon SN2 1EU
[0793–411500]

The Natural Environment Research Council was established in 1965, to encourage, plan and conduct research in the physical and biological sciences which relate to man's natural environment and its resources.
The Council carries out research and training through its own institutes and grant-aided institutes, and by grants, fellowships and post-graduate awards to universities and other institutions of higher education.
Chairman, Prof. J. Knill, PH.D., D.SC.
Secretary, Dr. Eileen Buttle.
Director of Earth Sciences, Prof. J. C. Briden, PH.D.
Director of Terrestrial and Fresh Water Sciences, P. B. Tinker, D.SC., PH.D.
Director of Marine and Atmospheric Sciences, J. D. Woods, PH.D.

RESEARCH INSTITUTES

British Antarctic Survey
Madingley Road, Cambridge CB3 0ET
[0223–61188]

Director, Dr. D. J. Drewry, PH.D.

British Geological Survey
Nicker Hill, Keyworth, Nottingham NG12 5GG
[06077–6111]

Director, F. G. Larminie, C.B.E.

Institute of Oceanographic Sciences
Deacon Laboratory, Wormley, nr. Godalming
GU8 5UB
[042879–4141]

Director, Dr. C. Summerhayes.

Plymouth Marine Laboratory
Prospect Place, The Hoe, Plymouth PL1 3DH
Citadel Hill, Plymouth PL1 2PB
[0752–222772]

Director, B. L. Bayne, PH.D.
Deputy Director, M. Whitfield.

Proudman Oceanographic Laboratory
Bidston, Birkenhead L43 7RA
[051–653 8633]

Director, B. S. McCartney, PH.D.

Sea Mammal Research Unit
c/o British Antarctic Survey,
[0223–311354]

Head of Unit, J. Harwood, PH.D.

Institute of Hydrology
Maclean Building, Crowmarsh Gifford,
Wallingford, Oxon. OX10 8BB
[0491–38800]

Director, Prof. B. Wilkinson.

Institute of Terrestrial Ecology (North)
Bush Estate, Penicuik, Midlothian EH26 0QB,
[031–445 4343]

Director, O. W. Heal, PH.D.

Institute of Terrestrial Ecology (South)
Monks Wood Experimental Station, Abbots Ripton,
Huntingdon PE17 2LS
[04873–381/8]

Director, Dr. M. Roberts.

Institute of Virology and Microbiology
Mansfield Road, Oxford OX1 3SR
[0865–512361]

Director, Prof. D. H. L. Bishop, PH.D.

GRANT-AIDED INSTITUTES

Institute of Freshwater Ecology
The Ferry House, Far Sawrey,
Ambleside, Cumbria LA22 0LP
[09662–2468/9]

Director, Prof. J. G. Jones, PH.D.

Dunstaffnage Marine Laboratory
P.O. Box 3, Oban, Argyll PA34 4AD
[0631–62244]

Director, Prof. J. B. L. Matthews.

Unit of Comparative Plant Ecology
Dept. of Plant Sciences, Sheffield University,
Sheffield S10 2TN
[0742–768555]

Head of Unit, Prof. I. H. Rorison, D.PHIL.

CENTRAL SERVICES

N.E.R.C. Scientific Services
Polaris House, North Star Avenue, Swindon,
Wilts. SN2 1EU
[0793–411000]

Director, B. J. Hinde.

Research Vessel Services
No. 1 Dock, Barry, S. Glamorgan
[0446–737451]

Head, Dr. C. Fay.

N.E.R.C. Computer Service
Holbrook House, Station Road,
Swindon, Wilts. SN1 1DE
[0793–411000]

Director, H. J. Down.

NATURE CONSERVANCY COUNCIL
Northminster House, Peterborough PE1 1UA
[0733–40345]

Establishes, maintains and manages National Nature Reserves, advises generally on nature conservation, gives advice to the Government on nature conservation policies and on how other policies may affect nature conservation, and supports, commissions and undertakes relevant research.
Chairman, Sir William Wilkinson.
Deputy Chairman, Sir John Burnett.
Director General, T. R. Hornsby.
Chief Scientist, Dr. P. Bridgewater.
Country Headquarters:
England: Northminster House, Peterborough PE1 1UA.—*Director*, Dr. F. B. O'Connor.
Scotland: 12 Hope Terrace, Edinburgh EH9 2AS.—*Director*, Dr. J. Francis.
Wales: Plas Penrhos, Penrhos Road, Bangor, Gwynedd LL57 2LQ.—*Director*, Dr. T. Pritchard.

NORTHERN IRELAND OFFICE
The Northern Ireland Office is the U.K. government department in which the Secretary of State for Northern Ireland has overall responsibility for the government of Northern Ireland. The Secretary of State is directly responsibile for constitutional developments, law and order, security and electoral matters. Under the Northern Ireland Act 1974, the Northern Ireland departments are also subject to the direction and control of the Secretary of State during direct rule.

Whitehall, SW1A 2AZ
[01–210 3000]
Secretary of State for Northern Ireland, THE RT. HON. PETER BROOKE, M.P.
Minister of State, THE RT. HON. JOHN COPE, M.P.
Parliamentary Under Secretaries of State, RICHARD NEEDHAM, M.P.; DR. BRIAN MAWHINNEY, M.P.; PETER BOTTOMLEY, M.P.; THE LORD SKELMERSDALE.
Permanent Under Secretary of State, Sir John Blelloch, K.C.B.
Second Permanent Under Secretary of State, Head of the NICS, Sir Kenneth Bloomfield, K.C.B.

Northern Ireland Civil Service
Stormont Castle, Belfast BT4 3TT
[0232–63011]

Department of Agriculture for Northern Ireland
Dundonald House, Upper Newtownards Road,
Belfast BT4 3SB
[0232–650111]

Department of Economic Development Northern Ireland
Netherleigh, Massey Avenue, Belfast BT4 2JP
[0232–63244]

Department of Education for Northern Ireland
Rathgael House, Balloo Road, Bangor,
Co. Down BT19 2PR
[0247–270077]

Department of the Environment for Northern Ireland
Stormont, Belfast BT4 3SS
[0232–63210]

Department of Finance and Personnel
Parliament Buildings, Stormont, Belfast BT4 3SW
[0232–63210]

Department of Health and Social Services Northern Ireland
Dundonald House, Upper Newtownards Road,
Belfast BT4 3SF
[0232–650111]

OMBUDSMAN, *see* **LOCAL COMMISSIONERS**, and **PARLIAMENTARY COMMISSIONER**

(For non-statutory Ombudsmen, *see* **Index)**

ORDNANCE SURVEY
Romsey Road, Maybush, Southampton SO9 4DH
[0703–792000]

The Ordnance Survey is the national mapping agency for Britain and it produces over 220,000 large scale maps of the country at three basic scales. These are 1:1,250 (50 inches to 1 mile) for urban areas; 1:2,500 (25 inches to 1 mile) for rural areas; and 1:10,000 (6 inches to 1 mile) for mountain and moorland. Additionally, Ordnance Survey produces a range of small scale maps and other products for general use.
Director-General, P. McMaster.
Directors:
 Surveys and Production, A. S. Macdonald.
 Marketing, Planning and Development, J. Leonard.
 Overseas Surveys, B. E. Furmston.
 Establishments and Finance, K. Nolan.
Heads of Functions:
 Production, E. Gilbert.
 Topographic Surveys, P. Wesley.
 Marketing, D. Toft.
 Research and Development, M. Sowton.
 Head of Finance, J. Evenett.
 Establishments, I. Lock.
 Information and Computer Service, B. W. Nanson.

OVERSEAS DEVELOPMENT ADMINISTRATION
Eland House, Stag Place, SW1E 5DH
[01–273 3000]
Abercrombie House, Eaglesham Road, East Kilbride,
Glasgow G75 8EA
[03552–41199]

The Overseas Development Administration deals with British development assistance to overseas countries. This includes both capital aid on concessional terms and technical assistance (mainly in the form of specialist staff abroad and training facilities in the United Kingdom), whether provided directly to developing countries or through the various multilateral aid organizations, including the United Nations and its specialized agencies.
(For **Salaries,** *see* page 293)

Minister for Overseas Development, THE RT. HON. LYNDA CHALKER, M.P.
 Private Secretary (G7), M. A. Wickstead.
 Parliamentary Private Secretary, D. French, M.P.
*Permanent Secretary (G1*A*),* T. P. Lankester.
 Private Secretary, Ms. S. A. Howes.
Deputy Secretary (G2), R. M. Ainscow, C.B.
Under Secretaries (G3), N. B. Hudson; J. L. F. Buist; B. R. Ireton; J. V. Kerby; Dr. J. M. Healey; R. G. Manning; A. J. Bennett.

Economic and Social Division

Head of the Economic Service (G3), Dr. J. M. Healey.
Senior Economic Advisers (G5), J. B. Wilmshurst; J. C. H. Morris; G. P. Sandersley; A. G. Coverdale; B. P. Thomson.
Economic Advisers (G7), P. J. Ackroyd; P. D. Balacs; B. Carstairs; Dr. F. C. Clift; J. G. Clarke; P. J. Dearden; M. G. Foster; K. E. Gubbins; Dr. G. Haley; E. Hawthorn; P. G. Hill; W. Kingsmill; P. J. A. Landymore; A. Moon; P. L. Owen; J. N. Stevens; Mrs. J. M. White.
Chief Statistician (G5), R. M. Allen.
Statisticians (G7), A. B. Williams; Miss M. O'Connor; J. R. B. King; P. J. Crook; Mrs. M. E. Frosztega; M. C. Walmsley.
Principal Finance and Management Adviser (G5), K. L. Sparkhall.
Senior Finance and Management Advisers (G6), E. A. Gill; D. W. Heffer.
Senior Social Development Adviser (G6), Dr. S. R. Conlin.
Social Development Adviser (G7), Dr. R. J. Eyben.

Information Department

Head of Information Dept. (G5), J. C. Machin.
Principal Information Officer (G7), Ms L. J. Sinclair.

Heads of Development Divisions (G5)

Caribbean (Bridgetown), M. G. Bawden; *East Africa (Nairobi).* M. C. McCulloch; *Pacific (Suva),* J. Hodges; *South-East Asia (Bangkok),* M. J. Dinham; *Southern Africa (Lilongwe),* Ms. S. E. Unsworth.
Assistant Secretaries (G5), Miss A. M. Archbold; G. A. Beattie; P. D. M. Freeman; R. M. Graham-Harrison; W. Hobman; C. R. O. Jones; Mrs. B. M. Kelly; J. C. Machin; V. J. McLean; R. G. Pettitt; M. A. Power; C. P. Raleigh; D. Sands Smith; D. L. Stanton; G. M. Stegmann; D. F. Turner; Mrs. P. M. Wilkinson; R. J. Wilson; R. W. Wootton.
Senior Principals (G6), D. G. Bell; F. Crampsey; L. E. Fitzpatrick; B. W. Hammond; S. Ray; G. A. Williams.
Principals (G7), J. D. Aitken; J. A. Anning; G. A. Armstrong; D. W. Baker; D. G. Bell; W. T. Birrell; H. Britton; W. A. Brownlie; P. J. Burton; R. O. Carter; J. H. S. Chard; P. H. Charters; D. J. Church; T. F. G. Connor; G. Crabtree; D. R. Curran; A. D. Davis; P. Dean; J. R. Drummond; J. R. Gilbert; K. D. Grimshaw; Ms. J. V. Hanna; Ms. V. M. Harris; Ms. P. J. Hilton; M. I. Holland; N. Hoult; W. Jardine; D. Lawless; G. G. Leader; G. H. Malley; C. A. Metcalf; J. C. Millett; J. D. Moye; G. A. Mustard; C. Myhill; P. T. Perris; B. G. Peskett; G. M. Porter; S. Ray; D. T. Richards; R. S. Ridgwell; S. R. J. Robbins; C. R. Roth; J. M. Scoular; R. J. Smith; M. J. Sexton; I. F. Stickels; I. D. Stuart; A. J. Sutherland; B. A. Thorpe; R. G. Toulmin; D. Trotter; Miss M. H. Vowles; C. W. Warren; S. A. Wheeler; C. J. White; R. S. White; D. M. White-

cross; M. A. Wickstead; J. M. Winter; A. K. C. Wood.

Advisory and Specialist Staff

Principal Education Adviser (G5), Dr. R. O. Iredale.
Senior Education Advisers (G6), M. D. Francis; Ms. M. Harrison; M. E. Seath; Dr. D. G. Swift.
Principal Engineering Adviser (G5), T. D. Pike.
Engineering Advisers (G6), J. N. Bulman; A. G. Colley; D. Gillett; B. Dolton; P. H. Hilton; H. B. Jackson; B. G. Little.
Engineering Advisers (G7), C. I. Ellis; R. J. Cadwallader; C. S. Reid; M. F. Sergeant; P. W. D. H. Roberts; A. Coulthart; A. Barker.
Senior Renewable Energy Adviser (G6), Dr. J. L. D. Harrison.
Electrical and Mechanical Engineering Adviser (G6), R. P. Jones.
Senior Architectural and Planning Adviser (G6), M. W. Parkes.
Senior Architectural and Physical Planning Adviser (G6), H. W. Housego-Woolgar.
Senior Medical Adviser (G6), Dr. P. Key, O.B.E.
Principal Nursing and Health Services Adviser, Miss M. Pollock.
Nursing and Health Services Adviser, Miss J. Isard.
Chief Natural Resources Adviser (G3), A. J. Bennett.
Deputy Chief National Resources Adviser (G5), R. H. Kemp.
Deputy Chief Natural Resources Adviser (G5), Dr. J. C. Davies (*Research*).
Senior Agricultural Advisers (G6), J. R. F. Hansell; R. W. Smith (*Research*); J. M. Scott; A. J. Tainsh; R. L. Waddell; M. F. Watson; M. J. Wilson.
Agricultural Advisers (G7), Dr. B. E. Grimwood; D. J. Salmon; D. A. Trotman.
Animal Health Advisers (G6), G. G. Freeland; Dr. A. D. Irvin.
Fisheries Adviser (G6), Dr. J. Tarbit.
Forestry Advisers (G6), R. H. Kemp; W. J. Howard.
Financial Management Advisers (G6), E. A. Gill; D. W. Heffer.
Senior Procurement Adviser (G6), R. C. Morgan.

Overseas Development Natural Resources Institute

Central Avenue, Chatham Maritime,
Chatham, Kent ME4 4TB
[0634–880088]

Director (G5), G. A. Beattie.

OFFICE OF THE PARLIAMENTARY COMMISSIONER AND HEALTH SERVICE COMMISSIONER

Church House, Great Smith Street, SW1P 3BW
[01–276 3000]

The Parliamentary Commissioner for Administration is responsible for investigating complaints referred to him by Members of the House of Commons from members of the public who claim to have sustained injustice in consequence of maladministration in connection with administrative action taken by or on behalf of Government Departments and certain non-departmental public bodies. Certain types of action by Government Departments or bodies are excluded from investigation. Actions taken by other public bodies (such as local authorities, the police, the Post Office and nationalized industries) are outside the Commissioner's scope.

The Health Service Commissioners for England, for Scotland and for Wales are responsible for investigating complaints against National Health Service authorities that are not dealt with by those authorities to the satisfaction of the complainant. Complaints can be referred direct by the member of the public who claims to have sustained injustice or

hardship in consequence of the failure in a service provided by a relevant body, failure of that body to provide a service or in consequence of any other action by that body. Certain types of action are excluded, in particular, action taken solely in consequence of the exercise of clinical judgment. The three offices are presently held by the Parliamentary Commissioner.

Parliamentary Commissioner and Health Service Commissioner, Sir Anthony Barrowclough, Q.C.
£72,000
Deputy Parliamentary Commissioner (G3), D. G. Allen, C.M.G.
Deputy Health Service Commissioner, R. A. Oswald.
Directors (G5), K. H. Green; Mrs. J. M. Fowler; M. D. Randall; J. E. Avery; J. C. Bateman; M. A. Johnson; M. P. Cornwell-Kelly.
Principals (G7), P. J. Belsham; G. M. Keil; Mrs. C. Bentley; Miss D. M. Pace; R. Paxton; T. J. Corkett; R. A. Bourley; D. S. Burn; A. C. Beer (*Establishment Officer*); Mrs. E. A. Cooper; F. J. Drummond; R. V. Siese; J. D. Jarvis; D. Hall; B. P. Jones; D. G. Tempest.

PARLIAMENTARY COUNSEL

36 Whitehall, SW1A 2AY
[01–210 6633]

Parliamentary Counsel draft all Government Bills (i.e. primary legislation) except common form ones and those relating exclusively to Scotland. They also advise on all aspects of parliamentary procedure in connection with such Bills and draft Government amendments to them as well as any motions (including financial resolutions) necessary to secure their introduction into, and passage through, Parliament.
First Counsel, Sir Henry de Waal, K.C.B., Q.C. £72,000
Second Counsel, P. Graham, C.B. £59,800
Counsel, J. D. M. Rennie, C.B.; J. C. Jenkins, C.B.; J. S. Mason, C.B.; Miss S. P. Burns, C.B.; D. W. Saunders, C.B.; E. G. Caldwell; E. G. Bowman; G. B. Sellers; E. R. Sutherland. *up to* £50,400

PAROLE BOARD

Abell House, John Islip Street, SW1P 4LH
[01–217 3000]

The Board was constituted under section 59 of the Criminal Justice Act, 1967.

The function of the Board is to advise the Secretary of State for the Home Department with respect to: (1) Release on licence under section 60 (i) or 61 and recall under section 62 of the Criminal Justice Act, 1967 of persons whose cases have been referred to the Board by the Secretary of State; (2) The conditions of such licences, and the variation and cancellation of such conditions; and (3) any other matter so referred which is connected with release on licence or recall of persons to whom section 60 or 61 of the Act applies.
Chairman, The Viscount Colville of Culross, Q.C.
Vice-Chairman, The Hon. Mr. Justice Garland.
Secretary, T. J. Wilkie.

PATENT OFFICE (and Industrial Property and Copyright Department)

Department of Trade and Industry,
State House, 66–71 High Holborn,
WC1R 4TP
[01–831 2525]
Sale Branch: Orpington, Kent

The duties of the Department consist in the administration of the Patent Acts, the Registered Designs Act and the Trade Marks Act and in dealing with questions relating to the Copyright Acts. The

Department also provides an information service about patent specifications. In 1986 the Office granted 16,206 patents and registered 7,167 designs and 17,089 trade marks.

Comptroller-General (G3), P. J. Cooper, C.B. ... £47,400
Assistant Comptrollers (G4), T. W. Sage; V. Tarnofsky.
Superintending Examiners, J. P. Britton; M. F. Vivian; A. Sugden; J. Sharrock; G. K. Lindsey; E. F. Blake; K. E. Panchen; W. J. Lyon; P. Ferdinando .... £32,826–£38,210
Principal Examiners, P. L. Eggington; Miss C. M. Edwards; D. R. Barratt; B. C. Faulkner; S. J. Rutland; E. J. Lawrence; B. J. Phillips; D. B. Johnson; C. G. M. Hoptroff; S. Southworth; B. G. Harden; M. W. Hills; L. Lewis; P. S. Michaelis; N. M. Miles; K. C. Thomas; R. S. Vidler; Miss Y. J. Pegler; M. F. Pilgrim; P. J. Herbert; J. K. Dugnolle; G. C. Brown; D. L. Wood; C. Corney; D. Davenport; I. R. Bloomfield; Mrs. J. A. Wilson; P. Haywood
£28,170–£35,415
Assistant Registrar (G5), *Trade Marks*, J. M. Myall.
Senior Principals (G6), A. Holt; J. F. H. Craven; N. A. Harkness; M. Tuck.

Manchester Office
Room 921A, Sunley Buildings,
Piccadilly Plaza, M1 4BA
[01–236 2171]

PAYMASTER GENERAL'S OFFICE
H.M. Treasury, Parliament Street, SW1P 3AG
[01–270 4350]
Sutherland House, Russell Way, Crawley, West
Sussex RH10 1UH
[0293–560999]

The Paymaster General's Office was formed by the consolidation in 1835 of various separate pay departments then existing, some of which dated back at least to the Restoration of 1660. Its function is that of paying agent for Government Departments, other than the Revenue Departments. Most of its payments are made through banks, to whose accounts the necessary transfers are made at the Bank of England. The payment of over one million public service pensions is an important feature of its work.

Paymaster General, THE EARL OF CAITHNESS.
Assistant Paymaster General (G5), L. A. Andrews.
Senior Principals (G6), D. R. L. Breed; K. Sullens.
Principals (G7), D. R. Alexander; Mrs. D. F. Ambrose; T. R. George; J. A. Payne; G. Thomas; C. A. Ulph; M. D. West.

POLICE COMPLAINTS AUTHORITY
10 Great George Street, SW1P 3AB
[01–273 6403]

The Police Complaints Authority was established under the Police and Criminal Evidence Act 1984 to introduce a further independent element into the procedure for dealing with complaints by members of the public against police officers in England and Wales. The Authority has powers to supervise the investigation of certain categories of serious complaints and certain statutory functions in relation to the disciplinary aspects of complaints.

Chairman, His Hon. Judge Petre.
Deputy Chairman (Discipline), Brig. J. Pownall.
Deputy Chairman (Investigations), Rt. Hon. R. Moyle.
Members, Air Vice-Marshal D. Clark; V. Clements; J. Crawford; B. A. Gillman; G. V. Marsh; B. V. Moore; P. W. Moorhouse; K. Singh; Capt. N. Taylor; Mrs. R. Vickers; Mrs. R. Wolff.

POLITICAL HONOURS SCRUTINY COMMITTEE
Cabinet Office, 53 Parliament Street, SW1A 2NG
[01–210 3000]

The function of the Political Honours Scrutiny Committee is set out in an Order in Council dated May 31, 1979. The Prime Minister submits certain particulars to the Committee about persons proposed to be recommended for honour for their political services. The Committee, after such enquiry as they think fit, report to the Prime Minister whether, so far as they believe, the persons whose names are submitted to them are fit and proper persons to be recommended.

Chairman, The Lord Shackleton, K.G., P.C., O.B.E.
Members, The Lord Grimond, T.D., P.C.; The Lord Pym, M.C., P.C.
Secretary, J. H. Thompson, C.B.

THE POLYTECHNICS AND COLLEGES FUNDING COUNCIL
Metropolis House, 22 Percy Street, W1P 9FF
[01–637 1132]

The Polytechnics and Colleges Funding Council (P.C.F.C.) was established as a result of the Education Act 1988 to oversee the sector of higher education formerly controlled by local authorities. The Council consists of 15 members appointed by the Secretary of State for Education and Science and meets five times a year.

The P.C.F.C. distributes over £1,000 million of public funds in England each year to all the polytechnics, the largest colleges of higher education, and a number of specialist colleges. It also funds certain higher education courses in further education colleges. In April 1989 the P.C.F.C. sector comprised 84 institutions serving nearly 350,000 students. The P.C.F.C. also advises the Secretary of State on the funding of higher education. For this it has established Programme Advisory Groups to review provision in nine subject areas. It also establishes *ad hoc* committees of enquiry on particular issues.

Chairman, Sir Ronald Dearing.
Chief Executive, W. H. Stubbs.
Director of Finance, R. McClure.
Secretary, A. R. Phillips.

OFFICE OF POPULATION CENSUSES AND SURVEYS
St. Catherine's House, 10 Kingsway,
WC2B 6JP
[01–242 0262]

The Office of Population Censuses and Surveys was created by a merger in May 1970 of the General Register Office and the Government Social Survey Department. The Registrar General controls the local registration service in England and Wales in the exercise of its registration and marriage duties. Copies of the original registrations of births, stillbirths, marriages and deaths are kept in London. A register of adopted children is held at Titchfield. Central indexes are compiled annually and certified copies of entries may be obtained on payment of certain fees. Since 1841 the Registrar General has been responsible for taking the census of population. She also prepares and publishes a wide range of statistics and appropriate commentary relating to population, fertility, births, still-births, marriages, deaths and cause of death, infectious diseases, sickness and injuries. The Registrar General also maintains, at Southport, a central register of persons on doctors' lists, for the purposes of the National Health Service.

Hours of public access, Mon.–Fri., 8.30 a.m.–4.30 p.m.

Director and Registrar General (G2), Mrs. G. T. Banks.
Deputy Directors (G3), B. J. Ellis (*Establishment Officer*); E. J. Thompson.
Chief Medical Statistician (G3), A. J. Fox, Ph.D.
Grade 5, R. Barnes; J. Craig; M. L. Pennington; J. V. Ribbins (*Deputy Registrar General*); I. K. G. Arnold; J. A. Rowntree; B. H. Mahon; B. S. Smith.
Senior Statisticians (Medical), J. S. A. Ashley; A. G. McCormick; A. J. Swerdlow £29,344
Grade 6, B. S. T. Alcock; R. J. Butcher; A. M. Clark; J. Denton; Mrs. K. H. Dunnell; W. Jenkins; I. B. Knight; D. L. Pearce; R. K. Thomas; R. McLeod.
Grade 7, R. I. Armitage; F. L. Ashwood; Mrs. P. E. Astbury; Ms J. Atkinson; N. E. Auckland; R. A. P. Bailey; E. Barton; N. Bateson; R. J. Beacham; D. E. Birch; Mrs. M. R. Bone; Mrs. B. J. Botting; M. J. Bradley; J. A. Brown; T. B. Bryson; L. Bulusu; D. Capron; R. J. Carpenter; J. Cloyne; C. J. Denham; T. L. F. Devis; J. M. Dixie; Mrs. J. C. Dobbs; Ms. P. Dodd; Miss C. M. Ellis; Ms. E. M. Goddard; I. Golds; Mrs. H. A. Green; Mrs. J. R. Gregory; P. C. Gregory; J. Haskey; P. J. Heady; A. F. Jones; B. G. Little; Miss C. S. J. Lloyd; W. F. Loomes; Mrs. S. M. McCartney; Miss E. M. McCrossan; Mrs. I. MacDonald-Davies; Miss M. Machin; A. J. Manners; Mrs. J. Martin; Ms. J. Matheson; B. W. Meakings; I. D. Mills; Mrs. J. S. Morris; R. M. Nicholls; A. Parr (*Chief Inspector of Registration*); M. Quinn; Mrs. I. Rauta; R. U. Redpath; Miss J. M. R. Rosenbaum; T. A. Russell; J. A. Salvetti; C. Shaw; D. Stewart; Mrs. D. M. Stobbart; Mrs. L. M. Street; A. W. Tester; Miss J. Todd; Mrs. M. J. Waggett; Miss S. Wallace (*Press Officer*); P. H. White.

PORT OF LONDON AUTHORITY
International House, World Trade Centre,
E1 9UN
[01–481 1954]

The Port of London Authority is a public trust constituted under the Port of London Act 1968 and a Harbour Revision Order of 1975. The Board comprises a Chairman and up to ten non-executive members appointed by the Secretary of State for Transport, and up to six executive members appointed by the Board.
Chairman, Sir Brian Kellett.
Vice-Chairman, R. Crawford.
Chief Executive, River, D. Jeffery.
Chief Executive, Property, J. C. Jenkinson, M.V.O.
Chief Executive Tilbury, J. S. McNab.
Secretary, G. E. Ennals.

THE POST OFFICE
33 Grosvenor Place, SW1X 1PX
[01–235 8000]

Crown services for the carriage of Government despatches were set up about 1516. The conveyance of public correspondence began in 1635 and the mail service was made a Parliamentary responsibility with the setting up of a Post Office in 1657. Telegraphs came under the Post Office control in 1870 and the Post Office Telephone Service began in 1880. The National Girobank service of the Post Office began in 1968. The Post Office ceased to be a Government Department on October 1, 1969 and responsibility for the running of the postal, telecommunications, and giro and remittance services was transferred to a public authority called the Post Office. The 1981 British Telecommunications Act separated the functions of the Post Office, making it solely responsible for postal services and Girobank. (The Government announced in 1988 that Girobank is to be privatized.)

The Chairman and members of the Post Office Board are appointed by the Secretary of State but responsibility for the running of the Post Office as a whole rests with the Board in its corporate capacity.

Financial Results

	1987–88 £m.	1988–89 £m.
Post Office Group		
Turnover	3,790·8	3,914·8
Trading profit before tax	212·2	169·7
Letters and Parcels		
Turnover	3,037·0	3,125·2
Trading profit before tax	151·3	107·9
Counters		
Turnover	769·2	798·4
Trading profit before tax	33·6	45·5
Girobank		
Income	190·9	234·2
Operating profit before tax . . .	23·5	21·6

Post Office Board

Chairman, Sir Bryan Nicholson.
Vice-Chairman and Member for Personnel and Corporate Resources, K. M. Young, C.B.E.
Members, W. Cockburn, C.B.E., T.D. (*Managing Director, Letters*); N. Nelson (*Managing Director, Parcels*); A. J. Roberts (*Managing Director, Counters*); R. Close (*Corporate Finance and Planning*); J. Baden.
Part-time Members, Miss E. M. L. Cole, C.B.E.; A. K. Gill; D. O. Gladwin, C.B.E.; D. Hodson.
Secretary, Miss M. MacDonald.

PRIVY COUNCIL OFFICE
Whitehall, SW1A 2AT
[01-270 3000]

The Office is responsible for the arrangements leading to the making of all Royal Proclamations and Orders in Council; for certain formalities connected with Ministerial changes; for considering applications for the grant (or amendment) of Royal Charters; the scrutiny and approval of bye-laws and statutes of Chartered Bodies; for the appointment of High Sheriffs and many Crown and Privy Council appointments to governing bodies.
Lord President of the Council (and Leader of the House of Commons), THE RT. HON. SIR GEOFFREY HOWE, Q.C., M.P.
Private Secretary, S. Catling.
Minister of State, THE RT. HON. RICHARD LUCE, M.P.
Clerk of the Council, G. I. de Deney, C.V.O. £42,900
Deputy Clerk of the Council, R. P. Bulling . . . £27,547
Senior Clerk, Miss J. Fairbairn £16,903

PUBLIC HEALTH LABORATORY SERVICE
61 Colindale Avenue, NW9 5DF
[01-200 1295]

The Public Health Laboratory Service comprises 52 regional or area laboratories distributed through England and Wales, the Central Public Health Laboratory and the Communicable Disease Surveillance Centre at Colindale, and the Centre for Applied Microbiology and Research, Porton Down. The P.H.L.S. gives a diagnostic microbiological service to hospitals, and provides reference facilities that are available nationally. It collates information on the incidence of infection, and when necessary it institutes special enquiries into outbreaks and the epidemiology of infectious disease. It also undertakes bacteriological surveillance of the quality of food and water for local authorities and others. The P.H.L.S.

is often called upon to advise central and local government and the hospital service on many aspects of infectious disease. It maintains close contact with veterinary organizations in areas of mutual interest, and collaborates with the World Health Organization and with national laboratory and epidemiological services overseas.

The Board

Chairman, Dr. M. P. W. Godfrey, C.B.E., F.R.C.P.
Members, D. F. R. Crofton; E. Doorbar; A. E. Eames; A. M. George; E. L. Harris, C.B., F.R.C.P.; P. Higham; Prof. Dame Rosalinde Hurley, D.B.E., M.D.; Prof. M. D. Lilly, Ph.D.; M. J. Painter; Prof. H. Smith, Ph.D., D.SC., F.R.S.; Prof. A. J. Zuckerman, D.SC., M.D., F.R.C.P.; J. Forsythe; N. E. Day, Ph.D.; J. Godfrey; A. Graham-Dixon; P. R. Grob, M.D.; H. H. John.
Staff Assessors, J. F. R. Graves; R. Gross; A. T. Willis.

Head Office
Colindale Avenue, NW9 5DF

Secretary, K. M. Saunders.
Deputy Secretary, J. M. Harker.
Director, J. W. G. Smith, M.D.
Deputy Directors, E. M. Cooke, M.D.; C. Roberts, M.D.

Central Public Health Laboratory
Colindale Avenue, NW9 5HT

Director, Dr. M. C. Timbury.
Division of Enteric Pathogens, B. Rowe, T.D.
Division of Hospital Infection, vacant.
Division of Microbiological Reagents and Quality Control, A. G. Taylor, Ph.D.
Food Hygiene Laboratory, R. J. Gilbert, Ph.D.
Hepatitis Epidemiology Unit (Division of Epidemiology), S. Polakoff, M.D.
Mycological Reference Laboratory, Prof. D. W. R. Mackenzie, Ph.D.
National Collection of Type Cultures, L. R. Hill, D.SC.
Virus Reference Laboratory, P. P. Mortimer, M.D.

Communicable Diseases Surveillance Centre
Colindale Avenue, NW9 5EQ

Director, Dr. C. L. R. Bartlett.

Centre for Applied Microbiology and Research
Porton Down, Salisbury, Wilts, SP4 0JG

Director, P. M. Sutton, M.D.
Director of Pathology Division, A. Baskerville, D.V.SC., Ph.D.
Director of Biologics Division, Prof. J. Melling, Ph.D.
Director of Biotechnology Division, Prof. A. Atkinson, Ph.D.

Other Special Laboratories and Units

Anaerobe Reference Unit, Public Health Laboratory, Luton.—A. T. Willis, M.D.
Gonococcus Reference Unit, Public Health Laboratory, Bristol.—A. E. Jephcott, M.D.
Leptospira Reference Unit, Public Health Laboratory, Hereford.—vacant.
Malaria Reference Laboratory, London School of Hygiene and Tropical Medicine, W.C.1.—Prof. D. J. Bradley, D.M.; Prof. W. Peters, M.D., D.SC.
Mycobacterium Reference Unit, Public Health Laboratory, Cardiff.—P. A. Jenkins, Ph.D.

Regional Laboratories

Birmingham, I. D. Farrell, M.D.; *Bristol*, A. E. Jephcott, M.D.; *Cambridge*, A. M. Rampling (*acting*);

Cardiff, C. D. Ribeiro (*acting*); *Leeds*, R. N. Peel; *Liverpool*, J. H. Pennington, M.D.; *Manchester*, D. M. Jones, M.D.; *Newcastle*, N. F. Lightson; *Oxford*, J. B. Selkon, T.D.; *Portsmouth*, O. A. Okubadejo, M.D.; *Sheffield*, P. Norman.

Area Laboratories

Ashford, C. Dulake; *Bath*, D. G. White; *Brighton*, B. T. Thom; *Carlisle*, M. A. Knowles; *Carmarthen*, H. D. S. Morgan; *Chelmsford*, R. E. Tettmar, D.Path.; *Chester*, P. Hunter; *Coventry*, P. R. Mortimer, M.D.; *Dorchester*, P. Burden; *Epsom*, S. A. Chambers; *Exeter*, J. G. Cruickshank; *Gloucester*, K. A. V. Cartwright; *Guildford*, Prof. R. Y. Cartwright; *Hereford*, I. R. Ferguson; *Hull*, S. L. Mawer; *Ipswich*, P. H. Jones; *Leicester*, C. J. Mitchell; *Lincoln*, J. G. Wallace; LONDON: *Central Middlesex Hospital*, D. A. McSwiggan; *Dulwich*, A. H. C. Uttley, Ph.D.; *Tooting*, R. Holliman (*acting*); *Whipps Cross*, B. Chattopadhyay, M.D.; *Luton*, A. T. Willis, M.D.; *Middlesbrough*, E. McKay-Ferguson, M.D.; *Norwich*, P. B. White; *Nottingham*, M. J. Lewis, M.D.; *Peterborough*, R. S. Jobanputra, M.D.; *Plymouth*, P. J. Wilkinson; *Poole*, W. L. Hooper; *Preston*, D. N. Hutchinson; *Reading*, J. V. Dadswell; *Rhyl*, D. N. Looker; *Salisbury*, S. Patrick; *Shrewsbury*, C. A. Morris, M.D.; *Southampton*, J. A. Lowes; *Stoke-on-Trent*, J. Gray; *Swansea*, D. H. M. Joynson; *Taunton*, J. V. S. Pether (*acting*); *Truro*, W. A. Telfer Brunton; *Watford*, M. T. Moulsdale; *Wolverhampton*, R. G. Thompson.

REGISTRAR OF PUBLIC LENDING RIGHT
Bayheath House, Prince Regent Street, Stockton-on-Tees, TS18 1DF
[0642–604699]

Under the Public Lending Right system, in operation since January 1983, payment is made from public funds to authors whose books are lent out from public libraries. Payment is made once a year (in February) and the amount each author receives is proportionate to the number of times (established from a sample) that each registered book was lent out during the previous year.

The Registrar of PLR, who is appointed by the Minister for the Arts, compiles the register of authors and books. Only living authors resident in the U.K. or West Germany are eligible to apply. (The term 'author' covers writers, illustrators, translators, and some editors/compilers.)

A payment of 1·45 pence was made in 1988–89 for each estimated loan of a registered book, up to a top limit of £6,000 for the books of any one registered author: the money for loans above this level is used to augment the remaining PLR payments.

In February 1989, the sum of £3,107,000 was made available for distribution to 13,211 registered authors and assignees as the sixth annual payment of PLR.

The PLR Advisory Committee advises the Minister for the Arts and the Registrar of Public Lending Right. Its members are appointed by the Minister.
Chairman of Advisory Committee, D. H. Whitaker.
Registrar, J. W. Sumsion.

PUBLIC RECORD OFFICE
See **Record Offices**

PUBLIC TRUST OFFICE
Stewart House, 24 Kingsway, WC2B 6JX
[01–269 7000]

The Public Trustee is a trust Corporation created to undertake the business of executorship and trusteeship; he can act as executor or administrator of the estate of a deceased person, or as trustee of a will or settlement. The Public Trustee is also responsible for the performance of all the administrative, but not the judicial, tasks required of the Court of Protection under Part VII of the Mental Health Act, 1983, relating to the management and administation of the property and affairs of persons suffering from mental disorder. The Public Trustee also acts as Receiver when so directed by the Court, usually where there is no other person willing or able so to act.

The Accountant General of the Supreme Court, through the Court Funds Office, is responsible for the investment and accounting of funds in court for persons under a disability, monies in Court subject to litigation and statutory deposits.

The Court Funds Office is at 22 Kingsway, WC2B 6LE (01-936 6000).

Public Trustee and Accountant General, J. A. Boland.
Assistant Public Trustee (Administration) and Deputy Accountant General, P. J. Farmer.
Assistant Public Trustee (Legal), H. N. Mather.

Client Services Sector

Head, E. J. Dober.
Receivership Division, R. A. Cunningham, T.D.
Protection Division, I. S. Price.

Internal Services Sector

Head, I. J. MacBean.
Court Funds Office, F. J. Eddy.
Investment Division, H. Stevenson.
Property, A. Nightingale.

PUBLIC WORKS LOAN BOARD
see **National Investment and Loans Office.**

COMMISSION FOR RACIAL EQUALITY
Elliot House, 10–12 Allington Street, SW1E 5EH
[01-828 7022]

Established on June 13, 1977, under the Race Relations Act 1976, to work towards elimination of discrimination and promote equality of opportunity and good relations between different racial groups generally.

Chairman, M. Day, O.B.E.
Deputy Chairman, Prof. B. Parekh.
Members, L. Crawford; Mrs. S. Sadeque; M. Skillicorn; K. R. Whitesides; Q. S. Anisuddin; Prof. B. Hepple; Mrs. E. Nam; D. A. C. Lambert; Dr. D. Ray; C. Lloyd; Mrs. B. Anderson; R. Singh.
Chief Executive, Dr. P. Sanders.

RECORD OFFICES, ETC.

THE PUBLIC RECORD OFFICE
Chancery Lane, WC2A 1LR
[01-876 3444]
Ruskin Avenue, Kew,
Richmond, Surrey TW9 4DU
[01-876 3444]

The Office, originally established in 1838 under the Master of the Rolls, was placed by the Public Records Act 1958 under the direction of the Lord Chancellor. He appoints a Keeper of Public Records, whose duties are to co-ordinate and supervise the selection of records of government departments and the English Law Courts for permanent preservation, to safeguard the records under his charge, and to make them available to the public.

The Office holds records of central government dating from *Domesday Book* (1086) to the present. Under the Public Records Act 1967 they are normally open to inspection when 30 years old, and are then available, without charge, in the reading rooms, Mon.–Fri., 9.30–5. The museum at Chancery Lane is open Mon.–Fri., 10–5.

Keeper of Public Records (G3), M. Roper.
Deputy Keeper (G5), C. D. Chalmers.
Records Administration Officer (G5), Dr. N. G. Cox.
Establishment Officer (G7), J. A. Keene.
Principal Assistant Keepers (G6), Mrs. J. M. Cox; N. E. Evans; Dr. A. A. H. Knightbridge; Mrs. A. E. Morton; Mrs. A. N. Nicol; Dr. J. B. Post; J. L. Walford.
Assistant Keepers (G7), Mrs. M. K. Banton; Miss G. L. Beech; Dr. A. S. Bevan; Dr. T. M. Chalmers; Miss M. M. Condon; C. R. H. Cooper; Miss A. Crawford; Dr. D. Crook; Dr. H. Forde; Dr. M. R. Foster; Dr. E. M. Hallam Smith; Ms. S. M. F. Healy; Dr. E. J. Higgs; Mrs. H. E. Jones; A. H. Lawes; A. J. McDonald; T. R. Padfield; Dr. N. A. M. Rodger; Dr. D. L. Thomas.
Head, Repository and Reprographic Services (G7), K. J. Smith.
Principal Inspecting Officer (G7), A. W. H. Medlicott.
Inspecting Officers (G7), D. Barlow; R. A. Blake; Miss C. J. Dimmer; J. S. Harley; F. McCall; Mrs. E. J. Baldwin; Mrs. M. A. Bull; C. J. Edwards; Mrs. H. R. Saw........................£14,549–£18,573
Head of Information Technology Unit (G7), Miss J. K. Lawlor.

ADVISORY COUNCIL ON PUBLIC RECORDS
Public Record Office, Chancery Lane, WC2A 1LR
[01-878 3666]

Council members are appointed by the Lord Chancellor, under the Public Records Act 1958, to advise him 'on matters concerning public records in general and, in particular, on those aspects of the work of the Public Record Office which affect members of the public who make use of the facilities provided by the Public Record Office'. The Council meets quarterly and produces an annual report which is published alongside the Report of the Keeper of Public Records as a House of Commons sessional paper.

Chairman, The Master of the Rolls.
Members, Prof. B. W. E. Alford; Miss S. Beesley; A. C. Carlile, Q.C., M.P.; Rt. Hon. Sir Frank Cooper, G.C.B., C.M.G.; Miss V. Cromwell; T. A. G. Davis, M.P.; A. Gomersall; J. S. W. Gibson; Prof. P. D. A. Harvey; M. A. Latham, M.P.; Prof. Shula Marks; Sir George Moseley, K.C.B.; Prof. H. Roseveare; Prof. W. Saunders; Prof. R. Skidelsky; D. G. Vaisey.
Assessors, M. D. Huebner; M. Roper.
Secretary, Dr. M. R. Foster.

HOUSE OF LORDS RECORD OFFICE
House of Lords, SW1A 0PW
[01-219 3074]

Since 1497, the records of Parliament have been kept within the Palace of Westminster. They are in the custody of the Clerk of the Parliaments, who in 1946 established a record department to supervise their preservation and their production to students. The Search Room of this office is open to the public Mon.–Fri., 9.30–5.

The records preserved number some 3,000,000 documents, and include Acts of Parliament from 1497, Journals of the House of Lords from 1510, Minutes and Committee proceedings from 1610, and Papers laid before Parliament from 1531. Amongst the records are the Petition of Right, the Death

Warrant of Charles I, the Declaration of Breda, and the Bill of Rights. The House of Lords Record Office also has charge of the Journals of the House of Commons (from 1547), and other surviving records of the Commons (from 1572), which include plans and annexed documents relating to Private Bill legislation from 1818. Among other documents are the records of the Lord Great Chamberlain, the political papers of certain members of the two Houses (including the papers of Lloyd George, Bonar Law and other statesmen previously preserved in the Beaverbrook Library), and documents relating to Parliament acquired on behalf of the nation. All the manuscripts and other records are preserved in the Victoria Tower of the Houses of Parliament. A permanent exhibition was established in the Royal Gallery in 1979.

Clerk of the Records, H. S. Cobb, F.S.A.
£29,920–£38,536
Deputy Clerk of the Records, D. J. Johnson, F.S.A.
£23,383–£34,576
Assistant Clerks of the Records, J. C. Morgan (*Sound Archives*); S. K. Ellison .... £19,110–£28,708

ROYAL COMMISSION ON HISTORICAL MANUSCRIPTS
Quality House, Quality Court, Chancery Lane, WC2A 1HP
[01–242 1198]

The Commission was set up by Royal Warrant in 1869 to enquire and report on collections of papers of value for the study of history in private hands. In 1959 a new warrant enlarged these terms of reference to include all historical records, wherever situated, outside the Public Records and gave it added responsibilities, as a central co-ordinating body, to promote, assist and advise on their proper preservation and storage. The Commission has published over 200 volumes of reports. It holds a further 32,000 unpublished reports in the National Register of Archives, available for consultation in its search room. It also administers the Manorial and Tithe Documents Rules on behalf of the Master of the Rolls.

Chairman, The Lord Blake, F.B.A.
Commissioners, The Lord Kenyon, C.B.E., F.S.A.; The Lord Fletcher, P.C., F.S.A.; J. P. W. Ehrman, F.B.A., F.S.A.; Prof. S. F. C. Milsom, F.B.A.; Sir John Habakkuk, F.B.A.; G. E. Aylmer, F.B.A.; P. T. Cormack, F.S.A., M.P.; H. M. Colvin, C.B.E., F.B.A., F.S.A.; Prof. G. W. S. Barrow, F.B.A.; Ms. V. L. Pearl, F.S.A.; The Marquess of Anglesey; Prof. Owen Chadwick, O.M., K.B.E., F.B.A.; D. G. Vaisey, F.S.A.; The Viscount of Arbuthnott, C.B.E., D.S.C.; The Lord Camoys; The Lord Egremont and Leconfield; Ms. J. Thirsk, F.B.A.
Secretary, B. S. Smith, F.S.A.

SCOTTISH RECORD OFFICE
H.M. General Register House, Edinburgh EH1 3YY
[031–556 6585]

The history of the national archives of Scotland can be traced back to the 13th century. The present headquarters of the Scottish Record Office, the General Register House, was founded in 1774. Here are preserved the administrative records of pre-Union Scotland, the registers of central and local courts of law, the public registers of property rights and legal documents, and many collections of local and church records and private archives. Certain groups of records, mainly the modern records of government departments in Scotland, the Scottish railway records, the plans collection, and private archives of an industrial or commercial nature are preserved in the branch repository at the West Register House in Charlotte Square. The Search

Rooms in both buildings open Mon.–Fri., 9–4.45. A permanent exhibition at the West Register House and changing exhibitions at the General Register House are open to the public on weekdays, 10–4. The National Register of Archives (Scotland), which is a branch of the Scottish Record Office, is based in the West Register House.
Keeper of the Records of Scotland, Dr. A. L. Murray.

CORPORATION OF LONDON RECORDS OFFICE
Guildhall, EC2P 2EJ
[01–260 1251]

Contains the municipal archives of the City of London which are regarded as the most complete collection of ancient municipal records in existence. Includes charters of William the Conqueror, Henry II, and later Kings and Queens to 1957; ancient custumals: Liber Horn, Dunthorne, Custumarum, Ordinacionum, Memorandorum and Albus, Liber de Antiquis Legibus, and collections of Statutes; continuous series of judicial rolls and books from 1252 and Council minutes from 1275; records of the Old Bailey and Guildhall Sessions from 1603, and financial records from the 16th century, together with the records of London Bridge from the 12th century and numerous subsidiary series and miscellanea of historical interest. A Guide was published in 1951. Readers' Room open Mon.–Fri., 9.30–4.45.
Keeper of the City Records, The Town Clerk.
City Archivist, J. R. Sewell.
Deputy City Archivist, Mrs. J. M. Bankes.

RED DEER COMMISSION
Knowsley, 82 Fairfield Road, Inverness IV3 5LH
[0463–231751]

Chairman, I. K. Mackenzie, O.B.E. £24,645
Secretary, N. H. McCulloch .... £13,318–£17,149

REVIEW BODIES

The secretariat for these bodies is provided by the Office of Manpower Economics (see page 339).

ARMED FORCES PAY

The Review Body on Armed Forces Pay was appointed in September 1971 to advise the Prime Minister on the pay and allowances of members of Naval, Military and Air Forces of the Crown and of any women's service administered by the Defence Council.

The members of the Review Body are: Sir Peter Cazalet (*Chairman*); P. Ball; D. P. M. Hudson; Mrs. J. Hughes; R. Sanderson, O.B.E.; Gen. Sir Richard Trant, K.C.B.; Prof. J. White, C.B.E.

DOCTORS' AND DENTISTS' REMUNERATION

The Review Body on Doctors' and Dentists' Remuneration was appointed in July 1971 to advise the Prime Minister on the remuneration of doctors and dentists taking any part in the National Health Service.

The members of the Review Body are: Sir Graham Wilkins (*Chairman*); Dr. Anne Hogg; D. G. Richards, C.B.E.; Prof. G. F. Thomason, C.B.E.; J. K. Warburton, C.B.E.

NURSING STAFF, MIDWIVES, HEALTH VISITORS AND PROFESSIONS ALLIED TO MEDICINE

The Review Body for nursing staff, midwives, health visitors and professions allied to medicine was set up in July 1983 to advise the Prime Minister on the remuneration of nursing staff, midwives and health visitors employed in the National Health Service; and physiotherapists, radiographers, remedial gymnasts, occupational therapists, orthoptists, chiropodists, dietitians and related grades employed in the National Health Service.

The members of the Review Body are: Sir James Cleminson, M.C. (*Chairman*); Sir John Herbecq, K.C.B. (*Deputy Chairman*); Mrs. M. Cameron; Miss B. Cooper, Q.C.; J. Hildreth; Miss A. Mackie, O.B.E.; I. H. Phillipps; Prof. G. F. Thomason, C.B.E.; Miss D. Whittingham.

TOP SALARIES

The Review Body on Top Salaries was appointed in May, 1971 to advise the Prime Minister on the remuneration of the higher judiciary and other judicial appointments; senior civil servants; and senior officers of the armed forces. Until August 1980 the remit also included the Chairmen and members of the Boards of nationalized industries. The Review Body has also been asked on a number of occasions to advise on the remuneration of Members of Parliament and of Ministers and on the level of parliamentary allowances.

The members of the Review Body are: Sir David Nickson, K.B.E. (*Chairman*); Sir Terence Beckett, K.B.E.; J. D. Birkin, T.D.; Ms. L. Botting; Sir Peter Cazalet; The Lord Chorley; H. S. Pigott; J. J. R. Pope, O.B.E.; Sir Thomas Skyrme, K.C.V.O., C.B., C.B.E., T.D.; Sir Anthony Wilson.

ROYAL BOTANIC GARDEN, EDINBURGH
Inverleith Row, Edinburgh EH3 5LR
[031–552 7171]

The Royal Botanic Garden Edinburgh, which originated as the Physic Garden established in 1670 beside the Palace of Holyroodhouse, became the direct responsibility of the Commissioners of Her Majesty's Works and Public Buildings (later the Department of Public Works) in 1889, transferring to the Department of Agriculture and Fisheries for Scotland in 1969. Since 1986, RBG Edinburgh has been administered by a Board of Trustees established under the National Heritage (Scotland) Act 1985.

RBG Edinburgh is an international centre for scientific research on plant diversity, maintaining collections of living plants and reference resources, including a herbarium of some 1.8 million specimens of preserved plants. Other statutory functions of RBG Edinburgh include provision of education and information on botany and horticulture, and the provision of public access to the living plant collections.

The Garden moved to its present site at Inverleith, Edinburgh in 1821. There are also three outstations of RBG Edinburgh: Younger Botanic Garden, Benmore, near Dunoon, Argyllshire; Logan Botanic Garden, near Stranraer, Wigtownshire; Dawyck Botanic Garden, near Stobo, Peeblesshire. Public opening hours: RBG Edinburgh – daily (except Dec. 25, Jan 1) 9 to sunset (1 hour earlier in summer) (Sun. 11 to sunset); outstations – April–Oct. 10–6.

Chairman of the Board of Trustees, Sir Peter Hutchison, Bt.
Regius Keeper, Prof. J. McNeill.
Assistant Keeper, vacant.

ROYAL BOTANIC GARDENS, KEW
Richmond, Surrey TW9 3AB
[01-940 1171]
Also at: Wakehurst Place, Ardingly, near Haywards Heath, West Sussex RH17 6TN
[0444–892701]

The Royal Botanic Gardens (RBG), Kew were founded in 1759 by H.R.H. Princess Augusta. In 1841, they became a public institution; in 1847, the Museums of Economic Botany were opened, and in 1852, the Herbarium and Library were established. The Jodrell Laboratory opened in 1876. In 1965, the garden at Wakehurst Place was acquired; it is owned by the National Trust and managed by RBG Kew. From 1903 to 1984, RBG Kew was part of the Ministry of Agriculture, Fisheries and Food. Under the National Heritage Act 1983, a Board of Trustees was set up to administer the Gardens which in 1984 became an independent body supported by a grant-in-aid.

The functions of RBG Kew are to carry out research into plant sciences, to disseminate knowledge about plants and to provide the public with the opportunity to gain knowledge and enjoyment from the Gardens' collections. There are extensive national reference collections of living and preserved plants and a comprehensive library and archive. The main emphasis is on tropical and subtropical plants.

Open daily, except Christmas Day and New Year's Day, from 9.30 a.m. The closing hour varies from 4 p.m. in mid-winter to 6.30 p.m. on week-days, and 8 p.m. on Sundays and Bank Holidays, in mid-summer. Admission, £1. Museums open 9.30 a.m.; Glasshouses, 9.30–4.30 (weekdays); to 5.30 p.m. (Sundays). No dogs except guide-dogs for the blind.

BOARD OF TRUSTEES

Chairman, Hon. J. D. Eccles, C.B.E.
Members, Sir Leslie Fowden, F.R.S.; Sir David Attenborough, C.B.E., F.R.S.; Prof. W. G. Chaloner, F.R.S.; Prof. E. C. D. Cocking, F.R.S.; Sir Philip M. Dowson, C.B.E.; Prof. G. E. Fogg, C.B.E.; R. A. E. Herbert; Mrs. A. Lennox-Boyd; P. J. D. Marshall; Prof. Elizabeth B. Robson, PH.D.; Cdr. L. M. Saunders Watson, R.N. (*ret*).
Director, Dr. G. T. Prance.

ROYAL COMMISSION FOR THE EXHIBITION OF 1851
Sherfield Building,
Imperial College of Science and Technology,
SW7 2AZ
[01–589 6483]

Incorporated by Supplemental Charter as a permanent Commission after winding up the affairs of the Great Exhibition of 1851. It has for its object the promotion of scientific and artistic education by means of funds derived from its Kensington Estate, purchased with the surplus left over from the Great Exhibition.

President, H.R.H. The Duke of Edinburgh, K.G., K.T., O.M., G.B.E., P.C.
Chairman, Board of Management, Sir Denis Rooke, C.B.E., F.R.S.
Secretary to Commissioners, M. C. Neale, C.B.

THE ROYAL MINT
Llantrisant, nr. Pontyclun,
Mid-Glamorgan CF7 8YT
[0443–222111]

Master Worker and Warden, The Chancellor of the Exchequer (*ex officio*).
Deputy Master and Comptroller, A. D. Garrett.

RURAL DEVELOPMENT COMMISSION
11 Cowley Street, SW1P 3NA
[01-276 6969]

The Rural Development Commission was formed in 1988 by the merger of the Development Commission for Rural England and the Council for Small Industries in Rural Areas. It is a statutory body funded by Government grant-in-aid which undertakes to alleviate economic and social problems in rural areas and advises the Government on related rural matters in England. It concentrates its resources in Rural Development Areas but some assistance is available both within and outside the RDAs.

Chairman, The Lord Vinson, L.V.O.
Other Commissioners, Mrs. P. Batty Shaw, C.B.E.; R. Best, O.B.E.; Prof. M. D. I. Chisholm; D. J. C. Davenport, C.B.E.; M. Schreiber; R. Thompson; A. Leavett; J. L. Thompson; G. P. Gray; M. B. Ferris; J. M. Galsworthy.
Chief Executive, R. Butt.

SCIENCE AND ENGINEERING RESEARCH COUNCIL
Polaris House, North Star Avenue,
Swindon, Wilts. SN2 1ET
[0793–411000]

The Science and Engineering Research Council (S.E.R.C.) is one of five research councils funded through the Department of Education and Science "to develop the natural and social sciences, including engineering, to maintain a fundamental capacity of research and scholarship and to support relevant postgraduate education". S.E.R.C.'s role is to encourage and support research and advanced training in U.K. universities and polytechnics in all the basic areas of science and engineering.

Chairman, Prof. E. W. J. Mitchell.
Members, Prof. Sir Michael Atiyah; Dr. R. F. Coleman; Prof. D. E. N. Davies; Prof. B. E. F. Fender; C. A. P. Foxell; Prof. C. J. Humphreys; Prof. M. A. Jeeves; Dr. C. Jordan; Dr. H. D. Law; D. Nash; Prof. E. R. Oxburgh; Prof. D. H. Perkins; Sir Charles Reece; D. T. Shore; Prof. J. M. Thomas; Prof. Sir Robert Wilson; Prof. A. Wolfendale.

SCOTTISH OFFICE
The Secretary of State for Scotland is responsible in Scotland for a wide range of statutory functions which in England and Wales are the responsibility of a number of departmental ministers. He also works closely with ministers in charge of Great Britain departments on topics of special significance to Scotland within their fields of responsibility. His statutory functions are administered by five main departments: Department of Agriculture and Fisheries for Scotland, Scottish Development Department, Scottish Education Department, Scottish Home and Health Department, and Industry Department for Scotland. These Departments (plus Central Services embracing the Solicitor's Office, the Scottish Information Office, Establishment, Liaison and Finance Divisions) are collectively known as the Scottish Office. In addition there are a number of other Scottish Departments for which the Secretary of State has some degree of responsibility: these include the Scottish Courts Administration, the Department of the Registrar General for Scotland (the General Register Office), the Scottish Record Office and the Department of the Registers of Scotland. The Secretary of State also bears Ministerial responsibility for the activities in Scotland of several statutory bodies whose functions extend throughout Great Britain such as the Training Agency and the Forestry Commission.
(For **Salaries**, *see* page 293)

Dover House, Whitehall, SW1A 2AU
[01–270 3000]

Secretary of State for Scotland, THE RT. HON. MALCOLM RIFKIND, Q.C., M.P.
Private Secretary (G5), D. J. Crawley
Assistant Private Secretaries, Miss U. M. Jamieson; L. Wright.
Ministers of State, IAN LANG, M.P. (*Industry, Local Government, and Education*); THE LORD SANDERSON OF BOWDEN (*Agriculture and Fisheries, Forestry, the Highlands and Islands, Tourism, and Rural Policy Co-ordination*).
Private Secretaries, D. C. Henderson (*I. Lang*); A. C. Maclaren (*Lord Sanderson of Bowden*).
Parliamentary Under Secretaries of State, LORD JAMES DOUGLAS–HAMILTON, M.P.; MICHAEL FORSYTH, M.P.*
Private Secretaries, Miss J. F. Waterman (*Lord James Douglas–Hamilton*); D. B. Binnie (*M. Forsyth*)*.
Parliamentary Clerk, I. D. Stage.
Permanent Under Secretary of State (G1), R. R. Hillhouse.
Private Secretary, R. M. Hay.
Liaison Staff:
Assistant Secretary (G5), E. W. Ferguson.
Principals (G7), I. A. Sneddon; A. C. King; E. B. Miller.

St. Andrew's House,
Edinburgh EH1 3DG
[031–556 8400]

MANAGEMENT GROUP SUPPORT STAFF
Principal (G7), G. S. Pearson.

CENTRAL SERVICES
Deputy Secretary (Central Services) (G2), I. D. Penman, C.B..

Establishment Division
16 Waterloo Place Edinburgh, EH1 3DN
[031–556 8400]

Principal Establishment Officer (G3), A. H. Bishop, C.B.
Assistant Secretaries (G5), D. J. Chalmers; G. N. Munro.
Senior Principals (G6), A. B. Fairweather, T.D.; I. C. Henderson; A. Stephenson; R. Tait.
Principals (G7), W. E. Bennet; D. A. Christie; J. H. F. Finnie; J. R. M. Flucker; C. D. Henderson; T. R. Macdonald; A. McNaughton; D. Murie; G. R. Pearson; Mrs. C. Peden; R. J. Walker.

Directorate of Information Technology
Broomhouse Drive, Edinburgh EH11 3XD
[031–556 8400]

Computer Services
Director (G5), J. Duffy.
Deputy Director (G6), I. W. Goodwin.
Principals (G7), W. Ferguson; A. R. McCowan; B. U. Pearson.

Telecommunications
St. Andrew's House, Edinburgh EH1 3DE
(031–556 8400)

Director (G6), A. F. Harrison.

---

*Based at New St. Andrew's House.

Finance Division
New St. Andrew's House, Edinburgh EH1 3SX
[031–556 8400]

Finance Group
Principal Finance Officer (G3), H. H. Mills.
Assistant Secretaries (G5), T. A. Cameron; T. E. McGreevy; A. J. Rushworth; A. M. Russell; W. T. Tait.
Principals (G7), E. G. J. Bee; D. I. Dalgetty; S. W. E. Davidson; D. A. Howe; T. Hunter; N. D. Ingrams; D. K. C. Jeffrey; W. A. Lamberton; I. A. McLeod; J. F. A. McMillan; D. R. Mayer; R. E. Merrall; G. S. Pearson; J. Porter; G. S. Smith; I. M. Smith.

Local Government Finance Group
Assistant Secretaries (G5), C. M. Baxter; G. Robson.
Principals (G6), M. T. Affolter; I. D. Bald; M. T. S. Batho; D. J. Christie; I. Melville.

Solicitor's Office
(For the Scottish Departments and certain U.K. services, including H.M. Treasury, in Scotland.)
Solicitor (G2), R. Brodie.
Deputy Solicitor (G3), N. W. Boe.
Divisional Solicitors (G5), J. B. Allan; †K. F. Barclay; G. C. Duke; R. M. Henderson; G. Jackson; J. L. Jamieson; †Mrs. L. A. Lilliker; H. F. Macdiarmid; T. G. Walters.
†Seconded to Scottish Law Commission

Scottish Information Office
(For the Scottish Departments and certain U.K. services)
Director (G5), C. F. Corbett.
Deputy Director (G6), D. C. M. Beveridge.

Statistics
Chief Statistician (G5), Dr. J. R. Cuthbert.

DEPARTMENT OF AGRICULTURE AND FISHERIES FOR SCOTLAND
Pentland House, 47 Robb's Loan, Edinburgh EH14 1TW
[031–556 8400]

Dover House, Whitehall, London, SW1A 2AU
[01–270 3000]

Secretary (G2), L. P. Hamilton, C.B.
Under Secretary (G3), D. J. Essery.
Fisheries Secretary (G3), W. A. P. Weatherston.
Assistant Secretaries (G5), R. S. B. Gordan; T. J. Kelly; L. V. McEwan; W. Moyes; J. A. Rennie; N. E. Sharp; G. M. D. Thomson; E. J. Weeple; I. M. Whitelaw.
Principals (G7), Ms. M. M. Arthur; D. H. Brown; J. G. Donnelly; J. H. B. Fleming, T.D.; A. W. Gladwin; R. A. Grant; A. Johnston; N. J. H. Kernohan; B. E. McAdam; I. F. McEwan; W. Malcolm; W. R. J. McQueen; B. Naylor; Miss J. Polley; J. Reid, M.B.E., W. B. Ritchie; A. B. Scott; Mrs. J. Scott; I. R. N. Stewart; N. A. Stewart; R. S. Stewart; T. A. Titterton.
Chief Agricultural Officer (G4), J. F. Hutcheson.
Deputy Chief Agricultural Officer (G5), W. A. Macgregor.
Assistant Chief Agricultural Officers (G6), D. R. J. Craven; J. A. Hardie; J. G. Muir; A. Robb; J. I. Woodrow.
Chief Agricultural Economist (G6), J. M. Dunn, D.Phil.
Chief Meat and Livestock Inspector (G7), J. Miller.
Chief Food and Dairy Officer (G7), M. E. M. Anderson.
Chief Surveyor (G6) N. Taylor.
Scientific Adviser (G5) A. M. Raven, Ph.D.
Senior Principal Scientific Officers (G6), R. J. Dowdell, Ph.D.; T. W. Hegarty, Ph.D.; D. Thornton.

Agricultural Scientific Services
East Craigs, Edinburgh EH12 8NJ
[031–556 8400]

Director (G5), D. C. Graham, Ph.D., F.R.S.E.
Deputy Director (G6), J. R. Cutler.
Senior Principal Scientific Officers (G6), J. L. Keppie; M. J. Richardson.

Fisheries Research Services
Marine Laboratory, P.O. Box 101,
Victoria Road, Torry, Aberdeen AB9 8DB
[0224–876544]

Director and Co-ordinator of Fisheries Research and Development, Prof. A. D. Hawkins, Ph.D
Deputy Director (G5), D. N. MacLennan.
Senior Principal Scientific Officers (G6), R. M. Cook, Ph.D.; J. M. Davies, Ph.D.; A. L. S. Munro, Ph.D.; P. A. M. Stewart, Ph.D.; C. S. Wardle, Ph.D.

Freshwater Fisheries Laboratory,
Faskally, Pitlochry, Perthshire PH16 5LB
[0796–2060]

Senior Principal Scientific Officers (G6), R. G. J. Shelton, Ph.D.; J. E. Thorpe, Ph.D.

Sea Fisheries Inspectorate
Chief Inspector of Sea Fisheries (G6), J. F. Fenton.
Inspector of Salmon and Freshwater Fisheries for Scotland (G7), R. B. Williamson.
Marine Superintendent, Capt. R. M. Mill Irving.

SCOTTISH DEVELOPMENT DEPARTMENT
St. Andrew's House, Edinburgh EH1 3DG
[031–556 8400]
Dover House, Whitehall, London, SW1A 2AU
[01–270 3000]

Secretary and Chief Economic Adviser (G2), Dr. R. C. L. McCrone, C.B., F.R.S.E.
Under Secretaries (G3), J. F. Laing; Miss E. A. MacKay.*
Director, Historic Buildings and Monuments, D. Connelly.
Assistant Secretaries (G5), Ms. L. Clare; R. S. Crofts; J. S. Graham; Mrs. M. B. Gunn; C. C. Macdonald; J. S. B. Martin; K. W. Moore; J. N. Randall; R. E. S. Robinson; Mrs. G. M. Stewart.
Principals (G7), J. S. Aldridge; I. R. Anderson; A. G. Beattie; D. S. Chalmers; I. G. Dewar; P. G. Drumm; M. A. Duffy; W. M. Giles; J. C. Halley; J. L. Helm; J. C. Henderson; I. W. Jardine; I. P. Hetherington; W. A. Howat; J. C. Judson; R. Levett; B. J. Lincoln; I. J. MacKenzie; Mrs. D. Mellon; Mrs. J. Niven; G. Paul; J. B. Rodden; P. D. Stephenson; J. Symington; Miss T. S. Teale; T. Tumilty; J. O. Wastle.

Professional Staff
Chief Engineer (G3), R. MacGillivray.
Deputy Chief Engineer (G5), A. C. Paton.
Assistant Chief Engineers (G6), T. Bolton; T. D. Macdonald; N. G. Semple.
Director of Building and Chief Architect (G3), J. E. Gibbons, Ph.D.
Deputy Director of Building and Deputy Chief Architect (G5), M. R. Miller.
Deputy Director of Building and Chief Quantity Surveyor (G5), D. C. Russell.
Deputy Director (G5), T. Birley.
Assistant Director and Deputy Chief Quantity Surveyor (G6), A. Duncan, O.B.E.
Assistant Directors (G6), G. Gray; H. R. McCallum.
Chief Planner (G3), A. Mackenzie.
Deputy Chief Planner (G5), D. R. Dare.
Assistant Chief Planners (G6), T. Williamson; A. W. Denham; I. R. Duncan; S. G. Fulton.
Chief Research Officer (G5), Dr. C. P. A. Levein.

*Based at New St. Andrew's House.

Senior Principal Research Officer (*G6*), C. L. Wood.
Chief Road Engineer (*G3*), J. A. L. Dawson.
Deputy Chief Engineer (Roads) (*G5*), G. S. Marshall.
Deputy Chief Engineer (Bridges) (*G5*), J. Innes.
Assistant Chief Engineers (*G6*), J. Patience; R. D. Udall; J. A. Howison.
H.M. Chief Industrial Pollution Inspector (*G5*), I. W. W. Wright.
Chief Estates Officer (*G6*), R. I. K. White.
Principal Inspector of Ancient Monuments for Scotland, I. MacIvor.
Principal Inspector of Historic Buildings, D. M. Walker.

Inquiry Reporters
16 Waterloo Place, Edinburgh EH1 3DN
[031–556 8400]

Chief Reporter (*G3*), A. G. Bell.
Deputy Chief Reporter (*G5*), W. D. Campbell.

INDUSTRY DEPARTMENT FOR SCOTLAND
New St. Andrew's House, Edinburgh EH1 3TA
[031–556 8400]
and
Dover House, Whitehall, SW1A 2AU
[01–270 3000]

Secretary (*G2*), J. A. Scott, C.B., L.V.O.
Under Secretaries (*G3*), A. D. F. Findlay; W. W. Scott.
Assistant Secretaries (*G5*), P. A. Brady; G. D. Calder; D. A. Campbell; J. D. Gallagher; Ms. S. Haird; Miss I. M. Low; D. N. G. Reid; Mrs. A. Robson.
Senior Economic Advisers (*G5*), J. A. Peat; W. M. McNie.
Principals (*G7*), J. A. Brown; C. H. Coulthard; M. J. Lowndes; J. Lugton; R. N. Irvine; A. McKean; A. K. MacLeod; N. MacLeod; B. R. Morgan; D. A. Stewart; M. R. Wilson.

Industrial Expansion
Alhambra House, 45 Waterloo Street, Glasgow
G2 6AT
[041–248 2855]

Under Secretary (*G3*), H. Morison.
Industrial Adviser, Dr. C. K. Benington.
Assistant Secretaries (*G5*), A. W. Fraser; S. F. Hampson.
Senior Principal (*G6*), J. McGhee.
Principals (*G7*), D. A. Brew; D. J. Fowles; D. M. McFadyen; A. H. Meldrum; Ms. J. E. Morgan.

Locate in Scotland
120 Bothwell Street, Glasgow G2 7JP
[041–248 2700]

Director, E. Frizzell.
Senior Principal (*G6*), W. Malone.
Principal (*G7*), R. Whyte.
R. Crawford (*U.S.A.*)

SCOTTISH EDUCATION DEPARTMENT
New St. Andrew's House,
Edinburgh EH1 3SY
[031–556 8400]
and
Dover House, Whitehall, London, SW1A 2AU
[01–270 3000]

Secretary (*G2*), G. R. Wilson.
Under Secretaries (*G3*), N. G. Campbell; P. MacKay, H. Robertson, M.B.E.
Assistant Secretaries (*G5*), D. A. Bennett; M. J. P. Cunliffe; E. C. Davison; M. Ewart; I. W. Gordon; J. W. L. Lonie; Miss M. MacLean; K. Macrae; E. C. Reavley; D. Salmond, Ph.D. (*Chief Statistician*); J. W. Sinclair; D. Wishart.
Senior Principal (*G6*), G. E. Brewerton.

Principals (*G7*), N. Atkinson; T. Blacklock; Mrs. M. Brannan; J. R. Brown; D. G. Campbell; W. Davidson; A. G. Dickson; M. Ewart; C. C. Forsyth; M. J. Hunter; J. Kirby; Mrs. E. Lewis; A. Lindsey; J. B. Lyall; G. A. McHugh; T. D. K. Meikle; Mrs. A. N. Menlowe; B. J. O'Connor; R. I. Perrett; D. R. Semple; B. W. Sharry; A. J. Stewart; D. Stewart; B. V. Surridge; I. M. Watt; G. P. Walker; R. Walker; A. W. Wallace.

H.M. Inspectors of Schools
Senior Chief Inspector (*G3*), T. N. Gallacher.
Deputy Senior Chief Inspectors (*G4*), D. W. Mack; S. E. McCelland, Ph.D.
Chief Inspectors (*G5*), W. T. Beveridge; W. F. L. Bigwood; J. P. Donaldson; G. P. D. Gordon; J. Howgego; J. J. McDonald; A. S. McGlynn; D. A. Osler; A. M. Rankin; D. B. Young.
Inspectors (*G6*), J. N. Alison; M. T. J. Axford; P. Banks; Mrs. W. Binnie; A. D. Blair; J. Boyes; Miss C. L. Boyle; M. J. Brown; Mrs. M. M. Browning; J. W. Burdin; D. C. Burgess; Miss G. C. Campbell; T. N. Carr; M. Q. Cramb; F. Crawford; A. H. B. Davidson; G. A. Dell; R. F. Dick; J. C. Dignan; G. H. C. Donaldson; D. W. Duncan; Miss K. M. Fairweather; B. Fryer; A. R. Gallon; K. G. Gavin; W. Geddes; A. B. Giovanazzi; G. D. Gray, Ph.D.; T. O. Greig; R. A. Hawke; K. A. Hope; L. A. Hunter; M. Jack; J. Jackson, Ph.D.; E. S. Kelly; D. E. Kelso; Ms. A. Kennedy; D. G. Kirkpatrick; I. Lawson; R. E. Lygo; M. McAllan; I. M. MacAskill; L. McCallum; H. K. McCorkindale; Mrs. M. A. Macfarlane; Ms. I. S. McGregor; H. M. MacLaren; C. R. MacLean; M. Macleod; A. J. Macpherson; A. Maltby; R. H. Manser; A. F. Marquis; H. L. Martin; G. Mathison; W. M. Mein; Mrs. J. M. Millar; A. Milne; J. Mitchell; Miss E. R. Mowat; R. H. Nelson; B. Nickerson, Ph.D.; I. P. Pascoe; W. M. Patterson; N. A. Pepin; J. Picken; R. B. Prescott; T. A. Rankin; S. A. Ritchie; W. M. Roach, Ph.D.; I. D. S. Robertson; Mrs. M. A. Robertson; A. L. Robson; M. Roebuck; I. S. Rowley; D. M. Russell; A. L. Small; E. P. Spencer; H. M. Stalker; A. M. Steele; W. Stevenson; A. Stewart; Mrs. J. A. Stewart; W. P. Stewart; T. Straiton, Ph.D.; J. W. Thomson; R. M. S. Tuck; R. S. Weir; Miss G. A. White; J. G. L. Wright; R. W. J. Young, Ph.D.

Social Work Services Group
43 Jeffrey Street, Edinburgh EH1 1DN
[031–556 8400]

The Social Work Services Group, which is attached to the Scottish Education Department, administers the provisions of the Social Work (Scotland) Act, 1968.
Under Secretary (*G3*), N. G. Campbell.
Assistant Secretaries (*G5*), D. A. Bennet; M. J. P. Cunliffe; J. W. Sinclair.
Principals (*G7*), J. R. Brown; M. J. Hunter; A. Lindsey; G. A. McHugh; D. Meikle; D. R. Semple; D. Stewart; R. Walker.
Chief Social Work Adviser, D. Colvin.
Senior Advisers, Ms. M. L. Hunt; F. A. O'Leary; I. C. Robertson; A. R. Sabine; J. I. Smith.

SCOTTISH HOME AND HEALTH DEPARTMENT
St. Andrew's House,
Edinburgh EH1 3DE
[031–556 8400]
Dover House, Whitehall, London, SW1A 2AU
[01–270 3000]

Secretary (*G2*), W. K. Reid, C.B.
Under Secretaries (*G3*), D. Belfall; J. E. Fraser; J. Hamill; K. J. MacKenzie.
Assistant Secretaries (*G5*), G. P. H. Aitken, T.D.; G. A.

Anderson; J. W. Barron; A. M. Burnside; W. J. Fearnley; I. G. F. Graft; J. W. H. Irvine; R. D. Jackson; C. M. A. Lugton; K. W. McKay; D. Macniven, T.D.; A. J. Matheson; Mrs. N. S. Munro; F. H. Orr; P. M. Russell; R. H. Scott; D. Stevenson.

Senior Principal (G6), vacant.

Principals (G7), A. G. Aitken; S. S. Anderson; J. Ballantyne; Mrs. E. E. R. Barnwell; J. Black; H. W. Bradford; D. H. Brown; J. T. Brown; L. C. Cunning; W. Davidson; D. H. F. Dee; Miss W. M. Doonan; L. P. S. Dunbar; Dr. N. Fojut; I. R. L. Gibson; J. Gilmour; Miss A. E. Hamilton; N. Harvey; D. M. Henderson; F. H. Hunter; S. M. Liddle; R. S. T. MacEwen; E. M. C. MacKay; H. M. MacKenzie; P. McLaren; D. C. Macnab; Mrs. V. M. Macniven; Miss M. M. Marshall; Mrs. C. M. Morgan; C. Naldrett; Mrs. J. Niven; D. J. Palmer; R. Patton; C. M. Reeves; D. A. Robertson; W. F. Robertson; D. M. Rowand; A. Simmen, O.B.E.; M. P. Sivell; I. A. Sneddon; T. Spence; D. Stephen; I. C. Stewart; R. Tait; B. F. Warren; A. G. Young.

Medical Services

Chief Medical Officer (G2), K. C. Calman.
Deputy Chief Medical Officer (G3), G. A. Scott.
Principal Medical Officers, J. V. Basson; G. Gilray; Margaret Hennigan; A. D. McIntyre; A. Rourke; A. B. Young.
Senior Medical Officers, R. E. G. Aitken, T.D.; P. W. Brooks; W. Dodd; D. C. Drummond; C. F. Fleming; G. I. Forbes; W. M. Gilmour; Dr. Margaret Halley; D. W. Sinclair; R. D. Skinner, Dr. Elizabeth Sowler; O. A. Thores; A. H. Watt.
Senior Regional Medical Officers, I. G. Conn; H. McBain.
Regional Medical Officers, I. Arthurson; P. I. Brown; Elspeth C. Carrick; T. E. S. Fergusson; G. W. G. Hunter; K. Inglis; G. McKay; A. S. Mackenzie; E. M. Melville; P. I. T. Walker.
Chief Scientist, Prof. R. D. Weir, O.B.E.
Chief Dental Officer, N. K. Colquhoun.
Deputy Chief Dental Officer, J. R. Wild.
Regional Dental Officers, Miss A. J. Power; G. A. Reid.
Chief Nursing Officer, Mrs. Y. Moores.
Chief Pharmacist (G6), G. Calder.

Miscellaneous Appointments

H.M. Chief Inspector of Constabulary, R. Sim, C.B.E., Q.P.M.
H.M. Chief Inspector of Prisons, T. B. Buyers, O.B.E.
Commandant, Scottish Police College, T. J. Whitson, O.B.E.
H.M. Chief Inspector of Fire Services, R. J. Knowlton, C.B.E., Q.F.S.M.
Commandant, Scottish Fire Service Training School, C. F. McManus, Q.F.S.M.
Secretary, Scottish Health Service Planning Council, W. J. Farquhar.

Prisons Group
Colton House, 5 Redheughs Rigg, Edinburgh EH12 9HW
[031–556 8400]

Director of Scottish Prison Service, P. McKinley.
Assistant Secretary, Deputy Director (Administration), F. H. Orr.
Assistant Controller, Deputy Director (Operations), W. McVey.
Deputy Director (Personnel) (G5), W. J. Fearnley.
Deputy Director (Regime Services and Supplies) (G6), T. Collinson.
Deputy Director (Co-ordinator), J. W. H. Irvine.

Prison Governors

Governor I £31,542*
Governor II £32,751

Governor III £28,158
*under review.

Aberdeen (III), L. C. McBain.
Barlinnie (I), A. R. Walker.
Barlinnie Special Unit (III), D. E. Gunn.
Castle Huntly Young Offenders Institution (III), E. J. Brownsmith.
Cornton Vale (II), A. Thomson.
Dumfries Young Offenders Institution (III), R. B. Carrick (acting).
Dungavel, Strathaven (III), W. G. McKinlay.
Edinburgh (I), J. Pearce.
Friarton Young Offenders Institution, J. A. Harker.
Glenochil Prison and Young Offenders Institution (I), R. A. Milne (acting).
Greenock (III), I. A. Bannatyne.
Inverness (III), W. G. Hewitson.
Longriggend Remand Institution (III), R. L. Houchim.
Low Moss (III), E. J. Campbell.
Noranside (III), J. C. Stuart.
Penninghame (IV), Mrs. M. Wood.
Perth (II), R. Kite.
Peterhead (I), A. G. Coyle.
Polmont Young Offenders Institution (II), G. R. Bond (acting).
Shotts (II), P. L. Abernethy.
Scottish Prison Service College (II), M. J. Milne.

Mental Welfare Commission for Scotland
25 Drumsheugh Gardens, Edinburgh EH3 7NS
[031–225 7034]

Chairman, P. C. Millar, O.B.E.
Commissioners, P. H. Brodie; Prof. T. D. Campbell; R. G. Davis; Dr. L. Dunbar; A. Findlay, M.B.E.; Mrs. A. M. Glen; Ms. A. M. Green; D. A. Macdonald, O.B.E.; Mrs. H. S. Mein; Dr. A. N. Munro; M. O'Reilly; Prof. P. Prophit; Mrs. A. J. Ritchie; J. G. Sutherland.
Medical Commissioners, W. Boyd; A. A. McKechnie.
Social Work Commissioner, J. H. L. Richards.
Secretary, D. Wishart.

Counsel to the Secretary of State for Scotland under the Private Legislation Procedure (Scotland) Act, 1936 (50 Frederick Street, Edinburgh.—(031–226 6499)).
Senior Counsel, G. S. Douglas, Q.C.
Junior Counsel, N. M. P. Morrison.

NATIONAL HEALTH SERVICE, SCOTLAND

Health Boards

Argyll and Clyde, Gilmour House, Paisley. *Chairman*, J. D. Ryan, C.B.E. *General Manager*, I. C. Smith.

Ayrshire and Arran, P.O. Box 13, Hunters Avenue, Ayr. *Chairman*, W. S. Fyfe, O.B.E. *General Manager*, J. M. Eckford.

Borders, Huntlyburn, Melrose, Roxburghshire. *Chairman*, Dr. D. H. Pringle, C.B.E. *General Manager*, D. A. Peters.

Dumfries and Galloway, Nithbank, Dumfries. *Chairman*, J. A. M. McIntyre, O.B.E.. *General Manager*, M. D. Cook.

Fife, Glenrothes House, North Street, Glenrothes. *Chairman*, Mrs. P. A. H. Ferguson. *General Manager*, Col. F. F. Gibb.

Forth Valley, 33 Spittal Street, Stirling. *Chairman*, Mrs. J. D. Isbister. *General Manager*, A. R. Robertson.

Grampian, 1–7 Albyn Place, Aberdeen. *Chairman,* J. Kyle, C.B.E. *General Manager,* H. Fullerton.

Greater Glasgow, The Royal Beatson Memorial Hospital, 132 Hill Street, Glasgow. *Chairman,* Dr. T. J. Thomson, C.B.E. *General Manager,* L. Peterken.

Highland, Reay House, 17 Old Edinburgh Road, Inverness. *Chairman,* J. McWilliam, O.B.E. *General Manager,* R. R. W. Stewart.

Lanarkshire, 14 Beckford Street, Hamilton, Lanarkshire. *Chairman,* Mrs. B. M. Gunn, O.B.E. *General Manager,* F. Clark.

Lothian, 11 Drumsheugh Gardens, Edinburgh. *Chairman,* R. B. Weatherstone, T.D. *General Manager,* W. J. Taylor.

Orkney, Balfour Hospital, New Scapa Road, Kirkwall, Orkney. *Chairman,* J. D. M. Robertson, O.B.E. *General Manager,* Dr. J. I. Cromarty.

Shetland, 28 Burgh Road, Lerwick. *Chairman,* Mrs. F. Grains. *General Manager,* D. C. March.

Tayside, P.O. Box 75, Vernonholme, Riverside Drive, Dundee. *Chairman,* D. B. Grant, C.B.E., T.D. *General Manager,* Dr. R. C. Graham.

Western Isles, 37 South Beach Street, Stornoway, Isle of Lewis. *Chairman,* Mrs. M. A. MacMillan. *General Manager,* J. J. Glover.

Common Services Agency
Trinity Park House, South Trinity Road, Edinburgh EH5 3SE

Chairman, D. F. Macquaker.
General Manager, J. T. Donald.

GENERAL REGISTER OFFICE (Scotland)
New Register House, Edinburgh EH1 3YT
[031–556 3952]

Registrar General (G4), Dr. C. M. Glennie.
Deputy Registrar General (G5), B. V. Philp.
Senior Principal (G6), D. A. Orr.
Principals (G7), I. G. Bowie; R. C. Lawson; D. M. Robertson.
Statisticians (G7), J. Arrundale; G. W. L. Jackson; F. G. Thomas.

SEA FISH INDUSTRY AUTHORITY
Sea Fisheries House, 10 Young Street, Edinburgh EH2 4JQ
[031–225 2515]

Chairman, B. Davies.
Chief Executive, C. H. Davies.
Deputy Chief Executive, P. D. Chaplin.
Administration and Finance Director, R. A. Davie.
Technical Director, A. G. Hopper.
Marketing Director, R. M. Kennedy.
Training Director, K. Waind.

SECURITIES AND INVESTMENTS BOARD
3 Royal Exchange Buildings, EC3V 3NL
[01–283 2474]
[*Central register of authorized firms:* 01–929 3652]

The Securities and Investments Board was formed in 1985 and is the designated agency, under the Financial Services Act 1986, to regulate the activities of investment businesses in the U.K. Although not a statutory body, the Board has transferred powers under the 1986 Act to recognize self-regulating organizations, professional bodies, investment exchanges and clearing houses, and directly to authorize firms to do investment business in the U.K. The Board also has the power to act as a prosecution authority in respect of persons carrying out authorizable business whilst unauthorized.

Members of the Board are appointed by agreement between the Secretary of State for Trade and Industry and the Governor of the Bank of England. The Chairman and Executive Directors are full-time Board members; the others are part-time and non-executive.

The Board

Chairman, D. A. Walker.
Deputy Chairmen, Sir Mark Weinberg; R. N. Quartano, C.B.E.
Members (part-time), A. V. Alexander, C.B.E.; D. M. Child, C.B.E.; J. Clement; R. G. Hodgson; P. J. Manser; W. Proudfoot; E. E. Ray, C.B.E.; G. Ross Russell; The Hon. W. G. Runciman, C.B.E.; Mrs R. Waterhouse, C.B.E.; R. B. Williamson, C.B.E.
Executive Directors, R. H. F. Croft, C.B.; D. E. Fellows.

Management

The Chairman.
The Executive Directors.
Directors of Divisions:
　Authorization, Compliance and Enforcement, J. D. Orme.
　Finance, R. P. A. Purcell.
　Financial Regulation, A. J. Thrall.
　Futures and Options, M. B. Gittins.
　Information Services, B. W. Smith.
　Intermediaries, A. Selman.
　International Securities, R. J. Britton.
　Investment Management, C. Bowe.
　Legal Services, M. C. Blair.
　Public Affairs, C. Bowe.
Deputy Directors:
　Authorization, Compliance and Enforcement, R. L. Devlin; J. M. Thomas.
　Futures and Options, P.E. Thompson.
　Intermediaries, R. B. Ferguson.
　International Securities, vacant.
　Investment Management, J. Hickman; M. Borland.
　Legal Services, A. Whittaker; J. Welch.
　Personnel and Administration, J. L. Clark.
　Secretary to the Board, T. E. Allen.
　Special Adviser, P. Jackson.

Recognized Bodies
(as at July 1, 1989)

Self-regulating Organizations

The Association of Futures Brokers and Dealers Ltd. (A.F.B.D.).
The Financial Intermediaries, Managers and Brokers Regulatory Association Ltd. (F.I.M.B.R.A.).
*The Investment Management Regulatory Organization Ltd. (I.M.R.O.).
*The Life Assurance and Unit Trust Regulatory Organization Ltd. (L.A.U.T.R.O.).
The Securities Association Ltd. (T.S.A.).
*These two bodies are also recognized self-regulating organizations for friendly societies.

International Securities Self-regulating Organization
(recognized by D.T.I.)

The Association of International Bond Dealers (A.I.B.D.)

Recognized Investment Exchanges

U.K. Exchanges
The Baltic Futures Exchange (B.F.E.).

The International Petroleum Exchange of London Ltd. (I.P.E.).

The International Stock Exchange of Great Britain and the Republic of Ireland Ltd. (I.S.E.).

The London Commodity Exchange (1986) Ltd. (London FOX).

The London International Financial Futures Exchange Ltd. (L.I.F.F.E.).

LIFFE Options P.L.C.

The London Metal Exchange Ltd. (L.M.E.).

Overseas Exchanges (recognized by the Secretary of State for Trade and Industry)

The National Association of Securities Dealers Automated Quotations System.

Sydney Futures Exchange Ltd.

Recognized Professional Bodies

The Institute of Chartered Accountants in England and Wales.

The Institute of Chartered Accountants of Scotland.

The Institute of Chartered Accountants in Ireland.

The Chartered Association of Certified Accountants.

The Institute of Actuaries.

The Insurance Brokers Registration Council.

The Law Society of England and Wales.

The Law Society of Scotland.

The Law Society of Northern Ireland.

Recognized Clearing Houses

International Commodities Clearing House Ltd. (I.C.C.H.).

GAFTA Clearing House Company Ltd.

SERIOUS FRAUD OFFICE
Elm House, 10–16 Elm Street, WC1X 0BJ
[01–833 1616]

The Serious Fraud Office is an independent department under the superintendence of the Attorney General. Its remit is to investigate and prosecute serious and complex fraud. The scope of its powers covers England, Wales and Northern Ireland. The staff includes lawyers, accountants and other support staff, and investigating teams work closely with the police.

Director (G2), J. Wood, C.B.
Deputy Director (G3), M. Chance.
Chief Accountant (G3), J. Knox.

DEPARTMENT OF SOCIAL SECURITY
Richmond House, 79 Whitehall, SW1A 2NS
[01-210 3000]

The Department was formed in July 1988 by the division of the Department of Health and Social Security into two separate departments. The Department of Social Security is responsible for the social security services in England, Wales and Scotland.

(For **Salaries,** *see* page 293)

Secretary of State for Social Security, THE RT. HON. ANTONY NEWTON, O.B.E., M.P.
  Private Secretary, J. S. Lord.
Minister of State, RT. HON. NICHOLAS SCOTT, M.B.E., M.P.
  Private Secretary, M. I. Rogers.
Parliamentary Under Secretary of State (Lords), THE LORD HENLEY.
  Private Secretary, Miss M. M. Dempster.
Parliamentary Under Secretary of State (Commons), MRS. GILLIAN SHEPHARD, M.P.
  Private Secretary, Ms. J. Rintoul.

Permanent Secretary (G1), M. J. A. Partridge, C.B.
  Private Secretary, J. Griffiths.

SOCIAL SECURITY OPERATIONS GROUP
Deputy Secretary (G2), N. E. Clarke.

Regional Directorate
Under Secretary (G3), R. A. Birch.
Assistant Secretaries (G5), O. C. L. Thorpe; J. F. Jones; J. C. Eversfield; Miss M. Moodie; Mrs. P. Hurley.

Information Technology Services Directorate
Director (G3*), F. J. Kenworthy.
Assistant Directors (G5), P. G. Dunn; A. Stott; R. Tilney.

North Fylde Central Office
Controller (G5), J. M. Bankier.

Newcastle upon Tyne Central Office
Controller (G3), S. Thorpe-Tracey.
Assistant Secretaries (G5), J. Wailes; A. Laurance.

SOCIAL SECURITY POLICY GROUP
Deputy Secretary (G2), Mrs. A. E. Bowtell, C.B.

Social Security Division A
Under Secretary (G3), Mrs. S. Maunsell.
Assistant Secretaries (G5), J. E. Knight; P. L. Adeane; Miss M. R. Edwards; J. W. White.

Social Security Division B
Under Secretary (G3), B. W. Taylor.
Assistant Secretaries (G5), D. Allsop; Miss K. E. W. Blunt.

Social Security Division C
Under Secretary (G3), Mrs. J. M. Firth.
Assistant Secretaries (G5), G. C. Fiegehen; S. Hewitt.
Senior Principal (G6), K. Milner.

Social Security Division D
Under Secretary (G3), M. L. Whippman.
Assistant Secretaries (G5), Mrs. U. Brennan; R. Brown; R. P. Cleasby; Mrs. L. M. Richards.

Medical Division (Social Security)
Chief Medical Adviser (G3), Dr. W. R. O. Eggington.
Principal Medical Officers, Dr. K. A. Cameron; Dr. P. Castaldi; T. J. G. Phillips; Dr. D. R. Findlay.

Information Division
Head of Information (G5), S. Reardon.
Press Officer (G7), H. Lumsden.

REGIONAL ORGANIZATION
Scotland
Argyle House, 3 Lady Lawson Street, Edinburgh
Controller (G4), R. Walton.

England and Wales
North Eastern, Government Buildings, Lawnswood, Leeds. *Regional Controller (G5),* P. Nelmes.
London North, Olympic House, Olympic Way, Wembley, Middx. *Regional Controller,* Mrs. M. A. Robinson (*Middx.*).
London South, Sutherland House, 29–37 Brighton Road, Sutton, Surrey and Grosvenor House, Basing View, Basingstoke, Hants. *Regional Controller,* M. F. Archer.
Wales and South Western, Gabalfa, Cardiff. *Regional Controller,* G. Griffiths.
Midlands, Five Ways Tower, Frederick Road, Edg-

baston, Birmingham. *Regional Controller*, J. T. Green.

North Western, St. Martin's House, Stanley Precinct, Bootle, Merseyside. *Regional Controller*, J. B. Griffin.

SOCIAL SECURITY ADVISORY COMMITTEE
New Court, Carey Street, WC2A 2LS
[01–831 6111]

The Social Security Advisory Committee (SSAC) was established by the Social Security Act 1980 to advise the Secretary of State for Social Security and the Department of Health and Social Services for Northern Ireland on all Social Security matters except those relating to benefits for industrial injuries and diseases and occupational pensions. The Social Security Housing Benefit Act 1982 added housing benefit to the Committee's responsibilities.
Chairman, P. M. Barclay, C.B.E.
Members, Prof. J. Cheetham; Mrs. E. A. Denholm; Dr. R. J. Donaldson, O.B.E.; Mrs. S. Flather; Rev. G. H. Good, O.B.E.; H. Hodge; J. Hughes; P. Jacques; P. F. Naish; Hon. Mrs. R. H. P. Price; Dr. A. V. Stokes, O.B.E.; Prof. Olive Stevenson; R. G. Wendt.
Secretary, N. Cockett.

SPORTS COUNCIL
16 Upper Woburn Place, WC1H 0QP
[01–388 1277]

The Sports Council exists to promote the development of sport and foster the provision of facilities for sport and recreation in Great Britain.
Chairman, P. G. Yarranton.

HER MAJESTY'S STATIONERY OFFICE
St. Crispins, Duke Street, Norwich NR3 1PD
[0603–622211]

Her Majesty's Stationery Office (HMSO) was established in 1786 and is the U.K. Government executive agency that provides printing, binding, office supplies and office machinery to the public service. HMSO is also the Government's publisher and has bookshops for the sale of Government publications in London, Edinburgh, Manchester, Bristol, Birmingham and Belfast, as well as appointed agents in other cities. HMSO obtains most of its supplies and printing from commercial sources by competitive tender, apart from about 20 per cent of its printing requirement, such as Hansard and Bills and Acts of Parliament, which are produced in its own printing works. HMSO is a self-financing Government trading fund and competes for its business with other commercial suppliers.
(For **Salaries**, *see* page 293)

Controller and Chief Executive (G2), P. I. Freeman.
  Executive Assistant, Mrs. J. B. Ward.
Deputy Chief Executive (G4), M. D. Lynn.
Director General of Corporate Services (G4), D. W. Ray.

Heads of Divisions
Publications (G5), C. J. Penn.
Supply (G5), P. J. Macdonald.
Production (G5), D. G. Forbes.
Print Procurement (G5), B. Ekers.
Corporate Development (G5), C. N. Southgate.
Finance (G5), V. G. Bell.
Personnel Services (G5), A. J. Davies.
Industrial Personnel (G5), D. J. Wintle.
Marketing Services (G6), G. A. H. Turner.
Information Technology (G5), D. C. Kerry.

Scotland
Bankhead Avenue, Edinburgh EH11 4AB
Bookshop: 71 Lothian Road, Edinburgh EH3 9AZ
Director Edinburgh (G7), G. W. Bedford.

Northern Ireland
IDB House, Chichester Street, Belfast BT1 4PS
Retail and Trade Bookshop: 80 Chichester Street, Belfast BT1 4JY
Director Belfast (G7), Miss V. J. Wilson.

London
Publications Centre: 51 Nine Elms Lane, SW8 5DR.
Bookshop: 49 High Holborn, WC1V 6HB.

Manchester
Broadway, Chadderton, Oldham, Lancs. OL9 9QH
Bookshop: 9–21 Princess Street, Manchester M60 8AS.

Bristol
Ashton Vale Road, Bristol BS3 2HN
Bookshop: Southey House, Wine Street, Bristol BS1 2BH.

Birmingham
Bookshop: 258 Broad Street, Birmingham B1 2HE.

STATUTE LAW COMMITTEE
House of Lords, SW1A 0PW

The Committee exercises a general supervision over the form of the statute law and of Statutory Instruments. It is also responsible for the publication of amended editions of the Statutes, including the current official revised edition of the Statutes in Force.
Chairman, The Lord Chancellor.
Vice-Chairman, The Hon. Mr. Justice Beldam.
Members, The Attorney General; The Lord Advocate; The Rt. Hon. J. Morris, Q.C., M.P.; The Rt. Hon. P. Archer, Q.C., M.P.; Sir Anthony Buck, Q.C., M.P.; Sir Derek Oulton, K.C.B.; D. Rippengal, C.B., Q.C.; H. Knorpel, C.B.; Sir Henry de Waal, K.C.B., Q.C.; N. J. Adamson, C.B., Q.C.; Sir John Sainty, K.C.B.; Sir Terence Heiser, K.C.B.; H. W. Gamon, C.B.E., M.C.; Sir Nicholas Lyell, Q.C., M.P.; Sir Robin Butler, K.C.B., C.V.O.; C. Boulton, C.B.; K. F. Barclay; M. H. Collon; R. Brodie; Sir Clive Whitmore, G.C.B., C.V.O.; J. Nursaw, C.B.; The Hon. Lord Davidson; H. M. Barclay; Rt. Hon. Sir Brian Hutton; The Lord Jauncey of Tullichettle, P.C.; Dr. P. Freeman.
Secretary, B. P. Keith.

OFFICE OF TELECOMMUNICATIONS
Atlantic House, Holborn Viaduct, EC1N 2HQ
[01–353 4020]

Oftel is a non-Ministerial Government Department headed by a Director General, which is responsible for supervising telecommunications activities in the U.K.

Its principal functions are to ensure that holders of telecommunications licences comply with their licence conditions; to maintain and promote effective competition in telecommunications; to promote, in respect of prices, quality and variety the interests of consumers, purchasers and other users of telecommunication services and apparatus.

The Director General has powers to deal with anticompetitive practices and monopoly situations. He also has a duty to consider all reasonable complaints and representations about telecommunication apparatus and services.
Director General, Prof. Sir Brian Carsberg.
Deputy Director General, W. R. B. Wigglesworth.

Director of P.T.O. Licensing, G. P. Knight.
Director of Apparatus Approval, Dr. H. Stewart.
Head of Information, D. C. Redding.

DEPARTMENT OF TRADE AND INDUSTRY
1–19 Victoria Street, SW1H 0ET
[01–215 5000]
[*Single European Market:* 01–200 1992]

The Department is responsible for:
(a) international trade policy, including the promotion of U.K. trade interests in the European Community, GATT, OECD, UNCTAD and other international organizations.
(b) under the direction of the British Overseas Trade Board, the promotion of U.K. exports and assistance to exporters.
(c) policy in relation to industry, including the general promotion of the interests of industry and assistance to industry; specific interest in all manufacturing and service industries apart from those covered by other Departments; regional policy, Inner Cities Initiative, enterprise and deregulation, and regional industrial assistance (some of this applying only to England); and policy in relation to the public bodies British Shipbuilders, the Post Office and the British Technology Group.
(d) competition policy and consumer protection, including relations with the Office of Fair Trading and the Monopolies and Mergers Commission, and the National Weights and Measures Laboratory.
(e) policy on science and technology and research and development matters, standards and designs, support for innovation, and the administration of the National Physical Laboratory, National Engineering Laboratory, Warren Spring Laboratory and the Laboratory of the Government Chemist.
(f) the administration of company legislation and the Companies House Executive Agency, the Insolvency Service; the regulation of the insurance industry; the regulation of radio frequencies; and the Patent Office.
(g) the Business Statistics Office.
(For **Salaries,** *see* page 293).

Secretary of State for Trade and Industry and President of the Board of Trade, THE RT. HON. NICHOLAS RIDLEY, M.P.
Principal Private Secretary, N. R. Thornton.
Minister for Industry and Enterprise, THE HON. DOUGLAS HOGG, M.P.
Minister for Trade, THE LORD TREFGARNE, P.C.
Private Secretaries, P. Smith; G. Williams.
Parliamentary Under Secretary of State for Industry and Consumer Affairs, ERIC FORTH, M.P.
Private Secretary, M. Carvell.
Parliamentary Under Secretary of State for Corporate Affairs, JOHN REDWOOD, M.P.
Private Secretary, S. Gill.
Permanent Secretary (G1), Sir Peter Gregson, K.C.B.
Private Secretary, T. Davy.
Deputy Secretaries (G2), D. M. Dell, C.B.; A. J. P. Macdonald, C.B.; Dr. R. F. Coleman (*Chief Engineer and Scientist*); R. Mountfield, C.B.; Miss E. M. Llewellyn-Smith, C.B.; C. W. Roberts, C.B.; R. Williams, C.B.; G. A. Hosker, C.B. (*The Solicitor*); W. M. Knighton, C.B. (*Principal Establishment and Finance Officer*).
Parliamentary Clerk, T. A. Hardbattle.

Central Unit
1 Victoria Street, SW1H 0ET
[01–215 5000]

Head of Unit (G3), J. A. Cooke.
Heads of Branch (G5), P. D. J. Makeham; S. Spivey.

External European Policy Division
1 Victoria Street, SW1H 0ET
[01–215 5000]

Under Secretary (G3), A. C. Hutton.
Heads of Branch (G5), M. D. C. Johnson; D. E. Love; Miss A. E. Stoddart.

Overseas Trade Divisions
1 Victoria Street, SW1H 0ET
[01–215 5000]

Division 1 (*Projects and Export Policy*)

Under Secretary (G3), C. C. W. Adams.
Heads of Branch (G5), Dr. C. A. Palmer; F. B. Wheeler; C. E. Blundell.

Division 2
(*N. America, N.E. and S.E. Asia, China, Hong Kong and Export Licensing Operation*)

Under Secretary (G3), J. Meadway.
Heads of Branch (G5), W. J. Hall; J. V. Hagestadt; E. W. Beston.

Division 3

Under Secretary (G3), P. Bryant.

Administration and Finance

Head of Branch (G5), I. Jones.

Exports to Europe Branch

Head of Branch (G5), K. D. Levinson.

Export Data Branch

Director (G6), A. Reynolds.

Fairs and Promotions Branch

Head of Branch (G5), G. J. Bradshaw.

Eastern Europe Branch

Head of Branch (G5), K. W. N. George.

Division 4
(*Middle East, India and Pakistan, Africa, Latin America, the Caribbean and Australasia*)

Under Secretary (G3), T. Muir.
Heads of Branch (G5), J. M. Bowder; M. Petter; M. A. S. Garrod.

Internal European Policy Division
1 Victoria Street, SW1H 0ET
[01–215 5000]

Under Secretary (G3), Miss M. T. Neville-Rolfe.
Heads of Branch (G5), A. W. C. Keddie; R. T. King; W. L. Stow.

Patent Office and Industrial Property and Copyright Department
see entry on pp. 351–2

Insurance Division
10–18 Victoria Street, SW1H 0NN
[01–215 5000]

Under Secretary (G3), A. C. Russell.
Heads of Branch (G5), D. W. Hellings; D. G. Hyde; M. G. Roberts.

Financial Services Division
10–18 Victoria Street, SW1H 0NN
[01–215 5000]

Under Secretary (G3), W. B. Willott.
Heads of Branch (G5), Dr. J. P. Compton; R. C. Dobbie; A. C. G. Lowry; K. M. Long.

Companies Division
10–18 Victoria Street, SW1H 0NN
[01–215 5000]

Under Secretary (G3), Mrs. S. E. Brown.
Heads of Branch (G5), M. J. C. Butcher; D. L. Gatland; N. Worman.

Companies House Executive Agency
Companies House, Crown Way, Maindy, Cardiff
CF4 3UZ
[0222–388588]

Registrar of Companies for England and Wales (G4),
S. R. Curtis.
London Search Room, 55–71 City Road, EC1Y 1BB
[01–253 9393]

102 George Street, Edinburgh EH2 3DJ
[031–225 5774]
Registrar for Scotland, J. D. Leithead.

**Manufacturing and Information Technologies
Division**
Ashdown House, 123 Victoria Street, SW1E 6RB
[01–215 5000]

Under Secretary (G3), J. E. Cammell.
Heads of Branch (G5), H. M. Lanyon; H. L. Evans; H. J. Ivey.

The Insolvency Service
Bridge Place, 88–89 Eccleston Square, SW1V 1PT
[01–215 5000]

Inspector General of the Insolvency Service, M. Clark.
Deputy Inspectors General, P. D. Pink; P. R. Joyce; A. K. Sales.
Head of Branch (G5), Miss A. J. Brimelow.

Consumer Affairs Division
10–18 Victoria Street, SW1H 0NN
[01–215 5000]

Under Secretary (G3), C. T. Newton.
Heads of Branch (G5), D. Jones; M. A. R. Lunn; R. E. Palmer.
Trading Standards Adviser (G5), M. Oldham.

Air Division
Ashdown House, 123 Victoria Street,
SW1E 6RB
[01–215 5000]

Under Secretary (G3), T. Nieduszynski.
Heads of Branch (G5), D. I. Richardson; D. Marsh.
Grade 6, M. O. Ralph; Dr. G. T. Coleman.

Research and Technology Policy Division
Ashdown House, 123 Victoria Street, SW1E 6RB
[01–215 5000]

Under Secretary (G3), B. Murray.
Heads of Branch (G5), Mrs. M. Bloom; J. H. Chapman; R. Foster; J. D. Howarth.

National Physical Laboratory
Teddington, Middx. TW11 0LW
[01–977 3222]

Director (G3), Dr. P. Dean, c.b.

Laboratory of the Government Chemist
Queens Road, Teddington, Middx. TW11 0LY
[01–943 7000]

Government Chemist (G3), A. Williams.

National Engineering Laboratory
East Kilbride, Glasgow G75 0QU
[03552–20222]

Director (G3), Dr. D. A. Bell.

Warren Spring Laboratory
Gunnels Wood Road, Stevenage, Herts SG1 2BX
[0438–741122]

Director (G3), Dr. J. S. S. Reay.

National Weights and Measures Laboratory
Teddington, Middx. TW11 0JZ
[01–977 3222]

(An Executive Agency within the Department of Trade and Industry.)
Director (G5), Dr. P. B. Clapham.

Competition Policy Division
1 Victoria Street, SW1H 0ET
[01–215 5000]

Under Secretary (G3), S. W. Treadgold.
Heads of Branch (G5), Mrs. C. E. D. Bell; G. C. Riggs; Mrs. A. Walker.

Enterprise and Deregulation Unit
1 Victoria Street, SW1H 0ET
[01–215 5000]

Director (G3), M. Baker.
Heads of Branch (G5), I. Freeman; R. Allpress.

Economic Management and Education Division
1 Victoria Street, SW1H 0ET
[01–215 5000]

Under Secretary (G3), G. Whiting.
Heads of Branch (G5), R. J. Brown; P. J. Goate; J. M. Healey; M. E. Stanley.

Engineering Markets Division
Ashdown House, 123 Victoria Street, SW1E 6RB
[01–215 5000]

Under Secretary (G3), C. B. Benjamin.
Heads of Branch (G5), D. R. Coates; A. C. Conway; P. Goodman; B. N. Steele; Dr. H. M. Sutton.

British National Space Centre
Millbank Tower, Millbank, SW1P 4QU
[01–217 3000]

Director General (G2), A. J. Pryor.
Heads of Branch (G5), Dr. J. E. Harries; A. C. Nicholas.

Enterprise Initiative and Standards Division
Kingsgate House, 66–74 Victoria Street,
SW1E 6SW
[01–215 5000]

Under Secretary (G3), A. R. Titchener.
Heads of Branches (G5), A. Berry; H. P. Brown; G. Kerfoot; S. Pride; R. M. Upson.

Telecommunications and Posts Division
Kingsgate House, 66–74 Victoria Street,
SW1E 6SW
[01–215 5000]

Under Secretary (G3), R. J. Priddle.
Heads of Branch (G5), Mrs. E. C. Jones; J. Phillips; P. Smith; S. R. Temple.

Radiocommunications Division
Waterloo Bridge House, Waterloo Road, SE1 8UA
[01–215 5000]

Under Secretary (G3), M. J. Michell.
Director (G4), Dr. K. C. Shotton.
Heads of Branch (G5), M. Goddard; M. P. Davies; M. V. Coolican; R. A. Bedford; P. Loughead; (G6) Dr. A. C. D. Whitehouse; Dr. A. F. Pollard.

Information Engineering Directorate
Kingsgate House, 66–74 Victoria Street,
SW1E 6SW
[01–215 5000]

Under Secretary (G3), Dr. J. C. J. Thynne.

Heads of Branches (G5), Prof. J. N. Buxton; C. Cheetham; M. Gibson; B. Nuttal; A. Wallard.

Industrial Materials Market Division
Ashdown House, 123 Victoria Street, SW1E 6RB
[01–215 5000]

Under Secretary (G3), S. Treadgold.
Heads of Branch (G5), V. F. Lane; Miss S. E. Harding; D. C. Jackson; R. C. McVickers; Dr. W. Vickers; Mrs. A. Wilks.

Consumer and Vehicles Market Division
Ashdown House, 123 Victoria Street, SW1E 6RB
[01–215 5000]

Under Secretary (G3), M. J. A. Cochlin.
Heads of Branch (G5), S. J. Bowen; M. S. Bremner; Miss V. Evans; J. C. Octon; P. Robinson.

Inner Cities Unit
1 Victoria Street, SW1H 0ET
[01–215 5000]

Director (G4), M. Gahagan.
Head of Branch (G5), Ms. S. Seymour.

Investment, Development and Accountancy Division
Kingsgate House, 66–74 Victoria Street,
SW1E 6SW
[01–215 5000]

Directors, I.D.A. (G3), J. Chastney; P. M. S. Corley; C. Crombie.
Heads of Branch (G5), R. H. S. Wells; G. M. Field; J. C. S. Priston; C. P. Hicks; K. Holt; Mrs. A. Taylor; *(G6)*, N. A. T. Hobbs.

DEPARTMENT OF TRADE AND INDUSTRY SERVICES ORGANIZATION

Deputy Secretaries (G2), G. A. Hosker, C.B. *(The Solicitor)*; W. M. Knighton, C.B. *(Principal Establishment and Finance Officer)*.

Personnel Management Division
Allington Towers,
17 Allington Street, SW1E 5EB
[01–215 5000]

Under Secretary (G3), N. F. Ledsome, C.B.
Heads of Branch (G5), P. S. Salvidge; D. W. F. Johnson; J. F. Bailes; T. Bryan.

Management Services and Manpower Division
29 Bressenden Place, SW1E 5DT
[01–215 5000]

Under Secretary (G3), R. M. Rumbelow.
Director of Information Technology (G4), N. Bernard.
Heads of Branch (G5), Miss D. Gane; Mrs. E. M. Ryle.

Finance and Resource Management Division
Ashdown House, 123 Victoria Street, SW1E 6RB
[01–215 5000]

Under Secretary (G3), D. R. C. Durie.
Heads of Branch (G5), P. R. S. Hartnack; D. M. Hoddinott; M. O'Shea.

Accounts Branch
P.O. Box 100, Government Buildings, Cardiff Road, Newport, Gwent NP9 1ZA
[0633–810636]

Director of Accounts, D. M. Hoddinott.

Internal Audit
29 Bressenden Place, SW1E 5DT
[01–215 5000]

Head of Internal Audit, A. C. Elkington.

SOLICITOR'S OFFICE
10–18 Victoria Street, SW1H 0NN
[01–215 5000]

The Solicitor (G2), G. A Hosker, C.B.
Grade 3, P. H. Bovey; C. S. Kerse.
Grade 4, J. M. Stanley.
Assistant Solicitors (G5), H. D. M. Bailey; Mrs. T. J. Dunstan; Miss P. A. E. Granados; R. Higgins, C.B.E.; D. S. Mangat; I. K. Mathers; Miss K. Morton; Miss E. N. O'Flynn; S. A. Parker; Miss J. Richardson; Miss J. V. Stokes; A. M. Susman; A. J. Woods.

Investigations Division
Ebury Bridge House,
2–18 Ebury Bridge Road, SW1W 8QD
[01–730 9678]

Head of Branch (G3), J. R. Mallinson.
Assistant Solicitors (G5), H. H. Bradshaw; A. W. G. Catto; E. A. Thompson; B. J. Welch; B. D. Winkett.

Information Division
1 Victoria Street, SW1H 0ET
[01–215 5000]

Head of Information (G4), A. E. Moorey.
Deputy Heads of Information Division (G5), S. Lyle-Smythe; *(G6)*, Miss A. MacLean; I. Cameron.

Micro-Economics Divisions
Ashdown House, 123 Victoria Street, SW1E 6RB
[01–215 5000]

Under Secretary (G3), J. R. Shepherd.
Heads of Branch (G5), B. M. Nonehebel; J. M. Barber; M. S. Bradbury; J. A. S. Robertson.

BRITISH OVERSEAS TRADE BOARD
1 Victoria Street, SW1H 0ET
[01–215 5000]

President, The Secretary of State for Trade and Industry.
Chairman, Sir James Cleminson, M.C.
Vice-Chairman, H.R.H. The Duke of Kent, K.G., G.C.M.G., G.C.V.O.
Members, J. M. Banham; N. P. Bayne, C.M.G.; Mrs. P. A. Beckett; A. B. Cleaver; D. M. Dell, C.B.; T. P. Frost; A. G. Gormly; Dr. A. Hayes; M. R. Hoffman; D. P. Hornby; Sir Philip Jones, C.B.; W. B. Jordan; The Earl of Limerick, K.B.E.; J. W. Parsons, C.B.E.; M. S. Perry, O.B.E.; M. G. Stephens; B. D. Taylor; G. S. Tucker, C.B.E.
Chief Executive, D. M. Dell, C.B.
Secretary (G5), I. Jones.

REGIONAL OFFICES

North East, Stanegate House, 2 Groat Market, Newcastle upon Tyne NE1 1YN. (091–232 4722).— *Regional Director (G3)*, R. W. Simpson.

North West, Sunley Tower, Piccadilly Plaza, Manchester M1 4BA. (061–236 2171).—*Regional Director (G3)*, J. H. Pownall.

Yorkshire and Humberside, Priestley House, Park Row, Leeds LS1 5LF. (0532 443171).—*Regional Director (G3)*, E. Wright.

West Midlands, Ladywood House, Stephenson Street, Birmingham B2 4DT. (021–631 6181).— *Regional Director (G3)*, N. H. Perry.

East Midlands, Severns House, 20 Middle Pavement, Nottingham NG1 7DW. (0602 506181).—*Regional Director (G3)*, R. M. Anderson.

South West, The Pithay, Bristol BS1 2PB. (0272–272666).—*Regional Director (G5)*, D. B. Lodge.

South East, Bridge Place, 88–89 Eccleston Square, SW1V 1PT. (01–215 5000).—*Regional Director (G5)*, A. J. Mantle. *Directors (G6)*, R. D. Dennis; D. J. Saunders; Dr. G. Thorpe.

TRAINING AGENCY
Head Office: Moorfoot, Sheffield S1 4PQ
[0742–753275]

The Training Agency is the U.K. national training authority. It operates as an Executive Agency within the Department of Employment and reports to the Secretary of State for Employment. The Agency develops and organizes the provision of the Government's training and vocational education programmes.
(For **Salaries**, *see* page 293)
Director General, R. Dawe, C.B., O.B.E.

Resources and Personnel Division

Director (G3), Mrs. V. Bayliss.
Heads of Branches (G5):
Resource Control, C. P. Thomas.
Internal Audit (G6), C. Williams.
Finance Control, N. L. Gregory.
Information Systems and Management Services, I. Turl.
Personnel and Staff Development, D. Grover.

Skills Training Agency

Chief Executive (G4), T. O'Conor.
Heads of Branches (G6):
Skillcentre Operations (G5), S. Bishell.
Financial and Accounting Services, T. Kent.
Product Development, P. Wells.
Marketing and Mobile Training, J. Davies.

Training Standards Advisory Service

Director (G5), J. D. Tinsley.

Information Services

Head (G5), A. J. Brookes.

POLICY AND PROGRAMMES DIVISION

Deputy Director General and Director, Policy and Programmes Division, I. Johnston.

Youth Training

Director (G3), D. Grover.
Heads of Branches (G5):
Youth Programmes, J. F. Smith.
Youth Development, R. Niven.
Commission Secretariat, M. Twomey.

Quality Standards and Methods

Director (G4), G. Kendall.
Heads of Branches (G5):
Industry Bodies, J. Wiltshire.
Programme Quality, J. K. Fuller.
Occupational Standards, A. T. Wisbey.
Psychological Services, Dr. M. Killcross.
Learning Technology, R. Wormald.

Education Programmes

Director (G3), Mrs. A. Jones.
Heads of Branches (G5):
T.V.E.I. (Policy), I. Fair.
T.V.E.I. (Operations), Mrs. R. Le Guen.
Higher Education, G. Macnair.
Further Education, I. Randall.
Compacts Support Unit, D. Main.

Adult Training Programmes

Director (G3), J. Surr.
Heads of Branches (G5):

Adult Training Special Needs, Miss S. Newton.
Employment Training Programmes, R. Lasko.
Employment Training Strategy and Resources, N. Schofield.

Systems and Strategy

Director (G3), R. Hillier.
Heads of Branches (G5):
Policy and Analysis, N. Davis.
Evaluation and Research, Mrs. J. Marquand.
Labour Market Information, A. Davies.
Human Resources Development Promotion, P. Gregory.
Learning Systems and Access, K. White.

Field Operations

Director (G4), J. Lambert.
Heads of Branches:
Field Support (G5), J. Franklin.
Field Development (G6), M. Christie.

DEPARTMENT OF TRANSPORT
2 Marsham Street, SW1P 3EB
[01–276 3000]

The Department of Transport has overall responsibility for land, sea and air transport. This entails general sponsorship of the transport industries, with particular responsibility for British Rail and London Regional Transport; domestic and international civil aviation policy; shipping policy and the ports industry; navigation lights; pilotage; H.M. Coastguard; oversight of road transport, including vehicle registration and licensing, driver licensing and road safety; responsibility for construction and maintenance of motorways and other trunk roads; and general oversight of the transport planning of local authorities, including payments of grant from central Government.

(For **Salaries**, *see* page 293).
Secretary of State for Transport, THE RT. HON. CECIL PARKINSON, M.P.
Private Secretary, R. J. Griffin.
Special Adviser, Miss E. Buchanan.
Minister of State for Public Transport, MICHAEL PORTILLO, M.P.
Private Secretary, S. L. Gooding.
Parliamentary Under Secretaries, ROBERT ATKINS, M.P.; PATRICK McLOUGHLIN, M.P.
Private Secretaries, G. Pendlebury; Miss E. A. Whatmore.
Lord in Waiting, The Viscount Davidson.
Private Secretary. Miss S. J. Smith.
Parliamentary Clerk, Mrs. L. C. Jones.
Permanent Under Secretary of State (G1), Sir Alan Bailey, K.C.B.
Private Secretary, M. J. Quinn.

Information

Head of Information (G5), Miss G. P. Samuel.

PUBLIC TRANSPORT AND RESEARCH

Deputy Secretary (G2), E. B. C. Osmotherly.

Railways

Under Secretary (G3), J. R. Coates.
Heads of Division (G5), A. Fortnam; S. K. Reeves; Mrs. R. M. Dixon; R. S. Peal.
Chief Inspecting Officer (G4), R. J. Seymour.
Deputy Chief Inspecting Officer (G5), A Cooksey.

Public Transport London and Metropolitan

Under Secretary (G3), A. J. Goldman.
Heads of Division (G4), F. Gale; (G5), Miss S. J. Lambert; M. N. Lambirth.

Transport and Road Research Laboratory

Director (G3), D. F. Cornelius *(temp.).*
Deputy Director (G4), D. I. Robertson *(temp.).*
Grade 5, P. H. Bly; G. Maycock; J. Porter; Dr. G. P. Tilly; K. Russam *(temp.).*
Grade 6, J. S. Yerrell.

Science and Research Policy and Programmes

Grade 5, P. G. O'Neill.

ROAD SAFETY AND LICENSING

Deputy Secretary and Principal Finance Officer (G2), R. C. M. Cooper, c.b.

Road and Vehicle Safety

Under Secretary (G3), Mrs. J. M. Bridgeman.
Heads of Division (G5), D. R. Instone; Dr. C. M. Woodman; P. H. Martin.
Grade 6, D. J. Spragg; J. David; K. Walton; D. Harvey.
Chief Mechanical Engineer (G4), E. Dunn.
Grade 6, R. J. White.

Driver and Vehicle Licensing

Director (G3), G. R. Wattley.
Deputy Director (G4), M. A. Robinson.
Heads of Division (G5), R. J. Verge; H. C. S. Derwent; P. G. Collis; J. K. Griffiths.
Grade 6, T. J. Horton.
Departmental Medical Adviser (G4), Dr. J. F. Taylor.

Vehicle Inspectorate Executive Agency

Chief Executive (G4), R. J. Oliver.

Freight

Under Secretary (G3), G. D. Crane.
Grade 5, L. Moyle.
Grade 6, J. Winder; D. J. Blackman.

Traffic Area Offices
Traffic Commissioners and Licensing Authorities

Eastern (Nottingham and Cambridge), Brig. C. M. Boyd.
Metropolitan (Acton), Air Vice-Marshal R. G. Ashford, c.b.e.
North Eastern (Newcastle upon Tyne and Leeds), F. Whalley.
North Western (Manchester), M. S. Albu.
Scottish (Edinburgh), K. R. Waterman.
South Eastern (Eastbourne), Brig. M. H. Turner.
West Midlands (Birmingham), J. M. C. Pugh.
Western (Bristol), Maj.-Gen. V. H. J. Carpenter, c.b., m.b.e.
South Wales (Cardiff), J. M. C. Pugh.

Finance

Under Secretary (G3), H. M. G. Stevens.
Grade 4, H. B. Wenban-Smith.
Heads of Division (G5), P. R. Smethurst; R. Bird; D. M. Smith; M. J. Fuhr; D. J. Rowlands.
Accounting Adviser (G5), A. R. Allum.

Internal Audit

Head of Branch (G6), J. Kingdom.

ECONOMICS AND STATISTICS

Chief Economic Adviser (G2), Dr. J. H. Rickard.
Grade 5, C. T. B. Smith; M. C. Mann; T. E. Worsley.

Statistics

Under Secretary (G3), D. W. Flaxen.
Grade 5, Miss B. J. Wood; H. Collings; G. R. Emes; R. P. Donachie.

HIGHWAYS AND TRAFFIC

Deputy Secretary (G2), D. Holmes, c.b.

Highways Policy and Programme

Under Secretary (G3), P. Wood.
Heads of Division (G5), B. R. A. Blaxall; B. J. Billington; P. E. Pickering; Ms. A. Munro; Miss P. A. Williams.
Grade 7, D. E. Gladding.

Highways, Contracts, Administration and Maintenance

Under Secretary (G3), P. Critchley.
Heads of Division (G5), P. R. Smith; J. H. Denning; P. G. Davies; J. B. W. Robins.

Highways Engineering

Chief Highway Engineer (G3), F. J. Parker.
Deputy Chief Highway Engineer (G4), D. A. Holland.
Grade 5, R. S. Wilson; P. H. Dawe; D. Kershaw; M. R. Nevard.
Grade 6, K. Softly.

Traffic Policy and London Regional

Under Secretary (G3), I. Yass.
Heads of Division (G5), R. M. C. Edridge; N. T. Rees; P. E. Butler; Dr. S. Chatterjee.

AVIATION, SHIPPING AND INTERNATIONAL

Deputy Secretary (G2), G. R. Sunderland.

Civil Aviation Policy

Under Secretary (G3), R. E. Clarke.
Grade 5, D. S. Evans; C. J. Harris; W. E. Kelly; E. C. Neve; S. C. Whiteley.

Shipping Policy and Emergency Planning

Under Secretary (G3), D. J. Lyness.
Heads of Division (G5), R. G. Jones; P. Kitchen.
Grade 6 J. R. Perrett.

Marine

Under Secretary (G3), J. D. Noulton.
Heads of Division (G5), J. R. Fells; M. W. Jackson.

Marine Emergency Operations and Marine Pollution Control Unit

Director (G4), Capt. W. H. H. McLeod.
Chief Coastguard (G5), Cdr. D. T. Ascona.
Surveyor General, G. Thompson.
Deputy Surveyors General (G5), P. J. Hambling; W. A. Graham; N. W. Scully.

Marine Accidents Investigation Branch

Chief Inspector of Marine Accidents (G5), Capt. P. B. Marriott.

International Aviation

Under Secretary (G3), D. C. Moss.
Heads of Division (G5), M. L. Fielder; Ms. E. A. Hopkins; G. J. Skinner.

Accidents Investigation Branch

Chief Inspector of Accidents (G4), D. A. Cooper.
Deputy Chief Inspector of Accidents (G5), K. P. R. Smart.

International Transport

Under Secretary (G3), J. D. Henes.
Grade 5, P. F. Emms; P. D. Burgess.

ESTABLISHMENTS
Lambeth Bridge House, SE1 7SB
[01–238 3000]

Principal Establishment Officer (G3), J. W. S. Dempster.
Grade 5, P. Stringfellow; G. D. Edmonds; A. S. D. Whybrow.
Grade 6, G. Bray; K. Wight; C. Payne.
Chief Librarian (G6), P. Kirwan.

REGIONAL OFFICES

West Midlands, Birmingham.—*Regional Director (G3)*, D. R. Ritchie; *Director (G4)*, T. A. Rochester; *Deputy Director (G5)*, N. E. Firkin.
Yorkshire and Humberside, Leeds.—*Regional Director (G3)*, J. F. Ballard; *Director (G4)*, A. J. Homer; *Deputy Director (G5)*, J. R. Wilkins.
North West, Manchester.—*Regional Director (G3)*, D. C. Renshaw; *Director (G4)*, vacant; *Deputy Director (G5)*, G. E. Hancock.
Northern, Newcastle upon Tyne.—*Regional Director (G3)*, J. A. Owen; *Director (G5)*, M. B. Constable; *Deputy Director (G6)*, J. A. Davidson.
South West, Bristol.—*Regional Director (G3)*, G. M. Wedd, C.B.; *Director (G4)*, W. E. Gallagher; *Deputy Directors (G5)*, A. P. Moss; M. A. Endacott (*temp.*).
East Midlands, Nottingham.—*Regional Director (G4)*, P. M. Hewitt, O.B.E.; *Director (G5)*, S. Rose.
South East, London.—*Regional Director (G3)*, D. Gruffydd Jones; *Director (G4)*, J. W. Fellows; *Deputy Director (G5)*, A. D. Rowland.
Eastern, London.—*Regional Director (G3)*, A. Whitfield; *Director (G4)*, B. Sperring; *Deputy Director (G5)*, P. E. Nutt.

THE TREASURY
Parliament Street, SW1P 3AG
[01–233 3000]

The Office of the Lord High Treasurer has been continuously in commission for well over 200 years: the Lord High Commissioners of H.M. Treasury consist of the First Lord of the Treasury (who is also the Prime Minister), the Chancellor of the Exchequer and five Junior Lords. This Board of Commissioners is assisted at present by the Chief Secretary, a Parliamentary Secretary who is the Chief Whip, a Financial Secretary, an Economic Secretary, a Minister of State, and by the Permanent Secretary.

The Prime Minister and First Lord is not primarily concerned in the day to day aspects of Treasury business. The Parliamentary Secretary and the Junior Lords are Government whips in the House of Commons. The management of the Treasury devolves upon the Chancellor of the Exchequer and, under him, the Chief Secretary, the Financial Secretary, the Economic Secretary and the Paymaster General.

The Chief Secretary is responsible for the control of public expenditure; public services and industry groups; overseas aid and export credit; efficiency in the public sector; and procurement policy.

The Financial Secretary discharges the traditional responsibility of the Treasury for the largely formal procedure for the voting of funds by Parliament. He also has responsibility for other Parliamentary financial business, Inland Revenue duties and taxes, privatization policy, and industrial casework.

The Economic Secretary has responsibility for monetary policy; the financial system (including banks, building societies and other financial institutions); HMSO, the Central Office of Information, the Government Actuary's Department, and the Civil Service catering organization; international financial business; North Sea fiscal regime; Department for National Savings, Registry of Friendly Societies

and the National Loans Office; Customs & Excise matters, and the Treasury research budget. The Paymaster General deals with European Community business; civil service pay; the Royal Mint, Central Computer and Telecommunications Agency, charities (non-tax aspects), profit-related pay, and the Paymaster General's Office. All Treasury Ministers are concerned in tax matters.

Prime Minister and First Lord of the Treasury, THE RT. HON. MARGARET THATCHER, M.P.
Chancellor of the Exchequer, THE RT. HON. NIGEL LAWSON, M.P. £34,479
  Principal Private Secretary, vacant.
  Private Secretary, J. M. G. Taylor.
  Parliamentary Private Secretary, N. Forman, M.P.
  Parliamentary Clerk, B. O. Dyer.
Chief Secretary to the Treasury, THE RT. HON. NORMAN LAMONT, M.P. £34,479
  Private Secretary, Miss G. C. Evans.
  Assistant Private Secretary, P. T. Wanless.
Paymaster General, THE RT. HON. THE EARL OF CAITHNESS £24,209
  Private Secretary, M. R. Buckler.
Financial Secretary to the Treasury, PETER LILLEY, M.P. £24,209
  Private Secretary, S. Flanagan.
Economic Secretary, RICHARD RYDER, O.B.E., M.P.
  .... £18,219
  Private Secretary, Miss. S. M. A. James.
Parliamentary Secretary to the Treasury and Government Chief Whip, THE RT. HON. DAVID WADDINGTON, Q.C., M.P. £28,589
  Private Secretary, M. Maclean.
Treasurer of H.M. Household and Deputy Chief Whip, TRISTAN GAREL-JONES, M.P. £24,209
Lord Commissioners of the Treasury, D. Lightbown, M.P.; K. Carlisle, M.P.; S. Dorrell, M.P.; J. Taylor, M.P.; D. Heathcoat-Amory, M.P. £15,349
Assistant Whips, M. Fallon, M.P.; The Hon. T. Sackville, M.P.; S. Chapman, M.P.; G. Knight, M.P.; I. Patnick, O.B.E., M.P. £15,349
(NOTE.—All salaries shown above do not include Parliamentary salary).
(For Civil Service **Salaries**, *see* page 293).

Permanent Secretary of the Treasury, Sir Peter Middleton, G.C.B.
  Private Secretary, S. D. H. Sargent.
Second Permanent Secretaries (G1A), N. L. Wicks, C.V.O., C.B.E. (*Overseas Finance*); J. Anson, C.B. (*Public Expenditure*); Dame Anne Mueller, D.C.B. (*Civil Service Management and Pay*).
Head of Government Economics Service and Chief Economic Adviser to the Treasury, Sir Terence Burns.
Head of Government Accountancy Service, A. J. Hardcastle.
Deputy Secretaries (G2), M. C. Scholar (*Public Finance*); H. P. Evans (*Overseas Finance*); H. Phillips, C.B. (*Public Services, and General Expenditure*); N. J. Monck, C.B. (*Industry*).
Deputy Chief Economic Adviser to the Treasury (G2), J. C. Odling-Smee.

INDUSTRY

Industry, Agriculture and Employment Group

Under Secretary (G3), I. P. Wilson.
Assistant Secretaries (G5), Miss J. Barber; T. J. Burr; D. Revolta.

Public Enterprises Group

Under Secretary (G3), D. J. L. Moore.
Assistant Secretaries (G5), R. Bent; M. L. Williams.

FINANCIAL MANAGEMENT: PUBLIC SERVICES
Financial Management Group

Under Secretary (G3), L. J. Harris.
Assistant Secretaries (G5), J. A. Barker; J. Dixon; G. Jordan.

Central Unit on Purchasing

Director, M. J. O. Willacy, C.B.E.
Deputy Director, M. J. Hoare.

Social Services and Territorial Group

Under Secretary (G3), Miss M. E. Peirson.
Assistant Secretaries (G5), J. P. McIntyre; R. B. Saunders; A. M. White.

Local Government Group

Under Secretary (G3), A. J. C. Edwards.
Assistant Secretaries (G5), B. H. Potter; S. N. Wood.

Home Transport and Education Group

Under Secretary (G3), Mrs. A. F. Case.
Assistant Secretaries (G5), C. Farthing; J. E. Mortimer.

Accounts and Purchasing

Under Secretary (G3), J. S. Beastall.
Assistant Secretary (G5), F. K. Jones.

Central Computer and Telecommunications Agency

Under Secretary (G3), W. A. Healey.
Assistant Secretaries (G5), W. Houldsworth; C. R. Muid; I. S. Thomson; R. E. Dibble; D. E. Thomas; A. R. Williams.

GENERAL EXPENDITURE
General Expenditure Policy Group

Under Secretary (G3), Mrs. J. R. Lomax.
Assistant Secretaries (G5), Mrs. R. Butler; A. J. T. MacAuslan; M. G. Richardson.

Defence Policy and Material Group

Under Secretary (G3), S. A. Robson.
Assistant Secretaries (G5), H. J. Bush; T. R. Fellgett.

OVERSEAS FINANCE
International Finance Group

Under Secretary (G3), A. C. S. Allan.
Assistant Secretaries (G5), C. L. Melliss; H. G. Walsh.

Aid and Export Finance Group

Under Secretary (G3), P. Mountfield.
Assistant Secretaries (G5), P. G. F. Davis; A. R. M. Bottrill.

European Community Group

Under Secretary (G3), R. I. G. Allen.
Assistant Secretaries (G5), Mrs. M. E. Brown; M. C. Mercer.

Accountancy Advice Group

Grade 4, D. Cooke.
Assistant Secretary (G5), D. Jamieson.
Senior Principals (G6), K. E. Bradley; R. Elias.

CHIEF ECONOMIC ADVISER'S DIVISIONS
Economic Assessment Group

Under Secretary (G3), P. N. Sedgewick.
Senior Economic Adviser (G5), J. S. Hibberd.

Medium Term and Policy Analysis

Under Secretary (G3), C. Riley.
Senior Economic Advisers (G5), N. J. Ilett; C. Kelly.

DEPUTY CHIEF ECONOMIC ADVISER'S DIVISIONS

Deputy Secretary (G2), J. C. Odling-Smee.
Assistant Secretary (G5), vacant.
Senior Economic Adviser (G5), S. W. Matthews.

Public Expenditure Economics and Operational Research

Under Secretary (G3), M. J. Spackman.
Assistant Secretaries (G5), A. J. Meyrick; D. Todd.
Deputy Chief Scientific Officer (G5), J. B. Jones.

PUBLIC FINANCE
Fiscal Policy Group

Under Secretary (G3), R. P. Culpin.
Assistant Secretary (G5), J. F. Gilhooly.

Monetary Group

Under Secretary (G3), D. L. C. Peretz.
Assistant Secretaries (G5), J. W. Grice; Miss M. O'Mara.

Financial Institutions and Markets Group

Under Secretary (G3), H. G. Walsh.
Assistant Secretaries (G5), N. J. Ilett, L. Watts.

Public Sector Finance

Assistant Secretary (G5), C. J. Mowl.
Economic Adviser (G7), P. S. F. Patterson.
Statistician (G7), Mrs. H. Wright.

PAY GROUP
Pay and Industrial Relations

Deputy Secretary (G3), C. W. Kelly.
Assistant Secretaries (G5), C. J. A. Chivers; I. Strachan; Ms. E. I. Young.
Grade 6, F. S. G. Easton; J. G. Graham.

Personnel Policy

Under Secretaries (G3), L. J. Harris; T. R. H. Luce.
Assistant Secretaries (G5), J. Dixon; Mrs. N. F. Haworth; G. H. B. Jordan.
Grade 6, J. A. Barker; D. G. Pain.

CENTRAL DIVISIONS
Establishment and Organization Division

Under Secretary (G3), B. M. Fox.
Assistant Secretaries (G5), C. C. Allan; E. I. Cooper.
Senior Economic Adviser (G5), R. B. Stannard.
Senior Principals (G6), D. E. G. Griffiths; R. N. Edwards.

Economic Briefing

Assistant Secrtetary (G5), A. W. Ritchie.

Information Division

Assistant Secretary (G5), E. J. W. Gieve.
Deputy Head of Division (G6), Miss J. C. Simpson.

TREASURY REPRESENTATIVES IN U.S.A.

Economic Minister and U.K. Representative IMF/IBRD, F. Cassell.

CIVIL SERVICE CATERING ORGANIZATION

Executive Director (G3), D. S. B. Simpson.

RATING OF GOVERNMENT PROPERTY DEPARTMENT
Jameson House, 69 Notting Hill Gate, W11 3JU

Treasury Valuer, J. F. Olney, c.b.e.
Deputy Treasury Valuer, T. J. Cundall.

THE TREASURY SOLICITOR
Department of H.M. Procurator-General and Treasury Solicitor
Queen's Chambers, 28 Broadway, SW1H 9JS
[01–210 3000]

The Treasury Solicitor's Department provides legal services for many Government Departments. Those that do not have their own lawyers are given legal advice, and both they and many other departments are provided with litigation and conveyancing services. The Department also deals with Bona Vacantia. The Treasury Solicitor is also the Queen's Proctor.

(For **Salaries**, *see* page 293).

Procurator-General and Treasury Solicitor (G1), J. Nursaw, c.b., q.c.
Deputy Treasury Solicitor (G2), (vacant).

Central Advisory Division

Principal Assistant Solicitor (G3), Miss J. L. Wheldon.
Assistant Solicitors (G5), M. A. Blythe; M. J. Hemming.
Grade 6, P. C. Jenkins; Mrs. P. Dayer; C. J. Gregory; M. Lewis; Ms. V. Selzer.

Litigation Divisions

Principal Assistant Solicitors (G3), T. J. G. Pratt; R. N. Ricks; J. H. Wilkinson.
Assistant Solicitors (G5), D. Brummell; J. E. Collins; I. Hood; A. S. W. Hyett; A. Leithead; C. G. Leonard; R. Lines; A. J. Sandal; S. Sargant; G. F. Sills.
Grade 6, Mrs. D. Babar; J. N. Desai; I. R. S. Falconer; Mrs. S. J. Hay; A. D. Lawton; P. Messer; D. Palmer; R. J. Phillips; D. A. Stalker; A. Turek; P. F. O. Whitehurst.
Senior Legal Assistants, A. P. M. Aylett; Miss P. J. Carroll; P. D. F. Grant; J. D. Howes.
Principals (G7), N. Ash; Miss J. L. C. Brooks; Miss R. M. Caudwell; N. M. Fleischman; A. K. Fraser; Miss J. A. Gensmantel; H. A. Kaya; Miss A. Lancaster; Miss E. Long; Miss M. A. McNally; N. Magyar; F. G. O'Connell; H. O. J. R. Shepheard; M. G. Truran; R. J. Walters; J. C. Youdell.

Queen's Proctor Division

Queen's Proctor, J. Nursaw, c.b., q.c.
Assistant Queen's Proctor, I. Hood.

Property Division

Principal Assistant Solicitor (G3), I. T. Lewis.

Assistant Solicitors (G5), M. H. M. Anderson; R. W. M. Cooper; P. L. Noble; M. F. Rawlins; A. M. Scarfe; J. Wyer.
Grade 6, R. L. Coward; M. Drayton; Miss R. C. Farmer; D. J. C. Garnett; Miss G. Gilder; J. B. Howe; P. F. Nockles; C. L. Oastler; R. M. Pierce; S. W. Rock; M. R. Rosenfeld; R. J. B. Stenhouse; Miss C. E. M. Troddyn.
Senior Legal Assistants, M. V. Cooper; T. Forrester; A. R. Lilleystone; Miss P. E. Slatter; T. J. Sylvester-Jones; B. D. Thurley; S. A. Tobin; W. F. Williams.
Grade 7, I. Adams; D. G. Ager; H. S. Davis; Mrs. A. M. Foxhuntley; R. D. Harris; C. R. Irving; J. H. McFarland; G. J. Norris; P. Page; A. W. Prior; A. M. H. Prosser; D. A. Reid; N. P. Rex; G. T. Tuttle; J. M. Williamson.

Statutory Publications Office

Editor (G5), J. M. Gibson.
Grade 6, C. E. J. Carey.

Establishment, Finance and General Services Division

Establishment and Legal Personnel Officer (G5), D. F. W. Pickup.
Deputy Establishment Officer (G7), Mrs. P. L. Woods.
Head of Costs Branch (G6), P. Moran.
Chief Accountant (G7), B. C. Shephard.

Bona Vacantia Division

Assistant Solicitor (G5), Miss S. L. Sargant.
Senior Legal Assistant, M. R. M. Davies.
Grade 7, Miss H. Donnelly.

Ministry of Defence Branch
Neville House, Page Street, SW1P 4LS
[01–218 4691]

Grade 4, R. P. Ellis.
Grade 6, J. R. G. Braggins; R. A. D. Jackson; Mrs. A. M. Morris; A. L. Norris; M. B. Sturdy.

Department of Education and Science Branch
Elizabeth House, York Road, SE1 7PH
[01–934 9958]

Principal Assistant Solicitor (G3), J. E. Coleman.
Assistant Solicitors (G5), D. J. Aries; F. L. Croft; M. Harris.
Grade 6, A. D. Preston; Miss M. Trefgarne.
Senior Legal Assistant, N. P. Beach.

Department of Employment Branch
Caxton House, Tothill Street, SW1H 9NF
[01–273 5851]

Principal Assistant Solicitor (G3), H. R. L. Purse.
Assistant Solicitors (G5), R. J. Baker; Mrs. A. Leale; S. G. Milligan; Miss V. Rice-Pyle.
Grade 6, R. H. Britten; Mrs. C. V. Fox; G. W. M. Galliford; C. House; N. A. D. Lambert; J. K. Winayak.
Senior Legal Assistant, J. Hall.
Grade 7, P. H. Kilgarriff.

Department of Energy Branch
Thames House South, Millbank, SW1P 4QJ
[01–211 6046]

Principal Assistant Solicitor (G3), G. B. Claydon.
Assistant Solicitors (G5), D. Hogg; D. H. M. Ingham; D. J. Ecclestone; D. F. Pascho.
Grade 6, M. R. Brocklehurst; F. D. W. Clarke; Miss V. F. Dewhurst; Mrs. C. V. Fox; R. C. Perkins.

Department of Transport Branch
2 Marsham Street, SW1P 3EB
[01–276 5107]

Principal Assistant Solicitor (G3), G. H. Beetham.
Assistant Solicitors (G5), R. G. Bellis; P. D. Coopman; C. W. M. Ingram; B. W. James; A. G. Jones.

Grade 6, Miss P. F. Henderson; Miss A. Lind-Smith; B. McHenry; N. C. Thomas,.
Senior Legal Assistants, B. J. Hammersley; A. K. Johnston.
Grade G7, S. T. Harker; A. W. Stewart.

COUNCIL ON TRIBUNALS
7th Floor, 22 Kingsway, WC2B 6LE
[01-936 7045]

The Council on Tribunals are an independent statutory body. They keep under review the constitution and working of the various tribunals which have been placed under their general supervision, and consider and report on administrative procedures relating to statutory inquiries. They must be consulted by Government departments on proposals for legislation affecting tribunals and inquiries and on proposals where the need for an appeals procedure may arise. They also offer advice on draft primary legislation.

Some 60 tribunals are currently under the Council's supervision. The matters with which they deal range from agriculture to immigration, pensions, road traffic, taxation, and the allocation of school places.

The Scottish Committee of the Council generally considers Scottish tribunals and matters relating only to Scotland.

Members of the Council are appointed by the Lord Chancellor and the Lord Advocate. The Scottish Committee is composed partly of members of the Council designated by the Lord Advocate and partly others appointed by him. The Parliamentary Commissioner for Administration is *ex officio* a member of both the Council and the Scottish Committee.
Chairman, Sir Cyril Philips.
Members, The Parliamentary Commissioner for Administration; D. Bruce; Miss S. M. Cameron, Q.C.; Mrs. M. P. Case; Prof. D. L. Foulkes; A. C. Heywood; Miss J. Horsham, C.B.E.; G. V. Hyde; W. N. Hyde; Mrs. J. U. Kellock; R. N. M. MacLean, Q.C.; M. E. J. Rush; Mrs. S. H. Spence; Prof. A. Webb.
Secretary, C. W. Dyment.

Scottish Committee
20 Walker Street, Edinburgh EH3 7HR
[031–220 1236]

Chairman, R. N. M. MacLean, Q.C.
Members, The Parliamentary Commissioner for Administration; D. Bruce; W. J. Campbell; Mrs. C. A. M. Davies; T. R. H. Godden; J. Langan; Mrs. E. Walker.
Secretary, Ms. L. Wilkie.

TRIBUNALS
(see pages 387–88)

UNIVERSITIES FUNDING COUNCIL
14 Park Crescent, W1N 4DH
[01–636 7799]

The Universities Funding Council was established under the provisions of the Education Reform Act 1988, and came into existence formally on April 1, 1989.
Chairman, The Lord Chilver, F.R.S.
Chief Executive, Sir Peter Swinnerton-Dyer, Bt., K.B.E., F.R.S.
Members, Prof. J. P. Barron; Prof. Gillian Brown; Mrs. R. Chapman; Prof. D. Dilks; Prof. Sir Colin Dollery; Prof. B. Follett, F.R.S.; Sir Kenneth Green; Prof. Marian Hicks; R. B. Horton; Sir Donald McCallum; Prof. G. Roberts, F.R.S.; Prof. H. Wood.
Secretary, N. T. Hardyman, C.B.

Assistant Secretaries (G5), E. C. Appleyard; I. C. H. Powell.

WELSH OFFICE
The Welsh Office has responsibility in Wales for ministerial functions relating to health and personal social services; education, except for terms and conditions of service, student awards and the University; the Welsh language and culture; local government; housing; water and sewerage; environmental protection; sport; agriculture and fisheries; forestry; land use, including town and country planning, countryside and nature conservation; new towns; ancient monuments and historic buildings; roads; tourism; a range of matters affecting the careers service and the activities of the Training Agency in Wales; financial assistance to industry; the urban programme in Wales; the operation of the European Regional Development Fund in Wales and other European Community matters; civil emergencies, and all financial aspects of these matters, including Welsh rate support grant. It has oversight responsibilities for economic affairs and regional planning in Wales.
(For **Salaries**, *see* page 293)

Gwydyr House, Whitehall, SW1A 2ER
[01–270 300]
Secretary of State for Wales, THE RT. HON. PETER WALKER, M.B.E., M.P.
Private Secretary, S. R. Williams.
Assistant Private Secretaries, M. E. Powell; E. K. Davies.
Parliamentary Private Secretary, C. Shepherd, M.P.
Minister of State, WYN ROBERTS, M.P.
Private Secretary, M. C. Hum.
Parliamentary Under-Secretary, IAN GRIST, M.P.
Private Secretary, W. H. Rees.
Parliamentary Clerk, V. R. Watkin.
Permanent Secretary (G1), Sir Richard Lloyd Jones, K.C.B.
Private Secretary, Mrs. A. M. Jackson.

Cathays Park, Cardiff CF1 3NQ
[0222–825111]
Deputy Secretaries (G2), J. W. Lloyd; J. W. Preston, C.B.

Establishment Group
Principal Establishment Officer (G3), G. C. G. Craig.
Heads of Divisions (G5), R. M. Abel; W. L. Chapman; L. L. Ginn.
Senior Economic Adviser (G5), O. T. Hooker.
Chief Statistician (G5), Dr. M. P. G. Pepper.
Head of Health Intelligence Unit (G6), G. J. Cockell.
Principals (G7), R. J. Callen; P. Davenport; C. Tudor.
Economic Adviser (G7), V. W. F. McPherson.
Principal Research Officers (G7), I. I. Thomas; E. Darwin; Mrs. M. A. J. Gronow.
Statisticians (G7), M. R. Brand; J. T. Fletcher; K. Francombe; Ms. C. Fullerton; P. J. Fullerton; E. Swires Hennessey; J. D. James; H. M. Jones; R. Jones; J. D. Kinder; Mrs. S. Stansfield.

Cadw: Welsh Historic Monuments
Brunel House, Fitzalan Road, Cardiff CF2 1UY
[0222–465511]
Director, E. A. J. Carr.
Conservation Architect (G6), J. D. Hogg.
Principal Inspector of Ancient Monuments and Historic Buildings, J. R. Avent.

Cathay Park, Cardiff CF1 3NQ
Inspectors of Ancient Monuments and Historic Buildings, J. K. Knight; A. D. McLees; Dr. S. E. Rees; R. C. Turner; M. J. Yates.

Finance Group

Principal Finance Officer (G3), J. F. Craig.
Heads of Divisions (G5), C. L. Jones; L. A. Pavelin; J. Shortridge; B. Wilcox.
Principals (G7), Dr. M. Dunn; M. G. Horlock; J. Kilner; P. G. C. Lunn; H. Rawlings; D. T. Richards; C. E. Taylor; B. O. Valentine.
Head of Internal Audit (G7), D. Howarth.
Head of N.H.S. Audit (G7), P. Brown.

Health Professional Group

Medical Officer .... £21,633–£29,280
Dental Officer .... £19,905–£28,154
Chief Medical Officer (G3), G. Crompton.
Deputy Chief Medical Officer (G4), A. M. George.
Senior Medical Officers (G5), G. J. Moses, O.B.E.; D. Ferguson Lewis; Ms. M. Cotter; D. E. Davies; D. Owen; H. G. Penrhyn Jones; Ms. R. Jacobs; Ms. A. K. Thomas.
Chief Dental Officer, D. M. Heap.
Medical Officers, J. D. Andrews; J. W. Crossley; T. I. Evans; Dr. L. Hamilton-Kirkwood; N. E. Thomas.
Dental Officers, M. Davies; J. D. O. Parkholm; T. A. Williams.
Scientific Adviser (G5), Dr. J. A. V. Pritchard.
Pharmaceutical Adviser (G6), Dr. G. B. A. Veitch.

Housing, Health and Social Services Policy Group

Head of Group (G3), R. W. Jarman.
Heads of Divisions (G5), D. Adams; R. J. Davies; S. H. Martin; A. Thornton; D. I. Westlake.
Chief Social Work Service Officer (G5), D. G. Evans.
Chief Architect (G6), C. Eyres (*acting*).
Deputy Chief Social Work Service Officer, J. K. Fletcher.
Principals (G7), L. Conway; C. Coombs; A. C. Elmer; P. Godden-Kent; D. B. Hilbourne; A. G. Huwes; Miss E. M. Jones; Mrs. C. Peat; M. Shannahan.
Social Work Service Officers (G7), D, Barker; D. A. Brushett; G. H. Davies; Miss R. E. Evans; I. Forster; J. F. Mooney; C. D. Vyvyan; Mrs. P. White; R. C. Woodward.
Principal Professional and Technology Officers (G7), R. Broad; T. A. Campden; G. N. Harding; W. Ross.

National Health Service Directorate

Director of the NHS in Wales, J. W. Owen.
Heads of Divisions (G5), W. G. Davies; G. T. Evans; P. R. Gregory; D. A. Pritchard; N. E. Thomas; Mrs. B. J. M. Wilson.
Head of Division (G6), G. T. Evans.
Principals (G7), Mrs. J. Annand; C. J. Burdett; W. M. Cooper; J. Duggan; M. Harper; N. S. Jones, I.S.O.; D. McGlinn; Miss C. Maddocks; K. Orchard; D. Quinlan; D. M. Rolph; M. F. Webb.
Ambulance Adviser (G7), P. J. Hunt.
Principal Professional and Technology Officer (G7), M. W. Grist.

Nursing Division

Chief Nursing Officer £34,969
Deputy Chief Nursing Officer £31,309
Nursing Officers .... £24,620–£28,280
Chief Nursing Officer, Miss M. Bull.
Deputy Chief Nursing Officer, Mrs. B. Melvin.
Nursing Officers, Miss G. Harris; Dr. D. Keyzer; Mrs. B. Melvin; M. F. Tonkin; Mrs. D. J. Vass; Mrs. A. Wakin.

Legal Division

Legal Adviser (G3), A. J. Beale.
Assistant Solicitors (G5), D. G. Lambert; P. J. Murrin.
Grade 6, J. D. H. Evans; A. K. Gillard; C. P. Jones; C. G. Longville; Mrs. T. C. Shellens; J. H. Turnball; A. J. Watkins; A. Widdrington.

Senior Legal Assistants (G7), A. J. Park; Mrs. A. T. Parkes; D. H. J. Williams.

Information Division

Director of Information (G5), H. G. Roberts.
Chief Press Officer (G7), E. M. Bowen, M.V.O.

Economic and Regional Policy Group

Head of Group (G3), O. Rees.
Heads of Divisions (G5), M. E. Bevan; Miss E. N. M. Davies; B. J. Mitchell; F. G. Watson.
Principals (G7), D. Beames; R. O. Evans; Ms. J. M. Gordon; R. D. Macey; Miss J. E. Paulett; Ms. J. H. Roberts; G. A. Thomas.

Industry Department

Director (G3), C. D. Stevens.
Industrial Director (G4), T. E. Morgan, M.B.E.
Heads of Divisions (G5), D. Jones; R. C. Williams.
Senior Principal Scientific Officer (G6), Dr. J. N. M. Firth.
Principals (G7), P. Bishop; J. A. Grimes; R. J. Masefield; D. Pugh (at Colwyn Bay); K. Smith; R. Waller; J. W. Wallington; G. S. Williams.
Principal Scientific Officers (G7), P. Bragg; G. A. Madden.

Education Department

Head of Department (G3), R. H. Jones, C.V.O.
Heads of Divisions (G5), H. Evans; M. L. Evans.
Head of Division (G6), R. C. Simpson.
Principals (G7), Mrs. J. Booker; D. A. Bullen; R. O. Evans; B. Hayward-Blake; Mrs. J. Hopkins; J. R. Howells; M. G. Richards; Mrs. H. Thomas; A. Whittaker; Dr. B. M. J. Wilson.

H. M. Inspectorate

Chief Inspector (G4), I. R. Lloyd.
Staff Inspectors (G5), S. J. Adams; R. L. James; W. R. Jenkins; T. E. Parry; P. Thomas; R. Thomas; M. J. F. Wynn.
H. M. Inspectors (G6), C. Abbott; G. Adams; R. A. Charles; Mrs. G. Briwnant Jones; R. G. Davies; D. G. Evans; J. R. N. Evans; N. B. Evans; Mrs. L. Gainsbury; G. C. Griffiths; J. Griffiths; M. G. Haines; A. Hamilton Jones; I. G. Higginbotham; A. Higgins; I. L. James; Mrs. R. James; M. John; G. D. Jones; A. R. Large; G. T. J. Jones; O. E. Jones; Mrs A. Keane; J. M. Laugharne; M. J. Law; J. R. Lewis; Miss S. Lewis; Mrs. M. E. R. Lloyd; A. Lowndes; A. Morgan; I. G. Morgan; Miss P. A. Nicholas; Miss E. Ogwen; T. G. Prosser; W. H. Raybould; D. G. H. Rees; Miss D. Selleck; Mrs. V. Scott; R. I. Swain; R. Taylor; G. Thomas; Mrs. I. Thomas; Miss L. Thomas; P. B. Walker; B. Wigley; E. L. Williams; D. P. Williams.

Transport, Planning, Water and Environment Group

Head of Group (G3), R. A. Wallace.
Director of Highways (G4), K. J. Thomas°.
Heads of Divisions (G5), A. H. H. Jones; J. C. Lewis; C. J. Curry (*Chief Planner*); H. R. Bollington°; Mrs. E. Taylor°; (*G6*), D. M. Timlin.
Superintending Engineers (G6), J. G. Evans°; B. H. Hawker*; R. Lober°.
Superintending Estates Officer (G6), G. K. Hoad.
Senior Principal (G6), P. R. Marsden.
Principals (G7), G. Davies; R. W. Jenkins°; A. V. Price; D. Powell°; G. R. Jones; D. Hadfield°; W. P. Roderick; D. Simpson.
Principal Planning Officers (G7), D. B. Courtier; J. O. Pryce; J. V. Spear.
Principal Research Officers (G7), A. S. Dredge; Ms. L. J. Roberts.
Principal Estates Officer (G7), R. W. Wilson.
Principal Scientific Officer (G7), R. A. Page.

Principal Professional and Technology Officers (G7), J. A. Atkins; H. R. Payne; J. E. Saunders.

Principal Professional and Technology Officers, Highways Directorate (G7), T. A. Dockerty°; P. Dunstan°; J. A. L. Harries*; A. L. Howcraft°; B. J. W. Martin°; S. D. Padfield°; R. H. Powell°; J. R. Rees°; D. P. Soane°; C. W. W. Smart°; J. Fitch*; J. Collins°; K. J. Alexander°; R. H. Hooper*.

Planning Inspectorate

Principal Planning Inspectors (G5), R. Pierce; D. Sheers.

Senior Housing and Planning Inspectors (G6), T. W. B. Barnes; J. H. Chadwick; D. Davey; R. Davies; Dr. D. L. R. Robins; G. Sloan; A. H. Vaughan.

H.M. Inspectorate of Pollution for Wales

Inspector, Radiation and Chemicals (G7), Dr. C. Hardman.

Inspector, Water (G7), A. A. Houlden.

Inspector, Hazardous Waste (G7), H. G. Taylor.

Agriculture Department

Head of Department (G3), J. I. Davies, M.B.E.

Heads of Divisions (G5), G. Podmore; D. R. Thomas; L. K. Walford.

Principals (G7), P. Finnigan†; J. C. Alexander; J. C. Carter *(acting)*; R. A. Norris; R. F. Patterson.

Divisional Executive Officers (G7), W. K. Griffiths *(Carmarthen)*; D. W. Evans *(Ruthin)*; E. Hughes *(Caernarfon)*; R. J. E. Wilcox *(Llandrindod Wells)*.

Based at:

°Ty Glas Road, Llanishen, Cardiff CF4 5PL (022–753271)

*Government Buildings, Pinerth Road, Rhos on Sea, Colwyn Bay LL28 4UL (0492–44261)

†Plas Crug, Aberystwyth SY23 1NG (0970–3162)

OFFICE OF WATER SERVICES

c/o Rivers House, 30–34 Albert Embankment, SE1 7TL

[01-820 0101]

The Office of Water Services was set up under the Water Act 1989 and came into being on Sept. 1, 1989. (The Office is to move to Birmingham in late 1989.) Its role is to support the Director General of Water Services who is the regulatory official for the industry. His main duties are to ensure that water companies comply with the terms of their appointments (or licences) and to protect the interests of water users. The Director General is independent of Ministerial control and directly accountable to Parliament.

Director General of Water Services, I. Byatt.

WOMEN'S NATIONAL COMMISSION

Government Offices, Horse Guards Road, SW1P 3AL

[01-270 5903]

The Women's National Commission is an advisory committee to Government whose terms of reference are to ensure by all possible means that the informed opinions of women are given their due weight in the deliberations of Government. The Commission's fifty members are all women who are elected or appointed by national organizations with a large and active membership of women. The organizations include the women's sections of the major political parties, trades unions, religious groups, professional women's organizations and other bodies broadly representative of women.

Government Co-Chairman, Mrs. Angela Rumbold, C.B.E., M.P. *(nominated by the Prime Minister 1986).*

Elected Co-Chairman, Mrs. Margaret Morrison *(elected 1989).*

Secretary, Ms. M. Jones.

LAW COURTS AND OFFICES

THE JUDICIAL COMMITTEE OF THE PRIVY COUNCIL

The Judicial Committee of the Privy Council is the final court of appeal from courts of the United Kingdom dependencies, courts of independent Commonwealth countries which have retained the right of appeal, courts of the Channel Islands and the Isle of Man, some professional and disciplinary committees, and church sources.

The Judicial Committee includes the Lord Chancellor, the Lords of Appeal in Ordinary (*see* below) and other members of the Privy Council who hold or have held high judicial office, and certain judges from the Commonwealth. Usually, only three or five hear each case.

Office, Downing Street, SW1.
Registrar of the Privy Council, D. H. O. Owen.
Chief Clerk, D. Rushton.

THE JUDICATURE OF ENGLAND AND WALES

The legal system of England and Wales is separate from those of Scotland and Northern Ireland and differs from them in law, judicial procedure and court structure, although there is a common distinction between civil law (disputes between individuals) and criminal law (acts harmful to the community).

The supreme judicial authority for England and Wales is the House of Lords, which is the ultimate Court of Appeal from all courts in Great Britain and Northern Ireland (except criminal courts in Scotland). As a Court of Appeal it consists of the Lord Chancellor and the Lords of Appeal in Ordinary (Law Lords). The Supreme Court of Judicature comprises the Court of Appeal, the Crown Court and the High Court of Justice. The High Court of Justice is the superior civil court and is divided into three Divisions. The Chancery Division is concerned mainly with equity, bankruptcy and contentious probate business; the Queen's Bench Division deals with commercial and maritime law, with civil cases not assigned to other courts; and the Family Division, which deals with matters relating to family law. Sittings are held at the Royal Courts of Justice in London or at 24 Crown Court centres outside the capital. High Court judges sit alone to hear cases at first instance. Appeals from lower courts are heard by two or three judges, or by single judges of the appropriate Division.

The decision to prosecute in cases tried on indictment and in summary cases of a serious nature rests with the Crown Prosecution Service, an independent prosecuting body established in 1986 to serve all of England and Wales (*see* p. 383–4). At the head of the Service is the Director of Public Prosecutions, who discharges his duties under the superintendence of the Attorney General. Certain categories of offence continue to require the consent for prosecution of the Attorney General.

Minor criminal offences (summary offences) are dealt with in magistrates' courts, which usually consist of three unpaid lay magistrates (justices of the peace) sitting without a jury, who are advised on points of law and procedure by a legally-qualified clerk to the justices: in busier courts a full-time, salaried and legally-qualified stipendiary magistrate presides alone. Cases involving people under 17 are heard in juvenile courts, specially constituted magistrates' courts which sit apart from other courts. Preliminary proceedings in a serious case to decide whether there is evidence to justify committal for

trial in the Crown Court are also held in the magistrates' courts. Appeals from magistrates' courts against sentence or conviction are made to the Crown Court. Appeals upon a point of law are made to the High Court, and may go on to the House of Lords.

The Crown Court sits in about 90 centres, divided into six circuits, and is presided over by High Court judges, full-time circuit judges, and part-time recorders, sitting with a jury in all trials which are contested. It deals with trials of the more serious criminal offences, the sentencing of offenders committed for sentence by magistrates' courts (when the magistrates' consider their own power of sentence inadequate), and appeals from lower courts. Magistrates usually sit with a circuit judge or recorder to deal with appeals and committals for sentence. Appeals from the Crown Court, either against sentence or conviction, are made to the Court of Appeal (Criminal Division), presided over by the Lord Chief Justice. A further appeal from the Court of Appeal to the House of Lords can be brought if a point of law of general public importance is considered to be involved.

Most minor civil cases are dealt with by the county courts, of which there are about 300. For cases involving small claims there are special arbitration facilities and simplified procedures: cases involving claims which exceed set limits may be tried in the county courts with the consent of the parties, or in certain circumstances on transfer from the High Court. Undefended divorce cases and, outside London, bankruptcy proceedings can be heard in designated county courts. Magistrates' courts can deal with certain classes of civil case, mostly those relating to the family, and committees of magistrates licence public houses, clubs and betting shops. Appeals in matrimonial, adoption and guardianship proceedings heard in the magistrates' courts go to the Family Division of the High Court: affiliation appeals and appeals from decisions of the licensing committees of magistrates to the Crown Court. Appeals from the High Court and county courts are heard in the Court of Appeal (Civil Division), presided over by the Master of the Rolls, and may go on to the House of Lords, the final court of appeal in civil cases.

Coroners' courts investigate violent and unnatural deaths or sudden deaths where the cause is unknown. Cases may be brought before a local coroner (a senior lawyer or doctor) by doctors, the police, various public authorities or members of the public. Where a death is sudden and the cause is unknown the coroner may order a post-mortem examination to determine the cause of death rather than holding an inquest in court.

THE HOUSE OF LORDS
(as final Court of Appeal)

The Lord High Chancellor (£91,500)
The Rt. Hon. the Lord Mackay of Clashfern
(*born* 1927, *apptd.* 1987).
Lords of Appeal in Ordinary (each £82,750)

	Apptd.
Rt. Hon. Lord Keith of Kinkel, *born* 1922	1977
Rt. Hon. Lord Bridge of Harwich, *born* 1917 ..	1980
Rt. Hon. Lord Brandon of Oakbrook, M.C., *born* 1920................................	1981
Rt. Hon. Lord Templeman, M.B.E., *born* 1920 ..	1982
Rt. Hon. Lord Griffiths, M.C., *born* 1923........	1985
Rt. Hon. Lord Ackner, *born* 1920	1986
Rt. Hon. Lord Oliver of Aylmerton, *born* 1921 ..	1986
Rt. Hon. Lord Goff of Chieveley, *born* 1926	1986
Rt. Hon. Lord Jauncey of Tullichettle, *born* 1925......................................	1987

Rt. Hon. Lord Lowry, *born* 1919 1988
Registrar: The Clerk of the Parliaments, Sir John Sainty, K.C.B.

SUPREME COURT OF JUDICATURE
COURT OF APPEAL

Ex officio Judges.—The Lord High Chancellor, the Lord Chief Justice of England, the Master of the Rolls, the President of the Family Division, and the Vice-Chancellor.
    The Master of the Rolls (£82,750)
The Rt. Hon. the Lord Donaldson of Lymington
    (*born* 1920, *apptd.* 1982).
Secretary, Miss V. Seymour; *Clerk*, K. H. L. Smeeton.

Lords Justices of Appeal (each £79,500)
                                              Apptd.
Rt. Hon. Sir Tasker Watkins, V.C., *born* 1918 . 1980
Rt. Hon. Sir Patrick O'Connor, *born* 1914 1980
Rt. Hon. Sir Michael Fox, *born* 1921 1981
Rt. Hon. Sir Christopher Slade, *born* 1927 1982
Rt. Hon. Sir Francis Purchas, *born* 1919 1982
Rt. Hon. Sir Brian Dillon, *born* 1923 1982
Rt. Hon. Sir Roger Parker, *born* 1923 1983
Rt. Hon. Sir David Croom-Johnson, D.S.C.,
    V.R.D., *born* 1914 1984
Rt. Hon. Sir Anthony Lloyd, *born* 1929 1984
Rt. Hon. Sir Brian Neill, *born* 1923 1985
Rt. Hon. Sir Michael Mustill, *born* 1931 1985
Rt. Hon. Sir Martin Nourse, *born* 1932 1985
Rt. Hon. Sir Iain Glidewell, *born* 1924 1985
Rt. Hon. Sir John Balcombe, *born* 1925 1985
Rt. Hon. Sir Ralph Gibson, *born* 1922 1985
Rt. Hon. Sir John Stocker, M.C., T.D., *born* 1918 1986
Rt. Hon. Sir Harry Woolf, *born* 1933 1986
Rt. Hon. Sir Donald Nicholls, *born* 1933 1986
Rt. Hon. Sir Thomas Bingham, *born* 1933 1986
Rt. Hon. Sir Patrick Russell, *born* 1926 1986
Rt. Hon. Dame Elizabeth Butler-Sloss, D.B.E.,
    born 1933 1988
Rt. Hon. Sir Peter Taylor, *born* 1930 1988
Rt. Hon. Sir Murray Stuart-Smith, *born* 1927 . 1988
Rt. Hon. Sir Christopher Staughton, *born* 1933 1988
Rt. Hon. Sir Michael Mann, *born* 1930 1988
Rt. Hon. Sir Donald Farquharson, *born* 1928 . 1989

Court of Appeal (Criminal Division)

Judges, The Lord Chief Justice of England, The Master of the Rolls, Lord Justices of Appeal and the Judges of the High Court of Justice.

Courts-Martial Appeal Court

Judges, The Lord Chief Justice of England, The Master of the Rolls, Lords Justice of Appeal, and Judges of the High Court of Justice.

HIGH COURT OF JUSTICE
CHANCERY DIVISION
President, The Lord High Chancellor
The Vice-Chancellor (£79,500)
The Rt. Hon. Sir Nicolas Browne-Wilkinson
    (*born* 1930, *apptd.* 1985)

Secretary (vacant); *Clerk*, W. Northfield, B.E.M.

Judges (each £72,000)   Apptd.
Hon. Sir John Vinelott, *born* 1923 1978
Hon. Sir Jean-Pierre Warner, *born* 1924 1981
Hon. Sir Peter Gibson, *born* 1934 1981
Hon. Sir Mervyn Davies, M.C., T.D., *born* 1918 . 1982
Hon. Sir Jeremiah Harman, *born* 1930 1982
Hon. Sir Richard Scott, *born* 1934 1983
Hon. Sir Leonard Hoffman, *born* 1934 1985
Hon. Sir John Knox, *born* 1925 1985

Hon. Sir Peter Millett, *born* 1932 1986
Hon. Sir Andrew Morritt, *born* 1938 1988
Hon. Sir William Aldous, *born* 1936 1988

High Court of Justice in Bankruptcy

Judges, The Master of the Rolls, The Vice-Chancellor, the Lord Justices, and other members of the Court of Appeal.

Companies Court

Judges, The Vice Chancellor; The Hon. Mr. Justice Vinelott; The Hon. Mr. Justice Warner; The Hon. Mr. Justice Mervyn Davies; The Hon. Mr. Justice Harman; The Hon. Mr. Justice Scott; The Hon. Mr. Justice Hoffman; The Hon. Mr. Justice Knox; The Hon. Mr. Justice Millett; The Hon. Mr. Justice Morritt.

Patent Court (Appellate Section)

Judges, The Hon. Mr. Justice Whitford; The Hon. Mr. Justice Falconer.

QUEEN'S BENCH DIVISION
The Lord Chief Justice of England (£89,500)
The Rt. Hon. the Lord Lane, A.F.C.
    (*born* 1918, *apptd.* 1980)

Secretary, Mrs. J. Simpson; *Clerk*, G. Curtis.

Judges (each £72,000)   Apptd.
Hon. Sir William Mars-Jones, M.B.E., *born*
    1915 1969
Hon. Sir Leslie Boreham, *born* 1918 1972
Hon. Sir Michael Davies, *born* 1921 1973
Hon. Sir Haydn Tudor Evans, *born* 1920 1974
Hon. Sir Kenneth Jupp, M.C., *born* 1917 1975
Hon. Sir Derek Hodgson, *born* 1917 1977
Hon. Sir Ronald Waterhouse, *born* 1926 1978
Hon. Sir Maurice Drake, D.F.C., *born* 1923 . . . 1978
Hon. Sir Barry Sheen, *born* 1918 1978
Hon. Sir David McNeill, *born* 1922 1979
Hon. Sir Christopher French, *born* 1925 1979
Hon. Sir Peter Webster, *born* 1924 1980
Hon. Sir Anthony McCowan, *born* 1928 1981
Hon. Sir Charles McCullough, *born* 1931 1981
Hon. Sir John Leonard, *born* 1926 1981
Hon. Sir Roy Beldam, *born* 1925 1981
Hon. Sir David Hirst, *born* 1925 1982
Hon. Sir John Stewart Hobhouse, *born* 1932 . . 1982
Hon. Sir Andrew Leggatt, *born* 1930 1982
Hon. Sir Michael Nolan, *born* 1928 1982
Hon. Sir Oliver Popplewell, *born* 1927 1983
Hon. Sir William Macpherson, T.D., *born* 1926 1983
Hon. Sir Philip Otton, *born* 1933 1983
Hon. Sir Paul Kennedy, *born* 1935 1983
Hon. Sir Michael Hutchison, *born* 1933 1983
Hon. Sir Simon Brown, *born* 1937 1984
Hon. Sir Anthony Evans, *born* 1934 1984
Hon. Sir Mark Saville, *born* 1936 1985
Hon. Sir Johan Steyn, *born* 1932 1985
Hon. Sir Christopher Rose, *born* 1937 1985
Hon. Sir Richard Tucker, *born* 1931 1985
Hon. Sir Robert Gatehouse, *born* 1924 1985
Hon. Sir Patrick Garland, *born* 1929 1985
Hon. Sir John Roch, *born* 1934 1985
Hon. Sir Michael Turner, *born* 1931 1985
Hon. Sir John Alliott, *born* 1932 1986
Hon. Sir Harry Ognall, *born* 1934 1986
Hon. Sir Konrad Schiemann, *born* 1937 1986
Hon. Sir John Owen, *born* 1925 1986
Hon. Sir Denis Henry, *born* 1931 1986
Hon. Sir Humphrey Potts, *born* 1931 1986
Hon. Sir Richard Rougier, *born* 1932 1986
Hon. Sir Ian Kennedy, *born* 1930 1986
Hon. Sir Nicholas Phillips, *born* 1938 1987

Hon. Sir Robin Auld, *born* 1937	1988
Hon. Sir Malcolm Pill, *born* 1938	1988
Hon. Sir Stuart McKinnon, *born* 1938	1988
Hon. Sir Mark Potter, *born* 1937	1988
Hon. Sir Henry Brooke, *born* 1936	1988
Hon. Sir Igor Judge, *born* 1941	1988
Hon. Sir Edwin Jowitt, *born* 1929	1988
Hon. Sir Michael Morland, *born* 1929	1989
Hon. Sir Mark Waller, *born* 1940	1989
Hon. Sir Roger Buckley, *born* 1939	1989

FAMILY DIVISION
President (£79,500)

Rt. Hon. Sir Stephen Brown
(*born* 1929, *apptd.* 1988).

Secretary, Mrs. S. Leung; *Clerk*, Mrs. S. Bell.

Judges (each £72,000)	Apptd.
Hon. Sir Kenneth Hollings, M.C., *born* 1918 ...	1971
Hon. Sir John Wood, M.C., *born* 1922	1977
Hon. Sir Gervase Sheldon, *born* 1913	1978
Hon. Sir Michael Eastham, *born* 1920	1978
Hon. Dame Margaret Booth, D.B.E., *born* 1933 .	1979
Hon. Sir Anthony Lincoln, *born* 1920	1979
Hon. Sir Anthony Ewbank, *born* 1925	1980
Hon. Sir John Waite, *born* 1932	1982
Hon. Sir Anthony Hollis, *born* 1927	1982
Hon. Sir Swinton Thomas, *born* 1931	1985
Hon. Sir Mathew Thorpe, *born* 1938	1988
Hon. Sir Edward Cazalet, *born* 1936	1988
Hon. Sir Alan Ward, *born* 1938	1988
Hon. Sir Scott Baker, *born* 1937	1988
Hon. Sir Robert Johnson, *born* 1933	1989
Hon. Sir Douglas Brown, *born* 1931	1989
Hon. Sir Donald Rattee, *born* 1937	1989

RESTRICTIVE PRACTICES COURT

Judicial Members, The Hon. Mr. Justice Lincoln (*Principal*); The Hon. Mr. Justice McNeill; The Hon. Mr. Justice Warner; The Hon. Lord Sutherland; The Hon. Mr. Justice Murray.
Lay Members, N. L. Salmon; I. G. Stewart; B. M. Currie; L. Robertson; R. Garrick; Z. A. Silberston.

OFFICIAL REFEREES' COURTS
St. Dunstan's House,
133–137 Fetter Lane,
EC4A 1HD

His Hon. Judge Hawser, Q.C.; His Hon. Judge Newey, Q.C.; His Hon. Judge Lewis, Q.C.; His Hon. Judge Davies, Q.C.; His Hon. Judge Fox-Andrews, Q.C.; His Hon. Judge Bowsher, Q.C. £62,700

LORD CHANCELLOR'S DEPARTMENT
See **Government and Public Offices.**

SUPREME COURT DEPARTMENTS AND OFFICES
Royal Courts of Justice, WC2A 2LL

Administrator, J. R. A. Hanratty, T.D.
£28,170–£31,602

Central Office of the Supreme Court
Royal Courts of Justice, WC2A 2LL

Senior Master of the Supreme Court (Q.B.D.), and Queen's Remembrancer, I. S. Warren £48,100
Masters of the Supreme Court (Q.B.D.), C. W. S. Lubbock; P. B. Creightmore; K. W. Topley; D. L. Prebble; A. A. Grant; G. H. Hodgson; R. L. Turner; J. Trench; M. Tennant £39,400
Chief Clerk (*Central Office*), C. F. Jones
£17,360–£22,606

Chief Clerk to the Q.B. Judges in Chambers, A. Foley .... £17,360–£22,606

Crown Office of the Supreme Court
Royal Courts of Justice, WC2A 2LL

Master of the Crown Office, and Queen's Coroner and Attorney, M. McKenzie £48,100

Court of Appeal (Civil Division) Office
Royal Courts of Justice, WC2A 2LL

Registrar, J. D. R. Adams £48,100

Criminal Appeal Office
Royal Courts of Justice, WC2A 2LL

Registrar, M. McKenzie £48,100
Deputy Registrar, Mrs. L. Knapman £28,170–£31,602
Chief Clerk, J. Read .... £17,360–£22,606

Courts-Martial Appeals Office
Royal Courts of Justice, WC2A 2LL

Registrar, M. McKenzie £48,100
Chief Clerk, J. Read.

Supreme Court Taxing Office

Chief Master, F. G. Berkeley £48,100
Masters of the Supreme Court, A. J. Wright; C. R. N. Martyn; M. N. Devonshire, T.D.; P. T. Hurst; C. A. Prince £39,400
Principal Taxing Officer, T. J. Ryan £17,360–£22,606

Examiners of the Court
(Empowered to take Examination of Witnesses in all Divisions of the High Court)
M. F. Meredith-Hardy; B. Rathbone; N. W. Briggs; R. Jacobs.

Chancery Chambers,
Royal Courts of Justice, WC2A 2LL

Chief Master of the Supreme Court, R. D. Munrow
£48,100
Masters of the Supreme Court, M. B. Cholmondeley Clarke; J. M. Dyson; J. S. Gowers; G. A. Barratt
£39,400
Chief Clerk, G. Robinson .... £17,360–£22,606
Conveyancing Counsel of the Supreme Court, J. Monckton; S. G. Maurice; M. J. Roth.

Bankruptcy Department
Thomas More Building, Royal Courts of Justice, Strand, WC2A 2LL

Chief Registrar, T. L. Dewhurst £48,100
Chief Clerk, T. Palmer.

Official Receivers' Department

Senior Official Receiver, P. D. Pink.
Official Receivers, D. E. Dolman; P. J. Chillery; M. J. Pugh; L. T. Cramp; M. W. A. Sanderson.

Companies Court
Thomas More Building,
Royal Courts of Justice, WC2A 2LL

Registrar, M. Buckley.
Chief Clerk, C. A. N. Edinboro ..... £17,360–£22,606
Senior Official Receiver, Companies Department, P. D. Pink.

Restrictive Practices Court
Thomas More Building,
Royal Courts of Justice, WC2A 2LL

Clerk of the Court, M. Buckley.
Chief Clerk, C. A. N. Edinboro.

Principal Registry (Family Division)
Somerset House, WC2R 1LP

Senior Registrar, C. F. Turner £48,100
Registrars, T. G. Guest; D. E. Morris; J. E. Artro-Morris; R. B. Rowe; G. B. N. A. Angel; B. P. F. Kenworthy-Browne; G. A. Terian; Mrs. K. T. Moorhouse; D. T. A. Davies; Mrs. N. Pearce; M. J. Segal; R. Conn £39,400
Secretary, G. J. Maple .... £17,360–£22,606

District Probate Registrars
Birmingham and Stoke-on-Trent, C. Marsh.
Brighton and Maidstone, M. N. Emery.
Bristol, Exeter and Bodmin, P. L. Speyer.
Ipswich, Norwich and Peterborough, E. R. Alexander.
Leeds, Lincoln and Sheffield, A. P. Dawson.
Liverpool, Lancaster and Chester, B. J. Thomas.
Llandaff, Bangor, Carmarthen and Gloucester, D. W. Jones.
Manchester and Nottingham, M. A. Moran.
Newcastle, Carlisle, York and Middlesbrough, A. Bertram.
Oxford, Miss M. L. Farmborough.
Winchester, A. K. Biggs.

Admiralty and Commercial Registry and Marshal's Office
Royal Courts of Justice, WC2A 2LL

Registrar, W. K. Topley £39,400
Marshal and Chief Clerk, V. E. Ricks
£17,360–£22,624

Court of Protection
Stewart House, 24 Kingsway, WC2B 6HD

Master, Mrs. A. B. Macfarlane £48,100

Official Solicitor's Department
Penderel House, 287 High Holborn, WC1

Official Solicitor to the Supreme Court, H. D. S. Venables .... £37,600–£47,600
Deputy Official Solicitor, H. J. Baker £37,425–£41,225
Chief Clerk, Mrs. V. J. Carter ...... £17,360–£22,606

OFFICE OF THE LORD CHANCELLOR'S VISITORS
Trevelyan House, 30 Great Peter Street, SW1

Legal Visitor, M. H. Fauvelle.
Medical Visitors, W. A. Heaton-Ward; E. Carr; F. E. Kenyon; R. J. Kerry; P. A. Morris; D. Parr.

OFFICE OF THE JUDGE ADVOCATE OF THE FLEET
The Law Courts, Barker Road, Maidstone ME16 8EQ

Judge Advocate of the Fleet, His Hon. Judge Waley, V.R.D., Q.C. £48,100

OFFICE OF THE JUDGE ADVOCATE GENERAL OF THE FORCES
(*Joint Service for the Army and the Royal Air Force*)
22 Kingsway, WC2B 6LE

Judge Advocate General, J. Stuart-Smith, C.B., Q.C.
£53,400
Vice Judge Advocate General, G. L. Chapman
£48,100
Assistant Judge Advocates General, C. G. Gould; E. G. Moelwyn-Hughes; A. P. Pitts; S. B. Spence; D. M. Berkson .... £28,170–£31,602
Deputy Judge Advocates, M. A. Hunter; T. R. King; J. P. Camp; T. G. Pontius .... £19,384–£26,378

HIGH COURT AND CROWN COURT CENTRES

First-tier centres deal with both civil and criminal cases and are served by High Court and Circuit Judges. Second-tier centres deal with criminal cases only but are served by both High Court and Circuit Judges. Third-tier centres deal with criminal cases only and are served only by Circuit Judges.

Midland and Oxford Circuit

First-tier—Birmingham, Lincoln, Nottingham, Oxford, Stafford, Warwick. *Second-tier*—Leicester, Northampton, Shrewsbury, Worcester. *Third-tier*—Coventry, Derby, Dudley, Grimsby, Peterborough, Stoke-on-Trent.
Circuit Administrator, R. E. K. Holmes, 2 Newton Street, Birmingham B4 7LU.
Courts Administrators, Birmingham Group, D. A. Warner; *Nottingham Group,* P. H. Martin; *Stafford Group,* A. F. Parker.

North Eastern Circuit

First-tier—Leeds, Newcastle upon Tyne, Sheffield, Teesside. *Second-tier*—York. *Third-tier*—Beverley, Doncaster, Durham, Huddersfield, Kingston-upon-Hull, Wakefield.
Circuit Administrator, S. W. L. James, West Riding House, 17th Floor, Albion Street, Leeds LS1 5AA.
Courts Administrators, Leeds Group, P. Delany; *Newcastle upon Tyne Group,* F. I. Lance; *Sheffield Group,* G. Bingham.

Northern Circuit

First-tier—Carlisle, Liverpool, Manchester, Preston. *Third-tier*—Barrow-in-Furness, Bolton, Burnley, Kendal, Lancaster.
Circuit Administrator, P. M. Harris, Aldine House, West Riverside, New Bailey Street, Salford M3 5EU.
Courts Administrators, Manchester Group, A. H. Howard; *Liverpool Group,* D. A. Beaumont; *Preston Group,* G. Davies.

South Eastern Circuit

First-tier—Greater London, Lewes, Norwich (The High Court in Greater London sits at the Royal Courts of Justice. The Crown Court in Greater London sits at the following locations: Acton, Central Criminal Court, Croydon, Inner London Sessions House, Isleworth, Kingston upon Thames, Knightsbridge, Middlesex Guildhall, Snaresbrook, Southwark and Wood Green). *Second-tier*—Chelmsford, Ipswich, Maidstone, Reading, St. Albans. *Third-tier*—Aylesbury, Bury St. Edmunds, Cambridge, Canterbury, Chichester, Guildford, King's Lynn, Southend.
Circuit Administrator, B. Cooke, New Cavendish House, 18 Maltravers Street, WC2.
Deputy Circuit Administrator, G. E. Calvett.
Courts Administrators, Chelmsford Group, P. Handcock; *Maidstone Group,* Mrs. H. Hartwell; *Kingston Group,* P. M. Thomas; *London (Civil),* K. Winberg; *London (Crime),* G. F. Addicott.

Wales and Chester Circuit

First-tier—Caernarfon, Cardiff, Chester, Mold, Swansea. *Second-tier*—Carmarthen, Newport, Welshpool. *Third-tier*—Dolgellau, Haverfordwest, Knutsford, Merthyr Tydfil, Warrington.
Circuit Administrator, D. Howe, Churchill House, Churchill Way, Cardiff.
Courts Administrators, Cardiff Group, G. Jones; *Chester Group,* E. R. Walter.

Western Circuit

First-tier—Bristol, Exeter, Truro, Winchester. *Second-tier*—Dorchester, Gloucester, Plymouth. *Third-tier*—Barnstaple, Bournemouth, Devizes, Newport (I.O.W.), Portsmouth, Salisbury, Southampton, Swindon, Taunton.

Circuit Administrator, G. Jones, Bridge House, Clifton, Bristol BS8 4BN.

Courts Administrators, Bristol Group, A. C. Butler; *Exeter Group,* (vacant); *Winchester Group,* K. Henderson.

CIRCUIT JUDGES
(*Senior Circuit Judges, £53,400; Circuit Judges, £48,100)

Midland and Oxford Circuit

W. A. L. Allardice; F. A. Allen; B. J. Appleby, q.c.; M. J. Astill; I. J. Black, q.c.; J. F. Blythe, t.d.; D. W. Brunning; F. L. Clark, q.c.; P. N. R. Clark; R. R. B. Cole; J. M. Coulson; P. F. Crane; P. J. Crawford, q.c.; R. H. Curtis, q.c.; A. de Piro, q.c.; T. M. Dillon, q.c.; J. F. Evans, q.c.; B. A. Farrer, q.c.; J. E. Fletcher; H. G. A. Gosling; M. K. Harrison-Hall; T. R. Heald; J. R. Hopkin; R. H. Hutchinson; J. E. M. Irvine; R. P. V. Jenkins; J. G. Jones; T. O. Kellock, q.c.; J. T. C. Lee; M. H. Mander; K. Matthewman, q.c.; R. G. May; P. W. Medd, o.b.e., q.c.; K. S. W. Mellor, q.c.; N. Micklem; A. J. H. Morrison; M. D. Mott; A. J. D. Nicholl; C. J. Pitchers; F. M. Potter; D. E. Roberts; J. A. O. Shand; J. R. S. Smyth; P. J. Stretton; C. S. Stuart-White; H. C. Tayler, q.c.; K. J. Taylor; R. J. Toyn; M. B. Ward; R. L. Ward, q.c.; D. J. R. Wilcox; D. H. Wild; H. Wilson; J. W. Wilson; B. Woods; G. H. Wootton; C. G. Young.

Northern Circuit

H. H. Andrew, q.c.; J. R. Arthur, d.f.c.; A. W. Bell; M. S. Blackburn; A. S. Booth, q.c.; R. Brown; I. B. Campbell; F. B. Carter, q.c.; D. Clarke; P. C. Clegg; G. P. Crowe, q.c.; J. M. Davies, q.c.; Miss A. E. Downey; B. Duckworth; S. B. Duncan; Miss A. M. Ebsworth; A. A. Edmondson; D. M. Evans, q.c.; S. J. D. Fawcus; D. M. Forster; D. G. F. Franks; J. Hall; R. G. Hamilton; J. A. Hammond; R. J. Hardy; T. D. T. Hodson; Miss M. Holt; G. W. Humphries; A. C. Jolly; H. A. Kershaw; H. L. Lachs; C. N. Lees; J. M. Lever, q.c.; R. Lockett; J. H. Lord; C. J. Mahon; I. H. Morris-Jones, q.c.; F. J. Nance; G. K. Naylor, t.d.; M. O' Donoghue; F. D. Paterson; R. E. I. Pickering; D. A. Pirie; *A. M. Prestt, q.c. (*Recorder of Manchester); A. J. Proctor; M. A. G. Sachs; N. W. M. Sellers, v.r.d.; H. S. Singer; J. A. Stannard; Miss A. H. Steel; I. R. Taylor, q.c.; *Sir Sanderson Temple, m.b.e., q.c. (*Recorder of Liverpool); J. P. Townsend; I. S. Webster.

North Eastern Circuit

T. G. F. Atkinson; G. Baker, q.c.; P. M. Baker, q.c.; J. M. A. Barker; G. N. Barr Young; H. G. Bennett, q.c.; D. R. Bentley, q.c.; D. M. A. Bryant; B. Bush; M. C. Carr; P. J. Charlesworth; Myrella Cohen, q.c.; G. J. K. Coles, q.c.; J. A. Cotton; J. Crabtree; M. T. Cracknell; W. H. R. Crawford, q.c.; P. J. Fox, q.c.; A. N. Fricker, q.c.; M. S. Garner; H. G. Hall; W. Hannah; G. F. R. Harkins; J. A. Henham; D. Herrod, q.c.; H. Hewitt; R. Hunt; V. R. Hurwitz; A. E. Hutchinson, q.c.; J. R. Johnson; G. M. Lightfoot; A. C. Macdonald; Miss M. B. M. MacMurray, q.c.; A. L. Myerson, q.c.; D. A. Orde; Miss H. E. Paling; R. A. Percy; J. Pickles; D. M. Savill, q.c.; A. Simpson; J. Stephenson; R. A. R. Stroyan, q.c.; R. C. Taylor; G. M. Vos; M. Walker; P. H. C. Walker.

South Eastern Circuit

M. F. Addison; F. J. Aglionby; A. K. Allen, o.b.e.; M. J. Anwyl-Davies, q.c.; J. A. Baker; J. B. Baker, q.c.; M. J. D. Baker; P. V. Baker, q.c.; A. F. Balston; R. M. N. Band, m.c., q.c.; C. J. A. Barnett, q.c.; R. A. Barr; N. G. A. Bathurst; P. T. S. Batterbury, t.d.; N. E. Beddard; F. E. Beezley; G. J. Binns; M. Birks; J. C. C. Blofeld, q.c.; J. Bolland; P. C. Bowsher, q.c.; P. N. Brandt; L. J. Bromley, q.c.; A. E. Brooks; G. N.

Butler, q.c.; *N. M. Butter, q.c.; H. J. Byrt, q.c.; C. V. Callman; B. E. Capstick, q.c.; A. W. Clark; D. J. Clarkson, q.c.; Patricia Coles, q.c.; C. C. Colston, q.c.; C. D. Compston; M. J. Cook; R. K. Cooke, o.b.e.; G. H. Coombe; M. R. Coombe; Margaret D. Cosgrave; P. H. Counsell; R. C. Cox; P. V. Crocker; D. L. Croft, q.c.; I. T. R. Davidson, q.c.; I. H. Davies, t.d.; L. J. Davies, q.c.; W. L. M. Davies, q.c.; W. N. Denison, q.c.; K. M. Devlin; G. L. S. Dobry, c.b.e., q.c.; C. M. Edwards; Q. T. Edwards, q.c.; F. P. L. Evans, m.c. & bar; q.c. Evans; P. R. Faulks, m.c.; A. L. Figgis; J. J. Finney; J. J. Fordham; G. C. F. Forrester; J. Fox-Andrews, q.c.; A. Garfitt; L. Gerber; S. A. Goldstein; P. W. Goldstone; M. B. Goodman; J. H. Gower, q.c.; M. Graham, q.c.; P. B. Greenwood; D. J. Griffiths; G. D. Grigson; R. B. Groves, t.d., v.r.d.; N. T. Hague, q.c.; P. J. Halnan; J. Hamilton; R. E. Hammerton; J. P. Harris, d.s.c., q.c.; C. L. Hawser, q.c.; J. D. W. Hayman; A. H. Head; M. R. Hickman; J. C. Hicks, q.c.; A. N. Hitching; D. Holden; A. C. W. Hordern, q.c.; Sir David Hughes-Morgan, Bt., c.b., c.b.e.; J. Hunter; H. J. Hyam; C. P. James; W. Kee; M. Kennedy, q.c.; A. M. Kenny; J. F. Kingham; C. F. Kolbert; L. G. Krikler; L. H. C. Lait; G. F. B. Laughland, q.c.; R. Laurie; T. Lawrence; C. G. Lea, m.c.; E. Lewis, q.c.; A. C. L. Lewisohn; A. Lipfriend; D. T. Lloyd; F. R. Lockhart; G. D. Lovegrove, q.c.; B. D. Lowe; R. H. Lownie; Mrs. N. M. Lowry; R. J. Lowry, q.c.; R. D. Lymbery, q.c.; K. M. McHale; K. A. Machin, q.c.; I. G. McLean; J. L. E. MacManus, t.d., q.c.; M. B. McMullan; M. J. P. Macnair; J. R. Main, q.c.; B. A. Marder, q.c.; O. S. Martin, q.c.; N. A. Medawar, q.c.; D. J. Mellor; J. H. E. Mendl; A. L. Mildon, q.c.; D. Q. Miller; Sir James Miskin, q.c. (*Recorder of London*); E. F. Monier-Williams; D. Morton Jack; J. I. Murchie; J. H. R. Newey, q.c.; C. W. F. Newman, q.c.; Mrs. M. F. Norrie; Suzanne F. Norwood; C. R. Oddie; A. Owen; D. A. Paiba; R. H. S. Palmer; M. C. Parker, q.c.; Miss V. A. Pearlman; F. H. L. Petre; A. J. Phelan; T. H. Pigot, q.c. (*Common Serjeant*); D. C. Pitman; P. B. Pollock; H. C. Pownall, q.c.; B. H. Pryor, q.c.; J. E. Pullinger; J. W. Rant, q.c.; E. V. P. Reece; G. K. Rice; K. A. Richardson, q.c.; G. Rivlin, q.c.; D. A. H. Rodwell, q.c.; G. H. Rooke, t.d., q.c.; P. C. R. Rountree; K. W. Rubin; J. H. Rucker; T. R. G. Ryland; R. B. Sanders; J. H. A. Scarlett; J. D. Sheerin; *G. J. Shindler, q.c.; D. R. A. Sich; M. Singh, q.c.; J. K. E. Slack, t.d.; P. M. J. Slot; F. B. Smedley, q.c.; R. J. Southan; *R. O. C. Stable, q.c.; E. Stockdale; C. J. Sumner; J. B. Taylor, m.b.e., t.d.; D. A. Thomas, m.b.e.; A. H. Tibber; A. M. Troup; S. Tumim; J. T. Turner; C. J. M. Tyrer; J. E. Van der Werff; L. J. Verney, q.c.; A. O. R. Vick, q.c.; R. W. Vick; B. J. Wakley, m.b.e.; A. F. Waley, v.r.d., q.c.; R. Walker; J. R. Warde; D. B. Watling, q.c.; V. B. Watts; Sir David West-Russell; F. J. White; J. E. Williams; S. M. Willis; G. N. Worthington; E. G. Wrintmore; K. H. Zucker, q.c.

Wales and Chester Circuit

T. R. Crowther, q.c.; G. H. M. Daniel; R. D. G. David, q.c.; Lord Elystan-Morgan; T. M. Evans, q.c.; W. N. Francis; M. Gibbon, q.c.; D. M. Hughes; G. J. Jones; G. E. Kilfoil; T. E. I. Lewis-Bowen; D. G. Morgan; T. H. Moseley, q.c.; D. A. Phillips; D. W. Powell; E. J. Prosser, q.c.; H. W. J. ap Robert; H. E. P. Roberts, q.c.; J. C. Rutter; S. M. Stephens, q.c.; D. B. Williams, t.d., q.c.; H. V. Williams, q.c.; R. G. Woolley.

Western Circuit

S. T. Bates, q.c.; G. B. Best; C. L. Boothman; Miss J. W. Bracewell, q.c.; M. J. L. Brodrick; R. D. H. Bursell, q.c.; Sir Jonathan Clarke; Hazel Counsell; J. A. Cox; J. W. Da Cunha; M. Dyer; P. Fallon, q.c.; P. D. Fanner; B. J. F. Galpin; I. S. Hill, q.c.; G. B. Hutton; J. H. Inskip, q.c.; A. C. Lauriston; Sir

Ian Lewis; D. McCarraher, V.R.D.; H. E. L. McCreery, Q.C.; Miss S. M. D. McKinney; I. S. McKintosh; J. G. McNaught; C. B. K. Mantell, Q.C.; E. G. Neville; J. N. P. Rudd; D. A. Smith, Q.C.; K. C. L. Smithies; H. J. M. Tucker, Q.C.; D. M. Webster, Q.C.; J. R. Whitley; K. M. Willcock, Q.C.; J. H. Wroath.

RECORDERS

J. R. S. Adams; I. D. G. Alexander; J. Altman; W. P. Andreae-Jones, Q.C.; Ms. L. E. Appleby, Q.C.; J. F. Appleton; J. F. A. Archer, Q.C.; Rt. Hon. P. K. Archer, Q.C., M.P.; A. J. Arlidge, Q.C.; R. Ashton; P. Ashworth, Q.C.; N. J. Atkinson; M. G. Austin-Smith; W. S. Aylen, Q.C.; P. Back, Q.C.; J. F. Badenoch; P. G. N. Badge; A. B. Baillie; N. R. J. Baker, Q.C.; G. S. Barham; A. Barker, Q.C.; B. J. Barker; D. Barker, Q.C.; R. O. Barlow; D. M. W. Barnes, Q.C.; T. P. Barnes, Q.C.; W. E. Barnett, Q.C.; Sir Anthony Barrowclough, Q.C.; J. E. Barry; J. C. T. Barton, Q.C.; K. Bassingthwaite; R. J. A. Batt; S. D. Batten, Q.C.; J. J. Baughan; J. F. Beashel; C. H. Beaumont; P. J. L. Beaumont, Q.C.; C. O. M. Bedingfield, T.D., Q.C.; R. W. Belben; R. E. Bell, Q.C.; The Hon. M. J. Beloff, Q.C.; D. P. Bennett; P. Bennett, Q.C.; R. C. W. Bennett; K. C. Bentall; H. L. Bentham; D. M. Berkson; Miss I. Bernstein; R. H. Bernstein, D.F.C., Q.C.; M. Bethel, Q.C.; J. P. V. Bevan; J. C. Beveridge, Q.C.; P. W. Birts; J. W. Black, Q.C.; D. M. Blair, Q.C.; J. A. Blair-Gould; A. N. H. Blake; C. Bloom, Q.C.; D. J. Blunt; J. G. Boal; G. T. K. Boney; L. A. F. Borrett; P. H. Bowers; I. R. Boyd; J. J. Boyle; R. W. A. Bray; D. J. Brennan, Q.C.; G. J. B. G. Brice, Q.C.; J. N. W. Bridges-Adams; A. J. Brigden; A. N. J. Briggs; P. J. Briggs; D. K. Brown; A. Bueno, Q.C.; J. M. Bull, Q.C.; J. W. M. Bullimore; D. L. Bulmer; J. P. Burgess; J. K. Burke, Q.C.; J. P. Burke, Q.C.; M. A. B. Burke-Gaffney, Q.C.; H. W. Burnett, Q.C.; M. R. Burr; M. J. Burton, Q.C.; A. J. Butcher, Q.C.; A. N. L. Butterfield, Q.C.; R. J. Buxton, Q.C.

Mrs. B. A. Calvert, Q.C.; D. Calvert-Smith; Miss S. M. C. Cameron, Q.C.; A. N. Campbell; The Lord Campbell of Alloway, Q.C.; J. Q. Campbell; B. J. Canham; G. M. C. Carey; A. C. Carlile, Q.C., M.P.; The Lord Carlisle of Bucklow, P.C., Q.C.; H. B. H. Carlisle, Q.C.; R. C. L. Carr; B. I. Caulfield; J. M. Chadwick, Q.C.; J. A. Chadwin, Q.C.; J. R. Chalkley; N. M. Chambers, Q.C.; F. A. Chapman; B. L. Charles, Q.C.; B. W. Chedlow, Q.C.; J. M. Cherry, Q.C.; C. H. Clark; A. P. Clarke, Q.C.; D. C. Clarke, Q.C.; R. N. B. Clegg, Q.C.; G. M. Clifton; C. D. Cochrane, Q.C.; P. J. Cockcroft; D. J. Cocks, Q.C.; J. J. Coffey; T. A. Coghlan; J. R. Cole; N. J. Coleman; N. B. C. Coles, Q.C.; S. H. Colgan; P. N. Collier; A. D. Collins, Q.C.; J. M. Collins; P. H. Collins; A. D. Colman, Q.C.; S. S. Coltart; Ms. M. Colton; J. S. Colyer, Q.C.; P. R. C. Coni, Q.C.; T. A. C. Coningsby, Q.C.; M. B. Connell, Q.C.; J. G. Connor; R. D. Connor; C. S. Cook; R. A. Cooke; Miss B. P. Cooper, Q.C.; A. Cooray; S. M. Corkhill; T. G. E. Corrie; E. Cotran; G. W. A. Cottle; Miss D. R. Cotton, Q.C.; J. S. Coward, Q.C.; B. R. E. Cox, Q.C.; P. J. Cox, D.S.C., Q.C.; C. J. Crespi, Q.C.; P. J. Cresswell, Q.C.; D. I. Crigman; M. L. S. Cripps; I. W. Crompton; F. P. Crowder, Q.C.; J. D. Crowley, Q.C.; E. J. R. Crowther, O.B.E.; W. R. H. Crowther, Q.C.; Miss E. A. M. Curnow, Q.C.; M. J. Curwen; S. C. Darwall-Smith; Mrs. S. P. Darwall-Smith; G. W. Davey; D. T. A. Davies; G. L. Davies; R. E. Davies, Q.C.; A. W. Dawson; D. H. Day, Q.C.; M. Dean, Q.C.; J. J. Deave; J. B. Deby, Q.C.; C. F. Dehn, Q.C.; P. N. De Mille; W. E. Denny, C.B.E., Q.C.; S. C. Desch, Q.C.; J. E. Devaux; M. N. Devonshire; A. E. J. Diamond, Q.C.; J. B. S. Diehl, Q.C.; A. D. Dinkin; A. M. Donne, Q.C.; D. P. Draycott, Q.C.; Sir John Drinkwater, Q.C.; R. Du Cann, Q.C.; S. M. Duffield; P. R. Dunkels; W. H. Dunn, Q.C.; C. H. Durman; A. H. Durrant; J. A. Dyson, Q.C.

D. Eady, Q.C.; T. K. Earnshaw; J. S. Eastwood; H. W. P. Eccles; D. E. H. Edwards; G. O. Edwards, Q.C.;

D. F. Elfer, Q.C.; G. Elias, Q.C.; B. J. Elliott; R. M. Englehart, Q.C.; G. A. Ensor; D. A. Evans, Q.C.; D. R. Evans, Q.C.; Miss M. A. P. Evans; S. J. Evans; E. C. Evans-Lombe, Q.C.; Sir Graham Eyre, Q.C.; W. D. Fairclough; D. J. Farnworth; D. J. Farrer, Q.C.; E. J. Faulks; M. H. Fauvelle; J. D. A. Fennell, O.B.E., Q.C.; R. Fernyhough, Q.C.; F. M. Ferris, T.D., Q.C.; P. Fingret; Miss E. N. Fisher; W. R. Fitch; G. D. Flather, Q.C.; P. E. J. Focke, Q.C.; T. J. Forbes, Q.C.; J. R. Foster, Q.C.; R. M. Foster; Ms. D. A. Freedman; N. H. Freeman; R. H. K. Frisby, Q.C.

W. M. Gage, Q.C.; M. Gale, Q.C.; J. R. B. Geake; R. Gee; L. N. H. George; R. J. H. Gibbs, Q.C.; L. Giovene; A. T. Glass, Q.C.; W. J. Glover, Q.C.; Miss A. F. Goddard, Q.C.; H. K. Goddard, Q.C.; Ms. L. S. Godfrey; J. B. Goldring, Q.C.; A. R. Goldsack; A. J. J. Gompertz, Q.C.; A. A. Gordon; C. G. M. Gordon; J. P. Gorman, Q.C.; J. B. Gosschalk; C. O. G. Gould; T. J. C. Gouldie, Q.C.; The Lord Grantchester, Q.C.; G. Gray, Q.C.; J. M. Gray; R. I. Gray, Q.C.; R. M. K. Gray, Q.C.; B. S. Green, Q.C.; H. Green, Q.C.; S. P. Grenfell; R. D. Grey, Q.C.; D. L. Griffiths; J. C. Griffiths, C.M.G., Q.C.; L. Griffiths; M. G. Grills; Mrs. H. M. Grindrod, Q.C.

A. S. Hacking, Q.C.; M. F. Haigh; V. E. Hall; Ms. H. C. Hallett, Q.C.; G. Hallon; A. W. Hamilton, Q.C.; G. M. Hamilton, T.D., Q.C.; J. Hampton; C. R. H. Hardy; Miss R. S. A. Hare, Q.C.; B. Hargrove, O.B.E., Q.C.; R. D. Harman, Q.C.; D. M. Harris, Q.C.; M. G. V. Harrison, Q.C.; R. M. Harrison, Q.C.; F. D. Hart, Q.C.; C. A. Hart-Leverton, Q.C.; C. S. Harvey, M.B.E., T.D.; M. L. T. Harvey, Q.C.; R. O. Havery, Q.C.; T. S. A. Hawkesworth, Q.C.; R. G. Hawkins, Q.C.; R. W. P. Hay; R. Hayward-Smith, Q.C.; M. Hedley; T. B. Hegarty; G. E. Heggs; R. A. Henderson, Q.C.; R. H. Q. Henriques, Q.C.; P. J. M. Heppel; R. B. Hickman; A. B. Hidden, Q.C.; B. J. Higgs, Q.C.; E. M. Hill, Q.C.; J. W. Hillyer; A. J. H. Hilton; Ms. E. J. Hindley; J. D. Hitchen; S. A. Hockman; C. R. Hodson; P. M. L. Hoffman; A. J. C. Hoggett, Q.C.; Ms. B. M. Hoggett, Q.C.; D. A. Hollis, V.R.D., Q.C.; A. T. Hoolahan, Q.C.; A. Hooper, Q.C.; The Lord Hooson, Q.C.; R. Houlker, Q.C.; M. Howard, Q.C., M.P.; M. J. Hubbard, Q.C.; A. P. G. Hughes; J. Hugill, Q.C.; J. G. Hull, Q.C.; P. J. Hunt, Q.C.; I. G. A. Hunter, Q.C.; B. A. Hytner, Q.C..

N. J. Inglis-Jones, Q.C.; The Lord Irvine of Lairg, Q.C.; F. C. Irwin, Q.C.; R. E. Jack, Q.C.; M. R. Jackson; P. J. E. Jackson; I. E. Jacob; C. E. F. James; N. F. B. Jarman, Q.C.; D. A. Jeffreys, Q.C.; J. Jeffs, Q.C.; D. B. Johnson, Q.C.; M. H. Johnson; E. S. Jones, Q.C.; G. R. Jones; H. D. H. Jones; N. H. Jones, Q.C.; T. G. Jones; W. H. Joss; P. S. L. Joyce; M. D. L. Kalisher, Q.C.; M. L. Kallipetis, Q.C.; J. W. Kay, Q.C.; M. R. Kay, Q.C.; D. St. J. Keane, Q.C.; M. L. Keane; R. W. M. Keeling; K. R. Keen; D. W. Keene, Q.C.; D. A. M. Kemp, Q.C.; T. D. Kent-Jones; P. M. Kershaw, Q.C.; G. M. Khayat; R. I. Kidwell, Q.C.; A. W. P. King; I. Kinnell, Q.C.; A. T. H. Kirkwood; R. C. Klevan, Q.C..

C. A. Lamb; D. G. Lane; P. Langan, Q.C.; J. B. R. Langdon; G. J. H. Langley, Q.C.; D. N. R. Latham, Q.C.; R. B. Latham; S. W. Lawler; I. J. Lawrence, Q.C., M.P.; J. G. M. Laws; M. H. Lawson; L. D. Lawton, Q.C.; D. Lederman; M. K. Lee, Q.C.; R. T. L. Lee; C. H. de V. Leigh, Q.C.; Sir Godfrey Le Quesne, Q.C.; A. P. Lester, Q.C.; B. H. Leveson, Q.C.; S. Levine; D. M. Levy, Q.C.; M. E. Lewer, Q.C.; A. K. Lewis, Q.C.; M. ap G. Lewis, Q.C.; R. S. Lewis; C. C. D. Lindsay, Q.C.; J. S. Lipton; B. J. E. Livesey; R. J. D. Livesey, Q.C.; G. Llewellyn-Jones; J. Lloyd-Eley, Q.C.; A. J. C. Lodge, Q.C.; A. G. Longden; D. C. Lovell-Pank; R. P. Lowden; G. W. Lowe; G. W. Lowther; F. D. L. Loy; J. A. T. Loyd, Q.C.; Sir Nicholas Lyell, Q.C., M.P.; D. Lynch; E. Lyons, Q.C.

A. G. MacDuff; D. D. McEvoy, Q.C.; E. A. Machin, Q.C.; N. R. B. Macleod, Q.C.; N. J. C. McLusky; J. B. MacMillan; K. C. Macrae; B. C. Maddocks; T. Maher; Miss V. H. Mairants; A. R. Malcolm; Miss A. Mallalieu, Q.C.; A. C. B. Markham-David; F. J. M.

Marr-Johnson; L. A. Marshall; R. G. Marshall-Andrews, Q.C.; D. N. N. Martineau; H. R. A. Martineau; C. G. Masterman; D. Matheson, Q.C.; P. B. Mauleverer, Q.C.; R. B. Mawrey, Q.C.; A. T. K. May, Q.C.; H. R. Mayor, Q.C.; M. Meggerson; J. T. Milford, Q.C.; R. A. Miller; T. J. Milligan; Mrs. B. J. L. Mills, Q.C.; J. B. M. Milmo, Q.C.; N. A. Miscampbell, Q.C., M.P.; S. G. Mitchell, Q.C.; J. E. Mitting, Q.C.; H. J. Montlake; H. M. Morgan; J. A. Morgan; W. G. O. Morgan, Q.C.; G. E. Moriarty, Q.C.; T. R. A. Morison, Q.C.; A. P. Morris; D. G. Morris; The Rt. Hon. J. Morris, Q.C., M.P.; J. I. Morris; W. P. Morris; D. C. Morton; A. G. Moses; P. C. Mott; J. Mulcahy, Q.C.; F. J. Muller, Q.C.; J. F. Mummery; M. J. A. Murphy; N. J. Mylne, Q.C.

Ms. N. F. Negus; M. H. D. Neligan; R. F. Nelson, Q.C.; R. E. Newbold; G. M. Newman, Q.C.; J. D. Newton; G. Nice; C. V. Nicholls, Q.C.; C. A. A. Nicholls, Q.C.; M. C. Nicholson; A. S. T. E. Nicol; B. Nolan; J. G. Nutting; D. P. O'Brien, Q.C.; P. W. O'Brien; E. M. Ogden, Q.C.; B. R. Oliver; S. J. L. Oliver, Q.C.; S. K. O'Malley; C. P. L. Openshaw; M. A. Oppenheimer; R. T. N. Orme; R. C. C. O'Rorke; J. F. F. Orrell; S. K. Overend; F. D. Owen; G. V. Owen, Q.C.; R. M. Owen, Q.C.; S. R. Page; D. C. J. Paget; A. W. Palmer, Q.C.; S. A. B. Parish; A. E. W. Park, Q.C.; J. F. Parker, Q.C.; T. C. Parkin; G. C. Parkins; G. E. Parkinson; E. O. Parry; N. S. K. Pascoe, Q.C.; A. Patience; J. G. Paulusz; Mrs. N. Pearce; D. H. Penry-Davey, Q.C.; J. R. Peppitt, Q.C.; Sir Ian Percival, Q.C.; D. S. Perrett, Q.C.; M. Pert; W. B. Phillips; C. J. Pitchford, Q.C.; A. P. Pitts; Miss E. F. Platt, Q.C.; J. R. Playford, Q.C.; R. F. D. Pollard; A. G. S. Pollock, Q.C.; D. A. Poole, Q.C.; L. R. Portnoy; M. J. Pratt, Q.C.; S. Pratt; R. J. C. V. Prendergast; T. W. Preston, Q.C.; J. E. Previté, Q.C.; J. A. Price, Q.C.; N. P. L. Price; P. J. Price, Q.C.; R. C. Pryor, Q.C.; G. V. Pugh, Q.C.; C. P. B. Purchas; R. M. Purchas, Q.C.; A. G. Purnell, Q.C.; N. R. Purnell, Q.C.; P. O. Purnell, Q.C.; J. R. Pyke.

D. A. Radcliffe; A. Rankin, Q.C.; A. D. Rawley, Q.C.; L. F. Read, Q.C.; A. R. F. Redgrave; P. Rees; J. R. Reid, Q.C.; R. E. Rhodes, Q.C.; M. S. Rich, Q.C.; D. W. Richards; H. A. Richardson; Miss S. A. Ritchie, Q.C.; S. D. Robbins; J. A. Roberts, Q.C.; J. H. Roberts; J. H. P. Roberts; J. M. G. Roberts, Q.C.; P. B. Roberts; P. E. Robertshaw; V. Robinson, Q.C.; D. E. H. Robson, Q.C.; G. W. Roddick, Q.C.; J. M. T. Rogers, Q.C.; J. W. Rogers, Q.C.; K. S. Rokison, Q.C.; J. J. Rowe, Q.C.; R. J. Royce, Q.C.; A. A. Rumbelow; R. R. Russell; G. C. Ryan, Q.C.

J. E. A. Samuels, Q.C.; M. P. Sayers, Q.C.; R. J. Scholes, Q.C.; R. M. Scott; A. F. B. Scrivener, Q.C.; R. J. Seabrook, Q.C.; C. Seagroatt, Q.C.; H. M. Self, Q.C.; M. R. Selfe; D. M. D. Selwood; D. Serota, Q.C.; R. M. Shawcross; S. J. Sher, Q.C.; M. D. Sherrard, Q.C.; L. S. Shields, Q.C.; J. M. Shorrock, Q.C.; S. R. Silber, Q.C.; A. G. Simmons; K. T. Simpson; P. R. Simpson; J. P. Singer, Q.C.; P. F. Singer; A. T. Smith, Q.C.; C. M. Smith, Q.C.; J. H. Smith, Q.C.; R. S. Smith, Q.C.; R. E. Snape; S. M. Solley, Q.C.; R. F. Solman; R. C. E. Southwell; Miss J. M. Southworth, Q.C.; M. H. Spence, Q.C.; S. B. Spence; D. H. Spencer, Q.C.; M. G. Spencer, Q.C.; S. M. Spencer, Q.C.; J. A. C. Spokes, Q.C.; R. W. Spon-Smith; S. A. Stamler, Q.C.; D. P. Stanley; D. H. Stembridge; J. S. H. Stewart, Q.C.; R. M. Stewart, Q.C.; G. J. C. Still; D. M. A. Stokes, Q.C.; E. D. R. Stone, Q.C.; P. L. Storr; T. M. F. Stow, Q.C.; M. Stuart-Moore; J. Stuart-Smith, Q.C.; G. C. Styler; F. R. C. Such; A. B. Suckling, Q.C.; J. M. Sullivan, Q.C.; D. M. Sumner; L. Swift, Q.C.; M. R. Swift, Q.C.

J. A. Tackaberry, Q.C.; A. B. Taylor; E. Taylor; N. Taylor, Q.C.; W. E. M. Taylor; A. D. Temple, Q.C.; V. B. A. Temple; M. I. Tennant; K. J. Tetley; D. M. Thomas, O.B.E., Q.C.; D. O. Thomas, Q.C.; Lord Thomas of Gwydir, P.C., Q.C.; R. J. L. Thomas, Q.C.; R. L. Thomas; R. U. Thomas, Q.C.; W. F. C. Thomas; A. A. R. Thompson, Q.C.; A. G. Y. Thorpe; J. Tiley; M. B.

Tillett; C. H. Tilling; R. N. Titheridge, Q.C.; J. K. Toulmin, Q.C.; R. G. Toulson, Q.C.; J. B. S. Townend, Q.C.; A. D. H. Trollope; S. L. Tuckey, Q.C.; H. W. Turcan; P. A. Twigg, Q.C.; C. J. M. Tyrer; A. R. Tyrrell, Q.C.; Mrs. A. P. Uziell-Hamilton; N. P. Valios; A. R. Vandermeer, Q.C.; M. J. D. Vere-Hodge; Miss M. S. Viner, Q.C.; C. D. Voelcker.

Rt. Hon. D. C. Waddington, Q.C., M.P.; J. P. Wadsworth, Q.C.; D. St. J. Wagstaff; R. M. Wakerley, Q.C.; W. H. Waldron, Q.C.; J. de G. Walford; R. Walker; R. J. Walker, Q.C.; T. E. Walker, Q.C.; J. J. Walker-Smith; B. Walsh, Q.C.; Sir James Watson, Bt.; C. D. G. Waud; P. A. Webster; M. Weisman; P. Weitzman, Q.C.; C. P. C. Whelon; C. H. Whitby, Q.C.; P. G. Whiteman, Q.C.; D. R. B. Whitehouse; P. J. M. Whiteman, T.D.; A. Whitfield, Q.C.; D. G. Widdicombe, Q.C.; J. A. J. Wigmore; A. D. F. Wilcken; S. R. Wilkinson; D. B. Williams; G. H. G. Williams, Q.C.; G. W. Williams, Q.C.; J. G. Williams, Q.C.; J. L. Williams, Q.C.; The Hon. J. M. Williams, Q.C.; S. W. Williamson, Q.C.; J. C. Willis; A. M. Wilson, Q.C.; N. A. R. Wilson, Q.C.; C. Wilson-Smith, Q.C.; G. W. Wingate-Saul, Q.C.; M. E. Wolff; H. Wolton, Q.C.; D. A. Wood, Q.C.; D. R. Wood; C. G. P. Woodford; L. G. Woodley, Q.C.; S. Woodley; B. Woodward; W. C. Woodward, Q.C.; D. R. Woolley, Q.C.; N. G. Wootton; A. M. Worrall; N. J. Worsley; P. F. Worsley; J. M. Wright, Q.C.; D. E. M. Young, Q.C.

STIPENDIARY MAGISTRATES
Provincial
(each £39,400)

Greater Manchester, W. D. Fairclough (1982); C. T. Latham, O.B.E. (1976).

Humberside, N. H. White (1985).

Merseyside, N. G. Wootton (1976).

Mid Glamorgan, D. P. Rowland (1961); B. R. Oliver (1983).

South Glamorgan, Sir Lincoln Hallinan (1976).

South Yorkshire, I. W. Crompton (1983); J. E. Barry (1985).

West Midlands, F. H. Hatchard (1981); W. M. Probert (1983); G. H. Kamil (1987).

West Yorkshire, F. D. L. Loy (1972); I. R. Boyd (1982).

Metropolitan

Chief Metropolitan Stipendiary Magistrate and Chairman of Committee of Magistrates for Inner London Area, Sir David Hopkin (*Bow Street*) £48,100

Committee of Magistrates for Inner London Area
3rd Floor, North West Wing,
Bush House, Aldwych, WC2B 4PJ

Principal Chief Clerk and Clerk to the Committee, I. Fowler £38,916
Chief Clerk (Training), J. W. Greenhill £33,787

Magistrates
(each £39,400)

Bow Street, The Chief Magistrate; R. D. Bartle; J. G. Connor; G. L. Wicks.

Camberwell Green, R. D. Connor; C. P. M. Davidson; P. Fingret; Mrs. H. Mitcham; A. W. Ormerod.

Clerkenwell, M. L. R. Romer; C. J. Bourke; M. A. Johnstone.

Greenwich and Woolwich, Miss P. M. Long; Mrs. K. R. Keating; vacant.

Highbury Corner, D. Barr; G. E. Parkinson; Miss D. Quick; vacant.

Horseferry Road, Sir Bryan Roberts, K.C.M.G., Q.C.; Mrs. N. F. Negus; A. R. Davies; vacant.

Marlborough Street, K. J. H. Nichols; J. Q. Campbell.

Marylebone, G. L. J. Noel; J. Q. Campbell; Miss D. A. Freedman; vacant.

Old Street, T. Maher; D. B. Meier.

South Western, S. G. Clixby; A. Cooray; M. H. D. Neligan.

Thames, P. G. N. Badge; B. J. Canham.

Tower Bridge, C. D. Voelcker; Mrs. J. R. Comyns; T. M. English.

Wells Street, Miss A. M. Jennings; D. M. Fingleton; K. L. Maitland-Davies; N. Crichton.

West London, H. J. Cook; D. Kennet Brown.

Unattached Magistrates, R. T. Moss; T. H. Workman; G. B. Breen.

CROWN PROSECUTION SERVICE

Headquarters: 4/12 Queen Anne's Gate, SW1H 9AZ
[01-273 8152: *Casework sections*, 01-222 7944]

Fraud Divisions
10 Furnival Street, EC4A 1PE
[01-831 3038]

The Crown Prosecution Service (C.P.S.) handles the prosecution of criminal proceedings instituted by police forces (excluding certain minor road traffic offences). The head of the C.P.S. is the Director of Public Prosecutions: day-to-day administration of the C.P.S. is handled by the Deputy Director. There are four Regional Directors responsible for the 31 areas: each area is headed by a Chief Crown Prosecutor.

Salaries

Grade 1	£72,000
Grade 2	£48,100–£59,800
Grade 3	£37,600–£47,600
Grade 4	£36,786–£41,255
Grade 5	£28,170–£41,225

London Weighting = £1,750 p.a.

Director of Public Prosecutions (G1), A. D. Green, Q.C.

Deputy Director and Chief Executive (G2), D. S. Gandy, C.B., O.B.E.

Principal Establishment and Finance Officer (G3), D. J. Wiblin.

Director, Headquarters Casework (G3), C. Newell.

Head, General Casework (G5), Mrs. V. Collins.

Head, Special Casework (G5), K. Horn.

Head, Policy Division (G5), K. Ashken.

Heads, Fraud Divisions (G5), T. Waring; G. Adams.

Head, Police Complaints Division (G5), C. Cleugh.

Head, Planning and Finance (G5), B. Spratt.

Head, Personnel and Training (G5), W. R. Mann.

Head, Office Services and Legal Costs (G6), B. Spear.

C.P.S. AREAS

Northern Region

Suite 101, Sunlight House, Quay Street
Manchester M3 3JU
Regional Director(G3), B. Crebbin

CHESHIRE, Hamilton House, Hamilton Place, Chester CH1 2BH.—*Chief Crown Prosecutor (G5)*, Mrs. N. E. Hollingsworth.

CLEVELAND/N. YORKSHIRE, Rydale Building, 60 Piccadilly, York YO1 1NS.—*Chief Crown Prosecutor (G5)*, D. M. Sharp.

GREATER MANCHESTER, P.O.Box 377, Sunlight House, Quay Street, Manchester M60 3LU.—*Chief Crown Prosecutor (G4)*, A. R. Taylor.

LANCASHIRE/CUMBRIA, Robert House, 2 Starkie Street, Preston, Lancs. PR1 3NY.—*Chief Crown Prosecutor (G5)*, J. V. Bates.

MERSEYSIDE, 7th Floor (South), Royal Liver Building, Liverpool L3 1HN.—*Chief Crown Prosecutor (G4)*, E. C. Woodcock.

NORTHUMBRIA/DURHAM, Cuthbert House, All Saints Centre, Newcastle upon Tyne NE1 2DW.—*Chief Crown Prosecutor (G5)*, G. Duff.

N. WALES/DYFED/POWYS, 491 Abergele Road, Old Colwyn, Colwyn Bay, Clwyd LL29 9AE.—*Chief Crown Prosecutor (G5)*, A. S. R. Clarke.

S. YORKSHIRE, Belgrave House, 47 Bank Street, Sheffield S1 2EH.—*Chief Crown Prosecutor (G4)*, M. J. Rose.

W. YORKSHIRE, Grove Hall, College Grove Road, Wakefield WF1 3RA.—*Chief Crown Prosecutor (G4)*, R. Otley.

Midland Region

1 King Edward Court, King Edward Street,
Nottingham NG1 1EL
Regional Director (G3), R. Williamson.

CAMBRIDGESHIRE/LINCOLNSHIRE, The River Mill, St Ives, Huntingdon, Cambs. PE17 4HJ.—*Chief Crown Prosecutor (G5)*, D. G. Lewis.

DERBYSHIRE, Celtic House, Heritage Gate, Friary Street, Derby DE1 1QX.—*Chief Crown Prosecutor (G5)*, D. R. K. Seddon.

HUMBERSIDE, Queens House, Paragon Street, Hull HU3 3DA.—*Chief Crown Prosecutor (G5)*, L. M. Bell.

LEICESTERSHIRE/NORTHAMPTONSHIRE, Leicester House, Lee Circle, Leicester LE1 3RE.—*Chief Crown Prosecutor (G5)*, P. J. M. Hollingworth.

NORFOLK/SUFFOLK, Saxon House, 1 Cromwell Square, Ipswich, Suffolk IP1 1TS.—*Chief Crown Prosecutor (G5)*, M. F. C. Harvey.

NOTTINGHAMSHIRE, 2 King Edward Court, King Edward Street, Nottingham NG1 1EL.—*Chief Crown Prosecutor (G5)*, D. C. Beal.

STAFFORDSHIRE/WARWICKSHIRE, Government Buildings, 11A Princes Street, Stafford ST16 2EU.—*Chief Crown Prosecutor (G5)*, D. V. Dickenson.

WEST MIDLANDS, The McClaren Building, Dale End, Birmingham B4 7LN.—*Chief Crown Prosecutor (G3)*, I. S. Manson.

South and West Region

Westminster House, 6 Little London Court,
Albert Street, Swindon, Wilts. SN1 3HY
Regional Director (G3), C. Hoad.

AVON/SOMERSET, Froomsgate House, Rupert Street, Bristol BS1 2PS.—*Chief Crown Prosecutor (G5)*, C. T. Jones.

DEVON/CORNWALL, 54 Mary Arches Street, Exeter EX4 3BA.—*Chief Crown Prosecutor (G5)*, R. J. Green.

DORSET/HAMPSHIRE, Black Horse House, 8–10 Leigh Road, Eastleigh, Hants. SO5 4FH.—*Chief Crown Prosecutor (G5)*, P. Boeuf.

GLOUCESTERSHIRE/WILTSHIRE, 7 Avon Reach, Monkton Hill, Chippenham, Wilts. SN15 1EE.—*Chief Crown Prosecutor (G5)*, R. A. Prickett.

S. WALES/GWENT, Pearl Assurance House, Greyfriars Road, Cardiff CF1 3PL.—*Chief Crown Prosecutor (G4)*, H. G. Wallace.

SUSSEX, Unit 3, Clifton Mews, Clifton Hill, Brighton, E. Sussex BN1 3HR.—*Chief Crown Prosecutor (G5)*, D. Thompson.

THAMES VALLEY, The Courtyard, Lombard Street, Abingdon, Oxon. OX14 5SE.—*Chief Crown Prosecutor (G5)*, P. D. F. Higginbottom.

WEST MERCIA, Orchard House, Victoria Square, Droitwich, Worcester WR9 8QT.—*Chief Crown Prosecutor (G5)*, D. R. Stott.

London and South East
Tolworth Tower (16th floor),
Surbiton, Surrey KT6 7DS
Regional Director (G3), R. Gwilliam.

ESSEX, Gemini Centre, 88 New London Road, Chelmsford, Essex CM2 0BR.—*Chief Crown Prosecutor (G5)*, J. J. Goodwin.

HERTFORDSHIRE/BEDFORDSHIRE, Queens House, 58 Victoria Street, St Albans AL1 3HZ.—*Chief Crown Prosecutor (G5)*, R. J. Chronnell.

KENT, Kent House, Lower Stone Street, Maidstone, Kent ME15 6JT.—*Chief Crown Prosecutor (G5)*, R. A. Crabb.

LONDON (INNER), New Portland House, Stag Place, SW1.—*Chief Crown Prosecutor (G4)*, B. McArdle.

LONDON (NORTH), Solar House, 1 Romford Road, Stratford E15 4LJ.—*Chief Crown Prosecutor (G4)*, G. D. Etherington.

LONDON (SOUTH)/SURREY, Tolworth Tower, Surbiton KT6 7DS.—*Chief Crown Prosecutor (G4)*, D. E. Dracup.

THE SCOTTISH JUDICATURE

Scotland has a legal system separate and differing greatly from the English legal system in enacted law, judicial procedure and the structure of courts.

There is in Scotland a system of public prosecution headed by the Lord Advocate which is independent of the police, who have no say in the decision to prosecute. The Lord Advocate, discharging his functions through the Crown Office in Edinburgh, is responsible for prosecutions in the High Court, sheriff courts and district courts. Prosecutions in the High Court are prepared by the Crown Office and conducted in court by one of the Law Officers or an advocate-depute. In the inferior courts the decision to prosecute is made and prosecution is preferred by procurators fiscal, who are lawyers and full-time civil servants, subject to the directions of the Crown Office. A permanent legally-qualified civil servant known as the Crown Agent is responsible for the running of the Crown Office and the organization of the Procurator Fiscal Service, of which he is the head.

Scotland is divided into six Sheriffdoms, each with a full-time Sheriff Principal. The Sheriffdoms are further divided into sheriff court districts, each of which has a legally-qualified, resident sheriff or sheriffs, who are the judges of the court.

In criminal cases sheriffs principal and sheriffs have the same powers: sitting with a jury of 15 members, they may try more serious cases on indictment, or, sitting alone, may try lesser cases under summary procedure. Minor summary offences are dealt with in district courts which are administered by the district and the islands local government authorities and presided over by lay justices of the peace, and, in Glasgow only, by stipendiary magistrates. Juvenile offenders (children under 16) may be brought before an informal children's hearing comprising three local lay people. The superior criminal court is the High Court of Justiciary which is both a trial and an appeal court. Cases on indictment are tried by a High Court Judge, sitting with a jury of 15, in Edinburgh and on circuit in other towns. Appeals from the lower courts against conviction or sentence are heard also by the High Court, which sits as an appeal court only in Edinburgh. There is no further appeal to the House of Lords in criminal cases.

In civil cases the jurisdiction of the sheriff court extends to most kinds of action. Appeal against decisions of the sheriff may be made to the Sheriff Principal and thence to the Court of Session, or direct to the Court of Session, which sits only in Edinburgh. The Court of Session is divided into the Inner and the Outer House. The Outer House is a court of first instance in which cases are heard by judges sitting singly, sometimes with a jury of 12. The Inner House, itself subdivided into two Divisions of equal status, is mainly an appeal court. Appeals may be made to the Inner House from the Outer House as well as from the sheriff court: an appeal may be made from the Inner House to the House of Lords.

The Judges of the Court of Session are the same as those of the High Court of Justiciary, the Lord President of the Court of Session also holding the office of Lord Justice General in the High Court.

The office of coroner does not exist in Scotland: the local procurator fiscal inquires privately into sudden and suspicious deaths and may report findings to the Crown Agent. In some cases a fatal accident inquiry may be held before the sheriff.

COURT OF SESSION (Established 1532) and HIGH COURT OF JUSTICIARY

The Lord President and Lord Justice General,
(£82,750)
The Rt. Hon. The Lord Emslie, M.B.E.
(*born* 1919, *apptd.* 1972)

INNER HOUSE
Lords of Session (each £79,500)

FIRST DIVISION

	Apptd.
The Lord President.	
Hon. Lord Brand (David William Robert Brand), *born* 1923	1972
Hon. Lord Allanbridge (William Ian Stewart), *born* 1925	1977
Hon. Lord Cowie (William Lorn Kerr Cowie), *born* 1926	1977

SECOND DIVISION

Lord Justice Clerk (£80,500), The Rt. Hon. Lord Ross, (Donald MacArthur Ross), *born* 1927	1985
Hon. Lord Dunpark (Alastair McPherson Johnston, T.D.), *born* 1915	1971
Rt. Hon. Lord Wylie (Norman Russell Wylie, V.R.D.), *born* 1923	1974
Rt. Hon. Lord Murray (Ronald King Murray), *born* 1922	1979

OUTER HOUSE
Lords of Session (each £72,000)

Hon. Lord Mayfield (Ian MacDonald, M.C.), *born* 1921	1981
Hon. Lord Davidson (Charles Kemp Davidson), (*seconded to Scottish Law Commission*) *born* 1929	1983
Hon. The Lord McCluskey, *born* 1929	1984
Hon. Lord Morison (Alastair Malcolm Morison), *born* 1931	1985
Hon. Lord Sutherland (Ranald Iain Sutherland), *born* 1932	1985
Hon. Lord Weir (David Bruce Weir), *born* 1931	1985
Hon. Lord Clyde (James John Clyde), *born* 1932	1985
Hon. Lord Cullen (William Douglas Cullen), *born* 1935	1986
Hon. Lord Prosser (William David Prosser), *born* 1934	1986
Hon. Lord Kirkwood (Ian Candlish Kirkwood), *born* 1932	1987
Hon. Lord Coulsfield (John Taylor Cameron), *born* 1934	1987

Hon. Lord Milligan (James George Milligan), *born*
1934....................................1988
Hon. Lord Dervaird (John Murray), *born* 1935..1988
Hon. The Lord Morton of Shuna, *born* 1930 1988
Hon. Lord Caplan (Philip Isaac Caplan), *born*
1929....................................1989
Rt. Hon. The Lord Cameron of Lochbroom, *born*
1931....................................1989

COURT OF SESSION AND HIGH COURT OF JUSTICIARY
Parliament House, Parliament Square, Edinburgh

Principal Clerk of Session and Justiciary, H. S.
Foley .... £28,170–£36,786
*Deputy Principal Clerk of Session and Principal
Extractor,* M. Weir .... £17,360–£26,958
Deputy Principal Clerk of Justiciary, J. Robertson
£17,360–£26,958
*Deputy Principal Clerk (Administration) and Keeper
of the Rolls,* M. G. Bonar .... £17,360–£26,958
Depute Clerks of Session and Justiciary, W. Gillon;
A. Hogg; N. J. Dowie; I. Smith; J. A. R. Cowie; T.
Higgins; E. A. Cumming; B. Watson; T. B. Cruick-
shank; Q. Oliver; F. Shannly; P. Crow; J. L.
Anderson; R. D. Sinclair; Mrs. A. Leighton; J.
Clark; T. M. Thomson; D. D. Mackay; A. S. Moffat;
E. G. Appelbe .... £13,969–£17,832

SCOTTISH COURTS ADMINISTRATION
26–27 Royal Terrace, Edinburgh EH7 5AH

Director, G. Murray.

SHERIFF COURT OF CHANCERY
16 North Bank Street, Edinburgh EH1 2NJ

Sheriff of Chancery, Sir Frederick O'Brien, Q.C.

H.M. COMMISSARY OFFICE
16 North Bank Street, Edinburgh EH1 2NJ

Commissary Clerk, D. B. White.

SCOTTISH LAND COURT
1 Grosvenor Crescent, Edinburgh

Chairman, The Hon. Lord Elliott, M.C. £48,100
Members, A. B. Campbell, O.B.E.; D. D. McDiarmid;
R. MacDonald.

SHERIFFDOMS
Salaries
Sheriff Principal £53,400
Sheriff £48,100
Regional Sheriff Clerk .... £21,633–£36,786
Sheriff Clerk .... £13,996–£36,786

GRAMPIAN, HIGHLAND AND ISLANDS
Sheriff Principal, R. D. Ireland, Q.C.
Regional Sheriff Clerk, J. S. Doig.

Sheriffs and Sheriff Clerks
Aberdeen and Stonehaven, A. M. G. Russell, C.B.E.,
Q.C.; A. L. Stewart; D. J. Risk; D. W. Bogie, D.
Kelbie; *Sheriff Clerks,* J. Rodden; W. A. Mouser.
Banff and Peterhead, A. J. Murphy; *Sheriff Clerk,* A.
H. Hempseed.
Elgin, N. McPartlin; *Sheriff Clerk,* A. Lynch.
*Inverness, Lochmaddy, Portree, Stornoway, Dingwall,
Tain, Wick and Dornoch,* W. J. Fulton; D. Booker-
Milburn; J. O. A. Fraser; E. Stewart; *Sheriff Clerks,*
J. S. Doig; W. Dunn.
Kirkwall and Lerwick, A. A. MacDonald; *Sheriff
Clerk,* J. Rodden.

Fort William, D. Noble (also *Oban and Campbeltown*);
Sheriff Clerk, J. S. Doig.

TAYSIDE, CENTRAL AND FIFE
Sheriff Principal, R. R. Taylor, Q.C., PH.D.
Regional Sheriff Clerk, B. J. Young.

Sheriffs and Sheriff Clerks
Arbroath and Forfar, S. O. Kermack; *Sheriff Clerks,*
B. T. McCabe; P. Dougan.
Dundee, G. L. Cox; E. F. Bowen; *Sheriff Clerk,* B. J.
Young.
Perth, J. F. Wheatley; C. Smith*; *Sheriff Clerk,* Miss
J. Telfer.
Falkirk, A. V. Sheehan; A. B. Wilkinson; *Sheriff
Clerk,* D. Nicoll.
Stirling, W. C. Henderson; R. E. G. Younger; *Sheriff
Clerk,* K. MacKenzie.
Alloa, R. E. G. Younger; *Sheriff Clerk,* R. G. Young.
Cupar, J. C. McInnes (also *Perth*); *Sheriff Clerk,* B.
Sullivan.
Dunfermline, J. S. Forbes; W. M. Reid; *Sheriff Clerk,*
J. Ross.
Kirkcaldy, W. J. Christie; C. R. Macarthur, Q.C.;
Sheriff Clerk, T. Fyffe.

LOTHIAN AND BORDERS
Sheriff Principal, Sir Frederick O'Brien, Q.C.
Regional Sheriff Clerk, D. B. White.

Sheriffs and Sheriff Clerks
Edinburgh, N. E. D. Thomson; J. L. M. Mitchell; P.
G. B. McNeill, PH.D.; Miss H. J. Aronson; R. G.
Craik, Q.C.; G. I. W. Shiach; Miss I. A. Poole; R. J.
D. Scott; I. D. MacPhail; G. W. S. Presslie; J. A.
Farrell*; I. A. Cameron; *Sheriff Clerk,* D. B. White.
Peebles, N. E. D. Thomson (also *Edinburgh*); *Sheriff
Clerk,* D. B. White.
Linlithgow, M. Stone; H. R. MacLean; *Sheriff Clerk,*
R. Sinclair.
Haddington, G. W. S. Presslie (also *Edinburgh*);
Sheriff Clerk, B. W. S. Manthorpe.
Jedburgh and Duns, J. V. Paterson; *Sheriff Clerk,* J.
R. Jenkins.
Selkirk, J. V. Paterson; *Sheriff Clerk,* J. R. Jenkins.

NORTH STRATHCLYDE
Sheriff Principal, R. C. Hay, C.B.E.
Regional Sheriff Clerk, A. A. Brown.

Sheriffs and Sheriff Clerks
Oban and Campbeltown, D. Noble (also *Fort William*);
Sheriff Clerks, N. R. Weir; A. A. Brown.
Dumbarton, J. T. Fitzsimons; C. W. Palmer; T. Scott;
F. H. Hamilton*; *Sheriff Clerk,* N. R. Weir.
Paisley, A. K. F. Hunter; R. G. Smith; C. N. Stoddart;
J. Spy; *Sheriff Clerk,* A. A. Brown.
Greenock, J. Irvine Smith (also *Rothesay*); Sir
Stephen Young; *Sheriff Clerk,* A. P. MacPherson.
Kilmarnock, T. M. Croan; D. B. Smith; T. F. Russell;
Sheriff Clerk, J. Shaw.
Dunoon, C. W. Palmer (also *Dumbarton*); *Sheriff
Clerk,* A. P. MacPherson.

GLASGOW AND STRATHKELVIN
Sheriff Principal, N. D. MacLeod, Q.C.
Regional Sheriff Clerk, C. McLay.

Sheriffs and Sheriff Clerks
Glasgow, A. C. Horsfall (*seconded to Scottish Lands
Tribunal*); J. J. Maguire; A. A. Bell, Q.C.; B.
Kearney; G. H. Gordon, Q.C.; A. C. McKay; A.
Lothian; J. C. M. Jardine; Mrs. D. J. B. Robertson;

B. A. Lockhart; I. G. Pirie; Miss A. L. A. Smith; W. G. Stevenson, Q.C.; G. J. Evans; E. H. Galt; F. J. Keane; A. C. Henry; A. M. Bell; J. K. Mitchell; A. G. Johnston; J. P. Murphy; *Sheriff Clerk,* C. McLay.

SOUTH STRATHCLYDE, DUMFRIES AND GALLOWAY

Sheriff Principal, J. S. Mowat, Q.C.
Regional Sheriff Clerk, H. Findlay.

Sheriffs and Sheriff Clerks

Hamilton, L. S. Lovat; A. C. MacPherson; W. F. Lunny; I. A. MacMillan, C.B.E.; V. J. Canavan (also *Airdrie*); W. E. Gibson; I. C. Simpson*; *Sheriff Clerk,* J. Cumming.
Lanark, J. D. Allan; *Sheriff Clerk,* A. S. Morwood.
Ayr, N. Gow, Q.C.; R. G. McEwan, Q.C.; *Sheriff Clerk,* T. D. McIntosh.
Stranraer and Kirkcudbright, J. R. Smith; *Sheriff Clerk,* L. McFarlane.
Dumfries, K. G. Barr; L. Cameron; *Sheriff Clerk,* P. McGonigle.
Airdrie, J. H. Stewart; J. S. Boyle; V. J. Canavan (also *Hamilton*); R. H. Dickson; *Sheriff Clerk,* H. Findlay.

*Floating Sheriff

CROWN OFFICE
Regent Road, Edinburgh EH7 5BL
[031-557 3800]

Crown Agent, I. Dean, C.B. £50,400
Deputy Crown Agent, A. C. Normand £35,415

PROCURATOR FISCAL SERVICE

Grampian, Highlands and Islands Region
Regional Procurator Fiscal, S. W. Lockhart, C.B.E. (*Aberdeen*).

Procurators Fiscal, J. D. McNaughton (*Stonehaven*); A. J. M. Colley (*Banff*); I. S. McNaughtan (*Peterhead*); A. Wither (*Elgin*); A. C. P. Reith (*Wick*); C. B. McClory (*Portree and Lochmaddy*); C. S. Mackenzie (*Stornoway*); H. T. Westwater (*Dornoch and Tain*); B. Heywood (*Inverness*); A. W. Wright (*Kirkwall*); Miss A. Thom (*Lerwick*); J. I. M. MacGillivray (*Fort William*); D. R. Hingston (*Dingwall*).

Tayside, Central and Fife Region
Regional Procurator Fiscal, D. R. Smith (*Dundee*).
Procurators Fiscal, C. D. G. Hillary (*Arbroath*); A. L. Ingram (*Forfar*); M. MacPhail (*Perth*); G. E. Scott (*Falkirk*); K. Valentine (*Stirling*); I. D. Douglas (*Alloa*); R. A. S. Brown (*Cupar*); R. T. Hamilton (*Dunfermline*); Mrs. I. Guild (*Kirkcaldy*).

Lothian and Borders Region
Regional Procurator Fiscal, J. D. Lowe (*Edinburgh*).
Procurators Fiscal, F. J. M. Brown (*Peebles*); H. R. Annan (*Linlithgow*); vacant (*Haddington*); J. C. Whitelaw (*Duns* and *Jedburgh*); D. McNeill (*Selkirk*).

North Strathclyde Region
Regional Procurator Fiscal, R. F. Lees (*Paisley*).
Procurators Fiscal, I. Henderson (*Campbeltown* and *Oban*); J. Cardle (*Dumbarton*); P. Docherty (*Greenock*); D. L. Webster (*Dunoon* and *Rothesay*); J. G. MacGlennan (*Kilmarnock*).

Glasgow and Strathkelvin Region
Regional Procurator Fiscal, A. S. Jessop (*Glasgow*).

South Strathclyde, Dumfries and Galloway Region
Regional Procurator Fiscal, W. G. Carmichael (*Hamilton*).
Procurators Fiscal, S. R. Houston (*Lanark*); N. G. O'Brien (*Ayr*); F. Walkingshaw (*Stranraer*); J. T. MacDougall (*Dumfries* and *Kirkcudbright*); A. T. Wilson (*Airdrie*).

NORTHERN IRELAND JUDICATURE

In Northern Ireland the legal system and the structure of courts closely resemble those of England and Wales; there are, however, often differences in enacted law.

The Supreme Court of Judicature of Northern Ireland comprises the Court of Appeal, the High Court of Justice and the Crown Court. The practice and procedure of these Courts is similar to those in England. The superior civil court is the High Court of Justice, from which an appeal lies to the Court of Appeal; the House of Lords is the final civil appeal court.

The decision to prosecute in cases tried on indictment and in summary cases of a serious nature rests in Northern Ireland with the Director of Public Prosecutions, who is responsible to the Attorney General. Minor summary offences are prosecuted by the police.

Minor criminal offences are dealt with in magistrates' courts by a full-time, legally qualified resident magistrate and, where an offender is under 17, by juvenile courts consisting of the resident magistrate and two lay members specially qualified to deal with juveniles (at least one of whom must be a woman). Appeals from magistrates' courts are heard by the county court. The Crown Court, served by High Court and county court judges, deals with criminal trials on indictment. Cases are heard before a judge and, except those involving offences specified under emergency legislation, a jury. Appeals from the

Crown Court against conviction or sentence are heard by the Northern Ireland Court of Appeal; the House of Lords is the final court of appeal.

Magistrates' courts in Northern Ireland can deal with certain classes of civil case but most minor civil cases are dealt with in county courts. Judgments of all civil courts are enforceable through a centralized procedure administered by the Enforcement of Judgments Office.

SUPREME COURT OF JUDICATURE
The Royal Courts of Justice
Belfast.

Lord Chief Justice of Northern Ireland (£82,750)
The Rt. Hon. Sir Brian Hutton
(*born* 1931, *apptd.* 1988)

Lords Justices of Appeal (each £79,500)

	Apptd.
Rt. Hon. Turlough O'Donnell, *born* 1924	1979
Rt. Hon. Sir Basil Kelly, *born* 1920	1984
Rt. Hon. Sir John MacDermott, *born* 1927	1987

Puisne Judges (each £72,000)

Hon. Sir Donald Murray, *born* 1923	1975
Hon. Sir John Higgins, *born* 1927	1984
Hon. Sir Robert Carswell, *born* 1934	1984
Hon. Sir Michael Nicholson, *born* 1933	1986
Hon. Sir William McCollum, *born* 1933	1987
Hon. Sir William Campbell, *born* 1936	1988

Lord Chief Justice's Office

Principal Secretary to the Lord Chief Justice and Clerk of the Crown for Northern Ireland, J. A. L. McLean, Q.C.
Legal Secretary to the Lord Chief Justice, R. T. Millar.
Heads of Departments of Supreme Court (£39,400):
Master, Central Office, V. A. Care, Q.C.
Master, Office of Care and Protection, F. B. Hall.
Master, Chancery Office, V. G. Bridges.
Master, Bankruptcy and Companies Office, J. B. C. Glass.
Master, Probate and Matrimonial Office, D. W. G. Heatly.
Master, Taxing Office, A. E. Anderson, C.B.E.
Accountant, Court Funds Office, vacant.

Master, High Court, J. W. Wilson.

Recorders

Belfast, Judge Pringle, Q.C. £53,400
Londonderry, Judge Hart, Q.C.

County Court Judges

Judge Babington, D.S.C., Q.C.; Judge Chambers, Q.C.; Judge Curran, Q.C.; Judge Gibson, Q.C.; Judge Hart, Q.C.; Judge McKee, Q.C.; Judge Petrie, Q.C.; Rt. Hon. Judge Sir Robert Porter, Q.C.; Judge Rowland, Q.C.; Judge Russell, Q.C.; Judge Watt, Q.C.; Judge Higgins, Q.C. £48,100

Crown Solicitor's Office
Royal Courts of Justice, Belfast

Crown Solicitor, H. A. Nelson.

Department of the Director of Public Prosecutions
Royal Courts of Justice, Belfast

Director of Public Prosecutions, A. Fraser, Q.C.
Deputy Director of Public Prosecutions, D. Magill.

ECCLESIASTICAL COURTS

Original jurisdiction is exercised by the Consistory Court of each Diocese in England, presided over by the Chancellor of that Diocese. Appellate jurisdiction is exercised by the Provincial Courts detailed below, and by the Court for Ecclesiastical Causes Reserved, and by Commissions of Review (the membership of these being newly constituted for each case).

Court of Arches
(Province of Canterbury)

Registry: 16 Beaumont Street, Oxford OX1 2LZ

Dean of the Arches, The Rt. Worshipful Sir John Owen.

Court of the Vicar-General of the Province of Canterbury

Registry: 16 Beaumont Street, Oxford OX1 2LZ

Vicar-General, The Rt. Worshipful Miss S. Cameron, Q.C.

Chancery Court of York

Registry: 1 Peckitt Street, York YO1 1SG

Auditor, The Rt. Worshipful Sir John Owen.

The Vicar-General of the Province of York

Registry: 1 Peckitt Street, York YO1 1SG

Vicar-General, The Rt. Worshipful T. A. C. Coningsby, Q.C.

Court of Faculties

Registry: 1 The Sanctuary, SW1P 3JT

Office for the issue of special and ordinary marriage licences, appointment of notaries public, etc. Office hours, Mon.–Fri., 10–4.
Master of the Faculties, The Rt. Worshipful Sir John Owen.

TRIBUNALS, ETC

Copyright Tribunal
Room 1509, State House, 66–71 High Holborn, WC1R 4TP

Chairman, J. M. Bowers.
Secretary, J. E. Owens.

Employment Appeal Tribunal

Central Office, 4 St. James's Square, SW1Y 4JU
Divisional Office, 11 Melville Crescent, Edinburgh, EH3 7LU.
President, The Hon. Mr. Justice Wood.
Registrar, Miss V. J. Selio.

The Industrial Tribunals
Central Office (England and Wales)
93 Ebury Bridge Road, SW1W 8RE

President, His Honour Judge Sir David West-Russell
£53,400

Central Office (Scotland)
St. Andrew House, 141 West Nile Street, Glasgow G1 2RU

President, I. M. Thomson, W.S. £53,400

Immigration Appellate Authorities
Thanet House, 231 Strand, WC2R 1DA

Immigration Appeal Tribunal
President, D. L. Neve £48,100
Vice-Presidents, G. W. Farmer; Prof. D. C. Jackson £48,100

Immigration Appeal Adjudicators
Chief Adjudicator, M. Patey, M.B.E. £48,100

Lands Tribunal
48–49 Chancery Lane, WC2A 1JR

President, V. G. Wellings, Q.C. £53,400
Members, W. H. Rees; C. R. Mallett; W. Hall, D.F.C., J. C. Hill, T.D.; Dr. T. Hoyes; His Hon. Judge B. Marder, Q.C. £48,100
Registrar, C. A. McMullan.

Lands Tribunal for Scotland
1 Grosvenor Crescent, Edinburgh EH12 5ER

President, The Hon. Lord Elliott, M.C. £53,400
Members, W. Hall, D.F.C.; Sheriff A. C. Horsfall, Q.C. (*full-time*); W. D. C. Andrews, C.B.E., W.S.; T. Finlayson; D. A. Shepherd (*part-time*) £48,100
Clerk, D. Pentland.

N.H.S. Tribunal

Inquires into representations that the continued inclusion of a family practitioner (doctor, dentist, pharmacist or optician) on a Family Practitioner Committee's list would be prejudicial to the efficiency of the services concerned. The Tribunal sits when required, about eight times a year, and usually in London.

Chairman, B. Hargrove, Q.C.
Clerk, I. D. Keith, Midtown House, 38–42 High Street, Crawley, W. Sussex RH10 1BW.

Pensions Appeal Tribunals
Central Office (England and Wales)
48–49 Chancery Lane, WC2A 1JR

Responsibility for hearing appeals in connection with War Pensions.

President, M. H. Fauvelle £39,400

Central Office (Scotland)
20 Walker Street, Edinburgh EH13 7HS

President, J. A. Cameron £39,400

The Office of the President of Social Security Appeal Tribunals, Medical Appeal Tribunals and Vaccine Damage Tribunals
Clements House, Gresham Street, EC2V 7DN

An independent statutory authority which exercises judicial and administrative control over social security appeal tribunals, medical appeal tribunals and vaccine damage tribunals.

President, His Hon. Judge J. Byrt, Q.C. £53,400
Secretary, J. Connelly.

The Office of the Social Security Commissioners
London: Harp House, 83–86 Farringdon Street, EC4A 4BL
Edinburgh: 23 Melville Street, EH3 7PW

The final statutory authority to decide social security and medical claims.

Chief Commissioner, Hon. Judge Bromley, Q.C. £53,400
Secretary, Mrs. M. Biggs (*London*); R. Lindsay (*Edinburgh*).

The Office of the Social Security Commissioners for Northern Ireland
Lancashire House, 5 Linenhall Street, Belfast BT2 8AA

Chief Commissioner, Hon. Judge Chambers, Q.C. £53,400

Secretary, J. Jackson.

The Solicitors' Disciplinary Tribunal
60 Carey Street, WC2A 2JB

Independent body with members appointed by the Master of the Rolls.

President, G. B. Marsh.
Clerk, Mrs. S. C. Elson.

Special Commissioners of Income Tax
Turnstile House, 98 High Holborn, WC1V 6LQ

Independent body appointed by the Lord Chancellor to hear appeals concerning income taxes, etc.

Presiding Special Commissioner, R. H. Widdows, C.B.
£48,100
Special Commissioners, B. M. F. O'Brien; T. H. K. Everett; D. A. Shirley £41,150
Deputy Special Commissioners, D. C. Potter, Q.C.; His Hon. Judge Medd, O.B.E., Q.C.
Clerk, R. P. Lester £19,611

Transport Tribunal
4th Floor, Golden Cross House, Duncannon Street, WC2N 4JF

President, Judge Inskip, Q.C.
Secretary, E. J. Thomas.

V.A.T. Tribunals
15–17 Great Marlborough Street, W1V 2AP

V.A.T. Tribunals are administered by the Lord Chancellor's Department (the Secretary of State in Scotland) and determine disputes concerning V.A.T.

President, His Hon. Judge Medd, O.B.E., Q.C. . £48,100
Vice-President, *Scotland*, R. A. Bennett, C.B.E., Q.C.
£39,400
Registrar, J. M. Busby.

Tribunal Centres
London (*including Belfast*), 15–17 Great Marlborough Street, W1V 2AP.
Edinburgh, 44 Palmerston Place, Edinburgh EH12 5BJ.
Manchester, Warwickgate House, Warwick Road, Old Trafford, Manchester M16 0GP.

Parliamentary and Local Government Election Petitions Office
Room 120, Royal Courts of Justice, Strand, WC2A 2LL

Prescribed Officer, I. S. Warren.
Chief Clerk, C. I. P. Denyer.

THE POLICE SERVICE

There are 52 police forces in the United Kingdom, each responsible for law enforcement in its area. Most forces' area is conterminous with an English or Welsh county or Scottish region, though there are several combined forces. Law enforcement in London is carried out by the Metropolitan Police and the City of London Police; in Northern Ireland by the Royal Ulster Police; and by the Isle of Man, States of Jersey, and Guernsey forces in their respective islands and bailiwicks.

Each police force is maintained by a police authority. The authorities of English and Welsh forces comprise committees of local councillors and magistrates; in Scotland, the regional and islands councils are the authorities. The authority for the Metropolitan Police is the Home Secretary. In Northern Ireland the Secretary of State appoints the police authority.

Police authorities are financed by central and local government. Subject to the approval of the Home Secretary and to regulations, they appoint the chief constable and, subject to regulations, decide the maximum size of the force and provide buildings and equipment.

The Home Secretary and the Secretaries of State for Scotland and Northern Ireland are responsible for the organization, administration and operation of the police service. They make regulations covering matters such as police ranks, discipline, hours of duty, and pay and allowances.

All police forces (including the Metropolitan Police at the request of the Commissioner) are subject to inspection by H.M. Inspectors of Constabulary, who report to the respective Secretary of State.

The investigation of a serious complaint against a police officer is supervised by the Police Complaints Authority in England and Wales. In Scotland, complaints are investigated by independent public prosecutors.

Basic rates of police pay
(since Sept. 1, 1989)

Chief Constable	£43,749–£55,608
Deputy Chief Constable	£38,535–£44,487
Assistant Chief Constable	£36,699
Chief Superintendent	£31,131–£33,054
Superintendent	£27,999–£30,405
Chief Inspector	£20,583–£22,896
Inspector	£18,129–£20,583
Sergeant	£15,804–£18,129
Constable	£9,900–£16,521

Metropolitan Police
(Including London Weighting and London Allowance for ranks below Commissioner)

Metropolitan Commissioner	£72,000*
Deputy Commissioner	£59,247
Assistant Commissioner	£52,269
Deputy Assistant Commissioner	£41,814
Commander	£36,699
Chief Superintendent	£33,331–£35,254
Superintendent	£30,913–£32,605
Chief Inspector	£23,770–£26,077
Inspector	£21,304–£23,770
Sergeant	£15,804–£18,129
Constable	£9,900–£16,521

*Since April 1, 1989.

METROPOLITAN POLICE FORCE
New Scotland Yard, Broadway, SW1H 0BG
[01–230 1212]
Establishment, 28,415

Commissioner, Sir Peter Imbert, Q.P.M.
Deputy Commissioner, J. A. Dellow, C.B.E.

Receiver, D. H. J. Hilary £50,400
Deputy Receiver, R. M. Gregory £35,415

Territorial Operations Department
Assistant Commissioner, G. D. McLean, C.B.E., Q.P.M.
Deputy Assistant Commissioner, D. Cree, Q.P.M.
Head of Administration, Miss B. Arnold
£21,633–£28,170
Commanders, G. E. Howlett, Q.P.M.; R. G. Monk; A. J. Speed.

Area Headquarters
Deputy Assistant Commissioners, T. J. Siggs, O.B.E.; C. J. Rideout, Q.P.M.; C. Pollard; W. E. Boreham; M. B. Taylor; R. Innes, Q.P.M.; R. B. Wells, Q.P.M.
Commanders, C. A. Couch; G. M. Ness; J. A. Coo; H. N. L. Blenkin; R. C. Marsh; M. G. Farbrother; D. N. Stevens; D. A. Ray; J. F. Purnell, G.M.; E. D. Humphrey, Q.P.M.; K. W. Masterson; J. E. Metcalf; D. Flanders; D. Y. Cooke; D. M. T. Kendrick.

Specialist Operations Department
Assistant Commissioner, J. A. Smith, Q.P.M.
Deputy Assistant Commissioners, J. H. Cracknell, L.V.O.; S. R. A. Crawshaw, Q.P.M.; P. Phelan, Q.P.M.
Commanders, M. R. Campbell; K. G. Churchill-Coleman, Q.P.M.; A. W. F. Hemingway, Q.P.M.; J. M. Allain, Q.P.M.; D. C. Veness; D. C. Gunn; R. A. Penrose; R. C. Adams, B.E.M.; J. A. Howley; D. C. Stockley; A. G. Fry, Q.P.M.; J. P. O'Connor.

Metropolitan Police Laboratory
Director, Dr. B. Sheard £33,162
Deputy Directors, G. J. O. Lee; M. R. Loveland; P. D. Martin; Dr. W. D. C. Wilson ..... £21,633–£28,170
Senior Principal Scientific Officer, B. B. Wheals
£21,633–£28,170

Personnel and Training Department
Assistant Commissioner, G. W. Jones, Q.P.M.
Deputy Assistant Commissioner, E. Mitchell, Q.P.M.
Commanders, M. J. Sulliven; Miss J. Hilton, Q.P.M.; L. T. Roach.
Welfare Officer, K. F. T. Rivers, M.B.E.
£17,360–£22,606

Metropolitan Police Cadet Corps
Commander, Miss J. Hilton, Q.P.M.

Medical and Dental Branch
Chief Medical Officer, Dr. E. C. A. Bott

Management Support Department
Assistant Commissioner, P. J. J. Winship, Q.P.M.
Deputy Assistant Commissioner, J. M. M. Huins, Q.P.M.
Commander, R. V. Franklin.

Complaints Investigation Bureau
Commander, J. G. Taylor.

Directorate of Public Affairs
Director of Public Affairs, M. S. D. Granatt
£28,170–£31,602
Deputy Director of Public Affairs, J. P. Stubbs
£21,633–£28,170

Directorate of Management Services
Director, N. E. Hand .... £28,170–£31,602
Deputy Directors, P. I. May; Mrs. S. M. Merchant
£21,633–£28,170

Force Inspectorate
Deputy Assistant Commissioner, R. A. Hunt, O.B.E.
Commanders, D. J. Osland; E. Jones.

POLICE AUTHORITIES IN THE UNITED KINGDOM

Police Force	Headquarters	Actual Strength	Chief Constable	Chairman of Police Authority/Committee
England				
Avon and Somerset	Bristol	3,083	D. Shattock, Q.P.M.	B. M. Tanner
Bedfordshire	Bedford	1,036	A. Dyer, Q.P.M.	*
Cambridgeshire	Huntingdon	1,174	I. H. Kane, Q.P.M.	K. Spink
Cheshire	Chester	1,868	D. J. Graham, Q.P.M.	J. H. Collins, O.B.E.
Cleveland	Middlesbrough	1,489	C. F. Payne, C.B.E.,Q.P.M.	I. Jeffrey
Cumbria	Penrith	1,136	L. Sharp, Q.P.M.	R. Watson
Derbyshire	Ripley	1,791	A. O. Smith, Q.P.M.	E. H. Swain
Devon and Cornwall	Exeter	2,834	J. S. Evans	D. L. C. Roberts
Dorset	Dorchester	1,247	B. H. Weight, Q.P.M.	Maj. Gen. H. M. G. Bond
Durham	Durham	1,348	F. W. Taylor, Q.P.M.	Mrs. J. Parkin
Essex	Chelmsford	2,766	J. H. Burrow, O.B.E.	G. C. Waterer, M.B.E.
Gloucestershire	Cheltenham	1,164	A. H. Pacey, Q.P.M.	C. P. Hay
Hampshire	Winchester	3,144	J. C. Hoddinott, Q.P.M.	Capt. B. L. P. Blacker
Hertfordshire	Welwyn Garden City	1,645	T. A. Morris, Q.P.M.	F. Cogan
Humberside	Hull	2,046	D. Hall, C.B.E., Q.P.M.	S. J. Bayes
Kent	Maidstone	2,968	P. Condon, Q.P.M.	R. Carr
Lancashire	Preston	3,163	R. B. Johnson, Q.P.M.	Mrs. R. B. Henig
Leicestershire	Leicester	1,755	M. J. Hirst, Q.P.M.	R. R. Angrave
Lincolnshire	Lincoln	1,186	S. W. Crump, Q.P.M.	M. D. Kennedy
Greater Manchester	Manchester 16	6,981	C. J. Anderton, C.B.E., Q.P.M.	S. Murphy
Merseyside	Liverpool 69	4,790	J. Sharples, Q.P.M.	G. Bundred
Norfolk	Norwich	1,354	G. Charlton, C.B.E., Q.P.M.	R. Chase
Northamptonshire	Northampton	1,105	D. J. O'Dowd, Q.P.M.	A. A. Morby
Northumbria	Newcastle upon Tyne	3,600	Sir Stanley Bailey, C.B.E., Q.P.M.	G. Gill
Nottinghamshire	Nottingham	2,294	R. Hadfield, Q.P.M.	F. Higgins
Staffordshire	Stafford	2,188	C. H. Kelly, C.B.E., Q.P.M.	Miss I. H. Moseley
Suffolk	Ipswich	1,179	A. T. Coe	Capt. R. J. Sheepshanks
Surrey	Guildford	1,649	B. Hayes, Q.P.M.	Mrs. D. James
Sussex	Lewes	2,929	R. Birch, C.B.E., Q.P.M.	Mrs. P. A. Drake
Thames Valley	Oxford	3,642	C. Smith, C.V.O., Q.P.M.	Lt. Col. J. C. Walton
Warwickshire	Warwick	969	P. D. Joslin, Q.P.M.	J. L. Findon
West Mercia	Worcester	1,955	A. A. Mullett, Q.P.M.	R. A. H. Lloyd, T.D.
West Midlands	Birmingham 4	6,761	G. J. Dear, Q.P.M.	D. M. Ablett
Wiltshire	Devizes	1,080	W. R. Girven, Q.P.M.	J. W. H. Archer
Yorkshire, North	Northallerton	1,357	D. M. Burke, Q.P.M.	J. H. G. Parfect, M.B.E.
Yorkshire, South	Sheffield	2,925	P. Wright, C.B.E.	Sir John Layden
Yorkshire, West	Wakefield	5,225	P. J. Nobes, Q.P.M.	K. Wilson
Wales				
Dyfed-Powys	Carmarthen	919	R. White	T. R. George, O.B.E.
Gwent	Cwmbran	993	J. E. Over, Q.P.M., C.P.M.	B. Sutton
North Wales	Colwyn Bay	1,325	D. Owen, Q.P.M.	T. M. Hughes
South Wales	Bridgend	3,137	W. R. Lawrence	H. J. Gough
Scotland				
Central Scotland	Stirling	597	I. T. Oliver, Q.P.M., Ph.D.	S. Conner
Dumfries and Galloway	Dumfries	346	G. Esson, Q.P.M.	K. A. Kelly
Fife	Kirkcaldy	754	W. M. Moodie, C.B.E., Q.P.M.	R. Gough
Grampian	Aberdeen	1,070	A. G. Lynn, C.B.E., Q.P.M.	W. A. Grant
Lothian and Borders	Edinburgh 4	2,420	Sir William Sutherland, Q.P.M.	W. G. Rankine
Northern	Inverness	611	H. C. MacMillan, Q.P.M.	J. S. Munro
Strathclyde	Glasgow 2	6,782	A. K. Sloan, Q.P.M.	W. Harley
Tayside	Dundee	1,009	J. W. Bowman, Q.P.M.	Mrs. P. Doran
Northern Ireland				
Royal Ulster Constabulary	Belfast 5	8,237	H. N. Annesley, Q.P.M.	T. Rainey
Islands				
Isle of Man	Douglas	200	R. E. N. Oake	Hon. E. G. Lowey, M.L.C.
States of Jersey	St. Helier	223	†D. Parkinson	R. J. Shenton
Guernsey	St. Peter Port	142	†M. Le Moignan	M. W. Torode

† Chief Officer   * Elected at every meeting

Solicitor's Department

Solicitor, C. S. Porteous £38,210
Assistant Solicitors, R. E. Marsh; P. A. Shawdon; P.
S. Hamilton . . . . £30,425–£34,095

The following departments are responsible to the Receiver through the Deputy Receiver.

"E" Department
Establishments and Secretariat

Establishment Officer, R. B. Jones . . £28,170–£31,602
Deputy Establishment Officers, D. F. F. Hannaford;
D. Wilson; A. M. J. Williams . . . . . £21,633–£28,170

"F" Department
Finance

Director of Finance, J. A. Crutchlow £28,170–£31,602
Deputy Directors of Finance, D. H. Burr; J. E. Tubb;
M. W. Maidment . . . . £21,633–£28,170

Supplies and Services Department

Director, N. N. I. Batten . . . . £21,633–£28,170

Catering Department

Director of Catering, R. J. Downing . £21,633–£28,170

Property Services Department

Director of Property Services, T. G. Lawrence
. . . . £28,170–£31,602
Deputy Directors, R. M. Boa; K. R. Sewell; D. F.
Hobart . . . . £21,633–£28,170

Chief Engineer's Department

Chief Engineer, N. Boothman . . . . . . £28,170–£31,602
Deputy Chief Engineers, D. A. Woolgar; G. C.
Sudbury; J. T. Clifton; R. J. Perham
. . . . £21,633–£28,170

Department of Computing Services

Director of Computing Services (acting), D. K.
Dunkin . . . . £28,170–£31,602
Deputy Directors of Computing Services, T. Egan;
(acting) M. J. Bloomfield . . . . £21,633–£28,170

CITY OF LONDON POLICE
26 Old Jewry, EC2R 8DJ
[01-601 2222]
Strength of Force (June 1989), 815

Commissioner, O. Kelly, Q.P.M. £52,629
Assistant Commissioner, W. Taylor £41,025
Commander, H. J. Moore £33,591
Chief Superintendents, E. Aggar (*Administration*), T.
Hillier (*Traffic & Communications*); G. Marshall
(*"B" Divn.*); R. Knevett (*"C" Divn.*); P. Gwynn
(*C.I.D.*); P. Nove (*C.I.D/Fraud*) . . £28,494–£30,729

BRITISH TRANSPORT POLICE
15 Tavistock Place, WC1H 9SJ
[01-388 7541]
Strength of Force (May 1989), 1,812

The Force provides a policing service to the British Railways Board and London Underground Ltd. Police posts are located throughout England, Wales and Scotland.

The Chief Constable reports to the British Transport Police Committee, a statutory body set up under the Transport Act 1962. The members of the Committee are appointed by the British Railways Board and London Regional Transport.

Chief Constable, D. O'Brien, O.B.E.
Deputy Chief Constable, G. E. Coles.

Assistant Chief Constables, T. H. S. Buckle (*Management Services*); W. I. McGregor (*Operations*); W. F. Palmer (*London Underground Division*); A. M. Mackenzie (*Scottish Division*).

MINISTRY OF DEFENCE POLICE
Ministry of Defence, Empress State Building,
Lillie Road, SW6 1TR
[01–385 1244]
Strength of Force (May 1989), 4,600

The Ministry of Defence Police are responsible chiefly for the policing of naval, military, R.A.F. establishments, etc. in Great Britain. The Chief Constable is responsible to the Secretary of State for Defence.

Chief Constable, J. Aspinall, Q.P.M.
Deputy Chief Constable, N. L. Chapple, Q.P.M.
Head of M.D.P. Secretariat, B. Aves.
Assistant Chief Constables, A. A. J. Scale (*Personnel and Training*); R. E. Murray (*Operations*); C. Bucke (*Support*); S. E. Edwards (*Inspectorate*); A. F. Grant (*Scotland*).

ROYAL PARKS CONSTABULARY
2 Marsham Street, SW1P 3EB
[01-276 3761/3]
Strength of Force (June 1989), 155

The Royal Parks Constabulary is maintained by the Department of the Environment and is responsible, through the Bailiff of the Royal Parks, for the policing of twenty Royal Parks and Gardens in and around London. These comprise an area in excess of 6,000 acres. Officers of the Force are appointed under the Parks Regulations Act 1872, as amended by the Parks Regulations (Amendment) Act 1974.

Chief Officer, P. H. Gilbert.
Deputy Chief Officer, M. J. Loader.

UNITED KINGDOM ATOMIC ENERGY AUTHORITY CONSTABULARY
11 Charles II Street, SW1Y 4QP
[01-930-5454]
Strength of Force (June 1989), 655

The Constabulary is responsible for policing United Kingdom Atomic Energy Authority and British Nuclear Fuels PLC establishments and for escorting nuclear material between establishments.

The Chief Constable is responsible, through the Atomic Energy Authority Police Committee, to the Secretary of State for Energy.

Chief Constable, J. Reddington, Q.P.M.
Deputy Chief Constable, H. J. McMorris.

STAFF ASSOCIATIONS

ASSOCIATION OF CHIEF POLICE OFFICERS OF ENGLAND, WALES AND NORTHERN IRELAND, Room 1133, New Scotland Yard, Broadway, SW1H 0BG.—Represents the Chief Constables, Deputy Chief Constables and Assistant Chief Constables of England, Wales and N. Ireland, and officers of the rank of Commander and above in the Metropolitan and City of London Police. *Gen. Sec.*, G. Maxted.

THE POLICE SUPERINTENDENTS' ASSOCIATION OF ENGLAND AND WALES, 67A Reading Road, Pangbourne RG8 7JD.—Represents officers of the rank of Superintendent and Chief Superintendent. *Sec.*, Chief Supt. T. G. Hewitt.

THE POLICE FEDERATION OF ENGLAND AND WALES, 15–17 Langley Road, Surbiton, Surrey KT6 6LP.—Represents officers up to and including the rank of Chief Inspector. *Gen. Sec.*, Insp. V. Nield (Miss).

ASSOCIATION OF CHIEF POLICE OFFICERS (SCOTLAND), Police Headquarters, Fettes Avenue, Edinburgh

EH4 1RB.—Represents the Chief Constables, Deputy Chief Constables and Assistant Chief Constables of the Scottish police forces. *Hon. Sec.,* Chief Constable Sir William Sutherland, Q.P.M.

THE ASSOCIATION OF SCOTTISH POLICE SUPERINTENDENTS, Hon. Secretary's Office, Strathclyde Police, Force Inspectorate, Police Headquarters, 173 Pitt Street, Glasgow G2 4JS.—Represents officers of the rank of Superintendent and Chief Superintendent. *Hon. Sec.,* Chief Supt. J. McNicol.

THE SCOTTISH POLICE FEDERATION, 5 Woodside Place, Glasgow G3 7PD.—Represents officers up to and including the rank of Chief Inspector. *Gen. Sec.,* A. W. A. Wallace.

THE SUPERINTENDENTS ASSOCIATION OF NORTHERN IRELAND, Ormiston House, Hawthornden Road, Belfast BT4 3JW.—Represents Superintendents and Chief Superintendents in the R.U.C. *Hon. Sec.,* W/Chief Supt. A. Donald.

THE POLICE FEDERATION FOR NORTHERN IRELAND, Royal Ulster Constabulary, Garnerville, Garnerville Road, Belfast BT4 2NX.—Represents officers up to and including the rank of Chief Inspector. *Gen. Sec.,* J. Elder.

POLICE FORCE STRENGTHS

Number

	1981	1982	1983	1984	1985	1986	1987
England and Wales							
Regular police							
Authorized establishment....	120,008	120,125	120,447	120,679	120,903	121,785	122,648
Strength:							
Men	107,379	108,517	108,519	108,102	107,960	108,225	109,773
Women..................	10,702	10,935	10,995	11,001	11,213	11,600	12,492
Seconded:							
Men	1,424	1,419	1,407	1,388	1,439	1,617	1,716
Women	70	80	82	82	90	108	121
Additional constables:							
Men	90	89	84	83	79	88	70
Women..................	1	1	2	—	1	1	—
Scotland							
Regular police							
Authorized establishment....	13,195	13,205	13,261	13,283	13,377	13,489	13,569
Strength:							
Men	12,379	12,433	12,435	12,415	12,455	12,504	12,470
Women..................	749	719	713	722	761	838	933
Central service:							
Men	54	55	65	61	69	70	73
Women..................	2	2	2	2	1	2	3
Seconded:							
Men	78	73	68	67	67	88	85
Women..................	5	4	3	3	3	4	5
Additional regular police:							
Authorized establishment..	67	62	60	88	88	86	73
Strength	71	66	62	60	88	86	73
Northern Ireland							
Royal Ulster Constabulary							
Strength:							
Men	6,622	7,017	7,328	7,487	7,610	7,581	7,591
Women..................	712	701	675	640	649	653	645

DEFENCE MANPOWER STRENGTHS

At April 1   Thousands

	1982	1983	1984	1985	1986	1987	1988
U.K. SERVICE PERSONNEL							
All services: total	327·6	320·6	325·9	326·2	322·5	319·8	316·8
Female	15·7	15·4	16·2	16·4	16·0	16·2	15·9
Royal Navy: total	65·1	64·0	63·7	62·8	60·3	58·7	58·2
Female	4·0	3·9	3·9	3·7	3·4	3·4	3·3
Royal Marines: total	7·9	7·8	7·6	7·6	7·6	7·8	7·8
Army: total	163·2	159·1	161·5	162·4	161·4	159·7	158·1
Female	6·0	6·1	6·6	6·8	6·6	6·5	6·3
Royal Air Force: total	91·5	89·8	93·1	93·4	93·2	93·6	93·3
Female	5·8	5·4	5·7	6·0	6·0	6·3	6·3
Personnel locally entered overseas:							
total	10·1	10·1	10·1	10·2	10·1	9·8	9·4
Regular Reserves: total	196·4	193·4	198·0	205·5	211·4	220·9	230·2
Royal Navy	24·8	23·9	23·5	23·3	24·2	24·5	24·7
Royal Marines	2·2	2·2	2·2	2·2	2·3	2·3	2·4
Army	140·2	138·3	143·2	150·1	153·8	160·4	167·7
Royal Air Force	29·3	28·9	29·0	29·8	31·2	33·7	35·4
Volunteer Reserves and Auxiliary							
Forces: total	86·3	87·5	85·9	88·6	95·4	96·8	92·8
Royal Navy	5·4	5·4	5·2	5·2	5·5	5·7	5·6
Royal Marines	1·0	1·1	1·1	1·1	1·2	1·2	1·3
Territorial Army	72·1	72·8	71·4	73·7	77·7	78·5	74·7
Ulster Defence Regiment	7·1	7·1	6·8	6·4	6·6	6·5	6·4
Home Service Force	–	0·3	0·3	0·9	3·0	3·3	3·1
Royal Air Force	0·6	0·8	1·1	1·2	1·4	1·6	1·8
Cadet Forces: total	148·7	149·0	146·5	144·7	143·4	145·7	144·6
Royal Navy	28·7	29·4	28·4	28·4	28·0	27·5	27·1
Army	74·1	74·5	73·8	72·1	70·9	71·2	69·3
Royal Air Force	45·9	45·1	44·3	44·1	44·5	47·0	48·3
Ministry of Defence civilians:							
total	251·7	242·7	232·5	206·5	201·7	196·1	175·1
U.K. based	216·9	208·9	199·1	174·1	169·4	164·0	143·3
Non-industrial	108·1	105·6	103·2	94·9	93·8	93·3	88·5
Industrial	108·8	103·3	95·9	79·1	75·6	70·7	54·8
Locally engaged overseas	34·8	33·8	33·4	32·4	32·2	32·1	31·8
Non-industrial	10·7	10·5	10·4	10·2	10·3	10·3	10·2
Industrial	24·1	23·3	23·0	22·2	22·0	21·8	21·6

Recruitment of U.K. Service personnel to each Service

Number

	1981–82	1982–83	1983–84	1984–85	1985–86	1986–87	1987–88
All Services: total	22,607	21,647	36,991	34,721	32,651	34,049	33,826
Female	1,419	2,305	3,231	2,645	2,244	2,902	2,611
Royal Navy: total	3,805	3,584	4,785	4,582	4,276	5,336	5,181
Female	452	506	562	351	289	545	580
Royal Marines: total		447	447	954	1,093	1,233	991
Army: total	14,	13,071	22,348	22,278	20,268	19,918	21,041
Female	601	1,392	1,537	1,364	1,095	1,200	1,146
Royal Air Force: total	3,899	4,545	9,411	6,907	7,014	7,562	6,613
Female	366	407	1,132	930	860	1,157	885

THE ARMED FORCES

MINISTRY OF DEFENCE
Main Building, Whitehall, SW1A 2HB
[01–218 9000]

Salaries

Secretary of State £34,479
Minister of State, Commons £24,209
Minister of State, Lords.................. £37,047
Parliamentary Under Secretaries £18,219
Grade 1 .... £72,000
Grade 1A £66,000
Grade 2 .... £48,100–£50,400
Grade 3 .... £37,600–£42,900
Grade 4 .... £34,095–£35,415
(For Services salaries, *see* pp. 404–9.)

Secretary of State for Defence, THE RT. HON. THOMAS KING, M.P.
  Private Secretary, B. R. Hawtin.
Minister of State for the Armed Forces, HON. ARCHIBALD HAMILTON, M.P.
  Private Secretary, Miss P. M. Aldred.
Parliamentary Under Secretary of State for the Armed Forces, MICHAEL NEUBERT, M.P.
  Private Secretary, Dr. A. Cowpe.
Minister of State for Defence Procurement, THE HON. ALAN CLARK, M.P.
  Private Secretary, C. E. V. Hain-Cole..
Parliamentary Under Secretary of State for Defence Procurement, THE EARL OF ARRAN.
  Private Secretary, H. D. Kernohan.
Permanent Under Secretary of State (G1), Sir Michael Quinlan, K.C.B.
  Private Sec., C. J. Wright.
Chief of Defence Staff, Marshal of the R.A.F. Sir David Craig, G.C.B., O.B.E.

Defence Staff

Vice Chief of the Defence Staff, Gen. Sir Richard Vincent, K.C.B., D.S.O.
Deputy Under Sec. of State (Policy) (G2), R. Mottram.
Deputy Chief of the Defence Staff (Commitments), Lt.-Gen. Sir Antony Walker, K.C.B.
Asst. Under Sec. of State (Commitments) (G3), N. Bevan.
Asst. C.D.S. (N.A.T.O./U.K.), Air Vice-Marshal M. J. D. Stear, C.B.E.
Asst. C.D.S. (Overseas), Rear-Adm. E. S. J. Larken, D.S.O.
Asst. C.D.S. (Logistics), Maj.-Gen. I. S. Baxter, C.B.E.
Deputy C.D.S. (Systems), Lt.-Gen. Sir Anthony Mullens, K.C.B., O.B.E.
Asst. C.D.S. (Concepts), Maj.-Gen. J. R. Templer, C.B., O.B.E.
Asst. C.D.S., Operational Requirements (Sea), Rear-Adm. C. L. Wood.
Asst. C.D.S., Operational Requirements (Land), Maj.-Gen. A. S. J. Blacker, C.B.E.
Asst. C.D.S., Operational Requirements (Air), Air Vice-Marshal G. C. Williams, A.F.C.
Asst. C.D.S. (C.C.C.I.S.), Air Vice-Marshal D. A. Saunders, C.B.E.
Asst. C.D.S. (Policy and Nuclear), Air Vice-Marshal J. F. Willis, C.B.E.
Asst. Under Sec. of State (Policy) (G3), H. Griffiths.
Deputy C.D.S. (Programmes and Personnel), Vice-Adm. B. N. Wilson.
Asst. C.D.S. (Programmes), Maj.-Gen. the Hon. T. P. J. Boyd-Carpenter, M.B.E.
Surgeon Gen. and Dir. Gen. Naval Medical Services, Vice-Adm. Sir Godfrey Milton-Thompson, K.B.E., Q.H.P.

Deputy Surgeon Gen. (Ops.), Dir. Gen. Medical Services (Army), Maj.-Gen. A. J. Shaw, C.B., C.B.E., Q.H.P.
Deputy Surgeon Gen. (Research and Training), Medical Dir. Gen. (R.A.F.), Air Vice-Marshal N. H. Mills, Q.H.P.

Naval Department

Chief of Naval Staff and First Sea Lord, Adm. Sir Julian Oswald, G.C.B.
Asst. Chief of Naval Staff, Rear-Adm. H. M. White, C.B.E.
Hydrographer of the Navy, Rear-Adm. R. O. Morris.
Cmdt. Gen. Royal Marines, Lt.-Gen. Sir Martin Garrod, K.C.B., O.B.E.
Chief of Naval Personnel and Second Sea Lord, Adm. Sir Brian Brown, K.C.B., C.B.E.
Naval Secretary, Rear-Adm. D. S. Dobson.
Dir. Gen., Naval Manpower and Training, Rear-Adm. N. Purvis.
Dir. Gen., Naval Personal Services, Rear-Adm. D. M. Dow.
Chief of Fleet Support, Vice-Adm. Sir Jock Slater, K.C.B., L.V.O.
Dir. Gen., Ship Refitting (G3), G. A. Allin.
Dir. Gen., Supplies and Transport (G3), J. T. Baugh.
Dir., Supplies and Transport (Armaments and Managements Services) (G4), W. N. Cooke.
Dir., Supplies and Transport (Stores, Moves and Victualling) (G4), G. E. Miller.
Dir. Gen., Fleet Support Policy and Services, Rear-Adm. R. T. Frere.
Dir. Gen., Aircraft (Navy), Rear-Adm. D. M. Pulvertaft.
Chaplain of The Fleet, Ven. M. H. G. Henley, Q.H.C.

Army Department

Chief of the General Staff, Gen. Sir John Chapple, G.C.B., C.B.E.
Asst. Chief of the General Staff, Maj.-Gen. R. H. Swinburn.
Dir., Military Survey, Maj.-Gen. P. F. Fagan, M.B.E.
Dir. Gen., T.A. and Organization, Maj.-Gen. C. A. Ramsay, C.B., O.B.E.
Dir. Gen., Training and Doctrine (Army), Maj.-Gen. A. J. G. Pollard, C.B.E.
Dir., Royal Armoured Corps, Maj.-Gen. N. G. P. Ansell, O.B.E.
Dir., Royal Artillery, Maj.-Gen. B. T. Pennicott.
Dir., Infantry, Maj.-Gen. J. D. G. Pank, C.B.
Dir., Army Air Corps, Maj.-Gen. L. F. H. Busk.
Engineer in Chief (Army), Maj.-Gen. R. L. Peck.
Signal Officer in Chief (Army), Maj.-Gen. R. F. L. Cook.
Military Secretary, Lt.-Gen. Sir John Learmont, K.C.B., C.B.E.
Adjutant-General, Gen. Sir Robert Pascoe, K.C.B., M.B.E.
Dir. Gen., Army Manning & Recruiting, Maj.-Gen. P. G. Brooking, C.B., M.B.E.
Paymaster in Chief, Maj.-Gen. P. S. Bray.
Dir. Gen., Personal Services (Army), Maj.-Gen. P. P. D. Stone, C.B.E.
Dir. Security (Army), Maj.-Gen. H. E. M. L. Garrett, C.B.E. (retd.).
Dir., Army Legal Services, Maj.-Gen. M. T. Fugard.
Dir., Army Education, Maj.-Gen. J. S. Lee, M.B.E.
Quartermaster General, Lt.-Gen. Sir Edward Jones, K.C.B., C.B.E.
Dir. Gen., Logistic Policy (Army), Maj.-Gen. P. W. E. Istead, C.B., O.B.E., G.M.

Dir. Gen., Transport and Movements, Maj.-Gen. C. E. G. Carrington, C.B.E.
Dir. Gen., Ordnance Services, Maj.-Gen. J. A. Hulme.
Dir. Gen., Electrical and Mechanical Engineering, Maj.-Gen. D. Shaw, C.B.E.
Chaplain General, Rev. J. Harkness, O.B.E., Q.H.C.

Air Force Department

Chief of the Air Staff, Air Chief Marshal Sir Peter Harding, K.C.B.
Asst. Chief of Air Staff, Air Vice-Marshal C. J. Thomson, C.B.E., A.F.C.
Cmdt. Gen. (R.A.F. Regt.) and Dir. Gen. of Security, Air Vice-Marshal J. H. Harris, C.B.E.
Controller of National Air Traffic Services, Air Marshal Sir Thomas Stonor, K.C.B.
Air Member for Personnel, Air Marshal Sir Laurence Jones, K.C.B., A.F.C.
Air Secretary, Air Vice-Marshal R. J. Honey, C.B.E.
Dir. Gen., R.A.F. Personal Services, Air Vice-Marshal D. O. Crwys-Williams.
Dir. Gen., Training, Air Vice-Marshal E. H. Macey, O.B.E., C.B.E.
Air Member for Supply and Organization, Air Chief Marshal Sir Brendan Jackson, K.C.B.
Dir. Gen., Communications, Information Systems and Organization, Air Vice-Marshal J. P. R. Browne, C.B.E.
Chief Engineer, Air Marshal Sir Frank Holroyd, K.B.E., C.B.
Dir. Gen., Supply, Air Vice-Marshal R. C. Allerton, C.B.
Chaplain-in-Chief, Rev. B. N. Halfpenny, Q.H.C.

Defence Scientific Staff

Chief Scientific Adviser (G1A), Prof. E. R. Oxburgh.
Deputy Chief Scientific Adviser (G2), Dr. G. G. Pope, C.B.
Asst. Chief Scientific Advisers (G3), D. E. Humphries (*Projects and Research*); Mrs. M. J. Bourne, O.B.E. (*Capabilities*); (*G4*) Dr. R. G. Ridley (*Nuclear*).
Dir., Defence Operational Analysis Establishment (G3), R. J. Poole.
Dir. Gen., Strategic Defence Initiative Participation Office (G3), Dr. S. Orman.

Office of Management and Budget

Second Permanent Under Secretary of State (G1A), K. C. Macdonald, C.B.
Deputy Under Secs. of State (G2), M. J. V. Bell (*Finance*); R. M. Hastie-Smith, C.B. (*Civilian Management*); R. L. L. Facer (*Personnel and Logistics*); C. T. McDonnell (*Resources and Programmes*).
Asst. Under Secs. of State (G3), T. J. Brack (*Naval Personnel*); T. F. W. B. Knapp (*Supply and Organization (Air)*); B. H. Cousins, C.B.E. (*General Finance*); M. J. Culham (*Civilian Management (Administrators)*); I. D. Dawson (*Resources*); N. Paren, (*Fleet Support*); M. Gainsborough (*Adj. Gen.*); K. W. B. Gooderham (*Security and Common Services*); Dr. M. J. Harte (*Personnel (Air)*); D. C. R. Heyhoe (*Dir. Gen. of Management Audit*); J. F. Howe (*Personnel and Logistics*); C. E. Johnson (*Dir. Gen. of Defence Accounts*); R. Jackling, C.B.E. (*Programmes*); D. B. Omand; D. J. L. Smith (*Civilian Management (Specialists)*); N. H. Nicholls (*Systems*); J. Roberts; B. F. Rule (*Dir. Gen. Information Technology Systems*); N. Beaumont (*Quartermaster*).

Public Relations

Chief of Public Relations (G4), H. B. Colver.
Dir. of Public Relations (Navy), Capt. A. Provest (R.N.).

Dir. of Public Relations (Army), Brig. C. B. Q. Wallace, O.B.E.
Dir. of Public Relations (R.A.F.), Air Cdre. M. Barnes.

PROCUREMENT EXECUTIVE

Chief of Defence Procurement, Sir Peter Levene, K.B.E. £110,000
Private Sec., S. French.

Procurement Executive Policy and Administration

Deputy Under Sec. of State (Defence Procurement) (G2), J. M. Stewart, C.B.
Asst. Under Sec. of State (International and Domestic Procurement), (G3), J. A. Galvin.
Dir. Gen. Defence Quality Assurance (G3), B. Miller.
Dir. Gen. Defence Contracts (G3), B. J. Slade.
Principal Dir. Accountancy Services (P.E.) (G4), J. V. A. Crawford.
Principal Dir. Technical Costs (G4), R. E. Rowe.
Principal Dir. of Patents (G4), E. J. Mansfield.

Research and Development Controllerate

Controller Establishments, Research and Nuclear Programmes (G3), W. F. Mumford, C.B.
Deputy Controller (Nuclear) (G3), J. C. Mabberley.
Deputy Controller (Research) (G3), Dr. T. Buckley.
Dir., Admiralty Research Establishment (G3), P. D. Ewins.
Dir., Royal Signals and Radar Establishment (G2), N. H. Hughes.
Dir., Atomic Weapons Establishment (G2), Dr. T. P. McLean.
Dir., Chemical Defence Establishment (G3), Dr. G. S. Pearson.
Dir., Royal Armament Research and Development Establishment (G2/3), Dr. A. C. Baynham.
Commandant, Aeroplane and Armament Experimental Establishment, Air Cdre. P. D. L. Gover.
Dir., Royal Aerospace Establishment (G2), M. T. Peters.
Chief Engineer, (G4), R. H. Lovell.

Sea Systems Controllerate

Controller of the Navy, Vice-Adm. K. J. Eaton.
Asst. Under Sec. of State (Material-Naval) (G3), J. K. Ledlie.
Principal Dir., Navy and Nuclear Contracts (G4), A. J. Figes.
Chief Strategic Systems Executive, Rear-Adm. I. H. Pirnie.
Deputy Chief Strategic Systems Executive, Cdre. J. S. Kelly, O.B.E.
Dir. Gen. Strategic Weapon Systems, Cdre. T. W. Craven.
Deputy Controller Warships, Vice-Adm. Sir Hugh Thompson, K.B.E.
Dir. Gen. Surface Ships (G3), R. V. Babbington.
Dir. Gen. Submarines (G3), W. G. Sanders.
Chief Naval Architect (G3), B. O. Wall.
Chief Naval Weapons System Engineer (G4), D. McArthur.
Deputy Controller Warship Equipment (G3), A. J. Creighton.
Dir. Gen. Surface Weapons (G4), H. Perkins.
Dir. Gen. Underwater Weapons (G4), R. McCaughan.
Dir. Gen. Marine Engineering, Chief Marine Systems Engineer, Rear-Adm. R. A. Issac, C.B.

Land Systems Controllerate

Master General of the Ordnance, Lt.-Gen. Sir John Stibbon, K.C.B., O.B.E.
Vice Master General of the Ordnance, Maj.-Gen. G. M. Hutchinson, C.B.

Asst. Under Sec. of State (Ordnance) (G3), Dr. A. Fox.
Principal Dir., Contracts (Ordnance) (G4), R. G. Woodman, C.B.E.
Dir. Gen., Guided Weapons and Electronics (G3), J. D. Maines.
Dir. Gen., Fighting Vehicles and Engineer Equipment, Maj.-Gen. R. J. Hayman-Joyce, O.B.E.
Dir. Gen., Weapons (Army), Maj.-Gen. E. G. Willmott, O.B.E.

Air Systems Controllerate

Controller Aircraft, D. M. Spiers, C.B., T.D.
Dep. Controller Aircraft, Air Marshal Sir Michael Simmons, K.C.B., A.F.C.
Asst. Under Sec. of State/Air (Procurement Executive) (G3), B. A. Taylor.
Principal Dir., Contracts/Air (G4), D. Grassby.
Dir. Gen. Aircraft 1, Air Vice-Marshal, R. M. Austin, A.F.C.
Dir. Gen. Aircraft 2, Air Vice-Marshal D. Cousins, A.F.C.
Dir. Gen. Aircraft 3, (G3), J. W. Britton.
Dir. Gen., Air Weapons Electronic Systems (G3), K. G. Hambleton.
Dir. Gen., Strategic Electronic Systems, Air Vice-Marshal M. J. D. Brown.

Defence Export Services Organization

Head of Defence Export Services, A. Thomas
£100,000

Military Deputy to Head of D.E.S., Maj.-Gen. C. N. Last, O.B.E.
Dir. Gen. Saudi Airforce Projects, Air Vice-Marshal R. I. Stuart-Paul, M.B.E.
Dir. Gen., Marketing (G3), R. J. Harding.
Asst. Under Sec. of State (D.E.S. Admin.) (G3), M. D. Tidy.

METEOROLOGICAL OFFICE

London Road, Bracknell, Berks.
[0344-420242]
The Meteorological Office is the State Meteorological Service. It forms part of the Ministry of Defence, the Director General being ultimately responsible to the Secretary of State for Defence.

Except for the common services provided by other government departments as part of their normal functions, the cost of the Meteorological Office is borne by Defence Votes.

Of the expenditure chargeable to Defence Votes about £35,000,000 represents expenditure associated with staff and £34,000,000 on stores, communications and miscellaneous services. About £25,500,000 is recovered from outside bodies for special services rendered, sales of meteorological equipment, etc.

Dir. Gen. (G2), Dr. J. T. Houghton, C.B.E., D.Phil., F.R.S.
Dir. of Services (G3), Dr. D. N. Axford.
Dir. of Research (G4), A. Gilchrist.

THE ROYAL NAVY

THE QUEEN

Admirals of the Fleet

H.R.H. The Prince Philip, Duke of Edinburgh, K.G., K.T., O.M., G.B.E., P.C., born June 10, 1921 ..... Jan. 15, 1953
Sir Varyl Begg, G.C.B., D.S.O., D.S.C., born Oct. 1, 1908 .... Aug. 12, 1968
The Lord Hill-Norton, G.C.B., born Feb. 8, 1915 .... March 12, 1971
Sir Michael Pollock, G.C.B., L.V.O., D.S.C., born Oct. 19, 1916 .... March 1, 1974
Sir Edward Ashmore, G.C.B., D.S.C., born Dec. 11, 1919 .... Feb. 9, 1977
The Lord Lewin, K.G., G.C.B., L.V.O., D.S.C., born Nov. 19, 1920 .... July 6, 1979
Sir Henry Leach, G.C.B., born Nov. 18, 1923 .... Dec. 1, 1982
Sir John Fieldhouse, G.C.B., G.B.E., born Feb. 12, 1928 .... Aug. 2, 1985
Sir William Staveley, G.C.B., born Nov. 10, 1928 .... May 25, 1989

Admirals

Oswald, Sir Julian, G.C.B., (First Sea Lord and Chief of Naval Staff).
Reffell, Sir Derek, K.C.B., (Controller of the Navy).
Bathurst, Sir Benjamin, K.C.B., (C.-in-C. Fleet, Allied C.-in-C. Channel and C-in-C. Eastern Atlantic Area).
Black, Sir Jeremy, K.C.B., D.S.O., M.B.E., (C.-in-C. Naval Home Command).
Thomas, Sir Richard, K.C.B., O.B.E., (U.K. Military Rep. H.Q. N.A.T.O.).
Brown, Sir Brian, K.C.B., C.B.E. (Second Sea Lord, Chief of Naval Personnel, and Admiral President Royal Naval College Greenwich).

Vice-Admirals

Symons, Sir Patrick, K.B.E., (Representative to SACLANT in Europe).
Webster, Sir John, K.C.B. (Flag Officer, Plymouth, Naval Base Commander Devonport, Commander Central Sub. Area, Eastern Atlantic and Plymouth Sub. Area Channel).
Thompson, Sir Hugh, K.B.E., (Deputy Controller Warships, Senior Naval Representative Bath and Chief Naval Engineer Officer).

Slater, Sir Jock, K.C.B., L.V.O., (Chief of Fleet Support).
Kerr, Sir John, K.C.B., (Chief of Defence Intelligence).
King, Sir Norman, K.B.E., (Chief of Staff to Commander, Allied Naval Forces Southern Europe).
Livesay, Sir Michael, K.C.B., (Flag Officer Scotland and N. Ireland, Commander Northern Sub. Area Eastern Atlantic, and Commander NORE Sub. Area Channel, and Naval Base Commander Rosyth).
Grose, Sir Alan, K.B.E., (Flag Officer Third Flotilla and Commander Anti-Sub. Warfare Striking Force).
Coward, J. F., D.S.O., (Flag Officer First Flotilla).
Weatherall, Sir James, K.B.E., (Deputy Supreme Allied Commander Atlantic).
Wilson, B. N., (Deputy C.D.S. (Programmes and Personnel)).
Eaton, K. J., (Controller of the Navy).

Rear-Admirals

Marsh, G. G. W., C.B., O.B.E., (Project Manager N.F.R.90)
Morris, R. O., (Hydrographer of the Navy).
Dingemans, P. G. V., D.S.O., (Chief of Staff to C.-in-C. Fleet).

Garnier, J., c.b.e., l.v.o., (*Flag Officer Royal Yachts*).

Sherval, D. R., c.b.

Balfour, H. M., l.v.o., (*Commander, Sultan of Oman's Navy*).

Grenier, P. F., c.b., (*Flag Officer Submarines and COMSUBEASTLANT*).

Wood, C. L., (*Asst. C.D.S. Operational Requirements (Sea Systems)*).

Layman, C. H., d.s.o., l.v.o., (*Asst. Dir. (Communications and Information Systems) on the I.M.S.*).

Isaac, R. A., c.b., (*Dir. Gen. Marine Engineering*).

Cole, M. C., (*Commander British Naval Staff Washington, Naval Attaché Washington and U.K. National Liaison Representative to SACLANT*).

Liardet, G. F., c.b.e., (*Cmdt. Joint Services Defence College*).

Purvis, N., (*Dir. Gen. Naval Manpower and Training*).

White, H. M., c.b.e., (*Asst. Chief of Naval Staff*).

Hill-Norton, N. J. (*Flag Officer Gibraltar, Gibraltar Naval Base Commander and COMGIBMED*).

Hill, R. C. F. (*Chief Staff Officer (Engineering) to C.-in-C. Fleet*).

Pulvertaft, D. M. (*Dir. Gen. Aircraft (Naval)*).

Larken, E. S. J., d.s.o. (*Asst. C.D.S. (Overseas)*).

Dobson, D. S., (*Naval Secretary*).

Woodhead, A. P., (*Flag Officer Second Flotilla*).

Allen, D., c.b.e. (*Defence Services Secretary and Chief Naval Supply and Secretariat Officer*).

Pirnie, I. H., (*Chief Strategic Systems Executive*).

Hilton, J. M. T., (*President of the Ordnance Board*).

Salt, J. F. T. G., (*Senior Naval Member of Directing Staff, Royal College of Defence Studies*).

Newman, R. T., (*Flag Officer Sea Training*).

Frere, R. T., (*Dir. Gen. Fleet Support Policy and Services*).

Layard, M. H. G., c.b.e., (*Flag Officer Naval Air Command*).

Dow, D. M., (*Dir. Gen. Naval Personal Services*).

Cooke-Priest, C. H. D. (*Deputy Asst. Chief of Staff (Operations) on the Staff of the Supreme Allied Commander Europe*).

Carine, J., (*Chief of Staff to C.-in-C. Naval Home Command*).

HER MAJESTY'S FLEET
(as at April 1, 1989)

Type/Class	No.	Operational or engaged in preparing for service or trials or training	No.	Undergoing restorative or major refit or conversion, on standby etc.
Submarines				
Polaris	3	*Repulse, Resolution, Revenge*	1	*Renown*
Fleet	13	*Conqueror, Courageous†, Sovereign, Swiftsure, Superb, Sceptre, Spartan†, Trafalgar, Turbulent, Tireless, Torbay, Trenchant†, Valiant†*	3	*Warspite, Churchill, Splendid*
Type 2400	1	*Upholder**		
Oberon Class	10	*Olympus, Odin, Onslaught, Otter, Otus, Ocelot, Onyx, Osiris, Oracle, Opossum*	1	*Opportune*
ASW Carriers	3	*Illustrious, Ark Royal, Invincible†*		
Assault Ships	1	*Intrepid*	1	*Fearless*
Guided-Missile Destroyers				
Type 82	1	*Bristol*		
Type 42	10	*Cardiff†, Birmingham, Glasgow†, Nottingham, Liverpool, Manchester, York, Gloucester, Edinburgh, Newcastle*	2	*Exeter, Southampton*
Frigates				
Type 23	1	*Norfolk*		
Type 22	12	*Boxer, Beaver, Brave, London, Sheffield, Cornwall†, Coventry†, Cumberland†, Campbeltown†, Chatham, Brilliant, Broadsword*	2	*Battleaxe, Brazen*
Type 21	5	*Amazon, Ambuscade, Active, Avenger, Alacrity*	1	*Arrow*
Leander Class	12	*Achilles, Charybdis, Penelope, Phoebe, Sirius, Danae, Andromeda, Scylla, Ariadne†, Cleopatra, Jupiter, Hermione*	2	*Minerva, Argonaut*
Navigation Training Ship			1	*Juno*
Offshore Patrol				
Castle Class	1	*Leeds Castle*	1	*Dumbarton Castle*
Island Class	7	*Alderney, Guernsey, Lindisfarne, Orkney, Shetland, Anglesey, Jersey*		
MCMVs				
Minesweepers	3	*Cuxton, Soberton, Upton*		
River Class**	12	*Waveney, Carron, Dovey, Helford, Humber, Blackwater, Itchen, Helmsdale, Orwell, Ribble, Spey, Arun*		
Minehunters Ton Class	8	*Brereton, Brinton, Iveston, Kedleston, Kellington, Hubberston, Sheraton, Wilton*	3	*Kirkliston, Gavinton, Nurton*

Type/Class	No.	Operational or engaged in preparing for service or trials or training	No.	Undergoing restorative or major refit or conversion, on standby etc.
Hunt Class	12	*Brecon, Ledbury, Cottesmore, Dulverton, Middleton, Chiddingford, Hurworth, Bicester, Atherstone, Berkeley, Quorn†, Cattistock*	1	*Brocklesbury*
Patrol Craft				
Bird Class	5	*Cygnet, Kingfisher†, Peterel, Sandpiper, Redpole*		
Coastal Training Craft†‡	15	*Attacker, Fencer, Hunter, Chaser, Striker, Archer, Biter, Smiter, Pursuer, Blazer, Dasher, Puncher, Charger, Ranger, Trumpeter*		
Peacock Class	3	*Peacock, Plover, Starling*		
Gibraltar Search and Rescue Craft	2	*Cormorant, Hart*		
Support Ships				
Submarine Tender	1	*Sentinel*		
Seabed Operations Vessel	1	*Challenger*		
Royal Yacht/Hospital Ship	1	*Britannia*		
Training Ships				
Fleet Tenders	3	*Manly†, Messina, Milbrook*	1	*Mentor*
Ice Patrol Ship	1	*Endurance*		
Survey Ships	7	*Fawn, Hecate, Herald, Gleaner, Hecla, Roebuck, Beagle*	1	*Bulldog*

Notes:
  (i) This table includes ships due for completion or disposal during the course of 1989–90; the numbers of each type are not therefore an accurate indication of the ships available at any one time. Ships solely engaged in harbour training duties are not included.
 (ii) Ships marked * were under construction on April 1, 1989 and are planned to enter service during 1989–90.
(iii) Ships marked † are engaged in trials or training.
 (iv) Vessels marked **, apart from H.M.S. *Blackwater*, are operated by the Royal Naval Reserve.
  (v) The Coastal Training Craft marked ‡ are operated by the Royal Naval Reserve and the University Royal Naval Units.
 (vi) All submarines, ASW Carriers, Assault Ships, Guided Missile Destroyers, Frigates, Offshore Patrol Ships and MCMVs are assigned to NATO. Other ships could be made available in support of NATO operations if national requirements permitted.
(vii) Ships approved during 1988–89 for disposal: *Abdiel, Apollo, Arethusa, Bronington, Diomede, Euryalus, Fox, Maxton, Plymouth, Swallow, Swift, Walkerton.*

Royal Naval Auxiliary Service.—The Royal Naval Auxiliary Service (R.N.X.S.) is a uniformed civilian volunteer service, administered by the Ministry of Defence and trained by the Royal Navy to operate at ports and anchorages, for duty in emergencies and war. R.N.X.S. units are situated on the coasts of the United Kingdom and organized and run by the Area Flag Officers. The role of the R.N.X.S. is to assist with the defence of ports and anchorages by manning local headquarters and supporting the Naval Control of Shipping Organization. The strength is 3,000.
Patron, H.R.H. Prince Michael of Kent.

ROYAL MARINES

The Corps of Royal Marines, about 7,000 strong, first formed in 1664, is part of the Naval Service. The Royal Marines provide Britain's sea soldiers and in particular 3 Commando Brigade Royal Marines, two thirds of which is trained and equipped for arctic warfare. Royal Marines also serve in H.M. Ships, provide landing craft crews, special boat sections and other detachments for naval and amphibious operations. They also provide the Naval Band Service.
The Royal Marines Reserve of about 1,350 volunteers consists of five main centres in London, Bristol, Liverpool, Newcastle and Glasgow.
Commandant General, Royal Marines, Lt.-Gen. Sir Martin Garrod, K.C.B., O.B.E.
Major-Generals, H. Y. La R. Beverley, O.B.E. (*Chief of Staff*); R. J. Ross, O.B.E. (*Training Reserve and Special Forces*); N. F. Vaux, C.B., D.S.O. (*Commando Forces*); P. T. Stevenson (*British Forces Falkland Is.*).

QUEEN ALEXANDRA'S ROYAL NAVAL NURSING SERVICE

The first nursing sisters were appointed to naval hospitals in 1884 and the Queen Alexandra's Royal Naval Nursing Service (Q.A.R.N.N.S.) gained its current title under the patronage of Queen Alexandra in 1902. Nursing ratings were introduced in 1960 and from 1982 a number of men have taken the opportunity to join Q.A.R.N.N.S. as both officers and ratings. Still largely based at the Royal Naval Hospitals, Q.A.R.N.N.S. continue their responsibility for the health and fitness of naval personnel. The strength is about 430.
Patron, H.R.H. Princess Alexandra.
Matron-in-Chief, Miss E. M. Northway, R.R.C., Q.H.N.S., Q.A.R.N.N.S.

WOMEN'S ROYAL NAVAL SERVICE

Originally founded in 1917, the Women's Royal Naval Service (W.R.N.S.) was temporarily disbanded between World Wars I and II. The contribution of the Service is now firmly established as a professional and integral part of the Royal Navy with personnel serving in the United Kingdom and abroad in a wide range of specialist roles. Although W.R.N.S. do not serve at sea, they provide an essential nucleus of about 3,000 trained personnel ashore in order to release men to H.M. Ships.

Chief Commandant, H.R.H. Princess Anne.

Director W.R.N.S., Commandant A. Larken, A.D.C., W.R.N.S.

THE ARMY

THE QUEEN

Field Marshals

H.R.H. The Prince Philip, Duke of Edinburgh, K.G., K.T., O.M., G.B.E., P.C., *born* June 10, 1921 ..... Jan. 15, 1953
Sir Richard A. Hull, K.G., G.C.B., D.S.O., *born* May 7, 1907 .... Feb. 8, 1965
Sir A. James H. Cassels, G.C.B., K.B.E., D.S.O., *born* Feb. 28, 1907 .... Feb. 29, 1968
The Lord Carver, G.C.B., C.B.E., D.S.O., M.C., *born* April 24, 1915 .... July 18, 1973
Sir Roland Gibbs, G.C.B., C.B.E., D.S.O., M.C., *born* June 22, 1921 .... July 13, 1979
The Lord Bramall, G.C.B., O.B.E., M.C., *born* Dec. 18, 1923 .... Aug. 1, 1982
Sir John W. Stanier, G.C.B., M.B.E., *born* Oct. 6, 1925 .... July 10, 1985
Sir Nigel Bagnall, G.C.B., C.V.O., M.C., A.D.C. (*Gen.*), *born* Feb. 10, 1927 .... Sept. 9, 1988

Generals

Vincent, Sir Richard, K.C.B., D.S.O., Col. Cmdt. R.A., (*Vice Chief of the Defence Staff*).

Chapple, Sir John, G.C.B., C.B.E., A.D.C. (*Gen.*), Col. 2 GR (*Chief of the General Staff*).

Akehurst, Sir John, K.C.B., C.B.E., Col. R. Anglian, (*D. SACEUR*).

Huxtable, Sir Charles, K.C.B., C.B.E., A.D.C. (*Gen.*), Col. D.W.R. (*C.-in-C. U.K.L.F.*).

Kenny, Sir Brian, K.C.B., C.B.E., Col. Cmdt. R.A.V.C., Col. Q.R.I.H., Col. Cmdt. R.A.C., (*C.-in-C. B.A.O.R. and Commander Northern Army Group, and D. SACEUR (desig.*)).

Pascoe, Sir Robert, K.C.B., M.B.E., A.D.C (*Gen.*), Col. Cmdt. 1 R.G.J., Col. Cmdt. R.A.C., (*Adjutant General*).

Palmer, Sir Patrick, K.B.E., Col. A. & S.H., (*C.-in-C AFNORTH*).

Stibbon, Sir John, K.C.B., O.B.E., Col. Cmdt. R.A.P.C., Col. Cmdt. R.P.C., Col. Cmdt. R.E., (*Master General of the Ordnance*).

Lieutenant-Generals

Walker, Sir Antony, K.C.B., Col. Cmdt. R.T.R., (*Deputy Chief of the Defence Staff (Commitments)*).

Ramsbotham, Sir David, K.C.B., C.B.E., Col. Cmdt. 2GR, (*Comd. U.K. Fd. Army and Inspec. Gen. T.A.*).

Inge, Sir Peter, K.C.B., Col. Green Howards, Col. Cmdt. R.M.P., (*Comd. 1 (B.R.) Corps. and C.-in-C. B.A.O.R. (desig.*)).

Billiere, Sir Peter de la, K.C.B., C.B.E., D.S.O., M.C., Col. Cmdt. The Light Division, (*G.O.C., S.E. District*).

MacMillan, Sir John, K.C.B., C.B.E., Col. Cmdt. The Scottish Division, (*G.O.C. Scotland and Governor Edinburgh Castle*).

Waters, Sir John, K.C.B., C.B.E., Col. Glosters, Col. Cmdt. P.O.W., (*G.O.C. & D. Mil. Ops. Northern Ireland*).

Jones, Sir Edward, K.C.B., C.B.E., Col. Cmdt. R.A.E.C., Col. Cmdt. 3 RGJ, (*Quartermaster General*)

Learmont, Sir John, K.C.B., C.B.E., Col. Cmdt. A.A.C., Col. Cmdt. R.A., (*Military Secretary*).

Mullens, Sir Anthony, K.C.B., O.B.E. (*Deputy Chief of the Defence Staff (Systems*)).

Johnson, G. D., O.B.E., M.C. (*Comd. Training and Arms Directors*).

Major-Generals

Pank, J. D. G., C.B., Col. L.I., (*Dir. Infantry*).

Cooper, S. C., (*G.O.C. London District and Maj.-Gen. Comd. The Household Divn.*).

Guthrie, C. R. L., L.V.O., O.B.E., Col. Cmdt. Int. Corps.

Jeapes, A. S., C.B., O.B.E., M.C., (*G.O.C. S.W. District*).

Ramsay, C. A., C.B., O.B.E., (*Dir. Gen., T.A. and Organization*).

Beckett, E. H. A., C.B., M.B.E., Col. Cmdt. The King's Division, (*Head of British Defence Staff, Washington*).

Brooking, P. G., C.B., M.B.E., (*Dir. Gen. Army Manning and Recruiting*).

Evans, J. A. M., C.B., (*Senior Army Member, Royal College of Defence Studies*).

Shaw, A. J., C.B., C.B.E., Q.H.P., (*D.G.A.M.S. and D.S.G. (Ops.*)).

Willmott, E. G., O.B.E., Col. Cmdt. R.E., (*Dir. Gen. Weapons (Army*)).

Fawcus, G. B., (*Chief of Staff LIVE OAK*).

Bonnet, P. R. F., M.B.E., (*G.O.C. W. District*).

Crowfoot, A. B., C.B.E., (*G.O.C. N.W. District*).

Quayle, T. D. G., (*Comd. Arty 1 (B.R.) Corps*).

Templer, J. R., C.B., O.B.E., (*Asst. Chief of Defence Staff (Concepts*)).

Busk, L. F. H., (*Dir. Army Air Corps*).

Fugard, M. T., (*Dir. Army Legal Services*).

Graham, P. W., C.B.E., Col. Gordons, (*Cmdt. R.M.A.S.*).

Pollard, A. J. G., C.B.E., Col. Comdt. S.A.S.C., Dep. Col. R. Anglian, (*Dir. Gen. Training and Doctrine*).

Ansell, N. G. P., O.B.E., (*Dir. Royal Armoured Corps*).

Baxter, I. S., C.B.E., (*Asst. Chief of Defence Staff (Logistics*)).

Davies, P. R., Col. King's, (*Comd. Comms. B.A.O.R.*).

Hodges, R. J., O.B.E., Col. Kings Own Border, (*C.L.F. and D.D. Ops. N. Ireland*).

Istead, P. W. E., C.B., O.B.E., G.M., (*Dir. Gen. Logistic Policy (Army*)).

Last, C. N., O.B.E., (*Mil. Dep. to the Head of Defence Export Services*).

Lee, J. S., M.B.E., (*Dir. Army Education*).

Blacker, A. S. J., C.B.E., Col. Cmdt. R.E.M.E., Col. Cmdt. R.T.R., (*Asst. Chief of the Defence Staff O.R. (Land*)).

Carlier, A. N., O.B.E., (*Chief Jt. Services Liaison Organization Bonn*).

Fagan, P. F., M.B.E., (*D. G. Mil. Svy.*).

Friedberger, J. P. W., C.B.E., (*Cdr. British Forces Cyprus and Admin. Sovereign Base Areas*).

Llewellyn, R. M., O.B.E., (*G.O.C. Wales*).

Naylor, D. M., M.B.E., (*G.O.C. N.E. District Comd. 2 Inf. Divn.*).

Rous, The Hon. W. E., O.B.E., (*Comd. 4 Armd. Divn.*).

Swinburn, R. H., (*Asst. Chief of the General Staff*).

Boyd-Carpenter, The Hon. T. P. J., M.B.E., (*Asst. Chief of Defence Staff (Programmes)*).

Hulme, J. A., (*Dir. Gen. Ordnance Services*).

Peck, R. L., (*Engineer-in-Chief (Army)*).

Shaw, D., C.B.E., (*Dir. Gen. Electrical and Mechanical Engineering*).

Carrington, C. E. G., C.B.E., (*Dir. Gen. Transport and Movements*).

Stone, P. P. D., C.B.E., Col. Cmdt. M.P.S.C., Dep. Col. R. Anglian, (*Dir. Gen. Personal Services (Army)*).

Wilsey, J. F. W., C.B.E., Col. Cmdt. A.C.C., (*Chief of Staff H.Q. U.K.L.F.*).

Corbett, R. J. S., (*G.O.C. Berlin (Br. Sector)*).

Hayman-Joyce, R. J., O.B.E., (*Dir. Gen. Fighting Vehicles and Equipment*).

Wilkes, M. J., C.B.E., (*Comd. 3 Armd. Divn.*).

Beale, P. J., Q.H.P., (*Comd. Med. U.K.L.F.*).

Bray, P. S., (*Paymaster in Chief (Army)*).

Cowan, S., C.B.E., (*Cmdt. R.M.C.S.*).

Hutchinson, G. M., C.B., (*Vice Master General of the Ordnance*).

Pennicott, B. T. (*Dir. Royal Artillery*).

Macphie, D. L., Q.H.S., (*Comd. Med. B.A.O.R.*).

Brown, M., Q.H.P., (*D.A. Med.*).

MacKenzie, J. J. G., O.B.E., (*Cmdt, Staff College*).

Coull, J. T., Q.H.S., (*D.A. Surg.*).

Barr, J. A. J. P., C.B.E., (*Dep. Chief of Staff (Support) AFNORTH*).

Cook, R. F. L., (*Signal Officer in Chief (Army)*).

Duffell, P. R., C.B.E., M.C., (*C.B.F. Hong Kong*).

Evans, W. A., (*G.O.C. E. District*).

Sugden, F. G., O.B.E., (*Chief of Staff H.Q. B.A.O.R.*).

Wheeler, R. N., C.B.E., (*Comd. 1 Armd. Div.*).

CONSTITUTION OF THE BRITISH ARMY

The Regular Forces include the following Arms, Branches and Corps. Soldiers' Record Offices are shown at the end of each group; records of officers are maintained at the Ministry of Defence.

The Arms

Household Cavalry.—The Life Guards; The Blues and Royals (Royal Horse Guards and 1st Dragoons). *Records,* Horse Guards, London, SW1.

Royal Armoured Corps.—Cavalry Regiments: 1st The Queen's Dragoon Guards; The Royal Scots Dragoon Guards (Carabiniers and Greys); 4th/7th Royal Dragoon Guards; 5th Royal Inniskilling Dragoon Guards; The Queen's Own Hussars; The Queen's Royal Irish Hussars; 9th/12th Royal Lancers (Prince of Wales's); The Queen's Own Hussars (Prince of Wales's Own), 13th/18th Royal Hussars (Queen Mary's Own); 14th/20th King's Hussars; 15th/19th The King's Royal Hussars; 16th/5th The Queen's Royal Lancers; 17th/21st Lancers; Royal Tank Regiment comprising four regular regiments. *Records,* Queen's Park, Chester.

Artillery.—Royal Regiment of Artillery. *Records,* Imphal Barracks, Fulford Road, York.

Engineers.—Corps of Royal Engineers. *Records,* Kentigern House, Brown Street, Glasgow.

Signals.—Royal Corps of Signals. *Records,* Kentigern House, Brown Street, Glasgow.

Infantry.—The Foot Guards and Regiments of Infantry of the Line are grouped in Divisions as follows:—

Guards Division—Grenadier, Coldstream, Scots, Irish and Welsh Guards. Divisional HQ: HQ Household Division, Horse Guards, SW1. *Depot:* Pirbright Camp, Brookwood, Surrey. *Records:* Imphal Barracks, Fulford Road, York.

Scottish Division—The Royal Scots (The Royal Regiment); The Royal Highland Fusiliers (Princess Margaret's Own Glasgow and Ayrshire Regiment); The King's Own Scottish Borderers; The Black Watch (Royal Highland Regiment); Queen's Own Highlanders (Seaforth and Camerons); The Gordon Highlanders; The Argyll and Sutherland Highlanders (Princess Louise's). *Divisional HQ,* The Castle, Edinburgh. *Depots,* Scottish Divisional Depots, Glencorse, Milton Bridge, Midlothian and Albemarle Barracks, Ouston, Newcastle. *Records,* Imphal Barracks, Fulford, York.

Queen's Division—The Queen's Regiment, The Royal Regiment of Fusiliers, The Royal Anglian Regiment. *Divisional HQ,* Bassingbourn Barracks, Royston, Herts. *Depot,* Bassingbourn Barracks, Royston, Herts. *Records,* Higher Barracks, Exeter, Devon.

King's Division—The King's Own Royal Border Regiment, The King's Regiment; The Prince of Wales's Own Regiment of Yorkshire; The Green Howards (Alexandra, Princess of Wales's Own Yorkshire Regiment); The Royal Irish Rangers (27th (Inniskilling) 83rd and 87th); The Queen's Lancashire Regiment; The Duke of Wellington's Regiment (West Riding). *Divisional HQ,* Imphal Barracks, York. *Depots,* The King's Division Depot (Yorkshire), Queen Elizabeth Barracks, Strensall, Yorks., and Albemarle Barracks, Ouston, Newcastle. The King's Division Depot (Royal Irish Rangers), St. Patrick's Barracks, Ballymena, Northern Ireland. *Records,* Imphal Barracks, Fulford, York.

Prince of Wales's Division—The Devonshire and Dorset Regiment; The 22nd (Cheshire) Regiment; The Royal Welch Fusiliers, The Royal Regiment of Wales (24th/41st Foot); The Gloucestershire Regiment; The Worcestershire and Sherwood Foresters Regiment (29th/45th Foot); The Royal Hampshire Regiment; The Staffordshire Regiment (The Prince of Wales's); The Duke of Edinburgh's Royal Regiment (Berkshire and Wiltshire). *Divisional HQ,* Whittington Barracks, Lichfield, Staffs. *Depots,* The Prince of Wales's Division Depot, Whittington Barracks, Lichfield, Staffs. *Records,* Imphal Barracks, Fulford, York.

Light Division—The Light Infantry; The Royal Green Jackets. *Divisional HQ,* Sir John Moore Barracks, Winchester, Hants., *Depot,* Sir John Moore Barracks, Winchester, Hants. *Records,* Higher Barracks, Exeter.

Brigade of Gurkhas—2nd King Edward VII's Own Gurkha Rifles (The Sirmoor Rifles); 6th Queen Elizabeth's Own Gurkha Rifles; 7th Duke of Edinburgh's Own Gurkha Rifles; 10th Princess Mary's Own Gurkha Rifles, The Queen's Gurkha Engineers, Queen's Gurkha Signals, Gurkha Transport Regt. *Brigade HQ,* H.M.S. *Tamar,* Hong Kong, B.F.P.O. 1. *Depot,* Training Depot, Brigade of Gurkhas, Malaya Lines, Sek Kong, B.F.P.O. 1. *Records,* Record Office, Brigade of Gurkhas, Hong Kong, B.F.P.O. 1.

The Parachute Regiment (Three regular battalions)—*Depot,* Browning Barracks, Aldershot, Hants. *Records,* Higher Barracks, Exeter.

Special Air Service Regiment—*Regimental HQ,* Duke of York's Headquarters, Sloane Square, SW3. *Depot,* Stirling Lines, Hereford. *Records,* Higher Barracks, Exeter, Devon.

Army Air Corps—Regimental H.Q. and Depot, Middle Wallop, Hants. *Records,* Higher Barracks, Exeter.

The Services

Royal Army Chaplain's Department—Regimental H.Q. and Depot, Bagshot Park, Surrey.

Royal Corps of Transport, *Records*, Kentigern House, Brown Street, Glasgow.

Royal Army Medical Corps, Royal Army Dental Corps, Queen Alexandra's Royal Army Nursing Corps, and Women's Royal Army Corps. *Records*, Queen's Park, Chester.

Royal Army Ordnance Corps, Corps of Royal Electrical and Mechanical Engineers. *Records*, Glen Parva Barracks, Saffron Road, Wigston, Leicester.

Small Arms School Corps. *Records*, Higher Barracks, Exeter.

General Service Corps. *Records*, Imphal Barracks, Fulford Road, York.

Corps of Royal Military Police, Royal Army Pay Corps, Royal Army Veterinary Corps, Royal Pioneer Corps, Intelligence Corps, Army Catering Corps, Military Provost Staff Corps, Royal Army Educational Corps, Army Physical Training Corps, Army Legal Corps, Sandhurst, Officers Training Corps. *Records*, Higher Barracks, Exeter, Devon.

———

The Ulster Defence Regiment (U.D.R.) was raised under authority of the U.D.R. Act 1969 and assists the Regular Army in Northern Ireland. H.Q., Magheralave Road, Lisburn, Co. Antrim. *Records*, Imphal Barracks, Fulford Road, York.

The Territorial Army.—The Territorial Army (T.A.) is designed to provide a highly trained and well equipped force which will complete the Regular Army order of battle in a time of national emergency. Its establishment is approximately 84,000 and it is planned that this will rise to 86,000 by 1990. A new element of the T.A., the Home Service Force, designed to produce a low cost guard force, is being expanded to some 5,000 posts by 1990.

QUEEN ALEXANDRA'S ROYAL ARMY NURSING CORPS

The Queen Alexandra's Royal Army Nursing Corps (Q.A.R.A.N.C.) was founded in 1902 as Queen Alexandra's Imperial Military Nursing Service (Q.A.I.M.N.S.) and gained its present title in 1949. The Q.A.R.A.N.C. has trained nurses for the register and roll since 1950 and has eight other employment categories. There was an introduction of a non-nursing officer element in 1959 for personnel work. The Q.A.R.A.N.C. provides service in military hospitals world-wide—United Kingdom (including N. Ireland), B.A.O.R., Hong Kong, Dhahran, Cyprus, Falkland Islands and Belize.

Colonel-in-Chief, H.R.H. Princess Margaret.

Matron-in-Chief (Army) and Director of Defence Nursing Services, Brig. J. Field, R.R.C., Q.H.N.S.

WOMEN'S ROYAL ARMY CORPS

The Women's Royal Army Corps (W.R.A.C.) was formed on February 1, 1949 as a Corps of the Regular Army. The Corps predecessors were Queen Mary's Army Auxiliary Corps (Q.M.A.A.C.) in World War I, and the Auxiliary Territorial Service (A.T.S.) in World War II. The present role of the W.R.A.C. is to be organized and trained, as an integral part of the Army, to carry out those tasks for which its members are best suited and qualified, so that it will contribute to the maximum efficiency of the Army as a whole. The Corps is approximately 8,500 (Regular and T.A.) and is employed by 36 sponsors in 30 employments in 500 units world-wide in the British Army.

Commandant-in-Chief, H.M. Queen Elizabeth The Queen Mother.

Controller Commandant, H.R.H. The Duchess of Kent, G.C.V.O.

Deputy Controller Commandant, Brig. A. Field, C.B.

Director, Women's Royal Army Corps, Brig. G. K. Ramsey, M.B.E.

THE ROYAL AIR FORCE

THE QUEEN

Marshals of the Royal Air Force

H.R.H. the Prince Philip, Duke of Edinburgh, K.G., K.T., O.M., G.B.E., P.C., *born* June 10, 1921 ...... Jan. 15, 1953
Sir Dermot A. Boyle, G.C.B., K.C.V.O., K.B.E., A.F.C., *born* Oct. 2, 1904 .... Jan 1, 1958
The Lord Elworthy, K.G., G.C.B., C.B.E., D.S.O., M.V.O., D.F.C., A.F.C., *born* March 23, 1911 .... April 1, 1967
Sir John Grandy, G.C.B., G.C.V.O., K.B.E., D.S.O., *born* Feb. 8, 1913 .... April 1, 1971
Sir Denis Spotswood, G.C.B., C.B.E., D.S.O., D.F.C., *born* Sept. 26, 1916 .... March 31, 1974
Sir Michael Beetham, G.C.B., C.B.E., D.F.C., A.F.C., *born* May 17, 1923 .... Oct. 15, 1982
Sir Keith Williamson, G.C.B., A.F.C., *born* Feb. 25, 1928 .... Oct. 15, 1985
Sir David Craig, G.C.B., O.B.E. (*Chief of Defence Staff*), *born* Sept., 17, 1929 .... Nov. 14, 1988

Air Chief Marshals

Harding, Sir Peter, G.C.B., (*Chief of the Air Staff*).

Hine, Sir Patrick, G.C.B., (*A.O.C.-in-C. Strike Command*).

Knight, Sir Michael, K.C.B., A.F.C., A.D.C., (*U.K. Military Representative, H.Q. N.A.T.O.*).

Armitage, Sir Michael, K.C.B., A.F.C., (*Cmdt. Royal College of Defence Studies*).

Skingsley, Sir Anthony, K.C.B., (*Deputy C.-in-C., Allied Forces Central Europe*).

Parry-Evans, Sir David, K.C.B., C.B.E.

Air Marshals

Duxbury, Sir Barry, K.C.B., C.B.E., (*A.O.C. No. 18 Group*).

Jackson, Sir Brendan, K.C.B., (*Air Member for Supply and Organization*).

Jones, Sir Laurence, K.C.B., A.F.C., (*Air Member for Personnel*).

Hayr, Sir Kenneth, K.C.B., C.B.E., A.F.C., (*Chief of Staff and Deputy C.-in-C. Strike Command*).

Holroyd, Sir Frank, K.B.E., C.B., (*Chief Engineer (R.A.F.)*).

Stonor, Sir Thomas, K.C.B., (*Controller National Air Traffic Services*).

Simmons, Sir Michael, K.C.B., A.F.C., (*Deputy Controller Aircraft*).

Graydon, Sir Michael, K.C.B., C.B.E., (*A.O.C.-in-C. R.A.F. Support Command*).

Palin, Sir Roger, K.C.B., O.B.E., (*C.-in-C. R.A.F. Germany and Cmdr. 2 ATAF*).

Air Vice-Marshals

Bennet, E. P., C.B., (*Commander Sultan of Oman's Air Force*).

Stuart-Paul, R. I., M.B.E., (*Dir. Gen. Saudi Air Force Project*).

Macey, E. H., O.B.E., (*Dir. Gen. of Training (R.A.F.)*).

Stear, M. J. D., C.B.E., (*Asst. Chief of Defence Staff (N.A.T.O./U.K.)*).

Alcock, R. J. M., C.B., (*Air Officer Engineering Strike Command*).

Campbell, K. A., C.B., (*Air Officer Maintenance, R.A.F. Support Command*).

Walker, J. R., C.B.E., A.F.C., (*Dir. Gen. Management and Support Intelligence*).

Kemball, R. J., C.B.E., (*Dir. Gen. of Intelligence (Rest of World)*).

Pilkington, M. J., C.B.E., (*Air Officer Training R.A.F. Support Command*).

Brown, M. J. D., (*Dir. Gen. of Strategic Electronic Systems*).

Roberts, A. L., C.B.E., A.F.C., (*Asst. Chief of Defence Staff (Concepts)*).

Wilson, R. A. F., A.F.C., (*Air Officer Commanding No. 1 Group*).

Thomson, C. J., C.B.E., A.F.C., (*Asst. Chief of the Air Staff*).

Honey, R. J., C.B.E., (*Air Secretary and Air Officer Commanding R.A.F. Personnel Management Centre*).

Williams, G. C., A.F.C., (*Asst. Chief of Defence Staff Operational Requirements (Air Systems)*).

Saunders, D. A., C.B.E., (*Asst. Chief of Defence Staff (Command, Control, Communications and Information Systems)*).

Allerton, R. C., C.B., (*Dir. Gen. of Supply (R.A.F.)*).

Austin, R. M., A.F.C., (*Dir. Gen. Aircraft 1*).

Wood, R. H., O.B.E., (*Air Officer Commanding and Cmdt. R.A.F. College, Cranwell*).

Woodford, A. A. G., C.B., (*Asst. Chief of Staff (Policy) Supreme H.Q. Allied Powers Europe*).

Harris, J. H., C.B.E., (*Cmdt. Gen. R.A.F. Regt. and Dir. Gen. of Security (R.A.F.)*).

Crwys-Williams, D. O., (*Dir. Gen. of Personal Services (R.A.F.)*).

Blackley, A. B., C.B.E., A.F.C., (*Deputy Chief of Staff (Operations) Allied Air Forces Central Europe*).

Johns, R. E., C.B.E., L.V.O., (*Senior Air Staff Officer, Strike Command*).

Evans, C. E., C.B.E., (*Senior Directing Staff, Royal College of Defence Studies*).

Willis, J. F., C.B.E., (*Asst. Chief of the Defence Staff (Policy and Nuclear)*).

Harding, P. J., C.B.E., A.F.C., (*Dep. Comd. R.A.F. Germany*).

Robinson, B. L., (*Air Officer Administration, Strike Command*).

Wratten, W. J., C.B.E., A.F.C., (*Air Officer Commanding No. 11 Group*).

Hunter, A. F. C., C.B.E., A.F.C., (*Cmdt. R.A.F. Staff College, Bracknell*).

Browne, J. P. R., C.B.E., (*Dir. Gen. of Communications, Information Systems and Organization (R.A.F.)*).

Dicken, M. J. C. W., (*Air Officer Administration, R.A.F. Support Command*).

Morris, J., C.B.E., (*Air Officer Scotland and Northern Ireland*).

Cousins, D., A.F.C., (*Dir. Gen. Aircraft 2*).

Emmerson, D., C.B.E., A.F.C., (*Chief of Staff H.Q. No. 18 Group*).

Jones, R. T. B., Q.H.S., (*Senior Consultant*).

Moran, M. F., Q.H.P., (*Dean of Air Force Medicine*).

Mills, N. H., Q.H.P., (*Dep. Surgeon General (Research and Training) and Dir. Gen. R.A.F. Medical Services*).

Johnson, A. T., Q.H.S., (*Principal Medical Officer, Strike Command*).

Davies, D. B. A. L., Q.H.P., (*Principal Medical Officer R.A.F. Support Command*).

Halfpenny, B. N., Q.H.C., (*Chaplain-in-Chief*).

Forman, G. N., C.B., (*Dir. of Legal Services (R.A.F.)*).

CONSTITUTION OF THE ROYAL AIR FORCE

The Royal Air Force consists of three Commands: Strike Command and Support Command in the United Kingdom, and R.A.F. Germany. Strike Command is responsible for providing the air defence of the United Kingdom and reinforcement forces for N.A.T.O.; its roles include strike/attack, air defence, control and reporting, maritime surveillance, air reconnaissance, air-to-air refuelling, offensive support, air transport, aero-medical facilities, and search and rescue. Support Command is responsible for air and ground training, communications, engineering support, logistics, hospitals and for providing a range of administrative support. R.A.F. Germany provides tactical air support in N.A.T.O.'s Central Region; its roles include strike/attack, interdiction, counter air operations, air defence, close air support of land forces, tactical reconnaissance and helicopter support.

To carry out its tasks, the Royal Air Force is equipped with Victor, Tornado, Buccaneer, Phantom, Harrier, Jaguar, Canberra, Nimrod, Shackleton, VC10, Tristar, Hercules, Hawk, Jet Provost, Tucano, Chipmunk and Bulldog aircraft; Puma, Wessex, Sea King and Chinook helicopters; miscellaneous communications aircraft, etc.; Bloodhound and Rapier missiles, and the Skyguard system.

Royal Auxiliary Air Force.—The Auxiliary Air Force was formed in 1924 as a corps of civilians who would serve their country in flying machines in their spare time. In recognition of their distinguished war record King George VI granted the prefix 'Royal' in 1947. Despite a major disbandment in the late fifties, there has been a renaissance since the late seventies and today the force is some 2,000 strong, serving in three Maritime Headquarters Units, six Regiment Field Squadrons, a Movements Squadron, an Aeromedical Evacuation Squadron, a short-range Air Defence Squadron and four Defence Flights.
Air Commodore-in-Chief, H.M. The Queen.

Royal Air Force Volunteer Reserve.—The Royal Air Force Volunteer Reserve (R.A.F.V.R.) was created in 1936 with the object of providing training for the increased number of aircrew who were required for reserve service. The R.A.F.V.R. was reconstituted in 1947 following war service and today consists of some 200 part-time officers, and a few airmen. They serve in specialist Reserve Flights whose roles are intelligence, photographic interpretation and public relations. Additionally, some R.A.F.V.R. personnel undertake operational flying duties with the R.A.F.

PRINCESS MARY'S ROYAL AIR FORCE NURSING SERVICE

The Princess Mary's Royal Air Force Nursing Service (P.M.R.A.F.N.S.) is open to suitable male and female candidates. Commissions are offered to those who are Registered General Nurses (R.G.N.) and possess a second qualification suitable to the needs of the service. R.G.N.s with no additional experience or qualification are also recruited as non-commissioned officers in the grade of Staff Nurse.
Air Chief Commandant, H.R.H. Princess Alexandra, G.C.V.O.
Matron-in-Chief, Princess Mary's R.A.F. Nursing Service, Group Captain E. A. I. Sandison, R.R.C., Q.H.N.S.

WOMEN'S ROYAL AIR FORCE

Formed on April 1, 1918, the Women's Royal Air Force (W.R.A.F.) was disbanded on April 1, 1920 and reformed on February 1, 1949 from the Women's Auxiliary Air Force, the World War II Service, which had been formed on June 28, 1939, and from the R.A.F. Companies of the Auxiliary Territorial Service.

W.R.A.F. officers and airwomen, respectively, serve in most of the R.A.F. ground branches and trades and also as Air Loadmaster aircrew. W.R.A.F. personnel are employed at R.A.F. stations and higher formations at home and abroad, and they compete, on equal terms, with their R.A.F. counterparts for appointments, promotion and places on training courses.
Commandant-in-Chief, H.M. Queen Elizabeth the Queen Mother.
Air Chief Commandant, H.R.H. Princess Alice, Duchess of Gloucester.
Director, Air Commodore, R. Montague.

ROYAL OBSERVER CORPS
Bentley Priory, Stanmore, Middlesex

Established 1925, the Royal Observer Corps is a uniformed voluntary civilian organization originally set up to identify and track the movement of aircraft in war. In 1955 the Corps assumed the modern role of detecting nuclear bursts and monitoring radioactive fall-out in support of the United Kingdom Warning and Monitoring Organization. The Corps is affiliated to the Royal Air Force and is administered by the Ministry of Defence.
Air Commodore-in-Chief, H.M. THE QUEEN.
Commandant, Air Commodore I. Horrocks

RELATIVE RANK—SEA, LAND AND AIR

ROYAL NAVY	ARMY	ROYAL AIR FORCE
1. Admiral of the Fleet.	1. Field Marshal.	1. Marshal of the R.A.F.
2. Admiral (Adm.).	2. General (Gen.).	2. Air Chief Marshal.
3. Vice-Admiral (Vice-Adm.).	3. Lieutenant-General (Lt.-Gen.).	3. Air Marshal.
4. Rear-Admiral (Rear-Adm.).	4. Major-General (Maj.-Gen.).	4. Air Vice-Marshal.
5. Commodore (1st & 2nd Class) (Cdre.).	5. Brigadier (Brig.).	5. Air Commodore (Air Cdre.).
6. Captain (Capt.).	6. Colonel (Col.).	6. Group Captain (Gp. Capt.).
7. Commander (Cdr.).	7. Lieutenant-Colonel (Lt.-Col.).	7. Wing Commander (Wg. Cdr.).
8. Lieutenant Commander (Lt. Cdr.).	8. Major (Maj.).	8. Squadron Leader (Sqn. Ldr.).
9. Lieutenant (Lt.).	9. Captain (Capt.).	9. Flight Lieutenant (Flt.-Lt.).
10. Sub-Lieutenant (Sub-Lt.).	10. Lieutenant (Lt.).	10. Flying Officer (F.O.).
11. Acting Sub-Lieutenant (Acting Sub-Lt.).	11. Second Lieutenant (2nd. Lt.).	11. Pilot Officer (P.O.).

SERVICE SALARIES AND PENSIONS

The following rates of pay have been introduced as part of the 1989 pay award for Service personnel. The Government accepted the recommendations of the Top Salaries Review Body (which advises on ranks above Brigadier) and the Armed Forces Pay Review Body (which advises on pay levels for all ranks) from April 1, 1989.

Salaries for the Women's Services reflect equal pay for equal work and conditions, but because the X-Factor addition for women is lower than for men (9 per cent compared to 10 per cent) women's rates approximate to 99·08 per cent of the rates for men.

Since 1970 the determining factor of the Review Bodies' recommendations has been the relation of forces' salaries to civilian earnings by a carefully detailed process of job evaluation.

ROYAL NAVY AND ROYAL MARINES
Normal Rates

Rank	Daily	Annual
	£	£
Midshipman		
On appointment.............	18·58	6,782
After 1 year.................	23·09	8,428
Sub-Lieutenant and Acting Lieutenant RM		
On appointment...............	26·47	9,661
After 2 years in rank	34·83	12,713
After 3 years in rank	37·59	13,720
Lieutenant		
On appointment.............	44·34	16,184
After 1 year in rank	45·54	16,622
After 2 years in rank	46·74	17,060
After 3 years in rank	47·94	17,498
After 4 years in rank	49·14	17,936
After 5 years in rank	50·34	18,374
After 6 years in rank	51·54	18,812
Lieutenant Commander/Captain RM		
On appointment.............	55·90	20,403
After 1 year in rank	57·28	20,907
After 2 years in rank	58·66	21,411
After 3 years in rank	60·04	21,912
After 4 years in rank	61·42	22,418
After 5 years in rank	62·80	22,922
After 6 years in rank	64·18	23,426
After 7 years in rank	65·56	23,929
After 8 years in rank	66·94	24,433
Commander/Major RM		
On appointment with less than 19 years service	76·85	28,050
After 2 years in rank or with 19 years service	78·87	28,787
After 4 years in rank or with 21 years service	80·89	29,525
After 6 years in rank or with 23 years service	82·91	30,262
After 8 years in rank or with 25 years service	84·93	30,999
Captain/Lieutenant-Colonel RM		
On appointment.............	88·62	32,346
After 2 years in rank	90·95	33,197
After 4 years in rank	93·28	34,047
With 6 years seniority/Colonel RM	106·16	38,748
Rear-Admiral/Major-General RM	118·08	43,100
Vice-Admiral/Lieutenant-General RM	138·08	50,400
Admiral/General RM	197·26	72,000
Admiral of the Fleet	245·20	89,500

ARMY
Normal Rates

Rank	Daily	Annual
	£	£
Second Lieutenant	26·47	9,661
Lieutenant		
On appointment.............	34·83	12,713
After 1 year in rank	35·75	13,049
After 2 years in rank	36·67	13,384
After 3 years in rank	37·59	13,720
After 4 years in rank	38·51	14,056
Captain		
On appointment.............	44·34	16,184
After 1 year in rank	45·54	16,622
After 2 years in rank	46·74	17,060
After 3 years in rank	47·94	17,498
After 4 years in rank	49·14	17,936
After 5 years in rank	50·34	18,374
After 6 years in rank	51·54	18,812
Major		
On appointment.............	55·90	20,403
After 1 year in rank	57·28	20,907
After 2 years in rank	58·66	21,411
After 3 years in rank	60·04	21,915
After 4 years in rank	61·42	22,418
After 5 years in rank	62·80	22,922
After 6 years in rank	64·18	23,426
After 7 years in rank	65·56	23,929
After 8 years in rank	66·94	24,433
Special List Lieutenant-Colonel	76·14	27,791
Lieutenant-Colonel		
On appointment with less than 19 years service	76·85	28,050
After 2 years in rank or with 19 years service	78·87	28,787
After 4 years in rank or with 21 years service	80·89	29,525
After 6 years in rank or with 23 years service	82·91	30,262
After 8 years or with 25 years service	84·93	30,999
Colonel		
On appointment.............	88·62	32,346
After 2 years in rank	90·95	33,197
After 4 years in rank	93·28	34,047
After 6 years in rank	95·61	34,898
After 8 years in rank	97·94	35,748
Brigadier......................	106·16	38,748
Major-General	118·08	43,100
Lieutenant-General	138·08	50,400
General	197·26	72,000
Field Marshal.................	245·20	89,500

ROYAL AIR FORCE, Normal Rates

Rank	Daily	Annual	Rank	Daily	Annual
	£	£		£	£
Acting Pilot Officer—On appointment..............	23·09	8,428	After 7 years in rank	65·56	23,929
After 6 months in the rank (aircrew officers only)......	23·62	8,621	After 8 years in rank	66·94	24,433
Pilot Officer	26·47	9,661	Wing Commander—On appointment with less than 19 years service	76·85	28,050
Flying Officer—On appointment	34·83	12,713	After 2 years in rank or with		
After 1 year in rank	35·75	13,049	19 years service	78·87	28,787
After 2 years in rank	36·67	13,384	After 4 years in rank or with		
After 3 years in rank	37·59	13,720	21 years service	80·89	29,525
After 4 years in rank	38·51	14,056	After 6 years in rank or with		
Flight Lieutenant—On			23 years service	82·91	30,262
appointment..............	44·34	16,184	After 8 years in rank or with		
After 1 year in rank	45·54	16,622	25 years service	84·93	30,999
After 2 years in rank	46·74	17,060	Group Captain—On		
After 3 years in rank	47·94	17,498	appointment..............	88·62	32,346
After 4 years in rank	49·14	17,936	After 2 years in rank	90·95	33,197
After 5 years in rank	50·34	18,374	After 4 years in rank	93·28	34,047
After 6 years in rank	51·54	18,812	After 6 years in rank	95·61	34,898
			After 8 years in rank	97·94	35,748
Squadron Leader—On appointment..............	55·90	20,403	Air Commodore	106·16	38,748
After 1 year in rank	57·28	20,907	Air Vice-Marshal	118·08	43,100
After 2 years in rank	58·66	21,411			
After 3 years in rank	60·04	21,912	Air Marshal	138·08	50,400
After 4 years in rank	61·42	22,418	Air Chief Marshal	197·26	72,000
After 5 years in rank	62·80	22,922			
After 6 years in rank	64·18	23,426	Marshal of the Royal Air Force .	245·20	89,500

ROYAL NAVY AND ROYAL MARINES SPECIAL DUTIES LIST OFFICERS, ARMY MALE OFFICERS COMMISSIONED FROM THE RANKS, ROYAL AIR FORCE BRANCH OFFICERS

Years of Commissioned Service	Years of Non-Commissioned Service from age 18					
	Less than 12 years		12 years but less than 15 years		15 years or more	
	Daily	Annual	Daily	Annual	Daily	Annual
	£	£	£	£	£	£
On appointment...................	47·33	17,275	49·83	18,188	52·33	19,100
After 1 year service..............	48·58	17,732	51·08	18,644	53·28	19,447
After 2 years service.............	49·83	18,188	52·33	19,100	54·23	19,794
After 3 years service.............	51·08	18,644	53·28	19,447	55·18	20,141
After 4 years service.............	52·33	19,100	54·23	19,794	56·13	20,487
After 5 years service.............	53·28	19,447	55·18	20,141	57·08	20,834
After 6 years service.............	54·23	19,794	56·13	20,487	58·03	21,181
After 8 years service.............	55·18	20,141	57·08	20,834	58·98	21,528
After 10 years service............	56·13	20,487	58·03	21,181	58·98	21,528
After 12 years service............	57·08	20,834	58·98	21,528	58·98	21,528
After 14 years service............	58·03	21,181	58·98	21,528	58·98	21,528
After 16 years service............	58·98	21,528	58·98	21,528	58·98	21,528

ROYAL NAVY—ARTIFICERS, MEDICAL AND COMMUNICATIONS TECHNICIANS
Daily rates of pay for those committed to serve for:

Rating	Less than 6 years Scale A	6 years but less than 9 years Scale B	9 years or more Scale C
	£	£	£
FCPO Artificer/Technician	49·54	48·84	50·29
CCPO Artificer/Technician	47·70	48·00	48·45
CPO Artificer/1st Class Technician—Scale I	45·86	46·16	46·61
CPO Artificer/1st Class Technician—Scale II	44·10	44·40	44·85
PO Artificer/2nd Class Technician	39·07	39·37	39·82
Probationary or Acting PO Artificer/3rd Class Technician	37·27	37·57	38·02
4th Class Technician (Leading)	32·55	32·85	33·30
Leading Artificer/Acting 4th Class Technician	30·52	30·82	31·27
Acting Leading Artificer..........................	27·54	27·84	28·29
5th Class Technician (Able)	25·75	26·05	26·50

ROYAL NAVY AND ROYAL MARINES—OTHER BRANCHES

Daily rates of pay for those committed to serve for:

Rank	Scale	Less than 6 years Scale A	6 years but less than 9 years Scale B	9 years or more Scale C
		£	£	£
Fleet Chief Petty Officer/Warrant Officer Class I	I	45·73	46·03	46·48
Chief Petty Officer	I	40·46	40·76	41·21
Chief Petty Officer	II	39·88	40·18	40·63
Petty Officer/Sergeant	I	36·19	36·49	36·94
Petty Officer/Sergeant	II	35·54	35·84	36·29
Leading Rating/Corporal	I	32·55	32·85	33·30
Leading Rating/Corporal	II	30·52	30·82	31·27
Able Rating/Marine 1st Class	I	25·75	26·05	26·50
Able Rating/Marine 1st Class	II	24·19	24·49	24·94
Able Rating/Marine 1st Class	III	21·08	21·38	21·83
Ordinary Rating/Marine 2nd Class	I	17·75	18·05	18·50
Ordinary Rating/Marine 2nd Class	II	16·31	16·61	17·06

ARMY

Daily rates of pay for those committed to serve for:

Rank	Less than 6 years Scale A			6 years but less than 9 years Scale B			9 years or more Scale C		
	Band 1	Band 2	Band 3	Band 1	Band 2	Band 3	Band 1	Band 2	Band 3
	£	£	£	£	£	£	£	£	£
Private Class IV ...	16·31	—	—	16·61	—	—	17·06	—	—
Class III ...	18·10	21·08	24·31	18·40	21·38	24·61	18·85	21·83	25·06
Class II	20·26	23·24	26·47	20·56	23·54	26·77	21·01	23·99	27·22
Class I	21·99	24·97	28·20	22·29	25·27	28·50	22·74	25·72	28·95
Lance Corporal									
Class III ...	21·99	24·97	28·20	22·29	25·27	28·50	22·74	25·72	28·95
Class II	23·75	26·73	29·96	24·05	27·03	30·26	24·50	27·48	30·71
Class I	25·58	28·56	31·79	25·88	28·86	32·09	26·33	29·31	32·54
Corporal Class II ...	27·54	30·52	33·75	27·84	30·82	34·05	28·29	31·27	34·50
Class I	29·57	32·55	35·78	29·87	32·85	36·08	30·32	33·30	36·53

	Band 4	Band 5	Band 6	Band 7	Band 4	Band 5	Band 6	Band 7	Band 4	Band 5	Band 6	Band 7
	£	£	£	£	£	£	£	£	£	£	£	£
Sergeant	32·32	35·54	39·07	—	32·62	35·84	39·37	—	33·07	36·29	39·82	—
Staff Sergeant	34·18	37·40	40·93	44·74	34·48	37·70	41·23	45·04	34·93	38·15	41·68	45·49
Warrant Officer Class II	36·55	39·77	43·30	47·11	36·85	40·07	43·60	47·41	37·30	40·52	44·05	47·86
Warrant Officer Class I	38·98	42·20	45·73	49·54	39·28	42·50	46·03	49·84	39·73	42·95	46·48	50·29

ROYAL AIR FORCE AIRMEN (GROUND TRADES, APPRENTICES AND P.M.R.A.F.N.S.)

Daily rates of pay for those committed to serve for:

Rank/Category	Less than 6 years Scale A			6 years but less than 9 years Scale B			9 years or more Scale C		
	Band 1	Band 2	Band 3	Band 1	Band 2	Band 3	Band 1	Band 2	Band 3
	£	£	£	£	£	£	£	£	£
Aircraftman over 17 on entry.	16·31	16·31	16·31	16·61	16·61	16·61	17·06	17·06	17·06
Leading Aircraftman	18·10	21·08	24·31	18·40	21·38	24·61	18·85	21·83	25·06
Senior Aircraftman	21·99	24·97	28·20	22·29	25·27	28·50	22·74	25·72	28·95
Junior Technician	25·58	28·56	31·79	25·88	28·86	32·09	26·33	29·31	32·54
Corporal	29·21	32·19	35·78	29·51	32·49	36·08	29·96	32·94	36·53

	Band 4	Band 5	Band 6	Band 7	Band 4	Band 5	Band 6	Band 7	Band 4	Band 5	Band 6	Band 7
	£	£	£	£	£	£	£	£	£	£	£	£
Sergeant	32·32	35·54	39·07	—	32·62	35·84	39·37	—	33·07	36·29	39·82	—
Chief Technician	33·83	37·05	40·58	44·39	34·13	37·35	40·88	44·69	34·58	37·80	41·33	45·14
Flight Sergeant	35·33	38·55	42·08	45·89	35·63	38·85	42·38	46·19	36·08	39·30	42·83	46·64
Warrant Officer	38·98	42·20	45·75	49·54	39·28	42·50	46·03	49·84	39·73	42·95	46·48	50·29

ROYAL AIR FORCE—AIRMEN (AIRCREW)
Daily rates for those committed to serve for:

Rank	Less than 6 years Scale A			6 years but less than 9 years Scale B			9 years or more Scale C		
	Band 5	Band 6	Band 7	Band 5	Band 6	Band 7	Band 5	Band 6	Band 7
	£	£	£	£	£	£	£	£	£
Pilot, Navigator, Air Electronics Operator and Air Engineer (A)									
Sergeant	—	39·07	—	—	39·37	—	—	39·82	—
Flight Sergeant ..	—	—	45·89	—	—	46·19	—	—	46·64
Master Aircrew ..	—	—	49·54	—	—	49·84	—	—	50·29
Air Signaller and Air Loadmaster									
Sergeant	35·54	—	—	35·84	—	—	36·29	—	—
Flight Sergeant ..	—	42·08	—	—	42·38	—	—	42·83	—
Master Aircrew ..	—	45·73	—	—	46·03	—	—	46·48	—

WOMEN'S SERVICES

OFFICERS OF W.R.N.S.

Rank	Daily	Annual
	£	£
Probationary 3rd Officer	26·23	9,574
Third Officer		
On confirmation	28·99	10,581
After 2 years..................	34·51	12,596
Second Officer		
On appointment...............	43·94	16,038
After 1 year in rank	45·13	16,472
After 2 years in rank	46·32	16,907
After 3 years in rank	47·50	17,337
After 4 years in rank	48·69	17,772
After 5 years in rank	49·88	18,206
After 6 years in rank	51·07	18,640
First Officer		
On appointment...............	55·39	20,217
After 1 year in rank	56·76	20,717
After 2 years in rank	58·13	21,217
After 3 years in rank	59·49	21,714
After 4 years in rank	60·86	22,214
After 5 years in rank	62·23	22,714
After 6 years in rank	63·60	23,214
After 7 years in rank	64·96	23,710
After 8 years in rank	66·33	24,210
Chief Officer		
On appointment with less than 19 years service	76·15	27,795
After 2 years in rank or with 19 years service	78·15	28,525
After 4 years in rank or with 21 years service...............	80·16	29,258
After 6 years in rank or with 23 years service...............	82·18	29,996
After 8 years in rank or with 25 years service...............	84·20	30,733
Superintendent		
On appointment...............	88·13	32,167
After 2 years in rank	90·46	33,018
After 4 years in rank	92·79	33,868
After 6 years in rank	95·12	34,719
After 8 years in rank	97·45	35,569
Director, W.R.N.S.	105·92	38,661

FEMALE OFFICERS OF Q.A.R.N.N.S.

Rank	Daily	Annual
	£	£
Nursing Officer		
On appointment..............	34·51	12,596
After 1 year in rank	35·42	12,928
After 2 years in rank	36·34	13,264
After 3 years in rank	37·25	13,596
After 4 years in rank	38·16	13,928
Senior Nursing Officer		
On appointment...............	43·94	16,038
After 1 year in rank	45·13	16,472
After 2 years in rank	46·32	16,907
After 3 years in rank	47·50	17,337
After 4 years in rank	48·69	17,772
After 5 years in rank	49·88	18,206
After 6 years in rank	51·07	18,640
Superintending Nursing Officer		
On appointment...............	55·39	20,217
After 1 year in rank	56·76	20,717
After 2 years in rank	58·13	21,217
After 3 years in rank	59·49	21,713
After 4 years in rank	60·86	22,214
After 5 years in rank	62·23	22,714
After 6 years in rank	63·60	23,214
After 7 years in rank	64·96	23,710
After 8 years in rank	66·33	24,210
Chief Nursing Officer		
On appointment with less than 19 years service	76·15	27,795
After 2 years in rank or with 19 years service	78·15	28,525
After 4 years in rank or with 21 years service	80·16	29,258
After 6 years in rank or with 23 years service	82·18	29,996
After 8 years in rank or with 25 years service	84·20	30,733
Principal Nursing Officer		
On appointment...............	88·13	32,167
After 2 years in rank	90·46	33,018
After 4 years in rank	92·79	33,868
After 6 years in rank	95·12	34,719
After 8 years in rank	97·45	35,569
Matron-in-Chief	105·92	38,661

OFFICERS OF W.R.A.C., AND Q.A.R.A.N.C.

Rank	Daily	Annual
	£	£
Second-Lieutenant	26·23	9,574
Lieutenant—On appointment	34·51	12,596
After 1 year in rank	35·42	12,928
After 2 years in rank	36·34	13,264
After 3 years in rank	37·25	13,596
After 4 years in rank	38·16	13,928
Captain—On appointment	43·94	16,038
After 1 year in rank	45·13	16,472
After 2 years in rank	46·32	16,907
After 3 years in rank	47·50	17,337
After 4 years in rank	48·69	17,772
After 5 years in rank	49·88	18,206
After 6 years in rank	51·07	18,640
Major—On appointment	55·39	20,217
After 1 year in rank	56·76	20,717
After 2 years in rank	58·13	21,217
After 3 years in rank	59·49	21,713
After 4 years in rank	60·86	22,214
After 5 years in rank	62·23	22,714
After 6 years in rank	63·60	23,214
After 7 years in rank	64·96	23,710
After 8 years in rank	66·33	24,210
Lieutenant-Colonel—On appointment with less than 19 years service	76·15	27,795
After 2 years in rank or with 19 years service...............	78·15	28,525
After 4 years in rank or with 21 years service...............	80·16	29,258
After 6 years in rank or with 23 years service...............	82·18	29,996
After 8 years in rank or with 25 years service...............	84·20	30,733
Colonel—On appointment........	88·13	32,167
After 2 years in rank	90·46	33,018
After 4 years in rank	92·79	33,868
After 6 years in rank	95·12	34,719
After 8 years in rank	97·45	35,569
Brigadier......................	105·92	38,661

OFFICERS OF W.R.A.F. AND FEMALE OFFICERS OF THE P.M.R.A.F.N.S.

Rank	Daily	Annual
	£	£
Acting Pilot Officer..............	22·88	8,351
Pilot Officer	26·23	9,574
Flying Officer—On appointment ..	34·51	12,596
After 1 year in rank	35·42	12,928
After 2 years in rank	36·34	13,264
After 3 years in rank	37·25	13,596
After 4 years in rank	38·16	13,928
Flight Lieutenant—On appointment..................	43·94	16,038
After 1 year in rank	45·13	16,472
After 2 years in rank	46·32	16,907
After 3 years in rank	47·50	17,337
After 4 years in rank	48·69	17,772
After 5 years in rank	49·88	18,206
After 6 years in rank	51·07	18,640
Squadron Leader—On appointment..................	55·39	20,217
After 1 year in rank	56·76	20,717
After 2 years in rank	58·13	21,217
After 3 years in rank	59·49	21,713
After 4 years in rank	60·86	22,214
After 5 years in rank	62·23	22,714
After 6 years in rank	63·60	23,214
After 7 years in rank	64·96	23,710
After 8 years in rank	66·33	24,210
Wing Commander—On appointment with less than 19 years service................	76·15	27,795
After 2 years in rank or with 19 years service................	78·15	28,525
After 4 years in rank or with 21 years service................	80·16	29,258
After 6 years in rank or with 23 years service................	82·18	29,996
After 8 years in rank or with 25 years service................	84·20	30,733
Group Captain—On appointment .	88·13	32,156
After 2 years in rank	90·46	33,018
After 4 years in rank	92·79	33,868
After 6 years in rank	95·12	34,719
After 8 years in rank	97·45	35,569
Air Commodore	105·92	38,661

W.R.N.S. RATINGS AND NAVAL NURSES
Daily rates for those who have served for:

Rank	Less than 6 years Scale A			6 years but less than 9 years Scale B			9 years or more Scale C		
	Band 1	Band 2	Band 3	Band 1	Band 2	Band 3	Band 1	Band 2	Band 3
	£	£	£	£	£	£	£	£	£
Ordinary Rating under 17½	11·92	—	—	—	—	—	—	—	—
Ordinary Rating at 17½..............	16·16	16·16	—	16·46	16·46	—	16·91	16·91	—
Able Rating Class III	17·94	20·89	24·09	18·24	21·19	24·39	18·69	21·64	24·84
Able Rating Class II	21·02	23·97	27·17	21·32	24·27	27·47	21·77	24·02	27·92
Able Rating Class I .	22·56	25·51	28·71	22·86	25·81	29·01	23·31	26·26	29·46
Leading Rating Class II	27·29	30·24	33·44	27·59	30·54	33·74	28·04	30·99	34·19
Leading Rating Class I	29·30	32·25	35·45	29·60	32·55	35·75	30·05	33·00	36·20

	Band 4	Band 5	Band 6	Band 7	Band 4	Band 5	Band 6	Band 7	Band 4	Band 5	Band 6	Band 7
	£	£	£	£	£	£	£	£	£	£	£	£
Petty Officer Class II	31·68	34·87	38·37	42·15	31·98	35·17	38·67	42·45	32·43	35·62	39·12	42·90
Petty Officer Class I	32·37	35·56	39·06	42·84	32·67	35·86	39·36	43·14	33·12	36·31	39·81	43·59
CPO Class II	34·11	37·30	40·80	44·58	34·41	37·60	41·10	44·88	34·86	38·05	41·55	45·33
CPO Class I	34·94	38·13	41·63	45·41	35·24	38·43	41·93	45·71	35·69	38·88	42·38	46·16
Warrant Officer Class I	38·62	41·81	45·31	49·09	38·92	42·11	45·61	49·39	39·37	42·56	46·06	49·84

W.R.A.C. and Q.A.R.A.N.C.
Daily rates of pay for those who have served for:

Rank	Less than 6 years			6 years but less than 9 years			9 years or more		
	Band 1	Band 2	Band 3	Band 1	Band 2	Band 3	Band 1	Band 2	Band 3
	£	£	£	£	£	£	£	£	£
Private Class IV Age 17–17½ ..	12·22	—	—	—	—	—	—	—	—
Class IV	16·16	—	—	16·46	—	—	16·91	—	—
Class III	17·94	20·89	24·09	18·24	21·19	24·39	18·69	21·64	24·84
Class II	20·08	23·03	26·23	20·38	23·33	26·53	20·83	23·78	26·98
Class I	21·79	24·74	27·94	22·09	25·04	28·24	22·54	25·49	28·69
Lance Corporal Class III	21·79	24·74	27·94	22·09	25·04	28·24	22·54	25·49	28·69
Class II	23·53	26·48	29·68	23·83	26·78	29·98	24·28	27·23	30·43
Class I	25·35	28·30	31·50	25·65	28·60	31·80	26·10	29·05	32·25
Corporal Class II	27·29	30·24	33·24	27·59	30·54	33·74	28·04	30·99	34·19
Class I	29·30	32·25	35·45	29·60	32·55	35·75	30·05	33·00	36·20

	Band 4	Band 5	Band 6	Band 7	Band 4	Band 5	Band 6	Band 7	Band 4	Band 5	Band 6	Band 7
	£	£	£	£	£	£	£	£	£	£	£	£
Sergeant	32·02	35·21	38·71	—	32·32	35·51	39·01	—	32·77	35·96	39·46	—
Staff Sergeant	33·87	37·06	40·56	44·34	34·17	37·36	40·86	44·64	34·62	37·81	41·31	45·09
Warrant Officer Class II	36·22	39·41	42·91	46·69	36·52	39·71	43·21	46·99	36·97	40·16	43·66	47·44
Class I	38·62	41·81	45·31	49·09	38·92	42·11	45·61	49·39	39·37	42·56	46·06	49·84

W.R.A.F. AIRWOMEN (Ground Trades) and P.M.R.A.F.N.S.
Daily rates of pay for those who have served for:

Rank/Category	Less than 6 years			6 years but less than 9 years			9 years or more		
	Band 1	Band 2	Band 3	Band 1	Band 2	Band 3	Band 1	Band 2	Band 3
	£	£	£	£	£	£	£	£	£
Aircraftwoman under age 17½	12·22	—	—	—	—	—	—	—	—
Aircraftwoman at age 17½	16·16	16·16	16·16	—	—	—	—	—	—
Leading Aircraftwoman	17·94	20·89	24·09	18·24	21·19	24·39	18·69	21·64	24·84
Senior Aircraftwoman	21·79	24·74	27·94	22·09	25·04	28·24	22·54	25·49	28·69
Junior Technician	25·35	28·30	31·50	25·65	28·60	31·80	26·10	29·05	32·25
Corporal	28·94	31·89	35·45	29·24	32·19	35·75	29·69	32·64	36·20

	Band 4	Band 5	Band 6	Band 7	Band 4	Band 5	Band 6	Band 7	Band 4	Band 5	Band 6	Band 7
	£	£	£	£	£	£	£	£	£	£	£	£
Sergeant	32·02	35·21	38·71	—	32·32	35·51	39·01	—	32·77	35·96	39·46	—
Chief Technician............	33·52	36·71	40·20	43·98	33·82	37·01	40·50	44·28	34·27	37·46	40·95	44·73
Flight Sergeant	35·01	38·20	41·70	45·47	35·31	38·50	42·00	45·77	35·76	38·95	42·45	46·22
Warrant Officer	38·62	41·81	45·31	49·09	38·92	42·11	45·61	49·39	39·37	42·56	46·06	49·84

CHARGES FOR MARRIED AND SINGLE QUARTERS

Married Quarters

Type of quarter	Annual charge*			
	Grade 1	Grade 2	Grade 3	Grade 4
	£	£	£	£
Officers				
I................	3,562	3,223	2,464	1,628
II	3,201	2,887	2,212	1,456
III	2,814	2,544	1,949	1,285
IV	2,435	2,201	1,705	1,110
V	2,150	1,949	1,486	996
Other Ranks				
D/WO	1,650	1,493	1,157	748
C	1,497	1,354	1,044	686
B	1,321	1,197	916	602
A	891	803	613	405

Single Quarters

Rank	Annual charge*			
	Grade 1	Grade 2	Grade 3	Grade 4
	£	£	£	£
Major and above	1,380	1,248	956	631
Captain and below	1,161	1,048	803	548
Warrant Officer and Senior N.C.O.	821	745	569	380
Corporal and below	442	398	303	201
Young serviceman receiving less than the minimum adult (i.e. Private IV) rate	332	296	226	153

*Annual charges are derived from daily rates in whole pence and rounded to the nearest £.

SERVICE RETIREMENT BENEFITS, ETC.

NOTE—Those who leave the Forces having served at least five years, but not long enough to qualify for the appropriate immediate pension, now qualify for a preserved pension and terminal grant both of which are payable at age 60. The tax-free resettlement grants shown below are payable on release to those who qualify for a preserved pension and who have completed 9 years service from age 21 (officers) or 12 years from age 18 (other ranks). The annual rates for the Army are given: these apply to the equivalent ranks in all Services, including the Nursing Services.

RETIREMENT BENEFITS (MEN) Officers*—All Services

No. of years reckonable service over age 21	Capt. (incl. Q.M.) and below	Major (incl. Q.M.)	Lt.-Col.	Col. (incl. Deputy Chaplain General)	Brigadier	Major-General	Lieutenant-General	General
	£p.a.	£p.a.	£p.a.	£p.a.	£p.a.	£p.a.	£p.a.	£p.a.
16	5,361	6,389	8,204					
17	5,607	6,692	8,584					
18	5,852	6,996	8,963	10,336				
19	6,098	7,299	9,343	10,774				
20	6,343	7,603	9,722	11,211				
21	6,589	7,906	10,102	11,649				
22	6,835	8,209	10,481	12,087	13,626			
23	7,080	8,513	10,861	12,524	14,057			
24	7,326	8,816	11,240	12,962	14,487	16,115		
25	7,571	9,120	11,620	13,399	14,918	16,594		
26	7,817	9,423	11,999	13,837	15,349	17,073		
27	8,063	9,726	12,379	14,275	15,779	17,552	20,524	
28	8,308	10,030	12,758	14,712	16,210	18,031	21,084	
29	8,554	10,333	13,138	15,150	16,640	18,510	21,644	
30	8,800	10,636	13,517	15,588	17,071	18,988	22,204	31,720
31	9,045	10,940	13,897	16,025	17,501	19,467	22,764	32,520
32	9,291	11,243	14,276	16,463	17,932	19,946	23,324	33,320
33	9,536	11,547	14,656	16,900	18,362	20,425	23,884	34,120
34	9,782	11,850	15,035	17,338	18,793	20,904	24,444	34,920

* Including those male officers holding equivalent ranks in the Q.A.R.N.N.S.

Ratings, Soldiers and Airmen*

Number of years reckonable service	Below Corporal	Corporal	Sergeant	Staff Sergeant	Warrant Officer Class II	Warrant Officer Class I
	£p.a.	£p.a.	£p.a.	£p.a.	£p.a.	£p.a.
22	3,081	3,980	4,379	4,964	5,105	5,592
23	3,189	4,119	4,532	5,137	5,286	5,793
24	3,296	4,258	4,685	5,311	5,466	5,994
25	3,404	4,397	4,838	5,484	5,647	6,195
26	3,511	4,535	4,990	5,657	5,827	6,397
27	3,619	4,674	5,143	5,830	6,008	6,598
28	3,727	4,813	5,296	6,004	6,198	6,799
29	3,834	4,952	5,449	6,177	6,369	7,000
30	3,942	5,091	5,602	6,350	6,550	7,201
31	4,049	5,230	5,755	6,523	6,730	7,402
32	4,157	5,369	5,908	6,697	6,911	7,603
33	4,265	5,508	6,061	6,870	7,092	7,804
34	4,372	5,646	6,213	7,043	7,272	8,006
35	4,480	5,785	6,366	7,216	7,453	8,207
36	4,587	5,924	6,519	7,390	7,633	8,408
37	4,695	6,063	6,672	7,563	7,814	8,609

* Including male nurses serving in the Q.A.R.N.N.S. holding equivalent rank.

RETIREMENT BENEFITS (WOMEN)

The annual rates for W.R.A.C. are given: these apply to equivalent ranks in all Services, including the Nursing Services.

OFFICERS (16–34 years' service).—Captain, £5,321–£9,709; Major, £6,341–£11,761; Lt.-Col., £8,142–£14,922; Colonel, £10,284–£17,251; Brigadier, £13,592–£18,746.

SERVICEWOMEN (22–37 years' service).—Below Corporal, £3,058–£4,660; Corporal, £3,950–£6,018; Sergeant, £4,346–£6,622; Staff Sergeant, £4,927–£7,506; Warrant Officer II, £5,067–£7,755; Warrant Officer I, £5,550–£8,544.

NOTES

Terminal grants are in each case three times the rate of retired pay or pension. There are special rates of retired pay for Chaplains, Flight Lieutenants (Specialist Aircrew), and certain other ranks not shown above. Deductions may be made in cases of voluntary retirement.

The normal rates of gratuity for officers with short service commissions are £1,825 (men) and £1,811 (women) for each year completed. Resettlement grants are: officers £6,271 (men) and £6,224 (women); non-commissioned ranks £4,149 (men), £4,118 (women).

THE CHURCHES
THE CHURCH OF ENGLAND

THE GENERAL SYNOD OF THE CHURCH OF ENGLAND
OFFICES.—Church House, Dean's Yard, SW1P 3NZ

The General Synod was constituted in 1970, under the Synodical Government Measure 1969, in succession to the former Church Assembly. There are in total some 574 members of the General Synod, divided into three distinct houses—the House of Bishops, the House of Clergy and the House of Laity. It is presided over jointly by the Archbishops of Canterbury and York and normally meets three times each year—in February, July and November.

The function of the General Synod is to consider and make provision for all matters concerning the Church of England, and to consider and express opinion on any other matters of religious or public interest. The Synod appoints a number of Committees, Boards and Councils which deal with, or advise the Synod on, a wide range of matters affecting the Church and its Ministry.

Under the Church of England Assembly (Powers) Act 1919 the General Synod has the power—delegated by Parliament—to frame Statute Law on any matter concerning the Church of England, which are known as Measures. A Measure, once approved by General Synod, must be laid before both Houses of Parliament who may accept or reject it but may not amend it. If the Measure is accepted it is then submitted for Royal Assent and when this has been given the Measure has the full force of Law just as an Act of Parliament.

The Synod also has the power to make Canons and other ecclesiastical regulations provided that they do not conflict with statutory law. Canons have to be submitted to the Crown before they can come into effect.

Presidents, The Archbishop of Canterbury; The Archbishop of York.
Sec. Gen., W. D. Pattinson.
THE HOUSE OF BISHOPS.—*Chairman*, The Archbishop of Canterbury; *Vice Chairman*, The Archbishop of York.
THE HOUSE OF CLERGY.—*Chairman*, The Archdeacon of Leicester; *Vice Chairman*, Canon P. H. Boulton.
THE HOUSE OF LAITY, *Chairman*, Prof. J. D. McClean; *Vice Chairman*, Mrs. J. Dann.

Stipends (from April 1989)
Archbishop of Canterbury	£34,130
Archbishop of York	£29,800
Bishop of London	£27,710
Bishop of Durham	£24,360
Bishop of Winchester	£20,170
Diocesan Bishop	£18,120
Dean or Provost	£14,750
Canons Residentiary	£11,190

Province of Canterbury

CANTERBURY

Stipendiary Male Clergy, 195; *Stipendiary Women Deacons*, 9.
102nd Archbishop and Primate of All England, Most Rev. and Rt. Hon. Robert Alexander Kennedy Runcie, M.C., *cons.* 1970, *trs.* 1980 (Lambeth Palace, SE1 7JU) [Signs Robert Cantuar] 1980

Bishops Suffragan
Dover, Rt. Rev. Richard Henry McPhail Third, *cons.* 1976 (Upway, St. Martin's Hill, Canterbury, CT1 1PR) 1980
Maidstone, Rt. Rev. David James Smith, *cons.* 1987 (Bishop's House, Pett Lane, Charing, Ashford TN27 0DL) 1987

Assistant Bishops
Rt. Rev. Ross Sydney Hook, M.C. (*cons.* 1965), 1986; Rt. Rev. William Alfred Franklin, O.B.E. (*cons.* 1972), 1987; Rt. Rev. Richard David Say, K.C.V.O. (*cons.* 1961), 1988.

Dean
Very Rev. John Arthur Simpson 1986

Canons Residentiary
J. H. R. De Sausmarez (1981); P. Brett (1983); Ven. M. Till (1986); C. A. Lewis (1987).
Organist, D. Flood (1988).

Archdeacons
Canterbury, Ven. M. Till 1986
Maidstone, Ven. P. Evans 1989
Vicar-General of Province and Diocese, Miss S. Cameron, Q.C.
Commissary General, J. H. R. Newey, Q.C. (1971).

Joint Registrars of the Province, F. E. Robson, 16 Beaumont Street, Oxford; B. J. T. Hanson, Church House, Dean's Yard, SW1P 3NZ.
Registrar of the Diocese of Canterbury, A. O. E. Davies, 9 The Precincts, Canterbury CT1 2EQ.

LONDON

Stipendiary Male Clergy, 580; *Stipendiary Women Deacons*, 41.
130th Bishop, Rt. Rev. and Rt. Hon. Graham Douglas Leonard, *cons.* 1964, *trs.* 1973 and 1981 (8 Barton Street, SW1P 3NE) [Signs Graham Londin] 1981

Area Bishops
Edmonton, Rt. Rev. Brian John Masters, *cons.* 1982 (13 North Audley Street, W1Y 1FW) 1984
Kensington, Rt. Rev. John Hughes, PH.D., *cons.* 1987 (19 Campden Hill Square, W8 7JY) 1987
Stepney, Rt. Rev. James Lawton Thompson, *cons.* 1978 (63 Coborn Road, E3 2DB) 1978
Willesden, Rt. Rev. Thomas Frederick Butler, PH.D., *cons.* 1985 (173 Willesden Lane, Brondesbury, NW6 7YN) 1985

Bishop Suffragan
Fulham, Rt. Rev. (Charles) John Klyberg, *cons.* 1985 (4 Cambridge Place, W8 5PB) 1985

Assistant Bishops
Rt. Rev. Maurice Wood, D.S.C. (*cons.* 1971), 1985; Rt. Rev. Michael Marshall (*cons.* 1975) 1984.

Dean of St. Paul's
Very Rev. Thomas Eric Evans 1988

Canons Residentiary

P. W. Ball (1984); Ven. G. Cassidy (1987); C. J. Hill (1989).
Organist, C. H. Dearnley, F.R.C.O. (1968).
Receiver of St. Paul's, P. Long.

Archdeacons

Charing Cross, Rt. Rev. C. J. Klyberg 1989
Hackney, Ven. R. E. D. Sharpley 1981
Hampstead, Ven. R. A. W. Coogan 1985
London, Ven. G. Cassidy 1987
Middlesex, Ven. T. J. Raphael 1983
Northolt, Ven. E. Shirras 1985
Chancellor and Commissary of the Dean and Chapter, G. H. Newsom, Q.C. (1971).
Registrar, D. W. Faull, 35 Great Peter Street, SW1P 3LR.

WESTMINSTER

The Collegiate Church of St. Peter—(A Royal Peculiar)
Dean, Michael Clement Otway Mayne 1986
Sub Dean and Archdeacon, A. E. Harvey (1987).

Canons of Westminister

S. Charles (1978); A. E. Harvey (1982); D. Gray (1987); C. Semper (1987).
Chapter Clerk and Receiver General, Rear-Adm. K. A. Snow, C.B. (1987).
Organist, M. Neary, F.R.C.O. (1988).
Legal Secretary, C. L. Hodgetts (1973).
Registrar, S. J. Holmes (1984), 20 Dean's Yard, SW1P 3PA.

WINCHESTER

Stipendiary Male Clergy, 263; *Stipendiary Women Deacons,* 5.
95th Bishop, Rt. Rev. Colin Clement Walter James, *cons.* 1973, *trs.* 1977 and 1985 (Wolvesey, Winchester SO23 9ND) [Signs Colin Winton] 1985

Bishops Suffragan

Basingstoke, Rt. Rev. Michael Richard John Manktelow, *cons.* 1977 (1 The Close, Winchester SO23 9LS) 1977
Southampton, Rt. Rev. John Freeman Perry, *cons.* 1989 (Jollers, Sparsholt SO21 2NS) 1989

Assistant Bishops

Rt. Rev. Hassan Dehqani-Tafti (*cons.* 1961), 1982;
Rt. Rev. Leslie Lloyd Rees (*cons.* 1980), 1986.

Dean

Very Rev. Trevor Randall Beeson 1987

Dean of Jersey (A Peculiar), Very Rev. Basil Arthur O'Ferrall, C.B., R.N. 1985
Dean of Guernsey (A Peculiar), Very Rev. Jeffrey Fenwick..................................1989

Canons Residentiary

E. G. Job (1979); P. A. Britton (1980); A. K. Walker (1987).
Organist, D. Hill, F.R.C.O. (1988).

Archdeacons

Basingstoke, Ven. T. G. Nash 1982
Winchester, Ven. A. G. Clarkson 1984
Chancellor, J. Spokes, Q.C. (1985).
Registrar and Legal Secretary, P. M. White, 19 St. Peter Street, Winchester SO23 8BU.

BATH AND WELLS

Stipendiary Male Clergy, 266; *Stipendiary Women Deacons,* 2.
75th Bishop, Rt. Rev. George Leonard Carey, PH.D., *cons.* 1987 (The Palace, Wells BA5 2PD)
[Signs George Bath & Wells]................1987

Bishop Suffragan

Taunton, Rt. Rev. Nigel Simeon McCulloch, *cons.* 1986 (Sherford Farm House, Sherford, Taunton TA1 3RF)..................................1986

Dean, (vacant).

Canons Residentiary

S. R. Cutt (1979); C. E. Thomas (1983); P. de N. Lucas (1988).
Organist, A. Crossland, F.R.C.O. (1970).

Archdeacons

Bath, Ven. J. E. Burgess 1975
Taunton, Ven. L. E. Olyott 1977
Wells, Ven. C. E. Thomas 1983
Chancellor, G. H. Newsom, Q.C. (1970).
Registrar, Sec. & Chapt. Clerk, N. M. Cavender, Diocesan Registry, Market Place, Wells BA5 2RE.

BIRMINGHAM

Stipendiary Male Clergy, 229; *Stipendiary Women Deacons,* 9.
7th Bishop, Rt. Rev. Mark Santer, *cons.* 1981 (Bishop's Croft, Harborne, Birmingham B17 0BG) [Signs Mark Birmingham] 1987

Bishop Suffragan

Aston, (vacant).

Provost

Very Rev. Peter Austin Berry 1986

Canons Residentiary

D. McLean (1972); L. M. Davies (1981); Ven. J. L. Cooper (1982).
Organist, M. R. Huxley, F.R.C.O. (1986).

Archdeacons

Aston, Ven. J. L. Cooper 1982
Birmingham, Ven. J. F. Duncan 1985
Chancellor, His Hon. Judge Aglionby (1970).
Registrar and Legal Secretary, M. B. Shaw, St. Philip's House, St. Philip's Place, Birmingham B3 2PP.

BRISTOL

Stipendiary Male Clergy, 160; *Stipendiary Women Deacons,* 19.
54th Bishop, Rt. Rev. Barry Rogerson, *cons.* 1979 (Bishop's House, Clifton Hill, Bristol BS8 1BW)
[Signs Barry Bristol] 1985

Bishop Suffragan

Malmesbury, Rt. Rev. Peter James Firth, *cons.* 1983 (7 Ivywell Rd., Bristol BS9 1NX) 1983

Dean

Very Rev. Wesley Arthur Carr 1987

Canons Residentiary

J. M. Free (1982); J. Rogan (1983); A. L. J. Redfern (1987); J. L. Simpson (1989).
Organist, M. Archer, F.R.C.O., A.R.C.M. (1983).

Archdeacons

Bristol, Ven. A. J. Balmforth 1979
Swindon, Ven. K. J. Clark 1982
Chancellor, D. C. Calcutt, Q.C. (1971).
Registrar and Sec., T. R. Urquhart, 30 Queen
Charlotte Street, Bristol BS13 8HE.

CHELMSFORD

Stipendiary Male Clergy, 477; *Stipendiary Women
Deacons*, 16.

7th Bishop, Rt. Rev. John Waine, cons. 1975
(Bishopscourt, Margaretting Ingatestone
CM4 0HD) [Signs John Chelmsford] 1986

Bishops Suffragan

Barking, Rt. Rev. James William Roxburgh, cons.
1983 (28A Connaught Avenue, Loughton, IG10
4DS) 1983
Bradwell, Rt. Rev. Charles Derek Bond, cons.
1976 (21 Elmhurst Avenue, Benfleet SS7
5RY) 1976
Colchester, Rt. Rev. Michael Edwin Vickers,
cons. 1988, (1 Fitzwalter Road, Lexden, Col-
chester CO3 3SS) 1988

Provost

Very Rev. John Henry Moses, PH.D. 1982

Canons Residentiary

P. G. Brett (1985); P. G. Southwell-Sander (1985);
T. Thompson (1988).
Organist, G. Elliott, PH.D., F.R.C.O. (1981).

Archdeacons

Colchester, Ven. E. C. F. Stroud 1983
Southend, Ven. J. S. Bailey 1982
West Ham, Ven. R. F. Sainsbury 1988
Chancellor, Miss S. M. Cameron, Q.C. (1970).
Diocesan Registrar, B. Hood, Guy Harlings, New
Street, Chelmsford CM1 1NG.

CHICHESTER

Stipendiary Male Clergy, 343; *Stipendiary Women
Deacons*, 5.

102nd Bishop, Rt. Rev. Eric Waldram Kemp, D.D.,
cons. 1974 (The Palace, Chichester PO19 1PY)
[Signs Eric Cicestr] 1974

Bishops Suffragan

Horsham, Rt. Rev. Ivor Colin Docker, cons. 1975
(Bishop's Lodge, Worth, nr. Crawley RH10
4RT) 1975
Lewes, Rt. Rev. Peter John Ball, cons. 1977
(Litlington Rectory, nr. Polegate BN26 5RB) .1977

Assistant Bishops

Rt. Rev. William Warren Hunt (cons. 1955), 1980;
Rt. Rev. Mark Green (cons. 1972), 1982; Rt.
Rev. Simon Wilton Phipps (cons. 1968), 1987;
Rt. Rev. Edward George Knapp-Fisher (cons.
1960), 1987; Rt. Rev. Morris Henry St. John
Maddocks (cons. 1972), 1987.

Dean

Very Rev. John David Treadgold 1989

Canons Residentiary

R. T. Greenacre (1975); J. F. Hester (1985).
Organist, A. J. Thurlow, F.R.C.O. (1980).

Archdeacons

Chichester, Ven. K. Hobbs 1981
Horsham, Ven. W. C. L. Filby, ... 1983
Lewes and Hastings, Rt. Rev. C. C. Luxmoore . . 1989
Chancellor, His Honour Judge Q. T. Edwards,
Q.C. (1978).

Legal Secretary to the Bishop, and Diocesan
Registrar, C. L. Hodgetts, 5 East Pallant,
Chichester PO19 1TS.

COVENTRY

Stipendiary Male Clergy, 159; *Stipendiary Women
Deacons*, 10.

7th Bishop, Rt. Rev. Simon Barrington-Ward,
cons. 1985 (The Bishop's House, 23 Davenport
Road, Coventry CV5 6PW) [Signs Simon
Coventry] 1985

Bishop Suffragan

Warwick, Rt. Rev. Keith Appleby Arnold, cons.
1980 (139 Kenilworth Rd., Coventry CV4 7AF)
. . . . 1980

Assistant Bishops

Rt. Rev. John Charles Sydney Daly (cons. 1935),
1968; Rt. Rev. Vernon Sampson Nicholls (cons.
1974), 1984.

Provost

Very Rev. John Fitzmaurice Petty 1987

Canons Residentiary

P. Oestreicher (1986); M. Sadgrove (1987); D. A.
Carrette (1988).
Organist, A. P. Wright, F.R.C.O. (1984).

Archdeacons

Coventry, (vacant).
Warwick, Ven. P. S. G. Bridges 1983
Chancellor, W. M. Gage (1980).
Registrar, D. J. Dumbleton, 8 The Quadrant,
Coventry CV1 2EL.

DERBY

Stipendiary Male Clergy, 220; *Stipendiary Women
Deacons*, 12.

5th Bishop, Rt. Rev. Peter Spencer Dawes, cons.
1988 (The Bishop's House, 6 King Street,
Duffield, Derby DE6 4EU) [Signs Peter Derby]
. . . . 1988

Bishop Suffragan

Repton, Rt. Rev. Francis Henry Arthur Richmond, cons. 1986 (Repton House, Lea, Matlock
DE4 5JP) 1986

Provost

Very Rev. Benjamin Hugh Lewers 1981

Canons Residentiary

Ven. R. S. Dell (1981); I. Gatford (1984); G. R.
Orchard (1986); G. A. Chesterman (1989).
Organist, P. Gould, F.R.C.O. (1982).

Archdeacons

Chesterfield, Ven. G. R. Phizackerley 1978
Derby, Ven. R. S. Dell 1973
Chancellor, J. W. M. Bullimore (1981).
Registrar, J. S. Battie, Derby Church House, Full
Street, Derby DE1 3DR.

ELY

Stipendiary Male Clergy, 165; *Stipendiary Women
Deacons*, 3.

66th Bishop, Rt. Rev. Peter Knight Walker, cons.
1972, trs. 1977 (The Bishop's House, Ely
CB7 4DW) [Signs Peter Ely] 1977
(Bishop Walker retires in Dec. 1989).

Bishop Suffragan

Huntingdon, Rt. Rev. William Gordon Roe, D.PHIL., *cons.* 1980 (Powchers Hall, The College, Ely CB7 4DL) 1980

Dean

Very Rev. William James Patterson 1984

Canons Residentiary

D. J. Green (1980); J. Rone (1989).
Organist, A. W. Wills, MUS.D., F.R.C.O. (1959).

Archdeacons

Ely, Ven. D. Walser 1981
Huntingdon, Ven. R. K. Sledge................1978
Wisbech, Ven. D. Fleming 1984
Chancellor, W. Gage, Q.C.
Registrar, W. H. Godfrey, 18 The Broadway, St. Ives, Huntingdon PE17 4BS.
Joint Registrar, P. F. B. Beesley, 1 The Sanctuary, SW1P 3JT.

EXETER

Stipendiary Male Clergy, 302; *Stipendiary Women Deacons*, 3.

69th Bishop, Rt. Rev. Geoffrey Hewlett Thompson, *cons.* 1974 (The Palace, Exeter EX1 1HY) [Signs Hewlett Exon] 1985

Bishops Suffragan

Crediton, Rt. Rev. Peter Everard Coleman, *cons.* 1984 (10 The Close, Exeter EX1 1EZ) 1984
Plymouth, Rt. Rev. Richard Stephen Hawkins, *cons.* 1988 (15 Stoneleigh Close, Pitt Hill Road, Newton Abbot TQ12 1PX) 1988

Assistant Bishops

Rt. Rev. Ronald Cedric Osbourne Goodchild (*cons.* 1964), 1983; Rt. Rev. Philip John Pasterfield (*cons.* 1974), 1984; Rt. Rev. Richard Fox Cartwright (*cons.* 1972), 1988.

Dean

Very Rev. Richard Montague Stephens Eyre ...1981

Canons Residentiary

J. A. Thurmer (1973); A. C. Mawson (1979); Ven. J. Richards (1981).
Organist, L. Nethsingha, F.R.C.O. (1972).

Archdeacons

Barnstaple, Ven. T. Lloyd 1989
Exeter, Ven. J. Richards 1981
Plymouth, Ven. R. G. Ellis....................1982
Totnes, Ven. A. F. Tremlett...................1988
Chancellor, D. C. Calcutt, Q.C. (1971).
Registrar, J. F. G. Michelmore, T.D., 18 Cathedral Yard, Exeter EX1 1HE.
Diocesan Secretary, Rev. R. R. Huddleson, Diocesan House, Palace Gate, Exeter EX1 1HX.

GIBRALTAR IN EUROPE

1st Bishop, Rt. Rev. John Richard Satterthwaite, *cons.* 1970 (5A Gregory Place, W8 4NG) [Signs John Gibraltar] 1970

Bishop Suffragan

In Europe, Rt. Rev. Edward Holland 1986

Auxiliary Bishops

Rt. Rev. E. M. H. Capper, O.B.E., (*cons.* 1967), 1973; Rt. Rev. D. de Pina Cabral, (*cons.* 1967), 1976; Rt. Rev. A. W. M. Weeks, C.B., (*cons.* 1977), 1988.
Vicar-General, Rev. Canon P. O. Deacon.
Bishop's Commissaries, Canon J. A. Taylor; Canon

L. Tyzack; Canon J. D. Beckwith; Canon D. H. Palmer.
Dean, Cathedral Church of the Holy Trinity, Gibraltar, Very Rev. B. W. Horlock, O.B.E.
Chancellor, Pro-Cathedral of St. Paul, Valletta, Malta, Canon K. W. A. Roberts.
Chancellor, Pro-Cathedral of the Holy Trinity, Brussels, Belgium, Ven. P. Cousins.

Archdeacons

Aegean, Ven. G. B. Evans.
N.W. Europe, Ven. J. Lewis.
N. France, Ven. M. B. Lea.
Gibraltar, Rt. Rev. D. de Pina Cabral.
Italy, Ven. G. L. C. Westwell.
Riviera, Ven. J. Livingstone.
Scandinavia, Ven. G. A. C. Brown.
Switzerland, Ven. P. J. Hawker.

Chancellor, D. Calcutt, Q.C.
Diocesan Registrar and Legal Secretary, J. G. Underwood, 37A Walbrook, EC4 8BS.

GLOUCESTER

Stipendiary Male Clergy, 195; *Stipendiary Women Deacons*, 8.

37th Bishop, Rt. Rev. John Yates, *cons.* 1972 (Bishopscourt, Gloucester GL1 2BQ) [Signs John Gloucestr] 1975

Bishop Suffragan

Tewkesbury, Rt. Rev. Geoffrey David Jeremy Walsh, *cons.* 1986 (Green Acre, Hempsted, Gloucester GL2 6LS) 1986

Dean

Very Rev. Kenneth Neal Jennings 1982

Canons Residentiary

D. C. St. V. Welander (1975); A. L. Dunstan (1978); R. D. M. Grey (1982); P. R. Greenwood (1986).
Organist, J. D. Sanders, F.R.C.O., A.R.C.M. (1967).

Archdeacons

Cheltenham, Ven. J. A. Lewis.................1988
Gloucester, Ven. C. J. H. Wagstaff 1982
Chancellor & Vicar-Gen., Rev. E. Garth Moore (1957).
Registrar, C. G. Peak, 34 Brunswick Road, Gloucester GL1 1JW.
Diocesan Secretary, R. Anderton, Church House, College Green, Gloucester GL1 2LY.

GUILDFORD

Stipendiary Male Clergy, 199; *Stipendiary Women Deacons*, 9.

7th Bishop, Rt. Rev. Michael Edgar Adie, *cons.* 1983 (Willow Grange, Woking Road, Guildford GU4 7QS) [Signs Michael Guildford] 1983

Bishop Suffragan

Dorking, Rt. Rev. David Peter Wilcox, *cons.* 1986 (13 Pilgrims Way, Guildford GU4 8AD) 1986

Assistant Bishop

Rt. Rev. Kenneth Evans, (*cons.* 1968) 1986

Dean

Very Rev. Alexander Gillan Wedderspoon 1987

Canons Residentiary

F. S. Telfer (1973); P. G. Croft (1983); A. S. Leak (1986).
Organist, A. T. S. Millington, F.R.C.O. (1983).

Archdeacons

Dorking, Ven. P. G. Hogben 1982
Surrey, Ven. J. S. Went 1989
Chancellor, M. B. Goodman.
Legal Secretary and Registrar, P. F. B. Beesley, 1 The Sanctuary, SW1P 3JT.

HEREFORD

Stipendiary Male Clergy, 138; Stipendiary Women Deacons, 3.

102nd Bishop, Rt, Rev. John Richard Gordon Eastaugh, cons. 1974 (The Palace, Hereford HR4 9BN) [Signs John Hereford]...........1974

Bishop Suffragan

Ludlow, Rt. Rev. Ian MacDonald Griggs, cons. 1987 (Halford Vicarage, Craven Arms, Shropshire SY7 9BT)...........................1987

Dean

Very Rev. Peter Haynes......................1982

Canons Residentiary

Ven. A. H. Woodhouse (1982); P. Iles (1983); J. Tiller (1984).
Organist, R. Massey, F.R.C.O. (1974).

Archdeacons

Hereford, Ven. A. H. Woodhouse 1982
Ludlow, Ven. J. H. R. Lewis 1987
Chancellor, J. M. Henty.
Joint Registrars, V. T. Jordan, 44 Bridge Street, Hereford; P. Beesley, 1 The Sanctuary, Westminster, SW1P 3JT.

LEICESTER

Stipendiary Male Clergy, 180; Stipendiary Women Deacons, 9.

4th Bishop, Rt. Rev. Cecil Richard Rutt, C.B.E., cons. 1966 (Bishop's Lodge, Leicester LE2 3BD) [Signs Richard Leicester] 1979

Assistant Bishops

Rt. Rev. John Ernest Llewelyn Mort, C.B.E. (cons. 1952) 1972; Rt. Rev. Godfrey Ashby, (cons. 1980) 1988.

Provost

Very Rev. Alan Christopher Warren 1978

Canons Residentiary

M. T. H. Banks (1988); M. Wilson (1988).
Organist, P. White, F.R.C.O. (1968).

Archdeacons

Leicester, Ven. R. D. Silk 1980
Loughborough, Ven. T. H. Jones 1986
Chancellor, N. H. Freeman (1979).
Registrar, G. K. J. Moore, 10 Friar Lane, Leicester LE1 5QD.

LICHFIELD

Stipendiary Male Clergy, 432; Stipendiary Women Deacons, 24.

97th Bishop, Rt. Rev. Keith Norman Sutton, cons. 1978 (Bishop's House, The Close, Lichfield WS13 7LG) [Signs Keith Lichfield] 1984

Bishops Suffragan

Shrewsbury, Rt. Rev. John Dudley Davies, cons. 1987 (Athlone House, 68 London Road, Shrewsbury SY2 6PG) 1987
Stafford, Rt. Rev. Michael Charles Scott-Joynt, cons. 1987 (Ash Garth, Broughton Crescent, Barlaston ST12 9DD) 1987

Wolverhampton, Rt. Rev. Christopher John Mayfield, cons. 1985 (61 Richmond Road, Wolverhampton WV3 9JH) 1985

Dean

Very Rev. John Harley Lang 1980

Canons Residentiary

Ven. R. B. Ninis (1974); A. N. Barnard (1977); W. J. Turner (1983); J. Howe (1988).
Organist, J. Rees-Williams, F.R.C.O. (1978).

Archdeacons

Lichfield, Ven. R. B. Ninis 1974
Salop, Ven. G. Frost 1987
Stoke on Trent, Ven. J. D. Delight 1982
Chancellor, (vacant).
Diocesan Registrar and Bishop's Sec., J. P. Thorneycroft, St. Mary's House, The Close, Lichfield WS13 7LD.

LINCOLN

Stipendiary Male Clergy, 261; Stipendiary Women Deacons, 11.

70th Bishop, Rt. Rev. Robert Maynard Hardy, cons. 1980 (Bishop's House, Eastgate, Lincoln LN2 1QQ) [Signs Robert Lincoln] 1987

Bishops Suffragan

Grantham, Rt. Rev. William Ind, cons. 1987 (Fairacre, Barrowby High Road, Grantham NG31 8NP) 1987
Grimsby, Rt. Rev. David Tustin, cons. 1979 (43 Abbey Park Road, Grimsby DN32 0HS) 1979

Assistant Bishops

Rt. Rev. Gerald Fitzmaurice Colin (cons. 1966), 1979; Rt. Rev. Harold Richard Darby (cons. 1975) 1989.

Dean

Very Rev. Brandon Donald Jackson 1989

Canons Residentiary

D. C. Rutter (1965); B. R. Davis (1977); J. S. Nurser, PH.D. (1977); Ven. J. H. C. Laurence (1985).
Organist, C. Walsh, F.R.C.O. (1988).

Archdeacons

Lincoln, Ven. M. P. Brackenbury 1988
Lindsey, Ven. J. H. C. Laurence 1985
Stow, Ven. D. Scott 1975
Chancellor, His Honour Judge M. B. Goodman (1971).
Registrar and Legal Secretary, D. M. Wellman, 28 West Parade, Lincoln LN1 1JT.

NORWICH

Stipendiary Male Clergy, 242; Stipendiary Women Deacons, 7.

70th Bishop , Rt. Rev. Peter John Nott, cons. 1977 (Bishop's House, Norwich, NR3 1SB) [Signs Peter Norvic] 1985

Bishops Suffragan

Lynn, Rt. Rev. David Edward Bentley, cons. 1986 (The Old Vic., Castle Acre, King's Lynn PE32 2AA) 1986
Thetford, Rt. Rev. Timothy Dudley-Smith, cons. 1981 (Rectory Meadow, Bramerton, Norwich NR14 7DW) 1981

Dean

Very Rev. John Paul Burbridge...............1983

Canons Residentiary

D. H. Bishop (1980); C. Beswick (1984); M. S. McLean (1986).
Organist, M. B. Nicholas, F.R.C.O. (1971).

Archdeacons

Lynn, Ven. A. C. Foottit 1987
Norfolk, Ven. P. Dawson 1977
Norwich, Ven. A. M. Handley 1981
Chancellor, His Hon. J. H. Ellison, V.R.D. (1955).
Registrar and Sec., B. O. L. Prior, M.B.E., T.D., 74 The Close, Norwich NR1 4DE.

OXFORD

Stipendiary Male Clergy, 453; *Stipendiary Women Deacons*, 22.

41st Bishop, Rt. Rev. Richard Douglas Harries, cons. 1987 (Diocesan Church House, North Hinksey, Oxford OX2 0NB) [Signs Richard Oxon] 1987

Area Bishops

Buckingham, Rt. Rev. Simon Hedley Burrows, cons. 1974 (Sheridan, Grimms Hill, Great Missenden HP16 9BD) 1974
Dorchester, Rt. Rev. Anthony Russell, cons. 1988 (The Rectory, Whitchurch, Stratford-on-Avon) 1988
Reading, Rt. Rev. John Frank Ewan Bone, cons. 1989 (Greenbanks, Old Bath Road, Sonning, Reading RG4 0SY) 1989

Assistant Bishops

Rt. Rev. Sydney Cyril Bulley, D.D. (cons. 1959), 1979; Rt. Rev. Albert Kenneth Cragg, D.D., (cons. 1970), 1982; Rt. Rev. Eric Wild, (cons. 1972), 1982; Rt. Rev. Leonard James Ashton, C.B., (cons. 1974), 1984; Rt. Rev. Richard Watson (cons. 1970), 1988.

Dean of Christ Church

Very Rev. Eric William Heaton 1979

Canons Residentiary

M. F. Wiles, (1970); J. C. Fenton (1978); Ven. F. V. Weston (1982); O. M. T. O'Donovan, D.Phil. (1982); R. D. Williams, D.Phil. (1985); J. M. Pierce (1987).
Organist, S. Darlington, F.R.C.O.

Archdeacons

Berkshire, Ven. D. Griffiths 1987
Buckingham, (vacant).
Oxford, Ven. F. V. Weston 1982
Chancellor, P. T. S. Boydell, Q.C. (1958).
Registrar and Legal Secretary, F. E. Robson, 16 Beaumont Street, Oxford OX1 2LZ.

WINDSOR

(*The Queen's Free Chapel of St. George within Her Castle of Windsor—A Royal Peculiar*)
Dean, Very Rev. Patrick Reynolds Mitchell, F.S.A. 1989

Canons Residentiary

J. A. White (1982); D. M. Stanesby (1985); A. A. Coldwells (1987).
Organist, C. J. Robinson, L.V.O., F.R.C.O. (1975).
Chapter Clerk, Maj.-Gen. R. L. C. Dixon, C.B., M.C. (1981).

PETERBOROUGH

Stipendiary Male Clergy, 188; *Stipendiary Women Deacons*, 7.

36th Bishop, Rt. Rev. William John Westwood, cons. 1975 (The Palace, Peterborough PE1 1YA) [Signs William Petriburg] 1984

Bishop Suffragan

Brixworth, Rt. Rev. Paul Everard Barber, cons. 1989 (4 The Avenue, Dallington, Northampton NN1 4RZ) 1989

Dean

Very Rev. Randolph George Wise 1981

Canons Residentiary

T. R. Christie (1980); J. Higham (1983); T. Willmott (1989).
Organist, C. S. Gower, F.R.C.O. (1977).

Archdeacons

Northampton, Ven. B. R. Marsh 1964
Oakham, Ven. B. Fernyhough 1977
Chancellor, (vacant).
Registrar and Legal Secretary, R. Hemingray, 10 Queen Street, Peterborough PE1 1PH.

PORTSMOUTH

Stipendiary Male Clergy, 138; *Stipendiary Women Deacons*, 4.

7th Bishop, Rt. Rev. Timothy John Bavin, cons. 1974 (Bishopswood, Fareham, Hants. PO14 1NT) [Signs Timothy Portsmouth] 1985

Provost

Very Rev. David Staffurth Stancliffe 1982

Canons Residentiary

S. G. Platten (1983); R. Eckersley (1984); M. J. Gudgeon (1987); M. D. Doe (1989).
Organist, A. Froggatt, F.R.C.O.

Archdeacons

Portsmouth, Ven. N. H. Crowder 1985
I. of Wight, Ven. A. H. M. Turner 1986
Chancellor, His Honour Judge Aglionby (1978).
Registrar, Miss H. A. G. Tyler, 132 High Street, Portsmouth PO1 2HR.

ROCHESTER

Stipendiary Male Clergy, 234; *Stipendiary Women Deacons*, 14.

105th Bishop, Rt. Rev. Anthony Michael Arnold Turnbull, cons. 1988 (Bishopscourt, Rochester ME1 1TS) [Signs Michael Roffen] 1988

Bishop Suffragan

Tonbridge, Rt. Rev. David Henry Bartleet, cons. 1982 (Bishop's Lodge, St. Botolph's Road, Sevenoaks TN13 3AG) 1982

Dean

Very Rev. Edward Shotter 1990

Canon Residentiary

E. R. Turner (1981); R. J. R. Lea (1988); J. Armson (1989); N. Warren (1989).
Organist, B. Ferguson, F.R.C.O. (1977).

Archdeacons

Bromley, Ven. E. R. Francis 1979
Rochester, Ven. N. L. Warren 1989
Tonbridge, Ven. R. J. Mason 1977
Chancellor, His Honour Judge M. B. Goodman (1971).

Registrar, O. R. Woodfield, The Precinct, Rochester ME1 1SZ.
Secretary, D. W. Faull, 35 Great Peter Street, SW1P 3LR.

ST. ALBANS

Stipendiary Male Clergy, 326; *Stipendiary Women Deacons*, 14.
8th Bishop, Rt. Rev. John Bernard Taylor, *cons.* 1980 (Abbey Gate House, St. Albans AL3 4HD) [Signs John St. Albans] 1980

Bishops Suffragan

Bedford, Rt. Rev. David John Farmbrough, *cons.* 1981 (168 Kimbolton Road, Bedford MK41 8DN).....................................1981
Hertford, (vacant).

Dean

Very Rev. Peter Clement Moore, D.Phil.........1973

Canons Residentiary

B. C. E. Pettifer; C. B. Slee (1982); C. Garner (1984); G. R. S. Ritson (1987); M. Sansom (1988).
Organist, B. Rose, F.R.C.O. (1988).

Archdeacons

Bedford, Ven. M. G. Bourke 1986
St. Albans, Ven. P. B. Davies 1987
Chancellor, G. H. Newsom, Q.C. (1958).
Registrar and Legal Sec., D. N. Cheetham, Holywell Lodge, 41 Holywell Hill, St. Albans AL1 1HE.

ST. EDMUNDSBURY AND IPSWICH

Stipendiary Male Clergy, 182; *Stipendiary Women Deacons*, 3.
8th Bishop, Rt. Rev. John Dennis, *cons.* 1979 (Bishop's House, Ipswich IP1 3ST) [Signs John St. Edmunds & Ipswich] 1986

Bishop Suffragan

Dunwich, Rt. Rev. Eric Nash Devenport, *cons.* 1980 (The Old Vicarage, Stowupland, Stowmarket IP14 4BQ) 1980

Provost

Very Rev. Raymond Furnell..................1981

Canons Residentiary

G. J. Tarris (1982); R. Garrard (1987).
Organist, P. Trepte, F.R.C.O. (1985).

Archdeacons

Ipswich, Ven. T. A. Gibson 1987
Sudbury, Ven. D. J. Smith 1984
Suffolk, Ven. N. Robinson 1987
Chancellor, His Honour Judge Blofeld, Q.C. (1974).
Registrar, J. D. Mitson, 22–28 Museum Street, Ipswich IP1 1JA.

SALISBURY

Stipendiary Male Clergy, 252; *Stipendiary Women Deacons*, 8.
76th Bishop, Rt. Rev. John Austin Baker, *cons.* 1982 (South Canonry, The Close, Salisbury SP1 2ER) [Signs John Sarum]..................1982

Bishops Suffragan

Ramsbury, Rt. Rev. Peter St. George Vaughan, *cons.* 1989 (Bishop's House, Urchfont, Devizes, Wilts., SN10 4QH) 1989

Sherborne, Rt. Rev. John Dudley Galtrey Kirkham, *cons.* 1976 (Little Bailie, Sturminster Marshall, Wimborne BH21 4AD) 1976

Assistant Bishop

Rt. Rev. John Kingsmill Cavell, (*cons.* 1972) 1988

Dean

Very Rev. the Hon. Hugh Geoffrey Dickinson ..1986

Canons Residentiary

I. G. D. Dunlop, F.S.A. (1972); R. G. Askew (1983); D. J. C. Davies (1985).
Organist, R. G. Seal, F.R.C.O. (1968).

Archdeacons

Dorset, Ven. G. E. Walton 1982
Sarum, Ven. B. J. Hopkinson 1986
Sherborne, Ven. J. K. Oliver 1985
Wilts, Ven. B. J. Smith 1980
Chancellor of the Diocese, His Hon. J. H. Ellison, V.R.D. (1955).
Registrar and Legal Secretary, F. M. Broadbent, 42 Castle Street, Salisbury SP1 3TX.

SOUTHWARK

Stipendiary Male Clergy, 399; *Stipendiary Women Deacons*, 29.
7th Bishop, Rt. Rev. Ronald Oliver Bowlby, *cons.* 1973, *trs.* 1980 (Bishop's House, 38 Tooting Bec Gardens, SW16 1QZ) [Signs Ronald Southwark] 1980

Bishops Suffragan

Croydon, Rt. Rev. Wilfred Denniston Wood, D.D., *cons.* 1985 (St. Matthew's House, George Street, Croydon CR0 1PE)..................1985
Kingston upon Thames, Rt. Rev. Peter Stephen Maurice Selby, PH.D., *cons.* 1984 (24 Albert Drive, SW19 6LS) 1984
Woolwich, Rt. Rev. Albert Peter Hall, *cons.* 1984 (8B Hillyfields Crescent, SE4 1QA) 1984

Assistant Bishops

Rt. Rev. Edmund Michael Hubert Capper, O.B.E. (*cons.* 1967), 1981; Rt. Rev. Archibald Ronald McDonald Gordon (*cons.* 1975), 1984; Rt. Rev. John Hughes (*cons.* 1956), 1986; Rt. Rev. Hugh William Montefiore (*cons.* 1970), 1987; Rt. Rev. Simon Wilton Phipps (*cons.* 1976), 1987.

Provost

Very Rev. David Lawrence Edwards 1983

Canons Residentiary

P. H. Penwarden (1971); I. G. Smith-Cameron (1972); J. S. Cox (1983); P. B. Price (1988).
Organist, P. Wright (1989).

Archdeacons

Croydon, Ven. F. R. Hazell....................1984
Lambeth, Ven. C. R. B. Bird 1988
Lewisham, Ven. G. Kuhrt 1989
Reigate, Ven. P. B. Coombs 1988
Southwark, Ven. D. L. Bartles-Smith 1985
Wandsworth, Ven. D. Gerrard 1989
Chancellor, Rev. E. Garth Moore (1948).
Registrar, D. W. Faull, 35 Great Peter Street, SW1P 3LR.

TRURO

Stipendiary Male Clergy, 150; *Stipendiary Women Deacons*, 2.
Bishop, (vacant).

Bishop Suffragan

St. Germans, Rt. Rev. Richard Llewellin, *cons.*
1986 (32 Falmouth Road, Truro TR1 2HX) ...1985

Assistant Bishop

Rt. Rev. R. F. Cartwright (*cons.* 1972)..........1982

Dean

Very Rev. David John Shearlock..............1982

Canons Residentiary

W. J. P. Boyd, ph.D. (1985); Ven. R. L. Ravenscroft
(1988); R. O. Osborne (1988).
Organist, D. J. Briggs, F.R.C.O. (1989).

Archdeacons

Cornwall, Ven. R. L. Ravenscroft 1988
Bodmin, Ven. R. D. C. Whiteman 1989
Chancellor, P. T. S. Boydell, Q.C. (1957).
Registrar and Secretary, M. J. Follett, 2 Princes
Street, Truro TR1 2EZ.

WORCESTER

Stipendiary Male Clergy, 145; *Stipendiary Women
Deacons*, 9.
111th Bishop, Rt. Rev. Philip Harold Ernest
Goodrich, *cons.* 1973 (The Bishop's House,
Hartlebury Castle, Kidderminster DY11 7XX)
[Signs Philip Worcester] 1982

Bishop Suffragan

Dudley, Rt. Rev. Anthony Charles Dumper, *cons.*
1977 (The Bishop's House, Brooklands, Halesowen Road, Cradley Heath B64 7JF)........1977

Assistant Bishops

Rt. Rev. David Howard Nicholas Allenby (*cons.*
1962), 1968; Rt. Rev. Oliver Stratford Tomkins
(*cons.* 1959), 1975; Rt. Rev. John Arthur
Arrowsmith Maund, C.B.E., M.C. (*cons.* 1950),
1984; Rt. Rev. Kenneth John Woollcombe
(*cons.* 1971), 1989.

Dean

Very Rev. Robert Martin Colquhoun Jeffery ...1987

Canons Residentiary

Ven. F. Bentley (1984); I. M. MacKenzie (1989).
Organist, D. Hunt, MUS.D., F.R.C.O. (1975).

Archdeacons

Dudley, Ven. J. Gathercole 1987
Worcester, Ven. F. Bentley 1984
Chancellor, P. T. S. Boydell, Q.C. (1959).
Registrar, Rev. Canon J. A. Dale, Diocesan
Registry, The Old Palace, Deansway, Worces-
ter WR1 2JE.

Province of York

YORK

Stipendiary Male Clergy, 315; *Stipendiary Women
Deacons*, 16.
95th Archbishop and Primate of England Most
Rev. and Rt. Hon. John Stapylton Habgood,
ph.D., *cons.* 1973, *trs.* 1983 (Bishopthorpe, York
YO2 1QE) [Signs John Ebor].................1983

Bishops Suffragan

Hull, Rt. Rev. Donald George Snelgrove, T.D.,
cons. 1981 (Hullen House, Woodfield Lane,
Hessle, Hull HU13 0ES) 1981
Selby, Rt. Rev. Clifford Conder Barker, T.D., *cons.*
1976 (8 Bankside Close, Upper Poppleton, York
YO2 6LH) 1983
Whitby, Rt. Rev. Gordon Bates, *cons.* 1983 (60
West Green, Stokesley, Middlesbrough
TS9 5BD) 1983

Assistant Bishops

Rt. Rev. George Eyles Irwin Cockin (*cons.* 1959),
1969; Rt. Rev. Richard Knyvet Wimbush (*cons.*
1963), 1977; Rt. Rev. Richard James Wood
(*cons.* 1973), 1985; Rt. Rev. Ronald Graham
Gregory Foley (*cons.* 1982), 1989.

Dean

Very Rev. John Eliot Southgate 1984

Canons Residentiary

R. A. Hockley (1976); R. Mayland (1982); J. Toy,
ph.D. (1983); R. Metcalfe (1988).
Organist, P. J. Moore, A.R.C.M., F.R.C.O.

Archdeacons

Cleveland, Ven. R. J. Woodley 1984
East Riding, Ven. H. F. Buckingham 1988
York, Ven. G. B. Austin 1988
Official Principal and Auditor of the Chancery
Court, J. A. D. Owen, Q.C.
Chancellor of the Diocese, T. A. C. Coningsby
(1977).

Vicar-General of the Province and Official Principal of the Consistory Court, T. A. C. Coningsby.
Registrar and Legal Secretary, L. P. M. Lennox,
1 Peckitt Street, York YO1 1SG.

DURHAM

Stipendiary Male Clergy, 279; *Stipendiary Women
Deacons*, 17.
92nd Bishop, Rt. Rev. David Edward Jenkins,
cons. 1984 (Auckland Castle, Bishop Auckland
DL14 7NR) [Signs David Dunelm]...........1984

Bishop Suffragan

Jarrow, Rt. Rev. Michael Thomas Ball, *cons.* 1980
(Melkridge House, Gilesgate, Durham
DH1 1JB)..................................1980

Dean

Very Rev. John Robert Arnold 1989

Canons Residentiary

Ven. M. C. Perry (1970); R. L. Coppin (1974);
Ven. J. D. Hodgson (1983); T. Hart (1983);
D. W. Hardy (1986).
Organist, J. B. Lancelot, F.R.C.O. (1985).

Archdeacons

Auckland, Ven. J. D. Hodgson 1983
Durham, Ven. M. C. Perry 1970
Chancellor, Judge R. D. H. Bursell, Q.C. (1989).
Registrar and Legal Secretary, D. M. Robertson,
Diocesan Registry, Auckland Castle, Bishop
Auckland DL14 7QJ (1988).

BLACKBURN

Stipendiary Male Clergy, 263; *Stipendiary Women
Deacons*, 2.
7th Bishop, Rt. Rev. Alan David Chesters, *cons.*
1989 (Bishop's House, Ribchester Road, Blackburn BB1 9EF) [Signs Alan Blackburn] 1989

Bishops Suffragan

Burnley, Rt. Rev. Ronald James Milner, *cons.* 1988 (Palace House, 458 Padiham Road, Burnley BB12 6TD) 1988
Lancaster, (vacant).

Provost

Very Rev. Lawrence Jackson 1973

Canons Residentiary

G. A. Williams (1965); J. M. Taylor (1976); B. M. Beaumont (1977); G. I. Hirst (1987).
Organist, D. A. Cooper, F.R.C.O. (1983).

Archdeacons

Blackburn, Ven. W. D. Robinson 1986
Lancaster, (vacant).
Chancellor, Q. T. Edwards, Q.C. (1977).
Registrar, L. Ranson, Diocesan Registry, Cathedral Close, Blackburn BB1 5AB (1954).

BRADFORD

Stipendiary Male Clergy, 134; *Stipendiary Women Deacons,* 8.
7th Bishop, Rt. Rev. Robert Kerr Williamson, *cons.* 1984 (Bishopscroft, Ashwell Road, Heaton, Bradford BD9 4AU) [Signs Robert Bradford]..................................1984

Assistant Bishop

Rt. Rev. David Richard John Evans (*cons.* 1978) 1988
Provost, (vacant).

Canons Residentiary

K. H. Cook (1977); C. J. Hayward (1983).
Organist, A. Horsey (1986).

Archdeacons

Bradford, Ven. D. H. Shreeve 1984
Craven, Ven. B. A. Smith.....................1987
Chancellor, D. M. Savill, Q.C. (1976).
Registrar and Secretary, J. G. H. Mackrell, 6–14 Devonshire Street, Keighley BD21 2AY (1977).

CARLISLE

Stipendiary Male Clergy, 187; *Stipendiary Women Deacons,* 4.
65th Bishop, Rt. Rev. Ian Harland, *cons.* 1985 (Rose Castle, Dalston, Carlisle CA5 7BZ), [Signs Ian Carliol] 1989

Bishop Suffragan

Penrith, Rt. Rev. George Lanyon Hacker, *cons.* 1979 (The Rectory, Great Salkeld, Penrith CA11 9NA) 1979

Dean

Very Rev. Henry Edward Champneys Stapleton 1988

Canons Residentiary

R. A. Chapman (1978); A. Smithson (1984); Ven. C. P. Stannard (1984); R. C. Johns (1989).
Organist, R. A. Seivewright, A.R.C.O. (1960).

Archdeacons

Carlisle, Ven. C. P. Stannard 1984
West Cumberland, Ven. T. R. B. Hodgson 1979
Westmorland and Furness, Ven. L. J. Peat 1989
Chancellor, His Hon. D. J. Stinson (1971).
Registrar and Secretary, I. S. Sutcliffe, Castle Street, Carlisle CA3 8TW (1964).

CHESTER

Stipendiary Male Clergy, 327; *Stipendiary Women Deacons,* 9.
39th Bishop, Rt. Rev. Michael Alfred Baughen, *cons.* 1982 (Bishop's House, Chester CH1 2JD) [Signs Michael Cestr] 1982

Bishops Suffragan

Birkenhead, Rt. Rev. Ronald Brown, *cons.* 1974 (Trafford House, Queen's Park, Chester CH4 7AX) 1974
Stockport, Rt. Rev. Frank Pilkington Sargeant, *cons.* 1984 (32 Park Gate Drive, Cheadle Hulme, Cheshire SK8 7DF) 1984

Dean

Very Rev. Stephen Stewart Smalley 1986

Canons Residentiary

W. H. Vanstone (1978); L. R. Barker (1984); C. D. Biddell (1986).
Organist, R. A. Fisher, F.R.C.O. (1967).

Archdeacons

Chester, Ven. M. F. Gear 1988
Macclesfield, Ven. J. S. Gaisford 1986
Chancellor, H. H. Lomas (1977).
Registrar and Legal Secretary, A. K. McAllester, Friars, 20 White Friars, Chester CH1 1XS.

LIVERPOOL

Stipendiary Male Clergy, 274; *Stipendiary Women Deacons,* 20.
6th Bishop, Rt. Rev. David Stuart Sheppard, *cons.* 1969 (Bishop's Lodge, Woolton Park, Liverpool L25 6DT) [Signs David Liverpool] ..1975

Bishop Suffragan

Warrington, Rt. Rev. Michael Henshall, *cons.* 1976 (Martinsfield, Elm Avenue, Great Crosby, Liverpool L23 2SX) 1976

Assistant Bishop

Rt. Rev. William Scott Baker (*cons.* 1943) 1968

Dean

Very Rev. R. D. C. Walters 1983

Canons Residentiary

M. M. Wolfe (1982); D. J. Hutton (1983); K. J. Riley (1983); H. Thomas (1988).
Organist, I. Tracey (1980).

Archdeacons

Liverpool, Ven. G. H. G. Spiers 1979
Warrington, Ven. C. D. S. Woodhouse.........1981
Chancellor, R. G. Hamilton.
Registrar and Cathedral Chapter Clerk, R. H. Arden, 1 Hanover Street, Liverpool L1 3DW.

MANCHESTER

Stipendiary Male Clergy, 368; *Stipendiary Women Deacons,* 9.
9th Bishop, Rt. Rev. Stanley Eric Francis Booth-Clibborn, *cons.* 1979 (Bishopscourt, Bury New Road, Manchester M7 0LE) [Signs Stanley Manchester] 1979

Bishops Suffragan

Bolton, Rt. Rev. David George Galliford, *cons.* 1984 (4 Sandfield Drive, Lostock, Bolton BL6 4DU) 1984
Hulme, Rt. Rev. Colin John Fraser Scott, *cons.* 1984 (1 Raynham Avenue, Didsbury, Manchester M20 0BW) 1984

Middleton, Rt. Rev. Donald Alexander Tytler, *cons.* 1982 (The Hollies, Manchester Road, Rochdale OL11 3QY) 1982

Assistant Bishops

Rt. Rev. Edward Ralph Wickham (*cons.* 1959), 1982; Rt. Rev. Kenneth Venner Ramsey (*cons.* 1953), 1975.

Dean

Very Rev. Robert Murray Waddington 1984

Canons Residentiary

Ven. R. B. Harris (1980); J. Nicholls (1983); J. R. Atherton, PH.D. (1984); B. Duncan (1986).
Organist, G. Stewart.

Archdeacons

Bolton, Ven. W. S. Brison 1985
Manchester, Ven. R. B. Harris 1980
Rochdale, Ven. D. Bonser 1982
Chancellor, G. C. H. Spafford (1976).
Registrar and Bishop's Secretary, M. Darlington, 90 Deansgate, Manchester M3 2GH (1986).

NEWCASTLE

Stipendiary Male Clergy, 179; *Stipendiary Women Deacons*, 4.
10th Bishop, Rt. Rev. Andrew Alexander Kenny Graham, *cons.* 1977 (Bishop's House, 29 Moor Road South, Gosforth, Newcastle upon Tyne NE3 1PA) [Signs A. Newcastle] 1981

Assistant Bishop

Rt. Rev. Kenneth Edward Gill (*cons.* 1972) 1980

Provost, (vacant).

Canons Residentiary

W. J. Thomas (1983); R. Langley (1985); P. R. Strange (1986); I. F. Bennett (1988).
Organist, T. Hone (1987).

Archdeacons

Lindisfarne, Ven. M. E. Bowering 1987
Northumberland, Ven. W. J. Thomas 1983
Chancellor, His Hon. A. J. Blackett-Ord, C.V.O. (1971).
Registrar and Secretary, R. R. V. Nicholson, 46 Grainger Street, Newcastle upon Tyne NE1 5LB.

RIPON

Stipendiary Male Clergy, 171; *Stipendiary Women Deacons*, 10.
11th Bishop, Rt. Rev. David Nigel de Lorentz Young, *cons.* 1977 (Bishop Mount, Ripon HG4 5DP) [Signs David Ripon] 1977

Bishop Suffragan

Knaresborough, Rt. Rev. Malcolm James Mennin, *cons.* 1986 (16 Shaftesbury Avenue, Roundhay, Leeds LS8 1DT) 1986

Assistant Bishops

Rt. Rev. John Howe (*cons.* 1955) 1983; Rt. Rev. Ralph Emmerson (*cons.* 1972) 1987.

Dean

Very Rev. Christopher Russell Campling 1984

Canons Residentiary

R. B. McFadden (1979); D. G. Ford (1980); P. J. Marshall (1985).
Organist, R. Perrin, F.R.C.O. (1966).

Archdeacons

Leeds, Ven. A. J. Comber 1982
Richmond, Ven. N. G. L. R. McDermid 1983
Chancellor, D. M. Savill, Q.C. (1987).
Registrar and Legal Secretary, J. R. Balmforth, York House, York Place, Knaresborough HG5 0AD.

SHEFFIELD

Stipendiary Male Clergy, 216; *Stipendiary Women Deacons*, 8.
5th Bishop, Rt. Rev. David Ramsay Lunn, *cons.* 1980 (Bishopscroft, Snaithing Lane, Sheffield S10 3LG) [Signs David Sheffield] 1980

Bishop Suffragan

Doncaster, Rt. Rev. William Michael Dermot Persson, *cons.* 1982 (Bishops Lodge, Rotherham S65 4PF) 1982

Assistant Bishop

Rt. Rev. Kenneth John Fraser Skelton, C.B.E. (*cons.* 1962) 1984

Provost

Very Rev. John Warren Gladwin 1988

Canons Residentiary

G. Lacey (1981); T. M. Page (1982); Ven. S. R. Lowe (1988); J. R. Giles (1988).
Organist, G. Matthews, F.R.C.O. (1967).

Archdeacons

Doncaster, Ven. D. Carnelley 1985
Sheffield, Ven. S. R. Lowe 1988
Chancellor, G. B. Graham, Q.C. (1971).
Registrar and Legal Secretary, P. T. Ward, 30 Bank Street, Sheffield S1 2DS.

SODOR AND MAN

Stipendiary Male Clergy, 20.
79th Bishop, Rt. Rev. Noel Debroy Jones, C.B., *cons.* 1989 (The Bishop's House, Quarterbridge Road, Douglas, I.o.M.) [Signs Noel Sodor and Man] 1989

Canons Residentiary

B. H. Kelly (1980); D. Baggaley (1980); J. D. Gelling (1980); B. H. Partington (1985).

Archdeacon

Isle of Man, Ven. D. A. Willoughby 1982
Vicar-General and Registrar, P. W. S. Farrant, 24 Athol Street, Douglas.

SOUTHWELL

Stipendiary Male Clergy, 213; *Stipendiary Women Deacons*, 12.
9th Bishop, Rt. Rev. Patrick Burnet Harris, *cons.* 1973 (Bishop's Manor, Southwell NG25 0JR) [Signs Patrick Southwell] 1988

Bishop Suffragan

Sherwood, Rt. Rev. Alan Wyndham Morgan, *cons.* 1989 1989

Provost

Very Rev. John Murray Irvine 1978

Canons Residentiary

D. P. Keene (1981); I. G. Collins (1985).
Organist, K. Beard, F.R.C.O. (1959).

Archdeacons

Newark, Ven. D. Leaning 1980
Nottingham, Ven. G. C. Handford 1984
Chancellor, J. Shand (1981).
Registrar, P. H. Mellors, Diocesan Office, Westgate, Southwell NG25 0JL (1970).

WAKEFIELD

Stipendiary Male Clergy, 205; *Stipendiary Women
Deacons*, 7.
10th Bishop, Rt. Rev. David Michael Hope,
D.Phil., cons. 1985 (Bishop's Lodge, Woodthorpe
Lane, Wakefield WF2 6JJ) [Signs David
Wakefield] 1985

Bishop Suffragan

Pontefract, Rt. Rev. Thomas Richard Hare, cons.
1971 (306 Barnsley Road, Wakefield WF2
6AX) 1971

Provost

Very Rev. John Edward Allen. 1982
Organist, J. L. Bielby, F.R.C.O. (1971).

Archdeacons

Halifax, (vacant).
Pontefract, Ven. K. Unwin 1981
Chancellor, G. B. Graham, Q.C. (1959).
Registrar and Sec., E. Chapman, Burton Street,
Wakefield WF1 2DA (1979).

THE CHURCH IN WALES

9th Archbishop of Wales, Most Rev. George Noakes (Bishop of St. David's), *elected* 1987.

BANGOR

79th Bishop, Rt. Rev. John Cledan Mears, b. 1922,
cons. 1982 (Tŷ'r Esgob, Bangor LL57 2SS)
[Signs Cledan Bangor] 1982

ST. ASAPH

74th Bishop, Rt. Rev. Alwyn Rice Jones, b., 1934,
cons. 1982 (Esgobty, St. Asaph, Clwyd
LL17 0TW) [Signs Alwyn St. Asaph] 1982

LLANDAFF

101st Bishop, Rt. Rev. Roy Thomas Davies, b.
1934, cons. 1985 (Llys Esgob, The Cathedral
Green, Llandaff, Cardiff CF5 2YE) [Signs Roy
Landav] 1985

ST. DAVID'S

124th Bishop and 9th Archbishop of Wales, Most
Rev. George Noakes, b. 1924, cons. 1982 (Llys
Esgob, Abergwili, Dyfed SA31 2JG) [Signs
George Cambrensis] 1982

MONMOUTH

7th Bishop, Rt. Rev. Royston Clifford Wright, b.
1922, cons. 1986 (Bishopstow, Stow Hill, Newport NP9 4EA) [Signs Clifford Monmouth] ...1986

SWANSEA AND BRECON

7th Bishop, Rt. Rev. Dewi Morris Bridges, b.
1933, cons. 1988 (Ely Tower, Brecon, Powys
LD3 9DE) [Signs Dewi Swansea & Brecon] ...1988

(Stipend of diocesan bishop of the Church in Wales is £18,756 p.a. from Jan. 1, 1990)

THE EPISCOPAL CHURCH IN SCOTLAND

Primus of the Episcopal Church in Scotland, Most Rev. Lawrence Edward Luscombe (Bishop of Brechin),
elected 1985.

The Rt. Rev. Bishops

Aberdeen and Orkney, Frederick Charles Darwent,
b. 1927, cons. 1978, apptd. 1978. Clergy 14.
Argyll and the Isles, George Kennedy Buchanan
Henderson, b. 1921, cons. 1977, apptd. 1977. Clergy
10.
Brechin, Lawrence Edward Luscombe, b. 1924, cons.
1975, apptd. 1975. Clergy 17.
Edinburgh, Richard Frederick Holloway, b. 1933,
cons. 1986, apptd. 1986. Clergy 65.

Glasgow and Galloway, Derek Alec Rawcliffe, O.B.E.,
b. 1921, cons. 1974, apptd. 1981. Clergy 42.
Moray, Ross and Caithness, George Minshull Sessford, b. 1928, cons. 1970, apptd. 1970. Clergy 17.
St. Andrews, Dunkeld and Dunblane, Michael Geoffrey Hare-Duke, b. 1925, cons. 1969, apptd. 1969.
Clergy 30.
Registrar of the Episcopal Synod, I.R. Guild, 16
Charlotte Square, Edinburgh EH2 4YS. Churches,
Mission Stations, etc., 338. Clergy 203; Communicants, 36,921.

(Stipend of diocesan bishop of the Episcopal Church in Scotland is £12,780).

THE CHURCH OF IRELAND

Central Office: Church of Ireland House, Church Avenue, Rathmines, Dublin 6.

Province of Armagh

Archbishop of Armagh and Primate of All Ireland,
Most Rev. Robert Henry Alexander Eames, PH.D.,
b. 1937, cons. 1975, trs. 1986: Clergy 52.

The Rt. Rev. Bishops

Clogher, Brian Desmond Anthony Hannon, b. 1936,
apptd. 1986: Clergy 32.
Connor, Samuel Greenfield Poyntz, b. 1926, apptd.
1978, trs. 1987: Clergy 109.

Derry and Raphoe, James Mehaffey, PH.D., b. 1931, apptd. 1980: *Clergy* 55.

Down and Dromore, Gordon McMullan, PH.D., b. 1934, apptd. 1980, trs. 1986: *Clergy* 105.

Kilmore, Elphin and Ardagh, William Gilbert Wilson, PH.D., b. 1918, apptd. 1981: *Clergy* 23.

Tuam, Killala and Achonry, John Robert Winder Neill, b. 1945, apptd. 1986: *Clergy* 10.

Province of Dublin

Archbishop of Dublin, Bishop of Glendalough, and Primate of Ireland, Most Rev. Donald Arthur

Caird, D.D., b. 1925, cons. 1970, apptd. 1985: *Clergy* 90.

The Rt. Rev. Bishops

Cashel and Ossory, Noel Vincent Willoughby, b. 1926, apptd. 1980: *Clergy* 35.

Cork, Cloyne and Ross, Robert Alexander Warke, b. 1930, apptd. 1988: *Clergy* 28.

Limerick and Killaloe, Edward Flewett Darling, b. 1933, apptd. 1985: *Clergy* 18.

Meath and Kildare, Most Rev. Walton Newcombe Francis Empey, b. 1934, cons. 1981, trs. 1985: *Clergy* 20.

St. Patrick's National Cathedral, Dublin: *Dean and Ordinary,* Very Rev. V. G. B. Griffin, PH.D.

ANGLICAN COMMUNION OVERSEAS

Sees   Apptd.

ANGLICAN CHURCH OF AUSTRALIA

Primate of Australia, (vacant).

Province of New South Wales

The Most Rev. Archbishop and Metropolitan

Sydney, Donald William Bradley Robinson, cons. 1973.......................................1982
Asst. Bps., J. R. Reid, (1972); K. H. Short, (1975); E. D. Cameron, (1975); R. H. Goodhew, (1982); P. R. Watson (1989).

The Rt. Rev. Bishops

Armidale, P. Chiswell, cons. 1976 1976
Bathurst, B. W. Wilson, cons. 1984.............1989
Canberra and Goulburn, O. D. Dowling, cons. 1981 1983
Grafton B. A. Schultz, cons. 1985 1985
Newcastle, A. C. Holland, cons. 1970 1978
Riverina, B. R. Hunter, cons. 1971 1971

Province of Queensland

The Most Rev. Archbishop and Metropolitan

Brisbane, (vacant).
Bp. for Southern Region, (vacant); Bp. for Western Region, A. O. Charles, (1983); Bp. for Northern Region, G. V. Browning, (1985).

The Rt. Rev. Bishops

Carpentaria, A. F. B. Hall-Matthews 1984
N. Queensland, H. J. Lewis 1971
N. Territory, C. M. Wood.
Rockhampton, G. A. Hearn 1981

Province of South Australia

The Most Rev. Archbishop and Metropolitan

Adelaide, Keith Rayner, PH.D., cons. 1969 1975

The Rt. Rev. Bishops

The Murray, G. H. Walden, cons. 1981 1989
Willochra, W. D. H. McCall, cons. 1987 1987

Province of Victoria

The Most Rev. Archbishop and Metropolitan

Melbourne, David John Penman, cons. 1982 1984
Bps. Coadj., J. A. Grant (1970); J. C. Stewart (1984); R. L. Butterss (1985); P. J. Hollingworth (1985); J. W. Wilson (1985); J. Bayton (1989).

Sees   Apptd.

The Rt. Rev. Bishops

Ballarat, J. Hazlewood, cons. 1975 1975
Bendigo, O. S. Heyward, cons. 1975 1975
Gippsland, C. D. Sheumack, cons. 1987 1987
Wangaratta, R. G. Beal, cons. 1985.............1985

Province of Western Australia

The Most Rev. Archbishop and Metropolitan

Perth, Peter Frederick Carnley, PH.D., cons. 1981 1981
Asst. Bps., M. B. Challen (1978); B. R. Kyme (1982); B. Wright (1988).

The Rt. Rev. Bishops

Bunbury, H. J. U. Jamieson, cons. 1974 1984
N. W. Australia, G. B. Muston, cons. 1971 1982

Extra-Provincial Diocese

Tasmania, P. K. Newell, cons. 1982 1982

EPISCOPAL CHURCH OF BRAZIL
(Igreja Episcopal Do Brasil)

The Most Rev. Primate

South Western Brazil, Olavo Ventura Luiz, cons. 1976 1986

The Rt. Rev. Bishops

Brasilia, A. Santos, cons. 1989 1989
Central Brazil, S. A. Ruiz, cons. 1985 1985
Northern Brazil, C. E. Rodrigues, cons. 1985 ...1986
Pelotas, L. O. P. Prado, cons. 1987 1989
South Central Brazil, S. Takatsu, cons. 1977 ...1977
Southern Brazil, C. V. S. Gastal, cons. 1984 1984
South Western Brazil, (see above) 1976

CHURCH OF THE PROVINCE OF BURMA

The Most Rev. Archbishop

Rangoon, Andrew Mya Han, cons. 1988 1988

The Rt. Rev. Bishops

Mandalay, T. Mya Wah, cons. 1984 1984
Myitkyina, A. Hla Aung, cons. 1988............1988
Pa'an, G. Kyaw Mya, cons. 1979...............1979
Sittwe, B. Theaung Hawi, cons. 1978 1980

CHURCH OF THE PROVINCE OF BURUNDI, RWANDA AND ZAIRE

The Most Rev. Archbishop

Butare, Justin Ndandali, cons. 1975 1982

Sees	Apptd.

The Rt. Rev. Bishops

Boga Zaire, P. Njojo 1980
Bujumbura, S. Sindamuka 1975
Bukavu, B. Dirokpa 1982
Butare, (see above).
  Asst. Bp. D. Nduhura 1985
Buye, S. Ndayisenga 1979
Gitega, J. Nduwayo 1985
Kigali, A. Sebununguri, (cons. 1965).
Kisangani, S. T. Mugera 1980
Shaba, K. Mbona, cons. 1980 1980
Shyira, A. Nshamihigo, (cons. 1984) 1984

ANGLICAN CHURCH OF CANADA

The Most Rev. Primate

Michael Geoffrey Peers, cons. 1977 1986

Province of British Columbia

The Most. Rev. Archbishop and Metropolitan

New Westminster, Douglas Walter Hambidge,
  cons. 1969 1981

The Rt. Rev. Bishops

British Columbia R. F. Shepherd, cons. 1984 1984
Caledonia, J. E. Hannen, cons. 1981 1981
Cariboo, J. S. P. Snowden, cons. 1975 1975
Kootenay, R. E. F. Berry, cons. 1971..........1971
Yukon, R. C. Ferris, cons. 1981 1981

Province of Canada

The Most Rev. Archbishop and Metropolitan

Montreal, Reginald Hollis, cons. 1974 1989

The Rt. Rev. Bishops

Central Newfoundland, M. Genge, cons. 1976 ...1976
Eastern Newfoundland and Labrador, M. Mate,
  cons. 1980...................................1980
Fredericton, G. C. Lemon, cons. 1989 1989
Montreal, (see above) 1975
Nova Scotia, A. G. Peters, cons. 1981 1982
Quebec, A. Goodings, cons. 1977 1977
Western Newfoundland, S. S. Payne, cons. 1978 .1978

Province of Ontario

The Most Rev. Archbishop and Metropolitan

Niagara, John Charles Bothwell, cons. 1971 1985

The Rt. Rev. Bishops

Algoma, L. E. Peterson, cons. 1983.............1983
Huron, D. D. Jones, cons. 1982 1984
Moosonee, C. J. Lawrence, cons. 1980 1980
Ontario, A. A. Read, cons. 1972...............1981
Ottawa, E. K. Lackey, cons. 1981 1981
Toronto L. S. Garnsworthy, cons. 1968 1972

Province of Rupert's Land

The Most Rev. Archbishop and Metropolitan

Rupert's Land, Walter Heath Jones, cons. 1970 .1988

The Rt. Rev. Bishops

Arctic, J. R. Sperry, cons. 1974 1974
Athabasca , G. F. Woolsey, cons. 1983 1983
Brandon, J. F. S. Conlin, cons. 1975...........1975
Calgary, J. B. Curtis, cons. 1983 1983
Edmonton, K. L. Genge, cons. 1988 1988
Keewatin, H. J. P. Allan, cons. 1974 1974
Qu' Appelle, E. Bays, cons. 1986 1986
Rupert's Land (see above).
Saskatchewan, T. O. Morgan, cons. 1985 1985
Saskatoon, R. A. Wood, cons. 1981 1981

Sees	Apptd.

CHURCH OF THE PROVINCE OF CENTRAL AFRICA

The Most Rev. Archbishop

Botswana, Walter P. K. Makhulu, cons. 1979 ...1980

The Rt. Rev. Bishops

Botswana (see above).
Central Zambia, C. W. H. Shaba, cons. 1984 1984
Harare, R. P. Hatendi, cons. 1979 1981
Lake Malawi, P. N. Nyanja, cons. 1978 1978
Lundi, J. Siyachitema, cons. 1981 1981
Lusaka, S. S. Mumba, cons. 1981...............1981
Manicaland, E. Masuko, cons. 1981.............1981
Matabeleland, T. T. Naledi, cons. 1987 1987
Northern Zambia, B. Malango, cons. 1988 1988
Southern Malawi, B. N. Aipa, cons. 1987 1987

CHURCH OF THE PROVINCE OF THE INDIAN OCEAN

The Most Rev. Archbishop

Seychelles, French Chang-Him................1984

The Rt. Rev. Bishops

Antananarivo, R. Rabenirina, cons. 1984 1984
Antsiranana, K. Benzies, cons. 1982 1982
Mauritius, R. Donat, cons. 1984 1984
Seychelles, (see above).
Toamasina, F. Razakariasy, cons. 1984.........1984

THE HOLY CATHOLIC CHURCH IN JAPAN
(Nippon Sei Ko Kai)

The Most Rev. Primate

Osaka, Christopher Ichiro Kikawada, cons.
  1975 1986

The Rt. Rev. Bishops

Chubu, S. W. Hoyo, cons. 1987 1987
Hokkaido, A. H. Amagi, cons. 1987.............1987
Kita Kanto, J. T. Yashiro, cons. 1985 1985
Kobe, P. K. Yashiro, cons. 1984 1984
Kyoto, St. George J. Yagi, cons. 1979 1979
Kyushu, J. N. Iida, cons. 1982 1982
Okinawa, P. S. Nakamura, cons. 1972 1972
Osaka, (see above) 1975
Tohoku, C. Y. Tazaki, cons. 1979 1979
Tokyo, J. M. Takeda, cons. 1988 1988
Yokohama, R. S. Kajiwara, cons. 1984 1984

THE EPISCOPAL CHURCH IN JERUSALEM AND THE MIDDLE EAST

President-Bishop, Rt. Rev. S. Kafity 1986
Jerusalem, S. Kafity 1984
Iran, H. B. Dehqani-Tafti.......................1961
Egypt, G. Abdel Malik 1984
Cyprus and the Gulf, J. Brown 1986

CHURCH OF THE PROVINCE OF KENYA

The Most Rev. Archbishop

Nairobi, Manasses Kuria, cons. 1970 1980

The Rt. Rev. Bishops

Eldoret, A. K. Muge, cons. 1983 1983
Machakos, B. N. P. Nzimbi, cons. 1985 1985
Maseno North, J. Mundia, cons. 1970 1970
Maseno South, J. H. Okullu, cons. 1974.........1974
Maseno West, D. J. Omolo, cons. 1982 1985
Mombasa, C. Nzano, cons. 1975 1981
Mount Kenya Central, J. Mahiaini, cons. 1984 .1984
Mount Kenya East, D. Gitari, cons. 1975 1975
Mount Kenya South, G. M. Njuguna, cons. 1984 .1985

Sees	Apptd.
Nairobi, (see above).	
Nakuru, L. Kamau, *cons*. 1984	1984
Nambale, I. Namango, *cons*. 1984	1987

CHURCH OF THE PROVINCE OF MELANESIA

The Most Rev. Archbishop

Central Melanesia, Amos Stanley Waiaru, *cons*. 1981 ... 1988

The Rt. Rev. Bishops

Central Melanesia, (see above).	
Malaita, W. A. Pwaisiho, *cons*. 1981	1981
Temotu, L. S. Munamua, *cons*. 1987	1987
Vanuatu, H. S. Tevi, *cons*. 1979	1980
Ysabel, E. L. Pogo, *cons*. 1981	1981

CHURCH OF THE PROVINCE OF NEW ZEALAND

The Most Rev. Primate and Archbishop

Wellington, Brian Newton Davis, *cons*. 1980 1986

The Rt. Rev. Bishops

Aotearoa, W. Vercoe, *cons*. 1981	1981
Auckland, B. C. Gilberd, *cons*. 1985	1985
Christchurch, M. J. Goodall, *cons*. 1984	1984
Dunedin, P. W. Mann, *cons*. 1976	1976
Nelson, P. E. Sutton, *cons*. 1965	1965
Polynesia, J. L. Bryce, *cons*. 1975	1975
Waiapu, P. G. Atkins, *cons*. 1983	1983
Waikato, R. A. Herft, *cons*. 1986	1986
Wellington, (see above).	

CHURCH OF THE PROVINCE OF NIGERIA

The Most Rev. Archbishop

Ibadan, (vacant).

The Rt. Rev. Bishops

Aba, (vacant).	
Akigwe/Orlu, S. C. N. Ebo	1985
Akoko, J. O. K. Olowokure	1986
Akure, E. B. Gbonigi	1983
Asaba, R. N. C. Nwosu	1977
Awka, M. S. C. Anikwenwa	1987
Benin, J. K. George	1985
Egba-Egbado, T. I. Akintayo	1977
Ekiti, C. A. Akinbola	1986
Enugu, G. N. Otubelu	1969
Ibadan, (vacant).	
Ijebu, I. O. B. Akintemi	1976
Ijebu Remo, E. O. I. Ogundana	1984
Ilesha, G. I. O. Olajide	1981
Jos, T. E. I. Adesola	1985
Kaduna, T. Ogbonyomi	1975
Kano, B. B. Ayam	1980
Kwara, H. Haruna	1974
Lagos, J. A. Adetiloye	1985
The Niger, J. A. Onyemelukwe.	
Niger Delta, S. O. Elenwa	1981
Ondo, S. O. Aderin	1981
Owerri, B. Chukuemeka.	
Owo, A. O. Awosan	1983
Warri, J. O. Dafiewhare	1980

ANGLICAN CHURCH OF PAPUA NEW GUINEA

The Most Rev. Archbishop

Popondota, George S. Ambo K.B.E., *cons*. 1960 .. 1984

The Rt. Rev. Bishops

Aipo Rongo, P. Richardson, *cons*. 1987	1987
Dogura, (vacant).	

Sees	Apptd.
New Guinea Is., B. S. Meredith, *cons*. 1967	1967
Popondota, (see above).	
Port Moresby, I. R. Gadebo, *cons*. 1983	1983

CHURCH OF THE PROVINCE OF SOUTHERN AFRICA

The Most Rev. Archbishop and Metropolitan

Cape Town, Desmond Mpilo Boy Tutu, *cons*. 1976 ... 1986

Bps. Suff., C. H. Albertyn, *cons*. 1983 (1983); A. G. Quinlan, *cons*. 1988 (1988); E. Mackenzie, *cons*. 1988 (1988).

The Rt. Rev. Bishops

Bloemfontein, T. S. Stanage, *cons*. 1978	1982
George, D. G. Damant, *cons*. 1985	1985
Grahamstown, D. P. H. Russell, *cons*. 1986	1986
Johannesburg, D. Buchanan, *cons*. 1986	1986
Bps. Suff., M. S. Ndwandwe, *cons*. 1978 (1978); J. S. Nkoane, *cons*. 1982 (1982).	
Kimberley & Kuruman, G. A. Swartz, *cons*. 1972	1983
Lebombo, D. S. Sengulane, *cons*. 1976	1976
Lesotho, P. S. Mokuku, *cons*. 1978	1978
Bp. Suff., D. P. Nestor, *cons*. 1979	1980
Namibia, J. H. Kauluma, *cons*. 1978	1981
Natal, M. Nuttall, *cons*. 1975	1982
Niassa, P. T. Manhique, *cons*. 1986	1986
Port Elizabeth, B. R. Evans, *cons*. 1975	1976
Pretoria, R. A. Kraft, *cons*. 1982	1982
Bp. Suff., J. H. G. Ruston, *cons*. 1983.	
St. Helena, J. N. Johnson, *cons*. 1985	1985
St. John's, J. Z. Dlamini, *cons*. 1980	1985
Bp. Suff., G. F. Davies, *cons*. 1987.	
St. Mark the Evangelist, R. P. J. Le Feuvre, *cons*. 1987.	
Swaziland, B. L. N. Mkhabela, *cons*. 1975	1975
Zululand, L. B. Zulu, *cons*. 1975	1975
Order of Ethiopia, S. Dwane, *cons*. 1983	1983

ANGLICAN CHURCH OF THE SOUTHERN CONE OF AMERICA

Presiding Bishop, Rt. Rev. David Leake.

The Rt. Rev. Bishops

Argentina and Uruguay, R. S. Cutts	1975
Chile, C. F. Bazley, *cons*. 1969	1977
Asst. Bp., I. A. Morrison	1977
Northern Argentina, D. Leake, *cons*. 1969	1980
Asst. Bp., M. L. Mariño	1975
Paraguay, J. Ellison.	
Peru, A. Winstanley.	

CHURCH OF THE PROVINCE OF THE SUDAN

The Most Rev. Archbishop, (vacant).

The Rt. Rev. Bishops

Bor, N. Garang.	
Juba, E. J. Ngalamu, *cons*. 1963	1976
Kadugli, M. Khamis.	
Kaji-Kaji, M. B. Dawidi.	
Khartoum, (vacant).	
Maridi, J. Marona.	
Mundri, E. Munda.	
Rumbek, B. W. Yugusuk, *cons*. 1971	1976
Yei, S. Solomona.	
Yambio, D. Zindo, *cons*. 1984	1984
Wau, (vacant).	

Sees	Apptd.

CHURCH OF THE PROVINCE OF TANZANIA

The Most Rev. Archbishop

Zanzibar and Tanga, John Acland Ramadhani, cons. 1980 1984

The Rt. Rev. Bishops

Central Tanganyika, G. Mhogolo, cons. 1989 ...1989
Dar es Salaam, C. Mlangwa, cons. 1984 1984
Kagera, C. Ruhuza, cons. 1985 1985
Mara, G. Nyaronga, cons. 1985 1985
Masasi, C. R. Norgate, cons. 1984 1984
Morogoro, D. Mageni, cons. 1987 1987
Mount Kilimanjaro, A. Mohamed, cons. 1982 ...1982
Ruvuma, (vacant).
South West Tanganyika, C. Mwaigoga, cons.
1983 1983
Tabora, F. Ntiruka, cons. 1989 1989
Victoria Nyanza, J. Rusibamayila, cons. 1976 ...1976
Western Tanganyika, G. E. Mpango, cons. 1983 .1983
Zanzibar and Tanga, (see above).

CHURCH OF THE PROVINCE OF UGANDA

The Most Rev Archbishop

Kampala, Dr. Yona Okoth cons. 1972 1984
Asst. *Bp.*, A. L. Gonahasa 1985

The Rt. Rev. Bishops

Bukedi, N. E. Okille 1984
Bunyoro-Kitara, Y. Rwakaikara 1981
Busoga, C. Bamwoze 1972
East Ankole, A. Betungura 1970
Kampala, (see above).
Karamoja, P. Lomongin 1987
Kigezi, (vacant).
Asst. *Bp.*, W. Rukirande 1975
Lango, M. Otim 1976
Asst. *Bp.*, W. Okodi 1979
Madi and West Nile, R. Ringtho, cons. 1976 1977
Mbale, A. M. Wesonga 1981
Mityana, Y. Mukasa 1977
Mukono, L. Mpalanyi-Nkoyoyo 1985
Namirembe, M. Kauma 1985
North Kigezi, Y. Ruhindi 1981
Northern Uganda, B. Ogwal-Abwang 1974
Asst. *Bp.*, G. Oboma 1979
Ruwenzori, E. Kamanyire 1981
Soroti, G. Ilukor 1976
West Ankole, Y. Bamunoba 1977
West Buganda, C. Senyonjo 1974

EPISCOPAL CHURCH IN THE U.S.A.

Presiding Bishop and Primate, Most Rev. Edmond Lee Browning, D.D., cons. 1986 installed1986

Rt. Rev. Bishops
(*Missionary Diocese)

Province I

Connecticut, Arthur E. Walmsley, cons. 1979 ...1981
Maine, Edward C. Chalfant, cons. 1984.........1986
Massachusetts, David E. Johnson, cons. 1985 ...1986
New Hampshire, Douglas E. Theuner, cons.
1986...1986
Rhode Island, George N. Hunt, cons. 1980 1980
Vermont, Daniel L. Swensen, cons. 1986.........1987
Western Massachusetts, Andrew F. Wissemann, cons. 1984..................................1984

Province II

Albany, David S. Ball, cons. 1984 1984
Central New York, O'Kelley Whitaker, cons.
1981...1983

Europe, Convocation of American Churches in,
A. Donald Davies.
Haiti, Luc A. J. Garnier, cons. 1971 .:.........1971
Long Island, Robert C. Witcher, cons. 1975 1977
New Jersey, G. P. Mellick Belshaw, cons. 1975 ..1983
New York, Paul Moore (Jnr.), cons. 1964 1972
Newark, John S. Spong, cons. 1976 1979
Rochester, William G. Burrill, cons. 1984 1984
Virgin Islands, Don. E. Taylor, cons. 1987 1987
Western New York, David C. Bowman, cons.
1986...1987

Province III

Bethlehem, J. Mark Dyer, cons. 1982..........1983
Central Pennsylvania, Charles F. McNutt, cons.
1980...1982
Delaware, C. Cabell Tennis, cons. 1986 1986
Easton, Elliott L. Sorge, cons. 1971 1983
Maryland, A. Theodore Eastman, cons. 1982....1986
Northwestern Pennsylvania, Donald. J. Davis, cons. 1973..................................1974
Pennsylvania, Allen L. Bartlett, cons. 1986 1987
Pittsburgh, Alden M. Hathaway, cons. 1981 1983
Southern Virginia, C. Charles Vaché, cons.
1976...1978
Southwestern Virginia, Arthur H. Light, cons.
1979...1979
Virginia, Peter J. Lee, cons. 1984 1985
Washington, John T. Walker, cons. 1971 1977
West Virginia, Robert P. Atkinson, cons. 1973 ..1976

Province IV

Alabama, Furman C. Stough, cons. 1971 1971
Atlanta, C. Judson Child, cons. 1978 1983
Central Florida, William H. Folwell, cons. 1970 .1970
Central Gulf Coast, Charles F. Duvall, cons.
1981...1981
East Carolina, B. Sidney Sanders, cons. 1979 ...1983
East Tennessee, William E. Sanders, cons. 1979 .1985
Florida, Frank S. Cerveny, cons. 1974 1975
Georgia, Harry W. Shipps, cons. 1984 1985
Kentucky, David B. Reed, cons. 1964 1974
Lexington, Don A. Wimberley, cons. 1984 1985
Louisiana, James B. Brown, cons. 1976.........1976
Mississippi, Duncan M. Gray (Jnr.), cons. 1974 .1974
North Carolina, Robert W. Estill, cons. 1980 ...1983
San Joaquin, Victor M. Rivera, cons. 1968 1968
South Carolina, C. FitzSimons Allison, cons.
1980...1982
Southeast Florida, Calvin O. Schofield (Jnr.),
cons. 1979......................................1980
Southwest Florida, E. Paul Haynes.
Tennessee, George L. Reynolds, cons. 1985......1985
Upper South Carolina, William A. Beckham, cons. 1979..................................1979
West Tennessee, Alex D. Dickson (Jnr.), cons.
1983...1983
Western Louisiana, Willis R. Henton.
Western North Carolina, William G. Weinhauer, cons. 1973..................................1975

Province V

Chicago, Frank T. Griswold III, cons. 1985 1987
Eau Claire, William C. Wantland, cons. 1980 ...1980
Fond Du Lac, William L. Stevens, cons. 1980 ...1980
Indianapolis, Edward W. Jones, cons. 1977 1977
Michigan, H. Coleman McGehee (Jnr.), cons.
1971...1973
Milwaukee, Roger J. White, cons. 1984.........1985
Missouri, William A. Jones (Jnr.), cons. 1975 ...1975
Northern Indiana, Francis C. Gray, cons. 1986 ..1987
Northern Michigan, Thomas K. Ray, cons. 1982 .1982

Sees	Apptd.
Ohio, James R. Moodey, *cons.* 1983	1984
Quincy, Donald J. Parsons, *cons.* 1973	1973
Southern Ohio, William G. Black, *cons.* 1979	1980
Springfield, Donald M. Hultstrand, *cons.* 1982	1982
Western Michigan, Harold S. Meeks.	

Province VI

Colorado, William C. Frey, *cons.* 1967	1973
Iowa, Walter C. C. Righter, *cons.* 1972	1972
Minnesota, Robert M. Anderson, *cons.* 1978	1978
Montana, Charles I. Jones, *cons.* 1986	1986
Nebraska, James D. Warner, *cons.* 1976	1976
North Dakota, Harold A. Hopkins, *cons.* 1980	1980
South Dakota, Craig B. Anderson, *cons.* 1984	1984
Wyoming, Bob G. Jones, *cons.* 1977	1977

Province VII

Arkansas, Herbert A. Donovan (Jnr.), *cons.* 1980	1981
Dallas, Donis D. Patterson, *cons.* 1983	1983
Fort Worth, Clarence C. Pope (Jnr.), *cons.* 1985	1986
Kansas, Richard F. Grein, *cons.* 1981	1981
Northwest Texas, Sam B. Hulsey, *cons.* 1980	1980
Oklahoma, Gerald N. McAllister, *cons.* 1977	1977
Rio Grande, Richard M. Trelease (Jnr.), *cons.* 1971	1972
Texas, Maurice M. Benitez, *cons.* 1980	1980
West Missouri, Arthur A. Vogel, *cons.* 1971	1973
West Texas, John H. MacNaughton, *cons.* 1986	1987
Western Kansas, John F. Ashby, *cons.* 1981	1981

Province VIII

Alaska, George C. Harris, *cons.* 1981	1981
Arizona, Joseph T. Heistand, *cons.* 1976	1979
California, William E. Swing, *cons.* 1979	1980
Central Philippines, Manuel C. Lumpias, *cons.* 1977	1978
Eastern Oregon, Rustin R. Kimsey, *cons.* 1980	1980
El Camino Real, C. Shannon Mallory, *cons.* 1972	1980
Hawaii, Donald P. Hart, *cons.* 1986	1986
Idaho, David B. Birney, *cons.* 1982	1982
Los Angeles, Frederick L. Borsch, *cons.* 1988	1988
*Navajoland Area Mission, Wesley Frensdorff.	
Nevada, Stewart C. Zabriskie, *cons.* 1986	1986
Northern California, John L. Thompson III, *cons.* 1978	1978
Northern Luzon, Richard A. Abellon, *cons.* 1975	1986
Northern Philippines, Robert L. O. Longid, *cons.* 1983	1983
Olympia, Robert H. Cochrane, *cons.* 1976	1976
Oregon, Robert L. Ladehoff, *cons.* 1985	1986
San Diego, C. Brinkley Morton, *cons.* 1982	1982
Southern Philippines, Narcisco V. Ticobay, *cons.* 1986	1986
Spokane, Leigh A. Wallace, *cons.* 1979	1979
Taiwan, Pui-Yeung Cheung.	
Utah, George E. Bates, *cons.* 1986	1986

*Province IX

Central and South Mexico, Jose G. Saucedo, *cons.* 1958	1958
Colombia, Bernardo Merino-Botero, *cons.* 1979	1979
Dominican Republic, Telesforo A. Isaac, *cons.* 1972	1972
Ecuador, Adrian D. Caceres-Villavicencio, *cons.* 1971	1971
El Salvador, James H. Ottley, *cons.* 1984	1989
Guatemala, Armando Guerra-Soria, *cons.* 1982	1982
Honduras, Leopold Frade, *cons.* 1984	1984
Nicaragua, Sturdie W. Downs-Higgs, *cons.* 1985	1985

Sees	Apptd.
Northern Mexico, German Martinez-Marquez, *cons.* 1987	1987
Panama, James H. Ottley, *cons.* 1984	1984
Western Mexico, Samuel Espinoza-Venegas, *cons.* 1981	1983

Extra-Provincial

Costa Rica, Cornelius J. Wilson, *cons.* 1978	1978
Puerto Rico, Francisco Reus-Froylan, *cons.* 1964	1964
Venezuela, Onell A. Soto, *cons.* 1987	1987

CHURCH OF THE PROVINCE OF WEST AFRICA

The Most Rev Archbishop

Liberia, George Daniel Browne, D.D., *cons.* 1970	1982

Bp. *Suff.*, Rt. Rev. Edward W. Neufville (1984).

The Rt. Rev. Bishops

Accra, F. W. B. Thompson, *cons.* 1983	1983
Bo, M. Keili, O.B.E., *cons.* 1981	1981
Cape Coast, J. Ackon.	
Freetown, P. E. S. Thompson, *cons.* 1981	1981
Gambia, (vacant).	
Guinea, W. Y. Macauley.	
Koforidua, R. G. Okine, *cons.* 1981	1981
Kumasi, E. K. Yeboah, *cons.* 1985	1985
Liberia, (see above)	
Sekondi, T. Annobil, *cons.* 1981	1981
Sunyani/Tamale, J. K. Dadson, *cons.* 1981	1981

As the Province of Nigeria came into being on Feb. 24, 1979, the rest of the Province of West Africa continues to function as the (On-going) Province of West Africa.

CHURCH IN THE PROVINCE OF THE WEST INDIES

The Most Rev. Archbishop

N.E. Caribbean and Aruba, Orland Lindsay, *cons.* 1970	1986

The Rt. Rev. Bishops

Barbados, D. W. Gomez, *cons.* 1972	1972
Belize, D. M. Smith, *cons.* 1989	1989
Guyana, R. O. George, *cons.* 1976	1980
Jamaica, N. W. de Souza *cons.* 1973	1979
Bps. *Suff.* (*Mandeville*), W. A. Murray (1976); (*Montego Bay*), A. C. Reid (1980)	
Nassau and the Bahamas, M. H. Eldon, C.M.G. *cons.* 1971	1972
N.E. Caribbean and Aruba (see above).	
Trinidad and Tobago, C. O. Abdulah *cons.* 1970	1970
Windward Islands, P. Elder, *cons.* 1966.	

OTHER CHURCHES AND EXTRA-PROVINCIAL DIOCESES

Under the Archbishop of Canterbury

The Rt. Rev. Bishops

Bermuda, (vacant).	
Kuching, John Leong Chee Yun.	
Lusitanian Church in Portugal, F. Soares	1971
Pusan, Bundo Kim	1988
Sabah, Chhoa Heng Sze	1971
Seoul, S. S. Kim.	
Singapore, M. Tay	1982
Spanish Reformed Episcopal Church, A. Sanchez	1982
Taejon, Paul Hwan Yoon	1988
West Malaysia, J. G. Savarimuthu	1973

THE PRESBYTERIAN CHURCH OF WALES

THE PRESBYTERIAN OR CALVINISTIC METHODIST CHURCH OF WALES is the only Church of purely Welsh origin, and embraces a large section of the Welsh-speaking population. Its form of government is Presbyterian, and it is a constituent of the World Alliance of Reformed Churches.

In 1989 the body numbered—chapels and other buildings, 1,050; ministers in pastoral charge, 146; elders, 4,554; communicants, 65,237; Sunday scholars, 20,949.

The *Association in the East* which includes nine of the English Presbyteries was formed in 1947.
Moderator of General Assembly (1989–90), R. M. Edwards, Oswestry.
Moderators of Associations (1989–90) *South Wales*, Dr. B. F. Roberts, Aberystwyth; *North Wales*, R. A. Roberts, Port Dinorwic; *East Wales*, Rev. J. E. Wynne Davies, Aberystwyth.
General Secretary, Rev. D. H. Owen, 53 Richmond Road, Cardiff CF2 3UP

THE CHURCH OF SCOTLAND

Church Office, 121 George Street, Edinburgh EH2 4YN

THE CHURCH OF SCOTLAND is Presbyterian in constitution, and is governed by Kirk Sessions, Presbyteries, Synods, and the General Assembly, which consists of both representative ministers and elders, in equal numbers from each of the Presbyteries. It is presided over by a Moderator chosen annually by the Assembly. The Sovereign, if not present in person, is represented by a Lord High Commissioner, who is appointed each year by the Crown. The country, for Church purposes, is divided into 12 Synods and 46 Presbyteries, and there are about 1,400 ministers and licentiates engaged in ministerial and other work. The figures at Dec. 31, 1987, were:—

Congregations, 1,727; total membership 838,659. There are 130 ministers and other personnel working with partner Churches and in expatriate charges in 26 countries.

LORD HIGH COMMISSIONER (1989–90), Capt. Sir Iain Tennant, K.T.
MODERATOR OF THE GENERAL ASSEMBLY (1989), Dr. W. G. G. McDonald.

Principal Clerk, Rev. J. L. Weatherhead.
Deputy Clerk, Rev. A. G. McGillivray.
Procurator, G. Penrose, Q.C.
Law Agent and Solicitor of the Church, R. A. Paterson.
Parliamentary Agent, I. McCulloch (London).
General Treasurer, W. G. P. Colledge.

THE PRESBYTERIAN CHURCH IN IRELAND

The largest of the Presbyterian churches in Ireland consists of 22 presbyteries, 413 ministers, 564 congregations, with 131,471 communicants, 123,283 families and 6,100 Sunday-school teachers. During the 12 months ended Dec. 31, 1987, there was contributed by congregational effort £4,214,060 plus IR£281,432 for religious, charitable, and missionary purposes. The total income for the period raised by congregations for all purposes was £19,567,540 plus IR£1,541,665.—
General Sec., Very Rev. Dr. T. J. Simpson, Church House, Belfast BT1 6DW.

UNITED REFORMED CHURCH

THE UNITED REFORMED CHURCH was formed by the union of the Congregational Church in England and Wales and the Presbyterian Church of England on October 5, 1972. The Re-formed Association of Churches of Christ were joined to the U.R.C. on September 26, 1981. It is divided into 12 Provinces, each with a Provincial Moderator, and 70 Districts. There are 126,000 members and 1,000 serving ministers of whom 190 are auxiliary and give voluntary service. It shares an international mission through the Council for World Mission and is a member of the British and World Council of Churches. Its ministers are trained at five recognized colleges.

General Sec., Rev. B. G. Thorogood, 86 Tavistock Place, WC1H 9RT

The Congregational Federation

The majority of those members of the Congregational Church who did not join the United Reformed Church comprise the Congregational Federation. This has about 9,800 members, 113 ministers and 286 churches.

Gen. Sec., G. A. Adams, The Congregational Centre, 4 Castle Gate, Nottingham NG1 7AS.

THE METHODIST CHURCH

THE METHODIST CHURCH was founded in 1739 by the two brothers Wesley and rapidly spread throughout the British Isles and to America before 1770. The Methodist Church in Great Britain was united in 1932 by the fusion of the Wesleyan Methodist Church (the original section), the Primitive Methodist Church (1810) and the United Methodist Church (a 1907 fusion of the Methodist New Connexion (1797), the Bible Christian Methodist Church (1815) and the United Methodist Free Churches (1828 and 1849)).

The World Methodist Council, founded 1881, reorganized 1951, associates Methodism throughout the world in 90 countries.

The Methodist Church in Great Britain is governed primarily by the Conference, secondarily by the

District Synods (held in the autumn and the spring), consisting of all the ministers and of selected laypeople in each district, over which a chairman, who is a minister, is appointed by the Conference; and thirdly by the circuit meeting of the ministers and lay officers of each circuit. The authority of both Synods and Circuit Meetings is subordinate to the Conference, which has the supreme legislative and judicial power in Methodism.

President of the Conference (July 1989–90), Rev. Dr. J. J. Vincent.
Vice-President of the Conference (July 1989–90), J. B. Hindmarsh.
Secretary of the Conference, Rev. B. E. Beck, 1 Central Buildings, Westminster, SW1H 9NH.
President Designate (1990–91), Rev. Dr. D. English.

Vice-President Designate (1990–91), Mrs. R. Wass.

Statistics.—In 1988 in association with the Conference in Great Britain there were 3,399 Ministers, 13,378 Local Preachers, 450,406 Members in 7,389 churches. (Statistics are published triennially.)

Methodist Church in Ireland

The Methodist Church in Ireland has 195 Ministers, 295 Lay Preachers, 20,094 Adult and 12,292 Junior Members.

President, (1989–90), Rev. George R. Morrison.

Secretary, Rev. C. G. Eyre, 3 Upper Malone Road, Belfast BT9 6TD.

Independent Methodists

Independent Methodists.—This body is Congregational in its organization, with an unpaid Ministry. Its first Conference was held in 1805. In 1989 there were in Great Britain 131 Ministers, 3,870 Members, 107 Churches and 3,315 Sunday scholars. *Gen. Sec.,* Rev. J. M. Day, The Old Police House, Croxton, Stafford ST21 6PE.

Wesleyan Reform Union

This Union is Methodist in doctrine, Congregational in government, with, if any church desires it, a paid ministry. It is the remnant of the original Reformers expelled from Wesleyan Methodism in 1849. The adherents are mainly in the Midland and Northern counties. In 1989 there were in Great Britain 23 Ministers, 145 Lay Preachers, 3,026 Members, 130 Churches and 1,829 Sunday School scholars.—*President,* M. T. Beasley, 2 Holsworthy Close, Hinckley Road, Nuneaton, Warks. CV11 6LS. *General Secretary,* Rev. D. A. Morris, Wesleyan Reform Church House, 123 Queen Street, Sheffield 1.

The Baptist Union

The Baptists have over 35,000,000 members in all countries. In Britain they are for the most part grouped in Associations of churches, and the majority of these belong to the Baptist Union, which was formed in 1812. Current statistics show that there are 2,111 churches and 167,466 members. There also exist separate Baptist Unions of Scotland (166 churches and 14,600 members); Wales (586 churches and 29,593 members); Ireland (92 churches and 8,550 members). *President of the Baptist Union of Great Britain,* (1989–90), Rev. Dr. John Biggs. *Secretary,* Rev. B. Green. *Office,* Baptist House, 129 Broadway, Didcot, Oxon. OX11 8RT.

LUTHERAN CHURCH

The Lutheran Church is one of the largest Protestant churches, with over 70 million members world-wide, although there are only about 27,000 adherents in Great Britain. The government and organization of the Lutheran Church varies from country to country, some having an episcopal and some a more congregational form.

Very few British people are Lutherans and services in Great Britain are held in many languages to serve members of different nationalities. English–language congregations in Great Britain are members either of the Lutheran Church in Great Britain— United Synod or of the Evangelical Lutheran Church of England. The United Synod and most of the "national churches" are members of the Lutheran Council of Great Britain and through the Council are related to the Lutheran World Federation.

LUTHERAN COUNCIL OF GREAT BRITAIN, 8 Collingham Gardens, SW5 0HW.—*Chairman,* Very Rev. R. J. Patkai.

ORTHODOX CHURCH

Greek Orthodox Church (Archdiocese of Thyateira and Great Britain), Most Rev. Archbishop Gregorios, 5 Craven Hill, W2 3EN.

Serbian Orthodox Church (Patriarchate of Serbia) Right Rev. Bishop Lavrentije, 89 Lancaster Road, W11 1QQ.

Russian Orthodox Church (Patriarchate of Moscow), Most Rev. Metropolitan Anthony of Sourozh, Russian Cathedral, Ennismore Gardens, SW7 1NH.

Russian Orthodox Church Outside Russia. His Grace Bishop Constantine, Dormition Cathedral, Emperor's Gate, SW7. *Mission Administrator,* Hegumen Seraphim, 14 St. Dunstan's Road, NW6.

The Poles, Ukrainians, Latvians, Byelorussians and Romanians also have congregations in this country.

OTHER RELIGIOUS DENOMINATIONS

The General Assembly of Unitarian and Free Christian Churches has about 95 ministers, 230 chapels and other places of worship in Great Britain and Ireland. *Gen. Sec.,* Dr. R. W. Smith, Essex Hall, 1–6 Essex Street, Strand, WC2R 3HY.

The Salvation Army, first known as the Christian Mission, was founded by William Booth in the East End of London in 1865. In 1878 it took its present name and adopted a quasi-military method of government. Since then it has become established in 90 countries of the world. The world leader, known as the General, is elected by a High Council, consisting of all active Commissioners and Territorial Commanders who have held the rank of Colonel for at least two years. In 1988 there were in Great Britain, 929 Corps (Churches), 135 Social Services Centres and 1,575 Officers engaged in evangelistic and social work. The latest world statistics (1988) are 14,397 Corps, 4,975 Social Services Centres (including institutions and schools) and 25,056 Officers.

General, Eva Burrows. *International Headquarters:*— 101 Queen Victoria Street, EC4P 4EP.

The Religious Society of Friends (Quakers), founded in the 17th century, has no separated ministry. There are in Great Britain 462 places of worship and 18,010 members (world membership 213,800). *Central Offices (Great Britain),* Friends House, Euston Road, NW1 2BJ; *(Ireland),* Swanbrook House, Morehampton Road, Dublin 4.

The First Church of Christ, Scientist, in Boston Massachusetts, U.S.A. (District Manager, Committees on Publication for Great Britain and Ireland, 108 Palace Gardens Terrace, W8), has about 230 branch churches and societies in Great Britain and Ireland.

The Free Church of England (otherwise called The Reformed Episcopal Church) has 29 churches and 1,657 adherents in England. *Gen. Sec.,* Rt. Rev. A. Ward, 28 Sedgebrook, Liden, Swindon, Wilts. SN3 6EY.

The Seventh Day Adventists (*Hdqrs.,* Stanborough Park, Watford, Herts. WD2 6JP), have more than 235 organized churches and companies and more than 17,000 members in the British Isles. *Executive Sec.,* D. W. McFarlane.

THE ROMAN CATHOLIC CHURCH

His Holiness Pope John Paul II (Karol Wojtyla), *born* in Wadowice, Poland, May 18, 1920; *ordained priest* November 1, 1946; appointed *Archbishop of Krakow* January 13, 1964, created *Cardinal* at a Consistory on June 26, 1967. Formally assumed Pontificate October 16, 1978.

The Sacred College of Cardinals, when complete, consisted of six Cardinal Bishops, fifty Cardinal Priests and fourteen Cardinal Deacons. This number was fixed by Pope Sixtus V in 1586. The number was increased by Pope John XXIII, who created 52 new Cardinals, and by Pope Paul VI, who created 141 new Cardinals; Pope John Paul II has created 86 new Cardinals (15 on June 30, 1979, 18 on Feb. 2, 1983, 28 on May 25, 1985, 25 on June 28, 1988). In Aug. 1988 there were 158 Cardinals. The Cardinals are advisers and assistants of the Sovereign Pontiff and form the supreme council or Senate of the Church. On the death of the Pope they elect his successor. The assembly of the Cardinals at the Vatican for the election of a new Pope is known as the Conclave in which, in complete seclusion, the Cardinals elect by secret ballot; a two-thirds majority is necessary before the vote can be accepted as final. When a Cardinal receives the necessary votes the Dean of the Sacred College formally asks him if he will accept election and the name by which he wishes to be known. On his acceptance of the office the Conclave is dissolved and the First Cardinal Deacon announces the election to the assembled crowd in St. Peter's Square. On the first Sunday or Holyday following the election the new Pope assumes the pontificate at High Mass in St. Peter's Square. A new pontificate is dated from the assumption of the pontificate.

Forms of Address: *Cardinal*, "His Eminence Cardinal . . ." (if an Archbishop, "His Eminence the Cardinal Archbishop of . . ."); *Archbishop*, "The Most Rev. Archbishop of . . ."; *Bishop*, "The Rt. Rev. Bishop of . . ."

THE CURIA

The Curia or governing body of the Roman Catholic Church is made up of various administrative departments headed by the Secretariat of State and the Sacred Council for the Public Affairs of the Church. Below these are congregations, secretariats and tribunals assisted by commissions and offices. All are headed by Cardinals who have as their British equivalent the Ministers or Secretaries of State heading the various government departments.

The Vatican State has, as with any nation, its own diplomatic service although its representatives are officially acknowledged in different ways throughout the countries of the world. Where the representation is only to the local churches and not to the government of that country then the man appointed is an Apostolic Delegate. However, where the representative is recognized as having diplomatic status by a particular government then he is known as either a nuncio, pro nuncio or inter nuncio. Nuncios are Papal Ambassadors who are given precedence over all other ambassadors by their appointed country and are the doyens of the diplomatic corps. In countries where precedence is not recognized, as in Britain, the papal representative is known as a pro nuncio.

THE BISHOPS' CONFERENCES

The Roman Catholic church in **England and Wales** is governed by:

1. **The Bishops' Conference** which consists of the local ordinaries (the Diocesan Bishops) of any rite; coadjutor bishops and auxiliaries; and titular bishops with special tasks. They are headed by the President, Cardinal Basil Hume, and Vice President, Archbishop Worlock, Archbishop of Liverpool.

2. **The Bishops' Standing Committee** made up of the Metropolitans (Archbishops) and department heads. It has general responsibility for continuity and policy between the Plenary Sessions of the Conference and for the preparation of the agenda and implementation of Conference decisions. This committee is serviced by the General Secretariat.

There are six departments, each with an episcopal chairman, which look after the life of the church within England and Wales. The departments and their heads are as follows:

(a) Department for Christian Life and Worship: Archbishop Bowen (*Southwark*).
(b) Department for Mission and Unity: Bishop Clark (*East Anglia*).
(c) Department for Christian Doctrine and Formation: Bishop Konstant (*Leeds*).
(d) Department for Social Responsibility: Bishop Harris (*Middlesbrough*).
(e) Department for Christian Citizenship: Bishop McCartie (*Auxiliary in Birmingham*).
(f) Department for International Affairs: Bishop O'Brien (*Hertfordshire*).

As well as the above, the Conference has agencies and consultative bodies affiliated to it and all are serviced by the General Secretariat headed by a General Secretary namely:

England & Wales—Mgr. Vincent Nichols, 39 Eccleston Square, SW1V 1PD.

Scotland—Right Rev. Maurice Taylor, Bishop of Galloway, Candida Casa, 8 Corsehill Road, Ayr, Scotland, KA7 26T.

Ireland—(Executive Secretary) Rev. Gerard Clifford, Iona, 67 Newry Road, Dundalk, Co. Louth.

GREAT BRITAIN

Apostolic Pro-Nuncio to the United Kingdom of Great Britain and Northern Ireland, The Most Rev. Luigi Barbarito.

England and Wales

The Most Revd. Archbishops	Cons.	Clgy.
Westminster, H.E. Cardinal Basil Hume		
(1976)	1976	926
Auxil., John Crowley	1986	
Auxil., Victor Guazzelli	1970	
Auxil., Philip Harvey	1977	
Auxil., Gerald Mahon	1970	
Auxil., James J. O'Brien	1977	
Birmingham, Maurice Couve de Murville		
(1982)	1982	526
Auxil., Joseph Cleary	1965	
Auxil., Patrick L. McCartie	1977	
Cardiff, John A. Ward (1983)	1981	186
Liverpool, Derek Worlock (1976)	1965	563
Auxil., Kevin O'Connor	1979	
Auxil., John Rawsthorne	1982	
Auxil., Vincent Malone	1989	
Southwark, Michael Bowen (1977)	1970	573
Auxil., Charles Henderson	1972	
Auxil., Howard Tripp	1980	
Auxil., John Jukes	1980	

The Rt. Revd. Bishops

Arundel and Brighton, Cormac Murphy-O'Connor	1977	331
Brentwood, Thomas McMahon (1980)	1980	214
Clifton, Mervyn Alexander (1975)	1972	246
East Anglia, Alan Clark (1976)	1969	125

	Cons.	Clgy.
Hallam, Gerald Moverley (1980)	1968	106
Hexham and Newcastle, Hugh Lindsay (1975)	1970	340
Auxil., Owen Swindelhurst	1977	
Lancaster, John Brewer (1971)	1985	265
Leeds, David Konstant (1985)	1977	299
Menevia (Wales), Daniel Mullins (1987)	1970	
Middlesbrough, Augustine Harris (1978)	1966	208
Auxil., Thomas O'Brien	1982	
Northampton, vacant.		
Nottingham, James McGuinness (1975)	1972	250
Plymouth, Christopher Budd	1986	187
Portsmouth, F. Crispian Hollis (1989)	1987	
Salford, Patrick Kelly	1984	490
Shrewsbury, Joseph Gray (1980)	1969	255
Wrexham (Wales), James Hannigan	1983	

Scotland

The Most Revd. Archbishops

	Cons.	Clgy.
St. Andrews and Edinburgh, Keith Patrick O'Brian	1985	250
Auxil., James Monaghan	1970	
Glasgow, Thomas Winning (1974)	1972	374
Auxil., John Mone	1984	
Auxil., Charles Renfrew	1977	

The Rt. Revd. Bishops

	Cons.	Clgy.
Aberdeen, Mario Conti	1977	57
Argyll and the Isles, Colin MacPherson	1969	39
Dunkeld, Vincent Logan	1981	75
Galloway, Maurice Taylor	1981	82
Motherwell, Joseph Devine	1977	203
Paisley, John A. Mone	1984	94

IRELAND

There is one hierarchy for the whole of Ireland. Several of the Dioceses have territory partly in the Republic of Ireland and partly in Northern Ireland. *Nuncio to Ireland*, Most Rev. Gaetano Alibrandi (Archbishop of Bindi)

The Most Revd. Archbishops

	Cons.	Clgy.
Armagh, H.E. Cardinal Thomas O'Fiaich	1977	290
Auxil., James Lennon	1980	
Cashel, Dermot Clifford	1986	
Dublin, Desmond Connell (1988)	1988	
Auxil., Joseph Carroll	1968	
Auxil., James Kavanagh	1973	
Auxil., Donal Murray	1982	
Auxil., Dermot O'Mahony	1975	
Auxil., Desmond Williams	1985	
Tuam, Joseph Cassidy (1987)	1979	182

The Rt. Revd. Bishops

	Cons.	Clgy.
Achonry, Thomas Flynn	1975	75
Ardagh and Clonmacnois, Colm O'Reilly	1983	115
Clogher, Joseph Duffy	1979	130
Clonfert, Joseph Kirby	1988	88
Cloyne, John Magee	1987	170
Cork and Ross, Michael Murphy	1976	389
Auxil., John Buckley	1984	
Derry, Edward Daly	1974	158
Auxil., Francis Lagan	1988	
Down and Connor, Cahal Daly	1967	329
Auxil., Anthony Farquhar	1983	
Auxil., Patrick Walsh	1983	
Dromore, Francis Brooks	1976	75
Elphin, Dominic Conway	1970	117
Ferns, Brendon Comiskey	1980	178
Galway and Kilmacduagh, Eamonn Casey	1969	162
Kerry, Dermot O'Sullivan	1985	167

	Cons.	Clgy.
Kildare and Leighlin, Laurence Ryan	1984	246
Killala, Thomas Finnegan	1970	55
Killaloe, Michael Harty	1967	204
Kilmore, Francis McKiernan	1972	139
Limerick, Jeremiah Newman	1974	247
Meath, John McCormack	1968	284
Auxil., Michael Smith	1984	
Ossory, Laurence Forristal	1980	149
Raphoe, Seamus Hegarty	1984	114
Waterford and Lismore, Michael Russell	1965	213

RESIDENTIAL ARCHBISHOPRICS THROUGHOUT THE WORLD

This list is set out with the name of the relevant country first; then the name of the diocese; and finally the Archbishop's name. It does not include England and Wales, Scotland or Ireland which are above.

Albania

Durrës, vacant. (Apostolic Administrator: Mgr. Nicola Troshani).
Shkodër, vacant. (Apostolic Administrator: Mgr. Ernesto Coba).

Algeria

Algiers, Henri Teissier.

Angola

Huambo, Francisco Viti.
Luanda, H.E. Cardinal Alexandre do Nascimento.
Lubango, Manuel Franklin da Costa.

Argentina

Bahia Blanca, Jorge Mayer.
Buenos Aires, H.E. Cardinal Juan Carlos Aramburu.
Córdoba, H.E. Cardinal Raúl Francisco Primatesta.
Corrientes, Fortunato A. Rossi.
La Plata, Antonio Quarracino.
Mendoza, Candido Genaro Rubiolo.
Paraná, Estanislao Esteban Karlich.
Resistencia, Juan J. Iriarte.
Rosario, Jorge Manuel López.
Salta, Moises J. Blanchoud.
San Juan de Cuyo, Italo Severino Di Stefano.
Santa Fe, Edgardo Gabriel Storni.
Tucumán, Horatio A. Bozzoli.

Australia

Adelaide, Leonard Anthony Faulkner.
Brisbane, Francis Roberts Rush.
Canberra, Francis P. Carroll.
Hobart, Joseph E. D'Arcy.
Melbourne, Thomas Francis Little.
Perth, William J. Foley.
Sydney, H.E. Cardinal Edward B. Clancy.

Austria

Salzburg, Georg Eder.
Vienna, H.E. Cardinal Hans Hermann Groer.

Bangladesh

Dhaka, Michael Rozario.

Belgium

Malines-Bruxelles, H.E. Cardinal Godfried Danneels.

Benin

Cotonou, Christophe Adimou.

Bolivia

Cochabamba, Rene Fernandez Apaza.
La Paz, Luis Sainz Hinojosa.
Santa Cruz de la Sierra, Luis Rodriguez Pardo.
Sucre, vacant.

Brazil

Aparecida, Geraldo Maria de Morais Penido.
Aracaju, Luciano José Cabral Duarte.
Bélem do Pará, Alberto Guadêncio Ramos.
Belo Horizonte, Serafim Fernandes de Araújo.
Botucatu, Vincent Marchetti Zioni.
Brasília, H.E. Cardinal Jose Freire Falcao.
Campinas, Gilberto Pereira Lopes.
Campo Grande, Vitorio Pavanello.
Cascavel, Armando Cirio.
Cuiaba, Bonifacio Piccinini.
Curitiba, Pedro Antonio Fedalto.
Diamantina, Geraldo Majelo Reis.
Florianópolis, Alfonso Niehues.
Fortaleza, H.E. Cardinal Aloisio Lorscheider.
Goiania, Antonio Ribeiro de Oliveira.
Juiz de Fora, Juvenal Roriz.
Londrina, Geraldo Majela Agnelo.
Maceió, Edvaldo G. Amaral.
Manaus, Clovis Frainer.
Mariana, Luciano Mendes de Almeida.
Maringá, Jaime Luis Coelho.
Natal, Alair V. Fernandes de Melo.
Niteroi, José Gonçalves da Costa.
Olinda & Recife, José Cardoso Sobrinho.
Paraiba, José M. Pires.
Porto Alegre, Claudio Colling.
Porto Velho, José Martins da Silva.
Pouso Alegre, José D'Angelo Neto.
Ribeirão Preto, Arnaldo Ribeiro.
São Luis do Maranhão, Paulo Eduardo Andrade Ponte.
São Paulo, H.E. Cardinal Paulo Evaristo Arns.
São Salvador da Bahia, H.E. Cardinal Lucas Moreira Neves.
São Sebastião do Rio de Janeiro, H.E. Cardinal Eugenio de Araújo Sales.
Teresina, Miguel F. Camara Filho.
Uberaba, Benedito de Ulhôa Vieira.
Vitória, Silvestre L. Scandian.

Burkina

Ouagadougou, H.E. Cardinal Paul Zoungrana.

Burma (Myanma)

Mandalay, Alphonse U. Than Aung.
Rangoon, Gabriel Thohey Mahn Gaby.

Burundi

Gitega, Joachim Ruhuna.

Cameroon

Bamenda, Paul Verdzekov.
Douala, Simon Tonyé.
Garoua, H.E. Cardinal Christian W. Tumi.
Yaoundé, Jean Zoa.

Canada

Edmonton, Joseph N. MacNeil.
Grouard-McLennon, Henri Légaré.
Halifax, James Martin Hayes.
Keewatin-Le Pas, Peter Alfred Sutton.
Kingston, Francis John Spence.
Moncton, Donat Chiasson.
Montreal, H.E. Cardinal Paul Grégoire.
Ottawa, Joseph Aurèle Plourde.
Quebec, H.E. Cardinal Louis-Albert Vachon.
Regina, Charles Halpin.
Rimouski, Gilles Ouellet.
St Boniface, Antoine Hacault.
St Johns, Newfoundland, Alphonsus L. Penney.
Sherbrooke, Jean Marie Fortier.
Toronto, H.E. Cardinal Gerald Emmett Carter.
Vancouver, James Francis Carney.
Winnipeg, Latin Rite–Adam Exner; Ukrainian Rite–Maxim Hermaniuk.

Central African Republic

Bangui, Joachim N'Dayen.

Chad

N'Djamena, Charles Vandame.

Chile

Antofagasta, Carlos Oviedo Cavada.
Concepción, vacant.
La Serena, Bernardino Pinera Carvallo.
Puerto Montt, Savino B. C. Bertollo.
Santiago de Chile, H.E. Cardinal Juan F. Fresno Larrain.

China

Ankang, Huai-Ning, vacant.
Canton, Dominic Tang Yee-Ming.
Changsha, vacant.
Chungking, vacant.
Foochow, Min-Hou, vacant.
Hangchow, vacant.
Hankow, vacant.
Kaifeng, vacant.
Kunming, vacant.
Kweiyang, vacant.
Lanchow, vacant.
Mukden, vacant.
Nanchang, vacant.
Nanking, vacant.
Nanning, vacant.
Peking, vacant.
Sian, vacant.
Suiyüan, Francis Wang Hsueh-Ming.
Taiyuan, vacant; Bishop Emeritus Dominic Luke Capozi (expelled April 11, 1946, now living in Nazareth, Israel).
Tsinan, vacant.

Colombia

Antioquia, Eladio Acosta Arteaga.
Barranquilla, Felix Maria Torres Parra.
Bogotá, H.E. Cardinal Mario Revollo Bravo.
Bucaramanga, Hector Rueda Hernández.
Cali, Pedro Rubiano Sáenz.
Cartagena, Carlos Jose Ruiseco Vieira.
Ibague, José Joaquin Flórez Hernández.
Manizales, José de Jesús Pimiento Rodriguez.
Medellin, H.E. Cardinal Alfonso López Trujillo.
Nueva Pamplona, Rafael Sarmiento Peralta.
Popayán, Samuel Silverio Buitrago Trujillo.
Tunja, Augusto Trujillo Arango.

Congo

Brazzaville, Barthélémy Batantu.

Costa Rica

San José, Román Arrieta Villalobos.

Côte d'Ivoire

Abidjan, H.E. Cardinal Bernard Yago.

Cuba

San Cristóbal de la Habana, Jaime Lucas Ortega y Alamino.
Santiago de Cuba, Pedro Meurice Estiu.

Cyprus

Cyprus, [Maronite Seat at Nicosia], Boutros Gemayel.

Czechoslovakia

Olomouc, vacant.
Praha, H.E. Cardinal František Tomášek.
Trnava, vacant.

Dominican Republic

Santo Domingo, Nicolás de Jesús López Rodriguez.

Ecuador

Cuenca, Alberto Luna Tobar.
Guayaquil, Bernardino Echeveria Ruiz.
Quito, Antonio J. González Zumárraga.

Equatorial Guinea

Malabo, Rafael Nze Abuy.

Ethiopia

Addis Ababa, H.E. Cardinal Paul Tzadua.

France

Aix, Bernard Panafieu.
Albi, Joseph Rabine.
Auch, Gabriel Vanel.
Avignon, Raymond Bouchex.
Besançon, Lucien Daloz.
Bordeaux, Marius Maziers.
Bourges, Pierre Plateau.
Cambrai, Jacques Delaporte.
Chambéry, Claude Feidt.
Lyon, H.E. Cardinal Albert Decourtray.
Marseilles, Robert Coffey.
Paris, H. E. Cardinal J. M. Lustiger.
Reims, Jean Balland.
Rennes, Jacques Jullien.
Rouen, Joseph Duval.
Sens, Eugene Ernoult.
Strasbourg, Charles Amarin Brand.
Toulouse, André Collini.
Tours, Jean Honoré.

French Polynesia

Papeete, Michel Coppenrath.

Gabon

Libreville, André Fernand Anguilé.

Germany (Federal Republic)

Bamberg, Elmar Maria Kredel.
Cologne, H.E. Cardinal Joachim Meisner.
Essen, H.E. Cardinal Franz Hengsbach.
Freiburg im Breisgau, Oskar Saier.
Munich & Freising, H.E. Cardinal Friedrich Wetter.
Paderborn, Johannes Joachim Degenhardt.

Ghana

Cape Coast, John Kodwo Amissah.
Tamale, Peter Poreiku Dery.

Greece

Athens, Nicholaos Foscolos.
Corfu, Antonio Varthalitis.
Naxos, Jean Perris.
Rhodes, vacant (Apostolic administrator: Michel Pierre Franzidis).

Guatemala

Guatemala, Prospero Penandos del Barrio.

Guinea

Conakry, Robert Sarah.

Haiti

Cap-Haitien, Francois Gayot.
Port au Prince, François-Wolff Ligondé.

Honduras

Tegucigalpa, Hector Enrique Santos Hernández.

Hong Kong

Hong Kong, H.E. Cardinal J. B. Wu Cheng Chung.

Hungary

Eger, Istvan Seregely.
Esztergom, H.E. Cardinal Laslo Paskai.
Kalocsa, Laszlo Danko.

India

Agra, Cecil de Sa.
Bangalore, Alphonsus Mathias.
Bhopal, Eugene D'Souza.
Bombay, H.E. Cardinal Simon Ignatius Pimenta.
Calcutta, Henry Sebastian D'Souza.
Changanacherry, Joseph Powathil.
Cuttack-Bhubaneswar, Raphael Cheenath.
Delhi, Angelo Innocent Fernandes.
Ernakulam, H.E. Cardinal Anthony Padiyara.
Goa and Daman, Raul Nicolau Gonsalves.
Hyderabad, Saminini Arulappa.
Madras and Mylapore, Casimir Gnanadickam.
Madurai, Marianus Arokiasamy.
Nagpur, Leobard D'Souza.
Pondicherry and Cuddalore, Venmani S. Selvanather.
Ranchi, Telesphore P. Toppo.
Shillong-Gauhati, Hubert D'Rosario.
Trivandrum, [Syrian Melekite Rite], Benedict Varghese Mar Gregorios Thangalathil.
Verapoly, Cornelius Elanjikal.

Indonesia

Ende, Donatus Djagom.
Jakarta, Leo Soekoto.
Medan, Alfred Gonti Pius Datubara.
Merauke, Jacobus Duivenvoorde.
Pontianak, Hieronymus Herculanus Bumbun.
Semarang, Julius R. Darmaatmadja.
Ujung Pandang, R. P. Francis van Roessel.

Iran

Ahváz, Hanna Zora.
Tehran, Youhannan Semaan Issayi.
Urmyā, Thomas Meram.

Iraq

Arbil, Stephane Babeka.
Baghdad, Paul Dahdah.
Basra, Yousif Thomas.
Kirkuk, André Sana.
Mosul, Georges Garmo.

Israel

Akka [Greek Melekite Catholic Rite], Maximos Salloum.

Italy

Acerenza, Michele Scandiffio.
Amalfi, Ferdinand Palatucci.
Ancona, Carlo Maccari.
Bari, Mariano Magrassi.
Benevento, Carlo Minchiatti.
Bologna, H.E. Cardinal Giacomo Biffi.
Brindisi, Settimio Todisco.
Cagliari, Otterino Pietro Alberti.
Camerino, vacant.
Campobasso-Boiano, Pietro Santoro.
Capua, Luigi Diligenza.
Catania, Luigi Bommarito.
Catanzaro, Antonio Cantisani.
Chieti, Antonio Valentini.
Conza, Antonio Nuzzi.
Cosenza, Dino Trabalzini.
Crotone-Santa Severina, Giuseppi Agostino.
Fermo, Cleto Bellucci.
Ferrara, Luigi Maverna.
Florence, H.E. Cardinal Silvano Piovanelli.
Foggia, Giuseppe Casale.
Gaeta, Vincenzo Farano.
Genoa, H.E. Cardinal Giovanni Canestri.
Gorizia and Gradisca, Antonio Vitale Bommarco.
Lanciano, Enzio d'Antonio.
L'Aquila, Mario Peressin.
Lecce, Cosmo F. Ruppi.

Lucca, Guiliano Agresti.
Manfredonia, Valentino Vailati.
Matera, Ennio Appignanesi.
Messina, Ignazio Cannavó.
Milan, H.E. Cardinal Carlo Maria Martini.
Modena, Santo B. Quadri.
Monreale, Salvatore Cassisa.
Naples, H.E. Cardinal Michele Giordano.
Oristano, Pier Luigi Tiddia.
Otranto, Vincenzo Franco.
Palermo, H.E. Cardinal Salvatore Pappalardo.
Perugia, Ennio Antonelli.
Pescara-Penne, Antonio Jannucci.
Pisa, Alessandro Plotti.
Potenza, Guiseppe Vairo.
Ravenna, Ersilio Tonini.
Reggio Calabria, Aurelio Sorrentino.
Rossano, Serafino Sprovieri.
Salerno, Guerino Grimaldi.
Sassari, Salvatore Isgrò.
Siena, Ismaele Mario Castellano.
Siracusa, Calogero Lauricella.
Sorrento, Felice Cece.
Spoleto, Antonio Ambrosiano.
Taranto, Salvatore De Giorgi.
Turin, Giovanni Saldarini.
Trani and Barletta, Giuseppe Carata.
Trento, Giovanni Sartori.
Udine, Alfredo Battisti.
Urbino, Donato U. Bianchi.
Vercelli, Albino Mensa.

Jamaica

Kingston, Samuel Emmanuel Carter.

Japan

Nagasaki, H.E. Cardinal Joseph Asajiro Satowaki.
Osaka, Paul Hisao Yasuda.
Tōkyō, Peter Seiichi Shirayanagi.

Jordan

Petra and Filadelfia [Greek Melekite Catholic Rite],
  Saba Youakim.

Kenya

Nairobi, H.E. Cardinal Maurice Otunga.

Korea

Kwangju, Victorinus Kong-Hi Youn.
Seoul, H.E. Cardinal Stephen Sou Hwan Kim.
Taegu, Paul Moun-Hi Ri.

Lebanon

Antelias [Maronite Rite], Joseph Mohsen Bechara.
Baalbek, Eliopoli [Greek Melekite Catholic Rite],
  Salim Bustros.
Beirut [Greek Melekite Catholic Rite], Habib Bacha;
  [Maronite Rite] Khalil Abinader.
Saïda [Greek Melekite Catholic Rite], Georges Kwaiter.
Tripoli [Maronite Rite], Antoine Joubeir; [Greek
  Melekite Catholic Rite], Elias Nijmé.
Tyre [Greek Melekite Catholic Rite], Jean A. Haddad;
  [Maronite Rite], Joseph Khoury.
Zahle and Furzol [Greek Melekite Catholic Rite],
  Andre Haddad.

Lesotho

Maseru, Alfonso Ligouri Morapeli.

Liberia

Monrovia, Michael Kpakala Francis.

Lithuania

Kaunas, H.E. Cardinal Vincentas Sladkevicius.
Vilna, Julijonas Steponavicius.

Luxembourg

Luxembourg, Jean Hengen.

Madagascar

Diego Suarez, Albert Joseph Tsiahoana.
Fianarantsoa, Gilbert Ramanantoanina.
Tananarive, H.E. Cardinal Victor Razafimahatratra.

Malaysia

Kuching, Peter Chung Hoan Ting.

Mali

Bamako, Luc Auguste Sangaré.

Malta

Malta, Joseph Mercieca.

Martinique

Fort de France, Maurice Marie-Sainte.

Mauritius

Port Louis, H.E. Cardinal Jean Margeot.

Mexico

Acapulco, Rafael Bello Ruiz.
Antequera, Bartolomé Carrasco Briseno.
Chihuahua, Adalberto Almeida Merino.
Guadalajara, Juan J.P. Ocampo.
Hermosillo, Carlos Quintero Arce.
Jalapa, Sergio Obeso Rivero.
Mexico City, H.E. Cardinal Ernesto Corripio Ahumada.
Monterrey, Adolfo Suarez Rivera.
Morelia, Estanislao Alcarez Figueroa.
Puebla de los Angeles, Rosendo Huesca Pacheco.
San Luis Potosi, Arturo A. Szymanski Ramirez.
Yucatán, Manuel Castro Ruiz.

Monaco

Monaco, Joseph-Marie Sardou.

Morocco

Rabat, Hubert Michon.
Tanger, Antonio J. Peteiro Freire.

Mozambique

Maputo, H.E. Cardinal Alexandre José Maria dos
  Santos.
Nampula, Manuel Vieira Pinto.

Netherlands

Utrecht, H.E. Cardinal Adrianus J. Simonis.

New Zealand

Wellington, H.E. Cardinal Thomas Stafford Williams.

Nicaragua

Managua, H.E. Cardinal Miguel Obando Bravo.

Nigeria

Kaduna, Peter Yariyok Jatau.
Lagos, Anthony Okogie.
Onitsha, Stephen Nweke Ezeanya.

Oceania

Agaña, Anthony Sablan Apuron.
Honiara, Adrian Thomas Smith.
Nouméa, Michel-Marie-Bernard Calvet.
Samoa, Apia and Tokelau, H.E. Cardinal Pio Taofino'u.
Suva, Petero Mataca.

Pakistan

Karachi, H.E. Cardinal Joseph Cordeiro.

Panama

Panama, Marcos Gregorio McGrath.

Papua New Guinea

Kerema, Paul John Marx.
Madang, Benedict To Varpin.
Mount Hagen, Michael Meier.
Port Moresby, Peter Kurongku.
Rabaul, Albert Bundervoet.

Paraguay

Asuncion, Ismael Blas Rolon Silvero.

Peru

Arequipa, Fernando Vargas Ruiz de Somocurcio.
Ayacucho o Huamanga, Federico Richter Fernandez-Prada.
Cuzco, Alcides Mendoza Castro.
Huancayo, Emilio Vallebuona Merea.
Lima, H.E. Cardinal Juan Landázuri Ricketts.
Piura, Oscar Rolando Cantuarias Pastor.
Trujillo, Manuel Prado Pérez-Rosas.

Philippines

Caceres, Leonardo Legazpi.
Cagayan de Oro, Jesus B. Tuquia.
Capiz, Onesimo C. Gordoncillo.
Cebu, Nome di Gesù, H.E. Cardinal Ricardo Vidal.
Cotabato, Philip Frances Smith.
Davao, Antonio Mabutas.
Jaro, Alberto J. Piamonte.
Lingayan-Dagupen, Federico G. Limon.
Lipa, Mariano Gaviola.
Manila, H.E. Cardinal Jaime L. Sin.
Nueva Segovia, Orlando Quevedo.
Ozamiz, Jesus Dosado.
Palo, Pedro R. Dean.
San Fernando, Paciano Aniceto.
Tuguegarao, Diosdado A. Talamayan.
Zamboanga, Francisco Raval Cruces.

Poland

Gniezno, H.E. Cardinal Józef Glemp. (See also Warsaw).
Kraków, H.E. Cardinal Franciszek Macharski.
Lwów, vacant.
Poznan, Jerzy Stroba.
Warsaw, H.E. Cardinal Józef Glemp.
Wroclaw, H.E. Cardinal Henryk Roman Gulbinowicz.

Portugal

Braga, Eurico Dias Nogueira.
Evora, Maurilio Jorge Quintal de Gouveia.

Puerto Rico

San Juan, H.E. Cardinal Luis Aponte Martinez.

Romania

Bucarest, vacant.

Rwanda

Kigali, Vincent Nsengiyumva.

El Salvador

San Salvador, Arturo Rivera Damas.

Senegal

Dakar, H.E. Cardinal Hyacinthe Thiandoum.

Sierra Leone

Freetown & Bo, Joseph Ganda.

Singapore

Singapore, Gregory Yong Sooi Nghean.

South Africa

Bloemfontein, Peter John Butelezi.
Cape Town, vacant.
Durban, Denis Eugene Hurley.
Pretoria, George Francis Daniel.

Spain

Barcelona, H.E. Cardinal Narciso Jubany Arnau.
Burgos, Theodoro C. Fernandez.
Granada, José Méndez Asensio.
Madrid, H.E. Cardinal Angel Suquia Goicoechea.
Oviedo, Gabino Diaz Merchán.
Pamplona, José Mariá Cirardo Lachiondo.
Santiago de Compostela, Antonio Rouco Varela.
Sevilla, Carlos Amigo Vallejo.
Tarragona, Ramon Torrella Cascante.
Toledo, H.E. Cardinal Marcelo González Martin.
Valencia, Miguel Roca Cabanellas.
Valladolid, José Delicado Baeza.
Zaragoza, Elíaz Yanez Alvarez.

Sri Lanka

Colombo, Nicholas Marcus Fernando.

Sudan

Khartoum, Gabriel Zubeir Wako.

Syria

Alep, Beroea, Halab [Greek Melekite Catholic Rite], Néophytes Edelby.
Baniyas, vacant.
Bosra, Bostra, Boulos Nassif Borkhoche.
Damascus [Greek Melekite Catholic Rite], vacant.
Hassaké-Nisibi, Georges Habib Hafouri.
Homs, Emesa [Syrian Catholic Rite], Jean Dahi.
Laodicea [Greek Melekite Catholic Rite], Michel Yatim.

Taiwan

Taipei, Joseph Ti-Kang.

Tanzania

Dar es Salaam, H.E. Cardinal Laurean Rugambwa.
Tabora, Mario E. A. Mgulunde.

Thailand

Bangkok, H.E. Cardinal Michael Michai Kitbunchu.
Tharé and Nonseng, Lawrence Khai Saen-Phon-On.

Togo

Lomé, Robert Casimir Dosseh-Anyron.

Trinidad

Port of Spain, Gordon Anthony Pantin.

Turkey

Diarbekir, Paul Karatas.
Istanbul (Constantinople), Jean Tcholakian.
Izmir, Giuseppe G. Bernardini.

Uganda

Kampala, H.E. Cardinal Emmanuel Nsubuga.

Uruguay

Montevideo, José Gottardi Cristelli.

U.S.A.

Anchorage, Francis Thomas Hurley.
Atlanta, Eugene A. Marino.
Baltimore, William Henry Keeler.
Boston, H.E. Cardinal Bernard F. Law.
Chicago, H.E. Cardinal Joseph L. Bernardin.
Cincinnati, Daniel E. Pilarczyk.
Denver, James Francis Stafford.
Detroit, H.E. Cardinal Edmund C. Szoka.
Dubuque, Daniel W. Kucera.
Hartford, John F. Whealon.
Indianapolis, Edward T. O'Meara.
Kansas City, Ignatius J. Strecker.
Los Angeles, Roger M. Mahony.
Louisville, Thomas C. Kelly.
Miami, Edward A. McCarthy.
Milwaukee, Rembert G. Weakland.

Mobile, Oscar H. Lipscomb.
Newark, Theodore E. McCarrick.
New Orleans, Francis B. Schulte.
New York, H.E. Cardinal John J. O'Connor.
Oklahoma City, Charles A. Salatka.
Omaha, Daniel E. Sheehan.
Philadelphia, Anthony J. Beuilacqua.
Pittsburgh, Stephen J. Kocisko.
Portland (Oregon), William J. Levada.
St Louis (Missouri), John L. May.
St Paul & Minneapolis, John Robert Roach.
San Antonio, Patrick F. Flores.
San Francisco, John R. Quinn.
Santa Fe, Robert F. Sanchez.
Seattle, Raymond G. Hunthausen.
Washington, H.E. Cardinal James A. Hickey.

U.S.S.R.

There is an **unnamed** Apostolic Administrator in the following Russian Dioceses: Mohilev, Moscow, Leningrad, Kharkov, Kazan, Samara and Simbirsk.

Venezuela

Barquisimeto, Julio Manuel Chirivella Varela.
Caracas, H.E. Cardinal José Ali Lebrún Moratinos.
Ciudad Bolivar, Medardo Luzardo Romero.
Maracaibo, Domingo Roa Pérez.
Mérida, Miguel Antonio Salas Salas.
Valencia, Luis Eduardo Henriquez Jiménez.

Vietnam

Hanoi, H.E. Cardinal Joseph-Marie Trinh văn Căn.
Hue, vacant.
Thanh-Phô Hôchiminh, Paul Nguyên Van Binh.

West Indies

Castries, Kelvin Edward Felix.

Yugoslavia

Bar, Petar Perkolić.
Belgrade, Franc Perko.
Ljubljana, Alojzij Suštar.
Rijeka-Senj, Josip Paulišić.
Split-Makarska, Ante Juric.
Vrhbosna, Marco Jozinović.
Zadar, Marijan Oblak.
Zagreb, H.E. Cardinal Franjo Kuharić.

Zaire

Bukavu, Mulindwa Mutabesha.
Kananga, Bakole wa Ilunga.
Kinshasa, vacant.
Kisangani, Laurent Monsengwo Pasinya.
Lubumbashi, Kabanga Songasonga.
Mbandaka-Bikoro, Etsou-Nzabi-Bamungwabi.

Zambia

Kasama, Elias Mutale.
Lusaka, Adrian Mungandu.

Zimbabwe

Harare, Patrick Chakaipa.

ARCHBISHOPS OF TITULAR SEES

Acrida, Mario Schierano.
Adana [Greek Melekite Catholic Rite]: Gregoire Haddad.
Amasya, James Patrick Carroll.
Amida, Flavien Zacharie Melkie.
Aquileia, Michele Cecchini.
Beroe, Victor Sartre.
Cadi, Stefan M. Marusyn.
Cesariana, H.E. Cardinal Angelo Felici.
Cesarea in Palaestina [Greek Melekite Catholic Rite]: Hilarion Capucci.
Claudiopolis in Honoriade, Alfredo Bruniera.
Corinthus, Gennaro Verolino.
Dara, Nicholas T. Elko.
Doclea, Pier Luigi Celata.
Drivastum, Traian Crisan.
Edessa in Osrhoëne [Greek Melekite Catholic Rite]: Pierre Rai; [Syrian Catholic Rite]: Gregoire Ephrem Jarjour.
Egina, Raffaele Forni.
Ephesus, John Henry Boccella.
Gabala, Gérard de Milleville.
Gangra, Antonio Ferreira de Macedo.
Gradum, José López Ortiz.
Hadrianopolis in Haemimonto, Lino Zanini.
Idicra, H.E. Cardinal Ferdinando Giuseppe Antonelli.
Kaškar, Emmanuel-Karim Delly.
Macra, John Dooley.
Marcianopolis, Teofilo Camomot Bastida.
Mesembria, Loris Francesco Capovilla.
Meta, Audrys J. Backis.
Nazareth, Giuseppe Carata.
Neapoli, H.E. Cardinal Jacques Martin.
Nicaea Parva, Paolino Limongi.
Nicosia, Aurelio Signora.
Novaliciana, Faustino Sainz Munoz.
Nubia, Paul Antaki.
Otriculum, Pietro Biggio.
Razia Ria, Marian Oles.
Rusellae, Lorenzo Antonetti.
Salamis, Joseph Kuo.
Scytopolis, Joseph Raya.
Selymbria, Emile Socquet.
Severiana, Luigi Bressan.
Silli, Jan Schotte.
Soteropolis, Ettore Cunial.
Tagora, H.E. Cardinal Eduardo M. Somalo.
Tarsus [Maronite Rite]: Abdallah Bared; [Greek Melekite Catholic Rite]: Loutfi Laham.
Tiburnia, Donato Squicciarini.
Velebusdo, Jose M. Estepa Llaurens.
Villamagna, Giulio Einaudi.
Viminacium, Franco Brambilla.

POPES FROM 1800

Sovereign Pontiff	Family Name	Elected
Pius VII	Chiaramonti	1800
Leo XII	della Genga	1823
Pius VIII	Castiglioni	1829
Gregory XVI	Cappellari	1831
Pius IX	Mastai-Ferretti	1846
Leo XIII	Pecci	1878
Pius X	Sarto	1903
Benedict XV	della Chiesa	1914
Pius XI	Ratti	1922

Sovereign Pontiff	Family Name	Elected
Pius XII	Pacelli	1939
John XXIII	Roncalli	1958
Paul VI	Montini	1963
John Paul I	Luciani	1978
John Paul II	Wojtyla	1978

Adrian IV (Nicholas Breakspear, the only Englishman elected Pope) was born at Langley, near St. Albans; elected Pope, on the death of Anastasius IV, 1154; died 1159.

EDUCATION IN THE UNITED KINGDOM

(For addresses of national education departments, *see* **Government and Public Offices**. For other addresses, *see* **Education Directory**.)

The Government's stated aims in education are to raise standards of achievement at all levels of ability; to increase parental choice; to secure the best possible return from the resources invested in the education service; and to widen access to further and higher education while linking them more closely to the needs of the economy. To achieve these objectives three major pieces of educational legislation have been introduced over the past three years, with similar measures proposed for Northern Ireland. Legislation is at present before Parliament for Scotland.

Recent legislation

The first of the recent measures was the Education Act 1986 which legislated for changes in the management of schools and the terms of employment of teachers.

The Education (No. 2) Act 1986 extended the legislation requiring appraisal and in-service training for teachers. It also made changes in the management and accountability of schools, introducing new arrangements for the composition of governing bodies which increase the influence of parents.

The Education Reform Act 1988 received the Royal Assent in July 1988. It provided for: the introduction of a national curriculum supported by attainment targets and systems of assessment; local education authorities to delegate control for their budgets to all secondary schools and larger primary schools; all secondary schools and the larger primary schools to have the choice to opt out of local authority control; and the establishment of City Technology Colleges and City Colleges for the Technology of the Arts.

These provisions apply to schools in England and Wales and similar measures are to be implemented for Northern Ireland. These will include: a curriculum common to all schools with six broad areas of study incorporating certain compulsory subjects; formal assessment of pupils; the provision for schools to become grant-maintained to apply to integrated schools only; the introduction of measures to facilitate the growth of integrated schools (*see* also p. 439); schools (initially secondary schools) and further education colleges to have control over their own budgets; changes to the composition of further education college boards to reflect the community served by the college.

In Scotland, the School Boards (Scotland) Act 1988 increased parental involvement in school management by instituting school boards with parent representation for state schools in Scotland. The Self-Governing Schools etc. (Scotland) Bill (expected to be enacted in October 1989) will create two new types of schools: self-governing schools, which will withdraw from local authority control although they will remain in the public sector; and Technology Academies, which will be set up in partnership with industry in deprived urban areas.

National administration of education

In the United Kingdom responsibility for education is largely decentralized. The Secretary of State for Education and Science has overall responsibility for all aspects of education in England, and for government policy and support for universities throughout Britain in consultation with the Secretaries of State for Wales and Scotland. Responsibility in Wales for nursery, primary and secondary education, and for all non-university institutions of higher and further education, the youth and community services, and adult education lies with the Secretary of State for Wales. The general supervision of the national system of education in Scotland, except for the universities, is the responsibility of the Secretary of State for Scotland acting through the Scottish Education Department. All aspects of education in Northern Ireland, schools, further education and universities, are the responsibility of the Secretary of State for Northern Ireland.

The main concerns of the education departments (the Department of Education and Science, the Welsh Office, the Scottish Education Department, and the Department of Education for Northern Ireland) are the formulation of national policies for education, and the maintenance of consistency in educational standards. They are responsible for the broad allocation of resources for education, for the rate and distribution of educational building and for the supply, training and superannuation of teachers. Hitherto, none of the education departments have run any schools or colleges directly, nor employed any teachers. However, under the provisions of the Education Reform Act 1988, the Department of Education and Science in England and Wales is to play a new role in funding individual schools which have opted out of local education authority control and applied for direct funding from the Secretary of State. In addition, the Department of Education and Science, in association with sponsors from industry, will fund the new City Technology Colleges and City Colleges for the Technology of the Arts.

Similar provisions are being introduced for Scotland under the Self-Governing Schools etc. (Scotland) Bill. This will allow schools to opt out of education authority control and be directly funded by central government. It will also provide for the institution of Technology Academies on a similar basis to City Technology Colleges in England and Wales.

Schools in Northern Ireland will be able to apply for grant-maintained status from the Department of Education for Northern Ireland only if they intend to provide integrated education.

Her Majesty's Inspectorate

Her Majesty's Inspectors (H.M.I.s) inspect state and independent schools and all other educational establishments apart from universities. H.M.I.s assess standards and trends and advise the Secretaries of State on the performance of the system in the United Kingdom. They identify and make more widely known good practice and promising developments, and draw attention to weaknesses needing consideration. They provide advice and help to those with responsibilities for, or in, the institutions through day-to-day contacts, contributions to training, and their publications. Inspection visits are the main way in which the H.M.I.s perform their functions. There were, in 1989–90, 481 H.M.I.s in England, 55 in Wales, 111 in Scotland, and 61 in Northern Ireland.

Expenditure

The Department of Education and Science (D.E.S.), the Welsh Office, the Scottish Office and the Northern Ireland Office act within a framework of estimates approved by Parliament.

In real terms expenditure on education by the Departments was as follows (£ million):

	1988–89 estimated outturn	1989–90 planned
D.E.S.	17,693	18,733
Welsh Office	939	984

S.E.D.	2,311	2,354
D.E.N.I.	823	903

In the United Kingdom in 1986–87, central government expenditure on education was apportioned as follows (£million):

Schools	465·1
Further and Higher education	1,953·3
Other education and related expenditure	220·3

Most of this expenditure is incurred by local authorities which make their own expenditure decisions according to their local situations and needs and which are also responsible for funding most further education courses. The bulk of direct expenditure by central government is by the D.E.S., which supports the universities in England, Wales and Scotland through the Universities Funding Council (U.F.C.). From April 1, 1989 the D.E.S. has also supported advanced courses in polytechnics and colleges of higher education in England through the Polytechnics and Colleges Funding Council (P.C.F.C.).

In Scotland, as in England and Wales, the bulk of expenditure on education is at a local level by the regional and islands councils. The main elements of central government expenditure are grant-aided special schools, student awards, and the capital and recurrent grants to central institutions and colleges of education.

The Department of Education for Northern Ireland finances higher education, teacher education, teacher salaries and superannuation, student awards and voluntary grammar schools. Remaining expenditure is by education and library boards at local level.

Local administration of education

The education service at present is a national service in which the provision of school education and post-school further education is locally administered and its administration is still largely decentralized.

England and Wales.—In England and Wales the education service is administered by local education authorities (L.E.A.s), which carry the day-to-day responsibility for providing state primary, secondary and some further education (but no longer advanced courses in the polytechnics and colleges of higher education) to meet the needs of their areas.

Each local education authority is required by statute to appoint an education committee, or committees, authorized to exercise on its behalf any of the authority's functions with respect to education except the power to borrow money or to raise a rate. Members of the council make up a majority of these committees, but a number of people with experience in education and knowledge of the local education situation are also included.

The L.E.A.s own and maintain schools and colleges, build new ones and provide equipment. Most of the public money spent on education is disbursed by the local authorities. L.E.A.s are financed largely from the rates and by rate support grants from the Department of the Environment in England and the Welsh Office in Wales.

The powers of local education authorities as regards the control of their schools have been modified in recent years. The Education (No. 2) Act 1986 legislated for equal numbers of parents and local authority representatives as governors in most maintained schools. This modification was continued by the Education Reform Act 1988, which delegated control of their budgets directly to secondary and larger primary schools. It also provided for schools with over 300 pupils to opt out of local authority control and to be funded directly by central government.

Scotland.—The duty of providing education locally in Scotland rests with the nine regional and three island councils. They are responsible for the construction of buildings, the employment of teachers and other staff, and the provision of equipment and materials. Their responsibility for the curricula taught in schools is delegated at the moment to individual headteachers, but discussions are taking place on the standardization of curricula to allow for new assessment procedures.

The powers of local authorities in educational institutions under their control are being reduced in Scotland as in England and Wales. Under the School Boards (Scotland) Act 1988, education authorities are required to establish school boards consisting of parents and teachers as well as co-opted members, responsible among other things for the appointment of staff. The Self-Governing Schools etc. (Scotland) Bill provides for schools to withdraw from local authority control and become self-governing; for the institution of Technology Academies directly funded by central government; and for the composition of further education college councils on which at least half the members are employers, and for the delegation of substantial functions to these new councils.

Northern Ireland.—Education is administered locally in Northern Ireland by five education and library boards. All grant-aided schools include elected parents and teachers on their boards of governors. Provision is being made for schools wishing to provide integrated education to apply for grant-maintained status and thus opt out of education authority control. It is also proposed, in line with England and Wales, to delegate the powers and responsibilities for their financial affairs to the boards of governors of schools (initially secondary schools) and colleges of further education.

SCHOOLS AND PUPILS

Schooling is compulsory in the United Kingdom for all children between 5 and 16 years. Some provision is made for children under 5 and many pupils remain at school after the minimum leaving age. No fees are charged in any publicly maintained school in England, Wales and Scotland. In Northern Ireland, however, fees are paid by pupils in preparatory departments of grammar schools, and a small number of pupils is admitted at present to grammar schools on a fee-paying basis. The latter is a consequence of the existence of a fixed quota for pupils transferring to grammar school, but as this is to be abolished by 1990, fees will no longer be appropriate.

In England, Wales and Scotland, parents have a right to express a preference for a particular school and have a right to appeal if dissatisfied. Parental choice has been increased by the introduction of a policy known as more open enrolment whereby schools are required to admit children up to the limit of their capacity if there is a demand for places.

Legislation to similar effect is also projected for Northern Ireland. However, schools may in exceptional cases seek permission from the Department of Education for Northern Ireland to enrol fewer pupils than their capacity where they consider the admission of certain pupils would not be in the pupils' best educational interests, considering the academic emphasis of the school.

Schools are now required to make available information about themselves and their examination results. Corporal punishment is no longer legal in publicly maintained schools in the United Kingdom.

Fall and rise in numbers

In primary education, and increasingly in secondary education, pupil numbers in the United Kingdom have declined. In primary schools pupil numbers peaked at around 5·6 million in the early 1970s and reached their lowest figure of 3·9 million in 1987. However, numbers are expected to increase gradually year by year until by 1998 they reach about 4·7 million. In secondary schools pupil numbers rose from 3·5 million in 1971 to 4·6 million in 1981. They are projected to decrease to 3·4 million in 1991, before rising to 3·6 million in 1998.

England and Wales

There are two main categories of school in England and Wales: those maintained by local education authorities (25,458), which charge no fees; and independent schools (2,340), which charge fees (*see* p. 440). To these categories may be added two more as a result of the Education Reform Act 1988, consisting of institutions funded directly by the Secretary of State. These comprise primary and secondary schools with over 300 pupils which, although still providing free education, have applied to opt out of local education authority control in favour of grant-maintained status; and City Technology Colleges (*see* below).

Maintained schools.—These are of two types: (i) county schools (17,592 in 1988) which are owned by L.E.A.s and wholly funded by them. They are non-denominational and provide primary and secondary education; (ii) voluntary schools (7,866 in 1988) which also provide primary and secondary education. Although the buildings are in many cases provided by the voluntary bodies (mainly religious denominations) they are financially maintained by an L.E.A.

All publicly maintained schools have a governing body usually made up of an equal number of parent representatives and governors appointed by the L.E.A., the headteacher (unless he or she chooses otherwise), and serving teachers. Parental involvement in the running of their children's schools has increased considerably in recent years, and parents have also been given the power to decide by ballot whether their child's school should opt out of local authority control. The responsibilities of governors under the Education (No. 2) Act 1986 were extended to cover the overall policies of schools and their academic aims and objectives. The governors also now control matters of school discipline and the appointment and dismissal of staff. The Education Reform Act 1988 delegated control of the administration of the major part of school budgets, including staffing costs, from L.E.A.s directly to the larger primary and secondary schools.

Voluntary schools are of three kinds: controlled (3,246), aided (4,528) and special agreement (85). In *controlled* schools the L.E.A. bears all costs. In *aided* schools the building is usually provided by the voluntary body. The managers or governors are responsible for repairs to the outside of the school building and for improvements and alterations to it, though the Department of Education and Science may reimburse part of approved capital expenditure. The L.E.A. pays for internal maintenance and other running costs. *Special agreement* schools are those where the L.E.A. may, by special agreement, pay between one-half and three-quarters of the cost of building a new, or extending an existing, voluntary school, almost always a secondary school. There are no special agreement schools in Wales. In voluntary schools the majority of the managers or governors are appointed by the voluntary body and at least one by the L.E.A. The managers or governors control the appointment of teachers. Expenditure is normally apportioned between the authority and the voluntary body.

City Technology Colleges (C.T.C.s) and City Colleges for the Technology of the Arts (C.C.T.A.s).—These schools are state-aided but independent of L.E.A.s. Their aim is to widen the choice of secondary education in disadvantaged urban areas and to teach a broad curriculum with an emphasis on science, technology, business understanding and arts technologies. Capital costs will be shared by government and sponsors from industry and commerce, and running costs will be covered by a per capita grant from the D.E.S. in line with comparable costs in an L.E.A. maintained school. The first city technology college opened in September 1988 in Solihull. By September 1990 there will be five: Nottingham and Teesside (opening September 1989), Middlesbrough, Bradford and Gateshead. The first C.C.T.A. will open in Croydon in 1990.

Scotland

Schools in Scotland fall into three main categories: (a) *education authority* schools (3,773) (known as public schools) which are financed and managed by the regional and islands councils; (b) *grant aided* schools (19), conducted by voluntary managers who receive grants direct from the Scottish Education Department; and (c) *independent* schools (153), which receive no direct grant and charge fees, but are subject to inspection and registration. An additional category would arise under the provisions of the Self Governing Schools etc. (Scotland) Bill, of schools opting to be managed entirely by a board of management consisting of the headmaster, parent and staff representatives and co-opted members. The change of status would require a ballot of parents and the publication of proposals by the board, and the achievement of self-government would be subject to a final decision by the Secretary of State. These schools would remain in the public sector and would be funded by direct government grant set to match the resources the school would have received under education authority management.

Under the School Boards (Scotland) Act 1988, education authorities are required to establish school boards to participate in the administration and management of schools. These boards consist of elected parents and staff members as well as co-opted members.

Technology Academies.—The Self-Governing Schools etc. (Scotland) Bill provides for setting up technology academies in areas of urban deprivation. These secondary schools are intended to be so placed as to draw on a wide catchment, and will offer a broad curriculum with an emphasis on science and technology. They are to be founded and managed in partnership with industrial sponsors, with central government meeting the running costs by grant-aid thereafter.

Northern Ireland

There are three main categories of grant-aided school in Northern Ireland: (a) *controlled* schools (701), which are controlled by the education and library boards with all costs paid from public funds; (b) *voluntary* schools (592), mainly under Roman Catholic management, which receive grants towards capital costs and running costs in whole or in part; and (c) *voluntary grammar* schools (59), which may be under Roman Catholic or non-denominational management and receive grants from the Department of Education for Northern Ireland. All grant-aided schools include elected parents and teachers on their boards of governors. There are also 12 independent schools in Northern Ireland.

An attempt is being made to encourage the integrated education of Protestant and Roman Catholic pupils in Northern Ireland by the introduction of legislation which may include provision for the setting up of an independent body assisted by public funds to help achieve this end. At present integrated education is provided by a small number of schools supported in part by charitable trusts. Provision is to be made for other schools to opt for grant-maintained integrated status (G.M.I.S), with financial help available in their early stages and priority given to capital projects to provide additional pupil places at such schools.

THE STATE SYSTEM

Nursery education.—Nursery education is for children from 2 to 5 years and is not compulsory. In the United Kingdom it takes place in nursery schools or nursery classes in primary schools. In January 1987, 680,700 pupils under 5 years of age were receiving education in maintained nursery and primary schools, an increase of 10,000 on the previous year. Of the total, 97,100 were in nursery schools, 537,400 in nursery classes in primary schools, and 37,000 in non-maintained nursery schools. Expressed as a percentage of the population aged 3 and 4 years, the 680,700 represented 47·6 per cent, compared to 46·7 per cent in the previous year.

Many children also attend pre-school playgroups organized by parents and voluntary bodies such as the Pre-School Playgroups Association.

Primary education.—Primary education begins at 5 years and is almost always co-educational. In England, Wales and Northern Ireland the transfer to secondary school is generally made at 11 years. In Scotland, the primary school course lasts for seven years and pupils transfer to secondary courses at about the age of 12.

Primary schools consist mainly of *infants' schools* for children aged 5 to 7, *junior schools* for those aged 7 to 11, and combined *junior and infant schools* for both age groups. In addition, *first schools* in some parts of England cater for ages 5 to 8, 9 or 10. (They are the first stage of a three-tier system: first, middle and secondary). Many primary schools provide nursery classes for children under 5 (*see* above).

The number of primary schools in the United Kingdom in 1987 was 24,609, which was 147 less than in 1986, with 4,567,000 full- and part-time pupils, of which 731,000 were under five. Between 1987 and 1994 primary school pupil numbers are projected to rise by 8·5 per cent.

Pupil teacher ratios in maintained primary schools in the United Kingdom are:

	1986	1987
England	22·1	22·0
Wales	22·1	22·0
Scotland	20·4	20·3
N. Ireland	23·4	23·5
U.K.	22·0	21·9

The average size of classes "as taught" has risen slightly from 25·5 in 1981 to 25·8 in 1987.

Middle schools.—Middle schools (which take children from first schools), mostly in England, cover varying age ranges between 8 and 14 and usually lead on to comprehensive upper schools.

Secondary education.—Secondary schools are for children aged 11 to 16 and for those who choose to stay on to 18. At 16, many students prefer to move on to tertiary or sixth form colleges (*see* p. 444). Most secondary schools in England, Wales and Scotland are co-educational. The largest secondary schools

have over 2,000 pupils but only 24·4 per cent of the schools take over 1,000 pupils.

In England and Wales the main types of secondary schools are: (a) *comprehensive* schools (85·8 per cent of pupils in England, 98·5 in Wales), whose admission arrangements are without reference to ability or aptitude; (b) *middle deemed secondary* schools for children aged variously between 8–14 years who then move on to senior comprehensive schools at 12, 13 or 14 (6·5 per cent of pupils in England, 0·1 per cent in Wales); (c) *secondary modern* schools (4·1 per cent of pupils in England, 0·6 per cent in Wales) providing a general education with a practical bias; (d) *secondary grammar* schools (3·1 per cent of pupils in England, 0·5 per cent in Wales) with selective intake providing an academic course from 11 to 16–18 years; and (e) *technical* schools (0·5 per cent) in England only providing an integrated academic and technical education.

In January 1987 there were in England and Wales 3,450,000 pupils in maintained secondary schools, including 62 per cent (England) and 63 per cent (Wales) who were 16 or over. After falling by 12 per cent between 1987 and 1991, numbers are projected to rise until 1998 by 8·7 per cent.

Pupil-teacher ratios have improved steadily from 16·6 in 1980–81 to 15·4 in 1988 in England and Wales. A steady annual decrease in class sizes in England resumed after a rise in 1985 (to 21·4); from to 20·9 in 1984 to 20·7 in 1988. In Wales the average class size in 1988 was 19·1.

In Scotland over 99 per cent of pupils in education authority secondary schools attend schools with a comprehensive intake. Most of these schools provide a full range of courses appropriate to all levels of ability from first to sixth year. In 1986–87 there were 327,700 pupils in education authority schools, of whom 54 per cent were 16 or over. Numbers are not expected to increase much between 1990 and 1995. Pupil-teacher ratios have improved from 14·4 in 1980–81 to 13·0 in 1988. The average class size in 1987 was 18·8.

In Northern Ireland entry at 11–12 years of age to a secondary (intermediate) school or grammar school is selective in most areas. However, the present transfer procedure is to be abolished. In future the type of secondary school to which a pupil transfers will normally be a matter of choice by parents, after consultation with primary teachers, and based on the information contained in the pupil's record of achievement. Grammar schools provide an academic type of secondary education with A-levels at the end of the seventh year, while secondary (intermediate) schools follow a curriculum suited to aptitudes and abilities leading to GCSE examinations.

In 1986–87 there were 109,000 pupils in public sector secondary schools, of whom 90,000 (88·5 per cent) attended secondary intermediate and 12,000 (11·5 per cent) attended grammar schools. Of these 63 per cent were 16 or over. Pupil-teacher ratios in Northern Ireland have improved from 15·2 in 1982 to 14·5 in 1988.

Special education.—Special education is provided for children with special educational needs, usually because they have a disability which either prevents or hinders them from making use of educational facilities of a kind generally provided for children of their age in schools within the area of the local authority concerned. Maintained special schools are run by education authorities which pay all the costs of maintenance. Non-maintained special schools are run by voluntary bodies; they may receive some grant from central government for capital expenditure and for equipment, but their current expenditure is met primarily from the fees charged to the education authorities for pupils placed in the schools. Some independent schools provide education wholly or mainly for children with special educational needs. The national curriculum also applies to children with a statement of special needs, but there is provision for them to be exempt from it, or for it to be modified to suit the individual child's capabilities.

In January 1987 in the United Kingdom there was a total of 120,400 full-time pupils in special schools (of whom 3,200 were in hospital schools). Of this total, 104,200 were in England, 4,000 in Wales, 9,800 in Scotland and 2,500 in Northern Ireland. Numbers have gone down since 1975–76 as education authorities in England, Wales and Northern Ireland must now ensure that children with special needs are educated as far as possible in ordinary schools with support teaching.

In Scotland, school placing is a matter of agreement between education authorities and parents. Parents have the right to say which school they want their child to attend, and a right of appeal where their wishes are not being met. Whenever possible, children with special needs are integrated into ordinary schools. However, for those who require a different environment or specialized facilities, there are special schools, both grant-aided and independent, and special classes within ordinary schools. The Self-Governing Schools etc. (Scotland) Bill will oblige education authorities to respond to reasonable requests for independent special schools, and provides for them to send children with special needs to schools outside Scotland if appropriate provision is not available within the country.

Alternative provision

There is no legal obligation on parents in the United Kingdom to educate their children at school provided that the local education authority is satisfied that the child is receiving full-time education suited to its age, abilities and aptitudes. The education authority need not be informed that a child is being educated at home unless the child is already registered at a state school. In this case the parents must arrange for the child's name to be removed from the school's register (by writing to the headteacher) before education at home can begin. Failure to deregister a child would leave the parents liable to prosecution for condoning non-attendance.

In most cases an initial visit is made by an education adviser or education welfare officer, and sometimes subsequent inspections are made, but practice varies according to the individual education authority. There is no requirement for parents educating their children at home to be in possession of a teaching qualification.

Further advice on educating children other than at school can be obtained from Education Otherwise.

INDEPENDENT SCHOOLS

Independent schools receive no grants from public funds. They charge fees, and are owned and managed under special trusts, with profits being used for the benefit of the schools concerned. There is a wide variety of provision, from kindergartens to large day and boarding schools, and from experimental schools to traditional institutions. A number of independent schools have been instituted recently by religious and ethnic minorities.

All independent schools in the United Kingdom are open to inspection by H.M. Inspectors (*see* above) and must register with the appropriate government education department. The education departments lay down certain minimum standards and can make schools remedy any unacceptable features of their building or instruction and exclude any unsuitable teacher or proprietor. Most independent schools offer a similar range of courses to state schools and enter pupils for the same public examinations.

The term public schools is often applied to those independent schools in membership of the Headmasters' Conference, the Governing Bodies Association or the Governing Bodies of Girls' Schools Association. Most public schools are single-sex (about half of them for girls) but there are some mixed schools and an increasing number of boys' schools admit girls to their sixth forms.

Preparatory schools are so called because they prepare children for the Common Entrance Examination to senior independent schools. Most cater for boys from about 7 to 13 years, but some are for girls and an increasing number are co-educational. The Common Entrance Examination is set by the Common Entrance Examination Board, but marked by the independent school to which the pupil intends to go. It is taken at 13 by boys, and from 11 to 13 by girls.

In 1988 there were in England 2,273 independent schools with 522,949 full-time pupils and a pupil-teacher ratio of 11·3.

In Wales in 1987–88 there were 67 independent schools, with 11,788 pupils and a pupil-teacher ratio of 10·3.

In Scotland in 1987–88 there were 153 registered independent schools with 35,200 pupils. Most independent schools in Scotland follow the English examination system, i.e. GCSE followed by A-levels, although some take the Scottish Education Certificate at Ordinary/Standard grade followed by Highers.

There are 12 independent schools in Northern Ireland with 901 pupils and a pupil-teacher ratio of 14·0.

Assisted Places Scheme

The Assisted Places Scheme enables children to attend independent secondary schools which their parents could not otherwise afford. The scheme provides help with tuition fees and other expenses, except boarding costs, on a sliding scale depending on the family's income. The take-up rate for places available at age 11 to 13 at the 286 participating schools in England and Wales is over 90 per cent, and the proportion of pupils receiving full fee remission is 40 per cent. Some 34,000 places were offered in England and Wales in the academic year 1988–89. The 40 participating schools in Scotland admitted 2,670 pupils on the scheme, which, unlike that in England and Wales, is cash-limited. The proportion of pupils receiving full fee remission is 49 per cent.

The scheme is administered and funded in England by the Department of Education and Science, in Wales by the Welsh Office, and in Scotland by the Scottish Education Department.

The scheme does not operate in Northern Ireland as the independent sector admits non-fee paying pupils. There is, however, a similar scheme known as the Talented Children's Scheme to help pupils gifted in music and dance.

Further information can be obtained from the Independent Schools Information Service.

THE CURRICULUM
England and Wales

Headteachers in England and Wales are responsible for determining the curriculum in their schools with due reference to their local education authority and their school governors. The Education Reform Act 1988 legislated for the progressive introduction from autumn 1989 of a national curriculum in primary and secondary schools. During the period of compulsory schooling for children aged 5 to 16 the curriculum will include mathematics, English and science as core subjects; and history, geography, technology, music, art, physical education and (for pupils in secondary schools) a modern foreign language as foundation subjects. For the core and foundation subjects there will be attainment targets and assessment procedures at the ages of 7, 11, 14 and 16, when the GCSE will be the main form of assessment. It is intended that pupils with special educational needs should have access to as much of the national curriculum as possible. Religious education is required to be available in schools, with the curriculum devised locally, but parents will have the right to remove their children if they wish.

In Wales the Welsh language is used as the main or secondary medium of instruction in many schools. Following the introduction of the national curriculum it will constitute a core subject in Welsh-speaking schools and a foundation subject in the others.

In England the National Curriculum Council, funded by the Department of Education and Science, is responsible for the promotion and support of curriculum development in addition to advising the Secretary of State on the national curriculum. In Wales this function is performed by the Curriculum Council for Wales, funded by the Welsh Office.

Scotland

The content and management of the curriculum in Scotland is the responsibility of education authorities and individual headteachers. Advice and guidance is provided by the Scottish Education Department and the Scottish Consultative Council on the Curriculum. Scotland effectively has a national curriculum for 14–16 year-olds, who are required to study English, mathematics and a science subject plus five other subjects. These form the core area, supplemented by other activities forming the elective area. There is a recommended percentage of class time to be devoted to each area over the two years. Provision is made for teaching in Gaelic in Gaelic-speaking areas.

The Scottish Consultative Council on the Curriculum, which is responsible for development and advisory work on the curriculum in Scotland, has been asked to undertake a major review of the balance of the primary curriculum, and to produce new guidelines for each of the subject areas for the age group 5–14. There will be new guidelines on assessment across the whole curriculum, and standardized tests will be introduced in English and mathematics for 9 and 12 year-olds. For 16–18 year-olds, there is available a modular system of vocational courses in addition to academic courses.

Northern Ireland

Major programmes of curriculum review and development are in progress in primary and secondary schools. A curriculum common to all schools is to be introduced, with six broad areas of study within which certain subjects will be compulsory; religious education will also be a compulsory part of the curriculum. All secondary school pupils will be obliged to study a European language, and the Irish language will be available as an additional modern language (broadly equivalent to the position of Welsh in schools in Wales) alongside the six areas of study. Arrangements for the assessment of pupils, broadly in line with those in England and Wales, are proposed at the ages of 8, 11, 14 and 16.

The Northern Ireland Curriculum Council advises the Government on all matters concerning the curriculum for grant-aided schools in Northern Ireland.

Records of achievement

Records of achievement are documents which set down the range of pupils' achievements and activities both inside and outside the classroom, including those not tested by examination. They are intended to inform potential employers and others about achievement, and it is proposed that by the mid-1990s all secondary school pupils in England and Wales should be provided with records of achievement on leaving school at 16+. There is a similar commitment for Northern Ireland.

Technical and Vocational Initiative

The Technical and Vocational Initiative (TVEI) operates across the curriculum within a framework of general education. It is intended to make the secondary curriculum more relevant to adult life and work. Following pilot projects, it is now a national scheme with newly established criteria which complement and are compatible with the requirements of the new national curriculum in England and Wales. Participation is voluntary, and is open to all maintained schools and colleges providing for young people of all abilities aged 14–18. TVEI is not an examination or a qualification.

THE EXAMINATION SYSTEM
England, Wales and Northern Ireland

Until the end of 1987 secondary school pupils at the end of compulsory schooling around the age of 16, and others, took the General Certificate of Education (G.C.E.) Ordinary-level or the Certificate of Secondary Education (C.S.E.). From 1988 these were replaced by a single system of examinations, the General Certificate of Secondary Education (GCSE), which is usually taken after five years of secondary education. The first examinations took place in summer 1988.

The GCSE differs from its predecessors in that there are: syllabuses based on national criteria covering course objectives, content and assessment methods; differentiated assessment (i.e. different papers or questions for different ranges of ability); and grade-related criteria (i.e. grades awarded on absolute rather than relative performance).

The GCSE certificates are awarded on a seven point scale, A to G. Grades A to C are the equivalent of the corresponding O-level grades A to C, or C.S.E. grade 1. Grades D, E, F and G record achievement at least as high as that represented by C.S.E. grades 2 to 5. There is no restriction on entry to any examination. All GCSE syllabuses, assessments and grading procedures are monitored by the School Examinations and Assessment Council (*see* below) to ensure that they conform to the national criteria.

Of school leavers in the United Kingdom who left school without A-levels or SCE H-grades in 1986–87, 37 per cent had achieved one or more graded G.C.E. O-level, C.S.E. or SCE O-grade results, compared to 24 per cent in 1980–81.

Certificate of Extended Education.—The Certificate of Extended Education (C.E.E.) comprises a number of single-subject examinations set and awarded by a number of GCSE examining boards and taken a year after GCSE. Apart from English and mathematics, subjects are non-traditional and include social, environmental, technological, business and health studies.

Advanced levels and Advanced Supplementary levels.—Advanced (A-level) examinations, taken by those who choose to continue their education two years after GCSE, continue as before although changes have been made to the grading system.

A-level courses last two years, and have traditionally provided the foundation for entry to higher education. A-levels are marked on a seven point scale, from A to E, N (narrow failure) and U (unclassified), which latter grade will not be certificated.

As an alternative and a complement to A-level examinations, Advanced Supplementary level (AS-level) examinations were introduced in September 1987, with the first examinations taking place in summer 1989. AS-levels are for full-time A-level students but also open to other students. An AS-level syllabus covers not less than half the amount of ground covered by the corresponding A-level syllabus and, where possible, is related to it. An AS-level course lasts two years and requires not less than half the teaching time of the corresponding A-level course, and two AS-levels are equivalent to one A-level. AS-level courses are intended to supplement and broaden A-level studies, and examinations are held at the same time as A-levels. AS-level passes are graded A to E, with grade standards related to the A-level grades.

A mixture of A-level courses in the subjects to be specialized in and AS-levels will form the standard for admission to higher education.

In the United Kingdom in 1986–87, 23 per cent of all 17 year olds (22 per cent of boys, 24 per cent of girls) achieved one or more A-level or SCE H-grade result, compared to 20 per cent in 1980–81. This figure includes those continuing their education in maintained further education establishments including tertiary colleges, as well as school leavers.

Of school leavers alone (442,000), 18·2 per cent achieved at least one A-level or SCE H-grade (18·0 per cent of boys, 18·5 per cent of girls). Of those in Great Britain obtaining two or more A-levels, or three or more SCE H-grades, 26 per cent studied sciences (36 per cent of boys, 16 per cent of girls), 39 per cent studied arts/social studies (30 per cent of boys, 39 per cent of girls), and 35 per cent (35 per cent of boys, 35 per cent of girls) studied science and arts/social studies.

S-levels.—Most examining boards allow the option of an additional paper of greater difficulty to be taken by A-level candidates to obtain what is known as a Special-level or Scholarship-level qualification. S-level papers are available in most of the traditional academic subjects and are marked on a three point scale, grade A or 1, grade B or 2, and unclassified.

Co-ordination and advisory body.—The School Examinations and Assessment Council (SEAC) has been set up to advise the Government on all school examinations and assessment matters in England and Wales. It is also responsible for the development of the assessment system for the national curriculum. The Council is funded wholly by the Department of Education and Science.

The Certificate of Pre-Vocational Education.—The Certificate of Pre-Vocational Education (CPVE) is a one-year full-time (or two years part-time) course available at schools and colleges in England, Wales and Northern Ireland. It is intended for a wide ability range at 16+, including pupils who might not go on to A-levels but would like to continue their education on completion of their secondary schooling. The qualification is offered by the Business and Technician Training Council and the City and Guilds of London Institute operating together as the Joint Board for Pre-Vocational Education.

There are no formal examinations but credits for work achieved during CPVE can be built up towards further study. Within guidelines laid down by the Board, schools and colleges design their own courses, which stress activity-based learning, basic numeracy and work experience. The CPVE is mainly for those who want to find out what aptitudes they may have

and to prepare themselves for work, but who are not yet committed to a particular occupation.

Scotland

The system of public examinations in Scotland is different from that in the rest of the United Kingdom. At the end of the fourth year of secondary education (equivalent to the fifth year in the rest of the United Kingdom), at about the age of 16, pupils take either the Ordinary grade of the Scottish Certificate of Education Examination (corresponding to the old G.C.E. Ordinary level) or the Standard grade. The Ordinary grade is gradually being replaced by the new Standard grade courses and examinations, which have been designed to suit every level of ability, with assessment against nationally determined standards of performance.

For most courses there are three separate examination papers at the end of the two-year Standard grade course. They are set at Credit (leading to awards at grade 1 or 2), General (leading to awards at grade 3 or 4) and Foundation (leading to awards at grade 5 or 6) levels. Grade 7 is available to those who, although they have completed the course, have shown no significant level of attainment. Normally pupils will take examinations covering two pairs of grades, either grades 1–4 or grades 3–6.

Pupils may attempt as many of a wide range of subjects as they are capable of, on either the Ordinary/Standard grades, or on the Higher grade which is normally taken one year after Ordinary/Standard grades, at the age of 17 or thereabouts. The shorter length of course means that Higher grades are normally studied to a lesser depth than Advanced levels; on the other hand it is common for pupils to be presented for four or more Higher grades at a single diet of the examination.

The Certificate of Sixth Year Studies (CSYS) is designed to give direction and purpose to sixth-year work by encouraging pupils who have completed their main subjects at Higher grade to study a maximum of three of these subjects in depth. Pupils may also use the sixth year to gain improved or additional Higher grades or Ordinary/Standard grades.

The Scottish Certificate of Education Examination and the Certificate of Sixth Year Studies are conducted by the Scottish Examination Board.

National Certificate.—The National Certificate was introduced in 1984–85 as an alternative or complement to Highers and CSYS. It is awarded to pupils over the age of 16 who have successfully completed a programme of vocational courses based on modular study units. It replaces the profusion of courses and certificates available in non-advanced further education, and the assessment system is based on national criteria. The modules are now being introduced in schools for pupils aged 14–16, and other short courses are being devised for use in schools. The National Certificate is validated by the Scottish Vocational Education Council (*see* also p. 444).

The International Baccalaureate

The International Baccalaureate is an internationally recognized two-year pre-university course and examination designed to facilitate the mobility of students and to promote international understanding. Candidates must offer one subject from each of six subject groups, at least three at higher level and the remainder at subsidiary level. Single subjects can be offered, for which a certificate is received. There are 17 schools and colleges in the United Kingdom which offer the International Baccalaureate diploma. Further information can be obtained from International Baccalaureate London.

TEACHERS
England and Wales

Teachers are appointed by local education authorities, school governing bodies, or school managers. Those in publicly maintained schools must be approved as "qualified" by the Department of Education and Science. To become a qualified teacher it is necessary to have successfully completed a course of initial teacher training. Teacher training is largely integrated with the rest of higher education, with training places concentrated in universities, polytechnics and institutes or colleges of education.

With certain exceptions the profession now has an all-graduate entry. Teachers in further education are not required to have qualified teacher status, though roughly half have a teaching qualification and most have industrial, commercial or professional experience.

A licensed teacher scheme has been introduced to attract into the teaching profession mature entrants without formal teaching qualifications but with relevant training and experience. All licensees will be required to have the equivalent of two years higher education in the United Kingdom in addition to the equivalent of grade C in GCSE maths and English. Local education authorities will be involved in devising a suitable training programme for any licensed teachers they may appoint to their schools; for grant-maintained schools and City Technology Colleges this will be a matter for the school itself.

Scotland

All teachers in maintained schools must be registered with the General Teaching Council for Scotland. They are registered provisionally for a two-year probationary period which can be extended if necessary. Only graduates are accepted as entrants to the teaching profession in Scotland.

Northern Ireland

Teacher training in Northern Ireland is provided by the two universities and two colleges of education. The colleges are concerned with teacher education mainly for the primary school sector. They also provide B.Ed. courses for intending secondary school teachers of religious education, commercial studies, and craft, design and technology. With these exceptions, the training of teachers for secondary schools is provided in the education departments of the universities.

Accreditation of training courses

The Council for the Accreditation of Teacher Education (CATE) has been reviewing all initial teacher training courses in England, Wales and Northern Ireland to ensure that they meet stringent conditions. In Scotland all training courses in colleges of education must be approved by the Scottish Education Department and a validating body.

Newly-trained teachers

Of teachers who in 1986 had successfully completed initial training courses in the United Kingdom, 8,600 had completed a postgraduate course and 7,000 a course for non-graduates.

In the year to January 1987, 11,467 teachers took up first full-time appointments, either permanently or for at least one term's duration, in maintained nursery, primary and secondary schools in England and Wales. In Scotland and Northern Ireland, figures for 1989 were 642 and 505 respectively.

Shortage subjects.—In recent years there have been shortages of teachers in a number of secondary subjects, particularly mathematics, the physical sciences, chemistry, and craft, design and technology. There is a tax-free bursary scheme worth £1,300 a year for trainee teachers in these four shortage areas for one- or two-year courses.

Serving teachers

In 1986–87 there were 620,000 teachers (full-time and full-time equivalent) in public sector schools and establishments of further education in the United Kingdom. Of these, 502,000 were in maintained schools and 117,000 in further education. There were 203,000 full-time teachers in public sector primary schools, 260,000 in public sector secondary schools and 19,000 in special schools.

In-service training of teachers.—A new scheme, known as INSET, was launched in 1987 for the in-service training of teachers and others employed in the education service. In 1988–89 local education authorities were planning to devote £280 million to the scheme.

Salaries

All qualified teachers in England, Wales and Northern Ireland other than heads and deputy heads, are paid on an 11 point scale ranging from £8,394 to £14,696. Entry points vary depending on qualification and according to the discretion of the appointing authority. In addition, incentive allowances are payable on a range of five rates. Headteachers' salaries range from £17,369 to £34,183, depending on the size of the school; deputy headteachers' salaries range from £16,555 to £24,932. There is a statutory superannuation scheme in maintained schools.

Teachers in Scotland are paid (1989 figures) on a ten point scale from £9,033 to £15,012. As in the rest of the United Kingdom, the entry point depends on type of qualification, and additional allowances are payable under certain circumstances. Headteachers are paid on a scale from £16,935 to £31,047 and depute headteachers from £17,781 to £23,706 depending on the size of school roll.

FURTHER EDUCATION

The term further education is sometimes loosely used for all post-compulsory education. However, the Education Reform Act 1988 defines it as all provision outside schools to people aged over 16 of an education up to and including A-level and its equivalent. All education authorities have a duty to secure provision for adequate facilities for further education in their area.

England and Wales

Responsibility for co-ordinating further education provision rests with ten **Regional Advisory Councils** set up by the local education authorities (L.E.A.s) in each region. There are nine for England, and the Welsh Joint Committee acts as the council for Wales. The councils operate in accordance with terms of reference agreed between the participating L.E.A.s, which meet staffing and other expenses. Members include representatives from L.E.A.s, polytechnics and universities, further education institutions, employers and employees in industry and commerce. H.M. Inspectors attend as assessors.

In England and Wales further education courses are taught at a variety of institutions. These range from polytechnics and colleges of further and higher education (most of which also offer higher education courses) to tertiary colleges and sixth form colleges, which concentrate on the provision of normal sixth form school courses as well as a range of vocational courses. A number of institutions specific to a particular form of training, e.g. the Royal College of Music, are also involved. All such courses are funded by local education authorities, with the exception of further education courses in polytechnics and colleges of higher education up to the end of the academic year 1989-90 (*see* also p. 447).

Every institution maintained by a local education authority and providing full-time further education under a further education scheme is required to appoint a board of governors. At least half the governors must represent employment interests or be people who are independent of local authority or college interests. Local authorities must delegate to these bodies extensive powers over the management of college budgets and the appointment of staff.

The position of teaching staff in further education establishments is similar to that in schools with respect to qualifications and regular appraisal of teachers' performance.

Much of the post-school provision outside the higher education sector is broadly vocational in purpose. It extends from lower level technical and commercial courses through advanced courses for those aiming at higher level posts in industry, commerce and administration, to professional courses. Facilities for GCSE courses, C.E.E. (Certificate of Extended Education), CPVE (Certificate of Pre-Vocational Education), AS-levels and A-level courses are also provided (*see* pp. 441–2). These courses are designated *non-advanced* further education, and can form the foundation for progress to *advanced* courses or courses of higher education (*see* below).

The main courses and examinations in the vocational field are offered by the following bodies, but there are also many others:

Business and Technician Education Council (BTEC) provides awards across a wide range of subject areas and three main qualifications, two at non-advanced and one at advanced level. Of the non-advanced courses, the BTEC First Certificate can be taken over one year part-time and the BTEC First Diploma over one year full-time or two years part-time. Neither requires any formal academic qualifications for entry. The BTEC National Certificate is taken over two years part-time and the BTEC National Diploma over two years full-time or over three years part-time or as a sandwich course. Both require certain academic qualifications for entry.

City and Guilds of London Institute (C.&G.) provides a variety of technical and vocational courses mostly lasting one or two years. Most C.&G. courses are part-time for students already in employment, but some full-time courses are available.

The City and Guilds of London Institute and the Business and Technician Education Council, operating together as the **Joint Board for Pre-Vocational Education**, are responsible for administering the Certificate of Pre-Vocational Education (*see* p. 442).

RSA (Royal Society of Arts) Examinations Board schemes cover the whole range of business and administrative occupations, plus language schemes and teacher qualifications. Many of the courses are offered at levels 1 to 3 along the lines drawn up by the NCVQ (*see* below). There are no set entry requirements and a policy of credit accumulation, so candidates can take a single certificate or complete qualifications.

There are 516 further education establishments in England and Wales with 2,632 adult education centres. In 1987–88 there were 375,686 full-time and sandwich students and 718,962 part-time students on non-advanced vocational courses of further education.

Scotland

Education authorities in Scotland provide further education comprising non-advanced courses up to S.C.E. Highers grade, G.C.E. A-level and SCOTVEC vocational courses. Courses are taught mainly at colleges of further education, including technical colleges, and in some schools.

Legislation is currently going through Parliament which will: ensure that at least half the members of further education college councils are employers; require education authorities to delegate substantial functions to the new councils; allow colleges to earn income from commercial activities and to be incorporated as companies with the agreement of the education authority and the Secretary of State.

The Scottish Vocational Education Council (SCOTVEC) provides national qualifications, known as the National Certificate, across a similar range of occupational sectors to the Business and Technician Education Council in England and Wales. The system is completely comprehensive and covers the whole range of non-advanced further education provision in Scotland. Students may study for the National Certificate on a full-time, part-time, or day- or block-release basis. The system is based on modules and National Certificate modules and modular programmes can be taken in further education colleges, central institutions or in secondary schools from the age of 16 onwards.

In 1986–87 there were 51,978 full-time and sandwich students, 132,992 part-time students on non-advanced vocational courses of further education in the 50 further education colleges, 12 central institutions and five colleges of education.

Northern Ireland

Education and library boards are obliged to prepare and submit for approval to the Department of Education for Northern Ireland, schemes setting out the principles to be applied by the boards in planning the further education provision to be made by colleges under their management.

Although the colleges of further education are maintained by the education and library boards, proposals along the lines of those in England and Wales are to be implemented for the delegation of financial powers and responsibilities to the boards of governors of the colleges. The composition of the boards themselves is to be changed to include 50 per cent membership from the professions, local business or industry, or other fields of employment relevant to the activities of the college.

On reaching school-leaving age, pupils may attend colleges of further education to pursue the same type of vocational courses as are provided in colleges in England and Wales, administered by the same examining bodies.

Northern Ireland has 26 institutions of further education with 231 out-centres. In 1986–87 there were 15,178 full-time students and 35,794 part-time students on non-advanced vocational courses of further education.

Applications for further education courses are generally made directly to the colleges concerned.

Information on further education courses in the United Kingdom and addresses of colleges can be found in the *Directory of Further Education* published annually by the Careers Research and Advisory Council.

National Council for Vocational Qualifications

The National Council for Vocational Qualifications (NCVQ) was set up by the Government in October 1986 to achieve a coherent national framework for vocational qualifications. The Council will not award qualifications but will work with and through the established examining and awarding bodies to reform the existing vocational qualifications system and introduce simplified arrangements. The new system should be fully operational in England, Wales and Northern Ireland by 1991. It does not apply to Scotland, where a reformed framework already exists under the SCOTVEC National Certificate (*see* below).

The name and style *National Vocational Qualification* will be accorded to qualifications accredited by NCVQ and awarded by bodies it has approved. The N.V.Q. framework is currently based on four levels incorporating qualifications up to and including the Higher National standard.

A *National Record of Vocational Achievement* has been introduced which allows small elements of competence acquired at different times and in different ways to be recorded in a standard form and to be built up into a full N.V.Q.

Further information can be obtained from the National Council for Vocational Qualifications.

HIGHER EDUCATION

The term higher education is used to describe education above A-level and Higher grade or their equivalent, which is provided in universities and on advanced courses in polytechnics and colleges of higher education.

The Education Reform Act 1988 legislated for important changes in the structure, national planning and funding of higher education (*see* below).

Students

In 1987–88, there were 578,000 full-time and sandwich students in higher education in the United Kingdom, of whom 58,000 were from overseas. The number of part-time students, including the Open University, in the United Kingdom was 329,000. The proportion of 18 and 19 year-olds entering full-time higher education in Great Britain rose from 13·2 per cent in 1983–84 to 14·6 per cent in 1987–88. The number of mature entrants to full-time higher education is up by 20 per cent on 1981–82. The number of full-time students on science courses in 1986–87 was 139,700, of which 47,600 were female, compared to 143,700 (49,600 female) in 1985–86.

Academic staff

Each university appoints its own academic staff on its own conditions, though there is a common salary structure and, except for Oxford and Cambridge, a common career structure. Most academic staff in British universities, usually well over 90 per cent, have tenure, i.e. after completing a probationary period they are confirmed in post until retirement age. However, the University Commissioners have been formally appointed under the Education Reform Act 1988 to secure changes in university statutes providing for dismissal for good cause and for redundancy.

The Education Reform Act 1988 has taken polytechnics and higher education colleges in England and Wales out of local education authority control, turning them into employers on their own account. The Polytechnics and Colleges Employers Forum has been set up to look after salary structures, which are being re-negotiated.

Teaching staff in higher education require no formal teaching qualification, but teacher trainers are required to spend a certain amount of time in schools to ensure that they have sufficient recent practical experience.

In 1987–88 there were 47,674 full-time and part-time academic staff in universities in the United Kingdom and 96,231 in public sector further and higher education.

The 1989–90 salary scales for non-clinical academic staff in universities were: lecturer grade A £9,816–£15,372; lecturer grade B £16,014–£20,469; senior lecturer £21,489–£26,253; professor £24,783 (minimum). The salaries of clinical academic staff are kept broadly comparable to those of doctors and dentists in the National Health Service.

UNIVERSITIES

Universities are self-governing institutions, usually established by Royal Charter, which are responsible for their own academic appointments, curricula and student admissions. The universities have freedom in academic matters but the Government, through the University Funding Council (*see* below), determines the total size of the university student population, its distribution between arts, science, medicine, etc., and the part which the university sector plays in the whole higher education system.

Overall responsibility for universities throughout Great Britain rests with the Secretary of State for Education and Science, who consults with the Secretaries of State for Scotland and Wales as necessary. Universities in Northern Ireland are the responsibility of the Secretary of State for Northern Ireland.

Advice to the Government on university matters is provided by the Universities Funding Council (U.F.C.), established under the Education Reform Act 1988 to replace the University Grants Committee. The U.F.C. acts as a buffer between the Government, from which it receives a block grant of money, and the universities, to which it allocates its grant. Its brief is to secure more effective use of public funds allocated to higher education.

There are 46 universities in the United Kingdom. Of these, 35 are in England, one (a federal institution) in Wales, eight in Scotland and two in Northern Ireland. In 1987–88 there was a total of 320,920 full-time students at universities in the United Kingdom (38,000 of these from overseas) and 46,062 part-time students. Women form 43 per cent of the full-time total and 60 per cent of the part-time total.

The non-residential **Open University** provides courses leading to degrees nationally. Teaching is through a combination of television and radio programmes, correspondence, tutorials, short residential courses and local audio-visual centres. No qualifications are needed for entry. The Open University offers undergraduate, post-experience and postgraduate courses. The University also has a programme of higher degrees: B.Phil., M.Phil. and Ph.D. through research, and M.A. and M.Sc. through taught courses. It is planned to introduce a Master of Business Administration (M.B.A.) degree course in 1989.

The Open University is grant-aided directly by the Department of Education and Science and does not come under the Universities Funding Council. For Open University purposes Northern Ireland is administered as a separate section of the United Kingdom and the cost is met by the Department of Education for Northern Ireland.

In 1987, 68,037 undergraduates were registered at the Open University, of whom 31,238 were women and 36,999 were men. Estimated cost (1989) of a B.A. general degree was over £1,280 and of a B.A. Hons. degree, £1,540. Applications should be made direct to The Open University, PO Box 71, Milton Keynes MK7 6AG.

The independent **University of Buckingham** provides a two-year course leading to a bachelor's degree and its tuition fees were £6,500 for 1989. It receives no capital or recurrent income from the Government but its students are eligible for mandatory awards from local education authorities. Its academic year consists of four terms of ten weeks each.

Courses

All universities award their own degrees and sometimes act as awarding and validating bodies for neighbouring colleges of higher education, though this function is increasingly being taken on by the Council for National Academic Awards (*see* below). With the exception of certain Scottish universities where Master is sometimes used for a first degree in arts subjects, undergraduate courses lead to the title of Bachelor—Bachelor of Arts (B.A.) and Bachelor of Science (B.Sc.) being the most common—and for a higher degree Master of Arts (M.A.), Master of Science (M.Sc.) (usually taught courses) and the research degrees of Master of Philosophy (M.Phil.) and Doctor of Philosophy (Ph.D. or, at a few universities, D.Phil.).

Most undergraduate programmes at British universities run for three years, except in Scotland and at the University of Keele where they may take four years. Professional courses in subjects such as medicine, dentistry and veterinary science take longer. Details of courses on offer and of entry requirements to first degree courses can be found in the annual handbook produced co-operatively by the universities, *University Entrance: The Official Guide*, published by the Association of Commonwealth Universities (for address, *see* p. 453).

Postgraduate programmes vary in length. Taught courses which lead to certificates, diplomas or master degrees usually take one year full-time or two years part-time. Research degrees take from two to three years full-time and much longer if completed on a part-time basis. Details of taught courses and research degree opportunities can be found in *Graduate Studies* published annually by the Careers Research and Advisory Council.

Post-experience short courses are forming an increasing part of university provision, reflecting the need to update professional and technical training. Most of these courses finance themselves.

Admission

Constraints are imposed by the Government on the number of home students which a university is able to admit, but the individual university decides which students to accept and which to reject. Students applying for admission to a first degree course at most universities do not apply direct but through a clearing-house, the Universities' Central Council on Admissions (UCCA). All universities in the United Kingdom participate in the UCCA scheme except the Open University which conducts its own admissions direct. The *UCCA handbook* is issued free for use in completing UCCA application forms, and is available from the Universities' Central Council on Admissions (for address, *see* p. 453).

For admission as a postgraduate student, universities normally require a good first degree in a subject related to the proposed course of study or research, but each candidate is considered on his or her merits. Application is normally to the institution direct.

Finance

Universities are being expected to look to a much wider range of funding sources than before, and to generate additional revenue in collaboration with industry.

In 1987–88 the total recurrent income of universities in the United Kingdom was £2,807 million. Exchequer grants have dropped from 75 per cent of total income in 1976–77 to 55·3 per cent in 1987–88. Income in 1987–88 from contracts with industry, commerce and public corporations rose by 15 per cent compared with the previous year. The exchequer grant of £1,553 million was, in real terms, seven per cent lower than in 1983–84. The total non-recurrent exchequer grant for 1987–88 was £121 million.

NON-UNIVERSITY SECTOR

England and Wales

Polytechnics, colleges of higher education, and other major establishments provide both advanced and non-advanced courses (*see* Further Education above) in England and Wales. *Advanced* courses comprise courses for the further training of teachers, and other courses which last full-time for at least four weeks or, if part-time, involve more than 60 hours of instruction. They include first degree and postgraduate courses (including research), courses for Diploma of Higher Education, Higher National Diploma and Higher National Certificate courses, courses in preparation for professional examinations and other courses of above G.C.E. A-level or Ordinary National Certificate standard. Facilities are available for full-time and part-time study, and day release, sandwich or block release courses are more commonly available than in universities. Advanced courses are offered in some 400 institutions outside the universities.

The **Diploma of Higher Education** (Dip.H.E.) is a two-year diploma usually intended to serve as a stepping-stone to a degree course or other further study. It has a normal entry requirement of two A-levels. The Dip.H.E. is usually awarded by the Council for National Academic Awards (*see* below).

The **BTEC Higher National Certificate** (H.N.C.) is awarded after two years part-time study. The **BTEC Higher National Diploma** (H.N.D.) is awarded after two years full-time, or three years sandwich or part-time study. Entry is with either a BTEC National Certificate or Diploma; or at least one G.C.E. A-level pass plus appropriate supporting GCSEs/G.C.E. O-levels or C.S.E. grade 1 passes; or BTEC Certificates of Achievement at appropriate levels and in relevant subjects; and/or appropriate on- or off-the-job training.

The **Council for National Academic Awards** (CNAA) was established by Royal Charter in 1964 as a self-governing body. It awards degrees to students taking courses approved by it in non-university institutions. More than 130 colleges in Britain conduct courses leading to its degrees: B.A., B.Ed., B.Sc., and higher degrees including M.A. and M.Sc.

(for postgraduate course work) and M.Phil. and Ph.D. (for research which may be undertaken jointly in industry and an academic institution). Some colleges of higher education have retained their traditional links with a university which validates and awards their degrees.

Until April 1989 all public sector higher education establishments were under local education authority control, except for institutions for teacher training and a few others which were grant-maintained directly from central government. However, the Education Reform Act 1988 legislated for the polytechnics and 55 higher education colleges in England to be removed from local education authority control and incorporated as independent institutions, each run by a Higher Education Corporation (H.E.C.). The H.E.C.s are responsible for providing higher education and carrying out research in these institutions. H.E.C.s are controlled by boards of governors appointed by the Secretary of State. At least half the members of each board must be drawn from industry, business, commerce and the professions.

The H.E.C.s are funded by the Polytechnics and Colleges Funding Council (PCFC), which succeeds the National Advisory Body for Public Sector Higher Education and takes over its functions of allocating funds between individual institutions for the provision of higher education (including further education courses for the transitional year 1988–89 only). The PCFC also advises the Secretary of State for Education on matters relevant to its sector. The independent higher education institutions are, like the universities, expected to supplement their income by undertaking consultancy work and exploiting commercial possibilities.

In November 1987, there was a total of 261,867 students enrolled at polytechnics: 248,006 (42 per cent of them women) were on advanced courses, and of this number, 170,870 (44 per cent of them women) were full-time or sandwich course students.

There are 486 major establishments of higher education (maintained, assisted by L.E.A.s, in receipt of direct grant from the D.E.S., or voluntary) in addition to the polytechnics. In England and Wales in 1987 they catered for 226,804 students on advanced courses including 97,148 on full-time or sandwich courses.

Admissions

Information on advanced courses in polytechnics can be found in the *Polytechnic Courses Handbook* available from the Committee of Directors of Polytechnics (for address, *see* p. 453).

The entry requirements to degree courses in this sector are much the same as those for universities, i.e. two or three GCSEs at grades A to C, or equivalent, and two or three A-levels. Polytechnics and colleges are, however, often more flexible than universities in accepting alternative entry qualifications, particularly technician-level awards.

The Polytechnics Central Admissions System (PCAS) acts as a clearing-house for all full-time and sandwich first degree, H.N.D. and Dip.H.E. courses at participating polytechnics and colleges, except for art and design (*see* below) and initial teacher training courses (*see* p. 472). Applicants can obtain a copy of the *Guide for Applicants* and the PCAS application form either from their school or college or from PCAS.

For CNAA first degree and postgraduate courses in art and design and BTEC H.N.D. courses in design and associated studies, applications should be made through the Art and Design Admissions Registry.

For polytechnic courses other than the above, applications are made to the institution direct, using the Polytechnic Standard Application Form, available in schools or colleges or from the Committee of Directors of Polytechnics. Applications for courses at colleges of higher education outside the clearing-house schemes are also made direct to the institutions.

Scotland

Advanced full-time courses outside the universities in Scotland are provided by the sixteen central institutions, five colleges of education and 50 education authority colleges. These are funded by central government mainly through the Scottish Education Department. Each is managed by an independent governing body which includes representatives of industrial, commercial, professional and educational interests. Most of the courses at the central institutions have a vocational orientation and are of the sandwich type. They are intended to complement provision in the universities. Most of the degrees are validated by the CNAA, though some degree courses such as agriculture, fine art and planning are run in collaboration with nearby universities which validate and award the degrees.

In 1986–87, 63,019 students were enrolled on advanced courses of higher education (35 per cent of them women): 32,978 at central institutions, 914 at colleges of education, and 27,127 at education authority colleges. Of the total number, 30,657 were on full-time or sandwich courses (46 per cent of them women).

Applications to the central institutions are made direct to the college concerned, with the exception of those courses offered by certain agricultural and art central institutions which are run in conjunction with universities. Application for these courses is made through UCCA. Further information can be obtained from the institutions themselves or from the Central Institutions Office.

Northern Ireland

In Northern Ireland advanced courses are provided by 26 institutions of further education and by the University of Ulster. As well as offering first and postgraduate degrees, the University runs courses leading to the BTEC Higher National Diploma and professional qualifications. Applications to undertake courses other than degree courses are made to the institutions direct.

In 1986–87, 2,357 students were enrolled on advanced courses of higher education in the institutions of further education (71 per cent of them women). There were 521 students on full-time or sandwich courses, including 373 women.

FEES

The tuition fees for students with mandatory awards (*see* p. 448) are paid by the grant-awarding body. Students from member states of the European Community pay fees at home student rates. Since 1980–81 students from outside the E.C. have paid fees that are meant to cover the cost of their education, but financial help is available under a number of schemes. Information about these schemes is available from British Council offices worldwide.

The recommended minimum fees at universities for students from non-E.C. countries in 1989–90 is £4,300 for arts students, £5,700 for science students and £10,500 for students following clinical courses in medicine, dentistry and veterinary science. These compare with home undergraduate fees of £607 for all courses.

The fees for home students and E.C. nationals on advanced courses at polytechnics and higher education colleges are £609 for all full-time courses in

1989–90 while the recommended minimum for non-E.C. overseas students is £4,017 for all courses.

GRANTS FOR STUDENTS

Students in the United Kingdom who plan to take a full-time or sandwich course of further study after leaving school may be eligible for a grant. A parental contribution is deductible on a sliding scale dependent on income. For married students this may be deducted from their spouse's income instead. However, parental contribution is not deducted from the grant to students over 25 years of age who have been self-supporting for at least three years. Tuition fees are paid in full for all students in receipt of a grant regardless of parental income.

Grants are paid by education authorities in England, Wales and Northern Ireland, and by the Scottish Education Department in Scotland. Applications are made to the authority in the area in which the student normally lives. Applications should not, however, be made earlier than the January preceding the start of the course.

Types of grant

Grants are of two kinds: mandatory and discretionary. *Mandatory* grants are those which awarding authorities must pay to students who are attending designated courses (*see* below) and who can satisfy certain other conditions. Such a grant is awarded normally to enable the student to attend only one designated course and there is no general entitlement to an award for any particular number of years. *Discretionary* grants are those for which each awarding authority has discretion to decide its own policy.

Designated courses are those full-time or sandwich courses leading to: a university or CNAA degree; the Diploma of Higher Education (Dip.H.E.); the Higher National Diploma (H.N.D.) of the Business and Technician Education Council; initial teacher-training courses including those for the postgraduate certificate of education and the art teachers' certificate or diploma; a university certificate or diploma course lasting at least three years; other qualifications which are specifically designated as being comparable to first degree courses; and the SCOTVEC Higher National Diploma.

Eligibility.—To be eligible for a mandatory grant, students admitted to a designated course must usually have been ordinarily resident in the United Kingdom for the three years immediately preceding the academic year in which the course begins; have not previously attended a course of advanced further education of more than two years' duration; and apply for the grant before the end of the first term of the course. (The local education authority should be consulted for advice about eligibility.)

Students taking designated courses who do not satisfy the residency condition may be eligible for a mandatory grant if they come from other member states of the E.C. and can establish migrant worker status, or their parents are migrant workers; or if they, or their spouse and children, are asylees or refugees.

Value.—A means-tested maintenance grant, usually paid once a term, covers periods of attendance during term as well as the Christmas and Easter vacations, but not the summer vacation. It is subject to deduction on account of the student's own income and her/his parents' or spouse's income. The basic grant rates (1989–90) are: £2,650 if living in a hall of residence or lodgings and studying within the London area; £2,155 as above but outside the London area; £1,710 if living at the parental home. Tuition fees in full are usually paid direct to the university or college by the education authority. Additional allowances are available if, for example, the course requires a period of study abroad.

Cost.—Education authority and Scottish Education Department expenditure on student maintenance in 1986–87 was £649·2 million.

Postgraduate awards

Unlike funding for undergraduates, which is mandatory for most degree and equivalent level courses, grants for postgraduate study are usually discretionary. Grants are also often dependent on the class of first degree, especially for research degrees.

A number of schemes of postgraduate bursaries or studentships for residents in England and Wales are funded by the Department of Education and Science, the five Government research councils, the Ministry of Agriculture, Fisheries and Food, and the British Academy which awards grants for study in the humanities.

In Scotland postgraduate funding is provided by the Department of Agriculture and Fisheries for Scotland, the Scottish Education Department, and the research councils as in England and Wales.

Awards in Northern Ireland are made by the Department of Education for Northern Ireland, the Department of Agriculture for Northern Ireland, and the Medical Research Council.

In 1986–87 in the United Kingdom 22,800 awards were made.

Value.—The national rates for twelve-month studentships in 1989–90 were: £3,970 in college or lodgings in London; £3,125 in college or lodgings outside London; £2,270 for those living with parents or spouse's parents. The rates for 30-week bursaries for 1989–90 were: £2,585 in college or lodgings in London; £2,090 in college or lodgings outside London; £1,575 if living with parents or spouse's parents.

ADULT AND CONTINUING EDUCATION

The term adult education covers a broad spectrum of educational activities ranging from non-vocational courses of general interest, through the acquiring of special vocational skills needed in industry or commerce, to study for a degree at the Open University.

Providers

Courses specifically designed for adults are funded and/or provided by many bodies. They include, in the statutory sector: local education authorities in England and Wales; the regional and islands education authorities in Scotland and the Scottish Educa-

tion Department; education and library boards in Northern Ireland; the Open University; the extra-mural departments of other universities and Birkbeck College of the University of London; residential colleges; the Open College; the B.B.C., I.B.A. and local radio stations. There are, in addition, a number of voluntary bodies.

The local education authorities in England and Wales operate through 'area' adult education centres (2,632 in 1987), institutes or colleges, and the adult studies departments of colleges of further education. The regional and islands education authorities in Scotland fund adult education including that provided by the universities and the Workers' Educational Association at vocational further education colleges (50 in 1988). In addition, the Scottish Education Department provides grants to a number of voluntary organizations. The education and library boards in Northern Ireland are responsible for the 26 further education colleges and a number of community schools.

More than 30 universities have extra-mural, adult education or continuing education departments which serve their local areas or regions, and Birkbeck College in the University of London caters solely for part-time students. The Open University, in partnership with the B.B.C., provides distance teaching leading to ordinary or honours first degrees, and also offers post-experience and higher degree courses (*see* p. 445–6). The Open College uses radio and television to provide open learning courses in all areas of vocational and technical competence, leading to nationally recognized qualifications or credits towards them.

Of the voluntary bodies, the biggest is the **Workers' Educational Association (W.E.A.)** which operates throughout the United Kingdom and comprises about 900 branches, organized into 20 districts, and nearly 1,500 affiliated educational and workers' organizations. It aims to stimulate and to satisfy the demands of workers for education, and to further the advancement of education generally, reaching about 180,000 adult students annually. The Department of Education and Science (D.E.S.), Scottish Education Department, Department of Education for Northern Ireland and local education authorities make grants towards expenses.

The **National Institute of Adult Continuing Education (England and Wales)** (NIACE) provides information and advice to organizations and individuals on all aspects of adult continuing education. It conducts enquiries into problems, organizes conferences and issues publications. The institute manages a number of agencies and special units, including the Adult Literacy and Basic Skills Unit, which receive funding from the D.E.S. and the Welsh Office. The Welsh committee, NIACE Cymru, receives financial support from the Welsh Office Education Department, and advises government, voluntary bodies and education providers on adult continuing education and training matters in Wales.

The **Scottish Institute of Adult and Continuing Education** (SIACE) advises on policy, conducts research, provides information, arranges conferences and produces publications. Its membership comprises all the major funders and providers of adult and continuing education in Scotland. SIACE publishes the *Scottish Handbook of Adult and Continuing Education*.

The **Northern Ireland Council for Continuing Education** has an advisory role. Its membership includes representatives of most organizations involved in the field, together with appointees of the Northern Ireland Minister responsible for education.

The **Universities Council for Adult and Continuing Education** consists of one or two representatives from each university in the United Kingdom.

It was established in 1947 for the interchange of ideas and the formulation of common policies on extra-mural education.

Among government initiatives run jointly by the D.E.S. and the Welsh Office are: the **Programme for the Adult Unemployed** (REPLAN), a major part of which is managed by NIACE; and the **Professional, Industrial and Commercial Updating Programme** (PICKUP) which, with contributions from the Training Agency, encourages the provision of short, flexible updating courses for adults in employment.

Courses

Although lengths vary, most courses are part-time. Long-term residential colleges, which are grant-aided by the D.E.S., the Welsh Office or the Scottish Office, provide full-time courses lasting one or two years.

Some colleges and centres offer short-term residential courses, lasting from a day or two to a few weeks, in a wide range of subjects. Local education authorities directly sponsor many of the colleges while others are sponsored by universities or voluntary organizations. A booklet listing courses, *Residential Short Courses*, is published by NIACE.

Grants

Although full-time courses at degree level attract mandatory awards regardless of the age of the student, for courses below that level all students over the age of 19 must pay a fee. However, discretionary grants may be available. Adult education bursaries for students at the long-term residential colleges of adult education are the responsibility of the colleges themselves. The awards are administered for the colleges by the Awards Officer of the Residential Colleges Committee for students resident in England; by the Welsh Office Education Department for those resident in Wales; by the Scottish Education Department for those resident in Scotland; and by the Department of Education for Northern Ireland for students resident there. The bursaries are paid in accordance with the rates and conditions set from time to time by the D.E.S. *Adult Education Bursaries* can be obtained from the Awards Officer, Adult Education Bursaries, c/o Ruskin College (for address, *see* p. 462).

Numbers

There are no comprehensive statistics covering all aspects of adult education. However, it is known that enrolments on evening courses of non-advanced education in further education establishments in the United Kingdom numbered 2,377,000 in 1986–87 (70 per cent women). This number included 1,663,000 students at adult education centres in England and Wales. In 1986–87, 299,269 students attended courses of liberal adult education provided by university extra-mural departments including joint courses with the W.E.A. in the United Kingdom.

EDUCATION DIRECTORY

LOCAL EDUCATION AUTHORITIES

ENGLAND

County Councils

AVON, P.O. Box 57, Avon House North, St. James Barton, Bristol BS99 7EB. (Tel: 0272-290777).—*Dir.*, (vacant).

BEDFORDSHIRE, County Hall, Bedford MK42 9AP. (Tel: 0234-63222).—*Dir.*, D. G. Wadsworth.

BERKSHIRE, Shire Hall, Shinfield Park, Reading RG2 9XE. (Tel: 0734-875444).—*Chief Education Officer*, S. R. Goodchild.

BUCKINGHAMSHIRE, County Hall, Aylesbury HP20 1UZ. (Tel: 0296-395000).—*Dir.*, E. S. Sharp.

CAMBRIDGESHIRE, Castle Court, Shire Hall, Cambridge CB3 0AP. (Tel: 0223-317111).—*Chief Education Officer*, G. H. Morris.

CHESHIRE, County Hall, Chester CH1 1SF. (Tel: 0244-602424).—*Dir.*, N. J. Fitton.

CLEVELAND, Woodlands Road, Middlesbrough TS1 3BN. (Tel: 0642-248155).—*County Education Officer*, A. H. R. Calderwood.

CORNWALL, County Hall, Truro TR1 3BA. (Tel: 0872-74282).—*Sec. of Education*, D. W. Fryer.

CUMBRIA, 5 Portland Square, Carlisle CA1 1PU. (Tel: 0228-23456).—*Dir.*, P. C. Boulter, C.B.E.

DERBYSHIRE, County Offices, Matlock DE4 3AG. (Tel: 0629-580000).—*Dir.*, J. G. Evans.

DEVON, County Hall, Exeter EX2 4QG. (Tel: 0392-77977).—*Chief Education Officer*, S. W. Jenkin.

DORSET, County Hall, Dorchester DT1 1XJ. (Tel: 0305-251000).—*Dir.*, P. L. Gedling.

DURHAM, County Hall, Durham DH1 5UJ. (Tel: 091-386 4411).—*Dir.*, K. B. Grimshaw.

ESSEX, Threadneedle House, Market Road, Chelmsford CM1 1LD. (Tel: 0245-492211).—*County Education Officer*, R. M. Sharpe.

GLOUCESTERSHIRE, Shire Hall, Gloucester GL1 2TP. (Tel: 0452-425000).—*Dir.*, K. D. Anderson.

HAMPSHIRE, The Castle, Winchester SO23 8UG. (Tel: 0962-841841).—*County Education Officer*, P. J. Coles.

HEREFORD AND WORCESTER, Castle Street, Worcester WR1 3AG. (Tel: 0905-763763).—*County Education Officer*, J. W. Turnbull.

HERTFORDSHIRE, County Hall, Hertford SG13 8DE. (Tel: 0992-555818).—*County Education Officer*, D. Fisher, C.B.E.

HUMBERSIDE, County Hall, Beverley HU17 9BA. (Tel: 0482-867131).—*Dir.*, Dr. M. W. Garnett.

ISLE OF WIGHT, County Hall, Newport PO30 1UD. (Tel: 0983-821000).—*Dir.*, R. O. Burton.

KENT, Springfield, Maidstone ME14 2LJ. (Tel: 0622-671411).—*Dir.*, R. Pryke.

LANCASHIRE, County Hall, Preston PR1 8XJ. (Tel: 0772-54868).—*Chief Education Officer*, A. J. Collier.

LEICESTERSHIRE, County Hall, Glenfield, Leicester LE3 8RF. (Tel: 0533-323232).—*Dir.*, K. H. Wood-Allum.

LINCOLNSHIRE, County Offices, Newland, Lincoln LN1 1YQ. (Tel: 0522-552222).—*Dir.*, A. M. Ridings, F.R.S.A.

NORFOLK, County Hall, Norwich NR1 2DH. (Tel: 0603-222222).—*Dir.*, M. H. Edwards.

NORTHAMPTONSHIRE, Northampton House, Wellington Street, NN1 2HX. (Tel: 0604-236250).—*County Education Officer*, J. R. Atkinson.

NORTHUMBERLAND, County Hall, Morpeth NE61 2EF. (Tel: 0670-514343).—*Dir.*, C. C. Tipple.

NOTTINGHAMSHIRE, County Hall, West Bridgford, Nottingham NG2 7QP. (Tel: 0602-823823).—*Dir.*, A. J. Fox.

OXFORDSHIRE, Macclesfield House, New Road, Oxford OX1 1NA. (Tel: 0865-792422).—*Chief Education Officer*, Mrs. J. Stephens.

SHROPSHIRE, The Shirehall, Abbey Foregate, Shrewsbury SY2 6ND. (Tel: 0743-254307).—*County Education Officer*, P. B. Cates.

SOMERSET, County Hall, Taunton TA1 4DY. (Tel: 0823-333451).—*Chief Education Officer*, Mrs. J. Wisker.

STAFFORDSHIRE, Tipping Street, Stafford ST16 2DH. (Tel: 0785-223121).—*Chief Education Officer*, Dr. P. J. Hunter.

SUFFOLK, St. Andrew House, County Hall, Ipswich IP4 1LJ. (Tel: 0473-230000).—*County Education Officer*, T. R. Cornthwaite.

SURREY, County Hall, Kingston upon Thames KT1 2DN. (Tel: 01-541 8800).—*County Education Officer*, M. C. Pinchin.

SUSSEX, EAST, P.O. Box 4, County Hall, St. Anne's Crescent, Lewes BN7 1SG. (Tel: 0273-481316).—*County Education Officer*, J. A. Carter.

SUSSEX, WEST, County Hall, Chichester PO19 1RQ. (Tel: 0243-777100).—*Dir.*, R. D. C. Bunker.

WARWICKSHIRE, P.O. Box 24, 22 Northgate Street, Warwick CV34 4SR. (Tel: 0926-410410).—*Dir.*, Ms. M. Maden.

WILTSHIRE, County Hall, Trowbridge BA14 8JN. (Tel: 0225-753641).—*Dir.*, I. M. Slocombe.

YORKSHIRE, NORTH, County Hall, Northallerton DL7 8AD. (Tel: 0609-780780).—*Dir.*, F. F. Evans.

Metropolitan District Councils

BARNSLEY, Berneslai Close, Barnsley. (Tel: 0226-733252).—*Dir.*, T. Brooks.

BIRMINGHAM, Council House, Margaret Street, B3 3BU. (Tel: 021-235 2590).—*Dir.*, D. Hammond.

BOLTON, Paderborn House, Civic Centre, BL1 1JW. (Tel: 0204-22311).—*Education Officer*, B. Hughes.

BRADFORD, Provincial House, BD1 1NP. (Tel: 0274-752500).—*Dir.*, W. R. Knight, C.B.E.

BURY, Athenaeum House, Market Street, BL9 0BN. (Tel: 061-705 5000).—*Education Officer*, M. Gray.

CALDERDALE.—Northgate House, Northgate, Halifax HX1 1UN. (Tel: 0422-57257).—*Education Officer*, A. Pickvance.

COVENTRY, New Council Offices, Earl Street, CV1 5RR. (Tel: 0203-831500).—*Education Officer*, C. Farmer.

DONCASTER, Princegate, Doncaster. (Tel: 0302-734104).—*Education Officer*, M. J. Pass.

DUDLEY, Westox House, 1 Trinity Road, DY1 1JB. (Tel: 0384-456000).—*Education Officer*, R. K. Westerby.

GATESHEAD, Civic Centre, Regent Street, NE8 1HH. (Tel: 091-477 1011).—*Dir.*, D. Arbon.

KIRKLEES, Oldgate House, 2 Oldgate, Huddersfield HD1 6QW. (Tel: 0484-537399).—*Education Officer*, P. G. Davies.

KNOWSLEY, Land and House Building, Huyton Hey Road, Huyton, Merseyside L36 5YH. (Tel: 051-480 5111).—*Education Officer*, A. Culley.

LEEDS, 110 Merrion House, Woodhouse Lane, LS2 8DR. (Tel: 0532-463000).—*Dir.*, R. S. Johnson, C.B.E.

LIVERPOOL, 14 Sir Thomas Street, L1 6BJ. (Tel: 051-227 3911).—*Dir.*, M. F. Cogley.

MANCHESTER, Cumberland House, Crown Square, M60 3BB. (Tel: 061-234 5000).—*Education Officer*, R. Jobson.

NEWCASTLE UPON TYNE, Civic Centre, NE1 8PU. (Tel: 091-232 8520).—*Education Officer*, W. B. Dauner.

NORTH TYNESIDE, The Chase, North Shields NE29 1RW. (Tel: 091-257 6621).—*Education Officer, J. F. Partington.*

OLDHAM, Old Town Hall, Chadderton, OL9 6JW. (Tel: 061-624 0505).—*Education Officer, W. R. Kneen, Ph.D.*

ROCHDALE, Municipal Offices, Smith Street, OL16 1YD. (Tel: 0706-47474).—*Education Officer, A. N. Naylor.*

ROTHERHAM, Norfolk House, Walker Place, Rotherham. (Tel: 0709-382121).—*Education Officer, K. Snowden.*

ST. HELENS, Century House, Victoria Square, St. Helens WA10 1RN. (Tel: 0744-24061).—*Dir.*, N. D. Nelson.

SALFORD, Chapel Street, M3 5LT. (Tel: 061-832 9751).—*Chief Education Officer, A. Lockhart.*

SANDWELL, P.O. Box 41, Shaftesbury House, 402 High Street, West Bromwich B70 9LT. (Tel: 021-525 7366).—*Dir.*, G. A. Brinsdon.

SEFTON, Town Hall, Bootle, Merseyside L20 7AE. (Tel: 051-922 4040).—*Education Officer, J. A. Marsden.*

SHEFFIELD, Leopold Street, S1 1RJ. (Tel: 0742-726341).—*Education Officer, W. Walton.*

SOLIHULL, P.O. Box 20, Council House, B91 3QU. (Tel: 021-704 6000).—*Dir.*, M. E. Sweet.

SOUTH TYNESIDE, Town Hall and Civic Offices, South Shields, NE33 2RL. (Tel: 091-427 1717).—*Education Officer, K. Stringer.*

STOCKPORT, Stopford House, Piccadilly, Stockport. (Tel: 061-480 4949).—*Education Officer, J. E. Hendy.*

SUNDERLAND, Town Hall and Civic Centre, Burdon Road, SR2 7DN. (Tel: 091-567 6161).—*Education Officer, D. A. Bowers.*

TAMESIDE, Council Offices, Wellington Road, Ashton-under-Lyne OL6 6DL. (Tel: 061-330 8355).—*Education Officer, A. M. Webster.*

TRAFFORD, Sale Town Hall, Tatton Road, Sale M33 1YR. (Tel: 061-872 2101).—*Chief Education Officer, C. J. Radley.*

WAKEFIELD, County Hall, WF1 2QW. (Tel: 0924-367111).—*Education Officer, A. Lenney.*

WALSALL, Civic Centre, Darwall Street, WS1 1DQ. (Tel: 0922-650000).—*Education Officer, Mrs D. M. Tuck.*

WIGAN, Gateway House, Standishgate, WN1 1XL. (Tel: 0942-44991).—*Education Officer, J. K. Hampson.*

WIRRAL, Municipal Buildings, Cleveland Street, Birkenhead L41 6NH. (Tel: 051-647 7000).—*Education Officer, M. G. Nichol.*

WOLVERHAMPTON, Civic Centre, St. Peter's Square, WV1 1RR. (Tel: 0902-27811).—*Education Officer, Dr. C. Saville.*

London

INNER LONDON EDUCATION AUTHORITY.—*Chief Executive*, H. Ouseley. *Education Officer*, D. Mallen.

The I.L.E.A. is to be abolished on April 1, 1990 and from that date the inner London boroughs(*) and the Corporation of the City of London will assume responsibility for the provision of education within their own areas.

BARKING, Town Hall, Barking, Essex IG11 7LU. (Tel: 01-592 4500).—*Education Officer*, (vacant).

BARNET, Town Hall, Friern Barnet, N11 3DL. (Tel: 01-368 1255).—*Education Officer*, N. M. Gill.

BEXLEY, Town Hall, Crayford, Kent DA1 4EN. (Tel: 01-303 7777).—*Education Officer*, G. Hall.

BRENT, Chesterfield House, Park Lane, Wembley, Middx. HA9 7RW. (Tel: 01-904 1244).—*Dir.*, G. Benham.

BROMLEY, Town Hall, Tweedy Road, Bromley, Kent BR1 1SB. (Tel: 01-464 3333).—*Education Officer*, G. Grainge.

*CAMDEN, 100 Euston Road, NW1. (Tel: 01-860 5882).—*Education Officer*, P. Mitchell.

*CITY OF LONDON, P.O. Box 270, Guildhall, EC2P 2EJ. (Tel: 01-606 3030).—*City Education Officer*, (vacant).

*CITY OF WESTMINSTER, City Hall, P.O. Box 240, Victoria Street, SW1E 6QP. (Tel: 01-828 8070).—*Education Officer*, G. Robins.

CROYDON, Taberner House, Park Lane, CR9 1TP. (Tel: 01-686 4433).—*Dir.*, P. Benians.

EALING, Hadley House, 79–81 Uxbridge Road, W5 5SU. (Tel: 01-579 2424).—*Dir.*, M. Barlow.

ENFIELD, P.O. Box 56, Civic Centre, Silver Street, EN1 3XQ. (Tel: 01-366 6565).—*Education Officer*, G. Hutchinson.

*GREENWICH, Wellington Street, Woolwich, SE18 6PU.—*Education Officer*, N. McClelland.

*HACKNEY, Edith Cavell School, Enfield Road, N1. (Tel: 01-254 9002/5).—*Education Officer*, G. John.

*HAMMERSMITH and FULHAM, Hammersmith Town Hall, W6 9JU. (Tel: 01-748 3020).—*Education Officer*, Ms. C. Whatford.

HARINGEY, 35 Station Road, N22. (Tel: 01-975 9700).—*Education Officer*, R. L. Jones.

HARROW, P.O. Box 2, Civic Centre, Harrow HA1 2UW. (Tel: 01-863 5611).—*Dir.*, H. Fielding.

HAVERING, Mercury House, Mercury Gardens, Romford RM1 3DR. (Tel: 0708-66999).—*Dir.*, B. H. Laister.

HILLINGDON, Civic Centre, Uxbridge, Middx. UB8 1UW. (Tel: 0895-50528).—*Education Officer*, T. Hinds.

HOUNSLOW, Civic Centre, Lampton Road, Hounslow, Middx. TW3 4DN. (Tel: 01-570 7728).—*Dir.*, J. D. Trickett.

*ISLINGTON, Town Hall, Upper Street, N1 2UD. (Tel: 01-354 7100).—*Education Officer*, C. Webb.

*KENSINGTON AND CHELSEA, Young Street, W8 5EH. (Tel: 01-938 5311).—*Education Officer*, M. Stoten.

KINGSTON UPON THAMES, Guildhall, KT1 1EU. (Tel: 01-546 2121).—*Education Officer*, W. Dickinson.

*LAMBETH, Town Hall, Brixton Hill, SW2 1RW. (Tel: 01-274 7722).—*Education Officer*, B. Burchell.

*LEWISHAM, 1 Aitken Road, Catford, SE6 2UL. (Tel: 01-697 8166).—*Education Officer*, L. Fullick.

MERTON, Crown House, London Road, Morden, Surrey SM4 5DX. (Tel: 01-543 2222).—*Dir.*, R. Davies.

NEWHAM, 383 High Street, E15 4RD. (Tel: 01-534 4545).—*Education Officer*, (vacant).

REDBRIDGE, Lynton House, 255–259 High Road, Ilford, IG1 1NN. (Tel: 01-478 3020).—*Dir.*, K. G. M. Ratcliffe.

RICHMOND UPON THAMES, Regal House, London Road, Twickenham TW1 3QB. (Tel: 01-891 1411).—*Education Officer*, G. Alexander.

*SOUTHWARK, 19 Grange Road, SE1 3BE. (Tel: 01-237 4551).—*Eductaion Officer*, G. Mott.

SUTTON, The Grove, Carshalton, Surrey SM5 3AL. (Tel: 01-661 5000).—*Dir.*, C. Melville.

*TOWER HAMLETS, Town Hall, Patriot Square, E2 9LN. (Tel: 01-980 4831).—*Education Officer*, Ms. A. Sofer.

WALTHAM FOREST, Municipal Offices, High Road, Leyton E10 5QJ. (Tel: 01-527 5544).—*Dir.*, J. M. Shepherd.

*WANDSWORTH, Town Hall, Wandsworth High Street, SW18 2PU. (Tel: 01-871 6000).—*Education Officer*, D. Naismith.

WALES

County Councils

CLWYD, Shire Hall, Mold CH7 6NB. (Tel: 0352-2121).—*Dir.*, H. K. Evans.

DYFED, Pibwrlwyd, Carmarthen SA31 2NH. (Tel: 0267-233333).—*Dir.*, W. J. Phillips.

GWENT, County Hall, Cwmbran NP44 2XG. (Tel:
06337-838838).—*Dir.*, G. V. Drought.
GWYNEDD, County Offices, Caernarfon LL55 1SH.
(Tel: 0286-4121).—*Dir.*, G. E. Humphreys.
MID GLAMORGAN, County Hall, Cathays Park, Cardiff
CF1 3NE. (Tel: 0222-820820).—*Dir.*, E. Roberts.
POWYS, County Hall, Llandrindod Wells LD1 5LG.
(Tel: 0597-826422).—*Dir.*, R. W. Bevan.
SOUTH GLAMORGAN, County Hall, Atlantic Wharf,
Cardiff CF1 5UW. (Tel: 0222-872000).—*Dir.*, D.
Orrell.
WEST GLAMORGAN, County Hall, Swansea SA1 3SN.
(Tel: 0792-471111).—*Dir.*, J. Beale.

SCOTLAND
Regional and Islands Councils

BORDERS, Regional Headquarters, Newtown St.
Boswells, Melrose TD6 0SA. (Tel: 0835-23301).—
Dir., J. McLean.
CENTRAL, Regional Council H.Q., Viewforth, Stirling
FK8 2ET. (Tel: 0786-73111).—*Dir.*, I. Collie.
DUMFRIES AND GALLOWAY, 30 Edinburgh Road,
Dumfries DG1 1JQ. (Tel: 0387-61234).—*Dir.*, W. C.
Fordyce.
FIFE, Fife House, North Street, Glenrothes KY7 5LT.
(Tel: 0592-754411).—*Dir.*, M. More.
GRAMPIAN, Woodhill House, Westburn Road, Aber-
deen AB9 2LU. (Tel: 0224-682222).—*Dir.*, J. A. D.
Michie.
HIGHLAND, Regional Buildings, Glenurquhart Road,
Inverness IV3 5NX. (Tel: 0463-234121).—*Dir.*, Dr.
C. E. Stewart.
LOTHIAN, 40 Torphichen Street, Edinburgh EH3 8JJ.
(Tel: 031-229 9166).—*Dir.*, W. D. C. Semple.
ORKNEY, Council Offices, Kirkwall KW15 1NY. (Tel:
0856-3535).—*Dir.*, R. L. Henderson.
SHETLAND, 1 Harbour Street, Lerwick. (Tel: 0595-
3535).—*Dir.*, R. A. B. Barnes.
STRATHCLYDE, 129 Bath Street, Glasgow G2 2SY.
(Tel: 041-227 2600).—*Dir.*, F. Pignatelli.
TAYSIDE, Tayside House, 28 Crichton Street, Dundee
DD1 3RA. (Tel: 0382-23281).—*Dir.*, D. G. Robertson.
WESTERN ISLES, Council Offices, Sandwick Road,
Stornoway, Isle of Lewis PA87 2BW. (Tel: 0851-
3773).—*Dir.*, N. R. Galbraith.

NORTHERN IRELAND
Education and Library Boards

BELFAST, Board Headquarters, 40 Academy Street,
Belfast BT1 2NQ. (Tel: 0232-329211).—*Chief Officer*,
T. G. J. Moag.
NORTH EASTERN, County Hall, 182 Galgorm Road,
Ballymena, Co. Antrim BT42 1HN. (Tel: 0266-
653333).—*Chief Officer*, R. A. Hamilton.
SOUTH EASTERN, 18 Windsor Avenue, Belfast
BT9 6EF. (Tel: 0232-381188).—*Chief Officer*, T. No-
lan.
SOUTHERN, 3 Charlemont Place, The Mall, Armagh
BT61 9AX. (Tel: 0861-523811).—*Chief Officer*, J. G.
Kelly.
WESTERN, 1 Hospital Road, Omagh, Co. Tyrone
BT79 0AW. (Tel: 0662-44431).—*Chief Executive*, M.
H. F. Murphy, O.B.E.

ISLANDS, ETC.

GUERNSEY, P.O. Box 32, La Couperderie, St. Peter
Port. (Tel: 0481-710821).—*Dir.*, M. D. Hutchings.
JERSEY, P.O. Box 142, St. Saviour. (Tel: 0534-71065).—
Dir., B. Grady.
ISLE OF MAN, Government Offices, Buck's Road,
Douglas. (Tel: 0624-26262).—*Dir.*, A. Davies.
ISLES OF SCILLY, Town Hall, St. Mary's TR21 0LW.
(Tel: 0720-22537).—*Sec. for Education*, L. W. Mich-
ell.

ADVISORY BODIES
Schools

EDUCATION OTHERWISE, 25 Common Lane, Hemming-
ford Abbots, Cambridge PE18 9AN. *Helpline*, tel:
0480-63130.
INTERNATIONAL BACCALAUREATE LONDON, 18 Wob-
urn Square, WC1H 0NS. (Tel: 01-637 1682).—*Dep-
uty Dir.-Gen.*, R. Blackburn.
SCHOOLS EXAMINATION AND ASSESSMENT COUNCIL,
Newcombe House, 4 Notting Hill Gate, W11 3JB.
(Tel: 01-229 1234).—*Chief Exec.*, P. Halsey, C.B.,
L.V.O.; *Sec.*, P. Dines.

Independent Schools

ASSISTED PLACES COMMITTEE, 26 Queen Anne's Gate,
SW1H 9AN. (Tel: 01-222 9595).—*Sec.*, Mrs. L. Shaw.
COMMON ENTRANCE EXAMINATION BOARD, Drax
House, Tilshead, Salisbury, Wilts. SP3 4SJ. (Tel:
0980-620473).—*Sec.*, Mrs. E. J. Twiston-Davies.
GOVERNING BODIES ASSOCIATION, Windleshaw Lodge,
Withyham, Nr. Hartfield, E. Sussex TN7 4BB.—
Sec., D. J. Banwell.
GOVERNING BODIES OF GIRLS' SCHOOLS ASSOCIATION,
Windleshaw Lodge, Withyham, Nr. Hartfield, E.
Sussex TN7 4BB.—*Sec.*, D. J. Banwell.
INDEPENDENT SCHOOLS INFORMATION SERVICE, 56
Buckingham Gate, SW1E 6AG. (Tel: 01-630 8793/
4).—*National Dir.*, D. J. Woodhead.

Further Education

NATIONAL COUNCIL FOR VOCATIONAL QUALIFICA-
TIONS, 222 Euston Road, NW1 2BZ. (Tel. 01-387
9898).

Regional Advisory Councils

EAST ANGLIAN REGIONAL ADVISORY COUNCIL FOR
FURTHER EDUCATION, 2 Looms Lane, Bury St.
Edmunds, Suffolk IP33 1HE. (Tel: 0284-764977).—
Sec., D. J. Lock.
EAST MIDLAND FURTHER EDUCATION COUNCIL, Robins
Wood House, Robins Wood Road, Aspley, Not-
tingham NG8 3NH. (Tel: 0602-293291).—*Sec.*, R.
Ainscough.
REGIONAL ADVISORY COUNCIL FOR FURTHER EDUCA-
TION, LONDON AND SOUTH EASTERN REGION, Tavis-
tock House South, Tavistock Square, WC1H 9LR.
(Tel: 01-388 0027).—*Dir.*, L. South.
NORTHERN COUNCIL FOR FURTHER EDUCATION, 5
Grosvenor Villas, Grosvenor Road, Newcastle upon
Tyne NE2 2RU. (Tel: 091-281 3242).—*Sec.*, J. F.
Pearce.
NORTH WESTERN REGIONAL ADVISORY COUNCIL FOR
FURTHER EDUCATION, Town Hall, Walkden Road,
Worsley, Manchester M28 4QE. (Tel: 061-702
8700).—*Sec.*, D. W. Brown.
SOUTHERN REGIONAL COUNCIL FOR FURTHER EDUCA-
TION, 26 Bath Road, Reading RG1 6NT. (Tel: 0734-
572120).—*Sec. (acting)*, B. J. Knowles.
REGIONAL COUNCIL FOR FURTHER EDUCATION FOR THE
SOUTH WEST, Bishops Hull House, Bishops Hull,
Taunton, Somerset TA1 5RA. (Tel: 0823-335491).—
Sec., F. S. Fisher.
WELSH JOINT EDUCATION COMMITTEE, 245 Western
Avenue, Cardiff CF5 2YX. (Tel: 0222-561231).—
Sec., G. Lloyd Jones.
WEST MIDLANDS ADVISORY COUNCIL FOR FURTHER
EDUCATION AND TRAINING, Norfolk House, Small-
brook Queensway, Birmingham B5 4NB. (Tel: 021-
643 8924).—*Chief Officer*, C. H. Smith.
YORKSHIRE AND HUMBERSIDE ASSOCIATION FOR FUR-
THER AND HIGHER EDUCATION, Bowling Green
Terrace, Leeds LS11 9SX. (Tel: 0532-440751).—*Sec.*,
M. Neale.

Higher Education

THE ASSOCIATION OF COMMONWEALTH UNIVERSITIES, John Foster House, 36 Gordon Square, WC1H 0PF. (Tel: 01-387 8572).—*Sec.-Gen.*, A. Christodoulou, C.B.E.

POLYTECHNICS AND COLLEGES FUNDING COUNCIL, Metropolis House, 22 Percy Street, W1P 9FF (*see* also Government Offices).

UNIVERSITIES' FUNDING COUNCIL, 14 Park Crescent, W1N 4DH (*see* also Government Offices).

WALES ADVISORY BODY FOR LOCAL AUTHORITY HIGHER EDUCATION, 24 Cathedral Road, Cardiff CF1 9LJ. (Tel: 0222-397844).—*Sec.*, Dr. B. L. Powell.

Curriculum Councils, etc.

NATIONAL CURRICULUM COUNCIL, 15–17 New Street, York YO1 2RA. (Tel: 0904-622533).—*Chief Exec.*, D. G. Graham, C.B.E.

NORTHERN IRELAND CURRICULUM COUNCIL, Stranmillis College, Stranmillis Road, Belfast BT9 5DY. (Tel: 0232-381414).—*Chief Exec.*, Mrs. C. Coxhead.

SCOTTISH CONSULTATIVE COUNCIL ON THE CURRICULUM, 17 St. John Street, Edinburgh EH8 8DG. (Tel: 031-557 4888).—*Chief Exec.*, D. R. McNicoll.

CURRICULUM COUNCIL FOR WALES, Castle Buildings, Womanby Street, Cardiff CF1 9SX. (Tel: 0222-344946/388150).—*Chief Exec.*, B. Jones.

TECHNICAL AND VOCATIONAL EDUCATIONAL DEVELOPMENT, TVEI Unit, Enquiry Point, The Training Agency, 236 Gray's Inn Road, WC1X 8HL. (Tel: 01-278 0363).

EXAMINING BODIES

GCSE

LONDON AND EAST ANGLIA GROUP, The Lindens, Lexden Road, Colchester CO3 3RL. (Tel: 0206-549595).—*Sec.*, Miss M. Thompson.

NORTHERN EXAMINING ASSOCIATION, c/o Joint Matriculation Board, Manchester M15 6EU. (Tel. 061-273 2565).—*Joint Sec.*, C. Vickerman.

NORTH REGIONAL EXAMINATIONS BOARD, Wheatfield Road, Westerhope, Newcastle upon Tyne NE5 5JZ. (Tel: 091-286 2711).—*Sec.*, D. Kelly

NORTH WEST REGIONAL EXAMINATIONS BOARD, Orbit House, Albert Street, Eccles, Manchester M30 0WL. (Tel: 061-788 9521).—*Sec.*, Ms. K. Tattersall.

SOUTHERN EXAMINING GROUP, Stag Hill House, Guildford, Surrey GU2 5XJ. (Tel. 0483-503123).—*Chief Exec.*, P. Burke.

WEST MIDLANDS EXAMINATIONS BOARD, Norfolk House, Smallbrook Queensway, Birmingham B5 4NJ. (Tel: 021-6312151).—*Sec.*, B. Swift.

NORTHERN IRELAND SCHOOLS EXAMINATIONS COUNCIL, Beechill House, 42 Beechill Road, Belfast BT8 4RS. (Tel. 0232-704666).—*Chief Officer*, J. Caves.

WELSH JOINT EDUCATION COMMITTEE, 245 Western Avenue, Cardiff CF5 2YX. (Tel. 0222-561231).—*Sec.*, G. Lloyd Jones.

A-level

ASSOCIATED EXAMINING BOARD, Stag Hill House, Guildford, Surrey GU2 5XJ. (Tel: 0483-506506).—*Sec.*, J. A. Day.

CAMBRIDGE UNIVERSITY LOCAL EXAMINATIONS SYNDICATE, Syndicate Buildings, 1 Hills Road, Cambridge CB1 2EU. (Tel: 0223-61111).—*Sec.*, J. L. Reddaway.

JOINT MATRICULATION BOARD, Manchester M15 6EU. (Tel: 061-273 2565).—*Sec.*, C. Vickerman.

OXFORD AND CAMBRIDGE SCHOOLS EXAMINATION BOARD, Brook House, 10 Trumpington Street, Cambridge CB2 1QB. (Tel: 0223-64326).—*Joint Sec.*, H. F. King.

OXFORD AND CAMBRIDGE SCHOOLS EXAMINATION BOARD, Elsfield Way, Oxford OX2 8EP. (Tel: 0865-54421).—*Joint Sec.*, K. Schoenenberger.

SOUTHERN UNIVERSITIES' JOINT BOARD, Cotham Road, Bristol BS6 6DD. (Tel: 0272-736042).—*Sec.*, Dr. S. T. Smith.

UNIVERSITY OF LONDON SCHOOL EXAMINATIONS BOARD, Stewart House, 32 Russell Square, WC1B 5DN. (Tel: 01-636 8000).—*Sec.*, A. R. Stephenson.

UNIVERSITY OF OXFORD DELEGACY OF LOCAL EXAMINATIONS, Ewert House, Ewert Place, Summertown, Oxford OX2 7BZ. (Tel: 0865-54291).—*Sec.*, J. Pailing.

Scotland

SCOTTISH EXAMINATION BOARD, Ironmills Road, Dalkeith, Midlothian EH22 1LE. (Tel: 031-663 6601).—*Dir.*, J. H. Walker, C.B.E., PH.D.

SCOTTISH VOCATIONAL EDUCATION COUNCIL, Hanover House, 24 Douglas Street, Glasgow G2 7NQ. (Tel: 041-248 7900).—*Chief Exec.*, T. J. McCool.

Further Education

BUSINESS AND TECHNICIAN EDUCATION COUNCIL, Central House, Upper Woburn Place, WC1H 0HH. (Tel: 01-388 3288).—*Chief Exec.*, J. E. Sellars.

CITY AND GUILDS OF LONDON INSTITUTE, 76 Portland Place, W1N 4AA. (Tel: 01-278 2468).— *Dir. Gen.*, J. Barnes.

JOINT BOARD FOR PRE-VOCATIONAL EDUCATION, The CPVE Unit, 46 Britannia Street, WC1X 9RG. (Tel: 01-278 3344).—*Head of Unit*, Ms. S. Fifer.

R.S.A. EXAMINATIONS BOARD, Westwood Business Park, Westwood Way, Coventry CV4 8HS. (Tel: 0203-470033).—*Chief Exec.*, M. F. Cross.

Higher Education

COUNCIL FOR NATIONAL ACADEMIC AWARDS, 344–354 Gray's Inn Road, WC1X 8BP. (Tel: 01-278 4411).—*Chairman*, Sir Bryan Nicholson; *Chief Exec.*, M. Frazer, PH.D.

ADMISSIONS INFORMATION

ART AND DESIGN ADMISSIONS REGISTRY, Penn House, 9 Broad Street, Hereford HR4 9AP. (Tel: 0432-266653).—*Registrar*, T. W. M. Gourdie.

CAREERS RESEARCH AND ADVISORY COUNCIL, 2nd Floor, Sheraton House, Castle Park, Cambridge CB3 0AX. (Tel: 0223-460277).

THE CENTRAL INSTITUTIONS INFORMATION OFFICE, c/o Paisley College of Technology, High Street, Paisley PA1 2BE. (Tel: 041-887 1241).

CENTRAL REGISTER AND CLEARING HOUSE LTD., 3 Crawford Place, W1H 2BN.—*Registrar*, Lt. Col. O. J. Massey.

COMMITTEE OF DIRECTORS OF POLYTECHNICS, Kirkman House, 12–14 Whitfield Street, W1P 6AX. (Tel: 01-637 9939).—*Sec.*, Dr. M. S. Lewis.

POLYTECHNICS CENTRAL ADMISSIONS SYSTEM, P.O. Box 67, Cheltenham, Glos. GL50 3AP. (Tel: 0242-227788).—*Chief Exec.*, T. Higgins.

UNIVERSITIES' CENTRAL COUNCIL ON ADMISSIONS, P.O. Box 28, Cheltenham, Glos. GL50 3SA. (Tel: 0242-222444).—*Gen. Sec.*, P. A. Oakley.

UNIVERSITIES

ASTON UNIVERSITY (1966)
Aston Triangle, Birmingham B4 7ET

Full-time Students (1988–89), 4,100.

Chancellor, Sir Adrian Cadbury (1979).

Vice-Chancellor Prof. Sir Frederick Crawford, PH.D., D.Eng., D.SC.

Registrar and Secretary, R. D. A. Packham.

UNIVERSITY OF BATH (1966)
Claverton Down, Bath BA2 7AY

Full-time Students (1988–89), 4,036.
Chancellor, The Lord Kearton, O.B.E., F.R.S. (1980).
Vice-Chancellor, Prof. J. R. Quayle, PH.D., F.R.S.
Secretary and Registrar, R. M. Mawditt, O.B.E., F.R.S.A.

THE UNIVERSITY OF BIRMINGHAM (1900)
P.O. Box 363, Birmingham B15 2TT

Full-time Students (1988-89), 9,851.
Chancellor, Sir Alexander Jarratt, C.B. (1983).
Vice-Chancellor, Prof. M. W. Thompson, D.SC.
Registrar and Secretary, D. R. Holmes.

UNIVERSITY OF BRADFORD (1966)
Bradford BD7 1DP

Full-time Students (1988–89), 4,402.
Chancellor, Sir John Harvey-Jones, M.B.E. (1986).
Vice-Chancellor, Prof. D. J. Johns, PH.D., D.SC. (1989).
Registrar and Secretary, D. W. Granger, M.B.E.

THE UNIVERSITY OF BRISTOL (1909)
Bristol BS8 1TH

Full-time Students (1988–89), 7,521.
Chancellor, Sir Jeremy Morse, K.C.M.G. (1989).
Vice-Chancellor, Sir John Kingman, F.R.S.
Registrar, Mrs. C. M. Cunningham.
Secretary, J. H. M. Parry.

BRUNEL UNIVERSITY (1966)
Uxbridge, Middx. UB8 3PH

Full-time Students (1988–89), 3,740.
Chancellor, The Earl of Halsbury, F.R.S. (1966).
Vice-Chancellor, Prof. R. E. D. Bishop, C.B.E., F.R.S.
Registrar and Secretary, D. Neave.

UNIVERSITY OF BUCKINGHAM (1983)
(Founded 1976 as University College at
Buckingham). Independent of state finance.
Buckingham MK18 1EG

Full-time Students (1988–89), 720.
Chancellor, The Lord Hailsham of St. Marylebone,
K.G., C.H., P.C., F.R.S. (1983).
Vice-Chancellor, Dr. A. M. Barrett, PH.D.
Registrar and Secretary, Dr. M. Lavis.

THE UNIVERSITY OF CAMBRIDGE

FULL TERMS, 1990
Lent, Jan. 16 to March 16; *Easter*, April 24 to June 15;
Michaelmas, Oct. 9 to Dec. 7

Number of Undergraduates in Residence 1988–89:
Men, 6,131; *Women*, 3,950

UNIVERSITY OFFICERS, etc.†   Elect.
Chancellor, H.R.H. The Duke of Edinburgh,
K.G., K.T., O.M., G.B.E., P.C. 1977
Vice-Chancellor, Prof. D. G. T. Williams (*Wolf-son*) 1989
High Steward, The Lord Devlin, P.C., F.B.A.
(*Christ's*) 1966
Deputy High Steward, The Lord Richardson of
Duntisbourne, P.C., M.B.E., T.D. 1983
Commissary, The Lord Salmon, P.C. (*Pembroke*) 1979

---

† Correspondence for the Vice-Chancellor and other
administrative officers should be sent to the *University Offices*, The Old Schools, Cambridge CB2 1TN.

Proctors, E. H. R. Ford, M.D. (*Selwyn*); C. F.
Forsyth, PH.D. (*Robinson*) 1989
Orator, J. Diggle, LITT.D. (*Queen's*) 1982
Registrary, S. G. Fleet, PH.D. (*Downing*) 1983
Deputy Registrary, R. F. Holmes (*Darwin*) 1972
Librarian, F. W. Ratcliffe, PH.D. (*Corpus Christi*) 1980
Treasurer, M. P. Halstead, PH.D. (*Caius*) 1985
Secretary General of the Faculties, J. R. G.
Wright (*St. Catharine's*) 1987
Director of the Fitzwilliam Museum, Prof.
A. M. Jaffé, LITT.D. (*King's*) 1973

Cambridge Colleges and Halls, etc.
(With dates of foundation)

Christ's (1505), *Master*, Prof. Sir Hans Kornberg,
SC.D., F.R.S. (1983).
Churchill (1960), *Master*, Prof. Sir Hermann Bondi,
K.C.B., F.R.S. (1982).
Clare (1326), *Master*, Prof. R. C. O. Matthews, C.B.E.,
F.B.A. (1975).
Clare Hall (1966), *President*, Prof. D. A. Low, PH.D.
(1987).
Corpus Christi (1352), *Master*, M. W. McCrum (1980).
Darwin (1964), *Master*, Prof. G. E. R. Lloyd, PH.D.,
F.B.A. (1989).
Downing (1800), *Master*, P. Mathias, C.B.E., LITT.D.,
F.B.A. (1987).
Emmanuel (1584), *Master*, Prof. D. S. Brewer, LITT.D.
(1977).
Fitzwilliam (1966), *Master*, Prof. G. C. Cameron (1988).
Girton (1869), *Mistress*, The Baroness Warnock, D.B.E.
(1984).
Gonville & Caius (1348), *Master*, Prof. P. Gray, SC.D.,
F.R.S. (1988).
Homerton (1824) (for B. Ed. Students), *Principal*, A.
G. Bamford (1985).
Hughes Hall (1885), (for post-graduate students),
President, T. D. Hawkins (1989).
Jesus (1496), *Master*, Prof. A. C. Renfrew, SC.D. (1986).
King's (1441), *Provost*, Prof. P. P. G. Bateson, SC.D.,
F.R.S. (1987).
Lucy Cavendish College (1965) (for women research
students and mature and affiliated undergradu-
ates), *President*, Dame Anne Warburton, D.C.V.O.,
C.M.G. (1985).
Magdalene (1542), *Master*, D. Calcutt, Q.C. (1985).
New Hall (1954), *President*, Mrs. V. L. Pearl, PH.D.
(1981).
Newnham (1871), *Principal*, Miss S. J. Browne, C.B.
(1983).
Pembroke (1347), *Master*, Prof. The Lord Adrian, M.D.,
F.R.S. (1981).
Peterhouse (1284), *Master*, Prof. H. Chadwick, K.B.E.,
D.D., F.B.A. (1987).
Queens' (1448), *President*, Rev. J. C. Polkinghorne,
SC.D., F.R.S. (1989).
Robinson (1977), *Warden*, Prof. The Lord Lewis of
Newnham, SC.D., F.R.S. (1977).
St. Catharine's (1473), *Master*, Prof. B. E. Supple,
PH.D. (1984).
St. Edmund's (1896), *Master*, R. M. Laws, C.B.E., PH.D.
(1986).
St. John's (1511), *Master*, Prof. R. A. Hinde, SC.D.,
F.R.S. (1989).
Selwyn (1882), *Master*, Prof. Sir Alan Cook, SC.D.,
F.R.S. (1983).
Sidney Sussex (1596), *Master*, Prof. D. H. Northcote,
PH.D., SC.D., F.R.S. (1976).
Trinity (1546), *Master*, Sir Andrew Huxley, O.M., F.R.S.
(1984).
Trinity Hall (1350), *Master*, Sir John Lyons, PH.D.
(1984).
Wolfson (1965), *President*, Prof. D. G. T. Williams
(1980).

---

* Colleges for women only.

THE CITY UNIVERSITY (1966)
Northampton Square, EC1V 0HB

Full-time Students (1987–88), 3,226.
Chancellor, The Rt. Hon. Lord Mayor of London.
Vice-Chancellor and Principal, Prof. R. N. Franklin,
D.Phil., D.Sc.
Registrar, A. H. Seville, PH.D.
Secretary, M. M. O'Hara.

THE UNIVERSITY OF DURHAM
(Founded 1832; re-organized 1908, 1937 and 1963)
Old Shire Hall, Durham DH1 3HP

Full-time Students (1988–89), 5,179.
Chancellor, Dame Margot Fonteyn de Arias (1982).
Vice-Chancellor and Warden, Prof. F. G. T. Holliday,
C.B.E., F.R.S.E.
Registrar and Secretary, J. C. F. Hayward.

Colleges

Collingwood.—Principal, G. H. Blake, PH.D.
Graduate Society.—Principal, M. Richardson, PH.D.
Grey.—Master, V. E. Watts.
Hatfield.—Master, J. P. Barber, PH.D.
St. Aidan's.—Principal, P. H. Clarke, PH.D.
St. Chad's.—Principal, D. Jasper, Ph.d.
St. Cuthbert's Society.—Principal, S. G. C. Stoker.
St. Hild and St. Bede.—Principal, J. V. Armitage,
PH.D.
St. John's.—Principal, Rev. A. C. Thiselton, PH.D.
St. Mary's.—Principal, Miss J. M. Kenworthy.
Trevelyan.—Principal, Miss D. Lavin.
University.—Master, E. C. Salthouse, PH.D.
Ushaw.—President, Rt. Rev. Mgr. P. F. J. Walton.
Van Mildert.—Principal, Ms. J. Turner, PH.D.

THE UNIVERSITY OF EAST ANGLIA (1963)
Norwich NR4 7TJ

Full-time Students (1987–88), 4,384.
Chancellor, Rev. Prof. W. O. Chadwick, O.M., K.B.E.,
F.B.A. (1985).
Vice-Chancellor, Prof. D. C. Burke, PH.D.
Registrar and Secretary, M. G. E. Paulson-Ellis.

THE UNIVERSITY OF ESSEX (1964)
Wivenhoe Park, Colchester CO4 3SQ

Full-time Students (1988–89), 3,312.
Chancellor, The Rt. Hon. Sir Patrick Nairne G.C.B.,
M.C. (1983).
Vice-Chancellor, Prof. M. Harris, PH.D.
Registrar, E. Newcomb.

THE UNIVERSITY OF EXETER (1955)
Exeter EX4 4QJ

Full-time Students (1988–89), 5,417.
Chancellor, Sir Rex Richards, D.SC., F.R.S. (1981).
Vice-Chancellor, D. Harrison, PH.D., SC.D.
Academic Registrar and Secretary, I. H. C. Powell.

THE UNIVERSITY OF HULL (1954)
Cottingham Road, Hull HU6 7RX

Full-time Students (1987–88), 4,910.
Chancellor, The Lord Wilberforce, C.M.G., O.B.E., P.C.
(1978).
Vice-Chancellor, Prof. W. Taylor, C.B.E., PH.D.
Registrar and Secretary, F. T. Mattison.

THE UNIVERSITY OF KEELE (1962)
Keele, Newcastle-under-Lyme, Staffs. ST5 5BG

Full-time Students (1988–89), 3,337.
Chancellor, Sir Claus Moser, K.C.B., C.B.E., F.B.A. (1986).

Vice-Chancellor, Prof. B. E. F. Fender, C.M.G., PH.D.
Registrar, D. Cohen, PH.D.

UNIVERSITY OF KENT AT CANTERBURY
(1965)
Canterbury CT2 7LX

Full-time Students (1988–89), 4,913.
Chancellor, The Lord Grimond, T.D., P.C. (1969).
Vice-Chancellor, D. J. E. Ingram, D.Phil., D.SC.
Registrar, A. D. Linfoot.

THE UNIVERSITY OF LANCASTER (1964)
Bailrigg, Lancaster LA1 4YW

Full-time Students (1988–89), 4,988.
Chancellor, H.R.H. The Princess Alexandra, G.C.V.O.
(1964).
Vice-Chancellor, Prof. H. J. Hanham, PH.D.
Registrar, M. D. Forster.
Secretary, G. M. Cockburn.

THE UNIVERSITY OF LEEDS (1904)
Leeds LS2 9JT

Full-time Students (1988–89), 11,161.
Chancellor, H.R.H. The Duchess of Kent, G.C.V.O.
(1966).
Vice-Chancellor, Sir Edward Parkes, PH.D., SC.D.
Registrar, J. J. Walsh.

THE UNIVERSITY OF LEICESTER (1957)
Leicester LE1 7RH

Full-time Students (1988–89), 5,126.
Chancellor, Prof. Sir George Porter, F.R.S., PH.D., SC.D.
(1985).
Vice-Chancellor, K. J. R. Edwards, PH.D.
Registrar, Prof. G. Bernbaum.

THE UNIVERSITY OF LIVERPOOL (1903)
P.O. Box 147, Liverpool L69 3BX

Full-time Students (1988–89), 8,360.
Chancellor, The Viscount Leverhulme, K.G., T.D.
(1980).
Vice-Chancellor, Prof. G. J. Davies, PH.D., SC.D.
Registrar, P. H. Gayward, O.B.E..
Academic Secretary, M. D. Carr.

THE UNIVERSITY OF LONDON (1836)
Senate House, WC1E 7HU

Internal Students (1987–88), 52,776, External Students, 24,856.
Visitor, H.M. The Queen in Council.
Chancellor, H.R.H. The Princess Royal, G.C.V.O., F.R.S.
(1981).
Vice-Chancellor, The Lord Flowers, F.R.S.
Chairman of the Court, The Lord Goff of Chieveley,
P.C., D.C.L.
Chairman of Convocation, Prof. J. P. Quilliam, O.B.E.,
D.SC.
Principal, P. Holwell.

Principal Officers

Clerk of the Court, P. J. Griffiths.
Clerk of the Senate, J. R. Davidson.
Academic Registrar, Mrs. G. F. Roberts.
Secretary to University Entrance and School Examinations Council, A. R. Stephenson.

Schools of the University

Birkbeck College, Malet Street, WC1E 7HX.—*Master*,
The Baroness Blackstone, PH.D.
Goldsmiths' College, Lewisham Way, New Cross,
SE14 6NW.—*Warden*, Prof. A. Rutherford.

Imperial College of Science, Technology and Medicine, South Kensington, SW7 2AZ.—*Rector,* Prof. E. A. Ash, C.B.E., Ph.D., F.R.S.

Institute of Education, 20 Bedford Way, WC1H 0AL.—*Dir.,* Sir Peter Newsam.

King's College London (includes former Chelsea College and Queen Elizabeth College), Strand, WC2R 2LS.—*Principal,* Prof. S. R. Sutherland, Ph.D.

London School of Economics and Political Science, Houghton Street, WC2A 2AE.—*Director,* Dr. I. Patel.

Queen Mary and Westfield College, Mile End Road, E1 4NS.—*Principal,* Prof. I. Butterworth, C.B.E., Ph.D., F.R.S.

Royal Holloway and Bedford New College, Egham Hill, Egham, Surrey TW20 0EX.—*Principal,* Prof. Dorothy E. C. Wedderburn, D. Litt.

Royal Veterinary College, Royal College Street, NW1 0TU.—*Principal and Dean,* Prof. L. E. Lanyon, Ph.D.

School of Oriental and African Studies, Malet Street, WC1E 7HP.—*Dir.,* M. D. McWilliam.

School of Pharmacy, 29–39 Brunswick Square, WC1N 1AX.—*Dean,* Prof. A. T. Florence, Ph.D., F.R.S.E.

University College, Gower Street, WC1E 6BT.—*Provost,* Dr. D. H. Roberts, C.B.E., F.R.S.

Wye College, Wye, Ashford, Kent TN25 5AH.—*Principal,* Prof. J. H. D. Prescott, Ph.D.

*Heythrop College, 11–13 Cavendish Square, W1M 0AN.—*Principal,* Rev. B. A. Callaghan, S.J.

Medical Schools

Charing Cross and Westminster Medical School, The Reynolds Building, St. Dunstan's Road, W6 8RP.—*Dean,* J. E. H. Pendower; *Secretary,* G. K. Buckley.

The London Hospital Medical College, Turner Street, E1 2AD.—*Dean,* Prof. R. Duckworth, C.B.E., M.D., F.R.C.S., F.R.C. Path. *Secretary,* J. W. Walmsley.

Royal Free Hospital School of Medicine, Rowland Hill Street, NW3 2PF.—*Dean,* Prof. A. J. Zuckerman, M.D., F.R.C.P.; *Secretary,* B. A. Blatch.

St. Bartholomew's Hospital Medical College, West Smithfield, EC1A 7BE.—*Dean,* Prof. L. H. Rees, M.D., F.R.C.P.; *Secretary,* D. J. Brown, M.B.E.

St. George's Hospital Medical School, Cranmer Terrace, Tooting, SW17 0RE.—*Dean,* Prof. A. W. Asscher, M.D., F.R.C.P.; *Secretary,* R. B. Hill.

United Medical and Dental Schools of Guy's and St. Thomas's Hospitals, Guy's: London Bridge, SE1 9RT; St. Thomas's: Lambeth Palace Road, SE1 7EH.—*Dean,* Prof. I. R. Cameron, D.M., F.R.C.P.; *Secretary,* C. S. Argles.

Postgraduate Medical Schools

London School of Hygiene and Tropical Medicine, Keppel Street WC1E 7HT.—*Dean,* Prof. R. G. Feachem, Ph.D.

Royal Postgraduate Medical School, Du Cane Road W12 0SH.—*Dean,* Prof. D. N. S. Kerr, F.R.C.P.

British Postgraduate Medical Federation (University of London), 33 Millman Street, WC1N 3EJ.—*Director,* Prof. M. J. Peckham, M.D., F.R.C.P.(G), F.R.C.R.

Comprises:—

Institute of Cancer Research, Royal Cancer Hospital, 17A Onslow Gardens SW7 3AL.—*Director,* Prof. R. A. Weiss, Ph.D.

Institute of Child Health, 30 Guilford Street, WC1N 1EH.—*Dean,* Prof. P. J. Graham, F.R.C.P.

Institute of Dental Surgery, Eastman Dental Hospital, Gray's Inn Road, WC1X 8LD.—*Dean,* Prof. G. B. Winter, D.Ch., F.D.S.

National Heart and Lung Institute, Fulham Road, SW3 6HP.—*Dean,* M. Green, D.M., F.R.C.P.

Hunterian Institute, Royal College of Surgeons of England, Lincoln's Inn Fields, WC2A 3PN.—*Master,* Prof. Sir Stanley Peart, F.R.S., F.R.C.P.; *Academic Dean,* Prof. G. P. Lewis, Ph.D.

Institute of Neurology, National Hospital, Queen Square, WC1N 3BG.—*Dean,* D. N. Landon.

Institute of Ophthalmology, Judd Street, WC1H 9QS.—*Dean,* R. K. Blach, M.D., F.R.C.S.

Institute of Psychiatry, De Crespigny Park, Denmark Hill, SE5 8AF.—*Dean,* Dr. R. M. Murray, M.D.

Senate Institutes

British Institute in Paris, 9–11 Rue de Constantine, 75007, Paris.—*Dir.,* Prof. C. L. Campos, L-ès-L., Ph.D. London office: Senate House, WC1E 7HU.

Courtauld Institute of Art, North Block, Somerset House, Strand, WC2R 2LS.—*Dir.,* Prof. C. M. Kauffman, Ph.D.

Institute of Advanced Legal Studies, Charles Clore House, 17 Russell Square, WC1B 5DR.—*Dir.,* Prof. T. C. Daintith.

Institute of Classical Studies, 31–34 Gordon Square, WC1H 0PY.—*Dir.,* Prof. J. P. Barron, F.S.A.

Institute of Commonwealth Studies, 27–28 Russell Square, WC1B 5DS.—*Dir.,* Prof. Shula E. Marks, Ph.D.

Institute of Germanic Studies, 29 Russell Square, WC1B 5DP.—*Hon. Dir.,* Prof. M. W. Swales, Ph.D.

Institute of Historical Research (including the Institute of United States Studies), Senate House, Malet Street, WC1E 7HU.—*Dir.,* Prof. F. M. L. Thompson, D.Phil., F.B.A.

Institute of Latin American Studies, 31 Tavistock Square, WC1H 9HA.—*Dir.,* Prof. L. M. Bethell, Ph.D.

School of Slavonic and E. European Studies, Senate House, WC1E 7HU.—*Dir.,* Prof. M. A. Branch, Ph.D.

Warburg Institute, Woburn Square, WC1H 0AB.—*Dir.,* Prof. J. B. Trapp, F.B.A.

Institutions having Recognized Teachers

Jews' College, 44A Albert Road, NW4 2SJ.—*Principal,* Rabbi Dr. J. Sacks, Ph.D.

London Business School, Sussex Place, NW1 4SA.—*Principal,* Prof. G. Bain.

Royal Academy of Music, Marylebone Road, NW1 5HT.—*Principal,* Sir David Lumsden, D.Phil., F.R.C.M.

Royal College of Music, Prince Consort Road, SW7 2BS.—*Director,* M. G. Matthews, F.R.S.A.

Trinity College of Music, Mandeville Place, W1M 6AQ.—*Principal,* P. Jones, C.B.E.

LOUGHBOROUGH UNIVERSITY OF TECHNOLOGY (1966)
Loughborough LE11 3TU

Full-time Students (1988–89), 5,800.
Chancellor, Sir Denis Rooke, C.B.E., F.R.S. (1989).
Vice-Chancellor, Prof. D. E. N. Davies, C.B.E., Ph.D., D.SC., F.R.S.
Registrar, D. E. Fletcher, Ph.D.

THE UNIVERSITY OF MANCHESTER
Oxford Road, Manchester M13 9PL
(Founded 1851; re-organized 1880 and 1903).

Full-time Students (1988–89), 16,372.
Chancellor, Prof. J. A. G. Griffith, F.B.A. (1986).
Vice-Chancellor, Sir Mark Richmond, Ph.D., SC.D., F.R.S.
Registrar and Secretary, K. E. Kitchen.

---

*Not in receipt of U.F.C. grants.

UNIVERSITY OF MANCHESTER INSTITUTE OF SCIENCE AND TECHNOLOGY
(1824)
P.O. Box 88, Manchester M60 1QD

Full-time Students (1988–89), 4,230.
President, Sir John Mason, C.B., D.SC., F.R.S. (1986).
Principal, Prof. H. C. A. Hankins, PH.D.
Secretary and Registrar, P. C. C. Stephenson.

THE UNIVERSITY OF NEWCASTLE UPON TYNE
(Founded 1852; re-organized 1908, 1937 and 1963)
6 Kensington Terrace, Newcastle upon Tyne
NE1 7RU

Full-time Students (1988–89), 8,062.
Chancellor, The Viscount Ridley, T.D. (1989).
Vice-Chancellor, Prof. L. W. Martin, PH.D.
Registrar, D. E. T. Nicholson.

THE UNIVERSITY OF NOTTINGHAM (1948)
University Park, Nottingham NG7 2RD

Full-time Students (1988–89), 7,500.
Chancellor, Sir Gordon Hobday, PH.D. (1979).
Vice-Chancellor, C. M. Campbell.
Registrar, G. E. Chandler.

THE UNIVERSITY OF OXFORD
FULL TERMS, 1990

Hilary, Jan. 14 to March 10; *Trinity*, April 22 to June 16; *Michaelmas*, Oct. 7 to Dec. 1

Number of Undergraduates in Residence 1988–89:
Men, 6,004; *Women*, 4,001

UNIVERSITY OFFICERS, etc.	Elect.
Chancellor, The Lord Jenkins of Hillhead, P.C. (*Balliol*)	1987
High Steward, The Lord Wilberforce, P.C., C.M.G., O.B.E. (*All Souls*)	1967
Vice-Chancellor, Sir Richard Southward, D.SC., F.R.S. (*Merton*)	1989
Proctors, P. C. Newell, D.Phil., D.SC. (*St. Peter's*); P. N. Mirfield (*Jesus*)	1989
Assessor, J. K. Aronson, D.Phil. (*Green*)	1989
Public Orator, G. W. Bond (*Pembroke*)	1980
Bodley's Librarian, D. G. Vaisey (*Exeter*)	1986
Keeper of Archives, J. Hackney (*Wadham*)	1988
Director of the Ashmolean Museum, C. J. White (*Worcester*)	1985
Registrar of the University, A. J. Dorey, D.Phil. (*Linacre*)	1979
Surveyor to the University, D. W. Bending	1985
Secretary of Faculties, A. P. Weale (*Worcester*)	1984
Secretary of the Chest and Chief Accountant, I. G. Thompson (*Merton*)	1986
Deputy Registrar (Admin.), D. W. Roberts (*Pembroke*)	
Deputy Registrar (General), P. W. Jones (*Worcester*)	1989

Oxford Colleges and Halls
(With dates of foundation)

All Souls (1438), *Warden*, Sir Patrick Neill, Q.C. (1977).
Balliol (1263), *Master*, B. S. Blumberg (1989).
Brasenose (1509), *Principal*, The Lord Windlesham, C.V.O., P.C. (1989).
Christ Church (1546), *Dean*, Very Rev. E. W. Heaton (1979).
Corpus Christi (1517), *President*, Prof. Sir Keith Thomas, F.B.A. (1986).
Exeter (1314), *Rector*, Sir Richard Norman, K.B.E., D.SC., F.R.S. (1987).

Green (1979), *Warden*, J. T. Hughes, D.Phil. (*acting*) (1989).
Hertford (1874), *Principal*, Prof. E. C. Zeeman, F.R.S. (1988).
Jesus (1571), *Principal*, Dr. P. M. North, C.B.E., D.C.L. (1984).
Keble (1868), *Warden*, G. B. Richardson, C.B.E. (1989).
Lady Margaret Hall (1878), *Principal*, D. M. Stewart (1979).
Linacre (1962), *Principal*, Sir Bryan Cartledge, K.C.M.G. (1988).
Lincoln (1427), *Rector*, Sir Maurice Shock (1987).
Magdalen (1458), *President*, A. D. Smith, C.B.E. (1988).
Merton (1264), *Warden*, J. M. Roberts, D.Phil. (1985).
New College (1379), *Warden*, H. McGregor, Q.C., D.C.L. (1985).
Nuffield (1937), *Warden*, Sir David Cox, F.R.S. (1988).
Oriel (1326), *Provost*, The Rt. Hon. Sir Zelman Cowen, A.K., G.C.M.G., G.C.V.O., Q.C., D.C.L. (1982).
Pembroke (1624), *Master*, Sir Roger Bannister, C.B.E., D.M., F.R.C.P. (1985).
Queen's (1340), *Provost*, J. Moffatt, D.Phil. (1987).
St. Anne's (1952) (Originally Society of Oxford Home-Students (1879)), *Principal*, Claire Palley, PH.D. (1984).
St. Antony's (1950), *Warden*, R. Dahrendorf, HON. K.B.E., PH.D., F.B.A. (1987).
St. Catherine's (1962), *Master*, E. B. Smith, D.SC. (1988).
St. Cross (1965), *Master*, R. C. Repp, D.Phil. (1987).
St. Edmund Hall (c. 1278), *Principal*, J. C. B. Gosling (1983).
*St. Hilda's (1938), *Principal*, Mrs G. M. Moore (1980).
St. Hugh's (1886), *Principal*, Miss M. R. Trickett (1973).
St. John's (1555), *President*, W. Hayes, D.Phil. (1987).
St. Peter's (1929), *Master*, Prof. G. E. Aylmer, D.Phil., F.B.A. (1978).
*Somerville (1879), *Principal*, Miss C. E. Pestell, C.M.G. (1989).
Trinity (1554), *President*, Sir John Burgh, K.C.M.G., C.B. (1987).
University (1249), *Master*, W. J. Albery, D.Phil., F.R.S. (1989).
Wadham (1612), *Warden*, Sir Claus Moser, K.C.B., C.B.E., F.B.A. (1984).
Wolfson (1966), *President*, Sir Raymond Hoffenberg, K.B.E., F.R.C.P. (1985).
Worcester (1714), *Provost*, The Lord Briggs, F.B.A. (1976).

Campion Hall (1896), *Master*, Rev. J. A. Munitiz (1989).
St. Benet's Hall (1897), *Master*, Rev. P. F. Cowper, O.S.B. (1989).
Mansfield (1886), *Principal*, D. J. Trevelyan, C.B. (1989).
Regent's Park (1810), *Principal*, Rev. P. S. Fiddes, D.Phil. (1989).
Greyfriars (1910), *Warden*, Rev. T. M. Mann (1981).

* Colleges for women only.

THE UNIVERSITY OF READING (1926)
Whiteknights, P.O. Box 217, Reading RG6 2AH

Full-time Students (1988–89), 7,060.
Chancellor, The Lord Sherfield, G.C.B., G.C.M.G., F.R.S. (1970).
Vice-Chancellor, E. S. Page, PH.D.
Registrar, T. Bottomley.

UNIVERSITY OF SALFORD (1967)
Salford M5 4WT

Full-time Students (1988–89), 4,100.
Chancellor, H.R.H. The Prince Philip, Duke of Edinburgh, K.G., K.T., O.M., G.B.E., P.C., F.R.S. (1967).
Chancellor-Elect (from 1990), H.R.H. The Duchess of York.

Vice-Chancellor, Prof. J. M. Ashworth, PH.D., D.SC.
Registrar, S. R. Bosworth, O.B.E.

THE UNIVERSITY OF SHEFFIELD (1905)
Western Bank, Sheffield S10 2TN

Full-time Students (1987–88), 7,914.
Chancellor, The Lord Dainton, PH.D., SC.D., F.R.S. (1979).
Vice-Chancellor, Prof. G. D. Sims, O.B.E., PH.D.
Registrar and Secretary, Dr. J. S. Padley.

THE UNIVERSITY OF SOUTHAMPTON (1952)
Highfield, Southampton SO9 5NH

Full-time Students (1988–89), 7,141.
Chancellor, The Earl Jellicoe, K.B.E., D.S.O., M.C., P.C. (1984).
Vice-Chancellor, G. R. Higginson, PH.D.
Secretary and Registrar, D. A. Schofield.
Academic Registrar, Miss A. E. Clarke.

UNIVERSITY OF SURREY (1966)
Guildford, Surrey GU2 5XH

Full-time Students (1988–89), 4,153.
Chancellor, H.R.H. The Duke of Kent, K.G., G.C.M.G., G.C.V.O. (1977).
Vice-Chancellor, Prof. A. Kelly, C.B.E., SC.D., F.R.S.
Registrar, G. Haigh, PH.D.
Secretary, L. J. Kail.

THE UNIVERSITY OF SUSSEX (1961)
Falmer, Brighton BN1 9RH

Full-time Students (1988–89), 4,935.
Chancellor, The Earl of March and Kinrara (1985).
Vice-Chancellor, Sir Leslie Fielding, K.C.M.G.
Registrar and Secretary, G. Lockwood, D.Phil.

THE UNIVERSITY OF WARWICK (1965)
Coventry CV4 7AL

Full-time Students (1988–89), 8,220.
Chancellor, Sir Shridath Surendranath Ramphal, C.M.G., Q.C. (1989).
Vice-Chancellor, C. L. Brundin, PH.D.
Registrar, M. L. Shattock, O.B.E.

THE UNIVERSITY OF YORK (1963)
Heslington, York YO1 5DD

Full-time Students (1988–89), 4,098.
Chancellor, The Lord Swann, PH.D., F.R.S., F.R.S.E. (1979).
Vice-Chancellor, Prof. S. B. Saul, PH.D.
Registrar, D. J. Foster.

CRANFIELD INSTITUTE OF TECHNOLOGY (1969)
Central Business Exchange,
Central Milton Keynes MK9 2EN

Under Royal Charter (1969) the Cranfield Institute of Technology grants degrees in applied science, engineering, technology and management.
Full-time Students (1988–89), 1,941.
Chancellor, The Lord Kings Norton, PH.D. (1969).
Vice-Chancellor, Prof. F. R. Hartley, D.SC.
Secretary and Registrar, J. K. Pettifer.

THE OPEN UNIVERSITY (1969)
Walton Hall, Milton Keynes MK7 6AA

Students and clients (1989), 176,760.
Tuition by correspondence linked with special radio and television programmes, video and audio cassettes, residential schools and a locally-based tutorial and counselling service. Under Royal Charter the University awards degrees of B.A., B.Phil., M.A., M.B.A., M.SC., M.Phil., PH.D., D.SC. and D.Litt. There are seven faculties—arts, education, mathematics, science, social sciences, technology and management and a wide range of continuing education courses and study packs.
Chancellor, The Lord Briggs, F.B.A. (1978).
Vice-Chancellor, J. H. Horlock, PH.D., SC.D., F.R.S.
Secretary, D. J. Clinch.

ROYAL COLLEGE OF ART (1837)
Kensington Gore, SW7 2EU

Under Royal Charter (1967) the Royal College of Art grants the degrees of Doctor, Doctor of Philosophy, Master of Arts and Master of Design (RCA).
Students (1988–89), 600 (all postgraduate).
Provost, The Earl of Gowrie, P.C. (1986).
Registrar, D. Bennington.

THE UNIVERSITY OF WALES (1893)
King Edward VII Avenue, Cathays Park,
Cardiff CF1 3NS

Chancellor, H.R.H. The Prince of Wales, K.G., K.T., G.C.B., P.C. (1976).
Pro-Chancellor, The Lord Cledwyn of Penrhos, C.H., P.C. (1985).
Vice-Chancellor, Prof. E. Sutherland, PH.D.
Registrar, M. A. R. Kemp, PH.D.

Colleges

University College of Wales, Aberystwyth.—*Princ.*, Prof. K. O. Morgan, D.Phil. (1979).
University College of North Wales, Bangor.—*Princ.*, Prof. E. Sunderland, PH.D. (1984).
University of Wales College of Cardiff, Cardiff.—*Princ.*, Sir Aubrey Trotman-Dickenson, PH.D., D.SC. (1968).
Lampeter (St. David's College).—Princ., Prof. B. R. Morris, D.Phil. (1980).
Swansea (University College).—Princ., Prof. B. L. Clarkson, PH.D., (1982).
University of Wales College of Medicine, Cardiff.—*Provost*, Prof. Sir Herbert Duthie, M.D., ch.M., F.R.C.S. (1979).

SCOTLAND

UNIVERSITY OF ABERDEEN (1495)
Regent Walk, Aberdeen AB9 1FX

Full-time Students (1988–89), 6,260.
Chancellor, Sir Kenneth Alexander, F.R.S.E. (1987).
Principal, Prof. G. P. McNicol, M.D., PH.D., F.R.S.E. (1981).
Secretary, N. R. D. Begg.
Rector, W. Pickard (1988–90).

UNIVERSITY OF DUNDEE (1967)
Dundee DD1 4HN

Full-time Students (1988–89), 4,020.
Chancellor, The Earl of Dalhousie, K.T., G.C.V.O., G.B.E., M.C. (1977).
Vice-Chancellor, Prof. M. J. Hamlin, LL.D.
Secretary, R. Seaton.
Rector, P. H. Scott, C.M.G. (1989–92).

UNIVERSITY OF EDINBURGH (1583)
Old College, South Bridge, Edinburgh EH8 9YL

Full-time Students (1988–89), 10,477.
Chancellor, H.R.H. The Prince Philip, Duke of Edinburgh, K.G., K.T., O.M., G.B.E., P.C., F.R.S. (1952).

Vice-Chancellor and Principal, Sir David Smith, D.Phil., F.R.S.
Secretary, A. M. Currie, O.B.E. (M. J. B. Lowe from Jan. 1990).
Rector, Ms. M. Gray (1988–91).

UNIVERSITY OF GLASGOW (1451)
Glasgow G12 8QQ

Full-time Students (1988–89), 11,015.
Chancellor, Sir Alexander Cairncross, K.C.M.G., F.B.A. (1972).
Vice-Chancellor, Sir William Fraser, G.C.B., F.R.S.E.
Registrar, J. M. Black.
Secretary, R. Ewen, O.B.E., T.D.
Rector, Mrs. W. Mandela, (1987–90).

HERIOT-WATT UNIVERSITY (1966)
Riccarton, Edinburgh EH14 4AS

Full-time Students (1988–89), 4,160.
Chancellor, The Lord Thomson of Monifieth, K.T., P.C., F.R.S.E. (1977).
Principal and Vice-Chancellor, Prof. A. G. J. Mac-Farlane, C.B.E., Ph.D., F.R.S. (1989).
Secretary, D. I. Cameron.
Registrar, D. Sturgeon.

UNIVERSITY OF ST. ANDREWS (1411)
College Gate, St. Andrews KY16 9AJ

Full-time Students (1988–89), 3,776.
Chancellor, Sir Kenneth Dover, D.Litt., F.R.S.E., F.B.A. (1981).
Vice-Chancellor, Prof. S. Arnott, Ph.D., F.R.S., F.R.S.E.
Registrar and Secretary, Dr. M. J. B. Lowe.
Rector, N. Parsons (1989–92).

UNIVERSITY OF STIRLING (1967)
Stirling FK9 4LA

Full-time Students (1988–89), 3,450.
Chancellor, The Lord Balfour of Burleigh, F.R.S.E. (1988).
Principal and Vice-Chancellor, Prof. A. J. Forty, Ph.D., D.SC., F.R.S.E.
Registrar, D. J. Farrington, D.Phil.
Secretary, R. G. Bomont.

UNIVERSITY OF STRATHCLYDE (1964)
16 Richmond Street, Glasgow G1 1XQ

Full-time Students (1987–88), 7,630.
Chancellor, The Lord Todd, O.M., D.SC., D.Phil., F.R.S (1965).
Principal and Vice-Chancellor, Sir Graham Hills, Ph.D., D.SC., F.R.S.E.
Registrar and Secretary, D. W. J. Morrell.

NORTHERN IRELAND

THE QUEEN'S UNIVERSITY OF BELFAST (1908)
Belfast BT7 1NN

Full-time Students (1988–89), 7,552.
Chancellor, Sir Rowland Wright, K.B., C.B.E., D.SC. (1984).
President and Vice-Chancellor, G. Beveridge, Ph.D., F.R.S.E.
Registrar, (vacant).
Secretary, Dr. G. A. Baird.

UNIVERSITY OF ULSTER (1984)
Cromore Road, Coleraine BT52 1SA
(Amalgamation of New University of Ulster and Ulster Polytechnic)

Full-time Students (1988–89), 10,550.
Chancellor, The Lord Grey of Naunton, G.C.M.G., G.C.V.O., O.B.E. (1985).
Vice-Chancellor, Sir Derek Birley.
Academic Registrar, P. J. Conway.
Secretary, J. A. Hunter.

NON-UNIVERSITY SECTOR

POLYTECHNICS

The number of students (full-time equivalent) for the academic year 1988–89 are shown in parenthesis.

BIRMINGHAM POLYTECHNIC, Perry Barr, Birmingham B42 2SU (8,300).—*Dir.,* P. C. Knight, D.Phil.; *Registrar,* Ms. M. Penlington.

BRIGHTON POLYTECHNIC, Moulsecoomb, Brighton BN2 4AT (6,325).—*Dir.,* Prof. G. R. Hall, C.B.E.; *Registrar,* A. F. Hussey.

BRISTOL POLYTECHNIC, Coldharbour Lane, Frenchay, Bristol BS16 1QY (6,180).—*Dir.,* A. C. Morris; *Registrar,* Mrs. H. K. Croft.

CITY OF LONDON POLYTECHNIC, 117–119 Houndsditch, EC3 7BU (c. 7,750).—*Dir.,* Prof. R. Floud, D.Phil.; *Registrar,* B. High.

COVENTRY POLYTECHNIC, Priory Street, Coventry CV1 5FB (6,750).—*Dir.,* M. Goldstein, Ph.D., D.SC., F.R.S.C.; *Registrar,* Ms. S. Haselgrove.

HATFIELD POLYTECHNIC, College Lane, Hatfield, Herts AL10 9AB (4,500).—*Dir.,* Prof. N. K. Buxton, Ph.D.

HUDDERSFIELD POLYTECHNIC, Queensgate, Huddersfield HD1 3DH (6,000).—*Rector,* Prof. K. J. Durrands; *Registrar,* M. Bond.

KINGSTON POLYTECHNIC, Penrhyn Road, Kingston upon Thames KT1 2EE (5,770).—*Dir.,* R. C. Smith, C.B.E., Ph.D.

LANCASHIRE POLYTECHNIC, Preston PR1 2TQ (5,850).—*Dir.,* E. E. Robinson; *Registrar,* D. Sharrocks.

LEEDS POLYTECHNIC, Calverley Street, Leeds LS1 3HE (8,198).—*Dir.,* C. Price; *Registrar,* (vacant).

LEICESTER POLYTECHNIC, P.O. Box 143, Leicester LE1 9BH (6,325).—*Dir.,* K. Barker.

LIVERPOOL POLYTECHNIC, Rodney House, 70 Mount Pleasant, Liverpool L3 5UX (8,706).—*Rector,* Prof. P. Toyne; *Registrar,* Miss P. Eastwood.

MANCHESTER POLYTECHNIC, All Saints, Manchester M15 6BH (13,378)—*Dir.,* Sir Kenneth Green; *Sec.,* R. O. Yeo.

MIDDLESEX POLYTECHNIC, Trent Park, Bramley Road, Barnet N14 4XS (7,134).—*Dir.,* R. M. W. Rickett, C.B.E., Ph.D.

NEWCASTLE UPON TYNE POLYTECHNIC, Newcastle upon Tyne NE1 8ST (9,126)—*Dir.,* Prof. L. Barden, Ph.D., D.SC.; *Registrar,* R. A. Bott.

NOTTINGHAM POLYTECHNIC, Burton Street, Nottingham NG1 4BU (9,217).—*Dir.,* Prof. R. Cowell, R.D.; *Registrar,* A. E. Foster.

OXFORD POLYTECHNIC, Headington, Oxford OX3 0BP (6,016).—*Dir.,* Dr. C. Booth; *Registrar,* R. Tulloch.

POLYTECHNIC OF CENTRAL LONDON, 309 Regent Street, W1R 8AL (4,828).—*Rector,* Prof. T. E. Burlin, D.SC., Ph.D.; *Registrar,* J. Worner.

POLYTECHNIC OF EAST LONDON, Romford Road, E15 4LZ (6,200).—*Dir.,* Prof. G. T. Fowler; *Registrar,* G. D. Miller.

POLYTECHNIC OF NORTH LONDON, Holloway Road N7 8DB (5,708)—*Dir.,* L. Wagner; *Registrar,* Dr. P. Holiday.

POLYTECHNIC SOUTH WEST, Drake Circus, Plymouth PL4 8AA (5,040).—*Dir.,* R. J. Bull.

PORTSMOUTH POLYTECHNIC, Ravelin House, Museum Road, Portsmouth PO1 2QQ (6,632).—*Pres.*, H. D. Law, PH.D.; *Registrar*, Brig. B. R. Biggs.

SHEFFIELD CITY POLYTECHNIC, Pond Street, Sheffield S1 1WB (9,700).—*Principal*, J. M. Stoddart; *Registrar*, Ms. J. Tory.

SOUTH BANK POLYTECHNIC, 103 Borough Road, London SE1 0AA (5,420).—*Dir.*, Mrs. P. Perry; *Registrar (acting)*, T. Harvey.

STAFFORDSHIRE POLYTECHNIC, College Road, Stoke-on-Trent, ST4 2DE (5,614).—*Dir.*, K. B. Thompson; *Academic Registrar*, Mrs. F. Francis.

SUNDERLAND POLYTECHNIC, Langham Tower, Ryhope Road, Sunderland SR2 7EE (4,725).—*Rector*, E. P. Hart, PH.D.; *Registrar*, S. Porteous.

TEESSIDE POLYTECHNIC, Middlesbrough, Cleveland TS1 3BA (4,487).—*Dir.*, M. D. Longfield, PH.D.; *Registrar*, M. McClintock.

THAMES POLYTECHNIC, Wellington Street, Woolwich, London SE18 6PF (6,500).—*Dir.*, N. Singer, PH.D.; *Registrar*, A. I. Mayfield.

WOLVERHAMPTON POLYTECHNIC, Molineux Street, Wolverhampton WV1 1SB (7,479).—*Dir.*, M. J. Harrison; *Registrar*, A. M. Cooper.

POLYTECHNIC OF WALES, Pontypridd, Mid Glamorgan CF37 1DL (4,500).—*Dir.*, J. D. Davies, O.B.E., PH.D., D.SC.

SCOTTISH CENTRAL INSTITUTIONS

DUNCAN OF JORDANSTONE COLLEGE OF ART, Perth Road, Dundee DD1 4HT.—*Principal*, R. Miller-Smith.

DUNDEE INSTITUTE OF TECHNOLOGY, Bell Street, Dundee DD1 1HG.—*Principal*, H. G. Cuming, C.B.E., PH.D.

EAST OF SCOTLAND COLLEGE OF AGRICULTURE, West Mains Road, Edinburgh EH9 3JG.—*Principal*, Prof. P. N. Wilson.

EDINBURGH COLLEGE OF ART, Lauriston Place, Edinburgh EH3 9DF.—*Principal (acting)*, W. F. Wood.

GLASGOW COLLEGE, Cowcaddens Road, Glasgow G4 0BA.—*Principal*, Dr. J. S. Mason.

GLASGOW SCHOOL OF ART, 167 Renfrew Street, Glasgow G3 6RQ.—*Director*, T. H. Pannell.

NAPIER COLLEGE, Colinton Road, Edinburgh EH10 5DT.—*Principal*, W. A. Turmeau, C.B.E., PH.D.

NORTH OF SCOTLAND COLLEGE OF AGRICULTURE, 581 King Street, Aberdeen AB9 1UD.—*Principal*, Prof. A. S. Jones, PH.D.

PAISLEY COLLEGE OF TECHNOLOGY, High Street, Paisley PA1 2BE.—*Principal*, Prof. R. W. Shaw.

QUEEN MARGARET COLLEGE, Clerwood Terrace, Edinburgh EH12 8TS.—*Principal*, D. F. Leach.

THE QUEEN'S COLLEGE, GLASGOW, 1 Park Drive, Glasgow G3 6LP.—*Principal*, G. A. Richardson, PH.D.

ROBERT GORDON'S INSTITUTE OF TECHNOLOGY, Schoolhill, Aberdeen AB9 1FR.—*Principal*, D. A. Kennedy, PH.D.

ROYAL SCOTTISH ACADEMY OF MUSIC AND DRAMA, 100 Renfrew Street, Glasgow G2 3BD.—*Principal*, P. Ledger, C.B.E.

SCOTTISH COLLEGE OF TEXTILES, Netherdale, Galashiels, Selkirkshire, TD1 3HF.—*Principal*, C. E. R. Maddox, PH.D.

THE WEST OF SCOTLAND COLLEGE, Auchincruive, Ayr KA6 5HW.—*Principal*, Prof. P. C. Thomas.

COLLEGES

It is not possible to name here all the colleges offering courses of higher or further education. The list of English colleges that follows is confined to those in the PCFC sector; there are many more colleges in England providing higher education courses, some with PCFC funding. The list of colleges in Wales, Scotland and Northern Ireland includes institutions providing at least one full-time course leading to a first degree granted by a university or by the Council for National Academic Awards (C.N.A.A.). It does not include colleges forming part of a polytechnic or a university, nor does it include Scottish central institutions.

ENGLAND

P.C.F.C. Sector

ANGLIA HIGHER EDUCATION COLLEGE, Victoria Road South, Chelmsford CM1 1LL.—*Director*, M. Salmon.

BATH COLLEGE OF HIGHER EDUCATION, Newton Park, Newton St. Loe, Bath BA2 9BN.—*Director*, B. L. Gomes da Costa.

BISHOP GROSSETESTE COLLEGE, Lincoln LN1 3DY.—*Principal*, Prof. L. Marsh, D.PHIL.

BOLTON INSTITUTE OF HIGHER EDUCATION, Deane Road, Bolton BL3 5AB.—*Principal*, R. Oxtoby, PH.D.

BRETTON HALL COLLEGE OF HIGHER EDUCATION, West Bretton, Wakefield, W. Yorks. WF4 4LG.—*Principal*, Prof. J. L. Taylor.

THE BUCKINGHAMSHIRE COLLEGE, Queen Alexandra Road, High Wycombe, Bucks. HP11 2JZ.—*Director*, D. J. Everett, LL.D.

CAMBORNE SCHOOL OF MINES, Pool, Redruth, Cornwall TR15 3SE.—*Principal*, P. Hackett, PH.D.

CENTRAL SCHOOL OF SPEECH AND DRAMA, Embassy Theatre, Eton Avenue, London NW3 3HY.—*Principal*, R. S. Fowler.

CHARLOTTE MASON COLLEGE OF EDUCATION, Rydal Road, Ambleside, Cumbria LA22 9BB.—*Principal*, J. Thorley, PH.D.

CHESTER COLLEGE, Cheyney Road, Chester CH1 4BJ.—*Principal*, Rev. E. V. Binks.

CHRIST CHURCH COLLEGE, North Holmes Road, Canterbury, Kent CT1 1QU—*Principal*, M. H. A. Berry, T.D.

COLLEGE OF RIPON AND YORK ST. JOHN, Lord Mayor's Walk, York YO3 7EX.—*Principal*, Dr. G. P. McGregor.

COLLEGE OF ST. MARK AND ST. JOHN, Derriford Road, Plymouth PL6 8BH.—*Principal*, J. E. Anderson.

COLLEGE OF ST. PAUL AND ST. MARY, The Park, Cheltenham, Glos. GL50 2RH.—*Principal*, Miss J. O. Trotter.

CREWE AND ALSAGER COLLEGE OF HIGHER EDUCATION, Crewe Road, Crewe CW1 1DU.—*Director*, Miss B. P. R. Ward, C.B.E.

DARTINGTON COLLEGE OF ARTS, Totnes, Devon TQ9 6EJ.—*Principal*, P. Hulton.

DERBYSHIRE COLLEGE OF HIGHER EDUCATION, Kedleston Road, Derby DE3 1GB.—*Director*, J. May, T.D., PH.D.

DORSET INSTITUTE, Wallisdown Road, Poole, Dorset BH12 5BB—*Director*, B. R. MacManus, PH.D.

EALING COLLEGE OF HIGHER EDUCATION, St. Mary's Road, Ealing, London W5 5RF—*Director*, N. Merritt.

EDGE HILL COLLEGE OF HIGHER EDUCATION, St. Helens Road, Ormskirk, Lancs. L39 4QP.—*Director*, Ms. R. Gee.

FALMOUTH SCHOOL OF ART AND DESIGN, Woodlane, Falmouth, Cornwall TR11 4RA—*Principal*, Prof. A. G. Livingston.

HARPER ADAMS AGRICULTURAL COLLEGE, Newport, Shropshire TF10 8NB.—*Principal*, A. G. Harris.

HOMERTON COLLEGE, Cambridge CB2 2PH.—*Principal*, A. G. Bamford.

HUMBERSIDE COLLEGE OF HIGHER EDUCATION, Cottingham Road, Hull HU6 7RT.—*Principal,* R. King.

INSTITUTE OF ADVANCED NURSING, Royal College of Nursing, 20 Cavendish Square, London W1M 0AB.—*Principal (acting),* J. C. A. Wells.

KENT INSTITUTE OF ART ANL DESIGN, Oakwood Park, Oakwood Road, Maidstone ME16 8AG (*also* New Dover Road, Canterbury CT1 3AN; Fort Pitt, Rochester ME1 1DZ).—*Director,* P. I. Williams.

KING ALFRED'S COLLEGE, Sparkford Road, Winchester SO22 4NR.—*Principal,* J. A. Cranmer.

LA SAINTE UNION COLLEGE OF HIGHER EDUCATION, The Avenue, Southampton SO9 5HB.—*Principal,* Sister Maria Bernard.

LIVERPOOL INSTITUTE OF HIGHER EDUCATION, P.O. Box 6, Stand Park Road, Liverpool L16 9JD.—*Rector,* J. Burke, O.B.E., Ph.D.

THE LONDON INSTITUTE, 388–396 Oxford Street, W1R 1FE.—*Rector,* J. McKenzie. Comprising:
Camberwell College of Arts, Peckham Road, SE5 8UF.
Central St. Martins College of Art and Design, Southampton Row, WC1B 4AP.
Chelsea College of Art and Design, Manresa Road, SW3 6LS.
College for the Distributive Trades, 30 Leicester Square, WC2H 7LE.
London College of Fashion, 20 John Prince's Street, W1M 9HE.
London College of Printing, Elephant and Castle, SE1 6SB.

LOUGHBOROUGH COLLEGE OF ART AND DESIGN, Redmoor, Loughborough, Leics. LE11 3BT—*Principal,* K. H. Smith.

LUTON COLLEGE OF HIGHER EDUCATION, Park Square, Luton LU1 3JU.—*Director,* A. J. Wood, Ph.D.

NENE COLLEGE, Moulton Park, Northampton NN2 7AL.—*Director,* Dr. S. M. Gaskell.

NEWMAN COLLEGE, Genners Lane, Bartley Green, Birmingham B32 3NT.—*Principal,* Joan S. Cuming, Ph.D.

NORTH RIDING COLLEGE, Filey Road, Scarborough, N. Yorks. YO11 3AZ.—*Principal,* F. W. Wright.

RAVENSBOURNE COLLEGE OF DESIGN AND COMMUNICATION, Walden Road, Chislehurst, Kent BR7 5SN.—*Director,* N. J. Frewing.

ROEHAMPTON INSTITUTE OF HIGHER EDUCATION, Senate House, Roehampton Lane, London SW15 5PU.—*Rector,* Prof. S. C. Holt, Ph.D.

ROSE BRUFORD COLLEGE OF SPEECH AND DRAMA, Lamorbey Park, Burnt Oak Lane, Sidcup, Kent DA15 9DF.—*Principal,* P. Robins.

ROYAL ACADEMY OF MUSIC, Marylebone Road, London NW1 5HT.—*Principal,* Sir David Lumsden, D.Phil.

ROYAL COLLEGE OF MUSIC, Prince Consort Road, London SW7 2BS.—*Director,* M. G. Matthews.

ROYAL NORTHERN COLLEGE OF MUSIC, 124 Oxford Road, Manchester M13 9RD.—*Principal,* Sir John Manduell, C.B.E.

S. MARTIN'S COLLEGE OF HIGHER EDUCATION, Bowerham, Lancaster LA1 3JD.—*Principal,* D. Edynbry, Ph.D.

ST. MARY'S COLLEGE, Strawberry Hill, Twickenham TW1 4SX.—*Principal,* Rev. Father D. A. Beirne.

SALFORD COLLEGE OF TECHNOLOGY, Frederick Road, Salford M6 6PU.—*Principal,* Dr. R. Allerton.

SOUTHAMPTON INSTITUTE OF HIGHER EDUCATION, East Park Terrace, Southampton SO9 4WW.—*Principal,* D. G. Leyland.

TRINITY AND ALL SAINTS' COLLEGE, Brownberrie Lane, Horsforth, Leeds LS18 5HD.—*Principal,* H. Mary Hallaway, O.B.E., D.Phil.

TRINITY COLLEGE OF MUSIC, 11–13 Mandeville Place, London W1M 6AQ.—*Principal,* P. Jones, C.B.E.

WESTHILL COLLEGE, Hamilton Building, Weoley Park Road, Selly Oak, Birmingham B29 6LL.—*Principal,* Rev. G. Benfield.

WEST LONDON INSTITUTE OF HIGHER EDUCATION, Lancaster House, Borough Road, Isleworth, Middlesex TW7 5DU.—*Principal,* J. E. Kane, Ph.D.

WESTMINSTER COLLEGE, North Hinksey, Oxford OX2 9AT.—*Principal,* Rev. Dr. K. B. Wilson.

WEST SURREY COLLEGE OF ART AND DESIGN, Falkner Road, The Hart, Farnham, Surrey GU9 7DS.—*Director,* N. J. Taylor.

WEST SUSSEX INSTITUTE OF HIGHER EDUCATION, The Dome, Upper Bognor Road, Bognor Regis, West Sussex PO21 1HR.—*Director,* J. F. Wyatt.

WINCHESTER SCHOOL OF ART, Park Avenue, Winchester, Hants. SO23 8DL.—*Principal,* M. Sadler-Forster.

WORCESTERSHIRE COLLEGE OF HIGHER EDUCATION, Henwick Grove, Worcester WR2 6AJ.—*Principal,* D. R. Shadbolt, O.B.E., D.Phil.

WALES

GWENT COLLEGE OF HIGHER EDUCATION, Clarence Place, Newport, Gwent NP9 0UW.—*Principal,* M. I. Harris, O.B.E.

COLLEGE OF LIBRARIANSHIP WALES, Aberystwyth, Dyfed SY23 3AS.—*Principal,* F. N. Hogg.

NORMAL COLLEGE, Bangor, Gwynedd LL57 2PX.—*Principal,* R. Williams.

THE NORTH EAST WALES INSTITUTE OF HIGHER EDUCATION, Kelsterton Road, Connah's Quay, Deeside, Clwyd CH5 4BR.—*Principal,* Prof. G. O. Phillips, Ph.D., D.SC.

SOUTH GLAMORGAN INSTITUTE OF HIGHER EDUCATION, Western Avenue, Llandaff, Cardiff CF5 2YB.—*Principal,* E. J. Brent, Ph.D.

TRINITY COLLEGE, Carmarthen, Dyfed, SA31 3EP.—*Principal,* D. C. Jones-Davies.

WELSH AGRICULTURE COLLEGE, Llanbadarn Fawr, Aberystwyth, Dyfed SY23 3AL.—*Principal,* J. R. Gill.

WELSH COLLEGE OF MUSIC AND DRAMA, Castle Grounds, Cathays Park, Cardiff CF1 3ER.—*Principal,* E. Fivet.

WEST GLAMORGAN INSTITUTE OF HIGHER EDUCATION, Townhill Road, Swansea SA2 0UT.—*Principal,* G. Stockdale, Ph.D.

SCOTLAND

CRAIGIE COLLEGE OF EDUCATION, Ayr KA8 0SR.—*Principal,* G. M. Wilson, Ph.D.

DUNFERMLINE COLLEGE OF PHYSICAL EDUCATION, Cramond Road North, Edinburgh EH4 6JD.—*Principal,* Miss J. A. Carroll.

GLASGOW COLLEGE OF BUILDING AND PRINTING, 60 North Hanover Street, Glasgow G1 2BP.—*Principal,* T. B. Wilson.

JORDANHILL COLLEGE OF EDUCATION, Southbrae Drive, Jordanhill, Glasgow G13 1PP.—*Principal,* T. R. Bone, C.B.E., Ph.D.

MORAY HOUSE COLLEGE OF EDUCATION, Holyrood Road, Edinburgh EH8 8AQ.—*Principal,* G. Kirk.

NORTHERN COLLEGE OF EDUCATION, Hilton Place, Aberdeen AB9 1FA; Gardyne Road, Dundee DD5 1NY.—*Principal,* D. A. Adams.

ST. ANDREW'S COLLEGE OF EDUCATION, Duntocher Road, Bearsden, Glasgow G61 4QA.—*Principal,* B. J. McGettrick.

NORTHERN IRELAND

ST. MARY'S COLLEGE, 191 Falls Road, Belfast BT12 6FE.—*Principal,* J. I. O'Connell.

STRANMILLIS COLLEGE, Stranmillis Road, Belfast BT9 5DY.—*Principal,* R. J. Rodgers, Ph.D.

ADULT AND CONTINUING EDUCATION

NATIONAL INSTITUTE OF ADULT CONTINUING EDUCA-
TION, 19B De Montfort Street, Leicester LE1 7GE.
(Tel: 0533-551451).—*Dir.*, A. Tuckett.

NIACE CYMRU, 245 Western Avenue, Cardiff CF5
2YX. (Tel: 0222-516231).—*Admin. Officer*, Ms. A.
Poole.

NORTHERN IRELAND COUNCIL FOR CONTINUING EDU-
CATION, Department of Education Northern Ireland, Rathgael House, Balloo Road, Bangor BT19
2PR. (Tel: 0247-270077).

OPEN COLLEGE, 101 Wigmore Street, W1H 9AB.

THE RESIDENTIAL COLLEGES COMMITTEE, c/o Ruskin
College, Oxford OX1 2HE. (Tel: 0865-56360).—
Awards Officer, Mrs. C. A. Gregory.

SCOTTISH INSTITUTE OF ADULT AND CONTINUING
EDUCATION, 30 Rutland Square, Edinburgh EH1
2BW. (Tel: 031-229 0331).—*Dir.*, Dr. Elisabeth
Gerver.

THE UNIVERSITIES COUNCIL FOR ADULT AND CONTIN-
UING EDUCATION, Department of Continuing Education, The University of Warwick, Coventry CV4
7AL. (Tel: 0203-24011).—*Hon. Sec.*, Prof. C. Duke,
ph.D.

THE WORKER'S EDUCATIONAL ASSOCIATION, Temple
House, 9 Upper Berkeley Street, W1H 8BY. (Tel:
01-402 5608).—*Gen. Sec.*, R. Lochrie.

Long term Residential Colleges for Adult Education

COLEG HARLECH, Harlech, Gwynedd LL46 2PU. (Tel:
0766-780363).—*Warden*, J. W. England.

CO-OPERATIVE COLLEGE, Stanford Hall, Loughborough, Leics. LE12 5QR. (Tel: 0509-822333).—*Principal*, Dr. R. Houlton.

FIRCROFT COLLEGE, 1018 Bristol Road, Selly Oak,
Birmingham B29 6LH. (Tel: 021-472 0116).—*Principal*, K. Jackson.

HILLCROFT COLLEGE, South Bank, Surbiton, Surrey
KT6 6DF. (Tel: 01-399 2688). (For women only).—
Principal, Ms. P. J. Lambert.

NEWBATTLE ABBEY COLLEGE, Dalkeith, Midlothian
EH22 3LL. (Tel: 031-662 1921).—*Principal*, A. D.
Reid.

NORTHERN COLLEGE, Wentworth Castle, Stainbor-
ough, Barnsley, S. Yorks. S75 3ET. (Tel: 0226-
285426).—*Principal*, R. H. Fryer.

PLATER COLLEGE, Pullens Lane, Oxford OX3 0DT.
(Tel: 0865-741676).—*Principal*, D. G. Chiles.

RUSKIN COLLEGE, Walton Street, Oxford OX1 2HE.
(Tel: 0865-54331).—*Principal*, S. Yeo.

PROFESSIONAL EDUCATION
(excluding *postgraduate* study)

NOTE.—References to courses at universities, polytechnics and colleges in the sections following are
not claimed to be comprehensive and cover only
full-time courses leading to first degrees. Full lists
appear in *University Entrance: The Official Guide*
and in *C.N.A.A. Directory of First Degree and
Diploma of Higher Education Courses*. Both are
produced annually.

Postgraduate Study and Research are not treated
here.

ACCOUNTANCY

(*See also* Business, Management and Administration).

First Degrees in *Accounting* or *Accountancy* are
granted by most universities. At several universities
one of these subjects can be combined with, e.g.,
Financial Administration, Finance or Economics.

Courses leading to first degrees in *Accounting,
Accountancy* or *Accounting and Finance* granted by
the C.N.A.A. are provided by most of the polytechnics.

The main bodies granting membership on examination after a period of practical work are:

INSTITUTE OF CHARTERED ACCOUNTANTS IN ENGLAND
AND WALES, Chartered Accountants' Hall, P.O.
Box 433, Moorgate Place, EC2P 2BJ.—*Sec.*, E. J. D.
Warne, c.b.

INSTITUTE OF CHARTERED ACCOUNTANTS OF SCOT-
LAND, 27 Queen Street, Edinburgh EH2 1LA.—*Sec.*,
I. F. Y. Marrian (*acting*).

CHARTERED ASSOCIATION OF CERTIFIED ACCOUN-
TANTS, 29 Lincolns Inn Fields, WC2A 3EE.—*Sec.*,
A. W. Sansom.

CHARTERED INSTITUTE OF MANAGEMENT ACCOUN-
TANTS, 63 Portland Place, W1N 4AB.—*Sec.*, Sir
George Vallings, K.C.B.

CHARTERED INSTITUTE OF PUBLIC FINANCE AND AC-
COUNTANCY, 3 Robert Street, WC2N 6BH.—*Sec.*,
N. P. Hepworth, O.B.E.

ACTUARIAL SCIENCE

First Degrees in *Actuarial Science* are granted by
the City University and the Universities of Kent and
London (London School of Economics and Political
Science); in *Actuarial Studies and Mathematics* by
Southampton University; and in *Actuarial Mathe-
matics and Statistics* by Heriot-Watt University.

Two professional organizations grant qualifications after examination:

INSTITUTE OF ACTUARIES, Staple Inn Hall, High
Holborn, WC1V 7QJ.—*Sec. Gen.*, C. D. A. Mackie.

FACULTY OF ACTUARIES IN SCOTLAND, 23 St. Andrew
Square, Edinburgh EH2 1AQ.—*Sec.*, W. W. Mair.

AERONAUTICS
and Aeronautical Engineering

First Degrees in *Aeronautical Engineering* are
granted by the Universities of Bath, Belfast, Bristol,
Cambridge, the City University, the Universities of
Glasgow, London (Imperial College of Science and
Technology, Queen Mary College, also *Avionics—
Aeronautical/Electrical*), Loughborough (*Aeronauti-
cal Engineering and Design*), Manchester, Salford
and Southampton (*Aeronautics and Astronautics* and
Aerospace Systems Engineering) and in *Air Transport
Engineering* by the City University.

First degrees in *Aeronautical Engineering* are
granted by the C.N.A.A.

AGRICULTURE

First Degrees in *Agriculture* or *Agricultural Sci-
ence(s)* are granted by the Universities of Aberdeen,
Belfast, Edinburgh, Glasgow, Leeds, London (Wye
College), Newcastle upon Tyne, Nottingham, Reading
and Wales (University Colleges of Aberystwyth and
Bangor); in *Agricultural Technology and Manage-
ment* by Cranfield Institute of Technology (Silsoe
College); and in *Horticulture* by Bath, London (Wye
College), Nottingham, Reading and Strathclyde.

First degrees in *Agriculture* are granted by the
C.N.A.A.

ARCHAEOLOGY

First Degrees in *Archaeology* or *Archaeological
Sciences/Studies* are granted by the Universities of

Belfast (also *Archaeological Conservation*), Birmingham, Bradford, Bristol, Cambridge, Durham, Edinburgh, Exeter, Glasgow, Lancaster, Leicester, Liverpool, London (University College, Institute of Archaeology, King's College, School of Oriental and African Studies), Manchester, Newcastle upon Tyne, Nottingham, Reading, Southampton, Wales (University College Cardiff, also *Archaeological Conservation*, Bangor U.C., St. David's U.C.) and York. At several other universities archaeology can be combined with another subject, e.g. ancient history, classics or anthropology.

First degrees in *Archaeology* are granted by the C.N.A.A.

ARCHITECTURE

(*See also* Building, and Town and Country Planning).

First Degrees in *Architecture/Architectural Studies* are granted by the Universities of Bath, Belfast, Cambridge, Dundee, Edinburgh, Glasgow, Heriot-Watt, Leeds, Liverpool, London (University College), Manchester, Newcastle upon Tyne, Nottingham, Sheffield, Strathclyde, Wales (Cardiff).

First degrees in *Architecture/Architectural Studies* are granted by the C.N.A.A.

Other schools of architecture include THE ARCHITECTURAL ASSOCIATION SCHOOL OF ARCHITECTURE, 34–36 Bedford Square, WC1.

THE ROYAL INSTITUTE OF BRITISH ARCHITECTS
66 Portland Place, W1N 4AD

The Education and Professional Development Committee of the Royal Institute of British Architects sets standards and guides the whole system of architectural education throughout the United Kingdom. Courses at Schools recognized by the R.I.B.A. exempt students from the R.I.B.A.'s own examinations.

Pres., M. Hutchison.
Dir.-Gen. The Rt. Hon. W. Rodgers.

ART AND DESIGN

First Degrees in *Art, Fine Art* or *History of Art* are granted by the Universities of Aberdeen, Cambridge, East Anglia, Edinburgh, Essex, Glasgow, Lancaster (*Visual Arts*),Leeds, Leicester, London (Courtauld Institute of Art, Birkbeck, University and Westfield Colleges, School of Oriental and African Studies, Goldsmiths' College), Loughborough (*Design and Technology*), Manchester, Manchester Institute of Science and Technology (*Textile Design and Design Management*), Newcastle upon Tyne, Nottingham, Oxford, Reading, St. Andrews, Sussex, Ulster, Wales (University College, Aberystwyth—*Visual Art*) and Warwick. At several other universities art or history of art can be combined with another subject. The degrees in *Art* granted by the Royal College of Art are higher degrees.

Courses leading to first degrees in *Art and Design, Fine Art, Graphic Design, Textiles/Fashion* or *Three-Dimensional Design* granted by the C.N.A.A. are provided by more than 40 colleges/schools of art and polytechnics some of which also offer C.N.A.A. degree courses in other subjects in the field of Art and Design, including *Furniture Design, Industrial Design* and *Interior Design*.

ASTRONOMY

First Degrees in *Astronomy* are granted by the Universities of Glasgow, London (University College), Newcastle, St. Andrew's, Sheffield; in *Astrophysics* by the Universities of Edinburgh, London (Queen Mary College, University College), Newcas-

tle, St. Andrews and Wales (University College, Cardiff); and in *Physics and Astronomy/Astrophysics* at the Universities of Birmingham, Glasgow, Leeds, Leicester, London (King's College, Queen Mary College, Royal Holloway & Bedford New College, University College), Manchester and Sussex. Various combinations of Astronomy and Astrophysics with other subjects are also available.

Astronomy may be taken as part of a C.N.A.A. degree course at certain polytechnics.

BANKING

First Degrees with specialization in *Banking and Finance* are granted by the Universities of Birmingham (*Money, Banking and Finance*), Loughborough, Ulster (*Banking and Finance*) and Wales (University College, Cardiff), Bangor University College (*Banking, Insurance and Finance*), and the City University (*Banking and International Finance*).

Banking may be taken as part of a C.N.A.A. degree course at certain polytechnics/colleges.

Professional organizations granting qualifications after examination:—

CHARTERED INSTITUTE OF BANKERS, 10 Lombard Street, EC3V 9AS.—*Sec. Gen.*, E. Glover.

INSTITUTE OF BANKERS IN SCOTLAND, 20 Rutland Square, Edinburgh EH1 2DE.—*Sec.*, C. W. Munn.

BIOLOGY, CHEMISTRY, PHYSICS

First Degrees in these subjects are granted by many universities. Courses leading to first degrees, granted by the C.N.A.A., are provided by many polytechnics. Professional qualifications are awarded by:—

INSTITUTE OF BIOLOGY, 20 Queensberry Place, SW7 2DZ.—*Gen. Sec.*, Dr. R. H. Priestley.

ROYAL SOCIETY OF CHEMISTRY, Burlington House, Piccadilly, W1V 0BN.—*Sec.*, J. S. Gow, PH.D., F.R.S.C., F.R.S.E.

INSTITUTE OF PHYSICS, 47 Belgrave Square, SW1X 8QX.—*Sec.*, L. Cohen, PH.D.

BREWING

First Degrees in *Brewing* are granted by Heriot-Watt University.

BUILDING

(*See also* Architecture, Estate and Land Management and Surveying)

First Degrees in *Building, Building Engineering* or *Building Technology* are granted by the following Universities: Bath, Heriot-Watt (also *Building Services Engineering* and *Building Economics and Quantity Surveying*), Liverpool (*Building Management & Technology, Building Services Engineering*), London (University College), Manchester (Manchester Institute of Science and Technology, also *Building Services Engineering* and *Construction Management*), Reading (*Building Construction Management, Quantity Surveying* and *Building Surveying*), Salford (*Building Surveying, Quantity Surveying*) Strathclyde (*Building Design Engineering*), and Ulster (also *Building Services Engineering* and *Quantity Surveying*).

First degrees in *Building, Building Services Engineering, Building Surveying, Construction* and *Environmental Enginering* are granted by the C.N.A.A.

Examinations are also conducted by:—

CHARTERED INSTITUTE OF BUILDING, Englemere, King's Ride, Ascot, Berks. SL5 8BJ.—*Chief Exec.*, K. Banbury.

INSTITUTE OF BUILDING CONTROL, 21 High Street, Ewell, Epsom, Surrey KT17 1SB.—*Sec.*, Ms. R. Raywood.

INSTITUTE OF CLERKS OF WORKS OF GREAT BRITAIN, 41 The Mall, Ealing, W5 3TJ.—*Sec.*, A. P. Macnamara.

BUSINESS, MANAGEMENT AND ADMINISTRATION

First Degrees in *Business, Management, Administration* or various aspects of these subjects are granted by all the Universities. A variety of combinations in these subjects are available at some of the universities and the subjects may also form part of other degree courses.

Courses leading to first degrees in *Business Studies, Business Administration*, or other aspects of business, granted by the C.N.A.A., are provided by all the polytechnics. The C.N.A.A. also grants first degrees in *Marketing*.

Professional bodies conducting training and/or examinations in Business, Administration, Management or Commerce include:

ROYAL INSTITUTE OF PUBLIC ADMINISTRATION, 3 Birdcage Walk, SW1H 9JH.—*Dir.-Gen.*, D. Falcon.

CAM FOUNDATION, Abford House, 15 Wilton Road, SW1V 1NJ.—*Registrar*, Mrs. S. J. Hurford.

CHARTERED INSTITUTE OF MARKETING, Moor Hall, Cookham, Maidenhead, Berks. SL6 9QH.—*Dir. Gen.*, P. B. Blood.

CHARTERED INSTITUTE OF TRANSPORT, 80 Portland Place, W1N 4DP.—*Dir. Gen.*, R. P. Botwood.

FACULTY OF SECRETARIES AND ADMINISTRATORS, 15 Church Street, Godalming, Surrey GU7 1EL.—*Sec.*, Mrs. D. M. Rummery.

INSTITUTE OF ADMINISTRATIVE MANAGEMENT, 40 Chatsworth Parade, Petts Wood, Orpington, Kent BR5 1RW.—*Chief Exec.*, M. J. Ainsworth.

INSTITUTE OF CHARTERED SECRETARIES AND ADMINISTRATORS, 16 Park Crescent, W1N 4AH.—*Sec.*, B. Barker, M.B.E.

INSTITUTE OF CHARTERED SHIPBROKERS, 24 St. Mary Axe, EC3A 8DE.—*Sec.*, J. H. Parker.

INSTITUTE OF EXPORT, Export House, 64 Clifton Street, EC2A 4HB.—*Sec.*, D. J. Langham.

INSTITUTE OF HEALTH SERVICES MANAGEMENT, 75 Portland Place, W1N 4AN.—*Dir.*, Ms. M. Dixon, PH.D.

INSTITUTE OF HOUSING, 9 White Lion Street, N1 9XJ.—*Asst. Dir., Education and Training*, Ms. A. Paterson.

INSTITUTION OF INDUSTRIAL MANAGERS, Rochester House, 66 Little Ealing Lane, W5 4XX.—*Chief Exec.*, G. J. Rawlins, O.B.E.

INSTITUTE OF PERSONNEL MANAGEMENT, IPM House, Camp Road, Wimbledon SW19 4UX.—*Dir.*, K. B. Ward Lilley.

INSTITUTE OF PRACTITIONERS IN ADVERTISING, 44 Belgrave Square SW1X 8QS.—*Sec.*, J. Raad.

INSTITUTE OF PURCHASING AND SUPPLY, Easton House, Easton on the Hill, Stamford, Lincs. PE9 3NZ.—*Dir.-Gen.*, I. G. S. Groundwater.

HENLEY—THE MANAGEMENT COLLEGE, Greenlands, Henley on Thames, Oxon., RG9 3AU.—*Princ.*, Prof. T. Kempner.

LONDON BUSINESS SCHOOL, Sussex Place, Regent's Park, NW1 4SA.—*Princ.*, Prof. G. Bain, PH.D.

MANCHESTER BUSINESS SCHOOL, Booth Street West, Manchester M15 6PB.—*Dir.*, Prof. T. Cannon.

SCOTTISH BUSINESS SCHOOLS, CONFEDERATION OF.—*Dir.*, M. Makower, c/o University of Stirling, Department of Business and Management, Stirling SK9 4LA.

LONDON CHAMBER OF COMMERCE AND INDUSTRY EXAMINATIONS BOARD, Marlowe House, Station Road, Sidcup, Kent DA15 7BJ.—*Dir.*, I. W. Bell.

COMPUTER SCIENCE

First Degrees covering various aspects of *Computer/Computing Science, Data Processing, Information Systems* and *Information Technology* are available at all universities.

Courses leading to first degrees in computer science subjects granted by the C.N.A.A. are provided by all the polytechnics.

These subjects also form part of other degree courses, often as *Mathematics/Statistics and Computer Science*, at many universities, polytechnics and colleges.

DANCE

(*See also* Recreation, Sport, etc.)

First degrees in *Dance in Society* are granted by the University of Surrey.

The University of Kent grants a first degree in *Contemporary Dance* for which courses are provided at the London Contemporary Dance School.

First degrees in *Dance Theatre* are granted by the C.N.A.A. and Dance also forms part of other C.N.A.A. degree courses, often called *Performing Arts* or *Creative Arts*, at several polytechnics and colleges.

ROYAL ACADEMY OF DANCING, 48 Vicarage Crescent, SW11 3LT.—*Directors*, D. Wall, C.B.E., Ms. P. Yates.

ROYAL BALLET SCHOOL, 155 Talgarth Road, W14 9DE, and White Lodge, Richmond Park, Surrey TW10 5HR.—*Dir.*, Dame Merle Park, D.B.E.

IMPERIAL SOCIETY OF TEACHERS OF DANCING, Euston Hall, Birkenhead Street, WC1H 8BE.—*Gen. Sec.*, M. J. Browne.

DEFENCE

First Degrees in *Peace Studies* are granted by the Universities of Bradford and Ulster, and in *Strategic Studies* by the Universities of Lancaster and Wales (University College, Aberystwyth).

Royal Naval Colleges

ROYAL NAVAL COLLEGE, Greenwich, SE10 9NN.—*Admiral President*, Adm. Sir Brian Brown, K.C.B., C.B.E.; *Dean of the College*, Prof. J. L. Head, PH.D.

BRITANNIA ROYAL NAVAL COLLEGE, Dartmouth, Devon TQ6 0HJ.—Initial officer training. *Captain*, Capt. J. R. Shiffner.

ROYAL NAVAL ENGINEERING COLLEGE, Manadon, Plymouth PL5 3AQ.—B.Eng., M.Sc. and specialist training in naval engineering. Students are selected uniformed officers of the Royal Navy, Commonwealth and foreign navies, and civilians. *Captain*, Capt. J. A. Marshall.
Dean, Capt. G. C. George.
Executive Officer, Cdr. C. D. de Burgh.

INSTITUTE OF NAVAL MEDICINE, Alverstoke, Gosport Hants. PO12 2DL.—Higher professional and postgraduate training for officers of all three services, and some civilians. *Medical Officer in Charge*, Surgeon Capt. A. Craig.

Military Colleges

STAFF COLLEGE, Camberley, Surrey GU15 4NP.—*Commandant*, Maj.-Gen. J. J. G. MacKenzie, O.B.E.

ROYAL MILITARY ACADEMY, Sandhurst, Camberley, Surrey GU15 4PQ.—*Commandant*, Maj.-Gen. P. W. Graham, C.B.E.

ROYAL MILITARY COLLEGE OF SCIENCE, Shrivenham, nr. Swindon, Wilts SN6 8LA.—Students from U.K. and overseas study from degree to post-graduate levels in management, science and technology.

There is an increasing range of research and consultancy activity as the College is now a Faculty of the Cranfield Institute of Technology.
Commandant, Maj.-Gen. S. Cowan, C.B.E.
Principal (acting), Prof. W. G. Townsend, PH.D.

INSTITUTE OF ARMY EDUCATION, Court Road, Eltham, SE9 5NR.—*Director*, Maj.-Gen. J. S. Lee, M.B.E.

Royal Air Force Colleges

ROYAL AIR FORCE STAFF COLLEGE, Bracknell, Berks, RG12 3DD.—Prepares selected senior officers for high-grade command and staff appointments. The majority of students are R.A.F. officers but officers from the other U.K. services and from foreign air forces also attend.
Air Officer Commanding and Commandant, Air Vice-Marshal A. F. C. Hunter, C.B.E., A.F.C.

ROYAL AIR FORCE COLLEGE, Cranwell, Sleaford, Lincs NG34 8HB.—Initial officer training for officers of the R.A.F., W.R.A.F. and P.M.R.A.F.N.S., and initial specialist training for officers of the Engineer and Supply Branches. Advanced specialist training is provided for officers of the General Duties, Engineer and Supply Branches and basic flying training for pilots of the General Duties Branch.
Air Officer Commanding and Commandant, Air Vice-Marshal R. H. Wood, O.B.E.

ROYAL AIR FORCE SCHOOL OF EDUCATION AND TRAINING SUPPORT, R.A.F. Newton, Nottingham NG13 8HL.—*Commanding Officer*, Gp. Capt. R. S. R. Lloyd.

DENTISTRY

First Degrees in Dentistry are granted by the Universities of Belfast, Birmingham, Bristol, Dundee, Edinburgh, Glasgow, Leeds, Liverpool, London (United Medical and Dental Schools of Guy's and St. Thomas's Hospitals, King's College School of Medicine and Dentistry, London Hospital Medical College, University College & Middlesex Hospital Medical School), Manchester, Newcastle upon Tyne, Sheffield, Wales (College of Medicine).

To be entitled to be registered in the Dentists Register, a person must hold the degree or diploma in dental surgery of a University in the United Kingdom or Republic of Ireland or the diploma of any of the licensing authorities (The Royal College of Surgeons of England, of Edinburgh and in Ireland, and the Royal College of Physicians and Surgeons of Glasgow). Nationals of an E.C. member state holding an appropriate European diploma, and holders of certain overseas diplomas, may also be registered. The Dentists Register is maintained by THE GENERAL DENTAL COUNCIL, 37 Wimpole Street, W1M 8DQ.

DIETETICS
(See also Food and Nutrition Science)

Courses in *Nutrition and Dietetics* leading to first degrees granted by the University of Wales are provided by South Glamorgan Institute of Higher Education. The University of Bradford grants a first degree in *Nutrition and Food Policy*.

First degrees in *Dietetics* and *Nutrition and Dietetics* are granted by the C.N.A.A.

The professional association is THE BRITISH DIETETIC ASSOCIATION, Daimler House, Paradise Circus, Queensway, Birmingham B1 2BJ. Full membership is open to dietitians holding a recognized qualification, who may also become State Registered Dietitians through the Council for Professions Supplementary to Medicine (q.v.).

DRAMA

First Degrees in *Drama* are granted by the Universities of Birmingham (*Drama and Theatre Arts*), Bristol, East Anglia, Exeter, Glasgow (*Theatre Studies*), Hull, Kent (*Drama and Theatre Studies*), Lancaster (*Theatre Studies*), London (Royal Holloway and Bedford New College, *Drama and Theatre Studies*), Loughborough, Manchester and Wales (University College of Aberystwyth) and Warwick (*Theatre Studies and Dramatic Arts*). Drama also forms part of degree courses in other universities.

First degrees in *Drama Studies, Theatre, Theatre Arts* and *Drama, Theatre and TV Studies* are granted by the C.N.A.A.

The national validating body for courses providing training in drama is THE NATIONAL COUNCIL FOR DRAMA TRAINING, 5 Tavistock Place, WC1H 9SS. It currently has accredited courses at the following: Academy of Live and Recorded Arts; Arts Educational Schools; Birmingham School of Speech Training & Dramatic Art; Bristol Old Vic Theatre School; Central School of Speech and Drama; Drama Centre, London; Drama Studio; Guildford School of Acting; Guildhall School of Music and Drama; London Academy of Music and Dramatic Art; Manchester Polytechnic School of Theatre; Mountview Theatre School; Rose Bruford College of Speech and Drama; Royal Academy of Dramatic Art; Royal Scottish Academy of Music and Drama; Webber Douglas Academy of Dramatic Art; Welsh College of Music and Drama. (The accreditation of a course in a school does not necessarily imply that other courses of different type or duration in the same school are also accredited.)

ECONOMICS

Almost all universities grant first degrees in Economics. Courses leading to first degrees in Economics granted by the C.N.A.A. are provided by some 20 polytechnics and colleges.

ENGINEERING
(See separate subjects below)

The Council of Engineering Institutions ceased operations in Sept. 1983 and its major functions are now carried on by THE ENGINEERING COUNCIL, 10 Maltravers Street, WC2R 3ER.—*Sec.*, L. Chelton. The fifteen principal qualifying bodies are:—

INSTITUTION OF CHEMICAL ENGINEERS, George E. Davis Building, 165–171 Railway Terrace, Rugby, Warwickshire CV21 3HQ.—*Gen. Sec.*, Dr. T. J. Evans.

INSTITUTION OF CIVIL ENGINEERS, Great George Street SW1P 3AA.—*Sec.*, J. C. McKenzie.

INSTITUTION OF ELECTRICAL ENGINEERS, Savoy Place, WC2R 0BL.—*Sec.*, Dr. J. C. Williams.

INSTITUTE OF ENERGY, 18 Devonshire Street, W1N 2AU.—*Sec.* C. Rigg, T.D.

INSTITUTION OF GAS ENGINEERS, 17 Grosvenor Crescent, SW1X 7ES.—*Sec.*, D. J. Chapman.

INSTITUTE OF MARINE ENGINEERS, The Memorial Building, 76 Mark Lane, EC3R 7JN.—*Sec.*, J. E. Sloggett.

INSTITUTION OF MECHANICAL ENGINEERS, 1 Birdcage Walk, SW1H 9JJ.—*Sec.* R. Mellor, C.B.E.

INSTITUTE OF METALS, 1 Carlton House Terrace, SW1Y 5DB.—*Sec.*, Dr. J. A. Catterall.

INSTITUTION OF MINING ENGINEERS, Danum House, 6A South Parade, Doncaster DN1 2DY.—*Sec.*, W. J. W. Bourne.

INSTITUTION OF MINING AND METALLURGY, 44 Portland Place, W1N 4BR.—*Sec.*, M. J. Jones.

INSTITUTION OF PRODUCTION ENGINEERS, Rochester House, 66 Little Ealing Lane, W5 4XX.—*Sec.*, Brig. P. V. Crooks.

INSTITUTION OF STRUCTURAL ENGINEERS, 11 Upper Belgrave Street, SW1X 8BH.—*Sec.*, D. J. Clark.

ROYAL AERONAUTICAL SOCIETY, 4 Hamilton Place, W1V 0BQ.—*Sec.*, R. J. Kennett.

ROYAL INSTITUTION OF NAVAL ARCHITECTS, 10 Upper Belgrave Street, SW1X 8BQ.—*Sec.*, P. W. Ayling.

ENGINEERING, GENERAL AND ENGINEERING SCIENCE

First Degrees in *General Engineering* or *Engineering Science* are granted by the Universities of Aberdeen, Aston, Cambridge, Durham, Edinburgh, Exeter, Hull, Lancaster, Leicester, Liverpool, London (Queen Mary College), Loughborough, Manchester, University of Manchester Institute of Science and Technology (*Integrated Engineering*), Oxford, Reading, Surrey, Sussex, Ulster, Wales (University College, Cardiff), and Warwick. Courses leading to first degrees in *Engineering* granted by the C.N.A.A. are provided by some 10 polytechnics and colleges.

Aeronautical Engineering

See main heading:
AERONAUTICS AND AERONAUTICAL ENGINEERING

Agricultural Engineering

First Degrees in *Agricultural Engineering* and *Agricultural Mechanization Management* are granted by the University of Newcastle upon Tyne. Courses in *Agricultural Engineering* and *Agricultural Technology & Management* leading to degrees granted by Cranfield Institute of Technology are provided at Silsoe College.

Chemical Engineering

First Degrees are granted by the Universities of Aston (*Chemical Process Engineering*), Bath, Belfast, Birmingham, Bradford, Cambridge, Edinburgh, Exeter, Heriot-Watt, Leeds, London (Imperial College of Science and Technology, University College), Loughborough, Manchester (Manchester Institute of Science and Technology), Newcastle upon Tyne (*Chemical & Process Engineering*), Nottingham, Sheffield (*Chemical Process Engineering*), Strathclyde, Surrey and Wales (University College, Swansea).

Courses leading to first degrees granted by the C.N.A.A. are provided by North East London Polytechnic, Polytechnic of the South Bank, Teesside Polytechnic and Polytechnic of Wales.

Civil & Mechanical Engineering

First Degrees in *Civil* (or *Civil and Structural*), and *Mechanical Engineering* are granted by the Universities of Aberdeen, Aston, Bath (*M.*), Belfast, Birmingham, Bradford, Bristol, Brunel, Cambridge, the City University, Cranfield Institute, the Universities of Dundee, Edinburgh, Exeter, Glasgow, Heriot-Watt, Lancaster, Leeds, Leicester, Liverpool, London (Imperial College of Science and Technology, King's College, Queen Mary College, University College), Loughborough, Manchester, Manchester Institute of Science and Technology, Newcastle upon Tyne, Nottingham, Reading (*E. & M.*), Salford, Sheffield, Southampton, Strathclyde, Surrey, Sussex, Ulster, Wales (University Colleges at Cardiff and Swansea, Institute of Science and Technology, Cardiff) and Warwick.

Some 28 polytechnics or colleges provide courses in one or more of civil and mechanical engineering leading to first degrees granted by the C.N.A.A.

Electrical & Electronic Engineering & Electronics

First Degrees in *Electronic Engineering* or *Electronics* or *Electrical and Electronic Engineering* or *Electrical Engineering (including Electronics)* are granted by all the universities.

Courses leading to first degrees in *Electronic Engineering* or in *Electrical and Electronic Engineering*, granted by the C.N.A.A. are provided by some 30 polytechnics or colleges.

Marine Engineering and Naval Architecture

First Degrees in *Marine Engineering* and *Naval Architecture and Shipbuilding* are granted by the University of Newcastle upon Tyne; in *Naval Architecture and Ocean Engineering* by the Universities of Glasgow and London (University College); in *Naval Architecture* by the University of Strathclyde; in *Maritime Engineering and Civil Engineering* by the University of Liverpool; in *Offshore Engineering* by Heriot-Watt University; in *Ship Science* by the University of Southampton, and in *Maritime Technology* by the University of Wales (University College, Cardiff).

First degrees in *Mechanical Engineering (Marine)* are granted by the C.N.A.A.

Nuclear Engineering

First Degrees in *Nuclear Engineering* are granted by the University of Manchester; and in *Nuclear Engineering and Mechanical Engineering* by the University of London (Queen Mary College).

Production Engineering

First Degrees in *Production Engineering, Manufacturing Engineering* or *Industrial Engineering* are granted by the Universities of Aston, Bath, Belfast, Birmingham (*Engineering Production*), Brunel, Cambridge, Dundee, Edinburgh (*Manufacturing Systems Engineering*), Exeter (*Engineering (Operations & Manufacturing)*), Hull (*Engineering Design and Manufacture*), Loughborough, Nottingham, Strathclyde, Ulster, Wales (Institute of Science and Technology) and Warwick (*Engineering (Manufacturing)*).

First degrees in *Production Engineering, Industrial Engineering, Manufacturing Engineering, Manufacturing Systems Engineering*, and *Plant Engineering* are granted by the C.N.A.A.

Structural Engineering

First Degrees in *Civil and Structural Engineering* are granted by the Universities of Aberdeen, Bradford, Heriot-Watt (*Structural Engineering*), Liverpool, London (University College, *Civil, Structural and Environmental Engineering*), Sheffield, and Sussex (*Structural Engineering*).

ESTATE AND LAND MANAGEMENT, AND SURVEYING
(*See also* Building)

First Degrees are granted by the Universities of Aberdeen (*Land Economy*), Cambridge (*Land Economy*), Heriot-Watt (*Estate Management*), Reading (*Land Management* and *Rural Land Management*), Stirling (*Countryside Management*—provisional) and Ulster (*Estate Management*).

First Degrees in *Surveying Science* are granted by the University of Newcastle upon Tyne; in *Building Economics and Quantity Surveying* and in *Building Surveying* by Heriot-Watt University; in *Quantity Surveying* by Ulster University; in *Property Valuation and Management* by the City University; in *Quantity Surveying* and *Building Surveying* by the Universities of Reading and Salford.

First degrees in *Estate Management, Housing, Housing Studies, Land Administration, Land Economics, Land Management, Minerals Estate Management, Quantity Surveying, Surveying and Mapping Sciences, Urban Estate Management, Urban Estate Surveying, Urban Land Administration, Urban Land Economics, Valuation and Estate Management* are granted by the C.N.A.A.

Qualifying professional bodies include:

ROYAL INSTITUTION OF CHARTERED SURVEYORS (incorporating The Institute of Quantity Surveyors), 12 Great George Street, SW1P 3AD.—*Sec. Gen.*, M. Pattison.

ARCHITECTS AND SURVEYORS INSTITUTE, 15 St. Mary Street, Chippenham, Wilts SN15 3JN.—*Chief Exec.*, B. A. Hunt.

INCORPORATED ASSOCIATION OF ARCHITECTS AND SURVEYORS, Jubilee House, Billing Brook Road, Weston Favell, Northampton NN3 4NW.—*Hon. Sec.*, W. A. Black.

RATING AND VALUATION ASSOCIATION, 41 Doughty Street, WC1N 2LF.—*Dir.*, C. Farrington.

INCORPORATED SOCIETY OF VALUERS AND AUCTIONEERS, 3 Cadogan Gate, SW1X 0AS.—*Sec.*, M. Astbury.

FOOD AND NUTRITION SCIENCE
(*See also* Dietetics, Home Economics and Hotelkeeping)

First Degrees in *Food Science* are granted by the Universities of Belfast (also *Food Technology*), Leeds, London (King's College), Newcastle (*Agricultural & Food Marketing*), Nottingham, Reading (also *Food Science, Food Economics & Marketing* and *Food Technology*), Strathclyde, Surrey (*Nutrition & Food Science*), Ulster (*Food Technology Management*) and Wales (University College, Aberystwyth, *Agricultural & Food Marketing*); in *Nutrition* by the Universities of London (King's College), Nottingham and Surrey; and in *Human Nutrition* by the University of Ulster.

First degrees in *Food Science;* Catering and Applied Nutrition; *Food and Accommodation Studies; Food Marketing Sciences; Food, Textiles & Consumer Studies; Industrial Food Technology; Nutrition and Dietetics* are granted by the C.N.A.A.

Scientific and professional bodies include:

INSTITUTE OF FOOD SCIENCE & TECHNOLOGY, 5 Cambridge Court, 210 Shepherd's Bush Road, W6 7NL.—*Exec. Sec.*, Ms. H. G. Wild.

NUTRITION SOCIETY, Grosvenor Gardens House, 35–37 Grosvenor Gardens, SW1W 0BS.—*Hon. Sec.*, Dr. R. F. Grimble.

FORESTRY AND TIMBER STUDIES

First Degrees in *Forestry* are granted by the Universities of Aberdeen, Edinburgh (also *Agriculture, Forestry & Rural Economy*), and Wales (University College, Bangor, also *Wood Science* and *Agroforestry*).

First degrees in *Timber Technology* are granted by the C.N.A.A.

Professional Organizations include:

ROYAL FORESTRY SOCIETY OF ENGLAND, WALES AND NORTHERN IRELAND, 102 High Street, Tring, Herts., HP23 4AH.—*Dir.*, J. E. Jackson, PH.D.

ROYAL SCOTTISH FORESTRY SOCIETY, 11 Atholl Crescent, Edinburgh EH3 8HE.—*Sec.*, W. B. C. Walker.

INSTITUTE OF CHARTERED FORESTERS, 22 Walker Street, Edinburgh EH3 7HR.—*Sec.*, Mrs. M. W. Dick.

COMMONWEALTH FORESTRY ASSOCIATION, c/o Oxford Forestry Institute, South Parks Road, Oxford OX1 3RB.—*Sec.*, M. T. Rogers.

FUEL AND ENERGY STUDIES
(*See also* Nuclear Engineering)

First Degrees in *Fuel and Combustion Science* and in *Fuel and Energy Engineering* are granted by the University of Leeds; in *Petroleum Engineering* by London (Imperial College of Science and Technology); in *Mining and Petroleum Engineering* by the University of Strathclyde; in *Chemical Process Engineering, Fuel Technology* by the University of Sheffield. These subjects may also form part of other degree courses.

First degrees in *Energy Engineering* and *Power Engineering* are granted by the C.N.A.A.

Courses leading to certificates and qualification by professional bodies are available at many Technical Colleges.

The principal professional bodies are:—

INSTITUTE OF ENERGY, 18 Devonshire Street, W1N 2AU.—*Sec.*, C. Rigg, T.D.

INSTITUTION OF GAS ENGINEERS, 17 Grosvenor Crescent, SW1X 7ES.—*Sec.*, D. J. Chapman.

INSTITUTE OF PETROLEUM, 61 New Cavendish Street W1M 8AR.—*Dir. Gen.*, A. E. H. Williams.

GEOLOGY

First Degrees in *Geology* or *Geological Sciences* or *Applied Geology* are granted by the Universities of Aberdeen (also *Petroleum Geology*), Aston, Belfast, Birmingham, Bristol, Cambridge, Durham, Edinburgh, Exeter, Glasgow, Hull, Keele, Leeds, Leicester (also *Mining Geology*), Liverpool, London (Birkbeck College, Imperial College of Science and Technology (also *Mining Geology*), Queen Mary College (*Earth Sciences*), Royal Holloway & Bedford New College, University College), Manchester, Newcastle upon Tyne, Nottingham, Oxford (*Earth Sciences*), Reading, St. Andrews, Sheffield, Southampton, Wales (University Colleges at Aberystwyth, Cardiff and Swansea).

Degree courses in *Geophysics* and *Geophysical Sciences* are provided by the Universities of East Anglia, Edinburgh, Lancaster, Leeds, Leicester, Liverpool, Newcastle, Southampton and Wales (University College, Cardiff).

First degrees in *Geology, Earth Sciences*, etc. are granted by the C.N.A.A.

HOME ECONOMICS AND CATERING, HOTELKEEPING AND INSTITUTIONAL MANAGEMENT
(*See also* Dietetics, and Food)

First Degrees in *Home Economics* are granted by the Universities of Ulster and Wales (University College, Cardiff); in *Hotel and Catering Management* by the Universities of Strathclyde, Surrey (also *Hotel Management*), Ulster (*Hotel and Tourism Management*, also *Catering Administration*) and Wales (University College, Cardiff, *Hotel and Institutional Management*).

First degrees are granted by the C.N.A.A. in *Catering, Catering Administration, Home Economics, Hotel and Catering Administration/Management/ Studies, Catering Systems, Catering and Accommodation Management/Studies, Catering and Applied Nutrition, Applied Consumer Science, Hotel, Catering and Institutional Administration, Institutional Management*, and *Home and Community Studies*.

Qualifying professional body in the subjects is:

HOTEL CATERING AND INSTITUTIONAL MANAGEMENT ASSOCIATION, 191 Trinity Road, SW17 7HN.—*Dir.*, Ms. E. Gadsby.

INDUSTRIAL RELATIONS

First Degrees in Industrial Relations are granted by the Universities of Kent and Wales (Cardiff University College). Industrial relations also forms part of degree courses at other universities.

INSURANCE

First Degrees in *Banking, Insurance and Finance* are granted by the University of Wales (University College, Bangor) and in *Industrial Economics with Insurance* by the University of Nottingham.

First degrees in *Risk Management* are granted by the C.N.A.A.

Organizations conducting examinations and awarding diplomas:—

ASSOCIATION OF AVERAGE ADJUSTERS, H.Q.S. "Wellington", Temple Stairs, Victoria Embankment, WC2R 2PN.—*Joint Secs.*, H. R. P. Skinner; D. W. Taylor.

CHARTERED INSURANCE INSTITUTE, 20 Aldermanbury, EC2V 7HY.—*Sec. Gen.*, P. V. Saxton.

CHARTERED INSTITUTE OF LOSS ADJUSTERS, Manfield House, 376 The Strand, WC2R 0LR.—*Dir.*, A. F. Clack.

JOURNALISM

Courses for trainee newspaper journalists are available at 11 centres. One-year full-time courses are available for selected students. Particulars of all these courses are available from the Director of the NATIONAL COUNCIL FOR TRAINING OF JOURNALISTS, Carlton House, Hemnall Street, Epping, Essex CM16 4NL.—*Dir.*, D. K. Hall. Short courses for experienced journalists are also arranged by the National Council.

For periodical journalists, there are four centres running courses approved by THE PERIODICALS TRAINING COUNCIL, Imperial House, 15–19 Kingsway, WC2B 6UN.—*Dir.*, A. R. Sumption.

LANGUAGES

First Degrees in English and in a very wide range of foreign languages (including Oriental and African languages) are granted by universities. Degrees in *Linguistics* are awarded by the Universities of Cambridge, East Anglia, Essex (also *Language Studies* and *Psycholinguistics*), Lancaster, Leeds (*Linguistics and Phonetics*), London (School of Oriental and African Studies, University College), Newcastle upon Tyne, Reading (also *Linguistics and Language Pathology*), Sussex and Wales (University College, Bangor, *Applied Linguistics* and *Theoretical Linguistics*); in *Applied Languages* by the University of Ulster; and in *Language and Linguistic Science* by the University of York. These subjects also form part of degree courses at many other universities.

Courses leading to first degrees in various foreign languages granted by the C.N.A.A. are provided by some 15 polytechnics and colleges.

LAW

First Degrees in Law are granted by most of the universities.

Courses leading to first degrees in Law granted by the C.N.A.A. are provided by most of the polytechnics.

THE BAR

Admission to the Bar of England and Wales is controlled by the Inns of Court, and admission to the Bar of Northern Ireland by the Honorable Society of the Inn of Court of Northern Ireland. Admission as an Advocate of the Scottish Bar is controlled by the Faculty of Advocates.

England and Wales

THE GENERAL COUNCIL OF THE BAR
11 South Square, Gray's Inn, WC1R 5EL

The governing body of the Barristers' branch of the legal profession, established in 1987 in succession to the Senate of the Inns of Court and the Bar.
Chairman, D. Fennell, O.B.E., Q.C.
Chief Executive, J. Mottram, C.B., L.V.O., O.B.E.

THE INNS OF COURT

THE INNER TEMPLE, EC4Y 7HL.—*Treasurer*, Rt. Hon. Sir Ian Percival, Q.C.; *Sub-Treasurer*, Capt. P. T. Sheehan, C.B.E., R.N.

THE MIDDLE TEMPLE, EC4Y 9AT.—*Treasurer*, L. Price, Q.C.; *Deputy Treasurer*, G. Darling, Q.C.

GRAY'S INN, WC1R 5EU.—*Treasurer*, The Lord Wigoder, Q.C.; *Under-Treasurer*, D. Machin.

LINCOLN'S INN, WC2A 3TL.—*Treasurer*, The Rt. Hon. Lord Justice Parker; *Under-Treasurer*, Capt. P. M. Carver, R.N.

The education and examination of students for the Bar of England and Wales is superintended by the COUNCIL OF LEGAL EDUCATION, Inns of Court School of Law, 4 Gray's Inn Place, WC1R 5DX.
Chairman, The Hon. Mr. Justice Hobhouse.
Dean, Inns of Court School of Law, Mrs. M. A. Phillips.

Scotland

FACULTY OF ADVOCATES, Advocates Library, Parliament House, Edinburgh EH1 1RF.—*Dean*, J. A. D. Hope, Q.C.; *Clerk*, P. B. Cullen.

Northern Ireland

THE HONORABLE SOCIETY OF THE INN OF COURT OF NORTHERN IRELAND, Royal Courts of Justice, Belfast BT1 3JF.—*Treasurer* (1989), H. P. Kennedy, Q.C.; *Under-Treasurer*, J. A. L. McLean, Q.C.

SOLICITORS

Qualifications for Solicitor are obtainable only from one of the Law Societies, which control the education and examination of articled clerks, and the admission of solicitors.

LAW SOCIETY OF ENGLAND AND WALES, 113 Chancery Lane, WC2A 1PL.—*President* (1989–90), D. Ward; *Vice-President* (1989–90), P. T. Ely; *Sec.-Gen.*, J. W. Hayes.

Courses for The Law Society examinations are provided by THE COLLEGE OF LAW, at Braboeuf Manor, St. Catherine's, Guildford, Surrey GU3 1HA; 33–35 Lancaster Gate, W2 3LU; 2 Breams Buildings, Chancery Lane, EC4A 1DP; Christleton Hall, Chester CH3 7AB; and Bishopthorpe Road, York YO2 1QA.

LAW SOCIETY OF SCOTLAND, Law Society's Hall, 26 Drumsheugh Gardens, Edinburgh EH3 7YR.—*President* (1989–90), A. C. Clark; *Sec.*, K. W. Pritchard.

LAW SOCIETY OF NORTHERN IRELAND, Law Society House, 90–106 Victoria Street, Belfast BT1 3JZ.—*Sec.*, M. Davey.

LIBRARIANSHIP AND INFORMATION SCIENCE

First Degrees are granted by the University of Belfast (*Information Studies*), Loughborough (*Library Studies*), and the University of Wales (Aberystwyth) (*Librarianship* with another subject) (jointly with the College of Librarianship, Wales).

First degrees in *Librarianship/Library Studies* or *Librarianship/Library Studies and Information Studies/Science* are granted by the C.N.A.A.

THE LIBRARY ASSOCIATION, 7 Ridgmount Street, WC1E 7AE, maintains the professional register of Chartered Members.—*Chief Exec.*, G. Cunningham.

MATERIALS STUDIES (including Metallurgy)

First Degrees in *Materials Science, Materials Technology, or Materials Science and Technology* are granted by the Universities of Bath, Birmingham, Brunel, Cambridge (*Metallurgy and Materials Science*), Leeds, Liverpool, London (Imperial College of Science and Technology, Queen Mary College), Manchester and Manchester Institute of Science and Technology, Sheffield (*Science and Engineering of Materials*), Strathclyde (*Science of Engineering Materials*), Surrey and Wales (University College, Swansea). First Degrees in *Polymer Science and Engineering* are granted by London (Queen Mary College) and Manchester Institute of Science and Technology (*Polymer Science and Technology*). First Degrees in *Ceramics Science and Engineering* are granted by the Universities of Leeds and Sheffield; and in *Science and Engineering of Glasses* by the University of Sheffield. First Degrees in *Metallurgy* and/or *Metallurgical Engineering* are granted by the Universities of Birmingham (*Metallurgy/Materials Engineering*), Brunel, Cambridge (*Metallurgy and Materials Science*), Leeds, Liverpool (*Metallurgy and Materials Science*), Manchester and Manchester Institute of Science and Technology, Oxford (*Metallurgy and Science of Materials*), Salford (*Engineering Metallurgy*), Sheffield (*Science and Engineering of Metals*), Strathclyde and Surrey.

First degrees in *Materials Science/Technology* or *Metallurgy* or *Metallurgy and Materials* or *Polymer Science* are granted by the C.N.A.A.

INSTITUTE OF METALS, 1 Carlton House Terrace SW1Y 5DB, is a qualifying body—*Sec.*, Dr. J. A. Catterall.

MATHEMATICS

First Degrees in *Mathematics* and/or *Applied Mathematics* are granted by all universities.

Courses leading to first degrees in *Mathematics* granted by the C.N.A.A. are provided by about 16 polytechnics and colleges.

MEDICINE

First Degrees in *Medicine* are granted by the Universities of Aberdeen, Belfast, Birmingham, Bristol, Cambridge, Dundee, Edinburgh, Glasgow, Leeds, Leicester, Liverpool, London medical schools/colleges (University College and Middlesex S.M., King's College S.M.D., St. Mary's H.M.S., and those listed on p. 456), Manchester, Newcastle upon Tyne, Nottingham, Oxford, Sheffield, Southampton, and University of Wales College of Medicine.

Licensing Corporations granting Diplomas

ROYAL COLLEGE OF PHYSICIANS OF LONDON AND THE ROYAL COLLEGE OF SURGEONS OF ENGLAND, Examining Board in England, 35–43 Lincoln's Inn Fields, WC2A 3PN.—*President*, I. P. Todd; *Sec.*, R. S. Johnson-Gilbert, O.B.E.

SOCIETY OF APOTHECARIES OF LONDON, Black Friars Lane, EC4V 6EJ.—*Clerk*, Maj. J. C. O'Leary; *Registrar*, D. H. C. Barrie.

ROYAL COLLEGE OF OBSTETRICIANS AND GYNAECOLOGISTS, 27 Sussex Place, Regent's Park, NW1 4RG.—*President*, G. D. Pinker, C.V.O.; *Sec.*, P. A. Barnett.

ROYAL COLLEGE OF PHYSICIANS OF EDINBURGH, 9 Queen Street, Edinburgh EH2 1JQ.—*President*, Prof. J. Richmond, M.D.; *Sec.*, Dr. J. L. Anderton.

ROYAL COLLEGE OF SURGEONS OF EDINBURGH, Nicolson Street, Edinburgh EH8 9DW.—*President*, Prof. G. D. Chisholm; *Sec.*, Prof. A. G. D. Maran.

ROYAL COLLEGE OF PHYSICIANS AND SURGEONS OF GLASGOW, 234–242 St. Vincent Street, Glasgow G2 5RJ.—*President*, J. McArthur; *Hon. Sec.*, Dr. A. D. Beattie.

SCOTTISH TRIPLE QUALIFICATION BOARD, Nicolson Street, Edinburgh EH8 9DW and 242 St. Vincent Street, Glasgow.

PROFESSIONS SUPPLEMENTARY TO MEDICINE

The standard of professional education in chiropody, dietetics, medical laboratory sciences, occupational therapy, orthoptics, physiotherapy and radiography is the responsibility of seven professional boards, which also publish an annual register of qualified practitioners. The work of the Boards is co-ordinated by THE COUNCIL FOR PROFESSIONS SUPPLEMENTARY TO MEDICINE, Park House, 184 Kennington Park Road, SE11 4BU. *Registrar*, R. Pickis.

Biomedical/Medical Laboratory Sciences

First Degrees in *Biomedical Sciences* are granted by the Universities of Bradford, London (King's College), and Ulster.

First degrees in *Biomedical Sciences* and *Medical Laboratory Science* are granted by the C.N.A.A.

Qualifications from higher or further education establishments and training in medical laboratories are required for progress to the professional examinations and qualifications of the INSTITUTE OF MEDICAL LABORATORY SCIENCES, 12 Queen Anne Street, W1M 0AU.

Chiropody

Professional qualifications are granted by THE SOCIETY OF CHIROPODISTS, 53 Welbeck Street, W1M 7HE, to students who have passed the qualifying examination after attending a course of full-time training for three years at one of the ten recognized schools in England and Wales, two in Scotland and one in Northern Ireland. Qualifications granted by the Society are approved by the Chiropodists Board for the purpose of State Registration, which is a condition of employment within the National Health Service. *Gen. Sec.*, J. G. C. Trouncer.

Dietetics

(*See* main heading, p. 465)

Occupational Hygiene

First degrees in *Occupational Hygiene* are granted by the C.N.A.A.

Occupational Therapy

First Degrees in *Occupational Therapy* are granted by the University of Ulster; first degrees in *Occupation Therapy* are granted by the C.N.A.A.

Professional qualifications are awarded by THE COLLEGE OF OCCUPATIONAL THERAPISTS, 20 Rede Place, W2 4TU, upon completion of one of the 23 training courses approved by the College.

Orthoptics

Orthoptists undertake the diagnosis and treatment of all types of squint and other anomalies of binocular vision, working in close collaboration with ophthalmologists. The training and maintenance of professional standards are the responsibility of the Orthoptists Board of the Council for the Professions Supplementary to Medicine. The examining and qualifying body is the BRITISH ORTHOPTIC SOCIETY, Tavistock House North, Tavistock Square, WC1H 9HX. Training consists of a three-year course at one of nine approved Orthoptic Schools in England and Wales and one in Scotland.

(*See also* main heading Ophthalmic Optics, p. 471)

Physiotherapy

First Degrees are granted by the University of Ulster.

First degrees in *Physiotherapy* are granted by the C.N.A.A.

Full-time three- or four-year degree or diploma courses are available at 32 recognised Schools in the U.K. Information about examinations leading to eligibility for Membership of The Chartered Society of Physiotherapy and to State Registration is available from THE CHARTERED SOCIETY OF PHYSIOTHERAPY, 14 Bedford Row, London WC1R 4ED.—*Sec.*, T. Simon.

Radiography and Radiotherapy

Examinations leading to qualification are conducted by THE COLLEGE OF RADIOGRAPHERS, 14 Upper Wimpole Street, W1M 8BN.

There are recognized training centres in radiography and radiotherapy at many cities and towns in England and Wales, Scotland and Northern Ireland.

METEOROLOGY

First Degrees in *Meteorology* are granted by the University of Reading. The subject is also included in degree courses at some other universities.

MINING AND MINING ENGINEERING

First Degrees in *Mining* or *Mining Engineering* are granted by the following universities: Leeds (also *Mineral Engineering*), London (Imperial College of Science and Technology), Newcastle upon Tyne, Nottingham, Strathclyde (*Mining and Petroleum Engineering*) and Wales (University College, Cardiff, also *Mineral Engineering*).

First degrees are granted by the C.N.A.A. in *Mining Engineering* and *Mineral Processing Engineering*.

Miscellaneous Authorities

ENGINEERING COUNCIL, 10 Maltravers Street, WC2R 3ER.

INSTITUTION OF MINING ENGINEERS, Danum House, 6A South Parade, Doncaster DN1 2DY—*Sec.*, W. J. W. Bourne.

MUSIC

First Degrees in *Music* are granted by the Universities of Aberdeen (also *History of Music*), Belfast, Birmingham, Bristol, Cambridge, the City University, the Universities of Durham, East Anglia, Edinburgh, Exeter, Glasgow (also *Music Education* and *Music Performance* in conjunction with Royal Scottish Academy of Music and Drama), Hull, Lancaster, Leeds, Leicester (*Musicianship*), Liverpool, London (King's College, Royal Holloway and Bedford New College; *also* Goldsmiths' College, Royal Academy of Music, Royal College of Music, and Trinity College of Music), Manchester, Newcastle upon Tyne, Nottingham, Oxford, Reading, Sheffield, Southampton, Surrey (*Academic & Practical Applications of Music*; *Music & Sound Recording (Tonmeister)*), Sussex, Ulster, Wales (University Colleges at Aberystwyth, Bangor and Cardiff; also at Welsh College of Music and Drama), and York.

Courses leading to first degrees in Music granted by the C.N.A.A. are provided by several polytechnics and colleges.

ASSOCIATED BOARD OF THE ROYAL SCHOOLS OF MUSIC, 14 Bedford Square, WC1B 3JG.—Conducts the local examinations in centres throughout the world in music and speech for the Royal Academy of Music and the Royal College of Music in London, the Royal Northern College of Music, Manchester and the Royal Scottish Academy of Music and Drama, Glasgow.

Chief Exec. and Dir. of Examinations, R. Smith.

ROYAL ACADEMY OF MUSIC, Marylebone Road, NW1 5HT.—*Principal*, Sir David Lumsden, D.Phil.

ROYAL COLLEGE OF MUSIC, Prince Consort Road, South Kensington, SW7 2BS.—*Director*, M. G. Matthews.

ROYAL NORTHERN COLLEGE OF MUSIC, 124 Oxford Road, Manchester M13 9RD.—*Principal*, Sir John Manduell, C.B.E.

ROYAL SCOTTISH ACADEMY OF MUSIC AND DRAMA, 100 Renfrew Street, Glasgow G2 3BD.—*Principal*, P. Ledger, C.B.E.

ROYAL COLLEGE OF ORGANISTS, Kensington Gore, SW7 2QS.—*Clerk*, K. B. Lyndon.

GUILDHALL SCHOOL OF MUSIC AND DRAMA, Silk Street, EC2Y 8DT.—*Principal*, I. Horsbrugh.

LONDON COLLEGE OF MUSIC, 47 Great Marlborough Street, W1V 2AS.—*Director*, J. McCabe, C.B.E.

TRINITY COLLEGE OF MUSIC, 11–13 Mandeville Place, W1M 6AQ.—*Principal*, P. Jones, C.B.E.

NAUTICAL STUDIES
(*See also* Marine Engineering)

The University of Wales grants first degrees in *Maritime Studies, Maritime Commerce* and *Maritime Geography* (courses at Institute of Science and Technology).

First degrees in *Maritime Studies* and *Nautical Studies* are granted by the C.N.A.A.

Merchant Navy Training Schools
For Officers

THE COLLEGE OF MARITIME STUDIES, Warsash, Southampton SO3 6ZL. *Dean*, Capt. M. Longman.

For Seamen

INDEFATIGABLE AND NATIONAL SEA TRAINING SCHOOL FOR BOYS, Plas Llanfair, Llanfairpwllgwyngyll, Gwynedd LL61 6NT.—*Captain Headmaster*, Capt. T. R. Beggs.

NATIONAL SEA TRAINING COLLEGE, Denton, Gravesend, Kent DA12 2HR.—*Princ.*, Capt. C. G. W. Hunter.

NURSING

Courses in which academic study leading to a degree at a University may be combined with nursing training/practical nursing in hospitals are provided by the University of Bradford (provisional), Brunel (*Mental Nursing*), the City University, the Universities of Edinburgh, Glasgow, Hull, Liverpool, London

(King's College), Manchester, Southampton, Surrey, Ulster and Wales (College of Medicine).

First degrees in *Nursing* are granted by the C.N.A.A.

Three-year courses are undertaken for State Registration in general, sick children's, mental and mental deficiency nursing. Two-year courses lead to State enrolment. There are training schools in many parts of Great Britain.

THE ROYAL COLLEGE OF NURSING
OF THE UNITED KINGDOM
20 Cavendish Square, W1M 0AB

The Royal College of Nursing, within its Institute of Advanced Nursing Education, provides education at post-basic level in hospital, occupational health and community health fields. Advanced courses are held in preparation for senior posts in management and teaching; and other short and special courses.
Director of Education and Principal of the Institute of Advanced Nursing Education, J. C. A. Wells (*acting*).

ENGLISH NATIONAL BOARD FOR NURSING, MIDWIFERY AND HEALTH VISITING, Victory House, 170 Tottenham Court Road, W1P 0HA.—*Chief Exec. Officer,* D. Jones, O.B.E.

WELSH NATIONAL BOARD FOR NURSING, MIDWIFERY AND HEALTH VISITING, Floor 13, Pearl Assurance House, Greyfriars Road, Cardiff CF1 3AG.—*Chief Exec. Officer,* D. A. Ravey.

NATIONAL BOARD FOR NURSING, MIDWIFERY AND HEALTH VISITING FOR SCOTLAND, 22 Queen Street, Edinburgh EH2 1JX.—*Chief Exec. Officer.,* Mrs. E. C. Mitchell.

NATIONAL BOARD FOR NURSING, MIDWIFERY AND HEALTH VISITING FOR NORTHERN IRELAND, R.A.C. House, 79 Chichester Street, Belfast BT1 4JE.—*Chief Exec. Officer,* J. J. Walsh.

OPHTHALMIC OPTICS

First Degrees in *Ophthalmic Optics* or *Optometry* are granted by the Universities of Aston, Bradford, the City University, Manchester (Manchester Institute of Science and Technology), and Wales (Institute of Science and Technology).

First degrees in *Ophthalmic Optics* are granted by the C.N.A.A.

THE BRITISH COLLEGE OF OPTOMETRISTS, 10 Knaresborough Place, SW5 0TG, grants qualifications as an optometrist.—*Gen. Sec.,* T. H. Collingridge.

THE ASSOCIATION OF BRITISH DISPENSING OPTICIANS, 6 Hurlingham Business Park, Sulivan Road, SW6 3DU, grants qualifications as a dispensing optician.—*Registrar.,* D. G. Baker.

PHARMACY

First Degrees in *Pharmacy* are granted by the Universities of Aston, Bath, Belfast, Bradford, London (King's College and the School of Pharmacy), Manchester, Nottingham, Strathclyde, Wales (Institute of Science and Technology).

First degrees in *Pharmacy* are granted by the C.N.A.A. Information may be obtained from The Secretary and Registrar, ROYAL PHARMACEUTICAL SOCIETY OF GREAT BRITAIN, 1 Lambeth High Street, SE1 7JN. *Sec. and Registrar,* J. Ferguson.

PHOTOGRAPHY, FILM AND TV STUDIES

First Degrees are awarded by the Universities of Glasgow (*Theatre Studies/Film & TV Studies*), Kent (*Drama/Film Studies*) and Stirling (*Film and Media Studies*). At some other universities these subjects may be studied as part of a first degree course.

First degrees in *Photography, Photographic Arts/Sciences/Studies* and various aspects of film, video and television are granted by the C.N.A.A.

BRITISH INSTITUTE OF PROFESSIONAL PHOTOGRAPHY, Amwell End, Ware, Herts. SG12 9HN.—*Chief Exec.,* A. M. Berkeley.

PRINTING

First Degrees in *Typography and Graphic Communication* are awarded by the University of Reading.

First degrees in *Printing and Packaging Technology* are granted by the C.N.A.A.

Courses in technical and general, design and administrative aspects of printing are available at technical colleges throughout the United Kingdom. Details can be obtained from the Institute of Printing and the British Printing Industries Federation (*see* below).

In addition to the examining and organizing bodies listed below, examinations are held by various independent regional examining boards in further education.

BRITISH PRINTING INDUSTRIES FEDERATION, 11 Bedford Row, WC1R 4DX.—*Dir.-Gen.,* C. Stanley.

INSTITUTE OF PRINTING, 8 Lonsdale Gardens, Tunbridge Wells, Kent TN11NU.—*Sec.,* C. F. Partridge.

RECREATION, SPORT, AND HUMAN MOVEMENT STUDIES
(*See also* Dance)

First Degrees are granted by the University of Birmingham (*Sport and Recreation Studies*), Glasgow (*Physical Education and Sports Science*), Liverpool (*Physical Education and Movement Science*), Loughborough (*Physical Education and Sports Science*; also *Physical Education, Sports Science and Recreation Management*) and Ulster (*Sport and Leisure Studies*). *Physical Education* and various aspects of Recreation may be studied as part of other first degree courses at several universities.

First Degrees in various aspects of Physical Education, Recreation and Sports Science/Studies are granted by the C.N.A.A.

Physical Education and *Sports Science/Studies* also form part of a degree course at many other colleges/polytechnics.

ROBOTICS

First Degrees in *Electronic Control and Robot Engineering* are granted by the University of Hull.

SOCIAL WORK

First Degrees in *Social Studies* or in *Social Sciences* are granted by most universities. Courses leading to first degrees in *Social Science* or *Social Sciences/Applied Social Science or Sociology* granted by the C.N.A.A. are provided by some 30 polytechnics and colleges.

CENTRAL COUNCIL FOR EDUCATION AND TRAINING IN SOCIAL WORK, Derbyshire House, St. Chad's Street, London WC1H 8AD.—*Dir.,* A. Hall. The Council validates and approves courses, schemes and programmes leading to the C.C.E.T.S.W.'s awards, including the Certificate of Qualification in Social Work, the Certificate in Social Service and the Diploma in Social Work.

SPEECH SCIENCE
(*See also* Languages)

First Degrees are awarded in *Speech Science* by the University of Sheffield; in *Speech Sciences* by the University of London (University College); in *Speech Pathology* by the University of Manchester; and in *Speech Therapy* by the University of Ulster.

First degrees in various aspects of Speech Therapy and Speech Pathology are granted by the C.N.A.A.

THE COLLEGE OF SPEECH THERAPISTS, Harold Poster House, 6 Lechmere Road, NW2 5BU, provides details of courses leading to qualification as a speech therapist. The College also sponsors advanced clinical courses. Associate Membership is available for professionals in other disciplines. A Directory of Members of the College is published triennially.

SURVEYING
(*See* Estate Management and Surveying)

TEACHING

To become a qualified teacher it is necessary to have successfully completed a course of initial teacher training.

Non-graduates usually qualify by way of a three- or four-year course leading to a Bachelor of Education (B.Ed.) honours degree, but some universities offer first degree courses (B.A., B.Sc.) taken concurrently with a certificate of education. Graduates take a one-year postgraduate certificate of education (PGCE).

Details of courses in England and Wales are contained in the *Handbook of Degree and Advanced Courses* published annually by the National Association of Teachers in Further and Higher Education.

Applications for B.Ed. courses in England and Wales for intending teachers are made through the Central Register and Clearing House Ltd., 3 Crawford Place, W1H 2BN, from which application forms can be obtained. For PGCE courses in England and Wales, applications are handled by the Graduate Teacher Training Registry at the same address.

Details of courses in Scotland can be obtained from the Scottish Education Department. Details of courses in Northern Ireland can be obtained from the Department of Education for Northern Ireland. Applications for teacher training courses in Scotland and Northern Ireland are made to the institutions direct.

Special arrangements exist for those wishing to teach craft design and technology.

TECHNICAL EDUCATION

First Degrees in one or more technologies are awarded by almost all universities; and many polytechnics and colleges of technology provide courses leading to first degrees granted by the C.N.A.A. Details are given under individual subject headings.

Industry Training Boards

AGRICULTURAL, Summit House, Glebe Way, West Wickham, Kent BR4 0RF.—*Dir.*, D. C. Newman.

CLOTHING AND ALLIED PRODUCTS, Richardshaw Lane, Pudsey, Leeds LS28 6BN.—*Chief Exec.*, J. W. Dearden.

CONSTRUCTION, Bircham Newton, Nr. King's Lynn, Norfolk PE31 6RH.— *Sec.*, M. Smith.

ENGINEERING, 54 Clarendon Road, Watford, Herts. WD1 1LB.—*Sec.*, E. P. Jones.

HOTEL AND CATERING, International House, High Street, Ealing, W5 5DB.—*Sec.*, W. A. Heaney.

LOCAL GOVERNMENT TRAINING BOARD, Arndale House, Arndale Centre, Luton, Beds. LU1 2TS.—*Dir.*, M. G. Clarke.

MAN-MADE FIBRES INDUSTRY TRAINING ADVISORY BOARD, Gable House, 40 High Street, Rickmansworth, Herts. WD3 1ER.—*Sec.*, P. Grice.

OFFSHORE PETROLEUM, Offshore Training Centre, Forties Road, Montrose, Angus DD10 9ET.—*Sec.*, P. J. Bing, O.B.E.

PLASTICS PROCESSING, Coppice House, Halesfield 7, Telford, Shropshire, TF7 4NA.—*Chief Exec.*, J. C. Shearman.

ROAD TRANSPORT, Capitol House, Empire Way, Wembley, Middx. HA9 0NG.—*Dir. Gen.*, D. C. Barnett.

TEXTILES

First Degrees are awarded by the Universities of Leeds (*Textile Chemistry* and *Textile Studies*) and Manchester (Manchester Institute of Science and Technology, *Textile Technology* and *Clothing Engineering*).

Courses leading to first degrees granted by the C.N.A.A. in various aspects of *Textiles/Fashion Clothing Studies*, and *Textile Marketing* are provided by some 25 polytechnics and colleges.

THE TEXTILE INSTITUTE, 10 Blackfriars Street, Manchester M3 5DR.—*Gen. Sec.*, R. G. Denyer.

THEOLOGY

First Degrees in *Theology, Divinity, Religious Studies*, or combinations of these subjects are granted by most universities.

Courses leading to first degrees in *Theology* or *Theological Studies* granted by the C.N.A.A. are provided by about half a dozen polytechnics and colleges.

Theological Colleges
Church of England and Church in Wales

CHICHESTER THEOLOGICAL COLLEGE, Chichester, W. Sussex PO19 1SG. (45).—*Princ.*, Rev. Canon J. Hind.

CRANMER HALL, St. John's College, Durham DH1 3RJ. (80).—*Warden*, Rev. I. P. M. Cundy.

LINCOLN THEOLOGICAL COLLEGE, Drury Lane, Lincoln LN1 3BP. (75).—*Warden*, Rev. Canon W. M. Jacob, PH.D.

OAK HILL COLLEGE, Chase Side, Southgate, N14 4PS. (106).—*Princ.*, Rev. Canon G. Bridger.

COLLEGE OF THE RESURRECTION, Mirfield, W. Yorks. WF14 0BW. (43).—*Princ.*, Rev. Fr. D. Lloyd.

RIDLEY HALL, Cambridge CB3 9HG. (63).—*Princ.*, Rev. Canon H. F. de Waal.

RIPON COLLEGE, Cuddesdon, Oxford OX9 9EX. (70).—*Princ.*, Rev. Canon J. H. Garton.

ST. DEINIOL'S LIBRARY, Hawarden, Deeside, Clwyd CH5 3DF.—*Princ.*, Rev. P. J. Jagger.

ST. JOHN'S COLLEGE, Bramcote, Nottingham NG9 3DS. (120).—*Princ.*, Rev. Dr. J. Goldingay.

ST. MICHAEL'S THEOLOGICAL COLLEGE, Llandaff, Cardiff CF5 2YJ. (32).—*Warden*, Rev. J. H. L. Rowlands.

ST. STEPHEN'S HOUSE, 16 Marston Street, Oxford OX4 1JX. (55).—*Princ.*, Rev. E. R. Barnes.

SALISBURY AND WELLS THEOLOGICAL COLLEGE, 19 The Close, Salisbury SP1 2EE. (62).—*Princ.*, Rev. P. A. Crowe.

TRINITY COLLEGE, Stoke Hill, Bristol BS9 1JP. (125).—*Princ.*, Rev. D. Gillett.

WESTCOTT HOUSE, Jesus Lane, Cambridge CB5 8BP. (50).—*Princ.*, Rev. Dr. R. W. N. Hoare.

WYCLIFFE HALL, 54 Banbury Road, Oxford OX2 6PW. (85).—*Princ.*, Rev. Dr. R. T. France.

Scottish Episcopal Church

THEOLOGICAL COLLEGE, Rosebery Crescent, Edinburgh EH12 5JT. (26).—*Princ.*, Rev. Canon K. Mason.

Church of Scotland

CHRIST'S COLLEGE, Aberdeen AB1 1YD. (187).—*Master*, Rev. H. R. Sefton, PH.D.

NEW COLLEGE, Mound Place, Edinburgh EH1 2LU. (282).—*Princ.*, Rev. Prof. D. B. Forrester.

TRINITY COLLEGE, 4 The Square, University of Glasgow, Glasgow G12 8QQ. (140).—*Princ.*, Rev. Prof. R. Davidson, D.D.

Presbyterian Church of Wales

UNITED THEOLOGICAL COLLEGE, Aberystwyth SY23 2LT. (42).—*Princ.*, Rev. Prof. E. ap Nefydd Roberts.

Presbyterian

UNION THEOLOGICAL COLLEGE, Belfast BT7 1JT. (96).—*Princ.*, R. F. G. Holmes.

Methodist

EDGHILL THEOLOGICAL COLLEGE/CHRISTIAN EDUCATION CENTRE, 9 Lennoxvale, Belfast BT9 5BY. (119).—*Princ.*, Rev. W. D. D. Cooke, PH.D.

WESLEY COLLEGE, Westbury-on-Trym, Bristol BS10 7QD. (66).—*Princ.*, Dr. H. McKeating.

WESLEY HOUSE, Cambridge CB5 8BJ. (34).—*Princ.*, Rev. Dr. I. H. Jones.

Baptist

BRISTOL BAPTIST COLLEGE, Woodland Road, Bristol BS8 1UN. (40).—*Princ.*, Rev. Dr. J. E. Morgan-Wynne.

NORTHERN BAPTIST COLLEGE, Martin Luther House, Brighton Grove, Rusholme, Manchester M14 5JP. (40).—*Princ.*, Rev. Dr. B. Haymes.

NORTH WALES BAPTIST COLLEGE, Ffordd Ffriddoedd, Bangor, Gwynedd LL57 2EH. (4).—*Princ.*, Rev. J. R. Rowlands.

REGENT'S PARK COLLEGE, Oxford OX1 2LB. (75).—*Princ.*, Rev. Dr. P. S. Fiddes.

THE SCOTTISH BAPTIST COLLEGE, 12 Aytoun Road, Glasgow G41 5RT. (20).—*Princ.*, Rev. I. J. N. Oakley.

SOUTH WALES BAPTIST COLLEGE, 54 Richmond Road, Cardiff CF2 3UR. (20).—*Princ.*, Rev. N. Clark.

SPURGEON'S COLLEGE, South Norwood Hill, London SE25 6DJ. (67).—*Princ.*, P. Beasley-Murray, PH.D.

United Reformed and Congregational

BALA-BANGOR INDEPENDENT COLLEGE, Bangor LL57 2EH. (15).—*Princ.*, R. T. Jones, D.Phil., D.D.

MANSFIELD COLLEGE, Mansfield Road, Oxford OX1 3TF. (23).—*Princ.*, D. J. Trevelyan, C.B.

MEMORIAL COLLEGE, Aberystwyth. (20).—*Princ.*, Rev. Dr. D. E. Davies.

NORTHERN COLLEGE, Luther King House, Brighton Grove, Rusholme, Manchester M14 5JP. (44).—*Princ.*, Rev. R. J. McKelvey, PH.D.

SCOTTISH CONGREGATIONAL COLLEGE, Rosebery Crescent, Edinburgh EH12 5YN. (14).—*Princ.*, Rev. Dr. J. W. S. Clark.

WESTMINSTER COLLEGE, Madingley Road, Cambridge CB3 0AA. (40).—*Princ.*, Rev. M. H. Cressey.

Unitarian

UNITARIAN COLLEGE, Luther King House, Brighton Grove, Rusholme, Manchester M14 5JP. (4).—*Principal*, Rev. G. Murphy.

Ecumenical

QUEEN'S COLLEGE, Somerset Road, Edgbaston, Birmingham B15 2QH. (75).—*Princ.*, Rev. Dr. J. B. Walker.

Non-Denominational

ST MARY'S COLLEGE, The University, St. Andrews, Fife KY16 9JU. (140).—*Princ.*, Rev. D. W. D. Shaw.

Roman Catholic

ALLEN HALL COLLEGE, 28 Beaufort Street, SW3 5AA. (75).—*Rector*, Rt. Rev. Mgr. P. O'Donoghue.

CAMPION HOUSE COLLEGE, 112 Thornbury Road, Isleworth, Middx. TW7 4NN. (40).—*Princ.*, Rev. M. Barrow, S.J.

CHESTERS COLLEGE, 2 Chesters Road, Bearsden, Glasgow. (50).—*Rector*, Very Rev. P. Tartaglia.

OSCOTT COLLEGE, Chester Road, Sutton Coldfield, W. Midlands B73 5AA. (77).—*Rector*, Very Rev. P. McKinney.

ST. JOHN'S SEMINARY, Wonersh, Guildford, Surrey GU5 0QX. (50).—*Rector*, Rt. Rev. Mgr. P. Smith.

ST. JOSEPH'S UPHOLLAND NORTHERN INSTITUTE FOR ADULT CHRISTIAN EDUCATION, Upholland, Skelmersdale, Lancs. WN8 0PZ. (Closed temporarily).

USHAW COLLEGE, Durham DH7 9RH. (135).—*Princ.*, Rt. Rev. Mgr. P. Walton.

Jewish

JEWS' COLLEGE, Albert Road, Hendon, NW4 2SJ. (102).—*Princ.*, Rabbi Dr. J. Sacks.

LEO BAECK COLLEGE, Sternberg Centre for Judaism, 80 East End Road, N3 2SY (20).—*Princ.* Rabbi Dr. J. Magonet.

TOWN AND COUNTRY PLANNING

First Degrees are granted by the Universities of Belfast (*Environmental Planning*), Dundee (*Town and Regional Planning*), East Anglia (*Development Studies*), Glasgow (*Planning*), Heriot-Watt (*Town Planning*), Kent (*Urban Studies*), London (University College, *Environmental Studies and Planning*), Manchester (*Town and Country Planning*), Newcastle upon Tyne (*Town and Country Planning*), Sheffield (*Urban Studies*), Stirling (*Urban Studies and Social Policy*), Strathclyde (*Planning*), Sussex (*Urban Studies*), and Wales (Institute of Science and Technology, *Town Planning Studies*).

First degrees in *Town Planning*, *Town and Country Planning*, *Environmental/Urban Planning*, and other aspects of Planning are granted by the C.N.A.A.

The ROYAL TOWN PLANNING INSTITUTE, 26 Portland Place, W1N 4BE, recognizes a number of degree and diploma courses in town planning.

TRANSPORT

First Degrees are granted by the Universities of Aston (*Transport Management*), Loughborough (*Transport Management and Planning*), Wales (Institute of Science and Technology: *International Transport*) and Ulster (*Transport Technology*). The City University awards a first degree in *Air Transport Engineering*.

First degrees in *Transportation Design*, *Transportation Engineering* and *Transport and Distribution* are granted by the C.N.A.A.

THE CHARTERED INSTITUTE OF TRANSPORT, 80 Portland Place, London W1N 4DP, conducts qualifying examinations in transport management leading to chartered professional status. *Dir. Gen.*, R. P. Botwood.

VETERINARY STUDIES

First Degrees in *Veterinary Science/Medicine and Surgery* are granted by the Universities of Bristol, Cambridge, Edinburgh, Glasgow, Liverpool and London (Royal Veterinary College).

INDEPENDENT SCHOOLS

The following pages list those independent schools whose Head is a member of the Headmasters' Conference, the Society of Headmasters of Independent Schools or the Girls Schools Association.

THE HEADMASTERS' CONFERENCE

Chairman (1990), D. J. Jewell (Haileybury); *Gen. Sec.*, J. S. Sutton, 130 Regent Road, Leicester LE1 7PG; *Deputy Sec.*, R. N. P. Griffiths. The annual meetings are, as a rule, held at the end of September.

In considering applications for election to membership the Committee will have regard to the scheme or other instrument under which the school is administered (taking particularly into consideration the degree of independence enjoyed by the Headmaster and the Governing Body); the number of pupils over thirteen years of age in the school and the number of pupils in proportion to the size of the school who are in the sixth form, i.e. engaged on studies at the Advanced Level of the General Certificate of Education.

The Headmasters of some maintained schools are by invitation Additional Members of the H.M.C. These include the following: Cavendish School; Easingwold School; High Wycombe Royal Grammar School; John Fisher School; Liskeard School; London Oratory School; Prescot School; Richard Huish College; Richmond School; Royal Grammar School, Lancaster; Royal High School, Edinburgh; St. Bartholomew's School; Watford Grammar School.

Name of School	Founded	No. of Pupils	B'ding	Day	Headmaster (With date of Appointment)
England and Wales					
Abbotsholme School, Staffs.	1889	250‡	£7,452	£4,968	D. J. Farrant (1984)
Abingdon School, Oxon.	1256	700	£6,270	£3,207	M. St. J. Parker (1975)
Aldenham School, Herts.	1597	370†	£8,091	£5,139	M. Higginbottom (1983)
Alleyn's School, SE22	1619	917‡	....	£3,600	D. A. Fenner (1976)
Allhallows School, Dorset	1515	300‡	£7,764	£4,080	P. S. Larkman, L.V.O. (1983)
Ampleforth College (*R.C.*), Yorks.	1802	720	£7,830	....	Rev. D. L. Milroy, O.S.B. (1980)
*Ardingly College, W. Sussex	1858	475‡	£7,680	£6,045	J. W. Flecker (1980)
Arnold School, Blackpool	1896	804‡	£4,779	£2,385	J. A. B. Kelsall (1987)
Ashville College, Harrogate	1877	495‡	£5,355	£2,910	M. H. Crosby (1987)
Bancroft's School, Essex	1727	712‡	....	£3,510	Dr. P. C. D. Southern (1985)
Barnard Castle School, Co. Durham	1883	509†	£4,326°	£2,316°	F. S. McNamara (1980)
Bedales School, Hants.	1893	408‡	£8,157	£5,847	E. A. M. MacAlpine (1981)
Bedford School	1552	738	£6,759	£3,951	Dr. I. P. Evans (1990)
Bedford Modern School	1566	975	£5,031	£2,736	P. J. Squire (1977)
Berkhamsted School, Herts.	1541	500	£6,414	£3,729	Rev. K. H. Wilkinson (1989)
Birkenhead School, Merseyside	1860	740	....	£2,355	S. J. Haggett (1988)
Bishop's Stortford College, Herts.	1868	356°	£6,078°	£4,317°	S. G. G. Benson (1984)
*Bloxham School, Oxon.	1860	369†	£7,245	£4,944	M. W. Vallance (1982)
Blundell's School, Devon	1604	480†	£7,620	£4,635	A. J. D. Rees (1980)
Bolton School	1524	850	....	£2,634	A. W. Wright (1983)
Bootham School, York.	1823	320‡	£6,222	£3,837	I. M. Small (1988)
Bradfield College, Berks.	1850	530†	£8,250	£6,190	P. B. Smith (1985)
Bradford Grammar School	1662	1011‡	....	£2,736	D. A. G. Smith (1975)
Brentwood School, Essex	1557	853†	£6,444	£3,684	J. A. E. Evans (1981)
Brighton College, E. Sussex	1845	498‡	£7,245	£4,770	J. D. Leach (1987)
Bristol Cathedral School	1542	462†	....	£2,445	C. S. Martin (1979)
Bristol Grammar School	1532	1000‡	....	£2,688	C. E. Martin (1986)
Bromsgrove School, Worcs.	1553	540°	£5,697°	£3,624°	T. M. Taylor (1986)
Bryanston School, Dorset	1928	660‡	£8,600	£5,750	T. D. Wheare (1983)
Bury Grammar School, Lancs.	1634	650	....	£2,070	J. Robson (1969)
Canford School, Dorset	1923	530°	£7,510°	£5,260°	M. Marriott (1976)
Caterham School, Surrey	1811	420°	£5,850°	£3,180°	R. Smith (1976)
Charterhouse, Surrey	1611	700†	£8,700	£7,230	P. J. Attenborough (1982)
Cheadle Hulme School, Cheshire	1855	870°	£5,200°	£2,500°	D. C. Firth (1977)
Cheltenham College, Glos.	1841	565†	£8,160	£6,120	R. M. Morgan (1978)
Chigwell School, Essex	1629	344†	£2,064	£1,357	A. R. M. Little (1989)
Christ College, Brecon	1541	336†	£5,580	£4,230	S. W. Hockey (1982)
Christ's Hospital, W. Sussex	1553	840‡	£7,100	....	R. C. Poulton (1987)
Churcher's College, Hants.	1722	460‡	£6,048	£3,258	G. W. Buttle (1988)
City of London, EC4	1442	850	....	£3,870	J. M. Hammond (1984)
City of London Freemen's School, Surrey	1854	360‡	£6,060	£3,900	D. C. Haywood (1987)
Clifton College, Bristol	1862	700‡	£8,310	£5,820	S. M. Andrews (1975)
Colfe's School, SE12	1652	690†	....	£3,030	V. S. Anthony (1976)
Colston's School, Bristol	1710	340†	£5,880	£3,555	S. B. Howarth (1988)
Coventry School	—	1659‡	....	£2,310	R. Cooke (*Director*) (1977)
Cranleigh School, Surrey	1863	560†	£8,550	£6,420	A. Hart (1984)
Culford School, Suffolk	1881	450‡	£6,309	£4,101	D. Robson (1971)

* A Woodard Corporation School.   ‡ Co-educational.   † Girls in VI form.   ° 1989 figure.

Name of School	Founded	No. of Pupils	Annual Fees B'ding	Annual Fees Day	Headmaster (With date of Appointment)
Dame Allan's School, Newcastle upon Tyne	1705	450†	....	£2,364	T. A. Willcocks (*Principal*) (1988)
Dauntsey's School, Wiltshire	1543	580‡	£6,870	£4,230	C. R. Evans (1985)
Dean Close School, Cheltenham	1884	440‡	£7,695	£5,025	C. J. Bacon (1979)
*Denstone College, Staffs.	1873	360‡	£6,990	£4,900	R. M. Ridley (1986)
Douai School (*R.C.*), Berks.	1903	295	£6,489	£4,086	Dom. G. Scott, o.s.b. (1987)
Dover College, Kent	1871	320‡	£6,825	£4,485	J. K. Ind (1981)
Downside School (*R.C.*), Somerset	1607	435	£7,206	£4,611	Dom. P. Jebb, o.s.b. (1980)
Dulwich College, SE21	1619	1430	£7,920	£3,690	A. C. F. Verity (*Master*) (1986)
Durham School	1414	380†	£7,563	£5,043	M. A. Lang (1982)
Eastbourne College, E. Sussex	1867	540†	£7,818	£5,754	C. J. Saunders (1981)
*Ellesmere College, Shropshire	1884	410†	£7,200	£5,100	D. R. du Croz (1988)
Eltham College, SE9	1842	530†	£7,296	£3,456	C. D. Waller, ph.d. (1983)
Emanuel School, W11	1594	760	....	£1,035	P. F. Thomson (1984)
Epsom College, Surrey	1855	650†	£7,680	£5,370	Dr. J. B. Cook (1982)
Eton College, Berks.	1440	1260	£8,496	....	Dr. W. E. K. Anderson (1980)
Exeter School	1633	676†	£6,867	£8,145	G. T. Goodall (1979)
Felsted School, Essex	1564	500†	£8,100	£6,390	E. J. H. Gould (1983)
Forest School, E17	1834	447†	£5,445	£3,693	J. C. Gough (*Warden*) (1983)
Framlingham College, Suffolk	1864	465‡	£6,357	£4,080	J. F. X. Miller (1989)
Frensham Heights, Surrey	1925	266‡	£8,160	£5,130	A. L. Pattinson (1973)
Giggleswick School, N. Yorks.	1512	320‡	£7,410	£4,950	P. Hobson (1986)
Gresham's School, Norfolk	1555	483‡	£7,275°	£4,995°	H. R. Wright (1985)
Haberdashers' Aske's School, Herts.	1690	1107	....	£3,702	K. Dawson (1987)
Haileybury, Herts.	1862	695†	£7,500	£4,800	D. J. Jewell (1987)
Hampton School, Middx.	1557	840	....	£2,925	G. G. Able (1988)
Harrow School, Middx.	1571	770	£8,850	....	I. D. S. Beer (1981)
Hereford Cathedral School	1384	602‡	£5,115	£2,985	Dr. H. C. Tomlinson (1987)
Highgate School, N6	1565	610°	£6,810°	£3,915°	R. C. Giles (1974)
Hulme Grammar School, Oldham	1611	750	....	£2,421	G. F. Dunkin (1987)
*Hurstpierpoint College, W. Sussex	1849	410	£7,485	£5,985	S. A. Watson (1986)
Hymers College, Hull	1889	700‡	....	£1,815°	B. G. Bass (1983)
Ipswich School, Suffolk	1390	610†	£5,496	£3,300	Dr. J. M. Blatchly (1972)
John Lyon School, Middx.	1876	500	....	£3,060	Rev. T. J. Wright (1986)
Kelly College, Devon	1877	350†	£7,530	£2,985	C. H. Hirst (1985)
Kent College, Canterbury	1885	550‡	£6,426	£3,600	R. J. Wicks (1980)
Kimbolton School, Cambs.	1600	530‡	£6,000	£3,300	R. V. Peel (1987)
King Edward VI School, Southampton	1553	944†	....	£2,985	C. Dobson (1971)
King Edward VII School, Lytham	1908	552	....	£2,145	D. Heap (1982)
King Edward's School, Bath	1552	685†	....	£2,665	J. P. Wroughton (1982)
King Edward's School, Birmingham	1552	730°	....	£2,430°	M. J. W. Rogers (*Chief Master*) (1982)
King Edward's School, Witley, Surrey	1553	525‡	£5,991	£4,425	R. J. Fox (1988)
*King's College, Taunton	1880	480†	£7,680	£5,712	R. S. Funnell (1988)
King's College School, SW19	1829	650	....	£3,735	R. M. Reeve (1980)
King's School, Bruton, Somerset	1519	335†	£7,560	£5,400	A. H. Beadles (1985)
King's School, Canterbury	600	700°‡	£7,350°	£5,145°	Rev. Canon A. C. J. Phillips (1986)
King's School, Chester	1541	450	....	£2,589	A. R. D. Wickson (1981)
King's School, Ely, Cambs.	970	430‡	£7,758	£4,944	H. Ward (1970)
King's School, Macclesfield	1502	850†	....	£2,865	A. G. Silcock (1987)
King's School, Rochester, Kent	604	430†	£6,615	£3,975	Dr. I. R. Walker (1986)
King's School, Worcester	1541	720†	£5,562	£3,372	Dr. J. M. Moore (1983)
Kingston Grammar School, Surrey	1561	571‡	....	£3,390	A. B. Creber (1987)
Kingswood School, Bath	1748	490‡	£7,155	£4,650	G. M. Best (1987)
*Lancing College, W. Sussex	1848	555‡°	£7,191°	£5,004°	J. S. Woodhouse (1981)
Latymer Upper School, W6	1624	935	....	£3,390	M. C. Pavey (1988)
Leeds Grammar School	1552	1044	....	£2,691	B. W. Collins (1986)
Leighton Park School, Reading	1890	360†	£7,074	£5,094	J. A. Chapman (1986)
The Leys School, Cambridge	1875	400†	£7,899	£5,865	T. G. Beynon (1986)
Liverpool College	1840	398†	£4,626	£2,445	R. V. Haygarth (1979)
Llandovery School, Dyfed	1848	250‡	£5,895	£3,597	Dr. C. E. Evans (1988)
Lord Wandsworth College, Hants.	1912	420†	£6,300	£4,920	G. A. G. Dodd (1982)
Loughborough Grammar School	1495	880	£5,355	£2,706	D. N. Ireland (1984)
Magdalen College School, Oxford	1480	500	£5,676	£2,967	W. B. Cook (*Master*) (1972)
Malvern College, Worcs.	1865	600	£8,085	£5,880	R. de C. Chapman (1983)
Manchester Grammar School	1515	1460	....	£2,490°	J. G. Parker (*High Master*) (1985)

* A Woodard Corporation School.   ‡ Co-educational.   † Girls in VI form.   ° 1989 figure.

Name of School	Founded	No. of Pupils	Annual Fees B'ding	Annual Fees Day	Headmaster (With date of Appointment)
Marlborough College, Wilts.........	1843	900‡	£8,100	£6,750	D. R. Cope (*Master*) (1986)
Merchant Taylors' School, Liverpool	1620	670	....	£2,637	S. J. R. Dawkins (1986)
Merchant Taylors' School, Middx. ..	1561	700	£7,050	£4,500	D. J. Skipper (1982)
Mill Hill School, NW7..............	1807	535†	£7,650	£5,070	A. C. Graham (1979)
Monkton Combe School, Bath	1868	340†	£7,725	£5,625	R. A. C. Meredith (1978)
Monmouth School, Gwent...........	1614	540	£5,610	£3,216	R. D. Lane (1982)
Mount St. Mary's College (*R.C.*), Derbys...........................	1842	300‡	£5,436	£3,672	Rev. J. F. Grumitt, s.j. (1976)
Newcastle-under-Lyme School	1874	1220†	....	£2,361	J. W. Donaldson (*Principal*) (1974)
Norwich School	1250	600	....	£2,865	C. D. Brown (1984)
Nottingham High School...........	1513	830	....	£2,700	D. T. Witcombe, ph.d. (1970)
Oakham School, Rutland	1584	750‡	£7,827	£4,191	G. Smallbone (1985)
The Oratory School (*R.C.*), Berks....	1859	380	£7,518	£5,259	M. K. Lynn (1989)
Oundle School, Northants..........	1556	730	£8,550	....	D. B. McMurray (1984)
Pangbourne College, Berks.	1917	320	£7,250	£5,100	A. B. E. Hudson (1988)
Perse School, Cambridge	1615	485	£5,430	£2,688	Dr. G. M. Stephen (1987)
Plymouth College	1877	690	£5,340	£4,485	A. M. Joyce (1983)
Pocklington School, York.	1514	720‡	£5,718	£2,925	A. D. Pickering (1981)
Portsmouth Grammar School	1732	750	....	£2,610	A. C. V. Evans (1983)
Prior Park College (*R.C.*), Bath	1830	394‡	£6,695	£3,704	J. W. R. Goulding (1989)
Queen Elizabeth G.S., Wakefield ...	1591	735	£4,458	£2,739	R. P. Mardling (1985)
Queen Elizabeth's G.S., Blackburn ..	1567	1060†	....	£2,490	P. F. Johnston (1978)
Queen Elizabeth's Hospital, Bristol..	1590	480	£4,740	£2,700	Dr. R. Gliddon (1985)
Queen's College, Taunton	1843	450‡	£5,985	£3,945	A. P. Hodgson (1979)
Radley College, Oxon..............	1847	600	£8,250	....	D. R. W. Silk (*Warden*) (1968)
Ratcliffe College (*R.C.*), Leicester ...	1844	427‡	£5,900	£3,800	Rev. L. G. Hurdidge (1985)
Reed's School, Surrey.............	1813	360†	£6,645	£4,800	D. E. Prince (1983)
Reigate Grammar School, Surrey ...	1675	860†	....	£3,033	J. G. Hamlin (1982)
Rendcomb College, Glos.	1920	260†	£6,750	....	J. Tolputt (1987)
Repton School, Derby	1557	570†	£7,110	£5,250	G. E. Jones (1986)
R.N.I.B. New College, Worcester	1987	117‡	£14,361	£9,576	Rev. B. R. Manthorp (1980)
Rossall School, Lancs.	1844	478‡	£7,704	£5,376	R. D. W. Rhodes (1987)
Royal Grammar School, Guildford ..	1552	800	....	£3,540	J. Daniel (1972)
Royal Grammar School, Newcastle upon Tyne	1545	963	....	£2,340	A. S. Cox (1972)
Royal Grammar School, Worcester ..	1291	748	£5,175	£2,925	T. E. Savage, t.d. (1978)
Rugby School, Warwicks.	1567	720†°	£7,575°	£4,525°	O. R. S. Bull (1985)
Rydal School, Clwyd	1885	350	£6,195	£4,710	P. F. Watkinson (1968)
Ryde School, Isle of Wight.........	1921	434‡	£5,166	£2,583	P. D. V. Wilkes (1984)
St. Albans School, Herts.	1570	665	....	£3,300	S. C. Wilkinson (1984)
St. Ambrose College, Cheshire	1946	640	....	£2,088	T. D. Coleman (1984)
St. Anselm's College (*R.C.*), Birkenhead.......................	1933	645	....	£2,136	Rev. Br. C. J. Sreenan, o.b.e. (1988)
St. Bede's College (*R.C.*), Manchester	1876	880‡	....	£2,562	J. Byrne (1983)
St. Bees School, Cumbria	1583	370‡	£7,110	£4,965	P. A. Chamberlain (1988)
St. Benedict's School (*R.C.*), W5.....	1902	580†	....	£2,900	Dr. A. J. Dachs (1987)
St. Dunstan's College (*R.C.*), SE6....	1888	670	....	£3,090	B. D. Dance (1973)
St. Edmund's College (*R.C.*), Herts...	1568	464‡	£6,174	£3,969	D. J. J. McEwen (1984)
St. Edmund's School, Canterbury ...	1749	310‡	£7,128	£4,863	J. V. Tyson (1978)
St. Edward's College (*R.C.*),Liverpool	1853	650†	....	£2,283	Rev. Br. B. D. Sassi (1984)
St. Edward's School, Oxford	1863	585†°	£7,350°	£5,520°	D. Christie (1988)
St. George's College, (*R.C.*), Surrey ..	1869	600†	£6,174	£4,182	Rev. J. W. Munton (1987)
St. John's School, Surrey	1851	450†	£6,450	£4,560	D. E. Brown (1985)
St. Lawrence College, Kent.........	1879	350‡	£7,110	£4,755	J. H. Binfield (1983)
St. Mary's College (*R.C.*), Merseyside	1919	570‡	....	£2,265	Rev. Br. P. E. Ryan (1987)
St. Paul's School, SW13	1509	780	£7,901	£4,969	Rev. Canon P. Pilkington (*High Master*) (1986)
St. Peter's School, York	627	490‡	£6,996	£4,872	R. N. Pittman (1985)
Sedbergh School, Cumbria	1525	495	£7,620	£5,340	Dr. R. G. Baxter (1982)
Sevenoaks School, Kent............	1418	906‡	£8,271	£5,238	R. P. Barker (1981)
Sherborne School, Dorset	1550	650	£8,400	£6,400	P. H. Lapping (1988)
Shrewsbury School	1552	660	£8,100	£5,715	F. E. Maidment (1988)
Silcoates School, W. Yorks..........	1820	409†	£5,628	£3,240	J. C. Baggaley (1979)
Solihull School, Warwicks	1560	837†	....	£2,568	A. Lee (1983)
Stamford School, Lincs.	1532	584	£5,280	£2,640	G. J. Timm (1978)
Stockport Grammar School.........	1487	1010‡	....	£2,637	D. R. J. Bird (1985)
Stonyhurst College (*R.C.*), Lancs. ...	1593	430	£7,413	£3,867	Dr. R. G. G. Mercer (1985)
Stowe School, Bucks.	1923	607†	£8,658	£6,060	J. G. L. Nichols (1989)

* A Woodard Corporation School.   ‡ Co-educational.   † Girls in VI form.   ° 1989 figure.

Name of School	Founded	No. of Pupils	Annual Fees B'ding	Annual Fees Day	Headmaster (With date of Appointment)
Sutton Valence School, Kent	1576	410‡	£7,236	£4,620	M. R. Haywood (1980)
Taunton School	1847	560‡	£7,680	£4,975	B. B. Sutton (1987)
Tettenhall College, Staffs.	1863	350‡	£5,568	£3,432	W. J. Dale (1968)
Tonbridge School, Kent	1553	660	£8,100	£5,700	C. H. D. Everett, C.B.E. (1975)
Trent College, Derbys.	1868	523†	£6,255	£3,726	J. S. Lee (1988)
Trinity School, Surrey	1596	825	....	£3,315	R. J. Wilson (1972)
Truro School	1879	849†	£5,445	£2,895	B. K. Hobbs (1986)
University College School, NW3	1830	520	....	£4,275	G. D. Slaughter (1983)
Uppingham School, Leics.	1584	680†	£8,550	....	N. R. Bomford (1982)
Warwick School	914	802	£6,090	£2,820	P. J. Cheshire (1989)
Wellingborough School, Northants .	1595	450‡	£6,105	£3,720	G. Garrett (1973)
Wellington College, Berks.	1856	810°	£6,480°	£4,710°	C. J. Driver (1989)
Wellington School, Somerset	1841	800‡	£5,190	£2,790	J. M. K. Kendall-Carpenter, C.B.E. (1973)
Wells Cathedral School, Somerset ...	1180	587‡	£5,904	£3,339	J. S. Baxter (1986)
West Buckland School, Devon	1858	446‡	£5,718	£3,105	M. Downward (1979)
Westminster School, SW1	1560	610†	£7,950°	£5,250	D. M. Summerscale (1986)
Whitgift School, Surrey	1596	900	....	£3,420	D. A. Raeburn (1970)
William Hulme's G.S., Manchester ..	1887	790‡	....	£2,835	P. D. Briggs (1987)
Winchester College, Hants.	1382	650	£8,658	£6,495	J. P. Sabben-Clare (1985)
Wolverhampton Grammar School	1512	635†	....	£3,084	P. H. Hutton (1978)
Woodbridge School, Suffolk	1662	550‡	£6,030	£3,480	Dr. D. Younger (1985)
Woodhouse Grove School, Bradford .	1812	560‡°	£4,905°	£2,994°	D. A. Miller (1972)
*Worksop College, Notts.	1895	410‡	£6,390	£4,320	A. H. Monro (1986)
Worth School (*R.C.*), W. Sussex	1959	310	£7,355	....	Rev. R. S. Ortiger (1983)
Wrekin College, Shropshire	1880	400‡	£7,395	£5,604	J. H. Arkell (1983)
Wycliffe College, Glos.	1882	330‡	£7,194	£4,683	A. P. Millard (1987)
Scotland					
Daniel Stewart's and Melville College, Edinburgh	1832	784	£5,300	£2,526	P. F. J. Tobin (1989)
Dollar Academy, Clackmannanshire	1818	887‡°	£5,046°	£2,352°	L. Harrison (*Rector*) (1984)
Dundee High School, Tayside	1239	750‡	....	£2,448	R. Nimmo (*Rector*) (1977)
The Edinburgh Academy	1824	584†	£6,945	£3,390	L. E. Ellis (*Rector*) (1977)
Fettes College, Edinburgh	1870	425‡	£7,455	£5,010	M. T. Thyne (1988)
George Heriot's School, Edinburgh . .	1659	1329‡	....	£2,580	K. P. Pearson (1983)
George Watson's College, Edinburgh	1741	1246‡	£5,346	£2,772	F. E. Gerstenberg (*Principal*) (1985)
Glasgow Academy	1845	550	....	£2,685	C. W. Turner (*Rector*) (1983)
Glenalmond College, Perth.	1841	370	£7,350	....	S. R. D. Hall (*Warden*) (1987)
Gordonstoun School, Moray	1934	477‡	£7,776	£4,995	M. B. Mavor, C.V.O. (1979)
The High School of Glasgow	1124	565‡	....	£2,670	R. G. Easton (1983)
Hutcheson's Grammar School, Glasgow	1641	1064‡	....	£2,259	D. R. Ward (*Rector*) (1987)
Kelvinside Academy, Glasgow	1878	500	....	£2,700	J. H. Duff (*Rector*) (1980)
Loretto School, E. Lothian	1827	300†°	£6,300°	£3,945°	Rev. N. W. Drummond (1984)
Merchiston Castle School, Edinburgh	1833	360	£7,680	£4,950	D. M. Spawforth (1981)
Morrison's Academy, Perthshire....	1860	600‡	£5,880	£2,265	H. A. Ashmall (*Rector*) (1979)
Robert Gordon's College, Aberdeen .	1729	1120‡	£5,400	£2,500	G. A. Allan (1978)
Strathallan School, Perth	1913	400‡	£7,650	....	C. D. Pighills (1975)
Northern Ireland					
Bangor Grammar School, Co. Down .	1856	900	....	£1,600	T. W. Patton (1979)
Belfast Royal Academy	1785	1296‡	....	£1,800	W. M. Sillery (1980)
Campbell College, Belfast	1894	414	£5,884	£2,725	Dr. R. J. I. Pollock (1987)
Coleraine Academical Institution ...	1856	950	£3,894	£1,750	R. S. Forsythe (1984)
Methodist College, Belfast	1868	1600‡	£4,000	£1,850	T. W. Mulryne (1988)
Portora Royal School, Enniskillen ..	1618	340‡	£4,200	£2,100	R. L. Bennett (1983)
Royal Belfast Academical Institution	1810	900	....	£1,800	T. J. Garrett (1978)
Channel Islands and Isle of Man					
Elizabeth College, Guernsey	1563	537	£3,780	£1,320	J. H. F. Doulton (1988)
Victoria College, Jersey	1852	580	£5,430	£1,140	M. H. Devenport (1967)
King William's College, Isle of Man .	1668	380	£2,210	£1,465	S. A. Westley (1989)

* A Woodard Corporation School. ‡ Co-educational. † Girls in VI form. ° 1989 figure.

H.M.C. SCHOOLS OVERSEAS
Fees are given in local currency.

Name of School	Founded	No. of Pupils	Annual Fees		Headmaster *(With date of Appointment)*
			B'ding	Day	
Africa					
Diocesan College, Rondesbosch, S.A.	1849	617†	R12,120	R6,920	J. B. Gardener (1988)
Falcon College, Esigodini, Zimbabwe	1954	450	Z$6,300	....	P. N. Todd (1985)
Hilton College, Natal, S.A.	1872	490†	R14,000	....	P. Marsh (1987)
Kamuzu Academy, Malawi	1981	360‡	K11,000	....	vacant
Peterhouse, Marondera, Zimbabwe	1955	550†	Z$7,260	....	Rev. Dr. A. J. Megahey (*Rector*) (1984)
St George's College, Harare, Zimbabwe	1896	840	Z$3,930	Z$1,560	J. C. Berry (1983)
St. John's College, Johannesburg, S.A.	—	602†	R12,387	R7,176	W. W. MacFarlane (1983)
St. Stithian's College, Randburg, S.A.	1953	633	R9,810	R5,475	D. Wylde (1989)
Australia					
Anglican Church G.S., Queensland	1912	1289	$A7,350	$A3,250	C. V. Ellis (1987)
Brighton G.S., Victoria	1882	1100	....	$A5,500	R. L. Rofe (1967)
Camberwell G.S., Victoria	1886	856	....	$A5,378	C. F. Black (1987)
Canberra G.S., A.C.T.	1929	878	$A9,412	$A4,096	T. C. Murray (1986)
Carey Baptist G. S., Victoria	1923	1100‡	....	$A5,781	Dr. R. H. Millikan (1990)
Caulfield G.S., Victoria	1881	2171‡	$A10,737	$A5,427	Rev. A. S. Holmes (*Principal*) (1977)
Cranbrook School, N.S.W.	1918	801	$A10,860	$A5,490	Dr. B. N. Carter (1985)
The Geelong College, Victoria	1861	996‡	$A11,900	$A5,900	A. P. Sheahan (1986)
Geelong G.S., Victoria	1855	880‡	$A12,444	$A5,836	J. E. Lewis (1980)
Guildford G.S., W. Australia	1896	775	$A9,320	$A4,320	J. M. Moody (1979)
Haileybury College, Victoria	1892	900	....	$A5,500	A. M. H. Aikman (*Principal*) (1974)
Hale School, W. Australia	1858	655	$A9,500	$A4,500	J. Inverarity, O.B.E. (1989)
King's School, Parramatta, N.S.W.	1831	906	$A8,205	$A4,605	J. A. Wickham (1984)
Kinross Wolaroi School, N.S.W.	1886	615‡	$A10,020	$A4,695	A. E. S. Anderson (1978)
Knox, G.S., N.S.W.	1924	1250	$A10,930	$A5,280	Dr. I. W. Paterson (1969)
Melbourne C. of E. G.S., Victoria	1856	1107	$A8,379	$A4,839	A. J. de V. Hill (1988)
Newington College, N.S.W.	1863	1130	$A12,090	$A6,390	A. J. Rae (1972)
The Peninsula School, Victoria	1961	1026	$A10,346	$A6,047	H. A. Macdonald (1971)
St. Peter's College, S. Australia	1847	790	$A10,920	$A5,100	Dr. A. J. Shinkfield (1978)
Scotch College, Adelaide, S. Australia	1919	750‡	$A12,280	$A5,950	W. M. Miles (1975)
Scotch College, Hawthorn, Victoria	1851	1398	$A11,661	$A5,886	Dr. F. G. Donaldson (1983)
Scotch College, Swanbourne, W. Australia	1897	745	$A9,220	$A4,360	W. R. Dickinson (1972)
Scots College, Sydney, N.S.W.	1893	1050°	$A10,500°	$A5,500°	G. A. W. Renney (*Principal*) (1980)
Sydney C. of E. G.S., N.S.W.	1889	963	$A10,599	$A5,325	R. A. I. Grant (1983)
Sydney G.S., N.S.W.	1857	1117	....	$A6,435	Dr. R. D. Townsend, D. Phil. (1989)
Wesley College, Melbourne, Victoria	1866	1960‡	....	$A5,810	D. H. Prest (*Principal*) (1972)
Canada					
Brentwood College School, Vancouver	1961	375‡°	C$13,675°	C$6,800°	W. T. Ross (1976)
Hillfield Strathallan College, Ontario	1901	958‡	....	C$6,985	M. B. Wansbrough (1969)
Pickering College, Ontario.	1842	165	C$13,800	C$6,900	S. H. Clark (1978)
St. Andrew's College, Ontario	1899	393	C$16,150	C$9,350	R. P. Bedard (1981)
Toronto French School, Ontario	1962	1244‡	C$14,280	C$7,505	A. S. Troubetzkoy (1987)
Trinity College School, Ontario	1865	403	C$16,350	C$9,000	R. C. N. Wright (1983)
Upper Canada College, Toronto	1829	620	C$16,350	C$8,900	E. A. Barton (*Principal*) (1988)
Europe					
Aiglon College, Switzerland	1949	260	Frs.37,530	Frs.25,620	P. Parsons (1976)
British School in the Netherlands.	1935	470‡	n/a	n/a	B. D. Davidson (1979)
British School of Brussels	1970	500‡	Frs.621,000	Frs.421,000	Dr. J. Jackson (1983)

† Girls in VI form.   ‡ Co-educational.   ° 1989 figures.

Name of School	Founded	No. of Pupils	Annual Fees B'ding	Annual Fees Day	Headmaster (With date of Appointment)
British School of Paris, France ...	1954	300‡	Frs.94,380	Frs.62,355	A. W. Livingstone-Smith (1986)
The English School, Nicosia, Cyprus	1900	820‡°	....	C£1,102°	A. M. Hudspeth (1988)
The International School of Paris .	1964	220‡	....	Frs.£64,000	N. M. Prentki (1988)
St. Columba's College, Dublin	1843	251‡	IR£4,500	IR£2,850	T. E. Macey (*Warden*) (1988)
St. George's English School, Rome	1958	787‡	....	L13,500,000	Dr. C. H. R. Niven (1988)
India					
Birla Public School, Pilani	—	360°	Rs.8,750°	Rs.2,800°	B. K. Sood (1973)
Edwardes College, Peshawar	n/a	n/a	n/a	n/a	Dr. T. L. Woolmer
Lawrence School, Ootacamund ...	1858	700‡	Rs.14,000	....	B. S. Bhatnagar (1986)
Lawrence School, Sanawar	1847	540°	Rs.13,000°	....	S. B. Singh (1988)
The Scindia School, Gualior	1897	556	Rs.13,500	....	Dr. S. D. Singh (1978)
Yadavindra Public School, Patiala	1947	1143°	Rs.9,740 °	Rs.4,020°	Dr. H. S. Dhillon (1987)
New Zealand					
Christ's College, Christchurch	1850	570	NZ$8,226	NZ$4,470	Dr. M. J. Rosser (1985)
Collegiate School, Wanganui	1854	490	NZ$10,141	NZ$5,490	T. S. McKinlay (1988)
King's College, Auckland	1896	770†	NZ$9,390	NZ$5,550	J. S. Taylor (1988)
St. Andrew's College, Christchurch	1916	629	NZ$8,940	NZ$4,905	Dr. A. J. Rentoul (*Rector*) (1982)
South America					
Markham College, Peru	1946	1600	....	US$1,000	W. J. Baker (1990)
St. Andrew's Scots School, Argentina	—	580‡	n/a	n/a	K. Prior (1982)
St. George's College, Argentina ...	1898	225‡°	A.4,800°	A.3,300°	G. R. Sims (1986)
St. Paul's School, Brazil	1926	240°	....	£1,500°	P. Gysin (1987)
United Arab Emirates					
Dubai College	1855	511†	....	Dh.18,000	H. J. Deelman (1987)
U.S.A.					
The Rivers School, Massachusetts	1915	260‡	....	$10,000	R. A. Bradley (1981)

‡Co-educational.   † Girls in VI form.   °1989 figures.

SOCIETY OF HEADMASTERS OF INDEPENDENT SCHOOLS

Hon. Secretary, A. E. R. Dodds, Green Garth, Horsell Rise, Woking, Surrey GU21 4AY.

The Society was founded in 1961 and, in general, represents smaller boarding schools. A Headmaster may be a member of both H.M.C. and S.H.M.I.S. This is the case for the Headmasters of the following schools, details of which appear in the H.M.C. list:

Abbotsholme School, Bedales School, Churcher's College, City of London Freemen's School, Colston's School, Frensham Heights, Lord Wandsworth College, Pangbourne College, Reed's School, Rendcomb College, Ryde School, St. George's College, Silcoates School, Tettenhall College, Wells Cathedral School, West Buckland School and Woodbridge School.

Name of School	Founded	No. of Pupils	Annual Fees B'ding	Annual Fees Day	Headmaster (With date of Appointment)
Ackworth School, W. Yorks	1779	385‡	£5,952	£3,345	D. S. Harris (1989)
Austin Friars School (*R.C.*), Carlisle	1951	296‡°	£3,927°	£2,145°	Rev. T. Lyons, o.s.a. (1981)
Bearwood College, Berks.	1827	340°	£6,150°	£3,600°	The Hon. M. C. Penney (1980)
Bedstone College, Shropshire	1948	220‡°	£5,295°	....	G. S. Wilson (1971)
Belmont Abbey (*R.C.*), Hereford	1926	240	£5,145	£3,135	Rev. D. C. Jenkins, o.s.b. (1988)
Bembridge School, Isle of Wight	1919	173‡	£5,295	£2,850	J. High (1986)
Bentham School, N. Yorks	1726	290‡	£5,385	£2,715	J. E. Rigg (1988)
Bethany School, Kent	1866	275	£6,150	£4,110	W. M. Harvey (1988)

‡Co-educational.   °1989 figure.

Name of School	Founded	No. of Pupils	Annual Fees B'ding	Day	Headmaster (With date of Appointment)
Box Hill School, Surrey	1959	265‡	£6,885	£3,945	Dr. R. A. S. Atwood (1987)
Carmel College (*Jewish*), Oxon.	1948	290‡	£9,030	£5,250	P. D. Skelker (1984)
Clayesmore School, Dorset	1896	301‡	£7,575	£5,325	D. J. Beeby (1986)
Cokethorpe School, Oxon.	1957	175†	£7,410	£5,340	D. G. Crawford (1989)
Cranbrook School, Kent	1518	720	£3,225	......	P. A. Close (1988)
Ewell Castle School, Surrey	1926	355†	......	£2,640	R. A. Fewtrell (1983)
Friends' School, Essex	1702	265‡	£6,048	£3,612	Miss S. H. Evans (1989)
Fulneck Boys' School, W. Yorks.	1753	312†	£5,550	£2,865	I. D. Cleland (1980)
*Grenville College, Devon	1954	360	£6,352	£3,148	Dr. D. C. Powell-Price, T.D. (1975)
Halliford School, Middx.	1956	308†	......	£2,670	J. R. Crook (1984)
Keil School, Dumbarton	1915	200‡	£5,784	£3,294	C. H. Tongue (1984)
Kingham Hill School, Oxon.	1886	240	£5,400	£3,300	D. Shepherd (1981)
King's School, Gloucester	1541	450‡	£5,442	£3,222	Rev. A. C. Charters (1983)
King's School, Tynemouth	1860	680†	......	£2,340	W. T. Gillen (1987)
Kirkham Grammar School, Lancs.	1549	512‡	£4,080	£2,220	M. J. Summerlee (1972)
Lindisfarne College, Clwyd	1891	220‡	£6,240	£3,345	T. R. Wilson (1986)
Lord Mayor Treloar College, Hants.	1908	284‡	£18,780	£14,095	A. M. Macpherson (1974)
Milton Abbey School, Dorset	1954	285	£7,650	......	R. H. Hardy (1987)
Oswestry School, Shropshire	1407	306‡	£5,160	£3,075	I. G. Templeton (1985)
Pierrepont School, Surrey	1947	265‡°	£5,964°	£3,579°	J. D. Payne (1983)
The Purcell School (music), Middx.	1962	175‡°°	£6,045°°	£3,075°°	K. J. Bain (1983)
Rannoch School, Perthshire	1959	255‡	£6,750	£3,990	M. Barratt (1982)
Reading Blue Coat School, Berks.	1646	517†	£5,790	£3,201	Rev. A. C. E. Sanders (1974)
Rishworth School, W. Yorks.	1724	491‡	£5,955	£3,180	A. J. Morsley (1986)
Rougemont School, Gwent	1919	280‡	......	£2,970	F. W. Edwards (1975)
Royal Hospital School, Ipswich	1712	700	£3,930	......	M. A. B. Kirk (1983)
Royal Russell School, Surrey	1853	430‡	£6,030	£3,165	R. D. Balaam (1981)
Royal School, Dungannon, N. Ireland	1614	575‡	£3,600	£1,650	P. D. Hewitt (1984)
Royal Wolverhampton School	1850	335‡°	£5,100°	£2,985°	P. Gorring (1985)
Ruthin School, Clwyd	1574	136†	£6,375	£4,215	F. R. Ullmann (1986)
St. David's College, Gwynedd	1965	250	£6,360	£4,110	B. T. C. Morris (1989)
Scarborough College, N. Yorks.	1898	400‡	£6,498	£3,483	D. S. Hempsall, Ph.D. (1985)
Seaford College, W. Sussex	1884	420	£6,195	......	Rev. Canon C. E. Johnson (1944)
Shebbear College, Devon	1841	300	£5,790	£3,120	R. J. Buley (1983)
Shiplake College, Oxon.	1959	350	£7,650	£5,010	N. V. Bevan (1988)
Sidcot School, Avon	1808	275‡	£6,570	£3,675	C. J. Greenfield (1986)
Stanbridge Earls School, Hants.	1952	165‡	£7,650	£5,355	H. Moxon (1984)
Warminster School, Wilts.	1707	325‡	£5,850	£3,510	D. M. Green (1984)

*A Woodard Corporation School.   ‡Co-educational.   †Girls in VI form.   °1989 figure.   °°1988 figure.

GIRLS' SCHOOLS ASSOCIATION

THE GIRLS' SCHOOLS ASSOCIATION, 130 Regent Road, Leicester LE1 7PG.—*President* (1990), Mrs. A. T. D. Macaire; *Sec.*, Miss A. C. Parkin.

Name of School	Founded	No. of Pupils	Annual Fees B'ding	Day	Headmistress (a) Headmaster (With date of Appointment)
Abbey School, Reading	1887	750°	......	£2,850	S. M. Hardcastle, M.B.E. (1960)
Abbots Bromley, Staffs	1874	255°	£5,970°	£3,760°	(a) A. Grigg (1989)
Abbot's Hill, Herts.	1912	153°°	£4,950°°	£3,375°°	Mrs. J. Kingsley (1979)
Adcote School, Shropshire	1907	117	£5,865	£3,480	Mrs. S. B. Cecchet (1979)
Alice Ottley School, Worcester	1883	570	£5,670	£2,940	C. Sibbit (1986)
All Hallows School, Suffolk	1864	97	£5,103	£3,213	A. C. Harris (1984)
Amberfield School, Ipswich	1952	150	......	£2,520	Mrs. P. F. Webb (1979)
Ashford School, Kent	1910	545	£5,814	£3,360	Mrs. A. T. D. Macaire (1984)
Assumption School, N. Yorks.	1852	150	£5,304	£2,955	Mrs. J. Coulthard (1988)
Atherley School, Southampton (CSC)	1926	350	......	£2,688	Mrs. M. Williams (1988)
Badminton School, Bristol	1858	300°	£6,150°	£3,450°	(a) C. J. T. Gould (1981)
‡Bath High School	1875	548	......	£2,388	M. A. Winfield (1985)

‡Girls Public Day School Trust.   °1989 figure.   °°1988 figure.

Name of School	Founded	No. of Pupils	Annual Fees B'ding	Annual Fees Day	Headmistress (a) Headmaster (With date of Appointment)
Battle Abbey School, E. Sussex	1912	140††	£5,970	£3,600	(a) D. J. A. Teall (1982)
Bedford High School	1882	805	£5,856	£3,066	Mrs. D. M. Willis (1987)
Bedgebury School, Kent	1860	265	£6,984	£4,140	Mrs. M. E. A. Kaye (1987)
‡Belvedere School, Liverpool	1880	530	....	£2,388	S. Downs (1972)
Benenden School, Kent	1923	400	£7,200	....	Mrs. G. D. duCharme (1985)
Beresford House School, E. Sussex .	1902	220	£7,500	£3,945	S. B. Jackson (1988)
Berkhamsted School, Herts.	1888	465	£5,364	£2,976	V. E. M. Shepherd (1980)
‡Birkenhead High School	1901	943	....	£2,388	Mrs. K. R. Irving (1986)
‡Blackheath High School, SE3	1880	551	....	£2,700	R. K. Musgrave (1989)
Bolton School, Lancs	1877	875	....	£2,858	Mrs. M. A. Spurr (1979)
Bradford Girls' Grammar School ...	1875	691	....	£2,448	Mrs. L. J. Warrington (1987)
‡Brighton and Hove High School ...	1876	744	£5,163	£2,388	R. A. Woodbridge (1989)
Brigidine Convent, Windsor	1948	320	....	£2,385	Mrs. M. B. Cairns (1986)
‡Bromley High School, Kent	1883	693	....	£2,700	Mrs. E. J. Hancock (1989)
Bruton School, Somerset	1900	511	£4,350	£2,550	Mrs. J. M. Wade (1987)
Burgess Hill School, W. Sussex	1906	306°	£5,370°	£3,060°	Mrs. B. H. Webb (1979)
Bury Grammar School, Lancs.	1884	810	....	£2,070	J. M. Lawley (1987)
Casterton School, Cumbria	1823	365	£5,958	£3,630	(a) A. F. Thomas (1990)
‡Central Newcastle High School	1895	781	....	£2,388	Mrs. A. M. Chapman (1985)
Channing School, N6	1885	300	....	£3,555	Mrs. I. R. Raphael (1984)
‡Charters-Ancaster School, E. Sussex	1906	200	£5,475	£2,700	Mrs. S. V. Chapman (1985)
Cheltenham Ladies' College, Glos...	1853	840	£7,950	£5,055	E. Castle (1987)
City of London School for Girls, EC2	1894	550	....	£3,375	Lady France (1986)
Clarendon School, Bedford	1898	220	£6,150°	£3,570°	J. L. Howell (1978)
Clifton High School, Bristol	1877	510	£5,295	£2,700	Mrs. J. D. Walters (1985)
Cobham Hall, Kent	1962	307	£7,755	£5,175	Mrs. R. J. McCarthy (1989)
Colston's Girls' School, Bristol	1891	642	....	£2,340	Mrs. J. P. Franklin (1989)
Combe Bank School, Kent	1868	245	£5,550	£3,240	Mrs. A. J. K. Austin (1982)
Commonweal Lodge School, Surrey	1916	150	....	£2,535	J. M. Brown (1982)
Cranborne Chase School, Wilts.....	1946	125	£7,275	£3,600	Mrs. M. Simmons (1983)
Cranford House School, Oxon.	1931	130	....	£2,670	T. A. Spencer (1980)
Croft House School, Dorset	1941	200	£6,270	£4,356	Mrs. S. Rawlinson (1985)
Croham Hurst School, Surrey	1899	352	....	£2,682	J. M. Shelmerdine (1986)
‡Croydon High School, Surrey	1874	1033	....	£2,388	A. M. Mark (1980)
Dame Alice Harpur School, Bedford	1882	824	....	£2,487	S. M. Morse (1970)
Dame Allan's Girls' School, Newcastle upon Tyne	1705	420	....	£2,364	(a) T. A. Willcocks (Principal) (1988)
Derby High School	1892	290	....	£2,955	(a) Dr. G. H. Goddard (1983)
Downe House, Berks.	1907	464	£7,590	£5,310	S. Cameron (1989)
Dunottar School, Surrey	1926	309	....	£2,715	J. Burnell (1985)
Durham High School	1884	269	....	£2,340	B. E. Stephenson (1978)
Edgbaston Church of England College	1886	310	....	£925	(a) I. J. Walkley (1979)
Edgbaston High School	1876	530	....	£2,718	Mrs. S. J. Horsman (1987)
Edgehill College, Devon	1884	360	£5,895	£3,225	Mrs. E. M. Burton (1987)
Ellerslie, Worcs.	1922	250	£6,450	£4,200	Mrs. E. M. Baker (1988)
Elmslie Girls' School, Lancs.......	1918	400	....	£2,280	E. M. Smithies (1978)
Eothen School, Surrey (CSC)	1892	200°	....	£2,637°	D. C. Raine (1973)
Farlington School, W. Sussex	1896	236	£5,850	£3,600	Mrs. P. Metham (1987)
Farnborough Hill, Hants.	1889	520	....	£2,850	Sr. E. McCormack (1988)
Farringtons, Kent.................	1911	301	£5,835	£3,195	Mrs. B. J. Stock (1986)
Felixstowe College, Suffolk	1929	320	£7,125	£4,365	Mrs. A. F. Woodings (1989)
Fernhill Manor School, Hants......	1890	188	£5,385	£3,435	(a) Rev. A. J. Folks (1985)
Francis Holland School, NW1.	1878	350	....	£3,240	Mrs. P. H. Parsonson (1988)
Francis Holland School, SW1	1881	170	....	£3,360	Mrs. J. A. Anderson (1982)
Gateways School, Leeds	1941	200	....	£4,230	L. M. Brown (1984)
Godolphin School, Wilts.	1726	320	£7,050	£4,185	E. A. S. Hannay (1980)
Godolphin and Latymer School, W6	1905	700	....	£3,450	M. Rudland (1986)
Greenacre School, Surrey	1933	365°°	£4,515°°	£2,370°°	M. E. Haggerty (1977)
The Grove School, Hindhead, Surrey	1877	200	£5,454	£3,294	(a) C. Brooks (1984)
Guildford High School (CSC)	1888	446	....	£3,171	J. E. Dutton (1977)
Haberdashers' Aske's School for Girls, Herts.	1873	835	....	£2,400	Mrs. S. Wiltshire (1974)
Haberdashers' Monmouth School, Gwent	1891	525	£4,845	£2,565	H. L. Gichard (1986)
Harrogate Ladies' College	1893	400	£6,030	£4,014	Mrs. J. C. Lawrance (1974)
Headington School, Oxford	1915	530	£5,535	£2,826	E. M. Tucker (1982)
Heathfield School, Ascot, Berks. ...	1900	215	£7,950	....	Mrs. S. E. Watkins (1982)

‡ Girls Public Day School Trust.   †† Co-educational.   ° 1989 figure.   °° 1988 figure.

Name of School	Founded	No. of Pupils	Annual Fees B'ding	Annual Fees Day	Headmistress (a) Headmaster (With date of Appointment)
‡Heathfield School, Pinner, Middx. .	1900	350	....	£2,700	Mrs. J. Merritt (1988)
Hethersett Old Hall School, Norwich	1928	268	£5,160	£2,730	Mrs. V. M. Redington (1983)
Highclare School, W. Midlands	1932	360†	....	£2,385	Mrs. C. A. Hanson (1974)
Holy Child School, Birmingham	1933	230	£5,340	£2,790	J. M. Johnson (1987)
Holy Trinity Convent School, Bromley.......................	1886	380	....	£2,670	Sr. B. Wetz (1986)
Holy Trinity School, Kidderminster	1903	385	....	£2,070	Mrs. K. S. Butwilowska (1986)
Howell's School, Denbigh, Clwyd...	1859	305	£6,810	£4,260	(a) J. H. Delany (1987)
‡Howell's School, Landaff, Cardiff..	1860	674	£5,247	£2,472	J. P. Turner (1978)
Hull High School (CSC)	1890	232	£4,119	£2,769	C. M. B. Radcliffe (1976)
Hulme Grammar School, Oldham ..	1895	475	....	£2,205°	Mrs. A. Groom (1985)
Hunmanby Hall School, N. Yorks..	1928	202	£5,898	£3,159	J. Rutherford (1986)
Huyton College, Liverpool	1894	260††	£6,105	£2,685	W. E. Edwards (1984)
‡Ipswich High School	1878	596	....	£2,388	P. M. Hayworth (1971)
James Allen's Girls' School, SE22 ..	1741	720	£6,060	£3,270	Mrs. B. Davies (1984)
School of Jesus and Mary, Suffolk ..	1860	186	....	£2,460	Mrs. E. A. McKay (1982)
Kent College.....................	1885	288	£6,600	£3,930	(a) Rev. J. C. A. Barrett (1983)
King Edward VI High School for Girls, Birmingham	1883	560	....	£2,640	E. W. Evans (1977)
King's H.S. for Girls, Warwick.....	1879	540	....	£2,412	Mrs. J. M. Anderson (1987)
Kingsley School, Warwicks........	1884	380	£5,310	£2,580	Mrs. M. A. Webster (1988)
Lady Eleanor Holles School, Middx.	1711	620	....	£2,940	E. M. Candy (1981)
La Retraite School, Wilts.	1953	250	....	£2,859	Mrs. M. Paisey (1986)
La Sagesse Convent High School, Newcastle upon Tyne	1906	350	....	£2,346	Mrs. D. C. Parker (1988)
La Sagesse Convent School, Hants..	1896	160	£4,116°	£1,900	Sr. Thomas Cox (1977)
Lavant House School, W. Sussex ...	1952	100	£6,000	£3,800	Mrs. B. M. Gay (1987)
Lawnside, Worcs.	1818	130	£7,020	£4,500	D. M. M. Stewar⁺ (1971)
Leeds Girls' High School	1876	961°	....	£2,316°	P. A. Randall (1977)
Leicester High School	1906	300	....	£2,550	Mrs. D. Buchan (1982)
Loughborough High School	1850	520	£4,170	£2,517	J. E. L. Harvatt (1978)
Luckley-Oakfield School, Berks. ..	1895	280	£5,385	£3,375	(a) R. C. Blake (1984)
Malvern Girls' College, Worcs.	1893	520	£6,480	£4,320	Dr. V. B. Payne (1986)
Manchester High School	1874	735°	....	£2,277°	M. M. Moon (1983)
Maynard School, Exeter	1877	396	....	£2,601	F. Murdin (1980)
Merchant Taylors' School, Liverpool......................	1888	550°	....	£2,460°	E. J. Panton (1988)
Micklefield School, E. Sussex	1910	170	£6,480	£3,750	(a) E. Reynolds (1987)
Moira House School, E. Sussex	1875	300	£7,065	£4,596	(a) A. R. Underwood (1975)
More House School, SW1	1953	240	....	£3,750	Mrs. M. E. Dodds (1989)
Moreton Hall, Shropshire	1913	350	£7,260	£4,815	(a) E. J. Cussell (1976)
Mount School, York	1831	286	£6,102	£4,158	B. J. Windle (1986)
Newcastle upon Tyne Church H.S. .	1885	380	....	£2,415	P. E. Davies (1974)
New Hall, Essex	1642	554	£7,260	£4,650	Sr. M. M. Horton (1986)
Northampton High School	1878	510	....	£2,376	Mrs. L. A. Mayne (1988)
North Foreland Lodge, Hants.	1909	186	£6,225	....	D. L. Matthews (1983)
North London Collegiate School ...	1850	689	....	£2,985	Mrs. J. L. Clanchy (1986)
Northwood College, Middx.	1878	478	£4,923	£2,919	Mrs. D. K. Dalton (1986)
‡Norwich High School	1875	759	....	£2,388	Mrs. V. C. Bidwell (1985)
‡Nottingham High School.........	1875	1054	....	£2,388	Mrs. C. Bowering (1984)
‡Notting Hill and Ealing High School	1873	766	....	£2,700	Mrs. C. J. Fitz (1983)
Oakdene, Beaconsfield, Bucks......	1911	275	£5,940	£3,450	A. M. Tippett (1987)
Ockbrook School, Derby	1799	205	£4,167	£2,169	Dr. M. Rennie (1987)
Old Palace School, Surrey	1887	600	....	£2,475	K. L. Hilton (1974)
‡Oxford High School	1875	640	....	£2,388	Mrs. J. Townsend (1981)
Palmers Green High School, N21 ...	1905	110	....	£2,535	Mrs. S. Grant (1989)
Park School, Somerset	1851	95	£5,280	£3,150	Mrs. M. J. Hannon (1987)
Parsons Mead, Surrey	1897	490	£5,640	£3,075	M. M. Dees (1979)
Penrhos College, Clwyd	1880	270	£5,820	£3,870	(a) N. C. Peacock (1974)
Perse School for Girls, Cambridge ..	1881	545	....	£2,784	H. S. Smith (1989)
Pipers Corner School, Bucks.	1930	265	£5,805	£3,225	Dr. M. M. Wilson (1986)
Polam Hall, Co. Durham	1848	330	£5,595	£2,745	Mrs. H. C. Hamilton (1987)
‡Portsmouth High School	1882	674	....	£2,388	Mrs. J. M. Dawtrey (1984)
Princess Helena College, Herts. ..	1820	183	£6,600	£4,770	(a) Dr. D. Clarke (1971)
Prior's Field, Surrey	1902	230	£6,225	£3,885	Mrs. J. M. McCallum (1987)
‡Putney High School, SW15	1893	792	....	£2,700	Mrs. P. A. Penney (1987)
Queen Anne's School, Berks.	1698	399	£5,985	£3,690	A. M. Scott (1977)

‡Girls Public Day School Trust.   †Boys in VI form.   °1989 figure.   ††Co-educational.

Name of School	Founded	No. of Pupils	Annual Fees B'ding	Annual Fees Day	Headmistress (a) Headmaster (With date of Appointment)
*Queen Ethelburga's School, Harrogate	1912	150	£6,405	£3,840	Mrs. J. M. Town (1988)
*Queen Margaret's School, York	1901	365	£6,750	£4,275	(a) C. S. McGarrigle (1983)
Queen Mary School, Lytham, Lancs.	1930	700	....	£2,145	M. C. Ritchie (1981)
Queen's College, W1	1848	400	£4,725	£2,925	Mrs. P. J. Fleming (1983)
Queen's Gate School, SW7	1891	159	....	£3,825	Mrs. A. M. Holyoak (1987)
Queen's School, Chester	1878	420	....	£2,268	Miss D. M. Skilbeck (1989)
Queenswood, Herts.	1894	400	£7,500	....	Mrs. A. M. B. Butler (1981)
Redland High School, Bristol	1882	450	....	£2,403	E. Hobbs (1986)
Red Maids' School, Bristol	1634	473	£5,100	£2,550	S. Hampton (1987)
Rickmansworth Masonic School, Herts.	1788	650	£5,325	£3,060	(a) D. L. Curtis (1980)
Roedean School, Brighton	1885	470	£8,475	....	Mrs. A. R. Longley (1984)
Rosemead, W. Sussex	1919	200°	£5,685°	£3,180°	Mrs. J. Bevis (*Principal*) (1987)
Royal Naval School, Surrey	1840	280°	£5,544°	£3,696°	Dr. J. L. Clough (1987)
Royal School, Bath	1864	320	£6,561	£4,125	Dr. J. McClure (1987)
Runton Hill School, Norfolk	1911	150	£6,300	£3,975	Mrs. A. Cardew, ph.d. (1987)
Rye St. Anthony School, Oxford	1930	359	£5,130	£2,775	P. M. Sumpter (1976)
Sacred Heart School (R.C.), Kent	1915	216	£6,900	£3,969	(a) Dr. J. A. Fallon (1979)
St. Albans High School, Herts.	1889	500	....	£3,000	E. M. Diggory (1983)
St. Andrew's School, Bedford	1897	185	....	£2,085	Mrs. S. E. Cooke (1987)
St. Anne's School, Cumbria	1863	302	£6,759	£4,428	(a) M. P. Hawkins (1986)
St. Antony's-Leweston School, Dorset	1891	401	£6,585	£4,200	Mrs. P. Cartwright (1983)
St. Audries School, Somerset	1906	140	£6,183	£3,603	Mrs. A. M. Smith (1988)
St. Brandon's School, Avon	1831	250	£6,255	£3,345	(a) J. S. Davey (1978)
St. Catherine's School, Surrey	1885	462	£5,625	£3,435	(a) J. R. Palmer (1982)
*School of St. Clare, Penzance	1889	130	£5,475	£2,925	(a) I. Halford (1986)
St. David's School, Middx.	1716	260	£5,769	£3,348	Mrs. J. G. Osborne (1985)
St. Dunstan's Abbey, Devon	1850	250	£4,365	£2,685	H. L. Abley (1970)
St. Elphin's School, Derbys.	1844	240	£6,390	£3,720	(a) A. P. C. Pollard (1979)
St. Felix School, Suffolk	1897	360°	£5,841°	£3,615°	M. A. Claydon (1987)
St. Francis' College (R.C.), Herts.	1933	245	£6,105	£3,150	Mrs. J. Frith (1987)
S. Gabriel's School, Berks.	1929	150	....	£3,273	Mrs. P. Gott (1980)
St. George's School, Ascot, Berks.	1923	276	£6,675	£3,750	Mrs. A. M. Griggs (1989)
School of S. Helen and S. Katharine, Oxon.	1903	500	£4,560	£2,385	Y. Paterson (1973)
St. Helen's School, Middx.	1899	568	£5,115	£2,715	Mrs. Y. A. Burne, ph.d. (1987)
*S. Hilary's School, Cheshire	1880	210	....	£2,700	Mrs. J. Tracey (1985)
St. Hilary's School, Sevenoaks, Kent	1942	170	....	£3,105	Mrs. P. Miles (1977)
St. James's and the Abbey, Worcs.	1896	162	£6,450	£4,305	E. M. Mullenger (1986)
St. Joseph's Convent School (R.C.), Berks.	1909	536	....	£2,565	M. Ball (1986)
St. Joseph's School, Lincoln	1905	200	£5,115	£2,640	Mrs. A. Scott (1983)
St. Leonards-Mayfield School, E. Sussex	1850	560	£6,405	£4,270	Sr. J. Sinclair (1980)
St. Margaret's School, Bushey, Herts	1749	470	£5,535	£3,420	Mrs. S. K. Law (1985)
*St. Margaret's School, Exeter	1904	370	£4,062	£2,484	Mrs. J. M. Giddings (1984)
St. Martin's School, Solihull	1941	350	....	£2,685	Mrs. S. J. Williams (1988)
St. Mary's Hall, Brighton	1836	310	£6,249	£3,915	Mrs. M. T. Broadbent (1988)
St. Mary's School (R.C.), Ascot, Berks.	1885	320	£8,085	£4,410	Sr. M. M. Orchard (1982)
St. Mary's School, Calne, Wilts.	1872	316	£7,260	£4,320	D. H. Burns (1985)
St. Mary's School, Cambridge	1898	550	£4,320	£2,430	M. Conway (1989)
St. Mary's School, Colchester	1908	300	....	£2,370	Mrs. G. M. G. Mouser (1981)
St. Mary's School, Gerrards Cross	1872	200	....	£3,105	Mrs. J. P. G. Smith (1984)
St. Mary's School (R.C.), Shaftesbury	1945	320	£6,255	£3,795	Sr. M. Campion Livesey (1985)
St. Mary's School, Wantage, Oxon.	1873	300	£6,900	....	Mrs. P. H. Johns (1980)
*S. Michaels Burton Park, W. Sussex	1844	200	£6,150	£4,050	V. G. Bolton (1988)
St. Michael's, Limpsfield, Surrey	1850	135	£6,105	£3,345	(a) Dr. M. Hustler, ph.d. (1989)
St. Paul's Girls' School, W6	1904	635	....	£4,131	Mrs. H. Williams (*High Mistress*) (1989)
St. Stephen's College, Kent	1867	87°	£5,490°	£3,390°	M. de Villiers (1987)
St. Swithun's School, Winchester	1884	405	£7,200	£4,425	J. E. Jefferson (1986)
Selwyn School, Glos.	—	220	£4,635	£2,340	H. S. Beswick (1986)

*Woodard Corporation School.   °1989 figure.

Name of School	Founded	No. of Pupils	Annual Fees B'ding	Day	Headmistress (a) Headmaster (With date of Appointment)
‡Sheffield High School	1878	687	. . . .	£2,388	Mrs. M. A. Houston (1989)
Sherborne School for Girls, Dorset .	1899	455	£7,395	£4,935	J. M. Taylor (1985)
‡Shrewsbury High School	1885	569	. . . .	£2,388	E. M. Gill (1982)
Sir William Perkins's School, Surrey	1725	490	. . . .	£2,400	Mrs. A. F. Darlow (1982)
‡South Hampstead High School, NW3	1876	667	. . . .	£2,700	Mrs. D. A. Burgess (1975)
Springfield Park, W Sussex	—	n/a	n/a	n/a	Mrs. H. D. Schofield
Stamford High School, Lincs.	1876	748	£5,250	£2,625	G. K. Bland (1978)
Stonar School, Wilts.	1921	330	£6,360	£3,510	Mrs. S. Hopkinson (1985)
Stover School, Devon	1932	265	£5,265	£2,742	Mrs. W. E. Lunel (1984)
Stratford House School, Kent	1912	250	. . . .	£2,850	Mrs. A. Williamson (1974)
‡Streatham Hill and Clapham High School, SW2	1887	513	. . . .	£2,700	G. M. Ellis (1979)
Sunderland Church High School (CSC)	1884	236†	. . . .	£2,670	Mrs. M. Thrush (1980)
Surbiton High School (CSC), Surrey	1884	426	. . . .	£3,000	Mrs. R. A. Thynne (1979)
‡Sutton High School, Surrey	1884	819	. . . .	£2,700	A. E. Cavendish (1980)
‡Sydenham High School, SE26	1887	641	. . . .	£2,700	Mrs. G. Baker (1988)
Talbot Heath, Dorset	1886	504	£5,160	£2,808	C. E. Austin-Smith (1976)
Teesside High School, Cleveland . . .	1970	400°	. . . .	£2,526°	Mrs. J. Coles (1982)
Tormead School, Surrey	1905	365	. . . .	£3,045	Mrs. J. Crouch-Smith (1977)
Truro High School	1880	408†	£4,905	£2,715	Mrs. J. F. Marshall (1982)
*Tudor Hall School, Oxon.	1850	250	£7,050	£4,500	N. Godfrey (1984)
Upper Chine, Isle of Wight	1799	186	£5,790	£3,030	(a) S. H. Monard (1989)
Ursuline Convent School, Kent	1904	310	£6,324	£3,201	Sr. M. Murphy (1977)
Ursuline High School, Ilford	1903	410	. . . .	£2,784	P. Dixon (1984)
Wadhurst College, E. Sussex	1930	200	£6,675	£4,185	R. Purdom (1989)
Wakefield Girls' High School	1878	931	. . . .	£2,646	Mrs. P. A. Langham (1987)
Walthamstow Hall, Kent	1838	399	£6,600	£3,030	Mrs. J. S. Lang (1984)
Wentworth Milton Mount, Dorset .	1962	344	£5,715	£3,420	M. Vokins (1982)
Westfield School, Newcastle upon Tyne	1962	214	. . . .	£2,628	(a) J. S. Taylor (1986)
West Heath, Kent	1867	164	£7,200	£5,100	Mrs. D. Cohn-Sherbok (1988)
Westholme School, Lancs.	1923	600	. . . .	£2,205	Mrs. L. Croston (1988)
Westonbirt, Glos.	1928	225	£7,110	£4,575	Mrs. G. Hylson-Smith (1986)
Westwood House School, Peterborough	1939	250	£5,070	£2,520	Mrs. A. J. V. Storey (1977)
‡Wimbledon High School, SW19	1880	700	. . . .	£2,700	Mrs. R. A. Smith (1982)
Wispers School, Surrey	1946	186	£5,265°	£3,240°	(a) L. H. Beltran (1978)
Withington Girls' School, Manchester	1890	460	. . . .	£2,415	Mrs. M. Kenyon (1986)
Woldingham School, Surrey	1842	440	£6,930	£4,200	Dr. P. Dineen (1985)
Wroxhall Abbey School, Warwick . .	1872	140	£6,699	£4,035	Mrs. I. D. M. Iles (1980)
Wychwood School, Oxford	1897	160	£4,950	£2,910	Mrs. M. L. Duffill (1981)
Wycombe Abbey School, Bucks.	1896	490	£7,920	. . . .	Mrs. J. M. Goodland (1989)
Wykeham House School, Fareham, Hants	1913	171	. . . .	£2,514	Mrs. E. M. Moore (1983)
York College for Girls (CSC)	1908	206	. . . .	£2,958	Mrs. J. L. Clare (1982)
Scotland					
Laurel Bank School, Glasgow	1903	400	. . . .	£2,619	L. G. Egginton (1984)
Mary Erskine School, Edinburgh . .	1694	560	£5,346	£2,772	P. J. F. Tobin (Principal) (1989)
Oxenfoord Castle School, Midlothian	1931	70	£7,335	£2,880	M. Carmichael (1979)
Park School, Glasgow	1880	300	. . . .	£2,673	Mrs. M. E. Myatt (1986)
St. Denis and Cranley School, Edinburgh	1858	185	£5,730	£2,850	Mrs. J. M. Munro (1984)
St. George's School, Edinburgh	1888	580	£5,565	£2,835	Mrs. J. G. Scott (1986)
St. Leonards School, St. Andrews . .	1877	360	£7,950	£4,050	Mrs. L. E. James (1988)
St. Margaret's School, Aberdeen . . .	1846	314	. . . .	£2,280	L. M. Ogilvie (1989)
St. Margaret's School, Edinburgh . .	1890	600	£5,220	£2,670	Mrs. M. J. Cameron (1984)
Wellington School for Girls, Ayr . . .	1849	340	£5,550	£2,730	Mrs. D. A. Gardner (1988)
Channel Islands					
The Ladies' College, Guernsey	1872	329	. . . .	£1,290	J. Honey (1976)

‡ Girls' Public Day School Trust, 26 Queen Anne's Gate, SW1H 9AN.   * Woodard Corporation School.
C.S.C. Church Schools Company, 1A Doughty Street, WC1N 2PH.   † Boys in VI form.   ° 1989 figure.

EVENTS OF THE YEAR
SEPT. 1, 1988—AUG. 31, 1989

THE ROYAL HOUSE

(1988). Sept. 4. The Princess of Wales attended a concert at the Royal Festival Hall to mark the opening of the Royal Marsden Hospital's International Conference on Cancer Nursing. 12. The Princess Royal left Gatwick Airport for Korea to attend the Olympic Games in Seoul. 13. The Princess of Wales opened the Kobler Centre at St. Stephen's Hospital, London. 17. The Duke of Edinburgh left Dyce Airport for a two-day visit to Norway. 21. The Duchess of York left Heathrow Airport for Australia. 30. Prince Edward attended a banquet at Earls Court to mark the 21st anniversary of BBC Radio 1.

Oct. 1. The Prince of Wales opened the new fishing port at Kinlochbervie, Sutherland. 3. The Princess Royal arrived at Heathrow Airport from Korea. 5. The Queen Mother opened the Little Theatre at the Old Mill, Thurso. 9. Prince Edward attended a gala at the Theatre Royal, Windsor, in aid of the Thames Valley Hospice. The Princess Royal attended the Academy Award ceremony at the Odeon, Leicester Square, London. 17. The Queen and the Duke of Edinburgh left Heathrow Airport for a five-day State visit to Spain. 26. The Queen opened the new building at Moorfields Eye Hospital, London. The Prince of Wales left Heathrow Airport for the Netherlands, returning the following day. 27. The Queen and other members of the Royal Family attended a performance of *The Tempest* at the National Theatre.

Nov. 1. The Queen attended a service in Westminster Abbey to celebrate the 400th anniversary of the Welsh Bible. 3. The Princess Royal left R.A.F. Lyneham for a six-day visit to Switzerland. 4. The Queen, accompanied by the Duke of Edinburgh and the Duchess of York, attended a service of dedication of the roof and vault of the restored south transept at York Minster. 6. The Duchess of York attended a charity performance in aid of the Sick Children's Trust at the Sadler's Wells Theatre. 7. The Duke of Edinburgh arrived at Heathrow Airport from Hong Kong. The Prince and Princess of Wales left R.A.F. Northolt for a five-day official visit to France. 8. The President of Senegal and Mme Abdou Diouf arrived on a four-day State visit. 9. The Queen, accompanied by the Duke of Edinburgh, opened the new chapter house of Southwark Cathedral. 12. The Queen and other members of the Royal Family attended the Royal British Legion Festival of Remembrance at the Royal Albert Hall. 13. The Queen and other members of the Royal Family laid wreaths at the Cenotaph on Remem-

brance Day. 16. The Queen and the Duke of Edinburgh visited the Bank of England, opening a new museum there, and later visited the British Museum. The Princess Royal left Heathrow Airport for a four-day visit to Canada. 17. The Princess of Wales attended the Champion Children's luncheon in London. 18. The Prince of Wales visited the Shepperton Film Studios. 22. The Queen, accompanied by the Duke of Edinburgh, opened the new session of Parliament. The Princess Royal visited Northern Ireland. 24. Prince Edward opened the new headquarters of the Boys' Brigade in London. The Queen Mother visited the Royal Foundation of St. Katherine, in Ratcliffe. The Princess of Wales visited Great Ormond Street Hospital, London. 25. The Prince of Wales visited the Wolferton Training Centre in Norfolk. 28. The Duke of Edinburgh left Heathrow Airport for Portugal, returning the following day. 29. The Duchess of York presented the 1988 Association for Business Sponsorship of the Arts Awards at the National Theatre. The Queen Mother visited the Royal College of Music.

Dec. 1. The Queen and the Duke of Edinburgh visited Greater Manchester. 5. The Duchess of York visited the Royal Marsden Hospital. 7. The Queen Mother visited the Royal Smithfield Show at Earls Court, London. 8. The Princess Royal visited Jersey. 9. The Duke of Edinburgh visited the Automobile Association headquarters at Basingstoke. 13. The Duchess of York visited St. George's Hospital, Tooting, and met survivors of the Clapham Junction rail crash. 14. The Queen visited Queen Mary College, London. The Duchess of York attended the Children of Courage awards at Westminster Abbey. 16. The Princess Royal visited King's College, London. 17. The Prince and Princess of Wales attended a concert in London to raise funds for the Armenian earthquake survivors. 20. The baptism of Princess Beatrice, daughter of the Duke and Duchess of York, took place in the Chapel Royal, St. James's Palace. 22. The Princess of Wales visited the Great Ormond Street Children's Hospital, London. 30. The New Year Honours list was published.

(1989) Jan. 11. The Prince of Wales visited Queen's Medical Centre in Nottingham to offer sympathy to the victims of the air crash on the M1 on Jan. 9. 20. The Duchess of York attended the Clapham Junction Railway Accident Memorial Service in Winchester Cathedral. 24. The Princess Royal visited Cardiff and subsequently left Heathrow Airport for Switzerland. The Prince of Wales visited Lockerbie and Glasgow. 26. The

Princess Royal arrived at Heathrow Airport from Switzerland. 31. The Duchess of York left R.A.F. Northolt for Megève, France. The Princess of Wales attended a reception in London to launch the Silver Jubilee appeal of the Turning Point charity.

Feb. 1. The Queen visited R.A.F. Marham. The Princess of Wales left Heathrow Airport for New York. **2.** The Princess Royal visited the Save the Children Fund headquarters in London. **3.** The Princess of Wales arrived at Heathrow Airport from New York. **4.** The Duchess of York arrived at R.A.F. Northolt from France. **5.** The Princess Royal attended the London Taxi-drivers Fund for Underprivileged Children's Christmas Party in London. **6.** The Princess Royal visited Paris. **9.** The Queen and the Duke of Edinburgh attended a dinner at the Royal Hospital, Chelsea. The Duchess of York attended the Sports Aid Foundation dinner in London. **13.** The Queen was present at the launch of Motability's campaign to convert cars to lead-free petrol at the Royal Mews, Buckingham Palace. **14.** The Duke of Edinburgh left Heathrow Airport to visit Nigeria, Kenya, Tanzania, and Japan where he attended the funeral of Emperor Hirohito on Feb. 24. **22.** The Princess Royal left Heathrow Airport for Tasmania and New Zealand. **24.** The Queen visited the 6th Queen Elizabeth's Own Gurkha Rifles at Church Crookham. The Princess of Wales visited the Mildmay Mission Hospital in London. **27.** The Duke of Edinburgh arrived at Heathrow Airport from Japan.

March 4. Prince Edward attended a sponsored 24-hour dance marathon at Basildon in aid of the Duke of Edinburgh's Trust. **6.** The Queen and the Duke of Edinburgh attended a reception given by the Association of County Councils at St. James's Palace. Prince Edward attended the 75th Anniversary dinner of the Performing Right Society in London. The Prince of Wales attended a dinner at the British Museum for heads of delegation attending the Save the Ozone Layer Conference. The Princess of Wales visited survivors of the British Rail accident at Purley, at the Mayday Hospital, Thornton Heath. **7.** The Princess Royal arrived at Heathrow Airport from New Zealand. **8.** The Queen and the Duke of Edinburgh left Heathrow Airport for Barbados. **12.** The Queen arrived at Heathrow Airport from Barbados. The Prince and Princess of Wales left Heathrow Airport on an official visit to Kuwait, Bahrain, the United Arab Emirates and Saudi Arabia. **13.** The Queen attended the Commonwealth Day Observance Service in Westminster Abbey. The Princess Royal left R.A.F. Northolt to visit the 1st Battalion The Royal Scots in Werl, West Germany. **14.** The Princess Royal arrived at R.A.F. Lyneham from West Germany. **17.** The Princess of Wales arrived at

Heathrow Airport from the United Arab Emirates. **18.** The Princess Royal left R.A.F. Lyneham to attend the France v Scotland rugby union match in Paris. **19.** The Prince of Wales arrived at R.A.F. Lyneham from Saudi Arabia. **22.** The Duke of Edinburgh arrived at Heathrow Airport from Canada. The Duchess of York visited the Isle of Wight. **23.** The Queen and the Duke of Edinburgh attended the Maundy Service at Birmingham Cathedral. The Princess of Wales attended a lunch to launch Capital Radio's 1989 Help a London Child appeal. **24.** The Princess Royal arrived at R.A.F. Lyneham from Hungary. **30.** The Duchess of York visited the 4th International Contemporary Art Fair in London.

April 3. The Princess Royal left Heathrow Airport for a 24-hour visit to West Germany. **7.** The Princess Royal was installed as President of the Council for National Academic Awards. The Queen Mother visited the Royal Horticultural Society's gardens at Wisley. **10.** The Queen and the Duke of Edinburgh attended the charity premiere in London of *Aspects of Love*, in aid of the Family Welfare Association. **14.** The Princess Royal left Gatwick Airport for the U.S.A. **15.** Prince Edward left R.A.F. Northolt for Moscow. **17.** The Princess Royal arrived at Gatwick Airport from the U.S.A. The Prince and Princess of Wales visited survivors of the Hillsborough stadium tragedy in Sheffield. **24.** The Duchess of York attended the Sony Radio Awards ceremony in London. **29.** The Duke and Duchess of Kent were present at the Hillsborough Memorial Service in Liverpool.

May 2. The Duke of Edinburgh visited H.M.S. *Ark Royal* at sea. **3.** The Queen and the Duke of Edinburgh attended a reception at Lancaster House, London, to mark the centenary of the Ministry of Agriculture, Fisheries and Food. **4.** The Queen and the Duke of Edinburgh visited the Ministry of Agriculture, Fisheries and Food and subsequently opened the British Food and Farming Exhibition in Hyde Park, London. **8.** The Prince of Wales opened the Museum of the River at Ironbridge, Telford. **9.** President Babangida of Nigeria and Mrs. Babangida arrived at Gatwick Airport on a State visit. **12.** President Babangida of Nigeria and Mrs. Babangida left Heathrow Airport at the conclusion of the State visit. **15.** The Queen Mother, at a ceremony in Aberdeen, inaugurated the joint Shell/Esso Tern and Eider oilfields in the North Sea. **18.** The Queen visited H.M.S. *Dolphin* at Gosport and H.M.S. *Invincible* at Portsmouth. The Princess Royal attended a symposium in London on alcohol and drugs at work. **22.** The Queen visited H.M.S. *Warrior* and the *Mary Rose* Exhibition and Ship Hall at Portsmouth. **24.** The Queen and the Duke of Edinburgh visited Alderney and Sark. **25.** The Queen and the Duke of Edinburgh visited Jersey. **27.** The Princess Royal attended the Save the Children Fund's 70th Birthday Party at Alton Towers.

June 3. The Prince of Wales visited the Isles of Scilly. **7.** The Queen, accompanied by other members of the Royal Family, visited Epsom Races. **16.** The Queen's Birthday Honours List was published. **17.** The Queen, and other members of the Royal Family, attended the Trooping of the Colour. **21.** The Queen and the Duke of Edinburgh visited Ascot Races. **26.** The Queen and the Duke of Edinburgh attended the Test Match between England and Australia at Lord's. **28.** The Queen of the Netherlands and Prince Claus of the Netherlands arrived in London. **29.** The Queen, accompanied by other members of the Royal Family, opened the first stage of the redevelopment of the Imperial War Museum. The Prince and Princess of Wales attended a Thanksgiving Service in Westminster Abbey for the Wishing Well Appeal for the Hospital for Sick Children, Great Ormond Street, London.

July 5. The Queen and the Duke of Edinburgh attended the Royal Agricultural Society of England Show at Stoneleigh, Warks. **8.** The Princess Royal visited the tall ships taking part in the Cutty Sark Tall Ships Race in London. **12.** Prince Edward took the Salute at the opening of the Royal Tournament at Earl's Court. **13.** The Duke and Duchess of York left Heathrow Airport for Canada. **17.** The Princess Royal opened the Institute of Molecular Medicines, University of Oxford. **18.** The President of the United Arab Emirates arrived at Heathrow Airport on a State visit. **20.** The Prince of Wales presented the *Financial Times* Architecture at Work Award for 1989 in London. **21.** The Princess of Wales opened the British Council exhibition 'British Fashion in the 80s' at the Royal College of Art, London. **26.** The Duke and Duchess of York arrived at Heathrow Airport from Canada. **29.** The President of the United Arab Emirates left Heathrow Airport at the end of his State visit. **31.** The Duke and Duchess of York visited the SS *Great Britain* at Bristol, and subsequently they visited the Merthyr Tydfil Heritage Trust's Ynfsach Engine House.

Aug. 3. The Princess Royal attended the YMCA 'Today' programme Best of British Youth Awards Luncheon at the Savoy Hotel. **4.** The Queen, accompanied by the Duke and Duchess of York, embarked on HMY *Britannia* at Portsmouth and sailed for Scotland. **5.** The Princess Royal opened the European Athletics Cup meeting at Gateshead. **8.** The Queen and the Duke of Edinburgh visited the Isle of Man. **14.** The Queen, with other members of the Royal Family, disembarked

from the HMY *Britannia* at Aberdeen and drove to Balmoral Castle. **29.** The Princess Royal left Heathrow Airport to attend a session of the International Olympic Committee in Puerto Rico. **31.** A statement from Buckingham Palace announced that the Princess Royal and Captain Mark Phillips would live separately in future, but had no plans to divorce.

BRITISH POLITICS

(1988). Sept. 8. Mr. Peter Palumbo was appointed the next chairman of the Arts Council. **12.** The Cuban ambassador to London and another diplomat at the Cuban Embassy were ordered to leave Britain within 24 hours following a shooting incident in London. **15.** The Government announced that the Training Commission would be abolished and its powers transferred to a new executive agency within the Department of Employment. **17–20.** The Social Democratic Party annual conference took place in Torquay. On Sept. 19, in his leadership speech, David Owen called on other opposition parties to join with the S.D.P. in a coalition to defeat the Government: this call was later rejected by the Labour Party and the Social and Liberal Democrats. **22.** Three Czechoslovak diplomats were expelled from Britain for spying. **24–29.** The Social and Liberal Democrat conference took place in Blackpool. On Sept. 26 delegates voted against a motion to debate constitutional amendments: delegates voted in favour of the use of "The Democrats" as their short working title. On Sept. 29, in his leadership speech, Paddy Ashdown attacked the Government and emphasized the importance of environmental issues in the future. **29.** The Polish Government asked Mrs. Thatcher to postpone a visit due to take place in October because of "pressing domestic problems".

Oct. 2–7. The Labour Party annual conference took place in Blackpool. Neil Kinnock and Roy Hattersley were re-elected as leader and deputy leader. On Oct. 5 delegates voted against a motion giving qualified acceptance to the Employment Training programme. On Oct. 6 delegates confirmed the party's commitment to unilateral nuclear disarmament. **9.** John Smith, the Shadow Chancellor, suffered a heart attack. **11–14.** The Conservative Party conference took place in Brighton. On Oct. 12 the Secretary of State for Energy (Cecil Parkinson) announced that the coal industry would be privatized in the next Parliament. The Home Secretary (Douglas Hurd) announced a pilot scheme to use electronic tagging of people out of prison on bail. On Oct. 13 the Secretary of State for Health (Kenneth Clark) announced that an extra £138 million would be made available to settle the nurses' pay dispute. On Oct. 14 Mrs.

Thatcher, in her conference speech, pledged herself to worldwide effort on environmental issues. **19.** Mr. Hurd announced a broadcasting ban on interviews with 11 terrorist organizations, including Sinn Fein. **20.** The Secretary of State for Northern Ireland (Tom King) announced plans to allow a criminal suspect's refusal to answer questions after his arrest to be used as evidence at his trial.

Nov. 1. The Chancellor of the Exchequer (Nigel Lawson) presented his Autumn Statement in the House of Commons. **2.** Mrs. Thatcher arrived in Poland for an official visit. **7.** The Home Secretary presented plans for changes to radio and television broadcasting in a White Paper. **10.** The Scottish National Party candidate, Jim Sillars, won the Glasgow Govan by-election with a majority of 19,500. **17.** Three members of the Iraqi Embassy in London were expelled for spying. **19.** The Government let it be known that it would veto any suggestion from the Soviet Union that the Queen should visit Russia. **22.** The State Opening of Parliament took place. **23.** The Security Service Bill was introduced in the House of Commons. The Bill proposes the establishment of an independent tribunal and an independent commissioner to review the operation of MI5 and provide redress to members of the public who feel they have been wrongly investigated or adversely affected by the activities of the security service. **30.** The Government introduced the Official Secrets Bill in the House of Commons.

Dec. 2. Mr. George Russell was appointed the next chairman of the Independent Broadcasting Authority. **6.** Forty-four Labour M.P.s defied their party leadership and voted against the Prevention of Terrorism (Temporary Provisions) Bill. **13.** The Labour M.P. for Pontypridd, Brynmor John, died. **15.** The Conservative candidate, Steven Norris, won the Epping by-election with a majority of 4,504. **16.** Edwina Currie (Under-Secretary of State for Health) resigned from her post following criticism of her statement about the extent of salmonella in egg production.

(1989) Jan. 11. The Commons select committee on agriculture began an inquiry into the scare over salmonella in eggs. **14.** A Minister of State at the Foreign Office, William Waldegrave, in a BBC radio interview, referred to the Israeli Prime Minister, Yitzhak Shamir, as a reformed terrorist. **16.** The Home Secretary (Douglas Hurd) ordered the Court of Appeal to re-examine the conviction of four people, known as the Guildford Four, for pub bombings in Guildford in 1974. **18.** Viraj Mendis, a Sinhalese supporter of Tamil separatists in Sri Lanka, was seized by police from the Manchester church where he had taken sanctuary for two years to avoid deportation. The Home Secretary said that the Government did not believe that

Mr. Mendis faced persecution if he returned to Sri Lanka and did not consider that he qualified for refugee status. Mr. Hurd said that Mr. Mendis would be deported to Sri Lanka unless a third country offered asylum: on Jan. 20 Mr. Mendis was returned to Sri Lanka. **19.** The Prime Minister and the Attorney General announced a reorganization of the Government legal service. **22.** The British and Turkish governments ordered inquiries into an alleged "kidneys for cash" trade involving a British private hospital. **25.** The Prime Minister said that Britain would not join the European Monetary System during the present Parliament. **26.** An independent inquiry cleared Thames Television of the criticisms levelled against its programme "Death on the Rock". The findings of the inquiry were rejected by the Prime Minister, the Foreign Office and the Ministry of Defence. **27.** The Labour Party leaked details of the White Paper on the National Health Service. **31.** The Government published a White Paper on the National Health Service.

Feb. 7. Mrs. Edwina Currie agreed to give evidence to the Commons select committee on agriculture about her warning about salmonella in eggs. **9.** The Labour leader (Neil Kinnock) in an interview on Thames Television's "This Week" programme, said that his party was developing policies for the next election which would be intended to appeal to the centre-ground voter. **16.** The Government announced pay settlements for one and a quarter million public servants. **23.** The Richmond (N. Yorks.) by-election was won by the Conservative candidate William Hague. The by-election at Pontypridd was won by the Labour candidate, Kim Howells.

March 4. The Social and Liberal Democrats began a two-day conference in Bournemouth. The party leader (Paddy Ashdown) received support from his party for his offer to the Social Democratic Party of by-election deals. **14.** The Chancellor of the Exchequer (Nigel Lawson) made his Budget statement to the House of Commons. **16.** The Transport Secretary (Paul Channon) rejected newspaper and Opposition criticism of the way he handled bomb warnings received before the Lockerbie air crash. On March 19 the Department of Transport admitted that the warning about bomb attacks had been drawn up on Dec. 19 but was not posted until after Christmas. On March 20 Mr. Channon was accused by the Labour Party of being responsible for leaking a story that the Lockerbie bomber had been arrested. **16.** The director-general of the Confederation of British Industry (John Banham) criticized the Government for the lack of investment and excessive consumption in Britain. **21.** The Monopolies and Mergers Commission published a report on the tied house system in the brewing industry which said that the concentration of the ownership of outlets predominantly in the hands of the six biggest breweries restricted competition in the price of beer. The Commission recommended that the number of outlets each brewery might own should be restricted. **22.** The Northern Ireland Secretary (Tom King) announced that he had approved a provisional agreement for a management buyout of the Harland and Wolff shipyard in Belfast. **27.** Mrs. Thatcher left London to visit Morocco, Nigeria, Zimbabwe and Mozambique. **28.** The Green Party announced that it would field candidates in all seats for election to the European Parliament in June. **30.** The Government took out a High Court injunction against the *Observer* newspaper to prevent it distributing a midweek issue carrying extracts from an unpublished Department of Trade and Industry report into the purchase of the House of Fraser stores group by the Al Fayed brothers. On March 31 Lonhro, the owners of the *Observer*, refused to return its copies of the D.T.I. report.

April 5. The Soviet President, Mr. Gorbachev, arrived at Heathrow Airport on an official visit: on April 7 the Queen accepted his invitation to visit the Soviet Union. **21.** The Home Office announced a non-governmental review of the law and practice governing standards of press reporting. **24.** Following allegations that Ulster loyalists were involved in arms trafficking with a South African arms dealer, the Foreign Secretary (Sir Geoffrey Howe) rejected calls from M.P.s to expel South African diplomats. **29.** The Comptroller and Auditor General (John Bourn) announced an inquiry into allegations that Britons with close contacts with the Government had received bribes in business dealings which led to the sale of Tornado fighter-bombers to Saudi Arabia.

May 2. The Government published a Defence White Paper. **3.** Mrs. Margaret Thatcher celebrated ten years as Prime Minister. **5.** Britain expelled three South African diplomats who had knowledge of arms deals with Belfast loyalists. The Labour Party candidate, John Smith, won the by-election at the Vale of Glamorgan. **9.** The National Executive Committee of the Labour Party voted by 17 votes to eight to accept a policy of multilateral disarmament. A High Court Judge, Mr. Justice McCowan, issued a temporary injunction to stop the Government distributing leaflets about the community charge. **13.** The Social Democratic Party, led by Mr. David Owen, announced that it would no longer attempt to organize on a national scale.

June 1. President Bush of the U.S.A. arrived in London for talks with the Government. **15.** The by-election at Vauxhall was won by the Labour candidate, Kate Hoey. The by-election at Glasgow Central was also won by the Labour candidate, Mike Watson.

July 24. The Prime Minister, Mrs. Thatcher, announced a reshuffle of her Cabinet. The major changes included replacing Sir Geoffrey Howe as Foreign Secretary by John Major. Sir Geoffrey became Leader of the House of Commons. Paul Channon and John Moore were dropped from the Cabinet, and Lord Young and George Younger both resigned their posts.

Aug. 18. Britain and Argentina agreed to an immediate upgrading of diplomatic relations and to meet in Madrid in October for further discussions. **23.** The Government announced that a free vote would be held in the House of Commons in the autumn to decide whether former Nazis now living in Britain should be brought to trial. **26.** The Ministry of Defence ordered a review of the Trident nuclear missile programme, which is to be carried out by Sir Francis Tombs.

IRELAND

(1988). Sept. 1. A report by the Committee on the Administration of Justice called for the disbanding of the Royal Ulster Constabulary and its replacement by a new body with the power to determine police policy. **5.** Sinn Fein and S.D.L.P. spokesmen announced that talks between their two parties had collapsed. **11.** Police in Belfast discovered two caches of weapons believed to belong to loyalist paramilitary groups. **12.** Two bombs severely damaged the home in Co. Down of Sir Kenneth Bloomfield, the head of the Northern Ireland Civil Service. In Belfast eight people were injured by a car bomb. **13.** Security forces uncovered an arms cache in Londonderry. **20.** The Home Secretary (Douglas Hurd) announced that legislation would be introduced in Parliament that will allow the police to investigate and the courts to freeze and confiscate the assets of the I.R.A. and other terrorist groups. **23.** A man was shot dead in Belfast by members of the loyalist Ulster Freedom Fighters. **25.** A part-time member of the Ulster Defence Regiment was shot dead by the I.R.A. in Armagh.

Oct. 4. A senior prison officer was killed in Belfast by a booby-trap bomb attached to his car. **16.** The Ulster Defence Association (U.D.A.) admitted that they had shot a loyalist man in Belfast for alleged co-operation with the I.R.A. and I.N.L.A.

Nov. 1. A loyalist paramilitary leader was sentenced to 19 years in prison after being caught with a cache of arms. **3.** Father Patrick Ryan, suspected of having acted as the I.R.A.'s quartermaster in Europe, went on hunger strike in Belgium after pleading not guilty at a hearing into a British extradition request. On Nov. 25 Ryan was released from prison in Brussels and flew to Dublin after the Belgian government decided not to grant Britain's extradition request. On Nov. 26 the British Government applied to the Irish authorities for Ryan to be extradited to the U.K. On Nov. 28 Ryan disappeared from Dublin before the Irish authorities had decided whether he should face extradition proceedings. **18.** An I.R.A. member sentenced to life imprisonment for murder was granted leave in the U.S.A. to apply for political asylum. **23.** Two civilians were killed and five injured when an I.R.A. bomb exploded outside a police station in Benburb, Co. Tyrone.

Dec. 13. The Irish authorities announced that the suspected terrorist Patrick Ryan would not be extradited to Britain. **29.** Police and troops discovered a 400 lb bomb near the main Belfast-Dublin railway line in south Armagh.

(1989) Jan. 1. Gerry Adams, president of Sinn Fein, criticized the I.R.A. for killing innocent people in the past year. **16.** An R.U.C. reservist, Harry Keyes, was murdered by I.R.A. gunmen at Ballintra, Co. Donegal. On Jan. 31 Irish detectives arrested five men and one woman in Bundoran, Co. Donegal, in relation to the killing of Mr. Keyes. **23.** The I.R.A. announced that a cross-border active service unit based in Co. Donegal had been disbanded because its explanations of the murder of two civilians had not been satisfactory. **27.** The I.R.A. issued death threats against employees of the removal firm Pickfords, because the company was alleged to undertake removals for the British army.

Feb. 12. A solicitor, Pat Finucane, who had represented several Republicans was shot dead at his North Belfast home by loyalist gunmen. **19.** Solicitors in Northern Ireland met to discuss a spate of death threats. **20.** Three I.R.A. bombs exploded at Clive Barracks near Shrewsbury, but members of the Parachute Regiment stationed there were alerted and there were no casualties. **22.** A soldier driving a school bus was shot dead by I.R.A. men in Londonderry. **26.** Unionist leaders refused an invitation for talks from the Irish Prime Minister, Charles Haughey.

March 7. Three Protestants were shot dead by members of the I.R.A. in Co. Tyrone. On March 8 the president of Sinn Fein (Gerry Adams) said that his party could "not condone the deaths of people who are non-combatants". **11.** Police in London discovered an I.R.A. sniper's deathlist, which included M.P.s and peers, and increased security cover for those named. **14.** Eighteen Royal Ulster Constabulary officers, implicated in the police shoot-to-kill allegations, were reprimanded at a disciplinary hearing. **20.** Two senior R.U.C. officers, Chief Supt. Harry Breen and Supt. Bob Buchanan, were ambushed and shot dead by I.R.A. members near Jonesborough in South Armagh. The two officers were returning from a meeting with senior Garda officers in the Irish Republic.

April 10. A former passport officer at the Irish embassy in London, Kevin McDonald, was extradited to Britain to face charges of conspiracy to obtain passports, and other crimes. **12.** A woman was killed and 34 people injured by an I.R.A. bomb in Warrenpoint, Co. Down. **21.** Three Ulster loyalists were arrested in Paris after trying to sell information about the British Blowpipe missile system to a South African arms dealer: on the 24th they were charged with arms offences.

May 4. Two men were killed in separate bomb attacks in Armagh. **26.** Police in Dublin thwarted a plan by loyalist extremists to carry out bomb attacks in the city. **31.** Sir John Hermon retired as Chief Constable of the Royal Ulster Constabulary: he was succeeded by Mr. Hugh Annesley.

June 1. Two Belfast men, Alex Murphy and Henry Maguire, were given life sentences for the murder of two British soldiers who drove into the path of a Republican funeral in March 1988. **19.** A workman at a British Army barracks in West Germany disturbed two I.R.A. terrorists placing bombs at the barracks.

July 2. An I.R.A. car bomb exploded in a residential area of Hanover, West Germany, killing a British Army corporal, Steven Smith. **17.** Three members of a suspected I.R.A. unit were arrested near the French-German border. A Northern Ireland businessman, John McAnulty, was abducted by the I.R.A. Mr. McAnulty's partly-clothed body was found in a ditch near Crossmaglen, Armagh, the following day.

Aug. 9. A 15 year-old boy, Seamus Duffy, died after being hit by a plastic bullet during a riot in Belfast. **15.** Martin Galvin, director of Noraid, the American fund-raising organization for the Irish Republican movement, was arrested in Londonderry after defying a Government exclusion order banning him from entering the U.K. **25.** The loyalist Ulster Freedom Fighters admitted to the murder of a Roman Catholic, John Maginn, who was shot in his home in Rathfriland, Co. Down. **28.** A British serviceman in West Germany discovered a bomb under his car: experts said the device was similar to ones used by the I.R.A. **30.** Loyalist paramilitary sources claimed that they had obtained information about republican suspects from the security forces in Northern Ireland.

ACCIDENTS AND DISASTERS

(1988). Sept. 4. Floods in Bangladesh left more than 20 million people homeless. **13.** Much of the Caribbean was devastated by Hurricane Gilbert, the strongest hurricane recorded in the Western hemisphere: worst hit were Jamaica and the Cayman Islands. On Sept. 14 the hurricane reached the Mexican coast and on Sept. 16 the evacuation of the north-east coast of Mexico was ordered. On Sept. 17 flash floods caused by the hurricane killed more than 180 people near Monterrey in Mexico. **22.** The North Sea oil rig Ocean Odyssey exploded: 66 men were rescued but one man was missing after the explosion.

Oct. 17. A Uganda Airlines jet crashed near Leonardo da Vinci airport, Rome, killing 30 people. **19.** Two separate air crashes in India caused 165 deaths. **21.** A Greek cruise ship, the *Jupiter*, sank in Piraeus harbour after colliding with an Italian freighter. The *Jupiter* was carrying 486 British schoolchildren on an educational cruise: one schoolchild died. **25.** Typhoon Ruby hit the Philippines and sank a ferry carrying 451 passengers and 67 crew.

Nov. 7. The Luxembourg-Paris express train ploughed into a group of railwaymen working on the track in north-east France and killed nine. **13.** A car crashed into children taking part in a Remembrance Day procession in Birmingham: 13 children and four adults were taken to hospital. **27.** Five days of tropical storms caused serious flooding in Thailand and killed more than 1,000 people. **29.** Tidal waves struck Bangladesh, leaving over 3,000 people drowned and 2,000 missing. **30.** Two InterCity trains collided outside Newcastle upon Tyne, injuring 15 passengers.

Dec. 8. An earthquake struck Armenia and President Gorbachev cut short an overseas visit to return to take charge of the disaster operations. On Dec. 9 the Soviet Health Minister (Yevgeny Chazov) estimated the dead at 100,000 and the homeless at 400,000. On Dec. 10 the Soviet Embassy in London issued an urgent appeal for medical supplies. **11.** A cargo jet carrying troops and relief supplies crashed on its approach to Leninakan airport in northern Armenia, killing all 78 people on board. **12.** A stationary commuter train carrying 906 passengers was hit by an express train near Clapham Junction. A third train crashed into the wreckage. The death toll in the crash was 33, with another passenger dying on Dec. 16: 111 people were injured. On Dec. 17 British Rail established that two signal faults were responsible for the crash. **21.** A Pan-Am jumbo jet crashed onto the Scottish town of Lockerbie, killing everyone on board and demolishing a street in the town. On Dec. 23 the death toll was estimated at 276, with at least 17 killed in Lockerbie itself. On Dec. 28 Ministry of Defence scientists found evidence that the jet was blown up in mid-air by a bomb.

(1989) Jan. 1. About 100 New Year revellers were feared dead after a boat sank near Rio de Janeiro, Brazil. **9.** A British Midland 737 aircraft suffered engine malfunction on a flight from London to Belfast and crashed on the M1 motorway in Leicestershire, ploughing into the motorway embankment. Forty-four of the 82 people on board were killed. **15.** More than 170 people died in a train crash near Dhaka, Bangladesh. **23.** An earthquake struck the Soviet Republic of Tajikistan, killing at least 1,000 people.

Feb. 8. A Boeing 707 aircraft crashed into a mountain in the Azores, killing all 144 people on board. **22.** A South Korean ship sank in the Atlantic with the loss of all 17 crew members. **24.** The forward cargo door of a United Airlines Boeing 747 blew off during a flight over the Pacific Ocean. Eleven people were sucked out of the plane and 17 were injured.

March 4. Five people were killed and more than 80 injured in a rail crash at Purley, Surrey. **6.** Two suburban trains crashed near Bellgrove station in Glasgow, leaving two dead and 52 injured. **9.** Four people were killed and ten injured in a multiple vehicle crash on the M6 motorway in Cheshire. **22.** A van carrying over 1,500 lb of explosive caught fire and exploded in Peterborough, killing a fireman. **31.** A two-year-old boy was savaged by a chimpanzee at the Port Lympne Zoo Park in Kent.

April 8. A Soviet nuclear-powered submarine sank off northern Norway; 42 of the 90 crew died. **14.** An 11 year-old girl was mauled to death by two rottweiler dogs near Dunoon, Argyll. **15.** At the F.A. Cup semi-final between Liverpool and Nottingham Forest at Hillsborough, Sheffield, 95 people were killed and 200 injured in a crush at the Leppings Lane end of the ground. The crush was caused by thousands of fans entering the stand when police opened a gate to ease pressure outside the ground. **18.** An explosion on the Cormorant Alpha oil platform in the North Sea caused the Brent oilfield pipeline system to be shut down. **19.** An explosion on board the American battleship *Iowa* killed 47 sailors. **26.** A tornado struck central Bangladesh, leaving thousands homeless and killing over 1,000 people.

May 15. Nine Royal Navy men were killed when a helicopter from the frigate H.M.S. *Brilliant* crashed near Vipingo, Kenya. **24.** Two teenagers were drowned when their rowing boat was swept away by a flash flood at Chorlton. A man was killed near Macclesfield when his car was carried away by a stream in flood.

June 4. More than 800 people were killed after a gas pipeline beside the Trans-Siberian railway line exploded, causing a fire that swept through two passing trains. **29.** A 12 year-old girl and a teacher were killed when a school coach crashed in West Sussex.

July 14. Floods in the Sichuan province of China killed more than 100 people. **17.** Three soldiers were found dead in a crater left by a controlled explosion at an army ammunition depot at Kineton, Warks. **20.** Six people were slightly injured when the Glasgow to Euston express train was derailed at Harrow and Wealdstone station, London.

Aug. 1. Four soldiers were killed and three others injured when a helicopter crashed during a training exercise near Bodney, Norfolk. **6.** Six British Rail coaches overturned and a locomotive caught fire when a train left the track just outside West Ealing station, London: British Transport Police said that the accident was caused by vandalism. **20.** A Thames pleasure boat, *The Marchioness*, sank after being hit by the dredger *Bowbelle*: the death toll was 57. On Aug. 31 the Transport Secretary (Cecil Parkinson) announced new safety rules for vessels on the Thames.

CRIMES, TRIALS, ETC.

(1988). Sept. 8. Customs officers recovered drugs from the cargo ship *Salton Sea* at Ramsgate. **13.** Eight men were jailed for a total of 37 years at Southwark Crown Court for a V.A.T. swindle involving krugerrands and scrap metal. **14.** An amateur rugby player, Steven Lloyd, was sentenced to 18 months imprisonment for assaulting an opposition player during a match in Bristol. **15.** Gunmen stole over £300,000 from a bank in Preston after kidnapping the manager, his wife and daughter. Nine members of a drugs smuggling ring were sentenced to a total of 91 years at Cardiff Crown Court. **20.** Four men were jailed at the Central Criminal Court for manufacturing amphetamine sulphate at an illegal laboratory in London. **28.** A doctor was jailed for ten years at Newcastle upon Tyne Crown Court for raping a patient after drugging her.

Oct. 3. An arms dealer who supplied arms to the I.R.A. and other terrorist groups was jailed for ten years at Chelmsford Crown Court. **13.** Three members of a gang of rapists were sentenced to a total of 44 years at the Old Bailey. **16.** Vandals destroyed saplings planted to replace six of the seven oak trees of Sevenoaks, Kent, felled in the 1987 storm. **17.** Liverpool footballer Jan Molby was jailed for three months for reckless driving at Liverpool Crown Court. **25.** Ciaran Collins, aged 13, was convicted of the murder of two-

year old Sharona Joseph at Chelmsford Crown Court. **28.** Three Irish terrorists were found guilty at Winchester Crown Court of conspiring to murder the Northern Ireland Secretary (Tom King) and sentenced to 25 years imprisonment each. Andrew Longmire, convicted for a series of rapes over seven years, was given eleven life sentences at Manchester Crown Court.

Nov. 3. Victor Miller, who murdered a boy with a rock, was sentenced to life imprisonment at Birmingham Crown Court. **18.** Five people from three families who were involved in a child sex abuse ring were jailed at the Old Bailey for a total of 240 years. **21.** French police arrested David Evans, wanted by North Wales police for questioning in connection with the disappearance of schoolgirl Anna Humphries. On Nov. 27 the body of Anna Humphries was recovered from the River Severn by police divers. **25.** Lorraine Miles, who brought the first civil action for rape, was awarded £25,108 damages at Chelmsford Crown Court. **30.** A girl of 13 was acquitted at Northampton Crown Court of the murder of Carol Baldwin, aged 13.

Dec. 2. Sara-Jane Goodwin, who falsely accused a former boyfriend of rape, received a three-year sentence at Lincoln Crown Court for attempting to pervert the course of justice. **9.** Alban Turner, convicted at Aylesbury Crown Court of killing Michael Galvin during the Notting Hill Carnival in 1987, was sentenced to life imprisonment. **12.** Former British Olympic athlete David Jenkins was jailed for seven years by a court in San Diego, California, for drug smuggling. **14.** Five people, including two detectives, were wounded during a police ambush outside a London post office: members of a robbery gang were arrested. **16.** A police hunt began for an armed gang who murdered one man, stabbed another, and were responsible for a series of crimes in an area south of London. **19.** An unarmed police constable was shot dead by armed robbers in Coventry. Following a chase one of the robbers was captured, the other committed suicide. **21.** An I.R.A. bomb factory was discovered in a south London flat and police began a hunt for the two men who had been living there. On Dec. 31 police raided a number of houses and detained several people for questioning. The mother and stepfather of 16-month old Doreen Mason were convicted at the Old Bailey of her manslaughter and sentenced to 12 years imprisonment each.

(1989) Jan. 1. Police in London began a murder inquiry after the body of an hour-old baby was found in a hospital incinerator plant. **9.** David John Evans, wanted by police in connection with the murder of Anna Humphries, was extradited from France to Britain. **12.** A couple, Victor and Audrey

Johnson, died in an arson attack on their flat in Brixton, London: fire officers were unable to rescue them in time because a metal security door impeded entry into the flat. Fourteen police officers were suspended from duty, and 24 serving and two former officers received summonses concerning offences committed during disturbances outside the News International plant in Wapping in 1987. **30.** A gang which carried out a £40 million armed robbery of a Kensington safe deposit centre in 1987 were found guilty at the Central Criminal Court.

Feb. 2. Nine adult members of the same family were jailed at Nottingham Crown Court for child abuse offences against their own children. **23.** A bomb planted by animal rights activists destroyed part of the Senate building at Bristol University.

March 3. Michael Stone, responsible for the Milltown cemetery killings, was found guilty of murdering six people and sentenced to life imprisonment in Belfast. Erwin Van Haarlem was found guilty of spying for Czechoslovakia and sentenced at the Central Criminal Court to ten years imprisonment. **8.** At the Central Criminal Court the 18-year-old leader of a gang of muggers, Simon Thomas, was ordered to be detained indefinitely at a secure mental hospital. **10.** Two Sikh extremists who murdered a rival religious leader were sentenced in London to life imprisonment. **14.** Ian Simms was sentenced to life imprisonment at Liverpool Crown Court for the murder of Helen McCourt. The body of Ms. McCourt had never been found. **17.** The Court of Appeal turned down an appeal by three men convicted of the murder of newspaper delivery boy Carl Bridgewater and upheld the convictions. **23.** Roy Garner was sentenced to 22 years imprisonment at the Central Criminal Court for drug smuggling.

April 3. In a raid on a London amusement arcade the raiders, who took £1,000, doused four people with petrol and set them on fire: two men died. **13.** Scotland Yard marksmen killed two armed men robbing a post office in London. At the Central Criminal Court Tony Maclean, known as the Notting Hill rapist, was sentenced to life imprisonment for each of three rapes. **16.** A police constable, Anthony Salt, was murdered while on duty outside an illegal drinking club in Bordesley Green, Birmingham. **20.** Jane Salvesen, accused of murdering Diana Maw with a crossbow, was freed by magistrates at Ealing after the prosecution offered no evidence against her. **26.** Police said that a commercial blackmailer was involved in the recent contamination of baby food: in the six weeks since threats began, 28 confirmed cases were reported. **28.** A Belgium court sentenced fourteen Liverpool soccer fans to three years imprisonment

each, half of each sentence being suspended, for their part in the Heysel Stadium tragedy in 1985. At Exeter Crown Court, John Cannan was found guilty of the murder of Shirley Banks and was sentenced to life imprisonment. **30.** A gunman in West Monkseaton, near Whitley Bay, killed one man and injured 13 other people.

May 1. Risley Remand Centre in Cheshire was sealed off by police after nearly 100 prisoners were involved in two separate demonstrations about conditions in the centre. **12.** Four men were convicted at the Central Criminal Court of the manslaughter of 14 year-old Jason Swift during a homosexual orgy. **23.** William Jennings was jailed for life at Leeds Crown Court for murdering his three-year-old son Stephen more than 26 years ago.

June 15. Four masked gunmen held six people hostage at a bank in Bloxham, Oxfordshire, and stole about £26,000. **22.** Summonses alleging manslaughter were issued against seven employees of the Townsend Thoresen ferry company over the sinking of the *Herald of Free Enterprise*. A further summons was issued against P. & O. European Ferries (Dover) Ltd., who took over Townsend Thoresen shortly before the accident. **26.** A man who chased an armed robber through London's South Bank complex was shot and was seriously wounded: the robber stole £15,000 from a Securicor guard. **28.** A police officer who was filmed as he assaulted a motorist was jailed for a month at Caernarvon Crown Court. Patrick Morley was sentenced to five life terms at the Central Criminal Court for the rape and torture of two prostitutes.

July 5. David Evans was jailed for life at Chester Crown Court for the murder of schoolgirl Anna Humphries. **6.** A husband and wife, Peter and Gwenda Dixon, were shot dead as they walked along the Pembrokeshire coastal footpath in south-west Wales. **16.** A security guard, Philip Wells, disappeared from Heathrow Airport with nearly £1 million in cash. **21.** The comedian Ken Dodd was cleared at Liverpool Crown Court of eight charges of tax fraud and false accounting. **26.** A 66-year old pensioner, Donald Kell, was shot dead as he tried to stop an armed robbery in Finchley, London. **31.** Lord Lane, the Lord Chief Justice, doubled the three-year sentence imposed on a man who admitted incest with his daughter. His Court of Appeal ruling stated that six years in prison was the starting point for such offences. Two police officers jailed for life for killing a former Welsh guardsman, were cleared of murder by the Court of Appeal. The court substituted manslaughter convictions for Hamish Montgomery and Patrick Shevlin.

Aug. 1. Baroness Susan de Stempel was cleared at Worcester Crown Court of the murder of her ex-husband, Simon Dale. **3.** A terrorist, believed to be linked to Middle Eastern groups, died when a bomb exploded at a London hotel. **12.** A couple, Brian and Ursula Watt, were found murdered in their home in Hilperton, Wilts. Their 21-year-old daughter Sarah was found seriously injured. **14.** The Chief Constable of the West Midlands police force said that he had moved 48 officers from the force's serious crimes squad and suspended two detectives because of doubts about the way evidence had been collected and the disappearance of key papers from police files. The Chief Constable asked the Police Complaints Authority to supervise an investigation into the work and practices of the squad. **18.** A kidnap victim, Victor Cracknell, was released after being held for five days for a ransom of £1 million: later four people were arrested in connection with the kidnapping. **25.** A supermarket assistant was killed in London when he tackled a robber. **28.** The final day of the Notting Hill Carnival in London ended with a violent confrontation between police and youths.

ECCLESIASTICAL

(1988). Sept. 11. The Archibishop of Canterbury (Dr. Robert Runcie) announced that he was setting up a commission to study the potential threat to Anglican unity posed by the proposed consecration of the first woman bishop in the Anglican church in the U.S.A. **25.** The Rev. Barbara Harris was elected the next suffragan bishop of Massachusetts, U.S.A.

Oct. 6. The main Christian denominations in England launched a national membership recruitment campaign. **16.** An inquiry was launched by the Bishop of London (Dr. Graham Leonard) into the activities of the St. Hilda's Community after it came to light that communion was being celebrated by women priests ordained overseas at services organized by the Community at a University of London chapel.

Nov. 4. The Lord Chancellor (Lord Mackay of Clashfern) was suspended as an elder of the Free Presbyterian Church of Scotland following his attendance at two Roman Catholic requiem masses. **7.** The General Synod opened its autumn meeting. The Archibishop of Canterbury announced that the Church of England would not recognize women bishops consecrated abroad. On Nov. 10 members approved a proposal to guarantee a minimum of 24 black and Asian members of the General Synod at the next synodical election in 1990.

(1989) Jan. 13. A weekend conference of leading Anglicans began at Launde Abbey, Leics., to discuss how the Church of England could avoid division over the ordination of women.

Feb. 2. A measure to guarantee a minimum of 24 black members in the General Synod of the Church of England was defeated, following a revolt by members of the House of Laity. **11.** The Rev. Barbara Harris was consecrated bishop in Boston, U.S.A., the world's first Anglican woman bishop. **17.** Cardinal Basil Hume announced that the Tridentine Mass, in Latin, would be said regularly on Sundays at three churches in the Westminster diocese.

March 9. Archbishop Paul Marcinkus was replaced as president of the Vatican Bank by a five-man board of directors. **25.** In a television interview, the Bishop of Durham (Dr. David Jenkins) said that Christ's resurrection was spiritual rather than physical. Several Conservative M.P.s called upon the Archbishop of Canterbury, Dr. Robert Runcie, to either reprimand or dismiss Dr. Jenkins. On March 26 Dr. Runcie, in his Easter Day sermon, declared that the Resurrection was a miracle.

May 5. A Sikh campaigner, Indarjit Singh, became the first non-Christian winner of the Templeton Prize. **25.** The Free Presbyterian Church of Scotland suspended the Lord Chancellor, Lord Mackay of Clashfern, because of his attendance at a Roman Catholic requiem mass.

July 4. In a letter to leading members of Britain's Muslim community the Minister of State at the Home Office, John Patten, said that the blasphemy law would not be extended to include Islam.

Aug. 1. The Archbishop of Canterbury, Dr. Robert Runcie, set up a joint working party with Muslim representatives to consider the role of the law in protecting religious sensibilities.

EDUCATION

(1988). Sept. 12. A report on equal opportunities in polytechnics and colleges stated that ethnic minorities, women and disabled people were not given equal opportunities in higher education. **14.** The Secretary of State for Education (Kenneth Baker) announced a cash limit of 5·1 per cent for teachers' pay increases in 1989.

Oct. 3. The Secretary of State for Scotland (Malcolm Rifkind) announced proposals to introduce standarized English and mathematics tests for Scottish primary schoolchildren. **20.** An Equal Opportunities Commission inquiry found that six schools in West Glamorgan discriminated against boys and girls by not offering them equal access to craft subjects. **24.** A report by H.M. Inspectors of Schools, *The New Teacher in School*, indicated that many new teachers enter the classroom without proper training.

Nov. 1. In the Autumn Statement the Chancellor of the Exchequer (Nigel Lawson) announced expenditure of more than £300 million over the next three years for science research. **4.** The first city technology college opened at Kingshurst, Solihull. **7.** St. James's Church of England school in Bolton became the first comprehensive to vote to opt out of local authority control. **9.** The Government published a White Paper *Top-up Loans for Students*. **15.** Mr. Baker called for a return to a prominent place in the curriculum for grammar.

Dec. 5. The National Curriculum Council published consultation reports on science and mathematics. **18.** Mr. Baker said that he would consider the idea of universities charging students all or part of the real cost of tuition, provided that people from poorer families were not discouraged. **19.** Mr. Baker accepted the National Curriculum Council's revisions of its proposals for mathematics and science courses in English and Welsh schools.

(1989) Jan. 19. The Government announced increased funding for the training of specialist computer teachers. **27.** Mr. Baker proposed an apprentice-style training scheme for trainee teachers as a means of easing staff shortages.

Feb. 14. A report by H.M. Inspectorate of Schools, *"Our Policeman" – Good Practice in Police/Schools Liaison*, accused schools and education authorities of hampering efforts to overcome anti-police attitudes in the classroom. **15.** Mr. Baker told a conference in London that he believed Britain should move towards a system of universal education up to the age of 19. **22.** Mr. Baker gave approval for the first two schools to opt out of local authority control, Skegness Grammar School, Lincs., and Audenshaw High School, Greater Manchester. **28.** The independent annual report by the Senior Chief Inspector of Schools in England warned that the education service could collapse unless there was an increase in qualified and competent teachers.

March 4. Mr. Baker warned the Treasury that Britain faces a critical shortage of teachers unless their pay is substantially improved. **12.** A report by the Hillgate Group, *Learning to Teach*, called on the Government to disband the present method of teacher-training and replace it with an apprenticeship scheme. **13.** The inquiry into school discipline, headed by Lord Elton, published its report.

April 6. Plans to close veterinary schools in Glasgow and Cambridge were dropped after the Universities' Funding Council asked the Ministry of Agriculture, Fisheries and Food to reassess the need for veterinary surgeons in Britain. **20.** Mr. Baker refused to allow Sir Thomas Altham School in Watford to opt out of local government control.

May 5. A Commission of Inquiry report into the government of Cambridge University proposed a major overhaul of the government of the University.

June 12. The London Borough of Wandsworth announced plans to turn its comprehensive schools into 'magnet schools', specializing in subjects such as languages and science.

July 12. The Universities' Funding Council agreed a scheme whereby universities will have to bid against each other for their funds in future.

Aug. 22. The Education Secretary (John MacGregor) agreed that general principles concerning the content of A-level syllabuses should be laid down centrally.

ENVIRONMENT AND LOCAL AFFAIRS

(1988). Sept. 1. The Department of the Environment announced that £500,000 a year would be spent on research into North Sea pollution. **16.** A West German wildfowl association warned that the virus that caused the death of seals in the North Sea was killing seagulls. **24.** The Ministry of Agriculture approved the testing of the Kavak ID vaccine, which could improve the resistance of seals to canine distemper virus.

Oct. 6. Delegates from 65 countries, including Britain, signed the London Dumping Convention, which is intended to introduce a global ban on burning chemicals at sea by 1994. **7.** The Natural Environment Research Council's marine science committee agreed to spend £1·7 million on research into the effects of ozone depletion in the atmosphere on the climate (the "greenhouse effect"). **16.** Scientists at the Animal Health Research Laboratory at Pirbright, Surrey, identified the virus that killed thousands of seals in the North Sea as seal plague. **29.** The Secretary of State for Energy (Cecil Parkinson) announced that electricity charges would increase by about 6 per cent in April 1989. The National Trust voted to continue to allow hunting on its property in England and Wales.

Nov. 11. Torbay district council decided to proceed with the sale of its entire housing stock despite an overwhelming vote against the sale by its tenants. **16.** The Government warned that measures to give Britain safer water, cleaner rivers and pollution-free beaches would lead to higher water charges. **23.** The Prime Minister announced that an international conference would be held in London in March 1989 to discuss the phasing out of chlorofluorocarbons (C.F.C.s). **27.** The Duke of Edinburgh, in an Advent address at St. George's Chapel, Windsor, said that the over-exploitation of the earth's resources could lead to the extinction of mankind.

Dec. 8. The Department of the Environment announced a £1,000 million programme to modernize sewage works.

(1989) Jan. 20. The Government announced a £50 million scheme to plant trees in central Scotland over the next twenty years.

Feb. 22. The European Commission publicized correspondence with the British Government over the legality of certain clauses in the water privatization Bill. The Commission said that the Environment Secretary (Mr. Ridley) did not have the powers to exempt temporarily English and Welsh water authorities from meeting European criteria on the cleanliness of water. Mr. Ridley said that it would cost £300 million to meet the European Commission standards. **28.** Hammersmith and Fulham Council announced that it was technically defaulting on repayment of loans taken out and then negotiated at different rates. The Council had been advised that it was acting outside its legal powers in its interest swap dealings but the Environment Secretary refused to sanction the Council's plan to continue repayments, saying that it would be wrong to prevent the district auditor from proceeding if he considered unlawful spending had been incurred.

March 3. The people of the village of Wargrave, Berks., won a private prosecution against the Thames Water Authority over excessive levels of pollution in the River Loddon which runs through the village. **5.** The Prime Minister opened the Saving the Ozone Layer Conference in London. **8.** The Commons select committee on the environment published a report saying that the Government had endangered public health by failing to maintain adequate controls on toxic and radioactive waste. **31.** Friends of the Earth launched a campaign for the reduction of carbon emissions from diesel-driven vehicles.

April 10. The Government announced a campaign to encourage the recycling of waste paper.

May 10. The London Borough of Brent agreed to make a compensation payment of £72,000 to the former head of its race relations department, Miss Soonu Engineer, in return for her agreement not to sue for unfair dismissal.

July 7. A 20-nation survey carried out for the United Nations found that 25 per cent of the forests in the United Kingdom were being killed partly by pollution. **11.** The Environment Secretary (Nicholas Ridley) announced a reorganization of various government agencies responsible for the protection of wildlife and the countryside. The major change will be the break-up of the Nature Conservancy Council.

Aug. 20. More than 2,000 gallons of crude oil leaked into the River Mersey from an underground pipeline linking a refinery in Ellesmere Port and the Tranmere oil terminal. The leak caused a 10-mile slick in the estuary, threatening wildlife and holiday beaches.

FINANCE

(1988). Sept. 16. Figures were published showing that inflation reached 5·7 per cent in August 1988. **18.** Following an official complaint by the Charterhouse Bank, the Takeover Panel were asked to investigate a proposed exchange of shares between Pearson and the Dutch group Elsevier. **23.** The first figures released by the liquidators of Barlow Clowes International indicated that only 37 per cent of investors' money would be recovered.

Oct. 4. The Secretary of State for Trade and Industry (Lord Young) ordered Kuwait to reduce its shareholding in British Petroleum from 21·6 per cent to 9·9 per cent within twelve months. **15.** The Association of British Insurers said that claims for damage caused by the storm in Oct. 1987 were £1,025 million, plus another £25 million claimed for damage to cars. **25.** An offer of £2,900 million by Minorco for Consolidated Gold Fields was referred to the Monopolies and Mergers Commission by Lord Young.

Nov. 4. Robert Maxwell completed the £1,470 million purchase of the American publishers Macmillan Inc. and put his British Printing and Communications Corporation up for sale. **14.** Shareholders of Abbey Life rejected a proposed merger with Lloyds Bank. **16.** The British company General Electric Company (G.E.C.) and the West German company Siemens made a joint hostile bid of £1,700 million for Plessey. **17.** A takeover offer for the publishing group William Collins was made by News International. **18.** Figures were published showing that inflation reached 6·4 per cent in October, the highest rate since July 1985. **23.** British Steel was priced at 125p per share for the forthcoming privatization. **25.** Bank base rates rose to 13 per cent.

Dec. 2. The sale of shares in British Steel by public subscription was completed. On Dec. 5 dealing in British Steel shares opened on the Stock Exchange.

(1989) Jan. 3. British Petroleum agreed to buy, for £1,950 million, Kuwait's 11.7 per cent shareholding in the company. **11.** The Abbey National Building Society announced that all the shares in its proposed flotation as a public limited company would go initially to its members. **12.** A bid for Plessey by G.E.C. and Siemens was referred to the Monopolies and Mergers Commission. **13.** G.E.C. linked up with the American company General Electric to form four joint businesses. **17.** The High Court ordered Lord Young to refer the purchase of the House of Fraser group by the Al Fayed brothers in 1985 to the Monopolies and Mergers Commission.

Feb. 2. The Trade and Industry Secretary Lord Young announced that the Minorco group could go ahead with its takeover bid for Consolidated Gold Fields.

March 7. The Abbey National Building Society was forced to unveil its plans for flotation earlier than intended after an error by the Post Office caused many copies of the voting pack to be delivered early. **13.** Shares on the London stock market reached their highest level since the crash of October 1987. **15.** The Rover Group, sold by the Government to British Aerospace in 1988 for £150 million, reported profits of £65 million in the past year and was revalued at £830 million. **21.** The takeover bid by Elders IXL for the Scottish & Newcastle Breweries was blocked by Lord Young after the Monopolies and Mergers Commission ruled that the takeover would not be in the public interest. **29.** Britain's trade figures for February were the third worst ever, with a deficit of £1,700 million.

April 11. Members of the Abbey National Building Society voted in favour of the society's flotation on the stock market.

May 14. A consultative document recommended major reforms to the International Stock Exchange. **24.** Interest rates rose to 14 per cent.

June 6. The Abbey National Building Society received permission to proceed with its flotation.

July 20. Department of Trade and Industry investigators presented their report into the involvement of County NatWest and County NatWest Securities in the takeover of Manpower by Blue Arrow in 1987. The investigators stated that 'the events referred to in this report give rise to concern'. The Serious Fraud Squad was considering possible prosecutions. On July 25 Lord Boardman, chairman of the National Westminster Bank, and three senior colleagues resigned.

Aug. 18. Figures for inflation in July showed that it had dropped to 8·2 per cent, the first fall since January 1988. **24.** Britain's largest brewer, Bass, made a successful £1,300 million bid for the Holiday Inn chain in the U.S.A.

LABOUR AND TRADE UNIONS

(1988). Sept. 3. The Post Office dispute which began on Aug. 31 spread, and on Sept. 5 all international post to and from Britain was suspended. On Sept. 12 the strike was called off after the Union of Communication Workers reached a settlement with Post Office officials. **5–9.** The Trade Union Congress annual conference took place in Bournemouth. The Electrical, Electronic, Telecommunications and Plumbing Union (E.E.T.P.U.) was expelled from the T.U.C. for refusing to withdraw from single-union deals. On Sept. 6 Mr. Arthur Scargill, president of the National Union of Mineworkers, lost his seat on the T.U.C. General Council. **26.** The Iron and Steel Trades Confederation turned down British Coal's proposal that its members should work the proposed Margam "superpit": the National Union of Mineworkers had already expressed their opposition to the development of the pit.

Oct. 4. Following a Government decision to dismiss or transfer 18 trade union members at the G.C.H.Q. communications centre, unions representing Civil Servants agreed to ballot members about a strike in protest. On Oct. 18 Civil Servants staged unofficial protests after the Government confirmed the dismissal of four of the 18 trade union members. **15.** Clive Jenkins, leader of the Manufacturing, Science, Finance (M.S.F.) union, announced that he was to take early retirement.

Nov. 7. Thousands of Civil Servants went on 24-hour strike in protest at the dismissal of trade union members at G.C.H.Q. **18.** The West Cumberland Hospital in Whitehaven called for volunteer help after catering staff and ancillary workers joined nurses in a strike. **19.** The Union of Democratic Mineworkers (U.D.M.) agreed a two-year pay deal with British Coal. **21.** The Secretary of State for Health (Kenneth Clarke) agreed to meet representatives of the Royal College of Nursing but refused to talk to the other two unions involved in a dispute over the regrading of nurses. On Nov. 22 Acas was asked to intervene in the dispute. **25.** A march by members of the National Union of Students in London was disrupted by violence and resulted in 69 arrests. 28. Forty-four midwives resigned from the North Middlesex hospital in London in protest at regrading. The U.D.M. signed an agreement with British Coal for the introduction of a six-day working week at the Asfordby mine in Leicestershire.

Dec. 6. The investment banking group Morgan Grenfell announced that 450 staff were to be made redundant. 7. The Minister of Trade and Industry (Tony Newton) announced the closure of North East Shipbuilders in Sunderland, with the loss of some 2,000 jobs. He also announced that Sunderland was to become an Enterprise Zone. 11. Members of the U.D.M. rejected a recommended revised pay offer made by British Coal. 17. Eddy Shah's newly-launched daily newspaper *The Post* ceased production after only 33 issues. Mr. Shah announced that he had sold all the titles in his Messenger chain of newspapers. 29. The Secretary of State for Employment (Norman Fowler) launched a publicity scheme intended to double the number of long-term unemployed involved in government training schemes.

(1989) Jan. 9. The Government appointed Eric Hammond of the E.E.T.P.U. to the National Economic Development Council, ending the T.U.C.'s right to nominate all trade union representatives on the Council. 30. Following the refusal by prison officers to accept new shift rotas at Wandsworth prison, police were brought in to run the jail.

Feb. 10. British Steel announced the closure of a plant in South Wales with the loss of 900 jobs.

March 17. The executive of the Association of University Teachers voted to recommend that members reject a 6 per cent pay offer. 29. Members of the National Association of Schoolmasters/Union of Women Teachers voted for strike action in support of a pay claim; members of the National Union of Teachers voted against industrial action.

April 6. The Government announced that the National Dock Labour Scheme was to be abolished as soon as the necessary legislation had been passed. 11. Leaders of the Transport and General Workers Union voted to ballot members about a national strike in defence of the National Dock Labour Scheme.

May 4. A High Court Judge granted London Underground an injunction preventing the National Union of Railwaymen from striking, on the grounds that the union's ballot papers were incorrectly worded. 8. British Rail announced that it would impose a 7 per cent pay rise on its workers. BBC workers began a 48-hour strike in support of a 16 per cent pay increase. 15. Underground

and bus services in London were disrupted by an unofficial strike, and some 16 per cent of Southern region trains were halted by an unofficial overtime ban by N.U.R. members. 19. Dockers voted in favour of an indefinite strike in protest at the Government's decision to abolish the National Dock Labour Scheme. 30. Passport office staff in Liverpool began an indefinite strike over manning levels.

June 1. University lecturers voted to accept a 6 per cent pay offer, ending a five-month dispute. 7. The Court of Appeal granted an injunction banning an official national dock strike: on June 8 thousands of dockers ignored the injunction and took unofficial strike action. 12. Members of the National Union of Railwaymen voted to take industrial action against British Rail and London Underground.

July 6. The train drivers' union ASLEF decided to ban rest-day and overtime working. 17. The National Union of Railwaymen rejected an offer of an 8·8 per cent pay increase and decided to continue their strike action; the other rail unions accepted the offer. On July 27 the N.U.R. called off their strike action; and accepted the 8·8 per cent offer. 7. Dock workers voted in favour of a national strike at 60 registered ports in support of a claim that a national agreement should replace the Dock Labour Scheme which the Government intends to abolish.

Aug. 1. The Transport and General Workers Union voted to end the national docks strike. 25. British Coal closed the last remaining colliery in Kent, at Betteshanger.

LEGAL

(1988). Sept. 6. The inquest opened in Gibraltar into the deaths of three I.R.A. members killed there by the S.A.S. in March 1988. On Sept. 30 the jury decided that the three terrorists were justifiably killed. 13. The Director General of Fair Trading, Sir Gordon Borrie, announced that he would be investigating possible changes in the legal system to allow lawyers to work on a "no win, no fee" basis. 19. Magistrates were issued with a table of amounts of compensation that they might consider ordering offenders to pay victims. 23. The Solicitor General, Sir Nicholas Lyell, announced that in future barristers would be allowed to appear without solicitors in certain Crown court cases.

Oct. 4. The inquest began in London into the deaths of 31 people in the King's Cross fire in November 1987. The public inquiry into the proposed building of a nuclear power station at Hinkley began at Cannington, Somerset. 11. The jury at the King's Cross fire inquest returned verdicts of accidental death on the 31 victims. **13.** The Law Lords ruled that the British media could comment on and publish material from *Spycatcher*, but that the author, Peter Wright, had a lifelong duty of confidentiality which could be used by the Government as the basis for legal action if the book were published in the U.K. **24.** A girl who suffered severe brain damage after an appendix operation was awarded damages of £800,000 in the High Court. **27.** The annual report of H.M. Chief Inspector of Prisons was highly critical of conditions in British prisons.

Nov. 3. The actress Koo Stark was awarded £300,000 libel damages and £50,000 costs over articles published in the *Sunday People* newspaper. **10.** The report of the inquiry into the King's Cross fire was published. **14.** The Director of Public Prosecutions dropped his appeal against a High Court ruling that his use of unqualified clerks to screen cases for trial was illegal. **30.** The Lord Chancellor (Lord Mackay of Clashfern) ordered a report on a decision by Judge Sir Harold Cassel not to jail a man convicted of child abuse.

Dec. 5. The Lord Chancellor supported a move to abolish the right to trial by jury for some minor offences. **12.** The pop singer Elton John received a £1 million settlement from the *Sun* newspaper over allegations about his private life: the judge, the Hon. Mr. Justice Davies, strongly criticised both the newspaper and Mr. John for allowing details of the settlement to be printed before it had been approved by the court. **14.** The inquest on the victims of the Clapham Junction rail disaster began in London.

(1989) Jan. 25. The Government published three Green Papers containing proposals for the reform of the legal profession.

Feb. 3. Three senior appeal court judges approved the sterilization of a 36-year-old woman with a mental age of five. **17.** The Bar launched a campaign against the Government's proposed reforms of the legal profession. **20.** The inquiry into the Clapham rail disaster, chaired by Anthony Hidden, Q.C., began at Westminster Central Hall.

March 8. The Lord Chancellor, Lord Mackay of Clashfern, announced a series of changes to the legal aid system. **23.** Food hygiene and safety summonses issued by Westminster City Council against Le Gavroche restaurant were dismissed at Wells Street magistrate court.

April 4. Dr Marietta Higgs, the paediatrician involved in the Cleveland child sex abuse controversy, failed in the High Court to stop the Northern Health Authority from disciplining her without a full N.H.S. enquiry. **7.** Members of the House of Lords condemned the Government's proposed reforms of the legal system. **18.** Lord Justice Taylor was appointed to head the judicial inquiry into the Hillsborough disaster. **21.** A 10 year-old girl who suffered brain damage because of a mistake by hospital doctors was awarded damages of £1,002,799 in the High Court.

May 1. The Law Society presented its final response to the Green Papers on legal reform; on May 2 the Bar Council published its response and on May 23 the judges presented their response. **3.** The Serious Fraud Office obtained an order preventing the reporting of proceedings in a civil court action involving the Barlow Clowes investment group. **8.** The *Independent*, the *Sunday Times* and the defunct *News on Sunday* were each fined £50,000 for publishing extracts from Peter Wright's book *Spycatcher* while injunctions against two other newspapers were still in force. **18.** Five Law Lords ruled that no fault could be found in the Department of Trade and Industry's decision not to publish its report on the takeover of the House of Fraser by the Al-Fayed brothers: details of the report had been leaked in the *Observer* in March. **24.** Mrs. Sonia Sutcliffe, wife of the 'Yorkshire Ripper', Peter Sutcliffe, was awarded record libel damages of £600,000 against *Private Eye* in the High Court. The inquiry into the Clapham rail crash ended.

June 12. The *Observer* was cleared of contempt of court over the publication of extracts from the Department of Trade and Industry report on the House of Fraser takeover by the Al-Fayed brothers.

July 14. The judicial inquiry into the Hillsborough Stadium disaster closed. **19.** The Government published a White Paper proposing reform of the legal system, *Legal Services: A Framework for the Future.*

Aug. 4. Lord Justice Taylor's interim report into the Hillsborough Stadium disaster was published.

SOCIAL

(1988). Sept. 7. The Secretary of State for Health (Kenneth Clarke) announced that he is to be the new chairman of the National Health Service management board. **10.** Government experts confirmed fears that children living near nuclear plants run an increased risk of developing cancer. **24.** Hundreds of cancer patients who had received treatment at the Royal Devon and Exeter Hospital were recalled for checks following fears that radiation overdoses may have been given. Two members of the hospital staff were dismissed for failing to observe stringent safety procedures.

Oct. 5. A doctor co-ordinating the Government campaign to vaccinate children against measles, mumps and rubella claimed that the campaign was chaotic because many health authorities did not have enough money and that there was a shortage of vaccines. **10.** Doctors at the Royal Free Hospital, London, revealed that they had started using genetically engineered blood-clotting agents to treat haemophilia, and thus had eliminated the threat of passing on Aids. **25.** Figures released by the Department of Social Security indicated that some 200,000 families are not claiming their Family Credit entitlement. **27.** The Secretary of State for Social Security (John Moore) announced in the House of Commons a series of changes to benefit payments. **30.** Dr. Marietta Higgs, one of the paediatricians involved in the Cleveland child sex abuse case, was permanently banned from working in the field of child sex abuse by the Northern Regional Health Authority.

Nov. 1. The Chancellor of the Exchequer (Nigel Lawson) announced in the Autumn Financial Statement Government plans to increase the 1989–90 budget for the National Health Service by £2,000 million. **5.** A scientific investigation indicated that the most popular oral contraceptive pills currently in use carry the greatest health risks. **8.** The number of deaths from Aids in Britain passed 1,000. **24.** The Government published the Children Bill, proposing several changes in child care law.

Dec. 1. Doctors from the Public Health Laboratory Service said that eggs contaminated with salmonella bacteria were causing an epidemic of food poisoning in Britain. On Dec. 4 in a television interview Edwina Currie (Under-Secretary of State for Health) claimed that most of Britain's egg production was infected with salmonella bacteria. On Dec. 9 the Government issued guidelines to commercial egg producers in an attempt to curb salmonella infection. On Dec. 15 a leading egg producer, Thames Valley Eggs, began legal proceedings against Mrs. Currie for losses caused by her remarks. On Dec. 16 Mrs. Currie resigned from her government post. On Dec. 19 the Minister of Agriculture (John MacGregor) announced a £19 million package to help the egg production industry recover from the salmonella scare. **6.** It was disclosed that at least 78 of the 207 cancer patients given radiation overdoses at the Royal Devon and Exeter Hospital had subsequently died. **7.** The Health Minister (David Mellor) announced that the Government was to set up a third review of child protection in Cleveland. **8.** A study carried out by the Royal College of General Practitioners indicated that women who had used the oral contraceptive pill for 10 years or more were four times more likely to contract cervical cancer. **20.** Dr. Geoffrey Wyatt, one of the paediatricians involved in the Cleveland child sex abuse case, was severely reprimanded by the Northern Regional Health Authority but told that he would be allowed to remain in his job as a consultant. **21.** Answering an emergency question in the House of Commons, the Agriculture Minister (John MacGregor) said that contaminated meat imported from Ireland had not entered the food chain. The question was prompted by the discovery by district health officers of imported sub-standard beef at a meat-packing factory in Cornwall.

(1989) Jan. 19. The Department of Health told 22 health district managers that they must cut waiting times for treatment or lose the performance-related part of their pay. **23.** Two unnamed flocks of hens were identified as the source of repeated epidemics of food poisoning caused by eggs. On Jan. 27 the Government banned the sale of eggs by farmers found to have infected flocks. **31.** The Government published a White Paper on the National Health Service.

Feb. 6. Surgeon Michael Bewick and consultant renal physician Raymond Crockett, were referred to the General Medical Council by the Bloomsbury Health Authority following allegations that donors had been paid to donate kidneys for transplant operations at the Humana Wellington Hospital, London. On Feb. 16 Dr. Crockett resigned as medical director of the National Kidney Centre. **9.** The Government announced a campaign to advise the public about food safety. **10.** The Government's Chief Medical Officer, Sir Donald Acheson, warned pregnant women not to eat soft ripened cheeses, to reduce the risk of infection with listeria. **20.** The Health Secretary, Kenneth Clarke, published eight papers giving more detailed findings of the National Health Service review and proposals than the White Paper published in Jan.

March 2. The British Medical Association launched a campaign against the Government's reforms of the National Health Service. **8.** Over 250 doctors in Leeds said that they would resign if the Government did not make radical changes to its plans for reorganizing the National Health Service. **16.** Following a ruling by the Monopolies and Mergers Commission, general practitioners may advertise their services in the media. The ruling was condemned by the B.M.A. **20.** The Government announced the names of 50 hospitals chosen to take part in the Government's resource management initiative. **27.** Dr. Chris Johnstone, a junior doctor at University College Hospital, London, issued a writ against Bloomsbury Health Authority for failing to safeguard his health by causing him to work excessive hours, and so endangering his patients.

April 16. The council of the Royal College of General Practitioners voted to reject the White Paper on the National Health Service. **24.** An eight-day-old baby died of listeria at a hospital in Stoke-on-Trent.

May 11. Mr. Clark announced that £40 million would be spent on new technology for the National Health Service. **17.** At a special meeting of the British Medical Association members voted overwhelmingly to block the implementation of the White Paper on N.H.S. reforms.

June 12. An outbreak of botulism poisoning caused ten people to be admitted to hospital. It was believed to have been caused by hazelnut yoghurt.

July 12. The Department of Health issued a warning about pâté following the discovery of high levels of listeria in pâté imported from Belgium. **25.** A major outbreak of salmonella food poisoning was feared in North Wales after 43 people became infected; on July 26 two elderly people died and the number of sufferers had risen to over 80.

Aug. 9. A batch of vaccine used at Colchester General Hospital in the national campaign against measles, mumps and rubella, was withdrawn for analysis following the death of an 11-year old boy from inflammation of the brain shortly after he had been vaccinated. **24.** A national survey ordered by the Department of Health found that listeria was present in 10 per cent of pâté.

SPORT

(1988). Sept. 5. Stephen Cooper, a member of Britain's Olympic wrestling team was killed in a motor accident while cycling during training. **6.** The Bruno-Tyson world heavyweight title fight was postponed after Tyson was injured in a car crash. **9.** India announced that it would not allow eight members of the England cricket squad into the country because they had had sporting contacts with South Africa, effectively forcing the Test and County Cricket Board (T.C.C.B.) to cancel the proposed tour. **16.** The 24th Olympic Games began in Seoul, South Korea. **26.** Ben Johnson of Canada, winner of the 100 metres at the Olympic Games, failed a drugs test and on Sept. 27 he was stripped of his gold medal. **29.** Two British Olympic competitors, Linford Christie and Kerrith Brown, failed drugs tests. On Sept. 30 Christie was cleared of drug abuse but Brown was stripped of his judo bronze medal. **29.** Paul Davis of Arsenal was suspended for nine weeks and fined £3,000 by the Football Association after punching Glenn Cockerill of Southampton during a match and fracturing his jaw.

Oct. 2. The Olympic Games in Seoul closed. **3.** The World Professional Billiards and Snooker Association (W.P.B.S.A.) fined Bill Werbeniuk £2,000 and banned him from one ranking tournament for using the banned drug Inderal. **10.** Alex Higgins was given a suspended fine of £1,500 and a severe reprimand by the W.P.B.S.A. at a disciplinary hearing. **18.** At an extraordinary meeting of the Football League, the League president, Philip Carter, and another committee member, David Dein, were both voted off the management committee. **24.** Ben Johnson was banned from domestic competition for two years by the Canadian Track and Field Association for taking drugs.

Nov. 7. Sugar Ray Leonard became the first boxer to win five world titles when he defeated Donny Lalonde in Las Vegas. **9.** The Minister for Sport (Colin Moynihan) announced that identity cards would be compulsory for football spectators in England and Wales from 1990. **10.** The W.P.B.S.A. fined snooker world champion Steve Davis £12,000 for refusing to attend media interviews at the Rothmans Grand Prix in October. **21.** Jack Dunnett was elected president of the Football League. **25.** Peter May resigned as chairman of the England cricket selectors.

Dec. 7. National Hunt trainer David Elsworth was fined £17,500 by the Jockey Club for administering steroids to one of his horses and for misleading race stewards. An England cricket tour to New Zealand was announced, replacing the cancelled tour of India. On Dec. 14 Pakistan refused to play against England during the tour of New Zealand. On Dec. 22 the tour was cancelled by the New Zealand cricket authorities. **15.** National Hunt jockey Peter Scudamore rode his one hundredth winner of the season and broke the record for the fastest 100 wins in a season.

(1989) Jan. 5. Welsh rugby union player Jonathan Davies joined the Rugby League club Widnes. **17.** The Government published the Football Spectators Bill, which will require football spectators to carry identity cards. **18.** Brian Clough, manager of Nottingham Forest, attacked supporters who ran onto the pitch following a game against Queen's Park Rangers. On Jan. 27 Mr. Clough was charged by the Football Association with bringing the game into disrepute and on Feb. 9 the Football Association banned him from the touchline for the rest of the season and fined him £5,000. **24.** The International Cricket Conference passed a resolution stating that, from April 1, 1989, cricketers who played or coached in South Africa would be banned from Test matches for up to five years.

Feb. 6. Conservative M.P. Andrew MacKay published a Private Member's Bill to legalize professional sport on Sundays. **7.** Peter Scudamore rode his 151st winner of the season at Warwick, breaking the record for the highest number of winners in a National Hunt season. **25.** The British boxer Frank Bruno lost his fight with American Mike Tyson for the world heavyweight title.

March 28. A judge in New York ruled that the United States victory in the 1988 America's Cup was invalid and awarded the trophy to New Zealand.

April 18. The Football Trust indicated that, in the wake of the Hillsborough disaster, money was available for clubs who wanted to install seats in stands at their grounds. **27.** Peter Scudamore became the first National Hunt jockey to ride 200 winners in a season when he rode Gay Moore to victory at Towcester.

May 12. The Wembley stadium authorities agreed to remove the perimeter fences for the Everton-Liverpool F.A. cup final. **15.** The Rugby Football Union announced that it would allow its players to visit South Africa to take part in celebrations of the game's centenary in that country.

June 5. John Lyall, the longest serving manager in the Football League, was sacked by his club, West Ham.

July 10. Maurice Johnstone became the first Roman Catholic player to join Glasgow Rangers when he transferred from F.C. Nantes for £1·5 million.

Aug. 1. It was announced that a party of British cricketers led by former England captain Mike Gatting would tour South Africa in the winter of 1989–90. On Aug. 8 two of the players, Phillip DeFreitas and Roland Butcher, withdrew from the party. **10.** The Australian opening batsmen, Geoff Marsh and Mark Taylor, became the first pair to bat through a full day's play in a test match in England. They scored 301 on the first day of the fifth test at Trent Bridge. **18.** Michael Knighton, a property developer, bought 50·06 per cent of the shares in Manchester United Football Club.

TRANSPORT

(1988). Sept. 9. British Rail appointed the merchant bankers Lazard Brothers to assess the potential for private development of the proposed high-speed link between London and the Channel Tunnel. **19.** Safety officers ordered tests on older Boeing 747 aircraft after a wing flap failed to close on a British Airways jet landing at Heathrow.

Oct. 11. The Transport Secretary (Paul Channon) announced at the Conservative Party conference a plan to create private sector roads. **17.** The Civil Aviation Authority (C.A.A.) announced that near air-misses and other safety concerns reported by air traffic controllers would in future be investigated independently. **28.** The International Maritime Organization (I.M.O.) announced new safety standards intended to make passenger vessels less likely to capsize.

Nov. 3. The National Audit Office published a report, *Road Planning*, which indicated that Department of Transport estimates of expected traffic flow were wrong for over 68 sections of road.

Dec. 8. British Rail unveiled plans for a new international terminal for Channel Tunnel trains at Waterloo Station. **14.** The C.A.A. announced plans to increase the amount of controlled airspace over London and the south-east.

(1989) Jan. 12. British Rail announced that the second Channel Tunnel terminal in London would be at King's Cross. **22.** 6,000 citizens of Kent marched through Maidstone in protest at the proposed rail link from London to the Channel Tunnel. **26.** The Transport Secretary Paul Channon announced a £3,000 million plan for modernizing and extending London's rail and Underground network.

Feb. 6. London Regional Transport published its response to the recommendations of the inquiry into the King's Cross fire.

March 2. A private consortium proposed that a fifth, high-speed, rail link be built between the Channel Tunnel, London and the north of England. **5.** The director of the British Road Federation, Peter Witt, called on the Government to spend an extra £500 million per year on trunk roads, and to introduce a strategic road plan. **8.** British Rail announced plans for a high-speed Channel Tunnel link from Folkestone to London. **21.** A report published by the Commons select committee on transport proposed that responsibility for air traffic control should be removed from the Civil Aviation Authority and that a second runway should be built at Gatwick airport. **29.** A report by the Confederation of British Industry claimed that London's inadequate transport system was costing the nation some £15,000 million a year.

April 11. Mr. Paul Channon announced that he had refused permission for British Rail to close the Settle-Carlisle railway line.

May 18. The Government published a White Paper, *Roads for Prosperity*, which indicated that spending on roads would be doubled.

June 20. Mr. Channon gave permission for a new underground railway line to be built in London, linking the docklands with the centre of the capital.

Aug. 17. British Rail's fleet of Class 90 InterCity electric locomotives were taken out of service for inspection following the discovery of a brake fault.

AFRICA

(1988). Sept. 1. Nelson Mandela, the leader of the African National Congress suffering from tuberculosis, was transferred from a hospital to a nursing home in Cape Town as his condition improved. **11.** Pope John Paul II arrived in Zimbabwe at the start of a visit to southern Africa. **12.** President Botha of South Africa made his first state visit to a black African country when he visited Mozambique. **14.** A bus taking Catholic nuns, children and teachers to see the Pope in Maseru, the capital of Lesotho, was hijacked by gunmen. After a siege a South African commando unit freed the hostages: three hijackers and one hostage were killed. **16.** Angolan troops captured five Unita rebel strongholds in central Angola. **18.** A fierce battle in the western Sahara between Moroccan troops and Polisario Front guerrillas left more than 250 dead. **21.** A bomb exploded at a Johannesburg bus depot injuring 19 people.

Oct. 5. The centre of Algiers was taken over by rioters protesting at the high cost of living and on Oct. 6 a curfew was imposed in Algiers. Police and rioters continued to clash and on Oct. 9 sources said that at least 200 people had been killed. On Oct. 10 President Bendjedid Chadli delivered a televised speech offering a package of reforms. On Oct. 12 the President announced plans for a national referendum after lifting the curfew. **9.** Seven blacks were killed in Natal in clashes between anti-apartheid groups. **19.** Three leading black anti-apartheid campaigners ended a 37-day sit-in at the American consulate in Johannesburg: they were protesting at detention without trial. **31.** Refugees from Somalia were reported to be moving into Ethiopia at the rate of 500 a day.

Nov. 1. The South African anti-apartheid newspaper *The Weekly Mail* was banned for a month. **4.** A referendum in Algeria resulted in a 92 per cent vote in support of President Chadli's planned constitutional reforms. **15.** Representatives from South Africa, Cuba and Angola reached agreement on the withdrawal of South African troops from Namibia and Cuban troops from Angola, and on a timetable for granting independence to Namibia. **17.** The South African Government banned the Blanke Bevrydingsbeweging, a white right-wing pressure group. **18.** Four black South

African activists were found guilty of treason in the Supreme Court in Pretoria. **23.** President Botha of South Africa reprieved the "Sharpeville Six", five men and a woman sentenced to death for complicity in the mob murder of a black official. **27.** Two black nationalists, Zephana Mothopeng and Harry Gwala, were released from prison in South Africa.

Dec. 4. Eleven black people died in a house in New Hanover, a South African township, in an attack by a rival anti-apartheid group. On Dec. 25 nine people were killed and 17 injured in renewed fighting in Natal: by Dec. 27 the death toll had risen to 35. **7.** The A.N.C. leader Nelson Mandela was moved from a nursing home to a house in prison grounds in Paarl, near Cape Town, South Africa. **9.** Four black activists were jailed for treason in Cape Town after a three year trial. **13.** Senior ministers from South Africa, Cuba and Angola signed a protocol in Brazzaville, Congo, that provided for the independence of Namibia from South Africa within a year. **20.** The Sudanese government declared a state of emergency in Khartoum before a planned rally in support of a peace agreement to end the civil war.

(1989) Jan. 10. Cuban troops began to withdraw from Angola in accordance with an agreement aimed at achieving independence for Namibia. **16.** Three African National Congress members were sentenced to imprisonment for treason and terrorism in Pretoria. **18.** President Botha of South Africa suffered a stroke. On Jan. 19 Mr. Chris Heunis was appointed acting president.

Feb. 2. President Botha of South Africa resigned as leader of the ruling National Party. Mr. F. W. de Klerk became the new leader of the party. **13.** A lawyer in Johannesburg claimed that clients had told him that Mrs. Winnie Mandela was involved in events which led to the abduction and beating of four black youths. On Feb. 16 Mrs. Mandela was disowned by South Africa's black community, who expressed outrage at the activities of her "bodyguards", who called themselves the "Mandela United football team". On Feb. 19 police raided Mrs. Mandela's home and arrested four youths living there. On Feb. 21 two of the youths were charged with murder. **14.** Seventeen political detainees were released in South Africa.

March 5. The Sudanese Cabinet resigned and the Prime Minister, Sadiq al-Mahdi, agreed to form a coalition government and introduce a peace plan to end the civil war. **21.** The South African Government said that four black activists who had escaped from detention and taken refuge in the West German Embassy in Pretoria would be allowed to go free if they left the Embassy.

April 2. Fighting between South African forces and SWAPO guerrillas in Namibia threatened the Namibian independence accord: on April 6 the United Nations presented a ceasefire proposal, and on April 21 the South African Foreign Minister, Pik Botha, said that all South African troops in Namibia would be confined to barracks for sixty hours, to allow SWAPO guerrillas to leave the country unhindered. **3.** President Zine Ben Ali of Tunisia was re-elected. **26.** Intercommunal violence in Senegal and Mauritania left at least 44 people dead and many more wounded.

May 1. A white South African rights activist, Dr. David Webster, was shot dead. **16.** Mrs. Helen Suzman, veteran South African liberal M.P., announced her retirement from Parliament after 36 years. **17.** An Ethiopian radio station announced that an attempted coup had been foiled and two of its leaders killed, but fighting continued in Addis Ababa and other parts of the country.

June 4. Over 50 people were killed in riots over government economic policies in Lagos, Nigeria. **30.** The Government of Sudan, led by Sadiq el Mahdi, was overthrown in a military coup.

July 12. Nelson Mandela, the imprisoned leader of the African National Congress, made his first public statement since his detention 25 years ago. Mr. Mandela defended his recent meeting with the South African President, P. W. Botha.

Aug. 14. The President of South Africa, P. W. Botha, resigned following a series of disagreements with his cabinet. On Aug. 15 F. W. de Klerk was sworn in as acting President.

THE AMERICAS

(1988). Sept. 1. General Pinochet of Chile announced that all political exiles would be allowed to return to the country. **2.** The U.S. Government fined 32 airlines more than $1 million for failing to conduct adequate security checks at airports. The Peruvian Government resigned to pave the way for the implementation of an austerity programme by President García. **11.** The Chamber of Deputies in Mexico ratified the election of Carlos Salinas de Gortari as the next President. **16.** Chilean police arrested 110 anti-government demonstrators in incidents related to the forthcoming presidential elections. **18.** The military government of Haiti, which took power in a coup in June 1988, was itself overthrown in a military coup. General Prosper Avril became the new President. **29.** The U.S.A. resumed manned space flight with the launch of the shuttle *Discovery* on a four-day mission.

Oct. 6. The Cabinet in Chile resigned following the defeat of President Pinochet in the first free elections for 15 years. **13.** Peru's biggest union federation led a one-day general strike over low wages and high inflation. **26.** In a response to the expulsion of eight American diplomats from Nicaragua, President Reagan ordered that no Nicaraguan officials be allowed to enter the U.S.A. Two of the three Californian grey whales trapped for three weeks in the Alaskan ice-pack were released through a channel cut to the sea by a Soviet ice-breaker: the third whale died. **27.** A one-day strike took place in Bogota, Colombia. **30.** Latin American leaders met in Uruguay to discuss ways of reducing the region's massive foreign debt. **31.** The Argentine appeal court confirmed a twelve-year prison sentence on former President Galtieri for his mismanagement of the Falklands war.

Nov. 7. The Presidential election took place in the U.S.A. On Nov. 8 Vice-President George Bush was declared the President-elect, defeating Michael Dukakis. **10.** Armed soldiers in Brazil entered the grounds of the National Steel Company's factory at Volta Redonda where 2,500 workers were striking: in the confrontation at least three workers died and 36 were wounded. **21.** The Progressive Conservative Party led by Brian Mulroney won a general election in Canada called over the issue of a free trade agreement with the U.S.A. due to come into effect in Jan. 1989.

Dec. 2. Troops loyal to the Argentine government surrounded an army base occupied by rebel officers and coastguard commandos who had attempted a military rebellion: on Dec. 4 the rebels, led by Colonel Mohammed Ali Seineldín, agreed to surrender. **5.** Carlos Andres Perez was elected President of Venezuela for the second time. **20.** In Peru the governing party elected Luis Alva Castro secretary general of the party, undercutting party support for President Alan García. **23.** A judge in Los Angeles upheld the rights of a group of Palestinians by ruling against a law that allows the deportation of aliens who express anti-American views.

(1989) Jan. 3. Michael Dukakis announced that he would not seek re-election as governor of Massachussetts. **15.** President Sarney of Brazil decreed an indefinite price freeze and a currency devaluation of 17 per cent as part of the effort to reduce inflation. **17.** A gunman killed five schoolchildren and then shot himself in Stockton, California. **20.** George Bush was inaugurated as the 41st President of the United States. **23.** Armed men who seized a military base outside Buenos Aires were defeated by army troops and police.

Feb. 2. President Perez of Venezuela was sworn in for his second term in office. **3.** President Alfredo Stroessner of Paraguay was overthrown in a military coup. On Feb. 6 the head of the new junta, General Andres Rodriguez, dissolved congress and called a presidential election for May. **10.** The People's National Party, led by Malcolm Manley, won the Jamaican general election. The ruling United Bermuda Party was returned to power in general elections in Bermuda. **28.** Twenty-five people were killed in rioting over new austerity measures in Caracas, Venezuela.

March 9. The U.S. Senate rejected the nomination of John Tower as Defence Secretary. On March 10 President Bush nominated Dick Cheney for the post and on March 17 Mr. Cheney's nomination was confirmed. **20.** The candidate of the right-wing Arena party, Alfredo Cristiani, won the presidential election in El Salvador. In pre-election violence at least 23 people were killed. **24.** President Bush announced that he had reached agreement with Congress on the provision of interim aid to the Nicaraguan Contra rebels, in return for committing the U.S.A. to supporting diplomatic peace moves in Central America. **27.** A state of emergency was declared in Alaska as 11 million gallons of crude oil from a damaged tanker, *Exxon Valdez*, spread to cover an area of 100 square miles.

April 2. An attempted coup in Haiti failed. **27.** President Pinochet of Chile dismissed his Cabinet following a row over constitutional reform.

May 1. Gen. Andrès Rodriguez was elected President in Paraguay. **4.** Oliver North, the former marine lieutenant-colonel involved in the Iran-Contra affair, was found guilty in Washington of three charges of falsifying and destroying documents. **9.** A military coup in Guatemala was foiled by loyal troops. The government of Panama, led by General Noriega, was accused of falsifying election results and the opposition claimed victory. **15.** Carlos Menem, the Peronist candidate, won the Argentine presidential election. **31.** Mr. Jim Wright, the Speaker of the U.S. House of Representatives, resigned his post after allegations of financial misconduct were made against him.

June 2. Thomas Foley was appointed the new Speaker of the U.S. House of Representatives. **26.** The United States Supreme Court ruled that states are free to execute juveniles and the mentally retarded.

July 5. Oliver North, a central figure in the Iran-Contra affair, was given a three-year

suspended prison sentence, fined $150,000 and ordered to do community work by a Washington court. **7.** General Arnaldo Ochoa Sanchez was sentenced to death in Havana, Cuba, for drug trafficking. **8.** Carlos Menem was sworn in as President of Argentina.

Aug. 8. The leaders of five Central American countries signed an accord in Honduras which called for the disbandment of the Nicaraguan Contra rebel movement. **25.** The United States announced that it would give $65 million in aid to Colombia to help the fight against drug traffickers.

ASIA

(1988). Sept. 1. Both houses of the Indian Parliament were suspended after government and opposition M.P.s exchanged blows. **4.** The People's Action Party, led by the Prime Minister Lee Kuan Yew, won all but one of the seats in the Singapore general election. **7.** Opponents of the government in Burma were warned that any violence would be met with a shoot-to-kill response from troops. **10.** The Burma Socialist Programme Party announced that free elections would be held, bringing one-party rule to an end. **18.** A military junta took control of Burma following a coup. On Sept. 19 rioters protesting against the coup fought with troops in the streets of Rangoon, leaving more than 400 dead. On Sept. 27 an alliance of opposition parties elected U Aung Gyi as its chair and called for an interim government to replace the military autocracy.

Oct. 2. In Pakistan masked gunmen rampaged through Karachi and Hyderabad, killing more than 230 people. **3.** Pakistan's Supreme Court ruled that the forthcoming elections should be held on a party basis, with candidates declaring any affiliation to a political party. **7.** Students clashed with riot police in Seoul, S. Korea, following demands for the arrest of former President Chun Doo Hwan. **10.** Forty-four members of the Sinhalese community were murdered by Tamil guerrillas in northern Sri Lanka. **11.** Members of four of India's opposition parties agreed to merge to create a new party, Janata Dal, in an attempt to win the forthcoming elections. **21.** Fourteen Indian soldiers were killed by Tamil guerrillas in incidents in eastern and northern Sri Lanka.

Nov. 3. The Maldives were invaded by 400 mercenaries. Indian troops moved in to put down the attempted coup. On Nov. 4 the mercenaries fled from the Maldives, taking 28 hostages. On Nov. 5 two of the hostages were killed. On Nov. 6 Indian troops captured one of the ships in which the mercenaries were escaping and released 20 hostages. Four of the remaining hostages had been killed and four were missing. **4.** The Soviet Union announced the suspension of its withdrawal of troops from Afghanistan. **10.** Fifteen people died when troops fired on demonstrators in three separate incidents in Sri Lanka: the deaths occurred the day after the Government warned protesters that they would be shot on sight. **14.** Tamil guerrillas ambushed a bus in eastern Sri Lanka, killing 25 people. **16.** A general election was held in Pakistan: on Nov. 17 the Pakistan People's Party, led by Benazir Bhutto, emerged as the winner of the election. **23.** Former President Chun of Korea went into exile in a mountain Buddhist temple after promising to surrender his personal fortune and apologising for corruption and repression during his eight-year regime.

Dec. 1. Benazir Bhutto was appointed Prime Minister of Pakistan by the acting President, Ghulam Ishaq Khan. On Dec. 12 Mr. Khan was elected President. **5.** President Roh of South Korea announced a Cabinet reshuffle and replaced 21 of the 24 ministers. **9.** Japan's Finance Minister and Deputy Prime Minister, Kiichi Miyazawa, resigned over his involvement in a share trading scandal. **11.** President Ershad of Bangladesh announced a Cabinet reshuffle. **19.** The Indian Prime Minister (Rajiv Gandhi) began a visit to China, the first Indian leader to do so for 34 years. **20.** Prime Minister Ranasinghe Premadasa was declared the winner in the Sri Lankan presidential elections. **26.** Riots in the Indian city of Vijayawada left 17 dead and 100 injured. **27.** The Japanese Prime Minister, Noboru Takeshita, announced a reshuffle of his Cabinet.

(1989). Jan. 1. Soviet and Afghan government forces began a unilateral ceasefire in Afghanistan. **2.** Mr. Ranasinghe Premadasa was sworn in as President of Sri Lanka. **6.** Two Sikh extremists were executed in New Delhi for the murder of Mrs. Indira Gandhi in 1984. **7.** Emperor Hirohito of Japan died; he was succeeded by his son, Akihito. **15.** Chinese and Vietnamese officials met in Peking, ending ten years of diplomatic deadlock. **19.** British nationals living in Afghanistan were advised to leave the country by the British charge d'affaires. On Jan. 24 American nationals were also advised to leave. On Jan. 30 all American diplomats left Kabul.

Feb. 5. Following the Soviet withdrawal from Afghanistan, President Najibullah called 30,000 civilians to arms. **6.** The Tibetan religious festival of Moinlam Genmo was cancelled by Chinese officials. **14.** The Union Carbide Corporation agreed to pay the victims of the industrial disaster at Bhopal, India, in 1984, a total of $470 million in compensation. **15.** The ruling United National Party won a majority of seats in the general election in Sri Lanka.

March 5. Eleven people were killed and more than 100 injured when police opened fire on the crowd during pro-independence riots in Lhasa, Tibet. On March 7 Chinese troops moved into Lhasa to enforce martial law. **8.** A former Japanese Deputy Minister of Labour, Takashi Kato, was arrested on suspicion of accepting bribes in connection with a stocks scandal. **23.** The Sri Lankan Foreign and deputy Defence Minister told the Parliament that the Criminal Investigation Department was to investigate claims that government forces were involved in some of the civilian deaths among 140 people killed in political violence that week.

April 13. A car bomb planted by Tamil extremists exploded in Trincomalee, Sri Lanka, killing at least 45 people and injuring 57 others. Enraged Buddhists killed five Tamils in retaliation. **15.** The Liberation Tigers of Tamil Eelam accepted President Premadasa of Sri Lanka's invitation to hold peace talks. **24.** The Indian government dismissed the opposition-ruled state government of Karnataka and invoked presidential rule. **25.** The Prime Minister of Japan, Noboru Takeshita, announced his resignation following months of rumour and speculation about his role in the Recruit bribery scandal.

May 2. The Vietnamese-backed government in the People's Republic of Kampuchea announced that the country was reverting to its original name of Cambodia. **11.** The first talks were held in Colombo between Sri Lankan ministers and representatives of the guerrilla group the Liberation Tigers of Tamil Eelem. **12.** The Burmese Army and Karen rebels fought on the Thai-Burmese border.

June 2. Sosuke Uno was sworn in as Prime Minister of Japan. **20.** An indefinite State of Emergency was declared in Sri Lanka.

July 19. During a religious festival in Sri Lanka, thirteen people were killed and more than 80 injured after extremists threw hand grenades into the crowds. **24.** The Japanese Prime Minister, Sosuke Uno, resigned following the defeat of his Liberal Democrat party in the Upper House elections. **29.** India began to withdraw its troops from Sri Lanka. **30.** An international conference to consider possible solutions to the situation in Kampuchea began in Paris.

Aug. 8. Mr. Toshiki Kaifu was elected Prime Minister of Japan. **17.** Tamil guerrillas killed 24 Indian soldiers in Sri Lanka.

CHINA.—**(1989). April 18.** In Beijing (Peking) police dispersed a crowd of 5,000 students who tried to enter the headquarters of the Chinese Communist Party. **20.** The authorities issued strong warnings against continued pro-democracy demonstrations as student protests spread to other cities.

May 15. Students and workers demanded greater democracy in a day-long demonstration in Beijing staged to coincide with the visit to China of President Gorbachev of the Soviet Union. **17.** Beijing and most of the provincial cities were brought to a halt by popular pro-democracy demonstrations. **19.** Troops were ordered to enter Beijing in an attempt to quell the demonstrations. **26.** In a purge of moderates in the government, the general secretary of the Chinese Communist Party, Zhao Ziyang, was placed under house arrest.

June 2. Troops attempted to clear protesters from Tiananmen Square in Beijing but were stopped by the people. **3.** Troops launched an assault on the square, killing and wounding thousands. **4.** The unofficial death toll was put at over one thousand. **10.** A wave of arrests took place in Beijing, mainly of student and worker leaders. **14.** The British Foreign Secretary, Sir Geoffrey Howe, acknowledged that Britain would have obligations to the people of Hong Kong in the event of a similar crackdown in the colony after it reverts to China in 1997. **22.** A series of executions took place in Shanghai and Beijing. **24.** Zhao Ziyang was dismissed as Party general secretary and replaced by Jiang Zemin.

July 7. The Chinese Communist Party presented a report to the National People's Congress detailing the case against the disgraced former party secretary, Zhao Ziyang, and giving its explanation of the causes of the mass protests in May and June.

AUSTRALASIA AND THE PACIFIC

(1988). Sept. 7. Gough Whitlam, the former Australian Prime Minister, attacked the British Government over the *Spycatcher* affair, claiming that the security of other nations had been damaged. **15.** Lindy and Michael Chamberlain, the Australian couple convicted of killing their baby daughter in what became known as the "dingo murder", had their convictions quashed by a court in Darwin, Australia. **30.** Anti-nuclear protesters and I.R.A. sympathizers demonstrated in Sydney, Australia, during the visit of the Duke and Duchess of York.

Nov. 6. Proposals for the political and economic development of New Caledonia were approved in a referendum held in France. **15.** Fourteen present or former members of the Queensland state government were accused of abusing ministerial expenses

for private purposes. **23.** Australia has been struck by a plague of 200 million rabbits.

Dec. 2. The Yugoslav consulate in Sydney, Australia, was closed and the entire staff declared *persona non grata* after the Yugoslavs refused to hand over to the Australian authorities a security guard who had allegedly shot a boy during a protest. **14.** The New Zealand Minister of Finance, Roger Douglas, resigned, saying that he could no longer work with Prime Minister David Lange. **21.** President George Sokomanu of Vanuatu was arrested on the orders of Prime Minister, Father Walter Lini, and charged with inciting mutiny.

(1989) Jan. 11. An Australian policeman, Assistant Commissioner Colin Winchester, was murdered outside his home in Canberra.

Feb. 2. An Australian royal commission investigating the high incidence of Aboriginal deaths in police custody published its first report.

March 7. The former president of Vanuatu, George Sokomanu, was jailed for his part in the failed attempt to oust the Prime Minister, Father Walter Lini, in December. **28.** Mr. Solomon Mamaloni was elected Prime Minister of the Solomon Islands and announced his intention to turn the state into a republic.

April 5. The former head of the National Safety Council of Australia, John Friedrich, was arrested near Perth in connection with an investigation into $A40 million missing from the Council's accounts.

May 4. The leader of the Kanak community in New Caledonia, Jean-Marie Tjibaou, was assassinated in an ambush.

Aug. 3. Roger Douglas, who resigned from the New Zealand cabinet in 1988, was re-elected to the Cabinet by the parliamentary Labour party. On Aug. 7 the Prime Minister, David Lange, resigned, alleging that his party had 'stabbed him in the back' over Mr. Douglas' appointment. **8.** Geoffrey Palmer was elected Prime Minister of New Zealand.

EUROPE

(1988). Sept. 1. Thousands of Polish workers ended a strike (begun in mid-August) in response to a government offer of talks on the legalization of the Solidarity trade union. **6.** The Dutch Defence Minister, William van Eekelen, resigned after a parliamentary inquiry found that he had bungled the introduction of a new passport while in a previous post. **8.** In Yugoslavia the Serbian Communist Party and the Serbian State Presidency rejected the demand of the federal Communist Party that they take steps to stop demonstrations against alleged intimidation of Serbs and Montenegrins by ethnic Albanians in the Kosovo province of Serbia. **17.** The coalition government of Iceland, led by Thorsteinn Pálsson, resigned after two coalition partners withdrew their support. **19.** The ruling Social Democrats won a general election in Sweden. The Polish government, led by Zbigniew Messner, resigned. On Sept. 26 Mr. Mieczyslaw Rakowski became Prime Minister. **21.** The Soviet government declared a state of emergency in the Nagorno-Karabakh region of Azerbaijan as protests continued over the status of Nagorno-Karabakh. **28.** Steingrímur Hermannsson became Prime Minister of Iceland and formed a new coalition government. **30.** Major changes in the Soviet Politburo included the retirement of President Andrei Gromyko and the dismissal of several other leading figures.

Oct. 3. President Erich Honecker of East Germany began an official visit to Spain, the first by an East German head of state. **6.** The leaders of the Vojvodina province in the Serbian republic in Yugoslavia resigned after a crowd of 100,000 protested in the province's capital at the Vojvodina leadership's opposition to proposed constitutional changes which would increase Serbia's authority in the Vojvodina and Kosovo provinces. **10.** The Czechoslovak Prime Minister, Lubomir Strougal, resigned. **12.** An Italian court sentenced 26 Red Brigade terrorists to life imprisonment. **13.** The Italian Parliament voted partially to stop the use of the secret ballot in parliament. **16.** Four members of the Yugoslav Communist Party's politburo resigned on the eve of a Central Committee emergency plenum to discuss the unrest in Serbia. **28.** Police in Prague broke up a celebration by 5,000 people of the 70th anniversary of Czechoslovak independence. **30.** A Spanish financier, Emiliano Revilla, was released by kidnappers after his family paid £5·5 million to E.T.A., the Basque separatist organization. **31.** The Polish government announced the closure of the Lenin shipyard in Gdansk.

Nov. 3. The Hungarian Communist Party issued a statement calling for the speeding up of economic reforms. **10.** Czechoslovak police arrested at least 20 dissidents before the opening of an historical symposium to be attended by Western academics and human rights activists. **11.** The President of the West German Bundestag, Philipp Jenninger, resigned following protests at a speech he made to the Bundestag on Nov. 10, the fiftieth anniversary of the Nazi Kristallnacht pogrom. **16.** The parliament of the Soviet Republic of Estonia voted to give itself sovereign rights to veto laws passed in Moscow. On Nov. 26 the Presidium of the Supreme Soviet found the declaration uncon-

stitutional and ruled it invalid. **19.** A soviet court sentenced an Azerbaijani to death for leading anti-Armenian riots. **23.** Two regions in Azerbaijan were placed under a state of emergency following ethnic clashes which led to the deaths of three Soviet soldiers. On Nov. 27 the Communist Party leaders of the two areas were removed from office. **29.** A session of the U.S.S.R. Supreme Soviet opened. It was called to debate constitutional changes. On Dec. 1 the Supreme Soviet approved amendments to the 1977 constitution allowing the creation of a new supreme representative body and an executive presidency in 1989.

Dec. 7. The Swiss Parliament elected Mr. Jean-Paul Delamuraz President and Mrs. Elisabeth Kopp Vice-President of Switzerland. On Dec. 12 Mrs. Kopp resigned from her post following investigation of her husband's connection with a drugs money laundering case. **14.** Swedish police detained a man on suspicion of murdering Prime Minister Olaf Palme nearly three years ago. **16.** Thousands of Spanish workers demonstrated in Madrid in protest at the Government's austerity drive. **21.** The Hungarian Parliament rejected government proposals for the budget in 1989. **28.** Italian trade union leaders announced plans for a general strike in protest against the Government's 1989 budget. **30.** After the Yugoslav Parliament rejected the budget for 1989, the government resigned. The son-in-law of Leonid Brezhnev, Yuri Churbanov, was jailed for 12 years for abuse of power and accepting bribes.

(1989) Jan. 10. The Czechoslovak Foreign Minister, Jaromir Johanes, announced that his country intended to stop exporting the plastic explosive Semtex. **11.** The Hungarian Parliament approved laws legalizing independent and opposition groups outside the Communist Party. **19.** Mr. Ante Markovic was designated Prime Minister of Yugoslavia and asked to form a government following the resignation of the Mikulic government on Dec. 30.

Feb. 6. Talks between the Government and opposition began in Warsaw. **9.** The West German Interior Minister Friedrich Zimmermann banned the neo-Nazi Nationale Sammlung group. **12.** The Hungarian Communist Party Central Committee voted to adopt a multi-party system. **14.** The former Belgian Prime Minister, Paul Vanden Boeynants, who was kidnapped by left-wing extremists on Jan. 14, was released following the payment of a substantial ransom. **21.** Czech playwright Vaclav Havel was sentenced to nine months in prison in Prague for incitement and failing to obey police orders. **20.** Ethnic-Albanian miners in the autonomous province of Kosovo (Yugoslavia) began an underground sit-in and hunger strike in protest at proposed changes to the Serbian republic's constitution which would allow Serbia more control over the autonomous provinces of Kosovo and Vojvodina. The strike spread and by Feb. 26 was general. **27.** Members of the Kosovo Communist Party leadership resigned and the miners called off their hunger strike. **28.** Serbs in Kosovo and Serbia demonstrated against the Communist leadership's capitulation to the demands of the Kosovar Albanians.

March 1. The Yugoslav Federal Assembly held an emergency session to discuss the situation in Kosovo. A member of the State Presidency claimed to have evidence that the unrest in Kosovo was a cover for a plot to secede from Yugoslavia to Albania. **2.** Azem Vlasi and other alleged ringleaders of unrest in Kosovo were arrested. On March 9 ethnic-Albanian miners began a strike in protest at Vlasi's arrest: the protest spread and by March 19 an estimated 50,000 workers were on strike. **9.** In Algiers Spanish envoys began talks with exiled leaders of E.T.A., the Basque separatist group, in an attempt to reach a settlement. **17.** The Greek Prime Minister, Andreas Papandreou, reshuffled the cabinet, attempting to restore confidence in the government after a few ministers were found to be linked to a financial scandal. **21.** The Soviet leader Mr. Gorbachev signed a decree reducing the size of the Soviet armed forces and of defence spending. A Czechoslovak appeal court reduced the sentence of Vaclav Havel by one month. **23.** The Kosovo Provincial Assembly endorsed changes to the Serbian constitution. Widespread demonstrations began and after a few days escalated into violent clashes which left 29 people dead. **26.** The first contested elections for 70 years took place in the Soviet Union. **28.** The Serbian Republican Assembly ratified constitutional changes reducing the autonomy in internal affairs of the Kosovo and Vojvodina Autonomous Provinces.

April 4. E.T.A., the Basque separatist movement, called off a ceasefire that had lasted for three months. **5.** The President of the Yugoslavian province of Kosovo, Ramzi Koljgeci, resigned his post. The Polish government and the Solidarity trade union signed an agreement on extensive political and economic reforms. **9.** Troops killed sixteen people and wounded hundreds more when dispersing 10,000 demonstrators in Tbilisi, the capital of the Soviet republic of Georgia. **10.** Andrei Sakharov and other pro-reform academics were nominated for the Soviet parliament by the Academy of Sciences. **14.** The leader of Georgia's Communist Party and the republic's Prime Minister and President resigned their posts. **17.** A Polish judge pronounced Solidarity a legal organization after over seven years of underground existence. **23.** Police in Moscow arrested 47 people following a demonstration by the self-styled Democratic Union opposition party. **25.** President Gorbachev, endorsed by the Central Committee plenum, secured the retirement of 110 officials from the highest ranks of the committee: amongst those retiring was Andrei Gromyko.

May 1. Turkish police fired at protesters who defied a ban on May Day marches. Police in Prague arrested many people during a Czechoslovak May Day parade. **3.** The Prime Minister of the Netherlands, Rund Lubbers, resigned his post. **17.** The Czechoslovak playwright Vaclav Havel was released from prison after serving only half of an eight-month sentence for taking part in a banned protest. **19.** The Italian Prime Minister, Ciriaco de Mita, resigned his post. **25.** At the opening day of the inaugural session of the new Soviet Parliament Mikhail Gorbachev was elected President of the U.S.S.R.

June 4. In elections in Poland candidates of the trade union Solidarity won a majority of the seats in which a free contest was allowed. **6.** Riots in the Soviet republic of Uzbekistan left 56 dead. **16.** In the general election in Ireland, the governing Fianna Fáil party won the most seats but failed to gain an overall majority.

July 2. Tzannis Tzannetakis was sworn in as the interim Prime Minister of Greece. **4.** Poland's first democratically elected M.P.s and Senators were sworn in. **16.** Ethnic unrest in Abkhazia, part of the Soviet republic of Georgia, left 11 dead and 127 injured: on July 18 a state of emergency and curfew was imposed in the Abkhazian towns of Suhumi, Tkvarceli and Gagra. **19.** Poland's Communist leader, Gen. Jaruzelski, was elected President by the National Assembly. **27.** A Stockholm court sentenced Christer Pettersson to life imprisonment for the murder of the Swedish Prime Minister, Olof Palme, in 1986.

Aug. 2. The Polish Parliament chose Gen. Czeslaw Kisczak as Prime Minister. On Aug. 14 Gen. Kisczak resigned, having been unable to form a government. On Aug. 19 President Jaruzelski invited Tadeusz Mazowiecki, of Solidarity, to become Prime Minister. **23.** More than two million people in the Soviet Union's Balkan republics formed a human chain across their countries to mark the 50th anniversary of the non-aggression treaty between Germany and the U.S.S.R. which led to the Soviet annexation of Estonia, Latvia and Lithuania.

EUROPEAN COMMUNITY

(1988). Sept. 18. The Maltese Prime Minister, Dr. Edward Fenech Adami, said that his country would formally apply for membership of the European Community by 1992. **20.** Mrs. Thatcher delivered a speech on the European Community to students at the College of Europe in Bruges, Belgium. **23.** The European Court of Justice decided that European M.P.s would be allowed to hold some plenary sessions of the European Parliament in Brussels. **28.** The President of the European Commission, Jacques Delors, and the Prime Minister of Belgium, Wilfried Martens, both attacked Mrs. Thatcher's Bruges speech on the European Community.

Oct. 14. The British Government expressed opposition to a proposed E.C.-wide statute harmonizing company law and guaranteeing employees' rights after 1992. **16.** E.C. foreign ministers agreed to promote democratic change in the Soviet bloc through increased trade and political dialogue. **21.** Mrs. Thatcher, in a speech in Italy, attacked the idea of a European central bank. Jacques Delors accused Mrs. Thatcher of obstructing the integration of the European Community.

Nov. 22. Britain urged the European Community to pull back from a trade war with the U.S.A. over the use of hormones in meat.

Dec. 2. The European Community summit began in Rhodes, Greece. **16.** The European Commission's 17 new commissioners-designate met at Villiers-le-Temple, France, to decide on individual portfolios. **20.** E.C. farm ministers abandoned talks at Brussels after failing to reach agreement on a package of measures covering meat and dairy produce imports from New Zealand.

(1989) Jan. 18. European M.P.s voted in favour of a resolution enabling them to transfer up to 1,000 staff from Luxembourg to Brussels and to hold exceptional plenary sessions other than in Strasbourg. **23.** The European Parliament's budget control committee began a three-day hearing in Brussels to investigate fraud and corruption within the E.C.

Feb. 2. The European Court of Justice ruled that France had denied Mr. Ian Cowan a basic right as an E.C. citizen by refusing to pay compensation on the grounds that he was a tourist after he was attacked and robbed in Paris. **7.** Mrs. Thatcher called for a crackdown on racketeering and embezzlement in the European Community, which is estimated to cost the E.C. up to £600 million each year.

March 2. At a meeting in Brussels E.C. environment ministers agreed to press for the withdrawal from use of all chlorofluorocarbons (C.F.C.s) by the end of the century. **14.** The European Commission welcomed the agreement by E.C. economic and finance ministers to launch a campaign against fraud and corruption in the Community.

April 12. The European Parliament voted in favour of reducing the permitted level of exhaust emissions by small cars in Europe. **17.** Proposals presented by a committee of central bankers and finance officials calling for economic and monetary union within the European Community, were rejected by the British Chancellor, Nigel Lawson: on April 20 the other members of the Community accepted the proposals. **18.** The European Court threatened to prosecute Britain if it failed to produce within two months a programme for bringing water quality up to E.C. standards more rapidly. **24.** The European Community broke off trade negotiations with Romania because of that country's human rights record.

May 10. The former Liberal Party leader, David Steel, announced that he was standing as a candidate for the Central region of Italy in the forthcoming European Parliament elections. **21.** The British Chancellor Nigel Lawson accepted the Delors report as a basis for progress towards economic and monetary union. He agreed to begin work immediately on stage one and to consider the next two stages.

June 15. Elections for the European Parliament took place in Denmark, Ireland, Spain, the Netherlands and the U.K. **18.** Elections for the European Parliament took place in Belgium, France, West Germany, Greece, Italy, Luxembourg and Portugal. **26–27.** A European Council meeting of heads of state and heads of government was held in Madrid.

July 25. Enrique Baron Crespo of Spain was elected President of the new European Parliament.

MIDDLE EAST

(1988). Sept. 5. The trial of Shabtai Kalmanovitch, accused of spying for the Soviet Union, began in Jerusalem. **6.** Israeli troops sealed off the West Bank town of Kalkilya in a move to round up Palestinian stone-throwers. **9.** The Islamic Resistance Movement enforced a strike in most towns of the occupied West Bank. **12.** A West German hostage, Rudolf Cordes, was released by pro-Iranian kidnappers in Lebanon after 20 months in captivity. **15.** Israeli troops shot dead a 10-year old Palestinian boy when a fire bomb was thrown at an army patrol in the Gaza strip. **16.** Kurdish rebels claimed that Iraq bombed with nerve gas a gorge in which 430 refugee families were sheltering, killing everyone.

20. A car bomb exploded in east Beirut, killing five people and wounding 25. **22.** Lebanon's warring factions failed for the second time in a month to agree on a successor to President Gemayel, whose term of office ended at midnight on Sept. 22.

Oct. 3. Lebanese kidnappers released Professor Mithileshwar Singh who had spent 21 months in captivity. **6.** Two Palestinians suspected of collaboration with Israel were shot dead in Israeli territory. **14.** Two Israeli gunboats and a helicopter sank three rubber dinghies off south Lebanon carrying Palestinians who were trying to reach Israel. A car bomb exploded in west Beirut, killing three people and injuring 33. **19.** Seven Israeli soldiers were killed when a car bomb exploded amongst their jeeps in south Lebanon. **21.** In retaliation for the killing of seven Israeli soldiers in south Lebanon, Israel attacked Lebanese and Palestinian guerrilla bases in south Lebanon, killing 15 people and wounding at least 35 others. **26.** Israeli jets attacked Palestinian guerrilla bases south of Beirut and near Sidon, killing 15 people.

Nov. 1. A general election was held in Israel. Neither of the main parties gained a clear majority. On Nov. 14 Mr. Shamir, leader of the Likud Party, agreed to attempt to form a government. **7.** An Israeli soldier was stabbed to death by a Palestinian worker, who was then shot dead by another soldier at the Massua settlement. **9.** Israeli troops shot dead a three-year old child during unrest in the Gaza strip. **11.** Israel imposed an indefinite curfew in the Gaza strip. **14.** The P.L.O. parliament-in-exile declared the formation of an independent State of Palestine and voted to endorse U.N. Resolution 242, which implicitly recognizes the State of Israel. **15.** The P.L.O. leader Yasser Arafat called on Israel and the U.S.A. to hold direct talks with the P.L.O. to seek a solution to the Middle East conflict. **18.** The Soviet Union gave qualified recognition to the declaration of a Palestinian state. **20.** Egypt granted full recognition to a Palestinian state.

Dec. 2. Five hijackers ordered the pilot of a Soviet transport plane to fly to Israel, where they surrendered to authorities. On Dec. 3 the hijackers were sent back to the Soviet Union. **7.** In Stockholm the P.L.O. leader Yasser Arafat said that his organization now accepted Israel's right to exist. **9.** In Israeli territory the first anniversary of the Palestinian uprising (*intifada*) was marked by demonstrations and a general strike. Israeli commandos attacked a Palestinian guerrilla base in Lebanon: one Israeli officer and six guerrillas were killed. **16.** Four Palestinians were shot dead by Israeli troops on the West Bank. A Swiss delegate of the International Red Cross, Peter Winkler, was released one

month after being kidnapped in southern Lebanon. **19.** The two main political parties in Israel, Likud and Labour, agreed to form a coalition government again, led by Yitzhak Shamir, the leader of the Likud Party. **27.** The Israeli Finance Minister, Shimon Peres, devalued the shekel by five per cent. **29.** Two French children, Virginie and Marie-Laure Valente, arrived in France via Libya, after having been held captive in Lebanon since Nov. 1987.

(1989) Jan. 11. Israeli jets bombed positions held by the Fatah Revolutionary Council south of Beirut. **17.** Israel punished Arab stone throwers in the West Bank by demolishing their homes. **23.** Peace proposals made by the Israeli Defence Minister Yitzhak Rabin were rejected by the P.L.O. and by the Israeli Prime Minister, Yitzhak Shamir. **25.** A truce between the rival Hizbollah and Amal militia in Lebanon broke down after only a few hours: on Jan. 30 Amal and Hizbollah signed a peace accord providing for an immediate ceasefire.

Feb. 5. Israeli soldiers killed five Palestinian gunmen in southern Lebanon. **10.** Fighting between Christian militiamen and Lebanese Army units loyal to Gen. Aoun broke out in Beirut's Christian-controlled areas. **22.** The Soviet Foreign Minister, Eduard Shevardnadze, held separate talks in Cairo with the Israeli Foreign Minister, Moshe Arens, and with the P.L.O. leader Yasser Arafat.

March 14. At least 40 people, many of them civilians, were killed in fierce fighting between Christian and Muslim militia in Beirut. **17.** A car bomb exploded outside a bakery in Beirut, killing at least 12 people. **28.** The leader-designate of Iran, Ayatollah Hosain Ali Montazeri, resigned from his position because of his unhappiness with the regime's extremist policies.

April 10. An Arab was shot dead and two others injured by an unknown gunman outside the Jaffa gate in Jerusalem. **16.** The Spanish Ambassador and members of his family were among 18 people killed by random shelling in Beirut, Lebanon. **19.** Security forces surrounded the Jordanian city of Maan after shooting broke out following demonstrations against government-imposed price rises. **24.** The Jordanian Prime Minister, Zaid Rifai, resigned his post: on April 27 King Hussein appointed Field Marshal Zeid bin Shaker Prime Minister.

May 2. Yassir Arafat, leader of the P.L.O., announced that the 1964 charter of the Palestine Liberation Organization which challenged the right of Israel to exist was null and void. **5.** Three West German aid workers were kidnapped in Sidon, Lebanon: two were later released. **11.** Yehuda Meir, an Israeli army colonel who ordered soldiers to break the limbs of Palestinian demonstrators, was severely reprimanded and dismissed from the army. **16.** The spiritual head of Lebanon's Sunni Muslim community, Grand Mufti Sheikh Hassan Khaled, and over 20 other people were killed when a car bomb exploded in West Beirut. **23.** Egypt formally rejoined the Arab League following a decade's suspension.

June 3. Ayatollah Khomeini died. **4.** President Ali Khameini was elected as the new spiritual leader of the Islamic Republic of Iran. **6.** After being displayed for 24 hours at the Friday prayers ground, Ayatollah Khomeini's body was buried at the Behesht cemetery in Tehran. **15.** A Belgian doctor, Jan Cools, was released after being held hostage in southern Lebanon for 13 months.

July 6. At least 14 Israelis were killed when a Palestinian grabbed the steering wheel of a bus and caused it to crash into a ravine. **17.** The Israeli Industry Minister, Ariel Sharon, called on the Government to 'liquidate' the P.L.O. chairman Yassir Arafat. **27.** At least 28 people were killed during an artillery battle in Beirut. **28.** Israeli commandos kidnapped a leading Shia Muslim, Sheikh Abdul Karim Obeid, from a village in southern Lebanon. On July 30 an unknown group threatened to hang an American hostage, William Higgins, if the Sheikh was not released. On July 31 the group, named as the Organization of the Oppressed of the World, released a video tape which appeared to show the hanging of Lt.-Col. Higgins. **30.** Ali Akbar Hashemi Rafsanjani was elected President of Iran.

Aug. 1. A Lebanese group, the Revolutionary Justice Organization, threatened to kill an American hostage, Joseph Cicippio, but then announced a delay of 48 hours in response to appeals. On Aug. 2 the U.S.A. redirected a number of its warships towards the Lebanese coast. There followed a series of diplomatic efforts to resolve the crisis. **13.** Fighting continued in Beirut, causing civilian casualties and extensive structural damage.

INTERNATIONAL RELATIONS

(1988). Sept. 20. The 43rd General Assembly of the United Nations began in New York. **28.** Czechoslovakia ordered two British officials to leave in retaliation for the expulsion of three Czech intelligence officers. **29.** The United Nations peace-keeping forces were awarded the 1988 Nobel Peace Prize. **30.** At a meeting in New York the British and Iranian Foreign ministers agreed to restore full diplomatic relations between the two countries.

Oct. 19. During a visit to London President Arias of Costa Rica called on European leaders to put economic and political pressure on Central American states to revive and implement the Central American peace plan of August 1987. **20.** The West German Foreign Minister (Hans Dietrich Genscher) called on Western European nations to help the Soviet Union and East European nations put their economies in order.

Nov. 2. The U.S.A. insisted that the Soviet Union's Krasnoyarsk radar complex was in violation of the 1972 Anti-Ballistic Missile Treaty and must be dismantled. **4.** The European Community and the Soviet Union reached agreement on an economic pact. **6.** The review in Vienna of the Conference on Security and Co-operation in Europe entered its third year. **10.** In Vienna British and Iranian diplomats signed a memorandum after negotiating the restoration of full diplomatic relations between the two countries. **14.** Spain and Portugal joined the Western European Union. **22.** The U.N. Secretary-General, Javier Pérez de Cuellar, transferred responsibility for mediation in Afghanistan, Cyprus and the Middle East from the Office of Special Political Affairs to his own Executive Office. **26.** The U.S.A. rejected Yasser Arafat's request for a visa so that he could address a session of the U.N. General Assembly in New York.

Dec. 2. The U.N. General Assembly voted to move to Geneva on December 13 in order to allow Yasser Arafat to take part in a debate on Palestine. **6.** The Soviet leader Mikhail Gorbachev arrived in New York on a three-day visit. On Dec. 7 Mr. Gorbachev addressed the U.N. General Assembly. On Dec. 8 he cut short his visit and returned to Moscow following a devastating earthquake in Armenia. **13.** Yasser Arafat gave an 80-minute address to the U.N. General Assembly in Geneva. **15.** The U.S.A. initiated talks with the P.L.O., ending a 13-year refusal to meet P.L.O. representatives. **19.** The Soviet Foreign Minister, Eduard Shevardnadze, visited Japan for talks to settle territorial disputes. **27.** Iran released a British citizen, Nicholas Nicola, who had been in prison in Tehran for two years. **28.** Kenya announced that it was to restore full diplomatic relations with Israel.

(1989) Jan. 1. The United States imposed trade sanctions against the European Community in response to an E.C. ban on importing hormone-treated meat from the U.S.A. **3.** Israel rebuffed E.C. plans for a Middle East peace conference involving the P.L.O. **4.** Two U.S. jets shot down two Libyan MiG fighters over the Mediterranean sea. **7.** An international conference on chemical weapons began in Paris. On Jan. 8 the Soviet Foreign Minister Eduard Shevardnadze announced

THE QUEEN AND PRESIDENT GORBACHEV

President Gorbachev of the Soviet Union met The Queen during his official visit to Britain in April.

In August Tadeusz Mazowiecki became the first non-Communist Prime Minister of Poland for forty years.

MASS PROTESTS IN THE U.S.S.R.

Nationalist protests in the U.S.S.R. culminated in August in the forming of a 380-mile human chain stretching across Estonia, Latvia and Lithuania to mark the fiftieth anniversary of the republics' annexation by the U.S.S.R.

A crash involving three trains at Clapham in December 1988 killed 34 people.

LOCKERBIE AIR DISASTER

A Pan-Am jet crashed onto the town of Lockerbie in December 1988, killing everyone on board and at least 17 townspeople.

HILLSBOROUGH STADIUM

Over 90 people were killed in a crush at Hillsborough stadium, Sheffield, during an F.A. Cup semi-final in April.

THE MARCHIONESS

Following a collision with another boat, a pleasure boat, the *Marchioness*, sank in the Thames in August, killing over 25 people.

Salman Rushdie's novel *The Satanic Verses* provoked protests from Muslims worldwide, and led to Rushdie being condemned to death by the Ayatollah Khomeini in February.

DEATH OF AYATOLLAH KHOMEINI

Millions of mourners flocked to the cemetery near Tehran where Ayatollah Khomeini was buried after his death in June.

CHINA

Hundreds of thousands of people took part in demonstrations throughout May to demand greater democracy in China.

CHINA

A man tries to stop tanks in the centre of Beijing in June, after thousands of demonstrators were killed by troops in Tiananmen Square.

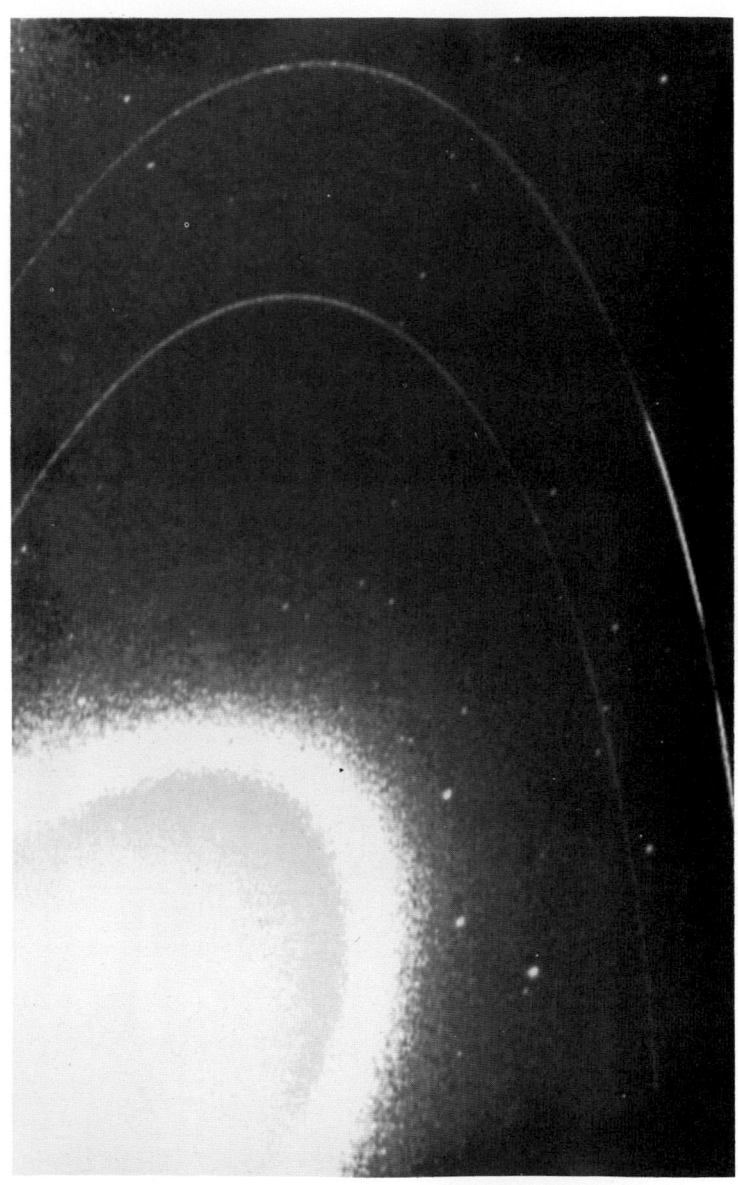

The Voyager 2 space craft passed Neptune in August, taking photographs of the planet's rings.

OBITUARIES

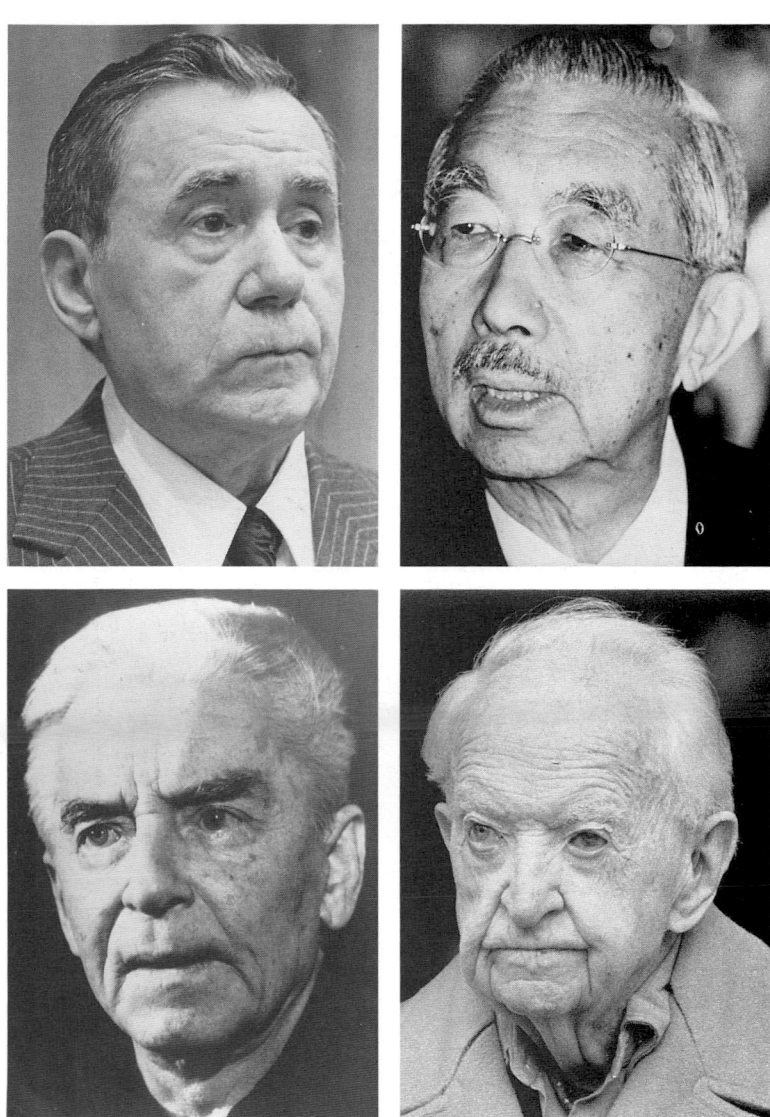

Andrei Gromyko (*top left*), Emperor Hirohito (*top right*), Herbert von Karajan (*bottom left*), Thomas Sopwith.

OBITUARIES

Daphne du Maurier (*top left*), Laurence Olivier (*top right*), Lucille Ball (*bottom left*), Salvador Dali.

Peter Scudamore rode more than 200 winners in the 1988–89 National Hunt season, an unparalleled record.

ATHLETICS VICTORY

The 100 metres relay team's victory contributed to Britain winning the European Cup in August.

that the Soviet Union would unilaterally start to destroy its chemical weapons. On Jan. 11 149 nations agreed to a total ban on chemical weapons. **13.** A 35-nation conference on security and co-operation began in Vienna. On Jan. 19 Mr. Shevardnadze announced that the Soviet Union would withdraw and dismantle some of its tactical nuclear force in Eastern Europe.

March 6. A new round of talks between Nato and Warsaw Pact countries on conventional forces in Europe began in Vienna.

April 20. The United Nations General Assembly condemned Israel's policies and practices in the occupied territories and asked the Security Council to consider ways of protecting Palestinians there. **28.** France expelled three South African diplomats for their involvement in arms trafficking in Paris with three loyalists from Northern Ireland.

May 5. The Speaker of the Iranian Parliament, Ali Akbar Hashemi Rafsanjani called on Palestinians to kill Westerners in revenge for Arab deaths in the Israeli-occupied territories: on May 10 Mr. Rafsanjani retracted his call. **11.** President Gorbachev of the Soviet Union said that he intended to withdraw unilaterally 500 short-range missiles from Europe by the end of 1989. **31.** President Bush of the U.S.A., in a speech in West Germany, called for the dismantling of the Berlin Wall.

June 22. The Soviet Union and Iran signed an agreement on economic, scientific and peaceful nuclear co-operation.

July 6. President Gorbachev addressed the Council of Europe: it was announced that the Soviet Union would be granted 18 permanent guest observers at the Council. **13.** Leaders of the seven major industrialized nations joined in the bicentenary celebrations of the French Revolution in Paris before attending an economic summit meeting. **17.** The United States offered to pay compensation of up to $250,000 for each of the 290 people who died when the U.S. Navy accidentally shot down an Iranian airliner over the Persian Gulf in 1988.

Aug. 31. In Algiers Libya and Chad signed a peace treaty ending their 17-year border dispute.

THE RUSHDIE AFFAIR.—**(1988) Oct. 5.** The novel *The Satanic Verses* by Salman Rushdie was banned by the Indian government.

(1989) Jan. 14. Muslims in Bradford burnt a copy of *The Satanic Verses*, claiming that the book was blasphemous. Similar protests occurred in Pakistan and India in which several people died.

Feb. 14. Ayatollah Khomeini of Iran urged Muslims to kill Salman Rushdie on the grounds that his novel was a blasphemy against Islam. **18.** Mr. Rushdie issued an apology to Muslims: this was rejected by Iran. **20.** Britain announced that it was recalling its four envoys in Tehran and asked Iran to withdraw its diplomats from London. The other E.C. countries agreed to support Britain by recalling their ambassadors to Iran.

March 11. Forty-five Islamic countries declared a ban on sales of the products of Penguin Books, the publisher of *The Satanic Verses*, because of the company's refusal to withdraw the book from sale. **16.** At a meeting in Riyadh, Saudi Arabia, of foreign ministers representing Islamic nations, Salman Rushdie was declared an apostate.

MISCELLANEOUS

(1988). Sept. 17. Tests on the Turin Shroud, believed to be the shroud in which Christ's body was wrapped, found it to be a medieval fake. **27.** The British Library bought an autograph manuscript by Jane Austen for £132,000.

Oct. 14. The Egyptian novelist Naguib Mahfouz became the first Arabic writer to win the Nobel Prize for Literature. **15.** The accommodation module of the Piper Alpha oil rig was lifted from the bed of the North Sea and on Oct. 17 started its journey by barge to Flotta in Orkney.

Nov. 13. Chinese archaeologists unearthed a collection of giant statues in the Alkat steppes in north-west China. **16.** Hereford Cathedral announced that it intended to sell the Mappa Mundi, a 13th century map of the world, to raise funds for the maintenance of the cathedral. **28.** A painting by Picasso sold at Christie's in London for £20·9 million, a world record.

Dec. 11. The Astra satellite, which will be used to provide at least eight new television channels in Britain, was launched from Kourou in French Guiana. **15.** A script of the only play written by George Orwell was sold at Sotheby's for £4,400.

(1989) Feb. 28. Hereford Cathedral abandoned its plan to auction the medieval Mappa Mundi.

March 20. American archaeologists announced the rediscovery of an ancient Assyrian city, Mashkanshapir, at Abu Duwari in Iraq. **23.** Prof. Stanley Pons of the University of Utah and Prof. Martin Fleischmann of Southampton University claimed that they had achieved nuclear fusion at room temperature in a test-tube experiment.

April 6. Archaeological workers at Luxor, Egypt, uncovered several statues dating from the New Kingdom (c. 1570–1080 B.C.).

May 4. A campaign was launched in London to save the Rose, an Elizabethan playhouse in Southwark threatened by building development: on May 15 the developers agreed to delay work for one month. **14.** An international team led by Robert Swan succeeded in walking to the North Pole.

June 5. Hereford Cathedral authorities launched an appeal to raise £2 million to save the Mappa Mundi.

Aug. 24. Twelve years after its launch, the Voyager spacecraft reached the planet Neptune.

DISTANCES FROM LONDON BY AIR

The list of the distances in statute miles from London, Heathrow, to various places abroad has been supplied by the publishers of *IATA/IAL Air Distances Manual*, Southall, Middx.

To	Miles	To	Miles	To	Miles
Abidjan	3,197	Detroit	3,754	Munich	588
Abu Dhabi	3,425	Dhaka	4,976	Nairobi	4,248
Addis Ababa	3,675	Doha	3,253	Naples	1,011
Aden	3,670	Dubai	3,414	Nassau	4,333
Algiers	1,035	Dublin	279	New York (J. F. Kennedy)	3,440
Amman	2,287	Durban	5,937	Nice	645
Amsterdam	230	Düsseldorf	310	Oporto	806
Ankara	1,770	Entebbe	4,033	Oslo (Fornebu)	723
Athens	1,500	Frankfurt	406	Ottawa	3,321
Auckland	11,404	Freetown	3,046	Palma, Majorca	836
Baghdad	2,551	Geneva	468	Paris	215; (Orly 227)
Bahrain	3,163	Gibraltar	1,084	Perth, Australia	9,008
Bangkok	5,928	Gothenburg (Landvetter)	664	Port of Spain, Trinidad	4,405
Barbados	4,193	Hamburg	463	Prague	649
Barcelona	712	Harare	5,156	Rangoon	5,582
Basle	447	Havana	4,647	Reykjavik	1,167
Beijing (Peking)	5,063	Helsinki (Vantaa)	1,147	Rhodes	1,743
Beirut	2,161	Hong Kong	5,990	Rio de Janeiro	5,745
Belfast	325	Honolulu	7,220	Riyadh	3,067
Belgrade	1,056	Istanbul	1,560	Rome (Fiumicino)	895
Berlin (Tegel)	588	Jeddah	2,947	Salzburg	651
Bermuda	3,428	Johannesburg	5,634	San Francisco	5,351
Berne	476	Karachi	3,935	Seoul	5,507
Bombay	4,478	Khartoum	3,071	Shannon	369
Brasilia	5,452	Kingston, Jamaica	4,668	Singapore	6,756
Brisbane	10,273	Kuala Lumpur	6,557	Sofia	1,266
Brussels	217	Kuwait	2,903	Stockholm (Arlanda)	908
Bucharest	1,307	Lagos	3,107	Sydney, Australia	10,568
Budapest	923	Larnaca, Cyprus	2,036	Tangier	1,120
Buenos Aires	6,915	Leningrad	1,314	Teheran	2,741
Cairo	2,194	Lima	6,303	Tel Aviv	2,227
Calcutta	4,958	Lisbon	972	Tokyo (Narita)	5,956
Canberra	10,563	Lomé	3,129	Toronto	3,545
Cape Town	6,011	Los Angeles	5,439	Tripoli	1,468
Caracas	4,639	Madrid	773	Tunis	1,137
Casablanca	1,300	Malta	1,305	Turin (Caselle)	570
Chicago (O'Hare)	3,941	Manila	6,685	Valencia	826
Cologne	331	Marseilles	614	Vancouver	4,707
Colombo	5,411	Mauritius	6,075	Venice (Tessera)	715
Copenhagen	608	Mexico City	5,529	Vienna (Schwechat)	790
Dakar	2,706	Milan	609	Warsaw	912
Damascus	2,223	Montego Bay	4,687	Washington	3,665
Dar-es-Salaam	4,662	Montevideo	6,841	Wellington	11,692
Darwin	8,613	Montreal (Mirabel)	3,241	Zagreb	848
Delhi	4,180	Moscow (Sheremetievo)	1,557	Zürich	490

OBITUARIES

SEPT. 1, 1988–AUG. 31, 1989

Abell, Sir George, K.C.I.E., O.B.E., former civil servant, *aged* 84—Jan. 11.

Acton, 3rd Baron, C.M.G., M.B.E., T.D., *aged* 81—Jan. 23.

Adamson, George, conservationist, *aged* 83—*killed*, Aug. 20.

Ailwyn, 4th Baron, T.D., *aged* 91—Sept. 27, 1988.

Alvarez, Prof. Luis, American physicist and Nobel laureate, *aged* 77—Sept. 1, 1988.

Anderson, Lt.-Col. Charles, V.C., *aged* 91—Nov. 11, 1988.

Andrewes, Sir Christopher, F.R.S., virologist, *aged* 92—Dec. 31, 1988.

Andrews, Harry, C.B.E., actor, *aged* 77—March 7.

Annigoni, Pietro, Italian painter, *aged* 77—Oct. 28, 1988.

Ayer, Sir Alfred, philosopher, *aged* 78—June 27.

Baker White, John, Conservative M.P. for Canterbury 1945–53, *aged* 86—Dec. 10, 1988.

Balfour of Inchrye, 1st Baron, M.C., P.C., Conservative politician, *aged* 90—Sept. 21, 1988.

Ball, Lucille, American comedienne, *aged* 77—April 27.

Basnett, Lord (David), trade unionist, *aged* 64—Jan. 25.

Biddulph, 4th Baron, *aged* 57—Nov. 3, 1988.

Biggs-Davison, Sir John, M.P., Conservative M.P. for Chigwell 1955–74 and Epping Forest since 1974, *aged* 70—Sept. 17, 1988.

Bowden, Lord PH.D., former civil servant, *aged* 79—July.

Boyd, Sir John, C.B.E., general secretary of the A.U.E.W. 1975–82, *aged* 71—April 30.

Brewis, John, Conservative M.P. for Galloway 1959–74, and Lord Lieutenant of Wigtown since 1981, *aged* 69—May 25.

Brewster, Kingman, former ambassador and Master of University College, Oxford since 1986, *aged* 69—Nov. 8, 1988.

Brown, Pamela, author, actress and producer, *aged* 64—Jan. 26.

Buhler, Robert, R.A., painter, *aged* 72—June 20.

Bush, Hon. Mr. Justice (Sir Brian), Judge of the High Court (Family Division) since 1976, *aged* 63—April 3.

Byron, 12th Baron, D.S.O., *aged* 89—June 15.

Cairns, Rear-Adm. (5th) Earl, G.C.V.O., C.B., Marshal of the Diplomatic Corps 1962–71, *aged* 79—March 21.

Carlsson, Bernt, U.N. Commissioner for Namibia since 1987, *aged* 50—*killed in Lockerbie air crash*, Dec. 21, 1988.

Carradine, John, American actor, *aged* 82—Nov. 27, 1988.

Cassavetes, John, American actor and director, *aged* 59—Feb. 3.

Cavan, 12th Earl of, *aged* 77—Nov. 17, 1988.

Chatwin, Bruce, author, *aged* 48—Jan. 18.

Chelwood, Lord, M.C. (Tufton Beamish), Conservative M.P. for Lewes 1945–74, *aged* 72—April 6.

Church, Charles, house builder, *aged* 46—*killed accidentally*, July 1.

Clanwilliam, 6th Earl of, *aged* 74—March 30.

Cooper of Stockton Heath, Lord, trade unionist, *aged* 80—Sept. 2, 1988.

Crofton, 6th Baron, *aged* 40—June 27.

Crook, 1st Baron, *aged* 88—March 10.

Cross, Rt. Rev. Stewart, Bishop of Blackburn 1982–88, *aged* 61—April 6.

Cross of Chelsea, Lord, P.C., Lord of Appeal 1971–75, *aged* 84—Aug. 4.

Dali, Salvador, Spanish artist, *aged* 84—Jan. 23.

Darwen, 2nd Baron, *aged* 73—Dec. 9, 1988.

Davis, Air Chief Marshal Sir John, *aged* 77—Feb. 3.

de Ferranti, Basil, Conservative M.E.P. for Hampshire West 1974–84 and Hampshire Central since 1984, *aged* 58—Sept. 24, 1988.

de Manio, Jack, broadcaster, *aged* 74—Oct. 28, 1988.

Devonshire, Dowager Duchess of, G.C.V.O., C.B.E., Mistress of the Robes to the Queen 1953–66 and Chancellor of Exeter University 1956–70, *aged* 93—Dec. 24, 1988.

Dexter, Keith, C.B., Second Crown Estate Commissioner since 1983, *aged* 61—April 8.

Dorati, Antal, composer and conductor, *aged* 82—Nov. 13, 1988.

Downshire, 7th Marquess, *aged* 94—March 28.

du Maurier, Dame Daphne, D.B.E., writer, *aged* 81—April 19.

Easton, Adm. Sir Ian, K.C.B., D.S.O., *aged* 71—June.

Elliot, Capt. Walter, Conservative M.P. for Carshalton 1960–74, *aged* 78—Sept. 1988.

Enniskillen, 6th Earl of, M.B.E., *aged* 70—May 30.

Evans, Albert, Labour M.P. for West Islington 1947–50 and South West Islington 1950–70, *aged* 85—Dec. 4, 1988.

ffolkes, Michael, cartoonist and illustrator, *aged* 63—Oct. 18, 1988.

Fletcher-Cooke, Sir John, C.M.G., Conservative M.P. for Southampton, Test 1964–66, *aged* 77—May 19.

Fraser, Tom, Labour M.P. for Hamilton 1943–67 and Minister of Transport 1964–65, *aged* 77—Nov. 21, 1988.

Fraser of Tullybelton, Lord, P.C., former law lord, *aged* 78—Feb. 17.

Gaitskill, Baroness (Dora), *aged* 88—July 1.

Gower, Sir Raymond, M.P., Conservative M.P. for Barry 1951–83 and for Vale of Glamorgan since 1983, *aged* 72—Feb. 22.

Graham, Sheilah, gossip columnist, *aged* 84—Nov. 17, 1988.

Gretton, 3rd Baron, *aged* 48—April 4.

Gromyko, Andrei, Soviet politician and diplomat, *aged* 79—July 2.

Guérisse, Maj.-Gen. Count Albert (Pat O'Leary), G.C., HON. K.B.E., D.S.O., Allied World War II escape-line organizer, *aged* 77—March 26.

Gurden, Sir Harold, Conservative M.P. for Birmingham Selly Oak 1955–74, *aged* 85—April 27.

Halliwell, Leslie, film reference book author, *aged* 59—Jan. 21.

Harding of Petherton, Field Marshal Lord (1st Baron), G.C.B., C.B.E., D.S.O., M.C., *aged* 92—Jan. 20.

Hargreaves, Roger, author of *Mr. Men* books, *aged* 53—Sept. 11, 1988.

Harvey, Joe, footballer, *aged* 70—Feb. 24.

Hawtrey, Charles, actor, *aged* 73—Oct. 27, 1988.

Hicks, Sir John, F.B.A., economist and Nobel laureate, *aged* 85—May 20.

Hill of Luton, Baron, P.C., M.D., wartime broadcaster, Conservative politician, chairman of the I.T.A. and the B.B.C., *aged* 85—Aug. 22.

Hirohito, Emperor of Japan 1926–1989, *aged* 87—Jan. 6.

Homewood, Bill, Labour M.P. for Kettering 1979–83, *aged* 68—Jan.

Hosking, Julian, ballet dancer, *aged* 36—March.

Household, Geoffrey, author, *aged* 87—Oct. 4, 1988.

Houseman, John, American film producer and actor, *aged* 86—Oct. 1988.

Hu Yaobang, former general secretary of the Chinese Communist Party, *aged* 73—April 15.

Huxley, Sir Leonard, K.B.E., physicist, *aged* 86—Sept. 3, 1988.

Hyde, H. Montgomery, author, politician and lawyer, *aged* 81—Aug. 10.

Inglewood, 1st Baron, T.D., Conservative politician, *aged* 80—June 22.

Issigonis, Sir Alec, C.B.E., F.R.S., car designer, *aged* 81—Oct. 2, 1988.

Jackley, Nat, comedian, *aged* 79—Sept. 17, 1988.

James, C.L.R., Trinidadian author and historian, *aged* 88—May 31.

James, Emrys, actor, *aged* 58—Feb.

John, Brynmor, M.P., Labour M.P. for Pontypridd since 1970 and a junior minister 1974–79, *aged* 54—Dec. 13, 1988.

Kádár, János, Hungarian leader 1956–88, *aged* 77—July 6.

Kahn, Lord, C.B.E., economist, *aged* 83—June 6.

Karajan, Herbert von, conductor, *aged* 81—July 16.

Kendrew, Maj.-Gen. Sir Douglas, K.C.M.G., C.B., C.B.E., D.S.O., Governor of Western Australia 1963–73, *aged* 78—Feb. 28.

Khomeini, Ayatollah Sayyed Ruhollah, Iranian leader, *aged* 86—June 3.

Kidd, Dame Margaret, D.B.E., Q.C., Scotland's first woman advocate, *aged* 89—March 22.

Kinnear, Roy, actor, *aged* 54—Sept. 20, 1988.

Laing, R.D., psychoanalyst and writer, *aged* 61—Aug. 23.

Lambert, 2nd Viscount, *aged* 79—May 24.

Langan, Peter, restaurateur, *aged* 47—Dec. 7, 1988.

Laroche, Guy, French couturier, *aged* 66—Feb. 17.

Layton, 2nd Baron, *aged* 76—Jan. 23.

Lee of Asheridge, Baroness (Jennie Lee), *aged* 84—Nov. 16, 1988.

Lemnitzer, Gen. Lyman, Supreme Allied Commander Europe 1963–69, *aged* 89—Nov. 12, 1988.

Lillie, Beatrice, comedienne, *aged* 94—Jan. 20.

Lindsay, 15th Earl, *aged* 63—Aug. 1.

Lorenz, Prof. Konrad, Austrian psychologist, *aged* 85—Feb. 27.

McAnally, Ray, actor, *aged* 63—June 15.

MacAndrew, 2nd Baron, *aged* 69—July 9.

McNair, 2nd Baron, deputy S.L.D. Whip in House of Lords, *aged* 74—*killed accidentally*, Aug. 6.

McTaggart, Robert, M.P., Labour M.P. for Glasgow Central since 1980, *aged* 43—March 23.

Marshall, Arthur, broadcaster and writer, *aged* 78—Jan. 27.

Martonmere, 1st Baron, G.B.E., K.C.M.G., P.C., Conservative M.P. 1931–64 and Governor of Bermuda 1964–72, *aged* 82—May 3.

Mee, Margaret, botanical artist, *aged* 79—*killed accidentally*, Nov. 30, 1988.

Merrison, Sir Alec, Vice-Chancellor of Bristol University 1969–84, *aged* 64—Feb. 19.

Midleton, 11th Viscount, *aged* 85—Oct. 30, 1988.

Milburn, Jackie, footballer, *aged* 64—Oct. 9, 1988.

Miles, Alfred, G.C., *aged* 89—May 27.

Mills, 2nd Viscount, *aged* 69—Dec. 6, 1988.

Monks, Connie, Conservative M.P. for Chorley 1970–74, *aged* 78—Feb. 4.

Moore, Ray, radio presenter, *aged* 47—Jan. 11.

Morony, Gen. Sir Thomas, K.C.B., O.B.E., *aged* 62—May 27.

Morris, Rev. Marcus, O.B.E., founder and editor of *Eagle*, *aged* 73—March 16.

Murray, Gen. Sir Horatius, G.C.B., K.B.E., D.S.O., *aged* 85—July 2.

Newcastle, 9th Duke of, O.B.E., *aged* 81—Nov. 4, 1988.

Newcastle, 10th Duke, entomologist, *aged* 68—Dec. 25, 1988.

Norstad, Gen. Lauris, Supreme Allied Commander Europe 1956–62, *aged* 81—Sept. 12, 1988.

Northumberland, 10th Duke, K.G., G.C.V.O., P.C., F.R.S., Lord Steward of H.M. Household since 1973, *aged* 74—Oct. 11, 1988.

Ogdon, John, pianist, *aged* 52—Aug. 1.

Olivier, Lord (Laurence), O.M., actor, *aged* 82—July 11.

Onassis, Christina, shipping heiress, *aged* 37—Nov. 19, 1988.

Orbison, Roy, pop singer, *aged* 52—Dec. 6, 1988.

Palmer, Col. Hon. Sir Gordon, K.C.V.O., O.B.E., T.D., Lord Lieutenant for Berkshire since 1978, *aged* 70—July 3.

Panchen Lama, Tibetan religious leader, *aged* 50—Jan. 28.

Parr, Gladys, opera singer, *aged* 97—Nov. 4, 1988.

Perkins, Sir Robert, Conservative M.P. for Stroud 1931–45 and Stroud and Thornbury 1950–55, *aged* 85—Dec. 8, 1988.

Petre, 17th Baron, *aged* 74—Jan. 1.

Powis, 6th Earl of, *aged* 84—Oct. 7, 1988.

Ranfurly, 6th Earl of, K.C.M.G., *aged* 75—Nov. 6, 1988.

Revie, Don, football mannager, *aged* 61—May 26.

Roberthall, Lord, K.C.M.G., C.B., former civil servant, *aged* 87—Sept. 17, 1988.

Robinson, 'Sugar' Ray, boxer, *aged* 67—April 12.

Russell-Smith, Dame Enid, D.B.E., former civil servant, *aged* 83—July 12.

Rutherford, Charles, V.C., *aged* 97—June 11.

St. Albans, 13th Duke, O.B.E., *aged* 73—Oct. 8, 1988.

Scott, Sir Peter, C.H., C.B.E., D.S.C., conservationist, *aged* 79—Aug. 29.

Scott, Sheila, O.B.E., aviator, *aged* 61—Oct. 21, 1988.

Segrè, Emilio, American physicist and Nobel laureate, *aged* 84—April 22.

Singh, Nagendra, President of the International Court of Justice since 1985, *aged* 74—Dec. 11, 1988.

Sitwell, Sir Sacheverell, Bt. C.H., author, *aged* 90—Oct. 1, 1988.

Smith, Doug, former jockey, *aged* 71—April 11.

Smith, Michael, cookery writer and television presenter, *aged* 61—Jan. 20.

Sopwith, Sir Thomas, C.B.E., aviator and aircraft designer, *aged* 101—Jan. 27.

Stephenson, Sir William, M.C., D.F.C., chief of British security co-ordination in U.S.A. 1940–46, *aged* 93—Jan. 31.

Stephenson, William, racehorse trainer, *aged* 77—Nov. 29, 1988.

Stone, Irving, American novelist, *aged* 86—Aug. 26.

Strathclyde & Campbell, 5th Baron, *aged* 86—Oct. 1988.

Strauss, Franz Josef, President of Bavaria since 1978, *aged* 73—Oct. 3, 1988.

Tait, Air Vice-Marshal Sir Victor, K.B.E., C.B., *aged* 96—Nov. 27, 1988.

Taylor, Sir Charles, T.D., Conservative M.P. for Eastbourne 1935–74, *aged* 79—March 29.

Thomas, Rt. Rev. Francis, R.C. Bishop of Northampton since 1982, *aged* 58—Dec. 25, 1988.

Thomas, Jeffrey, Q.C., Labour/S.D.P. M.P. for Abertillery 1970–83, *aged* 55—May 17.

Tinbergen, Prof. Nikolaas, F.R.S., naturalist and Nobel laureate, *aged* 81—Dec. 21, 1988.

Topolski, Feliks, artist and writer, *aged* 82—Aug. 24.

Trinder, Tommy, comedian, *aged* 80—July 10.

Tuchman, Barbara, American historian, *aged* 77—Feb.

Tuttle, Air Marshal Sir Geoffrey, K.B.E., C.B., D.F.C., *aged* 82—Jan. 11.

Urquhart, Maj.-Gen., R. E. (Roy), C.B., D.S.O., *aged* 87—Dec. 13, 1988.

Vreeland, Diana, fashion editor—Aug. 22.

Wade, Lord, Liberal M.P. 1950–64, *aged* 84—Nov. 6, 1988.

Walpole, 9th Baron, *aged* 75—Feb. 25.

Walsh, Dr. Tom, founder of Wexford Festival Opera, *aged* 76—Nov. 8, 1988.

Wankel, Felix, German engine designer, *aged* 86—Oct. 9, 1988.

Washbourne, Mona, actress, *aged* 84—Nov. 15, 1988.

Worth, Harry, comedian, *aged* 71—July 20.

Zita, Empress of Austria-Hungary 1916–18, *aged* 96—March 14.

CENTENARIES

One Hundred Years Ago (1890).—A selection follows of "Remarkable Occurrences" (as "Events of the Year" was then called) as printed in the 1891 and 1892 editions of *Whitaker's Almanack* covering the year 1890.

January

1. Robert Browning, the poet, buried in Westminster Abbey.

— Calamitious fire at Forest Gate Industrial School; 26 children perished by suffocation.

7. Strike of upwards of 200 men employed in the East India Dock tea warehouses.

— The Limerick and Waterford Railway Servants struck for increased wages, which were conceded.

10. Jubilee of Penny Postage.

12. Portugal having surrendered to the ultimatum of England on the East African question, the windows of the British Consulate at Lisbon were broken and the escutcheon torn down.

13. The Prince of Wales presided at a dinner to promote the creation of a fund for the relief of lepers in the British dominions.

21. Meeting in Birmingham in support of a movement to establish a bishopric for Birmingham and Coventry.

22. Opening of a miners' conference at Birmingham.

24. The first train, with directors and their friends, passed over the Forth Bridge.

26. Fierce gale throughout the United Kingdom. The passenger ship *Paris*, from Dieppe to Newhaven, reached Dover on the 27th, after a perilous passage of nearly 40 hours.

28. The electric light inaugurated in the British Museum.

30. A resolution in favour of free education passed by the London School Board.

February

3. The action of "Parnell *v.* Walter," in relation to the Piggott letters, settled by a payment of £5,000 to Mr. Parnell.

4. Commencement of the trial of the Bishop of Lincoln on charges of unlawful practices in the administration of the Sacrament.

6. Over 170 persons killed by an explosion in the Llanerch Colliery, near Newport.

7. The Duc d'Orléans having unexpectedly presented himself at the War Office in Paris, was arrested and charged with having entered France in violation of the law against pretenders.

11. Miss Cobden and Miss Cons take their seats in the London County Council.

12. The Duc d'Orléans sentenced to two years' imprisonment.

13 The Parnell Commission report issued.

17. A deputation of the Miners' National Federation received by the Home Secretary.

18. At a fire in Lambeth a woman was run over by an engine and a fireman killed by the fall of a wall.

— Lord R. Churchill received a deputation of the Miners' National Federation in regard to the Eight Hours Bill in Parliament.

24. The United States House of Representatives decide on Chicago as the site of the World's Fair in 1892.

25. Arguments concluded and judgment deferred in the case of the Bishop of Lincoln.

27. The Court of Appeal rejected an appeal against a fine imposed by Mr. Justice Butt for contempt in commenting on the divorce suit of O'Shea *v.* Parnell.

March

4. The Prince of Wales, accompanied by the Duke of Edinburgh and Prince George of Wales, opened the new Forth Railway Bridge.

6. Memorial to Sir Erskine May unveiled in the House of Commons.

7. A resolution opposing Imperial federation unanimously carried in the Quebec House of Assembly.

9. Great demonstration in Hyde Park to denounce the cruel treatment of prisoners in Siberia.

15. First sitting of the International Labour Conference at Berlin, the Prussian Minister of Commerce presiding.

17. Prince Bismarck resigned his offices and the Chancellorship of the German Empire.

— Many thousand colliers struck work in the northern counties.

19. General von Caprivi appointed to the Chancellorship of Germany.

20. Settlement of the great coal strike, the terms of the men being granted.

28. The steamer *City of Paris*, much overdue from New York, reached Queenstown in tow of another steamer.

— Publication of the new Education Code, abolishing payment by results.

April

7. Opening of a railway to be worked by water power between Lynton and Lynmouth.

9. Meeting of the Country Brewers' Society at Cannon Street Hotel to protest against the duty on beer.

15. The Earl of Carlisle opened the museum presented to Sheffield by Mr. Ruskin.

23. Rioting in Biala, in Galicia; 20 persons killed and others wounded.

25. Great strike of railway men in Ireland.

26. Arrival in London of Mr. H. M. Stanley.

May

2. Reception of Mr. H. M. Stanley at St. James's Hall.

3. End of the railway strike in Ireland.

4. Great labour demonstration in Hyde Park in favour of an eight hours' labour law.

5. Mr. H. M. Stanley received the Royal Geographical Society's gold medal at the Albert Hall.

6. The Queen received Mr. Stanley at Windsor Castle.

— A hundred women burnt to death in a lunatic asylum at Montreal.

19. Mr. J. Chamberlain re-elected President of the Birmingham Liberal Unionist Association.

21. The Queen's 72nd birthday celebrated.

23. The *Gazette* notified that the Queen had conferred a peerage on Prince Albert Victor under the title of Duke of Clarence and Avondale and Earl of Athlone.

26. First performance this year of the Oberammergau Passion Play.

28. Professor Tyndall delivered an animated speech at Guildford condemning Mr. Gladstone's Home Rule policy.

29. Fifteen Nihilists arrested in Paris charged with the manufacture of explosives.

June

3. The Duc d'Orléans released and conducted to the Swiss frontier.

7. Demonstration in Hyde Park against the Government Licensing Bill.

17. The *Official Gazette* of Berlin published the heads of an agreement between the British and German Governments in respect of their claims in Africa.

28. Mr. H. M. Stanley's book, "In Darkest Africa" published.

30. The cession of Heligoland announced.

July

1. The Anglo-German Convention with respect to Africa and Heligoland signed in Berlin.

7. Threatened strike of the Metropolitan Police: rioting in Bow Street, and dismissal of 40 men for insubordination.

— The men of the 2nd Battalion of Grenadier Guards, quartered in Wellington Barracks, complaining of excessive duty, refused to attend parade.

8. The Prince of Wales laid the foundation stone of the Royal College of Music at Kensington.

12. The new encampment of the National Rifle Association opened at Bisley Common, when the Prince of Wales fired the first shot.

— Wedding of Mr. Stanley at Westminster Abbey.

15. Celebration of the 25th anniversary of the Salvation Army held at the Crystal Palace; 100,000 persons assembled.

18. Court-martial opened at Wellington Barracks to inquire into the insubordination of the Grenadier Guards.

21. The Duke of Cambridge paraded the Guards at Wellington Barracks, and spoke warmly of the disgrace they had brought on themselves by the recent insubordination. Next day they embarked for Bermuda.

— News received in London of a war in Central America, the State of Guatemala having invaded the State of Salvador.

26. The Empress Dock at Southampton opened by the Queen.

— A revolution broke out at Buenos Aires, followed by three days' fighting, with the loss of upwards of 1,000 lives.

August

9. Heligoland formally transferred to Germany.

12. Miss Gladys Knowles awarded £10,000 damages for breach of promise against the proprietor of the *Matrimonial News*.

13. Strike of all the men employed on the Cardiff Railway.

17. Mass meeting of railway servants at Glasgow to obtain a reduction in working hours.

18. Davis Dalton, an American, swam from Cape Grisnez to Folkestone in 23½ hours.

19. Solemn requiem mass over the remains of Cardinal Newman in the Oratory Church at Edgbaston.

22. Publication of the Convention between England and Portugal in respect of Central Africa.

26. The British East Africa Equatorial Railway formally inaugurated at Mombassa.

29. The new Science and Art Museum at Dublin opened by the Lord Lieutenant.

September

1. Meeting of the annual Trade Union Congress at Liverpool.

4. At Liverpool the Trade Union Congress passed a resolution in favour of the Eight Hours movement.

8. Serious strike of dock labourers at Southampton.

11. Revolution in the Swiss Canton of Ticino; a provisional government set up to last only one day.

15. Alarming fire at Farringdon Street Station, on the Metropolitan Railway.

21. Revolution in Manipur, the Maharaja taking refuge in the British Residency.

23. Frank Slavin and J. M'Auliffe charged with being about to break the peace by engaging in a glove fight in Walworth.

27. The glove fight between Slavin and M'Auliffe resulted in the defeat of the latter after a brief contest.

28. A man shot himself in St. Paul's Cathedral during divine service.

October

4. The remains of the man who shot himself in St. Paul's Cathedral cremated at Woking.

9. Messrs. Dillon and O'Brien, having to appear on the morrow on the resumption of the Tipperary prosecutions, embarked in a small yacht and proceeded to Cherbourg, where they landed on the 15th.

13. An unusual service of "Reconciliation" held in St. Paul's Cathedral after its defilement by a suicide.

21. Mr. Gladstone commenced a tour in Midlothian, speaking at Edinburgh on the question of Ireland.

— The Dutch States General met to appoint a Regent in place of the King.

24. Strike of labourers in the Royal Albert Docks.

25. Messrs. Dillon and O'Brien embarked at Hâvre for New York.

27. Two judges in the Queen's Bench decided that Mr. Conybeare, M.P., was disqualified from the London School Board by reason of his conviction and imprisonment for conspiracy in Ireland.

29. The Dutch States General declared the King incapacitated, but deferred appointing a Regent.

November

2. Messrs. Dillon and O'Brien arrived in New York.

4. The Prince of Wales inaugurated a new underground railway to be worked by electricity between the City and Stockwell.

— Official notification published in the *Gazette* of an agreement with the Sultan of Zanzibar, placing his dominions under the Protectorate of England.

14–15. Panic in the Money Market; suspension of the house of Baring Bros. averted by the prompt action of the Bank of England, assisted by various other banks.

15. In a divorce suit of "O'Shea *v.* O'Shea and Parnell, M.P.," a decree *nisi* was granted, with costs against the respondent and co-respondent.

21. The Archbishop of Canterbury delivered judgement in the case of the Bishop of Lincoln:—that the mixed chalice is not unlawful if the mixture be not made in the sight of the congregation; that the adoption of the north side of the table is not illegal; that there is no illegality in having two lighted candles, but making the sign of the cross at the final benediction is not justifiable.

24. Judgment for £150 given agaist Miss Cobden for acting as a member of the London County Council, for which, being a woman, she was not qualified.

25–26. Meetings of the Irish Parliamentary party to discuss the expediency of Mr. Parnell's retirement from the position of leader.

28. Mr. Parnell issued a manifesto "To the People of Ireland."

December

3. Irish Roman Catholic Archbishops and Bishops met in Dublin and declared against Mr. Parnell.

4. King of the Netherlands buried—service held in Dutch Church, London.

8. Queen Emma of Holland took oaths as regent and as guardian of Queen Wilhelmina.

10. Enthusiastic reception of Mr. Parnell in Dublin; Mr. Parnell seized *United Ireland*.

— Guildhall meeting protested against Russian persecution of Jews.

15. Archbishop Walsh issued manifesto against Parnell.

18. City and South London Electrical Railway under the Thames opened.

22. Scottish railway strike began, 4,500 struck.

30. Conference at Boulogne between O'Brien and Parnell.

31. Skating on Thames at Windsor.

THE CENTENARIES OF 1990

1890
Deaths
July 29   Vincent van Gogh, Dutch artist.
Oct. 20   Sir Richard Burton, explorer.
Nov. 8   César Franck, French composer.

Births
Feb. 10   Boris Pasternak, Russian writer.
March 12   Vaslav Nijinski, Russian dancer.
Sept. 15   Dame Agatha Christie, writer.
Oct. 1   Stanley Holloway, entertainer.
Oct. 14   Dwight D. Eisenhower, American general and President.
Nov. 22   Charles de Gaulle, French general and President.

Events
March 4   Opening of Forth Railway Bridge.

1790
Deaths
March 5   Flora Macdonald.
April 17   Benjamin Franklin, American statesman and scientist.
July 17   Adam Smith, Scottish economist.

1690
July 1   Battle of the Boyne.

THE CENTENARIES OF 1991

1891
Deaths
Jan. 16   Léo Delibes, French composer.
April 7   Phineas T. Barnum, American showman.

Sept. 28   Herman Melville, American novelist and poet.
Oct. 6   Charles Stewart Parnell, Irish politician.

Births
April 2   Max Ernst, German artist.
April 23   Sergei Prokofiev, Russian composer.
Aug. 2   Sir Arthur Bliss, composer and Master of the Queen's Music 1953–1975.
Aug. 6   Field Marshal Viscount Slim.

1791
Deaths
March 2   John Wesley, founder of Methodism.
April 2   Comte de Mirabeau, French statesman.
May 2   Giacomo Meyerbeer, German composer.
Dec. 5   Wolfgang Amadeus Mozart, Austrian composer.

Births
Jan. 28   Louis Hérold, French composer.
April 27   Samuel Morse, American inventor of the electric telegraph and Morse code.
Sept. 22   Michael Faraday, physicist and chemist.

Events
Dec. 4   First publication of *The Observer*.

1691
Deaths
Dec. 30   Robert Boyle, chemist and philosopher.

1591
Bapt.
Aug. 24   Robert Herrick, poet.

1491
Births
*   Saint Ignatius Loyola, founder of the Jesuits.
June 28   Henry VIII.

1291
Events
Aug. 1   Swiss Confederation founded.

1191
Events
July 12   Capture of Acre by Crusaders.

* Exact date unknown.

WEDDING ANNIVERSARIES

First	Cotton	Twentieth	China
Second	Paper	Twenty-fifth	Silver
Third	Leather	Thirtieth	Pearl
Fourth	Fruit and Flower	Thirty-fifth	Coral
Fifth	Wood	Fortieth	Ruby
Sixth	Sugar	Forty-fifth	Sapphire
Seventh	Wool	Fiftieth	Gold
Tenth	Tin	Sixtieth	Diamond
Twelfth	Silk and Fine Linen	Seventieth	Platinum
Fifteenth	Crystal		

PRIME MINISTERS AND SPEAKERS

PRIME MINISTERS SINCE 1782

Marquess of Rockingham, *Whig*, March 27, 1782.
Earl of Shelburne, *Whig*, July 13, 1782.
Duke of Portland, *Coalition*, April 4, 1783.
William Pitt, *Tory*, Dec. 7, 1783.
Henry Addington, *Tory*, March 21, 1801.
William Pitt, *Tory*, May 16, 1804.
Lord Grenville, *Whig*, Feb. 10, 1806.
Duke of Portland, *Tory*, March 31, 1807.
Spencer Perceval, *Tory*, Dec. 6, 1809.
Earl of Liverpool, *Tory*, June 16, 1812.
George Canning, *Tory*, April 30, 1827.
Viscount Goderich, *Tory*, Sept. 8, 1827.
Duke of Wellington, *Tory*, Jan. 26, 1828.
Earl Grey, *Whig*, Nov. 24, 1830.
Viscount Melbourne, *Whig*, July 13, 1834.
Sir Robert Peel, *Tory*, Dec. 26, 1834.
Viscount Melbourne, *Whig*, March 18, 1835.
Sir Robert Peel, *Tory*, Sept. 6, 1841.
Lord John Russell, *Whig*, July 6, 1846.
Earl of Derby, *Tory*, Feb. 28, 1852.
Earl of Aberdeen, *Peelite*, Dec. 28, 1852.
Viscount Palmerston, *Liberal*, Feb. 10, 1855.
Earl of Derby, *Conservative*, Feb. 25, 1858.
Viscount Palmerston, *Liberal*, June 18, 1859.
Earl Russell, *Liberal*, Nov. 6, 1865.
Earl of Derby, *Conservative*, July 6, 1866.
Benjamin Disraeli, *Conservative*, Feb. 27, 1868.
W. E. Gladstone, *Liberal*, Dec. 9, 1868.
Benjamin Disraeli, *Conservative*, Feb. 21, 1874.
W. E. Gladstone, *Liberal*, April 28, 1880.
Marquess of Salisbury, *Conservative*, June 24, 1885.
W. E. Gladstone, *Liberal*, Feb. 6, 1886.
Marquess of Salisbury, *Conservative*, Aug. 3, 1886.
W. E. Gladstone, *Liberal*, Aug. 18, 1892.
Earl of Rosebery, *Liberal*, March 3, 1894.
Marquess of Salisbury, *Conservative*, July 2, 1895.
A. J. Balfour, *Conservative*, July 12, 1902.
Sir H. Campbell-Bannerman, *Liberal*, Dec. 5, 1905.
H. H. Asquith, *Liberal*, April 8, 1908.
H. H. Asquith, *Coalition*, May 26, 1915.
D. Lloyd-George, *Coalition*, Dec. 7, 1916.
A. Bonar Law, *Conservative*, Oct. 23, 1922.
S. Baldwin, *Conservative*, May 22, 1923.
J. R. MacDonald, *Labour*, Jan. 22, 1924.
S. Baldwin, *Conservative*, Nov. 4, 1924.
J. R. MacDonald, *Labour*, June 8, 1929.
J. R. MacDonald, *Coalition*, Aug. 25, 1931.
S. Baldwin, *Coalition*, June 7, 1935.
N. Chamberlain, *Coalition*, May 28, 1937.
W. S. Churchill, *Coalition*, May 11, 1940.
W. S. Churchill, *Conservative*, May 23, 1945.
C. R. Attlee, *Labour*, July 26, 1945.
Sir W. S. Churchill, *Conservative*, Oct. 26, 1951.
Sir A. Eden, *Conservative*, April 6, 1955.
H. Macmillan, *Conservative*, Jan. 13, 1957.
Sir A. Douglas-Home, *Conservative*, Oct. 19, 1963.

J. H. Wilson, *Labour*, Oct. 16, 1964.
E. R. G. Heath, *Conservative*, June 19, 1970.
J. H. Wilson, *Labour*, March 4, 1974.
L. J. Callaghan, *Labour*, April 5, 1976.
Mrs. M. H. Thatcher, *Conservative*, May 4, 1979.

SPEAKERS OF THE COMMONS SINCE 1660

PARLIAMENT OF ENGLAND

1660 Sir Harbottle Grimston.
1661 Sir Edward Turner.
1673 Sir Job Charlton.
1673 Sir Edward Seymour.
1678 Sir Robert Sawyer.
1679 Sir William Gregory.
1680 Sir William Williams.
1685 Sir John Trevor.
1688 Henry Powle.
1694 Paul Foley.
1698 Sir Thomas Lyttelton.
1700 Robert Harley (*Earl of Oxford and Mortimer*).
1702 John Smith.

PARLIAMENT OF GREAT BRITAIN

1708 Sir Richard Onslow (*Lord Onslow*).
1710 William Bromley.
1713 Sir Thomas Hanmer.
1715 Spencer Compton (*Earl of Wilmington*).
1727 Arthur Onslow.
1761 Sir John Cust.
1770 Sir Fletcher Norton.
1780 Charles Cornwall.
1788 Hon. William Grenville (*Lord Grenville*).
1789 Henry Addington (*Viscount Sidmouth*).

PARLIAMENT OF UNITED KINGDOM

1801 Sir John Mitford (*Lord Redesdale*).
1802 Charles Abbot (*Lord Colchester*).
1817 Charles M. Sutton (*Viscount Canterbury*).
1835 James Abercromby (*Lord Dunfermline*).
1839 Charles Shaw-Lefevre (*Viscount Eversley*).
1857 J. Evelyn Denison (*Viscount Ossington*).
1872 Sir Henry Brand (*Viscount Hampden*).
1884 Arthur Wellesley Peel (*Viscount Peel*).
1895 William C. Gully (*Viscount Selby*).
1905 James W. Lowther (*Viscount Ullswater*).
1921 John H. Whitley.
1928 Hon. Edward A. FitzRoy.
1943 Col. D. Clifton Brown (*Viscount Ruffside*).
1951 William S. Morrison (*Viscount Dunrossil*).
1959 Sir Harry Hylton-Foster.
1965 Horace M. King, PH.D. (*Lord Maybray-King*).
1971 Selwyn Lloyd (*Lord Selwyn-Lloyd*).
1976 George Thomas (*Viscount Tonypandy*).
1983 (Bruce) Bernard Weatherill.

NATIONAL PRODUCT
Categories of expenditure and factor incomes

£ million

	1983	1984	1985	1986	1987
Categories of expenditure at current market prices					
Consumers' expenditure	184,619	197,494	215,267	236,756	258,431
General government final consumption	65,873	69,884	73,995	79,685	85,772
of which: central government	40,661	43,165	45,976	49,089	51,689
local authorities	25,212	26,719	28,019	30,596	34,083
Gross domestic fixed capital formation	48,615	55,025	60,283	63,797	70,767
Value of physical increase in stocks and work in progress	1,465	1,561	569	572	627
Total domestic expenditure	300,572	323,964	350,114	380,810	415,597
Exports of goods and services	80,541	92,349	102,782	98,484	107,506
of which: Goods	60,698	70,263	77,988	72,678	79,422
Services	19,843	22,086	24,794	25,806	28,084
Total final expenditure	381,113	416,313	452,896	479,294	523,103
less imports of goods and services[1]	−77,895	−92,988	−99,166	−101,582	−112,030
of which: Goods	−61,773	−74,843	−80,334	−81,394	−89,584
Services	−16,122	−18,145	−18,832	−20,188	−22,446
Gross domestic product (expenditure based)[2]	303,218	323,325	353,730	377,712	411,073
Statistical discrepancy (expenditure adjustment)[3]	−270	775	527	1,103	3,382
Gross domestic product (average estimate)[2]	302,948	324,100	354,257	378,815	414,455
Net property income from abroad	2,847	4,433	2,800	5,079	5,523
Gross national product (average estimate)	305,795	328,533	357,057	383,894	419,978
Factor cost adjustment					
Taxes on expenditure	49,460	52,585	56,724	62,700	67,980
Subsidies	6,269	7,538	7,202	6,106	5,762
Factor cost adjustment (taxes less subsidies)	43,191	45,047	49,522	56,594	62,218
Factor incomes					
Income from employment	169,580	180,096	194,573	209,542	226,343
Income from self-employment[4]	24,523	27,149	28,302	30,485	32,959
Gross trading profits of companies[4,5]	39,810	45,085	53,500	51,358	65,596
Gross trading surplus of public corporations	9,918	8,267	7,020	8,016	6,623
Gross trading surplus of general government enterprises	50	−92	256	105	−177
Rent	18,775	19,849	21,619	23,261	24,798
Imputed charge for consumption of non-trading capital	2,473	2,594	2,808	3,067	3,235
Total domestic income[4]	265,129	282,948	308,078	325,834	359,377
less stock appreciation	−4,204	−4,206	−2,816	−2,005	−4,858
Gross domestic product (income-based)	260,925	278,742	305,262	323,829	354,519
Statistical discrepancy (income adjustment)[3]	−1,168	311	−527	−1,608	−2,282
Gross domestic product (average estimate) at factor cost	259,757	270,053	304,735	322,221	352,237
Net property income from abroad	2,847	4,433	2,800	5,079	5,523
Gross national product (average estimate)	262,604	283,486	307,535	327,300	357,760
less Capital consumption	−36,150	−38,686	−41,899	−45,165	−48,238
Net national product at factor cost (average estimate): "National income"	226,454	244,800	265,636	282,135	309,522
Value indices, at current prices (1985 = 100)					
Gross domestic product (expenditure-based)					
At market prices	85·7	91·4	100·0	106·8	116·2
At factor cost	85·5	91·5	100·0	105·6	114·7
Gross domestic product (income-based) at factor cost	85·5	91·3	100·0	106·1	116·1
Gross domestic product (average estimate)					
At market prices ("money GDP")	85·5	91·5	100·0	106·9	117·0
At factor cost	85·2	91·6	100·0	105·7	115·6

[1] Excluding taxes on expenditure levied on imports.
[2] Including taxes on expenditure levied on imports.
[3] The statistical discrepancies are each part of the residual error.
[4] Before providing for depreciation and stock appreciation.
[5] Including financial institutions.

GROSS DOMESTIC PRODUCT BY INDUSTRY

(Before depreciation but after stock appreciation)

£ million

	1981	1982	1983	1984	1985	1986	1987
Agriculture, forestry and fishing...	4,775	5,412	5,274	6,229	5,565	5,947	5,901
Energy and water supply..........	23,519	26,049	30,112	30,091	32,436	23,575	24,184
Manufacturing (revised definition)	54,498	59,165	61,725	66,424	72,688	78,222	85,552
Construction	12,837	14,116	15,643	16,896	18,101	19,380	21,524
Distribution; hotels and catering;							
repairs	27,247	30,223	33,174	36,300	40,907	45,673	48,963
Transport	10,244	10,724	11,629	12,436	13,233	14,483	16,227
Communication	5,648	6,530	6,654	7,367	8,142	8,886	9,688
Banking, finance, insurance,							
business services and leasing	27,962	32,068	36,056	40,188	47,475	55,590	63,903
Ownership of dwellings	13,895	15,044	15,944	16,734	17,963	19,170	20,180
Public administration, national							
defence and compulsory social							
security	16,247	17,376	18,815	20,184	21,598	23,068	24,895
Education and health services	20,586	21,308	23,351	24,483	25,959	28,858	31,681
Other services	11,990	13,330	15,029	16,492	18,017	20,223	22,366
Total	229,448	251,345	273,406	293,824	322,084	343,075	375,064
Adjustment for financial services ..	−11,732	−13,320	−12,481	−15,082	−16,822	−19,246	−20,545
Statistical discrepancy (income							
component)....................	93	−728	−1,168	311	−527	−1,608	−2,282
Gross domestic product (average							
estimate)	217,809	237,297	259,757	279,053	304,735	322,221	352,237

GENERAL GOVERNMENT CURRENT ACCOUNT

£ million

	1981	1982	1983	1984	1985	1986	1987
Receipts							
Taxes on income	36,249	40,392	43,484	46,791	51,603	52,158	55,601
Taxes on expenditure	42,465	46,467	49,460	52,585	56,724	62,700	67,980
Social security contributions	15,916	18,095	20,780	22,312	24,191	26,033	28,449
Gross trading surplus*	236	216	50	−92	256	105	−177
Rent, dividends and interest, etc. ..	9,171	10,149	9,933	10,501	11,786	9,968	10,172
Miscellaneous current transfers ...	177	187	222	217	229	262	317
Imputed charge for consumption of							
non-trading capital	1,935	1,999	2,056	2,162	2,350	2,582	2,732
Total..........................	106,149	117,505	125,985	134,476	147,139	153,808	165,074
Expenditure							
Final consumption	55,457	60,446	65,873	69,884	73,995	79,685	85,772
Subsidies	6,369	5,811	6,269	7,538	7,202	6,106	5,762
Social security benefits	27,002	31,677	32,434	34,483	37,620	40,830	41,826
Other current grants to personal							
sector	4,240	4,907	7,409	8,546	9,137	9,899	10,652
Current grants paid abroad (net)...	1,607	1,789	1,930	2,099	3,332	2,233	3,287
Debt interest	12,703	13,973	14,189	15,756	17,474	17,191	17,667
Total current expenditure	107,378	118,603	128,104	138,306	148,760	155,944	164,966
Balance: current surplus*	−1,229	−1,098	−2,119	−3,830	−1,621	−2,136	108
Total..........................	106,149	117,505	125,985	134,476	147,139	153,808	165,074

* Before depreciation.

HOME FINANCE

Central government funds and accounts transactions   £ million

| | Consolidated Fund | | | National Loans Fund | | | | Central government borrowing requirement |
| | | | | | Other transactions | | | |
	Revenue	Expenditure	Consolidated fund surplus/deficit	Receipts	Payments	Borrowing required	Other funds and accounts	
1985	104,193	110,497	−6,304	13,899	19,226	11,631	−173	11,804
1986	110,867	113,305	−2,438	14,984	20,397	7,851	−610	8,461
1987	119,517	120,712	−1,195	16,345	21,345	6,195	2,184	4,010
1988	129,738	125,865	3,873	17,697	21,532	−38	4,506	−4,544
Financial years								
1986–87	111,211	116,451	−5,240	15,614	21,251	10,877	−381	10,496
1987–88	122,969	120,562	2,407	16,406	20,538	1,725	843	882
1988–89	133,592	128,002	5,590	18,239	22,217	−1,612	5,284	−6,896
1989 1st quarter . .	40,183	34,011	6,172	5,274	6,739	−4,707	−341	−4,366
2nd quarter .	30,520†	32,076†	−1,556†	3,855†	4,876†	2,577†	571†	2,006†
1988 June	8,899	8,394	505	742	1,078	−169	−1,199	1,030
July	11,109	10,818	291	2,070	2,403	42	1,304	−1,262
August	10,024	12,070	−2,046	1,400	754	1,400	1,743	−343
September . .	11,148	10,024	1,124	1,674	1,535	−1,263	−2,436	1,173
October	11,489	11,380	109	1,519	2,272	644	1,582	−938
November . .	10,027	10,849	−822	1,737	2,131	1,216	396	820
December . .	10,740	9,977	763	794	1,067	−490	1,635	−2,125
1989 January . . .	18,937	10,629	8,308	2,135	2,293	−8,150	−1,346	−6,804
February . . .	10,234	10,150	84	557	2,606	1,965	1,503	462
March	11,012	13,232	−2,220	2,582	1,840	1,478	−498	1,976
April	10,008	9,586	422	419	2,223	1,382	1,755	−373
May	9,947	12,152	−2,205	2,555	2,003	1,653	360	1,293
June	10,565	10,338	227	881	650	−458	−1,544	1,086

Public sector borrowing requirement   £ million

	Total		Contributions by			Financed by				
						Non-bank private sector		Monetary sector/Overseas sector		
									External finance		
	Not Seasonally adjusted	Seasonally adjusted†	Central government*	Local authorities	Public corporations	Notes and coin	Other	Borrowing in sterling from banks	Foreign currency borrowing from banks	Direct external finance
1985	7,474	7,511	11,804	3,371	959	528	7,816	−2,408	403	1,811
1986	2,419	3,527	8,420	5,210	791	768	4,499	−972	44	533
1987	−1,463	−1,558	4,102	4,734	831	768	6,358	776	−365	−6,730
1988	−11,603	−11,773	−4,544	4,347	2,712	1,164	−7,057	−611	−571	−1,824
Financial years										
1986–87	3,395	3,395	10,452	5,734	1,323	−211	4,257	986	254	1,117
1987–88	−3,484	−3,499	882	2,860	1,506	1,786	4,367	−61	−1,342	−6,974
1988–89	−14,381	—	−6,896	4,525	2,960	530	−8,441	−3,348	299	−136
1988 1st quarter	−2,925	−1,733	−2,014	−389	1,300	362	−880	−567	−766	−1,297
2nd quarter	−1,565	−2,912	145	1,543	167	−103	479	−1,074	−132	428
3rd quarter	−2,108	−3,240	−432	886	790	431	−786†	−806	6	−803
4th quarter	−5,005	−3,888	−2,243	2,307	455	474	−5,870	1,836	321	−152
1989 1st quarter	−5,703	—	−4,366	−211	1,548	−272	−2,264	−3,304	104	391
2nd quarter	228	—	2,006	972	806	—	—	—	—	—

†Financial year constrained.   *An increase in debt is shown positive.

PERSONAL INCOME AND EXPENDITURE (£ million)

	1982	1983	1984	1985	1986	1987
Income before tax						
Income from employment:						
Wages and salaries	133,340	142,348	151,829	164,978	178,781	194,098
Pay in cash and kind of HM Forces	2,905	3,121	3,288	3,590	3,833	4,093
Total.........................	136,245	145,469	155,117	168,568	182,614	198,191
Employers' contributions:						
Social Security	9,344	10,536	11,268	12,244	13,362	14,657
Other	13,032	13,575	13,711	13,761	13,566	13,495
Total income from employment ...	158,621	169,580	180,096	194,573	209,542	226,343
Income from self-employment:						
After deducting stock						
appreciation	21,704	23,973	26,841	27,813	30,197	32,485
Stock appreciation	362	550	308	489	288	474
Total[1]	22,066	24,523	27,149	28,302	30,485	32,959
Rent, dividends and net interest:						
Receipts by life assurance and						
pension schemes	10,505	11,785	14,017	15,872	17,498	19,370
Imputed rent of owner-occupied						
dwellings.....................	10,160	11,181	11,917	12,783	13,810	14,632
Other receipts, net	2,297	2,503	833	664	−41	−108
Total.........................	22,962	25,469	26,767	29,319	31,267	33,894
Social security benefits and other current grants from general						
government	36,584	39,843	43,029	46,757	50,729	52,478
Current transfers from overseas	1,248	1,448	1,588	1,689	1,668	1,566
Current transfers to charities from						
companies	69	86	105	119	151	185
Imputed charge for capital consumption of private non-profit making						
bodies.........................	409	417	432	458	485	503
Total personal income[1]	241,959	261,366	279,166	301,217	324,327	347,928
Deductions from income						
U.K. taxes on income	31,396	33,230	34,612	37,559	40,918	44,074
Social security contributions	18,095	20,780	22,312	24,191	26,033	28,449
Current transfers abroad	1,200	1,179	1,261	1,436	1,615	1,782
Miscellaneous current transfers	187	222	217	229	262	317
Personal disposable income[2]	191,081	205,955	220,764	237,802	255,499	273,306
Expenditure						
Consumers' expenditure	168,545	184,619	197,494	215,267	236,756	258,431
Balance saving[2]	22,536	21,336	23,270	22,535	18,743	14,875
Total.........................	191,081	205,955	220,764	237,802	255,499	273,306
Memorandum items						
Saving ratio (per cent)[3]	*11.8*	*10.4*	*10.5*	*9.5*	*7.3*	*5.4*
Real personal disposable income[4]						
At 1985 prices...................	221,709	227,931	232,426	237,802	244,797	252,185
1985 = 100......................	93.2	95.8	97.7	100.0	102.9	106.0

[1] Before providing for depreciation and stock appreciation.
[2] Before providing for depreciation, stock appreciation and additions to tax reserves.
[3] Saving as a percentage of personal disposable income.
[4] Personable disposable income revalued by the implied consumers' expenditure deflator (1985 = 100).

HOUSEHOLDS AND THEIR EXPENDITURE[1]

(United Kingdom)

	1983	1984	1985	1986
Number of households supplying data	6,973	7,081	7,012	7,178
Total number of persons	18,532	18,557	18,206	18,330
Total number of adults[2]	13,401	13,618	13,401	13,554
Household percentage distribution by tenure				
Rented unfurnished	*35·8*	*35·4*	*34·9*	*33·9*
Rented furnished	*2·9*	*2·7*	*2·5*	*3·0*
Rent-free	*2·2*	*1·8*	*2·1*	*2·0*
Owner-occupied	*59·2*	*60·1*	*60·5*	*61·1*
Average number of persons per household				
All persons	2·658	2·621	2·596	2·554
Males	1·289	1·266	1·258	1·236
Females	1·369	1·355	1·339	1·317
Adults[2]	1·922	1·923	1·911	1·888
Persons under 65	1·562	1·572	1·552	1·526
Persons 65 and over	0·360	0·351	0·359	0·362
Children[2]	0·736	0·698	0·685	0·665
Children under 2	0·080	0·068	0·077	0·073
Children 2 and under 5	0·123	0·114	0·114	0·118
Children 5 and under 18	0·533	0·516	0·495	0·474
Persons working	1·172	1·179	1·164	1·160
Persons not working	1·485	1·442	1·433	1·394
Men 65 and over, women 60 and over	0·403	0·399	0·407	0·403
Others	1·082	1·043	1·026	0·991
Average weekly household expenditure on commodities and services (£)				
Housing[3]	23·99	24·06	26·63	29·92
Fuel, light and power	9·22	9·42	9·95	10·43
Food	29·56	31·43	32·70	34·97
Alcoholic drink	6·91	7·25	7·95	8·21
Tobacco	4·21	4·37	4·42	4·55
Clothing and footwear	10·00	11·10	11·92	13·46
Durable household goods	10·26	11·57	11·61	13·83
Other goods	10·81	11·89	12·59	13·87
Transport and vehicles	20·96	22·77	24·56	25·43
Services	16·09	17·41	19·48	22·67
Miscellaneous	0·58	0·64	0·68	0·74
Total	142·59	151·92	162·50	178·10
Expenditure on commodity or service as a percentage of total expenditure (per cent)				
Housing[3]	*16·8*	*15·8*	*16·4*	*16·8*
Fuel, light and power	*6·5*	*6·2*	*6·1*	*5·9*
Food	*20·7*	*20·7*	*20·1*	*19·6*
Alcoholic drink	*4·8*	*4·8*	*4·9*	*4·6*
Tobacco	*3·0*	*2·9*	*2·7*	*2·6*
Clothing and footwear	*7·0*	*7·3*	*7·3*	*7·5*
Durable household goods	*7·2*	*7·6*	*7·2*	*7·8*
Other goods	*7·6*	*7·9*	*7·8*	*7·8*
Transport and vehicles	*14·7*	*15·0*	*15·1*	*14·3*
Services	*11·3*	*11·5*	*12·0*	*12·7*
Miscellaneous	*0·4*	*0·4*	*0·4*	*0·4*
Total	*100·0*	*100·0*	*100·0*	*100·0*

[1] Information derived from the Family Expenditure Survey.

[2] Adults = all persons 18 and over and married persons under 18.
Children = all unmarried persons under 18.

[3] Excludes mortgage payments but includes imputed expenditure (i.e. the weekly equivalent of rateable value). Figures on housing for 1983 and 1984 are not comparable because of the introduction of the Housing Benefit Scheme.

VALUE OF UNITED KINGDOM IMPORTS (cif)
Analysis by sections and divisions (£ million)

	1984	1985	1986	1987*
Total U.K. imports	78,967·4	85,027·0	86,175·5	94,015·7
Food and live animals chiefly for food	7,820·4	8,106·5	8,718·6	8,724·8
Live animals chiefly for food	196·8	238·3	293·4	236·5
Meat and meat preparations	1,342·2	1,400·9	1,465·3	1,562·2
Dairy products and birds' eggs	604·6	606·3	653·2	617·8
Fish, crustaceans and molluscs, and preparations thereof	537·8	600·4	747·8	759·2
Cereals and cereal preparations	629·0	713·2	769·3	741·2
Vegetables and fruit	1,930·3	2,037·1	2,184·4	2,394·0
Sugar, sugar preparations and honey	524·3	508·1	530·3	521·2
Coffee, tea, cocoa, spices, and manufactures thereof	1,291·4	1,205·7	1,220·6	997·2
Feeding-stuff for animals (not including un-milled cereals)	501·5	487·4	527·3	506·5
Miscellaneous edible products and preparations	262·6	309·0	326·9	389·0
Beverages and tobacco	1,112·5	1,230·8	1,346·7	1,433·2
Beverages	705·5	843·6	1,007·9	1,105·4
Tobacco and tobacco manufactures	407·1	387·2	338·7	327·9
Crude materials, inedible, except fuels	4,884·9	4,856·8	4,622·4	5,183·5
Hides, skins and furskins, raw	235·3	238·9	216·4	264·1
Oil seeds and oleaginous fruit.................	234·8	238·8	271·3	255·0
Crude rubber (including synthetic and reclaimed)	223·5	228·3	203·5	227·1
Cork and wood	1,009·3	895·3	1,000·3	1,198·5
Pulp and waste paper	611·7	505·9	523·3	657·2
Textile fibres (other than wool tops) and their wastes (not manufactured into yarn or fabric)	596·7	662·8	546·9	633·5
Crude fertilizers and crude minerals (excluding coal, petroleum and precious stones)........	312·6	354·1	317·1	286·6
Metalliferous ores and metal scrap	1,343·8	1,371·8	1,139·5	1,222·9
Crude animal and vegetable materials	317·3	361·0	404·1	438·6
Mineral fuels, lubricants and related materials	10,333·8	10,663·6	6,400·4	6,117·0
Petroleum, petroleum products and related materials	8,219·8	8,316·2	4,461·3	4,493·3
Coal, coke, gas and electric current	2,114·0	2,347·4	1,939·1	1,623·7
Animal and vegetable oils, fats and waxes ..	533·2	531·5	365·1	427·0
Total manufactured goods	53,010·7	58,312·2	62,825·3	70,984·0
Chemicals and related products	6,322·1	6,900·8	7,345·3	8,330·4
Organic chemicals...........................	1,874·4	1,893·8	1,830·7	2,025·9
Inorganic chemicals	709·8	897·0	951·4	987·3
Dyeing, tanning and colouring materials	269·7	310·9	396·5	448·2
Medicinal and pharmaceutical products	542·3	590·4	679·7	786·3
Essential oils and perfume materials; toilet, polishing and cleansing materials	377·1	443·3	480·3	554·5
Fertilizers, manufactured	219·4	217·3	213·2	210·6
Explosives and pyrotechnic products	19·0	20·0	22·0	24·1
Artificial resins and plastic materials, and cellulose esters and ethers	1,609·4	1,763·5	1,985·2	2,415·9
Chemical materials and products, not elsewhere specified..................................	700·8	764·6	786·4	877·6

* provisional figures.

Value of United Kingdom Imports (cif) (£ million)—*Continued*

	1984	1985	1986	1987*
Total U.K. imports	78,967·4	85,027·0	86,175·5	94,015·7
Manufactured goods classified chiefly by material	13,447·4	14,342·3	15,328·1	16,970·3
Leather, leather manufactures, nes, and dressed furskins	245·1	250·3	247·9	299·4
Rubber manufactures, nes	457·1	527·4	589·2	682·5
Cork and wood manufactures (excluding furniture)	622·1	632·0	687·8	784·6
Paper, paperboard, and articles of paper pulp, of paper or of paperboard	2,280·4	2,532·0	2,702·8	3,238·2
Textile yarn, fabrics, made-up articles, nes, and related products	2,705·4	3,032·0	3,162·4	3,497·6
Non-metallic mineral manufactures, nes	2,269·3	2,242·6	2,661·7	2,747·6
Iron and steel	1,487·2	1,715·5	1,796·2	1,890·1
Non-ferrous metals	1,996·2	1,903·4	1,835·7	1,942·5
Manufactures of metal, nes	1,384·4	1,507·2	1,644·5	1,887·8
Machinery and transport equipment	23,781·7	26,937·5	28,765·7	32,795·2
Power generating machinery and equipment	1,782·4	1,997·5	2,237·3	2,513·3
Machinery specialised for particular industries	2,078·6	2,327·3	2,362·7	2,856·8
Metalworking machinery	432·7	525·1	645·7	567·7
General industrial machinery and equipment, nes, and machine parts, nes	2,249·9	2,603·9	2,757·2	3,012·2
Office machines and automatic data processing equipment	4,102·7	4,510·0	4,542·1	5,431·2
Telecommunications, sound recording and re-producing apparatus and equipment	1,848·3	2,130·6	2,401·6	2,801·4
Electrical machinery, apparatus and appliances, nes, and electrical parts thereof (including non-electrical counterparts, nes, of electrical household type equipment)	3,846·7	4,276·9	4,445·9	5,051·8
Road vehicles (including air cushion vehicles)	5,957·6	6,800·6	7,938·8	8,807·2
Other transport equipment	1,482·9	1,765·6	1,434·5	1,753·6
Miscellaneous manufactured articles	9,459·5	10,131·6	11,386·1	12,888·1
Sanitary, plumbing, heating and lighting fixtures and fittings, nes	151·2	177·2	216·6	254·5
Furniture and parts thereof	591·6	662·8	776·0	878·1
Travel goods, handbags and similar containers	161·9	174·9	199·9	230·9
Articles of apparel and clothing accessories	2,011·7	2,090·1	2,386·1	2,778·4
Footwear	642·0	671·1	734·4	799·3
Professional, scientific and controlling instruments and apparatus, nes	1,593·8	1,761·5	1,790·0	1,903·6
Photographic apparatus, equipment and supplies and optical goods, nes, watches and clocks	1,068·7	1,173·0	1,285·6	1,357·9
Miscellaneous manufactured articles, nes	3,238·7	3,420·9	3,997·5	4,685·4
Commodities and transactions not classified elsewhere	1,271·8	1,325·7	1,897·0	1,146·2

nes   not elsewhere specified.   * provisional figures.

VALUE OF UNITED KINGDOM EXPORTS (fob)
Analysis by sections and divisions (£ million)

	1984	1985	1986	1987*
Total U.K. exports	70,488·3	78,391·8	72,987·7	79,851·4
Food and live animals chiefly for food	3,114·8	3,252·4	3,745·8	3,730·4
Live animals chiefly for food	191·0	262·0	299·9	325·8
Meat and meat preparations	491·1	497·4	521·9	626·0
Dairy products and birds' eggs	246·6	281·3	331·5	314·1
Fish, crustaceans and molluscs, and preparations thereof	224·4	260·3	328·9	407·2
Cereals and cereal preparations	992·7	833·0	1,177·5	831·2
Vegetables and fruit	190·8	205·3	251·7	300·3
Sugar, sugar preparations and honey	165·7	220·8	170·4	218·6
Coffee, tea, cocoa, spices and manufactures thereof	363·4	390·8	364·0	377·5
Feeding-stuff for animals (not including un-milled cereals)	96·8	121·8	139·3	155·8
Miscellaneous edible products and preparations	152·3	179·7	160·6	173·9
Beverages and tobacco	1,577·9	1,719·1	1,737·9	1,861·4
Beverages	1,157·0	1,253·7	1,331·6	1,411·6
Tobacco and tobacco manufactures	420·9	465·4	406·3	449·8
Crude materials, inedible, except fuels	1,898·1	2,032·1	1,940·9	1,925·9
Hides, skins and furskins, raw	280·3	288·5	260·2	311·5
Oil seeds and oleaginous fruit.................	54·0	90·4	155·5	86·2
Crude fertilizers and crude minerals (excluding coal, petroleum and precious stones).........	249·1	269·2	271·9	340·6
Cork and wood	25·5	25·7	22·9	26·0
Pulp and waste paper	27·2	24·7	25·0	33·9
Textile fibres (other than wool tops) and their wastes (not manufactured into yarn or fabric)	427·9	419·4	373·0	397·0
Crude fertilisers and crude minerals (excluding coal, petroleum and precious stones).........	249·1	269·2	271·9	340·6
Metalliferous ores and metal scrap	591·4	645·8	538·9	451·1
Crude animal and vegetable materials	75·6	94·3	110·4	99·8
Mineral fuels, lubricants and related materials	15,308·4	16,795·5	8,671·9	8,769·0
Petroleum, petroleum products and related materials	14,851·8	16,133·9	8,207·9	8,465·8
Coal, coke, gas and electric current	456·8	661·6	464·0	303·1
Animal and vegetable oils, fats and waxes ..	91·0	95·9	105·3	263·5
Total manufactured goods	46,703·0	52,506·1	54,580·5	61,039·9
Chemicals and related products	8,216·8	9,411·7	9,676·8	10,519·7
Organic chemicals..........................	2,381·7	2,742·8	2,571·0	2,831·1
Inorganic chemicals	811·1	976·6	1,123·3	1,100·0
Dyeing, tanning and colouring materials	633·3	692·0	763·2	879·0
Medicinal and pharmaceutical products	1,222·4	1,427·0	1,532·7	1,620·7
Essential oils and perfume materials; toilet, polishing and cleansing materials	690·5	767·9	807·7	886·4
Fertilizers, manufactured	64·4	74·8	67·4	85·4
Explosives and pyrotechnic products	47·6	45·7	42·8	45·7
Artificial resins and plastic materials, and cellulose esters and ethers	1,179·8	1,330·7	1,401·1	1,553·1
Chemical materials and products, not elsewhere specified	1,186·0	1,351·3	1,367·5	1,518·1

* provisional figures.

Value of United Kingdom Exports (fob) (£ million)—*Continued*

	1984	1985	1986	1987*
Total U.K. exports	70,488·3	78,391·8	72,987·7	79,851·4
Manufactured goods classified chiefly by material	10,010·6	10,430·2	10,977·8	11,877·3
Leather, leather manufactures, nes, and dressed furskins	312·5	295·2	321·5	372·9
Rubber manufactures, nes	481·8	554·4	611·8	677·9
Cork and wood manufactures (excluding furniture)	104·6	84·1	77·2	85·6
Paper, paperboard, and articles of paper pulp, of paper or of paperboard	678·6	767·6	824·3	971·1
Textile yarn, fabrics, made-up articles, nes, and related products	1,484·8	1,709·1	1,711·5	1,886·2
Non-metallic mineral manufactures, nes	2,298·7	2,164·5	2,549·3	2,654·1
Iron and steel	1,528·9	1,856·2	1,866·5	2,186·0
Non-ferrous metals	1,656·7	1,379·6	1,551·3	1,502·2
Manufactures of metal, nes	1,464·1	1,619·6	1,464·5	1,541·3
Machinery and transport equipment	21,520·5	24,667·5	25,351·2	28,803·1
Power generating machinery and equipment	2,709·0	3,061·3	3,251·1	3,241·4
Machinery specialised for particular industries	2,676·8	3,077·6	3,101·1	3,300·5
Metalworking machinery	503·8	521·1	581·2	691·1
General industrial machinery and equipment, nes, and machine parts, nes	2,577·1	2,937·5	3,037·2	3,097·5
Office machines and automatic data processing equipment	3,046·6	3,746·7	3,561·9	4,483·2
Telecommunications and sound recording and reproducing apparatus and equipment	1,117·0	1,295·1	1,401·6	1,567·7
Electrical machinery, apparatus and appliances, nes, and electrical parts thereof (including non-electrical counterparts, nes, of electrical household type equipment)	2,805·3	3,380·1	3,382·6	3,786·1
Road vehicles (including air cushion vehicles)	3,318·8	3,910·6	3,953·5	4,876·8
Other transport equipment	2,766·1	2,737·4	3,080·9	3,758·9
Miscellaneous manufactured articles	6,955·0	7,996·8	8,574·7	9,839·8
Sanitary, plumbing, heating and lighting fixtures and fittings, nes	118·9	135·0	126·3	133·1
Furniture and parts thereof	282·0	357·7	356·3	394·7
Travel goods, handbags and similar containers	22·4	29·4	30·6	34·8
Articles of apparel and clothing accessories	996·3	1,171·7	1,228·2	1,428·8
Footwear	142·7	159·2	167·2	186·6
Professional, scientific and controlling instruments and apparatus, nes	1,777·6	2,151·7	2,283·7	2,328·5
Photographic apparatus, equipment and supplies and optical goods, nes, watches and clocks	694·2	817·3	843·3	976·2
Miscellaneous manufactured articles, nes	2,290·8	3,174·9	3,539·2	4,357·1
Commodities and transactions not classified elsewhere	1,795·3	1,990·7	2,205·5	2,261·3

nes not elsewhere specified.   * provisional figures.

EMPLOYMENT

Distribution of the workforce

Thousands

At mid-June	1983	1984	1985	1986	1987
United Kingdom					
Workforce[1]	26,610	27,265	27,797	27,985	28,206
Males	16,104	16,315	16,548	16,531	16,535
Females	10,506	10,950	11,249	11,454	11,671
Unemployed[2]	2,984	3,030	3,179	3,229	2,905
Males	2,145	2,120	2,197	2,217	2,023
Females	839	910	982	1,012	882
Workforce in employment[3]	23,626	24,235	24,618	24,756	25,301
Males	13,959	14,196	14,351	14,313	14,512
Females	9,667	10,040	10,267	10,442	10,789
HM Forces	322	326	326	322	319
Males	306	310	309	305	302
Females	16	16	16	16	16
Self-employed persons (with or without employees)[4]	2,221	2,496	2,610	2,627	2,861
Males	1,705	1,902	1,975	1,989	2,152
Females	516	594	635	637	709
Employees in employment	21,067	21,238	21,506	21,581	21,810
Males	11,940	11,888	11,966	11,891	11,881
Females	9,127	9,350	9,540	9,691	9,930
of whom					
Total, index of production and construction industries	7,217	7,062	6,977	6,766	6,650
Total, all manufacturing industries	5,525	5,409	5,366	5,236	5,145
Work Related Government Training Programmes[5]	16	175	176	226	311
Males	8	95	100	127	177
Females	8	80	76	99	134
Great Britain					
Workforce[1]	25,932	26,582	27,107	27,298	27,521
Males	15,693	15,903	16,133	16,118	16,125
Females	10,239	10,679	10,975	11,179	11,396
Unemployed[2]	2,871	2,911	3,057	3,103	2,780
Males	2,062	2,034	2,109	2,126	1,931
Females	809	877	948	978	848
Workforce in employment[3]	23,061	23,671	24,050	24,194	24,741
Males	13,631	13,869	14,023	13,993	14,193
Females	9,430	9,802	10,027	10,201	10,548
HM Forces	322	326	326	322	319
Males	306	310	309	305	302
Females	16	16	16	16	16
Self-employed persons (with or without employees)[4]	2,160	2,435	2,550	2,567	2,801
Males	1,652	1,850	1,923	1,937	2,099
Females	508	586	628	630	701
Employees in employment	20,572	20,741	21,006	21,088	21,289
Males	11,670	11,619	11,697	11,629	11,620
Females	8,901	9,123	9,309	9,460	9,669
of whom					
Total, index of production and construction industries	7,072	6,919	6,833	6,630	6,515
Total, all manufacturing industries	5,418	5,302	5,258	5,133	5,044
Work Related Government Training Programmes[5]	8	168	168	218	303
Males	3	91	94	122	171
Females	5	78	74	96	132

1. The workforce is the workforce in employment plus the claimant unemployed.
2. From April 1983 the figures of unemployment reflect the effects of the provisions in the Budget for some men aged 60 and over who no longer have to sign on at an unemployment office.
3. The workforce in employment comprises employees in employment, the self-employed, HM Forces and work-related government training programmes.
4. Estimates of the self-employed are based on the 1981 census and the results of the Labour Force Surveys.
5. Includes participants in the Youth Training Scheme except those who have contracts of employment, and participants in the Job Training Scheme. Additionally, for the UK this includes some participants on Northern Ireland Schemes: Youth Training Programme (excluding second year trainees in further education colleges); Job Training Programme; and Attachment Training Scheme participants and other management train scheme participants training with an employer.

RATES OF UNEMPLOYMENT[1]

Analysis by standard regions. Seasonally adjusted[2]   Percentages

Annual averages	1981	1982	1983	1984	1985	1986	1987
United Kingdom	8·5	9·8	10·8	11·0	11·2	11·4	10·2
Great Britain	8·4	9·7	10·6	10·9	11·1	11·2	10·0
North	12·2	13·6	14·9	15·6	15·7	15·4	14·3
Yorkshire and Humberside	9·4	10·7	11·7	12·0	12·3	12·7	11·6
East Midlands	7·7	8·8	9·8	10·1	10·1	10·3	9·2
East Anglia	6·6	7·7	8·3	8·2	8·2	8·4	7·0
South East	5·7	7·0	7·8	8·0	8·2	8·4	7·2
South West	7·1	8·1	9·0	9·3	9·6	9·8	8·4
West Midlands	10·4	12·2	13·1	13·0	13·0	12·8	11·3
North West	10·6	12·4	13·7	13·9	14·1	14·2	13·0
Wales	10·8	12·4	13·2	13·5	14·1	14·2	12·8
Scotland	10·4	11·7	12·6	13·0	13·3	13·7	13·3
Northern Ireland	13·1	14·7	15·8	16·2	16·4	17·9	17·9

1. The number of claimant unemployed as a percentage of the estimated total work force (the sum of claimant employees in employment, unemployed, self-employed, participants on work related government training programmes and HM Forces at mid-year.
2. Seasonally adjusted and excluding school leavers, consistent with current coverage.

Unemployment (Thousands)

	United Kingdom					
	Not seasonally adjusted		Seasonally adjusted*			
	Total	% rate	Males	Females	Total	% rate
1983................	3,104·7	11·7	2,012·3	778·1	2,790·5	10·4
1984................	3,159·8	11·7	2,058·2	862·4	2,920·6	10·7
1985................	3,271·2	11·8	2,114·3	921·4	3,035·7	10·9
1986................	3,289·1	11·8	2,148·3	958·9	3,107·2	11·1
1987................	2,953·4	10·6	1,971·0	851·3	2,822·3	10·1
1988................	2,370·4	8·7	1,607·2	687·3	2,294·5	8·2
1989 January	2,074·3	7·3	1,405·4	582·4	1,987·8	7·0
February	2,018·2	7·1	1,377·9	570·8	1,948·7	6·8
March	1,960·2	6·9	1,359·5	557·1	1,916·6	6·7
April	1,883·6	6·6	1,321·5	536·5	1,858·0	6·5
May	1,802·5	6·3	1,309·7	526·1	1,835·8	6·4
June	1,743·1	6·1	1,295·4	513·9	1,809·3	6·3

* The seasonally adjusted figures relate only to claimants aged 18 or over, in order to maintain the consistent series, available back to 1971, allowing for the effect of the change in benefit regulations for under 18 year-olds from September 1988.

Industrial Stoppages (Thousands)

	Workers beginning involvement in period in any dispute	Total working days lost						
		All industries and services	Coal, coke, mineral oil and natural gas	Metals, engineering and vehicles	Textiles, footwear and clothing	Construction	Transport and communication	All other industries and services
1983...............	573	3,754	591	1,420	32	68	295	1,348
1984...............	1,436	27,135	22,484	2,055	66	334	666	1,530
1985...............	643	6,402	4,143	590	31	50	197	1,391
1986...............	538	1,920	143	895	38	33	190	622
1987...............	884	3,546	217	458	50	22	1,705	1,095
1988...............	759	3,702	222	1,456	90	17	1,490	428
1989 January	13	42	4	9	—	1	17	11
February	18	59	2	15	5	6	16	16
March ...	21	74	2	36	—	3	—	33
April	36	89	5	26	—	10	20	28
May	32	171	4	68	5	14	38	42

HOUSING

Stock of dwellings (Great Britain)

	1984	1985	1986	1987*
Estimated annual gains and losses (thousands)				
Gains: New construction	203·4	188·7	198·0	202·8
Other	17·6	18·9	11·3	12·7
Losses: Slum clearance	12·4	12·1	9·1	10·1
Other	14·2	16·0	9·4	11·6
Net gain	194·4	179·5	190·8	193·8
Stock at end of year	21,716	21,896	22,093	22,287
Estimated tenure distribution at end of year (percentage)				
Owner occupied	*60·9*	*61·9*	*63·1*	*64·1*
Rented: From local authorities and new towns	*27·9*	*27·3*	*26·6*	*25·9*
From housing associations	*2·4*	*2·5*	*2·4*	*2·5*
From private owners including other tenures	*8·7*	*8·3*	*7·9*	*7·5*

*Provisional.

Permanent dwellings completed

	United Kingdom				England and Wales			
	Total	For local housing authorities	For private owners	Housing associations and other	Total	For local housing authorities	For private owners	Housing associations and other
1965	391,234	164,957	217,162	9,115	347,181	133,024	206,246	7,911
1975	321,936	150,526	154,528	16,882	278,694	122,857	140,381	15,456
1980	241,657	87,968	131,651	22,038	214,590	78,006	115,841	20,743
1981	206,542	68,139	118,507	19,896	179,759	58,215	103,929	17,615
1982	182,027	39,879	128,415	13,733	158,591	33,349	113,280	11,962
1983	206,513	38,830	151,035	16,648	178,980	31,300	132,886	14,794
1984	218,343	37,407	163,369	17,567	189,087	31,186	143,074	14,827
1985	202,912	30,292	159,006	13,614	173,735	24,248	137,617	11,870
1986	208,095	24,843	170,222	13,030	179,351	20,076	148,308	10,967
1987	212,652	21,279	178,283	13,090	185,173	16,876	156,919	11,378

	Scotland				Northern Ireland			
	Total	For local housing authorities	For private owners	Housing associations and other	Total	For local housing authorities	For private owners	Housing associations and other
1965	35,116	26,584	7,553	979	8,937	5,349	3,363	225
1975	34,323	22,784	10,371	1,168	8,919	4,885	3,776	258
1980	20,611	7,455	12,242	914	6,456	2,507	3,568	381
1981	20,015	7,065	11,021	1,929	6,768	2,859	3,557	352
1982	16,429	3,716	11,529	1,184	7,007	2,814	3,606	587
1983	17,941	3,486	13,178	1,277	9,592	4,044	4,971	577
1984	18,841	2,633	14,118	2,090	10,415	3,588	6,177	650
1985	18,376	2,811	14,449	1,116	10,801	3,233	6,940	628
1986	18,599	2,187	14,832	1,580	10,145	2,580	7,082	483
1987	17,810	2,639	13,913	1,258	9,669	1,764	7,451	454

AGRICULTURE

Estimated quantity of crops and grass harvested (thousand tonnes)

	1981	1982	1983	1984	1985	1986	1987
Cereals							
Wheat	8,710	10,320	10,800	14,970	12,050	13,910	n/a
Barley	10,230	10,960	9,980	11,070	9,740	10,010	n/a
Oats	620	575	465	515	615	505	n/a
Mixed corn for threshing	44	39	35	35	31	29	n/a
Rye for threshing	25	27	24	28	35	32	n/a
Potatoes							
Early crop‡	388	432	322	397	403	363	395*
Main crop‡	5,826	6,498	5,535	7,001	6,489	6,083	6,395*
Fodder crops							
Beans for stockfeeding	125	120	105	125	155	230	n/a
Turnips and swedes	4,795	4,575	3,655	3,960	3,300	3,855	n/a
Fodder beet and mangolds†	320	370	295	570	815	845	n/a
Maize for threshing or stockfeeding	635	635	550	580	770	915	n/a
Rape for stockfeeding, kale, cabbage, savoys and kohlrabi	2,195	1,985	1,660	1,805	1,555	1,380	n/a
Peas harvested dry for stockfeeding	—	—	85	170	215	330	n/a
Other crops							
Sugar beet	7,395	10,005	7,495	9,015	7,715	8,120	n/a
Rape grown for oilseed	325	580	565	925	895	965	n/a
Hops	9	10	9	8	6	5	5
Hay	6,775	6,550	6,000	5,700	4,650	4,675	n/a
Horticultural crops							
Vegetables grown in the open:							
Brussels sprouts	197	223	154	169	152	168	165
Cabbage (including savoys and spring greens)	546	610	518	670	683	688	690
Cauliflowers	325	353	298	344	356	360	384
Carrots	711	725	554	572	600	634	567
Parsnips	53	55	51	57	62	68	66
Turnips and swedes	109	145	135	142	142	163	159
Beetroot	97	105	94	115	114	95	94
Onions, dry bulb	232	231	175	238	268	247	305
Onions, salad	25	27	25	22	25	30	31
Leeks	40	43	44	53	60	71	77
Broad beans	17	19	17	21	19	14	11
Runner beans including French	69	92	65	77	66	67	50
Peas, green for market	25	28	23	27	26	20	19
Peas, green for processing	277	238	198	241	206	239	195
Celery	50	51	46	57	53	65	69
Lettuce	134	161	155	153	193	160	171
Rhubarb	41	39	29	26	26	28	29
Protected crops							
Tomatoes	125	118	118	129	116	137	132
Cucumbers	54	56	61	68	71	76	85
Lettuce	37	45	49	48	50	50	51
Fruit crops							
Total dessert apples	152	216	186	184	161	163	167
Total culinary apples	80	147	126	163	141	139	122
Pears	49	40	54	48	51	47	63
Plums	16	34	36	34	24	33	33
Cherries	3	7	3	5	5	4	4
Soft Fruit	105	109	124	114	111	109	110

‡ revised basis of calculation adopted in 1984 which prevents direct comparison with earlier years.
* provisional figures.
† from 1986 Scotland collected fodder beet separately.

Cattle, Sheep, Pigs and Poultry on Agricultural Holdings

Thousands

At June each year	1981	1982	1983	1984	1985	1986	1987
Cattle and calves: total	13,138	13,244	13,290	13,213	12,911	12,533	12,158
Dairy herd	3,191	3,250	3,333	3,281	3,150	3,138	3,042
Beef herd	1,420	1,389	1,358	1,351	1,333	1,308	1,343
Heifers in calf (first calf)	863	851	847	811	874	879	774
Bulls for service	84	84	83	80	78	76	74
Other cattle:							
Two years old and over	963	937	904	905	852	769	732
One year old and under two	3,041	3,057	3,059	3,069	3,012	2,819	2,749
Six months old and under one year	1,876	1,890	1,924	1,949	1,905	1,876	1,844
Under six months old	1,699	1,786	1,783	1,768	1,707	1,668	1,599
Sheep and lambs: total	32,097	33,067	34,069	34,802	35,628	37,016	38,701
Breeding ewes	12,528	12,909	13,310	13,648	13,893	14,252	14,780
Rams for service	358	366	383	393	406	419	437
Other sheep	3,584	3,748	3,764	3,680	3,763	3,961	4,107
Lambs under one year old	15,628	16,044	16,612	17,080	17,566	18,384	19,377
Pigs: total	7,828	8,023	8,174	7,689	7,865	7,937	7,942
Breeding herd	836	864	856	800	828	824	820
Boars for service	43	45	45	42	44	44	44
Gilts not yet in pig	87	89	82	77	80	79	81
Barren sows for fattening	11	12	15	12	12	12	11
Other pigs:							
110 kg and over	90	117	100	91	89	80	67
80 kg and under 110 kg	638	630	605	599	589	603	615
50 kg and under 80 kg	1,776	1,824	1,868	1,787	1,813	1,863	1,890
20 kg and under 50 kg	2,227	2,281	2,362	2,198	2,260	2,270	2,253
Under 20 kg	2,119	2,163	2,241	2,082	2,151	2,163	2,160
Poultry: total	132,286	135,363	127,618	127,507	128,968	—	—
Fowls: total	122,639	126,091	117,854	118,846	119,456	120,740	128,628
Growing pullets	14,219	14,766	11,828	12,536	12,503	12,502	12,230
Laying flock	44,473	44,792	41,127	40,573	39,538	38,096	38,498
Breeding flock	6,117	6,457	6,012	6,396	6,104	6,334	7,146
Table birds	57,830	60,075	58,887	59,341	61,311	63,807	70,754
Ducks*	1,333	1,443	1,566	1,566	1,648	1,741	1,735
Geese*	148	157	157				
Turkeys	8,167	7,672	8,198	7,134	7,864	—	—

*Excludes Scotland except from 1983 to 1986.

Agricultural land: area

Thousand hectares

	1981	1982	1983	1984	1985	1986	1987
Total tillage	5,071	5,127	5,124	5,196	5,265	5,287	5,312
All grasses under five years old	1,911	1,859	1,846	1,794	1,796	1,723	1,691
Total arable	6,982	6,986	6,970	6,990	7,061	7,010	7,003
All grasses five years old and over	5,103	5,097	5,107	5,105	5,019	5,077	5,112
Total crops and grass	12,085	12,083	12,078	12,095	12,080	12,088	12,115
Rough grazings							
Sole rights	5,021	4,984	4,927	4,895	4,872	4,829	4,743
Common (estimated)	1,214	1,214	1,212	1,212	1,216	1,216	1,214
Woodland on agricultural holdings	277	285	292	299	312	316	322
All other land on agricultural holdings	211	217	227	218	223	227	225
Total area of agricultural land	18,808	18,783	18,735	18,720	18,703	18,676	18,619
Total area of the United Kingdom	24,089	24,088	24,088	24,088	24,085	24,086	24,086

FISHERIES
Fishing fleet

Number

At December 31	1981	1982	1983	1984	1985	1986	1987p
England and Wales							
Trawlers	1,750	1,759	1,757	1,686	1,285	1,561	1,730
Seine nets	227	216	195	181	150	83	63
Lines	794	469	499	629	534	802	810
Purse seine	4	3	5	3	2	1	—
Other nets	133	89	111	114	99	257	183
Other and unknown	1,729	1,692	2,113	2,454	3,311	2,935	2,790
Scotland							
Total fishing vessels	2,370	2,233	2,214	2,180	2,198	2,183	2,263
Demersal trawl	339	315	291	244	253	235	253
Demersal pair trawl	72	70	76	104	116	122	132
Industrial trawl	9	19	17	12	10	6	6
Seine net	308	296	302	291	291	283	277
Lines	208	147	112	94	83	70	69
Purse seine	43	45	42	44	45	47	47
Pelagic trawl	35	34	26	23	20	12	7
Other nets*	22	27	43	48	46	43	32
Nephrops trawl	303	302	317	337	335	383	412
Other shellfishing†	1,031	978	988	983	999	982	1,028

p provisional figures only for England and Wales.
* Gill and cod nets, drift and ring nets.
† All shellfishing methods except nephrops trawl.

Landings of fish of British taking (Great Britain)

	Landed weight (Thousand tonnes)				Value (£ thousand)			
	1984	1985	1986	1987*	1984	1985	1986	1987*
Total all fish	733·7	762·1	716·9	788·3	297,863	323,825	361,680	434,906
Total wet fish	661·0	687·2	629·3	677·3	240,587	258,904	284,161	338,965
Demersal: total	395·0	402·3	383·2	379·3	211,713	227,175	256,705	304,068
Catfish	1·3	1·4	1·5	1·6	589	755	1,035	1,318
Cod	90·9	90·0	76·5	92·5	65,258	69,945	69,140	86,057
Dogfish	12·3	13·8	11·6	13·6	3,547	4,550	6,376	7,201
Haddock	107·5	132·2	131·0	102·1	64,204	67,757	79,019	78,080
Hake	2·5	2·7	3·0	3·2	2,794	3,851	4,549	5,540
Halibut	0·1	0·1	0·1	0·1	319	365	372	446
Lemon sole	5·7	5·7	5·0	5·1	5,972	7,137	8,265	9,021
Plaice	21·5	20·4	21·3	25·8	14,097	13,821	16,048	22,537
Redfish	0·4	0·2	0·1	0·2	98	75	56	62
Saithe (Coalfish)	12·1	14·4	17·7	15·3	2,759	3,874	6,361	7,078
Skate and ray	6·8	7·0	6·9	8·6	2,792	2,992	3,908	4,742
Sole	2·4	2·7	3·2	2·9	6,717	9,093	14,500	16,988
Turbot	0·5	0·5	0·6	0·7	1,660	1,976	2,607	3,611
Whiting	60·7	50·2	41·1	51·3	23,006	18,997	18,460	25,199
Livers	—	—	—	—	—	1	1	—
Roes	0·6	0·5	0·5	0·5	321	390	348	499
Other demersal	69·7	60·5	63·1	55·8	17,580	21,596	25,660	35,689
Pelagic: total	266·0	285·0	246·1	298·0	28,874	31,730	27,456	34,897
Herring	71·5	95·4	106·1	100·3	9,076	11,493	11,881	12,214
Mackerel	186·3	174·2	132·1	189·3	18,768	18,694	14,766	21,485
Other pelagic	8·2	15·4	7·9	8·3	1,030	1,543	809	1,198
Total shellfish	72·6	74·8	87·6	111·0	57,274	64,920	77,519	95,941
Cockles	5·4	7·8	19·4	39·0	311	476	1,165	4,286
Crab	14·0	13·5	12·6	13·5	8,422	8,557	9,599	11,399
Lobster	1·2	1·1	1·0	1·1	7,696	8,030	7,680	9,346
Mussels	4·3	5·8	6·3	4·9	314	467	541	543
Nephrop (Norway lobster)	22·2	24·8	25·4	24·2	24,545	31,548	39,119	43,010
Oysters	0·4	0·5	0·6	0·1	770	734	845	241
Shrimps	0·7	0·8	1·4	3·3	566	711	1,254	4,368
Whelks	2·2	1·6	2·0	2·7	456	355	418	665
Other shellfish	22·2	18·9	18·9	22·1	14,194	14,042	16,898	22,083

* Contains some provisional information.

MERCHANT SHIPPING

PRINCIPAL MERCHANT FLEETS OF THE WORLD. Source: *Lloyd's Register of Shipping*

Flag	1978 No.	1978 Gross Tonnage	1983 No.	1983 Gross Tonnage	1987 No.	1987 Gross Tonnage	1988 No.	1988 Gross Tonnage
Liberia	2,523	80,191,329	2,062	67,564,201	1,574	51,412,029	1,507	49,733,615
Panama	3,640	20,748,679	5,316	34,665,508	5,136	43,254,716	5,022	44,604,071
Japan	9,321	39,182,079	10,593	40,751,915	9,822	35,932,177	9,804	32,074,417
U.S.S.R.	7,991	22,261,927	7,753	24,549,350	6,705	25,232,091	6,741	25,783,869
Greece	3,666	33,956,993	3,169	37,477,642	1,948	23,559,852	1,874	23,788,820
*U.S.A.	4,746	16,187,636	6,437	19,358,496	6,427	20,172,236	6,442	20,832,137
Cyprus	793	2,985,829	1,593	3,870,941	1,541	15,650,207	1,352	18,390,642
China, People's Republic of	713	5,180,898	1,219	8,674,599	1,773	12,341,477	1,841	12,919,876
Norway	1,238	26,128,923	2,340	19,229,996	1,979	6,359,349	2,078	9,350,303
Philippines	577	1,264,995	884	2,964,472	1,394	8,681,227	1,483	9,311,555
Bahamas	93	84,989	122	860,952	469	9,105,182	572	8,962,893
United Kingdom	3,359	30,896,606	2,570	19,121,457	2,165	8,504,605	2,142	8,260,431
Italy	1,694	11,491,873	1,609	10,015,211	1,571	7,817,353	1,583	7,794,247
Korea (South)	1,148	2,975,389	1,733	6,386,002	1,899	7,214,070	1,930	7,333,704
Hong Kong	150	874,850	294	4,383,526	409	8,034,668	394	7,328,984
Singapore	954	7,489,205	855	7,009,106	700	7,098,116	715	7,208,498
India	591	5,759,224	677	6,226,646	803	6,725,776	797	6,160,773
Brazil	565	3,701,731	698	5,807,906	718	6,324,069	719	6,122,836
China, Republic of (Taiwan)	444	1,619,595	514	2,879,200	594	4,512,749	617	4,631,474
France	1,317	12,191,354	1,173	9,868,075	964	5,371,273	930	4,506,227
Denmark	1,397	5,530,408	1,112	5,115,097	1,256	4,873,485	1,240	4,401,122
Spain	2,753	8,056,080	2,589	7,504,690	2,350	4,249,487	2,343	4,336,609
Iran	208	1,194,675	220	1,594,942	375	4,949,873	375	3,917,257
Germany, Federal Republic of	1,999	9,956,667	1,769	6,994,961	1,414	4,317,616	1,233	3,774,298
Bermuda	99	1,814,655	67	819,450	105	1,925,297	116	3,726,464
Netherlands	1,238	5,181,392	1,287	4,939,806	1,307	3,908,231	1,265	3,560,736
Romania	239	1,428,041	379	2,390,764	430	3,263,823	462	3,489,449
Poland	796	3,490,587	812	3,686,127	719	3,469,670	714	3,476,354
Yugoslavia	468	2,365,630	479	2,546,638	498	3,164,893	499	3,281,153
Turkey	460	1,358,779	687	2,524,374	852	3,336,093	872	3,041,811
Gibraltar	4	832	48	231,122	113	2,827,098	107	2,902,394
Canada	1,289	2,954,499	1,300	3,384,677	1,238	2,971,155	1,225	2,685,888
Malta	47	101,541	147	906,736	271	1,725,984	356	2,365,923
Australia	426	1,531,739	578	2,022,481	690	2,404,559	709	2,269,398
Saudi Arabia	154	1,246,112	435	5,296,798	349	2,692,044	320	2,126,016
Indonesia	1,093	1,272,387	1,391	1,949,699	1,734	2,120,531	1,736	2,118,422
Belgium	268	1,684,692	322	2,273,503	350	2,268,383	344	2,116,079
Sweden	696	6,508,255	674	3,432,683	642	2,269,541	633	1,876,673
Argentina	432	2,000,879	532	2,469,686	434	1,901,026	451	1,608,155
Malaysia	182	552,466	376	1,475,048	498	1,688,523	499	1,448,335
Mexico	336	727,201	619	1,475,104	651	1,532,485	659	1,445,340
German Democratic Republic	452	1,539,994	427	1,461,177	377	1,584,039	389	1,392,381
Bulgaria	189	1,082,477	197	1,293,277	205	1,551,176	201	1,351,176
Egypt	205	456,291	351	662,567	428	1,074,192	431	1,226,725

*Including ships of the United States Reserve Fleet.

CLASSIFICATION WITH LLOYD'S REGISTER OF SHIPPING

Ships classed or to be classed with Lloyd's Register at June 30, 1988, totalled 8,711 with an aggregate of over 90 million gross tonnage.

MERCHANT SHIPPING

MERCHANT SHIPS COMPLETED IN THE WORLD DURING 1988

Source: *Lloyd's Register of Shipping*

Country of Build	Total No.	Gross Tonnage	For Registration in	Total No.	Gross Tonnage
Japan	598	4,040,199	Panama	93	2,980,306
Korea (South)	117	3,174,494	Liberia	42	1,389,674
Germany, Federal Republic of	55	521,156	Japan	480	1,042,149
China, Republic of (Taiwan)	8	452,896	Korea (South)	67	690,131
Denmark	38	376,886	Singapore	19	559,847
German Democratic Republic	27	292,221	U.S.S.R.	81	479,814
Poland	51	275,036	Bahamas	18	432,229
*China, People's Republic of	22	253,784	Denmark	45	426,868
Yugoslavia	22	251,043	United States of America	41	316,393
Finland	14	166,874	China, Republic of (Taiwan)	7	280,972
Spain	126	161,584	Poland	17	210,662
Italy	24	144,887	Norway	45	193,452
*Romania	8	91,146	Philippines	4	178,106
France	18	71,823	Italy	30	147,017
India	20	65,879	China, People's Republic of	20	129,148
Bulgaria	10	65,633	Spain	106	122,077
*U.S.S.R.	4	60,986	Germany, Federal Republic of	28	102,377
United Kingdom	31	59,975	Netherlands	53	96,000
Netherlands	74	59,232	Cyprus	5	94,750
Belgium	7	54,767	Mexico	5	92,759
Norway	56	52,589	Romania	7	87,268
Argentina	10	35,944	Greece	5	71,874
Sweden	22	28,037	Sweden	14	69,845
Brazil	13	25,419	India	33	67,724
Mexico	2	24,414	Finland	7	59,817
Austria	8	16,488	Belgium	10	57,042
Singapore	18	14,967	Kuwait	5	53,501
Turkey	14	12,207	France	24	52,175
Australia	41	10,858	Vanuatu	3	51,416
United States of America	60	10,765	German Democratic Republic	2	40,757
Portugal	12	10,669	Yugoslavia	5	38,720
Other Countries	45	26,522	Other Countries	254	294,470
WORLD TOTAL	1,575	10,909,340	WORLD TOTAL	1,575	10,909,340

Of the steamships and motorships completed in the world during the year 2,135,959 gross tonnage (19·6 per cent) is to be classed with Lloyd's Register.

* Information incomplete.

TRANSPORT

Goods transport in Great Britain

	1982	1983	1984	1985	1986	1987
Total tonne kilometres (thousand millions)	177·7	182·8	183·1	187·2	186·7	195·3
Road	93·8	95·5	100·3	103·3	105·7	113·3
Rail (British Rail only)	15·9	17·1	12·7	15·3	16·5	17·3
Water: coastwise oil products*	39·8	40·2	41·0	39·4	34·0	31·8
Water: other*	18·9	20·1	18·7	18·0	20·1	22·4
Pipelines (except gases)	9·3	9·9	10·4	11·2	10·4	10·5
Total (million tonnes)	1,733	1,719	1,701	1,804	1,840	1,909
Road	1,376	1,349	1,395	1,451	1,476	1,542
Rail (British Rail only)	142	145	78	122	140	141
Water: coastwise oil products*	54	53	53	50	45	43
Water: other*	83	90	87	92	99	100
Pipelines (except gases)	78	82	88	89	79	83

*'Coastwise' includes all sea traffic within the U.K., Isle of Man and Channel Islands. 'Other' means other coastwise plus inland waterway traffic and one-port traffic.

Seaport traffic of Great Britain

Million gross tonnes

	1982	1983	1984	1985	1986	1987
Foreign traffic						
Imports						
Bulk fuel traffic	49·1	42·0	60·0	57·2	61·7	57·3
Other bulk traffic	31·8	34·3	34·6	36·7	37·3	42·0
Container and roll-on traffic	23·4	26·0	28·1	29·8	31·1	34·0
Semi-bulk traffic	14·1	14·6	14·6	14·5	15·8	16·9
Conventional traffic	2·3	2·3	2·3	1·7	1·5	1·6
All imports	120·7	119·1	139·6	139·9	147·4	151·8
Exports						
Bulk fuel traffic	92·0	96·0	97·3	103·1	101·9	100·2
Other bulk traffic	15·3	16·3	18·7	17·7	21·1	20·4
Container and roll-on traffic	17·1	18·6	20·3	21·3	22·1	23·9
Semi-bulk traffic	3·0	3·5	3·6	4·1	4·0	5·1
Conventional traffic	2·9	2·1	1·8	1·6	1·2	1·2
All exports	130·3	136·5	141·7	147·8	150·4	150·7
Domestic traffic						
Bulk fuel traffic	129·0	130·7	123·2	119·9	112·2	108·1
Other bulk traffic	30·3	31·7	31·0	31·7	32·7	34·8
Container and roll-on traffic	5·1	5·4	5·4	5·9	6·2	7·3
Semi-bulk traffic	0·2	0·2	0·4	0·3	0·2	0·2
Conventional traffic	0·4	0·3	0·2	0·3	0·3	0·3
Non-oil traffic with UK offshore installations	2·1	2·2	3·2	3·6	2·9	3·1
All domestic traffic	167·2	170·4	163·5	161·6	154·5	153·8
Total foreign and domestic traffic	418·3	426·0	444·7	449·3	452·3	456·2

Passenger transport in Great Britain

Thousand million passenger kilometres

	1982	1983	1984	1985	1986	1987
Total	463	471	487	496	520	544
Air	3	3	3	4	4	4
Rail*	31	34	35	36	37	38
Road:						
Public service vehicles	41	42	42	42	41	41†
Cars and taxis	376	380	395	403	428	451
Motorcycles	7	7	7	6	6	6
Pedal cycles	5	5	5	5	4	4

*including London Regional Transport and Passenger Transport Executive railway systems.
†provisional.

BRITISH RAILWAYS

The British Railways Board was set up by the Transport Act, 1962, and assumed its responsibilities on January 1, 1963. (For members, see Government and Public Offices.)

The railway business is broken down into six distinct business sectors each with its own Director. The sectors focus on three passenger businesses of InterCity; Network SouthEast; and Provincial; together with the Railfreight and Parcels businesses. The sixth sector has been established to deal with international traffic through the Channel Tunnel. In addition for the purposes of management and operation the railways are divided into Regions. They cover the following areas:

London Midland Region—bounded by a line joining Carlisle, Oldham, Nottingham, Bedford, London, Banbury, Kidderminster, Aberystwyth.

Western Region—west of a line joining Yeovil, Westbury, Reading, London and the southern border of the L.M. Region.

Southern Region—south of a line joining Dorchester, Salisbury, London and the Thames.

Eastern Region—east of a line joining London, Peterborough, Sheffield, Bradford and Carlisle, but excluding Anglia Region.

Anglia Region—east of a line joining London with Hertford East, Meldreth and Whittlesea.

Scottish Region—north of a line joining Carlisle and Berwick.

Financial Results.—The Profit and Loss Account for 1988–89 showed a surplus of £107 million, £18·2 million after interest, compared with a surplus of £47·3 million after interest in 1987–88. The railway working surplus was £110·5 million compared with a surplus of £108·7 million for the previous year.

Railways	£ million 1988–89
Gross receipts:	
Passenger (including grants)	2,576·3
Freight (inc. parcels and mails)	806·7
TOTAL	3,383·0
Working expenses:	
Train services	1,331·9
Terminals	334·6
Miscellaneous traffic expenses	142·7
Track and signalling	621·7
General expenses	493·0
Provision for replacement of assets	167·6
TOTAL	3,091·5
Railway net surplus	18·2
Surplus from subsidiaries, operational and non-operational property letting	286·1
GROUP OPERATING SURPLUS	304·3

Staff.—On March 31, 1989, British Rail employed 128,476 staff (133,567 at March 31, 1988). Including B.R. Property Board, InterCity On Board Services, Transmark, B.R. Maintenance Ltd. and B.R. Pension Trustee Co. Ltd., the group total at March 31, 1989, was 135,243 (154,748 at March 31, 1988).

OPERATING STATISTICS

At March 31, 1989, British Rail had 23,530 miles of standard gauge lines and sidings in use, representing 10,314 miles of route of which 2,614 miles were electrified. Standard rail on main line has a weight of 110 lb. per yard. British Rail had 2,180 locomotives (diesel and diesel electric, 1,920 and electric, 260); 2,361 diesel multiple-unit vehicles, 7,256 electric multiple-unit vehicles and 2,595 locomotive-hauled passenger carriages.

Loaded train miles run in passenger service totalled 210·9m. 763·7m. passenger journeys were made during the year, including 365·2m. made by holders of season tickets. The average distance of each passenger journey on ordinary fare was 36·2 miles; and on season ticket, 18·9 miles. Passenger stations in use in 1989 numbered 2,435 and freight stations 126.

Freight.—There were 24,922 freight-vehicles and 1,334 other vehicles in the non-passenger-carrying stock. Train miles run in freight service totalled 32·2m.

Accidents on Railways

	1986	1987
Train accidents: total	1,171	1,164
Persons killed : total	27	10
Passengers	8	3
Railway staff	5	1
Others	14	6
Persons injured : total	510	396
Passengers	342	310
Railway staff	137	65
Others	31	21
Other accidents through movement of railway vehicles		
Persons killed	41	41
Persons injured	2,443	2,776
Other accidents on railway premises		
Persons killed	4	37
Persons injured	6,528	6,614
Trespassers and suicides		
Persons killed	312	132
Persons injured	78	46

AIR
Air Traffic Between the United Kingdom and Abroad*

Thousands

	1982	1983	1984	1985	1986	1987
Flights: total	511·4	518·5	566·3	579·3	615·8	675·7
United Kingdom airlines						
Scheduled services	143·5	141·9	151·3	170·8	177·5	188·5
Non-scheduled services	176·3	184·9	214·0	196·2	198·8	219·2
Overseas airlines†						
Scheduled services	154·3	155·2	160·9	172·8	195·8	222·8
Non-scheduled services	37·3	36·5	40·2	39·5	43·6	45·2
Passengers carried: total	44,131·9	46,284·9	51,154·8	52,862·7	51,608·1	66,578·6
United Kingdom airlines						
Scheduled services	12,214·7	12,140·0	13,174·2	14,854·3	15,082·9	17,473·8
Non-scheduled services	13,216·6	14,661·9	16,643·7	15,529·0	12,929·7	22,250·5
Overseas airlines†						
Scheduled services	15,520·5	16,065·6	17,623·0	18,815·6	19,409·5	22,441·5
Non-scheduled services	3,180·1	3,417·4	3,713·9	3,663·8	4,186·0	4,412·8

* Excludes travel to and from the Channel Islands.
† Includes airlines of overseas U.K. Territories.

Activity at Civil Aerodromes

	1982	1983	1984	1985	1986	1987
Movement of civil aircraft (thousands)	2,113	2,238	2,363	2,354	2,439	2,614
Commercial: total	1,072	1,243	1,179	1,205	1,238	1,312
Transport	974	1,019	1,079	1,097	1,125	1,193
Other	98	224	100	108	113	118
Non-commercial	1,041	995	1,184	1,149	1,201	1,303
Passengers handled (thousands): total	60,033	62,301	68,830	71,812	76,593	87,517
Terminal	58,778	61,099	67,572	70,434	75,161	86,041
Transit..............................	1,255	1,202	1,258	1,377	1,432	1,476
Commercial freight handled (tonnes): total	692,693	725,897	860,629	850,268	881,202	975,879
Set down	320,604	332,162	388,292	377,127	419,275	485,468
Picked up............................	372,088	393,737	472,335	473,140	461,927	490,412
Mail handled (tonnes): total	118,406	124,080	136,640	145,770	153,467	155,199
Set down	55,200	56,943	61,461	64,138	67,802	67,758
Picked up............................	63,206	67,138	75,179	81,632	85,665	87,441

Air Passengers by Type of Operator, 1987

Airport	Total terminal and transit	Scheduled U.K. and overseas		Charter U.K. and overseas	
		Terminal	Transit	Terminal	Transit
All U.K. airports: total	85,517,397	58,721,413	1,171,673	27,319,491	304,820
London area airports: total .	58,166,557	43,813,776	525,224	13,746,380	81,177
Battersea Heliport	9,459	—	—	9,459	—
Gatwick	19,587,281	8,351,913	174,366	11,029,310	31,692
Heathrow	35,079,755	34,670,262	334,048	72,641	2,804
London City†	15,403	15,403	—	—	—
Luton	2,611,321	471,658	682	2,112,797	26,184
Southend	123,602	83,998	—	38,741	863
Stansted	749,195	220,542	16,128	492,891	19,634
Other U.K. airports: total ...	29,341,381	14,907,637	646,449	13,563,652	223,643
Aberdeen..................	1,495,276	813,848	25,712	655,159	557
Barrow-in-Furness	7,050	6,037	—	1,004	9
Belfast	2,123,619	1,610,182	13	506,100	7,324
Belfast Harbour	279,574	278,467	—	1,107	—
Benbecula	30,907	28,422	1,585	900	—
Birmingham	2,725,853	1,145,392	54,019	1,493,199	33,243
Blackpool	127,560	77,015	912	49,633	—
Bournemouth..............	108,842	74,107	1,846	31,952	937
Bristol	657,382	104,406	8,796	540,800	3,380
Cambridge.................	18,539	12,104	—	6,403	32
Cardiff	690,325	58,498	18,858	593,444	19,525
Carlisle	7,251	4,174	1,311	1,755	11
Coventry	13,466	2,054	18	11,390	4
Dundee	10,640	7,758	1,228	1,638	16
East Midlands	1,297,373	392,216	2,657	895,007	7,493
Edinburgh.................	1,923,109	1,676,054	73,134	168,860	5,061
Exeter	176,105	87,175	8,648	79,853	429
Glasgow...................	3,411,341	2,070,606	40,513	1,293,996	6,226
Gloucester/Cheltenham.....	3,539	118	—	3,421	—
Hawarden	825	—	—	820	5
Humberside	141,224	74,646	28,134	38,112	332
Inverness	174,511	164,946	4,668	3,578	1,319
Islay	15,156	14,144	9	1,003	—
Isle of Man	426,416	394,089	26,688	5,639	—
Isles of Scilly–St. Mary's	94,177	91,660	—	2,517	—
–Tresco	14,013	13,484	529	—	—
Kirkwall	103,749	83,322	13,735	5,365	1,327
Leeds/Bradford	646,955	351,674	19,314	273,335	2,632
Lerwick (Tingwall).........	13,622	10,256	510	2,837	19
Liverpool..................	339,626	293,897	6,567	38,566	596
Londonderry	12,862	12,001	—	861	—
Lydd	1,086	207	—	875	4
Manchester................	8,745,859	3,059,383	85,149	5,549,231	52,096
Manston	8,518	3,145	292	4,177	904
Newcastle	1,422,358	523,268	69,794	812,178	17,118
Norwich	191,325	129,752	28,971	32,198	404
Penzance Heliport..........	86,416	84,416	—	—	—
Plymouth	126,553	109,867	15,137	1,549	—
Prestwick	405,042	235,699	71,502	64,159	33,682
Scateta...................	13,195	—	—	13,195	—
Shoreham	3,484	3,279	—	205	—
Southampton	439,157	427,499	4,166	6,983	509
Stornoway	65,564	64,045	97	1,379	43
Sumburgh	288,790	62,973	710	199,365	25,742
Swansea...................	1,587	—	—	1,567	20
Tees-side	313,452	221,321	21,198	69,370	1,563
Tiree.....................	6,441	4,557	1,569	315	—
Unst	101,253	2,283	—	97,908	1,062
Wick	30,414	21,191	8,460	744	19
Channel Is airports: total ...	2,659,578	2,567,974	55,700	35,259	645
Alderney	85,159	84,211	—	928	—
Guernsey..................	804,887	763,080	31,482	10,064	261
Jersey.....................	1,769,552	1,720,683	24,218	24,267	384

† Opened October 1987.

AERODROMES AND AIRPORTS

The following aerodromes in Great Britain, Northern Ireland, the Isle of Man and the Channel Islands are either State owned or licensed for use by civil aircraft. A number of unlicensed aerodromes not included in this list are also available for private use by permission of the owner or controlling authority.

Aerodromes designated as Customs airports are printed in **bold** type. Customs facilities are available at certain other aerodromes by special arrangement.

S = Owned and operated by the Government.
BAA = Owned by the British Airports Authority P.L.C.
M = Owned by the municipal authority.
HIAL = Operated by Highland and Islands Airports Ltd.

J = Military aerodromes available for civil use by prior permission.
H = Licensed helicopter aerodrome.

ENGLAND AND WALES

Aberporth, Dyfed. J
Abingdon, Oxon. J
Andrewsfield, Essex.
Barrow (Walney Island), Cumbria.
Bembridge, I.O.W.
Benson, Oxon. J
Biggin Hill, Kent.
Birmingham, W. Midlands. M
Blackbushe, Hants.
Blackpool, Lancs. M
Bodmin, Cornwall.
Bourn, Cambridge.
Bournemouth, Dorset. M
Bristol, Avon. M
Brize Norton, Oxford. J
Brough, N. Humberside. M
Caernarfon, Gwynedd.
Cambridge.
Cardiff, S. Glamorgan. M
Carlisle, Cumbria. M
Chichester (Goodwood), Sussex.
Chivenor, Devon. J
Church Fenton, N. Yorks. J
Clacton, Essex.
Compton Abbas, Dorset.
Cosford, Wolverhampton. J
Coventry, W. Midlands. M
Cranfield, Beds.
Cranwell, Lincs. J
Culdrose, Cornwall. J
Denham, Bucks.
Derby/Burnaston, Derby.
Dishforth, N. Yorks. J
Doncaster, S. Yorks.
Dunkeswell, Devon.
Dunsfold, Surrey. M
Duxford, Cambs. M
Eaglescott, Devon.
Earls Colne, Halstead.
East Midlands, Derbys. M
Elstree, Herts.
Exeter, Devon.
Fairoaks, Surrey.
Farnborough, Hants. S
Fenland, Lincs.
Filton, Bristol. M
Finningley, S. Yorks. J
Gloucester/Cheltenham (Staverton), Glos. M
Great Yarmouth (North Denes), Norfolk.
Halfpenny Green, Staffs.
Halton, Bucks. J
Hatfield, Herts.
Haverfordwest, Dyfed. M
Hawarden, Clywd.
Hucknall, Notts.
Humberside. M
Ipswich, Suffolk.
Isle of Wight/Sandown.
Kemble, Glos. J

Land's End (St. Just), Cornwall.
Lashenden, Headcorn, Kent.
Leavesden, Herts.
Leeds/Bradford, Yorks. M
Lee-on-Solent, Hants. J
Leicester, Leics.
Linton-on-Ouse, Yorks. J
Liverpool, Merseyside. M
Llanbedr, Gwynedd. J.
London/City.
London/Gatwick. BAA
London/Heathrow. BAA
London/Stansted. BAA
London/Westland Heliport. H
Luton, Beds. M
Lydd, Kent.
Lyneham, Wilts. J
Manchester. M
Manchester (Barton).
Manston, Kent. J
Netherthorpe, S. Yorks.
Newcastle, Tyne and Wear. M
Newton, Notts. J
Northampton (Sywell), Northants.
Northolt, Mddx. J
Norwich, Norfolk. M
Nottingham, Notts.
Old Sarum, Wilts.
Oxford (Kidlington), Oxfordshire.
Panshanger, Herts.
Penzance, Cornwall. H
Peterborough (Conington).
Peterborough (Sibson), Cambs.
Plymouth (Roborough), Devon.
Portland Naval, Dorset. JH
Redhill, Surrey.
Retford/Gamston, Notts.
Rochester, Kent.
St. Mawgan, Cornwall. J
Sandtoft, Humberside.
Scilly Isles (St. Mary's).
Seething, Norfolk.
Shawbury, Shropshire. J
Sherburn-in-Elmet, N. Yorks.
Shipdham, Norfolk.
Shobdon, Herefordshire.
Shoreham, W. Sussex. M
Silverstone, Northants.
Skegness (Ingoldmells), Lincs.
Sleap, Shropshire.
Southampton/Eastleigh, Hants.
Southend, Essex. M
Stapleford, Essex.
Sturgate, Lincs.
Swansea, W. Glam. M
Teesside, Cleveland. M
Thruxton, Hants.
Tresco, Isles of Scilly. H
Valley, Gwynedd. J
Warton, Lancs.
Wattisham, Suffolk. J

Wellesbourne Mountford, Warwick.
Weston, Avon. H
White Waltham, Berks.
Wickenby, Lincs.
Woodford, Gtr. Manchester.
Woodvale, Merseyside. J
Wycombe Air Park (Booker), Bucks.
Yeovil, Somerset.
Yeovilton, Somerset. J

SCOTLAND

Aberdeen (Dyce). BAA
Barra, Hebrides.
Benbecula, Hebrides. HIAL
Cumbernauld, Strathclyde.
Dounreay (Thurso). S
Dundee, Angus. M
Eday. M
Edinburgh. BAA
Fair Isle.
Fife/Glenrothes.
Flotta, Orkneys.
Glasgow. BAA
Inverness (Dalcross). HIAL
Islay (Port Ellen). HIAL
Isle of Skye. M
Kirkwall. HIAL
Lerwick (Tingwall). M
Machrihanish, Kintyre. J
North Ronaldsay, Orkneys. M
Papa Westray, Orkneys. M
Perth (Scone).
Prestwick, BAA
Sanday, Orkneys. M
Scatsta.
Stornoway, Hebrides. HIAL
Stronsay, Orkneys. M
Sumburgh, Shetlands. HIAL
Tiree. HIAL
Unst, Shetlands. M
West Freugh, Dumfries. S
Westray, Orkneys. M
Whalsay, Shetlands.
Wick. HIAL
Wigtown/Baldoon, Dumfries.

NORTHERN IRELAND

Belfast (Aldergrove). S
Belfast (Harbour).
Enniskillen (St. Angelo). M
Londonderry (Eglinton). M
Newtownards.

ISLE OF MAN

Ronaldsway. S

CHANNEL ISLANDS

Alderney. S
Guernsey. S
Jersey. S

ROADS

Highway Authorities

The powers and responsibilities of highway authorities in England and Wales are set out in the Highways Acts 1980: for Scotland there is separate legislation.

Responsibility for trunk road motorways and other trunk roads in Great Britain rests in England with the Secretary of State for Transport, in Scotland with the Secretary of State for Scotland, and in Wales with the Secretary of State for Wales. The costs of construction, improvement and maintenance are paid for by central government. The highway authority for non-trunk roads in England and Wales is, in general, the county council in whose area the roads lie, and in Scotland the regional or islands council. In Northern Ireland the Northern Ireland Department of the Environment is responsible for public roads and their maintenance and construction.

Expenditure

Transport Supplementary Grant (T.S.G.) is a block grant and was introduced in England and Wales on April 1, 1975, to replace a variety of specific grants paid towards local transport expenditure.

In England grant was paid towards capital and current spending on transport by county councils and the G.L.C. from 1975–76 to 1984–85. From April 1, 1985, T.S.G. has only been paid towards capital spending on highways and the regulation of traffic, current expenditure having been subsumed by Rate Support Grant. With the abolition of the G.L.C. and the Metropolitan County Councils on April 1, 1986, grant has become payable to London Boroughs, the Common Council of the City of London and Metropolitan District Councils. In Wales, grant was also paid to the Welsh County Councils towards current and capital expenditure on transport. Since April 1982, T.S.G. became payable on capital expenditure only; current expenditure having been subsumed into the Rate Support Grant. From April 1, 1985 eligibility of new transport schemes for T.S.G. has been confined to those costing over £5 million.

Grant rates are determined by the respective Secretaries of State; at present grant is paid at 50 per cent of expenditure accepted for grant in England and Wales.

For the financial year 1988–89 local authorities in England received £191 million in T.S.G. Total expenditure on building and maintaining motorways and trunk roads in 1988–89 was £1,000 million in England, of which new construction of national roads accounted for over £700 million.

In the financial year 1989–90, local authorities in Wales will receive £19·7 million in T.S.G. Total expenditure on roads in 1987–88 was £331 million in Wales, of which £134 million was spent on trunk roads and £197 million on local authority roads, including public lighting and road safety.

Total expenditure on roads during the financial year 1986–87 was £403 million in Scotland.

Road Lengths (miles)
(at April 1988)

	Public Roads	Trunk Roads (incl. motorways)	*Trunk Motorways
England	167,935	6,602	1,576
Wales	20,407	1,057	74
Scotland ...	31,818	1,953	145
N. Ireland ..	14,812	1,433	70
U.K.	234,972	11,045	1,865

*There were in addition 48 miles of local authority motorway in England and 15 miles in Scotland.

Motorways

The network in England and Wales is based on five main routes—London–Yorkshire (M1), London–South Wales (M4), Birmingham–Bristol–Exeter (M5), Birmingham–Carlisle (M6) and Lancashire–N. Humberside (M62).

Other important motorways in use include: Medway Towns (M2); London–Basingstoke (M3); London–Cambridge (M11); Rotherham–Goole (M18); London–Folkestone (M20); London orbital route (M25); London–Oxford (M40); North Cheshire (M56); and South Humberside (M180).

Motorways in use in Scotland include: Edinburgh–Glasgow–Greenock (M8); Edinburgh–Stirling (M9); Maryville–Mollisburn (M73); Millbank–Maryville (M74); Stirling–Haggs (M80); Friarton Bridge–Perth (M85); Inverkeithing–Perth (M90), and (M80)–Kincardine Bridge (M876).

Driving Tests

The number of driving tests conducted in Great Britain in 1988 was 22,072,966, of which 51·75 per cent resulted in a pass. In addition 85,269 H.G.V./P.S.V. tests were undertaken, of which 55 per cent. were successful. In 1988 3,206 Part I motorcycle tests were conducted by Departmental examiners (47 per cent. successful) and 42,768 by Approved Training Bodies (96 per cent. successful).

Motor Vehicles

The number of vehicles in Great Britain with current licences in 1987 was:

Private and light goods	19,249,000
Motor cycles, scooters, mopeds	978,000
Public transport vehicles	129,000
Heavy goods vehicles	609,000
Agricultural tractors	374,000
Others	68,000
TOTAL	22,152,000

There were 744,000 Crown vehicles and vehicles exempt from licensing.

Buses and Coaches 1987–88
(Great Britain)

No. of vehicles (average)	71,700
Vehicle kilometres (millions)	3,665
Passenger journeys (millions)	5,936
Passenger receipts (£ million)	2,388

Road Accidents 1987

Road accidents	239,063
Vehicles involved:	
Pedal cycles	27,010
Motor vehicles	387,521
Total casualties	311,473
Pedestrians	57,453
Vehicle users	254,020
Killed*	5,125
Pedestrians	1,703
Pedal cycles	280
All two-wheeled motor vehicles	723
Cars & taxis	2,206
Others	213

*Died within 30 days of accident.

Year	Killed	Injured	Year	Killed	Injured
1965	7,952	389,985	1984	5,599	318,715
1970	7,499	355,869	1985	5,165	312,359
1975	6,366	318,584	1986	5,382	316,069
1980	6,010	323,000	1987	5,125	306,348

VEHICLE LICENCES, ETC.

Since October 1, 1974, registration and first licensing of vehicles has been done through local offices (known as Vehicle Registration Offices) of the Department of Transport's Driver and Vehicle Licensing Centre in Swansea. The records of existing vehicles are held at Swansea. Local facilities for relicensing are available as follows:—

(i) with a licence reminder (form V11) in person at any Post Office which deals with vehicle licensing or post it to the Post Office, shown on the form.

(ii) with a vehicle licence renewal (form V10). You may normally apply in person at any licensing Post Office. You will need to take your vehicle registration document with you: if this is not available you must complete form V62 which is held at Post Offices. Postal applications can be made to the Post Offices shown on form V100, available at any Post Office. This form also provides guidance on registering and licensing vehicles.

Details of the present duties chargeable on motor vehicles are available at Post Offices and Vehicle Registration Offices. The Vehicles (Excise) Act, 1971 provides *inter alia* that any vehicle kept on a public road but not used on roads is chargeable to excise duty as if it were in use.

Rates of duty for motor car and motor cycle licences are shown below.

Type of Vehicle	Exceeding	Not Exceeding	12 Months	6 Months
Motor Cars			£	£
Those first constructed before January 1, 1947	—	—	60·00	33·00
Other than above	—	—	100·00	55·00
Motor Cycles				
With or without sidecar	—	150 c.c.	10·00	—
With or without sidecar	150 c.c.	250 c.c.	20·00	—
With or without sidecar	250 c.c.	—	40·00	22·00
If first constructed before 1 Jan. 1933 and weighs not more than 101·6 kgs.	250 c.c.	—	20·00	—
Three Wheelers				
Other than pedestrian-controlled	—	150 c.c.	10·00	—
Other than pedestrian-controlled	150 c.c.	—	40·00	22·00
Pedestrian-Controlled Vehicles				
(Other than mowing machines)				
Three wheeled	—	150 c.c.	10·00	—
Three wheeled	150 c.c.	—	20·00	—
More than three wheels	—	—	20·00	—
Hackney Carriages				
Seating less than 9 persons	—	—	100·00	55·00
Seating 9–16 persons	—	—	130·00	71·50
Seating 17–35 persons	—	—	200·00	110·00
Seating 36–60 persons	—	—	300·00	165·00
Seating over 60 persons	—	—	450·00	247·50

Driving Licences—Fees

On or after 1.11.88

FULL LICENCE

First full licence . . . . £17·00*

Changing a provisional to a full licence after passing a driving test — free

Renewal of full licence if last full licence was issued after 30·9·82 . . . . — free

New licence after a period of disqualification . . . . £5·00

PROVISIONAL LICENCE

First provisional licence . . . . £17·00*

First renewal of provisional licence issued before 1.10.82 . . . . £17·00

DUPLICATE LICENCE . . . . £5·00

EXCHANGE LICENCE . . . . £5·00

* Once you have paid the life fee for *either* a provisional *or* a full licence all renewals are free except where additional entitlement is required.

Driving Test—Fees

For cars . . . . £18·00

For motor cycles, part I . . . . £17·94*

      part II . . . . £24·00

*When conducted by the Department of Transport. Appointed motor cycle training organizations, who conduct the majority of part I tests within the framework of their own training courses, are free to set their own fee.

Driving tests for invalid carriages are free.

M.o.T. Testing

Cars, motor cycles, motor caravans, light goods and dual-purpose vehicles more than 3 years old must be covered by an effective vehicle test certificate (often called the M.o.T. certificate). Copies of the legislation governing M.o.T. testing can be obtained from any bookshop which stocks H.M.S.O. publications. The legislation comprises The Road Traffic Act 1972 (Sections 44 and 45), The Motor Vehicles (Test) Regulations 1981, The Motor Vehicles (Extension) Order 1981, and The Motor Vehicles (Production of Test Certificate) Regulations 1969.

FUEL AND POWER

Coal: supply and demand

Million tonnes

	1982	1983	1984	1985	1986	1987
SUPPLY						
Production of deep-mined coal.................	106·2	101·7	35·2	75·2	90·4	85·9
Production of opencast coal....................	15·3	14·7	14·3	15·6	14·3	15·8
Recovered slurry, fines, etc.....................	3·3	2·8	1·6	3·3	3·5	2·8
Imports......................................	4·1	4·5	8·9	12·6	10·6	9·8
Change in colliery stocks	+0·2	+1·2	−7·9	−5·3	+0·3	−1·1
Change in stocks at opencast sites	−0·4	+0·8	+4·7	−6·3	−0·8	−1·5
Total supply.............................	128·9	121·7	63·2	118·2	119·2	116·8
HOME CONSUMPTION						
Electricity supply industry	80·2	81·6	53·4	73·9	82·6	86·2
Coke ovens	10·4	10·4	8·2	11·1	11·1	10·9
Low temperature carbonization plants	1·2	1·2	1·1	1·4	1·0	1·0
Manufactured fuel plants	1·1	0·9	0·2	0·8	1·0	1·0
Railways.....................................	0·1	—	—	—	—	—
Collieries....................................	0·5	0·5	0·2	0·3	0·3	0·2
Industry (disposals to users)...................	7·1	7·2	6·1	7·4	8·1	7·9
Domestic (disposals to users)	8·6	8·0	6·5	8·6	8·4	7·2
Public services...............................	1·4	1·4	1·3	1·3	1·3	1·2
Miscellaneous	0·5	0·4	0·5	0·4	0·2	0·2
Total home consumption	111·0	111·4	77·3	105·4	114·2	115·9
Overseas shipments and bunkers	7·4	6·6	2·3	2·4	2·7	2·4
Total consumption and shipments	118·4	+118·0	79·6	107·8	120·9	118·2
Change in distributed stocks*	+10·3	+3·5	−17·1	+10·0	+4·0	−2·8
Balance†	+0·2	—	+0·7	+0·5	−1·8	+1·3

*Stock change excludes industrial and domestic stocks.
† This is the balance between supply and consumption, shipments and changes in known distributed stocks.

Fuel input and gas output; gas sales

	1982	1983	1984	1985	1986	1987
FUEL INPUT TO GAS INDUSTRY:			million tonnes			
Petroleum..................................	0·1	0·1	0·1	0·1	—	—
			million therms			
Petroleum gases†	52	33	30	28	36	6
Natural gas	—	—	—	—	—	—
Coke oven gas	—	—	—	—	—	—
Total to gas works	85	61	56	57	55	20
Natural gas for direct supply	16,667	17,153	17,739	18,988	19,215	20,198
Total fuel input..............................	16,752	17,214	17,794	19,046	19,270	20,218
GAS OUTPUT AND SALES			million therms			
Gas output:						
Town gas	26	23	21	20	18	13
Natural gas supplied direct	16,719	17,186	17,764	19,017	19,243	20,205
Gross total available	16,745	17,209	17,785	19,038	19,261	20,218
Own use	126	−121	−129	−140	−152	−137
Statistical difference*	+38	−244	−354	−508	−585	−708
Total sales..................................	16,657	16,844	17,302	18,390	18,524	19,373
Analysis of gas sales						
Power stations	76	77	178	197	75	79
Final users:						
Iron and steel industry	365	342	462	464	414	468
Other industries	5,319	5,295	5,258	5,319	4,677	5,275
Domestic	8,719	8,871	8,931	9,682	10,360	10,500
Public administration	1,003	1,050	1,071	1,183	1,279	1,326
Miscellaneous	1,175	1,210	1,337	1,474	1,652	1,665

† Butane, propane, ethane and refinery tail gases.
*Supply greater than recorded demand (−). Includes losses in distribution.

Electricity: production and fuel used

	1982	1983	1984	1985	1986	1987
Electricity generated: total (GWh)..........	256,090	261,082	266,645	280,602	282,913	283,321
England and Wales..........................	220,505	226,324	227,010	242,248	246,895	246,521
S. Scotland Electricity Board.................	23,276	20,332	22,938	25,771	23,748	25,814
N. Scotland Hydro-Electric Board	6,312	8,395	10,451	6,015	5,611	4,204
Northern Ireland	5,346	5,384	5,591	5,938	6,018	6,157
Railway and transport authorities............	651	647	655	630	641	625
Method of generation (GWh)						
Steam plant, nuclear	40,001	45,776	49,498	56,354	54,005	50,282
Steam plant, other	210,545	209,116	209,711	216,830	221,981	226,957
Gas turbines and oil engines	580	401	2,012	1,138	609	512
Hydro-electric plant other than pumped storage plant	3,884	3,892	3,368	3,447	3,925	3,312
Pumped storage plant	1,080	1,897	2,055	2,831	2,394	2,207
Fuel used (Thousand tonnes)						
Coal	79,816	81,437	53,411	73,940	82,647	86,174
Coke and coke breeze	69	33	19	—	—	—
Oil	6,232	4,746	21,313	10,638	6,097	4,812
Natural gas*	304	311	712	762	285	298
Electricity sales total (GWh).................	217,096	220,532	224,660	235,570	242,969	250,927
Domestic and farm premises..................	84,601	84,713	85,667	90,068	93,496	94,927
Domestic and commercial	2,014	1,980	1,987	1,712	1,417	1,408
Shops, offices, other commercial premises	46,134	49,055	51,113	55,459	59,242	62,012
Factories, other industrial premises	79,806	80,034	81,105	83,419	83,870	87,531
Public lighting	2,243	2,261	2,296	2,335	2,316	2,345
Traction	2,298	2,488	2,492	2,577	2,627	2,704

*Expressed in thousand tonnes of coal equivalent.

Electricity Council Finance 1986–88

	£ million	
	1986–87	1987–88
Turnover		
Electricity Supply	10,385·1	10,566·2
Contracting................	183·8	199·3
Appliance Marketing	549·7	601·0
TOTAL	11,118·6	11,366·5
Operating Costs		
Electricity Supply	9,266·7	9,749·8
Contracting................	174·8	189·9
Appliance Marketing	510·9	561·9
TOTAL	9,952·4	10,501·6
Operating profit/loss before monetary working capital adjustment		
Electricity Supply	1,118·4	816·4
Contracting................	9·0	9·4
Appliance Marketing	38·8	39·1
TOTAL	1,166·2	864·9
Monetary working capital adjustment	16·5	50·2
Profit/loss on ordinary activities before interest ..	1,149·7	814·7
Interest payable	436·3	301·8
Profit/loss before taxation ...	713·4	512·9
Taxation	126·5	356·2
Minority interest	—	2·1
Profit/loss for the year transferred to reserves	586·9	154·6

British Coal Corporation Finance (£million)

	1987–88	1988–89
Operating Profit		
Turnover	4,388	4,295
Operating profit/(loss):		
Deep mines and related activities	(55)	136
Opencast	252	272
Total mining...............	197	408
Non-mining activities	14	8
Profits from asset sales, etc....	50	82
TOTAL.....................	261	498
Results after Interest		
Operating profit.............	261	498
Interest charges.............	(368)	(432)
PROFIT (LOSS)	(107)	66
Overall result		
Profit (loss) after interest	(107)	66
Net restructuring costs	(387)	(269)
Taxation and extraordinary items.....................	(1)	—
OVERALL PROFIT (LOSS)	(495)	(203)
Government Grants		
Social cost grants	435	255
Contributions towards improved pension benefits ..	42	42
Total social grants...........	477	297
Deficit grant................	200	—
TOTAL.....................	677	297

BRITISH GAS P.L.C.
152 Grosvenor Road, SW1V 3JL
[01–821 1444]

British Gas was privatised following the Gas Act, 1986. Its primary activities are the purchase, distribution and sale of gas. It also explores for and produces hydrocarbons.
Chairman and Chief Executive, R. Evans, C.B.E.

Gas Regions

Scotland, Granton House, 4 Marine Drive, Edinburgh EH5 1YB.
Northern, P.O. Box 1GB, Killingworth, Newcastle upon Tyne NE99 1GB.
North Western, Welman House, Altrincham, Cheshire WA15 8AE.
North Eastern, New York Road, Leeds LS2 7PE.
East Midlands, P.O. Box 145, De Montfort Street, Leicester LE1 9DB.
West Midlands, Wharf Lane, Solihull, West Midlands B91 2JP.
Wales, Helmont House, Churchill Way, Cardiff CF1 4NB.
Eastern, Star House, Potters Bar, Herts. EN6 2PD.
North Thames, North Thames House, London Road, Staines, Middx. TW18 4AE.
South Eastern, Katherine Street, Croydon CR9 1JU.
Southern, 80 St. Mary's Road, Southampton SO9 5AT.
South Western, Riverside, Temple Street, Keynsham, Bristol BS18 1EQ.

British Gas P.L.C. **Finance (£ million)**

	1987	1988
Turnover		
Gas supply	6,967	6,679
Installation and contracting	310	347
Appliance trading	300	307
Exploration subsidiaries	189	224
Other activities	28	27
	7,794	7,584
Less: intra-group sales	(184)	(220)
TOTAL	7,610	7,364
Operating costs		
Gas prime materials	3,024	2,717
Gas levy	503	469
Salaries, wages, associated costs	1,180	1,139
Cost of sales adjustment.......	2	4
Monetary working capital adjustment	(27)	(14)
Current cost depreciation	779	789
Lease rentals	34	27
Exploration expenditure	22	61
Research, testing & development	74	77
Employee profit-sharing scheme	—	38
Auditor's remuneration	0·581	0·635
Current cost pre-tax profit	1,058	1,008
Gearing adjustment	(8)	(23)
Total funds generated from operations	1,492	1,485
New Loans	—	225
Proceeds from disposal of tangible fixed assets	23	51
Total funds generated	1,515	1,761
Taxation paid	410	553
Dividends paid	—	270

BRITISH OIL STATISTICS
(million tonnes)

	1983	1984	1985	1986	1987
Oil production†					
Land	0·3	0·3	0·4	0·5	0·6
Offshore	114·6	125·6	127·1	126·5	122·7
Refinery output	70·9	73·2	72·9	74·1	74·7
Deliveries of petroleum products for inland consumption	64·5	81·4	70·1	69·2	67·7
Exports (including re-exports):					
Crude petroleum	68·3	75·9	79·6	82·1	80·6
Refined petroleum products and process oils	15·9	16·4	18·9	20·2	18·5
Imports:					
Crude petroleum	22·8	25·0	26·9	32·6	33·1
Refined petroleum products and process oils	17·3	28·5	25·0	22·9	20·5

† Crude oil plus condensates and petroleum gases derived at onshore treatment plants.

WATER

ENGLAND AND WALES

In England the Secretary of State for the Environment is responsible for policy relating to water supply. This includes the conservation and distribution of water resources, the provision of sewerage and sewage disposal services, the quality of rivers and other inland waters, and the use of inland waters for navigation and recreation. Responsibility for policy relating to land drainage, flood protection, sea defences, and the protection and development of fisheries lies with the Minister of Agriculture, Fisheries and Food. In Wales, all aspects of policy relating to water are the responsibility of the Secretary of State for Wales.

Regional Water Authorities

At present (August 1989) nine regional water authorities in England and the Welsh Water Authority in Wales are responsible for water supply and the development of water resources, sewerage and sewage disposal, pollution control, freshwater fisheries, flood protection, water recreation, and environmental conservation. Under the Water Act 1989, which received Royal Assent on July 6, 1989, the regional water authorities are to be privatized towards the end of 1989 (see below).

Of the 99 per cent of the population of England and Wales who are connected to a public water supply, at present 75 per cent are supplied by the regional water authorities. The remaining 25 per cent are supplied by 29 statutory water companies which act as independent water supply agents to the regional authorities. The statutory water companies bear no responsibility for sewage disposal or land drainage. The status of the statutory companies will also change under the provisions of the Water Act 1989.

The regional water authorities (at Aug. 1989) are:

ANGLIAN WATER AUTHORITY, Ambury House, Huntingdon, Cambs. PE18 6NZ.

NORTHUMBRIAN WATER AUTHORITY, Northumbria House, Regent Centre, Gosforth, Newcastle upon Tyne NE3 3PX.

NORTH WEST WATER AUTHORITY, Dawson House, Liverpool Road, Great Sankey, Warrington WA5 3LW.

SEVERN TRENT WATER AUTHORITY, Abelson House, 2297 Coventry Road, Sheldon, Birmingham B26 3PS.

SOUTHERN WATER AUTHORITY, Guildborne House, Chatsworth Road, Worthing, W. Sussex BN11 1LD.

SOUTH WEST WATER AUTHORITY, Peninsula House, Rydon Lane, Exeter EX2 7HR.

THAMES WATER AUTHORITY, Nugent House, 71 Vastern Road, Reading RG1 8DB.

WESSEX WATER AUTHORITY, Wessex House, Passage Street, Bristol BS2 0JQ.

YORKSHIRE WATER AUTHORITY, West Riding House, 67 Albion Street, Leeds LS1 5AA.

WELSH WATER AUTHORITY, Cambrian Way, Brecon, Powys LD3 7HP.

The Water Act

The Water Act 1989 will create a privatized water industry under public regulation. The water industry's infrastructure and services will be provided by the private sector, while independent statutory bodies will set standards and regulate in the public interest.

The Water Act provides for the setting up of the National Rivers Authority (N.R.A.) and the appointment of a regulatory official, the Director General of Water Services (see below). It provides for the functions, property rights and liabilities of the water authorities to be transferred to their successor companies and the N.R.A. and ensures the appointment of water and sewerage services suppliers for all areas of England and Wales at all times after the transfer date (the date on which water authorities' functions, etc. are divided between their successor companies and the N.R.A.). Flotation of the regional water authorities is planned for late November 1989.

The Water Act provides for the statutory water companies to become water suppliers on the same basis as the privatized water authorities, and with the same relationship to the Director General of Water Services and the National Rivers Authority. Subject to Parliament's approval, the statutory water companies will be able to convert to public limited company status.

Regulatory Bodies

A Director General of Water Services has been appointed by the Secretaries of State for the Environment and for Wales. Independent of Ministers and directly accountable to Parliament, his main duties are to ensure that the water companies comply with the terms of their appointments (or licences) and to protect the interests of the consumer. The Office of Water Services, similar to the Office of Telecommunications and the Office of Gas Supply, has been set up to support his activities.

An independent national body, the National Rivers Authority (N.R.A.) was established under the Water Act 1989 to take over the regulatory and river management functions of the regional water authorities. Its responsibilities include monitoring the quality of inland, coastal and underground waters and controlling pollution, and the management of water resources, land drainage, flood protection and fisheries.

Methods of charging

In England and Wales, householders at present pay for domestic water supply and sewage disposal services through charges based on the rateable value of their property (domestic rates). Industrial and most commercial users are charged according to consumption, which is recorded by meter.

The replacement of domestic rates by the community charge in April 1990 necessitates new methods of charging the private consumer for water and sewage services. The Water Act 1989 gives the water companies until the end of the century to decide on and introduce a suitable method of charging. Two options under consideration by the water industry are a flat-rate licence fee and metering. Large-scale trials of domestic metering are currently taking place.

SCOTLAND

Overall responsibility for national water policy in Scotland rests with the Secretary of State for Scotland. Fisheries and certain aspects of land drainage are the responsibility of the Department of Agriculture and Fisheries for Scotland. The supply of water and the development of water resources are administered by separate authorities from those responsible for the control of water pollution.

Water supply and sewerage are local authority responsibilities and are among the functions of the nine Regional Councils and the three Islands Councils.

Seven river purification boards have the specific duty of restoring and maintaining the quality of water in Scotland's rivers, lochs and coastal waters, except in the three Islands Councils' regions. The Islands Councils of Orkney, Shetland and the Western Isles are responsible for the prevention of pollution within their own areas.

The Water (Scotland) Act 1967 brought into being a bulk water supply authority, the Central Scotland Water Development Board. The main statutory function of the board is to develop new sources of water supply for the purpose of providing water in bulk to water authorities whose limits of supply are within the board's area. Its area covers the limits of supply as water authorities of Central, Fife, Lothian, Strathclyde and Tayside Regional Councils.

The community charge, which was introduced in Scotland in April 1989, includes a community water charge set by each Regional and Islands Council.

CENTRAL SCOTLAND WATER DEVELOPMENT BOARD, Balmore, Torrance, Glasgow G64 4AJ.—*Director*, W. G. Mitchell

NORTHERN IRELAND

In Northern Ireland ministerial responsibility for water services lies with the Secretary of State for Northern Ireland. The Department of the Environment for Northern Ireland, operating through the Water Service, is responsible for policy and co-ordination with regard to supply and distribution of water, and provision and maintenance of sewerage services.

The Water Service is divided into four regions, the Eastern, Northern, Western and Southern Divisions. These are based in Belfast, Ballymena, Londonderry and Craigavon respectively.

On all major policy issues the Department of the Environment for Northern Ireland seeks the views of the Northern Ireland Water Council, a body appointed to advise the Department on the exercise of its water and sewerage functions. The Council includes representatives of agriculture, angling, industry, commerce, tourism, trade unions and local government.

Usually householders do not pay directly for water and sewerage services: the costs of these services are allowed for in the Northern Ireland regional rate. Water consumed by industry, commerce and agriculture in excess of 100 cubic metres (22,000 gallons) per half year is charged through meters.

ROYAL OBSERVATORIES

Royal Greenwich Observatory
Herstmonceux, East Sussex, BN27 1RP
[0323 833171]

The Royal Observatory was founded at Greenwich by Charles II in 1675. Because of smog and light pollution, the Observatory was moved to Herstmonceux in East Sussex after the Second World War. The traditional work in positional astronomy remains an important activity of the Observatory. It participates in the reduction of data from the European Space Agency's astrometric satellite, HIPPARCOS. The Observatory collaborates with Danish and Spanish astronomers to operate the Carlsberg Automatic Meridian Circle on the island of La Palma in the Canary Islands. The rate of rotation of the Earth and other geophysical parameters are monitored by the satellite laser ranging telescope at Herstmonceux. Various almanacs and other astronomical data are prepared by H.M. Nautical Almanac Office, which is part of the Royal Greenwich Observatory. However, as an establishment of the Science and Engineering Research Council, the main task of the Observatory now is the provision of facilities for research in optical astronomy for astronomers in the universities. In particular, this involves the running of the Isaac Newton group of telescopes with its associated instrumentation at the Roque de los Muchachos Observatory on La Palma. This group comprises the 4·2 m. William Herschel telescope, the 2·5 m. Isaac Newton telescope and the 1·0 m Jacobus Kapteyn telescope. The running of these is shared with the Netherlands, and, in the case of the Jacobus Kapteyn telescope, with the Republic of Ireland also.

At the U.K. headquarters, there are facilities for the processing of astronomical data obtained from the telescopes on La Palma and elsewhere; these include a node of the STARLINK computing network. The U.K. headquarters of the Royal Greenwich Observatory is moving from Herstmonceux to Cambridge during 1990.

Dir., Prof. A. Boksenberg, F.R.S.

Royal Observatory
Blackford Hill, Edinburgh EH9 3HJ
[031–668 8100]

The Observatory was founded by the Astronomical Institution in 1818 and its Royal Charter dates from 1822. It is now responsible for some major national astronomical facilities funded by the Science and Engineering Research Council, including a 15·0 m. millimetre-wave telescope and a 3·8 m. infra-red telescope in Hawaii and COSMOS, a fast automatic plate measuring machine, in Edinburgh. The Observatory is also part of the U.K. Starlink network for astronomical image and data processing. The Observatory specializes in the development of advanced technologies and the application of these to studies of the properties of matter in extreme environments in space.

Dir., and Astronomer Royal for Scotland, Prof. M. S. Longair.

LOCAL GOVERNMENT

ENGLAND AND WALES

The London Government Act, 1963, and the Local Government Acts of 1972 and 1985 have brought about the present system of local government in England and Wales. The system is based on two tiers of local authorities, county and district councils, in the non-metropolitan areas; and a single tier, of metropolitan district and London borough councils, in the six metropolitan areas of England and in London respectively.

Structures and Areas in England

England outside Greater London is divided into counties. Each county is divided into districts. Six *metropolitan counties* cover the main conurbations outside Greater London: Tyne and Wear, West Midlands, Merseyside, Greater Manchester, West Yorkshire and South Yorkshire. They are divided into 36 *metropolitan districts*, most of which have a population of over 200,000. There are 39 *non-metropolitan counties*; each of these is divided into *non-metropolitan districts*, of which there are 296. These districts have populations broadly in the range of 60,000 to 100,000: some however, have larger populations, because of the need to avoid dividing large towns, and some in mainly rural areas have smaller populations. Greater London is divided into 32 *London boroughs*, with populations between 134,000 and 390,000, and the *City*, with a daytime population of 340,000 but only 5,400 by night.

There are also about 10,000 parishes, in 219 of the non-metropolitan and 18 of the metropolitan districts.

A permanent Local Government Boundary Commission keeps the areas and electoral arrangements under review, and makes proposals to the Secretary of State for changes found necessary.

Constitution and Elections

For districts, non-metropolitan counties, London boroughs, the City, and for about 8,000 parishes, there are elected councils, consisting of directly elected councillors. Broadly, county councils range from 60–100 members; metropolitan district councils 50–80 members; non-metropolitan district councils 30–60 members. The councillors elect annually one of their number as chairman.

The general pattern in England is that councillors serve 4 years and there are no elections of district and parish councillors in county elections years. In metropolitan districts one-third of the councillors for each ward are elected each year except in the year of county elections. Non-metropolitan districts can choose whether to have elections by thirds or whole council elections. In the former case, one-third of the council, as nearly as may be, is elected in each year of metropolitan district elections. If whole council elections are chosen, these are held in the year midway between county elections. The London boroughs have whole council elections, in the year immediately following the county council election years. Local elections are normally held on the first Thursday in May.

Generally speaking, all British subjects or citizens of the Republic of Ireland of 18 years or over, resident on the qualifying date in the area for which the election is being held, are entitled to vote at local government elections. A register of electors is prepared and published annually by local electoral registration officers.

A returning officer has the overall responsibility for an election. Voting takes place at polling stations,

arranged by the local authority and under the supervision of a presiding officer specially appointed for the purpose. Candidates, who are subject to various statutory qualifications and disqualifications designed to secure that they are suitable persons to hold office, must be nominated by electors for the electoral area concerned.

Internal Organization

Local authorities increasingly are organized along party political lines and over 80 per cent are now controlled by groups of councillors having allegiance to one of the main political parties. However, the council as a whole is the final decision-making body within any authority. Councils are free to a great extent to make their own internal organizational arrangements. Normally, questions of major policy are settled by the full council, while the administration of the various services is the responsibility of committees of members. Day to day decisions are delegated to the council's officers, who act within the policies laid down by the members.

Functions

Local authorities are empowered or required by various Acts of Parliament to carry out functions in their areas. The legislation concerned comprises public general Acts and "local" Acts which local authorities have promoted as private bills. In non-metropolitan areas, functions are divided between the districts and counties, those requiring the larger area or population for their efficient performance going to the county. The metropolitan district councils, with the larger population in their areas, already had wider functions than non-metropolitan councils, and following abolition of the metropolitan county councils have now been given most of their functions also. A few functions continue to be exercised over the larger area by joint bodies, made up of councillors from each district.

The allocation of functions is as follows:

county councils: education; strategic planning; traffic, transport and highways; police; fire service; consumer protection; refuse disposal; smallholdings; social services; libraries.

non-metropolitan district councils: local planning; housing; highways (maintenance of certain urban roads and off-street car parks); building regulations; environmental health; refuse collection; cemeteries and crematoria.

metropolitan district and London borough councils: their functions are all those listed above, except that fire, civil defence (and in some cases, refuse disposal) in all areas and police and passenger transport in the metropolitan counties only are exercised by joint bodies. Education in inner London is the responsibility of a special authority.

Functions exercised *concurrently* by county and district councils and London boroughs: recreation (parks, playing fields, swimming pools); museums; encouragement of the arts, tourism and industry.

The sewerage and sewage disposal functions of local authorities have been transferred to nine water authorities in England and the Welsh Water Authority. Water authorities, however, are expected to make agreements whereby the new district councils discharge sewerage functions on an agency basis. Apart from these functions, the water authorities are responsible for water supply and conservation; river pollution control and river management; fisheries; land drainage; and use of water space for recreation and amenity purposes.

The personal health functions of local authorities were transferred in 1977 to area health authorities, whose areas were the same as non-metropolitan and Welsh counties and metropolitan districts. From April 1982 this two-tier structure was replaced by about 199 District Health Authorities. They work in close collaboration with local education, social services and environmental health authorities.

Residuary Bodies

Residuary bodies were set up in 1985 to deal with the business of the Greater London and Metropolitan County Councils which had not already devolved onto other bodies at the time of the Councils' abolition in 1986. Addresses and details of principal officers are given on page 579 (page 598 for Greater London).

Parishes

Parishes with 200 or more electors must generally have parish councils, and about three-quarters of the parishes have councils. A parish council comprises at least five members, the number being fixed by the district council. Elections are held every four years, in the year in which the local district councillor is elected. All parishes have parish meetings, comprising the electors of the parish. Where there is no council, the meeting must be held at least twice a year.

Parish council functions include: allotments; encouragement of arts and crafts; community halls, recreational facilities (e.g. open spaces, swimming pools), cemeteries and crematoria; and many minor functions. They must also be given an opportunity to comment on planning applications. They may, like county and district councils, spend limited sums for the general benefit of the parish. They precept on the district councils for their rate funds.

Civic Dignities

District councils may petition for a Royal Charter granting borough status to the district. In boroughs the chairman of the council is the mayor. The status "City" and the right to call the mayor "Lord Mayor" may also be granted by letters patent. Parish councils may call themselves "town councils", in which case their chairman is the "town mayor".

Charter trustees were established for those former boroughs which were too large to have parish councils when local government was reorganised in 1974 and they became part of districts without city or borough status. The charter trustees are the district councillors representing the area of the former borough and they elect a mayor, continue civic tradition, and look after the charters, insignia and civic plate of the former borough.

Local Commissioners for England and Wales

Commissioners for Local Administration in England and in Wales (*see* page 338) have been appointed with the duty of investigating complaints of maladministration in aspects of local government; they report to the local council concerned.

Wales

Since 1974 Wales, including the former Monmouthshire, has been divided into eight counties; Gwynedd; Clwyd; Powys; Dyfed; West, Mid and South Glamorgan; and Gwent. There are 37 districts in Wales, many of those in the less populated parts reflecting the areas of former Welsh counties.

The arrangements for Welsh counties and districts are generally similar to those for English non-metropolitan counties and districts. There are some differences in functions: Welsh district councils have refuse disposal as well as refuse collection functions and they may provide on-street as well as off-street car parks with the consent of the county council. A few districts have also been designated as library authorities.

In Wales parishes have been replaced by communities. Unlike England, where many areas are not in any parish, communities have been established for the whole of Wales; approximately 1,000 communities in all. Community meetings may be convened as and when desired. Community councils exist in about 770 communities and further councils may be established at the request of a community meeting. Community councils have broadly the same range of powers as English parish councils. Community councillors are elected *en bloc* on the same basis as parish councillors in England, i.e. at the same time as a district council election and for a term of four years.

Local Government Finance

Local government is financed from various sources.

(1) *Community charges.*—These will replace domestic rates from April 1, 1990 under the provisions of the Local Government Finance Act 1988. They are raised by the charging authorities (district councils and, in London, borough councils and the City Corporation). Liability to pay a community charge arises from an entry in the community charges register which is compiled by the community charges registration officer of each charging authority. Sums required by county and parish councils and joint boards for police, fire and transport will be included by the charging authority when calculating its community charge. There are three types of charge: the personal community charge, payable by people aged 18 or over (unless exempt); the collective community charge paid in respect of certain designated buildings whose occupants move frequently and are difficult to register, and who will therefore pay their community charge contributions to the landlord; and the standard community charge which is payable in respect of domestic property which is not occupied.

The Community Charges Benefits (General) Regulations 1989 makes provision for community charge rebates. These will be administered by charging authorities. Eligibility for a rebate depends chiefly on the net income of the charge-payer.

(2) *Non-domestic (business) rates.*—Collected from April 1, 1990 by charging authorities, i.e. by district councils, the Council of the Isles of Scilly and in London by the borough councils and the Common Council of the City of London. The Local Government Finance Act 1988 provides for liability for rates to be assessed on the basis of a poundage (multiplier) tax on the rateable value of property (hereditaments). The multiplier is to be set by central Government and rates collected by the charging authority for the area where a property is located. Rate income collected by charging authorities is paid into a central national non-domestic rating (N.N.D.R.) pool and redistributed to individual authorities on the basis of adult resident population. For the years 1990–91 to 1994–95 actual payment of rates in certain cases will be subjected to transitional arrangements, to phase in the larger increases and reductions in rates resulting from the combined effects of the 1990 revaluation and the introduction of a uniform national business rate (U.B.R.).

Rateable values for the rating lists come into force on April 1, 1990. They are derived from the rental value of property as at April 1, 1988 and determined on certain statutory assumptions by valuation officers of the Board of Inland Revenue. New property is added to the list, and significant changes to existing property necessitate amendments to the rateable value, on the same basis. Rating lists remain in force until the next general revaluation, which is scheduled for April 1, 1995.

Certain types of property are exempt from rates, e.g. agricultural land and buildings, and places of public religious worship. Charities and other nonprofit-making organizations may receive full or partial relief. Specified classes of empty property are liable to pay rates at 50 per cent.

(3) *Government grants.*—In addition to specific grants in support of revenue expenditure on particular services, central Government has paid rate support grant to local authorities. This grant consists of two elements: block grant and domestic rate relief grant. The block grant is paid to enable all local authorities to provide comparable standards of service whilst levying the same rate poundage. The domestic rate relief grant is payable to all rating authorities to reimburse them for the cost of giving the domestic rate relief prescribed for the year.

The 1989–90 rate support grant settlement provided for a total of £9,588 million in rate support grant to be paid to local authorities. Unlike previous years, when an authority's entitlement was determined by its actual spending during the year, this amount will be paid out in full.

On April 1, 1990 the Government is introducing a new local government finance system. Local authorities will continue to receive specific grants in support of particular services. Those authorities responsible for setting and collecting the community charge (charging authorities) will also receive revenue support grant. Grant entitlement will depend on the costs authorities providing services in the area would have to meet to provide a standard level of service. Payments of revenue support grant will be such that if all local authorities in a charging authority's area were to budget to spend at a level sufficient to provide the standard level of service, then the community charge paid by each individual in that area would equal a national standard amount (the community charge for standard spending).

Expenditure 1988–89

Forecasts of local authority relevant expenditure for 1988–89 in England adopted by the Government for rate support grant purposes were as follows. The amounts given are at 1988–89 cash prices.

Service	£m
Education	13,420
School meals and milk	450
Libraries, museums and art galleries	480
Personal social services and port health	3,035
Police	3,350
Fire	717
Other Home Office services	443
Local transport	1,950
Local environmental services	3,015
Agricultural services	137
Consumer protection and trading standards	76
Employment	103
Non-Housing Revenue Account housing	175
Housing benefits	187
Unallocated current expenditure	—
Total current expenditure	**27,538**

	£m
Rate fund revenue account contributions to capital outlay:	
Unallocated contributions to special funds, etc.	−483
Other	387
Loan charges (including leasing)	2,757
Rate fund revenue account contributions to Housing Revenue Account	279
Interest receipts	−632
Total relevant expenditure	**29,846**

The aggregate amount of Exchequer grants for 1988–89 was determined at £13,775 million. Of this, the specific grants and the transport and National Parks supplementary grants were estimated at £3,556 million, giving a total for rate support grants of £10,209 million, of which £9,482 million was in respect of the block grant and £727 million in respect of the domestic rate relief grant.

Rates and Rateable Values.—The total rateable value for England on April 1, 1987 was £7,729·5 million (figure for 1988 not yet available) and an estimate of the amount to be raised in rates, gross of rebates, in 1988–89 is £18,464 million.

Average Rates.—The estimated average rates levied in England in 1987–88 were: Inner London Boroughs, *domestic* rate 176·7p, *non-domestic* rate 181·9p; Outer London, 190·7p and 214·3p; Metropolitan Districts, 268·5p and 289·7p. The average rates levied in England were estimated at 228·9p (*domestic*) and 239·5p (*non-domestic*). In Wales the estimated average rates levied were, *domestic* rate 238·8p, *non-domestic* rate 257·6p.

SCOTLAND

Since 1975, mainland Scotland has been divided for local government purposes into nine regions within which there are 53 districts. Regional and district councils have separate responsibility for specific functions. In the three islands areas, Orkney, Shetland and the Western Isles, there are single tier Islands Councils responsible for most local authority functions.

Local Government Electors.—In 1989 the Register shows 3,932,897 electors in Scotland. Elections are next due to take place in 1990 for regional and island councils, and in 1992 for district councils.

Functions

Regional Councils are responsible for education; social work; strategic planning; the provision of infrastructure such as roads, water and sewerage; consumer protection; flood prevention; coast protection; and valuation and rating. They also have responsibility for the police and fire services; civil defence; and electoral registration, and in relation to public transport and registration of births, deaths and marriages.

District Councils deal with more local matters such as housing; leisure and recreation, including tourism, parks, libraries, museums and galleries; development control and building control; environmental health, including cleansing, refuse collection and disposal, food hygiene, inspection of shops, offices and factories, clean air, markets and slaughterhouses, burial and cremation; licensing, including liquor, cinemas and theatres, taxis, street traders, betting and gaming, and charitable collections; allotments; public conveniences; the administration of district courts.

Community Councils.—Unlike the parish councils of England or community councils of Wales, Scottish community councils are not local authorities. Their purpose as defined in statute is to ascertain and express the views of the communities which they represent, and to take in the interests of their communities such action as appears to be expedient or practicable. Schemes drawn up by district and islands councils provide for a possible total of 1,342 community councils, of which about 1,130 are in existence.

Rates

In 1987–88, the latest year for which final figures were available, a total of £2,133,647,795 was received from the general rates of local government in Scotland and £64,200,000 from domestic water rates. The rateable value on which rates were leviable was £3,219,546,252 on the general rates and £1,341,300,000 on the domestic water rates. The average general rate levied was 75·0p and the domestic water rate levied was 4·84p.

Provisional figures for 1988–89 show total receipts from general rates of £2,277,543,819 and £65,400,000 from domestic water rates. The average rate per £ levied for 1988–89 was 78·66p (general) and 4·94p (domestic water rate).

Domestic rates were abolished with effect from April 1, 1989 and were replaced by community charges. The average personal community charge payable in Scotland for 1989–90 is £280·20 and the average community water charge is £20·40.

Non-domestic rates remain and are set by the local authorities subject to a ceiling on the annual increase in poundage equal to the annual rate of inflation.

Local Commissioner

The Commissioner for Local Administration in Scotland is responsible for investigating complaints from members of the public against local authorities (*see* page 338).

NORTHERN IRELAND

For the purpose of local government Northern Ireland has a system of 26 single-tier district councils. There are 566 members of the councils, elected for periods of four years at a time on the principle of proportional representation.

The district councils all have the same three main roles. These are:

(a) an executive role in which the councils are responsible for a wide range of local services including the provision of recreational, social, community, and cultural facilities; environmental health; consumer protection; the enforcement of building regulations; the promotion of tourist development schemes; gas supply; street cleansing; refuse collection and disposal; litter prevention; and miscellaneous licensing and registration provisions, including dog control;

(b) a representative role in which they nominate representatives to sit as members of the various statutory bodies responsible for the administration of regional services such as education and libraries, health and personal social services, drainage, fire and electricity; and

(c) a consultative role in which they act as the media through which the views of local people are expressed on the operation in their area of other regional services, notably planning, roads, and conservation (including water supply and sewerage services) provided by those departments of central government which have an obligation, either statutorily or otherwise, to consult the district councils about proposals affecting their areas.

PARTY REPRESENTATION IN LOCAL GOVERNMENT
(as at end May 1989)

Abbreviations: *A.* = Liberal/SDP Alliance; *C.* = Conservative; *Com.* = Communist; *Dem.* = Democrat; *Grn.* = Green; *Ind.* = Independent; *Ind.C.* = Independent Conservative; *Ind.Lab.* = Independent Labour; *Lab.* = Labour; *Lib.* = Liberal; *Lib.Dem.* = Liberal Democrat; *MK* = Mebyon Kernow; *ND* = Non-Political/Non-Party; *PC* = Plaid Cymru; *RA* = Ratepayers'/Residents' Associations; *SDP* = Social Democratic Party; *SLD* = Social and Liberal Democrat; *SNP* = Scottish National Party.

ENGLAND

Counties

Avon ....*Lab.* 36, *C.* 33, *SLD* 7.
Bedfordshire........*C.* 35, *Lab.* 27, *SLD* 11.
Berkshire ....*C.* 38, *Lab.* 19, *SLD* 15, *Ind.* 1, *Ind.C.* 1, *RA* 1.
Buckinghamshire ...*C.* 50, *Lab.* 11, *SLD* 6, *Ind.* 2, *Lib.* 1, *SDP* 1.
Cambridgeshire .....*C.* 46, *Lab.* 20, *SLD* 9, *Ind.* 1, *Lib.* 1.
Cheshire ....*Lab.* 32, *C.* 29, *SLD* 10.
Cleveland ....*Lab.* 48, *C.* 19, *SLD* 10.
Cornwall ....*SLD* 31, *Ind.* 24, *C.* 14, *Lab.* 8, *Lib.*, *MK* 1.
Cumbria...........*C.* 37, *Lab.* 37, *SLD* 6, *Ind.* 3.
Derbyshire ....*Lab.* 52, *C.* 27, *SLD* 3, *Ind.* 2.
Devon.............*C.* 56, *Lab.* 13, *SLD* 11, *Ind.* 2, *SDP* 2, *Lib.* 1.
Dorset ....*C.* 43, *SLD* 22, *Ind.* 6, *Lab.* 6.
Durham ....*Lab.* 56, *C.* 7, *SLD* 5, *Ind.* 3.
Essex ....*C.* 57, *Lab.* 26, *SLD* 14, *Ind.* 1.
Gloucestershire .....*SLD* 23, *C.* 19, *Lab.* 16, *Ind.C.* 4, *RA* 1.
Hampshire ....*C.* 57, *SLD* 25, *Lab.* 19, *Ind.* 1.
Hereford and
Worcester ....*C.* 38, *Lab.* 22, *SLD* 11, *Ind.* 5.
Hertfordshire.......*C.* 45, *Lab.* 27, *SLD* 5.

Humberside ....*Lab.* 41, *C.* 31, *Lib.Dem.* 3.
Kent...............*C.* 55, *Lab.* 25, *SLD* 18, *SDP* 1.
Lancashire ....*Lab.* 50, *C.* 42, *Lib.Dem.* 7.
Leicestershire ......*C.* 38, *Lab.* 34, *SLD* 12, *Ind.* 1.
Lincolnshire........*C.* 39, *Lab.* 19, *SLD* 12, *Ind.* 4, *Ind.C.* 1, *SDP* 1.
Norfolk ....*C.* 47, *Lab.* 28, *SLD* 9.
Northamptonshire ..*C.* 34, *Lab.* 31, *SLD* 2, *Ind.* 1.
Northumberland ....*Lab.* 38, *C.* 17, *SLD* 8, *Ind.* 2, *NP* 1.
Nottinghamshire. ...*Lab.* 49, *C.* 34, *SLD* 4, (1 Vac.).
Oxfordshire ....*C.* 33, *Lab.* 23, *SLD* 13, *Ind.* 1.
Shropshire ....*C.* 31, *Lab.* 24, *SLD* 8, *Ind.* 3.
Somerset ....*C.* 32, *SLD* 17, *Lab.* 6, *Ind.* 1, *SDP* 1.
Staffordshire ....*Lab.* 50, *C.* 28, *RA* 2, *SLD* 2.
Suffolk ....*C.* 46, *Lab.* 26, *SLD* 5, *Ind.* 3.
Surrey ....*C.* 56, *SLD* 9, *Lab.* 7, *Ind.* 2, *RA* 2.
Sussex, East ....*C.* 38, *Lab.* 17, *SLD* 15.
Sussex, West........*C.* 46, *SLD* 15, *Lab.* 9, *SDP* 1.
Warwickshire ......*C.* 32, *Lab.* 24, *SLD* 4, *Ind.* 1, *RA* 1.
Wight, Isle of ....*SLD* 23, *C.* 15, *Ind.* 4, *Grn.* 1.
Wiltshire...........*C.* 35, *Lab.* 18, *SLD* 17, *Ind.* 2, *SDP* 2, *Lib.* 1.
Yorkshire, North ...*C.* 44, *Lab.* 22, *SLD* 21, *Ind.* 6, *SDP* 3.

Metropolitan District Councils
GREATER MANCHESTER

Bolton ....*Lab.* 38, *C.* 16, *SLD* 5, *Ind. Lab.* 1.
Bury ....*Lab.* 26, *C.* 22.
Manchester.........*Lab.* 76, *C.* 10, *SLD* 8, *Ind.* 4, (1 Vac.).
Oldham ....*Lab.* 42, *SLD* 13, *C.* 5.
Rochdale ....*Lab.* 34, *SLD* 13, *C.* 11, (2 Vac.).
Salford ....*Lab.* 54, *C.* 5, *Ind.* 1.
Stockport ....*SLD* 24, *C.* 21, *Lab.* 14, *RA* 3, (1 Vac.).
Tameside ....*Lab.* 45, *C.* 7, *SLD* 3, (2 Vac.).
Trafford ....*C.* 31, *Lab.* 27, *Dem.* 4, (1 Vac.).
Wigan ....*Lab.* 63, *SLD* 5, *C.* 3, *Ind. Lab.* 1.

MERSEYSIDE

Knowsley ....*Lab.* 59, *C.* 3, *Ind. Lab.* 2, *Lib.* 1, (1 Vac.).
Liverpool...........*Lab.* 56, *SLD* 39, *C.* 2, *SDP* 2.
St. Helens ....*Lab.* 39, *C.* 8, *SLD* 7.
Sefton..............*C.* 25, *Lab.* 24, *SLD* 20.
Wirral ....*Lab.* 29, *C.* 23, *SLD* 10, *Ind. Lab.* 3, (1 Vac.).

SOUTH YORKSHIRE

Barnsley ....*Lab.* 61, *C.* 2, *Ind.* 1, *RA* 1, (1 Vac.).
Doncaster ....*Lab.* 54, *C.* 9.
Rotherham ....*Lab.* 62, *SLD* 2, *C.* 1, *Ind.* 1.
Sheffield............*Lab.* 66, *C.* 12, *SLD* 9.

TYNE AND WEAR

Gateshead ....*Lab.* 58, *SLD* 5, *C.* 3.
Newcastle upon Tyne..............*Lab.* 60, *SLD* 11, *C.* 6, *SDP* 1.
North Tyneside .....*Lab.* 34, *C.* 16, *SLD* 6, *SDP* 3, *Ind. Lab.* 1.
South Tyneside .....*Lab.* 56, *C.* 3, *Others* 1.
Sunderland ....*Lab.* 63, *C.* 9, *Lib.* 3.

WEST MIDLANDS

Birmingham ....*Lab.* 67, *C.* 43, *SLD* 6, *SDP* 1.
Coventry ....*Lab.* 43, *C.* 10, *SLD* 1.
Dudley ....*Lab.* 41, *C.* 31.
Sandwell ....*Lab.* 56, *C.* 13, *Lib.* 2, (1 Vac.).
Solihull ....*C.* 28, *Lab.* 14, *SLD* 6, *Others* 3.
Walsall ....*Lab.* 31, *C.* 18, *Lib.* 8, *Ind.* 2, (1 Vac.).
Wolverhampton.....*Lab.* 31, *C.* 23, *SLD* 6.

WEST YORKSHIRE

Bradford ....*C.* 45, *Lab.* 43, *SDP* 2.
Calderdale ....*Lab.* 27, *C.* 18, *SLD* 9.
Kirklees............*Lab.* 34, *C.* 18, *Lib.* 17, (3 Vac.).
Leeds ....*Lab.* 59, *C.* 25, *Lib.* 10, *Ind.* 1, (4 Vac.).
Wakefield ....*Lab.* 57, *C.* 3, *SLD* 2, *Ind. Lab.* 1.

Non-Metropolitan District Councils
(* one-third of councillors of Councils so denoted retire each year, except in those years when County Council elections are held)

*Adur...............*SLD* 22, *C.* 15, *RA* 2.
Allerdale ....*Lab.* 24, *Ind.* 20, *C.* 11.
Alnwick...........*Lib.* 12, *C.* 3, *Ind.* 3, *Lab.* 2, *Ind. Lab.* 1, *SLD* 1, *Others* 7.
*Amber Valley ......*C.* 25, *Lab.* 14, *Ind.* 3, *SLD* 1.
Arun ....*C.* 50, *SLD* 4, *Lab.* 1, (1 Vac.).

Ashfield ....*Lab.* 27, *C.* 4, *SDP* 2.
Ashford ....*C.* 31, *SLD* 9, *Lab.* 7, *Ind.* 1, *Lib.* 1.
Aylesbury Vale ....*C.* 34, *SLD* 13, *Ind.* 7, *Lab.* 2, *SDP* 1, (1 Vac.).
Babergh ....*C.* 16, *Ind.* 12, *A.* 3, *Lab.* 3, *Lib.* 1, *Others* 7.
*Barrow-in-Furness .*Lab.* 20, *C.* 14, *Ind.* 2, (2 Vac.).
*Basildon ....*Lab.* 21, *C.* 13, *SLD* 8.
*Basingstoke and Deane............*C.* 33, *Lab.* 13, *SLD* 9, *Ind.* 4.
*Bassetlaw ....*Lab.* 25, *C.* 19, *Ind.* 6.
*Bath ....*C.* 27, *Lab.* 14, *Ind.C.* 7.
Berwick-upon-Tweed ....*SLD* 13, *Ind.* 9, *C.* 4, *Lab.* 1, (1 Vac.).
Beverley ....*C.* 34, *Lib.* 15, *Lab.* 2, *Ind.* 1, (1 Vac.).
Blaby ....*C.* 32, *Ind.* 3, *SLD* 3, *Others* 1.
*Blackburn ....*Lab.* 30, *C.* 24, *SLD* 4, *SDP* 1, (1 Vac.).
Blackpool ....*C.* 23, *Lab.* 15, *SLD* 6.
Blyth Valley ....*Lab.* 26, *SLD* 18, *SDP* 3.
Bolsover ....*Lab.* 30, *RA* 2, *SLD* 2, *C.* 1, *Ind.* 1, *Others* 1.
Boothferry ....*C.* 17, *Lab.* 10, *Ind.* 8.
Boston ....*C.* 16, *Ind.* 8, *Lab.* 5, *Lib.* 5.
Bournemouth......*C.* 37, *SLD* 12, *Lab.* 5, *Ind.* 3.
Bracknell Forest ...*C.* 40.
Braintree ....*C.* 30, *Lab.* 14, *Ind.* 6, *SLD* 6, *RA* 3, (1 Vac.).
Breckland ....*C.* 33, *Lab.* 7, *NP* 6, *Ind.* 5, *SDP* 2.
*Brentwood ....*C.* 23, *SLD* 13, *Lab.* 2, (1 Vac.).
Bridgnorth ....*Ind.* 16, *C.* 11, *Ind. Lab.* 2, *Lib.* 2, *SLD* 2.
*Brighton ....*Lab.* 27, *C.* 19, *SLD* 2.
*Bristol ....*Lab.* 38, *C.* 24, *SLD* 5, (1 Vac.).
*Broadland ....*C.* 35, *SLD* 7, *Ind.* 6, *SDP* 1.
Bromsgrove ....*C.* 29, *Lab.* 7, *SLD* 4, *RA* 1.
*Broxbourne ....*C.* 36, *Lab.* 5, *SLD* 1.
Broxtowe..........*C.* 32, *Lab.* 10, *SLD* 4, *SDP* 2, *Ind.* 1.
*Burnley ....*Lab.* 41, *SLD* 6, *C.* 5, *Lib.* 1.
*Cambridge ....*Lab.* 23, *C.* 12, *SLD* 7.
*Cannock Chase ....*Lab.* 25, *SLD* 14, *C.* 3.
Canterbury ....*C.* 33, *Lib. Dem.* 11, *Lab.* 5.
Caradon ....*Ind.* 25, *SLD* 8, *C.* 4, *RA* 3, *Lab.* 1.
*Carlisle ....*Lab.* 29, *C.* 19, *Lib.* 2, *Ind.* 1.
Carrick ....*SLD* 21, *C.* 15, *Ind.* 5, *Lab.* 4.
Castle Morpeth ....*SLD* 13, *Ind.* 10, *Lab.* 5, *C.* 4, *Others* 2.
Castle Point ....*C.* 39.
Charnwood ....*C.* 40, *Lab.* 9, *SLD* 2, *Ind.* 1.
Chelmsford ....*SLD* 28, *C.* 24, *Ind.* 3, *SDP* 1.
*Cheltenham ....*C.* 16, *SLD* 14, *Lab.* 2, *RA* 1.
*Cherwell ....*C.* 31, *Lab.* 14, *SLD* 3, *SDP* 2, *Ind.* 1, *Ind. C.* 1.
*Chester ....*C.* 30, *Lab.* 18, *SLD* 11, *Ind.* 1.
Chesterfield ....*Lab.* 35, *SLD* 7, *C.* 5.
Chester-le-Street ...*Lab.* 25, *Lib.* 4, *Ind.* 3, *C.* 1.
Chichester ....*C.* 35, *SLD* 12, *Ind.* 2, *RA* 1.
Chiltern ....*C.* 42, *A.* 6, *Lab.* 1, *RA* 1.
*Chorley ....*C.* 24, *Lab.* 20, *SLD* 3, *Ind.* 1.
Christchurch ......*C.* 16, *Ind.* 5, *Lab.* 3, *SLD* 1.
Cleethorpes ....*SLD* 16, *C.* 11, *Lab.* 11, *Ind.* 3.
*Colchester.........*C.* 24, *SLD* 24, *Lab.* 8, *RA* 3, *Ind.* 1.
*Congleton ....*SLD* 23, *C.* 15, *Lab.* 5, *SDP* 1, (1 Vac.).
Copeland ....*Lab.* 26, *C.* 21, *Ind.* 2, *RA* 2.
Corby ....*Lab.* 23, *C.* 3, *Ind. Lab.* 1.
Cotswold ....*C.* 9, *Ind.* 8, *Lib.* 2, *Lab.* 1, *Others* 25.
*Craven............*C.* 12, *SLD* 11, *Ind.* 7, *Lab.* 3, *Lib.* 1.

*Crawley .... *Lab.* 21, *C.* 10, *SLD* 1.
*Crewe and
Nantwich .... *C.* 27, *Lab.* 26, *SLD* 4.
Dacorum .... *C.* 40, *Lab.* 7, *SLD* 7, *SDP* 3, (1 Vac.).
Darlington .... *C.* 24, *Lab.* 24, *Ind.* 2, *SLD* 2.
Dartford .... *C.* 28, *Lab.* 17, *RA* 2.
*Daventry .... *C.* 19, *Lab.* 9, *Ind.* 5, *SLD* 2.
*Derby .... *C.* 24, *Lab.* 19, *Ind. Lab.* 1.
Derbyshire Dales ... *C.* 23, *SLD* 9, *Lab.* 3, *NP* 3, *Ind.* 1.
Derwentside .... *Lab.* 43, *Ind.* 9, *C.* 3.
Dover .... *C.* 33, *Lab.* 19, *SLD* 4.
Durham .... *Lab.* 28, *SDP* 14, *Ind.* 6, *Ind. Lab.* 1.
Easington .... *Lab.* 43, *Ind.* 4, *Lib.* 2, *Ind. Lab.* 1, *SDP* 1.
*Eastbourne .... *C.* 16, *SLD* 13, *Lab.* 1.
E. Cambridgeshire . *Ind.* 4, *SLD* 4, *C.* 3, *A.* 1, *Others* 24, (1 Vac.).
East Devon .... *C.* 53, *SLD* 7.
East Dorset .... *C.* 25, *SLD* 7, *Ind.* 4.
East Hampshire .... *C.* 23, *SLD* 12, *Ind.* 6, (1 Vac.).
East Hertfordshire . *C.* 33, *Ind.* 6, *SLD* 5, *RA* 4, *Ind. C.* 1, *Lab.* 1.
*Eastleigh .... *SLD* 22, *C.* 16, *Lab.* 6.
East Lindsey .... *NP* 27, *SLD* 11, *Ind.* 10, *C.* 9, *Lab.* 3.
East Northants. ..... *C.* 30, *Lab.* 19, *SLD* 1.
East Staffordshire .. *C.* 22, *Lab.* 21, *SLD* 2, *Ind.* 1.
East Yorkshire ..... *C.* 21, *Ind.* 11, *Lab.* 2, *SDP* 2, *SLD* 2, *Others* 5.
Eden .... *Ind.* 35, *C.* 1, *Ind. C.* 1.
*Ellesmere Port and
Neston .... *Lab.* 29, *C.* 12.
*Elmbridge .... *C.* 32, *RA* 15, *Lab.* 6, *SLD* 5, *Ind. C.* 1, *SDP* 1.
*Epping Forest...... *C.* 37, *Lab.* 10, *RA* 7, *SLD* 2, *Ind.* 1, *Ind. C.* 1, *SDP* 1.
Epsom and Ewell ... *RA* 35, *Lab.* 3, *SLD* 1.
Erewash........... *C.* 29, *Lab.* 20, *Ind.* 1, *Ind. C.* 1, *Ind. Lab.* 1.
*Exeter .... *C.* 15, *Lab.* 13, *SLD* 5, *SDP* 2, *Ind.* 1.
*Fareham .... *C.* 27, *SLD* 12, *Ind.* 1, *RA* 1, *SDP* 1.
Fenland .... *C.* 25, *Ind.* 5, *Lab.* 4, *Lib.* 3, *SLD* 3.
Forest Heath ...... *C.* 14, *Ind.* 9, *SDP* 1, *SLD* 1.
Forest of Dean ..... *Lab.* 14, *C.* 8, *SLD* 8, *Ind. Lab.* 6, *Ind.* 4, *RA* 1, *Others* 8.
Fylde .... *C.* 26, *RA* 11, *Ind.* 2, *Lab.* 1, *Lib.* 1, *Others* 8.
Gedling .... *C.* 43, *Lab.* 6, *SLD* 5, *Ind.* 1, *Ind. C.* 1, *Lib.* 1.
*Gillingham .... *C.* 22, *SLD* 13, *Lab.* 7.
Glanford .... *C.* 25, *Ind.* 13, *Lab.* 2, *SDP* 1.
*Gloucester........ *C.* 16, *Lab.* 9, *SLD* 7, *Ind.* 1.
*Gosport .... *C.* 16, *SLD* 9, *Lab.* 5.
Gravesham .... *C.* 22, *Lab.* 22.
*Great Grimsby ..... *Lab.* 29, *C.* 13, *SLD* 2, *Ind.* 1.
*Great Yarmouth ... *C.* 23, *Lab.* 21, *Ind. Lab.* 3, *Lib.* 1.
Guildford.......... *C.* 30, *SLD* 9, *Lab.* 6.
*Halton .... *Lab.* 40, *SLD* 4, *C.* 3, *SDP* 1, *Others* 1.
Hambleton .... *C.* 20, *Ind.* 19, *SDP* 4, *SLD* 2, *Ind. C.* 1, *Lab.* 1.
Harborough .... *C.* 17, *SLD* 12, *Lab.* 2, *Ind.* 1, *Others* 5.
*Harlow............ *Lab.* 35, *C.* 4, *Dem.* 3.
*Harrogate .... *C.* 30, *SLD* 21, *Ind.* 3, *Ind. C.* 3, *Lab.* 3, *Ind.* 2, *SDP* 1.
*Hart .... *C.* 16, *SLD* 10, *Ind.* 8, (1 Vac.).
*Hartlepool........ *Lab.* 34, *C.* 10, *SLD* 2, *Ind.* 1.
*Hastings .... *C.* 12, *SLD* 12, *Lab.* 8.
*Havant............ *C.* 22, *Lab.* 11, *SLD* 4, *Ind.* 3, *RA* 2.

*Hereford .... *SLD* 19, *Lab.* 4, *C.* 3, *Ind.* 1.
*Hertsmere .... *C.* 22, *Lab.* 12, *SLD* 4, *SDP* 1.
High Peak .... *Ind. C.* 21, *Lab.* 12, *SLD* 7, *Ind.* 4.
Hinckley and
Bosworth......... *C.* 21, *SLD* 8, *Lab.* 5.
Holderness .... *NP* 21, *SLD* 5, *Ind.* 4, *C.* 1.
Horsham .... *C.* 31, *SLD* 8, *Ind.* 4.
Hove .... *C.* 22, *Lab.* 4, *SLD* 3, *Ind.* 1.
*Huntingdonshire .. *C.* 46, *Lab.* 4, *Ind.* 2, *SLD* 1.
*Hyndburn .... *Lab.* 24, *C.* 17, *SLD* 6.
*Ipswich .... *Lab.* 34, *C.* 14.
Kennet............. *C.* 14, *NP* 12, *Ind.* 7, *SLD* 7.
Kerrier .... *SDP* 19, *Ind.* 5, *C.* 4, *Lab.* 4, *MK* 1. *Others* 9, (1 Vac.).
Kettering .... *C.* 16, *Lab.* 13, *SLD* 9, *Ind.* 7.
King's Lynn and
West Norfolk ..... *C.* 47, *Lab.* 11, *SLD* 1, (1 Vac.).
*Kingston upon Hull *Lab.* 55, *C.* 3, *SLD* 2.
Kingswood .... *C.* 26, *Lab.* 20, *Lib.* 2, *Ind.* 1, *SDP* 1.
Lancaster .... *C.* 29, *Lab.* 20, *SLD* 5, *RA* 1, *SDP* 1, *Others* 4.
Langbaurgh on Tees *Lab.* 27, *C.* 24, *SLD* 7, *Ind. Lab.* 2.
Leicester .... *Lab.* 33, *C.* 15, *SLD* 7, (1 Vac.).
*Leominster .... *Ind.* 23, *C.* 8, *A.* 2, *Ind. C.* 2, *Lib. Dem.* 1.
Lewes .... *C.* 33, *SLD* 12, *Ind.* 3.
Lichfield .... *C.* 42, *Lab.* 10, *Ind. Lab.* 3, *Ind.* 1.
*Lincoln .... *Lab.* 27, *C.* 6.
Luton .... *C.* 32, *Lab.* 13, *SLD* 3.
*Macclesfield .... *C.* 33, *SLD* 13, *Lab.* 6, *Ind.* 4, *RA* 3, *SDP* 1.
*Maidstone .... *SLD* 24, *C.* 21, *Lab.* 8, *Ind.* 2.
Maldon .... *C.* 14, *A.* 11, *Ind.* 3, *Ind. C.* 1, *Lab.* 1.
Malvern Hills ...... *A.* 16, *C.* 10, *Ind.* 9, *Lab.* 1, *Others* 15.
Mansfield.......... *Lab.* 37, *C.* 5, *Ind. C.* 2, *SLD* 2.
Medina............ *C.* 21, *SLD* 11, *Ind.* 2, *Lab.* 1, *Others* 1.
Melton .... *C.* 15, *SLD* 7, *Ind. C.* 4.
Mendip............ *SLD* 19, *C.* 17, *Ind.* 4, *Lab.* 2, *Lib.* 1.
Mid Bedfordshire .. *C.* 42, *Ind.* 5, *Lab.* 3, *SLD* 3.
Mid Devon .... *Ind.* 28, *SLD* 7, *Lib.* 5.
Middlesbrough..... *Lab.* 36, *C.* 12, *SLD* 4, *Ind.* 1.
Mid Suffolk .... *C.* 22, *Ind.* 8, *Lab.* 6, *SLD* 4.
*Mid Sussex .... *C.* 37, *SLD* 11, *Ind.* 6.
*Milton Keynes ..... *Lab.* 18, *C.* 13, *SLD* 13, *Ind.* 2.
*Mole Valley .... *C.* 17, *Ind.* 14, *SLD* 8, *Grn.* 1, *Lab.* 1.
Newark and
Sherwood .... *C.* 26, *Lab.* 24, *Ind.* 2, *SLD* 2.
Newbury .... *C.* 32, *SLD* 13.
*Newcastle under
Lyme .... *Lab.* 37, *C.* 10, *SLD* 9.
New Forest........ *C.* 34, *SLD* 16, *Ind.* 3, *SDP* 1, *Others* 4.
Northampton ...... *C.* 25, *Lab.* 16, *Lib.* 2.
Northavon .... *C.* 30, *SLD* 14, *Lab.* 8, *SDP* 4, *Ind.* 1.
*North Bedfordshire *C.* 25, *SLD* 14, *Lab.* 13, *Ind.* 1.
North Cornwall .... *SLD* 6, *C.* 2, *Others* 30.
North Devon ...... *Lib.* 17, *Ind.* 16, *C.* 9, *Others* 2.
North Dorset ...... *Ind.* 24, *SLD* 8, *C.* 1.
N.E. Derbyshire .... *Lab.* 30, *C.* 15, *Ind.* 5, *SLD* 1, (2 Vac.).
*North Hertfordshire *C.* 28, *Lab.* 13, *SDP* 4, *RA* 3, *SLD* 2.
North Kesteven .... *C.* 14, *Ind.* 13, *SLD* 5, *Lab.* 2, *Others* 5.
North Norfolk ..... *Ind.* 13, *C.* 10, *Lab.* 3, *SLD* 3, *Others* 17.
North Shropshire .. *NP* 27, *C.* 6, *Ind.* 5, *Lab.* 2.

N. Warwickshire ... *Lab.* 20, *C.* 12, *NP* 1, *SLD* 1.
N.W. Leicestershire *Lab.* 19, *C.* 14, *Ind.* 4, *A.* 3.
North Wiltshire .... *C.* 27, *SLD* 22, *Ind.* 1, *Lab.* 1, (1 Vac.).
*Norwich .... *Lab.* 37, *SLD* 9, *C.* 2.
Nottingham .... *C.* 27, *Lab.* 27, *Com.* 1.
*Nuneaton and
  Bedworth .... *Lab.* 35, *C.* 10.
*Oadby & Wigston .. *C.* 18, *SLD* 8.
Oswestry .... *NP* 14, *C.* 7, *Lab.* 5, *SLD* 3.
*Oxford .... *Lab.* 30, *C.* 10, *SLD* 5.
*Pendle .... *Lib.* 27, *Lab.* 19, *C.* 5.
*Penwith .... *C.* 16, *Ind.* 7, *Lab.* 7, *SLD* 2, *MK* 1, *SDP* 1.
*Peterborough ...... *Lab.* 22, *C.* 21, *Lib.* 5.
Plymouth .... *C.* 30, *Lab.* 23, *SDP* 6, *SLD* 1.
Poole .... *C.* 21, *SLD* 11. *Lib.* 2, *SDP* 2.
*Portsmouth .... *C.* 21, *Lab.* 8, *SLD* 4, *Ind.* *C.* 3, *Grn.* 1, *Ind.* 1, (1 Vac.).
*Preston .... *Lab.* 36, *C.* 16, *Lib.* 5.
*Purbeck .... *C.* 10, *Ind.* 6, *SLD* 3, *Lib.* 2, *RA* 1.
*Reading .... *Lab.* 25, *C.* 15, *Dem.* 5.
*Redditch .... *Lab.* 19, *C.* 8, *SLD* 2.
*Reigate and   *C.* 31, *Lab.* 10, *SLD* 3, *Ind.* 2,
  Banstead   *SLD* 2, *RA* 1.
Restormel .... *SLD* 23, *NP* 11, *C.* 5, *Ind.* 4, *Lab.* 1.
Ribble Valley ..... *C.* 32, *Lab.* 4, *Ind.* 2, *SLD* 1.
Richmondshire .... *Ind.* 27, *SDP* 5, *C.* 1, (1 Vac.).
Rochester upon   *C.* 29, *Lab.* 15, *SLD* 4, *Ind.* 1,
  Medway   *SDP* 1.
*Rochford .... *C.* 21, *Lib.* 13, *Lab.* 5, *Ind.* 1.
*Rossendale .... *Lab.* 21, *C.* 15.
Rother .... *C.* 28, *Ind.* 7, *SLD* 5, *RA* 3, *Lab.* 2.
*Rugby .... *C.* 24, *Lab.* 15, *RA* 6, *Ind.* 2, (1 Vac.).
*Runnymede ...... *C.* 25, *Lab.* 8, *Ind.* 3, *RA* 3, *SLD* 2, *SDP* 1.
Rushcliffe .... *C.* 46, *SLD* 6, *Lab.* 3.
*Rushmoor .... *C.* 32, *SLD* 8, *Lab.* 5.
Rutland .... *C.* 9, *Ind.* 7, *SLD* 3, (1 Vac.).
Ryedale .... *Ind.* 21, *SLD* 17, *C.* 4.
*St. Albans .... *C.* 32, *SLD* 16, *Lab.* 8, *SDP* 1.
St. Edmundsbury .. *C.* 31, *Lab.* 8, *SLD* 4, *Ind.* 1.
Salisbury .... *C.* 30, *Ind.* 9, *SLD* 9, *RA* 5, *SDP* 2, *Grn.* 1, *Lab.* 1, (1 Vac.).
Scarborough .... *C.* 21, *Ind.* 13, *Lab.* 8, *SLD* 7.
*Scunthorpe .... *Lab.* 29, *C.* 7, *SDP* 4.
Sedgefield .... *Lab.* 35, *Ind.* 4, *SLD* 4, *SDP* 3, *C.* 2, *NP* 1.
Sedgemoor .... *C.* 32, *SLD* 7, *Lab.* 5, *Ind.* 4, *Ind. Lab.* 1.
Selby.............. *C.* 24, *Ind.* 12, *Lab.* 9, *A.* 5.
Sevenoaks .... *C.* 35, *Ind.* 11, *SLD* 7.
Shepway .... *C.* 26, *SLD* 26, *Ind.* 3, (1 Vac.).
*Shrewsbury and   *C.* 19, *Lab.* 17, *SLD* 9, *Ind.* 2,
  Atcham   *SDP* 1.
*Slough .... *Lab.* 26, *C.* 8, *Lib.* 5.
*Southampton ...... *Lab.* 24, *C.* 17, *SLD* 4.
*South Bedfordshire . *C.* 38, *Lab.* 8, *SLD* 5, *RA* 2.
South Bucks. .... *C.* 30, *RA* 4, *SDP* 4, *Ind.* 3.
*South
  Cambridgeshire .. *Ind.* 29, *C.* 22, *Lab.* 3, *SLD* 1.
South Derbyshire . . *Lab.* 18, *C.* 11, *Ind.* 4, *Lib.* 1.
*Southend-on-Sea .. *SLD* 18, *C.* 16, *Lab.* 5.
South Hams .... *C.* 26, *Ind.* 6, *Lib.* 2, *Lab.* 1, *SLD* 1, *Others* 8.
*S. Herefordshire ... *NP* 17, *Ind.* 10, *C.* 4, *SLD* 2, *Lib.* 1, (1 Vac.).
South Holland ..... *C.* 13, *Ind.* 5, *SDP* 2, *Lab.* 1, *Others* 17.
South Kesteven .... *C.* 33, *Lab.* 10, *SLD* 8, *Ind.* 5, *Ind. C.* 1.
*South Lakeland .... *C.* 23, *SLD* 11, *Lab.* 5, *Others* 13.

South Norfolk ..... *C.* 26, *SLD* 16, *Ind.* 5.
South Northants. . . *C.* 28, *Ind.* 8, *Lab.* 2, *Others* 2.
South Oxfordshire . *C.* 36, *Lab.* 8, *Ind.* 6, *SDP* 6.
South Ribble .... *C.* 36, *Lab.* 10, *SLD* 7, (1 Vac.).
South Shropshire .. *SLD* 6, *C.* 5, *Ind.* 4, *Ind. Lab.* 1, *Others* 24.
South Somerset .... *SLD* 35, *C.* 15, *Ind.* 10.
South Staffordshire *C.* 43, *Lab.* 5, *Ind.* 2, *Others* 2.
South Wight .... *C.* 13, *Ind.* 5, *SLD* 5, *RA* 1.
Spelthorne .... *C.* 38, *Lab.* 2.
Stafford .... *C.* 31, *Lab.* 17, *SLD* 12.
Staffordshire   *C.* 27, *Lab.* 10, *Ind.* *C.* 6, *RA* 6,
  Moorlands   *Ind.* 5, *SDP* 1, *SLD* 1.
*Stevenage .... *Lab.* 27, *SLD* 9, *C.* 1, *Ind. Lab.* 1, *Others* 1.
Stockton-on-Tees .. *Lab.* 28, *C.* 18, *SLD* 9.
*Stoke-on-Trent ... *Lab.* 54, *C.* 6.
*Stratford-on-   *C.* 34, *SLD* 12, *Ind.* 6, *Lab.* 2,
  Avon   *Ind. C* 1.
*Stroud .... *C.* 22, *Lab.* 14, *SLD* 10, *Ind.* 7, *Grn.* 3.
Suffolk Coastal ..... *C.* 39, *SDP* 6, *Ind.* 5, *NP* 3, *Lab.* 2.
Surrey Heath ...... *C.* 36.
*Swale .... *C.* 21, *SLD* 14, *Lab.* 13, *SDP* 1.
*Tamworth .... *C.* 15, *Lab.* 15.
*Tandridge .... *C.* 25, *SLD* 12, *Lab.* 4, *Ind.* 1.
Taunton Deane .... *C.* 28, *Dem.* 8, *Lab.* 7, *SDP.* 7, *Ind.* 3.
Teesdale........... *Ind.* 22, *Lab.* 6, *C.* 1, *Ind. Lab.* 1, *Lib.* 1.
Teignbridge .... *C.* 28, *Ind.* 25, *SLD* 3, *Lab.* 2.
Tendring .... *C.* 30, *SLD* 16, *Lab.* 5, *RA* 5, *Ind.* 2, *Ind. C.* 1, (1 Vac.).
Test Valley .... *C.* 25, *SLD* 14, *Ind.* 2, *NP* 2, (1 Vac.).
Tewkesbury .... *C.* 17, *Ind.* 10, *NP* 7, *A.* 5, *Lab.* 1, *Others* 3, (1 Vac.).
*Thamesdown ...... *Lab.* 36, *C.* 11, *SLD* 4, *Ind.* 1, *SDP* 1, (1 Vac.).
Thanet .... *C.* 23, *Ind.* 13, *Lab.* 8, *SDP* 6, *Others* 4.
*Three Rivers ...... *SLD* 23, *C.* 17, *Lab.* 7.
*Thurrock.......... *Lab.* 29, *C.* 8, *Ind. Lab.* 2.
*Tonbridge and
  Malling .... *C.* 34, *SLD* 12, *Lab.* 6.
*Torbay .... *C.* 26, *SLD* 7, *SDP* 2, *Ind.* 1.
Torridge .... *Ind.* 23, *C.* 7, *Lab.* 3, *SLD* 3.
*Tunbridge Wells ... *C.* 36, *Lib.* 5, *SLD* 3, *SDP* 2, *Ind.* 1, *Lab.* 1.
Tynedale .... *C.* 16, *SLD* 13, *Ind.* 10, *Lab.* 8.
Uttlesford .... *C.* 25, *SLD* 8, *Ind.* 8, *Lab.* 1.
Vale of White
  Horse .... *C.* 42, *SLD* 7, *Ind.* 1, *Lab.* 1.
Vale Royal .... *C.* 28, *Lab.* 25, *Ind.* 3, *SLD* 3, *RA* 1.
Wansbeck .... *Lab.* 39, *Lib.* 7.
Wansdyke .... *C.* 28, *Lab.* 16, *Ind.* 3.
Warrington .... *Lab.* 37, *C.* 15, *SLD* 8.
Warwick .... *C.* 29, *Lab.* 7, *SLD* 6, *RA* 3.
*Watford .... *Lab.* 17, *C.* 11, *Ind. Lab.* 5, *Dem.* 3.
*Waveney .... *C.* 23, *Lab.* 20, *SLD* 4, *Ind.* 1.
Waverley.......... *C.* 42, *SLD* 9, *SDP* 3, *Ind.* 2, (1 Vac.).
Wealden .... *C.* 49, *SLD* 5, *RA* 3, *Ind.* 1.
Wear Valley .... *Lab.* 24, *Ind.* 6, *SLD* 4, *C.* 3, *Ind. Lab.* 1, *Others* 1, (1 Vac.).
Wellingborough.... *C.* 21, *Lab.* 9, *Ind.* 3, *Lib.* 1.
*Welwyn Hatfield ... *Lab.* 22, *C.* 19, *SLD* 2.
West Devon .... *Ind.* 14, *C.* 12, *Grn.* 1, *Lab.* 1, *SLD* 1, (1 Vac.).
West Dorset .... *NP* 27, *C.* 11, *SLD* 5, *Ind.* 4, *Ind. C.* 3, *Lib.* 3, *Lab.* 2.
*West Lancashire ... *C.* 30, *Lab.* 23, *SLD* 2.
*West Lindsey ...... *SLD* 16, *C.* 11, *Ind.* 9, *Lab.* 1.

*West Oxfordshire ..*C.* 26, *Ind.* 10, *SLD* 6, *Lab.* 4, *Ind. C.* 1, *Others* 2.
West Somerset .....*NP* 24, *C.* 5, *Ind.* 3.
West Wiltshire.....*C.* 30, *A.* 6, *Lab.* 3, *Ind.* 2, *Ind. C.* 1, *RA* 1.
*Weymouth and *Lab.* 13, *C.* 12, *Lib.* 5, *Ind.* 4, *RA*
Portland 1.
*Winchester ....*C.* 25, *SLD* 22, *Lab.* 6, *Ind.* 2.
Windsor and
Maidenhead ......*C.* 41, *SLD* 9, *RA* 7, *SDP* 1.
*Woking ....*C.* 15, *SLD* 14, *Lab.* 6.
*Wokingham ....*C.* 38, *SLD* 12, *Lab.* 2, (2 Vac.).
Woodspring ....*C.* 46, *SLD* 5, *Lab.* 4, *Ind. C.* 3, *Grn.* 1.
*Worcester ....*Lab.* 22, *C.* 14.
*Worthing ....*C.* 26, *SLD* 10.
Wrekin ....*Lab.* 30, *C.* 11, *Ind.* 3, *Dem.* 2.
Wychavon.........*C.* 31, *SLD* 9, *Ind.* 3, *Lab.* 3, *Ind. C.* 1, *Others* 2.
Wycombe..........*C.* 47, *Lab.* 5, *Ind.* 2, *SDP* 2, *SLD* 2, *Lib.* 1, *RA* 1.
Wyre ....*C.* 42, *Lab.* 8, *Lib.* 4, *Ind.* 1, *RA* 1.
*Wyre Forest ....*Lib. Dem.* 16, *C.* 13, *Lab.* 10, *Ind.* 3.
*York ....*Lab.* 28, *C.* 11, *S.L.D.* 6.

Greater London Boroughs

Barking ....*Lab.* 36, *SDP* 5, *C.* 3, *RA* 3, (1 Vac.).
Barnet ....*C.* 39, *Lab.* 18, *SLD* 3.
Bexley ....*C.* 37, *Lab.* 15, *SLD* 10.
Brent ....*Lab.* 40, *C.* 22, *SLD* 4.
Bromley ....*C.* 44, *Lab.* 10, *A.* 6.
Camden ....*Lab.* 44, *C.* 13, *SLD* 2.
City of Westminster .*C.* 32, *Lab.* 27, *Ind.* 1
Croydon............*C.* 44, *Lab.* 26.
Ealing ....*Lab.* 44, *C.* 23, *SLD* 3.
Enfield ....*C.* 40, *Lab.* 26.
Greenwich ....*Lab.* 41, *C.* 12, *SDP* 6, *SLD* 2, *Ind. Lab.* 1.
Hackney ....*Lab.* 50, *SLD* 5, *C.* 4, (1 Vac.).
Hammersmith ......*Lab.* 41, *C.* 9.
Haringey ....*Lab.* 39, *C.* 19, *SLD* 1.
Harrow ....*C.* 32, *Lib.* 17, *Lab.* 8, *RA* 4, *Ind. C.* 1, *Ind. Lab.* 1.
Havering ....*C.* 28, *Lab.* 20, *RA* 10, *SLD* 5.
Hillingdon..........*Lab.* 34, *C.* 28, *SLD* 7.
Hounslow ....*Lab.* 40, *C.* 17, *SLD* 3.
Islington ....*Lab.* 38, *SDP* 13, *Lib.* 1.
Kensington and
Chelsea ....*C.* 39, *Lab.* 14, (1 Vac.).
Kingston-upon- *C.* 25, *Lib. Dem.* 19, *Lab.* 4, *Ind.*
Thames .... 1.
Lambeth ....*Lab.* 40, *C.* 21, *SLD* 3.
Lewisham ....*Lab.* 49, *C.* 17, *SLD* 1.
Merton ....*C.* 29, *Lab.* 25, *SLD* 3.
Newham ....*Lab.* 59, *SLD* 1.
Redbridge ....*C.* 44, *Lab.* 17, *A.* 1, (1 Vac.).
Richmond upon
Thames ....*SLD* 46, *C.* 4, *SDP* 2.
Southwark ....*Lab.* 42, *SLD* 15, *C.* 7.
Sutton ....*SLD* 28, *C.* 21, *Lab.* 7.
Tower Hamlets......*Dem.* 25, *Lab.* 25.
Waltham Forest.....*Lab.* 29, *C.* 16, *SLD* 12.
Wandsworth........*C.* 31, *Lab.* 30.

WALES
County Councils

Clwyd..............*Lab.* 33, *Ind.* 19, *C.* 9, *SLD* 2, *Lib.* 1, *PC* 1, (1 Vac.).
Dyfed ....*Ind.* 32, *Lab.* 27, *Lib. Dem.* 4, *PC* 4, *Ind. Lab.* 1, *RA* 1.
Gwent ....*Lab.* 55, *C.* 7, *Ind.* 1.

Gwynedd ....*Ind.* 33, *PC* 13, *Lab.* 11, *SLD* 4, *C.* 1.
Mid Glamorgan .....*Lab.* 65, *PC* 5, *Ind.* 2, *SLD* 1, *RA* 1.
Powys.............*Ind.* 37, *Lab.* 5, *SLD* 3, *SDP* 1.
South Glamorgan ...*Lab.* 40, *C.* 13, *SLD* 6, *SDP* 2, *PC* 1.
West Glamorgan ....*Lab.* 44, *C.* 6, *Ind.* 6, *SLD* 2, *PC* 1.

District Councils

Aberconwy ....*A.* 11, *C.* 8, *Ind.* 5, *Lab.* 4, *PC* 1, *Others* 12.
Alyn & Deeside .....*Lab.* 24, *Ind.* 8, *C.* 5, *SLD* 4, *Ind. C.* 1, (1 Vac.).
Arfon ....*Ind.* 16, *Lab.* 11, *PC* 11, *SLD* 1.
Blaenau Gwent .....*Lab.* 34, *RA* 4, *Ind.* 2, *C.* 1, *Ind. Lab.* 1, *Lib.* 1, *PC* 1.
Brecknock..........*Ind.* 29, *Lab.* 13, *SLD* 2.
Cardiff ....*Lab.* 28, *C.* 24, *SLD* 13.
Carmarthen ....*Ind.* 27, *Lab.* 4, *RA* 2, *Lib.* 1, *PC* 1, (2 Vac.).
Ceredigion ....*Ind.* 22, *Lib.* 10, *A.* 6, *PC* 4, *Lab.* 2.
Colwyn ....*SLD* 15, *Ind.* 10, *C.* 3, *RA* 3, *Lab.* 2, (1 Vac.).
Cynon Valley ......*Lab.* 28, *PC* 5, *Com.* 1, *Ind.* 1, *Ind. Lab.* 1, (2 Vac.).
Delyn ....*Ind.* 20, *Lab.* 9, *A.* 5, *Ind. Lab.* 4, *C.* 3, *PC* 1.
Dinefwr ....*Lab.* 18, *Ind.* 11, *PC* 2, *Ind. Lab.* 1.
Dwyfor ....*PC* 6, *Others* 23.
Glyndŵr ....*Ind.* 29, *Lab.* 3, *SLD* 3.
Islwyn ....*Lab.* 25, *PC* 10.
Llanelli ....*Lab.* 25, *Ind. Lab.* 3, *SLD* 3, *Others* 4.
Lliw Valley ....*Lab.* 24, *Ind.* 5, *PC* 3, *C.* 1.
Meirionnydd ....*PC* 8, *Lab.* 6, *Ind.* 1, *Others* 26.
Merthyr Tydfil......*Lab.* 22, *RA* 7, *Ind.* 3, *PC* 1.
Monmouth ....*C.* 27, *Lab.* 11, *Ind.* 2.
Montgomeryshire ..*Ind.* 41, *Lib.* 2, *Lab.* 1, *PC* 1, (1 Vac.).
Neath ....*Lab.* 30, *SDP* 2, *Com.* 1, *PC* 1.
Newport ....*Lab.* 41, *C.* 6.
Ogwr ....*Lab.* 30, *C.* 17, *Ind.* 1, (1 Vac.).
Port Talbot ....*Lab.* 23, *RA* 4, *Ind.* 1, *SDP* 1, *SLD* 1, (1 Vac.).
Preseli
Pembrokeshire....*Ind.* 37, *C.* 1, *Lab.* 1, *SLD* 1.
Radnor............*Ind.* 27, *RA* 4, *Lab.* 1, (1 Vac.).
Rhondda ....*Lab.* 27, *RA* 3, *PC* 2, *Ind.* 1.
Rhuddlan ....*Ind.* 18, *C.* 7, *Lab.* 7.
Rhymney Valley ....*Lab.* 32, *PC* 7, *Ind. Lab.* 2, *Ind.* 1, *Lib.* 1, *Others* 3.
South Pembrokeshire *Ind.* 3, *Lab.* 2, *SLD* 1, *Others* 24.
Swansea............*Lab.* 29, *C.* 10, *SLD* 7, *Ind.* 3, *RA* 2.
Taff-Ely ....*Lab.* 22, *PC* 11, *Ind.* 4, *Lib.* 2, *RA.* 2, *C.* 1, *SDP* 1.
Torfaen ....*Lab.* 33, *Ind.* 6, *C.* 1, *Com.* 1, *Ind. Lab.* 1, *RA* 1, *SDP* 1.
Vale of Glamorgan ..*C.* 26, *Lab.* 14, *Ind.* 3, *PC* 3.
Wrexham Maelor ...*Lab.* 26, *C.* 9, *Ind.* 5, *A.* 3, *PC* 1, *Others* 1, (1 Vac.).
Ynys Môn ....*Ind.* 29, *Lab.* 4, *PC* 4, *C.* 1, *SLD* 1.

SCOTLAND
Scottish Regional Councils

Borders ....*Ind.* 7, *C.* 4, *NP* 4, *Lib.* 3, *SNP* 3, *SLD* 2.
Central ....*Lab.* 23, *SNP* 5, *C.* 4, *Ind.* 1, *SLD* 1.

Dumfries &   *Lab.* 9, *SNP* 6, *Ind.* 4, *A.* 2,
  Galloway ....   *Others* 14.
Fife ....*Lab.* 29, *SLD* 8, *C.* 3, *SNP* 3,
                 Ind. 2, *Others* 1.
Grampian ....*Lab.* 17, *C.* 15, *SLD* 12, *SNP* 8,
                 Ind. 4, *SDP* 1.
Highland ....*Ind.* 12, *Lab.* 7, *Lib.* 3, *SNP* 3,
                 C. 2, *Others* 25.
Lothian ....*Lab.* 32, *C.* 13, *SLD* 3, *SNP* 1.
Orkney ....*NP* 24.
Shetland ....*Ind.* 18, *Shetland Movement* 4,
                 Lab. 3.
Strathclyde.........*Lab.* 87, *C.* 6, *SLD* 5, *SNP* 3,
                 Ind. 2.
Tayside ....*Lab.* 19, *C.* 15, *SNP* 9, *Ind.* 2,
                 SLD 1.
Western Isles ....*Ind.* 30.

Scottish District Councils

Aberdeen...........*Lab.* 28, *SLD.* 14, *C.* 9, *SNP* 1.
Angus..............*SNP* 13, *C.* 6, *Ind.* 1, *Dem.* 1.
Annandale
  & Eskdale ....*NP.* 7, *SLD* 6, *Lab.* 2, (1 Vac.).
Argyll & Bute.......*Ind.* 8, *NP* 7, *SNP* 4, *C.* 3, *SLD*
                 3, *Lab.* 1.
Badenoch and
  Strathspey ....*Ind.* 10, *SNP* 1.
Banff & Buchan .....*Ind.* 10, *SNP* 8.
Bearsden and
  Milngavie ....*C.* 6, *SLD* 2, *Ind.* 1, *Lab.* 1.
Berwickshire ....*C.* 9, *Ind.* 2, *SLD* 1.
Caithness ....*Ind.* 13, *Lab.* 2, *Lib.* 1.
Clackmannan ....*Lab.* 10, *C.* 1, *SNP* 1.
Clydebank ....*Lab.* 11, *C.* 1.
Clydesdale..........*Lab.* 8, *SNP* 4, *Ind.* 2, *C.* 1, (1
                 Vac.).
Cumbernauld
  & Kilsyth ....*Lab.* 6, *SNP* 6.
Cumnock and
  Doon Valley ......*Lab.* 8, *Ind. Lab.* 1, *SDP* 1.
Cunninghame ......*Lab.* 24, *C.* 4, *Ind.* 2.
Dumbarton ....*Lab.* 7, *C.* 4, *SNP* 3, *Ind.* 1, *NP*
                 1.
Dundee ....*Lab.* 29, *C.* 10, *SNP* 5.
Dunfermline........*Lab.* 25, *C.* 3, *SLD* 3, *SNP* 3.
East Kilbride ....*Lab.* 14, *C.* 2.

East Lothian........*Lab.* 12, *C.* 4, *Ind. Lab.* 1.
Eastwood...........*C.* 8, *Ind.* 1, *Lab.* 1, *RA* 1, *SLD*
                 1.
Edinburgh..........*Lab.* 33, *C.* 23, *SLD* 4, *SNP* 2.
Ettrick and
  Lauderdale ....*Ind.* 13, *C.* 1, *Lab.* 1, *SNP* 1.
Falkirk ....*Lab.* 20, *SNP* 10, *C.* 3, *Ind.* 2,
                 Ind. Lab. 1.
Glasgow............*Lab.* 59, *C.* 4, *SLD* 2, (1 Vac.).
Gordon.............*SLD* 10, *Ind.* 6.
Hamilton ....*Lab.* 15, *SLD* 2, *C.* 1, *Ind. Lab.*
                 1, *SNP* 1.
Inverclyde..........*Lab.* 12, *SLD* 7, *C.* 1.
Inverness ....*Ind.* 12, *Lab.* 12, *Lib.* 1, *SLD* 1,
                 Others 2.
Kilmarnock and
  Loudoun ....*Lab.* 12, *C.* 3, *SNP* 3.
Kincardine and
  Deeside ....*Ind.* 6, *SLD* 3, *C.* 2, *SNP* 1.
Kirkcaldy ....*Lab.* 33, *C.* 2, *Ind.* 2, *SNP* 2,
                 SLD 1.
Kyle and Carrick ....*Lab.* 16, *C.* 7, *Ind.* *C.* 1, *Ind.*
                 Lab. 1.
Lochaber ....*Ind.* 8, *Lab.* 4, *Ind. Lab.* 3.
Midlothian ....*Lab.* 13, *C.* 1, (1 Vac.).
Monklands ....*Lab.* 18, *SNP* 2.
Moray ....*NP* 8, *SNP* 8, *Lab.* 2.
Motherwell ....*Lab.* 22, *SNP* 3, *C.* 2, *Ind. Lab.*
                 2, *NP* 1.
Nairn ....*Ind.* 9, *C.* 1.
Nithsdale...........*Lab.* 12, *Ind.* 7, *SNP* 6, *C.* 3.
N.E. Fife ....*Lib.* 12, *C.* 4, *Ind.* 2.
Perth and Kinross ...*C.* 11, *SNP* 9, *Lab.* 5, *Ind.* 2,
                 SLD 2.
Renfrew............*Lab.* 32, *C.* 6, *SNP* 4, *SLD* 2,
                 Lib. 1.
Ross & Cromarty ....*Ind.* 17, *Lab.* 2, *SNP* 2, *C.* 1.
Roxburgh ....*Ind.* 7, *SLD* 3, *NP* 2, *SNP* 2, *C.*
                 1, *Others* 1.
Skye & Lochalsh ....*Ind.* 10, *SLD* 1.
Stewartry ....*NP* 9, *Ind.* 3.
Stirling ....*Lab.* 10, *C.* 10.
Strathkelvin........*Lab.* 11, *C.* 2, *SLD* 1, (1 Vac.).
Sutherland ....*NP* 14.
Tweeddale ....*Ind.* 7, *C.* 1, *Lab.* 1, *SNP* 1.
West Lothian ....*Lab.* 13, *SNP* 8, *Ind.* 3.
Wigtown ....*Ind.* 11, *SNP* 2, *Lab.* 1.

THE KINGDOM OF ENGLAND

Position and Extent.—The Kingdom of England lies between 55° 46′ and 49° 57′ 30″ N. latitude (from a few miles north of the mouth of the Tweed to the Lizard), and between 1° 46′ E. and 5° 43′ W. (from Lowestoft to Land's End). England is bounded on the north by the Cheviot Hills; on the south by the English Channel; on the east by the Straits of Dover (Pas de Calais) and the North Sea; and on the West by the Atlantic Ocean, Wales and the Irish Sea. It has a total area of 50,363 sq. miles (land 50,070; inland water 293).

Population.—The population (1981 Census) was 46,362,836 (males 22,520,723; females 23,842,113). The average density of the population in 1981 was 915 per square mile. The population, mid-1987 estimate, was 47,407,000.

Relief.—There is a marked division between the upland and lowland areas of England. In the extreme north the Cheviot Hills (highest point, *The Cheviot*, 2,674 ft.) form a natural boundary with the Kingdom of Scotland. Running south from the Cheviots, though divided from them by the Tyne Gap, is the Pennine range (highest point, *Cross Fell*, 2,930 ft.), the main orological feature of the country. The Pennines culminate in the Peak District of Derbyshire (*Kinder Scout*, 2,088 ft.). West of the Pennines are the Cumbrian mountains, which include *Scafell Pike* (3,210 ft.), the highest peak in England, and to the east are the Yorkshire Moors, their highest point being *Urra Moor* (1,490 ft.).

In the west, the foothills of the Welsh mountains extend into the bordering English counties of Shropshire (the *Wrekin*, 1,334 ft.; *Long Mynd*, 1,694 ft.) and Hereford and Worcester (the Malvern Hills—*Worcestershire Beacon*, 1,394 ft.). Extensive areas of high land and moorland are also to be found in the south-western peninsula formed by Somerset, Devon and Cornwall: principally Exmoor (*Dunkery Beacon*, 1,704 ft.), Dartmoor (*High Willhays*, 2,038 ft.) and Bodmin Moor (*Brown Willy*, 1,377 ft.). Ranges of low, undulating hills run across the south of the country, including the Cotswolds in the Midlands and southwest, the Chilterns to the north of Greater London, and the North (Kent) and South (Sussex) Downs of the south-east coastal areas.

The lowlands of England lie in the Vale of York, East Anglia and the area around the Wash, the lowest lying being the Cambridgeshire Fens in the valleys of the Great Ouse and the River Nene, which are below sea-level in places; since the 17th century extensive drainage has brought much of the Fens under cultivation. The North Sea coast between the Thames and the Humber, low-lying and formed of sand and shingle for the most part, is subject to erosion and defences against further incursion have been built along many stretches.

Hydrography.—The *Severn* is the longest river in Great Britain, rising in the north-eastern slopes of Plinlimmon (Wales) and entering England in Shropshire with a total length of 220 miles from its source to its outflow into the Bristol Channel, where it receives on the east the Bristol Avon, and on the west the Wye, its other tributaries being the Vrynwy, Tern, Stour, Teme and Upper (or Warwickshire) Avon. The Severn is tidal below Gloucester, and a high bore or tidal wave sometimes reverses the flow as high as Tewkesbury (13½ miles above Gloucester). The scenery of the greater part of the river is very picturesque and beautiful, and the Severn is a noted salmon river, some of its tributaries being famous for trout. Navigation is assisted by the Gloucester and Berkeley Ship Canal (16¾ miles), which admits vessels of 350 tons to Gloucester. The *Severn Tunnel*, begun in 1873 and completed in 1886 (at a cost of £2,000,000) after many difficulties from flooding, is 4 miles 628 yards in length (of which 2¼ miles are under the river). The Severn road bridge between Haysgate, Gwent, and Almondsbury, Glos., with a centre span of 3,240 ft. was opened in 1966.

The longest river wholly in England is the *Thames*, with a total length of 215 miles from its source in the Cotswold hills to the Nore, and is navigable by ocean-going ships to London Bridge. The Thames is tidal to Teddington (69 miles from its mouth) and forms county boundaries almost throughout its course; on its banks are situated London, Windsor Castle, the home of the Sovereign, Eton College, the first of the public schools, and Oxford, the oldest university in the kingdom.

Of the remaining English rivers those flowing into the North Sea are the Tyne, Wear, Tees, Ouse and Trent from the Pennine Range, the Great Ouse (160 miles), which rises in Northamptonshire, and the Orwell and Stour from the hills of East Anglia. Flowing into the English Channel are the Sussex Ouse from the Weald, the Itchen from the Hampshire Hills, and the Axe, Teign, Dart, Tamar and Exe from the Devonian hills; and flowing into the Irish Sea are the Mersey, Ribble and Eden from the western slopes of the Pennines and the Derwent from the Cumbrian mountains. The English Lakes, noteworthy for their picturesque scenery and poetic associations, lie in Cumbria, the largest being *Windermere* (10 miles long), *Ullswater* and *Derwentwater*.

Islands.—The *Isle of Wight* is separated from Hampshire by the Solent; total area 147 sq. miles, population about 124,600. The climate is mild and healthy, making the island a popular holiday resort. Capital, Newport, at the head of the estuary of the Medina, Cowes (at the mouth) being the chief port; other centres are Ryde, Sandown, Shanklin, Ventnor, Freshwater, Yarmouth, Totland Bay, Seaview and Bembridge.

Lundy (= Puffin Island) 11 miles N.W. off Hartland Point, Devon, is about 2 miles long and about half a mile broad (average), with a total area of about 1,116 acres, and a population of about 20; it became the property of the National Trust in 1969 and is now principally a bird sanctuary.

(*See also* The Isles of Scilly, p. 624.)

Climate.—England has a generally mild and temperate climate. Because of the prevailing south-westerly winds, the weather day to day is variable, being affected mainly by depressions moving eastwards across the Atlantic Ocean. This maritime influence means that the west of the country tends to experience wetter but also milder weather than the east. Rainfall also increases with altitude, the mountainous areas of the north and west having more rain than the lowlands of the south and east. Rain is fairly well-distributed throughout the year in all areas but, on average, the driest months are March to June, and the wettest September to January.

The mean annual temperature reduced to sea-level varies from 11°C in the south-west to 9°C near Berwick-on-Tweed. In winter, temperatures tend to be higher in the south and west than in the east, while the warmest in summer are the south and inland areas. Latitude for latitude the mean annual temperature is lower in the east; the decrease of mean temperature with height is about 0·6°C per 100 metres.

EARLY INHABITANTS

Prehistoric Man.—Archaeological evidence suggests that England has been inhabited since at least the Palaeolithic period, though the extent of the various Palaeolithic cultures was dependent upon the degree of glaciation. The succeeding Neolithic and Bronze Age cultures have left abundant remains throughout the country, the best-known of these being the henges and stone circles of Stonehenge (10 miles north of Salisbury, Wilts.) and Avebury (Wilts.), both of which are believed to have been of religious significance. In the latter part of the Bronze Age the Goidels, a people of Celtic race, and in the Iron Age other Celtic races of Brythons and Belgae, invaded the country and brought with them Celtic civilization and dialects, place names in England bearing witness to the spread of the invasion over the whole kingdom.

The Roman Conquest.—The Roman conquest of Gaul (57–50 B.C.) brought Britain into close contact with Roman civilization, but although Julius Caesar raided the south of Britain in 55 B.C., and 54 B.C., conquest was not undertaken until nearly 100 years later. In A.D. 43 the Emperor Claudius dispatched Aulus Plautius, with a well-equipped force of 40,000, and himself followed with reinforcements in the same year. Success was delayed by the resistance of Caratacus (Caractacus), the British leader from A.D. 48–51, who was finally captured and sent to Rome, and by a great revolt in A.D. 61 led by Boudicca (Boadicea), Queen of the Iceni; but the south of Britain was secured by A.D. 70, and Wales and the area north to the Tyne by about A.D. 80.

In A.D. 122, the Emperor Hadrian visited Britain and built a continuous rampart, since known as Hadrian's Wall, from Wallsend to Bowness (Tyne to Solway). The work was entrusted to the Emperor Hadrian to Aulus Platorius Nepos, legate of Britain from 122 to 126, and it was intended to form the northern frontier of the Roman Empire.

The Romans administered Britain as a Province under a Governor, with a well-defined system of local government, each Roman municipality ruling itself and surrounding territory, while London was the centre of the road system and the seat of the financial officials of the Province of Britain. Colchester, Lincoln, York, Gloucester and St. Albans stand on the sites of five Roman municipalities, and Wroxeter, Caerleon, Chester, Lincoln and York were at various times the sites of legionary fortresses. Well-preserved Roman towns have been uncovered at (or near) Silchester (*Calleva Atrebatum*), 10 miles south of Reading, Wroxeter (*Viroconium Cornoviorum*), near Shrewsbury, and St. Albans (*Verulamium*) in Hertfordshire.

Four main groups of roads radiated from London, and a fifth (the Fosse) ran obliquely from Lincoln through Leicester, Cirencester and Bath to Exeter. Of the four groups radiating from London one ran S.E. to Canterbury and the coast of Kent, a second to Silchester and thence to parts of Western Britain and South Wales, a third (later known as Watling Street) ran through Verulamium to Chester, with various branches, and the fourth reached Colchester, Lincoln, York and the eastern counties.

In the 4th century Britain was subject to raids along the east coast by Saxon pirates, which led to the establishment of a system of coast defence from the Wash to Southampton Water, with forts at Brancaster, Burgh Castle (Yarmouth), Walton (Felixstowe), Bradwell, Reculver, Richborough, Dover, Lympne, Pevensey and Porchester (Portsmouth). The Irish (Scoti) and Picts in the north were also becoming more aggressive; from about A.D. 350 incursions became more frequent and more formidable. As the Roman Empire came under attack increasingly towards the end of the 4th century many troops were removed from Britain for service in other parts of the Empire. The island was eventually cut off from Rome by the Teutonic conquest of Gaul, and with the withdrawal of the last Roman garrison early in the 5th century, the Romano-British were left to themselves.

According to legend, the British King Vortigern called in the Saxons to defend him against the Picts, the Saxon chieftains being Hengist and Horsa, who landed at Ebbsfleet, Kent, and established themselves in the Isle of Thanet; but the events during the one and a half centuries between the final break with Rome and the re-establishment of Christianity are unclear. However, it would appear that in the course of this period the raids turned into large-scale settlement by invaders traditionally known as Angles (England north of the Wash and East Anglia), Saxons (Essex and southern England) and Jutes (Kent and the Weald), which pushed the Romano-British into the mountainous areas of the north and west, Celtic culture outside Wales and Cornwall surviving only in topographical names. Various kingdoms were established at this time which attempted to claim overlordship of the whole country, hegemony finally being achieved by Wessex (capital, Winchester) in the 9th century. This century also saw the beginning of raids by the Vikings (Danes), which were resisted by Alfred the Great (871–899), the greatest of the Wessex kings, who fixed a limit to the advance of Danish settlement by the Treaty of Wedmore (878), giving them the area north and east of Watling Street, on condition they adopt Christianity.

In the 10th century the Kings of Wessex recovered the whole of England from the Danes, but subsequent rulers were unable to resist a second wave of invaders. England paid tribute (*Danegeld*) for many years, and was invaded in 1013 by the Danes and ruled by Danish Kings from 1016 until 1042, when Edward the Confessor was recalled from exile in Normandy. In 1066 Harold Godwinson (brother-in-law of Edward and son of Earl Godwin of Wessex) was chosen King of England. After defeating (at Stamford Bridge, Yorkshire, Sept. 25) an invading army under Harald Hadraada, King of Norway (aided by the outlawed Earl Tostig of Northumbria, Harold's brother), Harold was himself defeated at the Battle of Hastings on Oct. 14, 1066, and the Norman Conquest secured the throne of England for Duke William of Normandy, a cousin of Edward the Confessor.

Christianity reached the Roman province of Britain from Gaul in the 3rd century (or possibly earlier); Alban, traditionally Britain's first martyr, was put to death as a Christian during the persecution of Diocletian (June 22, 303), at his native town Verulamium; and the Bishops of Londinium, Eboracum (York), and Lindum (Lincoln) attended the Council of Arles in 314. However, the Anglo-Saxon invasions submerged the Christian religion in England until the 6th century when conversion was undertaken in the north from 563 by Celtic missionaries from Ireland led by St. Columba, and in the south by a mission sent from Rome in 597 which was led by St. Augustine, who became the first archbishop of Canterbury. England appears to have been converted again by the end of the 7th century and followed, after the Council of Whitby in 663, the practices of the Roman Church, which brought the country into the mainstream of European thought and culture.

ENGLISH COUNTIES AND SHIRES
LORD LIEUTENANTS AND HIGH SHERIFFS

County or Shire	Lord Lieutenant	*High Sheriff, 1989–90
Avon	Sir John Wills, Bt., T.D.	Sir George White, Bt.
Bedfordshire	Lt. Col. H. C. Hanbury, L.V.O., M.C.	J. H Wells
Berkshire	J. R. Henderson.	Maj. G. R. Seymour, L.V.O.
Buckinghamshire	Cdr. the Hon. J. T. Fremantle.	T. A. Bird, O.B.E., D.S.O.
Cambridgeshire	M. B. M. Bevan	J. Odam
Cheshire	The Rt. Hon. the Viscount Leverhulme, T.D.	J. B. Lockett
Cleveland	The Rt. Hon. the Lord Gisborough	D. Hunter Peart
Cornwall	The Rt. Hon. the Viscount Falmouth	G. E. M. Trinick, O.B.E
Cumbria	Maj. Sir Charles Graham, Bt.	Maj. T. R. Riley
Derbyshire	Col. P. Hilton, M.C.	D. A. G. Shields
Devon	Lt.-Col. the Rt. Hon. the Earl of Morley	O. N. W. William-Powlett
Dorset	The Rt. Hon. the Lord Digby	Hon. Mrs. M. A. S. E. Marten, O.B.E.
Durham	D. J. Grant, C.B.E.	J. T. Brockbank
Essex	Adm. Sir Andrew Lewis, K.C.B.	L. A. Jordan
Gloucestershire	Col. M. St. J. V. Gibbs, C.B., D.S.O., T.D.	G. E. M. Vernon
Hampshire	Lt.-Col. Sir James Scott, Bt.	Capt. J. L. Jervoise
Hereford and Worcester	Capt. T. R. Dunne	Maj. D. J. C. Davenport
Hertfordshire	S. A. Bowes Lyon	Hon. Mrs. S. V. Blount
Humberside	R. A. Bethell	J. E. Spilman
Kent	The Rt. Hon. Robin Leigh-Pemberton	Hon. H. C. Maude
Lancashire	S. Towneley	C. J. Weld-Blundell
Leicestershire	T. G. M. Brooks	G. A. A. M. P. de Lisle
Lincolnshire	Capt. H. N. Neville	Mrs. B. K. Cracroft-Eley
Greater London	Field Marshal the Lord Bramall, G.C.B., O.B.E., M.C.	Mrs. J. E. Wheeler-Bennett
Greater Manchester	Col. J. B. Timmins, O.B.E., T.D.	Col. W. Elder
Merseyside	H. E. Cotton	Col. D. R. Morgan, O.B.E.
Norfolk	T. J. Colman	Brig. P. N. R. Stewart-Richardson, M.B.E.
Northamptonshire	J. L. Lowther, C.B.E.	Sir Gordon Roberts, C.B.E.
Northumberland	The Rt. Hon. the Viscount Ridley, T.D.	E. A. Wrangham
Nottinghamshire	Sir Gordon Hobday	R. A. Craven-Smith-Milnes
Oxfordshire	Sir Ashley Ponsonby, Bt., M.C.	C. G. A. Parker
Shropshire	J. R. S. Dugdale	D. R. B. Thompson
Somerset	Col. G. W. F. Luttrell, M.C.	R. W. Vivian-Neal
Staffordshire	Sir Arthur Bryan	D. H. Field
Suffolk	Sir Joshua Rowley, Bt.	R. J. D. Blois
Surrey	R. E. Thornton, O.B.E.	Gp. Capt. Sir Hugh S. L. Dundas
Sussex, East	Adm. Sir Lindsay Bryson, K.C.B.	D. O. Baker
Sussex, West	Her Grace Lavinia, Duchess of Norfolk, C.B.E.	J. R. B. Morgan-Grenville
Tyne and Wear	Sir Ralph Carr-Ellison, T.D.	D. Smith
Warwickshire	Sir Charles Smith-Ryland, K.C.V.O.	D. C. Rutherford
West Midlands	The Rt. Hon. the Earl of Aylesford	D. J. C. Johnson
Wight, Isle of	The Rt. Hon. the Lord Mottistone, C.B.E.	C. D. J. Bland
Wiltshire	Col. Sir Hugh Brassey, K.C.V.O., O.B.E., M.C.	B. N. Gibbs
Yorkshire, North	Sir Marcus Worsley, Bt.	Col. Hon. R. N. Crossley
Yorkshire, South	J. H. Neill, C.B.E., T.D.	J. A. Boddy
Yorkshire, West	The Rt. Hon. the Lord Ingrow, O.B.E., T.D.	V. H. Watson

* High Sheriffs are nominated by the Queen on November 12 and come into office after Hilary Term.

ENGLISH COUNTY COUNCILS
AREAS AND POPULATIONS

County	Administrative Headquarters	Area (hectares)	Estimated Resident Population 1987	Rateable Value 1989 £	Actual Rateable Value per head £
Avon	Avon House, The Haymarket, Bristol	134,614	951,200	133,384,327	139·49
Bedfordshire......	*Bedford	123,460	525,900	92,800,000	172·08
Berkshire	†Reading	125,890	740,600	146,542,565	200·29
Buckinghamshire .	*Aylesbury	188,284	621,300	117,010,000	183·48
Cambridgeshire ...	†Cambridge	340,892	642,400	101,177,123	158·00
Cheshire	*Chester	232,846	951,900	148,121,779	155·00
Cleveland	Municipal Buildings, Middlesbrough	58,308	554,500	80,777,713	146·05
Cornwall	*Truro	354,792‡	453,100	52,687,612	113·53
Cumbria..........	The Courts, Carlisle	681,012	486,900	55,398,000	113·06
Derbyshire	County Offices, Matlock	263,094	918,700	114,248,353	125·00
Devon............	*Exeter	671,088	1,010,000	125,925,335	178·00
Dorset	*Dorchester	265,375	648,600	97,481,689	148·06
Durham	*Durham	243,592	598,700	62,194,831	132·68
Essex	*Chelmsford	367,192	1,521,800	257,711,090	169·00
Gloucestershire ...	†Gloucester	264,266	522,200	73,000,000	232·50
Hampshire	The Castle, Winchester	377,698	1,537,000	239,000,000	210·20
Hereford and Worcester	*Worcester	392,650	665,100	97,633,376	144·49
Hertfordshire.....	*Hertford	163,415	986,800	186,229,973	186·94
Humberside	*Beverley, N. Humberside	351,212	846,500	106,473,202	126·00
Kent.............	*Maidstone	373,060	1,510,500	203,265,500	209·35
Lancashire	*Preston	306,346	1,381,300	156,847,399	112·06
Leicestershire	*Leicester	255,293	879,400	126,811,235	144·20
Lincolnshire......	County Offices, Lincoln	591,485	574,600	72,027,504	121·05
Norfolk	*Norwich	536,776	736,200	102,508,900	136·30
Northamptonshire	*Northampton	236,737	561,800	87,202,639	155·22
Northumberland ..	*Morpeth	503,165	300,900	35,133,000	155·00
Nottinghamshire..	*Nottingham	216,365	1,007,800	132,187,000	131·35
Oxfordshire	*Oxford	260,782	578,000	93,787,000	159·00
Shropshire	The Shirehall, Shrewsbury	349,014	396,500	50,369,172	125·39
Somerset	*Taunton	345,094	452,300	59,144,357	128·30
Staffordshire	County Buildings, Stafford	271,615	1,027,500	136,962,758	236·00
Suffolk	*Ipswich	379,663	635,100	89,044,279	140·75
Surrey	*Kingston upon Thames	167,924	1,000,400	191,024,165	194·00
Sussex, East	Pelham House, St. Andrew's Lane, Lewes	179,512	698,000	109,055,584	228·90
Sussex, West......	*Chichester	198,935	700,000	112,869,999	158·00
Warwickshire	†Warwick	198,053	484,200	76,171,361	158·46
Wight, Isle of	*Newport, I.O.W.	38,066	126,900	15,109,844	119·44
Wiltshire.........	*Trowbridge	348,070	550,900	69,631,130	309·22
Yorkshire, North .	*Northallerton	830,865	705,700	87,202,892°	121·00°

* County Hall.　　† Shire Hall.　　‡ Excluding Isles of Scilly.　　° 1988 figure.

CHIEF EXECUTIVES, TREASURERS AND CHAIRMEN

County or Shire	Chief Executive	County Treasurer	Chairman of County Council
Avon	N. J. L. Pearce	D. G. Morgan	R. Rosewarn
Bedfordshire........	V. F. Phillips (*acting*)	V. F. Phillips	J. P. B. Kinchella
Berkshire	A. J. Allen	D. J. Bowles	W. A. Wiseman
Buckinghamshire ...	C. M. Garrett	H. R. H. Spring-thorpe	Mrs. G. M. M. Miscampbell, O.B.E.
Cambridgeshire	A. G. Lister	D. Prince‡	Mrs. J. Brooks
Cheshire	R. G. Wendt	J. E. H. Whiteoak	J. T Humphreys
Cleveland	B. Stevenson	P. Riley†	J. Stokes
Cornwall	G. K. Burgess	A. L. Wilkes	D. L. C. Roberts
Cumbria............	J. R. Ford	R. Wirth	C. B. Ross
Derbyshire	J. S. Raine*	R. C. Beard	A. Morris
Devon..............	R. D. Clark	B. J. Weston	M. McGahey, O.B.E
Dorset	K. A. Abel, C.B.E.	D. M. Gasson	Sir Stephen Hammick, Bt.
Durham	K. W. Smith°	K. W. Smith	J. Graham
Essex	R. W. Adcock	K. D. Neale	P. E. W. White
Gloucestershire	M. G. Bichard	J. R. Cockroft	E. J. Radley
Hampshire	A. R. Hodgson	J. E. Scotford	C. M. Jones
Hereford and Worcester	G. A. Price	G. A. Price	R. J. Carrington, O.B.E.
Hertfordshire.......	M. J. Le Fleming	K. S. Cliff	R. H. Fielding
Humberside	J. A. Parkes	G. T. Southern‡	D. Spooner
Kent...............	P. R. Sabin	P. Martin‡	Sir John Grugeon
Lancashire	B. Hill	D. Morgan	J. Entwistle
Leicestershire	S. Jones	R. Hale	N. R. Hangar
Lincolnshire........	R. J. D. Procter	D. G. Barrett	D. C. Hoyes
Norfolk	B. J. Capon	C. A. Boar‡	J. O. C. Birkbeck
Northamptonshire ..	A. J. Greenwell	D. W. Cleggett	G. Pollard
Northumberland	C. B. Rodger	K. Morris	Mrs. E. Atkinson
Nottinghamshire....	A. Sandford	G. S. Luff	F. Warsop
Oxfordshire	J. Harwood	J. T. Vokins	B. H. Duggan
Shropshire	M. Suter	M. N. Davis	Mrs. J. A. Hayward
Somerset	J. E. Whittaker	B. M. Tanner	H. Hobhouse
Staffordshire	B. A. Price	B. Smith	J. O.'Leary
Suffolk	C. W. Smith	P. B. Atkinson	J. P. Patton
Surrey	D. J. Thomas	R. Wolstenholme	D. Robertson
Sussex, East	R. M. Beechey	M. R. Hancock	Mrs. J. M. Mont
Sussex, West........	J. R. Hooley	B. Fieldhouse	M. Long
Warwickshire	I. G. Caulfield	J. P. Hunt	S. W. T. Birch
Wight, Isle of	J. S. Horsnell	J. B. W. Proctor	B. M. Pratt, O.B.E
Wiltshire...........	I. A. Browning	A. F. Gould	Mrs. M. E. Salisbury
Yorkshire, North ...	H. J. Evans	D. Martin	Lt.-Col. H. Dawson

* County Director.   ° Principal Executive Officer.   ‡ Director of Finance.   † County Finance Officer.

Residuary Bodies

GREATER LONDON, (*see* page 598).

GREATER MANCHESTER.—The residuary body is to be wound up in October 1989.

MERSEYSIDE, 3rd Floor, Steers House, Canning Place, Liverpool.
Chairman, N. G. Brodrick.
Chief Executive, A. A. Thompson.
Treasurer, J. R. Smith.

TYNE AND WEAR.—The residuary body was wound up in October 1988.

WEST MIDLANDS, 1 Lancaster Circus, Queensway, Birmingham B4 7DJ (021–300 5151).
Chairman, Dr. M. Skillicorn.
Chief Executive, K. E. Rose.

SOUTH YORKSHIRE.—The residuary body was wound up in July 1989.

WEST YORKSHIRE, P.O. Box 22, Pearl Assurance House, Queen Street, Wakefield, WF1 2QN (0924–367111).
Chairman, T. McDonald.
Chief Executive, H. S. Hoare.

METROPOLITAN COUNCILS

A list of Metropolitan Borough and City Councils. Those accorded CITY status are in SMALL CAPITALS.

Metropolitan Boroughs	Estimated Resident Population 1987	Rateable Value 1989 £	Chief Executive	Mayor †Lord Mayor *Chairman 1989–90
GREATER MANCHESTER	2,580,100			
Bolton	262,300	30,060,133	K. P. Bounds	K. MacIvor
Bury	173,700	20,606,105	D. J. Burton	A. K. Matthews
MANCHESTER	450,100	81,133,220	G. Hainsworth	†S. A. Mambu
Oldham	219,500	24,091,863	C. Smith	Mrs. E. W. Shaw
Rochdale	206,700	22,499,056	J. F. D. Pierce	J. E. Littler
SALFORD	237,700	32,790,064	R. C. Rees	S. Turner
Stockport	291,100	41,317,726	A. L. Wilson	H. Whitehead
Tameside	216,000	22,694,824	D. Spiers	Mrs. K. W. Shaw
Trafford	216,100	40,495,564	W. A. Lewis	A. R. Coupe
Wigan	307,200	33,175,654	P. Johnson	Mrs. A. Bennett
MERSEYSIDE	1,456,800			
Knowsley	161,500	21,564,411	D. G. Henshaw	Mrs. A. Burke
LIVERPOOL	476,000	69,600,000	(vacant)	*Ms. D. Gavin
St. Helens	187,300	23,755,221	F. Kendall	M. Doyle
Sefton	297,300	37,989,624	A. G. Corless	Mrs. M. Fearn
Wirral	334,800	44,228,617	‡P. G. Manson	M. P. Cooke
SOUTH YORKSHIRE	1,295,600			
Barnsley	221,500	20,334,135	P. G. Thompson	A. Storey
Doncaster	290,100	30,902,793	C. B. Jeynes	R. Stockhill
Rotherham	251,700	24,562,142	J. Bell	R. J. Hughes
SHEFFIELD	532,300	66,163,727	Mrs. P. Gordon	†A. Damms
TYNE AND WEAR	1,135,800			
Gateshead	206,900	22,054,842	L. N. Elton	N. Lakey
NEWCASTLE UPON TYNE	282,700	43,198,283	G. N. Cook	†T. Cooney
North Tyneside	192,900	21,936,082	‡‡E. D. Nixon	Mrs. E. Bennett
South Tyneside	156,300	15,760,525	S. Clark	S. Forster
Sunderland	297,100	29,706,150	G. P. Key	R. Kirby
WEST MIDLANDS	2,642,300			
BIRMINGHAM	998,200	168,500,000	R. M. W. Taylor	†F. Chapman
COVENTRY	308,900	45,827,469	I. Roxburgh	†D. J. Cairns
Dudley	302,600	46,712,689	A. V. Astling	S. Davies
Sandwell	298,400	50,400,000	A. C. Griffin	J. W. McKenzie
Solihull	203,900	33,038,200	J. Scampion	W. Rees
Walsall	261,800	40,172,096	J. W. Hadley	R. Farrell
Wolverhampton	250,500	43,561,944	M. T. Lyons	R. Reynolds
WEST YORKSHIRE	2,052,400			
BRADFORD	462,500	47,049,825	R. Penn	†S. Hodgson
Calderdale	194,800	18,100,361	M. Ellison	J. Kneafsey
Kirklees	375,800	35,231,102	R. V. Hughes	C. Watson
LEEDS	709,000	96,300,000	D. A. Ansbro	†J. L. Carter
WAKEFIELD	310,300	36,198,800	J. G. Stanbury	F. Ward

‡ Borough Secretary.   ‡‡ Director of Administrative Services.

DISTRICT COUNCILS

A list of non-Metropolitan District Councils in England. Those accorded CITY status are in SMALL CAPITALS, those with Borough status are distinguished by having § prefixed.

District	Estimated Resident Population 1987	Rateable Value 1989 £	Chief Executive (*Clerk)	Chairman 1989–90 (a) Mayor (b) Lord Mayor
Adur, West Sussex	57,500	8,897,799	F. M. G. Staden	J. Brooks
Allerdale, Cumbria	96,100	9,650,931	A. G. Perry	J. Watson
Alnwick, Northumberland	30,000	3,331,537	A. G. A. Groome	A. Davidson
Amber Valley, Derbyshire	110,100	12,974,087	A. Dow	Mrs. J. Flowers
Arun, West Sussex	128,300	18,236,520	A. S. Potts	F. C. Lyons
Ashfield, Nottinghamshire	107,000	10,910,061	S. Beedham	Mrs. M. Drew

District	Estimated Resident Population 1987	Rateable Value 1989 £	Chief Executive (* Clerk)	Chairman 1989–90 (a) Mayor (b) Lord Mayor
§Ashford, Kent	93,900	13,058,552	E. H. W. Mexter	(a) J. B. Simpson
Aylesbury Vale, Bucks.	144,300	22,106,204	B. J. Quoroll	Gp. Capt. J. F. Stowart
Babergh, Suffolk	77,800	10,469,708	D. C. Bishop	T. M. Bailey-Smith
§Barrow in Furness, Cumbria	73,200	6,726,091	R. H. McCulloch	(a) S. M. Smart
Basildon, Essex	157,400	28,126,791	J. C. Rosser°	D. Marks
§Basingstoke and Deane, Hants.	138,400	23,801,415	D. W. Pilkington, R.D.	(a) Mrs. M. Weston
Bassetlaw, Notts.	104,900	17,573,093	R. D. Blair	R. F. Webster
BATH, Avon	84,800	11,750,114	N. C. Abbott	(a) Ms. A. McDonagh
§Berwick-upon-Tweed, Northumberland	27,100	3,251,809	J. V. Picking	(a) Mrs. C. Robson
§Beverley, Humberside	110,800	13,363,785	W. J. H. Thomas	(a) E. Gray
Blaby, Leics.	83,000	10,625,324	G. E. Phillips	F. G. B. Bisiker
§Blackburn, Lancs.	136,900	14,333,873	S. M. Jones	(a) W. G. Taylor
§Blackpool, Lancs.	144,100	19,514,891	D. Wardman	(a) Mrs. M. A. Barnes
§Blyth Valley, Northumberland	78,200	7,826,507	D. Crawford	(a) E. Breadin
Bolsover, Derbys.	69,400	6,288,401	C. A. Tucker	J. R. Allsop
§Boothferry, Humberside	62,500	5,761,872	J. W. Barber	(a) M. Crowther
§Boston, Lincs.	52,100	6,872,032	R. E. Coley	(a) R. G. M. Moulder
§Bournemouth, Dorset	154,200	26,313,812	K. Lomas	(a) H. Bostock
§Bracknell Forest, Berks.	95,000	17,074,810	A. J. Targett	(a) A. Cheney
Braintree, Essex	116,400	16,783,763	C. R. Daybell	Ms. K. Richards
Breckland, Norfolk	103,600	12,987,746	J. B. Heath	L. J. Potter
Brentwood, Essex	70,700	13,905,220	C. P. Sivell	P. Hodgson
Bridgnorth, Salop	51,400	6,264,473	A. L. Bain	P. M. Whiteman
§Brighton, East Sussex	140,900	26,229,594	(vacant)	(a) B. R. Fitch
BRISTOL, Avon	384,400	63,800,000	W. G. Miller (acting)	(b) Mrs. K. M. Mount-stephen
Broadland, Norfolk	102,500	11,927,147	J. H. Bryant	D. J. Hastings
Bromsgrove, Hereford and Worcs.	90,300	12,779,366	R. P. Bradshaw	J. D. Tracey
§Broxbourne, Herts.	82,800	13,458,038	M. J. Walker	(a) E. J. Rowland
§Broxtowe, Notts.	106,800	12,579,878	M. Brown	(a) T. Buckley
§Burnley, Lancs.	85,000	8,676,024	B. Whittle	(a) G. Halsted
CAMBRIDGE	98,400	23,937,302	G. G. Datson, O.B.E.	(a) J. R. Woodhouse
Cannock Chase, Staffs.	86,600	11,808,902	C. E. Evans	F. W. C. Allen
CANTERBURY, Kent	129,500	16,343,433	C. Gay	(a) A. Porter, T.D.
Caradon, Cornwall	73,300	7,499,545	J. O. Collins	A. Brooking
CARLISLE, Cumbria	101,500	12,280,827	R. Wilson, M.B.E.	(a) R. C. Hayhoe
Carrick, Cornwall	79,700	10,328,092	P. M. Talbot	F. J. Warne
§Castle Morpeth, Northumberland	50,500	6,947,943	M. Cole	(a) R. Errington
Castle Point, Essex	85,900	12,400,000	B. Rollinson	A. A. S. Patterson
§Charnwood, Leics.	146,800	21,126,527	R. M. Holroyd	(a) W. A. Danvers
§Chelmsford, Essex	151,200	27,121,347	R. M. C. Hartley	(a) Ms. J. C. Norton
§Cheltenham, Glos.	86,800	16,001,940	B. N. Wynn	(a) E. J. Phillips
Cherwell, Oxon.	122,600	18,331,341	A. M. Brace	V. S. H. Duclos, C.B.E., D.F.C.
CHESTER, Cheshire	116,900	19,229,684	P. F. Durham	(a) J. Price
§Chesterfield, Derbyshire	97,900	13,022,330	D. R. Shaw	(a) L. McCulloch
Chester-le-Street, Co. Durham	53,300	4,811,587	J. A. Greensmith	R. Allon
Chichester, West Sussex	104,900	15,471,157	P. Ryan	H. N. Allen
Chiltern, Bucks.	89,200	17,214,568	D. G. Sainsbury	M. J. Batt
§Chorley, Lancs.	96,100	9,791,434	J. W. Davies	(a) J. Meadows
§Christchurch, Dorset	40,300	7,223,247	C. H. Dewsnap	(a) J. Moss
§Cleethorpes, Humberside	68,900	9,191,930	R. W. Bull	(a) Mrs. M. W. Howes
§Colchester, Essex	147,200	21,591,095	J. Cobley	(a) J. G. Sanderson
§Congleton, Cheshire	85,900	11,424,158	R. H. Flint	(a) T. J. King
§Copeland, Cumbria	71,600	9,474,703	P. N. Denson	(a) Mrs. M. E. Stalker
Corby, Northants.	50,200	9,927,580	T. J. Simmons	P. McGowan
Cotswold, Glos.	74,300	10,343,984	D. A. Sketchley	I. M. Maitland-Hume
Craven, North Yorks	48,600	5,489,496	A. Howell*	Mrs. J. M. Bell
§Crawley, West Sussex	84,400	20,298,977	M. D. Sander	(a) Ms. L. Moffatt
§Crewe and Nantwich, Cheshire	96,600	13,859,717	R. Mather	(a) L. A. Turnock
§Dacorum, Herts.	132,600	25,098,719	R. H. Davis	(a) Mrs. W. Lees
§Darlington, Co. Durham	99,100	13,457,930	H. R. C. Owen	(a) J. B. Lamb
§Dartford, Kent	79,100	13,429,750	C. R. Shepherd	(a) K. R. Thurlow

° Town Manager.

District	Estimated Resident Population 1987	Rateable Value 1989 £	Chief Executive (*Clerk)	Chairman 1989–90 (a) Mayor (b) Lord Mayor
Daventry, Northants...........	62,300	9,836,350	R. J. Symons, R.D.	R. P. Fletcher
DERBY........................	215,800	32,336,473	R. H. Cowlishaw	(a) R. S. Baxter
Derbyshire Dales..............	67,000	7,741,351	D. Wheatcroft	B. Oldfield
Derwentside, Co. Durham	86,300	7,773,215	N. F. Johnson	Mrs. M. Armstrong
Dover, Kent	104,300	12,517,538	J. P. Moir, T.D.	P. A. Watkins
DURHAM.......................	86,200	9,757,087	C. G. Firmin	(a) J. A. Fearon
Easington, Co. Durham	95,700	8,062,092	T. Robinson†	C. Reynolds
§Eastbourne, East Sussex	80,400	14,913,971	C. A. Bloor	(a) A. F. Aldridge
East Cambridgeshire	59,300	6,603,438	T. T. G. Hardy	A. N. Wright
East Devon	116,600	13,841,580	F. J. Vallender	R. L. Gigg
East Dorset	79,100	11,758,762	A. Breakwell	G. W. Ridge
East Hampshire	100,200	13,842,430	B. P. Roynon	Mrs. D. K. Denston
East Hertfordshire	119,100	18,740,395	D. J. Anstey	P. A. Ruffles
§Eastleigh, Hants.	99,900	16,046,093	M. C. Brainsby	(a) E. C. B. Perry
East Lindsey, Lincs.	113,800	14,210,836	A. W. Silcox-Crowe	M. F. Capes
East Northamptonshire........	65,300	7,683,000	R. K. Heath	P. C. Chantrell
East Staffordshire	94,600	13,829,938	F. W. Saunders	S. Deeming
§East Yorkshire, Humberside ...	81,400	7,912,000	J. H. Gibson	(a) R. A. Owen
Eden, Cumbria	45,400	5,149,962	I. W. Bruce	J. M. Carlyle
§Ellesmere Port and Neston, Cheshire	79,500	17,443,291	S. Ewbank	(a) B. Jones
§Elmbridge, Surrey	107,900	24,183,021	D. W. L. Jenkins	(a) Mrs. I. M. Simmons
Epping Forest, Essex..........	113,000	19,934,848	A. V. Hackman	R. P. Braybrook
§Epsom and Ewell, Surrey	66,800	12,430,870	D. J. Smith	(a) Mrs. P. M. Ballard
§Erewash, Derbyshire..........	106,800	12,507,466	G. Coveyduck	(a) Mrs. M. Tumanow
EXETER, Devon	98,800	16,281,237	B. Frowd	(a) Mrs. D. Bess
§Fareham, Hants.	98,200	14,850,290	O. D. Ellis	(a) M. I. Nobes
Fenland, Cambs.	70,900	9,108,112	E. S. Thompson	M. Cotterell
Forest Heath, Suffolk	57,000	7,256,457	J. F. Gale	J. O. Wiggin
Forest of Dean, Glos...........	76,200	7,491,431	P. R. Starling	A. C. Cooper
§Fylde, Lancs.	72,500	9,618,996	J. P. Johnson	(a) W. Callon
§Gedling, Notts................	110,500	12,207,000	W. Brown	(a) T. G. Aslin
§Gillingham, Kent.............	96,100	11,514,669	Dr. R. Chilton	(a) J. A. Lee
§Glanford, Humberside	69,700	9,950,286	D. D. H. Cameron	(a) W. Woods
GLOUCESTER	90,500	13,854,505	H. R. T. Shackleton	(a) E. J. V. Ede
§Gosport, Hants.	77,400	10,165,510	W. D. Hooper	(a) Mrs. A. M. Ellis, M.B.E.
§Gravesham, Kent	91,700	13,278,899	E. V. J. Seager	(a) W. G. Dyke
§Great Grimsby, Humberside ...	89,900	12,223,981	R. S. G. Bennett	(a) D. A. Currie
§Great Yarmouth, Norfolk	87,000	12,411,689	K. G. Ward	(a) J. R. Shrimplin
§Guildford, Surrey	123,400	23,845,935	D. T. Watts	(a) B. Parke
§Halton, Cheshire	123,500	18,573,297	R. Turton	(a) D. Cargill
Hambleton, North Yorks.	75,800	8,727,316	C. Spencer	Mrs. M. Potter
Harborough, Leics.	65,000	8,860,068	J. Ballantyne	R. L. Freelove
Harlow, Essex.................	72,900	14,789,920	D. F. Byrne	R. Rowland
§Harrogate, North Yorks.	146,400	18,352,355	J. V. Lovell	(a) N. J. Nichol
Hart, Hants.	83,300	11,838,998	M. W. Tyler	D. D. Carrow
§Hartlepool, Cleveland	89,800	12,099,752	B. J. Dinsdale	(a) Mrs. M. Kellman
§Hastings, East Sussex	81,900	10,515,955	R. A. Carrier	(a) P. Smith
§Havant, Hants................	118,800	16,755,938	D. E. Ridley	(a) R. Beresford
HEREFORD	48,700	7,472,925	C. E. S. Willis	(a) J. W. Newman
§Hertsmere, Hertfordshire	88,100	17,292,443	J. N. Pearson	(a) M. Johnson
§High Peak, Derbyshire........	83,500	9,766,244	R. P. H. Brady	(a) J. A. T. Pritchard
§Hinckley and Bosworth, Leics..	94,600	12,984,560	F. Shaw	(a) Mrs. M. Aldridge
§Holderness, Humberside	49,200	5,423,763	A. Johnson	(a) R. L. Hunt
Horsham, West Sussex	107,000	16,283,827	M. J. Pearson	Mrs. B. J. Palmer
§Hove, East Sussex	90,400	15,647,749	G. H. Longden	(a) Mrs. M. Adams
Huntingdonshire, Cambs.	145,300	18,541,995	T. J. Gee	J. C. Mugglestone
§Hyndburn, Lancs.	79,800	7,001,936	M. J. Wedgeworth	(a) A. D. Lund
§Ipswich, Suffolk	116,500	19,491,603	J. D. Hehir	(a) Ms. S. A. Baguley
Kennet, Wilts.	67,000	7,220,890	P. L. Owens	G. A. Taylor
§Kerrier, Cornwall	86,000	9,126,092	G. G. Cox	T. G. V. Hart
§Kettering, Northants.	73,800	9,099,401	T. P. Williams	(a) A. C. C. Evans
King's Lynn and W. Norfolk ...	131,400	17,733,370	A. E. Pask	(a) A. L. Daubney
KINGSTON UPON HULL, Humberside	252,700	30,021,215	A. B. Wood	(b) J. Stanley
§Kingswood, Avon	89,200	9,453,083	A. Smith	(a) J. W. Lewis

†Principal Chief Officer.

District	Estimated Resident Population 1987	Rateable Value 1989 £	Chief Executive (* Clerk)	Chairman 1989–90 (a) Mayor (b) Lord Mayor
LANCASTER, Lancs.	130,400	15,872,987	W. Pearson*	(a) F. W. Wilcox
§Langbaurgh-on-Tees, Cleveland	145,600	23,157,777	K. Abigail	(a) D. Moore
LEICESTER	279,700	43,997,494	D. Mellor	(b) D. A. Taylor
Leominster, Hereford and Worcs.	38,900	4,025,441	G. A. Robson	G. B. Bray
Lewes, East Sussex	89,600	13,653,683	C. W. Mann	Gp. Capt. J. S. Palmer
Lichfield, Staffs.	92,900	13,511,692	J. T. Thompson	F. W. Lewis
LINCOLN	79,600	11,692,975	C. J. Thomas	(a) J. S. Robertson
§Luton, Beds.	165,300	33,730,767	J. C. Southwell	(a) F. S. Lester, O.B.E.
§Macclesfield, Cheshire	151,800	24,823,005	B. W. Longden	(a) J. K. Jackson
§Maidstone, Kent	134,500	18,947,458	J. D. Makepeace	(a) J. V. Banks
Maldon, Essex	53,300	8,209,533	T. K. Griffin	K. S. Munnion
Malvern Hills, Hereford and Worcs.	88,100	11,108,217	M. J. Jones	B. A. Wilcock
Mansfield, Notts.	100,100	10,539,862	R. P. Goad	E. Carter
§Medina, Isle of Wight	71,600	8,723,632	J. Sprake‡‡	(a) J. Ritchie
§Melton, Leics.	43,000	6,090,239	P. J. G. Herrick°	(a) A. M. Dames
Mendip, Somerset	93,200	11,198,180	G. Jeffs	R. Clark
Mid Bedfordshire	113,200	15,084,530	P. A. Freeman	M. J. Randall
Mid Devon	62,400	6,171,559	R. C. Greensmith	Air Vice-Marshal D. L. Attlee, C.B., L.V.O.
§Middlesbrough, Cleveland	143,300	18,322,988	J. R. Foster	(a) C. E. Robson
Mid Suffolk	76,600	9,371,529	H. McFarlane	P. T. Chapman
Mid Sussex	120,400	18,296,232	B. J. Grimshaw	Mrs. J. M. Mackelden
§Milton Keynes, Bucks.	170,800	30,564,891	M. J. Murray	(a) R. L. Bristow
Mole Valley, Surrey	76,800	13,721,179	A. A. Huggins	Sqn. Ldr. J. Findlay
Newark and Sherwood, Notts. . . .	103,400	11,380,000	V. G. Crawley	J. Baker
Newbury, Berks.	137,900	23,484,705	P. E. McMahon	A. D. Steel
§Newcastle under Lyme, Staffs. .	118,100	14,510,512	A. G. Owen	(a) J. H. Matthews
New Forest, Hants.	161,300	25,907,042	P. A. D. Hyde	D. S. Burdle
§Northampton	177,200	31,872,930	R. J. B. Morris	(a) M. F. Lloyd
Northavon, Avon	127,800	19,108,592	F. Maude	P. Arnold
§North Bedfordshire.	136,400	22,489,315	J. F. Hayward	(a) S. Gillard
North Cornwall	70,300	8,191,776	I. Whiting	H. S. Medland
North Devon	82,900	8,701,625	R. D. Hall	F. Purcell
North Dorset	53,100	6,060,191	A. J. Bridgeman	G. A. Pitt-Rivers
North East Derbyshire.	97,700	9,449,372	D. G. Hunt†	C. Robinson
North Hertfordshire.	111,700	20,338,533	K. Sutton	P. McCormack
North Kesteven, Lincs.	83,300	8,895,345	S. M. Peatfield	Mrs. M. H. Brighton
North Norfolk	92,700	11,727,739	T. V. Nolan	C. C. Durrant
North Shropshire	54,400	5,439,520	K. Flood	W. Sinker
§North Warwickshire	59,400	8,917,391	D. Monks	(a) T. A. Kenwright
North West Leicestershire	79,600	11,324,527	J. E. White	D. H. Wintle
North Wiltshire.	110,600	11,705,618	H. Miles	D. C. Hartley
NORWICH, Norfolk	118,600	23,882,733	J. R. Packer	(b) D. Fullman
NOTTINGHAM	276,800	44,236,121	M. H. F. Hammond	(b) J. Riley
§Nuneaton and Bedworth, Warwickshire	114,600	15,135,696	I. J. Clarke	(a) T. Hargreaves
§Oadby and Wigston, Leics.	51,800	7,346,798	J. B. Burton*	(a) R. Rudham
§Oswestry, Shropshire	31,800	3,416,989	D. A. Towers	(a) Mrs. B. Hughes
OXFORD	115,800	22,168,831	R. S. Block	(b) Mrs. P. Yardley
§Pendle, Lancs.	84,400	6,644,127	F. Wood	(a) A. F. Evans
Penwith, Cornwall	57,800	6,469,957	M. J. Furneaux††	J. F. W. Jago
PETERBOROUGH, Cambs.	151,200	24,475,972	P. B. Sidebottom	(a) D. J. Hedges
PLYMOUTH, Devon	255,800	32,621,371	M. S. Boxall	(b) D. H. Dicker
§Poole, Dorset.	129,300	22,517,086	I. K. D. Andrews*	(a) Mrs. M. Ballam
PORTSMOUTH, Hants.	186,800	28,430,066	R. Trist	(b) Miss G. Howard
§Preston, Lancs.	126,700	16,758,788	A. Owens	(a) R. Ball
Purbeck, Dorset	45,200	6,270,068	P. B. Croft	K. Marlow
§Reading, Berks.	133,300	30,281,654	G. Filkin	(a) Mrs. M. Lockey
§Redditch, Hereford and Worcs.	76,600	12,876,893	D. H. Phipps	(a) K. Smith
§Reigate and Banstead, Surrey .	113,700	20,909,579	C. T. Pollard	(a) Mrs. E. Dunsmore
§Restormel, Cornwall	84,000	11,053,457	D. Brown	(a) G. B. Down
§Ribble Valley, Lancs.	53,300	5,905,994	O. Hopkins	(a) J. D. Cliff
Richmondshire, North Yorks. . .	49,700	4,772,472	M. F. Tooze	J. R. Bell

‡‡ Borough General Manager.   °Borough Secretary.
†Chief Officer.   ††Director of Central Services.

District	Estimated Resident Population 1987	Rateable Value 1989 £	Chief Executive (*Clerk)	Chairman 1989–90 (a) Mayor (b) Lord Mayor
ROCHESTER UPON MEDWAY, Kent	146,400	24,894,379	R. I. Gregory	(a) B. G. Flack
Rochford, Essex	74,800	11,149,052	A. G. Cooke	Mrs. P. Cooke
§Rossendale, Lancs.	64,500	5,645,022	J. S. Hartley‡	(a) G. Bland
Rother, East Sussex	83,000	12,000,000	D. F. Powell	H. J. Penney
§Rugby, Warwicks.	85,200	13,550,436	J. S. R. Lawton	(a) Mrs. E. Humphreys
§Runnymede, Surrey	70,800	13,033,654	T. N. Williams	(a) Mrs. E. E. Price
§Rushcliffe, Notts.	98,400	13,874,935	J. Saxton	(a) Mrs. M. M. Males
§Rushmoor, Hants.	77,700	13,169,580	D. Hartley	(a) B. A. Oliver
Rutland, Leics.	36,000	4,392,091	A. S. Jowett	A. D. Makey
Ryedale, North Yorks.	90,300	8,904,631	D. Cudworth	Mrs. E. L. Shields
ST. ALBANS, Herts.	128,600	24,575,287	E. A. Hackford	(a) K. J. Davies
§St. Edmundsbury, Suffolk	92,000	13,387,593	G. R. N. Toft	(a) P. A. E. A. Rudge
Salisbury, Wilts.	101,400	14,067,469	D. R. J. Rawlinson	M. W. M. T. Newman
§Scarborough, North Yorks.	104,400	11,678,991	J. M. Trebble	(a) G. W. Allanson
§Scunthorpe, Humberside	61,500	12,614,996	I. M. Hutchinson	(a) W. L. Baker
Sedgefield, Co. Durham	88,400	9,923,053	A. J. Roberts	T. H. Conley
Sedgemoor, Somerset	95,200	12,195,375	D. D. Tremlett	M. J. W. Tingley
Selby, North Yorks.	89,000	16,743,686	J. C. Edwards	J. T. Deans
Sevenoaks, Kent	107,500	14,584,840	B. C. Cova, M.B.E.	A. C. Garner
Shepway, Kent	88,300	14,619,170	R. H. Summers	W. H. Payne
§Shrewsbury and Atcham	91,200	13,047,454	D. M. Clarke	(a) V. W. C. Evason
§Slough, Berks.	98,200	25,238,710	A. Bhattacharya*	(a) D. A. Hewitt
SOUTHAMPTON, Hants.	199,100	32,851,000	E. A. Urquhart	(a) N. Best, C.B.E.
South Bedfordshire	111,000	21,468,167	T. D. Rix	Mrs. I. M. Beesley
South Bucks.	60,500	14,871,079	S. R. Jobson	Mrs. P. H. Watkins
South Cambridgeshire	117,400	19,114,639	B. J. Hancock	Mrs. D. S. K. Spink
South Derbyshire	70,500	10,213,858	T. Day	I. Harper
§Southend-on-Sea, Essex	162,500	28,203,373	D. Moulson*	(a) J. F. Armitage
South Hams, Devon	74,000	8,989,276	F. G. Palmer	Mrs. N. M. K. Hart
South Herefordshire	50,100	5,701,019	A. Hughes	S. I. Williams
South Holland, Lincs.	65,100	7,658,699	C. J. Simpkins	R. Gaunt
South Kesteven, Lincs.	103,400	13,910,948	K. R. Cann	D. Fletcher
South Lakeland, Cumbria	99,000	12,115,632	A. F. Winstanley*	E. Proctor
South Norfolk	100,500	11,828,913	A. G. T. Kellett	N. G. Chapman
South Northamptonshire	67,300	8,437,102†	C. Nye	H. W. D. Tucker
South Oxfordshire	132,200	20,045,498	J. B. Chirnside	Miss N. Le. P. Blackmore
§South Ribble, Lancs.	98,600	11,318,198	J. B. R. Leadbetter	(a) G. Woods
South Shropshire	35,400	3,827,755	G. C. Biggs	Maj. A. H. Coles, T.D.
South Somerset	140,200	17,190,128	D. J. Ashford	Mrs. J. P. Clark
South Staffordshire	106,800	13,670,946	G. J. Haywood	Mrs. J. M. Burton
§South Wight, I.o.W.	55,300	6,416,174	D. W. Jaggar	(a) B. W. Coates-Evans
§Spelthorne, Surrey	87,000	23,737,276	M. B. Taylor	(a) A. W. Sawyer
§Stafford	117,900	17,348,065	J. K. M. Krawiec*	(a) W. J. Kemp
Staffordshire Moorlands	96,300	10,420,774	A. W. Law	C. B. Ellis
§Stevenage, Herts.	73,800	15,426,831	H. L. Miller	(a) Mrs. H. M. Lawrence
§Stockton-on-Tees, Cleveland	175,900	27,218,223	F. F. Theobalds*	(a) H. L. Davies
STOKE-ON-TRENT, Staffs.	246,700	32,885,875	S. W. Titchener	(b) S. J. Bate
Stratford-on-Avon, Warwicks.	107,200	17,553,452	I. B. Prosser	C. G. Corbett
Stroud, Glos.	108,900	13,088,079	(vacant)	Mrs. V. Gardiner
Suffolk Coastal	109,200	16,296,113	D. L. Blay	H. E. Brookes
§Surrey Heath	81,100	15,325,355	M. F. Orlik	(a) D. J. Bobbett
§Swale, Kent	112,500	13,469,921	W. Croydon, C.B.E.	(a) Mrs. J. M. Newman
§Tamworth, Staffs.	67,600	8,773,015	P. E. Thorpe	(a) P. F. Knowles
Tandridge, Surrey	75,500	10,749,329	C. W. Rockall	A. S. J. Wellman
§Taunton Deane, Somerset	92,900	12,355,255	P. F. Berman	(a) J. E. Richards
Teesdale, Co. Durham	24,900	2,353,723	C. E. Fell	G. K. Robinson
Teignbridge, Devon	107,500	12,497,022	P. B. Young	Mrs. M. Stanton
Tendring, Essex	126,200	17,145,941	D. Mitchell-Gears	V. Y. Pound
§Test Valley, Hants.	100,400	15,899,593	G. Blythe	(a) E. A. Sier
§Tewkesbury, Glos.	85,500	13,182,598	R. A. Wheeler	(a) B. R. Izett
§Thamesdown, Wilts.	166,100	25,187,990	D. M. Kent	(a) K. Savage
Thanet, Kent	126,900	15,562,355	I. G. Gill	W. H. Dawson
Three Rivers, Herts.	80,200	13,435,259	A. Robertson	G. Tither
§Thurrock, Essex	124,000	28,381,058	C. Ennis	(a) M. Bidmead
§Tonbridge and Malling, Kent	100,400	14,820,939	J. E. Sweetman (*acting*)	(a) Mrs. P. Sinclair-Lee
§Torbay, Devon	117,700	17,825,889	D. P. Hudson	(a) D. P. Hudson

†1988 figure.　　‡Borough Director.

District	Estimated Resident Population 1987	Rateable Value 1989 £	Chief Executive (*Clerk)	Chairman 1989-90 (a) Mayor (b) Lord Mayor
Torridge, Devon	50,500	4,396,623	R. K. Brasington	N. Sharrock
§Tunbridge Wells, Kent	99,100	13,396,388	R. J. Stone	(a) J. Perry
Tynedale, Northumberland	55,500	6,788,044	A. Baty	D. Elwell
Uttlesford, Essex	66,100	10,114,382	J. F. Vernon	R. P. Chambers
Vale of White Horse, Oxon	111,400	20,200,000	J. C. Neville Wood	J. Jones, O.B.E.
§Vale Royal, Cheshire	114,000	15,795,412	W. R. T. Woods	(a) Mrs. J. M. Salter
Wansbeck, Northumberland	59,600	8,072,050	A. G. White	C. Buglass
Wansdyke, Avon	80,300	9,346,716	P. May‡	Rev. K. B. Akin-Flenley
§Warrington, Cheshire	183,700	28,406,779	M. I. M. Sanders	(a) G. H. Syers
Warwick	117,800	20,852,199	M. J. Ward	Mrs. V. Davis
§Watford, Herts.	76,100	17,650,585	R. B. McMillan	(a) J. M. Watts
Waveney, Suffolk	105,900	12,780,555	M. Berridge	Mrs. B. I. Pointon
§Waverley, Surrey	110,900	18,607,491	G. W. Nuttall	(a) D. G. Kinsella, M.B.E.
Wealden, East Sussex	131,700	15,926,792	D. R. Holness	B. H. F. Trew
Wear Valley, Co. Durham	64,700	6,194,957	F. A. Dobson†	Mrs. E. M. Wilson
§Wellingborough, Northants.	65,800	10,130,504	W. B. Veal	(a) S. T. Partridge-Underwood
Welwyn Hatfield, Herts.	93,800	20,212,258	D. Riddle	T. Freeman
§West Devon	43,900	4,369,013	J. S. Ligo	(a) K. A. Charlton
West Dorset	84,100	10,542,707	R. C. Rennison	E. H. King
West Lancashire	106,700	13,846,700	J. Cowdall	C. A. Kells
West Lindsey, Lincs.	77,300	8,772,215	R. W. Nelsey	J. G. Stanley
West Oxfordshire	96,000	11,743,401	N. J. B. Robson	Mrs. M. I. Frost
West Somerset	30,900	6,091,473	H. Close	S. D. Wall
West Wiltshire	105,900	12,448,555	D. G. Latham	J. B. Bennett
§Weymouth and Portland, Dorset	63,300	7,077,338	M. N. Ashby	(a) Mrs. J. W. Nagel
WINCHESTER, Hants.	95,600	15,057,513	D. H. Cowan	(a) F. G. Allgood
§Windsor and Maidenhead, Berks.	129,900	27,656,445	G. B. Blacker	(a) A. W. Griffiths
§Woking, Surrey	86,600	17,531,953	P. Russell	(a) Mrs. A. Cartwright
Wokingham, Berks.	145,600	22,595,608	N. E. Butler	Maj. D. G. Goddard
Woodspring, Avon	184,700	21,478,307	R. H. Moon	J. C. Wiltshire
WORCESTER	79,900	14,346,418	R. G. Grant	(a) Miss B. Sheridan
§Worthing, West Sussex	97,400	15,444,955	M. J. Ball	(a) A. Dockerty
Wrekin, Shropshire	132,000	18,388,951	D. G. Hutchinson	P. A. Heighway
Wychavon, Hereford and Worcs	99,000	15,547,485	P. G. Rust, M.B.E.	R. G. Cartwright
Wycombe, Bucks.	156,500	32,013,316	L. Timms	Mrs. K. M. Peatey
§Wyre, Lancs.	102,200	31,547,965	M. Brown	(a) R. C. Williamson
Wyre Forest, Hereford and Worcs.	93,700	13,943,583	A. S. Dick	M. B. Kelly
YORK, North Yorks.	101,500	12,533,933	J. Cairns	(b) J. Archer

‡General Manager.   †Managing Director.

THE PRINCIPAL ENGLISH CITIES

BIRMINGHAM

BIRMINGHAM (West Midlands) is Britain's second city and the largest metropolitan district in the country. It is a focal point in national communications networks with a rapidly expanding International Airport.

The generally accepted derivation of "Birmingham" is the *ham* or dwelling-place of the *ing* or the family of *Beorma*, presumed to have been a Saxon. During the Industrial Revolution the town grew into a major manufacturing centre. In 1889 Birmingham was granted City status.

Despite the decline in manufacturing, Birmingham is still a major hardware trade and motor component industry centre. Recent development includes the National Exhibition Centre and the Aston Science Park. An Urban Development Agency has been set up.

The principal buildings are the Town Hall, built in 1832–34; the Council House (1879); Victoria Law Courts (1891); the University (1909); the 13th century Church of St. Martin (rebuilt 1873); the Cathedral (formerly St. Philip's Church) (1711) and the Roman Catholic Cathedral of St. Chad (1839–41).

BRADFORD

BRADFORD (West Yorkshire), 192 miles N.N.W. of London, is the administrative centre of the Metropolitan District of Bradford. The District covers an area of 91,444 acres and lies on the southern edge of the Yorkshire Dales National Park, including within its boundaries the village of Haworth, home of the Brontë sisters, and Ilkley Moor.

Originally a Saxon township, Bradford received a market charter in 1251 but developed only slowly until the industrialization of the textile industry brought rapid growth during the 19th century. The prosperity of that period is reflected in much of the city's architecture, particularly the public buildings—City Hall (1873), Wool Exchange (1867), St George's Hall (Concert Hall, 1853), Cartwright Hall

(Art Gallery, 1904) and Technical College (1882). Other chief buildings are the Cathedral (15th century) and Bolling Hall (14th century).

Textiles still play an important part in the city's economy but industry is now more broadly based, including engineering and micro-electronics. The city has a strong banking, insurance and building society sector, and a growing tourism industry.

BRISTOL

BRISTOL (Avon) is the largest non-metropolitan district in population in the country, and lies 119 miles W. of London. The present municipal area is 10,954 hectares.

Bristol's commercial port systems comprise the largest municipally owned port in the country. The Avonmouth dock complex, Royal Portbury Dock and Portishead Dock handle import and export cargoes. Principal imports include cocoa, timber, metals, animal feeding stuffs, oil products, chemicals, vehicles and molasses. The Royal Portbury Dock, opened by H.M. the Queen in Aug. 1977, is capable of accommodating up to six vessels of 70,000 d.w.t.

The chief buildings include the 12th century Cathedral (with later additions), with Norman chapter house and gateway, the 14th century Church of St. Mary Redcliffe, Wesley's Chapel, Broadmead, the Merchant Venturers' Almshouses, the Council House (1956), Guildhall, Exchange (erected from the designs of John Wood in 1743), Cabot Tower, the University and Clifton College. The Roman Catholic Cathedral at Clifton was opened in 1973.

The Clifton Suspension Bridge, with a span of 702 feet over the Avon, was projected by Brunel in 1836 but was not completed until 1864. Brunel's SS *Great Britain*, the first ocean going propeller driven ship, is now being restored in the City Docks from where she was launched in 1843. The docks themselves have been extensively restored and redeveloped.

Bristol was a Royal Borough before the Norman Conquest. The earliest form of the name is *Bricgstow*. In 1373 it received from Edward III a charter granting it county status.

CAMBRIDGE

CAMBRIDGE, a settlement far older than its ancient University, lies on the Cam or Granta, 51 miles north of London. It has an area of 10,060 acres.

The city is a county town and regional headquarters. Its industries include electronics, flour milling, cement making and the manufacture of scientific instruments. Among its open spaces are Jesus Green, Sheep's Green, Coe Fen, Parker's Piece, Christ's Pieces, the University Botanic Garden, and the Backs, or lawns and gardens through which the Cam winds behind the principal line of college buildings. East of the Cam, King's Parade, upon which stand Great St. Mary's Church, Gibbs' Senate House and King's College Chapel with Wilkins' screen, joins Trumpington Street to form one of the most beautiful throughfares in Europe.

University and college buildings provide the outstanding features of Cambridge architecture but several churches (especially St. Benet's, the oldest building in the City, and St. Sepulchre's, the Round Church) also are notable. The modern Guildhall (1939) stands on a site of which at least part has held municipal buildings since 1224.

CANTERBURY

CANTERBURY, the Metropolitan City of the Anglican Communion, has a history going back to prehistoric times. It was the Roman *Durovernum*

Cantiacorum and the Saxon Cant-wara-byrig (stronghold of the men of Kent). Here in 597 St. Augustine began the conversion of the English to Christianity, when Ethelbert, King of Kent, was baptized.

Of the Benedictine St. Augustine's Abbey, burial place of the Jutish Kings of Kent (whose capital Canterbury was) only extensive ruins remain. St. Martin's Church, on the eastern outskirts of the City, is stated by Bede to have been the place of worship of Queen Bertha, the Christian wife of King Ethelbert, before the advent of St. Augustine.

In 1170 the rivalry of Church and State culminated in the murder in Canterbury Cathedral, by Henry II's knights, of Archbishop Thomas Becket, whose shrine became a great centre of pilgrimage as described by Chaucer in his *Canterbury Tales*. After the Reformation pilgrimages ceased, but the prosperity of the City was strengthened by an influx of Huguenot refugees, who introduced weaving. The Elizabethan poet and playwright Christopher Marlowe was born and reared in Canterbury, and there are literary associations also with Defoe, Dickens, Joseph Conrad and Somerset Maugham.

The Cathedral, with architecture ranging from the 11th to 15th centuries, is world famous. Modern pilgrims are attracted particularly to the Martyrdom, The Black Prince's Tomb, the Warriors' Chapel and the many examples of medieval stained glass.

The medieval City Walls are built on Roman foundations and the 14th century West Gate is one of the finest buildings of its kind in the country.

The 1,000 seat Marlowe Theatre is the base for the Canterbury International Festival of the Arts each autumn.

CARLISLE

CARLISLE is situated at the confluence of the River Eden and River Caldew, 309 miles north west of London and a few miles from the Scottish border. It has an area of 254,955 acres, and was granted a charter in 1158.

The city stands at the western end of Hadrian's Wall and dates from the original Roman settlement of *Luguvalium*. Granted to Scotland in the 10th century, Carlisle is not included in the Domesday Book. William Rufus reclaimed the area in 1092 and the Castle and city walls were built to guard Carlisle and the western border; the Citadel is a Tudor addition to protect the south of the city. Until the Union of the Crowns in 1603, Carlisle changed hands several times and was frequently besieged. During the Civil War the city remained Royalist; in 1745 it supported the Young Pretender.

The Cathedral, originally a 12th century Augustinian priory, was enlarged in the 13th and 14th centuries after the diocese was created in 1133. To the south is a restored Tithe Barn and nearby the 18th century church of St. Cuthbert, the third to stand on a site dating from the 7th century.

Carlisle is the major shopping, commercial and agricultural centre for the area, and industries include the manufacture of metal goods, biscuits and textiles. However, the largest employer is the services sector, notably in retailing and transport. The city has an important communications position at the centre of a network of major roads, as an important stage on the main west coast rail services and with its own airport at Crosby.

CHESTER

CHESTER is situated on the River Dee, 189 miles north west of London. The city administers an area of 173 square miles and was granted Borough and City status in 1974.

Chester's recorded history dates from the 1st century when the Romans founded the fortress of *Deva*. The city's name is derived from the Latin *castra* (a camp or encampment). During the Middle Ages, Chester was the principal port of north west England but declined with the silting of the Dee estuary and competition from Liverpool. The city was also an important military centre, notably during Edward I's Welsh campaigns and the Elizabethan Irish campaigns. During the Civil War, Chester supported the King and was besieged from 1643–46. Chester's first charter was granted *c.* 1175 and the city was incorporated in 1506. The office of Sheriff is the earliest created in the country (*c.* 1120's), and the Mayor also enjoys the title "Admiral of the Dee".

The city's architectural features include the city walls (an almost complete two mile circuit), the unique Rows (covered galleries above the street level shops), the Victorian Gothic Town Hall (1869), the Castle (rebuilt 1788 and 1822) and numerous half-timbered buildings. The Cathedral was a Benedictine abbey until the Dissolution. Remaining monastic buildings include the chapter house, refectory and cloisters and there is a modern free-standing bell tower. The Norman church of St. John the Baptist was a Cathedral church in the early Middle Ages.

Chester is primarily a regional service centre and has considerable tourist appeal. In 1984 the city was awarded Development Area status which has attracted a range of nationally known companies to expand or locate in Chester.

COVENTRY

COVENTRY (West Midlands) is 92 miles N.W. of London, and an important industrial centre, producing cars, machine tools, agricultural machinery, man-made fibres, composite materials and telecommunications equipment.

The city owes its beginning to Leofric, Earl of Mercia and his wife Godiva who, in 1043, founded a Benedictine monastery. The guildhall of St. Mary dates from the 14th century, three of the city's churches date from the 14th and 15th centuries and 16th century almshouses may still be seen. Coventry's first cathedral was destroyed at the Reformation, its second in the 1940 blitz (its walls and spire remain) and the new cathedral designed by Sir Basil Spence, consecrated in 1962, now draws innumerable visitors.

Coventry is the home of the University of Warwick and its Science Park, the rapidly-expanding Westwood Business Park and the Museum of British Road Transport.

DERBY

DERBY stands on the banks of the River Derwent, 127 miles N.N.W. of London, and covers an area of 30 square miles. The name Derby dates back to 880 when the Danes settled in the locality and changed the original Saxon name of "Northworthy" to "Deoraby".

Derby has a wide range of industries: its products include aero engines, lawn mowers, pipework, specialized mechanical engineering equipment, textiles, chemicals, plastics and the Royal Crown Derby porcelain. The city is an established railway centre, the site of British Rail's Technical Centre with its research laboratories.

Buildings of interest include St Peter's Church and the Old Abbey Building (14th century), the Cathedral (1525), St Mary's Roman Catholic Church (1839) and the Industrial Museum, formerly the Old Silk Mill (1721). The traditional city centre is complemented by the new Eagle Centre and "out-of-centre" retail developments. In addition to the Derby

Playhouse, the Assembly Rooms are a multi-purpose venue.

The first charter granting a Mayor and Aldermen was that of Charles I in 1637. Previous charters date back to 1154. It was granted City status in 1977.

DURHAM

The city of DURHAM is a district in the county of Durham and covers an area of 73 square miles. The city is a major tourist attraction in the county because of its prominent Norman Cathedral and Castle set high on a wooded peninsula overlooking the River Wear. The Cathedral was founded as a shrine for the body of St. Cuthbert in 995. The present building dates from 1093 and among its many treasures is the tomb of the Venerable Bede (673–735). Durham's Prince Bishops had unique powers up to 1836, being lay rulers as well as religious leaders. As a palatinate Durham could have its own army, nobility, coinage and courts. The Castle was the main seat of the Prince Bishops for nearly 800 years; it is now used as a college by the University.

The University, founded on the initiative of Bishop William Van Mildert, is England's third oldest. Its students live in 14 colleges spread across the city.

Among other buildings of interest is the Guildhall in the Market Place which dates originally from the 14th century. Much work has been carried out to conserve this area, forming part of the city's major contribution to the Council of Europe's Urban Renaissance Campaign. Annual events include Durham's Regatta in June (claimed to be the oldest rowing event in Britain) and the Annual Gala (formerly Durham Miners' Gala) in July.

In the past 20 years the economy of Durham has undergone a significant change with the replacement of mining as the dominant feature by "white collar" employment. Although still a predominantly rural area, the industrial and commercial sector is growing and a wide range of manufacturing and service industries are based on industrial estates on and around the City area.

EXETER

EXETER lies on the River Exe 170 miles S.W. of London and 10 miles from the sea. It covers an area of 11,661 acres and was granted a Royal Charter by Henry II.

The Romans founded *Isca Dumnoniorum* in the 1st century A.D., and in the 3rd century a stone wall (most of which remains) was built, providing protection against Saxon, and then Danish invasions. After the Conquest, the city led resistance to William in the west, until reduced by siege. The Normans built the motte and bailey castle of Rougemont, the gatehouse and one tower of which remain, although the rest was pulled down in 1784. The first bridge across the Exe was built in the 13th century. The city's role as a port declined due to the silting of the river, but was somewhat restored by the construction in the 1560's of the first ship canal in England. Exeter was the Royalist headquarters in the West during the Civil War.

The diocese of Exeter was established by Edward the Confessor in 1050, although a church existed on the Cathedral site in the early 10th century. A new cathedral was built in the 12th century but the present building was begun *c.* 1275 in the Gothic style, although incorporating the Norman towers, and completed about a century later with the West Front. The Guildhall dates from the 12th century and there are many other medieval buildings in the city, as well as architecture in the Georgian and Regency styles (Custom House, The Quay). Damage suffered by bombing in 1942 led to the redevelopment of the city centre.

Exeter's prosperity from medieval times was based on trade in wool and woollen cloth (commemorated by Tuckers Hall), which remained at its height until the late 18th century when export trade was hit by the French Wars. Subsequently Exeter has developed as an administrative and commercial centre, notably in the distributive trades, light manufacturing industries and tourism.

KINGSTON UPON HULL

HULL (officially "Kingston upon Hull") lies in the mostly rural County of Humberside, at the junction of the River Hull with the Humber, 22 miles from the North Sea and 205 miles N. of London. The municipal area is 17,535 acres.

Hull is one of the great seaports of the United Kingdom. It has docks covering a water area of 172 acres, equipped to handle cargoes by unit-load techniques, and is a departure point for car ferry services to continental Europe. There is a great variety of industry and service industries, as well as increasing tourism and conference business.

The city, restored after very heavy air raid damage during World War II, has good office and administrative buildings, its municipal centre being the Guildhall, its educational centre the University of Hull and its religious centre the Parish Church of the Holy Trinity. The old Town area is being renovated and includes a new marina and a new shopping complex, to be opened in October 1990. Just west of the city is the Humber Bridge, the world's longest single span suspension bridge, which was officially opened by H.M. The Queen in July 1981.

Kingston upon Hull was so named by Edward I. City status was accorded in 1897 and the office of Mayor raised to the dignity of Lord Mayor in 1914.

LEEDS

LEEDS (West Yorkshire), a Metropolitan District from April 1, 1974, is a junction for road, rail, canal and air services and an important commercial centre, situated in the lower Aire Valley, 195 miles by road N.N.W. of London. The metropolitan area is 138,915 acres.

The main manufacturing industries are mechanical engineering, printing, publishing and clothing. However, 65 per cent of employment is in services, notably professional and scientific, particularly education and medicine, distributive trades, finance and banking.

The principal buildings are the Civic Hall (1933), the Town Hall (1858), the Municipal Buildings and Art Gallery (1884) with the Henry Moore Gallery (1982), the Corn Exchange (1863) and the University. The Parish Church (St. Peter's) was rebuilt in 1841; the 17th century St. John's Church has a fine interior with a famous English renaissance screen; the last remaining 18th century church is Holy Trinity, Boar Lane (1727). Kirkstall Abbey (about 3 miles from the centre of the city), founded by Henry de Lacy in 1152, is one of the most complete examples of Cistercian houses now remaining. Temple Newsam, birthplace of Lord Darnley, was acquired by the Council in 1922. The present house was largely re-built by Sir Arthur Ingram in about 1620. Adel Church, about 5 miles from the centre of the city, is a fine Norman structure.

Leeds was first incorporated by Charles I in 1626. The earliest forms of the name are *Loidis* or *Ledes*, the origins of which are obscure.

LEICESTER

LEICESTER is situated geographically in the centre of England, 100 miles N. of London. The City dates back to pre-Roman times and was one of the five Danish *Burhs*. In 1589 Queen Elizabeth I granted a Charter to the City and the ancient title was confirmed by Letters Patent in 1919. Under local government reorganization Leicester's area remained unchanged at 18,141 acres, and it retains its designation as a City.

The principal industries of the city are hosiery, and knitwear, footwear manufacturing and engineering. The growth of Leicester as a hosiery centre increased rapidly from the introduction there of the first stocking frame in 1670 and today it has some of the largest hosiery factories in the world, with much of the output being exported.

The principal buildings in the city are the Town Hall, the New Walk Centre, the University, Leicester Polytechnic, De Montfort Hall, one of the finest concert halls in the provinces seating over 2,750 persons, and the Granby Halls, a major indoor sports facility. The ancient Churches of St. Martin (now Leicester Cathedral), St. Nicholas, St. Margaret, All Saints, St. Mary de Castro, and buildings such as the Guildhall, the 14th century Newarke Gate, the Castle and the Jewry Wall Roman site still exist. The Haymarket Theatre, an integral part of a large shopping and car-parking complex, was opened in 1973.

LINCOLN

Situated 143 miles N. of London and 40 miles inland on the River Witham, LINCOLN derives its name from a contraction of *Lindum Colonia*, the settlement founded in A.D. 48 by the Romans to command the crossing of Ermine Street and Fosse Way. Sections of the 3rd century Roman city wall can be seen, including an extant gateway (Newport Arch), and excavations have discovered traces of a sewerage system unique in Britain. The Romans also drained the surrounding fenland and created a canal system, laying the foundations of Lincoln's agricultural prosperity, and also of the city's importance in the medieval wool trade as a port and Staple town. As one of the Five Boroughs of the Danelaw, Lincoln was an important trading centre in the 9th and 10th centuries and medieval prosperity from the wool trade lasted until the 14th century, enabling local merchants to build parish churches (of which three survive), and attracting in the 12th century a Jewish community (Jew's House and Court, Aaron's House). However, the removal of the Staple to Boston in 1369 heralded a decline from which the city only recovered fully in the 19th century when improved fen drainage made Lincoln agriculturally important, and improved canal and rail links led to industrial development, mainly in the manufacture of machinery, components and engineering products.

The Castle was built shortly after the Conquest and is unusual in having two mounds; on one mound stands a Keep (Lucy's Tower) added in the 12th century. The Cathedral was begun *c*.1073 when the first Norman bishop moved the see of Lindsey to Lincoln, but was mostly destroyed by fire and earthquake in the 12th century. Rebuilding was begun by St. Hugh and completed over a century later. The Wren library contains manuscripts including one of the four surviving originals of the Magna Charta. Other notable architectural features of the city are the 12th century High Bridge, the oldest in Britain still to carry buildings, and the Guildhall situated above the 15–16th century Stonebow gateway.

LIVERPOOL

LIVERPOOL (Merseyside) on the right bank of the river Mersey, 3 miles from the Irish Sea and 210 miles

N.W. of London, is the U.K.'s fourth most important port and the foremost for the Atlantic trade. The municipal area of 27,864 acres includes 2,840 acres in the bed of the river Mersey. Tunnels link Liverpool with Birkenhead and Wallasey.

There are 2,100 acres of dockland on both sides of the river and the Gladstone and Royal Seaforth Docks can accommodate the largest vessels afloat. Annual tonnage of cargo handled is approximately 10,500,000 tonnes. The main imports are crude oil, grain, ores, edible oils, timber, containers and break bulk cargo. Liverpool Free Port, Britain's largest, was opened in 1984.

Liverpool was created a free borough in 1207 and a city in 1880. From the early eighteenth century it expanded rapidly with the growth of industrialization and Atlantic trade. Surviving buildings from this date include the Bluecoat Chambers (1717, formerly the Bluecoat School), the Town Hall (1754, rebuilt to the original design, 1795), and buildings in Rodney Street, Canning Street and the suburbs. Notable from the 19th and 20th centuries are the Anglican Cathedral, built from the designs of Sir Giles Gilbert Scott (the foundation stone was laid in 1904, and the building was only completed in 1980), the Catholic Metropolitan Cathedral (designed by Sir Frederick Gibberd, consecrated 1967) and St. George's Hall, (1838–54), regarded as one of the finest modern examples of classical architecture. The recently refurbished Albert Dock (designed by Jesse Hartley) contains the Merseyside Maritime Museum and Tate Gallery, Liverpool. In 1852 an Act was obtained for establishing a public library, museum and art gallery: as a result Liverpool had one of the first public libraries in the country. The Brown, Picton and Hornby libraries now form one of the country's major libraries. The Victoria Building of Liverpool University, the Royal Liver, Cunard and Mersey Docks & Harbour Company buildings at the Pier Head, the Municipal Buildings and the Philharmonic Hall are other examples of the City's fine buildings.

Britain's first International Garden Festival was held in Liverpool in 1984.

MANCHESTER

MANCHESTER (the *Mamucium* of the Romans, who occupied it in A.D. 78) is 189 miles N.W. of London and covers about 43 square miles.

Manchester is a commercial and industrial centre with a population engaged in engineering, chemical, clothing, food processing and textile industries. Banking and insurance are among the prime commercial activities. The city is connected with the sea by the Manchester Ship Canal, opened in 1894, 35½ miles long, and accommodating ships up to 15,000 tons. Manchester Airport handles more than 5 million passengers yearly.

The principal buildings are the Town Hall, erected in 1877 from the designs of Alfred Waterhouse, R.A., together with a large extension of 1938; the Royal Exchange (1869, enlarged 1921) the Central Library (1934); Heaton Hall; the 17th century Chetham Library; the Rylands Library (1899), which includes the Althorp collection; the University precinct; the 15th century Cathedral (formerly the parish church) and the Free Trade Hall. Manchester is the home of the Hallé Orchestra, the Royal Northern College of Music, the Royal Exchange Theatre and seven public art galleries.

The town received its first charter of incorporation in 1838 and was created a city in 1853. The title of city was retained under local government reorganization.

NEWCASTLE UPON TYNE

NEWCASTLE UPON TYNE (Tyne and Wear) a Metropolitan District on the north bank of the River Tyne, is 8 miles from the North Sea, 272 miles N. of London and has an area of 27,640 acres. A Cathedral and University City, it is the administrative, commercial and cultural centre for north-east England and the principal port. It is an important manufacturing centre with a wide variety of industries.

The principal buildings include the Castle Keep (12th century), Black Gate (13th century), Blackfriars (13th century), West Walls (13th century), St. Nicholas's Cathedral (15th century, fine lantern tower), St. Andrew's Church (12th–14th century), St. John's (14th–15th century), All Saints (1786 by Stephenson), St. Mary's Roman Catholic Cathedral (1844), Trinity House (17th century), Sandhill (16th century houses), Guildhall (Georgian), Grey Street (1834–39), Central Station (1846–50), Laing Art Gallery (1904), University of Newcastle Physics Building (1962) and Medical Building (1985), Civic Centre (1963), Central Library (1969) and Eldon Square Shopping Development (1976). Open spaces include the Town Moor (927 acres) and Jesmond Dene. Eight bridges span the Tyne at Newcastle.

The City derives its name from the "new castle" (1080) erected as a defence against the Scots. In 1400 it was made a County, and in 1882 a City.

NORWICH

NORWICH (Norfolk) is an ancient City 110 miles N.E. of London. It grew from an early Anglo-Saxon settlement near the confluence of the Rivers Yare and Wensum, and now serves as provincial capital for the predominantly agricultural region of East Anglia. The name is thought to relate to the most northerly of a group of Anglo-Saxon villages or "wics". The present City has an area of 9,655 acres. The City's first known Charter was granted in 1158 by Henry II.

Norwich serves its surrounding area as a market town and commercial centre, banking and insurance being prominent among the City's businesses. From the 14th century until the Industrial Revolution, Norwich was the regional centre of the woollen industry, but now the biggest single industry is financial services and principal trades are engineering, printing, shoemaking, double glazing, and the production of chemicals, clothing, confectionery and other foodstuffs. Norwich is accessible to seagoing vessels by means of the River Yare, entered at Great Yarmouth, 20 miles to the east.

Among many historic buildings are the Cathedral (completed in the 12th century and surmounted by a 15th century spire 315 feet in height), the Keep of the Norman Castle (now a museum and art gallery), the 15th century flint-walled Guildhall (now a tourist information centre), some thirty medieval parish churches, St. Andrew's and Blackfriars' Halls, the Tudor houses preserved in Elm Hill and the Georgian Assembly House. The University of East Anglia has been established in Norwich on a spacious site at Earlham on the City's western boundary and received its first students in 1963.

NOTTINGHAM

NOTTINGHAM (Nottinghamshire) stands on the River Trent, 124 miles N.N.W. of London in one of the most valuable coalfields of the country connected by canal with the Atlantic and the North Sea. The municipal area is 18,364 acres.

The principal industries are hosiery, lace, bleaching, dyeing and spinning, tanning, engineering and cycle works, brewing and the manufacture of tobacco, chemicals, furniture, typewriters and mechanical products.

The chief buildings are the 17th century Nottingham Castle (restored in 1878, and now the City Museum and Gallery of Art), Wollaton Hall (1580–88) owned by the City Council and now a Natural History Museum, St. Mary's, St. Peter's, and St. Nicholas's Churches, the Roman Catholic Cathedral (Pugin, 1842–44), the Council House (1929), the Guildhall and Court House (1888), Shire Hall, Albert Hall, the University, Trent Polytechnic, Newstead Abbey, home of Lord Byron, the Theatre Royal (1865), the Playhouse (1963) and the Royal Concert Hall (1982).

Snotingaham or *Notingeham*, "the village or home of the sons of Snot" (the Wise), is the Anglo-Saxon name for the Celtic *Tuigogobauc*, "Cave Homes". The City possesses a Charter of Henry II, and was created a City in 1897. Under local government reorganization, the style of City was reaccorded from April, 1974.

OXFORD

OXFORD is a University City, an important industrial centre, and a market town, with an area of 8,785 acres. Industry played a minor part in Oxford until the motor industry was established in 1912.

It is for its architecture that Oxford is of most interest to the visitor, its oldest specimens being the reputed Saxon tower of St. Michael's church, the remains of the Norman castle and city walls and the Norman church at Iffley. It is chiefly famous however for its Gothic buildings, such as the Divinity Schools, the Old Library at Merton College, William of Wykeham's New College, Magdalen College and Christ Church and many other college buildings. Later centuries are represented by the Laudian quadrangle at St. John's College, the Renaissance Sheldonian Theatre by Wren, Trinity College Chapel, and All Saints Church; Hawksmoor's mock-Gothic at All Souls College, and the 18th century Queens' College. In addition to individual buildings, High Street and Radcliffe Square, just off it, both form architectural compositions of great beauty. Most of the Colleges have gardens, those of Magdalen, New College, St. John's (designed by "Capability" Brown) and Worcester being the largest.

PLYMOUTH

PLYMOUTH is situated on the borders of Devon and Cornwall at the confluence of the Rivers Tamar and Plym, 210 miles from London, with an area of 19,572 acres. The city has a long maritime history; it was the home port of Sir Francis Drake and the starting point for his circumnavigation of the world, as well as the last port of call for the *Mayflower* when the Pilgrim Fathers sailed for the New World in 1620. Today Plymouth is host to many international yacht races. The Barbican harbour area has many Elizabethan buildings, and on Plymouth Hoe stands the first lighthouse to be built on the Eddystone Rocks, some miles offshore.

Following extensive war damage, the city centre, comprising a large shopping centre, municipal offices, law courts and public buildings, has been re-built. The main employment is provided at the Naval Base, though many new industrial firms and service industries have become established in the post-war period and the city is a growing tourism centre. In 1982 the Theatre Royal was opened. In conjunction with the Cornwall County Council, the Tamar Bridge was constructed linking the City by road with Cornwall.

PORTSMOUTH

PORTSMOUTH occupies Portsea Island, Hampshire, with boundaries extending to the mainland. It has an area of 15½ sq. miles and is 70 miles S.W. of London.

Portsmouth is a centre of industry and commerce, including many high technology and manufacturing industries. It is the U.K. headquarters of a major computer company and two insurance companies. H.M. Naval Base still has a substantial work force, although this has decreased in recent years. The commercial port and Continental Ferry Port is owned and run by the City Council, and carries passengers and vehicles to France.

A major port since the 16th century, Portsmouth is also a thriving seaside resort catering for thousands of visitors and day-trippers annually. Among many historic attractions are Lord Nelson's flagship, H.M.S. *Victory*, the Tudor warship *Mary Rose*, Britain's first "ironclad", H.M.S. *Warrior*, the D-Day Museum, Charles Dickens' birthplace at 393 Old Commercial Road, the Royal Naval and Royal Marine museums, Southsea Castle (built by Henry VIII), the Round Tower and Point Battery, which for hundreds of years have guarded the entrance to Portsmouth Harbour, Fort Widley on Portsdown Hill and the Sealife Centre.

ST. ALBANS

Twenty-five miles N.W. of London and situated on the River Ver, ST. ALBANS' origins stem from the major Roman town of *Verulamium*. Named after the first Christian martyr in Britain, who was executed here, St. Albans has developed around the Norman Abbey and Cathedral Church (consecrated 1115), the second longest in Britain, built partly of materials from the old Roman city. The museums house Iron Age and Roman artefacts and the Roman Theatre, unique in Britain, has a stage as opposed to an amphitheatre. Archaeological excavations in the city centre continue also to reveal evidence of pre-Roman, Saxon and medieval occupation.

The town's significance grew to the extent that it was a signatory and venue for the drafting of the Magna Charta. It was also the scene of major riots during the Peasants' Revolt; the French King John was imprisoned there after the Battle of Poitiers, and heavy fighting took place during the Wars of the Roses; but it is as a Roman town that it is best recognized.

Previously controlled by the Abbot, the town achieved a Royal Charter in 1553 and City status in 1877. The street market, first established in 1553, is still an important feature of the city, as are many hotels and inns which survive from the days when St. Albans was an important coach stop. Tourist attractions include historic churches and houses, and a 15th century clock tower.

The advent of the railway saw the gradual expansion of the city, and the area now contains a wide range of firms, with special emphasis on microtechnology and electronics, particularly in the medical field. In addition, it is the home of the Royal National Rose Society, and of Rothamsted Park, the agricultural research centre.

In 1974 the City and District of St. Albans was formed, taking in the town of Harpenden and many villages, and it now covers an area of 63 square miles.

SHEFFIELD

SHEFFIELD (South Yorkshire), the centre of the special steel and cutlery trades, is situated 159 miles N.N.W. of London, at the junction of the Sheaf, Porter, Rivelin and Loxley with the River Don.

Sheffield has an area of 91,000 acres (nearly 150

square miles), including 4,619 acres of publicly owned parks and woodland. Though its cutlery, silverware and plate have long been famous, Sheffield has other and now more important industries—special and alloy steels, engineering and tool-making. Research in glass, metallurgy, radiotherapy and other fields is carried on.

The parish church of St. Peter and St. Paul, founded in the 12th century, became the Cathedral Church of the Diocese of Sheffield in 1914. The Roman Catholic Cathedral Church of St. Marie (founded 1847) was created Cathedral for the new diocese of Hallam in 1980. Parts of the present building date from *c.* 1435. The principal buildings are the Town Hall (1897, 1923 and 1977), the Cutlers' Hall (1832), the University (1905 and recent extensions, including 19-storey Arts Tower), City Hall (1932), Graves Art Gallery (1934), Castle Market Building (1959), the retail market (1973), Mappin Art Gallery and the Crucible Theatre.

Sheffield was created a city in 1893 and on April 1, 1974 became a Metropolitan District Council incorporating Stocksbridge and most of the Wortley Rural area, and retained city status.

Master Cutler (1988–89) of the Company of Cutlers in Hallamshire, G. A. Jowitt.

SOUTHAMPTON

SOUTHAMPTON is the leading British deep sea port on the Channel and is situated on one of the finest natural harbours in the world. The first Charter was granted by Henry II and Southampton was created a county of itself in 1447. In February, 1964, Her Majesty The Queen granted city status by Royal Charter. The city has an area of 12,071 acres excluding tidal waters.

There have been Roman and Saxon settlements on the site of the city, which has been an important port since the time of the Conquest due to its natural deep-water harbour. The oldest church is St. Michael's (1070) which has a black tournai marble font and an unusually tall spire built in the 18th century as a landmark for navigators of Southampton Water. Other buildings and monuments within the city walls are the Tudor House, God's House Tower, Bargate Museum, the Tudor Merchants Hall, the Weigh-house, West Gate, King John's House, Long House, Wool House, the ruins of Holy Rood Church, St. Julien's Church and the Mayflower Memorial. The medieval town walls, built for artillery, are among the most complete in Europe. Public open spaces total over 1,000 acres in extent and comprise 9 per cent of the city's area. The Common covers an area of 328 acres in the central district of the city and is mostly natural parkland.

STOKE-ON-TRENT

STOKE-ON-TRENT (Staffordshire), familiarly known as The Potteries, stands on the River Trent 157 miles N. of London. The present municipal area is 22,916 acres (36 square miles) and the city is the main centre of employment for the population of North Staffordshire. It is the largest clayware producer in the world (china, earthenware, sanitary goods, refractories, bricks and tiles) and has a considerable coal mining output drawn from one of the richest coalfields in Western Europe. The city has steelworks, foundries, chemical works, engineering plants, rubber works, paper mills, and a very wide range of manufactures. Extensive reconstruction has been carried on in recent years.

The City was formed by the federation in 1910 of the separate municipal authorities of Tunstall, Burslem, Hanley, Stoke-upon-Trent, Fenton, and Longton, all of which are now combined in the present City of Stoke-on-Trent.

WINCHESTER

WINCHESTER, the ancient capital of England, is situated on the River Itchen 65 miles S.W. of London and 12 miles N. of Southampton. Since local government reorganization in 1974, the style of City has been accorded to the whole of the new district of Winchester, which embraces an area of 162,921 acres of mid-Hampshire.

Winchester is rich in architecture of all types but the Cathedral takes pride of place. The longest Gothic cathedral in the world, it was built in 1079–93 and exhibits examples of Norman, Early English and Perpendicular styles. Winchester College, founded in 1382, is one of the most famous public schools, the original building (of 1393) remaining unaltered. St. Cross Hospital, another great medieval foundation, lies 1 mile south of the city. The Almshouses were founded in 1136 by Bishop Henry de Blois, and Cardinal Henry Beaufort added a new Alms House of "Noble Poverty" in 1446. The Chapel and dwellings are of great architectural interest, and visitors may still receive the "Wayfarer's Dole" of bread and ale.

Recent excavations have done much to clarify the origins and development of Winchester. Part of the forum and several of the streets of the Roman town have been discovered; and excavations in the Cathedral Close have uncovered the entire site of the Anglo-Saxon cathedral (known as the Old Minster) and parts of the New Minster, built by Alfred's son Edward the Elder, and the burial place of the Alfredian dynasty. The original burial place of St. Swithun, before his remains were translated to a site in the present cathedral, was also uncovered.

Excavations in other parts of the City have thrown much light on Norman Winchester, notably on the site of the Royal Castle, adjacent to which the new Law Courts have been built, and in the grounds of Wolvesey Castle, where the great house built by Bishops Giffard and Henry of Blois in the 12th century has been uncovered.

YORK

The City of YORK is a District in the County of North Yorkshire, and is an archiepiscopal seat.

The recorded history of York dates from A.D. 71, when the Roman Ninth Legion established a base under Petilius Cerealis which later became the fortress of *Eburacum*. In Anglo-Saxon times the city was the royal and ecclesiastical centre of Northumbria, and was captured by a Viking army in A.D. 866, after which it became the capital of the Viking kingdom of Jorvik. By the 14th century the city had become a great mercantile centre, chiefly owing to its control of the wool trade, and was used as the chief base against the Scots. Under the Tudors its fortunes declined, though Henry VIII made it the headquarters of the Council of the North. Recent excavations on many sites, including Coppergate, has greatly expanded knowledge of Roman, Viking and medieval urban life.

With its development as a railway centre in the 19th century the commercial life of York expanded. The principal industries are the manufacture of chocolate, railway coaches, scientific instruments, and sugar.

The City is rich in examples of architecture of all periods. The earliest church was built in A.D. 627 and in the 12th to the 15th centuries, the present Minster was built in a succession of styles. Other examples within the city are the medieval city walls and gateways, churches and guildhalls. Domestic architecture includes the Georgian mansions of The Mount, Micklegate and Bootham. Its museums include the Castle Museum, the National Railway Museum and the Jorvik Viking Centre.

THE CORPORATION OF LONDON

The City of London is the historic centre at the heart of London known as "the square mile" around which the vast metropolis has grown over the centuries. The City's residential population is 5,300 (1981 Census). The civic government is carried on by the Corporation of London through the Court of Common Council, a body consisting of the Lord Mayor, 24 other Aldermen and 132 Common Councilmen. The legal title of the Corporation is "the Mayor and Commonalty and Citizens of the City of London."

The City is the financial and business centre of London and includes the head offices of the principal banks, insurance companies and mercantile houses, in addition to buildings ranging from the historic interest of the Roman Wall and the 15th century Guildhall, to the massive splendour of St. Paul's Cathedral and the architectural beauty of Wrer.'s spires.

The City of London was described by Tacitus in 62 A.D. as "a busy emporium for trade and traders". Under the Romans it became an important administration centre and hub of the road system. Little is known of London in Saxon times when it formed part of the kingdom of the East Saxons. In 886 Alfred recovered London from the Danes and reconstituted it a burgh under his son-in-law. In 1066 the citizens submitted to William the Conqueror who in 1067 granted them a charter, which is still preserved, establishing them in the rights and privileges they had hitherto enjoyed.

The *Mayoralty* was established on the recognition of the corporate unity of the citizens by Prince John in 1191, the first Mayor being Henry Fitz Ailwyn who filled the office for 21 years and was succeeded by Fitz Alan (1212–14). A new charter was granted by King John in 1215, directing the Mayor to be chosen annually, which has ever since been done, though in early times the same individual often held the office more than once. A familiar instance is that of "Whittington, thrice Lord Mayor of London" (in reality four times, 1397, 1398, 1406, 1419); and many modern cases have occurred. The earliest instance of the phrase "Lord Mayor" in English is in 1414. It was used more generally in the latter part of the 15th century and became invariable from 1535 onwards. At Michaelmas the Liverymen in Common Hall choose two Aldermen who have served the office of Sheriff for presentation to the Court of Aldermen, and one is chosen to be Lord Mayor for the ensuing mayoral year.

Lord Mayor's Day.—The Lord Mayor of London was previously elected on the feast of St Simon and St Jude (Oct. 28), and from the time of Edward I, at least, was presented to the King or to the Barons of the Exchequer on the following day, except that day be a Sunday. The day of election was altered to Oct. 16 in 1346, and after some further changes was fixed for Michaelmas Day in 1546, but the ceremonies of admittance and swearing-in of the Lord Mayor continued to take place on Oct. 28 and 29 respectively until 1751. In 1752, at the reform of the Calendar (*see* page 114), the Lord Mayor was continued in office until Nov. 8, the "New Style" equivalent of Oct. 28. The Lord Mayor is now presented to the Lord Chief Justice at the Royal Courts of Justice on the second Saturday in November to make the final declaration of office, having been sworn in at Guildhall on the preceding day. The procession to the Royal Courts of Justice is popularly known as the *Lord Mayor's Show.*

Aldermen are mentioned in the 11th century and their office is of Saxon origin. They were elected annually between 1377 and 1394, when an Act of Parliament of Richard II directed them to be chosen for life. The *Common Council*, elected annually on the first Friday in December, was, at an early date, substituted for a popular assembly called the *Folkmote.* At first only two representatives were sent from each ward, but the number has since been greatly increased.

Sheriffs were Saxon officers: their predecessors were the *wic-reeves* and *portreeves* of London and Middlesex. At first they were officers of the Crown, and were named by the Barons of the Exchequer; but Henry I (in 1132) gave the citizens permission to choose their own Sheriffs, and the annual election of Sheriffs became fully operative under King John's charter of 1199. The citizens lost this privilege, as far as the election of Sheriff of Middlesex was concerned, by the Local Government Act, 1888; but the Liverymen continue, as heretofore, to choose two Sheriffs of the City of London, who are appointed on Midsummer Day, and take office at Michaelmas.

Officers.—The Recorder was first appointed in 1298. The office of Chamberlain is an ancient one, the first contemporary record of which is 1237. The Town Clerk (or Common Clerk) is mentioned in 1274 and the Common Serjeant in 1291.

Activities.—The work is assigned to a number of committees which present reports to the Court of Common Council. These Committees are:—City Lands and Bridge House Estates, Policy and Resources, Coal, Corn and Rates Finance, Planning and Communications, Central Markets, Billingsgate and Leadenhall Markets, Spitalfields Market, Police, Port and City of London Health and Social Services, Library (Library, Records, Art Gallery), Boards of Governors of Schools, Music (Guildhall School of Music and Drama), Establishment, Housing, Gresham (City side), Hampstead Heath Management, Epping Forest and Open Spaces, West Ham Park, Privileges, Barbican Residential and Barbican Centre (Barbican Arts and Conference Centre).

The Honourable the *Irish Society*, which manages the Corporation's Estates in Ulster, consists of a Governor and 5 other Aldermen, the Recorder, and 19 Common Councilmen, of whom one is elected Deputy Governor.

The *City's Estate*, in the possession of which the Corporation of London differs from other municipalities, is managed by the City Lands and Bridge House Estates Committee, the Chairmanship of which carries with it the title of "Chief Commoner."

The Right Honourable the Lord Mayor 1988–1989*

Sir Christopher Collett, G.B.E., *born* 1931; Alderman of *Broad Street,* 1979; *Sheriff of London,* 1985; *Lord Mayor,* 1988.

Secretary, Rear-Admiral A. J. Cooke, C.B.

Recorder, Sir James Miskin, Q.C., 1975; *Chamberlain,* Bernard Peter Harty, 1983; *Town Clerk,* Geoffrey William Rowley, C.B.E., 1982; *Common Serjeant,* Thomas Herbert Pigott, Q.C., 1984.

* The Lord Mayor for 1989–90 was elected on Michaelmas Day (*See* "Occurrences During Printing").

The Aldermen

Aldermen	Ward	Born	C.C.	Ald.	Shff.	Lord Mayor
Cdr. Sir Robin Danvers Penrose Gillett, Bt., G.B.E., R.D., R.N.R.	Bassishaw	1925	1965	1969	1973	1976
Sir Peter Drury Haggerston Gadsden, G.B.E.	Farringdon Wt.	1929	1969	1971	1970	1979
Sir Christopher Leaver, G.B.E.	Dowgate	1937	1973	1974	1979	1981
Dame Mary Donaldson, G.B.E.	Coleman St.	1921	1966	1975	1981	1983
Sir Alan Towers Traill, G.B.E.	Langbourn	1935	1970	1975	1982	1984
Sir William Allan Davis, G.B.E.	Cripplegate	1921	1971	1976	1982	1985
Sir David Kenneth Rowe-Ham, G.B.E.	Bridge	1935	....	1976	1984	1986
Sir Greville Douglas Spratt, G.B.E., T.D.	Castle Baynard	1927	....	1978	1984	1987
Sir Christopher Collett, G.B.E.	Broad Street	1931	1973	1979	1985	1988

All the above have passed the Civic Chair

	Ward	Born	C.C.	Ald.	Shff.	Lord Mayor
Hugh Charles Philip Bidwell	Billingsgate	1934	....	1979	1986	....
Alexander Michael Graham	Queenhithe	1938	1978	1979	1986	....
Brian Garton Jenkins	Cordwainer	1935	....	1980	1987	....
Francis McWilliams	Aldersgate	1926	1978	1980	1988	....
Paul Henry Newall, T.D.	Walbrook	1934	1980	1981	....	....
Christopher Rupert Walford	Farringdon Wn.	1935	....	1982	....	....
Roderic Neil Young	Bread Street	1933	1980	1982	....	....
Roger William Cork	Tower	1947	1978	1983	....	....
Bryan Edward Toye	Lime Street	1938	....	1983	....	....
Richard Everard Nichols	Candlewick	1938	1983	1984	....	....
Peter Anthony Bull	Cheap	1937	1968	1984	....	....
Sir Peter Keith Levene, K.B.E.	Portsoken	1941	1983	1984	....	....
Leonard John Chalstrey	Vintry	1931	1981	1984	....	....
Clive Haydn Martin, O.B.E., T.D.	Aldgate	1935	....	1985	....	....
David Howarth Seymour Howard	Cornhill	1945	1972	1986	....	....
James Michael Yorrick Oliver	Bishopsgate	1940	1980	1987	....	....

The Sheriffs 1989–1990

Paul Henry Newall, T.D. (*see above*) and Derek Edwards (*see below*), *elected* July 10; *assumed office* September 28, 1989.

THE COMMON COUNCIL OF LONDON

Alexander, Lady (1987)	*Farringdon Wt.*
Anstee, N. J. (1987)	*Aldersgate*
Archibald, W. W. (1986)	*Cornhill*
Arthur, G. F. (1988)	*Farringdon Wt.*
Ballard, K. A., M.C. (1969)	*Castle Baynard*
Balls, *Deputy* H. D. (1970)	*Cripplegate Wt.*
Barker, J. A. (1981)	*Cripplegate Wt.*
Barnes, H. M. F. (1986)	*Coleman Street*
Beale, M. J. (1979)	*Lime Street*
Bird, J. L. (1977)	*Bridge*
Biroum-Smith, P. L. (1988)	*Dowgate*
Block, S. A. A. (1983)	*Cheap*
Boreham, B. P. (1986)	*Dowgate*
Bramwell, F. M. (1983)	*Langbourn*
Brighton, R. L. (1984)	*Portsoken*
Brooks, W. I. B. (1988)	*Billingsgate*
Brown, *Deputy* D. T. (1971)	*Walbrook*
Cann, T. J. (1988)	*Cripplegate Wn.*
Cassidy, M. J. (1980)	*Aldersgate*
Catt, B. F. (1982)	*Farringdon Wn.*
Challis, G. H. (1978)	*Langbourn*
Chandler, *Deputy* E. G., C.B.E. (1982)	*Cornhill*
Clements, *Deputy* G. E. I. (1960)	*Farringdon Wt.*
Cohen, Mrs. C. M. (1986)	*Lime Street*
Cole, Lt.-Col., Sir Colin, K.C.V.O., T.D. (1964)	*Castle Baynard*
Colover, D. (1975)	*Bishopsgate*
Cope, Dr. J. (1963)	*Farringdon Wn.*
Coven, *Deputy* Mrs. E. O., C.B.E. (1972)	*Dowgate*
Currie, Miss S. E. M. (1985)	*Cripplegate Wt.*
David, C. P. (1984)	*Aldgate*
Delderfield, D. W. (1982)	*Aldersgate*
de Silva, D., Q.C. (1980)	*Farringdon Wt.*
Donnelly, T. A., M.B.E. (1982)	*Bread Street*
Duckworth, *Deputy* H., C.B.E. (1960)	*Lime Street*
Dunitz, A. A. (1984)	*Portsoken*
Durnin, J. C. (1976)	*Cordwainer*
Edwards, R. D. K. (1978)	*Bassishaw*
Eskenzi, A. N. (1970)	*Farringdon Wn.*
Evans, Mrs. J. (1975)	*Farringdon Wt.*
Eve, R. A. (1980)	*Cheap*
Everett, K. M. (1984)	*Candlewick*
Falk, F. A., T.D. (1984)	*Farringdon Wt.*
Farrow, M. W. W. (1987)	*Bishopsgate*
Farthing, R. B. C. (1981)	*Aldgate*
Fell, J. A. (1982)	*Queenhithe*
FitzGerald, R. C. A. (1981)	*Bread Street*
Floyd-Ewin, *Deputy* Sir David, L.V.O., O.B.E. (1963)	*Castle Baynard*
Frappell, C. E. (1973)	*Bread Street*
Fraser, W. B. (1981)	*Vintry*
Frazer, C. M. (1986)	*Farringdon Wt.*
Galloway, A. D. (1981)	*Broad Street*
Gass, *Deputy* G. J. (1967)	*Coleman Street*
Gold, R. (1965)	*Castle Baynard*
Graves, A. C. (1985)	*Bishopsgate*
Harding, N. H. (1970)	*Farringdon Wn.*
Hardwick, Dr. P. B. (1987)	*Aldgate*
Hart, *Deputy* M. G. (1970)	*Bridge*
Hatfield, A. F. R. (1968)	*Bishopsgate*
Haynes, J. E. H. (1986)	*Cornhill*
Henderson, *Deputy* J. S., O.B.E. (1975)	*Langbourn*
Henderson-Begg, M. (1977)	*Coleman Street*
Holland, *Deputy* J. (1972)	*Aldgate*
Horlock, *Deputy* H. W. S. (1969)	*Farringdon Wn.*
Humphrays, Mrs. R. (1976)	*Cripplegate Wt.*
Ide, W. R. (1972)	*Castle Baynard*
Jackson, L. St. J. T., (1978)	*Bassishaw*
James, A. J. (1973)	*Cordwainer*
Jennings, I. G. (1988)	*Cripplegate Wn.*
Keep, Mrs. B. (1987)	*Cripplegate Wn.*

Kellett, Mrs. M. W. F. (1986) . . . . *Tower*
Kemp, D. L. (1984) . . . . *Coleman Street*
Knowles, S. K. (1984) . . . . *Candlewick*
Lamport, J. C. (1987) . . . . *Cripplegate Wt.*
Langmead, A. D. G., T.D. (1982) . . . . . *Tower*
Lawrence, D. W. O., T.D. (1979) . . . . . *Bridge*
Lawson, G. C. H. (1971) . . . . *Portsoken*
McAuley, *Deputy* C. (1957) . . . . *Bread Street*
McNeil, I. D. (1977) . . . . *Lime Street*
Malins, J. H. (1981) . . . . *Farringdon Wt.*
Martin, R. C. (1986) . . . . *Queenhithe*
Mayhew, Miss J. (1986) . . . . *Queenhithe*
Mills, A. P. (1969) . . . . *Bassishaw*
Minshull-Fogg, J., T.D. (1986) . . . . *Walbrook*
Mitchell, C. R. (1971) . . . . *Castle Baynard*
Mizen, *Deputy* D. H. (1979) . . . . *Broad Street*
Mobsby, D. J. L. (1985) . . . . *Billingsgate*
Morgan, *Deputy* B. L., C.B.E. (1963) . . *Bishopsgate*
Murkin, *Deputy* C. H., O.B.E. (1969) . . *Vintry*
Nash, *Deputy* Mrs. J. C. (1983) . . . . . *Aldersgate*
Neary, J. E. (1982) . . . . *Aldgate*
Northall-Laurie, P. D. (1975) . . . . *Walbrook*
Olson, A. H. F. (1972) . . . . *Dowgate*
Owen, Mrs. J. (1975) . . . . *Langbourn*
Owen-Ward, J. R. (1983) . . . . *Bridge*
Packard, Brig. J. J. (1972) . . . . *Cripplegate Wn.*
Pembroke, *Deputy* Mrs. A. M. F.
　(1978) . . . . *Cheap*
Ponsonby of Shulbrede, The Lady
　(1981) . . . . *Farringdon Wt.*
Pulman, G. A. G. (1983) . . . . *Tower*
Ratner, R. A., T.D. (1981) . . . . *Broad Street*

Reed, *Deputy* J. L., M.B.E. (1967) . . . . . *Farringdon Wn.*
Revell-Smith, P. A. (1959) . . . . *Vintry*
Rigby, P. P. (1972) . . . . *Farringdon Wn.*
Rigg-Milner, Mrs. A. I. (1987) . . . . *Cripplegate Wt.*
Rodgers, Miss E. H. L. (1987) . . . . *Vintry*
Rodgers, S. C. (1969) . . . . *Farringdon Wt.*
Roney, E. P. T., C.B.E. (1974) . . . . *Bishopsgate*
Samuel, *Deputy* Mrs. I. (1971) . . . . *Portsoken*
Saunders, *Deputy* R. (1975) . . . . *Candlewick*
Savory, M. B. (1980) . . . . *Broad Street*
Scriven, R. G. (1984) . . . . *Candlewick*
Scrivener, M. J. H. (1986) . . . . *Cripplegate Wn.*
Shalit, D. M. (1972) . . . . *Farringdon Wn.*
Sharp, *Deputy* Mrs. I. M. (1974) . . . . . *Queenhithe*
Shindler, *Deputy* A. B. (1966) . . . . *Billingsgate*
Simpson, A. S. J. (1987) . . . . *Aldersgate*
Smithers, H. J. (1986) . . . . *Billingsgate*
Snyder, M. J. (1986) . . . . *Cordwainer*
Spanner, J. H., T.D. (1984) . . . . *Broad Street*
Stevenson, J. L. (1970) . . . . *Coleman Street*
Stitcher, *Deputy* G. M., C.B.E. (1966) . *Farringdon Wt.*
Swan, N. E. B. (1985) . . . . *Coleman Street*
Webb, C. J. (1986) . . . . *Bishopsgate*
White, J. W. (1986) . . . . *Cornhill*
Williams, G. M. E. (1985) . . . . *Aldersgate*
Willoughby, P. J. (1985) . . . . *Bishopsgate*
Wilmot, *Deputy* R. T. D. (1973) . . . . . *Cordwainer*
Wilson, A. B. C.B.E., (1984) . . . . *Cheap*
Wixley, G. R. A., T.D. (1964) . . . . *Bassishaw*
Woodward, *Deputy* C. D., O.B.E. (1971) *Cripplegate Wn.*
Wooldridge, F. D. (1988) . . . . *Farringdon Wn.*

Deputies.—In the preceding list each Common Councilman so described serves as *Deputy* to the Alderman of her/his Ward.

THE CITY GUILDS (LIVERY COMPANIES)

The Livery Companies of the City of London derive their name from the assumption of a distinctive dress or livery by their members in the 14th century.

The order of precedence (according to 2nd Report of Municipal Corporations' Commissioners, 1837), omitting extinct companies, is given in parentheses after the name of each Company.

About 23,146 Liverymen of the Guilds are entitled to vote at elections in Common Hall.

MERCERS (*1*). *Hall*, Ironmonger Lane, EC2V 8HE. *Livery*, 244.—*Clerk*, G. M. M. Wakeford; *Master*, The Earl of Selborne, K.B.E.

GROCERS (*2*). *Hall*, Princes Street, EC2R 8AD. *Livery*, 335.—*Clerk*, C. G. Mattingley, C.B.E.; *Master*, H. R. D. Billson.

DRAPERS (*3*). *Hall*, Throgmorton Street, EC2N 2DQ. *Livery*, 250.—*Clerk*, R. C. G. Strick; *Master*, F. M. W. R. Neville.

FISHMONGERS (*4*). *Hall*, London Bridge, EC4R 9EL. *Livery*, 363.—*Clerk*, M. R. T. O'Brien; *Prime Warden*, Lord Kindersley.

GOLDSMITHS (*5*). *Hall*, Foster Lane, EC2V 6BN. *Livery*, 273.—*Clerk*, R. D. Buchanan-Dunlop, C.B.E.; *Prime Warden*, Sir Hugo Huntington-Whiteley, Bt.

MERCHANT TAYLORS (*6* and *7*). *Hall*, 30 Threadneedle Street, EC2R 8AY. *Livery* 330.—*Clerk*, Capt. D. A. Wallis, R.N.; *Master*, G. P. Theobald.

SKINNERS (*6* and *7*). *Hall*, 8 Dowgate Hill, EC4R 2SP. *Livery*, 360.—*Clerk*, M. H. Glover; *Master*, R. N. Dobbs.

HABERDASHERS (*8*). *Hall*, Staining Lane, EC2V 7DD. *Livery*, 320.—*Clerk*, Capt. M. E. Barrow, D.S.O., R.N.; *Master*, D. A. H. Sime, O.B.E., M.C., T.D.

SALTERS (*9*). *Hall*, 4 Fore Street, EC2Y 5DE. *Livery*, 150.—*Clerk*, J. M. Montgomery; *Master*, Maj.-Gen. Sir Michael Palmer, K.C.V.O.

IRONMONGERS (*10*). *Hall*, Barbican, EC2Y 8AA. *Livery*, 104.—*Clerk*, R. B. Brayne, M.B.E.; *Master*, R. H. Stedall.

VINTNERS (*11*). *Hall*, Upper Thames Street, EC4V 3AN. *Livery*, 326.—*Clerk*, Brig. G. Read, C.B.E. *Master*, G. L. Gordon Clark, O.B.E.

CLOTHWORKERS (*12*). *Hall*, Dunster Court, Mincing Lane, EC3R 7AH. *Livery*, 185.—*Clerk*, C. M. Mowll; *Master*, Sir Peter Gadsden, G.B.E.

The above are the Twelve "Great" London Companies in order of Civic precedence.

ACCOUNTANTS, CHARTERED (86). *Livery*, 327.—*Clerk*, G. H. Kingsmill, The Grove, Hinton Parva, Swindon SN4 0DH; *Master*, D. B. Shaw.

ACTUARIES (91). *Livery*, 151.—*Clerk*, A. K. Tudor, 8 Madgeways Close, Great Amwell, Ware, Herts., SG12 9RU; *Master*, P. W. Parker, T.D.

AIR PILOTS AND AIR NAVIGATORS, GUILD OF (81). *Livery*, 400.—*Grand Master*, H.R.H. the Prince Philip, Duke of Edinburgh, K.G., K.T.; *Clerk*, Capt. P. Wilson, 291 Gray's Inn Road, WC1X 8QF; *Master*, F. S. Stringer.

APOTHECARIES, SOCIETY OF (58). *Hall*, Black Friars Lane, EC4V 6EJ. *Livery*, 1,150.—*Clerk*, Maj. J. C. O'Leary; *Master*, Dr. M. P. Godfrey.

ARBITRATORS (93). *Livery*, 190.—*Clerk*, B. W. Vigrass, O.B.E., V.R.D., 75 Cannon Street, EC4N 5BH; *Master*, A. B. Shindler.

ARMOURERS AND BRASIERS (22). *Hall*, 81 Coleman Street, EC2R 5BJ. *Livery*, 120.—*Clerk*, Lt. Col. R. R. F. Cowe; *Master*, G. C. Wintle.

BAKERS (19). *Hall*, Harp Lane, Lower Thames Street, EC3R 6DP. *Livery*, 410.—*Clerk*, P. F. Wilson, D.F.C.; *Master*, S. Wise.

BARBERS (17). *Hall*, Monkwell Square, EC2Y 5BL. *Livery*, 224.—*Clerk*, Col. A. B. Harfield, C.B.E.; *Master*, J. C. Smethers.

BASKETMAKERS (52). *Livery*, 500.—*Clerk*, D. J. Farrier, 5 The Spinney, Warren Road, Purley, Surrey CR2 1AB; *Prime Warden*, G. R. Redcliffe.

BLACKSMITHS (40). *Livery*, 250.—*Clerk*, D. T. Dresch, Hill House, Branksome Park Road, Camberley, Surrey GU15 2AE; *Prime Warden*, R. Lister.

BOWYERS (38). *Livery*, 97.—*Clerk*, A. Black, C.B.E., 2 Serjeants' Inn, Fleet Street, EC4Y 1LL; *Master*, R. H. Hardy, C.B.E.

BREWERS (14). *Hall*, Aldermanbury Square, EC2V 7HR. *Livery*, 92.—*Clerk*, Rear-Adm. M. L. T. Wemyss, C.B; *Master*, M. N. F. Cottrell.

BRODERERS (48). *Livery*, 120.—*Clerk*, S. G. B. Underwood, 11A Bridge Road, East Molesey, Surrey KT8 9EY; *Master*, K. Motley.

BUILDERS MERCHANTS (88). *Livery*, 200.—*Clerk*, Ms. S. Robinson, 14 Charterhouse Street, EC1M 6AX; *Master*, J. B. Jackson.

BUTCHERS (24). *Hall*, 87 Bartholomew Close, EC1A 7EB. *Livery*, 750.—*Clerk*, A. H. Emus; *Master*, R. W. Baker.

CARMEN (77). *Livery*, 482.—*Clerk*, Lt.-Col. G. T. Pearce, M.B.E., St. Olave's Rectory, 8 Hart Street, EC3R 7NB; *Master*, Maj. D. R. Baker.

CARPENTERS (26). *Hall*, 1 Throgmorton Avenue, EC2N 2JJ. *Livery*, 150.—*Clerk*, Capt. K. G. Hamon, R.N.; *Master*, P. C. Osborne.

CHARTERED SECRETARIES AND ADMINISTRATORS (87). *Livery*, 230.—*Hon. Clerk*, G. H. Challis, The Irish Chamber, Guildhall Yard, EC2V 5AE; *Master*, K. E. Parry.

CLOCKMAKERS (61). *Livery*, 281.—*Clerk*, Air Cdre. B. G. Frow, D.S.O, D.F.C., 2 Greycoat Place, SW1P 1SD; *Master*, A. W. Henn.

COACHMAKERS AND COACH-HARNESS MAKERS (72). *Livery*, 400.—*Clerk*, Maj. W. H. Wharfe, 149 Banstead Road, Ewell, Epsom, Surrey KT17 3HL; *Master*, G. A. Hepworth.

COOKS (35). *Livery*, 75.—*Clerk*, M. C. Thatcher, 49 Queen Victoria Street, EC4N 4SE; *Master*, L. C. Grainger.

COOPERS (36). *Hall*, 13 Devonshire Square, EC2M 4TH. *Livery*, 267.—*Clerk*, J. A. Newton; *Master*, I. Cooper.

CORDWAINERS (27). *Livery* 143.—*Clerk*, Cdr. C. Shears, C.V.O., O.B.E., Eldon Chambers, 30 Fleet Street, EC4Y 1AA; *Master*, G. Barrett, B.E.M.

CURRIERS (29). *Livery*, 92.—*Clerk*, I. R. McNeil, Nile House, P.O. Box 1034, Nile Street, Brighton BN1 1JB; *Master*, W. M. Westland.

CUTLERS (18). *Hall*, Warwick Lane, EC4M 7BR. *Livery*, 100.—*Clerk*, K. S. G. Hinde, T.D.; *Master*, I. A. Scott.

DISTILLERS (69). *Livery*, 300.—*Clerk*, B. Dehn, 60 Montford Place, Kennington Lane, SE11 5DF; *Master*, A. J. Macdonald-Buchanan.

DYERS (13). *Hall*, Dowgate Hill, EC4R 2ST. *Livery*, 132.—*Clerk*, J. R. Chambers; *Prime Warden*, J. Atkinson.

ENGINEERS (94). *Livery*, 290.—*Clerk*, Cdr. B. D. Gibson, 1 Carlton House Terrace, SW1Y 5DB; *Master*, G. Lee.

ENVIRONMENTAL CLEANERS (97). *Livery*, 126.—*Clerk*, S. J. Holt, Whitethorns, Rannoch Road, Crowborough, E. Sussex TN6 1RA; *Master*, B. G. C. Becker, V.R.D.

FAN MAKERS (76). *Hall*, St. Botolph's Hall, Bishopsgate, EC2. *Livery*, 215.—*Clerk*, Lt. Col. I. R. P. Green; *Master*, R. Scott-White.

FARMERS (80). *Hall*, 3 Cloth Street, EC1A 7LD. *Livery*, 300.—*Clerk*, C. M. Taylor; *Master*, R. M. Older.

FARRIERS (55). *Livery*, 375.—*Clerk*, H. W. H. Ellis, 37 The Uplands, Loughton, Essex IG10 1NQ; *Master*, W. D. Tavernor, PH.D.

FELTMAKERS (63). *Livery*, 225.—*Clerk*, R. M. Peel, 10 Carteret Street, SW1H 9DR; *Master*, C. F. C. Simeons.

FLETCHERS (39). *Hall*, 3 Cloth Street, EC1A 7LD. *Livery*, 114.—*Clerk*, J. R. Garnett; *Master*, P. P. Rigby.

FOUNDERS (33). *Hall*, 1 Cloth Fair, EC1A 7HT. *Livery*, 180.—*Clerk*, A. J. Gillett; *Master*, H. H. Draycott.

FRAMEWORK KNITTERS (64). *Livery*, 225.—*Clerk*, C. J. Eldridge, Apothecaries' Hall, Black Friars Lane, EC4V 6EL; *Master*, P. Corah.

FRUITERERS (45). *Livery*, 237.—*Clerk*, Cdr. M. T. H. Styles, Denmead Cottage, Chawton, Alton, Hants. GU34 1SB; *Master*, Rt. Hon. Sir Edward du Cann, K.B.E.

FUELLERS (95). *Livery*, 250.—*Clerk*, Wg. Cdr. H. F. C. Squire, O.B.E., 4 Maycross Avenue, Morden, Surrey SM4 4DA; *Master*, G. McGecham.

FURNITURE MAKERS (83). *Livery*, 249.—*Clerk*, Wg. Cdr. G. Acklam, M.B.E., 30 Harcourt Street, W1H 2AA; *Master*, J. Reid.

GARDENERS (66). *Livery*, 250.—*Clerk*, A. L. McGeachy, 14–15 Craven Street, WC2N 5AD; *Master*, G. H. Denney.

GIRDLERS (23). *Hall*, Basinghall Avenue, EC2V 5DD. *Livery*, 80.—*Clerk*, T. J. Straker; *Master*, P. F. D. Trimingham.

GLASS-SELLERS (71). *Livery*, 173.—*Clerk*, P. J. Willoughby, 25 New Street Square, EC4A 3LN; *Master*, R. F. B. Marshall.

GLAZIERS AND PAINTERS OF GLASS (53). *Hall*, 9 Montague Close, SE1 9DD. *Livery*, 280.—*Clerk*, P. R. Bachelor; *Master*, S. F. Peck.

GLOVERS (62). *Livery*, 300.—*Clerk*, Gp. Capt. D. G. F. Palmer, O.B.E., Glovers, Tismans Common, Rudgwick, W. Sussex RH12 3DU; *Master*, C. W. Lidstone, M.B.E..

GOLD AND SILVER WYRE DRAWERS (74). *Livery*, 350.—*Clerk*, J. R. Williams, 50 Cheyne Avenue, E18 2DR; *Master*, M. J. Hollins.

GUNMAKERS (73). *Livery*, 226.—*Clerk*, F. B. Brandt, The Proof House, 48–50 Commercial Road, E1 1LP; *Master*, Maj. D. H. L. Back.

HORNERS (54). *Livery*, 430.—*Clerk*, Dr. E. M. Hunt, 11 Hobart Place, SW1W 0HL; *Master*, B. Schavarien.

INNHOLDERS (32). *Hall*, College Street, Dowgate Hill, EC4R 2SY. *Livery*, 120.—*Clerk*, J. R. Edwardes Jones; *Master*, D. C. Robertson.

INSURERS (92). *Hall*, 20 Aldermanbury, EC2V 7HY. *Livery*, 333.—*Clerk*, V. D. Webb; *Master*, P. R. Dugdale.

JOINERS AND CEILERS (*41*). *Livery*, 128.—*Clerk*, D. A. Tate, Parkville House, Bridge Street, Pinner, Middx. HA5 3JD; *Master*, R. D. Peppiatt.

LAUNDERERS (*89*). *Hall*, London Bridge, SE1. *Livery*, 300.—*Clerk*, W. E. Kingsland; *Master*, O. E. Longshaw.

LEATHERSELLERS (*15*). *Hall*, 15 St. Helen's Place, EC3A 6DQ. *Livery*, 150.—*Clerk*, Capt. N. MacEacharn, C.B.E., R.N.; *Master*, M. W. Chester.

LIGHTMONGERS (*96*). *Livery*, 119.—*Clerk*, S. H. Birch, 53 Leithcote Gardens, SW16 2UX; *Master*, I. R. Bush.

LORINERS (*57*). *Livery*, 350.—*Clerk*, J. R. Williams, 50 Cheyne Avenue, E18 2DR; *Master*, R. Walker-Arnott.

MARKETORS (*90*). *Livery*, 170.—*Clerk*, B. F. Catt, 42 Tottenham Lane, N8 8QS; *Master*, H. F. Druce.

MASONS (*30*). *Livery*, 111.—*Clerk*, H. J. Maddocks, 9 New Square, WC2R 3QN; *Master*, R. G. St. J. Rowlandson.

MASTER MARINERS, HONOURABLE COMPANY OF (*78*). H.Q.S. *Wellington*, Temple Stairs, WC2R 2PN. *Livery*, 300.—*Clerk*, D. H. W. Field; *Admiral*, H.R.H. the Duke of Edinburgh, K.G., K.T.; *Master*, H.R.H. the Prince of Wales, K.G., K.T., G.C.B., P.C.

MUSICIANS (*50*). *Livery*, 261.—*Clerk*, M. J. G. Fletcher, 1 The Sanctuary, Westminster, SW1P 3JT; *Master*, Lt.-Col. Sir Vivian Dunn, K.C.V.O., O.B.E.

NEEDLEMAKERS (*65*). *Livery*, 230.—*Clerk*, M. G. Cook, 17 Southampton Place, WC1A 2EH; *Master*, P. W. Barrows.

PAINTER STAINERS (*28*). *Hall*, 9 Little Trinity Lane, EC4V 2AD. *Livery*, 400.—*Clerk*, Wg. Cdr. B. C. Pratt; *Master*, M. W. D. Northcott.

PATTENMAKERS (*70*). *Livery*, 250.—*Clerk*, P. Merritt, 25 Wellesley Road, W4 4BU; *Master*, G. W. Marshall.

PAVIORS (*56*). *Livery*, 275.—*Clerk*, R. F. Coe, Cutlers' Hall, Warwick Lane, EC4M 7BR; *Master*, D. H. Thornton.

PEWTERERS. (*16*). *Hall*, Oat Lane, EC2V 7DE. *Livery*, 110.—*Clerk*, Maj. J. M. Halford, R.M.; *Master*, N. G. Fazan.

PLAISTERERS (*46*). *Hall*, 1 London Wall, EC2Y 5JU. *Livery*, 205.—*Clerk*, H. Mott; *Master*, P. A. Girle.

PLAYING CARDS, MAKERS OF (*75*). *Livery*, 145.—*Clerk*, M. J. Smyth, 6 The Priory, Godstone, Surrey RH9 8NL; *Master*, G. D. Pannell.

PLUMBERS (*31*). *Livery*, 310.—*Clerk*, Col. E. M. P. Hardy, 3rd Floor, 21 Fleet Street, EC4Y 1AA; *Master*, L. Hill.

POULTERS (*34*). *Hall*, Armourers' Hall, 81 Coleman Street, EC2R 5BJ. *Livery*, 167.—*Clerk*, Lt.-Col. R. R. F. Cowe; *Master*, A. W. Scott.

SADDLERS (*25*). *Hall*, 40 Gutter Lane, EC2V 6BR. *Livery*, 70.—*Clerk*, Gp. Capt. K. M. Oliver; *Master*, Lt.-Col. G. E. Vere-Laurie.

SCIENTIFIC INSTRUMENT MAKERS (*84*). *Livery*, 225.—*Clerk*, F. G. Everard, 9 Montague Close, SE1 9DD; *Master*, C. G. R. Hall.

SCRIVENERS (*44*). *Livery*, 183.—*Clerk*, H. J. W. Harman, Chancery House, 53–64 Chancery Lane, WC2A 1QU; *Master*, C. J. Malim.

SHIPWRIGHTS (*59*). *Livery*, 500.—*Clerk*, Gp. Capt. R. C. Olding, C.B.E., D.S.C., Ironmongers' Hall, Barbican, EC2Y 8AA; *Permanent Master*, H.R.H. the Duke of Edinburgh, K.G., K.T.; *Prime Warden*, F. M. Everard.

SOLICITORS (*79*). *Livery*, 411.—*Clerk*, Miss S. H. Robinson, T.D., 14 Charterhouse Square, EC1M 6AX; *Master*, J. A. E. Young.

SPECTACLE MAKERS (*60*). *Livery*, 400.—*Clerk*, C. J. Eldridge, Apothecaries' Hall, Black Friars Lane, EC4V 6EL; *Master*, Sir Nigel Mobbs.

STATIONERS AND NEWSPAPER MAKERS (*47*). *Hall*, Ave Maria Lane, EC4M 7DD. *Livery*, 450.—*Clerk*, Capt. P. Hames, R.N.; *Master*, D. J. Ryman.

SURVEYORS, CHARTERED (*85*). *Livery*, 325.—*Clerk*, Mrs. A. L. Jackson, 16 St. Mary-at-Hill, EC3R 8EE; *Master*, J. R. T. Eve.

TALLOW CHANDLERS (*21*). *Hall*, 4 Dowgate Hill, EC4R 2SH. *Livery*, 180.—*Clerk*, Col. M. ff. Woodhead, O.B.E.; *Master*, J. N. Harrington.

TIN PLATE WORKERS Alias Wire Workers (*67*). *Livery*, 170.—*Hon. Clerk*, R. G. Vincent, 14 Talbot House, 98 St. Martin's Lane, WC2N 4AX; *Master*, D. J. K. Greggains.

TOBACCO PIPE MAKERS AND TOBACCO BLENDERS (*82*). *Livery*, 178.—*Clerk*, I. J. Kimmins, Bouverie House, 154 Fleet Street, EC4A 2HX; *Master*, J. W. Solomon.

TURNERS (*51*). *Livery*, 165.—*Clerk*, R. G. Woodwark, D.S.C., 33a Hill Avenue, Amersham, Bucks. HP6 5BX; *Master*, G. A. Todd.

TYLERS AND BRICKLAYERS (*37*). *Livery*, 130.—*Clerk*, F. A. G. Rider, 6 Martin Lane, Cannon Street, EC4R 0DP; *Master*, D. W. Fuller.

UPHOLDERS (*49*). *Livery*, 200.—*Clerk*, W. R. Wallis, Charrington House, The Causeway, Bishops Stortford CH23 2EW; *Master*, C. F. Hayman.

WAX CHANDLERS (*20*). *Hall*, Gresham Street, EC2V 7AD. *Livery*, 100.—*Clerk*, T. Wood; *Master*, R. C. Chaventré.

WEAVERS (*42*). *Livery*, 125.—*Clerk*, J. G. Ouvry, 1 The Sanctuary, Westminster, SW1P 3JT; *Upper Bailiff*, R. D. N. Day.

WHEELWRIGHTS (*68*). *Livery*, 256.—*Clerk*, M. R. Francis, Greenup, Milton Avenue, Gerrards Cross, Bucks. SL9 8QW; *Master*, E. J. Macey.

WOOLMEN (*43*). *Livery*, 150.—*Clerk*, D. R. L. Humble, R.D., Kingsmead House, 250 King's Road, SW3 5UE; *Master*, Dr. J. Scorey.

PARISH CLERKS (*No livery*.) (*Members*, 99).—*Clerk*, J. D. Hebblethwaite, General Synod Office, Church House, Great Smith Street, SW1P 3NZ; *Master*, L. A. Lewis.

WATERMEN AND LIGHTERMEN (*No livery*.) (*Craft Owning Freemen*, 300).—*Hall*, 18 St. Mary-at-Hill, EC3R 8EE.—*Clerk*, W. A. A. Wells, T.D.; *Master*, J. G. Adams.

NOTE.—In certain companies the election of Master or Prime Warden for the year does not take place till the autumn. In such cases the Master or Prime Warden for 1988–89 is given.

City or Borough (§Inner London Borough)	Municipal Offices	Estimated resident population 1987	Rateable Value 1989 £	Chief Executive (*Town Clerk) (a) Managing Director	Mayor or (a) Lord Mayor
GTR. LONDON .		6,775,200			
Barking and Dagenham....	°Dagenham, RM10 7BN.	147,800	27,227,458	D. C. J. Farr	J. Butler
Barnet	†The Burroughs, Hendon, NW4 4BG.	305,900	64,078,483	M. M. Caller	Mrs. D. Benson
Bexley	‡Bexleyheath, Kent DA6 7LB.	220,600	32,623,236	T. Musgrave	M. Ketley
Brent	†Forty Lane, Wembley, HA9 9HX.	256,600	52,963,719	C. Wood	L. R. Williams
Bromley........	°Bromley, BR1 3UH.	298,200	53,075,967	N. T. Palk	T. Ainsby
§Camden	†Euston Road, NW1 2RU.	184,900	124,588,723	F. Nickson	Ms. B. Hughes
§City of Westminster	City Hall, Victoria Street, SW1E 6QP.	173,400	338,607,393	(a) R. W. Phillips	(a) S. Mabey
Croydon........	Taberner House, Park Lane, Croydon CR9 3JS.	319,200	73,669,481	*F. S. H. Birch	D. Mead
Ealing	°Uxbridge Road, W5 2HL.	296,900	59,660,460	Ms. J. Hunt	Ms. H. J. Graham
Enfield	°Enfield, EN1 3XA.	261,500	51,180,189	B. A. McAndrew	D. Lewis
§Greenwich	†Wellington Street, SE18 6PW.	216,600	33,723,431	C. Roberts	B. Strong
§Hackney	†Mare St., E8 1EA.	187,400	44,116,014	Ms. P. Gordon	Ms. P. Edwards
§Hammersmith and Fulham ..	†King St., W6 9JU.	151,100	38,531,833	T. Eddison	I. Grey
Haringey	°Wood Green, N22 4LE.	193,700	37,551,528	G. Singh	F. Knight
Harrow	°Harrow, HA1 2UH.	200,100	36,678,104	A. G. Redmond	Mrs. P. Harkett
Havering	†Romford, RM1 3BD.	237,300	39,439,215	R. G. Smith (acting)	T. W. Orrin
Hillingdon......	°Uxbridge, UB8 1UW.	231,200	62,171,536	P. Johnson	K. T. Guy
Hounslow	°Lampton Rd., Hounslow, TW3 4DN.	194,000	53,375,700	R. D. Jefferies	J. Chatt
§Islington	†Upper St., N1 2UD.	168,700	56,198,392	E. W. Dear	Ms. C. Atherton
§Kensington and Chelsea (R.B.) .	†Hornton St., W8 7NX.	133,100	74,660,023	R. S. Webber	N. Freeman, O.B.E.
Kingston upon Thames (R.B.).	Guildhall, Kingston upon Thames KT1 1EU.	132,200	30,529,598	R. McCloy	Rev. M. Mannall
§Lambeth	†Brixton Hill, SW2 1RW.	243,200	67,187,000	A. J. George	R. Daley
§Lewisham	†Catford, SE6 4RU.	231,600	35,878,904	T. Hanafin	N. Taylor
Merton.........	Crown House, London Rd., Morden, SM4 5DX.	164,000	32,770,706	W. A. McKee	B. Edwards
Newham	†East Ham, E6 2RP.	206,500	36,513,752	J. Samuel	R. Massey
Redbridge	†Ilford, IG1 1DD.	230,100	37,365,722	G. U. Price	G. H. Brewer, T.D.
Richmond upon Thames	York House, Twickenham, TW1 3AA.	163,000	34,236,885	R. L. Harbord	G. R. Pope
§Southwark	†Peckham Rd., SE5 8UB.	216,800	46,666,796	Ms. A. Whyatt	A. Ritchie
Sutton	‡St. Nicholas Way, Sutton, SM1 1EA.	168,600	31,039,708	A. Taylor	T. Dutton
§Tower Hamlets .	†Patriot Square, E2 9LN.	159,000	56,109,060	J. McBride	J. Shaw
Waltham Forest .	†Forest Rd., Walthamstow, E17 4JF.	214,500	32,740,495	L. G. Knox	W. G. Anstey
§Wandsworth ...	†Wandsworth, SW18 2PU.	258,100	46,234,016	G. K. Jones	G. K. Jones

R.B. Royal Borough.   °Civic Centre.   †Town Hall.   ‡Civic Offices.

GREATER LONDON SERVICES

The abolition of the Greater London Council on April 1, 1986, led to the bulk of its work being passed to the London Boroughs, Government Departments and Government-appointed bodies, and to joint boards and committees.

The London Residuary Body (L.R.B.) was established by the Local Government Act, 1985, which abolished the G.L.C. Its brief was to wind up the affairs of the G.L.C. within a maximum life of five years. Its tasks have fallen mainly in three areas:

(i) to clear up functions of the G.L.C. which have not been transferred to other successor bodies. These include debt management, the preparation of the final accounts of the G.L.C., and payment of compensation to former G.L.C. staff made redundant. These responsibilities have now been completely discharged.

(ii) to dispose of former G.L.C. properties, other than those passing to other successor bodies.

(iii) to manage former G.L.C. services until new homes have been found for them.

Properties.—One of the L.R.B.'s major duties is the sale of ex-G.L.C. buildings and properties, the proceeds being distributed among the London Boroughs. Management of mortgages granted by the G.L.C. was transferred to the London Borough of Richmond upon Thames.

Most of the L. R. B.'s work on selling former G.L.C. property and finding homes for former G.L.C. responsibilities has been completed with a year to spare of its five-year life span.

Recreation, Parks, etc.—The arts facilities on the South Bank have been transferred to the South Bank Board and the Arts Council. Responsibility for historic buildings, parks, open spaces, etc. has passed to Borough Councils or bodies such as English Heritage.

Land Drainage and Flood Prevention.—This is now the responsibility of the Borough Councils and the Thames Water Authority.

Extension of L.R.B.'s Life.—With the announcement by the Government of its intention to abolish the Inner London Education Authority, the London Residuary Body has been given the task of dealing with residual ILEA affairs as it dealt with the G.L.C. This will prolong the life of the L.R.B. for three years beyond ILEA's abolition, until March 31, 1993.

Finance.—The boroughs and successor bodies finance the L.R.B. In Feb. 1989 the budget was £135,000,000; the reduction from the previous year's £199,000,000 reflects the transfer of services to the boroughs and other bodies as the L.R.B. winds down its former G.L.C. work. More than £500 million has been distributed amongst the boroughs.

LONDON RESIDUARY BODY, St. Vincent House, 30 Orange Street, WC2H 7HH. (01-633 5000).
Chairman, Sir Godfrey Taylor.
Director of Administration, J. Howes.
Director of Finance, P. Scales.

Education

The local education authority for an area corresponding with the area of the twelve inner London boroughs and the City of London is the Inner London Education Authority which took over responsibility for the education service from the G.L.C. on April 1, 1986. The first elections of the 58 members took place on May 8, 1986. The 20 outer London Borough Councils remain the education authorities for their Boroughs.

The total number of pupils on the rolls of the Authority's nursery, primary and secondary schools (including special schools for handicapped children) was 270,062. There are 946 schools, staffed by the equivalent of 18,647 full-time teachers. Vocational instruction, cultural studies and recreational activities for persons over compulsory school age are arranged at the various establishments for further education. Part-time classes are offered at 20 adult education and literary institutes, and 78 youth centres, including 2 drama centres.

The ILEA is to be abolished in April 1990, when responsibility for education in the inner London boroughs will pass to the Borough and City Councils (*see* **Education Directory**).

ILEA, County Hall, SE1 7PB (01-633 5000).

Transport

The G.L.C.'s responsibility, through the London Transport Executive, for transport services in London was transferred in June 1984 to the London Regional Transport board (*see* p. 338), which is responsible to the Secretary of State for Transport. Former G.L.C. responsibilities, including the maintenance of the Thames bridges, ferries and tunnels, have been passed to the Borough Councils and to the Department of Transport. Other services which have been transferred include traffic control (to the Secretary of State for Transport) and work on the North–South route.

Solid waste disposal

Responsibility for the disposal of London's household, commercial and civic amenity refuse lies with 16 Waste Disposal Authorities.

There are four statutory bodies—*West London Waste Authority* (Brent, Ealing, Harrow, Hillingdon, Hounslow, Richmond upon Thames), *North London Waste Authority* (Barnet, Camden, Enfield, Hackney, Haringey, Islington, Waltham Forest), *East London Waste Authority* (Barking and Dagenham, Havering, Newham, Redbridge) and *Western Riverside Waste Authority* (Hammersmith and Fulham, Kensington and Chelsea, Lambeth, Wandsworth).

Twelve boroughs are Waste Disposal Authorities in their own right and eleven of them have come together in voluntary groupings—*Central London Group* (City of London, City of Westminster, Tower Hamlets), *South London Group* (Bromley, Croydon, Kingston upon Thames, Merton, Sutton) and *South East London Group* (Greenwich, Lewisham, Southwark). The twelfth, Bexley, liaises with Kent County Council.

The London Waste Regulation Authority regulates and controls waste management activities in both the public and private sectors.

LONDON WASTE REGULATION AUTHORITY, County Hall, SE1 7PB (01-633 4149).

Fire Services

The authority for London's fire service is the London Fire and Civil Defence Authority (L.F.C.D.A.). The Fire Brigade is organized into five Area Commands, which coincide with Borough boundaries. The L.F.C.D.A.'s responsibilities also include petroleum licensing.

LONDON FIRE AND CIVIL DEFENCE AUTHORITY, London Fire Brigade Headquarters, 8 Albert Embankment, SE1 7SD (01-582 3811).

LONDON AND ITS ENVIRONS

(For National Art Galleries and Museums in London, see Index.)

Adelphi, Strand, WC2.—Adelphi Terrace and district commemorate the four Adam brothers, James, John, Robert and William, who laid out the district (formerly Durham House) at the close of the 18th century, though few 18th century buildings now remain. Four of the streets were formerly called after the brothers but are now Adam Street, John Adam Street, Robert Street and Durham House Street. In the neighbourhood of the Adelphi was York House, built by the Duke of Buckingham in 1625 (the Water Gate of which still stands in Embankment Gardens), the commemorative streets being Charles Street, Villiers Street, Duke Street, Buckingham Street.

Alexandra Palace and Park, Wood Green, N22 4AY.—Set in 200 acres of parkland. The Victorian Palace was severely damaged by fire in 1980 but has been restored and developed and reopened in January 1988. Alexandra Palace provides modern facilities for exhibitions, sports, conferences and leisure activities. The Palace is a charitable trust administered by the London Borough of Haringey.

Baltic Exchange, St. Mary Axe, EC3.—The world market for the chartering of cargo ships. The present Exchange was built in 1903 and the new wing opened by H.M. The Queen on Nov. 21, 1956.

Bank of England, Threadneedle Street, EC2. (Not open to the public)—The Bank of England, founded in 1694, has always been closely connected with the Government. The present building, completed in 1940 to the designs of Sir Herbert Baker, incorporates features reminiscent of the earlier architects, Sampson (1734), Sir Robert Taylor (1765) and Sir John Soane (1788).

Bank of England Museum (entrance in Bartholomew Lane).—The Museum charts the Bank's history since the granting of the Royal Charter in 1694. Open Mon.–Sat. and public holidays 10–6, Sun. 2–6. Admission free.

Banqueting House, Whitehall, SW1P 3EB.—The only important building left of the great Palace of Whitehall. The previous banqueting house was burnt down in 1619, and replaced by the present structure designed by Inigo Jones. In 1635 it was enriched with Rubens' ceiling paintings. Charles I was executed on a scaffold set up just in front of the present entrance. Open Tues.–Sat. 10–5, Sun. 2–5. Closed Mon. Admission (1989) £1·60, concessions £1·20.

Barbican Centre, Silk Street, EC2Y 8DS.— Owned, funded and managed by the Corporation of London, the Barbican Centre was opened on March 3, 1982 by H.M. The Queen, and is the largest complex of its kind in Western Europe. It houses the 1,166 seat Barbican Theatre, now the London base of the Royal Shakespeare Company, along with a smaller 200 seat studio theatre (The Pit), and the 2,026 seat Barbican Hall, the home of the London Symphony Orchestra. There are also three cinemas, an art gallery, a sculpture court, a large lending library, facilities for trade exhibitions and conferences, and bars and restaurants.

Blackheath, SE10.—272 acres of parkland. Morden College, founded in 1695 as a home for "decayed Turkey merchants", is near the S.E. corner. The building was designed by Wren and its Chapel doors have carvings attributed to Grinling Gibbons. Concerts and poetry recitals are held at Rangers House, a villa built c. 1700 which houses the Suffolk collection of English portraits from Larkin to Lely, and the Dolmetsch Collection of musical instruments. Open daily 10–5 (Nov.–Jan. 10–4). Closed Good Friday, Dec. 24, 25. Admission free.

Bridges.—The bridges over the Thames (from East to West) are: *Tower Bridge* (built by the Corporation of London and opened in 1894), with its bascules, operated now by new electrically-run machinery, walkway, opened to the public in 1982, and museum, opened in 1983; *London Bridge* (opened after rebuilding in 1831 by Rennie; the new London Bridge was completed in 1973 and opened by H.M. The Queen on March 16, 1973; *Southwark Bridge* (opened in 1819, also by Rennie; rebuilt by the Corporation of London, 1922); *Blackfriars Bridge* (opened in 1769, rebuilt, 1869, and widened by the Corporation of London in 1909); *Waterloo Bridge* (Rennie), opened in 1817, commanding a fine view of western London, rebuilt by L.C.C. and reopened 1944; *Hungerford Bridge,* 1863 (railway bridge with a footbridge); *Westminster Bridge* (built in 1750 and then presenting a view that inspired Wordsworth's sonnet; rebuilt and re-opened in 1862; width, 84 ft.) with Thomas Thornycroft's *Boadicea* at the north-eastern end; this bridge leads from Westminster Abbey and the Houses of Parliament to the County Hall and St. Thomas' Hospital; *Lambeth Bridge* (built 1862, rebuilt 1932) leading from Lambeth Palace to Millbank; *Vauxhall Bridge* (built in 1811–16, rebuilt in 1906), leading to Kennington Oval; *Chelsea Bridge,* leading from Chelsea Hospital to Battersea Park (reconstructed and widened, 1937) and *Albert Bridge* (1873); *Battersea Bridge* (opened in 1890); *Wandsworth Bridge* (opened in 1873; rebuilt and re-opened in 1940); *Putney Bridge* (built 1729, rebuilt 1884, widened in 1933), where the Oxford and Cambridge Boat Race is started for Mortlake; *Hammersmith Bridge* (rebuilt 1887); *Barnes Bridge* (for pedestrians only, 1933); *Chiswick Bridge* (opened in 1933); *King Edward VII Bridge,* Kew (rebuilt in 1902, opened 1903), leading to the Royal Botanic Gardens, Kew; *Twickenham Lock Bridge; Twickenham Bridge* (opened 1933); *Richmond Bridge* (opened in 1777); *Kingston Bridge* (built 1828 and widened 1914) and *Hampton Court Bridge* (rebuilt, 1933).

Buckingham Palace, SW1A 1AA. (Not open to the public.)—Purchased by King George III in 1762 from the heir of the Duke of Buckingham, the Palace has been the London home of the Sovereign since Queen Victoria's accession in 1837. It was altered by Nash for King George IV, and refronted in stone (part of the Queen Victoria Memorial) by Sir Aston Webb in 1913.

The Queen's Gallery, containing a changing selection of the finest pictures and works of art from all parts of the royal collection, was opened to the public on July 25, 1962. Open Tues.–Sat. and Bank Holidays 10.30–5, Sun. 2–5. Admission charges are payable, entering from Buckingham Palace Road.

The Royal Mews is open to visitors on Wed. and Thurs. throughout the year (except in Ascot Week), 2–4. Admission charges, the net proceeds of which are devoted to charities, are payable at the entrance.

Canada House, Trafalgar Square, SW1.—Designed by Sir Robert Smirke and built in 1824–7, it underwent major alterations to incorporate the former Royal College of Physicians building, also by Smirke, between 1964–67. Certain interior features of the original building, now housing the Canadian High Commission, are preserved, including the spacious, richly furnished room now occupied by the High Commissioner.

Canonbury Tower, N1.—The largest remaining part of a 16th century country house originally built by the Priors of St. Bartholomew, and since 1952 used as the headquarters of a non-professional theatre company.

Contains the "Spencer" and "Compton" oak-panelled rooms. Other relics of Canonbury House can be seen nearby.

Catholic Central Library, St. Francis Friary, 47 Francis Street, SW1P 1QR.—Founded as a private library in 1914, it was taken over in 1959 by the Franciscan Friars of the Atonement. It is an up-to-date lending and research library of over 55,000 volumes and 150 periodicals, for the general reader, student and ecumenist. Books are sent by post when required. Open Mon.-Fri. 10–5, Sat. 10–1.30.

Cemeteries.—In *Kensal Green Cemetery*, North Kensington, W10 (70 acres), are tombs of Thackeray, Trollope, Sydney Smith, Wilkie Collins, Tom Hood, George Cruikshank, John Leech, Leigh Hunt, I. K. Brunel and Charles Kemble (actor). In *Highgate Cemetery*, N6, are the tombs of George Eliot, Herbert Spencer, Faraday and Marx. In *Abney Park Cemetery*, Stoke Newington, N16, the tomb of General Booth, founder of the Salvation Army, and memorials to many Nonconformist Divines are to be found. In the *South Metropolitan Cemetery*, Norwood, SE27, are the tombs of Sir Henry Bessemer, Sir Hiram Maxim, Mrs. Beeton, Sir Henry Tate and Joseph Whitaker, F.S.A. (*Whitaker's Almanack*). In the churchyard of the former *Marylebone Chapel* are buried Charles Wesley and his son Samuel Wesley (musician). The chapel itself was demolished in 1949. *Crematoria.*—*Ilford* (City of London); *Norwood*; *Hendon*; *Streatham Park*; *Finchley* (St. Marylebone) and *Golders Green* (12 acres), near Hampstead Heath, with "Garden of Rest" and memorials to famous men and women.

Cenotaph, Whitehall, SW1.—(Literally "empty tomb".) Monument erected "To the Glorious Dead", as a memorial to all ranks of the Sea, Land and Air Forces who gave their lives in the service of the Empire during the First World War. Designed by Sir Edwin Lutyens. Erected as a temporary memorial in 1919 and replaced by a permanent structure in 1920. Unveiled by King George V on Armistice Day, 1920. An additional inscription was added after the 1939–45 War to commemorate those who gave their lives in that conflict.

Charterhouse, Sutton's Hospital, Charterhouse Square, EC1M 6AN.—A Carthusian monastery from 1371–1537, when it came into the possession of Sir Edward (later first Lord) North, who sold it in 1565 to the fourth Duke of Norfolk. After Norfolk's execution in 1572 following the Ridolfi Plot (hatched at Charterhouse), it was eventually granted by Queen Elizabeth I in 1587 to Norfolk's second son, Thomas Howard, later Earl of Suffolk. In 1611 he sold it to Thomas Sutton, who endowed it as a Hospital for aged men "of gentle birth" and a school for poor scholars (removed to Godalming in 1872). The buildings are partly 15th but mainly 16th and 17th century. Parts of the building were damaged by enemy action in 1941 but have been largely restored and now accommodate some 30 pensioners. Roger Williams, founder and governor of Rhode Island, was a scholar on the foundation. Among other famous pupils were John Wesley, Lord Baden-Powell, the poets and writers Crashaw, Lovelace and Thackeray, and more recently Lord Beveridge. Visitors are shown round on Wednesdays at 2.15 (April–July). Admission £1.50.
Master, E. E. Harrison, F.S.A.
Registrar and Clerk to the Governors, Lt.-Col. I. Macdonald.

Chelsea Physic Garden, 66 Royal Hospital Road, SW3 4HS.—A garden of general botanical research, maintaining a wide range of rare and unusual plants. The garden was established in 1673 by the Society of Apothecaries. Open on Wed. and Sun. p.m. during summer months. All enquiries to the Curator at above address.

City Business Library (Corporation of London), 106 Fenchurch Street, EC3M 5JB. Open Mon.-Fri. 9.30-5.00.

College of Arms or Heralds' College, Queen Victoria Street, EC4V 4BT.—Her Majesty's Officers of Arms (Kings, Heralds and Pursuivants of Arms) were first incorporated by Richard III, and granted Derby House on the site of the present College building by Philip and Mary. The building now in use dates from 1671–88. The powers vested by the Crown in the Earl Marshal (The Duke of Norfolk) with regard to State ceremonial are largely exercised through the College, which is also the official repository of English pedigrees and all Arms granted to subjects of the Queen (except in Scotland and (since 1988) Canada). Enquiry may be made to the Officer on duty in the Public Office, Mon.-Fri. 10–4.

The Heralds Museum at the Tower of London (admission charge included in the Tower's own charge) aims to explain what heraldry is about and traces its development over the centuries to its application and use in modern times. Open April-Sept.

Commonwealth Institute, Kensington High Street, W8 6NQ.—A cultural and educational centre opened on Nov. 6, 1962, by Her Majesty The Queen, replacing the former Imperial Institute opened in 1893 in S. Kensington. A distinctive feature of the building is its paraboloid copper-sheathed roof. The Institute contains, in 60,000 square feet arranged in three floors of circular galleries, a visual representation of the history, geography and ways of life of the Commonwealth countries and dependencies, as well as educational resource, information and conference centres, and a restaurant and craft/bookshop.
Open Mon.-Sat. 10–5, Sun. 2–5. Admission free. Closed Christmas Eve, Christmas Day, Boxing Day, New Year's Day, Good Friday and May Day.

County Hall, Westminster Bridge, SE1.—Formerly the headquarters of the Greater London Council, built on the Pedlar's Acre, Bishop's Acre, Four Acres and Float Mead, Lambeth, from the designs of Ralph Knott, with a river façade of 750 ft. The main building was completed in 1933. The North and South blocks were occupied in 1939 but not finally completed until 1963.

Courtauld Institute Galleries, University of London, Woburn Square, WC1.—The galleries of the University of London contain the Lee collection and the Gambier–Parry collections (14th century to 18th century old masters); the important Courtauld collection of Impressionist and Post-Impressionist paintings; the Roger Fry collection and the Witt and Spooner collections (old master drawings and English water-colours). A major new bequest, the Princes Gate collection of old master paintings and drawings, was opened to the public in July 1981. The Galleries will be moving to Somerset House in January 1990. Open weekdays 10–5, Sun. 2–5. Admission £1·50, concessions 50p.

Custom House, Lower Thames Street, EC3.—Built 1813–17, with a wide quay on the Thames. The Long Room is about 190 ft. long.

Design Museum, Butlers Wharf, SE1 2YD.—Comprising a study collection, temporary exhibitions, a review of new products, a library and a lecture theatre, the Museum attempts to increase the understanding of design by explaining how mass-produced consumer objects work and why they look as they do.

Open Tues.-Sun. and Bank Hols. 11.30–6.30. Admission £2, concessions £1.

Downing Street.—Number 10 Downing Street, SW1, is the official town residence of the Prime Minister, No. 11 of the Chancellor of the Exchequer and No. 12 is the office of the Government Whips. The street was named after Sir George Downing, Bt., soldier and diplomatist, who was M.P. for Morpeth from 1660 to 1684.

Chequers, a Tudor mansion in the Chilterns, about three miles from Princes Risborough, was presented together with a maintenance endowment by Lord and Lady Lee of Fareham in 1917 to serve, from Jan. 1, 1921, as a country residence for the Prime Minister of the day, the Chequers estate of 700 acres being added to the gift by Lord Lee in 1921. The mansion contains a famous collection of Cromwellian portraits and relics.

Dulwich, SE21.—Contains *Dulwich College* (founded by Edward Alleyn in 1619) and the *Dulwich Picture Gallery*, built by Sir John Soane to house the collection bequeathed by the artist Sir Francis Bourgeois. The gallery was damaged in the Second World War but rebuilt with the aid of a grant from the Pilgrim Trust and reopened in 1953. *Dulwich Village* retains many of the rural characteristics of the pre-suburban period.

Eltham, SE9.—Contains remains of 13th–15th century *Eltham Palace*, the birthplace of John of Eltham (1316), son of Edward II. The hall, built by Edward IV, has a hammer-beam roof of chestnut. In the churchyard of St. John the Baptist is the tomb of Thomas Doggett, the comedian and founder of the Thames Watermen's championship (Doggett's Coat and Badge).

Ely Place, Holborn Circus, EC1.—Previously the site of the London house of the Bishop of Ely, Ely Place is a private street (built in 1773) whose affairs are administered by Commissioners under a special Act of Parliament. The 14th century chapel, now St. Etheldreda's (R.C.) Church, is open daily until dusk.

Fulham Palace, Bishop's Avenue, Fulham, SW6.—The courtyard is 16th century, the remainder 18th and 19th century. Former residence of the Bishop of London.

Geffrye Museum, Kingsland Road, E2 8EA.—The Museum is housed in a building erected originally as almshouses in 1713. The exhibits are displayed in a series of period rooms dating from 1600 to 1939, showing the development of decorative art and design. A display of woodworking tools focuses on furniture-making, and the museum has an interesting picture collection. Events and temporary exhibitions are held. Special arrangements exist for children visiting the Museum in school parties (which must be booked in advance) and in their leisure time. Open on Tues.-Sat. 10–5, Sun. 2–5. Closed on Christmas Eve, Christmas Day, Boxing Day and New Year's Day and on Mondays except Bank Holidays. Admission free.
Director, D. Rodgers.

George Inn, Borough High Street, SE1.—Near London Bridge Station. Given to the National Trust in 1937. Last galleried inn in London, built in 1677. Open during licensed hours.

Greenwich, SE10.—*Greenwich Hospital* (since 1873, the Royal Naval College) was built by Charles II, largely from designs by John Webb, and by Queen Anne and William III, from designs by Wren. It stands on the site of an ancient royal palace, and of the more recent *Palace of Placentia*, an enlarged edition of the palace, constructed by Humphrey, Duke of Gloucester (1391–1447), son of Henry IV. Henry VIII, Queen Mary I and Queen Elizabeth I were born in the Royal Palace (which reverted to the Crown in 1447) and King Edward VI died there. In the principal quadrangle is a marble statue of George II by Rysbraeck. (For *National Maritime Museum, see* Index.) *Painted Hall* and *Chapel* closed until further notice. Visitors are also admitted to Sunday Service in the Chapel at 11 a.m., summer and winter, except during College vacations. *Greenwich Park* (196½ acres) was enclosed by Humphrey, Duke of Gloucester, and laid out by Charles II, from the designs of Le Nôtre. *The Queen's House*, begun in 1616, was designed for Anne of Denmark by Inigo Jones (closed for repairs until mid-1990). On a hill in Greenwich Park is the former Royal Observatory (founded 1675). Part of its buildings at Greenwich have been taken over by the Maritime Museum and named *Flamsteed House*, after John Flamsteed (1646–1719), first Astronomer Royal. Astronomical and navigational equipment is exhibited, and the time ball and zero meridian of longitude can also be seen. The Parish church of Greenwich (*St. Alfege*) was rebuilt by Hawksmoor (Wren's pupil) in 1728, and restored after severe damage during the Second World War. General Wolfe and Thomas Tallis are buried in the church. Henry VIII was christened in the former church. *Charlton House* was built in the early 17th century (1607–1612) for Adam Newton, tutor to Prince Henry, brother to Charles I. It is largely in the Jacobean style of architecture. *Cutty Sark*, the last of the famous tea clippers, which has been preserved as a memorial to ships and men of a past era is fully restored and re-rigged, with a museum of sail on board. Open weekdays 11–5 (summer 11–6), Sundays and Boxing Day 2.30–5. The yacht *Gipsy Moth IV* in which Sir Francis Chichester sailed single-handed round the world, 1966–67, is preserved alongside the *Cutty Sark*.

Guildhall, Gresham Street, City, EC2.—Scene of civic government for the City for more than a thousand years. Built *c.* 1440; façade built 1788–9; damaged in the Great Fire, 1666, and by incendiary bombs, 1940. The main hall and crypt (the most extensive medieval crypt in London) have been restored. Events in Guildhall include the annual election of Lord Mayor, election of Sheriffs, receptions in honour of Sovereigns and Heads of State, and the meetings of the Court of Common Council (*see* "Corporation of London"). Open weekdays and Sun. (May to Sept.) 10–5. Admission free.
Keeper of the Guildhall, J. H. Lucioni.

The Guildhall (reference) Library and the Library and Museum of the Clockmakers' Company are housed in new premises. Library open Mon.-Sat. 9.30–5, Museum open Mon.-Fri. 9.30–4.45. Admission free (entrance in Aldermanbury). The Library contains Plans of London, 1570; Deed of Sale with Shakespeare's signature; first, second and fourth folios of Shakespeare's plays etc. (*See also* City Business Library.)

Hampton Court Palace, East Molesey, Surrey.—Sixteenth-century palace built by Cardinal Wolsey, with additions by Sir Christopher Wren for William and Mary. Beautiful gardens with maze and grape vine (planted in 1769). State Apartments and collection of pictures. Tennis Court, built by King Henry VIII in 1530. Collection of Mantegna paintings. Gardens open daily until dusk, Maze and Palace open mid March–mid Oct. daily 9.30–6, mid Oct.–March 9.30–4.30. Admission charge for Maze and Palace. Gardens free.

Holland Park, W8.—55 acres including open air theatre and concerts, floodlit gardens, King George VI Memorial Youth Hostel and a restaurant.

Honourable Artillery Company's Headquarters, City Road, EC1Y 2BQ.—The H.A.C. received its charter of incorporation from Henry VIII in 1537, and has occupied its present ground since 1641. The Armoury House dates from 1735. The present castellated barracks date from 1860. Four of its members who emigrated in the 17th century, founded in 1638 the Ancient and Honorable Artillery Company of Massachusetts. The H.A.C. is the senior regiment of the Territorial Army Volunteer Reserves, and maintains a Headquarters, four squadrons, a gun troop, and two companies of the Home Service Force.
Chief Exec., Capt. G. C. Lloyd, C.B.E., R.N.

Horniman Museum and Library, London Road, Forest Hill, SE23 3PQ.—The Museum was presented in 1901 to the London County Council by the founder, Mr. F. J. Horniman, M.P. With the adjoining Gardens, it is now an independent charitable trust. The Museum has three main departments: ethnography, musical instruments and natural history. In the ethnography department the large collections include exhibits illustrating man's progress in the arts and crafts from prehistoric times. The natural history department includes an aquarium. Reference library (except Mondays). Education Service (adults and schoolchildren). Free concerts and lectures (autumn and spring). Special exhibitions. Open Mon.–Sat. 10.30–6, Sun. 2–6. Admission free.
Director, D. M. Boston, O.B.E.

Horse Guards, Whitehall, SW1.—Archway and offices built about 1753. The mounting of the guard (Life Guards, or the Blues and Royals) at 11 a.m. (10 a.m. on Sundays) and the dismounted inspection at 4 p.m. are picturesque ceremonies. Only those on the Lord Chamberlain's list may drive through the gates and archway into *Horse Guard's Parade* (230,000 sq. ft.), where the Colour is "trooped" on the Queen's Official Birthday.

The Houses of Parliament, Westminster, SW1.— An ordinance issued in the reign of Richard II stated that "Parliament shall be holden or kepid wheresoever it pleaseth the King" and at the present day the Sovereign summons Parliament to meet and prescribes the time and place of meeting. The royal palace of Westminster, originally built by Edward the Confessor (Westminster Hall (*q.v.*) being added by William Rufus), was the normal place of Parliament from about 1340. St. Stephen's Chapel was used from about 1550 for the meetings of the House of Commons, which had previously been held in the Chapter House or Refectory of Westminster Abbey. The House of Lords met in an apartment of the royal palace.

The fire of 1834 destroyed much of the palace and the present Houses of Parliament were erected on the site from the designs of Sir Charles Barry and Augustus Welby Pugin between 1840 and 1867. The Chamber of the House of Commons was destroyed by enemy action in 1941 and a new Chamber designed by Sir Giles Gilbert Scott was used for the first time on Oct. 26, 1950.

The Victoria Tower of the House of Lords is about 330 ft. high, and when Parliament is sitting the Union Flag flies by day from its flagstaff. *The Clock Tower* of the House of Commons is about 320 ft. high and contains "Big Ben", the hour bell said to be named after Sir Benjamin Hall, First Commissioner of Works when the original bell was cast in 1856. This bell, which weighed 16 tons 11 cwt., was found to be cracked in 1857. The present bell (13½ tons) is a recasting of the original and was first brought into use in July 1859. The dials of the clock are 23 ft. in diameter, the hands being 9 ft. and 14 ft. long (including balance piece). A light is displayed from the Clock Tower at night when Parliament is sitting.

For security reasons tours of the Houses of Parliament are available only to those who have made advance arrangements through a Member or Peer.

Admission to the Strangers' Gallery of the House of Lords is arranged by a Peer or by queue via St. Stephen's Entrance. Admission to the Strangers' Gallery of the House of Commons is by Members' order (Members' orders should be sought several weeks in advance), or by queue via St. Stephen's Entrance. Queues are usually shorter after 6 p.m., Mon.–Thurs. Overseas visitors may obtain cards of introduction from their Embassy or High Commission.

Inns of Court.—The *Inner* and *Middle Temple,* S. of Fleet Street, EC4, and N. of Victoria Embankment, to which the gardens extend, have occupied (since the early 14th century) the site of the buildings of the Order of Knights Templars. *Inner Temple Hall* (rebuilt in 1955 after bomb damage) is open Mon.–Fri. 10.30–11.30 and 3–4 on application to Treasurer's Office during law sittings. *Middle Temple Hall* (1562–70) is open when not in use, Mon.–Fri. 10–12 and 3–4, Sat. when staff are available. Closed on Public Holidays. In Middle Temple Gardens (not open to the public) Shakespeare (Henry VI, Part I) places the incident which led to the "Wars of the Roses" (1455–85).

Temple Church, EC4, was restored in 1958 after severe damage by bombing. The nave formed one of five remaining round churches in England (the others being at Cambridge, Northampton, Little Maplestead (Essex) and Ludlow Castle). Open weekdays 9.30–4.—Services: 8.30 and 11.15 a.m. except in August and September. *Master of the Temple,* Rev. Canon J. Robinson.

Lincoln's Inn, from Chancery Lane to Lincoln's Inn Fields, WC2, occupies the site of the palace of a former Bishop of Chichester and of a Black Friars monastery. Records show the Society as being in existence in 1422. The Hall and Library Buildings are of 1845, although the Library is first mentioned in 1474, the old Hall early 16th century and the Chapel was rebuilt c. 1619–23. Halls open by appointment, Chapel and Gardens, Mon.–Fri. 12–2.30. Tours weekdays mid March–mid Sept. 9.30–11.30, £2. Chapel services Sun. 11.30 a.m. during Law Terms. *Lincoln's Inn Fields* (7 acres). The Square, laid out by Inigo Jones, contains many fine old houses with handsome interiors.

Gray's Inn, Holborn/Gray's Inn Road, W.C.1. Early 14th century. Hall (1556–60). Chapel (largely rebuilt in 1698). Services 11.15 a.m. (during Law Dining Terms only.) Holy Communion 1st Sunday in every month except Aug.–Sept. Public welcome. Library (30,000 vols., mss. and printed books) may be viewed by appointment. Gardens open to the public May–Sept. 12–2.30. The Inn, although badly damaged during the last war, has been completely restored to its former beauty with gracious red brick buildings overlooking grass covered squares and gardens. Strong Elizabethan associations.

No other "Inns" are active, but what remains of *Staple Inn* is worth visiting as a relic of Elizabethan London; though heavy damage was done by a flying-bomb, it retains a picturesque gabled front on Holborn (opposite Gray's Inn Road). *Clement's Inn* (near St. Clement Danes' Church), *Clifford's Inn,* Fleet Street, and *Thavies Inn,* Holborn Circus, are all rebuilt. *Serjeant's Inn,* Fleet Street (damaged by bombing) and another (demolished 1910) of the same name in Chancery Lane, were composed of Serjeants-at-Law, the last of whom died in 1922.

Jewish Museum, Woburn House, Tavistock Square, WC1H 0EP.—Opened in 1932, the Museum contains a rich collection of ceremonial art, portraits and antiquities, illustrating Jewish life, history and religion. Open Tues.–Thurs. and Sun. (and Fri. in summer) 10–4, Fri. in winter 10–12.45. Closed on Public and Jewish Holidays. Group visits by arrangement with Secretary.

Kensington Palace, W8 4PX.—The original house was bought by William III in 1689 and enlarged by Christoper Wren. The birthplace of Queen Victoria in 1819. The State Apartments contain pictures and furniture from the royal collections. A suite of rooms devoted to the memory of Queen Victoria is also shown. The *Court Dress Collection* is also open, and includes three restored rooms: the Red Saloon, the Teck Saloon and the room where Queen Victoria is said to have been born. Both open weekdays 9–5, Sun. 1–5. Admission £3, concessions £2; £1·50.

Kenwood, NW3 7JR.—Nearly 200 acres forming the northern part of Hampstead Heath. Open air symphony concerts each summer. The Iveagh Bequest, in an Adam villa, includes valuable paintings and furniture. Recitals and poetry readings in the Orangery. House open daily, except Good Friday and Dec. 24, 25. Times vary seasonally. Admission free.

Kew, Surrey.—A favourite home of the early Hanoverian monarchs. Kew House, the residence of Frederick, Prince of Wales, and later of his son, George III, was pulled down in 1803, but the earlier Dutch House, now known as Kew Palace, survives. It was built in 1631 and acquired by George III as an annexe to Kew House in 1781. The famous Kew Gardens (*see* Index) were originally laid out as a private garden for Kew House for George III's mother in 1759 and were much enlarged in the 19th century, notably by the inclusion of the grounds of the former Richmond Lodge.

Kneller Hall, Twickenham, TW2 7DU.—Royal Military School of Music. A band of up to 120 instrumentalists gives concerts in the grounds on Wednesdays throughout the summer, commencing at 8 p.m. Admission charge. Season tickets and party bookings available.

Lambeth Palace, SE1.—The official residence of the Archbishop of Canterbury, on the south bank of Thames; the oldest part is 13th century, the house itself is early 19th century. For leave to visit the historical portions, applications should be made by letter to the Archbishop's Chaplain.

Livery Companies' Halls.—The Principal Companies (*see* Index) have magnificent halls but admission to view them has generally to be arranged beforehand. The following are among the finest or more interesting. *Goldsmiths' Hall,* Foster Lane. The present hall was completed in 1835, and contains some magnificent rooms. Exhibitions of plate have been shown here periodically in recent years. *Fishmongers' Hall,* London Bridge (built 1831–3), now admirably restored after severe bomb damage, also contains fine rooms. *Apothecaries' Hall,* Black Friars Lane, was rebuilt in 1670, after the Great Fire, and has library, hall and kitchen which are good examples of this period, together with a pleasant courtyard. *Vintners' Hall,* Upper Thames Street, was also rebuilt after the Great Fire, and its hall has very fine late 17th century panelling. The Watermen and Lightermen's Company is not, strictly speaking, a Livery Company, but its *Hall,* in St. Mary at Hill, is a good example of a smaller 18th century building, with pilastered façade. It was completed in 1780. *Stationers' Hall,* in Stationers' Hall Court, behind Ludgate Hill, another post-fire Hall, standing in its own court, has a particularly finely carved screen; its façade dates from 1800. *Barbers' Hall,* Monkwell Street, with a Hall attributed to Inigo Jones, was completely destroyed by bombing, but has now been rebuilt. The new hall was built some 30 ft. from the old site to enable one of the bastions and part of the wall of the Roman fort to remain exposed to view.

Lloyd's, Lime Street, EC3M 7HA.—Society of private underwriters which evolved during the 18th century from Lloyds Coffee House. Housed in the Royal Exchange for 150 years and in Leadenhall Street and Lime Street from 1928–1986. The present building was opened for business in May 1986, and houses the Lutine Bell. Underwriting is on four floors with a total area of 114,000 sq. ft. A visitors' gallery is open daily and incorporates an exhibition showing the history and operation of the insurance market at Lloyds.

London Planetarium, Marylebone Road, NW1 5LR.—Open daily (except Christmas Day), star shows 11–4.30. Admission charge.

London Transport Museum, Covent Garden, WC2E 7BB.—Housed in the former Flower Market, the Museum contains a collection of buses, trams, trolley-buses, trains, working displays and London Transport paraphernalia. There is a research library and lecture theatre. Open daily 10–6 (except Dec. 24, 25, 26). Admission £2·60, concessions £1·10.

Lord's Cricket Ground, St. John's Wood Road, NW8 8QN.—The headquarters (since 1814) of the Marylebone Cricket Club, the premier cricket club in England (founded 1787), Lord's is the scene of some of the principal matches of the season and Middlesex County headquarters. Real tennis court and squash courts in building behind members' pavilion.

The Cricket Memorial Gallery, a museum of cricket, open on match days 10.30–5. Admission £1, concessions 50p. In winter and on non-match days admission is by prior arrangement with the Curator.

Madame Tussaud's Exhibition, Marylebone Road NW1 5LR.—Open daily (except Christmas Day) 10–5.30. Admission charge.

Mansion House, City, EC4.—(Built 1739–53, reconstructed 1930–31.) The official residence of the Lord Mayor; the Egyptian Hall and Ballroom are the chief attractions. Admission by order from the Lord Mayor's Secretary.

Markets.—The London markets (administered by the Corporation of the City of London) provide foodstuffs for 8,500,000 to 9,000,000 people. *Central Meat, Fish, Fruit, Vegetable, and Poultry Markets,* Smithfield (built 1866) (now moved) the largest meat market in the world and site of St. Bartholomew's Fair from 9th to 19th century; *Leadenhall Market* (meat and poultry), built 1881, part recently demolished; *Billingsgate* (fish), Thames Street, built 1875, part recently demolished, a market site for over 1,000 years (moved to the Isle of Dogs in Jan. 1982); *Spitalfields,* E1 (vegetables, fruit, etc.), enlarged 1928, and opened by Queen Mary; *London Fruit Exchange,* Brushfield Street, built by Corporation of London 1928–29, faces Spitalfields Market; *Covent Garden* (vegetables, fruit, flowers, etc.), (now moved to Nine Elms) established under a charter of Charles II, in 1661; *Borough Market,* SE1 (vegetables, fruit, flowers, etc.).

Marlborough House, Pall Mall, SW1A 2AF.— Built by Wren for the first Duke of Marlborough and completed in 1711, the house finally reverted to the Crown in 1835. Prince Leopold lived there until 1831, and Queen Adelaide from 1837 until her death in 1849. In 1863 it became the London house of the Prince of Wales and was the London home of Queen Mary until her death in 1953. The Queen's Chapel, Marlborough Gate, begun in 1623 from the designs of Inigo Jones for the Infanta Maria of Spain, and completed for Queen Henrietta Maria, is open to the public for services on Sundays at 8.30 a.m. and 11.15 a.m. between

Easter Day and end July (*see also* St. James's Palace for winter services in The Chapel Royal). In 1959 Marlborough House was given by the Queen as a centre for Commonwealth Government conferences and it was opened as such in March, 1962.

London Monument (commonly called "The Monument"), Monument Street, EC3.—Built from designs of Wren, 1671–77, to commemorate the Great Fire of London, which broke out in Pudding Lane, Sept. 2, 1666. The fluted Doric column is 120 ft. high (the moulded cylinder above the balcony supporting a flaming vase of gilt bronze is 42 ft. in addition), and is based on a square plinth 40 ft. high, with fine carvings on W. face (making a total height of 202 ft.). Splendid views of London from gallery at top of column (311 steps). Open April–Sept., Mon.–Fri. 9–6, Sat. and Sun. 2–6. Oct.–March, Mon.–Sat. 9–4. Closed Christmas Day, Boxing Day and Good Friday. Admission charge.

Monuments.—*Albert Memorial,* South Kensington; *Royal Air Force,* Victoria Embankment; *Beaconsfield,* Parliament Square; *Beatty, Jellicoe* and *Cunningham,* Trafalgar Square; *Belgian Gratitude* (Reginald Blomfield), Victoria Embankment; *Boadicea* (or "Boudicca"), Queen of the Iceni, E. Anglia (Thomas Thornycroft), Westminster Bridge; *Brunel* (Marochetti), Victoria Embankment; *Burghers of Calais* (Rodin), Victoria Tower Gardens, Westminster; *Burns,* Embankment Gardens; *Carlyle* (Boehm), Cheyne Walk, Chelsea; *Cavalry,* Hyde Park; *Edith Cavell* (Frampton), St. Martin's Place; *Cenotaph* (Lutyens), Whitehall; *Charles I,* Trafalgar Square; *Charles II,* inside the Royal Exchange; *Churchill,* Parliament Square; *Cleopatra's Needle* (68½ ft. high *c.* 1500 B.C. erected on the Thames Embankment in 1877–8)—the Sphinxes are Victorian; *Clive,* Whitehall; *Captain Cook* (Brock), The Mall; *Crimean,* Broad Sanctuary; *Oliver Cromwell* (Thornycroft), outside Westminster Hall; *Duke of Cambridge,* Whitehall; *Duke of York* (124 ft.), Carlton House Terrace; *Edward VII* (Mackennal), Waterloo Place; *Elizabeth I* (1586, oldest outdoor statue in London) (from Ludgate), Fleet Street; *Eros* (Shaftesbury Memorial) (Gilbert), Piccadilly Circus; *Marechal Foch,* Grosvenor Gardens; *Charles James Fox,* Bloomsbury Square; *George III,* Cockspur Street; *George IV* (Chantrey), riding without stirrups, Trafalgar Square; *George V,* Old Palace Yard; *George VI,* Carlton Gardens; *Gladstone,* facing Australia House, Strand; *Guards'* (Crimea), Waterloo Place; (Great War), Horse Guards' Parade; *Haig* (Hardiman), Whitehall; *Irving* (Brock), N. side of National Portrait Gallery; *James II,* Trafalgar Square; *Samuel Johnson,* opposite St. Clement Danes; *Kitchener,* Horse Guards' Parade; *Abraham Lincoln,* Parliament Square; *Milton,* St. Giles, Cripplegate; *The Monument* (*see above*); *Mountbatten,* Foreign Office Green; *Nelson* (170 ft. 2 in.), Trafalgar Square, with Landseer's lions (cast from guns recovered from the wreck of the *Royal George*); *Florence Nightingale,* Waterloo Place; *Palmerston,* Parliament Square; *Peel,* Parliament Square; *Pitt* (Chantrey), Hanover Square; *Portal,* Embankment Gardens; *Prince Consort,* Holborn Circus; *Raleigh,* Whitehall; *Richard Coeur de Lion* (Marochetti), Old Palace Yard; *Roberts,* Horse Guards' Parade; *Franklin D. Roosevelt* (Reid Dick), Grosvenor Square; *Royal Artillery* (South Africa), The Mall; (Great War), Hyde Park Corner; *Captain Scott* (Lady Scott), Waterloo Place; *Shackleton,* Kensington Gore; *Shakespeare,* Leicester Square; *Smuts* (Epstein), Parliament Square; *Sullivan,* Victoria Embankment; *Trenchard,* Victoria Embankment; *Victoria Memorial,* in front of Buckingham Palace; *George Washington* (Houdon copy), Trafalgar Square; *Wellington,* Hyde Park Corner; *Wellington* (Chantrey) riding without stirrups, Royal Exchange;

John Wesley, City Road; *William III,* St. James's Square; *Wolseley,* Horse Guards' Parade.

Percival David Foundation of Chinese Art, 53 Gordon Square, WC1H 0PD.—Set up in 1950, the Foundation contains the collection of Chinese ceramics formed by Sir Percival David and his important library of books on Chinese art. To these was added a gift from the Hon. Mountstuart Elphinstone of part of his collection of Chinese monochrome porcelains. The Foundation is administered on behalf of the University of London by the School of Oriental and African Studies. Galleries, Mon.–Fri. 10.30–5. Closed weekends and Bank Holidays. Library available to ticket holders only; applications in writing to the *Curator,* Miss R. Scott.

Port of London.—The Port of London covers the tidal portion of the River Thames from Teddington to the seaward limit (Tongue light vessel), a distance of 150 km. The governing body is the Port of London Authority (P.L.A.), whose Head Office is at Europe House, World Trade Centre, E1 9AA. The enclosed dock at Tilbury is wholly-owned by the P.L.A. and is 40 km. below London Bridge. The docks have a comprehensive range of modern cargo-handling facilities and perform every type of cargo-handling operation. Tilbury is principally used by vessels to and from Australia, North and South America, India, Middle and Far East, Scandinavia, U.S.S.R. and continental Europe.

Privately owned cargo-handling facilities along the River Thames are an important part of the Port of London, handling some 40 million tonnes of cargo a year, 60 per cent. of which is crude oil and refined products. The combination of P.L.A. and privately-owned facilities makes the Port of London the U.K.'s largest non-oil port.

Passenger vessels and cruise liners can be handled at moorings at Greenwich, near Tower Bridge and at Tilbury Passenger Landing Stage. The latter provides accommodation for liners at all states of the tide.

Prince Henry's Room, 17 Fleet Street, EC4.—Early 17th century timber-framed house containing fine room on first floor with panelling and moulded plaster ceiling. Includes an exhibition on Samuel Pepys and the London in which he lived. Open Mon.–Fri. 1.45–5, Sat 1.45–4.30. Closed Christmas Day, Good Friday and Bank Holidays. Admission free. Available for morning or evening lettings on application to The Town Clerk, Guildhall, EC2.

Richmond, Surrey.—Contains the red brick gateway of *Richmond Palace* (Henry VII, 1485–1509) and buildings of the Jacobean, Queen Anne, and early Georgian periods, including *White Lodge* in Richmond Park, the former home of Queen Mary's mother (the Duke of Windsor was born there, June 23, 1894), and now the home of the Royal Ballet School. The *Star and Garter* Home for Disabled Soldiers, Sailors, and Airmen (the Women's Memorial of the Great War) was opened by Queen Mary in 1924. *Richmond Park* (2,469 acres) contains herds of fallow and red deer.

Roman London.—Although visible remains from this period are few, excavations carried out in the City on sites due for redevelopment often reveal Roman features. Sections of the City Wall are the most striking remains to be seen of Roman *Londinium,* although even these are largely medieval due to the Roman wall being rebuilt during the medieval period. Sections may be seen near the White Tower in the Tower of London; at Tower Hill; at Coopers' Row; at All Hallows, London Wall, its vestry being built on the remains of a semi-circular Roman bastion; at St. Alphage, London Wall, showing a striking succession of building repairs from Roman until the late medieval period, and at St. Giles, Cripplegate. Excavations in the Cripplegate area have revealed that a Roman fort was built there c. A.D.100–120. It was later incorporated into the city wall when this was built c. A.D.200.

The administrative centre of the Roman city was the great forum and basilica, more than 165 metres square, sections of which have been encountered during excavations in the area of Leadenhall, Grace-church Street and Lombard Street. Excavations during the past few years have revealed Roman activity along the river. Traces of a massive riverside wall, built in the late Roman period, have been found and a succession of Roman timber quays have been excavated along Lower and Upper Thames Street helping to prove that Roman London was a thriving commercial centre.

Other major buildings found are the *Provincial Governor's Palace* in Cannon Street; remains of a bath-building, preserved in Lower Thames Street; and the *Temple of Mithras* in Walbrook. The fine sculptures from this temple are displayed in the Museum of London (*see* Index) where many other relics from the Roman City may be seen. There is also an Ordnance Survey map of Roman London.

Royal Albert Hall, Kensington Gore, SW7 2AP.—The elliptical hall, one of the largest in the world, was completed in 1871, and since 1941 has been the venue each summer for the Promenade Concerts founded in 1895 by Sir Henry Wood. Also used for public meetings, concerts, sports and other entertainments. Guided tours are available in the summer months.
Chief Exec., P. Deuchar.

Royal Exchange, EC3V 3LS.—Founded by Sir Thomas Gresham, 1566, opened as "The Bourse" and proclaimed "The Royal Exchange" by Queen Elizabeth I, 1571, rebuilt 1667–69 and 1842–44. The building is occupied by the Guardian Royal Exchange Assurance Group and by the London International Financial Futures Exchange. It is administered by the Gresham Committee.
Clerk, Mercers' Hall, Ironmonger Lane, EC2.

Royal Geographical Society, Kensington Gore, SW7 2AR.—Map room open to public, admission free. Advice for scientific expeditions abroad, by appointment only.

Royal Hospital, Chelsea, Royal Hospital Road, Chelsea, SW3 4SL. Founded by Charles II, in 1682, and built by Wren; opened in 1692 for old and disabled soldiers. Great Hall, Chapel and Museum open daily 10–12, 2–4 (Museum closed on Sunday afternoons Oct.–March). The extensive grounds include the former Ranelagh Gardens, and are the venue for the Chelsea Flower Show held each May by the Royal Horticultural Society.
Governor, General Sir Roland Guy, G.C.B., C.B.E., D.S.O.
Lieut.-Governor and Secretary, Maj.-Gen. A. L. Watson, C.B.

Royal Opera House, Covent Garden, WC2E 7DD.—Home of The Royal Ballet (1931), The Royal Opera (1946) and Sadler's Wells Royal Ballet (1946) companies, the Royal Opera House is the third theatre to be built on the site, opening May 15, 1858: the first was opened Dec. 7, 1732. The season of the resident companies runs mid Sept.–Aug.
General Director, J. Isaacs.

Runnymede.—A meadow of about 100 acres, on the south bank of the Thames (part of the Crown Lands), between Windsor and Staines. From June 15 to 23, 1215, the hostile Barons encamped on this meadow during negotiations with King John, who rode over each day from Windsor. The 48 "Articles of the Barons" were accepted by the King on June

15, and were subsequently embodied in a charter, since known as *Magna Charta,* of which several copies were sealed on June 19. About half a mile N.E. of the meadow is *Magna Charta Island* (claimed as the actual site of the sealing), presented to the National Trust in 1930.

There is a memorial at *Cooper's Hill,* near Runnymede, to members of the Commonwealth air forces who lost their lives in the Second World War while serving from bases in the United Kingdom and north-western Europe and have no known grave. In May, 1965, a memorial was unveiled to President John F. Kennedy of the United States on ground nearby.

St. James's Palace, in Pall Mall, S.W.1.—(Closed to the public.) Built by Henry VIII; the Gatehouse and Presence Chamber remain, later alterations were made by Wren and Kent. The Chapel Royal is open for services on Sundays at 8.30 a.m. and 11.15 a.m. between beginning October and Good Friday (*see also* Marlborough House for summer services in The Queen's Chapel). Representatives of Foreign Powers are still accredited "to the Court of St. James's". *Clarence House* (1825) in the palace precinct is the home of H.M. The Queen Mother.

St. John's Gate, Clerkenwell, EC1.—Now the Chancery of the Order of St. John of Jerusalem, and formerly the entrance of the Priory of that Order, of which the gate house (early 16th century) and crypt of Church (12th century) alone survive. They may be inspected on application to the Curator.

St. Paul's Cathedral, EC4M 8AD.—Built 1675–1710, cost £747,660. The cross on the dome is 365 ft. above the ground level, the inner cupola 218 ft. above the floor. "Great Paul," in the south-west tower weighs 17 tons. Organ by Father Smith (enlarged by Willis and rebuilt by Mander) in a case carved by Grinling Gibbons (who also carved the choir stalls). The choir and high altar were restored in 1958 after war damage and the North Transept in 1962. The American War Memorial Chapel was consecrated in November, 1958. The chapel of the Most Excellent Order of the British Empire in the Crypt of the Cathedral was dedicated in 1960. Nave and transepts free. The following parts open weekdays 10–4.15 (Sat. 11–4.15). Admission: Ambulatory, 60p; Crypt, Treasury and historical display, 80p; whispering gallery, stone gallery, £1 (Children reduced price.)—Services: Sundays, 8, 10.30, 11.30 and 3.15. Weekdays, 7.30, 8, 12.30 and 5.

Sir John Soane's Museum, 13 Lincoln's Inn Fields, WC2A 3BP.—The house and galleries, built 1812–24, are the work of the founder, Sir John Soane (1753–1837) and contain his collections, arranged as he left them, in pursuance of an Act procured by him in 1833. Exhibits include the Sarcophagus of Seti 1 (c. 1290 B.C.), Classical vases and marbles, Hogarth's *Rake's Progress* and *Election* series, paintings by Canaletto, Reynolds, Turner, Lawrence, etc., and sculpture by Chantrey, Flaxman, etc. Soane's library of 8,000 vols, and collection of 40,000 architectural drawings are available for study by appointment. Open Tues.–Sat. 10–5. Closed Bank Holidays. Tours must be booked in advance.
Curator, P. Thornton, F.S.A.
Assistant Curator, Mrs M. Richardson.

Somerset House, Strand, WC2, and Victoria Embankment, WC2.—The beautiful river façade (600 ft. long) was built in 1776–86 from the designs of Sir William Chambers; the eastern extension, which houses part of King's College, was built by Smirke in 1829. Somerset House was the property of Lord Protector Somerset, at whose attainder in 1552 the palace passed to the Crown, and it was a royal residence until 1692.

South Bank, SE1.—The arts complex on the south bank of the River Thames includes the South Bank Centre, owned and managed by the South Bank Board, and consisting of the 2,903-seat *Royal Festival Hall* (opened in 1951 for the Festival of Britain), a major venue for concert and ballet seasons, with the adjacent 1,056-seat *Queen Elizabeth Hall* and 368-seat *Purcell Room*, accommodating smaller-scale performances.

The *National Film Theatre* (opened 1958), administered by the British Film Institute, has two auditoria showing films, television and video of outstanding historical, artistic or technical merit. The London Film Festival is held here every November.

The *National Theatre* opened in 1976 and stages classical, modern, new and neglected plays in its three auditoria: the 1,160-seat Olivier theatre (open stage), the 890-seat Lyttleton theatre (proscenium stage) and the experimental Cottesloe theatre (adaptable stage) which holds up to 400.

The *Museum of the Moving Image* charts the history of the moving image in cinema and television from the earliest devices through to disc technology. Open Tues.–Sat. 10–8, Sun. and Bank Holidays 10–6 (Oct.–May), 10–8 (June–Sept.). Admission £3·50, concessions £2·50.

Southwark Cathedral, SE1 9DA.—Mainly 13th century, but the nave is largely rebuilt. The tomb of John Gower (1330–1408) is between the Bunyan and Chaucer memorial windows in the north aisle: Shakespeare's effigy backed by a view of Southwark and the Globe Theatre in the south aisle; the altar screen (erected 1520) has been restored; the tomb of Bishop Andrewes (died 1626) is near the screen. The Early English Lady Chapel (behind the choir), restored 1930, was the scene of the Consistory Courts of the reign of Mary (Gardiner and Bonner) and is still used as a Consistory Court. John Harvard, after whom Harvard University is named, was baptized here in 1607, and the Chapel by the North Choir Aisle is his memorial chapel. Open 7.30–6, admission free.—Services: Sundays, 11, 3. Weekdays, 12.30, 12.45, 5.30 (sung on Tuesdays and Fridays), Saturdays, 12 noon.

Stock Exchange, EC2.—The market floor of the new Stock Exchange building in London opened for trading in June, 1973. Since "Big Bang" in 1986, the floor has been used solely by the London Traded Options Market. A tower, 331 feet high, and the new Market replace the complex of buildings started in 1801 on the same site. The new building is the headquarters of The Stock Exchange, following the amalgamation of all the Stock Exchanges in Great Britain and Ireland on March 25, 1973.

The Visitors Gallery is open Mon.–Fri., 9.30–5. Admission free and without ticket. Film show, advance bookings are advisable via the Public Information Unit (01-588 2355).

Thames Embankments.—The *Victoria Embankment*, on the N. side (from Westminster to Blackfriars), was constructed by Sir Joseph William Bazalgette for the Metropolitan Board of Works, 1864–70 (the seats, of which the supports of some are a kneeling camel, laden with spicery, and of others a winged sphinx, were presented by the Grocers' Company, and by Rt. Hon. W. H. Smith, M.P., in 1874); the *Albert Embankment*, on the S. side (from Westminster Bridge to Vauxhall), 1866–69; the *Chelsea Embankment*, 1871–74. The total cost exceeded £2,000,000. Bazalgette (1819–91) also inaugurated the London main drainage system, 1858–65. A medallion has been placed on a pier of the Victoria Embankment to commemorate the engineer of the Thames waterside improvements ("Flumini vincula posuit").

County Hall includes an embankment on the Surrey side.

Thames Flood Barrier.—Officially opened in May 1984, though first used in Feb. 1983, the Barrier consists of ten rising sector gates which span 570 yards from bank to bank of the Thames at Woolwich Reach. When not in use the gates lie horizontally, allowing shipping to navigate the river normally; when the Barrier is closed, the gates turn through 90 degrees to stand vertically more than 50 feet above the river bed. The Barrier took eight years to complete and can be raised within about 30 minutes.

Thames Tunnels.—The *Rotherhithe Tunnel*, constructed by the L.C.C. and opened in 1908, connects Commercial Road, E14, with Lower Road, Rotherhithe; the total length is 1 mile 332 yards, of which 474 yards are under the river. The cost of the tunnel and its approaches was £1,506,914. The first *Blackwall Tunnel* (pedestrians and vehicles) was constructed by the L.C.C. and opened in 1897, connecting East India Dock Road, Poplar, with Blackwall Lane, East Greenwich. The cost of the tunnel with its approaches was about £1,323,663. A second tunnel (for southbound vehicles only) was opened in August, 1967, at a cost of about £9,750,000 and the old tunnel was improved at a cost of about £1,350,000 and made one-way northbound. Both tunnels are for vehicles only. The relative lengths of the tunnels measured from East India Dock Road to the Gate House on the south side are 6,215 ft. (old tunnel) and 6,152 feet. *Greenwich Tunnel* (pedestrians only), constructed by the L.C.C. and opened in 1902, connects the Isle of Dogs, Poplar, with Greenwich. The length of the subway is 406 yards, and the cost was about £180,000. The *Woolwich Tunnel* (pedestrians only), constructed by the L.C.C. and opened in 1912, connects North and South Woolwich below the passenger and vehicular ferry from North Woolwich Station, E16, to High Street, Woolwich, SE18. The length of the subway is 552 yards, and its cost was about £86,000. The *Thames Tunnel* (1,300 feet) was opened in 1843 to connect Wapping with Rotherhithe. In 1866 it was closed to the public, and purchased by the East London Railway Company. The *Tower Subway* for pedestrians was opened in 1870, and has long been closed.

Tower Bridge Walkway and Museum, SE1 2UP.—Owned by the Bridge House Trust of the City of London and open daily April–Oct. 10–6·30, Nov.–March 10–4·45. Admission £2·50, concessions £1. Attractions include exhibitions, videos, the observation platform and walkway, engine rooms, working models and souvenir gift shop.

Tower Hill, EC1 and EC3, was formerly the place of execution for condemned prisoners from the Tower, the site of the scaffold being marked in the gardens of Trinity Square.

Tower of London, EC3.—Admission to a general view of the Tower, the White Tower (Armouries), the History, Oriental, Ordnance and 18th–19th century Galleries, and the Wall Walk Phases I and II.

The White Tower is the oldest and central building in Her Majesty's Royal Palace and Fortress of the Tower of London. It was built at the order of William I and constructed by Gundulph, Bishop of Rochester, in the years 1078–98. The Inner Wall, with thirteen towers, was constructed by Henry III in the 12th century. The Moat was extended and completed by Richard I and the Wharf first mentioned in 1228. The Outer Wall was completed in the reign of Edward I and now incorporates six towers and two bastions. The last Monarch to reside in the Tower of London was James I. The Crown Jewels came to the Tower in the reign of Henry III. All coinage used in Great

Britain was minted in the Outer Ward of the Tower of London until 1810 when the Royal Mint was formed. The Tower of London has had a military garrison since 1078. The Chapel Royal of St. John the Evangelist, within the White Tower (1080–1088) is the oldest Norman church in London. The chapel of St. Peter ad Vincula was built in the early 16th century.

Open weekdays March–Oct., 9.30–5, Nov.–Feb., 9.30–4; Sundays, March–Oct., 2–5. Tower closed Christmas Eve, Christmas Day, Boxing Day, New Year's Day and Good Friday. On Sundays throughout the year (except August) the public is admitted to Holy Communion, 9.15 a.m. and Morning Service, 11 a.m. Admission £4·80 (£3·50 when Jewel House closed for cleaning in Feb.); various concessions.

Constable, Field Marshal Sir Roland Gibbs, G.C.B., C.B.E., D.S.O., M.C.

Lieutenant, Lt.-Gen. Sir Derek Boorman, K.C.B.

Resident Governor and Keeper of the Jewel House, Maj.-Gen. C. Tyler, C.B.

Master of the Armouries, G. Wilson.

Chaplain at the Chapel Royal of St. Peter ad Vincula, Rev. N. A. Hood.

Waltham Abbey (or Waltham Holy Cross), Essex EN9 1UQ.—The Abbey ruins, Harold's Bridge (14th century), the Nave of the former cruciform Abbey Church *c.* 1120 and the traditional burial place of King Harold II (1066), and a Guild Chapel of Edward II, with crypt below, which houses a visitors centre with permanent exhibition. New evidence of four former churches on the site, and the shape of the east end of Harold's church, have been revealed in recent excavations. Lee Valley Regional Park Authority has a country centre in the Abbey grounds. At Waltham Cross, one mile from the Abbey, is one of the crosses (partly restored) erected by Edward I to mark a resting place of the corpse of Queen Eleanor on its way to Westminster Abbey. (Ten crosses were erected, but only those at Geddington, Northampton and Waltham remain; "Charing" Cross originally stood near the spot now occupied by the statue of Charles I at Whitehall.)

Wellington Museum, Apsley House, 149 Piccadilly, at Hyde Park Corner, W1.—Known as "No. 1 London", Apsley House was designed by Robert Adam for Lord Bathurst and built 1771–78. It was bought in 1817 by the Duke of Wellington, who in 1828–29 employed Benjamin Wyatt to enlarge it, face it with Bath stone and add the Corinthian portico. The museum contains many fine paintings, sculptures, services of porcelain and silver plate and personal relics of the 1st Duke of Wellington (1769–1852). The House was given to the Nation by the 7th Duke and was first opened to the public in 1952, under the administration of the Victoria and Albert Museum. Open daily 11–5. Closed Mon., Christmas Eve, Christmas Day, Boxing Day and New Year's Day. Admission £2, concessions £1.

Westminster Abbey, SW1.—Built 1050–1745. Chapel of Henry VII, Chapter House and Cloisters; King Edward the Confessor's shrine, A.D. 1269, tombs of kings and queens (Henry III, Edward I, Edward III, Henry V, Mary Queen of Scots, Elizabeth I), and many other monuments and objects of interest, including the grave of "The Unknown Warrior" and Poets' Corner. The Coronation Chair encloses the "Stone of Scone", which was removed from Scotland by Edward I in 1296. Open on weekdays 9–6 (9–7.45 Wed.). Admission to the Royal Chapels, Poets' Corner, Quire and Statesmen's Aisle £2, concessions £1/50p. Last admission Mon.–Fri. 4 p.m., Sat. 5 p.m. Wed. 6–8 p.m. free. Nave open on Sundays between services.—Services: Sundays, 8, 10, 11.15, 3, 6.30 (generally preceded by an organ recital). Monday–

Friday, 7.30, 8, 12.30 (Wednesdays, Lunch-hour Service), 5. Saturdays, 8, 9.20, 3.

Westminster Cathedral, Ashley Place, SW1P 1QW.—Built 1895–1903 from the designs of J. F. Bentley. The campanile is 283 feet high. Cathedral open 6.45 a.m.–8 p.m.—Masses: Sundays, 7, 8, 9, 10.30 (sung), 12, 5.30 and 7; Solemn Vespers and Benediction 3.30. Monday–Friday, 7, 8, 8.30, 9, 10.30, 12.30, 1.05 and 5.30 (sung). Morning Prayer 7.40, Vespers 5. Saturdays 7, 8, 8.30, 9, 10.30 (sung),12.30 and 6, Morning Prayer 7.40, Vespers 5.30. Holy days of obligation, Low Masses 7, 8, 8.30, 9, 10.30, 12.30, 1.05, 5.30 (sung) and 7.

Westminster Hall, SW1A 0AA.—The only part of the old Palace of Westminster to survive the fire of 1834, Westminster Hall is adjacent to and incorporated in the Houses of Parliament. Westminster Hall was built by William Rufus from 1097–99 and altered by Richard II, 1394–99. It is about 240 ft. long, 68 ft. wide and 92 ft. high; the hammerbeam roof of carved oak dates from 1396–98. The Hall was the scene of the trial of Charles I. Westminster Hall is included on the route followed by those who have arranged a visit to the Houses of Parliament with their M.P.

Whitechapel Art Gallery, Whitechapel High Street, E1 7QX.—Opened in 1901; administered by a charitable trust. There is no permanent collection; temporary exhibitions, mainly of modern art, are presented, and community and educational projects are run. Open Tues.–Sun. 11–5; Wed. 11–8.

Wimbledon Lawn Tennis Museum, SW19 5AE.—Exhibits include fashion, trophies, replicas and memorabilia representing the history of lawn tennis. A theatre shows films of great matches. Open Tues.–Sat. 11–5, Sun. 2–5. Admission £1·50, concessions 75p.

Windsor Castle (begun by William the Conqueror, A.D. 1066–87).—The Castle Precincts are open daily. Admission free. The *State Apartments* of Windsor Castle are open on a regular basis throughout the year. Admission £2, concessions £1. *Queen Mary's Doll's House, the Exhibition of Master Drawings* and the *Exhibition of The Queen's Presents and Royal Carriages* can be seen on the same days as the State Apartments; admission £1, concessions 50p. When the State Apartments are closed, the other exhibitions remain open to the public. The *Albert Memorial Chapel* is open throughout the year (closed on Sundays). Admission free. A fee is charged to visit *St. George's Chapel*.

The *Royal Mausoleum*, Frogmore Gardens, Home Park, is open annually on two days in early May in conjunction with the opening of Frogmore Gardens in aid of the National Garden Scheme. Also open on the Wednesday nearest to May 24 (Queen Victoria's birthday). Admission free.

Zoological Gardens, Regent's Park, NW1.—(Opened in 1828). Open daily (except Christmas Day) March–Oct. 9–6 or dusk (Bank Holidays and associated Suns. Easter–Aug. and Suns. July 12–Sept. 13, 9–7). Oct.–March opens 10. Admission £4·30, various concessions. Aquarium and Children's Zoo free.

[London Tourism Board and Convention Bureau.—Tourist Information Centre, Victoria Station Forecourt, SW1V 1JU. (01–730 3488).]

PARKS, SPACES AND GARDENS

The principal Parks and Open Spaces in the Metropolitan area are maintained as under:—

By the Crown

BUSHY PARK (1,099 acres).—Adjoining Hampton Court, contains avenue of horse-chestnuts enclosed in a four-fold avenue of limes planted by William III. "Chestnut Sunday" (when the trees are in full bloom with their "candles") is usually about May 1 to 15.

GREEN PARK (49 acres), W1.—Between Piccadilly and St. James's Park with Constitution Hill, leading to Hyde Park Corner.

GREENWICH PARK (196¼ acres), SE10.

HAMPTON COURT GARDENS (54 acres).

HAMPTON COURT GREEN (17 acres).

HAMPTON COURT PARK (622 acres).

HYDE PARK (341 acres).—From Park Lane, W1, to Kensington Gardens, W2, containing the Serpentine. Fine gateway at Hyde Park Corner, with Apsley House, the Achilles Statue, Rotten Row and the Ladies' Mile. To the north-east is the Marble Arch, originally erected by George IV at the entrance to Buckingham Palace and re-erected in the present position in 1851.

KENSINGTON GARDENS (275 acres), W2.—From western boundary of Hyde Park to Kensington Palace, containing the Albert Memorial.

KEW, ROYAL BOTANIC GARDENS *see* p. 357.

REGENT'S PARK and PRIMROSE HILL (464 acres), NW1.—From Marylebone Road to Primrose Hill surrounded by the Outer Circle and divided by the Broad Walk leading to the Zoological Gardens.

RICHMOND PARK (2,469 acres).

ST. JAMES'S PARK (93 acres), SW1.—From White-hall to Buckingham Palace. Ornamental lake of 12 acres. The original suspension bridge built in 1857 was replaced in 1957. The Mall leads from the Admiralty Arch to the Queen Victoria Memorial and Buckingham Palace, Birdcage Walk from Storey's Gate, past Wellington Barracks, to Buckingham Palace.

By the Corporation of London

BURNHAM BEECHES and FLEET WOOD, Bucks. (510 acres).—Purchased by the Corporation for the benefit of the public in 1880, Fleet Wood (65 acres) being presented in 1921.

COULSDON COMMON, Surrey (133 acres).

EPPING FOREST (6,000 acres).—Purchased by the Corporation for £250,000 and thrown open to the public in 1882. The present forest is 12 miles long by 1 to 2 miles wide, about one-tenth of its original area.

FARTHINGDOWN, Surrey (121 acres).

HAMPSTEAD HEATH (676 acres), NW3.—Including Golders Hill (36 acres) and Parliament Hill (271 acres), this was transferred to the Corporation on April 1, 1989.

HIGHGATE WOOD (70 acres).

KENLEY COMMON, Surrey (138 acres).

QUEEN'S PARK, Kilburn (30 acres).

RIDDLESDOWN, Surrey (90 acres).

SPRING PARK, West Wickham (51 acres).

WEST HAM PARK (77 acres).

WEST WICKHAM COMMON, Kent (25 acres).

With smaller open spaces within the City of London, including FINSBURY CIRCUS GARDENS.

Temporarily Maintained
by the London Residuary Body

When the G.L.C. was abolished in April 1986 the responsibility for some of its parks and open spaces had already been transferred to other bodies (indicated where known). Negotiating the transfer of the remainder to individual Boroughs has been the responsibility of the London Residuary Body since abolition.

SOUTH BANK (10 acres, including Jubilee Gardens), Belvedere Road, SE1, vested in the L.R.B. but to be managed by the South Bank Board.

ROMAN NAMES OF ENGLISH TOWNS AND CITIES

Bath	*Aquae Sulis*	Lincoln	*Lindum*
Canterbury	*Durovernum Cantiacorum*	London	*Londinium*
Carlisle	*Luguvalium*	Manchester	*Mamucium*
Chelmsford	*Caesaromagus*	Newcastle upon	*Pons Aelius*
Chester	*Deva*	Tyne	
Chichester	*Noviomagus Regnensium*	Pevensey	*Anderitium*
Cirencester	*Corinium Dobunnorum*	Rochester	*Durobrivae*
Colchester	*Camulodunum*	St. Albans	*Verulamium*
Doncaster	*Danum*	Salisbury	*Sorviodunum*
Dorchester	*Durnovaria*	(Old Sarum)	
Dover	*Dubris*	Silchester	*Calleva Atrebatum*
Exeter	*Isca Dumnoniorum*	Winchester	*Venta Belgarum*
Gloucester	*Glevum*	Wroxeter	*Viroconium Cornoviorum*
Leicester	*Ratae Corieltauvorum*	York	*Eburacum*

THE PRINCIPALITY OF WALES

Position and extent.—Wales (Cymru) occupies the extreme west of the central southern portion of the island of Great Britain, with a total area of 8,018 sq. miles (land 7,968; inland water 50); it is bounded on the N. by the Irish Sea, on the S. by the Bristol Channel, on the E. by the English counties of Cheshire, Shropshire, Hereford and Worcester, and Gloucester, and on the W. by St. George's Channel. Across the Menai Straits is the Welsh island of *Anglesey* or Ynys Môn (276 sq. miles), communication with which is facilitated by the Menai Suspension Bridge (1,000 ft. long), built by Telford in 1826 and by the tubular railway bridge (1,100 ft. long) built by Stephenson in 1850. Holyhead harbour, on Holy Isle (N.W. of Anglesey), provides accommodation for ferry services to Dublin (70 miles).

Population.—The population at the Census of 1981 was 2,791,851 (males 1,352,639; females 1,439,212). The average density of population in 1981 was 343 per square mile. The population, mid 1987 estimate, was 2,836,000.

Relief.—Wales is a country of extensive tracts of high plateau and shorter stretches of mountain ranges deeply dissected by river valleys. Lower-lying ground is largely confined to the coastal belt and the lower parts of the valleys. The highest mountains are those of Snowdonia in the north-west (*Snowdon*, 3,559 ft.), Berwyn (*Aran Fawddwy*, 2,971 ft.), Cader Idris (*Pen y Gadair*, 2,928 ft.), Dyfed (*Plynlimon*, 2,467 ft.), and the Black Mountain, Brecon Beacons and Black Forest ranges in the south-east (*Carmarthen Van*, 2,630 ft., *Pen y Fan*, 2,906 ft., *Waun Fâch*, 2,660 ft.).

Hydrography.—The principal river of those rising in Wales is the *Severn* (*see* England), which flows from the slopes of Plynlimon to the English border. The *Wye* (130 miles) also rises in the slopes of Plynlimon. The *Usk* (56 miles) flows into the Bristol Channel, through Gwent. The *Dee* (70 miles) rises in Bala Lake and flows through the Vale of Llangollen, where an aqueduct (built by Telford in 1805) carries the Pontcysyllte branch of the Shropshire Union Canal across the valley. The estuary of the Dee is the navigable portion, 14 miles in length and about 5 miles in breadth, and the tide rushes in with dangerous speed over the "Sands of Dee". The *Towy* (68 miles), *Teifi* (50 miles), *Taff* (40 miles), *Dovey* (30 miles), *Taf* (25 miles), and *Conway* (24 miles), the last named broad and navigable, are wholly Welsh rivers.

The largest natural lake in Wales is *Bala* (Llyn Tegid) in Gwynedd, 4 miles long and about 1 mile wide; *Lake Vyrnwy* is an artificial reservoir, about the size of Bala, and forms the water supply of Liverpool, and Birmingham is supplied from a chain of reservoirs in the Elan and Clærwen valleys.

The Welsh Language.—According to the 1981 Census results, the percentage of persons of three years and over able to speak Welsh were:

Clwyd	18·7	Powys	20·2
Dyfed	46·3	S. Glamorgan	5·8
Gwent	2·5	W. Glamorgan	16·4
Gwynedd	61·2		
Mid Glamorgan	8·4	**Wales**	18·9

The 1981 figure represents a slight decline from 20·8 per cent in 1971 (1961, 26 per cent; 1951, 28·9 per cent).

Flag.—A red dragon on a green and white field (per fess argent and vert a dragon passant gules). The flag was augmented in 1953 by a royal badge on a shield encircled with a riband bearing the words

Ddraig Goch Ddyry Cychwyn and imperially crowned. Only the unaugmented flag is flown on Government offices in Wales and, where appropriate, in London. Both flags continue to be used elsewhere.

EARLY HISTORY

Celts and Romans.—The earliest inhabitants of whom there is any record appear to have been subdued or exterminated by the *Goidels* (a people of Celtic race) in the Bronze Age, and a further invasion of Celtic *Brythons* and *Belgae* followed in the ensuing Iron Age. The *Roman* conquest of South Britain and Wales was for some time successfully opposed by *Caratacus* (Caractacus or Caradog), chieftain of the Catuvellauni and son of *Cunobelinus* (Cymbeline). South east Wales was subjugated and the legionary fortress at Caerleon-on-Usk established by about A.D. 75-77: the conquest of Wales was completed by Agricola about A.D. 78. Communications were opened up by the construction of military roads from Chester to Caerleon-on-Usk and Caerwent, and from Chester to Conway (and thence to Camarthen and Neath). *Christianity* was introduced (during the Roman occupation) in the 4th century.

The Anglo-Saxon Attacks.—The Anglo-Saxon invaders of South Britain drove the Celts into the mountain fastness of Wales, and into Strathclyde (Cumberland and S.W. Scotland) and Cornwall, giving them the name of *Waelisc*, or Welsh (= foreign). The West Saxons' victory of Deorham (577) isolated Wales from Cornwall and the battle of Chester (613) cut off communication with Strathclyde and northern Britain. In the 8th century the boundaries of the Welsh were further restricted by the annexations of Offa, King of Mercia, and counter-attacks were largely prevented by the construction of an artificial boundary from the Dee to the Wye (Offa's Dyke). In the 9th century Rhodri Mawr (844-78) united the country and successfully resisted further incursions of the Saxons by land and raids of Norse and Danish pirates by sea, but at his death his three provinces of *Gwynedd* (N.), *Powys* (Mid.) and *Deheubarth* (S.) were divided among his three sons—Anarawd, Mervyn and Cadell. Cadell's son Hywel Dda ruled a large part of Wales and codified its laws but the provinces were not united again until the rule of Llewelyn ap Seisyllt (husband of the heiress of Gwynedd) from 1018 to 1023.

The Norman Conquest.—After the Norman conquest of England, William I created Palatine counties along the Welsh frontier, and the Norman barons began to make encroachments into Welsh territory. The Welsh princes recovered many of their losses, however, during the civil wars of Stephen's reign and in the early 13th century Owen Gruffydd, prince of Gwynedd was the dominant figure in Wales. Under Llywelyn ap Iorwerth (1194-1240) the Welsh united in powerful resistance to English incursions and Llywelyn's privileges and *de facto* independence were recognized in Magna Carta. His grandson, Llywelyn ap Gruffydd, was the last native prince: he was killed in 1282 during hostilities between the Welsh and English, allowing Edward I of England to establish his authority over the country. On Feb. 7, 1301, Edward of Caernarvon, son of Edward I, was created *Prince of Wales*, a title which has subsequently been borne by the eldest son of the sovereign.

Strong Welsh national feeling continued, expressed in the early 15th century in the rising led by Owain Glyndŵr, but the situation was altered by the accession to the English throne in 1485 of Henry VII of the Welsh House of Tudor. Wales was politically assimilated to England under the Act of Union of 1535, which extended English laws to the Principality and gave it parliamentary representation for the first time.

Eisteddfod.—The Welsh are a distinct nationality, with a language and literature of their own, and the national bardic festival (Eisteddfod), instituted by Prince Rhys ap Griffith in 1176, is annually maintained. These *Eisteddfodau* (sessions) form part of the *Gorsedd* (assembly), which is believed to date from the time of Prydian, a ruling prince in an age many centuries before the Christian era.

LORD LIEUTENANTS AND HIGH SHERIFFS

County	Lord Lieutenant	High Sheriff (1989–90)
Clwyd	Sir William Gladstone, Bt.	D. Mars-Jones
Dyfed	D. C. Mansel Lewis	P. J. K. Speyer
Gwent	R. Hanbury-Tenison	P. A. Brown, M.B.E.
Gwynedd	The Most Hon. The Marquess of Anglesey	H. F. Richards
Mid Glamorgan	D. G. Badham, C.B.E.	H. J. Tamplin, O.B.E.
Powys...................	M. L. Bourdillon	T. G. Steadman
South Glamorgan	Mrs. S. E. Williams, M.B.E.	C. L. Pollard, O.B.E.
West Glamorgan	Lt.-Col. Sir Michael Llewllyn, Bt.	B. K. Davison, O.B.E.

WELSH COUNTY COUNCILS

AREAS AND POPULATIONS

County	Administrative Headquarters	Area (*hectares*)	Population	Rateable Value 1989 £	Actual Rateable Value per head £
Clwyd	Shire Hall, Mold	242,650	402,800	42,517,960	104·90
Dyfed	*Carmarthen	576,577	343,200	33,024,395	94·90
Gwent	*Cwmbran	137,599	443,100	48,127,037	108·61
Gwynedd	County Offices, Caernarfon	386,708	236,300	27,635,573	221·00
Mid Glamorgan ...	*Cardiff	101,867	534,700	42,323,364	79·15
Powys............	*Llandrindod Wells	507,741	113,300	10,913,922	96·33
South Glamorgan .	*Cardiff	41,629	399,400	57,411,618	144·03
West Glamorgan ..	*Swansea	81,657	363,200	39,934,605	109·95

* County Hall.

COUNTY OFFICIALS AND CHAIRMEN

County	Chief Executive	County Treasurer	Chairmen of C.C.
Clwyd	M. H. Phillips	A. Dalby	W. A. Jones
Dyfed	D. H. Davies	A. C. Williams	W. J. W. Evans
Gwent	M. J. Perry	J. P. Walsh	R. W. Jones
Gwynedd	I. B. Rees	T. D. Heald	R. C. Williams
Mid Glamorgan ...	D. H. Thomas*	L. D. Heycock	J. H. Davies
Powys............	M. J. Greenwood	M. J. Greenwood	F. E. D. Leach
South Glamorgan .	M. Boyce	R. G. Tettenborn	Mrs. L. S. Hughes
West Glamorgan ..	M. E. J. Rush, C.B.E.	S. G. Dunster	Mrs. E. Morgan

* County Clerk.

WELSH DISTRICT COUNCILS

Those accorded CITY Status are shown in SMALL CAPITALS; those with Borough Status are distinguished by having § prefixed.

District	Estimated resident population 1987	Rateable Value 1989 £	Chief Executive	Chairman 1989–90 (a) Mayor (b) Lord Mayor
§Aberconwy, Gwynedd	53,500	5,807,114	J. E. Davies	(a) S. R. Roberts
Alyn and Deeside, Clwyd	72,000	8,897,162	W. E. Rogers	J. A. Barker
§Arfon, Gwynedd	54,600	6,874,035	D. L. Jones	(a) G. Owen
§Blaenau Gwent, Gwent	77,300	5,968,619	R. Leadbeter	(a) R. Davies
§Brecknock, Powys	40,600	3,704,173	R. O. Doylend	(a) J. Morgan
CARDIFF, South Glamorgan......	281,500	42,442,021	R. E. Paine	(b) Mrs. B. Jones
Carmarthen, Dyfed	54,600	4,393,473	R. R. Morgan	C. W. Roberts
Ceredigion, Dyfed	65,300	5,445,768	D. Morgan	J. E. Davies
§Colwyn, Clwyd	53,400	5,667,862	D. Crump (acting)	(a) M. Pritchard
§Cynon Valley, Mid Glamorgan ..	64,900	4,521,937	G. W. Hosgood	(a) W. J. Pearson
§Delyn, Clwyd	64,800	6,350,309	P. J. McGreevy	(a) G. B. Roberts
§Dinefwr, Dyfed................	38,400	2,506,005	E. W. Harries	(a) H. B. L. Samways
Dwyfor, Gwynedd	26,700	2,739,965	E. Davies	O. W. Roberts
Glyndŵr, Clwyd	41,100	3,763,203	J. H. Parry	R. T. Roberts
§Islwyn, Gwent	65,800	4,736,784	B. Bird	(a) Mrs. Z. Creed
§Llanelli, Dyfed	73,600	6,298,144	A. B. Thomas	(a) D. H. R. Jones
§Lliw Valley, West Glamorgan ...	61,200	4,746,561	J. C. Howells	(a) D. Young
Meirionnydd, Gwynedd	31,300	4,233,358	G. W. Hughes	W. M. Meredith
§Merthyr Tydfil, Mid Glamorgan	58,500	4,825,386	R. V. Morris	(a) Mrs. C. Rogers
§Monmouth, Gwent	79,400	8,228,594	G. Cummings	(a) B. M. Cowles
Montgomeryshire, Powys	50,600	4,779,353	N. J. Bardsley	J. H. Evans
§Neath, West Glamorgan........	65,100	6,203,281	S. Penny	(a) Miss M. L. Lewis
§Newport, Gwent	129,500	19,710,666	C. Tapp	(a) R. J. M. Butler
§Ogwr, Mid Glamorgan	135,800	11,579,396	J. G. Cole	(a) M. Fitzgibbon
§Port Talbot, West Glamorgan ...	49,900	8,434,916	I. K. Lewis	(a) G. L. Cooper
Preseli Pembrokeshire, Dyfed	70,500	7,063,878	I. W. R. David	G. C. Grey
Radnor, Powys	22,100	2,410,396	G. C. Read	Mrs. E. M. Davies
§Rhondda, Mid Glamorgan	77,100	3,974,317	G. Evans	(a) T. J. D. Hughes
§Rhuddlan, Clwyd	55,700	6,365,527	E. O. Lake	(a) R. E. Davies
Rhymney Valley, Mid Glamorgan	104,700	7,853,122	P. A. Bennett	S. Blackwell
South Pembrokeshire, Dyfed	40,800	7,317,166	D. R. Jones	Mrs. E. Hodgson
SWANSEA, West Glamorgan	187,000	19,814,33	A. K. B. Boatswain	(b) H. J. Morgan
§Taff-Ely, Mid Glamorgan	93,600	9,569,206	D. Gethin	(a) R. Cann
§Torfaen, Gwent	91,200	9,459,019	M. B. Mehta	(a) B. J. Cunningham
§Vale of Glamorgan, South Glamorgan	118,100	14,969,597	J. R. Gau	(a) B. D. J. Edmunds
§Wrexham Maelor, Clwyd	115,800	12,430,961	R. J. Dutton	(a) F. V. Robinson
§Ynys Môn (Isle of Anglesey), Gwynedd	70,100	7,967,550	E. L. Gibson	(a) R. G. Parry

PRINCIPAL WELSH CITIES

CARDIFF

CARDIFF (South Glamorgan), at the mouth of the rivers Taff, Rhymney and Ely, is the capital City of Wales and one of Britain's major administrative, commercial and office centres. It has many industries, including steel works, cigars and a flourishing port with a substantial and varied trade. There are many fine buildings in the civic centre started early this century which includes the City Hall, the National Museum of Wales, University Buildings, Law Courts, Welsh Office, County Hall, Police Headquarters and the Temple of Peace and Health. Also in the city are Llandaff Cathedral, the Welsh National Folk Museum at St. Fagans, Cardiff Castle, the New Theatre, the Sherman Theatre and the Cardiff College of Music and Drama. New buildings include St. David's Hall, a 2,000-seat concert and conference hall, and the Welsh National Ice Rink.

SWANSEA

SWANSEA (in Welsh, Abertawe) is a City and a seaport of West Glamorgan with its own municipal airport. The beautiful Gower Peninsula was brought within the City boundary under local government reform on April 1, 1974. The trade of the port includes coal, patent fuel, ores, and the import and export of oil. The municipal area is 60,511 acres.

The principal buildings are the Norman Castle (rebuilt in 1330), the Royal Institution of South Wales, founded in 1835 (containing Museum and Library), the University College at Singleton and the Guildhall, containing the Brangwyn panels. New buildings include the Industrial and Maritime Museum, the new Maritime Quarter and Marina and the leisure centre. Swansea was chartered by the Earl of Warwick, c. 1158–1184, and further charters were granted by King John, Henry III, Edward II, Edward III and James II, 2 from Cromwell and 1 from the Marcher Lord William de Breos.

THE KINGDOM OF SCOTLAND

Position and Extent.—The Kingdom of Scotland occupies the northern portion of the main island of Great Britain and includes the Inner and Outer Hebrides, and the Orkney, Shetland, and many other islands. The Kingdom lies between 60° 51′ 30″ and 54° 38′ N. latitude and between 1° 45′ 32″ and 6° 14′ W. longitude, its southern neighbour being the Kingdom of England, with the Atlantic Ocean on the N. and W., and the North Sea on the E. The greatest length of the mainland (Cape Wrath to the Mull of Galloway) is 274 miles, and the greatest breadth (Buchan Ness to Applecross) is 154 miles. The customary measurement of the island of Great Britain is from the site of John o' Groats house, near Duncansby Head, Caithness to Land's End, Cornwall, a total distance of 603 miles in a straight line and (approximately) 900 by road. The total area of the Kingdom is 30,414 square miles (land 29,761; inland water 653).

Population.—The population (1981 Census) was 5,130,735 (males 2,466,437; females 2,664,298). The average density of the population in 1981 was 168 persons per square mile. The population, mid 1987 estimate, was 5,112,000.

Relief.—There are three natural orographic divisions of Scotland. The Southern Uplands have their highest points in Merrick (2,766 feet), Rhinns of Kells (2,669 feet), and Cairnsmuir of Carsphairn (2,614 feet), in the west; and the Tweedsmuir Hills in the east (*Hartfell* 2,651 ft., *Dollar Law* 2,682 ft., *Broad Law* 2,756 ft.). The Central Lowlands, formed by the valleys of the Clyde, Forth and Tay, divide the Southern Uplands from the Northern Highlands, which extend almost from the extreme north of the mainland to the central lowlands, and are divided into a northern and southern system by the *Great Glen*. The Grampian Mountains, which entirely cover the southern Highland area, include in the west *Ben Nevis* (4,406 ft.), the highest point in the British Isles, and in the east the Cairngorm Mountains (*Cairn Gorm* 4,084 ft., *Braeriach* 4,248 ft., *Ben Macdui* 4,296 ft.). The north-western Highland area contains in the mountains of Wester and Eastern Ross *Carn Eige* (3,880 ft.) and *Sgurr na Lapaich* (3,775 ft.).

Created, like the Central Lowlands, by a major geological fault, the *Great Glen* (60 miles long) runs between Inverness and Fort William, and contains Loch Ness, Loch Oich and Loch Lochy. These are linked to each other and to the north-east and south-west coasts of Scotland by the Caledonian Canal, providing a navigable passage between the Moray Firth and the Inner Hebrides.

Hydrography.—The western coast of Scotland is fragmented by peninsulas and islands, and indented by fjords (sea-lochs), the longest of which is *Loch Fyne* (42 miles long) in Argyll. Although the east coast tends to be less fractured and lower, there are several great drowned inlets (firths), e.g. Firth of Forth, Firth of Tay, Moray Firth, as well as the Firth of Clyde in the west.

The lochs are the principal hydrographic feature of the Kingdom. The largest in the Kingdom and in Great Britain is *Loch Lomond* (27 square miles), in the Grampian valleys; the longest and deepest is *Loch Ness* (24 miles long and 800 feet deep), in the Great Glen; and Lochs Shin (20 miles) and Maree in the northern Highlands.

The longest river in Scotland is the *Tay* (117 miles), noted for its salmon. It flows into the North Sea, with Dundee on the estuary, which is spanned by the *Tay Bridge* (10,289 ft.) opened in 1887 and the *Tay Road Bridge* (7,365 ft.) opened in 1966. Other noted salmon rivers are the *Dee* (90 miles) which flows into the North Sea at Aberdeen, and the *Spey* (110 miles), the swiftest flowing river in the British Isles, which

flows into Moray Firth. The *Tweed*, which gave its name to the woollen cloth produced along its banks, marks in the lower stretches of its 96-mile course the border between Scotland and England.

The most important river commercially is the *Clyde* (106 miles), formed by the junction of the Daer and Portrail water, which flows through the city of Glasgow to the Firth of Clyde. During its course it passes over the picturesque Falls of Clyde, *Bonnington Linn* (30 ft.), *Corra Linn* (84 ft.), *Dundaff Linn* (10 ft.) and *Stonebyres Linn* (80 ft.), above and below Lanark. The *Forth* (66 miles), upon which stands Edinburgh, the capital, is spanned by the *Forth* (*Railway*) *Bridge* (1890), which is 5,330 feet long, and the *Forth* (*Road*) *Bridge* (1964), which has a total length of 6,156 ft. (over water) and a single span of 3,000 ft.

The highest waterfall in Scotland, and the British Isles, is *Eas a'Chùal Aluinn* with a total height of 658 ft., which falls from Glas Bheinn in Sutherland. The *Falls of Glomach*, on a head-stream of the Elchaig in Wester Ross, have a drop of 370 ft.

Gaelic Language.—According to the 1981 Census, 82,620 people, mainly in the Highlands and western coastal regions, were able to speak, read or write the Scottish form of Gaelic.

THE SCOTTISH ISLANDS

The Hebrides did not become part of the Kingdom of Scotland until 1266, when they were ceded to Alexander III by Magnus of Norway. Orkney and Shetland fell to the Scottish Crown as a pledge for the unpaid dowry of Margaret of Denmark, wife of James III, in 1468, the Danish claims to suzerainty being relinquished in 1590 when James VI married Anne of Denmark.

Orkney.—The Orkney Islands (total area 375½ square miles) lie about six miles north of the mainland, separated from it by the Pentland Firth. Of the 90 islands and islets (holms and skerries) in the group, about one-third are inhabited. The total population at the 1981 Census was 19,040; the 1981 populations of the islands shown here include those of smaller islands forming part of the same civil parish.

Mainland	14,299	Shapinsay	345
Eday	154	South Ronaldsay	1,188
Hoy and Graemsay	80	Stronsay	462
Papa Westray	94	Walls and Flotta	761
Rousay and Egilsay	264	Westray	741
Sanday and North Ronaldsay	652		

The islands are rich in Pictish and Scandinavian remains, the most notable being the Stone Age village of Skara Brae, the burial chamber of Maeshowe, the many brochs (Pictish towers) and St. Magnus Cathedral. Scapa Flow, between the Mainland and Hoy, was the war station of the British Grand Fleet from 1914–19 and the scene of the scuttling of the surrendered German High Seas Fleet (June 21, 1919).

Most of the islands are low-lying and fertile, and farming (principally beef cattle) is the main industry. Flotta, to the south of Scapa Flow, is now the site of the oil terminal for the Piper, Claymore and Tartan fields in the North Sea.

Capital.—Kirkwall (population 6,881) on Mainland.

Shetland.—The Shetland Islands (total area, 551 square miles; population (1981 Census) 27,271) lie about 50 miles north of the Orkneys, with Fair Isle about half way between the two groups. Out Stack, off Muckle Flugga, one mile north of Unst, is the most northern part of the British Isles (60° 51′ 30″ N. lat.). There are over 100 islands, of which 16 are inhabited.

Mainland	22,184	Muckle Roe	101
Bressay	335	Out Skerries	79
East and West Burra,		Papa Stour	29
and Trondra	930	Unst	1,206
Fair Isle	69	Whalsay	1,026
Fetlar	102	Yell	1,168
Foula	39		

Shetland's many archaeological sites include Jarlshof, Mousa and Clickhimin, and its long connection with Scandinavia has resulted in a strong Norse influence on its place names and dialect.

Industries include fishing, knitwear and farming. In addition to the fishing fleet there are fish processing factories, while the traditional handknitting of Fair Isle and Unst is supplemented now with machine knitted garments,. Farming is mainly crofting, with sheep being raised on the moorland and hills of the islands. Latterly the islands have become an important centre of the North Sea oil industry, with pipelines from the Brent and Ninian fields running to the terminal at Sullom Voe, the largest of its kind in Europe. Lerwick is the main centre for supply services for offshore oil exploration and development.

Capital.—Lerwick (population 7,901) on Mainland.

The Hebrides.—Until the closing years of the 13th century "The Hebrides" included other Scottish islands in the Firth of Clyde, the peninsula of Kintyre (Argyllshire), the Isle of Man, and the (Irish) Isle of Rathlin. The origin of the name is stated to be the Greek *Eboudai*, latinized as *Hebudes* by Pliny, and corrupted to its present form. The Norwegian name *Sudreyjar* (Southern Islands) was latinized as *Sodorenses*, a name that survives in the Anglican bishopric of Sodor and Man.

There are over 500 islands and islets, of which about 100 are inhabited, though mountainous terrain and extensive peat bogs mean that only a fraction of the total area is under cultivation. Stone, Bronze and Iron Age settlement has left many remains, including those at Callanish on Lewis, and Norse colonization has influenced language, customs and place-names. Occupations include farming (mostly crofting and stock-raising), fishing and the manufacture of tweeds and other woollens. Tourism is also an important factor in the economy.

The **Inner Hebrides** lie off the west coast of Scotland and relatively close to the mainland. The largest and best-known is *Skye* (area 643 sq. miles; pop. 8,139; chief town, Portree), which contains the Cuillin Hills (*Sgurr Alasdair* 3,257 feet), the Red Hills (*Beinn na Caillich* 2,403 feet) as well as *Bla Bheinn* (3,046 feet) and *The Storr* (2,358 feet). Skye is also famous as the refuge of the Young Pretender in 1746. Other islands in the Highland Region include *Raasay* (pop. 182) *Rum, Eigg* and *Muck*. Islands in the Strathclyde Region include *Arran* (pop. 4,726) containing *Goat Fell* (2,868 feet); *Coll* and *Tiree* (pop. 933); *Colonsay and Oronsay* (pop. 137); *Islay* (area 235 sq. miles; pop. 3,997); *Jura* (area 160 sq. miles; pop. 239) with a range of hills culminating in the Paps of Jura (*Beinn-an-Oir*, 2,576 feet, and *Beinn Chaolais*, 2,477 feet); *Mull* (area 367 sq. miles; pop. 2,605; chief town Tobermory) containing *Ben More* (3,171 feet).

The **Outer Hebrides**, separated from the mainland by the Minch, now form the Western Isles Islands Council area (area 1,119 sq. miles; pop. (1981 Census) 31,842). The main islands are *Lewis with Harris* (area 770 sq. miles, pop. 23,390), whose chief town, Stornoway (pop. 13,409), is the administrative headquarters; *North Uist* (pop. 1,454); *South Uist* (pop. 2,223); *Benbecula* (pop. 1,988) and *Barra* (pop. 1,232). Other inhabited islands include *Bernera* (292), *Berneray*

(134), *Eriskay* (219), *Grimsay* (206), *Scalpay* (461) and *Vatersay* (108).

EARLY HISTORY

Prehistoric Man.—The Picts, believed to be of non-Aryan origin, seem to have inhabited the whole of North Britain and to have spread over the north of Ireland. Remains are most frequent in Caithness and Sutherland and the Orkney Islands. Celts arrived from Belgic Gaul during the latter part of the Bronze Age and in the early Iron Age, and except in the extreme north of the mainland and in the islands, the civilization and speech of the people were definitely Celtic at the time of the Roman invasion of Britain.

The Roman Invasion.—In A.D. 79–80 Julius Agricola extended the Roman conquests in Britain by advancing into *Caledonia* and building a line of fortifications across the isthmus between the Forth and Clyde, but after a victory at *Mons Graupius* he was recalled. Hadrian's Wall, mostly complete by A.D. 130, marked the frontier until about A.D. 143 when the frontier moved north to the Forth-Clyde isthmus and was secured by the Antonine Wall. From about A.D. 155 the Antonine Wall was damaged by frequent attacks and by the close of the second century the northern limit of Roman Britain had receded to Hadrian's Wall.

The Scots.—After the withdrawal (or absorption) of the Roman garrison of Britain there were many years of tribal warfare between the Picts and Scots (the Gaelic tribe then dominant in Ireland), the Brythonic Waelisc (Welsh) of Strathclyde (southwest Scotland and Cumberland), and the Anglo-Saxons of Lothian. The Waelisc were isolated from their kinsmen in Wales by the victory of the West Saxons at Chester (613), and towards the close of the 9th century the Scots under *Kenneth Macalpine* became the dominant power in Caledonia. In the reign of Malcolm I (943–954) Strathclyde was brought into subjection, the English lowland kingdom (Lothian) being conquered by Malcolm II (1005–1034). From the late 11th century until the middle of the 16th there were constant wars between Scotland and England, the outstanding figures in the struggle being William Wallace, who defeated the English at Stirling Bridge (1297) and Robert Bruce, who won the victory of Bannockburn (1314). James IV and many of his nobles fell at the disastrous battle of Flodden (1513).

The Jacobite Revolts.—In 1603 James VI of Scotland succeeded Elizabeth I on the throne of England (his mother, Mary Queen of Scots, was the great-granddaughter of Henry VII), his successors reigning as Sovereigns of Great Britain, although political union of the two countries did not occur until 1707. After the abdication (by flight) in 1688 of James VII and II, the crown devolved upon William III (grandson of Charles I) and Mary (daughter of James VII and II). In 1689 Graham of Claverhouse "roused the Highlands" on behalf of James VII and II, but died after a military success at Killiecrankie. After the death of Anne (second daughter of James VII and II) the throne devolved upon George I (great-grandson of James VI and I). In 1715, armed risings on behalf of James Stuart (the Old Pretender) led to the indecisive battle of Sheriffmuir, but the Jacobite movement died down until 1745, when Charles Stuart (the Young Pretender) defeated the Royalist troops at Prestonpans and advanced to Derby in England (1746). From Derby, the adherents of "James VIII and III" (the title claimed for his father by Charles Stuart) fell back on the defensive, and the movement was finally crushed at Culloden (April 16, 1746).

LORD LIEUTENANTS IN SCOTLAND

Region	Title	Name
Borders	Berwickshire	Maj.-Gen. Sir John Swinton, K.C.V.O., O.B.E.
	Roxburgh, Ettrick and Lauderdale	The Duke of Buccleuch and Queensberry, K.T., V.R.D
	Tweeddale	Lt. Col. A. M. Sprot of Haystoun, M.C.
Central	Clackmannan	The Earl of Mar and Kellie
	Stirling and Falkirk	Lt. Col. J. Stirling of Garden, C.B.E., T.D.
Dumfries & Galloway	Dumfries	Capt. J. G. M. Home, T.D.
	The Stewartry of Kirkcudbright	Sir Michael Herries, O.B.E., M.C.
	Wigtown	Maj. E. S. Orr Ewing
Fife	Fife	The Earl of Elgin and Kincardine, K.T.
Grampian	Aberdeenshire	Capt. C. A. Farquharson
	Banffshire	J. A. S. McPherson, C.B.E.
	Kincardineshire	The Viscount of Arbuthnott, D.S.C., F.R.S.E.
	Morayshire	Capt. Sir Iain Tennant, K.T.
Highland	Caithness	The Viscount Thurso
	Inverness	Lt. Comdr. L. R. D. Mackintosh of Mackintosh, O.B.E.
	Nairn	The Earl of Leven and Melville
	Ross and Cromarty	Capt. R. W. K. Stirling of Fairburn, T.D.
	Sutherland	Col. A. MacD. Gilmour, O.B.E., M.C.
Lothian	East Lothian	Sir Hew Hamilton-Dalrymple, Bt., K.V.C.O.
	Midlothian	Sir John Dutton Clerk of Penicuik, Bt., C.B.E., V.R.D.
	West Lothian	The Earl of Morton
Strathclyde	Argyll and Bute	The Lord Maclean, K.T., P.C., G.C.V.O., K.B.E.
	Ayr and Arran	Col. B. M. Knox, M.C., T.D.
	Dunbartonshire	Brig. A. S. Pearson, C.B., D.S.O., O.B.E., M.C., T.D.
	Lanarkshire	Col. The Lord Clydesmuir, K.T., C.B., M.B.E., T.D.
	Renfrewshire	Maj. J. D. M. Crichton Maitland
Tayside	Angus	The Earl of Airlie, K.T., G.C.V.O., P.C.
	Perth and Kinross	Maj. D. H. Butter, M.C.
Orkney	Orkney	Col. R. A. A. S. Macrae, M.B.E.
Shetland	Shetland	M. M. Shearer
Western Isles	Western Isles	The Earl Granville, M.C.

NOTE.—The Lord Provosts of the four city districts of Aberdeen, Dundee, Edinburgh and Glasgow are Lord Lieutenants for those districts *ex officio*.

PRECEDENCE IN SCOTLAND

THE SOVEREIGN.

The Prince Philip, Duke of Edinburgh.

The Lord High Commissioner to the General Assembly (while that Assembly is sitting).

The Duke of Rothesay (eldest son of the Sovereign).

The Sovereign's younger sons.

The Sovereign's cousins.

Lords Lieutenant of Counties, Lord Provosts of Counties of Cities, and Sheriffs Principal (successively—within their own localities and during holding of office).

Lord Chancellor of Great Britain.

Moderator of the General Assembly of the Church of Scotland.

The Prime Minister.

Keepers of the Great Seal and of the Privy Seal (successively—if Peers).

Hereditary Lord High Constable of Scotland.

Hereditary Master of the Household.

Dukes (successively) of England, Scotland, Great Britain and United Kingdom (including Ireland since date of Union).

Eldest sons of Dukes of the Blood Royal.

Marquesses, in same order as Dukes.

Dukes' eldest sons.

Earls, in order as Dukes.

Younger sons of Dukes of Blood Royal.

Marquesses' eldest sons.

Dukes' younger sons.

Keepers of the Great Seal and of the Privy Seal (successively if not Peers).

Lord Justice General.

Lord Clerk Register.

Lord Advocate.

Lord Justice Clerk.

Viscounts, in order as Dukes.

Earls' eldest sons.

Marquesses' younger sons.

Lord-Barons, in order as Dukes.

Viscounts' eldest sons.

Earls' younger sons.

Lord-Barons' eldest sons.

Knights of the Garter.

Privy Counsellors.

Senators of Coll. of Justice (Lords of Session).

Viscounts' younger sons.

Lord-Barons' younger sons.

Sons of Life Peers.

Baronets.

Knights of the Thistle.

Knights Grand Cross, Grand Commander, and Knight Commanders, as in England.

Solicitor-General for Scotland.

Lord Lyon King of Arms.

Sheriffs Principal (except as shown in column 1).

Knights Bachelor.

Sheriffs.

Companions of Orders, as in England.

Commanders of Royal Victorian and British Empire Orders.

Eldest sons of younger sons of Peers.

Companions of Distinguished Service Order.

Lieutenants of Royal Victorian Order.

Officers of British Empire Order.

Baronets' eldest sons.

Knights' eldest sons successively (from Garter to Bachelor).

Members, Royal Victorian Order.

Members, British Empire Order.

Baronets' younger sons.

Knights' younger sons.

Queen's Counsel.

Barons-feudal.

Esquires.

Gentlemen.

SCOTTISH REGIONAL AND ISLANDS COUNCILS

AREA AND POPULATION

Region	Administrative Headquarters	Area (*hectares*)	Population	Regional community charge per head 1989 £	Community water charge per head 1989 £
Borders	Newtown St. Boswells	467,158	102,592	174·00	31·00
Central	Stirling	263,609	272,077	198·00	15·00
Dumfries and Galloway ..	Dumfries	637,006	147,036	178·50	28·00
Fife	Glenrothes	130,700	344,590	220·00	18·00
Grampian	Aberdeen	870,400	502,863	189·00	30·00
Highland	Inverness	2,539,122	201,866	180·00	20·00
Lothian	Edinburgh	175,509	741,179	287·00	18·00
Orkney	Kirkwall	97,581	19,455	122·00	26·00
Shetland	Lerwick	143,268	22,939	90·76	23·40
Strathclyde	Glasgow	1,385,716	2,332,537	200·00	19·00
Tayside	Dundee	750,318	393,748	220·00	21·00
Western Isles	Stornoway, Lewis	7,717,381	21,413	137·00	34·00

CHIEF EXECUTIVES, DIRECTORS OF FINANCE AND CHAIRMEN

Region	Chief Executive	Director of Finance	Convener
Borders	K. J. Clark, C.B.E.	P. Jeary	T. Hunter, C.B.E.
Central	J. Broadfoot	S. C. Craig	C. Snedden, O.B.E.
Dumfries and Galloway	N. W. D. McIntosh	J. C. Stewart	J. V. M. Jameson
Fife	Dr. J. A. Markland	A. E. Taylor	R. Gough
Grampian	J. D. Macnaughton	A. McLean	Dr. G. Hadley
Highland	R. H. Stevenson	J. W. Bremner	A. J. Russell
Lothian	G. M. Bowie	D. B. Chynoweth	J. Cook
Orkney	R. H. Gilbert	R. H. Gilbert	E. R. Eunson
Shetland	M. A. Gerrard	M. E. Green	E. Thomason, O.B.E.
Strathclyde	R. Calderwood	A. Gillespie	J. Jennings
Tayside	J. A. Wallace	I. B. McIver	R. M. Tosh
Western Isles	Dr. G. Macleod	D. G. Macleod	A. Matheson

PRINCIPAL SCOTTISH CITIES

ABERDEEN

ABERDEEN, 130 miles north-east of Edinburgh, received its charter as a Royal Burgh from William the Lion in 1179. Scotland's third largest city, Aberdeen is the second largest Scottish fishing port and the main European centre for offshore oil exploration. It is also an ancient university town and distinguished research centre. Other industries include engineering, shipbuilding, food processing, textiles, paper manufacturing and chemicals. Places of interest: King's College, St. Machar's Cathedral, Brig o' Balgownie, Duthie Park and Winter Gardens, the Kirk of St. Nicholas, Mercat Cross, Marischal College and Anthropological Museum, Provost Skene's House, Art Gallery, James Dun's House (children's museum) and Provost Ross's House (maritime museum).

DUNDEE

DUNDEE, a Royal Burgh, is situated on the north bank of the Tay estuary. The city's port and dock installations are important to the offshore oil industry and the airport also provides servicing facilities. Principal industries include textiles, computers and other electronic industries, lasers, printing, tyre manufacture, food processing, carpets, engineering and clothing manufacture. Six sites have Enterprise Zone status, including the Technology Park, airport and port. The unique City Churches—three churches under one roof, together with the 15th century St. Mary's Tower—are the most prominent architectural feature. R.R.S. *Discovery*, the ship which took Captain Scott to the Antarctic and which was built in Dundee in 1901, is now berthed in Victoria Dock.

EDINBURGH

EDINBURGH, the capital of and seat of government in Scotland, has a municipal area of 100·6 sq. miles. The city is built on a group of hills and contains in Princes Street one of the most beautiful thoroughfares in the world. The principal buildings are the Castle, which includes St. Margaret's Chapel, the oldest building in Edinburgh, and near it, the Scottish National War Memorial; the Palace of Holyroodhouse; Parliament House, the present seat of the judicature; two universities (Edinburgh and Heriot-Watt); St. Giles' Cathedral (restored 1879–83); St. Mary's (Scottish Episcopal) Cathedral (Sir Gilbert Scott); the General Register House (Robert Adam): the National and the Signet Libraries; the National Gallery; the Royal Scottish Academy; and the National Portrait Gallery.

GLASGOW

GLASGOW, a Royal Burgh, is the principal commercial and industrial centre in Scotland. The city occupies the north and south banks of the Clyde, formerly one of the chief commercial estuaries in the world. The principal industries include engineering, aero and marine engines, chemicals, printing, etc. The city has also developed recently as a tourism and conference centre. The chief buildings are the 13th century Gothic Cathedral, the University (Sir Gilbert Scott), the City Chambers, Pollok House, the School of Art (Mackintosh), Kelvingrove Art Galleries, the Burrell Collection museum and the Mitchell Library. The city is home of the Scottish National Orchestra, Scottish Opera, Scottish Ballet, etc.

SCOTTISH DISTRICT COUNCILS

District	Administrative Headquarters	Population	District community charge per head 1989 £	Chief Executive	Chairman (a) Convener (b) Provost (c) Lord Provost
Aberdeen City (5)	Aberdeen	209,250	85·00	J. J. K. Smith‡	(c) R. A. Robertson
Angus (9)............	Forfar	94,822	52·00	P. B. Regan	(b) B. M. C. Milne
Annandale and Eskdale (3).........	Annan	36,416	47·00	J. A. Whitecross	(a) F. Park
Argyll and Bute (8) ...	Lochgilphead	65,993	58·00	M. A. J. Gossip	W. R. Hunter
Badenoch and Strathspey (6)......	Kingussie	10,807	35·00	H. G. McCulloch	J. A. McCook
Banff and Buchan (5) .	Banff	83,708	56·70	{ R. W. Jackson D. Urquhart§	(a) W. R. Cruick-shank
Bearsden and Milngavie (8)	Bearsden	40,365	79·00	I. C. Laurie	(b) Mrs. J. Cameron
Berwickshire (1)	Duns	18,833	31·00	R. A. Christie	Capt. J. Evans
Caithness (6).........	Wick	27,098	25·00	A. Beattie	(a) J. M. Young
Clackmannan (2)	Alloa	47,412	87·00	I. F. Smith	(a) W. G. Watt
Clydebank (8)	Clydebank	48,203	78·00	J. T. McNally	(b) D. S. Grainger
Clydesdale (8)	Lanark	58,324	82·00	P. W. Daniels	(a) Mrs. E. Logan
Cumbernauld and Kilsyth (8).........	Cumbernauld	62,489	56·00	J. Hutton	(b) Ms. R. McKenna
Cumnock and Doon Valley (8)..........	Cumnock	43,400	57·00	D. T. Hemmings, O.B.E.	(a) J. Hodge, B.E.M.
Cunninghame (8).....	Irvine	137,096	59·00	B. Devine	(a) J. Carson
Dumbarton (8)	Dumbarton	79,704	79·00	A. Nisbet	(b) W. Petrie
Dundee City (9)	Dundee	175,748	83·00	J. F. Hoey	(c) T. Mitchell
Dunfermline (4)	Dunfermline	129,049	55·00	G. Brown	(a) J. Cameron
East Kilbride (8)......	East Kilbride	81,700	99·00	D. J. Liddell	(b) Ms. H. Biggins
East Lothian (7)	Haddington	82,821	69·00	M. Duncan	G. M. Wanless
Eastwood (8)	Giffnock	57,613	63·00	M. D. Henry	(b) Mrs. J. Y. Macfie
Edinburgh City (7) ...	Edinburgh	438,232	87·00	A. Hepburn	(c) Rt. Hon. Eleanor T. McLaughlin
Ettrick and Lauderdale (1)	Galashiels	33,500	42·00	C. M. Anderson	(b) A. L. Tulley, M.B.E.
Falkirk (2)...........	Falkirk	143,500	46·00	J. P. H. Paton	(b) D. Goldie
Glasgow City (8)	Glasgow	715,621	87·00	S. F. Hamilton	(c) Rt. Hon. Susan Baird
Gordon (5)...........	Inverurie	73,000	44·00	M. C. Barron	(b) J. Lawrence
Hamilton (8)	Hamilton	106,200	72·00	A. Baird	(b) R. Gibb
Inverclyde (8)	Greenock	95,192	72·00	I. C. Wilson, O.B.E.	(b) F. A. McGlone
Inverness (6)........	Inverness	61,478	26·00	B. Wilson	(b) A. G. Sellar
Kilmarnock and Loudoun (8)	Kilmarnock	81,186	50·00	R. W. Jenner	(a) J. Mills
Kincardine and Deeside (5)........	Stonehaven	48,910	32·00	T. Hyder	(a) D. J. Mackenzie
Kirkcaldy (4)	Kirkcaldy	147,963	60·00	{ J. M. Smith H. Wilson§	(a) R. King
Kyle and Carrick (8) ..	Ayr	113,081	89·00	I. R. D. Smillie†	(b) D. MacNeill
Lochaber (6)	Fort William	19,000	37·00	D. A. B. Blair	D. P. MacFarlane
Midlothian (7)	Dalkeith	81,440	59·00	T. Muir	(a) D. Lennie
Monklands (8)	Coatbridge	104,818	74·00	M. V. P. Hart	(b) E. Cairns
Moray (5).............	Elgin	85,071	42·00	J. P. C. Bell	(a) E. Aldridge
Motherwell (8)	Motherwell	146,784	86·00	J. Bonomy	(b) J. Armstrong
Nairn (6)	Nairn	10,348	28·00	A. M. Kerr†	(b) S. A. Macarthur
Nithsdale (3)	Dumfries	57,384	39·00	W. W. Japp	(b) E. D. Gibson
North-East Fife (4) ...	Cupar	66,720	82·00	R. G. Brotherton	Dr. C. R. Sneddon
Perth and Kinross (9) .	Perth	124,671	58·00	J. E. D. Cormie	(b) A. Murray
Renfrew (8)	Paisley	200,194	76·00	A. I. Cowe*	(b) G. Murray
Ross and Cromarty (6)	Dingwall	47,897	39·00	D. Sinclair	(a) G. D. Finlayson
Roxburgh (1)	Hawick	35,060	42·00	K. W. Cramond	G. Yellowlees
Skye and Lochalsh (6).	Portree	11,435	25·00	D. H. Noble	J. F. Munro
Stewartry (3)	Kirkcudbright	23,136	37·00	J. C. Howie	(a) J. Nelson
Stirling (2)	Stirling	81,436	97·00	R. W. Black	(a) J. Hendry
Strathkelvin (8)......	Kirkintilloch	89,475	80·00	C. Mallon	(b) R. M. Coyle
Sutherland (6)	Golspie	13,199	6·00	J. Allison†	D. I. MacRae
Tweeddale (1)	Peebles	14,850	43·00	G. H. T. Garvie	M. A. R. Maher
West Lothian (7)	Bathgate	141,684	54·00	W. N. Fordyce	(a) D. McCauley
Wigtown (3)	Stranraer	30,410	40·00	A. Geddes	J. Brown

‡ Town Clerk.   § Joint Chief Officers.   † Director of Administration.   * Managing Director.
REGIONS.—(1) Borders; (2) Central; (3) Dumfries and Galloway; (4) Fife; (5) Grampian; (6) Highland; (7) Lothian; (8) Strathclyde; (9) Tayside.

CHIEFS OF CLANS AND NAMES IN SCOTLAND

THE ROYAL HOUSE: H.M. The Queen

AGNEW: Sir Crispin Agnew of Lochnaw, Bt., 6 Palmerston Road, Edinburgh.

ANSTRUTHER: Sir Ralph Anstruther of that Ilk, Bt., K.C.V.O., M.C., Balcaskie, Pittenweem, Fife.

ARBUTHNOTT: The Viscount of Arbuthnott, C.B.E., D.S.C., Arbuthnott House, Laurencekirk, Kincardineshire.

BARCLAY: Peter C. Barclay of that Ilk, Gatemans, Stratford St. Mary, Colchester, Essex.

BORTHWICK: The Lord Borthwick, T.D., Crookston, Heriot, Midlothian.

BOYD: The Lord Kilmarnock, Casa de Mondragon, Ronda (Malaga), Spain.

BOYLE: The Earl of Glasgow, Kelburn, Fairlie, Ayrshire.

BRODIE: Ninian Brodie of Brodie, Brodie Castle, Forres, Morayshire.

BRUCE: The Earl of Elgin and Kincardine, K.T., Broomhall, Dunfermline, Fife.

BUCHAN: David S. Buchan of Auchmacoy, Auchmacoy, Ellon, Aberdeenshire.

BURNETT: J. C. A. Burnett of Leys, Crathes Castle, Kincardineshire.

CAMERON: Col. Sir Donald Cameron of Lochiel, K.T., C.V.O., T.D., Achnacarry, Spean Bridge, Invernessshire.

CAMPBELL: The Duke of Argyll, Inveraray, Argyll.

CARMICHAEL: Richard J. Carmichael of Carmichael, Carmichael, Thankerton, Biggar, Lanarkshire.

CARNEGIE: The Earl of Southesk, K.C.V.O., Kinnaird Castle, Brechin.

CATHCART: Maj.-Gen. The Earl Cathcart, C.B., D.S.O., M.C., 2 Pembroke Gardens, W8.

CHARTERIS: The Earl of Wemyss and March, K.T., Gosford House, Longniddry, East Lothian.

CLAN CHATTAN: M. K. Mackintosh of Clan Chattan, Maxwell Park, Gwelo, Zimbabwe.

CHISHOLM: Alastair Chisholm of Chisholm (*The Chisholm*), Silver Willows, Bury St. Edmunds.

COCHRANE: The Earl of Dundonald, Lochnell Castle, Ledaig, Argyllshire.

COLQUHOUN: Sir Ivar Colquhoun of Luss, Bt., Camstraddan, Luss, Dunbartonshire.

CRANSTOUN: Lt.-Col. Alastair Cranstoun of that Ilk, M.C., Corehouse, Lanarkshire.

CRICHTON: Charles Crichton of that Ilk, Monzie, Perth.

DARROCH: Capt. Duncan Darroch of Gourock, The Red House, Branksome Park Road, Camberley, Surrey.

DRUMMOND: The Earl of Perth, P.C., Stobhall, Perth.

DUNBAR: Sir Jean Dunbar of Mochrum, Bt., 45–55 39th Street, Long Island City, New York.

DUNDAS: David D. Dundas of Dundas, 8 Derna Road, Kenwyn 7700, South Africa.

DURIE: Raymond V. D. Durie of Durie, Court House, Pewsey, Wilts.

ELIOTT: (vacant).

ERSKINE: The Earl of Mar and Kellie, Claremont House, Alloa.

FARQUHARSON: Capt. A. A. C. Farquharson of Invercauld, M.C., Invercauld, Braemar.

FERGUSSON: Sir Charles Fergusson of Kilkerran, Bt., Kilkerran, Maybole, Ayrshire.

FORBES: The Lord Forbes, K.B.E., Balforbes, Alford, Aberdeenshire.

FORSYTH: Alistair Forsyth of that Ilk, Ethie Castle, by Arbroath, Angus.

FRASER: The Lady Saltoun, Cairnbulg Castle, Fraserburgh, Aberdeenshire.

FRASER (OF LOVAT)*: The Lord Lovat, D.S.O., M.C., T.D., Balblair House, Beauly, Inverness-shire.

GAYRE: Lt.-Col. Robert Gayre of Gayre and Nigg, 1–3 Gloucester Lane, Edinburgh.

GORDON: The Marquess of Huntly, Aboyne Castle, Aberdeenshire.

GRAHAM: The Duke of Montrose, Auchmar, Drymen, Stirlingshire.

GRANT: The Lord Strathspey, 111 Elms Ride, West Wittering, W. Sussex.

HAIG: The Earl Haig, O.B.E., Bemersyde, Melrose, Roxburghshire.

HALDANE: Alexander N. C. Haldane of Gleneagles, Auchterarder, Perthshire.

HANNAY: Ramsey W. R. Hannay of Kirkdale and of that Ilk, Cardoness House, Gatehouse-of-Fleet, Kirkcudbrightshire.

HAY: The Earl of Erroll, Wolverton Farm, Wolverton, Basingstoke, Hants.

HENDERSON: John W. P. Henderson of Fordell, 7 Owen Street, Toowoomba, Queensland, Australia.

HUNTER: Neil A. Hunter of Hunterston, Tour d'Escas, Carretera d'Escas, La Massana, Andorra.

IRVINE OF DRUM: C. F. Irvine of Drum, 29 Forest Road, Hoylake, Wirral, Merseyside.

JARDINE: Sir Alexander Jardine of Applegirth, Bt., Ash House, Thwaites, Millom, Cumbria.

JOHNSTONE: The Earl of Annandale and Hartfell, Raehills, Lockerbie, Dumfriesshire.

KEITH: The Earl of Kintore, Glenton House, Rickarton, Stonehaven, Kincardineshire.

KENNEDY: The Marquess of Ailsa, O.B.E., Blanefield, Kirkoswald, Ayrshire.

KERR: The Marquess of Lothian, K.C.V.O., Monteviot, Ancrum, Roxburghshire.

KINCAID: Mrs. Heather V. Kincaid of Kincaid, 4A Bristol Gardens, Brighton, E. Sussex.

LAMONT: Peter N. Lamont of that Ilk, St. Patrick's College, Manley, N.S.W. 2095, Australia.

LEASK: Madam Leask of Leask, 1 Vincent Road, Sheringham, Norfolk.

LENNOX: Dennis P. H. Lennox of that Ilk, Pools Farm, Downton on the Rock, Ludlow, Shropshire.

LESLIE: The Earl of Rothes, Tanglewood, West Tytherley, Salisbury, Wilts.

LINDSAY: The Earl of Crawford and Balcarres, P.C., Balcarres, Colinsburgh, Fife.

LOCKHART: Angus H. Lockhart of the Lee, Newholme, Dunsyre, Lanark.

LUMSDEN: Gillem Lumsden of that Ilk and Blanerne, Kinderslegh, Bois Avenue, Chesham Bois, Amersham, Bucks.

MCBAIN: J. H. McBain of McBain, 7025, North Finger Rock Place, Tucson, Arizona, U.S.A.

MALCOLM (MACCALLUM): Robin N. L. Malcolm of Poltalloch, Duntrune Castle, Lochgilphead, Argyll.

MACDONALD: The Lord Macdonald (*The Macdonald of Macdonald*), Ostaig House, Skye.

MACDONALD OF CLANRANALD*: Ranald A. Macdonald of Clanranald, 55 Compton Road, N1.

MACDONALD OF SLEAT (CLAN HUSTEAIN)*: Sir Ian Bosville Macdonald of Sleat, Bt., Thorpe Hall, Rudston, Driffield, N. Humberside.

MACDONELL OF GLENGARRY*: Air Cdre. Aeneas R. MacDonell of Glengarry, C.B., D.F.C., Elonbank, Castle Street, Fortrose, Ross-shire.

MACDOUGALL: Madam Coline MacDougall of MacDougall, Dunollie, Argyll.

MACDOWELL: Fergus D. H. Macdowell of Garthland, 16 Tower Road, Nepean, Ontario, Canada.

MACGREGOR: Sir Gregor MacGregor of MacGregor, Bt., Bannatyne, Newtyle, Angus.

MACKAY: The Lord Reay, 11 Wilton Crescent, SW1.

MACKENZIE: The Earl of Cromartie, M.C., T.D., Castle Leod, Strathpeffer, Ross-shire.

MACKINNON: Madam Anne Mackinnon of Mackinnon, 16 Purleigh Road, Bridgewater, Somerset.

MACKINTOSH: The Mackintosh of Mackintosh, O.B.E., Moy Hall, Inverness.

MACLACHLAN: Madam Marjorie MacLachlan of MacLachlan, Castle Lachlan, Argyll.

MACLAREN: Donald MacLaren of MacLaren and Achleskine, British Military Government, Berlin (B.F.P.O. 45).

MACLEAN: The Lord Maclean, K.T., G.C.V.O., K.B.E., P.C., Duart Castle, Mull.

MACLENNAN: Ronald G. MacLennan of MacLennan, The Old Mill, Dores, Inverness.

MACLEOD: J. MacLeod of MacLeod, Dunvegan Castle, Skye.

MACMILLAN: George MacMillan of MacMillan, Finlaystone, Langbank, Renfrewshire.

MACNAB: J. C. Macnab of Macnab (*The Macnab*), Finlarig, Killin, Perthshire.

MACNAGHTEN: Sir Patrick Macnaghten of Macnaghten and Dundarave, Bt., Dundarave, Bushmills, Co. Antrim.

MACNEACAIL: Iain Macneacail of Macneacail and Scorrybreac, 12 Fox Street, Ballina, N.S.W., Australia.

MACNEIL OF BARRA: Ian R. Macneil of Barra (*The Macneil of Barra*), Kisimul Castle, Barra.

MACPHERSON: Hon. Sir William Macpherson of Cluny, T.D., Newtown Castle, Blairgowrie, Perthshire.

MACTHOMAS: Andrew P. C. MacThomas of Finegand, c/o The Clan MacThomas Society, 19 Warriston Avenue, Edinburgh 3.

MAITLAND: The Earl of Lauderdale, 12 St. Vincent Street, Edinburgh.

MAKGILL: The Viscount of Oxfuird, Hill House, St. Mary Bourne, Andover, Hants.

MAR: The Countess of Mar, St. Michael's Farm, Great Witley, Worcs.

MARJORIBANKS: William Marjoribanks of that Ilk, Kirklands of Forglen, Turriff, Aberdeenshire.

MATHESON: Sir Torquhil Matheson of Matheson, Bt., Sanderwick Court, Frome, Somerset.

MENZIES: David R. Menzies of Menzies, 20 Nardina Crescent, Dalkeith, Western Australia.

MOFFAT: Francis Moffat of that Ilk, Redacres, Moffat, Dumfriesshire.

MONCREIFFE: (vacant).

MONTGOMERIE: The Earl of Eglinton and Winton, The Dutch House, West Green, Hartley Wintney, Hants.

MORRISON: Dr. Iain M. Morrison of Ruchdi, Todhurst Farm, Lake Lane, Barnham, W. Sussex.

MUNRO: Patrick G. Munro of Foulis, T.D., Foulis Castle, Ross.

MURRAY: The Duke of Atholl, Blair Castle, Blair Atholl, Perthshire.

NICOLSON: The Lord Carnock, 90 Whitehall Court, SW1.

OGILVY: The Earl of Airlie, K.T., G.C.V.O., P.C., Cortachy Castle, Kirriemuir, Angus.

RAMSAY: The Earl of Dalhousie, K.T., G.C.V.O., G.B.E., M.C., Brechin Castle, Angus.

RATTRAY: James S. Rattray of Rattray, Craighall, Rattray, Perthshire.

ROBERTSON: Alexander G. H. Robertson of Struan (*Struan-Robertson*), The Breach Farm, Goudhurst Road, Cranbrook, Kent.

ROLLO: The Lord Rollo, Pitcairns, Dunning, Perthshire.

ROSE: Miss Elizabeth Rose of Kilravock, Kilravock Castle, Croy, Inverness.

ROSS: David C. Ross of that Ilk, The Old Schoolhouse, Fettercairn, Kincardineshire.

RUTHVEN: The Earl of Gowrie, P.C., Castlemartin, Kilcullen, Co. Kildare, Republic of Ireland.

SCOTT: The Duke of Buccleuch and Queensberry, K.T., V.R.D., Bowhill, Selkirk.

SCRYMGEOUR: The Earl of Dundee, Birkhill, Cupar, Fife.

SEMPILL: The Lady Sempill, Druminnor Castle, Rhynie, Aberdeenshire.

SHAW: John Shaw of Tordarroch, Newhall, Balblair, By Conon Bridge, Ross-shire.

SINCLAIR: The Earl of Caithness, Finstock Manor, Finstock, Oxon.

STIRLING: Fraser J. Stirling of Cader, 17 Park Row, Farnham, Surrey.

SUTHERLAND: The Countess of Sutherland, House of Tongue, Brora, Sutherland.

SWINTON: W. F. H. Swinton of that Ilk, 23301 8th Avenue S.S., Calgary, Alberta, Canada.

URQUHART: Kenneth T. Urquhart of that Ilk, 4713 Orleans Boulevard, Jefferson, Louisiana, U.S.A.

WALLACE: Lt.-Col. M. R. Wallace of that Ilk, Hilton of Gask, Auchterarder, Perthshire.

WEDDERBURN OF THAT ILK: The Master of Dundee, Birkhill, Cupar, Fife.

WEMYSS: David Wemyss of that Ilk, Invermay, Forteviot, Perthshire.

Only chiefs of *whole* Names or Clans are included, except certain special instances (marked *), who though not chiefs of a "whole name", were, or are, for some reason, independent. (*e.g.* the Macdonald forfeiture), independent. Under decision (*Campbell-Gray*, 1950) that a bearer of a "double or triple-barrelled" surname cannot be held chief of a part of such, several others cannot be included in the list at present.

NEW TOWNS IN GREAT BRITAIN

Commission for the New Towns. Glen House, Stag Place, SW1E 5AJ.—The Commission was established under the New Towns Act, 1959, its remit is to (a) take over and, with a view to its eventual disposal, to hold, manage and turn to account the property of Development Corporations transferred to the Commission and (b) as soon as it considers it expedient to do so, to dispose of property so transferred and any other property held by it. In carrying out its remit the Commission must have due regard to the convenience and welfare of persons residing, working or carrying on business there and, until disposal, the maintenance and enhancement of the value of the land held and return obtained from it. The Commission has such responsibilities in Basildon, Bracknell, Central Lancashire, Corby, Crawley, Harlow, Hatfield, Hemel Hempstead, Northampton, Peterborough, Redditch, Skelmersdale, Stevenage, Warrington and Runcorn, Washington and Welwyn Garden City. The Commission has minimal responsibilities (principally financial and litigation) in Aycliffe and Peterlee and Cwmbran following the wind-up of their Development Corporations in 1988.

Chairman, Sir Neil Shields, M.C.
Deputy Chairman, Sir Reginald Eyre.
Members, R. B. Caws, C.B.E.; W. J. Mackenzie, O.B.E.; P. M. Vine, C.B.E.; Sir Gordon Roberts, C.B.E.; The Lord Bellwin; E. G. Barratt; M. H. Mallinson; R. W. P. Luff.
Chief Executive, D. M. Woodhall.
Director of Estates and Technical Services, H. J. M. Thomas.
Director of Finance, Administrative and Legal Services, G. T. C. Probart.

BASILDON, Essex.—*Executive Officer,* H. Bacon. *Offices,* Gifford House, London Road, Bowers Gifford, Basildon SS13 2EX.

BRACKNELL, Berks.—Glen House, SW1E 5AJ.

CENTRAL LANCASHIRE, Lancs.—*Executive Officer,* B. Birtwistle. *Offices,* Cuerden Pavilion, Shady Lane, Bamber Bridge, Preston PR5 6AZ.

CORBY, Northants.—*Executive Officer,* J. G. Lloyd. *Offices,* Chisholm House, 9 Queen's Square, Corby NN17 1PA.

CRAWLEY, Sussex.—Glen House, SW1E 5AJ.

HARLOW, Essex.—Glen House, SW1E 5AJ.

HATFIELD, Herts.—Glen House, SW1E 5AJ.

HEMEL HEMPSTEAD, Herts.—Glen House, SW1E 5AJ.

NORTHAMPTON.—*Executive Officer,* I. McKay. *Offices,* Highfield House, Headless Cross Drive, Redditch B97 5EW.

PETERBOROUGH, Cambs.—*Executive Officer,* P. Way. *Offices,* Stuart House, City Road, Peterborough PE1 1UJ.

REDDITCH, Worcs.—*Executive Officer,* I. McKay. *Offices,* Highfield House, Headless Cross Drive, Redditch B97 5EU.

SKELMERSDALE, Lancs.—*Executive Officer,* J. Leigh. *Offices,* Pennylands, Skelmersdale WN8 8AR.

STEVENAGE, Herts.—Glen House, SW1E 5AJ.

WARRINGTON AND RUNCORN, Cheshire.—*Executive Officer,* J. Leigh. *Offices,* New Town House, Buttermarket Street, Warrington WA1 2LF.

WASHINGTON, Tyne and Wear.— *Executive Officer,* J. Edwards. *Offices,* Usworth Hall, Stephenson, District 12, Washington NE37 3HS.

WELWYN GARDEN CITY, Herts.—Glen House, SW1E 5AJ.

DEVELOPMENT CORPORATIONS

England and Wales

MILTON KEYNES, Bucks.—Formed 1967. *Chairman,* Lord Chilver, F.R.S. *General Manager,* F. C. Henshaw. *Offices,* Saxon Court, 502 Avebury Boulevard, Central Milton Keynes, Milton Keynes MK9 3HS. Area, 22,000 acres. Population, 143,000. Estimated eventual population, 200,000.

TELFORD, Shropshire.—Formed 1963. *Chairman,* F. J. Jones. *General Manager,* M. D. Morgan. *Offices,* Priorslee Hall, Telford, Salop TF2 9NT. Area, 19,300 acres. Population, 116,000. Estimated eventual population, 130,000

DEVELOPMENT BOARD FOR RURAL WALES.—Formed 1977. *Chairman,* G. Davies. *Offices,* Ladywell House, Newtown, Powys SY16 1JB.

Scotland

CUMBERNAULD, Strathclyde.—Formed 1956. *Chairman,* D. W. Mitchell, C.B.E.. *Chief Executive,* D. W. Anderson, C.B.E. *Headquarters,* Cumbernauld House, Cumbernauld G67 3JH. Area, 7,788 acres. Population, 49,200. Estimated eventual population, 55,000.

EAST KILBRIDE, Strathclyde.—Formed 1947. *Chairman,* J. A. Denholm. *Managing Director,* G. B. Young, C.B.E. *Offices,* Atholl House, East Kilbride, Glasgow G74 1LU. Area, 10,250 acres. Population, 69,200. Estimated eventual population not known.

GLENROTHES, Fife.—Formed 1948. *Chairman,* Prof. C. Blake. *Chief Executive,* W. M. Cracknell. *Offices,* Unicorn House, Falkland Place, Glenrothes KY7 5PD. Area, 5,765 acres. Population, 38,070. Estimated eventual population, 45,000.

IRVINE, Ayrshire.—Formed, 1966. *Chairman,* A. R. Belch, C.B.E. *Managing Director,* Brig. R. A. Rickets. *Offices,* Perceton House, Irvine, Ayrshire KA11 2AL. Area, 12,404 acres. Population, 56,000. Estimated eventual population, 65,000.

LIVINGSTON, West Lothian.—Formed, 1962. *Chairman,* R. S. Watt. *Chief Executive,* J. A. Pollock. *Offices,* Sidlaw House, Almondvale, Livingston, West Lothian EH54 6QA. Area, 6,868 acres. Population, 41,400. Estimated eventual population, 70,000.

NORTHERN IRELAND

(For geographical and historical notes on Ireland, see Index)

The usually resident population of Northern Ireland, as revised, at the 1981 Census was 1,556,039 (males, 761,882; females, 794,157) compared with a total population of 1,536,065 at the Census of 1971. (N.B. This revised figure takes account of the population effect of non-enumerated households, estimated at 74,000 persons.) In 1981 the number of persons in the various religious denominations (expressed as percentages of the total usually resident population) were: Roman Catholic, 28·0; Presbyterian, 22·9; Church of Ireland, 19·0; Methodist, 4·0; others 7·6; not stated, 18·5. Northern Ireland has a total area of 5,452 sq. miles (land, 5,206 sq. miles; inland water and tideways, 246 sq. miles) with a density of population of 282 persons per sq. mile in 1981. The population, mid 1987 estimate, was 1,575,200.

CONSTITUTION AND GOVERNMENT

A separate parliament and executive Government was established for Northern Ireland in 1921 by the Government of Ireland Act. The Northern Ireland Constitution Act, 1973, abolished the post of Governor and Parliament of Northern Ireland and provided for the transfer of certain legislative functions to a Northern Ireland Assembly and Executive. Devolved Government came into operation with effect from January 1, 1974 but when the Executive collapsed the Northern Ireland Assembly was prorogued on May 29, 1974. The Northern Ireland Act, 1974, which became law in July 1974, made provision for temporary arrangements for the government of Northern Ireland by the Secretary of State for Northern Ireland and also provided for the holding of elections and a Constitutional Convention. Direct Rule continues in being under the terms of the Northern Ireland Act 1974.

Attempts have been made by successive governments to find a way of restoring devolved government to Northern Ireland. The most recent attempt failed when the Northern Ireland Assembly (elected on October 20, 1982) was dissolved on June 23, 1986.

FLAG.—The national flag is that of the United Kingdom.

THE PRIVY COUNCIL

R. J. Bailie (1971); D. W. Bleakley (1971); R. H. Bradford (1969); W. Craig (1963); J. Dobson (1969); W. K. Fitzsimmons (1965); Lt. Col. the Lord Glentoran (1953); Sir Edward Jones (1965); Mr. Justice Kelly (1969); H. V. Kirk (1962); Capt. W. J. Long (1966); Lord Lowry (1971); R. W. B. McConnell (1964); W. B. McIvor (1971); W. J. Morgan (1961); The Lord Moyola (1966); Sir Ivan Neill (1950); The Lord O'Neill of the Maine (1956); Sir Robert Porter, Q.C. (1969); Lord Rathcavan (1969); R. Simpson (1969); J. D. Taylor (1970); H. W. West (1960).

FINANCE

Taxation in Northern Ireland is largely imposed and collected by the United Kingdom Government. After deducting the cost of collections and of Northern Ireland's contributions to the European Economic Community the balance, known as the Attributed Share of Taxation, is paid over to the Northern Ireland Consolidated Fund. Northern Ireland's revenue is insufficient to meet its expenditure and is supplemented by a grant in aid.

	1988–89*	1989–90**
	£	£
Public income.....	4,327,915,463	4,420,283,300
Public expenditure	4,327,814,598	4,420,183,000
	* Outturn	** Estimate

PRODUCTION

Industries.—The products of the engineering, shipbuilding and aircraft industries, which employed 29,000 persons, were valued at £823 million. The textile industries, employing about 10,000 persons, produced products valued at approximately £236 million. The food and drink industry, employing about 20,000 persons, produced goods valued at £2,446 million.

Minerals.—1,304 persons were employed in mining and quarrying operations in Northern Ireland in 1988 and the minerals raised (17,343,584 tonnes) were valued at £29,135,108.

COMMUNICATIONS

Seaports.—The total tonnage handled by N. Irish ports in 1987 was 13·7m. Regular ferry, freight and container services operate to ports in Great Britain and Europe from Belfast, Larne, Londonderry and Warrenpoint.

Road and Rail Transport.—The Northern Ireland Transport Holding Company is largely responsible for the supervision of the subsidiary companies, Ulsterbus and Citybus (which operate the public road passenger services) and Northern Ireland Railways. Road freight services are also provided by a large number of hauliers operating competitively under licence.

Air Transport.—Belfast International Airport is run by Northern Ireland Airports Ltd., a subsidiary of the Northern Ireland Transport Holding Company and provides scheduled and chartered services on domestic and international routes.

Scheduled services also operate from Belfast Harbour Airport to eleven British destinations and from Eglinton, Co. Londonderry, to Blackpool, Glasgow and Dublin.

BELFAST

BELFAST, the administrative centre of Northern Ireland, is situated at the mouth of the River Lagan at its entrance to Belfast Lough. The city grew, owing to its easy access by sea to Scottish coal and iron, to be a great industrial centre.

The principal buildings are of a relatively recent date and include the Parliament Buildings at Stormont, the City Hall, the Law Courts, the Public Library and the Museum and Art Gallery.

Belfast received its first charter of incorporation in 1613 and was created a city in 1888; the title of Lord Mayor was conferred in 1892.

LONDONDERRY

LONDONDERRY, situated on the River Foyle, was reputedly founded in 546 by St. Columba. Londonderry (formerly *Derry*) has important associations with the City of London. The Irish Society, under its royal charter of 1613, fortified the city and was for long closely associated with its administration.

The city is famous for the great siege of 1688–89, when for 105 days the town held out against the forces of James II until relieved by sea. The city walls are still intact and form a circuit of almost a mile around the old city. Interesting buildings are the Protestant Cathedral of St. Columb's (1633) and the Guildhall reconstructed in 1912 and containing a number of beautiful stained glass windows, many of which were presented by the livery companies of London.

COUNTIES OF NORTHERN IRELAND

Counties and ‡County Boroughs	Area* sq. miles	Lord Lieutenant	High Sheriff, 1989
Antrim..................	1,093	Capt. R. A. F. Dobbs	Lt.-Col. A. J. Cramsie
Belfast City‡..............	25	Sir Robin Kinahan, E.R.D.	(vacant)
Armagh..................	484	The Earl of Caledon	Col. W. F. Gillespie, O.B.E., T.D.
Down	945	Col. W. N. Brann, O.B.E., E.R.D.	R. P. Blakiston Houston
Fermanagh..............	647	The Earl of Erne	Dr. S. G. W. Kyle
Londonderry†	798	Col. M. W. McCorkell, O.B.E., T.D.	R. M. Palmer
Londonderry City‡........	3·4	J. T. Eaton, T.D.	D. St. C. Baird
Tyrone..................	1,211	The Duke of Abercorn	A. V. Cramsie

† Excluding the City of Londonderry.   * Excluding inland waters and tideways.

MUNICIPAL DIRECTORY OF NORTHERN IRELAND

District and §Borough Councils	Population (June 30, 1987)	Net Annual Value	Council Clerk	Mayor (†) or Chairman 1989
		£		
§Antrim, Co. Antrim	46,600	6,513,335	S. J. Magee	†J. Graham
§Ards, Co. Down	63,600	7,180,240	D. J. Fallows	†J. S. Hamilton
Armagh, Co. Armagh ...	50,700	4,677,142	D. R. D. Mitchell	D. Hutchinson
§Ballymena, Co. Antrim .	56,100	7,534,520	J. S. McIlroy	†A. Spence, M.B.E.
§Ballymoney, Co. Antrim	23,800	2,396,412	W. J. Williamson, M.B.E.	†J. A. Gaston
Banbridge, Co. Down ...	32,000	3,316,300	A. G. Waite (*acting*)	Mrs. J. Baird
Belfast, Co. Antrim and Co. Down	303,800	51,043,470	C. Ward, C.B.E.	R. Empey (*Lord Mayor*)
§Carrickfergus, Co. Antrim..............	29,300	4,535,074	R. Boyd	†J. Brown
§Castlereagh, Co. Down ..	57,900	7,408,177	A. D. Nicol	†E. S. Harpur
§Coleraine, Co. Londonderry	47,700	7,213,131	W. E. Andrews	†W. J. Watt
Cookstown, Co. Tyrone .	27,700	2,835,745	W. A. Bownes	A. Kane
§Craigavon, Co Armagh..	76,600	9,903,051	E. A. McKinley	†S. J. McCammick
Derry, Co. Londonderry	97,500	10,910,232	C. M. Geary	†T. Carlin
Down, Co. Down	56,400	5,420,047	S. Byrne	M. Boyd
Dungannon, Co. Tyrone	43,900	4,153,398	W. J. Beattie	N. R. D. Mulligan
Fermanagh, Co. Fermanagh	50,300	4,770,953	G. Burns, M.B.E.	C. McCaughrey
§Larne, Co. Antrim	28,700	3,699,924	G. McKinley	†Mrs. R. G. Armstrong
§Limavady, Co. Londonderry	29,600	2,611,704	J. K. Stevenson	R. Cartwright
§Lisburn, Co. Antrim and Co. Down	92,900	11,997,608	M. S. Fielding	†W. J. McAllister
Magherafelt, Co. Londonderry	33,300	3,127,147	W. R. S. McMaster	Mrs. M. K. McSorley, M.B.E.
Moyle, Co. Antrim	15,200	1,355,398	J. O'Kane	A. McAuley
Newry and Mourne, Co. Down and Co. Armagh .	87,100	7,432,529	K. O'Neill	A. Ruddy
§Newtownabbey, Co. Antrim..............	72,300	10,639,684	J. Campbell	†E. L. Herron
§North Down, Co. Down .	70,700	8,687,086	J. McKimm	†I. Thompson
Omagh, Co. Tyrone	45,800	4,013,140	J. P. McKinney	C. McFarland
Strabane, Co. Tyrone ...	35,700	2,818,197	J. T. Keanie	E. Turner
Northern Ireland	1,575,200	196,193,644		

NOTE.—Since the reorganization of local government, rates in Northern Ireland are collected by the Department of Environment and consist of two rates, a regional rate made by the Department of Finance and a district rate made by individual District Councils.

THE ISLE OF MAN
(ELLAN VANNIN)

An island in the Irish Sea, in lat. 54° 3'–54° 25' N. and long. 4° 18'–4° 47' W., nearly equidistant from England, Scotland, and Ireland. Although the early inhabitants were of Celtic origin, the Isle of Man was part of the Norwegian Kingdom of the Hebrides until 1266, when this was ceded to Scotland. Subsequently granted to the Stanleys (Earls of Derby) in the 15th century and later to the Dukes of Atholl, it was brought under the direct administration of the Crown in 1765. The island forms the bishopric of Sodor and Man.

The total land area is 141,263 acres (221 sq. miles). The report on the 1986 Census showed a resident population of 64,282 (males, 30,782; females, 33,500). In 1988 births numbered 781 and deaths 993. The main language in use is English. There are no remaining native speakers of Manx Gaelic but around 200 people are able to speak the language.

CAPITAL, ΨDouglas. Population (1986), 20,368; ΨCastletown (3,019) is the ancient capital; the other towns are ΨPeel (3,660), and ΨRamsey (5,778).

FLAG.—Three legs in white and gold armed conjoined on a red ground.

TYNWALD DAY.—July 5.

GOVERNMENT

The Isle of Man is a self-governing Crown dependency, having its own legal and administrative systems. The Lieutenant-Governor is the Queen's personal representative in the Island. The legislature, called the Tynwald, has two branches—the Legislative Council and the House of Keys. The Council consists of the Bishop of Sodor and Man, the Attorney-General and 8 members chosen by the House of Keys, one of whom is appointed President of the Council. The House of Keys, one of the most ancient legislative assemblies in the world, consists of 24 members, elected by the adult male and female population.

ECONOMY

Most of the income generated in the Island is earned in the services sector with financial and business services being considerably larger than the traditional industry of tourism. Manufacturing industry is also a major generator of income whilst the Island's other traditional industries of agriculture and fishing now play a minor role in the economy.

Under the terms of the Island's special relationship with the European Community the Island has free access to E.C. markets.

A twenty-acre Freeport has been developed adjacent to the main airport at Ronaldsway.

The Island's unemployment rate is approximately 2 per cent and price inflation is around 7 per cent per annum.

FINANCE

The Island's Budget for 1989–90 provided for gross expenditure of £230,005,590. The principal sources of Government revenue are taxes on income and expenditure. Income tax is payable at a rate of 15 per cent. on the first £8,000 of taxable income of resident individuals and 20 per cent. on the balance. The rate of income tax is 20 per cent. on the whole taxable incomes of non-residents and companies. By agreement with the United Kingdom Government, the Island keeps most of its rates of indirect taxation (Value Added Tax and duties) the same as those in the United Kingdom, but this agreement may be terminated by either party. A reciprocal agreement on National Insurance benefits and pensions exists between the Governments of the Isle of Man and the United Kingdom. Taxes are also charged on property (rates), but these are comparatively low.

The major Government expenditure items are health, social security and education, which account for 53 per cent. of the Government budget. The Island makes a voluntary annual contribution to the United Kingdom for defence and other external services.

Although the Island has a special relationship with the European Community it neither contributes money to nor receives funds from the E.C. Budget.

Lieutenant-Governor, His Excellency Maj.-Gen. Laurence A. W. New, C.B., C.B.E.
A.D.C. to the Lieutenant-Governor, Capt. C. P. Dawson.
President of the Legislative Council, R. J. G. Anderson.
Speaker, House of Keys, Sir Charles Kerruish, O.B.E.
His Honour the First Deemster and Clerk of the Rolls, J. W. Corrin.
Clerk of Tynwald and Secretary to the House of Keys, Prof. T. St. J. N. Bates.
Attorney-General, T. W. Cain, Q.C.
Chief Secretary, J. F. Kissack.
Chief Financial Officer, W. Dawson.

THE CHANNEL ISLANDS

The Channel Islands, situated off the north-west coast of France (at distances of from ten to thirty miles), are the only portions of the *Dukedom of Normandy* now belonging to the Crown, to which they have been attached ever since the Conquest. They consist of Jersey (28,717 acres), Guernsey (15,654 acres), and the dependencies of Guernsey—Alderney (1,962 acres), Brechou (74), Great Sark (1,035) Little Sark (239), Herm (320), Jethou (44) and Lihou (38)—a total of 48,083 acres, or 75 square miles. In 1986 the population of Jersey was 80,212; and of Guernsey, 54,380; Alderney, 2,000 and Sark, 604.

GOVERNMENT

The islands are Crown dependencies with their own legislative assemblies (the States in Jersey, Guernsey and Alderney, and the Court of Chief Pleas in Sark), and systems of local administration and of law, and their own courts. Acts passed by the States require the sanction of The Queen-in-Council. The British Government is responsible for defence and international relations.

In both Bailiwicks the Lieutenant-Governor and Commander-in-Chief, who is appointed by the Crown, is the personal representative of the Queen and the channel of communication between the Crown (via the Privy Council) and the insular government. The Bailiffs of Jersey and Guernsey, also appointed by the Crown, are President of the States and of the Royal Courts of their respective islands. The government of each Bailiwick is conducted by committees appointed by the States. Justice is administered by the

Royal Courts of Jersey and Guernsey, each consisting of the Bailiff and 12 elected Jurats.

Each Bailiwick constitutes a deanery under the jurisdiction of the Bishop of Winchester (*see* Index).

ECONOMY

A mild climate and good soil have led to the development of intensive systems of agriculture and horticulture, which form a significant part of the economy of the Channel Islands. Equally important are invisible earnings, principally from the tourist trade and from banking and finance, the low rate of income tax (20p in the £ in Jersey and Guernsey; no tax of any kind in Sark) and the absence of super-tax and death duties making the Channel Islands a popular tax-haven. Principal exports are agricultural produce and flowers; imports are chiefly machinery, manufactured goods, food, fuel and chemicals. Trade with the U.K. is regarded as internal trade.

British currency is legal tender in the Channel Islands but each Bailiwick issues its own coins, and some notes, of the same values as those of the U.K. They also issue their own postage stamps; U.K. stamps are not valid.

LANGUAGE

The official languages are English and French, but French is gradually being supplanted by English, which is the language in daily use. In country districts of Jersey and Guernsey and throughout Sark a Norman-French *patois* is also in use, though to a declining extent.

CHIEF TOWNS, Ψ St. Helier on the south coast of Jersey; Ψ St. Peter Port, on the east coast of Guernsey; and St. Anne's on Alderney.

JERSEY

Lieutenant-Governor and Commander-in-Chief of Jersey, His Excellency Adm. Sir William Pillar, G.B.E., K.C.B. (1985).
Secretary and A.D.C., Comdr. D. M. L. Braybrooke, L.V.O., R.N.
Bailiff of Jersey, Sir Peter Crill, C.B.E.
Deputy Bailiff, V. A. Tomes
Attorney-General and Receiver-General, P. M. Bailhache, Q.C.

Solicitor-General, T. C. Sowden, Q.C.
Greffier of the States, E. J. M. Potter.
States Treasurer, L. May.

Year to Dec. 31:	1987	1988
Revenue	£234,061,396	£258,281,219
Revenue Expenditure	177,041,020	201,673,508
Capital Expenditure	33,013,000	38,022,000
Public Debt	−1,166,690	−1,166,690

FLAG.—A white field charged with a red saltire, and coat of arms.

GUERNSEY AND DEPENDENCIES

Lieutenant-Governor and Commander-in-Chief of the Bailiwick of Guernsey and its Dependencies, His Excellency Lt.-Gen. Sir Alexander Boswell, K.C.B., C.B.E. (1985).
Secretary and A.D.C., Capt. D. P. L. Hodgetts.
Bailiff of Guernsey, Sir Charles Frossard.
Deputy Bailiff, G. M. Dorey.
H. M. Procureur and Receiver-General, de V. G. Carey, Q.C.
H. M. Comptroller, A. C. K. Day, Q.C.
States Supervisor, F. N. Le Cheminant.

Year to Dec. 31:	1987	1988
Revenue	£101,250,316	£117,243,209
Expenditure	83,161,418	97,645,270

FLAG.—White, bearing a red cross of St. George, with an argent a cross gules superimposed on the cross.

Alderney

President of the States, J. Kay-Mouat.
Clerk of the States, D. V. Jenkins.
Clerk of the Court, P. Beer.

Sark

Le Seigneur of Sark, J. M. Beaumont.
The Seneschal, L. P. de Carteret.
The Greffier, J. P. Hamon.

Brechou, Lihou and Jethou are leased by the Crown. Herm is leased by the States of Guernsey.

THE ISLES OF SCILLY

There are about 140 islands and skerries in the Scillies group (total area, 6 square miles) situated 28 miles south-west of Land's End, of which only five are inhabited; St. Mary's, St. Agnes, Bryher, Tresco and St. Martin's. The population is 1,978. The entire group has been designated an Area of Outstanding Natural Beauty, and given National Nature Reserve status by the Nature Conservancy Council because of its unique flora and fauna. Tourism and the winter/spring flower trade for the home market form the basis of the economy of the Isles. The island group is a recognised rural development area.

The islands are administered by the Council of the Isles of Scilly, a 21-member non-political body, which combines the powers and duties of a County Council and a District Council under the Local Government

Act 1972 and the Isles of Scilly Orders 1978. Legislation is specifically applied to the Isles of Scilly by Special Order. The Council is responsible for education, fire services, highways, planning and social services, and Cornwall County Council provides other services on an agency basis: the police service is administered by the Devon and Cornwall Police Authority, of which the Council is a member. The Isles are part of the St. Ives electoral division.

Administrative Headquarters, Town Hall, St. Mary's, Isles of Scilly, TR21 0LW.
Chairman of the Council, H. R. Duncan.
Clerk, Chief Executive and Chief Financial Officer, L. W. Michell.
Chief Technical Officer, B. M. Lowen.

PATRON SAINTS

ST. GEORGE

Patron Saint of England

St. George is believed to have been born in Cappadocia, of Christian parents, in the latter part of the 3rd century and to have served with distinction as a soldier under the Emperor Diocletian, including a visit to England on a military mission. When the persecution of Christians was ordered, St. George sought a personal interview to remonstrate with the Emperor and after a profession of faith resigned his military commission. Arrest and torture followed and he was martyred at Nicomedia on April 23, 303, a day ordered to be kept in remembrance as a national festival by the Council of Oxford in 1222, although it was not until the reign of Edward III that he was made patron saint of England.

St. George's connection with a dragon seems to date from the close of the 6th century and to be due to the transfer of his remains from Nicomedia to Lydda, close to the scene of the legendary exploit of Perseus in rescuing Andromeda and slaying the sea monster, credit for which became attached to the Christian martyr.

ST. DAVID

Patron Saint of Wales

St. David is believed to have been born near the beginning and to have died towards the end of the 6th century. St. David was an eloquent preacher, who founded the monastery at Menevia, now St.

David's. He became the patron of Wales, but there is no record of any papal canonization before 1181. His annual festival is observed on March 1.

ST. ANDREW

Patron Saint of Scotland

St. Andrew, one of the Christian Apostles and brother of Simon Peter, was born at Bethsaida on the Sea of Galilee and lived at Capernaum. He preached the Gospel in Asia Minor and in Scythia along the shores of the Black Sea and became the patron saint of Russia. It is believed that he suffered crucifixion at Patras in Achaea, on a *crux decussata* (now known as St. Andrew's Cross) and that his relics were removed from Patras to Constantinople and thence to St. Andrews, probably in the 8th century, since which time he has been the patron saint of Scotland. The festival of St. Andrew is held on November 30.

ST. PATRICK

Patron Saint of Ireland

St. Patrick was born, probably in England, about 389 and was carried off to Ireland as a slave about sixteen years later, escaping to Gaul at the age of 22. He was ordained deacon at Auxerre and having been consecrated Bishop in 432 was despatched to Wicklow to reorganize the Christian communities in Ireland. He founded the see of Armagh and introduced Latin into Ireland as the language of the Church. He died *c.* 461 and his festival is celebrated on March 17.

THE CINQUE PORTS

As their name implies the Cinque Ports were originally five in number, Hastings, New Romney, Hythe, Dover and Sandwich. They were in existence before the Norman Conquest and were the Anglo-Saxon successors to the Roman system of coast defence organized from the Wash to Spithead to resist Saxon onslaughts. William the Conqueror reconstituted them and granted peculiar jurisdiction, most of which was abolished in 1855. Only jurisdiction in Admiralty still survives.

At some time after the Conquest the "antient towns" of Winchelsea and Rye were added with equal privileges. The other members of the Confederation, known as Limbs, are Lydd, Faversham, Folkestone, Deal, Tenterden, Margate and Ramsgate.

The Barons of the Cinque Ports have the ancient privilege of attending the Coronation Ceremony and are allotted special places in Westminster Abbey.

Lord Warden of the Cinque Ports, H.M. Queen Elizabeth the Queen Mother.

Judge, Court of Admiralty, Gerald Darling, R.D., Q.C.

Registrar, I. G. Gill, P.O. Box 9, Margate, Kent CT9 1XZ.

Lord Wardens of the Cinque Ports since 1904

THE COMMONWEALTH

The Commonwealth is a free association of the 48 sovereign independent states listed below together with their associated states and dependencies.

ANTIGUA AND BARBUDA	NAURU
AUSTRALIA	NEW ZEALAND
BAHAMAS	NIGERIA
BANGLADESH	PAPUA NEW GUINEA
BARBADOS	SAINT CHRISTOPHER
BELIZE	AND NEVIS
BOTSWANA	SAINT LUCIA
BRUNEI	SAINT VINCENT AND THE
CANADA	GRENADINES
CYPRUS	SEYCHELLES
DOMINICA	SIERRA LEONE
GAMBIA, THE	SINGAPORE
GHANA	SOLOMON ISLANDS
GRENADA	SRI LANKA
GUYANA	SWAZILAND
INDIA	TANZANIA
JAMAICA	TONGA
KENYA	TRINIDAD AND TOBAGO
KIRIBATI	TUVALU
LESOTHO	UGANDA
MALAWI	UNITED KINGDOM
MALAYSIA	VANUATU
MALDIVES	WESTERN SAMOA
MALTA	ZAMBIA
MAURITIUS	ZIMBABWE

Area and Population.—The total area of the independent Commonwealth is estimated at over 19,500,000 sq. miles (50,504,000 sq. km.) (U.N. estimate 1985), over one third of the world total. The total population of the Commonwealth is estimated to be about one quarter of the world total. In 1985 this amounted to over 1,200,000,000 (U.N. estimate). Details of the areas and populations of the Member States and dependencies appear in the following pages.

History and Government.—The status and relationship of member nations was first defined by the Inter-Imperial Relations Committee of the 1926 Imperial Conference, under the chairmanship of Lord Balfour, in what came to be known as the "Balfour Declaration": "They are autonomous communities . . . equal in status, in no way subordinate one to another in any aspect of their domestic or external affairs, though united by a common allegiance to the Crown and freely associated as members of the British Commonwealth of Nations." This formula was given legal substance by the Statute of Westminster, 1931.

The concept of a group of countries owing allegiance to a single Crown changed in 1949 when India decided to become a republic, and her continued membership of the Commonwealth was agreed by the other members on the basis of her "acceptance of the King as the symbol of the free association of its independent member nations and as such the Head of the Commonwealth". Member nations agreed at the time of the accession of Queen Elizabeth II to recognize Her Majesty as the new Head of the Commonwealth. The position is not vested in the British Crown.

Most members of the Commonwealth are parliamentary democracies.

Queen Elizabeth II is Head of State of 17 member countries of the Commonwealth: Antigua and Barbuda, Australia, the Bahamas, Barbados, Belize, Britain, Canada, Grenada, Jamaica, Mauritius, New Zealand, Papua New Guinea, St. Christopher and Nevis, Saint Lucia, Saint Vincent and the Grenadines, Solomon Islands and Tuvalu. In each of these countries (except Britain) The Queen is personally represented by a Governor-General, who holds in all essential respects the same position in relation to the administration of public affairs in the realm as is held by Her Majesty in Britain (with the exception of certain constitutional functions which are performed by The Queen personally). The Governor-General is appointed by The Queen on the advice of the Government of the country concerned.

Twenty-five member countries are republics: Bangladesh, Botswana, Cyprus, Dominica, The Gambia, Ghana, Guyana, India, Kenya, Kiribati, Malawi, The Maldives, Malta, Nauru, Nigeria, Seychelles, Sierra Leone, Singapore, Sri Lanka, Tanzania, Trinidad & Tobago, Uganda, Vanuatu, Zambia and Zimbabwe. In Malaysia, the Head of State is elected from among the nine hereditary Malay rulers and holds office for five years. Brunei, Lesotho, Tonga, and Swaziland have their own monarchs. Western Samoa has a Head of State whose functions are analogous to those of a constitutional monarch.

Membership of the Commonwealth is subject only to the approval of existing members. Two countries, Nauru and Tuvalu, are special members, with the right to participate in all functional Commonwealth meetings and activities, but not to attend Meetings of Commonwealth Heads of Government.

Consultation.—Commonwealth Heads of Government meet every two years to discuss international developments and to consider co-operation among members. These meetings, the successors to the pre-war Imperial Conferences, have grown in importance as they are the only regular forum of leaders from both developed and developing countries, constituting a broad sample of the world community. Decisions are reached by consensus, and the views of the meeting are set out in a communiqué.

In addition, there are annual meetings of Finance Ministers, and frequent meetings of Ministers and officials in the fields of trade, education, health, law, science, agriculture, labour and employment, and youth affairs.

Defence.—The Commonwealth is not a military alliance and members make their own defence arrangements in the light of their particular requirements. Some are parties to multi-lateral treaties, for example A.N.Z.U.S. and N.A.T.O. Various members of the Commonwealth co-operate with each other in combined exercises, joint research organizations and exchanges of personnel and training facilities.

Law.—English common law forms the basis of the legal system in many Commonwealth countries, although in most cases it has been radically adapted by statute to suit the individual needs and aspirations of a country, and there are countries where other systems have been adopted—for example, the law of Quebec Province and of Mauritius is founded on that of France, and Roman Dutch law forms the basis in Sri Lanka and Lesotho. Of the non-realms in the Commonwealth, Brunei, Dominica, The Gambia, Kiribati, Singapore, and Trinidad and Tobago retain the right of appeal to the Judicial Committee of the Privy Council in the United Kingdom, which also hears appeals from a number of realms (Antigua and Barbuda, the Bahamas, Barbados, Belize, Jamaica, Mauritius, New Zealand, St. Christopher and Nevis, St. Lucia, St. Vincent and the Grenadines, Tuvalu) and the dependent territories.

Citizenship and Nationality.—Each member of the Commonwealth defines the citizenship and nationality of its own people and determines the status of other Commonwealth nationals within its own boundaries. Members of the Commonwealth differentiate, to a greater or lesser degree, as regards the grant of privileges, between citizens of the Commonwealth and aliens. The Republic of Ireland, which in 1949 ceased to be a member of the Commonwealth, is not regarded by the other Commonwealth nations as a foreign country nor her citizens as foreigners.

Finance and Development.—Complete financial autonomy is enjoyed by all members of the Commonwealth. In some countries, customs tariffs are lower for merchandise of Commonwealth origin than for imports from foreign countries. Developing countries, including those in the Commonwealth, obtain preference for exports of industrial goods and some agricultural exports from the developed countries under the Generalised Scheme of Preferences (G.S.P.). Many smaller Commonwealth countries are also party to the Lomé Convention which accords preferential access to the European Community. Many former Commonwealth preferences have been replaced by these arrangements.

British aid for the development needs of the Commonwealth countries and dependent territories are dealt with under the provisions of the Overseas Aid Act 1966, administered by the Overseas Development Administration. This Act succeeds the former Colonial Development and Welfare Acts. Those countries which are party to the Lomé Convention also receive aid under that Convention from the European Community.

Commonwealth Secretariat. Marlborough House, Pall Mall, SW1Y 5HX [01-839 3411]. —This was established by decision of Commonwealth Heads of Government in 1965, and is the main agency for multi-lateral communication between Commonwealth Governments on issues relating to the Commonwealth as a whole. It promotes consultation and disseminates information on matters of common concern, organizes meetings and conferences, co-ordinates Commonwealth activities and provides technical assistance for economic and social development through the Commonwealth Fund for Technical Cooperation. *Secretary General*, Shridath S. Ramphal, Kt., C.M.G., Q.C.

Commonwealth Institute.—See p. 600.

Dependent Territories and Associated States. —Britain, Australia and New Zealand have a number of dependent territories. New Zealand also has two associated states: Cook Islands (since 1965) and Niue (since 1974).

Member States of the Commonwealth
(with dates of independence)

1867* Canada
1901* Australia
1907* New Zealand
1947 India (Republic, 1950)
1948 Sri Lanka (Republic, 1972)
1957 Ghana (Republic, 1960)
   Federation of Malaya (Federation of Malaysia since 1963—indigenous monarchy)
1960 Cyprus (Republic on independence; joined Commonwealth 1961)
   Nigeria (Republic, 1963)
1961 Sierra Leone (Republic, 1971)

   Tanganyika (Republic, 1962; united 1964 with Zanzibar as TANZANIA)
1962 Western Samoa (Republic on independence; joined Commonwealth 1970)
   Jamaica
   Trinidad and Tobago (Republic, 1976)
   Uganda (Republic, 1967)
1963 Kenya (Republic, 1964)
   Singapore (as State in Federation of Malaysia; seceded as Republic, 1965)
1964 Malawi (Republic, 1966)
   Malta (Republic, 1974)
   Zambia (Republic on independence)
1965 The Gambia (Republic, 1970)
   Maldives (Republic, 1968; joined Commonwealth as a Special Member 1982; full member 1985)
1966 Guyana (Republic, 1970)
   Botswana (Republic on independence)
   Lesotho (indigenous monarchy)
   Barbados
1968 Mauritius
   Nauru (Republic on independence—Special Member)
   Swaziland (indigenous monarchy)
1970 Tonga (indigenous monarchy)
   Fiji (membership lapsed 1987)
1971 Bangladesh (Republic on independence; joined Commonwealth 1972)
1973 Bahamas
1974 Grenada
1975 Papua New Guinea
1976 Seychelles (Republic on independence)
1978 Solomon Islands
   Tuvalu (Special Member)
   Dominica (Republic on independence)
1979 Saint Lucia
   Kiribati (Republic on independence)
   Saint Vincent and the Grenadines (Joined as a Special Member; became a full member 1985)
1980 Zimbabwe (Republic on independence)
   Vanuatu (Republic on independence)
1981 Belize
   Antigua and Barbuda
1983 Saint Christopher and Nevis
1984 Brunei (indigenous monarchy)

* These are the effective dates of independence, given legal effect by the Statute of Westminster, 1931.

(The above member states are Realms of Queen Elizabeth II unless otherwise stated.)

Associated States

The Cook Islands and Niue are self-governing states in association with New Zealand, which likewise remains responsible for their external affairs and defence.

Countries which have left the Commonwealth

1949 Republic of Ireland
1961 South Africa
1972 Pakistan
Pakistan is to be formally invited to return to the Commonwealth at the Commonwealth Heads of Government conference at Kuala Lumpur in October 1989. (*See* **Occurrences During Printing.**)

CANADA

AREA AND POPULATION

Provinces or Territories (with official contractions)	Area (Sq. Miles). Land and Water	Population Census, 1981	Population Census, 1986
Alberta (*Alta.*)	255,285	2,237,724	2,365,825
British Columbia (*B.C.*)	365,944	2,744,467	2,883,365
Manitoba (*Man.*)	250,945	1,026,241	1,063,015
New Brunswick (*N.B.*)	28,355	696,403	709,440
Newfoundland and Labrador (*Nfld.*)	156,648	567,681	568,350
Nova Scotia (*N.S.*)	21,425	847,442	873,175
Ontario (*Ont.*)	412,578	8,625,107	9,101,690
Prince Edward Island (*P.E.I.*)	2,185	122,506	126,645
Quebec (*Que.*)	594,855	6,438,403	6,532,460
Saskatchewan (*Sask.*)	251,864	968,313	1,009,615
Yukon Territory (*Y.T.*)	186,660	23,153	23,505
Northwest Territories (*N.W.T.*)	1,322,900	45,741	52,240
Total	3,849,646	24,343,181	25,309,330

Of the total immigration of 160,143 in 1988, 6,518 were from the United States, 9,946 from the United Kingdom and Ireland, and 9,398 from the Caribbean.

Mother Tongues of the Population

	1981	1986
Sole Language		
English	14,684,365	15,334,085
French	6,127,530	6,159,740
Non-Official Languages	2,933,305	2,860,570
Native Indian Languages		
Cree	60,845	57,645
Inuktitut	18,650	21,050
Ojibway	17,605	16,380
Bi/Multi-Lingual		
English and French	208,245	332,610
English and non-official language(s)	325,530	525,720
French and non-official language(s)	22,255	36,310
English, French and non-official language(s)	29,475	46,585
Non-official languages	12,485	13,715
Total Population	24,343,180	25,309,330

PHYSIOGRAPHY

Canada was originally discovered by Cabot in 1497, but its history dates only from 1534, when the French took possession of the country. The first permanent settlement at Port Royal (now Annapolis), Nova Scotia, was founded in 1605, and Quebec was founded in 1608. In 1759 Quebec was captured by the British forces under General Wolfe, and in 1763 the whole territory of Canada became a possession of Great Britain by the Treaty of Paris of that year. Nova Scotia was ceded in 1713 by the Treaty of Utrecht, the Provinces of New Brunswick and Prince Edward Island being subsequently formed out of it. British Columbia was formed into a Crown colony in 1858, having previously been a part of the Hudson Bay Territory, and was united to Vancouver Island in 1866.

Canada occupies the whole of the northern part of the North American Continent (with the exception of Alaska), from 49° North latitude to the North Pole, and from the Pacific to the Atlantic Ocean. In Eastern Canada, the southernmost point is Middle Island in Lake Erie, at 41° 41′.

Relief.—The relief of Canada is dominated by the mountain ranges running north and south on the west side of the Continent, by the pre-Cambrian shield on the east, with, in between, the northern extension of the North American Plain. From the physiographic point of view Canada has six main divisions. These are: (1) Appalachian-Acadian Region, (2) the Canadian Shield, (3) the St. Lawrence-Great Lakes Lowland, (4) the Interior Plains, (5) the Cordilleran Region and (6) the Arctic Archipelago. The first region occupies all that part of Canada lying southeast of the St. Lawrence. In general, the relief is an alternation of highlands and lowlands and is hilly rather than mountainous. The great Canadian Shield comprises more than half the area. The interior as a whole is an undulating, low plateau (general level 1,000 to 1,500 feet), with the more rugged relief lying along the border between Northern Quebec and Labrador. Throughout the whole area water or muskeg-filled depressions separate irregular hills and ridges, 150 to 200 feet in elevation. Newfoundland, an outlying portion of the shield, consists of glaciated, low rolling terrain broken here and there by mountains.

The flat relief of the St. Lawrence-Great Lakes lowland varies from 500 feet in the east to 1,700 feet south of Georgian Bay. The most striking relief is provided by the eastward facing scarp of the Niagara escarpment (elevation 250 to 300 feet). The interior plains, comprising the Pacific Provinces, slope east-

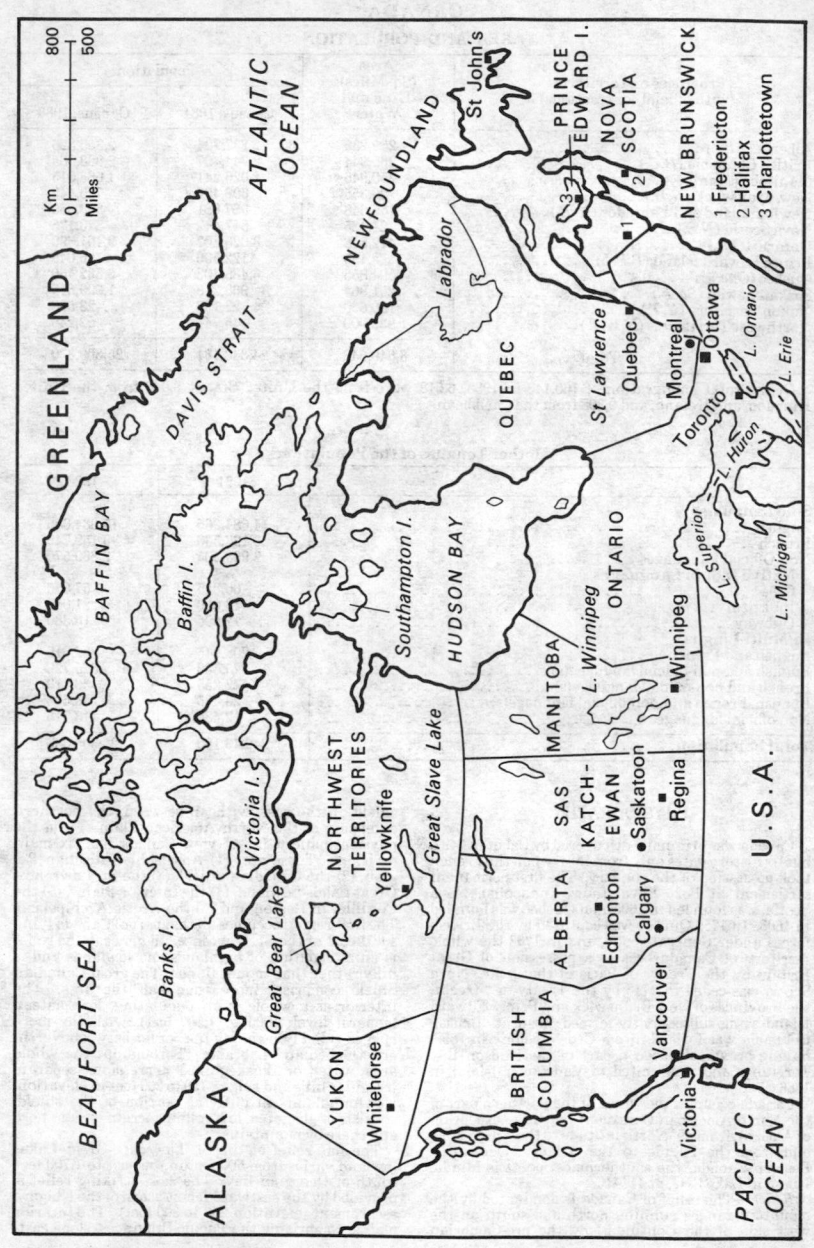

ward and northward a few feet per mile. The descent from west to east is made from 5,000 feet to less than 1,000 feet in three distinct levels, with each new level being marked by an eastward facing conteau or scarp. Five fairly well-developed topographic divisions mark out the Cordilleran region of western Canada. These are: (1) coastal ranges, largely above 5,000 feet with deep fjords and glaciated valleys, (2) the interior plateau, around 3,500 feet and comparatively level, (3) the Selkirk ranges, largely above 5,000 feet, (4) the Rocky Mountains with their chain of 10,000 to 12,000 feet peaks, and (5) the Peace River or Tramontane region with its rolling diversified country.

The Arctic Archipelago, with its plateau-like character has an elevation between 500 and 1,000 feet, though in Baffin Land and Ellesmere Island the mountain ranges rise to 8,500 and 9,500 feet. Two tremendous waterway systems, the St. Lawrence and the Mackenzie, providing thousands of miles of water highway, occupy a broad area of lowland with their dominant axis following the edge of the shield.

Climate.—The climate of the eastern and central portions presents greater extremes than in corresponding latitudes in Europe, but in the south-western portion of the Prairie Region and the southern portions of the Pacific slope the climate is milder. Spring, summer, and autumn are of about seven to eight months' duration, and the winter four to five months.

GOVERNMENT

The Constitution of Canada had its source in the British North America Act of 1867 which formed a Dominion, under the name of Canada, of the four provinces: Ontario, Quebec, New Brunswick and Nova Scotia; to this Federation the other Provinces have subsequently been admitted. Under this Act Canada came into being on July 1, 1867 (Dominion Day), and under the Statute of Westminster, which received the royal assent on Dec. 11, 1931, Canada and the Provinces were exempted (in common with other self-governing Dominions of the Common-wealth of Nations) from the operation of the Colonial Laws Validity Act, the Statute of Westminster having removed all limitations with regard to the legislative autonomy of the Dominions, except that the British North America Act could be amended in important respects only by Acts of the British Parliament.

Provinces admitted since 1867 are: Manitoba (1870), British Columbia (1871), Prince Edward Island (1873), Alberta and Saskatchewan (1905) and New-foundland (1949).

Agreement was reached in Nov. 1981 between the Federal and Provincial Governments (except Quebec) to patriate the Constitution so that it was amendable only in Canada. The inclusion in the Constitution of a Charter of Rights was also agreed. At the request of the Canadian Parliament, legislation was passed at Westminster and the Constitution formally pa-triated on 17th April 1982.

The Executive power is vested in a Governor-General appointed by the Sovereign on the advice of the Canadian Ministry, and aided by a Privy Council.

CURRENCY.—Canadian dollar (C$) of 100 cents.

FLAG.—Red maple leaf with 11 points on white square, flanked by vertical red bars one half the width of the square.

NATIONAL ANTHEM.—Oh Canada.

NATIONAL DAY.—July 1.

Governor General's Household

Governor General and Commander-in-Chief, Her Excellency The Rt. Hon. Jeanne Sauvé, C.C., C.M.M., C.D.

Secretary to the Governor General and Sec. Gen. of Honours, L. Amyot.

Deputy Secretaries, A. Smyth (Policy); J. M. Sévigny (Operations).

Asst. Sec. to the Chancellery, Lt.-Gen. F. Richard, C.D.

Honorary Historian, Dr. R. Hubbard.

Finance, Personnel and Administration Director, D. John, C.D.

Cultural Advisor, J.-N. Tremblay.

Director, Information Services, Mrs. M. de Belle-feuille-Percy.

Director, Programme Implementation, Health, Safety and Security Programme, C. A. Sangster, C.D.

Policy and Programme Director, Mrs. S. Orr.

Press Secretary, Miss M. Bender.

Hospitality Director, Ms. L. D'Ascanio.

Director, Protocol and Ceremonial, L. Lemieux.

Aides-de-Camp, Capt. P. Harrison; Lt. S. Nadeau; Capt. P. Sergerie.

Personal Asst. to the Governor General, Mlle. R. Langevin.

The Cabinet
(as at July 18, 1989)

Prime Minister, Rt. Hon. M. Brian Mulroney.

Secretary of State for External Affairs, Rt. Hon. C. Joseph Clark.

International Trade, Hon. John C. Crosbie.

Deputy P.M., President of the Queen's Privy Council for Canada and Minister for Agriculture, Hon. Donald F. Mazankowski.

Public Works and Minister for the purposes of the Atlantic Canada Opportunities Agency Act, Hon. Elmer M. MacKay.

Energy, Mines and Resources, Hon. A. Jacob Epp.

President of the Treasury Board, Hon. Robert R. de Cotret.

National Health and Welfare, Hon. H. Perrin Beatty.

Finance, Hon. Michael H. Wilson.

Regional Industrial Expansion and Minister of State for Science and Technology, Hon. Harvie Andre.

National Revenue, Hon. Otto J. Jelinek.

Fisheries and Oceans, Hon. Thomas E. Siddon.

Western Economic Diversification and Minister of State for Grains and Oilseeds, Hon. Charles J. Mayer.

National Defence, Hon. William H. McKnight.

Transport, Hon. Benoit Bouchard.

Communications, Hon. Marcel Masse.

Employment and Immigration, Hon. Barbara J. McDougall.

Veterans' Affairs, Hon. Gerald S. Merrithew.

Leader of the Government in the Senate and Minister of State for Federal-Provincial Relations, Hon. Lowell Murray.

Supply and Services, Hon. Paul W. Dick.

Indian Affairs and Northern Development, Hon. Pierre H. Cadieux.

Deputy Leader of the Government and Minister of State for Youth, and Fitness and Amateur Sport, Hon. Jean J. Charest.

External Relations, Hon. Monique Landry.

Consumer and Corporate Affairs, Hon. Bernard Valcourt.

Secretary of State of Canada and Minister of State for Multiculturalism and Citizenship, Hon. Gerry Weiner.

Leader of the Government in the House of Commons, Attorney General and Minister of Justice, Hon. Douglas G. Lewis.

Solicitor General and Minister of State for Agriculture, Hon. Pierre Blais.

Environment, Hon. Lucien Bouchard.

Associate Minister of National Defence, Hon. Mary Collins.

Ministers of State, Hon. Monique Vezina (*Employment and Immigration, and Seniors*); Hon. Frank Oberle (*Forestry*); Hon. Thomas Hockin (*Small Businesses and Tourism*); Hon. John H. McDermid (*Privatization and Regulatory Affairs*); Hon. Shirley Martin (*Transport*); Hon. Alan Redway (*Housing*); Hon. William C. Winegard (*Science and Technology*); Hon. Kim Campbell (*Indian Affairs and Northern Development*); Hon. Gilles Loiselle (*Finance*).

The Prime Minister receives remuneration of C$148,500; other ministers, C$125,700 each.

CANADIAN HIGH COMMISSION
Macdonald House, 1 Grosvenor Square, W1X 0AB
[01–629 9492]

High Commissioner, His Excellency Donald Macdonald (1988).
Deputy High Commissioner, (vacant).
Ministers, J. T. Boehm (*Political and Public Affairs*); R. J. L. Berlet (*Commercial/Economic*).
Minister-Counsellor, J. R. MacLachlan (*Immigration*).

BRITISH HIGH COMMISSION
80 Elgin Street, Ottawa K1P 5K7
[Ottawa 237-1530]

High Commissioner, His Excellency Brian James Proetel Fall, C.M.G.
Deputy High Commissioner, P. M. Newton.
Counsellor, R. T. Fell (*Economic and Commercial*).
Defence and Military Adviser, Brig. F. R. Maynard.
Naval Adviser, Cdr. J. J. Howard, M.B.E.
Air Adviser, Gp. Capt. M. A. Radnorth.
First Secretaries, D. J. Pugh, M.B.E. (*Administration*); A. Jordan; I. D. Kydd (*Commercial*); N. Penrhys-Evans; D. E. Donald (*Information*).
Cultural Affairs and British Council Representative, M. Evans.

THE LEGISLATURE

Parliament consists of a Senate and a House of Commons. The *Senate* consists of 104 members, nominated by the Governor General (age limit 75). They are distributed between the various provinces thus: 24 each for Ontario and Quebec, 10 each for Nova Scotia and New Brunswick, 6 each for Newfoundland, British Columbia, Manitoba, Alberta, and Saskatchewan and 4 for Prince Edward Island, 1 for Northwest Territories and 1 for Yukon; each Senator must be at least thirty years old, a resident in the province for which he is appointed, a natural-born or naturalized subject of the Queen, and the owner of a property qualification amounting to $4,000. The Speaker of the Senate is chosen by the Government of the day.

The *House of Commons* has 295 members and is elected every five years at longest. Representation by provinces is at present as follows: Newfoundland 7, Prince Edward Island 4, Nova Scotia 11, New Brunswick 10, Quebec 75, Ontario 99, Manitoba 14, Saskatchewan 14, Alberta 26, British Columbia 32, Yukon 1, Northwest Territories 2.

In every case—including the Prime Minister's—a sessional indemnity of C$58,300 per annum is paid to members of the House of Commons. In addition, Ministers and members of the House of Commons receive an expense allowance. Certain Members of Parliament for large northern constituencies have larger expense allowances.

THE SENATE

The state of the parties in the Senate as at January 29, 1989, was Liberals 56, Progressive Conservatives 36, Independent 5, Vacant 7.
Speaker of the Senate, Hon. Guy Chapbonneau, Q.C. C$99,700
Clerk of the Senate & Clerk of the Parliaments, C. A. Lussier.

THE HOUSE OF COMMONS

The state of parties in the House of Commons as at May 1, 1989, was Progressive Conservatives 167, Liberals 83, New Democratic Party 43, Reform Party 1, Independent 1.
Speaker of the House of Commons, Hon. John A. Fraser............................ C$122,200
Deputy Speaker, Marcel Danis........... C$101,000
Clerk of the House of Commons, Robert Marleau.

THE JUDICATURE

The Judicature is administered by judges following the Civil Law in Quebec Province and Common Law in other Provinces. Each Province has its Court of Appeal. All Superior, County and District Court Judges are appointed by the Governor General, the others by the Lieutenant Governors of the Provinces.

The highest federal court is the Supreme Court of Canada, composed of a Chief Justice and eight puisne judges, which exercises general appellate jurisdiction throughout Canada in civil and criminal cases, and which usually holds three sessions each year. There is one other federally constituted Court, the Federal Court of Canada, which has jurisdiction on appeals from its Trial Division, from Federal Tribunals and reviews of decisions and references by Federal Boards and Commissions. The Trial Division has jurisdiction in claims by or against the Crown, its officers or servants or Federal bodies. It also deals with inter-Provincial and Federal-Provincial disputes.

SUPREME COURT OF CANADA
Chief Justice of Canada, Rt. Hon. Brian Dickson, P.C. .... C$171,600
Puisne Judges, Hon. A. Lamer; Hon. Bertha Wilson; Hon. G. Le Dain; Hon. G. V. LaForest; Hon. Claire L'Heureux-Dube; Hon. J. Sopinka; Hon. C. Gonthier; Hon. P. Cory; Hon. Beverley McLachlin. ... each   C$158,900

FEDERAL COURT OF CANADA
Chief Justice, Hon. F. Iacobucci ...... C$146,400
Associate Chief Justice, Hon. J. A. Jerome .... C$146,400
Appeal Division Judges, Hon. L. Pratte; Hon. D. V. Heald; Hon. J. J. Urie; Hon. P. M. Mahoney, P.C.; Hon. L. Marceau; Hon. J. K. Hugesson; Hon. A. J. Stone; Hon. M. Mac-Guigan; Hon. B. Lacombe; Hon. Alice Desjardins .... each   C$133,800
Trial Division Judges, Hon. G. A. Addy; Hon. J.-E. Dubé; Hon. P. U. C. Rouleau; Hon. F. C. Muldoon; Hon. B. L. Strayer; Hon. J. C. McNair; Hon. Barbara J. Reed; Hon. P. Denault; Hon. Y. Pinard; Hon. L. M. Joyal; Hon. B. Cullen; Hon. L. A. Martin; Hon. M. A. Teitelbaum each   C$133,800

VITAL STATISTICS

BIRTHS, DEATHS AND MARRIAGES, 1987

Province	Births	Deaths	Marriages
Alberta	42,110	13,316	18,640
British Columbia .	41,814	21,814	23,395
Manitoba	16,953	8,710	7,994
New Brunswick ..	9,588	5,408	4,924
Newfoundland ...	7,769	3,540	3,481
Nova Scotia	12,110	7,112	6,697
Ontario	134,617	68,119	76,201
P.E.I.	1,955	1,116	924
Quebec..........	83,791	47,616	32,616
Saskatchewan ...	17,034	7,808	6,853
Yukon	478	108	189
N. W. Territories	1,523	197	237
Total......	369,742	184,953	182,151

Canada's birth rate per 1,000 population (1987) 14·4; Death Rate 7·2; Marriage Rate 7·1. Divorces 78,160 in 1986.

FINANCE

Federal Government gross general revenue and expenditure was (C$ millions):—

	1987–88	1988–89p
Total Revenue	110,438	117,241
Total Expenditure........	136,264	143,924
p – preliminary		

DEBT (C$ millions)

	1986–87	1987–88
Gross Public Debt	328,230	360,655
Net Public Debt	188,733	253,157

Banking.—There were 67 chartered banks on Dec. 31, 1988, with assets of C$506,920 m. Deposits were C$402,681 m. of which C$162,506 m. were personal savings.

NATIONAL DEFENCE

The Minister of National Defence has the control and management of the Canadian Armed Forces and all matters relating to National Defence establishments and works for the defence of Canada.

The Canadian Forces are organized on a functional basis to reflect the major commitments assigned by the government and are formed into National Defence Headquarters and five major Commands reporting to the Chief of the Defence Staff. The roles of the five Commands are: *Mobile Command*—Provision of ground forces for the protection of Canadian territory, combat forces in Canada for support of overseas commitments, and forces for support of United Nations or other peace-keeping operations. *Maritime Command*—Provision of sea forces for the defence of Canada, anti-submarine defence in support of NATO. Maritime Command also has operational control of Maritime aircraft. *Air Command*—Provision of operationally ready air forces to national, continental and international commitments. *Canadian Forces Communications Command*—Manages, operates and maintains strategic communications for the Canadian Forces. *Canadian Forces Europe*—Canadian Forces allocated to support NATO in Europe consisting of land and air elements.

National Defence expenditure for the fiscal year 1988–89 was estimated at C$11,200 million. Canadian Armed Forces strength at May 1989, 87,600 authorized force.

EDUCATION

Education is under the control of the Provincial Governments, the cost of the publicly controlled schools being met by local taxation, aided by provincial grants. In 1988–89 there were 16,017 publicly controlled elementary and secondary schools with 4,996,160 pupils. Of these, 1,380 were private schools with 234,100 pupils; 400 federal schools with 47,500 pupils and 21 special schools for the blind and deaf with 2,560 pupils.

In 1988–89 there were 68 degree-granting universities with a full-time enrolment of 497,450, as well as 321,400 students in 198 other post-secondary, non-university institutions.

PRODUCTION

Agriculture.—About 7 per cent of the total land area of Canada is classified as farm land and approximately half of this is under cultivation, the remainder being woodland or suitable only for grazing purposes. More than three-quarters of the land now cultivated is found in the prairie region of Western Canada. Farm cash receipts from the sale of farm products in 1988 were C$21,640,226,000. Livestock and animal products contributed C$10,632,304,000; field crops C$8,874,319,000.

	1987	1988
	('000 tonnes)	
Wheat	25,950·2	15,654·9
Oats	2,995·2	2,993·4
Barley	13,957·1	10,125·1
Rye	492·6	257·0
Flaxseed	729·0	413·9
Canola	3,846·5	4,243·0
Total.................	47,970·6	33,687·3

Livestock.—In July 1988 the livestock included 12,060,200 cattle, 696,700 sheep, 10,846,500 hogs and 22,421,000 chickens (layers).

Fur Production.—Canada in 1987–88 produced pelts valued at C$123,449,379. Wild life pelts made up 52·6 per cent of the total, with a value of C$64,903,166.

Fisheries.—The marketed value of catches in 1988 was C$3,185,180,000 (preliminary).

Forestry.—About 44 per cent of the total land area is in forests. The shipment value of forest products in 1986 was: standard newsprint C$5,179,601,000; paper (groundwood printing and speciality papers; wrapping, packaging and related paper) C$2,848,019,000; lumber C$6,018,613,000; wood pulp C$1,774,665,000.

Minerals.—Canada is the world's largest producer of zinc, nickel and uranium, and the second largest of asbestos, potash and gypsum. The country is also rich in many other minerals, including gold, silver, iron, copper, cobalt and lead.

	1987	1988
	('000 tonnes)	
Copper	794·1	721·6
Nickel	189·1	213·9
Lead	373·2	333·7
Molybdenum........	14·8	12·4
Zinc	1,157·9	1,253·6
Iron Ore...........	37,702·0	38,742·0
Asbestos............	665·0	705·0
Gypsum	9,094·0	8,522·0
Cement	12,603·0	12,611·0
Lime	2,330·0	2,535·0
Salt................	10,129·0	10,975·0
Potash	7,668·0	8,070·0

Production of gold was 127,843,000 grams in 1988 (115,818,000 in 1987) and of silver was 1,527,000 kg. (1,375,000 kg. in 1987). Uranium production in 1988 was 13,232,000 kilograms (13,612,000 kg. in 1987).

TRADE

Merchandise imports into Canada in 1988 were valued at C$131,554,027,000 and merchandise exports (including re-exports) at C$134,075,121,000. The main exports in 1987 were motor vehicles and parts, newsprint paper, wheat, crude petroleum, lumber, natural gas, woodpulp, petroleum and coal products, and television and telecommunication equipment. Trade with the U.S.A. accounts for 69.5 per cent of total trade in merchandise, although efforts are being made to develop alternative markets. Value of trade with Canada's largest trading partners in 1988 was as follows (C$'000):

Country	Imports	Domestic Exports
United States	86,509,012	98,218,792
Japan	9,264,609	8,686,256
United Kingdom ..	4,634,836	3,464,910
Germany, Fed. Rep. of	3,847,124	1,693,170
France	2,864,405	1,179,914
China	955,395	2,596,381
Korea, Rep. of	2,270,576	1,192,814
Taiwan	2,257,337	967,871
Italy	1,953,530	1,000,939
Netherlands	762,292	1,393,623
Hong Kong	1,153,384	986,836
Mexico	1,331,250	488,958
Belgium	588,128	1,149,030

COMMUNICATIONS

Railways.—The total track of railways in operation on Dec. 31, 1987, was 94,184 km.

	1987
Property Accounts	C$16,930,264,442
Operating Revenues	7,899,255
Operating Expenses	6,838,334

In 1987 revenue freight was 267,672,091,319 tonne-kilometres.

Shipping.—The registered shipping on Jan. 1, 1987 including inland vessels, was 38,363 vessels with gross tonnage 5,266,385. The volume of international shipping handled at Canadian ports in 1987 was 158,993,861 metric tonnes loaded and 68,025,360 metric tonnes unloaded.

Canals.—The bulk of canal shipping in Canada is handled through the two sections of the St. Lawrence Seaway, which provide access to the Great Lakes for ocean-going ships. In 1988, transits on the Montreal-Lake Ontario section numbered 3,142 for a total of 40,557,669 cargo tonnes; transits in the Welland Canal section numbered 3,909 for a total of 43,538,517 cargo tonnes. Principal commodities carried were iron ore, wheat, corn, barley, soybeans, fuel oil, manufactured iron and steel, coal and coke.

Civil Aviation.—The number of passengers carried in 1987 (all major Canadian carriers) was 31,863,203. 1,245,630,240 tonne-km of freight were carried in 1987.

Motor Vehicles.—Total motor vehicle registrations numbered 15,864,388 in 1987.

Post.—Post office revenue in the fiscal year 1987–88 was C$3,139 m.; total expenditure C$3,169 m.

FEDERAL CAPITAL

OTTAWA, the federal capital, 111 miles west of Montreal and 247 miles north-east of Toronto, is a city on the south bank of the Ottawa river. The city was chosen as the capital of the Province of Canada in 1857 and was later selected as the site of the Dominion capital. Ottawa contains the Parliamentary Buildings, the Public Archives, Royal Mint, several national museums, the National Art Gallery and the Dominion Observatory.

Manufacturing is also carried on, medical advancement, high technology (communications, defence), printing and publishing being of greatest importance. Ottawa is connected with Lake Ontario by the Rideau Canal. The City population was 300,763 at the Census of 1986; and Metropolitan Ottawa 819,263.

YUKON TERRITORY

The area of the Territory is 186,660 sq. miles (483,450 sq. km.), with a population (1988) of 25,300. Minerals and tourism are the chief industries, followed closely by transport, communications and other utilities industry.

Commissioner, J. K. McKinnon.

The Yukon Act, 1970, as amended, provides for the administration of the Territory by a Commissioner acting under instructions from time to time given by the Governor-in-Council or the Minister of Indian Affairs and Northern Development. Legislative powers, analogous to those of a provincial government, are exercised by a Legislative Assembly of 16 members elected from electoral districts in the Territory. The Executive Council of the Assembly consists of the government leader as chairman and four elected members.

EXECUTIVE COUNCIL

Government Leader, Minister of the Executive Council Office, Health and Human Resources, Minister responsible for the Yukon Development Corporation, Hon. Tony Penikett.

House Leader, Minister of Education, Finance, Economic Development, Mines and Small Business, Hon. Piers McDonald.

Justice, Minister responsible for the Public Service Commission, the Workers' Compensation Board, the Women's Directorate, Hon. Margaret Joe.

Renewable Resources, Tourism, and the Yukon Liquor Corporation, Hon. Art Webster.

Community and Transportation Services, Yukon Housing Corporation, Hon. Maurice Byblow.

Seat of Government, Whitehorse. Pop. 15,199 (1986).

NORTHWEST TERRITORIES

The area of the Northwest Territories is 1,322,900 sq. miles (3,426,320 sq. km.), with a population (1988 estimate) of 51,800. The chief industry is mining, with a total value of $492,000,000 in 1985. Lead, zinc, gold, silver, oil exploration and natural gas contributed about 32 per cent. of the total activities in the Northwest Territories.

The Northwest Territories are subdivided into the districts of Mackenzie, Keewatin and Franklin.

Commissioner, J. H. Parker.

The Northwest Territories Act, 1979, as amended, provides for a Legislative Assembly of 24 elected members, of which the Executive Council under the chairmanship of the government leader is the senior decision-making body of the government in the Territory.

EXECUTIVE COUNCIL

Government Leader, Minister responsible for the Executive, for the N.W.T. Science Institute, the Devolution Office and Minister of Intergovernmental Affairs, Hon. Dennis Patterson.

Culture and Communications, Renewable Resources, Associate Minister of Aboriginal Rights and Constitutional Development, Hon. Titus Allooloo.

House Leader, Minister of Finance, Justice and Public Utilities Board, Hon. Michael Ballantyne.

Health, Energy, Mines and Petroleum Resources, Public Works and Highways, Hon. Nellie Cournoyee.

Education, Aboriginal Rights and Constitutional Development, Safety and Public Services, Minister responsible for Workers' Compensation Board, Hon. Stephen Kakfwi.

Social Services, Personnel, Equal Employment Directorate, Women's Secretariat, and the Highway Transport Board, Hon. Jeannie Marie-Jewell.

Government Services, and the NWT Housing Corporation, Hon. Tom Butters.

Municipal and Community Affairs, Economic Development and Tourism, Transportation, Hon. Gordon Wray.

Seat of Government, Yellowknife. Pop. 11,753 (1986).

PROVINCES OF CANADA

ALBERTA

Area and Population.—The Province of Alberta has an area of 255,285 sq. miles (661,185 sq. km.), including about 6,485 sq. miles of water (16,796 sq. km.), with a population (April 1989) of 2,423,500.

Government.—The Government is vested in a Lieutenant Governor and Legislative Assembly composed of 83 members, elected for five years, representing 83 electoral districts in the Province. At a provincial election held on March 20, 1989, the Progressive Conservative party took 59 seats, the New Democratic Party 16 seats and the Liberal Party 8 seats.

Lt. Governor, Her Honour Helen Hunley.

EXECUTIVE
(as at June 30, 1989)

Premier, President of Executive Council, Hon. Don Getty................................ C$94,479*

Deputy Premier and Minister of Federal and Intergovernmental Affairs, Government House Leader, Hon. Jim Horsman.

Provincial Treasurer, Hon. Dick Johnston.

Transportation and Utilities, Hon. Al Adair.

Forestry, Lands and Wildlife, Hon. LeRoy Fjordbotten.

Economic Development and Trade, Hon. Peter Elzinga.

Energy, Hon. Rick Orman.

Agriculture, Hon. Ernie Isley.

Health, Hon. Nancy Betkowski.

Attorney General, Hon. Ken Rostad.

Technology, Research and Telecommunications, Hon. Fred Stewart.

Public Works, Supply and Services, Hon. Ken Kowalski.

Career Development and Employment, Hon. Connie Osterman.

Education, Hon. Jim Dinning.

Tourism, Hon. Don Sparrow.

Labour, Hon. Elaine McCoy.

Consumer and Corporate Affairs, Hon. Dennis Anderson.

Family and Social Services, Hon. John Oldring.

Associate Minister of Family and Social Services, Hon. Norm Weiss.

Occupational Health and Safety, Workers' Compensation Board, Hon. Peter Trynchy.

Advanced Education and Deputy House Leader, Hon. John Gogo.

Recreation and Parks, Hon. Steve West.

Associate Minister of Agriculture, Hon. Shirley McClellan.

Municipal Affairs, Hon. Ray Speaker.

Environment, Hon. Ralph Klein.

Solicitor General, Hon. Dick Fowler.

Culture and Multiculturalism, Hon. Doug Main.

Speaker of the Legislative Assembly, Hon. D. Carter................................ C$40,841†

*Includes Legislative Assembly Members' Annuity and Expense Allowances.

†Ministerial salary only.

London Office, Alberta House, 1, Mount Street, W1.

THE JUDICATURE

Court of Appeal of Alberta, Hon. J. H. Laycraft (*Chief Justice*).

Justices, Hons. S. S. Lieberman; D. C. Prowse; W. J. Haddad; J. W. McClung; A. M. Harradence; R. P. Kerans; R. H. Belzil; W. A. Stevenson; M. M. Hetherington; H. L. Irving; J. E. Cote; R. P. Foisy; J. J. Stratton.

Court of Queen's Bench of Alberta, Hon. W. K. Moore (*Chief Justice*); Hon. T. H. Miller (*Associate Chief Justice*).

ECONOMY

The Gross Domestic Product at factor cost in 1988 was

	millions p
Agriculture, fishing and trapping	C$2,750
Forestry (1)	172
Mining	9,873
Manufacturing	5,160
Construction	3,406
Transportation	4,650
Utilities	2,241
Trade	5,771
Finance	12,113
Services	11,730
Public Administration	3,544
Total G.D.P. at factor cost	61,411

p – preliminary

(1) Includes logging; excludes sawmills, pulp and paper mills which are included in manufacturing.

Mineral Production 1988
(preliminary estimates)

	(thousands)
Crude oil	C$7,724,165
Natural gas	4,415,169
Natural gas by-products	1,559,096
Coal	456,000
Sulphur (elemental)	420,582
Sand & gravel	133,875
Cement	126,545
Other	70,963
Total	14,906,395

Manufacturing.—The total value of manufacturing shipments (1988) was C$17,924,824,000. Number of industrial establishments 2,747 (1986), total employees 53,268 (1986). The leading industrial products are refined petroleum and coal products, meat and meat products, chemicals and chemical products, fabricated metal products, non-metallic mineral products and primary metals.

GOVERNMENT FINANCE
Budgetary Estimates C$ millions

	1988–89	1989–90
Revenue	9,129	10,181
Expenditure	10,867	11,674
Deficit	1,738	1,493

NOTE: The Budgetary revenue figure does not include funds allocated to the Alberta Heritage Savings Trust Fund.

CAPITAL.—Edmonton—city population (1988) 576,249, metropolitan area, 783,909. Other centres are Calgary (657,118), Lethbridge (66,610), Red Deer (54,839), Medicine Hat (42,290), St. Albert (38,318), Fort McMurray (34,949).

BRITISH COLUMBIA

Area and Population.—British Columbia has a total area estimated at 365,944 sq. miles (947,790 sq. km.), with a population of 2,935,000 (April 1987).

Government.—The Government consists of a Lieutenant Governor and an Executive Council together with a Legislative Assembly of 57 members.

The Social Credit Party formed a government after a General Election on October 22, 1986. The present standing in the Assembly is Social Credit Party 34, New Democratic Party 22, Independent 1.

Lt. Governor, His Honour Dr. David See-Chai Lam.

EXECUTIVE COUNCIL

Premier and President of the Council, Hon. William N. Vander Zalm.
Regional Development, Hon. Elwood Veitch.
Attorney-General, Hon. Stuart D. Smith, Q.C.
Forests and Lands, Hon. David F. H. Parker.
Finance and Corporate Relations, Hon. Melville B. Couvelier.
Agriculture and Fisheries, Hon. John Savage.
Energy, Mines and Petroleum Resources, Hon. John Davis, P.C.
Education, Hon. Anthony J. Brummet.
Labour and Consumer Services, Hon. Lyall Hanson.
Municipal Affairs, Hon. Rita M. Johnston.
Health, Hon. Peter A. Dueck.
Social Services and Housing, Hon. Claude H. Richmond.
Transportation and Highways, Hon. Neil Vant.
Environment, Hon. Bruce Strachan.
Parks, Hon. Terry Huberts.
Crown Lands, Hon. Howard Dirks.
Native Affairs, Hon. Jack Weisgerber.
International Business and Immigration, Hon. John Jansen.
Government Services, Hon. Cliff Michael.
Solicitor General, Hon. Angus Ree.
Tourism, Recreation and Culture, Hon. William E. Reid.
Advanced Education and Job Training, Hon. Stanley Hagen.

(The Premier receives a total salary of C$76,527; Members of the Executive Council receive a total salary of C$71,330.)
Speaker, Legislative Assembly, Hon. John D. Reynolds .... C$64,809

Agent-General in London, G. Gardom, Q.C., British Columbia House, 1 Regent Street, SW1.

THE JUDICATURE

Court of Appeal—Chief Justice of British Columbia, Hon. N. T. Nemetz.
Justices of Appeal, Hons. J. D. Taggart; P. D. Seaton; A. B. B. Carrothers; E. E. Hinkson; W. A. Craig; J. S. Aikins; J. D. Lambert; J. A. Macdonald; R. P. Anderson; H. E. Hutcheon; A. B. Macfarlane; W. A. Esson; B. M. McLachlin; W. J. Wallace; C. C. Locke.
Supreme Court—Chief Justice, Hon. A. McEachern.
Puisne Judges, Hons. K. E. Meredith; A. A. Mackoff; S. M. Toy; J. C. Bouck; L. G. McKenzie; G. L. Murray; H. P. Legg; W. J. Trainor; P. M. Proudfoot; H. A. Callaghan; A. G. MacKinnon; M. R. Taylor; P. D. Dohm; R. M. P. Paris; D. B. Hinds; A. A. W. Macdonell; J. E. Spencer; W. H. Davies; C. R. Lander; B. D. Macdonald; K. M. Lysyk; L. S. G. Finch; J. Wood; R. J. Gibbs; M. F. Southin; G. S.

Cumming; D. B. MacKinnon; W. T. Oppal; M. A. Rowles; B. I. Cohen; C. M. Huddart; J. J. Gow; D. W. Shaw; G. R. B. Coultas.

FINANCE

	1987–88	1988–89
Estimated Revenue	C$10,322·0 m.	C$11,440·0 m.
Estimated Expenditure	11,122·0 m.	11,835·0 m.
Net Guaranteed Debt ..	9,922·0 m.	9,418·7 m.

ECONOMY

Production and Industry.—Manufacturing activity is based largely on the processing of the output of the logging, mineral, fishing and agriculture industries. The principal manufacturing centres are Vancouver, New Westminster, Victoria, North Vancouver, Kelowna and Prince George. Forestry and forest-based industries form the most important economic activity, accounting for approximately 40 per cent of total production. British Columbia is the leading province of Canada in the quantity and value of its timber and sawmill products. Mining, the second most important non-service economic activity, is based on copper, zinc, lead, iron concentrates, molybdenum, coal, natural gas, crude petroleum, asbestos, gold and silver. Molybdenum production is approximately 99 per cent of the Canadian total.

The production levels for important industries were estimated for 1987 as follows:—

Lumber	37,455,600 cu. metres.
Paper	2,752,600 tonnes
Pulp	6,850,300 tonnes
Coal	21,964,200 tonnes
Natural Gas	9,281,300,000 cu. metres

Mineral production for 1987 was valued at C$3,402·0 million.

The most important agricultural products are livestock, eggs and poultry, fruits and dairy products. Salmon accounts for approximately 60 per cent of the value of fisheries. Other species include halibut, herring, sole, cod, flounder, perch, tuna and shellfish. In 1987 farm cash receipts were valued at C$1,056·3 million.

The economy is dependent upon markets outside the province for the disposal of most of the products of her industry. An estimated 55–60 per cent of production is exported to foreign markets. Manufacturing shipments in 1987 were valued at C$23,008·5 million.

Transport.—The Province has deep water harbours which are well serviced by railways and modern highways. Vancouver is the base for regular scheduled air routes to other parts of Canada, the United States, Europe, Mexico, South America, Hawaii, Fiji, Australia, Japan, Hong Kong and the Middle East.

CAPITAL.—ΨVictoria, Metropolitan population (1988) 266,385. ΨVancouver metropolitan population (1988) 1,452,358, is the western terminus of the Canadian Pacific Railway and the Canadian National Railways (the C.N.R. also has a terminus at Prince Rupert) and the southern terminus of the British Columbia Railway, and possesses one of the finest natural harbours in the world, servicing a variety of vessels, including large bulk cargo carriers. Other principal cities are Prince George, Kamloops, Kelowna and Nanaimo.

MANITOBA

Area and Population.—Manitoba, originally the Red River settlement, is the central province of Canada. The Province has a considerable area of prairie land but is also a land of wide diversity combining 400 miles of sea-coast, large lakes and rivers covering an area of 30,225 sq. miles and precambrian rock which covers about three-fifths of the

Province. The total area is 250,745 sq. miles (649,426 sq. km.), with a population (1987 estimate) of 1,082,800.

Government.—The Government is administered by a Lieutenant Governor, assisted by an Executive Council of Ministers, who are members of the Legislative Assembly of 57 members. Each member of the Legislative Assembly received an annual sessional indemnity totalling C$37,521 for the year ending July 1, 1987.

The Progressive Conservatives formed a minority government after a General Election held on April 26, 1988. The standing in the House at July 7, 1989 was: Progressive Conservatives 24, Liberal 21, New Democratic Party 12.

Lt. Governor, His Honour George Johnson.

EXECUTIVE

Premier, President of the Council and Minister of Federal-Provincial Relations, Hon. Gary A. Filmon.
Natural Resources, Hon. Harry J. Enns.
Northern and Native Affairs and Seniors, Hon. James E. Downey.
Health, Hon. Donald W. Orchard.
Highways and Transportation, and Government Services, Hon. Albert Driedger.
Finance, Hon. Clayton S. Manness.
Family Services, Hon. Charlotte L. Oleson.
Environment, Hon. James G. Cummings.
Attorney-General, Minister for Constitutional Affairs and Corrections, Hon. James C. McCrae.
Co-operative, Consumer and Corporate Affairs, Hon. Edward J. Connery.
Industry, Trade and Tourism, Hon. James A. Ernst.
Agriculture, Hon. Glen M. Findlay.
Education and Training, Hon. Leonard Derkach.
Urban Affairs and Housing, Hon. Gerald Ducharme.
Culture, Heritage and Recreation, Hon. Bonnie E. Mitchelson.
Rural Development, Hon. John Penner.
Energy and Mines, Hon. Harold J. Neufeld.
Labour, the Status of Women, Hon. Gerrie Hammond.

THE JUDICATURE

Court of Appeal:—
Chief Justice of Manitoba, Hon. A. M. Monnin	C$117,900
Puisne Judges, Hons. G. C. Hall; J. F. O'Sullivan; C. R. Huband; A. R. Philp; A. K. Twaddle; S. R. Lyon	108,700
Queen's Bench, Chief Justice, Q.B.D. Hon. A. S. Dewar	117,900
Associate Chief Justice (Family Division), Hon. A. C. Hamilton	117,900

ECONOMY

Finance.—The projected revenue for the province in the fiscal year 1989–90 is C$4,679 million while expenditures are forecast at C$4,766 million.

Agriculture.—The total land area in Manitoba is 135,342,565 acres, of which 19,126,517 acres are in occupied farms. The gross value of agriculture production in 1986 was estimated at C$2,200 million.

Manufactures.—Manufacturing enterprises employed about 57,000 persons on average in 1986. The chief manufacturing centres are Winnipeg, Brandon, Selkirk and Portage la Prairie. The largest manufacturing industry is the food and beverage industry, followed by the machinery and metal fabricating industries.

CAPITAL.—Winnipeg, population 595,000. Other cities are Brandon (38,708), Thompson (14,701), Portage la Prairie (13,198) and Flin Flon (7,243).

NEW BRUNSWICK

Area and Population.—New Brunswick is situated between 45°–48° N. lat. and 63° 47′–69° W. long. and comprises an area of 28,355 sq. miles (73,439 sq. km.), with a population (June 1986 Census) of 710,422. It was first colonized by British subjects in 1761, and in 1783 by inhabitants of New England, who had been dispossessed of their property in consequence of their loyalty to the British Crown. New Brunswick entered Confederation in 1867.

Government.—Government is administered by a Lieutenant Governor, an Executive Council, and a Legislative Assembly of 58 members elected by the people. The present Legislative Assembly of the Province was elected on Oct. 13, 1987 and has 58 members, all of whom are from the Liberal Party.

Lt. Governor, His Honour Gilbert Finn.

EXECUTIVE
(as at June 30, 1989)

Premier, Hon. Frank McKenna.
Justice, Hon. James Lockyer.
Transportation, Hon. Sheldon Lee.
Agriculture, Hon. Alan Graham.
Commerce and Technology, Hon. Al Lacey.
Health and Community Services, Hon. Raymond Frenette.
Minister of State for Child Services, Hon. Jane Barry.
Education, Hon. Shirley Dysart.
Advanced Education and Training, Hon. Russell King.
Labour, Hon. Michael McKee.
Finance, Hon. Allan Maher.
Environment, Hon. Vaughn Blaney.
Municipal Affairs, Hon. Hubert Seamans.
Fisheries and Aquaculture, Hon. Denis Losier.
Tourism, Recreation and Heritage, Hon. Roland Beaulieu.
Chairman, Board of Management, Hon. Gérald Clavette.
Supply and Services, Hon. Bruce Smith.
Natural Resources and Energy, Hon. Morris Green.
Minister of State for Mines, Hon. Edmond Blanchard.
Income Assistance, Hon. Laureen Jarrett.
Housing, Hon. Peter Trites.
Minister responsible for Intergovernmental Affairs, Hon Aldéa Landry.
Speaker of the House, Hon. Frank Branch.
Solicitor General, Hon. Joseph-Conrad Landry.

THE JUDICATURE

Court of Appeal

Chief Justice, Hon. S. G. Stratton.
Judges of Appeal, Hons. J. C. Angers; W. Hoyt; R. C. Rice; L. C. Ayles; P. A. A. Ryan.

Queen's Bench Division

Chief Justice, Hon. G. A. Richard.

ECONOMY

Finance.—The estimated revenue for the year ending March 31, 1988, was C$3,024,858,732 and ordinary expenditure, $3,131,700,768.

Manufactures.—New Brunswick's largest manufacturing group, in terms of shipments, is the paper and allied industries, followed by the food and wood industries. Together these industries accounted in 1988 for 61·8 per cent of the total value of manufacturing shipments of C$4,602·6 million. Saint John has a major ice-free port and is the principal manufacturing centre of the Province.

Agriculture.—Total land area 27,633 sq. miles; farms numbered 3,554 and averaged 284 acres each in 1986. Dairy products and potatoes are the leading agricultural products. Both industries together accounted for 44·7 per cent of total farm cash receipts in 1988. Farm cash receipts in 1988 totalled C$251,593,000.

Fisheries.—Fishing is an important industry, employing about 7,900 fishermen. The chief commercial fish are lobsters, herring, tuna, crab and cod. Landings reached 134,207 tonnes valued at C$108,655,000 in 1988.

Minerals.—Extensive zinc, lead and copper deposits are now being mined in the north-eastern part of the Province with New Brunswick being the third largest producer of zinc in Canada. A lead smelter, fertilizer plant and port facilities have been constructed at Belledune. Canada's only primary antimony producer is located at Lake George. There is exploration and development near Sussex and Salt Springs, where potash production continues to escalate. A potash terminal has been built at the port of St. John. Coal is mined at Grand Lake and exploration for other deposits is being undertaken. Total mineral production was valued at C$831,055,000 in 1988.

Tourism is of increasing value to the economy.

CAPITAL.—Fredericton: population (1986), 65,768. Other cities are ΨSaint John (121,265); Moncton (102,084); Bathurst (34,895); Edmundston (22,614); Campbellton (17,418).

NEWFOUNDLAND AND LABRADOR

Area and Population.—The Island of Newfoundland is situated between 46° 37'–51° 37' N. latitude and 52° 44'–59° 30' W. longitude, on the north-east side of the Gulf of St. Lawrence, and is separated from the North American continent by the Straits of Belle Isle on the N.W. and by Cabot Strait on the S.W. The island is about 317 miles long and 316 miles broad and is triangular in shape. It comprises an area of 43,008 sq. miles (111,390 sq. km.), with a population (1986 Census) (inclusive of Labrador) of 568,349.

Labrador forms the most easterly part of the North American continent, and extends from Point St. Charles, at the northeast entrance to the Straits of Belle Isle, on the south, to Cape Chidley, at the eastern entrance to Hudson's Straits on the north. It has an area of 113,641 sq. miles (294,328 sq. km), with a population (1986 Census) of 28,741. Labrador is noted for its cod fisheries and also possesses valuable salmon, herring, trout and seal fisheries.

Government.—On March 31, 1949 Newfoundland became the 10th Province of the Dominion of Canada. The Government is administered by a Lieutenant Governor, aided by an Executive Council and a Legislative Assembly of 52 members elected for a term of five years. A General Election was held on April 20, 1989. The standings in the current House of Assembly are: Liberals, 32; Progressive Conservatives, 20.

Lt. Governor, His Honour James A. McGrath.

EXECUTIVE
(as at June 30, 1989)

Premier, Hon. Clyde Wells.
Treasury Board President, Hon. Winston Baker.
Fisheries, Hon. Walter Carter.
Employment, Hon. Patt Cowan.
Health, Hon. Chris Decker.
Justice, Hon. Paul Dicks.
Social Services, Hon. John Efford.
Forestry, Hon. Graham Flight.
Development, Hon. Chuck Furey.
Mines and Energy, Hon. Rex Gibbons.
Works, Services and Transportation, Hon. Dave Gilbert.
Municipal and Provincial Affairs, Hon. Eric Gullage.
Environment and Lands, Hon. Paul Kelland.
Finance, Hon. Hubert Kitchen.
Education, Hon. Philip Warren.

Speaker of the House of Assembly, Hon. Dr. P. McNicholas.
Clerk of the Executive Council, H. M. Clarke.

ECONOMY

Finance.—The estimated gross capital and current account revenues for 1989–90 were C$2,894,581,000 and the gross current and capital account expenditures C$3,148,019,200.

Production and Industry.—The main primary industries are fishing, forestry and mining. In 1984 shipments of fish products were valued at C$450 million. In 1988 newsprint shipments from the three pulp and paper mills were valued at C$517 million, mining plus structural materials shipments were estimated at C$888·5 million (1988 provisional figs.), of which C$726·6 million was from the two iron ore mines in Labrador. Manufacturing shipments with the exclusion of fish and paper products totalled approximately C$750 million in 1988. The hydroelectric plant on the Churchill river is the largest underground plant in the world, with a capacity of 5,225,000 kw.

Petroleum and Natural Gas.—Over 137 wells have been drilled off Newfoundland since 1965. Discovery of oil was made in 1979 on the Grand Banks. Oil production is expected to begin in the 1990's, with a peak production of 110,000 barrels of oil a day. In 1988 (provisional figs.) offshore exploration expenditure was approximately C$175 million

Transport.—The Province is connected to mainland Canada by a ferry service from North Sydney, Nova Scotia to Port aux Basques and Argentina. An official agreement on June 20, 1988 signified the end of the railway in Newfoundland. Transport between various points on the island is by highway but the south coast and Labrador still rely on the coastal boat service.

CAPITAL.—ΨSt. John's (population 1986 Census, Greater St. John's 161,901) is North America's oldest city, and thus of historical interest and is the seat of the provincial legislature, the site of most provincial and federal government offices and the principal port for the island of Newfoundland. Newfoundland's second city of Corner Brook (population 1986 Census, 22,719) is situated on the west coast, its principal industry being its pulp and paper mill.

NOVA SCOTIA

Area and Population.—Nova Scotia is a peninsula between 43° 25'–47° N. lat. and 59° 40'–66° 25' W. long., and is connected to New Brunswick by a low fertile isthmus about 17·5 miles wide. It comprises an area of 21,425 sq. miles (55,490 sq. km.), including 1,023 sq. miles of lakes and rivers and 6,479 miles of shoreline. No place is more than 35 miles from the Atlantic Ocean. Population (April 1989 estimate) 885,700.

Government.—The Government consists of a Lieutenant Governor and a 52-member elected Legislative Assembly, from which the Executive Council is selected. The state of the parties in June 1989 was Conservatives 28, Liberals 21, New Democratic Party 2 and Independent 1.

The Lieutenant Governor represents the Queen and is appointed by the Governor-in-Council.

Lt. Governor, His Honour Lloyd R. Crouse, P.C.

EXECUTIVE COUNCIL
(as at June 30, 1989)

Premier, Hon. John M. Buchanan, P.C., Q.C.
Deputy Premier and Minister for Housing, Hon. Roger S. Bacon.
Mines and Energy, Hon. John A. MacIssac.
Tourism and Culture, Hon. Roland J. Thornhill.
Industry, Trade and Technology, Hon. Donald W. Cameron.

Small Business Development, Hon. Kenneth Streatch.

Education, Hon. Ronald C. Giffin, Q.C.

Management Board, Government Services, Hon. Terence R. B. Donahoe, Q.C.

Attorney General, Hon. Thomas J. McInnis.

Advanced Education and Job Training, Hon. Joel R. Matheson, Q.C.

Labour, Hon. Ronald S. Russell.

Finance, Hon. Greg Kerr.

Environment, Hon. John G. Leefe.

Transportation and Communications, Hon. George C. Moody.

Health and Fitness, Hon. David Nantes.

Community Services, Hon. Guy J. LeBlanc.

Municipal Affairs, Hon. Brian A. Young.

Fisheries, Hon. Donald P. McInnes.

Consumer Affairs, Hon. Colin D. Stewart.

Agriculture and Marketing,, Hon. George Archibald.

Lands and Forests, Hon. Charles W. MacNeil.

Solicitor General and Provincial Secretary, Hon. Neil J. LeBlanc.

Speaker of the House of Assembly, Hon. Arthur R. Donahoe, Q.C.

Clerk of the Executive Council, H. F. G. Stevens, Q.C.

During the calendar year 1988, a Member of the House of Assembly was entitled to an annual indemnity of C$28,695 together with an annual expense allowance of C$10,865, a total basic remuneration of C$39,560. In addition the Premier receives C$43,785; a Minister having charge of a Department C$33,935; and a Minister without Portfolio up to C$33,935.

Agent-General in London, Donald M. Smith, 14 Pall Mall, SW1Y 5LU.

The Judicature

Supreme Court—Appeal Division

Chief Justice, Hon. L. O. Clarke .... C$146,400
Judges, Hons. G. L. S. Hart; A. L. Macdonald; L. L. Pace; M. C. Jones; K. M. Matthews; D. R. Chipman............................C$133,800

Trial Division

Chief Justice, Hon. Constance R. Glube ... C$146,400
Judges, Hons. A. M. MacIntosh; W. J. Grant; J. D. Hallett; K. P. Richard; C. Denne Burchell; R. M. Rogers; H. Nathanson; M. Nunn; R. B. Macdonald; F. B. W. Kelly; G. Tidman; J. M. Davison .... C$133,800

Economy

Finance.—The revenue for the fiscal year ending March 31, 1988, was C$3,164,459 and expenditure was C$3,283,606. The net direct debt was C$3,755,603.

Manufacturing.—Manufacturing constitutes the most important goods producing sector of the economy. Shipments were worth C$4,356 million in 1988 with a total added value estimated to be about C$1,800 million. Manufacturing plants provide employment for 46,000 or 11 per cent of the labour force. Capital expenditure in the manufacturing sector has increased from C$599·4 million in 1988 to C$528·9 million in 1989.

Utilities.—Electric power in Nova Scotia is supplied by the Nova Scotia Power Corporation, a Crown corporation. The Corporation's generating stations, which are predominantly coal fired have a nameplate capacity of 1,964,305 kilowatts. The Corporation's generating system is made up of seven thermal plants, three gas turbines, 33 hydro stations scattered throughout the Province and one tidal power station.

Petroleum Activity.—By mid-1988 a total of 125 wells had been completed off-shore since drilling began in 1967, the drilling being done by five major operations. There was one well drilled onshore in 1988–89.

Mining.—The total value of mineral production in 1988 (preliminary) was estimated at C$504,560,000. Dollar value of production for specific minerals was:—

Coal .... C$213,449,000
Sand and gravel 36,000,000
Salt................................. 51,585,000
Limestone 1,640,900

Agriculture.—Farm cash receipts were about C$307 million in 1988. About 3 per cent of the total area, or 390,000 acres, is classified as farm land. Dairy, horticulture, cattle, hogs, fur and poultry products form the largest sectors.

Fishing.—A total of 519,600 tonnes of fish and shellfish was harvested in 1988 for a landed value of C$437, 650,000.

Forest Products.—The gross value of shipments in the manufacturing sector was C$840,436,000 in 1988. Forest lands total 10,800,000 acres or 84 per cent of the land area. About 71 per cent of forest land is privately owned. Forest based industries employed an average of 10,200.

Tourism.—Between May 15 and October 31, 1988, over 1·2 million visitors spent about C$276 million in the Province.

CAPITAL.—ΨHalifax, including the neighbouring city of Dartmouth, has a population of 178,820. In addition to a container-handling terminal in South Halifax a new terminal at the north end of Halifax Harbour was opened in 1981. A 90-acre autoport has been built at Port Halifax to handle both the export and import of motor vehicles. A shipyard, with drydock, can build and repair the largest ocean-going liners. The harbour, ice-free the year round, is the main Atlantic winter port of Canada. Other cities and towns include ΨSydney (27,754), ΨGlace Bay (20,467), Amherst (9,671) and New Glasgow (10,022).

Cape Breton Island

This has been part of Nova Scotia since 1819. It is the centre of the steel manufacturing and coal mining industries, and is also noted for its lakes and coastal scenery, making it a tourist attraction in Canada.

ONTARIO

Area and Population.—The Province of Ontario contains a total area of 412,578 sq. miles (1,068,572 sq. km.), with a population (1986 Census) of 9,113,515.

Government.—The Government is vested in a Lieutenant Governor and a Legislative Assembly of 125 members elected for five years.

After the last election on Sept. 10, 1987, there were 95 Liberals, 19 New Democrats and 16 Progressive Conservatives.

Lt. Governor, His Honour Lincoln Alexander, P.C., Q.C.

Executive Council

Premier and Minister of Intergovernmental Affairs, Hon David Peterson.

Deputy Premier, Minister of the Treasury, Economics and Financial Institutions, Hon. Robert Nixon.

Minister of Mines and Government House Leader, Hon. Sean Conway.

Environment, Hon. James Bradley.

Attorney General and Minister responsible for Native Affairs, Hon. Ian Scott.

Agriculture and Food, Hon. Jack Riddell.

Municipal Affairs, Hon. John Eakins.

Natural Resources, Hon. Vince Kerrio.

Tourism and Recreation, Hon. Hugh O'Neil.

Community and Social Services, Hon. John Sweeney.

Management Board, Chairman of Cabinet, Hon. Murray Elston.

Consumer and Commerical Relations, Hon. William Wrye.

Revenue and Francophone Affairs, Hon. Bernard Grandmaitre.

Skills Development, Hon. Alvin Curling.

Transportation, Hon. Edward Fulton.

Industry, Trade and Technology, Hon. Monte Kwinter.

Culture and Communications, Hon. Lily Munro.

Labour and Women's Issues, Hon. Gregory Sorbara.

Health, Hon. Elinor Caplan.

Northern Development, Hon. Rene Fontaine.

Correctional Services, Hon. David Ramsay.

Solicitor General, Hon. Joan Smith.

Education, Hon. Christopher Ward.

Housing, Hon. Chaviva Hosek.

Colleges and Universities, Hon. Lyn McLeod.

Governmental Services, Hon. Richard Patten.

Citizenship, Race Relations, Hon. Gerry Phillips.

Energy, Hon. Robert Wong.

Disabled Persons, Hon. Remo Mancini.

Senior Citizens, Hon. Mavis Wilson.

Secretary of the Cabinet and Clerk of the Executive Council, R. D. Caraman.

Speaker, Legislative Assembly, Hon. H. Edighoffer.

Agent-General in London, T. Wells, 13 Charles II Street, SW1.

JUDICATURE

Chief Justice of Ontario, Hon. W. G. C. Howland.

Chief Justice of the High Court, Hon. W. D. Pucker.

ECONOMY

Agriculture.—Ontario has the highest total of agricultural production in Canada with a gross value of C$5,520,000,000 and a total net farm income of C$5,460,000,000 in 1986.

Forestry.—Productive forested lands cover 377,000 sq. km. or 35·3 per cent of the land area of the Province. Paper and allied industries are by far the most important sector of Ontario's forest industry.

Minerals.—Ontario's natural resources include 15 basic minerals, such as copper, iron ore, zinc, sulphur, gold and platinum. The province has half the world's supply of nickel and the largest amount of uranium in the western world. Total value of the mineral production in 1986 was estimated at C$4,800,000,000.

Energy.—Total electrical energy generated in Ontario in 1985 was 121,000 million kWh (34 per cent hydro, 40 per cent nuclear and 26 per cent other conventional fossil fuels).

Manufacture.—Ontario is the chief manufacturing province in Canada, producing 50 per cent of all manufactured goods. During 1985 Ontario's exports totalled C$59,000 million, an increase in value of C$4,000 million over 1984. A C$4,200 million growth in the value of end products—the sector which contains the bulk of Ontario's manufactured exports—was also achieved.

CAPITAL.—ΨToronto (metropolitan population 1986, 2,192,721) has a wide range of manufacturing and service industries and is a centre of education, business and finance. Other major urban areas are: Ottawa, the national capital (300,763); ΨHamilton (306,140), with iron and steel industry, metal fabrication, machinery, electrical and chemical industries; London (283,140), a business and manufacturing centre; ΨWindsor (193,111); Kitchener (150,604) and Sudbury (88,717).

PRINCE EDWARD ISLAND

Area and Population.—Prince Edward Island lies in the southern part of the Gulf of St. Lawrence, between 46°–47° N. lat. and 62°–64° 30′ W. long. It is about 140 miles in length, and from 4 to 40 miles in breadth; its area is 2,185 sq. miles (5,659 sq. km.), and its population (1988) 128,800.

Government.—The Government is vested in a Lieutenant Governor, an Executive Council, and Legislative Assembly of 32 members elected for a term of up to 5 years, 16 as Councillors and 16 as Assemblymen. After the election of May 29, 1989 there were 30 Liberals and 2 Progressive Conservatives.

Lt. Governor, His Honour Lloyd G. MacPhail.

EXECUTIVE COUNCIL

Premier, President of the Executive Council, Minister of Justice and Attorney General, Hon. Joseph A. Ghiz, Q.C.

Finance and Environment, Hon. Gilbert R. Clements.

Community and Cultural Affairs, Fisheries and Aquaculture, Hon. Leonce Bernard.

Industry, Hon. Robert Morrissey.

Health and Social Services, Hon. Wayne Cheverie.

Transportation and Public Works, Hon. Gordon MacInnis.

Agriculture, Hon. Keith Milligan.

Education, Hon. Paul Connolly.

Energy and Forestry, Hon. Barry Hicken.

Tourism and Parks, Hon. Nancy Guptill.

Labour, Hon. Roberta Hubley.

Speaker of the Legislative Assembly Hon. Edward W. Clark.

Members of the Legislative Assembly received a salary of C$19,200 per annum *plus* C$9,300 expense allowance; in addition the Premier received C$46,000 per annum; a Minister, C$35,300 per annum; and the Speaker, C$10,000 per annum, as at July 1, 1989.

SUPREME COURT

Chief Justice, Hon. Norman H. Carruthers.

Justices, Appeal Division, Hons. G. E. Mitchell; G. R. McMahon.

Chief Justice, Trial Division, Hon. K. R. MacDonald.

Justices, Trial Division, Hons. A. B. Campbell; G. J. Mullally; J. R. Matheson.

Supernumerary Justice, Hon. C. R. McQuaid.

ECONOMY

Agriculture.—The major industrial activity is agriculture. Approximately 48 per cent of the total area of the Province is farmland. The value of farm cash receipts in 1988 was C$206.2 million, of which 30 per cent was from the sale of potatoes. Dairy, beef and hogs are also important agriculture products.

Finance.—The ordinary revenue of the Province in 1988–89 was C$598.6 million and the expenditure C$603.8 million.

Fisheries.—Fish landings were valued at C$78.3 million in 1988 of which 72 per cent was of lobster.

Manufacturing.—The total value of manufacturing shipments was C$357.5 million in 1988, of which approximately 53 per cent was in food (dairy, vegetable, fish and meat) products and beverages.

Tourism.—A major summer economic activity is tourism. Non-resident tourists spent C$90.0 million in the Province in 1988.

Education.—A university and a college of applied arts and technology were established in 1969, estimated full- and part-time enrolment for 1988–89 being 2,836 (University of Prince Edward Island), and 813 for the college of applied arts and technology (Holland College).

CAPITAL.—ΨCharlottetown (pop. July 1986 Census, 15,776), on the shore of Hillsborough Bay, which forms a good harbour.

QUEBEC

Area and Population.—The Province of Quebec contains an area estimated at 594,855 sq. miles (1,540,667 sq. km.) with a population (June, 1988 estimate), of 6,639,200.

Government.—The Government of the Province is vested in a Lieutenant Governor, a Council of ministers and a National Assembly of 122 members elected for five years. At May 1988, there were 99 Liberals, 20 Parti Quebecois, 1 Independent and 2 vacancies.

Lt. Governor, His Honour Gilles Lamontagne.

Executive

Prime Minister, Hon. Robert Bourassa.
Deputy Prime Minister and Minister for Cultural Affairs, Hon. Lise Bacon.
President of the National Assembly, Hon. Pierre Lorrain.
Parliamentary Leader of the Government and Minister for Tourism, Hon. Michel Gratton.
Manpower and Income Security, Hon. André Boubeau.
Energy and Resources, Hon. John Ciaccia.
Transport and Regional Development, Hon. Marc-Yvan Côté.
International Affairs, Hon. Paul Gobeil.
Health and Social Services, Hon. Thérèse Lavoie-Roux.
Agriculture, Fisheries and Food, Hon. Michel Pagé.
Finance, Hon. Gérard D. Levesque.
Communications, Hon. Robert Dutil.
Revenue and Labour, Hon. Yves Séguin.
Industry, Commerce and Technology, Hon. Pierre MacDonald.
Supply and Services, Hon. André Vallerand.
Justice, Hon. Gil Rémillard.
Municipal Affairs, Hon. Pierre Paradis.
Recreation, Hunting and Fishing, Hon. Yvon Picotte.
International Relations, Hon. Gil Rémillard.
Cultural Communities and Immigration, Hon. Louise Robic.
Education, and Higher Education and Science, Hon. Claude Ryan.
Minister-Delegates, Hon. Albert Côté (*Forests*); Hon. Raymond Savoie (*Mines and Aboriginal Affairs*); Hon. Robert Dutil (*Family, Health and Social Services*); Hon. Pierre Fortier (*Finance and Privatization*); Hon. Monique Gagnon-Trembley (*Status of Women*); Hon. Daniel Johnson (*Administration/President, Treasury Board*); Hon. André Vallerand (*International Affairs*); Hon. Gil Rémillard (Intergovernmental Affairs).
Solicitor General, Hon. Gérard Latulippe.
Agent-General in London, Patrick Hyndmann, 59 Pall Mall, SW1Y 5JH.

Judicature

Court of Appeal, Chief Justice of Quebec, Hon. Claude Bisson.
Superior Court, Chief Justice of Quebec (Montreal), Hon. Alan B. Gold.

Economy

Finance.—The revenue for the year 1986–87 was C$25,646,247,000; expenditure amounted to C$28,465,454,000. The net debt (March 31, 1987) was C$24,051,417,000.

Production and Industry.—The principal manufacturing centres are Montreal, Montreal East, Quebec, Trois-Rivières, Sherbrooke, Shawinigan Drummondville and Lachine. Forest lands cover 779,256 sq. km., of which 556,044 sq. km. are productive. Forest products in 1986 included wood pulp, 6,119,576 tonnes.

Total estimated value of shipments in the manufacturing industries in 1988 was C$72,780,000,000. Value of 1987 shipments in the chief industries:—

Food	C$9,009,000,000
Beverages	1,571,000,000
Paper and allied industries	8,405,000,000
Petroleum and coal products	3,042,000,000
Primary metal industries	7,135,000,000
Transportation equipment industries	6,155,000,000

Agriculture and Fisheries.—In 1988 total farm receipts were:

Crops	C$535,408,000
Livestock and livestock products	2,385,978,000
Other farm receipts	428,883,000

In 1988 89,150 tonnes of fish, to the value of C$97,610,000 were landed.

Mineral Production.—Minerals to the value of C$2,760,951,507 were mined in 1987. This included copper, $161,876,857; asbestos, C$171,860,187; and gold, C$562,326,956.

CAPITAL.—ΨQuebec. Population (Census 1986), 164,580; historic city visited annually by thousands of tourists, and one of the great seaport towns of Canada. ΨMontreal (1,015,420) is the commercial metropolis. Other important cities are Laval (284,164); Verdun (60,246), Sherbrooke (74,438), Montreal-Nord (90,303) and La Salle (75,621).

SASKATCHEWAN

Area and Population.—The Province of Saskatchewan lies between Manitoba to the east and Alberta to the west and has an area of 251,864 sq. miles (652,324 sq. km.), (of which the land area is 220,182 sq. miles), with a population (estimated, 1988) of 1,012,800. Saskatchewan extends along the Canada–U.S.A. boundary for 393 miles and northwards for 761 miles. Its northern width is 276 miles.

Government.—The Government is vested in the Lieutenant Governor, with a Legislative Assembly of 64 members. There is an Executive Council of 16 members. The Legislative Assembly is elected for 5 years and the state of the parties in June 1989 was: Progressive Conservative 38; New Democratic Party 26.

Lt. Governor, Her Honour Sylvia O. Fedoruk.

Executive Council

Premier, President of the Council, and Minister of Agriculture and Food, Hon. Grant Devine.
Deputy Premier, Provincial Secretary, Hon. Eric Berntson.
Attorney-General, Minister of Justice, Trade and Investment, Hon. Robert Andrew.
Economic Development and Tourism, Hon. Joan Duncan.
Education, Hon. Lorne Hepworth.
Energy and Mines, Hon. Patricia Smith.
Environment and Public Safety, Hon. H. Swan.
Finance and Telecommunications, Hon. Gary Lane.
Health, Hon. George McLeod.
Highways and Transportation, Indian and Native Secretariat, Hon. Grant Hodgins.
Human Resources, Labour and Employment, Social Services, Hon. Grant Schmidt.
Parks, Recreation and Culture, Hon. Colin Maxwell.
Public Participation, Hon. Graham Taylor.
Rural Development, Hon. Neal Hardy.
Science and Technology, Consumer and Commercial Affairs, Hon. R. Meiklejohn.
Urban Affairs, Hon. J. Klein.

Premier, C$72,867; Ministers, each C$63,538.

Agent-General in London.—P. Rousseau, 16 Berkeley Street, W1X 5AE.

Finance.—Combined* revenue for year ending March 1990 is C$4,083,400,000 and combined* expenditure C$4,309,460,000 (*Consolidated Fund and Heritage combined).

CAPITAL.—Regina. Population (1987 estimate), 189,400. Other cities: Saskatoon (204,000), Moose Jaw (35,073); Prince Albert (33,686) and Yorkton (15,574).

THE COMMONWEALTH OF AUSTRALIA
AREA AND POPULATION

States	Area (Sq. Miles)	Estimated Resident Population		
		June 30, 1981 (a)	June 30, 1987 (a)	Dec. 31, 1988
States				
New South Wales	309,433	5,234,900	5,612,244	5,738,600
Queensland	667,000	2,345,200	2,676,765	2,782,800
South Australia	380,070	1,318,800	1,394,154	1,415,600
Tasmania	26,383	427,200	447,941	449,300
Victoria	87,884	3,946,900	4,208,946	4,290,300
Western Australia	975,920	1,300,100	1,500,507	1,568,700
Territories				
Australian Capital Territory	939	227,600	266,088	275,300
Northern Territory	520,280	122,600	156,674	156,400
Total	2,967,909	14,923,300	16,263,319	16,676,800

Population of Aboriginal or Torres Strait Islander Origin (a)

States	1976 number			1981 number		
	Aboriginal	T.S.I.	Total	Aboriginal	T.S.I.	Total
States						
New South Wales	37,688	2,763	40,451	33,414	1,953	35,367
Queensland	31,948	9,396	41,344	33,966	10,732	44,698
South Australia	9,940	774	10,714	9,476	349	9,825
Tasmania	2,522	421	2,943	2,334	354	2,688
Victoria	12,415	2,345	14,760	5,283	774	6,057
Western Australia	25,565	560	26,125	30,749	602	31,351
Territories						
Australian Capital Territory	769	59	828	763	60	823
Northern Territory	23,535	215	23,750	28,680	408	29,088
Total	144,382	16,533	160,915	144,665	15,232	159,897

Inter-Censal Increases, 1961–1986

Year of Census	Population at Census			Inter-Censal Increase	Net Immigration during Period	
	Males	Females	Total			
1961	5,333,185	5,215,082	10,548,267	(b) 1,521,656	1954–1961 ..	584,754
1966	5,841,588	5,757,910	11,599,498	1,051,231	1961–1966 ..	395,485
1971 (a)	6,567,936	6,499,329	13,067,265	(c) 1,156,140	1966–1971 ..	521,139
1976 (a)	7,032,034	7,001,049	14,033,083	965,818	1971–1976 ..	281,074
1981 (a)	7,448,267	7,474,993	14,923,260	890,177	1976–1981 ..	370,865
1986 (a)	8,000,187	8,018,163	16,018,350	1,095,090	1981–1986 ..	449,960

(a) Based on Census counts, place of usual residence, adjusted for under-enumeration, and including an estimate of Australian residents temporarily overseas on Census night.
(b) Excludes full-blood Aboriginals.
(c) Based on 1971 Census figure as enumerated.

Births, Deaths, Marriages and Divorces
(Year ended June 30)

	1986	1987	1988*
Births	239,115	242,797	245,759
Deaths	116,069	116,139	120,316
Marriages	113,056	110,690	114,186
Divorces	39,417	39,725	40,998

*provisional

Migration
(Year ended June 30)

	1986	1987	1988
Permanent arrivals	92,590	113,540	143,470
Permanent departures	18,100	19,930	20,470

PHYSICAL FEATURES

Australia, including Tasmania, comprises a land area of 7,682,300 square kilometres lying between latitudes 10°41′S (Cape York) and 43°39′S (South East Cape, Tasmania) and longitudes 113°09′E (Steep Point) and 153°39′E (Cape Byron). The latitudinal distance between Cape York and South East Cape is about 3,680 kilometres and the longitudinal distance between Steep Point and Cape Byron is about 4,000 kilometres. (The latitudinal distance between Cape York and the most southerly point on the mainland South Point, Wilson's Promontory, is about 3,180 kilometres.)

Australia has three major landforms: the western plateau, the interior lowlands and the eastern uplands. The western half of the continent consists mainly of a great plateau of altitude 300–600 metres. The interior lowland includes the channel country of southwest Queensland (drainage to Lake Eyre) and the Murray-Darling river system to the south. The eastern uplands consist of a broad belt of varied width extending from north Queensland to Tasmania and composed largely of tablelands, ranges and ridges with only limited mountain areas above 1,000 metres. The highest point is Mt. Kosciusko (2,228 m.) and the lowest, Lake Eyre (−15 m.).

Australia's large area and latitudinal range have resulted in climatic conditions ranging from the alpine to the tropical. Two thirds of the continent is arid or semi-arid although good rainfalls (over 800 mm annually) occur in the northern monsoonal belt under the influence of the Australian Asian Monsoon and along the eastern and southern highland regions under the influence of the great atmospheric depressions of the Southern Ocean. The effectiveness of the rainfall is greatly reduced by marked alternations of wet and dry seasons, unreliability from year to year, high temperatures and high potential evaporation.

Fifty per cent of the area of Australia has a medium rainfall of less than 300 mm per year and 80 per cent has less than 600 mm. Extreme minimum temperatures are not as low as those recorded in other continents because of the absence of extensive mountain masses and because of the expanse of ocean to the south. However, extreme maxima are comparatively high, reaching 50 C. over the inland, mainly due to the great east–west extent of the continent in the vicinity of the Tropic of Capricorn.

Only one third of the Australian land mass drains directly to the ocean, mainly on the coastal side of the Main Divide and inland with the Murray-Darling system. With the exception of the Murray-Darling system, most rivers draining to the ocean are comparatively short and account for the majority of the country's average annual discharge.

GOVERNMENT

The Commonwealth of Australia was constituted by an Act of the Imperial Parliament dated July 9,

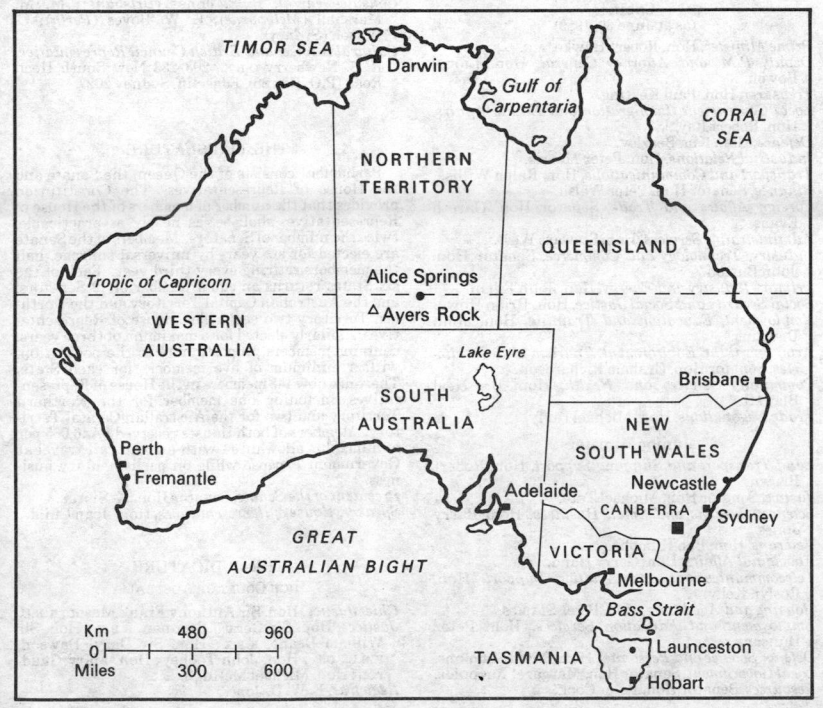

1900, and was inaugurated Jan. 1, 1901. The Government is that of a Federal Commonwealth within the British Commonwealth of Nations, the executive power being vested in the Sovereign (through the Governor General), assisted by a Federal Ministry of Ministers of State. Under the Constitution the Federal Government has acquired and may acquire certain defined powers as surrendered by the States, residuary legislative power remaining with the States. The right of a State to legislate on any matter is not abrogated except in connection with matters exclusively under Federal control, but where a State law is inconsistent with a law of the Commonwealth the latter prevails to the extent of the inconsistency.

CURRENCY.—Australian dollar ($A) of 100 cents.

FLAG.—The British Blue Ensign, consisting of a blue flag, with the Union Flag occupying the upper quarter next the staff, differenced by a large white star (representing the six States of Australia and the Territories of the Commonwealth) in the centre of the lower quarter next the staff and pointing direct to the centre of the St. George's Cross in the Union Flag and five white stars, representing the Southern Cross, in the fly.

NATIONAL ANTHEM.—Advance Australia Fair.

NATIONAL DAY.—January 26 (Australia Day).

Governor General and Staff

Governor General, His Excellency the Hon. Bill Hayden, A.C., *born* January 23, 1933; *assumed office*, February 16, 1989.

Official Secretary, D. I. Smith, A.O., C.V.O.

Deputy Official Secretary, Mrs L. Lawless.

Cabinet
(as at June 30, 1989)

Prime Minister, Hon. Robert Hawke, A.C.

Deputy P.M. and Attorney General, Hon. Lionel Bowen.

Treasurer, Hon. Paul Keating.

Local Government, Immigration and Ethnic Affairs, Hon. Robert Ray.

Defence, Hon. Kim Beazley.

Industrial Relations, Hon. Peter Morris.

Transport and Communications, Hon. Ralph Willis.

Finance, Senator Hon. Peter Walsh.

Foreign Affairs and Trade, Senator Hon. Gareth Evans.

Administrative Services, Hon. Stewart West.

Industry, Technology and Commerce, Senator Hon. John Button.

Primary Industry and Energy, Hon. John Kerin.

Social Security and Social Justice, Hon. Brian Howe.

Employment, Education and Training, Hon. John Dawkins.

Arts, Sport, the Environment, Tourism and Territories, Senator Hon. Graham Richardson.

Community Services and Health, Hon. Dr. Neal Blewett.

Trade Negotiations, Hon. Michael Duffy.

Junior Ministers

Land Transport and Shipping Support, Hon. Robert Brown.

Justice, Senator Hon. Michael Tate.

Science, Customs and Small Business, Hon. Barry Jones.

Veterans, Hon. Ben Humphreys.

Aboriginal Affairs, Hon. Gerry Hand.

Telecommunications and Aviation Support, Hon. Roslyn Kelly.

Housing and Aged Care, Hon. Peter Staples.

Employment and Education Services, Hon. Peter Duncan.

Defence Science and Personnel, Hon. David Simmons.

Local Government, Senator Hon. Margaret Reynolds.

Resources, Senator Hon. Peter Cook.

Arts, Tourism and Territories, Hon. Clyde Holding.

Consumer Affairs, Hon. Nick Bolkus.

AUSTRALIAN HIGH COMMISSION
Australia House, Strand, London, WC2B 4LA
[01–379 4334]

High Commissioner, His Excellency The Hon. Douglas McClelland.

Deputy High Commissioner, D. W. Evans.

Official Secretary, R. E. Taylor.

Ministers, R. G. Starr (*Political*); R. K. H. Lim (*Commercial*); E. F. Delofski (*Economic*).

Defence Adviser and Head of Defence Staff, Brig. I. J. C. Hearn.

BRITISH HIGH COMMISSION
Commonwealth Avenue, Canberra
[Canberra (062) 706666]

High Commissioner, His Excellency Sir John Coles, K.C.M.G. (1988).

Deputy High Commissioner, Head of Chancery, M. G. Dougal.

Defence and Naval Adviser and Head of British Defence Liaison Staff, Cdre. D. M. Oddie.

Counsellors, D. P. R. MacKilligin (*Economic and Commercial*); C. T. W. Skeate.

First Secretaries, D. Moorhouse (*Administration*); P. Reddicliffe; D. H. Cairns (*Commercial, Agriculture*); W. C. Patey; G. Burrows (*Defence Research*); J. Simmons (*Passports*); W. Talbot.

Military Adviser, Col. C. D. McCarthy.

Air Adviser, Gp. Capt. R. J. Coleman.

Consuls-General, B. S. Jones (*Brisbane*); M. M. Marshall (*Melbourne*); L. W. Boyes (*Perth*); C. Wilson (*Sydney*).

Cultural Adviser and British Council Representative, R. S. Newberry O.B.E., 203–233 New South Head Road (P.O. Box 88), Edgecliff, Sydney 2027.

THE LEGISLATURE

Parliament consists of the Queen, the Senate and the House of Representatives. The Constitution provides that the number of members of the House of Representatives shall be, as nearly as practicable, twice the number of Senators. Members of the Senate are elected for six years by universal suffrage, half the members retiring every third year. Each of the six States returns an equal number of 10 Senators, and the Australian Capital Territory and the Northern Territory two each. The House of Representatives, similarly elected for a maximum of three years, contains members proportionate to the population, with a minimum of five members for each State. There are now 148 members in the House of Representatives, including one member for the Northern Territory and two for the Australian Capital Territory. Members of both Houses received $A46,065 per annum, plus allowances, with air and rail travel at Government expense while on parliamentary business.

President of the Senate, Senator Hon. K. Sibraa.

Speaker, House of Representatives, Hon. Joan Child.

THE JUDICATURE
HIGH COURT OF AUSTRALIA

Chief Justice, Hon. Sir Anthony Frank Mason, K.B.E.

Justices, Hon. Sir Gerard Brennan, K.B.E.; Hon. Sir William Deane, K.B.E.; Hon. Sir Daryl Dawson, K.B.E., C.B.; Hon. John Toohey; Hon. Mary Gaudron; Hon. Michael McHugh.

Registrar, F. W. D. Jones.

FEDERAL COURT OF AUSTRALIA

Chief Justice, Hon. Sir Nigel Bowen, A.C., K.B.E.
Judges, Hons. C. A. Sweeney, C.B.E.; Sir Edward
Woodward, O.B.E.; R. M. Northrop; J. A. Keely; F.
R. Fisher; J. F. Gallop; J. D. Davies; J. S. Lockhart;
I. F. Sheppard; J. J. A. Kelly; T. R. Morling; K. J.
Jenkinson; A. R. Neaves; B. A. Beaumont; M. R.
Wilcox; J. E. J. Spender; P. R. A. Gray; C. W.
Pincus; J. C. S. Burchett; J. A. Miles; D. M. Ryan;
W. M. C. Gummow; R. S. French; M. R. Einfeld; T.
R. Hartigan; M. L. Foster; A. B. Nicholson; M. C.
Lee; H. W. Olney; J. W. von Doussa; D. G. Hill.
Registrar, J. T. Howard, R.F.D., E.D.

SUPREME COURT OF THE AUSTRALIAN
CAPITAL TERRITORY

Judges, Hons. J. A. Miles (*Chief Justice*); J. J. A.
Kelly; J. F. Gallop (*Resident Judges*); Sir Edward
Woodward, O.B.E.; R. M. Northrop; J. D. Davies; J.
S. Lockhart; I. F. Sheppard; T. R. Morling; K. J.
Jenkinson; B. A. Beaumont; M. R. Wilcox; J. E. J.
Spender; C. W. Pincus; M. L. Foster; D. M. Ryan;
J. W. von Doussa (*Additional Judges*).
Registrar, P. G. Dingwall.

SUPREME COURT OF THE NORTHERN TERRITORY

Chief Justice, Hon. K. J. A. Asche.
Judges, Hons. J. A. Nader; Sir William Kearney; P.
J. Rice; B. J. Martin; D. N. Angel.
Master, P. G. Lefevre.

DEFENCE

A single Department of Defence was created in
1973, following the abolition of the Departments of
the Navy, Army and Air, though the separate
identities of the three services have been retained.
The defence research and development elements of
the former Department of Supply, along with other
research groups on the three services, were incorporated in 1978 into the Defence, Science and Technology Organization. The Chief of Defence Force Staff
is responsible for command of the Defence Force
through the three Service Chiefs of Staff and is also
the principal military adviser to the Minister.

The Secretary to the Department of Defence is
responsible to the Minister for Defence for advice on
policy, resources and organization.

Total defence expenditure was $A 7,578,169,000 in
1986–87.

The personnel strengths of the Permanent Defence
Force at June 30, 1987 were:—

	Males	Females
Navy	14,345	1,458
Army	30,016	2,295
Air Force	20,161	2,486
Total	64,522	6,239

FINANCE

COMMONWEALTH GOVERNMENT FINANCE

Outlays and revenue of the Commonwealth Government were ($Amillion):

	1987–88*	1988–89†
Current outlays	75,084	78,044
Capital outlays	3,323	3,714
Revenue	80,765	87,539
Financing transactions	− 2,358	− 5,832

*preliminary †estimate

STATE GOVERNMENT FINANCE 1987–88(*)
($A million)

State	Outlay (current and capital)	Revenue and grants received	Financing transactions
N.S.W.	17,878	16,240	1,639
Victoria	14,147	11,892	2,255
Queensland	8,685	8,093	592
S. Australia	4,782	4,284	497
W. Australia	5,773	5,180	593
Tasmania	1,751	1,579	172
N.T.	1,242	1,107	135
Total	54,258	48,375	5,883

(*) preliminary

BANKING

In June 1987 the trading banks had total liabilities
of $A114,871 million including total deposits of
$A57,367 million; and total assets of $A126,844
million, including $A10,870 million of Commonwealth
Government securities.

PRODUCTION AND INDUSTRY

In 1985, 63·6 per cent of the Australian land area
consisted of agricultural establishments, with the
remainder being urban areas, State forests, mining
leases and unoccupied land. Crop-growing areas
constituted up to 4·32 per cent of the total agricultural
establishments, emphasizing the relative importance
of the livestock industries in Australia (sheep in the
warm, temperate, semi-arid lands and beef cattle in
the tropics).

The wide range of climatic and soil conditions over
the agricultural regions of Australia has resulted in
a diversity of crops being grown throughout the
country. Generally, cereal crops (excluding rice and
sorghum) are grown in all States over wide areas,
while other crops are confined to specific locations in
a few States. However, scanty or erratic rainfall,
limited potential for irrigation and unsuitable soils
or topography have restricted intensive agriculture.

The gross values of agricultural commodities ($A
million):—

	1986–87	1987–88*
Crops	7,618·0	7,676·6
Livestock slaughterings	4,611·0	5,021·6
Livestock products	4,915·6	7,283·0
Total agriculture	17,152·8	19,989·8
* provisional.		

AGRICULTURAL PRODUCTION
All crops gross value ($A million)

	1986–87	1987–88p
Cereals for grain		
Barley	432·6	455·1
Wheat	2,410·3	2,039·1
Total	3,330·2	3,079·5
Cotton	372·5	437·1
Crops for hay	79·1	89·0
Fruit		
Apples	204·5	198·7
Bananas	126·7	123·4
Grapes	272·2	337·9
Oranges	126·1	147·9
Sugar Cane*	586·4	633·6

	1986–87	1987–88p
Vegetables		
Potatoes	272·0	198·7
Tomatoes	115·0	121·5
Total pastures and grasses	419·3	403·4
Total crops	7,618·0	7,676·6

p preliminary
* cut for crushing

In 1987–88 the gross value (preliminary figures) of wool production was $A5,537·3 million (1986–87 was $A3,333·6 million).

Livestock Numbers at March 31 (in thousands)

	1985	1986	1987
Sheep and lambs	149,248	146,776	149,157
Cattle and calves	22,738	21,820	21,915
Pigs	2,463	2,512	2,611
Poultry	54,833	52,791	57,608

Mines and Minerals.—Significant mineral resources comprise bauxite, coal, copper, crude petroleum, gems, gold, ilmenite, iron ore, lead, limestone, manganese, nickel, rutile, salt, silver, tin, tungsten, uranium, zinc and zircon. Recently, geological exploration has significantly increased the mineral resources of the nation.

Australia now has fourteen oilfields in production: Alton, Bennett, Conloi, Kincora, Moonie and Trinidad in Queensland; Barracouta, Cobia, Halibut, Kingfish, Mackerel and Tuna in Victoria in the offshore Gippsland Basin and Dongara and Barrow Island in Western Australia.

In 1983–84, value added by the mining industry was $A8,825·4 million. Mine production of black coal was 116,346,000 tonnes, crude oil (incl. condensate) was 26,826 megalitres and natural gas 12,098 gigalitres. Production of principal metals was:—

Iron ore	76,478,000 tonnes	
Copper	249,282	,,
Lead-Zinc concentrate	37,932	,,
Gold	33,881 kg.	

Manufactures.—In 1983–84 there were in Australia 27,470 industrial establishments, employing 1,009,376 persons; wages paid amounted to $A17,461m; purchases, transfers in and selected expenses $A54,666m; value added by manufacture $A34,229m; and turnover $A88,632m.

Trade Unions.—On June 30, 1985, there were 323 reporting trade unions in Australia with a total membership of 3,154,200.

TRADE

	1986–87	1987–88
Imports	$A36,988,073,000	$A40,591,016,000
Exports	35,806,394,000	40,945,604,000

IMPORTS FROM ALL COUNTRIES, 1987–88
(by commodity classifications)

	$A'000
Food and live animals	1,668,580
Beverages and tobacco	344,545
Crude materials, inedible (except fuels)	1,321,723
Crude fertilizers, crude minerals (except coal, petroleum, precious stones)	248,255
Mineral fuels, lubricants, etc	2,050,033
Petroleum, petroleum products, etc	2,040,231
Animal and vegetable oils, fats and waxes	107,760
Chemical and related products, n.e.s.	4,274,475
Organic chemicals	1,106,443
Manufactured goods	7,125,755
Textile yarn, fabric, made-up articles, n.e.s., etc.	1,926,372
Machinery and transport equipment	16,368,660
Road vehicles	3,139,043
Miscellaneous manufactured articles	5,574,896
Imports not classified elsewhere	1,754,589
TOTAL IMPORTS	40,591,016

EXPORTS 1987–88
(by commodity classifications)

	$A'000
Food and live animals	8,099,631
Meat and meat preparations	2,558,917
Cereal grains and preparations	2,297,173
Beverages and tobacco	249,724
Crude materials, inedible (except fuels)	12,326,587
Textile fibres and their wastes	5,600,308
Metalliferous ores and metal scrap	5,283,611
Mineral fuels, lubricants, etc	7,021,824
Coal, coke and briquettes	4,834,363
Animal and vegetable oils, fats and waxes	138,329
Chemical and related products, n.e.s.	892,096
Manufactured goods	4,954,237
Non-ferrous metals	3,251,519
Machinery and transport equipment	2,731,593
Miscellaneous manufactured articles	1,026,169
Exports not classified elsewhere	3,505,414
TOTAL EXPORTS	40,945,604

MAIN TRADING PARTNERS 1987–88

Imports from:—	Value ($A m.)	Percentage of total trade
U.S.A.	8,529·8	21·0
Japan	7,816·7	19·3
U.K.	3,011·7	7·4
Germany, Fed. Rep.	2,918·0	7·2
Taiwan	1,743·9	4·3
New Zealand	1,732·5	4·3
Italy	1,329·5	3·3
Korea, Rep. of	1,020·0	2·5

Exports to:—	Value ($A m.)	Percentage of total trade
Japan	10,661·2	26·0
U.S.A.	4,652·1	11·4
New Zealand	2,181·8	5·3
Hong Kong	1,927·8	4·7
Korea, Rep. of	1,781·9	4·4
U.K.	1,771·2	4·3
Taiwan	1,374·5	3·4
China	1,277·5	3·1

FOOD EXPORTS TO U.K. 1987–88

	$A'000
Meat and meat preparations	67,001
Cereal and cereal preparations	1,125
Dairy products and birds' eggs	7,803
Vegetables and fruit	60,741
Sugar, sugar preparations and honey	6,830

COMMUNICATIONS

Railways.—There are six government owned railways systems, operated by the State Rail Authority of N.S.W., Victorian Railways, Queensland Government Railways, Western Australian Government Railways, the State Transport Authority of Southern Australia, and the Australian National Railways Commission. The A.N.R.C. incorporates the former Commonwealth Railways system, and the Tasmanian and non-metropolitan South Australian railways (urban rail services in Southern Australia remain the responsibility of the State Transport Authority). In 1985–86 there were 38,760 route-kilometres open.

Gross earnings 1985–86 were:	$A million
New South Wales	1,082·4
Victoria	335·0
Queensland	966·0
South Australia*	14·6
Western Australia	262·0
A.N.R.C.	283·3
Total	2,943·3

*Includes urban rail operations only.

In 1985–86 there were 377,520,000 rail passenger journeys on government railways and 171,841,000 tonnes of goods and livestock carried.

Shipping.—Total arrivals and departures (one arrival and one departure per voyage, irrespective of the number of ports visited) of vessels engaged in overseas trade at the various Australian ports in 1986–87 were: arrivals 6,707 (300,348,000 deadweight tonnes); departures 6,507 (296,952,000 deadweight tonnes).

Posts and Telegraphs.—In the year ended June 30, 1984, there were 4,790 post offices dealing with a total of 3,035,060 postal articles. Internal telegrams despatched numbered 3,668,907. At June 30, 1984, there were 53·6 telephones per 100 population.

Broadcasting and Television.—On June 30, 1984, the Australian Broadcasting Corporation operated 144 stations. Privately owned commercial broadcasting stations totalled 137. On June 30, 1984, 276 national and 152 commercial television and translator stations were in operation.

Motor Vehicles.—At June 30, 1987, there were 9,022,700 motor vehicles registered in Australia and 351,600 motor cycles.

Civil Aviation.—Figures for domestic and overseas services in 1985–86 are as follows:

	Domestic	Overseas
Paying passengers	12,057,000	2,671,000
Freight (tonnes)	150,369	91,961
Mail (tonnes)	17,997	4,869

FEDERAL CAPITAL

CANBERRA is the capital of Australia. It is situated in the Australian Capital Territory which has an area of 939 sq. miles (2,395 sq. km.) and was acquired from New South Wales in 1911. Canberra, which is the seat of the federal government, had a population (estimated) at June 30, 1986, of 281,000. Apart from Parliament House, the city also contains other national institutions, such as the Australian War Memorial, National Library, Royal Australian Mint and the Australian National University. Most Government departments have their headquarters in Canberra. An artificial lake is a central feature of this planned city, based on Walter Burley Griffin's design.

THE NORTHERN TERRITORY

The Northern Territory has a total area of 519,770 sq. miles (1,346,200 sq. km.), and lies between 129°–138° east longitude and 11°–26° south latitude. The estimated population in the Northern Territory at June 1987 was 158,400, of which about a quarter are Aboriginals.

The administration was taken over by the Commonwealth on January 1, 1911, from the government of the State of South Australia.

The Northern Territory (Self-Government) Act 1978 established the Northern Territory as a body politic as from 1 July 1978, with Ministers having control over and responsibility for Territory finances and the administration of the functions of government as specified by the Federal Government by regulations made pursuant to the Act. Proposed laws passed by the Legislative Assembly in relation to a transferred function require the assent of the Administrator. Proposed laws in all other cases may be assented to by the Administrator or reserved by the Administrator for the Governor General's pleasure. The Governor General may disallow any laws assented to by the Administrator within six months of the Administrator's assent.

The Northern Territory has federal representation electing one member to the House of Representatives and two members to the Senate.

Seat of Administration.—Darwin.
Administrator, His Honour the Honourable J. H. Muirhead, Q.C.

THE MINISTRY

Chief Minister and Treasurer, Hon. Marshall Perron.
Deputy Chief Minister, Minister for Mines and Energy, Industries and Development, Hon. Barry Coulter.
Attorney General, Lands and Housing, Conservation, Hon. Daryl Manzie.
Health and Community Services, Hon. Don Dale.
Education and Assisting on Constitutional Development, Hon. Tom Harris.
Transport and Works, Hon. Fred Finch.
Labour, Administrative Services and Local Government, Hon. Terry McCarthy.
Tourism, Assisting on Central Australian Affairs, Hon. Eric Poole.
Primary Industry and Fisheries, Hon. Mike Reed.

Various Aboriginal Land Trusts hold title to land previously called Reserves, totalling about one-fifth of the Northern Territory.

The Aboriginal Land Rights (N.T.) Act of 1976 provides for the investigation and determination of Aboriginal traditional claims to vacant Crown land or land already owned by or on behalf of Aboriginals. Successful land claims to date have increased Aboriginal ownership to 34 per cent of the Northern Territory whilst a further 13 per cent is the subject of claims.

A number of major Aboriginal communities previously administered by Church Mission Societies and the Federal Government are now controlled by the Aboriginal people themselves, through local Aboriginal Councils. A recent phenomenon is the voluntary movement of some Aboriginals to their traditional homeland areas where they feel that their culture will be better preserved.

ECONOMY

Northern Territory's economy is based on the exploitation of its natural resources of minerals, land, fisheries and tourist attractions. Following the introduction of a number of government measures designed to expand and diversify primary production, the Territory's agricultural and horticultural industries are also beginning to contribute an increasing amount to Territory rural output.

The beef cattle industry continues to be the major user of pastoral lands and cattle production in the financial year to 1988 was valued at $A109 million.

The buffalo population, estimated at 100,000 head, is confined to the Darwin and Gulf districts. Live buffalos and buffalo meat products are an important export, currently valued at $A9·9 million.

The Territory's six main crops are sorghum, maize, mung beans, soybeans, peanuts and rice. A total of 8,595 hectares was harvested in 1987–88 and was valued at $A1,789,600.

In 1988, 1,400 hectares were used for horticulture in the Territory, yielding crops valued at $A13·2 million. Crops include a wide range of temperate and tropical fruit and vegetables.

The annual gross value of production of the Northern Territory's fishing industry was approximately $A33·5 million in 1988. The industry is based on barramundi and prawn fisheries. Other resources, such as mud crab, shark, mackerel and offshore reef fish are becoming increasingly important. A mooring basin for protection of the fleet from cyclonic conditions has been constructed.

Mining has played a major part in the development of the Northern Territory and in the calendar year 1988 the industry produced minerals with a value of $A1,199 million. The Territory is a leading uranium producer, extracting 3,713,287 kg of uranium oxide in 1988 with a value of $A254 million. In 1988 1·97 million tonnes of manganese was sold, with a total value of about $A126 million. Gold production for 1988 was valued at $A195 million.

Tourism is of importance to the Territory's economy. It is a major growth industry and generates over $A300 million annually.

COMMUNICATIONS

The Northern Territory has three main ports—Darwin, managed by the Darwin Port Authority; and the private mining ports of Gove, operated by Nabalco Pty. Ltd., and Groote Eylandt, operated by Groote Eylandt Mining Co. Pty. Ltd.

The new standard gauge rail link between Southern Australia and Alice Springs was officially opened in October, 1980. The link between Alice Springs and Darwin is provided by a fully co-ordinated rail-road service.

The main population centres are linked by the Stuart Highway, which connects Alice Springs to Darwin via Tennant Creek and Katherine. Of special interest to the Northern Territory is the operation of "road trains". These are basically massive trucks hauling two or three trailers, having a net capacity of about 100 tonnes and measuring up to 45 metres in length.

Darwin is a port of call for international air services between Australia and Asia, and New Zealand. Within Australia, there are flights from Darwin to all Australian capital cities by two major domestic carriers, Australian Airlines and Ansett Airlines of Australia. Internally, the main Territory centres of Katherine, Tennant Creek, Alice Springs, Ayers Rock, Nhulunbuy and Groote Eylandt are linked by Ansett N.T. All the major centres can take jet passenger traffic.

AUSTRALIAN EXTERNAL TERRITORIES

ASHMORE AND CARTIER ISLANDS

Ashmore Islands (known as Middle, East and West Islands) and Cartier Island are situated in the Indian Ocean some 850 km. and 790 km. west of Darwin respectively. The islands lie at the outer edge of the continental shelf. They are small and low and are composed of coral and sand. Vegetation consists mainly of grass. Turtles are plentiful at certain times of the year and beche-de-mer is abundant. The islands are uninhabited.

Great Britain took formal possession of the Ashmores in 1878 and Cartier was annexed in 1909. By Imperial Order in Council of July 23, 1931, the islands were placed under the authority of the Commonwealth of Australia, and were accepted in 1933 under the name of the Territory of Ashmore and Cartier Islands. The territory was annexed to the Northern Territory of Australia. With the granting of self-government to the Northern Territory on July 1, 1978, responsibility for the administration of Ashmore and Cartier Islands became a direct responsibility of the Commonwealth Government. In 1983 Ashmore Reef was declared a national nature reserve.

In accordance with an agreement between the governments of Indonesia and Australia, Indonesian fishermen who have traditionally plied the area may engage in limited fishing activity within the territory but are prohibited from taking any products from the nature reserve. They can land to collect water at certain locations.

THE AUSTRALIAN ANTARCTIC TERRITORY

The Australian Antarctic Territory was established by an Order in Council, dated February 7, 1933, which placed under the government of the Commonwealth of Australia all the islands and territories, other than Adélie Land, which are situated south of the latitude 60° S. and lying between 160° E. longitude and 45° E. longitude. The Order came into force on August 24, 1936, after the passage of the Australian Antarctic Territory Acceptance Act, 1933. The boundaries of Terre Adélie were definitely fixed by a French Decree of April 1, 1938, as the islands and territories south of 60° S. latitude lying between 136° E. longitude and 142° E. longitude. The Australian Antarctic Territory Act 1954 declared that the laws in force in the Australian Capital Territory are, so far as they are applicable, in force in the Australian Antarctic Territory. The territory is administered by the Antarctic Division of the Department of Science, which, since its inception in 1947, has organized yearly expeditions to Antarctica, known as Australian National Antarctic Research Expeditions (ANARE).

On February 13, 1954, ANARE opened Mawson Station in Mac-Robertson Land at latitude 67° 36′ S. and longitude 62° 53′ E. Scientific research conducted at Mawson includes upper atmosphere physics, cosmic ray physics, meteorology, earth sciences, biology and medical science. Mawson is also a centre for coastal and inland exploration.

Davis Station was opened on the coast of Princess Elizabeth Land on January 13, 1957, at latitude 68° 35′ S. and longitude 77° 58′ E. Scientific programmes carried out at Davis include meteorology, biology, upper atmosphere physics, with field investigations in biology.

In February, 1959, the Australian Government accepted from the U.S. Government custody of Wilkes Station on the Budd Coast, Wilkes Land. The station was closed in February 1969, and activities were transferred to the nearby Casey Station at 66° 17′ S., 110° 32′ E. Scientific programmes carried out there include geophysics, meteorology with field programmes in glaciology, geology, etc.

Each of the stations on continental Antarctica are being replaced by new station buildings of advanced design, in a building programme which is expected to be completed in 1998.

Since 1948 ANARE has operated a station on Macquarie Island, a dependency of Tasmania, situated at 54° 30′ S. and 158° 57′ E., about 900 miles north of the Antarctic Continent.

Summer stations have been established in the Bunger Hills, 200 miles west of Casey, at Cape Denison in Commonwealth Bay, in the Larsemann Hills and on Heard Island.

CHRISTMAS ISLAND

Until the end of 1957 a part of the then Colony of Singapore, Christmas Island was administered as a separate colony until October 1, 1958, when it became an Australian territory. It is situated in the Indian Ocean about 224 miles S. of Java Head. Area 52 sq. miles. Population (estimated, June 30, 1988) is 1,100, consisting of former employees of the Phosphate Mining Corporation, and present employees of the Christmas Island Services Corporation, the Administration, and their families. There is no indigenous population.

The island is densely wooded and had extensive deposits of phosphates, the extraction of which has traditionally been the major economic activity. An Australian Government company, the Phosphate Mining Corporation of Christmas Island, which carried out the mining operation ceased operating on Dec. 31, 1987. Extensive deposits of low grade phosphate ore still remain but alternative economic development is being encouraged. The principal current development is a hotel complex.

The Administrator is responsible to the Australian Minister for Arts, Sport, the Environment, Tourism and Territories in Canberra. The second local elections were held in Oct. 1986 and nine members were elected to the Christmas Island Assembly. The Assembly is responsible for directing the operations of the Christmas Islands Services Corporation, which was established in 1984 to provide municipal functions and services.

Administrator, Hon. A. D. Taylor, O.B.E.

COCOS (KEELING) ISLANDS

The Cocos (Keeling) Islands were declared a British possession in 1857. All land in the islands was granted to George Clunies-Ross and his heirs by Queen Victoria in 1886. In 1955 the islands, which had been governed through the British colonies of Ceylon (from 1878), the Straits Settlements (1886) and Singapore (1903), were accepted as a Territory of Australia.

In 1978 the Australian Government purchased all Clunies-Ross land and property interests except for the family home and grounds. In 1979 ownership of the kampong area of Home Island was transferred to the Cocos (Keeling) Islands Council, the local government body established in 1979. Title to most of the remaining land purchased from Clunies-Ross in 1978 was transferred to the Council in 1984.

The Cocos (Keeling) Islands Act, 1955, provides the legal framework for the present political and administrative arrangements in the Territory. On April 6, 1984, the Cocos community, in a U.N. supervised Act of Self-Determination, chose to integrate with Australia. The Government's major commitment was that living standards would reach comparable mainland levels by 1994. The Commonwealth Grants Commission monitors the progress.

The islands are two separate atolls (North Keeling Island and, 24 km. to the south, the main atoll) comprising some 27 small coral islands with a total area of about 14 sq. km., situated in the Indian Ocean in latitude 12° 5′ South and longitude 96° 53′ East. The main islands of the southern atoll are West Island (the largest, about 9 km. from north to south) on which are the administrative centre, the aerodrome, and the Australian-based employees of government departments; Home Island, where the Cocos Malay community and the Clunies-Ross family live; Direction Island, Horsburgh and South Island.

The territory has no viable economic base at present. In 1986–87 the copra industry suffered severe losses and in 1987 ceased production. Tourism is being developed as a likely successor to the copra industry.

The climate is equable and pleasant, being usually under the influence of the south-east trade winds for about three-quarters of the year. A weekly air charter service operates between Perth, the Cocos (Keeling) Islands and Christmas Island. Population (June 30, 1988), 686. The islands are administered by the Australian Government through the Department of the Arts, Sport, the Environment, Tourism and Territories in Canberra. All proposed Ordinances, Regulations and By-laws for the islands must be submitted to the Islands Council (est. 1979) for its consideration.

Acting Administrator, Ms. D. Lawrie.

CORAL SEA ISLANDS TERRITORY

The Coral Sea Islands Territory lies east of Queensland between the Great Barrier Reef and longitude 156° 06′ E., and between latitudes 12° and 24° S. It comprises scattered islands, often little more than sandbanks, spread over a sea area of 780,000 sq. km. The islands are formed mainly of coral and sand. Some have grass or scrub cover but most are extremely small, with no permanent fresh water.

There is a manned metereological station in the Willis Group but the remaining islands are uninhabited. Large populations of sea birds nest and breed in the area, and two national nature reserves were designated in the Territory in 1982.

The Australian Government bases its claim to the islands on numerous acts of sovereignty since early this century and enacted the Coral Sea Islands Act 1969 which declares the islands a territory of the Commonwealth of Australia. The Department of the Arts, Sport, the Environment, Tourism and Territories, Canberra, is responsible for the administration of the territory.

HEARD ISLAND AND MCDONALD ISLANDS

The Heard and McDonald islands, about 4,100 km. south-west of Fremantle, comprise all the islands and rocks lying between 52° 30′ and 53° 30′ S. latitude and 72° and 74° 30′ E. longitude. Sovereignty over the islands was transferred by the U.K. to the Commonwealth of Australia in 1947. The Heard Island and McDonald Islands Act 1953 provides for the government of the islands as one territory. Under this Act the law operating there is that of the Australian Capital Territory. The islands are administered by the Department of the Arts, Sport, the Environment, Tourism and Territories. Under the Environment Protection and Management Ordinance 1987, a permit system regulates entry to the territory and a range of activities there.

NORFOLK ISLAND

Norfolk Island is situated in the South Pacific Ocean at latitude 29° 02′ S. and longitude 167° 57′ E., being about 1,042 miles from Sydney and 400 miles north of New Zealand. It is about five miles in length by three in breadth, with an area of 8,528 acres. The climate is mild and sub tropical. Resident population at the 1986 Census was 1,977.

The island, discovered by Capt. Cook in 1774, served as a penal colony from 1788 to 1814 and 1825 to 1855. In 1856, 194 descendants of the *Bounty* mutineers accepted an invitation to leave Pitcairn and settle on Norfolk Island, which led to Norfolk Island becoming a separate settlement under the jurisdiction of the Governor of N.S.W. In 1897 Norfolk Island became a dependency of N.S.W., and in 1914, pursuant to the Norfolk Island Act 1913, a territory of Australia. From that date, Norfolk Island has been regarded as an integral part of Australia.

In 1979 Norfolk Island gained a substantial degree of self-government, enabling the island to run its affairs to the greatest practical extent. Wide powers are exercised by a nine-member Legislative Assembly. The Act preserves the Commonwealth's responsibility for Norfolk Island as a territory under its authority, with the Minister for the Arts, Sport, the Environment, Tourism and Territories as the responsible Minister. In 1985, responsibility for a range of matters was transferred, and the transference of more is proceeding.

The island is a popular tourist resort, and a large proportion of the population depends on tourism and its ancillaries for employment. In 1987–88 there were 28,192 tourist arrivals on the Island. Regular air services operate from mainland Australia and New Zealand.

Seat of Government and Administration Offices.— Kingston.

Administrator, H. B. McDonald.

STATES OF THE COMMONWEALTH OF AUSTRALIA

NEW SOUTH WALES

The State of New South Wales is situated entirely between the 28th and 38th parallels of S. lat. and 141st and 154th meridians of E. long., and comprises an area of 309,433 sq. miles (801,427 sq. km.) (exclusive of 939 sq. miles of Australian Capital Territory which lies within its borders).

POPULATION.—Preliminary estimated resident population at Dec. 31, 1988 was 5,738,600.

Births, deaths and marriages of usually resident population were:

	1987	1988p
Births.................	85,650	84,139
Deaths	42,146	43,954
Marriages	38,380	38,741

p preliminary.

Annual rate per 1,000 of estimated resident population in 1988 (preliminary):—Births, 14·8; Deaths, 7·8; Marriages, 7·2. Deaths under 1 year per 1,000 live births, 9·0.

Religions

The members of the Roman Catholic Church in New South Wales, according to the Census of 1986, numbered 1,529,176, Anglican Church 1,519,806, Uniting (including Methodist) 327,360, Presbyterian 227,663, Orthodox 165,659, Baptist 67,187, Lutheran 31,890, other Christian 288,865, Muslim 57,551, Hebrew 28,236 and other religions 57,079. The religion of 1,101,409 persons was either not stated in the census schedules or was stated as "none".

PHYSIOGRAPHY

Natural features divide the State into four main zones extending from north to south, viz., the Coastal Districts; the Tablelands, which form the Great Dividing Range between the coastal districts and the plains; the Western Slopes of the Dividing Range; and the Western Plains. The highest points are Mounts Kosciusko, 7,314 ft., and Townsend, 7,251 ft. The western portion of the State is watered by the rivers of the Murray-Darling system. The Darling, the major part of whose 1,712 miles is in N.S.W., and the Murrumbidgee, 981 miles, are both tributaries of the Murray, part of which forms the boundary between the States of New South Wales and Victoria.

Climate.—New South Wales is situated entirely in the Temperate Zone. The climate is generally mild and mostly free from extremes of heat and cold. At Sydney the average mean shade temperature is 18° C with a range of 11°C between the hottest and coldest months. Rainfall varies widely over the State diminishing from an annual average of about 2,000 mm. in parts of the north coast to about 200 mm. in the far north west.

GOVERNMENT

New South Wales was first colonized as a British possession in 1788, and after progressive settlement a partly elective legislature was established in 1843. In 1855 Responsible Government was granted, the present Constitution being founded on the Constitution Act of 1902. New South Wales federated with the other States of Australia in 1901. The executive authority of the State is vested in a Governor (appointed by the Crown), assisted by a Council of Ministers.

GOVERNOR

Governor of New South Wales, His Excellency Rear-Adm. D. J. Martin, A.O., *assumed office* Jan. 20, 1989.

Lt. Governor, The Hon. Sir Laurence Whistler Street, K.C.M.G.

THE MINISTRY
(since June 8, 1988)

Premier, Treasurer and Minister for Ethnic Affairs, Hon. N. F. Greiner.

Deputy Premier, Minister for State Devlopment, and Public Works, Hon. W. T. J. Murray.

Health and Arts, Hon. P. E. J. Collins.

Agriculture and Rural Affairs, Hon. I. M. Armstrong, O.B.E.

Attorney General, Hon. J. R. A. Dowd.

Housing, Hon. J. J. Schipp.

Environment and Assistant Minister for Transport, Hon. T. J. Moore.

Chief Secretary and Minister for Tourism, Hon. G. B. West.

Police and Emergency Services, Vice-President of Executive Council, Hon. E. P. Pickering.

Sport, Recreation and Racing, Hon. R. B. R. Smith.

Family and Community Services, Hon. Virginia Chadwick.

Education and Youth Affairs, Hon. T. A. Metherell.

Transport, Hon. B. G. Baird.

Administrative Services and Assistant Minister for Transport, Hon. M. Singleton.

Business and Consumer Affairs, Hon. G. B. P. Peacocke.

Mineral Resources and Energy, Hon. N. E. W. Pickard.

Industrial Relations and Employment and Minister Assisting the Premier, Hon. J. J. Fahey.

Natural Resources, Hon. I. R. Causley.

Local Government and Planning, Hon. D. A. Hay.

Corrective Services, Hon. M. R. Yabsley.

The annual salaries of Ministers are: Premier, $A89,088; Deputy Premier, $A80,257; Leader of the Government members in the Legislative Council, $A81,155; (Deputy $A77,325); other Ministers $A75,808 each. Ministers also receive expense allowances and electoral allowances, and a special expense allowance is paid to Ministers who represent or reside in outlying electorates.

AGENT-GENERAL IN LONDON

Agent-General, Hon. K. J. Stewart, N.S.W. House, 66 Strand, WC2N 5LZ.

THE LEGISLATURE

The *Legislative Council* consists of 45 members, elected by popular vote and the *Legislative Assembly* consists of 109 members elected for a maximum period of 4 years. Party representation in the Council at June 8, 1988 was; Labor 21, Liberal 12, National 7, Australian Democrat 2, and Independent 3. Party representation in the Assembly at June 8, 1988 was: Liberal-National coalition 59 (Liberal 39, National 20), Labor 43, and Independent 7. The annual salary of members of the Legislative Council and Legislative Asssembly who are not Ministers is $A43,620. Members also receive expense and electoral allowances, and a special expense allowance is paid to members who reside in, or represent outlying electorates.

President of the Legislative Council, Hon. J. R. Johnson.

Speaker, Legislative Assembly, Hon. K. R. Rozzoli.

THE JUDICATURE

The judicial system includes a Supreme Court, Industrial Commission, District Court, Land and

Environment Court, Compensation Court, and Local Courts (Magistrates).

Chief Justice, Supreme Court, Mr. Justice Gleeson (+ *allce.* $A8,286)...................... $A117,533
President, Court of Appeal, Hon. Mr. Justice Kirby, c.m.g. (+ *allce.* $A6,681) $A107,147

GOVERNMENT FINANCES

	1986–87	1987–88p
	$A million	$A million
Current outlays 12,860		14,111
Capital outlays........ 4,282		3,767
Revenue and grants ... 14,262		16,240
Net financing 2,881		1,639
p preliminary.		

Banking, etc.—There were (March 1988) 29 trading banks with deposits of $A24,920 million. Savings bank depositors' balances amounted to $A18,571 million, representing $A3,313 per head of the population.

EDUCATION

Education.—Education is compulsory between the ages of 6 and 15 years. It is non-sectarian and free at all government schools. The enrolment in July 1987 in 2,210 government schools was 755,084. In addition there were 852 non-government schools, with an enrolment of 275,940 students. The six universities had an enrolment of 69,726 students at April 30, 1987. In addition, there were 57,478 students enrolled in advanced education courses (predominantly in colleges of advanced education) in 1987. Students enrolled in technical and further education colleges in 1986 numbered 402,572. State Government recurrent expenditure on education was $A3,620 million in the year ended June 30, 1986.

PRODUCTION AND INDUSTRY

Local value of production in 1986–87 was ($A million):—

Agricultural commodities	$A4,280·8
Crops	1,718·9
Livestock products	1,406·9
Slaughterings.....................	1,154·9
Value added ($A million)	
Mining and Quarrying (1985–86)	$A2,155·0
Manufacturing (1984–85).............	$A14,036·6

Crops.—Production in 1986–87 was (tonnes):

Wheat-grain.........................	4,855,244
Wheat-hay	55,456
Barley	613,646
Oats	635,185
Rice	589,074
Cotton	499,356
Oilseed	156,452
Potatoes...........................	121,573
Sugar-cane, crushed	1,276,084

611,733 kg. of dried leaf tobacco and 79,478,200 kg. of bananas were obtained; almost every kind of fruit and vegetable is grown.

Livestock and Livestock Products.—A large area is suitable for sheep-raising, the principal breed of sheep being the merino, which was introduced in 1797. At March 31, 1987, there were 4,868,047 cattle, 52,191,792 sheep and lambs, and 829,833 pigs. In 1986–87, 229,711,693 kg. of wool (in the grease) were produced, 829 tonnes of butter, 13,411 tonnes of cheese, and 26,062 tonnes of bacon and ham.

Mining Industry.—The principal minerals are coal, lead, zinc, gold, rutile, copper and zircon. The total value of minerals extracted in 1986–87 was $A3,436,916,000, of which the value of output of the coal mining industry was $A2,611,741,000 and of the silver-lead-zinc industry, $A329,732,000 and the con-

struction materials industry, including stone, gravel and sand, was $A304,845,000. The average number of persons employed in the mining industry during 1986–87 was 26,695. In 1986–87, 88,057,000 tonnes of coal were produced.

Manufacturing Industry.—At June 30, 1985, there were 10,238 manufacturing establishments (employing four or more persons). The average number of persons employed during 1984–85 was 364,847. Products include iron and steel, pipes, boilers, steel wire and wire netting, copper wire, copper and brass cables and tin-plate. Production of raw steel in 1986–87 was 5,080,000 tonnes.

OVERSEAS TRADE

	1987
Imports f.o.b.....................	$16,131,220,000
Exports f.o.b.....................	8,360,569,000

The chief exports in 1986–87 were coal and coke, wool, wheat, meat, non-ferrous metal and iron and steel. Chief imports were, office machines and data processing equipment, electrical machinery, road vehicles and general industrial machinery.

TRANSPORT AND COMMUNICATIONS

Shipping.—2,751 vessels entered the major ports of N.S.W. from overseas during the year ended June 30, 1987, the deadweight tonnage being 97,767,734. The shipping entries at Sydney were 1,185 vessels of 27,901,296 deadweight tonnage.

Roads and Bridges.—Expenditures by the State Government and the local authorities on road systems and regulation in 1986–87 was $A1,616·8 million.

Motor Vehicles.—At Dec. 31, 1987, there were 3,035,926 registered motor vehicles (cars, 1,910,986).

Railways.—The railways of New South Wales are controlled by the State Government. At June 30, 1987, the route kilometres of the State railways open for traffic was 9,909, revenue in the year 1986–87 being $A1,840·6 million.

Aviation.—Sydney is the principal overseas terminal in Australia. Overseas and local traffic at Sydney airport in 1987 were: passengers 9,889,680; freight 200,513 tonnes; aircraft, 110,477 (provisional figs.).

Postal and Telecommunication Services.—The postal and telecommunication services are administered by the Commonwealth Government.

Radio and Television.—At June 30, 1987, there were 33 Australian Broadcasting Corporation radio stations and 44 commercial radio stations operating under licence in N.S.W. There were also 30 licensed non-profit radio stations providing special interest services not catered for by the A.B.C. and commercial services. At June 30, 1987, there were 27 television stations (14 A.B.C., 13 commercial) in operation in the state.

TOWNS

ψSydney, the State capital and the largest city in Australia, stands on the shores of Port Jackson. Sydney Harbour extends inland for 21 km.: the total area of water is about 55 sq. km.

The preliminary estimated resident population at June 30, 1987 of the Sydney Statistical Division was 3,525,850. The Newcastle and Wollongong Statistical subdivisions contain populations of 418,960 and 233,650 respectively.

The populations of principal municipalities located outside the boundaries of these statistical areas are: Albury 39,610, Dubbo 31,290, Greater Taree 36,960, Hastings 42,220, Lismore 38,130, Orange 32,520, Shoalhaven 59,470, Tamworth 33,830, Wagga Wagga 50,930.

LORD HOWE ISLAND

Lord Howe Island, which is part of New South Wales, is situated 702 kilometres north-east of Sydney. Lat. 31° 33′ 4″ S., Long. 159° 4′ 26″ E. Area 6·37 sq. miles (16·5 sq. km.). Pop. June 30, 1987, 290. The island is of volcanic origin with Mount Gower reaching an altitude of 866 m. The affairs of the Island are administered by the Lord Howe Island Board.

QUEENSLAND

This State, situated in lat. 10° 40′–29° S. and long. 138°–153° 30′ E., comprises the whole north-eastern portion of the Australian continent.

Queensland possesses an area of 666,798 sq. miles (1,727,000 sq. km.).

POPULATION.—At June 30, 1988, the estimated resident population numbered 2,743,765.

Births, Deaths and Marriages were:

	1986	1987
Births	40,371	39,365
Deaths	17,861	18,861
Marriages	18,030	18,265

Annual rate per 1,000 of mean population in 1987: Births, 14·7; Deaths, 7·0; Marriages 6·8. Deaths under 1 year, 9·3 per 1,000 live births.

Religions

At the Census of 1986, there were 640,867 Anglican, 628,906 Catholics, 255,287 Uniting Church, 120,239 Presbyterians, 56,910 Lutherans, 30,089 Baptists, and 211,316 other Christians.

PHYSIOGRAPHY

The Great Dividing Range on the eastern coast of the continent produces a similar formation to that of New South Wales, the eastern side having a narrow slope to the coast and the western a long and gradual slope to the central plains, where the Selwyn and Kirby Ranges divide the land into a northern and southern watershed.

GOVERNMENT

Queensland was constituted a separate colony with responsible government in 1859, having previously formed part of New South Wales. The executive authority is vested in a Governor (appointed by the Crown), aided by an Executive Council of 18 members.

GOVERNOR

Governor of Queensland, His Excellency Hon. Sir Walter Benjamin Campbell, Q.C.

EXECUTIVE COUNCIL.

(H.E. the Governor presides)
(as at June 30, 1989)

Premier and Treasurer, and Minister for State Development and the Arts, Hon. M. J. Ahern.
Deputy Premier and Minister for Public Works, Housing and Main Roads, Hon. W. A. M. Gunn.
Health, Hon. I. J. Gibbs.
Land Management, Hon. W. H. Glasson.
Finance, Hon. B. D. Austin.
Employment, Training, and Industrial Affairs, Hon. V. P. Lester.
Mines, Energy and Northern Development, Hon. M. J. Tenni.
Primary Industries, Hon. N. J. Harper.
Environment, Conservation and Forestry, Hon. G. H. Muntz.
Transport, Hon. P. R. McKechnie.
Community Services and Ethnic Affairs, Hon. R. C. Katter.

Water Resources and Maritime Services, Hon. D. M. Neal.
Justice, Attorney-General and Minister for Corrective Services, Hon. P. J. Clauson.
Industry, Small Business, Technology and Tourism, Hon. R. E. Borbidge.
Local Government and Racing, Hon. J. H. Randell.
Emergency Services, Police and Administrative Services, Hon. T. R. Cooper.
Family Services, Hon. C. A. Sherrin.
Education, Youth and Sport, Hon. B. G. Littleproud.

AGENT-GENERAL IN LONDON

Agent-General, D. T. McVeigh, 392–393 Strand, WC2.

THE LEGISLATURE

Parliament consists of a *Legislative Assembly* of 89 members, elected by all persons aged 18 years and over. The Assembly, as at June 30, 1989, was composed of: National Party, 47; Liberal Party, 11; Australian Labor Party, 30; Independent, 1.
Speaker, Hon. L. W. Powell.
Chairman of Committees, E. C. Row.
Government Whip, A. A. Fitzgerald.
Leader of the Opposition, W. K. Goss.

THE JUDICATURE

There are a Supreme Court; District Courts; Children's Courts; an Industrial Court; a Land Court and a Medical Assessment Tribunal; a Local Government Court; the Industrial Conciliation and Arbitration Commission; Inferior Courts at all the principal towns, presided over by Stipendiary Magistrates; a Small Claims Tribunal; Small Debts Court; a Licensing Court and a Mining Warden's Court.
Chief Justice, Supreme Court, Hon. J. M. Macrossan.
Senior Puisne Judge, Hon. J. L. Kelly.

EDUCATION

Education is compulsory between the ages of 6 and 15 years and is provided free in Government schools. At July 1988 the State administered 1,078 primary, 69 primary/secondary, and 168 secondary schools with 237,309 primary students, and 143,011 secondary students.

Post-secondary education involves technical and further education (TAFE), advanced education, and university education. During 1987, 112,580 students were enrolled in TAFE courses, excluding 66,874 enrolled in adult education courses. At April 30, 1988, there were 18,106 full-time, 8,236 part-time, and 8,634 external students enrolled in advanced education courses. The three universities had enrolments of 18,287 full-time students, 8,236 part-time, and 2,085 external students at April 30, 1988.

PRODUCTION AND INDUSTRY

Agriculture and Livestock.—The provisional gross value of agricultural commodity production in 1987–88 was $A3,935,009,000 (including crops $A1,824,024,000, livestock disposals $A1,405,716,000, livestock products $A705,270,000).

The most important crops in 1987–88* were (tonnes):

Sugar cane	24,311,000
Wheat	738,000
Barley	269,000
Pineapples	145,100
Bananas	68,900

The livestock on March 31, 1988* included 8,795,000 cattle, 328,000 being dairy cattle, 14,306,000 sheep and 589,000 pigs.
*provisional figures.

Forestry.—Total Australian grown timber processed in 1987–88 amounted to 1,338,600 cubic metres (gross volume measure).

Minerals.—There are rich deposits of both metallic

and non-metallic minerals. Coal is mined extensively in Central Queensland and on a lesser scale in the Ipswich district.

Mineral Production Value (at mine), 1987–88

	$A'000
Bauxite	186,244
Coal	2,144,962
Copper concentrate	409,250
Crude oil, natural gas, etc.	269,965
Gold (various forms)	400,556
Lead concentrate	212,979
Mineral sands	89,118
Nickel ore	12,149
Tin concentrate	3,193
Zinc concentrate (incl. middlings)	102,752
Other	275,375
Total	4,106,543

Manufacturing.—In 1986–87 there were 4,090 establishments with four or more workers, employing 117,935 persons, and producing goods and services worth $A14,848 million. The value added was $A5,053 million. Much of the production was the processing of primary products, e.g. foodstuffs, timber and minerals. Included in other factory production were the products from engineering, transport equipment, basic and fabricated metal, chemical and fertilizer works, cement, paper and textile mills and oil refineries.

FINANCE

Government finance (Consolidated Revenue Fund) ($A'000) was:—

	1987	1988
Revenue	5,649,027	6,308,439
Expenditure	5,648,701	6,270,304
Gross Debt	2,477,500	2,444,925

Banking.—Advances made by Trading Banks (including the Commonwealth Trading Bank of Australia) at June 30, 1988, totalled $A7,642,464,000. The deposits at the same date amounted to $A8,672,061,000. Depositors' balances in Queensland savings banks at June 30, 1988, $A8,637,225,000, averaged $A3,149 for each inhabitant. There were 4,753,123 operative accounts.

OVERSEAS TRADE

	1986–87	1987–88
Imports	$A2,503,854,410	$A2,844,500,000
Exports	7,928,405,572	8,189,900,000

The chief overseas exports are coal, non-ferrous metals, meat, sugar, wool, and cereal grains.

COMMUNICATIONS

Road and Rail.—The State is served by 10,089 kilometres of railways. During 1987–88, 46,228,000 passengers and 74,893,000 tonnes of goods and livestock were carried. At June 30, 1988, there were 152,952 kilometres of formed roads in the State, and 1,616,200 motor vehicles were on the register.

Aviation.—Regular services operate between Brisbane, the main Queensland coastal and inland towns and the southern capitals. Brisbane, Townsville and Cairns are also ports of call on several international services.

Radio and Television.—On June 30, 1987, 11 national and 29 commercial sound broadcasting stations were operating in Queensland. There were seven public broadcasting stations.

CAPITAL.—ΨBrisbane, is situated on the Brisbane River, which is navigable by large vessels to the city, over 23 kilometres from Moreton Bay. The estimated resident population of the Brisbane Statistical Division at June 30, 1988 was 1,240,286. This area includes

the cities of Brisbane (739,794), Ipswich (74,987), Logan (134,031) and Redcliffe (47,177).

Other cities with population over 30,000 at June 30, 1988, are: ΨTownsville, 82,475; Gold Coast, 128,456; Toowoomba, 79,934; ΨRockhampton, 58,410; ΨCairns, 41,191; ΨCaloundra, 40,776; ΨThuringowa, 34,384; ΨBundaberg, 32,614.

SOUTH AUSTRALIA

The State of South Australia is situated between 26° and 38° S. lat. and 129° and 141° E. long., the total area being 380,070 sq. miles (984,376 sq. km.).

POPULATION.—At June 30, 1988, the resident population was estimated to be 1,407,984.

Births, deaths and marriages were:

	1987	1988
Births	19,235	19,231
Deaths	10,531	10,716
Marriages	9,695	10,128

Religions

Religion is free and receives no State aid. At the Census, 1986, the persons belonging to the principal religious denominations were as follows: Catholic, 267,137; Anglican, 242,722; Uniting Church, 176,980; Lutheran, 64,851; Orthodox, 37,149; Baptist, 21,415; Presbyterian, 18,566; Church of Christ, 16,629; and Pentecostal, 14,997.

PHYSIOGRAPHY

The most important physical features of South Australia are broad plains, divided longitudinally by four great secondary features, which form barriers to east-west movement, and which have thus largely determined the direction of roads and railways, the sites of towns and villages and the manner of distribution of the population. These four barriers are Spencer Gulf, Gulf St. Vincent, the Mt. Lofty-Flinders Ranges and the River Murray.

The north-western portion of the State is mostly desert, while north of latitude 32° S. the country is unpromising by comparison with the fertile land which surrounds the hill country of the east. The Murray, which flows for some 400 miles through the south-eastern corner, is the only river of importance.

The lack of rivers and fresh-water lakes in the settled areas has necessitated the building of a number of reservoirs, which are supplemented by pipelines from the River Murray.

Climate.—The mean annual temperature at Adelaide is 17·1°C, the winter temperature (June-August) averaging 11·9°C, and the summer (Nov.-Mar.) 22·3°C. During the summer months the maximum temperature at times exceeds 40°C, but is associated with a relatively low humidity. The average annual rainfall at Adelaide is 21 inches.

GOVERNMENT

South Australia was proclaimed a British Province in 1836, and in 1851 a partially elective legislature was established. The present Constitution rests upon a Law of Oct. 24, 1856, the executive authority being vested in a Governor appointed by the Crown, aided by a Council of 13 Ministers.

GOVERNOR

Governor of South Australia, His Excellency Lt. Gen. Sir Donald B. Dunstan, K.B.E., C.B. (1982).
Lt. Governor, The Hon. Sir Condor Laucke, K.C.M.G. (1982).

THE MINISTRY

Premier and Treasurer, Hon. John Bannon.
Deputy Premier, Minister of Health, Community Welfare, the Aged, Hon. Donald Hopgood.
Attorney General, Minister of Community Affairs, and Corporate Affairs, Hon. Christopher Sumner.
State Development and Technology, Agriculture, Fisheries and Ethnic Affairs, Hon. Lynn Arnold.
Education and Children's Services, Hon. Gregory Crafter.
Housing and Construction, Public Works, and Aboriginal Affairs, Hon. Terence Hemmings.
Transport, Correctional Services and Minister assisting the Treasurer, Hon. Frank Blevins.
Tourism and State Services, Hon. Barbara Wiese.
Employment and Further Education, Youth Affairs, Recreation and Sport, Hon. Kym Mayes.
Environment and Planning, Water Resources, Lands and Repatriation, Hon. S. Lenehan.
Emergency Services, Mines, Energy and Forests, Hon. J. Klunder.
Labour, Marine and Chief Secretary, Hon. R. Gregory.
Local Government and the Arts, Hon. J. Levy.

AGENT-GENERAL IN LONDON

Agent-General, G. Walls, South Australia House, 50 Strand, WC2.

THE LEGISLATURE

Parliament consists of a *Legislative Council* of 22 members elected for 8 years, one-half retiring every 4 years; and a *House of Assembly* of 47 members, elected for a maximum duration of 4 years. Election is by ballot, with universal adult suffrage for both the Legislative Council and the House of Assembly.

The representation in the House of Assembly is 27 Labor, 16 Liberals, 1 National Party and 3 Independent.

President of the Legislative Council, Hon.
Anne Levy $A75,498
Speaker of the House of Assembly, Hon. J.
P. Trainer $A75,498

THE JUDICATURE

Law and Justice.—The Supreme Court is presided over by the Chief Justice and 13 Puisne Judges.

EDUCATION

Education at the primary and secondary level is available at Government schools controlled by the Education Department and at non-government schools, most of which are denominational. In 1988 there were 715 Government schools with 184,766 students, and 178 independent schools with 55,245 students. Tertiary education is available through universities, colleges of advanced education, and technical and further education.

The two universities had, in 1987, a total enrolment of 11,706 full-time students.

FINANCE

Revenue and expenditure of the Consolidated Revenue Account and debt of South Australia (year ended June 30) was:—

	1987	1988
Revenue	3,788,253,000	4,867,400,000
Expenditure	3,778,336,000	4,833,100,000

Banking.—There are eleven trading banks in Adelaide, including the Commonwealth Trading Bank and the State Bank of South Australia, having total average deposits of $A4,521,140,000 in June 1988. The nine savings banks had deposits of $A3,807,801,000 at June 30, 1988.

PRODUCTION AND INDUSTRY

The gross value of primary production in 1987–88 was:—

Crops	$A963,763,000
Livestock products	690,570,000
Slaughterings...................	395,508,000
Fisheries	107,542,000

Agriculture.—Wheat harvest 1986–87, 2,255,000 tonnes; barley, 1,592,000 tonnes. Oranges, lemons, apples, apricots, peaches, and all stone fruits and olives are successfully grown, and a quantity of this fruit is dried. In 1987–88, 210,359,000 litres of wine and 5,115 tonnes of sultanas, currants and raisins were produced. Considerable quantities of fruits (fresh and dried), wine and brandy, are annually sent to overseas countries, and to other Australian States. Some areas of the State, particularly near Adelaide, are also very suitable for growing all kinds of root crops and vegetables.

Livestock (March 31, 1989).—There were 17,339,800 sheep, 949,268 cattle, 421,247 pigs. Wool production (1987–88), 112,361,000 kg.

Minerals.—Iron, pyrite, gypsum, salt, coal, limestone, clay, oil and gas, etc., are found. The total mineral output was valued at $A949,698,000 in 1987–88, including oil and gas valued at $A686,319,000.

OVERSEAS TRADE

	1986–87	1987–88
Imports	1,501,827,000	1,804,614,000
Exports	2,047,147,000	2,263,360,000

The principal exports are wool, wheat, barley, meat, lead and lead alloys, silver, zinc, iron and steel, petroleum products, rock lobster and prawns.

TRANSPORT AND COMMUNICATIONS

The State Transport Authority operated (in 1988) 127 km. of railway and 1,031 km. of tram and bus routes in the metropolitan area. Australian National operated 6,345 km. of railway in country areas. There are 95,979 km. of roads.

There are a number of excellent harbours, of which Port Adelaide is the most important. The number of vessels (exceeding 200 net tonnage) entering South Australia from overseas during 1986–87 was 828 with 1,889,509 import tonnes and leaving with 6,381,640 export tonnes.

Civil Aviation.—There are 36 Government and licensed airports; the largest of these, Adelaide airport, recorded 1,976,613 passenger movements during 1987–88.

Motor Vehicles.—The registration on June 30, 1988, totalled 846,400.

Radio and Television (June 1989)—Broadcasting stations 43; Television stations 50 (including translator and satellite fed stations).

CAPITAL.—ΨAdelaide, the chief city and capital, estimated resident population on June 30, 1988, 1,023,517 inclusive of suburbs. Other centres with 1988 populations) are: ΨWhyalla (27,317); ΨMt. Gambier (22,013); ΨPort Pirie (15,182); ΨPort Augusta (16,006); and ΨPort Lincoln (12,909).

TASMANIA

Tasmania is an island state of Australia situated in the Southern ocean off the south-eastern extremity of the mainland. It is separated from the Australian mainland by Bass Strait and incorporates King Island and the Furneaux group of islands which are in the Strait. It lies between 40° 38'–43° 39' S. lat. and 144° 36'–148° 23' E. long., and contains an area of 26,383 sq. miles (68,331 sq. km.).

POPULATION.—The estimated resident population at December 31, 1988 was 449,300.

Births, deaths and marriages were:

	1987	1988
Births	6,790	6,748
Deaths	3,637	3,527
Marriages	3,141	3,034

Vital Statistics.—The birth rate in 1988 was 15·05, death rate 7·8, marriage rate 6·7 per 1,000. Infant mortality (1988) 8·7 per 1,000 births.

Religions

In 1986 there were 154,748 members of the Anglican Church of Australia, 80,479 Catholics, 36,724 Uniting Church of Australia, 12,084 Presbyterians and 8,092 Baptists.

PHYSIOGRAPHY

The surface of the country is generally hilly and wooded, with mountains from 1,500 to 5,300 ft. in height, and expanses of level, open plains. There are numerous rivers, the South Esk, Gordon, Derwent and Huon being the largest. At Hobart the mean maximum temperature ranges from about 12°C in winter to 21°C in summer, the mean minimum from 5°C to 11°C. The western side of the island is very wet, the eastern side being much drier.

GOVERNMENT

The island was first settled by a British party from New South Wales in 1803, becoming a separate colony in 1825. In 1851 a partly elective legislature was inaugurated, and in 1856 responsible government was established. In 1901 Tasmania became a State of the Australian Commonwealth. The State executive authority is vested in a Governor (appointed by the Crown), but is exercised by Cabinet Ministers responsible to the Legislature, of which they are members.

GOVERNOR

Governor of Tasmania, Gen. Sir Phillip Bennett, K.B.E.

THE MINISTRY

Premier, Treasurer, Minister for State Development and Small Business, Status of Women, Science and Technology, Antarctic Affairs, Hon. Robin Gray.

Deputy Premier, Forests, Mines, Energy, Multicultural Affairs, Hon. Raymond Groom.

Attorney General, Minister for Lands, Parks and Wildlife, Sport and Recreation, Deregulation, Hon. John Bennett.

Education and the Arts, Employment and Training, Hon. Richard Beswick.

Main Roads, Primary Industry, Local Government, Water Resources, Racing, Hon. Ian Braid.

Police, Sea Fisheries, Licensing, Road Safety, Gaming, Hon. R. Cornish.

Tourism, Public Administration, Transport, Industrial Relations, Labour and Industry, Hon. Nicholas Evers.

Health, Community Welfare and the Elderly, Hon. Francis Groom.

Construction, Administrative Services, Environment, Inland Fisheries, Hon. Peter Hodgman.

Housing, Consumer Affairs, Youth Affairs, Hon. F. Madill.

THE LEGISLATURE

Parliament consists of two Houses, a *Legislative Council* of 19 members, elected for six years (3 retiring annually, in rotation, except in every sixth year, when four retire) and a *House of Assembly* of 35 members, elected by proportional representation for four years in five 7-member constituencies, the electors for both Houses being all Tasmanians of 18 years and over who have resided continuously in the State for at least 6 months. Elections for the Assembly are held every four years.

The election of May 13, 1989 resulted in a minority Liberal Government being sworn in on June 1, 1989. The state of the parties in the Legislative Council following the election was Independent 18, Labor 1. The state of parties in the House of Assembly in June 1989 was: Liberals 17, Labor 13, Independent 5.

President of the Legislative Council, Hon. A. J. Broadby.

Speaker of the House of Assembly, Hon. R. Cornish.

THE JUDICATURE

The Supreme Court of Tasmania, with civil, criminal ecclesiastical, admiralty and matrimonial jurisdiction, was established by Royal Charter on October 13, 1823.

Local Courts are held before Commissioners who are legal practitioners. Courts of General Sessions, constituted by a chairman who is a Justice of the Peace and at least one other Justice, are established in the municipalities and Courts of Petty Sessions are constituted by Magistrates sitting alone, or by two or more justices. A single justice may hear and determine certain matters.

Chief Justice, Supreme Court, Hon. Sir Guy Green, K.B.E.

EDUCATION

Government schools are of three main types: primary, secondary and secondary colleges. On July 1, 1988, there were 65,404 students enrolled in 257 government schools. There were also 65 independent schools with an enrolment of 17,795. The University of Tasmania at Hobart, established 1890, had 3,712 full-time students and 1,665 part-time (including external) students in 1988. The Tasmanian State Institute of Technology, offering degree and diploma courses, was established in 1972. Enrolments in 1988 were 1,798 full-time students and 1,305 part-time (including external) students.

FINANCE

Revenue and expenditure of the Consolidated Revenue Fund and debt of Tasmania at current rates of exchange (June 30) was:—

	1987–88
Revenue	\$A1,201,397,069
Expenditure	1,375,666,945
Debt	1,394,893,769

Banking.—The weekly average of depositors' balances at trading banks in December 1988 was \$A749,000,000; the savings bank balances were \$A1,761,000,000.

PRODUCTION AND INDUSTRY

Gross value of agricultural production in 1987–88 was \$A541m. Total value added in manufacturing in 1986–87 was \$A1,250·3m.; value added in mining was \$A177m. in 1986–87.

Agriculture and Livestock.—The principal crops are apples, potatoes, green peas, oil poppies, hops, barley, beans and onions.

The livestock included (March 31, 1988) 542,200 cattle, 4,746,400 sheep and 47,600 pigs. The shorn wool production (1987–88) was 23,519 tonnes.

Electrical Energy.—Tasmania, the smallest Australian state, ranks fourth as a producer of electrical energy—most of it derived from water power, with a total installed generator capacity of 2,171,400 kW. By reason of its low-cost electrical energy, Tasmania has large plants producing ferro-manganese and newsprint. A large aluminium plant is situated at Bell Bay and Tasmania is the source of the bulk of

Australian requirements of zinc and fine papers. The Hydro-Electric Commission has completed a network of 26 stations including a dual machine oil fired station at Bell Bay. Work is continuing on three hydro-electric developments in the remote western region of the State, which will increase the installed generator capacity to 2·54 million kW.

Forestry.—The quantity of timber (excluding firewood) of various species cut in 1987–88 was 4,784,500 cubic metres, including 3,892,000 cubic metres for woodchip and wood-pulp.

Minerals.—The chief ores mined are those containing copper, tin, iron, silver, zinc and lead.

Manufactures.—The chief manufactures for export are: refined metals, preserved fruit and vegetables, butter, cheese, textiles, paper, confectionery, wood chips and sawn timber. In 1986–87, 631 manufacturing establishments employed 24,600 persons, including working proprietors. Salaries and wages paid totalled $A531m.

OVERSEAS TRADE

	1986–87	1987–88
Imports	$A289,525,000	$A282,415,000
Exports	1,099,808,000	1,221,955,000

The principal overseas exports are ores and concentrates, refined metals, woodchips, greasy wool, meat, abalone, fresh fruit, cheese and hides and skins.

COMMUNICATIONS

Road and Rail.—Tasmania is served by a 1,067 mm. gauge Federal Government railway system of 856 route km. An additional 134 route km of the same gauge is privately operated. Regular passenger services no longer operate. At June 30, 1987 there were 22,715 kilometres of road normally open to traffic. Of this total 8,905 kilometres were sealed. Motor vehicles on the register at June 30, 1988 were: cars and station wagons, 209,400; commercial vehicles, 62,700 and motor cycles, 6,000.

Aviation.—Regular services operate between Tasmania and the other Australian States. During 1987–88 1,132,934 passengers were carried on these services. The main cities and towns in the State are served by regular internal services.

CAPITAL.—ΨHobart, founded 1804. Population (June 30, 1988), 179,910. Other towns (with population at June 30, 1988) are ΨLaunceston (63,250), ΨDevonport (25,290), Burnie-Somerset (21,060), Ulverstone (14,450).

VICTORIA

The State of Victoria comprises the south-east corner of Australia, at the part where its mainland territory projects farthest into the southern latitudes; it lies between 34°–39° S. latitude and 141°–150° E. longitude. Its extreme length from east to west is about 493 miles, its greatest breadth is about 290 miles, and its extent of coast-line is about 1,043 geographical miles, including the length around Port Phillip Bay, Western Port and Corner Inlet, the entire area being 87,876 sq. miles (227,597 sq. km.).

Population.—The estimated resident population at June 30, 1987 was 4,208,900.

Births, deaths and marriages were:

	1986	1987
Births........................	60,387	61,507
Deaths	30,062	31,549
Marriages	29,390	29,682

Annual rate per 1,000 of estimated resident population in 1987: Births, 14·65; Deaths, 7·50; Marriages, 7·1. Deaths under 1 year per 1,000 live births, 8·1.

Religions

At the Census in 1986, members of the Catholic Church numbered 1,104,044, Anglican, 715,414, Uniting (union of Presbyterian, Congregationalist and Methodist) 280,262, Presbyterian 138,000, Orthodox 177,565, and Baptist 39,784. The number of persons who did not state their religion was 589,132.

PHYSIOGRAPHY

The Australian Alps and the Great Dividing Range pass through the centre of the State, and divide it into a northern and southern watershed, the latter sloping down to the ocean and containing, especially in the south-east, well-wooded valleys. The length of the Murray River, which forms part of the northern boundary of Victoria, is about 1,196 miles along the Victorian bank. Melbourne, the capital city, stands upon the Yarra River, which rises in the southern slopes of the Dividing Range.

Climate.—The climate of Victoria is characterized by warm to hot summers and rather cold winters. The highest temperature ever recorded in the State is 50·8°C, the lowest being −12·8°C. Normally, rain falls at most places throughout the year, with a maximum in winter or spring. In Melbourne, the mean annual temperature is 14·8°C.

GOVERNMENT

Victoria was originally known as the Port Phillip District of New South Wales and was created a separate colony in 1851, with a partially elective legislature. In 1855 Responsible Government was conferred. The executive authority is vested in a Governor, appointed by the Crown, aided by an Executive Council of Ministers.

The Legislative Assembly (elected October 2, 1988) consists of Australian Labor Party (ALP) 46, Liberal Party 33, and National Party 9.

Governor of Victoria, His Excellency Rev. Dr. John Davis McCaughey, *assumed office* Feb. 18, 1986.

Lt. Governor, The Hon. Sir John McIntosh Young, K.C.M.G. (1974).

THE MINISTRY
(as at June 30, 1989)

Premier, Hon. John Cain.
Deputy Premier, Minister for Education, Hon. Joan Kirner.
Arts, Post-Secondary Education, Major Projects, Hon. E. Walker.
Industry, Technology and Resources, Hon. D. White.
Police and Emergency Services, Tourism, Corrections, Hon. S. Crabb.
Health, Hon. Caroline Hogg.
Treasurer, Hon. R. Jolly.
Transport, Hon. J. Kennan.
Local Government, the Aged, Hon. M. Lyster.
Attorney General and Minister for Ethnic Affairs, Hon. A. McCutcheon.
Labour and Youth Affairs, Hon. N. Pope.
Housing and Construction, Hon. B. Pullen.
Planning and Environment, Consumer Affairs, Aboriginal Affairs, Hon. T. Roper.
Agricultural and Rural Affairs, Hon. B. Rowe.
Conservation, Forests and Lands, Hon. Kay Setches.
Community Services and Prices, Hon. P. Spyker.
Sport and Recreation, the Olympic Games, Hon. N. Trezise.
Property and Services, Water Resources, Hon. R. Walsh.
Parliamentary Secretary of the Cabinet, Hon. M. Sandon.

AGENT-GENERAL IN LONDON

Agent-General, I. M. Haig, Victoria House, Melbourne Place, Strand, WC2B 4LG.

THE LEGISLATURE

Parliament consists of a *Legislative Council* of 44 members, elected for the 22 Provinces for two terms of the Legislative Assembly, one-half retiring every 4 years at a General Election; and a *Legislative Assembly* of 88 members, elected for a maximum duration of 4 years. Voting is compulsory.

President of the Legislative Council, Hon.
A. J. Hunt $A95,375
Speaker of the Legislative Assembly, Hon.
Dr. K. A. Coghill $A95,375

THE JUDICATURE

There is a Supreme Court with a Chief Justice and 21 Puisne Judges, a County Court and Magistrates' Courts.

Chief Justice, Supreme Court, Hon. Sir
John Young, K.C.M.G. $A117,547
Chief Judge, County Court, Hon. G. R. D.
Waldron $A103,785

EDUCATION

Primary education is compulsory, secular and free between the ages of 6 and 15. At July 1, 1987, there were 1,585 Government Primary Schools, 22 Primary–Secondary Schools and 399 Secondary Schools attended by 293,948 primary students and 238,824 secondary students. In addition there are technical and further education institutions and Colleges of Advanced Education.

At July 1, 1987, 253,086 pupils attended 729 non-Government schools, 502 of which were Roman Catholic.

There are four State-aided Universities.

FINANCE

Revenue and expenditure from the Consolidated Fund, and the debt of Victoria were:—

	1984–85	1985–86
Revenue	$A8,827,256,489	$A9,658,600,000
Expenditure	8,827,728,064	9,686,300,000
Debt	5,720,919,563	5,944,900,000

Banking, etc.—State Savings Bank deposits at June 30, 1987, amounted to $A9,197,400,000; in addition, deposits in the Commonwealth Savings Bank (in the State of Victoria) amounted to $A2,862,100,000, and in other savings banks $A7,610,600,000.

PRODUCTION AND INDUSTRY

The gross value of primary production (excluding mining and quarrying) in 1986–87 was $A4,020,600,000, crops $A1,494,600,000, livestock $A2,526,100,000. The local value of production of primary industries, excluding mining, was $A3,628,200,000. Wool, wheat, flour, butter, livestock, fruits, milk and cream, meats, poultry and eggs are staple products.

Livestock.—There were on establishments with agricultural activity on March 31, 1987, 28,102,000 sheep, 3,583,000 cattle, and 431,832 pigs. The quantity of wool produced in 1986–87 was valued at $A726,200,000.

Minerals.—Minerals raised include oil and natural gas, brown coal, limestone, clays and stone for construction material. Production of brown coal in 1986–87 amounted to 39,124,000 tonnes.

Crude Oil and Natural Gas.—In 1965 natural gas was first discovered in commercial quantities in the offshore waters of the Gippsland Basin in eastern Victoria and in 1966–67, three more valuable oilfields were located in the same general area. These fields are still the largest yet found in Australia. Following the development of the four fields, commercial gas and crude oil came on stream in October, 1969.

Production from the Victorian fields during 1987 was 151,571,000 barrels.

Secondary Industry.—At June 30, 1987 there were 9,108 manufacturing establishments in which 247,897 males and 108,641 females were employed. Value added in the course of manufacture by all manufacturing establishments with four or more persons employed was $A15,596 million.

OVERSEAS TRADE

The export trade (excluding inter-state trade) consists largely of agricultural and mining products, machinery and transport equipment. The principal overseas imports of the State are apparel and textiles, electrical and other machines and machinery, motor vehicles and tractors, metals and metal manufactures, iron and steel, chemicals, petroleum and petroleum products, artificial resins and plastic materials.

	1985–86	1986–87
Imports	$A12,408,800,000	$A13,743,000,000
Exports	6,819,300,000	7,398,000,000

TRANSPORT

Motor Vehicle Registration.—The number of vehicles on the register at June 30, 1987, was: cars and stationwagons, 2,010,200; utilities and panel vans, 200,200; trucks and buses, 234,500, and motor cycles, 84,500.

CAPITAL.—ΨMelbourne, had a resident population at June 30, 1987, estimated at 2,964,800. Other urban centres are ΨGeelong, 149,310; Ballarat, 79,770; Bendigo, 66,840; Shepparton-Mooroopna, 39,100; ΨWarrnambool, 23,800; Wodonga, 23,620.

WESTERN AUSTRALIA

Includes all that portion of the continent west of 129° E. long., the most westerly point being in 113° 9′ E. long. and from 13° 44′ to 35° 8′ S. lat. Its extreme length is 1,480 miles, and 1,000 miles from east to west; total area 975,920 sq. miles (2,527,621 sq. km.).

POPULATION.—At June 1988, the estimated resident population was 1,544,806.

Births, deaths and marriages were:—

	1987	1988p
Births...........................	23,271	25,316
Deaths	8,889	9,516
Marriages	10,150	10,578

p=preliminary

Religions

Census of 1986—Anglican Church 371,302, Roman Catholics 347,695, Uniting Church 82,876, and Presbyterians 31,641.

PHYSIOGRAPHY

Large areas of the State, for some hundreds of miles inland, are hilly and even mountainous, although the altitude, so far as ascertained, rises nowhere above that of Mount Meharry (4,097 ft.) in the north-west division or that of Bluff Knoll (3,640 ft.) in the Stirling Range in the south-west. The coastal regions are undulating, with an interior slope to the unsettled central portion of Australia. The Darling and Hamersley ranges of the west have a seaward slope to the Indian Ocean, into which flow many streams, notably the Preston, Collie, Murray, Swan, Murchison, Gascoyne, Ashburton, Fortescue and De Grey. In the north the Fitzroy flows from the King Leopold ranges into the Indian Ocean, and the Drysdale and Ord into the Timor Sea. The greater portion of the State may be described as an immense tableland, with an average elevation of 1,000 to 1,500 ft. above sea-level. The climate is one of the most temperate in the world. Of the total area two-thirds is suitable for pastoral purposes.

GOVERNMENT

Western Australia was first settled by the British in 1829, and in 1870 it was granted a partially elective legislature. In 1890 responsible government was granted, and the administration vested in a Governor, a Legislative Council, and a Legislative Assembly. The present constitution rests upon the Constitution Act, 1889, the Constitution Acts Amendment Act, 1899, and amending Acts. The Executive is vested in a Governor appointed by the Crown and aided by a Council of responsible Ministers.

The Legislative Assembly (elected February 4, 1989) is composed of Australian Labor Party 31, Liberal Party 20, National Party of Australia 6.

Governor of Western Australia, His Excellency Prof. Gordon Reid, A.C.

Lt. Governor and Administrator, Hon. Sir Francis Burt, A.C., K.C.M.G.

THE MINISTRY
(as at June 30, 1989)

Premier, Minister for Public Sector Management, Women's Interests, Hon. Peter Dowding.

Deputy Premier, Treasurer, Resources Development, the Arts, Hon. David Parker.

Attorney General, Budget Management, Corrective Services, Leader of the Government in the Legislative Council, Hon. Joseph Berinson.

Local Government, Lands, the Family, the Aged, Deputy Leader of the Government in the Legislative Council, Hon. Elsie Hallahan.

Housing and Planning, Hon. Pamela Beggs.

Agriculture, Water Resources, and the North-West, Hon. Ernest Bridge.

Mines, Fuel and Energy, and the Mid-West, Hon. Jeffrey Carr.

Racing and Gaming, Sport and Recreation, and Youth, Hon. Graham Edwards.

Economic Development and Trade, and Tourism, Hon. Julian Grill.

Consumer Affairs and Works and Services, Hon. Yvonne Henderson.

Regional Development, Fisheries, Multicultural and Ethnic Affairs, Hon. Gordon Hill.

Education, Aboriginal Affairs, Hon. Carmen Lawrence.

Transport, Environment, Parliamentary and Electoral Reform, Leader of the House in the Legislative Assembly, Hon. Robert Pearce.

Community Services, Justice, the South-West, Hon. D. Smith.

Police and Emergency Services, Conservation and Land Management, Waterways, Hon. Ian Taylor.

Labour, Employment and Training, Productivity, Hon. Gavan Troy.

Health, Hon. Keith Wilson.

Agent-General in London, R. Davies, Western Australia House, 115 The Strand, WC2R 0AJ.

THE LEGISLATURE

Parliament consists of a *Legislative Council* and a *Legislative Assembly,* elected by adult suffrage subject to qualifications of residence and registration. The qualifying age for electors for both the Legislative Council and Legislative Assembly is 18 years. There are 34 members in the Legislative Council, two from each province, for a period of 6 years, one member from each province retiring triennially. The Legis-

lative Assembly is composed of 57 members, who are elected for a term of 3 years.

President of the Legislative Council, Hon. C. E. Griffiths	\$A82,855
Speaker of the Legislative Assembly, Hon. M. Barnett	\$A82,855

THE JUDICATURE

Chief Justice, Hon. D. K. Malcolm	\$A126,500
Senior Puisne Judge, Hon. A. R. A. Wallace	\$A115,557
Puisne Judges, Hons. P. F. Brinsden; C. H. Smith; G. A. Kennedy; W. P. Pidgeon; B. W. Rowland; E. M. Franklyn; P. L. Seaman .... each	\$A112,057

EDUCATION

In 1988 there were 741 government and 243 non-government primary and secondary school campuses with 210,068 and 65,330 full time students respectively. The total recurrent and capital outlay expended on education (by State authorities) during the year ended June 30, 1988, was \$A1,225,100,000, including grants for higher education totalling \$A233,328,000. The principal higher education institutions are the University of Western Australia (10,063 enrolments in 1988), Murdoch University (5,196 enrolments in 1988), Curtin University (14,208 enrolments in 1988) and the Western Australian College of Advanced Education (12,719 enrolments in 1988).

PRODUCTION AND INDUSTRY

The gross value of agricultural production in 1987–88 was: crops \$A1,203,189,000; livestock slaughterings, etc., \$A440,067,000; livestock products \$A1,347,976,000. Gross value of fisheries in 1986–87 was \$A172,356,000.

Crops and Livestock.—The production of wheat for grain in 1987–88 was 3,882,000 tonnes. On March 31, 1988, the livestock included 1,705,000 cattle, 33,951,000 sheep, and 307,000 pigs. Wool production in 1987–88 was 188,527 tonnes in the grease.

Manufacturing Industries.—There were 4,063 manufacturing establishments operating in the State at June 30, 1987. The total number of persons employed (including working proprietors) by these establishments at the end of June, 1987 was 72,305.

Forestry.—The forests contain some of the finest hardwoods in the world. The total quantity of sawn timber produced during 1986–87 was 316,658 cubic metres.

Minerals.—The State has large deposits of a wide range of minerals, many of which are being mined or are under development for production. The ex-mine value of all minerals produced during 1986–87 was \$A5,009,886,500.

Communications.—On June 30, 1988, there were 5,553 km. of State government railway open for general and passenger traffic; and 731 km. (Kalgoorlie-W.A. border) of the Australian National Railway. In the year ended June 30, 1988, 2,614 vessels entered Western Australian ports direct from, and 2,567 were cleared direct to, overseas. The number of registered motor vehicles at June 30, 1988, was 935,761.

FINANCE

	1986–87	1987–88
	\$A	\$A
Revenue	3,284,233,136	3,810,401,671
Expenditure	3,277,526,154	3,807,340,069
Public Debt (June 30)	1,575,414,004	1,554,144,943

OVERSEAS TRADE

	1986–87	1987–88
Imports	\$A2,545,276,000	\$A3,151,907,000
Exports	6,673,720,000	7,350,387,000

Principal overseas exports in 1987–88 included iron ore and concentrates, wheat, wool, live sheep and lambs, petroleum and petroleum products, beef and veal, gold bullion, rock lobster tails.

Capital.—ΨPerth. Estimated resident population (estimate for June 30, 1988) of Perth Statistical Division, including the port of ΨFremantle, 1,118,772.

Perth stands on the right bank of the Swan River estuary, 12 miles from Fremantle.

NEW ZEALAND

AREA AND POPULATION

Islands	Area (Sq. Miles)	Population	
		Census Mar. 24, 1981†	Census Mar. 4, 1986†
(a) Exclusive of Island Territory:			
North Island	44,281	2,322,989	2,441,615
South Island	58,093	852,748	865,469
Stewart Island	670	600*	531*
Chatham Islands	372	751*	755*
Minor Islands:			
Inhabited—			
Kermadec Islands	13	5*	5(d)
Campbell Island	44	10*	10(d)
Uninhabited—			
Three Kings	3	..	..
Snares	1	..	..
Solander	½	..	..
Antipodes	24	..	..
Bounty	½	..	..
Auckland	234	..	..
Total exclusive of Island Territory	103,736	3,175,737	3,307,084
(b) Island Territory:			
Tokelau	5	1,572 (a)	1,690 (e)
(c) Niue¶	100	3,226 (b)	2,531 (f)
Cook Islands¶	93	17,754 (c)	17,185 (g)
Ross Dependency	175,000	..	..

* Included in North Island and South Island totals.
† Excluding members of the Armed Forces overseas—979 in 1981; 1,247 in 1986.
¶ The Cook Islands have had complete internal self-government since Aug. 4, 1965, as has Niue since Oct. 19, 1974, but Cook Islanders and Niueans remain New Zealand citizens.
(a) Nov. 2, 1981. (b) Jan. 1, 1981. (c) Dec. 1, 1981. (d) March 31, 1983. (e) Oct. 10, 1986. (f) Sept. 29, 1986. (g) Dec. 1, 1986.

Vital Statistics

Year	Births	Deaths	Natural Increase	Deaths of Infants under one year	Infant Mortality per 1,000 live births	Marriages
1980	50,542	26,676	23,866	650	12·86	22,981
1981	50,794	25,150	25,644	592	11·65	23,660
1982	49,938	25,532	24,406	587	11·75	25,537
1983	50,474	25,991	24,483	633	12·54	24,678
1984	51,636	25,378	26,258	597	11·56	25,272
1985	51,798	27,480	24,318	560	10·81	24,657
1986	52,824	27,045	25,779	592	11·21	24,037
1987	55,254	27,419	27,835	554	10·03	24,443
1988	57,546	27,408	30,138	620	10·77	23,485

Inter-Censal Increases

	Results of Census			Numerical Increase	Net Inflow or Outflow from Total Migration
Year	Males	Females	Total		
1966	1,343,743	1,333,176	2,676,919	261,935	+12,950
1971	1,430,856	1,431,775	2,862,631	185,712	+8,481
1976	1,562,042	1,567,341	3,129,383	266,752	+6,567
1981	1,578,927	1,596,810	3,175,737	46,354	−15,328
1986	1,616,004	1,645,782	3,261,786	131,347	−18,518

Excluding 1,936 members of the Armed Forces overseas at the time of the 1966 Census, 1,482 at the 1971 Census, 1,333 at the 1976 Census, 979 at the 1981 Census and 1,247 at the 1986 Census.

Races and Religions

Races	1981	1986	Religions	1981	1986
				per cent	per cent
European	2,696,568	2,612,958	Church of England	25·7	24·0
Maori	279,084	294,201	Presbyterian	16·7	18·0
Chinese	18,480	19,206	Roman Catholic	14·3	15·2
Polynesian (other than N.Z.			Methodist	4·7	4·7
Maori)	88,827	90,612	Baptist	1·6	2·1

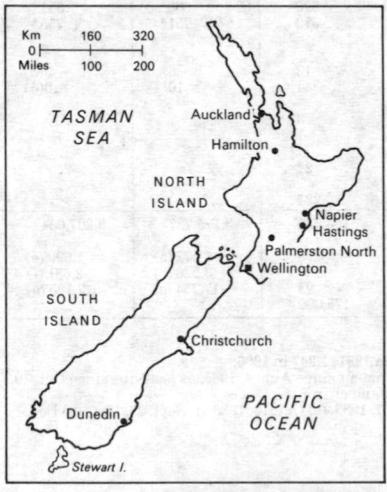

PHYSIOGRAPHY

New Zealand consists of a number of islands of varying size in the South Pacific Ocean, and has also administrative responsibility for the Ross Dependency in Antarctica. The two larger and most important islands, the North and South Islands of New Zealand, are separated by only a relatively narrow strait. The remaining islands are very much smaller and, in general, are widely dispersed over a considerable expanse of ocean. The boundaries, inclusive of the most outlying islands and dependencies, range from 33° to 53° South latitude, and from 162° East longitude to 173° West longitude.

Geographical Features.—The two principal islands have a total length of 1,040 miles, and a combined area of 102,344 sq. miles, (265,069 sq. km.). A large proportion of the surface is mountainous in character. The principal range is the Southern Alps, extending over the entire length of the South Island and having its culminating point in Mount Cook (12,349 ft.). The North Island mountains include several volcanoes, two of which are active, others being dormant or extinct. Mt. Ruapehu (9,175 ft.) and Mt. Ngauruhoe (7,515 ft.) are the most important. Of the numerous glaciers in the South Island, the Tasman (18 miles long by 1¼ wide), the Franz Josef and the Fox are the best known. The North Island is noted for its hot springs and geysers. For the most part the rivers are too short and rapid for navigation. The more important include the Waikato (270 miles in length), Wanganui (180), and Clutha (210). Lakes (Taupo, 234 sq. miles in area; Wakatipu, 113; and Te Anau, 133) are abundant, many of them of great beauty.

In addition to North, South, Stewart and Chatham Islands:—

The Three Kings (discovered by Tasman on the Feast of the Epiphany), in 34° 9′ S. lat. and 172° 8′ 8″ E. long. Auckland Islands, about 290 miles south of Bluff Harbour, in 50° 32′ S. lat. and 166° 13′ E. long. Antipodes Group, 40° 41′ 15″ S. lat. and 178° 43′ E. long. Bounty Islands, 47° 4′ 43″ S. lat., 170° 0′ 30″ E. long. Snares Islands and Solander. All these islands are uninhabited.

The Kermadec Group (population normally 9 or 10) between 29° 10′ to 31° 30′ S. lat., and 177° 45′ to 179° W. long., includes Raoul or Sunday, Macaulay, Curtis Islands, L'Esperance, and some islets. All the inhabitants are government employees at a meteorological station. Campbell Island (used as a weather station).

Climate.—New Zealand has a moist-temperate marine climate, but with abundant sunshine. A very important feature is the small annual range of temperature which permits some growth of vegetation, including pasture, all the year round. Very little snow falls on the low levels even in the South Island. The mean temperature ranges from 15° C. in the North to about 9° C. in the South. Rainfall over the more settled areas in the North Island ranges from 35 to 70 inches and in the South Island from 25 to 45 inches. The total range is from approximately 13 to over 250 inches.

CAPITAL.—ΨWellington, in the North Island (estimated population March 1988, Wellington urban area, 325,200.

Other large urban areas; ΨAuckland, 841,700; ΨChristchurch, 300,700; ΨDunedin, 106,600; Hamilton, 103,500; Ψ Napier-Hastings, 107,500.

CURRENCY.—New Zealand dollar (NZ$) of 100 cents.

FLAG: Blue ground, with Union Flag in top left quarter, four five-pointed red stars with white borders on the fly. On June 20, 1968, a naval ensign bearing the Southern Cross was adopted, replacing the British white ensign.

NATIONAL ANTHEM.—God Save The Queen/God Defend New Zealand.

NATIONAL DAY.—February 6 (Waitangi Day).

GOVERNMENT

The discoverers and first colonists of New Zealand were Polynesian people, ancestors of the Maori of today. Whether there was a single colonization, several, or many, is not known but the 9th century is generally considered to be the date of the first settlement. By the 13th or 14th century early exploration was over and there were well established Maori settlements.

The first European to discover New Zealand was a Dutch navigator, Abel Tasman, who sighted the coast on December 13, 1642 but did not land. It was the British explorer James Cook who circumnavigated New Zealand and landed in 1769. Traders, whalers and sealers made up the majority of Europeans in New Zealand from the end of the 18th century until the late 1830s, when the proportion of permanent European settlers became significant.

Largely as a result of increased British emigration, the country was annexed by the British Government in 1840. The British Lieutenant Governor, William Hobson, R.N., proclaimed sovereignty over the North Island by virtue of the Treaty of Waitangi, signed by him and many Maori chiefs, and over the South Island and Stewart Island by right of discovery.

On May 3, 1841, New Zealand was, by letters patent, created a separate colony distinct from New South Wales. Organized colonization on a large scale commenced in 1840 with the New Zealand company's settlement at Wellington. On Sept. 26, 1907, the designation was changed to *The Dominion of New Zealand*. The Constitution rests upon the Constitution Act of 1852, and other Imperial statutes such as the Bill of Rights. A 1986 Constitution Act brought a number of statutory constitutional provisions. The Statute of Westminster was formally adopted by New Zealand in 1947. The executive authority is entrusted to a Governor General appointed by the Crown and aided by an Executive Council, within a Legislature consisting of one chamber, the House of Representatives.

Governor General and Staff

Governor General and Commander-in-Chief of New Zealand, His Excellency The Most Rev. Sir Paul Alfred Reeves, G.C.M.G., *sworn in,* Nov. 20, 1985.
Official Secretary, Paul Canham.

The Executive Council
His Excellency the Governor General
(as at June 30, 1989)

Prime Minister and Minister of Education, Hon. David Lange.*
Deputy P.M., Attorney-General, Minister of Justice, and the Environment, Hon. Geoffrey Palmer.

Overseas Trade and Marketing, External Relations and Trade, Deputy Minister of Finance, Hon. Michael Moore.
Finance and Revenue, Hon. David Caygill.
State-Owned Enterprises, Labour, Immigration, State Services, Hon. Stan Rodger.
Maori Affairs, Hon. Koro Wetere.
Foreign Affairs and Pacific Island Affairs, Hon. Russell Marshall.
Housing, Health, Hon. Helen Clark.
Internal Affairs, Local Government, Civil Defence, Arts and Culture, Hon. Dr. Michael Bassett.
Minister of State and Leader of the House, Minister of Tourism, Hon. Jonathan Hunt.
Defence, Science and Technology, Hon. Bob Tizard.
Agriculture and Fisheries, Hon. Colin Moyle.
Employment and Youth Affairs, Hon. Phil Goff.
Women's Affairs, Consumer Affairs, Customs, and Statistics, Hon. Mrs. Margaret Shields.
Police, Forestry and Lands, Recreation and Sport, Hon. Peter Tapsell.
Social Welfare, Hon. Dr. Michael Cullen.
Transport, Civil Aviation, Works and Development, Hon. Bill Jeffries.
Commerce, Energy and Regional Development, Postmaster-General, Hon. David Butcher.

The Prime Minister receives NZ$147,000 per annum with an allowance of NZ$26,000 for expenses of his office and the Ministerial residence. The salary of each Minister holding a portfolio is NZ$103,000 with expense allowance of NZ$10,750 and that of each Minister without portfolio NZ$83,000, with NZ$8,500 expense allowance.

* David Lange resigned in Aug. 1989 and was replaced as Prime Minister by Geoffrey Palmer. Helen Clark subsequently replaced Mr. Palmer as Deputy P.M.

NEW ZEALAND HIGH COMMISSION
New Zealand House, Haymarket, SW1Y 4TQ
[01–930 8422]

High Commissioner, His Excellency Bryce Harland (1985).
Deputy High Commissioner, R. A. Farrell.
Minister, P. K. Munn (*Administration*); D. Walker (*Commercial*).
Head, Defence Liaison Staff, Brig. R. J. Andrews, C.B.E.

THE LEGISLATURE

Parliament consists of a House of Representatives consisting of 97 members elected for 3 years. There are four Maori electorates. Women have been entitled to vote since 1893, and to be elected Members of the House of Representatives since the passing of the Women's Parliamentary Rights Act, 1919. Following the General Election of August 15, 1987, the state of the parties in Parliament was Labour 57 and National Party 40.

Members of the House receive NZ$57,000 per annum, with an allowance of NZ$5,500 per annum for expenses, plus an electorate allowance. The Leader of the Opposition receives NZ$103,000 per annum and NZ$10,750 per annum for expenses, plus house and travelling allowances.
Speaker of the House of Representatives,
Hon. T. K. Burke (*plus expense allowance and residential quarters in Parliament House*) . . . . NZ$97,000

THE JUDICATURE

The judicial system comprises a High Court and a Court of Appeal; also District Courts having both civil and criminal jurisdiction.

Chief Justice, Rt. Hon. Sir Thomas Eichelbaum, G.B.E., P.C.	NZ$144,500
President, Court of Appeal, Rt. Hon. Sir Robin Cooke, K.B.E.	139,700
Judges, Rt. Hons. Sir Ivor Richardson; Sir Duncan McMullin; Sir Edward Somers; M. E. Casey; G. E. Bisson	134,900

High Court Puisne Judges, Hons. M. F. Chilwell; J. F. Jeffries; R. I. Barker; J. B. Sinclair; A. D. Holland; T. M. Thorp; L. M. Greig; M. Hardie-Boys; J. H. Wallace; P. G. Hillyer; R. G. Gallen; D. L. Tompkins; J. S. Henry; R. A. Heron; N. W. Williamson; A. A. T. Ellis; R. P. Smellie; R. E. Wylie; R. A. McGechan; J. A. Doogue; A. P. C. Tipping; N. C. Anderson; T. M. Gault; J. B. Robertson 130,100

High Court Administrative Divn., Rt. Hon. Sir Ronald Davison (*Chief Justice*); Hons. M. F. Chilwell; J. F. Jeffries; A. D. Holland; L. M. Greig; D. L. Tompkins.

Chief Judge, Labour Court, J. R. P. Horn.

POLICE

On March 31, 1988 the strength of the New Zealand Police Force was 5,114 of all ranks, equivalent to 1 for every 654 of the population. Total police expenditure for the year 1987–88 was NZ$379,000,000.

DEFENCE

A unified Ministry of Defence which retained the three single services was set up in 1964. The Minister of Defence is responsible for national defence, and, with the other members of the Defence Council, commands and administers the three services:

The *Royal New Zealand Navy* consisted of 2,610 officers and ratings as at March 31, 1988, as well as the Volunteer Reserve in four divisions. The strength is four frigates, one survey ship, one research vessel and one tanker, as well as patrol and inshore survey craft.

The *New Zealand Army* consists of the Regular Force, the Territorial Force and the Army Reserve. The strength of the Regular Force at March 31, 1988 was 6,061, and of the Territorial Force and Army Reserve, 7,351. The Army is structured to provide a Regular Force battalion group which is available for rapid deployment on military operations or civil assistance tasks, as well as a framework of integrated Regular Force/Territorial Force Units as a basis for expansion when required.

The *Royal New Zealand Air Force* had a Regular Force strength of 4,192 at March 31, 1988, with 1,075 in the Territorial and Reserve Forces. Operational units include fighter ground attack, maritime, medium and short-range transport, and helicopter squadrons, and flying training units.

FINANCE

Into the Consolidated Account (New Zealand's main public account) are paid the proceeds of income tax, goods and services tax, customs and excise duties and other taxes, also interest, profits from trading undertakings, and departmental receipts. Revenue from taxation is also paid into the National Roads Fund principally from a tax on motor spirits and registration and licence fees for motor vehicles.

Revenue and expenditure for year ended March 31 (NZ$'000):

	1987	1988
Revenue	18,992,500	23,583,800
Expenditure (net)	20,945,100	23,116,600

Revenue from taxation was (NZ$'000):

	1987	1988
Total	17,408,870	21,528,100
Consolidated Account	16,989,095	21,018,500
National Roads Fund	419,016	509,600

Gross expenditure includes (NZ$'000):

	1987	1988
Education	2,617,899	3,179,340
Social welfare	6,175,123	7,190,763
Health	2,961,132	3,397,077
Development of industry	11,531,500	2,095,800
Defence	1,095,961	1,278,488
Debt services	4,411,897	6,945,691
Law and order	622,022	816,222

DEBT

The gross Public Debt amounted on March 31, 1988, to NZ$39,111,400,000 of which NZ$7,204,180,000 was domiciled in Europe, NZ$4,771,571,000 in U.S.A. and NZ$5,152,530,000 in Japan; NZ$21,854,569,000 was held in New Zealand.

BANKING

As at March 31, 1988 there were 15 registered banks including four major trading banks. At September 1988 the assets of registered banks in relation to New Zealand business totalled NZ$38,319,000,000; savings institutions NZ$12,944,000,000; and other financial corporations NZ$17,279,000,000. New Zealand's official overseas reserves at September 1988 amounted to NZ$3,589,000,000.

The Reserve Bank of New Zealand notes and coins are legal tender. Value of notes in circulation on March 31, 1988 were NZ$908,065,000.

EDUCATION

Schools are free and attendance is compulsory between the ages of 6 and 15. At July 1987 there were 421,361 pupils attending public primary schools, and 11,611 pupils attending registered private primary schools. The secondary education of boys and girls in the cities and large towns is carried on in 314 state secondary schools, and 47 private secondary schools (27 also provide primary education). The total number of pupils receiving full-time secondary education in July 1987 was 232,307 and in addition there were 124,264 students attending technical classes including 34,802 receiving part-time tuition from the Technical Correspondence Institute. Almost all the students attending technical classes are part-time. There are seven universities with a total of 66,435 students in 1987. The university system is co-ordinated by the University Grants Committee.

The total expenditure on education out of public funds in 1987–88 was NZ$3,118,200,000 or 13·5 per cent of government expenditure.

PRODUCTION AND INDUSTRY

Gross Agricultural Production (Gross Output)

	Year ended March 1985–86	1986–87
	NZ$(million)	
Sheep	400	646
Wool	1,069	1,214
Cattle	779	974
Pigs	104	116
Dairy products	1,529	1,130
Crops and seeds	349	304
Fruit, nuts, oilseeds	424	621
Vegetables	266	364
Poultry products	176	170
Agricultural services	445	446
Other horticulture	173	208
Other products n.e.c.	151	179
Value of change in livestock	386	−34
Sales of live animals	630	607
Gross Output	6,878	6,945

Agricultural and Pastoral Production

	1987	1988
*Wheat, metric tons	336,800	206,000
*Wool, metric tons	350,000	346,000
†Butter, metric tons	223,600	242,000
‡Cheese, metric tons	115,200	128,400
‡Stock Slaughtered—		
Lambs, No.	31,656,000	30,389,000
Sheep, No.	9,295,000	7,931,000
Cattle, No.	2,318,000	2,218,000
Calves, No.	857,000	891,000
Pigs, No.	774,000	782,000

* Year ended June 30.
† Year ended May 31.
‡ Year ended Sept. 30.

Forestry.—The output of sawn timber for 1988 was 1,822,000 cubic metres, of which 1,737,000 cubic metres represented exotic varieties, mainly radiata pine.

Livestock.—Livestock on farms at June 30, 1988, included 3,200,000 dairy cattle, 4,858,000 beef cattle (of which 1,460,000 were beef breeding cows), and 414,000 pigs. Sheep numbered 64,600,000.

Minerals.—Non-metallic minerals such as coal, clay, limestone and dolomite are both economically and industrially more important than metallic ones. Coal output in 1988 was 2,720,000 tonnes (provisional). Of the metals, the most important is ironsand. Natural gas deposits in Taranaki are being used for electricity generation and as a premium fuel, piped to all the major North Island centres.

TRADE

	1986–87	1987–88
Imports (v.f.d.)	NZ$10,803,400,000	NZ$11,606,500,000
Exports (f.o.b.)	12,107,200,000	12,451,500,000

Trade with U.K.

	1987 ('000)	1988 ('000)
Imports from U.K.	NZ$1,060,700	NZ$1,014,600
Exports to U.K.	1,125,100	1,062,200

New Zealand produce exported to the U.K. in the 12 months ending June, 1988, included butter and cheese, valued at NZ$302,000,000; wool (NZ$144,400,000); lamb (NZ$288,000,000); hides, skins and leather (NZ$87,100,000).

COMMUNICATIONS

Railways.—The national railway system is owned and operated by the New Zealand Railways Corporation. In March, 1988, there were 4,202 km. of Government railway in operation.

Motor Vehicles.—At March 31, 1988 there were 2,179,005 licensed motor vehicles. These included 1,385,149 cars and 297,338 commercial vehicles.

Shipping.—During 1988 the vessels entered from overseas ports numbered 3,298 (gross tonnage 27,844,000) and those cleared for overseas 3,334 (gross tonnage 27,247,000).

Civil Aviation—Figures are for scheduled services in the year to end Dec. 1987:

	Domestic Flights	International Flights
Passengers carried ('000)	3,782	3,001
Freight carried (tonnes)	58,000	117,769
Mail carried (tonnes)	—	4,385

BRITISH HIGH COMMISSION
Reserve Bank of New Zealand Building,
2 The Terrace (P.O. Box 1812), Wellington, 1
[Wellington 726-049]

High Commissioner, His Excellency Ronald Archer Campbell Byatt, C.M.G. (1988).

Deputy High Commissioner, Head of Chancery, S. I. Soutar.

Defence Adviser, Gp. Capt. J. G. Sheldon.

First Secretaries, A. B. Cawthorn (*Agriculture and Food*); H. A. Payne (*Commercial*); J. R. Setterfield (*Chancery, Information*).

Second Secretaries, R. Leadbeater (*Consular and Administration*); T. A. Torlot (*Chancery*).

Attaché, S. Bailey (*Consular*).

British Council Representative, A. C. Ramsay.

BRITISH CHAMBER OF COMMERCE FOR AUSTRALIA AND NEW ZEALAND, P.O. Box 141, Manuka, A.C.T. 2603, Australia; U.K. OFFICE, Suite 615, 6th Floor The Linen Hall, 162/8 Regent Street, W1R 5TB.

THE TERRITORIES OF NEW ZEALAND

TOKELAU (OR UNION ISLANDS)

A group of atolls (Fakaofo, Nukunonu and Atafu) (population 1,690 at Oct. 10, 1986), proclaimed part of New Zealand as from Jan. 1, 1948.

THE ROSS DEPENDENCY

The Ross Dependency, placed under the jurisdiction of New Zealand by Order in Council dated July 30, 1923, and defined as all the islands and territories between 160° E. and 150° W. longitude which are situated south of the 60° S. parallel. The Ross Dependency includes Edward VII Land and portions of Victoria Land. Since 1957 a number of research stations have been established in the Dependency.

ASSOCIATED STATES

COOK ISLANDS

Included in the boundaries of New Zealand since June, 1901, the group consists of the islands of Rarotonga, Aitutaki, Mangaia, Atiu, Mauke, Mitiaro, Manuae, Takutea, Palmerston, Penrhyn or Tongareva, Manihiki, Rakahanga, Suwarrow, Pukapuka or Danger and Nassau. The total population of the group was 17,185 at December 1, 1986. The chief industries of the Cook Islands are tourism, financial services and the production of fruit juice, clothing, copra, bananas, citrus fruit and pulp, and pearl shell. The trade is chiefly with New Zealand, Australia, Japan, the U.K. and the U.S.A. The New Zealand Government continues to give financial aid to the Cook Islands.

The Queen's representative in the islands is Sir Tangaroa Tangaroa, K.B.E. There is also a representative of the New Zealand government. Since Aug. 4, 1965, the Islands have enjoyed complete internal self-government, executive power being in the hands of a Cabinet consisting of the Premier and five other ministers. The new Constitution Act was passed by the New Zealand Parliament in November 1964, but did not come into force until it had been endorsed by the 22-member Legislative Assembly of the Cook Islands, elected in April 1965.

The New Zealand citizenship of the Cook Islanders is embodied in the Constitution, and assurances have been given that the changed status of the Islands will in no way affect the consideration of subsidies or the right of free entry into New Zealand for exports from the group.

H.M. Representative, Sir Tangaroa Tangaroa, K.B.E.
New Zealand Representative, A. Simcock.

NIUE

The population of Niue was estimated at 2,155 at March 31, 1989.

A New Zealand Representative is stationed at Niue, which since October 1974 has been self-governing in free association with New Zealand, which is responsible for external affairs and defence, and continues to give financial aid. Executive power is in the hands of a Premier and a Cabinet of three drawn from the Assembly of 20 members.
New Zealand Representative, M. J. Taylor.

ANTIGUA AND BARBUDA
(State of Antigua and Barbuda)

AREA, POPULATION, ETC.—Antigua and Barbuda comprises the islands of Antigua (108 sq. miles (279 sq. km.)), Barbuda (62 sq. miles (160 sq. km.)) 25 miles north of Antigua, and Redonda (½ square mile; 1·2 sq. km.) 25 miles south-west of Antigua. Antigua is part of the Leeward Islands in the Eastern Caribbean and lies 17° 3′ N. and 61° 48′ W. It is distinguished from the rest of the Leeward group by its absence of high hills and forest, and a drier climate than most of the W. Indies. Barbuda, formerly a possession of the Codrington family, is very flat with a large lagoon and well wooded in the north east. Antigua was first settled by the English in 1632, and was granted to Lord Willoughby by Charles II. Antigua has a population of 80,000, (1985 U.N. estimate); Barbuda, 1,500, and Redonda is uninhabited.

CAPITAL.—♀St. John's. Population, 30,000. The town of Barbuda is Codrington.

CURRENCY.—East Caribbean dollar (EC$) of 100 cents.

FLAG.—Inverted triangle (centred on a red field) divided horizontally into three bands of black over blue over white; rising sun device in gold on black band.

NATIONAL ANTHEM.—"Fair Antigua and Barbuda".

NATIONAL DAY.—November 1 (Independence Day).

GOVERNMENT

Antigua became internally self-governing in 1967 and fully independent on Nov. 1, 1981, as a constitutional monarchy with H.M. The Queen as Head of State, represented by the Governor General. There is a Senate of 17 appointed members and a House of Representatives elected every 5 years. The Attorney-General may be appointed.

The Antigua Labour party led by Mr. Vere Bird won the general election of March 9, 1989 and a fourth successive term of office.

Governor General, Sir Wilfred Ebenezer Jacobs, G.C.M.G., G.C.V.O., O.B.E., Q.C.

Cabinet
(as at May 31, 1989)

Prime Minister, Defence, and Information, Rt. Hon. Vere C. Bird (Sr).
Deputy P.M. and Minister for Foreign Affairs, Economic Development, Tourism and Energy, Hon. Lester Bird.
Public Utilities and Aviation, Hon. Robin Yearwood.
Finance, Hon. John E. St. Luce.
Education, Culture and Youth Affairs and Sport, Hon. Reuben H. Harris.
Labour and Health, Hon. Adolphus Freeland.
Home Affairs, Hon. Christopher M. O'Mard.
Agriculture, Fisheries and Lands, Housing, Hon. Hilroy Humphreys.
Attorney General (apptd), Hon. Keith Ford.
Public Works, and Communications, Hon. V. C. Bird (Jnr).
Ministers within a Ministry:
  Foreign Affairs, Economic Development, Tourism and Energy, Hon. Hugh Marshall; Hon. Molwyn Joseph.
  Public Utilities and Aviation, Hon. Eustace Cochrane.
  Finance and Port Authority, Hon. Henderson St. Clair Simon.
  Prime Minister's Office, Senator Hon. Bernard Percival.

HIGH COMMISSION FOR
ANTIGUA AND BARBUDA
15 Thayer Street, W1M 5LD
[01–486 7073]

High Commissioner, His Excellency James Thomas (1987).

ECONOMY

Tourism is the main feature of the economy, with several hotels (and a number under construction) to take advantage of the many white sand beaches which made Antigua one of the first Caribbean islands to attract tourists.

For many years sugar was the dominant crop but is now produced primarily for local consumption. Areas of agricultural development include livestock, sea island cotton, corn (for cornmeal production) and improved vegetable and fruit production.

FINANCE

	1988	1989*
Revenue	EC$217,000,000	EC$236,720,991
Expenditure (recurrent) ...	231,700,000	263,579,351
*estimated		

Trade with U.K.

	1987	1988
Imports from U.K.	£19,334,000	£20,755,000
Exports to U.K.	4,271,000	10,845,000

BRITISH HIGH COMMISSION
38 St. Mary's Street (P.O. 483), St. John's
[St. John's 462 0008/9]

High Commissioner, (resides at Bridgetown, Barbados).
Resident Representative, B. Taylor (*First Secretary*).

THE BAHAMAS
(The Commonwealth of The Bahamas)

AREA, POPULATION, ETC.—The Bahama Islands are an archipelago lying in the North Atlantic Ocean between 20° 55′–25° 22′ N. lat; 72° 35′–79° 35′ W. long. They extend from the coast of Florida on the north-west almost to Haiti on the south-east. The group consists of 700 islands, of which 30 are inhabited and 2,400 cays comprising an area of more than 5,380 sq. miles, (19,935 sq. km.). The population, at the census of 1980 was 237,090. The principal islands include: Abaco, Acklins, Andros, Berry Islands, Bimini, Cat Island, Crooked Island, Eleuthera, Exumas, Grand Bahama, Harbour Island, Inagua, Long Island, Mayaguana, New Providence (on which is located the capital, Nassau), Ragged Island, Rum Cay, San Salvador and Spanish Wells. San Salvador was the first landfall in the New World of Christopher Columbus on October 12, 1492.

The Bahamas were settled by British subjects when the islands were deserted. The ownership of The Bahamas was taken over in 1782 by the Spanish, but the Treaty of Versailles in 1783 restored them to the British.

CAPITAL.—ΨNassau. Population (1980 census), 135,437.

CURRENCY.—Bahamian dollar (B$) of 100 cents.

FLAG.—Horizontal stripes of aquamarine, gold and aquamarine, with a black equilateral triangle on the hoist.

NATIONAL ANTHEM.—March on, Bahamaland.

NATIONAL DAY.—July 10 (Independence Day).

GOVERNMENT

The Bahamas gained independence on July 10, 1973. The Head of State is H.M. Queen Elizabeth II, represented in the islands by a Governor General. There is a Senate of 15 members and an elected House of Assembly of 49 members.

Acting Governor General, His Excellency Sir Henry Milton Taylor (1988).

Cabinet
(as at June 30, 1989)

Prime Minister and Minister of Finance, Rt. Hon. Sir Lynden Pindling, K.C.M.G.

Deputy P.M., Minister of Tourism and of Public Personnel, Hon. Sir Clement Maynard.

Education, National Security and Government Leader in the House of Assembly, Hon. Paul L. Adderley.

Works and Lands, Hon. Darrell E. Rolle.

Employment and Immigration, Hon. Alfred T. Maycock.

Transport and Local Government, Hon. Philip M. Bethel.

Health, Hon. Dr. Norman Gay.

Housing and National Insurance, Hon. George W. Mackey.

Agriculture, Trade and Industry, Hon. Ervin Knowles.

Foreign Affairs, Hon. Charles E. Carter.

Consumer Affairs, Hon. Dr. Bernard J. Nottage.

Youth, Sports and Community Affairs, Senator Hon. Peter J. Bethell.

Attorney General, Senator Hon. Sean G. McWeeny.

President of the Court of Appeal, Kenneth Henry.

Chief Justice, Rt. Hon. Philip Telford-Georges.

BAHAMAS HIGH COMMISSION
Bahamas House, 10 Chesterfield Street, W1X 8AH
[01-408 4488]

High Commissioner, Her Excellency Dr. Patricia Rodgers (1988).

ECONOMY

Tourism is the economic mainstay of The Bahamas, employing about two-thirds of the labour force. It provides about two-thirds of Government revenue and about half the country's foreign exchange earnings. The second main industry is international banking and trust business, The Bahamas' absence of any direct taxation and internal stability enabling the country to become one of the world's leading financial centres.

Agricultural production is mainly of fresh vegetables, fruit, meat and eggs for the domestic market, and crawfish, mostly for export. There are large reserves of aragonite, and reserves of limestone and salt, all of which are being commercially exploited. Freeport is the country's leading industrial centre, with a chemicals and a pharmaceutical plant, an oil trans-shipment and storage terminal, and port and bunkering facilities. There are also a brewery and a rum distillery on New Providence.

EDUCATION

Education is compulsory between the ages of 5 and 14. More than 60,000 students are enrolled in Ministry of Education and Independent schools in New Providence and the Family Islands.

COMMUNICATIONS

The main ports are Nassau (New Providence), Freeport (Grand Bahama), Mathew Town (Inagua). International air services are operated from Abaco, Bimini, Eleuthera, Exuma, Grand Bahama and New Providence. About 50 smaller airports and landing strips facilitate services between the islands, the services being provided by Bahamasair, the national carrier. There are roads on the larger islands, and roads are under construction on the smaller islands. There are no railways. Wireless and telephone services are in operation to all parts of the world.

FINANCE AND TRADE

	1987	1988p
Public revenue	B$436·1m	B$432·6m
Expenditure	462·0m	513·8m
p provisional		

Trade with U.K.

	1987	1988
Imports from U.K.	£27,063,000	£20,708,000
Exports to U.K.	15,943,000	24,781,000

The imports are chiefly foodstuffs, manufactured articles, building material, vehicles and machinery, chemicals and petroleum. The chief exports are rum, petroleum, hormones, salt, crawfish and aragonite.

BRITISH HIGH COMMISSION
Bitco Building, East St.
P.O. Box N7516, Nassau.
[Nassau 325-7471]

High Commissioner, His Excellency Colin Garth Mays, C.M.G. (1986).

Deputy High Commissioner, P. H. Johnson (*Head of Chancery*).

BANGLADESH
(Ghana Praja Tantri Bangladesh)

AREA, POPULATION, CLIMATE, ETC.—The People's Republic of Bangladesh consists of the territory which was formerly East Pakistan (the old province of East Bengal and the Sylhet district of Assam), covering an area of 55,598 sq. miles (143,998 sq. km.)

in the region of the Gangetic delta, and has a population (1989 estimate) of 110 million.

The country is crossed by a network of navigable rivers, including the eastern arms of the Ganges, the Jamuna (Brahmaputra) and the Meghna, flowing into the Bay of Bengal. The climate is tropical and monsoon; hot and extremely humid during the summer, and mild and dry during the short winter. The rainfall is heavy, varying from 50 inches to 135 inches in different districts and the bulk of it falls during monsoon season from June to September.

CAPITAL.—Dhaka. Population (1989 estimate), 5,000,000.

CURRENCY.—Taka (Tk) of 100 poisha.

FLAG.—Red circle on a bottle-green ground.

NATIONAL ANTHEM.—Amar Sonar Bangla.

NATIONAL DAY.—March 26 (Independence Day).

GOVERNMENT

Prior to becoming East Pakistan, the territory had been part of British India. It acceded to Pakistan in October, 1947, which became a Republic on March 23, 1956.

By a proclamation of March 26, 1971, Bangladesh purported to secede from the central government, and a government-in-exile was set up in April in Calcutta. The short war between India and Pakistan, in both the East and the West, and India's overwhelming defeat of the Pakistani Army in the East, brought about a *de facto* secession of the East wing. The Indo-Pakistan war was concluded on December 16, 1971, and Mr. Zulfiqar Ali Bhutto became President of Pakistan on December 20. Sheikh Mujib was sworn in as Prime Minister of Bangladesh on January 12, 1972. Pakistan and Bangladesh accorded one another mutual recognition in Feb. 1974 and established diplomatic relations in Jan. 1976.

From 1975 a non-political administration ran the country under martial law. A Presidential election was held on June 3, 1978, and President Zia was elected by a considerable majority. Martial law was subsequently lifted. Zia was assassinated in May 1981 in an unsuccessful coup, but the military, led by Lt.-Gen. Ershad, took over in March 1982 and martial law was again imposed. Following elections in May 1986 a civilian Cabinet was appointed. Presidential elections were held on Oct. 15, 1986 and Ershad gained a substantial majority. Martial law was subsequently lifted on Nov. 10 and the 1972 Constitution fully restored.

Parliament was dissolved by President Ershad on December 6, 1987 amid growing political turmoil. Parliamentary elections were held on March 3, 1988 and were boycotted by the country's main political parties. In the new Parliament which convened on April 25, the Jatiya Party of President Ershad had a two-thirds majority. In July 1989, Parliament passed a constitutional amendment withdrawing the provision of life presidency from President Ershad and limiting him to one further term of five years.

President, Hossain Mohammed Ershad.

Vice President and Minister for Justice, A. K. M. Nurul Islam.

Council of Ministers
(as at May 31, 1989)

Prime Minister and Minister for Industry, Moudud Ahmed.

Deputy P.M. and Minister for Health and Family Planning, Prof. M. A. Matin.

Deputy P.M., Political Adviser to the President, and Minister for Information, Kazi Zafar Ahmed.

Deputy P.M. and Minister for Labour and Manpower, Shah Moazeem Hossain.

Commerce, M. A. Sattar.

Finance, Wahidul Haque.

Energy and Mineral Resources, A. B. M. Gholam Mostafa.

Foreign Affairs, Anisul Islam Mahmud.

Jute, A. K. M. Mayeedul Islam.

Land Administration and Reform, Sunil Kumar Gupta.

Communications, Anwar Hossain.

Civil Aviation and Tourism, Ziauddin Ahmed.

Education and Establishment, Sheikh Shahidul Islam.

Agriculture, Maj.-Gen. Mohammad Abdul Munim.

Fisheries and Livestock, Sardar Amzad Hossain.

Planning, Air Vice Marshal A. K. Khondaker.

Shipping, Korban Ali.

Relief and Rehabilitation, Sirajul Hossain Khan.

Religious Affairs, Nazimuddin Al Azad.

Irrigation, Water Development and Flood Control, Mahbubur Rahman.

Textiles, Zafar Imam.

Works, Mostafa Jamal Haider.

Social Welfare and Women's Affairs, Rezwanul Huq Chowdhury.

Youth, Maj.-Gen. Iqbal Hossain Chowdhury.

Sports, Lt.-Col. H. M. A. Ghaffar.

Posts and Telecommunications, Kazi Feroz Rashid.

Cultural Affairs, Nur Muhammad Khan.

Tribal Affairs, Binoy Kumar Dewan.

Dhaka Municipal Corporation, Col. M. A. Malek.

The Bangladesh cabinet was reshuffled in Aug. 1989 but no further details were available at the time of going to press.

BANGLADESH HIGH COMMISSION
28 Queen's Gate, SW7 5JA
[01–584 0081–4/589 4842–4]

High Commissioner, His Excellency Maj.-Gen. K. M. Safiullah (1987).

RELIGION

The faith of over 90 per cent of the population is Islam. Islam has been constitutionally declared the state religion of Bangladesh.

LANGUAGE

The state language is Bengali. Use of Bengali is compulsory in all government departments. English, however, is understood and is used widely as an unofficial second language.

EDUCATION

Primary education is free but not universal. Most primary schools are under government management. The majority of secondary schools and colleges are privately managed, but many receive government grants. There are six universities. In 1981 literacy was estimated at 23·8 per cent of the whole of Bangladesh; 31 per cent of the male population and 16 per cent of the female population.

TRANSPORT AND COMMUNICATIONS

Principal seaports are Chittagong and Mongla. The Bangladesh Shipping Corporation has been set up by the Government to operate the Bangladesh merchant fleet. The principal airports are Dhaka, (Zia International) and Chittagong. The international airline, Bangladesh Biman, serves Europe, the Middle East, South and South-East Asia, and an internal network.

There are about 6,880 miles of roads in Bangladesh; 4,724 miles are metalled. There are 2,798 miles of railway track.

Radio Bangladesh is the main national broadcasting service. A television service was introduced in 1965 and colour transmissions began in 1981.

ECONOMY

Bangladesh is a principal producer of raw jute. Other agricultural products are rice, tea, oil seeds, pulses, and sugar cane. The chief industries are jute, cotton, tea, leather, pharmaceuticals, fertilizer, sugar, prawn fishing, natural gas and garment manufacture. Remittances sent home by Bangladeshi workers abroad have been of considerable support to the economy in recent years.

Aid

Bangladesh is a major recipient of bilateral and multilateral development aid. The total annual development plan for 1988–89 is budgeted at U.S. $1,423 million, of which U.S. $1,146 million will be financed from external sources as follows:

Project aid	U.S. $900 million
Commodity aid	445 million
Food aid	78 million

Trade with U.K.

	1987	1988
Imports from U.K.	£54,382,000	£64,018,000
Exports to U.K.	35,454,000	50,249,000

BRITISH HIGH COMMISSION
Abu Bakr House, Plot 7, Road 84, Gulshan Dhaka,
P.O. Box 6079
[Dhaka 600133/7]

High Commissioner, His Excellency Colin Henry Imray, C.M.G (1989).
Deputy High Commissioner, J. F. Holding.
British Council Representative, W. G. Harvey, 5 Fuller Road, (P.O. Box 161), Ramna, Dhaka 1000.

BARBADOS

AREA, POPULATION, ETC.—Barbados, the most easterly of the Caribbean islands, is situated in latitude 13° 14′ N. and longitude 59° 37′ W. The island has a total area of 166 sq. miles, (430 sq. km.), the land rising in a series of tablelands marked by terraces to the highest point, Mt. Hillaby (1,116 ft.). It is nearly 21 miles long by 14 miles broad. The climate is equable with annual average temperature 26·6°C. (79·8°F.) and rainfall varying from a yearly average of 75 inches in the high central district to 50 inches in some of the low-lying coastal areas.

POPULATION.—The population of Barbados (1985 U.N. estimate) was 253,000. There are eleven administrative areas (parishes); St. Michael; Christ Church; St. Andrews; St. George; St. James; St. John; St. Joseph; St. Lucy; St. Peter; St. Philip, and St. Thomas.

CAPITAL.—ΨBridgetown (population, estimated April, 1980, 7,466) in the parish of St. Michael. There are three other towns, Oistins in Christ Church, Holetown in St. James and Speightstown in St. Peter.

CURRENCY.—Barbados dollar (BD$) of 100 cents.

FLAG.—Three vertical stripes, dark blue, gold and dark blue, with trident devises on gold stripe.

NATIONAL ANTHEM.—In Plenty and in Time of Need.

NATIONAL DAY.—November 30 (Independence Day).

GOVERNMENT

The first inhabitants of Barbados were Arawak Indians but the island was uninhabited when first settled by the British in 1627. It was a Crown Colony from 1652 until it became an independent state within the Commonwealth on November 30, 1966. The Legislature consists of the Governor General, a Senate and a House of Assembly. The Senate comprises 21 Senators appointed by the Governor General, of whom 12 are appointed on the advice of the Prime Minister, 2 on the advice of the Leader of the Opposition and 7 by the Governor General at his discretion to represent religious, economic or social interests in the Island or such other interests as the Governor General considers ought to be represented. The House of Assembly comprises 27 members elected every five years by adult suffrage. The last General Election took place on May 28, 1986 and, as a result, seats in the House of Assembly were distributed as follows: Democratic Labour Party 24, Barbados Labour Party 3.

Governor General, Sir Hugh Springer, G.C.M.G., G.C.V.O., C.B.E. (1984).

Cabinet
(as at May 31, 1989)

Prime Minister, Minister of Economic Affairs and Finance, Rt. Hon. L. Erskine Sandiford.
Deputy P.M., Minister of International Transport, Telecommunications, and Immigration, Hon. Philip M. Greaves, Q.C.
Attorney General and Minister of Legal Affairs, Hon. Maurice A. King, Q.C.
Agriculture, Food and Fisheries, Hon. Warwick O. Franklin.
Employment, Labour Relations and Community Development, Hon. N. Keith Simmons.
Trade, Industry and Commerce, Hon. E. Evelyn Greaves.
Foreign Affairs and Leader of the Senate, Senator Hon. Sir James Tudor, K.C.M.G.
Health, Hon. Branford M. Taitt.
Housing and Lands, Hon. Harold A. Blackman.
Transport and Works, Hon. Dr. Donald G. Blackman.
Tourism and Sport, Hon. Wesley W. Hall.
Education and Culture, Hon. Cyril V. Walker.
Minister of State, Finance, Senator Hon. Dr. Carl Clarke.
Minister of State for the Civil Service, Senator Hon. L. V. Harcourt Lewis.
President of the Senate, Senator Hon. Frank Walcott, O.B.E.
Speaker, House of Assembly, Hon. Lawson Weekes.

BARBADOS HIGH COMMISSION
1 Great Russell Street, WC1B 3NH
[01–631 4975]

High Commissioner, new appointment awaited.

JUDICATURE

There is a Supreme Court of Judicature consisting of a High Court and a Court of Appeal. In certain cases a further appeal lies to the Judicial Committee of H.M. Privy Council. The Chief Justice and Puisne Judges are appointed by the Governor-General on the recommendation of the Prime Minister and after consultation with the Leader of the Opposition.
Chief Justice, The Hon. Sir Denys Ambrose Williams, K.B.

EDUCATION

Primary and secondary education is free in Government schools. There are 105 primary schools, 21 Government secondary schools and 15 approved Government secondary schools.

COMMUNICATIONS

Barbados has some 965 miles of roads, of which about 917 miles are asphalted. The Grantley Adams International airport is situated at Seawell, 12 miles from Bridgetown, and frequent scheduled services connect Barbados with the major world air routes. Bridgetown, the only port of entry, has a deep-water harbour with berths for 8 ships, but oil is pumped ashore at Spring Gardens and at an Esso installation on the West Coast. Barbados has a colour television service, three radio broadcasting services, and a wired broadcasting service.

FINANCE

	1987–88*
Current revenue	BD$698,071,077
Current expenditure	711,636,404
Capital expenditure	176,518,229
* estimated.	

ECONOMY

The economy of the island is based on tourism, sugar and light manufacturing. In 1986, 369,770 tourists visited Barbados and 145,335 cruise ship passengers. Chief exports are sugar and its by-products (15·7 per cent of exports in 1986), electrical components (52·1 per cent) and clothing (8·4 per cent).

	1985 BD$	1986 BD$
Total imports	1,221·5 m	1,181·0 m
Total exports	707·7 m	552·3 m

Trade with U.K.

	1987	1988
Imports from U.K.	£33,067,000	£32,061,000
Exports to U.K.	23,320,000	19,487,000

BRITISH HIGH COMMISSION
Lower Collymore Rock, P.O. Box 676,
Bridgetown
[Bridgetown 436 6694]

High Commissioner, His Excellency Kevin Francis Xavier Burns, C.M.G. (1986).

BELIZE

AREA, POPULATION, ETC.—Belize lies on the east coast of Central America, bounded on the north and north-west by Mexico, and on the west and south by Guatemala. The total area (including offshore islands) is about 8,867 sq. miles (22,965 sq. km.), with a length and breadth of 174 miles and 68 miles respectively. The climate is sub-tropical, with a mean annual temperature of 20°C, but is tempered by sea breezes. There are two dry seasons, the main one from March to May and the other (the Maugre season) from August to September. The country is occasionally affected by hurricanes.

The coastal areas are mostly flat and swampy but the country rises gradually towards the interior. The northern and western districts are hilly, and in the south the Maya Mountains and the Cockscombs form the backbone of the country, reaching a height of 3,800 feet at Victoria Peak.

The population is 166,000 (1985 U.N. estimate), of which the main racial groups are Creole, Mestizo (Maya-Spanish) and Carib, plus a number of East Indian and Spanish descent. The races are now heavily inter-mixed. The majority of the population is Christian, about 60 per cent Catholic and most of the remainder Protestant.

The early history of Belize is little known, although the numerous ruins in the area indicate that it was heavily populated by the Maya Indians. The first British settlement was established in 1638 but was subject to repeated attacks by the Spanish, who claimed sovereignty over the area, until the decline of Spanish power in the Americas in the 19th century. In 1862 the area was recognized by Britain as a colony and called British Honduras. On June 1, 1973 the colony was officially renamed Belize, and was granted independence on September 21, 1981. The long-standing territorial dispute with Guatemala, which had delayed independence earlier, remains unresolved despite efforts to reach a settlement.

CAPITAL.—Belmopan (estimated population, 1980, 2,935). The largest city and the former capital is ΨBelize City (population, 1980 census, 39,771). Other towns are Corozal (6,899), San Ignacio (5,616), Dangriga (6,661), Orange Walk (8,439), Punta Gorda (2,396).

CURRENCY.—Belize dollar (BZ$) of 100 cents. The Belize dollar is tied to the U.S. dollar—BZ$2 = U.S.$1.

FLAG.—Blue ground with red band along top and bottom edges, and in centre a white disc containing the coat of arms surrounded by a green garland.

NATIONAL ANTHEM.—Land of the Gods.

NATIONAL DAY.—September 21 (Independence Day).

GOVERNMENT

The Queen is Head of State, represented in Belize by a Governor General, who is a citizen of the country, appointed in consultation with the Prime Minister of Belize. There is a National Assembly, comprising a House of Representatives (28 members elected for 5 years) and a Senate (8 members appointed by the Governor General). Executive power is vested in the Cabinet, which is responsible to the National Assembly.

Governor General, Her Excellency Dame Minita Elmira Gordon, G.C.M.G., G.C.V.O.

The Cabinet
(as at May 31, 1989)

Prime Minister and Minister of Finance, Hon. Manuel Esquivel.
Deputy Prime Minister and Minister of Home Affairs, Hon. Curl Thompson.
Commerce, Industry and Tourism, Hon. Eduardo Juan (Jr.).
Education, Youth and Sports, Hon. Elodio Aragon.
Health, Hon. Israel Alpuche.
Natural Resources, Hon. Charles Wagner.
Attorney General, Foreign Affairs and Economic Development, Hon. Dean Barrow.
Electricity, Transport, and Communications, Hon. Derek Aikman.
Works and Housing, Hon. Hubert Elrington.
Agriculture, Hon. Dean Lindo.
Labour and Social Services, Hon. Philip Goldson.

BELIZE HIGH COMMISSION
200 Sutherland Avenue,
W9 1RX
[01-266 3486]

High Commissioner, His Excellency Sir Edney Cain, O.B.E.

ECONOMY

About 42 per cent of the population is engaged in agriculture. Corn (maize), rice, red kidney beans, root crops and fruit are the main food crops, although main agricultural exports are sugar, bananas and citrus products. The country is more or less self-sufficient in fresh beef, pork and poultry, but processed meat and dairy products are imported. About 25 per cent of timber production (mostly mahogany) is exported, and there is a large U.S. market for lobster, conch and scale fish. Tourism is also a valuable source of income.

FINANCE

	1987–88	1988–89p
Revenue	BZ $114·2 m	BZ $132·2 m
Expenditure	134·6 m	131·3 m
Deficit	− 20·4 m	0·9 m

p = provisional

TRADE

	1986	1987
Total imports	BZ $243·9 m	BZ $285·9 m
Total exports	185·2 m	205·7 m

Trade with U.K.

	1987	1988
Imports from U.K.	£7,543,000	£12,064,000
Exports to U.K.	22,757,000	22,461,000

EDUCATION

Education is compulsory from 5 to 14 years of age. In 1985 primary education was provided by 225 schools, most of which are government aided. Enrolment totalled 38,512. Secondary education is provided by 29 secondary and post-secondary institutions with an enrolment of 7,441. Plans are underway for Ferris State College of Michigan, U.S.A., to establish an affiliate university in Belize. The Government also offers scholarships for students to go abroad. There is an extra-mural faculty of the University of the West Indies, with a resident tutor.

COMMUNICATIONS

There is a Government-operated radio service but no official television service in the country. An automatic telephone service operated by Belize Telecommunications Ltd. covers the whole country.

The principal airport is at Belize City and various airlines operate international flights to U.S. and other Central American states. The main port is also Belize City, where construction of deep water quays was recently completed. There are 1,865 miles of road, including four main highways, but there is no railway system.

BRITISH HIGH COMMISSION
P.O. Box 91, Belmopan.
[Belmopan 2146/7]
High Commissioner, His Excellency Peter Alexander Bremner Thomson, C.V.O. (1987).
Deputy High Commissioner, J. Bentley.

BOTSWANA
(The Republic of Botswana)

AREA, POPULATION, ETC.—Botswana (formerly the British Protectorate of Bechuanaland) lies between latitudes 18° and 26° S. and longitudes 20° and 28° W. and is bounded by the Cape and Transvaal Provinces of South Africa on the south and east, by Zimbabwe, the Zambezi and Chobe (Linyanti) Rivers on the north and north-east and by South West Africa on the west. Botswana has a total area of 224,607 sq. miles (581,730 sq. km.). The climate of the country is generally sub-tropical, but varies considerably with latitude and altitude. A plateau at a height of about 4,000 feet divides Botswana into two main topographical regions. To the east of the plateau streams flow into the Marico, Notwani and Limpopo Rivers; to the west lies a flat region comprising the Kgalagadi

Desert, the Okavango Swamps and the Northern State Lands area. Large areas of the country support only herds of game. Elephant numbers have been estimated at 15–30,000.

POPULATION.—Botswana has an estimated population (1988) of 1,200,000. The eight principal Botswana tribes are Bakgatla, Bakwena, Bangwaketse, Bamalete, Bamangwato, Barolong, Batawana and Batlokwa. The principal languages in use in Botswana are Setswana and English.

CAPITAL.—Gaborone, estimated population 110,000. Other centres are Francistown (52,000), Lobatse (25,000), and Selebi-Phikwe (46,000).

CURRENCY.—Pula (P) of 100 thebe. P1 = US$0·5166 (Dec. 1988).

FLAG.—Horizontal bands of blue, white, blue, with a black stripe on the white band.

NATIONAL ANTHEM.—Fatshe La Rona.

NATIONAL DAY.—September 30.

GOVERNMENT

On September 30, 1966, Bechuanaland became a Republic within the Commonwealth under the name Botswana. The President of Botswana is Head of State and appoints as Vice President a member of the National Assembly who is his principal assistant and leader of Government business in the National Assembly. The Assembly consists of the President, 34 members elected on a basis of universal adult suffrage, 4 specially elected members, the Attorney-General (non-voting) and the Speaker. There is also a House of Chiefs.

President, His Excellency Dr. Q. K. J. Masire.

Cabinet
(as at May 31, 1989)

Vice President, Minister of Finance and Development Planning, Hon. P. S. Mmusi.
External Affairs, Hon. Dr. G. K. T. Chiepe, M.B.E.
Presidential Affairs and Public Administration, Hon. P. H. K. Kedikilwe.
Health, Hon. J. T. Mothibamele.
Agriculture, Hon. D. K. Kwelagobe.
Local Government and Lands, Hon. P. K. Balopi.
Works and Communications, Hon. C. J. Butale.
Commerce and Industry, Hon. M. P. K. Nwako.
Education, Hon. K. P. Morake.
Mineral Resources and Water Affairs, Hon. A. M. Mogwe, M.B.E.
Home Affairs, Hon. E. M. K. Kgabo.
Assistant Minister, Finance and Development Planning, Hon. I. O. Chilume.
Assistant Minister, Local Government and Lands, Hon. M. R. Tshipinare.
Assistant Minister, Agriculture, Hon. G. M. Oteng.

BOTSWANA HIGH COMMISSION
6 Stratford Place, WIN 9AE
[01–499 0031]
High Commissioner, Her Excellency Mrs. Margaret Nasha (1989).

ECONOMY

Botswana is predominantly a pastoral country. The national herd is normally around 3 million cattle and 1 million sheep and goats but drought conditions during the past 6 years have reduced the number of cattle to around 2·5 million.

Cattle rearing accounts for about 85 per cent of agricultural output and livestock products, particularly beef, are a major source of foreign exchange earnings. The Government has a number of programmes to improve land use and cattle and crop production, and schemes to provide financial assistance for farmers.

Mineral extraction and processing is now the major source of income for the country following the opening of large mines for diamonds and copper-nickel. Botswana is one of the largest producers of diamonds in the world. Large deposits of coal have been discovered and are being mined on a small scale. Much of the country has yet to be fully prospected. Manufacturing industry is growing and will continue to do so as communications improve but it is still a small sector of the economy.

EDUCATION

There are over 500 primary schools (enrolment 230,890), 70 community junior secondary schools (enrolment 22,000) and 23 government and government-aided senior secondary schools (enrolment 7,000). The government embarked on a massive expansion of secondary education in January 1984 aimed at providing universal access to junior secondary education; over 50 more schools are being opened by 1990. There are 5 teacher training establishments (total enrolment 1,540) including one for secondary teachers (enrolment 340), one Polytechnic with 770 students and the University of Botswana with 1,850 undergraduates. Further expansion of the technical education system is planned via a network of vocational training centres.

COMMUNICATIONS

The railway from Cape Town to Zimbabwe passes through eastern Botswana. The main roads in the country are the north-south road, which closely follows the railway, and the road running east-west that links Francistown and Maun. A new road from Nata to Kazungula provides a direct link to Zambia from Botswana. Air services are provided on a scheduled basis between the main towns, linking with services from South Africa, Swaziland, Zambia, Zimbabwe, Malawi, Kenya, Mozambique, Tanzania and the United Kingdom.

FINANCE

	1986–87	1987–88
Actual Revenue (Recurrent and development)	P1,548 m	P2,226 m
Actual Expenditure	1,009 m	1,312 m

TRADE

Principal exports are diamonds, copper-nickel matte, and beef and beef products.

	1987	1988
Imports	P1,572 m	P1,851 m
Exports	2,672 m	2,703 m

Trade with U.K.

	1987	1988
Imports from U.K.	£10,275,000	£26,763,000
Exports to U.K.	11,836,000	6,942,000

BRITISH HIGH COMMISSION
Private Bag 0023, Gaborone
[Gaborone 352841]

High Commissioner, His Excellency Brian Smith, O.B.E. (1989).
British Council Representative, S. Moss, O.B.E.

BRUNEI
(Negara Brunei Darussalam)

Brunei is situated on the north-west coast of the island of Borneo, total area of 2,226 sq. miles (5,765 sq.

km.), population (1988 estimate) 241,000 of whom 68 per cent are of Malay, 18 per cent Chinese and 5 per cent other indigenous races. The country has a humid tropical climate.

CAPITAL.—Bandar Seri Begawan, with a population of 58,000 (1981).

CURRENCY.—Brunei dollar (B$) of 100 sen. It is fully interchangeable with the currency of Singapore.

FLAG.—Yellow, with diagonal bands of white over narrow black band (from top by staff), with red device on diagonal bands.

NATIONAL ANTHEM.—Ya Allah Lanjutkan Lah Usia Duli Tuanku (Oh God, long live our Majesty the Sultan).

NATIONAL DAY.—February 23.

GOVERNMENT

In 1959, the Sultan of Brunei promulgated the first written Constitution, which provides for a Privy Council, a Council of Ministers and a Legislative Council. On January 1, 1984 Brunei resumed full independence. A ministerial system of government was established at independence, the seven Ministers being appointed by the Sultan and responsible to him. The Sultan presides over the Privy Council and the Council of Ministers. The Legislative Council was disbanded in Feb. 1984.

Sultan, H.M. Sultan Haji Hassanal Bolkiah Mu'izzaddin Waddaulah, Sultan and Yang Di-Pertuan, *acceded* 1967, *crowned* Aug. 1, 1968.

The Government

Prime Minister, Minister of Defence, H.M. The Sultan.
Foreign Affairs, H.R.H. Prince Mohammed.
Finance, H.R.H. Prince Jefri.
Special Adviser to the Sultan and Minister for Home Affairs, Pehin Dato Haji Isa.
Education, Pehin Dato Abdul Aziz.
Law, Pengiran Bahrin.
Industry and Primary Resources, Pehin Dato Abdul Rahman.
Religious Affairs, Pehin Dato Mohammed Zain.
Development, Pengiran Dato Dr. Ismail.
Culture, Youth and Sports, Pehin Dato Haji Hussein.
Health, Dato Dr. Johar.
Communications, Dato Haji Zakaria.

BRUNEI DARUSSALAM HIGH COMMISSION
49 Cromwell Road, SW7 2ED
[01–581 0521]

High Commissioner, His Excellency Pengiran Setia Raja Pengiran Haji Jaya (1984).

FINANCE

	1985 (forecast)
Revenue	B$4,500 million
Expenditure*	2,600 million
*Including development expenditure.	

Trade with U.K.

	1987	1988
Imports from U.K.	£204,129,000	£171,556,000
Exports to U.K.	34,144,000	142,461,000

BRITISH HIGH COMMISSION
Hong Kong and Shanghai Bank
Building (3rd floor), Bandar
Seri Begawan
[Bandar Seri Begawan 22231]

High Commissioner, His Excellency Roger Westbrook (1986).
British Council Representative, J. Robson, P.O. Box 3049, Bandar Seri Begawan.

CYPRUS
(Kypriaki Dimokratia/Kibris Cumhuriyeti)

AREA, CLIMATE AND POPULATION.—Cyprus with an area of 3,572 sq. miles (9,251 sq. km.), is the third largest island in the Mediterranean Sea. Its greatest length is 140 miles and greatest breadth 60 miles, situated at latitude 35°N. and longitude 33° 30′E. It is about 40 miles distant from the nearest point of Asia Minor, 60 miles from Syria and 240 miles from Port Said.

Cyprus has a Mediterranean climate with a hot dry summer and a variable warm winter, while the intermediate seasons are short and transitional.

In 1988 the population (estimate) was 691,700. There are two major communities, Greek Cypriots (80·1 per cent) and Turkish Cypriots (18·6 per cent); and minorities of Armenians, Maronites and others.

CAPITAL.—Nicosia, near the centre of the island, with a population of 166,900 (in the Government controlled area); the other principal towns are ΨLimassol, ΨFamagusta, ΨLarnaca, Paphos and Kyrenia.

CURRENCY.—Cyprus pound (C£) of 100 cents.

FLAG.—Gold map of Cyprus on a white ground, surmounting crossed olive branches (green).

NATIONAL ANTHEM.—Ode to Freedom.

NATIONAL DAY.—October 1 (Independence Day).

GOVERNMENT

Cyprus passed under British administration from 1878. Cyprus was formally annexed to Great Britain on Nov. 5, 1914, on the outbreak of war with Turkey. From 1925 to 1960 it was a Crown Colony administered by a Governor, assisted by an Executive Council and also for a time by a partly-elected Legislative Council. Following the launching in April 1955 of an armed campaign by EOKA in support of union with Greece, a state of emergency was declared in November, 1955, which lasted for four years. After a meeting at Zürich between the Prime Ministers of Greece and Turkey, a conference was held in London and an agreement was signed on February 19, 1959, between the United Kingdom, Greece, Turkey and the Greek and Turkish Cypriots which provided that Cyprus would be an independent Republic.

Under the Cyprus Act, 1960, the island became an independent sovereign republic on August 16, 1960. The constitution provided for a Greek Cypriot President and a Turkish Cypriot Vice-President elected for a five-year term by the Greek and Turkish communities respectively. The House of Representatives, elected for five years by universal suffrage of each community separately, was to consist of 35 Greek and 15 Turkish members. The 1960 Constitution proved unworkable in practice and led to intercommunal troubles. The U.N. Peace Keeping Force in Cyprus (UNFICYP) was set up in March 1964: its mandate was last renewed on June 10, 1989.

On July 15, 1974, mainland Greek officers of the Greek Cypriot National Guard launched a coup d'état against President Makarios and installed a former EOKA member, Nikos Sampson, in his place. Turkey reserved to itself the right to maintain constitutional order and the independence and territorial integrity of the island, invaded Northern Cyprus and occupied over a third of the island. In Feb. 1975 a "Turkish Federated State of Cyprus" under Mr. Rauf Denktash was declared in this area, its constitution being approved by referendum in July 1975. In Nov. 1983 a "Declaration of Statehood" was issued which purported to establish the "Turkish Republic of Northern Cyprus". The declaration was condemned by the U.N. Security Council and only Turkey has recognized the new "state". In May 1985 a referendum in the north of Cyprus approved a constitution for the "Turkish Republic of Northern Cyprus": in June 1985 Mr. Denktash was elected President of the "state" and a General Election was held.

Since 1974 attempts to reach a settlement have focused on intercommunal talks under the auspices of the U.N. The latest talks began in August 1988.

A general election was held for the Greek House of Representatives on Dec. 8, 1985, resulting in the parties gaining the following number of seats: Democratic Rally (Right Wing) 19; Democratic Party (Centre) 16; AKEL (Communist) 15; EDEK (Socialist) 6.

President, George Vassiliou, *elected* Feb. 21, 1988.

COUNCIL OF MINISTERS
(as at June 30, 1989)

Foreign Affairs, George Iacovou.
Interior, Christodoulos Veniamin.
Finance, George Syrimis.
Education, Andreas Philippou.
Justice, Christodoulos Chrysanthou.
Defence, Andreas Aloneftis.
Communications & Works, Nakos Protopapas.
Health, Panicos Papageorghiou.
Commerce and Industry, Takis Nemitsas.
Labour and Social Insurance, Takis Christofides.
Agriculture and Natural Resources, Andreas Gavrielides.

CYPRUS HIGH COMMISSION
93 Park Street, W1Y 4ET
[01-499 8272]

High Commissioner, His Excellency Tasos Panayides (1979).

ECONOMY

Although agriculture still occupies a prime position in the Cyprus economy it is unlikely to expand further. Main products are citrus fruits, grapes and vine products, potatoes and other vegetables. Manufacturing, construction, distribution and other service industries are other major employers. Tourism is the main growth industry with over 1 million long-stay tourists producing C£380 million (estimate) in foreign exchange earnings in 1988. Some 4,700 foreign firms and individuals have registered as offshore companies in Cyprus, which supports Cyprus' claim to be a centre for Middle East trade.

Britain continues to be the country's most important trading partner, taking some 21·6 per cent of its exports in 1988 and supplying 13·9 per cent of its imports. Cyprus is seeking to diversify its export markets and until recently sold almost half its exports to the Middle East. However, these traditional markets are now drying up, and Cyprus is looking more towards Europe. A Customs Union between Cyprus and the E.C. came into force on Jan. 1, 1988.

There is a large visible trade deficit (C£535·9 million in 1988), which is offset by invisible earnings, particularly from tourism (C£380 million in 1988). The current account overall showed a surplus of C£6 million in 1988.

FINANCE

	1987	1988
Total Revenue	C£416·2 m	C£436·7 m
Ordinary Expenditure	581·4 m	579·8 m

TRADE

	1987	1988
Imports	C£711·4 m	C£866·8 m
Exports (including re-exports)	297·9 m	330·9 m

Trade with U.K.

	1987	1988
Imports from U.K.	C£101·6 m	C£120·3 m
Exports to U.K.	66·5 m	71·4 m

BRITISH HIGH COMMISSION
Alexander Pallis Street (P.O. Box 1978)
Nicosia
[Nicosia 02-473131]

High Commissioner, His Excellency The Hon. Humphrey Maud, C.M.G. (1988).
British Council Representative, C. Mogford, P.O. Box 5654, 3 Museum Street, Nicosia.

BRITISH SOVEREIGN AREAS

The United Kingdom retained full sovereignty and jurisdiction over two areas of 99 square miles in all—Akrotiri–Episkopi–Paramali and Dhekelia–Pergamos–Ayios Nicolaos–Xylophagou—and use of roads and other facilities. The British Administrator of these areas is appointed by the Queen and is responsible to the Secretary of State for Defence.
Administrator of the British Sovereign Areas, Maj.-Gen. J. P. W. Friedberger, C.B.E.

DOMINICA
(The Commonwealth of Dominica)

AREA, POPULATION, ETC.—Dominica, the loftiest of the Lesser Antilles, lies in the Windward Group, between 15° 20′ and 15° 45′ N. lat. and 61° 13′ and 61° 30′ W. long., 95 miles S. of Antigua. It is about 29 miles long and 15 broad comprising an area of 290 sq. miles (751 sq. km.). The island is of volcanic origin and very mountainous, and the soil is very fertile. The temperature varies, according to the altitude, from 13°–29°C. The climate is healthy, and during the winter months is very pleasant. The population is 76,000 (1985 U.N. estimate).
CAPITAL.—ΨRoseau, on the south-west coast, population, 8,346. The other principal town is Portsmouth, population, 2,220.
CURRENCY.—East Caribbean dollar (EC$) of 100 cents.
FLAG.—Green ground with a cross overall of yellow, white and black stripes, and in the centre a red disc charged with a Sisserou parrot in natural colours within a ring of 11 green stars.
NATIONAL DAY.—November 3 (Independence Day).
NATIONAL ANTHEM.—Dominica Day Song.

GOVERNMENT

The island was discovered by Columbus in 1493, when it was a stronghold of the Caribs, who remained virtually the sole inhabitants until the French established settlements in the 18th century. It was captured by the British in 1759 but passed back and forth between France and Britain until 1805, after which British possession was not challenged. From 1871–1939 Dominica was part of the Leeward Islands Colony, then from 1940 the island was a unit of the Windward Islands group. Internal self-government from 1967 was followed on Nov. 3, 1978 by independence as a republic with the name The Commonwealth of Dominica. Executive authority is vested in the President, who is elected by the House of Assembly for not more than two terms of five years. Parliament consists of the President and the House of Assembly (representatives elected by universal adult suffrage) and nine Senators, who may be appointed by the President or elected. Parliament has a life of five years.

President, His Excellency Sir Clarence Seignoret, G.C.B., O.B.E.

Cabinet
(as at June 30, 1989)

Prime Minister and Minister for Finance, Economic Development, and Foreign Affairs, Establishment and Security, Hon. M. Eugenia Charles.
Attorney General and Minister for Legal Affairs, and Labour, Hon. Brian Alleyne.
Agriculture, Lands, Trade, Industry and Tourism, Hon. Charles Maynard.
Communications and Works, Hon. Alleyne Carbon.
Education and Sports, Hon. Henry George.
Health, Hon. Ronan David.
Community Development, Housing and Social Affairs, Hon. Heskeith Alexander.

HONORARY CONSULTATE FOR THE COMMONWEALTH
OF DOMINICA
1 Collingham Gardens, SW5 0HW
[01–370 5194/5]

High Commissioner, His Excellency Franklin A. Baron (1986) (resident in Roseau).

FINANCE

	1985–86 revised	1986–87 estimated
Recurrent Revenue .	EC$83·6 m	EC$88·2 m
Recurrent Expenditure	81·1 m	91·6 m
Capital Revenue	37·9 m	49·3 m
Capital Expenditure .	45·3 m	57·2 m

ECONOMY

Agriculture is the principal occupation, with tropical and citrus fruits the main crops. Products for export are bananas, lime juice, lime oil, bay oil, copra and rum. Forestry and fisheries are being encouraged. The only commercially exploitable mineral is pumice, used chiefly for building purposes. Manufacturing consists largely of the processing of agricultural products.

TRADE

	1985
Imports	EC$149,376,000
Exports	76,766,000

Trade with U.K.

	1987	1988
Imports from U.K.	£10,431,000	£8,416,000
Exports to U.K.	37,083,000	32,423,000

BRITISH HIGH COMMISSION

High Commissioner, (resides at Bridgetown, Barbados).

THE GAMBIA
(The Republic of the Gambia)

AREA, POPULATION, ETC.—The Gambia takes its name from the Gambia River, which it straddles for over 200 miles inland from the west coast of Africa. It is a narrow strip, surrounded by the Republic of Senegal, except at the coast, lying between 13° 10′–13° 45′ N. and 13° 90′–16° 50′ W. The area is 4,361 sq. miles (11,295 sq. km.), of which one fifth is the river. Except during the rainy season from June to October, when it sometimes becomes uncomfortably humid, Banjul's climate is very pleasant. Rainfall is 32–40 inches a year.
The population comprises mainly Wolof, Mandinka and Fula peoples who originally migrated there from the north and east. Population (1983 Census) was 695,886.
The Gambia River basin was part of the region

dominated in the 10th–16th centuries by the strong Songhai and Mali kingdoms centred on the upper Niger. The first recorded Europeans to reach the Gambia River were the Portuguese in 1447. In 1588 Queen Elizabeth I gave the first charter to English merchants to trade along the river. Merchants from France, Courland (now part of Latvia) and the Netherlands also established trading posts there. The English presence was strongly challenged by the French, who were dominant further north up the coast, but in 1783 the Treaty of Versailles acknowledged English rights. In 1816, after the Napoleonic Wars, and in order to enforce abolition of the slave trade, the British stationed a garrison on a low sandy island called Banjul at the river mouth. Renamed Bathurst, this became the capital of a small British-administered colony, initially under the Governor of Sierra Leone. Negotiations with France continued sporadically until 1889 when it was agreed that the British rights along the upper river should extend 10 km on either bank. British administration was extended from the Colony to this Protectorate. The Gambia became independent within the Commonwealth on February 18, 1965, and a Republic on April 24, 1970.

The Gambia's relationship with Senegal has always been an important factor in political and economic policy. Moves towards a closer association were accelerated after an abortive coup in The Gambia in July 1981 was put down with the help of Senegalese troops. In February 1982 the Senegambia Confederation was formally instituted based on certain joint institutions and integration of policies, but each country remains sovereign and independent.

CAPITAL.—ψBanjul. Population (1983 Census) of island of Banjul was 44,536; and of adjacent Kombo St. Mary district 102,858. Total population of Banjul/Kombo St. Mary, 147,394.

CURRENCY.—Dalasi (D) of 100 butut.

FLAG.—Horizontal stripes of red, blue and green, separated by narrow white stripes.

NATIONAL ANTHEM.—For The Gambia, Our Homeland.

NATIONAL DAY.—February 18 (Independence Day).

GOVERNMENT

The constitution is democratic and Parliamentary, with an executive President elected for five years. The House of Representatives has 35 elected members, 5 elected Chiefs Representatives and up to 8 nominated members plus the Attorney General (ex-officio). The Vice President and other Ministers are appointed by the President. Parliament must be dissolved after five years. The last general elections were held in March 1987. The present state of the parties for elected members is PPP (People's Progressive Party) 31; NCP (National Convention Party) 5.

President and Cabinet
(as at May 31, 1989)

President and Minister of Defence, His Excellency Alhaji Sir Dawda Kairaba Jawara, G.C.M.G.
Vice-President and Minister of Education, Youth, Sports and Culture, Hon. Bakary Bunja Darbo.
Attorney-General and Minister of Justice, Hon. Hassan B. Jallow.
Finance and Trade, Hon. Sheriff Saikouba Sisay.
External Affairs, Hon. Alhaji Omar Baru Sey.
Interior, Hon. Lamin Kiti Jabang.
Agriculture, Hon. Alhaji Saihou S. Sabally.
Local Government and Lands, Hon. Landing Jallow Sonko.
Water Resources, Forestry and Fisheries, Hon. Omar Amadou Jallow.

Health, Environment, Labour and Social Welfare, Hon. Mrs. Louise A. N'Jie.
Works and Communications, Hon. Alhaji Muhammadu Cadi Cham.
Economic Planning and Industrial Development, Hon. Mbemba Jatta.
Information and Tourism, Hon. Dr. Lamin Kebba Saho.

Chief Justice, Hon. E. Olayinka Ayoola.
Speaker, Alhaji Hon. M. B. N'Jie.

GAMBIA HIGH COMMISSION
57 Kensington Court, W8 5DG
[01-937 6316–8]

High Commissioner, His Excellency Horace R. Monday (Jr.) (1987).

COMMUNICATIONS

There is an international airport at Yundum, 17 miles from Banjul, with scheduled services flying to other West African states and to the U.K. Banjul is the main port. Internal communication is by road and river. There is no railway system. There are two broadcasting stations and a U.H.F. telephone service linking Banjul with the principal towns in the provinces. There is no television service.

EDUCATION

There are 24 secondary schools (eight high and 16 technical) with a total enrolment of 15,635 students. Two High Schools provide 'A' level education. Gambia College provides post-secondary courses in education, agriculture, public health and nursing. There are seven vocational training institutions with a total enrolment of 1,400. Higher education and advanced training courses are taken outside The Gambia, currently by over 200 students.

PRODUCTION

Eighty-five per cent of the population depend for their livelihood on agriculture (40 per cent of G.D.P.). The chief product, groundnuts, is also the most important export item, forming over 90 per cent of all domestic exports. Other crops are rice, millet, sorghum, maize and cotton. Fishing and livestock industries are being developed. Thirty per cent of the country's basic food requirements are imported. There are no significant deposits of minerals. Manufactures are limited to groundnut processing, minor metal fabrications, paints, furniture, soap and bottling. Tourism is developing quickly, with 98,248 visitors in 1987–88. The entrepôt trade through The Gambia, re-exporting imported goods to neighbouring countries, is an important element in the national economy.

FINANCE

	1984–85	1985–86
Recurrent Revenue ...	D172,600,000	D218,000,000
Recurrent Expenditure	180,900,000	203,000,000

Over 80 per cent of capital expenditure comes from external aid grants and loans. The Five Year Development Plan 1981–86 envisaged an annual GDP growth rate of 5·1 per cent or 2·5 per cent per capita (at 1980–81 prices).

TRADE

	1986–87	1987–88
Total imports	D797,600,000	D844,900,000
Total exports	523,800,000	576,600,000

Trade with U.K.

	1987	1988
Imports from U.K.	£19,765,000	£19,236,000
Exports to U.K.	3,038,000	2,927,000

BRITISH HIGH COMMISSION

48 Atlantic Road, Fajara (P.O. Box 507), Banjul [Banjul 95133]

High Commissioner, His Excellency Alec Ibbott, C.B.E. (1988).

GHANA
(The Republic of Ghana)

AREA AND POPULATION.—Ghana (formerly known as the Gold Coast) is situated on the Gulf of Guinea, between 3° 07′ W. long. and 1° 14′ E. long. (about 334 miles), and extends 441 miles north from Cape Three Points (4° 45′ N.) to 11° 11′ N. It is bounded on the north by Burkina, on the west by the Côte d'Ivoire, on the east by Togo, and on the south by the Atlantic Ocean. Although a tropical country, Ghana is cooler than many countries within similar latitudes.

Ghana has a total area of 92,099 sq. miles (238,537 sq. km.). The population at the Census of 1984 was 12,205,574. A 1985 U.N. estimate gave a figure of 13,588,000. Almost all Ghanaians are Sudanese Negroes, although Hamitic strains are common in Northern Ghana. The official language is English. The principal indigenous language group is Akan, of which Twi and Fanti are the most commonly used. Ga, Ewe and languages of the Mole–Dagbani group are common in certain regions.

CAPITAL.—ΨAccra. Population of the Greater Accra Region (including Tema) was (1984 Census) 1,420,066. Other towns are Kumasi, Tamale, ΨSekondi-Takoradi, ΨCape Coast, Sunyani, Ho, Koforidua, Tarkwa and ΨWinneba.

CURRENCY.—Cedi of 100 pesewas.

FLAG.—Equal horizontal bands of red over yellow over green; five-point black star on gold stripe.

NATIONAL ANTHEM.—Hail the Name of Ghana.

NATIONAL DAY.—March 6 (Independence Day).

GOVERNMENT

There is no recorded history of the Gold Coast region before the coming of Europeans in the fifteenth century. The constituent parts of the State came under British administration at various times, the original Gold Coast Colony (the coastal and Southern areas) being first constituted in 1874; Ashanti in 1901; and the Northern Territories Protectorate in 1901. The territory of Trans-Volta-Togoland, part of the former German colony of Togo, was mandated to Britain by the League of Nations after the First World War, and remained under British administration as a United Nations Trusteeship after the Second World War. After a plebiscite in May, 1956, under the auspices of the United Nations, the territory was integrated with the Gold Coast Colony.

The former Gold Coast Colony and associated territories became the independent state of Ghana and a member of the British Commonwealth on March 6, 1957 and adopted a Republican constitution on July 1, 1960. A coup in June 1979 led to the formation of an Armed Forces Revolutionary Council chaired by Flt.-Lt. Jerry Rawlings. Civilian rule was restored in Sept. 1979 but overthrown on Dec. 31, 1981, when another coup brought back into power Flt.-Lt. Rawlings.

Provisional National Defence Council

Chairman, Flt.-Lt. Jerry J. Rawlings.

Vice-Chairman, Justice Daniel Annan.

Members, Mrs. Aanaa Enin; Ebo Tawiah; Alhaji Mahama Iddrisu; P. V. Obeng; Capt. Kojo Tsikata (retd); Lt.-Gen. Arnold Quainoo; Maj.-Gen. W. M. Mensa-Wood.

P.N.D.C. Secretaries
(as at May 31, 1989)

Foreign Affairs, Obed Y. Asamoah.
Internal Affairs, Nii Okaija Adamafio.
Finance and Economic Planning, Dr. Kwesi Botchwey.
Defence, Alhaji Mahama Iddrisu.
Fuel and Power, Ato Ahwoi.
Trade and Tourism, (vacant).
Local Government, K. Ahwoi.
Education and Culture, K. B. Asante.
Youth and Sports, K. Saarah-Mensah.
Transport and Communications, E. O. Donkor.
Works and Housing, E. Appiah-Korang.
Industries, Science and Technology, Dr. Francis Acquah.
Justice and Attorney-General, E. G. Tanoh.
Agriculture, Cdre. Steve Obimpeh.
Information, Kofi Totobi Quakyi (*acting*).
Lands and Natural Resources, Kwame Peprah.
Roads and Highways, Lt.-Col. Mensah Gbedemah.
Committee for the Defence of the Revolution, W. H. Yeboah.
Health, Nana A. Sarpong.
Mobilization and Productivity, Huudu Yahaya.

GHANA HIGH COMMISSION
13 Belgrave Square, SW1X 8PR
[01-235 4142]

High Commissioner, His Excellency Dr. J. L. S. Abbey (1986).

PRODUCTION, ETC.

Agriculture.—Agriculture forms the basis of Ghana's economy, employing 70 per cent of the working population. Crops of the Forest Zone include cocoa, which is the largest single source of revenue, rice and a variety of other foodstuff crops grown on mixed-crop farms. Fruits such as avocado pears, oranges and pineapples are grown. Cassava is the most important crop of the Coastal Savannas Zone, of the lower Volta area. Production of pulses such as groundnuts is widespread. Near the Togo border oil palms, yams, maize, cassava, fruit and vegetables are produced. Livestock is raised in the uncultivated areas. The Northern Savanna Zone is Ghana's principal cattle rearing area and other livestock production there is important for home consumption. Corn and millet crops are produced in the far north and maize, yams, rice and groundnut crops in more southerly parts of the Zone.

Attempts are being made to diversify agricultural production, with cash crops being extensively cultivated for export and to provide raw materials for local industry.

Fisheries.—Fishing is important in coastal areas and in the Volta itself. However production cannot meet demand and there are considerable imports of fish products. About 80 per cent of home supply is obtained from sea fisheries, but production from the Volta Lake and other inland fisheries is increasing.

Mineral Production.—The area within a 60 mile radius of Dunkwa produces 90 per cent of Ghana's mineral exports. Manganese production from Nsuta ranks among the world's highest and gold, industrial diamonds and bauxite are also produced. Some 30,000 persons are employed by the mining companies.

Manufactures.—Examples of the small-scale traditional industries are tailoring, goldsmithing and carpentry. Priority has been given in recent years to the establishment of a number of "Pioneer Industries" including timber products, vehicle and refrigerator assembly, cigarettes, boatbuilding, food processing, cotton textiles, clothing, footwear, printing and other light industries. A modern industrial complex is growing in the Accra-Tema area.

Volta River Project.—Since 1966 the Volta Dam at Akosombo has generated hydro-electric power for the processing of bauxite and fed a power transmission network for the Accra-Kumasi-Takoradi area. Electricity is now also sent to Togo and Benin.

COMMUNICATIONS

Accra Airport is an international airport and Ghana Airways Corporation is the national airline. There are also internal airports at Takoradi, Kumasi and Tamale.

There are 20,000 miles of motorable roads, of which 2,335 miles are bituminized. There are 600 miles of railway, linking Accra and the principal ports of Takoradi and Tema with their hinterlands, and with each other.

Takoradi Harbour consists of seven quay berths—one is leased specially for manganese exports. Tema Harbour has 10 berths for larger ocean going vessels and the largest dry dock on the West African coast. An oil berth has also been built to serve the Ghaip refinery which has been constructed at Tema.

Trade with U.K.

	1987	1988
Imports from U.K.	£138,081,000	£126,148,000
Exports to U.K.	113,859,000	106,314,000

Principal exports are cocoa, timber and gold. Principal imports are road vehicles, manufacturing equipment, petroleum and raw materials.

BRITISH HIGH COMMISSION
P.O. Box 296, Osu Link, Accra
[Accra 221665]

High Commissioner, His Excellency Anthony Michael Goodenough (1989).

British Council Representative, J. M. Day, Liberia Road (P.O. Box 771), Accra, and an office in *Kumasi*.

GRENADA
(The State of Grenada)

AREA, POPULATION.—Grenada is situated between the parallels of 12° 13′–11° 58′ N. lat. and 61° 20′–61° 35′ W. long., and is about 80 miles north of Trinidad, 68 miles S.S.W. of St. Vincent, and about 120 miles S.W. of Barbados. The island is about 21 miles in length and 12 miles in breadth, with an area of 133 sq. miles (344 sq. km.). Also included in the territory of Grenada are some of the Grenadines islets, the largest of which is Carriacou, 13 square miles in area. The population was estimated at 112,000 (1985 U.N. estimate). The country is mountainous and very picturesque, and the climate is healthy.

CAPITAL.—ΨSt. George's (population 7,500) lies on the southwest coast, and possesses a good harbour.

CURRENCY.—East Caribbean dollar (EC$) of 100 cents.

FLAG.—Rectangle formed of yellow triangles top and bottom, and green triangles at side, with yellow five-pointed star on red circle in centre, and a nutmeg in green triangle nearest the fly; all on a red ground with three yellow five-pointed stars at top and bottom.

NATIONAL DAY.—February 7 (Independence Day).

GOVERNMENT

Grenada was discovered by Columbus in 1498, and named Conception. It was originally colonized by the French, and was ceded to Great Britain by the Treaty of Versailles in 1783. It became an Associated State in 1967 and an independent nation on Feb. 7, 1974.

The government of Sir Eric Gairy was overthrown on March 13, 1979 by the New Jewel Movement and a People's Revolutionary Government was set up. Disagreements within the P.R.G. led, in Oct. 1983, to violence and the death of the Prime Minister, whose government was replaced by a Revolutionary Military Council. These events prompted the intervention of Caribbean and U.S. forces. The Governor General installed an advisory council in Nov. 1983 to act as an interim government until a General Election was held, on Dec. 3, 1984. The New National Party (NNP) won 14 of the 15 seats in the House of Representatives and, following the dissolution of the advisory council, its leader, Mr. Herbert Blaize, was sworn in as Prime Minister. A phased withdrawal of U.S. forces was completed in June 1985.

Defections from the NNP reduced their number of seats in Parliament to 9 by April 1987. The defectors formed their own political party, the National Democratic Congress. The next General Election must take place by March 28, 1990.

Governor General, Sir Paul Scoon, G.C.M.G., G.C.V.O., O.B.E. (1978).

Cabinet
(as at June 30, 1989)

Prime Minister, National Security, Home Affairs, Carriacou and Petit Martinique Affairs, Information, Energy, Finance, Trade, Industry and Economic Planning, Rt. Hon. Herbert A. Blaize.

Deputy P.M., External Affairs, Agriculture, Lands, Forestry and Tourism, Hon. Benjamin Jones.

Attorney General, Legal Affairs, Health, Housing, Physical Planning, Hon. Daniel Williams.

Education, Social Security, Labour, Culture, Youth Affairs, Sport, Local Government, Fisheries, Hon. George McGuire.

Communications, Works, Public Utilities, Co-operatives, Community Development, Women's Affairs, Aviation, Hon. Dr. Keith Mitchell.

Ministers of State, Hon. Pauline Andrew (*Agriculture and Tourism*); Hon. Grace Duncan (*Women's Affairs and Community Development*); Hon. Alleyne Walker (*Works and Co-operatives*); Hon. Felix Alexander (*Information, Finance, Trade, Industry and Energy*); Senator the Hon. Lawrence Joseph (*Legal Affairs and National Security*); Senator the Hon. Ben Andrew (*Education, Culture, Youth Affairs and Fisheries*).

GRENADA HIGH COMMISSION
1 Collingham Gardens, SW5 0HW
[01–373 3800/3808]

High Commissioner, His Excellency Oswald M. Gibbs, C.M.G. (1984).

ECONOMY

The economy is principally agrarian, with cocoa, nutmegs and bananas the major crops. Fruit and vegetables are grown and a little livestock raised for domestic consumption. The fishing industry is being developed. Manufacturing is mostly confined to processing agricultural products.

Tourism has prospered since the opening in 1984 of the Point Salines International Airport. British Airways began regular weekly flights in April 1987. A hotel expansion programme is planned. The number of cruise ships visiting Grenada in 1988 was 234.

Total value of imports in 1988 was EC$248·6 million. Principal domestic exports for 1988 were cocoa (EC$8·75m), nutmeg (EC$31·3m), mace (EC$7·3m) and fruit (EC$3·8m).

Trade with U.K.

	1987	1988
Imports from U.K.	£8,772,000	£7,162,000
Exports to U.K.	6,302,000	6,115,000

BRITISH HIGH COMMISSION
14 Church Street, St. George's.
[St. George's 440-3222]

High Commissioner, (resides at Bridgetown, Barbados).
Resident Representative, G. Roberts (*First Secretary*).

GUYANA
(The Co-operative Republic of Guyana)

AREA, POPULATION, ETC.—Guyana, the former colony of British Guiana, which includes the Counties of Demerara, Essequibo and Berbice, is situated on the north-east coast of South America, bordering on Venezuela, Brazil and Suriname. It has a total area of 83,000 sq. miles (214,969 sq. km.). While the 1985 U.N. estimate puts the population at 790,000, 750,000 is generally considered to be a more representative figure. There are three distinct areas. (1) A narrow alluvial coastal belt 10 to 40 miles deep, the eastern part of which is intensively cultivated and contains some 90 per cent of the population. Much of this is below the level of the sea and is drained and irrigated by an intricate system of canals constructed by the Dutch. (2) A mountainous area of dense rain forest behind the coastland, still partly unexplored, which reaches its highest point at *Mount Roraima* (9,000 ft.) on the junction of the Guyana–Brazil–Venezuela borders. (3) The open savanna country of the Rupununi in the south-west where cattle ranching is practised and oil deposits have been discovered.

The entire country is intersected by numerous large rivers, though these are of limited navigational use because of rapids and waterfalls, the most notable of which are the *Kaieteur Fall* on the Potaro River with a sheer drop of 741 ft., the *Horse Shoe Falls* on the Essequibo and the *Marina Fall* on the Ipobe River.

Climate.—The two dry seasons normally last from mid February to end April, and from mid August to end November. In the Aug.–Oct. period it is hot. The mean temperature is 27°C., the usual extremes being 21°C and 32°C. In the interior the mean temperature is higher—28°C., its extremes ranging from 19°C to 40°C. The yearly rainfall is subject to marked variation, its mean on the coast lands averaging about 90 inches with an average of 58 inches on the savannas.

CAPITAL.—ΨGeorgetown. Estimated population, including environs, 185,000. Other towns are: Linden (population 29,000); ΨNew Amsterdam (population 23,000); Corriverton (population 17,000).

CURRENCY.—Guyana dollar (G$) of 100 cents.

FLAG.—Red triangle with black border, pointing from hoist to fly, on a yellow triangle with white border, all on a green field.

NATIONAL ANTHEM.—"Dear Land of Guyana".

NATIONAL DAYS.—May 26 (Independence Day); February 23 (Republic Day).

GOVERNMENT

Guyana became independent on May 26, 1966, with a Governor General appointed by the Queen. It became a Co-operative Republic on Feb. 23, 1970. Under the Independence Constitution the Prime Minister and Cabinet were responsible to a National Assembly elected by secret ballot every 5 years. The last election under this Constitution was in 1973 and the term of that Assembly was later extended to October 1980.

A new Constitution was passed into law in February 1980 and promulgated in October 1980. It provides for an Executive President, a National Assembly of 65 members, and also for a National Congress of Local Democratic Organs responsible for local government. The Supreme Congress of the People consists of all members of these two assemblies.

The electoral system is a Proportional Representation or "single list" system, each voter casting his vote for a party list of candidates. The voting age is 18.

Executive President, H. Desmond Hoyte, *took office* Aug. 1985, *sworn in* Dec. 12, 1985 for five-year term.

Cabinet
(as at June 30, 1989)

Executive President (*with responsibility for Home Affairs, Co-operatives, Regional Development*), H. D. Hoyte.
First Vice President and Prime Minister, Hamilton Green.
Vice President (*Culture and Social Development*) *and Deputy P.M.*, Mrs. Viola Burnham.
Attorney-General and Minister for Legal Affairs, Keith Massiah.
Deputy P.M. (*Public Utilities*), Robert H. O. Corbin.
Deputy P.M. (*Planning and Development*), William H. Parris.

SENIOR MINISTERS

Foreign Affairs, Rashleigh Jackson.
Finance, Carl Greenidge.
Planning and Development, Seeram Prashad.
Trade and Tourism, Winston Murray.

GUYANA HIGH COMMISSION
3 Palace Court, Bayswater Road, W2 4LP
[01-229 7684]

High Commissioner, His Excellency Mr. Cecil Stanley Pilgrim (1986).

JUDICATURE

The Supreme Court of Judicature consists of a Court of Appeal and a High Court. There are also Courts of Summary Jurisdiction. The Court of Appeal consists of the Chancellor as President, the Chief Justice and such number of Justices of Appeal as may be prescribed by Parliament.

The High Court consists of the Chief Justice, as President, and nine Puisne Judges. It is a court with unlimited jurisdiction in civil matters and exercises exclusive jurisdiction in probate, divorce and admiralty, and certain other matters.

Chancellor, K. M. George.
Chief Justice, R. Harper.

PRODUCTION, ETC.

The economy is based almost entirely on the main export items of sugar, rice, bauxite and alumina. Diamonds and gold are also mined, timber and rum are produced and there is some cattle ranching. The fishing industry is being expanded. Industry is fairly small-scale.

COMMUNICATIONS

Georgetown and New Amsterdam are the principal

ports, though bauxite ships also sail to Linden, on the R. Demerara, and Everton, on the R. Berbice. There are no public railways and the few roads are confined mainly to the coastal areas. Air transport is the easiest form of communication between the coast and the interior. There is a state-owned radio broadcasting station which operates two channels; there is a fledgling television service.

EDUCATION

The Government assumed total control of the education system in September 1976 and made education free from nursery to university level. The Government trains teachers for primary and secondary schools at its own institutions. In 1982 there were 368 nursery schools with 29,958 pupils, 423 primary schools with 130,003 pupils, and 414 secondary schools with 73,762 students.

Approximately 1,800 students were enrolled at the University of Guyana in degree programmes and certificate and diploma courses in 1986.

There are several technical and vocational institutions, as well as some 30 adult education schools (with an enrolment of 13,500). There are also a number of technical and vocational institutions not under the aegis of the Ministry of Education.

Trade with U.K.

	1987	1988
Imports from U.K.	£15,371,000	£10,590,000
Exports to U.K.	58,502,000	43,518,000

BRITISH HIGH COMMISSION
44 Main Street (P.O. Box 10849),
Georgetown
[Georgetown 65881/4]

High Commissioner, His Excellency David Purvis Small, C.M.G., M.B.E. (1987) (also Ambassador to Suriname).

INDIA
(The Republic of India)

AREA AND POPULATION.—The Republic of India has an area of 1,269,346 sq. miles (3,287,590 sq. km.), composed of three well-defined regions: the mountain range of the Himalayas; the Indo-Gangetic plain; and the Southern Peninsula. The main mountain ranges are the Himalayas in the north (over 29,000 feet) and the Western and Eastern Ghats (over 8,000 feet). Major rivers include the Ganges, Indus, Krishna, Godavari and Mahanadi.

There are four seasons: the cold season (Dec.–March); the hot season (April–May); the rainy season (June–Sept.); and the season of the retreating S.W. monsoon (Oct.–Nov.). Temperatures vary over the whole country, between averages of about 10° C and 33° C, reaching over 38° C in some parts during the hot season. There are similar variations in rainfall, from only a few inches a year falling in the western Thar Desert to over 400 inches in Meghalaya.

India is the second most populous country in the world. The population at the 1981 Census was 685,184,692, of which slightly more than 20 per cent was urban. A 1985 U.N. estimate gave a figure of 750,900,000. The majority of the population are Hindu (82 per cent), the rest being Muslim (11 per cent), Christian (2·5 per cent), Sikh (1·8 per cent), Buddhist (0·7 per cent) and Jain (0·5 per cent). The official languages are Hindi in the Devanagari script and English, though 14 regional languages also are recognized for adoption as official State languages.

HISTORY.—The Indus civilization was fully developed by c. 2,500 B.C. but collapsed c. 1,750 B.C., subsequently being replaced by an Aryan civilization spread from the west. The first Arab invasions of the north west began in the seventh century and Muslim, Hindu and Buddhist states developed until the establishment of the Mogul dynasty in 1526. The British East India Company established settlements throughout the 17th century; clashes with the French and native princes led to the British government taking control of the company in 1784. The separate dominions of India and Pakistan became independent within the Commonwealth in 1947 and India became a Republic in 1950.

CAPITAL.—Delhi (population in 1981 was 6,220,000). Populations of other principal cities (1981 figures) were ΨCalcutta, 9,166,000; ΨBombay (Mumbai), 8,202,000; ΨMadras, 4,277,000; Bangalore, 2,914,000; Hyderabad, 2,566,000; Ahmedabad, 2,124,000; Kanpur, 1,685,000; Pune, 1,685,000; Lucknow, 1,007,000.

CURRENCY.—Indian rupee (Rs) of 100 paisa.

FLAG.—The National Flag is a horizontal tricolour with bands of deep saffron, white and dark green in equal proportions. In the centre of the white band appears an Asoka wheel in navy blue.

NATIONAL ANTHEM.—Jana-gana-mana.

NATIONAL DAY.—January 26 (Republic Day).

STATES AND TERRITORIES OF THE UNION

There are 25 States and seven Union Territories. Each State is governed by a Governor appointed by the President who holds office for five years, and a Council of Ministers. All States have a Legislative Assembly, and some have also a Legislative Council, elected directly by adult suffrage for a maximum period of five years. The judges of the High Court of a State are appointed by the President.

The Union Territories are administered, except where otherwise provided by Parliament, by the President acting through an Administrator or Lieutenant Governor, or other authority appointed by him.

GOVERNMENT

The Constitution of India came into force in 1950. Executive power is vested in the President, who is elected for a five year term by an electoral college consisting of the elected members of the Union and State Legislatures. He appoints the Prime Minister and, on the latter's advice, the Ministers, and can dismiss them. The Council of Ministers is collectively responsible to the *Lok Sabha* (Lower House). The Vice President is ex-officio chairman of the *Rajya Sabha* (Upper House).

Legislative power rests with the President, the *Rajya Sabha* (which has up to 250 members) and the *Lok Sabha* (which has up to 544 members). Twelve members of the *Rajya Sabha* are nominated by the President, the rest are indirectly elected representatives of the State and Union Territories. They hold office for six years. The 525 members of the *Lok Sabha* representing the States are directly elected by universal adult franchise, and 17 representatives of the Union Territories are chosen, for a maximum term of five years. Subject to the provisions of the Constitution, the Union Parliament can make laws for the whole of India and the State legislatures for their respective units.

The Supreme Court consists of the Chief Justice and not more than 17 other judges, appointed by the President. It is the highest court in respect of all constitutional matters and the final Court of Appeal.

President of the Republic of India, Ramaswami Venkataraman, *elected* July 16, 1987.

Vice-President, Shankar Dayal Sharma.

States and Territories (Capitals)	Area (sq. km.)	Population (1981 Census)	Governor	Chief Minister
States				
Andhra Pradesh (Hyderabad)...	275,100p	53,549,673	Miss K. Joshi	N. T. Rama Rao
Arunachal Pradesh (Itanagar)..	83,700p	631,839	R. D. Pradhan	Gegong Apang
Assam (Dispur)	78,400	19,896,843†	H. Joshi	P. K. Mahanta
Bihar (Patna)	173,900p	69,914,734	J. Paharia	S. N. Sinha
Goa (Panaji)	3,701	1,000,000†	K. A. Khan	P. S. Rana
Gujurat (Gandhinagar)	196,000p	34,085,799	R. K. Trivedi	Amarsinh Chaudhary
Haryana (Chandigarh).........	44,200p	12,922,618	B. M. Brari	Devi Lal
Himachal Pradesh (Shimla)	55,700	4,280,818	Vice-Adm. (retd) R. K. S. Ghandi	Virbhadra Singh
Jammu and Kashmir* (Srinagar/Jammu).........	222,200p	5,987,389	Gen. K. V. Krishna Rao	Dr. Farooq Abdullah
Karnataka (Bangalore)	191,800	37,135,714	P. Venkatasubbiah	(President's rule)
Kerala (Trivandrum)	38,900p	25,453,680	Mrs. R. D. Sinha	E. K. Nayanar
Madhya Pradesh (Bhopal)	443,500p	52,178,844	Mrs. S. Grewal	Motilal Vora
Maharashtra (Bombay Mumbai)	307,700p	62,784,171	K. B. Reddy	Sharad Pawar
Manipur (Imphal)	22,300	1,420,953	C. Panigrahi	R. K. Jaichandra Singh
Meghalaya (Shillong)	22,400p	1,335,819	H. Joshi	P. A. Sangma
Mizoram (Aizawl)	21,100	493,757	H. Saikia	Lal Thanhawla
Nagaland (Kohima)	16,600	774,930	Dr. Gopal Singh	S. C. Jamir
Orissa (Bhubaneswar)	155,700	26,370,271	S. Nurul Hasan	J. B. Patnaik
Punjab (Chandigarh)	50,400	16,788,915	S. S. Ray	(President's rule)
Rajasthan (Jaipur)	342,200	34,261,862	S. Prasad	S. C. Mathur
Sikkim (Gangtok)	7,100	316,385	S. K. Bhatnagar	N. B. Bhandari
Tamil Nadu (Madras)	130,100p	48,408,077	Dr. P. C. Alexander	M. Karunanidhi
Tripura (Agartala)	10,500	2,053,058	Sultan Singh	S. R. Majumdar
Uttar Pradesh (Lucknow)	294,400p	110,862,013	M. Usman Arif	N. D. Tiwari
West Bengal (Calcutta)	88,800p	54,580,647	T. V. Rajeshwar	Jyoti Basu
Union Territories			*Lt. Governor*	
Andaman and Nicobar Is. (Port Blair)	8,200	188,741	Lt.-Gen. T. S. Oberoi	
Chandigarh	100	451,610	S. S. Ray	
Dadra and Nagar Haveli (Silvassa)	500	103,676	K. A. Khan	
Daman and Diu	112	51,602†	K. A. Khan	
Delhi	1,500	6,220,406	Romesh Bhandari	
Lakshadweep (Kavaratti)	30	40,249	W. Habibullah	
Pondicherry	500	604,471	Lt.-Gen. R. S. Dyal	

p provisional figure   † estimated figure

* Jammu and Kashmir is an area disputed between India, Pakistan and China, all three controlling a part of the territory. The area figure includes those parts occupied by Pakistan and China, which are claimed by India, but the population figure excludes the population of these areas, where the census was not taken. The state's capital is at Srinagar in winter and Jammu in summer.

Cabinet
(as at June 30, 1989)

Prime Minister, Science and Technology, Atomic Energy, Space Personnel, Rajiv Gandhi.
External Affairs, P. V. Narasimha Rao.
Finance, S. B. Chavan.
Commerce, Dinesh Singh.
Human Resource Development, P. Shiv Shankar.
Home Affairs, Buta Singh.
Steel and Mines, M. L. Fotedar.
Defence, K. C. Pant.
Planning and Programme Implementation, Madhav Singh Solanki.
Urban Development, Mrs. Mohsina Kdwai.
Industry, J. Vengal Rao.
Agriculture, Bhajan Lal.
Parliamentary Affairs, with additional charge of Information and Broadcasting, H. K. L. Bahagat.
Energy, Vasant Sathe.
Law and Justice, with additional charge of Water Resources, B. Shnkaranand.
Labour, Bindeshwari Dubey.
Textiles, Ram Niwas Mirdha.
Environment and Forests, Z. R. Ansari.
In addition to the members of the Council of Ministers there are ten Ministers of State with independent charge and 32 Ministers of State.

INDIAN HIGH COMMISSION
India House, Aldwych, WC2B 4NA
[01–836 8484]

High Commissioner, His Excellency Maharaj Krishna Rasgotra (1988).
Deputy High Commissioner, S. S. Haider.

DEFENCE

The supreme command of the armed forces is vested in the President. Administrative and operational control resides in the Army, Navy and Air Headquarters under the supervision of the Ministry of Defence.
The *Army* has five Commands, Southern, Eastern, Northern, Western and Central.

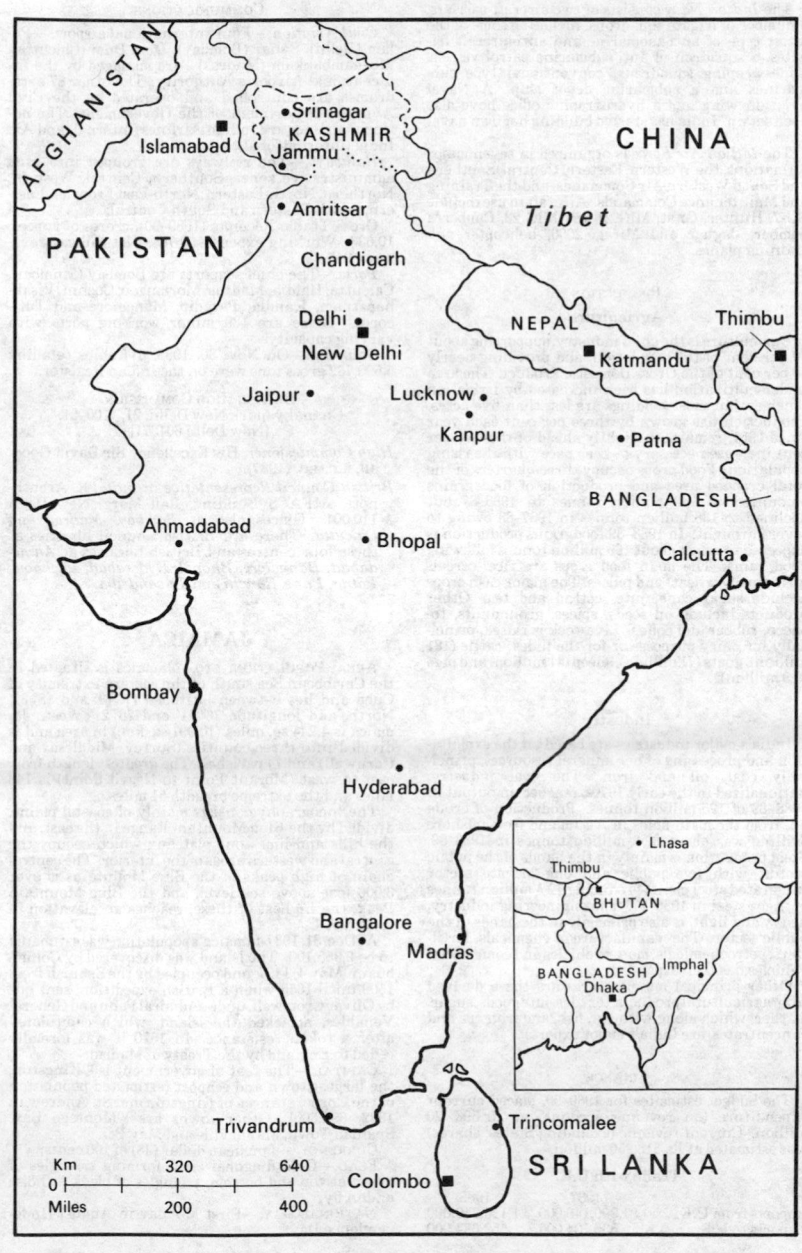

The *Indian Navy* consists of two aircraft-carriers, a number of frigate squadrons, including some of the latest type of anti-submarine and anti-aircraft frigates, a squadron of anti-submarine patrol vessels, minesweeping squadrons, conventional type submarines and a submarine depot ship. A Naval aviation wing and a hydrographic office have also been set up. India has started building her own naval craft.

The *Indian Air Force* is organized in seven major formations, the Western, Eastern, Central, Southern and South Western Air Commands, and the Training and Maintenance Commands. Aircraft in use include SU-7, Hunter, Gnat, MiG 21 and MiG 23, Canberra bomber, Jaguar and Mirage-2000, helicopter and training planes.

PRODUCTION

Agriculture

Agriculture is the chief industry, supporting about 70 per cent of the population, and providing nearly 40 per cent of the Gross Domestic Product. The area under cultivation has been increased by irrigation schemes, but most holdings are less than five acres. Production has grown by three per cent each year since 1951, remaining slightly ahead of the two per cent increase necessary to keep pace with the rising population. Food crops occupy three-quarters of the total cropped area and production of food grains amounted to 143 million tonnes in 1986–87 but declined to 138 million tonnes in 1987–88 owing to severe drought. In 1988–89 foodgrains production is expected to reach about 169 million tonnes following good rains. The main food crops are rice, cereals (principally wheat) and pulses. The major cash crops include sugar cane, jute, cotton and tea. Other products include oil seeds, spices, groundnuts, tobacco, rubber and coffee. Livestock is raised, principally for dairy purposes or for the hides: cattle (181 million), goats (71 million), sheep (41 million) and pigs (9·9 million).

Industry

India's major industries are based on the exploitation and processing of her mineral resources, principally coal, oil and iron. The coal industry, nationalized in the early 1970s, reached an output in 1988–89 of 195 million tonnes. Production of crude oil, from the main fields in Assam and from offshore drilling was about 32·2 million tonnes in 1988–89. Steel production is mainly in the hands of the public sector, with five public and one private sector integrated steel plants producing 12·4 million tonnes of ingot steel in 1986–87. The engineering industry, heavy and light, is also primarily in the hands of the public sector. The manufacture of chemicals, fertilizers, petrochemicals, motor vehicles and commercial vehicles has been expanded.

Other principal manufactures are those derived from agricultural products, textiles, jute goods, sugar, leather, which along with tea, fish, and iron ore and concentrates, are India's major exports.

FINANCE

The budget estimates for 1989–90, placed current expenditure (on revenue account) at Rs.596,420 million. Current revenue (excluding States' shares) was estimated at Rs.518,950 million.

Trade with U.K.

	1987	1988
Imports from U.K.	£1,090,146,000	£1,110,740,000
Exports to U.K.	536,704,000	559,684,000

COMMUNICATIONS

Civil Aviation.—Four international airports—Palam (Delhi), Sahar (Bombay), Dum Dum (Calcutta), Meenambakkam (Madras)—are managed by the International Airports Authority. The other 87 aerodromes are controlled and operated by the Civil Aviation Department of the Government. The national airlines are Indian Airlines (internal) and Air India (international).

Railways.—The railways are grouped into nine administrative zones, Southern, Central, Western, Northern, North-Eastern, North-East Frontier, Eastern, South-Eastern and South-Central.

Gross Traffic Receipts (1989–90), crores of rupees, 10,633. Working expenses, 9,788. Net railway revenues, 945.

Ports.—The chief seaports are Bombay (Mumbai), Calcutta, Haldia, Madras, Mormugao, Cochin, Visakhapatnam, Kandla, Paradip, Mangalore and Tuticorin. There are 139 minor working ports with varying capacity.

Shipping.—On Nov. 30, 1988, 377 ships totalling 5,590,752 gross tons were on the Indian Register.

BRITISH HIGH COMMISSION

Chanakyapuri, New Delhi, 21, 1100–21.
[New Delhi 601371]

High Commissioner, His Excellency Sir David Goodall, K.C.M.G. (1987).

British Council Representative in India, R. Arbuthnott, AIFACS Building, Rafi Marg, New Delhi 110 001. Offices also at *Bombay, Madras* and *Calcutta.* There are British Council libraries at these four centres and British libraries at *Ahmedabad, Bangalore, Bhopal, Hyderabad, Lucknow, Patna, Pune, Ranchi* and *Trivandrum.*

JAMAICA

AREA, POPULATION, ETC.—Jamaica is situated in the Caribbean Sea south of the eastern extremity of Cuba and lies between latitudes 17° 43′ and 18° 32′ North, and longitude 76° 11′ and 78° 21′ West. Jamaica is 4,244 sq. miles (10,991 sq. km.) in area and is divided into three counties (Surrey, Middlesex and Cornwall) and 14 parishes. The greatest length from east to west (Morant Point to Negril Point) is 146 miles and the extreme breadth 51 miles.

The topography consists mainly of coastal plains, divided by the Blue Mountain Range in the east, and the hills and limestone plateaux which occupy the central and western areas of the interior. The central chain of high peaks of the Blue Mountains is over 6,000 feet above sea level, and the Blue Mountain Peak, the highest of these, reaches an elevation of 7,402 feet.

At Dec. 31, 1987 Jamaica's population was estimated to be 2,355,100. The island was discovered by Columbus on May 4, 1494, and occupied by the Spanish from 1509 until 1655 when a British expedition, sent out by Oliver Cromwell, under Admiral Penn and General Venables, attacked the island, which capitulated after a token resistance. In 1670 it was formally ceded to England by the Treaty of Madrid.

CAPITAL.—The seat of government is ΨKingston, the largest town and seaport (estimated population of the Corporate area of Kingston and St. Andrew in 1982, 696,300). Other towns are ΨMontego Bay, Spanish Town, Mandeville and May Pen.

CURRENCY.—Jamaican dollar (J$) of 100 cents.

FLAG.—Gold diagonal cross forming triangles of green at top and bottom, triangles of black at hoist and in fly.

NATIONAL DAY.—First Monday in August (Independence Day).

GOVERNMENT

Jamaica became an independent state within the Commonwealth on Aug. 6, 1962. The Legislature consists of a Senate of 21 nominated members and a House of Representatives consisting of 60 members elected by universal adult suffrage. The Senate has no power to delay money bills for longer than one month or other bills for longer than seven months against the wishes of the House of Representatives. The Constitution provides for a Leader of the Opposition.

At the General Election of February 9, 1989, the People's National Party won 45 seats and the Jamaica Labour Party won 15.

Governor General, His Excellency Sir Florizel Glasspole, G.C.M.G., G.C.V.O.

Cabinet
(as at May 31, 1989)

Prime Minister, Hon. Michael Manley.
Deputy P.M. and Minister of Production and Planning, Hon. P. J. Patterson, Q.C.
Foreign Affairs and Foreign Trade, Senator the Hon. David Coore, Q.C.
Finance and the Public Service, Hon. Seymour Mullings.
National Security, Hon. K. D. Knight.
Attorney General and Minister for Justice, Hon. Carl Rattray, Q.C.
Education, Senator the Hon. Carlyle Dunkley.
Health, Hon. Easton Douglas.
Labour, Welfare and Sports, Hon. Portia Simpson.
Construction, Hon. O. D. Ramtallie.
Public Utilities and Transport, Hon. Robert Pickersgill.
Agriculture, Hon. Horace Clarke.
Local Government, Hon. Ralph Brown.
Tourism, Senator the Hon. Frank Pringle.
Mining and Energy, Hon. Hugh Small, Q.C.
Industry and Commerce, Hon. Claude Clarke.
Youth, Culture and Community Development, Hon. Dr. Douglas Manley.
Ministers without Portfolio, Hon. Dr. Ken McNeil (*Leader of the House of Representatives*); Senator the Hon. Dr. Paul Robertson.

JAMAICAN HIGH COMMISSION
1–2 Prince Consort Road, SW7 2BZ
[01–823 9911]

High Commissioner, (new appointment awaited).

JUDICATURE

Chief Justice and Keeper of Records, Hon. E. Zacca.
Judges of the Court of Appeal, Hon. I. D. Rowe (*President*); Hons. B. M. Carey; M. L. Wright; U. V. Campbell; I. X. Forte; H. E. Downer; M. E. Morgan.

COMMUNICATIONS

There are several excellent harbours, Kingston being the principal port. The island has 2,944 miles of main roads and over 7,000 miles of subsidiary roads. There are about 204 miles of railway. Telegraph stations and post offices are established in every town and in very many villages.

There are two international airports capable of handling the largest civil jet aircraft, the Norman Manley International Airport on the south coast serving Kingston, and Sangster Airport on the north coast serving the major tourist areas. In addition there are licensed aerodromes at Port Antonio, Ocho Rios, Mandeville and Negril. There are 16 privately owned, seven public and two military airstrips.

Air Jamaica, the national airline, operates international services; Trans-Jamaica Airlines operates scheduled internal services.

PRODUCTION

Agriculture.—Most of the staple products of tropical climates are grown; sugar, bananas, pimento, coffee and citrus fruit. Some of the sugar is used to produce rum and molasses. Main products exported in 1987 were sugar (US$74·1 million), bananas (US$19·1 million), citrus fruit and citrus products (US$6·1 million).

Industry.—Jamaica is the fourth largest producer of bauxite in the world; output for 1985 was 5,975,000 tonnes of which 1,513,000 tonnes were processed into alumina before being exported. In 1987 exports of bauxite and alumina were valued at US$336·5 million. Cement is manufactured locally, the output being 232,800 long tons in 1985.

In the last decade, manufacturing has grown from the processing of a few agricultural products into the production of a whole range of commodities such as textiles, clothing, footwear, and construction materials. Jamaica is a popular tourist resort, attracting visitors mainly from the U.S.A. In 1985 the total number of visitor arrivals was 846,716, and expenditure was estimated at US$406·8 million.

FINANCE

	1985–86*	1986–87**
Revenue	J$3,078·4m	J$3,942·9m
Expenditure	3,830·9m	4,688·5m

*provisional   **estimates

National External Debt at Dec. 1985 US$1,841·3 million.

TRADE

	1986	1987
Total imports	J$5,322·2m	J$6,788·65m
Total exports	3,089·2m	3,896·20m

Trade with U.K.

	1987	1988
Imports from U.K.	£54,644,000	£48,855,000
Exports to U.K.	85,655,000	89,693,000

BRITISH HIGH COMMISSION
P.O. Box 575, Trafalgar Road, Kingston 10.
[Kingston 926-9050]

High Commissioner, His Excellency Derek Francis Milton (1989).

KENYA
(Jamhuri ya Kenya)

AREA, POPULATION, ETC.—Kenya is bisected by the equator and extends approximately from latitude 4° N. to latitude 4° S. and from longitude 34° E. to 41° E. From the coast of the Indian Ocean in the east, the borders of Kenya are with Somalia in the east and Ethiopia and Sudan in the north and north-west. To the west lie Uganda and Lake Victoria. On the south is Tanzania. The total area is 224,961 sq. miles (582,646 sq. km.), including 5,171 square miles of water. The country is divided into 8 provinces (Nyanza, Rift Valley, Nairobi, Central, Coast, Western, Eastern and North-Eastern). The population is 20,333,000 (1985 U.N. estimate). The main tribal groups are the Kikuyu, Luhya, Luo, Kamba, Kalenjin and Masai. The official languages are Swahili, which is generally understood throughout Kenya, and English: numerous indigenous languages are also spoken.

CAPITAL.—Nairobi, population 1,103,554 (1984 estimate).

CURRENCY.—Kenya shilling (Ksh) of 100 cents.

FLAG.—Three equal horizontal bands of black over red over green; red and white spears and shield device in centre.

NATIONAL ANTHEM.—Kenya, Land of the Lion.

NATIONAL DAY.—December 12 (Independence Day).

GOVERNMENT

Kenya became an independent state and a member of the British Commonwealth on December 12, 1963, after six months of internal self-government. Kenya became a Republic on Dec. 12, 1964. In 1982 the Government introduced amendments to the constitution and election law, making the country a one-party (K.A.N.U.) state. There is a uni-cameral National Assembly of 202 members.

President and C.-in-C. Armed Forces, Hon. Daniel T. arap Moi, *took office*, Oct. 14, 1978.

Cabinet
(as at May 1, 1989)

Vice-President and Minister for Finance, Hon. Prof. George Saitoti.

Environment and Natural Resources, Hon. Jeremiah Nyagah.

Lands and Settlement, Hon. Darius Mbele.

Water Development, Hon. Ndolo Ayah.

Planning and National Development, Hon. Z. Onyonka.

Transport and Communications, Hon. J. J. Kamotho.

Energy, Hon. K. N. K. Biwott.

Local Government and Physical Planning, Hon. William ole Ntimama.

Foreign Affairs and International Co-operation, Hon. Dr. Robert J. Ouko.

Commerce, Hon. Arthur K. Magugu.

Tourism and Wildlife, Hon. Noah K. Ngala.

Culture and Social Services, Hon. James Njiru.

Agriculture, Hon. Mwai Kibaki.

Public Works, Hon. Timothy arap Mibei.

Co-operative Development, Hon. John Cheruiyot.

Labour, Hon. Peter Habenga Okondo.

Education, Hon. Peter Oloo Aringo.

Information and Broadcasting, Hon. Waruru Kanja.

Livestock Development, Hon. Elijiah W. Mwangale.

Industry, Hon. Dalmas Anyango Otieno.

Research, Science and Technology, Hon. George Muhoho.

Supplies and Marketing, Hon. Wycliffe Musalia Mudavadi.

Technical Training and Applied Technology, Hon. Sam K. Ongeri.

Manpower Development and Employment, Hon. Paul Ngei.

Reclamation and Development of Arid, Semi-Arid and Waste Land, Hon. George Ndotto.

Regional Development, Hon. J. Okwanyo.

KENYA HIGH COMMISSION
45 Portland Place, W1N 4AS
[01–636 2371]

High Commissioner, Her Excellency Dr. Sally Jemng-'Etich Kosgei (1987).

PRODUCTION

Agriculture provides about 52 per cent of total export earnings (excluding processed oil products). The great variation in altitude and ecology provide conditions under which a wide range of crops can be grown. These include wheat, barley, pyrethrum, coffee, tea, sisal, coconuts, cashew nuts, cotton, maize and a wide variety of tropical and temperate fruits and vegetables. The total area of well-farmed land on which concentrated mixed farming can be practised is small and the remainder is arid or semi-arid country but population pressure and the need to increase agricultural production for export has led to attempts to develop such areas.

Prospecting and mining are carried on in some parts of the country, the principal minerals produced being soda ash, salt and limestone.

Hydro-electric power has been developed, particularly on the Upper Tana River. Kenya is now almost self-sufficient in electric power generation but the connection with Owen Falls in Uganda is still in being.

There has been considerable industrial development over the last 15 years and Kenya has a wide variety of industries processing agricultural produce and manufacturing an increasing range of products from local and imported raw materials. New industries have recently come into being such as steel, textile mills, dehydrated vegetable processing and motor tyre manufacture as well as many smaller schemes which have added to the country's already considerable consumer goods. There is an oil refinery in Mombasa supplying both Kenya and Uganda, and a fuel pipeline now connects Mombasa and Nairobi.

COMMUNICATIONS

The Kenya Railways Corporation has 1,300 miles of railway open to traffic. There are also 31,000 miles of road, of which 2,700 are bitumen surfaced. Transborder links with Tanzania were re-opened in 1985 with rail services for freight and steamer services for passengers and freight.

The principal port is Mombasa, operated by the Kenya Ports Authority.

International air services operate from airports at Nairobi and Mombasa.

TRADE

Principal exports are coffee and tea, which account for 33 per cent of total export earnings. Also exported are fruit, vegetables, and crude animal and vegetable material. Petroleum products account for about 37 per cent of imports; other imports are manufactured goods, particularly machinery, transport equipment, metals, pharmaceuticals and chemicals.

Trade with U.K.

	1987	1988
Imports from U.K.	£199,059,000	£202,094,000
Exports to U.K.	129,236,000	142,455,000

BRITISH HIGH COMMISSION
Bruce House, Standard Street, P.O. Box 30465
Nairobi
[Nairobi 335944]

High Commissioner, His Excellency Sir John Rodney Johnson, K.C.M.G. (1986).

British Council Representative, T. Edmundson, (P.O. Box 40751) ICEA Building, Kenyatta Avenue, Nairobi. There are offices at *Kisumu* and *Mombasa*.

KIRIBATI
(Ribaberikin Kiribati)

AREA, POPULATION, ETC.—Kiribati, the former Gilbert Islands, became an independent Republic in 1979. Kiribati comprises 36 islands—the Gilberts Group (17) including Banaba, formerly Ocean Island; the Phoenix Islands (8); and the Line Islands (11) — situated in the South West Central Pacific around the point at which the International Date Line cuts the Equator. The total land area of 281 sq. miles (728 sq. km), is spread over some 2 million square miles of ocean. Few of the atolls are more than half a mile in width or more than 12 feet high. The vegetation consists mainly of coconut palms, breadfruit trees and pandanus. The population (1985 Census) was approx. 63,800. The population is predominantly Christian.

CAPITAL.—Tarawa (Population estimated at 24,400).

CURRENCY.—Kiribati uses the Australian dollar ($A) of 100 cents.

FLAG.—Red, with blue and white wavy lines in base, and in the centre a gold rising sun and a flying frigate bird.

NATIONAL ANTHEM.—Teirake Kain Kiribati (Stand Kiribati).

NATIONAL DAY.—July 12 (Independence Day).

GOVERNMENT

The President is Head of State as well as Head of Government and is elected nationally. There is an elected House of Assembly (36 members); executive authority is vested in the Cabinet.

Cabinet
(as at May 31, 1989)

President and Minister of Foreign Affairs, Hon. Ieremia Tabai, G.C.M.G..
Vice-President and Minister of Finance, Hon. Teatao Teannaki.
Works and Energy, Hon. Ieruru Karotu.
Natural Resources Development, Hon. Taomati T. Iuta.
Home Affairs and Decentralization, Hon. Babera Kirata, O.B.E.
The Line and Phoenix Islands, Hon. Tekinaiti Kaiteie.
Trade, Industry and Labour, Hon. Raion Bataroma.
Transport and Communications, Hon. Uera Rabaua.
Health and Family Planning, Hon. Rotaria Ataia.
Education, Hon. Ataraoti Bwebwenibure.
Attorney-General, Hon. Michael N. Takabwebwe.
Chief Justice, Hon. V. Maxwell.

ECONOMY

Most people still practise a semi-subsistence economy, the main staples of their diet being coconuts and fish.

Estimated recurrent revenue for 1987 is $A17,756,000. United Kingdom budgetary assistance ceased in 1985. The principal imports are foodstuffs, consumer goods, machinery and transport equipment. The principal exports are copra, which earned $A1,173,000, and fish, income from which was around $A823,000 in 1987. Total value of exports in 1987 was $A2,869,000.

COMMUNICATIONS

Air communication exists between most of the islands, and is operated by Air Tungaru, a statutory corporation. Air Marshall Islands operate a weekly service between Majuro/Tarawa/Funafuti and Nandi. Inter-island shipping is operated by a statutory corporation, the Shipping Corporation of Kiribati.

SOCIAL WELFARE

The Government maintains a teacher training college and a secondary school. Four junior second-

ary schools are maintained by missions. Throughout the Republic there are about a hundred primary schools. The total enrolment of children of school age is about 14,000. The Marine Training School at Tarawa trains seamen for service with overseas shipping lines. There is a general hospital at Tarawa. The other inhabited islands have dispensaries.

Trade with U.K.

	1987	1988
Imports from U.K.	£301,000	£522,000
Exports to U.K.	8,000	128,000

BRITISH HIGH COMMISSION
P.O. Box 61, Bairiki, Tarawa
[Bairiki 21327]

High Commissioner, His Excellency Charles Thompson, O.B.E. (1983).

LESOTHO
('Muso oa Lesotho)

Lesotho is a landlocked mountainous state entirely surrounded by the Republic of South Africa. Of the total area of 11,720 sq. miles, (30,355 sq. km.), a belt between 20 and 40 miles in width lying across the western and southern boundaries and comprising about one-third of the total is classed as lowlands, being between 5,000 and 6,000 ft. above sea level. The remaining two-thirds are classed as foothills and highlands, rising to 11,425 ft. The population was 1,443,853 (1986 Census).

CAPITAL.—Maseru, population, (1986 Census) 288,951.

CURRENCY.—Loti (M) of 100 lisente.

FLAG.—Diagonally white over blue over green with the white of double width, and an assegai and knobkerrie on a Basotho shield in brown in the upper hoist.

NATIONAL ANTHEM.—Pina ea Sechaba.

NATIONAL DAY.—October 4 (Independence Day).

GOVERNMENT

Lesotho became a constitutional monarchy within the Commonwealth on October 4, 1966. The independence constitution was suspended in January 1970, when the country was governed by a Council of Ministers, until the establishment of a nominated National Assembly in April 1974. The Government was overthrown in Jan. 1986: all legislative and executive authority is now vested in the King acting on advice from a Military Council and with the assistance of a Council of Ministers.

The country is divided into ten administrative districts. In each district there is a District Co-ordinator who co-ordinates all Government activity in the area, working in co-operation with hereditary chiefs.

Head of State, H.M. King Moshoeshoe II.

Military Council

Chairman, Maj. Gen. Justin Metsing Lekhanya.
Members, Col. Elias P. Ramaema; Col. Aloysieus K. Mosoeunyane; Col. Michael N. Ts'otetsi; Col. Thaabe S. Letsie; Col. J. Sekhobe N. Letsie.

Council of Ministers
(as at May 31, 1989)

Chairman, Minister of Defence and Internal Security, H.E. Maj.-Gen. Justin Metsing Lekhanya.
Foreign Affairs, H.E. Col. Thaabe S. Letsie.

Law, Public Service, Constitutional and Parliamentary Affairs, Hon. B. M. Khaketla (*acting*).
Finance, Hon. E. R. Sekhonyana.
Works, Hon. L. B. Monyake.
Justice and Prisons, Hon. B. M. Khaketla.
Information and Broadcasting, Hon. V. M. Malebo.
Employment, Social Welfare and Pensions, Hon. M. M. Tiheli.
Planning and Economic Manpower Development, Hon. Dr. M. M. Sefali.
Agriculture, Co-operatives and Marketing, Hon. Dr. D. R. Phozozo.
Transport and Communications, Hon. Col. P. M. Mokhants'o.
Tourism, Sports and Culture, Hon. M. L. Mathealire.
Water, Energy and Mining, Hon. Col. A. L. Jane.
Highlands, Water and Energy Affairs, Hon. M. M. Lebotsa.
Interior and Chieftainship Affairs and Rural Development, Hon. Morena M. Seeiso.
Education, Hon. Prof. L. B. J. Machobane.
Trade and Industry, Hon. M. Mokoroane
Health, Hon. Dr. S. T. Makenete.

JUDICIARY

The Lesotho Courts of Law consist of the Court of Appeal, the High Court, Magistrates' Courts, Judicial Commissioners' Court, Central and local Courts. Magistrates' and higher courts administer the laws of Lesotho. They also adjudicate appeals from the Judicial Commissioner's and Subordinate Courts.
Chief Justice, Hon. B. P. Cullinan.

LESOTHO HIGH COMMISSION
10 Collingham Road, SW5 0NR
[01–373 8581]

High Commissioner, new appointment awaited.

EDUCATION

Most schools are mission-controlled, the Government providing grants for salaries and buildings. There are over 1,000 primary and over 100 secondary schools; few areas lack a school and there is a high literacy rate of about 70 per cent. Increasing emphasis is being laid on agricultural and vocational education. The National University of Lesotho at Roma was established in 1975.

COMMUNICATIONS

A tarred road of 110 miles links Maseru to several of the main lowland towns, and this is being extended in the south of the country. The mountainous areas are linked by 1,300 miles of gravelled and earth roads and tracks. Roads link border towns in South Africa with the main towns in Lesotho. Maseru is connected by rail with the main Bloemfontein–Natal line of the South African Railways. Scheduled international air services are operated daily between Maseru and Johannesburg and other scheduled international flights are to Manzini and Maputo. There are around 30 airstrips. Internal scheduled services are operated by the Lesotho Airways Corporation.

The telephone network is fully automated in all urban centres. Radio telephone communication is used extensively in the remote rural areas.

PRODUCTION

The economy of Lesotho is based on agriculture and animal husbandry, and the adverse balance of trade (mainly consumer and capital goods) is offset by the earnings of the large numbers of the population who work in South Africa. Apart from some diamonds, Lesotho has few natural resources and only small-scale industrial development. The Lesotho National Development Corporation was set up to promote the development of industry, mining, trade and tourism. Work has commenced on the Highlands Water Scheme designed to provide water for the Vaal industrial zone in South Africa and hydro-electricity for Lesotho. Drilling is being carried out for oil. A National Park has been established at Sehlabathebe in the Maluti mountains. A number of light manufacturing and processing industries have recently been established.

FINANCE AND TRADE

The main sources of revenue are customs and excise duty. Estimates of expenditure and revenue (1986) are recurrent revenue M241·2 million; recurrent expenditure M265·3 million; capital revenue M144 million; capital expenditure M198 million.

Trade with U.K.

	1987	1988
Imports from U.K.	£1,112,000	£1,260,000
Exports to U.K.	486,000	977,000

BRITISH HIGH COMMISSION
P.O. Box 521, Maseru
[Maseru 313961]

High Commissioner, His Excellency John Coates Edwards, C.M.G. (1988).
British Council Representative, A. D. Bates, Hobson's Square, P.O. Box 429, Maseru, 100.

MALAWI
(Mfuko La Malawi)

AREA, POPULATION, ETC.—Malawi comprises Lake Malawi (formerly Lake Nyasa) and its western shore, with the high table-land separating it from the basin of the Luangwa River, the watershed forming the western frontier with Zambia; south of the lake, Malawi reaches almost to the Zambezi and is surrounded by Mozambique, the frontier lying on the west on the watershed of the Zambezi and Shire Rivers, and to the east on the Ruo, a tributary of the Shire, and Lakes Chiuta and Chirwa. This boundary reaches the eastern shore of Lake Malawi and extends up to the mid-point of the lake for about half its length where it returns to the eastern and northern shores to form a frontier with Tanzania. Malawi has a total area of 45,747 sq. miles (118,484 sq. km.). The population, according to the Census held in 1987 was 7,982,607. The official languages are Chichewa and English.

CAPITAL.—Lilongwe (population (1987) 175,000). The city of Blantyre in the Southern Region, incorporating Blantyre and Limbe (population (1987) 289,000), is the major commercial and industrial centre. Other main centres are: Mzuzu, Thyolo, Mulanje, Mangochi, Salima, Dedza and Zomba, the former capital.

CURRENCY.—Kwacha (K) of 100 tambala.

FLAG.—Horizontal stripes of black, red and green, with rising sun in the centre of the black stripe.

NATIONAL ANTHEM.—O God Bless Our Land of Malawi.

NATIONAL DAY.—July 6 (Independence Day).

GOVERNMENT

Malawi became a republic on July 6, 1966, having assumed internal self-government on February 1, 1963, and achieved independence on July 6, 1964. There is a Cabinet consisting of the Life President and other Ministers. The Parliament consists of 112 members, each elected by universal suffrage. Under the 1981 Amendment to the Constitution, the Life President has the power to nominate as many Members of Parliament as he wishes. Being a one-party State (the Malawi Congress Party), all elected members are required to be members of the Party. The Parliament, which usually meets three times a year, is presided over by a Speaker.

President, Minister of External Affairs, Agriculture, Justice, Works, Supplies, Dr. H. Kamuzu Banda, *elected 1966, sworn in as President for Life*, July 6, 1971.

Cabinet
(as at May 31, 1989)

Trade, Industry and Tourism, Hon. Robson Chirwa.
Transport and Communications, Hon. Dalton Katopola.
Health, Hon. Edward Bwanali.
Finance, Hon. Louis Chimango.
Labour, Wadson Bini Deleza.
Education and Culture, Hon. Michael Mlambala.
Community Services, Hon. E. C. Katola Phiri.
Forestry and Natural Resources, Hon. Stanford Demba.
Local Government, Hon. M. M. Mwakikunga.
Minister without Portfolio, Hon. Maxwell Pashane.

JUDICIARY

Chief Justice, Hon. F. L. Makuta.

MALAWI HIGH COMMISSION
33 Grosvenor Street, W1X 0DE
[01-491 4172/7]

High Commissioner, His Excellency Mr. Bernard B. Mtawali (1987).

EDUCATION

Primary education is the responsibility of local authorities in both urban and rural areas, although policy, curricula and inspection are the responsibility of the Ministry of Education and Culture. The Ministry is also responsible for secondary schools, technical education and primary teacher training. Religious bodies, with Government assistance, still play an important part in these fields. The University of Malawi was opened in 1965 and has four constituent colleges.

COMMUNICATIONS

A single-track railway runs from Mchinji on the Zambian border, through Lilongwe and Salima on Lake Malawi (itself served by two passenger and a number of cargo boats) through Blantyre to the southern frontier into Mozambique, and connecting with the Mozambique port of Beira. There are 12,215 km. of roads in Malawi of which about 21·8 per cent are bituminized.

There is an international airport 26 km. from Lilongwe, which handles regional and inter-continental flights.

FINANCE
(excluding Development Account)

	1986–87	1987–88
Revenue	K512m	K583m
Expenditure	547m	823m

ECONOMY

The economy is largely agricultural, with maize the main subsistence crop. Tobacco, sugar, tea, groundnuts and cotton are the main cash crops and principal exports. There are two sugar mills and total production in 1987 was 167,925 tonnes. A number of light manufacturing industries have been established recently.

TRADE

	1986	1987
Imports	K478m	K621m
Exports	462m	615m

Trade with U.K.

	1987	1988
Imports from U.K.	£18,069,000	£27,618,000
Exports to U.K.	44,223,000	30,183,000

BRITISH HIGH COMMISSION
Lingadzi House (P.O. Box 30042),
Lilongwe 3
[Lilongwe 731544]

High Commissioner, His Excellency Dr. Denis Osborne (1987).
Deputy High Commissioner and Head of Chancery, J. Wilde.
British Council Representative, S. Newton, (P.O. Box 30222), Lilongwe. There is also a library at Blantyre.

MALAYSIA
(Persekutuan Tanah Malaysia)

AREA, POPULATION, ETC.—Malaysia, comprising the 11 states of peninsular Malaya plus Sabah and Sarawak, forms a crescent well over 1,000 miles long between latitudes 1° and 7° N. and longitudes 100° and 119° E. It occupies two distinct regions—the Malay peninsula which extends from the isthmus of Kra to the Singapore Strait and the north-west coastal area of the island of Borneo. Each is separated from the other by 400 miles of the South China Sea. The total area of Malaysia, including the Federal Territories of Kuala Lumpur and Labuan, is approx. 127,317 sq. miles, (329,749 sq. km.), containing a population of 16,921,300 (1988 Census). The principal racial groups are the Malays, the Chinese and those of Indian and Sri Lankan origin, as well as the indigenous races of Sarawak and Sabah. Bahasa Malaysia (Malay) is the sole official language, but English, various dialects of Chinese, and Tamil are also widely spoken. There are a few indigenous languages widely spoken in Sabah and Sarawak.

RELIGION.—Islam is the official religion of Malaysia, each Ruler being the head of religion in his State, though the Heads of State of Sabah and Sarawak are not heads of the Muslim religion in their States. The Yang di-Pertuan Agung is the head of religion in Malacca and Penang. The Constitution guarantees religious freedom.

CLIMATE.—The year is commonly divided into the Southwest and Northwest monsoon seasons. Rainfall averages about 100 inches throughout the year, though the annual fall varies from place to place. The average daily temperature throughout Malaysia varies from 21° C. to 32° C., though in higher areas temperatures are lower and vary widely.

CAPITAL.—Kuala Lumpur was proclaimed Federal Territory on February 1, 1974. Its population is (1985) 1,103,200.

CURRENCY.—Malaysian dollar (ringgit) (M$) of 100 sen.

FLAG.—Equal horizontal stripes of red (7) and white (7); 14 point yellow star and crescent in blue canton.

NATIONAL ANTHEM.—Negara-Ku.

NATIONAL DAY.—August 31 (*Hari Kebangsaan*).

STATES OF THE FEDERATION

The 13 States of the Federation of Malaysia (State capitals in brackets) and their populations at the 1988 Census are:

ΨJohore (Johore Bahru)	2,007,300
Kedah (Alor Setar)	1,353,500
Kelantan (Kota Bahru)	1,150,400
ΨMelaka (Melaka)	560,700
Negri Sembilan (Seremban)	694,100
ΨPahang (Kuantan)	1,001,200
ΨPenang (Georgetown)	1,103,200
Perak (Ipoh)	2,143,200
Perlis (Kangar)	179,700
ΨSabah (Kota Kinabalu)	1,371,000
ΨSarawak (Kuching)	1,591,000
ΨSelangor (Shah Alam)	1,878,300
ΨTerengganu (Kuala Terengganu)	705,200

Ψ Seaport

FEDERAL TERRITORIES

The two Federal Territories and their population at the 1988 Census are:

Kuala Lumpur	} 1,182,700
Labuan	

GOVERNMENT

The Federation of Malaya became an independent country within the Commonwealth on August 31, 1957, as a result of an agreement between H.M. the Queen and the Rulers of the Malay States. On Sept. 16, 1963, the Federation was enlarged by the accession of the states of Singapore, Sabah (formerly British North Borneo) and Sarawak, and the name of Malaysia was adopted from that date. On Aug. 9, 1965, Singapore seceded from the Federation.

The Constitution was designed to ensure the existence of a strong Federal Government and also a measure of autonomy for the State Governments. It provides for a constitutional Supreme Head of the Federation (H.M. the *Yang di-Pertuan Agung*) to be elected for a term of five years by the Rulers from among their number, and for a Deputy Supreme Head (H.R.H. *Timbalan Yang di-Pertuan Agung*) to be similarly elected. The Malay Rulers are either chosen or succeed to their position in accordance with the custom of the particular state. In other states of Malaysia choice of the Head of State is at the discretion of the *Yang di-Pertuan Agung* after consultation with the Chief Minister of the State.

The Federal Parliament consists of two houses, the Senate and the House of Representatives. The Senate (*Dewan Negara*) consists of 68 members, under a President (*Yang di-Pertua Dewan Negara*), 26 elected by the Legislative Assemblies of the States (2 from each) and 42 appointed by the *Yang di-Pertuan Agung*. The House of Representatives (*Dewan Rakyat*), consists of 177 members (Peninsular Malaysia, 134; Sarawak, 24; and Sabah, 20). Members are elected on the principle of universal adult suffrage with a common electoral roll.

The Constitution provides that each State shall have its own Constitution not inconsistent with the Federal Constitution, with the Ruler or Governor acting on the advice of an Executive Council appointed on the advice of the Chief Minister and a single chamber Legislative Assembly. The State Secretary, the State Legal Adviser and the State Financial Officer sit in the Executive Council as *ex-officio* members. The Legislative Assemblies are fully elected on the same basis as the Federal Parliament.

Supreme Head of State, H.M. Sultan Azlan Muhibuddin Shah Ibni-Almarhum Sultan Yusuff Izzuddin Ghafarullahu-Lahu Shah (Sultan of Perak), sworn in April 26, 1989.

Deputy Supreme Head of State, H.R.H. Tuanku Saafar Ibni Al-Marhum Tuanku Abdul Rahman (Yang Dipertuan Besar of Negeri Sembilan).

MINISTRY
(as at June 30, 1989)

Prime Minister and Minister of Home Affairs, Datuk Seri Dr. Mahathir Muhammad.

Deputy P.M. and Minister of National and Rural Development, Ghafar Baba.

Labour, Datuk Lim Ah Lek.

Welfare Services, Encik Mustaffa Muhammad.

Youth and Sports, Datuk Najib Tun Razak.

Land and Regional Development, Datuk Kasitah Gadam.

Works, Datuk Leo Moggie.

Health, Datuk Ng Cheng Kiat.

Finance, Datu Paduka Daim Zainuddin.

Foreign Affairs, Datuk Haji Abu Hassan Omar.

Education, Anwar Ibrahim.

Information, Datuk Muhammad Rahmat.

Transport, Datuk Ling Liong Sik.

Trade and Industry, Datuk Seri Rafidah Aziz.

Defence, Tengku Ahmad Rithaudden.

Agriculture, Datuk Seri Sanusi Junid.

Public Enterprises, Datuk Napsiah Omar.

Primary Industries, Datuk Lim Kheng Yaik.

Science, Technology and Environment, Datuk Stephen Yong.

Energy, Telecommunications and Posts, Datuk S. Sammy Vallu.

Housing and Local Government, Leo Kim Sai.

Tourism and Culture, Datuk Hj Sabaruddin Chik.

Ministers in Prime Minister's Department, Datuk Dr. Sulaiman Daud (*Justice Minister*); Datuk Dr. Yusoff Noor.

NOTE.—The words "Tunku/Tengku", "Tun", "Tan Sri", and "Datuk" are titles. The word "Tunku/Tengku" is equivalent to "Prince". "Tun" denotes membership of a high Order of Malaysian Chivalry and "Tan Sri" and "Datuk" ("Datuk Seri" in Perak and "Datu" in Sabah) are each the equivalent of a knighthood. The wife of a "Tun" is styled "Toh Puan", that of a "Tan Sri" is styled "Puan Sri" and of a "Datuk" "Datin". The honorific "Tuan" or "Encik" is equivalent to "Mr." and the honorific "Puan" is equivalent to "Mrs.". The words "Al-Haj" or "Haji" indicate that the person so named has made the pilgrimage to Mecca.

MALAYSIAN HIGH COMMISSION
45 Belgrave Square, SW1X 8QT
[01–235 8033]

High Commissioner, His Excellency Dato Mon Bin Jamaluddin (1988).

JUDICATURE

The Judicial System consists of a Supreme Court and two High Courts, one in Peninsular Malaysia and one for Sabah and Sarawak (sitting alternately in Kota Kinabalu and Kuching).

The Supreme Court comprises a President, the two Chief Justices of the High Courts and other judges. It possesses appellate, original and advisory jurisdiction.

Each of the High Courts consists of a Chief Justice and not less than 4 other judges. The Federal Constitution allows for a maximum of twelve such judges for Malaya and eight for Borneo. In Peninsular Malaysia the Subordinate Courts consist of the Sessions Courts and the Magistrates' Courts. In Sabah/Sarawak the Magistrates' Courts constitute the Subordinate Courts.

DEFENCE

The Malaysian Armed Forces consist of the Army, Navy and Air Force, together with volunteer forces for each arm. The defence of the country is largely borne by the army in its role of providing defence against external threat and counter-insurgency operations and also to assist the police in the performance of public order duties. The Royal Malaysian Navy (RMN) has the responsibility of defending the 3,000 miles of the country's coastline and maintaining constant patrol of 500 miles of the high seas that separate Sabah and Sarawak from the mainland. The Royal Malaysian Air Force (RMAF) is capable of providing close strategic and tactical support to the army and police in the defence and internal security of the country.

FINANCE	M$million	
	1988	1989
Revenue	21,448	22,742
Expenditure	21,340	22,286

PRODUCTION AND TRADE

The agricultural sector continues to be the mainstay of the Malaysian economy. However, diversification of crops and rapid growth in the manufacturing sector has made Malaysia less vulnerable to fluctuations in the price of its primary crop, natural rubber.

Malaysia is the largest exporter of natural rubber, tin, palm oil and tropical hardwoods. Other major export commodities are manufactured and processed products, petroleum, oil, and other minerals, palm kernel oil, tea and pepper.

Exports of major commodities were (percentage of total exports):

	1987	1988
Primary commodities	31·9	34·0
Petroleum	15·2	17·8
Manufactured goods	44·2	44·9

Another commodity which is produced throughout Malaysia is rice, the staple food, and efforts are being made to achieve self-sufficiency.

Imports consist mainly of machinery and transport equipment, manufactured goods, foods, mineral fuels, chemicals and inedible crude materials for her growing population and to accelerate the pace of her economic growth and development.

	M$million	
	1987	1988
Imports	31,983	42,880
Exports	45,176	54,422

Trade with U.K.

	1987	1988
Imports from U.K.	£257,970,000	£310,462,000
Exports to U.K.	397,122,000	525,017,000

BRITISH HIGH COMMISSION
185 JLN Ampang
(P.O. Box 11030), 50732 Kuala Lumpur
[Kuala Lumpur 03–2482122]

High Commissioner, His Excellency John Nicholas Teague Spreckley, C.M.G. (1986).

British Council Representative, A. Johnson, C.B.E. Jalan Bukit Aman, 50480, Kuala Lumpur 10–01; offices at *Kota Kinabalu* (Sabah) and *Kuching* (Sarawak), and a library in Penang.

THE MALDIVES
(Divehi Jumhuriya)

AREA, POPULATION, ETC.—The Maldives are a chain of coral atolls, some 400 miles to the south-west of Sri Lanka, stretching from just south of the equator for about 600 miles to the north. There are about 20 coral atolls comprising over 1,200 islands, 202 of which are inhabited. Total area of the islands is 115 sq. miles (298 sq. km.). No point in the entire chain of islands is more than 8 feet above sea-level. The population of the islands (1988) is 200,000. The people are Sunni Muslims and the Maldivian language is akin to Elu or old Sinhalese.

CAPITAL.—ΨMalé (population, 1985, 46,334). There is an international airport at Malé.

CURRENCY.—Rufiyaa of 100 laaris.

FLAG.—Green field bearing a white crescent, with wide red border.

NATIONAL ANTHEM.—Qawmee Salaam.

NATIONAL DAY.—July 26.

GOVERNMENT

Until 1952 the islands were a Sultanate under the protection of the British Crown. Internal self-government was achieved in 1948 and full independence in 1965. In 1982 the Republic of the Maldives became a special member of the Commonwealth, and a full member in 1985.

The Maldives form a Republic which is elective. There is a Parliament (the *Citizens' Majlis*) with representatives elected from all the atolls. The life of the Majlis is 5 years. The Government consists of a Cabinet, which is responsible to the Majlis.

President, His Excellency Maumoon Abdul Gayoom, *elected* 1978, 1983, *re-elected* September 1989 (also *Minister of Defence and National Security*).

Cabinet

Foreign Affairs, Hon. Fathulla Jameel.
Justice, Hon. Mohamed Rasheed Ibrahim.
Home Affairs and Sports, Hon. Umar Zahir.
Education, Hon. Mohamed Zahir Hussain.
Health and Welfare, Hon. Abdul Sattar Moosa Didi.
Fisheries and Agriculture, Hon. Abdulla Jameel.
Transport and Shipping, Hon. Abbas Ibrahim.
Atolls Administration, Hon. Abdulla Hameed.
Trade and Industries, Hon. Ilyas Ibrahim.
Tourism, Hon. Ahamed Mujuthaba.
Public Works and Labour, Hon. Abdulla Kamaaludeen.
Attorney General, Hon. Ahamed Zaki.
Speaker of Majlis, Hon. Abdulla Hameed.
Chief Justice, Hon. Moosa Sathy.

PRODUCTION

The vegetation of the islands is coconut palms with some scrub. Hardly any cultivation of crops is possible and nearly all food to supplement the basic fish diet has to be imported. The principal industry is fishing and considerable quantities of fish are exported to Japan. Dried fish is exported to Sri Lanka, where it is a delicacy. The tourist industry is expanding very rapidly. Maldives Shipping Ltd. has a fleet of some 30 merchant ships.

Trade with U.K.

	1987	1988
Imports from U.K.	£2,772,000	£1,689,000
Exports to U.K.	440,000	1,859,000

BRITISH HIGH COMMISSION
High Commissioner, (resident at Colombo).

MALTA
(Repubblika Ta'Malta)

AREA, POPULATION, ETC.—Malta lies in the Mediterranean Sea, 58 miles from Sicily and about 180 miles from the African coast, about 17 miles in length and 9 in breadth, and having an area of 94·9 square miles. Malta includes also the adjoining islands of *Gozo* (area 25·9 sq. miles), *Comino* and minor islets. The estimated population at 1987 was 345,636.

Maltese and English are the official languages of administration and Maltese is ordinarily the official language in all the courts of law and the language of general use in the islands.

Malta was in turn held by the Phoenicians, Greeks, Carthaginians, Romans and Arabs. In 1090 it was conquered by Count Roger of Normandy. In 1530 it was handed over to the Knights of St. John, who made it a stronghold of Christianity. In 1565 it sustained the famous siege, when the last great effort of the Turks was successfully withstood by Grandmaster La Valette. The Knights expended large sums in fortifying the island and carrying out many magnificent works, until they were expelled by Napoleon in 1798. The Maltese rose against the French garrison soon afterwards, and the island was subsequently blockaded by the British fleet. The Maltese people freely requested the protection of the British Crown in 1802 on condition that their rights and privileges would be preserved and respected. The islands were finally annexed to the British Crown by the Treaty of Paris in 1814.

Malta was again closely besieged in the last war. From June, 1940, to the end of the war, 432 members of the garrison and 1,540 civilians were killed by enemy aircraft, and about 35,000 houses were destroyed or damaged. The island was awarded the George Cross in 1942.

CAPITAL.—ΨValletta. Population (Census 1985), 9,239. Valletta Grand Harbour is one of the finest in the world; it is very deep, and large vessels can anchor alongside the shore. It is an important port of call and ship repairing centre for vessels, being half-way between Gibraltar and Port Said.

CURRENCY.— Maltese lira (LM) of 100 cents and 1,000 mils.

FLAG.—Two equal vertical stripes, white at the hoists and red at the fly. A representation of the George Cross is carried edged in red in the top corner of the white stripe.

NATIONAL ANTHEM.—Lil Din I-Art Helwa.
NATIONAL DAY.—March 31.

GOVERNMENT

On Sept. 21, 1964, under the Malta Independence Order, 1964, Malta became an independent state within the Commonwealth; on December 13, 1974, Malta became a republic within the Commonwealth.

Elections are held every five years by a system of proportional representation. Seats are obtained by the highest number of votes in the respective districts. The party with the highest number of votes forms the government, with extra members being co-opted if necessary.

President.—Dr. Vincent Tabone.

Cabinet
(as at May 31, 1989)

Prime Minister and Minister for Foreign Affairs, Hon. Dr. Edward Fenech Adami.
Deputy P.M. and Minister of the Interior and Justice, Hon. Dr. Guido De Marco.
Education, Hon. Dr. Ugo Mifsud Bonnici.
Social Policy, Hon. Dr. Louis Galea.
Finance, Hon. Dr. G. Bonello Du Puis.

Infrastructure Development, Hon. Michael Falzon.
Productive Development, Hon. Lawrence Gatt.
Tertiary Sector Development, Hon. Dr. Emmanuel Bonnici.
Gozo, Hon. Anton Tabone.
Health, Hon. Dr. George Hyzler.
Elderly, Hon. Dr. John Rizzo Naudi.
Housing, Hon. Dr. Joe Cassar.
Water, Electricity and Energy, Hon. Anthony Zammit.
Post and Telecommunications, Hon. Pierre Muscat.
Industry, Hon. John Dalli.
Tourism, Hon. Dr. Michael Refalo.
Maritime Affairs, Hon. Dr. Joe Fenech.

MALTA HIGH COMMISSION
16 Kensington Square, W8 5HH
[01–938 1712]

High Commissioner, His Excellency John A. Manduca (1987).

EDUCATION

In June 1987 there were 92 Government Primary Schools with 26,324 pupils and 43 Secondary Schools and new Lyceums, with a total of 14,478 pupils.

The Government also runs 24 Technical/Trade Schools (with an enrolment of 6,610 students). Schools of Art, Music, Secretarial Studies, Catering, Nursing and Dramatic Art are sponsored by the Government. Tertiary education is available at the University of Malta, which had 1,449 students in 1987.

A number of private schools offer more or less the same facilities that exist in Government schools. All state education is free.

The Maltese are mainly Roman Catholic. The Maltese language is of Semitic origin and held by some to be derived from the Carthaginian and Phoenician tongues.

AGRICULTURE

Agriculture plays a significant role in the economy. There are 2,920 full time farmers and about 12,400 part time farmers. The yearly crop production is about 104,270 tonnes consisting mainly of tomatoes, potatoes, onions, cabbages and cauliflowers, and some 6,576 tonnes of fruit. Grape is the largest fruit crop. Flowers and cuttings are produced for export markets.

INDUSTRY

The island's leading industry is the state-owned Malta Drydocks, employing about 5,000 people. The main port of Grand Harbour handled traffic (excluding mineral oils) of 1,837,522 tonnes in 1987.

At the end of 1988 manufacturing firms employed some 28,271 people. The wide range of produce includes food processing, textiles and clothing, plastics and chemical products, electronic equipment and components. The gross output of the manufacturing industry in 1987 was LM351·3 million, of which LM188·3 million were export sales.

Tourism has assumed primary importance, with over 574,189 tourists visiting the island in 1987, and Marsamxett Harbour is being further developed by the extension of a yacht centre. Gross income from this industry stood at LM113 million.

FINANCE

	1987	1988
Revenue	LM241,000,000	LM304,225,000
Expenditure	269,000,000	270,786,000

TRADE

The principal imports for home consumption are foodstuffs—mainly wheat, meat and bullocks, milk and fruit—fodder, beverages and tobacco, fuels, chemicals, textiles and machinery (industrial, agricultural and transport). The chief domestic exports are processed food, electronics, textiles, and other manufactures.

	1987	1988
Imports	LM392,900,000	LM447,100,000
Exports	208,600,000	235,700,000

Trade with U.K.

	1987	1988
Imports from U.K. ...	£107,941,000	£121,696,000
Exports to U.K.	52,105,000	40,189,000

BRITISH HIGH COMMISSION
7 St. Anne Street, Floriana, Malta
[233134/8]

High Commissioner, His Excellency Brian Hitch, C.M.G., C.V.O. (1988).

MAURITIUS

AREA, POPULATION, ETC.—Mauritius is an island group lying in the Indian Ocean, 550 miles east of Madagascar, between 57° 17′–57° 46′ E. long. and 19° 58′–20° 33′ S. lat., and comprising with its dependencies an area of 790 square miles (2,045 sq. km.). The population (Dec. 1988 estimate) was 1,036,000 made up of Asiatic races (Hindus 52·6 per cent, Muslims 16·5 per cent), and persons of European (mainly French extraction), mixed and African descent (28·3 per cent).

English is the official language but French may be used in the Legislative Assembly and lower law courts. However, Creole is the mostly commonly used language.

CLIMATE.—Mauritius enjoys a sub-tropical maritime climate, with a wide range of rainfall and temperature resulting from the mountainous nature of the island. Humidity is rather high throughout the year and rainfall is sufficient to maintain a green cover of vegetation, except for a brief period in the driest districts.

CAPITAL.—Ψ Port Louis, population (1985), 138,272; other centres are Beau Bassin-Rose Hill (93,059); Curepipe (64,072); Vacoas-Phoenix (55,330) and Quatre Bornes (65,405).

CURRENCY.—Mauritius rupee of 100 cents.

FLAG.—Red, blue, yellow and green horizontal stripes.

NATIONAL ANTHEM.—Glory to the Motherland.

NATIONAL DAY.—March 12.

GOVERNMENT

Mauritius was discovered in 1511 by the Portuguese; the Dutch visited it in 1598, and named it Mauritius, after Prince Maurice of Nassau. From 1638 to 1710 it was held as a small Dutch colony and in 1715 the French took possession but did not settle it until 1721. Mauritius was taken by a British Force in 1810. A British garrison remained on the island until June 1960. The French language and French law were preserved under British rule.

A Crown Colony for 158 years, Mauritius became an independent state within the Commonwealth on March 12, 1968. The Constitution defined by Order in Council in 1964 was slightly altered in 1966 on the recommendation of the Banwell Commission, the effect being to increase the membership of the Legislative Assembly to 70, 62 elected by block voting in multi-member constituencies (including 2 members for Rodrigues) and 8 specially-elected members. Of the latter, 4 seats go to the "best loser" of whichever communities in the island are under-represented in the Assembly after the General Election and the four remaining seats are allocated on the basis of both party and community. The Constitution provides for the appointment of a Governor General who acts on the advice of the Council of Ministers, collectively responsible to the Legislative Assembly.

In the August 1987 General Election, the Mouvement Socialiste Militant (MSM), allied with the Labour Party (MLP), the Parti Mauricien Social Democrate and the Organisation du Peuple Rodriguais (OPR), defeated the Mouvement Mauricien Militant and formed the Government, with a majority of 22 seats. The Parti Mauricien Social Democrate left the alliance in August 1988.

Governor General, His Excellency Sir Veerasamy Ringadoo, G.C.M.G., Q.C.

Council of Ministers
(as at August 1988)

Prime Minister, Minister of Defence and Internal Security, Information, Internal and External Communications and the Outer Islands, Rt. Hon. Sir Anerood Jugnauth, K.C.M.G., Q.C. (*MSM*).

Deputy P.M., Attorney General and Minister of Justice, External Affairs and Emigration, Hon. Sir Satcam Boolell, Q.C. (*MLP*).

Deputy P.M. and Minister of Finance, Hon. Seetanah Lutchmeenaraidoo (*MSM*).

Deputy P.M. and Minister of Economic Planning and Development, Dr. the Hon. Beergoonath Ghurburrun (*MSM*).

Education, Arts and Culture, Hon. Armoogum Parsuramen (*MSM*).

Trade and Shipping, Hon. Dwarkanath Gungah (*MSM*).

Energy, Water Resources and Postal Services, Hon. Mahyendrah Utchanah (*MSM*).

Social Security, National Solidarity, and Reform Institutions, Dr. the Hon. Dineshwar Ramjuttun (*MSM*).

Housing, Lands and the Environment, Hon. Sir Ramesh Jeewoolall (*MLP*).

Labour and Industrial Relations, Women's Rights and Family Welfare, Hon. Mrs. Sheilabai Bappoo (*MSM*).

Youth, Sports and Tourism, Hon. Michael Glover (*MSM*).

Rodrigues, Hon. Serge Clair (*OPR*).

Co-operatives, Hon. Vishwanath Sajadah (*MLP*).

Health, Hon. Jagdishwar Goburdhun (*MSM*).

Agriculture, Fisheries and Natural Resources, Hon. Murlidas Dulloo (*MSM*).

Industry, Hon. Clarel Malherbe (*MLP*).

Works, Hon. Ramduthsing Jaddoo (*MSM*).

Local Government, Hon. Regis Finnette (*MSM*).

Civil Service Affairs and Employment, Hon. Mrs. France Roussety (*MLP*).

MAURITIUS HIGH COMMISSION
32–33 Elvaston Place, SW7 5NW
[01–581 0294]

High Commissioner, His Excellency Dr. Boodhun Teelock (1989).

EDUCATION

Primary education is free and in 1987 was provided for 137,935 children at 273 primary schools. Although education is not compulsory it is estimated that about 90 per cent of children of primary age attend school. At post-primary level there are a total of 69,825 students attending secondary schools: fees and teachers' salaries in the private secondary schools are paid by government. There are a number of Training Facilities offering training in engineering and mechanical trades, nursing, building, seamanship, hotel and catering etc. The College of Education trains primary school teachers. The Institute of Education is responsible for training secondary school teachers and for curriculum development. The University of Mauritius consists of Schools of Agriculture, of Administration and of Industrial Technology. Estimated expenditure on education in 1987–88 was Rs.791,700,000.

COMMUNICATIONS

Port Louis, on the N.W. coast, handles the bulk of the island's external trade. A bulk sugar terminal capable of handling the total crop began operating in 1980. The international airport is located at Plaisance in the southeast of the island about 5 miles from Mahébourg. There are 6 daily newspapers and 5 weeklies, mostly in French, and 2 Chinese daily papers and one weekly paper. The Mauritius Broadcasting Corporation has a monopoly of radio broadcasting in the country: television was introduced in 1965. There is a satellite communications ground station near Port Louis.

PRODUCTION

In 1988 the manufacturing sector employed 105,784, while the sugar industry employed 39,698.

About 55 per cent of the total sugar crop is produced on a plantation scale, while smaller owners (cultivating less than 10 acres) cultivate about 24 per cent of the land under cane. Tea and tobacco are also grown commercially but on a smaller scale than sugar.

	1987	1988
	tonnes	
Sugar	691,134	634,224
Tea (manufactured)	7,147	6,857
Tobacco (leaves)	912	970

In 1988 production of molasses, mainly for export, was 160,000 tonnes. Other products include alcohol, rum, denatured spirits, perfumed spirits and vinegar.

The bulk of the island's requirements in manufactured products still has to be imported. However, the Mauritius Export Processing Zone (M.E.P.Z.) scheme, introduced in 1971, has attracted investment from overseas and the number of export-orientated enterprises has risen from ten in 1971 to 591 at the end of 1988, employing 89,100 people. The biggest firms are in clothing manufacture, particularly woollen knitwear, but the range of goods produced includes toys, plastic products, leather goods, diamond cutting and polishing, watches, television sets and telephones.

Tourism is a major source of income for Mauritius, with an estimated 240,000 tourists in 1988. Earnings from tourism in 1987 are estimated to be Rs2,374 million (£95 million), compared with Rs1,175 million (£57 million) in 1986. The neighbouring French island of Réunion is the most important source of tourists, followed closely by mainland France.

FINANCE

The main sources of Government revenue are private and company income tax, customs and excise duties, mainly on imports, but also on sugar exports.

	1986–87	1987–88 p
Public revenue	Rs.5,126 m	Rs.5,892 m
Public expenditure	5,235 m	6,560 m
p–provisional		

TRADE

Most foodstuffs and raw materials have to be imported from abroad. Apart from local consumption (about 36,500 tonnes per annum), the sugar produced is exported, mainly to Britain.

	1987	1988
Total imports	Rs.13,042 m	Rs.17,247 m
Total exports	11,927 m	13,904 m

Trade with U.K.

	1987	1988
Imports from U.K.	Rs.1,058 m	Rs.1,259 m
Exports to U.K.	4,055 m	4,799 m

BRITISH HIGH COMMISSION
King George V Avenue, Floreal.
[Floreal 865795/9]

High Commissioner, His Excellency Michael Edward Howell, C.M.G., O.B.E.

RODRIGUES AND DEPENDENCIES OF MAURITIUS

Rodrigues, formerly a dependency but now part of Mauritius, is about 350 miles east of Mauritius. Area, 40 square miles. Population (1987) 36,537. Cattle, salt fish, sheep, goats, pigs and onions are the principal exports. The island is administered by an Island Commissioner.

Island Commissioner, Claude Wong So.

The islands of Agalega and St. Brandon are dependencies of Mauritius. Other small islands, formerly Mauritian dependencies, have since 1965 constituted the British Indian Ocean Territory (*see* p. 709).

REPUBLIC OF NAURU

The Republic of Nauru is an island of 8·2 sq. miles (21 sq. km.) in size, situated in 166° 55′ E. longitude and 0° 32′S. of the Equator. It has a population (Census May 1983) of 8,042 (Nauruans 4,964; other Pacific Islanders 2,134; Asians 682; Caucasians 262). About 43 per cent of Nauruans are adherents of the Nauruan Protestant Church and there is a Roman Catholic Mission on the island. The main languages are English and Nauruan.

CURRENCY.—Nauru uses the Australian dollar of 100 cents as legal tender.

FLAG.—Twelve-point star (representing the 12 original Nauruan tribes) below a gold bar (representing the Equator), all on a blue ground.

NATIONAL DAY.—January 31 (Independence Day).

GOVERNMENT

From 1888 until the First World War Nauru was administered by Germany, in 1920 becoming a British mandated territory under the League of Nations administered by Australia. A Trusteeship superceding the Mandate was approved in 1947 by the U.N. and Nauru continued to be administered by Australia until it became an Independent State on February 1, 1968. It was announced in November, 1968, that a limited form of membership of the Commonwealth had been devised for Nauru at the request of its Government.

Parliament has eighteen members including the Cabinet and Speaker. Voting is compulsory for all Nauruans over 20 years of age, except in certain specified instances. Elections are held every three years. The Cabinet is chosen by the President and comprises not fewer than five nor more than six members including the President.

President and Minister for External Affairs, Internal Affairs, Island Development and Industry, Civil Aviation Authority and the Public Service, His Excellency Hon. Hammer DeRoburt, G.C.M.G., O.B.E.

Cabinet
(as at May 31, 1989)

Works and Community Services and Minister Assisting the President, Hon. R. B. Detudamo.
Finance, Hon. K. Clodumar.
Health and Education, Hon. R. Kun.
Justice, Hon. B. Dowiyogo.

The government fell in August 1989; elections are planned for December.

JUDICIARY

A Supreme Court of Nauru is presided over by the Chief Justice. The District Court, which is subordinate to the Supreme Court, is presided over by a Resident Magistrate. Both the Supreme Court and the District Court are Courts of Record. The Supreme Court exercises both original and appellate jurisdiction.

EDUCATION AND WELFARE

Nauru has a hospital service and other medical and dental services. There is also a maternity and child welfare service. Education is available in 9 primary and 2 secondary schools on the island with a total enrolment of about 1,600 pupils receiving primary education and 500 secondary education.

PRODUCTION, ETC.

The only fertile areas are the narrow coastal belt and local requirements of fruit and vegetables are mostly met by imports. The economy is heavily dependent on the extraction of phosphate, of which the island has one of the world's richest deposits. About 1·5 million tonnes of phosphate are mined each year, providing employment for over 1,000 people. The industry has been run since 1970 by the Nauru Phosphate Corporation. Considerable investments have been made abroad with the royalties on phosphate exports to provide for a time when production declines.

The Nauru Pacific Line owns six ships: the Government-owned Air Nauru normally operates air services throughout the Pacific region and to Australia, New Zealand, Japan, Singapore and the Philippines. Scheduled services have ceased since December 1988.

Trade with U.K.

	1987	1988
Imports from U.K........	£394,000	£759,000
Exports to U.K.	674,000	642,000

British High Commissioner, (resident at Suva, Fiji).

NIGERIA
(Federal Republic of Nigeria)

AREA, POPULATION, ETC.—The Republic of Nigeria is situated on the west coast of Africa. It is bounded on the south by the Gulf of Guinea, on the west by the Republic of Benin, on the north by Niger and on the east by Cameroon. It has an area of 356,669 sq. miles (923,768 sq. km.), with a population presently estimated at around 100,000,000. The population is almost entirely African. The main ethnic groups are Hausa/Fulani, Yoruba and Ibo, and the principal languages are English, Hausa, Yoruba and Ibo. Over half the population are Muslim, these being concentrated in the north and west. In the southern areas in particular there are many Christians.

A belt of mangrove swamp forest 10–60 miles in width lies along the entire coastline. North of this there is a zone 50–100 miles wide of tropical rain forest and oil-palms. North of this the country rises and the vegetation changes to open woodland and savanna. In the extreme north the country is semi-desert. There are few mountains, but in Northern Nigeria the central plateau rises to an average level of 4,000 feet. The Niger, Benue, and Cross are the main rivers.

The climate varies with the types of country described above, but Nigeria lies entirely within the tropics and temperatures are high. The rainy season is from about April to October; rainfall varies from under 25 inches a year in the extreme north to 172 inches on the coast line. During the dry season the *harmattan* wind blows from the desert; it is cool and laden with fine particles of dust.

CAPITAL.—ΨLagos, estimated population, 3,000,000. Other important towns are Ibadan, Kaduna, Kano, Benin City, Enugu and ΨPort Harcourt. Movement of Federal Ministries to a new capital at Abuja has begun.

CURRENCY.—Naira (N) of 100 kobo.

FLAG.—Three equal vertical bands, green, white and green.

NATIONAL ANTHEM.—Arise, O Compatriots.

NATIONAL DAY.—October 1 (Republic Day).

GOVERNMENT

The Federation of Nigeria attained independence as a member of the Commonwealth on Oct. 1, 1960 and became a republic in 1963. On Jan. 15, 1966 the military took power, suspended the Constitution and dissolved the legislature. In 1979 civil rule was restored under a new constitution similar to that of the United States after elections at National and State level. After similar elections in 1983 the new administration was removed by the military on Dec. 31, this regime itself being overthrown in Aug. 1985. A 28-member Armed Forces Ruling Council was sworn in on Aug. 30. It is the country's most senior decision-making body. The Council of Ministers is the third most senior body after the A.F.R.C. and the National Council of States, which comprises the 21 State Governors.

Originally regional in structure the Federation was divided into 12 states in 1967. It was divided again into 19 states in 1976, and a further two states were created in 1987.

On May 3, 1989 Gen. Babangida promulgated the new draft constitution paving the way for a return to civilian rule by 1992. He also announced that a ban on political parties was to be lifted, leading to the formation of a large number of parties.

Head of State, Commander-in-Chief of the Armed Forces, Chairman of the Armed Forces Ruling Council, Maj.-Gen. Ibrahim Babangida.

Armed Forces Ruling Council

Chairman, General Ibrahim Badamasi Babangida.
Members, Vice-Adm. A. Aikhomu; Lt.-Gen. D. Y. Bali; Lt.-Gen. S. Abacha; Vice-Adm. P. S. Koshoni; Air Marshal I. Alfa; A. M. A. Gambo; Maj.-Gen. M. G. Nasko; Maj.-Gen. P. Omu; Air Vice-Marshal M. Yahaya; Maj.-Gen. P. Adomokhai; Maj.-Gen. D. O. Ajayi; Maj.-Gen. A. B. Mamman; Maj.-Gen. S. O. Ifere; Maj.-Gen. G. Duba; Brig. O. Diya; Brig. J. N. Dogonyaro; Cdre. M. A. B. Elegbede; Cdre. N. Kanu;

Cdre. S. Aluko; Rear-Adm. A. Nyako; Air Vice-Marshal N. Yusuf; Air Cdre. L. Koinyan; Air Vice-Marshal N. M. Imam; Col. J. N. Shagaya; Col. H. Akilu; Col. D. Mark; Maj.-Gen. Y. Y. Kure; Maj.-Gen. S. Sami.

Council of Ministers
(as at May 31, 1989)

Agriculture, Water Resources and Rural Development, Maj.-Gen. G. Nasko.
Communications, Col. D. Mark.
Defence, Maj.-Gen. D. Y. Bali.
Education, Prof. J. Aminu.
Employment, Labour and Productivity, A. A. Umar.
External Affairs, Maj.-Gen. I. O. S. Nwachukwu.
Federal Capital Territory, Abuja, Air Cdre. H. Abdullahi.
Finance and Economic Development, Dr. C. S. P. Okongwu.
Health, Prof. K. Ransome-Kuti.
Information and Culture, Prince Tony Momoh.
Internal Affairs, Col. J. N. Shagaya.
Industry, Lt.-Gen. A. I. Akinrinade.
Justice, Prince Bola Ajibola.
Mines, Power and Steel, Alhaji Bunu Sheriff Musa.
Petroleum Resources, Alhaji Rilwanu Lukman.
Science and Technology, Prof. E. Emovon.
Social Development, Youth and Sports, Air Cdre. B. Lawal.
Trade, Alhaji Samaila Mamman.
Transport, Dr. K. I. Kalu.
Aviation, Air Vice-Marshal T. Okpere.
Works and Housing, Brig. Kontagora.
Special Duties, Air Vice-Marshal A. I. Shekarri.

NIGERIA HIGH COMMISSION
Nigeria House, 9 Northumberland Avenue, WC2N 5BX
[01–839 1244]

High Commissioner, His Excellency Mr. George Dove-Edwin (1986).

EDUCATION

A programme was introduced in September 1976 intended to achieve universal primary education. Numbers of pupils in 1982–83 were: 15·4 million in primary schools, 3·5 million in secondary schools, 53,766 in polytechnics and 88,636 in universities. There are 24 universities.

COMMUNICATIONS

The Nigerian railway system, which is controlled by the Nigerian Railway Corporation, is the most extensive in West Africa. There are 2,178 route miles of lines. The principal international airlines operating from Lagos, Kano and Port Harcourt bring Nigeria within about six hours of the Western European capitals. There are also services to other parts of Africa and to the United States. A network of internal air services connects the main centres. The principal seaports are served by a number of shipping lines, including the Nigerian National Line. A nationwide television and radio network is being developed, with each State eventually having its own television and radio station. There is a network of meteorological reporting stations.

PRODUCTION AND INDUSTRY

Nigeria was a predominantly agricultural country until the early 1970s with agriculture contributing over 60 per cent of export revenue and 45 per cent of G.N.P. Tin and calumbite mining on the Jos plateau, textiles and coal mining were also important. The

major exports were ground nuts, palm products, tin, cocoa, rubber and timber. Recently oil has provided over 90 per cent of exports revenue and agricultural exports have greatly declined. Though agriculture still employs half the labour force it contributes only 20 per cent of G.N.P., exceeded by trading and oil. The construction sector is twice as large as the manufacturing sector and industries dependent on imported raw materials such as vehicle assembly have faltered recently. Three oil refineries are in operation at Port Harcourt, Warri and Kaduna. A steel plant has been opened near Warri and a larger one is being completed at Ajaokuta. Other projects include natural gas liquifaction, petro-chemicals, fertilizers and several power stations plus the Abuja Federal Capital. Several large irrigation schemes have been completed and more are planned.

TRADE

Oil revenues have been falling since 1981 and are now restricted by an OPEC production quota and lower prices to half their peak level. In March 1982 imports curbs and payments restrictions were introduced but exchange reserves fell and debts increased. Austerity measures were introduced, and continue, while the present Government attempts to stimulate greater self-reliance in the economy by encouraging non-oil exports and the use of local rather than imported raw materials.

Trade with U.K.

	1987	1988
Imports from U.K....	£481,568,000	£390,476,000
Exports to U.K.	159,386,000	128,123,000

BRITISH HIGH COMMISSION
Eleke Crescent, Victoria Island, Lagos
[Lagos 619531]

High Commissioner, His Excellency Jeremy Richard Lovering Varcoe, C.M.G. (1989).

British Council Representative, D. M. Waterhouse, 11 Kingsway Road, Ikoyi, (P.O. Box 3702), Lagos. Branch offices at *Kano, Kaduna* and *Enugu*.

PAKISTAN
(see **Foreign Countries** section)

PAPUA NEW GUINEA

AREA, POPULATION, ETC.—Papua New Guinea extends from the equator to Cape Baganowa in the Louisiade Archipelago at 11° S. latitude and from the border with Irian Jaya to 160° E. longitude. The total area of Papua New Guinea is 178,260 sq. miles, (461,691 sq. km.), of which approximately 152,420 sq. miles form the mainland, on the island of New Guinea. The country has many island groups, principally the Bismarck Archipelago, a portion of the Solomon Islands, the Trobriands, the D'Entrecasteaux Islands and the Louisade Archipelago. The main islands of the Bismarck Archipelago are New Britain, New Ireland and Manus. Bougainville is the largest of the Solomon Islands within Papua New Guinea.
Papua New Guinea lies within the tropics and has a typically monsoonal climate. Temperature and humidity are uniformly high throughout the year. The average rainfall is about 80 inches per year but there are wide variations—from 47 inches at Port Moresby to over 200 inches in mountainous western areas.
The estimated population in 1987 was 3,500,000. The inhabitants of the country comprise a great

diversity of physical types and a large number of linguistic groups.

CAPITAL.—ΨPort Moresby. Estimated population (1985), 139,300. Other major towns are Lae, Rabaul, Madang, Wewak, Goroka and Mount Hagen.

CURRENCY.—Kina (K) of 100 toea.

FLAG.—A rectangle divided diagonally from the top of the hoist to the bottom of the fly, the upper segment scarlet and containing a soaring yellow bird of paradise. The lower segment is black charged with five white five-pointed stars representing the Southern Cross.

NATIONAL ANTHEM.—Arise All You Sons.

NATIONAL DAY.—September 16 (Independence Day).

GOVERNMENT

New Guinea was sighted by Portuguese and Spanish navigators in the early sixteenth century, but remained largely isolated from the rest of the world. In 1884, a British Protectorate was proclaimed over the southern coast of New Guinea (Papua) and the adjacent islands. British New Guinea, as the Protectorate was called, was annexed outright in 1888. In 1906 the Territory of British New Guinea was placed under the authority of the Commonwealth of Australia. Also in 1884 Germany had formally taken possession of certain northern areas, which later came to be known as the Trust Territory of New Guinea. In 1914 the German areas were occupied by Australian troops and remained under military administration until 1921, when the League of Nations conferred on Australia a mandate for their government.

New Guinea was administered under the Mandate and Papua under the Papua Act until the invasion by the Japanese in 1942 when the civil administration was suspended until the surrender of the Japanese in 1945.

The first House of Assembly for the whole country met in 1964 and included an elected majority and ten nominated official members. After 1970 there was a gradual assumption of powers by the Papua New Guinea Government, culminating in formal self-government in December 1973. Final reserve powers held by Australia over defence and foreign relations were relinquished to Papua New Guinea in March 1975, and Papua New Guinea achieved full independence on September 16, 1975.

Elections are held every five years. The Parliament comprises 109 elected Members, 20 from Regional electorates, the remainder from Open electorates. There are 19 provinces, which have their own provincial governments with certain legislative and administrative powers.

Governor General, His Excellency Sir Ignatius Kilage, G.C.M.G., C.B.E.

National Executive Council
(CABINET)
(as at July 15, 1989)

Prime Minister, Rabbie Namaliu.

Deputy P.M. and Minister for Public Service, Akoka Doi.

Finance and Planning, Paul Pora.

Civil Aviation, Bernard Vogae.

Communications, (vacant).

Labour and Employment, Peter Garong.

Justice, Bernard Narokobi.

Lands and Physical Planning, Kala Swokin.

Police, Mathias Ijape.

Provincial Affairs, John Momis.

Administrative Services, Theo Tuya.

Education, Jack Genia.

Environment and Conservation, Jim Waim.

Foreign Affairs, Michael Somare.

Forests, Karl Stack.

Health, Robert Suckling.

Home Affairs, Timothy Bonga.

Defence, Ben Sabumei.

Culture and Tourism, G. Beona.

Trade and Industry, John Giheno.

Minister for State, Ted Diro.

Housing, Gerard Sigulogo.

Minerals and Energy, Patterson Lowa.

Corrective Institutions, Melchor Pep.

Transport, Anthony Temo.

Works, Paul Wanjik.

Fisheries, Allan Ebu.

Agriculture and Livestock, Galang Lang.

PAPUA NEW GUINEA HIGH COMMISSION
3rd Floor, 14 Waterloo Place, SW1Y 4AR
[01-930 0922/6]

High Commissioner, His Excellency Philip Bouraga (1989).

COMMUNICATIONS

Road communications are very limited, the most important road being that linking Lae with the populous highlands.

Air Niugini (the national airline) and Qantas operate regular air services between Port Moresby and Australia. Air Niugini also operates services to Manila (Philippines), Honiara (Solomon Islands), Jayapura (Indonesia), Honolulu and Singapore. Internal air services are operated by Air Niugini, Douglas Airways, and Talair.

Several shipping companies operate cargo services between Papua New Guinea and Australia, Europe, the Far East and U.S.A. There are very limited cargo and passenger services between Papua New Guinea main ports, outports, plantations and missions.

Papua New Guinea is linked by international cable to Australia, Guam, Hong Kong, Kota Kinabalu, the Far East and U.S.A. Telecommunications are widely available.

ECONOMY

Until the 1970s the Papua New Guinea economy was based almost entirely on agriculture. At the beginning of the 20th century copra plantations formed the basis of the cash economy. Further crops which have been introduced over the years are cocoa, tea, coffee, palm oil, rubber, groundnuts, spices and timber. A variety of commercial agricultural developments now co-exist with the traditional informal rural economy. Government expenditure is still reliant on Australian budgetary support, to the extent of just under 30 per cent in 1983.

In 1972, Bougainville Copper Pty Ltd (BCL) began mining in the North Solomons Province, producing copper, silver and gold. However, the Bougainville Copper Mine closed indefinitely in May 1989. There are extensive mineral deposits throughout Papua New Guinea, including nickel, chromite, bauxite and possibly commercial deposits of oil and gas. The most important new development is the exploitation of large copper and gold deposits on the Ok Tedi, in the Western Province.

In 1984 the Papua New Guinea economy was influenced by good prices for agricultural commodities, offset by low prices for copper and gold. New developments to promote export crops and increase employment, typically involving foreign investment, are planned for the future.

Industry includes processing of primary products, and brewing, bottling and packaging, paint, plywood, and metal manufacturing and the construction industries.

Although the formal economy is still dominated by non-Papua New Guineans, the participation of Papua New Guineans is increasing.

Trade with U.K.

	1987	1988
Imports from U.K.	£16,693,000	£20,520,683
Exports to U.K.	46,045,000	44,291,211

BRITISH HIGH COMMISSION
P.O. Box 4778, Boroko, Port Moresby
[Port Moresby 212500]

High Commissioner, His Excellency Edward John Sharland (1989).

ST. CHRISTOPHER AND NEVIS
(The Federation of St. Christopher and Nevis)

The State of St. Christopher and Nevis is located at the northern end of the Eastern Caribbean. It comprises the islands of St. Christopher (St. Kitts) (65 sq. miles: 168 sq. km.; population about 35,700) and Nevis (36 sq. miles: 93·2 sq. km.; population about 9,400).

St. Christopher, lat. 17° 18′ N. and long. 62° 48′ W. was the first island in the British West Indies to be colonized (1623). The central area of the island is forest-clad and mountainous, rising to the 3,792 ft. Mount Liamuiga.

Nevis, lat. 17° 10′ N. and long. 62° 35′ W. is separated from the southern tip of St. Christopher by a strait two miles wide and is dominated by the central Nevis Peak, 3,232 ft. Chief town of Nevis is ΨCharlestown (pop. 1,200), which is a port of entry.

CAPITAL—ΨBasseterre (estimated population, 15,000).

CURRENCY.—East Caribbean dollar (EC$) of 100 cents.

FLAG—Three diagonal bands, green, black and red; each colour separated by a stripe of yellow. Two white stars on the black band.

NATIONAL ANTHEM.—Our Land of Beauty.

NATIONAL DAY.—September 19 (Independence Day).

GOVERNMENT

The Territory of St. Christopher and Nevis became a State in Association with Britain on Feb. 27, 1967. The State of St. Christopher and Nevis became an independent nation on Sept. 19, 1983, with a new constitution under which Great Britain relinquished its responsibility for defence and external affairs. Under the new Constitution, H.M. The Queen is Head of State, represented in the islands by the Governor General. There is a central Cabinet Government with a Ministerial system, the Head of which is the Prime Minister of St. Christopher and Nevis, and a National Assembly located on St. Christopher. On Nevis there is a Nevis Island Administration, the Head being styled Premier of Nevis, and a Nevis Island Assembly.

Governor General, His Excellency Sir Clement Athelston Arrindell, G.C.M.G., G.C.V.O., Q.C. (1983).

Cabinet
(as at May 31, 1989)

Prime Minister and Minister of Finance, Home Affairs and Foreign Affairs, Rt. Hon. Dr. Kennedy A. Simmonds.

Deputy P.M. and Minister of Labour and Tourism, Rt. Hon. Michael O. Powell.

Education, Youth and Community Affairs, Communications, Works and Public Utilities, Hon. Sydney E. Morris.

Agriculture, Lands, Housing and Development, Hon. Hugh C. Heyliger.

Health and Women's Affairs, Hon. Constance Mitcham.

Trade and Industry, Hon. Fitzroy P. Jones.

In Ministry of Finance, Hon. Richard L. Caines.

Attorney-General, Hon. S. W. Tapley Seaton, C.V.O.

Cabinet Secretary, C. Farier.

ST. KITTS HIGH COMMISSION
10 Kensington Court, W8 5DL
[01-937 9522]

High Commissioner for the Eastern Caribbean States, His Excellency Richard Gunn (1987).

FINANCE

	1987	1988
Revenue	EC$72,927,410	EC$79,275,862
Expenditure	69,456,759	78,453,932

ECONOMY

The economy of the islands has been based on sugar for over three centuries. Tourism and light industry are now being developed. The economy of Nevis centres on small peasant farmers, but a sea-island cotton industry is being developed for export.

COMMUNICATIONS

Basseterre is a port of registry and has deep water harbour facilities. Golden Rock airport, on St. Kitts, can take most large jet aircraft; Newcastle airstrip on Nevis can take small aircraft and has night landing facilities.

The sea ferry route from Basseterre to Charlestown is 11 miles.

Trade with U.K.

	1987	1988
Imports from U.K.	£7,041,000	£8,025,000
Exports to U.K.	4,677,000	4,271,000

ST. LUCIA

St. Lucia, the second largest of the Windward group, situated in 13° 54′ N. lat. and 60° 50′ W. long., at a distance of about 21 miles N. of St. Vincent, and 24 miles S. of Martinique, is 27 miles in length, with an extreme breadth of 14 miles. It comprises an area of 238 sq. miles (616 sq. km.), with an estimated population (1986) of 138,000. It possesses perhaps the most interesting history of all the smaller islands. Fights raged hotly around it, and it constantly changed hands between the English and the French. It is mountainous, its highest point being Mt. Gimie (3,145 feet) and for the most part it is covered with forest and tropical vegetation.

CAPITAL.—ΨCastries (estimated population 1988, 55,000) is recognized as being one of the finest ports in the West Indies on account of its reputation as a safe anchorage in the hurricane season.

CURRENCY.—East Caribbean dollar (EC$) of 100 cents.

FLAG.—Blue, bearing in centre a device of yellow over black over white triangles having a common base.

NATIONAL ANTHEM.—"Sons and Daughters of Saint Lucia."

NATIONAL DAY.—February 22 (Independence Day).

GOVERNMENT

St. Lucia became independent within the Commonwealth on Feb. 22, 1979. The Head of State is H.M. The Queen, represented in the island by a St. Lucian Governor General, and there is a bicameral legislature. The Senate has 11 members, 6 appointed by the ruling party, 3 by the Opposition and 2 by the Governor General. The House of Assembly, which has a life of five years, has 17 elected Members and a Speaker, who may be elected from outside the House.

Acting Governor General, His Excellency Stanislaus James, O.B.E.

Cabinet
(as at June 30, 1989)

Prime Minister, Minister of Finance, Foreign Affairs, Development and Home Affairs, Rt. Hon. John G. M. Compton.

Deputy P.M. and Minister of Trade, Industry and Tourism, Hon. George Mallet.

Communications, Works and Transport, Hon. Senator Desmond Fostin.

Health, Housing, Labour, Information and Broadcasting, Hon. Romanus Lansiquot.

Youth, Community Development, Social Affairs, Sport, Hon. Stephenson King.

Attorney General and Minister for Legal Affairs, Hon. Senator Parry Husbands.

Agriculture, Lands, Fisheries and Co-operatives, Hon. Ferdinand Henry.

Education and Culture, Hon. Louis George.

ST. LUCIA HIGH COMMISSION
10 Kensington Court, W8 5DL.
[01–937 9522]

High Commissioner for the Eastern Caribbean States, His Excellency Richard Gunn (1987).

ECONOMY

The economy is mainly agrarian, with manufacturing based on the processing of agricultural products. Principal crops are bananas, coconuts, cocoa, mangoes, avocado pears, breadfruit, spices, root crops such as cassava and yams, and citrus fruit. Attempts are being made to diversify the economy, in particular through greater industrialization; tourism is also of increasing importance, with 181,915 visiting the island in 1988.

The principal exports are bananas, coconut products (copra, edible oils, soap), cardboard boxes, beer, and textile manufactures. The chief imports are flour, meat, machinery, building materials, motor vehicles, cotton piece goods, petroleum and fertilizers.

Trade with U.K.

	1987	1988
Imports from U.K.	£13,196,000	£19,750,000
Exports to U.K.	40,908,000	58,385,000

OFFICE OF THE BRITISH HIGH COMMISSION
Columbus Square, P.O. Box 227, Castries.
[Castries 22484]

High Commissioner, (resides at Bridgetown, Barbados).

Resident Representative, C. H. Woodland.

ST. VINCENT AND THE GRENADINES

The territory of the State of St. Vincent includes certain of the Grenadines, a chain of small islands stretching 40 miles across the Caribbean Sea between Grenada and St. Vincent, some of the larger of which are Bequia, Canouan, Mayreau, Mustique, Union Island, Petit St. Vincent and Prune Island. The whole territory extends 150 sq. miles (388 sq. km.).

The main island, St. Vincent, is situated between 13° 6′ and 14° 35′ N. latitude and 61° 6′ and 61° 20′ W. longitude, approximately 21 miles south west of St. Lucia and 100 miles west of Barbados. The island is 18 miles long and 11 miles wide at its extremities comprising an area of 133 sq. miles (344 sq. km.), and a population (1985 U.N. estimate) of 104,000. St. Vincent was discovered by Christopher Columbus in 1498. It was granted by Charles I to the Earl of Carlisle in 1627 and after subsequent grants and a series of occupations alternately by the French and English, it was finally restored to Britain in 1783.

CAPITAL.—ΨKingstown, population approximately 33,694.

CURRENCY.—East Caribbean dollar (EC$) of 100 cents.

FLAG.—Three vertical bands, of blue, yellow and green, with three green diamonds in the shape of a "V" mounted on the yellow band.

NATIONAL ANTHEM.—St. Vincent, Land So Beautiful.

NATIONAL DAY.—October 27 (Independence Day).

GOVERNMENT

St. Vincent and the Grenadines achieved full independence within the Commonwealth on Oct. 27, 1979.

St. Vincent has a constitution under which there is a Governor General who is Her Majesty's Representative. Except where otherwise provided, the Governor General is required to act in accordance with the advice of the Prime Minister.

The House of Assembly consists of 15 elected members and 6 Senators appointed by the Government (4) and the Opposition (2). It is presided over by a Speaker elected by the House from within or without it. All 15 seats were won by the governing New Democratic Party at the election held on May 16, 1989.

Acting Governor General, His Excellency Henry Williams, *sworn in* Feb. 29, 1988.

Cabinet
(as at May 31, 1989)

Prime Minister, Minister of Finance and Foreign Affairs, Rt. Hon. James Mitchell.

Attorney General and Minister of Justice, Information and Culture, Hon. Parnell Campbell, C.V.O.

Education, Youth and Women's Affairs, Hon. John Horne.

Agriculture, Industry and Labour, Hon. Allan Cruickshank.

Trade and Tourism, Hon. Herbert Young.

Health and the Environment, Hon. Burton Williams.

Housing, Local Government, Community Development and Social Welfare, Hon. Louis Jones.

Communications and Works, Hon. Jeremiah Scott.

Ministers of State, Hon. Mrs. Yvonne Gibson (*Education, Youth and Women's Affairs*); Hon. Jonathan Peters (*Trade and Tourism*).

ST. VINCENT AND THE GRENADINES
HIGH COMMISSION
10 Kensington Court, W8 5DL
[01-937 9522]

High Commissioner for the Eastern Caribbean States, His Excellency Richard Gunn (1987).

ECONOMY

This is based mainly on agriculture but the tourist and manufacturing industries have been expanding. The main products are bananas, arrowroot, coconuts, sugar, cocoa, spices and various kinds of food crops. The main imports are foodstuffs (meat, rice, beverages), textiles, lumber, cement and other building materials, fertilizers, motor vehicles and fuel.

EDUCATION

Primary and secondary education in Government schools is free but not compulsory. In 1982 there were 24,651 enrolments in state primary schools and 5,501 enrolments in state secondary schools.

Trade with U.K.

	1987	1988
Imports from U.K.	£8,529,000	£8,011,000
Exports to U.K.	20,208,000	29,709,000

OFFICE OF THE BRITISH HIGH COMMISSION
Granby Street (P.O. Box 132), Kingstown.
[St Vincent 71701]

High Commissioner, (resides at Bridgetown, Barbados).
Resident Representative, G. Greaves.

SEYCHELLES
(The Republic of Seychelles)

The Republic of Seychelles, in the Indian Ocean, consists of 115 islands with a total land area of 108 sq. miles (280 sq. km.), spread over 400,000 square miles of ocean. There is a relatively compact granitic group, 32 islands in all, with high hills and mountains (highest point about 2,990 ft.), of which Mahé is the largest and most populated (90 per cent of the population live on Mahé): and the outlying coralline group, for the most part, only a little above sea-level. Although only 4° S. of the Equator, the climate is pleasant though tropical. The population was estimated (mid 1988) to be 66,745.

CAPITAL.—ΨVictoria (population, 1982, 24,733), on the N.E. side of Mahé.
CURRENCY.—Seychelles rupee (Rs) of 100 cents.
FLAG.—Red over green, divided by wavy white band.
NATIONAL ANTHEM.—Fyer Seselwa (Proud Seychellois).
NATIONAL DAY.—June 5.

GOVERNMENT

Proclaimed as French territory in 1756, the Mahé group began to be settled as a dependency of Mauritius from 1770, was captured by a British ship in 1794, changed hands several times between 1803 and 1814, when it was finally assigned to Great Britain. By Letters Patent of September, 1903, these islands, together with the coralline group, were formed into a separate Colony. On June 29, 1976, the islands became an independent republic within the Commonwealth. A coup d'état took place on June 5, 1977.

A new constitution making Seychelles a one-party state came into force in June 1979. The executive power lies with the President, who is elected by universal suffrage for a five year term. Legislative power lies with the President and the People's Assembly which has 23 elected members and two nominated by the President.

President, France Albert René, *assumed office* June 5, 1977; *elected* June 26, 1979; *re-elected* June 18, 1984, and June 12, 1989.

Council of Ministers
(as at Aug. 1, 1989)

Legal Affairs, Industry, Environment and Defence, The President.
Finance, James Michel.
Tourism and Transport, Jacques Hodoul.
Labour and Social Services, Joseph Belmont.
Community Development, Esme Jumeau.
Foreign Relations, Danielle de St. Jorre.
Health, Ralph Adam.
Agriculture and Fisheries, Jeremie Bonnelame.
Employment, William Herminie.
Education, Simone Testa.
Information and Culture, Sylvette Frichot.

SEYCHELLES HIGH COMMISSION
Box No. 4PE, 50 Conduit Street, W1A 4PE
[01–439 0405]

High Commissioner, His Excellency Robert F. Delpech (1987).

ECONOMY

The economy is based on tourism, fishing, small-scale agriculture and manufacturing, and the re-export of fuel for aircraft and ships. Copra and cinnamon bark have lost their importance as exports.

Deep sea tuna fishing by foreign fleets under licence, improved trans-shipment and other port facilities at Victoria, exports from a tuna canning factory opened in 1987 and the export of fresh and frozen fish, attract growing revenues.

TRADE

	1985	1986
Imports	Rs.718,700,000	Rs.686,600,000
Exports	19,500,000	14,500,000
Re-exports......	177,200,000	94,200,000

The principal imports are foodstuffs, beverages, tobacco, mineral fuels, manufactured items, building materials, machinery and transport equipment.

Trade with U.K.

	1987	1988
Imports from U.K.	£10,770,000	£10,478,000
Exports to U.K.	880,000	1,297,000

BRITISH HIGH COMMISSION
Victoria House, P.O. Box 161,
Victoria, Mahé.
[Victoria 23055]

High Commissioner, His Excellency Guy William Pulbrook Hart, O.B.E. (1989).

SIERRA LEONE
(The Republic of Sierra Leone)

AREA, POPULATION, ETC.—Sierra Leone, with a total land area of 27,699 sq. miles (71,740 sq. km.), is on the west coast of Africa, between Guinea and Liberia. A Census of December 1985 put the population at 3,700,000. The origins of the country date back to the late 18th century when a project was begun to settle destitute Africans from England on Freetown peninsula. In 1808 the settlement was declared a Crown Colony and became the main base in West Africa for enforcing the 1807 Act outlawing the slave trade. The Colony was also used as a settlement for Africans from North America and the West Indies, and great numbers of Africans rescued from slave ships, also settled there. Their descendants, known as Creoles, still live on Freetown peninsula. The southern half of Sierra Leone is inhabited by peoples whose languages fall into the Mende group; the northern half by the Temne, and smaller groups such as the Limba, Loko, Koranko and Susu.

CAPITAL.—ΨFreetown (population at 1985 Census, 470,000).

CURRENCY.—Leone (Le) of 100 cents.

FLAG.—Three horizontal stripes of leaf green, white and cobalt blue.

NATIONAL ANTHEM.—"High We Exalt Thee, Realm of the Free."

NATIONAL DAY.—April 27 (Independence Day).

GOVERNMENT

Sierra Leone became a fully independent state within the Commonwealth on April 27, 1961. On April 19, 1971 a Republican Constitution was adopted and Dr. Siaka Stevens became the first Executive President. In June 1978 Sierra Leone became a one-Party State, following approval by Parliament and a Referendum. The first General Election under the one party system was held on May 1, 1982. The Parliament now comprises 85 elected members and 12 Paramount Chiefs, plus nine nominated members, two of whom are the Army Commander and the Inspector General of Police.

President, His Excellency Maj.-Gen. Joseph Saidu Momoh, *sworn in* Nov. 28, 1985.

Cabinet
(as at June 30, 1989)

President and Minister of Defence with responsibility for Public Services, His Excellency Maj.-Gen. J. S. Momoh.
First Vice-President, Hon. Abu Bakarr Kamara.
Second Vice-President, Hon. Salia Jusu Sheriff.
Finance, Hon. Hassan Gbessay Kanu.
Attorney-General and Minister of Justice, Hon. Dr. Abdulai Conteh.
Foreign Affairs, Hon. Abdul Karim Koroma.
Economic Planning and National Development, Hon. Dr. Sheka Kanu.
Agriculture, Natural Resources and Forestry, Hon. M. O. Bash-Taqi.
Trade, Hon. Joseph Bandabla Dauda.
Education, Cultural Affairs and Sports, Hon. Dr. Moses Dumbuya.
Transport and Communications, Hon. Philipson Kamara.
Mines, Hon. Birch Conteh.
Health, Hon. Dr. Wiltshire Johnson.
Works, Hon. J. E. Laverse.
Energy and Power, Hon. Dr. Shekou Sesay.
Information and Broadcasting, Hon. V. J. V. Mambu.
Tourism, Hon. Abdul Iscandari.
Internal Affairs, Hon. Ahmed Sesay.
Rural Development, Social Services and Youth, Hon. Alhaji Musa Kabia.
Industry and State Enterprises, Hon. Ben Kanu.
Labour, Hon. M. L. Sidique.
Lands, Housing and Environment, Hon. Dominic Musa.
Ministers of State, Hon. E. R. Ndomahina (*Leader of the House*); Hon. Maj.-Gen. M. Sheku Tarawallie (*Force Cdr.*); Hon. James Bambay Kamara (*Inspector General of Police*); Hon. E. T. Kamara (*Party Affairs*).

SIERRA LEONE HIGH COMMISSION
33 Portland Place, W1N 3AG
[01–636 6483–6]

High Commissioner, His Excellency Caleb B. Aubee (1987).

COMMUNICATIONS

Since the phasing out of the railway system in 1974 the road network has been developed considerably and there are now 5,000 miles of roads in the country, over 2,000 miles being surfaced. A bridge has been constructed over the Mano River linking Sierra Leone and Liberia.

The Freetown international airport is situated at Lungi, across the Sierra Leone River from Freetown. The main port is Freetown, which has one of the largest natural harbours in the world, and where there is a deep water quay providing about six berths for medium sized ships. There are smaller ports at Pepel, Bonthe and Niti.

Radio and television are operated by the Department of Broadcasting of the Sierra Leone Government. There are two shortwave transmitting and receiving stations in Freetown. Broadcasts are made in several of the more important indigenous languages in addition to English. There is also a weekly broadcast in French.

EDUCATION

In 1988 there were 2,294 primary schools in Sierra Leone and 205 secondary schools. Technical education is provided in the two Government Technical Institutes, situated in Freetown and Kenema, in two Trade Centres and in the technical training establishments of the mining companies. Teacher training is carried out at the university, six colleges in the Provinces and in the Milton Margai Training College near Freetown. The University of Sierra Leone (1967), consists of Fourah Bay College (1827), the Institute of Public Administration and Management (1980), the College of Medicine and Allied Health Sciences (1988) and Njala University College (1964).

PRODUCTION AND TRADE

On the Freetown peninsula, farming is largely confined to the production of cassava and garden crops, such as maize and vegetables, for local consumption. In the hinterland, the principal agricultural product is rice, which is the staple food of the country, and cash crops such as cocoa, coffee, palm kernels, and ginger.

The economy depends largely on mineral exports; mainly diamonds, gold, bauxite and rutile. Iron ore production ceased in March 1985. Diamond exports provided Le447m in 1986. Total imports for 1988 were Le5,215m and exports were Le3,317·1m.

Trade with U.K.

	1987	1988
Imports from U.K.	£16,221,019	£14,256,000
Exports to U.K.	12,678,907	14,462,000

BRITISH HIGH COMMISSION
Standard Bank of Sierra Leone Building
Lightfoot Boston Street, Freetown
[Freetown 23961/5]

High Commissioner, His Excellency Derek William Partridge, C.M.G. (1986).
British Council Representative, Theresa Harvey, P.O. Box 124, Tower Hill, Freetown.

SINGAPORE

AREA, POPULATION, ETC.—The Republic of Singapore consists of the island of Singapore and 57 smaller islands, covering a total area of 224 sq. miles (581 sq. km.). Singapore island is 26 miles long and 14 miles in breadth and is situated just north of the Equator off the southern extremity of the Malay Peninsula, from which it is separated by the Straits of Johore. A causeway, carrying a road, railway and a water pipeline, crosses the three-quarters of a mile to the mainland. The highest point of the island is 581 feet above sea level. The climate is hot and humid and there are no clearly defined seasons. Rainfall averages 240 cm. a year and temperature ranges from 24°–32° C (76°–89° F).

In June 1987, the population was 2,612,800. (Chinese, 1,988,600; Malays, 393,800; Indians, 169,100; others (Europeans, Eurasians, etc.), 61,300. Malay, Mandarin, Tamil and English are the official languages. At least 8 Chinese dialects are used.

CURRENCY.—Singapore dollar (S$) of 100 cents.

FLAG.—Horizontal bands of red over white; crescent with five five-point stars on red band near staff.

NATIONAL ANTHEM.—Majulah Singapura.

NATIONAL DAY.—August 9.

GOVERNMENT

Singapore, where Sir Stamford Raffles had first established a trading post under the East India Company in 1819, was incorporated with Penang and Malacca to form the Straits Settlements in 1826. The Straits Settlements became a Crown Colony in 1867. Singapore fell into Japanese hands in 1942 and civil government was not restored until 1946, when it became a separate colony. Internal self-government and the title "State of Singapore" were introduced in 1959. Singapore became a state of Malaysia when the Federation was enlarged in September, 1963, but left Malaysia and became an independent sovereign state within the Commonwealth on August 9, 1965. Singapore adopted a Republican constitution from that date, the Yang di-Pertuan Negara being restyled President. There is a Cabinet collectively responsible to a fully-elected Parliament of 81 members.

After the General Election of Sept. 3, 1988 the People's Action Party (PAP) had 80 seats in Parliament. The other seat was taken by the Singapore Democratic Party (SDP).

HEAD OF STATE

President, Wee Kim Wee, *elected* Aug. 30, 1985.

Cabinet
(as at June 30, 1989)

Prime Minister, Lee Kuan Yew, G.C.M.G., C.H..

First Deputy P.M. and Minister for Defence, Goh Chok Tong.

Second Deputy P.M., Ong Teng Cheong.

National Development, S. Dhanabalan.

Education, Dr. Tony Tan Keng Yam.

Environment, Dr. Ahmad Mattar.

Communications and Information, Dr. Yeo Ning Hong.

Law and Home Affairs, Prof. S. Jayakumar.

Finance, Dr. Richard Hu Tsu Tau.

Labour, Lee Yock Suan.

Foreign Affairs and Community Development, Wong Kan Seng.

Trade and Industry, Lee Hsien Loong.

Health (acting), Yeo Cheow Tong.

Speaker of Parliament, Tan Soo Khoon.

SINGAPORE HIGH COMMISSION
2 Wilton Crescent, SW1X 8RW
[01–235 8315]

High Commissioner, His Excellency Abdul Aziz Mahmood (1988).

COMMUNICATIONS

Singapore is one of the largest and busiest seaports in the world, with deep water wharves and ship repairing facilities. Ships also anchor in the roads,

unloading into lighters. In 1988, 90,600,000 freight tonnes of seaborne cargo was discharged and 64,100,000 freight tonnes loaded. More than 500 shipping lines use the port, with 35,966 ship arrivals in 1988. The international airport is at Changi, in the east of the island. There are 25·75 km. of metric gauge railway connected to the Malaysian rail system by the causeway across the Straits of Johore, and 2,760 kilometres of roads. There are both wireless and wired broadcasting services carrying commercial advertising. There are three television channels. The Singapore Broadcasting Authority Corporation was established in February 1980.

ECONOMY

Historically Singapore's economy was largely based on the sale and distribution of raw materials from surrounding countries and on entrepot trade in finished products. In the last decade, however, new manufacturing industries have been introduced, including ship building and repairing, iron and steel, textiles, footwear, wood products, micro-electronics, scientific instruments, detergents, confectionery, pharmaceuticals, petroleum products, etc. Singapore has also become a financial centre with 137 commercial banks and 63 merchant banks established in the Republic, and an oil-refining centre.

Projects now being undertaken include the improvement of public utilities (electricity and gas supply, sewage system); the natural gas pipeline from the Straits of Johore to Senoko power station; the Jurong port expansion project; the new container terminal at Pulai Brani; a submarine telephone cable system; building projects; computerization in schools and government departments; and the near completion of the Mass Rapid Transit Rail system and the second passenger terminal at Changi Airport.

Finance (estimates)

	1988–89	1989–90
Revenue	S$11,560·0m	S$13,274·3m
Expenditure	12,470·0m	12,634·9m

Trade

	1987	1988
Total imports	S$68,415·2m	S$88,226·7m
Total exports	60,265·7m	79,051·3m

Trade with U.K.

	1987	1988
Imports from U.K.	£602,627,000	£632,452,000
Exports to U.K.	473,814,000	579,368,000

BRITISH HIGH COMMISSION
Tanglin Road, Singapore 1024
[Singapore 4739333]

High Commissioner, His Excellency Michael Edmund Pike, C.M.G. (1987).

British Council Representative, D. R. Howell, O.B.E., 30 Napier Road, Singapore 1025.

SOLOMON ISLANDS

Forming a scattered archipelago of mountainous islands and low-lying coral atolls, the Solomon Islands stretches about 900 miles in a south-easterly direction from Bougainville, in Papua New Guinea, to the Santa Cruz islands. The archipelago covers an area of about 249,000 square nautical miles while the land area is 10,938 sq. miles (28,446 sq. km.). Solomon Islands lies between the east longitudes 155° 30′ and 170° 30′ and between south latitudes 5° 10′ and 12° 45′. The six biggest islands are: Choiseul, New Georgia, Santa Isabel, Guadalcanal, Malaita and Makira. They are characterized by precipitous, thickly-forested mountain ranges intersected by deep, narrow valleys, and vary between 90 to 120 miles in length and between 20 to 30 miles in width.

Distribution of population at the Census of 1986 was: Melanesian 268,536; Polynesian 10,661; Micronesian 3,929; European 1,107; Chinese 379; Others 564. Total 285,176.

CAPITAL.—ΨHoniara (population (1986), 30,499).

CURRENCY.—Solomon Islands dollar (SI$) of 100 cents.

FLAG.—Blue over green divided by a diagonal yellow band, with five white stars in the top left quarter.

NATIONAL ANTHEM.—God Bless our Solomon Islands.

NATIONAL DAY.—July 7 (Independence Day).

GOVERNMENT

The origin of the present Melanesian inhabitants is uncertain. European discovery of the islands began in the mid-16th century and continued intermittently for about 300 years, when the inauguration of sugar plantations in Queensland and Fiji (which created a need for labour) and the arrival of missionaries and traders led to increased European interest in the region. Great Britain declared a Protectorate in 1893 over the Southern Solomons, adding the Santa Cruz group in 1898 and 1899. The islands of the Shortland groups were transferred by treaty from Germany to Great Britain in 1900.

The Solomon Islands achieved internal self-government in 1976, and became independent in July 1978. The Solomon Islands is a constitutional monarchy, H.M. The Queen being represented locally by the Governor General. Legislative power is vested in a unicameral National Parliament of 38 members, elected for a four-year term. The executive authority is exercised by the Cabinet.

Governor General, (new appointment awaited).

Cabinet

Prime Minister, Hon. Solomon Mamaloni.
Deputy P.M. and Minister for Home Affairs, Danny Philip.
Agriculture and Lands, Abraham Kapei.
Education and Human Resources Development, Albert Laore.
Finance and Economic Planning, Christopher Columbus Abe.
Foreign Affairs and Trade Relations, Sir Baddeley Devesi, G.C.M.G., G.C.V.O.
Health and Medical Services, Nathaniel Supa.
Housing and Government Services, Allan Qurusu.
Natural Resources, Allen Paul.
Police and Justice, Allen Kemakeza.
Post and Communications, Ben Gale.
Provincial Government, Nathaniel Waena.
Tourism and Aviation, Victor Ngele.
Transport, Works and Utilities, Michael Maena.
Commerce and Primary Industries, Edmund Andressen.

JUDICIARY

The High Court of Solomon Islands, constituted by the Solomon Islands Independence Order, consists of a Chief Justice and not fewer than two nor more than three Puisne Judges. The Court of Appeal Act was enacted on May 8, 1978.

COMMUNICATIONS

Solomon Islands Airways Ltd. serves 28 airstrips throughout the country, four of which are designated international airports. It also has combined services with Quantas making two flights each way weekly

between Honiara and Brisbane and one each way between Honiara and Nadi. Air Niugini has a weekly combined service with Solomon Islands Airways.

There are about 52 miles of secondary and minor roads in the urban areas of Honiara, Auki and Gizo. About 18 miles of road in and around Honiara and one mile in Auki and Gizo are bitumen sealed, the remainder being coral or gravel surfaced. In the rural areas there are some 800 miles of road, including those in private plantations, forestry areas and roads built and maintained by councils. All main islands have transreceivers to maintain communications with Honiara and there is a telephone link between Honiara and Auki, Gizo and Tulagi.

Telekom, a company jointly owned by Cable and Wireless Limited and Solomon Islands Government operates the international telephone circuits from a ground station in Honiara via the Intelsat Pacific Ocean communication satellite.

FINANCE AND TRADE

Revenue (1985), SI$63,567,000.

The main imports are foodstuffs, consumer goods, machinery and transport materials. Principal exports are timber, fish, copra, and palm oil. Other exports include cocoa and marine shells.

Trade with U.K.

	1987	1988
Imports from U.K.	£1,566,000	£2,576,000
Exports to U.K.	4,461,000	5,153,000

BRITISH HIGH COMMISSION
Telekom House, Mendana Avenue, (P.O. Box 676), Honiara.
[Honiara 21705]

High Commissioner, His Excellency (David) Junor Young (1988).

SRI LANKA
(Sri Lanka Prajatantrika Samajawadi Janarajaya)

AREA, POPULATION, ETC.—Sri Lanka (formerly Ceylon) is an island in the Indian Ocean, off the southern tip of the peninsula of India and separated from it by a narrow strip of shallow water, the Palk Strait. Situated between 5° 55′–9° 50′ N. latitude and 79° 42′–81° 52′ E. longitude, it has an area of 25,332 sq. miles (65,610 sq. km.), including 33 square miles of inland water. Its greatest length is from north to south, 270 miles; and its greatest width 140 miles, no point in Sri Lanka being more than 80 miles from the sea.

The population at the 1981 census was 14,800,001. (A 1985 U.N. estimate gave a figure of 15,837,000.) Of these 74 per cent were Sinhalese, 12·6 per cent Sri Lankan Tamils, 5·6 per cent Indian Tamils, 7·1 per cent Sri Lankan Moors and 0·7 per cent Burghers, Malays and others. The religion of the great majority of inhabitants is Buddhism, introduced from India, according to ancient Sinhalese chronicles, in 247 B.C. After Buddhism (69·3 per cent), Hinduism has the largest following (15·5 per cent); 7·6 per cent of the population are Muslims and 7·5 per cent Christians. The national languages are Sinhalese, Tamil and English.

Forests, jungle and scrub cover the greater part of the island, often being intermingled. In areas over 2,000 feet above sea level grasslands (*patanas* or *talawas*) are found. One of the highest peaks in the central massif is Adam's Peak (7,360 ft), a place of pilgrimage for Buddhists, Hindus and Muslims.

The climate of Sri Lanka is warm throughout the

year, with a high relative humidity. In the hills the climate is more temperate. Temperatures average 27° C. in the lowlands, and 16° C. at elevations over 6,000 ft. Day humidity is over 70 per cent and night humidity over 85 per cent. Rainfall is generally heavy, with marked regional variations. The two main monsoon seasons are mid-May to September (south-west) and November to March (north-east).

CAPITAL.—ΨColombo, population (1981) 585,776. 1984 estimate 643,000. Other principal towns are ΨJaffna (118,215), Kandy (101,281), ΨGalle (77,183), ΨNegombo (51,376) and ΨTrincomalee (44,913).

CURRENCY.—Sri Lankan rupee of 100 cents.

FLAG.—On a dark red field, within a golden border, a golden lion passant holding a sword in its right paw, and a representation of a *bo*-leaf, issuing from each corner; and to its right, two vertical stripes of saffron and green also placed within a golden border, to represent the minorities of the country.

NATIONAL ANTHEM.—Namo Namo Matha (We all stand together).

NATIONAL DAY.—February 4 (Independence Commemoration Day).

GOVERNMENT

Early in the sixteenth century the Portuguese landed in Ceylon and founded settlements, eventually conquering much of the country. Portuguese rule in Ceylon lasted 150 years, but in 1658, following a twenty-year period of decline, Portuguese rule gave way to that of the Dutch East India Company which was to exploit Ceylon with varying fortunes until 1796.

The Maritime Provinces of Ceylon were ceded by the Dutch to the British on February 16, 1798, becoming a British Crown Colony in 1802 under the terms of the Treaty of Amiens. With the annexation of the Kingdom of Kandy in 1815, all Ceylon came under British rule.

On February 4, 1948, Ceylon became a self-governing state and a member of the British Commonwealth of Nations. A republican Constitution was adopted on May 22, 1972, providing for a unicameral legislature, the National State Assembly, which has a six year term, and the country was renamed the Republic of Sri Lanka (meaning 'Resplendent Island'). On Sept. 5, 1978 a new Constitution introduced the title the Democratic Socialist Republic of Sri Lanka and a system of proportional representation. Legislative power is exercised by Parliament, the executive power being exercised by the President. A referendum in Dec. 1982 extended the life of the 1977 Parliament by six years from Aug. 1983.

A Bill providing for the holding of the Provincial Council elections was passed on Jan. 22, 1988. President Jayewardene issued a proclamation on Sept. 8, 1988, merging the Northern and Eastern Provinces, as envisaged under the Indo-Sri Lanka Agreement. The Eelam People's Revolutionary Liberation Front (E.P.R.L.F.) gained a clear majority in the Northern-Eastern Provincial Council, while the ruling United National Party (UNP) gained an absolute majority in elections to the seven other newly formed Provincial Councils.

In the General Election of February 15, 1989 the United National Party gained a decisive victory. The results were as follows: United National Party 125 seats, Sri Lanka Freedom Party 67, Independent Tamils 14, Tamil United Liberation Front 10, Sri Lanka Muslim Congress 3, United Socialist Alliance 3, Mahajana Eksath Peramuna 3.

President, His Excellency Ranasinghe Premadasa *elected* Dec. 20, 1988, *sworn* in Jan. 2, 1989 (*also Minister of Defence, Policy Planning and Implementation, and Buddha Sasana*).

Cabinet
(as at June 30, 1989)

Prime Minister and Minister of Finance, Hon. D. B. Wijetunge.
Transport and Highways, Hon. Wijayapala Mendis.
Higher Education, Science and Technology, Hon. A. C. S. Hameed.
Plantation Industries, Hon. Gamini Dissanayake.
Justice and Parliamentary Affairs, Hon. M. Vincent Perera.
Agriculture, Food and Co-operatives, Hon. Lalith Athulathmudali.
Power and Energy, Hon. Festus Perera.
Textiles and Rural Industrial Development, Hon. S. Thondaman.
Leader of the House and Minister of Industries, Hon. Ranil Wickramasinghe.
Labour and Social Welfare, Hon, Ranjith Atapattu.
Lands, Irrigation and Mahaweli Development, Hon. P. Dayaratne.
Fisheries and Aquatic Resources, Hon. Joseph Michael Perera.
Education, Cultural Affairs, and Information, Hon. W. J. M. Lokubandara.
Posts and Telecommunications, Hon. Alick Aluvihare.
Youth Affairs and Sports, Hon. C. Nanda Mathew.
Trade and Shipping, Hon. A. R. Munsoor.
Public Administration, Provincial Councils and Home Affairs, Hon. U. B. Wijekoon.
Health and Women's Affairs, Hon. Renuka Herath.
Tourism, Hon. A. M. S. Adikari.
Housing and Construction, Hon. B. Sirisena Cooray.
Foreign Affairs, Hon. Ranjan Wijeratne.

SRI LANKAN HIGH COMMISSION
13 Hyde Park Gardens, W2 2LU
[01–262 1841]

High Commissioner, His Excellency Chandra Monerawela (1984).

THE JUDICATURE

The Judicial System provides for a Supreme Court, a Court of Appeal, a High Court and other Courts of First Instance.

COMMUNICATIONS

There are over 15,660 miles of motorable roads in Sri Lanka and a government-run railway system with 984 miles of lines.

There is a satellite earth station at Padukka, in south-west Sri Lanka, which provides telecommunication links via satellite with any part of the globe.

The principal airports are at Katunayake, 19 miles north of Colombo, and Ratmalana, nine miles south of the capital. Air Lanka operates on 76 flights weekly to the Gulf States, the Maldives, Western Europe and throughout the Far East.

PRODUCTION

Agriculture.—The staple products of the island are tea, rubber, copra, spices and gems. There is increasing emphasis on local production of food, especially rice, and plans for the large-scale production of sugar cane, cotton and citrus fruits.

Industry.—Factories are established for the manufacture or processing of ceramic ware, vegetable oils and by-products, paper, tobacco, tanning and leather goods, plywood, cement, chemicals, sugar, flour, salt, textiles, ilmenite, tiles, tyres, fertilizers, clothing, jewellery and hardware and there is a petroleum refinery.

Trade with U.K.

	1987	1988
Imports from U.K........	£84,680,000	£92,528,000
Exports to U.K.	53,817,000	56,661,000

BRITISH HIGH COMMISSION
Galle Road, Kollupitiya (P.O. Box 1433),
Colombo 3
[Colombo 27611/9]

High Commissioner, His Excellency David Arthur Steuart Gladstone, C.M.G. (1987).

British Council Representative, R. A. K. Baker, 49 Alfred House Gardens, Colombo 3. Office also in *Kandy*.

SWAZILAND
(Umbuso we Swatini)

AREA, POPULATION, ETC.—Surrounded by South Africa on its northern, western and southern borders and by Mozambique to the east, this small land-locked country is geographically and climatically divided into three principal areas. The broken mountainous Highveld along the western border with an average altitude of 4,000 feet is densely forested mainly with conifers and eucalyptus; the Middleveld, averaging about 2,000 feet, is a mixed farming area including cotton and pineapples; and the Lowveld in the east, which was mainly scrubland until the introduction of large sugar cane plantations west of the Lubombo mountain range and the Mozambique border. Four rivers, the Komati, Usutu, Mbuluzi and Ngwavuma, flow from west to east. The total area of Swaziland is 6,704 sq. miles (17,363 sq. km.), and the population is estimated at some 731,000.

CAPITAL.—Mbabane (population, estimated 30,000), the headquarters of the Government, is situated at an average altitude of 3,800 ft. Other main townships are: Manzini (population, estimated 30,000), Big Bend, Mhlambanyati, Mhlume, Nhlangano, Pigg's Peak and Simunye.

CURRENCY.—Lilangeni (E) of 100 cents. South African currency is also in circulation. Swaziland is a member of the Common Monetary Area and its unit of currency *Emalangeni* (singular *Lilangeni*) has a par value with the South African Rand.

FLAG.—Five horizontal bands, crimson, bearing shield and spears device, bordered by narrow yellow bands; blue bands at top and foot.

NATIONAL ANTHEM.—Elwatini.

NATIONAL DAY.—September 6 (Independence Day).

GOVERNMENT

The Kingdom of Swaziland came into being on April 25, 1967, under a new internal self-government constitution and became an independent kingdom, headed by H.M. Sobhuza II, in membership of the Commonwealth on September 6, 1968.

A new electoral law was introduced in 1978, under which each of the 40 traditional Tinkhundla elect two members to the electoral college who elect 40 members to the House of Assembly. The King nominates 10 members to the House of Assembly, making 50 in all, who then elect 10 members (not of their own number) to the Senate. To these are added 10 senators nominated by the King, bringing the full membership of the Senate to 20. Under the Establishment of the Parliament of Swaziland Order, 1978, the Head of State, advised by the Swazi National Council, continues to reserve a large measure of executive, legislative and judicial authority.

Head of State, H.M. King Mswati III, *inaugurated* April 25, 1986.

Cabinet
(as at May 31, 1989)

Prime Minister, H. E. the Hon. Sotsha E. Dlamini.
Foreign Affairs, Hon. Senator George Mamba, G.C.V.O.
Labour and Public Service, Hon. Ben Nsibandze.
Defence and Youth, (vacant).
Justice, Hon. Reginald Dhladhla.
Education, Hon. Chief Sipho Shongwe.
Agriculture and Co-operatives, Hon. Sipho Hezekiel Mamba.
Finance, Hon. Barnabas Sibusiso Dlamini.
Commerce, Industry, Mines and Tourism, Hon. Nkomeni Douglas Ntiwane.
Natural Resources, Land Utilisation and Energy, H.R.H. the Hon. Prince Nqaba Dlamini.
Interior and Immigration, Hon. Enzenjani Enoch Shabalala.
Health, Hon. Dr. Fanie Friedman.
Works and Communications, Hon. Wilson Mkhonta.

KINGDOM OF SWAZILAND HIGH COMMISSION
58 Pont Street, SW1X 0AE
[01–581 4976/8]

High Commissioner, His Excellency Mboni N. Dlamini (1988).

EDUCATION

In 1982, there were 125,303 pupils enrolled at 470 primary schools and 26,576 at 86 secondary schools. The University of Swaziland was founded in 1976.

COMMUNICATIONS

Swaziland's railway is about 150 miles long and runs from Ngwenya in the west to the Mozambique border near Goba in the east, and thence to the Mozambique port of Maputo. A southern link from Phuzumoya in central Swaziland joins up with the South African railway network to Richards Bay. A rail link from Mpaka in central Swaziland to the north-west border opened in 1986 and provides a link to Komatipoort.

Most passenger and goods traffic is carried by privately-owned motor transport services. There are daily scheduled air services by Royal Swazi National Airways to Johannesburg and scheduled routes to Durban, Harare, Lusaka, Gaborone, Nairobi and Dar es Salaam. International telecommunications and television services are provided through a satellite earth station opened in 1983. There is also a national telephone network through a series of microwave links.

FINANCE

Government revenue for 1987–88 is estimated at E284,783,000, of which E134,928,000 (or 47·4 per cent) is anticipated revenue from the South African Common Customs Union with South Africa, Botswana and Lesotho. A local sales tax introduced from Sept. 1984 is expected to yield E38,412,000 in 1987–88. Total Government-financed recurrent and capital expenditure in 1987–88 is estimated at E295,857,000.

Trade with U.K.

	1987	1988
Imports from U.K........	£2,257,000	£1,564,000
Exports to U.K.	36,901,000	27,973,000

BRITISH HIGH COMMISSION
Allister Miller Street, Mbabane
[Mbabane 42581]

High Commissioner, His Excellency John Gerrard Flynn (1987).

TANZANIA
(Jamhuri ya Mwungano wa Tanzania)

AREA, POPULATION, ETC.—Tanganyika, the mainland part of the United Republic of Tanzania (Tanganyika and Zanzibar), occupies the east-central portion of the African continent, between 1°–11° 45′ S. lat. and 29° 20′–40° 38′ E. long. It is bounded on the N. by Kenya and Uganda; on the S.W. by Lake Malawi, Malawi and Zambia; on the S. by Mozambique; on the W. it is bounded by Rwanda, Burundi and Zaire; on the E. the boundary is the Indian Ocean. Tanzania has an area of 364,900 sq. miles (945,087 sq. km.). The greater part of the country is occupied by the Central African plateau from which rise, among others, Mt. Kilimanjaro (19,340 ft.), the highest point on the continent of Africa, and Mt. Meru (14,974 ft.). The Serengeti National Park, which covers an area of 6,000 sq. miles in the Arusha, Mwanza and Mara Regions, is famous for its variety and number of species of game.

The African population consists mostly of tribes of mixed Bantu race. The total population of Tanzania at the Census held in August, 1978 was 17,551,925; a 1985 estimate put the figure at 21,733,000. Africans form a very large majority, while Europeans, Asians, and other non-Africans form a small minority. Swahili is the national and official language. The use of English is widespread both for educational and government purposes.

Zanzibar.—Formerly ruled by the Sultan of Zanzibar, and a British Protectorate until Dec. 10, 1963. Zanzibar consists of the islands of Zanzibar, Pemba and Latham.

CAPITAL.—ΨDar es Salaam (population 1,096,000 1985 estimate). Other towns (1978 population) are ΨTanga (103,409); Mwanza (110,611); Arusha (55,281); Moshi (52,223); Morogoro (61,890); Dodoma (45,703); Tabora (67,392) and ΨMtwara (48,510). ΨZanzibar (population, 110,669) is the chief town and seaport of the island.

CURRENCY.—Tanzanian shilling of 100 cents.

FLAG.—Green (above) and blue; divided by diagonal black stripe bordered by gold, running from bottom (next staff) to top (in fly).

NATIONAL ANTHEM.—Mungu Ibariki Afrika (God Bless Africa).

NATIONAL DAY.—April 26 (Union Day).

GOVERNMENT

Tanganyika became an independent state and a member of the British Commonwealth on December 9, 1961, and a Republic, within the Commonwealth, on December 9, 1962, with an executive President, elected by universal suffrage as the Head of State and Head of the Government. On Dec. 10, 1963, Zanzibar became an independent state within the Commonwealth and on April 26, 1964, Tanganyika united with Zanzibar to form the United Republic of Tanzania.

Tanzania became a one-party state on July 10, 1965 but with the Tanganyika African National Union (TANU) and the Afro-Shirazi Party (ASP) remaining the ruling parties in Tanganyika and Zanzibar respectively. On Feb. 5, 1977 these two parties merged to form the Chama Cha Mapinduzi (CCM) (Revolutionary Party).

A new constitution was introduced on April 26, 1977 and revised in Oct. 1984. There is a President and two Vice-Presidents, one the President of Zanzibar and the other the Prime Minister. The President may only serve two five year terms and if he comes from Zanzibar the Prime Minister will be the First Vice-President and must come from Tanganyika. If the President comes from Tanganyika the President of Zanzibar will be the First Vice President. In a

Presidential election a single Presidential candidate nominated by the CCM has to obtain an affirmative majority of the votes cast, failing which a fresh candidate must be nominated. The National Assembly contains 243 members, of whom 118 are elected from mainland constituencies and 50 from Zanzibar, 25 are ex-officio, 15 nominated and 35 indirectly elected. The Speaker may either be elected from among the members or be an additional member. Constituency members are elected by popular vote at a general election held at a maximum of five-yearly intervals in which the CCM nominates two candidates to contest each seat.

A new constitution was also approved in 1984 for Zanzibar providing for an elected President and House of Representatives. Although Zanzibar has its own government and Chief Minister, Tanganyika is governed by the government of the Union. Overall policy is decided by the CCM whose chairman, Julius Nyerere, was re-elected in 1987 by the Party National Conference for a 5 year term.

President of the United Republic, H.E. Hon. Ali Hassan Mwinyi, *b.* 1925; *elected* Oct. 27, 1985; *sworn in* Nov. 5, 1985.
First Vice-President of the United Republic and Prime Minister, Hon. Joseph Sinde Warioba.
Second Vice-President of the United Republic and President of Zanzibar, H.E. Idris Abdul Wakil.

Cabinet
(as at June 30, 1989)

Deputy Prime Minister and Minister of Defence, Hon. Salim Ahmed Salim.
Without Portfolio, Hon. Rashidi Kawawa; Hon. Gertrude Mongella.
Foreign Affairs, Hon. Benjamin Mkapa.
Finance, Economic Affairs and Planning, Hon. Cleopa Msuya.
Communications and Works, Hon. Stephen Kibona.
Local Government Co-operatives and Marketing, Hon. Paul Bomani.
Agriculture and Livestock Development, Hon. Jackson Makwetta.
Labour and Manpower Development, Hon. Christian Kisanji.
Home Affairs, Hon. Brig. Muhidin Kimario.
Energy and Minerals, Hon. Al-Noor Kassum.
Lands, Natural Resources and Tourism, Hon. Arcado Ntagazwa.
Industry and Trade, Hon. Joseph Rwegasira.
Education, Hon. Amran Mayagilo.
Health and Social Welfare, Hon. Aaron Chiduo.
Justice, and Attorney-General, Hon. Damian Lubuva.
Water, Hon. Pius Ng'wandu.
Community Development, Culture, Youth and Sport, Hon. Fatima Saidi Ali.

TANZANIA HIGH COMMISSION
43 Hertford Street, W1Y 7TF
[01–499 8951]

High Commissioner, (new appointment awaited).

EDUCATION

Education, almost entirely under state control, is characterised by official insistence that education must serve the aims of overall Government policy and planning. All Tanzanian secondary schools are expected to include practical subjects in the basic course. All who receive secondary (or equivalent) education are called up for a period of National Service. The school system is administered in Swahili but the Government is making efforts to improve English standards for the purposes of secondary and higher education. For higher education Tanzanian students go to the University of Dar es Salaam, Sokoine University of Agriculture in Morogoro, other East African universities, or to universities and colleges outside East Africa, including Britain.

COMMUNICATIONS

The main port is Dar es Salaam, and there are other ports on the coast at Tanga, Mtwara, Zanzibar, Mkoani and Wete, in addition to Mwanza, Musoma and Bukoba on Lake Victoria and Kigoma on Lake Tanganyika. Coastal shipping services connect the mainland to Zanzibar, and lake services are operated on Lake Tanganyika and Lake Malawi with neighbouring countries.

The principal international airports are Dar es Salaam and Kilimanjaro. Other airports include Zanzibar, Arusha, Mwanza and Tanga.

There are two railway systems; one connecting Dar es Salaam to Zambia; and the second having two main lines running from Dar es Salaam, one to northern Tanzania and Kenya and the other to Lake Tanganyika and Victoria.

PRODUCTION AND TRADE

The economy is based mainly on the production and export of primary produce and the growing of foodstuffs for local consumption. The islands of Zanzibar and Pemba produce a large part of the world's supply of cloves and clove oil; and coconuts, coconut oil and copra are also produced. The mainland's chief export crops are coffee, cotton, sisal, tea, tobacco, cashew nuts and diamonds. The most important minerals are diamonds. Hides and skins are another valuable export. Industry is at present largely concerned with the processing of raw material for either export or local consumption. There are also secondary manufacturing industries, including factories for the manufacture of leather and rubber footwear, knitwear, razor blades, cigarettes and textiles, and a wheat flour mill.

Trade with U.K.

	1987	1988
Imports from U.K.	£91,874,000	£88,686,000
Exports to U.K.	26,400,000	26,386,000

BRITISH HIGH COMMISSION

Hifadhi House, Samora Avenue (P.O. Box 9200),
Dar es Salaam.
[Dar es Salaam 29601]

High Commissioner, His Excellency John Thorold Masefield, C.M.G. (1989).
British Council Representative, J. Mayatt, O.B.E., Samora Avenue, (P.O. Box 9100), Dar es Salaam.

TONGA
(Kingdom of Tonga)

Tonga, or the Friendly Islands, comprises a group of islands situated in the Southern Pacific some 450 miles to the E.S.E. of Fiji, with an area of 270 sq. miles (699 sq. km.), and population (1985 U.N. estimate) of 97,000. The largest island, Tongatapu, was discovered by Tasman in 1643. Most of the islands are of coral formation, but some are volcanic (Tofua, Kao and Niuafoou or "Tin Can" Island). The limits of the group are between 15° and 23° 30′ S., and 173° and 177° W.

CAPITAL.—ΨNuku'alofa (28,899), on Tongatapu.
CURRENCY.—Pa'anga (T$) of 100 seniti.
FLAG.—Truncated red cross on rectangular white ground (next staff) on a red field.

NATIONAL ANTHEM.—E, 'Otua Mafimafi (Oh, Almighty God Above).
NATIONAL DAY.—June 4 (Independence Day).

GOVERNMENT

The Kingdom of Tonga is an independent constitutional monarchy within the Commonwealth. Prior to June 4, 1970 it had been a British-protected state for 70 years. The constitution provides for a Government consisting of the Sovereign, a privy council and cabinet, a legislative assembly and a judiciary. The legislative assembly has 29 members, with a Speaker, and includes the Ministers of the Crown, the two Governors of Island groups, and the representatives of the Nobles and of the people (nine of each), who are elected triennially.

Head of State, H.M. King Taufa'ahau Tupou IV, G.C.M.G., G.C.V.O., K.B.E., *acceded* Dec. 16, 1965.
Heir, H.R.H. Crown Prince Tupouto'a.

Cabinet

Prime Minister and Minister of Agriculture, H.R.H. Prince Fatafehi Tu'ipelehake, K.B.E.
Labour, Commerce and Industries, Baron Vaea.
Health, Hon. Dr. S. Tapa.
Finance, Hon. J. C. Cocker.
Education, Works and Civil Aviation, Hon. Dr. S. L. Kavaliku.
Police, Hon. 'Akau'ola.
Foreign Affairs and Defence, H.R.H. Crown Prince Tupouto'a.
Justice, and Attorney General, Hon. Tevita Tupou.
Minister without portfolio, Hon. Ma'afu Tuku'i'aulahi.
Lands, Hon. Dr. Ma'afu Tupou (*acting*).
Governor of Vava'u, Hon. Tu'i'afitu (*acting*).
Governor of Ha'apai, Hon. Fakafanua.

TONGA HIGH COMMISSION

New Zealand House, Haymarket, SW1Y 4TE
[01–839 3287]

High Commissioner, His Excellency S. M. Tuita (1989).

ECONOMY

The economy is primarily agricultural; the main crops are coconuts, bananas, vanilla, yams, taro, cassava, groundnuts and other fruits. Fish is an important staple food though recent shortfalls have led to canned fish being imported. Industry is based on the processing of agricultural produce, and the manufacture of foodstuffs, clothing and sports equipment. The principal exports are copra, other coconut products, tropical root crops and bananas.

TRADE

	1984	1985
Total imports	T$46,614,000	T$58,900,000
Total exports	9,995,000	7,700,000

Trade with U.K.

	1987	1988
Imports from U.K.	£2,013,000	£856,000
Exports to U.K.	100,000	145,000

BRITISH HIGH COMMISSION

P.O. Box 56, Nuku'alofa
[Nuku'alofa 21020]

High Commissioner, His Excellency (Andrew) Paul Fabian (1987).

TRINIDAD AND TOBAGO
(The Republic of Trinidad and Tobago)

AREA, POPULATION, ETC.—*Trinidad*, the most southerly of the West Indian islands, lies close to the north coast of S. America, the nearest point being Venezuela, 7 miles distant. The island is situated between 10° 2′–11° 12′ N. lat. and 60° 30′–61° 56′ W. long., and is about 50 miles in length by 37 miles in width, with an area of 1,864 sq. miles (4,827 sq. km.). Two mountain systems, the Northern and Southern Ranges, stretch across almost its entire width and a third, the Central Range, lies diagonally across its middle portion; otherwise the island is mostly flat. The climate is tropical with temperatures averaging 82° F. (27·8° C) by day and 74° F. (23·3° C) by night, and a rainfall averaging 82 inches a year. There is a well-marked dry season from January to May, and a wet season from June to December broken by a short dry season (the Petite Careme) in September and October. The island was discovered by Columbus in 1498, was colonized in 1532 by the Spaniards, capitulated to the British under Abercromby in 1797, and was ceded to Britain under the Treaty of Amiens (March 25, 1802).

Tobago lies between 11° 9′ and 11° 21′ N. lat. and between 60° 30′ and 60° 50′ W. long., 19 miles northeast of Trinidad. The island is 32 miles long at its widest point, and 11 wide, and has an area of 116 sq. miles (300 sq. km.). It is a popular tourist resort. It was ceded to the British Crown in 1814 and amalgamated with Trinidad in 1888.

In 1985 the population of Trinidad and Tobago was estimated at 1,185,000.

Other Islands.—Corozal Point and Icacos Point, the N.W. and S.W. extremities of Trinidad, enclose the Gulf of Paria. West of Corozal Point lie several islands, of which Chacachacare, Huevos, Monos and Gaspar Grande are the most important.

CAPITAL.—ΨPort of Spain (population approximately 59,649 in 1985) is the administrative centre of the islands. About 33 miles south of the capital is San Fernando (population approximately 34,300 in 1985), a town of growing importance which is emerging as the industrial centre of Trinidad, and which is in close proximity to a number of large industrial plants. The main town of Tobago is ΨScarborough.

CURRENCY.—Trinidad and Tobago dollar (TT$) of 100 cents.

FLAG.—Black diagonal stripe bordered with white stripes, running from top by staff, all on a red field.

NATIONAL DAYS.—August 31 (Independence Day); September 24 (Republic Day).

GOVERNMENT

The Territory of Trinidad and Tobago became an independent state and a member of the British Commonwealth on August 31, 1962, and a Republic in 1976. The President is elected for 5 years by all members of the Senate and the House of Representatives. The House of Representatives has 36 members, elected by universal adult suffrage, and the Senate has 31, of whom 16 are appointed on the advice of the Prime Minister, 6 on the advice of the Leader of the Opposition and 9 at the discretion of the President. Legislation was passed in Sept. 1980 which afforded Tobago a degree of self-administration through the 12-member Tobago House of Assembly.

President, His Excellency Noor Mohammed Hassanali.

Cabinet
(as at May 31, 1989)

Prime Minister and Minister for Finance and the Economy, Hon. Arthur Robinson.
Finance, Hon. Selby Wilson.

Justice and National Security, Hon. Selwyn Richardson.
Environment and National Service, Hon. Lincoln Myers.
Education, Hon. Clive Pantin.
External Affairs and International Trade, Hon. Sahadeo Basdeo.
Health, Hon. Emmanuel Hosein.
Industry, Enterprise, and Tourism, Hon. Kenneth Gordon.
Labour, Employment and Manpower Resources, Hon. Albert Richards.
Energy, Hon. Herbert Atwell.
Planning and Mobilization, Hon. Winston Dookeran.
Youth, Sports, Culture and Creative Arts, Hon. Jennifer Johnson.
Works, Infrastructure and Decentralization, Hon. Carson Charles.
Attorney General, Hon. Anthony Smart.
Social Development and Family Services, Hon. Gloria Henry.
Settlements and Public Utilities, Hon. Pamela Nicholson.
Food Production and Marine Exploitation, Hon. Brinsley Samaroo.
Minister without portfolio, Hon. Bhoe Tewarie.

TRINIDAD AND TOBAGO HIGH COMMISSION
42 Belgrave Square, SW1X 8NT
[01–245 9351]

High Commissioner, His Excellency Mervyn I. Assam (1987).

EDUCATION

The education system provides for free education at all state-owned and government-assisted denominational schools and certain faculties at the University of the West Indies. In addition there are various private teaching establishments. Attendance is compulsory for children aged 6–12 years, after which attendance at free secondary schools is determined by success in the common entrance examination at 11 years. There are three technical institutes, two teachers' training colleges, and one of the three branches of the University of the West Indies is located in Trinidad, at the St. Augustine campus. A medical teaching complex was built at Mt. Hope, and operates in collaboration with the University of the West Indies.

COMMUNICATIONS

There are some 6,436 km. of all-weather roads in Trinidad and Tobago. The only general cargo port is Port of Spain but there are specialized port facilities elsewhere for landing crude oil, loading refinery products and sugar, and for storing and transmitting bauxite and cement. Regular shipping services call here and many inter-island craft use the port. Another, rapidly growing, port is at Port Lisas where new industries powered by local natural gas are located.

International scheduled airlines, including the national airline, Trinidad and Tobago Airways (BWIA) Corporation, use Piarco International Airport outside Port of Spain. The airline also flies between Piarco and Crown Point Airport in Tobago.

Two commercial broadcasting stations and one commercial television station operate in Trinidad and Tobago. The internal telephone system and the external telephone and telegraph connections are operated by state-owned companies.

PRODUCTION

Trinidad and Tobago's main source of revenue is from oil. Production of domestic crude in 1985 was

10·2 million cu. metres. The two major oil refineries increased production in 1985 to an average throughput of 12,538 cu. metres per day, and refined both local and imported crude. Trinidad has large reserves of natural gas, estimated at 18,000,000 million cu. feet, and in 1985 production was 7,413 million cu. metres. An integrated steel plant, an anhydrous ammonia plant and a methanol plant have been constructed at Point Lisas.

Fertilizers, tyres, clothing, soap, furniture and foodstuffs are manufactured locally while motor vehicles, radios, TV sets, and electro-domestic equipment are assembled from parts, mainly from Japan.

Finance

	1985	1986
Revenue	TT$6,766·7m	TT$5,239·9m
Expenditure	7,684·1m	8,004·4m
Gross public debt	3,640·7m	3,605·4m

TRADE

	1985	1986
Imports	TT$3,739·0m	TT$4,027·2m
Exports	5,247·1m	4,249·8m

In Jan. 1987, the exchange rate was unified at TT$1·00 = US$0·27778.

Trade with U.K.

	1987	1988
Imports from U.K.	£57,016,000	£39,868,000
Exports to U.K.	38,600,000	35,728,000

BRITISH HIGH COMMISSION
Furness House, 90 Independence Square
(P.O. Box 778) Port of Spain
[Port of Spain 62528616]

High Commissioner, His Excellency Sir Martin Berthoud, K.C.V.O., C.M.G.

TUVALU

Tuvalu, formerly the Ellice Islands, formed part of the Gilbert and Ellice Islands Colony until October 1, 1975, when separate constitutions came into force. Separation from the Gilbert Islands was implemented on January 1, 1976.

Tuvalu comprises nine coral atolls situated in the South West Pacific around the point at which the International Date Line cuts the Equator. The total land area is only about 10 sq. miles. Few of the atolls are more than 12 ft above sea level or more than half a mile in width. The vegetation consists mainly of coconut palms. The resident population in 1985 was 8,229, but it is estimated that about 1,500 Tuvaluans work overseas, mostly in Nauru, or as seamen. The people are almost entirely Polynesian. The principal languages are Tuvaluan and English. The entire population is Christian and is predominantly Protestant.

CAPITAL.—ΨFunafuti. Estimated population 2,856. The capital has a grass strip airfield from which a service operates regularly to Fiji and Kiribati, and is also the only port.

CURRENCY.—Tuvalu uses the Australian dollar ($A) of 100 cents as legal tender.

FLAG.—Blue ground with Union Flag in top left quarter and nine five-pointed gold stars in the fly.

NATIONAL ANTHEM.—Tuvalu Mo Te Atua (Tuvalu for the Almighty).

NATIONAL DAY.—October 1 (Independence Day).

GOVERNMENT

On October 1, 1978, Tuvalu became fully independent as a sovereign state within the Commonwealth. The Constitution provides for a Prime Minister and four other Ministers who must be members of the 12-member elected Parliament. The Prime Minister presides at meetings of the Cabinet, which consists of the five Ministers, and is attended by the Attorney General. Local Government services are provided by elected Island Councils.

Governor General, His Excellency Sir Tupua Leupena, G.C.M.G., M.B.E., *sworn in* March 1, 1986.

Cabinet
(as at May 31, 1989)

Prime Minister, Rt. Hon. Dr. Tomasi Puapua.
Minister for Finance and Economic Development, Hon. Kitiseni Lopati, M.B.E.
Commerce and Natural Resources, Hon. Lale Seluka.
Works and Communications, Hon. Metia Tealofi.
Health and Education, Hon. Bikeni Paeniu.
Secretary to Government (acting), Semu Taafaki.
Attorney-General, David Ballantyne.

EDUCATION AND WELFARE

There are eight primary schools in Tuvalu and a church secondary school run jointly with the Government. The total of enrolled children of school age in 1985 was 1,300. A Maritime Training School started in 1979 now caters for 60 boys per annum.

There is a 30-bed hospital at Funafuti. All islands are served by a dispensary and a primary school.

ECONOMY

Most people still practise a subsistence economy, the main staples of their diet being coconuts and fish. The main imports are foodstuffs, consumer goods and building materials. The only export is copra (333 tons in 1985), but philatelic sales provide a major source of revenue and handicraft sales are increasing. The unit of currency is the Australian dollar. In addition there are Tuvalu dollar and cent coins in circulation.

TRADE

	1984
Imports	$A3,954,000
Exports	307,917

Trade with U.K.

	1987	1988
Imports from U.K.	£106,000	£105,000
Exports to U.K.	2,000	1,000

British High Commissioner, (resident at Suva, Fiji).

UGANDA
(Republic of Uganda)

AREA, POPULATION, ETC.—Situated in Eastern Africa, Uganda is flanked by Zaire, the Sudan, Kenya and on the south by Tanzania and Rwanda. Large parts of Lakes Victoria, Edward and Albert (Mobuto) are within its boundaries, as are Lakes Kyoga, Kwania, George and Bisina (formerly Salisbury) and the course of the River Nile from its outlet from Lake Victoria to the Sudan frontier post at Nimule. Uganda has an area of 91,259 sq. miles (236,036 sq. km.) (water and swamp 16,400 sq. miles) and population (1989 estimate) of 16,398,000. The official language of Uganda is English. The main local vernaculars are of Bantu, Nilotic and Hamitic origins. Ki-Swahili is generally understood in trading centres.

Despite its tropical location, the climate is tempered

by its situation some 3,000 ft. above sea level, and well over that altitude in the highlands of the Western and Eastern Regions. In South Uganda, temperatures seldom rise above 85° F. (29° C.) or fall below 60° F. (15° C.). The rainfall averages about 50 inches a year. Uganda has three National Parks and a fourth (Lake Mburo) has been designated.

CAPITAL.—Kampala (population of Greater Kampala, 631,000). Other principal towns are Jinja (45,000), Mbale (28,000) and Masaka (29,000).

CURRENCY.—Uganda shilling of 100 cents.

FLAG.—Six horizontal stripes of black, yellow and red (repeated) with a crested crane emblem on a white orb in the centre.

NATIONAL ANTHEM.—"Oh Uganda".

NATIONAL DAY.—October 9 (Independence Day).

GOVERNMENT

Uganda became an independent state and a member of the Commonwealth on October 9, 1962, after some 70 years of British rule. A Republic was instituted on September 8, 1967, under an executive President, assisted by a Cabinet of Ministers.

Early in 1971 an army coup took place and Maj.-Gen. Idi Amin, the Army Commander, proclaimed himself Head of State. In 1979, following risings and military intervention by Tanzania, President Amin was overthrown. Following elections in 1980, Dr. Milton Obote became President. A military coup on July 27, 1985 ousted Dr. Obote and installed a military council which attempted to negotiate a power-sharing agreement with the National Resistance Movement led by Yoweri Museveni. However, the National Resistance Army captured Kampala in late Jan. 1986, securing control of the rest of the country in the following few months. Yoweri Museveni was sworn in as President on Jan. 29, 1986; subsequently the Prime Minister and a 24-member National Resistance Council were appointed, and a government was formed.

President, H. E. Yoweri Museveni, *sworn in* Jan. 29, 1986.

Cabinet
(as at March 31, 1989)

President and Minister of Defence, Lt.-Gen. Yoweri Museveni.
Prime Minister, Dr. Samson Kisseka.
1st Deputy P.M., Eriya Kategaya.
2nd Deputy P.M. and Minister for Foreign Affairs, Paul Ssemogerere.
3rd Deputy P.M., Abu Bakar Mayanja.
Internal Affairs, Ibrahim Mukiibi.
Finance, Dr. Crispus Kiyonga.
Planning and Economic Development, Prof. Yoweri Kyesimira.
Agriculture and Forestry, Mrs. Victoria Ssekitoleko.
Industry and Technology, Prof. Stanley Tumwine.
Commerce, Paul Etiang.
Local Government, Amanya Mushega.
Animal Industries and Fisheries, Prof. George Mondo Kagonyera.
Youth, Culture and Sports, Dr. Edward Kakonge.
Public Services and Cabinet Affairs, Tom Rubale.
Regional Co-operation, Joseph Mulenga.
Information and Broadcasting, Ali Kirunda Kivejinja.
Education, Joshua Mayanja-Nkangi.
Land and Surveys, Ben Luwum.
Minerals and Water Development, Robert Kitariko.
Justice and Attorney General, George Kanyeihamba.
Constitutional Affairs, Sam Njuba.
Co-operatives and Marketing, James Wapakabulo.
Labour, Stanislaus Okurut.

Transport and Communications, Dr. Ruhakana-Rugunda.
Energy, Jaberi Bidandi-Ssali.
Tourism and Wildlife, Brig. Moses Ali.
Works, Daniel Kigozi.
Health, Dr. Adoko Nekyon.
Housing and Urban Development, John Ssebana-Kizito.
Environment, Joseph Okune.
Relief and Social Rehabilitation, B. Chango-Machyo.

UGANDA HIGH COMMISSION
Uganda House, 58–59 Trafalgar Square, WC2N 5DX
[01–839 5783]

High Commissioner, His Excellency William S. K. Matovu (1988).

EDUCATION

Education is a joint undertaking by the Government, local authorities and, to some extent, voluntary agencies. In 1981 Uganda had 4,276 primary schools with an enrolment of 1,421,615 children. Secondary schools numbered 199 with 78,727 students enrolled; and 4,979 students in various technical training institutions.

The National University is Makerere University, Kampala, founded as a trade school in 1921 and becoming an independent university in 1970.

COMMUNICATIONS

There is an international airport at Entebbe, with direct flights to destinations in Africa and Europe. There are 8 other airfields in Uganda. Having no sea coast, Uganda is heavily dependent upon rail and road links to Mombasa for her trade. There are 2,226 kilometres of bituminized and 25,310 kilometres of gravel roads. Roads are poor but many are being rebitumenized. A railway network joins the capital to the western, eastern and northern centres.

TRADE, ETC.

The principal export earner is coffee (over 90 per cent of all exports), which earned $397 million in 1986. Attempts are being made to increase production of cotton and tea for export. Hydro-electricity is produced from the Owen Falls power station which generated 539 kW in 1987, 217 kW of which was exported to Kenya. The principal food crops are plantains, bananas, cassava, sweet potatoes, potatoes and sorghum.

Trade with U.K.

	1987	1988
Imports from U.K.	£38,500,000	£35,340,000
Exports to U.K.	37,100,000	30,487,000

BRITISH HIGH COMMISSION
10/12 Parliament Avenue, P.O. Box 7070, Kampala
[Kampala 257054/9]

High Commissioner, His Excellency Sir Derek March, K.B.E. (1986).
British Council Representative, T. L. G. Mullen.

VANUATU
(Ripablik Blong Vanuatu)

AREA, POPULATION, ETC.—Vanuatu, the former Anglo-French Condominium of the New Hebrides, is situated in the South Pacific Ocean, between 13° and 21° S. and 166° and 170° E. It includes 13 large and some 70 small islands, of coral and volcanic origin, including the Banks and Torres Islands in the North, and has a total land area of 4,706 sq. miles

(12,190 sq. km.). The principal islands are Vanua Lava, Espiritu Santo, Maewo, Pentecost, Aoba, Malekula, Ambrym, Epi, Efate, Erromango, Tanna and Aneityum. Most islands are mountainous and there are active volcanoes on several. The climate is oceanic tropical, moderated by the south-east trade winds which blow between May and October. At other times winds are variable and cyclones may occur. Temperatures range between 17° C. and 28° C, with annual rainfall averaging 90 in. to the south and 155 in. to the north.

A 1986 estimate showed a population of 140,154. A national census took place in May 1989. No results have thus far been published. About 95 per cent of the population are Melanesian, the rest being made up largely of Micronesians, Polynesians and Europeans. The national language is Bislama, but English and French are also official languages.

SEAT OF ADMINISTRATION—ΨVila, Efate, population (1986), 14,184. The only other town is Luganville (population, 1986, 5,621), on Espiritu Santo.

CURRENCY.—Vatu of 100 centimes.

FLAG.—Red over green with a black triangle in the hoist, the three parts being divided by fimbriations of black and yellow, and in the centre of the black triangle a boar's tusk overlaid by two crossed fern leaves.

NATIONAL ANTHEM.—"Nasinal Sing sing long Vanuatu."

NATIONAL DAY.—July 30 (Independence Day).

GOVERNMENT

The Condominium of the New Hebrides became an independent republic within the Commonwealth under the name of Vanuatu on July 30, 1980.

President, His Excellency Frederick Karlomuana Timakata, *elected* 1989.

Council of Ministers
(as at May 31, 1989)

Prime Minister and Minister of Planning, Hon. Father Walter Lini, C.B.E.

Education, Hon. S. J. Regenvanu.

Finance and Housing, Hon. S. Molisa.

Lands, Minerals and Rural Water Supply, Hon. W. Mahit.

Foreign Affairs and Judicial Services, Hon. D. Kalpokas.

Health, Hon. J. M. Chilia.

Agriculture, Forestry and Fisheries, Hon. J. Hopa.

Home Affairs, Hon. I. Abbil.

Trade, Commerce, Industry, Co-operatives and Energy, Hon. H. Qualao.

Transport, Public Works and Tourism, Hon. E. Natapei.

Chief Justice, Hon. Mr. Justice F. G. Cooke.

Attorney-General, S. Hakwa.

ECONOMY

Most of the population is employed on plantations or in subsistence agriculture. Subsistence crops include yams, taro, manioc, sweet potato and breadfruit; principal cash crops are copra, cocoa and coffee. Large numbers of cattle are kept on the plantations and beef is the second largest export after copra.

Principal exports are copra, meat (frozen, tinned and chilled), timber and cocoa.

Tourism is an important revenue earner, and the absence of direct taxation has led to growth in the finance and associated industries.

Trade with U.K.

	1987	1988
Imports from U.K.	£1,058,000	£991,000
Exports to U.K.	15,000	5,000

BRITISH HIGH COMMISSION
Melitco House, Rue Pasteur, Vila.
[Vila 3100]

High Commissioner, His Excellency John Thompson, M.B.E. (1988).

WESTERN SAMOA
(Malotuto'atasi o Samoa i Sisifo)

Western Samoa lies in the south Pacific Ocean between latitudes 13° and 15° S. and longitudes 171° and 173° W. It consists of the islands of Savai'i (662 sq. miles) and of Upolu, which, with seven other islands (Apolima, Manono, Fanuatapu, Namua, Nuutele, Nuulua and Nuusafee) has an area of 435 sq. miles (1,714 sq. km.). All the islands are mountainous. Upolu, the most fertile, contains the harbours of ΨApia and ΨSaluafata, and Savai'i the harbour of ΨAsau. The population at the 1981 census was 158,130, the largest numbers being on Upolu (114,980) and Savai'i (43,150): a 1985 U.N. estimate put the figure at 163,000. The Samoans are a Polynesian people, though the population also includes other Pacific Islanders, Euronesians, Chinese and Europeans. The main languages spoken are Samoan and English. The islanders are Christians of different denominations.

CAPITAL.—ΨApia, on Upolu (population (1981 census) 33,100). Robert Louis Stevenson died and was buried at Apia in 1894.

CURRENCY.—Tala (WS$) of 100 sene.

FLAG.—Five white stars (depicting the Southern Cross) on a quarter royal blue at top next staff, and three quarters red.

NATIONAL ANTHEM.—The Banner of Freedom.

NATIONAL DAY.—January 1 (Independence Day).

GOVERNMENT

Formerly administered by New Zealand (latterly with internal self-government), Western Samoa became, on January 1, 1962, the first fully-independent Polynesian State. The State was treated as a member country of the Commonwealth until its formal admission on August 28, 1970.

The 1962 Constitution provides for a Head of State to be elected by the Legislative Assembly for a five year term. However, it was decided that initially two of the four Paramount chiefs should jointly hold the office of Head of State for life. When one of the chiefs died in April 1963, Malietoa Tanumafili II became the holder of the office of Head of State for life. The Head of State's functions are analogous to those of a constitutional monarch. Executive government is carried out by a Cabinet of Ministers.

Head of State, H. H. Malietoa Tanumafili II, G.C.M.G., C.B.E. (April 15, 1963).

Deputy Head of State, Hon. Mataafa Faasuamaleaui Puela.

Cabinet
(as at April 30, 1989)

Prime Minister and Minister of Foreign Affairs, Hon. Tofilau Eti Alesana.

Finance, Hon. Tuilaepa Sailele.

Agriculture, Hon. Pule Lameko.

Economic Development, Hon. Tanuvasa Livi.

Lands and Survey, Hon. Sifuiva Sione.

Education, Hon. Patu Afaese.

Health, Hon. Polataivao Fosi.
Post Office, Transport and Civil Aviation, Hon. Jack Netzler.
Public Works, Hon. Leiataua Vaiao.

ECONOMY

Agriculture is the basis of Western Samoa's economy, the principal cash crops (and exports) being coconuts (copra), cocoa and bananas. Other agricultural exports include coffee, timber, tropical fruits and seeds. Efforts are being made to develop fishing on a commercial scale. Manufacturing is very small in scope and concerned largely with processing agricultural products, but is being encouraged by the Government. Tourism is increasing rapidly.

Trade with U.K.

	1987	1988
Imports from U.K.	£1,650,000	£757,000
Exports to U.K.	531,000	1,323,000

BRITISH HIGH COMMISSION (*see* New Zealand)

ZAMBIA
(Republic of Zambia)

AREA, POPULATION, ETC.—The Republic of Zambia lies on the plateau of Central Africa between the longitudes 22° E. and 33° 33′ E. and between the latitudes 8° 15′ S. and 18° S. It has an area of 290,586 sq. miles (752,614 sq. km.) within boundaries 3,515 miles in length and a population (U.N. estimate, 1985) of 6,666,000, including about 50,000 non-Africans.

With the exception of the valleys of the Zambezi, the Luapula, the Kafue and the Luangwa Rivers, and the Luano valley, elevations vary from 3,000 to 5,000 feet above sea level, but in the north-east the plateau rises to occasional altitudes of over 6,000 feet.

Although Zambia lies within the tropics, and fairly centrally in the African land mass, its elevation relieves it from extremely high temperatures and humidity.

CAPITAL.—Lusaka, situated in the Central Province. Population (estimated, 1980), 641,000. Other centres are Livingstone, Kabwe, Chipata, Mazabuka, Mbala, Kasama, Solwezi, Mongu, Mansa, Ndola, Luanshya, Mufulira, Chingola, Chililabombwe, Kalulushi and Kitwe, the last six towns being the main centres on the Copperbelt.

CURRENCY.—Kwacha (K) of 100 ngwee.

FLAG.—Green with three small vertical stripes, red, black and orange (next fly); eagle device on green above stripes.

NATIONAL ANTHEM.—Stand and Sing of Zambia, Proud and Free.

NATIONAL DAY.—October 24 (Independence Day).

GOVERNMENT

At the dissolution of the Federation of Rhodesia and Nyasaland, on December 31, 1963, Northern Rhodesia (as Zambia was then known) achieved internal self-government under a new constitution. Zambia became an independent republic within the Commonwealth on October 24, 1964—75 years after coming under British rule and nine months after achieving internal self-government.

In July 1973, a new Constitution was introduced, making the United National Independence Party (U.N.I.P.) the only party.

President, Dr. Kenneth David Kaunda, *assumed office* Oct. 24, 1964; *re-elected,* Dec. 1973, Dec. 1978, Oct. 1983 and Oct. 1988.

Cabinet
(as at June 30, 1989)

Prime Minister, Gen. Rt. Hon. Malimba Masheke.
UNIP Secretary General, Hon. A. Grey Zulu.
Secretary of State for Defence and Security, Hon. Alex K. Shapi.
Defence, Hon. Frederick Hapunda.
Home Affairs, Gen. the Hon. Kingsley Chinkuli.
Agriculture and Co-operatives, Hon. Justin J. Mukando.
Water, Lands and Natural Resources, Hon. Paul Malukutila.
Foreign Affairs, Hon. Luke J. Mwananshiku.
Attorney General and Minister for Legal Affairs, Hon. Frederick M. Chomba.
Information and Broadcasting Services, Hon. Arnold Simuchimba.
Commerce and Industry, Hon. Ottema Musuka.
Finance, Hon. Gibson G. Chigaga.
Mines, Hon. Bernard N. Fumbelo.
Power, Transport and Communications, Brig. Gen. the Hon. Enos Haimbe.
Tourism, Hon. Pickson Chitambala.
Higher Education, Science and Technology, Prof. the Hon. Lameck K. H. Goma.
General Education, Youth and Sport, Dr. the Hon. Eli Mwanang'onze.
Health, Hon. Alina Nyikosa.
Labour, Social Development and Culture, Hon. Lavu Mulimba.

ZAMBIA HIGH COMMISSION
2 Palace Gate, W8 5NG
[01–589 6655]

High Commissioner, new appointment awaited.

JUDICATURE

There is a Chief Justice appointed by the President, all other judges being appointed on the recommendation of the Judicial Service Commission consisting of the Chief Justice, the chairman of the Public Service Commission, a senior Justice of Appeal and one Presidential nominee.

PRODUCTION

Principal products are maize, sugar, groundnuts, cotton, livestock, vegetables and tobacco.

Mineral production was valued at K8,390,765,000 in 1987, of which copper production (of 483,100 tonnes) accounted for K6,870,386,000.

FINANCE AND TRADE

Gross Domestic Product (current prices) was K18,079·8m in 1987. G.D.P. per capita (current prices) was K2,486·9.

	1986	1987
Imports	K4,447,687	K6,627,473
Exports	3,074,357	8,058,595

Trade with U.K.

	1987	1988
Imports from U.K....	£75,178,000	£85,746,000
Exports to U.K.	30,310,000	24,822,000

BRITISH HIGH COMMISSION
Independence Avenue (P.O. Box 50050), Lusaka
[Lusaka 228955]

High Commissioner, His Excellency John Michael Willson, C.M.G. (1988).
British Council Representative, J. Mulholland, O.B.E., Heroes Place, Cairo Road, (P.O. Box 34571), Lusaka. There is also a library in *Ndola*.

ZIMBABWE
(Republic of Zimbabwe)

AREA, POPULATION, ETC.—Zimbabwe, the former Southern Rhodesia (named after Cecil Rhodes) comprising eight provinces (Manicaland, Masvingo, Matabeleland North, Matabeleland South, Midlands, Mashonaland West, Central and East), lies south of the Zambezi river. The political neighbours are Zambia and Mozambique on the N., South Africa and Botswana on the S. and W., and Mozambique on the E. It has a total area of 150,804 sq. miles (390,580 sq. km.), and a population (estimated 1989) of 9,000,000.

CAPITAL.—Harare (formerly Salisbury) situated on the Mashonaland plateau, population (August 1982) 658,364. Bulawayo—the largest town in Matabeleland, population (August 1982) 495,317. Other centres are, Chitungwiza, Mutare, Gweru, Kadoma, Kwe Kwe, Masvingo and Hwange.

CURRENCY.—Zimbabwe dollar (Z$) of 100 cents.

FLAG.—Seven horizontal stripes (green, gold, red, black, red, gold, green) with white triangle at the hoist containing the Zimbabwe bird superimposed on red five-point star.

NATIONAL ANTHEM.—Ishe Komborerai Africa.
NATIONAL DAY.—April 18 (Independence Day).

GOVERNMENT

Southern Rhodesia was granted responsible government in 1923. An illegal declaration of independence on November 11, 1965 was finally terminated on December 12, 1979. Following elections in February 1980 the country obtained independence on April 18, 1980 as the Republic of Zimbabwe, a member of the British Commonwealth. The Parliament consists of a House of Assembly of 100 members and a Senate of 40 Senators and has a maximum life of five years. A Constitutional Amendment Bill designed to replace the 20 reserved white seats with nominated members from any race, was approved in Sept. 1987.

On Oct. 30, 1987 a Constitutional Amendment Bill was passed providing for the creation of an executive presidency. On Dec. 30, 1987 Mr. Robert Mugabe was elected by M.P.s and Senators as the first President. The Bill provides for a President to be popularly elected every six years. The President has the power to appoint a Cabinet and to veto parliamentary bills.

A merger agreement between the ZANU (PF) and ZAPU parties was signed on Dec. 22, 1987 which will lead to the eventual creation of a one-party state. The new party is known as ZANU-PF.

Executive President, Hon. Robert Gabriel Mugabe, elected Dec. 30, 1987.

Cabinet
(as at May 31, 1989)

President, Robert Mugabe.
Vice President, Simon Muzenda.
Ministers in the President's Office, Joshua Nkomo; Dr. Bernard Chidzero (*Finance, Economic Planning and Development*).

Foreign Affairs, Dr. Nathan Shamuyarira.
Telecommunications, Dr. Witness Mangwende.
Higher Education, (vacant).
Primary and Secondary Education, Fay Chung.
Industry and Technology, (vacant).
Trade and Commerce, Oliver Munyaradzi.
Transport, Simbarashe Mumbengegwi.
Construction and National Housing, Joseph Msika.
Mines, Richard Hove.
Lands, Agriculture and Rural Settlement, David Karimanzira.
Youth, Sport and Culture, David Kwidini.
Community Development, Co-operatives and Women's Affairs, Teurai Ropa Joyce Mujuru.
Justice, Legal and Parliamentary Affairs, Emmerson Munangagwa.
National Supplies, Simbi Mubako.
Health, Brig. Felix Muchemwa.
Energy, Water Resources and Development, Kumbirai Kangai.
Labour, Manpower Planning and Social Welfare, John Nkomo.
Home Affairs, Moven Mahachi.
Natural Resources and Tourism, Victoria Chitepo.
Local Government, Rural and Urban Development, Enos Chikowore.
Ministers of State in the President's Office, Christopher Anderson (*Public Service*); Dr. Sydney Sekeremayi (*National Security and Minister of Defence (acting)*); Joseph Culverwell (*National Scholarships*).

ZIMBABWE HIGH COMMISSION
Zimbabwe House, 429 Strand, WC2R 0SA
[01-836 7755]

High Commissioner, His Excellency Dr. Herbert M. Murerwa (1984).

EDUCATION

Since independence, a policy of free primary education and accelerated expansion at secondary level has resulted in rapidly expanding enrolment. In 1986 there were 2,260,367 primary school and 545,841 secondary school pupils in both Government and Government aid schools. Over 80 per cent of schools are government aided schools. The University of Zimbabwe was founded in 1955.

ECONOMY

The country is endowed with minerals, water, forests, wildlife and other resources. The agricultural sector is well developed with both commercial and communal farmers. Tobacco remains the most important crop in terms of export and maize the most important for domestic consumption. Other crops include wheat, cotton, and sugar. Good quality beef is exported to the E.C. Production can be severely affected by drought.

The manufacturing sector has a high degree of inter-dependency and many industries depend on the agricultural sector for their raw materials. Industry is dependent on vital imports e.g. fuel oil, steel products and chemicals, as well as heavy machinery and items of transport. The mining sector, although contributing a relatively small portion to G.D.P. (7·6 per cent in 1984) is important to the economy as a foreign exchange earner (26 per cent of total in 1984). Almost all mineral production is exported. Gold is the most important mineral, others are asbestos, silver, nickel, copper, chrome ore, tin, iron ore and cobalt. There is a successful ferro-chrome industry and a substantial steel works which has been heavily subsidized by Government.

A high domestic budget deficit combining with a high external debt service ratio has put the economy into decline. The 1986–87 drought made this worse.

GOVERNMENT FINANCE

	1984-85	1985–86
Revenue	Z$2,212·3m	Z$2,616·2m
Expenditure	2,923·0m	3,307·8m

Trade with U.K.

	1987	1988
Imports from U.K.	£63,181,000	£58,077,000
Exports to U.K.	79,771,000	86,268,000

BRITISH HIGH COMMISSION
Stanley House, Stanley Avenue,
(PO Box 4490), Harare
[Harare 793781]

High Commissioner, His Excellency (Walter) Kieran Prendergast (1989).
British Council Representative, N. M. Ross, 23 Stanley Avenue, (P.O. Box 664), Harare.

Dependent Territories, etc.

ANGUILLA

Anguilla is a flat coralline island, about 16 miles in length, 3½ miles in breadth at its widest point and its area is about 35 sq. miles (91 sq. km.). It lies approximately 18° N. latitude and 63° W longitude, to the north of the Leeward Islands group.

The island is covered with low scrub and fringed with some of the finest white coral-sand beaches in the Caribbean. The climate is pleasant and healthy with temperatures in the range of 24-30° C. throughout the year. The population (U.N. 1985 estimate) is about 7,000.

CAPITAL.—The Valley (population 500).
CURRENCY.—East Caribbean dollar (EC$) of 100 cents.

GOVERNMENT

Anguilla has been a British colony since 1650. For most of its history it has been linked administratively with St. Christopher, but three months after the Associated State of Saint Christopher (St. Kitts)-Nevis-Anguilla came into being in 1967 the Anguillans repudiated government from St. Kitts. A Commissioner was installed in 1969 and in 1976 Anguilla was given a new status and separate constitution. Final separation from St. Kitts and Nevis was effected on Dec. 19, 1980 and Anguilla reverted to a British Dependency. A new Constitution was introduced in 1982, providing for a Governor, an Executive Council comprising four elected Ministers and two ex-officio members (Attorney General and Permanent Secretary, Finance), and an 11-member legislative House of Assembly presided over by a Speaker.

Governor, His Excellency B. G. J. Canty (1989).

Executive Council

Chief Minister and Minister of Home Affairs, Tourism and Community Development, Hon. Emile Gumbs.
Lands, Agriculture and Fisheries, Health and Prisons, Hon. Eric Reid.
Communications, Public Utilities and Works, Hon. Kenneth Harrigan.
Finance, Education, Economic Development, Osbourne Fleming.
Permanent Secretary (Finance), Hon. Franklin Connor, O.B.E.
Attorney-General, Hon. Alan Hoole.

ECONOMY

Low rainfall limits agricultural output and export earnings are mainly from sales of lobsters. Tourism has developed rapidly in recent years and accounts for most of the islands economic activity. In 1988 there were 28,000 tourists and a further 42,000 day visitors.

FINANCE

	1988	1989*
Revenue	EC$26,800,000	EC$28,200,000
Expenditure	22,800,000	26,764,000
Capital Expenditure		
*estimate	5,700,000	2,956,000

Trade with U.K.

	1987	1988
Imports from U.K.	£1,328,000	£1,372,000
Exports to U.K.	188,000	68,000

ASCENSION
See ST. HELENA

BERMUDA

The Bermudas, or Somers Islands, are a cluster of about 100 small islands (about 20 only of which are inhabited) situated in the west of the Atlantic Ocean, in 32° 18′ N. lat. and 64° 46′ W. long., the nearest point of the mainland being Cape Hatteras in North Carolina, about 570 miles distant. The colony derives its name from Juan Bermudez, a Spaniard, who sighted it before 1515, but no settlement was made until 1609, when Sir George Somers, who was shipwrecked here on his way to Virginia, colonized the islands.

The total area is approximately 20·59 sq. miles (53 sq. km.), which includes 2·3 sq. miles leased to the U.S.A. The civil population was 56,000 in 1985 (U.N. estimate).

CAPITAL.—ΨHamilton (population, 1984, 1,669).
CURRENCY.—Bermuda dollar of 100 cents.

GOVERNMENT

Internal self-government was introduced on June 8, 1968. There is a Senate of 11 members and an elected House of Assembly of 40 members. The Governor retains responsibility for external affairs, defence, internal security and the police, although administrative matters for the Police Service have been delegated to the Minister of Home Affairs.

At the General Election of Feb. 9, 1989 the United Bermuda Party gained 23 seats, the Progressive Labour Party 15, National Liberal Party 1, and Independent Environmentalist 1.

Governor and Commander-in-Chief, His Excellency Sir Desmond Langley, K.C.V.O., M.B.E. (1988).
Deputy Governor, B. Canty, O.B.E.

Cabinet
(as at Jan. 31, 1989)

Premier, Hon. J. W. Swan.
Deputy Premier and Minister of Finance, Dr. Hon. C. James.
Tourism, Hon. J. Irving Pearman.
Education, Hon. G. D. E. Simons.
Works and Housing, Hon. Q. L. Edness.
Health and Social Services, Hon. A. F. Cartwright DeCouto.
Transport, Hon. S. Stallard.
Environment, Hon. T. H. Davis.
Labour and Home Affairs, Hon. Sir John Sharpe.
Community and Cultural Affairs, Hon. R. Barritt.
Youth, Sport and Recreation, Hon. M. A. Burgess.
Legislative Affairs, with responsibility for Telecommunications, Sen. Hon. C. T. M. Collis.

President of the Senate, Hon. A. S. Jackson, M.B.E.
Speaker of the House of Assembly, Hon. F. J. Barritt, C.B.E.
Chief Justice, Hon. Sir James R. Astwood.
Puisne Judges, Hon. L. Austin Ward, Q.C.; Hon. M. Ward; Hon. D. Hull.

ECONOMY

Locally manufactured concentrates and pharmaceuticals are now the colony's leading exports. Little food is produced except vegetables and fish, other foodstuffs being imported.

The islands' economic structure is based on tourism, the major industry, and international company business, attracted by the low level of taxation and sophisticated telecommunications system. In 1987 a total of 613,628 visitors arrived by air and cruise ship. Cruise ships dock at Hamilton, Somerset and St. George's.

Free elementary education was introduced in 1949. Free secondary education was introduced in 1965 for those children in the aided and maintained schools who were below the upper limit of the statutory school age of 16 (from 1969 onwards).

There are 5 radio and one television station, one daily and 2 weekly newspapers and overseas telephone and telegraph services are maintained.

FINANCE

	1987–88	1988–89
Public revenue	$251,550,300	$279,639,200
Public expenditure	220,172,000	245,542,700

Trade with U.K.

	1987	1988
Imports from U.K.	£25,383,000	£24,995,000
Exports to U.K.	1,208,000	8,767,000

THE BRITISH ANTARCTIC TERRITORY

The British Antarctic Territory was designated in 1962 and consists of the areas south of 60°S. latitude which were previously included in the Falkland Islands Dependencies. The territory lies between longitudes 20° and 80°W., south of latitude 60°S. and includes the South Orkney Islands, the South Shetland Islands, the mountainous Antarctic Peninsula (highest point *Mount Jackson,* 13,620ft, in Palmer Land) and all adjacent islands, and the land mass extending to the South Pole. The territory has no indigenous inhabitants and the British population consists of the scientists and technicians who man the British Antarctic Survey stations. The number averages about 60 to 70 in winter, but increases considerably in the summer months with the arrival of field workers; Argentina, Brazil, Chile, China, Poland, U.S.A., U.S.S.R. and Uruguay also have scientific stations in the territory.

The first two British Antarctic Survey stations were established in the South Shetland Islands in 1944, and by 1956 the number of stations had risen to twelve. Due to the completion of field work in some areas and increased mobility, the number has now been reduced to five. These are Signy (Signy Island, S. Orkney Islands), Faraday (Argentine Islands, Graham Coast), Rothera (Adelaide Island), Halley (Caird Coast) and, in summer only, Fossil Bluff (George VI Sound). Fifteen other stations have been established but are at present unoccupied.

The territory is administered by a High Commissioner, resident in the Falkland Islands.

High Commissioner, His Excellency William Hugh Fullerton, C.M.G. (1988).

(*See also index for* the Antarctic)

THE BRITISH INDIAN OCEAN TERRITORY

The British Indian Ocean Territory was established by an Order in Council in 1965 and included islands formerly administered from Mauritius and the Seychelles. After the independence of both, the territory was redefined in 1976 as comprising only the islands of the Chagos Archipelago.

The Chagos Archipelago consists of six main groups of islands situated on the Great Chagos Bank and covering some 21,000 sq. miles (54,389 sq. km.). The largest and most southerly of the Chagos Islands is *Diego Garcia,* a sand cay with a land area of about 17 square miles approximately 1,100 miles east of Mahé, used as a joint naval support facility by Britain and U.S.A.

The other main island groups of the archipelago, *Peros Banhos* (29 islands with a total land area of 4 sq. miles) and *Salomon* (11 islands with a total land area of 2 sq. miles) are uninhabited. The islands have a typical tropical maritime climate, with average temperatures between 25°C and 29°C in Diego Garcia, and rainfall in the whole archipelago of 90–100 inches a year.

Commissioner and Administrator, R. Edis.

THE BRITISH VIRGIN ISLANDS

The Virgin Islands are a group of islands at the eastern extremity of the Greater Antilles, divided between Great Britain and the U.S.A. Those of the group which are British number 46, of which 11 are inhabited, and have a total area of about 59 sq. miles, (153 sq. km.). The principal are Tortola, the largest (situated in 18° 27′ N. lat. and 64° 40′ W. long., area, 21 sq. miles), Virgin Gorda (8¼ sq. miles), Anegada (15 sq.miles) and Jost Van Dyke (3¼ sq. miles). The 1980 Census showed a total population of 10,985 (Tortola (9,119); Virgin Gorda (1,443); Anegada (169); Jost

Van Dyke (136); and other islands (82). A 1985 U.N. estimate gave a figure of 13,000. Apart from Anegada, which is a flat coral island, the British Virgin Islands are hilly, being an extension of the Puerto Rico and the U.S. Virgin Islands archipelago. The highest point is Sage Mountain on Tortola which rises to a height of 1,780 feet. Tourism is the main industry, but there is some cattle raising and fishing. Other products are vegetables, fruit, charcoal and rum.

The islands lie within the Trade Winds belt and possess a pleasant and healthy sub-tropical climate. The average temperature varies from 22°–28° C. in winter and 26°–31° C. in summer. The summer heat is tempered by sea breezes and the temperature usually falls by about 6° C. at night. Average rainfall is 53 inches.

CAPITAL.—ΨRoad Town, on the south-east of Tortola. Population, 2,479.

CURRENCY.—The U.S. dollar (US$) of 100 cents is legal tender in the British Virgin Islands.

GOVERNMENT

Under the 1977 Constitution, the Governor, appointed by the Crown, remains responsible for defence and internal security, external affairs and the civil service but in other matters acts in accordance with the advice of the Executive Council. The Executive Council consists of the Governor as Chairman, one ex officio member (the Attorney-General), the Chief Minister and three other ministers. The Legislative Council consists of a Speaker chosen from outside the Council, one ex officio member (the Attorney-General), and nine elected members returned from nine one-member electoral districts.

Governor, His Excellency (John) Mark (Ambrose) Herdman, L.V.O. (1986).
Deputy Governor, E. Georges, O.B.E.
Financial Secretary, R. Mathavious.

The Executive Council

Chairman, The Governor.
Chief Minister and Minister of Finance, Hon. H. Lavity Stoutt.
Natural Resources and Labour, Hon. Ralph O'Neal.
Communications and Works, Hon. Oliver Cills.
Health, Education and Welfare, Hon. Louis Walters, M.B.E.
Attorney-General, Hon. Karl S. Atterbury.

Puisne Judge (resident), Hon. Miss Sylvia Bertrand.

COMMUNICATIONS

The principal airport is on Beef Island, linked by bridge to Tortola, and an extended runway of 3,600 ft enables larger aircraft to call. There is a second airfield on Virgin Gorda and a third on Anegada. There are direct shipping services to the United Kingdom and the United States and fast passenger services connect the main islands by ferry.

FINANCE

	1986	1987
Revenue	U.S.$22,297,000	U.S.$26,702,000
Expenditure	22,971,000	24,869,000

ECONOMY

Tourism is the main industry but other industries include a rum distillery, three stone-crushing plants and factories manufacturing concrete blocks and paint. The major export items are fresh fish, gravel, sand, fruit and vegetables: exports are largely confined to the U.S. Virgin Islands. Chief imports are building materials, machinery, cars and beverages.

Trade with U.K.

	1987	1988
Imports from U.K.	£3,310,000	£7,108,000
Exports to U.K.	752,000	4,030,000

THE CAYMAN ISLANDS

The Cayman Islands, between 79° 44′ and 81° 26′ W. and 19° 15′ and 19° 46′ N., consist of three islands, Grand Cayman, Cayman Brac, and Little Cayman, with a total area of 100 sq. miles (259 sq. km.). Population (1988 estimate), 24,900.

CAPITAL.—ΨGeorge Town, in Grand Cayman, population (1988) 11,000.

CURRENCY.—Cayman Islands dollar (CI$) of 100 cents.

GOVERNMENT

The constitution provides for a Governor, Legislative Assembly and an Executive Council, and effectively allows a large measure of self-government. Unless there are exceptional reasons, the Governor must take the advice of the Executive Council, which comprises three official members and four others elected from the 12 elected members of the Assembly. The Governor retains control over the police, civil service, defence and external affairs. He presides over the Assembly, in which the three official members also sit, though there is provision for the appointment of a Speaker if the members request it. The normal life of the Assembly is four years, with a general election next due in November 1992.

Governor, His Excellency Alan James Scott, C.V.O., C.B.E.

Executive Council
(as at May 31, 1989)

President, The Governor.
Financial Secretary, Hon. T. C. Jefferson, O.B.E.
Administrative Secretary, Hon. J. L. Hurlston.
Attorney-General, Hon. R. W. Ground, Q.C.
Member for Education, Recreation and Culture, Hon. B. O. Ebanks, O.B.E.
Member for Communications, Works and Natural Resources, Hon. L. Pierson.
Member for Tourism, Aviation and Trade, Hon. W. N. Bodden, O.B.E.
Member for Health and Social Services, Hon. E. Miller.

LONDON OFFICE
Cayman Islands Government Office,
100 Brompton Road, SW3 1EX.
[01–581 9418]

Government Representative, T. Russell, C.M.G., C.B.E.

ECONOMY

Based on a complete absence of direct taxation, the Cayman Islands have been successfully promoted over the past 25 years as an offshore financial centre. At the end of 1988 there were 527 banks and trust companies and 391 insurance companies licensed, and over 18,250 companies registered. Promotion of tourism, with an emphasis on scuba diving, has also been successful, and there were 218,709 visitors by air and 315,585 cruise ship callers in 1988. The two industries support a heavy imbalance in trade resulting from the need to import most of what is consumed and used on the Islands. Import duty and fees from financial centre operations have provided revenue enabling the government to undertake heavy investment in education, health and other social programmes.

FINANCE

	1988	1989*
Revenue	CI$91·34m	CI$97·04m
Expenditure	72·60m	83·50m

*estimated

At end 1988, public debt totalled CI$24·84 million, compared to CI$18·17 million at end 1987.

TRADE

	1986	1987
Total imports	CI$134m	CI$162·6m
Total exports	2·2m	2·2m

Trade with U.K.

	1987	1988
Imports from U.K........	£6,442,000	£5,051,000
Exports to U.K.	1,318,000	9,858,000

FALKLAND ISLANDS

The Falkland Islands, the only considerable group in the South Atlantic, lie about 300 miles east of the Straits of Magellan, between 52° 15′–53° S. lat. and 57° 40′–62° W. long. They consist of East Falkland (area 2,610 sq. miles; 6,759 sq. km.), West Falkland (2,090 sq. miles; 5,413 sq. km.) and upwards of 100 small islands in the aggregate. Mount Usborne (E. Falkland), the loftiest peak, rises 2,312 feet above the level of the sea.

The climate is cool. At Stanley the mean monthly temperature varies between 9° C. in January and 2° C. in July. The islands are chiefly moorland.

The Falklands were sighted first by Davis in 1592, and by Hawkins in 1594: the first known landing was by Strong in 1690. A settlement was made by France in 1764; this was subsequently sold to Spain, but the latter country recognized Great Britain's title to a part at least of the group in 1771. After Argentina declared independence from Spain, the Argentine government in 1820 proclaimed its sovereignty over the Falklands and a settlement was founded in 1826. The settlement was destroyed by the Americans in 1831. In 1833 occupation was resumed by the British for the protection of the seal-fisheries, and the islands were permanently colonized as the most southerly organized colony of the British Empire. Argentina continued to claim sovereignty over the islands (known to them as las Islas Malvinas), and in pursuance of this claim invaded the islands on April 2, 1982 and also occupied South Georgia. A Task Force despatched from Great Britain recaptured South Georgia on April 25, and after landing at San Carlos Bay on May 21, recaptured the islands from the Argentines, who surrendered on June 14, 1982. A British naval and military presence remains in the area.

The population was 1,916 at Dec. 31, 1986 and is almost totally British.

CHIEF TOWN.—ΨStanley, population 1,231 (1986). Stanley is distant from England about 8,103 miles.

CURRENCY.—Falkland pound of 100 pence.

GOVERNMENT

Under the 1985 Constitution, the Governor is advised by an Executive Council consisting of three elected members of the Legislative Council and two ex-officio members, the Chief Executive and the Financial Secretary. The Legislative Council consists of eight elected members and the same two ex-officio members.

Governor, His Excellency William Hugh Fullerton, C.M.G. (1988).
Commander, British Forces, Falkland Islands, Air Vice-Marshal D. O. Crwys-Williams.
Acting Chief Executive, R. Sampson.
Financial Secretary, J. Buckland-James.
Attorney General, D. G. Lang, Q.C.

LONDON OFFICE

Falkland Islands Government Office,
Falkland House, 14 Broadway, SW1H 0BH
[01-222 2542]

Government Representative, D. L. Clifton.

FINANCE

	1987–88*	1988–89*
Public Revenue	£39,762,000	£35,761,000
Expenditure	24,592,000	28,646,000

*Estimated.

ECONOMY

The economy was formerly based solely on agriculture, principally sheep-farming with a little dairy farming for domestic requirements and crops for winter fodder. Since the establishment of an interim conservation and management zone around the islands and the consequent introduction on Feb. 1, 1987 of a licensing regime for vessels fishing within the zone the economy has diversified and income from the associated fishing activities is now the largest source of revenue. Chief imports are provisions, alcoholic beverages, timber, clothing and hardware.

Trade with U.K.

	1987	1988
Imports from U.K........	£7,353,000	£9,037,000
Exports to U.K.	8,148,000	4,209,000

GIBRALTAR

Gibraltar is a rocky promontory, 2¾ miles in length, three-quarters of a mile in breadth and 1,396 ft. high at its greatest elevation, near the southern extremity of Spain, with which it is connected by a low isthmus. It is about 14 miles distant from the opposite coast of Africa. In a total area of 2¼ sq. miles (6 sq. km.), the population at the census of Nov. 1981 was 28,719. At the end of 1988, it stood at 30,077.

Gibraltar is a naval base of strategic importance to Great Britain. It was captured in 1704, during the war of the Spanish Succession, by a combined Dutch and English force, under Sir George Rooke, and was ceded to Great Britain by the Treaty of Utrecht, 1713. Several attempts have been made to retake it, the most celebrated being the great siege, 1779–83, when General Eliott, afterwards Lord Heathfield, held it for three years and seven months against a combined French and Spanish force. The town stands at the foot of the promontory on the W. side.

CURRENCY.—Gibraltar pound of 100 pence.

GOVERNMENT

The Constitution of Gibraltar, approved in 1969, made formal provision for certain domestic matters to devolve on Ministers appointed from among elected members of the House of Assembly then set up to replace the former Legislative Council. The House of Assembly consists of an independent Speaker, 15 elected members, the Attorney-General and the Financial and Development Secretary.

Governor and Commander-in-Chief, His Excellency Air Chief Marshal Sir Peter Terry, G.C.B., A.F.C.
Flag Officer, Gibraltar, and Admiral Supr., H.M. Naval Base, Gibraltar, Rear-Adm. N. J. Hill Norton.
Deputy Governor, W. E. Quantrill £34,000
Financial and Development Secretary, B. Traynor
£30,344
Attorney-General, E. Thistlethwaite, Q.C. . . . £30,344
Chief Justice, A. Kneller £34,000

Chief Minister, J. Bossano.
Speaker, Mayor R. J. Peliza, O.B.E.

ECONOMY

Gibraltar enjoys the advantages of an extensive shipping trade and is a popular shopping centre. The chief sources of revenue are the port dues, the rent of the Crown estate in the town, and duties on consumer items. The free port tradition of Gibraltar is still reflected in the low rates of import duty. The gradual change from a fortress city to a holiday centre has led to a flourishing tourist trade.

A total of 2,762 merchant ships (44,112,541 gross registered tons aggregate) entered the port during 1988. Of these 2,068 were deep-sea ships (43,922,873 gross registered tons aggregate). In addition 5,014 yachts (152,678 gross registered tons) called at the port. There are 26·75 miles of roads.

EDUCATION

Education is compulsory and free for children between the ages of 4 and 15 whose parents are ordinarily resident in Gibraltar. Scholarships are available for higher education in Britain. The total enrolment in Government schools was 4,459 in Dec. 1988.

FINANCE AND TRADE

	1986–87	1987–88
Revenue	£74,216,000	£76,553,000
Expenditure	71,051,000	78,216,000

	1987	1988
Total imports	£140,962,000	£144,717,000
Total exports	51,731,000	46,093,000

Trade with U.K.

	1987	1988
Imports from U.K.	£49,986,000	£67,944,000
Exports to U.K.	3,367,000	4,537,000

HONG KONG

Hong Kong, consisting of a number of islands and of a portion of the mainland (Kowloon and the New Territories), on the south-eastern coast of China, is situated at the eastern side of the mouth of the Pearl River, between 22° 9′ and 22° 37′ N. lat. and 113° 52′– 114° 30′ E. long. The total area of the territory (including recent reclamation) is 413 sq. miles (1,071 sq. km.) with a population which at the end of 1988 was 5,700,000.

The island of Hong Kong is about 11 miles long and from two to five miles broad, with a total area of 29 sq. miles; at the eastern entrance to the harbour it is separated from the mainland by a narrow strait. The island was first occupied by Great Britain in January, 1841, and formally ceded by the Treaty of Nanking in 1842; Kowloon was subsequently acquired by the Peking Convention of 1860; and the New Territories, consisting of a peninsula in the southern part of the Guangdong province, together with adjacent islands, by a 99-year lease signed June 9, 1898.

Climate.—Hong Kong enjoys unusually varied weather for a tropical area. The mean monthly temperature ranges from 15° C. to 29° C., though summer temperatures can exceed 33° C and winter temperatures drop below 10° C. The average annual rainfall is 2,225 mm., of which nearly 80 per cent falls between May and September. Tropical cyclones passing at various distances from Hong Kong occur between July and September, causing high winds and heavy rain.

CAPITAL.—ΨVictoria, situated on the island of Hong Kong, is about 81 miles S.E. of Canton and 40 miles E. of the Portuguese province of Macao at the other side of the Pearl River. It lies along the northern shore of the island and faces the mainland; the harbour (23 sq. miles water area) lies between the city and the mainland.

CURRENCY.—Hong Kong dollar (HK$) of 100 cents.

GOVERNMENT

Hong Kong is administered by the Hong Kong Government, at the head of which is the Governor, and its administration has developed from the basic pattern applied to all British-governed territories overseas. Under the terms of the Joint Declaration of the British and Chinese Governments, which entered into force on May 27, 1985, Hong Kong will become with effect from July 1, 1997, a Special Administrative Region of the People's Republic of China. However, the social and economic systems in the S.A.R. will remain unchanged for 50 years.

The Governor governs aided by an Executive Council, consisting of four ex-officio and ten appointed members, and a Legislative Council, which consists of three ex-officio and seven official members, 20 appointed members, 12 elected by the Electoral College and 14 by the functional constituencies.

There is also an Urban Council which provides services relating to public health and sanitation, culture and recreation in the urban area. A Regional Council was also set up in 1986 to provide similar services in the New Territories. Both Councils are financially autonomous.

Governor, His Excellency Sir David Wilson, K.C.M.G. (1987).
Chief Secretary, Hon. Sir David Ford, K.B.E., L.V.O.
Commander, British Forces, Maj.-Gen. Hon. G. D. Johnson, O.B.E., M.C.
Financial Secretary, Hon. Sir Piers Jacobs, K.B.E.
Attorney-General, Hon. J. F. Mathews, C.M.G
Secretary for Trade and Industry, J. Chan, L.V.O., O.B.E
Secretary for District Administration, Hon. D. Liao, C.B.E.
Secretary for Economic Services, Mrs. Anson Chan.
Secretary for Security, Hon. G. T. Barnes, C.B.E.
Secretary for Lands and Works, Hon. G. Barnes, C.B.E.
Secretary for Education and Manpower, Yeung Kai-yin.
Secretary for Health and Welfare, Hon. Chak Tak-hay.
Secretary for Administrative Services and Information, Hon. P. K. Y. Tsao, C.B.E, C.P.M.
Secretary for Transport, Hon. M. Leung.
Secretary for Monetary Affairs, D. A. C. Nendick.
Secretary for the Civil Service, H. S. Grewal, E.D.
Secretary for Municipal Services, A. K. Chui.
Secretary (General Duties), E. B. Wiggham.
Chief Justice, Hon. Sir Ti Liang Yang.
British Council Representative, J. Davey, Easey Commercial Building, 225 Hennessy Road, Hong Kong.

LONDON OFFICE
Hong Kong Government Office
6 Grafton Street, W1X 3LB
[01-499 9821]

Commissioner, John Yaxley.

COMMUNICATIONS

Hong Kong, one of the world's finest natural harbours, possesses excellent wharves. The Kwai Chung container terminal has eight berths which can accommodate eight "third-generation" container ships simultaneously. An ocean terminal pier with an overall length of 381 m. can accommodate large liners and cargo vessels. Vessels up to 550 metres length and 16·5 metres draught can be berthed. Mooring buoys in the harbour are available to vessels of up to 12 metres draught. Excellent dockyard facilities are available and include five floating drydocks, the largest of which has a lifting capacity of over 40,000 tonnes. In 1988 some 17,089 ocean-going vessels and 94,931 river-trade vessels called at Hong Kong and loaded and discharged more than 81 million tonnes of cargo.

Hong Kong International Airport, Kai Tak, situated to the east of the Kowloon peninsula, is an important link on the main air routes of the Far East. It is regularly used by over 37 international airlines, providing some 1,400 frequent scheduled passenger and cargo services each week between Hong Kong and the United Kingdom, the People's Republic of China, North and South America, Europe, East and South Africa, the Middle East, Australia, the South Pacific region, and Asian countries. In addition, several other airlines operate about 230 non-scheduled services a week.

During 1988, over 87,000 aircraft on international flights arrived and departed, carrying 15·3 million passengers and 694,000 tonnes of freight.

EDUCATION

In Sept. 1988 there were 2,115 day schools with 1,228,786 pupils. Free education for children up to the age of 15 was made compulsory in 1979. Post-secondary education is provided by two universities, two polytechnics, the Hong Kong Baptist College and two approved post-secondary colleges. The Hong Kong Polytechnic and City Polytechnic of Hong Kong have about 8,208 and 3,376 full-time students respectively. There are also eight technical institutes and four teacher-training colleges.

FINANCE

	1986–87	1987–88
Public revenue	HK$48,602m	HK$60,875m
Public expenditure	42,702m	48,375m

TRADE AND INDUSTRY

The manufacturing sector is the mainstay of Hong Kong's economy, contributing about 22 per cent to the G.D.P and accounting for about 35 per cent of total employment. Up to 90 per cent of Hong Kong's manufacturing output is eventually exported.

Hong Kong's manufacturing industries produce mainly light consumer goods. In the past ten years or so, industries like electronics, plastics, electrical products, and watches and clocks have grown significantly—they accounted for 39 per cent of Hong Kong's total domestic exports in 1988. The corresponding share of textiles and clothing, Hong Kong's traditional leading industries, was 38 per cent in 1988.

Diversification in terms of products and markets continues to be the main feature of recent industrial development, as are industrial partnerships with overseas companies. The economy of Hong Kong is based on export rather than the domestic market. In 1988, the total value of visible trade (including domestic exports, re-exports and imports) amounted to 233 per cent of the G.D.P. Hong Kong's visible

trade account attained in 1988 a surplus of HK$5,729 million. Taking visible and invisible trade together, there was a combined surplus of HK$24,542 million, compared with HK$23,703 million in 1987. In 1988, Hong Kong's principal customers for its domestic products, in order of value of trade, were U.S.A., China, the Federal Republic of Germany, the United Kingdom, Japan, Canada and Singapore. China was its principal supplier.

	1987	1988
	HK$	HK$
Total Exports	378,034m	493,069m
Total Imports	377,948m	498,798m

Trade with U.K.

	1987	1988
Imports from U.K.	£1,013,038,000	£1,030,725,000
Exports to U.K.	1,531,681,000	1,788,631,000

MONTSERRAT

Situated in 16° 45′ N. lat. and 61° 15′ W. long., 27 miles S.W. of Antigua, the island is about 11 miles long and seven wide, with an area of 38 sq. miles (98 sq. km.), and a population (1988), of 11,900. Discovered by Columbus in 1493, it was settled by Irishmen in 1632, conquered and held by the French for some time, and finally assigned to Great Britain in 1783. Fertile and green, it is volcanic with several hot springs. About two-thirds of the island is mountainous, the rest capable of cultivation.

CHIEF TOWN.—ΨPlymouth. Population 3,000.

CURRENCY.—East Caribbean dollar (EC$) of 100 cents.

GOVERNMENT

A Ministerial system was introduced in Montserrat in 1960. The Executive Council is presided over by the Governor and is composed of four elected members (the Chief and three other Ministers) and two ex-officio members (the Attorney-General and the Financial Secretary). The four Ministers are appointed from the members of the political party holding the majority in the Legislative Council. The Legislative Council consists of the Speaker, two ex-officio members (the Attorney General and the Financial Secretary), two nominated unofficial members and seven elected members.

Governor, His Excellency Christopher John Turner, O.B.E. (1987).

Executive Council
(as at May 31, 1989)

President, The Governor.

Chief Minister and Minister of Finance, Hon. J. A. Osborne.

Communications and Works, Hon. J. B. Chalmers.

Education, Health and Community Services, Hon. V. K. Jeffers.

Agriculture, Trade, Lands and Housing, Hon. N. Tuitt.

Attorney-General, Hon. O. Adams.

Financial Secretary, J. E. Ryan.

Speaker of the Legislative Council, Hon. H. A. Fergus, O.B.E.

ECONOMY

The economy is dominated by tourism, related construction activities and offshore business services. The chief export in 1987 was electronic components assembled on the island, but attempts are being made to expand sea island cotton, agriculture, data processing and some other island-based exports. The island has also established a computer centre to reinforce its position as a regional information technology, telecommunications and media communications base.

FINANCE		
	1986	1987
Revenue	EC$25,843,338	EC$27,734,100
Expenditure	25,156,090	27,241,000

Trade with U.K.

	1987	1988
Imports from U.K....	£2,432,000	£2,524,000
Exports to U.K.	139,000	125,000

PITCAIRN ISLANDS

Pitcairn, a small volcanic island, 1·9 sq. miles (5 sq. km.), in area, is the chief of a group of islands situated about midway between New Zealand and Panama in the South Pacific Ocean at longitude 130° 06′ W. and latitude 25° 04′ S.

The island rises in cliffs to a height of 1,100 feet and access from the sea is possible only at Bounty Bay, a small rocky cove, and then only by surf boats. Mean monthly temperatures vary between 66° F. (19°C) in August and 75° F. (24°C) in February and the average annual rainfall is 80 inches. With an equable climate, the island is very fertile and produces both tropical and sub-tropical trees and crops.

The small community, numbering 52 (1988), are descendants of the Bounty mutineers and their Tahitian companions who did not wish to remain on Norfolk Island when the entire community was transferred there in 1856, and returned to Pitcairn three years later.

Pitcairn became a British Settlement under the British Settlement Act, 1887, and was administered by the Governor of Fiji from 1952 until 1970, when the administration was transferred to the British High Commission in New Zealand and the British High Commissioner was appointed Governor. The local Government Ordinance of 1964 provides for a Council of ten members of whom four are elected.

Governor of Pitcairn, Henderson, Ducie and Oeno Islands, His Excellency R. A. C. Byatt, C.M.G. (*British High Commissioner to New Zealand*).
Island Magistrate and Chairman of Island Council, B. Young.
Education Officer and Government Adviser, L. Buckley.

The islanders live by subsistence gardening and fishing, and their limited monetary needs are satisfied by the manufacture of wood carvings and other handicrafts which are sold to passing ships and to a few overseas customers. Other than small fees charged for gun and driving licences there are no taxes and Government revenue is derived almost solely from the sale of postage stamps. Communication with the outside world is maintained by cargo vessels travelling between New Zealand and Panama which call at irregular intervals; and by means of telephone telegraphic links with New Zealand.

The New Zealand Education Department provides assistance in recruiting a teacher for the sole-charge school. Education is compulsory between the ages of five and fifteen. Secondary education in New Zealand is encouraged by the Administration which provides scholarships and bursaries for the purpose. Medical care is provided by a registered nurse when a doctor is not present. Since 1887 the islanders have all been adherents of the Seventh Day Adventist Church.

The other three islands of the group (Henderson

lying 105 miles E.N.E. of Pitcairn, Oeno lying 75 miles N.W. and Ducie lying 293 miles E.) are all uninhabited. Henderson Island is occasionally visited by the Pitcairn Islanders to obtain supplies of "miro" wood which is used for their carvings. Oeno is visited for excursions of about a week's duration every two years or so.

ST. HELENA

Probably the best known of all the solitary islands in the world, St. Helena is situated in the South Atlantic Ocean, 955 miles S. of the Equator, 702 S.E. of Ascension, 1,140 from the nearest point of the African Continent, 1,800 from the coast of S. America, 1,694 from Cape Town (transit 5 days), in 15° 55′ S. lat. and 5° 42′ W. longitude. It is 10½ miles long, 6½ broad, and encloses an area of 47 sq. miles (122 sq. km.), with a population of 5,564 (end 1987).

St. Helena is of volcanic origin, and consists of numerous rugged mountains, the highest rising to 2,700 feet, interspersed with picturesque ravines. Although within the tropics, the south-east "trades" keep the temperature mild and equable. St. Helena was discovered by the Portuguese navigator, Juan da Nova Castella, in 1502 (probably on St. Helena's Day) and remained unknown to other European nations until 1588. It was used as a port of call for vessels of all nations trading to the East until it was annexed by the Dutch in 1633. It was never occupied by them, however, and the English East India Company seized it in 1659. In 1834 it was ceded to the Crown. During the period 1815 to 1821 the island was lent to the British Government as a place of exile for the Emperor Napoleon Bonaparte who died in St. Helena on May 5, 1821. It was formerly an important station on the route to India, but its prosperity decreased after the construction of the Suez Canal. Since the collapse of the New Zealand flax industry in 1965, there have been no significant exports. ΨSt. James's Bay, on the north-west of the island, possesses a good anchorage. There is as yet no airport or airstrip.

CAPITAL.—ΨJamestown. Population (1987), 1,330.
CURRENCY.—St. Helena pound (£) of 100 pence.

GOVERNMENT

The government of St. Helena is administered by a Governor, with the aid of a Legislative Council, consisting of the Governor, two ex-officio members (Chief Secretary and Financial Secretary) and twelve elected members. Five committees of the Legislative Council are responsible for general oversight of the activities of Government Departments and have in addition a wide range of statutory and administrative functions. The Governor is also assisted by an Executive Council of the two ex-officio members and the Chairmen of the Council committees.

Governor, His Excellency Robert F. Stimson (1988).
Chief Secretary, (vacant).
Financial Secretary, M. Rosling.
Senior Medical Officer, Dr. R. Grant.
Dir. of Agriculture and Natural Resources, V. Hart.
Chief Education Officer, B. George.
Dir. of Works, A. Rennie.
Social Services Officer, I. Ellick.

FINANCE AND TRADE

	1986–87	1987–88
Local revenue	£2,205,400	£2,866,300
Budgetary	3,650,000	3,015,200
Recurrent expenditure	5,563,200	5,734,900
Development aid	2,081,700	2,595,300
Total imports	5,049,000	5,656,000
Total exports	73,000	100,000

ASCENSION

The small island of Ascension lies in the South Atlantic (7° 56′ S., 14° 22′ W.) some 700 miles north-west of the island of St. Helena. It is a rocky peak of purely volcanic origin, the highest point (Green Mountain) some 2,817 ft. is covered with lush vegetation. Ascension Island Services operate a farm of some 10 acres on the mountain, producing vegetables and livestock. The island is famous for turtles, which land on the beaches from January to May to lay their eggs. It is also a breeding area for the sooty tern, or wideawake, large numbers of which settle on the south-western coastal section every eighth month to hatch their eggs. Other wild life on the island includes feral donkeys and cats, rabbits and francolin partridge. All wildlife except rabbits and cats is protected by law. The ocean surrounding the island abounds with shark, barracuda, tuna, bonito and many other fish.

Ascension is said to have been discovered by Juan da Nova Castella, on Ascension Day, 1501, and two years later was visited by Alphonse d'Albuquerque, who gave the island its present name. It was uninhabited until the arrival of Napoleon in St. Helena in 1815 when a small British naval garrison was stationed on the island. It remained under the supervision of the Board of Admiralty until 1922, when it was made a dependency of St. Helena by Royal Letters Patent.

The British Foreign Secretary appoints the Administrator who is responsible to the Governor resident in St. Helena. There is a small Police Force and Post Office. The British organizations through Ascension Island Services (AIS) provide and operate various common services for the island (school, hospital, public works etc).

Ascension Island is a main relay point of the coaxial submarine cable system laid between South Africa, Portugal and the United Kingdom, which is operated by the South Atlantic Cable Company. Cable & Wireless PLC operates the international telephone and cable services and maintains an internal telephone service. The B.B.C. opened its Atlantic relay station broadcasting to Africa and South America in 1967.

The resident population in March 1989 totalled 1,081, of whom 704 were from St. Helena, 177 from the U.K., 187 from the U.S.A. and 13 from the Republic of South Africa. The residents consist of the employees and families of the British organizations, of the contractors of the U.S. Air Force and N.A.S.A. (Computer Sciences Raytheon and Bendix Field Engineering Corporation) and of the St. Helena Government. (N.A.S.A./Bendix were due to leave on Sept. 30, 1989).

British forces returned to the island in April 1982 in support of operations in the Falkland Islands. At present there are about 160 R.A.F. personnel on the island supporting the air link to the Falklands.

Capital.—Georgetown.

Administrator, J. J. Beale.

TRISTAN DA CUNHA

Tristan da Cunha is the chief of a group of islands of volcanic origin lying in lat. 37° 6′ S. and long. 12° 2′ W., discovered in 1506 by a Portuguese admiral (Tristão da Cunha), after whom they are named. They have a total area of 40 sq. miles (104 sq. km.).

Population (1988) 311. The main island, with a peak rising to 6,760 ft., is about 1,500 miles W. of the Cape of Good Hope, 3,600 miles N.E. of Cape Horn, and about 1,320 miles S.S.W. of St. Helena. It was the resort of British and American sealers from the middle of the 18th century, and in 1760 a British naval officer visited the group and gave his name to Nightingale Island. On August 14, 1816, the group was annexed to the British Crown and a garrison was placed on Tristan da Cunha, but this force was withdrawn in 1817, William Glass, a corporal of artillery (*died* 1853), remaining at his own request, with his wife and two children. This party, with five others, formed a settlement. In 1827 five women from St. Helena, and afterwards others from Cape Colony, joined the party.

The islands form a dependency of St. Helena, being administered by the Foreign and Commonwealth Office through a resident Administrator, with headquarters at the settlement of Edinburgh. Under a new constitution introduced in 1969, he is advised by an elected Island Council of 8 members of whom one must be a woman, and three appointed members, with universal suffrage at 18. The population numbered 294 persons in 1986, plus five expatriate Government officers and their families, and a resident chaplain.

In October, 1961, a volcano, believed to have been extinct for thousands of years, erupted and the danger of further volcanic activity led to the evacuation of inhabitants to the United Kingdom. An advance party returned to Tristan da Cunha in the spring of 1963, and subsequently the main body of the islanders returned to the island.

A boat harbour was completed in 1967. The first freezing factory was re-established in 1966. There are no taxes on Tristan, income being derived from royalties paid by the fishing company and from the sale of stamps and handicrafts. The Camogli Hospital was opened early in 1971 and a new school in 1975.

Capital.—Edinburgh.

Administrator, R. Perry.

INACCESSIBLE ISLAND is a lofty mass of rock with sides 2 miles in length; the island is the resort of penguins and sea-fowl. Cultivation was started in 1937, but has been abandoned.

THE NIGHTINGALE ISLANDS are three in number, of which the largest is 1 mile long and ¾ mile wide, and rises in two peaks, 960 and 1,105 ft. above sea-level respectively. The smaller islands, Stoltenhoff and Middle Isle, are little more than huge rocks. Seals, innumerable penguins, and vast numbers of sea-fowl visit these islands.

GOUGH ISLAND (or Diego Alvarez), in 40° 20′ S. and 9° 44′ W., lies about 250 miles S.S.E. of Tristan da Cunha. The island is about 8 miles long and 4 miles broad, with a total area of 40 square miles, and has been a British possession since 1816. The island is the resort of penguins and sea-elephants and has valuable guano deposits. There is no permanent population, but there is a meteorological station maintained on the island by the South African Government and manned by South Africans.

SOUTH GEORGIA AND THE SOUTH SANDWICH ISLANDS

South Georgia is an island 800 miles east-south-east of the Falkland group, with an area of 1,450 sq. miles. The population comprises an army unit at King Edward Point, and staff of the British Antarctic Survey at Bird Island, in the north-west of S. Georgia.

The South Sandwich Islands lie some 470 miles S.E. of South Georgia. The group is a chain of uninhabited, actively volcanic islands about 150 miles long, with a wholly Antarctic climate.

The present constitution came into effect on Oct. 3, 1985. It provides for a Commissioner who, for the time being, shall be the officer administering the Government of the Falkland Islands.

Commissioner for South Georgia and the South Sandwich Islands, William Hugh Fullerton, C.M.G. (1988).

TURKS AND CAICOS ISLANDS

The Turks and Caicos Islands are situated between 21° and 22° N. latitude and 71° and 72° W. longitude, about 100 miles north of the Dominican Republic and 50 miles south-east of the Bahamas of which they are geographically an extension. There are over 30 islands of which eight are inhabited covering an estimated area of 166 sq. miles (430 sq. km.). The principal is Grand Turk. The population in 1988 was estimated to be 14,000 (Grand Turk 3,146).

The Islands lie in the Trade Wind but with an excellent climate. The average temperature varies from 24°–27° C. in the winter and 29°–32° C. in the summer and humidity is generally low. Average rainfall is 21 inches per annum.

GOVERNMENT

A new Constitution was introduced in 1988, providing for an enlarged Executive Council and Legislative Council. The Executive Council is presided over by the Governor and comprises the Chief Minister and four elected Ministers, together with the Chief Secretary, the Attorney General and the Financial Secretary ex-officio.

At the General Election of March 3, 1988, the People's Democratic Movement won 11 seats and the People's National Party 2 seats in the Legislative Council.

Governor, His Excellency Michael John Bradley, Q.C. (1987).

Executive Council
(as at May 31, 1989)

President, The Governor.
Chief Secretary, Hon. A. N. Hoole.
Attorney-General, Hon. I. S. Lamb.
Financial Secretary, Hon. A. Robinson, M.B.E.
Members, Hon. O. O. Skippings (*Chief Minister*); Hon. L. N. A. Handfield; Hon. W. L. Swann; Hon. S. I. Harvey; Hon. D. H. Taylor.

The principal airports are on the islands of Grand Turk, Providenciales and South Caicos. There are direct shipping services to the U.S.A. (Miami). There is an air service between Miami, Providenciales and Grand Turk, and between South Caicos and the Bahamas. An internal air service provides a twice daily service between the principal islands. A comprehensive telephone and telex service is provided by Cable and Wireless (W.I.) Ltd.

The most important industries are fishing, tourism and offshore finance.

FINANCE

	1986–87	1987–88
Local Revenue	U.S.$10,895,915	U.S.$12,992,896
Expenditure	13,269,795	14,770,808
Budgetary Aid	3,016,000	2,022,000

Trade with U.K.

	1987	1988
Imports from U.K....	£496,000	£710,000
Exports to U.K.	31,000	66,000

FOREIGN COUNTRIES

The following articles have been revised under the direction of the various Governments or of the British Representatives at foreign capitals and by the Foreign and Commonwealth Office in London, whom the Editor warmly thanks. The Editor is also greatly indebted to the Embassies and Consulates-General in London for various corrections and additions.

AFGHANISTAN
(Da Afghanistan Jamhuriat)

President of the Republic of Afghanistan, Najibullah.
Vice Presidents, Abdul Rahim Hatif; Col.-Gen. Mohammad Rafie; Abdul Hamid Mohtat; Abdul Wahid Sorabi.

COUNCIL OF MINISTERS
(as at February 1989)

Prime Minister, Dr. Mohammad Hassan Sharq.
Deputy Prime Ministers, Sayed Amanuddin Amin; Mohammad Sarwar Mangal; Mahbubullah Koshani.
Finance, Hamidullah Tarzi.
Interior, Gen. Sayed Mohammad Gulabzoi.
Higher and Vocational Education, Mohammad Esmail Danesh.
State Security, Gen. Ghulam Faruq Yaqubi.
Public Health, Sayed Amir Zara.
Foreign Affairs, Abdul Wakil.
Commerce, Borhanoddin Ghiasi.
Planning, Sultan Hussain.
Agriculture and Land Reform, Mohammad Ghafran.
Tribal Affairs, Sulaiman Laeq.
Repatriates, Sayd Ekram Paygir.
Education, Dr. Ghulum Rasul Rasuli.
Civil Aviation, Sher Jan Mazduryar.
Transport, Mohammad Aziz.
Mines and Industries, Mohammad Ishaq Kawa.
Water and Power, Raz Mohammad Paktin.
Construction, Nazar Mohammad.
Communications, Mohammad Aslam Watanjar.
Rehabilitation and Rural Development, Mohammad Asif Zahir.
Light Industry and Foodstuffs, Abdollah Bahar.
Justice, Mohammad Bashir Baghlani.
Information and Culture, Ahmad Bashir Roigar.
Without Portfolio, Nehmat ullah Pazhwak; Sarjang Zazi; Faqir Mohammad Yaqubi; Fazil-ul-Haq Khalikyar; Shah Mohammad Dost; Noor Ahmad Barets.
Chairman of National Assembly, Khalil Ahmad Abawi.
Chairman of Senate, Mahmoud Habibi.

PEOPLE'S DEMOCRATIC PARTY OF AFGHANISTAN

Politburo:
Secretary General, Najibullah.
Secretary, Sultan Ali Keshtmand.
Full Members, Noor Ahmad Noor; Saleh Mohammad Zeary; Gen. Mohammad Rafie; Mohammad Aslam Watanjar; Sulaiman Laeq; Gen. Ghulam Faruq Yaqubi; Abdul Zohur Razmjo; Abdul Wakil; Gen. Sayed Mohammad Gulabzoi; Najmuddin Kawyani; Niaz Mohammad Mohmand; Haider Massoud.
Alternate Members, Nazar Mohammad; Mir Saheb Karwal; Farid Ahmad Mazdak; Lt. Gen. Shahnawaz Tanai.
Central Committee Secretariat, Noor Ahmad Noor; Saleh Mohammad Zeary; Niaz Mohammad Mohmand; Mir Saheb Karwal; Najmuddin Kawyani; Haider Massoud; Mohammad Daoud Razmyar; Abdul Zohur Razmjo.

EMBASSY OF THE REPUBLIC OF AFGHANISTAN
31 Prince's Gate, SW7 1QQ
[01–589 8891/2]

Chargé d'Affaires, Ahmad Sarwar.

Afghanistan lies to the N. and W. of Pakistan. Its ancient name was Aryana, by which title it is referred to by Strabo, the Greek geographer who lived in the 1st century B.C. The estimated area is 250,000 sq. miles (647,497 sq. km.), and the population 18,136,000 (1985 U.N. estimate), although it is estimated that over four million have become refugees in Pakistan and over one million in Iran since the Soviet invasion. The population is very mixed. The most numerous race is the Pushtoons who predominate in the South and West, the Tadjiks, a Persian-speaking people mainly cultivators and small traders, Uzbeks and Turkomen in the North, Hazaras in the centre, Baluchis in the South-West and Nuristanis, who live near the Chitral border. All are Sunni Muslims, except the Hazaras and Kizilbashes, who belong to the Shia sect.

Afghanistan is bounded on the W. by Iran, on the S. by Pakistan, on the N. by the U.S.S.R., and on the E. by Pakistan and China.

Mountains, chief among which are the Hindu Kush, cover three-quarters of the country, the elevation being generally over 4,000 feet. There are three great river basins, the Oxus, Helmand, and Kabul. The climate is dry, with extreme temperatures.

Government.—The constitutional monarchy, introduced by the 1964 Constitution, was overthrown by a coup on July 17, 1973. The country was ruled by Presidential decree until February 1977 when a constitution was approved by a Loya Jirgah (Grand Assembly). Mohammad Daoud was elected President of the Republic but was overthrown on April 27, 1978, by the Armed Forces and power handed to the People's Democratic Party of Afghanistan (PDPA). In December 1979 Soviet troops invaded Afghanistan and installed Babrak Karmal as Secretary General of the PDPA, President of the Revolutionary Council and Head of State. Karmal was replaced as Secretary General of the PDPA by Najibullah in May 1986. A peace agreement in April 1988 led to the withdrawal of Soviet troops which was completed by February 1989. A new Constitution, approved in Nov. 1987, provides for a President, a Council of Ministers, a National Assembly and a Senate.

President Najibullah declared a State of Emergency on Feb. 19, 1989. The Supreme Council for the Defence of the Homeland was established to take control of the country's affairs during the State of Emergency.

Seghbatullah Mujjaddedi was elected President of an interim government-in-exile on Feb. 23, 1989.

Afghanistan is divided into 30 provinces each under a centrally appointed governor.

Judiciary.—The Constitution introduced in 1965 provided for the creation of a legal code, and for a new structure of courts, consisting of a lower court in each *woleswali* (sub province), and a court of appeal in each province, with a Supreme Court in Kabul. The complete separation of executive and judiciary in this constitution was abolished by Presidential Decree in July, 1973. In late 1976 and early 1977 new Penal and Civil Codes were published. The new Constitution leaves the judicial system largely untouched.

Defence.—The Army, which numbered about 80,000 before the Soviet invasion, has been greatly depleted by desertions. Men between the ages of 18 and 40 are liable to four years' military service. A military academy and military colleges are located in Kabul; some regular officers are trained in the U.S.S.R. A small Air Force is maintained. All military and air force equipment is now of Russian pattern.

Production.—Agriculture and sheep raising are the principal industries. There are generally two crops a year, one of wheat (the staple food), barley, or lentils, the other of rice, millet, maize, and dal. Sugar beet and cotton are grown. Afghanistan is rich in fruits. Sheep, including the Karakuli, and transport animals are bred. Silk, woollen and hair cloths and carpets are manufactured. Salt, silver, copper, coal, iron, lead, rubies, lapis lazuli, gold, chrome, barite, uranium, and talc are found.

Main roads run from Kabul to Kandahar, Herat, Maimana via Mazari-Sharif and Faizabad via Khanabad. The road from Kabul to the North was shortened by the completion in 1964 of the Salang pass. Roads cross the border with Pakistan at Chaman and via the Khyber Pass, and there are roads from Herat to the Russian and Iranian borders. A network of minor roads fit for motor traffic in fine weather links up all important towns and districts.

In 1982 the Afghan and Soviet shores of the River Oxus were linked by a road and rail bridge which joins the Afghan port of Hairatan and the Soviet port of Termez. A network of internal air services operates between the main towns.

Language and Literature.—The principal languages of the country are Dari (a form of Persian) and Pushtu, although a number of minority languages are also spoken in various provinces. All schoolchildren learn both Persian and Pushtu. Education is free and nominally compulsory, elementary schools having been established in most centres; there are secondary schools in large urban areas and two universities, one in Kabul (established 1932) and one in Jalalabad (established early 1970's).

Trade.—Exports are mainly Persian lambskins (Karakul), dried fruits, nuts, cotton, raw wool, carpets, spice and natural gas, while the imports are chiefly oil, cotton yarn and piece goods, tea, sugar, machinery and transport equipment.

Trade with U.K.

	1987	1988
Imports from U.K.	£10,735,000	£12,109,000
Exports to U.K.	11,289,000	11,501,000

CAPITAL, Kabul (about 2,000,000). The chief commercial centres are Kabul and Kandahar (185,000). Other provincial capitals are Herat (145,000), Mazar-i-Sharif (105,000), Jalalabad (55,000).

CURRENCY.—Afghani (Af) of 100 puls.

FLAG.—Black, red and green horizontal stripes with a device in top left-hand corner.

NATIONAL ANTHEM.—Soroud-e-Melli.

NATIONAL DAY.—April 27.

BRITISH EMBASSY
Karte Parwan, Kabul
[Kabul 30511/3]

Staff temporarily withdrawn from post.

ALBANIA
(Republika Popullore Socialiste e Shqipërisë)

Chairman of the Presidium of the People's Assembly (i.e. Head of State), Ramiz Alia, *assumed office*, Nov. 22, 1982; *re-elected*, Feb. 19, 1987.

Deputy Chairmen, Rita Marko; Xhafer Spahiu; Emine Guri.

Secretary, Sihat Tozaj.

COUNCIL OF MINISTERS
(as at June 2, 1989)

Prime Minister, Adil Çarçani.

Deputy Prime Ministers, Pali Miska; Manush Myftiu; Simon Stefani.

Agriculture, Pali Miska.

Communal Economy, Xhemal Tafaj.

Construction, Ismail Ahmeti.

Education, Skender Gjinush.

Energy, Industry and Mining, Besnik Bekteshi.

Finance, Andrea Nako.

Food Industry, Jovan Bardhi.

Foreign Affairs, Reiz Malile.

Foreign Trade, Shane Korbeci.

Internal Affairs, Simon Stefani.

Internal Trade, Osman Murati.

Light Industry, Ms. Vito Kapo.

People's Defence, Prokop Murra.

Public Health, Ahmet Kamberi.

Transportation, Hajredin Celiku.

Minister to the Presidium of the Council of Ministers, Farudin Hoxha.

Minister Secretary General of the Council of Ministers, Enver Halili.

Chairman of State Planning Commission, Niko Gjyzari.

Chairman of State Control Commission, Manush Myftiu.

Albanian Workers' Party (AWP)

Politbureau of the Central Committee, R. Alia; M. Asllani; B. Bekteshi; F. Cami; A. Çarçani; H. Celiku; Ms. L. Cuko; H. Isai; R. Marko; P. Miska; P. Murra; M. Myftiu; S. Stefani (*full members*); V. Cerava; L. Gegprifti; P. Kondi; Q. Mihali; K. Mustaqi (*candidate members*).

Secretariat of the Central Committee, R. Alia (*First Secretary*); F. Çami; Ms. L. Cuko; H. Isai.

Chairman of the Party Control Commission, P. Peristeri.

Situated on the Adriatic Sea, Albania is bounded on the north and east by Yugoslavia and on the south by Greece. The area of the Republic is estimated at 11,099 sq. miles (28,748 sq. km.), with a population (1988 estimate) of 3,410,000.

Albania was under Turkish suzerainty from 1468 until 1912, when independence was declared. After a period of unrest, a republic was declared in 1925, and in 1928 a monarchy. The King went into exile in 1939 when the country was occupied by the Italians: Albania was liberated in Nov. 1944. Elections in Dec. 1945 resulted in a Communist-controlled Assembly: the King was deposed in absentia and a republic declared in Jan. 1946. United Kingdom diplomatic relations with Albania ceased due to the invasion in 1939 and although U.K. recognized the provisional government of Enver Hoxha in 1945, relations were broken off in 1946 after a mine sunk a British warship in Albanian waters. They have so far not been restored.

Much of the country is mountainous and nearly a half is covered by forest. There are fertile areas along the Adriatic coast and the Koritza Basin and there have been land reclamation and irrigation programmes. The main crops are wheat, maize, sugarbeet, potatoes and fruit.

All industry is nationalized. The principal industries are agricultural product processing, textiles, oil products and cement. Output is small at present but the chemical and engineering industries are being built up and the country's considerable mineral resources are being increasingly exploited.

Exports include crude oil, minerals (bitumen, chrome, nickel, copper), tobacco, fruit and vegetables.

Trade with U.K.

	1987	1988
Imports from U.K.	£2,565,000	£1,126,000
Exports to U.K.	91,000	2,764,000

CAPITAL, Tirana, pop. 210,757 (1984).
CURRENCY.—Lek (Lk) of 100 qindarka.
FLAG.—Black two-headed eagle surmounted by yellow outline star, all on a red field.
NATIONAL DAY.—January 11.

ALGERIA
(Al-Jumhuriya al-Jazairiya ad-Dimuqratiya ash-Shabiya)

President of State, Secretary-General of the Party, Chadli Bendjedid, *elected,* Feb. 1979, *re-elected,* Jan. 1984 and Dec. 1988.

GOVERNMENT
(as at May 31, 1989)

Prime Minister, Kasdi Merbah.
Foreign Affairs, Boualem Bessaih.
Interior and Environment, Aboubakr Belkaid.
Religious Affairs, Boualem Baki.
Ex-Combatants, Mohamed Djeghaba.
Justice, Ali Benflis.
Labour, Employment and Social Affairs, Mohamed Nabi.
Transport, El-Hadi Khediri.
Information and Culture, Mohamed Ali Ammar.
Finance, Sid Ahmed Ghozali.
Trade, Mourad Medelci.
Hydraulics, Ahmed Benfreha.
Agriculture, Nourredine Kadra.
Public Works, Aissa Abdellaoui.
Construction and Town Planning, Nadir Benmaati.
Light Industry, Mohamed Tahar Bouzeghoub.
Heavy Industry, Mohamed Ghrib.
Energy and Petro-Chemical Industries, Sadek Boussena.
Health, Messaoud Zitouni.
Higher Education, Abdelhamid Aberkane.
Education and Training, Slimane Chikh.
Youth and Sports, Cherif Rahmani.
Posts and Telecommunications, Yacine Fergani.

ALGERIAN EMBASSY
54 Holland Park, W11 3RS
[01–221 7800]

Ambassador Extraordinary and Plenipotentiary, His Excellency Hadj Benabdelkader Azzout (1988).

Algeria lies between 8° 45′ W. to 12° E. longitude 27° 6′ N. to a southern limit about 19° N. Area, 919,595 sq. miles (U.N. estimate). The population (1987 Census) totals 22,971,558.
Government.—Algiers surrendered to a French force on July 5, 1830, and Algeria was annexed to France in Feb. 1842. From 1881 the three northern departments of Algiers, Oran and Constantine formed an integral part of France. The Southern Territories of the Sahara, formerly a separate colony, became an integral part of Algeria on the attainment of independence. An armed rebellion led by the Muslim *Front de Liberation Nationale* (*F.L.N.*) against French rule broke out on Nov. 1, 1954. French control of Algeria came to an end when President de Gaulle declared Algeria independent on July 3, 1962; by October 1963, all agricultural land held by foreigners had been expropriated and by 1965 more than 80 per cent of the French population had left Algeria.

Ben Bella was elected President of the Republic in Sept., 1963, but was deposed and a Council of the Revolution presided over by Col. Boumediène assumed power on June 19, 1965. A new constitution

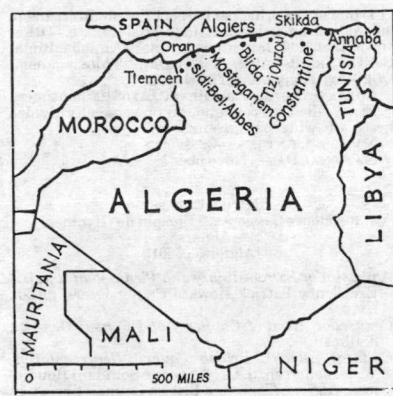

was established by referendum on Nov. 19, 1976, and on Dec. 10, 1976 President Boumediène was elected for a six-year term of office. Elections for a national popular assembly were held in Feb. 1977. Following President Boumediène's death in December 1978, M. Chadli Bendjedid was elected President in February 1979. A new Constitution was agreed by referendum in Feb. 1989 which moves Algeria away from a one-party socialist system to a more pluralist political system.

Development in Algeria is regulated by a series of national development plans. The 1970–73 Plan placed emphasis on industrial development, and the 1974–77 Plan on infrastructure development and social services. The 1980–84 Plan concentrated on housing, water supply and agriculture. The 1985–89 Plan continues with these objectives and also includes food and processing industries. Agrarian reform started in 1987. The 4,000 state farms have been broken up into 23,000 units. Following riots in October 1988, economic reform was speeded up and now endorses the industrial and financial sectors. The aim is to decentralize planning and devolve management. The private sector is also receiving official encouragement.

Algeria's main industry is the hydrocarbons industry. Oil and natural gas are pumped from the Sahara to terminals on the coast before being exported; the gas is first liquefied at liquefaction plants at Skikda and Arzew, although pipelines serve Libya and Italy direct.

Other major industries being developed include a steel industry, motor vehicles, building materials, paper making, chemical products and metal manufactures. Most major industrial enterprises are still under State control.

Trade with U.K.

	1987	1988
Imports from U.K.	£73,115,000	£86,615,000
Exports to U.K.	172,927,000	159,748,000

Algeria's main exports are crude oil and liquefied natural gas. Principal imports from the United Kingdom are capital plant, equipment for industrial use and foodstuffs.

Algeria has a rapidly expanding network of roads and railways. Considerable sums are also being spent on the development of the State airline, the national shipping company and telecommunications.
CAPITAL.—ΨAlgiers, population 3,250,000 (approx).

It is one of the principal ports of the Mediterranean as well as an important industrial centre. Other towns include ΨOran; Constantine; ΨAnnaba; Blida; Setif; Sidi-Bel-Abbès; Tlemcen; ΨMostaganem; ΨSkikda; ΨBejaia and Tizi Ouzou.

CURRENCY.—Algerian dinar (DA) of 100 centimes.

FLAG.—Red crescent and star on vertically divided green and white background.

NATIONAL ANTHEM.—Qassaman.

NATIONAL DAY.—November 1.

BRITISH EMBASSY
Résidence Cassiopée, 7 Chemin de Glycines,
Algiers.
[Algiers 605601]

Ambassador Extraordinary and Plenipotentiary, His Excellency Patrick Howard Caines Eyers, C.M.G., L.V.O.

Counsellor, Head of Chancery and Consul General, J. Illman.

Cultural Attaché, British Council Representative, W. M. Jefferson, O.B.E., 6 Avenue Souidani Boudjemaa, Algiers. There is a British Council library in Algiers.

ANDORRA
(Principat d'Andorra)

Viguier Français, M. Louis Deblé.
Viguier Episcopal, Sr. Francesc Badia.
Head of Government, Sr. Josep Pintat Solens.

A small, neutral principality (formed by a treaty in 1278), situated on the southern slopes of the Pyrenees between Spain and France, with an approximate area of 175 sq. miles (453 sq. km.), and population of about 40,000, less than one fifth of whom are native Andorrans. It is surrounded by mountains of 6,500 to 10,000 feet. Andorra is divided into seven Parishes, each of which has four Councillors elected by vote to the Valleys of Andorra Council of twenty-eight. The Council appoints the head of the executive government, who designates the members of his government. Constitutionally, the sovereignty of Andorra is vested in two "Co-Princes", the President of the French Republic and the Spanish Bishop of Urgel. These two "co-princes" can veto certain decisions of the Council of the Valleys but cannot impose their own decisions without the consent of the Council. They are represented by Permanent Delegates of whom one is the French Prefect of the Pyrenees Orientales Department at Perpignan and the other is the Spanish Vicar-General of the Diocese of Urgel. They are in turn represented in Andorra la Vella by two resident "Viguiers" known as the Viguier Français and the Viguier Episcopal, who have a joint responsibility for law and order and overall administration policy, together with judicial powers as members of the Supreme Court.

The language of the country is Catalan, but French and Spanish (Castilian) are also spoken. Spanish pesetas and French francs are the accepted currency and the Budget is expressed in pesetas. The estimated national revenue (1988) was US$754 million, with a per capita income of $15,403. The climate is cold for six months, but mild in spring and summer. Potatoes are produced in the highlands and tobacco in the valleys. The mountain slopes have been developed for skiing, and it is estimated that 10,000,000 tourists visit the Valleys during the year. The economy is largely based on tourism, commerce, tobacco, construction and forestry; a third of the country is classified as forest in which pine, fir, oak, birch and box-tree predominate. Andorra is negotiating a commercial agreement with the European Community which will regulate future trade with and through neighbouring countries.

A good road into the Valleys from Spain is open all year round, and that from France is closed only occasionally in winter. An airport at Seo d'Urgell just outside Andorra provides very limited air connections. There are two radio stations in Andorra, one privately-owned and one operated by a French Government corporation. Both pay dues to the Council of the Valleys.

Trade with U.K.

	1987	1988
Imports from U.K.	£10,976,000	£10,780,000
Exports to U.K.	200,000	46,000

CAPITAL.—Andorra la Vella (population 16,000).

CURRENCY.—French francs and Spanish pesetas are both in use.

FLAG.—Three vertical bands, blue, yellow, red; Andorran coat of arms frequently imposed on central (yellow) band but not essential.

NATIONAL DAY.—September 8.

H.M. Consul-General, D. Joy, C.B.E. (*resident at Barcelona*) (Tel. 3–322 2151).

ANGOLA
(República Popular de Angola)

President, Jose Eduardo Dos Santos.

COUNCIL OF MINISTERS
(as at June 30, 1989)

Interior, Lt.-Gen. Francisco Magalhaes Paiva.
State Security, Kundi Paihama.
Defence, Col. Gen. Pedro Tonha.
Foreign Affairs, Col. Pedro de Castro Van-Dunem.
Planning, Antonio Henriques da Silva.
Trade, Dumilde das Chagas Simoes Rangel.
Justice, Fernando França van Dunem.
Petroleum and Energy, Zeferino Cassa Yombo.
Industry, (vacant).
Health, Flavio Joao Fernandes.
Labour and Social Security, Diogo Jorge de Jesus.
Construction, Joao Garcia.
Fisheries, Francisco Jose Ramos Da Cruz.
Agriculture, Fernando Faustino Muteka.
Transport and Communications, Carlos Antonio Femandes.
Education, Augusto Teixeira.
Finance, Augusto Teixeira de Matos.
Youth and Sport, Marcolino Jose Carlos Moco.

EMBASSY OF THE PEOPLE'S REPUBLIC OF ANGOLA
87 Jermyn Street, SW1.
[01–839 5743]

Ambassador Extraordinary and Plenipotentiary, His Excellency Luis Antonio Neto Kiambata (1989).

Angola, which has an area of 481,354 sq. miles (1,246,700 sq. km.), lies on the western coast of Africa; its population in 1985 was estimated at 8,754,000.

After a Portuguese presence of at least four centuries, and an anti-colonial war since 1961, Angola became independent on Nov. 11, 1975 in the midst of civil war. Soviet-Cuban military assistance to the Popular Movement for the Liberation of Angola (M.P.L.A.) enabled it to defeat its rivals early in 1976. However, the M.P.L.A. government remains under pressure from the U.N.I.T.A. guerrilla movement (led by Dr. Jonas Savimbi) which now controls up to one-third of the country and operates freely in another third. On Aug. 8, 1988 it was announced that a ceasefire between South African, Cuban and Angolan forces had taken place pending talks on withdrawal from Angola. The ceasefire agreement was signed, and came into effect, on Aug. 22. In Dec. 1988 an agreement providing for the withdrawal of the 50,000 Cuban troops by July 1991, was signed in Cuba.

The M.P.L.A., a Marxist-Leninist party, is the sole legal party. The Constitution provides for a President, who appoints a Council of Ministers to assist him, and a National People's Assembly.

Angola has valuable oil and diamond deposits and exports of these two commodities account for over 90 per cent of total exports.

Principal agricultural crops are cassava, maize, bananas, coffee, palm oil and kernals, cotton and sisal. Coffee, sisal, maize and palm oil are exported: exports also include mahogany and other hardwoods from the tropical rain forests in the north of the country.

Trade with U.K.

	1987	1988
Imports from U.K........	£29,573,000	£26,154,000
Exports to U.K.	2,312,000	10,036,000

CAPITAL.—ΨLuanda (Est. over 1 million in 1984).
CURRENCY.—Kwanza (Kz) of 100 lwei.
FLAG.—Red and black with a yellow star, machete and cog-wheel.
NATIONAL ANTHEM.—Angola Avante.
NATIONAL DAY.—November 11. (Independence Day).

BRITISH EMBASSY
Rua Diogo Caõ 4 (Caixa Postal 1244), Luanda.
[Luanda 334582/3]

Ambassador Extraordinary and Plentipotentiary, His Excellency Michael John Carlisle Glaze, C.M.G., (1987).

ARGENTINA
(República Argentina)

President, Dr. Carlos Saúl Menem, *took office* July 8, 1989.
Vice President, Dr. Eduardo Alberto Dunalde.

CABINET
(as at July 15, 1989)

Interior, Dr. Eduardo Bauzá.
Foreign Affairs, Dr. Domingo Cavallo.
Labour, Sr. Jorge Triaca.
Economy, (vacant).
Education and Justice, Dr. Antonio Salonia.
Defence, Dr. Italo Luder.
Health and Social Welfare, Sr. Julio Corzo.
Public Works, Sr. Roberto Dromi.

EMBASSY IN LONDON
The Embassy closed after the Argentine invasion of the Falkland Islands. Argentine interests in Great Britain are currently handled by the Brazilian Embassy.

Argentina occupies the greater portion of the southern part of the South American Continent, and extends from Bolivia to Cape Horn, a total distance of nearly 2,300 miles; its greatest breadth is about 930 miles. It is bounded on the north by Bolivia, on the north-east by Paraguay, Brazil and Uruguay, on the south-east and south by the Atlantic, and on the west by Chile, from which it is separated by the Cordillera de los Andes. On the west the mountainous Cordilleras, with their plateaux, extend from the northern to the southern boundaries: on the east are the great plains.

The Republic consists of 22 provinces, one territory

(Tierra del Fuego) and one federal district (Buenos Aires), comprising in all an area of 1,068,302 sq. miles (2,766,889 sq. km.), with a population of 30,564,000 (1985, U.N. estimate).

Government.—The estuary of La Plata was discovered in 1515 by Juan Díaz de Solís, but it was not until 1534 that Pedro de Mendoza founded Buenos Aires. This city was abandoned and later re-founded by Don Juan de Garay in 1580. In 1810 (May 25) Spanish rule was defied, and in 1816 (July 9), after a long campaign of liberation conducted by General José de San Martín, the independence of Argentina was declared by the Congress of Tucumán.

In 1946 Juan Domingo Perón became President until overthrown in 1955. There followed eighteen years of political and economic instability, and eventually in 1973, Perón was recalled from exile. Elected President he died within a year and was succeeded by his widow, Vice President María Estela Martínez de Perón. However, warring factions in the Perónist movement and increasing terrorist activity eventually led to a coup by the armed forces on March 24, 1976. A Junta, consisting of the three commanders of the Armed Forces, was established with one of their number as President. Following the Falkland Islands defeat in 1982 the President, Gen. Galtieri, resigned and the Army appointed Gen. Bignone as President. The Navy and Air Force withdrew from the Junta but this was reconstituted shortly afterwards. Elections for a civilian government to replace the military one were held on October 30, 1983 and the Radical Party's candidate, Raúl Alfonsín, was elected President. Presidential elections in May 1989 were won by the Peronist candidate Carlos Menem.

Agriculture.—Of a total land area of approximately 700 million acres, farms occupy about 425 million. About 60 per cent. of the farmland is pasture, 10 per cent. annual crops, 5 per cent. permanent crops and the remaining 25 per cent. forest and wasteland. A large proportion of the land is still held in large estates devoted to cattle raising but the number of small farms is increasing. The principal crops are wheat, maize, oats, barley, rye, linseed, sunflower seed, alfalfa, sugar, fruit and cotton. Argentina is pre-eminent in the production of beef, mutton and wool, and pastoral and agricultural products provide about 85 per cent. of Argentina's exports.

Mineral Production.—Oil is found in various parts of the Republic and the production of oil is of first importance to her industries and, to some extent, to her economic and financial development. Total petroleum output for 1986 was 450,000 b.p.d. There is a refinery in San Lorenzo (Santa Fé province). Natural gas is also produced in a number of provinces.

Coal, lead, zinc, tungsten, iron ore, sulphur, mica and salt are the other chief minerals being exploited. There are small worked deposits of beryllium, manganese, bismuth, uranium, antimony, copper, kaolin, arsenate, gold, silver and tin. Coal production in 1984 was 500,000 tonnes; this is produced at the Rio Turbio mine in the province of Santa Cruz. The output of other materials is not large but greater attention is now being paid to the development of these natural resources, especially copper for which the Government and private companies are carrying out exploration.

Industries.—Meat-packing is one of the principal industries; flour-milling, sugar-refining, and the wine industry are also important. In recent years progress has been made by the textile, plastic and machine tool industries and engineering, especially in the production of motor vehicles and steel manufactures.

Communications.—There are 25,386 miles of railways, which are State property. Plans are in hand for complete re-organization of the railways in order

indigenous literature before the break from Spain, but all branches have flourished since the latter half of the nineteenth century. About 450 daily newspapers are published in Argentina, including 7 major ones in the city of Buenos Aires. The English language newspaper is the *Buenos Aires Herald* (daily). There are several other foreign language newspapers.

Trade with U.K.

	1987	1988
Imports from U.K.	£10,267,000	£12,991,000
Exports to U.K.	64,595,000	66,281,000

CAPITAL.—ΨBuenos Aires, Pop. (1988), Metropolitan area 3,323,000; with suburbs, 9,677,200. Other large towns are: ΨRosario de Santa Fé (798,292), Córdoba (798,663), ΨLa Plata (408,300), ΨMar del Plata (317,444), San Miguel de Tucumán (326,000), ΨSanta Fé (312,427) and Mendoza (118,568).

CURRENCY.—Austral (A) of 100 centavos or 1,000 pesos.

FLAG.—Horizontal bands of blue, white, blue; gold sun in centre of white band.

NATIONAL ANTHEM.—Oid Mortales! El Grito Sagrado, Libertad (Hear, oh mortals! The sacred cry, freedom).

NATIONAL DAY.—May 25.

BRITISH EMBASSY

The British Embassy was closed after the Argentine invasion of the Falkland Islands. British interests are currently handled by a section at the Swiss Embassy, Dr. Luis Agote 2412 52, 1425, Buenos Aires. BRITISH CHAMBER OF COMMERCE, Av. Corrientes 457, 10 piso, 1043 Buenos Aires.

to improve their operating efficiency and reduce a very large financial deficit. The combined national and provincial road network totals approximately 137,000 miles of which 23,180 miles are surfaced. There are air services between Argentina and all the neighbouring republics, Europe, Asia, Canada, the U.S.A. and South Africa. Total tonnage entering Argentine ports in 1979 was 13,879,391.

Defence.—The Army consists of four corps organized into 12 brigades, including mountain, jungle, airborne and armoured troops. It numbers about 47,000, consisting of 20,000 officers and N.C.O.s and 27,000 conscripts who serve for between 6 months and 1 year.

The Navy consists of 1 aircraft carrier, 6 destroyers, 6 corvettes, 4 submarines, 6 minesweepers and ancillary craft. Strength is about 27,000, consisting of 19,500 officers and N.C.O.s and 7,500 conscripts.

The Air Force consists of 9 brigades and a training force, with a strength of 12,000, consisting of 6,900 officers and N.C.O.s and 5,100 conscripts.

Education.—Education is compulsory for the 7 grades of primary school (6 to 13). Secondary schools (14 to 17+) are available in and around Buenos Aires and in most of the important towns in the interior of the country. Most secondary schools are administered by the Central Ministry of Education in Buenos Aires, while primary schools are administered by the Central Ministry or by Provincial Ministries of Education. Private schools, of which there are many, are also loosely controlled by the Central Ministry. Teacher training now takes place at post school level, courses lasting from 2 to 5 years. Many new universities have been created in recent years. The total is now over 50 with 24 national, 25 private and a small number of provincial universities.

Language and Literature.—Spanish is the language of the Republic and the literature of Spain is accepted as an inheritance by the people. There is little

AUSTRIA
(Republik Österreich)

President of the Republic of Austria, Dr. Kurt Waldheim, *born* 1918; *elected* June 8, 1986.

CABINET
(as at May 31, 1989)

Chancellor, Dr. Franz Vranitzky (*SPÖ*).
Vice-Chancellor and Minister for the Constitution and Federalism, Josef Riegler (*ÖVP*).
Foreign Affairs, Alois Mock (*ÖVP*).
Interior, Franz Löschnak (*SPÖ*).
Justice, Dr. Egmont Foregger (*Ind.*).
Finance, Ferdinand Lacina (*SPÖ*).
Nationalized Industries and Transport, Dr. Rudolf Streicher (*SPÖ*).
Agriculture and Forestry, Franz Fischer (*ÖVP*).
Defence, Dr. Robert Lichal (*ÖVP*).
Science and Research, Dr. Erhard Busek (*ÖVP*).
Employment and Social Affairs, Walter Geppert (*SPÖ*).
Education, Arts and Sports, Dr. Hilde Hawlicek (*SPÖ*).
Economic Affairs, Wolfgang Schüssel (*ÖVP*).
Environment, Youth and Family, Dr. Marilies Flemming (*ÖVP*).
Ministers at Federal Chancellery, Harald Ettl (*SPÖ*) (*Civil Servants and Health*); Günter Stummvoll (*Finance*); Johanna Dohnal (*SPÖ*) (*Women's Affairs*).
SPÖ: Socialists; *ÖVP*: People's Party (Conservatives).

AUSTRIAN EMBASSY
18 Belgrave Mews West, SW1X 8HU
[01–235 3731]

Ambassador Extraordinary and Plenipotentiary, His Excellency Dr. Walter F. Magrutsch (1987).

Austria is a country of Central Europe bounded on the north by Czechoslovakia, on the south by Italy and Yugoslavia, on the east by Hungary, on the north-west by the Federal Republic of Germany and on the west by Switzerland and Liechtenstein. Its area is 32,374 sq. miles (83,849, sq. km.), and its population is 7,557,000 (1987, estimate).

Government.—The Republic of Austria comprises nine provinces (Vienna, Lower Austria, Upper Austria, Salzburg, Tyrol, Vorarlberg, Carinthia, Styria and Burgenland) and was established in 1918 on the break-up of the Austro-Hungarian Empire. On March 13, 1938, as a result of the *Anschluss*, Austria (*Österreich*) was incorporated into the *Deutsches Reich* under the name *Ostmark*. After the liberation of Vienna in 1945, the Republic of Austria was reconstituted within the frontiers of 1937 and a freely-elected Government took office on December 20, 1945. The country was divided at this time into four zones occupied respectively by the U.K., U.S.A., U.S.S.R. and France, while Vienna was jointly occupied by the four Powers. On May 15, 1955, the Austrian State Treaty was signed in Vienna by the Foreign Ministers of the four Powers and of Austria. This Treaty recognized the re-establishment of Austria as a sovereign, independent and democratic state, having the same frontiers as on January 1, 1938.

There is a national assembly of 183 Deputies. After the elections of Nov. 1986, the Socialists formed a coalition with the People's Party.

The state of the parties in the Nationalrat (Lower House) in Nov. 1986, was:

Socialist Party (Social Democrat)	80
People's Party (Conservative)	77
Freedom Party (Liberal)	18
Green Party	8

In the Bundesrat (Upper House) in March 1988 the People's Party held 32 seats, the Socialist Party 30 and the Liberal Party 1 seat.

Religion and Education.—The predominant religion is Roman Catholic. Education is free and compulsory between the ages of 6 and 15 and there are good facilities for secondary, technical and professional education. There are 12 state-maintained Universities and six colleges of art.

Language and Literature.—The language of Austria is German, but the rights of the Slovene- and Croat-speaking minorities in Carinthia, Styria and Burgenland are protected. The press is free.

Communications.—Internal communications in Austria are partly restricted because of the mountainous nature of the country, although there has been an extensive programme to increase the number of motorways, many of which are tunnelled through the mountains. There were, in 1985, 37,501 km. of roads, including a network of *autobahn* between major cities which also links up with the West German and Italian networks. The railways in Austria are state-owned and in 1985 had 5,766 km. of track, over half of which is electrified. Of the 425 km. of waterways, 355 km. are navigable and there is considerable trade through the Danube ports by both local and foreign shipping. There are six commercial airports catering for 4,872,922 passengers in 1985.

Tourism.—In 1986, 15,092,200 tourists visited Austria. Foreign exchange receipts from tourism were 101,555 million Schilling—a major contribution to the balance of payments.

PRODUCTION AND INDUSTRY

The origin of Gross Domestic Product in 1986 was as follows (in per cent.):

Agriculture and forestry	4·7
Mining and material goods production	30·8

Energy and water supply	3·2
Construction	6·3
Commerce, hotels, restaurants	16·4
Transport and communications	6·4
Asset management	12·6
Other services and producers	16·7
Import duties and other items	2·9

The value of G.D.P. in 1986 (at current prices) was Schilling 1,441,100 million: G.D.P. per capita (at current prices) was Schilling 190,627.

Agriculture.—The arable land produces wheat, rye, barley, oats, maize, potatoes, sugar beet, turnips, and miscellaneous crops. Many varieties of fruit trees flourish and the vineyards produce excellent wine. The pastures support horses, cattle and pigs. Timber forms a valuable source of Austria's indigenous wealth, about 40·7 per cent. of the total land area consisting of forest areas. Coniferous species predominate (75 per cent. of afforested area).

Energy.—Energy production in 1986 was:—

Crude oil

—production	1,116,000	tonnes
—imports	6,188,000	„
(from Libya	2,113,202	„)
(from Algeria	838,647	„)

Natural gas

—production	1,112m. cu. metres	
—imports	4,055m. cu. metres	
(from U.S.S.R.	3,956m. cu. metres)	

Electric power

—output	44,652m. kWh.
—imports	5,962m. kWh.
—exports	7,426m. kWh.

A 700 mw nuclear power station had already been constructed when in November 1978 the Austrian people decided by a very small margin in a national referendum not to allow the introduction of nuclear power stations in Austria.

Mining.—Production was (tonnes):—

	1985	1986
Lignite	3,081,071	2,968,978
Iron/manganese ore	3,270,000	3,120,000
Raw magnesite	1,255,043	1,084,360
Lead/zinc ore	643,255	400,246
Crystal salt	437,584	485,513
Graphite	30,764	36,167

In addition 2,306,706 cu. metres of brine was produced in 1985 and 2,335,067 cu. metres in 1986.

Industry.—Heavy industry production in 1986 included pig iron 3,348,600 tonnes, raw steel 4,291,895 tonnes and rolled steel 3,461,545 tonnes. In addition, petroleum, non-ferrous metals and chemicals are processed in quantity and construction materials, industrial machinery, vehicles, paper and textiles are produced.

FINANCE

	1986	1987
	Schilling, million	
Federal Budget:		
Revenue	391,675	409,556
Expenditure	498,380	514,461
Gross Budget Deficit	106,705	104,905

Federal Budget expenditure (S million):—

	1985	1986
Agriculture, forestry	12,493·0	13,622·0
Defence	17,147·3	18,495·0
Education	39,733·6	42,452·0
Internal security, justice	14,583·4	15,365·0
Public services	7,892·8	6,479·0
Roads	15,927·8	16,682·0
Science and research	14,110·8	17,162·0
Health and Social welfare	113,686·3	119,949·0
Transportation	89,369·4	97,668·0

	1985	1986
Expenditure on debts	69,654·0	75,707·0
Other purposes	69,883·6	74,782·0

TRADE

Main exports are processed goods (iron and steel, textiles, paper and cardboard products), machinery and transport equipment, other finished goods (including clothing), raw materials and foodstuffs. Main imports are machinery and transport equipment, processed goods, chemical products, foodstuffs, fuel and energy.

	1986	1987
	Schilling, million	
Imports	407,954	411,859
Exports	342,479	342,433

Over 80 per cent. of all trade is with other European countries, E.C. countries accounting for about 60 per cent., Eastern Europe for about 9 per cent. and E.F.T.A. members for 9 per cent.

Trade with U.K.

	1987	1988
Imports from U.K.	£463,187,000	£509,991,000
Exports to U.K.	781,986,000	874,430,000

CAPITAL, Vienna, on the Danube, population 1,531,346. Other towns are Graz (243,166), Linz (199,910), Innsbruck (117,287), Salzburg (139,426), and Klagenfurt (87,321).

CURRENCY.—Schilling of 100 Groschen.

FLAG.—Horizontal stripes of red, white, red, with eagle crest on white stripe.

NATIONAL ANTHEM.—Land der Berge, Land am Strome (Land of mountains, land of streams).

NATIONAL DAY.—October 26.

BRITISH EMBASSY
Jauresgasse 12, 1030 Vienna
[Vienna 7131575]

Ambassador Extraordinary and Plenipotentiary, His Excellency Brian Lee Crowe, C.M.G. (1989).

Counsellor, Consul General and Head of Chancery, R. P. Nash, L.V.O.

Counsellors, D. H. Cecil; P. A. S. Wise.

First Secretaries, S. J. O'Flaherty; S. G. Ratcliffe (*Commercial*); J. Moorby, M.B.E. (*H.M. Consul*); A. N. King, L.V.O. (*Administration*); M. G. Dalton (*Economic*); R. Dear (*Chancery*/*Information*); S. G. Barnes.

Defence Attaché, Lt.-Col. J. M. Craster.

There is a British Consular Office at *Vienna*, and Honorary Consulates at *Bregenz, Graz, Innsbruck* and *Salzburg*.

British Council Representative, T. Sandell, Schenkenstrasse 4, A-1010 Vienna.

BAHRAIN
(Dawlet al-Bahrein)

Amir, H.H. Shaikh Isa bin Sulman Al Khalifa, G.C.M.G., *born* 1932; *acceded* Dec. 16, 1961.

Crown Prince and C.-in-C., Bahrain Defence Force, H.E. Shaikh Hamad bin Isa Al Khalifa, K.C.M.G.

CABINET
(as at May 31, 1989)

Prime Minister, H.E. Shaikh Khalifa bin Sulman Al-Khalifa.

Foreign Affairs, Shaikh Mohammed bin Mubarak Al-Khalifa.

Defence, Maj.-Gen. Shaikh Khalifa bin Ahmed Al Khalifa.

Justice and Islamic Affairs, Shaikh Abdullah bin Khalid Al-Khalifa.

Development and Industry, and Cabinet Affairs, Yusuf Ahmad Shirawi.

Education, Dr. Ali Fakhro.

Health, Jawad Salim Al-Arayyed.

Transportation, Ibrahim Mohammed Humaidan.

Interior, Shaikh Mohammed bin Khalifa Al-Khalifa.

Information, Tariq Abdulrahman Al Moayed.

Labour and Social Affairs, Shaikh Khalifa bin Sulman bin Mohammed Al-Khalifa.

Works, Power and Water, Majid Jawad Al-Jishi.

Housing, Shaikh Khalid bin Abdullah Al-Khalifa.

Finance and National Economy, Ibrahim Abdul Karim.

Commerce and Agriculture, Habib Ahmed Kassim.

Minister of State, Legal Affairs, Dr. Hussain Al-Baharna.

EMBASSY OF THE STATE OF BAHRAIN
98 Gloucester Road, SW7 4AU
[01–370 5132]

Ambassador Extraordinary and Plenipotentiary, His Excellency Salman Abdul Wahab Al Sabbagh (1984).

Area and Population.—Bahrain consists of a group of low-lying islands situated about half-way down the Gulf, some 20 miles off the east coast of Arabia. The largest of these, Bahrain island itself, is about 30 miles long and 10 miles wide at its broadest. The capital, Manama, is situated on the north shore of this island. The next largest, Muharraq, with the town and Bahrain International Airport, is connected to Manama by a causeway 1½ miles long.

The population (1987 estimate) is 457,600, of whom 154,800 are foreign. About 35 per cent. of the Bahrainis are Sunni Muslims, the remaining 65 per cent. being Shias; the ruling family and many of the most prominent merchants are Sunnis.

Climate.—The climate is humid all the year round, with rainfall of about 3 in. concentrated in the mild winter months, December to March; in summer, May to October, temperatures can exceed 110°F. (44°C).

Government.—Bahrain has been a fully independent state since 1971. Government takes the form of a constitutional monarchy, in which traditional consultative procedures continue to play an important role.

Economy.—The largest sources of revenue are oil production and refining. The Bahrain field, discovered in 1932, is wholly owned by the Bahrain National Oil Co. Production in 1988 stood at about 42,000 b.p.d. The Sitra refinery derives about 70 per cent. of its crude oil by submarine pipeline from Saudi Arabia. Bahrain also has a half share with Saudi Arabia in the profits of the offshore Abu Sa'afa field. A reservoir of unassociated gas has recently been developed on Bahrain island.

Heavy industry is currently limited to the Aluminium Bahrain (ALBA) smelter, producing 170,000 tonnes p.a.; the Gulf Petrochemical Industries Co. (GPIC) producing 375,000 tonnes p.a. of ammonia and 395,000 tonnes p.a. of methanol in 1988, the Gulf Aluminium Rolling Mill (GARMCO), and the Arab Shipbuilding and Repair Yard (ASRY), operating dry dock facilities up to 500,000 tons.

There are a number of small to medium sized industrial units.

The state has developed as a financial centre. Apart from commercial banks, led by the National Bank of Bahrain, the Standard Chartered Bank, the British Bank of the Middle East and the Bank of Bahrain and Kuwait, many international banks have been licensed as "offshore banking units"; there are also money brokers and merchant banks.

Trade with U.K.

	1987	1988
Imports from U.K.	£125,189,000	£138,150,000
Exports to U.K.	60,687,000	75,786,000

Communications.—Bahrain International airport is the main air traffic centre of the Gulf; it is the headquarters of Gulf Air, and a stopping point on routes between Europe and Australia and the Far East for other airlines. A causeway linking Bahrain to Saudi Arabia was opened in Nov. 1986.

A world-wide telephone and telex service, by satellite and cable, is operated by Bahrain Telecommunications Company.

CAPITAL.—ΨManama; population (1981 Census), 121,986.

CURRENCY.—Bahrain dinar (BD) of 1,000 fils.

FLAG.—Red, with vertical serrated white bar next to staff.

NATIONAL DAY.—December 16.

BRITISH EMBASSY
21 Government Avenue,
Manama 306, P.O. Box 114
[Manama 254002]

Ambassador Extraordinary and Plenipotentiary, His Excellency John Alan Shepherd, C.M.G. (1988).
First Secretaries, W. I. Rae, M.B.E. (*Commercial and Head of Chancery and Consul*); J. C. A. Rundall.
Second Secretary, D. Leith (*Commercial*).
British Council Representative, J. Wright, 21 Government Avenue (P.O. Box 452), Manama 306.

BELGIUM
(Royaume de Belgique)

King of the Belgians, H.M. King Baudouin, K.G., *born* Sept. 7, 1930; *succeeded* July 17, 1951, on the abdication of his father, King Leopold III, after having acted as Head of the State since August 11, 1950; *married* Dec. 15, 1960, Doña Fabiola de Mora y Aragòn.
Heir Presumptive, H.R.H. Prince Albert, *born* June 6, 1934, *brother* of the King; *married* July 2, 1959, Donna Paola Ruffo di Calabria, and has *issue* Prince Philippe Léopold Louis Marie, *b.* April 15, 1960; Princess Astrid Josephine-Charlotte Fabrizia Elisabeth Paola Marie, *b.* June 5, 1962; Prince Laurent, *b.* Oct. 20, 1963.

CABINET
(as at July 31, 1989)

Prime Minister, Dr. Wilfried Martens (*CVP*).
Deputy P.M. and Minister for the Brussels Region, and Institutional Reform (French sector), Philippe Moureaux (*PS*).
Deputy P.M. and Minister for Economic Affairs and Planning, and National Education (Flemish Sector), Willy Claes (*SP*).
Deputy P.M. and Minister of Communications, and Institutional Reform (Dutch sector), Jean-Luc Dehaene (*CVP*).
Deputy P.M. and Minister of Justice, and the Middle Classes, Melchior Wathelet (*PSC*).
Deputy P.M. and Minister for the Budget and Scientific Policy, Hugo Schiltz (*VU*).
Foreign Affairs, Mark Eyskens (*CVP*).
Finance, Philippe Maystadt (*PSC*).
Foreign Trade, Robert Urbain (*PS*).
Public Affairs, Michel Hansenne (*PSC*).
Posts and Telecommunications, Marcel Colla (*SP*).
Social Affairs, Philippe Busquin (*PS*).
Defence, Guy Coëme (*PS*).

Public Works, Paula D'Hondt-Van Opdenbosch (*CVP*).
Interior, Modernization of Public Services and National Scientific and Cultural Institutions, Louis Tobback (*SP*).
National Education (French Sector), Yvan Ylieff (*PS*).
Co-operation and Development, André Geens (*VU*).
Pensions, Alain Van Der Biest (*PS*).
Employment and Work, Luc Vanden Brande (*CVP*).

CVP—Christian Social Party (Flemish); *PS*—Socialist Party (Francophone); *SP*—Socialist Party (Flemish); *PSC*—Christian Social Party (Francophone); *VU*—Flemish Peoples' Union.

BELGIAN EMBASSY
103 Eaton Square, SW1W 9AB
[01–235 5422]

Ambassador Extraordinary and Plenipotentiary, His Excellency Jean-Paul van Bellinghen (1984).
Minister Plenipotentiary, L. Willems.
Minister Counsellor, R. Vandemeulebroucke (*Economic*).
Military, Naval and Air Attaché, Capt. G. H. A. Busard.

A Kingdom of Western Europe, with a total area of 11,781 sq. miles (30,513 sq. km.), and a population, (1986) of 9,858,895 (Greater Brussels, 976,536; Flanders, 5,676,194; Wallonia, 3,206,165, of whom 66,445 are German-speaking). The majority of Belgians are Roman Catholics. The Kingdom of Belgium is bounded on the N. by the Kingdom of the Netherlands, on the S. by France, on the E. by the Federal Republic of Germany and Luxembourg, and on the W. by the North Sea.

Belgium has a frontier of 898 miles, and a seaboard of 41 miles. The Meuse and its tributary, the Sambre, divide it into two distinct regions, that in the west being generally level and fertile, while the table-land of the Ardennes, in the east, has for the most part a poor soil. The polders near the coast, which are protected by dykes against floods, cover an area of 193 sq. miles. The highest hill, Signal de Botranges, rises to a height of 2,276 feet, but the mean elevation of the whole country does not exceed 526 feet. The principal rivers are the Scheldt and the Meuse.

Government.—The kingdom formed part of the "Low Countries" (Netherlands) from 1815 until Oct. 14, 1830, when a National Congress proclaimed its independence, and on June 4, 1831, Prince Leopold of Coburg was chosen hereditary king. The separation from the Netherlands and the neutrality and inviolability of Belgium were guaranteed by a Conference of the European Powers, and by the Treaty of London (April 19, 1839), the famous 'Scrap of Paper,' signed by Austria, France, Great Britain, Prussia, The Netherlands, and Russia. On Aug. 4, 1914, the Germans invaded Belgium, in violation of the terms of the treaty. The kingdom was again invaded by Germany on May 10, 1940. The whole kingdom eventually fell and was occupied by Nazi troops until liberated by the Allies in September 1944.

According to the Constitution of 1831 the form of government is a constitutional representative and hereditary monarchy with a bicameral legislature, consisting of the King, the Senate and the Chamber of Deputies. The parliamentary term is four years.

The last general election was held on December 13, 1987. The results were as follows (seats):

Chamber of Deputies: CVP, 43; PS, 40; SP, 32; PVV (Flemish Freedom and Progress Party), 25; PRL (Liberal Reform Party (Francophone)), 23; PSC, 18; VU, 16; Agalev (Flemish Environmental Party), 6; Ecolo (Francophone Ecology Party), 3; FDF (Francophone Democratic Front), 3; Vlaams Blok (Flemish Nationalist Party), 2.

Senate: (as at Dec. 1987), CVP, 22; PS, 20; SP, 17; PRL, 12; PVV, 11; PSC, 9; VU, 8; Ecologists, 5; FDF, 1; Vlaams Blok, 1. Besides these directly elected representatives the Senate also includes 51 members who are elected by the Provincial Councils and 26 who are co-opted in the proportions of the directly elected seats. H.R.H. Prince Albert is a "sénateur de droit".

Regional Governments.—The 1980 regionalization law made provision for the establishment of three Regional Community Parliaments (Assemblies) with executive councils which were set up in November 1981 and became effective in January 1982. The executives are autonomous from the central government, and their members are elected by the members of the Assemblies to whom they are responsible. They prepare Bills within the limits of their regional/community competences, and once these Bills have been passed by the regional assembly and published in the *Moniteur Belge*, they have the force of law.

The Flemish Community Assembly (186 members) and Executive (a President and 8 Regional Ministers) covers the provinces of Antwerp, East and West Flanders, Limbourg and the Flemish *arrondissements* (Halle, Vilvoorde, Leuven) in the province of Brabant, and is also responsible for the Flemish population of Brussels. The Walloon Regional Assembly (104 members) and Executive (a President and 6 Regional Ministers) covers the provinces of Hainaut, Liège, Luxembourg and Namur, and the *arrondissement* of Nivelles in the province of Brabant. The French Community Assembly (132 members) and Executive (a President and 3 Community Ministers) has no fixed territory but is responsible for the francophone population of Brussels and, in concert with the Walloon Regional Assembly, deals with certain Walloon regional affairs. The German-speaking community (about 66,000) also has an Assembly, which gained autonomy in 1984. It is based in Eupen.

Since June 1989 there has been a 75-member Brussels Regional Council with a 5-member Executive: 2 Flemings, 2 Francophones and a President.

An Arbitration Court was set up in 1984 to resolve conflicts between laws made by the various legislative bodies.

Language and Literature.—Belgium is divided between those who speak Dutch (the Flemings) and those who speak French (the Walloons). Dutch is spoken in the provinces of West Flanders, East Flanders, Antwerp, Limburg, and the northern half of Brabant, and French in the provinces of Hainault, Namur, Luxembourg, Liège and the southern half of Brabant. Dutch is recognized as the official language in the northern areas and French in the southern (Walloon) area and there are guarantees for the respective linguistic minorities. Brussels is officially bi-lingual. There is a small German-speaking area (Eupen and Malmedy) along the German border, east of Liège.

The literature of France and the Netherlands is supplemented by an indigenous Belgian literary activity, in both French and Dutch. Maurice Maeterlinck (1862–1949) was awarded the Nobel Prize for Literature in 1911. Emile Verhaeren (1855–1916) was a poet of international standing. Of contemporary Belgian writers, perhaps the most celebrated was Georges Simenon (1903–89). There are 39 daily newspapers in Belgium (23 in French, 15 in Dutch and 1 in German).

Education.—The nursery schools provide free education for the 2½ to 6 age group. There are over 8,000 primary schools (6 to 12 years) of which approximately 5,000 are administered by the State, province or commune and the remainder are free institutions (predominantly Roman Catholic). There are more than 1,100 secondary schools offering a general academic education slightly over half of which are free institutions (predominantly Roman Catholic but subsidized by the State) and the remainder official institutions. The official school leaving age is 18.

Production.—Belgium is a manufacturing country. With no natural resources except coal, annual production of which was approximately 6 million tonnes in 1986, industry is based largely on the processing for re-export of imported raw materials. Gross National Product per capita in 1986 was B.Fr.439,992. Principal industries are steel and metal products, chemicals and petrochemicals, textiles, glass, and foodstuffs.

FINANCE

Budget	1987	1988
	B. Fr. (millions)	
Revenue	1,449,699	1,491,124
Expenditure	1,859,334	1,892,341

External trade figures relate to Luxembourg as well as Belgium since the two countries formed an Economic Union in 1921.

TRADE

	1986	1987
	B. Fr. (millions)	
Total Imports	3,065,239	3,099,209
Total Exports	3,070,327	3,093,069

Trade with U.K. (Belgium and Luxembourg)

	1987	1988
Imports from U.K.	£9,713,881,000	£9,835,241,000
Exports to U.K.	11,510,499,000	13,235,784,000

Communications.—In 1983, there were 3,920 kilometres of normal gauge railways operated by the Belgian National Railways, of which 1,763 kilometres were electrified. The Belgian National Light Railways (SNCV) also operated 27,671 kilometres of regular bus routes. In 1984 there were 2,930,000 telephone subscribers in Belgium.

Ship canals include *Ghent-Terneuzen* (18 miles, of which half is in Belgium and half in the Netherlands) which permits the passage to Ghent of ships up to 60,000 tons; the Canal of *Willebroek Rupel-Brussels* (20 miles, by which ships drawing 18 ft reach Brussels from the sea; opened in 1922); and *Bruges* (from Zeebrugge on the North Sea to Bruges, 6½ miles). The *Albert Canal* (79 miles), links Liège with Antwerp; it was completed in 1939 and accommodates barges up to 1,350 tons. The modernization of the port of Antwerp is well advanced. Inland waterway approaches to Antwerp are also to be improved. The river Meuse from the Dutch to the French frontiers, the river Sambre between Namur and Monceau, the river Scheldt from Antwerp to Ghent and the Brussels-Charleroi Canal are being widened or deepened to take barges up to 1,350 tons. Most of the maritime trade of Belgium is carried in foreign shipping.

In 1986 there were 14,260 km. of trunk roads of which about 1,550 km. are motorways.

The Belgian National Airline *Sabena* operates regular services between Brussels and London, and many continental centres, as well as overseas services to Northern and Central America, Africa, Middle East, Far East, etc. Many foreign airlines call at Brussels.

CAPITAL.—Brussels, has a population (1986) of 976,536. Other towns are ΨAntwerp, the chief port (918,963); ΨGhent (484,295); Liège (592,732); Charleroi (430,767); Bruges (258,917); ΨOstend (134,215); Malines (293,050).

CURRENCY.—Belgian franc of 100 centimes (centiemen).

FLAG.—Three vertical bands, black, yellow, red.

NATIONAL ANTHEM.—La Brabançonne.

NATIONAL DAY.—July 21 (Accession of King Leopold I, 1831).

BRITISH EMBASSY.
Britannia House, 28 rue Joseph II,
1040 Brussels.
[Brussels 2179000]

Ambassador Extraordinary and Plenipotentiary, His Excellency Robert (Robin) James O'Neill, C.M.G. (1989).

Counsellors, M. G. D. Evans (*Head of Chancery*); B. Attewell (*Commercial*).

Defence and Military Attaché, Col. K. Woodrow.

Naval and Air Attaché, Wing Cdr. B. A. Horton, R.A.F.

There are British Consular Offices at *Brussels, Antwerp* and *Liège.*

British Council Representative to Belgium and Luxembourg, K. McGuinness, 30 rue Joseph II, 1040 Brussels (Council Library at *Brussels*).

BRITISH CHAMBER OF COMMERCE FOR BELGIUM AND LUXEMBOURG (INC.), 30 rue Joseph II, 1040 Brussels.

BENIN
(République Populaire du Benin)

President of the Military Revolutionary Government and Head of State, Brig.-Gen. Ahmed Mathieu Kerekou; *assumed office,* Oct. 26, 1972, *re-elected,* July 31, 1984.

NATIONAL EXECUTIVE COUNCIL
(as at July 31, 1988)

President of the Council and Minister of Defence, Brig.-Gen. Ahmed Mathieu Kerekou.

Minister-Delegate to the Presidency (Interior, Security, Territorial Administration), Maj. Edouard Zodehougan.

Minister-Delegate to the Presidency (Planning, Statistics), Simon Ifede Ogouma.

Rural Development and Co-operative Action, Gandonou Kodja.

Equipment and Transport, Martin Dohou Azonhiho.

Finance, Didier Dassi.

Commerce, Crafts and Tourism, Girigissou Gado.

Primary Education, Capt. Philippe Akpo.

Secondary and Higher Education, Vincent Guedzodje.

Culture, Youth and Sports, Ali Houdou.

Labour and Social Affairs, Irenee Zinsou.

Public Health, Soule Dankoro.

Information and Communications, Ousmane Batoko.

Foreign Affairs and Co-operation, Guy Landry Hazoume.

Justice, and Inspection of Parastatal Enterprises, Saliou Abdoudou.

Industry and Energy, Justin Gnidehou.

A republic situated in West Africa, between 2° and 3° W. and 6° and 12° N., Benin (formerly known as Dahomey) has a short coastline of 78 miles on the Gulf of Guinea but extends northwards inland for 437 miles. It is flanked on the west by Togo, on the north by Burkina and Niger and on the east by Nigeria. It has an area of 43,484 sq. miles (122,622 sq. km.), and a population of 4,444,000 (1988 estimate). Although poor in resources, Benin is one of the most heavily populated areas in West Africa, with a high standard of education. It is divided into four main regions running horizontally: a narrow sandy coastal strip, a succession of inter-communicating lagoons, a clay belt and a sandy plateau in the north.

Government.—The first treaty with France was signed by one of the kings of Abomey in 1851 but the country was not placed under French administration until 1892. Benin became an independent republic within the French Community on Dec. 4, 1958; full independence outside the Community was proclaimed on August 1, 1960. In October, 1963, a popular revolution led to the fall of the government and the Army held power until a civilian government was formed. The government's life was very short, however, and in the subsequent 8–9 years successive governments were overthrown by the military after only a short term in office until a coup d'état of October 26, 1972 brought to power a Military Revolutionary Government, headed by Lt.-Col. Kerekou. Although now a one-party state, a general election was held in Nov. 1979, and a new Constitution and National Assembly were established.

Benin is a member of the Conseil de l'Entente, the Organisation Commune Africaine et Malgache (OCAM), the Organization of African Unity (O.A.U.) and the Economic Community of West African States (ECOWAS). The official language is French.

Trade.—The principal exports are cotton, palm products, ground nuts, shea-nuts, and coffee. Small deposits of gold, iron and chrome have been found; oil production started in 1983.

Trade with U.K.

	1987	1988
Imports from U.K.	£7,207,000	£8,169,000
Exports to U.K.	2,930,000	2,450,000

CAPITAL.—ΨPorto Novo (population (1982 estimate) 208,258). Political capital and principal commercial town and port, ΨCotonou (popn. (1982) 487,020).

CURRENCY.—Franc C.F.A. of 100 centimes.

FLAG.—Green, with five pointed red star in the top left corner.

NATIONAL DAY.—November 30.

British Embassy (*resident at* Lagos, Nigeria).

BHUTAN
(Druk-yul)

King of Bhutan, H.M. Jigme Singye Wangchuk, *born* Nov. 11, 1955; *succeeded his father,* July, 1972; *crowned,* June 2, 1974; *heir,* Crown Prince Jigme

Gesar Namgyal Wangchuk, *designated*, Oct. 31, 1988.

COUNCIL OF MINISTERS
(as at May 31, 1989)

H.M. Representative in the Ministry of Finance, H.R.H. Ashi S. C. Wangchuk.
H.M. Representative in the Ministry of Agriculture, H.R.H. Ashi D. W. Wangchuk.
Home Affairs, Trade, Industry and Forests, H.R.H. Namgyal Wangchuk.
Foreign Affairs, Lyonpo Dawa Tshering.
Social Services, Lyonpo Sangye Penjor.
Communications, Tourism and Social Services, Lyonpo Dr. T. Tobgyal.
Deputy Minister of Defence, Maj.-Gen. Lam Dorji.
Speaker of the National Assembly, Lyonpo Tamji Jagar.

Bhutan is a small Himalayan Kingdom situated between Tibet (to the north) and India (to the west, south and east). The total area is about 18,147 sq. miles (47,000 sq. km.), with a mountainous northern region which is infertile and sparsely populated, a central zone of upland valleys where most of the population and cultivated land is found, and in the south the densely forested foothills of the Himalayas, which are mainly inhabited by Nepalese settlers and indigenous tribespeople.

The population of Bhutan is estimated at 1,417,000 (1985, U.N. estimate), about three-quarters of whom are Buddhists. The remainder (mostly the Nepali Bhutanese) are Hindu. The official language, for administrative and religious purposes, is Dzongkha, a variant of Tibetan, which functions as a lingua franca amongst a variety of languages and dialects. It is government policy to make the study of Dzongkha compulsory in schools, although English is the medium of instruction and has become widely used within the administration.

In 1949, a treaty was concluded with the Government of India under which the Kingdom of Bhutan agreed to be guided by the Government of India in regard to its external relations, but it still retains independence, issues its own passports, has its own diplomatic representatives and is a member of the U.N. and other international and regional organizations. It also receives from the Government of India an annual payment of Rs.500,000 as compensation for portions of its territory annexed by the British Government in India in 1864.

Government.—Bhutan has a 150-member National Assembly which meets twice a year. The ten-member Royal Advisory Council, nominated by the King and the National Assembly, acts as a consultative body when the National Assembly is not in session. The King is also assisted by a Council of Ministers.

Economy.—The sixth 5-year Plan (1987–92) has a projected expenditure of Nu 9,485m. Economic emphasis is on the infrastructure, especially roads and telecommunications. The economy is based on agriculture and animal husbandry, which engage over 90 per cent of the workforce in what is largely a self-sufficient rural society. The principal food crops are rice, wheat, maize and barley. Vegetables and fruit are also produced. Bhutan is the world's largest producer of cardamon, which forms its principal export to countries other than India. Mineral resources include dolomite and small amounts of coal, which are exported to India. A modest industrial base is being developed. A distillery and cement, chemicals and food processing plants are in production: a forestry industries complex is being expanded. Tourism and postage stamps are increasingly important sources of foreign exchange. Over 90 per cent of foreign trade is with India. Principal exports are agricultural products, timber, cement and coal; main imports are textiles, cereals and consumer goods. Bhutan's airline, Druk Air, flies between Paro and Calcutta.

Trade with U.K.

	1987	1988
Imports from U.K.	£411,000	£12,464,000
Exports to U.K.	14,000	175,000

CAPITAL.—Thimphu (Population estimate 1987, 15,000).
CURRENCY.—Ngultrum of 100 chetrums. Indian currency is also legal tender.
FLAG.—Saffron yellow and orange-red divided diagonally, with dragon device in centre.
NATIONAL DAY.—December 17.

BOLIVIA
(República de Bolivia)

President of the Republic, Jaime Paz Zamora, inaugurated, Aug. 6, 1989.
Vice President, Sr. Julio Garret Ayllón.

CABINET
(as at May 31, 1989)

Foreign Affairs, Dr. Valentin Abecia.
Interior, Dr. Eduardo Perez Beltran.
Defence, Alfonso Revollo Thenier.
Finance, Ramiro Cahezas.
Planning, Fernando Romero.
Education, Enrique Ipiña Melgar.
Transport and Communications, Alfonso Balderama.
Industry and Commerce, Luis Fernando Palerque.
Labour, Dr. Alfonso Pera Rueda.
Health, Dr. Joaquin Asce Serra.
Mines and Metallurgy, Jaime Villalobos.
Agriculture, José Guillermo Justiniano.
Energy and Hydrocarbons, Fernando Illánes.
Housing, Roberto Roca Isiaste.
Information, Herman Antelo Louckling.
Aeronautics, Gen. Jaime Zegada Hurtado.
Secretary General, Dr. Walter Zuleta Roncal.
Secretary to the Presidency, Johnny Nogales.

BOLIVIAN EMBASSY
106 Eaton Square, SW1W 9AD
[01–235 2257/4248]

Ambassador Extraordinary and Plenipotentiary, (new appointment awaited).
Minister Counsellor, J. Loayza.
First Secretary, Srta. Marta Bosacoma Bonel.

The land-locked Republic of Bolivia extends between lat. 10° and 23° S. and long. 57° 30′ and 69° 45′ W. It has an area estimated at 424,165 sq. miles (1,098,581 sq. km.), with a population (1985 U.N. estimate) of 6,429,000. The Republic derives its name from its liberator, Simon Bolivar (1783–1830).

The chief topographical feature is the great central plateau (65,000 square miles) over 500 miles in length, at an average altitude of 12,500 feet above sea level, between the two great chains of the Andes, which traverse the country from south to north. The total length of the navigable streams is about 12,000 miles, the principal rivers being the Itenez, Beni, Mamore and Madre de Dios.

Language and Literature.—The official language of the country is Spanish, but many of the Indian inhabitants (about two-thirds of the population) speak Quechua or Aymará, the two linguistic groups being more or less equal in numbers.

The Roman Catholic religion was disestablished in 1961 but relations between it and the State are good. Elementary education is compulsory and free and there are secondary schools in urban centres. Provision is also made for higher education; in addition to St. Francisco Xavier's University at Sucre, founded in 1624, there are six other universities, the largest being the University of San Andres at La Paz. There are nine principal daily newspapers in Bolivia.

Production.—Mining, natural gas, petroleum and agriculture are the principal industries. The ancient silver mines of Potosí are now worked chiefly for tin, but gold, partly dug and partly washed, is obtained on the Eastern Cordillera of the Andes; the tin output is one of the largest in the world, and together with other minerals (copper, antimony, lead, zinc, asbestos, wolfram, bismuth salt and sulphur), provides over half of Bolivia's exports.

In 1982 Bolivia produced 1·4 million cubic metres of oil, sufficient for internal consumption. Gas (currently providing about a quarter of Bolivia's export income) is piped to Argentina and there are plans to build a pipeline to São Paulo, Brazil. Bolivia's agricultural produce consists chiefly of rice, barley, oats, wheat, sugar-cane, maize, cotton, indigo, rubber, cacao, potatoes, cinchona bark, medicinal herbs, brazil nuts etc.

Transport and Communications.—There are 2,200 miles of railways in operation including the lines from Corumbá to Santa Cruz (312 miles). There are about 10,950 miles of telegraphs, and microwave telephone communications between La Paz, Santa Cruz, Cochabamba, Oruro and Sucre. Most other towns of any size have radio/telephone communication with the main cities. There is direct railway communication to the sea at Antofagasta (32 hours), Arica (10 hours), and Mollendo (2 days), and also to Buenos Aires (3¼ days). Communication with Peru is by road from La Paz via Copacabana and thence to the railhead at Puno.

Commercial aviation in Bolivia is conducted by the national airline, Lloyd Aereo Boliviano and Transporte Aereo Militar between the major towns, and Lloyd Aereo Boliviano and a number of foreign airlines provide international flights to the U.S.A., South and Central America and Europe.

Bolivia is without a coastline, having been deprived of the ports of Tocopilla, Cobija, Mejillones and Antofagasta by the "Pacific War" of 1879–1884.

FINANCE

The economy has deteriorated since 1977, with disappointing petroleum reserves, a large external debt, and the collapse of world tin prices (Oct. 1985). Tin prices began to increase once more from April 1989. The peso was replaced in Jan. 1987 with the Boliviano of 1,000,000 old pesos in an effort to stem inflation. The inflation rate at the end of 1988 was about 20 per cent. Total exports (c.i.f.) in 1985 were U.S. $672·5 million.

Trade with U.K.

	1987	1988
Imports from U.K.	£3,658,000	£6,029,000
Exports to U.K.	14,799,000	13,224,000

Mineral exports represent about 94 per cent of these totals. A large part of Bolivia's minerals were shipped to U.K. for smelting and re-export, but Bolivia is now developing her own smelters and will in future be exporting metals. The chief imports are wheat and flour, iron and steel products, machinery, vehicles and textiles.

CAPITAL.—La Paz (Population, 1,000,000). Other large centres are Cochabamba (250,000), Oruro (180,000), Santa Cruz (380,000), Potosí (90,000), Sucre, the legal capital and seat of the judiciary (80,000) and Tarija (45,000).

CURRENCY.—Boliviano ($b) of 100 centavos.

FLAG.—Three horizontal bands; red, yellow, green.
NATIONAL ANTHEM.—"Bolivianos, El Hado Propicio" (Oh Bolivia, our long-felt desires).
NATIONAL DAY.—August 6 (Independence Day).

BRITISH EMBASSY
Avenida Arce 2732–2754,
(Casilla 694) La Paz.
[La Paz 329401/4]

Ambassador Extraordinary and Plenipotentiary, His Excellency Michael Francis Daly, C.M.G. (1989).
First Secretary, A. W. Shave (*Commercial and Head of Chancery*).

BRITISH CONSULAR OFFICES

There is a British Consulate at *Santa Cruz.*

BRAZIL
(República Federativa do Brasil)

President, José Sarney, *inaugurated*, April 22, 1985.
Vice-President, (vacant).

CABINET
(as at August 3, 1989)

Planning, Joao Batista de Abreu.
Finance, Mailson da Nobrega.
Mines and Energy, Vicente Fialho.
Agriculture, Iris Rezende.
Industrial Development, Science and Technology, Roberto Cardoso Alves.
Justice, Saulo Ramos.
Foreign Affairs, Roberto de Abreu Sodre.
Transport, Jose Reinaldo Tavares.
Communications, Antonio Carlos Magalhaes.
Interior, Joao Alves Filho.
Urban Development and Environment, Luiz Humberto Prisco Vianna.
Army, Gen. Leonidas Pires Goncalves.
Navy, Adm. Henrique Saboya.
Air Force, Brig. Octavio Moreira Lima.
Chief of Military Staff at Presidency, Gen. Ruben Bayma Denys.
Chief of Civilian Staff at Presidency, Ronald Costa Couto.
Chief of National Information Service, Gen. Ivan de Souza Mendes.
Armed Forces Chief of Staff, Adm. Valber Lisieux Medeiros de Figueiredo.
Health, Seigo Tsuzuki.
Social Security, Jader Barbalho.
Education, Carlos Sant'anna.
Culture, Jose Aparecido de Oliveira.
Labour, Dorothea Werneck.

BRAZILIAN EMBASSY
32 Green Street, W1Y 4AT
[01–499 0877]

Ambassador Extraordinary and Plenipotentiary, His Excellency Senhor Celso de Souza e Silva (1986).
There are also a Brazilian Consulate-General in *London* and honorary consular offices at *Cardiff* and *Glasgow.*

Area and Population.—Brazil, discovered in 1500 by Portuguese navigator Pedro Alvares Cabral, is bounded on the north by the Atlantic Ocean, the Guianas, Colombia and Venezuela; on the west by Peru, Bolivia, Paraguay, and Argentina; on the south by Uruguay; and on the east by the Atlantic Ocean. Brazil extends between lat. 5° 16′ N. and 33° 45′ S. and long. 34° 45′ and 73° 59′22″ W. The Republic comprises

an area of 3,286,488 sq. miles (8,511,965 sq. km.), with a population (1985 U.N. estimate) of 135,564,000.

The northern States of Amazonas and Pará are mainly wide, low-lying, forest-clad plains. The central states of Mato Grosso are principally plateau land and the eastern and southern States are traversed by successive mountain ranges interspersed with fertile valleys. The principal ranges are *Serra do Mar*, the *Serra da Mantiqueira* and the *Serra do Espinhaco* along the east coast. The River *Amazon* with a total length of some 4,000 miles has tributaries which are themselves great rivers, and flows from the Peruvian Andes to the Atlantic. Its principal northern tributaries are the *Rio Branco, Rio Negro,* and *Japurá*; its southern tributaries are the *Juruá, Purus, Madeira* and *Tapajós,* while the *Xingú* meets it within 200 miles of its outflow into the Atlantic. The *Tocantins* and *Araguaia* flow northwards from Mato Grosso and Goiás to the Gulf of Pará. The *Parnaiba* flows from Piauí into the Atlantic. The *São Francisco* rises in the South of Minas Gerais and flows to the eastern coast. The *Paraguai,* rising in the south-west of Mato Grosso, flows through Paraguay to its confluence with the *Paraná,* which rises in the mountains of that name and divides Brazil from Paraguay.

Government.—Brazil was colonized by Portugal in the early part of the sixteenth century, and in 1822 became an independent empire under Dom Pedro, son of the refugee King Joao VI of Portugal. On Nov. 15, 1889, Dom Pedro II, second of the line, was dethroned and a republic was proclaimed.

The Federative Republic of Brazil is made up of the Federal District, 23 States and 3 Territories (the most under-developed frontier regions). By the end of 1989 there will be elections to a new state called Tocantins. The two territories of Amapá and Roraima are due to become states in 1990, and the territory of Fernando de Noronha is already a part of Pernambuco state.

The constitution of January 1967 draws on the same conceptual basis as that of the United States, and envisages an equal distribution of power between the executive, the legislature and the judiciary. Under the existing constitutional provisions the President, who heads the executive, is indirectly elected for a five-year term.

The Congress consists of a Senate (3 Senators per State elected for an 8-year term) and a Chamber of Deputies which is re-elected every 4 years. (The number of Deputies per State depends upon the State's population). Each State has a Governor, and a Legislative Assembly with a 4-year term.

The new Brazilian Constitution was promulgated after its approval by the Constituent Assembly on Oct. 5, 1988.

Production.—There are large and valuable mineral

deposits including among others, iron ore (hematite), manganese, bauxite, beryllium, chrome, nickel, tungsten, cassiterite, lead, gold, monazite (containing rare earths and thorium) and zirconium. Diamonds and precious and semi-precious stones are also found. The mineral wealth is being exploited to an increasing extent. The iron ore deposits of Minas Gerais are exceeded by those of the Amazon region, principally in the Carajás areas where deposits are estimated at 35,000 million tonnes. Mining operations began in Feb. 1985.

Electric power production in 1987 was 202,287 Gwh. In the same year, the total output of steel was 22,227 million tonnes. Production of oil was 566,000 b.p.d. Of these 487,000 b.p.d. were produced from offshore fields.

Agriculture production was (tonnes):

	1986	1987
Black Beans	2,221,000	2,019,000
Cassava	25,542,000	23,399,000
Cocoa	459,000	337,000
Coffee	2,007,000	4,220,000
Cotton	2,314,000	1,672,000
Maize	20,510,000	26,787,000
Peanuts	216,000	196,000
Potatoes	1,834,000	2,343,000
Rice	10,399,000	10,422,000
Soya	13,335,000	16,814,000
Tobacco	386,000	398,000
Wheat	5,433,000	5,889,000

Defence.—The peace-time strength of the Army is 192,000. The Navy consists of 1 aircraft carrier, 7 submarines, 10 destroyers, 6 frigates, 9 patrol vessels, 5 river patrol ships, 1 river monitor, 1 river transport, 6 coastal mine sweepers, 7 survey ships, and 29 other vessels. The strength of the Navy is 49,000. The Air Force, with a strength of 45,000, has 680 aircraft, of which 151 are fast-jet.

Education.—Primary education is compulsory and is the responsibility of State governments and municipalities. At this level approximately 10 per cent attend private schools. Secondary education is largely the responsibility of State and municipal governments, although a small number of very old foundations (the Pedro II Schools) remain under direct federal control. Over 50 per cent. of all pupils at this level attend private schools. Higher education is available in Federal, State, municipal and private universities and faculties.

Language and Literature.—Portuguese is the language of the country, but Italian, Spanish, German, Japanese and Arabic are spoken by immigrant minorities, and newspapers of considerable circulation are produced in those languages. English and French are currently spoken by educated Brazilians.

Public libraries have been established in urban centres and there is a flourishing national press with widely circulated daily and weekly newspapers.

Communications.—In 1983 there were 1,552,463 km. of highways. The route-length of railways in 1980 was 35,100 km. Internal air services are highly developed. There are 21,944 miles of navigable inland waterways. During 1982, 9,574 vessels entered Rio de Janeiro and Santos, the two leading ports.

FINANCE

	1987	1988*
	Cruzados	
Revenue	1,203,001 m.	10,519 m.
Expenditure	1,392,120 m.	15,511 m.

* A new Cruzado worth 1,000 old Cruzados was introduced in 1989.

At Dec. 1987 Brazil's foreign debt stood at U.S.$121,264 million. Reserves in Dec. 1987 were $6,799 million.

TRADE

Principal imports are fuel and lubricants, machinery, chemicals, wheat, metals and metal manufactures. Principal exports are coffee, iron ore, soya, meat, steel and orange juice. In 1987 the Brazilian automobile industry produced 920,300 vehicles. Of these, 339,900 vehicles were exported.

	1987	1988
Total imports	US$26,224 m.	US$33,784 m.
Total exports	15,052 m.	14,688 m.

Trade with U.K.

	1987	1988
Imports from U.K.	£347,916,000	£304,735,000
Exports to U.K.	636,675,000	742,145,000

CAPITAL.—Brasilia (inaugurated on April 21, 1960). Population (1985 estimate), 1,576,657. Other important centres (1980 Census) were São Paulo (8,490,763); the former capital ΨRio de Janeiro (5,094,396); Belo Horizonte (1,774,712); ΨRecife (1,204,794); ΨSalvador (1,017,591); ΨPorto Alegre (1,125,091); ΨFortaleza (1,308,859); and Belem (934,330).

CURRENCY.—Novo (new) Cruzado (NCz$).

FLAG.—Green, with yellow lozenge in centre; blue sphere with white band and stars in centre of lozenge.

NATIONAL ANTHEM.—Ouviram do Ipirangas Margens (From peaceful Ypiranga's banks).

NATIONAL DAY.—September 7 (Independence Day).

BRITISH EMBASSY
Setor de Embaixadus Sul, Quadra 801, Conjunto K, 70.408 Brasilia, D.F.
[Brasilia 225–2710]

Ambassador Extraordinary and Plenipotentiary, His Excellency Michael John Newington, C.M.G. (1987).

There are British Consulates-General at *Rio de Janeiro* and *São Paulo*.

British Council Representative, J. Lawrence, SCRN 708/9-BLF Nos 1/3 (Caixa Postal 6104), 70,740 Brasilia D.F. Tel. 272–3060. Regional Directors in *Recife, Rio de Janeiro* and *São Paulo*.

BRITISH AND COMMONWEALTH CHAMBER OF COMMERCE IN SÃO PAULO, Rua Barão de Itapetininga 275, 7th Floor, 01042, São Paulo (*Postal Address*, P.O. Box 1621, 01000 São Paulo) and Rua Real Grandeza 99, 22281 Rio de Janeiro.

BULGARIA
(Narodna Republika Bulgaria)

COUNCIL OF STATE

Chairman of the Council of State, Todor Zhivkov, *elected*, July 7, 1971; *re-elected*, June 1981 and June 1986 (*Head of State*).
First Deputy Chairman, Petur Tanchev.
Deputy Chairmen, Georgi Dzhagarov; Yaroslav Radev.
Secretary, Nikola Manolov.

COUNCIL OF MINISTERS
(as at July 31, 1989)

Chairman (Prime Minister), Georgi Atanasov.
Deputy Chairman, Grigor Stoichkov.
Culture, Science and Education, Georgi Yordanov.
Economy and Planning, Stoyan Ovcharov.
Agriculture and Forests, Georgi Menov.
Foreign Economic Relations, Andrei Lukanov.
Foreign Affairs, Petur Mladenov.
Internal Affairs, Georgi Tanev.
Justice, Mrs. Svetla Daskalova.
National Defence, Gen. Dobri Dzhurov.

Public Health and Social Welfare, Mincho Peychev.
Transport, Trifon Pashov.
Minister, Ambassador to the U.S.S.R., Georgi Pankov.
Chairman, Committee on State and People's Control,
Georgi Georgiev.

THE COMMUNIST PARTY

Politbureau of the Central Committee, T. Zhivkov; P.
Kubadinski; G. Filipov; I. Panev; D. Stoyanov; D.
Dzhurov; P. Mladenov; M. Balev; Y. Yotov; G.
Atanasov (*full members*); A. Lukanov; G. Yorda-
nov; P. Dyulgerov; G. Stoichkov; P. Danchev; S.
Orcharov (*candidate members*).
Secretariat of the Central Committee, Todor Zhivkov
(*Secretary General*); D. Stanishev; M. Balev; V.
Tsanov; E. Khristov; D. Stoyanov; G. Filipov; Y.
Yotov.

EMBASSY OF THE PEOPLE'S REPUBLIC OF BULGARIA
186–188 Queen's Gate, SW7 5HL
[01–584 9400/9433]

Ambassador Extraordinary and Plenipotentiary, His
Excellency Dimitar Zhulev (1987).

The Republic of Bulgaria is bounded on the north
by Romania, on the west by Yugoslavia, on the east
by the Black Sea, and on the south by Greece and
Turkey. The total area is 42,823 sq. miles (110,912 sq.
km.), with a population at the Dec. 1985 Census of
8,948,388. The largest religion of the Bulgarians is
the Bulgarian Orthodox Church.

A Principality of Bulgaria was created by the
Treaty of Berlin (July 13, 1878) and in 1885 Eastern
Roumelia was added to the newly-created principality. In 1908 the country was declared to be an
independent kingdom. In 1912–13 a successful war of
the Balkan League against Turkey increased the size
of the kingdom, but in August, 1913, a short campaign
against the remaining members of the League reduced
the acquired area, and led to the surrender of
Southern Dobrudja to Romania. On Oct. 12, 1915,
Bulgaria entered the War on the side of the Central
Powers by declaring war on Serbia. She thus became
involved in the defeats of 1918, and on Sept. 29, 1918,
made an unconditional surrender to the Allied
Powers. On Nov. 29, 1919, she signed the Treaty of
Neuilly, which ceded to the Allies her Thracian
territories (later handed over to Greece) and some
territory on the western frontier to Yugoslavia.

Nazi troops entered the country on March 3, 1941,
and occupied Black Sea ports, but Bulgaria was not
at war with the Soviet Union. On August 26, 1944,
the government declared Bulgaria to be "neutral in
the Russo-German war" and sought terms of peace
from Great Britain and the United States. The Soviet
Union refused to recognize the so-called "neutrality"
and called upon Bulgaria to declare war against
Germany, and no satisfactory reply being received
on Sept. 5, 1944, the U.S.S.R. declared war on
Bulgaria. Bulgaria then asked for an armistice and
on Sept. 7 declared war on Germany, hostilities with
U.S.S.R. ending on Sept. 10. The armistice with the
Allies was signed in Moscow, Oct. 28, 1944. The Peace
Treaty with Bulgaria was signed on Feb. 22, 1947,
and came into force on Sept. 15, 1947. It recognized
the return of Southern Dobrudja to Bulgaria.

On Sept. 9, 1944 a coup d'état gave power to the
Fatherland Front, a coalition of Communists, Agrar-
ians, Social Democrats and officers and intellectuals.
In August, 1945, the main body of Agrarians and
Social Democrats left the Government. On Sept. 8,
1946, a referendum was held, which led to the
abolition of the monarchy and the setting up of a
Republic. On Oct. 27, 1946, a general election to a
Grand National Assembly (with power to make a

constitution) was held; the Opposition won 101 seats
out of 465. The opposition Agrarian Party was
suppressed in 1947, but its remnant was later revived
as the Agrarian Union which now constitutionally
shares power with the Communist Party.

A new Constitution was adopted in 1971 according
to which the legislature is a single chamber National
Assembly or *Subranie* elected by adult suffrage for a
maximum term of 5 years and consisting of 400
deputies representing constituencies of equal size.
This Constitution also established the Council of
State, being the supreme permanent body of the
National Assembly with both legislative and executive functions.

Production.—Until 1939 Bulgaria was a predominantly agricultural country, but has since pursued
an elaborate programme of industrialization. About
90 per cent of the country's agriculture has been
turned over to co-operatives, and a smaller proportion
mechanized. The principal crops are wheat, maize,
beet, tomatoes, tobacco, oleaginous seeds, fruit,
vegetables and cotton. The livestock includes cattle,
sheep, goats, pigs, horses, asses, mules and water
buffaloes.

There is now a substantial engineering industry
which accounts for about two-thirds of Bulgaria's
exports; and considerable production of ferrous and
non-ferrous metals. In 1985 production of electricity
was 41,621 million kilowatt-hours, of steel 2,926,000
tons and of coal 32,450,000 tons (of which about one-
quarter was soft coal).

There are mineral deposits of varying importance.
Bulgaria's heavy industry includes the Kremikovtsi
Steel Plant near Sofia and the Lenin steel mill at
Pernik, the chemical complex at Devnia, the petro-
chemical plant at Bourgas and various other chemical
and metallurgical works situated around the country.
The Soviet-designed nuclear power station at Kozlo-
dui has four reactors, each with a capability of
producing 880 million kilowatt/hours.

Defence.—Under the Peace Treaty signed between
Bulgaria and the Allies, the Bulgarian Army is
limited to 55,000 men, but the peacetime strength of
the ground forces is at present estimated to be 100,000.

Education.—Free basic education is compulsory
for children from 7 to 15 years inclusive. The
Bulgarian educational system was reorganized on
Soviet lines in September, 1950, providing kindergartens and educational establishments for primary and
secondary education including vocational, technical
and other specialized schools for secondary age pupils.
There are three Universities (at Sofia, Plovdiv and
Veliko Turnovo) and 21 higher educational establishments.

Language and Literature.—Bulgarian is a Southern Slavonic tongue, closely allied to Serbo-Croat
and Russian with local admixtures of modern Greek,
Albanian and Turkish words. There is a modern
literature, chiefly educational and popular. The
alphabet is Cyrillic. In 1983 there were 8 daily
newspapers in Sofia.

Finance.—Planned budget revenue for 1989 is
24,287·8 million leva, expenditure 24,286·3 million
leva.

TRADE

The principal imports are industrial and agricultural machinery, industrial raw materials, machine
tools, chemicals, dyestuffs, pharmaceuticals, rubber,
paper. The principal exports are non-ferrous metals,
electric trucks and motors, pumps, ships, accumula-
tors and machine tools, cereals, tobacco, fruit, vegetables, oil seeds, fats, textiles, eggs, chemicals and oils
including attar of roses. In 1986, 79·2 per cent of
Bulgaria's foreign trade was within the C.M.E.A.,
including 59·2 per cent with the Soviet Union.

Trade with U.K.

	1987	1988
Imports from U.K.	£88,761,000	£82,156,000
Exports to U.K.	24,249,000	28,068,000

CAPITAL.—Sofia, Pop. (1985), 1,114,759, at the foot of the Vitosha Range, the capital and commercial centre is on the main railway line to Istanbul, 338 miles from the Black Sea port of ΨVarna (302,211) and 125 miles from Lom (32,121), on the Danube; ΨBourgas (182,549) is also a Black Sea Port. Other important trading and industrial centres are Plovdiv (342,131), Rousse (183,746), Pleven (129,766), Stara Zagora (150,803), Pernik (94,758), Sliven (102,423), Yambol (90,215), Khaskovo (97,763) and Tolbukhin (109,066).

CURRENCY.—Lev of 100 stotinki.

FLAG.—3 horizontal bands, white, green, red; national emblem on white stripe near hoist.

NATIONAL DAY.—September 9 (Day of Freedom).

BRITISH EMBASSY
Boulevard Marshal Tolbukhin, 65–67, Sofia.
[Sofia 885361/2]

Ambassador Extraordinary and Plenipotentiary, His Excellency Richard Thomas (1989).

First Secretaries, M. E. Frost, L.V.O. (*Consul and Head of Chancery*); Miss C. M. Laidlaw (*Commercial*); J. B. Macpherson (*Political/Economical/Press*).

Cultural Attaché and British Council Representative, P. Lyner.

BURKINA
(République Démocratique Populaire de Burkina Faso)

President of the Popular Front and Head of State, Capt. Blaise Compaoré, *assumed office*, October 1987.

COUNCIL OF MINISTERS
(as at April 25, 1989)

Defence and Security, Cmdt. Boukari Jean-Baptiste Lingani.
Economic Promotion, Capt. Henri Zongo.
Foreign Affairs, Issouf Go.
Health and Social Work, Kanidoua Naboho.
Higher Education and Scientific Research, Mouhoussine Nacro.
Planning and Co-operation, Pascal Zagré.
National Education and Literacy, Mme. Alice Tiendrebeogo.
Peasants' Affairs, Laurent Sédgo.
Information and Culture, Mme. Beatrice Damiba.
Environment and Tourism, Maurice Dieu Boné.
Trade and Supply, Frederic Korsagha.
Transport and Communications, Thomas Sanon.
Territorial Administration, John-Léonard Compaoré.
Justice, Antoine Komy Sambo.
Equipment, Com. Daprou Kambou.
Sport, Kilimite Hien.
Labour, Social Security and Public Works, Salif Sampebogo.
Finance, Bintou Sanogo.
Agriculture and Livestock, Albert Guigma.
Water, Alfred Nombre.
Secretaries of State, Celestin Tiendrebeogo (*Budget*); Alimata Salemberé (*Culture*); Joseph Kaboré (*Housing and Town Planning*); Elie Saré (*Social Work*); Ju'es Boleo (*Secondary Education*); Amadou Giao (*Livestock*).
Secretary General, Prosper Vokouma.

Burkina (formerly Upper Volta) is an inland savanna state in West Africa, situated between 9° and 15°N. and 2°E. and 5°W. with an area of 105,869 sq. miles (274,200 sq. km.), and a population of 8,846,929

(1985 estimate). It has common boundaries with Mali on the west, Niger and Benin on the east and Togo, Ghana and the Côte d'Ivoire on the south. The largest tribe is the Mossi whose king, the Moro Naba, still wields a certain moral influence.

Burkina was annexed by France in 1896 and between 1932 and 1947 was administered as part of the Colony of the Ivory Coast. It decided on December 11, 1958, to remain an autonomous republic within the French Community; full independence outside the Community was proclaimed on August 5, 1960. The official language is French.

The 1960 constitution provided for a presidential form of government with a single chamber National Assembly, but in January, 1966, the Army assumed power. A new constitution allowing for a partial return to civilian rule but with the Army still in effective control was adopted in 1970, but in 1974 this was suspended. Full legislative and presidential elections were held again in 1978. In a military coup in Nov. 1980, Col. Zerbo assumed power. He was overthrown in Nov. 1982 by Maj. Ouedraogo, who was himself overthrown in Aug. 1983 by radical Army officers led by Capt. Sankara. On Oct. 15, 1987 Capt. Sankara was overthrown and killed in a military coup led by Capt. Blaise Compaoré. The present government is a broad-based coalition (the Popular Front). The future form of the Burkinabè Government will be considered by a National Congress of the Popular Front in late 1989. New constitutional arrangements are likely to be drawn up in 1990.

Trade.—The 1988 Budget totalled Franc CFA 90,300 million.

The principal industry is the rearing of cattle and sheep and the chief exports are livestock, groundnuts, shea-nuts and cotton. Small deposits of gold, manganese, copper, bauxite and graphite have been found. Trade in 1985 was valued at imports, CFA 95,158 m., exports, CFA 23,065 m.

Trade with U.K.

	1987	1988
Imports from U.K.	£4,168,000	£3,732,000
Exports to U.K.	462,000	546,000

CAPITAL.—Ouagadougou (375,001). Other principal towns; Bobo-Dioulasso (211,538) and Koudougou (52,431).

CURRENCY.—Franc C.F.A.

FLAG.—Equal bands of red over green, with a yellow star in centre.

NATIONAL DAY.—August 4.

BRITISH REPRESENTATION

British Ambassador (resident in Abidjan, Côte d'Ivoire).

BURMA (MYANMA)
(Pyidaungsu Socialist Thammada Myanma Naingngandaw)

STATE LAW AND ORDER RESTORATION COUNCIL (SLORC)
(as at May 31, 1989)

Prime Minister and Minister for Defence and Foreign Affairs, Gen. Saw Maung.
Planning and Finance, Energy, and Mines, Rear-Adm. Maung Maung Khin.
Transport and Communications, and Construction, Maj.-Gen. Tin Tun.
Home and Religious Affairs, Information and Culture, Maj.-Gen. Phone Myint.
Education, Social Welfare and Labour, Brig.-Gen. Aung Ye Kyaw.
Industry, Maj.-Gen. Sein Aung.

Co-operatives, Livestock Breeding and Fisheries, and Agriculture, Maj.-Gen. Chit Swe.
Trade, Col. Abel.
Health, Dr. Pe Thein.

EMBASSY OF THE UNION OF BURMA
19A Charles St., Berkeley Square, W1X 8ER
[01–629 6966]

Ambassador Extraordinary and Plenipotentiary, His Excellency U Tin Hlaing (1989).

Area and Population.—Burma forms the western portion of the Indo-Chinese district of the continent of Asia, lying between 9° 58′ and 28° N. latitude and 92° 11′ and 101° 9′ E. longitude, with an extreme length of approximately 1,200 miles and an extreme width of 575 miles. It has a sea coast on the Bay of Bengal to the south and west and a frontier with Bangladesh along the Naaf River (defined in 1964) and India to the north-west (defined in 1967). In the north and east the frontier with China was determined by a treaty with the People's Republic in October, 1960, and has since been demarcated; there is a short frontier with Laos in the east, while the long finger of Tenasserim stretches southward along the west coast of the Malay Peninsula, forming a frontier with Thailand to the east. The total area of the Union is 261,218 sq. miles (676,552 sq. km.), with a population of 37,153,000 (1985 U.N. estimate).

Physical Features.—Burma falls into four natural divisions. Arakan (with the Chin Hills region), the Irrawaddy basin, Tenasserim, including the Salween basin and extending southwards to the Burma-Thailand peninsula, and the elevated plateau on the east. Mountains enclose Burma on three sides, the highest point being Hka-kabo Razi (19,296 ft.) in the northern Kachin hills. Mt. Popa, 4,981 ft., in the Myingyan district is an extinct volcano and a well-known landmark in Central Burma. The principal river systems are the Kaladan-Lemro in Arakan, the Irrawaddy-Chindwin and the Sittang in Central Burma, and the Salween which flows through the Shan Plateau.

Races, Language and Religions.—The indigenous inhabitants who entered Burma from the north and east are of similar racial types and speak languages of the Tibeto-Burman, Mon-Khmer and Thai groups. The three important non-indigenous elements are Indians, Chinese and those from the former East Pakistan. Burmese is the official language, but minority languages include Shan, Karen, Chin, Kayah and the various Kachin dialects. English is spoken in educated circles. Buddhism is the religion of 85 per cent of the people, with 5 per cent Animists, 4 per cent Muslims, 4 per cent Hindus and less than 3 per cent Christians.

Government.—Burma became an independent republic outside the British Commonwealth on January 4, 1948, and remained a parliamentary democracy for 14 years.   On March 2, 1962 the army took power, and suspended the parliamentary Constitution. A Revolutionary Council of senior officers under General Ne Win took measures to create a Socialist State.

In January 1974 a new Constitution was adopted under which the highest authority was the People's Assembly (476 representatives) with a Council of State (29 members) and the senior executive body being the Council of Ministers.

After months of popular demonstrations and rioting and a series of Presidents throughout the summer of 1988, Gen. Saw Maung, leader of Burma's armed forces, assumed power in September 1988. The People's Assembly, the Council of State and the Council of Ministers were abolished and replaced by the State Law and Order Restoration Council

(SLORC) headed by Gen. Saw Maung as Prime Minister.

A People's Assembly Election Law was published in March 1989 committing the State Law and Order Restoration Council to hold multi-party elections. These elections have been promised by May 1990.

Political Divisions.—Burma is comprised of seven States (Chin, Kachin, Karen, Kayah, Mon, Rakhine, Shan) and seven Divisions (Irrawaddy, Magwe, Mandalay, Pegu, Rangoon, Sagaing, Tenasserim).

Education.—The literacy rate is high compared to other Asian countries, there is no caste system and women engage freely in social intercourse and play an important part in agriculture and retail trade.

Most Burmese children attend primary school, and about four million are currently enrolled; in middle and high schools, 11 million. There are two universities, at Rangoon and Mandalay, and in 1986–87 the numbers graduating were 9,981. A number of autonomous institutes of university standard award their own degrees. Under the two universities are three affiliated Degree Colleges and the Workers' College, Rangoon. There are also 14 two-year colleges affiliated to the universities, spread throughout the country.

There are three Teachers' Training Institutes for middle and primary schools, and 13 Teachers' Training Schools for primary only. Seven Government Technical Institutes offer post-secondary technical training courses and 14 Technical High Schools train semi-skilled tradesmen. Six Agricultural Institutes offer training courses in agriculture and veterinary science; nine Agricultural High Schools train semi-skilled agriculturists. There are 34 Vocational Schools for weaving, handicrafts, etc.

Finance.—The chief sources of revenue are profits on state trading, income-tax, customs duties, commercial taxes and excise duties; the chief heads of expenditure are general administration, defence, education, police and development. The budget estimates for 1988–89 were: Revenue, K31,083,000,000; Expenditure, K30,042,000,000.

Production, Industry and Commerce.—Three-quarters of the population depend on agriculture; the chief products are rice, oilseeds (sesamum and groundnut), maize, millet, cotton, beans, wheat, grain, tea, sugarcane, Virginia and Burmese tobacco, jute and rubber. Rice has traditionally been the mainstay of Burma's economy and the quantity of rice and by-products available for export was 900,000 tons in 1986–87. The principal export after rice is teak, of which 190,000 cubic tons was exported in 1986–87.

Burma is rich in minerals, including petroleum, lead, silver, tungsten, zinc, tin, wolfram and gemstones. Of these, petroleum products are the most important. Oil is now being produced from oilfields in Myanaung, Prome and Shwepyitha and at Chauk, Yenangyaung, Mann, and Letpando. Production of crude oil in 1986–87 totalled 10,103,000 U.S. barrels. There is a refinery at the main oilfield, Chauk, another at Syriam near Rangoon and a third is being built at Mann. There has been a slight decline in Burma's oil production in recent years and the country is no longer self-sufficient. Onshore exploration continues. There has also been some offshore oil exploration on a small scale. Major reserves of natural gas have been discovered in the Martaban Gulf, which Burma is hoping to develop.

All industrial activity of any size is in the public sector. Under development plans, projects completed or under construction with overseas financial and technical assistance include the production of cement, bricks and tiles, sheet glass, steel sections, jute bags and twine, cotton yarns, cotton and cotton mixture cloth, pharmaceuticals, sugar, paper, plywood, urea fertilizers, soda ash, tractors and tyres;

also a hydro-electric scheme and various irrigation works. Japan continues to be the major individual donor of soft loans and grant aid in the industrial and agricultural sectors. West Germany has also been an important contributor of soft loans.

Loans amounting to US$450 million have been extended by the World Bank. As a member of the Colombo Plan since 1952 Burma continues to receive technical assistance from a number of countries and international agencies. Faced with a serious foreign exchange shortage, Burma has applied for Least Developed Country status (LLDC) at the U.N.

Trade with U.K.

	1987	1988
Imports from U.K........	£24,715,000	£11,685,000
Exports to U.K.	3,826,000	4,427,000

Communications.—The Irrawaddy and its chief tributary, the Chindwin, form important waterways, the main stream being navigable beyond Bhamo (900 miles from its mouth) and carrying much traffic.

The chief seaports are Rangoon, Moulmein, Akyab and Bassein.

The Burma Railways network covers 2,764 route miles, extending to Myitkyina, on the Upper Irrawaddy. There were 2,452 miles of Union highways and 11,767 miles of other main roads in 1982–83. The airport at Mingaladon, about 13 miles north of Rangoon, only handles limited international air traffic.

CAPITAL.—The chief city of Lower Burma, and the seat of the government of the Union is ΨRangoon (Yangon), on the left bank of the Rangoon river, about 21 miles from the sea. The city contains the Shwe Dagon pagoda, much venerated by Burmese Buddhists. Population (1983): Rangoon District, 3,973,872; city population, 2,458,712.

Mandalay is the chief city of Upper Burma, population (1983): Mandalay district, 4,580,923; city, 532,985; Moulmein of 219,991 and Bassein of 144,092. Pagan, on the Irrawaddy, S.W. of Mandalay, contains many sacred buildings.

CURRENCY.—Kyat (K) of 100 pyas.

FLAG.—The Union flag is red, with a canton of dark blue, inside which are a cogwheel and two rice ears surrounded by 14 white stars.

NATIONAL DAY.—January 4.

BRITISH EMBASSY
80 Strand Road (Box No. 638), Rangoon
[Rangoon 81700]

Ambassador Extraordinary and Plenipotentiary, His Excellency Martin Robert Morland C.M.G. (1986).
First Secretaries, D. G. Alexander, M.B.E. (*Head of Chancery and Consul*); F. A. Wilson, M.B.E. (*Commercial*).
Cultural Attaché and British Council Representative, R. H. Isaacs.

BURUNDI
(République de Burundi)

President and Minister for National Defence, Major Pierre Buyoya, *elected* Sept. 9, 1987, *sworn in* Oct. 2, 1987.

COUNCIL OF MINISTERS
(w.e.f. Oct. 19, 1988)

Prime Minister and Minister for Planning, Adrien Sibomana.
Foreign Affairs and Co-operation, Cyprien Mbonimpa.
Agriculture, Jumiane Hussein.
Finance, Gerard Nihigira.
Rural Development, Gabriel Toyi.

Justice, Evariste Niyonkuru.
Interior, Aloys Kadoyi.
Commerce and Industry, Bonaventure Kidwingira.
Primary and Secondary Education, Gamayel Ndaruzaniye.
Higher Education and Scientific Research, Nicholas Myugi.
Transport, Posts and Telecommunications, Maj. Simon Rusuka.
Public Works and Urban Development, Evariste Simbarakira.
Energy and Mines, Gilbert Midende.
Public Health, Norbert Ngendabanyikwa.
Civil Service, Didace Rudargi.
Labour and Professional Training, Charles Karikuruba.
Family and Women's Affairs, Mme. Pia Ndayiragwe.
Social Affairs, Mme. Julie Ngiriye.
Information, Frederic Ngenzebuhoro.
Youth, Sport and Culture, Adolphe Nahayo.
Development, Tourism and the Environment, Basile Sindaharaye.

Formerly a Belgian trusteeship under the United Nations, Burundi was proclaimed an independent State on July 1, 1962. Situated on the east side of Lake Tanganyika, the State has an area of 10,747 sq. miles (27,834 sq. km.) and a population (1985 U.N. estimate) of 4,718,000. The majority of the population are of the Bahutu ethnic group, but power rests in the hands of the minority Batutsi ethnic group.

Burundi became independent as a constitutional monarchy but this was overthrown on November 28, 1966 and the country became a republic. On Nov. 1, 1976, the government of President Micombero was overthrown and a Supreme Revolutionary Council led by Col. Jean-Baptiste Bagaza took power. In 1980 the S.R.C. was replaced by a political bureau and central committee as part of a process of political normalization, which continued with elections to the National Assembly, a 65-member legislature. On Sept. 3, 1987 the government of President Bagaza was overthrown by a Military Committee of National Redemption led by Major Pierre Buyoya.

The chief crop is coffee, representing about 80 per cent of Burundi's export earnings. Cotton is the second most important crop. Mineral, tea, hide and skin exports are also important.

Trade with U.K.

	1987	1988
Imports from U.K......	£2,867,000	£2,922,000
Exports to U.K.	1,330,000	1,807,000

CAPITAL.—Bujumbura (formerly Usumbura), with about 150,000 inhabitants. Kitega (18,000 inhabitants) is the only other sizeable town. Official languages are Kirundi, a Bantu language, and French. Kiswahili is also used.

CURRENCY.—Burundi franc of 100 centimes.

FLAG.—White diagonal cross on green and red quarters, with a circular white panel in the centre.

NATIONAL DAY.—July 1.

British Ambassador (resident at Kinshasa, Zaire).

CAMEROON
(République Unie du Cameroun)

President, Head of State, Government and Commander in Chief of the Armed Forces, His Excellency Paul Biya, *acceded* Nov. 6, 1982, *elected* Jan. 14, 1984, *re-elected* April 24, 1988, *sworn in* May 13, 1988.

MINISTRY
(as at May 31, 1989)

At the Presidency, Paul Tessa (*Secretary General*);

Michel Meva'a M'Eboutou *Minister Delegate for Defence*); Prof. Titus Edzoa (*Special Adviser*); Adolphe Moudiki (*Dir. of Civil Cabinet*); Ogork Ebot Ntui (*Special Missions*).
Ministers:
Territorial Administration, Ibrahim Mbombo Njoya.
Women's Affairs and Social Welfare, Aissatou Yaou.
Agriculture, John Niba Ngu.
Industrial and Commercial Development, Joseph Tsanga Abanda.
National Education, Prof. Georges Ngango.
Animal Husbandry, Fisheries and Animal Industries, Hamadjoda Abjoudji.
Higher Education, Scientific Research, Public Contracts, and Computer Services, Abdoulaye Babale.
Finance, Sadou Hayatou.
Public Service and State Control, Prof. Joseph Owono.
Information and Culture, Henri Bandolo.
Youth and Sports, Dr. Joseph Fofe.
Justice, Benjamin Itoe.
Lands, Water and Energy, Francis Wainchom Nkwain.
Planning and Territorial Development, Elisabeth Tankeu.
Posts and Telecommunications, Sanda Oumarou.
External Relations, Jacques Roger Booh Booh.
Public Health, Prof. Joseph Mbedi.
Public Works and Transport, Claude Tchepannou.
Labour and Social Welfare, Jean Baptiste Bokam.
Town Planning and Housing, Ferdinand Leopold Oyono.

EMBASSY OF THE REPUBLIC OF CAMEROON
84 Holland Park, W11 3SB
[01–727 0771]

Ambassador Extraordinary and Plenipotentiary, His Excellency Dr. Gibering Bol-Alima (1987).

The Republic of Cameroon lies on the Gulf of Guinea between Nigeria to the west, Chad and the Central African Republic to the east and Congo and Gabon and Equatorial Guinea to the south. It has an area of 183,569 sq. miles, (475,442 sq. km.) and a population of 10,927,000 (1987 estimate).
The whole territory was administered by Germany from 1884 to 1916. From 1916 to 1959, the former East Cameroon was administered by France as a League of Nations (later U.N.) trusteeship. On Jan. 1, 1960 it became independent as the Republic of Cameroon. The Republic was joined on October 1, 1961, by the former British administered trust territory of the Southern Cameroons, after a plebiscite held under United Nations auspices. Cameroon became a Federal Republic with separate East and West Cameroon state governments. Subsequently, after a plebiscite held in May, 1972, Cameroon became a United Republic.
Cameroon is the only country in Africa where French and English are both official languages enjoying equal status, and the government's declared long-term objective is to achieve complete 'bilingualism' and 'biculturalism'.
The main economic emphasis is on agricultural development, both through encouraging small-scale peasant agriculture, and through the development of large-scale agro-industrial complexes, with the aim of making the country agriculturally self-sufficient and a major food exporter.
Principal products are cocoa, coffee, bananas, cotton, timber, ground-nuts, aluminium, rubber and palm products. There is an aluminium smelting plant at Edéa with an annual capacity of 50,000 tons. Oil is now also one of Cameroon's principal products with an estimated production of 9·2m. tonnes during 1984–5.

TRADE

	1985	1986
		CFA million
Total imports	508,756	590,439
Total exports	321,751	271,639

Trade with U.K.

	1987	1988
Imports from U.K.	£28,057,000	£20,472,000
Exports to U.K.	14,201,000	16,180,000

CAPITAL.—Yaoundé (1984 estimate, 522,000). Ψ Douala (1984 estimate, 763,000) is the commercial centre.
CURRENCY.—Franc C.F.A. of 100 centimes.
FLAG.—Vertical stripes of green, red and yellow with single five-pointed yellow star in centre of red stripe.
NATIONAL ANTHEM.—O Cameroun, Berceau de Nos Ancêtres (O Cameroon, cradle of our forefathers).
NATIONAL DAY.—May 20.

BRITISH EMBASSY
Avenue Winston Churchill, B.P. 547
Yaoundé
[Yaoundé 220545]

Ambassador Extraordinary and Plenipotentiary, His Excellency Martin Reith (1987).
First Secretary, B. Donaldson (*Head of Chancery and Commercial*).
Second Secretaries, R. O. Arrowsmith (*Commercial/ Aid*); R. W. Hyde, M.B.E. (*Administration and Vice Consul*).
British Council Representative, P. Ellwood, Les Galéries, Avenue J. F. Kennedy, (B.P. 818), Yaoundé. Tel. 223172.

CAPE VERDE
(República de Cabo Verde)

President, Aristides Pereira, *born* 1924, *assumed office*, July 5, 1975, *re-elected*, Jan. 13, 1986.

COUNCIL OF MINISTERS
(as at June 30, 1989)

Prime Minister, Minister of Co-operation and Planning, and Minister for Finance, M. Pedro Pires.
Justice, Dr. José E. F. Araujo.
Foreign Affairs, Col. Silvino M. Da Luz.
Civil Aeronautics, Tourism and Communications, Maj. Osvaldo L. da Silva.
Armed Forces and Security, Maj. Julio de Carvalho.
Agriculture and Fisheries, Maj. João P. Silva.
Education, André C. Tolentino.
Local Government and Town Planning, Tito L. S. de O. Ramos.
Information, Culture and Sport, Dr. David H. Almada.
Health, Labour and Social Services, Dr. Irineu Gomes.
Industry and Energy, Adão Rocha.
Public Works, Adriano de O. Lima.

The Cape Verde Islands, off the west coast of Africa, consist of two groups of islands, *Windward* (Santo Antão, São Vicente, Santa Luzia, São Nicolau, Boa Vista and Sal) and *Leeward* (Maio, São Tiago, Fogo and Brava) with a total area of 1,557 sq. miles (4,033 sq. km.). The population (1985 U.N. estimate) was 326,000, the majority of whom are Roman Catholic.
The Islands, colonized in *c.* 1460, achieved independence from Portugal on July 5, 1975, under the nationalist party of Guinea Bissau and Cape Verde. A federation of the islands with Guinea Bissau was planned (till 1879 Guinea-Bissau and the Islands were

a single administrative unit) but this was dropped following the 1980 coup in Guinea Bissau.

The Republic is a one-party (the P.A.I.C.V.) state with a President elected by the National Assembly. He has a mandate of 5 years, as do Assembly deputies, who are elected by universal adult suffrage.

The islands have had little rain since 1969, and agriculture is mostly confined to irrigated inland valleys, the chief products being bananas and coffee (for export), maize, sugarcane and nuts. Fish and shellfish are important exports. Salt is obtained on Sal, Boa Vista and Maio; volcanic rock is also mined for export. The main ports are Praia and Mindelo, and there is an international airport on Sal.

Trade with U.K.

	1987	1988
Imports from U.K.	£1,207,526	£1,812,000
Exports to U.K.	300,905	132,000

CAPITAL, Ψ Praia (1980, 57,748).

CURRENCY.—Escudo Caboverdiano of 100 centavos.

FLAG.—Horizontal band of yellow over green, with a vertical red band in the hoist charged with a black star over a garland of maize sheaves, two corn cobs and a clam shell.

NATIONAL DAY.—July 5. (Independence Day.)

British Ambassador (resident at Dakar, Senegal.)

CENTRAL AFRICAN REPUBLIC
(République Centrafricaine)

Head of State, Gen. André Kolingba, *assumed office* Sept. 1, 1981, *re-elected* Nov. 21, 1986.

COUNCIL OF MINISTERS
(w.e.f. Jan. 7, 1987)

President, Prime Minister, Minister of Defence, Gen. André Kolingba.
Economy, Finance, Planning and International Co-operation, Dieudonné Wazoua.
Foreign Affairs, Michel Gbezera Bria.
Rural Development, Theodore Bagua-Yambo.
Energy, Mines, Geology and Water Resources, Michel Salle.
Public Health and Social Affairs, Jean Willibiro-Sako.
Interior and Territorial Administration, Christophe Grelombe.
Justice, Thomas Mapouka.
Public Works and Territorial Development, Jacques Kithe.
National and Higher Education, Jean-Louis Psimhis.
Post Office and Telecommunications, Hugues Dobozendi.
Transport and Civil Aviation, Pierre Gonifei Gaibonanou.
Trade and Industry, and Small and Medium Enterprises, Thimothée Marboua.
Civil Service, Labour, Social Security and Vocational Training, Daniel Sehoulia.
Tourism, Water, Forests, Wildlife and Fishing, Raymond Mbitikon.
Communications, Arts and Culture, David N'Guindo.
Cabinet Secretariat and Relations with Parliament, Edouard Franck.

The Republic lies just north of the Equator between the Cameroon Republic, the Republic of Chad, the southern part of Sudan and Zaire. The Republic has an area of 240,535 sq. miles (622,984 sq. km.), and a population (1985 U.N. estimate) of 2,608,000.

On December 1, 1958, the French colony of Ubanghi Shari elected to remain within the French Community and adopted the title of the Central African Republic. It became fully independent on August 17, 1960. The first President of the Central African Republic, M. David Dacko, held office from 1960 until Jan. 1, 1966, when he was replaced by the then Col. Bokassa after a coup d'état. On Dec. 4, 1976, President Bokassa proclaimed himself Emperor and a new constitution (Parliamentary Monarchy) was introduced, the country being known as the Central African Empire. On Sept. 20, 1979, Emperor Bokassa was deposed by M. David Dacko in a bloodless coup and the country reverted to a Republic. President Dacko surrendered power on September 1 1981 to army commander Gen. André Kolingba in a bloodless coup. On Sept. 21, 1985 President Kolingba dissolved the Military Committee for National Recovery (C.M.R.N.) and appointed a civilian-dominated cabinet. Moves towards democratization have been made and on Nov. 21, 1986, a referendum was held whereby voters approved a new Constitution and the establishment of a one-party state. Legislative elections are to be held in the near future.

Economy.—A programme of economic reconstruction is under way, concentrating on agricultural production and private investment. Cotton, diamonds, coffee and timber are the major exports.

Trade with U.K.

	1987	1988
Imports from U.K.	£1,127,000	£733,000
Exports to U.K.	233,000	195,000

CAPITAL.—Bangui, near the border with Zaire, 473,817 (1984 est.).

CURRENCY.—Franc C.F.A. of 100 centimes.

FLAG.—Four horizontal stripes, blue, white, green, yellow, crossed by central vertical red stripe with a yellow five-pointed star in top left-hand corner.

NATIONAL DAY.—December 1.

British Ambassador, (resident at Yaoundé, Cameroon).

CHAD REPUBLIC
(Republique du Tchad)

Head of State, Hissène Habré, *took office* June 1982.

COUNCIL OF MINISTERS
(w.e.f. March 3, 1989)

President and Minister of Defence, Veterans and War Victims, Hissène Habré.
Minister of State, Djidingar Dono Ngardoum.
Foreign Affairs, Acheikh Ibn Oumar.
Territorial Administration, Ibrahim Mahamat Itno.
Justice, Wadal Abdelkader Kamougue.
National Education, Mahamat Senoussir.
Finance and Data Processing, Mbailim Bana Ngarnayal.
Transport and Civil Aviation, Djibril Negue Djogo.
Civil Service, Oudalbaye Naham.
Livestock, Animal Resources and Rural Hydraulics, Mahamat Nour Mallaye.
Agriculture, Gouara Lassou.
Mines, Petroleum and Energy, Mahamat Senoussi Khatir.
Public Health, Alphonse Kotiga Guerina.
Public Works, Abdoulaye Douto.
Social Affairs & Women's Advancement, Ruth Yeneko Romba.
Labour and Employment, Capt. Routouang Yoma Galom.
Food, Security and Afflicted Groups, Seid Bauche.
Post and Telecommunications, Kassire Delwa Koumakoye.
Planning and Co-operation, Soumaila Mahamat.
Culture, Youth and Sport, Djibrine Grinky.
Trade and Industry, Moussa Raouiengar.

Presidential Adviser, Ouangmoutching Homsala.
Information and Civil Orientation, Adoum Moussa
  Seif.
Higher Education and Scientific Research, Tibenoua
  Nemachoda.
National Education, Assilek Hazlata.
Territorial Development, Urbanism and Housing,
  Blial Soubiane.
Minister Delegate to the Presidency, Inspector General
  and Comptroller of State, Korom Ahmed.

Situated in north-central Africa, the Chad Republic extends from 23° N. latitude to 7° N. latitude and
is flanked by the Republics of Niger and Cameroon
on the west, by Libya on the north, by the Sudan on
the east and by the Central African Republic on the
south. It has an area of 495,755 sq. miles (1,284,000 sq.
km.) and a population (1985 U.N. estimate) of
5,018,000.

Chad became a member state of the French
Community on Nov. 28, 1958, and was proclaimed
fully independent on August 11, 1960. On April 14,
1962, a new Constitution was adopted involving a
presidential-type regime. This was suspended on
April 13, 1975 when President Tombalbaye was killed
in a military coup. The country was run by a Supreme
Military Council, under General Felix Malloum until
his overthrow in February 1979. A Transitional
Government of National Unity, headed by Goukouni
Oueddei, was replaced in June 1982 by the government of Hissène Habre. A ceasefire between Chad
and Libya was agreed in Sept. 1987. In May 1988,
Libya formally recognized the government of Habré
and offered to help in the reconstruction of northern
Chad. The war was formally ended on Oct. 3, 1988.

About 90 per cent of the workforce is occupied in
agriculture, fishing and forestry. There is an oilfield
in Kanem and salt is mined around Lake Chad, but
the most important activities are cotton growing
(mostly in the south) and animal husbandry in
central areas). Raw cotton and meat are the main
exports.

Trade with U.K.

	1987	1988
Imports from U.K	£1,006,000	£639,000
Exports to U.K.	1,101,000	1,764,000

CAPITAL.—Ndjaména (formerly known as Fort
Lamy) south of Lake Chad (402,000).
CURRENCY.—Franc C.F.A. of 100 centimes.
FLAG.—Vertical stripes, blue, yellow and red.
NATIONAL DAY.—April 13.

British Ambassador (resident in London).

CHILE
(República de Chile)

Head of State, Army Commander-in-Chief and Presi-
  dent of the Republic, General Augusto Pinochet
  (Ugarte), born, November 25, 1915.
Junta Members, Adm. José T. Merino (C.-in-C. Navy);
  Gen. Fernando Matthei (C.-in-C. Air Force); Gen.
  Rodolfo Stange (Dir.-Gen. of Carabineros); Lt.-
  Gen. Humberto Gordon (Army).

CABINET
(as at April 30, 1989)

Foreign Affairs, Hernan Felipe Errázuriz Correa.
Interior, Carlos Cáceres.
Defence, Vice-Adm. Patricio Carvajal.
Education, (vacant).
Finance, Enrique Sequel Morel.
Justice, Hugo Rosende.
Public Works, Brig.-Gen. Bruno Siebert.
Transport and Communications, Carlos Silva Echi-
  buru.

Agriculture, Jaime de la Sota Benavente.
National Property, Armando Alvarez Marin.
Labour and Social Security, Guillermo Arturo Errá-
  zuriz.
Health, Juan Giaconi.
Housing, Gustavo Montero Saavedra.
Economy, Development and Reconstruction, Pablo
  Barahona Urzúa.
Planning, Gen. Sergio Valenzuela.
Energy, Gen. Hernan Brady.
Secretary General of the Government, Oscar Varbas
  Guzman.

EMBASSY OF CHILE
12 Devonshire Street, W1N 2FS
[01–580 6392/4]

Ambassador Extraordinary and Plenipotentiary, His
  Excellency Juan Carlos Délano (1987).

A state of South America lying between the Andes
and the shores of the South Pacific, Chile extends
coastwise from just north of Arica to Cape Horn
south, between lat. 17° 15′ and 55° 59′ S. and long.
66° 30′ and 75° 48′ W. Extreme length of the country
is about 2,800 miles, with an average breadth, north
of 41°, of 100 miles. The great chain of the Andes runs
along its eastern limit, with a general elevation of
5,000 to 15,000 feet above the level of the sea; but
numerous summits attain a greater height. The
chain, however, lowers considerably towards its
southern extremity. The Andes form a boundary
with Argentina, and at the head of the pass where
the international road from Chile to Argentina
crosses the frontier, has been erected a statue of
Christ the Redeemer, 26 feet high, made of bronze
from old cannon, to commemorate the peaceful
settlement of a boundary dispute in 1902. There are
no rivers of great size, and none of them is of much
service as a navigable highway. In the north the
country is arid. The total area of the Republic is
292,258 sq. miles, (756,945 sq. km.), with a population
(1985 U.N. estimate) of 12,074,000.

Among the island possessions of Chile are the Juan
Fernandez group (3 islands) about 360 miles distant
from Valparaiso. One of these islands is the reputed
scene of Alexander Selkirk's (Robinson Crusoe)
shipwreck. Easter Island (27° 8′ S. and 109° 28′ W.),
about 2,000 miles distant in the South Pacific Ocean,
contains stone platforms and hundreds of stone
figures, the origin of which has not yet been
determined. The area of the island is about 45 sq.
miles, (116·5 sq. km.).

Chile is divided into 12 regions and the Metropolitan Area. The disputed boundary with Argentina
in the Beagle Channel was settled by a treaty ratified
in May 1985.

The Chilean population has four main sources:
(a) indigenous Araucanian Indians, Fuegians, and
Changos; (b) Spanish settlers and their descendants;
(c) mixed Spanish Indians; and (d) European immigrants. Only the few remaining indigenous Indians
and some originally Bolivian Indians in the north
are racially separate. Following extensive intermar-
riage there is no effective distinction among the
remainder.

Government.—Chile was discovered by Spanish
adventurers in the 16th century and remained under
Spanish rule until 1810, when a revolutionary war,
culminating in the Battle of Maipu (April 5, 1818),
achieved the independence of the nation.

At a general election held on Sept. 4, 1970, the
Marxist candidate Dr. Allende was elected President
by a narrow margin. After severe industrial unrest
and widespread violent incidents, Allende was overthrown on September 11, 1973, in a coup carried out
by leaders of the Armed Forces and National Police.

After a national plebiscite, the Constitution of 1925

was replaced early in 1981 and Gen. Pinochet was sworn in as President, to serve until 1989. Gen. Pinochet was defeated in a plebiscite of Oct. 5, 1988 regarding his term of office being extended for a further eight years. He resisted calls for his resignation. Another plebiscite on July 30, 1989 was held on changes to the 1980 Constitution. Presidential and Congressional elections have been scheduled for Dec. 14, 1989.

Production.—Cereals, legumes, sugar beet, vegetables, fruit, tobacco, hemp and vines are grown extensively (especially in the central zone) and livestock accounts for nearly 40 per cent of agricultural production. Sheep farming predominates in the extreme south. There are large timber tracts in the central and southern zones of Chile, some types of which are exported, along with wood derivatives such as cellulose and pulp. Industrial-scale fishing, which exceeds 5·5 million tonnes p.a., makes Chile the third largest nation in terms of catch. The principal end product is fish meal.

The mineral wealth is considerable, the country being particularly rich in copper-ore, iron-ore and nitrate. Chile also produces iodine, manganese ore, coal, mercury, molybdenum, zinc, lead and a small quantity of gold. Uranium is also said to have been discovered in small quantities. The rainless north is the scene of the only commercial production of nitrate of soda (Chile saltpetre) from natural resources in the world. The country has also large deposits of high grade sulphur, but mostly around high extinct volcanoes in the Andes Cordillera, difficult of access. Oil was struck in Magallanes (Tierra del Fuego) in December, 1945, and oil and natural gas are produced in the Magallanes area from on- and off-shore wells. This domestic production, despite declining, covers approximately 50 per cent of total oil requirement, and imported crude oil is refined at Concon and San Vicente in the central part of the country. There is a steel plant at Huachipato, near Concepción.

Production figures for 1987 were:

Copper (tonnes)	1,398,263
Potassium and sodium nitrate (tonnes)	795,268
Coal (tonnes)	1,515,604
Steel ingots (tonnes)	744,468
Crude oil (cu. metres)	1,736,500
Natural gas (cu. metres)	4,352,600,000

Industry is based on the processing of mineral, forestry, fish and agricultural products, and the manufacture of consumer goods.

Communications.—Chilean ships have a virtual monopoly in the coastwide trade, though, with the improvement of the roads, an increasing share of internal transportation is moving by road and rail. The Chilean mercantile marine numbers 57 vessels (of over 100 tons gross) with a total deadweight tonnage of 1,125,200 (1987).

There are 6,575 miles of railway track. A metre-gauge line (the *Longitudinál*) runs from La Calera, just north of Santiago, to Iquique: however, road transport has caused a reduction in rail traffic along this route. The wide gauge railway runs from Valparaiso through La Calera, 60 miles inland, and after passing through Santiago ends at Puerto Montt.

With the completion of a section of 435 miles from Corumba, Brazil, to Santa Cruz, Bolivia, the Trans-Continental Line will link the Chilean Pacific port of Arica with Rio de Janeiro on the Atlantic. Another line from Antofagasta to Salta (Argentina) was opened in 1948. Further south, the Trans-Andine Railway connects Valparaiso on the Pacific with Buenos Aires, crossing the Andes at 11,500 ft. However services have now been suspended due to financial difficulties.

Chile is served by about 20 international airlines. The domestic traffic is carried by the state-owned Linea Aerea Nacional and the privately-owned LADECO, which also operate internationally, and smaller regional carriers.

Chile's road system is about 65,000 kilometres in length, but only an estimated 7,000 kilometres are first-class paved highways.

Defence.—Military service is compulsory, but not all those who are liable are required. Recruitment for the Navy is mostly voluntary, but there are some conscripts. The Navy consists of 1 cruiser, 10 destroyers, frigates and escorts, 6 patrol vessels and FPBs and 4 submarines. There is a support force of transports, tankers, 1 submarine depot ship and ancillary small craft. The strength of the Navy is 28,000 (3,000 conscripts) including men of the Marine Force. The Army's total strength is 53,000, which includes 3,000 officers and 30,000 conscripts (2 years). In addition there is a police force of Carabineros of 28,000 officers and men. The Air Force total strength is 15,000 with a strength of 120 aircraft.

Education.—Elementary education is free, and has been compulsory since 1920. There are 8 Universities (3 in Santiago, 2 in Valparaiso, 1 in Antofagasta, 1 in Concepción and 1 in Valdivia). The religion is Roman Catholic.

Language and Literature.—Spanish is the language of the country, with admixtures of local words of Indian origin. Recent efforts have reduced illiteracy and have thus afforded access to the literature of Spain, to supplement the vigorous national output. The Nobel Prize for Literature was awarded in 1945 to Señorita Gabriela Mistral, for Chilean verse and prose, and in 1971 to the poet Pablo Neruda. There are over 100 newspapers and a large number of periodicals.

FINANCE

	1986	1987
Total revenue	US$3,841·4 m.	US$8,469·8 m.
Total expenditure	4,232·0 m.	8,421·6 m.

Foreign debt at December 31, 1987 was provisionally quoted at U.S. $19,100 million.

EXTERNAL TRADE
($U.S. ,000)

	1986	1987
Total imports	3,156,900	4,023,300
Total exports	4,222,400	5,101,900

Trade with U.K.

	1987	1988
Imports from U.K.	£105,838,000	£80,901,000
Exports to U.K.	112,843,000	179,628,000

The principal exports are metallic and non-metallic minerals (copper represented 41 per cent of total export earnings in 1987), sawn timber, cellulose and other wood derivatives, some metal products, fish products, vegetables, fruit and wool. The principal imports are sugar and other food products, industrial raw materials, machinery, equipment and spares, oil fuels, lubricants and transportation equipment.

CAPITAL, Santiago, 4,132,293 (Greater Santiago), Other large towns are:—ΨValparaiso (500,000), Concepción (170,000), Temuco (110,000), ΨAntofagasta (110,000), Chillán (79,461), ΨTalcahuano (75,643), Talca (75,354); ΨValdivia (70,000), ΨIquique (50,000), ΨPunta Arenas (50,000). Punta Arenas on the Straits of Magellan, is the southernmost city in the world.

CURRENCY.—Chilean peso of 100 centavos.

FLAG.—Two horizontal bands, white, red; in top sixth a white star on blue square, next staff.

NATIONAL ANTHEM.—Canción Nacional de Chile.

NATIONAL DAY.—September 18 (National Anniversary).

BRITISH EMBASSY
Avenida La Concepción 177, Santiago 9
(Casilla 72-D)
[Santiago 2239166]

Ambassador Extraordinary and Plenipotentiary, His
Excellency Alan White, C.M.G., O.B.E. (1987).
Counsellor, Head of Chancery and Consul-General, G.
M. Baker.
Defence Attaché, Capt. T. Leland, R.N.

BRITISH CONSULAR OFFICES

There are British Consular Offices at *Santiago,
Arica, Punta Arenas, Valparaiso.*

BRITISH COUNCIL

Cultural Attaché and British Council Representative,
W. Campbell, Eliodoro Yañez 832, Santiago (Casilla
15-T). The Council supplies books to the libraries
of the *Instituto Chileno-Britanico* in *Santiago, Viña
del Mar/ Valparaiso* and *Concepción.*

BRITISH-CHILEAN CHAMBER OF COMMERCE
Luis Thayer Ojeda 0115 O.F. 3021 Santiago
(*Postal Address*, Casilla 536, Santiago).

CHINA
(Zhonghua Renmin Gongheguo—
The People's Republic of China)

President of the People's Republic of China, Yang
Shangkun, *elected* April 1988.
Vice President, Wang Zhen.
*Chairman of the Standing Committee of the Seventh
National People's Congress*, Wan Li.
Chairman of the Central Military Commission, Deng
Xiaoping.

STATE COUNCIL
(as at July 15, 1989)

Premier, Li Peng.
Vice-Premiers, Yao Yilin; Tian Jiyun; Wu Xueqian.
State Councillors, Li Tieying; Qin Jiwei; Wang
Bingqian; Song Jian; Wang Fang; Zou Jiahua; Li
Guixian; Chen Xitong; Chen Junsheng.

Ministers:
Aeronautics and Astronautics Industry, Lin Zong-
tang.
Agriculture, He Kang.
Chemical Industry, Gu Xiulian.
Civil Affairs, Cui Naifu.
Commerce, Hu Ping.
Communications, Qian Yongchang.
Construction, Lin Hanxiong.
Culture, Wang Meng.
Energy Resources, Huang Yicheng.
Finance, Wang Bingqian.
Foreign Affairs, Qian Qichen.
Foreign Economic Relations and Trade, Zheng Tuo-
bin.
Forestry, Gao Dezhan.
Geology and Mineral Resources, Zhu Xun.
Justice, Cai Cheng.
Labour, Ruan Chongwu.
Light Industry, Zeng Xianlin.
Machine Building and Electronics Industry, Zou
Jiahua.
Metallurgical Industry, Qi Yuanjing.
National Defence, Qin Jiwei.
Personnel, Zhao Dongwan.
Posts and Telecommunications, Yang Taifang.
Public Health, Chen Minzhang.
Public Security, Wang Fang.
Radio, Film and Television, Ai Zhisheng.
Railways, Li Senmao.

State Security, Jia Chunwang.
Supervision, Wei Jianxing.
Textile Industry, Wu Wenying.
Water Resources, Yang Zhenhuai.

MINISTERS IN CHARGE OF STATE COMMISSIONS

Education, Li Tieying.
Family Planning, Peng Peiyun.
Nationalities Affairs, Ismail Amat.
Physical Culture and Sports, Wu Shaozu.
Planning, Yao Yilin.
Restructuring Economy, Li Peng.
*Science, Technology and Industry for National Def-
ence*, Ding Henggao.
Science and Technology, Song Jian.
Auditor General, Lu Peijian.
Secretary General, Luo Gan.

President of the People's Bank of China, Li Guixian.

THE CHINESE COMMUNIST PARTY

General Secretary, Jiang Zemin.
The Politburo Standing Committee, Jiang Zemin; Li
Peng; Qiao Shi; Yao Yilin; Li Ruihuan; Song Ping.
The Politburo of the Central Committee, Wan Li; Tian
Jiyun; Qiao Shi; Jiang Zemin; Li Tieying; Li
Ruihuan; Li Ximing; Yang Rudai; Yang Shang-
kun; Wu Xueqian; Song Ping; Hu Qili; Yao Yilin;
Qin Jiwei; Li Peng (*full members*); Ding Guangen
(*alternate member*).
The Secretariat of the Central Committee, Li Ruihuan;
Ding Guan'Gen; Qiao Shi (*full members*); Wen
Jiabao (*alternate member*).
The Advisory Commission, Chen Yun (*Chairman*);
Bo Yibo; Song Renqiong; (*Vice Chairmen*).
The Discipline Inspection Commission, Secretary,
Qiao Shi; *Deputy Secretaries*, Chen Zuolin; Li
Zhengting; Xiao Hongda.
Membership, 42,000,000.

EMBASSY OF THE PEOPLE'S REPUBLIC OF CHINA
49–51 Portland Place, W1N 3AH
[01–636 9375]

Ambassador Extraordinary and Plenipotentiary, His
Excellency Ji Chaozhu (1987).

AREA AND POPULATION.—The area of China is
3,705,408 sq. miles, (9,596,961 sq. km.). A nationwide
census (the third) was held in July 1982, which
recorded a total population of 1,008,175,288. According to the P.R.C. State Statistical Bureau, the
population at the beginning of 1989 was 1,160,000,000.
China is anxious to control the growth of the
population and has introduced stringent policies
intended to result in a population of 1,200 million by
the year 2000. About 6 per cent of the population
belong to around 55 ethnic minorities. Among the
largest are the Zhuang of Guangxi, the Uygurs of
Xinjiang, the Tibetans and the Mongols.

THE PROVINCES OF CHINA
(1988 estimated population figures)

Anhui	53,770,000
Beijing	10,810,000
Fujian	28,450,000
Gansu	21,360,000
Guangdong	59,280,000
Guangxi Zhuang Autonomous Region	40,880,000
Guizhou	31,270,000
Hainan	6,280,000
Hebei	57,950,000
Heilongjiang	34,660,000
Henan	80,940,000
Hubei	51,850,000
Hunan	58,900,000
Jiangsu	64,380,000
Jiangxi	36,090,000

Jilin	23,730,000
Liaoning	38,200,000
Nei Monggol Autonomous Region	20,940,000
Ningxia Hui Autonomous Region	4,450,000
Qinghai	4,340,000
Shaanxi	31,350,000
Shandong	80,610,000
Shanghai	12,620,000
Shanxi	27,550,000
Sichuan	105,760,000
Tianjin	8,430,000
Tibet Autonomous Region	2,120,000
Xinjiang Uygur Autonomous Region	14,260,000
Yunnan	35,940,000
Zhejiang	41,700,000
Armed Forces	4,238,210

Government.—On October 10, 1911, the party of reform forced the Imperial dynasty to a 'voluntary' abdication, and a Republic was proclaimed at Wuchang.

On September 30, 1949, the Chinese People's Political Consultative Conference (C.P.P.C.C) met in Peking and appointed the National People's Government Council under the Chairmanship of Mao Zedong (Mao Tse-tung). On October 1, Mao proclaimed the inauguration of the Chinese People's Republic.

The regime was recognized by all the Communist bloc countries in quick succession, and soon after by the Asian countries of the Commonwealth, the United Kingdom and by a number of other countries. Others, led by the United States, continued to recognize the Chiang Kai-shek regime on Taiwan as the rightful Government of China. In 1971 the People's Republic won acceptance into the United Nations on the expulsion of Taiwan. Since then many more countries have accorded recognition.

A new Constitution was adopted in December 1982, under which the National People's Congress is the highest organ of state power. It is elected for a term of five years and is supposed to hold one session a year. It is empowered to amend the Constitution, make laws, select the President and Vice-President and other leading officials of the state, approve the national economic plan, the state budget and the final state accounts, and to decide on questions of war and peace. The State Council is the highest organ of the state administration. It is composed of the Premier, the Vice Premiers, the State Councillors, heads of Ministries and Commissions, the Auditor General and the Secretary General. Command over the armed forces is vested in the Central Military Commission, of which Deng Xiaoping is the Chairman.

Deputies to congresses at the primary level are 'directly elected' by the voters 'through a secret ballot after democratic consultation'. This is now being extended to county level. These Congresses elect the Deputies to the Congress at the next higher level. Deputies to the National People's Congress are elected by the People's Congresses of the provinces, autonomous regions and municipalities directly under the Central Government, and by the armed forces.

Local government is conducted through People's Governments at provincial, municipal and county levels. Autonomous regions, prefectures and counties exist for national minorities and are described as self-governing. The system prevailing is that found elsewhere, i.e. People's Congresses and People's Governments. Beijing, Shanghai and Tianjin continue to come directly under the central government.

Following the deaths of Mao Zedong and Zhou Enlai in 1976 the disgraced Vice-Premier Deng Xiaoping was recalled. At the 11th Party Congress in 1977 Deng was elected Vice-Chairman and has since become the dominant force within the Party by eliminating leftist influence, rehabilitating fallen leaders and adjusting Maoist policies to permit economic liberalization. Deng's policies were reaffirmed at the 12th Congress in 1982. The Congress also elected a new Party leadership dominated by Deng and his supporters. The post of Chairman of the Party was abolished. The Party leader now holds the post of General Secretary. The 13th Party Congress in 1987 reaffirmed open-door policies. Most of the old revolutionary generation were removed, in elections, from the top posts.

Student-led pro-democracy demonstrations throughout April and May ended on June 3–4, 1989 when the People's Liberation Army took control of Beijing, killing thousands of protesters (*see also* Events of the Year).

Armed Forces.—All three military arms in China are parts of the People's Liberation Army (P.L.A.) The size of this body has not been formally given, but it is estimated that China has approximately 3·5 million men under arms, with a further 12 million (or perhaps many more) reserves who take part in militia activities. In June 1985 a planned reduction of over 1 million in the course of a year was officially announced. In 1955 compulsory military service was introduced for all men between the ages of 18 and 40. This service was on a selective basis. The present length of service for those conscripted is three years in the Army, four years in the Air Force and five years in the Navy. With effect from June 1, 1965, the rank structure was abolished, together with all marks of distinction of branch of service. Both are expected to be reinstated.

Religion.—The indigenous religions of China are Confucianism (which includes ancestor worship), Taoism (originally a philosophy rather than a religion) and, since its introduction in the first century of the Christian era, Buddhism. There are also Chinese Muslims (officially estimated at about 12 million) and Christians (unofficially estimated at about 50 million). Religious freedoms, severely curtailed during the Cultural Revolution, are reviving slightly under more liberal policies.

Education.—The Cultural Revolution caused considerable disruption to the educational system and since 1976 attempts have been made to raise academic standards. Primary education now lasts five years, and has a claimed enrolment of 146,000,000 pupils. Secondary education lasts five years (three years in Junior Middle School and two years in Senior Middle School). There were 47,000,000 Middle School pupils in 1986. The proportion of illiterates and semi-illiterates in 1982 was 23·5 per cent, but efforts are being made to expand secondary education, particularly in the rural areas. Particular attention is being paid to higher education where there are over 1,000 universities, colleges and institutes with an enrolment of 1,700,000 students. In May 1985 the Central Committee of the Party announced the abolition of free higher education except for teacher training, and the aim of providing all children with junior secondary education within 10 years.

Language and Literature.—The Chinese language has many dialects, notably Cantonese, Hakka, Amoy, Foochow, Changsha, Nanchang, Wu (Shanghai) and the northern dialect. The Common Speech or *Putonghua* (often referred to as Mandarin) which is being taught throughout the country is based on the northern dialect. The Communists have promoted it as the national language and made intensive efforts to propagate it throughout the country. Since the most important aspect of this policy is the use of the spoken language in writing, the old literary style and ideographic form of writing has fallen into disuse.

In 1956, after some 4 years of study, the Government decided to introduce 230 simplified characters with a view to making reading and writing easier. The list was enlarged and there are now over 2,000 simplified

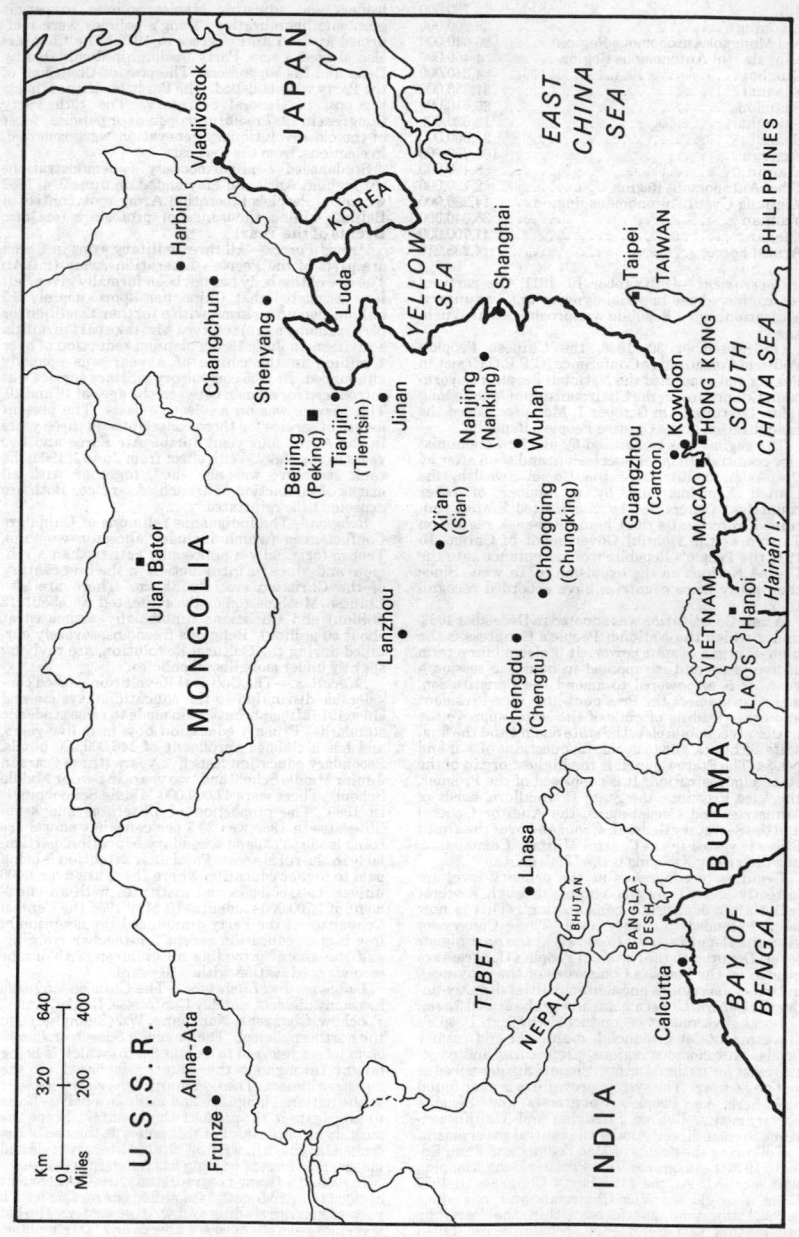

characters in use. In Jan. 1956, all Chinese newspapers and most books began to appear with the characters printed horizontally from left to right, instead of vertically reading from right to left, as previously.

In Feb. 1958 The National People's Congress adopted a system of Romanization, known as pinyin, using 25 of the letters of the Latin alphabet (not v). This has been used within the country largely for assisting schoolchildren and others to learn the pronunciation of characters in *Putonghua*, and is now used for Chinese names in foreign-language publications.

Chinese literature is one of the richest in the world. Paper has been employed for writing and printing for nearly 2,000 years. The Confucian classics which formed the basis of the traditional Chinese culture date from the Warring States period (4th–3rd centuries B.C.) as do the earliest texts of the rival tradition, Taoism. Histories, philosophical and scientific works, poetry, literary and art criticism, novels and romances survive from most periods. Many have been translated into English. In the past all this considerable literature was available only to a very small class of *literati*, but with the spread of literacy in the 20th century, a process which has received enormous impetus since the Communists took over in 1950, the old traditional literature has been largely superseded by modern works of a popular kind and by the classics of Marxism and modern developments from them.

The most important among the newspapers and magazines are the People's Daily and the twice-monthly Red Flag, the communist party organs.

Production and Industry.—China is essentially an agricultural and pastoral country: peasants constitute about 80 per cent of the population. People's communes gave way to townships as the basic level of State administration in rural districts under the 1982 Constitution.

New agricultural policies, designed to give greater incentives to the rural population, have meant that the responsibility for agricultural production has been devolved down to individual households, whereas previously work was generally assigned on a collective basis.

Wheat, barley, maize, millet and other cereals, with peas and beans, are grown in the northern provinces, and rice and sugar in the south. Rice is the staple food of the inhabitants. Cotton (mostly in valleys of the Yangtze and Yellow Rivers), tea (in the west and south), with hemp, jute and flax, are the most important crops.

Livestock is raised in large numbers. Silkworm culture is one of the oldest industries. Cottons, woollens and silks are manufactured in large quantities. The mineral wealth of the country is very great. Coal of excellent quality is produced. Iron ore, tin, antimony, wolfram, bismuth and molybdenum are also abundant. Oil is produced in several northern provinces, particularly in Heilongjiang and Shandong, and off-shore deposits are being sought in co-operation with Western and Japanese companies.

The Chinese State Statistical Bureau issues production figures annually. The following are of note for 1987:

Grain (tons)	402,410,000
Pork, beef, mutton (tons)	19,210,000
Tea (tons)	497,000
Cotton (tons)	4,190,000
Timber (cu. metres)	68,430,000
Crude oil (tons)	134,000,000
Steel (tons)	56,020,000
Electric power (KWh)	496 billion
Machine tools	146,000
Motor vehicles	472,000

The State Statistical Bureau valued the national income for 1987 at Yuan 915·3 billion, an increase of 9·3 per cent over 1986. The Gross National Product in 1987 was Yuan 1,092 billion, a 9·3 per cent. increase over 1986. The total value of agricultural output rose by 4·7 per cent. over the 1986 figure to Yuan 444·7 billion. The total value of industrial output rose by 16·5 per cent. to Yuan 1,378 billion.

In 1982 China set itself the aim of quadrupling the 1980 gross agricultural and industrial output value by the year 2000. The focus of its reform programme was switched to industry in 1984. Wide-ranging reforms have been introduced to make the industrial sector more efficient by narrowing the scope of central planning and broadening enterprise decision-making, material incentives and the role of the market.

Foreign trade and external economic relations have expanded quickly since the open-door policy, adopted in the late 1970's. The principal articles of export are animals and animal products; oil; textiles; ores, metals, tea and manufactured goods. The principal imports are motor vehicles; machinery; chemical fertilizer plants; aircraft; books, paper and paper-making materials; chemicals; metals and ores; and dyes.

Trade with U.K.

	1987	1988
Imports from U.K.	£416,012,000	£411,563,000
Exports to U.K.	391,766,000	443,698,000

Communications.—Of the total area of China over half consists of tableland and mountainous areas where communications and travel are generally difficult. The country has more than 52,000 kilometres of railway trunk and branch lines and some 926,746 kilometres of highway. In addition, internal civil aviation has been developed, with routes now totalling more than 340,000 kilometres. As a result the communications network now covers most of the country.

In the past where roads did not exist the principal means of communication east to west was provided by the rivers, the most important of which are the Yangtze (Changjiang) (3,400 miles long), the Yellow River (Huanghe) (2,600 miles long) and the West River (Xihe) (1,650 miles). These, together with the network of canals connecting them are still much used, but their overall importance is less than it was. Coastal port facilities are being improved and the merchant fleet expanded. In the past 10 years great progress has been made in developing postal services and telecommunications. It is now claimed that 95 per cent of all rural communes are on the telephone and that postal routes reach practically every production brigade headquarters.

CAPITAL.—Beijing (Peking), population (1988), 9,957,000.

Population of major cities in 1986:

ΨShanghai	*12,620,000	Harbin	2,670,000
Tianjin	5,460,000	Chengdu	2,640,000
Shenyang	4,290,000	Xian	2,390,000
Wuhan	3,490,000	Nanjing	*2,433,000
Guangzhou		Taiyuan	1,930,000
(Canton)	3,360,000	Kunming	1,520,000
Chongqing	2,700,000	Lanzhou	1,390,000

* 1988 figures.

CURRENCY.—The currency is called Renminbi (RMB). The unit of currency is the yuan of 10 jiao or 100 fen.

FLAG.—Red, with large gold five-point star and four small gold stars in crescent, all in upper quarter next staff.

NATIONAL ANTHEM.—March of the Volunteers.

NATIONAL DAY.—October 1 (Founding of People's Republic).

BRITISH EMBASSY
11 Guang Hua Lu,
Jian Guo Men Wai, Beijing.
[Beijing 521961/5]

Ambassador, His Excellency Sir Alan Ewen Donald, K.C.M.G. (1988).
Counsellors, Miss A. J. K. Bailes; J. K. Chapman (*Commercial*); D. Marler, O.B.E. (*Cultural, and British Council Representative*).
Defence, Military and Air Attaché, Col. C. A. Lees.
First Secretaries, Dr. J. E. Hoare (*Head of Chancery and Consul General*); P. Wood (*Economic*); G. R. Duff (*Administration and Consul*); P. Davies (*Consul*); P. Clark (*Chancery*); S. Prince (*Commercial*); C. O. Piggott (*Chancery*); S. S. Calder (*Energy*); I. A. Seaton (*Cultural ELO*); Dr. J. P. Eyres (*Cultural/ Science*).

There is also a Consulate-General in *Shanghai.*

TIBET

Tibet is a plateau seldom lower than 10,000 feet, which forms the northern frontier of India (boundary imperfectly demarcated), from Kashmir to Burma, but is separated therefrom by the Himalayas. The area is estimated at 463,000 square miles with a population of 2,120,000 in 1988.

From 1911 to 1950, Tibet was virtually an independent country though its status was never officially so recognized. In October 1950, Chinese Communist forces invaded Eastern Tibet. On May 23, 1951, an agreement was reached whereby the Chinese army was allowed entry into Tibet. A Communist military and administrative headquarters was set up. In 1954 the Government of India recognized that Tibet was an integral part of China, in return for the right to maintain trade and consular representation there.

A series of revolts against Chinese rule over several years culminated on March 17, 1959, in a rising in Lhasa. Heavy fighting continued for several days before the rebellion was suppressed by Chinese troops and military rule imposed. The Dalai Lama fled to India where he and his followers were granted political asylum. On March 28, 1959, the Chinese Premier issued an order dissolving the Tibetan Government. In its place the 16-member Preparatory Committee for the Tibetan Autonomous Region, originally set up in 1955 with the Dalai Lama as Chairman, was to administer Tibet under the State Council. The Preparatory Committee was to have the Panchen Lama as Acting Chairman and also to include 4 Chinese Officials. Elections were held to choose local People's Congresses in Tibet, thus indicating that the government organization there no longer differed significantly from that of any ordinary province in China.

In December, 1964, the Dalai Lama was declared to be a traitor, and both he and the Panchen Lama were dismissed. The position of Acting Chairman of the Preparatory Committee was assumed by Ngapoi Ngawang Jigmi, who had long been the most prominent secular figure in Tibet. This move marked the end of the period of co-operation by the Chinese Government with the traditional religious authorities, and the eclipse of the latter. The Preparatory Committee completed its work with the setting up of Tibet as an Autonomous Region of China on Sept. 9, 1965. The Panchen Lama was rehabilitated as an official of the C.P.P.C.C., but died in 1989. The

Chinese have invited the Dalai Lama to return from exile.

TAIWAN (REPUBLIC OF CHINA)
(Ta Chung-Hwa Min-Kwo)

President, Lee Teng-hui, *elected,* Jan. 13, 1988.
Vice-President, (vacant).
Premier, Lee Huan (May 29, 1989).

An island of some 13,800 sq. miles, (35,742 sq. km.), in the China Sea, Taiwan, formerly Formosa, lies 90 miles east of the Chinese mainland in latitude 21° 45′N.–25° 38′N. The population (19,460,000 in 1986), is almost entirely Chinese in origin and includes about 2,000,000 mainlanders who came to the island with Chiang Kai-shek in 1947–49. The territories administered by the Chinese Nationalists include the Pescadores Islands (50 sq. miles), some 35 miles west of Taiwan, as well as Quemoy (68 sq. miles) and Matsu (11 sq. miles) which are only a few miles from the mainland. Settled for centuries by the Chinese, the island was administered by Japan from 1895 to 1945. General Chiang Kai-shek withdrew to Taiwan in 1949, towards the end of the war against the Communist regime, accompanied by 500,000 Nationalist troops, after which the territory continued under his presidency until his death on April 5, 1975. A mutual defence treaty between the United States and Taiwan Governments was signed in 1954 but this was terminated when the United States recognized the People's Republic of China on January 1, 1979. Martial law was lifted in July 1987, after 38 years. Chiang Kai-shek's son Chiang Ching-kuo died in Jan. 1988 and was succeeded by Vice President Lee Teng-hui, a native Taiwanese.

The eastern part of the main island is mountainous and forest covered. Mt. Morrison (Yu Shan) (13,035 ft.) and Mt. Sylvia (Tz'ukaoshan) (12,972 ft.) are the highest peaks. The western plains are watered by many rivers and the soil is very fertile, producing sugar, rice, sweet potatoes, tea, bananas, pineapples and tobacco. Coal, sulphur, iron, petroleum, copper and gold are mined. There are important fisheries. The principal seaports ΨKeelung and ΨKaohsiung are situated in the northern and southern sections of the island.

Trade with U.K.

	1987	1988
Imports from U.K.	£292,275,000	£355,786,000
Exports to U.K.	1,006,880,000	1,150,392,000

CAPITAL.—Taipei (population 1985, 2,507,620). Other towns are ΨKaohsiung (1,314,364); Tainan (572,590); Taichung (585,205); and ΨKeelung (345,392).

CURRENCY.—New Taiwan dollar (NT$) of 100 cents.
FLAG.—Red, with blue quarter at top next staff, bearing a twelve-point white sun.
NATIONAL DAY.—October 10.

COLOMBIA
(República de Colombia)

President, Dr. Virgilio Barco Vargas, *assumed office,* August 7, 1986.

CABINET
(as at July 31, 1989)

Home Affairs, Rafael Orejuela Bueno.
Foreign Affairs, Julio Londoño Paredes.
Finance, Luis Fernando Alarcón Mantilla.

National Defence, Gen. Oscar Botero Restrepo.
Public Works and Transport, Priscila Ceballos Ordo-
nez.
Justice, Monica de Greiff.
Labour and Social Security, Maria Teresa Forero de
Saade.
Agriculture, Gabriel Rosas Vega.
Health, Eduardo Diaz Uribe.
Mines, Margarita Mena de Quevedo.
Communications, Carlos Lemos Simmonds.
Education, Manuel Francisco Becerra.
Government, Orlando Vasquez Velasquez.
Mayor of Bogotá, Andres Pastrana Arango.
National Planning Department, Maria Mercedes
Cuellar de Martinez.
Attorney General, Alfonso Gomez Mendez.
Comptroller General, Rodolfo Gonzalez Garcia.

CsLOMBIAN EMBASSY
3 Hans Crescent, SW1X 0LR
[01–589 9177]

Ambassador Extraordinary and Plenipotentiary, His
Excellency Dr. Fernando Cepeda (1988).

The Republic of Colombia lies in the extreme north-
west of South America, having a coastline on both
the Caribbean Sea and Pacific Ocean. It is situated
between 4° 13′ S. to 12° 30′ N. lat. and 68° to 79° W.
long., with an area of 439,737 sq. miles (1,138,914 sq.
km.), and a population (census 1985) of 26,525,670.

The country is divided into a narrow coastal strip
in the west and extensive plains in the east by the
Cordillera de los Andes. The Eastern Cordillera
consists of a series of vast tablelands. This temperate
region is the most densely peopled portion of the
Republic. The principal rivers are the Magdalena,
Guaviare, Cauca, Atrato, Caquetá, Putumayo and
Patia.

Government.—The Colombian coast was visited in
1502 by Christopher Columbus, and in 1536 a Spanish
expedition under Jiménez de Quesada penetrated to
the interior and established on the site of the present
capital a government which continued under Spanish
rule until the revolt of the Spanish–American
colonies of 1811–1824. In 1819 Simón Bolívar (1783–
1831) established the Republic of Colombia, consisting
of the territories now known as Colombia, Panama,
Venezuela and Ecuador. In 1829–1830 Venezuela and
Ecuador withdrew from the association of provinces,
and in 1831 the remaining territories were formed
into the Republic of New Granada. In 1858 the name
was changed to the Granadine Confederation and in
1861 to the United States of Colombia. In 1866 the
present title was adopted. In 1903 Panama seceded
from Colombia, and became a separate Republic.

During the early nineteen-fifties Colombia suffered
a period of virtual civil war between the supporters
of the traditional political parties, the Conservatives
and the Liberals. From 1957–1974 the country was
governed under the 'National Front' agreement with
the presidency alternating between the two parties
every four years and ministerial posts being shared
equally by the parties. The alternation of the
presidency was ended in 1974 and parity in appointments in 1978. Thereafter, the constitution lays
down that Government portfolios and administrative
appointments shall be divided among the two majority parties in Congress in an adequate and equitable
manner. However, after a General Election in 1986,
the Liberal Party won a large majority. The Liberals
are now known as the majority and the Conservatives, the Opposition.

Defence.—The Army peace effective strength is
60,000; war effective, approx. 400,000. The Navy,
with 9,000 personnel including approximately 5,000
marines, has four corvettes, one destroyer, one

frigate, one sail training ship, two submarines and a
number of patrol boats. The Air Force, with 6,000
personnel, is equipped with Mirage fighters, 837B's,
C47's and a number of support helicopters.

Production.—Much of Colombia's natural resources in coal, natural gas and hydro-electricity
remain largely unexploited. Development of coal is
being given priority but no new hydro projects are
likely to be started for the next 4–5 years. Annual
coal production is increasing from the recent peak of
5·5 million tonnes now that the Cerrejón Norte
coalfield is being fully worked. This is essentially for
export. Proven coal reserves stand at 16,000 million
tonnes. Estimated natural gas reserves are 3,788,000
million cu. ft., with daily use at 381,772 million B.t.u.
Proven crude oil reserves stand at 1,300 million
barrels. Colombia is again a net exporter of oil. In
1987 exports averaged 152,000 b.p.d. and are expected
to rise to 282,000 b.p.d. by 1989.

The hydrocarbon sector accounts for over half of
the mining output with precious metals (gold, platinum and silver) and iron ore accounting for the
remainder. Iron ore production in 1982 was 450,000
tons. Other mineral deposits include nickel (a
processing plant started operating in 1982), bauxite,
copper, gypsum, limestone, phosphates, sulphur and
uranium. Colombia is also the world's largest producer of emeralds and has deposits of other precious
and semi-precious stones.

Because of the range of climate, a wide variety of
crops can be grown, and the country is close to self-
sufficency in food. The principal agriculture products
are coffee (Colombia is second only to Brazil as the
world's largest coffee producer) and other major cash
crops are sugar, bananas, cut flowers and cotton.
Cattle are raised in large numbers, and meat and
cured skins and hides are also exported.

Industry.—The Government has encouraged diversification to reduce dependence on coffee as the
major export and this has led to the growth of new
export-orientated industries, particularly textiles,
paper products and leather goods. Stimulus to the
economy has been provided by large loans from the
World Bank and IADB for project development,
particularly in the power sector (in which hydroelectric projects have predominated) and for telecommunications.

Communications.—The massive ranges of the Andes make surface transport difficult therefore air
transport is used extensively. There are daily passenger and cargo air services between Bogotá and all the
principal towns, as well as daily services to the
U.S.A., frequent services to other countries in South
America, and to Europe. The 'Atlantic Railway'
links the departmental lines running down to the
river, and completes the connection between Bogotá
and Santa Marta. Although the railways generally
are in a poor state there are about 2,600 miles of rail
in use at present. The total road network (1985)
consists of 105,201 km. of roads of all types, of which
21,800 km. are classified as main trunk and transver-
sal roads.

Large appropriations have been made for modernization of the country's telecommunication system.
There are 485 radio stations (1983) and two national
television channels with several regional ones.

Language and Literature.—Spanish is the language
of the country and education has been free since
1870. Great efforts have been made in reducing
illiteracy and estimates (1980) put the literacy rate
at 77·6 per cent of those over 10 years of age. In
addition to the National University with headquarters at Bogotá there are 26 other universities. There
is a flourishing press in urban areas and a national
literature supplements the rich inheritance from the
time of Spanish rule.

Roman Catholicism is the established religion.

TRADE

Colombia's principal export is still coffee although other products, principally bananas, cut flowers, clothing and textiles, ferro-nickel and coal are important exports.

	1984 $U.S.	1985 $U.S.
Total imports (c.i.f.)	4,492m.	4,688m.
Total exports (f.o.b.)	3,483m.	3,763m.

Trade with U.K.

	1987	1988
Imports from U.K........	£61,385,000	£53,132,000
Exports to U.K.	65,331,000	61,835,000

CAPITAL, Bogotá, population (census, 1985) 3,967,988. Bogotá is an inland city in the Eastern Cordilleras, at an elevation of 8,600 to 9,000 ft. above sea level. Other centres are Medellín (1,500,000); Cali (1,350,000); ΨBarranquilla (900,000); ΨCartagena (530,000); Bucaramanga (350,000); ΨBuenaventura (130,000) is the country's major port.

CURRENCY.—Colombian peso of 100 centavos.

FLAG.—Broad yellow band in upper half, surmounting equal bands of blue and red.

NATIONAL ANTHEM.—"Oh gloria inmarcesible".

NATIONAL DAY.—July 20 (National Independence Day).

BRITISH EMBASSY

Torre Propaganda Sancho, Calle 98, No. 9–03, Piso 4, Bogotá
[Bogota 2185111]

Ambassador Extraordinary and Plenipotentiary, His Excellency Richard A. Neilson, C.M.G., L.V.O. (1987).
There are British Consular Offices at *Barranquilla, Bogotá, Cali* and *Medellín.*
British Council Representative, J. Coope, Calle 87, No. 12–79, Bogotá D.E.

COLOMBO-BRITISH CHAMBER OF COMMERCE, Apartado Aereo 054 728, CVA. 13 No. 82-20, Bogotá D.E.

THE COMOROS
(Republique Fédérale Islamique des Comores)

Head of State, President Ahmed Abdallah Abdermane, *took office* May 1978; *elected,* Oct. 22, 1978; *re-elected,* Sept. 30, 1984.
Prime Minister, Ahmed Abdallah Abdermane.
Director of the President's Office, Ali Nassor.
Secretary General of the Presidency and Government, Said Ahmed Cheikh.

COUNCIL OF GOVERNMENT
(as at July 31, 1989)

Interior, Information and Press, Omar Tamou.
Vocational Training, Culture, Youth and Sports, Education, Salim Idarousse.
Production, Industry, Economy and Trade, Tourism and Crafts, Mohamed Ali.
Economics and Trade, Management, Control of State Companies, Commercial and Public Organisations, Said Ahmed Said Ali.
Environment, Urban Planning, Housing, Mikidache Abdourahim.
Foreign Affairs and Co-operation, Said Kafe.
Finance and Budget, Said Ahmed Ali.
Public Health and Population, Ali Hassan Ali.
Justice, Civil Service, Employment and Professional Training, Dr. Ben Ali Bacar.

The Comoro archipelago includes the islands of Great Comoro, Anjouan, Mayotte and Moheli and certain islets in the Indian Ocean with an area of 838 sq. miles (2,171 sq. km.) and a population (1985 U.N. estimate) of 444,000, most of whom are Muslim. The islanders voted for independence from France in December 1974 and three islands became independent on July 6, 1975. (The island of Mayotte was against independence and has remained under French administration.) On October 1, 1978 the three islands voted in a referendum to adopt a new Constitution which provides for a President, directly elected for a six year term. The Council of Government, consisting of a Prime Minister and up to nine other Ministers, is appointed by the President. There is a 39-member Federal Assembly elected for 5 years. Each island is administered by a Governor, assisted by up to four Commissioners whom he appoints, and has an elected Legislative Council.

The most important products are vanilla, copra, cloves and essential oils, which are the principal exports; cacao, sisal and coffee are also cultivated. Great Comoro is well forested and produces some timber.

Trade with U.K.

	1987	1988
Imports from U.K........	£527,000	£333,000
Exports to U.K.	91,000	33,000

CAPITAL.—Moroni, on Great Comoro (pop. 17,267).

CURRENCY.—Comorian franc of 100 centimes. The Comoros also use the Franc C.F.A. of 100 centimes.

FLAG.—Green ground with a crescent and four stars all in white in the half by the hoist.

NATIONAL DAY.—July 6 (Independence Day).

British Ambassador, (resident in Mauritius).

CONGO
(République Populaire du Congo)

President, Gen. Denis Sassou-Nguesso, *appointed* 1979, *re-elected,* July 30, 1984 (also holds *Defence and Security Portfolios*).

COUNCIL OF MINISTERS
(as at May 31, 1989)

Prime Minister, A. E. Poungui.
Rural Development, I. O. Lekoundzou.
Territorial Administration and Local Government, Benoit Moundele-Ngolo.
Transport and Civil Aviation, R. D. Ngollo.
Planning, Finance and the Economy, P. Moussa.
Foreign Affairs and Co-operation, A. Ndinga Oba.
Health and Social Affairs, B. Combo Matsiona.
Public Works, Construction, Town Planning and Housing, Col. F. Ntsiba.
Higher Education, Culture and the Arts, J. B. Tati Loutard.
Industry, Fisheries and Crafts, H. Mounthault.
Mines and Energy, Posts and Telecommunications, A. E. Yoka.
Primary Education and Literacy, P. D. Boussoukou Boumba.
Labour, Social Security and Justice, D. Kimbembe.
Trade, and Small and Medium Enterprises, A. Poaty Souchlaty.
Forestries, A. Noumazalay.
Secondary and Higher Education, R. Adada.
Scientific Research and the Environment, O. Douniam.
Information, P. Ngatse.
Tourism, Sport and Recreation, J. C. Ganga.

The Republic lies on the Equator between Gabon on the west and Zaire on the east, the River Congo and its tributary the Ubangui forming most of the eastern boundary of the state. The Congo has a short Atlantic coastline. Area of the Republic of Congo is 132,047 sq. miles (342,000 sq. km.), with a population of 1,740,000 (1985 U.N. estimate). Formerly the French colony of Middle Congo, it became a member state of the French Community on November 28, 1958, and was proclaimed fully independent on August 17, 1960.

In 1968, conduct of affairs was assumed by a National Council of Army officers. The Parti Congolais du Travail (*PCT*) was created by the Congress of December 29–31, 1969 and the People's Republic of the Congo was established. Under the present Constitution, approved by referendum in 1979, executive power is vested in the President, who is elected by the Congress of the P.C.T. (the only legal party). The Council of Ministers is appointed and led by the President.

Congo has its own oil deposits, producing about 6 million tonnes annually. It also produces lead, zinc and gold. The principal agricultural products are timber, cassava, sugar cane and yams. Imports are mainly of machinery.

Trade with U.K.

	1987	1988
Imports from U.K.	£19,218,901	£8,521,000
Exports to U.K.	1,930,030	2,018,000

CAPITAL.—Brazzaville (600,000); Ψ Pointe Noire (350,000).

CURRENCY.—Franc C.F.A. of 100 centimes.

FLAG.—Red, with hammer and hoe in wreath of leaves in top corner.

NATIONAL DAY.—August 15.

BRITISH EMBASSY
B.P. 1038, Brazzaville
[Brazzaville 834944]

Ambassador Extraordinary and Plenipotentiary, His Excellency (Alfred) Ian Glasby (1988).

COSTA RICA
(República de Costa Rica)

President, Dr. Oscar Arias Sánchez, *took office*, May 8, 1986.

MINISTERS
(as at Dec. 31, 1988)

Vice Presidents, J. Manuel Dengo; Sra. V Garrón de Doryan.
Minister for the Presidency, R. Arias Sánchez.
Foreign Affairs and Worship, R. Madrigal Nieto.
Interior and Police, Guido Fernández Saborio.
Justice, L. Paulino Mora.
Public Security, H. Garrón Salazar.
Finance, Dr. F. Naranjo Villalobos.
Agriculture, A. Esquival Volio.
Economy, Industry and Commerce, L. D. Escalante Vargas.
Natural Resources, Energy and Mines, Calixto Chavez Zamora.
Public Works and Transport, Dr. G. Constenla Umaña.
Education, F. Antonio Pacheco.
Health, Dr. E. Mohs Villalta.
Culture, Youth and Sports, C. Echeverría Salgado.
Labour and Social Security, Edwin León.
Planning, O. Solís Fallas.
Housing and Urban Development, Dr. F. Zumbado Jiménez.

Foreign Trade, J. M. Figueres.
Science and Technology, R. Zeledón Araya.

COSTA RICAN EMBASSY
Flat 1, 14 Lancaster Gate, W2 3LH
[01–723 1772/9630]

Ambassador Extraordinary and Plenipotentiary, His Excellency Miguel T. Yamuni (1989).

The Republic of Costa Rica in Central America extends across the isthmus between 8° 17′ and 11° 10′ N. lat. and from 82° 30′ to 85° 45′ W. long., has an area of 19,575 sq. miles (50,700 sq. km.), and a population (1988 estimate) of 2,816,558. The population is basically of European stock, in which Costa Rica differs from most Latin American countries. The Republic lies between Nicaragua and Panama and between the Caribbean Sea and the Pacific Ocean. The coastal lowlands by the Caribbean Sea and Pacific have a tropical climate but the interior plateau, with a mean elevation of 4,000 feet, enjoys a temperate climate.

For nearly three centuries (1530–1821) Costa Rica formed part of the Spanish-American dominions, the seat of government being at Cartago. In 1821 the country obtained its independence, although from 1824 to 1839 it was one of the United States of Central America.

On Dec. 1, 1948, the Army was abolished, the President declaring it unnecessary, as the country loved peace.

Economy.—Agriculture is the chief industry and the principal products are coffee, bananas, sugar and cattle (for meat), all of which are important exports. Other crops are cocoa, rice, maize, potatoes and hemp. Industrial activity is principally in the manufacturing sector and manufactured goods are the largest category of exports. The main goods are foodstuffs, textiles and clothing, plastic goods, pharmaceuticals, fertilizers and electrical equipment.

Communications.—The chief ports are Limón, on the Atlantic coast, through which passes most of the coffee exported, and Caldera on the Pacific coast, currently under construction with Japanese aid. In 1982, 1,236 ships entered Costa Rican ports handling imports and exports of approximately 2,666,386,811 tons of goods. The railway system is nationalized. About 500 miles of railroad are open. LACSA is the national airline, operating flights throughout Central and South America, the Caribbean and U.S.A., besides internal flights to local airports by SANSA.

Language, etc.—Spanish is the language of the country. Education is compulsory and free. The literacy rate is the highest in Latin America.

FINANCE

	1987 Colones
Revenue	35,665·3m
Expenditure	42,500·6m

TRADE

The chief exports were manufactured goods and other products, coffee, bananas, cocoa and sugar. The chief imports were machinery, including transport equipment, manufactures, chemicals, fuel and mineral oils and foodstuffs.

	1986	1987
	(US$ '000)	
Total imports	1,163	1,385
Total exports	1,085	1,113

Trade with U.K.

	1987	1988
Imports from U.K.	£14,407,000	£11,390,000
Exports to U.K.	16,752,000	16,902,000

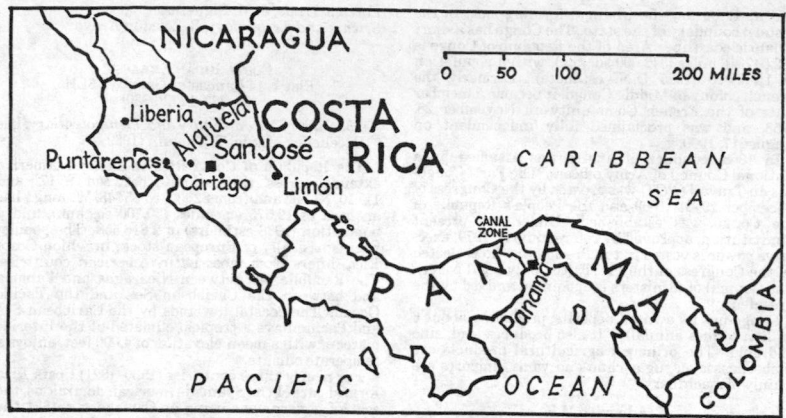

CAPITAL.—San José, pop. (estimate 1988) 1,031,102; Alajuela (499,623); Cartago (316,379); Heredia (197,575); Guanacaste (227,950); ΨPuntarenas (313,541); ΨLimón (200,638). (Populations shown are of provinces, cantons and districts.)

CURRENCY.—Costa Rican colón (₵) of 100 céntimos.

FLAG.—Five horizontal bands, blue, white, red, white, blue (the red band twice the width of the others with emblem near staff).

NATIONAL ANTHEM.—Himno Nacional de Costa Rica.

NATIONAL DAY.—September 15.

BRITISH EMBASSY
Apartado 815, Edificio Centro Colon 1007, San José.
[San José 215566]

Ambassador Extraordinary and Plenipotentiary and Consul-General, His Excellency William Marsden (1989).

CÔTE D'IVOIRE
(République de Côte d'Ivoire)

President, Félix Houphouët-Boigny, *elected* for five years in 1960; *re-elected* 1965, 1970, 1975, 1980 and 1985.

CABINET
(as at May 31, 1989)

Ministers of State, August Denise; Mathieu Ekra; Camille Alliali; Maurice Séri Gnoléba; Emile Kei Boguinard; Lazéni N. P. Coulibaly; Paul Gui Dibo; Lamine Diabaté.

Ministers:
Defence and the Navy, Jean Konan Banny.
Foreign Affairs, Siméon Aké.
Information, Laurent Dona Fologo.
Interior, Léon Konan Koffi.
Internal Security, Issouf Koné.
Economy and Finance, Abdoulayé Koné.
Agriculture and Rural Development, Denis Bra Kanon.
Technical Education and Vocational Training A. F. Barry-Battesti.
Public Works and Transport, Aoussou Koffi.
Secondary and Higher Education, Balla Keita.
Justice, Noël Nemin.
Fight Against Drugs, Oumar N'Daw.

Labour, Albert Vanié Bi Tra.
Health and Population, Mady Alphonse Djédjé.
Women's Affairs, Hortense Aka Anghui.
Commerce, Angba Nicolas Kouandi.
Public Service, Jean-Jacques Béchio.
Social Affairs, Yaya Ouattara.
National Assembly, Emile Brou.
Plan and Industry, Oumar Diarra
Construction and Town Planning, Vamoussa Bamba.
Scientific Research, Alhassane N'Diaye.
Budget, Moïse Koumoué Koffi.
Pre-School and Primary Education, Odette Kouamé N'Guessan.
Mines, Yed Esaïe Angoran.
Posts and Telecommunications, Vincent Tieko Djedje.
Animal Production, Christophe Gboho.
Water Resources and Forests, Vincent-Pierre Lokrou.
Culture, Sadia Duon.
Youth and Sport, Bernard K. Ehui.
Tourism, Jean-Claude Delafosse.

President of the National Assembly, Henri Konan Bédie.

President of the Economic and Social Council, Philippe Yacé.

EMBASSY OF THE REPUBLIC OF CÔTE D'IVOIRE
2 Upper Belgrave Street, SW1X 8BJ
[01–235 6991]

Ambassador Extraordinary and Plenipotentiary, new appointment awaited.
First Counsellor, G. G. Ballou.

The Côte d'Ivoire is situated on the Gulf of Guinea between 5° and 10° N. and 3° and 8° W. and is flanked on the west by Guinea and Liberia, on the north by Mali and Burkina and on the east by Ghana. It has an area of 124,503 sq. miles (322,463 sq. km.)—tropical rain forest in the southern half and savanna in the northern—and a population of 10,056,000 (1985 estimate) divided into a large number of ethnic and tribal groups.

Although French contact was made in the first half of the 19th century, the Côte d'Ivoire became a colony only in 1893 and was finally pacified in 1912. It decided on December 5, 1958 to remain an autonomous republic within the French Community; full independence outside the Community was proclaimed on August 7, 1960. Special agreements with France, covering financial and cultural matters, technical assistance, defence, etc., were signed in Paris on April 24, 1961. The official language is French.

The Côte d'Ivoire has a presidential system of government modelled on that of the United States and the French Fifth Republic. The single Chamber National Assembly of 175 members was elected in 1985. The defence of the Constitution which was promulgated on Nov. 3, 1960, is vested in a Supreme Court.

BUDGET

	1988
Current Expenditure	CFA493,500m.
Investment and Equipment	143,600m.

Trade.—The principal exports are coffee, cocoa, timber, palm oil, pineapples, bananas, and cotton. Diamonds are exported. There are a few deposits of minerals including manganese and iron.

TRADE

	1985	1986
Imports	CFA772,987m.	CFA709,040m.
Exports	1,318,059m.	1,160,400m.

Trade with U.K.

	1987	1988
Imports from U.K.	£26,834,000	£31,172,000
Exports to U.K.	90,246,000	64,041,000

CAPITAL, ΨAbidjan (population, 3,000,000) which is also the main port. In March 1983 the National Assembly ratified a decision to transfer the political and administrative capital from Abidjan to Yamoussoukro.

CURRENCY.—Franc C.F.A. of 100 centimes.

FLAG.—Three vertical stripes, orange, white and green.

NATIONAL ANTHEM.—L'Abidjanaise.

NATIONAL DAY.—December 7.

BRITISH EMBASSY
Immeuble Les Harmonies, 01 B.P. 2581,
Abidjan 01.
[Abidjan 226850]

Ambassador Extraordinary and Plenipotentiary, Her Excellency Veronica Evelyn Sutherland, C.M.G. (1987).

Head of Chancery and Consul, P. W. Chandley, M.V.O.
First Secretary (Education) and British Council Representative, C. J. Hickey.

BRITISH BUSINESSMEN'S ASSOCIATION, c/o Barclays Bank P.L.C., Immeuble Alpha 2000, 01 BP 522 Abidjan 01 (Tel. 322804).

CUBA
(Republica de Cuba)

President of Council of State and Head of Government, Dr. Fidel Castro Ruz, *appointed* Nov. 2, 1976.

COUNCIL OF STATE
(as at June 30, 1989)

President, Dr. Fidel Castro Ruz.
First Vice-President, Raúl Castro Ruz.
Vice-Presidents, Juan Almeida Bosque; Osmany Cienfuegos Gorriarán; José Ramón Machado Ventura; Pedro Miret Prieto; Carlos Rafael Rodríguez.
Secretary, José M. Miyar Barrueco.

COUNCIL OF MINISTERS

President, Dr. Fidel Castro Ruz.
First Vice-President, Raúl Castro Ruz.
Vice-Presidents, Dr. Carlos Rafael Rodríguez; Pedro Miret Prieto; Diocles Torralba González; José Ramón Fernández Alvarez; José A. López Moreno; Osmany Cienfuegos Gorriarán; Antonio Esquivel Yedra; Raul Cabrera Nunez; Joel Domenech Benítez; Antonio Rodriguez Maurell.
Secretary, Osmany Cienfuegos Gorriarán.
Presidents of State Committees: Jose A. Lopez Moreno *(Central Planning Board)*; Hector Rodriguez Llompart *(National Bank)*; Levi Farah Balmaseda *(Construction Materials Industry)*; Ernesto Melendez Bachs *(Economic Co-operation)*; Rodrigo J. Garcia Leon *(Finance)*; Francisco Linares Calvo *(Labour and Social Security)*; Sonia Rodriguez Cardona *(Material and Technical Supply)*; Arturo Guzman Pascual *(Prices)*; Ramón Darias Rodés *(Standardization)*; Fidel Emilio Vascos Gonzalez *(Statistics)*.
Ministers, Adolfo Diaz Suarez *(Agriculture)*; Marcos J. Portal Leon *(Basic Industry)*; Manuel Castillo Rabasa *(Communications)*; Homero Crabb *(Construction)*; Levi Farah Balmaseda *(Construction Materials Industry)*; Armando Enrique Hart Davalos *(Culture)*; Manuel Vila Sosa *(Domestic Trade)*; José Ramon Fernandez Alvarez *(Education)*; Jorge A. Fernandez Cuervo-Vinent *(Fishing)*; Alejandro Roca Iglesias *(Food Industry)*; Isidoro Octavio Malmierca Peoli *(Foreign Relations)*; Ricardo Cabrisas Ruiz *(Foreign Trade)*; Fernando Vecino Alegret *(Higher Education)*; Abelardo Colome Ibarra; Juan Escalona Reguera *(Justice)*; Antonio Esquivel Yedra *(Light Industry)*; Julio Jesus Teja Pérez *(Public Health)*; Raul Castro Ruz *(Revolutionary Armed Forces)*; Marcos Lage Coello *(Steel Industry)*; Juan Ramon Herrera Machado *(Sugar Industry)*; Jose Alberto Naranjo Morales; Raul Cabrera Nunez *(Ministers without Portfolio)*.

EMBASSY OF THE REPUBLIC OF CUBA
167 High Holborn, WC1V 6PA
[01–240 2488]

Ambassador Extraordinary and Plenipotentiary, new appointment awaited.

Cuba, the largest island in the Caribbean, lies between 74° and 85° W. long., and 19° and 23° N. lat., with a total area of 42,804 sq. miles (110,861 sq. km.). The country is divided into 14 provinces. The estimated total population in 1987 was 10,356,400.

The island of Cuba was visited by Christopher Columbus during his first voyage, on Oct. 27, 1492, and was then believed to be part of the western mainland of India. Early in the 16th century the island was conquered by the Spanish, to be used later as a base of operations for the conquest of Mexico and Central America, and for almost four centuries Cuba remained under a Spanish Captain-General. [The island was under British rule for one year, 1762–1763, when it was returned to Spain in exchange for Florida.] Separatist agitation culminated in the closing years of the 19th century in open warfare. In 1898 the government of the United States intervened and on April 20, 1898, demanded the evacuation of Cuba by the Spanish forces. A short Spanish–American war led to the abandonment of the island, which was occupied by U.S. troops. Cuba was under U.S. military rule from Jan. 1, 1899 until May 20, 1902, when an autonomous government was inaugurated with an elected President, and a legislature of two houses. The island was, however, again the prey of revolution from Aug. to Sept., 1906, when the U.S. Government resumed control. On Jan. 28, 1909, a republican government was again inaugurated.

A revolution led by Dr. Fidel Castro overthrew the Government of General Batista on January 1, 1959. In October, 1965, the Communist Party of Cuba was formed to succeed the United Party of the Socialist Revolution. It is the only authorized political party.

The new Socialist Constitution came into force on February 24, 1976 and indirect elections to the National Assembly of People's Power were subsequently held.

Production.—The Government has carried out programmes of land and urban reform and of nationalization; by March, 1968, virtually all industrial and commercial enterprises were nationalized. About 85 per cent of the cultivated land is in state farms or State-controlled co-operatives. Private smallholders, who own the remainder, have to sell all their produce to the state.

Although efforts are being made to diversify the economy, sugar is still its mainstay and principal source of foreign exchange. In 1986–87 the harvest was 7·2 million tons. Cuba's other main exports are oil, nickel, seafood, citrus fruits, tobacco and rum.

Despite increased trade with Western Europe and Japan, the Communist countries, particularly the Soviet Union, form Cuba's main trading partners, covering about 86 per cent of imports and exports. In addition, the U.S.S.R. offers substantial aid through a system of subsidies which has recently been estimated to amount to $4,500 million.

There are 12,700 kms. of railway track, of which 5,000 kms. are in public service. In 1986 there were 13,247 kms. of road. At present scheduled international air services run to North, Central and South American countries and Europe.

Language and Literature.—Spanish is the language of the island. English, formerly widely understood, is now spoken less. Education is compulsory and free. In 1964 illiteracy was officially declared to be completely eliminated. The press and broadcasting and television are under the control of the Government.

	1986	1987
	\multicolumn{2}{c}{Pesos million}
Imports	7,569·0	7,611·5
Exports	5,325·0	5,401·0

Trade with U.K.

	1987	1988
Imports from U.K.	£41,510,000	£31,162,000
Exports to U.K.	12,776,000	28,489,000

CAPITAL.—ΨHavana (pop., est. 1986), 2,100,000; other towns are ΨSantiago (429,800), Santa Clara (198,800), Camagüey (279,800), Holgüin (254,300), and ΨCienfuegos (124,600).

CURRENCY.—Cuban peso of 100 centavos.

FLAG.—Five horizontal bands, blue and white (blue at top and bottom) with red triangle, close to staff, charged with 5-point star.

NATIONAL ANTHEM.—"Al Combate, Corred Bayameses" (To battle, men of Bayamo).

NATIONAL DAY.—January 1 (Day of Liberation).

BRITISH EMBASSY
Edificio Bolívar, Cárcel 101–103,
e Morro y Prado, Apartado 1069, Havana.
[Havana 615681/4]

Ambassador Extraordinary and Plenipotentiary, His Excellency (Anthony) David Brighty, C.M.G., C.V.O. (1989).
Counsellor, N. R. Jarrold, (*Head of Chancery*).
First Secretary, R. Daly (*Commercial and H.M. Consul*).

CZECHOSLOVAKIA
(Československá Socialistická Republika)

President, Gustáv Husák, *born* Jan. 10, 1913; *elected* May 29, 1975, *re-elected* May, 1980, 1985.

Federal Government

Prime Minister, Ladislav Adamec.
First Deputy P.M. and Chairman of the State Commission for Scientific, Technical and Investment Development, Pavol Hrivnák.
Deputy Prime Ministers, Matej Lučan; Jaromír Obzina; František Pitra (*P.M. of the Czech Republic*); Ivan Knotek (*P.M. of the Slovak Republic*).
First Deputy P.M. and Chairman of the State Planning Commission, Bohumil Urban.
Deputy Prime Minister and Minister for Metallurgy and Engineering, Karel Juliš.

Ministers
(as at May 31, 1989)

Agriculture and Food, Jaromír Algayer.
Finance, Jan Stejskal.
Foreign Affairs, Jaromír Johanes.
Foreign Trade, Jan Štěrba.
Fuel and Power, Antonin Krumnikl.
Interior, František Kincl.
Labour and Social Affairs, Miloslav Boďa.
National Defence, Milán Václavík.
Minister-Chairman of People's Control Committee, František Ondřich.
Transport and Communications, František Podlena.
Price Office, Jaromír Žák.
Minister without Portfolio, Marian Čalfa.

CZECHOSLOVAK COMMUNIST PARTY

Presidium of the Central Committee, L. Adamec; J. Fojtík; K. Hoffman; G. Husák; A. Indra; M. Jakeš; I. Janák; J. Lenárt; K. Urbánek; F. Pitra; M. Štěpán; I. Knotek; M. Zavadil (*full members*); M. Hruškovič; J. Haman; V. Herman (*candidate members*).

Secretariat of the Central Committee, J. Fojtík; K. Hoffman; M. Jakeš; J. Lenárt; F. Hanus (*secretaries*); M. Kabrhelová; Z. Hořeni; V. Mohorita; J. Poledník; R. Rohlíček; J. Mevald (*members*).

CZECHOSLOVAK EMBASSY
25 Kensington Palace Gardens, W8 4QY
[01–229 1255]

Ambassador Extraordinary and Plenipotentiary, His Excellency Jan Fidler (1986).
Counsellor, R. Hronek.
Commercial Counsellor, S. Žiak.
Military and Air Attaché, Col. Jaromír Široký.
Commercial Attachés, J. Slánský; J. Navara.

Area and Population.—Czechoslovakia, formerly part of the Austro-Hungarian Empire, declared its independence on Oct. 28, 1918 (Czechoslovak Independence Day). It has an area of 49,370 sq. miles (127,869 sq. km.). The population of Czechoslovakia (1985 U.N. estimate) was 15,500,000.

Government.—The Communist Party came to power in Czechoslovakia in February, 1948, and Communist control of the country is now unqualified. On July 11, 1960, a new constitution was proclaimed, replacing that of 1948 and the official title of the State was accordingly changed to The Czechoslovak Socialist Republic.

In January, 1968, pressures for reform of the system led to the proposal of new legislation, which envisaged the democratization of the country's political life, greater guarantees of fundamental liberties and the establishment of a federal system.

The implications for the internal development of the other communist regimes in Eastern Europe and the Soviet Union, as well as for the system of alliances among these countries, alarmed the Soviet Union. On the night of August 20, Czechoslovakia was invaded by Soviet, Polish, East German, Hungarian and Bulgarian troops, the capital and all major towns being occupied. The Czechoslovak leadership was forced to modify its policies and to legalize the presence of Soviet troops on Czechoslovak territory. With the exception of the Federal system of government, the reforms of 1968 were abandoned when Gustáv Husák became leader of the Communist party in April 1969.

Czechoslovakia now consists of the Czech Socialist Republic and the Slovak Socialist Republic, each of which has its own government responsible to its legislative body—the National Council. Areas such as the constitution, defence, foreign affairs, state material reserves and currency are the responsibility of the Federal Administration. The Federal Government is responsible to the Federal Assembly, which is composed of two Chambers, the Chamber of the People, whose deputies are elected throughout the Federation, and the Chamber of the Nations, consisting of an equal number of Czech and Slovak Deputies. The federal system was not extended to the organization of the Communist Party.

The Economic System.—Under the present political system industry is state-owned, and nearly all agricultural land is cultivated by state or co-operative farms. Economic planning is centralized, and state economic plans have the force of law. In Jan. 1987 a programme of 'reconstruction' was announced, aimed at increasing the efficiency of the economy by a measure of decentralization and relaxation of controls.

Czechoslovakia is not rich in minerals, although significant quantities of coal, brown coal and lignite are mined. Principal agricultural products are sugar-beet, potatoes and cereal crops; the timber industry is also very important. The country has long been highly industrialized, and machinery, industrial consumer goods and raw materials are major exports. The 8th Five Year Plan (1986–90) aims to raise national income by 18–19 per cent over the five years.

Language and Literature.—Czech and Slovak are the official languages, each having its own literature. The Reformation gave a wide-spread impulse to Czech literature, the writings of Jan Hus (martyred in 1415 as a religious and social reformer) familiarizing the people with Wyclif's teaching. This impulse endured to the close of the 17th century when Jan Amos Komensky or Comenius (1592–1670) was expelled from the country. Under Austrian rule and with the persistent pursuit of Germanization, there was a period of stagnation until the national revival in the first half of the 19th century. Authors of international reputation include Jaroslav Hašek (1883–1923), Jaroslav Seifert (1901–1986, Nobel Prize for Literature, 1985), Václav Havel (b. 1936) and Milan Kundera (b. 1929). Many of the best Czechoslovak authors are either in exile or in disfavour at home.

Education.—Education is compulsory and free for all children from the ages of 6 to 16. The number of pupils in basic nine-year schools is 1,992,000 (1983). There are 175,198 students in the secondary grammar schools and the number given for technical schools of all kinds is 290,038. There are five universities in Czechoslovakia of which the most famous is Charles University in Prague (founded 1348), the others being situated at Bratislava, Brno, Olomouc and Košice. In addition there are a considerable number of other institutions of university standing, technical colleges, agricultural colleges, etc.

Trade with U.K.

	1987	1988
Imports from U.K.	£114,101,000	£130,420,000
Exports to U.K.	141,472,000	148,248,000

CAPITAL.—Prague (Praha), on the Vltava (Moldau), the former capital of Bohemia with a population (1985) of 1,190,576. Other towns are Brno (Brünn), capital of Moravia (381,000), Bratislava (Pressburg),

capital of Slovakia (401,000), Ostrava (324,000), Košiče (214,000) and Plzen (Pilsen) (174,000).

CURRENCY.—Koruna (Kčs) or Czechoslovak crown of 100 Haléru (Heller).

FLAG.—Two equal horizontal stripes, white (above) and red; a blue triangle next to staff.

NATIONAL ANTHEM.—Kde Domov Můj (Where is my Motherland).

NATIONAL DAY.—May 9.

BRITISH EMBASSY
Thunovská 14, 11800 Prague 1.
[Prague 533347]

Ambassador Extraordinary and Plenipotentiary, His Excellency (Peter) Laurence O'Keeffe, C.M.G., C.V.O. (1988).
Counsellor, J. M. Macgregor (*Head of Chancery*).
Defence and Military Attaché, Col. R. J. M. Drummond, O.B.E.
Air Attaché, Wing-Cdr. B. Blackford.
Cultural Attaché, J. R. Potts (*British Council Representative*).

DENMARK
(Kongeriget Danmark)

Queen, Margrethe II, eldest daughter of King Frederik IX, *born* April 16, 1940, *succeeded* Jan. 14, 1972, *married* June 10, 1967, Count Henri de Monpezat (Prince Henrik of Denmark) and *has issue* Crown Prince Frederik *born* May 26, 1968; and Prince Joachim, *born* June 7, 1969.

CABINET
(as at May 31, 1989)

Prime Minister, Poul Schlüter (*C*).
Foreign Affairs, Uffe Ellemann-Jensen (*V*).
Finance, Palle Simonsen (*C*).
Justice, Hans Peter Clausen (*C*).
Economy, Niels Helveg Petersen (*RL*).
Environment, Lone Dybkjaer (*RL*).
Education and Research, Bertel Haarder (*V*).
Social Affairs, Aase Olesen (*RL*).
Ecclesiastical Affairs and Communications, Torben Rechendorff (*C*).
Energy, Jens Bilgrav-Nielsen (*RL*).
Fisheries, Lars Gammelgaard (*C*).
Labour, Henning Dyremose (*C*).
Interior and Nordic Co-operation, Thor Pedersen (*V*).
Culture, Ole Vig Jensen (*RL*).
Industry, Nils Wilhjelm (*C*).
Transport, Knud Ostergaard (*C*).
Taxation, Anders Fogh Rasmussen (*V*).
Health, Elsebeth Kock-Petersen (*V*).
Agriculture, Laurits Toernaes (*V*).
Defence, Knud Enggaard (*V*).
Housing, Agnete Laustsen (*C*).

C, Conservative Party; *V,* Venstre (Liberals); *RL,* Radical Liberal Party.

ROYAL DANISH EMBASSY
55 Sloane Street, SW1X 9SR
[01–235 1255]

Ambassador Extraordinary and Plenipotentiary, His Excellency R. A. Thorning-Petersen (1989).
Minister Counsellors, H. M. Kofoed-Hansen; P. Essemann (*Commercial*); F. A. Axmark (*Press and Culture*); S. R. Nielsen (*Economic and Consular Affairs*).
Defence Attaché, Capt. E. Faage-Pedersen.

Area and Population.—A Kingdom of Northern Europe, consisting of the islands of Zeeland, Funen, Lolland, etc., the peninsula of Jutland, and the outlying island of Bornholm in the Baltic, the Faröes and Greenland. Denmark is situated between 54° 34′

and 57° 45' N. lat., 8° 5'–15° E. 12' long., with an area of 16,629 sq. miles (43,069 sq. km.), and a population estimated (1987) of 5,124,794.

Government.—Under the Constitution of the Kingdom of Denmark Act of June 5, 1953, the legislature consists of one chamber, the *Folketing*, of not more than 179 members, including 2 for the Faröes and 2 for Greenland. The voting age is 18.

The new coalition government of Mr. Poul Schlüter was formed in June 1988 after the General Election on May 10.

Education is free and compulsory. Special schools are numerous, commercial, technical and agricultural predominating. There are Universities at Copenhagen (founded in 1479), Aarhus (1933), Odense (1966), Roskilde (1972) and Aalborg (1974). A further University at Esbjerg is planned.

Language and Literature.—The Danish language is akin to Swedish and Norwegian. Danish literature, ancient and modern, embraces all forms of expression, familiar names being Hans Christian Andersen (1805–1875), Sören Kierkegaard (1813–1855) and Karen Blixen (1885–1962). Some 48 newspapers are published in Denmark; 2 daily papers are published in Copenhagen.

Production and Industry.—Of the labour force, in 1988, 1·8 per cent was engaged in agriculture, fishing, forestry, etc.; 27·5 per cent in manufacturing, building and construction; 15·4 per cent in commerce, 0·2 per cent in liberal professions and 53·2 per cent in administration, transport and the financial services. The chief agricultural products are pigs, cattle, dairy products, poultry and eggs, seeds, cereals and sugar beet; manufactures are mostly based on imported raw materials but there are also considerable imports of finished goods.

Communications.—Mercantile marine (ships above 100 gross tonnage) at beginning of 1988, totalled 618 ships. In 1985 there was 2,471 km. of state-owned railway and 494 km. of privately-owned railway systems.

Finance (Budget Estimates)

	1988	1989
Revenue	Kr. 201,280m.	Kr. 221,008m.
Expenditure	212,823m.	222,179m.

Denmark's balance of payments on current account showed a deficit for 1988 of Kr.12,200 million (1987, Kr.20,700 million).

Merchandise Trade

The principal imports are industrial raw materials, consumer goods, construction inputs, machinery, raw materials, vehicles and textile products. The chief exports are miscellaneous manufactured articles, agricultural and dairy products.

	1987	1988
	Kr. million	
Total Imports	174,066	178,269
Total Exports	175,302	187,381

Trade with U.K.

	1987	1988
Imports from U.K.	£1,231,097,000	£1,170,853,000
Exports to U.K.	1,873,495,000	2,028,089,000

CAPITAL.—ΨCopenhagen, pop. (1988), 467,850; Greater Copenhagen, 1,495,736. Ψ Aarhus, 259,493; ΨOdense 174,948; ΨAalborg, 154,547; ΨEsbjerg, 81,480; ΨRanders, 61,094; ΨKolding, 57,128; ΨHelsingør, 56,754; ΨHorsens, 54,940; Ψ Vejle, 50,879; Roskilde, 48,996; Ψ Fredericia, 45,992.

CURRENCY.—Danish krone (Kr.) of 100 øre.

FLAG.—Red, with white cross.

NATIONAL ANTHEM.—Kong Kristian.

NATIONAL DAY.—April 16 (The Queen's Birthday).

British Embassy

36–40 Kastelsvej, DK-2100 Copenhagen.
[Copenhagen 264600]

Ambassador Extraordinary and Plenipotentiary, His Excellency Nigel Christopher Ransome Williams, C.M.G. (1989).

Counsellors, J. W. Hodge (*Head of Chancery*); P. Longworth (*Commercial*).

Defence Attaché, Cmdr. R. Woolgar, R.N.

There are Consulates at *Aabenraa, Aalborg, Aarhus, Esbjerg, Fredericia, Herning, Odense, Rønne* (Bornholm) and at *Tórshavn* (Faröe Islands).

British Council Representative and Cultural Attaché, Dr. M. Sørensen-Jones, Møntergade 1, Copenhagen.

Outlying Parts of the Kingdom

THE FARÖES, or Sheep Islands (540 sq. miles; 1,399 sq. km.; pop. (1985) 46,000), capital, Thorshavn, are governed by a *Lagting* of 26 members, a *Landsstyre* of 4 members which deals with special Faröes affairs, and send 2 representatives to the *Folketing* at Copenhagen. On Sept. 14, 1946, the *Lagting*, with the consent of the Danish Government, for its own guidance held a plebiscite on the Faröes. About one-third of the electors did not, however, take part in the voting: of the rest a little more than half the votes cast were in favour of separation from Denmark and the establishment of a republic. At the subsequent general election for the *Lagting* a great majority voted in favour of remaining part of the Kingdom of Denmark with a certain measure of home rule and in 1948 the Faröes received this. The Faröes are not part of the E.C.

Prime Minister, Atli Dam.

GREENLAND (ice-free portion about 132,000 sq. m., total area about 840,000 sq. m., population (1985) 52,940) is divided into 3 provinces (West, North and East). Greenland (capital, Nuuk (Godthåb)) has a *Landsraad* of 17 members and sends 2 representatives to the *Folketing* at Copenhagen. Greenland attained a status of internal autonomy on May 1, 1979. The trade of Greenland is mainly under the management of the Royal Greenland Trade Department. Following a plebiscite Greenland negotiated its withdrawal from the E.C., but without discontinuing relations with Denmark, and left on Feb. 1, 1985. Mineral and oil prospecting revealed deposits of lead, zinc, iron ore, oil, gas and uranium. Commercial exploitation of these resources has already begun. The United States of America has acquired certain rights to maintain air bases in Greenland.

Premier, Jonathan Motzfeldt.

DJIBOUTI
(Jumhouriyya Djibouti)

President, Hassan Gouled Aptidon.

CABINET
(as at May 31, 1989)

Prime Minister and Minister for Port Affairs, Barkat Gourad Hamadou.

Justice, Omar Kamil Warsama.

Foreign Affairs and Co-operation, Moumin Bahdon Farah.

Interior, Posts and Telecommunications, Youssouf Ali Chirdon.

Defence, Moussa Boúraleh Robleh.

Finance, Mohamed Djaha Elabeh.

Commerce, Transport and Tourism, Moussa Bouraleh Robleh.

Education, Youth and Sports, Souleiman Farah Lodon.

Public Health, Mohamed Adabo Kako.

Labour, Mohamed Del Waiss.

Civil Service and Administrative Reform, Helem Houmed.

Public Works, Town Planning and Housing, Bourhan Ali Warki.

Industry, Salem Abdou Yaya.

Rural Development, Ahmed Hassan Liban.

Formerly known as French Somaliland and then the French Territory of the Afars and the Issas, the country became independent on June 27, 1977. Djibouti is situated on the north-east coast of Africa (i.e. the Horn of Africa) and has an area of 8,494 sq. miles (22,000 sq. km.). It has an estimated population (1985) of 430,000. The climate is harsh and much of the country is semi-arid desert. The French continue to maintain army, navy and air force bases. Djibouti has an excellent port, international airport and a railway line runs to Addis Ababa.

Trade with U.K.

	1987	1988
Imports from U.K. ...	£12,501,000	£8,479,000
Exports to U.K.	175,000	169,000

CAPITAL.—Ψ Djibouti (1985, 200,000).

CURRENCY.—Djibouti franc of 100 centimes.

FLAG.—Blue over green with white triangle in the hoist containing a red star.

NATIONAL DAY.—June 27 (Independence Day).

BRITISH CONSULATE

P.O. Box 81, 9–11, Rue de Geneve, Djibouti.

Honorary Consul, E. Vandendriessche.

DOMINICAN REPUBLIC
(República Dominicana)

President, Dr. Joaquin Balaguer, *took office,* Aug. 16. 1986.

Vice-President, Carlos Morales Troncoso.

CABINET
(w.e.f. August 1988)

Defence, Interior and Police, Elias Wessin y Wessin.

Secretary for the Presidency, Rafael Bello Andino.

Administrative Secretary of the Presidency, Luis Toral.

Secretary of the Presidency (Technical), Guillermo Caram.

External Relations, Dr. Donald Reid Cabral.

Finance, Roberto Martinez Villanueva.

Education, Dr. Pedro C. Pichardo.

Agriculture, Agronomo Manuel Amezquita.

Public Works and Communications, A. Subero Sajuin.

Labour, Dr. José Carlos Isaias.

Public Health and Social Welfare, Dr. Ney Arias Lora.

Industry and Commerce, Juan Valerio Sanchez.

Sport, Temiztocles Metz.

Tourism, Fernando Rainieri.

Secretaries of State without Portfolio, Simon Tomás Fernandéz; Manuel Guaroa Liranzo.

HONORARY CONSULATE
6 Queen's Mansions, Brook Green, W6 7EB
[01–602 1885]

Honorary Consul, Mrs. J. De Wardener.

There are also Consular Offices at *Liverpool, Birmingham, Manchester, Grimsby, Southampton, Cardiff* and *Plymouth.*

The Dominican Republic, formerly the Spanish portion of the island of Hispaniola, is the oldest settlement of European origin in America. The western part of the island forms the Republic of Haiti. The island lies between Cuba on the west and Puerto Rico on the east and the Republic covers an area of 18,816 sq. miles (48,734 sq. km.), with a population (1984 Census) of 6,416,000. The climate is tropical in the lowlands and semi-tropical to temperate in the higher altitudes.

Spanish is the language of the Republic.

Government.—Santo Domingo was discovered by Christopher Columbus in December, 1492, and remained a Spanish Colony until 1821. In 1822 it was subjugated by the neighbouring Haitians who remained in control until 1844 when the Dominican Republic was proclaimed. The country was occupied by American marines from 1916 until the adoption of a new Constitution in 1924. From 1930 until May 30, 1961 (when he was assassinated) Generalissimo Rafael Trujillo ruled the country.

President Juan Bosch held office from Dec. 1962 to Sept. 1963, when he was deposed by a military junta. A revolt in favour of ex-President Bosch in April, 1965, developed into civil war lasting until September the same year when a provisional President was elected. On June 1, 1966, Dr. Joaquin Balaguer was elected President and in Nov. 1966 a new Constitution was introduced.

Executive power is vested in the President, who is elected by direct vote and serves for four years. The President forms his cabinet without reference to the Congress.

Legislative power is exercised by the Congress, which has a term of four years concurrent with the Presidency. The Upper Chamber is the Senate of 27 senators, one for each province and one for Santo Domingo. The lower is the Chamber of Deputies which has 120 members, one for each 50,000 inhabitants in each province, with the provision that no province has less than two members. Judicial power is exercised by the Supreme Court of Justice.

Communications.—According to local classification there are 2,932 miles of first class and 1,392 miles of second class and inter-communal roads in the Republic. There is a direct road from Santo Domingo to Port-au-Prince, the capital of Haiti, but that part of it in the border area has fallen into disuse. The frontier has been closed since Sept., 1967, except for that section crossed by the main road linking the two capitals. A telephone system connects practically all the principal towns of the republic and there is a telegraph service with all parts of the world. There are more than 90 commercial broadcasting stations and six television stations.

The Republic is served by two national and six foreign airlines, and an international airport 18 miles to the east of the capital is in operation. Another has been built near Puerto Plata on the north coast.

Economy.—Sugar, coffee, cocoa, and tobacco are the most important crops. Other products are peanuts, maize, rice, bananas, molasses, salt, cement, ferro-nickel, gold, silver, cattle, sisal products, honey and chocolate. There is a growing number of light industries producing beer, tinned foodstuffs, glass products, textiles, soap, cigarettes, construction materials, plastic articles, shoes, papers, paint, rum, matches, peanut oil and other products.

FINANCE

	1986
Expenditure	RD$2,251m
Revenue	2,113m

TRADE

The chief imports are machinery, food stuffs, iron and steel, cotton textiles and yarns, mineral oils (including petrol), cars and other motor vehicles, chemical and pharmaceutical products, electrical equipment and accessories, construction material, paper and paper products, and rubber and rubber products. The chief exports are sugar, coffee, cocoa, tobacco, chocolate, molasses, bauxite, ferro-nickel and gold. Tobacco and tobacco manufactures are the principal exports to the U.K.

	1984	1985
Imports	RD$1,459,000,000	RD$1,285,900,000
Exports	1,211,100,000	739,300,000

Trade with U.K.

	1987	1988
Imports from U.K.	£23,887,000	£17,235,000
Exports to U.K.	8,637,000	8,523,000

CAPITAL.—Ψ Santo Domingo, population of the Capital District (1981 census), 1,313,172. Other centres, with populations (1981 census); Santiago de los Caballeros (550,372); La Vega (385,043); San Francisco De Macoris (235,544); San Juan (239,957); San Cristóbal (446,132).

CURRENCY.—Dominican Republic peso (RD$) of 100 centavos.

FLAG.—Red and blue, with white cross bearing an emblem at centre.

NATIONAL ANTHEM.—"Quisqueyanos Valientes, Alcemos" (Brave men of Quisqueya, let's raise our song).

NATIONAL DAY.—February 27 (Independence Day, 1844).

BRITISH AMBASSADOR, (*resident at* Caracas, Venezuela).

ECUADOR
(Republica del Ecuador)

President, Rodrigo Borja Cevallos, *took office* Aug. 10, 1988.

CABINET
(as at July 31, 1989)

Interior and Police, Andrés Vallejo.
Foreign Affairs, Diego Cordovéz.
Education and Culture, Alfredo Vera Arrata.
Social Welfare, Raul Baca Carbo.
Health, Plutarco Naranjo.
Agriculture and Livestock, Enrique Delgado.

Public Works, Juan Neira.
Finance, Jorge Gallardo Zavala.
Industry and Commerce, Juan José Pons.
Energy and Mines, Diego Tamariz.
Employment, César Verduga.
Defence, Gen. Jorge Félix.

EMBASSY OF ECUADOR
Flat 3b, 3 Hans Crescent, SW1X 0LS
[01–584 1367/2648]

Ambassador Extraordinary and Plenipotentiary, His Excellency Jose Antonio Correa (1989).

Area and Population.—Ecuador is an equatorial state of South America, the mainland extending from lat. 1° 38′ N. to 4° 50′ S., and between 75° 20′ and 81° W. long., comprising an area reduced by boundary settlements with Peru (Jan. 29, 1942) to about 109,484 sq. miles (283,561 sq. km.).

The Republic of Ecuador is divided into 20 provinces. It has a population (1985 U.N. estimate) of approximately 9,378,000, mostly descendants of the Spanish, aboriginal Indians, and Mestizoes. The territory of the Republic extends across the Western Andes, the highest peaks in Ecuador being Chimborazo (20,408 ft.) and Ilinza (17,405 ft.) in the Western Cordillera; and Cotopaxi (19,612 ft.) and Cayambe (19,160 ft.) in the Eastern Cordillera. Ecuador is watered by the Upper Amazon, and by the rivers Guayas, Mira, Santiago, Chone, and Esmeraldas on the Pacific coast. There are extensive forests.

Government.—The former Kingdom of Quito was conquered by the Incas of Peru in the latter part of the 15th century. Early in the 16th century Pizarro's conquests led to the inclusion of the present territory of Ecuador in the Spanish Vice-royalty of Peru. The independence of the country was achieved in a revolutionary war which culminated in the battle of Mount Pichincha (May 24, 1822).

After seven years of military rule, Ecuador returned to democracy in 1979. The present constitution, introduced in 1978, provides for an elected President and Vice-President who serve for a four year term. (Neither may stand for re-election.) There is a Chamber of Representatives with 71 members elected every four years, 12 of whom are elected on a national basis and the rest by the provinces. The Chamber meets for two months every year (Aug.–Oct.) but can be convoked at any time for extraordinary sessions. Four Legislative Commissions meet through the year.

Voting is compulsory for all literate and (since 1980) voluntary for all illiterate citizens over the age of 18. Sixteen political parties took part in the 1988 elections.

Agriculture and Industry.—Agriculture is the most important sector of the economy, supporting nearly 50 per cent of the population (particularly the poorest) and contributing 14·5 per cent of the Gross Domestic Product and 19·5 per cent of exports. The main products for export are fish (mainly shrimps, tuna and sardines), which had become the largest agricultural export by early 1982; bananas, which provide a third of agricultural exports; cocoa and coffee. Other important crops are sugar, corn, soya, rice, cotton, African palm (for oil), vegetables, fruit and timber, the temperate crops being produced mostly in the highlands.

The economy was transformed by the discovery in 1972 of major oil fields in the Oriente area, and oil accounted for two thirds of 1981 export earnings. The economy grew rapidly in the 1970s but is now faced with reduced growth, due mainly to the fall in the price of oil. The oil deposits in the Oriente are estimated at between 10,000 and 15,000 million barrels, and further exploration and development is taking place. The oil is evacuated by a trans-Andean pipeline to the port of Balao (near Esmeraldas).

Communications.—There are 23,256 km. of permanent roads and 5,044 km. of roads which are only open during the dry season. There are about 750 miles of railway, including the railway from Quito to Guayaquil. Ten commercial airlines operate international flights, linking Ecuador with major foreign cities and there are internal services between all important towns.

Defence.—The standing Army has a strength of about 38,000. There is an Air Force of some 120 aircraft of various kinds and 4,800 personnel. The Navy is 4,500 strong.

Language, etc.—Spanish is the principal language of the country but Quechua is also a recognized language and is spoken by the majority of the Indian population. As a result of an intensive national education programme more than 75 per cent of the population are now literate. Elementary education is free and compulsory. There are 9 Universities, at Quito (2), Guayaquil (3), Cuenca, Machala, Loja and Portoviejo, Polytechnic Schools at Quito and Guayaquil and 8 technical colleges in other provincial capitals. 2 daily newspapers are published at Quito and 4 at Guayaquil.

Finance.—The estimated government budget in 1986 was: revenue 186,824 million sucres; expenditure 216,466 million sucres.

TRADE

Import licences are required for all merchandise and these are issued by the Central Bank of Ecuador.

	1985	1986
Imports	US$1,614·5m.	US$1,631·1m.
Exports	2,904·6m.	2,185·8m.

Trade with U.K.

	1987	1988
Imports from U.K.	£37,934,000	£50,417,000
Exports to U.K.	14,002,000	13,120,000

Manufactured goods and machinery are the main imports.

CAPITAL.—Quito. Population (1985 estimate), 1,003,875; Ψ Guayaquil (1,000,000) is the chief port; Cuenca (110,000).

CURRENCY.—Sucre of 100 centavos.

FLAG.—Three horizontal bands, yellow, blue and red (the yellow band twice the width of the others); emblem in centre.

NATIONAL DAY.—August 10 (*Independence Day*).

BRITISH EMBASSY
Calle Gonzalez Suarez, 111 (Casilla 314),
Quito.
[Quito 560669]

Ambassador Extraordinary and Plenipotentiary, His Excellency Frank Basil Wheeler (1989).

There is a British Consular Office at *Guayaquil*.

British Council Representative, Ms. G. B. Marsh, Av. Amazonas 1646 (Casilla 8829), Quito.

The GALÁPAGOS (Giant Tortoise) ISLANDS forming the province of the Archipelago de Colón, were annexed by Ecuador in 1832. The archipelago lies in the Pacific, about 500 miles from Saint Elena peninsula, the most westerly point of the mainland. There are 12 large and several hundred smaller islands with a total area of about 3,000 sq. miles and an estimated population (1982) of 6,119. The capital is San Cristobal, on Chatham Island. Although the archipelago lies on the equator, the temperature of the surrounding water is well below equatorial average owing to the Antarctic Humbolt Current. The province consists for the most part of National Park Territory, where unique marine birds, iguanas, and the giant tortoises are conserved. There is some local subsistence farming; the main industry, apart from tourism, is tuna and lobster fishing.

EGYPT
(Al-Jumhuriyat Misr al-Arabiya)

President, Muhammad Hosni Mubarak, *elected*, Oct. 13, 1981 re-elected, 1987.

COUNCIL OF MINISTERS
(as at June 30, 1989)

Prime Minister, Dr. Atef Muhammad Naguib Sidqi.

Presidential Assistant, Muhammad Abdul Halim Abu Ghazala.

Defence and Military Production, Gen. Youssef Sabri Abu Taleb.

Deputy P.M. and Foreign Minister, Dr. Ahmed Ismat Abdul Magid.

Deputy P.M. and Minister of Planning and International Co-operation, Dr. Kamal Ahmed al-Ganzuri.

Deputy P.M. and Minister of Agriculture and Land Reclamation, Dr. Yussif Amin Wali.

Economy and Foreign Trade, Dr. Yussri Ali Mustafa.

Finance, Dr. Muhammad Ahmed el-Razzaz.

Interior, Maj.-Gen. Zaki Badr.

Oil and Mineral Wealth, Abdul-Hadi Muhammad Qandil.

Tourism and Civil Aviation, Fouad Abdul Latif Sultan.

Justice, Farouq Saif al-Nasr.

Culture, Farouq Hosni.

Industry, Muhammad Mahmoud Abdul Wahhab.

Parliamentary and Shura Council Affairs, Dr. Ahmed Salama.

Supply and Internal Trade, Dr. Mohammed Galaleddin Abdul-Dahab.

Public Works and Water Resources, 'Issam Abdul Hamid Radi.

Manpower and Vocational Training, Assem Abdul Haq.

Education, Dr. Ahmed Fathi Sorour.

Transport, Communications and Marine Transport, Suliman Metwalli Suliman.

Scientific Research, Dr. Adel Abul-Hamid 'Ezz.

Health, Dr. Mohammed Ragheb Dawidar.

Information, Muhammad Safwat al-Sharif.

Cabinet Affairs and Administrative Development, Dr. 'Atif Mohammad 'Ebeid.

Religious Affairs (Waqfs), Dr. Muhammad Ali Mahgoub.

Social Affairs and Social Insurance, Dr. Amal Abdul Rahim Osman.

Electricity and Energy, Mohammad Mahir Osman Abaza.

Housing, New Communities and Public Utilities, Hasaballah Mohammad al-Kafrawi.

Ministers of State, Dr. Boutros Yussef Boutros-Ghali (*Foreign Affairs*); Gamal al-Sayyid Ibrahim (*Military Production*); Dr. Fouad Iskander (*Immigration and Egyptians living abroad*); Dr. Mouris Makramallah (*International Co-operation*).

EGYPTIAN EMBASSY
26 South Street, W1Y 8EL
[01–499 2401]

Ambassador Extraordinary and Plenipotentiary, His Excellency Mohamed I. Shaker (1988).

AREA AND POPULATION.—The total area of Egypt is 386,662 sq. miles (1,001,449 sq. km.), only three per cent of which is cultivated land, with a population now officially estimated (1987) at 52,000,000.

There are three distinct elements in the native population. The largest, or 'Egyptian' element, is a Hamito-Semite race, known in the rural districts as *Fellahin* (*fellâh*—ploughman, or tiller of the soil). A

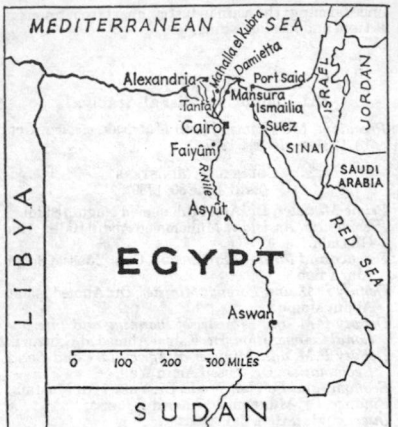

second element is the *Bedouin*, or nomadic Arabs of the Western and Arabian deserts, of whom about one-seventh are real nomads, and the remainder semi-sedentary tent-dwellers on the outskirts of the cultivated area of the Nile Valley and the Fayûm. The third element is the *Nubian* of the Nile Valley between Aswân and Wadi-Halfa of mixed Arab and Negro blood. Over 90 per cent of the population are Muslims of the Sunni denomination, and most of the rest Coptic Christians.

The territory of Egypt comprises (1) Egypt Proper, forming the N.E. corner of the African continent, divisible into (*a*) the valley and delta of the Nile, (*b*) the Western Desert, and (*c*) the Arabian or Eastern Desert; (2) The Peninsula of Sinai, forming part of the continent of Asia; and (3) a number of islands in the Gulf of Suez and Red Sea, of which the principal are Jubal, Shadwan, Gafatin and Zeberged (or St. John's Island). This territory lies between 22° and 32° N. lat. and 24° and 37° E. long. The northern boundary is the Mediterranean, and in the south Egypt is conterminous with the Sudan. The western boundary runs from a point on the coast 10 kilometres N.W. of Sollûm to the latitude of Siwa and thence due S. along the 25th meridian. The E. boundary follows a line drawn from Rafa on the Mediterranean (34° 15′ E. long.) to the head of the Gulf of 'Aqaba.

Physical Features.—The country is mainly flat but there are mountainous areas in the south-west, along the Red Sea coast and in the south of the Sinai peninsula, rising in some places to peaks of over 6,000 ft. The highest mountain in Egypt is Mt. Catherina (8,668 ft). Most of the land is desert but the Nile valley and delta are covered with silt 20–30 feet deep, and areas of desert are increasingly being reclaimed by irrigation and fertilization.

The Nile has a total length of 4,145 miles. In the 960 miles of its course through Egypt it receives not a single tributary stream. The river formerly had a regular yearly rise and fall of about 13 feet at Cairo, but since the completion of the Aswan High Dam in 1965, there has been no flood downstream of the dam and the water level remains almost constant throughout the year. The area of fertile land, a 5–15 mile wide strip in the Nile valley and some 6,000 square miles of the Nile delta, has been increased by the opening of the Aswan Dam. This has allowed the reclamation of about 1,300,000 acres, and a further

700,000 acres have been converted from basin to perennial irrigation. Westward from the Nile Valley stretches the Western desert, containing some depressions, whose springs irrigate small areas known as Oases, of which the principal, from S.E. to N.W., are known as Kharga, Dakhla, Farafra, Baharia and Siwa.

In the Eastern Desert between the Nile and the mountains along the Red Sea coast, are plateaux of sandstones and limestones, dissected by wadis (dry water-courses), often of great length and depth, with some wild vegetation and occasional wells and springs.

History.—The unification of the Kingdoms of Lower and Upper Egypt under the Pharaohs in *c.* 3,100 B.C. marked the establishment of the Egyptian state, with Memphis as its capital. Egypt was ruled for nearly 2,800 years by a succession of Pharaonic dynasties (31 in all), which built the pyramids at Gizeh. The oldest of these is that of Zoser, built *c.* 2,700 B.C., and the highest the Great Pyramid of Cheops, at 451 feet; nearby is the Sphinx, 189 feet long. A period of Hellenic rule began in 332 B.C., after the conquest of Egypt by Alexander the Great, followed by a period of rule by Rome (30 B.C. to A.D. 324) and then by the Byzantine Empire. In A.D. 640 Egypt was subjugated by Arab Muslim invaders, becoming a province of the Eastern Caliphate. In 1517 the country was incorporated in the Ottoman Empire under which it remained until early in the 19th century.

A British Protectorate over Egypt declared on Dec. 18, 1914, lasted until Feb. 28, 1922, when Sultan Ahmed Fuad was proclaimed King of Egypt. In July, 1952, following a military coup d'état, King Farouk abdicated in favour of his infant son, who became King Ahmed Fuad II. In June, 1953, however, Gen. Neguib's military council deposed the young king, and Egypt became a Republic.

In 1956, as a result of Egypt's trade agreements with Communist countries, Britain and U.S.A. withdrew offers of financial aid and in retaliation Pres. Nasser seized the assets of the Suez Canal Company. An Egyptian invasion of the Canal Zone while repulsing an Israeli attack provoked military action by Britain and France in support of their Suez Canal Company interests. A ceasefire and Anglo-French withdrawal were negotiated by the U.N.

The Israeli invasion of 1956 overran the Sinai peninsula but six months later Israel withdrew and a U.N. peace-keeping force was established in the area. However, mounting tension culminated in a second invasion of Sinai (the Six Day War of June 1967) and occupation of the peninsula by Israel. Egypt's attempt to recapture the territory (the Yom Kippur War of October 1973) was unsuccessful but Sinai was returned to Egypt in April 1982, under the treaty of 1979 which resulted from the Camp David talks between Pres. Sadat and Mr. Begin and formally terminated a 31-year old state of war between the two countries. Pres. Hosni Mubarak came to power on Oct. 13, 1981 after the assassination of Pres. Sadat by Muslim fundamentalists.

Government.—The Constitution of 1971 provides for an executive President who appoints Ministers to the Cabinet. The President determines policy which the Cabinet implements and Ministers are responsible to him. The Legislature consists of the People's Assembly (458 members, 448 of whom are elected, the remaining 10 nominated by the President); the Shura Council, or Consultative Assembly (258 members) has an advisory role. The Constitution guarantees also the independence of the Judiciary. Religious courts were abolished in 1956 and their functions transferred to the national court system. Freedom of the press is guaranteed under the Constitution.

Agriculture.—Despite increasing industrialization, agriculture remains the most important economic activity, employing over 45 per cent of the labour force and contributing to 17 per cent of the country's exports. Agricultural output has been increased as a result of land reclamation programmes and the introduction of more efficient methods, e.g. the change from basin to perennial irrigation which yields 2–3 crops per year instead of one, the pivotal sprinkling irrigation system which uses water more efficiently, and the increasing mechanization and use of fertilizers. Egypt is still a net importer of foodstuffs, especially grain, and a food security programme has been set up with the aim of achieving self-sufficiency through the use of more advanced technology. Estimates suggest that an additional 3 million acres of land could be reclaimed by the end of the century.

The main cash crop is cotton, of which Egypt is one of the world's main producers. Production in 1986 was 403,000 tons. Other important summer crops are (1986 figures) maize 2,908,000 tons, rice 2,445,000 tons, and sugar cane 9,684,000 tons. Important winter crops are wheat 1,929,000 tons, and beans 382,000 tons. Citrus fruit and other fruits and vegetables are also grown.

Energy.—With its considerable reserves of petroleum and natural gas in Sinai, the Nile Delta and the Western Desert, and the hydro-electric power produced by the Aswan and High Dams, Egypt is self-sufficient in energy. Electricity has been provided to almost all of the country and there are plans to extend the natural gas network to all major cities.

Industry.—The production of petroleum provides Egypt with its major export (60–65 per cent. of total exports), and supports a growing refining industry. Steel production is another important heavy industry. The major manufacturing industries are in food processing, motor cars and electrical goods, chemical products and yarns and textiles.

FINANCE

	1986–87	1987–88
Estimated revenue ..	£E12·4m.	£E14·2m.
Total expenditure ...	19·9m.	21·7m.

TRADE

The main imports are wheat and flour, wood and trucks. The main exports are crude petroleum, cotton, cotton yarn, oranges, rice and cotton textiles.

	1986–87
Imports	£E7·8m.
Exports	2·6m.

Trade with U.K.

	1987	1988
Imports from U.K.	£342,195,000	£289,309,000
Exports to U.K.	127,261,000	163,038,000

Communications.—The road and rail networks link the Nile Valley and Delta with the main development areas to east and west of the river.

The Suez Canal was re-opened in 1975 and a two-stage development project begun to widen and deepen the canal to allow the passage of larger shipping and to permit two-way traffic. Port Said and Suez have been reconstructed and the port of Alexandria is being improved.

CAPITAL.—Cairo (population, estimated in 1986 at 14,000,000), stands on the E. bank of the Nile, about 14 miles from the head of the Delta. Its oldest part is the fortress of Babylon in old Cairo, with its Roman bastions and Coptic churches. The earliest Arab building is the Mosque of 'Amr, dating from A.D. 643, and the most conspicuous is the Citadel, built by Saladin towards the end of the 12th century and containing in its walls the Mosque of Mohamed Ali built in the 19th century.

ΨAlexandria (estimated population in 1986 of 5,000,000), founded 332 B.C. by Alexander the Great, was for over 1,000 years the capital of Egypt and a centre of Hellenic culture which vied with Athens herself. Its great *pharos* (lighthouse), 480 feet high, with a lantern burning resinous wood, was one of the Seven Wonders of the World. Other towns are: Ismailia (400,000); ΨPort Said (285,000); Mansura (120,000); Asyût (300,000); Faiyûm (180,000); Tanta (150,000); Mahalla el Kubra (130,000); ΨSuez; ΨDamietta (100,000).

CURRENCY.—Egyptian pound (£E) of 100 piastres and 1,000 millièmes.

FLAG.—Horizontal bands of red, white and black, with an eagle in the centre of the white band.

NATIONAL DAY.—July 23 (Anniversary of Revolution in 1952).

BRITISH EMBASSY
Ahmed Ragheb Street, Garden City, Cairo
[Cairo 354–0850]

Ambassador Extraordinary and Plenipotentiary, His Excellency (William) James Adams, C.M.G. (1987).
British Council Representative, G. Tindale, O.B.E., 192 Sharia el Nil, Agouza, Cairo. There is also a library in *Alexandria*.

EQUATORIAL GUINEA
(República de Guinea Ecuatorial)

President, Col. Teodoro Obiang Nguema Mbasogo, *took office*, Aug. 1979, *re-elected* June 1989.

MINISTERS
(as at May 31, 1989)

Minister of Defence, Security and Political Affairs, The President.
Prime Minister and Minister for Health, C. Seriche Bioko.
Deputy P.M., Minister of Territorial Administration and National Security, Monsuy Andeme.
Public Works, Housing, Town Planning, Alejandro Envoro Ovono.
Economic Planning, Hilario Nsue Alene.
Education and Sport, Fortunato Nzambi Michinde.
Information and Tourism, Leandro Mbomio Nsue.
Labour, Anacleto Ejapa Bolekia.
Communications and Transport, Demetrio Elo Ndongo Nsefumu.
Agriculture, Alfredo Abero Nvono.
Industry and Commerce, Francisco Pascual Obama Eyegue.
Justice and Religion, Angel Ndong Micha.
Civil Service, Massoko Mecheba Ikaka.
Secretary-General to the Presidency, Martin Mka Esono.
Territorial Administration, Isidoro Eyi Monsuy Andeme.
Energy, Juan Olo Mba Nseng.
Water Resources and Forestry, Angel Alogo Nchama.
Foreign Affairs, Marcelino Nguema Onguene.
Finance, Felipe Inestroca Ikaka.
Relations with the House of Reps, Eloy Elo Nve Mbengono.
Deputy Minister of Defence, Maj. Melanio Ebendeng Nsomo.

Equatorial Guinea (formerly Spanish Guinea) consists of the island of Biogo (formerly Macias Nguema), in the Bight of Biafra about 20 miles from the west coast of Africa, Pagalu Island (formerly Annobon) in the Gulf of Guinea, the Corisco Islands (Corisco, Elobey Grande and Elobey Chico) and Rio Muni, a mainland area between Cameroon and Gabon. It has a total area of 10,830 sq. miles (28,051 sq. km.), and a population (1985 U.N. estimate) of 392,000.

Government.—Formerly colonies of Spain, the territories now forming the Republic of Equatorial Guinea were constituted as two provinces of Metropolitan Spain, in 1960, became autonomous in 1964 and fully independent in 1968. Serious disorders in Rio Muni early in 1969 caused many of the Spanish community to leave. Following Nigerian allegations of continuing mistreatment, most of the Nigerian labour force, on whom cocoa production largely depended, were repatriated in late 1975 and early 1976.

In Aug. 1979, President Macias was deposed by a revolutionary military council headed by his nephew Col. T. Obiang Nguema. The first parliamentary elections since 1968 were held on Aug. 28, 1983, under a new constitution approved by a referendum in Aug. 1982. Forty-one representatives were elected to the National Assembly for a five-year term.

Economy.—The chief products are cocoa, coffee and wood (which is exported almost entirely from Rio Muni). Production has declined and except for cocoa, there is little commercial agriculture and the economy is now heavily dependent on outside aid, principally from Spain. Equatorial Guinea entered the 'Franc zone' in 1985.

TRADE

	1984
Total Imports	US$18·7m.
Total Exports	30·0m.

Trade with U.K.

	1987	1988
Imports from U.K.	£1,572,000	£1,029,000
Exports to U.K.	—	—

CAPITAL.—ΨMalabo on the island of Bioco (population 1983 estimate, 34,980). ΨBata is the principal town and port of Rio Muni.

CURRENCY.— Franc C.F.A. of 100 centimes.

FLAG.—Three horizontal bands, green over white over red; blue triangle next staff; coat of arms in centre of white band.

NATIONAL DAY.—October 12.

British Ambassador, (resides at Yaoundé).

ETHIOPIA
(Hebretesebawit Ityopia)

President of the People's Democratic Republic, Mengistu Haile Mariam, *elected* Sept. 10, 1987.

Vice President, Lt.-Col. Fisseha Desta.

STATE COUNCIL

Vice Presidents, Emanuel Amde-Mikhail; Debela Dinsa; Yusuf Ahmed.

Secretary, Embibe Ayele.

Members, Capt. Fikre Selassie Wogderess; Lt.-Gen. Tesfaye Gebre Kidan; Lt.-Col. Berhanu Bayih; Addis Tedla; Hailu Yimenu; Alemu Abebe; Fasika Sidelil; Tesfaye Dinka; Shewandagn Belete; Endalle Tessema; Ashagre Yigletu; Tefera Wonde; Kasaye Aragaw; Tadese Tamirat; Abdela Sonesa; Haile Gabriel Dagne; Asegedech Bizuneh; Getachew Robele.

COUNCIL OF MINISTERS
(as at May 31, 1989)

Prime Minister, Capt. Fikre Selassie Wogderess.

Agriculture, Geremew Debele.

Coffee and Tea Development, Tekola Dejene.

Construction, Kassa Gebre.

Culture, Youth and Sports, Maj. Girma Yilma.

Defence, (vacant).

Domestic Trade, Mersha Wodajo.

Education, Dr. Yaherad Kitaw.

Finance, Wole Chekol.

Foreign Affairs, Lt.-Col. Berhanu Bayeh.

Foreign Trade, Tadesse Gebre Kidan.

Health, Brig.-Gen. Gizan Tseha.

Industry, (vacant).

Information and National Guidance, Abdul Hafis Yusuf.

Internal Affairs, Col. Tesfaye Wolde Selassie.

Labour and Social Affairs, Shimelis Adugna.

Law and Justice, Wondayin Mehretu.

Mines, Energy and Water Resources, Tekeze Shoa Aytenfisu.

State Farms, Yoseph Muleta.

Transport and Communications, Asegid Wolde Amanuel.

Urban Development and Housing, Tesfaye Maru.

Ministers in President's Office, Dr. Feleke Gedle-Giorgis (*Foreign Relations*); Maj.-Gen. Kefelegn Yibza (*Chief Inspector of Military Affairs*); Neguse Wolde Mikael (*Chief Inspector of Economic, Social and Administrative Affairs*); Maj.-Gen. Seyoum Mekonen (*Chief of Defence and Security*).

EMBASSY OF THE PEOPLE'S DEMOCRATIC REPUBLIC OF ETHIOPIA
17 Prince's Gate, SW7 1PZ
[01–589 7212]

Ambassador Extraordinary and Plenipotentiary, His Excellency Ato Teferra Haile-Selassie (1985).

Position and Extent.—Ethiopia is in North-Eastern Africa, bounded on the north-west by the Sudan; on the south by Kenya; on the east by Djibouti and the Republic of Somalia: and on the north-east by the Red Sea. The area is 471,778 sq. miles (1,221,900 sq. km.), with a population (1985) of 43,350,000. About one-third are of the dominant race of Semitic origin (Amharas and Tigreans) and the remainder mainly Gallas (about 40 per cent of the population), Somalis and Afar.

Ethiopia has a large central plateau (average height, 6,000–7,000 ft.) which rises to nearly 15,000 ft. at Ras Dashan in the north. The plateau drops to the Nile basin in the west and the Red Sea in the east. To the north (Eritrea) and east (Ogaden) the land is mostly desert. The chief river is the Blue Nile, issuing from Lake Tana; the Atbara and many other tributaries of the Nile also rise in the Ethiopian highlands.

Those of Semitic origin (Amharas and Tigreans), and many of the Gallas, are Christians of the Ethiopian Orthodox Church, which was formerly led by the head of the Coptic Church, the Patriarch at Alexandria. Since 1959, however, the Ethiopian Church has been autocephalous and the new Patriarch, Abuna Markarious, was enthroned in Sept. 1988. The Afar people, who inhabit lowland Eritrea, Wollo, Hararghe and Bale provinces, and the Somalis, in the south-east, are Muslim. The Falashas, to be found principally in Gandar and Tigre provinces, practise Judaism. Between autumn 1984 and February 1985 a secret airlift ("Operation Moses") took 7,000 of the estimated 25,000 Falashas to Israel, via Sudan.

History.—The basic Hamitic culture was heavily influenced by Semitic immigration from Arabia in the centuries about the time of Christ. Christianity was introduced in the 4th century. The empire expanded sporadically, attaining a zenith in the 6th century under the Axum rulers, but subsequently checked by Islamic expansion from the east. Modern Ethiopia dates from 1855 when Theodore succeeded in establishing supremacy over the various tribes. The last Emperor was Haile Selassie who reigned from 1930, though in exile from 1936–1941 during the Italian occupation. After considerable military and civil unrest the armed forces assumed power in Sept. 1972 and deposed the Emperor. A Worker's Party on the Soviet model was formed in Sept. 1984, with Mengistu as General-Secretary.

The civilian government of the People's Democratic Republic of Ethiopia was established in Sept. 1987 with Lt.-Col. Mengistu being elected the first President. A new constitution was established and provides for the *Shengo* (National Assembly) of 835 seats. The *Shengo* votes on the membership of the 24-member State Council.

Eritrea was administered by Great Britain from the end of the Second World War until September 15, 1952, when it was federated with Ethiopia. It was incorporated as a province of Ethiopia in 1962. An armed campaign for independence started in 1962 and has intensified since the early 1970's.

Due to the lack of spring rains both the harvests of 1983 and 1984 failed. A famine relief programme launched in October 1984 drew world-wide attention to the problem, and airlifts of food began almost immediately. In two of the worst hit areas, the provinces of Tigre and Eritrea, the situation was exacerbated by the difficulty of supplying food and other aid to areas experiencing guerrilla activity.

In July 1977, Somalia, claiming the Ogaden region of Ethiopia in support of Western Somalia Liberation Front guerrillas, invaded the region. Ethiopia, with Soviet arms, and the aid of Cuban troops, was able to defeat the Somalis. In April 1988 both governments agreed to re-establish diplomatic relations and to withdraw troops from their common border.

The Tigrean province, which lies south of Eritrea, seeks to establish greater autonomy : the activities of the Tigrean People's Liberation Front have escalated since the early 1980s, and the T.P.L.F. claims to control and administer large areas of the province.

Production and Industry.—The principal pursuit is agriculture, which accounts for approximately 40 per cent of G.D.P., 85 per cent of exports and 80 per cent of total employment. Land was nationalized in 1975 and tenants given rights of use to the land they had tilled : large private holdings became state farms. The major food crops are teff, maize, barley, sorghum, wheat, pulses and oil seeds. Coffee, the principal export crop generates over 50 per cent of the country's export earnings.

Manufacturing industry accounts for less than 9 per cent of G.D.P. and is heavily dependent on agriculture. Ethiopia's known, but as yet largely unexploited, natural resources include gold, platinum, copper and potash. Traces of oil and natural gas have been found.

Communications.—With the aid of loans from the IBRD, China and the African Development Bank, a network of roads has been built in rural areas and link the major cities with each other, and with the Sudanese and Kenyan borders and the Red Sea coast. Transport links have suffered during the secessionist wars and under the heavy burden of famine relief traffic. The two roads to the north are usable only under heavy military escort in Tigre and Eritrea. There is a railway link from Addis Ababa to Djibouti although this is vulnerable to guerrilla activity. The narrow gauge line in Eritrea has been closed by conflict. Ethiopian Airlines maintains regular services from Addis Ababa to many provincial towns. External services are operated throughout Africa and to Europe.

Defence.—Under the Ministry of Defence the armed forces comprise the Army, the Air Force and the Navy. The Army strength totals 250,000–300,000 personnel (including a People's Militia) divided into 28 divisions.

The Air Force comprises a transport squadron, a reconnaissance squadron, five fighter squadrons, a training squadron, and two helicopter squadrons. There are 150 fighter planes, all of Russian manufacture. The Air Force headquarters is situated at Debre Zeit.

The Navy has a headquarters in Addis Ababa with a main base at Massawa and a smaller one at Assab.

National Military Service was established on May 4, 1983 and came into effect in May 1984.

Education.—Elementary education is provided without religious discrimination by Government schools in the main centres of population ; there are also Mission schools, and cadet-schools for the Army, Navy, Air Force, and Police. Government secondary schools are found mainly in Addis Ababa, but also in most of the provincial capitals. The National University (founded 1961) co-ordinates the institutions of higher education (University College, Engineering, Building and Theological Colleges in Addis Ababa, Agricultural College at Alemaya, near Harar, and Public Health Centre in Gondar, etc.). It is intended to develop the provincial colleges to university level and status. Amharic is the official language of instruction, with English as the first foreign language and main language of instruction from secondary level upwards. Arabic is taught in Koran Schools ; and Ge'ez (the ancient Ethiopic) in Christian Church Schools, which abound.

FINANCE

	1987–88
Revenue	US$1,709·5m.
Expenditure	2,226·4m.

Trade.—The chief imports by value are machinery and transport equipment, manufactured goods and chemicals (from U.K.) ; the principal exports by value being coffee, oilseeds, hides and skins, and pulses.

TRADE

	1987–88
Total Imports	US$1,083·6m.
Total Exports	393·7m.

Trade with U.K.

	1987	1988
Imports from U.K.	£46,146,000	£47,661,000
Exports to U.K.	12,875,000	8,451,000

CAPITAL.— Addis Ababa (population, 1985 estimate, 1,464,901), also capital of the province of Shoa ;

Asmara (population 250,000) is the capital of the Province of Eritrea. Dire Dawa is the most important commercial centre after Addis Ababa and Asmara, ΨMassawa and ΨAssab (recently enlarged) are the two main ports. There are ancient architectural remains at Aksum, Gondar, Lalibela and elsewhere.

CURRENCY.—Ethiopian birr (EB) of 100 cents.

FLAG.—Three horizontal bands; green, yellow, red.

NATIONAL ANTHEM.—Ityopya, Ityopya Kidemi.

NATIONAL DAY.—September 12 (People's Revolution Day).

BRITISH EMBASSY
Fikre Mariam Abatechan Street (P.O. Box 858),
Addis Ababa
[Addis Ababa 612354]

Ambassador Extraordinary and Plenipotentiary, His Excellency Harold Berners Walker, C.M.G. (1986).

There is a British Consular Office at *Addis Ababa.*

British Council Representative, B. Nightingale, Artistic Building, Adwa Avenue (P.O. Box 1043), Addis Ababa. There is also a library in *Asmara.*

FIJI
(Matanitu Ko Fiti—Republic of Fiji)

President, Ratu Sir Penaia Ganilau, G.C.M.G., K.V.C.O., K.B.E., D.S.O., *apptd.* Dec. 5, 1987.

Cabinet
(as at June 30, 1989)

Prime Minister and Foreign Affairs, Ratu Sir Kamisese Mara, G.C.M.G., K.B.E.

Home Affairs, National Youth Service and Auxiliary Army Services, Maj.-Gen. Sitiveni Rabuka.

Fijian Affairs, Col. Vatiliai Navunisaravi.

Finance and Economic Planning, Josefata Kamikamica.

Education, Filipe Bole, C.B.E.

Primary Industry, Viliame Gonelevu.

Trade and Commerce, Berenado Vunibobo.

Health, Apenisa Kurisaqila.

Communications, Works and Transport, Apisai Tora.

Attorney-General and Justice, Sailosi Kepa.

Tourism, Civil Aviation and Energy, David Pickering, C.B.E.

Youth and Sport, Col. Ilaisa Kacisolomone.

Rural Development, and Rural Housing, Col. Apolosi Biuvakaloloma.

Indian Affairs, Mrs. Irene Jai Narayan.

Forestry, Ratu Sir Josaia Tavaiqia, K.B.E.

Employment and Industrial Relations, Taniela Veitata.

Co-operatives and National Marketing Authority, Ishwari Bajpai.

Women's Affairs and Social Welfare, Adi Finau Tabakaucoro.

Housing and Urban Development, Tomasi Vakatora.

Lands and Mineral Resources, Ratu William Tonganivalu.

Information, Ratu Inoke Kubuabola.

EMBASSY OF FIJI
34 Hyde Park Gate, SW7 5BN
[01-584 3661/2]

Ambassador Extraordinary and Plenipotentiary, His Excellency Brig.-Gen. Ratu Epeli Nailatikau, L.V.O., O.B.E. (1988).

Area, Population, etc.—Fiji is made up of about 332 islands and over 500 islets (including numerous atolls and reefs) in the South Pacific Ocean, about 1,100 miles north of New Zealand. About 100 islands are permanently inhabited. The gross area of the group,

which extends 300 miles from east to west, and 300 north to south, between 15° 45'—21° 10' S. lat. and 176° E.—178° W. long. is 7,055 sq. miles (18,274 sq. km.). The International Date Line has been diverted to the east of the island group. The largest islands are Viti Levu and Vanua Levu. The main groups of islands are Lomaiviti, Lau and Yasawas. Most of the larger islands are mountainous with sharp peaks and crags, but also have conspicuous areas of flat land and many of the rivers have built extensive deltas. The climate is tropical, without extremes of heat and temperatures rarely exceed 32°C. and seldom fall below 15°C.

The population (Census 1986) was 715,373 comprising 48·6 per cent. Indians, 46·2 per cent. Fijians, and 5·2 per cent. other races.

Government.—Fiji was a British colony from 1874 until October 10, 1970, when it became an independent state and a member of the Commonwealth.

A coalition of the left under Dr. Timoci Bavadra defeated the Alliance Party of Ratu Sir Kamisese Mara in a General Election on April 12, 1987. The new Government, drawing its support mainly from the Indian population, was overthrown in a military coup on May 14 by Lt.-Col. Sitiveni Rabuka. In the wake of the constitutional crisis an Advisory Council of 19 members was set up by the Governor General as an interim government to consider constitutional reform.

A second coup occurred on Sept. 25, 1987. On Oct. 7 Rabuka declared Fiji to be a republic; the Governor General resigned on Oct. 15 and Fiji's Commonwealth membership lapsed. An Executive Council of Ministers, with Rabuka at its head, assumed control until Dec. 5 when Ratu Sir Penaia Ganilau was appointed President. The President called upon Ratu Sir Kamisese Mara to form another interim administration to work for a resolution to the political crisis.

FINANCE

	1987	1988 (est)
Public Income	F$342,000,000	F$358,000,000
Public Expenditure . . .	416,000,000	399,000,000

Economy.—The economy is primarily agrarian, with about 600,000 acres under cultivation. The principal cash crop is sugar cane, which is the main export, followed by coconuts, ginger and copra. A variety of other fruit, vegetables and root crops are also grown, and self-sufficiency in rice is a major aim. Forestry, fishing and beef production are being encouraged in order to diversify the economy. The processing of agricultural, marine and timber products are the main industries, along with gold mining. A policy of tax concessions for export-oriented manufacturing has encouraged expansion of the garment industry.

Tourism is also a major factor in the economy, second only to sugar as a money-earner.

TRADE

	1987	1988
Total Imports	F$465,583,000	F$570,700,000
Total Exports (including Re-exports)	408,815,000	493,800,000

Trade with U.K.

	1987	1988
Imports from U.K.	£7,381,000	£6,358,000
Exports to U.K.	53,062,000	65,273,000

The chief imports are foodstuffs, machinery, mineral fuels, chemicals, beverages, tobacco and manufactured articles. Chief exports are sugar, coconut oil, gold, lumber, garments, molasses, ginger and canned fish.

Communications.—Fiji is one of the main aerial crossroads in the Pacific, providing services to New

Zealand, Australia, Tonga, Western Samoa, Vanuatu, the Solomon Islands, Kiribati, Tuvalu, New Caledonia and American Samoa.

Fiji has three ports of entry, at Suva, Lautoka and Levuka.

CAPITAL.—ΨSuva, in the island of Viti Levu. Population (1985) 75,000.

CURRENCY.—Fiji dollar (F$) of 100 cents.

FLAG.—Light blue ground with Union flag in top left quarter and the shield of Fiji in the fly.

NATIONAL ANTHEM.—Hail to Fiji.

NATIONAL DAY.—October 10 (Fiji Day).

BRITISH EMBASSY
Victoria House, 47 Gladstone Road,
P.O. Box 1355, Suva
[Suva 311033]

Ambassador Extraordinary and Plenipotentiary, His Excellency (Alexander Basil) Peter Smart (1989).

FINLAND
(Suomen Tasavalta)

President, Dr. Mauno Koivisto, *born*, 1923, *elected*, Jan 26, 1982, *re-elected*, March 1, 1988.

CABINET
(as at May 31, 1989)

Prime Minister, Harri Holkeri (*NCP*).
Foreign Affairs, Pertti Paasio (*SDP*).
Cabinet, Ilkka Kanerva (*NCP*).
Foreign Trade, Pertti Salolainen (*NCP*).
Justice, Matti Louekoski (*SDP*).
Interior, Jarmo Rantanen (*SDP*).
Defence, Ole Norrback (*SPP*).
Finance, Erkki Liikanen (*SDP*).
Deputy Minister of Finance, Ms. Ulla Puolanne (*NCP*).
Education, Christoffer Taxell (*SPP*).
Deputy Minister of Education, Mrs. Anna-Liisa Kasurinen (*SDP*).
Agriculture and Forestry, Toivo T. Pohjola (*NCP*).
Transport and Communications, Pekka Vennamo (*FRP*).
Trade and Industry, Ilkka Suominen (*NCP*).
Social Affairs and Health, Ms. Helena Pesola (*NCP*).
Deputy Minister of Social Affairs and Health, Ms. Tarja Halonen (*SDP*).
Labour, Matti Puhakka (*SDP*).
Environment, Kaj Bärlund (*SDP*).

(*NCP*= National Coalition Party, *SDP*=Social Democratic Party, *SPP*=Swedish People's Party of Finland, *FRP*= Finnish Rural Party).

FINNISH EMBASSY AND CONSULATE
38 Chesham Place, SW1X 8HW
[01–235 9531]

Ambassador Extraordinary and Plenipotentiary, His Excellency Ilkka Pastinen, K.C.M.G. (1983).
Minister Counsellor, J. Leino.
Counsellors, Dr. H. Markala; J. Muttonen; R.Pöntynen.
Defence Attaché, Col. T. Aaltonen.

Area and Population.—A country situated on the Gulfs of Finland and Bothnia, with a total area of 137,851 sq. miles (337,032 sq. km.), of which 65 per cent is forest, 8 per cent cultivated, 9 per cent lakes and 18 per cent waste and other land. The population (December, 1985) was 4,954,000, of whom 90·3 per cent are Lutheran, 1·1 per cent Greek Orthodox and 8·4 per cent others.

The Åland Archipelago (Ahvenanmaa), a group of small islands at the entrance to the Gulf of Bothnia, covers about 572 square miles, with a population (December, 1985) of 23,600 (95·2 per cent Swedish-

speaking). The islands have a semi-autonomous status.

Government.—Under the Constitution there is a single Chamber (*Eduskunta*) composed of 200 members, elected by universal suffrage. The legislative power is vested in the Chamber and the President. The highest executive power is held by the President who is elected for a period of 6 years.

The present government came into office on April 30, 1987. The four parties in the coalition are the National Coalition Party (conservative), the Social Democratic Party, the Swedish People's Party of Finland, and the Finnish Rural Party.

Defence.—By the terms of the Peace Treaty (Feb. 10, 1947) with U.K. and U.S.S.R., the Army is limited to a force not exceeding 34,400. The Navy is limited to a total of 10,000 tons displacement with personnel not exceeding 4,500. The Air Force, including naval air arm, is limited to 60 machines with a personnel not exceeding 3,000. Bombers or aircraft with bomb-carrying facilities are expressly forbidden. The Defence Forces contain a cadre of regular officers and N.C.O.'s, but their bulk is provided by conscripts who serve for 8–11 months. Total strength of trained and equipped reserves is over 700,000, 16,500 of whom have served in the U.N. peacekeeping force.

Education.—Primary education (co-educational comprehensive school) is compulsory for children from 7 to 16 years, and free of charge. In the autumn of 1986, there were 678,463 in comprehensive schools (388,465 at basic stage and 289,998 at upper stage), and 113,117 in vocational institutions of senior level. There are 21 universities or other schools of academic level, and enrolment was (1985) 92,230.

Language and Literature.—There are two official languages in Finland. 93·5 per cent of the population speak Finnish as their first language, 6·3 Swedish (1979). The remaining 0·2 per cent. speak other languages (mainly Lapps who number about 2,500 and live in the Far North). Both Finnish and Swedish are used for administration and education; newspapers, books, plays and films appear in both languages. There is a vigorous modern literature. F. E. Sillanpää, who died in 1964, was awarded the Nobel prize for

Literature in 1939. Best known among the living authors are Väinö Linna, Veijo Meri and Paavo Haavikko. There are 99 daily newspapers in Finland which appear on 4 or more days per week (12 Swedish).

Production and Industry.—Finland is a highly industrialized country producing a wide range of capital and consumer goods. Timber and the products of the forest-based industries remain the backbone of the economy, accounting for 40 per cent of her export earnings, but the importance of the metal-working, shipbuilding and engineering industries has been growing. This sector in 1986 accounted for 30 per cent of Finland's exports. The textile industry is well developed and Finland's glass, ceramics and furniture industries enjoy international reputations. Other important industries are rubber, plastics, chemicals and pharmaceuticals, footwear, foodstuffs and electronic equipment.

Communications.—There are 9,000 kilometres of railroad, a railway connection with Sweden and U.S.S.R., passenger boat connection with Sweden, Federal Republic of Germany, Poland and U.S.S.R. Vessels on the London to Leningrad route call at Helsinki. There are also passenger/cargo services between Britain and Helsinki, Kotka and other Finnish ports. External civil air services are maintained by most European airlines. The merchant fleet at the end of Dec. 1986 totalled 1,900,000 tons gross.

FINANCE

	1983	1984
	Finnmarks	
Revenue (*Budget*)	64,938,000	75,395,000
Expenditure (*Budget*)	76,590,000	86,095,000

TRADE

The principal imports are raw materials, machinery and manufactured goods. The exports are principally the output of the paper and other forest industries, engineering, metal industry (e.g. paper-working machinery and ships) and chemicals.

	1986	1987
	Finnmarks	
Total Imports	77,600,000	86,690,000
Total Exports	82,570,000	87,560,000

Trade with U.K.

	1987	1988
Imports from U.K.	£797,236,000	£824,951,000
Exports to U.K.	1,539,011,000	1,813,549,000

CAPITAL.—ΨHelsinki (Helsingfors). Population (Jan. 1986), 485,626; other towns are Tampere (Tammerfors), 169,153; ΨTurku (Åbo), 161,508; Espoo (Esbo), 156,851; Vantaa (Vanda), 143,986; ΨOulu (Oleåborg), 97,329; Lahti (Lahtis), 94,467; ΨPori (Björneborg), 78,365.

CURRENCY.—Markka (Mk) of 100 penniä.

FLAG.—White with blue cross.

NATIONAL DAY.—December 6 (Day of Independence).

BRITISH EMBASSY
Uudenmaankatu 16–20
00120 Helsinki 12
[Helsinki 647922]

Ambassador Extraordinary and Plenipotentiary, His Excellency Neil Smith (1989).
Counsellor (Commercial), J. Noss.
First Secretaries, G. S. Hand (*Head of Chancery*); A. J. Marlowe; A. R. Powell.
Defence, Naval, Military and Air Attaché, Lt.-Col. J. M. F. Thomson.

There are British Consular offices at *Helsinki, Tampere, Turku, Pori, Kotka, Oulu, Vaasa, Jyväskylä* and *Kuopio.*
British Council Representative, G. Coe, Erottajankatu 7B, 00130 Helsinki 13.

FRANCE
(La République Française)

President of the French Republic, François Mitterrand, *elected* May 10, 1981, *re-elected* May 8, 1988.

COUNCIL OF MINISTERS
(as at July 31, 1989)

Prime Minister, Michel Rocard (*PS*).
National Education, Research and Sport, Lionel Jospin (*PS*).
Economy, Finance and Budget, Pierre Bérégovoy (*PS*).
Civil Service and Administrative Reform, Michel Durafour (*UDF*).
Foreign Affairs, Roland Dumas (*PS*).
Justice, Pierre Arpaillange.
Defence, Jean-Pierre Chevènement (*PS*).
Interior, Pierre Joxe (*PS*).
European Affairs, Roger Fauroux.
Equipment and Housing, Transport, Sea, Michel Delebarre (*PS*).
Labour and Employment, Jean-Pierre Soisson (*UDF*).
Co-operation and Development, Jacques Pelletier (*UDF*).
Culture and Communications, Major Public Works, and Bicentenary, Jack Lang (*PS*).
Overseas Departments and Territories, Louis Le Pensec (*PS*).
Agriculture and Forests, Henri Nallet (*PS*).
Posts and Telecommunications, and Space, Paul Quilès (*PS*).
Relations with Parliament, Jean Poperen (*PS*).
Solidarity, Health, Social Protection, Government Spokesman, Claude Evin (*PS*).
Research and Technology, Hubert Curien (*PS*).
Foreign Trade, Jean-Marie Rausch (*UDF*).

(*PS,* Parti socialiste; *UDF,* Union pour la démocratie française.)

In presidential elections held on April 24 and May 8, 1988 François Mitterrand was re-elected. M. Michel Rocard was appointed Prime Minister, after the resignation of M. Jacques Chirac, and appointed a socialist-dominated cabinet. However, as the socialists did not have a majority in the National Assembly, the Assembly was dissolved and elections followed in June. A hung parliament resulted, but with the support of the Communist Party the socialist Laurent Fabius was elected President of the National Assembly. Michel Rocard formed his second cabinet on June 28.

FRENCH EMBASSY
58 Knightsbridge, SW1X 7JT
[01–235 8080].

Ambassador Extraordinary and Plenipotentiary, His Excellency Vicomte Luc de La Barre de Nanteuil (1986).

Area and Population.—The largest state in Central Europe, extending from 42° 20′ to 51° 5′ N. lat., and

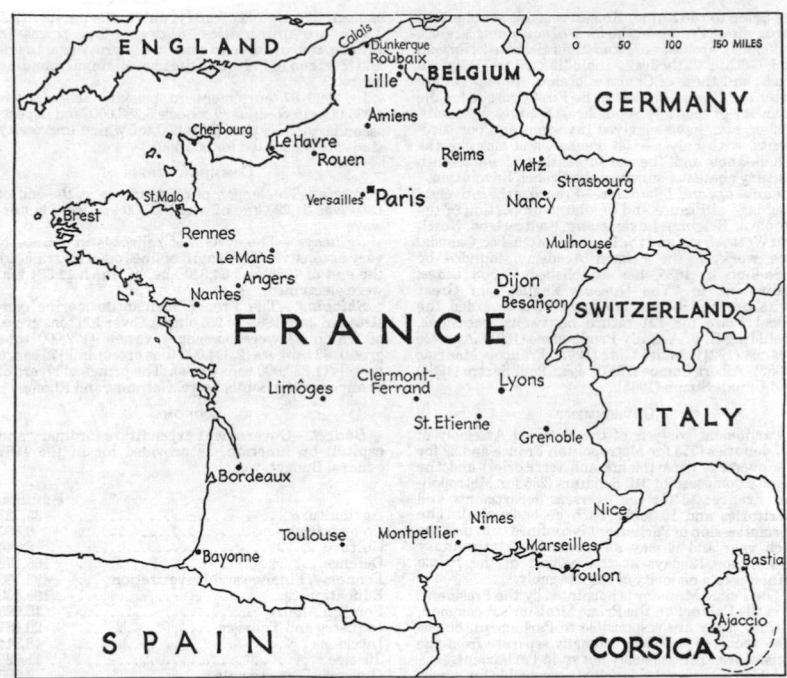

from 7° 85′ E. to 4° 45′ W. long. Its area is estimated at 211,208 sq. miles (547,026 sq. km.), divided into 95 departments, including the island of Corsica, in the Mediterranean, off the west coast of Italy. The population of France in 1987 was 55,600,000.

POPULATION OF THE REGIONS 1987
(Names of Departments in brackets)

Alsace (Bas-Rhin, Haut-Rhin)	1,605,000
Aquitaine (Dordogne, Gironde, Landes, Lot-et-Garonne, Pyrénées-Atlantiques)	2,708,000
Auvergne (Allier, Cantal, Haute-Loire, Puy-de-Dôme)	1,329,000
Basse-Normandie (Calvados, Manche, Orne)	1,374,000
Bourgogne (Côte-d'Or, Nièvre, Saône-et-Loire, Yonne)	1,604,000
Bretagne (Côtes-du-Nord, Finistère, Ille-et-Vilaine, Morbihan)	2,767,000
Centre (Cher, Eure-et-Loir, Indre, Indre-et-Loire, Loir-et-Cher, Loiret)	2,333,000
Champagne-Ardenne (Ardennes, Aube, Marne, Haute-Marne)	1,359,000
Corse (Corse-du-Sud, Haute-Corse)	243,000
Franche-Comté (Doubs, Haute-Saône, Jura, Territoire-de-Belfort)	1,099,000
Haute-Normandie (Eure, Seine-Maritime)	1,685,000
Île-de-France (Essonne, Hauts-de-Seine, Seine-et-Marne, Seine-St-Denis, Val-de-Marne, Val-d'Oise, Ville de Paris, Yvelines)	10,290,000
Languedoc-Roussillon (Aude, Gard, Hérault, Lozère, Pyrénées-Orientales)	2,072,000
Limousin (Corrèze, Creuse, Haute-Vienne)	735,000
Lorraine (Meurthe-et-Moselle, Meuse, Moselle, Vosges)	2,320,000
Midi-Pyrénées (Ariège, Aveyron, Haute-Garonne, Gers, Lot, Hautes-Pyrénées, Tarn, Tarn-et-Garonne)	2,370,000
Nord-Pas-de-Calais (Nord, Pas-de-Calais)	3,923,000
Pays de la Loire (Loire-Atlantique, Maine-et-Loire, Mayenne, Sarthe, Vendée)	3,013,000
Picardie (Aisne, Oise, Somme)	1,787,000
Poitou-Charentes (Charente, Charente-Maritime, Deux-Sèvres, Vienne)	1,601,000
Provence-Alpes-Côte d'Azur (Alpes-de-Haute-Provence, Alpes-Maritime, Bouches-du-Rhône, Haute-Alpes, Var, Vaucluse)	4,116,000
Rhône-Alpes (Ain, Ardèche, Drôme, Isère, Loire, Rhône, Savoie, Haute-Savoie)	5,177,000

Archaeology, etc.—There are dolmens and menhirs in Brittany, prehistoric remains and cave drawings in Dordogne and Ariège, and throughout France various megalithic monuments erected by primitive tribes, predecessors of Iberian invaders from Spain (now represented by the Basques), Ligurians from northern Italy and Celts or Gauls from the valley of the Danube. Julius Cæsar found Gaul "divided into three parts" and described three political groups—Aquitanians south of the Garonne, Celts between the Garonne and the Seine and Marne, and Belgae from the Seine to the Rhine. Roman remains are plentiful throughout France in the form of aqueducts, arenas, triumphal arches, etc., and the celebrated Norman and Gothic Cathedrals, including Notre Dame in Paris, and those of Chartres, Reims, Amiens (where Peter the Hermit preached the First Crusade for the recovery of the Holy Sepulchre), Bourges, Beauvais, Rouen, etc., have survived invasions and bombardments, with only partial damage, and many of the renaissance and the seventeenth and eighteenth century chateaux survived the French Revolution.

Language and Literature.—French is the universal language of France and of a large proportion of the people of Belgium, Luxembourg, Switzerland, North and West Africa, and the Province of Quebec, Canada. The work of the French Academy, founded by Richelieu in 1635, has established *le bon usage*, equivalent to "The Queen's English" in Great Britain. French authors have been awarded the Nobel Prize for Literature on twelve occasions, including R. F. A. Sully-Prudhomme (1901), Anatole France (1921), André Gide (1947), François Mauriac (1952), Albert Camus (1957), Jean Paul Sartre (1964) and Claude Simon (1985).

GOVERNMENT

Parliament consists of the National Assembly of 577 deputies (555 for Metropolitan France and 22 for the overseas departments and territories) and the Senate composed of 319 Senators (296 for Metropolitan France; 13 for the overseas departments and territories and 10 for French dependencies). The normal session of Parliament is confined to 5½ months each year and it may also meet in extraordinary session for 12 days at the request of the Prime Minister or a majority of the Assembly.

The Prime Minister is appointed by the President, as is the Cabinet on the Prime Minister's recommendation. They are responsible to Parliament, but as the executive is constitutionally separate from the legislature Ministers may not sit in Parliament.

A Constitutional Council is responsible for supervising all elections and referenda and must be consulted on all constitutional matters and before the President of the Republic assumes emergency powers.

DEFENCE

The personnel of the Defence Forces in 1985 totalled 464,000. National nuclear forces include medium-range ballistic missiles, submarine-launched ballistic missiles and *Mirage* IV medium bombers. The Army has a variety of new French-made equipment in service, including medium tanks, field and anti-aircraft SP guns, trucks and radio equipment. Defence Budget for 1988, 174,276 million francs.

EDUCATION

The educational system is highly centralized and is administered by the Ministry of National Education. Local Administration comprises 25 Territorial Academies, with inspecting staff for all grades, and Departmental Councils presided over by the *Préfet*, and charged especially with primary education.

Primary and secondary education are compulsory, free and secular, the school age being from 6 to 16. Schools may be single-sex or co-educational. Primary education is given in nursery schools, primary schools and *collèges d'enseignement général* (4-year secondary modern course); secondary education in *collèges d'enseignement technique*, *collèges d'enseignement secondaire* and *lycées* (7-year course leading to one of the five *baccalauréats*). Special schools are numerous.

There are many *Grandes Ecoles* in France which award diplomas in many subjects not taught at university, especially applied science and engineering. Most of them are State institutions but have a competitive system of entry, unlike the universities. There are universities in twenty-four towns in France, two or three in some major provincial towns and thirteen in Paris and the immediate surrounding district.

In 1986–87 enrolment in primary schools was 4,335,000; in secondary schools 5,388,000, and in post-secondary education 1,234,800 (of which university students accounted for 903,500).

COMMUNICATIONS

Roads.—The length of roads in use at the end of 1986 was 34,293 km. of which 6,300 km. were motorways.

Railways.—The system of railroads in France is very extensive. The length of lines open for traffic at the end of 1986 was 34,640 km., of which 11,584 km. were electrified.

Shipping.—The French mercantile marine consisted in Jan. 1988, of 261 ships of over 100 tons gross, of which 27 were passenger vessels (172,000 tons gross), 62 tankers (2,394,000 tons gross) and 172 cargo vessels (1,823,000 tons gross). The principal rivers of France are the Seine, Loire, Garonne, and Rhône.

ECONOMY

Budget.—Government expenditure (ordinary and capital) by function, as provided for in the 1987 general Budget, was:

	F million
Agriculture	35,723
Co-operation	6,830
Culture	8,844
Defence	165,176
Economy, Finance and Privatization	493,765
Education	195,830
Foreign Affairs	10,095
Industry and Tourism	20,687
Interior	48,811
Justice	11,927
Overseas Departments	2,090
Prime Ministerial	2,515
The Sea	5,823
Social Affairs and Employment	111,990
Town Planning and Housing	51,136
Transport	42,762
Veterans	26,226
Youth and Sports	2,120
Total	1,242,350

PRODUCTION

Agriculture.—Approximately 31,444,000 hectares of land is used for agricultural purposes, 14,618,000 hectares is forested. Production in 1987 included wheat, 27,414,700 tonnes; sugar-beet, 25,739,160 tonnes; maize, 12,040,300 tonnes; barley, 10,489,020 tonnes; and potatoes 6,719,970 tonnes.

The vine is extensively cultivated, regions famous for their wines including Bordeaux, Burgundy and Champagne. Production of wine in 1985 was 15,918,121 hectolitres. Cognac, liqueurs and cider are also important products.

Energy.—France produces its own oil, the greater part coming from fields in the Landes area, but is a net importer of crude oil, for processing by its important oil-refining industry. Natural gas is produced in the foothills of the Pyrenees. Electricity production was 359,900 GWh in 1987, of which 19·9 per cent was hydro-electric, 69·9 per cent nuclear, and 10·2 per cent thermal power.

Industry.—France's heavy industries include oil-refining and the production of iron and steel, and aluminium. In 1987 production of steel was 16,500,000 tonnes, cement 23,600,000 tonnes and paper products 5,700,000 tonnes. Other important industries produce chemicals, tyres, aluminium, textiles, and processed food. Engineering products include motor vehicles, and television and radio sets.

TRADE

The principal imports are raw materials for the heavy and manufacturing industries (e.g. oil, minerals, chemicals), machinery and precision instruments, agricultural products and vehicles. Raw materials, semi-manufactured and manufactured goods are also France's principal exports. Other member countries of the E.C. are France's main trading partners.

TOTAL TRADE

	1986	1987
	Francs	Francs
Imports	887,502 m.	944,900 m.
Exports	825,417 m.	857,800 m.

Trade with U.K.

	1987	1988
Imports from U.K.	£7,781,546,000	£8,270,408,000
Exports to U.K.	8,381,984,000	9,390,207,000

CAPITAL.—Paris, on the Seine. Population (census, 1982), 2,176,243 (town); 8,706,963 (incl. suburbs).

The largest conurbations (populations, 1982) are ΨMarseilles (1,111,000); Lyons (1,221,000); Toulouse (541,000); Lille (936,000) and ΨBordeaux (640,000).

The chief towns of Corsica are ΨAjaccio (55,279) and ΨBastia (45,081).

CURRENCY.—French franc of 100 centimes.

FLAG.—The tricolour, three vertical bands, blue, white, red (blue next to flagstaff).

NATIONAL ANTHEM.—La Marseillaise.

NATIONAL DAY.—July 14 (Bastille Day, 1789).

BRITISH EMBASSY

35 rue du Faubourg St. Honoré, 75383 Paris Cedex 08
[Paris 42 66 91 42]

Ambassador Extraordinary and Plenipotentiary, His Excellency Sir Ewen Alastair John Fergusson, K.C.M.G. (1987).

Minister, M. J. Llewellyn Smith, C.M.G.

Defence and Air Attaché, Air Cdre. B. N. J. Speed, O.B.E.

Counsellor and Head of Chancery, J. Q. Greenstock.

Consul-General, J. Daly.

BRITISH CONSULAR OFFICES

There are British Consulates-General in Metropolitan France at *Bordeaux, Lille, Lyons, Marseilles* and *Paris.*

BRITISH COUNCIL

Representative in Paris, P. J. Prescott, 9 rue de Constantine, 75007 Paris.

There are British Council libraries at *Bordeaux, Lille, Lyons, Marseilles* and *Paris.*

FRANCO-BRITISH CHAMBER OF COMMERCE
8 rue Cimarosa, 75116 Paris

President, R. Mitchell.

Vice-Presidents, R. Lyon; R. King.

OVERSEAS DEPARTMENTS

Legislation passed in Dec. 1982 by the French Parliament granted greater powers of self-government to four of the five overseas departments—French Guiana, Guadeloupe, Martinique and Réunion. These former colonies had enjoyed departmental status since 1947 and the status of regions of France since 1974. Elections to their new directly-elected Assemblies were held in each department in Feb. 1983 and the Assemblies will operate in parallel with the existing, indirectly constituted Regional Councils. The French government is represented by a Commissioner.

French Guiana.—Situated on the north-eastern coast of South America, French Guiana is flanked by Suriname on the west and by Brazil on the south and east. Area, 34,749 sq. miles (90,000 sq. km.). Population (1986 estimate), 86,000. Capital, ΨCayenne (38,135). Under the administration of French Guiana is a group of islands (St. Joseph, Ile Royal and Ile du Diable), known as Iles du Salut. On Devil's Isle, Captain Dreyfus was imprisoned from 1894 to 1899.

Commissioner, J. Dewatre.

Guadeloupe.—A number of islands in the Leeward Islands group of the West Indies, consisting of the two main islands of Guadeloupe (or Basse-Terre) and Grande-Terre, with the adjacent islands of Marie-Galante, La Désirade and Îles des Saintes, and the islands of St. Martin and St. Barthélemy over 150 miles to the north-west. Area, 687 sq. miles (1,779 sq. km.). Population (1986 estimate), 334,000. Capital Ψ Basse Terre (15,778) in Guadeloupe. Other towns are ΨPointe à Pitre (23,889) on Grande-Terre and Ψ Grand Bourg (6,611) in Marie Galante.

Commissioner, Y. Bonnet.

Martinique.—An island situated in the Windward Islands group of the West Indies, between Dominica in the north and St. Lucia in the south. Area, 425 sq. miles (1,102 sq. km.). Population (1986), 331,000. Capital ΨFort de France (100,576). Other towns are ΨTrinité (11,214) and ΨMarin (6,104).

Commissioner, E. Lacroix.

Réunion.—Réunion, which became a French possession in 1638, lies in the Indian Ocean, about 569 miles east of Madagascar and 110 miles S.W. of Mauritius. Area, 969 sq. miles (2,510 sq. km.). Population (1986 estimate), 555,000. Capital, St. Denis (109,072).

Commissioner, J. Anciaux.

Also lying in the Indian Ocean adjacent to Madagascar are the smaller, uninhabited islands of Bassas da India, Europa, Îles Glorieuses, Juan de Nova and Tromelin, which are administered from Réunion.

TERRITORIAL COLLECTIVITÉS

Mayotte.—Area, 144 sq. miles (372 sq. km.). Population (1985 estimate), 67,000. Capital, Mamoundzou (12,000). Part of the Comoros Islands group, Mayotte remained a French dependency when the other 3 islands became independent as the Comoros Republic in 1975. Since 1976 the island has been a *collectivité territoriale*, an intermediate status between Overseas Department and Overseas Territory.

Commissioner, A. Khider.

St. Pierre and Miquelon—Area, 93 sq. miles (242 sq. km.). Population (1987), 6,500. Two small groups of Islands off the coast of Newfoundland. Became a *collectivité territoriale* in June 1985.

Commissioner, J.-R. Garnier.

OVERSEAS TERRITORIES

French Polynesia.—Five archipelagos in the south Pacific, comprising the Society Islands (Windward Islands group includes Tahiti, Moorea, Makatea, Mehetia, Tetiaroa, Tubai Manu, etc: Leeward Islands group includes Huahine, Raiatea, Tahaa, Bora-Bora, Maupiti, etc.), the Tuamotu Islands (Rangiroa, Hao, Turéia, etc.), the Gambier Islands (Mangareva, etc.), the Tubuai Islands (Rimatara, Rurutu, Tubuai, Raivavae, Rapa, etc.) and the Marquesas Islands (Nuku-Hiva, Hiva-Oa, Fatu-Hiva, Tahuata, Ua Huka, etc.). Area, 1,544 sq. miles (4,000 sq. km.). Population (1985 estimate) 172,000. Capital, ΨPapeete (22,967) in Tahiti. Economy based on tourism and exports of copra, coffee, vanilla, citrus fruits and cultured pearls.

High Commissioner, J. Montpezat.

New Caledonia.—A large island in the Western Pacific, 700 miles E. of Queensland. Dependencies are the Isles of Pines, the Loyalty Islands (Mahé, Lifou, Urea, etc.), the Bélep Archipelago, the Chesterfield Islands, the Huon Islands and Walpole. New Caledonia was discovered in 1774 and annexed by France in 1854; from 1871 to 1896 it was a convict settlement. A referendum in 1987 on the question of independence for New Caledonia was boycotted by the indigenous Kanaks, and New Caledonia therefore voted to remain French. However, a new independence referendum has been promised for 1998. Area, 7,358 sq. miles (19,058 sq. km.). Population (1985 U.N. estimate), 153,000. Capital ΨNoumea (60,112). It is one of the world's largest producers of nickel.

High Commissioner, B. Grasset.

Southern and Antarctic Territories.—Created in 1955 from the former Réunion dependencies, the territory comprises the islands of New Amsterdam (25 sq. miles) and St. Paul (2·7 sq. miles), the Kerguelen Islands (2,700 sq. miles) and Crozet Islands (116 sq. miles) archipelagos and Adélie Land (116,800 sq. miles) in the Antarctic continent. The only population are members of staff of the scientific stations.

Wallis and Futuna Islands.—Two groups of islands (the Wallis Archipelago and the Îles du Hooru) in the central Pacific, N.E. of Fiji. Area, 106 sq. miles (274 sq. km.). Population (estimate 1985) 13,100. Capital, Mata-Utu on Urea, the main island of the Wallis group.

THE FRENCH COMMUNITY

The Constitution of the fifth French Republic promulgated on Oct. 6, 1958, envisaged the establishment of a French Community of States closely linked with common institutions. A number of the former French States in Africa have seceded from the Community but for all practical purposes continue to enjoy the same close links with France as those that remain formally members of the French Community. The Community Institutions in fact never operated as envisaged. Nevertheless, with the exception of Guinea, which opted out of the Community in the 1958 referendum, all the former French African colonies are closely linked to France by a series of financial, technical and economic agreements.

FRANCOPHONE COUNTRIES

In the following countries French is either the official or national language or the language of instruction; where there is another national language the name of it is shown after the name of the country:—Algeria (*Arabic*); Belgium (*Flemish*); Benin; Burkina; Burundi (*Kirundi*); Cameroon (*English*); parts of Canada (in Quebec, parts of Ontario and New Brunswick) (*English*); Central African Republic (*Sangho*); Chad; Congo; Côte d'Ivoire; France; Gabon; Guinea; Haiti (*Creole*); Kampuchea (*Khmer*); Laos (*Laotian*); Lebanon (*Arabic*); Luxembourg (*German and Letzeburgesch*); Madagascar (*Malagasy*); Mali; Morocco (*Arabic*); Mauritania (*Arabic*); Niger; Rwanda (*Kinyarwanda*); Senegal; Switzerland (1,000,000 French speaking); Togo; Tunisia (*Arabic*); Vietnam (*Vietnamese*); Zaire. French is also spoken in the Overseas Departments (*see* above).

GABON
(République Gabonaise)

President, El Hadj Omar Bongo, *assumed office*, Dec. 1967, *re-elected*, Feb. 1973, Dec. 1979 and Nov. 1986.

MINISTERS
(since Aug. 1988)

Prime Minister, L. Mébiame.
First Deputy P.M., Minister for Transport, Water, Forests and Social Communications, G. Rawiri.
Second Deputy P.M., Minister for Mines and Hydrocarbons, E.-G. Mouvagha Tchioba.
Third Deputy P.M., Minister for the Civil Service and Administrative Reform, E. Kassa Mapsi.
Fourth Deputy P.M., Minister for Housing and Town Planning, S. Essimengane.
Foreign Affairs and Co-operation, M. Bongo.
Public Lands and Registration, and Law of the Sea, H. Minko.
Secretary General to the Presidency, R. R. Coniquet.
Higher Education and Scientific Research, J. B. Ogouliguende.
Industry and Consumer Affairs, E. Moussirou.
Territorial Administration, Local Collectives and Immigration, R. Nguema Bekale.
Commerce, Technology Transfer and Rationalization, J.-F. Ntoutoume-Emane.
Culture and Arts, F. Owono-Nguema.
Defence, Veterans' Affairs and Public Security, J. Mpouho-Epigat.
Justice, Mrs. S. Ngwamassana.
Information, Post and Telecommunications, Z. Myboto.
Finance, Budget and State Shareholdings, J.-P. Lemboumba-Le-Pandou.
Public Works and Construction, Gen. J.-B. Assele.
Planning and Economy, P. Nze.
Agriculture, Livestock and Rural Development, M. Anchouey.
Education, G. Nzouba.
Labour and Employment, L.-G. Mayila.
Civil and Commercial Aviation, M. Essonghe.
Public Health and Population, J.-P. Okias.
Social Affairs, Natural Disasters and Social Security, S. Oyouomi.
Youth and Sports, V. Afene.
State Control, E. Mbot.
Professional Training and Handicrafts, J.-J. Amiar Nganga.
Energy and Water Resources, D. Di Dinge.
Small and Medium-Sized Enterprises, E. Nze-Bekale.
Environment and Conservation, Dr. H. Moutsinga.
Tourism, A. Sambat.

EMBASSY OF THE REPUBLIC OF GABON
48 Kensington Court, W8 5DB
[01–937 5285/6]

Ambassador Extraordinary and Plenipotentiary, His Excellency Charles Mamadou Diop (1986).

Gabon lies on the Atlantic coast of Africa at the Equator and is flanked on the north by Equatorial Guinea and Cameroon and on the east and south by the People's Republic of Congo. It has an area of 103,347 sq. miles (267,667 sq. km.) and a population (1985 U.N. estimate) of 1,151,000. Gabon elected on Nov. 28, 1958, to remain an autonomous republic within the French Community and was proclaimed fully independent on August 17, 1960.

The Constitution provides for an Executive President directly elected for a seven-year term, who appoints the Council of Ministers. There is a unicameral National Assembly comprising 84 members directly elected for a five-year term and nine members nominated by the President. The sole legal party is the *Parti democratique gabonais*.

Gabon's economy remains heavily dependent on oil, and, to a much lesser extent, other mineral resources, including manganese and uranium. Gabon has considerable timber reserves (particularly Okoumé) although production in this industry has stagnated in recent years.

The economy, which experienced considerable growth in real terms from the mid-1970s onwards, has since 1986 been adversely affected by the fall in oil prices. As a result government spending is expected to remain at a reduced level until 1989.

Gabon is a full member of OPEC.

Trade with U.K.

	1987	1988
Imports from U.K.	£11,962,000	£18,808,000
Exports to U.K.	5,357,000	5,091,000

CAPITAL.—ΨLibreville (251,000).
CURRENCY.—Franc C.F.A. of 100 centimes.
FLAG.—Horizontal bands, green, yellow and blue.
NATIONAL ANTHEM.—"La Concorde".
NATIONAL DAY.—August 17.

BRITISH EMBASSY
B.P. 476, Libreville
[Libreville 74 31 83]

Ambassador Extraordinary and Plenipotentiary, His Excellency Mark Aubrey Goodfellow (1986).
Second Secretary, I. M. Thom.

GERMANY
* Deutsches Reich (German Realm)

The term "deutsch" (German) probably began to be used in the 8th century and initially described the language spoken in the eastern part of the Frankish realm which reached its apogee in Charlemagne's reign, subsequently being divided into an eastern and western realm whose political and linguistic borders coincided. Then the term was transferred from the language to its speakers, and ultimately to the region they lived in. The first German realm was the Holy Roman Empire, established in A.D. 962 when Otto I of Saxony was crowned Emperor. The Empire endured until 1806, but from as early as the 12th century the achievement of a national state was prevented by territorial fragmentation into small principalities and dukedoms, the gradually increasing autonomy of their rulers weakening the central power.

The Holy Roman Empire was replaced by a loose association of the individual sovereign states known as the German Confederation, which survived until 1866 when it was dissolved and replaced by the Prussian-dominated North German Federation. Prussia, directed by its Prime Minister (later Chancellor) Otto von Bismarck, had translated its earlier economic predominance amongst the German states into political hegemony by the annexation of the duchies of Schleswig and Holstein from Denmark in 1864 and a decisive defeat of Austria in 1866 (the Seven Weeks' War) which ended Austrian influence over German politics. After the Franco-Prussian War of 1870–71 resulted in the defeat of France and the cession of Alsace and Lorraine, the south German principalities united with the northern federation to form a second German Empire, the King of Prussia being proclaimed Emperor at Versailles on Jan. 18, 1871.

Germany's defeat in the 1914–18 War led to the abdication of the Emperor and the princes, and the country became a Republic. The 1919 Treaty of Versailles returned Alsace and Lorraine to France, large areas in the east of the country were lost to the newly created state of Poland, and all German colonies placed under the administration of other countries. The world economic crisis of 1929 led to

---

* Nazi historians referred to the National Socialist regime as *Drittes Reich*.

the collapse of the Weimar Republic and the subsequent rise to power of the National Socialist movement of Adolf Hitler, who became Chancellor in 1933.

THE WAR OF 1939–1945.—After concluding a Treaty of Non-Aggression with Soviet Russia (Aug. 24, 1939), Germany invaded Poland (Sept. 1, 1939), thus precipitating war with France and Great Britain, which had (March 31) given a pledge to support Poland against aggression.

Hitler committed suicide on April 30, 1945. On May 8, 1945, the unconditional surrender of all German forces was accepted by representatives of the Western Allied and Soviet Supreme Commanders.

THE POST WAR PERIOD.—After the surrender the Allied Powers exercised supreme authority in Germany on lines laid down in the Potsdam agreement (August 1945) between the U.K., U.S.A. and U.S.S.R. Power was exercised by the Commanders-in-Chief, each in his own zone of occupation and jointly in matters affecting Germany as a whole through a Control Council. Berlin was governed jointly by the four occupying powers. The agreement also provided for the total disarmament and demilitarization of Germany, the destruction of the National Socialist German Workers' Party, the decentralization of the economy and the construction of a democratic constitution. No central German government was permitted but central German administration was established in the fields of finance, industry, foreign trade, transport and communications as support organs for the Control Council. The Potsdam agreement was to have been confirmed or revised by a peace treaty but no treaty has been drawn up. Some provisions of the Potsdam agreement were carried out but differences in interpretation among the Allies made it impossible to implement in full and the system of quadripartite control broke down when the Russians withdrew from the Control Council in March 1948.

FEDERAL REPUBLIC OF GERMANY
(Bundesrepublik Deutschland)

Federal President, Dr. Richard von Weizsäcker, *born* 1920, *elected* May 22, 1984, *re-elected* May 23, 1989, *sworn in*, July 1, 1989, *for five years*.

CABINET

Federal Chancellor, Dr. Helmut Kohl (*CDU*).
Foreign Minister and Vice-Chancellor, Hans Dietrich Genscher (*FDP*).
Interior, Wolfgang Schäuble (*CDU*).
Justice, Hans Engelhard (*FDP*).
Finance, Theodor Waigel (*CSU*).
Economics, Helmut Haussmann (*FDP*).
Food, Agriculture and Forestry, Ignaz Kiechle (*CSU*).
Intra-German Relations, Dr. Dorothee Wilms (*CDU*).
Labour and Social Affairs, Dr. Norbert Blüm (*CDU*).
Defence, Dr. Gerhard Stoltenberg (*CDU*).
Youth, Family Affairs, Women and Health, Prof. Dr. Ursula Lehr (*CDU*).
Transport, Dr. Friedrich Zimmermann (*CSU*).
Environment, Nature Conservation and Reactor Safety, Prof. Klaus Töpfer (*CDU*).
Posts and Telecommunications, Dr. Christian Schwarz-Schilling (*CDU*).
Regional Planning, Building and Urban Development, Gerda Hasselfeldt (*CSU*).
Research and Technology, Dr. Heinz Riesenhuber (*CDU*).
Education and Science, Jürgen Möllemann (*FDP*).
Economic Co-operation, Dr. Jürgen Warnke (*CSU*).
Federal Minister at the Chancellery, Rudolf Seiters (*CDU*)

Federal Minister and Government Spokesman, Dr. Hans Klein (*CSU*).

CDU = Christian Democratic Union; *CSU* = Christian Social Union; *FDP* = Free Democratic Party.

EMBASSY OF THE FEDERAL REPUBLIC OF GERMANY
23 Belgrave Square, SW1X 8PZ
[01–235 5033]

Ambassador Extraordinary and Plenipotentiary, His Excellency Baron Hermann von Richthofen (1988).
Minister Plenipotentiary, Helmut Wegner.
Minister-Counsellor, Dr.Klaus-Peter Klaiber, C.M.G.
First Counsellors, B. Weber (*Head of Press Dept.*); Dr. O. Roever (*Head of Economic Dept.*); E.-O. Bitzegeio (*Defence Research*); D. Greineder (*Scientific Affairs*); Dr. R. Peters (*Agriculture*).

NOTE.—Except where otherwise indicated statistical data on the Federal Republic of Germany include Berlin (West).

Area and Population.—The area of the Federal Republic is approximately 95,976 sq. miles (248,577 sq. km.). Total population of the Federal Republic at April 1987 was 61,149,000. Distribution of the population among the *Länder* at end 1987 was:

Baden-Württemberg	9,327,000
Bavaria	11,026,000
Berlin (West)	1,879,000
Bremen	654,000
Hamburg	1,571,000
Hesse	5,544,000
Lower Saxony	7,196,000
North Rhine Westphalia	16,677,000
Rhineland Palatinate	3,611,000
Saarland	1,042,000
Schleswig-Holstein	2,613,000

Vital Statistics.—There were 10·8 live births per 1,000 inhabitants in the Federal Republic in 1988.

Government.—The Federal Republic grew out of the fusion of the three western zones. The economic union of the U.K. and U.S. zones was later joined by the French zone and in 1948–49 Parliamentary Council, elected by the parliaments of the *Länder* in the three zones, drafted a provisional democratic federal constitution for Germany. This Basic Law came into force in the three western zones on May 23, 1949. When the Federal Government took office the Allied Military Governors were replaced by High Commissioners. In 1952 a contractual agreement was signed between the Federal Republic and the western

Allies, whereby the Republic, in return for certain promises regarding a defence contribution, a foreign debt settlement, and the continuation of allied policies concerning decartelization, democratization, restitution, etc., regained virtual sovereignty in May, 1955, after ratification by all the parties concerned. The High Commissioners then became Ambassadors.

The Basic Law provides for a President, elected for a five-year term, a Lower House (*Bundestag*), with a four-year term of office, elected by direct universal suffrage, and an Upper House (*Bundesrat*) composed of 45 delegates of the *Länder*, without a fixed term of office.

The results of the elections held for the lower House (*Bundestag*) on Jan. 25, 1987, were as follows:

Party	Numbers
Social Democrats	186
Christian Democratic Union	174
Christian Social Union	49
Free Democrats	46
The Greens	42

with an additional 22 representatives of Berlin elected by the House of Representatives of Berlin (CDU 11; SPD 7; FDP 2; Alternative Liste 2).

The Prime Ministers of the *Länder* governments in July 1989, were:

Ministers-President

Baden-Württemberg.—Lothar Späth.
Bavaria.—Max Streibl.
Berlin.—Walter Momper (*Governing Mayor*).
Bremen.—Klaus Wedemeier (*Mayor*).
Hamburg.—Henning Voscherau (*First Mayor*).
Hesse.—Dr. Walter Wallmann.
Lower Saxony.—Dr. Ernst Albrecht.
North Rhine-Westphalia.—Johannes Rau.
Rhineland-Palatinate.—Ludwig Wagner.
Saarland.—Oskar Lafontaine.
Schleswig-Holstein.—Björn Engholm.

Law and Justice.—Judicial authority is exercised by the Federal Constitutional Court, the Federal courts provided for in the Basic Law and the courts of the Länder.

The death sentence has been abolished.

ECONOMY

Despite the difficulties arising from the division of Germany, which cut off from the Federal Republic the main food-producing areas of Eastern Germany and some of the principal centres of light industry, Germany has regained her position as the main industrial power on the Continent, and is the most economically powerful member of the European Community. The Gross National Product at current prices in 1988 was estimated at DM2,121,500 million, an increase of 5 per cent in nominal terms over 1987. In real terms GNP grew by 3·4 per cent, after a 1·8 per cent growth in 1987. Forecasts for real growth in 1989 range from 2·5 to 3 per cent.

Agriculture.—In 1987 total area of farmland was 11,956,000 hectares, of which 7,269,700 hectares were arable land. Forest areas cover 7,360,000 hectares.

Crop yields were (tonnes):

	1986	1987
Rye	1,768,300	1,599,000
Wheat	10,406,200	9,931,600
Maslin	49,400	45,700
Barley	9,377,100	8,571,300
Oats	2,276,000	2,008,000
Potatoes	7,390,300	6,836,100
Sugar beet	20,260,000	19,049,000
Colza and rape	968,900	1,264,600
Fruit	3,478,527	2,043,897

Milk production in 1987 was 24,436,000 tonnes. Total yield of fisheries was 159,616 tonnes, valued at DM229,508,000.

Industrial Production.—The Federal Republic has a predominantly industrial economy. Principal industries are coal mining, iron and steel production, machine construction, the electrical industry, the manufacture of steel and metal products, chemicals and textiles, and the processing of foodstuffs. The index of industrial net production adjusted for irregularities of the calendar (1985 = 100) is as follows:

	1987	1988
Mining	91·6	87·4
Manufacturing industry	102·6	106·8
(i) Basic materials	99·3	105·6
(ii) Capital goods	104·8	108·4
(iii) Consumer goods	103·2	106·2
(iv) Foodstuffs	100·3	102·3
Power (electricity and gas)	103·0	105·2
Construction	105·7	110·6
Total industry	102·6	106·3

Annual production figures were:

	1987	1988
	Tonnes '000	
Hard coal	76,300	73,304
Brown coal	108,799	108,563
Crude petroleum	3,800	3,937
Pig iron	27,333	31,388
Raw steel	35,916	40,668
Rolled steel	27,440	30,385
Fuel oils	31,757	34,332
Petrol	18,598	19,662
Chemical fibres	985	996
Cement	25,243	26,412
	Number	
Passenger cars	4,008,000	3,978,000
Televisions	3,454,000	3,706,000

Labour.—Labour figures, in annual averages, were:

	1987	1988
Employment	26,007,000	26,160,000
Unemployed	2,229,000	2,242,000
Men	1,207,000	1,199,000
Youths under 20	128,000	106,000
Foreign Workers	1,577,000	n/a

FINANCE

Federal Finance Plan 1988–1990

	1988 Plan	1989 Draft	1990
	DM billion		
Expenditure	275·40	288·15	293·8
Percentage increase on previous year	+2·40	+4·60	+2·0
Revenue	236·80	256·18	257·8
Tax revenue	217·90	234·00	233·7
Other revenue	18·86	22·18	24·1
Bundesbank	0·24	5·00	7·0
Privatization	2·50	0·30	—
Mint revenue	0·50	0·90	0·7
Borrowing requirement	38·60	31·97	36·0

TRADE

	1987	1988
	DM million	
Total imports	409,641·3	439,768·1
Total exports	527,376·7	567,750·1

Of 1988 imports, 12·1 per cent were foodstuffs and 6·3 per cent industrial raw materials in 1988. Main trading partners in 1988 were (figures shown as percentage of total trade):

	Imports	Exports
France	12·1	12·6
Netherlands	10·3	8·7
Italy	9·1	9·1
U.K.	6·9	9·3
Belg./Lux.	7·1	7·4
U.S.A.	6·6	8·0
Japan	6·5	2·3

Trade with U.K.

	1987	1988
Imports from U.K	£9,404,257,000	£9,521,851,000
Exports to U.K.	15,783,904,000	17,667,097,000

Communications.—At the end of 1986 the state-owned railways of the Federal Republic (*Deutsche Bundesbahn*) measured 27,500 kilometres of which 11,426 kilometres were electrified, and the privately owned railways 2,918 kilometres, a total of 30,418 kilometres. Railway rolling stock included, in 1986, 2,620 electric locomotives, 4,295 diesel locomotives and 253,200 goods waggons; in 1986 the railways handled 316·8 million tonnes of goods. Classified roads measured 173,478 kilometres in 1987, of which motorways were 8,437 kilometres. The total number of motor vehicles registered at the beginning of 1989 was 30 million. Ocean-going shipping under the German flag in Dec., 1986, amounted to 5,290,000 tons gross. Inland waterways handled 229,494,000 tonnes of goods in 1986.

Social Welfare.—There is compulsory insurance against sickness, accident, old age and unemployment. Children's allowances are payable in respect of all children. Pension schemes for widows and orphans of public servants are in operation. Public assistance is given to persons unable to earn their living, or with insufficient income to maintain a decent standard of living.

Education.—School attendance is compulsory for all children and juveniles between the ages of 6 and 18 and comprises 9 years full-time compulsory education at primary and main schools (*Grund und Hauptschulen*) and 3 years of compulsory vocational education on a part-time basis. In autumn, 1986, there were in the Federal Republic 21,119 primary and main schools (*Grund und Hauptschulen*) with 3,722,748 pupils. Secondary modern schools (*Realschulen*) numbered 2,609 with 975,485 pupils. There were 2,808 other general secondary schools (*Gymnasien* including *Gesamtschulen*) with 1,893,866 pupils.

There were also 2,824 special schools (*Sonderschulen*) for retarded, physically and mentally handicapped and socially maladjusted children in the Federal Republic with 261,461 pupils.

The secondary school leaving examination (*Abitur*) entitles the holder to a place of study at a university or another institution of higher education.

Children below the age of 18 who are not attending a general secondary or a full-time vocational school are obliged to take a three-year course (part-time) at a vocational school. In November, 1986, there were 2,830 full and part-time vocational schools (*Berufsschulen*) with 1,972,139 pupils and 298 vocational extension schools (*Berufsaufbauschulen*) with 8,132 pupils, 2,316 full-time vocational schools (*Berufsfachschulen*) with 318,640 pupils, 969 schools for secondary technical studies (*Fachoberschulen/Fachgymnasien*) with 196,206 students.

Results for the winter term 1987–88 show a total of 1,410,789 students at institutions of higher education, of whom 953,839 were attending universities. The largest universities are in Munich, Berlin, Hamburg, Bonn and Cologne.

Language and Literature.—Modern (or New High) German has developed from the time of the Reforma-

tion to the present day, with differences of dialect in Austria and Alsace and in the German-speaking cantons of Switzerland. The literary language is usually regarded as having become fixed by Luther and Zwingli at the Reformation, since which time many great names occur in all branches, notably philosophy, from Leibnitz (1646–1716) to Kant (1724–1804), Fichte (1762–1814), Schelling (1775–1854) and Hegel (1770–1831); the drama from Goethe (1749–1832) and Schiller (1759–1805) to Gerhart Hauptmann (1862–1946); and in poetry, Heine (1797–1856). German authors have received the Nobel Prize for Literature on seven occasions—Theodor Mommsen (1902), R. Eucken (1908), P. Heyse (1909), Gerhart Hauptmann (1912), Thomas Mann (1929), N. Sachs (1966) and Heinrich Böll (1972). In 1985 there were 382 daily papers.

Religion.—In 1970 there were 29,696,571 Protestants in the Republic, 27,060,826 Roman Catholics, 31,684 Jews and 3,861,518 others.

CAPITAL.—Bonn, in North Rhine Westphalia, 15 miles distant from Cologne. Population 291,400 (end Dec. 1986).

The population of the principal cities and towns in the Federal Republic at end Dec. 1986, was:

Berlin (West)	1,879,200	Dortmund ...	568,200
ψHamburg...	1,571,300	Stuttgart	565,500
Munich	1,274,700	Düsseldorf ...	560,600
Cologne	914,300	ψBremen	522,000
Essen	615,400	Duisburg	514,600
Frankfurt am		Hanover	505,700
Main......	592,400	Nuremberg ..	467,400

CURRENCY.—Deutsche mark (DM) of 100 pfennig.

FLAG.—Horizontal bars of black, red and gold.

NATIONAL ANTHEM.—"Einigkeit und Recht und Freiheit" (Unity, right and freedom).

NATIONAL DAY.—May 23.

BRITISH EMBASSY
Friedrich-Ebert-Allee 77, 5300 Bonn 1
[Bonn 23 40 61]

Ambassador Extraordinary and Plenipotentiary, His Excellency Sir Christopher Leslie George Mallaby, K.C.M.G. (1988).

Minister, Miss L. P. Neville Jones, C.M.G.

Counsellors, C. Budd (*Head of Chancery*); B. H. Dinwiddy; Miss A. Walker (*Defence Supply*); D. S. Broucher (*Economic*); R. F. Escritt (*Science and Technology*); A. L. Free-Gore (*Administration*); Mrs. A. Le Sage (*Labour*).

First Secretaries, D. M. Bell; R. E. Brinkley; R. W. Barnett; R. Weaver; V. Evans; D. J. Grieg; M. Uden; E. Jenkinson; M. Evans; P. Cunningham; D. A. Drake.

Legal Adviser, J. O. Hill.

Defence and Military Attaché, Brig. A. P. Sims.

Asst. Military Attaché, Lt. Col. J. D. Colson.

Naval Attaché, Capt. W. K. Hutchinson, R.N.

Asst. Naval Attaché, Lt. Cdr. T. J. Lankester.

Air Attaché, Air Cdre. B. T. Sills.

Head of Visa Section (Düsseldorf), P. Faulkner.

Chaplain, Rev. J. Newsome.

There are British Consulates-General at *Berlin, Düsseldorf, Frankfurt, Hamburg* and *Munich.*

BRITISH COUNCIL

Representative, T. Rutter, O.B.E., Hahnenstrasse 6, 5000 Cologne 1. Offices at *Berlin, Hamburg* and *Munich* and British Council libraries at all four centres.

BRITISH CHAMBER OF COMMERCE
Neumarkt 14, D-5000 Cologne 1.

Director, J. Parr.

G.O.C. British Sector, Maj.-Gen. R. J. S. Corbett.

Minister and Deputy Commandant, M. St. E. Burton, C.V.O.

Counsellor, R. H. Smith (*Political Adviser and Head of Chancery*).

GERMAN DEMOCRATIC REPUBLIC
(Deutsche Demokratische Republik)

COUNCIL OF STATE

Chairman, Erich Honecker.

Deputy Chairmen, Dr. Manfred Gerlach; Günter Maleuda; Gerald Götting; Prof. Heinrich Homann; Horst Sindermann; Willi Stoph; Egon Krenz; Günter Mittag.

Members, P. Florin; Prof. K. Hager; Frau B. Hanke; F. Kind; Prof. L. Kolditz; W. Krolikowski; Frau M. Müller; A. Pisnik; B. Quandt; Dr. K. Sorgenicht; P. Strauss; Frau I. Thiele; H. Tisch; Prof. J. Töpfer; Frau R. Walther; K. Anclam; W. Seifert.

Secretary, H. Eichler.

Head of the Chairman's Chancery, F.-J. Herrmann.

COUNCIL OF MINISTERS
(as at June 2, 1989)

Chairman, Willi Stoph.

Deputy Chairmen, Günther Kleiber; Alfred Neumann (*First Deputy Chairmen*); M. Flegel; H-J. Heusinger; W. Rauchfuss; Dr. H. Reichelt; G. Schürer; R. Schulze; H. Sölle; Dr. H. Weiz.

Agriculture, Forestry, and the Food Industry, Bruno Lietz.

Chemical Industry, Guenther Wyschofsky.

Coal and Energy, Wolfgang Mitzinger.

Construction Industry, Wolfgang Junker.

Culture, Hans-Joachim Hoffmann.

Defence, Heinz Kessler.

District-managed Industry and District-managed Food Industry, Udo-Dieter Wange.

Electrical Engineering and Electronics, Felix Meier.

Environmental Protection and Water Management, Hans Reichelt.

Finance, Ernst Hoefner.

Foreign Affairs, Oskar Fischer.

Foreign Trade, Gerhard Beil.

General Machinery, Agricultural Machinery and Equipment, Gerhard Trautenhahn.

Geology, Manfred Bochmann.

Glass and Ceramics, Karl Gruenheid.

Health, Ludwig Mecklinger.

Heavy Machinery and Equipment, Hans Joachim Lauck.

Interior, Friedrich Dickel.

Justice, Hans-Joachim Heusinger.

Light Industry, Werner Buschmann.

Machine Tools and Processing Machinery Manufacturing, Rudi Georgi.

Management of Materials, Wolfgang Rauchfuss.

Ore Mining, Metallurgy, and Potash, Kurt Singhuber.

Post and Telecommunications, Rudolph Schulze.

Public Education, Margot Honecker.

Science and Technology, Herbert Weiz.

State Security, Erich Mielke.

Trade and Supply, Gerhard Briksa.

Transportation, Otto Arndt.

University and Technical School Affairs, Hans-Joachim Böhme.

SOCIALIST UNITY PARTY OF GERMANY

Politbureau of the Central Committee, H. Axen; H.-J. Böhme; H. Dohlus; W. Eberlein; Prof. K. Hager; J. Herrmann; E. Honecker; W. Jarowinski; Gen. H. Kessler; G. Kleiber; E. Krenz; W. Krolikowski; S. Lorenz; E. Mielke; G. Mittag; E. Mückenberger; A. Neumann; G. Schabowski; H. Sindermann; W. Stoph; H. Tisch (*full members*); Frau I. Lange; G. Müller; Frau M. Müller; G. Schürer; W. Walde (*candidate members*).

Secretariat of the Central Committee, E. Honecker (*Secretary General*); H. Axen; H. Dohlus; Prof. K. Hager; J. Herrmann; W. Jarowinski; E. Krenz; W. Krolikowski; I. Lange; G. Mittag; G. Schabowski (*secretaries*).

EMBASSY OF THE G.D.R.
34 Belgrave Square, SW1X 8QB
[01–235 9941]

Ambassador Extraordinary and Plenipotentiary, His Excellency Dr. Joachim Mitdank (1989).

Counsellors, S. Reichel; H. Vorpahl (*Commercial*); Dr. A. Schaller; M. Rudolph.

First Secretaries, K. Pfenning; Dr. H. Kluge; J. Döring.

Area and Population.—The German Democratic Republic comprises the five former German *Länder* of Brandenburg, Mecklenburg, Saxony, Saxony-Anhalt and Thuringia (an area of 41,768 sq. miles; 108,178 sq. km.). The seat of Government is the Soviet sector of Berlin (eastern part of Berlin) (156 sq. miles). The population of the Republic, including East Berlin (end of 1987) was 16,661,423. In 1952 the former *Länder* were replaced by fourteen *Bezirke* (regions): Potsdam, Cottbus and Frankfurt (formerly Brandenburg); Rostock, Schwerin and Neubrandenburg (formerly Mecklenburg); Karl-Marx-Stadt, Dresden and Leipzig (formerly Saxony); Halle and Magdeburg (formerly Saxony-Anhalt); Erfurt, Gera and Suhl (formerly Thuringia.)

Government.—The present Constitution, which defines the G.D.R. as a Socialist state, came into force on April 9, 1968 after endorsement by a referendum. It replaced the first Constitution of October 7, 1949. The supreme organ of State power is the *Volkskammer*, which has power to elect and dismiss the Council of State, the Council of Ministers, the Chairman of the National Defence Council, the Supreme Court and the Procurator-General. The Council of State retains the presidential powers which it has exercised since the abolition of the office of President on September 12, 1960, together with responsibility for the organization of defence with the help of the National Defence Council. The Council of Ministers is responsible to the *Volkskammer* for the conduct of State policy. The present *Volkskammer* is that elected in April 1986.

As with other communist countries, effective power lies with the ruling Marxist-Leninist Party, in this case the Socialist Unity Party of Germany (SED). The other parties and mass organizations are members of the SED-controlled National Front.

ECONOMY

The G.D.R. economy, including the control of industry and foreign trade, is centrally planned and administered. The State Planning Commission, which is subordinate to the Council of Ministers, is responsible for drawing up the 5- and 1-Year Plans. The 5-Year Plans determine the future development and structure of the economy; the 1-Year Plans have to achieve these aims. The implementation of these plans is the responsibility of the State Production Enterprises under the supervision of the economic and industrial Ministries. The economy is very closely integrated with those of other member countries of C.M.E.A. and particularly with the U.S.S.R.

The Budget forecast for 1989 is: revenue, M275,214·8 million; expenditure, M275,059·4 million.

Agriculture.—Land is cultivated mostly on state or collective farms, though some is cultivated independently. Crop yields in 1987 were: potatoes 12,228,000 tonnes; sugar-beet 7,683,000 tonnes; corn (green and silage) 16,329,000 tonnes; grain 11,224,000 tonnes, and oilseeds 378,000 tonnes.

Industry.—Almost all industry is nationally or co-operatively owned with less than 2 per cent. of the working population engaged in private enterprise. G.D.R. is the leading world producer of lignite, production in 1987 was 309,000,000 tonnes, and the iron and steel industry is also important. Other highly developed industries include basic chemicals and petro-chemicals, machine tools and industrial plant, ship-building and transport equipment, electronic and engineering equipment, precision tools and optical instruments.

Trade with U.K.

	1987	1988
Imports from U.K. . . .	£81,489,000	£113,239,000
Exports to U.K.	180,299,000	152,977,000

Principal cities and towns (population, mid-1987): East Berlin (1,246,872); Leipzig (549,229); Dresden (519,524); Karl-Marx-Stadt (313,347); Magdeburg (289,627); Rostock (250,727); Halle (Saale) (235,730); Erfurt (217,961); Potsdam (141,662).

CURRENCY.—Mark der Deutschen Demokratischen Republik (M) of 100 pfennig.

FLAG.—Horizontal bands of black, red, gold; hammer, compasses and corn device at centre.

NATIONAL ANTHEM.—Auferstanden Aus Ruinen (Risen from ruins).

NATIONAL DAY.—October 7.

BRITISH EMBASSY
108 Berlin, Unter den Linden 32/34
[Berlin 220–2431]

Ambassador Extraordinary and Plenipotentiary, His Excellency Nigel Hugh Robert Allen Broomfield, C.M.G. (1988).
Counsellor, C. Munro.
First Secretaries, R. M. Sands (*Head of Chancery*); G. Deane (*Information*); D. J. Peate, O.B.E. (*Commercial*).
Second Secretaries, A. R. Weeks (*Administration and Consul*); J. W. Lawson; W. A. F. Ridout.
Third Secretary, R. C. Morton.
Cultural Attaché, M. G. Holcroft (*British Council Representative*).

GREECE
(Elliniki Dimokratia)

President of the Hellenic Republic, Christos Sartzetakis, *born* 1927, *elected* March 29, 1985.

CABINET
(as at August 1, 1989)

Prime Minister and Minister for Foreign Affairs, and Tourism, Tzannis Tzannetakis.
Minister in charge of P.M.'s Office, Athanasios Kanellopoulos.
Interior, Nikolaos Konstantopoulos.
National Defence, Ioannis Varvitsiotis.
National Economy, George Souflias.
Finance, Antonios Samaras.
Agriculture, Stavros Dimas.
Labour, Theocharis Papamargaris.
Health and Welfare, Miltiades Evert.
Justice, Fotios Kouvelis.
Education and Religion, Vassilios Kontoyannopoulos.
Culture, George Mylonas.
Public Order, Ioannis Kefaloyannis.

Macedonia and Thrace, Panayotis Hatzinikolaou.
Aegean, Emmanuel Kefaloyannis.
Environment, Regional Planning and Public Works, Sotirios Kouvelas.
Industry, Energy and Technology, Michael Papakonstantinou.
Commerce, Andreas Andrianopoulos.
Transport and Communications, Nikolaos Gelestathis.
Merchant Marine, Aristotelis Pavlidis.

EMBASSY OF GREECE
1A Holland Park, W11 3TP
[01–727 8040]

Ambassador Extraordinary and Plenipotentiary, new appointment awaited.
Defence Attaché, Capt. S. Gouleas.
Counsellors, D. Vidouris; A. Agathocles; A. Mitsialis (*Consular Affairs*); G. Protonotarios (*Economic and Commercial*); I. Staikos (*Education*); A. Xerikos (*Labour*); G. Arzoglou (*Press*).
Tourist Adviser, A. Kimissis.

There are Honorary Consuls at *Belfast, Birmingham, Edinburgh, Falmouth, Glasgow, Leeds* and *Southampton*.

A maritime State in the south-east of Europe, bounded on the N. by Albania, Yugoslavia and Bulgaria, on the S. and W. by the Ionian and Mediterranean seas, and on the E. by Turkey, with an estimated area of 50,944 sq. miles (131,944 sq. km.). Population (1987 estimate) is given as 10,002,000.

The main areas of Greece are: *Macedonia* (which includes Mt. Athos and the island of Thasos), *Thrace* (including the island of Samothrace), *Epirus, Thessaly, Continental Greece* (which includes the island of Euboea and the Sporades or 'scattered islands' of which the largest is Skyros), the *Peloponnese* (or *Morea*), the *Dodecanese* or *Southern Sporades* (12 islands occupied by Italy in 1911 during the Italo-Turkish War and ceded to Greece by Italy in 1947) consisting of Rhodes, Astypalaia, Karpathos, Kassos, Nisyros, Kalymnos, Leros, Patmos, Kos, Symi, Khalki and Tilos, the *Cyclades* (a circular group numbering about 200, with a total area of 923 sq. miles; the chief islands are Syros, Andros, Tinos, Naxos, Paros, Santorini, Milos and Serifos), the *Ionian Islands* (Corfu, Paxos, Levkas, Ithaca, Cephalonia, Zante and Cerigo), the *Aegean Islands* (Chios, Lesbos, Limnos and Samos). In *Crete* there was for over 1,500 years (3000 to 1400 B.C.) a flourishing civilization which spread its influence far and wide throughout the Aegean, and the ruins of the palace of Minos at Knossos afford evidence of astonishing comfort and luxury. Greek civilization emerged about 1300 B.C. and the poems of Homer, the blind poet of Chios, which were probably current about 800 B.C., record the 10-year struggle between the Achaeans of Greece and the Phrygians of Troy (1194–1184 B.C.).

Language and Literature.—The spoken language of modern Greece is descended by a process of natural development from the Common Greek of Alexander's empire. *Katharevousa*, a conservative literary dialect evolved by Adamantios Corais (Diamant Coray), who lived and died in Paris (1748–1833) and used for official and technical matters, is to be phased out over the next few years. Novels and poetry are mostly composed in *dimotiki*, a progressive literary dialect which owes much to John Psycharis (1854–1929). The poets Solomos, Palamas, Cavafis, Sikelianos, Seferis and Elytis have won a European reputation.

Religion.—Over 97 per cent of the people are adherents of the Greek Orthodox Church, which is the State religion, all others being tolerated and free from interference. The Church of Greece recognizes the spiritual primacy of the Œcumenical Patriarch of Constantinople, but is otherwise a self-governing body administered by the Holy Synod under the Presidency of the Archbishop of Athens and All Greece. It has no jurisdiction over the Church of Crete, which has a degree of autonomy under the Œcumenical Patriarch, nor over the Monastic Community of Mount Athos and the Church in the Dodecanese, both of which come directly under the Œcumenical Patriarch.

Government.—A military coup on April 21, 1967, suspended parliamentary government and, following an unsuccessful royal counter-coup on December 13, 1967, King Constantine went into voluntary exile in Rome. On June 1, 1973 the monarchy was abolished and a republic established under the Presidency of George Papadopoulos.

The overthrow of Archbishop Makarios, President of Cyprus, on July 15, 1974, by a military coup led by Greek officers of the Cypriot National Guard caused an international crisis, in the wake of which the heads of the Greek armed forces decided, on July 23, to relinquish power. Konstantinos Karamanlis, Prime Minister between 1955 and 1963, returned from his self-imposed exile in Paris to form a provisional Government, and the first elections for ten years were held on November 17, 1974.

The constitutional position of the King, who was still in exile, remained unsettled until December 8, when by a referendum, the Greek people rejected 'crowned democracy' by 69·2 per cent to 30·8 per cent and Greece became a republic. A new constitution came into force on June 11, 1975.

A general election, under a new system of proportional representation, was held on June 18, 1989 and the results were as follows: New Democracy Party, 145 seats; Pasok (Socialists), 125 seats; Left Coalition, 28 seats; Diana (Democratic Renewal), 1 seat; Others 1.

The Left Coalition and New Democracy agreed to form an interim coalition government with Tzannis Tzannetakis as Prime Minister. A fresh general election was announced for Oct. 1989.

Defence.—The strength of the Army is 130,000 backed up by some 50,000 in the National Guard. The Navy consists of 19,500 men and is equipped with a fleet of destroyers, submarines, patrol boats and amphibious warfare vessels, mostly of U.S., French, Dutch and German origin. The Air Force consists of 25,000 men and is equipped with aircraft disposed in 14 combat squadrons supported by the necessary transport, training, helicopter and reconnaissance squadrons. National service is 2 years on average.

Communications.—The 2,650 kilometres of Greek railways are State-owned with the exception of the Athens–Piraeus Electric Railway. Greek roads total somewhat over 35,500 kilometres, of which about 25 per cent are classified as national highways and just under 30,000 km. are classified as provincial roads. The road connection with Albania was reopened in 1985.

On Dec. 31, 1986, the Greek Mercantile fleet numbered 2,138 ships with a total tonnage of 24,792,516 tons gross. On the same day Greek-owned ships registered under foreign flags numbered 276 with a total tonnage of 5,176,347 tons gross. (N.B. These figures exclude Greek-owned vessels under 100 tons gross.) Athens has direct airline links with Australasia, North America, most countries in Europe, Africa and the Middle East.

Education.—Education is free and compulsory from the age of 6 to 15 and is maintained by State grants. There are six Universities, Athens, Salonika, Patras, Thrace, Ioannina and Crete. There are several other institutes of higher learning, mostly in Athens.

Production.—Though there has in recent years been a substantial measure of industrialization, agriculture still employs about a quarter of the working population. The most important agricultural products are tobacco, wheat, cotton, sugar and rice. The most important of the fruit trees are the olive, peach, vine, orange, lemon, fig, almond and currant-vine, and now exports of Greek fresh fruit and vegetables have established themselves as an important contributor to the economy and have considerable growth potential. Currants, grown mainly around Patras, remain one of Greece's main exports, the United Kingdom being the principal purchaser.

The principal minerals mined in Greece are nickel, bauxite, iron ore, iron pyrites, manganese magnesite, chrome, lead, zinc and emery, and prospecting for petroleum is being carried on. Oil refineries are in operation near Athens and at Salonika, where there is also a petro-chemical plant. The chief industries are textiles (cotton, woollen and synthetics), chemicals, cement, glass, metallurgy, shipbuilding, domestic electrical equipment and footwear. In recent years new factories have been opened for the production of aluminium, nickel, iron and steel products, tyres, chemicals fertilizers and sugar (from locally-grown beet). Food processing and ancillary industries have also grown up throughout the country. The development of the country's electric power resources, irrigation and land reclamation schemes and the exploitation of Greece's lignite resources for fuel and industrial purposes are also being carried out. Tourism has developed rapidly, but is now slowing down.

TRADE

	1986	1987
Total imports ...	Drs 1,587,214·0m.	Drs 1,758,951·1m.
Total exports ...	789,994·6m.	880,958·2m.

Trade with U.K.

	1987	1988
Imports from U.K. ...	£444,500,000	£468,032,000
Exports to U.K. ...	355,320,000	356,974,000

CAPITAL.—Athens. Population (including ΨPiraeus and suburbs), 3,027,331 (1981 Census). Other large towns are ΨSalonika (706,180); ΨPatras (154,596), ΨVolos (107,407); Larissa (102,426); and ΨKavalla (56,705).

Larger towns in the islands are: in Crete—Ψ Heraklion or Candia (102,398), ΨCanea (47,451), and ΨRethymnon (18,190); in the Ionian Islands—ΨCorfu (36,901); in the Dodecanese—ΨRhodes (41,425); in the Cyclades— ΨSyros Hermoupolis (13,877); in Lesbos—ΨMytilene (24,991); in Chios—ΨChios (24,070).

CURRENCY.—Drachma of 100 leptae.

FLAG.—Blue and white stripes with a white cross on a blue field in the canton.

NATIONAL ANTHEM.—Imnos Eis Tin Eleftherian (Hymn to Freedom).

NATIONAL DAY.—March 25 (Independence Day).

BRITISH EMBASSY
1 Ploutarchou Street, 10675 Athens.
[Athens 7236–211/9]

Ambassador Extraordinary and Plenipotentiary, His Excellency Sir (Henry) David (Alastair Capel) Miers, K.B.E., C.M.G. (1989).

Counsellors, J. B. Donnelly (*Political and Consul-General*); B. S. T. Eastwood (*Economic and Commercial*); W. V. Fell; Dr. R. T. Taylor (*Cultural Affairs*).

Defence and Military Attaché, Brig. G. R. A. Evans.

Naval and Air Attaché, Capt. R. Evans, L.V.O.

Hon. Attaché, H. W. Catling, O.B.E., D.Phil. (*Director, British School of Archaeology*).

BRITISH CONSULAR OFFICES

There are British Consular Offices at *Athens, Corfu, Samos, Rhodes, Salonika, Heraklion* (Crete) and *Patras.*

BRITISH COUNCIL
17 Plateia Philikis Etairias (P.O. Box 3488), 10673 Athens.

Representative, Dr. R. T. Taylor.

There is also an office at *Salonika* and British Council libraries at both centres.

BRITISH-HELLENIC CHAMBER OF COMMERCE
25 Vas. Sofias Avenue, GR-106 74 Athens.
[72 10 361]

GUATEMALA
(República de Guatemala)

Head of State, President Marco Vinicio Cerezo Arévalo, *inaugurated,* Jan. 14, 1986.

CABINET
(as at July 31, 1989)

Vice President, Roberto Carpio Nicolle.

Minister of Government, Juan Jose Rodil Peralta.

Foreign Affairs, Alfonso Cabrera Hidalgo.

National Defence, Gen. Héctor Alejandro Gramajo Morales.

Finance, Dr. Rudolfo Paiz Andrade.

Communications, Mario Lopez Estrada.

Education, Eduardo Meyev Maldonado.

Agriculture, Rodolfo Augusto Estrada.

Economy, Lizardo Arturo Sosa Lopez.

Public Health and Social Welfare, Carlos Gehelert Matta.

Labour and Social Insurance, Rodolfo Maldonado.

Energy and Mines, Roland Castillo Contoux.

Special Affairs, Sara Mishaan Rossell.

Urban and Rural Development, Rene Armando De-Léon Schlotter.

Culture and Sport, Ana Isabel Prera Flores de Lobo.

EMBASSY OF GUATEMALA
13 Fawcett Street, SW10 9HN
[01–351 3042]

Ambassador Extraordinary and Plenipotentiary, His Excellency Dr. Erwin Blandon (1987).

Guatemala, in Central America, is situated in N. lat. from 13° 45′ to 17° 49′, and in W. long. from 88° 12′ 49″ to 92°13′ 43″, and has an area of 42,042 sq. miles (108,889 sq. km.), and a population (1985 U.N. estimate) of 7,963,000.

The Republic is divided into 22 departments, and is traversed from W. to E. by an elevated mountain chain, containing several volcanic summits rising to 13,000 feet above sea level; earthquakes are frequent. The country is well watered by numerous rivers; the climate is hot and malarial near the coast, temperate in the higher regions. The rainfall in the capital averages 57 in. per annum. The chief seaports are San José de Guatemala and Champerico on the Pacific and Santo Tomás de Castilla and Puerto Barrios on the Atlantic side.

Language and Literature.—Spanish is the language of the country, but 40 per cent of the population speak an Indian language. Since the establishment of the University in the capital, education has received a marked impulse and the high figure of illiteracy is being reduced. The National library contains about 80,000 volumes in Spanish.

Government.—The constitutionally elected president, Gen. Miguel Ydigoras Fuentes, was overthrown on March 31, 1963, by the Army, which handed executive and legislative powers to the Minister of Defence, Col. Enrique Peralta Azurdia. Important changes were included in a new constitution promulgated on Sept. 15, 1965, and elections for a new Congress and for President and Vice-President took place on March 6, 1966. The constitution was suspended 'for as long as the situation demands' following a military coup in March 1982. An amnesty for guerrillas was unsuccessful and the Army was fully occupied dealing with the proliferating subversive groups throughout the country.

Elections for a Constituent Assembly were held on July 1, 1984, as promised by Gen. Mejía Víctores when he overthrew Gen. Ríos Montt in 1983. The Assembly drew up a new Constitution, promulgated in June 1985, and a new electoral law, paving the way for Presidential, Governmental and Municipal elections which took place on Nov. 3 and Dec. 8, 1985. The elections were won by the Christian Democratic party and Vinicio Cerezo Arévalo was elected President.

Finance.—The Central Government revenue in 1988 was Quetzales 2,500 million, and expenditure Quetzales 3,000 million.

TRADE		
	1985	1986
Imports (c.i.f.)...	U.S.$1,755 m.	U.S.$1,261 m.
Exports (f.o.b.) ..	1,112 m.	1,210 m.

Trade with U.K.		
	1987	1988
Imports from U.K.	£13,926,000	£15,387,000
Exports to U.K.	7,536,000	10,678,000

The principal export is coffee, other articles being manufactured goods, sugar, bananas, cotton, beef and essential oils. The chief imports are petroleum, vehicles, machinery and foodstuffs.

CAPITAL.—Guatemala City. Population: 1,300,000. Quezaltenango has a pop. of over 100,000. Other towns are ΨPuerto Barrios (23,000), Mazatenango (21,000), and Antigua (30,000).

CURRENCY.—Quetzal (Q) of 100 centavos.

FLAG.—Three vertical bands, blue, white, blue; coat of arms on white stripe.

NATIONAL ANTHEM.—Guatemala Feliz (Guatemala be praised).

NATIONAL DAY.—September 15.

BRITISH EMBASSY
Centro Financiero Torre II (7th Floor), Seventh
Avenue 5–10 Zone 4, Guatemala City.
[Guatemala City 321601]

*Ambassador Extraordinary and Plenipotentiary, His
Excellency Bernard Everett.*

GUINEA
(République de Guinée)

President, Brig. Gen. Lansana Conté, *took power*,
April 3, 1984.

COUNCIL OF MINISTERS
(as at June 30, 1989)

Ministers of the Presidency, Cmdt. Henri Tofani
(*National Defence and Security*); Hervey Bangoura
(*Information, Culture and Tourism*); Cmdt. Henri
Foulah (*Economy and Finance*); Réné Gomez
(*Secretary General*).
Permanent Secretary to CMRN, Cmdt. Babacar
Ndiaye.
Foreign Affairs, Cmdt. Jean Toure.
Planning and International Co-operation, Ibrahima
Sylla.
Economy and Finance, Edouard Benjamin.
Administrative Reform and the Civil Service, Ma-
mouna Bangoura.
Interior and Decentralization, Cmdt. Mamadou Bal-
det.
Agriculture and Animal Resources, Capt. Abdourah-
mane Diallo.
Natural Resources and the Environment, Cmdt.
Mohamed Traore.
Post and Telecommunications, Lamine Bolivogui.
Town Planning and Housing, Bahna Sidibe.
Public Health and Population, Dr. Madigbé Fofana.
Transport and Public Works, Cmdt. Facinet Toure.
Industry, Trade and Handicrafts, Ousmane Sylla.
*National Education, Higher Education and Scientific
Research*, Saliou Coumbassa.
Justice, Bassirou Barry.
Social Affairs and Employment, Cmdt. Jean Kolipé
Lamah.
Youth and Sports, Capt. Joseph Zoumanigui.
Regional Ministers, Cmdt. Abou Camara (*Maritime
Guinea*); Cmdt. Alpha Oumar Barou Diallo (*Upper
Guinea*); Lt.-Col. Sory Doumbouya (*Middle
Guinea*); Cmdt. Alhousseny Fofana (*Forest Re-
gion*).

Formerly part of French West Africa, Guinea has
a coastline on the Atlantic Ocean between Guinea-
Bissau and Sierra Leone and in the interior is
adjacent to Senegal, Mali, Côte d'Ivoire, Liberia and
Sierra Leone. Area, 94,926 sq. miles (245,857 sq. km.).
The population (1985 U.N. estimate) was 6,075,000,
mostly the Fullah, Malinké and Soussou tribes.

Government.—Guinea was separated from Senegal
in 1891 and administered by France as a separate
colony until 1958. In a referendum held in Sept. 1958,
Guinea rejected the new French Constitution and
on Oct. 2, 1958, became an independent republic
governed by a Constituent Assembly. M. Sékou
Touré, Prime Minister in the Territorial Assembly,
assumed office as head of the new Government.
Under a provisional constitution, adopted on Nov.
12, 1958, powers of government are exercised by a
president assisted by the Cabinet. The President,
eligible for a term of 7 years and for re-election, is
head of state and of the armed forces. M. Sékou Touré
was elected President of the Republic in January,
1961. Pres. Sékou Touré died in March 1984: a few
days later there was a military coup. Guinea is now
ruled by a military government, which is directed by
a Military Committee for National Recovery

(C.M.R.N.). The country's foreign policy is one of
non-alignment.
Guinea withdrew from the Franc Zone on March
1, 1960, and established her own currency. Guinea is
in receipt of economic aid and technical assistance
from a number of countries, including the United
States, Canada, Federal Republic of Germany, Yugoslavia, the Soviet Union and China.
Production, etc.—The principal products of Guinea
are bauxite, alumina, iron-ore, palm kernels, millet,
rice, coffee, bananas, pineapples and rubber. At
Sangaredi in the mountainous hinterland, where the
rivers Senegal, Gambia and Niger have their sources,
large deposits of bauxite are mined. Deposits of iron
ore, gold, diamonds and uranium have also been
discovered. Principal imports are cotton goods,
manufactured goods, tobacco, petroleum products,
sugar, rice, flour and salt; exports, bauxite, alumina,
iron-ore, diamonds, coffee, hides, bananas, palm
kernels and pineapples.

Trade with U.K.

	1987	1988
Imports from U.K.	£10,675,000	£10,106,000
Exports to U.K.	19,538,000	7,582,000

CAPITAL.—ΨConakry (763,000). Other towns are
Kankan, which is connected with Conakry by a
railway, Kindia, N'Zérékoré, Mamou, Siguiri and
Labé.
CURRENCY.—Guinea franc of 100 centimes.
FLAG.—Three vertical stripes of red, yellow and
green.
NATIONAL DAY.—October 2 (Anniversary of Pro-
clamation of Independence).

BRITISH EMBASSY
British Ambassador (*resident at* Dakar, Senegal).

GUINEA-BISSAU
(República da Guiné-Bissau)

President of the Council of State (*Head of State*), Gen.
João Bernardo Vieira, *took power*, Nov. 1980;
elected for a five-year term, June 1989.

COUNCIL OF MINISTERS
(as at May 31, 1989)

Minister of State for the Armed Forces, Col. Iafai
Camara.
*Minister of State for Rural Development and Agricul-
ture*, Carlos Correia.
*Minister of State at the Presidency and Minister for
Fisheries*, Tiago Aleluia Lopes.
*Minister of State at the Presidency charged with
Social Affairs*, Fidelis Cabral d'Almada.
Economic Co-ordination, Commerce and Tourism,
Manuel Maria Santos.
Minister for the Northern Province, Mario Cabral.
Natural Resources and Industry, Filinto de Barros.
Foreign Affairs, Julio Semedo.
Public Health, Alexandre Nunes Correia.
Minister for the Eastern Province, Malam Bacai
Sanha.
Minister for the Southern Province, Luis Oliveira
Sanca.
Justice, Nicandro Pereira Barreto.
Finance, Victor Freire Monteiro.
Governor of the National Bank, Pedro Godinho
Gomes.
Information and Telecommunications, Mussa Djassi.
Planning, Bernardino Cardoso.
Public Works, Avito José Da Silva.
Civil Service and Labour, Henriqueta Godinho
Gomes.
Education, Manuel Ramout Barcelos.

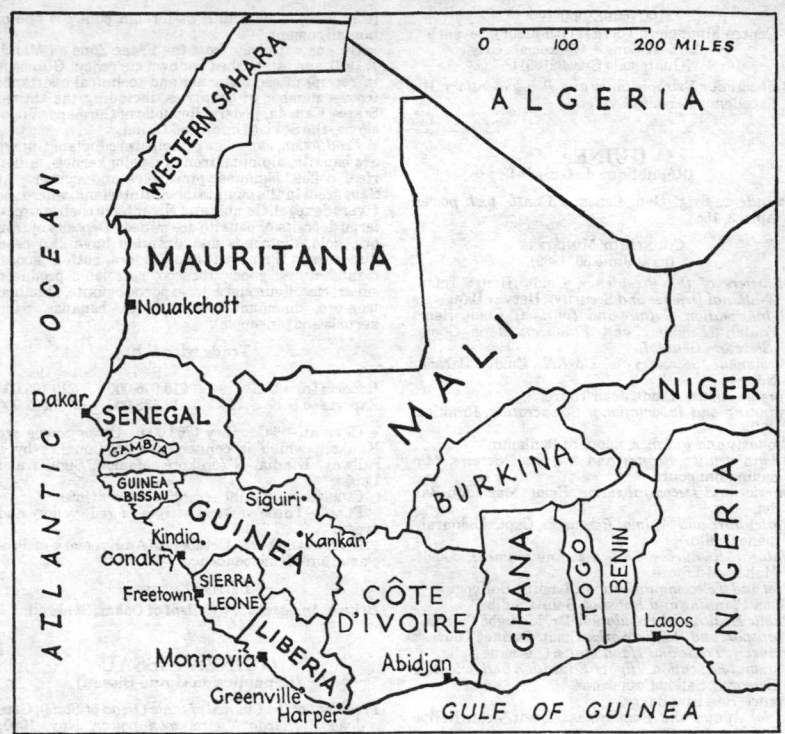

Guinea-Bissau, formerly Portuguese Guinea, lies in Western Africa, between Senegal and Guinea; it has an area of 13,948 sq. miles (36,125 sq. km.), and had a population (1985 U.N. estimate) of 890,000. The main ethnic groups are the Balante, Malinké, Fulani, Mandjako and Pepel.

Guinea-Bissau achieved independence on Sept. 10, 1974. Sr. Luis Cabral was ousted in a coup led by Maj. (now Gen.) Vieira in November, 1980. Following the coup the Assembly was suspended, and a Revolutionary Council was established. Under a new constitution adopted in April 1984 the Revolutionary Council became a 15-member Council of State, and a parliament was set up. An attempted coup to overthrow President Vieira was defeated in November 1985.

Economy.—The country produces rice, coconuts, ground-nuts and palm oil products. Cattle are raised, and there are bauxite deposits in the south.

Trade with U.K.

	1987	1988
Imports from U.K. . . .	£1,152,043	£925,000
Exports to U.K.	16,660	22,000

CAPITAL.—ΨBissau (census 1979, 109,486), also the chief port.

CURRENCY.—Guinea-Bissau peso of 100 centavos.

FLAG.—Horizontal bands of yellow over green with vertical red band in the hoist charged with a black star.

NATIONAL DAY.—September 24 (Independence Day).

BRITISH EMBASSY
British Ambassador, (resident at Dakar, Senegal).

HAITI
(République d'Haiti)

President of the Military Government, Lt.-Gen. Prosper Avril.

CABINET
(as at May 31, 1989)

Interior and Defence, Col. Acédius Saint-Louis.
Foreign Affairs, Yvon Perrier.
Information and Public Relations, Mrs. Rosemarie Nazon.
Economy and Finance, Léonce Thélusma.
Justice, Augustin Romain Ceme.
Public Health and Population, Dr. Serge Pinthro.
Public Works, Transport and Communications, Mines and Energizing Resources, Franck Paultre.
Agriculture, National Resources and Rural Development, Frédéric Agénor.

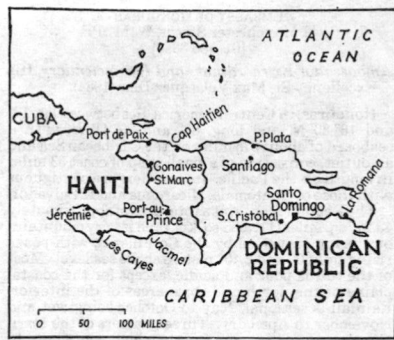

Education, Youth and Sports, Rémy Zamor.
Social Affairs, Arnault Guerrier.
Trade and Industry, Jean Gérard Louisias.
Administration and Public Affairs, Wilner Dessources.
Planning and External Co-operation, Théophile Roche.

The London Embassy of the Republic of Haiti closed on March 30, 1987.

The Republic of Haiti occupies the western third of the island of Hispaniola, which, after Cuba, is the largest island in the West Indies.

The area of the Republic, including off-shore islands, is 10,714 sq. miles (27,750 sq. km.) (of which about three-quarters is mountainous), with a population (1985 U.N. estimate) of 6,585,000, 85 per cent of whom live in rural areas. The people are mainly negroes but there are numbers of mulattoes and others with some admixture of European blood.

Climate.—The climate is tropical with comparatively little difference in the temperatures between the summer (March–Oct.) and the winter (Nov.–Feb.). Humidity is high, especially in the autumn.

Language.—Following the new constitution of March 1987 both French and Creole are regarded as the official languages of Haiti. French is the language of the government and the press, but it is only spoken by the educated minority. The usual language of the people is Creole.

Haiti was a French colony under the name of Saint-Domingue from 1697. The slave population, estimated at 500,000, revolted in 1791 under the leadership of Toussaint L'Ouverture, who was born a slave and made himself Governor General of the colony. He capitulated to the French in 1802 and died in captivity in 1803. Resistance was continued by Jean Jacques Dessalines, also a former negro slave, who, on January 1, 1804, declared the former French colony to be an independent state. It was at this time that the name Haiti, an aboriginal word meaning mountainous, was adopted. Dessalines became Emperor of Haiti, but was assassinated in 1806. In 1915, following a period of political upheaval, the country was occupied by a force of U.S. marines. The occupation came to an end in 1934, and U.S. control of the revenue of Haiti officially ended on October 1, 1947.

Dr. Duvalier was installed as President in 1957 and held the position until his death in 1971. He was succeeded as President for life on the same day by his son, Jean Claude Duvalier, whom he had nominated as his successor. President Duvalier fled to France on Feb. 7, 1986 in the face of sustained popular unrest, and a council headed by Gen. Henri Namphy assumed power. In March 1987, by popular referendum, a new Constitution was agreed and Presidential elections scheduled for Nov. 29. These elections were aborted following violence in the capital. The elections held on Jan. 17, 1988, were boycotted by a number of leading candidates but Leslie Manigat eventually won after a very low turnout. President Manigat was inaugurated on Feb. 7, 1988, but he and his government were ousted on June 19 by Gen. Henri Namphy. Manigat was deported to the Dominican Republic and Namphy set up a military government until he in turn was replaced in a coup by Lt.-Gen. Prosper Avril on Sept. 18, 1988.

Production.—In recent years measures for agricultural rehabilitation have been taken with the aim of a gradual restoration of productivity, which had declined after the ending of the colonial plantation system. The main project is a scheme for the irrigation of more than 70,000 acres of the Artibonite valley.

Coffee accounts for about 32 per cent of total exports, worth approximately U.S.$55 million in 1986. Cocoa is the second largest export earner at U.S.$4·5 million. Corn, 110,000 tonnes (1985), sorghum, 108,000 tonnes (1985), and rice are also grown. Increased production of tropical fruits and vegetables is being encouraged.

Industry.—Export assembly industries account for about 30 per cent of the total manufacturing industry in Haiti, employing an estimated 40,000 people. Items such as leather goods, textiles, electronic components and sports equipment are manufactured, using imported raw materials, for re-export, primarily to the U.S.A. Principal imports are raw materials for the export assembly sector, foodstuffs, machinery, vehicles, mineral oils and textiles.

Communications.—The main roads are asphalted and secondary roads are fair. Internal air services are maintained between the capital and the principal provincial towns. International air-services connect Port-au-Prince with the U.S.A. and other Caribbean and South American cities. The principal towns and villages are connected by telephone and/or telegraph. The telephone company is state owned (51 per cent) and the service both in Port-au-Prince and Inter-urban has been greatly improved. External telegraph, telephone and postal services are normal. There are several commercial radio stations and two television stations at Port-au-Prince.

Regular passenger liner services to New York have ceased, but cruise ships call occasionally. Freight sailings are frequent for the U.S.A., Canada, Europe, Latin America (except Cuba) and the main Caribbean ports.

Education.—Education is free but estimates of illiteracy are as high as 85 per cent.

Trade.—Value of imports 1984 U.S.$ 474·1 million; exports 1984 U.S.$ 219·4 million.

Trade with U.K.

	1987	1988
Imports from U.K.	£5,327,000	£6,760,000
Exports to U.K.	621,000	844,000

CAPITAL.—Ψ Port-au-Prince. Population estimated at about 1 million. Other centres are: Ψ Cap Haitien (54,691); Gonaives (36,736); Les Cayes (27,222); Jérémie (25,117); St. Marc (20,504); Jacmel (16,449); Ψ Port de Paix (21,733).

CURRENCY.—Gourde of 100 centimes.

FLAG.—Horizontal blue over red with national arms on a white square in the centre.

NATIONAL ANTHEM.—La Dessalinienne.

NATIONAL DAY.—January 1.

British Ambassador, (*resident at* Kingston, Jamaica).

HOLY SEE
(see, VATICAN CITY STATE)

HONDURAS
(Republica de Honduras)

President of the Republic, José Azcona del Hoyo, *assumed office,* 27 Jan. 1986.

CABINET
(as at May 31, 1989)

Interior and Justice, Dr. Enrique Ortez Colindres.
Foreign Affairs, Carlos López Contreras.
Defence, Col. Luiz Alonzo Cardona.
Education, Elisa Valle de Martinez.
Finance, Carlos Falck.
Economy, Reginaldo Panting.
Communications, Public Works and Transport, Alejandro Castro Ruiz.
Health, Dr. Rubén Villeda Bermúdez.
Labour and Social Security, Armando Blanco Paniagua.
Natural Resources, Rodrigo Castillo.
Culture and Tourism, Dr. Arturo Rendón Pineda.
Economic Planning, Francisco Figueroa.
Director of National Agrarian Institute, Raul Flores Gomez.
Minister for the Presidency, Celeo Arias Moncada.

EMBASSY OF HONDURAS
47 Manchester Street, W1M 5PB
[01–486 3380]

Ambassador Extraordinary and Plenipotentiary, His Excellency Sr. Max Velásquez-Diaz (1984).

Honduras, in Central America, lies between lat. 13° and 16° 30′ N. and long. 83° and 89° 41′ W. with a seaboard of about 375 miles on the Caribbean Sea and an outlet, consisting of a small strip of coast 63 miles in length on the Pacific. Its frontiers are contiguous with those of Guatemala, Nicaragua and El Salvador.

The Republic contains a total area of approximately 43,277 sq. miles (112,088 sq. km.) and is very mountainous, being traversed by the Cordilleras, with peaks rising to 1,500 and 2,400 metres above sea level. Most of the soil is poor and acidic, except for the coastal plains of the north and some areas of the interior. Rainfall is seasonal, May to October being wet and November to April dry. Three-quarters of the territory is covered by pine forests which contribute to much of the country's wealth in natural resources. The population (1985 U.N. estimate) of 4,372,000 is of mixed Spanish and Indian blood. There is a negro (West Indian) element in Northern Honduras who are known as Garifunas.

The language of the country is Spanish, although English is the first language of many in the islands and on the North coast. Primary and secondary education is free, primary education being compulsory, and the Government have launched a campaign to eradicate illiteracy.

Government.—Originally discovered and settled by

the Spanish at the beginning of the sixteenth century Honduras formed part of the Spanish American Dominions for nearly three centuries until 1821 when independence was proclaimed. Under military government from 1972–81, the present Liberal government was elected in Nov. 1985 and took office in Jan. 1986.

The Republic is divided into 18 departments, the newest of which, Gracias a Dios, formed in Feb. 1957, is now the home of thousands of Miskito Indian refugees from Nicaragua.

Production.—Agriculture is mainly confined to the large and fertile valleys on the wide Caribbean plain, and the extensive valleys found in the Comayagua and Olancho regions of the interior. Reaching inland from the Caribbean towards the eastern border with Nicaragua a vast tropical forest area called the Mosquitia provides valuable reserves of timber. Lead, zinc and silver are mined on a small scale.

The chief exports are coffee, bananas and timber, the most important woods being pine, mahogany and cedar. Cattle raising and the exporting of frozen meat is an important industry, and exports of shrimps and lobsters are increasing. Other products are tobacco, beans, maize, rice, cotton, palm oil, sugar cane, cement and tropical fruits. There are large tracts of uncultivated land.

Communications.—There are about 1,004 km. of railway in operation, chiefly to serve the banana plantations and the Caribbean ports. There are 17,947 km. of roads, of which 2,173 are paved, excluding some 250 kms of new major highways recently inaugurated. Improvements are being made and new roads built. There are 33 smaller airstrips and three international airports, Tegucigalpa, San Pedro Sula and La Ceiba.

Ψ The chief ports are Puerto Cortes, Tela and La Ceiba on the North Coast, through which passes the bulk of the trade with the United States and Europe. Peurto Castilla is being developed as a deep-water container port, and San Lorenzo is also experiencing rapid growth.

TRADE

	1986	1987
	Lempiras	
Imports	2,571·2 m.	2,646·1 m.
Exports	2,044·3 m.	1,986·9 m.

Trade with U.K.

	1987	1988
Imports from U.K.	£10,449,000	£7,891,000
Exports to U.K.	4,703,000	8,295,000

CAPITAL.—Tegucigalpa. Pop. 640,900 (1987 est.); other towns are San Pedro Sula (429,300), ΨLa Ceiba (66,000), ΨPuerto Cortes (42,100), Choluteca (64,500) and ΨTela (27,800).

CURRENCY.—Lempira of 100 centavos.

FLAG.—Three horizontal bands, blue, white, blue (with five blue stars on white band).

NATIONAL ANTHEM.—Tu Bandera Es Un Lampo De Cielo (Your flag is a heavenly light).

NATIONAL DAY.—September 15.

BRITISH EMBASSY
Apartado Postal 290, Tegucigalpa.
[Tegucigalpa 32–0612/8]

Ambassador Extraordinary and Plenipotentiary, His Excellency Peter John Streams, C.M.G. (1986).

HUNGARY
(Magyar Népköztársaság)

President of the Presidential Council of the Republic, Bruno Ferenc Straub, *elected* June 1988.

COUNCIL OF MINISTERS
(as at May 31, 1989)

Prime Minister, Miklós Németh.

Deputy P.M. and Chairman of Planning and Economic Committee, Péter Medgyessy.

Agriculture and Food, Csaba Hütter.

Construction, Transport and Telecommunications, Andras Cerzsi.

Culture and Education, Ferenc Glatz.

Defence, Lt.-Gen. Ferenc Kárpáti.

Environment and Water, Dr László Maróthy.

Finance László Bekesi.

Foreign Affairs, Gyûla Horn.

Industry, Ferenc Horváth.

Interior, István Horváth.

Justice, Kálman Kulcsar.

Social and Health Affairs, Dr. Judit Csehák.

Trade, Tamas Beck.

President, Technical Development Committee, Dr. Pál Tétényi.

President, Central People's Control Commission, Lászlo Ballai.

President, National Planning Office, Ernö Kemenes.

THE COMMUNIST PARTY

Politbureau of the Central Committee, K. Grósz (*Gen Sec.*); Cs. Hámori; P. Ivanyi; M. Jasso; M. Nemeth; R. Nyers; I. Pozsgay; I. Tatai; P. Vastagh.

Secretariat of the Central Committee, K. Grósz (*Gen. Sec.*); G. Lázár (*Deputy Gen. Sec.*); J. Berecz; F. Havasi; I. Horváth; L. Pál; M. Ovári; M. Szürös.

EMBASSY OF THE HUNGARIAN PEOPLE'S REPUBLIC
35 Eaton Place, S.W.1.
[01–235 4048, 7191; *Consulate*: 01–235 2664]

Ambassador Extraordinary and Plenipotentiary, new appointment awaited.

Counsellors, G. Bródi; Dr. P. Kallós (*Consul*); T Antalpéter (*Commercial*).

Defence, Military and Air Attaché, Col. G. Demeter.

Area and Population.—The area of Hungary is 35,919 sq. miles (93,030 sq. km.) with a population (1985) of 10,658,000.

Government.—Hungary was reconstituted a kingdom in 1920 after having been declared a republic on Nov. 17, 1918. She joined the Anti-Comintern Pact on Feb. 24, 1939, and entered the 1939–45 War on the side of Germany in 1941. On Jan. 20, 1945, a Hungarian provisional government of liberation, which had been set up during the preceding December, signed an armistice under the terms of which the frontiers of Hungary were withdrawn to the limits existing in 1937.

After the liberation, a coalition of the Smallholder, National Peasant, Social Democrat and Communist parties carried out major land reform and mines, heavy industry, banks and schools were nationalized. By 1949 the Communists had succeeded in gaining a monopoly of power. A campaign was opened to collectivize agriculture and by 1952 practically the entire economy had been 'socialized'. The Party formulates policy and the function of the Government is mainly executive.

The period from July 1956 to the outbreak of the national revolution on Oct. 23 was marked by growing ferment in intellectual circles and increased discord within the Party. The withdrawal of Soviet troops from the country and free elections were among the demands put forward. Fighting broke out on the night of Oct. 23 between demonstrators, who had been joined by large numbers of factory workers, and the State Security Police (A.V.H.). Soviet forces intervened in strength early the next morning. By Oct. 30 Soviet troops had withdrawn from Budapest and on Nov. 3 an all-party coalition government under Imre Nagy was formed. This government was overthrown and the revolution suppressed as the result of a renewed attack by Soviet forces on Budapest in the early hours of Nov. 4. Simultaneously the formation of a new Hungarian Revolutionary Worker Peasant Government under the leadership of Mr. Kádár was announced.

Economy.—Since 1968 the Hungarian economy has been run according to a system which allows more decentralized decision-making than in some other Eastern European countries, although central control in vital areas such as the allocation of fuels and raw materials has remained. Industrialization has made considerable progress in the last decade and now produces 68 per cent of national income. Industry is mainly based on imported raw materials but Hungary has her own coal (mostly brown), bauxite, considerable deposits of natural gas (some not yet under full exploitation), some iron ore and oil. Output figures in 1985 (1,000 tons), coal, 24,042; bauxite, 2,815; rolled steel 2,860; crude oil, 2,000; cement, 3,678. Natural gas production totalled 7,441 million cubic metres.

Agriculture still occupies an important place in the Hungarian economy. Ten and a half per cent. of the entire land area is owned by State farms and a further 63·8 per cent is within co-operative farms. Production in 1987 was (tons):

Wheat	5,674,000
Rye	185,000
Barley	781,000
Maize	6,987,000
Oats	95,000
Sugar beet	4,224,000

In 1983, national income grew by only 0·5 per cent. Consumption and, particularly, investment continued to be squeezed by the adjustment measures necessitated by Hungary's hard currency debts. Retail prices rose by just under 8 per cent, whilst real incomes stagnated.

Religion and Education.—About two-thirds of the population are Roman Catholics, and the remainder mostly Calvinist. There are five types of schools under the Ministry of Education—kindergartens 3–6, general schools 6–14 (compulsory), vocational schools (15–18), secondary schools (15–18), universities and adult training schools (over 18).

Language and Literature.—Magyar, or Hungarian, is one of the Finno-Ugrian languages. Hungarian literature began to flourish in the second half of the sixteenth century. Among the greatest writers of the nineteenth and twentieth centuries are Mihály Vörösmarty (1800–1855), Sándor Petöfi (1823–1849), János Arany (1817–1882), Imre Madach (1823–1864), Kálmán Mikszáth (1847–1910), Endre Ady (1877–1918), Attila József (1905–1937), Mihály Babits (1883–1941) and Dezsö Kosztolányi (1885–1936).

Finance.—The budget estimates for the year 1986 were: Revenue, Forints 681,000 million; Expenditure, Forints 706,000 million.

TRADE

	1986	1987
	Forints	
Imports	439,700 m	463,100 m
Exports	420,300 m	450,100 m
	forints)	

Trade with U.K.

	1987	1988
Imports from U.K.	£101,300,000	£131,212,000
Exports to U.K.	83,267,000	98,288,000

CAPITAL.—Budapest, on the Danube; population (1985), 2,072,000. Other large towns are: Miskolc (212,000); Debrecen (210,000); Szeged (181,000) and Pecs (175,000).

CURRENCY.—Forint of 100 fillér.

FLAG.—Red, white, green (horizontally).

NATIONAL ANTHEM.—Isten Aldd Meg A Magyart (God Bless the Hungarians).

NATIONAL DAY.—April 4 (Anniversary of Liberation, 1945).

BRITISH EMBASSY
Harmincad Utca 6, Budapest V
[Budapest 182–888]

Ambassador Extraordinary and Plenipotentiary, His Excellency John Allan Birch, C.M.G. (1989).

Counsellor, P. G. Harborne (*Head of Chancery*).

Defence and Military Attaché, Col. F. N. J. Davies.

Air Attaché, Wg.-Cdr. O. J. A. Knight.

First Secretary and British Council Representative, D. J. Harvey.

Consul, F. A. Blogg.

ICELAND
(Island)

President, Vigdís Finnbogadóttir, *born* 1930, *elected* June 29, 1980, *re-elected,* July 1984 and June 1988.

CABINET
(since Sept. 1988)

Prime Minister, Steingrímur Hermannsson (*Pr.*).

Foreign Affairs and Trade, Jón Baldvin Hannibalsson (*SDP*).

Finance, Ulafur Ragnar Grímsson (*PA*).

Justice, and Ecclesiastical Affairs, and Fisheries, Halldór Asgrímsson. (*Pr*).

Education and Culture, Svavar Gestsson (*PA*).

Social Affairs, Jóhanna Sigurthardóttir (*SDP*).

Health and Social Security, Guthmundur Bjarnason (*Pr*).

Commerce, Industry and Nordic Co-operation, Jón Sigurthsson (*SDP*).

Agriculture and Communications, Steingrímur Sigfusson (*PA*).

(*Pr.*—Progressive Party; *SDP.*—Social Democrat Party; *PA.*—People's Alliance).

EMBASSY OF ICELAND
1 Eaton Terrace, SW1W 8EY
[01–730 5131]

Ambassador Extraordinary and Plenipotentiary, His Excellency Ólafur Egilsson (1986).

Minister Counsellor, T. Karlsson.

Iceland is a large volcanic island in the North Atlantic Ocean, extending from 63° 23′ to 66° 33′ N. lat., and from 13° 22′ to 24° 35′ W. long., with an estimated area of 39,768 sq. miles (103,000 sq. km.). The population was 247,024 on Dec. 1, 1987.

Iceland was uninhabited before the ninth century, when settlers came from Norway. For several centuries a form of republican government prevailed, with an annual assembly of leading men called the *Althing*, but in 1241 Iceland became subject to Norway, and later to Denmark. During the colonial period, Iceland maintained its cultural integrity but a deterioration in the climate, together with frequent volcanic eruptions and outbreaks of disease led to a serious fall in the standard of living and to a decline in the population to little more than 40,000. In the nineteenth century a struggle for independence began which led first to home rule for Iceland under the Danish Crown (1918), and later to complete independence under a republican form of rule in 1944.

Government.—The parliamentary (*Althing*) elections in April 1987 gave the Independence Party 18 seats, Progressives 13, Social Democratic Party 10, People's Alliance 8, Citizens' Party 7, Women's Alliance 6 and Independent 1. The coalition government resigned on Sept. 18, 1988 and on Sept. 28 Steingrímur Hermannsson formed a new government.

Language and Literature.—The ancient Norraena (or Northern tongue) presents close affinities to Anglo-Saxon and as spoken and written in Iceland today differs little from that introduced into the island in the ninth century. There is a rich literature with two distinct periods of development, from the mid-11th to the late 13th century and from the early 19th century to the present.

Production.—Iceland has considerable resources of hydro-electric and geothermal energy. It is estimated that exploited water power (4,000 Gigawatt hours/a) represents only about 9 per cent of that economically exploitable, whereas only 5 per cent of the estimated 80,000 Gigawatt hours/a of available geothermal power has so far been harnessed. Energy-intensive heavy industry includes an aluminium smelter, a nitrogen fertilizer factory, a diatomite plant and a ferro-silicone plant.

The principal exports are frozen fish fillets, salt fish, stock fish, fresh fish on ice, frozen scampi, fishmeal and oil, skins and aluminium; the imports consist of almost all the necessities of life, the chief items being petroleum products, transport equipment, textiles, foodstuffs, animal feeds, timber, and alumina.

At January 1, 1988, the mercantile marine consisted of 639 vessels of under 100 gross tons and 398 ships of 100 gross tons and over; a total of 1,037 vessels (187,829 gross tons), of which 899 (117,452 gross tons) are decked fishing vessels. There are regular shipping services between Reykjavík and Felixstowe, Humber ports and the Continent.

A regular air service is maintained between Glasgow and London and Reykjavík. There are also air services from the island to Scandinavia, U.S.A., Germany, France and Luxembourg.

Road communications are adequate in summer but greatly restricted by snow in winter. Only roads in town centres and key highways are metalled the rest being of gravel, sand and lava dust. The climate and terrain make first-class surfaces for highways out of the question. There are no railways.

FINANCE

	1986	1987
	Krónur (millions)	
Revenue	38,235	48,963
Expenditure	40,111	51,668

TRADE

	1986	1987
	Krónur (millions)	
Exports	44,968	53,053
Imports	45,910	61,237

Trade with U.K.

	1987	1988
Imports from U.K.	£84,866,000	£87,100,000
Exports to U.K.	178,314,000	198,365,000

CAPITAL: ΨReykjavík. Population (Dec. 1, 1987), 93,270.

Other centres in approximate order of importance are ΨAkureyri, Kópavogur, ΨHafnarfjördur, Keflavík, Westmann Islands, Akranes, Isafjördur and ΨSiglufjördur.

CURRENCY.—Icelandic króna (Kr) of 100 aurar.

FLAG.—Blue, with white-bordered red cross.

NATIONAL ANTHEM.—O Gud Vors Lands (Our Country's God).

NATIONAL DAY.—June 17.

BRITISH EMBASSY
Laufásvegur 49, Reykjavik
[Reykjavik 15883/4]

Ambassador Extraordinary and Plenipotentiary and Consul-General, His Excellency Richard Radford Best, C.B.E. (1989).

First Secretary, Head of Chancery and Consul, S. C. Parris.

Vice Consul and Attaché (Commercial), J. N. L. Burgess.

BRITISH CONSULAR OFFICES

There are Consular Offices at *Reykjavík* and *Akureyri.*

INDONESIA
(Republik Indonesia)

President, General Suharto, *born* June 9, 1921. *Acting President,* March 12, 1967; *confirmed as President,* Mar. 28, 1968, *re-elected for a term of 5 years,* March, 1973, March 1978, March 1983 and March 1988.

Vice-President, Lt.-Gen. Sudharmono, *elected* March 1988.

CABINET
(as at June 30, 1989)

Co-ordinating Ministers, Adm. Sudomo (*Political and Security Affairs*); Dr. Radius Prawiro (*Economy, Finance, Industry and Development Supervision*); Gen. Supardjo Rustam (*Public Welfare*).

Ministers, Gen. Rudini (*Internal Affairs*); Ali Alatas (*Foreign Affairs*); Gen. L. B. Murdani (*Defence and Security*); Lt.-Gen. Ismail Saleh (*Justice*); Mr. Harmoko (*Information*); Dr. J. B. Sumarlin (*Finance*); Dr. Arifin Siregar (*Trade*); Mr. Hartarto (*Industry*); Mr. Wardoyo (*Agriculture*); Air Vice Marshal Ginandjar Kartasasmita (*Mines and Energy*); Radinal Mochtar (*Public Works*); Maj.-Gen. Azwar Anas (*Communications*); Maj.-Gen. Bustanil Arifin (*Co-operatives*); Cosmas Batubara (*Manpower*); Lt.-Gen. Sugiarto (*Transmigration*); Gen. Susilo Sudarman (*Tourism, Posts and Telecommunications*); Prof. Fuad Hassan (*Education and Culture*); Dr. Adhyatma (*Health*); Haji Munawir Sjadzali (*Religious Affairs*); Prof. Haryati Subadio (*Social Affairs*); Hasjrul Harahap (*Forestry*).

Ministers of State, Maj.-Gen. Murdiono (*State Secretary*); Dr. Saleh Afif (*National Development Planning*); Siswono Judo Husodo (*Housing*); Prof. Emil Salim (*Population and Environment*); Sarwono Kusumaatmadja (*Administrative Reform*); Prof.

B. J. Habibie (*Research and Technology*); Mrs. A. Sulasikin Murpratomo (*Women's Affairs*); Akbar Tandjung (*Sport and Youth Affairs*).

INDONESIAN EMBASSY
38 Grosvenor Square, W1X 9AD
[01–499 7661]

Ambassador Extraordinary and Plenipotentiary, new appointment awaited.
Minister, Hidayat Soemo (*Deputy Chief of Mission*).

Situated between latitudes 6° North and 11° South and between longitudes 95° and 141° East, Indonesia comprises the islands of *Java, Madura,* and *Sumatra,* the *Riouw-Lingga Archipelago* (which with Karimon, Anambas, Natuna Islands, Tambelan, and part of Sumatra, forms the province of Riau), the islands of *Bangka* and *Billiton,* part of the island of *Borneo* (Kalimantan), *Sulawesi* (formerly *Celebes*) *Island,* the *Molucca Islands* (Ternate, Tidore, Halmahera, Buru, Seram, Banda, Timor-Laut, Larat, Bachiam, Obi, Kei, Aru, Babar, Leti and Wetar), the island of *Bali* and the islands of *Lombok, Sumbawa, Sumba, Flores, Timor* and others comprising the provinces of East and West *Nusa Tenggara* and the western half of the island of New Guinea (*Irian Jaya*), with a total area of 735,358 sq. miles (1,904,569 sq. km.), and a population (1985) of about 165,030,000.

From the early part of the 17th century much of the Indonesian Archipelago was under Netherlands rule. Following the World War 1939–45, during which the Archipelago was occupied by the Japanese, a strong nationalistic movement manifested itself and after sporadic fighting the formal transfer of sovereignty by the Netherlands of all the former Dutch East Indies except W. New Guinea took place on December 27, 1949.

Western New Guinea became part of Indonesia in 1963 under the name West Irian (now Irian Jaya), this interpretation being confirmed in an "Act of Free Choice" in July, 1969, of which the United Nations took note in November 1969. Following a unilateral declaration of independence by the Fretilin, Indonesia took over the former Portuguese colony of East Timor, which in July 1976 was declared the 27th province of Indonesia.

Following a three-week period of unrest and violent student demonstrations the Minister of the Army, General Suharto, took over effective political power in March, 1966.

General Suharto was made Acting President with full powers, on March 11, 1967, and on March 28, 1968, appointed full President for a period of five years.

In the general election of April 1987, Golkar obtained 299 seats, the Muslim United Development Party 61 seats and the Indonesian Democratic Party 40 seats. President Suharto was subsequently re-elected in March 1988.

Production.—Nearly 70 per cent. of the population of Indonesia is engaged in agriculture and related production. Copra, kapok, nutmeg, pepper and cloves are produced, mainly by smallholders; palm oil, sugar, fibres and cinchona are produced by large estates. Rubber, tea, coffee and tobacco are also produced by both in large quantities. Rice is a traditional staple food for the people of Indonesia and the islands of Java, Sulawesi and Sumatra are important producers. Production has risen rapidly in recent years to 25 million tons and the country is now self sufficient.

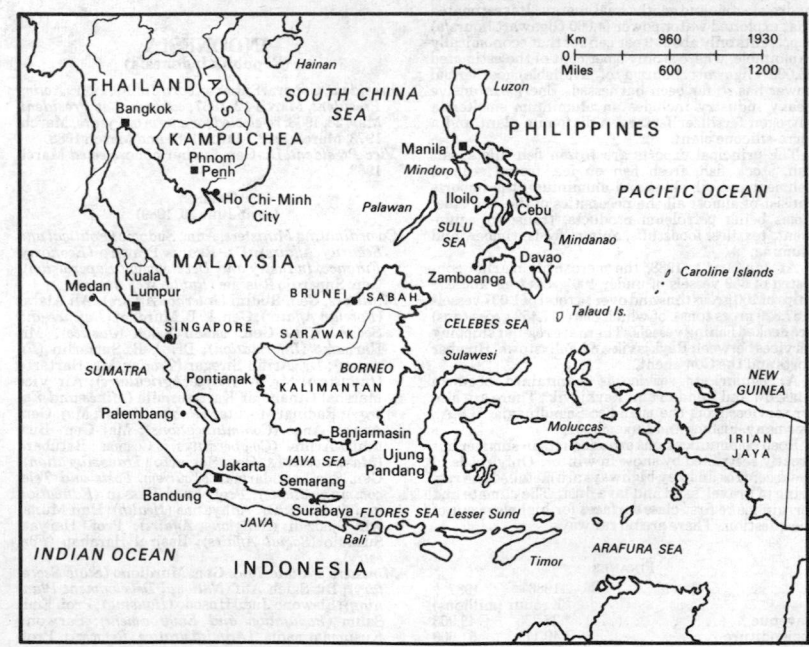

Oil and LNG are the most important assets, the export of which in 1985–86 earned about U.S. $11,000 million (about 80 per cent. of Indonesia's exports), but more recent developments have underscored the vulnerability of the economy to depressed international markets and weak oil prices. Timber is the second largest foreign exchange earner after oil. Strenuous efforts have been made to develop non-oil exports.

Indonesia is rich in minerals, particularly tin, of which the country is the world's third biggest producer; petroleum, coal, nickel and bauxite are the other principal products; there are also considerable deposits of gold, silver, manganese phosphates and sulphur. Aid to Indonesia is channelled through the Inter-Governmental Group on Indonesia (IGGI). Indonesia received about US$4 billion in 1988.

Indonesia's Fourth Development Programme started in 1984 and its main objectives are the elimination of poverty, agricultural and urban problems, and the continued growth of installed power generation.

Finance.—The drop in oil prices led in March 1983 to the rupiah being devalued by 27 per cent, and a rescheduling of major projects was undertaken. More recently an increase in foreign reserves has meant that several of these projects could be re-instated.

Trade with U.K.

	1987	1988
Imports from U.K.	£236,027,000	£203,275,000
Exports to U.K.	144,819,000	233,807,000

Principal exports to the United Kingdom are rubber, timber, non-ferrous metals, tea, coffee, spices, and crude oil for refinement. Imports from the United Kingdom are mainly of machinery, transport equipment and electrical equipment.

Transport.—In Java a main line connects Jakarta with Surabaya in the East of Java and there are several branches. In Sumatra the important towns of Medan, Padang and Palembang are the centres of short railway systems.

Sea communications in the archipelago are maintained by the State-run shipping companies Djakarta-Lloyd (ocean-going) and Pelni (coastal and inter-island) and other small concerns. Transport by small craft on the rivers of the larger islands plays an important part in trade. Air services in Indonesia are operated by Garuda Indonesian Airways and other local airlines, and Jakarta is served by various international services. There are approximately 50,000 miles of roads.

CAPITAL.—ΨJakarta (population 6,503,449). Other important centres are: (Java) ΨSurabaya (2,027,913), ΨSemarang (1,026,671), Bandung (1,462,637); (Sumatra) Palembang (787,187), Medan (1,378,955); (Sulawesi), ΨUjung Pandang (formerly *Makassar*) (709,038); (Kalimantan) Banjarmasin (381,286), ΨPontianak (304,778), ΨBalikpapan (280,675); (Moluccas) Ambon (208,898); (Bali) Denpasar, Singaraja (for whole island 2,174,105); (Nusa Tenggara) Kupang (329,371); (Irian Jaya) Jayapura (107,184).

CURRENCY.—Rupiah (Rp) of 100 sen.

FLAG.—Equal bands of red over white.

NATIONAL ANTHEM.—Indonesia Raya (Great Indonesia).

NATIONAL DAY.—August 17 (Anniversary of Proclamation of Independence).

BRITISH EMBASSY
Jalan M. H. Thamrin 75, Jakarta 10310
[Jakarta 330904]

Ambassador Extraordinary and Plenipotentiary, His Excellency (William) Kelvin (Kennedy) White, C.M.G. (1988).

BRITISH CONSULAR OFFICES

There are British Consular Offices at *Jakarta*, *Medan* and *Surabaya*.

British Council Representative, Dr. J. C. Blackwell, C.B.E., S Widjojo Centre, Jalan Jendral Sudirman, 71, Jakarta. There are also libraries at *Bandung* and *Medan*.

INDONESIA BRITAIN ASSOCIATION

c/o Mr. R. A. M. Ramsay, Sarinah Building, 13th Floor, J1. M. H. Thamrin 11, Jakarta.

IRAN
(Jomhori-e-Islami-e-Iran)

Leader of the Islamic Republic, Ayatollah Seyed Ali Khamenei, *appt.* June 1989.
President, Hojjatoleslam Ali Akbar Hashemi Rafsanjani, *elected* July 28, 1989.
Foreign Affairs, Dr. Ali Akbar Velayati.
Education, Mohammad Ali Najafi.
Islamic Culture and Guidance, Hojjatoleslam Seyed Mohammad Khatami.
Commerce, (vacant).
Health Care and Training, Dr. Ali Reza Marandi.
Plan and Budget, Masoud Roghani Zanjani.
Post, Telephone and Telegraph, Mohammad Gharrazi.
Justice, Dr. Hassan Habibi.
Defence, Brig.-Gen. Mohammad Hossein Jalali.
Roads and Transport, Mohammad Saidi-Kia.
Industry, Gholam Reza Shafei.
Higher Education, Dr. Mohammad Farhadi.
Mines and Metals, Mohammad Reza Ayatollahi.
Labour and Social Affairs, Abolqasem Sarhadizadeh.
Interior, Hojjatoleslam Ali Akbar Mohtashami.
Agriculture, Isa Kalantari.
Housing in Urban Development, Serajuddin Kazeruni.
Energy, Bijan Namdar Zanganeh.
Oil, Gholamreza Agazadeh.
Economic and Finance, Mohammad Javad Iravani.
Heavy Industries, Engineer Behzad Nabavi.
Revolutionary Guards, Ali Shamkhani.
Construction Crusade, Gholamreza Foruzesh.
Intelligence, Hojjatoleslam Mohammad Mohammadi Reyshahri.

The above Cabinet held office until a new Cabinet was chosen by President Rafsanjani. This was approved on Aug. 29 but further details were not available at the time of going to press.

DIPLOMATIC REPRESENTATION

Following the breaking off of diplomatic relations with Iran on March 7, 1989, an Iranian Interests section has been set up at the Embassy of Pakistan.

Area and Population.—Iran has an area of 636,296 sq. miles (1,648,000 sq. km.), with a population of over 52 million. It is mostly an arid table-land, encircled, except in the east, by mountains, the highest in the north rising to 18,934 ft. The central and eastern portion is a vast salt desert.

The Iranians are mostly Shi'ah Muslims but among them are Zoroastrians, Bahais, Sunni Muslims and Armenian and Assyrian Christians. Emigration has much reduced the once substantial Jewish community.

Language and Literature.—Persian, or Farsi, the language of Iran, and of some other areas formerly under Persian rule, is an Indo-European tongue with many Arabic elements added; the alphabet is mainly Arabic, with writing from right to left. Among the great names in Persian literature are those of Abu'l Kásim Mansúr, of Firdausi (A.D. 939–1020), Omar Khayyám, the astronomer-poet (died A.D. 1122),

Muslihu'd-Din, known as Sa'di (born A.D. 1184) and Shems-ed-Din Muhammad, or Hafiz (died A.D. 1389).

Government.—Iran was ruled from the end of the 18th century by Shahs of the Qajar Dynasty. A nationalist movement became active in Dec., 1905, and in Aug., 1906, the Shah, Muzaffer-ud-Din, admitting the need for reforms, granted a Constitution. After the war of 1914–18, the subsequent troubles and the signature of the Soviet-Iranian Treaty of 1921, a vigorous Prime Minister, Reza Khan re-established general order. On Oct. 31, 1925, the last representative of the Qajar Dynasty, Sultan Ahmed Shah was deposed in his absence by the National Assembly, which handed over the government to the Prime Minister, Reza Khan, who was elected Shah on Dec. 13, 1925, by the Constituent Assembly, and took the title Reza Shah Pahlavi. On September 16, 1941, Reza Shah abdicated in favour of the Crown Prince, who ascended the throne under the title of Mohammed Reza Shah Pahlavi.

Following widespread and persistent opposition to his regime, the Shah departed from Iran in January, 1979. Ayatollah Khomeini, the main spiritual leader of the Shi'ah Muslims, returned to Iran from exile on February 1. Following a national referendum, Iran was declared an Islamic Republic by Ayatollah Khomeini on April 1, 1979. A new constitution, providing for a President, Prime Minister and Consultative Assembly, and also for overall leadership by Khomeini, was approved by referendum in December 1979. The government's severe measures suppressed violent opposition. In June 1989 Khomeini died and President Khamenei (whose term of office expires in Oct. 1989) was appointed Leader of the Islamic Republic.

Iran was at war with Iraq following the Iraqi invasion of Iran in Sept. 1980. Both sides carried out attacks on neutral shipping in the Gulf and in 1987 several foreign navies entered the Gulf to escort neutral merchant shipping. International efforts to end the fighting focused on United Nations Security Council Resolution 598 of July 1987, and a ceasefire came into effect on Aug. 20, 1988. A U.N. Observer Peace-Keeping Force was sent to the Gulf to monitor the ceasefire whilst peace talks continued.

Defence.—The Army has a strength of about 150,000 men, in 4 armoured divisions, 4 infantry divisions and one airborne division. The Air Force has a strength of about 35,000, with some 70 combat aircraft. The Navy has a strength of about 20,000 and consists of 3 destroyers, 3 frigates, 4 corvettes, 5 minesweepers, and patrol boats, support ships, landing craft and hovercraft. The Islamic Revolutionary Guards Corps numbers about 500,000 men. Total armed forces personnel including paramilitary forces number over one million.

Education.—Since 1943 primary education has been compulsory and free, but there is large scale absenteeism, particularly outside the towns. There are 22 universities in Iran (8 in Tehran, 14 in the provinces). The educational system has been reformed following the revolution.

Finance.—The budget for the Iranian year beginning March 21, 1988, was revenue Rials. 9,800,290 million; expenditure Rials. 9,800,290 million.

Agriculture.—While petroleum is the principal product and by far the greatest export, Iran is otherwise largely an agricultural and pastoral country. After the 1979 revolution the Government announced its intention of giving greater emphasis to the development of agriculture with a view to reducing Iran's dependence on food imports, but it has so far had only limited success. Some redistribution of land has taken place, but agreement has not been reached on basic land reform.

Wheat is the principal crop; other important crops are barley, rice, cotton, sugar beet, fruit, nuts and

vegetables. Wool is also a major product. There are extensive forests in the north and west, the conservation of which is a continuing problem.

Industry.—Under the Shah, great emphasis was given to the development of industry. Apart from oil, the principal industrial products are carpets, textiles, sugar, cement and other construction materials, ginned cotton, vegetable oil and other food products, leather and shoes, metal manufactures, pharmaceuticals, motor vehicles, fertilizers and plastics. Industrial output was severely curtailed by the 1979 revolution, as a result of which many industrialists left the country. In July 1979 the Government nationalized a wide range of major industrial concerns, having nationalized the banks and the insurance companies the previous month. Foreign trade is controlled by the State, although formal legislation to this effect has yet to be passed and the private sector plays an increasingly important role.

Energy.—The oilfields, which lie in South Western Iran, were nationalized in 1951. From 1957 until the 1979 revolution a consortium of eight oil companies (one British, one French, one Dutch, and five U.S.) was responsible for the production, refining and sale of oil. In July 1979 the National Iranian Oil Company assumed full control of the oil industry. In addition to that extracted from the onshore wells, oil is also produced from a number of off-shore oilfields. Oil production by June 1979 had reached an average of 3·5 million b.p.d., but is now approximately 2·2 million b.p.d., of which some 1·5 million b.p.d. is exported. Iran is a member of O.P.E.C.

Communications.—Tehran is at the centre of a network of highways linking the capital with other major towns, the ports and the frontiers with Turkey, U.S.S.R., Afghanistan and Pakistan, and with the Caspian Sea. The Trans-Iranian Railway runs from Bandar Turcoman, on the Caspian Sea, via Tehran to Bandar Khomeini, on the Persian Gulf. Other lines link Tehran with Tabriz and with Mashad. There are also railways from Tabriz to Julfa and from Zahedan to Quetta, and a branch line from Ahwaz to Khorramshahr. An extension from Qom to Yazd via Kashan is now in operation, as is one from Bandar Turcoman to Gorgan. An extension from Yazd to Kerman is partially complete. The Iranian rail system is linked to the Turkish system via Van. There is an international airport at Tehran (Mehrabad), and airports at all the major provincial centres. The national airline, Iranair, is government-owned and operates international and domestic routes.

TRADE

Imports to Iran declined dramatically at the beginning of 1979 as a result of the economic disruption caused by the revolution. Iran's aggressive oil sales policy during 1982 enabled foreign exchange reserves to recover from the 1981 low level and made possible increased imports. However, the drop in world oil prices in 1986 again affected Iran's foreign exchange earnings, and her level of imports declined.

Imports into Iran consist mainly of industrial and agricultural machinery, motor vehicles and motor vehicle components for assembly, iron and steel (including manufactures), electrical machinery and goods, meat, various other foods, and certain textile fabrics and yarns. The principal exports, apart from oil, are cotton, carpets, dried fruit, nuts, hides and skins, mineral ores, wool, gums, caviare, cumin seed and spices. Federal Republic of Germany, Japan and the U.K. are Iran's leading suppliers.

	1984	1985
Imports	US$15,343 m.	US$11,145 m.
Exports	15,136 m.	13,952 m.

Trade with U.K.

	1987	1988
Imports from U.K. ...	£307,853,000	£247,768,000
Exports to U.K.	187,572,000	140,207,000

CAPITAL: Tehran, population (1986 estimate) over 6 million. Other large towns are Tabriz (853,296), Isfahan (1,000,000) Meshed (500,000), Shiraz (300,000), Resht (150,000), Kerman (100,000), Hamadan (130,000), Yazd (70,000), Kermanshah (152,000), Ahwaz (175,000).

CURRENCY.—Rial of 100 dinars.

FLAG.—Equal horizontal bands of green, white and red; with an emblem of the Islamic Republic.

NATIONAL ANTHEM.—Sorood-e Jomhoori-e Eslami.

NATIONAL DAY.—February 11.

BRITISH DIPLOMATIC REPRESENTATION

Diplomatic relations were broken off by Iran in March 1989, and British interests are handled by the Swedish Embassy.

IRAQ
(Al-Jumhouriya al-'Iraqia)

REVOLUTIONARY COMMAND COUNCIL

Chairman, President of the Republic, and *Supreme Commander of the Armed Forces,* Saddam Hussain, *assumed office* July 16, 1979.

Members, Izzat Ibrahim (*RCC Vice-Chairman*); Taha Muhiddin Ma'aruf (*Vice-President of the Republic*); Taha Yasin Ramadhan (*First Deputy Prime Minister*); Dr. Sa'doun Hammadi (*Deputy Prime Minister*); Tariq 'Aziz (*Deputy Prime Minister and Foreign Minister*); Sa'doun Shakir; Hassan Ali.

Secretary General, Khalid Abdul Mun'im Rasheed (*acting*).

In addition to those members of the R.C.C. holding departmental portfolios listed above, there are 17 other Ministers and one Minister of State.

EMBASSY OF THE REPUBLIC OF IRAQ
21 Queen's Gate, SW7 5JG
[01–584 7141/6]

Ambassador Extraordinary and Plenipotentiary, new appointment awaited.

Area, etc.—Traversed by the Rivers Euphrates and Tigris, Iraq extends from Turkey on N. and N.E. to the Gulf on the S. and S.E. and from Iran on E. to Syria and Arabian Desert on W., the approximate position being between 37¼° to 48¼° E. long., and 37¼° to 30° N. lat. (*see* MAP, p. 784). The area of Iraq is 167,925 sq. miles (434,924 sq. km.), of which 37 per cent. is desert land. About 35 to 40 per cent. of the remainder is potentially cultivable either by rainfall or by irrigation.

The *Euphrates* (which has a total length of 1,700 miles from its source to its outflow in the Persian Gulf) is formed by two arms, of which the Murad Su (415 miles) rises in eastern Erzurum, and flows westwards to a junction with the Kara Su, or Frat Su (275 miles); the other arm rises in the north-west of Erzurum in the Dumlu Dagh. The *Tigris* has a total length of 1,150 miles from its source to its junction with the Euphrates at Qurna, 70 miles from the Gulf, and rises in two arms south of the Taurus mountains, in Kurdistan, uniting at Til, where the boundaries of the districts of Diarbekir, Van and Bitlis conjoin.

Population.—At the Census of October 1987 Iraq had a total population of 16,278,316.

Language.—The language is mainly Arabic and English is widely used in commerce, science and the arts.

Antiquities.—In 1944 excavations at Tell Hassuna, near Shura (on the Tigris in North Iraq) unearthed abundant traces of culture dating back to 5000 B.C. Excavations in 1948 at Tel Abu Shahrain, south of 'Ur of the Chaldees,' confirm Eridu's claim to be the most ancient city of the Sumerian world. Hillah, the ancient city on the left bank of the Shatt el Hillah, a branch of the Euphrates, about 70 miles south of Baghdad, is near the site of Babylon and of the 'house of the lofty-head' or 'gate of the god' (Tower of Babel). Mosul Governorate covers a great part of the ancient kingdom of *Assyria,* the ruins of Ninevah, the Assyrian capital, being visible on the banks of the Tigris, opposite Mosul. Qurna, at the junction of the Tigris and Euphrates, is traditionally supposed to be the site of the *Garden of Eden.*

Government.—Under the Treaty of Lausanne (1923), Turkey renounced sovereignty over Mesopotamia. A provisional Arab Government was set up in Nov., 1920, and in Aug., 1921, the Emir Faisal was elected King of Iraq. The country was a monarchy until July, 1958, when King Faisal II was assassinated. From 1958 Iraq has been under Presidential rule. The ruling Party is the Arab Ba'ath Socialist Party, which came to power on July 17, 1968.

Iraq has been engaged in hostilities with Iran since September 1980, originally over control of the Shatt-al-Arab waterway. In July 1982 Iranian forces moved across the border into Iraq, and since that time a series of inconclusive battles have been fought along the borders. Both sides carried out attacks on neutral shipping and in the summer of 1987 foreign navies entered the Gulf to escort neutral merchant shipping.

International efforts to end the fighting focused on United Nations Security Council Resolution 598 of July 1987, and a ceasefire came into effect on Aug. 20, 1988. A U.N. Observer Peace-Keeping Force was sent to the Gulf to monitor the ceasefire whilst peace talks continued.

Communications and Trade.—New roads are being rapidly built, and communications between Baghdad and the provincial capitals are being improved and secured. Facilities at the port of Basra have been improved but the port has not been used since the outbreak of hostilities with Iran in Sept. 1980. Continuous dredging of the Shatt-al-Arab has also been suspended by hostilities and the channel has seriously silted. The port of Um Qasr near the Kuwaiti border has been developed for freight and sulphur handling and a container terminal is ready for operation but not in use due to the port's proximity to the war zone. Road routes from Turkey and the Mediterranean are well used, and carry through traffic to Kuwait and the south. The border between Syria and Iraq was closed in late 1977, reopened in November, 1978 and closed again in April 1982.

There is an international airport at Baghdad. Iraqi Airways provide flights between Baghdad and London, and other international airlines operate to Europe. Iraqi Republican Railways provide regular passenger and goods services between Basra, Baghdad and Mosul, and links up through Syria and Turkey with the Mediterranean and the Bosphorus, though no through traffic has used the line since the Syrian government cut the rail link in April 1982. There is also a metre gauge line connecting Baghdad with Khanaqin, Kirkuk and Arbil.

Agriculture and Industry.—Apart from the valuable revenues to be derived from oil, agricultural development makes a valuable contribution to the wealth of the country and two harvests can usually be gathered in the year. Production fluctuates from year to year according to rainfall. The Government's concern with agricultural development is shown in the large financial allocations made to the sector. Salinity and soil erosion, caused by a high water table, inadequate irrigation and drainage and traditional farming methods, are the major problems now being addressed by development planners.

Increasing industrialization is taking place. Since 1987 the Government has been encouraging increased private and mixed sector involvement in the economy. Priority is being given to petro-chemicals, food industries, construction industries and engineering. Existing industries include cement, building materials, steel fabrications, food processing and the manufacture of consumer goods, as well as the development of mineral resources.

Iraq's major industry is oil production. It was nationalized on June 1, 1972 and accounts for approximately 98 per cent. of the total government revenue and 45 per cent. of the Gross National Product. Production was some 3·5 million barrels per day in 1979 but the effects of war damage on the Basra terminals and the closure of the trans-Syria pipeline reduced production until new pipelines were built via Turkey and Saudi Arabia. Total revenues from oil are estimated at $11,000–14,000 million in 1988, although they are difficult to calculate due to fluctuations in price.

FINANCE

	1981*
Total revenue	ID19,434,856,809
Total expenditure	19,250,261,450

* Estimates.

TRADE

	1984
Total Imports	$11,260,000
Total Exports	11,720,000

Trade with U.K.

	1987	1988
Imports from U.K.	£271,655,000	£412,091,000
Exports to U.K.	33,871,000	43,406,000

The principal imports are iron and steel, cement and other building materials, mechanical and electrical machinery, motor vehicles, textiles and clothing, essential foodstuffs, grain, tinned foods and raw industrial materials. The chief exports are crude petroleum, dates, raw wool, raw hides and skins and raw cotton.

CAPITAL.—Baghdad. Population of the governorate (Census 1977) 3,205,645. Other towns of importance are Ψ Basra, Mosul and Kirkuk.

CURRENCY.—Iraqi dinar (ID) of 1,000 fils.

FLAG.—Horizontal stripes of red, white and black, with three green stars on the white stripe.

NATIONAL DAY.—July 17 (Revolution Day).

BRITISH EMBASSY
Zukaq 12, Mahala 218,
Hai Al Kheloud, Baghdad
[Baghdad 5372121/5]

Ambassador Extraordinary and Plenipotentiary, His Excellency Terence Joseph Clark, C.M.G., C.V.O. (1985).

Counsellor, R. A. Kealy (*Head of Chancery and Consul General*).

First Secretary, A. R. Brown, M.V.O. (*Commercial*).

Defence Attaché, Col. J. C. Cochrane, O.B.E.

British Council Representative, P. Elborn, Waziriya, 301, Street 3, (P.O. Box 298), Baghdad.

IRELAND

Position and Extent.—Ireland lies in the Atlantic Ocean, to the W. of Great Britain, and is separated from Scotland by the North Channel and from Wales by the Irish Sea and St. George's Channel. The area of the island is 32,588 sq. miles (84,402 sq. km.), and its geographical position between 51° 26′ and 55° 21′ N. latitude and from 5° 25′ to 10° 30′ W. longitude. The greatest length of the island, from N.E. to S.W. (Torr Head to Mizen Head), is 302 miles, and the greatest breadth, from E. to W. (Dundrum Bay to Annagh Head), is 174 miles. On the N. Coast of *Achill Island* (Co. Mayo) are the highest cliffs in the British Isles, 2,000 feet sheer above the sea. Ireland is occupied for the greater part of its area by the *Central Plain*, with an elevation 50 to 350 ft. above mean sea level, with isolated mountain ranges near the coastline. The principal mountains, with their highest points, are the *Sperrin Mountains* (Sawel 2,240 ft.) of County Tyrone; the *Mountains of Mourne* (Slieve Donard 2,796 ft.) of County Down, and the *Wicklow Mountains* (Lugnaquilla 3,039 ft.); the *Derryveagh Mountains* (Errigal 2,466 ft.) of County Donegal; the *Connemara Mountains* (Twelve Pins 2,695 ft.) of County Galway; *Macgillicuddy's Reeks* (Carrantuohill 3,414 ft., the highest point in Ireland); and the *Galtee Mountains* (3,018 ft.) of County Tipperary, and the *Knockmealdown* (2,609 ft.) and *Comeragh Mountains* (2,470 ft.) of County Waterford. The principal river of Ireland (and the longest in the British Isles) is the *Shannon* (240 miles), rising in County Cavan and draining the central plain; the Shannon flows through a chain of loughs to the city of Limerick, and thence to an estuary on the western Atlantic seaboard. The *Slaney* flows into Wexford Harbour, the *Liffey* to Dublin Bay, the *Boyne* to Drogheda, the *Lee* to Cork Harbour, the *Blackwater* to Youghal Harbour, and the *Suir*, *Barrow* and *Nore*, to Waterford Harbour. As in Scotland, the principal hydrographic feature is the *Loughs*, of which Lough *Neagh* (150 sq. miles) in the north-east is the largest in Ireland and the British Isles, others being the Shannon Chain of *Allen, Boderg, Forbes, Ree* and *Derg*, and the Erne Chain of *Gowna, Oughter, Lower Erne*, and *Erne; Melvin, Gill, Gara* and *Conn* in the north-west; and *Corrib* and *Mask* (joined by a hidden channel) in the west. In County Kerry, to the east of Macgillicuddy's Reeks, are the famous *lakes of Killarney*.

Primitive Man.—Although little is known concerning the earliest inhabitants of Ireland, there are many traces of neolithic man throughout the island; a grave containing a polished stone axehead assigned to 2,500 B.C. was found at Linkardstown, Co. Carlow, in 1944, and the use of bronze implements appears to have become known about the middle of the 17th century B.C. In the later Bronze Age a Celtic race of *Goidels* appears to have invaded the island, and in the early Iron Age *Brythons* from South Britain are believed to have effected settlements in the south-east, while *Picts* from North Britain established similar settlements in the north. Towards the close of the Roman occupation of Britain, the dominant tribe in the island was that of the *Scoti*, who afterwards established themselves in Scotland.

History.—According to Irish legends, the island of Ierne was settled by a Milesian race, who came from Scythia by way of Spain, and established the *Kingdom of Tara*, about 500 B.C. The supremacy of the *Ardri* (high king) of Tara was acknowledged by eight lesser kingdoms (Munster, Connaught, Ailech, Oriel, Ulidia, Meath, Leinster and Ossory) ruled by descendants of the eight sons of Miled. The basalt columns on the coast of Antrim, eight miles from Portrush, known as the *Giant's Causeway*, are connected with the legendary history of Ireland as the remnants of a bridge built in the time of Finn M'Coul (Fingal) to connect Antrim with Scotland (Staffa).

Hibernia was visited by Roman merchants but never by Roman legions, and little is known of the history of the country until the invasions of *Northmen* (Norwegians and Danes) towards the close of the 8th century A.D. The Norwegians were distinguished as Findgaill (White Strangers) and the Danes as Dubgaill (Black Strangers), names which survive in "Fingall," "MacDougall" and "MacDowell," while the name of the island itself is held to be derived from the Scandinavian *Ira-land* (land of the Irish), the names of the Provinces being survivals of Norse dialect forms (Ulaids-tir, Laiginstir, Mumans-tir and Kunnak-tir). The outstanding events in the encounters with the Northmen are the *Battle of Tara* (980), at which the Hy Neill king Maelsechlainn II defeated the Scandinavians of Dublin and the Hebrides under the king Amlaib Cuarán; and the *Battle of Clontarf* (1014) by which the Scandinavian power was completely broken. After Clontarf the supreme power was disputed by the O'Briens of Munster, the O'Neills of Ulster, and the O'Connors of Connaught, with varying fortunes. In 1152 Dermod MacMurrough (Diarmit MacMurchada), the deposed king of Leinster, sought assistance in his struggle with Rauidhri O'Connor (the high king of Ireland), and visited Henry II, the Norman king of England. Henry authorized him to obtain armed support in England for the recovery of his kingdom, and Dermod enlisted the services of Richard de Clare, the Norman Earl of Pembroke, afterwards known as *Strongbow*, who landed at Waterford (Aug. 23, 1170) with 200 knights and 1,000 other troops for the reconquest of Leinster, where he eventually settled, after marriage with Dermod's daughter. In 1172 (Oct. 18) Henry II himself landed in Ireland. He received homage from the Irish kings and established his capital at Dublin. The invaders subsequently conquered most of the island and a feudal government was created. In the 14th and 15th centuries, the Irish recovered most of their lands, while many Anglo-Irish lords became virtually independent, royal authority being confined to the "Pale," a small district round Dublin. Though, under Henry VII, Sir Edward Poynings, as Lord Deputy, had passed at the *Parliament of Drogheda* (1494) the act later known as *Poynings' Law*, subordinating the Irish Legislature to the Crown, the Earls of Kildare retained effective power until, in 1534, Henry VIII began the reconquest of Ireland. Parliament in 1541 recognized him as King of Ireland and by 1603 English authority was supreme.

Christianity.—Christianity did not become general until the advent of St. Patrick. *St. Patrick* was born in Britain about 389, and was taken to Ireland as a slave about sixteen years later escaping to Gaul at the age of 22. In 432 he was consecrated Bishop of Auxerre and landed in Wicklow to establish and organize the Christian religion throughout the island.

REPUBLIC OF IRELAND
(Poblacht Na L'Eireann)

Uachtarán-na-hÉireann (*President*), Patrick J. Hillery, *born* 1923, *assumed office*, Dec. 3, 1976, *sworn in for 2nd term*, Dec. 3, 1983.

CABINET
(as at July 15, 1989)

Taoiseach and Minister for the Gaeltacht, Charles J. Haughey (*FF*).
Tánaiste and Minister for Defence, Brian Lenihan (*FF*).
Foreign Affairs, Gerry Collins (*FF*).
Finance, Albert Reynolds (*FF*).
Industry and Commerce, Des O'Malley (*PD*).
Labour, Bertie Ahern (*FF*).
Justice and Communications, Ray Burke (*FF*).
Energy, Bobby Molloy (*PD*).
Marine, John Wilson (*FF*).
Agriculture and Food, Michael O'Kennedy (*FF*).
Social Welfare, Michael Woods (*FF*).
Environment, Padraig Flynn (*FF*).
Health, Rory O'Hanlon (*FF*).
Education, Mrs. Mary O'Rourke (*FF*).
Attorney General, John Murray (*FF*).
Tourism and Transport, Seamus Brennan (*FF*).

The present coalition Government was formed by the Fianna Fail Party (*FF*) and the Progressive Democrat Party (*PD*) following a general election on June 15, 1989.

IRISH EMBASSY
17 Grosvenor Place, SW1X 7HR
[01-235 2171]

Ambassador Extraordinary and Plenipotentiary, His Excellency Andrew O'Rourke (1987).

Area and Population.—The Republic has a land area of 27,136 sq. miles (70,283 sq. km.), divided into the four Provinces of *Leinster* (Carlow, Dublin, Kildare, Kilkenny, Laoighis, Longford, Louth, Meath, Offaly, Westmeath, Wexford and Wicklow); *Munster* (Clare, Cork, Kerry, Limerick, Tipperary and Waterford); *Connacht* (Galway, Leitrim, Mayo, Roscommon and Sligo); and part of *Ulster* (Cavan, Donegal and Monaghan).

The estimated population of the Republic in 1987 was 3,543,000. Figures also showed 58,864 births, 18,149 marriages and 31,219 deaths in the year 1987 (provisional).

GOVERNMENT

The Constitution.—The constitution, approved by a plebiscite on July 1, 1937, came into operation on December 29, 1937. The Constitution declares the national territory to be the whole island of Ireland, its islands and the territorial seas. Pending the reintegration of the national territory, and without prejudice to the right of the Parliament and the Government established by the Constitution to exercise jurisdiction over the whole of the national territory, the laws enacted by that Parliament shall have the like area and extent of application as those of the Irish Free State, which did not include the six counties of Northern Ireland.

The Irish language, being the national language, is

the first official language. The English language is recognized as a second official language.

The President (*Uachtarán na hEireann*) is elected by direct vote of the people for a period of seven years. A former or retiring President is eligible for a second term. The President summons and dissolves Dáil Éireann on the advice of the *Taoiseach* (Head of the Government). He signs and promulgates laws. The supreme command of the Defence forces is vested in him, its exercise being regulated by law. He has the power of pardon. The President, in the exercise and performance of certain of his constitutional powers and functions, is aided and advised by a Council of State.

The National Parliament (*Oireachtas*) consists of the President and two Houses: a House of Representatives (*Dáil Éireann*) and a Senate (*Seanad Éireann*).

Dáil Éireann is composed of 166 members elected by adult suffrage on a basis of proportional representation by means of the single transferable vote. All citizens, and such other persons in the state as may be determined by law, who have reached the age of 18 years and are not disqualified by law have the right to vote. Each Dáil may continue for a period not exceeding five years from the date of election.

Seanad Éireann is composed of 60 members, of whom 11 are nominated by the Taoiseach and 49 are elected; six by institutions of higher education, and 43 from panels of candidates, established on a vocational basis.

Members of Dáil Éireann are paid an allowance of IR£23,177 per annum (and members of Seanad Éireann IR£12,946). They are allowed travelling facilities between Dublin and their constituencies and are, subject to certain restrictions, granted free telephone and postal facilities from Leinster House and allowances for overnight stays in Dublin.

The executive authority is exercised by the Government subject to the Constitution. The Government is responsible to Dáil Éireann, meets and acts as a collective authority, and is collectively responsible for the Departments of State administered by the Ministers.

The Taoiseach is appointed by the President on the nomination of Dáil Éireann. The other members of the government are appointed by the President on the nomination of the Taoiseach with the previous approval of Dáil Éireann. The Taoiseach appoints a member of the Government to be the *Tánaiste* who acts for all purposes in the place of the Taoiseach in the event of the death, permanent incapacitation, or temporary absence of the Taoiseach. The Taoiseach, the Tánaiste and the Minister for Finance must be members of Dáil Éireann. The other members of the Government must be members of Dáil Éireann or Seanad Éireann, but not more than two may be members of Seanad Éireann.

The result of the general election on June 15, 1989 was as follows: *Fianna Fáil*, 77; *Fine Gael*, 55; *Labour*, 15; *Workers' Party*, 7; *Progressive Democrats*, 6; *Independent*, 6. Total membership including the *Ceann Comhairle* (Chairman), 166.

JUDICIAL SYSTEM

The judicial system comprises Courts of First Instance and a Court of Final Appeal called the Supreme Court (*Cúirt Uachtarach*). The Courts of First Instance include a High Court (*Ard-Chúirt*) and Courts of local and limited jurisdiction, with a right of appeal as determined by law. The High Court alone has original jurisdiction to consider the question of the validity of any law having regard to the provisions of the Constitution. The Supreme Court has appellate jurisdiction from all decisions of the High Court, with such exceptions and subject to such regulations as may be prescribed by law.

Chief Justice, Hon. Thomas A. Finlay .... IR£62,413
President of the High Court, Hon. Liam Hamilton .... IR£54,156
Judges, Supreme Court, Hon. Brian Walsh; Hon. Francis Griffin; Hon. Anthony Hederman; Hon. Niall J. McCarthy .... IR£51,058
Judges, High Court, Hon. Donal Barrington; Hon. John M. Gannon; Hon. Rory O'Hanlon; Hon. Declan Costello; Hon. Ronan Keane; Hon. Ms. Mella Carroll; Hon. Henry D. Barron; Hon. Francis D. Murphy; Hon. Kevin Lynch; Hon. Seamus Egan; Hon. Robert Barr; Hon. Gerard Lardner; Hon. John J. Blayney; Hon. John P. McKenzie; Hon. Richard Johnson; Hon. Thomas F. Roe (*ex officio*) .... IR£45,895
Attorney-General, John Murray.

RELIGION
(Census of 1981)

Catholic	3,204,476
Church of Ireland	95,366
Presbyterians	14,255
Methodists	5,790
Others	123,518
Total	3,443,405

DEFENCE

Establishments provide at present for a Permanent Defence Force of approximately 17,980 all ranks, including the Air Corps and the Naval Service. Recruitment is on a voluntary basis. Minimum term of enlistment is three years in the Permanent Defence Force followed by six years in the Reserve Defence Force. Establishments also provide for a Reserve Defence Force of 22,214 all ranks. Recruitment is also on a voluntary basis; minimum term of enlistment is three years. The Defence Estimate for the year ending Dec. 31, 1989 provides for an expenditure of IR£264,487,000.

FINANCE

	1988 (*Provisional Out-turn*)	1989 (*Post-Budget Estimate*)
	IR£m.	IR£m.
Total Current Revenue	7,690	7,331
Total Current Expenditure .	8,007	8,150
Current Revenue		
Customs	108	121
Excise Duties	1,481	1,535
Capital Taxes	62	45
Stamp Duties	198	212
Income Tax	3,055	2,697
Income Levy		
Corporation Tax	334	320
Value-Added Tax	1,805	1,815
Agricultural Levies (E.C.) ..	13	13
Motor Vehicle Duties	140	146
Employment and Training Levy*	126	105
Total Tax Revenue	7,322	7,009
Non-Tax Revenue	368	322
Total Current Revenue ..	7,690	7,331

*Formerly Youth Employment Levy.

	1988 (Provisional Out-turn) IR£m.	1989 (Post-Budget Estimate) IR£m.
Current Expenditure		
Debt Service	2,141	2,244
Industry and Labour	214	201
Agriculture	232	237
Fisheries	13	14
Forestry	7	13
Tourism	28	21
Roads and Transport	20	27
Sanitary Services	3	3
Health	1,002	1,041
Education	1,073	1,143
Social Welfare	1,606	1,617
Housing	32	28
Subsidies	172	166
Defence	296	300
Garda	266	277
Prisons...................	48	55
Legal, etc.	47	44
Other	807	719
Total (excluding Local Loans Fund Subsidies)	8,007	8,150
Add back:		
Local Loans Fund Subsidies	—	—
Total (including Local Loans Fund Subsidies)	8,007	8,150

Note: The figures do not take account of Departmental balances.

The Gross Debt at end 1987 was IR£23,690,800,000.

EDUCATION

Primary education is directed by the State, with the exception of 60 private primary schools with an enrolment of 8,508 in 1987–88.

There were 3,383 State-aided primary schools with an enrolment of 565,485.

In 1987-88 there were 500 recognized secondary schools with 214,485 pupils under private management (mainly religious orders), and 254 vocational schools with 84,868 pupils. Vocational schools are controlled by 38 statutory local Vocational Education Committees. There were 16 State comprehensive schools in 1987–88 with a total enrolment of 8,859 students, and 45 community schools with an enrolment of 31,031 students. There were also other miscellaneous second-level schools and the total full-time enrolment at second-level for 1987–88 was 342,641.

Third-level education is catered for by five University Colleges, two National Institutes for Higher Education, and also by third-level courses offered by the Technical Colleges and Regional Technical Colleges and other miscellaneous third-level institutions. There were 59,500 full-time third-level students in 1987–88, of whom 27,484 were attending university courses.

The estimated State expenditure on education in 1989, excluding administration and inspection, is first-level education IR£449,353,000; second-level education IR£461,840,000. The vote for third-level education amounted to IR£214,506,000.

MINERALS AND FISHERIES

Minerals.—238 persons were employed in the coal mines in 1988 (provisional) and 41,700 tons of coal were produced.

Sea Fisheries.—An estimated 7,750 persons were employed in the fisheries in 1987. Total value of all fish landed in 1987 was IR£78,878,105.

COMMUNICATIONS

Railways.—In the year ended Dec. 31, 1987, there were 1,944 kms of railway; 24,895,000 passengers and 3,014,000 tonnes of merchandise were conveyed; the receipts were IR£132,083,000 and expenditure IR£133,329,000. These figures are in respect of railway working by *Iarnród Eireann.*

Road Motor Services.—In 1987 road motor vehicles carried 228,116,110 passengers, the gross receipts being IR£123,984,350.

Shipping.—In 1987 the number of ships with cargo which arrived at Irish ports was 11,724 (22,557,000 net registered tons); of these 2,518 (5,479,000 net registered tons) were of Irish nationality.

CIVIL AVIATION

Shannon Airport, 15 miles W. of Limerick, is on the main transatlantic air route. In 1988 the airport handled 1,394,194 passengers.

Dublin Airport, 6 miles N. of Dublin, serves the cross-channel and European services operated by the Irish national airline *Aer Lingus* and other airlines. In 1988 the airport handled 4,418,356 passengers.

Cork Airport, 5 miles S. of Cork serves the cross Channel and European services operated by *Aer Lingus* and other airlines. In 1988 the airport handled 541,524 passengers.

Trade with U.K.

	1987 IR£	1988 IR£
Imports from U.K.	3,815,916,879	4,301,859,205
Exports to U.K.	3,662,629,824	4,349,094,183

OVERSEAS TRADE

	1987 IR£	1988 IR£
Imports	9,155,206,963	10,213,064,564
Exports	10,723,497,879	12,300,705,135
Trade balance	1,568,291,016	2,087,640,571

PRINCIPAL ARTICLES

Principal imports in 1988 were:

	IR£
Live animals	75,743,000
Food, drink and tobacco............	1,116,290,000
Petrol and petroleum products	387,530,000
Chemicals	1,292,744,000
Machinery	2,909,445,000
Transport equipment	606,491,000
Metal and manufactures	643,937,000
Textiles and clothing	862,569,000
Paper, paperboard and manufactures	347,551,000
Professional, scientific etc. goods....	243,196,000

Principal exports in 1988 were:

	IR£
Live animals	229,266,000
Meat and meat preparations	763,617,000
Other food, drink and tobacco	2,157,671,000
Machinery and transport equipment	3,837,825,000
Clothing, headgear and footwear ...	234,565,000
Textiles	414,953,000
Metal ores and scrap	230,069,000
Metal and manufactures	311,474,000
Non-metallic mineral manufactures .	172,464,000
Chemicals	1,612,787,000
Professional, scientific etc., goods ...	473,442,000

CAPITAL.—Dublin (*Baile Atha Cliath*) is a City and County Borough on the River Liffey at the head of Dublin Bay. In April 1986 the population (1986 Census) was 502,749.

Other cities and towns with their populations at the Census of 1986 are ΨCork (133,271); ΨLimerick (56,279); ΨDun Laoghaire (54,715); ΨWaterford (39,529); Ψ Galway (47,104); and ΨDundalk (26,669).

CURRENCY.—Punt (IR£) of 100 pence.

FLAG.—Equal vertical stripes of green, white and orange.

NATIONAL ANTHEM.—Amhrán na BhFiann (The Soldier's Song).

NATIONAL DAY.—March 17 (St. Patrick's Day).

BRITISH EMBASSY
31 Merrion Road, Dublin 4
[Dublin 695211]

Ambassador Extraordinary and Plenipotentiary, His Excellency Sir Nicholas Maxted Fenn, K.C.M.G. (1986).

Counsellor and Head of Chancery, J. Thorp.

First Secretaries, D. F. B. Edye (*Commercial*); W. M. L. Dickinson; G. M. Johnston; G. Fergusson; Miss B. M. Pugh; P. M. Innes.

ISRAEL
(Medinat Israel)

President of Israel, Chaim Herzog, *born* 1918, *elected* 1983, *re-elected* Feb. 20, 1988, *inaugurated*, May 8, 1988.

CABINET
(as at Dec. 1988)

Prime Minister and Minister for Labour, Yitzhak Shamir (*Lik*).

Vice-Premier and Finance Minister, Shimon Peres (*Lab*).

Foreign Affairs, Moshe Arens (*Lik*).

Defence, Yitzhak Rabin (*Lab*).

Second Vice Premier and Minister for Housing, David Levy (*Lik*).

Deputy Prime Minister and Minister for Education and Culture, Yitzhak Navon (*Lab*).

Transport, Moshe Katzav (*Lik*).

Police, Chaim Bar-Lev (*Lab*).

Trade, Ariel Sharon (*Lik*).

Energy, Moshe Shahal (*Lab*).

Justice, Dan Meridor (*Lik*).

Agriculture, Avraham Katz-Oz (*Lab*).

Tourism, Gideon Patt (*Lik*).

Health, Yaacov Tsur (*Lab*).

Economics Planning, Yitzhak Modai (*Lik*).

Communications, Gad Yaacobi (*Lab*).

Interior, Arie Deri (*Shas*).

Immigration, Yitzhak Peretz (*Shas*).

Science, Ezer Weizman (*Lab*).

Environmental Quality, Ronni Milo (*Lik*).

Without Portfolio, Moshe Nissim (*Lik*); Ehud Olmert (*Lik*); Mordechai Gur (*Lab*); Rafi Edri (*Lab*).

Lik = Likud Party; *Lab* = Labour; *Shas* = (Oriental Jew Religions).

EMBASSY OF ISRAEL
2 Palace Green, Kensington, W8 4QB
[01–937 8050]

Ambassador Extraordinary and Plenipotentiary, His Excellency Yoav Biran (1988).

Area and Population.—Israel lies on the western edge of the continent of Asia at the eastern extremity of the Mediterranean Sea, between lat. 29° 30′–33° 15′ N. and longitude 34° 15′–35° 40′ E. Its political neighbours are Lebanon on the North, Syria on the North and East, Jordan on the East and the Egyptian province of Sinai on the South West.

The area is estimated at 8,019 sq. miles (20,770 sq. km.). The population was estimated at the end of 1987 at 4,404,000. During the upheavals of 1948–49 a large number of Arabs left the country as refugees and settled in neighbouring countries.

Hebrew and Arabic are the official languages of Israel. Arabs are entitled to transact all official business with Government Departments in Arabic, and provision is made in the *Knesset* for the simultaneous translation of all speeches into Arabic.

Physical Features.—Israel comprises four main regions: (*a*) the hill country of Galilee and Judea and Samaria, rising in places to heights of nearly 4,000 ft.; (*b*) the coastal plain from the Gaza strip to North of Acre, including the plain of Esdraelon running from Haifa Bay to the south-east, and cutting in two the hill region; (*c*) the Negev, a semi-desert triangular-shaped region, extending from a base south of Beersheba, to an apex at the head of the Gulf of 'Aqaba; and (*d*) parts of the Jordan valley, including the Hula Region, Tiberias and the south-western extremity of the Dead Sea. The principal river is the Jordan, which rises from three main sources in Israel, the Lebanon and Syria, and flows through the Hula valley and the canals which have replaced Lake Hula, drained in 1958. Between Hulata and Tiberias (Sea of Galilee) the river falls 926 ft. in 11 miles and becomes a turbulent stream. Lake Tiberias is 696 ft. below sea-level and liable to sudden storms. Between it and the Dead Sea the Jordan falls 591 ft. The other principal rivers are the Yarkon and Kishon. The largest lake is the *Dead Sea* (shared between Israel and Jordan); area 393 sq. miles, 1,286 feet below sea-level, 51·5 miles long, with a maximum width of 11 miles and a maximum depth of 1,309 ft.; it receives the waters of the Jordan and of six other streams, and has no outlet, the surplus being carried off by evaporation. The water contains an extraordinarily high concentration of mineral substances. The highest mountain peak is Mount Meron, 3,962 ft. above sea-level, near Safad, Upper Galilee.

Climate.—The climate is variable, similar to that of Lower Egypt, but modified by altitude and distance from the sea. The summer is hot but tempered in most parts by daily winds from the Mediterranean. The winter is the rainy season lasting from November to April, the period of maximum rainfall being January and February.

Antiquities.—The following are among the principal historic sites in Israel: *Jerusalem*: the Church of the Holy Sepulchre: the Al Aqsa Mosque and Dome of the Rock, standing on the remains of the Temple Mount of Herod the Great, of which the Western (wailing) Wall is a fragment; the Church of the Dormition and the Coenaculum on Mount Zion; Ein Karem: Church of the Visitation, Church of St. John the Baptist. *Galilee*: The Sea; Church and Mount of the Beatitudes, ruins of Capernaum and other sites connected with the life of Christ. *Mount Tabor*: Church of the Transfiguration. *Nazareth*: Church of the Annunciation and other Christian shrines associated with the childhood of Christ. There are also numerous sites dating from biblical and medieval days, such as Ascalon, Caesarea, Atlit, Massada, Megiddo and Hazor. Other antiquities in the West Bank of Jordan and the Golan Heights at present occupied by Israel can now be visited from Israel. In accordance with the terms of the peace treaty signed between Egypt and Israel on March 26, 1979, Israel withdrew in April 1982 to the pre-1967 boundary, returning the Sinai area to Egyptian sovereignty.

Government.—There is a Cabinet and a single-chamber Parliament (*Knesset*) of 120 members. A general election is held at least once every four years. The last General Election was held in Nov. 1988.

Immigration.—The Declaration of Independence of May 14, 1948, laid down that 'the State of Israel

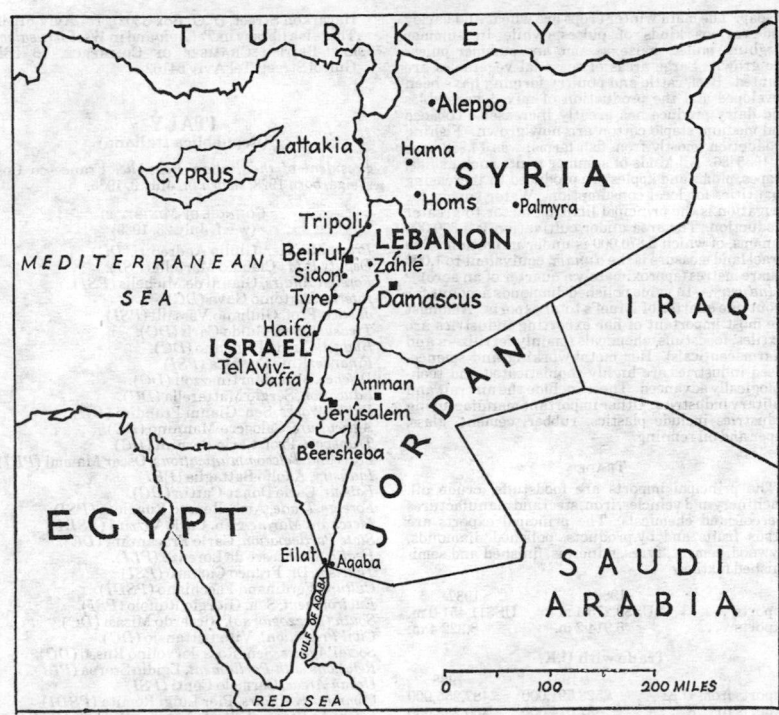

will be open to the immigration of Jews from all countries of their dispersion.' The Law of Return, passed by the *Knesset* on July 5, 1950, provides that an immigrant visa shall be granted to every Jew who expresses his desire to settle in Israel. From the establishment of the State until April 1978, about 1·7 million immigrants had entered Israel from over 100 different countries.

Education.—Elementary education for all children from 5 to 15 years is free, though secondary education is not compulsory. The law also provides for working youth, age 15–18 who for some reason have not completed their primary education, to be exempted from work in order to do so.

In 1985–86 enrolment in all educational establishments was 1,383,838: kindergartens 277,200; elementary education, 622,056; secondary education, 348,262; post-secondary, 98,420.

Finance.—Government expenditure in 1986 was 25,399,234,000 new Shekels at market prices. GNP at market prices was 40,354,955,000 new Shekels.

COMMUNICATIONS

Railways and Roads.—Israel State Railways started operating in August 1949. Towns now served are Haifa, Tel Aviv, Jerusalem, Lod, Nahariya, Beersheba, Dimona, Ashdod and intermediate stations. In 1986 the total railway network amounted to 528 km. There were 12,823 km. of paved road and in 1986 819,102 licensed vehicles.

Shipping.—Israel's merchant marine had reached

a total of 2,805,000 tons deadweight by December, 1985.

The chief ports are Haifa, a modern harbour, with a depth of 30 ft. alongside the main quay; the harbour on the Red Sea at Eilat, inaugurated in September 1965, has a capacity of 10,000 tons a day; Acre has an anchorage for small vessels; the deep-water port at Ashdod, 20 miles south of Tel Aviv, which started operations at the end of 1965, handled 8,006,000 tons of cargo in 1986. In the same year Israel's three main ports handled 17,048,000 tons of cargo.

Civil Aviation.—In 1986, 3,098,000 passengers passed through Ben Gurion airport, of which 230,146 arrived by charter flight.

PRODUCTION AND INDUSTRY

Agriculture.—The country is generally fertile and climatic conditions vary so widely that a large variety of crops can be grown, ranging from temperate crops, such as wheat and cherries, to subtropical crops such as sorghum, millet and mangoes. The famous 'Jaffa' orange is produced in large quantities mostly in the coastal plain for export: high-profit export crops such as strawberries and cut flowers are increasingly important. The citrus yield during the 1985–86 season was 1,308,700 tons. Specialized glasshouse crops for export, such as flowers, tomatoes and strawberries, are becoming increasingly popular and exports of flowers in 1985 earned US$75,454,000. Olives are cultivated, mainly for the production of oil used for edible purposes and for the manufacture of soap. The main winter crops are wheat and barley and various kinds of pulses, while in summer sorghum, millet, maize, sesame and summer pulses are grown. Large areas of seasonal vegetables are planted. Beef, cattle and poultry farming have been developed and the production of mixed vegetables and dairy produce has greatly increased. Tobacco and medium staple cotton are now grown. Fishing production (mostly from fish farms) was 14,958 tons in 1985–86. All kinds of summer fruits such as figs, grapes, plums and apples are produced in increasing quantities for local consumption. Water supply for irrigation is the principal limiting factor to greater production. The area under cultivation is 4,370,000 dunams, of which 2,370,000 is under irrigation. The Israel land measure is the *dunam*, equivalent to 1,000 square metres (approximately a quarter of an acre).

Industry.—In value polished diamonds account for about one quarter of Israel's total exports. Amongst the most important of her exporting industries are textiles, foodstuffs, chemicals (mainly fertilizers and pharmaceuticals). Her metal-working and science-based industries are highly sophisticated and technologically advanced. These include the aircraft and military industries. Other important manufacturing industries include plastics, rubber, cement, glass, paper and oil refining.

TRADE

The principal imports are foodstuffs, crude oil, machinery and vehicles, iron, steel and manufactures thereof, and chemicals. The principal exports are citrus fruits and by-products, polished diamonds, plywood, cement, tyres, minerals, finished and semi-finished textiles.

	1986	1987
Imports	US$9,275·4 m.	US$11,451·0 m.
Exports	6,914·2 m.	8,222·4 m.

Trade with U.K.

	1987	1988
Imports from U.K. ...	£523,591,000	£487,255,000
Exports to U.K.	437,014,000	460,289,000

CAPITAL.—Most of the Government departments are in Jerusalem (population, 1984, 506,200). A resolution proclaiming Jerusalem as the capital of Israel was adopted by the Israel parliament on Jan. 23, 1950. It is not, however, recognized as the capital by the United Nations. Other principal towns (1986) were ΨTel Aviv and district (1,624,100); ΨHaifa and district (393,000) and Beersheba and district (115,000).

CURRENCY.—Shekel of 100 agora.

FLAG.—White, with two horizontal blue stripes, the Shield of David in the centre.

NATIONAL ANTHEM.—Hatikvah (The Hope).

JERUSALEM

Until 1967 Jerusalem was divided between Israel and Jordan, two of the 36 recognized Christian Holy Places (in the New City) being under Jewish administration, the remainder under Arab administration in the Old City. At the conclusion of hostilities between Israel and the surrounding Arab countries in 1967 the entire city was under Israeli control.

BRITISH EMBASSY

192 Hayarkon Street, Tel Aviv.
[Tel Aviv 249171/8]

Ambassador Extraordinary and Plenipotentiary, His Excellency Mark Elliott, C.M.G.
Counsellor, S. W. J. Fuller (*Head of Chancery, Consul-General and Counsellor*).
Defence and Military Attaché, Col. E. C. Loden, M.C.

British Council Representative, P. Sandiford, 140

Hayarkon Street, (P.O. Box 3302), Tel Aviv 61032. There is a library in *Tel Aviv* and in *West Jerusalem.*
ISRAEL-BRITISH CHAMBER OF COMMERCE, 76 IBN Guirol Street, Tel Aviv 64162.

ITALY
(Repubblica Italiana)

President of the Italian Republic, Francesco Cossiga, *born* 1928, *sworn in,* July 3, 1985.

COUNCIL OF MINISTERS
(w.e.f. July 23, 1989)

Prime Minister, Giulio Andreotti (*DC*).
Deputy P.M., Claudio Martelli (*PSI*).
Foreign Affairs, Gianni de Michelis (*PSI*).
Interior, Antonio Gava (*DC*).
Justice, Prof. Giuliano Vassalli (*PSI*).
Treasury, Sen. Guido Carli (*DC*).
Budget, Cirino Pomicino (*DC*).
Finance, Rino Formica (*PSI*).
Defence, Mino Martinazzoli (*DC*).
Education, Sergio Mattarella (*DC*).
Public Works, Sen. Gianni Prandini (*DC*).
Agriculture, Calogero Mannino (*DC*).
Transport, Prof. Carlo Bernini (*DC*).
Posts and Telecommunications, Oscar Mammi (*PRI*).
Industry, Adolfo Battaglia (*PRI*).
Labour, Carlo Donat-Cattin (*DC*).
Foreign Trade, Amb. Renato Ruggiero (*PSI*).
Merchant Marine, Sen. Carlo Vizzini (*PSDI*).
State Participation, Carlo Fracanzani (*DC*).
Health, Francesco de Lorenzo (*PLI*).
Tourism, Dr. Franco Carraro (*PSI*).
Culture, Ferdinand Facchiano (*PSDI*).
Environment, Sen. Giorgio Ruffolo (*PSI*).
South (Mezzogiorno), Riccardo Misasi (*DC*).
Civil Protection, Vito Lattanzio (*DC*).
Social Affairs, Sen. Rosa Jervolino Russo (*DC*).
Relations with Parliament, Egidio Sterpa (*PLI*).
Urban Areas, Carmelo Conti (*PSI*).
Community Affairs, Pier Luigi Romita (*PSDI*).
Scientific Research, Prof. Antonio Ruberti (*PSI*).
Regional Affairs and Institutional Reforms, Dr. Antonio Maccanico (*PRI*).
Public Administration, Remo Gaspari (*DC*).

DC—Christian Democrat Party; *PSI*—Socialist Party; *PLI*—Liberal Party; *PSDI*—Social Democratic Party; *PRI*—Republican Party.

ITALIAN EMBASSY

14 Three Kings Yard, Davies Street, W1Y 2EH
[01–629 8200]

Ambassador Extraordinary and Plenipotentiary, Boris Biancheri (1987).
Minister-Counsellor, Livio Muzi-Falconi.
First Counsellors, E. Augelli; F. Pigliapoco; N. Cappello; L. Visconti di Modrone.
There are also consular offices in *Bedford, Edinburgh* and *Manchester.*

Italy is a Republic in the south of Europe, consisting of a peninsula, the large islands of Sicily and Sardinia, the island of Elba and about 70 other small islands. Italy is bounded on the N. by Switzerland and Austria, on the S. by the Mediterranean, on the E. by the Adriatic and Yugoslavia, and on the W. by France and the Ligurian and Tyrrhenian Seas. The total area is about 116,304 sq. miles (301,225 sq. km.).

The peninsula is for the most part mountainous, but between the Apennines, which form its spine, and the East coastline are two large fertile plains: of Emilia/Romagna in the north and of Apulia in the south. The Alps form the northern limit of Italy, dividing it from France, Switzerland, Austria and

Yugoslavia. Mont Blanc (15,771 ft.), the highest peak, is in the French Pennine Alps, but partly within the Italian borders are Monte Rosa (15,217 ft.), Matterhorn (14,780 ft.) and several peaks from 12,000 to 14,000 ft.

The chief rivers are the Po (405 miles), which flows through Piedmont, Lombardy and the Veneto, and the Adige (Trentino and Veneto) in the north, the Arno (Florentine Plain) and the Tiber (flowing through Rome to Ostia). The Rubicon, a small stream flowing into the Adriatic near Rimini, formed the boundary between Italy and Cisalpine Gaul: 'crossing the Rubicon' (as Caesar did in 49 B.C., thus 'invading' Italy in arms) is used to indicate definite committal to some course of action.

Population.—In Feb. 1986 Italy's population was 57,193,708.

Government.—Italian unity was accomplished under the House of Savoy, after a struggle from 1848 to 1870, in which Mazzini (1805–72), Garibaldi (1807–82) and Cavour (1810–61) were the principal figures. It was completed when Lombardy was ceded by Austria in 1859 and Venice in 1866, and through the evacuation of Rome by the French in 1870. In 1871 the King of Italy entered Rome, and that city was declared to be the capital.

Benito Mussolini, known as *Il Duce* (The Leader) was continuously in office as Prime Minister from Oct. 30, 1922, until July 25, 1943, when the Fascist regime was abolished. He was captured by Italian partisans while attempting to escape across the Swiss frontier and was put to death on April 28, 1945.

In fulfilment of a promise given in April, 1944, that he would retire when the Allies entered Rome, a decree was signed on June 5, 1944, by King Victor Emmanuel III under which Prince Umberto, the King's son, became 'Lieutenant General of the Realm.' The King remained head of the House of Savoy and retained the title King of Italy until his abdication on May 9, 1946, when he was succeeded by the Crown Prince.

A general election was held on June 2, 1946, together with a referendum on the future of the monarchy. The result showed a majority in favour of replacing the monarchy with a Republic. The Royal Family left the country on June 13, and on June 28, 1946, a Provisional President was elected.

Constitution.—The constitution of the Republic of Italy, approved by the Constituent Assembly on December 22, 1947, provides for the election of the President by an electoral college which consists of the two Houses of Parliament (the Chamber of

Deputies and the Senate) sitting in joint session together with three delegates from each region (one in the case of the Valle d'Aosta). The President, who must be over 50 years of age, holds office for 7 years. He has numerous carefully defined powers, the main one of which is the right to dissolve one or both Houses of Parliament, after consultation with the Speakers.

Defence.—The Armed Forces are largely manned by conscripts, who serve for 12 months. The Army has approx. 295,000 men, of whom 40,000 are regular officers and N.C.O.s. In addition, the elite paramilitary *Carabinieri* force, which is part of the Army, has over 96,000 men, most of whom are regulars. The Army, which has three Corps concentrated in the North, is equipped with Leopard 1 and M60 tanks and M113 armoured personnel carriers. There is also a parachute brigade, 5 alpine brigades, a missile brigade, and a Light Aviation Arm with over 300 helicopters. The Navy consists of one helicopter carrier, 3 cruisers, 4 destroyers, 9 submarines, 24 frigates and corvettes and 24 mine warfare ships. Manpower strength is approx. 45,000. The Air Force has 70,000 men and 347 combat aircraft. It is largely a tactical air force, equipped with Tornado, F104 and G91 aircraft, but also has transport, anti-submarine and helicopter search and rescue units. There is a large Reserve Force of ex-conscripts under the age of 35.

REGIONS OF ITALY

Rome and Central Italy.—Rome was founded, according to legend, by Romulus in the year now known as 753 B.C. It was the focal point of Latin civilization and dominion under the Republic and afterwards under the Roman Empire, and became the capital of Italy when the Kingdom was established in 1871. The capital is concerned mainly with tourism and government, but its importance as a business centre is steadily increasing, and it is reportedly the third largest industrial centre in the country.

Lombardy and Milan.—In the Lombardy region are to be found some 15·7 per cent of Italy's commercial and banking services and some 21·9 per cent of her manufacturing industry. The whole range of Italian industry is represented, most important being the steel, machine tool and motor car factories.

Turin and Piedmont.—Turin between 1861 and 1865 was Italy's first capital as the home of the Piedmontese Royal Family. Now it is the headquarters of Europe's largest manufacturer of motor cars, produces 75 per cent of Italy's motor vehicles and over 80 per cent of its roller bearings. Turin is also Italy's second largest steel producing city. Piedmont is the centre of the Italian textile industry based mainly on Biella.

Genoa and the Ligurian Riviera.—Genoa has been one of Europe's major ports since the Middle Ages, and handles one-third of Italy's foreign trade. About 80 per cent of the goods handled are imports.

Venice and the North-East.—Venice is primarily a tourist attraction of unique beauty. It was founded in the middle of the 5th century by refugees from the mainland fleeing attacks, and by the 16th century it was one of the strongest and richest states of Europe, dominating Eastern Mediterranean trade. It lost its independence in 1797 when Napoleon handed it over to Austria. Industry (paper and stationery, mechanical equipment, consumer goods, electrical appliances, woollens) is now developing in the Venice area, particularly on the autostrada linking Venice with her historical and now developing rivals, Verona, Vicenza, Padua and in the areas around Treviso and Pordenone. Near Trieste, is the modern Monfalcone shipyard.

Tuscany, Emilia and Romagna.—Florence, the capital of Tuscany, was one of the greatest cities in Europe from the 11th to the 16th centuries, and the cradle of the Renaissance. Under the Medici family in the 15th century flourished many of the greatest names in Italian art, including Filippo Lippi, Botticelli, Donatello and Brunelleschi and in the 16th century great Florentine artists like Michelangelo and Leonardo da Vinci. These regions were the agricultural centre of Italy but the post-war period has seen the development of large industrial centres at Bologna, Florence, Modena, Pistoia and Ravenna. Most of the new firms are small or medium-sized. The footwear industry is based in Florence, textiles in Prato, reproduction furniture at Cascina and Poggibonsi, ceramics at Sassuolo, and glass and pottery at Empoli and Montelupo. Bologna is an important centre for the food industry.

Naples and the Toe of Italy.—Naples, formerly the capital and administrative centre of the Kingdom of Naples and Sicily, remains the dominant city in the area, but it is beset with great problems of unemployment and the need for modernization. Around it, however, helped by Government incentives, industry is slowly developing, northwards to Caserta, southwards to Salerno and eastwards to Benevento.

Puglia.—Bari has always been a commercial centre and now industrial development is also taking place in the areas of Taranto, Brindisi and Foggia. At Taranto there are a highly-mechanized steel-works and a modern oil refinery. The Bari industrial zone has factories producing electronic and pneumatic valves, specialized vehicle bodies and tyres, etc. The main industry of Brindisi is a petro-chemical plant. At Foggia there is a textile factory.

Sicily.—The main source of income is agriculture, particularly citrus fruits, almonds and tomatoes, but this faces severe competition. Oil in small quantities has been found off the southern shore of the island and drilling continues, while onshore there are growing oil-refining, natural gas and petrochemical industries. Small and medium sized industries, benefiting from the Government's incentives, are developing, and tourism is bringing an increasing amount of revenue to the island.

Sardinia.—Sardinia is an autonomous region, with its capital at Cagliari. Six main industrial development areas have been officially designated. The major industries are aluminium production (there is a smelting plant at Porto Vesme), petrochemicals, lead and zinc mining; and the tourist industry is flourishing.

THE ECONOMY

Italian gross domestic product in 1986 was L.894,362,000 million. The economy has recovered from the setbacks of the early seventies, reversing the balance of payments and halving inflation, but this was accompanied by stagnation and increasing unemployment. The rate of inflation for 1985–86 was 5·9 per cent.

Industry.—The general index of industrial production (1980 = 100) stood at +2·7 per cent in 1985–86. The State-owned sector of Italian industry is important, dominated by the holding companies IRI (mechanical, steel, airlines), ENI (petro-chemicals) and ENEL (electricity).

Mineral Production.—Italy is generally poor in mineral resources but since the war deposits of natural methane gas and small deposits of oil have been discovered and rapidly exploited. Production of lignite has also increased. Other minerals produced in significant quantities include iron ores and pyrites, mercury (over one-quarter of the world production), lead, zinc and aluminium. Marble is a traditional product of the Massa Carrara district.

Agriculture.—Agriculture accounted for 5·2 per cent of gross domestic product in 1984. The agricultural labour force was 2,242,000 in 1986.

Tourist Traffic.—In 1986 an estimated 18 million foreign tourists visited Italy, and in 1986 foreigners spent an estimated L14,691,000 million. The net balance on tourism was about L10,579,000 million.

Communications.—The main railway system is State-run by the *Ferrovia dello Stato.* A network of motorways (*autostrade*) covers the country, built and operated mainly by the IRI State-holding company and ANAS the State highway authority. The auto-strada network covered 5,176 km. in 1974. *Alitalia*, the principal international and domestic airline, is also State-controlled by the IRI group. Other smaller companies, including ATI (an *Alitalia* subsidiary) and Air Mediterranea operate on domestic routes. The Italian mercantile marine totalled 7,587,117 tons in December, 1985.

FOREIGN TRADE

The balance of trade in 1987 showed a deficit of 11,138 billion lira, compared with 3,722 billion lira in 1986.

The main markets for Italian exports in 1987 were the O.E.C.D. countries, which accounted for almost 80 per cent of the total, and the E.C. markets with 56 per cent of the total. Imports came principally from the Federal Republic of Germany, France and the U.S.A.

Trade with U.K.

	1987	1988
Imports from U.K.	£4,145,659,000	£4,057,046,000
Exports to U.K.	5,216,751,000	3,878.530,000

Language and Literature.—Italian is a Romance language derived from Latin. It is spoken in its purest form in Tuscany, but there are numerous dialects, showing variously French, German, Spanish and Arabic influences. Sard, the dialect of Sardinia, is accorded by some authorities the status of a distinct Romance language. Italian literature (in addition to Latin literature, which is the common inheritance of Western Europe) is one of the richest in Europe, particularly in its golden age (Dante, 1265–1321; Petrarch, 1304–1374; Boccaccio, 1313–1375) and in the renaissance (Ariosto, 1474–1533; Machiavelli, 1469–1527; Tasso, 1544–1595). Modern Italian literature has many noted names in prose and verse, notably Manzoni (1785–1873), Carducci (1835–1907) and Gabriele d'Annunzio (1864–1938). The Nobel Prize for Literature has been awarded to Italian authors on five occasions—G. Carducci (1906), Signora G. Deledda (1926), Luigi Pirandello (1934), Salvatore Quasimodo (1959) and Eugenio Montale (1975). In 1985, there were 48 daily newspapers published in Italy, of which 6 were published in Rome and 7 in Milan.

Education.—Education is free and compulsory between the ages of 6 and 14; this comprises five years at primary school and three in the 'middle school', of which there are about 8,000. Pupils who obtain the middle school certificate may seek admission to any 'senior secondary school', which may be a lyceum with a classical or scientific or artistic bias, or an institute directed at technology (of which there are eight different types), trade or industry (including vocational schools), or teacher-training. Courses at the lyceums and technical institutes usually last for five years and success in the final examination qualifies for admission to university. There are 35 State and 14 private universities, some of ancient foundation; those at Bologna, Modena, Parma and Padua were started in the 12th century. University education is not free, but entrants with higher qualifications are charged reduced fees according to a sliding scale. In general, schools, lyceums and universities are financed by local taxation and central government grants.

ISLANDS.—*Pantelleria Island* (part of Trapani Province) in the Sicilian Narrows, has an area of 31 sq. miles and a population of 9,601. The *Pelagian Islands* (Lampedusa, Linosa and Lampione) are part of the Province of Agrigento and have an area of 8 sq. miles, pop. 4,811. The Tuscan Archipelago (including Elba), area 293 sq. km., pop. 31,861; Pontine Archipelago (including Ponza, area 10 sq. km., pop. 2,515); Flegrean Islands (including Ischia, area 60 sq. km., pop. 51,883); Capri; Eolian Islands (including Lipari, area 116 sq. km., pop. 18,636); Tremiti Islands (area 3 sq. km., pop. 426).

CAPITAL.—Rome. Population of the commune (1986) 2,821,420.

1986 estimates of the population of the communes of the principal cities and towns are Milan, 1,511,193; ΨNaples, 1,204,959; Turin, 1,034,007; ΨGenoa, 733,990; Bologna, 436,570; Florence, 429,865; *Sicily*, ΨPalermo, 719,960; *Sardinia*, ΨCagliari, 223,021.

CURRENCY.—Lira of 100 centesimi.
FLAG.—Vertical stripes of green, white and red.
NATIONAL ANTHEM.—"Inno di Mameli".
NATIONAL DAY.—June 2.

BRITISH EMBASSY
Via XX Settembre 80a, 00187 Rome
[Rome 475–5441]

Ambassador Extraordinary and Plenipotentiary, His Excellency Sir Derek Morison David Thomas, K.C.M.G. (1987).

Ministers, T. C. Wood, C.M.G.; J. R. Goldsack, M.B.E. (*FAO*).

Defence and Military Attaché, Brig. M. J. Hague.
Naval Attaché, Capt. N. R. Harris, R.N.
Air Attaché, Group-Capt. A. R. Tolcher, R.A.F.
Counsellors, M. J. Williams, C.V.O., O.B.E. (*Head of Chancery*); J. P. Watson; M. Perceval (*Commercial*).

First Secretaries, A. McGuffog (*Labour*); N. E. Cole, O.B.E. (*Administration*); Miss C. M. T. Elmes (*Economic*); R. Godfrey (*Consul*); M. C. Adams (*Commercial*); D. B. A. Evans (*Agriculture*); Miss K. Coombs (*Information*); N. J. L. Martin (*Chancery*); J. A. Towner (*Political*); J. Ashton.

There are British Consular Offices at *Milan, Rome, Naples, Genoa, Florence, Venice, Trieste* and *Cagliari* and a trade representative at *Turin.*

British Council Representative, D. T. Ricks, O.B.E., Palazzo del Drago, Via Quattro Fontane 20, 00184, Rome.

There are *British Council Offices* at *Milan* and *Naples*, each with a library.

BRITISH CHAMBER OF COMMERCE, Via San Paolo 7, 20121 Milan.

JAPAN
(Nihon Koku—Land of the Rising Sun)

Emperor of Japan, His Majesty Akihito, *born* Dec. 23, 1933; *married* April 10, 1959, Miss Michiko Shoda and has issue Prince Naruhito Hironomiya (*Crown Prince*), *born* Feb. 23, 1960, Prince Fumihito, *born* Nov. 30, 1965 and Princess Sayako, *born* April 18, 1969.

THE CABINET
(as at Aug. 13, 1989)

Prime Minister, Toshiki Kaifu.
Justice, Masao Goto.
Foreign Affairs, Taro Nakayama.
Finance, Ryutaro Hashimoto.
Health, Saburo Toida.
Education, Kazuya Ishibashi.
Trade, Hikaru Matsunaga.

Agriculture, Michihiko Kano.
Home Affairs, Kozo Watanabe.
Defence, Juro Matsumoto.
Economy, Mrs. Sumiko Takahara.
Environment, Mrs. Mayumi Moriyama.

EMBASSY OF JAPAN
101–104 Piccadilly, W1V 9FN
[01-465 6500]

Ambassador Extraordinary and Plenipotentiary, His
Excellency Kazuo Chiba (1988).
Ministers, Hiroshi Hashimoto; Shotaro Miyake (*Fi-
nancial*); Hikoharu Kure (*Commercial*).
Counsellors, I. Fujisaki (*Political*); H. Ando (*Infor-
mation*); W. Hayashi (*Economic*); S. Shiga (*Finan-
cial*); S. Miyamoto (*Agricultural*); Dr. N. Tode
(*Medical Attaché*); T. Sugiyama; I. Aoki (*Labour*);
T. Kitamura (*Commercial*).
Defence Attaché, Capt. Isamu Kyoda.

Area and Population.—Japan consists of 4 large
islands: *Honshū* (or Mainland), 230,448 sq. km. (88,839
sq. m.), *Shikoku,* 18,757 sq. km. (7,231 sq. m.), *Kyūshū,*
42,079 sq. km. (16,170 sq. m.), *Hokkaido,* 78,508 sq. km.
(30,265 sq. m.), and many small islands situated in the
North Pacific Ocean between longitude 128° 6′ East
and 145° 49′ East and between latitude 26° 59′ and 45°
31′ N., with a total area of 145,834 sq. miles (377,708

sq. km.), and a population (1988) of 121,870,000. In
1987 the birth rate was 11·1 per 1,000, and the death
rate 6·2 per 1,000.

Physiography.—The coastline exceeds 17,000 miles
and is deeply indented, so that few places are far from
the sea. The interior is very mountainous, and
crossing the mainland from the Sea of Japan to the
Pacific is a group of volcanoes, mainly extinct or
dormant. Mount Fuji, the loftiest and most sacred
mountain of Japan, about 60 miles from Tokyo, is
12,370 ft. high and has been dormant since 1707, but
there are other volcanoes which are active, including
Mount Aso in Kyūshū. There are frequent earthquakes, mainly along the Pacific coast near the Bay
of Tokyo. Japan proper extends from sub-tropical in
the south to cool temperate in the north. Heavy
snowfalls are frequent on the western slopes of
Hokkaidō and Honshū, but the Pacific coasts are
warmed by the Japan current. There is a plentiful
rainfall and the rivers are short and swift-flowing
offering abundant opportunities for the supply of
hydro-electric power.

Government.—According to Japanese tradition,
Jimmu, the First Emperor of Japan, ascended the
throne on Feb. 11, 660 B.C. Under the *Meiji* constitution of Feb. 11, 1889, the monarchy was hereditary in
the male heirs of the Imperial house.

After the unconditional surrender to the Allied
Nations (Aug. 14, 1945), Japan was occupied by Allied

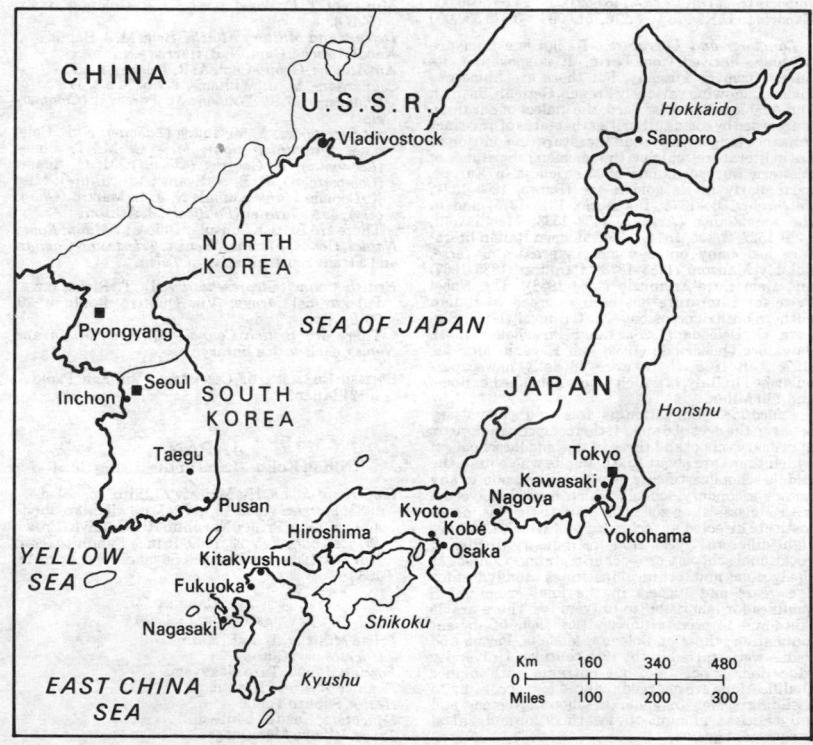

forces under General MacArthur (Sept. 15, 1945). A Japanese peace treaty conference opened at San Francisco on Sept. 4, 1951, and on Sept. 8, 48 nations signed the treaty, which became effective on April 28, 1952. Japan then resumed her status as an independent power.

A new constitution came into force on May 3, 1947. Legislative authority rests with *The Diet*, which is bicameral, consisting of a *House of Representatives* and a *House of Councillors*, both Houses being composed of elected members. Executive authority is vested in the Cabinet which is responsible to the Legislature.

The conservatives have governed Japan almost without interruption since World War II. Since 1955, when it was formed, the Liberal Democratic Party has maintained an absolute majority in the House of Representatives. In June 1987 the strength of the Parties was: Liberal Democratic Party, 303; Japan Socialist Party, 87; Komeito, 57; Democratic Socialist, 29; Japan Communist Party, 27; Independents, 5. (Four vacant seats).

The House of Councillors whose powers are subordinate to the House of Representatives, re-elects half of its members every three years. In June, 1987, the strength of the Parties was: Liberal Democratic Party, 142; Japan Socialist Party, 42; Komeito, 24; Japan Communist Party, 16; Democratic Socialist Party, 12; Shimsei Club, 4; Niim Club, 4; Salaryman Party, 3; Independents, 4. (Two vacant seats).

Agriculture and Livestock.—Owing to the mountainous nature of the country not more than one-sixth of its area is available for cultivation. The forest land includes Cryptomeria japonica, Pinus massoniana, Zeikowaskeaki, and Paulownia imperialis, in addition to camphor trees, mulberry, vegetable wax tree and a lacquer tree which furnishes the celebrated lacquer of Japan. The soil is only moderately fertile, but intensive cultivation secures good crops. Tobacco, tea, potato, rice, wheat and other cereals are all cultivated: rice is the staple food of the people, about 10,627,000 tonnes being produced in 1987. Fruit is abundant, including the mandarin, persimmon, loquat and peach; European fruits such as apples, strawberries, pears, grapes and figs are also produced. There is a small-scale beef industry and pigs and chickens are widely reared.

Minerals.—The country has mineral resources, including gold and silver, and copper, lead, zinc, iron chromite, white arsenic, coal, sulphur, petroleum, salt and uranium, but iron ore, coal and crude oil are among the principal post-war imports to supply deficiencies at home.

Industry.—Japan is the most highly industrialized nation in the Far East, with the whole range of modern light and heavy industries, including motor vehicles, electronics, metals, machinery, chemicals, textiles (cotton, silk, wool and synthetics), cement, pottery, glass, rubber, lumber, paper, oil refining and shipbuilding. The labour force of Japan in 1987 (average) was 60,840,000, of which around 2·8 per cent (1,730,000) are permanently unemployed. Of the total labour force, over 15 per cent are over 65 and this rate is increasing. Industrial, manufacturing and services workers numbered 53,430,000 and agricultural, forestries and fisheries workers 5,090,000 in 1985.

Communications.—There were 1,120,051 km. of road and 44,297 km. of rail road (steam and electric) in 1984. Also new Shinkansen (bullet train) tracks are currently being expanded. Japan National Railways was privatized on April 1, 1987 and is known as Japan Railways (JR). There are six regional companies and one goods company. The merchant fleet (oceangoing ships over 100 tons gross) totalled an aggregate of 64·16m. tons in 1985. The opening in 1988 of the Seikan rail tunnel and the Seto Ohashi

rail bridge means that the four major islands are now linked for the first time.

Armed Forces.—After the unconditional surrender of August, 1945, the Imperial Army and Navy were disarmed and disbanded.

Although the Constitution of Japan prohibits the maintenance of armed forces, internal security forces came into being in 1950, and 1952. In July, 1954, the mission of the forces was extended to include the defence of Japan against direct and indirect aggression.

The defence budget allocated for the fiscal year 1986–87 amounted to Yen 3,343,549 million, equivalent to 6·18 per cent of the General Account budget. The authorized uniformed strength was: Ground Self-Defence Force (GSDF) 180,000 (Reserve 43,000); Maritime Self-Defence Force (MSDF) 43,897 (Reserve 600); Air Self-Defence Force (ASDF) 46,204. Actual strengths of all three services are slightly below their authorized figure.

The GSDF is organized into five regional Armies, totalling thirteen Divisions, one of which is an Armoured Division. Major equipment includes tanks, APC's, towed and SP guns and rocket launchers, Hawk AA missiles, and 425 aircraft. Equipment is now largely manufactured in Japan.

The MSDF has 164 warships and auxiliaries including four DDH, four TARTAR-equipped GMDs, 42 destroyers, 14 submarines and 99 others, 205 fixed-wing aircraft and 97 helicopters.

The ASDF has 820 aircraft including 375 trainers; 43 transports and 75 support aircraft (including helicopters). There are 6 groups of Nike SAM missiles and one training unit of Patriot.

Religion.—All religions are tolerated. The principal religions of Japan are Mahayana Buddhism and Shinto. About 1 per cent of Japanese are Christians. The Roman Catholic Church has 2 archbishops and 16 bishops. The Nippon Seikokai (Holy Catholic Church of Japan) has 11 Japanese bishops (1987) and is an autonomous branch of the Anglican communion. There is also a United Protestant Church.

Education.—Under the Education Law of 1987, education at elementary (6 year course) and lower secondary (3 year course) schools is free, compulsory and co-educational. The (3 year) upper secondary schools are attended by 94 per cent of the age group. They have courses in general, agricultural, commercial, technical, mercantile marine, radio-communication and home-economics education, etc. 33 per cent of the population aged between 18 and 21 were enrolled in higher education in 1984. There are 2 or 3 year junior colleges and 4 year universities. Some of the 4 year universities have graduate schools. In 1987 there were 1,003 universities and junior colleges, the vast majority of which are privately maintained. The most prominent universities are the seven State Universities of Tokyo, Kyoto, Tohoku (Sendai), Hokkaido (Sapporo), Kyushu (Fukuoka), Osaka and Nagoya, and the two private universities, Keio and Waseda.

Language and Literature.—Japanese is said to be one of the Uro-Altaic group of languages and remained a spoken tongue until the fifth-seventh centuries A.D., when Chinese characters came into use. Japanese who have received school education (99·8 per cent of the population) can read and write the Chinese characters in current use (about 1,800 characters) and also the syllabary characters called Kana. English is the best known foreign language. It is taught in all middle and high schools and universities. There are 125 daily newspapers in Japan.

FINANCE

The Budget for the financial year 1989 for revenue

and expenditure on the general account was Yen 60,414,200 million.

PRODUCTION AND TRADE

Being deficient in natural resources, Japan has had to develop a complex foreign trade. Principal imports in 1988 consisted of mineral oils (20·5 per cent), raw materials (8·7 per cent) e.g. metal ores and scrap, 4·5 per cent, timber, 3·8 per cent, foodstuffs (15·5 per cent) (e.g. wheat and sugar), machinery (14·2 per cent), chemicals (7·9 per cent) and textiles (5·7 per cent).

Principal exports consist of steel (5·8 per cent), ships (1·5 per cent), motor vehicles (18·4 per cent), electric machinery and appliances (18·4 per cent), non-electric machinery (21·2 per cent), chemicals (4·5 per cent) and textile goods (2·6 per cent).

FOREIGN TRADE

	1987	1988
	($1,000)	
Total imports	149,515,113	187,353,686
Total exports	229,221,230	264,916,803

Trade with U.K.

	1987	1988
Imports from U.K..	£1,495,111,000	£1,742,747,000
Exports to U.K. ...	5,463,116,000	6,509,137,000

CAPITAL.—Tokyo. Population, (March 1988) 11,680,282. The other chief cities had the following populations:
Ψ Osaka (2,543,520); Ψ Nagoya (2,099,564); Ψ Yokohama (3,121,601); Kyoto, the ancient capital (1,419,390); Ψ Kobé (1,426,838); Kita-Kyushu (1,035,053); Sapporo (1,582,073); Ψ Kawasaki (1,114,173); Ψ Fukuoka (1,157,111).
CURRENCY.—Yen of 100 sen.
FLAG.—White, charged with sun (red).
NATIONAL ANTHEM.—"Kimigayo."
NATIONAL DAY.—December 23.

BRITISH EMBASSY
No. 1 Ichiban-cho, Chiyoda-ku, Tokyo 102
[Tokyo 265–5511]

Ambassador Extraordinary and Plenipotentiary, His Excellency Sir John Stainton Whitehead, K.C.M.G., C.V.O. (1986).
Minister, E. J. Field
Counsellors, S. J. Gomersall (*Economic*); M. R. J. Guest (*Commercial*); D. G. Raikes (*Financial*); J. A. Barnett, C.B.E., (*Cultural*); G. Fry (*Head of Chancery*); Dr. R. Hinder (*Science and Technology*); R. Mrowicki (*Atomic Energy*); D. Pragnell (*Administration*); J. R. H. Walker (*Chancery*).
First Secretaries, S. D. M. Jack; R. R. Hoggard; G. Williams; N. K. Hook (*Commercial*); K. J. Pocknell (*Science and Technology*); D. Powell; E. Hewlett (*Consul*); P. Sprunt (*Chancery*); A. T. MacDermott (*Information*).
Defence and Air Attaché, Gp. Capt. A. Terrett.
Naval Attaché, Capt. N. Tobin, R.N.

There is a British Consulate-General at *Osaka* and an Honorary Consulate at *Fukuoka*.

British Council Representative, J. A. Barnett, C.B.E., 2 Kagurazaka, 1-Chome, Shinjuku-ku, Tokyo 162. There is also an office and library in *Kyoto*.

BRITISH CHAMBER OF COMMERCE
No. 16 Kowa Building, 1–9–20 Akasaka, Minato-ku, Tokyo 107.

JORDAN
(Al-Mamlaka al Urduniya al-Hashemiyah)

King of the Jordan, Hussein, G.C.V.O., *born* November 14, 1935, *succeeded* on the deposition of his father, King Talal, Aug. 11, 1952, *assumed constitutional powers*, May 2, 1953, on coming of age.

Crown Prince, Prince Hassan, third son of King Talal of Jordan, *born* 1948, *appointed Crown Prince*, April 1, 1965.

CABINET
(w.e.f. April 27, 1989)

Prime Minister and Minister of Defence, Sharif Zaid bin Shaker.
Deputy P.M. and Minister of Interior, Salem Masa'deh.
Deputy P.M. and Minister for Economic Affairs, Taher Masri.
Deputy P.M. and Minister for Foreign Affairs, Marwan Al Qasem.
Agriculture, Dr. Adnan Badran.
Awqaf and Islamic Affairs, Sheikh Abdul Aziz Khayyat.
Culture and Information, Nasouh Majali.
Education, Dr. Abdullah Nsour.
Energy and Mineral Resources, Dr. Hisham Al Khatib.
Finance, Basil Jardaneh.
Health and Social Development, Dr. Zuhair Malhas.
Higher Education, Dr. Nasreddin Al Asad.
Industry and Trade, Ziyad Annab.
Justice, Rateb Al Wazani.
Labour, Dr. Jawad Bdour.
Municipal and Rural Affairs and the Environment, Yousef Hamdan Al Jaber.
Planning, Dr. Ziad Fariz.
Public Works and Housing, Shafiq Zawaideh.
Minister of State for Cabinet Affairs, Ibrahim Izzadin.
Supply, Ibrahim Ayoub.
Transport and Communications, Hikmat Khammash.
Tourism and Antiquities, Yanal Hikmat.
Water and Irrigation, Mohammad Saleh Kilani.
Youth, Dr. Awad Khleifat.

EMBASSY OF THE HASHEMITE KINGDOM OF JORDAN
6 Upper Phillimore Gardens, W8 7HB
[01-937 3685/7]

Ambassador Extraordinary and Plenipotentiary, His Excellency Dr. Albert Butros.
Counsellor, Dr. Issa Dabbah.
Defence Attaché, Col. I. Al-Khatib.
Service Office: 16 Upper Phillimore Gardens, W8. (01–937–9611).

Area and Population.—The Hashemite Kingdom of the Jordan, which covers 37,738 sq. miles (97,740 sq. km.), is bounded on the north by Syria, on the west by Israel, on the south by Saudi Arabia and on the east by Iraq. Since the hostilities of June, 1967, that part of the country lying to the west of the Jordan River has been under Israeli occupation. The majority of the population are Sunni Muslims and Islam is the religion of the State, freedom of belief is, however, guaranteed by the Constitution. Total population on the East Bank of the Jordan was estimated (1988) to be 2,910,000.

History.—After the defeat of Turkey in the First World War the Amirate of Transjordan was established in the area east of the River Jordan as a state under British mandate. The mandate was terminated after the Second World War and the Amirate, still ruled by its founder, the Amir Abdullah, became the Hashemite Kingdom of Jordan. Following the 1948 war between Israel and the Arab States, that part of Palestine remaining in Arab hands (but excluding Gaza) was incorporated into the Hashemite Kingdom.

King Abdullah was assassinated in 1951; his son Talal ruled briefly but abdicated in favour of the present King, Hussein, in 1952.

All of Jordan west of the River has been under Israeli occupation since 1967. In 1988 Jordan severed its legal and administrative ties with the occupied West Bank, but did not formally renounce sovereignty over the area. As a result of the wars of 1948 and 1967 there are about 991,000 refugees and displaced persons living in East Jordan, about 200,000 of whom live in refugee and displaced persons camps established by the U.N. Relief and Works Agency (UNRWA). In addition there are some 300,000 entirely self-supporting Palestinian members of the East Jordanian community.

Government.—The present constitution of the Kingdom came into force in 1952. It provides for a senate of 30 members (all appointed by the King) and an elected House of Representatives. Until 1988, the House of Representatives had 60 members representing both the East and West Banks. Legislation passed in 1989 stipulated that in future elections, seats would be contested on the East Bank only. The first parliamentary elections since 1967 have been called for Nov. 1989.

The King appoints the members of the Council of Ministers. Crown Prince Hassan normally acts as Regent when King Hussein is away from Jordan.

Production and Industry.—The main agricultural areas are the Jordan Valley, the hills overlooking the valley and the flatter country to the south of Amman and around Madaba and Irbid, though several large farms, which depend for irrigation on water pumped from deep aquifers, have been established in the Southern desert area. The rest of the country is desert and semi-desert. The principal crops are wheat, barley, vegetables, olives and fruit (mainly grapes and citrus fruits). Agricultural production has increased considerably in recent years due to improvements in production and irrigation techniques, and exports to Europe and elsewhere are increasing.

Important industrial products are raw phosphates (1988: 5·6 million tons) and potash (1988: 1·3 million tons), most of which is exported. The Trans-Arabian oil pipeline (Tapline) runs through North Jordan on its way from the eastern province of Saudi Arabia to the Lebanese port of Sidon. A branch pipeline, together with oil trucked by road from Iraq, feeds a refinery at Zerqa (production 1988: 2·3 million tons) which meets most of Jordan's requirements for refined petroleum products. Sufficient reserves of natural gas have been discovered in the north-east to produce electricity for the national grid (generators were commissioned in May 1989). Despite extensive efforts no significant reserves of oil have been found.

Tourism has steadily developed. International-class hotels cater for businessmen and tourists in Amman and Aqaba. A spa hotel has been opened by hot springs close to the Dead Sea and a hotel complex is planned at the Dead Sea.

Communications.—The trunk road system is good. Amman is linked to Aqaba, Damascus, Baghdad and Jeddah by roads which are of considerable importance in the overland trade of the Middle East. The former Hejaz Railway enters Jordan from Syria east of Ramtha and runs through Zerqa and Amman to Ma'an with a spur to the top of the Ras al-Naqb escarpment. It is little used, mainly for freight between Amman and Damascus. The Aqaba railway carries phosphate rock from the mines of al Hasa and al Abiad to Aqaba. A total of 2,583 vessels called at Aqaba in 1988, and 20,096,200 tons of cargo were handled. The Royal Jordanian Airline operates from Amman to Aqaba and has an extensive network of routes to the Middle East, Europe, North America and the Far East.

FINANCE

	1987	1988
	JD ('000)	
Revenue	869,969	917,562
Expenditure	965,808	1,045,680
Surplus/Deficit	−95,839	−128,118

Trade with U.K.

	1987	1988
Imports from U.K.	£188,998,000	£183,555,000
Exports to U.K.	29,285,000	21,310,000

CAPITAL.—Amman. Population, 1,100,000 (1988 estimate).

CURRENCY.—Jordanian dinar (JD) of 1,000 fils.

FLAG.—Black, white and green horizontal stripes, surcharged with white seven-point star on red triangle.

NATIONAL ANTHEM.—Long Live the King.

NATIONAL DAY.—May 25 (Independence Day).

BRITISH EMBASSY
Abdoun (P.O. Box 87),
Amman
[Amman 823100]

Ambassador Extraordinary and Plenipotentiary, His Excellency Anthony Reeve, C.M.G. (1988).

Counsellors, H. G. Hogger (*Head of Chancery and Consul-General*); P. J. F. Mansley.

Defence Attaché, Col. A. E. Cornick.

Air Attaché, Wing-Cdr. P. W. Mayes.

First Secretaries, M. Thomas (*Commercial*); D. H. Whitbread (*Information*); M. J. H. Tobin (*Consul and Administration*).

Second Secretaries, M. Ives (*Development*); Miss G. Little.

British Council Representative, M. Roddis, Rainbow Street, (P.O. Box 634), Jebel Amman, Amman.

KAMPUCHEA

COALITION GOVERNMENT OF
DEMOCRATIC KAMPUCHEA

President, Prince Norodom Sihanouk (*resigned* July 1988) *and again in* Aug. 1989 *after previously resuming the Presidency in* Feb. 1989.

Vice-President responsible for Foreign Affairs, Khieu Samphan.

Prime Minister, Son Sann.

PEOPLE'S REPUBLIC OF KAMPUCHEA ('State of Cambodia')

Head of State, Heng Samrin.

Chairman of Council of Ministers and Foreign Minister, Hun Sen.

Area and Population.—Situated between Thailand and the south of Vietnam and extending from the border with Laos on the north to the Gulf of Thailand, Kampuchea covers an area of 69,898 sq. miles, (181,035 sq. km.). It has a population (1985 U.N. estimate) of 7,284,000. The climate is tropical monsoon with a rainy season from May to October.

Fifty per cent of the total land area is forest or jungle. Around the Tonlé Sap lake in the centre of the country and along the Mekong river, which traverses the country, there is ample fertile land for the support of the population in times of peace.

History.—Once a powerful kingdom, which, as the Khmer Empire, flourished between the tenth and fourteenth centuries, Cambodia became a French protectorate in 1863 and was granted independence within the French Union as an Associate State in 1949. Full independence was proclaimed on November 9, 1953, and the process was completed when, in

January, 1955, the Kingdom of Cambodia became financially and economically independent not only of France but also of Laos and Vietnam. For the next fifteen years the political life of the country was dominated by Prince Norodom Sihanouk, first as King, then as Head of Government after he had abdicated in favour of his father and finally (following his father's death in 1960) as Head of State.

On March 18, 1970, during his absence from the country, Prince Sihanouk was deposed as Head of State by a vote of the National Assembly. A Republic was declared on October 9, 1970, and the name of the country changed to the Khmer Republic.

In April 1970 widespread fighting developed between communist insurgents and government forces which gradually developed into a general civil war. In April 1975 Phnom Penh fell to the North Vietnamese-backed Khmer Rouge. Prince Sihanouk returned to Cambodia on September 9, as nominal Head of State. However, a new Constitution was promulgated in Jan. 1976 and elections to a People's Representative Assembly were held in March. Prince Sihanouk resigned as Head of State in April, and Khieu Samphan was elected President of the State Presidium. A Government led by Pol Pot, the leader of the Khmer Rouge (Communist) party, was appointed and the state was renamed Democratic Kampuchea. During the years of Khmer Rouge rule thousands of Cambodians died or fled into exile. Relations between the Khmer Rouge regime and their Vietnamese backers deteriorated sharply, and on Dec. 25, 1978 Vietnamese troops invaded Cambodia in support of an uprising. The Cambodian capital, Phnom Penh, fell on Jan. 7, 1979. The following day the Cambodian National United Front for National Salvation established a People's Revolutionary Council, recognized by Vietnam, U.S.S.R. and by other, chiefly Soviet-aligned, countries. The state was renamed The People's Republic of Kampuchea. The Government, backed by an occupation army of Vietnamese troops, more or less controls Kampuchea, but is challenged by the guerrilla forces of the Coalition Government of Democratic Kampuchea, which was formed in June 1982 by the Khmer Rouge and non-communist groups. Vietnam has reduced its troop strength and has promised to withdraw completely by Sept. 26, 1989. Talks between the rival groups have produced some elements of compromise. As part of the rapprochement the regime in Phnom Penh has renamed the country The State of Cambodia, and has taken some measures to liberalize its constitution. The C.G.D.K. occupies Kampuchea's seat at the U.N.

Economy.—Kampuchea has an economy based on agriculture, fishing and forestry, the bulk of its people being rice-growing farmers. In addition to rice, which is the staple crop, the major products are rubber, livestock, maize, timber, pepper, palm sugar, fresh and dried fish, kapok, beans, soya and tobacco. Rice and rubber used to be the main exports though production was brought to a standstill by the hostilities. Following the Khmer Rouge victory, the populations of Phnom Penh and other towns were forcibly evacuated to the country to work on the land, and re-establish the plantations producing such crops as cotton, rubber and bananas. Following the Vietnamese invasion of 1978 the towns were repopulated and commerce revived; currency was reintroduced. Factories, in particular textile mills, iron smelting works and cement works were put back in production.

Trade with U.K.

	1987	1988
Imports from U.K.	£435,000	£322,000
Exports to U.K.	268,000	55,000

Communications.—The country had over 5,000

kilometres of roads, of which nearly half were hard-surfaced and passable in the rainy season, although now in a state of disrepair. There are two railways, one from Phnom Penh to the Thai border; the other from Phnom Penh to Kampot and Kompong Som, but operations and repairs are hindered by the continuing fighting. Phnom Penh is on a river capable of receiving ships of up to 2,500 tons all the year round. The deep water port at Kompong Som on the Gulf of Thailand can receive ships up to 10,000 tons. The port is linked to Phnom Penh by a modern highway.

Religion and Education.—The state religion was Buddhism of the 'Little Vehicle'. The constitution guaranteed religious freedom, but in practice Buddhism was suppressed by the Khmer Rouge. There has been some revival recently and Buddhism has been re-established as the state religion. There were also small Muslim and Christian communities, but many members of them died or fled the country during Khmer Rouge rule. The national language is Khmer. In the years preceding the civil war considerable efforts were devoted to the development of education and new schools, colleges and technical institutes had been established. Until April 1975 there was a Buddhist University in Phnom Penh, and several residential teachers' training colleges were in operation. However, most of the country's educated elite died under the Khmer Rouge regime, which closed all institutions of higher education. The University was re-opened in 1988.

CAPITAL.—Phnom Penh, pop. 500,000 (1983 estimate).

CURRENCY.—Riel of 100 sen.

FLAG.—(C.G.D.K.) Red, with a yellow three-towered temple in the middle. ('State of Cambodia') Red upper half and blue lower half with a yellow five-towered temple in the middle.

NATIONAL DAY.—(C.G.D.K.) April 17; ('State of Cambodia') January 7.

KOREA

Korea is situated between 124° 11″ and 130° 57′ E. long., and between 33° 7′ and 43° 1″ N. lat. It has an area of 84,565 sq. miles (219,022 sq. km.), with an estimated population of approx. 62 million, of whom about 42 million live south of the present dividing line. The southern and western coasts are fringed with innumerable islands, of which the largest, forming a province of its own, is Cheju.

History.—The last native dynasty (Yi) ruled from 1392 until 1910, in which year Japan formally annexed Korea. The country remained an integral part of the Japanese Empire until the defeat of Japan in 1945, when it was occupied by troops of the U.S.A. and the U.S.S.R., the 38th parallel being fixed as the boundary between the two zones of occupation. The U.S. Government endeavoured to reach agreement with the Soviet Government for the creation of a Korean Government for the whole country and the withdrawal of all Russian and American troops. These efforts met with no success, and in September, 1947, the U.S. Government laid the whole question of the future of Korea before the General Assembly of the United Nations. The Assembly in November, 1947, resolved that elections should be held in Korea for a National Assembly under the supervision of a temporary Commission formed for that purpose by the United Nations and that the National Assembly when elected should set up a Government. The Soviet Government refused to allow the Commission to visit the Russian Occupied Zone and in consequence it was only able to discharge its function in that part of Korea which lies to the south of the 38th parallel.

A general election was held on May 10, 1948, and the first National Assembly met in Seoul on May 31.

The Assembly passed a constitution on July 12, and on July 20 elected Dr. Syngman Rhee as the first President of the Republic of Korea. On August 15, 1948, the Republic was formally inaugurated and American Military Government came to an end.

Meanwhile in the Russian-occupied zone north of the 38th parallel the Democratic People's Republic had been set up with its capital at Pyongyang; a Supreme People's Soviet was elected in September 1948, and a Soviet-style Constitution adopted.

The Korean War.—The country remained effectively divided into two along the line of 38th parallel until the aggression of June 25, 1950, when the North Korean forces invaded South Korea. An emergency meeting of the U.N. Security Council adopted a Resolution calling for an immediate cease-fire and the withdrawal of North Korean forces. This was ignored and the communist advance continued. In response to Security Council recommendations that United Nations members should furnish assistance to repel the attack, 16 nations, including the U.S.A. and the U.K., came to the aid of the Republic of Korea. However, the communist advance could not be contained until eventually a front was established around Pusan. Later, following a successful U.S. marine landing at Inchon, the communist forces were driven beyond the 38th parallel and U.S. forces reached as far north as the Yalu River. At this point the Chinese 'volunteers' joined the campaign and although the U.N. forces were initially driven back beyond Seoul they regrouped and threw the communist forces back to approximately the old dividing line. The fighting was ended by an Armistice Agreement signed by the U.N. Commander-in-Chief and the Commander of the North Korean army and the Chinese People's 'volunteers' on July 27, 1953. By this Agreement (which was not signed by the representatives of the Republic of Korea) the line of division between North and South Korea remained in the neighbourhood of the 38th parallel. The Geneva Conference discussed Korea in 1954, but failed to agree on measures for re-unifying the country. Talks between North and South Korea on the reunification of the country have taken place intermittently.

Language and Literature.—Despite the great cultural influence of the Chinese, Koreans have developed and preserved their own cultural heritage. The Korean language is of the Ural-Altaic Group. Its script, Hangul, was invented in the 15th century; prior to this Chinese characters alone were used. Also invented around this time was the first metal movable printing type. The first works translated into Hangul were Buddhist, Confucian and other classics and it was only in the late 19th century that the European influence first began to be felt.

REPUBLIC OF KOREA
(Daehan minkuk)

President, Roh Tae Woo, *took office* February 24, 1988.

CABINET
(as at June 30, 1989)

Prime Minister, Kang Young Hoon.
Deputy P.M. and Head of the Economic Planning Board, Cho Soon.
Foreign Affairs, Choi Ho Joong.
Home Affairs, Lee Han Dong.
Finance, Lee Kyu Sung.
Justice, Huh Hyung Koo.
Defence, Lee Sang Hoon.
Education, Chong Won Shik.
Sports, Kim Jip.
Agriculture and Fisheries, Kim Shik.
Energy and Resources, Lee Bong Suh.

Trade and Industry, Han Seung Soo.
Construction, Park Seung.
Health and Social Affairs, Moon Tae Joon.
Labour, Chang Young Choi.
Transport, Kim Chang Kun.
Communication, Choi Young Choi.
Culture and Information, Choi Byung Yol.
Government Administration, Kim Young Rae.
Science and Technology, Lee Sang Hee.
Unification, Lee Hong Koo.
Political Affairs I, Chung Chong Taek.
Political Affairs II, Kim Young Chong.
Legal Affairs, Hyon Hong Choo.
Veterans' Affairs, Lee Sang Yon.
Dir. of National Security Planning Agency, Park Sei Jik.

KOREAN EMBASSY
4 Palace Gate, W8 5NF
[01–581 0247]

Ambassador Extraordinary and Plenipotentiary, His Excellency Jay Hee Oh (1987).
Minister, Keun Bae Choi.

The Republic of Korea has been officially recognized by the Governments of the United States, France, United Kingdom, and most other countries but, until recently, not by any Communist bloc country. On Feb. 1, 1989 Hungary established diplomatic relations with the Republic of Korea.

President Syngman Rhee was overthrown by a popular rising in 1960. After a year of unstable government a new regime was set up on May 16, 1961 by an army officers' coup led by Major General Park Chung Hee. On March 22, 1962 he took over as acting President. He was elected President in December 1963 and again in 1967, 1971, 1972 and 1978, but was assassinated on October 26, 1979. The country was placed under partial martial law. The then Prime Minister Choi Kyu Hah was elected President that December but resigned in August 1980 to be succeeded by Gen. Chun Doo Hwan. The constitution was revised and new elections held. President Chun was re-elected and his Democratic Justice Party gained a majority in the National Assembly after elections in March 1981. Following extensive political unrest a new constitution was agreed in October 1987. Roh Tae Woo became President in Feb. 1988. In elections to the new 299-seat National Assembly the largest number of seats (125) were won by the Democratic Justice Party but it failed to achieve an overall majority.

Constitution.—The President, who is Head of State, Chief of the Executive and Commander-in-Chief of the Armed Forces, is directly elected for a single term of five years. He appoints the Prime Minister with the consent of the National Assembly, and members of the State Council on the recommendation of the Prime Minister. The President is also empowered to take wide-ranging measures in an emergency, including the declaration of martial law, but must obtain the agreement of the National Assembly. The National Assembly is directly elected for a four-year term.

Armed Forces.—The Republic of Korea has an army of about 542,000, a small navy mostly for coastal patrol and protection duties, an air force with over 500 combat aircraft and a marine corps which is incorporated in the navy. About five per cent of the nation's G.N.P. is currently spent on defence.

Education and Religion.—Primary education is compulsory for six years from the age of seven. Secondary and higher education is extensive. The national illiteracy rate is among the lowest in Asia. There is freedom of religion. Buddhism has the most followers (13 million) followed by Protestantism (8 million) and Confucianism (4·7 million). Catholics number 2·2 million.

Agriculture and Fisheries.—The soil is fertile but the arable land is limited by the mountainous nature of the country. Staple agricultural products are rice, barley and other cereals, beans, tobacco and hemp. Fruit growing and sericulture are also practised. Ginseng, a medicinal root much used by both the Chinese and Koreans, forms a useful source of revenue. The Korean fishing industry is a major contributor to both food supply and exports.

Minerals.—The Republic of Korea is deficient in mineral resources, except for deposits of coal on the East Coast and tungsten. There are some prospects of discovering oil in the sea between Korea and Japan.

Finance.—The budget for 1988 totals about U.S.$24,330 million.

Trade and Industry.—Since the beginning of 1962 a series of successful five-year plans resulted in real economic growth averaging around 10 per cent a year. The 6th economic development plan (1987–91) envisages a growth rate of 7·5 per cent. Annual per capita G.N.P. is U.S.$4,000.

Since the 1960s the Republic of Korea has industrialized rapidly on the basis of greatly expanded exports. Important exports include cars, electrical and electronic equipment, footwear, ships, railway rolling stock and iron and steel products.

TRADE

	1987	1988
Imports	U.S.$38,585 m.	U.S.$48,105 m.
Exports	46,244 m.	59,666 m.

Trade with U.K.

	1987	1988
Imports from U.K.	£427,229,000	£450,924,000
Exports to U.K.	936,038,000	1,135,107,000

Communications and Transport.—In 1980 there were 15,599 km. of paved road. Seoul has a subway system and there are national railway and airline systems. Korean Air operates regular flights to Europe, the United States, the Middle East and South East Asia. Pusan and Inchon are the major ports with Pusan serving the industrial areas of the south-east. Inchon, 28 miles from Seoul, serves the capital, but development and operation at Inchon are hampered by a tidal variation of 9–10 metres.

CAPITAL.—Seoul, population (Nov. 1987), 9,991,089. Other main centres are Ψ Pusan (3,654,097), Taegu (2,165,954) and Ψ Inchon (1,526,435).

CURRENCY.—Won of 100 jeon.

FLAG.—White, with red over blue device in centre, three black parallel bars, some broken, in each quarter.

NATIONAL ANTHEM.—"Aegukka".

NATIONAL DAY.—August 15 (Independence Day).

BRITISH EMBASSY

No. 4, Chung-Dong, Chung-Ku, Seoul 100
[Seoul 735–7341/3]

Ambassador Extraordinary and Plenipotentiary, His Excellency Lawrence John Middleton, C.M.G. (1986).

Counsellor, R. M. Jackson, C.V.O. (*Commercial*).

Defence and Military Attaché, Brig. D. S. Williams.

First Secretaries, W. Morris (*Head of Chancery and Consul*); A. V. Hill (*Commercial/Information*).

Cultural Attaché and British Council Representative, D. G. Rogers, O.B.E., Room 401 Anglican Church Annex, 3/7 Chung Dong, Chung-ku, Seoul. There is an Honorary British Consul at *Pusan*.

BRITISH CHAMBER OF COMMERCE, c/o Chartered Bank,

1st and 2nd Floors, Samsung Building, 50, 1-Ka Ulchi Ro, Chung-Ku, Seoul.

DEMOCRATIC PEOPLE'S REPUBLIC OF KOREA
(Chosun Minchu-chui Inmin Kongwa-guk)

Politburo of the Central Committee, Kim Il-sung; Kim Chong-il; O Chin-u (*full members and members of the presidium*); Yi Chong-ok; Pak Song-choi; So Chol; Kim Yong-nam; Yon Hyong-muk; Kye Ling-tae; Kang Song-san; So Yun-sok; Ho Tam; Hong Song-nam; Chon Pyong-ho (*full members*). Choe Kwang; Cho Se-ung; Chong Chun-ki; Hyon Mu-kwang; Kang Hui-won; Han Song-yong; Kim Pok-sin; Hong Si-hak; Yi Son-sil (*alternate members*).

Secretariat of the Central Committee, Kim Il-sung (*General Secretary*); Kim Chong-il; Hwang Chang-yop; Ho Chong-suk; So Kwan-hui; Ho Tam; Pak Nam-ki; Kye Ung-tae; Chon Pyong-ho; Choe Tae-pok; Kim Chung-nin; Han Song-yong.

The area of North Korea is 46,540 sq. miles (120,538 sq. km.), with a population of about 20,385,000 (1985 U.N. estimate). North Korea is rich in minerals and industry has been developed, but the economy has stagnated in recent years because of poor planning and a shortage of foreign exchange. The armed forces are believed to number about 840,000 men.

Government.—The Constitution of the Democratic People's Republic of Korea provides for a Supreme People's Assembly, presently consisting of 615 deputies, which is elected every four years by universal suffrage. The Assembly elects a President, and the Central People's Committee. In turn, the Central People's Committee directs the Administrative Council which implements the policy formulated by the Committee. The Administrative Council (37 members), formally the government of N. Korea, includes the Prime Minister and various ministers. In practice, however, the country is ruled by the Communist Party which elects a Central Committee; this in turn appoints a Politburo. The Senior Ministers of the Administrative Council are all members of the Communist Central Committee and the majority are also members of the Politburo.

Trade with U.K.

	1987	1988
Imports from U.K.	£2,198,000	£3,125,000
Exports to U.K.	641,000	824,000

CAPITAL.—Pyongyang (population, approx. 1,500,000).

CURRENCY.—Won of 100 chon.

FLAG.—Broad red horizontal band bordered by white lines bearing a five-point red star on a white disc in centre; blue horizontal bands at top and bottom.

NATIONAL DAY.—September 8.

NATIONAL ANTHEM.—A Chi Mun Bin No Ra I Gang San (Shine bright, oh dawn, on this land so fair).

KUWAIT
(Dowlat al- Kuwait)

Amir, H. H. Sheikh Jaber Al Ahmad Al Sabah, *born* 1928; acceded Jan. 1, 1978.

CABINET
(as at June 30, 1989)

Prime Minister, H.H. Crown Prince, Sheikh Saad Al-Abdullah.

Deputy Premier and Minister of Foreign Affairs, Sheikh Sabah Al-Ahmed Al Jaber.

Education, Anwar Abdulla Al Nouri.
Social Affairs, and Labour, Sheikh Nasser Mohammed al Ahmed al Sabah.
Finance, Jasem Mohammed Al Khorafi.
Awqaf and Islamic Affairs, Khalid Ahmed Al Jassar.
Communications, Abdul Mohsen Al-Sharahan.
Minister of State for Cabinet, Rashed Abdul Aziz Al Rashed.
Defence, Sheikh Nawaf Al Ahmen Al Jaber.
Minister of State for Foreign Affairs, Saoud Mohammed Al Osaimi.
Justice and Legal Affairs, Dhari Abdulla Al Othman.
Public Works, Abdul Rahman Ibrahim Al Houti.
Minister of State for Municipality Affairs, Mohammad Abdul Mohsin al Rifai.
Public Health, Abdul Razzaq Youssef.
Oil, Sheikh Ali Al-Khalifa Al-Athbi.
Minister of State for Services Affairs, Issa Mohammed Al Mazeidi.
Commerce and Industry, Faisal Abdul Razaq Al Khalid.
Planning, Abdul Rahman Abdullah al Awadhi.
Electricity and Water, Hamoud Abdulla Al-Raqba.
Interior, Sheikh Salem Sabah Al Salem.
Minister of State for Housing Affairs, Naser Abdulla Al Rodhan.
Information, Sheikh Jaber Mubarak al Sabah.
Higher Education, Dr. Ali al Shamlan.
Amiri Diwan Affairs, Sheikh Khaled Al Ahmad Al Jasser al Sabah.

EMBASSY OF THE STATE OF KUWAIT
45–46 Queen's Gate, SW7.
[01–589 4533]

Ambassador Extraordinary and Plenipotentiary, His Excellency Ghazi M. A. Al-Rayes (1980).

Area and Population.—Kuwait extends along the shore of the Persian Gulf from Iraq to Saudi Arabia, with an area of 6,880 sq. miles (17,818 sq. km.). Kuwait has a dry, desert climate with a summer season extending from April to September. The mean temperature varies between 29–45° C. in summer, and 8–18° C. in winter. Humidity rarely exceeds 60 per cent except in July and August. The population is 1,695,128 (census 1985), of which about 42 per cent are Kuwaiti citizens, the remainder being large numbers of other Arab peoples, Iranians, Indians and Pakistanis. The total European and American population is about 12,500. The gross population growth rate is 6·4 per cent, a growth rate of 3·5 per cent for Kuwaiti citizens.

The official language is Arabic, and English is widely spoken as a second language. Islam is the official religion, though religious freedom is constitutionally guaranteed.

Government.—Although Kuwait had been independent for some years, the 'exclusive agreement' of 1899 between the Sheikh of Kuwait and the British Government was formally abrogated by an exchange of letters dated June 19, 1961. This exchange was immediately followed by Iraqi claims to sovereignty over Kuwait, but on Oct. 4, 1963, Iraq recognized Kuwait's independence although the Kuwait-Iraqi border has not yet been determined formally. Under the Constitution legislative power is vested in the Amir and the 50-member National Assembly, and executive power in the Amir and the Cabinet. The sixth National Assembly was dissolved on July 3, 1986.

Education, etc.—As a result of the very considerable oil revenues, the Kuwait Government embarked on a large scale development scheme and plans for social services. Education and medical treatment are free. New hospitals and schools continue to be built. Kuwait University was opened in 1966, and in 1987–

88 had 15,602 students. In 1987–88 there were over 489,000 pupils at government and private schools.

Public Utilities.—Kuwait has a domestic water supply from water distillation plants which operate on natural gas from the oil fields. These plants can produce over 118,000,000 gallons of fresh water daily. Total water storage capacity, in reservoirs and water towers, amounts to over 1,201 million gallons. A natural source of fresh water, discovered at Raudhatain in the north of the State, has been developed to produce up to 3,000,000 gallons per day for at least 20 years and a pipeline has been built to carry the water to Kuwait town.

Electricity is produced by six power stations in Kuwait. Production in 1987 was 18,092 million Kwh.

Communications.—Ships of British, Dutch, Kuwaiti and other lines make regular calls at Kuwait. Several international and Middle Eastern airlines operate regular air services, and other companies make non-scheduled flights to Kuwait under charter. There is a network of dual-carriageway roads and more are under construction. Telecommunications and postal services are conducted by the Kuwait Government, which has built an earth satellite station.

Finance.— Revenue for the financial year 1987–88 was KD2,915 m and expenditure was KD4,566 m. Oil revenues constitute 91·8 per cent. of total revenue. There are a large number of investment banks in some of which the Government holds equity. The banking system is controlled by the Central Bank of Kuwait.

Production.—The G.D.P. of Kuwait in 1987 was estimated at KD5,444·5 million.

Despite the desert terrain, 8·4 per cent of land is under cultivation, fruit and vegetables being the main crops. Shrimp fishing is becoming important.

The Government of Kuwait began to participate in the ownership of the British- and American-owned Kuwait Oil Company in 1974 and an agreement was signed in November 1975 which brought 100 per cent government ownership. After a reorganization of the national oil industry in 1980, all the business was taken over by the Kuwait Petroleum Corporation.

The centre of Kuwait oil production is at Burgan, south of Kuwait City. Oil is also lifted in the Kuwait/Saudi Arabia Partitioned Zone (Wafra) south of the State. Oil is exported through a specially constructed port at Mina al Ahmadi. Production of crude oil in 1987 was approximately 1·2 million barrels per day. About 3,000 people are employed, including Kuwaitis, British, Americans, Indians, Pakistanis and citizens of other Arab countries.

Trade.—Oil exports constitute about 88 per cent of Kuwait's total exports. Non-oil exports include chemical fertilizers, ammonia and other chemicals, metal pipes, shrimps and building materials; re-exports accounted for 73 per cent of non-oil exports in 1982. Major trading partners are Asian countries, followed by E.C. countries and Arab states.

	1986
Imports	KD1,661m
Exports	251m*

* excluding oil.

Trade with U.K.

	1987	1988
Imports from U.K.	£225,168,000	£237,515,000
Exports to U.K.	81,530,000	72,318,000

CAPITAL.— Ψ Kuwait (population, excluding suburbs, 400,000).
CURRENCY.—Kuwaiti dinar (KD) of 1,000 fils.
FLAG.—Three horizontal stripes of green, white and red, with black trapezoid next to staff.
NATIONAL DAY.—February 25.

BRITISH EMBASSY
P.O. Box Safat 2,
Arabian Gulf Street, Kuwait
[Kuwait 2432046/9]

Ambassador Extraordinary and Plenipotentiary, His
Excellency Peter Robert Mossom Hinchcliffe,
C.M.G., C.V.O. (1987).
Counsellor, I. L. Blackley.
First Secretaries, T. Millson (*Head of Chancery*); L.
Banks (*Consul*); A. J. Paice (*Chancery*); D. A. R
Macauley (*Commercial*); J. Brand; A. Young.

British Council Representative, D. Brown, O.B.E., P.O.
Box 345, 2 al Arabi Street, Mansouriyah. There is
a library in *Kuwait*.

LAOS
(Sathalamalid Pasathu' Paait)

President, Phoumi Vongvichit (*acting*).
President of the Supreme People's Assembly, Sisom-
phone Lovansay (*acting*).
Deputy President, Khamsouk Keola.

COUNCIL OF MINISTERS
(as at June 30, 1989)

Prime Minister, Kaysone Phomvihan.
First Deputy P.M., Nouhak Phoumsavan (*responsi-
bility for Economic Matters*).
Deputy P.M.s, Phoumi Vongvichit (*responsibility for
Education, Culture, Health and Justice*); Phoun
Sipaseut (*Minister, Foreign Affairs*); Khamtai Si-
phandone (*Minister of Defence*); Sali Vongkhamsao
(*Minister of Economics, Planning and Finance*).
Ministers attached to the P.M.'s Office, Ma Khaykham-
phithoune (*Special Affairs*); Souli Nanthavong
(*Chairman, State Commission for Science and
Technology*); Thongchan Ouplavan (*Prices*); Soth
Phetrasi (*Mapping and Frontiers*).
Agriculture, Forestry, Irrigation and Co-operatives,
Inkong Mahavong.
Construction, Khemphon Phouipaseut.
Culture, Thongsing Thammavong.
Education, Bounthiam Phitsamai.
Finance, Yao Phonvantha.
Public Health, Khamlieng Pholsena.
Industry and Handicrafts, Soulivang Daravong.
*Chairman, Committee for Economic Relations with
Foreign Countries and State Commerce*, Phao
Bounnaphon.
Interior, Sisavath Keobounphan.
*Chairman, Information, Press, Radio and Television
Committee*, Son Khamvanvongsa.
Justice, Kou Souvannamethi.
Chairman, State Bank, Nouphan Sitprasai.
Chairman, Nationalities Committee, Nhiaveu Lob-
liayao.
Chairman, Social Welfare and Veterans Committee,
Khambou Sounisai.
Trade, Vanthong Sengmuong.
Transport, Posts and Construction, Oudom Khat-
tigna.

Position and Extent.—The People's Democratic
Republic of Laos is in the northerly part of Indo-
China, lying between China and Vietnam, on the
north and east, and Burma (Myanma) and Thailand
on the west. Laos has a common boundary with
Kampuchea to the south. The area of the country is
91,429 sq. miles (231,800 sq. km.), with a population
(1985 U.N. estimate) of 4,117,000.
History.—The Kingdom of Lane Xang, the Land of
a Million Elephants, was founded in the 14th century,
but broke up at the beginning of the 15th century
into the separate kingdoms of Luang Prabang and

Vientiane and the Principality of Champassac, which
together came under French protection in 1893. In
1945 the Japanese executed a coup and suppressed
the French administration. Under a Constitution of
1947 Laos became a constitutional monarchy under
King Sisvang Vong of the House of Luang Prabang,
and an independent sovereign state in 1949. The next
twenty-five years in Laos were marked by power
struggles and civil war.
After the fall of Saigon in April 1975, internal
resistance to the *Pathet Lao* (communists) crumbled;
Communist troops occupied the whole country and,
though still paying lip-service to the 1973 ceasefire
agreement and maintaining a façade of coalition, the
Pathet Lao took over the government and began to
implement an authoritarian regime with policies of
austerity and economic self-sufficiency. On December
2, 1975, following the abdication of the King, Laos
was declared a People's Democratic Republic and the
Pathet Lao assumed full charge of the country.
Economy.—There is no significant industrial base
in Laos, an estimated 85 per cent of the work force
being engaged in agriculture, largely concerned with
rice cultivation. Rice production in 1984 amounted
to 1·3 million tonnes, thus rendering the country
theoretically self-sufficient in this staple food.
In 1984, exports amounted to US$36·2 m. and
imports to US$98·4 m. Hydro-electric power was 88·3
per cent of exports, timber 8·5 per cent. and coffee 1·2
per cent. Clearing agreements have been signed with
certain socialist countries and the trade gap is largely
financed by foreign aid, of which some 60 per cent is
provided by socialist countries.
Laos' economic performance so far has been poor
and shows no signs of early recovery, the free market
rate for the dollar is much higher than the official
rate and prices of consumer items continue to
increase.
Currency.—In January 1980 a 'new' Kip replaced
the former currency. In July 1983 the non-commer-
cial rate of exchange was rectified by the State Bank.

Trade with U.K.

	1987	1988
Imports from U.K.	£1,742,000	£1,332,000
Exports to U.K.	621,000	2,000

CAPITAL.—Vientiane, population (estimated 1984)
120,000.
CURRENCY.—Kip (K) of 100 at.
FLAG.—Blue background with a central white
circle, framed by 2 horizontal red stripes.
NATIONAL DAY.—December 2.

BRITISH AMBASSADOR, *resides at* Bangkok, Thailand.

LEBANON
(Al-Jumhouriya al-Lubnaniya)

President of the Republic of Lebanon, Amin Gemayel,
elected, Sept. 21, 1982.
Prime Minister, Selim Hoss (*acting*).

(as at Nov. 30, 1988)

CHRISTIAN GOVERNMENT (EAST BEIRUT)

Prime Minister, Minister for Defence and Information,
Gen. Michel Aoun.
*Deputy P.M., Minister for Posts and Communications,
Housing and Co-operatives, Economy and Trade*,
Col. Islam Abu Jamrah.
Finance, Health, Social Affairs, Industry and Oil,
Brig. Gen. Adgar Ma'luf.

MUSLIM GOVERNMENT (WEST BEIRUT)

Prime Minister, Dr. Selim al-Hoss.
Deputy P.M. and Minister of the Interior, Abdullah al-Rassi.
Justice and Hydroelectric Resources, Nabbi Berri.
Defence and Agriculture, Adel Osseirane.
Public Works, Transport and Tourism, Walid Jumblatt.

LEBANESE EMBASSY IN LONDON
21 Kensington Palace Gardens, W8 4QM
[01–229 7265/6]

Ambassador Extraordinary and Plenipotentiary, His Excellency Gen. Ahmed El-Hajj (1983).
First Secretaries, Michel El-Khoury ; Mohammed Dib.
Consular Section, 15 Palace Gardens Mews, W8 (01–727 6696)

Area and Population.—Lebanon forms a strip about 120 miles in length and varying in width from 30 to 35 miles, along the Mediterranean littoral, and extending from the Israel frontier on the south to the Nahr al Kebir (15 miles north of Tripoli) on the north; its eastern boundary runs down the Anti-Lebanon range and then down the Great Central depression, the *Beqaa*, from which flow the rivers Orontes and Litani. It is divided into 5 districts, North Lebanon, Mount Lebanon, Beirut, South Lebanon and Beqaa. The seaward slopes of the mountains have a Mediterranean climate and vegetation. The inland range of Anti-Lebanon has the characteristics of steppe country. There is a mixed Arabic-speaking population of Christians, Muslims and Druses. The total area of Lebanon is 4,015 sq. miles, (10,400 sq. km.), population (1985 U.N. estimate), 2,668,000.

Government.—Lebanon became an independent state on Sept. 1, 1920, administered under French Mandate until Nov. 22, 1943. Powers were transferred to the Lebanese Government from Jan. 1, 1944, and French troops were withdrawn in 1946.

In April 1975, serious fighting broke out in Beirut between members of the predominantly Christian Phalangist Party and mainly Muslim militias later supported by Palestinian guerrillas based in Lebanon. The fighting continued and increased throughout 1975 and 1976. In the autumn of 1976 the Arab Deterrent Forces composed mainly of Syrian troops, imposed an effective ceasefire. In March 1978, Israeli forces invaded but withdrew some months later, handing over their positions, except for a belt in the south, to the U.N. Interim Force in Lebanon (UNIFIL). Major bouts of fighting took place in October 1978 and April/May 1981, interspersed with regular clashes on a smaller scale. In the summer of 1982 Israeli forces again invaded the country, penetrating as far as Beirut. Following negotiations, Palestine Liberation Organization guerrillas left Beirut for various Arab countries.

The north-east of the country is currently occupied by Syrian and Palestinian forces. Although the bulk of Israeli troops withdrew from southern Lebanon in 1985, a buffer zone controlled by Israeli-backed Christian militias has been established along the Israeli-Lebanon border.

Reconciliation talks in Geneva and Lausanne, Switzerland, in March 1984, failed to produce any lasting agreement. Attempts to impose a Syrian-brokered accord in December 1985 failed when the main Christian militia overthrew the leadership which had signed it.

In Sept. 1988 President Gemayel appointed a Christian-led military government. A rival Muslim government led by Dr. Selim Hoss was at the same time set up in West Beirut. In March 1989 Gen. Aoun announced a 'War of Liberation' against the Syrians.

Production.—Fruits are the most important products and include citrus fruit, apples, grapes, bananas and olives. There is some light industry, mostly for the production of consumer goods, but most factories have been adversely affected by the instability of the past fourteen years. There is little remaining of the famous cedars of Lebanon.

Communications.—A railway runs from Beirut to Damascus, connecting at Rayak with a branch line which runs from Tripoli through Homs, Hama and Aleppo to the Turkish frontier, from Nusaybin to the Iraq frontier at Tel Kotchek. A railway also runs up the coast from Nakowia to Tripoli. The railways are not functioning as a result of the civil war. There is an international airport at Beirut, served by the national carrier MEA and a few others from East Europe. Operations can be disrupted by fighting in the city.

Archaeology, etc.—Lebanon has some important historical remains, notably Baalbek (Heliopolis) which contains the ruins of first to third century Roman temples and Jubail (Biblos), one of the oldest continuously inhabited towns in the world, and ancient Tyre.

Language and Literature.—Arabic is the official language, and French and English are also widely used.

Education.—There are six universities in Beirut, the American and the French (R.C.) Universities established in the last century, and the Lebanese National University, the Beirut University College, the Kaskik Saint Esprit University and the Arab University which are recent foundations in the early stages of development. There are several institutions for vocational training, some of which have been rendered inoperative by the civil war, and there is a good provision throughout the country of primary and secondary schools, among which are a great number of private schools.

Finance.—No reliable statistics have been published for some time. The country is known to have a deficit, and the Lebanese pound has lost much of its value against foreign currencies.

Trade.—Principal imports are gold and precious metals, machinery and electrical equipment, textiles and yarns, vegetable products, iron and steel goods, and motor vehicles. There has been a gradual decline in the overall amount of imports, as a result of continued instability.

Principal exports include gold and precious metals, fruits and vegetables, textiles, building materials, furniture, plastic goods, foodstuffs, tobacco and wine.

At one time there was a considerable transit trade through Beirut into the Arab hinterland. Lebanon is the terminal for two oil pipe lines, one formerly belonging to the Iraq Petroleum Company, debouching at Tripoli, the other belonging to the Trans Arabian Pipeline Company, at Sidon. These lines have not functioned for some years, for political/security considerations.

Trade with U.K.

	1987	1988
Imports from U.K.	£40,707,000	£55,675,000
Exports to U.K.	9,528,000	14,172,000

CAPITAL.— ΨBeirut (population, 702,000). Other towns are ΨTripoli (175,000), Zahlé (46,800), ΨSidon (24,740), ΨTyre (14,000).

CURRENCY.—Lebanese pound (£L) of 100 piastres.

FLAG.—Horizontal bands of red, white and red with a green cedar of Lebanon in the centre of the white band.

NATIONAL ANTHEM.—Kulluna Lil Watan Lil'ula Lil'alam (We all belong to the homeland).

NATIONAL DAY.—November 22.

BRITISH EMBASSY
Shamma Building, Raouché, Ras Beirut, Beirut
[Beirut 417007]

Ambassador Extraordinary and Plenipotentiary, His
Excellency Allan John Ramsay, C.M.G. (1988).

LIBERIA
(Republic of Liberia)

President and Commander-in-Chief, Dr. Samuel Kanyon Doe.

CABINET
(as at May 31, 1989)

Defence, Maj. Gen. Gray D. Allison.
Finance, David Farhat.
Justice, Jenkins Scott.
Internal Affairs, Edward Sackor.
Public Works, Yudu Gray.
Posts and Telecommunications, Morris Dukuly.
Planning and Economic Affairs, Dr. Elijah Taylor.
Agriculture, Scott Gblorzuo Toweh.
Health and Social Welfare, Martha Sendolo Belleh.
Commerce and Industry, Wisseh McClain.
Lands, Mines and Energy, William Freeman.
Minister of State for Presidential Affairs, Alvin Jones.
Rural Development, Samuel Brownell.
Youth and Sports, Haven Grigsby.
Education, Othello Gongar.
Foreign Affairs, Rudolph Johnson.
Information, Culture and Tourism, Emmanuel Bowier.
Labour, Peter Naigow.
National Security, Patrick Minikon.
Transport, Macleod Darpoh.
Minister of State without Portfolio, John Beh.
Director General of the Cabinet, Momolu Getaweh.

EMBASSY OF THE REPUBLIC OF LIBERIA
2 Pembridge Place, W2 4XB
[01–221 1036]

Ambassador Extraordinary and Plenipotentiary, His
Excellency Willie A. Givens (1985).

An independent republic of West Africa, occupying
that part of the coast between Sierra Leone and the
Côte d'Ivoire, which is between the rivers Mano in
the N.W. and Cavalla in the S.E., a distance of about
350 miles, with an area of about 43,000 sq. miles
(111,369 sq. km.), and extending to the interior to
latitude 8° 50′, a distance of 150 miles from the
seaboard. It was founded by the American Colonization Society in 1822 as a colony for freed American
slaves, and has been recognized since 1847 as an
independent State. The population at the Census of
1974 was 1,481,524; a 1988 estimate put the figure at
2,300,000.

William V. S. Tubman, President of Liberia since
1944, died in 1971 and was succeeded by Dr. Tolbert.
The Constitution was suspended following a military
coup on April 12, 1980 led by M/Sgt. Samuel K. Doe,
who then became Head of State. Executive power is
now vested in the Head of State assisted by an
appointed Cabinet. A new Constitution was endorsed
by a referendum on July 3, 1984 and on July 22 the
People's Redemptive Council was dissolved and
replaced by an interim National Assembly, comprising the Council and 35 civilian members, which will
oversee the country's return to civilian rule. Presidential and legislative elections were held in Oct.
1985; and on Jan. 6, 1986 the Interim Assembly was
dissolved and replaced by a Legislative Assembly.

The Army of Liberia consists of one division of 2
brigades of militia, three regular infantry battalions,
one engineer battalion and a small coastguard.

The artificial harbour and free port of Monrovia
was opened on July 26, 1948. There are 9 ports of
entry, including 3 river ports. International and
African airlines call at Robertsfield, 35 miles from
Monrovia. Spriggs Payne airfield, on the outskirts of
Monrovia, is used for internal flights.

Liberia is receiving assistance from a number of
countries, including the United Kingdom, and from
the E.C. and various international agencies. This aid
is mainly directed towards the implementation of
Liberia's National Socio-Economic Development
Plan.

FINANCE

	1987	1988
Revenue	$183,800,000	$207,100,000
Expenditure	345,740,000	356,084,000

$ = US Dollar

TRADE

The principal exports are iron ore, crude rubber,
timber, uncut diamonds, palm kernels, cocoa and
coffee. The chief imports are manufactured goods of
all kinds, transport and iron-ore mining equipment
and foodstuffs.

	1987	1988
Imports	$307,600,000	$282,530,000
Exports	382,200,000	416,920,000

$ = US Dollar

Trade with U.K.

	1987	1988
Imports from U.K.	£13,538,000	£11,684,000
Exports to U.K.	7,284,000	9,574,000

The language of the Republic is English. American
weights and measures are used.

CAPITAL, Ψ Monrovia. Est. pop. (1984) 425,000.
Other ports are Ψ Buchanan, Ψ Greenville (Sinoe) and
Ψ Harper (Cape Palmas).

CURRENCY.—Liberian dollar (L$) of 100 cents.

FLAG.—Alternate horizontal stripes (5 white, 6
red), with 5-pointed white star on blue field in upper
corner next to flagstaff.

NATIONAL ANTHEM.—All Hail, Liberia, Hail.

NATIONAL DAY.—July 26.

BRITISH EMBASSY
Mamba Point (P.O. Box 120), Monrovia
[Monrovia 221055]

*Ambassador Extraordinary and Plenipotentiary, and
Consul-General,* His Excellency Michael Edward
John Gore (1988).
Consul and Head of Chancery, S. J. Seaman.

LIBYA
(Al-Jamahiriya Al-Arabiya
Al-Libya Al-Shabiya Al-Ishtirakiya)

*Leader of the Revolution and Supreme Commander of
the Armed Forces,* Col. Muammar al-Gadaffi.

(as at July 30, 1989)

SECRETARIAT OF THE GENERAL PEOPLE'S CONGRESS

Secretary, Dr. Miftah al Usta Umar.
Asst. Secs., Ibrahim Abu Khizam; Salmin Ali al
Uraybi.
Sec. (Affairs of People's Congresses), Umar Ishkal.
Sec. (Affairs of People's Committees), Sulayman Sasi
al-Shuhumi.
Sec. (Affairs of Professional Congresses), Bashir
Huwayj Humaydi.

GENERAL PEOPLE'S COMMITTEE

Secretary, Umar Mustafa al-Muntasir.

Sec. for Foreign Liaison, Jadallah Azzuz al-Talhi.
Sec. for Petroleum, Fawzi al-Shakshuki.
Sec. for Communications and Maritime Transport, Mubarak al-Shamikh.
Sec. for Higher Education, Ahmad Muhammad Ibrahim.
Sec. for Economy and Foreign Trade, Dr. Farhat Sharnanah.
Sec. for Planning, Dr. Muhammad Lutfi Farhat.
Sec. for Health, Dr. Mustafa Muhammad al-Zaydi.
Sec. for Strategic Industries, Dr. Fathi Ahmad bin Shatwan.
Sec. for the Treasury, Muhammad al Madani al Bukhari.
Sec. for Information and Culture, Dr. Rajab Miftah Abu Dabbus.
Sec. for Marine Wealth, Miftah Muhammad Ku'aybah.
Sec. for Vocational Training, Ma'tuq Muhammad Ma'tuq.
Sec. for Mass Mobilization and Revolutionary Guidance, Ali al Sha'iri.
Sec. for Scientific Research, Nuri al-Fayturi al Madani.
Sec. for Agrarian Reform and Land Reclamation, Abd al-Majid al-Qa'ud.
Sec. for Justice, Izz al-Din al Hinshiri.
Sec. for Education, Fatimah Abd al-Hafiz Muktar.
Sec. for Light Industries, Amin Halimi Othman Kamil.

LIBYAN DIPLOMATIC MISSION IN LONDON

Following the break of diplomatic relations with Libya in April 1984, the Royal Embassy of Saudi Arabia has handled Libyan interests in Britain.

Libya, on the Mediterranean coast of Africa, is bounded on the East by Egypt and the Sudan, on the South by the Republics of Chad and Niger, and on the West by Algeria and Tunisia. It consists of the three former provinces of Tripolitania, Cyrenaica and the Fezzan, with a combined area of 679,362 sq. miles (1,759,540 sq. km) and a population (1989 estimate) of 3,500,000. The people of Libya are principally Arab with some Berbers in the West and aboriginal tribes in the Fezzan. Islam is the official religion of Libya, but other religions are tolerated. The official language is Arabic.

Vast sand and rock deserts, almost completely barren, occupy the greater part of Libya. The southern part of the country lies within the Sahara Desert. There are no rivers, and, as rainfall is irregular good harvests are rare. The ancient ruins in Cyrenaica, at Cyrene, Ptolemais (Tolmeta) and Apollonia, are outstanding, as are those at Leptis Magna near Homs, 70 miles from Tripoli and at Sabratha, 40 miles west of Tripoli. An Italian expedition found in the S.W. of the Fezzan a series of rock-paintings more than 5,000 years old.

Production and Industry.—Agriculture is confined mainly to the coastal areas of Tripolitania and Cyrenaica, where barley, wheat, olives, almonds, citrus fruits and dates are produced, and to the areas of the oases, many of which are well supplied with springs supporting small fertile areas. Among the important oases are Jaghbub, Ghadames, Jofra, Sebha, Murzuq, Brak, Ghat, Jalo and the Kufra group in the South-East. The main industry is oil and gas production. There are pipelines from Zelten to the terminal at Mersa Brega, from Dahra to Ras-es-Sider, from Amal to Ras Lanuf and from the Intisar field to Zuetina. Since 1984 average production of crude oil has been about 1 million barrels per day. A major petrochemical complex is under construction at Ras Lanuf where a refinery and ethylene plant began operations in early 1985. The construction of an iron and steel plant at Misurata is under way, though its completion has been slower than expected. Economic constraints have delayed some projects, particularly since Libya decided in 1983 to go ahead with a major irrigation scheme, the 'Great Man-Made River'.

Exports from Libya are dominated by crude oil, but some wool, cattle, sheep and horses, olive oil, and hides and skins are also exported. Principal imports are foodstuffs, including sugar, tea and coffee and most constructional materials and consumer goods. In recent years the private sector has been virtually eliminated and Libya is now a state trading country with imports controlled by state monopolies. In early 1988, however, reforms were proposed which will allow a small private sector to be re-established.

Communications in Libya are good. Besides the coastal road running from the Tunisian frontier through Tripoli to Benghazi, Tobruk and the Egyptian border, which serves the main population centres, main roads now link the provincial centres, and the oil-producing areas of the south with the coastal towns. There are airports at Tripoli and Benghazi (Benina), Tobruk, Mersa Brega, Sebha, Ghadames and Kufra regularly used by commercial airlines, and military airfields near Tobruk, near Tripoli and at Al Watiya, south of Zuara.

Government.—Libya was occupied by Italy in 1911-12 in the course of the Italo-Turkish War, and under the Treaty of Ouchy (Oct. 1912) the sovereignty of the province was transferred by Turkey to Italy. In 1939 the four Provinces of Libya (Tripoli, Misurata, Benghazi and Derna) were incorporated in the national territory of Italy as *Libia Italiana*. After the Second World War Tripolitania and Cyrenaica were placed provisionally under British and the Fezzan under French administration, and in conformity with a resolution of the U.N. General Assembly on Nov. 21, 1949, Libya became on Dec. 24, 1951, the first independent state to be created by the United Nations. The monarchy was overthrown by a revolution on Sept. 1, 1969, and the country was declared a republic. It was ruled by the Revolutionary Command Council (RCC) under the leadership of Colonel Muammar Gadaffi.

In March 1977 a new form of direct democracy, the 'Jamahiriya' (state of the masses) was promulgated and the official name of the country was changed to Socialist People's Libyan Arab Jamahiriya. At local level authority is now vested in about 1,500 Basic and 14 Municipal People's Congresses which appoint Popular Committees to execute policy. Officials of these Congresses and Committees, together with representatives from unions and other organizations, form the General People's Congress, which normally meets for about a week early each year. This is the highest policy-making body in the country. The General People's Congress appoints its own General Secretariat and the General People's Committee, whose members head the 13 government departments which execute policy at national level. The Secretary of the General People's Committee has functions similar to those of a Prime Minister.

Since a reorganization in March 1979 neither Col. Gadaffi nor his former RCC colleagues have held formal posts in the administration. Gadaffi continues to hold the ceremonial title 'Leader of the Revolution'.

Libya has technical assistance agreements with a number of countries, and also employs large numbers of foreign labourers and experts.

Trade with U.K.

	1987	1988
Imports from U.K.	£220,626,000	£235,957,000
Exports to U.K.	133,649,000	111,812,000

CAPITAL—ΨTripoli, pop. 1989, about 1,000,000. The principal towns are: ΨBenghazi (500,000); ΨMisurata (200,000); Sirte (100,000).

CURRENCY.—Libyan dinar (LD) of 1,000 dirhams.
FLAG.—Libya uses a plain emerald green flag.
NATIONAL DAY.—September 1.

BRITISH EMBASSY

Diplomatic relations between the U.K. and Libya were broken in April 1984. British interests are currently handled by a section at the Italian Embassy, 1 Sharia Oran, Tripoli.

LIECHTENSTEIN
(Fürstentum Liechtenstein)

Prince, Franz Josef II., *born* Aug. 16, 1906; *succeeded*, July 26, 1938; *married* March 7, 1943, Countess Gina von Wilczek.
Heir, Crown Prince Hans Adam, *born* Feb. 14, 1945; *married* July 30, 1967, Countess Marie Kinsky; and has issue, Prince Alois, *b.* June 11, 1968; Prince Maximilian, *b.* May 16, 1969; Prince Constantin, *b.* March 15, 1972; Princess Tatjana, *b.* April 10, 1973.

From Aug. 26, 1984, Prince Hans Adam took over official duties and executive authority; Prince Franz Josef II remains titular Head of State.

MINISTRY
(as at June 30, 1989)

Prime Minister, Hans Brunhart (*Head of Government 'Presidium', Foreign Affairs, Education, Finance, Construction*).
Deputy P.M., Dr. Herbert Wille (*Interior, Agriculture, Forestry and Environment, Culture, Youth and Sport, Justice*).
Government Councillors, René Ritter (*Economy*), Dr. Peter Wolff (*Social and Health Services*), Wilfried Büchel (*Communications*).

Liechtenstein is represented in diplomatic and consular matters in the United Kingdom by the Swiss Embassy, *q.v.*

Liechtenstein is a Principality on the Upper Rhine, between Vorarlberg (Austria) and Switzerland, with an area of 61 sq. miles (158 sq. km.), and a population in 1988 of 28,181. The language of the Principality is German.

At the General Election on March 5, 1989, the Patriotic Union Party won 13 seats and Progressive Citizens' Party 12.

The main industries are high and ultra-high vacuum engineering, semi-conductor industry, roller bearings, fastenings and securing systems, artificial teeth, heating and hot water equipment, synthetic fibres, woollen and homespun fabrics.

FINANCE

	1987	1988
Revenue	F318,401,301	F319,016,168
Expenditure	308,306,099	321,229,914

(F = Swiss francs)

CAPITAL, Vaduz. Pop. (1988), 4,919.
CURRENCY.—Swiss franc of 100 rappen (or centimes).
FLAG.—Equal horizontal bands of blue over red; gold crown on blue band near staff.
NATIONAL ANTHEM.—Oben Am Jungen Rhein (High on the Rhine).
NATIONAL DAY.—August 15.
British Consul General, Anthony Hugh Morgan (*office* at Dufourstrasse 56, 8008 Zürich).

LUXEMBOURG
(Grand-Duché de Luxembourg)

Grand Duke, H.R.H. Jean, *born* Jan. 5, 1921, *married*, April 9, 1953, Princess Joséphine-Charlotte of Belgium, and has issue, 3 sons and 2 daughters; *succeeded* (on the abdication of his mother) Nov. 12, 1964.
Heir Apparent, Prince Henri, *born* April 16, 1955, *married* February 14, 1981, Maria Teresa Mestre, and has issue, Prince Guillaume, *b.* Nov. 11, 1981; Prince Felix, *b.* June 3, 1984; Prince Louis, *b.* Aug. 3, 1986.

CABINET
(w.e.f. July 14, 1989)

Christian Socialists:
Minister of State, President of the Government, Minister of the Treasury and Cultural Affairs, M. Jacques Santer.
Interior, M. Jean Spautz.
The Family, Social Solidarity, Women's Affairs and the Retired, M. Fernand Boden.
Budget, Finance and Labour, M. Jean-Claude Juncker.
Education, Justice and the Civil Service, M. Marc Fischbach.
Agriculture and Viticulture, Rural Development and Scientific Research, M. Rene Steichen.

Socialists:
Vice-President of the Government, Minister of Foreign Affairs, Foreign Trade and Aid, and Defence, M. Jacques Poos.
Public Health and Social Security, Physical Education and Sports, and Youth Affairs, M. Johny Lahure.
Economy, Transport and Public Works, M. Robert Goebbels.
Environment, Regional Development, Posts and Telecommunications, Energy and Information Technology, M. Alex Bodry.
State Secretary for Social Security, Health, Sports and Youth Affairs, Mady Delvaux-Stehres.
State Secretary for Foreign Affairs, Overseas Trade, Aid and Defence, M. Georges Wohlfart.

EMBASSY OF LUXEMBOURG
27 Wilton Crescent, SW1X 8SD
[01–235 6961]

Ambassador Extraordinary and Plenipotentiary, His Excellency Edouard Molitor (1989).

Luxembourg is a Grand Duchy in Western Europe, bounded by the Federal Republic of Germany, Belgium, and France. The area is 998 sq. miles (2,586 sq. km.), the population (Dec. 1984) 365,900, nearly all Roman Catholics. The country is well wooded, with many deer and wild boar. The language is Letzeburgesch but French is the official language; most speak German and many English.

Established as an independent State under the sovereignty of the King of the Netherlands as Grand Duke by the Congress of Vienna in 1815, it formed part of the Germanic Confederation, 1815–66, and was included in the German 'Zollverein'. In 1867 the Treaty of London declared it a neutral territory. On the death of the King of the Netherlands in 1890 it passed to the Duke of Nassau. The territory was invaded and overrun by the Germans at the beginning of the war in 1914, but was liberated in 1918. By the Treaty of Versailles, 1919, Germany renounced her former agreements with Luxembourg in respect of the customs union, etc., and in 1921 an economic union was made with Belgium. The Grand Duchy was again invaded and occupied by Germany on May 10, 1940. The constitution of the Grand Duchy was modified on April 28, 1948, and the stipulation of permanent neutrality was then abandoned. Luxembourg is now a fully effective member of the Western association of powers and a signatory of the Brussels and North Atlantic Treaties, and also a member of the European Communities. Luxembourg is a member of the Belgium–Netherlands–Luxembourg Customs Union (Benelux, 1960).

The Court of the European Communities has its seat in Luxembourg, as does the Secretariat of the European Parliament, the European Investment Bank, the European Audit Court and the European Monetary Co-operation Fund.

There is a Chamber of 64 Deputies, elected by universal suffrage for 5 years. Legislation is submitted to the Council of State.

The Grand Duchy was rich in iron-ore and possesses an important iron and steel industry with an annual productive capacity over 5,700,000 tons. Government revenue for 1987 was estimated at L.F. 79,600 million, expenditure L.F. 79,700 million. The Luxembourg franc has at present the same value as the Belgian franc.

There are 170 miles of railway.

Trade with U.K.

	1986	1987
Imports from U.K.	£58,507,000	£70,492,000
Exports to U.K.	148,811,000	134,077,000

CAPITAL.—Luxembourg, pop. (1987), 77,500, is a dismantled fortress.

CURRENCY.—Luxembourg franc (LF) of 100 centimes. Belgian currency is also legal tender.

FLAG.—Three horizontal bands, red, white and blue.

NATIONAL ANTHEM.—Ons Hémécht (Our homeland).

NATIONAL DAY.—June 23.

BRITISH EMBASSY
14 Boulevard F. D. Roosevelt, P.O. Box 874, L-2018, Luxembourg
[Luxembourg 29864]

Ambassador Extraordinary and Plenipotentiary, Her Excellency Juliet Jeanne Campbell, C.M.G. (1988).

MADAGASCAR
(Repoblika Demokratika n'i Madagaskar)

President, Didier Ratsiraka, *took office* 1975, *re-elected* 1982 and March 12, 1989 for a seven-year term.

COUNCIL OF MINISTERS
(w.e.f. Feb. 12, 1989)

Prime Minister, Lt.-Col. Victor Ramahatra.
Finance and Economy, Pascal Rakotomavo.
Agricultural Production, Jose Michel Andrianoelison.
Animal Production, Water and Forests, Joseph Randrianasolo.
Trade, Georges Solofoson.
Industry, Energy and Mines, Jose Rakotomavo.
Population and Social Condition, Youth and Sports, Jean André Ndremanjary.
Revolutionary Art and Culture, Gisèle Rabesahala.
Posts and Telecommunications, Rakotovoa Andriantiana.
Justice, Joseph Bedo.
Transport, Meteorology and Tourism, Cmdt. Jean Emile Tsaranazy.
Civil Service and Labour, Georges Ruphin.
Defence, Gen. Mahasampa Raveloson.
Health, Dr. Jean-Jacques Séraphin.
Interior, Ampy Portos.
Primary and Secondary Education, Charles Zeny.
Higher Education, Ignace Rakoto.
Scientific Research, Antoine Zafera.
Information, Pierre Simon.
Foreign Affairs, Jean Bemananjara.
Public Works, Andrianaivomanana Razafindramisa.

HONORARY CONSULATE IN LONDON
16 Lanark Mansions, Pennard Road, W12 8DT
[01-746 0133]

Honorary Consul, S. Hobbs.

Madagascar lies 240 miles off the east coast of Africa and is the fourth largest island in the world. It has an area of 226,669 sq. miles (587,041 sq. km.), and a population (1988 estimate) of 11,000,000. The people are of mixed Polynesian, Arab and Negro origin. The languages spoken are Malagasy and French. There are sizeable French, Chinese and Indian communities.

Government.—It became a French protectorate in 1895, and a French colony in 1896 when the former queen was exiled. Republican status was adopted on October 14, 1958, and independence was proclaimed on June 26, 1960.

The post-independence civilian government was replaced by a military government in Jan. 1975 and the following month martial law was declared. A Supreme Council of the Revolution of 18 members under Capitaine de Frégate (now Admiral) Didier Ratsiraka was established on June 15, 1975.

In December 1975 a new constitution was approved in a referendum, which vested executive power in the President. He appoints a Council of Ministers to assist him, with the guidance of the Revolutionary Supreme Council. There is a 137-member National People's Assembly elected for a 5-year term by universal suffrage,

Revised agreements with France, signed on June 4, 1973, provided for the withdrawal of the French forces stationed in the country after independence. The French naval base at Diégo Suarez (now called Antsiranana) was turned into a civilian ship repair yard. Madagascar also withdrew from the Franc Zone and announced a claim to the islands of Juan de Nova, Glorieuses, Isle de l'Europe, Bassa da India and Tromelin which had remained integral parts of the French Republic after independence.

The island's economy is still largely based on agriculture, which accounts for three-quarters of its exports. Development plans have placed emphasis on increasing agricultural and livestock production, the improvement of communications, the exploitation of mineral deposits and the creation of small industries.

TRADE

	1985	1986
Imports	$US 400·54 m.	$US 441·54 m.
Exports	274·23 m.	351·18 m.

Trade with U.K.

	1987	1988
Imports from U.K.	£6,382,000	£4,747,000
Exports to U.K.	6,925,000	7,154,000

CAPITAL.—Antananarivo (population about 1,000,000). Other main towns are the chief port ΨToamasina (55,000); ΨMahajanga (50,000); Fianarantsoa (47,000); ΨAntsiranana (41,000).

CURRENCY.—Franc Malgache (Malagasy franc) (FMG) of 100 centimes.

FLAG.—Equal horizontal bands of red (above) and green, with vertical white band by staff.

NATIONAL DAY.—June 26 (Independence Day).

BRITISH EMBASSY
(BP 167, Antananarivo)
[Antananarivo 277 49]

Ambassador Extraordinary and Plenipotentiary, His Excellency Anthony Victor Hayday (1987).
Second Secretary, J. J. Macadie.

MALI
(République du Mali)

Secretary-General of the U.D.P.M., President of the Government, and Minister of Defence, Gen. Moussa Traore, *born* 1937, *assumed office* Nov. 20, 1968, *elected* June 19, 1979, *re-elected* June 9, 1985.

GOVERNMENT MINISTERS
(w.e.f. June 8, 1989)

Secretary General to the Presidency, Diango Cissoko.
National Education, Gen. Sékou Ly.
Territorial Administration and Basic Development, Col. Issa Ongoiba.
Sports, Art and Culture, Bakary Traore.
Public Works, Urbanism and Construction, Cheikh Oumar Doumbia.
Agriculture, Moulaye Mohamed Haidara.
Finance and Commerce, Tiéna Coulibaly.
Environment and Livestock, Morifing Kone.
Employment and the Civil Service, Mme. Diallo Lalla Sy.
Foreign Affairs and International Co-operation, Dr. N'Golo Traore.
Transport and Tourism, Zeini Moulaye.
Information and Telecommunications, Naimanto Diarra.
Planning, Souleymane Dembele.
Justice, Mamadou Sissoko.
Industry, Hydraulics and Energy, Amadou Deme.
Public Health and Social Affairs, Dr. Abdoulaye Diallo.
Minister delegate to the Ministry of Defence, Gen. Abdoulaye Ouologuem.

The Republic of Mali, an inland state in north-west Africa, has an area of 478,791 sq. miles (1,240,000 sq. km.), and a population (1985 U.N. estimate) of 8,206,000. The principal rivers are the Niger and the Senegal.

Formerly the French colony of Soudan, the territory elected on Nov. 24, 1958, to remain as an autonomous republic within the French Community. It associated with Senegal in the Federation of Mali which was granted full independence on June 20, 1960. The Federation was effectively dissolved on August 22 by the secession of Senegal. The title of the Republic of Mali was adopted on Sept. 22, 1960.

Government.—The regime of Modibo Keita was overthrown on Nov. 19, 1968, by a group of Army officers who formed a National Liberation Committee and appointed a Prime Minister. Moussa Traore assumed the functions of Head of State. A new civil constitution came into being in 1979. The new government formed on May 4, 1978 contained a majority of civilians. On June 19, 1979, elections were held for an 82-member National Assembly. Presidential elections held on the same day confirmed Traore as President.

Economy.—Mali's principal exports are groundnuts (raw and processed), cotton fibres, meat and dried fish. The Republic rejoined the CFA Franc Zone on June 1, 1984 when measures were taken to convert the Franc Malien at the rate of 2FM : 1 Franc CFA.

Trade with UK.

	1987	1988
Imports from UK	£5,573,000	£12,732,000
Exports to U.K.	6,937,000	2,240,000

CAPITAL.—Bamako (600,000). Other towns are Gao, Kayes, Mopti, Sikasso, Segou and Timbuktu (all regional capitals).
CURRENCY.—Franc C.F.A. of 100 centimes.
FLAG.—Vertical stripes of green (by staff), yellow and red.
NATIONAL DAY.—September 22.

BRITISH EMBASSY
British Ambassador, resident at Dakar, Senegal.

MAURITANIA
(République Islamique de Mauritanie)

President, Col. Maaouya Ould Sid' Ahmed Taya, *took power* Dec. 12, 1984 (*also holds portfolios of Prime Minister and Defence*).

GOVERNMENT MINISTERS
(as at June 30, 1989)

Foreign Affairs and Co-operation, Cmdt. Cheikh Sid Ahmed Ould Baba.
Justice, Mouhamed Salem Ould Mohamed Lemine.
Interior, Post and Telecommunications, Col. Djibril Ould Abdallahi.
Finance, Mohamed Ould Nani.
Fisheries and Marine Economy, Lt.-Col. Sidina Mohamed Ould Sidiya.
Industry and Mining, Ahmed Ould Khalifa Ould Jiddou.
Equipment, Lt.-Col. Oumar Dieng Harouna.
National and Higher Education, Ba Aliou Ibra Hasni Ould Didi.
Civil Service, Employment, Youth and Sport, Mohammed Ould Haimer.
Hydraulics and Energy, Mohamed Lemine Ould Abdi Soumare Oumar.
Rural Development, Hamoud Ould Ely.
Health and Social Affairs, Cmdt. N'Diaye Kane.
Trade and Transport, Hamdi Samba Diop.
Information and Sec. of State for Literacy and Basic Teaching, Mohamed Lemine Ould Ahmed.
Planning and Employment, Moustaphe Ould Abderahman.
Women's Issues, Handicrafts and Tourism, Mme. Abderrahmane Khadijetou Mint Ahmed.
Culture and Islamization, Mohamed Saloum Ould Addoud.
State Security, Ethmane Sid'Ahmed Yessa.
Secretary General, Barro Abdoulaye.
Asst. Sec. Gen., Ba Alassane Yero.
Controller General, Boullaha Ould Mogueya Ethmane Ould Yessa.

Mauritania lies on the north-west coast of Africa immediately to the north of Senegal. It is bounded on the east by the Republic of Mali. To the north it is bounded by Morocco and the Western Sahara. Mauritania and Morocco took possession of that territory in February 1976 when Spain formally relinquished all right to it and in April 1976 agreed on a new frontier dividing the territory between them. In August 1979, Mauritania relinquished all claim to the southern sector of the Western Sahara after a three-year war against the Polisario front guerrilla army. Area 397,955 sq. miles (1,030,700 sq. km.). The population was estimated at 1,888,000 in 1985. The Republic of Mauritania elected on November 28, 1958, to remain within the French Community as an autonomous republic. It became fully independent on Nov. 28, 1960. In 1972 Mauritania broke with the franc zone and established its own unit of currency, the Ouguiya, equal in value to 5 francs CFA.

Mauritania's main source of potential wealth lies in rich deposits of iron ore around Zouérate, in the north of the country. Exports began in 1963, via a railway laid for the purpose from the mine to the port of Nouadhibou. The deposits are being exploited under the aegis of the *Société Nationale Industrielle Miniere* following the nationalization in 1974 of the internationally based company MIFERMA. There are copper deposits at Akjoujt which are being exploited by SOMIMA, a company nationalized on Feb. 25, 1975; the mine was closed in 1978, but reopened in 1981.

Trade with U.K.

	1987	1988
Imports from U.K.	£3,862,000	£3,048,000
Exports to U.K.	8,724,000	7,259,000

CAPITAL.—Nouakchott (500,000).
CURRENCY.—Ouguiya of 5 khoums.
FLAG.—Yellow star and crescent on green ground.
NATIONAL DAY.—November 28.

British Ambassador, resident at Dakar, Senegal.

MEXICO
(Estados Unidos Mexicanos)

President (1988–94), Lic. Carlos Salinas de Gortari, *elected,* June 4, 1988, *took office,* Dec. 1, 1988.

THE CABINET
(as at June 1989)

Interior, Lic. Fernando Gutiérrez Barrios.
Foreign Affairs, Lic. Fernando Solana Morales.
Finance and Public Credit, Dr. Pedro Aspe Armella.
Defence, Gral de División D.E.M. Antonio Riviello Bazán.
Navy, E. M. N. Mauricio Shleskes.
Budget and Planning, Dr. Ernesto Zedillo Ponce de León.
Energy, Mines and Parastatal Industries, Sr. Fernando Hiriart Balderrama.
Trade and Industrial Development, Dr. Jaime Serra Puche.
Agriculture and Water Resources, Jorge de la Vega Domínguez.
Communications and Transport, Andrés Caso Lombardo.
Education, Lic. Manuel Barlett Díaz.
Urban Development and Ecology, Patricio Chirinos C.
Health, Jesús Kumante Rodríguez.
Labour and Social Security, Sr. Arsenio Farell Cubillas.
Agrarian Reform, Victor Cervera Pacheco.
Tourism, Carlos Hank González.
Fisheries, María de los Angeles Moreno.
Attorney-General, Enrique Alvarez del Castillo.
Attorney-General of Federal District, Ignacio Morales Lechuga.
Comptroller-General, María Elena Vazquez Nava.
Mayor of Mexico City, Lic. Manuel Camacho Solís.

MEXICAN EMBASSY
8 Halkin Street, SW1X 7DW
[01-235 6393/6]

Ambassador Extraordinary and Plenipotentiary, His Excellency Bernardo Sepulveda (1989).

Area and Population.—Mexico occupies the southern part of the continent of North America, with an extensive seaboard to both the Atlantic and Pacific Oceans, extending from 14° 33′ to 32° 43′ N. lat. and 86° 46′ to 117° 08′ W. long., and comprising one of the most varied zones in the world. It contains 31 states and the federal district of Mexico, making in all 32 political divisions, covering an area of 761,605 sq. miles (1,972,547 sq. km.). At the 1980 Mexican General Census, the total population was 67,383,000, but a 1985 U.N. estimate gives a figure of 78,524,000.

The two great ranges of North America, the Sierra Nevada and Rocky Mountains, are prolonged from the north to a convergence towards the narrowing isthmus of Tehuantepec, their course being parallel to the west and east coasts. The surface of the interior consists of an elevated plateau between the two ranges, with steep slopes both to the Pacific and Atlantic (Gulf of Mexico). In the west is the peninsula of Lower California, with a mountainous surface,

separated from the mainland by the Gulf of California. The Sierra Nevada, known in Mexico as the *Sierra Madre,* terminates in a transverse series of volcanic peaks, from Colima on the west to Citlaltepetl (El Pico de Orizaba) on the east. The low-lying lands of the coasts form the *Tierra Caliente,* or tropical regions (below 3,000 ft.), the higher levels form the *Tierra Templada,* or temperate region (from 3,000 to 6,000 ft.), and the summit of the plateau with its peaks is known as *Tierra Fria,* or cold region (above 6,000 ft.). The only considerable rivers are the *Rio Grande del Norte* which forms part of the northern boundary, and is navigable for about 70 miles from its mouth in the Gulf of Mexico, and the *Rio Grande de Santiago,* the *Rio Balsas* and *Rio Papaloapan.* The largest fresh-water lakes are *Chapala* (70 miles long and 20 miles wide), and *Pátzcuaro.*

History and Archaeology.—The present Mexico and Guatemala were once the centre of a remarkable indigenous civilization, which had unknown beginnings in the centuries before Christ, flowered in the periods from A.D. 500 to 1100 and A.D. 1300 to 1500 and collapsed before the little army of Spanish adventurers under Hernán Cortés in the years following 1519. Pre-Columbian Mexico was divided between different but connected Indian cultures, each of which has left distinctive archaeological remains: the best-known of these are Chichén Itzá, Uxmal, Bonampak and Palenque, in Yucatán and Chiapas (Maya); Teotihuacon, renowned for the Pyramid of the Sun (216 feet high) in the Valley of Mexico (Teotihuacáno); Monte Albán and Mitla, near Oaxaca (Zapotec); El Tajín in the State of Veracruz (Totonac); and Tula in the State of Hidalgo (Toltec). The last and most famous Indian culture of all, the Aztec, based on Tenochitlán, suffered more than the others from the Spanish and only very few Aztec monuments remain.

A few years after the Conquest, the Spanish built Mexico City on the ruins of Tenochitlán, and appointed a Viceroy to rule their new dominions, which they called New Spain. The country was largely converted to Christianity, and a distinctive colonial civilization, representing a marriage of Indian and Spanish traditions, developed and flourished, notably in architecture and sculpture. In 1810 a revolt began against Spanish rule. This was finally successful in 1821, when a precarious independence was proclaimed. Friction with the United States in Texas led to the war of 1845–48, at the end of which Mexico was forced to cede the northern provinces of Texas, California and New Mexico. In 1862 Mexican insolvency led to invasion by French forces which installed Archduke Maximilian of Austria as Emperor. The empire collapsed with the execution of the Emperor in 1867 and the austere reformer, Juárez, restored the republic. Juárez's death was followed by the dictatorship of Porfirio Diaz, which saw an enormous increase of foreign, particularly British and United States, investment in the country. In 1910 began the Mexican Revolution which reformed the social structure and the land system, curbed the power of foreign companies and ushered in the independent industrial Mexico of today.

Government.—Under the Constitution of Feb. 5, 1917 (as subsequently amended), Congress consists of a Senate of 64 members, elected for six years, and of a Chamber of Deputies, at present numbering 400, elected for three years. Presidents, who wield full executive powers, are elected for six years; they cannot be re-elected.

There are nine political parties registered in Mexico, of which by far the largest and most influential is the *Partido Revolucionario Institucional* (P.R.I.) which has for many years constituted the governing party. The Mexican Communists allied with several like-minded smaller parties to form the Mexican United Socialist Party (P.S.U.M.) in 1982.

Communications.—Veracruz, Tampico and Coatzacoalcos are the chief ports of the Atlantic, and Guaymas, Mazatlán, Puerto Lázaro Cárdenas, Acapulco, Salina Cruz and Puerto Madero on the Pacific. Work is proceeding on the reorganization and re-equipment of the whole system; help in this has been forthcoming from the World Bank, the Export-Import Bank and private sources in the United States. The railways were completely nationalized in 1970.

Mexico City may be reached by at least three highways (with 14 entry points) from the United States, and work is complete on roads southward from Mexico City to Yucatán as well as on two principal highways to the Guatemalan border (with three entry points).

International telegraph services to the United States frontier are provided by the government-owned Mexican Telegraph Company and then through the United States to Canada and Europe.

Teléfonos de México, a state-controlled company, controls about 98 per cent of all telephone services. Satélite Latinoamericano, S.A. (SATELAT) is a joint government/private sector venture disseminating television programmes to Latin America through Intelsat IV satellite facilities leased by the Mexican Government.

There is a good national and international network of air services. There are 1,113 airports and landing fields in Mexico, of which eighteen are equipped to handle long-distance flights. There are 166 airline companies, including two of the major national airlines—*Mexicana de Aviación* and *Aeroméxico.* Passenger traffic is growing by about 14 per cent yearly, while cargo is increasing by a similar percentage.

Production.—The principal agricultural crops are maize, beans, rice, wheat, sugar cane, coffee, cotton, tomatoes, chili, tobacco, chick-peas, groundnuts, sesame, alfalfa, vanilla, cocoa and many kinds of fruit, both tropical and temperate. The maguey, or Mexican cactus, yields several fermented drinks, mezcal and tequila (distilled) and pulque (undistilled). Another species of the same plant supplies sisal-hemp (henequen). The forests abound in mahogany, rosewood, ebony and chicle trees. Agriculture employs an estimated 30 per cent of the working population.

The principal industries are mining and petroleum, but over the last twenty years there has been very considerable expansion of both light and heavy industries. Exports of manufactured goods now average about 20 per cent of total exports. The steel industry expanded steadily until recently and current production is around 6·5 m. tons. The mineral wealth is great, and principal minerals are gold, silver, copper, lead, zinc, quicksilver, iron and sulphur. Substantial reserves of uranium have been found. In the non-metals sector, Mexico continues to produce 25 per cent of the world's supply of fluorspar.

The total proven petroleum reserves were 72 billion barrels in 1983. Crude oil production is currently about 2,600,000 barrels. Daily production of natural gas is approximately 3 billion cubic feet. Oil reserves have increased substantially due to important discoveries in the Gulf of Campeche. A new refinery at Tula, State of Hidalgo, is the nation's largest; and new refineries in Monterrey, State of Nuevo Leon, and Salina Cruz, State of Oaxaca, are under construction.

Textile production is led by the artificial fibres sector, which comprised 66 per cent of the industry's output in 1983.

Defence.—Supreme command is vested in the President, exercised through the Ministries of Defence (for Army and Air Force) and Marine.

The country is divided into 36 zones in which the regular army (106,000) and part-time conscripts (250,000) are trained. The Army in 1985 had three HQ Brigades, five Artillery Regiments, 26 mechanized and one Horse Cavalry Regiments, Transport, Engineering and Signals Regiments, and 78 Infantry Battalions. In addition, there is a Rural Defence Militia of some 12,000 men.

The Navy has a strength of about 38,500 officers and men including the Naval Air Force and Marines. It is equipped with three destroyers, five frigates, six OPVs, 19 corvettes, 17 minesweepers, 31 coastal craft patrol, 12 inshore and river patrol boats, 13 transports and tugs, and one sail training ship. Many vessels are non-operational. The Marine Infantry has 10 battalions (4,300 officers and men). The Naval Air Force consists of four squadrons and 49 aircraft.

The Air Force has an approximate strength of 5,500 officers and men and 298 aircraft, including tactical/training aircraft, reconnaissance aircraft/helicopters and transport aircraft. There is a Parachute Brigade consisting of three Parachute battalions (approx. 2,000 men).

Language and Literature.—Spanish is the official language of Mexico and is spoken by about 95 per cent of the population. In addition to Spanish, there are five basic groups of Indian languages spoken in Mexico. The 1970 Census showed that of the 3,111,415 inhabitants speaking an Indian language, 25·7 per cent spoke Náhuatl; 14·6 per cent Maya; 9·1 per cent Zapotec; 7·1 per cent Otomí; 7·5 per cent Mixtec and 36 per cent one or other of the 59 dialects derived from these basic languages.

Education.—Education is divided into primary, secondary, preparatory and university. Primary education is free, secular and nominally compulsory.

Trade with U.K.

	1987	1988
Imports from U.K.	£198,992,000	£190,011,000
Exports to U.K.	244,719,000	144,947,000

Imports consist largely of transport, sound-recording and power-generating equipment, chemicals, industrial machinery, pharmaceuticals and specialized appliances. Principal exports are oil, fertilizers, minerals, metallic ores and scrap, sugar, honey, textiles and power-generating equipment.

CAPITAL.—Mexico City, metropolitan area 18,748,000 (est. pop. 1986). Other cities (est. pop. 1986) are:

Guadalajara	2,587,000	Puebla	1,217,600
Monterrey	2,335,000	León	946,800
Torréon	729,800	Ciudad	
San Luis		Juarez	595,700
Potosì	601,900	Mérida	580,300

CURRENCY.—Peso of 100 centavos.

FLAG.—Three vertical bands in green, white, red, with the Mexican emblem (an eagle on a cactus devouring a snake) in the centre.

NATIONAL ANTHEM.—Mexicanos, Al Grito De Guerra (Mexicans, to the war cry).

NATIONAL DAY.—September 16 (Proclamation of Independence).

BRITISH EMBASSY
Calle Río Lerma 71, Colonia Cuauhtémoc,
06500 Mexico City, D.F.
[Mexico City 207 20 89]

Ambassador Extraordinary and Plenipotentiary, His Excellency Michael Keith Orlebar Simpson-Orlebar, C.M.G. (1989).

There are British Consular Offices at *Mexico City, Acapulco, Guadalajara, Mérida, Monterrey, Tampico* and *Cuidad Juarez*.

British Council Representative.—R.Watkins, Maestro Antonio Caso 127, Col. San Rafael (P.O. Box 30-588), Mexico 06470, D.F.

BRITISH CHAMBER OF COMMERCE, British Trade Centre, Rio Tiber 103–60, Mexico 5 D.F.—*Manager*, J. Carral.

MONACO
(Principautē de Monaco)

Sovereign Prince, H.S.H. Rainier III Louis-Henri-Maxence Bertrand, *born* May 31, 1923, *succeeded his grandfather* (H.S.H. Prince Louis II), May 9, 1949; *married* April 19, 1956, Miss Grace Patricia Kelly (died Sept. 14, 1982) and *has issue* Prince Albert Alexandre Louis Pierre, *born* March 14, 1958, Princess Caroline Louise Marguerite, *born* January 23, 1957; and Princess Stephanie Marie Elisabeth, *born* Feb. 1, 1965.

President of the Crown Council, M. Jean-Charles Marquet.

President of the National Council, M. Jean-Charles Rey.

Minister of State, Jean Ausseil, *appointed* 1985.

CONSULATE-GENERAL IN LONDON
4 Audley Square, W1Y 5DR
[01–629 0734]

Consul-General, I. B. Ivanovic.

A small Principality on the Mediterranean, with land frontiers joining France at every point, and consisting of the old town of Monaco, La Condamine, Fontvielle and Monte Carlo, the location of the famous casino. The Principality comprises a narrow strip of country about 2 miles long (area approx. 195 hectares), with approximately 27,063 inhabitants (1989) and a yearly average of over 250,000 visitors.

The principality, ruled by the Grimaldi family since the late 13th century, was abolished during the French Revolution and re-established in 1815 under the protection of the Kingdom of Sardinia. In 1861 Monaco came under French protection. The 1962 Constitution, which can be modified only with the approval of the National Council, maintains the traditional hereditary monarchy and guarantees freedom of association, trade union freedom and the right to strike. Legislative power is held jointly by the Prince and a uni-cameral, 18 member National Council elected by universal suffrage. Executive power is exercised by the Prince and a four-member Council of Government, headed by a Minister of State. The judicial code is based on that of France.

The whole available ground is built over, so that there is no cultivation, though there are some notable public and private gardens. Monaco has a small harbour (30 ft. alongside quay) and the import duties are the same as in France.

CAPITAL.—Monaco-ville (1,234).

CURRENCY.—Monaco uses the French franc of 100 centimes as legal tender.

FLAG.—Two equal horizontal stripes, red over white.

NATIONAL ANTHEM.—Hymne Monegasque.

NATIONAL DAY.—November 19.

H.M. Consul-General, T. E. J. Mound, C.V.O., O.B.E. (*resident at Marseilles*).

MONGOLIA
(Mongolian People's Republic—
Bugd Nairamdakh Mongol Ard Uls)

President: J. Batmunkh.
Prime Minister: D. Sodnom.

MONGOLIAN PEOPLE'S REVOLUTIONARY
(= *Communist*) PARTY

Politburo of the Central Committee, J. Batmunkh; D. Sodnom; D. Molomjamts; B. Dejid; B. Altangerel; B. Lamjav; Ts. Namsrai (*full members*); P. Damdin (*candidate member*).

Secretariat of the Central Committee, J. Batmunkh (*General Secretary*); D. Molomjamts; Ts. Namsrai; B. Dejid; P. Damdin; Ts. Balkhaajav.

Chairman, Council of Ministers, D. Sodnom.

First Deputy Chairman, B. Altangerel.

Deputy Chairmen, Ch. Suren; M. Peljee; P. Jasrai; S. Gungadorj.

EMBASSY OF THE MONGOLIAN PEOPLE'S REPUBLIC
7 Kensington Court, W8 5DL
[01–937 0150]

Ambassador Extraordinary and Plenipotentiary, His Excellency Ishetsogyin Ochirbal (1987).

Third Secretary, B. Chimiddorjiin.

Attaché, B. N. Javyn.

Area and Population.—The Mongolian People's Republic is a large and sparsely populated country to the north of China. Its area is 604,250 sq. miles (1,565,000 sq. km.). Its population (July 1988) is about 2,000,000. However, this total constitutes only part of the Mongolians of Asia, a number of whom are to be found in China and in the neighbouring regions of the Soviet Union (especially the Mongolian Buryat Autonomous Region). This country, which is almost nowhere below 1,000 metres above sea level, forms part of the Central Asiatic Plateau and rises towards the west in the high mountains of the Mongolian Altai and Khanggai Ranges. The Khentai Mountain Range, situated to the north-east of the capital Ulan Bator, is less high. The Gobi region covers much of the southern half of the country. It contains some sand deserts, but between these less hospitable areas there is semi-desert which provides pasture for great numbers of sheep, goats, camels and horses (the latter is still the characteristic means of transport for the rural population) and some cattle. In the steppe areas to the north pasturage is better and livestock more abundant. Even further north, in the better watered provinces, grain, fodder and vegetable crops are increasingly grown. There are several long rivers and many lakes, but good water is scarce since much of the lake water is salty. The climate is harsh, with a short mild summer giving way to a long winter when temperatures can drop as low as minus 50° C.

History.—Mongolia, under Genghis Khan the conqueror of China and much of Asia, was for many years a buffer state between Tsarist Russia and China, although it was under general Chinese suzerainty. The outbreak of the Chinese Revolution in 1911 led to a declaration of autonomy under

Chinese suzerainty which was confirmed by the Sino-Russian Treaty of Kiakhta (1915), but cancelled by a unilateral Chinese declaration in 1919. Later the country became a battleground of the Russian Civil War, and Soviet and Mongolian troops occupied Ulan Bator in 1921: this was followed by another declaration of independence. However, in 1924 the Soviet Union in a Treaty with China again recognized the latter's sovereignty over Mongolia; but this was never properly exercised because of China's pre-occupation with internal affairs, and later by the war with Japan. The Mongolian People's Republic was formally established in 1924. Under the Yalta Agreement, Chiang Kai-shek agreed to a plebiscite, held in 1945, in which the Mongolians declared their desire for independence and this was formally recognized by Nationalist China. The country entered the United Nations in 1961. The heroes of Mongolian history during the earlier part of the century were Sukhebator, who died in 1923, and the Communist Choibalsan (died 1952), who did much to turn the country into the Communist state it is today, and carried out a systematic destruction of the power of the Lamas and the old princely houses which had previously been the dominant force in both the economy and the government.

Production, etc.—The total of Mongolia's livestock was 23 million in 1988. Traditionally the Mongolian is a herdsman, tending his flock of sheep, goats and horses, cows and camels and leading a totally nomadic life. With the coming of the Communist regime (under the Mongolian People's Revolutionary Party) and especially since 1952, great efforts have been made to settle the population, but a large proportion still live nomadically or semi-nomadically in the traditional *ger* (circular tent). The pastoral population was collectivized at the end of the 1950s into huge *negdels* (co-operatives) and State farms which have hastened the process of settlement, but within these the herdsmen and their families still move with their *gers* from pasture to pasture as the seasons change. The country, and three city districts (Ulan Bator, Darkhan and Erdenet), is today divided into 18 *aimaks* (provinces) and beneath these into 258 *somons* (districts), and these form the basis of the State organization of the country, parallel with which runs the apparatus of the Revolutionary Party.

Membership of the Communist bloc has brought Mongolia considerable quantities of aid from other Socialist countries, especially Czech, Polish and East German aid to supplement the massive assistance from the Soviet Union. Soviet and Bloc aid is hastening the process of industrialization; for although the economy remains predominantly based on the herds of animals, and the principal exports of the country are still animal by-products (especially wool, hides and furs) and cattle, factories serving the needs of the country have been started up and the coal and electricity industries are being developed to provide an industrial base. A joint Mongolian/Soviet enterprise for copper and molybdenum mining was opened in 1978, at Erdenet in northern Mongolia. It is now in full production and processes 16 million tonnes of ore annually. A major geological survey is being carried out by the CMEA countries, in order to prepare for the extraction of the considerable mineral deposits known to exist in Mongolia. Coal production in 1980 was 4·5 million tons and was expected to rise to 6·8 million tons by 1985.

Ulan Bator, which contains over a quarter of the country's population, is the main seat of industry. The second largest industrial centre is at Darkhan (pop. 80,000), north of the capital, near the Soviet frontier. Its industries include lime, cement and building materials, a flour mill and a power station. Choibalsan, in the east, is also being developed

industrially. Agriculture, formerly little practised, is now being extended. Average cereal production for 1976–80 was 347,000 tons, but by 1983 had risen to 800,000 tonnes. Communication is still difficult in the country as there are very few tarmac roads. The trans-Mongolian railway, following the line of the old north-south trade route, was opened in 1955 and links Mongolia with both China and Russia. Mongolia's fundamental difficulty is its very small population and labour force.

Foreign trade is dominated by the Soviet Union, with the eastern European countries taking most of what is left. Trade with western countries and Japan is developing slowly although the pace has increased recently as Mongolia embarks on its own version of perestroika.

Trade with U.K.

	1987	1988
Imports from U.K.	£941,000	£1,637,000
Exports to U.K.	3,847,000	1,857,000

CAPITAL.—Ulan Bator. (Pop. 505,000.)

CURRENCY.—Tugrik of 100 möngö.

FLAG.—Vertical tri-colour red, blue, red and in the hoist the traditional Soyombo symbol in gold.

NATIONAL DAY.—July 11 (Anniversary of the Mongolian People's Republic).

BRITISH EMBASSY
30 Enkh Taivny Gudamzh (P.O. Box 703)
Ulan Bator 13
[Ulan Bator 51033/4]

Ambassador Extraordinary and Plenipotentiary, His Excellency David Keith Sprague, M.V.O. (1989).
Second Secretary, D. A. Slinn (*Head of Chancery*).
Attachés, I. Grant; C. G. Bain.

MOROCCO
(Al-Mamlaka Al-Maghrebia)

King, H.M. King Hassan II (Moulay Hassan Ben Mohammed), *born* July 9, 1929; *acceded* February 26, 1961, *on the death of his father,* King Mohammad V. *Heir,* Crown Prince Sidi Mohamed, *b.* August 21, 1963.

MINISTERS
(as at July 31, 1989)

Prime Minister, Azeddine Laraki.
Ministers of State, Hadj M'hamid Bahnini; Moulay Ahmed Alaoui.
Justice, Moulay Mustapha Belarbi Alaoui.
Interior and Information, Driss Basri.
Foreign Affairs and Co-operation, Abdellatif Filali.
National Education, Prof. Taieb Chkili.
Health, Tayeb Bencheikh.
Religious Endowments and Islamic Affairs, Abdelke-bir Alaoui M'Daghri.
Equipment, Training of Cadres and Professional Training, Mohamed Kabbaj.
Finance, Mohamed Berrada.
Tourism, Moussa Saadi.
Traditional Industry and Social Affairs, Mohamed Abied.
Transport, Mohamed Bouamoud.
Energy and Mines, Mohamed Fettah.
Youth and Sport, Abdellatif Semlali.
Fisheries and Merchant Shipping, Bensalem Smili.
Secretary General of the Government, Abbès Kaissi.
Culture, Mohamed Benaissa.
Environment, Abderrahmane Boufettass.
Posts and Telecommunications, Mohamed Laensar.
Agriculture and Agricultural Reform, Othman Demnati.
Trade and Industry, Abdellah Al Azmani.

Employment, Hassan Abbadi.
Prime Minister's Office, Moulay Zine Zahidi (*Economic Affairs*); Khali Hanna Ould Errachid (*Development of the Sahara Provinces*); Rachidi Ghazouani (*the Plan*); Abdeslem Baraka (*Relations with Parliament*); Abderrahim Ben Abdeljalil (*Administrative Affairs*).

EMBASSY OF THE KINGDOM OF MOROCCO
49 Queen's Gate Gardens, SW7 5NE
[01–581 5001/4]

Ambassador Extraordinary and Plenipotentiary, His Excellency Abdeslam Zenined, G.C.V.O. (1987).
Military, Naval and Air Attaché, Col. M. Jabrane.

Area and Population.—Morocco is situated in the north-western corner of the African continent between latitude 27° 40'–36° N. and longitude 1°–13° W. with an area estimated at 172,414 sq. miles (446,550 sq. km.), and a population (1989 estimate) of approx. 27,000,000. It is traversed in the north by the Rif mountains and in a general S.W. to N.E. direction, by the Middle Atlas, the High Atlas, the Anti-Atlas and the Sarrho ranges. The northern flanks of the Middle and High Atlas mountains are well wooded but their southern slopes, exposed to the dry desert winds, are generally arid and desolate. The north-westerly point of Morocco is the peninsula of Tangier which is separated from the continent of Europe by the narrow strait of Gibraltar. The Jebel Mousa dominates the promontory and, with the rocky eminence of Gibraltar, was known to the ancients as the Pillars of Hercules, the western gateway of the Mediterranean.

Western Sahara.—Formerly the Spanish Sahara, the territory was split between Morocco and Mauritania in 1976 after Spain withdrew in Dec. 1975. In 1979 Mauritania renounced its claim to its share of the territory, which was added by Morocco to its area. Morocco's annexation has been opposed by Polisario guerrillas, who want the territory to become an independent state. On August 30, 1988, Morocco and the Polisario Front accepted a U.N. peace plan. Under the plan a ceasefire will come into effect, and a referendum to determine the future of the area will be held.

Climate.—The climate of Morocco is generally good and healthy, especially on the Atlantic coast (where a high degree of humidity is, however, prevalent), the country being partially sheltered by the Atlas mountains from the hot winds of the Sahara. The rainy season may last from November to April. The plains of the interior are intensely hot in summer. Average summer and winter temperatures for Rabat are 27° C. and 7° C.

Government.—Morocco became an independent sovereign state in 1956, following joint declarations made with France on March 2, 1956, and with Spain on April 7, 1956. The Sultan of Morocco, Sidi Mohammad ben Youssef, adopted the title of King Mohammad V.

Following serious disturbances in Casablanca in March, 1965, attempts were made by King Hassan, in consultation with all political parties, to form a government of national union. These efforts were unsuccessful and on June 7, 1965, the King proclaimed a 'state of exception' and suspended Parliament. Assuming himself the office of Prime Minister, he announced the formation of a new government and indicated that constitutional changes were to follow. A revised constitution was approved by a national referendum on July 24, 1970 and brought into effect soon after. It was superseded by another constitution, also approved by a national referendum, on March 1, 1972. This provides that not only political parties, but trade unions, chambers of commerce and professional bodies will participate in the organization of

the State and representation of the people; specifies that the King is the supreme representative of the people; makes changes in the composition of the Regency Council and the Sovereign's rights and establishes a unicameral legislature. The Chamber has 306 members, 204 elected by direct universal suffrage (including 5 representing overseas workers) and 102 members elected by electoral colleges representing local government, industry, agriculture and working class groups. There were elections in Sept.–Oct. 1984 and the new Parliament began its 6 year term on Oct. 12. A new government was named in April 1985 which included members of three political parties, though over half the portfolios went to non-political appointees.

Defence.—The Moroccan army, formed in 1956, is about 200,000 strong. A Moroccan air force was formed in 1959 and a navy in 1960. Their strengths are about 13,500 and 8,000 respectively. The armed forces possess quantities of French, Spanish and American equipment, including aircraft, as well as a little Soviet-supplied hardware.

Production and Trade.—Morocco's main sources of wealth are agricultural and mineral. The Five Year Plan (1981–85) for economic development placed particular emphasis on social improvement. Other priority sectors were industrial development, fisheries, agriculture and tourism. The next development plan (1987 onwards) is similar to the last. The world recession and high energy prices, coupled with a fall in the price of phosphates and poor harvests due to low rainfall have created problems for the economy since the end of the 1970s. However, rains in the winter of 1985–6 ended the long drought and the 1986 harvest was good. The 1988 harvest was excellent and the 1989 one is expected to be good also. Similarly the fall in oil prices, the value of the dollar and interest rates have helped.

Agriculture employs more than 40 per cent of the working population and accounts for about 36 per cent of Morocco's exports. The main agricultural exports are fruit and vegetables. Cork and wood-pulp are the most important commercial forest products. Esparto grass is also produced. There is a fishing industry and substantial quantities of canned fish, mainly sardines and fishmeal, are exported. Manufacturing industries are centred in Casablanca, Fez, Tangier and Safi.

Morocco's mineral exports are phosphates, fluorite, barite, manganese, iron ore, lead, zinc, cobalt, copper and antimony. Morocco possesses nearly three-quarters of the world's estimated reserves of phosphates. There are oil refineries at Mohammedia and Sidi Kacem handling about four million tonnes of crude oil per year, but no significant quantities of hydrocarbons have been found.

Tourism is of increasing importance to the Moroccan economy with development concentrated in Agadir and Marrakesh.

Morocco's main import requirements are petroleum products, motor vehicles, building materials, agricultural and other machinery, chemical products, sugar, green tea and other foodstuffs.

The trade of Morocco is chiefly with France, U.S.A., the Federal Republic of Germany, Italy, the United Kingdom, Spain, Canada, Iraq, Benelux and Kuwait.

	1985	1986
Imports	DH 78,376m.	DH 78,686m.
Exports	48,132m.	50,718m.

Trade with U.K.

	1987	1988
Imports from U.K.	£94,486,589	£79,017,000
Exports to U.K.	61,108,450	78,896,000

Communications.—The railway runs south from Tangier to Sidi Kacem. From this junction, one line runs eastwards through Fez to Oujda, and another continues southwards, through Rabat and Casablanca, to Marrakesh. A line running due south from Oujda skirts the Morocco-Algeria frontier and reaches Bouarfa. Moroccan railroads cover 1,250 miles and traction is electric or diesel. An extensive network of well-surfaced roads covers all the main towns in the kingdom.

British Airways and Royal-Air-Maroc operate services between Casablanca and London. There are air services between Tangier, Agadir (seasonal), Marrakesh and London, and also between Tangier and Gibraltar connecting with London. Royal-Air-Maroc operates internal services. There are also regular services by many airlines in many parts of the world.

Language.—Arabic is the official language. Berber is the vernacular mainly in the mountain regions. French and Spanish are also spoken mainly in the towns. The national daily press consists of 6 Arabic and 5 French newspapers.

Education.—There are government primary, secondary and technical schools. At Fez there is a theological university of great repute in the Muslim world. There is a secular university at Rabat. Schools for special denominations, Jewish and Catholic, are permitted and may receive government grants. American schools operate in Rabat and Casablanca.

CAPITAL.—ΨRabat (population 1,123,000, including Salé). Regional capitals, with municipal population figures as at 1989, are: ΨCasablanca (2,904,000); Marrakesh (1,425,000); Fez (933,000); Oujda (895,000); Meknes (1,425,000); Ψ Agadir (700,000). The towns of Fez, Marrakesh and Meknes were capitals at various times in Morocco's history.

CURRENCY.—Dirham (DH) of 100 centimes.

FLAG.—Red, with green pentagram (the Seal of Solomon).

NATIONAL DAY.—March 3 (Anniversary of the Throne).

BRITISH EMBASSY
17 Boulevard de la Tour Hassan (B.P. 45), Rabat
[Rabat 20905]

Ambassador Extraordinary and Plenipotentiary, His Excellency John William Richmond Shakespeare, C.M.G., L.V.O. (1987).

First Secretary, S. R. H. Pease (*Head of Chancery/ Commercial, and Consul*).

Defence Attaché, Lt.-Col. R. Chetwyn-Stapylton.

Vice Consul (Tangier), W. A. T. Pulleyblank, O.B.E.

There is a British Consulate/Commercial Office at *Casablanca* and an Honorary Consul at *Agadir.*

British Council Representative, P. Taylor, (P.O. Box 427), 22 Avenue Moulay Youssef, Rabat.

BRITISH CHAMBER OF COMMERCE, 291 Boulevard Mohamed V, Casablanca (Tel: 30 37 60).

MOZAMBIQUE
(República Popular de Moçambique)

President, Joaquim Alberto Chissano, *sworn in,* November 1986.

COUNCIL OF MINISTERS
(as at May 31, 1989)

Prime Minister, Mario da Graca Machungo.
Foreign Affairs, Pascoal Mocumbi.
National Defence, Alberto Joaquim Chipande.
Chief of Staff of the Armed Forces, Lt.-Gen. Antonio Hama Thai.
Co-ordination, Jacinto Veloso.
Minister in the Presidency, Feliciano Gundana.
State Administration, Jose Oscar Monteiro.

Education, Aniceto dos Muchangos.
Interior, Manuel Antonio.
Security, Mariano de Araujo Matsinha.
Transport and Communications, Armando Emilio Guebuza.
Finance, Abdul Magid Osman.
Health, Dr. Leonardo Simao.
Information, Teodato Hunguana.
Construction and Water, Joao Salomao.
Trade, Gabriel Tembe.
Agriculture, Alexandre Jose Zandamela.
Industry and Energy, Antonio Branco.
Mineral Resources, John Kachamila.
Justice, Ossumane Ali Dauto.

EMBASSY OF THE PEOPLE'S REPUBLIC OF MOZAMBIQUE
159 New Bond Street, W1Y 9PA
[01–491 8146]

Ambassador Extraordinary and Plenipotentiary, His Excellency Armando Alexandre Panguene (1988).

Area and Population.—The People's Republic of Mozambique lies on the east coast of Africa, and is bounded by Swaziland in the south, South Africa in the south and west, Zimbabwe in the west, Zambia and Malawi in the north-west and Tanzania in the north. It has an area of 309,495 sq. miles (801,590 sq. km.), with a population estimated at 14,000,000 (1986). The official language is Portuguese.

Government.—Mozambique, discovered by Vasco de Gama in 1498, and colonized by Portugal, achieved complete independence from Portugal on June 25, 1975. The date had been agreed in September 1974 by Portugal and *Frelimo (Frente de Libertação de Moçambique),* the Marxist liberation movement.

Constitution.—The country is governed by a Council of Ministers and by the Permanent Political Committee of the *Frelimo* Party; membership of these two bodies virtually overlaps. No other political parties are permitted. The principal legislative body, the People's Assembly, consists of 216 members nominated by *Frelimo.*

The basis of the economy is subsistence agriculture, but there is an industrial sector based mainly in Beira and Maputo. After giving priority to the development of collective farms and state enterprises in all sectors, the government is now encouraging the private sector and foreign investment, particularly in agriculture and consumer goods production. Main exports are sugar, cashew nuts, copra, cotton, tea and sisal. There are substantial coal deposits in Tete province. Mozambique has a range of aid and co-operation agreements with a number of countries in Eastern Europe and in the West. An agreement of non-aggression and good neighbourliness with South Africa was signed on March 16, 1984 (the Nkomati Accord).

Trade with U.K.

	1987	1988
Imports from U.K.	£21,168,000	£24,200,000
Exports to U.K.	6,580,000	5,600,000

CAPITAL.—Ψ Maputo (pop. 1,000,000). Other main ports are ΨBeira and ΨNacala.

CURRENCY.—Metical (MT) of 100 centavos.

FLAG.—From top, three lateral bands of green, black and yellow separated by white stripes, and red half diamond pointing to centre of flag over which is superimposed a yellow star, book, and crossed rifle and hoe.

NATIONAL DAY.—June 25 (Independence Day).

BRITISH EMBASSY
C.P. 55, Av. V. I. Lenine, 310, Maputo.
[Maputo 420111/2/5/6/7]

Ambassador Extraordinary and Plenipotentiary, Her Excellency Maeve Geraldine Fort (1989).

First Secretary, D. S. Gordon-MacLeod (*Head of Chancery and Consul*); J. M. Winter (*Aid/Commercial*); C. A. Pagett (*Chancery*).
Second Secretary, Miss E. A. Rose, M.B.E.

NEPAL

Sovereign, H.M. King Birendra Bir Bikram Shah Dev, *born* Dec. 28, 1945; *succeeded* Jan. 31, 1972; *crowned* Feb. 24, 1975; *married,* Feb. 1970, H.M. Queen Aishwara Rajya Laxmi Devi Shah. *Heir,* H.R.H. Crown Prince Dipendra Bir Bikram Shah Dev, *born,* June 27, 1971.

COUNCIL OF MINISTERS
(as at Oct. 31, 1988)

Prime Minister, Royal Palace and Defence, Rt. Hon. Marich Man Singh Shrestha.
Foreign Affairs, Rt. Hon. Shailendra Kumar Upadhaya.
Panchayat and Local Development, Rt. Hon. Prakash Bahadhur Singh.
Industry, Rt. Hon. Rabindra Nath Sharma.
Water Resources, Rt. Hon. Hari Bahadur Basnyat.
Housing and Physical Planning, Rt. Hon. Dr. Prakash Chandra Lohani.
Labour and Social Welfare, Rt. Hon. Lila Raj Bista.
Education and Culture, Rt. Hon. Parshu Narayan Choudhary.
Finance, Rt. Hon. Bharat Bahadur Pradhan.
Tourism, Rt. Hon. Dr. Mohammed Mohsin.
Agriculture, Rt. Hon. Krishna Charan Shrestha.
Works and Transport, Rt. Hon. Dipak Bohra.
Law and Justice, Rt. Hon. Badri Prasad Mandal.

ROYAL NEPALESE EMBASSY
12A, Kensington Palace Gardens, W8 4QU
[01–229 1594/6231]

Ambassador Extraordinary and Plenipotentiary, His Excellency Maj.-Gen. Bharat Kesher Simha (1988).
First Secretary, Badri Prasad Khanal.
Military Attaché, Lt.-Col. C. B. Gurung.
Attachés, Baikuntha Prasad Arjyal; Ghanashyam Lall Joshi; Rameswor Paudel.

Area and Population.—Nepal lies between India and the Tibet Autonomous Region of China on the slopes of the Himalayas, and includes Mount Everest (29,028 ft). It has a total area of 54,342 sq. miles (140,747 sq. km.), and a population estimated (1988) at about 18 million. The country comprises three distinct horizontal formations. In the south, joining the Indian plains, is the Terai, a fair proportion of which was covered with jungle. It has recently been more widely cultivated but wild life is preserved in parts. The region represents 23 per cent of the total land area and nearly 44 per cent of the population live there. The central belt of the country is hilly, but with many fertile valleys, leading up to the snowline at about 14,000 feet. The hills account for 42 per cent of the area of the country and about 48 per cent of the population. The remainder of the country, the Himalayan Region, consists of high mountains which are sparsely inhabited. The country is drained by three great river systems rising within and beyond the Himalayan mountain ranges and eventually flowing into the Ganges in India.

The inhabitants are of mixed stock, with Mongolian characteristics prevailing in the North and Indian in the south. The official religion is Hinduism: 89·5 per cent of the population are Hindus and 6 per cent are Buddhist. Gautama Buddha was born in Nepal.

History and Government.—The country was originally divided into numerous hill clans and petty principalities, but Nepal emerged as a nation in the middle of the 18th century when its component parts were unified by the warrior Raja of Gorkha, Prithvi Narayan Shah, who founded the present Nepalese dynasty. In 1846 power was seized by Jung Bahadur Rana after a massacre of nobles, and he was the first of a line of hereditary Rana Prime Ministers who ruled Nepal for 104 years. During this time the role of the Monarchs was mainly ceremonial.

In 1950–51 a revolutionary movement achieved its aim of breaking the hereditary power of the Ranas and restoring the Monarchy to its former position. After 10 years, during which various parties and individuals tried their hand at government, the late King Mahendra proscribed all political parties and assumed direct powers on December 16, 1960, with the object of leading a united country to democracy. In 1962 he introduced a new Constitution embodying a tiered, partyless system of panchayat (council) democracy, under which there were elected councils at village level which in turn elect members to district council and thence to zonal councils; a referendum in May 1980 decided in favour of retaining the panchayat system, with some reforms; namely, election to the Rastriaya Panchayat (National Parliament) by universal adult franchise (over 21 years old); selection of the Prime Minister by the Rastriaya Panchayat and responsibility of his government to that body. The King retains certain reserve powers. The Rastriaya Panchayat has 112 members elected from the 75 districts of Nepal. The King appoints 28 other members, making a total of 140. The last election was in May 1986.

Economy.—Nepal exports carpets, jute, handicrafts, garments, hides and skins, medicinal herbs, cardamom, pulses etc., and imports textiles, machinery and parts, transport equipment, medicine, construction materials etc. Tourism is the single largest commercial earner of foreign exchange (U.S.$55·9 million in 1986–87).

The budget for the fiscal year 1988–89 is estimated at NRs. 19,520·2 million, of which NRs. 6,152,139 million is allocated to regular and NRs. 13,368,061 million to development expenditures. Revenue is estimated at NRs. 9,300 million, foreign aid and grants NRs. 8,890·2 million, and domestic borrowing NRs. 1,330 million.

Trade with U.K.

	1987	1988
Imports from U.K.	£8,707,000	£4,968,000
Exports to U.K.	8,331,000	9,384,000

A State Bank was inaugurated on April 26, 1956, to issue bank notes, regulate the Nepalese currency, fix foreign exchange rates and help in the preparation of a national budget. There are three commercial banks with branches throughout Nepal and three further banks, based only in Kathmandu, established since 1984 with approximately 49 per cent foreign bank participation.

Communications.—Kathmandu is connected with India by a road, the mountain section of which was built by India under the Colombo Plan, and to Tibet by a road to Kodari on the border which was built by the Chinese and opened on May 26, 1967. The Indian-aided Sunauli-Pokhara road (128 miles) was inaugurated in April 1972, and a road between Pokhara and Kathmandu, constructed by the Chinese, was opened in 1973. A link road between Mugling and Naryanghat, completed by the Chinese in 1981, has further improved communications between Kathmandu and the Terai. The East-West Highway (Mahendra Raj Marg) running along the entire length of the country is complete except for the Kohalpur-Mahahali section. The total length of roads in Nepal in 1987–88 was 6,525 km. British assistance has included major road projects, agriculture, education and forestry.

Telecommunication services, both domestic and international, are available from the Central Telegraph Office or hotels. There are international subscriber dialling facilities from Nepal to 35 countries. Nepal Television was introduced in Aug. 1984.

Royal Nepal Airlines operates an extensive network of domestic flights, and there are international flights to India, Pakistan, Bangladesh, Burma, Singapore, Thailand, West Germany, and the Middle East.

CAPITAL.—Kathmandu, population (1981) 235,000. Other towns of importance are Biratnagar (94,000), Lalitpur (81,000) and Bhaktapur (50,500) and Pokhara (48,500).

CURRENCY.—Nepalese rupee of 100 paisa.

FLAG.—Double pennant of crimson with blue border on peaks; white moon with rays in centre of top peak; white quarter sun, recumbent in centre of bottom peak.

NATIONAL ANTHEM.—May Glory Crown Our Illustrious Sovereign.

NATIONAL DAY.—February 18 (National Democracy Day).

BRITISH EMBASSY
(Lainchaur Kathmandu, P.O. Box 106)
[Kathmandu 411583]

Ambassador Extraordinary and Plenipotentiary, His Excellency Richard Eagleson Gordon Burges Watson, C.M.G. (1987).
First Secretary, A. Maclean (*Head of Chancery and Consul*).
Defence and Military Attaché, Col. M. G. Allen.
Vice-Consul, B. Mason.
British Council Representative, P. Moss, (P.O. Box 640), Kanti Path, Kathmandu.

THE NETHERLANDS
(Koninkrijk der Nederlanden)

Queen of the Netherlands, Her Majesty Queen Beatrix Wilhelmina Armgard, K.G., G.C.V.O., *born* Jan. 31, 1938; *married* March 10, 1966, H.R.H. Prince Claus George Willem Otto Frederik Geert of the Netherlands, Jonkheer van Amsberg; *and has issue*, Prince Willem Alexander, *b.* April 27, 1967; Prince Johan Friso, *b.* Sept, 25, 1968; Prince Constantijn Christof, *b.* Oct. 11, 1969; *succeeded*, April 30, 1980, upon the abdication of her mother Queen Juliana.

CABINET
(as at July 31, 1989)

Prime Minister and Minister of General Affairs, Ruud Lubbers (*C.D.A.*).
Deputy P.M. and Minister for Economic Affairs, Dr. Rudolf de Korte (*V.V.D.*).
Social Affairs and Employment, and Netherlands Antillean and Aruban Affairs, Dr. Jan de Koning (*C.D.A.*).
Defence, Frits Bolkenstein (*V.V.D.*).
Finance, Dr. Herman Ruding (*C.D.A.*).
Transport and Waterways, Mrs. Neelie Smit-Kroes (*V.V.D.*).
Education and Science, Dr. Wim Deetman (C.D.A.).
Welfare, Public Health and Culture, Elco Brinkman (*C.D.A.*).
Development Co-operation, Piet Buckman (*C.D.A.*).
Agriculture and Fisheries, Gerrit Braks (*C.D.A.*).
Housing, Physical Planning and Environment, Ed Nijpels (*V.V.D.*).
Justice, Frits Korthals Altes, (*V.V.D.*).
Home Affairs, Cees van Dijk, (*C.D.A.*).

Foreign Affairs, Hans van den Broek (*C.D.A.*).

(*C.D.A.* = Christian Democrats; *V.V.D.* = Liberals.) There was a general election on Sept. 6, 1989.

ROYAL NETHERLANDS EMBASSY
38 Hyde Park Gate, SW7 5DP
[01–584 5040]

Ambassador Extraordinary and Plenipotentiary, His Excellency Hans Jonkman, G.C.V.O. (1987).
Ministers Plenipotentiary, E. J. P. Roberts; R. R. Smit.
Counsellors, D. Vries; A. D. H. Simonsz; A. E. Moses; A. Verduyn.
First Secretaries, Baroness H. J. C. M. van Lynden; A. C. Brouwer; R. G. de Vos.
Defence, Naval and Air Attaché, Capt. A. H. A. G. Remmen.
Military Attaché, Col. J. Smit.

Area and Population.—The Kingdom of the Netherlands is a maritime country of Western Europe, situated on the North Sea, in lat. 50° 46'–53° 34' N. and long. 3° 22'–7° 14' E., consisting of 12 provinces (Eastern and Southern Flevoland being amalgamated to form the twelfth province) and containing a total area of 15,770 sq. miles (40,844 sq. km). The population (1988 estimate) is 14,669,000. The live birth rate in Jan., 1984 was 12·1 per 1,000 of the population, and the death-rate was 8·3.

The land is generally flat and low, intersected by numerous canals and connecting rivers—in fact, a network of water courses. The principal rivers are the Rhine, Maas, Yssel and Scheldt.

Language and Literature.—Dutch is a West-Germanic language of Saxon origin, closely akin to Old English and Low German. It is spoken in the Netherlands and the northern part of Belgium. It is also used in the Netherlands Antilles. Afrikaans, one of the two South African languages, has Dutch as its origin, but differs from it in grammar and pronunciation. There are six national papers, four of which are morning papers, and there are many regional daily papers.

Government.—In 1815 the Netherlands became a constitutional Kingdom under King William I, a

Prince of Orange-Nassau, a descendant of the house which had taken a leading part in the destiny of the nation since the 16th century. The States-General consists of the *Eerste Kamer* (First Chamber) of 75 members, elected for 4 years by the Provincial Council; and the *Tweede Kamer* (Second Chamber) of 150 members, elected for 4 years by voters of 18 years and upwards. Members of the *Tweede Kamer* are paid.

Production.—The chief agricultural products are potatoes, wheat, rye, barley, sugar beet, cattle, pigs, milk and milk products, cheese, butter, poultry, eggs, beans, peas, vegetables, fruit, flower bulbs, plants and cut flowers and there is an important fishing industry. Among the principal industries are engineering, both mechanical and electrical, electronics, nuclear energy, petro-chemicals and plastics, road vehicles, aircraft and defence equipment, shipbuilding repair, steel, textiles of all types, electrical appliances, metal ware, furniture, paper, cigars, sugar, liqueurs, beer, clothing etc.

In 1985 the production of crude oil was 3,729 million kg and refined oil products 61,000 million kg; steel (1984) 5,739 million kg, and natural gas 80,721 million cubic metres.

Defence.—The armed forces are almost entirely committed to NATO. All ground and air units are assigned to the NATO Central Region, and naval forces to the Atlantic and Channel commands. Total armed forces number 106,183, which includes 48,720 conscripts and 1,495 women. In addition there are over 176,000 reservists. There is compulsory military service of 14–17 months.

Education.—Primary and secondary education is given in both denominational and State schools, the denominational schools being eligible for State assistance on equal terms with the State schools. Attendance at primary school is compulsory. The principal Universities are at Leiden, Utrecht, Groningen, Amsterdam (2), Nijmegen (R.C.) and Rotterdam, and there are technical Universities at Delft (polytechnic); Eindhoven (polytechnic), Enschede (polytechnic) and Wageningen (agriculture). Illiteracy is practically non-existent.

Communications.—The total extent of navigable rivers including canals, was 4,845 km. at Jan. 1, 1985, and of metalled roads 97,189 km. In 1985 the total length of the railway system amounted to 2,867 km., of which 1,810 km. were electrified. The mercantile marine in January 1985 consisted of 550 ships of total 3,461,000 gross registered tons. The total length of air routes covered by K.L.M. (Royal Dutch Airlines) in 1985 was 370,640 km.

FINANCE

	1986
Budget Revenue	D.fl. 175,610 m
Budget Expenditure	194,493 m

TRADE

The Dutch are traditionally a trading nation. Entrepot trade, banking and shipping are of particular importance to the economy. The geographical position of the Netherlands, at the mouths of the Rhine, Meuse and Scheldt, brings a large volume of transit trade to and from the interior of Europe to Dutch ports.

Principal trading partners are the Federal Republic of Germany and Belgium/Luxembourg. U.K. supplied 10 per cent of Netherlands imports in 1985 and took 9·5 per cent of Netherlands exports.

Excluding the building industry, the index of industrial production in the Netherlands (1980 = 100) was 101 in 1984 and the index of industrial production per worker (1980 = 100) was 122 in 1984.

	1984	1985
Imports	D.fl. 198,922 m.	D.fl. 215,467 m.
Exports	210,691 m.	225,568 m.

Trade with U.K.

	1986	1987
Imports from U.K.	£5,442,503,000	£5,856,164,000
Exports to U.K.	6,615,581,000	7,148,036,000

CAPITAL.—ΨAmsterdam, 1,031,000 (urban agglomeration). SEAT OF GOVERNMENT, The Hague (Den Haag or, in full, 's-Gravenhage). Pop. 443,456. Other principal cities; ΨRotterdam, 571,081; Utrecht, 229,969; Eindhoven, 191,675; Haarlem, 151,025; Groningen, 168,119; Tilburg, 153,812.

CURRENCY.—Netherlands guilder or florin of 100 cents.

FLAG.—Three horizontal bands of red, white and blue.

NATIONAL ANTHEM.—"Wilhelmus".

BRITISH EMBASSY
Lange Voorhout, 10, The Hague, 2514 ED
[The Hague 64 58 00]

Ambassador Extraordinary and Plenipotentiary, His Excellency Michael Romilly Heald Jenkins, C.M.G. (1988).
Counsellors, G. Archer; L. G. Faulkner (*Commercial/Agriculture*).
Defence and Naval Attaché, Capt. R. N. Blair, R.N.
Military and Air Attaché, Lt. Col. P. Cook.
First Secretary and Head of Chancery, P. J. Sullivan.
British Council Representative, J. Andrews, Keizersgracht 343, Amsterdam (Library).

NETHERLANDS-BRITISH CHAMBER OF COMMERCE, The Dutch House, 307–308 High Holborn, WC1V 7LS; U.K. OFFICE, Holland Trade House, Bezuidenhoutseweg 181, 2594 AH The Hague.

OVERSEAS TERRITORIES

Aruba covers an area of 75 sq. miles (193 sq. km.) with a population (1988 estimate) of 62,500. The island of Aruba was from 1828 part of the Dutch West Indies and from 1845 part of the Netherlands Antilles. On Jan. 1, 1986 it became a separate territory within the Kingdom of the Netherlands. The 1983 Constitutional Conference agreed that Aruba's separate status would last for ten years from 1986, after which the island would become fully independent.

The economy of Aruba is based largely on tourism. In 1986 there were over 180,000 tourists.

Governor, F. B. Tromp.
Prime Minister, J. Henny Eman.

Trade with U.K.

	1987	1988
Imports from U.K.	£5,652,000	£7,315,000
Exports to U.K.	296,000	133,000

CAPITAL.—ΨOranjestad (pop. 20,000); and Sint Nicolaas (17,000).
CURRENCY.—Aruban florin.

Netherlands Antilles comprise certain islands in the West Indies (Curaçao, Bonaire, part of St. Martin, St. Eustatius, and Saba). The islands cover an area of 308 sq. miles (800 sq. km.) with a population (1986 estimate) of 188,000. The Netherland Antilles (which have a federal parliament) are largely self-governing under the terms of the Realm Statute which took effect on December 29, 1954.

The economy of the Netherlands Antilles is based on small manufacturing industries. The soil is too poor to permit large-scale agriculture and most products for consumption, and industrial raw materials must be imported.

Governor, Dr. R. A. Römer (1983).
Prime Minister, Mrs. Maria Liberia Peters.

Trade with U.K.

	1987	1988
Imports from U.K.	£19,635,000	£20,089,000
Exports to U.K.	5,133,000	7,823,000

CAPITAL.—ΨWillemstad (on Curaçao) (pop. 50,000).
CURRENCY.—Netherlands Antilles guilder of 100 cents.

NICARAGUA
(República de Nicaragua)

President, Cmdt. Daniel Ortega Saavedra, *inaugurated*, Jan. 10, 1985.
Vice-President, Dr. Sergio Ramírez Mercado.

COUNCIL OF MINISTERS
(as at May 31, 1989)

Foreign, Fr. Miguel d'Escoto.
Defence, Gen. Humberto Ortega.
Minister of the Interior, Cmdt. Tomás Borge.
External Co-operation, Cmdt. Henry Ruiz.
Agriculture, Cmdt. Jaime Wheelock.
Economy, Industry and Commerce, Cmdt. Luis Carrión.
Minister of the Presidency, René Núñez Téllez.
Vice Minister of the Presidency, Cmdt. Mónica Baltodano.
Secretariat of Planning and Budgeting, Dr. Alejandro Martínez.
Finance, William Hupper.
Construction, Transport and Housing, Cmdt. Mauricio Valenzuala.
Health, Cmdt. Dora María Téllez.
Education and Culture, Fr. Fernando Cardenal.
Justice, Dr. Rodrigo Reyes.
Labour, Benedicto Meneses.

EMBASSY OF NICARAGUA
8 Gloucester Road, SW7 4PP
[01–584 4365]

Ambassador Extraordinary and Plenipotentiary, His Excellency Señor Francisco d'Escoto (1981).

Nicaragua is the largest State of Central America, with a long seaboard on both the Atlantic and Pacific Oceans, situated between 10° 45'–15° N. lat. and 83° 40'–87° 38' W. long., containing an area of 50,193 sq. miles (130,000 sq. km.). It has a population (1987 U.N. estimate) of 3,500,000, of whom about three-quarters are of mixed blood. Another 15 per cent are white, mostly of pure Spanish descent and the remaining 10 per cent are Indians or negroes. The latter group includes the Mosquitos, who live on the Atlantic coast and were formerly under British protection.

Government.—The eastern coast of Nicaragua was touched by Columbus in 1502, and in 1518 was overrun by Spanish forces under Davila, and formed part of the Spanish Captaincy-General of Guatemala until 1821, when its independence was secured. In 1927, Augusto Cesar Sandino began a guerrilla war against the occupation of Nicaragua by U.S. Marines, which continued until they were expelled in 1933. Sandino was assassinated by Anastasio Somoza, Director of the National Guard, and in 1936 Somoza assumed the Presidency. He was succeeded in power by his sons Luis and Anastasio Somoza, until 1979 when the family and the National Guard were overthrown by guerrillas of the Sandinista National Liberation Front. A Junta of National Reconstruction subsequently took power.
Elections for President, Vice-President and a

National Assembly were held on Nov. 4, 1984, and on Jan. 10, 1985 they replaced the Junta and the Council of State. Distribution of seats in the National Assembly was: Sandinista National Liberation Front 61; Democratic Conservative Party 14; Independent Liberal Party 9; People's Christian Social Party 6; Communist Party 2; Socialist Party 2; Marxist–Leninist Popular Action Movement 2.
On Jan. 9, 1987, President Ortega signed the new constitution but almost immediately re-introduced the state of emergency. Presidential and parliamentary elections are to take place in 1990.

Agriculture and Industry.—The country is mainly agricultural. The major crops are cotton, coffee (30 per cent of total export earnings), sugar cane, tobacco, sesame and bananas. Beans, rice, maize and ipecacuanha, livestock and timber production are also important. However, fishing, forestry, grain and cattle production have been hit by the civil war in the main growing areas. Nicaragua possesses deposits of gold and silver.

Communications.—There are 252 miles of railway, all on the Pacific side and approximately 5,500 miles of telegraph. There are 51 radio stations and two television stations in Managua. An automatic telephone system has been installed in the capital and extended to all major cities. A ground station for satellite communication was inaugurated in 1973. Transport except on the Pacific slope, is still attended with difficulty but many new roads have either been opened or are under construction. The Inter-American Highway runs from the Honduras frontier in the north to the Costa Rican border in the south; the inter-oceanic highway runs from the Corinto on the Pacific coast via Managua to Rama, where there is a natural waterway to Bluefields on the Atlantic. The country's main airport is at Managua. The chief port is Corinto on the Pacific.

Language and Literature.—The official language of the country is Spanish and the majority profess Catholicism, although the English language and the Moravian Church are widespread on the Atlantic coast. There are three daily newspapers published at Managua, apart from the official Gazette (*La Gaceta*). A national literacy campaign in 1980 has reduced illiteracy to 12 per cent. There are universities at León and Managua.

Trade with U.K.

	1987	1988
Imports from U.K.	£7,883,000	£6,856,000
Exports to U.K.	717,000	725,000

Considerable quantities of foodstuffs are imported as well as cotton goods, jute, iron and steel, machinery and petroleum products. The chief exports are cotton, coffee, beef, gold, sugar, cottonseed and bananas.
CAPITAL.—Managua, population 615,000. The centre was almost totally destroyed in the earthquake of December 1972. León, 158,577; Granada, 72,640; Masaya, 78,308; Chinandega, 144,291.
CURRENCY.—Córdoba (C$) of 100 centavos.
FLAG.—Horizontal stripes of blue, white and blue, with the Nicaraguan coat of arms in the centre of the white stripe.
NATIONAL DAY.—September 15.
NATIONAL ANTHEM.—Salve A Ti Nicaragua (Hail, Nicaragua).

BRITISH EMBASSY
P.O. Box A-169, Reparto Los Robles, Primera Etapa, De la entrada principal, la 4ª casa a mano derecha,
Managua, Nicaragua.
[Managua 70034]

British Ambassador and Consul-General, (*resides at* San José, Costa Rica).

NIGER
(République du Niger)

President, Col. Ali Saibou (*also holds Defence and Interior portfolios*).

MINISTERS
(as at Oct. 31, 1988)

Prime Minister, Hamid Algabid.
Finance, Beidari Mamadou.
Public Health and Social Affairs, Bare Mainassara Ibrahim.
Public Works and Housing, Oumarou Coulibali.
Post and Telecommunications, Issa Amsa.
Transport and Tourism, Amadou Moussa Gros.
Youth, Sport and Culture, Abdourahamane Seydou.
Higher Education and Technical Research, Yahaya Tounkara.
Minister delegate for Interior, Amadou Fiti Maiga.
Mines and Energy, Allele Elhadj Habibou.
Planning, Almoustapha Soumaila.
Foreign Affairs and Co-operation, Sani Bako.
Public Establishments, State Enterprises, and Parastatals, Maina Boukar Moussa.
National Education, Amadou Madougou.
Labour, Aboubacar Abdou.
Trade, Industry and Workers, Madou Mahamadou.
Agriculture and Environment, Amadou Mamadou.
Information, Sahidou Alou.
Animal Resources and Hydraulics, Mahamadou Danda.
Justice, Soli Abdourahamane.

Situated in West Central Africa, between 12° and 24° N. and 0° and 16° E., Niger has common boundaries with Algeria and Libya in the north, Chad, Nigeria, Benin, Mali and Burkina.

It has an area of about 489,191 sq. miles (1,267,000 sq. km.), with a population (estimate, 1985) of 6,317,550. Apart from a small region along the Niger Valley in the south-west near the capital the country is entirely savanna or desert. The main ethnic groups are the Hausa (54 per cent) in the south, the Songhai and Djerma in the south-west, the Fulani, the Beriberi-Manga, and the nomadic Tuareg in the north. The official language is French.

The first French expedition arrived in 1891 and the country was fully occupied by 1914. It decided on December 18, 1958, to remain an autonomous republic within the French Community; full independence outside the Community was proclaimed on August 3, 1960. Special agreements with France, covering financial and cultural matters, technical assistance, defence, etc., were signed in Paris on April 24, 1961. These are now being revised.

The constitution of Niger, adopted on November 8, 1960, provided for a presidential system of government, modelled on that of the United States and the French Fifth Republic, and a single Chamber National Assembly. In April 1974 Lt.-Col. Seyni Kountché seized power, suspended the Constitution, dissolved the National Assembly, and suppressed all political organizations. He then set up a Supreme Military Council with himself as President. President Kountché died on Nov. 10, 1987 and was succeeded peacefully by his cousin, Col. Ali Saibou.

Since coming to power, Col. Saibou has restored a measure of normal political life. There is a single political party, the Mouvement National de la Société de Developpement (MNSD). A draft constitution will be the subject of a referendum in Sept. 1989, and presidential and legislative elections will be held in Dec. 1989.

Finance.—The 1987 General Budget allocation was CFA 198,100 million.

Trade.—The cultivation of ground-nuts and the production of livestock are the main industries and provide two of the main exports. A company formed by the Government, the French Atomic Energy Authority and private interests is exploiting uranium deposits at Arlit, and this is the main export.

Trade with U.K.

	1987	1988
Imports from U.K.	£7,026,000	£7,562,000
Exports to U.K.	10,556,000	1,359,000

CAPITAL.—Niamey (pop. 399,100).
CURRENCY.—Franc C.F.A. of 100 centimes.
FLAG.—Three horizontal stripes, orange, white and green with an orange disc in the middle of the white stripe.
NATIONAL DAY.—December 18.

British Ambassador, (*resident at* Abidjan, Côte d'Ivoire).

NORWAY
(Kongeriket Norge)

King, Olav V, K.G., K.T., G.C.B., G.C.V.O., b. July 2, 1903; *succeeded*, Sept. 21, 1957, on death of his father King Haakon VII; *married* March 21, 1929, Princess Märtha of Sweden (*born* March 28, 1901; *died* April 5, 1954); having issue, Prince Harald (*see below*), Princess Ragnhild (b. 1930), and Princess Astrid (b. 1932).

Heir-Apparent, H.R.H. Prince Harald, G.C.V.O., b. Feb. 21, 1937; *m.* Aug. 29, 1968, Sonja Haraldsen, and has issue Princess Märtha Louise, b. Sept. 22, 1971; and Prince Haakon Magnus, b. July 20, 1973.

CABINET
(as at June 30, 1989)

Prime Minister, Ms. Gro Harlem Brundtland.
Foreign Affairs, Thorvald Stoltenberg.
Cultural and Scientific Affairs, Hallvard Bakke.
Environment, Ms. Sissel Rønbeck.
Industry, Finn Kristensen.
Petroleum and Energy, Arne Øien.
Local Government and Labour, Kjell Borgen.
Development Co-operation, Ms. Kirsti Kolle Grøndahl.
Trade, Jan Balstad.
Fisheries, Bjarne Mørk Eidem.
Defence, Johan Jørgen Holst.
Transport and Communications, William Engseth.
Justice, Ms. Helen Bøsterud.
Finance, Gunnar Berge.
Church and Education, Ms. Mary Kvidal.
Health and Social Affairs, Ms. Tove Strand Gerhardsen.
Agriculture, Ms. Gunhild Øyangen.
Consumer Affairs and Government Administration, Ms. Oddrun Pettersen.

(A General Election is to take place on Sept. 11, 1989.)

ROYAL NORWEGIAN EMBASSY
25 Belgrave Square, SW1X 8QD
[01–235 7151]

Ambassador Extraordinary and Plenipotentiary, His Excellency Kjell Eliassen (1989).
Minister-Counsellor, Haakon B. Hjelde.
Counsellors, Paul Moe (*Press and Cultural*); Marius Hauge (*Fisheries*); Eva Bugge (*Economic*); Viggo Smestad (*Commercial*).
First Secretaries, K. Harald Dalen (*Political*); T. S. Kijewski (*Consul*); R. Aasheim (*Economic*).
Second Secretaries, A. Rikter-Svendsen (*Press, Information and Cultural*).

Area and Population.—Norway is a kingdom in the northern and western portion of the Scandinavian

peninsula, and was founded in 872. It is 1,752 km. in length, its greatest width about 430 km. The length of the coastline is 2,542 km., and the frontier between Norway and the neighbouring countries is 2,542 km. (Sweden 1,619 km., Finland 727 km. and U.S.S.R. 196 km.). It is divided into 19 counties (*fylker*) and comprises an area of 149,282 sq. miles (386,638 sq. km.), of which Svalbard and Jan Mayen have a combined area of 24,101 sq. km., with a population (April 1989) of 4,224,606.

The Norwegian coastline is extensive, deeply indented with numerous fjords, and fringed with an immense number of rocky islands. The surface is mountainous, consisting of elevated and barren tablelands, separated by deep and narrow valleys. At the North Cape the sun does not appear to set from the second week in May to the last week in July, causing the phenomenon known as the Midnight Sun; conversely, there is no apparent sunrise from about Nov. 18 to Jan. 23. During the long winter nights are seen the multiple coloured Northern Lights or Aurora Borealis, which have a maximum intensity in a line crossing North America from Alaska to Labrador and Northern Europe to the Arctic coast and Siberia.

Language and Literature.—Old Norse literature is among the most ancient and richest in Europe. Norwegian in both its present forms is closely related to other Scandinavian languages. Independence from Denmark (1814) and resurgent nationalism led to the development of 'new Norwegian' based on dialects, which now has equal official standing with 'bokmål', in which Danish influence is more obvious. This was formed in the time of the Reformation, and Ludvig Holberg (1684–1754) is regarded as the father of Norwegian literature, though the modern period begins with the patriotic and romantic writings of Henrik Wergeland (1808–1845). Some of the famous names are Henrik Ibsen (1828–1906), Bjørnstjerne Bjørnson (1832–1910), Nobel Prizewinner in 1903, and the novelists Jonas Lie (1833–1908), Alexander Kielland (1849–1906), Knut Hamsun (1859–1952) and

Sigrid Undset (1882–1949), the latter two both Nobel Prizewinners, and the latter a champion of Norwegian womanhood. In 1989 there were 153 daily newspapers.

Government.—From 1397 to 1814 Norway was united with Denmark, and from Nov. 4, 1814, with Sweden, under a personal union which was dissolved on June 7, 1905, when Norway regained complete independence. Under the constitution of May 17, 1814, the *Storting* (Parliament) itself elects one-quarter of its members to constitute the *Lagting* (Upper Chamber), the other three-quarters forming the *Odelsting* (Lower Chamber). Legislative questions alone are dealt with by both parts in separate sittings.

The three-party coalition government fell on May 1, 1986, when it lost a vote of confidence, and was succeeded by a minority Labour government which took office on May 9, 1986.

Production.—The cultivated area is about 8,636 sq. km. (2·3 per cent of total surface area); forests cover nearly 25 per cent; the rest consists of highland pastures or uninhabitable mountains.

The *Gulf Stream* pours from 140 to 170 million cubic feet of warm water per second into the sea around Norway and causes the temperature to be higher than the average for the latitude. It brings shoals of herring and cod into the fishing grounds and causes a warm current of air over the west coast, making it possible to cultivate potatoes and barley in latitudes which in other countries are perpetually frozen. In normal years the quantity of fish caught by Norwegian fishing vessels is greater than that of any other European country except U.S.S.R. In 1987 the total catch amounted to 1,867,720 tonnes.

The chief industries are manufactures, agriculture and forestry, fisheries, mining, production of metals and ferro-alloys and shipping. Also in recent years industries providing both manufactured products and services for the development of North Sea oil and gas resources have assumed growing importance. In 1988, the total workforce was 2,163,000 of which 324,000 persons were employed in Norwegian industry. Manufactures are aided by great resources of hydro-electric power. Actual production in 1988 amounted to 110,063 Gwh.

Defence.—Norway is a member of the North Atlantic Treaty Organization, and the Headquarters of Allied Forces, Northern Europe, is situated near Oslo. The period of compulsory national service is 15 months (without refresher training) in the Navy and Air Force, and 12 months (with refresher training) in the Army. In March 1978 Norway committed an infantry battalion with additional support to the U.N. Interim Force in the Lebanon.

Education from 7 to 16 is free and compulsory in the 'basic schools' maintained by the municipalities with State grants-in-aid. The majority of the pupils receive post-compulsory schooling at 'upper secondary' schools, colleges of education (19) regional colleges akin to polytechnics (12), universities (4) and other university-level specialist institutions.

Communications.—The total length of railways open at the end of 1988 was 4,070 km., excluding private lines. There are 87,603 km. of public roads in Norway (including urban streets). At the end of 1988, 2,893,639 road motor vehicles were registered.

Scheduled internal air services are operated by Scandinavian Airlines System (SAS) on behalf of Det Norske Luftfartselskap (DNL), by Braathens South American and Far East Airtransport (SAFE), and by Widerøes Flyveselskap A.S.

The Mercantile Marine, 1988, consisted of 1,532 vessels of 12,921,932 gross tons (vessels above 100 gross tons, excluding fishing boats, floating whaling factories, tugs, salvage vessels, icebreakers and similar types of vessel).

FINANCE

	1987	1988
Total Revenue	K321,677,000	K342,900,000
Total Expenditure	282,648,000	309,717,000

TRADE

	1987	1988
	million Kroner	
Total imports	211,794	217,455
Total exports	199,731	213,117

Trade with U.K.

	1987	1988
Imports from U.K.	£1,220,844,000	£1,053,613,000
Exports to U.K.	3,290,339,000	3,074,312,000

The chief imports are raw materials, motor vehicles, chemicals, motor spirit, fuel and other oils; coal, ships and machinery; together with manufactures of silk, cotton and wool. The exports consist chiefly of crude oil and gas, manufactured goods, fish and products of fish (as canned fish, whale oils), pulp, paper, iron ore and pyrites, nitrate of lime, stone, calcium carbide, aluminium, ferro-alloys, zinc, nickel, cyanamide, etc.

CAPITAL.—ΨOslo (incl. Aker). Pop. (Jan. 1987), 450,808. Other towns are ΨTrondheim, 135,542; ΨBergen, 209,912; ΨStavanger, 96,316; ΨKristiansand, 63,637; ΨDrammen, 51,807; ΨTromsø, 49,358.

CURRENCY.—Krone of 100 øre.

FLAG.—Red, with white-bordered blue cross.

NATIONAL ANTHEM.—Ja, Vi Elsker Dette Landet (Yes, we love this country).

NATIONAL DAY.—May 17 (Constitution Day).

BRITISH EMBASSY
Thomas Heftyesgate 8, 0264 Oslo 2.
[Oslo 55 24 00]

Ambassador Extraordinary and Plenipotentiary, His Excellency John Adam Robson, C.M.G. (1987).

Counsellors, R. G. Short, M.V.O. (*Head of Chancery and Consul General*); Dr. C. P. Burdess, L.V.O. (*Economic*).

First Secretaries, J. Venning; D. O. Hay-Edie (*Economic and Commercial*); P. S. Dickson (*Administration*).

Defence and Air Attaché, Wg. Cdr. S. A. Wrigley, R.A.F.

Naval Attaché, Cdr. H. L. Foxworthy, R.N.

Military Attaché, Lt. Col. R. M. Gamble.

BRITISH CONSULAR OFFICES

There is a British Consular Office at *Oslo* and Honorary Consulates at *Bergen, Tromsø, Alesund, Kristiansund, Stavanger, Trondheim, Kristiansand, Haugesund* and *Harstad*.

British Council Representative, P. A. Thompson, Fridtjof Nansens Plass 5,0160, Oslo 1.

TERRITORIES

SVALBARD. By Treaty (Feb. 9, 1920) the sovereignty of Norway over the Spitsbergen (Pointed Mountain) Archipelago was recognized by the Great Powers and other interested nations, and on Aug. 14, 1925, Norway assumed sovereignty. In September, 1941, Allied forces (British, Canadian and Norwegian) landed on the main island. After destruction of the accumulated stocks of coal and dismantling of mining machinery and the wireless installation, the Norwegian inhabitants (about 600) were evacuated to a British port and the Russians (about 1,500) to the U.S.S.R. After the war the Norwegian mining plants were rebuilt. 288,000 metric tons of coal were extracted from Norwegian mines in Svalbard in 1980. The Svalbard Archipelago lies between 74°–81° N.

lat. and between 10°–35° E. long., with an estimated area of 24,295 square miles. The archipelago consists of a main island, known as Spitsbergen (15,200 sq. miles); North East Land, closely adjoining and separated by Hinlopen Strait; the Wiche Islands, separated from the mainland by Olga Strait; Barents and Edge Islands, separated from the mainland by Stor Fjord (or Wybe Jansz Water); Prince Charles Foreland, to the W.; Hope Island, to the S.E.; Bear Island (68 square miles) 127 miles to the S.; with many similar islands in the neighbourhood of the main group. In addition to those engaged in coal-mining, the archipelago is also visited by hunters for seals, foxes and polar bears.

South Cape is 355 miles from the Norwegian Coast. Ice Fjord is 520 miles from Tromsø, 650 miles from Murmansk, and 1,300 miles from Aberdeen. Transit from Tromsø to Green Harbour 2 to 3 days; from Aberdeen 5 to 6 days.

JAN MAYEN, an island in the Arctic Ocean (70° 49'–71° 9' N. lat. and 7° 53'–9° 5' W. long.) was joined to Norway by law of Feb. 27, 1930.

Norwegian Antarctic

BOUVET ISLAND (54° 26' S. lat. and 3° 24' E. long.) was declared a dependency of Norway by law of Feb. 27, 1930.

PETER THE FIRST ISLAND (68° 48' S. lat. and 90° 35' W. long.), was declared a dependency of Norway by resolution of Government, May 1, 1931.

PRINCESS RAGNHILD LAND (from 70° 30' to 68° 40' S. lat. and 24° 15' to 33° 30' E. long.) has been claimed as Norwegian since Feb. 17, 1931.

QUEEN MAUD LAND.—On Jan. 14, 1939, the Norwegian Government declared the area between 20° W. and 45° E., adjacent to Australian Antarctica, to be Norwegian territory.

OMAN
(The Sultanate of Oman)

Sultan, Qaboos Bin-Said, succeeded on deposition of Sultan Said bin Taimur, July 23, 1970.

(The Sultan acts as his own Prime Minister, Minister of Foreign Affairs, Defence and Finance.)

COUNCIL OF MINISTERS
(as at June 30, 1989)

Agriculture and Fisheries, H.E. Muhammad bin Abdullah bin Zahir al Hinai.

Commerce and Industry, H.E. Col. Salim bin Abdullah al Ghazali.

Communications, H.E. Hamoud bin Abdullah al Harthi.

Deputy P.M., Security and Defence, H.H. Sayyid Fahr bin Taimur Al Said.

Office of the Personal Representative of H.M. The Sultan, H.H. Sayyid Thuwaini bin Shihab Al Said.

Education and Youth Affairs, H.E. Yahya bin Mahfuth al Manthari.

Electricity and Water, H.E. Khalfan bin Nasr al Wahaibi.

Environment, H.H. Sayyid Shabib bin Taimur Al Said.

Deputy P.M., Financial and Economic Affairs, H.E. Qais bin Abdul Munim al Zawawi.

Minister of State for Foreign Affairs, H.E. Yusuf bin Alawi bin Abdullah.

Health, H.E. Dr. Ali bin Muhammad bin Musa.

Housing, H.E. Malik bin Sulaiman al Ma'mari.

Information, H.E. Abdul Aziz bin Muhammad al Rowas.

Interior, H.E. Sayyid Badr bin Saud bin Harib al Bu Saidi.

Justice, Awqaf and Islamic Affairs, H.E. Sayyid Hilal Bin Saud bin Hamad Al Bu Saidi.

Deputy Prime Minister for Legal Affairs, H.H. Sayyid Fahd bin Mahmoud Al Said.

National Heritage and Culture, H.H. Sayyid Faisal bin Ali Al Said.

Petroleum and Minerals, H.E. Said bin Ahmad bin Said al Shanfari.

Posts, Telegraphs and Telephones, H.E. Ahmad bin Suwaidan al Balushi.

Regional Municipalities, H.E. Sheikh Muhammad bin Ali al Qutbi.

Social Affairs and Labour, H.E. Sheikh Mustahail bin Ahmad al Mashani.

President, Consultative Council of the State, H.E. Sheikh Abdullah Bin Ali Bin Muhammad Al Qutbi.

Office of the Minister of State and Wali of Dhofar, H.E. Sayyid Musallim Bin Ali Al Bu Saidi.

President, Diwan of Royal Court Affairs, H.E. Sayyid Saif bin Hamad bin Saud.

First ADC to H.M. The Sultan and President of the Palace Office, H.E. Maj.-Gen. Ali bin Majid al Mamari.

Civil Service, H. E. Ahmad Bin Abdul Nabi Macki.

Secretary to the Council of Ministers, H.E. Sayyid Hamoud bin Faisal Al Bu Saidi.

EMBASSY OF THE SULTANATE OF OMAN
44A/B Montpelier Square, SW7 1JJ
[01–584 6782/3/4]

Ambassador Extraordinary and Plenipotentiary, new appointment awaited.

The independent Sultanate of Oman lies at the eastern corner of the Arabian Peninsula. Its seaboard is nearly 1,000 miles long and extends from near Tibat on the west coast of the Musandam Peninsula round to Ras Darbat Ali, with the exception of the stretch between Dibba and Kalba on the east coast which belongs to Sharjah and Fujairah of the United Arab Emirates. Ras Darbat Ali marks the boundary between the Sultanate and the People's Democratic Republic of Yemen. The Sultanate extends inland to the borders of the Rub al Khali, or Empty Quarter of the Arabian Desert.

The area of Oman has been estimated at 82,030 sq. miles (212,457 sq. km.), and the population at 1,500,000 (1986). The inhabitants of the North are for the most part Arab but along the coast there is a strong infusion of negro blood, while in the Capital Area which stretches from Muscat to Seeb there are large communities of Hindus, Khojas and Baluch, in addition to Zanzibaris of Omani origin. In Dhofar there is also an infusion of negro blood around Salalah, but in the mountains the inhabitants are either of pure Arab descent or belong to tribes of pre-Arab origin, the Qarra and Mahra, who speak their own dialects of semitic origin.

Physically and historically modern Oman can be split into two main parts, the North and the South, divided by a large tract of desert. *Northern Oman* has three main sections. The *Batinah*, the coastal plain, varies in width from 30 miles in the neighbourhood of Suwaiq to almost nothing at Muscat where the mountains descend abruptly to the sea. The plain is fertile, with date gardens extending over its full length of 150 miles. The *Hajjar*, a mountain spine running from north west to south east, reaching nearly 10,000 feet in height on Jabal Akhdar. For the most part the mountains are barren, but numerous valleys penetrate the central massif of Jabal Akhdar and in these there is considerable cultivation irrigated by wells or a system of underground canals called *falajs* which tap the water table. The two plateaus leading from the western slopes of the mountains, the *Dhahirah*, in the north and the *Sharqia* in the south east also have centres of settlements and cultivation. They fall from an average height of 1,000 feet into the sands of the Empty Quarter. The north is separated from the south by nearly 400 miles of inhospitable country crossed by one trunk road, the only land link. *Dhofar*, the southern province, is the only part of the Arabian Peninsula to be touched by the south-west monsoon. Temperatures are more moderate than in the north and sugar cane and coconuts are grown on the coastal plain, while cattle are bred on the mountains.

Government.—A Consultative Council for the State was established by Sultanic decree on October 18, 1981. The Council is a nominated body consisting of 55 members (36 representing the public and 19 representing the government). The Council's jurisdiction is confined to economic affairs and social development.

Commerce and Trade.—Trade is mainly with the United Kingdom, Japan, the Netherlands, U.S., Federal Republic of Germany, France and India. Total imports for the year 1987 were OR 700,730,000. Chief imports were machinery, cars, building materials, refined petroleum and food and telecommunications equipment.

Trade with U.K.

	1987	1988
Imports from U.K.	£249,916,000	£344,875,000
Exports to U.K.	3,951,000	146,751,000

Production.—Petroleum Development (Oman) Ltd. (owned 60 per cent by Oman Government and 34 per cent by Shell) began exporting oil in 1967. Concessions (off and on shore) are held by several major international companies. The current level of oil production is about 650,000 barrels per day.

Development.—For many years the Sultanate was a poor country with a total annual income of less than £1,000,000. The advent of oil revenues since 1967 and the change of regime in 1970 led to the initiation of a wide-ranging development programme, especially concerned with health, education and communications. New hospitals have been completed in the main provincial centres and there are now 40 hospitals with 2,861 beds, and 696 schools, with 272,018 pupils, were in operation in 1987. A gas turbine power station operates at Rusail, where there is also a 200 plot industrial estate. There is a desalination plant near Muscat and flour, animal feed, cement and copper production facilities.

Communications.—Since 1972 ships have been using Port Qaboos at Matrah, where eight deep water berths have been constructed as part of the new harbour facilities.

The telegraph office, an automatic telephone service in Muscat and Matrah and an international telephone service are operated by the General Telecommunications Organization. There are now good tarmac roads linking most main population centres of the country with the coast and with the towns of the U.A.E. There is now over 4,000 km. of asphalted road in the Sultanate.

CAPITAL.—Ψ Muscat, population (estimated), 400,000. The commercial centre has grown around Mutrah, 3 miles away and the main port, and Ruwi. The main towns on the northern coast are ΨSur, ΨBarka and ΨSohar. The main town of Dhofar is Salalah.

CURRENCY.—Rial Omani (OR) of 1,000 baiza.

FLAG.—Red, green and white with crossed daggers in red sector.

NATIONAL DAY.—November 18.

BRITISH EMBASSY
P.O. Box 300, Muscat
[Muscat 738501/5]

Ambassador Extraordinary and Plenipotentiary, His Excellency Robert John Alston, C.M.G. (1986).

Counsellor, A. M. Layden (*Head of Chancery*).
Defence Attaché, Brig. M. J. Smith.
Naval and Air Attaché, Cdr. K. Harris, O.B.E., R.N
First Secretaries, D. S. Watson; B. Baldwin.
British Council Representative, R. A. Steedman, P.O. Box 7090, Mutrah, Oman.

PAKISTAN
(Islami Jamhuriya-e-Pakistan)

President, Ghulam Ishaq Khan, *elected* Dec. 12, 1988 *for a four-year term.*
Prime Minister, Minister for Establishment, O. & M. Division, Defence, Production, Information and Broadcasting, Minority Affairs, Finance, Economic Affairs, Planning and Development, Ms. Benazir Bhutto, *sworn in* Dec. 2, 1988.
Chairman of the Senate, Sen. Wasim Sajjad.
Deputy Chairman of the Senate, Sen. Mohammad Fazal Agha.
Speaker, National Assembly, Malik Meraj Khalid.
Deputy Speaker, National Assembly, Dr. Mrs. Ashraf Abbasi.

MINISTERS
(as at July 31, 1989)

Senior Minister without Portfolio, Begum Nusrat Bhutto.
Interior, Aitzaz Ahsan.
Labour, Manpower and Overseas Pakistanis, Mukhtar Awan.
Communications, Makhdoom Mohammad Amin Faheem.
Culture and Tourism, Agha Tariq Khan.
Food, Agriculture and Co-operatives, Rao Sikander Iqbal.
Commerce, Local Government and Rural Development, Syed Faisal Saleh Hayat.
Health, Special Education and Social Welfare, Syed Amir Haider Kazmi.
Science and Technology, Petroleum and Natural Resources, Jahangir Badar.
Foreign Affairs, Sen. Sahabzada Yaqub Khan.
Housing and Works, Mohammad Hanif Khan.
Law and Justice, Sen. Syed Iftikhar Gillani.
Water and Power, Sardar Farooq Ahmad Khan Leghari.
Education, Syed Ghulam Mustafa Shah.
Railways, Haji Zaffar Ali Leghari.
Industries, Ali Nawaz Shah.
Religious Affairs, Khan Bahadur Khan.
Parliamentary Affairs, Ahmad Tariq Rahim.
Youth, Syed Pervez Ali Shah Jillani.
States and Frontier Regions, and Kashmir Affairs, Mir Baz Mohammad Khan Khetran.
Tourism, Yousaf Raza Gillani.
Attorney General, Yahya Bakhtiar.

EMBASSY OF PAKISTAN
35 Lowndes Square, SW1X 9JN
[01–235 2044]

Ambassador Extraordinary and Plenipotentiary, His Excellency Shaharyar M. Khan (1987).
Ministers, Karam Elahi (*Deputy Head of Mission*); Khurshid Anwar (*Political*).
Defence Attaché, Brig. Saeed Ismat.

Area and Population.—The Islamic Republic of Pakistan consists of country situated to the northwest of the Indian sub-continent, bordered by Iran, Afghanistan, the disputed territory of Kashmir, and India. It covers a total area of 307,374 sq. miles (746,045 sq. km.). Running through Pakistan are five great rivers, the Indus, Jhelum, Chenab, Ravi and Sutlej. The upper reaches of these rivers are in Kashmir, and their sources in the Himalayas.

The Government of Pakistan census in 1981 showed a population figure of 83,780,000 (1985 U.N. estimate, 96,180,000). Of these, about 95 per cent are Muslims, about 1 per cent Hindus, 3·5 per cent Christians, and 0·5 per cent Buddhists.

Government.—Pakistan was constituted as a Dominion under the Indian Independence Act, 1947, which received Royal Assent on July 18, 1947. In terms of the Act the Dominion of Pakistan consisted of former territories of British India. The States of Bahawalpur and Khairpur (in Punjab and Sind), with a Muslim population of almost 80 per cent and with Muslim rulers, acceded to Pakistan in October, 1947. The following States also acceded to Pakistan: the Baluchistan States of Kalat, Mekran, Las Bela and Kharan, and the North-West Frontier States of Amb, Chitral, Dir and Swat. (The States of Junagadh and Manavadar which had acceded to Pakistan were occupied by India on November 8, 1947.) Boundaries of the Provinces of East Bengal and of Punjab (West Punjab) were defined by a Boundary Commission. Thus, until 1972 when East Pakistan seceded, Pakistan consisted of two geographical units, West and East Pakistan, which were separated by about 1,100 miles of Indian territory.

Pakistan became a Republic on March 23, 1956, when a Parliamentary Constitution came into force. On October 7, 1958, however, this Constitution was abrogated and Pakistan came under martial law.

The first general elections ever held in Pakistan on a basis of 'one man, one vote', were held in Dec. 1970 and Jan. 1971. The Awami League in East Pakistan, led by Sheikh Mujibur Rahman, and the Pakistan People's Party in West Pakistan, led by Zulfikar Ali Bhutto, won large majorities. Following the elections there was total disagreement between the two main parties on the question of a new Constitution for Pakistan, Sheikh Mujibur insisting on complete autonomy for East Pakistan. The proposed opening of the National Assembly at Dacca on March 25, 1971, was postponed and civil war broke out. East Pakistan seceded by unilateral declaration the following day. Fighting continued until Dec. 1971 when a ceasefire was arranged, and 'The Democratic Government of Bangladesh' was formally proclaimed on April 17, 1972.

Following general elections in March 1977 and allegations of vote-rigging the armed forces under Gen. Zia-ul-Haq assumed power on July 5, 1977 and imposed martial law throughout the country. The military government scheduled new general elections for October 1977, but these were postponed. Gen. Zia declared himself President on Sept. 16, 1978. In Dec. 1984 Gen Zia got a five-year mandate as a civilian President through a national referendum. Martial law was lifted on Dec. 30, 1985. On May 29, 1988, Zia dissolved the National Assembly and the Cabinet and announced fresh elections. A caretaker cabinet was announced on June 9. Zia was killed in a plane crash on Aug. 17, 1988, and the Senate Chairman, Ghulum Ishaq Khan, assumed the office of President. The Pakistan People's Party won the election to the National Assembly and Benazir Bhutto became Prime Minister on Dec. 2, 1988. The legislature then elected President Ghulam Ishaq Khan as a constitutional President.

Education.—Formal education in Pakistan is organized into five stages. These are five years of primary education (5–9 years), three years of middle or lower secondary (general or vocational), two years of upper secondary, two years of higher secondary (intermediate) and two to five years of higher education in colleges and universities. Education is free to upper secondary level. It was expected that primary education would become universal for boys by mid-1985 and for girls by mid-1988.

At primary level enrolment had increased to 6·5

million in 1984–85, and the number of schools to 75,000. At the middle level enrolment had increased to 1·7 million in 1984–85, and the number of schools to 6,200. At the upper secondary level enrolment increased to 570,000 in 1984–85.

Provincial Governments are responsible for the total financial support of the government institutions and for grants to non-government institutions. But policy making is authorized by the national Government, which makes annual grants. In 1986, 24 per cent of adults were estimated as being literate.

Production.—Pakistan's economy is chiefly based on agriculture. The principal crops are cotton, rice, wheat, sugar cane, maize and tobacco. There are large deposits of rock salt. Pakistan has one of the longest irrigation systems in the world. The total area irrigated is 33 million acres.

Pakistan also produces hides and skins, leather, wool, fertilizers, paints and varnishes, soda ash, paper, cement, fish, carpets, sports goods, surgical appliances and engineering goods, including switch-gear, transformers, cables and wires.

Trade.—Pakistan imported manufactured goods and raw materials to the value of US$5,792 million in 1986–87 and exported mainly agricultural products valued at US$3,498 million. Principal imports are listed as: petroleum products, machinery, fertilizers, transport equipment, edible oils, chemicals and ferrous metals. Principal exports are raw cotton, cotton yarn and cloth, carpets, rice, petroleum products, synthetic textiles, leather, and fish.

Trade with U.K.

	1987	1988
Imports from U.K.	£252,978,000	£263,300,000
Exports to U.K.	167,315,000	175,337,000

Finance.—The 1989–90 Budget anticipated net federal revenues of Rs.127,407·4 million and current expenditure (excluding development expenditure) of some Rs.124,878·5 million.

Communications.—The main seaport is Karachi. The main airport at Karachi occupies an important position on international trunk routes and is equipped with modern facilities and equipment. Pakistan International Airlines (P.I.A.) operates air services between the principal cities within the country as well as abroad.

Post and telegraph facilities are available to every country in the world.

CAPITAL.—Islamabad, pop. 350,000. ΨKarachi (pop. est. 6,500,000) is the largest city and seaport; Lahore has a population of about 3,500,000.

CURRENCY.—Pakistan rupee of 100 paisa.

FLAG.—Dark green ground, with white vertical stripes at the mast, the green portion bearing a white crescent in the centre and a five-pointed heraldic star.

NATIONAL ANTHEM.—'Quami Tarana.'

NATIONAL DAYS.—March 23 (Pakistan Day), August 14 (Independence Day).

BRITISH EMBASSY
Diplomatic Enclave, Ramna 5,
P.O. Box 1122, Islamabad.
[Islamabad 822131/5]

Ambassador Extraordinary and Plenipotentiary, His Excellency Nicholas John Barrington, C.M.G., C.V.O. (1987).

There is a British Consulate-General at *Karachi* and a Consulate at *Lahore.*

British Council Representative, R. F. Budd, P.O. Box 1135, Islamabad. There are regional offices at *Karachi* and *Lahore*, and a library in *Peshawar.*

PANAMA
(República de Panamá)

Minister in Charge of the Presidency, Gen. Francisco Rodriguez, *apptd.* Sept. 1, 1989.

MINISTERS OF STATE
(as at June 30, 1989)

Government and Justice, Rodolfo Chiari de León.
Foreign Affairs, Dr. Jorge Eduardo Ritter.
Treasury and Finance, Dr. Orville Goodin.
Agricultural Development, Armando Ayala Walter.
Public Works, René Bultrón.
Commerce and Industry, Mario Rognoni.
Labour and Social Welfare, Dr. César Martans.
Health, Dr. José Renan Esquivel.
Housing, Ricardo Bermúdez.
Planning and Economic Policy, Gustavo González.
Education, Dr. Rolando Murgas.
Presidency, Nander Pitty Velásquez.

EMBASSY OF THE REPUBLIC OF PANAMA
119 Crawford Street, W1H 1AF
[01–487 5633]

Ambassador Extraordinary and Plenipotentiary, His Excellency Lic. Guillermo Vega (1984).
Minister-Counsellor, Prof. Dionisio Johnson.

CONSULATE
24 Tudor Street, EC4Y 0JD
[01–353 4792/3].

There is also a Consular Office of the Republic at *Liverpool.*

Panama lies on the isthmus of that name which connects N. and S. America. The area of the Republic is 29,762 sq. miles (77,082 sq. km.), the population (1986 estimate) 2,227,254. After a revolt (Nov. 3, 1903) it declared its independence from Colombia and established a separate Government.

After 1968 control of Panama was increasingly taken over by Gen. Omar Torrijos, Commander of the National Guard, following a military coup. In 1972 General Torrijos was designated as 'Leader of the Revolution' with wide overriding powers. In October 1978 he withdrew from the government, and Dr. Aristides Royo was elected President by the Assembly of Representatives. In a Presidential election in May 1984, Dr. Nicolas Barletta was elected president and took office in Nov. 1984. However, he resigned in Sept. 1985 after disagreements with military leaders and was succeeded by his Vice-President, Eric Arturo Delvalle. An attempt in Feb. 1988 by President Delvalle to remove Gen. Noriega as Commander of the Defence Forces failed. Noriega, using the legislative body dominated by his supporters, ousted Delvalle and replaced him with Manuel Solis Palma. The U.S. Government continues to recognize President Delvalle and has broken off diplomatic relations with Panama. Presidential elections were held on May 7, 1989, but many observers felt them to be fraudulent. Gen. Noriega annulled the results, which had appeared to give victory to the opposition.

The Panama Canal Zone.—With effect from Oct. 1, 1979 the Canal Zone (647 sq. miles) was disestablished, with all areas of land and water within the Zone reverting to Panama. By the 1977 treaty with the U.S.A., the U.S.A. is allowed the use of operating bases for the Panama Canal, together with several military bases, but the Republic of Panama is sovereign in all such areas. Control of the Canal will revert to Panama in the year 2000.

The soil is moderately fertile, but nearly one-half of the land is uncultivated. The chief crops are bananas, sugar, coconuts, cacao, coffee and cereals. The shrimping industry plays an important role in the Panamanian economy. A railway 47 miles in length joins the Atlantic and Pacific oceans.

Education is compulsory and free from 7 to 15 years.

Language and Literature.—The official language is Spanish. There are five Spanish language and one English language newspapers published daily in the capital but in 1988 the opposition press was banned.

TRADE

Republic of Panama	1987	1988
Imports	US$1,211 m	US$735 m
Exports	338 m	279 m

Colon Free Zone.......	1987	1988
Imports	US$2,044 m	US$1,843 m
Exports	2,285 m	2,119 m

Trade with U.K.†

	1987	1988
Imports from U.K.......	£40,020,000	£32,497,000
Exports to U.K.	4,919,000	12,230,000

† Including Colon Free Zone.

The imports are mostly manufactured goods, machinery, lubricants, chemicals and foodstuffs; exports are bananas, petroleum products, shrimps, sugar, meat and fishmeal.

CAPITAL, ΨPanama City. Population (1985 est.), 608,890.

CURRENCY.—Balboa of 100 centésimos. US notes are also in circulation.

FLAG.—Four quarters; white with blue star (top, next staff), red (in fly), blue (below, next staff) and white with red star.

NATIONAL ANTHEM.—"Alcanzamos Por Fin La Victoria" (Victory is ours at last).

NATIONAL DAY.—November 3.

Dependencies of Panama.—Taboga Island (area 4 sq. miles) is a popular tourist resort of some 12 miles from the Pacific entrance to the Panama Canal. Tourist facilities have also been developed in the Las Perlas Archipelago in the Gulf of Panama, particularly on the island of Contadora. There is a penal settlement at Guardia on the island of Coiba (area 19 sq. miles) in the Gulf of Chiriqui.

BRITISH EMBASSY

Torre Swiss Bank, Urb. Marbella,
Calle 53, piso 4 & 5, Panama City
(P.O. Box 889) Panama 1
[Panama City 69–0866]

Ambassador Extraordinary and Plenipotentiary, Her Excellency Mrs. Margaret Bryan, C.M.G. (1986).
First Secretary and Consul, N. J. Bown.
Defence, Naval, Military and Air Attaché, Lt.-Col. R. J. Lawson.

There is a British consular office at *Panama City*.

PARAGUAY
(República del Paraguay)

President, General Andrés Rodriguez, *elected* May 1, 1989.

CABINET MINISTERS
(as at June 30, 1989)

Foreign Affairs, Dr. Luis Maria Argaña.
Interior, Gen. Orlando Machuca Vargas.
Finance, Enzo Debernardi.
Education and Worship, Prof. Dr. Dionisio González Torres.
Agriculture and Livestock, Hernando Bertoni.
Public Works and Communications, Gen. Porfirio Pereira Ruiz Diaz.
Defence, Gen. Adolfo Samaniego.

Public Health and Social Welfare, Dr. Juan Manuel Cano Melgarejo.
Justice and Labour, Dr. Alexis Frutos Vaesken.
Industry and Commerce, Sr. Pedro Antonio Zuccolillo.
Without portfolio, Dr. Juan Ramón Cháves.
President of the Central Bank, Dr. Crispiniano Sandoval.

EMBASSY OF PARAGUAY

Braemar Lodge, Cornwall Gardens, SW7 4AQ
[01–937 1253; *Consulate*: 01-937 6629]

Ambassador Extraordinary and Plenipotentiary, new appointment awaited.
Counsellor and Consul General, Rubén Alvarenga-Cabañas.

Area and Population.—Paraguay is an inland subtropical state of South America, situated between Argentina, Bolivia and Brazil.

The area is estimated at 157,048 sq. miles (406,752 sq. km.), with a population (1988 estimate) of 4,000,000.

Paraguay is a country of grassy plains and dense forest, the soil being marshy in many parts and liable to floods; while the hills are covered for the most part with immense forests. The streams flowing into the Alto Paraná descend precipitously into that river. In the angle formed by the Paraná-Paraguay confluence are extensive marshes, one of which, known as Neembucú, or endless, is drained by Lake Ypoa, a large lagoon, south-east of the capital. The Chaco, lying between the rivers Paraguay and Pilcomayo and bounded on the north by Bolivia, formed the subject of a long-standing dispute with that country and led to war between Paraguay and Bolivia from 1932 to 1935. The Chaco is a flat plain, rising uniformly towards its western boundary to a height of 1,140 feet; it suffers much from floods and still more from drought, but the building of dams and reservoirs has converted part of it into good pasture for cattle raising.

Government.—In 1535 Paraguay was settled as a Spanish possession. In 1811 it declared its independence of Spain.

The constitution provides for a two-chamber parliament consisting of a 36-member Senate and a 72-member Chamber of Deputies. Two-thirds of the seats in each chamber are allocated to the majority party and the remaining one-third shared among the minority parties in proportion to the votes cast. Voting is compulsory for all citizens over 18.

The President is elected for 5 years and may be re-elected for a further term. He appoints the Cabinet, which exercises all the functions of government. During parliamentary recess it can govern by decree through the Council of State, the members of which are representative of the Government, the armed forces and various other bodies. The state of siege, in force since 1947, was lifted on April 8, 1987.

Production.—About three-quarters of the population are engaged in agriculture and cattle raising. Cotton, soya beans, tobacco, edible and essential oils, sugar, coffee and timber are the main exports. The forests contain many varieties of timber which find a good market abroad. Paraguay's hydroelectric power station at Acaray produced in 1985, 1,118 Kwh. of which a surplus is exported to Argentina and Brazil.

At Itaipú the largest hydroelectric dam in the world, a joint project by Paraguay and Brazil, was inaugurated in 1982. It is expected to be completed in 1990 when it will have a capacity of over 12 million kw. Work is also under way on a hydroelectric project with Argentina at Yacyretá which it is hoped will be in operation by the end of the decade.

Communications.—A railway, 985 miles in length, connects Asunción with Buenos Aires. The journey takes 55 hours. Train ferries enable the run to be accomplished without break of bulk. River steamers also connect Buenos Aires and Asunción (3 to 5 days). This service is liable to cancellation without warning when the river is low or in flood. There are direct shipping services to Asunción from Britain, Western Europe and the U.S.A. Eight airlines operate services from Asunción.

There are 1,176 km. of asphalted roads in Paraguay, connecting Asunción with São Paulo (26 hrs.) via the Bridge of Friendship and Foz de Yguazú and with Buenos Aires (24 hrs.) via Puerto Pilcomayo, and about 4,050 miles of earth roads in fairly good condition, but liable to be closed or to become impassable in wet weather. A 1,000 km. road, of which 300 km. are paved, links Asunción with the Bolivian border. There are services to Buenos Aires, São Paulo and Paranagua, a port on the Brazilian coast.

Defence.—There is a permanent military force of about 25,000 all ranks, most of whom are conscripts doing their military service; and about 6,500 armed police (again mostly conscripts). Three gunboats and a number of small armed launches patrol inland waters.

Language and Literature.—Spanish is the official language of the country but outside the larger towns *Guarani*, the language of the largest single unit of original Indian inhabitants, is widely spoken. Four daily, one weekly and one bi-weekly newspapers are published in Asunción. There are 48 AM, 15 FM and three TV stations in the country.

Education.—Education is free and compulsory. In 1984 there were 3,209 government primary schools and 587 private schools with 559,080 pupils and 22,091 teachers. There are 713 secondary schools with 149,019 pupils and 2,448 teachers. The National University in Asunción had in 1984 20,343 students. The Catholic University had 10,971 students.

BUDGET 1989
(in million guaranies)

	Central Government	Decentralized Bodies
Expenditure	376·5	919·8

Trade.—Total value of imports (US$) in 1988 was $441,000,000. The chief imports were machinery ($80,295,000); fuels and lubricants ($67,792,000); transport and accessories ($35,340,000); and drinks and tobacco ($37,147,000). Total value of exports in 1988 was $720,421,000. The chief exports were soya bean ($158,714,000); cotton fibres ($158,816,000); sawn wood ($12,138,000); and processed meat ($13,196,000).

Trade with U.K.

	1987	1988
Imports from U.K.	£25,409,000	£22,024,000
Exports to U.K.	1,409,000	1,950,000

CAPITAL, Asunción, about 1,000 miles up the River Paraguay from Buenos Aires. Pop. (census, 1985), 729,307; other centres being Ciudad Presidente Stroessner (98,491); Encarnación (31,445); Concepción (25,607); P. Juan Caballero (41,475).

CURRENCY.—Guaraní (Gs) of 100 céntimos.

FLAG.—Three horizontal bands, red, white, blue with the National seal on the obverse white band and the Treasury seal on the reverse white band.

NATIONAL ANTHEM.—"Paraguayos, Republica O Muerte" (Paraguayans, republic or death).

NATIONAL DAY.—May 14.

BRITISH EMBASSY
Calle Presidente Franco 706,
(PO Box 404)
[Asuncion 444472]

Ambassador Extraordinary and Plenipotentiary and

Consul-General, His Excellency Terence Harry Steggle (1989).

PERU
(República del Perú)

President, Sr. Dr. Alan García Pérez, *assumed office,* July 28, 1985.

CABINET
(as at May 31, 1989)

President of the Council of Ministers and Minister of the Presidency, Dr. Luis Alberto Sánchez.
Foreign Affairs, Guillermo Larco.
Interior, Máximo Agustín Mantilla.
Agriculture, Juan Manuel Coronado.
Defence, Julio Velásquez.
Economy and Finance, César Vasquez.
Education, Mercedes Cabanillas Llanos de la Mata.
Energy and Mines, Mario Samamé.
Health, Dr. David Tejada.
Housing and Construction, Antenor Orrego.
Industry, Internal Commerce, Tourism and Integration, Carlos Raffo.
Justice, Dr. César Augusto Delgado.
Labour and Social Development, Dr. Oreste Rodriguez.
Fisheries, Almirante Willy Harm.
Transport and Communications, Luis Gabriel Heysen.

PERUVIAN EMBASSY
52 Sloane Street, SW1X 9SP
[01–235 1917/2545]

Ambassador Extraordinary and Plenipotentiary, Felipe Valdivieso-Belaúnde (1989).
Counsellor, Julio Florián.
Minister, Gilbert Chauny.
Air Attaché, Maj. Gen. Juan Morante.

Area and Population.—Peru is a maritime Republic of South America, situated between 0° 00′ 48″ and 18° 21′ 00″ S. latitude and between 68° 39′ 27″ and 81° 20′ 13″ W. longitude. The area of the Republic is 496,225 sq. miles (1,285,216 sq. km.), with a population estimated (1985) at 19,700,000.

Physical Features.—The country is traversed throughout its length by the Andes, running parallel to the Pacific coast, the highest points in Peru being *Huascaran* (22,211 ft), *Huandoy* (20,855 ft), *Ausangate* (20,235 feet), *Misti* volcano (18,364 ft), *Hualcan* (20,000 ft), *Chachani* (19,037 ft), *Antajasha* (18,020 ft), *Pichu-pichu* (17,724 ft), and *Mount Meiggs* (17,583 ft).

There are three main regions, the *Costa*, west of the Andes, the *Sierra* or mountain ranges of the Andes, which include the *Punas* or mountainous wastes below the region of perpetual snow and the *Montaña*, or *Selva*, which is the vast area of jungle stretching from the eastern foothills of the Andes to the eastern frontiers of Peru. The coastal area, lying upon and near the Pacific, is not tropical, though close to the Equator, being cooled by the Humboldt Current. It contains the capital, Lima, and most of the white population.

In the mountains, where most of the Indians live, are to be found minerals in great richness and variety, and cattle, sheep, llamas and alpacas are bred there.

Language and Literature.—Spanish, the language of the original Spanish stock from which the governing and professional classes are mainly recruited, was formerly the only official language of the country. However, in May 1975, the Quechua language was declared the second official tongue. Quechua and Aymará are widely spoken by more than half the population of the country. Before the arrival of Pizarro, the Incas had attained a high state of culture, some traces of which survived three centuries of Spanish rule. Modern Peruvian literature includes a national drama in the Spanish tongue and many Peruvian writers have attained international fame.

Government.—Peru was conquered in the early 16th century by Francisco Pizarro (born 1478, died 1541). He subjugated the Incas (the ruling caste of the Quechua Indians), who had started their rise to power some 500 years earlier, and for nearly three centuries Peru remained under Spanish rule. A revolutionary war of 1821–1824 established its independence, declared on July 28, 1821. The constitution rests upon the fundamental law of Oct. 18, 1856, and is that of a democratic Republic. A new constitution was drawn up and approved in July 1979.

Production.—The chief products of the coastal belt are cotton, sugar and petroleum. There are large tracts of land suitable for cultivation and stock raising on the eastern slopes of the Andes, and in the mountain valleys maize, potatoes and wheat are grown. The jungle area is a source of timber and petroleum. Other major crops are fruit, vegetables, rice, barley, grapes and coffee. Mineral exports include lead, zinc, copper, iron ore and silver. Peru is normally the world's largest exporter of fishmeal.

Communications.—In recent years the coastal and sierra zones have been opened up by means of roads and air routes and there is air communication, as well as communication by protracted land routes, with the tropical and little known eastern zones, which lie east of the Andes towards the borders of Brazil. The completion in 1944 of the trunk road of the Andean Highway from the Pacific port of Callao, via Lima to Pucallpa, the river port on the Ucayali, forms a link between the Pacific, the Amazon and the Atlantic. The Panamerican Highway runs along the Peruvian coast connecting it with Ecuador and Chile. The Inter-Ocean Corridor linking the port of Matarani and Buenos Aires will be opened soon.

The first railway was opened in 1850 and the 2,400 miles of track are now administered by the Government. There is also steam navigation on the Ucayali and Huallaga, and in the south on Lake Titicaca. Air services are maintained throughout Peru, and many international services call at Lima.

Defence.—The Army is recruited by voluntary enlistment, supplemented by conscription (2 years), and numbers about 45,000 of all ranks. Armoured units are equipped with American, Russian and French vehicles. Engineer units are employed on the construction of roadways in Peru using American equipment. The main Naval base is in Callao and supports all ships of the Fleet. There are training establishments in Callao and La Punta. The Naval Air Arm consists of U.S. and French helicopters; U.S. anti-submarine aircraft and DC3's. The Air Force is equipped with British, U.S. and French aircraft and U.S. and French helicopters. There are military airfields at Talara, Piura, Chiclayo, Lima, Pisco, Joya, Iquitos and Arequipa plus a seaplane base at Iquitos. The National Police is made up of the Republican Guard, the Civil Guard and the Police of Investigation.

Education.—Education is compulsory and free for both sexes between the ages of 6 and 15.

Trade.—Import trade of Peru in 1987 totalled US$2,520 million and exports US$2,605 million.

Trade with U.K.

	1987	1988
Imports from U.K.	£49,324,000	£31,384,000
Exports to U.K.	91,689,000	90,844,000

The principal imports are machinery and chemicals and pharmaceutical products. The chief exports are minerals and metals, fishmeal, sugar, cotton and coffee.

CAPITAL.—Metropolitan Lima (including ΨCallao), population (1983) 5,258,600. Other major cities (with pop. census, 1981) are: Arequipa (561,338) Iquitos (540,560), ΨChiclayo (533,266).

CURRENCY.—Inti of 100 céntimos.

FLAG.—Three vertical bands, red, white, red; coat of arms on white band.

NATIONAL ANTHEM.—Somos Libres, Seámoslo Siempre (We are free, let us remain so forever).

NATIONAL DAY.—July 28 (Anniversary of Independence).

BRITISH EMBASSY

Natalio Sánchez 125 Piso 12, Sanata Beatriz (P.O. Box 854), Lima 100.
[Lima 334738]

Ambassador Extraordinary and Plenipotentiary, His Excellency Adrian John Beamish, C.M.G. (1987).

First Secretaries, B. B. Low (*Head of Chancery and Consul*); G. Chalder (*Commercial*); J. Blount (*Chancery and Economic*).

Defence Attaché, Col. P. R. Rostron, M.B.E.

There are British Consular Offices at *Lima* and *Arequipa*.

British Council Representative, A. Moore, P.O. Box No. 14.0114, Calle Alberto Lynch 110, San Isidro, Lima 27.

THE PHILIPPINES
(Repúblika ng Pilipinas)

President, Corazon C. Aquino *b*. 1933, *elected* Feb. 7, 1986, *assumed office* Feb. 25, 1986.

CABINET SECRETARIES
(as at June 30, 1989)

Foreign Affairs, Raul Manglapus.
Finance, Vicente Jayme.
Justice, Sedfrey Ordonez.
Agriculture, Carlos Dominguez.
Public Works and Highways, Fiorello Estuar.
Education, Culture and Sports, Lourdes Quisumbing.
Labour, Franklin Drilon.
Health, Alfredo Bengzon.
Trade and Industry, Jose Concepcion.

Social Services and Development, Mita Pardo de Tavera.
Economic Planning, (vacant).
Agrarian Reform, (vacant).
Special Counsel, Teodoro Locsin Jr.
Local Government, Luis Santos.
Tourism, Pedro Garrucho.
Natural Resources, Fulgenio Factóran.
Budget, Guillermo Carague.
Transportation and Communications, Rainerio Reyes.
National Defence, Fidel Ramos.
Executive Secretary, Catalino Macaraig Jr.
Muslim Affairs and Cultural Communities, Dimas Pundato.
Chairman, Presidential Commission on Good Government, Mateo Caparas.
Science and Technology, Ceferino Follosco.
Presidential Press Secretary, Adolfo Azcuna.
Presidential Adviser on National Security, Rafael Illeto.
Cabinet Secretary, Jose de Jesus.

EMBASSY OF THE PHILIPPINES
9A Palace Green, W8 4QE
[01–937 1600/9]

Ambassador Extraordinary and Plenipotentiary, His Excellency Tomas T. Syquia (1989).
Deputy Chief of Mission and Consul General, Edmundo Libid.
Commercial Counsellor, S. Ileto.

Area and Population.—The Philippines are situated between 21° 20′–4° 30′ N. Lat. and 116° 55′–126° 36′ E. long., and are distant about 500 miles from the south-east coast of the continent of Asia. (For MAP, see p. 760.)

The total land area of the country is 115,831 sq. miles (300,000 sq. km.). There are eleven larger islands and 7,079 other islands.

The principal islands are:—

	sq. miles		sq. miles
Luzon	40,422	Mindoro	3,759
Mindanao	36,538	Leyte	2,786
Samar	5,050	Cebu	1,703
Negros	4,906	Bohol	1,492
Palawan	4,550	Masbate	1,262
Panay	4,446		

Other groups in the Republic are the Sulu islands (capital, Jolo), Babuyanes and Batanes; the Catanduanes; and Culion Islands.

The population of the Philippines was estimated (1988) at 58,700,000.

The inhabitants, known as Filipinos, are basically all of Malay stock, with a considerable admixture of Spanish and Chinese blood in many localities, and about 90 per cent of them are Christians, predominantly Roman Catholics. Most of the remainder are Muslims, in the south, and Animists and pagans, mainly in the north. There is a Chinese minority estimated at 500,000, and other much smaller foreign communities, notably Spanish, American and Indian.

History.—The Portuguese navigator Magellan came to the Philippines in 1521 and was slain by the natives of Mactan, a small island near Cebu. In 1565 Spain undertook the conquest of the country which was named Filipinas, after the son of the King of Spain, and in 1571 the city of Manila was founded by the conquistador Legaspi, who subdued the inhabitants of almost all the islands, their conversion being undertaken by the Augustinian friars in Legaspi's train. In 1762 Manila was occupied by a British force, but in 1764 it was restored to Spain. In the Spanish-American War of 1898, Manila was captured by American troops with the help of Filipinos and the Islands were ceded to the United States by the Treaty

of Paris of Dec. 10, 1898. Despite a rebellion against the U.S. government between 1899 and 1902, the Americans remained in control of the country until 1946.

The Republic of the Philippines came into existence on July 4, 1946 with a presidential form of government based on the American system.

Martial law was imposed on September 21, 1972. This was lifted, except in two southern provinces, on January 17, 1981.

The assassination on Aug. 21, 1983 of Marcos' main political opponent, Benigno Aquino, and a subsequent financial crisis caused a weakening in Marcos' position. Although Marcos gained a majority of votes in the official count of a Presidential election in Feb. 1986, the election was marred by widespread electoral abuse and his rival, Mrs Corazon Aquino, launched a series of non-violent civil disturbance actions.

On Feb. 22, Defence Minister Enrile and Vice Chief of Staff Ramos broke away from the Marcos government and declared their support for Mrs. Aquino. Thousands of people took to the streets to support their revolt and they were joined by a large section of the Armed Forces. On Feb. 25, Marcos, his family and aides left for Hawaii. Mrs Aquino took over as President. On March 25, she abolished the Batasan (legislature) and promulgated a Freedom (Provisional) Constitution.

An appointed Constitutional Convention drafted a new Constitution with a Congressional system of government, having a senate of 24 members and a House of Representatives with 250 members. This was overwhelmingly approved by a referendum in Feb. 1987. Elections to the Congress were held in May and the new Constitution came into force on July 27, 1987.

There is unrest in many of the islands due to insurgency. Muslim insurgents, the Moro National Liberation Front, operate in western Mindanao and the Sula archipelago. Most of the current activity is due to the Communist New People's Army, which is strongest in eastern Mindanao, Negros, Samar, Bicol, the mountains of northern Luzon, and Bataan. As of June 1987 the ceasefire agreed between the Government and the Moro National Liberation Front was still holding, unlike the ceasefire with the Communists which ended in Feb. 1987.

Language and Literature.—The official languages are Filipino and English. Filipino, the national language, is based on Tagalog, one of the Malay-Polynesian languages and the language of the part of Luzon surrounding Metro Manilla. Filipino is spoken by 29·66 per cent of the total number of households, but local languages and dialects are strong and Cebuano is spoken by 24·20 per cent of total households. English, which is the language of government and of instruction in secondary and university education, is spoken by at least 44 per cent of the population. Spanish, which ceased to be an official language in 1973, is now spoken by a very small minority. 89 per cent of the population are literate.

Education.—Secondary and higher education is extensive and there are 37 private universities recognized by the Government, including the Dominican University of Santo Tomas (founded in 1611); there are also 296 state-supported colleges and universities, including the University of the Philippines, founded 1908. Students at private and state colleges and universities in 1984–85 numbered 13,814,359.

Roads and Railways.—The highway system covered 161,709 kilometres in 1985 and there was a total of 1,120,172 registered road vehicles. The Philippine National Railway operates 740 km. of track on Luzon Island.

Shipping.—There are 94 ports of entry in the Philippines and 164,404 vessels of various types totalling 50,467,000 tons, are engaged in inter-island traffic.

Civil Aviation.—There 82 national airports and 137 privately operated airports. Philippine Air Lines have regular flights throughout the Far East, to the U.S.A. and Europe, in addition to inter-island services.

	1987	1988
Total imports	$6,736,969,000	$8,159,378,000
Total exports	5,720,238,000	6,994,425,000

Trade with U.K.

	1987	1988
Imports from U.K.	£113,784,000	£175,685,000
Exports to U.K.	202,707,000	328,013,000

The Philippines is a predominantly agricultural country, the chief products being rice, coconuts, maize, sugar-cane, abaca (manila hemp), fruits, tobacco and lumber. There is, however, an increasing number of manufacturing industries and it is the policy of the Government to diversify its economy.

Principal exports are sugar, coconut oil, copper concentrate, lumber and copra.

CAPITAL.—ΨManila, in the island of Luzon: population (1980): City area, 1,630,485; Manila with suburbs (incl. Quezon City, Pasay City, Caloocan City, Makati, Parañaque, San Juan Mandaluyong and Navotas), 6,720,050. The next largest cities are ΨCebu (490,281), ΨDavao (610,375), ΨIloilo (244,027), ΨZamboanga (343,722), and Bacolod (262,415).

CURRENCY.—Philippine peso (P) of 100 centavos.

FLAG.—Equal horizontal bands of blue (above) and red; gold sun with three stars on a white triangle next staff.

NATIONAL ANTHEM.—"Pambansang Awit".

NATIONAL DAY.—June 12 (Independence Day).

BRITISH EMBASSY
Locsin Building, 6752 Ayala Avenue Corner, Makati Avenue, Makati, Metro Manila
(P.O. Box 1970)
[Manila 853002/9]

Ambassador Extraordinary and Plenipotentiary, His Excellency Keith Gordon MacInnes, C.M.G. (1987).

Counsellor, P. J. Priestley.

Defence Attaché, Col. J. P. Clough.

First Secretaries, A. E. Huckle (*Head of Chancery*); P. R. Nelson.

Second Secretaries, D. Curran; E. J. McEvoy (*Commercial*); N. May (*Consul*); Miss H. C. Brown (*Administration*); Miss A. E. Conroy (*Information/Aid*).

Cultural Attaché, H. Salmon (*British Council Representative*).

POLAND
(Polska Rzeczpospolita Ludowa)

President, Gen. Wojciech Jaruzelski, *elected* July 20, 1989 *for a six-year term.*

COUNCIL OF MINISTERS
(as at Sept. 13, 1989)

Prime Minister, Tadeusz Mazowiecki (S).

Deputy P.M.s, Leszek Balcerowicz (S) (*Finance*); Czeslaw Kizczak (C) (*Interior*); Czeslaw Janicki (UPP) (*Agriculture*); Jan Janowski (D) (*Scientific Development*).

Defence, Florian Siwicki (C).

Foreign, Krzysztof Skubiszewski (*Ind.*).

Justice, Aleksander Bentkowski (UPP).

Industry, Tadeusz Syryjczyk (S).

Council of Ministers, Jacek Ambroziak (S).

Environment, Bronislaw Kaminski (UPP).

Housing, Aleksander Paszynski (S).

Transport, Adam Wieladek (C).

Domestic Trade, Aleksander Mackiewicz (D).

Labour and Social Policy, Jacek Kuron (S).

Education, Henryk Samsonowicz (S).

Health, Andrzej Kosiniak-Kamysz (UPP).

Foreign Trade, Marcin Swiecicki (C).

Culture, Izabella Cywinska (S).

Communications, Marek Kucharski (D).

Head of Central Planning, Jerzy Osiatynski (S).

Chairman of Economic Council, Witold Trzeciakowski (S).

Agricultural Development, Artur Balazs (S).

Contacts with non-Parliamentary opposition, Alexander Hall (S).

(S—Solidarity; C—Communist; UPP—United Peasants' Party; D—Democrats)

POLISH UNITED WORKERS' PARTY (P.U.W.P.)

Politbureau, W. Baka; K. Cypryniak; M. Gorywoda; C. Kiszczak; J. Kubasiewicz; I. Lubowska; Z. Michalek; L. Miller; W. Pyrkosz; M. F. Rakowski; G. Rembisz; J.Reykowski; F. Siwicki; Z. Swiatek (*full members*); Z. Balicki; M. Holdakowski; Z. Sobotka (*alternate members*).

Secretariat, M. F. Rakowski (*First Secretary*); M. Krol; Z. Michalek; L. Miller; W. Natorf; M.Stepien, M. Swiecicki; S. Wiatr (*Secretaries*); B. Kolodziejczak (*member*).

EMBASSY OF THE POLISH PEOPLE'S REPUBLIC
47 Portland Place, W1N 3AG
[01-580 4324]

Ambassador Extraordinary and Plenipotentiary, His Excellency Dr. Zbigniew Gertych (1987).

Area and Population.—Poland adjoins the German Democratic Republic in the west, the boundary being formed by the rivers Oder and Neisse, Czechoslovakia in the south, and the U.S.S.R. in the east. (The present frontiers were established at the end of the Second World War.) To the north is the Baltic Sea. The country has an area of 120,725 sq. miles (312,677 sq. km.), and a population (1985 U.N. estimate) of 37,203,000. Roman Catholicism is the religion of 95 per cent of the inhabitants and was legalized in May 1989.

Government.—The Polish Commonwealth ceased to exist in 1795 after three successive partitions in 1772, 1793 and 1795, in which Prussia, Russia and Austria shared. The Republic of Poland (reconstituted within the limits of the old Polish Commonwealth) was proclaimed at Warsaw in November, 1918, and its independence guaranteed by the signatories of the Treaty of Versailles.

German forces invaded Poland on Sept. 1, 1939; on Sept. 17, Russian forces invaded eastern Poland, and on September 21, 1939, Poland was declared by Germany and Russia to have ceased to exist. A line of demarcation was established between the areas occupied by German and Russian forces. At the end of the war a Coalition Government was formed in which the Polish Workers' Party played a large part. In December 1948, the Polish Workers' Party and the Polish Socialist Party fused in the new Polish United Workers' Party. A new Constitution modelled on the Soviet Constitution of 1936 was adopted on July 22, 1952, and was modified in February 1976. It changed the title of the country to the Polish People's Republic (*Polska Rzeczpospolita Ludowa*). It made no provision for a President of the Republic, whose functions were to be jointly exercised by a Council of State. Private ownership of land and freedom of religion were recognized. Church and State were to be separate.

Despite the guarantee of religious freedom in the Constitution, a campaign of encroachment in 1953 culminated in the arrest of the Primate of the Roman Catholic Church, and dissatisfaction with the regime and conditions of life have led periodically to unrest. The expression of severe popular discontent in December 1970 led to substantial government and Party changes. In July 1980 steep rises in food prices but static wages led to widespread strikes. The strikes continued throughout August, obliging the government to agree to allow independent trade unions, the right to strike, the easing of censorship and other political and economic demands. The independent trade union movement, Solidarity, led by Lech Walesa, became a powerful force but many of its leaders, including Walesa, were detained and union activity suspended when martial law was declared on Dec. 13, 1981. Initially there was some passive resistance to martial law, which was suspended on Dec. 31, 1982, and finally lifted in July 1983.

Solidarity continued as an underground movement until 1988 when a wave of strikes and the call for the legalization of Solidarity resulted in talks between Walesa and the Communist Party early in 1989. By April plans for political and economic reforms had been drawn up. These included the restoration of the legal status of Solidarity (April 17); the introduction of a bi-cameral parliamentary system and an Executive Presidency; and democratic elections to be held in the summer of 1989.

The lower house (Sejm) of 460 seats has 299 reserved for approved groups: the P.U.W.P. has 173 seats, the Democratic Party, 27, Catholic organizations, 23, and the United Peasants' Party, 76. In elections to the remaining seats in the new National Assembly, held on June 4 and 18, Solidarity, in its political form as the Solidarity Citizens' Committee, won all 161 seats. In elections to the upper house (Senate) 99 of the 100 seats were won by the Solidarity Citizens' Committee. After the first four-year parliamentary term the reserved seats system will be abolished and elections to both houses will be free.

General Jaruzelski was elected President by Poland's M.P.S on July 20, and on August 20, 1989, Tadeusz Mazowiecki became the first non-communist Prime Minister since 1945. Under the new constitution the Prime Minister can appoint all members of the Council of Ministers but the defence and interior portfolios must remain in the hands of the Communist Party.

Education.—Elementary education (ages 7–15) is compulsory and free. Secondary education is optional and free. There are universities at Kraków, Warsaw, Poznan, Lódź, Wroclaw, Lublin and Toruń and a considerable number of other towns.

Language and Literature.—Polish is a western Slavonic tongue (*see* U.S.S.R.), the Latin alphabet being used. Polish literature developed rapidly after the foundation of the University of Kraków (a printing press was established there in 1474 and there Copernicus died in 1543). A national school of poetry and drama survived the dismemberment and the former era of romanticism, whose chief Polish exponent was Adam Mickiewicz, was followed by realistic and historical fiction, including the works of Henryk Sienkiewicz (1846–1916), Nobel Prize-winner for Literature in 1905, Boleslaw Prus (1847–1912), and Stanislaw Reymont (1868–1925), Nobel Prize-winner in 1924.

Production and Industry.—On January 3, 1946, a decree was issued to provide for the nationalization of mines, petroleum resources, water, gas and electricity services, banks, textile factories and large retail stores. At present over 99 per cent of Polish industry is stated to be 'socialized', but 68 per cent of agricultural land is privately farmed.

Trade with U.K.

	1987	1988
Imports from U.K.	£181,451,000	£175,685,000
Exports to U.K.	303,418,000	328,013,000

CAPITAL.—Warsaw, on the Vistula, pop. (1984) 1,644,626. Other large towns are Lódź (849,000); Kraków (735,000); Wroclaw (632,000); Poznan (571,000); Gdansk (464,000); Szczecin (389,000); Katowice (361,000); Bydgoszcz (358,000).

CURRENCY.—Zloty of 100 groszy.

FLAG.—Equal horizontal stripes of white (above) and red.

NATIONAL ANTHEM.—Jeszcze Polska Nie Zginela (Poland has not yet been destroyed).

NATIONAL DAY.—July 22.

BRITISH EMBASSY
No. 1 Aleja Róz, 00-556 Warsaw
[Warsaw 281001]

Ambassador Extraordinary and Plenipotentiary, His Excellency Stephen Jeremy Barrett, C.M.G. (1988).
Counsellor, G. G. Wetherall (*Head of Chancery*).
Defence and Air Attaché, Gp.-Capt. M. R. Killick.
Naval and Military Attaché, Lt.-Col. R. C. Eyres.
British Council Representative, R. H. Alford, O.B.E., Al. Jerozolimskie 59, 00–697 Warsaw.

PORTUGAL
(República Portuguesa)

President of the Republic, Dr. Mario A. Nobre Lopes Soares, *elected*, February 16, 1986.

MINISTERS
(as at June 30, 1989)

Prime Minister, Prof. Anibal Cavaco Silva.
Deputy P.M. and Defence, Eurico de Melo.
Minister at the P.M.'s Office and Minister for Justice, Dr. Fernando Nogueira.
Parliamentary Affairs, Dr. Albino Azevedo Soares.
Finance, Dr. Miguel Ribeiro Cadilhe.
Planning and Territorial Administration, Prof. Luis Valente de Oliveira.
Internal Administration, Dr. José Silveira Godinho.
Foreign, Prof. João de Deus Pinheiro.
Agriculture, Fisheries and Food, Alvaro Barreto.
Industry and Energy, Luis Mira Amaral.
Education, Dr. Roberto Carneiro.

Public Works, Transport and Communications, João Oliveira Martins.

Health, Leonor Beleza.

Employment and Social Security, Dr. José Silva Peneda.

Trade and Tourism, Joaquim Ferreira do Amaral.

Youth, Antonio Couto dos Santos.

PORTUGUESE EMBASSY
11 Belgrave Square, SW1X 8PP
[01–235 5331]

Ambassador Extraordinary and Plenipotentiary, His Excellency Antonio Vaz-Pereira (1989).

Minister Counsellor, Sr. Manuel Corte Real, C.B.E.

First Secretary, Sra Ana Barata, O.B.E.

Area and Population.—Continental Portugal occupies the western part of the Iberian Peninsula, covering an area of 34,317 sq. miles (88,880 sq. km.). It lies between 36° 58'–42° 12' N. lat. and 6° 11' 48"–9° 29' 45" W. long., being 362 miles in length from N. to S., and averaging about 117 in breadth from E. to W. The population (including the Azores and Madeira) was estimated at 10,229,000 in 1985.

Language and Literature.—Portuguese is a Romance language with admixtures of Arabic and other idioms. It is the language of Portugal and Brazil, and is the *lingua franca* of Angola, Mozambique and Guinea-Bissau. Portuguese language and literature reached the culminating point of their development in the *Lusiadas* (dealing with the voyage of Vasco da Gama) and other works of Camoens (Camões) (1524–1580).

Government.—From the eleventh century until 1910 the government of Portugal was a monarchy, and for many centuries included the Vice-Royalty of Brazil, which declared its independence in 1822. In 1910 an armed rising in Lisbon drove King Manuel II and the Royal family into exile, and the National Assembly of Aug. 21, 1911, sanctioned a Republican form of government. A period of great political instability ensued until eventually the military stepped in. The Constitution of 1933 gave formal expression to the corporative 'Estado Novo' (New State) which was personified by Dr. Salazar, Prime Minister from 1932–68. Dr. Caetano succeeded Salazar as Prime Minister in 1968 but his failure to liberalize the regime or to conclude the wars in the African colonies resulted in his government's overthrow by a military coup on April 25, 1974. The next two years were characterized by great political turmoil with no fewer than six provisional governments between April 1974 and July 1976 but with the failure of an attempted coup by the extreme left in November 1975 the situation began to become more stable.

Constitutional reforms introduced in Aug. 1982 have reduced the President's scope for day-to-day intervention in government but the decision to dissolve the Assembly is still largely the President's. The revisions also ended the military's capacity for political interference, and created two new organs of state, the Constitutional Tribunal and the Council of State, to advise the President. Further constitutional reforms have been under discussion during 1989.

In the General Election held on July 19, 1987, the Social Democratic Party (*P.S.D.*) won 148 of the 250 seats; the Socialist Party (*P.S.*) 60 seats; the Communist Party (*P.C.P.*) 31 seats, the Democratic Renewal Party (*P.R.D.*) 7 seats and the Christian Democrats (*C.D.S.*) 4 seats.

Defence.—Most physically fit males are liable for military service but conscription is becoming increasingly selective as the armed forces were greatly reduced following the end of the colonial wars, and reorganized and re-equipped for a conventional national defence role. The present strength of the Army is about 43,000. One brigade is earmarked for N.A.T.O. service. The Navy consists of about 14,800 officers and men, including 2,500 marines, manning about 60 craft of various types. The present serving strength of the Air Force is about 12,600, (including 2,200 paratroops) and about 80 combat aircraft plus helicopters and transport and training aircraft.

Education is free and compulsory for nine years from the age of 6. Secondary education is mainly conducted in State lyceums, commercial and industrial schools, but there are also private schools. There are also military, naval, technical, polytechnic and other special schools. There are old established Universities at Coimbra (founded in 1290), Oporto and Lisbon. New Universities have been established at Lisbon, Braga, Aveiro and in the Azores.

Newspapers and Broadcasting.—There are now five morning and three evening daily newspapers in Lisbon and three morning papers in Oporto, and six main weekly newspapers. There are two TV channels (broadcasting in colour) and four radio stations (three state controlled) broadcasting nationwide.

Civil aviation is controlled by the Administração Nacional Aeronaútica. There is an international airport at Portela, about 5 miles from Lisbon, and the airport of Pedras Rubras near Oporto is also used for scheduled international services. There are direct flights between London and Faro in the Algarve.

Agriculture.—The chief agricultural products are cork, cereals, rice, vegetables, olives, figs, citrus fruits, almonds, timber, port wine and table wines. There are extensive forests of pine, cork, eucalyptus and chestnut covering about 20 per cent of the total area of the country.

Minerals.—The principal mineral products are pyrites, wolfram, tin, iron ores, copper and sodium and calcium minerals.

Industry.—The country is so far only moderately industrialized, but is fairly rapidly extending its industries. The principal manufactures are textiles, clothing and footwear, machinery (including electric machinery and transport equipment), foodstuffs (tomato concentrates and canned fish), chemicals, fertilizers, wood, cork, furniture, cement, glassware and pottery. There is a modern steelworks, and two modern and very large shipbuilding and repair yards at Lisbon and Setúbal working mainly for foreign ship-owners. There are several hydro-electric power stations and a new thermal power station.

Finance.—Portugal is a member of the European Monetary Agreement, the World Bank, the International Monetary Fund and the International Finance Corporation. The country has substantial gold and foreign exchange reserves.

Trade.—Portugal joined the E.C. on January 1, 1986.

The principal imports are cereals, meat, raw and semi-manufactured iron and steel, industrial machinery, chemicals, crude oil, motor vehicles and raw materials for textiles.

The principal exports are textiles, footwear, timber, cork, electrical and other machinery, and chemicals.

	1987	1988
Total imports	£3,500,000 m	£6,164,627 m
Total exports	2,600,000 m	4,230,727 m

Trade with U.K.

	1987	1988
Imports from U.K. ..	£699,915,000	£810,537,000
Exports to U.K.	847,980,000	928,015,000

The British share of the Portuguese market was 8·16 per cent in 1988 and the U.K. was the fifth largest market for Portuguese exports.

CAPITAL.—ΨLisbon. Population (estimated, 1984) 807,937. ΨOporto 327,368; ΨSetúbal 77,885.

CURRENCY.—Escudo (Esc) of 100 centavos.

FLAG.—Vertical band of green (next staff) and square of red, bearing arms of the Republic, framed.

NATIONAL ANTHEM.—A Portuguesa.

NATIONAL DAY.—June 10.

BRITISH EMBASSY
35–37 Rua de S. Domingos à Lapa,
1200 Lisbon
[Lisbon 661191]

Ambassador Extraordinary and Plenipotentiary, His Excellency Hugh James Arbuthnott, C.M.G. (1989).

There are British Consulates in *Oporto*, *Portimão*, *Funchal* (Madeira) and *Ponta Delgada* (Azores).

British Council Representative, J. Mallon, O.B.E., The British Institute, Rua Cecilio de Sousa 65, 1294 Lisbon.

BRITISH PORTUGUESE CHAMBER OF COMMERCE, Rua da Estrela 8, 1200 Lisbon and Rua Sa de Bandeira 784–20E, Frente, 4000 Oporto.

MADEIRA AND THE AZORES

Madeira and The Azores are two administratively autonomous regions of Portugal, having locally elected Assemblies and Governments.

Madeira is a group of islands in the Atlantic Ocean about 520 miles south-west of Lisbon, and consists of Madeira, Porto, Santo and 3 uninhabited islands (Desertas). The total area is 314 sq. miles (813 sq. km.), with a population of 264,800 (1984). ΨFunchal in Madeira, the largest island (270 square miles), is the capital, with a population of 44,111; Machico (10,905).

The Azores are a group of 9 islands (Flores, Corvo, Terceira, São Jorge, Pico, Faial, Graciosa, São Miguel and Santa Maria) in the Atlantic Ocean, with a total area of 922 sq. miles (2,387 sq. km.), and a population of 250,700 (1984). ΨPonta Delgada, on São Miguel, is the capital of the group; population is 21,347. Other ports are ΨAngra, in Terceira, (16,476) and ΨHorta (2,509).

MACAO

Macao, situated at the mouth of the Pearl River, comprises a peninsula and the islands of Coloane and Taipa, having an area of six sq. miles (15·5 sq. km.), with a population (1987 estimate) of 450,000. Portuguese trade with China began early in the 16th century and Macao became a Portuguese colony in 1557: in a Sino-Portuguese treaty of Dec. 1887 China recognised Portugal's sovereignty over, and government of, Macao. In 1974 Portugal changed Macao's status from that of an Overseas Province to 'a territory under Portuguese administration'. Following the Sino-British Joint Declaration on Hong Kong in 1984, Sino-Portuguese negotiations on the transfer of administration began on June 30, 1986. The agreement on the transfer of the Administration of Macao to the Chinese authorities was signed on April 13, 1987. Macao will become a 'special administrative region' of China when transferred on Dec. 20, 1999.

Macao is subject to Portuguese constitutional law but otherwise enjoys administrative, economic and financial autonomy. The Governor is appointed by the Portuguese President and since 1976 there has been a 17 member legislative assembly, which has a three year term. The assembly comprises 12 elected deputies appointed by the Governor. A new electoral system which came into effect February 28, 1984, gave equal voting rights to all residents, thus enfranchising the Chinese population.

Macao's major industry is textile manufacturing which accounts for 62 per cent of all exports. Port Macao is served by British, Portuguese and Dutch shipping lines and has regular services to Hong Kong, some 35 miles away.

Governor, (vacant).

Trade with U.K.

	1987	1988
Imports from U.K.	£5,617,000	£4,348,000
Exports to U.K.	45,896,000	41,116,000

QATAR
(Dawlat Qatar)

Amir of Qatar, H.H. Sheikh Khalifa Bin Hamad Al-Thani, G.C.M.G.; *assumed power* February 22, 1972 *(also Prime Minister)*.

COUNCIL OF MINISTERS
(as at May 31, 1989)

Heir Apparent, Minister of Defence and Commander-in Chief of the Qatar Armed Forces, H.H. Sheikh Hamad Bin Khalifa Al-Thani, K.C.M.G.

Education, H.E. Shaikh Mohammad Bin Hamad Al-Thani.

Foreign, (vacant).

Finance and Petroleum Affairs, H.E. Shaikh Abdul Aziz Bin Khalifa Al-Thani.

Municipal Affairs, (vacant).

Economy and Commerce, (vacant).

Justice (vacant).

Electricity and Water, H.E. Shaikh Jasem Bin Moh'd Al-Thani.

Interior, H.E. Shaikh Khalid Bin Hamad Al-Thani.

Industry and Agriculture, H.E. Shaikh Faisal Bin Thani Al-Thani.

Public Health, H.E. Sayed Khalid Bin Mohammed al-Mana.

Public Works, H.E. Sayed Khaled Bin Abdullah al-Attiyah.

Labour and Social Welfare Affairs, H.E. Sayed Ali Bin Ahmed Al-Ansari.

Communications and Transport, H.E. Sayed Abdullah Bin Naser al-Suwaidi.

Information, H.E. Sayed Issa Ghanim al-Kawari.

Minister of State for Foreign Affairs, H.E. Shaikh Ahmed bin Saif Al-Thani.

Adviser to H.H. The Amir, Dr. Hassan Kamel.

Secretary-General of the National Planning Council, Saleh Abu Daoud al-Mohannadi.

EMBASSY OF THE STATE OF QATAR
27 Chesham Place, SW1X 8HG
[01–235 0851/4]

Ambassador Extraordinary and Plenipotentiary, new appointment awaited.

The state of Qatar covers the peninsula of Qatar from approximately the northern shore of Khor al Odaid to the eastern shore of Khor al Salwa. The area is about 4,247 sq. miles (11,000 sq. km.), with a population estimated in 1988 at about 380,000. The great majority of the population is concentrated in the urban district of the capital Doha. Only a small minority still pursue the traditional life of the semi-nomadic tribesmen and fisherfolk.

Until 1971, Qatar was one of the nine independent Emirates in the Arabian Gulf in special treaty relations with the U.K. In that year, with the withdrawal of H.M. Forces from the area, these special treaty relations were terminated. On April 2, 1970 a Provisional Constitution for Qatar was proclaimed, providing for the establishment of a Council of Ministers and for the formation of a Consultative Council to assist the Council of Ministers in running the affairs of the State. The first

Cabinet was formed of 10 members on May 29, 1970. Qatar is a member of the Arab League as well as of the United Nations.

Production.—Although Qatar is a desert country, there are gardens and smallholdings near Doha and to the north and encouragement is being given to the development of agriculture.

The Qatar General Petroleum Corporation is the state-owned company controlling Qatar's interests in oil, gas and petrochemicals. The corporation is responsible for Qatar's oil production onshore and offshore. The production level for Qatar agreed in O.P.E.C. is currently 312,000 b.p.d. Explorations continue for further oil. The large reserves of natural gas in the North Field are expected to come into production by 1991. A 50,000 b.p.d. oil refinery was commissioned in 1984 to increase domestic refinery capacity.

Current industries include a steel mill, a fertilizer plant, a cement factory, a petrochemical complex and two natural gas liquids plants. With the exception of the cement works, which is at Umm Bab, all these industries are at Umm Said, about 30 miles south of Doha. There are tentative plans for new industry, including an aluminium smelter, a second ammonia plant and a methanol plant, downstream of the North Field. Qatar is also expanding its infrastructure including electrical generation and water distillation, roads, houses, and Government buildings, although reduced demand for crude oil in international markets has led to a downturn in the economy and a slower rate of development than hitherto.

Communications.—Doha is an expanding town with an airport built to international standards. Regular air services connect Qatar with Bahrain and the United Arab Emirates, Kuwait, Muscat, Saudi Arabia, Jordan, Syria, Lebanon, Egypt, the Indian sub-continent, Africa and Europe. The Qatar Broadcasting Service transmits on medium, shortwave, and V.H.F. Regular television transmissions in colour began in 1974 and a second channel opened in 1982.

Trade with U.K.

	1987	1988
Imports from U.K.	£105,087,000	£88,920,000
Exports to U.K.	13,765,000	3,888,000

CAPITAL.—ΨDoha. Population (estimated) 220,000. Other towns include Khor, Dukhan, Wakra and ΨUmm Said.

CURRENCY.—Qatar riyal of 100 dirhams.

FLAG.—White and maroon, white portion nearer the mast; vertical indented line comprising 17 angles divides the colours.

NATIONAL DAY.—September 3.

BRITISH EMBASSY
P.O. Box 3, Doha
[Doha 421991]

Ambassador Extraordinary and Plenipotentiary, His Excellency Patrick Michael Nixon, C.M.G., O.B.E. (1987).

First Secretary, J. G. Rice (*Commercial*).

Second Secretary, G. D. Cole (*Consul and Administration*).

Third Secretary, S. T. Harrison.

Attaché, P. D. G. Cook (*Commercial*).

Vice Consul, R. J. Clark.

British Council Representative, Dr. C. W. R. Long, Ras Abu Aboud Road (P.O. Box 2992), Doha.

ROMANIA
(Republica Socialistă România)

President of the Republic, Nicolae Ceauşescu, *first elected*, 1967; *latest re-election*, March 28, 1985.

STATE COUNCIL

President, N. Ceauşescu.

Vice-Presidents, Manea Mănescu; Gheorghe Rădulescu; Maria Ghitulica; Árpád Páll.

Counsellors, Emilian Dobrescu; Eugen Florescu; Gheorghe Fulea; Constantin Mitea; Ilie Vaduva.

Secretary, Dumitru Apostoiu.

Members, Ioan Anton; Constantin Arseni; Cameluta Beldie; Maria Ciocan; Silviu Curticeanu; Gheorghe Dinu; Tamara Dobrin; Eduard Eisenburger; Virginia Gemescu; Diamanta Laudoniu; Constantin Olteanu; Ion Popescu-Puturi; Doina Vasilescu; Dumitru Velicu; Vasile Vilcu.

COUNCIL OF MINISTERS
(as at July 31, 1989)

Prime Minister, Constantin Dascalescu.

First Deputy Prime Ministers, Elena Ceauşescu; Ion Dinca; Gheorghe Oprea.

Deputy Prime Ministers, Ludovic Fazekas; Cornel Pacoste; Stefan Andrei; Lina Ciobanu; Ion Radu.

Acquisition of Farm Produce, Constantin Zanfir.

Agriculture, Gheorghe David.

Chemical and Petrochemical Industry, Ion Nicolae.

Domestic Trade, Ana Muresan.

Education and Instruction, Ion Teoreanu.

Electrical Engineering, Nicolae Vaidescu.

Electricity, Petre Fluture.

Finance, Ion Patan.

Food Industry, Paula Prioteasa.

Foreign Affairs, Ioan Totu.

Foreign Trade and International Economic Co-operation, Ioan Ungar.

Forestry Administration, Eugen Tarhon.

Geology Department, Ioan Folea.

Health, Victor Ciobanu.

Industrial Construction, Alexandru Dimitriu.

Internal Affairs, Tudor Postelnicu.

Justice, Maria Bobu.

Labour, Maxim Berghianu.

Light Industry, Maria Flucsa.

Machine-Building Industry, Eugen Radulescu.

Metallurgy, Marin Enache.

Mining, Irimie Catargiu.

National Defence, Vasile Milea.

Oil, Nicolae Amza.

Technical Material Supply and Control of Fixed Assets, Gheorghe Stoica.

Tourism, Ion Stanescu.

Transportation and Telecommunications, Pavel Aron.

Wood Industry and Building Materials, Gheorghe Constantinescu.

Minister, Chairmen of Central Bodies, Gheorghe Pana (*Committee of People's Councils' Affairs*); Decebal Urdea (*State Prices Committee*); Cornel Mihulecea (*State Committee for Nuclear Power*); Radu Balan (*State Planning Committee*); Miu Dobrescu (*Central Council of General Confederation of Trade Unions*); (vacant) (*1st Vice-Chairman, Council of Economic and Social Organizations*); Suzana Gadea (*Council for Socialist Culture and Education*); Elena Ceauşescu (*National Council of Science and Technology*); Ion Ursu (*1st Vice-Chairman, National Council of Science and Technology*); Ion Badea (*National Council for Water Resources*); Ana Muresan (*National Council of Women*); Traian Girba (*National Union of Agricultural Production Co-operatives*); Ion Ceauşescu (*1st Vice-Chairman, State Planning Committee*).

Minister, Secretaries of State, F. Nagy (*Agriculture*); F. Gruia (*Agriculture and Head of State Agricultural Department*); A. Duma (*Foreign Affairs*); C. Panzaru; A. Necula (*Foreign Trade and International Economic Co-operation*); (vacant) (*Technical Material Supply and Control of Fixed Assets*); Col.

Gen. I. Vlad (*Internal Affairs and State Security Department*); V. Bulucea (*State Planning Committee*); M. Florescu (*National Council of Science and Technology*).

THE COMMUNIST PARTY

Political Executive Committee, N. Ceauşescu; E. Bobu; V. Cazacu; E. Ceauşescu; L. Ciobanu; I. Coman; N. Constantin; C. Dascalescu; I. Dinca; M. Dobrescu; L. Fazekąs; M. Mănescu; P. Niculescu; C. Olteanu; G. Oprea; G. Pana; I. Pătan; D. Popescu; G. Rădulescu (*full members*); S. Andrei; R. Balan; N. Ceauşescu; G. David; S. Gadea; M. Gere; M. Ghitulica; N. Giosan; N. Ibanescu; M. Marina; I. Matei; V. Milea; I. Moga; A. Mureşan; E. Nae; C. Pacoste; T. Postelnicu; C. Radu; I. Radu; I. Stoian; I. Szasz; I. Totu; I. Ursu; R. Winter (*alternate members*).

Permanent Bureau of the Political Executive Committee, N. Ceauşescu; E. Bobu; E. Ceauşescu; C. Dascalescu; M. Mănescu; G. Oprea; G. Rădulescu.

Secretariat of the Central Committee, N. Ceauşescu (*Secretary General*); I. Coman; E. Bobu; S. Curticeanu; I. Stoian; V. Barbulescu; I. Sarbu; C. Olteanu; C. Radu.

EMBASSY OF THE SOCIALIST REPUBLIC OF ROMANIA
4 Palace Green, W8 4QD
[01-937 9666]

Ambassador Extraordinary and Plenipotentiary, His Excellency Mr. Stan Soare (1986).

Area and Population.—Romania is a republic of South-Eastern Europe, formerly the classical *Dacia* and *Scythia Pontica*, having its origin in the union of the Danubian principalities of *Wallachia* and *Moldavia* under the Treaty of Paris (April 1856). The area of Romania is 91,699 sq. miles (237,500 sq. km.) and the population (1986 estimate) is 22,823,500.

Government.—The principalities remained separate entities under Turkish suzerainty until 1859, when Prince Alexandru Ion Cuza was elected Prince of both, still under the suzerainty of Turkey. Prince Cuza abdicated in 1866 and was succeeded by Prince Charles of Hohenzollern-Sigmaringen, in whose successors the crown was vested. By the Treaty of Berlin (July 13, 1878) the Principality was recognized as an independent State, and part of the Dobrudja (which had been occupied by the Romanians) was incorporated. On March 27, 1881, it was recognized as a Kingdom.

The outcome of the War of 1914–18 added Bessarabia, the Bukovina, Transylvania, The Banat and Crisana-Maramures, these additions of territory being confirmed in the Treaty of St. Germain, 1919, and the Treaty of Petit Trianon, 1920.

On June 27, 1940, in compliance with an ultimatum from U.S.S.R., Bessarabia and Northern Bukovina were ceded to the Soviet Government, and in August, 1940, Romania ceded to Bulgaria the portion of Southern Dobrudja taken from Bulgaria in 1913.

Romania became 'The Romanian People's Republic' in December, 1947, on the abdication of King Michael. A new Constitution, modelled on the Soviet Constitution of 1936, was adopted unanimously on September 24, 1952, by the Grand National Assembly. The Assembly was later dissolved and elections were held for a new Grand National Assembly on November 30, 1952; in each constituency there was only one candidate for election, representing the People's Democratic Front, now the Socialist and Democratic Unity Front (S.D.U.F.) A new Constitution was approved by the Grand National Assembly in 1965 when the name of the state was changed to The Socialist Republic of Romania. The Constitution states (Art. 3) that the leading political force of the

whole society is the Romanian Communist Party. The Constitution was modified in March, 1974.

Agriculture.—Wallachia, Moldavia and Transylvania are potentially among the most fertile areas in Europe, and agriculture and sheep and cattle raising are the principal industries of Romania, although the intense winter cold and summer heat, and fierce summer drought sometimes have adverse effects on crops. These are principally cereal crops, legumes and other vegetables, flax and hemp. Vines and fruits are also grown. The forests of the mountainous regions are extensive, and the timber industry is important.

Socialization of agriculture was completed when collectivization was achieved in the spring of 1962.

Natural Resources and Industry.—Before the war petroleum and agriculture were the backbone of the Romanian economy but rapid industrialization since 1948 has meant that they no longer hold the same dominant position. There are plentiful supplies of natural gas, together with various mineral deposits including coal, iron ore, bauxite, lead, zinc, copper and uranium in quantities which allow a substantial part of the requirements of industry to be met from local resources. Production of crude oil was put at about 10,125,000 tonnes in 1986.

The economy has faced increasing problems since the late 1970s, the result of over investment in energy-intensive heavy industry and neglect of agriculture, which has led to food shortages. The effects of these policies were aggravated by the international recession and by high interest rates, and Romania was severely in debt by the early 1980s. The government has sought to alleviate the situation by reducing borrowing and cutting imports. The economy is centrally organized on the basis of Five-Year Plans which cover all branches of national activity including investment and production.

Language and Literature.—Romanian is a Romance language with many archaic forms and with admixtures of Slavonic, Turkish, Magyar and French words. The folk-songs and folklore, transmitted orally through many centuries and collected in the 19th century, form one of the most interesting of such collections. The publication of all books and reviews is controlled and authorized by the Council for Socialist Culture and Education, which has the status of a Ministry. The leading religion is that of the Romanian Orthodox Church; the Roman Catholics and some Protestant denominations are of importance numerically. The Jewish community has declined through emigration.

Education is free and nominally compulsory. There are Universities at Bucharest, Iasi, Cluj, Timişoara, Craiova and Braşov, polytechnics at Bucharest, Timişoara, Cluj, Braşov, Galati and Iasi, two commercial academies at Bucharest and Braşov, and agricultural colleges at Bucharest, Iasi, Cluj, Craiova and Timişoara.

Communications.—In 1979 there were 11,113 km. of railway open for traffic. The mercantile marine had a gross tonnage of 13,220,000 tons in 1979. The principal ports are Constanta (on the Black Sea), Sulina (on the Danube Estuary), Galati, Braila, Giurgiu and Turnu Severin. The Danube and the Black Sea are linked by a canal completed in 1984. Romania is a member of the Danube Commission whose seat is at Budapest.

TRADE

In 1986 combined imports and exports totalled Lei 300·6 billion, compared with Lei 340·7 billion in 1985. Imports are chiefly semi-manufactured goods, raw materials, machinery and metals; export consists principally of maize, wheat, barley, oats, petroleum, timber, cattle, machines and industrial equipment.

Trade with U.K.

	1987	1988
Imports from U.K.	£55,688,000	£50,111,000
Exports to U.K.	92,526,000	100,906,000

CAPITAL, Bucharest, on the Dimbovita, population 1,961,189. Other large towns are:

Brașov	 290,722	Ψ Galati	 254,636
Constanța	 284,801	Craiova	 243,117
Cluj-Napoca	. . . 270,820	Ploiești	 215,500
Iasi	 265,176	Ψ Brăila	 214,561
Timișoara	 261,950		

CURRENCY.—Leu (Lei) of 100 bani.

FLAG.—Three vertical bands, blue, yellow, red, with the emblem of the Republic in the centre band.

NATIONAL ANTHEM.—Trei Culori (Three colours).

NATIONAL DAY.—August 23 (Liberation Day, 1944).

BRITISH EMBASSY
24 Strada Jules Michelet, Bucharest
[Bucharest 111634/6]

Ambassador Extraordinary and Plenipotentiary, new appointment awaited.
Counsellor, A. R. Clark (*Head of Chancery*).
Defence, Naval and Military Attaché, Lt.-Col. W. J. Chesshyre.
Cultural Attaché and British Council Representative, A. Pattison.

RWANDA
(Republika y'u Rwanda)

President, Maj. Gen. Juvénal Habyarimana, *assumed office*, July 5, 1973, *elected*, Dec. 24, 1978, *re-elected*, Dec. 19, 1983 and Dec. 17, 1988.

MINISTERS
(as at Jan. 15, 1989)

Minister of Defence, The President.
Commerce and Consumption, Juvénal Uwilingiyimana.
Finance, Benoit Ntezilyayo.
Industry and Crafts, Col. Aloys Nsekalije.
Public Works, Energy and Water, Joseph Nzirorera.
Transport and Communications, André Ntagerura.
Health, Dr. Placidé Ngendahayo.
Primary and Secondary Education, Daniel Mbangura.
Higher Education and Scientific Research, Charles Nyandwi.
Youth and Sport, Lt.-Col. Augustin Ndindiliyimana.
Interior and Community Development, Jean-Marie Vianey Mugemana.
Civil Service and Professional Training, François Habiyakare.
Justice, Théoneste Mujyanama.
Institutional Relations, Antoine Ntashamaje.
Planning, Callixte Nzabonimana.
Foreign Affairs and International Co-operation, Dr. Casimir Bizimungu.
Minister at the Presidency, Simeon Nteziryayo.

Rwanda, formerly part of the Belgian-administered trusteeship of Ruanda-Urundi, has an area of 10,169 sq. miles (26,338 sq. km.), and a population (1985 U.N. estimate) of 6,070,000, mainly of the Bahutu tribe, with Batutsi and Batwa minorities.

A referendum held in September, 1961, showed the majority of the population were opposed to the retention of the monarchy which was accordingly abolished on Oct. 2, 1961. Rwanda became an independent Republic on July 1, 1962, with Gregoire Kayibanda as Head of State and Head of the Government. He was deposed in 1973, and replaced by a military government under Maj.-Gen. Juvénal Habyarimana.

Coffee (the chief cash crop), tea and sugar are grown. Tin, hides, bark of quinine and extract of pyrethrum flowers are also exported.

The National University of Rwanda is situated at two campuses, Butare and Ruhengeri.

In 1987 total imports were valued at US$351·7 m.; total exports, US$112·3 m.

Trade with U.K.

	1987	1988
Imports from U.K.	£2,526,000	£1,636,000
Exports to U.K.	4,291,000	8,434,000

CAPITAL.—Kigali (156,000).

CURRENCY.—Rwanda franc of 100 centimes.

FLAG.—Three vertical bands, red, yellow and green with letter R on yellow band.

NATIONAL DAY.—July 1.

British Ambassador (resident at *Kinshasa*, Zaire).

EL SALVADOR
(República de El Salvador)

President, Alfredo Felix Cristiani Burkard, *elected* March 19, 1989, *assumed office*, June 1, 1989.

CABINET
(as at July 15, 1989)

Vice-President and Interior Minister, Francisco Merino.
Minister of the Presidency, Col. Jose Antonio Martinez Varela.
Secretary of Information, Mauricio Sandoval.
Planning and Co-ordination of Economic and Social Development, Mirna Lievano de Marquez.
Justice, Dr. Oscar Santamaria.
Finance, Dr. Rafael Alvarado Cano.
Economy, Dr. Arturo Zablah.
Education, Dr. Rene Hernandez Valiente.
Defence and Public Security, Gen. Humberto Larios.
Labour and Social Security, Mauricio Gonzalez Dubon.
Agriculture, Antonio Cabrales.
Public Works, Mauricio Stubig.
Health, Col. Dr. Lisandro Vasquez Sosa.

EMBASSY OF EL SALVADOR
9 Welbeck House, 62 Welbeck Street, W1
[01-486 8182]

Ambassador Extraordinary and Plenipotentiary, His Excellency Dr. Maurico Rosales-Rivera.
First Secretary and Consul General, Snrta Carolina Calderón.

Area and Population.—The Republic of El Salvador extends along the Pacific coast of Central America for 160 miles with a general breadth of about 50 miles, and contains an area of 8,124 sq. miles (21,041 sq. km.), with a population (1985 estimate) of 5,480,000. It is divided into 14 Departments.

The surface of the country is very mountainous, many of the peaks being extinct volcanoes. The highest are the Santa Ana volcano (7,700 ft.) and the San Vicente volcano (7,200 ft.). Much of the interior has an average altitude of 2,000 feet. The lowlands along the coast are generally hot, but towards the interior the altitude tempers the severity of the heat. There is a wet season from May to October, and a dry season from November to April. Earthquakes have been frequent in the history of El Salvador, the most recent being that of Oct. 10, 1986, when considerable damage was done to San Salvador.

The principal river is the Rio Lempa. There is a large volcanic lake (Ilopango) a few miles to the east of the capital, while farther away and to the west lies the smaller lake of Coatepeque, which appears to have been formed in a vast crater flanked by the Santa Ana volcano.

Government.—El Salvador was conquered in 1526 by Pedro de Alvarado, and formed part of the Spanish vice-royalty of Guatemala until 1821.

After two years of government by a Junta headed by José Napoleon Duarte, elections for a Constituent Assembly were held in March 1982, ending decades of military rule. Presidential elections, although boycotted by the guerrilla movement, were held in March 1984 and in the run-off between the two largest parties, Sr. Duarte, the Christian Democrat leader, won with a 54 per cent majority over the ARENA candidate, Roberto d'Aubuisson. Alfredo Cristiani (ARENA) won the presidential elections in March 1989 with 54 per cent of the vote. The FMLN guerrillas again boycotted the elections. ARENA also overturned a Christian Democrat majority in the National Assembly and since the March 1988 elections have held 32 of the 60 seats.

Agriculture.—The principal cash crops are coffee, which is grown principally on the slopes of the volcanoes, cotton, which is cultivated on the coastal plains, and sugarcane and shrimps. (However, cotton and sugar production have decreased as a result of the civil war.) Also cultivated are maize, sesame, indigo, rice, balsam, etc. In the lower altitudes towards the east, sisal is produced and used in the manufacture of coffee and cereal bags. Land reforms, announced in March 1980, have largely been implemented. The Salvadorean Coffee Company, sugar exports and the banking system are nationalized but Pres. Cristiani has announced his intention to privatize these industries and/or introduce competition.

Industry.—Existing factories make textiles, clothing, constructional steel, furniture, cement and household items. El Salvador is a member of the Central American Common Market. The first trade zone was inaugurated in November 1974 and others are planned.

Education.—The illiteracy rate has risen since 1980 when the figure was 30·5 per cent. Primary education is nominally compulsory, but the number of schools and teachers available is too small to enable education to be given to all children of school age.

Language and Literature.—The language of the country is Spanish. Indigenous literature has not yet produced work of international repute. There are five daily newspapers published at the capital, and four in the provinces.

Communications.—The Executive Autonomous Port Commission (CEPA) administers the port of Cutuco, at La Union and the principal port of Acajutla, and the railways through FENADESAL. There is a railway line between San Salvador and Guatemala City and Puerto Barrios on the Caribbean coast but it is subject to interruption. The roads are paved and in good condition but some bridges are temporary structures following guerrilla action. There are good roads between Acajutla and the capital (60 miles), and between the capital and Guatemala City. The Pan-American Highway from the Guatemalan frontier follows this route and continues to the Honduran frontier. The El Salvador international airport can receive jet aircraft with daily flights to other Central American capitals, Mexico, and five U.S. cities.

There are post and telegraph offices throughout the country. There are 100 broadcasting stations and six television stations.

BUDGET

	1988
Revenue	₡2,843·8 m
Expenditure	3,042·2 m

Trade with U.K.

	1987	1988
Imports from U.K.	£9,595,000	£8,186,000
Exports to U.K.	1,890,000	2,961,000

There is foreign exchange control. There is also a parallel market in U.S. dollars.

Other exports are sugar, shrimps, sisal (in the form of bags used for exporting coffee, sugar, etc.), balsam, meat, towels, hides and skins. The chief imports are chemicals, fertilizers, pharmaceutical goods, petroleum, manufactured goods, industrial and electronic machinery and equipment, vehicles and consumer goods.

CAPITAL.—San Salvador. Population of metropolitan area, est. 2,000,000. Other towns are Santa Ana (204,570), San Miguel (157,838), Ψ La Union (Cutuco), Ψ La Libertad and Ψ Acajutia.

CURRENCY.—El Salvador colón (₡) of 100 centavos. 5 colones = 1 US$.

FLAG.—Three horizontal bands, light blue, white, light blue; coat of arms on white band.

NATIONAL ANTHEM.—Saludemos La Patria Orgullosos (Let us proudly hail the Fatherland).

NATIONAL DAY.—September 15.

BRITISH EMBASSY
P.O. Box 1591, San Salvador

British Ambassador, (*resident at* Tegucigalpa, Honduras).

Chargé d'affaires a.i., I. R. Murray (*First Secretary*).
Vice Consul, P. D. Evans.

SAN MARINO
(Repubblica di San Marino)

Regents, Two "Capitani Reggenti".

CONSULATE GENERAL IN LONDON
166 High Holborn, WC1V 6TT
[01–836 7744]
Consul-General, The Lord Forte.

A small Republic in the hills near Rimini, on the Adriatic, founded, it is stated, by a pious stonecutter of Dalmatia in the 4th century. The Republic always resisted the Papal claims, and those of neighbouring dukedoms, during the 15th–18th centuries, and its integrity and sovereignty is recognized and respected by Italy. The Republic is governed by a State Congress of 10 members, under the Presidency of two Heads of State, who are elected at six-monthly intervals. The Great and General Council, a legislative body of 60 members, is elected by a universal suffrage for a term of 5 years. A Council of Twelve forms in certain cases a Supreme Court of Justice. The area is approximately 23 sq. miles (61 sq. km.), the population (April 30, 1985) was 22,361. The city of San Marino, on the slope of Monte Titano, has three towers, a fine church and Government palace, a theatre and museums. The principal products are wine, cereals, and cattle, and the main industries are tourism, ceramics, lime, concrete, cotton yarns, colour and paints. A Treaty of Extradition between the Governments of Great Britain and the Republic of San Marino has been in force since 1899.

CURRENCY.—Italian currency is in circulation.

FLAG.—Two horizontal bands, white, blue (with coat of arms of the Republic in centre).

NATIONAL DAY.—September 3.

BRITISH CONSULATE-GENERAL
Consul-General, Miss M. L. Croll (resides at Florence).

SÃO TOMÉ AND PRÍNCIPE
(República Democrática de São Tomé e Príncipe)

President, Dr. Manuel Pinto da Costa.

COUNCIL OF MINISTERS
(w.e.f. Jan. 1988)

Prime Minister, Celestino Rocha da Costa.
Defence and Internal Security, Raul Braganca Neto.
Foreign Affairs, Carlos da Graca.
Justice and Public Affairs, Francesco Fortunato Pires.
Planning and Trade, Teotonio d'Alva Torres.
Agriculture and Fisheries, Oscar Aguiar Sacramento e Sousa.
Co-operation, Guillermo Posser da Costa.
Education and Culture, Ligia do Espirito Santo Costa.
Health, Labour and Social Security, Armindo Vaz de Almeida.
Equipment, Environment, Transport and Communications, Carlos Ferreira.
Ministers Delegate, Manuel Quaresma Costa (*Príncipe Islands*); Manuel Vaz Alfonso Fernades (*Secretary General*).

The islands of São Tomé and Príncipe are situated in the gulf of Guinea, off the west coast of Africa. They have an area of 372 sq. miles (964 sq. km.), and a population (1985 U.N. estimate) of 108,000.

Following Portugal's decision to grant independence, a transitional government was installed on Dec. 21, 1974, and the islands became an independent democratic republic on July 12, 1975.

Cacao is the main product.

Trade with U.K.

	1987	1988
Imports from U.K.	£329,000	£416,000
Exports to U.K.	205,000	20,000

CAPITAL.—ΨSão Tomé (25,000).
CURRENCY.—Dobra of 100 centavos.
FLAG.—Horizontal stripes of green, yellow, green, the yellow of double width and bearing two black stars; and a red triangle in the hoist.
NATIONAL DAY.—July 12 (Independence Day).

British Ambassador (resident in *Luanda,* Angola).

SAUDI ARABIA
(Al Mamlaka al Arabiya as-Sa'udiyya)

Custodian of the Two Holy Mosques and King of Saudi Arabia, H.M. King Fahd bin Abdul Aziz, born, 1921, ascended the throne June 1, 1982.
Crown Prince, H.R.H. Amir Abdullah bin Abdul Aziz.

COUNCIL OF MINISTERS
(as at July 31, 1989)

Prime Minister, H.M. King Fahd bin Abdul Aziz.
First Deputy Prime Minister and Commander of the National Guard, H.R.H. Prince Abdullah bin Abdul Aziz.
Second Deputy Prime Minister, Defence and Aviation, H.R.H. Prince Sultan bin Abdul Aziz.
Public Works and Housing, H.R.H. Prince Mit'ab bin Abdul Aziz.
Interior, H.R.H. Prince Naif bin Abdul Aziz.
Foreign Affairs, H.R.H. Prince Saud al-Faisal bin Abdul Aziz.
Finance and National Economy, Muhammad Aba al-Khail.
Agriculture and Water, Dr. Abdul Rahman bin Abdul Aziz bin Hassan Al al-Shaikh.
Municipal and Rural Affairs, Ibrahim bin Abdullah al-Angari.

Commerce, Dr Sulaiman al-Solaim.
Communications, Dr. Hussain Mansouri.
Petroleum and Mineral Resources, Hisham Nazer (*and acting Minister of Planning*).
Labour and Social Affairs, Dr. Mohamed Ali al-Faiz.
Information, Ali Sha'er.
Health, Faisal bin Abdul Aziz al Hejailan.
Pilgrimage and Endowments, Abdul Wahhab Ahmed Abdul Wasi.
Education, Dr. Abdul Aziz Al-Abdullah al-Khuwaiter (*and acting Minister of Higher Education*).
Posts, Telegraphs and Telephones, Dr. Alawi Darwish Kayyal.
Industry and Electricity, Abdul Aziz al-Zamil.
Ministers of State, Muhammad Ibrahim Mas'oud; Dr. Muhammad Abdul Latif al-Melhem; Omar Abdul Qader Faqih; Dr. Fayez Ibrahim Badr; Turki bin Khalid Al Sudairi; Mohammed bin Abdulaziz Bin Zar'a; Mohammed bin Ibrahim Bin Jubeir (*acting Minister of Justice*).

ROYAL EMBASSY OF SAUDI ARABIA
30 Belgrave Square, SW1X 8QB
[01–235 0831]

Ambassador Extraordinary and Plenipotentiary, His Excellency Sheikh Nasser Almanqour, G.C.V.O. (1980).
Ministers Plenipotentiary, Ibrahim M. Mosly; Saud Ahmed M. Alyahya, L.V.O.

The Kingdom of Saudi Arabia is a personal union of two countries, the Sultan of Nejd becoming also King of the Hejaz. Great Britain recognized Abdul Aziz Ibn Saud as an independent ruler, King of the Hejaz and of Nejd and its Dependencies, by the Treaty of Jeddah (May 20, 1927). The name was changed to the Kingdom of Saudi Arabia in Sept. 1932.

The total area of the Kingdom is about 830,000 sq. miles (2,149,640 sq. km.), with a population (1985 est.) of 12,400,000, of whom perhaps 3 million are non-Saudis. Islam is the established and only permitted religion.

In the 18th century Nejd was an independent state governed from Diriya (now in ruins, 25 km. from Riyadh) and the stronghold of the Wahhabis, a puritanical Islamic sect. It subsequently fell under the Turkish yoke, but in 1913 Abdul Aziz Ibn Saud threw off Turkish rule and captured the Turkish province of Al Hasa. In 1920 he captured the Asir, and in 1921, by force of arms, he added to his dominions the Jebel Shammar territory of the Rashid family. In 1925 he completed the conquest of the Hejaz.

Saudi Arabia comprises almost the whole of the Arabian peninsula, with the exception of the small states in the extreme south (N. and S. Yemen), south-east (Oman and the U.A.E.) and east (Qatar). In the north-west it borders Jordan and in the north-east Iraq and Kuwait, while to the west lies the Red Sea and to the east the Gulf. The Nejd ('Plateau'), now the Central Province, extends over the centre of the peninsula, including the Nafud and Dahna deserts. The Hejaz ('the Boundary'), now the Western Province, extends along the Red Sea coast to Asir and contains the holy towns of Mecca and Medina. The former, about 60 km. east of Jeddah, is the birthplace of the Prophet Mohammed, and contains the Great Mosque, within which is the Kaaba or sacred shrine of the Muslim religion. This is the focus of the annual Hajj ('Pilgrimage') performed by 3·4 million in 1986. The latter, Medina Al Munawwarah ('The City of Light') some 300 km. north of Mecca, is celebrated as the first city to embrace Islam and as the Prophet Mohammed's burial place (he died there on Rabia 12, 11 AH, corresponding to June 7, 632 AD).

Asir ('Inaccessible') is named for its mountainous terrain, and, with the coastal plain of the Tihama, lies along the southern Red Sea coast from Hejaz to the border with Yemen. It is the only region to enjoy substantial rainfall. Water supplies are, however, supplemented by dams and irrigation. The east and south-east of the country are lower-lying and largely desert. Outside the manufacturing centres which have grown up around some of the towns, most of the population are engaged in agriculture. The productivity of traditional dryland farming is increasingly supplemented by irrigation.

Industry.—Oil was first found in commercial quantities in Dhahran, near Dammam, in 1938. Total production of crude oil peaked at 9·9 m.b.d. in 1980, and in 1986 was 4·8 m.b.d. About 97 per cent of the total is extracted by the Arabian-American Oil Company. Recoverable reserves stood at about 167 billion barrels at the end of 1986, equivalent to about 95 years' production at the 1986 rate. Aramco's 66-year lease will terminate in 1999 but the company was effectively nationalized in 1980. Aramco operates a deepwater oil terminal at Ras Tanura.

The Government actively encourages the establishment of manufacturing industries in the country. The policy includes the provision of industrial estates and loans covering 50 per cent of capital investment. By the end of 1984 3,310 private industrial licences had been granted, and 650 were in production. These establishments were concentrated in the fields of construction materials, metal fabrication, simple machinery and electrical equipment, food and beverages, chemicals and plastics. The Government is trying to encourage future investment in industrial gases, intermediate petrochemicals, light engineering, machinery and all kinds of spare parts. A new pharmaceutical plant is scheduled for completion by 1989.

The Government has also established two industrial poles at Jubail and Yanbu, financed by the state agency Saudi Arabian Basic Industries Corp., to be the focus of heavy industrial development. Linked by gas and oil pipelines, both are to have petrochemical complexes producing, initially, ethylene and methanol, six of the seven plants now on-stream are joint ventures with American and Japanese companies. In addition an integrated steel complex and a urea fertilizer factory are in production in Jubail with West German and Taiwanese partners. Complete new cities are being built at each pole: Jubail will eventually house 300,000 and Yanbu 190,000. The state agency Petromin operates three domestic refineries and two lubricant plants and the last of three joint-venture export refineries came on-stream in 1986. Total refining capacity is now approximately 1,950,000 b.p.d.

Communications.—The railway from the port of Dammam to the oilfields at Abqaiq and through Hofuf to Riyadh was opened in 1951, and a direct Dammam-Riyadh line opened in 1985. An extension to Jeddah via Medina and the reopening of the Hejaz railway are planned. Metalled roads connect all the cities and main towns: the network consisted of 28,500 km. in 1985. The principal port of the Gulf is Dammam which has 39 berths and an annual capacity of 9·1 million tons. Jeddah is the centre of commercial traffic on the Red Sea and has 51 piers, giving an annual capacity of 17 million tons. The Government-owned Saudi Arabian Airlines (Saudia) operate scheduled services to 19 domestic airports. There are international class airports at Dhahran, Jeddah and Riyadh. Work has begun on the new King Fahd International Airport in Eastern Province, due to be completed in 1990. Saudia have an extensive overseas operation, and a large number of international airlines operate into the country. Telecommunications are being rapidly expanded. By the end of 1985 60,000 telex and 1,216,000 telephone lines were installed; telephone and telex exchanges will be able to handle 2·25 million lines by 1990. The Government is a major participant in the Arab Satellite Communications Organization.

Education.—With the exception of a few schools for expatriate children, all schools are government supervised and segregated for boys and girls. By mid-1985 there were a total of 1,692,300 schoolchildren in 5,323 primary and 1,219 intermediate and 418 secondary schools. There are Universities in Jeddah, Mecca, Riyadh (branches in Abha and Qassim), Dammam (branch at Hofuf) and Dhahran, and there are Islamic universities in Medina and Riyadh. In addition there is great emphasis on vocational training, provided at 24 literacy and artisan skill training centres and 21 more advanced industrial, commercial and agricultural education institutes. Education in government-owned institutes is free at all levels.

Finance and Trade.—Oil remains the main source of receipts in the balance of payments. As a result, Government revenues have been markedly affected by oil prices and volume of production, and fell away from a peak of SR368,000 million in 1981–82 to SR133,600 million in 1985–86. The 1987 budget provided for expenditure of SR170,000 million. There is no public debt. There are no restrictions on foreign exchange transactions. The currency is strong, backed by gold and foreign exchange reserves, and maintained on a close parity to the U.S. dollar.

There is a total ban on the importation of alcohol, pork products, firearms and items regarded as non-Islamic or pornographic. The Arab boycott list also applies. In addition, certain chemicals now require import licences and fresh food items require radiation-free certificates. The leading suppliers of imports are U.S.A., Japan, West Germany, the U.K., Italy and France and the chief customers for exports are Japan, France, U.S.A. and Singapore.

	1985	1986
Total imports	SR99,645m	SR75,000m
Total exports	85,500m	70,800m

Trade with U.K.

	1987	1988
Imports from U.K.	£1,978,440,000	£1,713,423,000
Exports to U.K.	383,143,000	614,144,000

CAPITAL.—Riyadh, population about 1 million. Other major centres are Jeddah (pop. approx. 1 million), Dammam, Buraydah, Hofuf and Tabuk.

CURRENCY.—Saudi riyal (SR) of 20 qursh or 100 halala.

FLAG.—Green oblong, white Arabic device in

centre: "There is no God but God, Muhammad is the Prophet of God," and a white scimitar beneath the lettering.

NATIONAL ANTHEM.—"Long live our beloved King".

BRITISH EMBASSY
P.O. Box 94351, Riyadh 11693.
[Riyadh 488 0077]

Ambassador Extraordinary and Plenipotentiary, His Excellency Alan Gordon Munro, C.M.G. (1989).
Counsellors, D. J. Plumbly (*Head of Chancery and Consul-General*); P. W. Ford (*Commercial*).
Defence and Military Attaché, Brig. P. Sincock, M.B.E.
Air Attaché, Wing-Cdr. J. Ambler.
Naval Attaché, Cdr. N. Kerr.
First Secretaries, M. J. Crawford (*Chancery*); D. E. Lyscom (*Economic*); H. Formstone (*Commercial*); J. B. Midgley (*Consul General*); D. G. Lloyd (*Commercial*).

Consul General, Jeddah, H. J. Tunnell, P.O. Box 393, Jeddah 21411.
British Council Representative, C. P. Smith, Mura'aba, P.O. Box 2701, Riyadh 11461. There is also an office in Jeddah.

SENEGAL
(République du Sénégal)

President and Head of Government, Abdou Diouf, *installed*, Jan. 1, 1981, *elected for 5-year term*, Feb. 27, 1983; *re-elected* Feb. 28, 1988.

MINISTERS
(as at July 15, 1989)

Minister of State and Secretary General of the Presidency, Jean Collin.
Armed Forces, Médoune Fall.
Justice, Seydou Madani Sy.
Foreign Affairs, Ibrahima Fall.
Interior, André Sonko.
Economy and Finance, Serigne Lamine Diop.
Planning and Co-operation, Djibo Ka.
Communications, Robert Sagna.
Higher Education, Sakhir Thiam.
National Education, Ibrahima Niang.
Equipment, Alassane Dialy Ndiaye.
Rural Development, Cheikh Abdoul Khadre Cissokho.
Industrial Development and Handicrafts, Famara Ibrahima Sagna.
Trade, Seydina Oumar Sy.
Hydraulics, Samba Yela Diop.
Public Health, Mme. Thérèse King.
Youth and Sport, Abdoulaye Makhtar Diop.
Civil Service and Employment, Moussa Ndoye.
Tourism, El-Hadji Malick Sy.
Culture, Moustapha Ka.
Social Development, Mme. Ndioro Ndiaye.
Urban Affairs and Housing, Mamadou Abbas Ba.
Ministers Delegate, Mme. Fatou Ndongo Dieng (*Emigration*); Farba Lo (*Relations with National Assembly*); Moussa Toure (*Economy and Finance*); Mbaye Diouf (*Animal Resources*); Moctar Kebe (*Environmental Protection*).

EMBASSY OF THE REPUBLIC OF SENEGAL
11 Phillimore Gardens, W8 7QG
[01–937 0925/6]

Ambassador Extraordinary and Plenipotentiary, His Excellency Gen. Idrissa Fall, G.C.V.O., M.B.E. (1984).

Senegal lies on the west coast of Africa between Mauritania in the north, Mali in the east, and Guinea-Bissau and Guinea in the south. The Gambia lies entirely within Senegal, except for its sea-coast. (*For* MAP, *see* p. 776.) It has an area of 75,750 sq. miles (196,192 sq. km.), and a population (1985 estimate) of 6,540,000.

Formerly a French colony, Senegal elected on Nov. 25, 1958, to remain within the French Community as an autonomous republic. In March, 1963 (after an attempted coup d'état by the then Prime Minister in the previous December) a new constitution was approved giving executive powers to the President, on the lines of the present French constitution. The process of political liberalization continued; there are now 16 political parties officially recognized. Six parties contested the General Election in Feb. 1988. The P.S. took 103 seats and the P.D.S. 17.

In Feb. 1982, after an attempted coup in The Gambia in July 1981 had been put down with the aid of Senegalese troops, the Senegambia Confederation was established, based on certain joint institutions and the integration of defence, security and some other matters. Each country remains sovereign and independent. The President of Senegal is President of the Confederation and the President of The Gambia is Confederal Vice-President.

Senegal's principal exports are groundnuts (raw and processed) and phosphates. Tourism is also of growing importance as a revenue earner.

Trade with U.K.

	1987	1988
Imports from U.K.	£11,877,708	£14,840,000
Exports to U.K.	11,307,022	11,284,000

CAPITAL—ΨDakar (1,000,000).
CURRENCY.—Franc C.F.A. of 100 centimes.
FLAG.—Three vertical bands, green, yellow and red; a green star on the yellow band.
NATIONAL DAY.—April 4.

BRITISH EMBASSY
B.P. 6025, Dakar.
[Dakar 237392]

Ambassador Extraordinary and Plenipotentiary, His Excellency John Esmond Campbell Macrae, C.M.G. (1985).
First Secretary, R. S. Dewar (*Head of Chancery and Consul*).
Second Secretary, Miss J. M. Pearce.
Third Secretary, N. J. Enescott (*Vice Consul*).
Cultural Attaché (*British Council Representative*), Dr. M. Cooper.

SOMALIA
(Jamhuuriyadda Diimoqraadiga ee Soomaaliya)

President and Sec. Gen. of Somali Revolutionary Socialist Party, Maj.-Gen. Mohamed Siad Barre, *assumed office* Oct. 21, 1969.

COUNCIL OF MINISTERS
(as at May 31, 1989)

Prime Minister, Lt.-Gen. M. A. Samantar.
Planning, Maj.-Gen. H. K. Afrah.
Interior, Brig.-Gen. A. S. Abdullah.
Industry, Col. A. M. Farah.
Defence, Dr. Hussein Abdirahman Mattan.
Foreign Affairs, Dr. Abdirahmam Jama Barre.
Finance and Revenues, Brig.-Gen. Mohamed Sheikh Osman.
Commerce, Dr. Abdiqassim Salad Hassan.
Agriculture, Col. Bileh Rafleh Guleid.
Education, A. M. Mireh.
Livestock, Forestry and Range, Col. Abdirazak Mohamoud Abubakar.
Information, Yasin Haji Ismail Jirde.
Juba Valley Development, H. A. Habib.

Land, Air, Transport, Mohamed Sheikh Osman Jawari.
Minerals and Water Development, Col. Mireh Awareh Jama.
Health, Dr. M. A. Munassar.
Posts and Telecommunications, Y. H. Elmi.
Public Works and Housing, Osman Jama Ali.
Labour, Sports and Social Affairs, Col. Abdi Warsameh Issak.
Marine Transport and Ports, Brig.-Gen. Mohamoud Gelleh Yusuf.
Culture and Higher Education, Dr. Abdisalam Sheikh Hussein.
Fisheries and Marine Resources, Aden Mohamed Ali.
Tourism and Hotels, Dr. Abdirashid Sheikh Ahmed.
Justice and Religious Affairs, Mohamed Said Mohamed.

There are also eight Ministers in the Presidency.

Chairman, People's Assembly, Brig.-Gen. M. I. Ahmed.

EMBASSY OF THE SOMALI DEMOCRATIC REPUBLIC
60 Portland Place, W1N 3DG
[01–580 7148]

Ambassador Extraordinary and Plenipotentiary, His Excellency Ahmed Jama Abdulle (1988).

The Somali Democratic Republic occupies part of the north-east horn of Africa, with a coast-line on the Indian Ocean extending from the boundary with Kenya (2° South latitude) to Cape Guardafui (12° N.); and on the Gulf of Aden to the boundary with Djibouti. Somalia is bounded on the west by Djibouti, Ethiopia and Kenya and covers an area of approximately 246,201 sq. miles (637,657 sq. km.). The population, of which a large proportion is nomadic, is estimated (1987) at 5,800,000.

Government.—The Somali Democratic Republic, consisting of the former British Somaliland Protectorate and the former Italian trust territory of Somalia, was established on July 1, 1960. British rule in Somaliland lasted from 1887 until 1960 except for a short period in 1940–41 when the Protectorate was occupied by Italian forces. Somalia, formerly an Italian colony, was occupied by British forces in 1941. In 1950 it was placed under Italian administration by a resolution of the U.N.; this trusteeship lasted until independence. Following the assassination of President Shermake on October 15, 1969, the armed forces, assisted by the police, took over the Government without resistance and a Revolutionary Council under Siad Barre assumed control of the country. A new constitution was introduced following a referendum in 1979. This provides for an elected People's Assembly of 171 seats. The Assembly met for the first time in January 1980. A multi-party poll is to be held by the end of 1990. Following a dispute with Ethiopia over territory, which lasted many years, a peace agreement between the two countries was signed on April 3, 1988 in Mogadishu.

Civil war broke out in May 1988 between the Government and the opposition Somali National Movement. The situation is still confused but there was great damage to property and a significant number of casualties. There are now 400,000 refugees in Ethiopia. Most of southern Somalia is now under de facto military rule.

Livestock raising is the main occupation in Somalia and there is a modest export trade in livestock on the hoof, skins and hides. Italy, the Gulf States and Saudi Arabia import the bulk of the banana crop, the second biggest export.

Trade with U.K.

	1987	1988
Imports from U.K.	£11,417,000	£10,379,000
Exports to U.K.	825,000	1,151,000

CAPITAL.—ΨMogadishu, population (estimated 1987), 1,000,000. Other towns are Hargeisa (20,000), Boroma (65,000), ΨKisimayu (60,000), Ψ Berbera (15,000) and Burao (15,000).
CURRENCY.—Somali shilling of 100 cents.
FLAG.—Five-pointed white star on blue ground.
NATIONAL DAY.—October 21.

BRITISH EMBASSY
(PO Box No. 1036) Mogadishu
[Mogadishu 20288/9]

Ambassador Extraordinary and Plenipotentiary, His Excellency Ian McCluney (1989).
First Secretary and Consul, R. C. Huxley (*Head of Chancery*).

SOUTH AFRICA
(Republiek van Suid-Afrika)

State President, Frederick Willem de Klerk, *sworn in,* Sept. 20, 1989.

CABINET
(as at Sept. 18, 1989)

Foreign Affairs, Pik Botha.
Constitutional Development and National Education, Gerrit Viljoen.
Defence, Magnus Malan.
Mineral and Energy Affairs and Public Enterprises, Dawie de Villiers.
Justice, Kobie Coetsee.
Finance, Barend du Plessis.
Manpower, Eli Louw.
Law and Order, Adriaan Vlok.
Environment and Water Affairs, Gert Kotze.
Education and Development Aid, Stoffel van der Merwe.
Home Affairs, Gene Louw.
Trade, Industry and Tourism, Kent Durr.
Transport, George Bartlett.
Planning and Provisional Affairs, Hernus Kriel.
Health and Population Development, Rina Venter.
Agriculture, Jacob de Villiers.
Administration and Privatization, Wim de Villiers.
President's Council, Willie van Niekerk.

EMBASSY OF THE REPUBLIC OF SOUTH AFRICA
South Africa House, Trafalgar Square, WC2N 5DP
[01–930 4488]

Ambassador Extraordinary and Plenipotentiary, His Excellency P. R. (Rae) Killen (1987).
Minister, J. De Goede.
Counsellor (Press & Information), R. Ballard-Tremeer.
Minister (Trade), J. H. C. Engelbrecht.

There is a consulate-general at Golden Cross House, 8 Duncannon Street, W.C.2. [01–839 2211]

Area and Population.—The Republic, comprising the Provinces of the Cape of Good Hope, Natal, the Transvaal and the Orange Free State, occupies the southernmost part of the African continent from the courses of the Limpopo, Molopo and Orange Rivers (34° 50′ 22″ South latitude) to the Cape of Good Hope, with the exception of Lesotho, Botswana and Swaziland, and part of Mozambique. It has a total area of 471,445 sq. miles (1,221,031 sq. km.) and a total population (U.N. estimate, 1985) of 32,392,000 (of which approx. 18 per cent are white).

The southernmost province contains many parallel ranges, which rise in steps towards the interior. The south-western peninsula contains the famous *Table Mountain* (3,582 ft.), while the *Great Swartberg* and *Langeberg* run in parallel lines from west to east of the Cape Province. Between these two ranges and the *Roggeveld* and *Nuweveld* ranges to the north is

the Great Karoo Plateau, which is bounded on the east by the *Sneeuberg*, containing the highest summit in the province (Kompasberg, 7,800 ft.). In the east are ranges which join the *Drakensberg* (11,000 ft.) between Natal and the Orange Free State.

The Orange Free State presents a succession of undulating grassy plains with occasional hills or kopjes. The Transvaal is also mainly an elevated plateau with parallel ridges in the *Magaliesberg* and *Waterberg* ranges of no great height. The eastern province of Natal has pastoral lowlands and rich agriculture land between the slopes of the Drakensberg and the coast, the interior rising in terraces as in the southern provinces. The *Orange*, with its tributary the *Vaal*, is the principal river of the south, rising in the Drakensberg and flowing into the Atlantic between Namibia and the Cape Province. The *Limpopo*, or Crocodile River, in the north, rises in the Transvaal and flows into the Indian Ocean through Mozambique. Most of the remaining rivers are furious torrents after rain, with partially dry beds at other seasons.

Government.—The self-governing colonies of the Cape of Good Hope, Natal, the Transvaal and the Orange River Colony became united on May 31, 1910, under the South Africa Act, 1909, in a legislative union under the name of the Union of South Africa, the four colonies becoming Provinces of the Union. The Union of South Africa continued as a member of the British Commonwealth until 1961. After a referendum held among white voters on October 5, 1960, the Union of South Africa became a republic on May 31, 1961, and withdrew from the Commonwealth.

A new Constitution came into effect on Sept. 30, 1984, which provided for an executive President and a three-chamber Parliament; the House of Assembly (178 members) representing Whites, the House of Representatives (85 members) representing Coloureds, and the House of Delegates (45 members) representing Indians. The black population has no representation. There is joint parliamentary responsibility for 'general' affairs (foreign policy, defence, finance, law and order, justice, transport, manpower, commerce and industry, agriculture), and each chamber has separate responsibility for the 'own' affairs of the population group it represents (housing, social welfare, health, education, local government and some aspects of agriculture). Disputes between the chambers may be referred by the President to the President's Council (60 members—20 White, 10 Coloured, 5 Indian elected by their respective chambers, 15 nominated by the President, 10 nominated by Opposition parties).

The President is chosen by an 88-member electoral college (in the proportion 4 White : 2 Coloured : 1

Indian) of the majority parties of the three chambers. The President appoints the Cabinet from all three communities, and also appoints each community's ministerial council for 'own' affairs.

The promulgation of the new Constitution on Sept. 3, 1984 coincided with rioting in the black townships and the continuing unrest led to the declaration on July 20, 1985 of a State of Emergency in 36 districts.

A nationwide State of Emergency was declared on June 12, 1986; it was renewed in June 1987 and 1988, and extended again for up to a further twelve months in June 1989.

Elections to the House of Assembly took place on Sept. 6, 1989 and the results were: National Party, 93; Conservative Party 39; Democratic Party 33. One seat was undecided and is to be recontested after a tied vote.

Elections to the House of Representatives and House of Delegates took place on Sept. 6, 1989. The Coloured Labour Party (led by the Rev. H. J. Hendrickse) and the Indian National Peoples Party (led by Mr. A. Rajbansi) won the majority of seats respectively.

The Black Homelands.—The homelands are areas set aside for occupation by blacks. Six areas— Gazankulu, Lebowa, KwaNdbele, KaNgwane, Qwaqwa and KwaZulu—are designated self-governing national states. A further four areas—Bophuthatswana, Ciskei, Transkei and Venda—are regarded as independent republics by the South African government but they are not recognized as such by the United Nations.

Education.—The Provinces have been relieved of all vocational education (technical and industrial), and the Department of National Education under the Minister is concerned with universities, technical colleges, schools of industries, reformatories and State technical, housecraft and commercial high schools, State-aided vocational schools and State and State-aided special schools for the physically handicapped.

Communications.—The State-owned and controlled South African Transport Services operates the national railway system, the principal harbours, most long-distance passenger and freight road transport services, the South African Airways airline and a network of pipelines for petroleum products.

There are international airports at Johannesburg (Jan Smuts), Durban (Louis Botha) and Cape Town (D. F. Malan), with another under construction at La Mercy, Natal. South African Airways operates international services to Europe, North and South America, Australia, the Far East and the Middle East, as well as to neighbouring countries, and it is the principal operator of domestic flights.

The largest sea-port is Durban, Natal. Other major ports are Cape Town, Port Elizabeth, East London, Saldanha Bay and Mossel Bay in Cape Province and Richards Bay, Natal.

Production.—Mining is of the greatest importance to the South African economy, contributing 14·3 per cent to G.D.P. in 1982 (of which gold mining accounted for 10 per cent). Principal minerals produced are: gold, coal, iron ore, diamonds, copper, manganese, lime and limestone and asbestos.

Agriculture, forestry and fishing account for 6·2 per cent of G.D.P. Over 50 per cent of land is pasture so livestock farming is widespread with meat and wool important products. Principal crops are maize, sugar-cane, fruits and vegetables, wheat, sorghum, sunflower seed and groundnuts. Cotton is widely grown because of its suitability to the climate, and viticulture is also widespread.

Industries, concentrated most heavily around Johannesburg, Pretoria and the major ports, process foodstuffs, metals and non-metallic mineral products, and also produce beverages and tobacco, motor vehicles, chemicals and chemical products, machinery, textiles and clothing, and paper and paper products.

Trade.—Principal exports are: gold, base metals and metal products, diamonds, food (especially fruit), chemicals, machinery and transport equipment, and wool. Principal imports are: machinery, chemicals, motor vehicles, metals and metal products, food, inedible raw materials and textiles.

Trade with U.K.

	1987	1988
Imports from U.K. . . .	£948,584,000	£1,074,826,000
Exports to U.K.	658,162,000	807,669,000

Finance.—Estimated revenue for 1988–89 was R47,460 million, and estimated expenditure was R56,556 million.

CAPITAL.—The administrative seat of the Government is Pretoria, Transvaal; population (1985 estimate), 822,925; the seat of the Legislature is ΨCape Town, population (1985) 1,911,521. Other large towns (1985 figures) are Johannesburg, Transvaal (1,609,408); ΨDurban, Natal, the largest seaport (634,301); ΨPort Elizabeth, Cape (651,993); Bloemfontein, capital of Orange Free State (232,984); ΨEast London, Cape (167,992); and Pietermaritzburg, capital of Natal (192,417).

CURRENCY.—Rand (R) of 100 cents.

FLAG.—Three horizontal stripes of equal width; from top to bottom, orange, white, blue; in the centre of the white stripe, the old Orange Free State flag hanging vertical, towards the pole the Union Flag horizontal, away from the pole the old Transvaal Vierkleur, all spread full.

NATIONAL ANTHEM.—Die Stem Van Suid-Afrika (The Call of South Africa).

NATIONAL DAY.—May 31.

BRITISH EMBASSY
255 Hill Street, Pretoria
[Pretoria 433121]
91 Parliament Street, Cape Town (Jan.–June)
[Cape Town 4617220]

Ambassador Extraordinary and Plenipotentiary, His Excellency Sir Robin (William) Renwick, K.C.M.G. (1987).
Counsellors, J. Poston (*Head of Chancery*); M. G. Thickett.
First Secretaries, R. J. Sawers; C. G. Crawford; P. Haggie; A. E. Gay (*Administration*).
Cultural Attaché and British Council Representative, W. L. Radford, 4th Flr. Federated Building, 38 Ameshoff St., (P.O. Box 30637), Braamfontein 2017, Johannesburg (Tel. 339 3715).

There are British Consular Offices at *Cape Town, Johannesburg* and *Durban*; and Honorary Consuls at *Port Elizabeth* and *East London*.

NAMIBIA

Administrator General, Louis Pienaar.

Namibia (South West Africa) stretches from the southern border of Angola (lat. 17° 23′ S.) to part of the northern (Orange River) and north-western borders of the Cape Province of the Republic of South Africa; and from the Atlantic Ocean in the west to Botswana in the east. The average rainfall over 70 per cent of the Territory is below 400 mm. per annum.

The territory has an area of 318,261 sq. miles (824,292 sq. km.), including the area of Walvis Bay (434 sq. miles) which is claimed by South Africa. The population was estimated at 1,184,000 in 1986 and the main population groups are: Ovambo (587,000), Whites (78,000), Damara (89,000), Kavango (110,000), Herero (89,000), Nama (57,000), Coloured (48,000),

Caprivians (44,000), Bushmen (34,000), Rehoboth Baster (29,000), Tswana (7,000).

Government.—A German protectorate from 1880 to 1915, South West Africa was administered until the end of 1920 by the Union of South Africa. In terms of the Treaty of Versailles the Territory was entrusted to South Africa with full powers of administration and legislation over the Territory. After the dissolution of the League of Nations and in the absence of a trusteeship agreement, South Africa informed the United Nations that she would continue to administer South West Africa in the spirit of the Mandate. Since the establishment of the United Nations, South West Africa has been the subject of dispute.

On June 21, 1971, the International Court of Justice at The Hague delivered an advisory opinion as requested by the U.N. Security Council on the legal consequences for States of the continued presence of South Africa in Namibia (South West Africa). The Court decided by 13 votes to 2, that (*inter alia*) 'the continued presence of South Africa being illegal, South Africa is under obligation to withdraw its administration from Namibia immediately and thus put an end to its occupation of the Territory'. The South African Government rejected this opinion, but accepted the principle that the territory should attain independence. In September 1975 constitutional talks (known as the Turnhalle Conference) were begun in Windhoek between delegates from the 11 ethnic groups of the territory in order to determine the future of South West Africa. But their representative nature was contested by, *inter alia*, SWAPO, a liberation movement with substantial international support and when, in April 1977, it became clear that independence based on the Turnhalle would not solve the problem, the Five Western members of the U.N. Security Council at that time drew up a plan, later incorporated into Security Council Resolution 435, for a peaceful settlement. The plan involves free and fair elections under U.N. supervision leading to independence. The plan has been accepted by all the parties to the Namibia question and attempts to implement the plan are continuing.

Meanwhile, the South African Government appointed an Administrator-General in 1977 to establish a central administration there for those functions previously administered from Pretoria. In December 1978, the South Africans organized an election for a constituent assembly which SWAPO and most of the internal political parties boycotted. The resultant assembly was transformed into a National Assembly with legislative powers in May 1979, and a Council of Ministers was established in 1980 but both were abolished in Jan. 1983 and the territory again came under direct rule. However, in May 1985 legislative powers and executive authority were restored under a Transitional Government of National Unity intended to hold office while South Africa and the U.N. negotiate Namibia's independence.

After a series of talks between Cuba, Angola, South Africa and the U.S.A., agreement was reached in Dec. 1988 for the withdrawal over 27 months of the Cuban troops in Angola in exchange for Namibian independence under U.N. Security Council Resolution 435. Resolution 435 began to be implemented on April 1, 1989: the Administrator General resumed control of the territory, the South West Africa Territory Force was gradually demobilized and the South African Defence Force presence in Namibia was gradually cut to 1,500 personnel, restricted to base. The U.N. Secretary General sent his Special Representative, Martti Ahtisaari, to Namibia to oversee the seven-month run-up to elections and a 4,500 strong United Nations Transition Assistance Group (UNTAG) was deployed to monitor South

African withdrawal and the conduct of the parties. Elections to a Constituent Assembly are due to be held in Nov. 1989. The Assembly will then decide on a constitution, which must be approved by a two thirds majority.

Production.—Mining, agriculture and fisheries are important. Animal husbandry accounts for 99 per cent of the total gross output of commercial agriculture.

Trade with U.K.

	1987	1988
Imports from U.K.	£3,909,000	£3,259,000
Exports to U.K.	7,681,000	10,729,000

CAPITAL.—Windhoek (population, 1987 estimate, 110,000). The only port of any size is Ψ Walvis Bay.
CURRENCY.—South African rand (R) of 100 cents.

BRITISH LIAISON OFFICE
116A Leutwein Street, Windhoek
[Windhoek 223022]

Head of Mission, P. G. Wallis.
First Secretary, R. S. G. Clarke.

SPAIN
(España)

Head of the Spanish State, King Juan Carlos I de Borbón y Borbón, K.G., *born* Jan. 5, 1938, *acceded to the throne,* Nov. 22, 1975, *married* May 14, 1962, Princess Sophie of Greece *and has issue,* Infante Felipe Juan Pablo Alfonso Todos Los Santos (Prince of Asturias, *and heir to the throne*) *born* Jan. 30, 1968; Infanta Elena Maria Isabel Dominica, *born* Dec. 20, 1963; and Infanta Christina Frederica Victoria, *born* June 13, 1965.

CABINET

(as at July 15, 1989)

Prime Minister, Felipe González.
Deputy P.M., Alfonso Guerra.
Foreign Affairs, Francisco Fernández Ordóñez.
Justice, Enrique Múgica.
Defence, Narcis Serra Serra.
Economy and Finance, Carlos Solchaga.
Interior, José Luis Corcuera.
Transport, Tourism and Communications, José Barrionuevo.
Public Works and Urban Planning, Javier Sáenz de Coscullela.
Education and Science, Javier Solana.
Labour and Social Security, Manuel Chaves.
Industry and Energy, José Claudio Aranzadi.
Agriculture, Fisheries and Food, Carlos Romero Herrera.
Public Administration, Joaquín Almunia.
Culture, Jorge Semprún.
Health and Consumer Affairs, Julián García Vargas.
Cabinet Secretary and Parliamentary Relations, Virgilio Zapatero.
Social Welfare, Matilde Fernández.
Chief Government Spokeswoman, Rosa Conde.

SPANISH EMBASSY
24 Belgrave Square, SW1X 8QA
[01-235 5555]

Ambassador Extraordinary and Plenipotentiary, His Excellency José Joaquin Puig de la Bellacasa, G.C.V.O. (1983).
Minister-Counsellor, Sr. D. J. I. Carbajal, C.V.O.

Area and Population.—Situated in the south-west of Europe, between 36°–43° 45′ N. lat. and 4° 25′ E.–9° 20′ W. long., Spain is bounded on the south and east by the Mediterranean, on the west by the Atlantic and Portugal, and on the north by the Bay of Biscay and France, from which it is separated by the Pyrenees. Continental Spain occupies about eleven-thirteenths of the Iberian peninsula, the remaining portion forming the Republic of Portugal. Its coastline extends 1,317 miles—712 formed by the Mediterranean and 605 by the Atlantic—and it comprises a total area of 194,897 sq. miles (504,782 sq. km.), with a population (1986 estimate) of 38,818,355.

Physical Features.—The interior of the Iberian Peninsula consists of an elevated tableland surrounded and traversed by mountain ranges—the Pyrenees, the Cantabrian Mountains, the Sierra Guadarrama, Sierra Morena, Sierra Nevada, Montes de Toledo, etc. The principal rivers are the Duero, the Tajo, the Guadiana, the Guadalquivir, the Ebro and the Miño.

Government.—Spain was a monarchy until April 1931, when King Alfonso XIII left the country and a Republic was proclaimed and a Provisional Government, drawn from the various Republican and Socialist parties, was formed. On July 18, 1936, a counter-revolution broke out in many military garrisons in Spanish Morocco and spread rapidly throughout Spain. The principal leader was General Francisco Franco Bahamonde, formerly Governor of the Canary Islands. The struggle, in its later phases, threatened to embroil other European countries, those of Nazi-Fascist tendency lending aid to General Franco (leader of the Military-Fascist fusion, or *Falange*) while those of Communist views supported the Azaña (*Popular Front*) government. In October, 1938, many of the supporting troops were withdrawn, and on March 29, 1939, the Civil War was declared to have ended, the Popular Front Governments in Madrid and Barcelona surrendering to the *Nationalists* (as General Franco's followers were then named). On June 5, 1939, the Grand Council of the *Falange Española Tradicionalista y de las Juntas Ofensivas Nacional-Sindicalistas,* met at Burgos to legislate for the reorganization of the country under the Presidency of General Franco, who had assumed the title of *Caudillo* (*Leader*) *of Spain and Chief of the State.* In the Civil War of 1936–39 over 1,000,000 lives were lost.

On July 22, 1969, General Franco nominated Prince Juan Carlos (Alfonso) of Bourbon (grandson of the late King Alfonso XIII) to succeed him as head of state at his death or retirement. The nomination was approved in the *Cortes* by a large majority. Following the death of General Franco, on November 20, 1975, Juan Carlos acceded to the throne on Nov. 22, 1975.

Under the Constitution drawn up in 1977–78 there is a bi-cameral *Cortes* comprising a 350-member Congress of Deputies elected for 4 years by universal adult suffrage, and a Senate consisting of directly elected representatives of the provinces, islands, autonomous regions and Ceuta and Melilla.

In the regional and municipal elections of May 1983, the P.S.O.E. won the majority of the votes. In elections held in the Basque country in February, and in Cataluña in April 1984, local nationalist parties (P.N.V. and C.I.U.) retained their majorities and formed autonomous governments. At the General Election on June 22, 1986, P.S.O.E. won 184 seats; C.P., 105; C.D.S., 19; and I.U., 7 seats.

Regions.—Since the promulgation of the 1978 Constitution, 17 autonomous regions have been established, with their own parliaments and governments. These are Andalucia, Aragon, Asturias, Balaerics, the Basque country, Canaries, Castilla-La Mancha, Castilla-Leon, Cantabria, Cataluña, Extremadura, Galicia, Madrid, Murcia, Navarre, La Rioja and Valencia.

Defence.—Army: There are in Spain 1 armoured, 1 mechanized, 1 motorized and 2 mountain divisions; 1 artillery brigade, 2 cavalry brigades, 1 air-transportable brigade, 1 helicopter brigade, 1 coastal artillery brigade. The *Guardia Civil* operates as a gendarmerie in the rural areas under the control of the Ministry of Defence.

The active Spanish *Navy* consists of 1 aircraft carrier, 9 destroyers, 12 frigates and corvettes, 12 minesweepers, 6 major amphibious vessels, 8 submarines, 12 fast patrol craft, 6 hydrographic vessels, 1 tanker, and many smaller patrol craft and auxiliaries. The Navy also has 50 helicopters and 10 Harrier aircraft.

The *Air Force* is divided geographically into 3 regions covering Spain plus an Air Zone for the Canaries. There are also functional Combat, Tactical and Transport Commands. The Air Force consists of 2 attack squadrons, 9 air defence squadrons, 1 maritime squadron, 7 transport squadrons, 3 search and rescue squadrons, 9 training squadrons and 1 fire-fighting squadron.

Spain became a member of N.A.T.O. in May 1982. Her continued membership (linked to non-military integration) was confirmed in a referendum in March 1986. The present government has also initiated reorganization of the military structure.

Education.—Under the Education Law 1985 free education for all children aged 6 to 16 is guaranteed. Under the new law, private schools (30 per cent of primary and 60 per cent of secondary schools) will have to fulfill certain criteria to receive government maintenance grants.

There are 32 state universities, the oldest of which, Salamanca, was founded in 1230. Other ancient foundations are Valencia (1245), Oviedo (1317), Valladolid (1346), Barcelona (1450), Zaragoza (1474), Santiago (1501), Seville (1502), Granada (1526), and Madrid (1590). New universities in 1989–90 include Universidad Pública de Navarra and Carlos III (Madrid). Private universities are Deusto in Bilbao, and Navarra in Pamplona. Student numbers in the universities have risen to over 960,000.

Language and Literature.—Castilian is the language of more than three-quarters of the population of Spain. Basque, reported to have been the original language of Iberia, is spoken in the rural districts of Vizcaya, Guipuzcoa and Alava. Catalan is spoken in Provençal Spain, and Galician, spoken in the northwestern provinces, is akin to Portuguese; the govern-

ments of these regions actively encourage use of their local languages.

The literature of Spain is one of the oldest and richest in the world, the *Poem of the Cid*, the earliest and best of the heroic songs of Spain, having been written about A.D. 1140. The outstanding writings of its golden age are those of Miguel de Cervantes Saavedra (1547–1616), Lope Felix de Vega Carpio (1562–1635) and Pedro Calderón de la Barca (1600–1681). The Nobel Prize for Literature has four times been awarded to Spanish authors—J. Echegaray (1904), J. Benavente (1922), Juan Ramón Jimenez (1956) and Vicente Aleixandre (1977).

Production and Industry.—The expansion of the Spanish economy and accession to the E.C. have led to changes in Spanish agriculture. It accounts for over 5 per cent of G.D.P. and employs over 13 per cent of the working population (down from 28 per cent in 1970). Between 1970 and 1985 the net value of agricultural production increased by 56 per cent in real terms.

The country is generally fertile, and well adapted to agriculture and the cultivation of heat-loving fruits—olives, oranges, lemons, almonds, pomegranates, bananas, apricots, tomatoes, peppers, cucumbers and grapes. The agricultural products include wheat, barley, oats, rice, hemp and flax. The orange crop is exported mainly to Germany, France and the United Kingdom. The vine is cultivated widely; in the southwest, Jerez, the well-known sherry and tent wines are produced. The fishing industry is important.

Spain's mineral resources of coal, iron, wolfram, copper, zinc, lead and iron ores are variously exploited. Output of coal in 1988 was 15·5 million tonnes; output of steel (1988) 11·9 million tonnes.

The principal goods produced are cars, steel, ships, manufactured goods, textiles, chemical products, footwear and other leather goods. In 1988 an estimated 54,172,000 tourists visited Spain.

TRADE

	1987	1988
	million pesetas	
Imports	6,029,838	7,039,516
Exports	4,193,388	4,686,376

The balance of payments on current account showed a deficit of $3,350m. in 1988 and reserves stood at $39,784 million, a 32 per cent increase on the previous year.

Trade with U.K.
(inc. Canary Islands)

	1987	1988
Imports from U.K.	£2,164,221,000	£2,691,662,000
Exports to U.K.	2,099,139,000	2,482,360,000

The principal imports are cotton, tobacco, cellulose, timber, coffee and cocoa, food products, fertilizers, dyes, machinery, motor vehicles and agricultural tractors, wool and petroleum products. The principal exports include cars, petroleum products, iron ore, cork, salt, vegetables, fruits, wines, olive oil, potash, mercury, pyrites, tinned fruit and fish, tomatoes and footwear.

CAPITAL, Madrid. Population (1986) 4,731,224. Other large cities are ΨBarcelona (4,597,429), ΨValencia (2,078,812), Seville (1,594,250), Zaragoza (824,781), ΨMálaga (1,137,782), Bilbao (1,179,148); Murcia (1,006,788).

CURRENCY.—Peseta of 100 céntimos.

FLAG.—Three horizontal bands, red, yellow and red, with coat of arms on yellow band.

NATIONAL ANTHEM.—"Marcha Real Española".

NATIONAL DAY.—October 12.

BRITISH EMBASSY
Calle Fernando el Santo, 16, Madrid 4
[Madrid 419 0200]

Ambassador Extraordinary and Plenipotentiary, His
Excellency Lord Nicholas Gordon Lennox, K.C.M.G.,
K.C.V.O. (1984).

Minister, I. V. Roberts.

Counsellor, D. R. Christopher (*Commercial*).

Defence and Military Attaché, Brig. A. D. Morland,
M.B.E.

Head of Political Section, G. C. Gillham.

There are Consulates General in *Barcelona, Bilbao;* Consulates in *Tenerife, Alicante, Seville,
Malaga, Palma de Mallorca, Las Palmas, Santander, Tarragona, Vigo* and *Lanzarote,* and Vice
Consulates in *Algeciras, Ibiza* and *Menorca.*

British Council Representative, R. T. Joscelyne, Plaza
de Santa Barbara 10, Madrid 28004. There is also a
regional office in Seville and offices with English
language institutes in Bilbao, Granada, Palma de
Mallorca, Las Palmas and Vigo.

BRITISH CHAMBER OF COMMERCE, Plaza de Santa
Barbara 10, 1st Floor, 28004 Madrid, also Paseo de
Gracia 11, Barcelona 7 and Alameda de Mazarredo
5, Bilbao 1.

The BALEARIC ISLES form an archipelago off the
east coast of Spain. There are four large islands
(Majorca, Minorca, Ibiza and Formentera), and seven
smaller (Aire, Aucanada, Botafoch, Cabrera, Drago-
nera, Pinto and El Rey). The islands were occupied
by the Romans after the destruction of Carthage and
provided contingents of the celebrated Balearic
slingers. The total area is 1,935 sq. miles (5,011 sq.
km.), with a population of 685,088. The archipelago
forms a province of Spain, the capital being ΨPalma
in Majorca, pop. 304,422; ΨMahon (Minorca), pop.
22,926.

The CANARY ISLANDS are an archipelago in the
Atlantic, off the African coast, consisting of 7 islands
and 6 mostly uninhabited islets. The total area is
2,807 sq. miles (7,270 sq. km.), with a population of
1,444,626. The Canary Islands form two Provinces of
Spain.—*Las Palmas* (Gran Canaria, Lanzarote
(38,500), Fuerteventura (19,500) and the islets of
Alegranza, Roque del Este, Roque del Oeste, Graciosa,
Montaña Clara and Lobos), with seat of administration at ΨLas Palmas (pop. 366,454) in Gran Canaria,
where major oil companies have installations for re-
fueling shipping; and *Santa Cruz de Tenerife* (Tenerife, La Palma (76,000), Gomera (31,829), and Hierro
(10,000)), with seat of administration at ΨSanta Cruz
in Tenerife, pop. 190,784.

ISLA DE FAISANES is an uninhabited Franco-
Spanish condominium, at the mouth of the Bidassoa
in La Higuera bay.

ΨCEUTA is a fortified post on the Moroccan coast,
opposite Gibraltar. The total area is 5 sq. miles (13 sq.
km.), with a population of 70,864.

ΨMELILLA is a town on a rocky promontory of the
Rif coast, connected with the mainland by a narrow
isthmus. Melilla has been in Spanish possession since
1492. Population 58,449. Ceuta and Melilla are parts
of Metropolitan Spain.

OVERSEAS TERRITORIES

Spanish settlements on the Moroccan seaboard
are:—

Peñon de Alhucemas, the bay of that name includes
six islands: population 366.

Peñon de la Gomera (or *Peñon de Velez*) is a
fortified rocky islet about 40 miles west of Alhucemas
Bay; population 450.

The Chaffarinas (or Zaffarines) are a group of three

islands near the Algerian frontier, about 2 miles
north of Cape del Agua; population 610.

The former provinces of Spanish Guinea, Fernando
Póo and Rio Muni achieved independence on October
12, 1968, under the title of Equatorial Guinea.

The protectorate of Spanish Morocco was incorporated in Morocco on the latter's independence in
1956. Ifni, the former enclave in Morocco, was
incorporated by treaty, on June 30, 1969, and the
Spanish Sahara came under joint Moroccan and
Mauritanian control in November 1975.

SUDAN
(Al-Jamhuryat es-Sudan Al-Democratia)

CABINET
(as from July 9, 1989)

Prime Minister and Minister for Defence, Lt.-Gen.
Omar Hassan Ahmad al-Bashir.

Deputy P.M., Brig.-Gen. Zubir Mohammed Saleh.

Presidential Affairs, Lt.-Col. Tayib Ibrahim Mohammed Khayr.

Foreign Affairs, Ali Sahlul.

Interior, Brig.-Gen. Faisal Ali Abu Salih.

Justice and Attorney General, Hassan Ismail al-Billi.

Culture and Information, Ali Mohammad Shumo.

Finance and National Economic Planning, Sayed Ali
Zaki.

Agriculture and Natural Resources, Ahmad Ali al-
Gunayfikh.

National Guidance and Orientation, Abdella Deng
Danyal.

*Local Government and Co-ordination of Provincial
Affairs*, Natali Yanku Ambu.

Irrigation, Yacoub Abu Shura Musa.

Energy and Mining, Abdel Munim Khujali.

Industry, Mohammed Omar Abdullah.

Education, Mahjub Badawi Mohammed.

Housing, Construction and Public Utilities, Maj.-Gen.
Mohammed al-Hadi Mamun al-Mardi.

Relief and Refugee Affairs, Peter Awur Adur.

Transport and Communications, Ali Ahmad Ibrahim.

Labour and Social Security, George Kinga.

Commerce, Co-operation and Supply, Faruq al-
Bushra.

Health and Social Welfare, Shakir al-Sarraj.

EMBASSY OF THE REPUBLIC OF THE SUDAN
3 Cleveland Row, SW1A 1DD
[01-839 8080]

Ambassador Extraordinary and Plenipotentiary, His
Excellency Sayed Ibrahim Mohamed Ali (1985).

Area and Population.—The Sudan extends from
the southern boundary of Egypt, 22° N. lat., to the
northern boundary of Uganda, 3° 36′ N. lat., and
reaches from the Republic of Chad about 21° 49′ E. (at
12° 45′ N.) to the north-west boundary of Ethiopia in
38° 35′ E. (at 18° N.). On the east lie the Red Sea and
Ethiopia; on the south lie Kenya, Uganda and Zaire;
and on the west the Central African Republic, Chad,
and Libya. The greatest length from north to south
is approximately 1,300 miles, and east to west 950
miles.

The *White Nile* enters from Uganda at Nimule as
the *Bahr el Jebel*, and leaves the Sudan at Wadi
Halfa. The *Blue Nile* flows from Lake Tana on the

Ethiopian Plateau. Its course in the Sudan is nearly 500 miles long, before it joins the White Nile at Khartoum. The next confluence of importance is at Atbara where the main Nile is joined by the River Atbara. Between Khartoum and Wadi Halfa lie five of the six *Cataracts*.

The estimated area is about 967,500 sq. miles (2,505,813 sq. km.), with a population of 21,550,000, partly Arabs, partly negroes, and partly of mixed Arab-Negro blood, with a small foreign element. The Arabs are mostly Muslims. The Nilotics of the Bahr el Ghazal and Upper Nile Valleys are generally Animists, but some have been converted to Christianity and others are Muslims. There are some 1 million refugees in the Sudan.

Government.—The Anglo-Egyptian Condominium over the Sudan which had been established in 1899 ended when the Sudan House of Representatives, on Dec. 19, 1955, voted unanimously a declaration that the Sudan was a fully independent sovereign state. A Republic was proclaimed on Jan. 1, 1956, and was recognized by Great Britain and Egypt, a Supreme Commission being sworn in to take over sovereignty. The Sudan was under military rule from Nov., 1958, until 1964 when a new civilian Cabinet was appointed. Government of the country was taken over on May 25, 1969, by a ten-man revolutionary council headed by Col. Gaafar Mohamed El Nimeri. In February 1972 an agreement was signed at Addis Ababa which brought to an end nearly 17 years of insurrection and civil war in the six southern provinces, and which recognized southern regional autonomy within a unified Sudanese State. Insurrection broke out again in 1983. In April 1985 the Army command assumed power after popular demonstrations, deposed Nimeri and appointed transitional government which undertook to hand over power to a democratically elected government. Elections were held in April 1986 and a new government formed, a coalition of Umma and D.U.P. members. A new broad-based coalition was formed in May 1988 with representatives from the Umma, D.U.P., National Islamic Front and Southern parties.

The government of Sadiq al Mahdi was overthrown in a military coup led by Brig.-Gen. Omar Hassan Ahmad al-Bashir on June 30, 1989. The Constitution was suspended and parliament was replaced by a 15-member ruling junta who have de facto control over a cabinet of 21 ministers.

Education.—School education is free for most children, but not compulsory, beginning with six years primary education, followed by three years secondary education at general secondary schools, the more academic higher secondary schools or vocational schools. The medium of instruction is Arabic. English is taught as the principal foreign language in all schools.

Khartoum University has 10 faculties. There is a branch of Cairo University in Khartoum, an Islamic University at Omdurman and universities at Wad Medani and Juba.

In addition to the universities there are various technical post-secondary institutes as well as professional and vocational training establishments.

Production.—The principal grain crops are *dura* (great millet) and wheat, the staple food of the people in the Sudan. Sesame and ground-nuts are other important food crops, which also yield an exportable surplus and a promising start has been made with castor seed. The principal export crop is cotton. Traditionally a major producer of long-staple cotton, Sudan has in recent years grown more short and medium-staple cotton. These grades now account for more than half total production. Production in 1987–88 is estimated to have been around 837,000 bales. The Sudan also produces the bulk of the world's supply of gum arabic. Sugar is an increasingly important crop. The Sudan still has to achieve self sufficiency in sugar production. Livestock is the mainstay of the nomadic Arab tribes of the desert and the negro tribes of the swamp and wooded grassland country in the South. Production has, however, been affected by drought, famine and flooding.

Sudan's agriculture production provided employment for over 60 per cent of the labour force and contributed 37 per cent to G.D.P. in 1986–87. It is based on large and medium sized public sector irrigation projects with small scale private irrigation schemes providing mostly fruit and vegetables. Mechanised and traditional agriculture is practised in areas of sufficient rainfall.

The manufacturing sector contributed less than 8 per cent to G.D.P. in 1986–87 and provided employment for 4 per cent of the work force. The main manufacturing enterprises are concentrated in the areas of food processing, textiles, shoes, cigarettes and batteries.

Communications.—The railway system has a route length of about 3,200 miles, linking Khartoum with Wadi Halfa, Karima, Port Sudan, Wad Medani, Sennar, El Damazin, Kosti, El Obeid and Nyala. A line branches out southwards to Wau from the Sennar/Nyala western line. Nile river services between Khartoum and Juba have been interrupted by the southern insurrection. ΨPort Sudan is a well-equipped modern seaport. Sudan Airways fly services from Khartoum to many parts of the Sudan and to other African states, Europe and the Middle East.

FINANCE

	1986–87
Revenue	£S2,741·1 m
Expenditure	6,100·7 m
Deficit	2,527·6 m
Deficit financing	2,527·6 m

TRADE

	1985–86*	1986–87*
Total Imports ...	US$1,055·2 m	US$832·3 m
Total Exports ...	497·2 m	481·6 m
*Estimates		

Trade with U.K.

	1987	1988
Imports from U.K. ...	£75,322,000	£86,480,000
Exports to U.K.	18,850,000	9,910,000

The principal exports are cotton, livestock, gum arabic and other agricultural produce. The chief imports are petroleum goods and other raw materials, machinery and equipment, transport and equipment, medicines and chemicals.

CAPITAL.—Khartoum. The town contains many mosques, a Catholic cathedral and an Anglican cathedral, and the University with extensive government buildings. The combined population of Khartoum, Khartoum North and Omdurman (excluding refugees and displaced people) is just over 2,000,000.

CURRENCY.—Sudanese pound (£S) of 100 piastres and 1,000 millièmes.

FLAG.—Three horizontal stripes of red, white and black with a green triangle next to the hoist.

NATIONAL ANTHEM.— "Nahnu Djundullah" (We are the army of God).

NATIONAL DAY.—January 1 (Independence Day).

BRITISH EMBASSY
(P.O. Box 801)
Khartoum
[Khartoum 70760/7]

Ambassador Extraordinary and Plenipotentiary, His Excellency John Lewis Beaven, C.M.G., C.V.O. (1987).

Counsellor, D. I. Lewty (*Head of Chancery and Consul General*).

Defence and Military Attaché, Col. R. J. M. Carson, O.B.E.

British Council Representative, P. B. M. Early, P.O. Box 1253, Khartoum. The British Council has a sub-office in *Juba* and there are libraries at *El Obeid*, and *Omdurman*.

SURINAME
(Nieuwe Republick van Suriname)

President, Ramsewak Shankar, *sworn in* Jan. 25, 1988.

Head of the National Military Council, Cmdr. Desi Bouterse.

COUNCIL OF MINISTERS
(as at June 30, 1989)

Vice President, Chairman of Council of Ministers, Henk A. E. Arron.

Foreign Affairs, Dr. E. Sedoc.

Finance and Planning, Subhes Chandra Mungra.

Natural Resources and Energy, Pretaapnarian Radhakishun.

Home Affairs, District Administration and Mobilization, Evelyn Alexander-Vanenburg.

Public Works, Telecommunications and Construction, H. Jankipersadsing.

Health, Henk Ali Mahumed.

Education, Science, Culture, Sport and Youth Affairs, Roland Venetiann.

Transport, Trade and Industry, W. Grep.

Labour, Romeo Van Russel.

Agriculture, Livestock, Fisheries and Forestry, S. Redjosenpeno.

Housing and Social Affairs, Willy Soemita.

Justice and Police, J. Adjodhia.

Army, Maj. A. Sheikkariem.

Suriname is situated on the north coast of South America and is bounded by French Guiana in the east, Brazil in the south and Guyana in the west. It has an area of 63,037 sq. miles (163,265 sq. km.), with a population (1988 estimate) of 410,000.

Formerly known as Dutch Guiana, Suriname remained part of the Netherlands West Indies until November 25, 1975, when it achieved complete independence. Suriname had received autonomy in domestic affairs under the Realm Statute which took effect on December 29, 1954. The civilian government was ousted by the military in Feb. 1980, who appointed the predominantly civilian Cabinet. A National Assembly of 31 members was appointed on Jan. 1, 1985 to draft a new constitution. A referendum held on Sept. 30, 1987 voted for the new constitution and in elections held on Nov. 25 a coalition of three opposition parties won a landslide victory over Cmdr. Bouterse's N.D.P. party. President Shankar and Vice-President Arron were sworn in on Jan. 25, 1988, and a new Council of Ministers was installed on Jan. 26.

Suriname has large timber resources. Rice and sugar cane are the main crops. Bauxite is mined, and is the principal export.

TRADE

	1985
Imports	US$ 359·5 m
Exports	337·3 m

Trade with U.K.

	1987	1988
Imports from U.K.	£7,974,000	£6,107,000
Exports to U.K.	12,488,000	11,256,000

CAPITAL.—ΨParamaribo (population 1971, 110,000).

CURRENCY.—Suriname guilder of 100 cents.

FLAG.—Horizontal stripes of green, white, red, white, green, with a five pointed yellow star in the centre.

NATIONAL DAY.—November 25.

British Ambassador (resides at *Georgetown*, Guyana).

British Consulate, c/o V.S.H. United Buildings, Van't Hogerhuystraat, P.O. Box 1300, Paramaribo.

Honorary Consul, J. J. Healy, M.B.E.

SWEDEN
(Konungariket Sverige)

King of Sweden, Carl XVI Gustaf, *born* April 30, 1946, *succeeded* September 15, 1973, *married* June 19, 1976 Fräulein Silvia Renate Sommerlath *and has issue*, Crown Princess Victoria Ingrid Alice Désirée, Duchess of Västergötland, *born* July 14, 1977; Prince Carl Philip Edmund Bertil, Duke of Värmland, *born* May 13, 1979; Princess Madeleine Thérèse Amelie Josephine, Duchess of Hälsingland and Gästrikland, *born* June 10, 1982.

COUNCIL OF MINISTERS
(as at May 31, 1989)

Prime Minister, Ingvar Carlsson.

Justice, Laila Freivalds.

Foreign Affairs, Sten Andersson.

Agriculture, Mats Hellström.

Finance, Kjell-Olof Feldt.

Housing, Ulf Lönnqvist.

Labour, Ingela Thalén.

Education and Culture, Bengt Göransson.

Industry, Ivar Nordberg.

Health and Social Affairs, Sven Hulterström.

Equality and Immigration, Majlis Lööw.

Energy and the Environment, Birgitta Dahl.

Public Sector, and Wages and Salaries, Bengt K. A. Johansson.

Foreign Trade, Anita Gradin.

Defence, Roine Carlsson.

Health and Social Affairs (*Deputy Minister*), Bengt Lindqvist.

Communications, Georg Andersson.

Aid, Lena Hjelm-Wallén.

Sport, Youth and Tourism, Margot Wallström.

Education (Deputy Minister), Göran Persson.
Finance (Deputy Minister), Odd Engström.

SWEDISH EMBASSY
11 Montagu Place, W1H 2AL
[01-724 2101]

Ambassador Extraordinary and Plenipotentiary, His Excellency Leif Leifland, G.C.V.O. (1982).
Minister Plenipotentiary, P. O. Jödahl.
Counsellors, A. Alsterdal (*Press*); P. Bruce (*Commodities*); P. Järborg (*Consular and Administration*); N. Daag (*Political*).
Defence and Naval Attaché, Cmdr. J. Bring.
Military and Air Attaché, Col. E. J. Hjelm.
Trade Commissioner, M. Nilsson (73 Welbeck Street, W1M 8AN.).

Area and Population.—Sweden occupies the eastern area of the Scandinavian peninsula in N.W. Europe and comprises 24 local government districts, '*Län*', with a total area of 173,732 sq. miles (449,964 sq. km.), and population Dec. 31, 1985 of 8,358,139. In 1985 the birth rate was 11·79 per 1,000 inhabitants, the death rate 11·26 per 1,000 inhabitants and infant mortality rate was 6·8 per 1,000 live births.

Government.—Under the Act of Succession of June 6, 1809 (with amendments) the throne is hereditary in the House of Bernadotte. (A 1979 amendment vested the succession in the monarch's eldest child, irrespective of sex.) Jean-Baptiste Jules Bernadotte, Prince of Ponte Corvo, a Marshal of France, was invited to accept the title of Crown Prince, with succession to the throne. He succeeded Charles XIII in 1818. There is a unicameral Diet (*Riksdag*) of 349 members elected for 3 years. The Council of Ministers (*Statsråd*) is responsible to the *Riksdag*.

Production and Industry.—The country's industrial prosperity is based on an abundance of natural resources in the form of forests, mineral deposits and water power. The forests are extensive, covering about half the total land surface, and sustain flourishing timber, pulp and paper milling industries. The mineral resources include iron ore, lead, zinc, sulphur, granite, marble, precious and heavy metals (the latter not exploited) and extensive deposits of low grade uranium ore. Industries based on mining, principally iron and steel, aluminium and copper are important but it is the general engineering industry that provides the basis of Sweden's exports. Growth areas are largely in the specialized machinery and systems and chemical industries. The relative importance of agriculture has declined and in 1983 only 5·4 per cent of the population was engaged in farming.

Apart from water power Sweden has no significant indigenous resources of conventional hydrocarbon fuels and relies to a high degree upon imported oil. Much of Sweden's electricity is generated by nuclear power but as a result of a referendum in 1980 the nuclear programme is to be discontinued by 2010. Small supplies of natural gas are imported from Denmark into southern Sweden, with the pipeline being extended to Gothenburg.

Communications.—The total length of Swedish railroads is 11,745 km. The number of passenger cars in use on December 31, 1985 was 3,151,195.

The mercantile marine amounted on December 31, 1985 to 2,619,625 gross tonnage. The Board of Civil Aviation under the control of the Ministry of Communications handles civil aviation matters. Regular domestic air traffic is maintained by the Scandinavian Airlines System and by A. B. Linjeflyg. Regular European and inter-continental air traffic is maintained by the Scandinavian Airlines System.

Defence.—Based on the policy of non-alignment in peace leading to neutrality in war Sweden maintains a Total Defence intended to make any attack on her costly. Total Defence includes peacetime organizations for civil, economic and psychological defence as well as compulsory national service for all acceptable males. Some 50,000 national servicemen are called up for 7–15 months training each year and most are recalled every fourth year for refresher training. On mobilization the Army strength totals 4 armoured brigades, 1 mechanized brigade and 23 infantry and winter warfare brigades. The Navy has 12 submarines, 48 fast attack craft, a number of minor craft and auxiliaries and 5 coast artillery units. The Air Force has modern supersonic aircraft of Swedish manufacture forming a standing force of 220 air defence, 150 attack and 55 reconnaissance with support aircraft and a modern air defence radar system. Facilities exist for rapid dispersal from main bases in war.

Religion.—The State religion is Lutheran Protestant, to which over 95 per cent of the people officially adhere.

Language and Literature.—Swedish belongs, with Danish and Norwegian, to the North Germanic language group. Swedish literature dates back to King Magnus Eriksson, who codified the old Swedish provincial laws in 1350. With his translation of the Bible, Olaus Petri (1493–1552) formed the basis for the modern Swedish language. Literature flourished during the reign of Gustavus III, who founded the Swedish Academy in 1786. Swedish literature is studded with names such as Almquist (1795–1866), Strindberg (1849–1912) and Lagerlöf (1858–1940), Nobel Prize Winner in 1909. Contemporary authors include Lagerquist (1891–1974), Nobel Laureate in 1951, Martinson (1904–1978) and Johnson (1900–1976), Nobel Laureates jointly in 1974. The Swedish scientist Alfred Nobel (1833–1896) founded the Nobel Prizes for Literature, Science and Peace.

Education.—Tuition within the State system, which is maintained by the State and by local taxation, is free. It provides 9 years' compulsory schooling from the age of 7 to 16 in the comprehensive elementary schools; further education of 2, 3 or 4 years in the upper secondary schools; a unified higher education system administered in 6 regional areas containing one of the universities—Uppsala (founded 1477); Lund (1668); Stockholm (1878); Gothenburg (1887); Umeå (1963) and Linköping (1967). At present there are 33 institutions of higher education including three technical universities in Stockholm, Gothenburg and Luleå, and the Karolinska Institute in Stockholm, which specializes in medicine and dentistry.

FINANCE

	1985–86	1986–87
	Kronor million	Kronor million
Revenue	275,638	293,190
Expenditure	327,177	336,392

TRADE

	1985	1986
	Kronor million	Kronor million
Imports	243,974·4	231,444·9
Exports	259,985·1	265,039·7

Trade with U.K.

	1987	1988
Imports from U.K.	£2,322,235,000	£2,195,032,000
Exports to U.K.	2,952,453,000	3,366,524,000

Sweden's main imports from Britain are crude oil and petroleum products, machinery and parts, road vehicles and components, clothing and textiles and steel. Britain's main imports from Sweden are paper and board, road vehicles, machinery, wood, steel and pulp.

CAPITAL.—ΨStockholm. Population (1985): City 659,030; Greater Stockholm, 1,435,474; ΨGothenburg

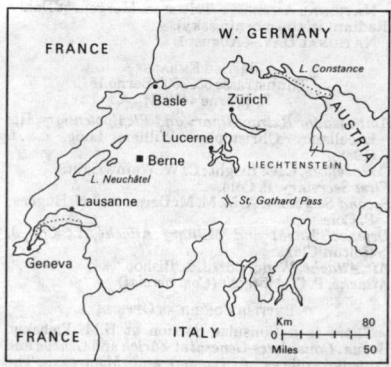

(Göteborg) (425,495); ΨMalmö (229,936); Uppsala (154,859).

CURRENCY.—Swedish krona of 100 øre.

FLAG.—Yellow cross on a blue ground.

NATIONAL ANTHEM.—"Du Gamla, Du Fria" (Thou ancient, thou freeborn).

NATIONAL DAY.—June 6 (Day of the Swedish Flag).

BRITISH EMBASSY
Skarpögatan 6–8, 115 27 Stockholm
[Stockholm 6670140]

Ambassador Extraordinary and Plenipotentiary, His Excellency Sir John Ure, K.C.M.G., L.V.O. (1987).
British Council Representative, Dr. S. M. Lewis.

BRITISH CONSULAR OFFICE
There is a British Consular Office at *Stockholm*.

BRITISH-SWEDISH CHAMBER OF COMMERCE, Grevgatan 34, 11453 Stockholm.

SWITZERLAND
(Schweizerische Eidgenossenschaft—
Confédération Suisse—Confederazione
Svizzera.)

FEDERAL COUNCIL

President of the Swiss Confederation (1989) *and Head of Public Economy*, Jean-Pascal Delamuraz.
Vice-President (1989) *and Head of Justice and Police*, Arnold Koller.
Military, Kaspar Villiger.
Transport, Energy and Communications, Adolf Ogi.
Foreign Affairs, René Felber.
Interior, Flavio Cotti.
Finance, Otto Stich.

EMBASSY OF SWITZERLAND
16–18 Montagu Place, W1H 2BQ
[01–723 0701]

Ambassador Extraordinary and Plenipotentiary, His Excellency Franz E. Muheim (1989).
Ministers, C. M. W. Faessler; Milan J. A. Lusser (*Economic and Financial*).
Counsellor, H. Hofer (*Commodities and Agriculture*).
Defence, Military, Naval and Air Attaché, Maj.-Gen. G. de Loës.
Consul General and Head of Administration, A. Mehr.

There is a Swiss Consulate-General in *Manchester*.

Area and Population.—Switzerland, the Helvetia of the Romans, is a federal republic of central Europe, situated between 45° 50′–47° 48′ N. lat. and 5° 58′–10° 3′ E. long. It is composed of 23 Cantons, 3 subdivided, making 26 in all, and comprises a total area of 15,943 sq. miles (41,293 sq. km.), with a population (Dec. 31, 1987) of 6,566,800. In 1987 there were 76,505 live births, 59,511 deaths and 43,063 marriages. Of the total population in 1980, 44·3 per cent of the population was Protestant, 47·6 per cent Roman Catholic and 0·3 per cent Jewish.

Physical Features.—Switzerland is the most mountainous country in all Europe. The Alps, covered with perennial snow and from 5,000 to 15,217 feet in height, occupy its southern and eastern frontiers, and the chief part of its interior; and the Jura mountains rise in the north-west. The Alps occupy 61 per cent, and the Jura mountains 12 per cent, of the country. The *Alps* are a crescent-shaped mountain system situated in France, Italy, Switzerland, Bavaria and Austria, covering an area of 80,000 square miles from the Mediterranean to the Danube (600 miles). The highest peak, Mont Blanc, Pennine Alps (15,782 ft.) is partly in France and Italy; Monte Rosa (15,217 ft.) and Matterhorn (14,780 ft.) are partly in Switzerland and partly in Italy. The highest wholly Swiss peaks are Dufourspitze (15,203 ft.), Finsteraarhorn (14,026), Aletschhorn (13,711), Jungfrau (13,671), Mönch (13,456), Eiger (13,040), Schreckhorn (13,385), and Wetterhorn (12,150) in the Bernese Alps, and Dom (14,918), Weisshorn (14,803) and Breithorn (13,685).

The Swiss lakes are famous for their beauty and include Lakes Maggiore, Zürich, Lucerne, Neuchâtel, Geneva, Constance, Thun, Zug, Lugano, Brienz and the Walensee. There are also many artificial lakes.

Government.—The legislative power is vested in a Parliament, consisting of two Chambers, a National Council (*Nationalrat*) of 200 members, and a States Council (*Ständerat*) of 46 members; both Chambers united are called the Federal Assembly, and the members of the National Council are elected for four years, an election taking place in October. The executive power is in the hands of a Federal Council (*Bundesrat*) of seven members, elected for four years by the Federal Assembly and presided over by the President of the Confederation. Each year the Federal Assembly elects from the Federal Council the President and the Vice-President. Not more than one of the same canton may be elected member of the Federal Council; on the other hand, there is a tradition that Italian and French-speaking areas should between them be represented on the Federal Council by at least two members.

Defence.—All Swiss males must undertake military service in the Army or the Air Force, which is part of the Army. Swiss Army equipment includes some British items, such as Centurion tanks, Bloodhound missiles, Vampire and Hunter aircraft, the Medium Girder Bridge and the Rapier guided missile. The Hawk aircraft is being delivered.

Production and Industry.—Agriculture is followed chiefly in the valleys and all over the Mittelland, where cereals, flax, hemp, and tobacco are produced, and nearly all temperate zone fruits and vegetables as well as grapes are grown. Dairying and stock-raising are the principal industries, about 3,000,000 acres being under grass for hay and 2,000,000 acres pasturage. The forests cover about one-quarter of the whole surface. The chief manufacturing industries comprise engineering and electrical engineering, metal-working, chemicals and pharmaceuticals, textiles, watchmaking, woodworking, foodstuffs and footwear. Banking, insurance and tourism are major industries.

Communications.—There are 5,020 km of railway tracks (Swiss Federal Railways, 2,990 km; Swiss privately owned railways 2,030 km). At the end of

1988 the number of telephones amounted to 5,879,200 and the network was fully automatic throughout the country. At the same time there were 2,590,200 licensed radio receivers and 2,338,300 television receivers.

At the end of 1987 the total length of motorways was 1,451 km. The number of motor vehicles licensed in 1987 was 6,139,268 (2,737,817 cars, 2,462 privately owned buses, 3,398,989 motorcycles).

A merchant marine, established in 1940, consisted at the end of 1987 of 25 vessels with a total gross tonnage of 571,161 tonnes. In 1987, goods handled at Basle Rhine ports amounted to 8,207,900 tonnes. In 1987 163 lake and river vessels (excluding the Rhine) transported 10,608,200 passengers and 500 tonnes of freight. Swiss airlines have a network covering 327,022 km and in 1987 carried 7,393,900 passengers. Swissair, the State airline, which owned 53 aircraft in 1988, flies to and from the Swiss airports at Zürich, Geneva and Basle.

Education.—Control by cantonal and communal authorities. No central organization. Illiteracy practically unknown. (i) *Primary:* Free and compulsory. School age varies, generally 7 to 14. (ii) *Secondary:* Age 12–15 for boys and girls. Schools numerous and well-attended, and there are many private institutions. (iii) *Special schools* make a feature of commercial and technical instruction. (iv) *Universities:* Basle (founded 1460), Berne (1834), Fribourg (1889), Geneva (1873), Lausanne (1890), Zürich (1832), and Neuchâtel (1909), and the technical Universities of Lausanne and Zürich and commercial University of St. Gall.

Language and Literature.—There are four official languages: French, German, Italian and Romansch. German is the dominating language in 19 of the 26 cantons; French in Fribourg, Jura, Geneva, Neuchâtel, Valais and Vaud; Italian in Ticino, and Romansch in parts of the Grisons.

Many modern authors, alike in the German school and in the Suisse Romande, have achieved international fame. Karl Spitteler (1845–1924) and Hermann Hesse (1877–1962) were awarded the Nobel Prize for Literature, the former in 1919, the latter in 1946.

FINANCE

	1987	1988	1989*
Revenue	SFr.24,902m	SFr.27,219m	SFr.28,031m
Expenditure	23,861m	26,000m	27,555m

*estimate.

TRADE

	1986	1987
Total Imports	SFr.73,512m	SFr.75,171m
Total Exports	67,004m	67,477m

Trade with U.K.
(including Liechtenstein)

	1987	1988
Imports from U.K.	£1,835,851,000	£1,854,918,000
Exports to U.K.	3,298,009,000	3,840,643,000

The principal imports are machinery, electrical and electronic equipment, textiles, motor vehicles, non-ferrous metals, chemical elements, clothing, food, medicinal and pharmaceutical products. The principal exports are machinery, chemical elements, nonferrous metals, watches, electrical and electronic equipment, textiles, dyeing, tanning and colouring equipment. Switzerland is a member of E.F.T.A.

CAPITAL.—Berne. Population, 135,000 (city). Other large towns are Zürich (359,084), Basle (173,147), Geneva (160,668), Lausanne (127,839), Winterthur (86,992), St. Gallen (70,817), Lucerne (62,400).

CURRENCY.—Swiss franc of 100 rappen or centimes.

FLAG.—Red, with white cross.

NATIONAL ANTHEM.—Trittst im Morgenrot Daher (Radiant in the morning sky).

NATIONAL DAY.—August 1.

BRITISH EMBASSY
Thunstrasse 50, 3000 Berne 15
[Berne 445021]

Ambassador Extraordinary and Plenipotentiary, His Excellency Christopher William Long, C.M.G. (1988).
Counsellors, C. C. Bright; C. W. Wainwright.
First Secretary, P. Cole.
Second Secretary, A. M. M. McDermott; I. N. Hughes; P. Cole.
Defence, Naval and Military Attaché, Lt.-Col. J. Bolton-Clark.
Air Attaché, Wing. Cdr. J. L. Bishop.
Attaché, P. C. Albrecht (*Commercial*).

BRITISH CONSULAR OFFICES

There is a Consular Section at H.M. Embassy, Berne; *Consulates-General* at *Zürich* and *Geneva* and Consular offices at *Lugano* and *Montreux*. The Directorate of British Export Promotion in Switzerland is in the Consulate-General Office in *Zürich*.

BRITISH-SWISS CHAMBER OF COMMERCE, Freiestrasse 155, 8032 Zürich.

SWISS-BRITISH SOCIETIES:
Berne.—*President*, Dr. H. Beriger.
Zürich.—*President*, J.-P. Müller.
Basle.—*President*, G. Simons.

SYRIA
(Al-Jamhouriya Al-Arabia as-Souriya)

President, Lt.-Gen. Hafez el Assad, *b.* 1930, *assumed office* March 14, 1971, *re-elected*, Feb. 1978, March 13, 1985.
Vice-Presidents, Abdul Halim Khaddam, Rifaat Al Assad, Zuhair Mashariqa.

MINISTERS
(as at July 31, 1989)

Prime Minister, Mahmoud Al Zubi.
Deputy Prime Minister and Minister for Defence, Gen. Mustafa Tlass.
Deputy Prime Minister for Public Services, Mahmoud Qaddur.
Deputy Prime Minister for Economic Affairs, Dr. Salim Yassin.

SYRIAN EMBASSY IN LONDON

The Syrian Embassy has been closed since Oct. 31, 1986, when Syria and the U.K. broke off diplomatic relations. The Lebanese Embassy represents Syrian interests in the U.K.

Area and Population.—Syria is in the Levant, covering a portion of the former Ottoman Empire, with an estimated area of 71,498 sq. miles (185,180 sq. km.), and a population (at Jan. 1988) of 11,338,000, most of whom are Arabic-speaking and Muslim. The Orontes flows northwards from the Lebanon range across the northern boundary to Antakya (Antioch, Turkey). The Euphrates crosses the northern boundary near Jerablus and flows through north-eastern Syria to the boundary of Iraq.

Archaeology, etc.—The region is rich in historical remains. Damascus (*Dimishq ash-Sham*) is said to be the oldest continuously inhabited city in the world (although Aleppo disputes this claim), having an existence as a city for over 4,000 years. It is situated on the river Barada, in an oasis at the eastern foot of the Anti-Lebanon, and at the edge of the wide sandy desert which stretches to the Euphrates. The city contains the Omayed Mosque, the Tomb of Saladin, and the 'Street Called Straight' (Acts ix. 11), while to the north-east is the Roman outpost of Dmeir and further east is Palmyra.

On the Mediterranean coast at Amrit are ruins of the Phoenician town of Marath, where the well has been found and is being excavated and also ruins of Crusaders' fortresses at Markab, Sahyoun, and Krak des Chevaliers. At Tartous (also on the coast) the cathedral of Our Lady of Syria, built by the Knights Templars in the 12th and 13th centuries has been restored as a museum. One of the oldest alphabets in the world has been discovered at Ugarit (Ras Shamra), a Phoenician village near the port of Latakia.

Hittite cities dating from 2,000 to 1,500 B.C., have recently been explored on the west bank of the Euphrates at Jerablus and Kadesh.

Government.—Syria, which had been under French mandate since the 1914–18 war, became an independent Republic during the 1939–45 war. The first independently elected Parliament met on August 17, 1943, but foreign troops were in part occupation until April, 1946. Syria remained an independent Republic until February, 1958, when it became part of the United Arab Republic. It seceded from the United Arab Republic on Sept. 28, 1961.

A new Constitution was promulgated in March 1973; this declared that Syria is a 'democratic, popular socialist State', and that the Ba'ath Party, which has been the ruling party since 1963, is 'the leading party in the State and society'. Elections to the 195-seat Peoples' Council in February 1986 resulted in a large majority for the Ba'ath Party, who had 129 seats, Arab Socialist Union 9, Arab Socialist Unionist Movement 8, Arab Socialist Party 5, Syrian Communist Party 9, and Independents 35.

Production and Industry.—Agriculture is the principal source of production; wheat and barley are the main cereal crops, but the cotton crop is the highest in value. Tobacco is grown in the maritime plain in Sahel, the Sahyoun and the Djebleh district of Latakia. Large new areas are coming under irrigation and cultivation in the north-east of the country as a result of the Thawra dam. Skins and hides, leather goods, wool and silk, textiles, cement, vegetable oil, glass, soap, sugar, plastics and copper and brass utensils are produced. There are an increasing number of light assembly plants as Syria's industrialization programme develops. Oil has been found at Karachuk and other parts in the north-eastern corner of the country and production of high quality reserves is proceeding in the region of Deir ez Zor. Syria produces about 350,000 barrels of oil per day at present. A pipeline has been built to the Mediterranean port of Banias, via Homs. Two oil refineries are in production at Homs and Banias. Another pipeline from the Iraq oilfields was closed in April 1982. Syria also has deposits of phosphate and rock salt, and produces asphalt.

Language and Literature.—Arabic is the principal language, but Kurdish, Turkish and Armenian are spoken among significant minorities and a few villages still speak Aramaic, the language spoken by Christ and the Apostles. There are 3 daily newspapers and several periodicals in Arabic published in Damascus, and also a daily newspaper in English. English has taken over from French as the main foreign language, especially among the young.

Education.—Education in Syria is under State control and, although a few of the schools are privately owned, they all follow a common system and syllabus. Elementary education is free at State Schools, and is compulsory from the age of seven. Secondary education is not compulsory and is free only at the State Schools. Because of the shortage of places, entry to these State Schools is competitive. Damascus University, founded in 1924, has nine faculties and a Higher Teachers' Training College.

The number of students has risen to over 60,000. There are also about 20,000 students at Aleppo University (founded 1961), over 10,000 at Tishrin University, Latakia (founded 1975) and 6,000 at Ba'ath University, Homs. Approximately 10 per cent of all students receive scholarships, and at the present time Palestinian refugees are admitted free. The rest pay fees.

Communications.—Although railway lines run from Damascus to both Beirut and Amman, train services go only as far as the border towns. A track has been opened connecting Homs with Damascus. A track links Homs, Hamah, Aleppo and Qamishliye to the Iraq frontier. Branch lines connect the ports of Tartous and Latakia to the system and another line runs from Aleppo down Euphrates valley to Deir ez Zor and thence north to Qamishliye, with a branch going to the Euphrates Dam. All the principal towns in the country are connected by roads which vary from modern dual carriageways to narrow country lanes. An internal air service operates between all major towns. The main International Airport is at Damascus and there are also flights to Eastern Europe, Turkey, Greece and Armenia from Aleppo.

Trade.—The principal imports are foodstuffs (fruit, vegetables, cereals, meat and dairy products, tea, coffee and sugar), mineral and petroleum products, yarn and textiles, iron and steel manufactures, machinery, chemicals, pharmaceuticals, fertilizers and timber. Exports include raw cotton, oil, cereals, fruit, phosphates, livestock and dairy products, other foodstuffs, textiles and raw wool.

Trade with U.K.

	1987	1988
Imports from U.K.	£34,053,000	£24,647,000
Exports to U.K.	24,937,000	36,100,000

CAPITAL.—Damascus (population estimated) 1,168,000). Other important towns are Aleppo, Homs and Hama, and the principal port is ΨLatakia.

CURRENCY.—Syrian pound (S£) of 100 piastres.

FLAG.—Red over white over black horizontal bands, with two green stars on central white band.

NATIONAL DAY.—April 17.

BRITISH INTERESTS SECTION
Quartier Malki, 11 rue Mohammad Kurd Ali, Imm. Kotob, Damascus.
[Damascus 712561]

Following the break in diplomatic relations with Syria in October 1986, Australia has been representing British interests in Syria.

THAILAND
(Prathes Thai)

King, His Majesty Bhumibol Adulyadej, *born* 1927; *succeeded his brother*, June 9, 1946; *married* Princess Sirikit Kitiyakara, April 28, 1950; *crowned* May 5, 1950; *and has issue*, Princess Ubolratana, *born*, April 6, 1951; Crown Prince Vajiralongkorn, *born*, July 28, 1952; Princess Sirindhorn, *born*, April 2, 1955; Princess Chulabhorn *born*, July 4, 1957.

CABINET
(as at Jan. 1989)

Prime Minister and Minister of Defence, Gen. Chatichai Choonhavan (*CT*).

Deputy P.M.s, Pong Sarasin (*SAP*); Bhichai Rattakul (*Democrat*); Gen. Thienchai Sirisamphan (*R*).

Ministers attached to the Prime Minister's Office, Meechai Ruchupan (*appointed*); Boon-eua Prasertsuwan (*CT*); Korn Tapparangsee (*CT*); Anuwat Wattanapongsiri (*CT*); Chaisiri

Ruangkanchanases (*SAP*); Mrs. Supatra Masdit (*Democrat*); Col. Phol Roengprasertvit (*UDP*); Pol. Capt. Chalerm Yubamrung (*MC*).

Agriculture, Lt.-Col. Sanan Khachornprasart (*Democrat*).

Commerce, Dr. Subin Pinkhayan (*SAP*).

Communications, Montri Pongpanich (*SAP*).

Education, Gen. Mana Rattanakoses (*R*).

Finance, Pramual Sabbavasu (*CT*).

Foreign Affairs, Siddhi Savetsila (*SAP*).

Industry, Banharn Silpa-archa (*CT*).

Interior, Maj.-Gen. Pramarn Adireksarn (*CT*).

Justice, Lt.-Gen. Chamras Mangkalarat (*CT*).

Public Health, Chuan Leekpai (*Democrat*).

Science, Technology and Energy, Prachuab Chaiyasarn (*Democrat*).

University Affairs, Tavich Klinprathum.

(*CT*—Chart Thai; *MC*—Muan Chon; *R*—Rassadorn Party; *SAP*—Social Action Party; *UDP*—United Democracy Party.)

ROYAL THAI EMBASSY IN LONDON
29–30 Queen's Gate, SW7 5JB
[01–589 0173]

Ambassador Extraordinary and Plenipotentiary, His Excellency Mr. Sudhee Prasasvinitchai (1986).

Area and Population.—The Kingdom of Thailand, formerly known as Siam, has an area of 198,457 sq. miles (514,000 sq. km.), with a population (estimated 1988) of 54,536,000. The population growth rate averages 2·4 per cent. per year. It has a common boundary with Malaysia in the south, is bounded on the west by Burma and on the north-east and east by Laos and Kampuchea. Although there is no common boundary between Thailand and China, the Chinese province of Yunnan is separated from the Thai northern border only by a narrow stretch of Burmese and Laotian territory.

Thailand is divided geographically into four regions, namely: central, north eastern, northern and southern. The capital, Bangkok, is situated in the south of the central plain area. To the north-east there is a plateau area and to the north-west mountains. The south of Thailand consists of a narrow mountainous peninsula. The principal rivers are the Chao Phraya in the central plains, and the Mekong on the northern and north-eastern borders.

Language and Religion.—Thai is basically a monosyllabic, tonal language, a branch of the Indo-Chinese linguistic family, but its vocabulary especially has been strongly influenced by Sanskrit and Pali. It is written in an alphabetic script derived from ancient Indian scripts. The principal religion is Buddhism. In 1985 94·95 per cent. of the population were Buddhists, 3·91 per cent Muslims, 0·53 per cent Christians and 0·61 per cent other religions.

Government.—Thailand became a Constitutional Monarchy in 1932. The Constitution promulgated in December 1978 provides for a National Assembly consisting of a Senate appointed by the King and a House of Representatives elected by universal adult suffrage. There are 260 Senate seats and 347 House seats. Each senator is appointed for six years and each M.P. for four years.

A General Election was held on July 24, 1988, following the dissolution of the House after two years. The results were: Chart Thai, 87; Social Action, 54; Democrat, 48; Ruam Thai, 35; Prachakorn Thai, 31; Rassadorn, 21; Prachachon, 19; Puangchon Chao Thai, 17; Palang Dharma, 14; Community Action, 9; Progressive, 8; Muan Chon, 5; United Democratic, 5; Liberal, 3; Others, 1.

Education.—Primary education is compulsory and free and secondary education in Government Schools is free. In 1986 there were 37,616 schools and training colleges, with a total of 10,720,780 pupils and 560,787 teachers. Private universities and colleges are playing an increasing role in higher education. In 1984 the Government agreed to upgrade four private colleges to universities. Out of 43 universities and other similar higher institutes of learning, 21 are private and attended by some 53,708 students. In 1986 their total enrolment was 171,438 students.

Agriculture and Industry.—The agricultural sector provides just under half the national income and employs 67·5 per cent of the labour force, which in 1985 was estimated at 26·8 million. Rice remains the most important crop, accounting for 60 per cent of the area planted. After rice the main crops are sugar, maize, rubber, tobacco, kenaf and jute. In recent years the production of livestock and poultry, especially pigs and chickens for export, has gained importance. There is a large fishing industry with more than 20,000 vessels registered. Fish farming is popular in many inland areas. A ban on hardwood export has resulted in the decline of the forestry industry.

The discovery of onshore oil and offshore gas in the late 1970s ushered in a new economic era. Crude production which began in 1983 stood at around 20,000 barrels per day in mid-1985, or about 10 per cent of the country's need. At the same time gas and condensate output stood at over 350 million cubic feet per day. It was estimated that by the end of 1985 indigenous oil and gas supplies should account for about half of Thailand's petroleum demand. The predicted surplus of natural gas has led the Government to designate an area on the east coast as the future centre of the petrochemical industry. Another energy resource becoming more important is lignite which is found mainly in the north and is being used increasingly for electricity production.

Mineral resources are mainly tin, tungsten, lead, antimony and iron. Among these, tin is the most important, with exports totalling 18,455 tons in 1984. In addition, about 60,000 tons of zinc ingots a year are expected to be produced by a zinc refinery which was opened in early 1984.

Industry is divided into two main categories: service and manufacturing. Since 1982 tourism has replaced rice as the country's top foreign exchange earner. There were 3,482,958 overseas visitors in 1987, generating an estimated 45,000 million baht for the country. The banking system is large and contributes much to the economy, especially employment. There are over 1,800 bank branches in the country employing some 72,000 workers.

Since 1960 the Government has actively promoted industrial investments by means of tax relief and other incentives to local and foreign investors; in 1985, 74·6 per cent of this investment was in Thai projects. Most of the industries established under this scheme in early years were import-substituting. However, there has been an increasing shift to export-oriented industries, taking advantages of low-wage labour and available domestic resources. Manufacturing now accounts for about 21·8 per cent of the national income. Crops contribute 12·1 per cent of G.D.P.

Communications.—The importance of rivers and canals as the traditional mode of transportation has been replaced by highways and roads. The existing road and highway network, totalling 34,701 kilometres in 1984, reaches all parts of the country. Most of the smaller towns and bigger villages are now served by paved roads.

Navigable waterways have a length of about 1,100 km. in the dry season and 1,600 km. in the wet season. About 3,825 km of State-owned railways were open to traffic in 1984. Main lines run from Bangkok to Aranya Prathet on the Kampuchean border via Korat to Ubon and to Nong Khai, the ferry terminal on the River Mekong opposite Vientiane, capital of

Laos; to Chiang Mai and to Hat Yai, whence lines go down the eastern and western sides of the Malay peninsula, via Sungei Galok and Penang respectively, to Singapore. A new line to Sattahip on the east coast is being constructed.

Bangkok is an important international air centre and has direct flights to most of the world's major cities. The airports at Chiang Mai, Phuket and Hat Yai also receive international flights. Most major provincial towns have airports. Thai International and Thai Airways merged in April 1988. Now named THAI, the airline is state-owned.

Thailand has an extensive network of telecommunications services, and the telephone service though still poor is being improved. All major cities and towns are linked by direct long-distance calls. Thailand has two mobile telephone networks, AMPS (urban), and NMT (rural) presently covering only the central area but expanding rapidly.

There are two important ports in the country. Bangkok, which is a river port, can serve vessels up to 27 ft. draught. The deep-sea port at Sattahip caters for larger vessels. Phuket and Songkhla deep water ports have already been completed and are the first to be managed privately under a ten-year concession. Construction of Laem Chabang deep water port started in 1988.

TRADE

Thailand's main exports are rice, tapioca and tapioca products, garments, rubber, integrated circuit boards, precious stones, pearls and other ornaments, maize, canned sea food, fabrics, sugar and tin. Main imports are crude oil, chemicals and pharmaceuticals, electrical and non-electrical machinery and spare parts, industrial machinery, iron and steel, diesel oil and other fuel oil, vehicle and transport equipment.

	1986	1987p
	Baht	
Total imports	245·9m	337·0m
Total exports	231·5m	291·0m

p = preliminary.

Trade with U.K.

	1987	1988
Imports from U.K.	£206,571,000	£279,717,000
Exports to U.K.	239,430,000	321,241,000

CAPITAL.—ΨBangkok (population 5,400,000 (1985)); at the mouth of the River Chao Phraya. Other centres are Chiang Mai, Phitsanuloke, Chon Buri, Korat, Khon Kaen, Surat Thani, Hat Yai and ΨPhuket but none approaches Bangkok in size or importance.

CURRENCY.—Baht of 100 satang.

FLAG.—Five horizontal bands, red, white, dark blue, white, red (the blue band twice the width of the others).

NATIONAL ANTHEM.—"Sanrasern Pra Barami".

NATIONAL DAY.—December 5 (The King's Birthday).

BRITISH EMBASSY
Wireless Road, Bangkok, 10500
[Bangkok 253 0191]

Ambassador Extraordinary and Plenipotentiary, His Excellency Michael Ramsay Melhuish, C.M.G. (1985).

British Council Representative, E. C. Pugh, 428 Rama 1 Road, Siam Square, Bangkok 10500.

BRITISH CHAMBER OF COMMERCE,
302 Silom Road, Bangkok 10500

TOGO
(République Togolaise)

President and Minister of Defence, Gen. Gnassingbé Eyadéma, *born* 1937, *assumed office*, April 14, 1967; *re-elected for seven-year term*, Dec. 23, 1986.

(as at June 30, 1989)

Justice and Interior, Gen. Yao Mawulikplimi Amegi.
Planning and Mines, Barry Moussa Barque.
Rural Development, Koffi Walla.
Minister Delegate to the Presidency (Information), Gbegnon Amegboh.
Equipment, Posts and Telecommunications, Nassirou Ayeva.
National Education and Scientific Research, Tchaa-Kozah Tchalim.
Public Health, Social and Women's Affairs, Aissah Agbetra.
Youth, Sports and Culture, Mensah Agbeyomé Kodjo.
Foreign Affairs and Co-operation, Yaovi Adodo.
Industry and State Enterprises, Koffi Djondo.
Technical Instruction and Professional Training, Koffi Edoh.
Economy and Finance, Komla Alipui.
Labour and Civil Service, Bitokotipou Yagninim.

EMBASSY OF TOGO
30 Sloane Street, SW1.
[01–235 0147/9]

Ambassador Extraordinary and Plenipotentiary, His Excellency Assiongbon Agbenou (1986).
Counsellor and chargé d'affaires a.i., Djibril Akanga.

The Republic is situated in West Africa between 0°–2° W. and 6°–11° N., with a coastline only 35 miles long on the Gulf of Guinea, and extends northward inland for 350 miles. It is flanked on the west by Ghana, on the north by Burkina Faso and in the east by Benin. It has an area of 21,925 sq. miles (56,785 sq. km.), and a population (estimate, 1985) of 3,030,000, including people of several African races. The official language is French.

The first President of Togo, Sylvanus Olympio, assassinated on January 13, 1963, was succeeded by Nicolas Grunitzky, who was himself overthrown by an army coup d'état on January 13, 1967. On April 14, 1967, the Commander-in-Chief of the Togolese army, Lt. Colonel (later promoted General) Eyadéma named himself President.

Production and Trade.—Although the economy of Togo remains largely agricultural, exports of phosphates have superseded agricultural products as the main source of export earnings. Other exports include palm kernels, copra and manioc. The production of phosphates entirely for export was taken over completely by the government in February 1974.

Trade with U.K.

	1987	1988
Imports from U.K.	£15,431,000	£22,231,000
Exports to U.K.	2,579,000	690,000

CAPITAL.—ΨLomé, population (1983), 366,476.

CURRENCY.—Franc C.F.A. of 100 centimes.

FLAG.—Five alternating green and yellow horizontal stripes; a quarter in red at top next staff bearing a white star.

NATIONAL DAY.—January 13 (National Liberation Day).

BRITISH EMBASSY
British Ambassador, (resides at *Accra, Ghana*).

TUNISIA
(Al-Djoumhouria Attunusia)

President, Zine el-Abidine Ben Ali *took office* Nov. 7, 1987, *re-elected* April 2, 1989.

CABINET
(as at June 30, 1989)

Prime Minister, Hedi Baccouche.
Justice, Hamed Karoui.
Foreign Affairs, Abdelhamid Escheikh.
Secretary General of the Presidency, Mohamed el Jeri.
National Defence, Abdallah Kallel.
Interior, Chedli Neffati.
Governor of the Central Bank, Ismail Khelil.
Planning and Finance, Mohammed Ghannouchi.
National Economy, Moncef Belaid.
Agriculture, Nouri Zorgati.
Equipment and Housing, Ahmed Friaa.
Transport, Ahmed Smaoui.
Tourism and Handicrafts, Mohamed Jegham.
Communications, Sadok Rabah.
Education, Higher Education and Scientific Research, Mohamed Charfi.
Culture and Information, Habib Boulares.
Public Health, Daly Jazi.
Social Affairs, Moncer Rouissi.
Youth and Childhood, Hammouda Ben Slama.
Secretary General for the Government, Taoufik Cheikhrouhou.

TUNISIAN EMBASSY
29 Prince's Gate, SW7 1QG
[01–584 8117]

Ambassador Extraordinary and Plenipotentiary, His Excellency Abdelwaheb Abdallah (1988).

Area and Population.—Tunisia lies between Algeria and Libya and extends southwards to the Sahara Desert, with a total area of 63,170 sq. miles (163,610 sq. km.), and an estimated population in 1985 of 7,205,106.

Government.—A French Protectorate from 1881 to 1956, Tunisia became an independent sovereign State with the signing on March 20, 1956, of an agreement whereby France recognized Tunisia's independence and right to conduct her own foreign policy and to form a Tunisian Army.

Following a first general election held on March 25, 1956, a Constituent Assembly met for the first time on April 8. On July 25, 1957, the Constituent Assembly deposed the Bey, abolished the monarchy and elected M. Bourguiba first President of the Republic. On June 1, 1959, the Constitution was promulgated and on December 7, 1959, the National Assembly held its first session. In March 1975 the National Assembly proclaimed M. Bourguiba as President for life. On Nov. 7, 1987 M. Bourguiba was deposed and succeeded by President Zine el-Abidine Ben Ali. Presidential and legislative elections were held in April 1989. The RCD (Rassemblement Constitutionnel Democratique) won all 141 seats in the National Assembly. Seven political parties contested the election. Pres. Ben Ali was re-elected with 99 per cent of the vote.

The country is divided into 22 regions (*gouvernorats*) each administered by a Governor.

Production, Trade, etc.—The valleys of the northern region support large flocks and herds, and contain rich agricultural areas, in which wheat, barley, and oats are grown. The vine and olive are extensively cultivated.

The chief exports are crude oil, phosphates, olive oil, finished textiles, and fruit. The chief imports are machinery and equipment, foodstuffs, petroleum products, and textiles. Some oil has been discovered and production reached an annual rate of 5 million tons in 1987. Gas has also been discovered off the east coast but exploitation is not viable at present. Tourists numbered almost 1·8 million in 1987.

	1986	1987
Total Imports	TD2,294,400	TD2,509,100
Total Exports	1,403,600	1,770,700

France remains the main trading partner, supplying 27·6 per cent of the country's imports and purchasing 22·9 per cent of Tunisia's exports.

Trade with U.K.

	1987	1988
Imports from U.K.	£24,942,830	£30,780,000
Exports to U.K.	14,713,628	36,062,000

Tunisia became an associate member of the E.C. early in 1969, and signed a new agreement with the E.C. in 1976. In 1977 the introduction of import quota measures by the E.C. on some textile goods resulted in a reduction of growth in this important sector of the Tunisian market. The quotas for some textile products was renegotiated and increased in 1982.

CAPITAL.—Ψ Tunis, connected by canal with La Goulette on the coast, had a population (1984) of 1,394,749. The ruins of ancient Carthage lie a few miles from the city. Other towns of importance are: Ψ Sfax (577,992); Ψ Sousse (322,491); Ψ Bizerta (394,670); Kairouan; Gabes; Menzel Bourguiba.

CURRENCY.—Tunisian dinar of 1,000 millimes.

FLAG.—Red crescent and star in a white orb, all on a red ground.

NATIONAL ANTHEM.—"Himat Al Hima".

NATIONAL DAY.—March 20.

BRITISH EMBASSY
Place de la Victoire, Tunis
[Tunis 245100]

Ambassador Extraordinary and Plenipotentiary and Consul-General, His Excellency Stephen Peter Day, C.M.G. (1987).
First Secretary, S. P. Collis (*Head of Chancery*).
Second Secretary, C. Innes-Hopkins (*Commercial and Consul*).
British Council Representative, D. Handforth.
There is a British Council Library in *Tunis*.

TURKEY
(Türkiye Cumhuriyeti)

President, Gen. Kenan Evren, *assumed power*, Sept. 12, 1980; *elected for 7-year term*, Nov. 1982.

GOVERNMENT
(as at May 31, 1989)

Prime Minister, Turgut Özal.
Deputy P.M., Ali Bozer.
Ministers of State, Güneş Taner; Isin Celebi; Ismet Özaslan; Saffet Sert; Ercüment Konukman; Ilhan Askin; Mehmet Yazar; Kamran Inan; Cemil Cicek.
Justice, Oltan Sungurlu.
Defence, Safa Giray.
Interior, Abdulkadir Aksu.
Foreign, Mesut Yilmaz.
Finance and Customs, Ekrem Pakdemirli.
Education, Avni Akyol.
Public Works and Housing, Cengiz Altinkaya.
Health, Halil Sivgin.
Transport, Cengiz Tuncer.
Agriculture, Lütfullah Kayalar.
Labour and Social Security, Imren Aykut.
Industry and Commerce, Sükrü Yürür.
Energy and Natural Resources, Fahrettin Kurt.
Tourism, Ilhan Aküzüm.
Culture, Namik Kemal Zeybek.

TURKISH EMBASSY
43 Belgrave Square, SW1X 8PA
[01–235 5252]

Ambassador Extraordinary and Plenipotentiary, His Excellency Nurver Nures (1989).

Area and Population.—People of Turkic stock are to be found scattered throughout a wide belt extending from China through the Soviet Union, Afghanistan and Iran to the present day Turkish State, and into Bulgaria.

Turkey itself extends from Edirne (Adrianople) to Transcaucasia and Iran, and from the Black Sea to the Mediterranean, Syria and Iraq. Total population at the Census of 1985 was 51,428,514, of which 6,942,780 were in Europe and 44,485,734 in Asia.

Turkey in Europe consists of Eastern Thrace, including the cities of Istanbul and Edirne, and is separated from Asia by the Bosphorus at Istanbul and by the Dardanelles—about 40 miles in length with a width varying from 1 to 4 miles—the political neighbours being Greece and Bulgaria on the west.

Turkey in Asia comprises the whole of Asia Minor or Anatolia and extends from the Aegean Sea to the western boundaries of Georgia, Soviet Armenia and Iran, and from the Black Sea to the Mediterranean and the northern boundaries of Syria and Iraq.

Government.—On October 29, 1923, the National Assembly declared Turkey a Republic and elected Gazi Mustafa Kemal (later known as Kemal Ataturk) President. In 1945 a multi-party system was introduced but in 1960 the government was overthrown by the Turkish Armed Forces which ruled through the Committee of National Union, a body of military officers. A new constitution was adopted in July 1961 and in October, after a general election, a civilian government took office. Civilian governments remained in power until Sept. 1980 when mounting problems with the economy and terrorism led the military to assume legislative powers. A civilian technocratic government was appointed later that month.

A new Constitution, extending the powers of the President, was approved by a referendum on Nov. 7, 1982. It provided for the separation of powers between the legislature, executive and judiciary, and the holding of free elections to the unicameral Grand National Assembly, which has 400 members elected every five years. Following the General Election on Nov. 6, 1983 the military leadership handed over power to a newly elected civilian government.

Party representation at end May 1989 was: Motherland Party, 289; Social Democratic Populist Party, 99; Correct Way Party, 56; Independent, 1; Vacant, 5.

Turkey is divided for administrative purposes into 67 *il* with subdivisions into *kaza* and *nahiye*. Each *il* has a governor (*vali*) and elective council.

Religion and Education.—On April 10, 1928, the Grand National Assembly passed a law in virtue of which Islam ceased to be the State religion of the Republic. However, 98·99 per cent of the population are Muslims. The main religious minorities, which are concentrated in Istanbul and on the Syrian frontier, are: Greek Orthodox, 10,000; Armenians, 42,000; Syriani Christians, 42,000; Others, 6,000. (Total Christians, 100,000); Jewish, 44,000. Education is free, secular and compulsory at primary level. There are elementary, secondary and vocational schools.

There are 27 universities in Turkey, including four in Istanbul, four in Ankara, two in Izmir, and one each in Erzurum and Trabzon.

The expenditure allocated to education in the 5th Five Year Plan (1985–89) was TL326,500,000, compared with TL76,000,000,000 in the 4th Five Year Plan (1979–83).

Language and Literature.—Until 1926, Turkish was written in Arabic script, but in that year the Roman alphabet was substituted for use in official correspondence and in 1928 for universal use, with Arabic numerals as used throughout Europe. Ancient Turkish literature aped the Arabic manner, but the revolution of 1908 led to the introduction of a native literature free from foreign influences and adapted to the understanding of the people. The leading Turkish newspapers are centred in Istanbul and Ankara, although most provincial towns have their own daily papers. There are foreign language papers in French, Greek, Armenian and English and numerous magazines and weeklies on various subjects, but few trade commercial publications.

Agricultural Production.—In 1985 agricultural production accounted for some 16 per cent of the gross domestic product at constant factor prices. About 50 per cent of the working population are in the rural sector. Estimated production figures for the principal crops in 1988 were ('000 tons):

Wheat	20,500	Olives	1,100
Barley	7,500	Tea (wet leaves)	756
Rice	263	Hazlenuts	362
Tobacco	212	Citrus fruit	1,445
Sugar beet	11,534	Grapes and figs	3,750

With the important exception of wheat, which is mostly grown on the arid Central Anatolian Plateau, most of the crops are grown on the fertile littoral. Tobacco, sultana and fig cultivation is centred around Izmir, where substantial quantities of cotton are also grown. The main cotton area is in the Cukurova Plain around Adana. The forests which lie between the littoral plain and the Anatolian Plateau, contain beech, pine, oak, elm, chestnut, lime, plane, alder, box, poplar and maple. During recent years the Government has attempted, so far not altogether successfully, to combat the depredations of peasant and goat which threaten to destroy the existing forests within the next 25 years.

Industry.—After agriculture, Turkey's second most important industry is based on her considerable mineral wealth which is, however, as yet comparatively unexploited. The main export minerals are chromite and boron. Production in 1988 was (tons):

Coal	6,688,000
Lignite	38,425,000
Crude petroleum	2,564,000
Crude iron	4,462,000
Boron minerals	2,032,000

The progress made in the manufacture of sugar, cotton, woollen and silk textiles, and cement, has been such that the bulk of the country's requirements can now be produced locally, while other industries contributing substantially to local needs include vehicle assembly, paper, glass and glassware, iron and steel, leather and leather goods, sulphur refining, canning and rubber goods, soaps and cosmetics, pharmaceutical products, prepared foodstuffs and a host of minor industries.

In common with other developing countries, Turkey's economy was adversely affected by the steep rises in oil prices from 1973 onwards. This led to a succession of economic crises and high inflation culminating in Jan. 1980 in the introduction of an economic stability programme. Exports have since risen dramatically, topping $11,846 million in 1988. Inflation, however, remains high (43 per cent in 1985) and as a result investment is low. Turkey's current account deficit has been reduced to about $1,503 million. G.N.P. growth for 1989 was about 3·4 per cent and unemployment remains high.

COMMUNICATIONS

Railways.—The complete network became the property of the State Railways Administration in

1948. The total length of lines in operation is 8,193 kilometres.

Roads.—At the end of 1985 there were 59,300 km. of national roads (55,296 of which were macadamized). The estimated number of vehicles in 1984 was 2,159,417.

The Bosporus is spanned by a single bridge, opened in 1973. Work on a second bridge was completed in 1988, and plans are being drawn up for a third fixed link between the two continents.

Shipping.—In August 1980 there were 343 merchant ships over 300 gross tons, 79 passenger ships and 73 tankers, giving a total draft weight of 1,545,062 tons.

Civil Aviation.—The State airlines (T.H.Y.) operate all internal services and have services to Europe and the Middle East. Most of the leading European airlines, including British Airways, operate services to Istanbul and some also to Ankara.

FINANCE

	1988
Estimated Expenditure	TL20,881·9m
Estimated Revenue	18,425·5m

TRADE

	1987	1988
Total imports ...	US$14,157·8m	US$14,339·7m
Total exports ...	10,190·0m	11,662·1m

Most imports are no longer subject to licence. The main imports are machinery, crude oil and petroleum products, iron and steel, vehicles, medicines and dyes, chemicals, fertilizers and electrical appliances. Agricultural commodities (cotton, tobacco, fruits, nuts, livestock) represent 47 per cent of total exports. Other exports are minerals, textiles, glass and cement.

Trade with U.K.

	1987	1988
Imports from U.K.	£513,479,000	£477,539,000
Exports to U.K.	579,366,000	509,636,000

CAPITAL.—Ankara (Angora), an inland town of Asia Minor, about 275 miles E.S.E. of Istanbul, with a population (1980) of 3,196,460. Ankara (or Ancyra) was the capital of the Roman Province of *Galatia Prima*, and a marble temple (now in ruins), dedicated to Augustus, contains the *Monumentum* (*Marmor*) *Ancyranum*, inscribed with a record of the reign of Augustus Caesar. Ψ Istanbul (4,870,747), the former capital, was the Roman city of Byzantium. It was selected by Constantine the Great as the capital of the Roman Empire about A.D. 328 and renamed Constantinople. Istanbul contains the celebrated church of St. Sophia, which, after becoming a mosque, was made a museum in 1934; it also contains Topkapi, former Palace of the Ottoman Sultans, which is also a museum. Other cities are Ψ Izmir (1,968,614); Adana (1,467,346); Bursa (1,161,553); Gaziantep (387,093); and Eskişehir (543,733).

CURRENCY.—Turkish lira (TL) of 100 kurus.

FLAG.—Red, with white crescent and star.

NATIONAL ANTHEM.—"Istikâl Marşi" (The Independence March).

NATIONAL DAY.—October 29 (Republic Day).

BRITISH EMBASSY
Sehit Ersan Caddesi 46/A, Cankaya, Ankara
[Ankara 274310/4]

Ambassador Extraordinary and Plenipotentiary, His Excellency Sir Timothy Lewis Achilles Daunt, K.C.M.G. (1986).

Counsellor, C. T. Humfrey.

First Secretaries, P. J. Westmacott (*Head of Chancery*); R. H. J. Ashton (*Chancery*); L. E. Walker

L.V.O., O.B.E. (*Commercial*); C. P. M. Harrison (*Cultural Affairs*); A. J. Mounford (*Cultural Affairs*); Ms. R. L. Varley (*Cultural Affairs*); J. M. Brown (*Administration*).

Defence and Military Attaché, Brig. S. T. Anderson, O.B.E., M.C.

Naval and Air Attaché, Cmdr. B. Jones, O.B.E.

BRITISH CONSULAR OFFICES

There is a British Consulate-General at *Istanbul*, a Vice-Consulate at *Izmir* and an Hon. British Consulate at *Iskenderun*.

British Council Representative, E. Marsden, Kirklangic Sokak 9, Gazi Osman Pasa, Ankara 06700.—There is also a centre and library at *Istanbul* and a library at *Ankara*.

BRITISH CHAMBER OF COMMERCE OF TURKEY INC., Mesrutiyet Caddessi No. 34, Tepebaşi Beyoğlu, Istanbul (Postal Address, P.O. Box 190 Karaköy, Istanbul).

UNION OF SOVIET SOCIALIST REPUBLICS
(Soyuz Sovetskikh Sotsialisticheskikh Respublik)

THE COMMUNIST PARTY OF THE SOVIET UNION
(K.P.S.S. = Kommunisticheskaya Partiya Sovetskogo Soyuza)

Politbureau, V. M. Chebrikov; M. S. Gorbachev; E. K. Ligachev; V. A. Medvedev; V. P. Nikonov; N. I. Ryzhkov; V. V. Shcherbitsky; E. A. Shevardnadze; N. N. Slyunkov; V. I. Vorotnikov; A. N. Yakovlev; L. N. Zaikov (*full members*); A. P. Biryukova; A. I. Lukyanov; Yu. D. Maslyukov; G. P. Razumovsky; Yu. F. Soloviev; N. V. Talyzin; A. I. Vlasov; D. T. Yazov (*candidate members*).

Secretariat, Mikhail Sergevich Gorbachev (*General Secretary since* March 11, 1985); O. D. Baklanov; V. M. Chebrikov; E. K. Ligachev; V. A. Medvedev; V. P. Nikonov; G. P. Razumovsky; N. N. Slyunkov; A. N. Yakovlev; L. N. Zaikov.

Committee of Party Control, B. K. Pugo (*Chairman*).

Komsomol (*Young Communist League*) V. I. Mironenko (*First Secretary*).

STATE STRUCTURE OF THE U.S.S.R.

The Supreme Soviet of the U.S.S.R.

Chairman (= *President of the U.S.S.R.*), M. S. Gorbachev, *since* May 25, 1989.

First Deputy Chairman, A. I. Lukyanov.

Chairman of the Council of the Union, E. M. Primakov.

Chairman of the Council of Nationalities, R. Nishanov.

The Council of Ministers of the U.S.S.R. (The Government)

Chairman, N. I. Ryzhkov.

FIRST DEPUTY CHAIRMEN OF THE COUNCIL OF MINISTERS

Director of Gosplan, Yu. D. Maslyukov.

General Responsibilities, L. A. Voronin.

DEPUTY CHAIRMEN OF THE COUNCIL OF MINISTERS

Head, Economic Reform Commission, L. I. Abalkin.

Head, Commission for Military Industrial Questions, I. S. Belousov.

Head, Buro for Social Development, A. P. Biryukova.

Head, Emergency Commission, V. K. Doguzhiev.

Head, the Buro for the Chemical-Timber Complex, V. K. Gusev.

Chairman, State Committee for Science and Technology, N. P. Laverov.
Chairman, State Committee for Material and Technical Supplies, P. I. Mostovoi.
Head, Buro for the Fuel and Energy Complex, L. D. Ryabev.
Head, Buro for the Machine Building Complex, I. S. Silaev.

ALL-UNION MINISTRIES

Aviation Industry, A. S. Systsov.
Automobile and Agricultural Machine Building, N. A. Pugin.
Atomic Energy and Industry, V. F. Konovalov.
External Economic Relations, K. F. Katushev.
Water Management Construction, (vacant).
Geology, G. A. Gabrielyants.
Civil Aviation, A. N. Volkov.
Medical Industry, V. A. Bykov.
Metallurgy, S. V. Kolpakov.
Maritime Fleet, Yu. M. Volmer.
Oil and Gas Industry, (vacant).
Defence Industry, B. M. Belousov.
Defence, D. T. Yazov.
General Machine Building, O. N. Shishkin.
Railways, (vacant).
Radio Industry, V. I. Shimko.
Fish Industry, N. I. Kotlyar.
Tool Building and Instrument Industry, N. A. Panichev.
Oil and Gas Construction, V. G. Chirskov.
Ship Building Industry, I. V. Koksanov.
Transport Construction, V. A. Brezhnev.
Heavy Machine Building, V. M. Velichko.
Coal Industry, M. I. Shchadov.
Chemical and Oil Refining Industry, N. V. Lemayev.
Electronics Industry, V. G. Kolesnikov.
Electrotechnical Industry and Equipment Building, O. G. Anfimov.

UNION REPUBLICAN MINISTRIES

Internal Affairs, B. V. Bakatin.
Health, E. I. Chazov.
Foreign Affairs, E. A. Shevardnadze.
Culture, (vacant).
Timber Industry, (vacant).
Assembly and Special Building Work, A. I. Mikhalchenko.
Communications, E. K. Pervyshin.
Trade, K. Z. Tekekh.
Finance, V. S. Pavlov.
Energy and Electrification, Yu. K. Semenov.
Justice, V. F. Yakovlev.

ALL-UNION STATE COMMITTEES

Science and Technology, N. P. Laverov.
Quality Control and Standards, V. V. Sychev.
Computer Technology and Information, B. L. Tolstykh.
Hydrometeorology, Yu. A. Izrael.

UNION REPUBLICAN STATE COMMITTEES

State Planning Committee (Gosplan), Yu. D. Maslyukov.
Material Technical Supply, P. I. Mostovoi.
State Building Committee (Gosstroi), V. M. Serov.
Labour and Social Questions, V. I. Shcherbakov.
State Price Committee, (vacant).
Statistics, V. N. Kirichenko.
Education, G. A. Yagodin.
Television and Radio (Gostelradio), M. F. Nenashev.
Cinematography, A. I. Kamshalov.
The Press, N. I. Efimov.
Forestry, A. S. Isaev.
Nature Conservation (Goskompriroda), (vacant).
Physical Culture and Sport, (vacant).
State Security Committee, V. A. Kryuchkov.

OTHER POSTS

Chairman, U.S.S.R. State Bank (Gosbank), (vacant).
Council of Ministers' Business Manager, M. S. Shkabardnya.
Chairman of Committee for Light Industry attached to Gosplan, L. E. Davletova.
First Deputy Chairman of Gosplan, V. A. Durasov.

Ministries.—There are three groups of departmental ministries, with a total of 56 ministers—26 All Union Ministries, i.e. federal ministries, 11 Union Republican Ministries (co-ordinating ministries of individual republics) and 19 State Committees whose Chairmen rank as Ministers. The Prime Ministers of the 15 constituent republics belong to the Council ex officio.

EMBASSY OF THE U.S.S.R.
13 Kensington Palace Gardens, W8 4QX
[01–229 3628]

Ambassador Extraordinary and Plenipotentiary, His Excellency Leonid M. Zamyatin (1986).

AREA AND POPULATION

The total area of the U.S.S.R. is 8,649,461 sq. miles (22,402,000 sq. km.); the total population: (Jan. 1, 1989) 286,700,000. The proportion of women to men is 53 to 47. In 1987 the birth-rate was 19·0 and the mortality rate, 10·2. In 1987 66 per cent of the population lived in urban areas.

Area and population (January, 1987) of the constituent Republics of the U.S.S.R. with their date of incorporation into the Union:

Republic	Sq. miles	Population
Armenia (1936)	11,306	3,412,000
Azerbaijan (1936)	33,436	6,811,000
Belorussia (1922)	80,300	10,078,000
Estonia (1940)	17,413	1,556,000
Georgia (1936)	26,911	5,266,000
Kazakhstan (1936)	1,064,980*	16,244,000
Kirghizia (1936)	76,642	4,143,000
Latvia (1940)	24,695	2,647,000
Lithuania (1940)	26,173	3,641,000
Moldavia (1940)	13,912	4,185,000
R.S.F.S.R. (1922)	6,593,391	145,300,000
Tadjikistan (1929)	54,019	4,807,000
Turkmenistan (1924)	188,417	3,361,000
Ukraine (1922)	252,046	51,200,000
Uzbekistan (1924)	157,181*	19,026,000

* (Adjusted to include transfer of 3 border regions—888 sq. miles and 162,000 inhabitants—by Uzbek S.S.R., Kazakh S.S.R. and U.S.S.R. decrees of May–June 1971.)

Before the outbreak of the Second World War (1941–45 in U.S.S.R.), the U.S.S.R. consisted of 11 Republics. In August 1940, the major part of *Bessarabia* ceded by Romania in June was joined to the Moldavian A.S.S.R. to form a Moldavian S.S.R. The same month, the three independent Baltic States, *Estonia, Latvia* and *Lithuania,* were forcibly incorporated into the Soviet Union. In October, 1944, *Tannu-Tuva,* until the Second World War a nominally independent state lying to the north-west of Outer Mongolia, became the autonomous province of *Tuva* and, in 1961, the Autonomous Republic of Tuva, within the R.S.F.S.R.

In July, 1956, the Karelo-Finnish Republic (formed in 1940 from the Karelian A.S.S.R. and land ceded by Finland) reverted to the status of an Autonomous *(Karelian)* Republic within the R.S.F.S.R.

Main Nationalities
(1979 Census)

The most numerous national groups of U.S.S.R. are: Russian, 137 m. and Ukrainian, 42 m. There are between 6 and 12 million Kazakhs, Tatars,

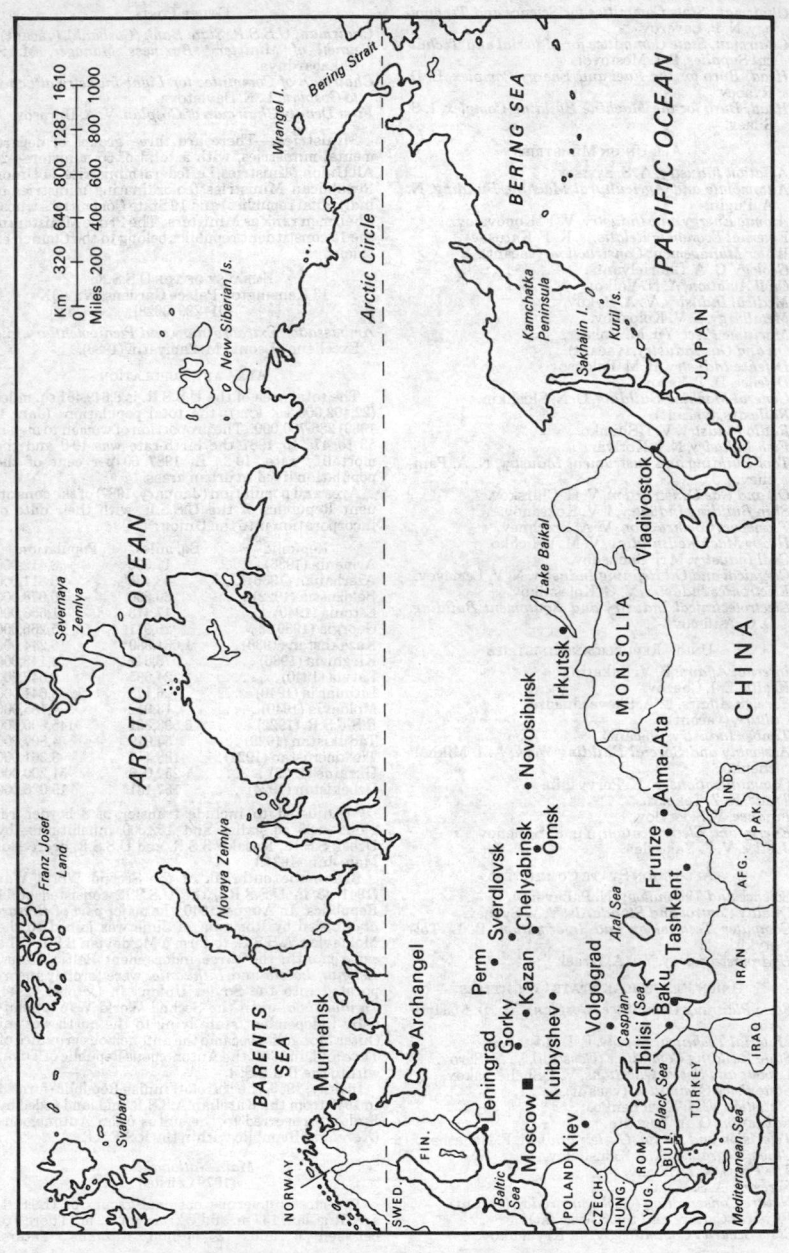

Belorussians, and Uzbeks respectively. Azerbaidjani, Armenians and Georgians number between 3·5 and 5·5 million each group. There are some 1·9 to 2·9 million Lithuanians, Kirghizians, Turkmens, Germans, Moldavians and Tadjiks. In each of the following nationality groups the population numbers between 1·02 and 1·8 millions: Chuvashes, Latvians, Poles, Mordovians, Bashkirs, Estonians, Dagestanis and Jews.

The 1979 census revealed a marked difference between the growth rates of individual nationalities: while the Slav nations showed an annual increase of under one per cent, certain Central Asian and Caucasian (mostly Muslim) nations recorded an annual net growth of 2·5 to 3·5 per cent.

Chronological System.—On February 14, 1918, the Soviet Government adopted the Gregorian (Western) Calendar. In 1981 Summer Time was introduced between April 1 and October 1, but there are some geographical anomalies in its application. The country is divided into 10 time zones (Moscow time is 3 hours ahead of G.M.T.).

LANGUAGE, LITERATURE AND ARTS

Language and Literature.—Russian is a branch of the Slavonic family of languages which is divided into the following groups: *Eastern*, including Russian, Ukrainian and White Russian; *Western*, including Polish, Czech, Slovak and Sorbish (or Lusatian Wendish); and *Southern*, including Serbo-Croat, Slovene, Macedonian and Bulgarian. The Western group and part of the Southern group are written in the Latin alphabet, the others in the Cyrillic, said to have been instituted by SS. Cyril and Methodius in the ninth century, and largely based on the Greek alphabet. Before the Westernization of Russia under Peter the Great (1682–1725), Russian literature consisted mainly of folk ballads (*byliny*), epic songs, chronicles and works of moral theology. The eighteenth and particularly the nineteenth centuries saw a brilliant development of Russian poetry and fiction. Romantic poetry reached its zenith with Alexander Pushkin (1799–1837) and Mikhail Lermontov (1814–1841). The 20th century produced great poets like Alexander Blok (1880–1921), the 1958 Nobel Prize laureate Boris Pasternak (1890–1960), Vladimir Mayakovsky (1893–1930) and Anna Akhmatova (1888–1966). Realistic fiction is associated with the names of Nikolai Gogol (1809–1852), Ivan Turgenev (1818–1883), Fedor Dostoyevsky (1821–1881) and Leo Tolstoy (1828–1910), and later with Anton Chekhov (1860–1904), Maxim Gorky (1868–1936), Ivan Bunin (1870–1953) and Alexander Solzhenitsyn (b. 1918).

Great names in music include Glinka (1804–1857), Borodin (1833–87), Mussorgsky (1839–1881), Rimsky-Korsakov (1844–1908), Rubinstein (1829–1894), Tchaikovsky (1840–1893), Rakhmaninov (1873–1943), Skriabin (1872–1915), Prokofiev (1891–1953), Stravinsky (1882–1971) and Shostakovich (1906–1975). Performers include Igor Oistrakh, M. Rostropovich, S. Richter and the famous conductor G. Rozhdestvensky.

THE CONSTITUTION

On October 7, 1977 a new Constitution was adopted to replace the 1936 Constitution. Amendments to the 1977 Constitution were adopted on Dec. 1, 1988, creating a new parliamentary structure.

The Constitution is divided into a preamble and 9 Sections. The preamble describes the Soviet Union as a 'developed Socialist society', which is said to be a logical stage on the road to communism. The highest aim of the Soviet state is said to be the building of a classless communist society.

Section I covers the bases of the social-political and economic system. The economic system is based on

'socialist ownership of the means of production' (Article 9). The economy is managed on the basis of state plans (Article 15).

This section also contains chapters on social development and culture, foreign policy, and the defence of the socialist Fatherland. The foreign policy of the U.S.S.R. is said to be 'directed to ensuring favourable international conditions for the building of communism in the U.S.S.R.' (Article 28).

Section II is devoted to the state and the individual. This includes a long chapter on the basic rights, freedoms and duties of citizens of the U.S.S.R., all of which are subject to the proviso that 'exercise by citizens of rights and freedoms must not injure the interests of society and state, and the rights of other citizens' (Article 39). The rights are listed in Articles 40–50. Freedom to profess or not profess a religion, and Church-State relations are dealt with in Article 52. Section II also includes a list of obligations (Articles 59–68).

Section III on the national-state structure of the U.S.S.R. describes it as a 'unitary federal multi-national state, formed as a result of the free self-determination of nations and the voluntary union of equal Soviet Socialist Republics' (Article 69). 'Each Union Republic shall retain the right freely to secede from the U.S.S.R.' (Article 71).

Section IV on the Soviets of people's deputies and the procedure for electing them provides for the U.S.S.R. Congress of People's Deputies, the Congresses of People's Deputies of Union Republics and local Soviets to be elected for a term of 5 years. (Articles 89 and 90). The minimum voting age is 18 (Article 96).

Under Section V, the higher organs of State power and administration of the U.S.S.R., the U.S.S.R. Congress of People's Deputies, is the highest organ of State power (Article 108). Regular sessions of the U.S.S.R. Congress of People's Deputies are held twice a year. The Congress of People's Deputies elects the U.S.S.R. Supreme Soviet and the Chairman of the U.S.S.R. Supreme Soviet from among its deputies (Article 108).

The U.S.S.R. Supreme Soviet is defined as the 'standing legislative, administrative and monitoring body of U.S.S.R. state authority' (Article 117). It consists of two chambers, a Council of the Union and a Council of Nationalities, and is convened for two annual sessions, each lasting 3–4 months. (Article 112). The Congress of People's Deputies and the Supreme Soviet are represented between sessions by the Presidium of the Supreme Soviet (Article 118). The Chairman of the Supreme Soviet is head of state.

The highest executive organ of the State is the Council of Ministers of the U.S.S.R. (Article 127). The Council of Ministers is accountable to the U.S.S.R. Congress of People's Deputies and the U.S.S.R. Supreme Soviet (Article 130). A smaller body, the Presidium of the Council of Ministers, acts as the permanent organ of the Council of Ministers (Article 131).

Constitutionally, the highest executive organ of the C.P.S.U. is its Central Committee, as elected by the Party Congress. The current Central Committee was elected at the XXVIIth Party Congress in March, 1986 but at a plenum of the Central Committee in April 1989 a number of members retired. It now consists of 251 full members and 133 candidate members with a consultative voice. The *Central Revision Commission* currently has 70 members. The real power in the Party is vested, however, in the Politbureau, the Secretariat and the permanent Departments of the Central Committee.

DEFENCE

Defence expenditure in the U.S.S.R. for 1988 was set officially at 20,244 million roubles (or 4·6 per cent of total budget). It has been admitted that this covers only manpower costs, not weapon procurement, etc. The overall defence budget was officially stated in May 1989 to be 77,300 million roubles (15·6 per cent of the total Soviet budget). Despite the I.N.F. Treaty with the U.S.A. of December 1987, which will eliminate a whole class of land-based nuclear weapons, and progress towards a START accord, there is a continuing reliance on nuclear weapons while improving the levels and capabilities of conventional arms.

The basic military service is two years in the Army and Air Force and two to three years in the Navy and Border Guards.

The total size of the Soviet regular forces was estimated at the beginning of 1989 to be about 5,130,000, excluding some 1,135,000 Border Guard, internal security, railway and construction troops (mainly uniformed civilians), but including some 1,500,000 command and general support troops not otherwise listed. Late in 1988 it was announced that within the next two years there would be unilateral cuts in Soviet conventional forces of 500,000 men and 10,000 tanks. Withdrawals of Soviet forces from Hungary, Czechoslovakia, the G.D.R. and Mongolia have begun and more may follow. This complicates the individual force levels but in 1988 the position was as follows:

Operational ICBMs, i.e. Inter-Continental Ballistic Missiles, totalled about 1,400. SLBMs numbered 983. The number of MRBMs and IRBMs deployed was 553. The operational personnel of the Strategic Rocket Forces totalled 298,000 (not including 112,000 assigned from Air and Navy).

The total strength of all Soviet air elements (including helicopters) was some 19,000. Of these, 10,000 can be classified as combat aircraft. The total strength of the Air Forces, excluding the Naval Air Force (68,000) and the bomber forces of the Aviation Armies (100,000), was about 450,000 men. The total personnel of the separate Air Defence Command, now merged with the Air Defence Troops of the Ground Forces, was estimated at 630,000 men.

The total size of the Soviet Army was estimated at 1,991,000. It is thought to be organized in 194 divisions, distributed as follows: 30 divisions in Central and Eastern Europe, 63 in European U.S.S.R., 30 in Southern Theatre, 53 in Far Eastern Theatre, and 18 in the Central Strategic Reserve.

The total strength of the Soviet Navy and Naval Air Force was 451,000 men. In total tonnage, it is the second largest navy in the world, and its main strength lies in the submarine fleet. There were in 1988/early 1989 277 cruise missile and attack submarines (118 nuclear-powered, 145 diesel-powered submarines, with a further 14 converting to other roles including SSN), and 84 attack submarines in reserve.

The Soviet Navy has 269 major surface combat vessels, including five aircraft carriers, 36 cruisers and 61 destroyers and some 180 frigates. The landbased Naval Air Force comprises about 915 combat aircraft, 395 of which are bombers, and some 300 helicopters.

The para-military forces number 570,000, including 230,000 border troops and 340,000 internal security troops. There are also DOSAAF members (claimed active membership, 80 million) who participate in such activities as athletics, flight training, shooting, parachuting and pre-military training.

Minister of Defence, Army Gen. D. T. Yazov.
Chief of General Staff, Army Gen. M. A. Moiseev.
Chief, Political Administration, Soviet Army and Navy, Army Gen. A. D. Lizichev.

On May 14, 1955, a Treaty of Friendship, Mutual Assistance and Co-operation was signed in Warsaw between the Soviet Union and its European associates (Bulgaria, East Germany, Hungary, Poland, Romania, and Czechoslovakia) (and Albania which left the Pact in Sept. 1968) to serve as a counterpoise to NATO. A united military command was set up in Moscow, *C.-in-C.*, Army Gen. P. G. Lushev; *Chief of Staff*, Army Gen. V. N. Lobov. The Treaty (Warsaw Pact), due to have expired in June 1985, was extended by Protocol in its existing form for a further 20 years, with provision for a further 10 year extension thereafter, at a meeting of Pact leaders in Warsaw on April 26, 1985. The Pact came into force on May 31, 1985.

INDUSTRY AND AGRICULTURE

One of the most remarkable aspects of the Soviet economy has been the transformation of an essentially agricultural country into the second-strongest industrial power in the world. The 1988 output amounted to 163 million tonnes of steel, 116 million tonnes of rolled metal, 772 million tonnes of coal, 624 million tonnes of crude oil, 139 million tonnes of cement, 1,705,000 million kW/h of electricity and 1,300,000 cars.

Agricultural development has been slower, mainly owing to lack of incentives among peasants organized in *kolkhozy* (collective farms). Repeated droughts, such as in 1980-81, were a contributing factor to a shortage of grain. The 1988 harvest was 195 million tonnes. Stock breeding has also suffered from the general mismanagement of farming, and from shortages of fodder in recent years. The livestock at Jan. 1, 1989 included 42,000,000 cows, 77,400,000 pigs and 147,300,000 sheep and goats. Besides *kolkhozy* (collective farms) and *sovkhozy* (state farms) a significant contribution to agricultural production is made by the private plots cultivated by individual peasants. The cultivation of these plots is encouraged by the Soviet authorities. The level of productivity remains very low. Forests cover nearly 40 per cent of the whole area of the Union and form a considerable source of wealth.

Trade with U.K.

	1987	1988
Imports from U.K.	£491,615,000	£511,653,000
Exports to U.K.	875,431,000	732,115,000

COMMUNICATIONS

European Russia is relatively well served by railways, Leningrad and Moscow being the two main focal points of rail routes. The centre and south have a good system of north-south and east-west lines, but the eastern part (the Volga lands), traversed as it is by trunk lines between Europe and Asia which enter Siberia via Sverdlovsk, Chelyabinsk, Magnitogorsk and Ufa, lacks north-south routes. In Asia, there are still large areas of the U.S.S.R., notably in the Far North and Siberia, with few or no railways. Railways built since 1928 include the Turkestan-Siberian line (*Turksib*) which has made possible a large-scale industrial exploitation of Kazakhstan, a number of lines within the system of the *Trans-Siberian Railway* (Magnitogorsk-Kartaly-Troitsk, Sverdlovsk-Kurgan, Novosibirsk-Proyektnaya, etc.), which are of great importance for the industrial development in the east, the Petropavlovsk-Karaganda-Balkhash line which has made possible the development of the Karaganda coal basin and of the Balkhash copper mines, and the Moscow-Donbass trunk line. In the northern part of European Russia, the North Pechora Railway has been completed, while in the Far East a recently completed second Trans-Siberian line (the Baikal-Amur Railway) is partially in use; it follows a more northerly alignment than the earlier Trans-Siberian and terminates in the Pacific port of Sovetskaya Gavan.

Sea Ports and Inland Waterways.—The most important ports (Odessa, Nikolayev, Batumi, Taganrog, Rostov, Kerch, Sevastopol and Novorossiisk) lie around the Black Sea and the Sea of Azov. The northern ports (Leningrad, Murmansk and Archangel) are, with the exception of Murmansk, icebound during winter. Several ports have been built along the Arctic Sea route between Murmansk and Vladivostok and are in regular use every summer. The great Far Eastern port of Vladivostok, the Pacific naval base of the U.S.S.R., is kept open by icebreakers all the year round. Inland waterways, both natural and artificial, are of great importance in the country, although some of them are icebound in winter (from 2½ months in the south to 6 months in the north). The great rivers of European Russia flow outwards from the centre, linking all parts of the plain with the chief ports, an immense system of navigable waterways which carried about 632,600,000 tons of freight in 1985. They are supplemented by a system of canals which provide a through traffic between the White, Baltic, Black and Caspian Seas. The most notable of them are the *White Sea-Baltic Canal*, the *Moscow-Volga Canal* and the *Volga-Don Canal* linking the Baltic and the White Seas in the north to the Caspian, the Black Sea and the Sea of Azov in the south.

CURRENCY.—Rouble of 100 kopeks.

FLAG.—Red, with five-pointed star above hammer and sickle.

NATIONAL DAY.—November 7 (commemorating the October Bolshevik Revolution of 1917).

NATIONAL ANTHEM.—Soyuz Nerushimy Respublik Svobodnykh (Indissoluble union of free republics).

BRITISH EMBASSY
Naberezhnaya Morisa Toreza 14, Moscow
[Moscow 2318511]

Ambassador Extraordinary and Plenipotentiary, His Excellency Sir Rodric Braithwaite, K.C.M.G. (1988).
Minister, N. H. Marshall, C.M.G.

There is a Consular Section attached to the Embassy.

ARMENIA

First Secretary of the Party Central Committee, S. G. Arutyunyan.
Chairman of the Presidium of the Supreme Soviet, G. M. Voskanyan.
Chairman of the Council of Ministers, V. S. Markaryants.

The Armenian S.S.R. occupies the south-western part of Transcaucasia: it was formed in 1920. In 1922 it joined the Transcaucasian Federation, and on its liquidation in 1936 became a Union Republic. In the south it borders on Turkey. It is a mountainous country consisting of several vast tablelands surrounded by ridges. The population and the economic life are concentrated in the low-lying part of Armenia, the Aras valley and the Erevan hollow; the climate is continental, dry and cold, but the Araks valley has a long, hot and dry summer. Irrigation is essential for agriculture. Industrial and fruit crops are grown in the low-lying districts, grain in the hills. Armenia is traditionally noted for her wine. There are large copper ore and molybdenum deposits and other minerals. The Armenian Church centred in Etchmiadzin is the oldest established Christian Church, Christianity having been recognized as the State religion in A.D. 300.

Nearly 90 per cent of the population is Armenian.

CAPITAL.—Erevan. Population, 1,185,000 (Jan. 1, 1987).

AZERBAIJAN

First Secretary of the Party Central Committee, A. Kh. Vezirov.
Chairman of the Presidium of the Supreme Soviet, E. M. Kafarova.
Chairman of the Council of Ministers, A. N. Mutalibov.

The Azerbaijan S.S.R. occupies the eastern part of Transcaucasia, on the shore of the Caspian Sea, and borders on Iran. It was formed in 1920. Between 1922 and 1936 it formed part of the Transcaucasian Federation. In 1936 it became a Union Republic. It includes the Nakhichevan Autonomous Republic and the Nagorno-Karabakh Autonomous Province.

The north-eastern part of the Republic is taken up by the south-eastern end of the main Caucasus ridge, its south-western part by the smaller Caucasus hills, and its south-eastern corner by the spurs of the Talysh Ridge. Its central part is a depression irrigated by the Kura and by the lower reaches of its tributary Araks. Sheltered by the mountains from the humid west winds blowing from the Black Sea, Azerbaijan has a continental climate. The land requires artificial irrigation. Industry is dominated by oil and natural gas extraction and related chemical and engineering industries centred on Baku and Sumgait. A large power station on the Araks was completed in 1969, in conjunction with Iran. Azerbaijan is also important as a cotton growing area. The Azerbaijani (Turkic) make up more than three-quarters of the population of the Republic, Armenians, about 8 per cent, and Russians, 8 per cent.

CAPITAL.—Ψ Baku. Population 1,741,000 (Jan. 1, 1987).

BELORUSSIA

First Secretary of the Party Central Committee, E. E. Sokolov.
Chairman of the Presidium of the Supreme Soviet, G. G. Tarazevich.
Chairman of the Council of Ministers, M. V. Kovalev.

The Belorussian S.S.R., lying in the western part of the European area of the U.S.S.R., was formed early in 1919. It now consists of six provinces (Brest, Gomel, Grodno, Minsk, Mogilev and Vitebsk). Belorussians make up four-fifths of the population, with Russians and Poles coming next. It is largely a plain with many lakes, swamps and marshy land. Before the revolution of 1917 the area was one of the most backward parts of European Russia. Since then, agriculture has been greatly developed, thanks to draining of swamps. Most of the Republic's industry is also of recent growth. Woodworking is of great importance, but engineering has also been greatly extended with several major plants built in Gomel and Minsk.

The main rivers are the upper reaches of the Dnieper, of the Niemen and of the Western Dvina.

CAPITAL.—Minsk. Population 1,566,000 (Jan. 1, 1987).

ESTONIA

First Secretary of the Party Central Committee, V. Valyas.
Chairman of the Presidium of the Supreme Soviet, A. F. Ryuitel.
Chairman of the Council of Ministers, I. Kh. Toome.

Estonia, formerly a Baltic province of the Russian Empire, was proclaimed an independent Republic in 1918. In 1940, it was forcibly incorporated into the U.S.S.R. It lies on the shores of the Baltic and of the Finnish Gulf in the north and of the Gulf of Riga in the south-west. Some 800 islands, among them Dagö and Ösel, form part of Estonian territory.

The country forms a low-lying plain with many lakes, among them the Chud (or Pskov) Lake, on the border with the R.S.F.S.R. Forests take up about one-fifth of the territory. Agriculture and dairy-farming are the chief industries, rye, oats, barley, flax and potatoes being the chief crops, and butter, bacon and eggs the chief products of dairy farming. There are important manufactures, including textiles, engineering, shipbuilding, woodworking, etc.

The population consists of Estonians (64·7 per cent) and Russians (27·9 per cent).

CAPITAL.—Ψ Tallinn (formerly Reval). Population, 494,000 (Jan. 1, 1987).

GEORGIA

First Secretary of the Party Central Committee, G. G. Gumbaridze.

Chairman of the Presidium of the Supreme Soviet, O. E. Cherkeziya.

Chairman of the Council of Ministers, N. A. Chitanava.

The Georgian S.S.R., occupying the north-western part of Transcaucasia, lies on the shore of the Black Sea and borders in the south-east on Turkey. It was formed in 1921; in 1922 it joined the Transcaucasian Federation which, in its turn, adhered to the U.S.S.R. in the same year. After the liquidation of the Transcaucasian S.F.S.R. in 1936 Georgia became a Union Republic. It contains two Autonomous Republics (Abkhazia and Adjaria) and the South-Osetian Autonomous Province. Georgia is a country of mountains, with the Greater Caucasus in the north and the Lesser Caucasus in the south. A relatively low-lying land between these two ridges is divided into two parts by the Surz Ridge: Western Georgia with a mild and damp climate and Eastern Georgia with a more continental and dry climate. The Black Sea shore and the Rioni lowland are subtropical in their climatic character. The most important mineral deposits are manganese (Chiatura), coal (Tkibuli and Tkvarcheli) and oil (Kakhetia). Georgia is a leading producer of manganese in the U.S.S.R. There are also many oil refineries. Viniculture, tea and tobacco-growing are the three main agricultural industries. The Black Sea harbours many famous holiday resorts. Georgians make up 68·8 per cent of the population, the remainder being largely composed of Armenians (9 per cent), Russians, Azerbaijanis and Osetians.

CAPITAL.—Tbilisi (Tiflis), population 1,197,000 (Jan. 1, 1987).

KAZAKHSTAN

First Secretary of the Party Central Committee, N. A. Nazarbaev.

Chairman of the Presidium of Supreme Soviet, M. R. Sagdiev.

Chairman of the Council of Ministers, (vacant).

The Kazakh S.S.R., the second-largest Union-Republic, stretching from the lower reaches of the Volga and the Caspian in the west to the Altai and Tienshan in the east, and bordering on China, was formed in 1920 as an autonomous republic (under the name of the Kazakh A.S.S.R.) within the R.S.F.S.R., and was constituted a Union Republic in 1936. It consists of 17 Provinces: Aktyubinsk, Alma-Ata, Chimkent, Dzhambul, Dzhezkazgan, East-Kazakhstan, Guryev, Karaganda, Kokchetav, Kustanay, Kzyl-Orda, North-Kazakhstan, Pavlodar, Semipalatinsk, Taldy-Kurgan, Tselinograd and Uralsk.

Kazakhstan is a country of arid steppes and semideserts, flat in the west, hilly in the east and

mountainous in the south-east (Southern Altai and Tienshan). The climate is continental and very dry. The main rivers are the (Upper) Irtysh, the Ural, the Syr-Darya and the Ili. Kazakhstan is very rich in minerals: copper in Kounrad and Dzhezkazgan, lead and zinc in the Altai and Karatau mountains, iron ore in Radryg and Lisakovsk, coal in Ekibastuz and Karaganda and oil and natural gas in the Mangyshlak peninsula. Major centres of metal industry exist in the Altai Mountains, in Chimkent, north of the Balkhash Lake and in Central Kazakhstan. Stockraising is highly developed, particularly in the central and south-western parts of the Republic. Grain is grown in the north and north-east and cotton in the south and south-east.

The Kazakhs (a Turkic people) are in a minority in the Republic named after them; they constitute only 36 per cent of its population, Russian settlers make up 41 per cent and Ukrainians 6 per cent.

CAPITAL.—Alma-Ata (formerly Verny). Population 1,113,000 (Jan. 1, 1987). Karaganda, a major mining centre, has a population of 633,000 (Jan. 1, 1987).

KIRGHIZIA

First Secretary of the Party Central Committee, A. M. Masaliev.

Chairman of the Presidium of the Supreme Soviet, T. Akmatov.

Chairman of the Council of Ministers, A. Dzhumagulov.

The Kirghiz S.S.R. occupies the north-eastern part of Soviet Central Asia and borders in the south-east on China. In 1924, a Kara-Kirghiz Autonomous Province was formed within the R.S.F.S.R. In 1926 it became a Kirghiz Autonomous Republic, and in 1936 a Union Republic. It contains three provinces, Issyk-Kul, Naryn and Osh. The Kirghiz Republic is a mountainous country, the major part being covered by the ridge of the Central Tienshan, while mountains of the Pamir-Altai system occupy its southern part. There are a number of spacious mountain valleys, the Alai, Susamyr, the Issyk-Kul lake and others. The majority of the population is concentrated in plains, lying at the foot of mountains—Chu, Talass, part of the Ferghana Valley where agriculture prospers. Crops include sugar beet and cotton, and sheep are important in the mountains. Industry is being developed and some mining is done. The Kirghiz constitute 47·9 per cent of the population, the Russians 25·9 per cent. The Uzbeks (in Eastern Ferghana) amount to 12·1 per cent.

CAPITAL.—Frunze (formerly Pishpek). Population, 641,000 (Jan. 1, 1987).

LATVIA

First Secretary of the Party Central Committee, Ya. Ya. Vagris.

Chairman of the Presidium of the Supreme Soviet, A. V. Gorbunov.

Chairman of the Council of Ministers, V.-E. G. Bresis.

The Latvian S.S.R., lying on the shores of the Baltic and of the Gulf of Riga, was formerly a Baltic Province of the Russian Empire. It was proclaimed an independent state in 1918 and was forcibly incorporated into the U.S.S.R. in August 1940.

The surface of the country is generally flat, interspersed by occasional chains of hills. The climate is moderately continental. The main rivers are the lower reaches of the Western Dvina and its tributaries. Forests occupy 20 per cent of the total territory.

The Latvians make up 53·7 per cent of the Republic's population, Russians 32·8 per cent.

Latvian industry was always highly developed,

with shipbuilding, engineering, chemical industry, textile industry, wood-working and dairying being the chief occupations. Both Riga and Liepaja (Libava, Libau) are important sea-ports.

CAPITAL.—Ψ Riga. Population, 900,000 (Jan. 1, 1987).

LITHUANIA

First Secretary of the Party Central Committee, A.-M. K. Brazauskas.
Chairman of the Presidium of the Supreme Soviet, V. S. Astrauskas.
Chairman of the Council of Ministers, V. V. Sakalauskas.

Lithuania, formerly a Province of the Russian Empire, was declared an independent Republic at Vilna in 1918 and was incorporated into the U.S.S.R. in August, 1940. The Republic forms a plain with a large number of lakes and swamps. The forests occupy 19 per cent of the whole area. The main river is the Niemen with its tributaries.

The chief industries are agriculture and forestry, the chief products being rye, oats, wheat, barley, flax, sugar-beet and potatoes.

The Lithuanians make up four-fifths of the population, Russians and Poles, 7–9 per cent each.

CAPITAL.—Vilnius (Vilna). Population 566,000 (Jan. 1, 1987).

MOLDAVIA

First Secretary of the Party Central Committee, S. K. Grossu.
Chairman of the Presidium of the Supreme Soviet, A. A. Mokanu.
Chairman of the Council of Ministers, I. P. Kalin.

Moldavia, occupying the south-western corner of the U.S.S.R., borders in the west on Romania with the Pruth forming the frontier. In 1918, Romania seized the Russian Province of Bessarabia, but in 1940 the U.S.S.R. forced Romania to give back Bessarabia, the major part of which was merged with the Moldavian A.S.S.R. (formed in 1924) to create the Moldavian S.S.R.

The northern part of the Republic consists of flat steppe lands, now all under plough. Some forests skirt the Dniester. Further south, around Kishinev, there are woody hills and further south again, low-lying steppe lands. The climate is moderate. The main river is the Dniester, navigable along the whole course.

The main industry is agriculture (viniculture, fruit-growing and market-gardening). Industry is insignificant in both parts of Moldavia, but the Republic has the densest population in the U.S.S.R. Moldavians make up 64 per cent of the population, with Ukrainians (14·2 per cent), and Russians (12·8 per cent) next.

CAPITAL.—Kishinev (Chisinau). Population, 672,000 (Jan. 1, 1987).

R.S.F.S.R.

(The Russian Soviet Federal Socialist Republic)

Chairman of the Presidium of the Supreme Soviet, V. I. Vorotnikov.
Chairman of the Council of Ministers, A. S. Vlasov.

The R.S.F.S.R. has no central Communist Party organization of its own.

The R.S.F.S.R., the largest and the most important of the Republics, occupies the major half of the European part of the U.S.S.R. and the major northern portion of its Asiatic part and makes up 77 per cent of the total territory of the U.S.S.R. with 53 per cent

of the total population. (About 83 per cent of the population are Russians.) It consists of 16 Autonomous Republics (the Bashkir, Buryat, Checheno-Ingush, Chuvash, Daghestan, Kabardin-Balkar, Kalmyk, Karelian, Komi, Mari, Mordovian, North-Osetian, Tatar, Tuva, Udmurt and Yakut, A.S.S.R.s); 6 regions (Altai, Khabarovsk, Krasnodar, Krasnoyarsk, Maritime and Stavropol) containing in their turn 5 autonomous provinces; 49 provinces (Amur, Archangel, Astrakhan, Belgorod, Bryansk, Chelyabinsk, Chita, Gorky, Irkutsk, Ivanovo, Kalinin, Kaliningrad, Kaluga, Kamchatka, Kemerovo, Kirov, Kostroma, Kuibyshev, Kurgan, Kursk, Leningrad, Lipetsk, Magadan, Moscow, Murmansk, Novgorod, Novosibirsk, Omsk, Orel, Orenburg, Penza, Perm, Pskov, Rostov, Ryazan, Sakhalin, Saratov, Smolensk, Sverdlovsk, Tambov, Tomsk, Tula, Tyumen, Ulyanovsk, Vladimir, Volgograd, Vologda, Voronezh and Yaroslavl).

There are three principal geographic areas: a low-lying flat Western part stretching eastwards up to the Yenisei and divided in two by the Ural ridge; an eastern part, between the Yenisei and the Pacific, consisting of a number of tablelands and ridges, and a southern mountainous part. Climatically, the R.S.F.S.R. extends from Arctic and tundra belts to the sub-tropical in the south. It has a very long coastline, including the longest Arctic coastline in the world (about 17,000 miles). The most important rivers are the Volga, the Northern Dvina and the Pechora, the Neva, the Don and the Kuban in the European part, and in the Asiatic part, the Ob, the Irtysh, the Yenisei, the Lena and the Amur, and, further north, Khatanga, Olenek, Yana, Indigirka, Kolyma and Anadyr. Lakes are abundant, particularly in the north-west. The huge Baikal Lake in Eastern Siberia is the deepest lake in the world. There are also two large artificial water reservoirs within the Greater Volga canal system, the Moscow and Rybinsk 'Seas'.

Minerals.—The Republic has some of the richest mineral deposits in the world. Coal is mined in the Kuznetsk area, in the Urals, south of Moscow, in the Donets basin (its Eastern part lies in the R.S.F.S.R.) and in the Pechora area in the North. Oil is produced in the Northern Caucasus, in the area between the Volga and the Ural and in Western Siberia, which also has large deposits of natural gas. Coal and gas deposits in Siberia and the Far East (especially Yakutia) are currently being developed, now that some deposits in the western parts of the U.S.S.R. are approaching exhaustion. The Ural mountains contain a unique assortment of minerals—high-quality iron ore, manganese, copper, aluminium, gold, platinum, precious stones, salt, asbestos, pyrites, coal, oil, etc. Iron ore is also mined near Kursk, Tula, Lipetsk, in several areas in Siberia and in the Kola Peninsula. Non-ferrous metals are found in the Altai, in Eastern Siberia, in the Northern Caucasus, in the Kuznetsk-Basin, in the Far East and in the Far North. Nine-tenths of all U.S.S.R. forests are located in the R.S.F.S.R.

Production and Industry.—The vastness of the territory of the Republic and the great variety in climatic conditions cause great differences in the structure of agriculture from north to south and from west to east. In the far north reindeer breeding, hunting and fishing are predominant. Further south, timber industry is combined with grain growing. In the southern half of the forest zone and in the adjacent forest-steppe zone, the acreage under grain crops is far larger and the structure of agriculture more complex. An extensive programme of land improvement mainly involving this zone aims to double its total agricultural output by 1990. In the eastern part of this zone, between the Volga and the Urals, cericulture is predominant (particularly summer wheat), with cattle breeding next. Beyond the

Urals is another important grain-growing and stock-breeding area in the southern part of the Western-Siberian plain. The southern steppe zone is the main wheat granary of the U.S.S.R., containing also large acreages under barley, maize and sunflower. In the extreme south cotton is now cultivated. Vine, tobacco and other southern crops are grown on the Black Sea shore of the Caucasus.

Industrially, the R.S.F.S.R. occupies the first place among the Soviet Republics. Moscow and Leningrad are still the two largest industrial centres in the country, but new industrial areas are being developed in the Urals, the Kuznetsk basin, and more recently in Siberia and the Far East. Most of the oil produced in the U.S.S.R. now comes from the R.S.F.S.R., half annual output comes from Tyumen Oblast in Western Siberia. All industries are represented in the R.S.F.S.R., including iron and steel and engineering.

CAPITAL.—Moscow. Population 8,815,000 (Jan. 1, 1987). Moscow, founded about A.D. 1147 by Yuri Dolgoruki, became first the centre of the rising Moscow principality and in the 15th century, the capital of the whole of Russia (Muscovy). In 1325, it became the seat of the Metropolitan of Russia. In 1703 Peter the Great transferred the capital to the newly built St. Petersburg, but on March 14, 1918, Moscow was again designated as the capital. ΨLeningrad (before the First World War St. Petersburg and from 1914–1924 Petrograd) has a population of 4,948,000 (Jan. 1, 1987).

Other towns with populations exceeding 1,000,000 are:—

Gorky (Nizhny-Novogorod)	1,425,000
Novosibirsk (Novonikolayevsk)	1,423,000
Sverdlovsk (Yekaterinburg)	1,331,000
Kuibyshev (Samara)	1,280,000
Omsk	1,134,000
Chelyabinsk	1,119,000
Ufa	1,092,000
Perm (Molotov)	1,075,000
Kazan	1,068,000
Rostov-on-Don	1,004,000

TADJIKISTAN

First Secretary of the Party Central Committee, K. Makhkamov.
Chairman of the Presidium of the Supreme Soviet, G. Pallaev.
Chairman of the Council of Ministers, I. Khaeev.

The Tadjik S.S.R. lies in the extreme south-east of Soviet Central Asia and borders in the south on Afghanistan and in the east on China. It was originally formed in 1924 as an Autonomous Republic within the Uzbek S.S.R. and became a Union Republic in 1929. It includes the Gorno-Badakhshan Autonomous Province and the Kulyab and Leninabad Provinces.

The country is mountainous: in the east lie the Pamir highlands with the highest point in the U.S.S.R., Pik Kommunizma (24,590 feet), in the centre the high ridges of the Pamir-Altai system. Plains are formed by wide stretches of the Syr-Darya valley in the north and of the Amu-Darya in the south.

Like the other Central-Asiatic Republics, Tadjikistan is a cotton-growing country. Its climatic conditions favour the cultivation of Egyptian cotton. Irrigation is of great importance. Of the population 58·8 per cent are Tadjiks (linguistically and culturally akin to the Persians), 23 per cent Uzbeks, the rest Russians and others.

CAPITAL.—Dushanbe (formerly Stalinabad; Dyushambe). Population, 591,000 (Jan. 1, 1987).

TURKMENISTAN

First Secretary of the Party Committee, S. A. Niyazov.

Chairman of the Presidium of the Supreme Soviet, R. A. Bazarova.
Chairman of the Council of Ministers, A. Khodzhamuradov.

Turkmenia occupies the extreme south of Soviet Central Asia, between the Caspian and the Amu-Darya, and borders in the south on Iran and Afghanistan. It was formed in 1924 and contains five Provinces: Ashkhabad, Chardjou, Krasnovodsk, Mary and Tashauz. The country is a low-lying plain, fringed by hills in the south. Ninety per cent of the plain is taken up by the arid Kara-Kum desert. Of all Central-Asiatic Republics, Turkmenia is the lowest and driest. The cultivation of cotton, stock-raising and mineral extraction are the principal industries. The republic produces about 16 per cent of the Soviet Union's natural gas, as well as astrakhan furs and carpets. Most of the land under plough is artificially irrigated. The oil and silk industries are of old standing. There are also some fisheries in the Caspian.

Turkmens make up 68·4 per cent of the population, Russians 12·6 per cent, and Uzbeks 8·5 per cent.

CAPITAL.—Ashkhabad (formerly Askhabad, Poltoratsk). Population, 386,000 (Jan. 1, 1987).

UKRAINE

First Secretary of the Party Central Committee, V. V. Shcherbitsky.
Chairman of the Presidium of the Supreme Soviet, V. S. Shevchenko.
Chairman of the Council of Ministers, V. A. Masol.

This Republic, second largest in population, lying in the south-western part of the European half of the U.S.S.R., was formed in December, 1917. Ukrainians make up nearly 75 per cent of the population, with 21 per cent Russians. It consists of 25 provinces—Cherkassy, Chernigov, Chernovtsy, Crimea, Dnepropetrovsk, Donetsk, Ivano-Frankovsk, Kharkov, Kherson, Khmelnitsky, Kiev, Kirovograd, Lvov, Nikolayev, Odessa, Poltava, Rovno, Sumy, Ternopol, Transcarpathia, Vinnitsa, Volhynia, Voroshilovgrad, Zaporozhye and Zhitomir.

Physical Features.—The larger part of the Ukraine forms a plain with small elevations. The Carpathian mountains lie in the south-western part of the Republic. The climate is moderate, with relatively mild winters (particularly in the south-west) and hot summers. The main rivers are the Dnieper with its tributaries, the Southern Bug and the Northern Donets (a tributary of the Don).

Production and Industry.—The main centre of Soviet coal mining and iron and steel industry is situated in the southern part of the Ukraine. In 1980, the Ukraine provided 36 per cent of the total Soviet steel, 51 per cent of iron ore and 27 per cent of coal. The engineering and chemical industries are also of importance. The central forest-steppe region (mainly on the right bank of the Dnieper) is the greatest sugar-producing area in the U.S.S.R. The Ukraine also leads in grain-growing and stock-raising.

There are large deposits of coal and salt in the Donets Basin, of iron ore in Krivoy Rog and near Kerch in the Crimea, of manganese in Nikopol, and of quicksilver in Nikitovka.

CAPITAL (since 1934).—Kiev, one of the oldest cities in the U.S.S.R., founded in the 6th–7th century A.D., was the capital of the Russian State from 865 to 1240. Population (Jan. 1, 1987), 2,558,000. Other towns are:—

Kharkov	1,587,000
Dnepropetrovsk (Yekaterinoslav)	1,182,000
Ψ Odessa	1,141,000
Donetsk (Stalino; Yuzovka, i.e. Hughesovka)	1,090,000

UZBEKISTAN

First Secretary of the Party Central Committee, I. A. Karimov.
Chairman of the Presidium of the Supreme Soviet, M. I. Ibragimov.
Chairman of the Council of Ministers, G. Kh. Kadyrov.

The Uzbek S.S.R. was formed in 1924 and consists of the Kara-Kalpak A.S.S.R. and of 12 provinces (Andizhan, Bokhara, Dzhizak, Ferghana, Kashka-darya, Khorezm, Namangan, Navoi, Samarkand, Surkhan-darya, Syr-darya and Tashkent). It lies between the high Tienshan Mountains and the Pamir highlands in the east and south-east and sandy lowlands in the west and north-west. The major part of the territory is a plain with huge waterless deserts and several large oases, which form the main centres of population and economic life. The largest is the Ferghana valley, watered by the Syr-Darya. Other oases include Tashkent, Samarkand, Bokhara and Khorezm. The climate is continental and dry. Minerals include gold, natural gas, oil, copper, lead, zinc and coal.

The Uzbeks, a Turkic people, make up 68·7 per cent of the population, the Russians (10·8 per cent), Tatars (4·2 per cent) and Kazakhs (4 per cent) come next.

There are major agricultural and textile machinery plants and several chemical combines. Uzbekistan is the main cotton-growing area of the U.S.S.R. producing more than 60 per cent of all Soviet cotton. Irrigation has always been of decisive importance in this area, and the Soviet Government has done much in this field, including the construction of the Great Ferghana Canal (230 miles).

CAPITAL.—Tashkent. Population 2,131,000 (Jan. 1, 1987). Samarkand (population (1987), 388,000) contains the Gur-Emir (Tamerlane's Mausoleum), completed A.D. 1400 by Ulugbek, Tamerlane's astronomer-grandson, and a 15th-century observatory.

UNITED ARAB EMIRATES
(Al-Imarat Al-Arabiya Al-Muttahida)

President, Shaikh Zaid bin Sultan al Nahayyan (*Abu Dhabi*).

MINISTERS
(as at June 30, 1989)

Vice-President and Prime Minister, Shaikh Rashid bin Said al Maktum.
Deputy Prime Ministers, Shaikh Maktum bin Rashid al Maktum; Shaikh Hamdan bin Muhammad al Nahayyan.
Interior, Shaikh Mubarak bin Muhammad al Nahayyan.
Finance and Industry, Shaikh Hamdan bin Rashid al Maktum.
Defence, Shaikh Muhammad bin Rashid al Maktum.
Minister of State for Foreign Affairs, Sayyid Rashid Abdullah al Nu'aimi.
Petroleum and Mineral Resources, Dr. Mana Said al Otaiba.
Economy and Commerce, Sayyid Saif al Jarwan.
Information and Culture, Shaikh Ahmad bin Hamid bin Butti.
Communications, Sayyid Muhammad Said al Mulla.
Public Works and Housing, Sayyid Muhammad Khalifa al Kindi.
Education, Sayyid Faraj Fadel al Mazroui.
Planning, (vacant).
Justice, Islamic Affairs and Awqaf, Shaikh Mohammad bin Hassan al Khazraji.
Agriculture and Fisheries, Sayyid Said al Raqabani.
Water and Electricity, Sayyid Humaid Nasser al Owais.

Labour and Social Affairs, Sayyid Khalfan al Roumi.
Health, Sayyid Hamad Abdul Rahman al Madfa.

EMBASSY IN LONDON
30 Prince's Gate, SW7 1PT
[01–581 1281]

Ambassador Extraordinary and Plenipotentiary, Dr. Khaifa Mohamed Sulaiman (1988).
Chargé d'Affaires, Ali Mubarak Ahmed Al Mansoori.

Area and Population.—The approximate area of the U.A.E. is 32,278 sq. miles (83,600 sq. km.), and the population in 1985 was estimated at about 1·6 million.
The United Arab Emirates (formerly the Trucial States) is composed of seven Emirates (Abu Dhabi, Ajman, Dubai, Fujeirah, Ras al Khaimah, Sharjah and Umm al Qaiwain) which came together as an independent state on December 2, 1971, when they ended their individual special treaty relationships with the British Government (Ras al Khaimah joined the other six on February 10, 1972).
The British Government, by virtue of a treaty made in 1892, had been responsible for the external affairs of the states through the British Political Resident in the Persian Gulf and the British Political Agents in each state, but on independence the Union Government assumed full responsibility for all internal and external affairs apart from some internal matters that remained the prerogative of the individual Emirates. Six of the Emirates lie on the shore of the Gulf between the Musandam peninsula in the East and the Qatar peninsula in the West while the seventh, Fujeirah, lies on the gulf of Oman.
Security in the area is maintained by the U.A.E. Armed Forces. The Ministry of Defence is located in Dubai with a General Headquarters in Abu Dhabi. Most of the separate police forces have also been merged.
Revenue is chiefly derived from oil, re-exports and customs dues on imports. A substantial amount is spent on overseas aid, where commitments in 1980 totalled £154·8 million, doubling those of 1979.

Trade with U.K.

	1987	1988
Imports from U.K.	£478,997,000	£463,344,000
Exports to U.K.	94,989,000	84,217,000

CURRENCY.—U.A.E. dirham of 100 fils.
FLAG.—Horizontal stripes of green over white over black with vertical red stripe in the hoist.
NATIONAL DAY.—December 2.

Abu Dhabi

Abu Dhabi is the largest Emirate of the U.A.E. in area, stretching from Khor al Odaid in the west to the borders with Dubai in the Jebel Ali area. It includes six villages in the Buraimi oasis, the other three being part of the Sultanate of Oman, and a number of settlements in the Liwa Oasis system. Following negotiations with Saudi Arabia, some adjustment of the border has now been made in the Khor al Odaid region, but the agreement has not yet been ratified. The population of the Emirate is now about 670,000
The Abu Dhabi Government controls oil, gas and petrochemical operations in the Emirate through the Abu Dhabi National Oil Company (ADNOC) which has majority shareholdings in the several oil operating and gas treatment companies. ADNOC also has majority shareholdings in oil industry-related companies covering drilling, refining, distribution, chemical manufacture and investment. Offshore production began in 1962, the most important fields being Umm Shaif and Lower Zakum, near Das Island, site of a large associated gas liquefaction plant. The Upper Zakum field came on stream in late 1982, and

four other offshore fields are being developed, one near Abu Dhabi city and three near Delma. Production of oil onshore began in 1963 from the Murban field. A large onshore associated gas liquefaction project based at Ruwais started production in 1981. Other large natural gas finds in recent years will consolidate Abu Dhabi's position as a holder of some of the largest reserves of natural gas in the world. Abu Dhabi's crude oil production in 1987 was approximately 1 million barrels per day.

With its oil wealth the Emirate has seen a decade of growth (which is currently slowing down), not only at Abu Dhabi, now a modern city of about 450,000 people, but also at Al Ain in the Buraimi Oasis and at the new petro-chemical city at Ruwais. An international airport opened in 1982 at Abu Dhabi and another is under construction at Al Ain. There are airfields at Das Island and Jebel Dhanna. The port and harbour on Abu Dhabi island are now completed and there are port facilities at Ruwais.

Ajman and Umm al Qaiwain

Ajman and Umm al Qaiwain are the smallest Emirates, having populations of approx. 64,000 and 29,000 respectively. Both lie on the Gulf coast although Ajman has two inland enclaves at Manama and Masfut. Exploration work continues in both Emirates for oil and gas but so far only Umm Al Qaiwain has experienced any success, with the offshore discovery of natural gas, but the field has yet to be commercially developed. The discovery of onshore gas in nearby Sharjah has increased hopes of similar discoveries in both Ajman and Umm Al Qaiwain.

Dubai

Dubai is the second largest Emirate both in size and in population, which is now about 419,000. The town of Dubai is the main port for the import of goods into the U.A.E. and has a wide re-export trade to the other Gulf States. Dubai's prosperity was established by this trade long before the discovery of oil. Oil was discovered in 1966 and production began in September 1969. The producer in Dubai's offshore oilfields is Dubai Petroleum Company, operated by CONOCO. Production is in excess of 350,000 b.p.d. In 1982 an ARCO-Britoil joint venture discovered an extensive gas and condensate field onshore. A small amount of condensate is produced from the onshore Margam field.

Oil income has been used to finance Dubai's infrastructure and major construction projects include an international airport, a dry dock complex and an international trade and exhibition centre. There is also a 66 berth port at Jebel Ali, forming the heart of an industrial complex which includes an aluminium smelter with an associated de-salination plant and a gas processing plant. The port and its immediate area is a free trade zone which is expected to attract more industry.

Fujeirah

Fujeirah, with a population of 40,000, is the most remote of the seven Emirates lying on the Gulf of Oman coast, and only connected by a metal road to the rest of the country since the end of 1975. Largely agricultural, its population is spread between the slopes of the inland Hajar mountain range and the town of Fujeirah itself, together with a number of smaller settlements on the comparatively fertile plain on the coast. Although exploration work continues, there have been no hydrocarbon discoveries in the Emirate. However, there are some chrome and other mineral deposits. Fujeirah has a new general cargo port.

Ras al Khaimah

Ras al Khaimah has a population of 116,000 of whom more than half live in the town. An ancient sea-port, near to which archaeological remains have been found, Ras al Khaimah is developing as the most agricultural of the Emirates, producing vegetables, dates, fruit and tobacco. In 1982 Ras al Khaimah announced the discovery of oil and gas offshore and this field currently produces approximately 5,000 b.p.d. An industrial area has been developed to the north of the Emirate, which includes 2 cement works. Ras al-Khaimah has an international airport and has also expanded its port. A new international airport is nearing completion. A new trade centre has just been completed and it is hoped that more industry will be attracted to the emirate.

Sharjah

Sharjah, with a present population of approx. 269,000, has declined from its position 50 years ago as principal town in the area. It became the third oil producing Emirate in the summer of 1974, following the discovery of oil offshore. The field declined over the years and by 1982 was yielding less than 6,000 b.p.d. However, new oil and gas discoveries were made in 1982 in the northern emirates and production now stands at about 50,000 b.p.d. Sharjah is well connected by metalled roads to all the other northern Emirates. It experienced a construction boom in the mid-1970's including an ambitious layout of roads and flyovers within the town. A new container port has been constructed on the Gulf of Oman at Khor Fakkan. The international airport was officially opened in 1979.

BRITISH EMBASSY
P.O. Box 248, Abu Dhabi

[Dubai 326600]

Ambassador Extraordinary and Plenipotentiary, His Excellency Michael Logan Tait, C.M.G., L.V.O. (1986).
British Council Representative, Dr. P. Clark, P.O. Box 248, Abu Dhabi.

(Dubai)

Counsellor and Consul General, J. C. Kay.
British Council Representative, A. Swales, P.O. Box 1636, Dubai.

UNITED STATES OF AMERICA

PHYSIOGRAPHY

The conterminous States of the Republic occupy nearly all that portion of the North American Continent between the Atlantic and Pacific Oceans, in latitude 25° 07′–49° 23′ North and longitude 66° 57′–124° 44′ West, its northern boundary being Canada and the southern boundary Mexico. The separate State of Alaska reaches a latitude of 71° 23′ N., at Point Barrow (2,502 miles from the U.S. geographic centre).

The general coastline of the 50 States has a length of about 2,069 miles on the Atlantic, 7,623 miles on the Pacific, 1,060 miles on the Arctic, and 1,631 miles on the Gulf of Mexico.

The principal river is the mighty Mississippi-Missouri-Red, traversing the whole country from north to south, and having a course of 3,710 miles to its mouth in the Gulf of Mexico, with many large affluents, the chief of which are the Yellowstone, Platte, Arkansas, and Ohio rivers. The rivers flowing into the Atlantic and Pacific Oceans are comparatively small; among the former may be noticed the Hudson, Delaware, Susquehanna, Potomac, James, Roanoke and Savannah; of the latter, the Columbia-Snake, Sacramento, and Colorado. The Nueces, Brazos, Trinity, Pearl, Mobile-Tombigbee-Alabama, Apalachicola-Chattahoochee, Suwannee and Colorado of Texas fall into the Gulf of Mexico, also the Rio Grande, a long river partly forming the boundary with Mexico. The areas of the water-basins have been estimated as follows:—Rivers flowing to the Pacific, 647,300 square miles; to the Atlantic, 488,877; and to the Gulf of Mexico, 1,683,325 square miles, of which 1,234,600 are drained by the Mississippi-Missouri-Red. The chain of the Rocky Mountains separates the western portion of the country from the remainder, communications being carried on over certain elevated passes, several of which are now traversed by railroads and major highways; west of these, bordering the Pacific coast, the Cascade Mountains and Sierra Nevada form the outer edge of a high tableland, consisting in part of stony and sandy desert and partly of grazing land and forested mountains, and including the Great Salt Lake, which extends to the Rocky Mountains. In the Eastern States (which form the more settled and most thickly inhabited portion of the country) large forests of valuable timber, as beech, birch, maple, oak, pine, spruce, elm, ash, walnut; and in the south, live oak, water-oak, magnolia, palmetto, pine, tulip-tree, cypress, etc., still exist, the remnants of the forests which formerly extended over all the Atlantic slope, but into which great inroads have been made by the advance of civilization. The mineral kingdom produces ore of iron, copper, lead, zinc, and aluminium, the non-metallic minerals include large quantities of coal, petroleum, stone, phosphate rock, and salt. The highest point is Mount McKinley (Alaska), 20,320 ft. above sea level and the lowest point of dry land is in Death Valley (Inyo, California), 282 ft. below sea-level.

AREA AND POPULATION

	Area, 1980 (sq. miles)		Population	
	Total	Land	Census 1970	Census 1980
The United States (a)	3,618,770	3,539,289	203,302,031*	226,545,805
Puerto Rico	3,515	3,459	2,712,033	3,196,520
Outlying areas under U.S. jurisdiction	1,176	1,176	314,657*	368,856
Territories	459	459	179,519**	235,927
Guam	209	209	84,996	105,979
Virgin Islands of U.S.	132	132	62,468	96,569
American Samoa	77	77	27,159	32,297
Midway Islands	2	2	2,220	453
Wake Island	3	3	1,647	302
Canton Island and Enderbury Island	27	27	—	—
Johnston Atoll (b)	0·5	0·5	1,007	327
Other (c)	9	9	—	—
Pacific Islands Trust Territory (excluding N. Mariana Is.)	533	533	81,300	116,149
N. Mariana Islands	184	184	9,640	16,780
Population abroad (d)			1,737,836†	995,546
Armed Forces			1,057,776	515,408
Total	**3,543,924**	**3,623,461**	**208,066,557**	**231,106,727**

(a) The 50 States and the Federal District of Columbia.
(b) Formerly listed as Johnston and Sand Island. Sand Island uninhabited at time of enumeration.
(c) Navassa, Baker, Howland and Jarvis Islands, Kingman Reef, and Palmyra Atoll.
(d) Excludes U.S. citizens temporarily abroad on private business.
* Includes population of Swan Islands (22) and Panama Canal Zone (44,198). Jurisdiction over the Swan Islands was transferrred to Honduras in 1972. Due to the 1978 Treaty, the Census is no longer conducted in the Canal Zone.
** Includes population of Swan Islands (22).
† Includes U.S. citizens abroad for long periods who were not connected with the U.S. government (236,336) and crews of U.S. merchant vessels (15,910).

Immigrants by Place of Birth, 1951–87

(1951–76, year ends June 30: from 1977, year ends Sept. 30)

Place of Birth	1951–60	1961–70	1971–80	1987
Europe	1,492,200	1,238,600	801,300	61,174
Asia	159,000	445,300	1,633,800	257,684
North America	769,200	1,351,100	1,645,000	216,550
Canada	274,900	286,700	114,800	11,876
Mexico	319,300	443,300	637,200	72,351
West Indies	122,900	519,600	759,800	102,899
Central America	44,600	97,700	132,400	29,296
South America	72,200	228,300	284,400	44,385
Africa	14,800	39,300	91,500	17,724
Australia	4,600	9,800	14,300	1,253
New Zealand	1,700	3,700	5,300	591
Other countries	1,800	5,500	17,700	2,155
TOTAL	3,277,200	3,321,700	4,493,300	601,516

From 1820 to 1986, 53,122,000 immigrants were admitted to the United States.

Resident Population by Race 1980
(in thousands)

White	188,372
Black	26,495
American Indian*	1,420·4
Chinese	806
Filipino	774·7
Japanese	701
Asian Indian	361·5
Korean	354·6
Vietnamese	261·7
Spanish origin**	14,609
Cuban	803
Mexican	8,740
Puerto Rican	2,014
Other Spanish	3,051
All other races	6,999·2
TOTAL	226,546

*Includes Eskimo and Aleut.
**Persons of Spanish origin may be of any race.

REGISTERED BIRTHS AND DEATHS

	Live Births		Deaths	
Calendar Year	Number	Rate per 1,000	Number	Rate per 1,000
1983	3,638,933	15·5	2,019,201	8·6
1984	3,669,141	15·5	2,039,369	8·6
1985	3,760,561	15·8	2,086,440	8·7
1986	3,756,547	15·6	2,105,361	8·7
1987*	3,829,000	15·7	2,127,000	8·7
1988*	3,913,000	15·9	2,171,000	8·8

For 1983–84 births based on 100 per cent sample in most states and 50 per cent sample in remaining states. Beginning with 1985 sample base was 100 per cent.

Note.—Figures tabulated are for the United States. Deaths exclude foetal deaths. Rates are based on the population as estimated on July 1.
* Provisional.

MARRIAGE AND DIVORCE

Laws of marriage and of divorce are within the exclusive jurisdiction of each State. Each State legislature enacts its own laws prescribing rules and qualifications pertaining to marriage and its dissolution.

Year	Marriages	Per 1,000 Pop.§	Estimated Divorces	Per 1,000 Pop.§
1983	2,445,604	10·5	1,158,000	4·9
1984	2,477,192	10·5	1,169,000	5·0
1985	2,412,625	10·1	1,190,000	5·0
1986*	2,400,000	10·0	1,159,000	4·8
1987*	2,421,000	9·9	1,157,000	4·8
1988*	2,389,000	9·7	1,183,000	4·8

§ Population as estimated on July 1.
* Provisional.

Largest Cities 1986 (estimated populations)

Ψ New York, N.Y.	7,262,700
Ψ Los Angeles, California	3,259,340
Ψ Chicago, Illinois	3,009,530
Ψ Houston, Texas	1,728,910
Ψ Philadelphia, Pennsylvania	1,642,900
Ψ Detroit, Michigan	1,086,220
Ψ San Diego, California	1,015,190
Dallas, Texas	1,003,520
San Antonio, Texas	914,350
Phoenix, Arizona	894,070
Ψ Baltimore, Maryland	752,800
Ψ San Francisco, California	749,000
Ψ Indianapolis, Indiana	719,820
San Jose, California	712,080
Memphis, Tennessee	652,640
Washington, D.C.	626,000
Jacksonville, Florida	609,860
Ψ Milwaukee, Wisconsin	605,090
Ψ Boston, Massachusetts	573,600
Columbus, Ohio	566,030
Ψ New Orleans, Louisiana	554,500
Ψ Cleveland, Ohio	535,830
Denver, Colorado	505,000
El Paso, Texas	491,800
Ψ Seattle, Washington	486,200

Ψ Seaport

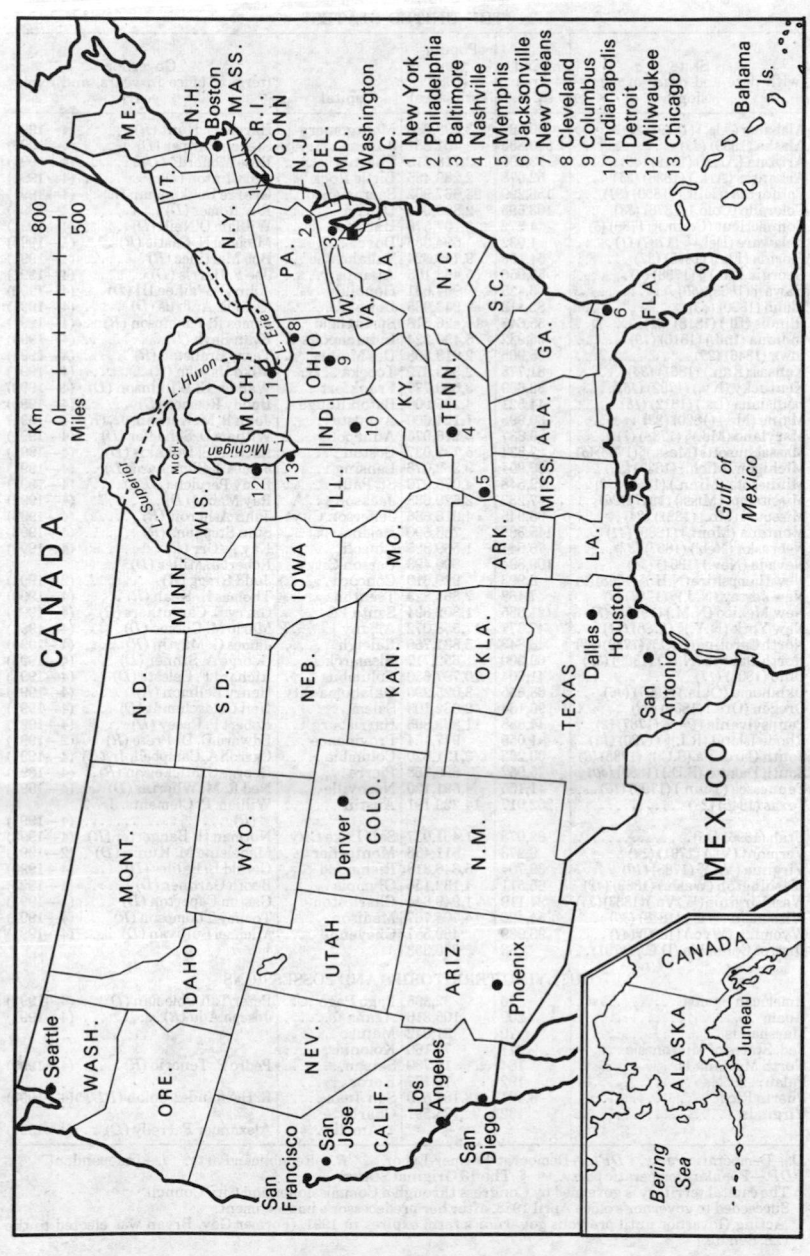

THE UNITED STATES

State (with date and *order* of admission)	Land Area sq. m.	Population, (1986 estimates)	Capital	Governor (term of office in years, and expiry year)
Alabama (Ala.) (1819) (*22*)	50,767	3,893,888	Montgomery..	Harold G. Hunt (*R*) (4—1991)
Alaska (1959) (*49*)	570,833	401,851	Juneau	Steven Cowper (*D*) (4—1990)
Arizona (Ariz.) (1912) (*48*)	113,508	2,718,215	Phoenix	Rose Mofford* (*D*) (4—1991)
Arkansas (Ark.) (1836) (*25*)	52,078	2,286,435	Little Rock ...	Bill Clinton (*D*) (4—1991)
California (Calif.) (1850) (*31*)	156,299	23,667,902	Sacramento ...	George Deukmejian (*R*) .. (4—1991)
Colorado (Colo.) (1876) (*38*)	103,595	2,889,964	Denver	Roy Romer (*D*) (4—1991)
Connecticut (Conn.)§(1788) (*5*) .	4,872	3,107,576	Hartford	William O'Neill (*D*) (4—1991)
Delaware (Del.) § (1787) (*1*)	1,932	594,338	Dover	Michael N. Castle (*R*) (4—1993)
Florida (Fla.) (1845) (*27*)	54,153	9,746,324	Tallahassee ..	Bob Martinez (*R*) (4—1991)
Georgia (Ga.) § (1788) (*4*)	58,056	5,463,105	Atlanta	Joe F. Harris (*D*) (4—1991)
Hawaii (1959) (*50*)	6,425	964,691	Honolulu	John D. Waihee III (*D*)... (4—1990)
Idaho (1890) (*43*)	82,412	943,935	Boise	Cecil D. Andrus (*D*) (4—1991)
Illinois (Ill.) (1818) (*21*)	55,645	11,426,518	Springfield ..	James R. Thompson (*R*) .. (4—1991)
Indiana (Ind.) (1816) (*19*)	35,932	5,490,224	Indianapolis .	Evan Bayh (*D*) (4—1993)
Iowa (1846) (*29*)	55,965	2,913,808	Des Moines ..	Terry Branstad (*R*) (4—1991)
Kansas (Kan.) (1861) (*34*)	81,778	2,363,679	Topeka	Mike Hayden (*R*) (4—1991)
Kentucky (Ky.) (1792) (*15*)	39,669	3,660,777	Frankfort ...	Wallace G. Wilkinson (*D*) (4—1992)
Louisiana (La.) (1812) (*18*)	44,521	4,205,900	Baton Rouge..	Buddy Roemer (*D*) (4—1992)
Maine (Me.) (1820) (*23*)	30,995	1,124,660	Augusta	John R. McKernan, Jr. (*R*) (4—1991)
Maryland (Md.)§ (1788) (*7*)	9,837	4,216,975	Annapolis ...	William D. Schaefer (*D*).. (4—1991)
Massachusetts (Mass.)§ (1788) (*6*)	7,824	5,737,037	Boston	Michael S. Dukakis (*D*) .. (4—1991)
Michigan (Mich.) (1837) (*26*)	56,954	9,262,078	Lansing	James J. Blanchard (*D*) .. (4—1991)
Minnesota (Minn.) (1858) (*32*)	79,548	4,075,970	St. Paul	Rudy Perpich (*DFL*) (4—1991)
Mississippi (Miss.) (1817) (*20*)	47,233	2,520,638	Jackson	Ray Mabus (*D*) (4—1992)
Missouri (Mo.) (1821) (*24*)	68,945	4,916,686	Jefferson City.	John Ashcroft (*R*) (4—1993)
Montana (Mont.) (1889) (*41*)	145,388	786,690	Helena	Stan Stephens (*R*) (4—1993)
Nebraska (Neb.) (1867) (*37*)	76,644	1,569,825	Lincoln	Kay A. Orr (*R*) (4—1991)
Nevada (Nev.) (1864) (*36*)	109,894	800,493	Carson City ..	Robert J. Miller (*D*)**
New Hampshire (N.H.)§ (1788) (*9*)	8,993	920,610	Concord	Judd Gregg (*R*) (2—1991)
New Jersey (N.J.)§ (1787) (*3*)	7,468	7,364,823	Trenton	Thomas H. Kean (*R*) (4—1990)
New Mexico (N.M.) (1912) (*47*)	121,335	1,302,894	Santa Fé	Garry E. Carruthers (*R*) . (4—1991)
New York (N.Y.)§ (1788) (*11*) ...	47,377	17,558,072	Albany	Mario M. Cuomo (*D*) (4—1991)
North Carolina (N.C.)§ (1789) (*12*)	48,843	5,881,766	Raleigh	James G. Martin (*R*) (4—1993)
North Dakota (N.D.) (1889) (*39*)	69,300	652,717	Bismarck ...	George A. Sinner (*D*) (4—1993)
Ohio (1803) (*17*)	41,004	10,797,630	Columbus	Richard F. Celeste (*D*) ... (4—1991)
Oklahoma (Okla.) (1907) (*46*)	68,655	3,025,290	Oklahoma City	Henry Bellmon (*R*) (4—1991)
Oregon (Ore.) (1859) (*33*)	96,184	2,632,105	Salem	Neil Goldschmidt (*D*) .... (4—1991)
Pennsylvania (Pa.)§ (1787) (*2*) ..	44,888	11,863,895	Harrisburg ..	Robert P. Casey (*D*) (4—1991)
Rhode Island (R.I.)§ (1790) (*13*) .	1,055	947,154	Providence ...	Edward D. Di Prete (*R*) .. (2—1991)
South Carolina (S.C.)§ (1788) (*8*)	30,203	3,121,820	Columbia	Carroll A. Campbell, Jr.(*R*) (4—1991)
South Dakota (S.D.) (1889) (*40*) .	75,952	690,768	Pierre	George S. Mickelson (*R*).. (4—1991)
Tennessee (Tenn.) (1796) (*16*) ...	41,155	4,591,120	Nashville	Ned R. McWherter (*D*) ... (4—1991)
Texas (1845) (*28*)	262,017	14,229,191	Austin	William P. Clements, Jr. (*R*) (4—1991)
Utah (1896) (*45*)	82,073	1,461,037	Salt Lake City	Norman H. Bangerter (*R*) (4—1993)
Vermont (Vt.) (1791) (*14*)	9,273	511,456	Montpelier ...	Madeleine M. Kunin (*D*) . (2—1991)
Virginia (Va.)§ (1788) (*10*)	39,704	5,346,818	Richmond	Gerald L. Baliles (*D*) (4—1990)
Washington (Wash.) (1889) (*42*)	66,511	4,132,156	Olympia	Booth Gardner (*D*) (4—1993)
West Virginia (W. Va.) (1863)(*35*)	24,119	1,949,644	Charleston ...	Gaston Caperton (*D*) (4—1993)
Wisconsin (Wis.) (1848) (*30*)	54,426	4,705,767	Madison	Tommy Thompson (*R*) .... (4—1991)
Wyoming (Wyo.) (1890) (*44*)	96,989	469,557	Cheyenne	Michael Sullivan (*D*) (4—1991)
Dist. of Columbia (D.C.) (1791)..	63	638,333		†

OUTLYING TERRITORIES AND POSSESSIONS

American Samoa	76	32,395	Pago Pago	Peter Tali Coleman (*D*) .. (4—1993)
Guam	209	105,816	Agaña	Joseph Ada (*R*) (4—1991)
Marshall Is.	70	31,042	Majuro	
Fed. States of Micronesia	271	73,160	Kolonia	..
North Mariana Is.	184	16,780	Saipan	Pedro P. Tenorio (*R*) (4—1990)
Palau	192	12,177	Koror	..
Puerto Rico	3,421	3,187,570	San Juan	R. Hernandez-Colon (*PDP*)(4—1993)
Virgin Is.	132	95,591	Charlotte Amalie	Alexander Farrelly (*D*) .. (4—1991)

D.—Democratic Party. *DFL.*—Democrat-Farmer-Labor. *R.*—Republican Party. *I.*—Independent.
PDP.—Popular Democratic party. § The 13 Original States.
† The capital territory is governed by Congress through a Commissioner and City Council.
* Succeeded to governor's office April 1988, after her predecessor's impeachment.
** Acting Governor until previous governor's term expires in 1991. (Former Gov. Bryan was elected to the U.S. Senate.)

THE PRESIDENTS OF THE UNITED STATES OF AMERICA

Name (*with Native State*)	Party	Born	Inaug.	Died	Age
George Washington, *Va*	Fed.	1732, Feb. 22	1789	1799, Dec. 14	67
John Adams, *Mass.*	,,	1735, Oct. 30	1797	1826, July 4	90
Thomas Jefferson, *Va.*	Rep.	1743, April 13	1801	1826, July 4	83
James Madison, *Va.*	,,	1751, Mar. 16	1809	1836, June 28	85
James Monroe, *Va.*	,,	1758, April 28	1817	1831, July 4	73
John Quincy Adams, *Mass.*	,,	1767, July 11	1825	1848, Feb 23	80
Andrew Jackson, *S.C.*	Dem.	1767, Mar. 15	1829	1845, June 8	78
Martin Van Buren, *N.Y.*	,,	1782, Dec. 5	1837	1862, July 24	79
William Henry Harrison†, *Va.*	Whig.	1773, Feb. 9	1841	1841, April 4	68
John Tyler (*a*), *Va.*	,,	1790, Mar. 29	1841	1862, Jan. 17	71
James Knox Polk, *N.C.*	Dem.	1795, Nov. 2	1845	1849, June 15	53
Zachary Taylor†, *Va.*	Whig.	1784, Nov. 24	1849	1850, July 9	65
Millard Fillmore (*a*), *N.Y.*	,,	1800, Jan. 7	1850	1874, Mar. 8	74
Franklin Pierce, *N.H.*	Dem.	1804, Nov. 23	1853	1869, Oct. 8	64
James Buchanan, *Pa.*	,,	1791, April 23	1857	1868, June 1	77
Abraham Lincoln†§, *Ky.*	Rep.	1809, Feb. 12	1861	1865, April 15	56
Andrew Johnson (*a*), *N.C.*	,,	1808, Dec. 29	1865	1875, July 31	66
Ulysses Simpson Grant, *Ohio*	,,	1822, April 27	1869	1885, July 23	63
Rutherford Birchard Hayes, *Ohio*	,,	1822, Oct. 4	1877	1893, Jan. 17	70
James Abram Garfield†§, *Ohio*	,,	1831, Nov. 19	1881	1881, Sept. 19	49
Chester Alan Arthur (*a*), *Vt.*	,,	1830, Oct. 5	1881	1886, Nov. 18	56
Grover Cleveland, *N.J.*	Dem.	1837, Mar. 18	1885	1908, June 24	71
Benjamin Harrison, *Ohio*	Rep.	1833, Aug. 20	1889	1901, Mar. 13	67
Grover Cleveland, *N.J.*	Dem.	1837, Mar. 18	1893	1908, June 24	71
William McKinley†§, *Ohio*	Rep.	1843, Jan. 29	1897	1901, Sept. 14	58
Theodore Roosevelt (*a*), *N.Y.*	,,	1858, Oct. 27	1901	1919, Jan. 6	60
William Howard Taft, *Ohio*	,,	1857, Sept. 15	1909	1930, Mar. 8	72
Woodrow Wilson, *Va.*	Dem.	1856, Dec. 28	1913	1924, Feb. 3	67
Warren Gamaliel Harding†, *Ohio*	Rep.	1865, Nov. 2	1921	1923, Aug. 2	57
Calvin Coolidge (*a*), *Vt.*	,,	1872, July 4	1923	1933, Jan. 5	60
Herbert Clark Hoover, *Iowa.*	,,	1874, Aug. 10	1929	1964, Oct. 20	90
Franklin Delano Roosevelt†‡, *N.Y.*	Dem.	1882, Jan. 30	1933	1945, April 12	63
Harry S. Truman (*a*), *Missouri*	,,	1884, May 8	1945	1972, Dec. 26	88
Dwight David Eisenhower, *Texas*	Rep.	1890, Oct. 14	1953	1969, Mar. 28	78
John Fitzgerald Kennedy, *Mass.*†§	Dem.	1917, May 29	1961	1963, Nov. 22	46
Lyndon Baines Johnson (*a*), *Texas*	,,	1908, Aug. 27	1963	1973, Jan. 22	64
Richard Milhous Nixon, *California*	Rep.	1913, Jan. 9	1969	..	..
Gerald Rudolph Ford (*a*), *Nebraska*	,,	1913, July 14	1974	..	..
James Earl Carter, *Georgia*	Dem.	1924, Oct. 1	1977	..	..
Ronald Wilson Reagan, *Illinois*	Rep.	1911, Feb. 6	1981	..	..
George Herbert Walker Bush, *Mass.*	,,	1924, June 12	1989	..	..

† Died in office.   § Assassinated.   (*a*) Elected as Vice-President.
‡ Re-elected Nov. 5, 1940, the first case of a third term; re-elected for a fourth term Nov. 7. 1944.

GOVERNMENT

The United States of America is a Federal Republic consisting of 50 States and 1 Federal District (of which 13 are Original States, 7 were admitted without previous organization as Territories, and 30 were admitted after such organization), and of organized Territories. Hawaii formally entered the Union as the 50th State on Aug. 21, 1959, from which date the flag of the United States has 13 stripes and 50 stars in 9 horizontal rows of six and five alternatively.

NATIONAL ANTHEM.—The Star-Spangled Banner.
NATIONAL DAY.—July 4 (Independence Day).

THE CONSTITUTION.—By the Constitution of Sept. 17, 1787 (to which ten amendments were added on Dec. 15, 1791 and eleventh to twenty-sixth, Jan. 8, 1798, Sept. 25, 1804, Dec. 18, 1865, July 28, 1868, March 30, 1870, Feb. 25, 1913, May 31, 1913, Jan. 16, 1920, Aug. 26, 1920, Feb. 6, 1933, Dec. 5, 1933, Feb. 26, 1951, March 29, 1961, Jan. 23, 1964, Feb. 10, 1967 and June 30, 1971), the government of the United States is entrusted to three separate authorities—the Executive, the Legislative, and the Judicial.

THE EXECUTIVE

THE executive power is vested in a President, who is elected every four years. The mode of electing the President is as follows:—Each State elects (on the first Tuesday after the first Monday in November of the year preceding the year in which the Presidential term expires), a number of electors, equal to the whole number of Senators and Representatives to which the State may be entitled in the Congress; but no Senator or Representative, or anyone holding office under Government, shall be appointed an elector. The electors for each State meet in their respective States on the first Monday after the second Wednesday in December following, and there vote for a President by ballot. The ballots are then sent to Washington, and opened on the *sixth day of January* by the President of Senate in presence of Congress, and the candidate who has received a majority of the whole number of electoral votes cast is declared President for the ensuing term. If no one has a majority, then from the highest on the list (not exceeding three) the House of Representatives elects a President, the votes being taken by States, the representation from each State having one vote. There is also a Vice-President, who, on the death of the President, becomes President for the remainder of the term. Under the XXth Amendment to the Constitution the terms of the President and Vice-President end at noon on the 20th day of January of the years in which such terms would have ended if the Amendment had not been ratified, and the terms of their successors then begin. In case of the removal or death of both President and Vice-President, a statute provides for the succession. Under the XXIInd Amendment to the Constitution, the tenure of the Presidency is limited to two terms.

Executive duties:—(1) He is Commander-in-Chief of the Army and of the Navy (and of the Militias when they are in Federal service), and he commissions all officers therein. (2) With the consent of the Senate, he appoints the Cabinet officers and all the chief (and many minor) officials. (3) He exercises a general supervision over the whole Federal Administration and sees that the Federal Laws are duly carried out. Should disorder arise in any state which the authorities thereof are unable to suppress, the aid of the President is invoked. (4) He conducts the foreign policy of the Republic, and has power, "by and with the Advice and Consent of the Senate, to make Treaties, provided two thirds of the senators present concur." The declaration of war rests with Congress. (5) He makes recommendation of a general nature to Congress, and when laws are passed by Congress he may return them to Congress with a veto. But if a measure so vetoed is again passed by both Houses of Congress by two-thirds majority in each House, it becomes law, notwithstanding the objection of the President. The President must be at least 35 years of age and a native citizen of the United States. He receives a taxable salary of $200,000 with a taxable expense allowance of $50,000 and a non-taxable travelling allowance not exceeding $100,000.

President of the United States, GEORGE HERBERT WALKER BUSH, *born* June 12, 1924, *sworn in* January 20, 1989. Republican.

Vice-President, DAN QUAYLE, *born* Feb. 4, 1947, *sworn in* Jan. 20, 1989.

THE CABINET

Secretary of State, James Baker.
Secretary of the Treasury, Nicholas Brady.
Attorney General, Richard Thornburgh.
Secretary of Defence, Richard Cheney.
Secretary of the Interior, Manuel Lujan.
Secretary of Agriculture, Clayton Yeutter.
Secretary of Commerce, Robert Mosbacher.
Secretary of Labour, Elizabeth Dole.
Secretary of Health and Human Services, Dr. Louis Sullivan.
Secretary of Housing and Urban Development, Jack Kemp.
Secretary of Transportation, Samuel Skinner.
Secretary of Energy, James Watkins.
Secretary of Education, Dr. Lauro Cavazos.
Veteran's Affairs, Edward Derwinski.

Other top positions:
Director of C.I.A., William Webster.
Dir., Office of National Drug Control Policy, William Bennett.
White House Chief of Staff, John Sununu.
National Security Adviser, Brent Scowcroft.
Dir., Office of Management and Budget, Richard Darman.

UNITED STATES EMBASSY
24 Grosvenor Square W1A 1AE
[01-499 9000]

Ambassador Extraordinary and Plenipotentiary, The Honourable Henry E. Catto (1989).
Minister, Hon. Raymond G. H. Seitz.
Minister for Economic Affairs, Richard M. Ogden.
Minister Counsellors, Edward Kreuser (*Consular Affairs*); Lawrence D. Russell (*Administrative Affairs*); David K. Diebold (*Commercial Affairs*); Lester P. Slezak (*Political/Labour Affairs*); Rolland E. Anderson (*Agricultural Affairs*); Miles S. Pendleton (*Political Affairs*); Charles E. Courtney (*Public Affairs*).

Defence Attaché, Col. Keith N. Lacey II.
Army Attaché, Col. James T. Hennessey, Jr.
Naval Attaché, Cpt. Joseph R. McCleary.

CAPITAL OF THE UNITED STATES

In 1790 Congress ratified the cession of 100 sq. miles by the States of Maryland and Virginia as a site for a Federal City to be the national capital of the United States. In 1791 it was decided to name the capital Washington and in 1793 the foundation-stone of the Capitol building was laid. In 1800 the seat of Government was removed to Washington, which was chartered as a city in 1802. In 1846 the Virginia portion was retroceded and the present area of the District of Columbia (with which the City of Washington is considered co-extensive) is 63 sq. miles, with a resident population (mid-1986 estimate) of 626,000.

The District of Columbia is governed by an elected mayor and City Council.

The City of Washington is situated on the west central edge of Maryland, opposite the State of Virginia, on the left bank of the Potomac at its confluence with the Anacostia. The population of the metropolitan area in 1986 was estimated at 3,563,000.

THE CONGRESS

The Legislative power is vested in two Houses, the Senate and the House of Representatives, the President having a veto power, which may be overcome by a two-thirds vote of each House. The Senate is composed of two Senators from each State, elected by the people thereof for the term of six years, and each Senator has one vote. Representatives are chosen in each State, by popular vote, for two years. The average number of persons represented by each Congressman is 1 for 550,000. The Senate consists of 100 members. The salary of a Senator is $89,500 per annum. The House of Representatives consists of 435 Representatives, a resident commissioner from Puerto Rico and a delegate from American Samoa, the District of Columbia, Guam and the Virgin Islands. The salary of a Representative is $89,500 per annum. By the XIXth Amendment, sex is no disqualification for the franchise. The Bureau of the Census estimated that there were 182,628,000 persons of voting age, excluding members of the armed forces overseas as of November 1988.

THE HUNDRED AND FIRST CONGRESS

President of the Senate, Dan Quayle (*Vice President of the United States*).
Speaker of the House of Representatives, Thomas S. Foley, *Washington.*
Secretary of the Senate, Walter J. Stewart, *Dist. of Columbia.*
Clerk of the House of Representatives, Donnald K. Anderson, *California.*

Members of the 101st Congress were elected on Nov. 8, 1988.

The 101st Congress is constituted as follows:
Senate.—Democrats 55; Republicans, 45; Total, 100.
House of Representatives.—Democrats, 257; Republicans, 175; Vacancies, 3. Total, 435 (July 1, 1989).

THE JUDICATURE

The Federal Judiciary consists of three sets of Federal Courts: (1) The Supreme Court at Washington, D.C., consisting of a Chief Justice and eight Associate Justices, with original jurisdiction in cases affecting Ambassadors, etc., or where a State is a party to the suit, and with appellate jurisdiction from inferior Federal Courts and from the judgments of the highest Courts of the States. (2) The United States Courts of Appeals, dealing with appeals from District Courts and from certain federal administrative agencies, and consisting of all the Circuit Judges within the circuit. (3) The 94 United States District Courts served by 700 District Court Judges.

THE SUPREME COURT
(U.S. Supreme Court Building, Washington, D.C., 20543)

Chief Justice, William H. Rehnquist, *Ariz., born* Oct. 1, 1924, *appointed* 1986.

ASSOCIATE JUSTICES

Name	Born	Apptd
William J. Brennan, Jr., *N.J.*	1906	1956
Byron R. White, *Colo.*	1917	1962
Thurgood Marshall, *N.Y.*	1908	1967
Harry Blackmun, *Minn.*	1908	1970
John Paul Stevens, *Ill.*	1920	1975
Sandra Day O'Connor, *Ariz.*	1930	1981
Antonin Scalia, *Va.*	1936	1986
Anthony M. Kennedy, *Calif.*	1936	1988

Clerk of the Supreme Court, Joseph F. Spaniol, Jr.

CRIMINAL STATISTICS, U.S.

Crime	No. of offences	
	1987	1988
Murder and Non-negligent Manslaughter	20,096	20,675
Forcible Rape	91,111	92,486
Robbery	517,704	542,968
Aggravated Assault	855,088	910,092
Burglary	3,236,184	3,218,077
Larceny—Theft	7,499,851	7,711,872
Thefts of Motor Vehicles	1,288,674	1,432,916
Total	13,508,708	13,929,086

DEFENCE
Department of Defence

Secretary of Defence (in the Cabinet), Richard B. Cheney.
Secretary of the Army, John O. Marsh, Jr.
Secretary of the Navy, H. L. Garrett.
Secretary of the Air Force, D. B. Rice.
Chairman, Joint Chief of Staff, Gen. Colin Powell.
Vice Chairman, Gen. Robert T. Herres.

The Department of Defence includes the Secretary of Defence as its head, the Deputy Secretary of Defence, the Defence staff offices, the Joint Chiefs of Staff and the Joint Staff, the three military departments and the military services within those departments, the unified and specified commands, and other Department of Defence agencies as the Secretary of Defence establishes to meet specific requirements. The Defence staff offices and the joint Chiefs of Staff, although separately organized, function in full co-ordination and co-operation. They include the offices of the Director of Defence Research and Engineering, the Assistant Secretaries of Defence, the General Counsel of the Department of Defence and such other staff offices as the Secretary of Defence may establish. The Joint Chiefs of Staff, as a group, are directly responsible to the Secretary of Defence for the functions assigned to them. Each member of the Joint Chiefs of Staff, other than the Chairman and Vice Chairman, is responsible for keeping the Secretary of his military department fully informed on matters considered or acted upon by the Joint Chiefs of Staff.

Each military department is separately organized under its own Secretary and functions under the direction, authority and control of the Secretary of Defence.

The Department of Defence maintains and employs armed forces: (1) to support and defend the Constitution of the United States against all enemies, foreign and domestic; (2) to insure, by timely and effective military action, the security of the United States, its possessions, and areas vital to its interests; (3) to uphold and advance the national policies and interest of the United States; and (4) to safeguard the internal security of the United States. All functions in the Department of Defence and its component agencies are performed under the direction, authority and control of the Secretary of Defence.

Commanders of unified and specified commands are responsible to the President and the Secretary of Defence for the accomplishment of military missions assigned to them.

Unified Defence Commands
COMMANDERS-IN-CHIEF

U.S. European Command, Brussels.—Gen. Crosbie Saint (*U.S. Army*) (concurrently *N.A.T.O. Supreme Allied Commander*).
U.S. Southern Command, Quarry Heights, Panama Canal Zone.—Lt.-Gen. Frederick F. Woerner (*U.S. Army*).
U.S. Atlantic Command, Norfolk, Virginia.—(vacant) (concurrently *N.A.T.O. Supreme Allied Commander, Atlantic*).
U.S. Pacific Command, Hawaii.—Adm. Ronald J. Hays (*U.S. Navy*).
U.S. Space Command, Gen. John L. Piotrowski (*U.S.A.F.*).
**Strategic Air Command,* Omaha.—Gen. John T. Chain (*U.S.A.F.*).
**U.S. Transportation Command,* Gen. Duane H. Cassidy (*U.S.A.F.*).
U.S. Special Operations Command, MacDill A.F.B., Florida.—Gen. James J. Lindsay (*U.S. Army*).
U.S. Central Command, Gen. George B. Crist (*U.S. Marine Corps*).
* A specified command.

Army.—The U.S. Army had a strength on March 31, 1989, of 764,259. Stationed in Germany were four divisions.
Chief of the Staff of the Army, Gen. Carl E. Vuono.
Navy.—The strength of the Navy (including Marine Corps) on March 31, 1989 was 581,050 active duty personnel.
The U.S. Navy had in service at Sept. 30, 1987, 568 active fleet ships (Surface vessels, 429; Submarines, 139).
Chief of Naval Operations, Adm. Carlisle A. H. Trost.
Marine Corps.—Established 1775. Strength on March 31, 1989 was 194,860 active duty personnel.
Commandant, Gen. Alfred M. Gray.
Air.—The United States Air Force was established as a separate organization on September 18, 1947. On March 31, 1989, there were 575,604 officers and airmen on active duty.
The Air Force has up to 30 per cent of the strategic bomber and tanker forces maintaining constant alert as well as 1,000 inter-continental ballistic missiles in silos. In addition, the Air Force maintains the capability to carry out limited war and special warfare operations, with more than 9,300 strategic, tactical and support aircraft. In March, 1961, the Air Force was assigned primary responsibility for the Department of Defence space development programmes and projects.
Chief of Staff of the U.S. Air Force, Larry D. Welch.

THE UNITED STATES BUDGET
(fiscal year; in millions of US$)

Receipts by Source	1987 (*actual*)	1988 (*estimated*)
Individual income taxes	392,600	393,400
Corporation income taxes	83,900	105,600
Social insurance taxes and contributions	303,300	331,500
Excise taxes	32,500	35,300
Estate and gift taxes	7,500	7,600
Customs duties	15,100	16,400
Miscellaneous	19,300	19,400
Total	854,100	909,200
Outlays by Function		
National defence	282,000	285,400
International affairs	11,600	9,900
Income security	123,300	129,600
Health	40,000	44,500
Social security and medicare	282,500	298,600
Veterans' benefits and services	26,800	27,700
Education, training, employment and social services	29,700	33,700
Commerce and housing credit	6,200	12,400
Transportation	26,200	27,200
Natural resources and environment	13,400	15,100
Energy	4,100	2,700
Community and regional development	5,100	6,300
Agriculture	27,400	22,400
Net interest	138,600	147,900
General science, space and technology	9,200	10,900
General government	7,600	8,800
General purpose fiscal assistance	1,600	1,800
Administration of justice	7,500	9,000
Undistributed offsetting receipts	−36,500	−36,100
Total	1,004,600	1,055,904

FINANCE

SOCIAL WELFARE EXPENDITURE

Total expenditure by programme was ($ millions):

	1985	1986
Social insurance	372,529	390,404
Education	166,418	178,518
Public aid	96,777	103,079
Health and medical	41,060	44,334
Veterans' programmes	27,042	27,445
Other social welfare	13,946	14,705
Housing	12,627	12,036
TOTAL	730,399	770,521

Expenditure per capita was ($):

Social insurance	1,528	1,587
Education	685	728
Public aid	398	421
Health and medical	169	181
Veterans' programmes	111	111
Other social welfare	57	60
Housing	52	49
TOTAL	3,001	3,137

PUBLIC DEBT

At the end Sept. 1988 the total gross Federal Debt of the United States stood at $2,614,581 million.

COST OF LIVING IN U.S.A.

The Consumer Price Index for all urban consumers (CPI-U) with prices collected in 91 areas across the U.S.A. was measured for the year 1988 at 117·0 (1982–84 = 100), versus 112·5 for 1987.

GROSS NATIONAL PRODUCT

Gross National Product by industry in 1987 was ($ million):—

All industries, total	4,461,200
Agriculture, forestry, fisheries	98,800
Mining	95,300
Construction	208,700
Manufacturing	861,200
Transportation and public utilities	406,900
Trade	740,600
Finance, insurance, real estate	755,100
Services	757,900
Government and government enterprises	541,200
Rest of the world	27,400

G.N.P., national and personal income in 1987 were ($ million):—

Gross national product	3,821,000
Net national product	3,362,300
National income	3,045,700
Corporate profits	304,700
Net interest	337,100
Personal income	3,746,500
Personal tax and non-tax payments	564,800
Disposable personal income	3,181,700
Personal outlays	3,062,700
Personal saving	119,000

Personal consumption expenditure in 1987 was $2,497,200 million, of which durable goods accounted for $388,200 million, non-durable goods $878,100 million and services $1,230,900 million. Gross private domestic investment in 1986 was $671,000 million.

UNITED STATES STOCK OF CURRENCY AND COIN

The U.S. unit of currency is the Dollar ($) of 100 cents.

U.S. stock of currency and coin at March 31, 1988 was:—

	$ million
Gold	11,062·5
Dollars	340·1
Subsidiary Coin	93·8
Minor Coin	20·7
Silver Certificates	198·6
U.S. Notes	322·5
Federal Reserve Notes	255,200·3
TOTAL	267,238·5

AGRICULTURE AND LIVESTOCK

The total number of farms in 1988 was 2,158,800, with a total area of land in farms of 998,692,000 acres, and an average acreage per farm of 463 acres. The total number of people employed on farms during the week of April 9–15, 1989, was 2,805,000, of whom 1,777,000 were unpaid workers, 830,000 hired workers and 198,000 agricultural service workers.

Principal crops are corn for grain, soybeans, wheat hay, cotton, tobacco, grain sorghums, potatoes, oranges and barley.

Livestock on farms on Jan. 1, 1987 and 1988 was:—

	1987 (000's)	1988 (000's)
All cattle	102,000	98,994
Milk cows	10,502	10,307
Sheep and lambs	10,334	10,774
Hogs and pigs*	50,920	53,795
Chickens*	369,131	377,516

Gross income from farming in 1987 was $169,765 million, of which cash receipts from marketing were $138,094 million and Government payments $16,747 million. Cash income from all crops in 1987 was $61,876 million and from livestock and livestock products $76,218 million.

NONFUEL MINERALS

The value of nonfuel raw mineral production in the United States in 1987 totalled an estimated $26,346 million compared with $23,480 million in 1986.

Trading Figures

	1985	1986
Imports	$29,380m	$31,693m
Exports	13,080m	11,558m

Production Figures
('000 tonnes)

	1987	1988p
Aluminium	3,343	3,900
Iron Ore†	46,817	58,400
Phosphate rock*	40,954	46,000
Zinc Ore	217	245
Refined Copper	1,561	1,900
Refined Lead	1,084	1,089

* marketable production
† measured in long tons
p = preliminary

ENERGY

Energy Summary
(*Quadrillion (10^{15}) Btu*)

	1986	1987	1988
Production	64·22	64·82	65·84
Consumption	74·23	76·76	79·94
Imports	14·43	15·75	16·95
Exports	4·05	3·85	4·44

Breakdown of Production and Consumption
(*Quadrillion (10^{15}) Btu*)

	1987	1988
Production		
Crude Oil	17·67	17·25
Coal	20·14	20·93
Natural Gas (dry)	17·05	17·15
Natural Gas Plant Liquids	2·21	2·26
Hydroelectric	2·59	2·31
Nuclear	4·90	5·67
Other*	0·24	0·23
Total	64·82	65·84
Consumption		
Petroleum	32·86	33·95
Natural Gas (dry)	17·66	18·59
Coal	18·00	18·82
Hydroelectric	3·06	2·61
Nuclear	4·90	5·67
Other*	0·25	0·27
Total	76·76	79·94

* Includes geothermal power, photovoltaic solar power and electricity produced from wood and waste.

During 1987 oil and gas drilling rigs in operation averaged 936 and the number of well completions in 1987 totalled 33,430. Seismic exploration work in progress involved a total (average) of 176 crews, 24 in offshore areas and 153 on shore. Domestic crude oil production in 1988 averaged 8,129,000 barrels per day and total petroleum imports averaged 7,172,000 barrels per day. Production of dry natural gas in 1988 was 16,642 billion cubic feet (Bcf). Stocks of gas available for withdrawal were estimated at 2,140 Bcf in 1988. Production of coal in 1988 was 958,912,000 short tons. In 1988 U.S. nuclear power generators produced 526,901 million net kilowatt-hours of electricity, accounting for 19·5 per cent of domestic electricity generation. Operable reactors at end Dec. 1988 totalled 108, with a net summer capacity of 95·08 million net kilowatts.

LABOUR

Organized Labour.—16,913,000 persons were members of labour organizations in 1987.

Work Stoppages.—There were 46 stoppages involving 1,000 or more workers in 1987. They resulted in 4,481,000 man-days of idleness, representing 0·02 per cent. of estimated working time of all non-agricultural workers.

Employment and Unemployment.—The civilian labour force (working population) was 120,978,000 in May 1988. This includes self-employed wage and salary-earners, and unpaid family workers, employed and unemployed. Unemployment was estimated at 6,783,000 in May 1988 (5·6 per cent.) (it was 6·3 per cent in May 1987).

Wages.—In March 1988, gross average weekly earnings in industry ranged from $711·47 per week in malt beverage industry (42·4 hours and $16·78 average hourly earnings) to $113·85 in eating and drinking places (25·3 hours and $4·50 average hourly earnings). The average for all manufacturing was $411·86 compared with $403·27 in March 1987.

On Jan. 1, 1981, the minimum wage set by federal law became $3·35. The law requires at least time and a half of an employee's regular rate of pay for all hours over 40 a week for most covered workers.

The Fair Labour Standards Act covers all employees of certain enterprises having workers engaged in interstate commerce, producing goods for interstate commerce, or handling, selling, or otherwise working on goods or materials that have been moved in or produced for such commerce by any person.

There are certain exemptions from these requirements in specific occupations and industries.

In addition to cash wages, almost all workers are covered by legally required social security, unemployment insurance and workers' compensation insurance. Also though not required by law, most workers receive some type of 'fringe' benefits—the most common forms being paid vacations, and public holidays, various types of retirement plans, insurance and health benefits financed by the employer or by employer and employees jointly.

EXTERNAL TRADE OF THE UNITED STATES

	1986	1987
	\$ million	
General Imports:		
c.i.f. value	387,082·0	424,082·3
customs value	369,961·0	405,900·6
Exports and re-exports:		
f.a.s. value†	217,292·0	252,852·7
Trade balance:		
f.a.s. exports: c.i.f.		
imports	−169,790·0	−171,229·6
f.a.s. exports: customs		
imports	−152,669·0	−153,048·0

† Excluding military aid.

EXPORTS BY PRINCIPAL COMMODITIES OF DOMESTIC ORIGIN, 1987

Commodity	Value
	\$ (million)
Food and Live Animals	19,178·8
Grain and cereal preparations	8,058·1
Beverages and Tobacco	3,666·7
Crude materials (inedible) except fuel .	20,416·3
Raw cotton	1,630·8
Metal ores, concentrates, scrap	3,018·3
Mineral fuels, lubricants, etc..........	7,713·1
Coal (bituminous)	3,322·7
Oils and Fats (animal and vegetable) ..	961·4
Chemicals and products	26,380·9
Machinery and Transport Equipment .	108,596·0
Electronic computers, parts, etc.	17,494·8
Electrical machinery, appliances,	
etc.	16,637·2
Motor vehicles and parts	20,878·8
Other Manufactured Goods	19,409·0
Unclassified Commodities	20,380·7

U.S. IMPORTS BY PRINCIPAL COMMODITIES, 1987

Commodity	Value
	\$ (million)
Food and Live Animals	20,547·1
Fish and fish preparations..........	5,590·0
Vegetables and fruit	4,475·9
Coffee—crude......................	2,705·8
Beverages and Tobacco	4,104·9
Crude materials (inedible), except fuels	11,525·7
Mineral fuels, lubricants, etc..........	64,219·5
Crude petroleum	29,320·5
Petroleum products	12,208·9
Oils and Fats (animal and vegetable) ..	568·1
Chemicals and products	16,213·4
Machinery and Transport Equipment .	177,808·7
Telecommunications, sound record-	
ing apparatus	20,820·5
Electrical machinery, parts.........	24,428·3
Motor vehicles	57,023·8
Other Manufactured Goods	66,183·1
Unclassified Commodities	12,373·4

U.S. FOREIGN TRADE BY ECONOMIC CLASS 1987

	\$ million	
Class	Imports	Exports*
Crude Materials...	38,645	11,973
Crude Foodstuffs ..	10,123	10,197
Manufactured		
Foods	14,225	10,312
Semi-manufactures	44,820	41,594
Finished		
Manufactures...	298,088	167,323
Total..........	405,901	241,399

*Excluding the total military grant-aid of \$228,280 million.

U.S. FOREIGN TRADE BY PRINCIPAL AREAS AND COUNTRIES, 1987

Area/Country	Exports and Re-exports to	General Imports from
	\$ million	
Africa..................	6,283	11,939
Asia	73,268	174,452
Japan	28,249	84,575
Saudi Arabia	3,373	4,433
Taiwan	7,418	24,622
Korea, Rep. of.........	8,099	16,987
Hong Kong	3,983	9,854
Oceania	6,526	4,136
Australia..............	5,495	3,007
Europe	71,917	97,419
Germany, Fed. Rep. of .	11,748	27,069
U.K.	14,114	17,341
Other E.C.............	34,713	36,778
Other O.E.C.D.........	8,516	13,447
Communist bloc	2,200	1,923
N. & Central America....	81,758	97,591
Canada	59,814	71,085
Mexico	14,582	20,271
S. America	13,036	20,363

COMMUNICATIONS

RAILWAYS

Data on Class I line-haul railroads (dollars in thousands)

	1986	1987
Operating Revenues		
Freight	25,343,911	25,797,002
Passenger	107,717	93,559
Total.......	26,204,122	26,622,482
Total operating		
expenses	24,896,015	23,878,116
Net working		
capital	742,739	34,081
Average number of		
employees	275,817	248,526

ROADS

In 1987 there were 3·87 million miles of public roads and streets in the United States, of which 3·16 million miles were in rural areas and 710,188 miles were in urban areas. Surfaced roads and streets account for 3·50 million miles, or 90·4 per cent, of the total; 371,325 miles, or 9·6 per cent, were unimproved or graded and drained.

An estimated total of \$62,987 million was spent in 1987 for roads and streets in the United States. Capital outlay accounts for 48·7 per cent of the total expenditure; 29·9 per cent was spent for maintenance, and 7·9 per cent for administration; 9·3 per cent for highway police and safety; and 4·4 per cent for interest on highway bonds.

Motor Vehicles and Taxation.—The number of motor vehicles registered in 1987 in the United States was 179,044,449, an increase of 1·9 per cent over the 1986 total of 175,700,214. In 1987 the State governments received $24,596,000,000 in State Highway-User Tax Receipts, including road and crossing tolls, and $12,618,000,000 in Federal Highway-User Tax Receipts.

Accidents.—In 1987 there were 46,385 deaths caused by motor vehicle accidents. The death rate per 100,000,000 vehicle-miles of travel was 2·41 in 1987 compared with 2·51 in 1986.

SHIPPING

The ocean-going Merchant Marine of the U.S. on April 1, 1989, consisted of 676 vessels of 1,000 gross tons and over, of which 425 were privately owned and 251 were government-owned ships. Of the 425 privately owned vessels, 378 were active including 3 combination passenger and cargo ships, 34 freighters, 16 bulk carriers, 175 tankers, 15 tug-barge units, 10 liquefied natural gas carriers and 125 intermodal

ships. There were 240 ships in the National Defence Reserve Fleet of inactive government-owned vessels.

AIR TRANSPORT

United States domestic and international scheduled airlines in 1984 carried 344,460,600 passengers over 304,987,288,000 revenue passenger miles. Cargo revenue ton-miles totalled 8,200,000,000, an increase of 8·0 per cent over 1983. Air cargo ton-miles were distributed as follows: freight 6,500,000,000 (up 7·7 per cent); express 64,400,000 (up 2·8 per cent); and air mail 1,600,000,000 (up 9·3 per cent).

Total operating revenues of all U.S. scheduled airlines were $43,800,000,000 in 1984, an increase of 13·5 per cent from 1983.

Total operating expenses rose to $41,700,000,000 in 1984, a 9·0 per cent increase over 1983. Scheduled operations showed a net operating profit of $2,100,000,000 in 1984, compared with a net operating profit of $361,700,000 in 1983.

Three principal classes of commercial air carriers have been established in the United States based on annual operating revenues. They are: Majors, with annual operating revenues of over $1,000 million; Nationals, with annual operating revenues of $75–1,000 million; and Regionals, with annual operating revenues of up to $75,999,000.

U.S. Scheduled Airline Industry Statistics, 1984 (Thousands)

	Majors	Nationals	Regionals	System
Revenue Passenger Carried	250,150	80,337	13,974	344,461
Revenue Passengers Miles	252,295,400	43,820,182	8,871,706	304,987,288
Air Mail Ton Miles	1,402,063	199,028	15,841	1,616,932
Express Ton Miles	60,255	2,024	131	62,410
Freight Ton Miles	3,905,550	2,445,897	145,714	6,497,161
Revenue Ton Miles	30,597,429	7,028,968	1,048,857	38,675,254
Revenue Plane Miles	2,391,806	579,533	159,890	3,131,229

EDUCATION
State School Systems

All the 50 States and the District of Columbia have compulsory school attendance laws. In general, children are obliged to attend school from 7 to 16 years of age. Officers of local administrative units, usually known as truant or attendance officers, are charged with enforcing the compulsory attendance laws.

In the autumn of 1987, 45,900,000 children were enrolled in regular elementary and secondary day schools in the United States, of whom 5·7 million or 12·4 per cent attended private schools.

The following percentages of the school-age population were estimated to be enrolled in school in the autumn of 1986; of 5- and 6-year-olds, 95 per cent; of 7- to 13-year-olds, 99 per cent; of 14- to 17-year-olds, 95 per cent; and of 18- to 24-year-olds, 32 per cent.

During the 1986–87 school year, the average daily attendance in regular public elementary and secondary day schools was 36,951,000. In the 1986–87 school year 2,428,000 students graduated from regular public high schools, 265,000 graduated from private high school. In addition some 25,000 graduated from evening schools and adult education programmes, and an estimated 400,000 received high school equivalency certificates. Public school teachers numbered 2,423,000, with an average salary of $26,534.

Most of the revenue for public elementary and secondary school purposes comes from the Federal, State, and local governments. Less than ½ per cent comes from gifts from tuition and transportation fees. Estimated revenue receipts during 1986–87

amounted to $162,453,000,000; 6·6 per cent from the Federal Government, 49·6 per cent from State governments, and 43·8 per cent from local sources. Estimated current expenditure in the 1986–87 school year was $149,099 million; for sites, buildings, furniture and equipment expenditures, $9,210 million; for interest in school debt $2,956 million.

Institutions of Higher Education

In the autumn of 1987, total enrolment in universities, colleges, professional schools, and two-year schools numbered 12,544,000.

Degrees conferred during the academic years 1985–86 and 1986–87 were:—

Degree	1985–86	1986–87
Bachelor's	987,823	987,000
First-Professional	73,910	73,000
Master's	288,567	291,000
Doctorates	33,653	34,200

During 1985–86 the major fields for bachelor's degrees were business and management (238,160), engineering (95,953) and social sciences (93,703). First-profession degrees in law (35,844) and medicine (15,938) predominated. Master's degrees were heavily concentrated in education (76,353) and business and management (67,137). The most popular fields of study for doctorates were education (7,110) and life sciences (3,358).

During the 1986–87 academic year, the 3,406 colleges and universities employed about 717,000 (full-time equivalent) instructional faculty. Total expenditures for colleges and universities during the 1986–87 academic year were $115,900 million.

Particulars of some of the Universities (with opening autumn enrolment figures, 1985) are: *Harvard* (20,711 students, including 7,747 women), founded at Cambridge, Mass. on Oct. 28, 1636, and named after John Harvard of Emmanuel College, Cambridge, England, who bequeathed to it his library and a sum of money in 1638; *Yale* (10,809 students, including 4,740 women), founded at New Haven, Connecticut, in 1701; *Bowdoin*, Brunswick, Me. (founded 1794; 1,446 students including 626 women); *Brown*, Providence, R.I. (founded 1764; 7,277 students, including 3,398 women); *Columbia*, New York, N.Y. (founded 1754; 23,556 students, including 12,393 women); *Cornell* (founded at Ithaca, N.Y., 1865; 19,680 students, including 8,626 women); *Dartmouth*, Hanover, N.H. (founded 1769, 4,519 students, including 1,826 women); *Georgetown*, Washington, D.C. (founded 1789; 11,985 students, including 5,484 women); *North Carolina*, Chapel Hill, N.C. (founded in 1789; 22,066 students, including 12,504 women); *Pennsylvania*, Philadelphia, Pa. (founded 1740; 21,870 students, including 9,926 women); *Princeton*, N.J. (founded 1746; 6,293 students and 2,215 women); and *William and Mary*, Williamsburg, Va. (founded 1693; 6,676 students, including 3,448 women).

WEIGHTS AND MEASURES

The weights and measures in common use in the United States are of British origin, and date back to the American Revolution when practically all the standards were intended to be equivalent to those used in England at that period. Divergencies in these weights and measures were, however, quite common, due no doubt to the fact that the system of weights and measures in England was not itself well established, and hence the copies brought to the United States were often adjusted to different standards. Because of these discrepancies, the system of weights and measures in the United States (U.S. inch-pound system) is not identical with the British system.

The U.S. ton (short) = 2,000 pounds (British Imperial ton = 2,240 pounds, or 1 U.S. long ton). The U.S. gallon = 231 cubic inches (277·42 cubic inches in U.K.) or 128 fluid ounces (160 fluid ounces in U.K.). In the British system the units of dry measure are the same as those of liquid measure. In the United States these two are not the same, the gallon and its subdivisions being used in the measurement of liquids, while the bushel, with its subdivisions, is used in the measurement of certain dry commodities. The U.S. gallon is divided into 4 liquid quarts and the U.S. bushel into 32 dry quarts.

The International System of Units—officially abbreviated SI—is a modernized version of the metric system. It was established by international agreement to provide a logical and interconnected framework for all measurements in science, industry and commerce.

In 1971, a study recommended a concerted, coordinated, but voluntary national effort to make the SI the predominant form of measurement in the United States. In December 1975, legislation was passed which established the United States Metric Board to coordinate voluntary conversion to the metric system. Since 1982 this function has been assumed by the Office of Metric Programmes of the U.S. Department of Commerce.

TERRITORIES, ETC. OF THE UNITED STATES

The territories and the principal islands and island groups under the sovereignty of the United States of America comprise the Commonwealth of Puerto Rico, the Commonwealth of the Northern Mariana Islands, and the following territories: Guam; American Samoa; U.S. Virgin Islands; Johnston Atoll; Midway Islands; Wake Islands.

Johnston Atoll (formerly Johnston and Sand Islands) comprises two small islands, less than 1 sq. mile in area, to the south-west of Hawaii which are administered by the U.S. Air Force. The two Midway Islands (area, 2 sq. miles; population (1970), 2,200), at the western end of the Hawaiian chain, are administered by the U.S. Navy. The Wake Islands have an area of about 3 sq. miles and a population (1979) of 300. They lie about 2,300 miles west of Hawaii and are administered by the U.S. Air Force.

Under the terms of a Treaty of Friendship between the United States and Kiribati, signed in 1979 and subsequently ratified by the U.S. Senate, the United States renounced its claim to Canton and Enderbury Islands.

There are certain small guano islands, rocks, or keys which, in pursuance of action taken under the Act of Congress, August 18, 1856, subsequently embodied in Sections 5570–5578 of the Revised Statutes are considered as appertaining to the United States. Responsibility for territorial affairs generally is centred in the Office of the Assistant Secretary, Territorial and International Affairs, Dept. of the Interior, Washington, D.C. Puerto Rico was removed from the Department of the Interior's administrative jurisdiction with the acquisition of Commonwealth status in 1952.

THE COMMONWEALTH
OF PUERTO RICO

Puerto Rico (Rich Port) is an island of the Greater Antilles group in the West Indies, and lies between 17° 50′–18° 30′ N. lat. and 65° 30′–67° 15′ W. long., with a total area of 3,421 sq. miles (8,860 sq. km.), and an estimated population (1985) of 3,451,000. The majority of the inhabitants are of Spanish descent and Spanish and English are the official languages. The island is about 111 miles from west to east, and 36 miles from north to south. The capital is 1,600 miles distant from New York, and 1,000 miles from Miami.

Puerto Rico was discovered in 1493 by Christopher Columbus and explored by Ponce de Léon in 1508. It continued as a Spanish possession until Oct. 18, 1898, when the United States took formal possession as a result of the Spanish-American War. It was ceded by Spain to the United States by the Treaty ratified on April 11, 1899.

The Constitution approved by the Congress and the President of the United States, which came into force on July 25, 1952, establishes the Commonwealth of Puerto Rico with full powers of local government. Legislative functions are vested in the Legislative Assembly, which consists of 2 elected houses; the Senate of 27 members (2 from each of 8 senatorial districts and 11 at large) and the House of Representatives of 51 members (1 from each of 40 representative districts and 11 at large). Membership of each house may be increased slightly to accommodate minority representatives. The term of the Legislative Assembly is 4 years. The selection of the Secretary of State must be approved also by the House of Representatives.

The Governor is popularly elected for a term of 4 years. A Supreme Court of 7 members is appointed by the Governor, with the advice and consent of the Senate. The Governor appoints all Judges. Residents of Puerto Rico are U.S. citizens. Puerto Rico is represented in Congress by a Resident Commissioner, elected for a term of 4 years, who has a seat in the House of Representatives, but not a vote, although he has a right to vote on those committees of which he is a member.

Preliminary 1983 figures for the Commonwealth Government's budget were Receipts, $4,948 million (of which $1,180 million were transfers from the Federal Government) and Expenditures, $4,111 million (including payments of $135 million to the Federal Government). Manufacturing added $5,765 million to net Commonwealth income in 1983 (preliminary figures), trade $1,743 million, finance, insurance and real estate $1,841 million and agriculture $435 million. Principal crops are sugar cane, coffee, vegetables, fruits and tobacco. Most valuable areas of manufacturing are chemicals and allied products, metal products and machinery. Public and private schools are established throughout—enrolment in 1985–86 was 686,914. Enrolment in private colleges and universities for 1985–86 was 98,402.

CAPITAL.—ΨSan Juan, population of the municipality, 1,816,300; Other major towns are: ΨPonce (188,500); Bayamón (205,800); ΨMayagüez (99,800); and ΨArecibo (83,300).

Governor, Rafael Hernández Colón.
Secretary of State, Hector Luis Acevedo.
Resident Commissioner, Jaime Fuster.
Chief Justice, Victor Pons.

TRADE

	1985	1986
Total Imports	$10,113 m.	$10,108 m.
Total Exports	10,543 m.	11,588 m.

Trade with U.K.

	1987	1988
Imports from U.K.	£39,405,000	£38,877,000
Exports to U.K.	76,347,000	91,909,000

GUAM

Guam, the largest of the Ladrone or Mariana Islands in the North Pacific Ocean, lies in 13° 26′ N. lat. and 144° 39′ E. long., at a distance of about 1,506 miles east of Manila. The area of the island is estimated at 209 sq. miles (541 sq. km.), with an estimated population (1987) of 127,675.

The Guamanians are of Chamorro stock mingled with Filipino and Spanish blood. The Chamorro language belongs to the Malayo-Polynesian family, but has had considerable admixture of Spanish. English is the language used throughout the island, although Chamorro is also used in Guamanian homes.

Guam was occupied by the Japanese in Dec. 1941 but was recaptured and occupied throughout by U.S. forces before the end of July, 1944. Under the Organic Act of Guam of August 1, 1950 (Public Law 630 of the 81st Congress), Guam has statutory powers of self-government, and Guamanians are United States citizens. A 21-member unicameral legislature is elected biennially. The Governor and Lieutenant Governor are popularly elected. A non-voting Delegate is elected to serve in the U.S. House of Representatives. There is also a District Court of Guam, with original jurisdiction in cases under federal law.

CAPITAL.—Agaña. Port of entry, ΨApra.

Governor, Joseph Ada.
Lt. Governor, Frank Blas.

AMERICAN SAMOA

American Samoa consists of the island of Tutuila, Anu'u, Ofu, Olesega, Ta'u, Rose and Swains Islands, with a total area of 76 sq. miles (197 sq. km.) and an estimated population of 37,450 in 1988.

Tutuila, the largest of the group, has an area of 52 square miles and contains a magnificent harbour at ΨPago Pago. The remaining islands have an area of about 24 square miles. Tuna and copra are the chief exports.

American Samoans are U.S. nationals, but some have acquired citizenship through service in the United States armed forces or other naturalization procedure.

The 1960 Constitution grants American Samoa a measure of self-government, with certain powers reserved to the U.S. Secretary of the Interior. There is a bicameral legislature with popularly elected Representatives and Governors, and a popularly-elected Governor. A non-voting Delegate is elected to serve in the U.S. House of Representatives.

The constitution of American Samoa designates the village of Fagatogo as the seat of government.

Governor, Peter T. Coleman.
Lt. Governor, Galea' I. Poumele.

VIRGIN ISLANDS

Purchased by the United States from Denmark for the sum of $25 million, and proclaimed, January 25, 1917. The total area of the islands is 132 sq. miles (342 sq. km.), with an estimated population (1988) of 106,000. There are three main islands, St. Thomas (28 sq. miles), St. Croix (84 sq. miles), St. John (20 sq. miles) and about 50 small islets or cays, mostly uninhabited.

The government of the Virgin Islands is organized under the provisions of the Revised Organic Act of the Virgin Islands, enacted by the Congress of the United States on July 22, 1954. Legislative power is vested in the Legislature of the Virgin Islands, a unicameral body composed of 15 senators popularly elected for two-year terms. Virgin Islanders are citizens of the United States. From the elections of November, 1970, the Governor has been popularly elected. A non-voting Delegate is elected to serve in the U.S. House of Representatives. The Virgin Islands are now a favourite tourist area in the Caribbean. The climate of the islands is delightful at all times, and particularly so during the winter months.

CAPITAL.—ΨCharlotte Amalie on St. Thomas.

Governor, Alexander Farrelly.
Lt. Governor, Derek M. Hodge.

NORTHERN MARIANA ISLANDS

The land area of the Northern Mariana Islands is 184 sq. miles (476 sq. km.) with an estimated population (1987) of 22,000.

A law enacted by Congress on March 24, 1976 provides a Covenant to establish a Commonwealth of the Northern Mariana Islands. The provisions of the Covenant became fully effective upon termination of the Trusteeship Agreement on Nov. 3, 1986. Most of the residents became U.S. citizens. There is a popularly elected bicameral legislature and a popularly elected Governor.

Governor, Pedro P. Tenorio.
Lt. Governor, Pedro A. Tenorio.

MARSHALL ISLANDS

The land area of the Marshall Islands is 70 sq. miles (181 sq. km.), with an estimated population of 45,000. The capital is Majuro with 15,000 inhabitants.

In May 1979 Constitutional Government was installed in the Marshall Islands which provides for a bicameral legislature comprising a Senate and a House of Assembly. A Compact of Free Association with the United States was signed on June 25, 1983, becoming law on Jan. 14, 1986. This allows the

Marshall Islands self government and vests in the United States full responsibility for the defence of the Marshall Islands for 15 years.

President, Amata Kabua.

FEDERATED STATES OF MICRONESIA

The Federated States of Micronesia comprise the four states of Kosrae, Ponape, Truk and Yap, which have a combined area of 271 sq. miles (701 sq. km.) and an estimated population of 100,000. The capital is Kolonia, on Ponape, with an estimated population of 6,000.

Constitutional government was installed in the Federated States of Micronesia in May 1979 and provides for a unicameral 14-member National Congress comprising members from the four states. Each state also elects its own Governor and legislature.

A Compact of Free Association with the United States was signed on Oct. 1, 1982, becoming law on Jan. 14, 1986. The Federated States enjoy full self-government and the responsibility for their defence is vested fully in the United States for 15 years.

President of the Federated States of Micronesia, John R. Haglelgam.
Vice President, Hiroshi Ismael.

REPUBLIC OF PALAU

Palau consists of more than 200 Pacific Ocean islands of which eight are permanently inhabited. The Palau archipelago stretches over 400 miles. The land area is 191 sq. miles (494 sq. km.), with an estimated population of 14,000. The major island is Koror with a population of 8,100.

Palau and the U.S.A. signed a Compact of Free Association on Aug. 26, 1982, which, when approved by the U.S. Congress, will recognize the Republic of Palau to be a self-governing state. The U.S.A. is responsible for financial support, and for the defence of Palau for 50 years.

Constitutional government was installed in Palau in Jan. 1981 and provides for a bicameral legislature. The President and Vice President are directly elected.

President, Ngiratkel Etpison.
Vice President, Kuniwo Nakamura.

THE PANAMA CANAL

As a result of the Panama Canal Treaty, 1977, the Canal Zone was disestablished, with all areas of land and water within the former Canal Zone reverting to Panama with effect from October 1, 1979. Under the treaty, the United States is allowed the use of operating areas for the Panama Canal, together with several military bases, although the Republic of Panama is sovereign in all such areas. The Panama Canal Commission, an arm of the U.S. Government, will continue to operate the canal until the year 2000.

TOTAL OCEAN GOING TRAFFIC

Fiscal Year	No. of Transits	Canal, Net Tons	Cargo Tons
1981	13,884	188,656,491	171,221,762
1982	14,009	202,884,207	185,452,332
1983	11,707	169,503,918	145,590,759
1984	11,230	162,335,342	140,470,818
1985	11,515	168,941,997	138,643,243
1986	11,925	182,750,830	139,945,181
1987	12,230	186,406,530	148,690,380
1988	12,234	191,478,087	156,482,641

The canal is fifty statute miles long (44·08 nautical miles), and the channel is from 500 to 1,000 feet wide

at the bottom. It contains 12 locks in twin flights; 3 steps at Gatun on the Atlantic side, 1 step at Pedro Miguel and 2 at Miraflores on the Pacific side. Each lock chamber is 1,000 feet long and 110 feet wide. Transit from sea to sea takes on average 8 to 10 hours. The least width is in Gaillard Cut, and the greatest in Gatun Lake.

BRITISH EMBASSY
3100 Massachusetts Avenue, N.W.
Washington, D.C. 20008
[Washington D.C. 462 1340]

Ambassador Extraordinary and Plenipotentiary, His Excellency Sir Antony Acland, G.C.M.G., K.C.V.O., (1986).
Ministers, F. Cassell (*Economic*); A. J. H. Ward (*Defence Equipment*); C. J. R. Meyer, C.M.G. (*Commercial*); B. J. P. Fall, C.M.G.; P. Lo.
Head of British Defence Staff and Defence Attaché, Maj.-Gen. E. H. A. Beckett, C.B., M.B.E.
Naval Attaché, Rear Adm. M. C. Cole.
Military Attaché, Brig. R. D. Grist, O.B.E.
Air Attaché, Air Cdre. R. G. Peters, R.A.F.
Counsellors, R. B. Bone (*Head of Chancery*); A. Pover (*Admin. and H.M. Consul-General*); R. C. Pratt (*Economic*); D. J. Hall (*Commercial*); J. A. L. Faint (*Overseas Development*); Mrs. S. S. Lee-Birch (*Hong Kong Commercial Affairs*); A. J. Hunt (*Civil Aviation and Shipping*); A. W. R. Allcock (*Science, Technology and Energy*); R. F. Cornish, L.V.O. (*Information*); R. P. Ralph; M. L. H. Doyle; J. D. Hansen; J. D. N. R. Clibborn; B. J. Limbert (*Defence Supply*); K. R. Tebbit; Mrs. C. J. Valentine.
Cultural Attaché and British Council Representative, J. W. Daniel.

There are British Consulates General in *Atlanta, Boston, Chicago, Houston, Los Angeles, New York* and *San Francisco*.

There are British Consulates in *Anchorage, Cleveland, Dallas, Kansas City, Miami, New Orleans, Norfolk, Philadelphia, Portland, St. Louis, Seattle* and *Puerto Rico*.

BRITISH-AMERICAN CHAMBER OF COMMERCE, 275 Madison Avenue, New York 10016; U.K. OFFICE, Suite 201, High Holborn, WCIV 6RR.

URUGUAY
(República Oriental del Uruguay)

President, Dr. Julio María Sanguinetti, *took office*, March 1, 1985.
Vice President, Sr. Enrique Tarigo.

CABINET
(as at May 31, 1989)

Interior, Dr. Antonio Marchesano.
Foreign Affairs, Dr. Luis Barrios Tassano.
Economy and Finance, Cr. Ricardo Zerbino.
Transport and Public Works, Sr. Jorge Sanguinetti.
Public Health, Dr. Raúl M. Ugarte.
Labour and Social Security, Sr. Luis Brezzo.
Agriculture and Fisheries, Sr. Pedro Bonino.
Education, Culture and Justice, Dra. Adela Reta.
National Defence, Hugo Medina.
Industry and Energy, Dr. Jorge Presno.
Planning and Budget Office, Cr. Ariel Davrieux.
Tourism, Sr. José Villar.

EMBASSY OF THE ORIENTAL REPUBLIC OF URUGUAY
48 Lennox Gardens, SW1X 0DL
[01–589 8835; *Consulate* 01–589 8735]

Ambassador Extraordinary and Plenipotentiary, His Excellency Dr. Luis Alberto Solé-Romeo (1987).

Area and Population.—The smallest Republic in South America, on the east coast of the Rio de la Plata situated in lat. 30°–35° S. and long. 53° 15′–57° 42′ W., with an area of 68,037 sq. miles (176,215 sq. km.), and an estimated population (1985) of 3,012,000, almost entirely white and predominantly of Spanish and Italian descent. Many Uruguayans are Roman Catholics. There is complete freedom of religion and no church is established by the State.

Physical Features.—The country consists mainly of undulating grassy plains. The principal chains of hills are the Cuchilla del Haedo, which cross the Brazilian boundary and extend southwards to the Cuchilla Grande of the south and east. In no case do the peaks exceed 2,000 feet.

The principal river is the *Rio Negro* (with its tributary the Yi), flowing from north-east to south-west into the *Rio Uruguay*. The boundary river *Uruguay* is navigable from its estuary to Salto, about 200 miles north, and the Negro is also navigable for a considerable distance. Smaller rivers are the Cuareim, Yaguaron, Santa Lucia, Queguay and the Cebollati.

The climate is reasonably healthy. The summer is warm, but the heat is often tempered by the breezes of the Atlantic. The winter is, on the whole, mild, but cold spells, characterized by winds from the South Polar regions, are experienced in June, July and August. Rainfall is regular throughout the year, but there are occasional droughts. Floods also occur.

Government.—Uruguay—or the *Banda Oriental*, as this territory lying on the eastern bank of the Uruguay River was then called—resisted all attempted invasions of the Portuguese and Spanish until the beginning of the 17th century, and 100 years later the Portuguese settlements were captured by the Spanish. From 1726 to 1814 the country formed part of Spanish South America and underwent many vicissitudes during the Wars of Independence. In 1814 the armies of the Argentine Confederation captured the capital and annexed the province, and it was afterwards annexed by Portugal and became a province of Brazil. In 1825, the country threw off the Brazilian yoke. This action led to war between Argentina and Brazil which was settled by the mediation of the United Kingdom, Uruguay being declared an independent state in 1828. In 1830 a Republic was inaugurated.

According to the Constitution the President appoints a council of 11 ministers and a Secretary (Planning and Budget Office), and the Vice-President presides over Congress. The legislature consists of a Chamber of 99 deputies and a Senate of 30 members (plus the Vice-President), elected for five years by a system of proportional representation. Voting is obligatory and extends to all citizens of good repute and certain long standing residents who are not citizens, from the age of 18. General elections held in Nov. 1984 marked the return to democracy after 11 years of presidential rule with military support. The new government took office on March 1, 1985 and the provisions of the 1967 Constitution now prevail.

The Republic is divided into 19 Departments each with a chief of police and a Departmental Council.

Production and Industry.—Wheat, barley, maize, linseed, sunflower seed and rice are cultivated. The wealth of the country is obtained from its pasturage, which supports large herds of cattle and sheep, the wool of which is of excellent quality. There are just over 9 million cattle and just under 24 million sheep. In addition to meat packing, other foodstuffs (citrus, wine, beer), fishing and textile industries are of importance.

The development of local industry continues and, in addition to the greatly augmented textile industry, marked expansion in local production is notable in respect of tyres, sheet-glass, three-ply wood, cement,

leather-curing, beet-sugar, plastics, household consumer goods, edible oils and the refining of petroleum and petroleum products.

Mineral Deposits.—There are some ferrous minerals, not extracted at present. Non-ferrous exploited minerals include clinker, dolomite, marble and granite.

Communications.—There are about 9,899 km. of national highways, and about 12,083 km. of telegraph and 48,375 miles of telephone communications.

There are about 2,987 km. of standard gauge railway in use in Uruguay. Passenger rail services were cancelled in Jan. 1988. Services are now limited to cargo transport. A State Autonomous Entity was formed to administer the railway systems purchased by the Government from four British companies in 1948.

An airline, PLUNA, which is owned by the State, runs daily services to southern Brazil, Paraguay and Argentina, and two flights a week to Madrid. The principal capitals of the interior and a limited freight service are connected to Montevideo by TAMU, another State owned airline, using principally military aircraft and personnel. International passenger and freight services are maintained by American, South American and European airlines. The international airport of Carrasco lies 12 miles outside Montevideo.

Education and Social Services.—Uruguay is one of the most advanced of the South American states, with old-age pensions, maternity and child welfare centres, accident insurance, etc. Primary education is compulsory and free, and technical and trade schools and evening courses for adult education are state controlled. There are about 322,053 pupils in the 2,362 state schools. The University at Montevideo (founded in 1849) has about 18,000 students enrolled in its ten faculties.

Language and Literature.—Spanish is the language of the Republic. Modern literature has provided some authors with international reputations and the literature of Spain is accessible in all public libraries. Five daily newspapers are published in Montevideo with an estimated total circulation of 150,000. Most of them are distributed throughout the country.

FINANCE

	1987	1988
Revenue	N$270,939·2 m	N$456,675·2 m.
Expenditure	292,987·7 m	510,651·4 m.

The external debt at Sept. 1988 was U.S.$6,117·3 million. Central Bank reserves (March 1989) were US$1,027 million.

TRADE

	1987	1988
Total exports	US$1,189,100,000	US$1,404,527,000
Total imports	1,141,900,000	1,176,945,000

The major exports are meat and by-products, wool and by-products, hides and bristle and agricultural products. The principal imports are raw materials, construction materials, oils and lubricants, automotive vehicles, kits and machinery.

Trade with U.K.

	1987	1988
Imports from U.K.	£26,484,000	£34,999,000
Exports to U.K.	40,474,000	35,410,000

The principal export items to the U.K. are wool and beef, the main imports are chemicals, machinery, raw materials, metals and beverages.

CAPITAL.—ΨMontevideo. Population (1984) 1,355,312. Other centres (with 1967 estimates) are Salto (60,000), Ψ Paysandu (60,000), Mercedes

(34,000), Minas (34,000), Melo (30,000), and Rivera (40,000).

CURRENCY.—New Uruguayan peso of 100 centésimos.

FLAG.—Four blue and five white horizontal stripes surcharged with sun on a white ground in the top corner, next flagstaff.

NATIONAL ANTHEM.—Orientales, La Patria O La Tumba (Uruguayans, the fatherland or death).

NATIONAL DAY.—August 25 (Declaration of Independence, 1825).

BRITISH EMBASSY
Calle Marco Bruto 1073 Montevideo
[Montevideo 723533]

Ambassador Extraordinary and Plenipotentiary, His Excellency Colum John Sharkey, C.M.G., M.B.E. (1989)
First Secretary, P. Hunt (*Head of Chancery and Consul*).
Second Secretaries, B. McIntyre (*Commercial*); W. A. Allan; R. Graham; R. S. Dillow.
Defence Attaché, Capt. J. W. Porter.

BRITISH CONSULAR OFFICES
There is a British Consular Office at *Montevideo*.

ANGLO-URUGUAYAN CULTURAL INSTITUTE, San José 1426, Montevideo. There are branch Institutes throughout Uruguay.
BRITISH-URUGUAYAN CHAMBER OF COMMERCE, Avenida Labertador Brig. Gen., Lavalleja 1641, P2-OF 201, Montevideo.

VATICAN CITY STATE
(Stato della Città del Vaticano)

Sovereign Pontiff, His Holiness Pope John Paul II (Karol Wojtyla), *born* at Wadowice (Krakow, Poland), May 18, 1920, *elected* Pope (in succession to Pope John Paul I), Oct. 16, 1978.
Secretary of State, Cardinal Agostino Casaroli, *appointed* April, 1979.

APOSTOLIC NUNCIATURE
54 Parkside, SW19 5NF
[01-946 1410]

Apostolic Pro Nuncio, His Excellency Archbishop Luigi Barbarito (1986).
Counsellor, Mons. Abraham Kattumana.

The office of the ecclesiastical head of the Roman Catholic Church (Holy See) is vested in the Pope, the Sovereign Pontiff. For many centuries the Sovereign Pontiff exercised temporal power, but by 1870 the Papal States had become part of unified Italy. The temporal power of the Pope was in suspense until the treaty of Feb. 11, 1929, which recognized the full and independent sovereignty of the Holy See in the City of the Vatican. The area of the Vatican City is 108 acres and its population in 1985 was 1,000.

Trade with U.K.

	1987	1988
Imports from U.K. ...	£813,000	£447,000
Exports to U.K.	31,000	111,000

CURRENCY.—Italian currency is legal tender.
FLAG.—Square flag; equal vertical bands of yellow (next staff) and white; crossed keys and triple crown device on white band.
NATIONAL DAY.—October 22 (Inauguration of present Pontiff).

BRITISH EMBASSY TO THE HOLY SEE
91 Via Condotti, 00187 Rome
[Rome 678 9462]

Ambassador Extraordinary and Plenipotentiary, His Excellency John Kenneth Elliott Broadley, C.M.G. (1988).
First Secretary, P. J. McCormick.

VENEZUELA
(La Republica de Venezuela)

President, Carlos Andrés Pérez, *elected* Dec. 4, 1988, *inaugurated*, Feb. 2, 1989.

COUNCIL OF MINISTERS
(w.e.f. Feb. 2, 1989)

Interior, Alejandro Izaguirre.
Foreign Affairs, Enrique Tejera Paris.
Finance, Eglee Iturbe de Blanco.
Defence, Gen. Italo de Valle Alliegro.
Transport and Communications, Gustavo Rada.
Urban Development, Luis Penzini Fleuri.
Energy and Mines, Celestino Armas.
Development, Moises Naim.
Environment and Natural Resources, Enrique Colmenares Finol.
Health and Social Welfare, Felipo Bello.
Agriculture and Livestock, Fanny Bello.
Education, Gustavo Rossen.
Labour, Marisela Padron.
The Family, Teresa Albanez.
Justice, Luis Beltran Guerra.
Secretariat of the Presidency, Reinaldo Figueroa Planchart.
Science and Technology, Dulce Arnao.
Culture, Jose Antonio Abreu.
Co-ordination and Planning, Miguel Rodriguez.
Guyana Development, Leopoldo Sucre Figarella.

VENEZUELAN EMBASSY
1 Cromwell Road, SW7 2HW
[01-584 4206/7]

Ambassador Extraordinary and Plenipotentiary, His Excellency Dr. Francisco Kerdel-Vegas, C.B.E. (1988).
Minister Counsellor, E. González-Urrutia.

There is also a Consulate-General at *Liverpool*.

Area and Population.—A South American Republic, situated approximately between 0° 45′ S. lat. and 12° 12′ N. lat. and 59° 45′–73° 09′ W. long. It consists of one Federal District, 20 states and 2 territories. Venezuela has a total area of 352,144 sq. miles (912,050 sq. km.) and a population (1985) of 17,323,000.

Venezuela lies on the north of the South American continent, and is bounded on the north by the Caribbean Sea, west by the Republic of Colombia, east by Guyana, and south by Brazil. Included in the area of the Republic are 72 islands off the coast, with a total area of about 14,650 square miles, the largest being Margarita, which is politically associated with Tortuga, Cubagua and Coche to form the State of *Nueva Esparta*. Margarita has an area of about 400 square miles.

Physical Features.—The Eastern Andes from the south-west cross the border and reach to the Caribbean Coast, where they are prolonged by the Maritime Andes of Venezuela to the Gulf of Paria on the north-east. The main range is known as the Sierra Nevada de Merida, and contains the highest peaks in the country in Pico Bolivar (16,411 feet) and Picacho de la Sierra (15,420 feet). Near the Brazilian border the Sierras Parima and Pacaraima, and on the eastern border the Sierras de Rincote and de Usupamo, enclose the republic with parallel northward spurs, between which are valleys of the Orinoco tributaries. The slopes of the mountains and foothills are covered with dense forests, but the basin of the Orinoco is mainly llanos, or level stretches of open prairie, with occasional woods.

The principal river is the Orinoco, with innumerable affluents, the main river exceeding 1,600 miles in length from its rise in the southern highlands of the republic to its outflow in the deltaic region of the north-east. The Orinoco is navigable for large steamers from its mouth for 700 miles, and by smaller vessels as far as the Maipures Cataract, some 200 miles farther up-stream. Dredging operations have opened the Orinoco to ocean-going ships, of up to 40 ft. draft, as far as Ciudad Guayana (about 150 miles up-stream). Among the many tributaries of the main stream are the Ventuari, Apure (with its tributary the Portuguesa), Arauca, Meta, and Guaviare from the west, the Meta and Guaviare being principally Colombian rivers. The upper waters of the Orinoco are united with those of the Rio Negro (a Brazilian tributary of the Amazon) by a natural river or canal, known as the Casiquiare.

The coastal regions of Venezuela are much indented and contain many lagoons and lakes, of which Maracaibo, with an area of 8,296 square miles, is the largest lake in South America. Other lakes are Zulia (290 square miles), south-west of Maracaibo, and Valencia (216 square miles) about 1,400 ft. above sea-level in the Maritime Andes.

The climate is tropical and, except where modified by altitude or tempered by sea breezes, is unhealthy, particularly in the coastal regions and in the neighbourhood of lowland streams and lagoons. The hot, wet season lasts from April to October, the dry, cooler season from November to March.

Language and Literature.—Spanish is the language of the country. There are 61 daily newspapers in Venezuela, of which ten are published in Caracas, and about 60 to 70 weekly news magazines. There are also a large number of fortnightly, monthly and quarterly publications.

Education is free and compulsory between the ages of 7 and 13. There are ten universities in Venezuela, five in Caracas and the others in Maracaibo, Mérida, Valencia, Cumaná and Barquisimeto.

Production and Industry.—Products of the tropical forest region include: orchids, wild rubber, timber, mangrove bark, balata gum and tonka beans: of agricultural areas, cocoa beans, coffee, cotton, rice, maize, sugar, sesame, groundnuts, potatoes, tomatoes, other vegetables, sisal and tobacco. There is an extensive beef and dairy farming industry. Despite substantial improvements in agriculture, Venezuela is heavily reliant upon food imports, which constitute about 60 per cent of total consumption.

The principal industry is that of petroleum, which in 1986 contributed 83 per cent of Venezuela's foreign exchange income. Daily production in the oilfields (nationalized 1976) has steadily declined since 1973 in line with Venezuela's conservation policies, reaching 1·7 mbd in 1986 (1973—3·366 mbd). There are refineries at Punta Cardon, Amuay, Caripitó, San Lorenzo, Puerto La Cruz, Tucupeido, El Chaure and El Palito. Development of the Orinoco heavy oil belt is now moving ahead with the inauguration of the Lagovén continuous steam injection pilot plant at El Jobo in southern Monagas. It has been estimated conservatively that there might exist recoverable resources of 70,000 million barrels in the Orinoco region, but the initial aim of the Lagovén project is the production of 125,000 and 500,000 bpd of upgraded crude by 1988 and 2000 respectively.

Aluminium is the second highest source of foreign exchange after petroleum. The Venezuelan state now holds the majority stake in both the principal producing companies, Venalum and Alcasa, and is moving towards a consolidation of the aluminium industry, with both companies sharing their resources and adopting general policies of marketing and procurement of supplies. Output in 1980 was 222,100 tons, with 151,250 tons exported.

Rich iron ore deposits in Eastern Venezuela have been developed. Secondary processes for pelletizing and briqueting ore for export have been installed. The government-owned steel mill at Matanzas in the Guayana uses local iron ore and obtains its electric power from hydro-electric installations on the Caroni River. It produces seamless steel tubes, billets, wire and profiles. The production of more steel products is planned over the next few years. A mill at Ciudad Guayana for the production of centrifugally-cast iron pipe came into operation at the end of 1970, with an annual capacity of 30,000 tons.

Other industries include petrochemicals, gold, diamonds and asbestos; textiles, clothing and footwear; plastics; manufacture or preparation of foodstuffs, alcoholic and non-alcoholic beverages; manufacture of paper, cement, glass, tyres, cigarettes, soap, animal feeding concentrates, simple steel products, tins, jewellery, rope, furniture, sacks, paint and motor-vehicle assembly; preparation of pharmaceutical goods; pearl fishing, sanitary ware, electric home appliances, pumps, toys, agricultural machinery, bicycles, electronic components, cosmetics and many others.

Communications.—There are about 62,449 km. of roads, 22,975 km. of them paved. The State has now acquired all but a very few of the railway lines, whose total length is only some 372 kilometres. Road and river communications have made railways of negligibile importance in Venezuela except for carrying iron ore in the south-east. However, the government is restoring the Puerto Cabello-Barquisimeto line and expanding it to Turén in the agricultural heartland of Venezuela. A new line connecting Caracas with La Guaira and the Litoral is planned, and in 1983 the Caracas Metro came into operation. British, U.S. and European airlines provide Venezuela with a wide range of services. There are three Venezuelan airlines (two of them state-owned) which between them have a comprehensive network of internal lines and also connect Caracas with the United States, Central and South America, the Caribbean and Europe. Foreign vessels are not permitted to engage in the coast trade. The telegraph, radio-telegraph and radio-telephone services are state-owned. There are two government-controlled, 150 commercial and one cultural, FM, broadcasting stations. There are four television stations in Venezuela, all in Caracas. Two are government controlled.

TRADE

	1985	1986
Total imports	US$7,388 m	US$7,600 m
Total exports	14,178 m	8,880 m

Trade with U.K.

	1987	1988
Imports from U.K.	£157,760,000	£177,787,000
Exports to U.K.	91,749,000	76,563,000

CAPITAL.—Caracas, population (1981), 1,816,901. Other principal towns are Ψ Maracaibo (870,000), Barquisimeto (495,000), Valencia (495,000), Maracay (322,000), San Cristobal (164,000), Cumaná (135,000) and Ciudad Guayana (250,000).

CURRENCY.—Bolivar (BS) of 100 céntimos.

FLAG.—Three horizontal bands, yellow, blue, red (with seven white stars on blue band and coat of arms next staff on yellow band).

NATIONAL ANTHEM.—Gloria Al Bravo Pueblo (Glory to the brave people).

NATIONAL DAY.—July 5.

BRITISH EMBASSY

Apartado 1246, Caracas 1010-A.
[Caracas 911255]

Ambassador Extraordinary and Plenipotentiary, His Excellency Giles Eden FiztHerbert, C.M.G. (1987).
Counsellor, A. R. Murray. *(Head of Chancery)*.
Defence Attaché, Capt. J. B. Lean, R.N.

BRITISH CONSULAR OFFICES

There are British Consular Offices at *Caracas, Maracaibo, Puerto La Cruz* and *Valencia*.

British Council Representative, Dr. V. A. Atkinson, Aparto 1246, Caracas 1010-A.

BRITISH-VENEZUELAN CHAMBER OF COMMERCE, Apartado 5713 Edificio Blandin, Piso I Oficina I-C, Plaza Chacaito, Caracas.

VIETNAM
(Công Hòa Xã Hôi Chu Nghĩa Viêt Nam)

COUNCIL OF STATE
(as at June 30, 1989)

Chairman, Vo Chi Cong.
Deputy Chairmen, Nguyen Huu Tho; Huynh Tan Phat; Le Quang Dao; Nguyen Quyet; Dam Quang Trung; Mrs. Nguyen Thi Dinh.
Gen. Secretary, Nguyen Viet Dung.
Members, Y-Ngong Nie-kdam; Pham The Duyet; Tran Do; Nguyen Xuan Huu; Vu Mao; Hoang Bich Son; Nguyen Dinh Tu.

COUNCIL OF MINISTERS

Chairman, Do Muoi.
Vice Chairmen, Vo Van Kiet; Nguyen Co Thach; Dong Sy Nguyen; Vo Nguyen Giap; Nguyen Khanh *(General Secretary)*; Tran Duc Luong.
Members, all Ministers, and Chairmen of most State Committees (around 35 in all).

VIETNAMESE COMMUNIST PARTY

Politburo of the Central Committee, Nguyen Van Linh *(General Secretary)*; Vo Chi Cong; Do Muoi; Vo Van Kiet; Le Duc Anh; Nguyen Duc Tam; Nguyen Co Thach; Dong Sy Nguyen; Tran Xuan Bach; Nguyen Thanh Binh; Doan Khue; Mai Chi Tho; Dao Duy Tung *(full members)*.

EMBASSY OF THE SOCIALIST REPUBLIC OF VIETNAM
12–14 Victoria Road, W8 5RD
[01–937 1912]

Ambassador Extraordinary and Plenipotentiary, His Excellency Tran Van Hung (1986).
Second Secretaries, Bui Xuan Khoa; Nguyen Thi Yen.

Vietnam, with an area of 127,242 sq. miles (329,556 sq. km.), and an estimated population (1989) of 64,500,000, is bordered on the north by China and the west by Laos and Kampuchea.

Government.—Following the end of the war in Vietnam in 1975, and the establishment of a Provisional Revolutionary Government to administer South Vietnam, a National Assembly representing the whole of Vietnam was elected on April 25, 1976. The Assembly met in Hanoi on June 24, and on July 2 approved the reunification of North and South Vietnam under the name of the Socialist Republic of Vietnam. The national flag, anthem and capital of North Vietnam were unanimously adopted for the Socialist Republic, and Saigon was renamed Ho Chi Minh City.

Effective power lies with the ruling Party, the Vietnamese Communist Party (*V.C.P.*), its highest executive body being the Central Committee, elected by a Party Congress on a national basis.

The Sixth Party Congress of the V.C.P. in December 1986 elected a new Central Committee. It is the Politburo and the Secretariat of the Central Committee which exercises real power and rules Vietnam.

Economy.—During the last nine years, Vietnam's economy has faced considerable problems. These include serious agricultural losses because of adverse weather, major reductions in Western aid (as a result of Vietnam's invasion and occupation of neighbouring Kampuchea), border hostilities with China, and the continued allocation of resources to military expenditure. Efforts to integrate the economies of the North and South have not been very successful.

Although food production has substantially increased (over 19 million tonnes of grain in 1988) as has G.D.P. in general, Vietnam's overall economic position at the end of 1988 was not good. Food production has not kept pace with the increase in population. There was little foreign exchange because of minimal exports to hard currency areas. Vietnam was in default of repayments to the international banking world from the I.M.F. to major commercial and merchant banks and therefore received very few long term credits. Some attempted reforms of the economic system in 1985, including devaluation and a currency change, were implemented disastrously and inflation increased rapidly in late 1985 and early 1986. Despite massive assistance from the Soviet Union (estimated at US$2·3 billion p.a. in 1987) and other member countries of C.M.E.A. (of which Vietnam is a member), Vietnam's economy continued to decline. Economic reforms were instituted in the wake of the sixth Party Congress (Dec. 1986), and have begun to take effect. Inflation is down to single figures per month; the exchange rate has been rationalized, subsidies removed and much greater economic activity allowed in both the countryside and the cities. Foreign investment is being actively encouraged.

Trade with U.K.

	1987	1988
Imports from U.K.	£2,598,000	£2,213,000
Exports to U.K.	357,000	492,000

CAPITAL.—Hanoi (population (1984), City, 925,000; Province, 2,800,000).
CURRENCY.—Dông of 10 hao or 100 xu.
FLAG.—Red, with yellow five-point star in centre.

NATIONAL ANTHEM.—Tien Quan Ca (The troops are advancing).

NATIONAL DAY.—September 2.

BRITISH EMBASSY
16 Pho Ly Thuong Kiet, Hanoi
[Hanoi 52349]

Ambassador Extraordinary and Plenipotentiary, His Excellency Emrys Thomas Davies, C.M.G. (1987).

First Secretary, C. D. Partridge.

Attaché (Commercial) and Vice Consul, Miss R. L. Foxwell.

YEMEN ARAB REPUBLIC
(North Yemen)
(Al-Jamhuriya Al-Arabiya Al-Yamaniya)

President and Commander of the Armed Forces, Col. Ali Abdullah Saleh, *elected* July 19, 1978, *re-elected* May 23, 1983 and July 17, 1989.

Prime Minister, Abdul Aziz Abdul Ghani.

Deputy Premiers, Dr. Hassan Mohammed Makki; Dr. Abdul Karim Aliryani (*Foreign Affairs*); Dr. Mohamed Saeed Alattar (*Development, and Chairman of Central Planning Organization*); Lt.-Col. Mujahid Abu Sha'warib (*Internal Affairs*).

Public Works and Transport, Abdullah Al Kurshumi.

Awqaf and Guidance, Qadi Ali Al Samman.

Economy, Supply and Trade, Dr. Abdul Wahab Muhmood.

Agriculture and Fisheries, Dr. Nasser Abdulla Alaulaqi.

Legal Affairs and Parliament, Ismail Ahmed Al Wazir.

Finance, Alwi Saleh as Salami.

Communications, Mohamed Alkhadim Alwajih.

Interior, Col. Abdullah Hussein Barakat.

Information and Culture, Hassan Al Lawzi.

Labour and Social Affairs, Mohammed Ahmed Luqman.

Oil and Mineral Resources, Ahmed Ali Al Mohanni.

Youth and Sports, Dr. Mohammed Al Kabab.

Electricity, Water and Sewerage, Jamal Mohammed Abdo.

Civil Service and Administrative Reform, Mohammed Abdullah Al Jaifi.

Justice, Mohsin Mohammed Alulafi.

Minister of State for Unity Affairs, Yahya Hussein Al Arashi.

Minister of State, Chairman of L.C.C.D.s, Sadeq Amin Abu Rass.

Health, Dr. Mohammed Ali Moqbil.

Education, Ahmed Mohammed Alanisi.

Housing and Municipalities, Mohsin Ali Alhamdani.

EMBASSY OF THE YEMEN ARAB REPUBLIC
41 South Street, W1Y 5PD
[01–629 9905/8]

Ambassador Extraordinary and Plenipotentiary, His Excellency Ahmed Daifellah Alazeib (1981).

Yemen, the *Arabia Felix* of the ancients, occupies the S.W. corner of Arabia between the kingdom of Saudi Arabia and the People's Democratic Republic of Yemen, with an estimated area of 75,290 sq. miles (195,000 sq. km.). The highlands and central plateau of Yemen, and the highest portions of the maritime range, form the most fertile part of Arabia, with an abundant but irregular rainfall. The ruins of Marib, the ancient Sabaean capital, and its dam are in the Yemen.

The population is (1987 Census) 9,250,000.

Government.—A General Popular Conference was established in Aug. 1982, consisting of 700 elected members and 300 appointed members. It agreed a new National Charter and elected a Permanent Council of 75 members (50 elected, 25 appointed), with a General Council and four sub-committees (economic; political; administrative and public works; cultural and reform).

The General Popular Conference meets every two years and is re-elected every four. The Permanent Council meets regularly for two months, followed by a two-month break. The General Council and sub-committees meet regularly. In 1986 the total membership of the General Popular Conference was expanded to 22,250, comprising elected and appointed members.

Economy.—The main exports are cotton, coffee, hides and skins. Oil has been produced at Marib since Dec. 1987. Production averages 175,000 b.p.d.

Trade with U.K.

	1987	1988
Imports from U.K.	£55,334,000	£42,564,000
Exports to U.K.	2,306,000	1,532,000

CAPITAL.—Sana'a (pop. 427,185). Other main cities are Taiz (178,043), Hodeida (155,110), Ibb (48,806) and Dhamar (47,733).

CURRENCY.—Yemeni riyal of 100 fils.

FLAG.—Horizontal bands of red, white and black, with 5-point green star in centre of white band.

NATIONAL DAY.—September 26.

BRITISH EMBASSY
P.O. Box 1287, Sana'a
[Sana'a 215630/3]

Ambassador Extraordinary and Plenipotentiary, His Excellency Mark Anthony Marshall (1987).

First Secretaries, G. Kirby (*Head of Chancery and Aid*); R. Kay, M.B.E. (*Commercial*).

British Council Representative, J. McGrath, Beit Al-Mottahar, Al-Bonia Street, Harat Handhal (P.O. Box 2157), Sana'a.

PEOPLE'S DEMOCRATIC REPUBLIC OF YEMEN
(South Yemen)
(Al-Jumhurijah Al-Yemen Al-Dimugratiyah Al Sha'abiyah)

President, Haider Abubaker Al-Attas, *assumed power* January 1986, *elected* Nov. 6, 1986 *for a 5-year term.*

Prime Minister, Dr. Yassin Saeed No'man.

EMBASSY OF THE PEOPLE'S DEMOCRATIC REPUBLIC OF YEMEN
57 Cromwell Road, SW7 2ED
[01–584 6607/9]

Ambassador Extraordinary and Plenipotentiary, His Excellency Ahmed Abdo Rageh (1987).

Area and Population.—The Democratic Republic of Yemen lies at the southern end of the Arabian peninsula, having a frontier with the Yemen Arab Republic, Saudi Arabia and the Sultanate of Oman, and a coastline extending 700 miles from the Red Sea eastwards along the Gulf of Aden. The area is largely composed of mountains and desert. Rainfall is generally scarce and unpredictable. The population outside Aden is concentrated in the fertile districts. In the more extensive desert and near-desert areas nomadic communities depend on their livestock for a livelihood.

Included in the State are the offshore islands of Perim (in the Bab al-Mandeb Straits) and Socotra. Sovereignty over the island of Kamaran (area 70 sq. miles) in the Red Sea is under dispute following its occupation by forces of the Yemen Arab Republic during border conflicts in October, 1972. The area of the People's Democratic Republic is 128,560 sq. miles (332,968 sq. km.), with a population (1985 estimate) of 2,500,000.

Government.—The People's Republic of South Yemen was set up on Nov. 30, 1967 when the British government ceded power to the National Liberation Front, thus bringing to an end 129 years of British rule in Aden and some years of protectorate status in the hinterland. Its name was changed to People's Democratic Republic of Yemen on Nov. 30, 1970. Territory of the Republic is that of the former Federation of South Arabia and the Aden Protectorates, consisting of the State of Aden and some 17 sultanates and emirates. It is now divided into six Governorates. Under a constitution promulgated on Nov. 30, 1970, there is a Supreme People's Council of 101 members and an 11-member Presidium. The Chairman of the Presidium is head of state.

In Jan. 1986, severe rivalries within the regime led to a fierce outbreak of fighting in Aden and the temporary evacuation of the foreign community. The President, Ali Nasser Mohammed, escaped abroad and a new government was set up continuing the existing Marxist regime.

The Government receives substantial development from the World Bank, Kuwait and Abu Dhabi (Arab Development Funds). Other aid is provided by China, the E.C., U.S.S.R. (including military aid) and other Socialist Bloc countries.

Production.—Agriculture is the main occupation of the inhabitants outside Aden. This is largely of a subsistence nature, sorghum, sesame and millets being the chief crops, with wheat and barley widely grown at the higher elevations. Disastrous floods in 1983 caused major damage to the principal agricultural areas.

Yemen is not an oil producing country but significant traces of hydrocarbons were found during exploration activities offshore in 1982. The Aden Refinery Company has a refining capacity of 8 m. tons per annum but for a number of years output has not exceeded a rate equivalent to 5 m. tons annually. Several Western companies are now involved in oil exploration and production is expected to begin in late 1988. The exact reserves and estimated production levels are unknown.

Under the Five Year Development Plan 1974–79 much importance was attached to the development of agricultural and fisheries projects. Under the second Five Year Plan (1981–85) emphasis shifted to industrial development, which was allocated 29 per cent of the total investment budget (YD508m); agricultural development was allocated 12 per cent. Light industries are being established which will replace imports and use locally produced raw materials.

Expenditure in 1986 was severely affected by the January fighting and had to be diverted to repair the considerable material damage.

Communications.—Following the closure of the Suez Canal in 1967 the once prosperous trading economy of Aden fell into a steady decline, which has not been reversed by the re-opening of the Canal. In the main harbour, cargo handling for larger vessels is by lighter, but wharves at Maalla can accommodate alongside vessels up to 300 feet in length and 18 feet in draught.

There are no railways in the Republic. Yemen has 760 miles of good roads and construction of a further 300 miles is in hand. A system of undeveloped but motorable roads links the towns and villages outside Aden. There is an international airport at Aden (Khormaksar) into which a limited number of international airlines operate.

FINANCE

	1986	1987
G.D.P.	YD 204·6m	YD215·6m
Per capita income	92·2m	94·5m

Trade with U.K.

	1987	1988
Imports from U.K.	£28,271,000	£20,862,000
Exports to U.K.	1,056,000	1,827,000

CAPITAL.—Ψ Aden (population, 270,000). Other towns are Ψ Mukalla, Seiyoun, Shabwa, Beihan, Lawdar, Shuqra, Dhala and Lahes.

CURRENCY.—Yemeni dinar (YD) of 1,000 fils.

FLAG.—A tricolour, red, white and black horizontal bands, with a triangle of light blue at the hoist pointing towards the fly and charged with a five pointed red star.

NATIONAL DAYS.—November 30 (Independence Day); October 14 (Revolution Day).

BRITISH EMBASSY
Khormaksar, Aden
[Aden 32711/6]

Ambassador Extraordinary and Plenipotentiary, His Excellency (Robert) Douglas Gordon (1989).
Second Secretary, M. S. T. Morgan (*Vice-Consul*).

YUGOSLAVIA
(Socijalistička Federativna Republika Jugoslavije)

President of the Presidency (1989–90), Janez Drnovšek (*Slovenia*).
Vice-President of the Presidency (1989–90), Borisav Jović (*Serbia*).
Members of the Presidency, Janez Drnovšek (*Slovenia*); Borisav Jović (*Serbia*); Stipe Šuvar (*Croatia*); Nenad Bućin (*Montenegro*); Dragutin Zelenović (*Vojvodina*); Riza Sapunxhiu (*Kosovo*).

FEDERAL EXECUTIVE COUNCIL
(as at May 31, 1989)

President, Ante Markovic.
Vice-Presidents, Aleksandar Mitrovic; Zivko Pregl.
Foreign Affairs, Budimir Lončar.
National Defence, Veljko Kadijević.
Internal Affairs, Petar Gracanin.
Finance, Branko Zekan.
Foreign Trade, Franc Horvat.
Trade and General Economic Affairs, Nazmi Mustafa.
Justice and Organization of Federal Administration, Vlado Kambovski.
Agriculture, Stevo Mirjanic.
Transport and Communications, Joze Slokar.
Labour, Health and Social Security, Questions concerning War Veterans and Disabled Veterans, Radisa Gacic.
Energy and Industry, Stevan Santo.

President of the SFRY Assembly, Slobodan Gugonijevic.
President of the Socialist Alliance of the Working People, Jelena Nicojevic.

LEAGUE OF COMMUNISTS OF YUGOSLAVIA
Presidency of the Central Committee
President of the Presidency, Milan Pancevski (*elected for one year in June* 1989).
Secretary, Stefan Korošec (*elected for two years in June* 1988).
Members, Ivan Brigic; Ugljesa Uzelac; Ivica Racan; Jusuf Zejnulahu; Milan Pancevski; Vasil Tupurkovski; Miomir Grbovic; Perko Vukotic; Dusan Ckrebic; Petar Skundric; Stefan Korosec; Boris Muzevic; Stanko Radmilovic.

EMBASSY OF THE SOCIALIST FEDERAL REPUBLIC OF
YUGOSLAVIA
5–7 Lexham Gardens W8 5JU
[01–370 6105]

Ambassador Extraordinary and Plenipotentiary, new
appointment awaited.
Minister Counsellors, Branko Brankovic; Dr. Milisav
Stanković *(Economic)*.
Counsellor, Nikola Mišljenović *(Press and Culture)*.
Defence Attaché, Col. Dragoljub Milovanovic.

Area and Population.—Yugoslavia is a Federation
comprising the Socialist Republics of Serbia, Croatia,
Slovenia, Montenegro, Bosnia and Hercegovina, and
Macedonia. Serbia includes the Socialist Autonomous Provinces of Vojvodina and Kosovo. The area
of Yugoslavia is estimated at 98,766 sq. miles (255,804
sq. km.). The population was estimated (1985) at
23,123,000; the latest Census (April 1981) broke down
the population into 8,140,000 Serbs, 4,430,000 Croats,
1,750,000 Slovenes, 1,730,000 Albanians, 1,341,000
Macedonians and 1,220,000 'Yugoslavs', as well as a
variety of other minorities.

Government.—On Nov. 29, 1945, the Constituent
Assembly of Yugoslavia at a joint session of the
Skupština and the House of Nationalities, proclaimed
Yugoslavia a Republic.

The official name of the country, 'The Socialist
Federal Republic of Yugoslavia', was adopted by the
1963 Constitution.

Several amendments to the Constitution were
made in 1971. The most important formed a new
ruling body called the Presidency, which has 8
members, one from each Republic and Autonomous
Province. Since the death of President Tito in May
1980, its members take it in turns according to a fixed
order of succession to become President of the
Presidency of the Republic for a period of 12 months
each. A new Constitution was proclaimed in 1974
followed by the reconstitution of the Federal Assembly into two chambers consisting of the Federal
Chamber (220 delegates) and the Republican/Provin-
cial Chamber (88 delegates). A new Federal Executive
Council (i.e. government) was also formed. The
current Council was elected in May 1986 with a 2
year renewable mandate. The first election of the
S.F.R.Y. Presidency since Pres. Tito's death occurred
in May 1984; each new member has a five-year
mandate.

The political party in Yugoslavia, the 'League of
Communists of Yugoslavia' has within each Republic
and Province its own separate L.C.Y. organization.
There is a formal separation of State and Party; no-
one may hold a post in the Federal or Republican/
Provincial governments and a paid L.C.Y. post
simultaneously. Political and economic decisions on
many issues are devolved from Federal to Republican/
Provincial level. Yugoslavia has a 'self-management'
form of industrial organization under which the
workforce have the constitutional right to own and
control their own enterprises.

Defence.—The Army, Navy and Air Force on a
peace footing consist of 250,000 officers and men.

Religion and Education.—The three main religions
are the Orthodox, Catholic and Islamic, and freedom
to practice is constitutionally guaranteed. Religion
is separated from the State and no religious instruction is allowed in state schools.

Education.—Eight years' elementary education is
compulsory and all education is free. There are 18
universities.

Language and Literature.—The language mainly
used throughout Yugoslavia and in the Federal
Government is Serbo-Croat but Slovenian and Ma-
cedonian (also South-Slav tongues) and Albanian,
Bulgarian, Romanian, Italian, Slovak, Ruthenian,
Hungarian and Turkish are also spoken in certain

areas. There is, however, no official language since
all are constitutionally equal, except in the Armed
Forces where Serbo Croat is obligatory. In Serbia,
Macedonia and Montenegro the Cyrillic script is
used and in the rest of the country the Latin. There
are 4 Serbian daily newspapers in Belgrade, 2 Slovene
dailies in Ljubljana, 2 Croat dailies in Zagreb, and
many other dailies published in other towns. There
are also many local newspapers and radio programmes
in the different 'minority' languages.

Production and Industry.—The share of industry
in Gross Domestic Product (average annual rate in
real terms of 6·5 per cent in 1981) is now 40 per cent,
while agriculture is 14 per cent. In industry the high
level of investment of recent years is being cut back
and present efforts are directed towards development
of high priority areas such as mining, energy
resources and transport and communications. Agricultural policy is directed towards substantially
increased production, to make the country self-
sufficient and to provide significant exports of
foodstuffs. Some 80 per cent of land is still privately
owned.

The main crops are wheat, maize, sugar beet,
sunflower and soya. Yields in 1985 were (tons):
wheat, 6·3 m; maize, 7·7 m; sugar beet, 9·5 m. According to Yugoslav official estimates, the livestock
population in 1988 was approximately as follows:
cattle, 9,881,000; sheep, 7,824,000; pigs, 8,323,000;
poultry, 78,589,000.

Minerals are an important source of wealth particularly in the central and south-eastern regions.
Production in 1987 included the following (tons):—

Coal	71,873,000
Coke	2,960,000
Iron ore	5,983,000
Pig iron	3,297,000
Steel	4,367,000
Crude oil	3,867,000

Smaller quantities of copper, zinc and mercury are
produced.

Communications.—In 1984 there were 9,279 kms of
standard and narrow gauge railway and approximately 116,600 kms of classified roads. In 1987 there
were 3,909,000 telephones in use in the country. The
principal ports on the long Adriatic seaboard of
Yugoslavia are Rijeka, Bakar, Šibenik, Split, Zadar,
Kardeljeva (formerly Ploče), Dubrovnik, Bar, Kotor
(Cattaro) and Koper. The Danube forms a great
commercial highway and the tributary rivers Sava
and Tisa provide other shipping routes.

FINANCE

	1983 million Dinars	1984 million Dinars
Revenue	1,140,000	374,000
Expenditure	1,140,000	374,000

The rate of exchange is variable. On June 6, 1980
the dinar was devalued against all convertible
currencies and there have been several devaluations
since then.

Trade with U.K.

	1987	1988
Imports from U.K.	£206,932,000	£203,066,000
Exports to U.K.	175,301,000	197,254,000

CAPITAL.—Belgrade, population (1981) 1,455,000.
Other towns are Zagreb (763,000); Skopje (503,000);
Ljubljana (253,000); Sarajevo (447,000); Novi Sad
(169,000); Priština (1971) (153,000); Ψ Split (152,000);
Ψ Rijeka (133,000); Titograd (95,000).
CURRENCY.—Yugoslav dinar of 100 paras.
FLAG.—Five-point red star outlined by narrow
yellow stripe, on a ground of three horizontal bars,
blue, white and red.

NATIONAL ANTHEM.—Hej, Slaveni, Jošte Živi Reč Naših Dedova (Oh! Slavs, our ancestors' words still live).

NATIONAL DAY.—November 29.

BRITISH EMBASSY
General Ždanova 46, Belgrade.
[Belgrade 645055]

Ambassador Extraordinary and Plenipotentiary, His Excellency Andrew Marley Wood, C.M.G., (1985).

Counsellor, D. C. A. Madden.

Defence and Military Attaché, Col. A. E. F. Cowan, O.B.E.

Naval and Air Attaché, Wg. Cdr. M. B. M. Canavan.

First Secretaries, R. J. Campbell (*Economic*); H. D. Marcelin (*Admin. and Consular*); J. D. Clark (*Commercial*).

Second Secretary, R. J. A. Huxter (*Chancery and Information*).

BRITISH CONSULAR OFFICES

There are British Consular Offices at *Belgrade, Dubrovnik, Split* and *Zagreb*.

British Council Representative, D. Gunton, O.B.E. Generala Ždanova 34, (P.O. Box 248), 11001 Belgrade. British Council Reading Room, Knez Mihajlova 45, Belgrade. There are also a centre and library at *Zagreb*.

ZAIRE
(République du Zaïre)

President of the Republic and National Security, Marshal Mobutu Sésé Séko, *born* Oct. 30, 1930; *assumed office* November 25, 1965; *elected* Nov. 5, 1970; *re-elected for third term*, July 28, 1984.

EXECUTIVE COUNCIL
(as at May 12, 1989)

Prime Minister, Kengo wa Dondo.

Deputy P.M. charged with Political, Administrative and Social Affairs and State Commissioner for Human Rights, Me Nimy Mayidika Ngimbi.

Deputy P.M. charged with Economic, Fiscal and Monetary Affairs and State Commissioner for Rural Development, Mwando Nsimba.

Deputy P.M. charged with Territorial Administration and Decentralization, Mozagba Ngbuka.

Territorial Security, Singa Boyenge Mosamboyi.

Foreign Affairs, Nguz a Karl-I-Bond.

International Co-operation, Nyiwa Mobutu.

Information and the Press, Sakombi Inongo.

Plan, Bieme Ngalisame.

Finance, Katanga Mukumadi ya Mutumba.

Budget, Kasereka Kasai.

Agricualture, Takizal Luyan Muis Mbingin.

National Economy and Industry, Selemani Mzana Yile.

Parastatals, Mvutukidi Ngindu Kagbia.

Mines and Energy, Bayeye Djem.

Public Works and Territorial Development, Kibangula Kia Makonga.

Transport and Communications, Mokolo wa Mpumbo.

Foreign Trade, Ntanda Buana Kalemba.

Land, Environment and Conservation, Pendje Demodetdo.

Higher Education, Universities and Scientific Research, Lombeya Bosongo.

Primary and Secondary Education, Nzege Alaziambina.

Public Health, Ngandu Kabeya.

Town Planning and Housing, Ileo Itambala.

Social Affairs, Kisolokele Wamba.

Labour and Social Security, Muduka Inyanza.

Civil Service, Ntawiniga Baleza.

Post, Telephones and Telecommunications, Okuka wa Katako.

Sport and Leisure, Kibassa Maliba.

Culture, Arts and Tourism, Ngongo Kamanda.

President of the Judicial Council, N'Singa Undjuu Ongwankebi Untumbe.

EMBASSY OF THE REPUBLIC OF ZAIRE
26 Chesham Place, SW1X 8HG
[01–235 6137]

Ambassador Extraordinary and Plenipotentiary, His Excellency Citoyen Kitshodi Nzekele (1987).

The State of the Congo, founded in 1885, became a Belgian Colony on Nov. 15, 1908, and was administered by Belgium until 1960, when it became the Democratic Republic of the Congo. In October 1971 the name changed to the Republic of Zaire. Situated between long. 12°–31° E. and lat. 5° N.–13° S., the Republic of Zaire comprises an area of 905,567 sq. miles (2,345,409 sq. km.), with a population (1985 Census) of 34,671,607.

Climate.—Apart from the coastal district in the West which is fairly dry, the rainfall averages between 60 and 80 inches. The average temperature is about 27°C., but in the South the winter temperature can fall nearly to freezing point. Extensive forest covers the central districts.

Government.—On June 30, 1960, the Belgian Congo became an independent unitary state under the Presidency of M. Kasavubu with a provisional constitution drawn up by the metropolitan Belgian Parliament. On July 11, M. Moise Tshombe announced the independence of the State of Katanga although he failed to obtain international recognition. Katanga did not come under the Government at Leopoldville until January 14, 1963.

The constitutional and political situation remained unsettled, the United Nations having mixed forces in the country until 1964. By the middle of 1965, the Congolese Government formed by M. Tshombe in July, 1964, had succeeded in gaining control of all the towns from the rebels and depriving them of military aid from outside the Congo. Gen. Joseph-Désiré Mobutu, Commander-in-Chief of the Congolese National Army, announced on November 25, 1965 that he had assumed the Presidency.

A Presidential regime was instituted by the 1967 Constitution, subsequently amended in 1974 and totally revised in Feb. 1978. The Mouvement Populaire de la Révolution is the sole political party. The President changed his name to Mobutu Sésé Séko Kuku Ngbendu Wa Za Banga in 1972, but is usually known by the first three of these names only.

Provinces.—There are 11 regions, each under a Governor and provincial administration (names of capitals in brackets) Bas-Zaire *(Matadi)*; Bandundu *(Bandundu)*; Equateur *(Mbandaka)*; Haut-Zaire *(Kisangani)*; Kinshasa *(Kinshasa)*; Maniema *(Kindu)*; Nord-Kivu *(Goma)*; Sud-Kivu *(Bukavu)*; Shaba, formerly Katanga *(Lubumbashi)*; East Kasai *(Mbuji-Mayi)*; West Kasai *(Kananga)*.

Language, Religion and Education.—The people are mainly of Bantu-Negro stock, divided into semi-autonomous tribes, each speaking a Bantu tongue. Swahili, a Bantu dialect with an admixture of Arabic, is the nearest approach to a common language in the East and South, while Lingala is the language of a large area along the river and in the north, and Kikongo of the region between Kinshasa and the sea. French is the language of administration. The National University of Zaire has campuses in Kinshasa, Kisangani and Lubumbashi, with approximately 28,000 students (1978–79).

Production.—The cultivation of oil palms is widespread, palm oil being the most important agricultural cash product though it is no longer exported. Coffee, rubber, cocoa and timber are the most important agricultural exports. The production of cotton, pyrethrum and copal fell sharply on independence but is now increasing. The country is rich in minerals, particularly Shaba (ex-Katanga) province. Copper is widely exploited, and industrial diamonds and cobalt are also produced. Oil deposits are exploited off the Zaire estuary and reef-gold is mined in the north-east of the country.

There is a wide variety of small secondary industries, the main products being: cotton fabrics, blankets, sacks, footwear, beer, cigarettes, cement, paint, sugar, furniture, metal goods and tyres, and local assembly of motor vehicles. There are very large reserves of hydro-electric power and the huge Inga dam on the river Zaire supplies electricity to Matadi, Kinshasa and Shaba.

The chief exports are copper, crude oil, coffee, diamonds, rubber, cobalt, gold, cassiterite, zinc and other metals.

Communications. There are approximately 20,500 km of roads (earth-surfaced) of national importance, and 6,000 km of railways. The country has two international and 40 principal airports.

Trade with U.K.

	1987	1988
Imports from U.K.	£26,142,000	£26,132,000
Exports to U.K.	8,544,000	7,542,000

CAPITAL.—Kinshasa (formerly Leopoldville), population (Census, 1985) 2,778,281. Principal towns, Lubumbashi (formerly Elisabethville) (403,623); Kisangani (formerly Stanleyville) (310,705); Likasi (146,394); Kananga (601,239); Ψ Matadi (143,598); and Mbandaka (134,495).

CURRENCY.—Zaïre of 100 makuta.

FLAG.—Dark brown hand and torch with red flame in yellow roundel on green background.

NATIONAL DAY.—November 24.

BRITISH EMBASSY
B.P. 8049, Kinshasa
[Kinshasa 23483/6]

Ambassador Extraordinary and Plenipotentiary, His Excellency Robert Linklater Burke Cormack, C.M.G. (1987).

First Secretaries, T. I. Hay-Campbell; (*Head of Chancery and H.M. Consul*); F. Geere (*Commercial*).

CURRENCIES OF THE WORLD
and Exchange Rates against £ sterling

NOTE:—Franc C.F.A. = Franc de la Communauté financière africaine; Franc C.F.P. = Franc des Comptoirs français du Pacifique.

Country	Monetary Unit	Middle Rate to £ September 1, 1988	Average Rate to £ September 4, 1989
Afghanistan	Afghani (Af) of 100 puls	—	Af 99·25
Albania	Lek (Lk) of 100 qindarka	—	Lk 9·7912
Algeria	Algerian dinar (DA) of 100 centimes	DA 10·91	DA 11.90276
Andorra	French and Spanish currencies are both in use	—	—
Angola	Kwanza (Kz) of 100 lwei	—	Kz 47·786
Antigua and Barbuda	East Caribbean dollar (EC$) of 100 cents	—	EC$ 4·19445
Argentina	Austral (A) of 100 centavos or 1,000 pesos	A 20·1705	A 1014·98
Aruba	Aruban florin	—	Florins 2·78077
Australia	Australian dollar ($A) of 100 cents	$A 2·1094	$A 2·0388
Austria	Schilling of 100 Groschen	Schilling 22·1589	Schilling 21·635
Azores	Currency is that of Portugal	—	Esc. 256$80
Bahamas	Bahamian dollar (B$) of 100 cents	B$ 1·6900	B$ 1·5540
Bahrain	Bahrain dinar (BD) of 1,000 fils	—	BD 0·5845
Balearic Isles	Currency is that of Spain	—	Pesetas 191·90
Bangladesh	Taka (Tk) of 100 poisha	—	Tk 48·40
Barbados	Barbados dollar (BD$) of 100 cents	BD$ 3·3931	BD$ 3·1246
Belgium	Belgian franc (or frank) of 100 centimes (centiemen)	Francs 66·03	Francs 64·25
Belize	Belize dollar (BZ$) of 100 cents	BZ$ 3·3740	BZ$ 3.107
Benin	Franc C.F.A.	—	Francs 518·5
Bermuda	Bermuda dollar of 100 cents	$ 1·6900	$ 1·5540
Bhutan	Ngultrum of 100 chetrum (Indian currency is also legal tender)	—	Ngultrum 25·60
Bolivia	Boliviano ($b) of 100 centavos	$b 4·25	$b 4·2954
Botswana	Pula (P) of 100 thebe	—	P 3·21
Brazil	Cruzado (CZ$) of 1,000 cruzeiros	CZ$ 475·45	CZ$ 4·3478
British Virgin Islands	U.S. dollar ($) (£ sterling and EC$ also circulate)	—	$ 1·5540
Brunei	Brunei dollar of 100 sen (fully interchangeable with Singapore currency)	—	$ 3·0665
Bulgaria	Lev of 100 stotinki	Leva 1·4461	Leva 1·4344
Burkina	Franc C.F.A.	—	Francs 518·5
Burma (Myanma)	Kyat (K) of 100 pyas	K 11·2754	K 10·7780
Burundi	Burundi franc of 100 centimes	—	Francs 252·7475
Cameroon	Franc C.F.A.	—	Francs 518·5
Canada	Canadian dollar (C$) of 100 cents	C$ 2·0761	C$ 1·8350
Canary Islands	Currency is that of Spain	—	Pesetas 191·90
Cape Verde	Escudo Caboverdiano of 100 centavos	—	Esc. 119$627
Cayman Islands	Cayman Islands dollar (CI$) of 100 cents	—	CI$ 1·2894
Central African Republic	Franc C.F.A.	—	Francs 518·5
Chad	Franc C.F.A.	—	Francs 518·5
Chile	Chilean peso of 100 centavos	Pesos 415·47	Pesos 413·9255
China	Yuan of 10 jiao or 100 fen	Yuan 6·2939	Yuan 5·8381
Colombia	Colombian peso of 100 centavos	Pesos 523·29	Pesos 618·19
Comoros	Comorian franc of 100 centimes (Franc C.F.A. also in circulation)	—	Francs 518·5
Congo	Franc C.F.A.	—	Francs 518·5
Costa Rica	Costa Rican colón (₡) of 100 céntimos	₡ 129·81	₡ 122·9595
Côte d'Ivoire	Franc C.F.A.	—	Francs 518·5
Cuba	Cuban peso of 100 centavos	Pesos 1·2848	Pesos 1·183
Cyprus	Cyprus pound (C£) of 100 cents	C£ 0·8145	C£ 0·791
Czechoslovakia	Koruna (Kčs) of 100 haléru	Kčs 9·2419	Kčs 24·22
Denmark	Danish krone of 100 øre	Kroner 12·1079	Kroner 11·92
Djibouti	Djibouti franc of 100 centimes	—	Francs 274·97
Dominica	East Caribbean dollar (EC$) of 100 cents	—	EC$ 4·19445
Dominican Republic	Dominican Republic peso (RD$) of 100 centavos	—	RD$ 9·9579
Ecuador	Sucre of 100 centavos	Sucres 420·78	Sucres 835·81
Egypt	Egyptian pound (£E) of 100 piastres or 1,000 millièmes	£E 3·9000	£E 3·984

Country	Monetary Unit	Middle Rate to £ September 1, 1988	Average Rate to £ September 4, 1989
Equatorial Guinea	Franc C.F.A.	—	Francs 518·5
Ethiopia	Ethiopian birr (EB) of 100 cents	EB 3·4678	EB 3·19145
Falkland Islands	Falkland pound of 100 pence	(at parity with £ sterling)	
Faroe Islands	Currency is that of Denmark	—	Kroner 11·92
Fiji	Fiji dollar (F$) of 100 cents	—	F$ 2·3607
Finland	Markka (Mk) of 100 penniä	Mk 7·4794	Mk 6·9503
France	Franc of 100 centimes	Francs 10·7017	Francs 10·37
French Guiana	Currency is that of France	—	Francs 10·37
French Polynesia	Franc C.F.P.	—	Francs 187·54
Gabon	Franc C.F.A.	—	Francs 518·5
Gambia	Dalasi (D) of 100 butut	—	D 9·554
Germany, East	Mark der Deutschen Demokratischen Republik (M) of 100 Pfennig	M 3·1400	M 3·075
Germany, West	Deutsche Mark (DM) of 100 Pfennig	DM 3·1519	DM 3·075
Ghana	Cedi of 100 pesewas	Cedi 383·07	Cedi 431·3170
Gibraltar	Gibraltar pound of 100 pence	(at parity with £ sterling)	
Greece	Drachma of 100 leptae	Drachmae 254·54	Drachmae 264·40
Greenland	Currency is that of Denmark	—	Kroner 11·92
Grenada	East Caribbean dollar (EC$) of 100 cents	—	EC$ 4·19445
Guadeloupe	Currency is that of France	—	Francs 10·37
Guam	Currency is that of U.S.A.	—	$ 1·5540
Guatemala	Quetzal (Q) of 100 centavos	Q 1·6900	Q 4·4318
Guinea	Guinea franc of 100 centimes	Francs 506·10	Francs 466·05
Guinea-Bissau	Guinea-Bissau peso of 100 centavos	—	Pesos 1,009·775
Guyana	Guyana dollar (G$) of 100 cents	—	G$ 46·635
Haiti	Gourde of 100 centimes	Gourdes 8·4350	Gourdes 7·7675
Honduras	Lempira of 100 centavos	Lempiras 3·3730	Lempiras 3·11
Hong Kong	Hong Kong dollar (HK$) of 100 cents	HK$ 13·0944	HK$ 12·1398
Hungary	Forint of 100 fillér	Forints 91·6637	Forints 95·8284
Iceland	Icelandic króna (Kr) of 100 aurar	Kr 78·82	Kr 95·85
India	Indian rupee (Rs) of 100 paisa	Rs 24·1172	Rs 25·60
Indonesia	Rupiah (Rp) of 100 sen	Rp 2,887·23	Rp 2,787·485
Iran	Rial of 100 dinars	Rials 120·50	Rials 116·30
Iraq	Iraqi dinar (ID) of 1,000 fils	ID 0·5247	ID 0·4843
Ireland, Republic of	Punt (IR£) of 100 pence	—	IR£ 1·1510
Israel	Shekel of 100 agora	Shekels 2·780	Shekels 3·115
Italy	Lira of 100 centesimi	Lire 2,345·70	Lire 2,202·00
Jamaica	Jamaican dollar (J$) of 100 cents	J$ 9·1150	J$ 8·4720
Japan	Yen of 100 sen	Yen 229·29	Yen 226·75
Jordan	Jordanian dinar (JD) of 1,000 fils	JD 0·6360	JD 1·0081
Kampuchea	Riel of 100 sen	—	Riel 115·40
Kenya	Kenya shilling (Ksh) of 100 cents	Ksh 30·80	Ksh 33·30
Kiribati	Australian dollar ($A) of 100 cents	—	$A 2·0388
Korea, North	Won of 100 jun	—	Won 1·5069
Korea, South	Won of 100 jeon	—	Won 1041·72
Kuwait	Kuwaiti dinar (KD) of 1,000 fils	KD 0·47875	KD 0·46550
Laos	Kip (K) of 100 at	—	K 887·049
Lebanon	Lebanese pound (L£) of 100 piastres	L£ 621·42	L£ 838·89
Lesotho	Loti (M) of 100 lisente	—	M 4·3330
Liberia	Liberian dollar (L$) of 100 cents	—	L$ 1·5540
Libya	Libyan dinar (LD) of 1,000 dirhams	LD 0·4992	LD 0·4715
Liechtenstein	Swiss franc of 100 Rappen (or centimes)	—	Francs 2·6575
Luxembourg	Luxembourg franc (LF) of 100 centimes (Belgian currency is also legal tender)	—	LF 64·25
Macao	Pataca of 100 avos	—	Pataca 12·5265
Madagascar	Franc malgache (FMG) of 100 centimes	FMG 2,110·00	FMG 2,384·75
Madeira	Currency is that of Portugal	—	Esc. 256$80
Malawi	Kwacha (K) of 100 tambala	K 4·5050	K 4·4120
Malaysia	Malaysian dollar (ringgit) (M$) of 100 sen)	M$ 4·4963	M$ 4·1958
Maldives	Rufiyaa of 100 laaris	—	Rufiyaa 13·0649
Mali	Franc C.F.A.	—	Francs 518·5
Malta	Maltese lira (LM) of 100 cents or 1,000 mils	LM 0·5743	LM 0·5620
Martinique	Currency is that of France	—	Francs 10·37
Mauritania	Ouguiya (UM) of 5 khoums	—	UM 133·756
Mauritius	Mauritius rupee of 100 cents	—	Rs 24·56

Country	Monetary Unit	Middle Rate to £ September 1, 1988	Average Rate to £ September 4, 1989
Mayotte	Currency is that of France	—	Francs 10·37
Mexico	Peso of 100 centavos	Pesos 3,681·04	Pesos 3,897·73
Monaco	French franc of 100 centimes	—	Francs 10·37
Mongolia	Tugrik of 100 möngö	—	Tugriks 5·2128
Montserrat	East Caribbean dollar (EC$) of 100 cents		EC$ 4·19445
Morocco	Dirham (DH) of 100 centimes	DH 14·1050	DH 13·36
Mozambique	Metical (MT) of 100 centavos	—	1,186 MT 24
Namibia	South African rand (R) of 100 cents	—	R 4·3330
Nauru	Australian dollar ($A) of 100 cents	—	$A 2·0388
Nepal	Nepalese rupee of 100 paisa	—	Rs 37·284
Netherlands	Gulden (guilder) or florin of 100 cents	Guilders 3·5594	Guilders 3·465
Netherlands Antilles	Netherlands Antilles guilder of 100 cents	Guilders 3·02	Guilders 2·7963
New Caledonia	Franc C.F.P.	—	Francs 187·54
New Zealand	New Zealand dollar (NZ$) of 100 cents	NZ$ 2·7842	NZ$ 2·6255
Nicaragua	Córdoba (C$) of 100 centavos	C$ 134·92	C$ 33,121·50
Niger	Franc C.F.A.	—	Francs 518·5
Nigeria	Naira (N) of 100 kobo	N 7·7167	N 11·1428
Norway	Krone of 100 øre	Kroner 11·6398	Kroner 11·1775
Oman	Rial Omani (OR) of 1,000 baiza	—	OR 0·5969
Pakistan	Pakistan rupee of 100 paisa	Rs 30·5116	Rs 32·00
Panama	Balboa of 100 centésimos (U.S. notes are also in circulation)	—	Balboa 1·5540
Papua New Guinea	Kina (K) of 100 toea	—	K 1·3547
Paraguay	Guaraní (Gs) of 100 céntimos	Gs 539·68	Gs 1,963·96
Peru	Inti of 100 céntimos	Inti 55·65	Inti 5,667·97
Philippines	Philippine peso (P) of 100 centavos	P 34·40	P 32·50
Poland	Złoty of 100 groszy	Złotys 786·59	Złotys 1,726·00
Portugal	Escudo (Esc) of 100 centavos	Esc 258$73	Esc 256$80
Puerto Rico	Currency is that of U.S.A.	—	$ 1·5540
Qatar	Qatar riyal of 100 dirhams	—	Riyals 5·6471
Réunion	Currency is that of France	—	Francs 10·37
Romania	Leu (Lei) of 100 bani	Lei 14·781	Lei 14·78
Rwanda	Rwanda franc of 100 centimes	—	Francs 127·706
St. Christopher and Nevis	East Caribbean dollar (EC$) of 100 cents		EC$ 4·19445
St. Helena	St. Helena pound (£) of 100 pence	At parity with £ sterling	
St. Lucia	East Caribbean dollar (EC$) of 100 cents		EC$ 4·19445
St. Pierre and Miquelon	Currency is that of France	—	Francs 10·37
St. Vincent and the Grenadines	East Caribbean dollar (EC$) of 100 cents		EC$ 4·19445
El Salvador	El Salvador colón (₡) of 100 centavos	₡ 8·4325	₡ 7·775
San Marino	Italian currency is in circulation	—	Lire 2,202·00
São Tomé and Príncipe	Dobra of 100 centavos	—	Dobra 167·042
Saudi Arabia	Saudi riyal (SR) of 20 qursh or 100 halala	SR 6·2914	SR 5·1890
Senegal	Franc C.F.A.	—	Francs 518·5
Seychelles	Seychelles rupee of 100 cents	—	Rs 8·89
Sierra Leone	Leone (Le) of 100 cents	—	Le 98·30
Singapore	Singapore dollar (S$) of 100 cents	—	S$ 3·0665
Solomon Islands	Solomon Islands dollar (SI$) of 100 cents	—	SI$ 3·7155
Somalia	Somali shilling of 100 cents	—	Shillings 636·935
South Africa	Rand (R) of 100 cents	R 4·1090	R 4·3330
Spain	Peseta of 100 céntimos	Pesetas 208·76	Pesetas 191·90
Sri Lanka	Sri Lankan rupee of 100 cents	—	Rs 58·50
Sudan	Sudanese pound (£S) of 100 piastres or 1,000 millièmes	£S 7·5915	£S 6·99075
Suriname	Suriname guilder of 100 cents	—	Guilders 2·77299
Swaziland	Lilangeni (E) of 100 cents (South African currency also in circulation)	—	E 4·3330
Sweden	Swedish krona of 100 öre	Kronor 10·8753	Kronor 10·36
Switzerland	Swiss franc of 100 Rappen (or centimes)	Francs 2·6563	Francs 2·6575
Syria	Syrian pound (S£) of 100 piastres	S£ 35·427	S£ 32·6235
Taiwan	New Taiwan dollar (NT$) of 100 cents	—	NT$ 41·45

Country	Monetary Unit	Middle Rate to £ September 1, 1988	Average Rate to £ September 4, 1989
Tanzania	Tanzanian shilling of 100 cents	Shillings 176·00	Shillings 224·30
Thailand	Baht of 100 satang	Baht 42·70	Baht 40·00
Togo	Franc C.F.A.	—	Francs 518·5
Tonga	Pa'anga (T$) of 100 seniti	—	T$ 2·0388
Trinidad and Tobago	Trinidad and Tobago dollar (TT$) of 100 cents	TT$ 7·1698	TT$ 6·602375
Tunisia	Tunisian dinar of 1,000 millimes	Dinars 1·5319	Dinars 1·51255
Turkey.................	Turkish lira (TL) of 100 kurus	TL 2,585·17	TL 3,484·89
Tuvalu	Australian dollar ($A) of 100 cents	—	$A 2·0388
Uganda	Uganda shilling of 100 cents	Shillings 251·11	Shillings 310·743
Union of Soviet Socialist Republics.............	Rouble of 100 kopeks	Roubles 1·0377	Roubles 1·0082
United Arab Emirates ...	UAE dirham of 100 fils	—	Dirham 5·6978
United Kingdom	Pound sterling (£) of 100 pence	£ 1·00	£ 1·00
United States of America	U. S. dollar ($) of 100 cents	$ 1·6770	$ 1·5540
Uruguay	New Uruguayan peso of 100 centésimos	Pesos 641·71	Pesos 1,014·63
Vanuatu	Vatu of 100 centimes	—	Vatu 185·00
Vatican City State	Italian currency is legal tender	—	Lire 2,202·00
Venezuela	Bolívar (Bs) of 100 céntimos	Bs 59·3986	Bs 59·09
Vietnam	Dông of 10 hào or 100 xu	Dông 620·82	Dông 6,990·75
Virgin Islands (U.S.).....	Currency is that of U.S.A.	—	$ 1·5540
Western Samoa	Tala (WS$) of 100 sene	—	WS$ 3·64
Yemen, North	Riyal of 100 fils	Riyals 17·29	Riyals 15·12
Yemen, South..........	Yemeni dinar (YD) of 1,000 fils	—	YD 0·53285
Yugoslavia	Dinar of 100 paras	Dinars 4,700·20	Dinars 42,456·56
Zaire	Zaïre of 100 makuta	Zaïre 339·984	Zaïre 652·68
Zambia	Kwacha (K) of 100 ngwee	K 13·10	K 24·20
Zimbabwe	Zimbabwe dollar (Z$) of 100 cents	—	Z$ 3·4650

INTERNATIONAL ORGANIZATIONS

THE UNITED NATIONS

The foundations of the Charter of the United Nations were laid at the Conference of Foreign Ministers in Moscow in 1943, and upon those foundations a structure was built at the meetings at Dumbarton Oaks, Washington, D.C., from Aug. 21 to Oct. 7, 1944. The design was discussed and criticized at San Francisco from April 25 to June 26, 1945, on which date representatives of 50 Allied Nations appended their signatures to the Charter.

The United Nations formally came into existence on October 24, 1945. It was later decided that its seat should be in the United States. Permanent headquarters have been erected at Manhattan, New York. October 24 has been designated "United Nations Day".

The following 159 states are members of the United Nations:—

Afghanistan
Albania
Algeria
Angola
Antigua and Barbuda
*Argentina
*Australia
Austria
Bahamas
Bahrain
Bangladesh
Barbados
*Belgium
Belize
Benin
Bhutan
*Bolivia
Botswana
*Brazil
Brunei
Bulgaria
Burkina
Burundi
*Byelorussian S.S.R.
Cameroon
*Canada
Cape Verde
Central African Rep.
Chad
*Chile
*China
*Colombia
Comoros
Congo
*Costa Rica
Côte d'Ivoire
*Cuba
Cyprus
*Czechoslovakia
*Denmark
Djibouti
Dominica
*Dominican Rep.
*Ecuador
*Egypt
Equatorial Guinea
*Ethiopia
Fiji
Finland
*France
Gabon
Gambia
German Democratic Rep.
Germany, Federal Rep. of
Ghana
*Greece
Grenada

*Guatemala
Guinea
Guinea-Bissau
Guyana
*Haiti
*Honduras
Hungary
Iceland
*India
Indonesia
*Iran
*Iraq
Ireland, Rep. of
Israel
Italy
Jamaica
Japan
Jordan
Kampuchea
Kenya
Kuwait
Laos
*Lebanon
Lesotho
*Liberia
Libya
*Luxembourg
Madagascar
Malawi
Malaysia
Maldives
Mali
Malta
Mauritania
Mauritius
Myanma (Burma)
*Mexico
Mongolia
Morocco
Mozambique
Nepal
*Netherlands
*New Zealand
*Nicaragua
Niger
Nigeria
*Norway
Oman
Pakistan
*Panama
Papua New Guinea
*Paraguay
*Peru
*Philippines
*Poland
Portugal
Qatar
Romania
Rwanda

St. Christopher and Nevis
St. Lucia
St. Vincent and the Grenadines
*El Salvador
São Tomé and Príncipe
*Saudi Arabia
Senegal
Seychelles
Sierra Leone
Singapore
Solomon Is.
Somalia
*South Africa
Spain
Sri Lanka
Sudan
Suriname
Swaziland
Sweden
*Syria
Tanzania
Thailand

Togo
Trinidad and Tobago
Tunisia
*Turkey
Uganda
*Ukrainian S.S.R.
*Union of Soviet Socialist Republics
United Arab Emirates
*United Kingdom
*United States of America
*Uruguay
Vanuatu
*Venezuela
Vietnam
Western Samoa
Yemen Arab Rep.
Yemen, People's Dem. Rep. of
*Yugoslavia
Zaire
Zambia
Zimbabwe

*Original member (i.e. from 1945). (From October 25, 1971, 'China' was taken to mean the People's Republic of China.)

The principal organs of the United Nations are:—
(1) The General Assembly; (2) The Security Council; (3) The Economic and Social Council; (4) The Trusteeship Council; (5) The International Court of Justice; (6) The Secretariat.

1. The General Assembly

The General Assembly consists of all the Members of the United Nations. Each Member is entitled to be represented at its meetings by five representatives, but has only one vote. The General Assembly meets once a year in regular session beginning on the third Tuesday in September. A new President is elected by the General Assembly at the start of every annual session. Special Sessions may also be held.

The work of the General Assembly is divided among seven Main Committees, on each of which every Member has the right to be represented:—(1) Disarmament and related security questions; (2) Economic and Financial; (3) Social, Humanitarian and Cultural; (4) Decolonization (including Non-Self Governing Territories); (5) Administrative and Budgetary; (6) Legal. There is also a Special Political Committee, to relieve the burden on the first Committee.

The Main Committees consider items referred to them by the General Assembly and recommend draft resolutions for submission to the Assembly's plenary meetings.

The Assembly has two procedural committees—a General Committee and a Credentials Committee; and three standing committees—an Advisory Committee on Administrative and Budgetary Questions, a Committee on Contributions and a Disarmament Commission.

The General Assembly appoints such ad hoc committees as may be required from time to time for special purposes. The Assembly is also assisted in its work by subsidiary bodies such as the Board of

Auditors, the Committee on Conferences, the International Law Commission, etc. In 1964 the General Assembly set up the United Nations Conference on Trade and Development (UNCTAD) as a permanent body.

The United Nations Industrial Development Organization was set up on Jan. 1, 1967, to promote industrialization and co-ordinate United Nations activities in this field.

President of the United Nations General Assembly, Peter Florin (*G.D.R.*) (1987).

2. The Security Council

The Security Council consists of fifteen Members, each of which has one representative and one vote. There are five permanent Members and ten non-permanent Members elected for a two-year term.

The Security Council bears the primary responsibility for the maintenance of peace and security. Decisions on procedural questions are made by an affirmative vote of nine Members. On all other matters the affirmative vote of nine Members must include the concurring votes of the permanent Members, and it is this clause which makes the Veto possible.

The General Assembly, any member of the United Nations, or the Secretary-General, can bring to the Council's attention any matter considered to threaten international peace and security. A non-member State can bring a dispute before the Council provided it accepts in advance the U.N. Charter obligations for peaceful settlement.

The Security Council also establishes ad hoc committees and commissions which may be required from time to time for special purposes.

The five permanent Members are China, France, U.K., U.S.A., and U.S.S.R. The ten non-permanent Members in 1989 are: Algeria, Brazil, Nepal, Senegal and Yugoslavia (*term expires Dec. 31, 1989*); Canada, Colombia, Ethiopia, Finland and Malaysia (*term expires Dec. 31, 1990*).

3. The Economic and Social Council

This body is responsible under the General Assembly for carrying out the functions of the United Nations with regard to international economic, social, cultural, educational, health and related matters.

The Council has 54 members who are elected for three-year terms by the General Assembly.

It has established the following Commissions: Statistical, Human Rights, Social Development, Status of Women, Narcotic Drugs, Population, Regional Economic Commissions for Europe, Asia and the Pacific, Western Asia, Latin America and Africa. The Council also makes recommendations for the co-ordination of the policies and activities of 15 specialized agencies and other organizations in the U.N. system.

4. Trusteeship Council

The Trusteeship Council now consists of five members: the U.S.A. (administering authority of Micronesia, the only remaining trust territory of the original 11), and the other four permanent members of the Security Council, China, France, U.K. and U.S.S.R. China does not participate in the Trusteeship Council's work

The Trusteeship Council considers reports from administering authorities; examines petitions in consultation with the administering authority; makes periodic inspection visits; and checks conditions with an annual questionnaire on the political, economic, social, and educational advancement of the inhabitants of trust territories.

5. International Court of Justice

The International Court of Justice is the principal judicial organ of the United Nations. The Statute of the court is an integral part of the Charter and all Members of the United Nations are *ipso facto* parties to it. The Court is composed of 15 judges, elected by both the General Assembly and the Security Council. Judges hold nine-year terms, which end on Feb. 5 of the year indicated below. The Court is based at The Hague.

If any party to a case fails to adhere to the judgment of the Court, the other party may have recourse to the Security Council.

President, Jose Maria Ruda (*Argentina*) (1991).
Vice-President, K. Mbaye (*Senegal*) (1991).
Judges, M. Lachs (*Poland*) (1994); T. O. Elias (*Nigeria*) (1994); S. Oda (*Japan*) (1994); R. Ago (*Italy*) (1997); M. Shahabuddeen (*Guyana*) (1997); S. Schwebel (*U.S.A.*) (1997); Sir Robert Jennings (*U.K.*) (1991); M. Bedjaoui (*Algeria*) (1997); Ni Zhengyu (*China*) (1994); J. Evensen (*Norway*) (1994); N. K. Tarassov (*U.S.S.R.*) (1997); G. Guillaume (*France*) (1991); R. S. Pathak (*India*) (1991).

(The judges are listed in order of precedence.)

THE SECRETARIAT

Secretary General, Javier Pérez de Cuellar (*Peru*).
Director General, Development and International Economic Co-operation, Antoine Bianca (*France*).

U.N. Office and Information Centre, Ship House, 20 Buckingham Gate, SW1 (Tel: 01-630 1981).

OTHER ORGANS

The U.N. Centre for Human Settlements (Habitat), Nairobi; U.N. Children's Fund (UNICEF), New York; U.N. Conference on Trade and Development (UNCTAD), Geneva; U.N. Development Programme (UNDP), New York; U.N. Disaster Relief Office (UNDRO), Geneva; U.N. Environment Programme (UNEP), Nairobi; U.N. Fund for Population Activities (UNFPA), New York; U.N. High Commissioner for Refugees (UNHCR), Geneva; U.N. Institute for Training and Research (UNITAR), New York; International Research and Training Institute for the Advancement of Women (INSTRAW); U.N. Relief and Works Agency for Palestine Refugees in the Near East (UNRWA), Vienna; U.N. University (UNU), Tokyo; World Food Council (WFC), Rome; World Food Programme (WFP), Rome.

These programmes are supported by voluntary contributions from governments, non-governmental organizations and individuals. The U.N. programmes receiving the largest total contributions in 1983 were: the U.N. Development Programme (UNDP.—$714m); the U.N. Children's Fund (UNICEF.—$297m), and the U.N. Fund for Population Activities (UNFPA.—$310m). The World Food Programme (WFP), jointly administered by the U.N. and FAO, provided aid worth $900m in 1983.

BUDGET OF THE UNITED NATIONS

The budget adopted at the 43rd session for the biennium 1988–89 was slightly over U.S.$1,769,000,000. The scale of assessment contributions of 78 U.N. members is set at 0·01 per cent., that of a further 11 at 0·02 per cent., and a further five at 0·03 per cent. The ten largest assessments are as follows: U.S.A., 25 per cent.; U.S.S.R., 11·82 per cent.; Japan, 10·84 per cent.; West Germany, 8·26 per cent.; France, 6·37 per cent.; U.K., 4·67 per cent.; Italy, 3·79 per cent.; Canada, 3·06 per cent.; Spain, 2·03 per cent. and Netherlands, 1·74 per cent.

U.K. MISSION TO THE
UNITED NATIONS
845 Third Avenue, New York, NY 10022

Permanent Representative to the United Nations and Representative on the Security Council, Sir Crispin Tickell, G.C.M.G., K.C.V.O. (1987).
Deputy Permanent Representative, T. L. Richardson.
Counsellors, C. O. Hum (*Head of Chancery*); A. I. Aust (*Legal Adviser*); J. F. R. Martin (*Economic and Social Affairs*); J. R. Leeland (*Administration*); R. A. Fulton; R. Kinchen, M.V.O..

U.K. MISSION TO THE U.N. AND OTHER
INTERNATIONAL ORGANIZATIONS IN
GENEVA
37–39 rue de Vermont, 1211 Geneva 20

Ambassador, Permanent U.K. Representative, John Anthony Sankey, C.M.G. (1985).
Deputy Permanent Representatives, G. W. Hewitt (*Head of Chancery*); P. W. M. Vereker (*Economic Affairs*).

SPECIALIZED AGENCIES

Sixteen other independent international organizations, each with its own membership, budget and headquarters, carry out their responsibilities in co-ordination with the U.N. under agreements made with the Economic and Social Council. These agencies set standards and provide technical assistance in economic, social and cultural and technical fields.

Food and Agriculture Organization of the United Nations (FAO), Via delle Terme di Caracalla, 00100 Rome.—Established on October 16, 1945, to raise levels of nutrition and standards of living, to secure improvements in the efficiency of the production and distribution of all food and agricultural products and to better the condition of rural populations, thus contributing to the expansion of world economy and ensuring man's freedom from hunger. Among its many activities the Organization promotes the global exchange of information in the fields of agriculture, forestry and fisheries, facilitates international agreement in these fields and provides technical assistance in such subjects as nutrition and food management, soil erosion control, re-afforestation, the establishment of paper industries, irrigation engineering, control of infestation of stored foods, production of fertilizers, control of crop pests and diseases, and improvement of fishing vessels, fish distribution and marketing.

FAO's regular programme is financed by its 158 member nations according to a scale of contributions set by the biennial FAO Conference, the Organization's governing body. At the 1987 Conference, funding for the 1988–1989 biennium was set at US$492 million.

During 1988, FAO carried out 1,539 field projects involving an expenditure of US$314.6 million funded by the UN Development Programme (UNDP) and other aid programmes, including various trust fund arrangements with both donor and recipient countries. In addition, 523 field projects were carried out under the Technical Co-operation Programme (TCP), financed from FAO's own budget.

The policy of the Organization is directed by a two-yearly Conference of the 158 member countries. A council of 49 member nations acts for the Conference between its sessions.
Director General, Edouard Saouma (*Lebanon*).
Permanent U.K. Representative, J. Goldsack.

International Bank for Reconstruction and Development (IBRD), Washington, D.C. 20433; *European office,* 66 Ave. d'Iéna, 75116, Paris, France;

Tokyo office, Kokusai Building 1–1, Marunouchi 3-Chome, Chiyoda-ku, Tokyo 100.—(Together with IDA known as the World Bank). Established on Dec. 27, 1945, to help raise standards of living in developing countries by the provision of financial resources through loans made for productive purposes to a government, or guaranteed by the government concerned. Loans are directed towards developing countries at more advanced stages of economic and social growth.

The Bank, which is owned by the governments of 151 countries and whose capital is subscribed by its member countries, finances its lending operations primarily from its own borrowing in the world capital markets, and derives a substantial contribution to its resources from its retained earnings and the repayment of loans. The interest rate on its loans is calculated in relation to its cost of borrowing; loans generally have a grace period of five years and are repayable over 20 years or less. The loans made by the Bank since its inception to June 30, 1988, totalled $155,048.8 million to 110 countries. Subscribed capital, $91,435.6 million.

The Board of Governors consists of one Governor and one alternate appointed by each of the member countries. Twenty-two Executive Directors exercise all powers of the Bank except those reserved to the Board of Governors. The President, selected by the Executive Directors, conducts the business of the Bank, with the assistance of an international staff.
President, B. B. Conable (*U.S.A.*).
U.K. Executive Director, F. Cassell.

International Civil Aviation Organization (ICAO), 1,000 Sherbrooke Street, W., Montreal, Quebec, Canada H3A 2R2.—ICAO was established on April 4, 1947, to study problems of international civil aviation, to establish international standards and recommended practices for civil aviation in areas such as airworthiness, personnel licensing, aeronautical charts, rules of the air, etc. ICAO encourages the use of safety measures, uniform regulations or operation, and simpler procedures at international airports. It promotes the use of new technical methods and equipment. With the co-operation of members, it has evolved a pattern for meteorological services, traffic control, telecommunications, search and rescue organization, and other facilities required for safe international flight. It has secured much simplification of government customs, immigration, and public health regulations as they apply to international air transport. 160 states are now members of ICAO.

An Assembly of delegates from member states meets at least once every three years. A Council of 33 members is elected by the Assembly, taking into account the countries of chief importance in air transport: countries which make the largest contribution to the provision of facilities for international civil air transport and those ensuring representation of the main geographical areas of the world. The Council is the executive body, working through subsidiary committees.
President of Council, Dr. Assad Kotaite (*Lebanon*).
Secretary General, Dr. Shivinder Singh Sidhu (*India*).

International Development Association (IDA), Washington, D.C. 20433; *European office,* 66 Ave. d'Iéna, 75116 Paris, France; *Tokyo office,* Kokusai Building 1–1, Marunouchi 3-Chome, Chiyoda-ku, Tokyo 100.—The IDA is an affiliate of the IBRD (the two together comprising the World Bank) and was established in September 1960 to provide assistance for the same purposes as the IBRD but primarily in the poorer developing countries and on terms that bear less heavily on their balance of payments than IBRD loans. Assistance is concentrated on the very poor countries, i.e. those with an annual per capita GNP of less than $940 (in 1987 dollars); more than 50 countries are eligible.

Membership is open to all members of IBRD and 137 have joined to date. Funds, called credits to distinguish them from IBRD loans, come mostly in the form of subscriptions and contributions by IDA's richer members, and transfers from the net earnings of the IBRD. The term of IDA credits, which are made to governments only, are ten-year grace periods, 35 or 40 year maturities, and no interest. By June 30, 1988, IDA had extended development credits totalling $47,766.7 million in 95 countries.

Although legally and financially distinct from the IBRD, IDA is administered by the same staff, and the Board of Governors and Executive Directors are the same as those holding equivalent positions in the IBRD.

International Finance Corporation (IFC), 1818 H Street, Washington, D.C. 20433; *European Representative,* New Zealand House, Haymarket, SW1.—The IFC was established in 1956 as an affiliate of the World Bank to assist developing member countries by promoting the growth of the private sector of their economies and helping to mobilize domestic and foreign capital for this purpose. Membership of the IBRD is a prerequisite for membership in the IFC, which has 133 members. Legally and financially the IFC and IBRD are separate entities; the Corporation has its own operating and legal staff, but draws upon the Bank for administrative and other services. IFC's subscribed share capital was $1,300 million at June 30, 1988, and it is also empowered to borrow up to four times the amount of its unimpaired subscribed capital and accumulated earnings for use in its lending programme. At the end of June 1988, IFC had made approved investments totalling more than $10,500 million in over 90 countries.
President, B. B. Conable (*U.S.A*).

International Fund for Agricultural Development (IFAD), 107 Via del Serafico, 00142 Rome, Italy.—The establishment of the Fund was proposed by the 1974 World Food Conference and it began operations in December 1977. The Fund's purpose is to mobilize additional funds for agricultural and rural development in developing countries through projects and programmes directly benefiting the poorest rural populations.

The Fund's operations are directed by the Governing Council, consisting of the entire membership. It has an 18-member Executive Board. Its governing structure provides for equal voting rights among the three groups of member countries, namely, the developed countries, the oil-exporting developing countries and other developing countries.
President, Idriss Jazairy (*Algeria*).

International Labour Organization (ILO), Geneva (*London Branch Office,* Vincent House, Vincent Square, SW1P 2NB).—Established with the League of Nations in 1919 under the Treaty of Versailles, the ILO became in 1946 the first specialized agency associated with the United Nations. In May, 1988 the Organization had 150 member States. The aim of the ILO is to promote lasting peace through social justice, and to this end it works for better economic and social conditions everywhere. It was awarded the Nobel Peace Prize in 1969.

The ILO establishes international labour standards, which set guidelines for improving working conditions and protecting basic human rights; runs a world-wide programme of technical assistance to developing countries; conducts research and disseminates information on the human aspects of economic activity, with a view to improving social and

economic well-being. Through its World Employment Programme, the ILO is attacking unemployment and its associated ills by aiding national and international efforts to provide productive work for the world's fast-growing population. It is also developing an international programme for the improvement of working conditions and the working environment.

The ILO is financed by contributions from its member states. A proportion of its budget is devoted to its technical assistance programme, but this is financed mainly by funds from UNDP and other sources. The I.L.O. budget for 1986–87 amounted to U.S.$324,860,000.

The International Labour Conference, composed of national delegations of two government delegates, one worker delegate and one employer delegate, meets annually. It formulates international labour standards and broad policies of the Organization, provides a forum for discussion of world labour and social problems, and approves the ILO's work programme and budget, which is financed by member States.

A 56-member Governing Body, composed of 28 government members, 14 worker members and 14 employer members, acts as the Organization's executive council. Ten governments hold seats on the Governing Body because of their industrial importance.

The International Labour Office, the secretariat of the Organization, collects and distributes information, assists governments on request in drafting legislation on the basis of international labour standards, directs technical co-operation activities, and issues publications.
Director General, Michel Hansenne (*Belgium*).

International Maritime Organization (IMO), Albert Embankment, SE1 7SR.—A United Nations Specialized Agency established on March 17, 1958, to provide means for co-operation and exchange of information among governments on technical matters related to international shipping, especially with regard to safety at sea and preventing marine pollution caused by ships. IMO is responsible for calling maritime conferences and drafting maritime agreements. It has produced numerous technical codes relating to the carriage of various types of cargo such as chemicals, ores, and dangerous goods and to the construction and equipment of ships, e.g., gas and chemical carriers. In June, 1989, 133 nations were in membership. Budget, 1988–89, $21,627,200. (The Organization changed its name from the Inter-Governmental Maritime Consultative Organization (IMCO) on May 22, 1982.)
Secretary General, C. P. Srivastava (*India*).

International Monetary Fund (IMF), 700 19th Street N.W., Washington, D.C. 20431.—Established on Dec. 27, 1945, the Fund exists to promote international monetary co-operation and the expansion of international trade; to promote exchange stability, maintain orderly exchange arrangements and avoid competitive exchange depreciations; and to assist in the establishment of a multilateral system of payments in respect of current transactions between members and in the elimination of foreign exchange restrictions which hamper world trade. 151 countries were in membership of the Fund in June, 1988.

The Fund's financial assistance takes the form of a foreign exchange transaction. The member pays to the Fund an amount of its own money equivalent to the amount of foreign currency it wishes to purchase. The member is expected to 'repurchase' its own currency from the Fund, usually within three to five years, with a payment of SDRs (Special Drawing Rights) or dollars or usable currency acceptable to the Fund. These arrangements are subject to certain charges.

Currencies drawn from the Fund may be used in a flexible way to relieve the member's payments difficulty, and usually the member is expected to undertake policy changes, where needed, to correct the payment imbalance.

Each member of the Fund is assigned a quota which determines its voting power and the amount of resources that it may draw from the Fund. The subscription of each member is equal to its quota, and is payable in the member's own currency and SDRs.
Managing Director, Michel Camdessus *(France)*.
U.K. Executive Director, F. Cassell.

International Telecommunication Union (ITU), Place des Nations, Geneva.—Founded at Paris in 1865 as the International Telegraph Union. ITU became a U.N. Specialized Agency in 1947. ITU exists to set up international regulations for telegraph, telephone and radio services to further their development and extend their utilization by the public, at the lowest possible rates; to promote international co-operation for the improvement and rational use of telecommunications of all kinds; the development of technical facilities and their most efficient operation. ITU allocates the radio frequency spectrum and registers radio frequency assignments. It studies, recommends, collects and publishes information on telecommunication matters, including space radio communications. The Budget for 1990 is S. Fr. 127,106,000.
Secretary General, P. Tarjanne *(Finland)*.

United Nations Educational, Scientific and Cultural Organization (UNESCO), 7 Place de Fontenoy, Paris 75700.—Under its constitution, the Organization makes its contribution to peace and security by promoting collaboration among its Member States in the fields of education, science, culture and communication. It aims at furthering a universal respect for justice, for the rule of law and for human rights, without distinction of race, sex, language or religion, in accordance with the Charter of the United Nations.

The Organization is composed of three organs: (i) the *General Conference*, consisting of representatives of Member States, which meets biennially to decide the programme and budget; (ii) the *Executive Board*, composed of 51 members elected by the General Conference to supervise the execution of the approved programme and (iii) the *Secretariat*, which is responsible for Unesco's day-to-day functioning and the execution of the programme. In most Member States National Commissions serve as a link with Unesco and help to carry out the programme. Member States in June 1986, 158 and three Associate Members (British Eastern Caribbean group, Netherlands Antilles and the British Virgin Islands).

The U.K. withdrew from Unesco on Dec. 31, 1985. At its 124th session the Executive Board of Unesco decided to grant to the U.K. the observer facilities requested.
Director General, Federico Mayor Zaragoza *(Spain)*.

United Nations Industrial Development Organization (UNIDO), Wagramerstrasse 5, P.O. Box 300, 1400 Vienna, Austria.—Established as an organ of the U.N. General Assembly in Nov. 1966, as an action-oriented body, replacing the Centre for Industrial Development, which had been operating since July 1961. It became a U.N. specialized agency on Jan. 1, 1986, with the aim of promoting the industrialization of developing countries, with special emphasis upon the mobilization of the manufacturing sector. UNIDO provides help on formulation of planning policies, and technical advice and assistance to Third World countries. UNIDO's principal policy-making body is the Industrial Development Board, with 53 members each serving a four year term.
Director General, Domingo Siazon *(Philippines)*.

Universal Postal Union (UPU), Weltpoststrasse 4, 3000 Berne 15.—Established on October 9, 1874, by the postal Convention of Berne and in operation from July 1, 1875, UPU exists to form a single postal territory of all the countries, members of the Union, for the reciprocal exchange of correspondence in order to secure the organization and improvement of the various postal services and to promote in this sphere the development of international collaboration. Every member agrees to transmit the mail of all other members by the best means used for its own mail. The Union includes almost all the countries of the world. Budget, 1990, S.Fr. 24,389,550. A Universal Postal Congress meets at five-yearly intervals. The last was held in Hamburg in June-July 1984, and the next is scheduled to take place in Washington in the autumn of 1989.
Director General, A.C. Botto de Barros *(Brazil)*.

World Bank (*see* International Bank for Reconstruction and Development *and* International Development Association).

World Health Organization (WHO), 1211 Geneva 27.—Established on April 7, 1948, the aim of the World Health Organization is the attainment by all peoples of the highest possible level of health. It co-operates with its member governments in their efforts to develop health manpower, streamline health services, control communicable diseases, promote family health—including mother and child care, family planning, nutrition and health education—and strengthen environmental health. It promotes biomedical and health services research through some 850 collaborating research centres in different parts of the world. Its other services include the International Pharmacopoeia, drug evaluation and monitoring, biological standardization, epidemiological surveillance and scientific publications. Approved budget for 1990 and 1991, $654,000,000. Membership (May 1989), 166.

Organs are a World Health Assembly meeting annually to frame policy, an Executive Board (31 members), meeting at least twice a year, and a Secretariat.
Director General, Dr. H. Nakajima *(Japan)*.

World Intellectual Property Organization (WIPO), 34 chemin des Colombettes, 1211 Geneva 20, Switzerland.—Established by a 1967 convention to succeed the United International Bureau for the Protection of Intellectual Property. Became a specialized agency of the United Nations in 1974, and has 123 members. The World Intellectual Property Organization is the United Nations specialized agency for intergovernmental co-operation in "industrial property" (patents and other rights in technological inventions, rights in trademarks, industrial designs, appellations of origin, etc.) and "copyright and neighbouring rights" (in literary, musical and artistic works, in films, performances of performing artists, phonograms, etc.). WIPO carries out a substantial programme of activities to promote creative intellectual activity and to facilitate the transfer of technology, especially to and among developing countries.

The Conference and the General Assembly control the International Bureau (or secretariat). The Bureau provides the necessary documentation and other services for meetings and carries out projects for the promotion of increased international co-operation among member states.
Director General: Arpad Bogsch *(U.S.A.)*

World Meteorological Organization (WMO), Geneva.—Came into existence in 1951. The present membership is 155 States and 5 Territories. WMO exists to facilitate world-wide co-operation in establishing networks of stations making observations related to meteorology and hydrology, and to promote the establishment and maintenance of centres providing meteorological and related services; to promote the establishment of systems for the rapid exchange of weather information; to promote standardization of meteorological observations and to ensure their uniform publication; to further the application of meteorology to aviation, shipping, water problems, agriculture, and other human activities; to promote activities in operational hydrology and to further close co-operation between meteorological and hydrological services; to encourage research and training in meteorology and to co-ordinate their international aspects. Budget (1988–91), S. Fr. 170,000,000. A World Meteorological Congress meets at least once every four years. An Executive Council (36 members), meeting at least annually, carries out the resolutions of the Congress, initiates studies and makes recommendations on matters requiring international action. Other organs are six Regional Meteorological Associations (Africa, Asia, S. America, N. and Central America, Europe and South-West Pacific), eight technical commissions and a Secretariat.

Secretary General, G. O. P. Obasi (*Nigeria*).

RELATED ORGANIZATIONS

International Atomic Energy Agency, Vienna International Centre, P.O. Box 100, A–1400, Vienna.—Set up on July 29, 1957, to accelerate and enlarge the contribution of atomic energy to peace, health and prosperity throughout the world and to ensure that assistance provided by it or under its supervision is not used to further any military purpose. Agreements have been reached concerning the Agency's working relationship with the United Nations and some of the specialized agencies. In June, 1988, 113 states were members.

A General Conference of all members meets in regular annual session and in such special session as may be necessary. A Board of Governors (35 members) carries out the functions of the Agency and meets usually four times a year. The Regular Budget for 1989 amounted to $157,540,000.

Director General, Hans Blix (*Sweden*).
Permanent U.K. Representative, G. E. Clark.

General Agreement on Tariffs and Trade (GATT), Centre William Rappard, Rue de Lausanne 154, CH-1211 Geneva 21.—A multilateral treaty, in operation since 1948, to which 96 countries are party, and one acceded provisionally; a further 28 countries apply GATT de facto. Its rules thus govern nearly 90 per cent of world trade. Objectives of GATT are to expand international trade and promote economic development. GATT provides a permanent forum for discussion and solution of particular international trade problems, and for multilateral negotiations to reduce tariffs and other obstacles to the expansion of international trade. Special attention is given to trade problems of developing countries. In November 1979, participating countries concluded the Tokyo Round of multilateral trade negotiations with agreements covering tariff reductions, non-tariff measures, an improved legal framework for the conduct of international trade, bovine meat, dairy products, tropical products, civil aircraft, and a revised GATT anti-dumping code. The Uruguay Round of multilateral trade negotiations was launched in October 1986 and is expected to last four years. The 105 participating countries in the eighth GATT Round are conducting negotiations on tariffs, non-tariff measures, tropical products, textiles, agriculture, subsidies, safeguards, etc. An International Trade Centre, set up by GATT in 1964 to aid developing countries in export promotion, is now operated jointly by GATT and UNCTAD.

Director General, A. Dunkel (*Switzerland*).

EUROPEAN COMMUNITY

The twelve member states: Belgium, Denmark, France, Federal Republic of Germany, Greece, Republic of Ireland, Italy, Luxembourg, The Netherlands, Portugal, Spain, the United Kingdom.

The beginnings of the European Community date from May 9, 1950, when Robert Schuman, France's Foreign Minister, proposed that France and Germany should pool their coal and steel industries under an independent ("supranational") High Authority, in a Community open to the membership of any other European country wishing to join. Not only West Germany, but also Italy, Belgium, the Netherlands, and Luxembourg accepted this invitation.

The Coal and Steel Community (E.C.S.C.), European Economic Community and Euratom share a single institutional framework: a Commission, Council of Ministers, Parliament and Court of Justice. The core of the Community policymaking process is the "dialogue" between the Commission, which initiates and implements policy, and the Council of Ministers, which takes major policy decisions. The beginnings of democratic control are exercised by the European Parliament, while the Court of Justice ensures the rule of law and is the final arbiter in all matters arising from the Community Treaties.

Since the start of the European Economic Community and Euratom in 1958, the Parliament and Court of Justice have been common to all three Communities. Up to July, 1967, each Community had its own executive body (the E.E.C. and Euratom Commissions, and the E.C.S.C. High Authority) and its own Council of Ministers.

In April, 1965, the Six signed a treaty providing for the merger of the three executive bodies in a single Commission and the three Councils in a single Council, with a view to the eventual merger of the three Communities themselves. The merger treaty came into force on July 1, 1967; the single Commission and single Council then took office. They enjoy the same powers under the three Community Treaties as did their predecessors.

On December 1 and 2, 1969, the Heads of State or Government of the Six met at the Hague and decided on the completion, strengthening, and, provided that other European countries wished to accept the Treaties of Rome, enlargement of the Community. They instructed the Commission to draw up a plan for economic and monetary union, and the Foreign Ministers to report by the end of July on possible moves towards political unification. They also resolved to intensify the co-ordination of research and development programmes.

In accordance with the Hague decisions the Council of Ministers agreed in April, 1970, that as from 1975 the Community would have its own revenue, independent of national contributions. The

Foreign Ministers agreed (May, 1970) to hold formal political consultations twice a year.

In June, 1970, the Six invited Britain, the Irish Republic, Denmark and Norway to open negotiations on June 30 at Luxembourg on their applications to join the Community. Negotiations continued in 1971 and were concluded with the United Kingdom Government for all major questions by the end of June; on July 8, H.M. Government issued a White Paper on the results. On Jan. 22, 1972, the four applicant countries signed the Treaty of Accession in Brussels. Norway conducted a referendum on its Common Market entry and as a result withdrew its application. The enlarged Community of the Nine came into existence on Jan. 1, 1973.

With the advent of a Labour Government in the U.K. in 1974, there followed a period of renegotiation of the terms of Britain's entry into the Community, culminating in a referendum on June 5, 1975, as to whether or not the country should remain a member of the E.C. The result of the referendum showed two to one in favour of staying in. British Labour Party representatives who had hitherto boycotted the European Parliament then took up their 18 allotted seats.

In January 1976 the European Parliament approved a Report urging direct elections to the Parliament in 1978. On July 12–13, 1976, the Heads of Government or State, meeting in European Council, decided to approve a 410 member Parliament with Britain, France, West Germany and Italy allocated 81 seats each; the Netherlands 25, Belgium 24, Denmark 16, Ireland 15 and Luxembourg 6. Because some countries (including Britain) had not passed the relevant legislation in time, the date of European Elections was postponed until June 1979. When Greece joined the E.C. in January 1981, she was allocated 24 seats in the Parliament, bringing the total number to 434. When Spain and Portugal became members in 1986, they took an additional 84 seats; Spain taking 60 and Portugal 24 making the total 518.

The European Council, an addition to the institutionalized meetings provided under the Treaties, evolved from the summit conference of December 1974, when the Heads of Government decided to meet at least three times a year in order to discuss Community problems and matters requiring political co-operation.

<small>OFFICE OF THE UNITED KINGDOM PERMANENT REPRESENTATIVE TO THE EUROPEAN COMMUNITIES</small>
Rond-point Robert Schuman 6, 1040 Brussels

Ambassador and U.K. Permanent Representative, Sir David Hannay, K.C.M.G. (1985).

The Commission

On July 1, 1970, the Commission was reduced from 14 members to nine, two each from Germany, France and Italy, and one each from Belgium, the Netherlands and Luxembourg. Following the 1973 enlargement, the number rose to 13, with two seats each from Britain, France, Germany, and Italy and one each for the other members. The admission of Greece in 1981, with 1 seat, brought the total to 14 Commissioners. When the Community was again enlarged in 1986, the total number of Commissioners grew to 17, two being appointed from Spain and one from Portugal.

The members of the Commission are appointed by agreement among the twelve member governments for a four-year renewable term; the president and vice-presidents are appointed from among the members for a two-year term, also renewable.

The members of the Commission are pledged to independence of the governments and of national or other particular interests. They accept joint respon-

sibility for their decisions, which are taken by majority vote.

In addition to being the initiator of Community action and having specific powers, the Commission acts as a mediator between the member governments in Community affairs and is the guardian of the Community Treaties.

Commission of the European Communities
200 Rue de la Loi, 1049 Brussels

President

Jacques Delors (France) (*Secretariat General; Legal Services; Monetary Affairs; Spokesman's Service; Joint Interpreting and Conference Service; Think Tank; Security Office*).

Vice-Presidents

Frans Andriessen (Netherlands) (*External Relations and Trade Policy; Co-operation with other European Countries*).

Henning Christophersen (Denmark) (*Economic and Financial Affairs; Co-ordination of Structural Instruments; Statistical Office*).

Manuel Marin (Spain) (*Co-operation and Development; Fisheries*).

Filippo Maria Pandolfi (Italy) (*Research and Science; Telecommunications; Information Technology and Innovation; Joint Research Centre*).

Martin Bangemann (Fed. Rep. of Germany) (*Internal Market and Industrial Affairs; Relations with the European Parliament*).

Sir Leon Brittan (U.K.) (*Competition Policy; Financial Institutions*).

Members

Carlo Ripa Di Meana (Italy) (*Environment; Nuclear Safety; Civil Protection*).

Antonio Cardoso E. Cunha (Portugal) (*Personnel and Administration; Energy; Euratom Supply Agency; Policy on Small and Medium Sized Enterprises; Tourism; Social Economy*).

Abel Matutes (Spain) (*Mediterranean Policy; Relations with Latin America; North-South Relations*).

Peter Schmidhuber (Fed. Rep. of Germany) (*Budget; Financial Control*).

Christiane Scrivener (France) (*Taxation; Customs Union; Questions relating to Obligatory Levies*).

Bruce Millan (U.K.) (*Regional Policy*).

Jean Dondelinger (Luxembourg) (*Audio-Visual Policy; Cultural Affairs; Information and Communication Policy; Citizens' Europe; Office for Official Publications*).

Ray MacSharry (Rep. of Ireland) (*Agriculture, Rural Development*).

Karel Van Miert (Belgium) (*Transport; Credit, Investments and Financial Instruments; Consumer Protection*).

Vasso Papandreou (Greece) (*Social Affairs and Employment; Education and Training; Human Resources*).

Secretary General, D. Williamson (U.K.).

The Commission maintains information offices in London (8 Storey's Gate, SWIP 3AT. Tel: 01-222 8122), Edinburgh (7 Alva Street EH2 4PH), Cardiff (4 Cathedral Road), Belfast (Windsor House, 9/15 Bedford Street), Dublin (39 Molesworth Street), Washington (2100 M. Street, N.W. (Suite 707), Washington, D.C. 20037), New York (1 Dag Hammarskjöld Plaza, 245 East 47th Street, New York, N.Y. 10017), Ottawa (Inn of the Provinces, Office Tower (Suite 1110), 350 Sparks Street, Ontario, KIR 7S8), and other cities.

The Council of the European Communities
170 Rue de la Loi, 1048 Brussels

This consists of ministers from the governments of each of the twelve member states, the ministers concerned depending on the subject under discussion. A single Council exists for the three European Communities. It is the main decision-taking body within the Community legislative process. The Council acts, in almost all cases, on the basis of proposals submitted by the Commission, which is present at Council sessions to participate in the shaping of the measures taken. Before examining Commission proposals the Council normally obtains the opinions of the European Parliament and the Economic and Social Committee on them.

As prescribed by the E.C. treaty, under which the great majority of the Council's business falls, decisions are taken by majority vote, qualified majority vote (a system in which the members' votes are weighted) or by unanimity. The Council acts under the E.C. treaty by issuing (*a*) regulations, which are binding in their entirety and directly applicable in all member states; (*b*) directives, which are binding as to the result to be achieved but leave open to national governments the method of attaining this result; (*c*) decisions, which bind those addressed; (*d*) recommendations; and (*e*) opinions, which have no binding force. The Euratom treaty has the same system of voting and taking action; the E.C.S.C. system differs in certain respects.

The Presidency of the Council is held in rotation for periods of six months. The sessions of the Council are prepared by a Committee of Permanent Representatives of the member states. The Council and its committees are serviced by a general secretariat.

European Parliament

Secretariat: Centre Européen, Kirchberg, Luxembourg.

U.K. Information Office, 2 Queen Anne's Gate, SW1H 9AA (Tel: 01-222 0411).

The first direct elections to the European Parliament were held in mid-1979, the second in 1984 and the latest in June 1989. Of 518 seats, the United Kingdom, France, Germany and Italy have 81 each, Spain 60, the Netherlands 25, Belgium, Greece, and Portugal 24, Denmark 16, Ireland 15 and Luxembourg 6. The Parliament meets in Strasbourg and its Committees in Brussels.

Set up in 1952 under the European Coal and Steel Community Treaty of 1951, the Parliament's authority was extended by the 1957 Convention on Common Institutions to cover the European Economic Community and Euratom. It must be consulted on all major issues and has the right to dismiss the Commission by a vote of censure.

On the bulk of legislation concerning the European Single Market due to be completed by the end of 1992, the Parliament enjoys additional powers under the 'co-operation procedure' introduced by the Single European Act in July 1987. Apart from general powers of supervision and consultation, it questions the Commission and the Council of Ministers and has a measure of control over the Community's annual budget including its final adoption. It can reject the budget as a whole and can amend items of non-obligatory expenditure (i.e. expenditure not specified in the original treaties or derived legislation—amounting to some 27 per cent. of the total budget).

The Members of the Parliament serve on specialized committees and sit in political groupings as follows: Socialists, 180; European People's Party, 121; Liberal Democratic Reformist, 49; European Democratic Group, 34; Green, 30; European United Left, 28; European Democratic Alliance, 20; European Right, 17; Coalition Left, 14; Rainbow Group, 13; Independent, 12.

President, Enrique Baron Crespo (*Spain*).

European Court of Justice
L–2925 Luxembourg

The European Court superseded the Court of Justice of E.C.S.C. and is common to the three European Communities. It exists to safeguard the law in the interpretation and application of the Community treaties, to decide on the legality of decisions of the Council of Ministers or the Commission and to determine violations of the Treaties. Cases may be brought to it by the member States, the Community institutions, firms or individuals. Its decisions are directly binding in the member countries. The thirteen judges and six advocates-general of the Court are appointed for renewable six-year terms by the member Governments in concert. During 1988, 373 new cases were lodged at the court and 238 judgments were delivered.

(w.e.f. October 7, 1988)

Judges, O. Due (*President*); R. Joliet (*President of 1st and 5th Chambers*); T. F. O'Higgins (*President of the 2nd Chamber*); F. Grevisse (*President of the 3rd Chamber*); T. Koopmans (*President of the 4th and 6th Chambers*); Sir Gordon Slynn; G. F. Mancini; C. N. Kakouris; F. A. Schockweiler; J. C. Moitinho de Almeida; G. C. Rodriguez Iglesias; M. Diez de Velasco; M. Zuleeg.

Advocates-General, J. Mischo (*1st Advocate-General*); C. O. Lenz; M. Darmon; W. Van Gerven; F. Jacobs; G. Tesauro.

The European Investment Bank
100 Boulevard Konrad Adenauer,
L–2950 Luxembourg

The European Investment Bank (E.I.B.) was set up in 1958 under the terms of the Treaty of Rome to finance capital investment projects promoting the balanced development of the European Community.

It grants long-term loans to private enterprises, public authorities and financial institutions, to finance projects which further: the economic development of less advanced regions (Assisted Areas); improve communication systems between Member States; environmental protection; attainment of the Communities energy policy objectives; modernization of enterprises; and co-operation between undertakings in the different Member States.

E.I.B. activities have also been extended outside member countries under the terms of different association or cooperation agreements with twelve countries in the Mediterranean region and, under the Lomé Conventions, 66 in Africa, the Caribbean and the Pacific.

The Bank's total financing operations in 1988 amounted to 10,175 million E.C.U.,* of which 9,475 million were for investments in the European Community and 700 million for outside the Community. Between 1973 and 1988 the E.I.B. had made available a total of £6,624 million E.C.U. for investment in the U.K.

The members of the European Investment Bank are the twelve member states of the Community, who have all subscribed to the Bank's capital, of 28,000 million E.C.U. (of which 2,596 E.C.U. is the paid in or due to be paid in portion). The bulk of the funds required by the Bank to carry out its tasks are borrowed on the capital markets of the Community and non-member countries, and on the international market.

As it operates on a non-profit-making basis, the interest rates charged by the E.I.B. reflect the cost of

* The financial statements of the European Investment Bank are drawn up in European currency unit (E.C.U.) which at June 30, 1989 equalled ± £0·68, U.S.$1·06.

the Bank's borrowings and closely follow conditions on world capital markets.

The Board of Governors of the European Investment Bank consists of one Minister nominated by each of the member countries, usually the Finance Minister, who lay down general directives on the policy of the Bank and appoint members to the Board of Directors (21 nominated by the member states, 1 by the Commission of the European Communities), which takes decisions on the granting and raising of loans and the fixing of interest rates. A Management Committee, also appointed by the Board of Governors, is responsible for the day-to-day operations of the Bank.

President, Ernst-Günther Bröder.

Vice-Presidents, Lucio Izzo; Alain Prate; Miguel A. Arnedo Orbañanos; Erling Jørgensen; Ludovicus Meulemans; Roger Lavelle.

(The President and Vice-Presidents also preside as Chairman and Vice-Chairmen at meetings of the Board of Directors.)

U.K. Office: 68 Pall Mall, SW1Y 5ES.

EUROPEAN COAL AND STEEL COMMUNITY

This, the first of the European Communities, was established in 1952. Since then, for coal, iron ore and scrap, it has abolished customs duties, quantitative restrictions, the dual pricing system whereby prices charged on exported coal or steel differed from those charged to home consumers, currency restrictions and discrimination in transport rates based on the nationality of customers and the special frontier charges which made international transport of these goods dearer within the Community than transport within national frontiers. It has applied rules for fair competition and a harmonized external tariff for the whole Community.

THE TREATY OF ROME

Discussions were held at Messina, Sicily, in 1955 between the foreign ministers of the six member states of E.C.S.C. (Belgium, France, Federal Republic of Germany, Italy, Luxembourg and The Netherlands) on proposals for further advances towards economic integration in Europe, and after intensive study of these proposals, a treaty was signed at Rome on March 25, 1957, setting up the European Economic Community.

The Treaty aimed to lay the foundations of an enduring and closer union between the European peoples by gradually removing the economic effects of their political frontiers. The Treaty provides for the elimination of customs duties and quotas in trade between member states; the establishment of a common customs tariff and a common trade policy towards third countries; the abolition of the obstacles to free movement of persons, services and capital between member states; the inauguration of common policies for agriculture and transport; the establishment of a system ensuring that competition shall not be distorted in the Common Market; the co-ordination of economic policies; the harmonization of social and economic legislation to the extent necessary in order to enable the Common Market to work; the creation of a European Social Fund in order to improve the possibilities of employment for workers and to contribute to the raising of their standard of living; the establishment of an Economic and Social Committee which must be consulted on major proposals, consisting of representatives of employers, workers, consumers and other groups; the establishment of a European Investment Bank intended to aid

investment in underdeveloped areas and help to finance modernization; and the association of overseas countries and territories with the Community with a view to increasing trade and to pursuing jointly their effort towards economic and social development.

ENLARGEMENT OF THE COMMUNITY

The question of possible enlargement of the Community played an important part in its development from the autumn of 1961 when Britain, the Irish Republic, Denmark and Norway first sought membership, and Austria, Sweden, Switzerland, Spain and Cyprus sought association with the Community. The negotiations were vetoed by France in January, 1963. In May, 1967, Britain, the Irish Republic and Denmark formally submitted applications for Community membership. In July Norway followed suit and Sweden announced that it would seek to participate in the enlargement of the Community on terms compatible with its neutrality. These applications made very slow progress and appeared to come to a standstill when in December, 1967, France declared that Britain's economy would have to be strengthened before negotiations could begin. But shortly after taking office as President of France, Georges Pompidou stated in July, 1969, that there was no objection in principle to the admission of Britain to the Community. At the Hague "summit" meeting in December, 1969, the Six decided that provided that the completion of the Community was not prejudiced, and provided that the Community was strengthened to provide for enlargement, then the entry of other European countries would be desirable. After deciding on a common negotiating position, the Six invited Britain and the other applicants to begin negotiations for membership.

A single overall transitional period of five years, during which the Three were to adopt Community rules and regulations, started on January 1, 1973, giving time for the gradual integration of the economies of the Three with the Six by the end of 1977.

The first 40 per cent alignment on the Community's Common External Tariff (C.E.T.)—i.e. 40 per cent of the difference between the new members' tariffs and the C.E.T.—was made at the beginning of 1974, and three further alignments of 20 per cent each followed.

Negotiations with Greece were concluded and the Treaty of Accession signed on May 28, 1979. Greece became the tenth member of the Community on January 1, 1981. Portugal and Spain applied to join the Community and became the eleventh and twelfth members on January 1, 1986.

Following a plebiscite, Greenland negotiated its withdrawal from the E.C. (but without discontinuing relations with Denmark) and formally left on February 1, 1986.

EUROPEAN ATOMIC ENERGY COMMUNITY (EURATOM)

A second treaty, arising from the Messina discussions between the E.C.S.C. powers on additional means of co-operation, was signed in Rome on March 25, 1957, setting up the European Atomic Energy Community. The task of Euratom, defined in detail in the Treaty, is to create within a short period the technical and industrial conditions necessary to utilize nuclear discoveries and especially to produce nuclear energy on a large scale. The United Kingdom, Denmark and Ireland joined Euratom on Jan. 1, 1973, Greece on Jan. 1, 1981, and Spain and Portugal on Jan. 1, 1986.

OTHER INTERNATIONAL ORGANIZATIONS

ASIAN DEVELOPMENT BANK
2330 Roxas Boulevard, 1300 Metropolitan Manila
Philippines

The Asian Development Bank began operations in December 1966. It has 47 member countries, 32 countries from the Asia–Pacific region and 15 from Europe and North America.

The aim of the Bank is to promote the economic and social progress of its developing member countries. It makes loans and equity investments; provides technical assistance for development programmes and advisory services; promotes public and private investment in development schemes; and co-ordinates development plans and policies.

The Bank's highest policy-making body is the board of Governors, which meets annually. Each member country appoints one governor and one alternate governor. The President, who is elected by the Board of Governors for a term of five years, acts as the Chairman of the Board of Directors. The twelve-man Board of Directors is responsible for the direction of the Bank's operations.

President, Masao Fujioka *(Japan)*.

ASSOCIATION OF SOUTH EAST ASIAN NATIONS
Jakarta, Indonesia

Formed in 1967, the main aims of the Association of South East Asian Nations (A.S.E.A.N.) are the acceleration of economic growth, social progress and cultural development, the promotion of collaboration and mutual assistance in matters of common interest, and the continuing stability of the South East Asian region.

The Heads of Government of the member countries are the highest authority and give directions to A.S.E.A.N. as and when necessary. The main policy-making body is the annual meeting of foreign ministers of the member countries. The members of the Association are Brunei, Indonesia, Malaysia, the Philippines, Singapore and Thailand.

Sec. Gen., Roderick Yong *(Brunei)*.

BANK FOR INTERNATIONAL SETTLEMENTS
Centralbahnplatz 2, 4051 Basle, Switzerland

The objectives of the Bank for International Settlements (founded in 1930) are to promote the co-operation of central banks; to provide facilities for international financial operations; and to act as trustee or agent in international financial settlements entrusted to it. The London agent is the Bank of England, and the Governor of the Bank of England is a member of the Board of Directors, in which administrative control is vested.

Chairman of the Board of Directors and President of the Bank for International Settlement, Dr. W. S. Duisberg *(Netherlands)* (1988).

C.A.B. INTERNATIONAL
Wallingford, Oxon. OX10 8DE
[0491-32111]

C.A.B. International (formerly the Commonwealth Agricultural Bureaux) was founded in 1929. It consists of four Institutes and eleven Bureaux under the control of an Executive Council comprising representatives of the countries which contribute to its funds. The functions of C.A.B.I. are to provide a scientific information service, identification of pests, biological control services and mutual assistance.

Each Institute and Bureau acts as an effective clearing house for the collection, collation and dissemination of information in its particular branch of agricultural science.

Director General, D. Mentz.

CARIBBEAN COMMUNITY AND COMMON MARKET
P.O. Box 10827, Georgetown, Guyana

The Caribbean Community and Common Market (CARICOM) was established on 1973 with three objectives: economic co-operation through the Caribbean Common Market; the co-ordination of foreign policy among the independent member states; the provision of common services and co-operation in functional matters such as health, education and culture, communications and industrial relations. The principal organs are the Conference of Heads of Government, which determines policy, and the Common Market Council of Ministers, consisting of Ministers of Government (usually Ministers of Trade) designated by each member state, which is responsible for the development and smooth running of the Common Market and for the settlement of any problems arising out of its functioning. The principal administrative arm is the Secretariat, based in Guyana.

The 13 member states are Antigua and Barbuda, The Bahamas (which is not a member of the Common Market), Barbados, Belize, Dominica, Grenada, Guyana, Jamaica, Montserrat, St. Christopher and Nevis, St. Lucia, St. Vincent and the Grenadines and Trinidad and Tobago. The Dominican Republic, Suriname and Haiti have observer status.

Sec. Gen., Roderick Rainford *(Jamaica)*.

CONFERENCE ON DISARMAMENT
Palais des Nations, CH-1211, Geneva 10, Switzerland

The Conference on Disarmament (C.D.) was constituted in its original form as the 18-nation Committee on Disarmament in 1962. The present title of the organization was adopted in 1984. The membership stood at 40 nations in June 1989.

The Conference holds two regular sessions per year, Feb.–April and June–August. The work of the Conference is conducted both in plenary meetings and in ad hoc committees set up with the consent of all members to deal with specific items of the agenda. Currently on the agenda are, *inter alia*, negotiations towards a global ban on chemical weapons.

The Conference on Disarmament is regarded by the U.N. as the single multilateral disarmament negotiating forum.

Secretary General, His Excellency Miljan Komatina.

U.K. Delegation to the Conference on Disarmament, 37–39 rue de Vermont, 1211 Geneva 20, Switzerland.—*Leader of U.K. Delegation*, Miss T. A. H. Solesby, C.M.G.

COUNCIL FOR MUTUAL ECONOMIC ASSISTANCE
56 Kalinin Avenue, Moscow G–205, U.S.S.R

Established in 1949, the aim of the Council for Mutual Economic Assistance (C.M.E.A. or COMECON) is to promote the development of the national economies of the member states and the development of socialist economic integration, through the co-operation of members in the most rational use of resources and the acceleration of economic and technical progress, industrialisation and productivity. The highest body is the Session of the Council, which consists of delegations from all member states, usually led by the heads of government. The Executive Committee consists of representatives of member states at the level of deputy heads of government, and is responsible for the implementation of the tasks set by the Session of the Council and for directing the work of the Committees, Standing Commissions, Secretariat and other bodies. In 1988 the C.M.E.A. established official relations with the E.C.

The member countries are Bulgaria, Cuba, Czechoslovakia, German Democratic Republic, Hungary, Mongolia, Poland, Romania, U.S.S.R. and Vietnam. Yugoslavia participates in the work of some C.M.E.A. bodies. There are also co-operation agreements with Afghanistan, Angola, Ethiopia, Finland, Iraq, Mexico, Mozambique, Nicaragua, the People's Democratic Republic of Yemen, and Yugoslavia.

Secretary, V. Sytchev (U.S.S.R.).

THE COUNCIL OF EUROPE
67006 Strasbourg, France

The Council of Europe was founded in 1949. Its aim is to achieve greater unity between its members to safeguard their European heritage and to facilitate their economic and social progress through discussion and common action in economic, social, cultural, educational, scientific, legal and administrative matters and in the maintenance and furtherance of human rights and fundamental freedoms.

The 23 members are Austria, Belgium, Cyprus, Denmark, Finland, France, the Federal Republic of Germany, Greece, Iceland, the Republic of Ireland, Italy, Liechtenstein, Luxembourg, Malta, Netherlands, Norway, Portugal, San Marino, Spain, Sweden, Switzerland, Turkey and the U.K.

The organs are the Committee of Ministers, consisting of the Foreign Ministers of member countries, who meet twice yearly, and the Parliamentary Assembly of 177 members, elected or chosen by the national parliaments of member countries in proportion to the relative strength of political parties. There is also a Joint Committee of Ministers and Representatives of the Parliamentary Assembly.

The Committee of Ministers is the executive organ of the Council. The majority of its conclusions take the form of international agreements (known as European Conventions) or recommendations to governments. Decisions of the Ministers may also be embodied in partial agreements to which a limited number of member governments are party. Member governments accredit Permanent Representatives to the Council in Strasbourg, who are also the Ministers' Deputies. The Committee of Deputies meets every month to transact business and to take decisions on behalf of Ministers.

The Parliamentary Assembly holds three weeklong sessions a year. It debates reports on, *inter alia*, political, economic, agricultural, social, educational, legal and regional planning affairs, and also reports received annually from the O.E.C.D., other European organizations and certain specialized agencies of the United Nations. Its 13 permanent committees meet, normally in private, once or twice between each public plenary session of the Assembly. The Standing Conference of Local and Regional Authorities of Europe each year brings together mayors and municipal councillors in the same numbers as the members of the Parliamentary Assembly.

One of the principal achievements of the Council of Europe is the European Convention of Human Rights (1950) under which was established the European Commission and the European Court of Human Rights. 131 other conventions and agreements have now been concluded. They include the European Social Charter, the European Social Security Code, and conventions on extradition, the legal status of migrant workers, conservation, and the transfer of sentenced prisoners.

Non-member states take part in certain Council of Europe activities on a regular or ad hoc basis; thus the Holy See and Yugoslavia participate in all the educational, cultural and sports activities. The European Youth Foundation funds events in both Eastern and Western European countries and in some outside Europe, while nationals of these countries attend courses and seminars at the European Youth Centre.

Secretary General, Catherine Lalumière *(France)*.
Permanent U.K. Representative, His Excellency Colin McLean, C.M.G., M.B.E.

EUROPEAN FREE TRADE ASSOCIATION
9–11 rue de Varembé, 1211 Geneva 20, Switzerland

The members of the European Free Trade Association (E.F.T.A.), which was established on May 3, 1960, are Austria, Finland (an associate from 1960 to 1985 and a member since Jan. 1, 1986), Iceland (since March 1, 1970), Norway, Sweden and Switzerland.

In 1973 all the E.F.T.A. Member States entered into a new relationship with the E.C. Two—Denmark and the United Kingdom—withdrew from E.F.T.A. at the end of December 1972 to become members of the E.C. on January 1, 1973. Agreements establishing industrial free trade between most of the other E.F.T.A. Member States and the enlarged E.C. came into force on that same date. Similar agreements with Norway and Finland came into force on July 1, 1973, and Jan. 1, 1974, respectively. On Jan. 1, 1986 Portugal became a member of the E.C. The free trade agreements therefore now apply to trade between the six countries remaining in E.F.T.A. and Portugal.

E.F.T.A.'s first objective was free trade between its original members and this was realized at the end of 1966. Its second objective was the creation of a single market to include all Western European countries, achieved through the free trade agreements.

The final abolition of tariffs on E.F.T.A.–E.C. trade was marked by a meeting in Luxembourg in April 1984 when ministers from all E.F.T.A. and E.C. countries met. They agreed on general guidelines for greatly increased co-operation between their countries. The emphasis was on the removal of technical barriers to trade and the simplification of the origin rules which determine which products may be traded free of duty. A start was made towards multilateral co-operation in research and development as a means of strengthening the industrial potential of Western Europe, and multilateral efforts to protect the environment are under discussion.

All E.F.T.A. and E.C. countries have co-operated in a successful attempt to simplify border formalities for trade in goods in Western Europe: multilateral conventions now provide for the use of a single administrative document for customs purposes and for the introduction of a common transit procedure.

The Council of E.F.T.A. meets every two weeks at the level of the heads of the permanent national delegations to E.F.T.A. and usually twice a year at the level of ministers. Each state has a single vote and recommendations must normally be unanimous. Decisions of the Council are binding on member countries.

Secretary General, Georg Reisch *(Austria)*.

EUROPEAN ORGANIZATION FOR NUCLEAR RESEARCH (C.E.R.N.)
1211 Geneva 23, Switzerland

The Convention establishing the European Organization for Research (C.E.R.N.) came into force in 1954. The Organization promotes European collaboration in nuclear research of a purely scientific nature. It is not concerned with research of a military nature.

The member countries are Austria, Belgium, Denmark, France, Federal Republic of Germany, Greece, Italy, Netherlands, Norway, Portugal, Spain, Sweden, Switzerland and the U.K. The following have observer status: Poland, Turkey, Yugoslavia, the E.C. Commission and UNESCO.

The Council is the highest policy-making body and is made up of two delegates from each member state. There is also a Committee of the Council comprising a single delegate from each member state (who is also a Council member) and the chairmen of the scientific policy and finance advisory committees. The Council is chaired by a President who is elected by the Council in Session. The Council also elects the Director General, the person responsible for the internal organization of C.E.R.N. The Director General heads a workforce of approximately 3,500, including physicists, craftsmen, technicians and administrative staff. At present over 5,000 physicists use C.E.R.N.'s facilities.

The member countries contribute to the budget directly in proportion to their net national revenue. The 1989 budget was S. Fr. 809.5 million.

President of the Council, J. Rembser (*Federal Republic of Germany*).

Director General, C. Rubbia (1989–1993).

EUROPEAN SPACE AGENCY
8–10 rue Mario Nikis, 75738 Paris, France

The European Space Agency (E.S.A.) was set up on May 31, 1975. It was formed from two earlier space organizations—the European Space Research Organization (E.S.R.O.) and the European Launcher Development Organization (E.L.D.O.). Its aims include the advancement of space research and technology, the implementation of a long-term European space policy and the co-ordination of national space programmes.

The member countries are Austria, Belgium, Denmark, France, Federal Republic of Germany, Republic of Ireland, Italy, Netherlands, Norway, Spain, Sweden, Switzerland and the United Kingdom. Finland is an associate member and Canada a co-operating state.

The agency is directed by a Council composed of the representatives of the member states, and its chief officer is the Director General.

Director General, Prof. Dr. Reimar Lüst.

INTERNATIONAL CONFEDERATION OF FREE TRADE UNIONS
37–41 rue Montagne aux Herbes Potageres, 1000 Brussels, Belgium

Formed in 1949 the International Confederation of Free Trade Unions (I.C.F.T.U.) was created to promote free trade unionism worldwide. It aims to establish, maintain and develop free trade unions, particularly in economically under-developed countries.

Affiliated to the I.C.F.T.U. are 142 individual unions and representative bodies in 97 countries and territories: on May 17, 1989 there were over 88 million members.

The supreme authority of the organization is the Congress which convenes at least every four years. It is composed of delegates from the affiliated trade organizations. The Congress elects an Executive Board of 35 members which meets at least twice a year. The Board establishes the budget and receives suggestions and proposals from affiliates as well as acting on behalf of the Confederation. The Congress also elects the General Secretary.

General Secretary, John Vanderveken.

U.K. Affiliate, T.U.C., Congress House, 23–28 Great Russell Street, WC1B 3LS.

INTERNATIONAL CRIMINAL POLICE ORGANIZATION
26 rue Armengaud, 92210 Saint-Cloud, France

The International Criminal Police Commission (INTERPOL) was set up in 1923 to establish an international criminal records office and to harmonize extradition procedures. In 1956 a revised Constitution was adopted and the organization adopted its present name. On Jan. 1, 1988 the organization comprised 146 member states.

INTERPOL's aims are to ensure and promote mutual assistance between all criminal police authorities, and to support government agencies concerned with combatting crime, whilst respecting the national sovereignty of members. INTERPOL is financed by annual contributions from the governments of member states.

INTERPOL's policy is decided by the General Assembly which meets annually: it is composed of delegates appointed by the member states. The 13-member Executive Committee is elected by the General Assembly from among the member states' delegates, and is chaired by the President, who has a four-year term of office. The permanent administrative organ is the General Secretariat, headed by the Secretary General, who is appointed by the General Assembly.

President, John Simpson.

U.K. Office, Criminal Investigation Department, New Scotland Yard, SW1H 0BG.—*U.K. Representative*, J. A. Smith, Q.P.M.

INTERNATIONAL ENERGY AGENCY
Chateau de la Muette, 2 rue Andre-Pascal, 75775 Paris, France

The International Energy Agency (I.E.A.), founded in November 1974, is an autonomous agency within the framework of the Organization for Economic Co-operation and Development (O.E.C.D.). The I.E.A. had 21 member countries at May 1989.

The I.E.A.'s objectives include improvement of energy supply and demand worldwide, increased efficiency, development of alternative energy sources and the promotion of relations between oil producing and oil consuming countries. The I.E.A. also maintains an emergency system to alleviate the effects of severe oil supply disruptions.

The main decision-making body is the Governing Board composed of senior energy officials from member countries. Various standing groups and special committees exist to facilitate the work of the Board. The I.E.A. Secretariat, with a staff of energy experts, carries out the work of the Governing Board and its subordinate bodies. The Executive Director is appointed by the Board.

Executive Director, Mrs. Helga Steeg (*Federal Rep. of Germany*).

INTERNATIONAL MARITIME SATELLITE ORGANIZATION
40 Melton Street, London NW1 2EQ

The International Maritime Satellite Organization (INMARSAT) was founded in July 1978 and began operations on Feb. 1, 1982. INMARSAT operates a system of satellites to provide telephone, telex, data and facsimile transmission, as well as distress and safety communication services to the world's shipping, aviation and offshore industries.

INMARSAT comprises three bodies: The Assembly is composed of representatives of all member countries, each with one vote. It meets every two years to review activities and objectives, to make recommendations to the Council. The Council is the main decision-making body and consists of representatives of the 18 members with the largest investment shares. Four others who represent the interests of developing countries are elected to the Council on the basis of geographical representation. The Council meets at least three times a year and oversees the activities of the Directorate, the permanent staff of INMARSAT.

As at May 1989 there were 56 member countries.
Director General, Oluf Lundberg.

INTERNATIONAL RED CROSS AND RED CRESCENT MOVEMENT

17 avenue de la Paix, 1202 Geneva, Switzerland

The International Red Cross and Red Crescent Movement is composed of three elements. The International Committee of the Red Cross (I.C.R.C.) is the founding body of the Red Cross and was formed in 1863. It is a neutral intermediary negotiating between warring parties. It also ensures the application of the Geneva Conventions with regard to prisoners of war and internees.

The League of Red Cross and Red Crescent Societies, founded in 1919, is the international federation which exists to contribute to humanitarian activities such as co-ordinating relief work, caring for refugees, training personnel and furthering medical research. There are also national Red Cross and Red Crescent Societies in 146 countries with a global membership of 250 million.

The International Red Cross meets every four years at the International Red Cross Conference, which is also attended by nations bound by the Geneva Conventions.

President of the I.C.R.C., Cornelio Sommaruga.
British Red Cross Society, 9 Grosvenor Crescent, SW1X 7EJ.—*Director*, J. C. Burke-Gaffney.

INTERNATIONAL TELECOMMUNICATIONS SATELLITE ORGANIZATION

3400 International Drive, N.W., Washington D.C. 20008–3098, U.S.A.

Formed in 1964, the International Telecommunications Satellite Organization (INTELSAT) owns and operates the world-wide commercial communications satellite system. The system is composed of a network of thirteen satellites and more than 800 antennas which link together over 700 member and non-member users.

INTELSAT provides an international telephony service; an international television service; the Intelsat Business Service (I.B.S.); Intelnet (a digital service designed for data collection and distribution); domestic telecommunications services and the Vista service providing telecommunications to remote communities.

Each of the 117 national signatories contributed to the capital costs of the organization in proportion to its investment share. The investment share is based on the relative usage of the system by member countries.

There is a four-tier hierarchy: the Assembly of Parties to the agreement meets every two years to consider long-term objectives. It is composed of representatives of the member governments: the Meeting of Signatories consider annually the financial, technical and operational aspects of the system: the Board of Governors, which has 28 members: the Executive Organ is the permanent staff of Intelsat and is headed by a Director General who reports to the Board of Governors.

LEAGUE OF ARAB STATES

37 Av. Khereddine Pacha, Tunis, Tunisia

The purpose of the League of Arab States (founded 1945) is to ensure co-operation among member states and protect their independence and sovereignty, to supervise the affairs and interests of Arab countries and to control the execution of agreements concluded among the member states. The League considers itself a regional organization and is an observer at the United Nations.

Member states are Algeria, Bahrain, Djibouti, Iraq, Jordan, Kuwait, Lebanon, Libya, Mauritania, Morocco, Oman, Palestine, Qatar, Saudi Arabia, Somalia, Sudan, Syria, Tunisia, United Arab Emirates, Arab Republic of Yemen and Democratic Republic of Yemen. (The re-admission of Egypt, a founder state, was announced in May 1989.)

Secretary General, Chedli Klibi (*Tunisia*).
U.K. Office—Arab Information Centre, 52 Green Street, WIY 3RH.

NORTH ATLANTIC TREATY ORGANIZATION

Brussels 1110, Belgium

The North Atlantic Treaty was signed on April 4, 1949, by the Foreign Ministers of twelve nations. The twelve are Belgium, Canada, Denmark, France, Iceland, Italy, Luxembourg, the Netherlands, Norway, Portugal, the United Kingdom and United States. Greece and Turkey acceded to the Treaty in 1952, the Federal Republic of Germany in 1955, and Spain in 1982. The North Atlantic Council, chaired by the Secretary General, is the highest authority of the Alliance and is composed of permanent representatives of the sixteen member countries. It meets at ministerial level (Foreign Ministers) at least twice per year. The permanent representatives (Ambassadors) head national delegations of advisers and experts.

Defence matters are dealt with in the Defence Planning Committee (D.P.C.), composed of representatives of all member countries, except France. Within the specialized field of defence, the D.P.C. has the same functions and authority as the Council. Like the Council it meets regularly at ambassador level and twice a year in ministerial sessions, when the nations are represented by their Defence Ministers.

The Council/D.P.C., as a unique forum for confidential and constant inter-governmental consultation and as the main decision-making body within the North Atlantic Alliance, is assisted by an International Staff, divided into five divisions: Political Affairs; Defence Planning and Policy; Defence Support; Infrastructure, Logistics and Civil Emergency Planning; Scientific Affairs.

U.K. Permanent Representative, His Excellency Vice Adm. Sir Richard Thomas, K.C.B., O.B.E.

The senior military authority in N.A.T.O., under the Council and D.P.C., is the Military Committee composed of the Chief of Defence of each member country except France and Iceland. The Military Committee, which is assisted by an international military staff, functions in permanent session with permanent military representatives and is responsible for making recommendations to the Council and Defence Planning Committee on measures considered necessary for the common defence of the N.A.T.O. area and for supplying guidance on military matters to the major N.A.T.O. Commanders.

Chairman of the Military Committee, Gen. Vikgleik Eide (*Norway*).

The strategic area covered by the North Atlantic Treaty is divided among three Commands (European, Atlantic and Channel) and a Regional Planning Group (Canada and the United States).

The Major N.A.T.O Commanders are responsible for the development of defence plans for their respective areas, for the determination of force requirements and for the deployment and exercise of the forces under their command. The Major N.A.T.O. Commanders report to the Military Committee.

The three Major N.A.T.O Commanders are:
Supreme Allied Commander, Europe, Gen. John R. Galvin (*U.S.*).
Supreme Allied Commander, Atlantic, Adm. Frank B. Kelso II (*U.S.*).
Commander-in-Chief, Channel, Adm. Sir Benjamin Bathurst, K.C.B. (*U.K.*).
Secretary General, Manfred Wörner (*Federal Rep. of Germany*).

ORGANIZATION FOR ECONOMIC CO-OPERATION AND DEVELOPMENT
2 rue André-Pascal, 75116 Paris

Formed on September 30, 1961, the Organization for Economic Co-operation and Development (O.E.C.D.) replaced the Organization for European Economic Co-operation. The O.E.C.D. is the instrument for international co-operation among industrialized member countries on economic and social policies. Its objectives are to assist its member governments in the formulation and co-ordination of policies designed to achieve high, sustained economic growth while maintaining financial stability, to contribute to world trade on a multilateral basis and to stimulate members' aid to developing countries.

The following countries belong to the O.E.C.D.: Australia, Austria, Belgium, Canada, Denmark, Federal Republic of Germany, Finland, France, Greece, Iceland, Republic of Ireland, Italy, Japan, Luxembourg, the Netherlands, New Zealand, Norway, Portugal, Spain, Sweden, Switzerland, Turkey, U.K. and U.S.A. (Yugoslavia participates with a special status).

The Council is the supreme body of the Organization. Composed of one representative for each member country, it meets at Permanent Representative level under the Chairmanship of the Secretary General, or at Ministerial level (usually once a year) under the Chairmanship of a Minister elected annually. Decisions and recommendations are adopted by mutual agreement of all members of the Council. Fourteen members of the Council are chosen annually to form an Executive Committee to assist the Council. However, most of the O.E.C.D.'s work is undertaken in over 200 specialized committees and working parties. Five autonomous or semi-autonomous bodies are related in varying degrees to the Organization: the Nuclear Energy Agency, the International Energy Agency, the Development Centre, the Centre for Educational Research and Innovation, and the European Conference of Ministers of Transport. These bodies, the committees and the Council are serviced by an international Secretariat headed by the Secretary General of the Organization.
Secretary General, Jean-Claude Paye (*France*).
U.K. Permanent Representative, John Walton David Gray, C.M.G., 19 rue de Franqueville, Paris 75116.

ORGANIZATION OF AFRICAN UNITY
P.O. Box 3243, Addis Ababa, Ethiopia

The Organization of African Unity (O.A.U.) was established in 1963 and has 50 members. It aims to further African unity and solidarity, to co-ordinate political, economic, social and defence policies, and to eliminate colonialism in Africa.

The chief organs are the Assembly of heads of state or government and the Council of Foreign Ministers.

The main administrative body is the Secretariat, based in Addis Ababa.
Sec. Gen., Salim Ahmed Salim (*Tanzania*).

ORGANIZATION OF AMERICAN STATES
17th Street and Constitution Ave. N.W., Washington D.C. 20006, U.S.A.

Originally founded in 1890 for largely commercial purposes, the Organization of American States (O.A.S.) adopted its present name and charter in 1948. Its aims are to strengthen the peace and security of the continent; to prevent possible causes of difficulties and to ensure the pacific settlement of disputes that may arise among the member states; to provide for common action on the part of those states in the event of aggression; to seek the solution of political, judicial and economic problems that may arise among them; and to promote, by co-operative action, their economic, social and cultural development. The O.A.S. is a regional organization within the United Nations.

Policy is determined by the annual General Assembly. Meetings of Ministers of Foreign Affairs consider urgent problems, and advise in cases of armed attack and threats to peace.

The 32 member states are Antigua and Barbuda, Argentina, Bahamas, Barbados, Bolivia, Brazil, Chile, Colombia, Costa Rica, Cuba, Dominica, Dominican Republic, Ecuador, Grenada, Guatemala, Haiti, Honduras, Jamaica, Mexico, Nicaragua, Panama, Paraguay, Peru, St. Christopher and Nevis, St. Lucia, St. Vincent and the Grenadines, El Salvador, Suriname, Trinidad and Tobago, U.S.A., Uruguay and Venezuela.
Secretary General, João Clemente Baena Soares (*Brazil*).

ORGANIZATION OF ARAB PETROLEUM EXPORTING COUNTRIES
P.O. Box 20501 Safat, 13066 Kuwait

The Organization of Arab Petroleum and Exporting Countries (O.A.P.E.C.) was founded in Jan. 1968. The objectives of the organization are to promote co-operation in economic activities; to safeguard members' interests; to unite efforts to ensure the flow of oil to consumer markets; and to create a favourable climate for the investment of capital and expertise.

The Ministerial Council is composed of oil ministers from the member countries and meets twice a year to determine policy, to direct activities and to approve the budgets and accounts of the General Secretariat and the Judicial Tribunal. The Judicial Tribunal is composed of nine part-time judges who rule on disputes between member nations and disputes between nations and oil companies. The executive organ of O.A.P.E.C. is the General Secretariat.

The member countries of O.A.P.E.C. are Algeria, Bahrain, Egypt, Iraq, Kuwait, Libya, Qatar, Saudi Arabia, Syria and the United Arab Emirates. (The suspension of Egypt's membership has been lifted in May 1989. Tunisia's membership has been inactive since 1987).
Acting Secretary General, Abdelaziz Alwattari.

ORGANIZATION OF THE PETROLEUM EXPORTING COUNTRIES
Obere Donaustrasse 93, A-1020 Vienna, Austria

The Organization of the Petroleum Exporting Countries (O.P.E.C.) was created in 1960 as a permanent intergovernmental organization with the aims of unifying and co-ordinating the pertroleum policies of members and determining the best means of protecting their interests, individually and collectively.

The supreme authority is the Conference of Ministers of Oil, Mines and Energy of member countries which meets at least twice a year and formulates policy. The Board of Governors, nominated by member countries, directs the management of O.P.E.C. and implements Conference resolutions. The Secretariat, based in Vienna, carries out executive functions under the direction of the Board of Governors.

The 13 member countries are Algeria, Ecuador, Gabon, Indonesia, Iran, Iraq, Kuwait, Libya, Nigeria, Qatar, Saudi Arabia, U.A.E. and Venezuela.
Secretary General, Dr. Subrota (*Indonesia*).

SOUTH PACIFIC COMMISSION
Anse Vata, Noumea, New Caledonia

The South Pacific Commission is a technical assistance agency with an advisory and consultative role in such fields as marine resources, rural management and technology, and community and education services. The management committee is involved with the day-to-day running of the organization and is headed by the Secretary General. The other members are the Director and the Deputy Director of Programmes.

The South Pacific Commission was established in February 1947 following the signing of the Canberra Agreement by the governments of Australia, France, the Netherlands, New Zealand, the U.K. and the U.S.A. The aim was to promote the economic and social stability of the islands in the region.

In 1983, the South Pacific Conference adopted a resolution that the Conference's 27 governments and administrations should have full and equal membership. Since 1967 the Conference has met annually to discuss the future policy of the Commission, to adopt the budget and to nominate the officers of the Commission.
Secretary General, Atanraoi Baiteke (*Kiribati*).
Director of Programmes, Jon Jonasson (*Cook Is.*).
Deputy Director of Programmes, Hélène Courte (*New Caledonia*).

THE WORLD COUNCIL OF CHURCHES
150 route de Ferney, CH–1211 Geneva 20,
Switzerland

The World Council of Churches (W.C.C.) was constituted in Amsterdam in 1948 to promote unity among the many different Christian churches. The 307 member churches of the W.C.C. have adherents in more than 100 countries. With the exception of Roman Catholicism, virtually all Christian traditions are included in the W.C.C. membership.

The policies of the Council are determined by delegates of the member churches meeting in Assembly, about every 8 years, the next Assembly being in Canberra, Australia, in 1991. More detailed decisions are taken by a 150-member Central Committee which is elected by the Assembly and meets, with the seven W.C.C. Presidents, annually. The Central Committee in turn appoints a smaller Executive Committee and also nominates commissions and working groups, to guide the various programmes. The implementation of the policies laid down by the churches and the co-ordination of the 14 programmes are the responsibility of the General Secretariat.
General Secretary, Dr. Emilio Castro (*Uruguay*).
British Council of Churches, 35–41 Lower Marsh, SE1 7RL.

WORLD FEDERATION OF TRADE UNIONS
Vinohradska 10, 12147 Prague 2, Czechoslovakia

The World Federation of Trade Unions (W.F.T.U.) was founded in October 1945. In Jan. 1949 a number of members withdrew and founded the International Confederation of Free Trade Unions. The W.F.T.U. now has 94 affiliated federations with 214 million members, mainly in Eastern Europe and the developing nations.

The Congress, which is comprised of delegates from member nations, meets every four years to review W.F.T.U.'s work and to elect the General Council and Bureau. The General Council is elected from members of national federations and meets once a year. Each affiliated organization has one member and one deputy. The Bureau of 40 members is elected by the General Council and carries out the executive work of the W.F.T.U.
General Secretary, Ibrahim Zakaria (*Sudan*).

BROADCASTING

BRITISH BROADCASTING CORPORATION
(*see also* entry on page 301)

Radio

BBC Radio broadcasts four national services to the United Kingdom, Isle of Man and the Channel Islands plus a fifth tier consisting of national regional services in Wales, Scotland and Northern Ireland and local radio services in England and the Channel Islands. In Wales there are two regional services based on the Welsh and English languages respectively.

The four national services are:

Radio 1: ("Pop" and "rock" network)—5 a.m.–2 a.m. daily. Frequencies: VHF-FM 98–99 MHz, coverage 86%; MW 1053 kHz/285m and 1089 kHz/275m, plus two local fillers giving population coverage 96% (day) and 57% (night).

Radio 2: (Light music, entertainment and sport)—24 hours a day. Frequencies: VHF-FM 88–90·2 MHz, coverage 97%; MW 693 kHz/433m and 909 kHz/330m, plus three local fillers giving population coverage 98% (day) and 65% (night).

Radio 3: (Serious music, drama and documentaries, poetry, and cricket in season)—6.55 a.m.–12 midnight daily. Frequencies: VHF-FM 90·2–92·4 MHz, population coverage 97%. MW (main centres of population only), 1215 kHz/247m, plus four local fillers on 1197 kHz/251m, coverage 87% (day) and 38% (night).

Radio 4: (News, documentaries, drama and entertainment)—5.50 a.m. to 12.45 a.m. daily. Frequencies: VHF-FM England, C.I. and I.o.M. plus part of Wales, Scotland and N. Ireland 92·4–95·8 MHz, coverage 92%; LW 198kHz/1515m, plus eight local fillers on MW giving population coverage 98% (day) and 91% (night).

The national regional services are:

Radio Scotland: Frequencies: MW 810 kHz/370m plus two local fillers, coverage 95% (day) and 87% (night); VHF-FM 92–95 MHz, coverage 94%.

Local programmes on VHF-FM 92–95 MHz: *Radio Aberdeen* (also MW 990 kHz/303m); *Radio Highland*; *Radio nan Eilean*; *Radio nan Gaidheal*; *Radio Orkney*; *Radio Shetland*; *Radio Solway* (also MW 585 kHz/513m); *Radio Tweed.*

Radio Ulster: Frequencies: MW 1341 kHz/224m, plus one local filler, coverage 96% (day) and 80% (night); VHF-FM 92–95 MHz, coverage 97%.

Radio Foyle: Frequencies: MW 792 kHz/379m; VHF-FM 92–95 MHz.

Radio Wales: Frequency: MW 882 kHz/340m and 1125 kHz plus two local fillers giving coverage 96% (day) and 63% (night).

Radio Clwyd: Frequency: MW 657 kHz/457m.

Radio Cymru (Welsh-language): Frequencies: VHF-FM 92–95 MHz, coverage 91%.

Local Radio: There are 35 local stations serving England and the Channel Islands (*see* below).

Television

The BBC's experiments in television broadcasting started in 1929 and in 1936 the BBC began the world's first public service of high-definition television from Alexandra Palace.

The BBC broadcasts two national television services, BBC 1 (BBC Wales in Wales, BBC Scotland in Scotland, BBC Northern Ireland in Northern Ireland) and BBC 2. These are broadcast in colour on 625-lines and UHF from a network of transmitting stations planned and built jointly with the Independent Broadcasting Authority. All stations (with a few exceptions) carry four channels including the two IBA channels.

Transmissions from 50 main stations and more than 800 relays are available to more than 99 per cent of the population.

World Service

The World Service broadcasts over 770 hours of programmes a week in 37 languages including the English Service. One hundred and one transmitters are used, 49 of them in the U.K. and 52 at relay stations overseas. In addition the World Service supplies many recorded programmes to other radio stations.

World Service in English, 24 hours a day, directed to all parts of the world, and with additional streams of programmes specially designated for audiences in Africa and South Asia at appropriate peak listening times.

African Service, which broadcasts in Swahili, Somali and Hausa.

Arabic Service, on the air for 9 hours a day to Middle East and North Africa.

Eastern Service, which broadcasts in Bengali, Burmese, Hindi, Nepali, Pashto, Persian, Tamil and Urdu.

Far Eastern Service, in Chinese (Cantonese and Mandarin), Indonesian, Japanese, Malay, Thai and Vietnamese.

Latin American Service, in Spanish and Portuguese.

French and Portuguese Service, directed to Europe and Africa.

German Service, directed to West and East Germany, Austria, and German-speaking Switzerland.

Central European Service, in Czech and Slovak, Hungarian, Polish and Finnish.

Russian Service, on the air for 6½ hours a day in Russian to the U.S.S.R.

South-East European Service, in Bulgarian, Romanian, Serbo-Croat, Slovene, Greek and Turkish.

Topical Tapes provides a variety of programmes on tape for overseas radio stations and produces the twice-weekly 'Calling the Falklands' programme.

BBC English by Radio and Television teaches English to learners outside Britain through radio, television and a wide range of published courses.

Transcription Service produces and sells to overseas radio stations recorded programmes drawn from the whole range of BBC Radio.

Monitoring Service provides regional summaries and a teleprinted news service from the output of overseas radio stations.

BBC Local Radio Stations

BEDFORDSHIRE, P.O. Box 476, Hastings Street, Luton LU1 5BA. (Tel: 0582-459111). *Wavelengths:* 258/476m, 1161/630 kHz, 95·5/103·8 VHF-FM.

BRISTOL, 3 Tyndalls Park Road, Bristol BS8 1PP. (Tel: 0272-741111). *Wavelengths:* 194/227m, 1548/1323 kHz, 94·9/95·5/104·6 VHF-FM.

CAMBRIDGESHIRE, Broadcasting House, Hills Road, Cambridge CB2 1LD. (Tel: 0223-315970). *Wavelengths:* 207/292m, 1449/1026 kHz, 96·0/95·7 VHF-FM.

CLEVELAND, P.O. Box 1548, Broadcasting House, Newport Road, Middlesbrough, Cleveland TS1 5DG. (Tel: 0642-225211). *Wavelengths:* 194m, 1548 kHz, 95·0/95·8 VHF-FM.

CORNWALL, Phoenix Wharf, Truro, Cornwall TR1 1UA. (Tel: 0872-75421). *Wavelengths*: 476/457m, 630/657 kHz, 95·2/96·0/103·9 VHF-FM.

CUMBRIA, Hilltop Heights, London Road, Carlisle CA1 2NA. (Tel: 0228-31661). *Wavelengths*: 397/206/ 358m, 756/1458/837 kHz, 95·2/95·6/96·1/104·2 VHF-FM.

DERBY, 56 St. Helen's Street, Derby DE1 3HL. (Tel: 0332-361111). *Wavelengths*: 269m, 1116 kHz, 104·5/ 94·2/95·3 VHF-FM.

DEVON, P.O. Box 100, St. David's Hill, Exeter EX4 4DB. (Tel: 0392-215651). *Wavelengths*: 351/303/206/ 375m, 855/990/1458/801 kHz, 103·4/97·0/96·0/95·8/ 94·8 VHF-FM.

ESSEX, 198 New London Road, Chelmsford CM2 9AB. (Tel:0245-262393). *Wavelengths*:392/196/412m, 765/ 729/1530 kHz, 103·5/95·3 VHF-FM.

GLOUCESTERSHIRE, London Road, Gloucester GL1 1SW. (Tel: 0452-308585). *Wavelengths*: 603 kHz, 95·0/104·7 VHF-FM.

GLR (GREATER LONDON RADIO), 35A Marylebone High Street W1A 4LG. (Tel: 01-224 2424). *Wavelengths*:206m, 1458 kHz, 94·9 VHF-FM.

GMR (GREATER MANCHESTER RADIO), P.O. Box 90, New Broadcasting House, Oxford Road, Manchester M60 1SJ. (Tel: 061-228 3434). *Wavelengths*: 206m, 1458 kHz, 95·1 VHF-FM.

HEREFORD AND WORCESTER, 43, Broad Street, Hereford HR4 9HH; and Hylton Road, Worcester WR2 5WW. (Tel: 0905-748485). *Wavelengths*: 819 kHz (Hereford); 738 kHz (Worcester); 104·0/ 94·7 VHF-FM.

HUMBERSIDE, 63 Jameson Street, Hull HU1 3NU. (Tel: 0482-23232). *Wavelengths*: 202m, 1485 kHz, 95·9 VHF-FM.

KENT, Sun Pier, Chatham, Kent ME4 4EZ. (Tel: 0634-830505). *Wavelengths*: 290/388/187m, 1035/774/1602 kHz, 96·7/104·2 VHF-FM.

LANCASHIRE, 20–26 Darwen Street, Blackburn BB2 2EA. (Tel: 0254-62411). *Wavelengths*: 351/193m, 855/ 1557 kHz, 95·5/104·5/103·9 VHF-FM.

LEEDS, Broadcasting House, Woodhouse Lane, Leeds LS2 9PN. (Tel: 0532-442131). *Wavelengths*: 388m, 774 kHz, 92·4/95·3/195·3 VHF-FM.

LEICESTER, Epic House, Charles Street, Leicester LE1 3SH. (Tel: 0533-516688). *Wavelengths*: 358m, 837 kHz, 104·9/95·1 VHF-FM.

LINCOLNSHIRE, Radion Buildings, P.O. Box 219, Newport, Lincoln LN1 3XY. (Tel: 0522-511411). *Wavelengths*: 219m, 1368 kHz, 94·9 VHF-FM.

MERSEYSIDE, 55 Paradise Street, Liverpool L1 3BP. (Tel: 051-708 5500). *Wavelengths*: 202m, 1485 kHz, 95·8 VHF-FM.

NEWCASTLE, Broadcasting Centre, Barrack Road, Fenham, Newcastle upon Tyne NE99 1RN. (Tel: 091-232 4141). *Wavelengths*: 206m, 1458 kHz, 95·4/ 104·4/96·0 VHF-FM.

NORFOLK, Norfolk Tower, Surrey Street, Norwich NR1 3PA. (Tel: 0603-617411). *Wavelengths*: 351/ 344m, 855/873 kHz, 95·1/104·4 VHF-FM.

NORTHAMPTON, P.O. Box 1107, Abington Street, Northampton NN1 2BE. (Tel: 0604-239100). *Wavelengths*: 271m, 1107 kHz, 104·2/103·6 VHF-FM.

NOTTINGHAM, York House, Mansfield Road, Nottingham NG1 3HZ. (Tel: 0602-415161). *Wavelengths*: 197/189m, 1521/1584 kHz, 103·8/95·5 VHF-FM.

OXFORD, 269 Banbury Road, Oxford OX2 7DW. (Tel: 0865-311444). *Wavelengths*: 202m, 1485 kHz, 95·2 VHF-FM.

SHEFFIELD, Ashdell Grove, 60 Westbourne Road, Sheffield S10 2QU. (Tel: 0742-686185). *Wavelengths*: 290m, 1035 kHz, 104·1/88·6 VHF-FM.

SHROPSHIRE, 2–4 Boscobel Drive, Shrewsbury SY1 3TT. (Tel: 0743-248484). *Wavelengths*: 189/397m, 1584/756 kHz, 95·0/96·0 VHF-FM.

SOLENT, South Western House, Canute Road,

Southampton SO9 4PJ. (Tel: 0703-631311). *Wavelengths*: 300m, 999 kHz, 96·1 VHF-FM, 221m, 1359 kHz.

STOKE ON TRENT, Conway House, Cheapside, Hanley, Stoke-on-Trent ST1 1JJ. (Tel: 0782-208080). *Wavelengths*: 200m, 1503 kHz, 94·6 VHF-FM.

SUSSEX, Marlborough Place, Brighton BN1 1TU (Tel: 0273-680231). *Wavelengths*: 202/258/219m, 1485/ 1161/1368 kHz, 95·3/104·5/104·0 VHF-FM.

WILTSHIRE SOUND, Broadcasting House, 56–58 Prospect Place, Swindon SN1 3RW. (Tel: 0793-512715). *Wavelengths*: 1332/1368 kHz, 103·6/104·3/103·5 VHF-FM.

WM (WEST MIDLANDS), P.O. Box 206, Pebble Mill Road, Birmingham B5 7SD. (Tel: 021-414 8484). *Wavelengths*: 206/362m, 1458/828 kHz, 95·6 VHF-FM.

YORK, 20 Bootham Row, York YO3 7BR. (Tel: 0904-641351). *Wavelengths*: 450/238m, 666/1260 kHz, 103·7/104·3/95·5 VHF-FM.

Two Stations outside the UK :—

GUERNSEY, Commerce House, Les Banques, St. Peter Port, Guernsey. (Tel: 0481-28977). *Wavelengths*: 269m, 1116 kHz, 93·2 VHF-FM.

JERSEY, Broadcasting House, Rouge Bouillon, St. Helier, Jersey. (Tel: 0534-70000). *Wavelengths*: 292m, 1026 kHz, 88·8 VHF-FM.

INDEPENDENT BROADCASTING AUTHORITY

(*see also* entry on pages 330–1)

Independent Television Programme Companies, etc.

ANGLIA TELEVISION (*East of England*), Anglia House, Norwich. (Tel: 0603-615151).

BORDER TELEVISION (*The Borders*), Television Centre, Carlisle. (Tel: 0228-25101).

CENTRAL INDEPENDENT TELEVISION (*East and West Midlands*), Central House, Broad Street, Birmingham. (Tel: 021-643 9898).

CHANNEL TELEVISION (*Channel Islands*), The Television Centre, St. Helier, Jersey. (Tel: 0534-73999).

GRAMPIAN TELEVISION (*North Scotland*), Queen's Cross, Aberdeen. (Tel: 0224-646464).

GRANADA TELEVISION (*North-West England*), Granada TV Centre, Manchester. (Tel: 061-832 7211).

HTV (*Wales and West of England*), HTV Wales, Television Centre, Cardiff CF5 6XJ. (Tel: 0222-590590).

LONDON WEEKEND TELEVISION (*London* [weekends]), South Bank Television Centre, SE1 9LT. (Tel: 01-261 3434).

SCOTTISH TELEVISION (*Central Scotland*), Cowcaddens, Glasgow. (Tel: 041-332 9999).

THAMES TELEVISION (*London* [weekdays]), Thames Television House, 306–316 Euston Road, NW1. (Tel: 01-387 9494).

TSW (TELEVISION SOUTH WEST) (*South-West England*), Derry's Cross, Plymouth. (Tel: 0752-663322).

TVS (TELEVISION SOUTH) (*South and South-East England*), Television Centre, Southampton. (Tel: 0703-34211).

TYNE TEES TELEVISION (*North-East England*), The Television Centre, City Road, Newcastle upon Tyne. (Tel: 091-261 0181).

ULSTER TELEVISION (*Northern Ireland*), Havelock House, Ormeau Road, Belfast. (Tel: 0232-228122).

YORKSHIRE TELEVISION (*Yorkshire*), The Television Centre, Leeds. (Tel: 0532-438283).

TV-AM, Hawley Crescent, NW1. (Tel: 01-267 4300).

CHANNEL FOUR TELEVISION COMPANY LTD, 60 Charlotte Street, W1. (Tel: 01-631 4444).

WELSH FOURTH CHANNEL AUTHORITY (Sianel Pedwar Cymru), Sophia Close, Cardiff CF1 9XY. (Tel: 0222-43421).

INDEPENDENT TELEVISION COMPANIES ASSOCIATION LTD., Knighton House, 56 Mortimer Street, W1. (Tel: 01-636 6866).

INDEPENDENT TELEVISION NEWS LTD, ITN House, 48 Wells Street, W1. (Tel: 01-637 2424).

ORACLE TELETEXT LTD., Craven House, 25–32 Marshall Street, W1. (Tel: 01-434 3121).

[NOTE: It has only been possible to give one address for each of the Programme Companies].

Independent Local Radio Stations

LBC (London Broadcasting Company Ltd.), Communications House, Gough Square, EC4. (Tel: 01-353 1010). *Wavelengths*: 261m, 1152 kHz, 97·3 VHF-FM.

CAPITAL RADIO P.L.C., Euston Tower, NW1. (Tel: 01-388 1288). *Wavelengths*: 194m, 1548 kHz, 95·8 VHF-FM.

RADIO CLYDE LTD., Clydebank Business Park, Clydebank, Glasgow. (Tel: 041-941 1111). *Wavelengths*: 261m, 1152 kHz, 95·1 VHF-FM.

BRMB RADIO, (Birmingham Broadcasting Ltd.), P.O. Box 555, Radio House, Aston Road North, Aston, Birmingham. (Tel: 021-359 4481/9). *Wavelengths*: 261m, 1152 kHz, 96·4 VHF-FM.

PICCADILLY RADIO LTD., 127-131 The Piazza, Piccadilly Plaza, Manchester. (Tel: 061-236 9913). *Wavelengths*: 261m, 1152 kHz, 103·0 VHF-FM.

METRO RADIO (North East Broadcasting Company Ltd.), Radio House, Long Rigg, Swalwell, Newcastle upon Tyne. (Tel: 091-488 3131). *Wavelengths*: 261m, 1152 kHz, 97·1 VHF-FM.

LEICESTER SOUND, Granville House, Granville Road, Leicester LE1 7RW. (Tel: 0533 551616). *Wavelengths*: 238m, VHF-FM 103·2 MHz.

SWANSEA SOUND LTD., Victoria Road, Gowerton, Swansea. (Tel: 0792-893751). *Wavelengths*: 257m, 1170 kHz, 95·1 VHF-FM.

RADIO HALLAM LTD., P.O. Box 194, Hartshead, Sheffield. (Tel: 0742-71188). *Wavelengths*: 194m, 1548 kHz, 96·1 VHF-FM (Rotherham), 97·4 VHF-FM (Sheffield), 302m, 990 kHz, 103·4 VHF-FM (Doncaster).

RADIO CITY (Sound of Merseyside Ltd.), P.O. Box 194, 8–10 Stanley Street, Liverpool. (Tel: 051-227 5100). *Wavelengths*: 194m, 1548 kHz, 96·7 VHF-FM.

RADIO FORTH LTD., Forth House, Forth Street, Edinburgh. (Tel: 031-556 9255). *Wavelengths*: 194m, 1548 kHz, 97·3 VHF-FM.

PLYMOUTH SOUND LTD., Earl's Acre, Alma Road, Plymouth. (Tel: 0752-27272). *Wavelengths*: 261m, 1152 kHz, 96·0 VHF-FM.

RADIO TFM (Sound Broadcasting (Teesside) Ltd.), 74 Dovecot Street, Stockton-on-Tees, Cleveland. (Tel: 0642-615111). *Wavelengths*: 257m, 1170 kHz, 96·6 VHF-FM.

RADIO TRENT LTD., 29–31 Castle Gate, Nottingham. (Tel: 0602-581731). *Wavelengths*: 301m, 999 kHz, 96·2 VHF-FM.

PENNINE RADIO, (Bradford Community Radio Ltd.), P.O. Box 235, Pennine House, Forster Square, Bradford. (Tel: 0274-390417). *Wavelengths*: 235/196m, 1278/1530 kHz, 97·5 VHF-FM (Bradford, Huddersfield, Halifax) 102·5 VHF-FM.

OCEAN SOUND LTD., 43–44 Bedford Place, Southampton. *Wavelengths*: 257m, 1170 kHz, 103·2 VHF-FM (Southampton), 97·5 VHF-FM (Portsmouth).

RADIO ORWELL LTD., Electric House, Lloyds Avenue, Ipswich. (Tel: 0473-216971). *Wavelengths*: 257m, 1170 kHz, 97·1 VHF-FM.

RADIO 210 THAMES VALLEY (Thames Valley Broadcasting Ltd.), P.O. Box 210, Reading, Berkshire. (Tel: 0734-413131). *Wavelengths*: 210m, 1431 kHz, 97·0 VHF-FM.

DOWNTOWN RADIO (Community Radio Services Ltd.), P.O. Box 293, Kiltonga Industrial Estate, Newtownards, Northern Ireland. (Tel: 0247-815555). *Wavelengths*: 293m, 1026 kHz, 97·4 VHF-FM.

BEACON RADIO (Beacon Broadcasting Ltd.), P.O. Box 303, 267 Tettenhall Road, Wolverhampton. (Tel: 0902-757211). *Wavelengths*: 303m, 990 kHz, 97·2 VHF-FM.

MERCIA SOUND (Midland Community Radio Ltd.), Hertford Place, Coventry. (Tel: 0203-28451). *Wavelengths*: 220m, 1359 kHz, 95·9 VHF-FM.

HEREWARD RADIO LTD., P.O. Box 225, 114 Bridge Street, Peterborough. (Tel: 0733-46225). *Wavelengths*: 225m, 1332 kHz, 102·7 VHF-FM.

TWO COUNTIES RADIO LTD., 5–7 Southcote Road, Bournemouth. (Tel: 0202-294881). *Wavelengths*: 362m, 828 kHz, 97·2 VHF-FM.

RADIO TAY (Tay Sound Broadcasting Ltd.), P.O. Box 123, Dundee. (Tel: 0382-29551). *Wavelengths*: 258m, 1161 kHz, 95·8 VHF-FM (Dundee); 189m, 1584 kHz, 96·4 VHF-FM (Perth).

SEVERN SOUND (Gloucestershire Broadcasting Company Ltd.), P.O. Box 388, Old Talbot House, 67 Southgate Street, Gloucester. (Tel: 0452-423791). *Wavelengths*: 388m, 774 kHz, 102·4 VHF-FM.

DEVONAIR RADIO, The Studio Centre, 35–37 St. David's Hill, Exeter EX4 4DA. (Tel: 0392-30703). *Wavelengths*: 450m, 666 kHz, VHF-FM 97·0 (Exeter); 314m, 954 kHz, VHF-FM 96·4 (Torbay).

NORTH SOUND (North of Scotland Radio Ltd.), 45 Kings Gate, Aberdeen. (Tel: 0224-632234). *Wavelengths*: 290m, 1035 kHz, 96·9 VHF-FM.

RADIO AIRE (West Yorkshire Broadcasting P.L.C.), P.O. Box 362, 51 Burley Road, Leeds. (Tel: 0532-452299). *Wavelengths*: 362m, 828 kHz, 96·3 VHF-FM.

ESSEX RADIO P.L.C., Radio House, Clifftown Road, Southend-on-Sea. (Tel: 0702-333711). *Wavelengths*: 210m, 1431 kHz, 96·3 VHF-FM (Southend), 220m, 1359 kHz, 102·6 VHF-FM (Chelmsford).

CHILTERN RADIO P.L.C., Chiltern Radio, Dunstable, Bedfordshire. (Tel: 0582-666001). *Wavelengths*: 362m, 828 kHz, 97·6 VHF-FM (Luton), 379m, 792 kHz, 96·9 VHF-FM (Bedford).

WEST SOUND (Radio Ayrshire Limited), Radio House, 54 Holmston Road, Ayr. (Tel: 0292-283662). *Wavelengths*: 290m, 1035 kHz, 96·7 VHF-FM (Ayr), 97·1 97·5 VHF-FM (Girvan).

GWR RADIO WEST P.L.C., P.O. Box 963, Watershed, Canons Road, Bristol. (Tel: 0272-279900). *Wavelengths*: 238m, 1260 kHz, 96·3 VHF-FM.

MORAY FIRTH RADIO LTD., P.O. Box 271, Inverness. (Tel: 0463-224433). *Wavelengths*: 271m, 1107 kHz, 97·4 VHF-FM.

RADIO WYVERN P.L.C., 5–6 Barbourne Terrace, Worcester. (Tel: 0905-612212). *Wavelengths*: 314m, 954 kHz, 97·6 VHF-FM (Hereford), 196m, 1530 kHz, 102·8 VHF-FM (Worcester).

RED ROSE RADIO P.L.C., P.O. Box 301, St. Paul's Square, Preston, Lancashire. (Tel: 0772-556301). *Wavelengths*: 301m, 999 kHz, 97·3 VHF-FM.

GWR (Wiltshire Radio) P.L.C., Old Lime Kiln, High Street, Wootton Bassett, Swindon. (Tel: 0793-853222). *Wavelengths*: 258m, 1161 kHz, 97·2 VHF-FM (Swindon), 321m, 936 kHz, 102·6 VHF-FM (West Wiltshire).

SAXON RADIO LTD. IN ASSOCIATION WITH RADIO ORWELL LTD., Long Brackland, Bury St. Edmunds, Suffolk. (Tel: 0284-701511). *Wavelengths*: 240m, 1251 kHz, 96·4 VHF-FM.

COUNTY SOUND P.L.C., The Friary, Guildford. (Tel: 0483-505566). *Wavelengths*: 203m, 1476 kHz, 96·4 VHF-FM.

RED DRAGON RADIO, Radio House, West Canal Wharf,

Cardiff. (Tel: 0222-384041). *Wavelengths*: 230m, 1305 kHz, 97·4 VHF-FM.

SOUTHERN SOUND P.L.C., Radio House, Franklin Road, Portslade. (Tel: 0273-422288). *Wavelengths*: 225m, 1332 kHz, 103·4 MHz.

MARCHER SOUND/SAIN-Y-GORORAU, The Studios, Mold Road, Gwersyllt, Wrexham, Clwyd. (Tel: 0978-752202). *Wavelengths*: 238m, 1260 kHz, 95·4 VHF-FM.

SIGNAL RADIO, 67–73 Stoke Road, Stoke-on-Trent. (Tel: 0782-417111). *Wavelengths*: 257m, 1170 kHz, 102·6 VHF-FM.

VIKING RADIO LTD., Commercial Road, Hull. (Tel: 0482-25141). *Wavelengths*: 258m, 1161 kHz, 96·9 VHF-FM.

RADIO MERCURY, Broadfield House, Brighton Road, Crawley, W. Sussex. (Tel: 0293-519161). *Wavelengths*: 197m, 1521 kHz, 102·7, 97·5 VHF-FM (Horsham).

INVICTA RADIO P.L.C. (incorporating Northdown Radio), 15 Station Road East, Canterbury, Kent. (Tel: 0227-58761). *Wavelengths*: 242m, 1242 kHz, 103·1 VHF-FM.

INVICTA RADIO P.L.C. (incorporating Network East Kent), 15 Station Road East, Canterbury, Kent. (Tel: 0227-58761). *Wavelengths*: 497m, 603 kHz, 97·0 VHF-FM (Dover), 95·9 VHF-FM (Thanet), 102·8 VHF-FM (Canterbury), 96·1 MHz (Ashford).

RADIO BROADLAND, P.O. Box 260, Norwich. (Tel: 0603-660926). *Wavelengths*: 260m, 1152 kHz, 97·6 MHz.

NORTHANTS 96 (Hereward Radio) P.L.C., P.O. Box 193, 73 Abington Street, Northampton. (Tel: 0733-46225). *Wavelengths*: 193m, 1557 kHz, 96·6 VHF-FM.

SERVICES SOUND AND VISION CORPORATION
(Incorporating B.F.B.S.)
Chalfont Grove, Gerrards Cross, Bucks. SL9 8TN
[02407–4461]

The Services Sound and Vision Corporation (S.S.V.C.) is the official organization providing the Ministry of Defence, H.M. Forces and their families with radio and television broadcasting, audio-visual and electronic training and educational support, training film production, and entertainment. The S.S.V.C. is a private limited company and registered charity with 1,100 employees and an annual turnover approaching £40 million; financial surpluses are donated to Services' welfare.

The Corporation's radio arm (British Forces Broadcasting Service) operates stations in London, Germany, Gibraltar, Cyprus, the Falklands, Hong Kong, Brunei and Belize. B.F.B.S. provides programmes from London for inclusion with local input by its overseas staff, and broadcasts to overseas stations by satellite throughout the year. Cassettes are provided for H.M. Ships at sea.

S.S.V.C. television broadcasts its own, B.B.C. and I.T.V. programmes in Germany, Cyprus and the Falkland Islands. Up to 50 isolated detachments of H.M. Forces (including ships at sea and the Service Children's Education Authority schools overseas), receive daily T.V. programmes on cassette.

In-flight films on R.A.F. long-haul passenger services are organized by S.S.V.C., and Combined Services Entertainment provides stage shows to such isolated garrisons and units as the Falklands and Ascension Islands. S.S.V.C. also operates cinemas around the world.

Audio-visual rentals and sales are provided through S.S.V.C.'s Sound and Vision Centre shops in Germany and at home.

Training films for the three Armed Services are produced, distributed to units and sold to other governments by S.S.V.C., which has its own crews and studios. Audio-visual and electronic training and educational equipment is assessed, issued to British Forces' units, and maintained by S.S.V.C. staff.

All S.S.V.C. services are available to other organizations and are provided to overseas governments and many U.K. companies.

Managing Director, S.S.V.C., A. Protheroe, M.B.E., T.D.

THE BROADCASTING COMPLAINTS COMMISSION
Grosvenor Gardens House, 35–37 Grosvenor Gardens, SW1W 0BS
[01–630 1966]

The Broadcasting Complaints Commission's function and authority derive from the Broadcasting Act 1981 and the Cable and Broadcasting Act 1984. Their task is to consider and adjudicate upon complaints of unjust or unfair treatment in sound or television programmes broadcast by the B.B.C. or the I.B.A. on or after June 1, 1981; or upon complaints of unjust or unfair treatment in programmes included in a licensed cable programme service on or after January 1, 1985 otherwise than by the reception and immediate re-transmission of broadcasts made by a broadcasting body; or upon complaints of unwarranted infringement of privacy in, or in connection with the obtaining of material included in such programmes. This function extends to all sound, television and cable programmes, including advertisements and teletext transmissions and programmes broadcast by the B.B.C.'s World Services.

The Members of the Commission are appointed by the Home Secretary.

Chairman, Lady Anglesey, D.B.E.
Members, T. Christopher, C.B.E.; D. Holmes; H. M. Johnston, C.B.; Mrs. B. Wells.
Legal Adviser, Sir Basil Hall, K.C.B., M.C., T.D.
Secretary, R. D. Hewlett.

PRINCIPAL NEWSPAPERS

DAILY NEWSPAPERS

National

Daily Express, Ludgate House, 245 Blackfriars Road, SE1 9UX.

Daily Mail, Northcliffe House, EC4Y 0JA.

Daily Mirror, Holborn Circus, EC1P 1DQ.

Daily Sport, 50 Eagle Wharf Road, N1 7ED

Daily Telegraph, 181 Marsh Wall, Peterborough Court, E14 9SR.

Financial Times, 1 Southwark Bridge, SE1 9HL.

The Guardian, 119 Farringdon Road, EC1R 3ER.

The Independent, 40 City Road, EC1Y 2DB.

Morning Star, 74 Luke Street, EC2A 4PY.

Racing Post, 120 Coombe Lane, Raynes Park, SW20 0BA.

The Sporting Life, Orbit House, 1 New Fetter Lane, EC4A 1AR.

The Star, Great Ancoats Street, Manchester M60 4HB.

The Sun, Virginia Street, E1 9BD.

The Times, 1 Pennington Street, E1 9XN.

Today, 70 Vauxhall Bridge Road, SW1V 2RP.

ABERDEEN—Press and Journal, and Evening Express, P.O. Box 43, Lang Stracht, Mastrick, AB9 8AF.

BARROW-IN-FURNESS—North-West Evening Mail, Newspaper House, Abbey Road, LA14 5QS.

BATH—Bath and West Evening Chronicle, 33–34 Westgate Street, BA1 1EW.

BELFAST—Belfast Telegraph, 124–144 Royal Avenue, BT1 1EB; Irish News and Belfast Morning News, 113–117 Donegall Street, BT1 2GE; News Letter, 51–59 Donegall Street, BT1 2GB.

BIRMINGHAM—The Birmingham Post, and Birmingham Evening Mail, P.O. Box 18, 28 Colmore Circus, Queensway, B4 6AX (Birmingham Evening Mail B4 6AY).

BLACKBURN—Lancashire Evening Telegraph, Telegraph House, High Street, BB1 1HT.

BLACKPOOL—West Lancashire Evening Gazette, P.O. Box 20, FY4 4AU.

BOLTON—Bolton Evening News, Newspaper House, Churchgate, BL1 1DE.

BOURNEMOUTH—Evening Echo, Richmond Hill, BH2 6HH.

BRADFORD—Telegraph and Argus, P.O. Box 234, Hall Ings, BD1 1JR.

BRIGHTON—Evening Argus, Argus House, 89 North Road, BN1 4AU.

BRISTOL—Bristol Evening Post, and Western Daily Press, Temple Way, BS99 7HD.

BURTON-ON-TRENT—Burton Mail, 65–68 High Street, DE14 1LE.

CAMBRIDGE—Cambridge Evening News, 51 Newmarket Road, CB5 8EJ.

CARDIFF—South Wales Echo, and Western Mail, Thomson House, Havelock Street, CF1 1WR.

CHATHAM—Kent Evening Post, New Hythe Lane, Larkfield, ME20 6SG.

CHELTENHAM—Gloucestershire Echo, 1 Clarence Parade, GL50 3NZ.

COLCHESTER—Evening Gazette, Oriel House, 43–44 North Hill, CO1 1TZ.

COVENTRY—Coventry Evening Telegraph, Corporation Street, CV1 1FP.

DARLINGTON—Northern Echo, Priestgate, DL1 1NP.

DERBY—Derby Evening Telegraph, Northcliffe House, Meadow Road, DE1 2DW.

DUNDEE—Courier and Advertiser, and Evening Telegraph and Post, 7 Bank Street, DD1 9HU.

EDINBURGH—The Scotsman, and Evening News, 20 North Bridge, EH1 1YT.

EXETER—Express and Echo, Sidwell House, Sidwell Street, EX4 6RS.

GLASGOW—Daily Record, 40 Anderston Quay, G3 8DA; Glasgow Herald, and Evening Times, 195 Albion Street, G1 1QP.

GLOUCESTER—The Citizen, St. John's Lane, GL1 2AY.

GREENOCK—Greenock Telegraph, 2 Crawfurd Street, PA15 1LH.

GRIMSBY—Grimsby Evening Telegraph, 80 Cleethorpe Road, DN31 3EH.

GUERNSEY—Guernsey Evening Press and Star, P.O. Box 57, Braye Road, Vale.

HALIFAX—Evening Courier, P.O. Box 19, Courier Buildings, HX1 2SF.

HARTLEPOOL—Hartlepool Mail, Pennywell Industrial Estate, Sunderland, SR4 9ER.

HUDDERSFIELD—Huddersfield Daily Examiner, Ramsden Street, HD1 2TD.

HULL—Hull Daily Mail, 84–86 Jameson Street, HU1 3LF.

IPSWICH—East Anglian Daily Times, and Evening Star, 30 Lower Brook Street, IP4 1AN.

JERSEY—Jersey Evening Post, P.O. Box 582, Five Oaks, St. Saviour.

KETTERING—Northamptonshire Evening Telegraph, Northfield Avenue, NN16 9JN.

LEAMINGTON SPA—Leamington & District Morning News, P.O. Box 45, Tachbrook Road, CV31 3EP.

LEEDS—Yorkshire Evening Post, and Yorkshire Post, Wellington Street, LS1 1RF.

LEICESTER—Leicester Mercury, St. George Street, LE1 9FQ.

LINCOLN—Lincolnshire Echo, Brayford Wharf East, LN5 7AT.

LIVERPOOL—Daily Post, and Liverpool Echo, P.O. Box 48, Old Hall Street, L69 3EB.

LONDON—The London Evening Standard, Northcliffe House 2 Derry Street, W8 5HY.

MANCHESTER—Manchester Evening News, 164 Deansgate, M60 2RD.

MIDDLESBROUGH—Evening Gazette, Gazette Building, Borough Road, TS1 3AZ.

NEWCASTLE UPON TYNE—Evening Chronicle, and The Journal, Thomson House, Groat Market, NE1 1ED.

NEWPORT—South Wales Argus, Cardiff Road, Maesglas, NP9 1QW.

NORTHAMPTON—Chronicle and Echo, Upper Mounts, NN1 3HR.

NORWICH—Eastern Daily Press, and Eastern Evening News, Prospect House, Rouen Road, NR1 1RE.

NOTTINGHAM—Evening Post, Forman Street, NG1 4AB.

NUNEATON—Nuneaton Evening Tribune, Watling House, Whitacre Road, CV11 6BJ.

OLDHAM—Evening Chronicle, 172 Union Street, OL1 1EQ.

OXFORD—Oxford Mail, Newspaper House, Osney Mead, OX2 0EJ.

PAISLEY—Paisley Daily Express, Hellenic House, 87–97 Bath Street, Glasgow, G2 2DZ.

PETERBOROUGH—Peterborough Evening Telegraph, Telegraph House, Priestgate, PE1 1JW.

PLYMOUTH—Western Morning News, and Western Evening Herald, 65 New George Street, PL1 1RE.

PORTSMOUTH—The News, The News Centre, Hilsea, PO2 9SX.

PRESTON—Lancashire Evening Post, 127 Fishergate, PR1 2DN.

READING—Evening Post, 8 Tessa Road, RG1 8NS.

SCARBOROUGH—Scarborough Evening News, 17–23 Aberdeen Walk, YO11 1BB.

SCUNTHORPE—Scunthorpe Evening Telegraph, Telegraph House, Doncaster Road, DN15 7RE.

SHEFFIELD—The Star, York Street, S1 1PU.

SOUTH SHIELDS—Shields Gazette, Chapter Row, NE33 1BL.

SOUTHAMPTON—Southern Evening Echo, 45 Above Bar, SO9 7BA.

STOKE-ON-TRENT—Evening Sentinel, Sentinel House, Etruria, ST1 5SS.

SUNDERLAND—Sunderland Echo, Pennywell Industrial Estate, SR4 9ER.

SWANSEA—South Wales Evening Post, Adelaide Street, SA1 1QT.

SWINDON—Evening Advertiser, Newspaper House, 100 Victoria Road, SN1 3BE.

TELFORD—Shropshire Star, Ketley, TF1 4HU.

TORQUAY—Herald Express, Harmsworth House, Barton Hill Road, TQ2 8JN.

WEYMOUTH—Dorset Evening Echo, 57 St. Thomas Street, DT4 8EU.

WOLVERHAMPTON—Express and Star, 51–53 Queen Street, WV1 3BU.

WORCESTER—Evening News, 3rd Floor, Haswell House, St. Nicholas Street, WR1 1UW.

YORK—Yorkshire Evening Press, 15 Coney Street, YO1 1YN.

SUNDAY NEWSPAPERS

The Mail on Sunday—Northcliffe House, EC4Y 0JA.

News of the World—Virginia Street, E1 9XR.

The Observer—Chelsea Bridge House, Queenstown Road, SW8 4NN.

The People—Holborn Circus, EC1P 1DQ.

Scotland on Sunday—20 North Bridge, Edinburgh EH1 1YT.

Sunday Correspondent—21 Clerkenwell Close, EC1R 0AA.

Sunday Express—Ludgate House, 245 Blackfriars Road, SE1 9UX.

Sunday Mail—40 Anderston Quay, Glasgow G3 8DA.

Sunday Mirror—Holborn Circus, EC1P 1DQ.

Sunday News—51–59 Donegall Street, Belfast BT1 2GB.

Sunday Post—Courier Place, Dundee DD1 9QJ.

Sunday Sport—50 Eagle Wharf Road, N1 7ED.

Sunday Telegraph—181 Marsh Wall, Peterborough Court, E14 9SR.

The Sunday Times—1 Pennington Street, E1 9XW.

RELIGIOUS PAPERS

[*W.* = Weekly; *M.* = Monthly; *Q.* = Quarterly]

Baptist Times—4 Southampton Row, WC1B 4AB. *W.*

Catholic Herald—Herald House, Lambs Passage, Bunhill Row, EC1Y 8TQ. *W.*

Challenge—the Good News Paper—Revenue Buildings, Chapel Road, Worthing, West Sussex BN11 1BQ. *M.*

Christian Herald—Herald House, 96 Dominion Road, Worthing, West Sussex BN14 8JP. *W.*

Christian Week—11 Carteret Street, SW1H 9DJ. *W.*

Church of England Newspaper—11 Carteret Street, SW1H 9DJ. *W.*

Church of Ireland Gazette—48 Bachelor's Walk, Lisburn, Co. Antrim, BT28 1XN. *W.*

Church Times—7 Portugal Street, WC2A 2HP. *W.*

English Churchman—Mill Lane House, Margate, Kent CT9 1ND. *Alt. W.*

The Friend—Drayton House, 30 Gordon Street, WC1H 0BQ. *W.*

The Inquirer—1–6 Essex Street, WC2R 3HY. *Alt. W.*

Jewish Chronicle—25 Furnival Street, EC4A 1JT. *W.*

Jewish Gazette—27 Bury Old Road, Prestwich, Manchester M25 8EY. *W.*

Jewish Telegraph—Telegraph House, 11 Park Hill, Bury Old Road, Prestwich, Manchester M25 8HH. *W.*

Leadership Today—37 Elm Road, New Malden, Surrey KT3 3HB. *M.*

Life and Work—Church of Scotland, 121 George Street, Edinburgh EH2 4QS. *M.*

Methodist Recorder—122 Golden Lane, EC1Y 0TL. *W.*

Orthodox News—64 Prebend Gardens, W6 0XU. *M.*

Reform—86 Tavistock Place, WC1H 9RT. *M.*

The Tablet—48 Great Peter Street, SW1P 2HB. *W.*

The Universe—33–39 Bowling Green Lane, EC1R 0AB. *W.*

The War Cry—101 Queen Victoria Street, EC4P 4EP. *W.*

PERIODICALS, MAGAZINES AND REVIEWS

[*Alt.* = Alternate; *M.* = Monthly; *Q.* = Quarterly; *W.* = Weekly]

Amateur Gardening—Westover House, West Quay Road, Poole, Dorset BH15 1JG. *W.*

Amateur Photographer—Prospect House, 9–13 Ewell Road, Cheam, Surrey SM1 4QQ. *W.*

Angler's Mail—King's Reach Tower, Stamford Street, SE1 9LS. *W.*

Antiquaries Journal—Oxford University Press, Walton Street, Oxford OX2 6DP. *Three times a year.*

The Antique Collector—National Magazine House, 72 Broadwick Street, W1V 2BP. *M.*

Apollo Magazine—22 Davies Street, W1Y 1LH. *M.*

Arena—The Old Laundry, Ossington Buildings, Moxon Street, W1M 3XH. *Alt. M.*

The Artist—Caxton House, 63–65 High Street, Tenterden, Kent TN30 6BD. *M.*

Autocar and Motor—38–42 Hampton Road, Teddington, Middlesex TW11 0JE. *W.*

Bella—2nd Floor, Shirley House, 25–27 Camden Road, NW1 9LL. *W.*

Best—10th Floor, Portland House, Stag Place, SW1E 5AU. *W.*

Blitz—40–42 Newman Street, W1P 3PA. *M.*

Boxing News—P.O. Box 94, W4 2ER. *W.*

Brain—Oxford University Press, Walton Street, Oxford OX2 6DP. *Alt. M.*

Brides & Setting up Home—Vogue House, Hanover Square, W1R 0AD. *Alt. M.*

British Birds—Fountains, Park Lane, Blunham, Bedford MK44 3NJ. *M.*

British Book News—The British Council, 65 Davies Street, W1Y 2AA. *M.*

The Burlington Magazine—6 Bloomsbury Square, WC1A 2LP. *M.*

Buses—Coombelands House, Addlestone, Weybridge, Surrey KT15 1HY. *M.*

Cage and Aviary Birds—Prospect House, 9–13 Ewell Road, Cheam, Surrey SM1 4QQ. *W.*

Camping & Caravanning—11 Lower Grosvenor Place, SW1W 0EY. *M.*

Caravan Magazine—Link House, Dingwall Avenue, Croydon CR9 2TA. *M.*

Chat—195 Knightsbridge, SW7 1RE. *W.*

Classical Quarterly—Oxford University Press, Walton Street, Oxford OX2 6DP. *Twice a Year.*

Classical Review—Oxford University Press, Walton Street, Oxford OX2 6DP. *Twice a Year.*

Coal News—Hobart House, Grosvenor Place, SW1X 7AE. *M.*

Coin and Medal News—Crossways Road, Grayshott, Hindhead, Surrey GU26 6HF. *M.*

Coin Monthly—Sovereign House, Brentwood, Essex CM14 4SE. *M.*

Company—72 Broadwick Street, W1V 2BP. *M.*

Contemporary Review—61 Carey Street, WC2A 2JG. *M.*

Cosmopolitan—72 Broadwick Street, W1V 2BP. *M.*

Country Homes and Interiors—25 Newman Street, W1P 3HA. *M.*

Country Life—King's Reach Tower, Stamford Street, SE1 9LS. *W.*

Country Living—72 Broadwick Street, W1V 2BP. *Alt. M.*

The Countryman—23–27 Tudor Street, EC4Y 0HR. *Q.*

Cricketer International—Beech Hangar, Ashurst, Tunbridge Wells, Kent TN3 9ST. *M.*

Criminologist—Little London, Chichester, West Sussex PO19 1PG. *Q.*

Cycling Weekly—Prospect House, 9–13 Ewell Road, Cheam, Surrey SM1 4QQ. *W.*

Daltons Weekly—C.I. Tower, St. George's Square, New Malden, Surrey KT3 4JA. *W.*

Dance and Dancers—248 High Street, Croydon CR0 1NF. *M.*

Dancing Times—Clerkenwell House, 45–47 Clerkenwell Green, EC1R 0BE. *M.*

Dog World—9 Tufton Street, Ashford, Kent TN23 1QN. *W.*

Do It Yourself—Link House, Dingwall Avenue, Croydon CR9 2TA. *M.*

Drama—British Theatre Association, Regent's College, Inner Circle, Regent's Park, NW1 4NW. *Q.*

Economic Journal—108 Cowley Road, Oxford OX4 1JF. *Q.*

Economica—London School of Economics and Political Science, Houghton Street, WC2A 2AE. *Q.*

The Economist—25 St. James's Street, SW1A 1HG. *W.*

Edinburgh Gazette (*Official*)—H.M.S.O., Publications Centre, P.O. Box 276, London SW8 5DT. *Twice a week.*

Elle—Rex House, 4–12 Lower Regent Street, SW1Y 4PE. *M.*

Encounter—44 Great Windmill Street, W1V 7PA. *Ten times a year.*

The English Historical Review—Longman House, Burnt Mill, Harlow, Essex CM20 2JE. *Q.*

Essentials—King's Reach Tower, Stamford Street, SE1 9LS. *M.*

Everywoman—34A Islington Green, N1 8DU. *M.*

Exchange and Mart—25 West Street, Poole, Dorset BH15 1LL. *W.*

The Face—The Old Laundry, Ossington Buildings, Moxon Street, W1M 3HX. *M.*

Family Circle—King's Reach Tower, Stamford Street, SE1 9LS. *Thirteen times a year.*

The Field—10 Sheet Street, Windsor, Berks SL4 1BG. *W.*

Garden News—Bushfield House, Orton Centre, Peterborough PE2 0UW. *W.*

Geographical Magazine—27 Kensington Court, W8 5DN. *M.*

Golf Illustrated—47 Dartford Road, Sevenoaks, Kent TN13 3TE. *Alt. W.*

Golf Monthly—1 Park Circus, Glasgow G3 6AS. *M.*

Good Housekeeping—72 Broadwick Street, W1V 2BP. *M.*

Good Motoring—352 Lewisham High Street, SE13 6LE. *Alt. M.*

Gramophone—177–179 Kenton Road, Harrow, Middx. HA3 0HA. *M.*

Granta—44A Hobson Street, Cambridge, CB1 1NL. *Q.*

Greece and Rome—Oxford University Press, Walton Street, Oxford OX2 6DP. *Twice a year.*

Guiding—17–19 Buckingham Palace Road, SW1W 0PT. *M.*

Hansard—*see* Parliamentary Debates.

Harpers and Queen—72 Broadwick Street, W1V 2BP. *M.*

Hello—44A Floral Street, WC2E 9DE. *W.*

High Magazine—Springfield House, The Parade, Oadby, Leics. LE2 5BF. *M.*

History—59A Kennington Park Road, SE11 4JH. *Three times a year.*

History Today—83–84 Berwick Street, W1V 3PJ. *M.*

Homes and Gardens—King's Reach Tower, Stamford Street, SE1 9LS. *M.*

Homoeopathy—27A Devonshire Street, W1N 1RJ. *Alt. M.*

Horse and Hound—King's Reach Tower, Stamford Street, SE1 9LS. *W.*

House and Garden—Vogue House, Hanover Square, W1R 0AD. *M.*

I-D Magazine—27–29 Macklin Street, WC2B 5LX. *M.*

Ideal Home—King's Reach Tower, Stamford Street, SE1 9LS. *M.*

Illustrated London News—Laurence House, 91–93 Southwark Street, SE1 0HX. *Q.*

In Britain—B.T.A., Thames Tower, Black's Road, W6 9EL. *M.*

International Affairs—P.O. Box 63, Westbury House, Bury Street, Guildford GU2 5BH. *Q.*

Irish Post—Lex House, 77 South Road, Middx. UB1 1SQ. *W.*

Jazz Journal International—35 Great Russell Street, WC1B 3PP. *M.*

Just Seventeen—52–55 Carnaby Street, W1V 1PF. *W.*

Kennel Gazette—1 Clarges Street, W1Y 8AB. *M.*

Labour Research— 78 Blackfriars Road, SE1 8HF. *M.*

The Lady—39–40 Bedford Street, WC2E 9ER. *W.*

Land and Liberty—177 Vauxhall Bridge Road, SW1V 1EU. *Alt. M.*

Light—College of Psychic Studies, 16 Queensberry Place, SW7 2EB. *Three times a year.*

The Listener—199 Old Marylebone Road, NW1 5QS. *W.*

Literary Review—51 Beak Street, W1R 3LF. *M.*

Living Magazine—King's Reach Tower, Stamford Street, SE1 9LS. *Thirteen times a year.*

Local Government Chronicle—122 Minories, EC3N 1NT. *W.*

London Gazette (*Official*)—H.M.S.O. Publications Centre, P.O. Box 276, SW8 5DT. *Four times a week.*

London Review of Books—Tavistock House South, Tavistock Square, WC1H 9JZ. *Alt. W.*

London Weekly Diary of Social Events—25 Park Row, SE10 9NL. *W.*

Marie Claire—2 Hatfields, SE1 9PG. *M.*

Melody Maker (MM)—King's Reach Tower, Stamford Street, SE1 9LS. *W.*

Meteorological Magazine—H.M.S.O., St. Crispins, Duke Street, Norwich NR3 1PD. *M.*

Mind—Oxford University Press, Walton Street, Oxford OX2 6DP. *Q.*

Model Boats—P.O. Box 35, Wolsey House, Wolsey Road, Hemel Hempstead, Herts. HP2 4SS *M.*

Modern Languages—10 Holt Park Way, Leeds LS16 7QR. *Q.*

Month—114 Mount Street, W1Y 6AH. *M.*

Monthly Digest of Statistics (*Official*)—H.M.S.O., P.O. Box 276, SW8 5DT. *M.*

Mother—12–18 Paul Street, EC2A 4JS. *M.*

Motor Cycle News—P.O. Box 11, Huxloe Place, High Street, Kettering, Northants. NN16 8SS. *W.*

Municipal Review and AMA News—35 Great Smith Street, SW1P 3BJ. *Ten times a year.*

Museums Bulletin—34 Bloomsbury Way, WC1A 2SF. *M.*

Music and Letters—Oxford University Press, Walton Street, Oxford OX2 6DP. *Q.*

My Weekly—80 Kingsway East, Dundee DD4 8SL. *W.*

Nature—4 Little Essex Street, WC2R 3LF. *W.*

Nautical Magazine—4–10 Darnley Street, Glasgow G41 2SD. *M.*

Navy International—Hunters Moon, Hogspudding Lane, Newdigate, Dorking, Surrey RH5 5DS. *M.*

N.M.E.—King's Reach Tower, Stamford Street, SE1 9LS. *W.*

New Scientist—Commonwealth House, 1–19 New Oxford Street, WC1A 1NG. *W.*

New Statesman and Society—Foundation House, Perseverance Works, 38 Kingsland Road, E2 8DQ. *W.*

19—King's Reach Tower, Stamford Street, SE1 9LS. *M.*

Notes and Queries—Oxford University Press, Walton Street, Oxford OX2 6DP. *Q.*

Nursery World—The Schoolhouse Workshop, 51 Calthorpe Street, WC1X 0HH. *Alt. W.*

Opera—1A Mountgrove Road, N5 2LU. *M.*

Options—25 Newman Street, W1P 3HA. *M.*

Our Dogs—5 Oxford Road, Station Approach, Manchester M60 1SX. *W.*

Parents—Victory House, Leicester Place, WC2H 7NB. *M.*

Parliamentary Debates (Lords) (Hansard)— H.M.S.O., P.O. Box 276, SW8 5DT. *Daily or weekly during Session.*

Parliamentary Debates (Commons) (Hansard)— H.M.S.O., P.O. Box 276, SW8 5DT. *Daily or weekly during Session.*

People's Friend—80 Kingsway East, Dundee DD4 8SL. *W.*

Philosophy—Cambridge University Press, The Edinburgh Building, Shaftesbury Road, Cambridge CB2 2RU. *Q.*

Pins and Needles—4th Floor, 4 Brandon Road, N7 9TP. *M.*

Plays and Players—248 High Street, Croydon CR0 1NF. *M.*

Poetry Review—21 Earl's Court Square, SW5 9DE. *Q.*

Political Quarterly—108 Cowley Road, Oxford OX4 1JF. *Q.*

Pony—296 Ewell Road, Surbiton, Surrey KT6 7AQ. *M.*

Poultry World—Carew House, Wallington, Surrey SM6 0DX. *M.*

Practical Boat Owner—Westover House, West Quay Road, Poole, Dorset BH15 1JG. *M.*

Practical Caravan—38–42 Hampton Road, Teddington, Middx. TW11 0JE. *M.*

Practical Gardening—Bushfield House, Orton Centre, Peterborough PE2 0UW. *M.*

Practical Householder—Greater London House, Hampstead Road NW1 7QQ. *M.*

Practical Photography—Bushfield House, Orton Centre, Peterborough PE2 0UW. *M.*

Prima—Portland House, Stag Place, SW1E 5AU. *M.*

Private Eye—6 Carlisle Street, W1V 5RG. *Alt. W.*

Progress (*Braille type*)—338–346 Goswell Road, EC1V 7JE. *M.*

Punch—23–27 Tudor Street, EC4 0HR. *W.*

Racing Calendar—The Jockey Club, Weatherbys, Sanders Road, Wellingborough, Northants. NN8 4BX. *W.*

Radio Control Models and Electronics—Wolsey House, Wolsey Road, Hemel Hempstead, Herts. HP2 4SS. *M.*

Radio Times—35 Marylebone High Street, W1M 4AA. *W.*

Railway Magazine—Prospect House, 9–13 Ewell Road, Cheam, Surrey SM1 4QQ. *M.*

Railway World—Coombelands House, Addlestone, Weybridge, Surrey KT15 1HY. *M.*

Reader's Digest—25 Berkeley Square, W1X 6AB. *M.*

Riding—Corner House, Foston, Grantham Lincs NG32 2JU. *M.*

Ritz Newspaper—35 Britannia Row, N1 8QH. *M.*

Scots Independent—51 Cowane Street, Stirling FK8 1JW. *M.*

Scottish Field—7th Floor, The Plaza Tower, East Kilbride, Glasgow G74 1LW. *M.*

Scouting—Baden-Powell House, Queen's Gate, SW7 5JS. *M.*

The Seafarer—202 Lambeth Road, SE1 7JW. *Q.*

She—72 Broadwick Street, W1V 2BP. *M.*

Shoot—King's Reach Tower, Stamford Street, SE1 9LS. *W.*

Shooting Times and Country Magazine—10 Sheet Street, Windsor, Berks. SL4 1BG. *W.*

Slimming Magazine—Victory House, Leicester Place, WC2H 7NB. *Alt. M.*

The Social Democrat—4 Cowley Street, SW1P 3NB. *Alt. W.*

Sociological Review—11 New Fetter Lane, EC4P 4EE. *Q.*

Spare Rib—27 Clerkenwell Close, EC1R 0AT. *M.*

The Spectator—56 Doughty Street, WC1N 2LL. *W.*

The Strad—8 Lower James Street, W1R 4DN. *M.*

Studio International—Tower House, Southampton Street, WC2E 7LS. *Q.*

Tatler—Vogue House, Hanover Square, W1R 0AD. *M.*

Tennis World—Chiltern House, 184 High Street, Berkhamsted, Herts. HP4 3AP. *M.*

This England—Alma House, Rodney Road, Cheltenham, Glos. GL50 1YQ. *Q.*

Time—Time and Life Building, New Bond Street, W1Y 0AA. *W.*

The Times Educational Supplement—Priory House, St. John's Lane, EC1M 4BX. *W.*

The Times Higher Education Supplement—Priory House, St. John's Lane, EC1M 4BX. *W.*

The Times Literary Supplement—Priory House, St. John's Lane, EC1M 4BX. *W.*

Tribune—308 Gray's Inn Road, WC1X 8DY. *W.*

Trout and Salmon—Bretton Court, Bretton, Peterborough PE3 8DZ. *M.*

True Romances—12–18 Paul Street, EC2A 4JS. *M.*

True Story—12–18 Paul Street, EC2A 4JS. *M.*

TV Times—247 Tottenham Court Road, W1P 0AU. *W.*

Vacher's Parliamentary Companion—113 High Street, Berkhamsted, Herts. HP4 2DJ. *Q.*

Vogue—Vogue House, Hanover Square, W1R 0AD. *M.*

Weather—James Glaisher House, Grenville Place, Bracknell, Berks. RG12 1BX. *M.*

Weekend—Carmelite House, Carmelite Street, EC4Y 0JA. *W.*

Welsh Nation—51 Cathedral Road, Cardiff CF1 9HD. *M.*

West Africa—Cambridge House, 373–375 Euston Road, NW1 3AR. *W.*

Which?—2 Marylebone Road, NW1 4DX. *M.*

Woman—King's Reach Tower, Stamford Street, SE1 9LS. *W.*

Woman and Home—King's Reach Tower, Stamford Street, SE1 9LS. *M.*

Woman's Journal—King's Reach Tower, Stamford Street, SE1 9LS. *M.*

Woman's Own—King's Reach Tower, Stamford Street, SE1 9LS. *W.*

Woman's Realm—King's Reach Tower, Stamford Street, SE1 9LS. *W.*

Woman's Weekly—King's Reach Tower, Stamford Street, SE1 9LS. *W.*

Woman's World—25 Newman Street, W1P 3HA. *M.*

The World Today—Chatham House, 10 St. James's Square, SW1Y 4LE. *M.*

Yachting Monthly—King's Reach Tower, Stamford Street, SE1 9LS. *M.*

Yachting World—Prospect House, 9–13 Ewell Road, Cheam, Surrey SM1 4QQ. *M.*

Yachts and Yachting—196 Eastern Esplanade, Southend-on-Sea, Essex SS1 3AB. *Alt. W.*

Your Model Railway—P.O. Box 35, Wolsey House, Wolsey Road, Hemel Hempstead, Herts. HP2 4SS. *M.*

TRADE, PROFESSIONAL AND BUSINESS JOURNALS

[*W.* = Weekly; *M.* = Monthly; *Q.* = Quarterly]

Accountancy—40 Bernard Street, WC1N 1LD. *M.*

The Accountant—Axe & Bottle Court, 70 Newcomen Street, SE1 1YT. *M.*

Accountants' Magazine—27 Queen Street, Edinburgh EH2 1LA. *M.*

Administrator—2nd Floor, Caxton House, Wellesley Road, Ashford, Kent. *M.*

Agriculture International—Yew Tree House, Horne, Horley, Surrey RH6 9JP. *M.*

Antique Dealer and Collectors' Guide—King's Reach Tower, Stamford Street, SE1 9LS. *M.*

Antiques Trade Gazette—17 Whitcomb Street, WC2H 7PL. *W.*

Architects' Journal—9 Queen Anne's Gate, SW1H 9BY. *W.*

Architectural Review—9 Queen Anne's Gate, SW1H 9BY. *M.*

The Author—84 Drayton Gardens, SW10 9SB. *Q.*

Bakers' Review—Turret House, 171 High Street, Rickmansworth, Herts. WD3 1SN. *M.*

The Banker—102–108 Clerkenwell Road, EC1M 5SA. *M.*

Banking World—Headway House, 66–73 Shoe Lane, EC4P 4AB. *M.*

The Bookseller—12 Dyott Street, WC1A 1DF. *W.*

Brewers' Guardian—209 Central Markets, Smithfield, EC1A 9LH. *M.*

British Baker—P.O. Box 109, Maclaren House, 19 Scarbrook Road, Croydon CR9 1QH. *W.*

British Business—2 Bentinck Court, Bentinck Road, West Drayton, Middx. UB7 7RQ. *W.*

British Clothing Manufacturer—100 Avenue Road, NW3 3TP. *Q.*

British Dental Journal—B.M.A. House, Tavistock Square, WC1H 9JR. *Alt. W.*

British Food Journal—M.C.B. University Press Ltd., 62 Toller Lane, Bradford BD8 9BY. *Alt. M.*

British Jeweller—10–11 Vyse Street, Hockley Birmingham B18 6LT. *M.*

British Journal for the Philosophy of Science—Oxford University Press, Walton Street, Oxford OX2 6DP. *Q.*

British Journal of Photography—244–249 Temple Chambers, Temple Avenue, EC4Y 0DT. *W.*

British Medical Journal—B.M.A. House, Tavistock Square, WC1H 9JR. *W.*

British Printer—Maclean Hunter House, Chalk Lane, Cockfosters Road, Barnet, Herts. EN4 0BU. *M.*

British Sugar Beet Review—P.O. Box 26, Oundle Road, Peterborough PE2 9QU. *Q.*

British Tax Review—11 New Fetter Lane, EC4P 4EE. *Alt. M.*

British Veterinary Journal—24–28 Oval Road, NW1 7DX. *Alt. M.*

Building Trade & Industry—Industry House, 74 West Street, Bristol BS3 3LL. *M.*

Building Trade News—100 Avenue Road, NW3 3TP. *Q.*

Cabinet Maker and Retail Furnisher—Sovereign Way, Tonbridge, Kent TN9 1RW. *W.*

Campaign—30 Lancaster Gate, W2 3LY. *W.*

Carpet and Floorcoverings Review—Sovereign Way, Tonbridge, Kent TN9 1RW. *Alt. W.*

Caterer and Hotelkeeper—Quadrant House, The Quadrant, Sutton, Surrey SM2 5AS. *W.*

Chemist and Druggist—Sovereign Way, Tonbridge, Kent TN9 1RW. *W.*

Chemistry and Industry—14 Belgrave Square, SW1X 8PS. *Alt. W.*

Chemistry in Britain—Burlington House, Piccadilly, W1V 0BN. *M.*

Child Education—Marlborough House, Holly Walk, Leamington Spa, Warwickshire CV32 4LS. *M.*

Chiropodist—53 Welbeck Street, W1M 7HE. *M.*

Civil Engineering—Morgan-Grampian House, 30 Calderwood Street, SE18 6QH. *M.*

Club Mirror—Maclaren House, Scarbrook Road, Croydon CR9 1QH. *M.*

Colliery Guardian—Queensway House, 2 Queensway, Redhill, Surrey RH1 1QS. *M.*

Commercial Motor—Quadrant House, The Quadrant, Sutton, Surrey SM2 5AS. *W.*

Computer Survey—U.T.P. House, 33–35 Bowling Green Lane, EC1R 0DA. *Alt. M.*

Concrete—Devon House, 12–15 Dartmouth Street, SW1H 9BL. *M.*

Containerisation International—72 Broadwick Street, W1V 2BP. *M.*

Contract Journal—Carew House, Wallington, Surrey SM6 0DX. *W.*

Control and Instrumentation—Morgan-Grampian House, 30 Calderwood Street, SE18 6QH. *M.*

C.S.E. News—Camping and Sports Equipment Ltd., Exhibition House, 4 Spring Street, W2 3RB. *M.*

Dairy Farmer—Wharfedale Road, Ipswich IP1 4LG. *M.*

Dairy Industries International—U.T.P. House, 33–35 Bowling Green Lane, EC1R 0DA. *M.*

Design—The Design Centre, 28 Haymarket, SW1Y 4SU. *M.*

Director—10 Belgrave Square, SW1X 8PH. *M.*

Dock and Harbour Authority—20 Harcourt Street, W1H 2AX. *M.*

D.R. The Fashion Business—100 Avenue Road, NW3 3TP. *W.*

Education—21–27 Lamb's Conduit Street, WC1N 3NJ. *W.*

Education Equipment—Sovereign Way, Tonbridge, Kent TN9 1RW. *M.*

Electrical and Radio Trading—Quadrant House, The Quadrant, Sutton, Surrey SM2 5AS. *W.*

Electrical Review—Quadrant House, The Quadrant, Sutton, Surrey SM2 5AS. *W.*

Electrical Times—Quadrant House, The Quadrant, Sutton, Surrey SM2 5AS. *W.*

Electronic Engineering—Morgan-Grampian House, 30 Calderwood Street, SE18 6QH. *M.*

Electronics Weekly—Quadrant House, The Quadrant, Sutton, Surrey SM2 5AS. *W.*

Embroidery—P.O. Box 42B, East Molesey, Surrey KT8 9BB. *Q.*

The Engineer—Morgan-Grampian House, 30 Calderwood Street, SE18 6QH. *W.*

Engineering—28 Haymarket, SW1Y 4SU. *M.*

Engineer's Digest—Catalyst House, 159–160 High Street, Clapham, SW4 7SS. *Ten times a year.*

Estates Gazette—151 Wardour Street, W1V 4BN. *W.*

Fairplay International Shipping Weekly—20 Ullswater Crescent, Coulsdon, Surrey CR3 2HR. *W.*

Farmers Weekly—Carew House, Wallington, Surrey SM6 0DX. *W.*

Fire—Queensway House, 2 Queensway, Redhill, Surrey RH1 1QS. *M.*

Fire and Security Protection—Stanley House, 9 West Street, Epsom, Surrey KT18 7RL. *M.*

Fish Friers Review—289 Dewsbury Road, Leeds LS11 5HW. *M.*

Fish Trader—Queensway House, 2 Queensway, Redhill, Surrey RH1 1QS. *W.*

Flight International—Quadrant House, The Quadrant, Sutton, Surrey SM2 5AS. *W.*

Food Trade Review—29 High Street, Green Street Green, Orpington, Kent BR6 6LS. *M.*

Forestry and British Timber—Sovereign Way, Tonbridge, Kent TN9 1RW. *M.*

Foundry Trade Journal—Queensway House, 2 Queensway, Redhill, Surrey RH1 1QS. *Alt. W.*

Frozen and Chilled Foods—Queensway House, 2 Queensway, Redhill, Surrey RH1 1QS. *M.*

Fuel—P.O. Box 63, Westbury House, Bury Street, Guildford GU2 5BH. *M.*

Funeral Service Journal—43 Stockens Green, Knebworth, Herts. SG3 6DQ. *M.*

Fur Weekly News—4 Great Saint Thomas Apostle, EC4V 2BH. *W.*

Gas Marketing—Sovereign Way, Tonbridge, Kent TN9 1RW. *M.*

Gas World—Sovereign Way, Tonbridge, Kent TN9 1RW. *M.*

Gifts International—Sovereign Way, Tonbridge, Kent TN9 1RW. *M.*

Glass—Queensway House, 2 Queensway, Redhill, Surrey RH1 1QS. *M.*

The Grocer—5–7 Southwark Street, SE1 1RQ. *W.*

The Grower—50 Doughty Street, WC1N 2LP. *W.*

Hair and Beauty—Quadrant House, The Quadrant, Sutton, Surrey SM2 5AS. *M.*

Hairdressers' Journal International—Quadrant House, The Quadrant, Sutton, Surrey SM2 5AS. *W.*

Handy Shipping Guide—230–234 Long Lane, SE1 4QE. *W.*

Hardware Today—20 Harborne Road, Birmingham B15 3AB. *M.*

Harpers Sports & Leisure—Unit 2, Mill Hill Industrial Estate, Flower Lane, NW7 2HU. *Every three weeks.*

Harpers Wine and Spirit Gazette—Harling House, 47–51 Great Suffolk Street, SE1 0BS. *W.*

Health Visitor—BMA House, Tavistock Square, WC1H 9JR. *M.*

Heating and Ventilating Engineer—177 Hagden Lane, Watford, Herts. WD1 8LW. *Alt. M.*

Ice Cream and Frozen Confectionery—90–94 Gray's Inn Road, WC1X 8AH. *M.*

Investors Chronicle—Greystoke Place, Fetter Lane, EC4A 1ND. *W.*

Journal of The Chemical Society—Burlington House, Piccadilly, W1V 0BN. *Six parts each M.*

The Journalist—Acorn House, 314 Gray's Inn Rd., WC1X 8DP. *M.*

Justice of the Peace—East Row, Little London, Chichester, W. Sussex PO19 1PG. *W.*

Knitting and Haberdashery Review—80A South Street, Romford RM1 1RX. *Alt. M.*

The Lancet—46 Bedford Square, WC1B 3DP. *W.*

Law Quarterly Review—11 New Fetter Lane, EC4P 4EE. *Q.*

The Law Reports—3 Stone Buildings, Lincoln's Inn, WC2A 3XN. *M.*

Law Society's Gazette—113 Chancery Lane, WC2A 1PL. *W.*

Leather—Sovereign Way, Tonbridge, Kent TN9 1RW. *M.*

The Legal Executive Journal—Kempston Manor, Kempston, Beds. MK42 7AB. *M.*

Library Review—62 Toller Lane, Bradford BD8 9BY. *Q.*

Litho Week—38–42 Hampton Road, Teddington, Middx. TW11 0JE. *W.*

Lloyd's Loading List—Sheepen Place, Colchester, Essex CO3 3LP. *W.*

Lloyd's Shipping Index—Sheepen Place, Colchester, Essex CO3 3LP. *D.*

Locomotive Journal—9 Arkwright Road, NW3 6AA. *M.*

London Corn Circular—54 Wentworth Crescent, Ash Vale, Aldershot, Hants. GU12 5LF. *W.*

Machinery and Production Engineering—Franks Hall, Franks Lane, Horton Kirby, Dartford, Kent DA4 9LL. *Alt. W.*

Machinery Market—6 Blyth Road, Bromley, Kent BR1 3RX. *W.*

Management Accounting—63 Portland Place, W1N 4AB. *M.*

Management Decision—62 Toller Lane, Bradford BD8 9BY. *Alt. M.*

Management Today—30 Lancaster Gate, W2 3LP. *M.*

Manufacturing Chemist—Morgan-Grampian House, 30 Calderwood Street, SE18 6QH. *M.*

Marketing—22 Lancaster Gate, W2 3LY. *W.*

Materials Reclamation Weekly—P.O. Box 109, Maclaren House, 19 Scarbrook Road, Croydon CR9 1QH. *W.*

Meat Trades' Journal—100 Avenue Road, NW3 3TP. *W.*

Medico-Legal Journal—5 New Square, Lincoln's Inn, WC2A 3RJ. *Q.*

Men's Wear—100 Avenue Road, NW3 3TP. *W.*

Metal Bulletin—Park House, Park Terrace, Worcester Park, Surrey KT4 7HY. *Twice a week.*

Metallurgia—Queensway House, 2 Queensway, Redhill, Surrey RH1 1QS. *M.*

Milk Industry—19 Cornwall Terrace, NW1 4QP. *M.*

Mining Journal—60 Worship Street, EC2A 2HD. *W.*

Mining Magazine—60 Worship Street, EC2A 2HD. *M.*

Model Engineer—P.O. Box 35, Wolsey House, Wolsey Road, Hemel Hempstead, Herts. HP2 4SS. *Alt. W.*

Modern Law Review—11 New Fetter Lane, EC4P 4EE. *Alt. M.*

Modern Railways—Coombelands House, Addlestone, Weybridge, Surrey KT15 1HY. *M.*

Motor Boat and Yachting—Quadrant House, The Quadrant, Sutton, Surrey SM2 5AS. *M.*

Motorcycle Trader—177 Hagden Lane, Watford, Herts. WD1 8LW. *M.*

Motor Trader—Quadrant House, The Quadrant, Sutton, Surrey SM2 5AS. *W.*

Motor Transport—Quadrant House, The Quadrant, Sutton, Surrey SM2 5AS. *W.*

The Musical Times—8 Lower James Street, W1R 4DN. *M.*

National Builder—82 New Cavendish Street, W1M 8AD. *M.*

Natural Gas—Sovereign Way, Tonbridge, Kent TN9 1RW. *Alt. M.*

New Law Journal—9–12 Bell Yard, WC2A 2JR. *W.*

Nuclear Engineering International—Quadrant House, The Quadrant, Sutton, Surrey SM2 5AS. *M.*

Nurseryman & Garden Centre—Monchelsea Farm, Boughton Monchelsea, Maidstone, Kent ME17 4JD. *Alt. W.*

Nursing Times & Nursing Mirror—4 Little Essex Street, WC2R 3LF. *W.*

Off-Licence News—5–7 Southwark Street, SE1 1RQ. *W.*

Optician—Quadrant House, The Quadrant, Sutton, Surrey SM2 5AS. *W.*

Optometry Today—Bridge House, 233–234 Blackfriars Road, SE1 8NW. *Alt. W.*

Packaging—177 Hagden Lane, Watford, Herts. WD1 8LW. *M.*

Packaging Week—Sovereign Way, Tonbridge, Kent TN9 1RW. *W.*

Paint & Resin—177 Hagden Lane, Watford, Herts. WD1 8LW. *Alt. M.*

Painting and Decorating Journal—177 Hagden Lane, Watford, Herts. WD1 8LW. *Alt. M.*

Paper—Sovereign Way, Tonbridge, Kent TN9 1RW. *Alt. W.*

Personnel Management—1 Hills Place, W1R 1AG. *M.*

Pharmaceutical Journal—1 Lambeth High Street, SE1 7JN. *W.*

The Photographer—1 Gayford Road, W12 9BY. *M.*

Physics Bulletin—Techno House, Redcliffe Way, Bristol BS1 6NX. *M.*

Physics Education—Techno House, Redcliffe Way, Bristol BS1 6NX. *Alt. M.*

Physics in Technology—Techno House, Redcliffe Way, Bristol BS1 6NX. *Alt. M.*

Plumbing and Heating Equipment News—Peterson House, Northbank, Berryhill Industrial Estate, Droitwich, Worcs. WR9 9BL. *M.*

Police Review—14 St. Cross Street, EC1N 8FE. *W.*

Power Farming—Carew House, Wallington, Surrey SM6 0DX. *M.*

Practical Wireless—Enefco House, The Quay, Poole, Dorset B15 1PP. *M.*

Practical Woodworking—King's Reach Tower, Stamford Street, SE1 9LS. *M.*

The Practitioner—Morgan-Grampian House, 30 Calderwood Street, SE18 6QH. *M.*

Precision Toolmaker—QueenswayHouse, 2 Queensway, Redhill, Surrey RH1 1QS. *Q.*

Printing World—Sovereign Way, Tonbridge, Kent TN9 1RW. *W.*

Product Finishing—127 Stanstead Road, SE23 1JE. *M.*

Public Law—11 New Fetter Lane, EC4P 4EE. *Q.*

The Public Ledger—Turret House, 171 High Street, Rickmansworth, Herts. WD3 1SN. *Daily* and *W.*

Public Service—1 Mabledon Place, WC1H 9AJ. *M.*

Quarry Management—7 Regent Street, Nottingham NG1 5BY. *M.*

Quarterly Journal of Experimental Psychology—Chancery House, 319 City Road, EC1V 1LJ. *Q.*

Quarterly Journal of Medicine—Oxford University Press, Walton Street, Oxford OX2 6DP. *M.*

Railway Gazette International—Quadrant House, The Quadrant, Sutton, Surrey SM2 5AS. *M.*

Rating & Valuation Reporter—2 Paper Buildings, Temple, EC4Y 7ET. *M.*

Resale Weekly—1–23 Queen's Road West, E13 0PE. *W.*

Retail Jeweller—100 Avenue Road, NW3 3TP. *Alt. W.*

Retail Newsagent Tobacconist Confectioner—60–66 Saffron Hill, EC1N 8QX. *W.*

The Review: Worldwide Reinsurance—U.T.P. House, 33–35 Bowling Green Lane, EC1R 0DA. *Twenty-two times a year.*

Review of English Studies—Oxford University Press, Walton Street, Oxford OX2 6DP. *Q.*

Safety at Sea—Queensway House, 2 Queensway, Redhill, Surrey RH1 1QS. *M.*

The Scottish Farmer—7th Floor, The Plaza Tower, East Kilbride, Glasgow G74 1LW. *W.*

Scottish Grocer—36 North Frederick Street, Glasgow G1 2BT. *M.*

Service Station—1A Dunvegan Road, Eltham, SE9 1RZ. *M.*

Sheet Metal Industries—Queensway House, 2 Queensway, Redhill, Surrey RH1 1QS. *M.*

Shipping World & Shipbuilder—4 Hubbard Road, Houndsmill, Basingstoke, Hants. RG21 2UH. *M.*

Shoe & Leather News—100 Avenue Road, NW3 3TP. *W.*

Soap, Perfumery and Cosmetics—U.T.P. House, 33–35 Bowling Green Lane, EC1R 0DA. *M.*

Solicitors' Journal—21–27 Lamb's Conduit Street, WC1N 3NJ. *W.*

Sports Retailing—Sovereign Way, Tonbridge, Kent TN9 1RW. *Alt. W.*

The Stage—47 Bermondsey Street, SE1 3XT. *W.*

Structural Engineer—11 Upper Belgrave Street, SW1X 8BH. *M. (Part A), Q. (Part B).*

Surveyor—Carew House, Wallington, Surrey SM6 0DX. *W.*

Tableware International—Queensway House, 2 Queensway, Redhill, Surrey RH1 1QS. *M.*

Taxation—Tolley House, Addiscombe Road, Croydon, Surrey CR9 5AS. *W.*

The Teacher—Derbyshire House, Lower Street, Kettering, Northants. NN16 8BB. *W.*

Teaching History—108 Cowley Road, Oxford OX4 1JF. *Three times a year.*

Television—King's Reach Tower, Stamford Street, SE1 9LS. *M.*

Textile Horizons—10 Blackfriars Street, Manchester M3 5DR. *M.*

Textile Month—Caiden House, Canal Road, Timperley, Altrincham, Cheshire WA14 1TD. *M.*

Timber Trades Journal & Wood Processing—Sovereign Way, Tonbridge, Kent TN9 1RW. *W.*

Tobacco—Queensway House, 2 Queensway, Redhill, Surrey RH1 1QS. *M.*

Town and Country Planning—17 Carlton House Terrace, SW1Y 5AH. *M.*

Town Planning Review—Liverpool University Press, P.O. Box 147, Liverpool L69 3BX. *Q.*

Toy Trader—177 Hagden Lane, Watford, Herts. WD1 8LW. *M.*

Trade Marks Journal—25 Southampton Buildings, WC2A 1AY. *W.*

Traffic Engineering and Control—29 Newman Street, W1P 3PE. *M.*

U.K. Press Gazette—Mitre House, 44 Fleet Street, EC4Y 1BS. *W.*

Ultrasonics—P.O. Box 63, Westbury House, Bury Street, Guildford, Surrey GU2 5BH. *Alt. M.*

Weekly Law Reports—3 Stone Buildings, Lincoln's Inn, WC2A 3XN. *W.*

Welding and Metal Fabrication—Queensway House, 2 Queensway, Redhill, Surrey RH1 1QS. *Five times a year.*

Whitaker's Books of the Month and Books to Come—12 Dyott Street, WC1A 1DF. *M.*

Whitaker's Classified Monthly Book List—12 Dyott Street, WC1A 1DF. *M.*

Wire Industry—110–112 Station Road East, Oxted, Surrey RH8 0QA. *M.*

Woodworker—1 Golden Square, W1R 3AB. *M.*

World's Fair—2 Daltry Street, Oldham OL1 4BB. *W.*

REPORTING AND NEWS AGENCIES IN LONDON

The Associated Press Ltd.—12 Norwich Street, EC4A 4BP. (01–353 1515).

Brenard Press Ltd.—Building 221, Heathrow Airport, Hounslow, Middx. TW6 2BU. (01–759 1235).

Central Press Features Ltd.—131 Aldersgate Street, Barbican, EC1A 4JA (01–600 4502).

The Exchange Telegraph Co. Ltd.—Extel House, East Harding Street, EC4P 4HB. (01–353 1080).

Hayters—4–5 Gough Square, EC4A 3DE. (01–353 0971).

Parliamentary and Common Market News Services—19 Kingsdowne Road, Surbiton, Surrey KT6 6JZ. (01–399 2049).

Press Association Ltd.—85 Fleet Street, EC4P 4BE. (01–353 7440).

Reuters Ltd.—85 Fleet Street, EC4P 4AJ. (01–250 1122).

United Press International (U.K.) Ltd.—8 Bouverie Street, EC4Y 8BB. (01–353 2282).

Universal News Service, Ltd.—Communications House, Gough Square, Fleet Street, EC4 4DP. (01–353 5200).

PRINCIPAL BOOK PUBLISHERS AND THEIR ADDRESSES

More than 10,000 firms, individuals and societies have published one or more books in recent years. The list which follows is a selective one comprising, in the main, those firms whose names are most familiar to the general public. An interleaved list, *Publishers in the United Kingdom and Their Addresses*, containing some 2,000 names and addresses is issued annually in April by the publishers of *Whitaker's Almanack*.

Abelard-Schumann, 7 Leicester Place, WC2H 7BP.

Allan (Ian), Terminal House, Station Approach, Shepperton, Middx. TW17 8AS.

Allen (J. A.), 1 Lower Grosvenor Place, SW1W 0EL.

Allen (W. H.), 175 St. John Street, EC1V 4LL.

Angus & Robertson, 16 Golden Square, W1R 4BN.

Apple Press, 79 Great Titchfield Street, W1P 7FN.

Argus Books, Argus House, Boundary Way, Hemel Hempstead, Herts. HP2 7ST.

Arlington Books, 15 King Street, SW1Y 6QU.

Armada Books, 8 Grafton Street. W1X 3LA.

Arms & Armour Press, Artillery House, Artillery Row, SW1P 1RT.

Arnold (Edward), 41 Bedford Square, WC1B 3DQ.

Arnold (E. J.) & Son, Parkside Lane, Leeds LS11 5TD.

Arrow Books, 62 Chandos Place, WC2N 4NW.

Athlone Press, 1 Park Drive, NW11 7SG.

Aurum Press, 33 Museum Street, WC1A 1LD.

B.B.C. Books, 80 Wood Lane, W12 0TT.

Baillière, Tindall, 24 Oval Road, NW1 7DX.

Bantam Bks., 61 Uxbridge Road, W5 5SA.

Barker (Arthur), 91 Clapham High Street, SW4 9TA.

Barrie & Jenkins, 289 Westbourne Grove, W11 2QA.

Bartholomew & Son, 12 Duncan Street, Edinburgh EH9 1TA.

Batsford, 4 Fitzhardinge Street, W1H 0AH.

Benn (Ernest), 35 Bedford Row, WC1R 4JH.

Bingley (Clive), 7 Ridgmount Street, WC1E 7AE.

Black (A. & C.), 35 Bedford Row, WC1R 4JH.

Blackie, Bishopbriggs, Glasgow G64 2NZ.

Blackwell (Basil), 108 Cowley Rd., Oxford OX4 1JF.

Blandford Press, Artillery House, Artillery Row, SW1P 1RT.

Blond (Anthony), 62 Chandos Place, WC2N 4NW.

Bloomsbury Publishing, 2 Soho Square, W1V 5DE.

Bodley Head, 32 Bedford Square, WC1B 3EL.

Boxtree, 36 Tavistock Street, WC2E 7PB.

Boyars (Marion), 24 Lacy Road, SW15 1NL.

Bracken Books, 50 Eastcastle Street, W1N 7AP.

British Museum, 46 Bloomsbury Street, WC1B 3QQ.

Brown, Son & Ferguson, 4 Darnley Street, Glasgow G41 2SD.

Butterworth & Co., Borough Green, Sevenoaks TN15 8PH.

Calder (John), 18 Brewer Street, W1R 4AS.

Cambridge Univ. Press, Shaftesbury Road, Cambridge CB2 2RU.

Cape (Jonathan), 32 Bedford Square, WC1B 3EL.

Cassell, Artillery House, Artillery Row, SW1P 1RT.

Centaur Press, Fontwell, Arundel, Sussex BN18 0TA.

Century Hutchinson, 62 Chandos Place, WC2N 4NW.

Century Publishing Co., *see* Century Hutchinson

Chambers (W. & R.), 43 Annandale Street, Edinburgh EH7 4AZ.

Chapman & Hall, 11 New Fetter Lane, EC4P 4EE.

Chapman (Geoffrey), Artillery House, Artillery Row, SW1P 1RT.

Chatto & Windus, 30 Bedford Square, WC1B 3SG.

Chivers Press, Windsor Bridge Road, Bath BA2 3AX.

Church House Publishing, Dean's Yard, SW1P 3NZ.

Churchill Livingstone, 1–3 Baxter's Place, Leith Walk, Edinburgh EH1 3AF.

Collins (William), 8 Grafton Street, W1X 3LA.

Constable & Co., 10 Orange Street, WC2H 7EG.

Consumers' Association, 2 Marylebone Road, NW1 4DX.

Corgi Books, 61 Uxbridge Road, W5 5SA.

Darton, Longman & Todd, 89 Lillie Road, SW6 1UD.

David & Charles, Brunel House, Newton Abbot, Devon TQ12 4PU.

Dean & Son, *see* Hamlyn.

Dent (J. M.) & Sons, 91 Clapham High Street, SW4 9TA.

Deutsch (A.), 105 Gt. Russell Street, WC1B 3LJ.

Dorling Kindersley, 9 Henrietta Street, WC2E 8PS.

Doubleday, 61 Uxbridge Road, W5 5SA.

Duckworth & Co., 43 Gloucester Crescent, NW1 7DY.

Elliot Right Way Books, Kingswood Bldg., Kingswood, Tadworth, Surrey KT20 6TD.

Encyclopaedia Britannica, Carew House, Station Approach, Wallington, Surrey SM6 0DA.

Epworth Press, 1 Central Bldgs., SW1H 9NR.

Evans Bros., 2A Portman Mansions, Chiltern Street, W1M 1LE.

Eyre & Spottiswoode, North Way, Andover, Hants. SP10 5BE.

Faber & Faber, 3 Queen Square, WC1N 3AU.

Fontana, 8 Grafton Street, W1X 3LA.

Foulis (G. T.), Sparkford, Yeovil, Somerset BA22 7JJ.

Foulsham & Co., Yeovil Rd., Slough SL1 4JH.

Fountain Press, 45 The Broadway, Tolworth, Surbiton, Surrey KT6 7DW.

French (Samuel), 52 Fitzroy Street, W1P 6JR.

Futura, *see* Macdonald & Co.

Gee & Co., 7 Swallow Place, W1R 8AB.

Geographia, 12 Duncan Street, Edinburgh EH9 1TA.

Gibbons (Stanley), 5 Parkside, Christchurch Road, Ringwood, Hants. BH24 3SH.

Gibson (Robert), 17 Fitzroy Place, Glasgow G3 7SF.

Ginn & Co., Prebendal House, Parson's Fee, Aylesbury, Bucks. HP20 2QZ.

Glasgow (Mary), 131 Holland Park Avenue, W11 4UT.

Gollancz (Victor), 14 Henrietta Street, WC2E 8QJ.

Gower Publishing Co., Croft Road, Aldershot, Hants. GU11 3HR

Grafton Books, 8 Grafton Street, W1X 3LA.

Graham (Frank), 6 Queen's Terrace, Newcastle NE2 2PL.

Green (W.), 2 St. Giles Street, Edinburgh EH1 1PU.

Guinness Publishing, 33 London Road, Enfield, Middx. EN2 6DJ.

H.M. Stationery Office, 51 Nine Elms Lane, SW8 5DR.

Hale (Robert), 45 Clerkenwell Green, EC1R 0HT.

Hamlyn, 81 Fulham Road, SW3 6RB.

Harcourt Brace Jovanovich, 24 Oval Road, NW1 7DX.

Harlequin, 18 Paradise Road., Richmond, Surrey TW9 1SR.

Harper & Row, 34 Cleveland Street, W1P 5FB.

Harrap, 19 Ludgate Hill, EC4M 7PD.

Hart-Davis, 8 Grafton Street, W1X 3LA.

Harvester Wheatsheaf, Wolsey House, Wolsey Road, Hemel Hempstead HP2 4SS.

Haynes (J. H.), Sparkford, Yeovil, Somerset BA22 7TJ.

Headline Book Publishing, 79 Great Titchfield Street, W1P 7FN.

Heinemann (Wm.), 81 Fulham Road, SW3 6RB.

Hodder & Stoughton, 47 Bedford Square, WC1B 3DP.

Hogarth Press, 30 Bedford Square, WC1B 3SG.

Holmes McDougall, 137 Leith Walk, Edinburgh EH6 8NS.

Hutchinson, 62 Chandos Place, WC2N 4NW.

Jane's Information Group, 163 Brighton Road, Coulsdon CR3 2NX.

Jarrold Colour, Barrack Street, Norwich NR3 1TR.

Johnston & Bacon, P. O. Box 1, Stirling.

Jordan & Sons, 21 St. Thomas Street, Bristol BS1 6JS.

Joseph (Michael), 27 Wright's Lane, W8 5TZ.

Kaye & Ward, 81 Fulham Road, SW3 6RB.

Kegan Paul International, P.O. Box 256, WC1B 3SW.

Kelly's Directories, East Grinstead House, East Grinstead, Sussex RH19 1XB.

Kimber (Wm.), Denington Estate, Wellingborough NN8 2QD.

Kimpton Medical, 205 Great Portland Street, W1N 6LR.

Kingsway Publications, 1 St. Anne's Road, Eastbourne, E. Sussex, BN21 3UN.

Kogan Page, 120 Pentonville Road, N1 9JN.

Ladybird, Beeches Road, Loughborough LE11 2NQ.

Lawrence & Wishart, 144a Old South Lambeth Road, SW8 1XX.

Letts (Charles), 77 Borough Road, SE1 1DW.

Lewis (H. K.), 136 Gower Street, WC1E 6BS.

Lion Publishing, Peter's Way, Littlemore, Oxford OX4 5HG.

Longman Group, Burnt Mill, Harlow, Essex CM20 2JE.

Lund Humphries, 16 Pembridge Road, W11 3HL.

Lutterworth Press, P.O. Box 60, Cambridge CB1 2NT.

Macdonald & Co., 66 Shoe Lane, EC4P 4AB.

Macdonald & Evans, 128 Long Acre, WC2E 9AN.

McGraw-Hill, Shoppenhangers Road, Maidenhead, Berks. SL6 2QL.

Macmillan Publishers, 4 Little Essex Street, WC2R 3LF.

Mandarin, 81 Fulham Road, SW3 6RB.

Marshall Cavendish, 58 Old Compton Street, W1V 5PA.

Marshall Pickering, 34 Cleveland Street, W1P 5FB.

Mayflower, 8 Grafton Street, W1X 3LA.

Methodist Publishing, 20 Ivatt Way, Peterborough PE3 7PG.

Methuen London, 81 Fulham Road, SW3 6RB.

Mills & Boon, 18 Paradise Rd., Richmond, Surrey TW9 1SR.

Mitchell Beazley, 14 Manette Street, W1V 5LB.

Mowbray, Artillery House, Artillery Row, SW1P 1RT.

Muller (Frederick), 62 Chandos Place, WC2N 4NW.

Murray (John), 50 Albemarle Street, W1X 4BD.

National Christian Education Council, Robert Denholm Ho., Nutfield, Redhill RH1 4HW.

Nelson (T.), Mayfield Rd., Walton-on-Thames KT12 5PL.

New English Library, 47 Bedford Square, WC1B 3DP.

Nisbet & Co., 78 Tilehouse St., Hitchin, Herts. SG5 2DY.

Novello & Co., Borough Green, Sevenoaks, Kent.

Octopus Books, 81 Fulham Road, SW3 6RB.

Oliver & Boyd, Longman House, Burnt Mill, Harlow, Essex, CM20 2JE.

O'Mara (Michael) Books, 20 Queen Anne Street, W1N 9FB.

Owen (Peter), 73 Kenway Road, SW5 0RE.

Oxford Univ. Press, Walton Street, Oxford OX2 6DP.

Paladin Books, 8 Grafton Street, W1X 3LA.

Pan Books, 18 Cavaye Place, SW10 9PG.

Panther, 8 Grafton Street, W1X 3LA.

Paul (Stanley), 62 Chandos Place, WC2N 4NW.

Pelham Books, 27 Wright's Lane, W8 5TZ.

Penguin Books, Harmondsworth, Middx. UB7 0DA.

Pergamon Press, Headington Hill Hall, Oxford OX3 0BW.

Phaidon Press, Musterlin House, Jordan Hill Road, Oxford OX2 8DP.

Pharmaceutical Press, 1 Lambeth High Street, SE1 7JN.

Philip (George), 59 Grosvenor Street, W1X 9DA.

Piatkus Books, 5 Windmill Street, W1P 1HF.

Piccadilly Press, 5 Canfield Place, NW6 3BT.

Pitkins, North Way, Andover, Hants. SP10 5BE.

Pitman Publishing, 128 Long Acre, WC2E 9AN.

Price Stern Sloan, John Clare House, The Avenue, Cliftonville, Northampton NN1 5BT.

Putnam & Co., 24 Bride Lane, EC4Y 8DR.

Quartet Books, 27 Goodge Street, W1P 1FD.

Quiller Press, 46 Lillie Road, SW6 1TN.

Random House, 30 Bedford Square, WC1B 3SG.

Ravette Books, 3 Glenside Estate, Star Road, Partridge Green, Horsham, W. Sussex, RH13 8RA.

Reader's Digest, 25 Berkeley Square, W1X 6AB.

Religious & Moral Education Press, Hennock Road, Exeter EX2 8RP.

Rider & Co., 62 Chandos Place, WC2N 4NW.

Routledge, 11 New Fetter Lane, EC4P 4EE.

S.C.M. Press, 26 Tottenham Road, N1 4BZ.

S.P.C.K., Holy Trinity Church, Marylebone Road, NW1 4DU.

St. Andrew Press, 121 George Street, Edinburgh EH2 4YN.

Scripture Union, 130 City Road, EC1V 2NJ.

Secker & Warburg, 81 Fulham Road, SW3 6RB.

Severn House, 35 Manor Road, Wallington, Surrey, SM6 0BW.

Sheed & Ward, 2 Creechurch Lane, EC3A 5AQ.

Sheldon Press, Holy Trinity Church, Marylebone Road, NW1 4DU.

Sidgwick & Jackson, 1 Tavistock Chambers, WC1A 2SG.

Simon & Schuster, Wolsey House, Wolsey Road, Hemel Hempstead HP2 4SS.

Smythe (Colin), P.O. Box 6, Gerrards Cross, Bucks. SL9 8XA.

Souvenir Press, 43 Great Russell Street, WC1B 3PA.

Sphere Books, 27 Wright's Lane, W8 5TZ.

Spon (E. & F. N.), 11 New Fetter Lane, EC4P 4EE.

Stanford Maritime, 59 Grosvenor Street, W1X 9DA.

Stephens (Patrick), Denington Estate, Wellingborough, Northants. NN8 2QD.

Stevens & Sons, 183 Marsh Wall, E14 9FT.

Sweet & Maxwell, 183 Marsh Wall, E14 9FT.

Thames & Hudson, 30 Bloomsbury Street, WC1B 3QP.

Thorsons, Denington Estate, Wellingborough, Northants. NN8 2RQ.

Times Books, 16 Golden Square, W1R 4BN.

Turnstone Books, Denington Estate, Wellingborough, Northants. NN8 2RQ.

University of Wales Press, Gwennyth Street, Cardiff CF2 4YD.

Unwin Hyman, 15 Broadwick Street, W1V 1FP.

Vallentine Mitchell, 11 Gainsborough Road, E11 1RS.

Viking, 27 Wright's Lane, W8 5TZ.

Virago Press, 20–23 Mandela Street, NW1 0HQ.

Walker Books, 87 Vauxhall Walk, SE11 5HJ.

Ward Lock, 8 Clifford Street, W1X 1RB.

Ward Lock Educational Co., TR House, Christopher Road, East Grinstead, W. Sussex, RH19 3BT.

Warne, 27 Wright's Lane, W8 5TZ.

Webb & Bower, 5 Cathedral Close, Exeter EX1 1EZ.

Weidenfeld & Nicolson, 91 Clapham High Street, SW4 9TA.

Wheaton (A.), Hennock Road, Exeter EX2 8RP.

Whitaker (J.), 12 Dyott Street, WC1A 1DF.

Wildwood House, Gower House, Croft Road, Aldershot, Hants. GU11 3HR.

Wisden (John), Station Road, Robertsbridge TN32 5DH.

Witherby (H. F. & G.), 14 Henrietta Street, WC2E 8QJ.

Wolfe Publishing, 2 Torrington Place, WC1E 7LT.

World's Work, see Heinemann (Wm.).

Wright (John), P.O. Box 63, Guildford GU2 5BH.

Zomba Books, 165 High Road, NW10 2SG.

BOOKS PUBLISHED IN GREAT BRITAIN IN 1988

This table shows the books published in 1988 with the number of new editions, translations and limited editions. Books and pamphlets priced at less than 12p have been omitted, as are also all Government publications except the more important issued by H.M. Stationery Office.

Classification	Total	Reprints and New Editions	Translations	Limited Editions
Aeronautics	258	54	1	—
Agriculture and Forestry	457	91	6	—
Architecture	378	86	6	—
Art	1,703	292	58	4
Astronomy	136	27	—	—
Bibliography and Library Economy	811	124	2	2
Biography	2,131	594	79	8
Chemistry and Physics	839	163	10	—
Children's Books	5,063	1,203	151	7
Commerce	2,033	514	15	2
Customs, Costumes, Folklore	189	40	9	2
Domestic Science	830	220	9	—
Education	1,429	204	5	—
Engineering	1,604	354	13	—
Entertainment	668	150	37	—
Fiction	6,496	3,076	270	3
General	961	131	7	—
Geography and Archaeology	520	152	3	1
Geology and Meteorology	259	52	1	—
History	2,153	412	76	4
Humour	286	33	1	—
Industry	456	99	7	1
Language	747	198	8	—
Law and Public Administration	1,932	441	13	—
Literature	1,574	216	44	3
Mathematics	927	185	21	—
Medical Science	3,423	729	29	—
Military Science	316	100	6	—
Music	421	100	14	—
Natural Sciences	1,199	194	8	2
Occultism	413	108	12	—
Philosophy	752	141	45	—
Photography	204	24	5	2
Plays	280	67	36	3
Poetry	834	97	68	23
Political Science and Economics	4,307	778	68	1
Psychology	887	156	19	—
Religion and Theology	2,047	331	117	2
School Textbooks	2,007	332	16	—
Science, General	91	20	2	—
Sociology	1,284	168	27	—
Sports and Outdoor Games	888	200	7	1
Stockbreeding	317	74	5	—
Trade	472	123	—	1
Travel and Guidebooks	1,333	426	17	—
Wireless and Television	199	47	2	—
Totals	56,514	13,326	1,355	72

BOOK PRODUCTION AND BOOK EXPORTS

These figures for book production and exports are issued by the Department of Trade and Industry. The totals for the years 1973 to 1988 are shown below:

Year	Total value of books produced in U.K. £ million	Total value of books exported from U.K. £ million	Year	Total value of books produced in U.K. £ million	Total value of books exported from U.K. £ million
1973	230·1	95·9	1981	738·0	234·5
1974	281·5	119·4	1982	759·1	232·8
1975	342·4	138·6	1983	831·9	261·1
1976	408·3	175·8	1984	937·2	307·3
1977	467·0	203·9	1985	1044·0	340·9
1978	521·4	211·8	1986	1068·3	315·4
1979	580·4	215·3	1987	1191·2	342·2
1980	666·9	213·7	1988 (provisional)	1296·3	358·8

ANNUAL REFERENCE BOOKS

Advertiser's Annual.—East Grinstead House, East Grinstead, W. Sussex RH19 1XE. £55·00.

Allied Dunbar Investment Guide.—Fourth Avenue, Harlow, Essex CM19 5AA. £14·99.

Allied Dunbar Tax Guide.—Fourth Avenue, Harlow, Essex CM19 5AA. £13·99.

Annual Register of World Events.—Fourth Avenue, Harlow, Essex, CM19 5AA. £62·00.

Antique Shops of Britain, Guide to the.—5 Church Street, Woodbridge, Suffolk IP12 1DS. £9·95.

Art Sales Index.—1 Thames Street, Weybridge, Surrey KT1 8JG. £90·00.

Association of Consulting Engineers Who's Who & Year Book.—178–202 Great Portland Street, W1N 6NH. £31·00.

Astronomical Almanac.—H.M.S.O., 51 Nine Elms Lane, SW8 5DR. (Aug.) £14·50.

Automobile Year.—Unit 6, Pilton Estate, Croydon, Surrey CR0 3RY. £22·95.

Baily's Hunting Directory.—1 Lower Grosvenor Place, SW1W 0EL. (Oct.) £25·00.

Banker's Almanac & Year Book.—East Grinstead House, East Grinstead, W. Sussex RH19 1XE. (Feb.) 2 v. £135·00.

Benedictine Year Book.—Ampleforth Abbey, York YO6 4EN. £1·00.

Benn's Direct Marketing Services.—P.O. Box 20, Sovereign Way, Tonbridge, Kent TN9 1RQ. £75·00.

Benn's Hardware & Do-it-Yourself Buyer's Guide.— P.O. Box 20, Sovereign Way, Tonbridge, Kent TN9 1RQ. £32·00.

Benn's Media Directory.—P.O. Box 20, Sovereign Way, Tonbridge, Kent TN9 1RQ. 2v. ea £75·00.

Birmingham Post & Mail Year Book & Who's Who.— Colmore Circus, Birmingham B4 6AX. (July) £13·25.

Britain: An Official Handbook.—H.M.S.O., 51 Nine Elms Lane, SW8 5DR. (Jan.) £13.95.

Britannica Book of the Year.—Carew House, Station Approach, Wallington, Surrey SM6 0DA. (Apr.) £40.00.

British Clothing Industry Year Book.—Westbury House, 701–705 Warwick Road, Solihull B91 3DA. £30·00.

British Music Year Book.—241 Shaftesbury Avenue, WC2H 8EH. £10·95.

British Plastics & Rubber Directory.—Catalyst House, 159 Clapham High Street, SW4 7SS. £10·00.

Brown's Nautical Almanack.—4–10 Darnley Street, Glasgow G41 2SD. (Sept.) £24·00.

Building Societies Year Book.—7 Swallow Place, WIR 8AB. £34·00.

Buses Yearbook.—Coombelands House, Addlestone, Weybridge, Surrey KT15 1HY. £7·50.

Carpet Annual.—P.O. Box 20, Sovereign Way, Tonbridge, Kent TN9 1RQ. £58·00.

Catholic Directory.—18 Crosby Road North, Liverpool L22 4QF. £17·50.

Charities Digest.—501–505 Kingsland Road, E8 4AU. £8·95.

Chemical Industry Directory.—P.O. Box 20, Sovereign Way, Tonbridge, Kent TN9 1RQ. £72·00.

Chemist & Druggist Directory.—P.O. Box 20, Sovereign Way, Tonbridge, Kent TN9 1RQ. £65·00.

Christies' Review of the Season.—Musterlin House, Jordan Hill Road, Oxford OX2 8DP. (Dec.) £30·00.

Church of England Year Book.—Church House, Dean's Yard, Westminster, SW1P 3NZ. (Jan.) £14·50.

Church of Scotland Year Book.—121 George Street, Edinburgh EH2 4YN. (Apr.) £8·95.

City of London Directory & Livery Companies Guide.—Fairfax House, Causton Road, Colchester CO1 1RJ. £15·50.

Civil Aviation Review.—Coombelands House, Addlestone, Weybridge, Surrey KT15 1HY. £8·00.

Civil Service Year Book.—H.M.S.O., 51 Nine Elms Lane, SW8 5DR. (Feb.) £15·95.

Commonwealth Universities Year Book.—36 Gordon Square, WC1H 0PF. (Sept.) £98·00.

Commonwealth Year Book.—H.M.S.O., 51 Nine Elms Lane, SW8 5DR. (May) £18.50.

Computer Users' Year Book.—32–34 Broadwick Street, W1A 2HG. £87·50.

Concrete Year Book.—Thomas Telford House, 1 Heron Quay, E14 9XF. £40·00.

Coventry Evening Telegraph Year Book and Who's Who.—Coventry Newspapers Ltd., Corporation Street, Coventry CV1 1FP. (Nov.) £8·50.

Current Law Year Book.—11 New Fetter Lane, EC4P 4EE. £60·00.

Daily Mail Year Book.—New Carmelite House, Fleet Street, EC4Y 0JA. (Dec.) £3·95.

Diplomatic Service List.—H.M.S.O., 51 Nine Elms Lane, SW8 5DR. (April) £17·50.

Directory of Directors.—East Grinstead House, East Grinstead, W. Sussex RH19 1XE. (Apr.) £95·00.

Directory of Official Architecture & Planning.— Fourth Avenue, Harlow, Essex CM19 5AA. £45·00.

Directory of Opportunities for Graduates.—Newpoint House, St. James's Lane, N10 3DF. 7v. each £8·95.

Dod's Parliamentary Companion.—Hurst Green, Etchingham, E. Sussex TN19 7PX. £52·00.

Education Authorities' Directory and Annual.— Derby House, Bletchingley Road, Merstham, Surrey RH1 3DN. (Jan.) £40·00.

Education Year Book.—Fourth Avenue, Harlow, Essex CM19 5AA. £47·50.

Electrical & Electronics Trades Directory.—P.O. Box 26, Station House, Nightingale Road, Hitchin, Herts. SG5 1SA. (Feb.) £49·00.

Electricity Supply Handbook.—Quadrant House, The Quadrant, Sutton, Surrey SM2 5AS. (Feb.) £15·00.

Engineer Buyers' Guide.—40 Beresford Street, SE18 6BQ. £35·00.

Europa World Year Book.—18 Bedford Square, WC1B 3JN. 2 v. £180·00.

European Glass Directory & Buyer's Guide.—2 Queensway, Redhill, Surrey RH1 1QS. £39·00.

Fairplay World Shipping Year Book.—P.O. Box 96, Coulsdon, Surrey CR3 2TE. £33·00.

Farm and Garden Equipment Data Book.—63 Ulcombe Gardens, Canterbury, Kent CT2 7QZ. £10·95.

Flight International Directory of British Aviation.— P.O. Box 1315, Potters Bar, Herts. EN6 1PU. £30·00.

Food Industry Directory.—48 Poland St., WIV 4PP. £36·00.

Frozen & Chilled Foods Year Book.—2 Queensway, Redhill, Surrey RH1 1QS. £32·50.

Furnishing Trade, Directory to the.—P.O. Box 20, Sovereign Way, Tonbridge, Kent TN9 1RQ. £70·00.

Gas Industry Directory.—P.O. Box 20, Sovereign Way, Tonbridge, Kent TN9 1RQ. (Jan.) £55·00.

Gibbons' Stamps of the World Catalogue.—5 Parkside, Christchurch Road, Ringwood, Hants. BH24 3SH. (Oct.) 2v. each £14·50.

Good Food Guide.—P.O. Box 6, Mill Road, Dunton Green, Sevenoaks, Kent TN13 2XX. £10·95.

Good Hotel Guide.—P.O. Box 6, Mill Road, Dunton Green, Sevenoaks, Kent TN13 2XX. £11·95.

Government & Municipal Contractors Register.—55 High Street, Epsom, Surrey KT19 8DW. (Jan.) £30·00.

Guinness Book of Records.—33 London Road, Enfield EN2 6DJ. (Oct.) £10·95.

Historic Houses, Castles and Gardens in Great Britain and Ireland.—East Grinstead House, East Grinstead, W. Sussex RH19 1XA. (Jan.) £4·50.

Hollis Press and P.R. Annual.—Contact House, Lower Hampton Road, Sunbury-on-Thames, TW16 5HG. (Oct.) £59·50.

Hospitals & Health Services Yearbook & Directory of Hospital Suppliers.—75 Portland Place, W1N 4AN. £55·00.

Hotel, Restaurant & Catering Supplies.—55 High Street, Epsom, Surrey KT19 8DW. £30·00.

Hutchins' Priced Schedules.—33 Station Road, Bexhill-on-Sea, E. Sussex TN40 1RG. £26·00.

Independent Schools Year Book.—35 Bedford Row, WC1R 4JH. 2v. £13·95, £9·50.

Insurance Directory & Yearbook.—The Butts, Half Acre, Brentford TW8 8BN. £55·00.

International Paper Directory, Philips'.—P.O. Box 20, Sovereign Way, Tonbridge, Kent TN9 1RQ. £80.00.

International Yearbook & Statesman's Who's Who.—East Grinstead House, East Grinstead, W. Sussex RH19 1XE. (Apr.) £95·00.

Jane's All The World's Aircraft.—Sentinel House, 163 Brighton Road, Coulsdon, Surrey CR3 2NX. (Oct.) £100·00.

Jane's Armour & Artillery.—Sentinel House, 163 Brighton Road, Coulsdon, Surrey CR3 2NX. (Nov.) £85·00.

Jane's Containerization Direct.—Sentinel House, 163 Brighton Road, Coulsdon, Surrey CR3 2NX. (Nov.) £80·00.

Jane's Fighting Ships.—Sentinel House, 163 Brighton Road, Coulsdon, Surrey CR3 2NX. £100·00.

Jane's High Speed Marine Craft & Air Cushion Vehicles.—Sentinel House, 163 Brighton Road, Coulsdon, Surrey CR3 2NX. £85·00.

Jane's Infantry Weapons.—Sentinel House, 163 Brighton Road, Coulsdon, Surrey CR3 2NX. (Aug.) £95·00.

Jane's Weapon Systems.—Sentinel House, 163 Brighton Road, Coulsdon, Surrey CR3 2NX. £95·00.

Jane's World Railways.—Sentinel House, 163 Brighton Road, Coulsdon, Surrey CR3 2NX. £100·00.

Jewish Year Book.—25 Furnival Street, EC4A 1JT. (Jan.) £11·50.

Kelly's Business Directory.—East Grinstead House, East Grinstead, W. Sussex RH19 1XB. £110·00.

Kelly's Post Office London Business Directory.—East Grinstead House, East Grinstead, W. Sussex RH19 1XB. 2v, £125·00.

Kelly's U.K. Exports.—East Grinstead House, East Grinstead, W. Sussex RH19 1XB. £50·00.

Kempe's Engineers Year Book.—40 Beresford Street, SE18 6BQ. £75·00.

Kemp's International Film & T.V. Year Book.—Westbury House, 701–705 Warwick Road, Solihull B91 3DA. (May) £35·00.

Kemp's International Music & Recording Industry Year Book.—Westbury House, 701–705 Warwick Road, Solihull B91 3DA. £19·00.

Kemp's Property Industry Year Book.—Westbury House, 701–705 Warwick Road, Solihull B91 3DA. (Feb.) £17·50.

Kime's International Law Directory.—P.O. Box 67, Carlisle CA4 9DE. (June) £24·00.

Laxton's National Building Price Book.—East Grinstead House, East Grinstead, W. Sussex RH19 1XE. £51·00.

Library Association Yearbook.—7 Ridgmount Street, WC1E 7AE. (May) £25·00.

Lloyd's List of Shipowners.—71 Fenchurch Street, EC3M 4BS. (Sept.) £70·00.

Lloyd's Maritime Directory.—Sheepen Place, Colchester CO3 3LP. (Jan.) £95·00.

Lloyd's Nautical Year Book.—Sheepen Place, Colchester CO3 3LP. (Sept.) £19·50.

Lloyd's Register of Ships.—71 Fenchurch Street, EC3M 4BS. (July). £275·00.

London Chamber of Commerce and Industry Directory.—3rd Floor, Albany House, Hurst Street, Birmingham B5 4BD. (Sept.) £45·00.

Lyle's Official Antiques Review.—Glenmayne, Galashiels TD1 3NR. £14·95.

Lyle's Official Arts Review.—Glenmayne, Galashiels TD1 3NR. £14·95.

Macmillan & Silk Cut Nautical Almanack.—Little Essex Street, WC2R 3LF. £15·95.

Magistrates' Court Guide.—Borough Green, Sevenoaks, Kent TN15 8PH. £16·95.

Medical Annual.—P.O. Box 63, Westbury House, Bury Street, Guildford, Surrey GU2 5BH. (July). £29·50.

Medical Directory.—Fourth Avenue, Harlow, Essex CM19 5AA. (Apr.) 2v, £105·00.

Medical Register.—44 Hallam Street, W1N 6AE. (Mar.) 3v. £65·00.

Middle East & North Africa.—18 Bedford Square, WC1B 3JN. (Oct.) £80·00.

Military Aviation Review.—Coombelands House, Addlestone, Weybridge, Surrey KT15 1HY. £7·00.

Miller's Antiques Price Guide.—Sissinghurst Court, Sissinghurst, Kent TN17 2JA. £16·95.

Mining Annual Review.—P.O. Box 10, Edenbridge, Kent TN8 5NE. £35·00.

Mining International Year Book.—Fourth Avenue, Harlow, Essex CM19 5AA. (June) £90·00.

Motor Industry of Great Britain World Automotive Statistics.—Forbes House, Halkin Street, SW1X 7DS. (Oct.) £60·00.

Municipal Yearbook & Public Services Directory, 178 Great Portland Street, W1N 6NH. (Dec.) 2v. £75·00.

Museums and Galleries in Great Britain and Ireland.—East Grinstead House, East Grinstead, W. Sussex RH19 1XA. (Nov.) £3·50.

Nautical Almanac.—H.M.S.O., 51 Nine Elms Lane, SW8 5DR. (Oct.) £10·95.

Old Moore's Almanac.—Yeovil Road, Slough, Bucks. SL1 4JH. (July) £0·65.

Owen's Africa Business Directory.—18 Farndon Road, Oxford OX6 2RT. £65·00.

Owen's Arabian Year Book.—18 Farndon Road, Oxford OX6 2RT. £90·00.

Packaging Industry Directory.—P.O. Box 20, Sovereign Way, Tonbridge, Kent TN9 1RQ. £49·00.

Pears Cyclopedia.—27 Wright's Lane, W8 5TZ. £11·95.

Photography Year Book.—45 The Broadway, Tolworth, Surbiton, Surrey KT6 7DW. £16·95.

Polymers, Paint & Colour Year Book.—2 Queensway, Redhill, Surrey RH1 1QS. £36·50.

Ports of the World.—Sheepen Place, Colchester, Essex CO3 3LP. £80·00.

Printers' Year Book.—11 Bedford Row, WC1R 4DX. £40·00.

Printing Trades Directory.—P. O. Box 20, Sovereign Way, Tonbridge, Kent TN9 1RQ. £72·00.

Publishing, Directory of.—Artillery House, Artillery Row, SW1P 1RT. (Oct.) £26·00.

R.A.C. Continental Hotel Guide.—P.O. Box 100, R.A.C. House, Lansdowne Road., Croydon CR9 2JA. (Jan.) £5·95.

R.A.C. Hotel Guide.—P.O. Box 100, R.A.C. House, Lansdowne Road., Croydon CR9 2JA. (Apr.) £8·95.

R.U.S.I. & Brassey's Defence Year Book.—Heading-ton Hill Hall, Oxford OX3 0BW. £35·00.

Railway Directory & Year Book.—Quadrant House, The Quadrant, Sutton, Surrey SM2 5AS. (Dec.) £34·00.

Railway World Year Book.—Coombelands House, Addlestone, Weybridge, Surrey KT15 1HY. £8·00.

Reed's Nautical Almanac & Tide Tables.—80 Coombe Road, New Malden, Surrey KT3 4QS. (Oct.) £15·95.

RIBA Directory of Practices.—Royal Institute of British Architects, 39 Moreland Street, EC1V 8BB. (Oct.) £35·00.

Rothmans Football Year Book.—Headway House, 66–73 Shoe Lane, EC4P 4AB. (Aug.) £11.95.

Royal Society Year Book.—6 Carlton House Terrace, SW1Y 5AG. (Feb.) £12·50.

Ruff's Guide to the Turf & Sporting Life Annual.—P.O. Box 54, Desborough, Northants. NN14 2LU. (Dec.) £50·00.

Salvation Army Year Book.—117–121 Judd Street, WC1H 9NN. (Apr.) £7·95, £3·95.

Scottish Current Law Year Book.—2 St. Giles Street, Edinburgh EH1 1PU. £115·00.

Scottish Law Directory.—59 George Street, Edinburgh EH2 2LQ. £25·00.

Screen International Film & Television Year Book.—6 Great Chapel Street, W1V 3AG £31·00.

Screen World.—Brookmount House, 62–65 Chandos Place, WC1N 4NW. £16·95.

Sell's Aerospace Europe.—55 High Street, Epsom, Surrey KT19 8DW. £40·00.

Sell's British Exporters.—55 High Street, Epsom, Surrey KT19 8DW. £30·00.

Sell's Building Index.—55 High Street, Epsom, Surrey KT19 8DW. £30·00.

Sell's Directory of Products and Services.—55 High Street, Epsom, Surrey KT19 8DW. (July) £40·00.

Sell's Health Service Buyers Guide.—55 High Street, Epsom, Surrey KT19 8DW. £30·00.

Sheet Metal Industries Year Book.—2 Queensway, Redhill, Surrey RH1 1QS. £39·00.

Shipowners, Shipbuilders & Marine Engineers, Directory of.—Quadrant House, The Quadrant, Sutton, Surrey SM2 5AS. £50·00.

Solicitors & Barristers Directory.—P.O. Box 55, Oyez House, 27 Crimscott Street, SE1 5TS. £30·00.

Specification.—9–13 Queen Anne's Gate, SW1H 9BY. (May) 6v. £52·00.

Spon's Architects' & Builders' Price Book.—11 New Fetter Lane, EC4P 4EE. £37·50.

Spon's Mechanical & Electrical Services Prices Book.—11 New Fetter Lane, EC4P 4EE. £40·00.

Statesman's Yearbook.—4 Little Essex Street, WC2R 3LF. (Aug.) £29·95.

Stock Exchange Official Year Book.—4 Little Essex Street, WC2R 3LF. £125·00.

Stone's Justices' Manual.—Borough Green, Sevenoaks, Kent TN15 8PH. 3v. (May) £120·00.

Stores, Shops, Hypermarkets Retail Directory.—48 Poland Street, W1V 4PP. £86·00.

Tanker Register.—12 Camomile Street, EC3A 7BP. (May) £110·00.

Timber Trades Journal Telephone Address Book.—Sovereign Way, Tonbridge, Kent TN9 1RQ. £37·00.

Training Directory.—120 Pentonville Road, N1 9JN. £20·00.

Travel Trade Directory.—40 Beresford Street, SE18 6BQ. (July) £35·00.

U.K. Kompass Register of British Industry & Commerce.—East Grinstead House, East Grinstead, W. Sussex RH19 1XD. v. 1–3, £260·00, v. 4, £110·00.

Unit Trust Year Book.—7th Floor, 50–64 Broadway, SW1H 0DB. (Mar.) £37·50.

United Reformed Church Year Book.—86 Tavistock Place, WC1H 9RT. (Sept.) £7·00.

Veterinary Annual.—Borough Green, Sevenoaks, Kent TN15 8PH. £40·00.

Water Services Year Book.—2 Queensway, Redhill, Surrey RH1 1QS. (Oct.) £33·00.

Whitaker's Almanack.—12 Dyott Street, WC1A 1DF. (Nov.) £29·95, £17·95, £9·50.

Whitaker's Books in Print.—12 Dyott Street, WC1A 1DF. (Sept.) £128·00.

Whitaker's Publishers in the United Kingdom and their Addresses.—12 Dyott Street, WC1A 1DF. (Mar.) £4·50.

Who Owns Whom?.—26–32 Clifton Street, EC2P 2LY. 2v. £189·00.

Who's Who.—35 Bedford Row, WC1R 4JH. £60·00.

Who's Who, International.—18 Bedford Square, WC1R 4JH. (Sept.) £85·00.

Willing's Press Guide.—East Grinstead House, East Grinstead, W. Sussex RH19 1XE. (Feb.) £54·00.

Wisden Cricketers' Almanack.—13–14 Eldon Way, Lineside Estate, Littlehampton, W. Sussex BN17 7HE. £16·95; £14·95.

World Advertising Review.—Artillery House, Artillery Row, SW1P 1RT. £40·00.

World Hotel Directory.—Fourth Avenue, Harlow, Essex CM19 5AA. £55·00.

World Insurance Year Book.—Fourth Avenue, Harlow, Essex CM19 5AA. £85.00.

World of Learning.—18 Bedford Square, WC1B 3JN. (Jan.) 2v. £110·00.

Writers' & Artists' Year Book.—35 Bedford Row, WC1R 4JH. (Jan.) £6·95.

SYMBOLS FOR CORRECTING PROOFS

Supplied by William Clowes Ltd, Beccles, Suffolk, printers of "Whitaker's Almanack"

Letter(s) or word(s) requiring alteration should be struck through IN INK in the text and the substitution should be written in the nearest margin followed by / (the symbol used to denote that the marginal mark is concluded). Insertions should be indicated by / or ∧ at the conclusion of the marginal mark *and* at the desired place in the text.

Alteration required	Mark in margin	Mark in text	Alteration required	Mark in margin	Mark in text
Delete (take out)	ℛ or ℛ	/ or Vertical stroke to delete one or two letters; horizontal line to delete more	Take letter(s) or word(s) from beginning of one line to end of preceding line	*back* or *take back*	
Delete and close up	ℛ or ℛ	Strike out letter(s) not required and add "close up" mark above and below	Begin a new paragraph	*n. p.*	before first word of new paragraph
Close up: delete space between letters	⌢	⌢ linking letters or words	No new para. here or run on previous matter with later matter	*run on*	between paras. or other matter
Use ligature (fi, fl, ffl, etc.) or diphthong (æ, œ)	*enclosing ligature or diphthong required*	enclosing letters to be altered	Spell out in full the abbreviation, contraction, or figure	*spell out*	Encircle, words, etc., or figures concerned
Insert space between letters or words	#		Insert omitted portion of copy	*out - see copy*	Attach the relevant copy to the proof, indicating omitted portion
Leave as printed (i.e. a cancellation of previous marking)	*stet*	•••• under letter(s) or word(s) crossed out but to be retained	Inserted or substituted letter(s), figure(s), or sign(s) under which this is placed to be superscript (i.e. high alignment)[1]	⟋ (see footnote)	∧ for insertions For substitutions encircle letter(s). figure(s). or sign(s) to be altered
Invert type (of letter(s) upside down)	↺	Encircle letter(s) to be altered	Inserted or substituted letter(s), figure(s), or sign(s) over which this is placed to be subscript (low alignment)[2]	⟋ (see footnote)	∧ for insertions For substitutions encircle letter(s), figure(s), etc., to be altered
"Battered" letter(s) to be replaced by similar but undamaged characters	✕	Encircle letter(s) or word(s) to be replaced and write the correct letter(s) in the margin	Change to lower case	*l. c.*	Encircle letter(s) to be altered
Push down space or "high" letter(s) or word(s)	⊥	Encircle space, letter(s), or word(s) affected	Replace "wrong fount" by letter(s) of correct fount	*w. f.*	Encircle letter(s) or word(s) to be altered
Transpose	*tr.* or *trs.*	between letters or words, numbered when necessary	Change to capital letters	*caps.*	≡ under letter(s) or word(s) to be altered
Take letter(s) or word(s) from end of one line to beginning of next line	*take over* or *over*		Change to small capitals	*s. c.*	≡ under letter(s) or word(s) to be altered

⟍ indicates a superior (superscript) figure one   ⟋ indicates an inferior (subscript) figure two

Alteration required	Mark in margin	Mark in text	Alteration required	Mark in margin	Mark in text
Use capital letters for initial letter(s) (as desired) and small capitals for rest of word(s)	*caps* & *s.c.*	under initial letter(s) and under the remainder of the word(s)	Move lines to the left		at right side of group of lines to be moved (indicating approx. position)
Change to bold type	*bold* ~~~	Draw wavy line under letter(s) or word(s) to be altered	Move portion of matter so that it is positioned as indicated	[ ]	at limits of required position
Change to roman type	*rom.*	Encircle letter(s) or word(s) to be altered	Raise lines	*raise* ↑	over lines to be raised
Change to italic type	*italic*	Draw this straight line under letter(s) or word(s) to be altered	Lower lines	*lower* ↓	under lines to be lowered
			Correct the vertical alignment	‖ ‖	
Letter(s) or word(s) to be underlined	*underline*	under letter(s), word(s), etc., to be underlined	Straighten lines	═ ═	through lines to be straightened
Equalize space between words	*eq. #*	between words	Insert parentheses (round-shaped brackets)	(/) or (/)/	
Reduce space	*less #*	between words			
Space to be inserted between lines or paragraphs	#>	*Amount of space should be indicated*	Insert [square] brackets	[/] or [/]/	
To be placed in centre of line, etc.	*centre*	Position to be indicated by	Insert hyphen	/-/	
Indent one en (approx. space occupied by n of type in use)	*en*	indicating approximate position	Insert en (= half-em) rule (*see above*)	*en*/	
Indent one em (approx. space occupied by M of type in use)	*em*	Ditto	Insert one-em rule (*see above*)	*em*/	
Indent two ems (approx. space occupied by MM of type in use)		Ditto	Insert two-em rule (*see above*)	*2em*/	
Move to the left		Ditto	Insert apostrophe	⸓	
Move to the right		Ditto	Insert single quotation marks	⸌ ⸍	
			Insert double quotation marks	⸌⸌ ⸍⸍	
Move lines to the right	[	at left side of group of lines to be moved (indicating approx. position)	Insert ellipsis	.../	
			Insert leader (*visual guide to alignment in contents pages, etc.*)	••• •• •	(*three, two, or one dot*)
			Insert oblique stroke	(/)	

Punctuation

PRINCIPAL LONDON CLUBS

ALPINE (1857), 74 South Audley Street, W1Y 5FF.—*Hon. Sec.*, S. W. Town.

AMERICAN (1919), 95 Piccadilly, W1V 0BS.—*Sec.*, A. M. Cook.

AMERICAN WOMEN'S (1899), 95 Piccadilly, W1V 0BS.—*Sec.*, Ms. M. Dougan.

ANGLO-BELGIAN (1955), 60 Knightsbridge, SW1X 7LF.—*Hon. Sec.*, Baron de Gerlache de Gomery, L.V.O.

ARMY AND NAVY (1837), 36–39 Pall Mall, SW1Y 5JN.—*Sec.*, Col. D. O. O'Reilly.

ARTS (1863), 40 Dover Street, W1X 3RB.—*Sec.*, Lt.-Col. C. Miers.

ARTS THEATRE (1927), 7 Great Newport Street, WC2.—*Sec.*, Miss C. Dowling.

THE ATHENAEUM (1824), 107 Pall Mall, SW1Y 5ER.—*Sec.*, R. R. T. Smith.

AUTHORS' (1892), 40 Dover Street, W1X 3RB.—*Sec.*, Mrs. H. Ridgway.

BEEFSTEAK (1876), 9 Irving Street, WC2H 7AT.—*Sec.*, E. Pool, M.C.

BOODLE'S (1762), 28 St. James's Street, SW1A 1HJ.—*Sec.*, R. J. Edmonds.

BROOKS'S (1764), St. James's Street, SW1A 1LN.—*Sec.*, M. A. Roberts.

BUCK'S (1919), 18 Clifford Street, W1X 1RG.—*Sec.*, R. C. Eggleshaw.

CALEDONIAN (1891), 9 Halkin Street, SW1X 7DR.—*Sec.*, P. J. Varney.

CANNING (1910), 42 Half Moon Street, W1Y 8DS.—*Sec.*, T. M. Harrington.

CARLTON (1832), 69 St. James's Street, SW1A 1PJ.—*Sec.*, R. N. Linsley.

CAVALRY AND GUARDS (1893), 127 Piccadilly, W1V 0PX.—*Sec.*, L. D. de Pinna.

CHALLONER (1949), 59–61 Pont Street, SW1 0BG—*Gen. Manager*, G. W. Jago.

CHELSEA ARTS (1891), 143 Old Church Street, SW3 6EB.—*Sec.*, Hon. D. Winterbottom.

CITY LIVERY (1914), Sion College, Victoria Embankment, EC4Y 0DN.—*Hon. Sec.*, B. L. Morgan, C.B.E.

CITY OF LONDON (1832), 19 Old Broad Street, EC2N 1DS.—*Hon. Sec.*, G. S. Chisholm.

CITY UNIVERSITY (1895), 50 Cornhill, EC3V 3PD.—*Sec.*, Miss R. C. Graham.

EAST INDIA (1849), 16 St. James's Square, SW1Y 4LH.—*Sec.*, J. G. F. Stoy.

FARMERS (1842), 3 Whitehall Court, SW1A 2EL.—*Sec.*, Lt.-Col. G. B. Murray.

FLYFISHERS' (1884), 24a Old Burlington Street, W1X 1RG.—*Sec.*, Cdr. N. T. Fuller (*retd.*).

GARRICK (1831), 15 Garrick Street, WC2E 9AY.—*Sec.*, M. J. Harvey.

GREEN ROOM (1877), 9 Adam Street, WC2N 6AA.—*Sec.*, J. Booth.

GRESHAM (1843), 15 Abchurch Lane, EC4N 7BB.—*Sec.*, Mrs. J. S. Downing.

GROUCHO (1985), 45 Dean Street, W1V 5AP.—*Sec.*, Ms. A. Howarth.

HURLINGHAM (1869), Ranelagh Gardens, SW6 3PR.—*Sec.*, P. H. Covell.

KEMPTON (1878), Kempton Park Racecourse, Sunbury-on-Thames, Middx., TW16 5AQ.—*Sec.*, Miss D. Taylor.

KENNEL (1873), 1 Clarges Street, W1Y 8AB.—*Sec.*, Maj.-Gen. M. H. Sinnatt, C.B.

LANSDOWNE (1934), 9 Fitzmaurice Place, W1X 6JD.—*Sec.*, Lt.-Cdr. T. P. Havers (*retd.*).

LONDON ROWING (1856), Embankment, Putney, SW15 1LB.—*Hon. Sec.*, N. A. Smith.

LONDON THAMES FENCING (1848), 83 Perham Road, W14 9SY.—*Hon. Sec.*, G. Morrison.

M.C.C. (MARYLEBONE CRICKET CLUB) (1787), Lord's Cricket Ground, NW8 8QN.—*Sec.*, Lt.-Col. J. R. Stephenson, O.B.E.

MINING (1910), 3 London Wall Buildings, EC2.—*Sec.*, Miss P. Warner.

NATIONAL (1845), c/o Carlton Club (*q.v.*).—*Sec.*, I. E. Nash.

NATIONAL LIBERAL (1882), Whitehall Place, SW1A 2HE.—*Sec.*, G. Snell.

NAVAL (1946), 38 Hill Street, W1X 8DP.—*Gen. Sec.*, Cdr. C. R. Parkes, R.D.

NAVAL AND MILITARY (1862), 94 Piccadilly, W1V 0BP.—*Gen. Manager*, A. Hickey.

NEW CAVENDISH (1984), (formerly V.A.D.), 44 Great Cumberland Place, W1H 8BS.—*Sec.*, Miss H. Bateman.

ORIENTAL (1824), Stratford House, Stratford Place, W1N 0ES.—*Sec.*, S. C. Doble.

PORTLAND (1816), 42 Half Moon Street, W1Y 7RD.—*Sec.*, R. B. Little.

PRATT'S (1841), 14 Park Place, SW1A 1LP.—*Sec.*, Capt. P. W. E. Parry, M.B.E.

QUEEN'S (1886), Palliser Road, W14 9EQ.—*Sec.*, J. A. S. Edwardes.

RAILWAY (1899), Keen House, 4 Calshot Street, N1 9DA.—*Hon. Sec.*, C. F. Wells.

REFORM (1836), 104–105 Pall Mall, SW1Y 5EW.—*Sec.*, R. A. M. Forrest.

ROEHAMPTON (1901), Roehampton Lane, SW15 5LR.—*Sec.*, R. W. Varley.

ROYAL AIR FORCE (1918), 128 Piccadilly, W1V 0PY.—*Sec.*, Sqn. Ldr. J. Swaffield.

ROYAL AUTOMOBILE (1897), 89–91 Pall Mall, SW1Y 5HS.—*Sec.*, J. N. Cranfield.

ROYAL COMMONWEALTH SOCIETY (1868), 18 Northumberland Avenue, WC2N 5BJ.—*Sec. Gen.*, Sir Michael Scott, K.C.V.O., C.M.G.

ROYAL OCEAN RACING (1925), 20 St. James's Place, SW1A 1NN.—*Sec.*, E. A. Green.

ROYAL OVER-SEAS LEAGUE (1910), Over-Seas House, Park Place, St. James's Street, SW1A 1LR.—*Gen. Manager*, R. F. Newell.

ROYAL THAMES YACHT (1775), 60 Knightsbridge, SW1X 7LF.—*Sec.*, Capt. A. R. Ward, C.B.E., R.N.

ST. STEPHEN'S CONSTITUTIONAL (1870), 34 Queen Anne's Gate, SW1H 9AB.—*Sec.*, L. D. Mawby.

SAVAGE (1857), 9 Fitzmaurice Place, W1X 5DE.—*Hon. Sec.*, D. Coomber, O.B.E.

SAVILE (1868), 69 Brook Street, W1Y 2ER.—*Sec.*, P. Aldersley.

SKI CLUB OF GREAT BRITAIN (1903), 118 Eaton Square, SW1W 9AF.—*Sec.*, Air Vice-Marshal J. M. Jones, C.B. (*retd.*).

THAMES ROWING (1860), Embankment, Putney, SW15 1LB.—*Hon. Sec.*, F. S. Beardmore.

TRAVELLERS' (1819), 106 Pall Mall, SW1Y 5EP.—*Sec.*, M. S. Allcock.

TURF (1868), 5 Carlton House Terrace, SW1Y 5AQ.—*Sec.*, Col. J. G. B. Rigby, O.B.E.

UNITED NURSING SERVICES (1921), 40 South Street, W1.—*Sec.*, W. Oakes.

UNITED OXFORD AND CAMBRIDGE UNIVERSITY (1972), 71 Pall Mall, SW1Y 5HD.—*Gen. Sec.*, D. McDougall.

UNIVERSITY WOMEN'S (1886), 2 Audley Square, W1Y 6DB.—*Sec.*, Mrs. P. J. Gray.

VICTORIA (1863), 1 North Court, Great Peter Street, SW1P 3LL.—*Sec.*, Ms. H. David.

VICTORY SERVICES (1907), 63–79 Seymour Street, W2 2HL.—*Gen. Manager*, Capt. G. F. Taylor.

WHITE'S (1693), 37–38 St. James's Street, SW1A 1JG.—*Sec.*, W. H. West.

WIG AND PEN (1908), 229–230 Strand, WC2R 1BA.—*Sec.*, J. Reynolds.

PRINCIPAL CLUBS OUTSIDE LONDON

Aldershot.—ROYAL ALDERSHOT OFFICERS CLUB (1856), Farnborough Road, Aldershot, Hants.—*Sec.*, Lt. Col. A. F. J. Channon, M.B.E.

Bath.—BATH AND COUNTY CLUB (1865), Queens Parade, Bath, BA1 2NJ.—*Sec.*, Mrs. G. M. Jones.

Birmingham.—BIRMINGHAM CLUB (1872), Winston Churchill House, 8 Ethel Street, Birmingham B2 4BG.—*Hon. Sec.*, T. R. Pepper.

ST. PAUL'S CLUB (1859), 34 St. Paul's Square, Birmingham B3 1QZ.—*Hon. Sec.*, J. S. Scott, T.D.

Bishop Auckland.—THE CLUB (1868), 1 Victoria Avenue, Bishop Auckland, Co. Durham DL14 7JH.—*Hon. Sec.*, L. Cooke.

Bristol.—BEAUFORT CLUB (1885), Marsh Street, Bristol BS1 4BG.—*Sec.*, M. Lansdell.

CLIFTON CLUB (1882), 22 The Mall, Clifton, Bristol BS8 4DS.—*Hon. Sec.*, H. B. Peckham.

Cambridge.—AMATEUR DRAMATIC CLUB (1855), A.D.C. Theatre, Park Street, Cambridge.—*Hon. Sec.*, B. Ball.

HAWKS CLUB (1874).—*Pres.*, M. Risman, Emmanuel College, Cambridge.

THE UNION (1815), Bridge Street, Cambridge CB2 1UB.—*Chief Clerk*, B. Thoday.

UNIVERSITY PITT CLUB (1835), Jesus Lane, Cambridge CB5 8BA.—*Joint Hon. Secs.*, S. d'O. Duckworth; G. Rowan-Hamilton.

Canterbury.—KENT AND CANTERBURY CLUB (1868), 17 Old Dover Road, Canterbury CT1 3JB.—*Sec.*, F. T. Bedingham.

Cheltenham.—NEW CLUB (1874), Montpellier Parade, Cheltenham GL50 1UD.—*Hon. Sec.*, J. A. Warhurst, O.B.E.

Chester.—CITY CLUB (1807), St. Peter's Churchyard, Chester CH1 2AG.—*Sec.*, C. Hodkinson.

Chichester.—WEST SUSSEX COUNTY CLUB (1872), 5 Stirling Road, Chichester, W. Sussex PO19 2EW.—*Sec.*, Mrs. P. Green.

Colchester.—THE CLUB (1874), 3–5 Culver Street West, Colchester, Essex.—*Sec.*, N. Duncan.

Devizes.—DEVIZES AND DISTRICT CLUB (1932), 27 St. John Street, Devizes, Wilts. SN10 1BN.—*Sec.*, D. J. J. Cox.

Durham.—COUNTY CLUB (1890), 52 Old Elvet, Durham.—*Sec.*, Mrs. C. Arnot.

DURHAM UNION SOCIETY (1842), North Bailey Club, 24 North Bailey, Durham.—*Sec.*, Mrs. E. M. Hardcastle.

Eastbourne.—DEVONSHIRE CLUB (1872), Hartington Place, Eastbourne, Sussex BN21 3RN.—*Hon. Sec.*, D. G. Matthews.

Exeter.—EXETER AND COUNTY CLUB (1871), 5 Cathedral Close, Exeter EX1 1EZ.—*Sec.*, Miss M. J. Toogood.

Guildford.—COUNTY CLUB, 158 High Street, Guildford GU1 3HF.—*Hon. Sec.*, R. W. D. Hemingway.

Harrogate.—THE CLUB (1857), 36 Victoria Avenue, Harrogate, N. Yorks.—*Hon. Sec.*, C. L. Leslie.

Henley-on-Thames.—LEANDER CLUB (1818), Henley-on-Thames, Oxon. RG9 2LP.—*Hon. Sec.*, K. Hylton-Smith.

PHYLLIS COURT CLUB (1906), Marlow Road, Henley, Oxon. RG9 2HT.—*Sec.*, R. I. Bulloch.

Hove.—HOVE CLUB (1882), 28 Fourth Avenue, Hove, E. Sussex BN3 2PJ.—*Sec.*, Sqn. Ldr. G. A. Inverarity, D.F.C.

Leamington.—TENNIS COURT CLUB (1846), 50 Bedford Street, Leamington, Warks. CV32 5DT.—*Hon. Sec.*, O. D. R. Dixon.

Leeds.—LEEDS CLUB (1850), 3 Albion Place, Leeds LS1 6JL.—*Administrator*, Mrs. D. Kavanagh.

Leicester.—LEICESTERSHIRE CLUB (1873), 9 Welford Place, Leicester LE1 6ZH.—*Manager*, J. A. Evans.

Liverpool.—THE ATHENAEUM (1797), Church Alley, Liverpool L1 3DD.—*Hon. Sec.*, S. Christie.

Manchester.—ST. JAMES'S CLUB, St. James's House, Charlotte Street, Manchester M1 4DZ.—*Hon. Sec.*, M. Deeble-Rogers.

Newcastle upon Tyne.—NORTHERN CONSTITUTIONAL CLUB (1882), 37 Pilgrim Street, Newcastle upon Tyne NE1 6QE.—*Hon. Sec.*, J. L. Browne.

Northampton.—NORTHAMPTON AND COUNTY CLUB (1873), George Row, Northampton NN1 1DF.—*Sec.*, Maj. G. D. Denholm, B.E.M.(retd.).

Norwich.—NORFOLK CLUB (1770), 17 Upper King Street, Norwich NR3 1RB.—*Sec.*, A. J. M. Williamson.

Nottingham.—NOTTINGHAM AND NOTTS. UNITED SERVICES CLUB (1920), Newdigate House, Castle Gate, Nottingham NG1 6AF.—*Hon. Sec.*, A. C. Ready.

Oxford.—FREWEN CLUB (1869), 98 St. Aldate's, Oxford OX1 1BT.—*Hon. Sec.*, W. H. Miller, B.E.M.

OXFORD UNION SOCIETY (1823), Frewin Court, Oxford OX1 3JB.—*Sec.*, S. Green.

VINCENT'S CLUB (1863), 1A King Edward Street, Oxford OX1 4HS.—*Sec.*, T. S. Bishop.

Paignton.—PAIGNTON CLUB (1882), The Esplanade, Paignton, Devon TQ4 6ED.—*Hon. Sec.* P. Grafton.

Peterborough.—CITY AND COUNTIES CLUB (1867), Priestgate, Peterborough PE6 7LT.—*Sec.*, J. R. Fillingham.

Reading.—BERKSHIRE ATHENAEUM CLUB (1972), 53 Blagrave Street, Reading, Berks.—*Hon. Sec.*, W. J. Stuck.

Rye.—DORMY HOUSE CLUB (1896), Rye, E. Sussex TN31 7LD.—*Hon. Sec.*, M. J. O'Brien.

Shrewsbury.—SALOP CLUB (1974), The Old House, Dogpole, Shrewsbury SY1 1EP.—*Hon. Sec.*, T. P. Roberts.

Teddington.—ROYAL CANOE CLUB (1866), Trowlock Island, Teddington, Middx. TW11 9QZ.—*Hon. Sec.*, Mrs. J. Williams.

Worcester.—UNION AND COUNTY CLUB (1861), 40 Foregate Street, Worcester.—*Sec.*, M. G. Maton.

York.—YORKSHIRE CLUB (1839), 17 Museum Street, York YO1 2DW.—*Hon. Sec.*, D. E. Gabbitas.

Wales

Cardiff.—CARDIFF AND COUNTY CLUB (1866), Westgate Street, Cardiff CF1 1DA.—*Hon. Sec.*, A. G. Robertson.

Scotland

Ayr.—COUNTY CLUB (1872), Savoy Park Hotel, Ayr KA7 2XA.—*Hon. Sec.*, J. K. Templeton.

Edinburgh.—CALEDONIAN CLUB (1825), 32 Abercromby Place, Edinburgh EH3 6QE.—*Sec.*, I. Harvey.

NEW CLUB (1787), 86 Princes Street, Edinburgh EH2 2BB.—*Sec.*, A. D. Orr Ewing.

Glasgow.—GLASGOW ART CLUB (1867), 185 Bath Street, Glasgow G2 4HU.—*Sec.*, L. J. McIntyre.

ROYAL SCOTTISH AUTOMOBILE CLUB (1899), 11 Blythswood Square, Glasgow G2 4AG.—*Sec.*, H. Dewar.

WESTERN CLUB (1825), 32 Royal Exchange Square, Glasgow G1 3AB.—*Sec.*, D. H. Gifford.

Northern Ireland

Belfast.—ULSTER REFORM CLUB (1885), 4 Royal Avenue, Belfast BT1 1DA.—*Sec.*, Miss M. P. Mackintosh.

Enniskillen.—FERMANAGH COUNTY CLUB (1883), 20 Church Street, Enniskillen, N. Ireland BT74 6DF.—*Hon. Sec.*, P. Little.

Channel Islands

Jersey.—VICTORIA CLUB (1853), Beresford Street, St. Helier, Jersey.—*Sec.*, Gp. Capt. J. W. E. Holmes, D.F.C., A.F.C.

YACHT CLUBS

Bembridge.—BEMBRIDGE SAILING CLUB (1886), Embankment Road, Bembridge, I.o.W., PO35 5NR.—*Sec.*, N. McLean.

Birkenhead.—ROYAL MERSEY YACHT CLUB (1844), Bedford Road East, Rock Ferry, Birkenhead, Merseyside L42 1LS.—*Hon. Sec.*, C. P. Broad.

Bridlington.—ROYAL YORKSHIRE YACHT CLUB (1847), 1 Windsor Crescent, Bridlington, N. Humberside YO15 3HX.—*Sec.*, I. Harness.

Burnham-on-Crouch.—ROYAL CORINTHIAN YACHT CLUB (1872), Burnham-on-Crouch, Essex CM0 8AX.—*Sec.*, N. R. Wynn.

Cowes.—ROYAL YACHT SQUADRON (1815), The Castle, Cowes, I.o.W., PO31 7QT.—*Sec.*, Maj. R. P. Rising, R.M.

ROYAL LONDON YACHT CLUB (1838), The Parade, Cowes, I. o. W., PO31 7QS.—*Sec.*, M. White.

Dover.—ROYAL CINQUE PORTS YACHT CLUB (1872), 5 Waterloo Crescent, Dover, Kent CT16 1LA.—*Sec.*, G. M. Cartwright.

Fishbourne.—ROYAL VICTORIA YACHT CLUB (1844), Fishbourne Lane, Ryde, I. o. W., PO33 4EU.—*Hon. Sec.*, R. M. Young.

Fowey.—ROYAL FOWEY YACHT CLUB (1881), Fowey, Cornwall PL23 1BH.—*Hon. Sec.*, E. P. Warren.

Harwich.—ROYAL HARWICH YACHT CLUB (1843), Woolverstone, Ipswich IP9 1AT.—*Sec.*, D. E. Gooch.

Kingswear.—ROYAL DART YACHT CLUB (1866), Priory Street, Kingswear, Dartmouth, Devon TQ6 0AB.—*Hon. Sec.*, P. J. C. Youd.

Leigh-on-Sea.—ESSEX YACHT CLUB (1890), H.Q.S. Bembridge, Foreshore, Leigh-on-Sea, Essex.—*Hon. Sec.*, A. Manning.

London.—THE CRUISING ASSOCIATION (1908), Ivory House, St. Katharine Dock, E1 9AT.—*Gen. Sec.*, Mrs. L. Hammett.

ROYAL CRUISING CLUB (1880), c/o Naval and Military Club, 42 Half Moon Street, W1Y 8DS.—*Hon. Sec.*, C. Buckley.

Lowestoft.—ROYAL NORFOLK AND SUFFOLK YACHT CLUB (1859), Royal Plain, Lowestoft, Suffolk NR33 0AQ.—*Sec.*, Lt.-Cdr. M. Dowsett (*retd.*).

Lymington.—ROYAL LYMINGTON YACHT CLUB (1922), Bath Road, Lymington, Hants. SO41 9SE.—*Sec.*, Gp. Capt. J. D. Hutchinson (*retd.*).

Plymouth.—ROYAL WESTERN YACHT CLUB (1827), 9 Grand Parade, Plymouth PL1 3DG.—*Sec.*, A. Miller.

ROYAL PLYMOUTH CORINTHIAN YACHT CLUB (1877), Madeira Road, Plymouth PL1 2NY.—*Hon. Sec.*, V. J. de Boo.

Poole.—EAST DORSET SAILING CLUB (1875), 352 Sandbanks Road, Poole, Dorset BH14 8HY.—*Hon. Sec.*, R. W. Howard.

PARKSTONE YACHT CLUB (1895), Pearce Avenue, Parkstone, Poole, Dorset BH14 8EH.—*Sec.*, J. Shore.

POOLE HARBOUR YACHT CLUB (1949), 38 Salterns Way, Lilliput, Poole, Dorset BH14 8JR.—*Sec.*, J. N. J. Smith.

POOLE YACHT CLUB (1865), New Harbour Road West, Hamworthy, Poole, Dorset BH15 4AQ.—*Sec.*, Miss L. Clark.

Portsmouth.—ROYAL NAVAL CLUB AND ROYAL ALBERT YACHT CLUB (1867), 17 Pembroke Road, Portsmouth PO1 2NT.—*Sec.*, Cdr. T. C. C. Greaves, O.B.E. (*retd.*).

Ramsgate.—ROYAL TEMPLE YACHT CLUB (1857), 6 Westcliff Mansions, Ramsgate, Kent CT11 9HY.—*Hon. Sec.*, G. F. Randell.

Southampton.—ROYAL AIR FORCE YACHT CLUB (1932), Riverside House, Rope Walk, Hamble, Southampton SO3 5HD.—*Sec.*, Miss R. M. Clements.

ROYAL SOUTHERN YACHT CLUB (1837), Hamble, Southampton SO3 5HB.—*Sec.*, C. R. Mannall.

Southend.—ALEXANDRA YACHT CLUB (1873), Clifton Terrace, Southend-on-Sea SS1 1DT.—*Hon. Sec.*, D. C. Osborn.

Westcliff-on-Sea.—THAMES ESTUARY YACHT CLUB (1895), 3 The Leas, Westcliff-on-Sea, Essex SS0 7ST.—*Hon. Sec.*, J. G. Davison (until Dec. 1989).

Weymouth.—ROYAL DORSET YACHT CLUB (1875), 11 Custom House Quay, Weymouth, Dorset DT4 8BG.—*Sec.*, Mrs. J. B. Cannon.

Windermere.—ROYAL WINDERMERE YACHT CLUB (1860), Fallbarrow Road, Bowness-on-Windermere, Cumbria LA23 3DJ.—*Hon. Sec.*, M. C. Bentley.

Yarmouth.—ROYAL SOLENT YACHT CLUB (1878), Yarmouth, I. o. W., PO41 0NS.—*Admin. Sec.*, Mrs. S. Tribe.

Wales

Beaumaris.—ROYAL ANGLESEY YACHT CLUB (1802), 6–7 Green Edge, Beaumaris, Gwynedd LL58 8AL.—*Hon. Sec.*, V. G. Keep.

Caernarvon.—ROYAL WELSH YACHT CLUB (1847), Porth-Yr-Aur, Caernarvon, Gwynned LL55 1SW.—*Hon. Sec.*, J. N. L. Thomas.

Penarth.—PENARTH YACHT CLUB (1880). The Esplanade, Penarth, S. Glamorgan CF6 2AU.—*Hon. Sec.*, W. H. Jones.

Swansea.—BRISTOL CHANNEL YACHT CLUB (1875), 744 Mumbles Road, Mumbles, Swansea SA3 4EL.—*Hon. Sec.*, R. L. Burrell.

Scotland

Dundee.—ROYAL TAY YACHT CLUB (1885), 34 Dundee Road, Broughty Ferry, Dundee DD5 1LX.—*Hon. Sec.*, T. Black.

Edinburgh.—ROYAL FORTH YACHT CLUB (1868), Middle Pier, Granton Harbour, Edinburgh, EH5 1HF.—*Hon. Sec.*, A. R. Woods.

Glasgow.—ROYAL WESTERN YACHT CLUB (1875), 42 Methil Street, Glasgow G14 0AN.—*Hon. Sec.*, Mrs. N. Simpson.

Oban.—ROYAL HIGHLAND YACHT CLUB (1881), Whins, 8 Grianach Gardens, Oban, Argyll PA34 4LZ.—*Sec.*, M. Bolton.

Rhu.—ROYAL NORTHERN AND CLYDE YACHT CLUB (1978), Rhu, Helensburgh, Dunbartonshire G84 8NG.—*Hon. Sec.*, J. S. Holgate.

Northern Ireland

Bangor.—ROYAL ULSTER YACHT CLUB (1866), 101 Clifton Road, Bangor, Co. Down BT20 5HY.—*Hon. Sec.*, T. O'Hara.

Channel Islands

Jersey.—ROYAL CHANNEL ISLANDS YACHT CLUB (1862), Le Boulevard, Bulwarks, St. Aubin, Jersey.—*Hon. Sec.*, A. K. Jackson.

PRINCIPAL BRITISH SOCIETIES AND INSTITUTIONS

THE ROYAL ACADEMY OF ARTS (1768), Burlington House, W1V 0DS—*President*, Roger de Grey, P.R.A., (1984); *Keeper*, Prof. N. Adams, R.A.; *Treas.*, Sir Philip Powell, C.H., O.B.E., R.A.; *Sec.* Piers Rodgers.

Royal Academicians

1972 Adams, Norman	1984 Hogarth, Paul
1988*Agar, Eileen	1986 Jones, Allen
1988 Aitchison, Craigie	1986 Kenny, Michael
1956*Bawden, Edward, C.B.E.	1988 King, Phillip, C.B.E.
1976 Blackadder, Elizabeth, O.B.E.	1974 Kneale, Bryan
1981 Blake, Peter, C.B.E.	1986*Lessore, Helen
1975 Blamey, Norman	1986 Levene, Ben
1978 Blow, Sandra	1956*Machin, Arnold, O.B.E.
1975 Bowey, Olwyn	1979 Manasseh, Leonard, O.B.E.
1981 Bowyer, William	1985*Martin, Sir Leslie
1971 Bratby, John R.	1985*Medley, Robert
1972 Brown, Ralph	1979*Moynihan, Rodrigo, C.B.E.
1972 Butler, James	1979 Paolozzi, Sir Eduardo, C.B.E.
1975*Cadbury-Brown, H. T., O.B.E.	1988 Partridge, John, C.B.E.
1984 Camp, Jeffery	1983*Pasmore, Victor, C.H., C.B.E.
1970*Casson, Sir Hugh, C.H., K.C.V.O.	1981 Philipson, Sir Robin
1976 Clarke, Geoffrey	1977 Powell, Sir Philip, C.H., O.B.E.
1973 Clatworthy, Robert	1973 Roberts-Jones, Ivor, C.B.E.
1972 Coker, Peter	1984 Rogers, Richard
1972 Cooke, Jean E.	1969 Rosoman, Leonard, O.B.E.
1974 Cuming, Frederick	1983*Rothenstein, Michael
1983 Dannatt, Trevor	1961*Sanders, Christopher C.
1969 de Grey, Roger	1984 Scott, William, C.B.E.
1976 Dickson, Jennifer	1969*Soukop, Willi
1985 Dowson, Sir Philip, C.B.E.	1954*Spear, Ruskin, C.B.E.
1955*Dring, William	1986 Stephenson, Ian
1968 Dunstan, Bernard	1988 Sutton, Philip
1953*Eurich, Richard, C.B.E.	1979 Tindle, David
1986 Eyton, Anthony	1965 Ward, John S., C.B.E.
1985 Fraser, Donald Hamilton	1965*Weight, Carel, C.B.E.
1977 Frink, Dame Elisabeth, D.B.E.	1974 Williams, Kyffin, O.B.E.
1972 Gore, Frederick, C.B.E.	
1977 Green, Anthony	
1960*Greenham, Peter, C.B.E.	
1981 Harpley, Sydney	
1970 Hayes, Colin	
1961*Hepple, Norman	

Associates

1989 Abrahams, Ivor	1985 Hockney, David
1988 Ackroyd, Norman	1983 Howard, Ken
1989 Armfield, Diana	1983 Hoyland, John
1982 Ayres, Gillian, O.B.E.	1987 Huxley, Paul
1986 Bellany, John	1989 Jacklin, Bill
1980 Christopher, Ann	1989 Kiff, Ken
1982 Crosby, Theo	1984 Kitaj, R. B.
1989 Cullinan, Edward	1986 Koralek, Paul, C.B.E.
1987 Flanagan, Barry	1982 Lawson, Sonia
1983 Foster, Norman	1987 McComb, Leonard
1978 Gowing, Sir Lawrence, C.B.E.	1987 Nolan, Sir Sidney
	1984 Phillips, Tom

* Senior.

1982 Sandle, Michael	1986 Titchell, John
1985 Stirling, James	1980 Whishaw, Anthony
1983 Symons, Patrick	1983 Wragg, John
1985 Tilson, Joe	

Former Presidents of the Royal Academy

Sir J. Reynolds, 1768	Sir F. Dicksee, 1924
Benjamin West, 1792	Sir W. Llewellyn, 1928
James Wyatt, 1805	Sir E. Lutyens, 1938
Benjamin West, 1806	Sir A. J. Munnings, 1944
Sir T. Lawrence, 1820	Sir G. F. Kelly, 1949
Sir M. A. Shee, 1830	Sir A. E. Richardson, 1954
Sir C. Eastlake, 1850	Sir C. Wheeler, 1956
Sir F. Grant, 1866	Sir T. Monnington, 1966
Lord Leighton, 1878	
Sir J. Millais, 1896	Sir Hugh Casson, 1976
Sir E. Poynter, 1896	
Sir A. Webb, 1919	

THE ROYAL CAMBRIAN ACADEMY OF ART (1882), Plas Mawr, High Street, Conwy, Gwynedd LL32 8DE—*Pres.*, R. Fields; *Hon. Sec.*, Ms. A. Hind; *Curator and Sec.*, L. H. S. Mercer.

THE ROYAL SCOTTISH ACADEMY (1826), Princes Street, Edinburgh EH2 2EL—*Pres.*, Sir Anthony Wheeler, O.B.E., R.S.A.; *Sec.*, R. R. Steedman, R.S.A.; *Treas.*, W. J. L. Baillie, R.S.A.; *Librarian*, P. Collins, R.S.A.; *Admin. Sec.*, W. T. Meikle.

Senior Academicians

1958 Armour, Mrs. M.	1967 Lorimer, Hew
1956 Fleming, Ian	1977 Whiston, Peter
1981 Glover, J. Hardie, O.B.E.	1957 Patrick, J. McIntosh
1967 Gordon, Esmé	1966 Peploe, Denis
1966 Johnston, Ninian	1986 Reiach, Alan

Royal Scottish Academicians

1979 Baillie, W. J. L.	1972 Michie, David
1972 Blackadder, Elizabeth, O.B.E.	1963 Morocco, Alberto
1986 Bushe, Fred	1989 Morris, James
1977 Butler, Vincent	1962 Philipson, Sir Robin
1971 Cameron, Gordon S.	1976 Reeves, Philip
1981 Campbell, Alex	1989 Richards, John, C.B.E.
1974 Collins, Peter	1989 Robertson, James D.
1974 Crosbie, William	1977 Robertson, R. Ross
1970 Cumming, James	1984 Scott, Bill
1962 Donaldson, David A.	1987 Smith, Ian McKenzie
1989 Evans, David	1985 Snowden, Michael (elect.)
1989 Fraser, Alexander	1979 Steedman, R. R.
1989 Harvey, Jake	1975 Wheeler, Sir Anthony, O.B.E.
1972 Houston, John	1982 Walker, Frances
1979 Knox, John	
1973 Littlejohn, W.	
1971 McClure, David	
1976 Malcolm, Ellen	

Associates

Arnott, Ian	Busby, John
Balmer, Barbara	Cairns, Joyce
Boys, John	Campbell, A. Buchanan
Brotherston, William	Clifford, J. G.
Brown, Neil Dallas	Cocker, Douglas
Bryce, Gordon	Crowe, Victoria
Buchan, Dennis	Dean, Fiona

Docherty, Michael
Donald, George
Fairgrieve, James
Gasson, Barry
The Earl Haig
Howard, Ian
Johnstone, John
Law, Graham C.
Low, Bet
McIntosh, Iain R.
Maclean, William J.
MacMillan, Andrew
MacPherson, George
Main, Kirkland
Merrylees, Andrew
Metzstein, Isi

Mooney, John
Morrison, James
Onwin, Glen
Pelly, Frances
Pottinger, Frank
Rae, Barbara
Renton, James S., o.b.e.
Ross, Alastair
Shanks, Duncan F.
Smart, Alastair
Squire, Geoffrey
Stenhouse, Andrew
Stiven, Fred
Watson, Arthur
Wedgwood, Roland

Non-Resident Associates, Charles Pulsford, Peter Womersley, Leon Morrocco.

ROYAL IRISH ACADEMY (1786), 19 Dawson Street, Dublin 2.—*Pres.*, Prof. J. C. I. Dooge; *Treas.*, Prof. A. F. Hegarty; *Sec.*, Prof. G. Watson.

ABBEYFIELD SOCIETY, 186–192 Darkes Lane, Potters Bar, Herts. EN6 1AB.—Housing for elderly people. 1,000 houses nationwide.—*Chief Exec.*, B. Palmer.

ACCOUNTANTS, INSTITUTE OF CHARTERED, IN ENGLAND AND WALES (1880), P.O. Box 433, Chartered Accountants' Hall, Moorgate Place, EC2P 2BJ.

ACCOUNTANTS, CHARTERED ASSOCIATION OF CERTIFIED (1904), 29 Lincoln's Inn Fields, WC2A 3EE.—*Sec.*, A. W. Sansom.

ACCOUNTANTS OF SCOTLAND, THE INSTITUTE OF CHARTERED (1854), 27 Queen Street, Edinburgh EH2 1LA.—*Sec.*, I. F. Y. Marrian.

ACCOUNTANTS IN IRELAND, INSTITUTE OF CHARTERED (1888), Chartered Accountants House, 87–89 Pembroke Road, Dublin 4.—*Dir.*, R. F. Hussey.

ACCOUNTANTS, SOCIETY OF COMPANY AND COMMERCIAL (1974), 40 Tyndalls Park Road, Bristol BS8 1PL.—*Sec. Gen.*, B. T. Banks.

ACCOUNTING TECHNICIANS, ASSOCIATION OF (1980), 154 Clerkenwell Road, EC1R 5AD.—*Sec.*, J. Hanson.

ACTION RESEARCH FOR THE CRIPPLED CHILD (1952), Vincent House, North Parade, Horsham, W. Sussex RH12 2DA.—*Dir. Gen.*, Col. A. N. Brearley-Smith, O.B.E.

ACTORS' BENEVOLENT FUND (1882), 6 Adam Street, WC2N 6AA.—*Gen. Sec.*, Mrs. R. Stevens.

ACTORS' CHARITABLE TRUST (1896), 19–20 Euston Centre, NW1 3JH.—*Gen. Sec.*, Ms. A. Stewart.

ACTORS' CHURCH UNION (1899), St. Paul's Church, Bedford Street, WC2E 9ED.—*Senior Chaplain*, Rev. W. Hall.

ACTUARIES IN SCOTLAND, THE FACULTY OF (1856), 23 St. Andrew Square, Edinburgh EH2 1AQ.—*Sec.*, W. W. Mair.

ACTUARIES, INSTITUTE OF (1848), Staple Inn Hall, High Holborn, WC1V 7QJ.—*Sec. Gen.*, C. D. A. Mackie.

ADMINISTRATIVE MANAGEMENT, INSTITUTE OF (1915), 40 Chatsworth Parade, Orpington, Kent BR5 1RW.—*Chief Exec.*, M. J. Ainsworth.

ADULT SCHOOL ORGANIZATION, NATIONAL (1899), Norfolk House, Smallbrook Queensway, Birmingham B5 4LJ.—*Gen. Sec.*, W. J. Scarle.

ADVERTISING BENEVOLENT SOCIETY, NATIONAL (1913), 3 Crawford Place, W1H 1JB.—*Dir.*, Mrs. D. Larkin.

ADVERTISING, INSTITUTE OF PRACTITIONERS IN (1927), 44 Belgrave Square, SW1X 8QS.—*Dir. Gen.*, N. Phillips.

ADVERTISING STANDARDS AUTHORITY (1962), Brook House, 2–16 Torrington Place, WC1E 7HN.—*Dir. Gen.*, E. Cassin (*acting*).

AERONAUTICAL SOCIETY, ROYAL (1866), 4 Hamilton Place, W1V 0BQ.—*Sec.*, R. J. Kennett.

AFRICAN INSTITUTE, INTERNATIONAL (1926), Lionel Robbins Building, 10 Portugal Street, WC2A 2HD.—*Dir.*, Prof. P. Lloyd.

AFRICAN MEDICAL AND RESEARCH FOUNDATION, London House, 68 Upper Richmond Road, SW15 2RP.—*Exec. Dir.*, Mrs. E. Young.

AGE CONCERN ENGLAND (1940), Bernard Sunley House, 60 Pitcairn Road, Mitcham, Surrey, CR4 3LL.—*Dir.*, Ms. S. Greengross.

AGE CONCERN NORTHERN IRELAND (1976), 6 Lower Crescent, Belfast, BT2 7BG.—*Chief Exec.*, J. A. O'Neill.

AGE CONCERN SCOTLAND (1943), 54A Fountainbridge, Edinburgh EH3 9PT.—*Dir.*, M. Cairns.

AGE CONCERN WALES, 4th Floor, 1 Cathedral Road, Cardiff, CF1 9SD.—*Chief Officer*, D. Haydn Thomas.

AGED POOR SOCIETY (1708), St. Joseph's House, 42 Brook Green, W6 7BW.—*Sec.*, Flt. Lt. W. Watson.

AGEING, CENTRE FOR POLICY ON (1947), 25–31 Ironmonger Row, EC1V 3QP.—*Dir.*, Dr. E. Midwinter, D.Phil.

AGEING, RESEARCH INTO (1978), 49 Queen Victoria Street, EC4N 4SA.—*Dir.*, J. Allfrey.

AGRICULTURAL BENEVOLENT INSTITUTION, ROYAL (1860), Shaw House, 27 West Way, Oxford OX2 0QH.—*Chief Exec.*, Maj. Gen. P. L. Spurgeon, C.B.

AGRICULTURAL BENEVOLENT INSTITUTION, ROYAL SCOTTISH (1897), Ingliston, Edinburgh, EH28 8NB.—*Organizing Sec.*, I. G. Cumming, T.D.

AGRICULTURAL SOCIETY, EAST OF ENGLAND, East of England Showground, Peterborough PE2 0XE.—*Sec.*, R. W. Bird, M.B.E..

AGRICULTURAL SOCIETY OF ENGLAND, ROYAL (1838), National Agricultural Centre, Stoneleigh, Kenilworth, Warks. CV8 2LZ.—*Chief Exec.*, R. E.Hicks.

AGRICULTURAL SOCIETY OF THE COMMONWEALTH, ROYAL (1957), 55 Sleaford Street, SW8 5AB.—*Hon. Sec.*, F. R. Francis, L.V.O., M.B.E.

AGRICULTURAL SOCIETY, ROYAL ULSTER (1826), The King's Hall, Balmoral Show Grounds, Belfast BT9 6GW.—*Chief Exec.*, W. H. Yarr.

AGRICULTURE, ASSOCIATION OF (1947), Victoria Chambers, 16–20 Strutton Ground, SW1P 2HP.—*Gen. Sec.*, Miss J. H. D. Bostock, M.B.E.

AIR LEAGUE, THE (1909), Grey Tiles, Kingston Hill, Kingston upon Thames, Surrey KT2 7LW.— *Sec. Gen.*, Air Cdre. C. A. Alldis, C.B.E., D.F.C., A.F.C.

ALCOHOLICS ANONYMOUS (1947), P.O. Box 1, Stonebow House, Stonebow, York YO1 2NJ.—*Gen. Sec.*, J. Gow.

ALEXANDRA ROSE DAY COMMITTEE (1912), 1 Castelnau, Barnes, SW13 9RP.—*Nat. Organizing Sec,* Mrs. L. Weston.

ALLOTMENT AND LEISURE GARDENERS LIMITED, NATIONAL SOCIETY OF (1930), Hunters Road, Corby, Northants. NN17 1JE.—*Sec.*, G. W. Stokes.

ALMSHOUSES, NATIONAL ASSOCIATION OF (1946), Billingbear Lodge, Wokingham, Berks. RG11 5RU.—*Dir.*, D. M. Scott.

AMNESTY INTERNATIONAL (1961), International Secretariat, 1 Easton Street, WC1X 8DJ.—*Sec. Gen.*, I. Martin.

ANAESTHETISTS OF GREAT BRITAIN AND IRELAND, ASSOCIATION OF (1932), 9 Bedford Square, WC1B 3RA.—*Hon. Sec.*, Dr. W. L. M. Baird.

ANCIENT BUILDINGS, SOCIETY FOR THE PROTECTION OF (1877), 37 Spital Square, E1 6DY.—*Sec.*, P. Venning.

ANCIENT MONUMENTS SOCIETY (1924), St. Andrew-by-the-Wardrobe, Queen Victoria Street, EC4V 5DE.—*Sec.*, M. Saunders.

ANGLO-ARAB ASSOCIATION (1961), The Arab British Centre, 21 Collingham Road, SW5 0NU.—*Exec. Dir.*, D. R. Collard, O.B.E.

ANGLO-BELGIAN SOCIETY (1982).—*Hon. Sec.*, Mrs. S. G. Ault, 46 Belgrave Manor, Brooklyn Road, Woking, Surrey GU22 7TW.

ANGLO-BRAZILIAN SOCIETY (1943), 32 Green Street, W1Y 3FD.—*Sec.*, Mrs. M. J. Fyfe.

ANGLO-DANISH SOCIETY (1924), 25 New Street Square, EC4A 3LN.—*Chairman*, Sir Andrew Stark, K.C.M.G., C.V.O.

ANGLO-NORSE SOCIETY (1918), 25 Belgrave Square, SW1X 8QD.—*Chairman*, Mrs. A. Dixon.

ANGLO-POLISH SOCIETY (1832), London H.Q., c/o S.P.C.K., 238–246 King Street, W6 0RF.—*Hon. Sec.*, Mrs. K. Szymaniak.

ANGLO-THAI SOCIETY (1962).—*Hon. Sec.*, Lt.-Col. H. Docherty, O.B.E., 22 Ulster Court, Albany Park Road, Kingbaston, Surrey KT2 5SS.

ANIMAL CONCERN (SCOTLAND) (1988), 121 West Regent Street, Glasgow G2 2SD.—*Organizing Sec.*, J. F. Robins.

ANIMAL HEALTH TRUST (1942), P.O. Box 5, Newmarket, Suffolk CB8 7DW.—*Dir.*, A. J. Higgins, PH.D.

ANTHROPOLOGICAL INSTITUTE, ROYAL (1843), 50 Fitzroy Street, W1P 5HS.—*Dir.*, J. C. M. Benthall.

ANTHROPOSOPHICAL SOCIETY IN GREAT BRITAIN (1923), Rudolf Steiner House, 35 Park Road, NW1 6XT.—*Gen. Sec.*, N. C. Thomas.

ANTI-COMMON MARKET CAMPAIGN, BRITISH (1976), 81 Ashmole Street, SW8 1NF.—*Hon. Sec.*, Sir Robin Williams, Bt.

ANTIQUARIES, SOCIETY OF (1717), Burlington House, Piccadilly, W1V 0HS.—*Dir.*, G. J. Wainwright, PH.D.

ANTIQUARIES OF SCOTLAND, SOCIETY OF (1780), Royal Museum of Scotland, Queen Street, Edinburgh EH2 1JD.—*Sec.*, Miss C. R. Wickham-Jones.

ANTI-SLAVERY SOCIETY FOR THE PROTECTION OF HUMAN RIGHTS (1839), 180 Brixton Road, SW9 6AT.—*Dir.*, P. D. Lowes.

ANTI-VIVISECTION: BRITISH UNION FOR THE ABOLITION OF VIVISECTION (1898), 16A Crane Grove, N7 8LB.—*Sec.*, A. Cheeseman.

ANTI-VIVISECTION SOCIETY, THE NATIONAL (1875), 51 Harley Street, W1N 1DD.—*Gen. Sec.*, Ms. J. Creamer.

APOSTLESHIP OF THE SEA (1920), Stella Maris, Atlantic House, New Strand, Bootle, Merseyside L20 4TQ.—For active seafarers. *Nat. Dir.*, Very Rev. Mgr. A. Stringfellow.

APOTHECARIES OF LONDON, SOCIETY OF (1617), Black Friars Lane, EC4V 6EJ.—*Clerk*, Maj. J. C. O'Leary; *Registrar*, D. H. C. Barrie.

ARBITRATORS, THE CHARTERED INSTITUTE OF (1915), 75 Cannon Street, EC4N 5BH.—*Sec.*, K. R. K. Harding.

ARCHAEOLOGICAL ASSOCIATION, BRITISH (1843), 24 Lower Street, Harnham, Salisbury SP2 8EY.—*Asst. Sec.*, M. Cowan.

ARCHAEOLOGICAL ASSOCIATION, CAMBRIAN (1846), Lleifior, 60 Dan-y-Coed, Aberystwyth, Dyfed SY23 2HA.—*Gen.Sec.*, G. L. Jones.

ARCHAEOLOGICAL INSTITUTE, ROYAL (1843), c/o Society of Antiquaries of London, Burlington House, Piccadilly, W1V 0HS.—*Sec.*, J. G. Coad.

ARCHAEOLOGY, COUNCIL FOR BRITISH (1944), 112 Kennington Road, SE11 6RE.—*Dir.*, Dr. H. F. Cleere.

ARCHITECTS, THE ROYAL INSTITUTE OF BRITISH (1834), 66 Portland Place, W1N 4AD.—*Pres.*, M. Hutchinson; *Dir. Gen.*, The Rt. Hon. W. Rodgers.

ARCHITECTS AND SURVEYORS, INCORPORATED ASSOCIATION OF (1925), Jubilee House, Billing Brook Road, Weston Favell, Northampton NN3 4NW.—*Hon. Sec.*, W. A. Black.

ARCHITECTS AND SURVEYORS INSTITUTE, 15 St. Mary Street, Chippenham, Wilts. SN15 3JN.—*Chief Exec.*, B. A. Hunt.

ARCHITECTS BENEVOLENT SOCIETY (1850), 66 Portland Place, W1N 4AD.—*Hon. Sec.*, R. J. Double.

ARCHITECTS IN SCOTLAND, ROYAL INCORPORATION OF (1922), 15 Rutland Square, Edinburgh EH1 2BE.—*Sec.*, C. A. McKean, F.R.S.A.

ARCHITECTS REGISTRATION COUNCIL OF THE UNITED KINGDOM (1931), 73 Hallam Street, W1N 6EE.—*Registrar*, K. J. Forder.

ARCHITECTURAL ASSOCIATION (INC.) (1847), 34–36 Bedford Square, WC1B 3EG.—*Sec.*, E. Le Maistre.

ARCHITECTURAL HERITAGE FUND, THE (1976), 17 Carlton House Terrace, SW1Y 5AW.—*Sec.*, Lady Weir.

ARCHIVISTS, SOCIETY OF (1947), Suffolk Record Office, County Hall, Ipswich IP4 2JS.—*Hon. Sec.*, Ms. A. J. E. Arrowsmith.

ARMY BENEVOLENT FUND (1944), 41 Queen's Gate, SW7 5HR.—*Controller*, Maj.-Gen. G. M. G. Swindells, C.B.

ARMY CADET FORCE ASSOCIATION (1930), Cheltenham Terrace, SW3 4RR.—*Gen. Sec.*, Brig. R. B. Mac-Gregor-Oakford, C.B.E., M.C.

ART-COLLECTIONS FUND, NATIONAL (1903), 20 John Islip Street, SW1P 4JX.—*Dir.*, Sir Peter Wakefield, K.B.E., C.M.G.

ARTHRITIS AND RHEUMATISM COUNCIL (1936), 41 Eagle Street, WC1R 4AR.—*Gen. Sec.*, J. Norton.

ARTHRITIS CARE (1949), 5 Grosvenor Crescent, SW1X 7ER.—*Sec.*, J. R. Collins.

ARTISTS, FEDERATION OF BRITISH, 17 Carlton House Terrace, SW1Y 5BD.—*Chief Exec.*, O. Warman.

ARTISTS' GENERAL BENEVOLENT INSTITUTION (1814) AND ARTISTS' ORPHAN FUND (1871), Burlington House, Piccadilly, W1V 0DJ.—*Sec.*, C. M. Rees.

ARTISTS, ROYAL SOCIETY OF BRITISH, 17 Carlton House Terrace, SW1Y 5BD.— *Sec.*, R. Morgan.

ART LIBRARIES SOCIETY (ARLIS) (1969), Central School of Art and Design, Southampton Row, WC1B 4AP.—*Sec.*, S. M. Price.

ART WORKERS' GUILD (1884), 6 Queen Square, WC1N 3AR.—*Sec.*, Hugh Krall.

ASLIB (The Association for Information Management) (1924), Information House, 26–27 Boswell Street, WC1N 3JZ.—*Dir.*, Dr. D. A. Lewis.

ASSISTANT MASTERS AND MISTRESSES ASSOCIATION (1978), 7 Northumberland Street, WC2N 5DA.—*Joint Gen. Secs.*, Miss J. E. L. Baird; P. Smith.

ASTHMA RESEARCH COUNCIL (1927), 300 Upper Street, N1 2XX.—*Chairman*, Prof. M. Turner-Warwick.

ASTRONOMICAL ASSOCIATION, BRITISH (1890), Burlington House, Piccadilly, W1V 9AG. Meetings at 23 Savile Row, W1X 1AB.— *Asst. Sec.*, Miss P. M. Barber

ASTRONOMICAL SOCIETY, ROYAL (1820), Burlington House, Piccadilly, W1V 0NL.—*Pres.*, Prof. R. J. Tayler; *Exec. Sec.*, J. A. Steff-Langston.

A.T.S. and W.R.A.C. BENEVOLENT FUNDS (1964), Queen Elizabeth Park, Guildford, Surrey GU2 6QH.—*Sec.*, Mrs. E. Laurence-Smith.

AUDIT BUREAU OF CIRCULATIONS LTD. (1931), 13 Wimpole Street, W1M 7AB.—*Dir.*, J. G. Holmes.

AUTHORS, THE SOCIETY OF (1884), 84 Drayton Gardens, SW10 9SB.—*Gen. Sec.*, M. Le Fanu.

AUTOMOBILE ASSOCIATION (1905), Fanum House, Basingstoke, Hants. RG21 2EA.—*Dir. Gen.*, S. Dyer.

AVICULTURAL SOCIETY (1894), Warren Hill, Hulford's Lane, Hartley Wintney, Hants. RG27 8AG.—*Hon. Sec.*, H. J. Horswell.

AYRSHIRE CATTLE SOCIETY OF GREAT BRITAIN AND IRELAND (1877), P.O. Box 8, 1 Racecourse Road, Ayr KA7 2DE.—*Gen. Sec.*, S. J. Thomson.

BALTIC AIR CHARTER ASSOCIATION (1949), The Baltic Exchange, St. Mary Axe, EC3A 8BU.—*Hon. Exec.*, D. Shepherd.

BALTIC EXCHANGE LTD. (1903), 14–20 St. Mary Axe, EC3A 8BU.—*Sec.*, D. J. Walker.

BALTIC EXCHANGE CHARITABLE SOCIETY (1978), 14–20 St. Mary Axe, EC3A 8BU.—*Sec.*, R. T. Wheelans.

BALZAN FOUNDATION, INTERNATIONAL (1956), Piazzetta U. Giordano 4, Milan 20122, Italy. Awards prizes for Literature, Moral Sciences and the Arts, Physical, Mathematical and Natural Sciences, Medicine, Humanity, Peace and Brotherhood.—*Sec. Gen.*, Dr. F. M. Tedeschi.

BANKERS, THE CHARTERED INSTITUTE OF (1879), 10 Lombard Street, EC3V 9AS.—*Sec. Gen.*, E. Glover.

BANKERS IN SCOTLAND, THE INSTITUTE OF (1875), 20 Rutland Square, Edinburgh EH1 2DE.—*Sec.*, C. W. Munn.

BAPTIST MISSIONARY SOCIETY (1792), Baptist House, 129 Broadway, Didcot, Oxon. OX11 8RT.—*Gen. Sec.*, Rev. R. G. S. Harvey.

BAR ASSOCIATION FOR LOCAL GOVERNMENT AND THE PUBLIC SERVICE (1945), 23 Wentworth Way, Bletchley, Milton Keynes MK3 7RW.—*Chairman*, P. G. Stivadoros.

BARNARDO'S (1866), Tanners Lane, Ilford, Essex IG6 1QG. Helps over 22,000 children and young people each year, many of them with special needs, in the United Kingdom, Republic of Ireland, Australia and New Zealand.—*Senior Dir.*, R. Singleton.

BARONETAGE, STANDING COUNCIL OF THE (1898).—*Sec.*, Sir Tobias Clarke, Bt. (*acting*), Church House, Bibury, Cirencester, Glos. GL7 5NR.

BARRISTERS' BENEVOLENT ASSOCIATION, THE (1873), 14 Gray's Inn Square, WC1R 5JP.—*Sec.*, Miss K. M. Hopper.

BEECHAM TRUST, SIR THOMAS (1946), Denton House, Denton, Harleston, Norfolk IP20 0AA.—*Sec.*, Shirley, Lady Beecham.

BEE-KEEPERS' ASSOCIATION, BRITISH (1874), National Agricultural Centre, Stoneleigh, Kenilworth, Warks. CV8 2LZ.—*Gen. Sec.*, vacant.

BIBLE CHURCHMEN'S MISSIONARY SOCIETY (1922), 251 Lewisham Way, SE4 1XF.—*Gen. Sec.*, Rev. Canon J. M. Ball.

BIBLE SOCIETY, BRITISH AND FOREIGN (1804), Stonehill Green, Westlea, Swindon SN5 7DG.—*Exec. Dir.*, R. Worthing-Davies.

BIBLIOGRAPHICAL SOCIETY (1892), British Library, Humanities and Social Sciences, Great Russell Street, WC1B 3DG.—*Hon. Sec.*, Dr. M. M. Foot.

BIBLIOGRAPHICAL SOCIETY, EDINBURGH (1890), c/o New College Library, Mound Place, Edinburgh EH1 2LU.—*Hon. Sec.*, M. C. T. Simpson.

BIOCHEMICAL SOCIETY (1911), 7 Warwick Court, High Holborn, WC1R 5DP.—*Exec. Sec.*, G. D. Jones.

BIOLOGICAL COUNCIL, THE (1945), c/o Institute of Biology, 20 Queensberry Place, SW7 2DZ.—*Hon. Sec.*, Prof. M. Sandler.

BIOLOGICAL ENGINEERING SOCIETY (1960), Royal College of Surgeons, Lincoln's Inn Fields, WC2A 3PN.—*Hon. Sec.*, Dr. R. E. Trotman.

BIOLOGY, THE INSTITUTE OF (1950), 20 Queensberry Place, SW7 2DZ.—*Gen. Sec.*, Dr. R. H. Priestley.

BIRD PRESERVATION, INTERNATIONAL COUNCIL FOR (BRITISH SECTION) (1922), c/o Flora and Fauna Preservation Society, 79–83 North Street, Brighton BN1 12A.—*Exec. Sec.*, J. R. Wilson.

BIRMINGHAM AND MIDLAND INSTITUTE (1854) and PRIESTLEY LIBRARY (1779), Margaret Street, Birmingham B3 3BS.—*Admin.* J. Hunt.

BIRTHDAY TRUST FUND, NATIONAL (1928), 27 Sussex Place, NW1 4RG. For extension of maternity services.—*Sec.*, Mrs. M. C. Matthews.

BLIND, GUIDE DOGS FOR THE, *see* GUIDE DOGS FOR THE BLIND ASSOCIATION.

BLIND, INCORPORATED ASSOCIATION FOR PROMOTING THE GENERAL WELFARE OF THE (1854), 37–55 Ashburton Grove, N7 7DW.—*Chief Exec.*, G. P. Robinson; *Sec.*, A. W. Cairns.

BLIND, LONDON ASSOCIATION FOR THE (1857), 14–16 Verney Road, SE16 3DZ.—*Deputy Dir.*, Mrs. E. Howard.

BLIND, NATIONAL LIBRARY FOR THE (1882), Cromwell Road, Bredbury, Stockport, Cheshire SK6 2SG. Over 300,000 volumes available.—*Dir. Gen.*, A. Leach.

BLIND, ROYAL LONDON SOCIETY FOR THE (1838), 105–109 Salusbury Road, NW6 6RH.—*Sec. Gen.*, R. J. Pocock.

BLIND, ROYAL NATIONAL COLLEGE FOR THE (1872), College Road, Hereford HR1 1EB.—*Principal*, L. Marshall.

BLIND, ROYAL NATIONAL INSTITUTE FOR THE (1868), 224 Great Portland Street, W1N 6AA.—*Dir. Gen.*, I. Bruce.

BLIND, ROYAL SCHOOL FOR THE (1799), Leatherhead, Surrey KT22 8NR.—*Dir.*, Rev. B. A. E. Coote.

BLOOD TRANSFUSION ASSOCIATION, SCOTTISH NATIONAL (1940), 29 Abercromby Place, Edinburgh EH3 6UE.—*Sec.*, P. C. Taylor.

BLUE CROSS (1897), Home Close Farm, Shilton Road, Burford, Oxon. OX8 4PF.—*Sec.*, P. Hannon.

BODLEIAN, FRIENDS OF THE (1925), Bodleian Library, Oxford OX1 3BG.—*Sec.*, G. Groom.

BOOKSELLERS ASSOCIATION OF GREAT BRITAIN AND IRELAND (1895), 154 Buckingham Palace Road, SW1W 9TZ.—*Dir.*, T. E. Godfray.

BOOK TRADE BENEVOLENT SOCIETY (1967), Dillon Lodge, The Retreat, Kings Langley, Herts. WD4 8LT.—*Exec. Sec.*, Mrs. A. R. Brown.

BOOK TRUST (1986), Book House, 45 East Hill, SW18 2QZ.—*Chief Exec.*, K. McWilliams.

BOTANICAL SOCIETY OF THE BRITISH ISLES (1836), British Museum (Natural History), Cromwell Road, SW7 5BD.—*Hon. Gen. Sec.*, Mrs. M. Briggs, M.B.E.

BOTANICAL SOCIETY OF EDINBURGH, Royal Botanic Garden, Inverleith Row, Edinburgh EH3 5LR.— *Hon. Gen. Sec.*, Dr. I. Edwards.

BOY SCOUTS ASSOCIATION, *see* SCOUT ASSOCIATION, THE.

BOYS' BRIGADE, THE (1883), 1 Kings Terrace, Galena Road, W6 0LT. Membership worldwide: 400,000 in 60 countries.—*Brigade Sec.*, S. Jones.

BOYS' CLUBS, NATIONAL ASSOCIATION OF (1925), 369 Kennington Lane, SE11 5QY. Has affiliated to it 2,000 clubs.—*Nat. Dir.*, D. P. Harris.

BOYS' CLUBS, NORTHERN IRELAND ASSOCIATION OF (1940), Bryson House, 28 Bedford Street, Belfast BT2 7FE.—*Gen. Sec.*, K. Culbert

BREWING, INSTITUTE OF (1886), 33 Clarges Street, W1Y 8EE.—*Sec.*, Capt. K. A. Leppard, C.B.E., R.N.

BRIDEWELL ROYAL HOSPITAL (1553), Witley, Surrey GU8 5SG.—*Clerk to the Governors*, Mrs. A. C. R. Mitchell.

BRITAIN-NEPAL SOCIETY (1960).—*Hon. Sec.*, Mrs. C. Brown, 1 Allen Mansions, Allen Street, W8 6UY.

BRITISH ACADEMY, THE (1901), 20–21 Cornwall Terrace, NW1 4QP.—*President*, Dr. A. J. P. Kenny; *Sec.*, P. W. H. Brown.

BRITISH AND FOREIGN SCHOOL SOCIETY (1808), Richard Mayo Hall, Eden Street, Kingston upon Thames, Surrey KT1 1HZ.—*Sec.*, S. M. A. Banister.

BRITISH ATLANTIC COMMITTEE (1952), 5 St. James's Place, SW1A 1NP.—*Dir.*, Maj.-Gen. C. J. Popham, C.B.

BRITISH INSTITUTE IN EASTERN AFRICA (1959), 1 Kensington Gore, SW7 2AR.—*London Sec.*, Mrs. J. Moyo.

BRITISH INSTITUTE OF ARCHAEOLOGY AT ANKARA (1948), c/o The British Academy, 20–21 Cornwall Terrace, NW1 4QP.—*London Sec.*, Ms. F. Chapman-Purchas.

BRITISH INSTITUTE OF PERSIAN STUDIES (1961), 13 Cambrian Road, Richmond, Surrey TW10 6JQ.— *Sec.*, Mrs. M. E. Gueritz, M.B.E.

BRITISH INTERPLANETARY SOCIETY (1933), 27–29 South Lambeth Road, SW8 1SZ.—*Exec. Sec.*, L. J. Carter.

BRITISH ISRAEL WORLD FEDERATION (1919), 6 Buckingham Gate, SW1E 6JP.—*Sec.*, A. E. Gibb.

BRITISH LEGION, ROYAL (1921), 48 Pall Mall, SW1Y 5JY.—*Gen. Sec.*, Lt.-Col. P. C. E. Creasy.

BRITISH LEGION SCOTLAND, ROYAL (1921), New Haig House, Logie Green Road, Edinburgh EH7 4HR.— *Sec.*, Brig. R. W. Riddle, O.B.E.

BRITISH MEDICAL ASSOCIATION (1832), B.M.A. House, Tavistock Square, WC1H 9JP.—*President*, Prof. J. B. L. Howell, PH.D.; *Sec.*, I. T. Field.

BRITISH SCHOOL OF ARCHAEOLOGY IN JERUSALEM (1919), The British Academy, 20 Cornwall Terrace, NW1 4QP.—*Pres.*, The Rev. Prof. H. Chadwick, K.B.E., F.B.A. *Dir.*, Dr. R. P. Harper.

BRUSH MANUFACTURERS' ASSOCIATION, BRITISH (1908), 35 Billing Road, Northampton NN1 5DD.— *Sec.*, A. N. Nisbet.

BTVC (BRITISH TRUST FOR CONSERVATION VOLUNTEERS) (1970), 36 St. Mary's Street, Wallingford, Oxon. OX10 0EU.—*Chief Exec.*, R. Morley.

BUDDHIST SOCIETY, THE (1924), 58 Eccleston Square, SW1V 1PH.—*Gen. Sec.*, R. C. Maddox.

BUDGERIGAR SOCIETY, THE (1925), 49–53 Hazelwood Road, Northampton NN1 1LG.—*Gen. Sec.*, A. C. Crook.

BUILDING, CHARTERED INSTITUTE OF (1834), Englemere, Kings Ride, Ascot, Berks. SL5 8BJ.—*Chief Exec.*, K. Banbury.

BUILDING SERVICES ENGINEERS, CHARTERED INSTITUTION OF (1897), Delta House, 222 Balham High Road, SW12 9BS.—*Sec.*, A. V. Ramsay.

BUILDING SOCIETIES ASSOCIATION (1936), 3 Savile Row, W1X 1AF.—*Dir. Gen.*, M. J. Boléat.

BUSINESS AND PROFESSIONAL WOMEN, UNITED KINGDOM FEDERATION OF (1938), 23 Ansdell Street, W8 5BN.—*Sec.*, Mrs. R. Bangle.

BUSINESS ARCHIVES COUNCIL (1934), 185 Tower Bridge Road, SE1 2UF.—*Sec. Gen.*, S. Kelly.

BUTCHERS' AND DROVERS' CHARITABLE INSTITUTION (1828), 61 West Smithfield, EC1A 9EA.—*Sec.*, J. A. Fordyce.

CADET FORCE ASSOCIATION, COMBINED (1952), 'E' Block, The Duke of York's H.Q., SW3 4RR.—*Sec.*, Brig. R. B. MacGregor-Oakford, C.B.E., M.C.

CALOUSTE GULBENKIAN FOUNDATION (1956), 98 Portland Place, W1N 4ET.—*Dir.*, B. Whitaker.

CAMBRIDGE PRESERVATION SOCIETY (1929), Wandlebury Ring, Gog Magog Hills, Babraham, Cambridge CB2 4AE.—*Sec.*, Mrs. K. Wright.

CAMERA CLUB, THE (1885), 8 Great Newport Street, WC2H 7JA.—*Sec.*, D. Pincham.

CAMERON FUND, THE (1971), Tavistock House North, Tavistock Square, WC1H 9JP.—*Sec.*, Mrs. J. Martin.

CAMPAIGN FOR NUCLEAR DISARMAMENT (C.N.D.) (1958), 22–24 Underwood Street, N1 7JG.—*Gen. Sec.*, Ms. M. Beresford.

CANCER RESEARCH CAMPAIGN, 2 Carlton House Terrace, SW1Y 5AR.—*Dir. Gen.*, D. de Peyer.

CANCER RELIEF, NATIONAL SOCIETY FOR (MACMILLAN FUND) (1911), Anchor House, 15–19 Britten Street, SW3 3TZ.—*Dir.*, D. Scott.

CANCER RESEARCH FUND, IMPERIAL (1902), P.O. Box 123, Lincoln's Inn Fields, WC2A 3PX.—*Sec.*, Maj.-Gen. A. W. Dennis, C.B., O.B.E.

CANCER RESEARCH, THE INSTITUTE OF, Royal Cancer Hospital, 17A Onslow Gardens, SW7 3AL.—*Sec.*, J. Defries.

CAREER TEACHERS, ASSOCIATION OF (1975), Hillsboro., Castledine Street, Loughborough, Leics. LE11 2DX.—*Gen. Sec.*, Miss P. Yaffé.

CARNEGIE DUNFERMLINE TRUST (1903), Abbey Park House, Dunfermline KY12 7PB (Social and cultural purposes in Dunfermline).—*Sec.*, F. Mann.

CARNEGIE HERO FUND TRUST (1908). Abbey Park House, Dunfermline KY12 7PB. Makes grants and allowances to people injured or the dependants of people killed in saving human life within the British Isles and territorial waters.— *Sec.*, F. Mann.

CARNEGIE UNITED KINGDOM TRUST (1913), Comely Park House, Dunfermline, KY12 7EJ.—*Sec.*, G. Lord.

CATHEDRALS ADVISORY COMMISSION FOR ENGLAND (1949), 83 London Wall, EC2M 5NA.—*Sec.*, P. A. T. Burman.

CATHOLIC FUND FOR OVERSEAS DEVELOPMENT (CAFOD) (1962), 2 Romero Close, Stockwell Road, SW9 9TY.—*Dir.* J. Filochowski.

CATHOLIC MARRIAGE ADVISORY COUNCIL (1946), Clitherow House, 1 Blythe Mews, Blythe Road, W14 0NW.—*Chief Exec.*, Mrs. J. C. Judge.

CATHOLIC RECORD SOCIETY (1904), c/o 114 Mount Street, W1Y 6AH.—*Hon. Sec.*, Miss R. Rendel.

CATHOLIC TRUTH SOCIETY (1868), 38–40 Eccleston Square, SW1V 1PD.—*Gen. Sec.*, D. Murphy.

CATHOLIC UNION OF GREAT BRITAIN (1872), St. Maximilian Kolbe House, 63 Jeddo Road, W12 9EE.—*Pres.*, The Duke of Norfolk, K.G., G.C.V.O., C.B., C.B.E., M.C.; *Hon. Sec.*, Mrs. J. Stuyt, M.B.E.

CATTLE BREEDERS' ASSOCIATION, NATIONAL, 24 Courtenay Park, Newton Abbot, Devon TQ12 2HB.—*Sec.*, J. H. Pappin.

CATTLE BREEDER'S CLUB, LTD. (1945), Lavenders, Isfield, Uckfield, E. Sussex TN22 5TX.—*Sec.*, C. R. Stains.

CECIL HOUSES (Inc.) (1926), 2 Priory Road, Kew, Richmond, Surrey TW9 3DG. (Housing Association).—*Sec.*, D. S. Cottrell.

CENTRAL BUREAU (for educational visits and exchanges) (1948), Seymour Mews House, Seymour Mews, W1H 9PE.—*Dir.* A. H. Male.

CERAMICS, INSTITUTE OF (1955), Shelton House, Stoke Road, Shelton, Stoke-on-Trent ST4 2DR.—*Pres.*, Dr. D. W. F. James.

CHADWICK TRUST (1895), Department of Civil Engineering, University College London, Gower Street, WC1E 6BT. (For the promotion of health and prevention of disease).—*Sec to the Trustees*, D. Kasher.

CHANTREY BEQUEST (1875), Royal Academy of Arts, Burlington House, Piccadilly, W1V 0DS.—*Sec.*, P. Rodgers.

CHARTERED SECRETARIES AND ADMINISTRATORS, INSTITUTE OF (1891), 16 Park Crescent, W1N 4AH.—*Sec.*, B. Barker, M.B.E.

CHEMICAL ENGINEERS, INSTITUTION OF (1922), George E. Davis Building, 165–171 Railway Terrace, Rugby, Warks. CV21 3HQ.—*Gen. Sec.*, Dr. T. J. Evans.

CHEMICAL INDUSTRY, SOCIETY OF, 14–15 Belgrave Square, SW1X 8PS.—*Pres.*, Dr. L. Fernandez; *Gen. Sec.*, Dr. P. P. King, F.R.S.C.

CHEMISTRY, THE ROYAL SOCIETY OF, Burlington House, Piccadilly, W1V 0BN.—*Pres.*, Prof. J. M Ward; *Sec. Gen.*, Dr. J. S. Gow, F.R.S.E.

CHESHIRE (LEONARD) FOUNDATION, *see* LEONARD CHESHIRE FOUNDATION.

CHESS FEDERATION, BRITISH (1904), 9A Grand Parade, St. Leonards-on-Sea, E. Sussex TN38 0DD.—*Office Man.*, Ms. G. White.

CHEST, HEART AND STROKE ASSOCIATION (1899), Tavistock House North, Tavistock Square, WC1H 9JE.—*Dir. Gen.*, Sir David Atkinson, K.B.E.

CHILDBIRTH TRUST, NATIONAL (1956), Alexandra House, Oldham Terrace W3 6NH.—*Nat. Sec.*, Mrs. H. Corbishley.

CHILDREN'S HOME, NATIONAL (1869), 85 Highbury Park, N5 1UD. Provides services to over 10,000 disadvantaged and disabled children and their parents annually in Great Britain and the Third World.—*Principal*, Rev. M. Newman.

CHILDREN'S SOCIETY, THE (1881), Edward Rudolf House, Margery Street, WC1X 0JL.—*Dir.*, I. Sparks.

CHINA ASSOCIATION (1889), Swire House, 59 Buckingham Gate, SW1E 6AJ.—*Exec. Dir.*, Brig. B. G. Hickey, O.B.E., M.C.

CHIROPODISTS, SOCIETY OF (1945), 53 Welbeck Street, W1M 7HE.—*Gen. Sec.*, J. G. C. Trouncer.

CHOIRS SCHOOLS ASSOCIATION (1921), King's School, College Green, Worcester WR1 2LH.—*Hon. Sec.*, Dr. J. M. Moore.

CHRISTIAN ACTION, St. Peter's House, 308 Kennington Lane, SE11 5HY.—*Dir.*, Canon E. James.

CHRISTIAN AID (1945), P.O. Box 100, SE1 7RT.—*Dir.*, Rev. M. H. Taylor.

CHRISTIAN EDUCATION COUNCIL, NATIONAL (1809), Robert Denholm House, Nutfield, Redhill RH1 4HW.—*Exec. Officer*, E. A. Thorn.

CHRISTIAN EDUCATION MOVEMENT (1965), Royal Buildings, Victoria Street, Derby DE1 1GW.—*Gen. Sec.*, Rev. Dr. S. Orchard.

CHRISTIAN EVIDENCE SOCIETY (1870), St. Stephen's House, St. Stephen's Crescent, Brentwood, Essex CM13 2AT.—*Hon. Sec.*, Mrs. G. M. Ryeland.

CHRISTIAN KNOWLEDGE, SOCIETY FOR PROMOTING (S.P.C.K.) (1698), Holy Trinity Church, Marylebone Road, NW1 4DU.—*Gen. Sec.*, P. N. G. Gilbert.

CHRISTIANS AND JEWS, COUNCIL OF (1942), 1 Dennington Park Road, NW6 1AX.—*Exec. Dir.*, Rev. Canon J. Richardson.

CHURCH ARMY (1882), Independents Road, SE3 9LG.—*Chief Sec.*, Rev. M. Rees.

CHURCH BUILDING SOCIETY, INCORPORATED (1818), Fulham Palace, SW6 6EA.—*Sec.*, Maj. R. I. Radford, M.B.E.

CHURCH EDUCATION CORPORATION, Bedgebury School, Goudhurst, Cranbrook, Kent TN17 2SH.—*Sec.*, R. P. Gilbert.

CHURCH HOUSE, THE CORPORATION OF (1888), Dean's Yard, SW1P 3NZ.—*Sec.*, Capt. P. W. E. Parry, M.B.E.

CHURCH LADS' AND CHURCH GIRLS' BRIGADE (1891), 2 Barnsley Road, Wath upon Dearne, Rotherham, S. Yorks. S63 6PY.—*Gen. Sec.*, Wg. Cdr. J. S. Cresswell.

CHURCH MISSIONARY SOCIETY (1799), Partnership House, 157 Waterloo Road, SE1 8UU.—*Gen. Sec.*, Rt. Rev. H. W. Moore.

CHURCH MUSIC, ROYAL SCHOOL OF (1927), Addington Palace, Croydon CR9 5AD.—*Sec.*, V. Waterhouse.

CHURCH OF ENGLAND PENSIONS BOARD (1926), 7 Little College Street, SW1P 3SF.—*Sec.*, R. G. Radford.

CHURCH OF ENGLAND SOLDIERS', SAILORS' AND AIRMEN'S CLUBS (1891), 1 Shakespeare Terrace, 126 High Street, Portsmouth PO1 2RH.—*Chairman*, Rear-Adm. A. G. Watson, C.B.

CHURCH UNION (1859), Faith House, 7 Tufton Street, SW1P 3QN.—*Gen. Sec.*, Father R. E. Thompson.

CHURCHES, BRITISH COUNCIL OF (1942), Inter-Church House, 35–41 Lower Marsh, SE1 7RL.—*Gen. Sec.*, Rev. Dr. P. Morgan.

CHURCHES, COUNCIL FOR THE CARE OF (1921), 83 London Wall, EC2M 5NA.—*Sec.*, P. A. T. Burman.

CHURCHES, FRIENDS OF FRIENDLESS (1957), 12 Edwardes Square, W8 6HG.—*Hon. Sec.*, L. E. Jones.

CHURCHES MAIN COMMITTEE (1941), Fielden House, Little College Street, SW1P 3JZ.—*Sec.*, B. M. Thimont, C.B.

CITIZENS' ADVICE BUREAUX, NATIONAL ASSOCIATION OF (1931), Myddelton House, 115–123 Pentonville Road, N1 9LZ.—*Chief Exec. Officer*, M. White.

CITY PAROCHIAL FOUNDATION (1891), 10 Fleet Street, EC4Y 1AU.—*Clerk*, T. Cook.

CIVIC TRUST, THE (1957), 17 Carlton House Terrace, SW1Y 5AW.—*Dir.*, M. C. Bradshaw.

CIVIL DEFENCE, INSTITUTE OF (1938), Bell Court House, 11 Blomfield Street, EC2M 7AY.—*Hon. Gen. Sec.*, T. B. Schofield.

CIVIL ENGINEERS, INSTITUTION OF (1818), Great George Street, SW1P 3AA.—*Sec.*, J. C. McKenzie.

CIVIL LIBERTIES, NATIONAL COUNCIL FOR (1934), 21 Tabard Street, SE1 4LA.—*Gen. Sec.*, Ms. S. Spencer.

CLASSICAL ASSOCIATION (1903).—*Hon. Treas.*, R. Wallace, Dept. of Classics, University of Keele, Keele, Newcastle, Staffs. ST5 5BG.

CLASSICAL TEACHERS, JOINT ASSOCIATION OF (1962), 31–34 Gordon Square, WC1H 0PY.—*Exec. Sec.*, Mrs. L. Kellett.

CLEAN AIR, NATIONAL SOCIETY FOR (1899), 136 North Street, Brighton BN1 1RG.—*Sec. Gen.*, J. Langston, C.B.E..

CLERGY ORPHAN CORPORATION (1749), 57B Tufton Street, SW1P 3QL.—*Sec.*, J. Buncher.

CLERKS OF WORKS OF GREAT BRITAIN INC., INSTITUTE OF (1882), 41 The Mall, Ealing, W5 3TJ.—*Sec.*, A. P. Macnamara.

COACHING CLUB (1871), 8 Parthenia Road, SW6 4BD.—*Sec.*, D. H. Clarke.

COMMERCE, ASSOCIATION OF BRITISH CHAMBERS OF (1860), Sovereign House, 212 Shaftesbury Avenue, WC2H 8EW.—*Dir. Gen.*, R. G. Taylor, C.B.E.

COMMERCE, ASSOCIATION OF SCOTTISH CHAMBERS OF, 30 George Square, Glasgow G2 1EQ.—*Sec.*, E. Marwick.

COMMERCE AND INDUSTRY, LONDON CHAMBER OF (1881), 69 Cannon Street, EC4N 5AB.—*Dir.*, A. M. W. Platt.

COMMERCE AND MANUFACTURES, EDINBURGH CHAMBER OF (1786), 3 Randolph Crescent, Edinburgh EH3 7UD.—*Chief Exec.*, D. M. Mowat.

COMMERCE AND MANUFACTURERS, GLASGOW CHAMBER OF (1783), 30 George Square, Glasgow G2 1EQ.—*Sec.*, E. Marwick.

COMMERCE, CANADA UNITED KINGDOM CHAMBER OF (1921), 3 Regent Street, SW1Y 4NZ.—*Exec. Dir.*, G. F. Bacon.

COMMERCIAL AND INDUSTRIAL EDUCATION, BRITISH ASSOCIATION FOR (BACIE) (1919), 16 Park Crescent, W1N 4AP.—*Dir.*, B. V. Murphy.

COMMERCIAL TRAVELLERS' BENEVOLENT INSTITUTION (1849).—*Sec.*, M. N. Bown, Gable End, Mill Hill Road, Arnesby, Leics. LE8 3WG.

COMMISSIONAIRES, THE CORPS OF (1859), provides employment for ex-members of H.M. forces and ex-police, fire service and merchant navy men and prison officers, *Headquarters*, 76 Bedford Court Mansions, Bedford Avenue, WC1B 3AE. Divisions in Belfast, Birmingham, Bristol, Edinburgh, Glasgow, Leeds, Liverpool, London, Manchester, Newcastle upon Tyne. Total strength, 3,000.—*Commandant*, Col. R. B. Robertson; *Deputy Commandant*, Brig. The Hon. H. E. C. Willoughby.

COMMONWEALTH TRUST (linking the Royal Commonwealth Society and the Victoria League for Commonwealth Friendship), Commonwealth House, Northumberland Avenue, WC2N 5BJ.—*Sec. Gen.*, Sir David Thorne.

COMPLEMENTARY MEDICINE, INSTITUTE FOR (1856), 21 Portland Place, W1N 3AF.—*Dir.*, A. Baird.

COMPOSERS' GUILD OF GREAT BRITAIN, THE (1945), 34 Hanway Street, W1P 9DE.—*Gen. Sec.*, Ms. E. Yeoman.

COMPUTER SOCIETY, BRITISH (1957), 13 Mansfield Street, W1M 0BP.—*Chief Exec.*, J. R. Brookes.

CONSERVATION OF HISTORIC AND ARTISTIC WORKS, INTERNATIONAL INSTITUTE FOR (1950), 6 Buckingham Street, WC2N 6BA.—*Sec. Gen.*, Prof. H. W. M. Hodges.

CONSULTING ECONOMISTS' ASSOCIATION, INTERNATIONAL (1986), 363 Upper Richmond Road West, SW14 7NX.—*Chairman*, Hon. Maureen Hadfield.

CONSULTING ENGINEERS, ASSOCIATION OF (1913), Alliance House, 12 Caxton Street, SW1H 0QL.—*Sec.*, Brig. H. Woodrow.

CONSULTING SCIENTISTS, ASSOCIATION OF (1958), 11 Rosemont Road, NW3 6NG.—*Hon. Sec.*, W. G. Simpson.

CONSUMERS' ASSOCIATION (1957), 2 Marylebone Road, NW1 4DX.—*Dir.*, J. Beishon.

CONTEMPORARY APPLIED ARTS (1948), 43 Earlham Street, WC2H 9LD.—*Dir.*, Ms. T. Marsden.

CONVEYANCERS, COUNCIL FOR LICENSED (1986), Golden Cross House, Duncannon Street, WC2N 4JF.—*Sec.*, N. R. Osner.

CO-OPERATIVE SOCIETIES AND ASSOCIATIONS:—

Co-operative Party, 158 Buckingham Palace Road, SW1W 9UB.—*Sec.*, D. Wise, O.B.E.

Co-operative Union Ltd. (1869), Holyoake House, Hanover Street, Manchester M60 0AS.—*Chief Exec. and Gen. Sec.*, D. L. Wilkinson.

Co-operative Wholesale Society (C.W.S.) (1863), P.O. Box 53, New Century House, Manchester M60 4ES.—*Chief Exec.*, Sir Dennis Landau.

Co-operative Women's Guild (1883), 342 Hoe Street, E17 9PX.—*Nat. Officer.*, Ms J. Motyka.

Fisheries Organization Society, Ltd. (1914), Lancastrian House, Derry's Cross, Plymouth PL1 2SG.—*Sec.*, W. H. Williams, M.B.E.

Plunkett Foundation for Co-operative Studies (1919), 23 Hanborough Business Park, Long Hanborough, Oxford OX7 2LH.—*Dir.*, E. Parnell.

COPYRIGHT COUNCIL, BRITISH (1953), 29–33 Berners Street, W1P 4AA.—*Sec.*, G. V. Adams.

CORONERS' SOCIETY OF ENGLAND AND WALES (1846).—*Hon. Sec.*, Dr. J. D. K. Burton, C.B.E., 7 Orchard Rise, Richmond, Surrey TW10 5BX.

CORPORATE TREASURERS, ASSOCIATION OF (1979), 12 Devereux Court, WC2R 3JJ.—*Sec.*, Ms. G. Pierpoint.

CORPORATE TRUSTEES, ASSOCIATION OF (1974), 2 Withdean Rise, Brighton BN1 6YN.—*Sec.*, L. C. Howes.

CORRESPONDENCE COLLEGES, ASSOCIATION OF BRITISH (1955), 6 Francis Grove, SW19 4DT.—*Sec.*, Mrs. M. Coren.

COTTON GROWING ASSOCIATION, BRITISH (1904), 3 Shortlands, W6 8RT.—*Man. Dir.*, M. T. G. Davies.

COUNCIL FOR THE PROTECTION OF RURAL ENGLAND (CPRE), *see* RURAL.

COUNSEL AND CARE FOR THE ELDERLY (1954), Twyman House, 16 Bonny Street, NW1 9LR.—*Gen. Sec.*, J. H. Hobart.

COUNTRY HOUSES ASSOCIATION LTD. (1955), 41 Kingsway, WC2B 6UB.—*Chief Exec.*, R. D. Bratby.

COUNTRY LANDOWNERS' ASSOCIATION (1907), 16 Belgrave Square, SW1X 8PQ.—*Dir. Gen.*, J. M. Douglas, C.B.E.

COUNTY CHIEF EXECUTIVES, ASSOCIATION OF (1974).—*Hon. Sec.*, R. W. Adcock, County Hall, Chelmsford, Essex CM1 1LX.

COUNTY COUNCILS, ASSOCIATION OF (1890), Eaton House, 66A Eaton Square, SW1W 9BH.—*Sec.*, Sir P. Newsam.

COUNTY EMERGENCY PLANNING OFFICERS' SOCIETY (1966).—*Hon. Sec.*, J. A. M. Holloway, Hampton House, 20 Albert Embankment, SE1 7SS.

COUNTY SECRETARIES, SOCIETY OF (1974).—*Hon. Sec.*, A. Fraser, County Secretary, Cumbria County Council, The Courts, Carlisle CA3 8LZ.

COUNTY SURVEYORS' SOCIETY (1884).—*Hon. Sec.*, J. J. Stansfield, Suffolk County Council, St. Edmunds House, Rope Walk, Ipswich IP4 1LZ.

COUNTY TREASURERS, SOCIETY OF (1903).— *Hon. Sec.*, D. G. Barrett, County Offices, Newland, Lincoln LN1 1YG.

CRUELTY TO ANIMALS, ROYAL SOCIETY FOR THE PREVENTION OF, *see* ROYAL and SCOTTISH SOCIETY.

CRUELTY TO CHILDREN, *see* NATIONAL and ROYAL SCOTTISH.

CULTURAL EXCHANGE, ASSOCIATION FOR (1958), Babraham, Cambridge CB2 4AP.—*Gen. Sec.*, P. B. Barnes.

CURWEN INSTITUTE (1875), 17 Primrose Avenue, Chadwell Heath, Romford RM6 4QB.—*Gen. Sec.*, H. Jones.

CWMNI URDD GOBAITH CYMRU (1922), Swyddfa'r Urdd, Aberystwyth, Dyfed SY23 1EN.—*Dir.*, J. E. Williams.

CYCLISTS' TOURING CLUB (1878), Cotterell House, 69 Meadrow, Godalming, Surrey GU7 3HS.—*Sec.*, A. J. Leng.

CYMMRODORION, THE HONOURABLE SOCIETY OF (1751), 30 Eastcastle Street, W1N 7PD.

CYSTIC FIBROSIS RESEARCH TRUST (1964), Alexandra House, 5 Blyth Road, Bromley BR1 3RS.—*Dir.*, Mrs. B. Bentley.

DAIRY ASSOCIATION, UNITED KINGDOM (1950), Giggs Hill Green, Thames Ditton, Surrey KT7 0EL.—*Sec.*, Mrs. J. M. Newton.

DAIRY FARMERS, ROYAL ASSOCIATION OF BRITISH (1876), 55 Sleaford Street, SW8 5AB.—*Chief Exec.*, P. M. Gilbert.

DAIRY TECHNOLOGY, SOCIETY OF (1943), 72 Ermine Street, Huntingdon, Cambs. PE18 6EZ.—*Nat. Sec.*, Mrs. R. Gale.

D-DAY AND NORMANDY FELLOWSHIP (1968).—*Hon. Sec.*, Mrs. L. R. Reed, 9 South Parade, Southsea, Hants. PO5 2JB.

DEAF ASSOCIATION, BRITISH (1890 *formerly* BRITISH DEAF AND DUMB ASSOCIATION), 38 Victoria Place, Carlisle CA1 1HU.—*Gen. Sec.*, Ms. E. Wincott.

DEAF CHILDREN, ROYAL SCHOOL FOR (1792), Victoria Road, Margate, Kent CT9 1NB.—*Sec.*, D. E. Downs.

DEAF, COMMONWEALTH SOCIETY FOR THE (1959), 105 Gower Street, WC1E 6AH.—*Chairman*, C. Holborow, T.D., M.D.

DEAF, ROYAL NATIONAL INSTITUTE FOR THE (1911), 105 Gower Street, WC1E 6AH.—*Chief Exec.*, M. Whitlam.

DEAF PEOPLE, FOLEY HOUSE RESIDENTIAL HOME FOR (1851), Foley House, 115 High Garrett, Braintree, Essex CM7 5NU.—*Dir.*, Mrs. N. Hartard.

DEAF PEOPLE, ROYAL ASSOCIATION IN AID OF (1841), 27 Old Oak Road, W3 7HN.—*Chief Exec.*, Ms. R. Brotherwood.

DEER MANAGEMENT SOCIETIES, THE FEDERATION OF (1975).—*Chairman.*, J. Hotchkis, Stede Court, Biddenden, Ashford, Kent TN27 EJG.

DEER SOCIETY, BRITISH, Church Farm, Lower Basildon, Reading RG8 9NH.

DEFENCE STUDIES, ROYAL UNITED SERVICES INSTITUTE FOR (1831), Whitehall, SW1A 2ET.—*Dir.*, Gp. Capt. D. Bolton.

DENTAL ASSOCIATION, BRITISH (1880), 64 Wimpole Street, W1M 8AL.—*Sec.*, N. H. Whitehouse.

DENTAL COUNCIL, GENERAL (1956), 37 Wimpole Street, W1M 8DQ.—*Registrar*, N. T. Davies, M.B.E.

DENTAL HOSPITALS OF THE UNITED KINGDOM, ASSOCIATION OF (1942).—*Hon. Sec.*, Mrs. P. Harrington, Birmingham Dental Hospital, St. Chad's Queensway, Birmingham B4 6NN.

DESIGN AND INDUSTRIES ASSOCIATION (1915).—*Chairman*, R. Moxley, Lawn Crescent, Kew Gardens, Surrey TW9 3NR.

DESIGNERS FOR INDUSTRY, FACULTY OF ROYAL (1936), R.S.A., 8 John Adam Street, WC2N 6EZ.—*Sec.*, C. Lucas.

DESIGNERS, THE CHARTERED SOCIETY OF (1930), 29 Bedford Square, WC1B 3EG.—*Dir.*, Ms. P. Rees Cummings.

DIABETIC ASSOCIATION, BRITISH (1934), 10 Queen Anne Street, W1M 0BD.—*Sec. Gen.*, Capt. D. G. Armytage, C.B.E., R.N.

DICKENS FELLOWSHIP (1902), Dickens House, 48 Doughty Street, WC1N 2LF.—*Hon. Gen. Sec.*, A. S. Watts.

DIRECTORS, INSTITUTE OF (1903), 116 Pall Mall, SW1Y 5ED.—*Dir. Gen.*, P. Morgan.

DISABILITY AND REHABILITATION, ROYAL ASSOCIATION FOR, *see* RADAR.

DISPENSING OPTICIANS, ASSOCIATION OF BRITISH (1925), 6 Hurlingham Business Park, Sulivan Road, SW6 3DU.—*Registrar*, D. S. Baker.

DISTRESSED GENTLEFOLKS' AID ASSOCIATION (1897), Vicarage Gate House, Vicarage Gate, W8 4AQ.— *Gen. Sec.*, J. A. Marshall, C.B.

DISTRICT COUNCILS, ASSOCIATION OF (1974), 9 Buckingham Gate, SW1E 6LE.—*Sec.*, G. McCartney.

DISTRICT MEDICAL OFFICERS, ASSOCIATION OF (1982).—*Hon. Sec.*, Dr. J. A. Sorrell, Burton District Hospital Centre, Belvedere Road, Burton upon Trent, Staffs. DE13 0RB.

DISTRICT SECRETARIES, ASSOCIATION OF (1974), 9 Margaret Road, Bishopsworth, Bristol BS13 9DQ.—*Hon. Sec.*, D. C. Lunn.

DITCHLEY FOUNDATION, Ditchley Park, Enstone, Oxford OX7 4ER.—*Dir.*, Sir John Graham, Bt., G.C.M.G.

DOCKLAND SETTLEMENTS (1895), Rotherhithe Street, SE16 1LJ.—*Chief Exec.*, J. B. Faul.

DOMESTIC SERVANTS' BENEVOLENT INSTITUTION (1846), Royal Bank of Scotland P.L.C., 7 Burlington Gardens, W1A 3DD.—*Sec.*, A. J. Gibson.

DOWSERS, BRITISH SOCIETY OF (1933).—*Sec.*, M. D. Rust, Sycamore Cottage, Tamley Lane, Hastingleigh, Ashford, Kent TN25 5HW.

DRAINAGE AUTHORITIES, ASSOCIATION OF (1937).— *Sec.*, D. Noble, The Mews, 3 Royal Oak Passage, High Street, Huntingdon, Cambs. PE18 6EA.

DRINKING FOUNTAIN AND CATTLE TROUGH ASSOCIATION, METROPOLITAN (1859).—*Sec.* D. R. W. Randall, 105 Wansunt Road, Bexley, Kent DA5 2DN.

DRIVING SOCIETY, BRITISH (1957), 27 Dugard Place, Barford, Warwick CV35 8DX.—*Sec.*, Mrs. J. M. Dillon.

DRUG DEPENDENCE, INSTITUTE FOR THE STUDY OF (1968), 1–4 Hatton Place, EC1N 8ND.—*Dir.*, J. Woodcock, O.B.E.

DUKE OF EDINBURGH'S AWARD SCHEME (1956), 5 Prince of Wales Terrace, W8 5PG. 61,455 awards gained world-wide.—*Dir.*, Maj.-Gen. M. F. Hobbs, C.B.E.

DYERS AND COLOURISTS, SOCIETY OF (1884), Perkin House, P.O. Box 244, 82 Grattan Road, Bradford BD1 2JB.—*Gen. Sec.*, M. Tordoff, PH.D.

EARL HAIG'S (BRITISH LEGION) APPEAL FUND, *see* BRITISH LEGION, ROYAL.

EARLY CHILDHOOD EDUCATION, BRITISH ASSOCIATION FOR (1923), 111 City View House, 463 Bethnal Green Road, E2 9QY.— *Sec.*, Mrs. B. Boon.

ECCLESIASTICAL HISTORY SOCIETY (1961).—*Sec.*, Dr. V. G. Davies, Dept. of History, Westfield College, Kidderpore Avenue, NW3 7ST.

ECCLESIOLOGICAL SOCIETY (1839).—*Hon. Sec.*, S. C. Humphrey, 1 Cornish House, Otto Street, SE17 3PE.

EDUCATION IN ART AND DESIGN, NATIONAL SOCIETY FOR (1888), 7A High Street, Corsham, Wilts. SN13 0ES.—*Gen. Sec.*, J. Steers.

EDUCATION OFFICERS, SOCIETY OF (1971), 21–27 Lambs Conduit Street, WC1N 3NJ.—*Gen. Sec.*, D. J. Hatfield.

EDUCATION OFFICERS' SOCIETY, COUNTY (1889).—*Hon. Sec.*, N. J. Fitton, Director of Education, County Hall, Chester CH1 1SQ.

EDUCATIONAL CENTRES ASSOCIATION (1921), Chequer Centre, Chequer Street, EC1Y 8PL.—*Gen. Sec.*, D. Delahunt.

EDUCATIONAL INSTITUTE OF DESIGN, CRAFT AND TECHNOLOGY (1891), 852 Melton Road, Thurmaston, Leicester LE7 8BW.—*Administrator*, C. Grimes.

EDUCATIONAL MANAGEMENT AND ADMINISTRATION SOCIETY, BRITISH (1977).—*Sec.*, Miss M. E. Hewitt, Buxton Girls' School, Buxton, Derbys. SK17 6RB.

EDUCATIONAL RESEARCH IN ENGLAND AND WALES, NATIONAL FOUNDATION FOR (1946), The Mere, Upton Park, Slough SL1 2DQ.—*Dir.*, C. Burstall, PH.D, D.SC.

EGYPT EXPLORATION SOCIETY (1882), 3 Doughty Mews, WC1N 2PG.—*Sec.*, Dr. P. A. Spencer.

ELECTORAL REFORM SOCIETY OF GREAT BRITAIN AND IRELAND, 6 Chancel Street, SE1 0UU.—*Pres.*, Lord Blake, F.B.A.

ELECTRICAL ENGINEERS, INSTITUTION OF (1871), Savoy Place, WC2R 0BL.—*Sec.*, Dr. J. C. Williams.

ELECTRICITY CONSUMERS' COUNCIL, Brook House, 2–16 Torrington Place, WC1E 7LL.—*Dir.*, T. Boorman.

ELGAR FOUNDATION (1973).— *Sec to the Trustees*, B. Edgington, Nether End, 18 Town Close, Dartmouth, Devon TQ6 9ES.

ELGAR SOCIETY (1951).—*Sec.*, Mrs. C. Holt, 20 Geraldine Road, Malvern, Worcs. WR14 3PA.

ENERGY, INSTITUTE OF (1927), 18 Devonshire Street, W1N 2AU.—*Sec.*, C. Rigg, T.D.

ENGINEERING COUNCIL, THE, 10 Maltravers Street, WC2R 3ER.—*Sec.*, L. Chelton.

ENGINEERING DESIGNERS, INSTITUTION OF (1945), Courtleigh, Westbury Leigh, Westbury, Wilts. BA13 3TA.—*Sec.*, M. J. Osborne.

ENGINEERING, FELLOWSHIP OF (1976), 2 Little Smith Street, SW1P 3DL.—*Exec. Sec.*, V. J. Osola, C.B.E.

ENGINEERING INDUSTRIES ASSOCIATION (1941), 16 Dartmouth Street, SW1H 9BL—*Dir.*, Col. W. T. Williams.

ENGINEERS AND SHIPBUILDERS, N.E. COAST INSTITUTION OF (1884), 12 Windsor Terrace, Jesmond, Newcastle upon Tyne NE2 4HE.—*Sec.*, Mrs. A. J. Rainsford.

ENGINEERS, INSTITUTION OF BRITISH (1928), Royal Liver Building, 6 Hampton Place, Brighton BN1 3DD.—*Sec.*, Mrs. D. Henry.

ENGINEERS, SOCIETY OF (INCORPORATED) (1854), Parsifal College, 527 Finchley Road, NW3 7BG.—*Sec.*, P. A. Lancaster.

ENGLISH ASSOCIATION, THE (1906), The Vicarage, Priory Gardens, W4 1TT.—*Sec.*, Dr. R. Fairbanks-Joseph.

ENGLISH FOLK DANCE AND SONG SOCIETY (1932), Cecil Sharp House, 2 Regent's Park Road, NW1 7AY.— *Chairman* , D. Purves.

ENGLISH PLACE-NAME SOCIETY (1923).—*Hon. Director*, Prof. K. Cameron, C.B.E., F.B.A., Dept. of English, The University, Nottingham NG7 2RD.

ENGLISH-SPEAKING UNION OF THE COMMONWEALTH (1918), 37 Charles Street, W1X 8AB.—*Dir. Gen.*, Rear-Adm. R. Heaslip, C.B.

ENTOMOLOGICAL SOCIETY OF LONDON, ROYAL (1833), 41 Queen's Gate, SW7 5HU.—*Registrar*, G. G. Bentley.

ENVIRONMENTAL HEALTH OFFICERS, INSTITUTION OF (1883), Chadwick House, Rushworth Street, SE1 0QT.—*Sec.*, A. M. Tanner.

ENVIRONMENT COUNCIL (1969), 80 York Way, N1 9AG.—*Chief Exec.*, S. Robinson.

EPILEPSY ASSOCIATION, BRITISH (1949), Anstey House, 40 Hanover Square, Leeds LS3 1BE.—*Chief Exec.*, T. J. O'Leary (*acting*)

EPILEPSY, THE NATIONAL SOCIETY FOR (1892), Chalfont Centre for Epilepsy, Chalfont St. Peter, Gerrards Cross, Bucks. SL9 0RJ.—*Chief Exec.*, Col. D. W. Eking.

EQUESTRIAN FEDERATION, BRITISH (1972), British Equestrian Centre, Kenilworth, Warks. CV8 2LR.—*Dir. Gen.*, M. C. R. Wallace.

ESPERANTO ASSOCIATION OF BRITAIN (1977), 140 Holland Park Avenue, W11 4UF—.*Hon. Sec.*, W. Green.

ESTATE AGENTS, NATIONAL ASSOCIATION OF (1962), Arbon House, 21 Jury Street, Warwick CV34 4EH.—*Gen. Sec.*, A. B. Clark.

EUGENICS SOCIETY *see* GALTON INSTITUTE.

EVANGELICAL ALLIANCE (1846), Whitefield House, 186 Kennington Park Road, SE11 4BT.—*Gen. Dir.*, Rev. C. R. Calver.

EVANGELICAL LIBRARY, THE (1928), 78A Chiltern Street, W1M 2HB.—*Librarian*, Miss F. S. Wright.

EXAMINERS UNDER SOLICITORS (SCOTLAND) ACT (1980), Law Society's Hall, 26 Drumsheugh Gardens, Edinburgh EH3 7YR.—*Sec.*, K. W. Pritchard.

EXECUTIVES ASSOCIATION OF GREAT BRITAIN LTD. (1929), Suite 87–89, The Hop Exchange, 24 Southwark Street, SE1 1TY.—*Sec.*, Lt.-Col. J. J. Langdon-Mudge.

EXPORT-FINANCE ADVISORY COUNCIL, BRITISH (1981), 1 Grosvenor Place, SW1X 7JB.—*Chairman*, C. D. Hankes-Drielsma.

EXPORT, INSTITUTE OF, Export House, 64 Clifton Street, EC2A 4HB.—*Sec.*, D. J. Langham.

EX-SERVICES LEAGUE, BRITISH COMMONWEALTH (1921), 48 Pall Mall, SW1Y 5JG.—*Sec. Gen.*, Brig. M. J. Doyle, M.B.E.

EX-SERVICES MENTAL WELFARE SOCIETY (1919), Broadway House, The Broadway, SW19 1RL.—*Gen. Sec.*, Brig. A. K. Dixon.

FABIAN SOCIETY (1884), 11 Dartmouth Street, SW1H 9BN.—*Gen. Sec.*, J. Willman.

FAIR ISLE BIRD OBSERVATORY TRUST (1948), 21 Regent Terrace, Edinburgh EH7 5BT.—*Hon. Sec.*, Miss V. M. Thom.

FAMILY CONCILIATION COUNCIL, NATIONAL (1982), 34 Milton Road, Swindon SN1 5JA.—*Chairman*, Mrs. K. Begg (*acting*).

FAMILY HISTORY SOCIETIES, FEDERATION OF (1974).— *Administrator*, Mrs. P. A. Saul, c/o The Benson Room, Birmingham and Midland Institute, Margaret Street, Birmingham B3 3BS.

FAMILY PLANNING ASSOCIATION (1939), 27–35 Mortimer Street, W1N 7RJ.—*Dir.*, Ms D. E. Massey.

FAMILY WELFARE ASSOCIATION (1869), 501–505 Kingsland Road, E8 4AU.—*Dir.*, R. E. Morley.

FAUNA AND FLORA PRESERVATION SOCIETY (1903), 79–83 North Street, Brighton BN1 1ZA.—*Administrator*, Miss A. Hillier.

FELLOWSHIP HOUSES TRUST (1937), Clock House, Byfleet, Weybridge, Surrey KT14 7RN.—*Sec.*, L. P. Leech.

FIELD SPORTS SOCIETY, BRITISH (1930), 59 Kennington Road, SE1 7PZ.—*Dir.*, Maj.-Gen. J. Hopkinson, C.B.

FIELD STUDIES COUNCIL (1943), Preston Montford, Montford Bridge, Shrewsbury SY4 1HW.—*Dir.*, A. D. Thomas.

FILM CLASSIFICATION, BRITISH BOARD OF (1912), 3 Soho Square, W1V 5DE.—*Dir.*, J. Ferman.

FILM INSTITUTE, BRITISH (1933), 21 Stephen Street, W1P 1PL.—*Dir.*, W. Stevenson.

FINANCIAL ACCOUNTANTS, INSTITUTE OF (1916), Burford House, 44 London Road, Sevenoaks, Kent TN13 1AS.—*Chief Exec.*, D. Gurney.

FIRE ENGINEERS, INSTITUTION OF (1918), 148 New Walk, Leicester LE1 7QB.—*Gen. Sec.*, Mrs. C. E. Mackwood.

FIRE PROTECTION ASSOCIATION (1946), 140 Aldersgate Street, EC1A 4HX.—*Dir.*, S. Kidd.

FIRE SERVICES ASSOCIATION, BRITISH (1949), 86 London Road, Leicester LE2 0QR.—*Gen. Sec.*, T. A. Plummer.

FIRE SERVICES NATIONAL BENEVOLENT FUND (1943), Marine Court, Fitzalan Road, Littlehampton, W. Sussex BN17 5NF.—*Gen. Man.*, R. A. Spackman.

FLEET AIR ARM OFFICERS ASSOCIATION (1957), 94 Piccadilly, W1V 0BP.—*Chairman*, W. J. Hanks.

FOLKLORE SOCIETY, c/o University College London, Gower Street, WC1E 6BT.—*Hon. Sec.*, A. R. Vickery.

FOOD SCIENCE AND TECHNOLOGY, INSTITUTE OF (1964), 5 Cambridge Court, 210 Shepherd's Bush Road, W6 7NL.—*Exec. Sec.*, Ms. H. G. Wild.

FOOD FROM BRITAIN (1983), 301–344 Market Towers, New Covent Garden Market, SW8 5NQ.—*Chairman*, W. Goldsmith.

FORCES HELP SOCIETY AND LORD ROBERTS WORKSHOPS (1899), 122 Brompton Road, SW3 1JE.— *Comptroller and Sec.*, Col. A. W. Davis, M.B.E.

FOREIGN BONDHOLDERS, COUNCIL OF (1873), 35 High Street, Bromley BR1 1LE.—*Manager*, E. J. French.

FOREIGN PRESS ASSOCIATION IN LONDON (1888), 11 Carlton House Terrace, SW1Y 5AJ.—*Sec.* Mrs D. Crole.

FORENSIC SCIENCES, BRITISH ACADEMY OF (1959).— *Sec. Gen.*, Dr. P. J. Flynn, Anaesthetic Unit, The London Hospital Medical College, Turner Street, E1 2AD.

FORESTERS, INSTITUTE OF CHARTERED (1982), 22 Walker Street, Edinburgh EH3 7HR.—*Sec.*, Mrs. M. W. Dick.

FORESTRY ASSOCIATION, COMMONWEALTH (1921), c/o Oxford Forestry Institute, South Parks Road, Oxford OX1 3RB.—*Sec.*, M. T. Rogers.

FORESTRY SOCIETY OF ENGLAND, WALES AND NORTHERN IRELAND, ROYAL (1882), 102 High Street, Tring, Herts. HP23 4AH.—*Dir.*, Dr. J. E. Jackson.

FORESTRY SOCIETY, ROYAL SCOTTISH (1854), 11 Atholl Crescent, Edinburgh EH3 8HE.—*Sec.* W. B. C. Walker.

FOUNDRYMEN, INSTITUTE OF BRITISH (1904), 3rd Floor, Bridge House, 121 Smallbrook Queensway, Birmingham B5 4JP.—*Sec.*, G. A. Schofield.

FRANCO-BRITISH SOCIETY (1924), Room 636, Linen Hall, 162–168 Regent Street, W1R 5TB.—*Exec. Sec.*, Mrs. M. Clarke.

FREE CHURCH FEDERAL COUNCIL (1940), 27 Tavistock Square, WC1H 9HH.—*Gen. Sec.*, Rev. D. Staple.

FREEDOM ASSOCIATION (1975), 35 Westminster Bridge Road, SE1 7JB.—*Chairman*, N. D. McWhirter.

FREEMASONS, GRAND LODGE OF ANTIENT FREE AND ACCEPTED MASONS OF SCOTLAND (1736), Freemasons' Hall, 96 George Street, Edinburgh EH2 3DH.—*Grand Master Mason of Scotland*, Brig. Sir Gregor MacGregor of MacGregor, Bt.; *Grand Sec.*, A. O. Hazel.

FREEMASONS, UNITED GRAND LODGE OF ENGLAND (1717), Freemasons' Hall, Great Queen Street, WC2B 5AZ.—*Grand Master*, H.R.H. the Duke of Kent, K.G., G.C.M.G., G.C.V.O.; *Grand Sec.*, Cdr. M. B. S. Higham.

FREEMEN OF ENGLAND (1966).—*Sec.*, H. B. Pate, 611 Old Chester Road, Rock Ferry, Birkenhead, Merseyside L42 4NN.

FREEMEN'S GUILDS:—
Freemen's Guild of Berwick-upon-Tweed, 9 Church Street, Berwick-upon-Tweed TD15 1EF.—*Clerk*, J. R. Reay.
Freemen and Guilds of the City of Chester.—The Guildhall, Chester.
City of Coventry Freemen's Guild (1946).—*Hon. Clerk*, H. J. McCranor, 89 Brinklow Road, Binley, Coventry CV3 2JB.
Guild of Freemen of the City of London (1908), P.O. Box 153, 40A Ludgate Hill, EC4M 7DE.—*Clerk*, Col. D. Ivy.
Gild of Freemen of the City of Newcastle upon Tyne.—*Hon. Sec.*, F. P. M. Cook, 79 Holly Avenue, Jesmond, Newcastle upon Tyne NE2 7QB.
Gild of Freemen of the City of York (1953).—*Hon. Clerk*, R. Lee, 29 Albemarle Road, York YO2 1EW.

FRIENDLY SOCIETIES, NATIONAL CONFERENCE OF (1887), Room 313, Victoria House, Vernon Place, WC1B 4DP.—*Sec.*, P. M. Madders.

FRIENDS OF CATHEDRAL MUSIC (1956), c/o Addington Palace, Croydon, Surrey CR9 5AD.—*Hon. Gen. Sec.*, vacant.

FRIENDS OF THE CLERGY CORPORATION, THE (1972), 27 Medway Street, SW1P 2BD.—*Sec.*, J. M. Greany.

FRIENDS OF THE ELDERLY AND GENTLEFOLK'S HELP (1905), 42 Ebury Street, SW1W 0LZ.—*Gen. Sec.*, Rev. J. Schofield.

FRIENDS OF THE NATIONAL LIBRARIES (1931), The British Library, WC1B 3DG.—*Hon. Sec.*, J. F. Fuggles.

FURNITURE HISTORY SOCIETY (1964), c/o Dept. of Furniture and Interior Design, Victoria and Albert Museum, SW7 2RL.—*Hon. Sec.*, Dr. B. Austen.

GALLIPOLI ASSOCIATION (1915).—*Hon. Sec.*, J. C. Watson-Smith, Berry Cottage, Nuptown, Bracknell, Berks. RG12 6HP.

GALTON INSTITUTE, THE (*formerly* The Eugenics Society) (1907), 19 Northfields Prospect, SW18 1PE.—*Gen. Sec.*, Mrs. L. Brooks.

GAME CONSERVANCY, THE (1969), Fordingbridge, Hants. SP6 1EF.—*Dir.*, R. M. Van Oss.

GARDEN HISTORY SOCIETY (1965), 5 The Knoll, Hereford HR1 1RU.—*Hon. Membership Sec.*, Mrs. A. Richards.

GARDENERS' ASSOCIATION, THE GOOD (1968), Two Mile Lane, Higham, Glos. GL2 8DW.—*Hon. Dir.*, R. Shewell-Cooper.

GARDENERS' ROYAL BENEVOLENT SOCIETY (1839), Bridge House, 139 Kingston Road, Leatherhead, Surrey KT22 7NT.—*Sec.-Administrator*, C. R. C. Bunce.

GAS CONSUMERS COUNCIL (1986), 6th Floor, Abford House, 15 Wilton Road, SW1V 1LT.—*Dir.*, I. W. Powe.

GAS ENGINEERS, INSTITUTION OF (1863), 17 Grosvenor Crescent, SW1X 7ES.—*Sec.*, D. J. Chapman.

GEMMOLOGICAL ASSOCIATION OF GREAT BRITAIN (1931), St. Dunstan's House, Carey Lane, EC2V 8AB.—*Sec.*, J. P. Brown.

GENEALOGICAL RESEARCH SOCIETY, IRISH (1936).—*Hon. Sec.*, Miss R. McCutcheon, c/o The Challoner Club, 61 Pont Street, SW1 0BG.

GENEALOGISTS AND RECORD AGENTS, ASSOCIATION OF (1968), 1 Woodside Close, Caterham, Surrey CR3 6AU.—*Sec.*, Mrs. J. Tooke.

GENEALOGISTS, SOCIETY OF (1911), 14 Charterhouse Buildings, Goswell Road, EC1M 7BA.—*Dir.*, A. J. Camp.

GENERAL PRACTITIONERS, ROYAL COLLEGE OF (1952), 14 Princes Gate, Hyde Park, SW7 1PU.—*Gen. Administrator*, Mrs. S. Irvine.

GENTLEPEOPLE, GUILD OF AID FOR (1904), 10 St. Christopher's Place, W1M 6HY.—*Sec.*, Mrs. G. A. Burgess.

GEOGRAPHICAL ASSOCIATION, 343 Fulwood Road, Sheffield S10 3BP.—*Sen. Administrator*, Miss M. R. Barlow.

GEOGRAPHICAL SOCIETY, ROYAL (1830), 1 Kensington Gore, SW7 2AR.—*Pres.*, Lord Chorley.

GEOGRAPHICAL SOCIETY, ROYAL SCOTTISH (1884), 10 Randolph Crescent, Edinburgh EH3 7TU.—*Sec.*, A. B. Cruickshank.

GEOLOGICAL SOCIETY (1807), Burlington House, Piccadilly, W1V 0JU.—*Pres.*, Prof. D. J. Blundell.

GEOLOGISTS' ASSOCIATION (1858), Burlington House, Piccadilly, W1V 9AG.—*Hon. Gen. Sec.*, Mrs. S. M. Dellow.

GEOLOGISTS, THE INSTITUTION OF (1977), Burlington House, Piccadilly, W1V 9AG.—*Sec.*, Dr. J. A. Seymour.

GEORGIAN GROUP (1937), 37 Spital Square, E1 6DY.—*Sec.*, R. White.

GIFTED CHILDREN, NATIONAL ASSOCIATION FOR (1966), 1 South Audley Street, W1Y 5DQ.—*Dir.*, Ms. P. G. Miles (*acting*).

GILBERT AND SULLIVAN SOCIETY (1924), 273 Northfield Avenue, W5 4UA.

GIRL GUIDES ASSOCIATION (1910), 17–19 Buckingham Palace Road, SW1W 0PT. In 1987 the total membership in the United Kingdom was 749,362.—*Chief Commissioner*, Dr. June Paterson-Brown; *Gen. Sec.*, Miss M. W. Hayter.

GIRLS' BRIGADE, THE, Girls' Brigade House, 62 Foxhall Road, Didcot, Oxon. OX11 7BQ.—*Brigade Sec. for England and Wales*, Miss D. M. Cosser.

GIRLS' FRIENDLY SOCIETY AND TOWNSEND FELLOWSHIP (1875), 126 Queens Gate, SW7 5LQ.—*Gen. Sec.*, Miss H. G. Smith.

GIRLS' VENTURE CORPS AIR CADETS (1964), Redhill Aerodrome, Kings Mill Lane, South Nutfield, Redhill RH1 5JY.—*Sec. Gen.*, Miss H. P. Prosper.

GLASS ENGRAVERS, THE GUILD OF (1975).—*Sec.*, Mrs. K. Coleman, 49 Crediton Hill, NW6 1HS.

GLASS TECHNOLOGY, SOCIETY OF (1916), Thornton, 20 Hallam Gate Road, Sheffield S10 5BT.—*Hon. Sec.*, W. Simpson.

GLIDING ASSOCIATION, BRITISH (1930), Kimberley House, Vaughan Way, Leicester LE1 4SE.—*Gen. Sec.*, B. Rolfe.

GOAT SOCIETY, BRITISH (1879), 34–36 Fore Street, Bovey Tracey, Newton Abbot, Devon TQ13 9AD.—*Sec.*, Mrs. S. Knowles.

GRAPHIC FINE ART, SOCIETY OF (1919), 9 Newburgh Street, W1V 1LH.—*Sec.*, Miss L. A. Robinson.

GRAPHOLOGISTS, THE BRITISH INSTITUTE OF (1983), 4th Floor, Bell Court House, 11 Blomfield Street, EC2M 7AY.—*Chairman*, J. E. Blomfield.

GREATER LONDON PLAYING FIELDS ASSOCIATION (1926), 25 Ovington Square, SW3 1LQ.—*Sec.*, Mrs. H. Hays.

GREEK INSTITUTE (1969), 34 Bush Hill Road, N21 2DS.—*Dir.*, Dr. K. Tofallis.

GREEN PARTY, THE (1973), 10 Station Parade, Balham High Road, SW12 9AZ.—*Office Manager*, J. Bishop.

GROCERS ASSOCIATION, BRITISH INDEPENDENT (1890), Federation House, 17 Farnborough Street, Farnborough, Hants. GU14 8AG.—*Nat. Sec.*, I. A. McKee.

GUIDE DOGS FOR THE BLIND ASSOCIATION (1931), Alexandra House, Park Street, Windsor, Berks. SL4 1JR.—*Dir. Gen.*, J. C. Oxley.

GULBENKIAN FOUNDATION, *see* CALOUSTE GULBENKIAN FOUNDATION.

GREENPEACE (1971), 30 Islington Green, N1 8XE.—*Gen. Sec.*, Lord Melchett.

HAKLUYT SOCIETY (1846), c/o Map Library, The British Library, Great Russell Street, WC1B 3DG.—*Joint Hon. Secs.*, Dr. T. E. Armstrong; Mrs. S. Tyacke.

HANSARD SOCIETY FOR PARLIAMENTARY GOVERNMENT (1944), 16 Gower Street, WC1E 6DP.—*Dir.*, D. Harris.

HARD OF HEARING, BRITISH ASSOCIATION OF THE (1948), 7–11 Armstrong Road, W3 7JL.—*Chairman*, P. J. Phillips.

HARVEIAN SOCIETY OF EDINBURGH (1782), Dept. of Medicine, The Royal Infirmary, Edinburgh EH3 9YW.—*Joint Secs.*, Dr. A. D. Toft; A. B. MacGregor.

HARVEIAN SOCIETY OF LONDON (1831), 11 Chandos Street, W1M 0EB.—*Exec. Sec.*, Maj. T. Tudor-Williams.

HEAD TEACHERS, NATIONAL ASSOCIATION OF (1897).—*Gen. Sec.*, D. M. Hart, O.B.E., 1 Heath Square, Boltro Road, Haywards Heath, W. Sussex RH16 1BL.

HEALTH AUTHORITIES, NATIONAL ASSOCIATION OF (1974), Garth House, 47 Edgbaston Park Road, Birmingham B15 2RS.—*Dir.*, P. Hunt.

HEALTH CARE ASSOCIATION, BRITISH (1931), 41 St. Paul's Street, Leeds LS1 2JL.—*Nat. Sec.*, G. K. Waite.

HEALTH EDUCATION, INSTITUTE OF (1962).—*Hon. Sec.*, Prof. L. Baric, 14 High Elm Road, Hale Barns, Altrincham, Cheshire WA15 0HS.

HEALTH, GUILD OF (1904), Edward Wilson House, 26 Queen Anne Street, W1M 9LB.—*Nat. Dir.*, W. R. Booth.

HEALTH SERVICES MANAGEMENT, INSTITUTE OF (1902), 75 Portland Place, W1N 4AN.—*Dir.*, Ms. M. Dixon, PH.D.

HEART FOUNDATION, BRITISH (1963), 102 Gloucester Place, W1H 4DH.—*Dir. Gen.*, Brig. M. C. Thursby Pelham, O.B.E.

HEDGEHOG PRESERVATION SOCIETY, BRITISH (1982), Knowbury House, Knowbury, Ludlow, Salop. SY8 3LQ.—*Sec.*, Mrs. A. Jenkins.

HELP THE AGED (1960), St. James's Walk, EC1R 0BE.—*Dir. Gen.*, J. Mayo, O.B.E.

HELLENIC STUDIES, SOCIETY FOR THE PROMOTION OF (1879), 31–34 Gordon Square, WC1H 0PP.—*Hon. Sec.*, Prof. J. P. Barron.

HENRY GEORGE FOUNDATION, 177 Vauxhall Bridge Road, SW1V 1EU.—*Company Sec.*, Mrs. B. P. Sobrielo.

HERALDIC AND GENEALOGICAL STUDIES, INSTITUTE OF (1961), 79–82 Northgate, Canterbury, Kent CT1 1BA.—*Sec.*, C. H. Schofield.

HERALDRY SOCIETY, THE (1947), 44–45 Museum Street, WC1A 1LY.—*Sec.*, Marian Miles, M.B.E.

HERALDRY SOCIETY OF SCOTLAND (1977).—*Sec.*, Dr. M. C. Stanton, 9 Priestden Park, St. Andrews, Fife KY16 8DL.

HERPETOLOGICAL SOCIETY, BRITISH (1947), c/o Zoological Society of London, Regent's Park, NW1 4RY.—*Sec.*, Mrs. M. Green.

HIGHWAYS AND TRANSPORTATION, INSTITUTION OF (1930), 3 Lygon Place, Ebury Street, SW1W 0JS.—*Sec.*, Miss P. A. Steel.

HISPANIC AND LUSO BRAZILIAN COUNCIL (1943), Canning House, 2 Belgrave Square, SW1X 8PJ.—*Dir. Gen.*, Sir Kenneth James, K.C.M.G.

HISTORICAL ASSOCIATION, THE (1906), 59A Kennington Park Road, SE11 4JH.—*Sec.*, Mrs. M. Stiles.

HISTORICAL SOCIETY, ROYAL (1868), University College London, Gower Street, WC1E 6BT.—*Pres.*, Prof. F. M. L. Thompson; *Exec. Sec.*, Mrs. J. N. McCarthy.

HOMEOPATHIC ASSOCIATION, BRITISH (1902), 27A Devonshire Street, W1N 1RJ.—*Gen. Sec.*, Mrs. E. Segall.

HONG KONG ASSOCIATION (1961), Swire House, 59 Buckingham Gate, SW1E 6AJ.—*Exec. Dir.*, Brig. B. G. Hickey, O.B.E., M.C.

HORATIAN SOCIETY (1933), 4 Stone Buildings, Lincolns Inn, WC2A 3XT.—*Hon. Sec.*, C. P. Sydenham.

HOROLOGICAL INSTITUTE, BRITISH (1858), Upton Hall, Upton, Newark, Notts. NG23 5TE.—*Sec.*, W. M. G. Evans.

HOROLOGICAL SOCIETY, ANTIQUARIAN (1953), New House, High Street, Ticehurst, Wadhurst, E. Sussex TN5 7AL.—*Acting Sec.*, Mrs. M. R. Janes.

HORSE SOCIETY, BRITISH (1947) (incorporating THE PONY CLUB), British Equestrian Centre, Kenilworth, Warks. CV8 2LR.—*Dir.*, Col. T. Eastwood.

HOSPITAL FEDERATION, INTERNATIONAL (1947), 2 St. Andrew's Place, NW1 4LB.—*Dir. Gen.*, Dr. E. N. Pickering.

HOSPITAL SATURDAY FUND, THE (1873), 192–198 Vauxhall Bridge Road, SW1V 1EE.—*Chief Exec.*, K. R. Bradley.

HOSPITAL SAVING ASSOCIATION, THE, Hambleden House, Andover, Hants. SP10 1LQ.—*Gen. Sec.*, J. A. Young.

HOTEL, CATERING AND INSTITUTIONAL MANAGEMENT ASSOCIATION (1971), 191 Trinity Road, SW17 7HN.—*Dir.*, Miss E. Gadsby.

HOTELS, RESTAURANTS AND CATERERS ASSOCIATION, BRITISH (1907), 40 Duke Street, W1M 6HR.—*Chief Exec.*, R. Lees, C.B., M.B.E.

HOUSE OF ST. BARNABAS IN SOHO (1846), 1 Greek Street, W1V 6NQ. For homeless women in London.—*Dir.*, Gp. Capt. H. A. Lax.

HOUSING, INSTITUTE OF, 9 White Lion Street, N1 9XJ.—*Dir.*, P. McGurk.

HOUSING AID SOCIETY, CATHOLIC (1956), 189A Old Brompton Road, SW5 0AR.—*Dir.*, Ms. R. Rafferty.

HOUSING AND TOWN PLANNING COUNCIL, NATIONAL (1900), 14–18 Old Street, EC1V 9AB.—*Dir.*, R. Walker.

HOUSING ASSOCIATION FOR OFFICERS' FAMILIES (1916), Alban Dobson House, Green Lane, Morden, Surrey SM4 5NS.—*Gen. Sec.*, J. B. Holt.

HOVERCRAFT SOCIETY, THE (1971), 24 Jellicoe Avenue, Alverstoke, Gosport, Hants. PO12 2PE.—*Chairman*, B. J. Russell.

HOWARD LEAGUE FOR PENAL REFORM, THE (1866), 322 Kennington Park Road, SE11 4PP.—*Dir.*, Ms. F. Crook.

HUGUENOT SOCIETY OF GREAT BRITAIN AND IRELAND (1885), The Huguenot Library, University College, Gower Street, WC1E 6BT.—*Sec.*, Mrs. M. Bayliss.

HUMANE RESEARCH TRUST, (1974), Brook House, 29 Bramhall Lane South, Bramhall, Stockport, Cheshire SK7 2DN.—*Chairman*, R. MacAlastair Brown.

HYDROGRAPHIC SOCIETY (1972), c/o Polytechnic of East London, Longbridge Road, Dagenham, Essex RM8 2AS.—*Hon. Sec.*, V. J. Abbott.

HYMN SOCIETY OF GREAT BRITAIN AND IRELAND (1936).—*Sec.*, Rev. M. Garland, St. Nicholas Rectory, Glebe Fields, Curdworth, Sutton Coldfield, W. Midlands B76 9ES.

INDEPENDENT SCHOOL BURSARS' ASSOCIATION (1933).—*Sec.*, D. J. Bird, Woodlands, Closewood Road, Denmead, Portsmouth PO7 6JD.

INDEPENDENT SCHOOLS CAREERS ORGANIZATION (1942), 12A–18A Princess Way, Camberley, Surrey GU15 3SP.—*Dir.* G. W. Searle.

INDEPENDENT SCHOOLS INFORMATION SERVICE (I.S.I.S.) (1972), 56 Buckingham Gate, SW1E 6AG.—*Dir.*, D. J. Woodhead.

INDEPENDENT SCHOOLS JOINT COUNCIL (1974), 25 Victoria Street, SW1H 0EX.—*Gen. Sec.*, Dr. A. G. Hearnden.

INDEXERS, SOCIETY OF (1957).—*Sec.*, Mrs. C. Troughton, 16 Green Road, Birchington, Kent CT7 9JZ.

INDUSTRIAL CHRISTIAN FELLOWSHIP (1877), St. Katharine Cree Church, 86 Leadenhall Street EC3A 3DH.—*Dir.*, D. Arthur.

INDUSTRIAL MANAGERS, INSTITUTION OF (1931), Rochester House, 66 Little Ealing Lane, W5 4XX.—*Chief Exec.*, G. J. Rawlings, O.B.E.

INDUSTRIAL MARKETING RESEARCH ASSOCIATION (1963), 11 Bird Street, Lichfield, Staffs. WS13 6PW.—*Dir. Gen.*, E. Barnsley.

INDUSTRIAL PARTICIPATION ASSOCIATION (1884), 85 Tooley Street, SE1 2QZ.—*Dir.*, B. C. Stevens.

INDUSTRIAL SOCIETY, THE (1918), Robert Hyde House, 48 Bryanston Square, W1H 7LN.—*Dir.*, A. Graham.

INDUSTRY AND PARLIAMENT TRUST, 25 Victoria Street, SW1H 0EX. Aims to bridge the gap in understanding between industry and parliament.—*Dir.*, F. R. Hyde-Chambers.

INFANT DEATHS, THE FOUNDATION FOR THE STUDY OF (1971), 15 Belgrave Square, SW1X 8PS.—*Chief Exec.*,Ms. E. De'Ath.

INFORMATION SCIENTISTS, INSTITUTE OF (1958), 44 Museum Street, WC1A 1LY.—*Exec. Sec.*, Mrs. S. A. Carter.

INNER WHEEL CLUBS IN GREAT BRITAIN AND IRELAND, ASSOCIATION OF (1934), 51 Warwick Square, SW1V 2AT.—*Gen. Sec.*, Miss J. Dobson.

INSURANCE AND INVESTMENT BROKERS' ASSOCIATION, BRITISH, BIIBA House, 14 Bevis Marks, EC3A 7NT.—*Dir. Gen.*, J. C. T. Hackett.

INSURANCE BROKERS REGISTRATION COUNCIL, 15 St. Helen's Place, EC3A 6DS.—*Registrar*, Miss E. J. Rees.

INSURANCE INSTITUTE, CHARTERED (1897), 20 Aldermanbury, EC2V 7HY.—*Sec. Gen.*, P. V. Saxton.

INSURERS, ASSOCIATION OF BRITISH (1985), Aldermary House, 10–15 Queen Street, EC4N 1TT.—*Chief Exec.*, M. A. Jones.

INTERCON (INTERCONTINENTAL CHURCH SOCIETY) (1823), 175 Tower Bridge Road, SE1 2AQ.—*Gen. Sec.*, Rev. Canon D. R. Irving.

INTERNATIONAL AFFAIRS, ROYAL INSTITUTE OF (1920), Chatham House, 10 St. James's Square, SW1Y 4LE.—*Dir.*, Adm. Sir James Eberle, G.C.B.

INTERNATIONAL FRIENDSHIP LEAGUE (1931), 3 Creswick Road, W3 9HE.—*Sec.*, Mrs. B. Macdonald.

INTERNATIONAL LAW ASSOCIATION (1873), 3 Paper Buildings, Temple, EC4Y 7EU.—*Hon. Sec. Gen.*, B. Mauleverer, Q.C..

INTERNATIONAL POLICE ASSOCIATION (British Section) (1950), 1 Fox Road, West Bridgford, Nottingham NG2 6AJ.—*Chief Exec. Officer*, K. H. Robinson.

INTERNATIONAL SHIPPING FEDERATION (1909), 30–32 St. Mary Axe, EC3A 8ET.—*Sec.*, D. A. Dearsley.

INTERNATIONAL STUDENTS HOUSE (1962), 229 Great Portland Street, W1N 5HD.—*Sec.*, W. R. Murray.

INTERNATIONAL TIN RESEARCH INSTITUTE (1932).—*Dir.*, Dr. B. T. K. Barry, Kingston Lane, Uxbridge, Middx. UB8 3PJ.

INTERNATIONAL VOLUNTARY SERVICE (1920), 162 Upper New Walk, Leicester LE1 7QA.—*Sec.*, P. Ticher.

INTERSERVE (*formerly* B.M.M.F.) (1852), Whitefield House, 186 Kennington Park Road, SE11 4BT.—*Gen. Sec.*, A. M. S. Pont.

INTER VARSITY CLUBS, ASSOCIATION OF (1946), 26 Chesswood Road, Worthing, W. Sussex BN11 2AD.—*Sec.*, M. A. Rooke-Matthews.

INVALID CHILDREN'S AID NATIONWIDE (I CAN) (1888), Allen Graham House, 198 City Road, EC1V 2PH.—*Dir.*, J. McKinnon.

INVALIDS-AT-HOME (1966).—*Hon. Sec.*, Mrs. E. Pierce, 23 Farm Avenue, NW2 2BJ. Helps seriously disabled people living at home.

INVISIBLE EXPORTS COUNCIL, BRITISH (1983), Windsor House, 39 King Street, EC2V 8DQ.—*Dir. Gen.*, D. P. Thomson.

IRAN SOCIETY (1936), 2 Belgrave Square, SW1X 8PJ.—*Hon. Sec.*, J. R. H. James, O.B.E.

IRISH SOCIETY, THE HONOURABLE THE (1613), Irish Chamber, Guildhall Yard, EC2V 5AE.—*Sec.*, B. E. Manning; *Representative* (*Ireland*), Cmdr. P. C. D. Campbell, M.V.O.

JAPAN ASSOCIATION (1950), Swire House, 59 Buckingham Gate, SW1E 6AJ.—*Exec. Dir.*, Brig. B. G. Hickey, O.B.E., M.C.

JERUSALEM AND THE MIDDLE EAST CHURCH ASSOCIATION, THE (1887), The Old Gatehouse, Castle Hill, Farnham, Surrey GU9 0AE—*Gen. Sec.*, Rev. E. Lewis.

JEWISH HISTORICAL SOCIETY OF ENGLAND (1893), 33 Seymour Place, W1H 5AP.—*Hon. Sec.*, C. M. Drukker.

JEWISH WELFARE BOARD (1859).—*Exec. Dir.*, M. I. Carlowe, 221 Golders Green Road, NW11 9DW.

JEWISH YOUTH, ASSOCIATION FOR (1899), A.J.Y. House, 50 Lindley Street, E1 3AX.—*Exec. Dir.*, M. Shaw.

JEWS, CHURCH'S MINISTRY AMONG THE (1809), 30C Clarence Road, St. Albans, Herts. AL1 4JJ.—*Gen. Dir.*, Rev. J. M. V. Drummond.

JOHN INNES INSTITUTE (1910), Colney Lane, Norwich NR4 7UH.—*Dir.*, Prof. R. B. Flavell, PH.D.

JOURNALISTS, THE INSTITUTE OF (1883), Suite 2, Dock Offices, Surrey Quays, Lower Road, SE16 2XL.—*Joint Gen. Secs.*, C. Underwood; W. Tadd.

JUSTICE (British Section of the International Commission of Jurists) (1957), 95A Chancery Lane, WC2A 1DT.—*Dir.*, Ms. L. Levin.

JUSTICES' CLERKS' SOCIETY (1839), The Court House, Homer Road, Solihull, W. Midlands B91 3RD.—*Hon. Sec.*, A. R. Heath.

KING EDWARD'S HOSPITAL FUND FOR LONDON (THE KING'S FUND) (1897), 14 Palace Court, W2 4HT.—Makes grants to hospitals and related organizations both within and outside the N.H.S. in the Greater London area.—*Sec.*, R. J. Maxwell, PH.D.

KING GEORGE'S FUND FOR SAILORS (1917), 1 Chesham Street, SW1X 8NF. Supports all seafarers or their dependants in need. Distributes over £1,400,000 in grants annually.—*Dir. Gen.*, Hon. H. Lawson.

KIPLING SOCIETY, THE (1927), 18 Northumberland Avenue, WC2N 5BJ.—*Hon. Sec.*, N. Entract.

LADIES IN REDUCED CIRCUMSTANCES, SOCIETY FOR THE ASSISTANCE OF (1886), Lancaster House, 25 Hornyold Road, Malvern, Worcs. WR14 1QQ.

LANCASTRIANS IN LONDON, ASSOCIATION OF (1892), Burnley House, 129 Kingsway, WC2B 6NJ.—*Hon. Sec.*, J. D. Dwyer.

LANDSCAPE INSTITUTE (1929), 12 Carlton House Terrace, SW1Y 5AH.—*Registrar*, P. R. Broadbent, O.B.E.

LAND VALUE TAXATION AND FREE TRADE, INTERNATIONAL UNION FOR, 177 Vauxhall Bridge Road, SW1V 1EU.—*Sec.*, Mrs. B. Sobrielo.

LAND-VALUE TAXATION LEAGUE, 177 Vauxhall Bridge Road, SW1V 1EU.—*Pres.*, V. G. Saldji.

LANGUAGE LEARNING, ASSOCIATION OF (1990), Regent's College, Inner Circle, Regent's Park, NW1 4NS.—*Gen. Sec.*, Mrs. C. Wilding.

LAW REPORTING FOR ENGLAND AND WALES, INCORPORATED COUNCIL OF (1865), 3 Stone Buildings, Lincoln's Inn, WC2A 3XN.—*Sec.*, B. Symondson.

LEAGUE OF THE HELPING HAND (1908), Baileys, Church Street, Charlbury, Oxford OX7 3PR.—*Sec.*, Mrs. D. R. Colvin.

LEAGUE OF WELLDOERS (1893), 119–121 Limekiln Lane, Liverpool L5 8SN.—*Warden and Sec.*, K. H. Stanton.

LEATHER AND HIDE TRADES' BENEVOLENT INSTITUTION (1860), 60 Wickham Hill, Hurstpierpoint, Hassocks, W. Sussex BN6 9NP.—*Sec.*, Mrs. G. M. Stapleton, M.B.E.

LEGAL EXECUTIVES, INSTITUTE OF (1892), Kempston Manor, Kempston, Bedford MK42 7AB.—*Sec. Gen.*, L. A. Evans.

LEONARD CHESHIRE FOUNDATION (1955), Leonard Cheshire House, 26–29 Maunsel Street, SW1P 2QN. 78 residential care and nursing homes and 28 family support services in the U.K. and affiliated to a further 165 homes worldwide.—*Dir.*, A. L. Bennett.

LEPROSY MISSION, THE (England and Wales) (1874), Goldhay Way, Orton Goldhay, Peterborough, PE2 0GZ.—*Chairman*, Dr. D. Moore.

LEUKAEMIA RESEARCH FUND (1962), 43 Great Ormond Street, WC1N 3JJ.—*Dir.*, G. J. Piller, O.B.E.

LIBRARY ASSOCIATION (1877), 7 Ridgmount Street, WC1E 7AE.—*Chief Exec.*, G. Cunningham.

LIFEBOATS, *see* ROYAL NATIONAL LIFEBOAT INSTITUTION.

LIGHT HORSE BREEDING SOCIETY, NATIONAL (1885), 96 High Street, Edenbridge, Kent TN8 5AR.—*Sec.*, G. W. Evans.

LINGUISTS, INSTITUTE OF (1910), 24A Highbury Grove, N5 2EA.—*Gen. Sec.*, vacant.

LINNEAN SOCIETY OF LONDON (1788), Burlington House, Piccadilly, W1V 0LQ.—*Pres.*, Prof. M. F. Claridge.

LIONS CLUBS INTERNATIONAL (British Isles & Ireland) (1949), 5 Vine Terrace, The Square, Harborne, Birmingham B17 9PU.—*Gen. Sec.*, P. Jay.

LLOYD'S, Lime Street, EC3M 7HL.—*Chief Exec.*, A. Lord, C.B.

LLOYD'S PATRIOTIC FUND (1803), Lloyd's, Lime Street, EC3M 7HA.—*Sec.*, Mrs. J. H. Bright.

LLOYD'S REGISTER OF SHIPPING (1760), 71 Fenchurch Street, EC3M 4BS.—*Sec.*, W. T. Leadbetter.

LOCAL AUTHORITIES, INTERNATIONAL UNION OF (British Section) (1913), (*also* COUNCIL OF EUROPEAN MUNICIPALITIES AND REGIONS (British Section) (1951)), 35 Great Smith Street, SW1P 3BJ.—*Sec. Gen.*, P. N. Bongers.

LOCAL AUTHORITY CHIEF EXECUTIVES, SOCIETY OF (1974).—*Hon. Sec.*, S. Jones, County Hall, Glenfield, Leicester LE3 8RA.

LOCAL COUNCILS, NATIONAL ASSOCIATION OF (1947), 108 Great Russell Street, WC1B 3LD.—*Sec.*, J. Clark.

LONDON APPRECIATION SOCIETY (1932), 17 Manson Mews, SW7 5AF.—*Hon. Sec.*, B. Peers, PH.D.

LONDON BOROUGHS ASSOCIATION (1964), 23 Buckingham Gate, SW1E 6LB.—*Hon. Sec.*, R. G. Brooke.

LONDON CITY MISSION (1835), 175 Tower Bridge Road, SE1 2AH.—*Gen. Sec.*, Rev. D. M. Whyte.

LONDON COURT OF INTERNATIONAL ARBITRATION (1892), 75 Cannon Street, EC4N 5BH.—*Pres.*, The Rt. Hon. Sir Michael Kerr; *Registrar*, B. W. Vigrass, O.B.E., V.R.D.

LONDON FLOTILLA (1937). (Association of Reserve and Retired Officers of The Royal Navy).—*Hon. Sec.*, Lt. Cdr. P. A. G. Norman R.D., R.N.R., Marden Rise, 81 Lower Road, Fetcham, Leatherhead, Surrey KT22 9HG.

LONDON LIBRARY, THE (1841), 14 St. James's Square, SW1Y 4LG.—*Librarian*, D. Matthews.

LONDON MAGISTRATES' CLERKS' ASSOCIATION (1889), Hampstead Magistrates' Court, Downshire Hill, NW3 1PA.— *Hon. Sec.*, Miss C. M. Glenn.

'LONDON OVER THE BORDER' CHURCH FUND (1878), 53 New Street, Chelmsford CM1 1NG.—*Sec.*, J. C. Reddington.

LONDON PLAYING FIELDS SOCIETY, THE (1890), Boston Manor Playing Field, Boston Gardens, Brentford, Middx. TW8 9LR.—*Sec.*, D. C. Northwood.

LONDON SOCIETY, THE (1912), Room U722, The City University, Northampton Square, EC1V 0HB.—*Hon. Sec.*, Mrs. J. E. Vernau.

LORD'S DAY OBSERVANCE SOCIETY (1831), 120 Wandle Road, Morden, Surrey SM4 6AE.—*Gen. Sec.*, J. G. Roberts.

LORD'S TAVERNERS, THE (1950), 1 Chester Street, SW1X 7HP.—*Dir.*, Capt. J. A. R. Swainson, O.B.E., R.N.

LOTTERIES COUNCIL, THE (1979), 81 Mansel Street, Swansea SA1 5TT.—*Hon. Sec.* J. H. Solly.

MAGISTRATES' ASSOCIATION, THE (1920), 28 Fitzroy Square, W1P 6DD.—*Sec.*, T. R. P. Rudin.

MAIL USERS' ASSOCIATION (1976), P.O. Box 500, Lavington Street, SE1 0NH.—*Chairman*, J. Blackwell.

MALAYSIAN RUBBER PRODUCERS' RESEARCH ASSOCIATION (1938), Tun Abdul Razak Laboratory, Brickendonbury, Hertford SG13 8NL.—*Dir.*, C. S. L. Baker.

MALCOLM SARGENT CANCER FUND FOR CHILDREN (1968).—*Gen. Administrator*, Miss S. Darley, O.B.E., 14 Abingdon Road, W8 6AF.

MALONE SOCIETY (for the publication of scholarly editions and facsimiles of early English dramatic texts).—*Hon. Sec.*, Dr. Lois Potter, Dept. of English, University of Leicester LE1 7RH.

MANAGEMENT, BRITISH INSTITUTE OF (1947), 64–78 Kingsway, WC2B 6BL.—*Dir. Gen.*, P. Benton.

MANAGEMENT CONSULTANCIES ASSOCIATION (1956), 11 West Halkin Street, SW1X 8JL.—*Exec. Dir.*, B. O'Rorke.

MANAGEMENT AND PROFESSIONAL STAFFS, ASSOCIATION OF (1972), Parkgates, Bury New Road, Prestwich, Manchester M25 8JX.—*Exec. Sec.*, Mr. A. J. Casey.

MANAGEMENT SERVICES, INSTITUTE OF, 1 Cecil Court, London Road, Enfield, Middx. EN2 6DD.—*Dir. and Gen. Sec.*, E. A. King.

MANORIAL SOCIETY OF GREAT BRITAIN (1906), 104 Kennington Road, SE11 6RE.—*Hon. Chairman*, R. A. Smith.

MANPOWER SOCIETY (1969).—*Administrator*, Mrs. B. Hurley, 2 Woodbine Cottages, Headington Hill Top, Oxford OX3 0BT.

MARIE CURIE CANCER CARE (Marie Curie Memorial Foundation) (1948), 28 Belgrave Square, SW1X 8QG.—*Dir. Gen.*, Maj. Gen. M. E. Carleton-Smith, C.B.E. *Scottish Office*, 21 Rutland Street, Edinburgh EH1 2AH.

MARINE ARTISTS, ROYAL SOCIETY OF (1939), 17 Carlton House Terrace, SW1V 4DG.—*Sec.*, M. Myers.

MARINE BIOLOGICAL ASSOCIATION OF THE U.K. (1884), Citadel Hill, Plymouth PL1 2PB.—*Sec.*, Dr. M. Whitfield.

MARINE BIOLOGICAL ASSOCIATION, SCOTTISH (1914), P.O. Box 3, Oban, Argyll PA34 4AD.—*Dir.*, Prof. J. B. L. Matthews.

MARINE ENGINEERS, INSTITUTE OF (1889), The Memorial Building, 76 Mark Lane, EC3R 7JN.—*Sec.*, J. E. Sloggett.

MARINE SOCIETY, THE (1756), 202 Lambeth Road, SE1 7JW.—*Gen. Sec.*, Lt. Cdr. R. M. Frampton.

MARIO LANZA EDUCATIONAL FOUNDATION (for singers) (1976),—*Hon. Sec.*, Miss P. Barron, 7 Lionfields Avenue, Allesley Village, Coventry CV5 9GN.

MARKET AUTHORITIES, NATIONAL ASSOCIATION OF BRITISH (1948).—*Sec.*, B. Ormshaw, 19 Derwent Avenue, Milnrow, Rochdale, Lancs. OL16 3UD.

MARKETING, INSTITUTE OF (1911), Moor Hall, Cookham, Maidenhead, Berks. SL6 9QH.—*Dir. Gen.*, T. McBurnie.

MARKET TRADERS' FEDERATION, NATIONAL (1899), Hampton House, Hawshaw Lane, Hoyland, Barnsley S74 0HA.—*Gen. Sec.*, R. J. Toller.

MARK MASTER MASONS, GRAND LODGE OF (1856), Mark Masons' Hall, 86 St. James's Street, SW1A 1PL.—*Grand Master*, H.R.H. Prince Michael of Kent; *Grand Sec.*, P. G. Williams.

MARRIAGE GUIDANCE, *see* RELATE.

MASONIC BENEVOLENT INSTITUTION, ROYAL (1842), 20 Great Queen Street, WC2B 5BG.—*Sec.*, N. A. Grout.

MASONIC BENEVOLENT INSTITUTIONS IN IRELAND, 17–19 Molesworth Street, Dublin 2.—*Sec.*, M. R. McWilliam.

MASONIC TRUST FOR GIRLS AND BOYS (1985), 31 Great Queen Street, WC2B 5AG.—*Sec.*, Col. R. K. Hind.

MASTER BUILDERS, FEDERATION OF (1941), Gordon Fisher House, 14–15 Great James Street, WC1N 3DP.—*Dir. Gen.*, W. S. Hilton.

MASTERS OF FOXHOUNDS ASSOCIATION (1881).—*Sec.*, A. H. B. Hart, Parsloes Cottage, Bagendon, Cirencester, Glos. GL7 7DU.

MASTERS OF WINE, THE INSTITUTE OF (1955), Five Kings House, 1 Queen Street Place, EC4R 1QS.—*Exec. Dir.*, D. F. Stevens.

MATERNAL AND CHILD WELFARE, NATIONAL ASSOCIATION FOR (1911), 1 South Audley Street, W1Y 6JS.—*Gen. Sec.*, W. H. L. Hedley.

MATHEMATICAL ASSOCIATION (1871), 259 London Road, Leicester LE2 3BE.—*Exec. Sec.*, F. A. Wood.

MATHEMATICS AND ITS APPLICATIONS, INSTITUTE OF (1964), Maitland House, Warrior Square, Southend-on-Sea SS1 2JY.—*Sec. and Registrar*, Miss C. M. Richards.

MEASUREMENT AND CONTROL, INSTITUTE OF (1944), 87 Gower Street, WC1E 6AA.—*Sec. and Chief Exec.*, M. J. Yates.

MECHANICAL ENGINEERS, INSTITUTION OF (1847), 1 Birdcage Walk, SW1H 9JJ.—*Sec.*, R. W. Mellor, C.B.E..

MEDIC-ALERT FOUNDATION, 17 Bridge Wharf, 156 Caledonian Road, N1 9UU. For the protection, in emergencies, of those with a hidden medical condition or allergy.—*Sec. Gen.*, Mrs. M. L. Stanton.

MEDICAL COUNCIL, GENERAL (1858), 44 Hallam Street, W1N 6AE.—*Registrar*, P. L. Towers.

MEDICAL SOCIETY OF LONDON (1773), 11 Chandos Street, W1M 0EB.—*Registrar*, Maj. T. Tudor-Williams.

MEDICAL WOMEN'S FEDERATION (1917), Tavistock House North, Tavistock Square, WC1H 9HX.—*Hon. Sec.*, Dr. Patricia Price.

MEDIEVAL ARCHAEOLOGY, SOCIETY FOR (1957).—*Hon. Sec.*, A. Vince, PH.D., C.L.A.U., The Lawn, Union Road, Lincoln LN1 3BG.

MEN OF THE TREES (1922), Sandy Lane, Crawley Down, Crawley, W. Sussex RH10 4HS.—*Exec. Sec.*, Mrs. E. Sandwell.

MENTAL AFTER CARE ASSOCIATION (1879), Bainbridge House, Bainbridge Street, WC1A 1HP.—*Dir.*, B. G. Garner.

MENTAL HEALTH FOUNDATION, THE (1949), 8 Hallam Street, W1N 6DH.—*Dir.*, Maj. Gen. R. B. Loudoun, C.B., O.B.E.

MERCHANT NAVY WELFARE BOARD (1948), 19–21 Lancaster Gate, W2 3LN.—*Gen. Sec.*, J. I. K. Walker.

METALS, THE INSTITUTE OF (1985), 1 Carlton House Terrace, SW1Y 5DB.—*Sec.*, Dr. J. A. Catterall.

METAL TRADES BENEVOLENT SOCIETY, ROYAL (1843), Kelvin House, 1 Totteridge Avenue, High Wycombe, Bucks. HP13 6XG.—*Gen. Sec.*, A. Whittle, M.B.E..

METEOROLOGICAL SOCIETY, ROYAL (1850), James Glaisher House, Grenville Place, Bracknell, Berks. RG12 1BX.—*Exec. Sec.*, R. P. C. Swash.

METROPOLITAN AND CITY POLICE ORPHANS FUND (1870), 30 Hazlewell Road, SW15 6LH.—*Sec.*, R. Duff-Cole, B.E.M.

METROPOLITAN AUTHORITIES, ASSOCIATION OF (1974), 35 Great Smith Street, SW1P 3BJ.—*Sec.*, A. Gronow.

METROPOLITAN HOSPITAL-SUNDAY FUND (1872), 40 High Street, Teddington, Middx. TW11 8EW. In 1988, £30,800 was distributed to N.H.S. hospitals. £269,400 was distributed to hospitals outside the N.H.S., and £9,200 to other medical charities.—*Sec.*, D. A. B. Lynch.

METROPOLITAN PUBLIC GARDENS ASSOCIATION (1882).—*Sec.*, Mrs. J. Bellamy, 3 Mayfield Road, Thornton Heath, Croydon CR4 6DN.

MIDDLE EAST ASSOCIATION, THE (1961), Bury House, 33 Bury Street, SW1Y 6AX.—*Dir.-Gen.*, Sir James Craig, G.C.M.G..

MIDWIVES, ROYAL COLLEGE OF (1881), 15 Mansfield Street, W1M 0BE.—*Gen. Sec.*, Miss R. M. Ashton.

MIGRAINE ASSOCIATION, BRITISH (1958), 178A High Road, Byfleet, Weybridge, Surrey KT14 7ED.—*Hon. Sec.*, Mrs. J. Liddell.

MIGRAINE TRUST (1965), 45 Great Ormond Street, WC1N 3HD.—*Dir.*, P. Hodgkins.

MILITARY HISTORICAL SOCIETY, National Army Museum, Royal Hospital Road, SW3 4HT.—*Hon. Sec.*, J. Gaylor.

MIND (National Association for Mental Health), 22 Harley Street, W1N 2ED.—*Dir.*, C. Heginbotham.

MINERALOGICAL SOCIETY (1876), 41 Queen's Gate, SW7 5HR.—*Hon. Gen. Sec.*, Dr. M. G. Bown.

MINES OF GREAT BRITAIN, FEDERATION OF SMALL, Northcote Chambers, 13A King Street, Newcastle under Lyme, Staffs. ST5 1ER.—*Sec.*, R. W. Bladen.

MINIATURE PAINTERS, SCULPTORS AND GRAVERS, ROYAL SOCIETY OF (1895).—*Exec. Sec.*, Mrs. S. M. Burton, 15 Union Street, Wells, Somerset BA5 2PU.

MINIATURISTS, SOCIETY OF (1895), Castle Gallery, Castle Hill, Ilkley, W. Yorks. LS29 9DT.—*Dir.*, L. Simpson.

MINING INSTITUTE OF SCOTLAND, c/o British Coal Corporation, Green Park, Greenend, Edinburgh, EH17 7PZ.—*Sec.*, E. R. Rodger.

MISSION TO DEEP SEA FISHERMEN, ROYAL NATIONAL (1881), 43 Nottingham Place, W1M 4BX.—*Chief Exec.*, A. D. Marsden.

MISSIONS TO SEAMEN, THE (1856), St. Michael Paternoster Royal, College Hill, EC4R 2RL.—*Gen. Sec.*, Rev. Canon W. J. D. Down.

MODERN CHURCHPEOPLE'S UNION (1898), for the advancement of liberal religious thought—*Hon. Sec.*, Rev. R. C. Truss, The Rectory, Church Square, Shepperton, Middx. TW17 9JY.

MONUMENTAL BRASS SOCIETY (1887).—*Hon. Sec.*, W. Mendelsson, 57 Leeside Crescent, NW11 0HA.

MORAVIAN MISSIONS, LONDON ASSOCIATION IN AID OF (1817), Moravian Church House, 5–7 Muswell Hill, N10 3TJ.—*Sec.*, Rev. F. J. C. Smith.

MOTHERS' UNION, THE (1876), Mary Sumner House, 24 Tufton Street, SW1P 3RB.—*Central Sec.*, Mrs. M. Chapman.

MOTOR INDUSTRY, THE INSTITUTE OF THE, Fanshaws, Brickendon, Hertford SG13 8PQ.—*Sec.*, F. W. Janes.

MOUNTBATTEN MEMORIAL TRUST (1979), 1 Grosvenor Crescent, SW1X 7EF.— *Dir.*, J. Boyd-Brent.

MOUNTBATTEN TRUST, THE EDWINA (1960), 1 Grosvenor Crescent, SW1X 7EF.—*Sec.*, J. Boyd-Brent.

MULTIPLE SCLEROSIS SOCIETY (1953), 25 Effie Road, SW6 1EE.—*Gen. Sec.*, J. Walford.

MUNICIPAL ENGINEERS, ASSOCIATION OF, 1–7 Great George Street, SW1P 3AA.—*Dir.*, K. J. Marchant.

MUSEUMS ASSOCIATION (1889), 34 Bloomsbury Way, WC1A 2SF.—*Dir. Gen.*, G. Farnell.

MUSIC HALL SOCIETY, BRITISH (1963), Brodie and Middleton Ltd., 68 Drury Lane, WC2B 5SP.—*Hon. Sec.*, Mrs. J. D. Masterton.

MUSICIANS BENEVOLENT FUND (1921), 16 Ogle Street, W1P 7LG.—*Sec.*, M. B. M. Williams.

MUSICIANS, INCORPORATED SOCIETY OF (1882), 10 Stratford Place, W1N 9AE.—*Gen. Sec.*, D. E. Padgett-Chandler.

MUSICIANS OF GREAT BRITAIN, ROYAL SOCIETY OF (1738), 10 Stratford Place, W1N 9AE.—*Sec.*, Mrs. M. E. Gleed, M.B.E.

MUSIC INFORMATION CENTRE, BRITISH (1967), 10 Stratford Place, W1N 9AE.—*Administrator*, Ms. E. Yeoman.

MUSIC SOCIETIES, NATIONAL FEDERATION OF (1935), Francis House, Francis Street, SW1P 1DE.—*Administrator*, R. Jones.

MYALGIC ENCEPHALOMYELITIS ASSOCIATION (1976), P.O. Box 8, Stanford-le-Hope, Essex SS17 8EX.—*Dir.*, E. Liddell.

NATIONAL AND UNIVERSITY LIBRARIES, STANDING CONFERENCE OF (SCONUL) (1950), 102 Euston Street, NW1 2HA.—*Sec.*, A. J. Loveday.

NATIONAL BENEVOLENT INSTITUTION (1812), 61 Bayswater Road, W2 3PG.—*Sec.*, Gp. Capt. D. St. J. Homer.

NATIONAL COUNCIL FOR VOLUNTARY ORGANIZATIONS (1919), 26 Bedford Square, WC1B 3HU.—*Dir.*, Ms. U. Prashar.

NATIONAL COUNCIL OF WOMEN OF GREAT BRITAIN (1895), 36 Danbury Street, N1 8JU.—*Pres.*, Mrs R. Preston.

NATIONAL SOCIETY, THE, (1811), Church House, Great Smith Street, SW1P 3NZ. For promoting religious education.—*Gen. Sec.*, C. Alves.

NATIONAL SOCIETY FOR THE PREVENTION OF CRUELTY TO CHILDREN (1884), 67 Saffron Hill, EC1N 8RS.—*Dir.*, C. Brown.

NATIONAL TRUST, THE (1895), 36 Queen Anne's Gate, SW1H 9AS.—*Dir. Gen.*, A. Stirling.

NATIONAL TRUST FOR SCOTLAND (1931), 5 Charlotte Square, Edinburgh EH2 4DU.

NATIONAL UNION OF STUDENTS (1922), Nelson Mandela House, 461 Holloway Road, N7 6LJ.—*Nat. Sec.*, R. Hawkes.

NATIONAL VIEWERS' AND LISTENERS' ASSOCIATION (1964).—*Pres.*, Mrs. M. Whitehouse, C.B.E, Ardleigh, Colchester CO7 7RH.

NATIONAL WOMEN'S REGISTER (1960), 245 Warwick Road, Solihull, W. Midlands B92 7AH.—*Nat. Organizer*, Mrs. H. Bushill.

NATION'S FUND FOR NURSES (1917), 3 Albermarle Way, EC1V 4JB.—*Administrator*, P. E. Starr.

NATURALISTS' ASSOCIATION, BRITISH (1905).— *Hon. Mem. Sec.*, Mrs. Y. H. Griffiths, 23 Oak Hill Close, Woodford Green, Essex IG8 9PH.

NATURE CONSERVATION, ROYAL SOCIETY FOR (1912), The Green, Nettleham, Lincoln LN2 2NR.—*Chief Exec.*, T. S. Cordy.

NAUTICAL RESEARCH, SOCIETY FOR (1911), c/o National Maritime Museum, Greenwich, SE10 9NF.—*Hon. Sec.*, Mrs. A. Shirley.

NAVAL, MILITARY AND AIR FORCE BIBLE SOCIETY (1780), Radstock House, Eccleston Street, SW1W 9LZ.—*Gen. Sec.*, R. Kennedy.

NAVAL ARCHITECTS, ROYAL INSTITUTION OF (1860), 10 Upper Belgrave Street, SW1X 8BQ.—*Sec.*, P. W. Ayling, O.B.E.

NAVIGATION, ROYAL INSTITUTE OF (1947), 1 Kensington Gore, SW7 2AT.—*Dir.*, Rear Adm. R. M. Burgoyne, C.B.

NAVY RECORDS SOCIETY (1893), c/o Public Record Office, Chancery Lane, WC2A 1LR.—*Hon. Sec.*, Dr. N. A. M. Rodger.

NEEDLEWORK, ROYAL SCHOOL OF (1872), 5 King Street, WC2 8HN.—*Dir. of Ed.*, Mrs. J. Fitzgerald Bond.

NEWCOMEN SOCIETY (1920), Science Museum, SW7 2DD. For the study of the history of engineering and technology.—*Exec. Sec.*, A. Smith.

NEW ENGLISH ART CLUB (1886), 17 Carlton House Terrace, SW1Y 5BD.—*Sec.*, W. Bowyer, R.A.

NEWSPAPER EDITORS, GUILD OF BRITISH (1946), Bloomsbury House, Bloomsbury Square, 74–77 Great Russell Street, WC1B 3DA.—*Sec.*, C. Gordon Page.

NEWSPAPER PRESS FUND (1864), Dickens House, 35 Wathen Road, Dorking, Surrey RH4 1JY.—*Dir.*, P. W. Evans.

NEWSPAPER SOCIETY (1836), Bloomsbury House, Bloomsbury Square, 74–77 Great Russell Street, WC1B 3DA.—*Dir.*, D. Nisbet-Smith.

NEWSVENDORS' BENEVOLENT INSTITUTION (1839), P.O. Box 306, Dunmow, Essex CM6 1HY.—*Dir.*, C. S. Jones.

NOISE ABATEMENT SOCIETY (1959), P.O. Box 8, Bromley BR2 0UH.—*Chairman*, J. Connell.

NON-SMOKERS, NATIONAL SOCIETY OF, *see* QUIT.

NORWOOD CHILD CARE (1795), Stuart Young House, 221 Golders Green Road, NW11 9DL. Jewish welfare organization for Jewish children.—*Exec. Dir.*, S. Brier.

NOTARIES' SOCIETY (1907), P.O. Box 102, Amersham, Bucks. HP7 0QB.—*Sec.*, P. D. Leonard.

NUCLEAR ENERGY SOCIETY, BRITISH (1962), 1–7 Great George Street, SW1P 3AA.—*Exec. Officer*, P. Bacos.

NUFFIELD FOUNDATION (1943), 28 Bedford Square, WC1B 3EG.—*Dir.*, R. Hazell.

NUFFIELD PROVINCIAL HOSPITALS TRUST (1939), 3 Prince Albert Road, NW1 7SP.—*Gen. Sec.*, Dr. M. Ashley-Miller.

NUMISMATIC SOCIETY, BRITISH (1903).—*Hon. Sec.*, W. Slayter, 63 West Way, Edgware, Middx. HA8 9LA.

NUMISMATIC SOCIETY, ROYAL (1836), c/o Dept. of Coins and Medals, The British Museum, Great Russell Street, WC1B 3DG.—*Hon. Sec.*, Dr. A. M. Burnett.

NURSES ASSOCIATION, ROYAL BRITISH (1887), 94 Upper Tollington Park, N4 4NB.—*Hon. Sec.*, Mrs. H. M. Vorsterman, M.B.E.

NURSES', RETIRED, NATIONAL HOME (1934), Riverside Avenue, Bournemouth BH7 7EE.—*Chairman*, E. V. Cornell.

NURSES, ROYAL NATIONAL PENSION FUND FOR, Burdett House, 15 Buckingham Street, WC2N 6ED.—*Gen. Man.*, V. G. West.

NURSING, MIDWIFERY AND HEALTH VISITING, U.K. CENTRAL COUNCIL FOR, 23 Portland Place, W1N 3AF.—*Registrar and Chief Exec.*, C. Ralph.

England.—Victory House, 170 Tottenham Court Road, W1P 0HA.

Wales.—Floor 13, Pearl Assurance House, Greyfriars Road, Cardiff CF1 3AG.

Scotland.—22 Queen Street, Edinburgh EH2 1JX.

N.Ireland—R.A.C House, 79 Chichester Street, Belfast BT1 4JE.

NURSING, ROYAL COLLEGE OF, 20 Cavendish Square, W1M 0AB.

NUTRITION FOUNDATION, BRITISH (1967), 15 Belgrave Square, SW1X 8PG.—*Dir. Gen.* Prof. D. M. Conning.

NUTRITION SOCIETY (1941), Grosvenor Gardens House, 35–37 Grosvenor Gardens, SW1W 0BS.—*Hon. Sec.*, Dr. R. F. Grimble.

OBSTETRICIANS AND GYNAECOLOGISTS, ROYAL COLLEGE OF (1929), 27 Sussex Place, NW1 4RG.—*Pres.*, G. D. Pinker, C.V.O.; *Sec.*, P. A. Barnett.

OCCUPATIONAL SAFETY AND HEALTH, INSTITUTION OF (1946), 222 Uppingham Road, Leicester LE5 0QG.—*Sec.*, J. R. Barrell.

OFFICERS' ASSOCIATION, THE (1920), 48 Pall Mall, SW1Y 5JY. Assists former officers of the Armed Forces, their widows and dependants.—*Gen. Sec.*, Brig. P. D. Johnson.

OFFICERS' FAMILIES FUND (1899), 48 Pall Mall, SW1Y 5JY.—*Sec.*, Mrs. I. C. Riley.

OFFICERS' PENSIONS SOCIETY LTD. (1946), 15 Buckingham Gate, SW1E 6NS.—*Gen. Sec.*, Maj. Gen. L. W. A. Gingell, C.B., O.B.E.

OIL PAINTERS, ROYAL INSTITUTE OF (1883).—*Sec.*, Mrs. J. Easterling, 76 Coniston Road, Bromley BR1 4JB.

OILSEED, OIL AND FEEDINGSTUFFS TRADES BENEVOLENT ASSOCIATION, 14–20 St. Mary Axe, EC3A 8BU.—*Sec.*, R. T. Wheelans.

ONE PARENT FAMILIES, NATIONAL COUNCIL FOR, 255 Kentish Town Road, NW5 2LX.—*Dir.*, Miss S. Slipman.

OPEN-AIR MISSION, THE (1853), 19 John Street, WC1N 2DL.—*Sec.*, A. J. Greenbank.

OPEN SPACES SOCIETY (Commons, open spaces and footpaths preservation society) (1865), 25A Bell Street, Henley-on-Thames, Oxon. RG9 2BA.—*Gen. Sec.*, Miss K. Ashbrook.

OPERATIC AND DRAMATIC ASSOCIATION, NATIONAL (1899), NODA House, 1 Crestfield Street, WC1H 8AU.—*Gen. Administrator*, B. Clarke.

OPTICAL COUNCIL, GENERAL (1958), 41 Harley Street, W1N 2DJ.—*Registrar*, R. Wilshin.

OPTOMETRISTS, BRITISH COLLEGE OF, 10 Knaresborough Place, SW5 0TG.—*Gen. Sec.*, T. H. Collingridge.

ORDERS AND MEDALS RESEARCH SOCIETY (1942).—*Gen. Sec.*, N. G. Gooding, 123 Turnpike Link, Croydon CR0 5NU.

ORIENTAL CERAMIC SOCIETY (1921), 31B Torrington Square, WC1E 7LJ.—*Sec.*, Vice-Adm. Sir John Gray, K.B.E., C.B.

ORNITHOLOGISTS' CLUB, SCOTTISH (1936), 21 Regent Terrace, Edinburgh EH7 5BT.—*Sec.*, Ms. M. R. Williams.

ORNITHOLOGISTS' UNION, BRITISH (1858), c/o British Museum (Natural History), Sub-dept. of Ornithology, Tring, Herts. HP23 6AP.—*Hon. Sec.*, Mrs. G. Bonham.

ORNITHOLOGY, BRITISH TRUST FOR (1932), Beech Grove, Tring, Herts. HP23 5NR.—*Dir. of Services*, S. M. Dorward.

ORTHOPAEDIC ASSOCIATION, BRITISH (1918), The Royal College of Surgeons, 35–43 Lincoln's Inn Fields, WC2A 3PN.—*Hon. Sec.*, M. A. Edgar.

OSTEOPATHIC MEDICINE, LONDON COLLEGE OF, 8–10 Boston Place, NW1 6QH.

OUTWARD BOUND TRUST LTD. (1941), Chestnut Field, Regent Place, Rugby, Warks. CV21 2PJ.—*Dir.*, I. L. Fothergill.

OVERSEAS DEVELOPMENT INSTITUTE (1960), Regent's College, Inner Circle, Regent's Park, NW1 4NS.—*Dir.*, Prof. J. Howell.

OVERSEAS SERVICE PENSIONERS' ASSOCIATION (1960), 63 Church Road, Hove, E. Sussex BN3 2BD.—*Sec.*, C. D. Stenton.

OVERSEAS SETTLEMENT, CHURCH OF ENGLAND BOARD FOR SOCIAL RESPONSIBILITY (1925), Great Smith Street, SW1P 3NZ.—*Admin. Sec.*, Miss P. J. Hallett.

OXFAM (1942), 274 Banbury Road, Oxford OX2 7DZ.—*Dir.*, F. Judd.

OXFORD PRESERVATION TRUST (1927), 10 Turn Again Lane, St. Ebbes, Oxford OX1 1QL.—*Sec.*, Mrs. H. E. Turner.

OXFORD SOCIETY (1932), 8 Wellington Square, Oxford OX1 2HY.—*Sec.*, Dr. H. A. Hurren.

PAEDIATRIC ASSOCIATION, BRITISH (1928), 5 St. Andrew's Place, NW1 4LB.—*Hon. Sec.*, Dr. R. MacFaul.

PAINTER-ETCHERS AND ENGRAVERS, ROYAL SOCIETY OF (1880), Bankside Gallery, 48 Hopton Street, SE1 9JH.—*Sec.*, M. Spender.

PAINTERS IN WATER COLOURS, ROYAL INSTITUTE OF (1831), 17 Carlton House Terrace, S.W.1.—*Sec.*, R. Spurrier.

PALAEONTOGRAPHICAL SOCIETY (1847) c/o British Geological Survey, Keyworth, Nottingham NG12 5GG.—*Sec.*, S. P. Tunnicliff.

PALAEONTOLOGICAL ASSOCIATION (1957).—*Sec.*, Dr. P. Wallace, The Croft Barn, Church Street, East Hendred, Wantage, Oxon. OX12 8LA.

PARKINSON'S DISEASE SOCIETY (1969), 36 Portland Place, W1N 3DG.—*Exec. Dir.*, C. A. A. Kilmister.

PARLIAMENTARY AND SCIENTIFIC COMMITTEE (1939), 16 Great College Street, SW1P 3RX.—*Sec.*, A. Butler.

PASTORAL PSYCHOLOGY, GUILD OF (1936).—*Hon. Sec.*, Mrs. M. Ditchfield, 37 Hogarth Hill, NW11 6AY.

PATENT AGENTS, CHARTERED INSTITUTE OF (1882), Staple Inn Buildings, High Holborn, WC1V 7PZ.—*Sec.*, Miss M. E. Poole.

PATENTEES AND INVENTORS, INSTITUTE OF (1919), Triumph House, 189 Regent Street, W1R 7WF.—*Sec.*, J. R. Kay.

PATHOLOGISTS, ROYAL COLLEGE OF, 2 Carlton House Terrace, SW1Y 5AF.—*Sec.*, K. Lockyer.

PATIENTS ASSOCIATION (1963), 18 Victoria Park Square, E2 9PF.— *Chairman*, Rabbi Julia Neuberger.

PEACE COUNCIL, NATIONAL (1908), 29 Great James Street, WC1N 3ES.—*Co-ordinator*, A. L. McLeod.

PEAK AND NORTHERN FOOTPATHS SOCIETY (1894).— *Hon. Gen. Sec.*, D. Taylor, 15 Parkfield Drive, Tyldesley, Manchester M29 8NR.

PEARSON'S HOLIDAY FUND, 2A Amity Grove, Raynes Park, SW20 0LH.—*Gen. Sec.*, G. P. Holloway.

PEDESTRIANS ASSOCIATION (1929), 1 Wandsworth Road, SW8 2XX.—*Chairman*, C. Myerscough.

P.E.N., INTERNATIONAL (1921), 38 King Street, WC2E 8JT. World association of writers.—*International Sec.*, A. Blokh.

PENSION FUNDS LTD, NATIONAL ASSOCIATION OF (1923), 12–18 Grosvenor Gardens, SW1W 0DH.— *Dir. Gen.*, M. A. Elton.

PEOPLE'S DISPENSARY FOR SICK ANIMALS (1917), PDSA House, South Street, Dorking, Surrey RH4 2LB.— *Gen. Sec.*, M. R. Curtis, M.B.E.

PERFORMING RIGHT SOCIETY LTD. (1914), 29–33 Berners Street, W1P 4AA.—*Chief Exec.*, M. J. Freegard.

PERIODICAL PUBLISHERS ASSOCATION LTD. (1913), Imperial House, 15–19 Kingsway, WC2B 6UN.— *Chief Exec.*, I. Locks.

PESTALOZZI CHILDREN'S VILLAGE TRUST (1959), Sedlescombe, Battle, E. Sussex TN33 0RR.—*Warden*, A. G. Hatter.

PETROLEUM, INSTITUTE OF (1913), 61 New Cavendish Street, W1M 8AR.—*Dir. Gen.*, A. E. H. Williams.

PHARMACEUTICAL SOCIETY OF GREAT BRITAIN, ROYAL (1841), 1 Lambeth High Street, SE1 7JN.—*Sec. and Registrar*, J. Ferguson.

PHARMACOLOGICAL SOCIETY, BRITISH (1931).—*Hon. Gen. Sec.*, Dr. A. R. Green, Astra Neuroscience Research Unit, 1 Wakefield Street, WC1N 1PJ.

PHILOLOGICAL SOCIETY (1842).—*Hon. Sec.*, Prof. T. Bynon, School of Oriental and African Studies, University of London, Thornhaugh Street, Russell Square, WC1H 0XG.

PHILOSOPHY, ROYAL INSTITUTE OF (1925), 14 Gordon Square, WC1H 0AG.—*Dir.*, Prof. A. Phillips Griffiths.

PHOTOGRAMMETRIC SOCIETY (1952).—*Hon. Sec.*, Dr. A. S. Walker, Kern Instruments Ltd., Revenge Road, Lordswood, Chatham, Kent ME5 8TE.

PHOTOGRAPHY, BRITISH INSTITUTE OF PROFESSIONAL (1901), Amwell End, Ware, Herts. SG12 9HN.— *Chief Exec.*, A. M. Berkeley.

PHYSICAL EDUCATION ASSOCIATION OF GREAT BRITAIN AND N. IRELAND, 162 King's Cross Road, WC1X 9DH.—*Gen. Sec.*, (vacant).

PHYSICAL RECREATION, CENTRAL COUNCIL OF (1935), Francis House, Francis Street, SW1P 1DE.—*Gen. Sec.*, P. Lawson.

PHYSICIANS, ROYAL COLLEGE OF (1518), 11 St. Andrew's Place, NW1 4LE.—*Registrar*, D. A. Pyke, C.B.E., M.D.

PHYSICIANS AND SURGEONS, ROYAL COLLEGE OF (Glasgow) (1599), 234–242 St. Vincent Street, Glasgow G2 5RJ.—*Hon. Sec.*, Dr. A. D. Beattie.

PHYSICIANS OF EDINBURGH, ROYAL COLLEGE OF (1681), 9 Queen Street, Edinburgh EH2 1JQ.—*Sec.*, Dr. J. L. Anderton.

PHYSICS, INSTITUTE OF (1874), 47 Belgrave Square, SW1X 8QX.—*Sec.*, L. Cohen, PH.D.

PHYSIOLOGICAL SOCIETY (1876).—*Hon. Sec.*, Prof. R.

A. Chapman, Dept. of Physiology, School of Veterinary Science, Park Row, Bristol BS1 5LS.

PHYSIOTHERAPY, THE CHARTERED SOCIETY OF (1894), 14 Bedford Row, WC1R 4ED.—*Sec.*, T. Simon.

PIG BREEDERS ASSOCIATION, NATIONAL (1884), 7 Rickmansworth Road, Watford, Herts. WD1 7HE.—*Chief Exec.*, G. E. Welsh.

PILGRIM TRUST, THE (1930), Fielden House, Little College Street, SW1P 3SH.—*Sec.*, Hon. A. H. Millar.

PILGRIMS OF GREAT BRITAIN, THE (1902), Savoy Hotel WC2R 0EU.—*Hon. Sec.*, Lt. Col. S. W. Chant-Sempill, O.B.E., M.C.

PLANT ENGINEERS, INSTITUTION OF, 138 Buckingham Palace Road, SW1W 9SG.—*Sec. Gen.*, R. S. Pratt.

PLASTICS AND RUBBER INSTITUTE, THE (1921), 11 Hobart Place, SW1W 0HL.—*Sec. Gen.* G. W. Stockdale.

PLAYING CARD SOCIETY, THE INTERNATIONAL (1972), 188 Sheen Lane, SW14 8LF.—*Sec.*, C. C. Rayner.

PLAYING FIELDS ASSOCIATION, NATIONAL (1925), 25 Ovington Square, SW3 1LQ.—*Dir.*, A. M. Watson.

P.N.E.U., WORLD-WIDE EDUCATION SERVICE OF THE (1888), Strode House, 44–50 Osnaburgh Street, NW1 3NN.—*Dir.*, H. Boulter.

POETRY SOCIETY (1909), 21 Earl's Court Square, SW5 9DE.—*Dir. and Gen. Sec.*, vacant.

POLICY STUDIES INSTITUTE (1978), 100 Park Village East, NW1 3SR—*Dir.*, W. W. Daniel

POLIO FELLOWSHIP, BRITISH (1939), Bell Close, West End Road, Ruislip, Middx. HA4 6LP.—*Gen. Sec.*, L. P. Jackson.

POLYTECHNICS, COMMITTEE OF DIRECTORS OF (1970), Kirkman House, 12–14 Whitfield Street, W1P 6AX.—*Chairman*, Prof. G. T. Fowler; *Sec.*, Dr. M. S. Lewis.

POLYTECHNIC TEACHERS, ASSOCIATION OF (1973), Caxton Chambers, 81 Albert Road, Southsea, Hants. PO5 2SG.—*Chief Exec.*, C. Cheesman.

PORTRAIT PAINTERS, ROYAL SOCIETY OF (1891), 17 Carlton House Terrace, SW1Y 5BD.—*President*, D. Poole.

POST OFFICE USERS' NATIONAL COUNCIL (1970), Waterloo Bridge House, Waterloo Road, SE1 8UA.—*Sec.*, B. J. Jones.

POULTRY CLUB OF GREAT BRITAIN, THE (1877).—*Sec.*, Mrs. M. A. Carefoot, Cliveden, Sandy Bank Farm, Chipping, Preston, Lancs. PR3 2GA.

PRAYER BOOK SOCIETY, THE (1975), St. James Garlickhythe, Garlick Hill, EC4 2AL.—*Hon. Sec.*, Mrs. M. Thompson.

PRECEPTORS, COLLEGE OF, (1846), Coppice Row, Theydon Bois, Epping, Essex CM16 7DN. Membership is open to practising educationalists.—*Chief Membership Officer*, N. Matthews.

PREPARATORY SCHOOLS, INCORPORATED ASSOCIATION OF, 138 Kensington Church Street, W8 4BN.—*Sec.*, J. M. C. Coates.

PRE-SCHOOL PLAYGROUPS ASSOCIATION, 61–63 Kings Cross Road, WC1X 9LL.—*Nat. Administrator*, Ms. M. Lochrie.

PRESS ASSOCIATION (1868), 85 Fleet Street, EC4P 4BE.—*Sec.*, E. G. Rhodes.

PRESS UNION, COMMONWEALTH (1909), Studio House, 184 Fleet Street, EC4A 2DU.—*Dir.*, J. Rajepakse.

PREVENTION OF ACCIDENTS, ROYAL SOCIETY FOR THE (1916), Cannon House, Priory Queensway, Birmingham B4 6BS.—*Dir. Gen.*, R. M. Warburton, O.B.E.

PRINCESS LOUISE SCOTTISH HOSPITAL (Erskine Hospital) (1916), Bishopton, Renfrewshire PA7 5PU. For disabled ex-servicemen and women.—*Commandant*, Col. W. K. Shepherd.

PRINTERS' CHARITABLE CORPORATION (1827), Victoria House, Harestone Valley Road, Caterham, Surrey CR3 6HY—*Dir.*, Cpt. D. J. Bradby, R.N.

PRINTING HISTORICAL SOCIETY (1964), St. Bride Institute, Bride Lane, EC4Y 8EE.—*Hon. Sec.*, C. L. Hicks.

PRINTING, INSTITUTE OF (1961), 8 Lonsdale Gardens, Tunbridge Wells, Kent TN1 1NU.—*Sec.*, C. F. Partridge.

PRISON VISITORS, NATIONAL ASSOCIATION OF (1922), 46B Hartington Street, Bedford MK41 7RP.—*Gen. Sec.*, Mrs. A. G. McKenna.

PRIVATE LIBRARIES ASSOCIATION (1957).—*Hon. Sec.*, F. Broomhead, Ravelston, South View Road, Pinner, Middx. HA5 3YD.

PROCURATORS IN GLASGOW, ROYAL FACULTY OF (1600), 12 Nelson Mandela Place, Glasgow G2 1BT.—*Clerk*, J. H. Sinclair.

PRODUCTION CONTROL, INSTITUTE OF, Elmcroft House, Tiddington Road, Tiddington, Stratford upon Avon, Warks. CV37 7AQ.—*Gen. Sec.*, K. Roberts.

PRODUCTION ENGINEERS, INSTITUTION OF, Rochester House, 66 Little Ealing Lane, W5 4XX.—*Sec.*, Brig. P. V. Crooks.

PROFESSIONAL CLASSES AID COUNCIL (1921), 10 St. Christopher's Place, W1M 6HY.—*Sec.*, Mrs. G. A. Burgess.

PROFESSIONAL ENGINEERS, U.K. ASSOCIATION OF (1969), Hayes Court, West Common Road, Bromley BR2 7AU.—*Sec.*, C. K. Hickling.

PROFESSIONAL FOOTBALLERS' ASSOCIATION, 2 Oxford Court, Bishopsgate, Manchester M2 3WQ.—*Sec.*, G. Taylor.

PROFESSIONS SUPPLEMENTARY TO MEDICINE, COUNCIL FOR, Park House, 184 Kennington Park Road, SE11 4BU.—*Registrar*, R. Pickis.

PROTESTANT ALLIANCE, THE (1845), 112 Colin Gardens, NW9 6ER.—*Gen. Sec.*, Rev. A. G. Ashdown.

PSORIASIS ASSOCIATION (1968), 7 Milton Street, Northampton NN2 7JG.—*Nat. Sec.*, Mrs. L. Henley.

PSYCHIATRISTS, ROYAL COLLEGE OF (1971), 17 Belgrave Square, SW1X 8PG—*Sec.*, Mrs. V. Cameron.

PSYCHICAL RESEARCH, SOCIETY FOR (1882), 1 Adam and Eve Mews, W8 6UG.—*Pres.*, Dr. A. Gauld.

PSYCHOLOGICAL SOCIETY, THE BRITISH (1901), St. Andrews House, 48 Princess Road East, Leicester LE1 7DR.—*Exec. Sec.*, C. V. Newman, Ph.D.

PUBLIC ADMINISTRATION, ROYAL INSTITUTE OF (1922), 3 Birdcage Walk, SW1H 9JH.—*Dir. Gen.*, D. Falcon.

PUBLIC FINANCE AND ACCOUNTANCY, CHARTERED INSTITUTE OF (1885), 3 Robert Street, WC2N 6BH.—*Dir.*, N. P. Hepworth, O.B.E.

PUBLIC HEALTH AND HYGIENE, THE ROYAL INSTITUTE OF (1937), 28 Portland Place, W1N 4DE.—*Sec.*, Rear-Adm. W. A. Waddell, C.B., O.B.E.

PUBLIC HEALTH ENGINEERS, INSTITUTION OF, *see* WATER AND ENVIRONMENTAL MANAGEMENT.

PUBLIC RELATIONS, INSTITUTE OF (1948), Gate House, St. John's Square, EC1M 4DH.—*Exec. Dir.*, J. B. Lavelle.

PUBLIC TEACHERS OF LAW, SOCIETY OF (1908).—*Hon. Sec.*, Prof. D. B. Casson, University of Buckingham, MK18 1EG.

PURCHASING AND SUPPLY, INSTITUTE OF (1967), Easton

House, Easton on the Hill, Stamford, Lincs. PE9 3NZ.—*Dir. Gen.*, I. G. S. Groundwater.

PURE WATER ASSOCIATION, NATIONAL (1960).—*Sec.*, N. Brugge, Meridan, Cae Goody Lane, Ellesmere, Salop. SY12 9DW.

QUALITY ASSURANCE, INSTITUTE OF, 10 Grosvenor Gardens, SW1 0DQ.—*Sec. Gen.*, Dr. J. Davies.

QUARRIER'S HOMES (1871), Bridge of Weir, Renfrewshire PA11 3SA.—*Chief Exec.*, Dr. J. R. Minto, O.B.E.

QUARRYING, INSTITUTE OF (1917), 7 Regent Street, Nottingham NG1 5BY.—*Sec.*, R. Oates.

QUEEN ELIZABETH'S FOUNDATION FOR THE DISABLED (1967), Leatherhead, Surrey KT22 0BN.—*Dir.*, M. B. Clark, Ph.D.

QUEEN VICTORIA CLERGY FUND (1897), Church House, Dean's Yard, SW1P 3NZ—*Sec.*, Capt. P. W. E. Parry, M.B.E.

QUEEN VICTORIA SCHOOL (1908), Dunblane, Perthshire FK15 0JY.—*Headmaster*, J. D. Hankinson.

QUEEN'S ENGLISH SOCIETY, THE (1972).—*Hon. Sec.*, A. I. Thompson, 2 South Side, Pulborough, Sussex RH20 2DH.

QUEEN'S NURSING INSTITUTE (1887), 3 Albemarle Way, EC1V 4JB.—*Dir.*, P. E. Starr.

QUEKETT MICROSCOPICAL CLUB (1865).—*Hon. Business Sec.*, A. V. Dodge, 61 Pewley Way, Guildford GU1 3PZ.

QUIT (National Society of Non-Smokers) (1926), Latimer House, 40–48 Hanson Street, W1P 7DE.—*Hon. Sec.*, T.W. Hurst.

RADAR, THE ROYAL ASSOCIATION FOR DISABILITY AND REHABILITATION (1977), 25 Mortimer Street, W1N 8AB.—*Dir.* G. Wilson, C.B.E.

RADIOLOGISTS, ROYAL COLLEGE OF (1934), 38 Portland Place, W1N 3DG.—*Sec.*, A. J. Cowles.

RADIOLOGY, BRITISH INSTITUTE OF (1897), 36 Portland Place, W1N 4AT.—*Gen. Sec.*, Miss S. M. Johnstone.

RAILWAY BENEVOLENT INSTITUTION (1858), 67 Ashbourne Road, Derby DE3 3FY.—*Exec. Officer and Gen. Sec.*, W. W. K. Humphreys.

RAINER FOUNDATION (1876), 227–239 Tooley Street, SE1 2JX. Helps young people at risk or in need; administers the Intermediate Treatment Fund on behalf of the government.—*Dir.*, R. Kay.

RAMBLERS' ASSOCIATION (1935), 1–5 Wandsworth Road, SW8 2XX.—*Dir.*, A. Mattingly.

RANFURLY LIBRARY SERVICE (1954), 2 Coldharbour Place, 39–41 Coldharbour Lane, SE5 9NR.—*Chairman*, J.D. Smith.

RATEPAYERS' ASSOCIATIONS, NATIONAL UNION OF (1921), 4 Eysham Court, Station Road, Barnet, Herts. EN5 1PS—*Hon. Gen. Sec.*, Mrs. D. E. Pannell.

RATING AND VALUATION ASSOCIATION (1882), 41 Doughty Street, WC1N 2LF.—*Dir.*, C. Farrington.

RECORD SOCIETY, SCOTTISH (1897), Dept. of Scottish History, University of Glasgow, Glasgow G12 8QQ.—*Hon. Sec.*, Dr. J. Kirk.

RECORDS ASSOCIATION, BRITISH (1932), 18 Padbury Court, E2 7EH.—*Hon. Sec.*, J. Davies.

RED CROSS SOCIETY, BRITISH (1870), 9 Grosvenor Crescent, SW1X 7EJ.—*Dir. Gen.*, J. C. Burke-Gaffney.

RED POLL CATTLE SOCIETY (1888), 6 Church Street, Woodbridge, Suffolk IP12 1DH.—*Sec.*, P. Ryder-Davies.

REFRIGERATION, INSTITUTE OF (1899), Kelvin House, 76 Mill Lane, Carshalton, Surrey SM5 2JR.—*Sec.*, M. J. Horlick.

REFUGEE COUNCIL, BRITISH (1981), Bondway House, 3–9 Bondway, SW8 1SJ.—*Dir.*, A. Dubs.

REGIONAL STUDIES ASSOCIATION (1965), 29 Great James Street, WC1N 3ES.—*Dir.*, Mrs. S. Hardy.

REGULAR FORCES EMPLOYMENT ASSOCIATION (1885), 25 Bloomsbury Square, WC1A 2LN. Finds employment for non-commissioned ex-Regulars.—*General Manager*, Maj.-Gen. D. T. Crabtree, C.B.

RELATE MARRIAGE GUIDANCE (1938), Herbert Gray College, Little Church Street, Rugby, Warks. CV21 3AP.—*Dir.*, D. French.

RENT OFFICERS, INSTITUTE OF (1966).—*Hon. Sec.*, M. R. Webber, Musgrave House, Musgrave Row, Exeter EX4 3TW.

RESEARCH DEFENCE SOCIETY (1908), Grosvenor Gardens House, Grosvenor Gardens, SW1W 0BS.—*Exec. Dir.*, Dr. M. Matfield.

RETAIL BOOK, STATIONERY AND ALLIED TRADES EMPLOYEES' ASSOCIATION (1919), 8–9 Commercial Road, Swindon SN1 5RB.—*Gen. Sec.*, J. Windust.

RETIREMENT PENSIONS ASSOCIATIONS, NATIONAL FEDERATION OF (1938), 14 St. Peter Street, Blackburn BB2 2HD.—*Sec.*, G. Dunn.

RICHARD III SOCIETY (1924), 4 Oakley Street, SW3 5NN.—*Sec.*, Miss E. M. Nokes.

ROAD SAFETY OFFICERS, INSTITUTE OF (1971).—*Sec.*, E. M. Marsh, 31 Dyers Close, West Buckland, Wellington, Somerset TA21 9JU.

ROAD TRANSPORT ENGINEERS, INSTITUTE OF (1945), 1 Cromwell Place, SW7 2JF.—*Exec. Sec.*, A. F. Stroud.

ROMAN STUDIES, SOCIETY FOR PROMOTION OF (1910), 31–34 Gordon Square, WC1H 0PP.—*Sec.*, Dr. H. M. Cockle.

ROTARY INTERNATIONAL IN GREAT BRITAIN AND IRELAND (1914), Kinwarton Road, Alcester, Warks. B49 6BP.—*Sec.*, G. S. Larcie.

ROUND TABLES OF GREAT BRITAIN AND IRELAND, NATIONAL ASSOCIATION OF (1927), Floor 7, The Rotunda, 150 New Street, Birmingham B2 4QB.—*Gen. Sec.*, R. H. Renold.

ROYAL AFRICAN SOCIETY (1901), 18 Northumberland Avenue, WC2N 5BJ.—*Sec.*, Mrs. L. Allan.

ROYAL AIR FORCE BENEVOLENT FUND (1919), 67 Portland Place, W1N 4AR.—*Controller*, Air Chief Marshal Sir Thomas Kennedy, G.C.B., A.F.C.

ROYAL AIR FORCES ASSOCIATION (1943), 43 Grove Park Road, W4 3RX.—*Sec. Gen.*, M. G. Tomkins, M.B.E.

ROYAL ALEXANDRA AND ALBERT SCHOOL (1758), Gatton Park, Reigate, Surrey RH2 0TW.—*Sec.*, Capt. A. J. Walsh, R.N.

ROYAL ALFRED SEAFARERS' SOCIETY (1865), Weston Acres, Woodmansterne Lane, Banstead, Surrey SM7 3HB.—*Gen. Sec.*, J. H. Moore.

ROYAL ARMOURED CORPS WAR MEMORIAL BENEVOLENT FUND (1946), R.H.Q. R.T.R., Bovington Camp, Wareham, Dorset BH20 6JA.—*Sec.*, Maj. R. Clooney.

ROYAL ARTILLERY ASSOCIATION, Artillery House, Connaught Barracks, Grand Depot Road, SE18 6SL.—*Gen. Sec.*, Lt.-Col. M.J. Darmody.

ROYAL ASIATIC SOCIETY (1823), 60 Queen's Gardens, W2 3AF.—*Sec.*, Miss L. Collins.

ROYAL CALEDONIAN SCHOOLS (1815), Bushey, Herts. WD2 3TS.—*Master*, Capt. R. E. Wilson, C.B.E., D.F.C., R.N.

ROYAL CELTIC SOCIETY (1820), 23 Rutland Street, Edinburgh EH1 2RN.—*Sec.*, J. G. S. Cameron.

ROYAL CHORAL SOCIETY (1871), International House, 2–4 Wendell Road, W12 9RT.—*Gen. Man.*, M. Heyland.

ROYAL ENGINEERS ASSOCIATION, R.H.Q. Royal Engineers, Brompton Barracks, Chatham, Kent ME4 4UG.—*Controller*, Maj. C. F. Cooper, M.B.E.

ROYAL ENGINEERS, THE INSTITUTION OF (1875), Brompton Barracks, Chatham, Kent ME4 4UG.—*Sec.*, Col. G. W. A. Napier.

ROYAL HIGHLAND AND AGRICULTURAL SOCIETY OF SCOTLAND (1784), Edinburgh Exhibition and Trade Centre, Ingliston, Edinburgh EH28 8NF.—*Sec.*, J. R. Good.

ROYAL HORTICULTURAL SOCIETY (1804), P.O. Box 313, 80 Vincent Square, SW1P 2PE.—*Sec.*, J. R. Cowell.

ROYAL HOSPITAL AND HOME, PUTNEY (1854), West Hill, SW15 3SW.—*Chief Exec.*, Col. B. E. Blunt.

ROYAL HUMANE SOCIETY (1774), Brettenham House, Lancaster Place, WC2E 7EP. Gives bravery awards for saving and attempting to save human life.—*Sec.*, Maj. A. J. Dickinson.

ROYAL INSTITUTION, THE (1799), 21 Albemarle Street, W1X 4BS.—*Pres.*, H.R.H. The Duke of Kent, K.G., G.C.M.G., G.C.V.O.; *Dir.*, Prof. J. M. Thomas, F.R.S.; *Sec.*, Prof. D. C. Bradley, F.R.S.

ROYAL LIFE SAVING SOCIETY, U.K. (1891), Mountbatten House, Studley, Warks. B80 7NN.—*Dir.*, C. J. Godsall.

ROYAL LITERARY FUND (1790), 144 Temple Chambers, Temple Avenue, EC4Y 0DT. Grants to necessitous authors of some published work of approved literary merit or to their immediate dependants.—*Sec.*, Mrs. F. M. Clark.

ROYAL MEDICAL BENEVOLENT FUND (1836), 24 King's Road, SW19 8QN.—*Sec.*, P. G. Gordon-Smith.

ROYAL MEDICAL SOCIETY (1737), Students Centre, 5-5 Bristo Square, Edinburgh EH8 9AL.—*Sec.*, S. Wanless.

ROYAL MICROSCOPICAL SOCIETY (1839), 37–38 St. Clements, Oxford OX4 1AJ.—*Administrator*, P. B. Hirst.

ROYAL MUSICAL ASSOCIATION (1874).—*Sec.*, P. Owens, 135 Purves Road, NW10 5TH.

ROYAL NATIONAL LIFEBOAT INSTITUTION, (1824), West Quay Road, Poole, Dorset BH15 1HZ.—263 lifeboats are maintained on the coasts of Great Britain and Ireland. In 1988 the lifeboats launched 4,224 times and saved 1,366 lives. The net cost of running the RNLI in 1989 is over £36m.—*Chairman*, M. Vernon.

ROYAL NAVAL AND ROYAL MARINES CHILDREN'S TRUST (1834), H.M.S. *Nelson*, Portsmouth, PO1 3HH.—*Sec.*, Mrs. M. Bateman.

ROYAL NAVAL ASSOCIATION (1950), 82 Chelsea Manor Street, SW3 5QJ.—*Gen. Sec.*, Capt. J. W. Rayner.

ROYAL NAVAL BENEVOLENT SOCIETY (1739), 1 Fleet Street, EC4Y 1BD.—*Sec.*, Capt. M. Murray, R.N.

ROYAL NAVAL BENEVOLENT TRUST (1922), 1 High Street, Brompton, Gillingham, Kent ME7 5QZ.—*Gen. Sec.*, Lt.-Cdr. D. C. Lawrence.

ROYAL NAVY OFFICERS, ASSOCIATION OF (1920), 70 Porchester Terrace, W2 3TP.—*Sec.*, Lt.-Cdr. I. M. P. Coombes.

ROYAL OVER-SEAS LEAGUE (1910), Over-Seas House, Park Place, St. James's Street, SW1A 1LR.—*Dir. Gen.*, Capt. J. B. Rumble, R.N.

ROYAL PATRIOTIC FUND CORPORATION (1854), Golden Cross House, Duncannon Street, WC2 4JR. Administers funds for the benefit of widows, children and other dependants of deceased officers and servicemen of the Armed Forces.—*Sec.*, Brig. D. C. Blomfield-Smith, M.B.E.

ROYAL PHOTOGRAPHIC SOCIETY (1853), The Octagon, Milsom Street, Bath BA1 1DN.—*Sec.*, K. R. Warr.

ROYAL PINNER SCHOOL FOUNDATION, 110 Old Brompton Road, SW7 3RB. Assists in the education of children of sales representatives.—*Sec.*, S. Thurtell.

ROYAL SAILORS' RESTS (1876), 2A South Street, Gosport, Hants. PO12 1ES.—*Sec.*, A. A. Lockwood.

ROYAL SCOTTISH SOCIETY FOR PREVENTION OF CRUELTY TO CHILDREN (1884), Melville House, 41 Polwarth Terrace, Edinburgh EH11 1NU.—*Gen. Sec.*, A. M. M. Wood, O.B.E.

ROYAL SIGNALS INSTITUTION (1950), 56 Regency Street, SW1P 4AD.—*Sec.*, Col. A. N. de Bretton-Gordon.

ROYAL SOCIETY, THE (1660), 6 Carlton House Terrace, SW1Y 5AG.—*Pres.*, Sir George Porter; *Treas. and Vice-Pres.*, Prof. R. W. K. Honeycombe; *Secretaries and Vice-Presidents*, Prof. R. J. Elliott, Prof. B. K. Follett, Prof. M. A. Epstein; *Executive Sec.*, Dr. P. T. Warren.

ROYAL SOCIETY FOR ASIAN AFFAIRS (1901), 2 Belgrave Square, SW1X 8PJ.—*Sec.*, Miss M. FitzSimons.

ROYAL SOCIETY FOR THE ENCOURAGEMENT OF ARTS, MANUFACTURES AND COMMERCE (Royal Society of Arts) (1754), 8 John Adam Street, WC2N 6EZ.—*Chairman*, Prof. C. B. Handy.

ROYAL SOCIETY FOR THE PREVENTION OF CRUELTY TO ANIMALS (1824), Causeway, Horsham, W. Sussex RH12 1HG.—*Chief Exec.*, A. J. Richmond, C.B.

ROYAL SOCIETY FOR THE PROTECTION OF BIRDS (1889), The Lodge, Sandy, Beds. SG19 2DL.—*Dir. Gen.*, I. Prestt, C.B.E.

ROYAL SOCIETY OF EDINBURGH (1783), 22–24 George Street, Edinburgh EH2 2PQ.—*Pres.*, Prof. C. Kemball; *Gen. Sec.*, Dr. C. D. Waterston.

ROYAL SOCIETY OF HEALTH, THE (1876), R.S.H. House, 38A St. George's Drive, SW1V 4BH.—*Sec.*, D. Goad.

ROYAL SOCIETY OF LITERATURE (1823), 1 Hyde Park Gardens, W2 2LT.—*Sec.*, Mrs. P. M. Schute.

ROYAL SOCIETY OF MEDICINE (1805), 1 Wimpole Street, W1M 8AE.—*Exec. Dir.*, R. N. Thomson.

ROYAL SOCIETY OF ST. GEORGE, THE (1894), Dartmouth House, 37 Charles Street, W1X 8AB.—*Gen. Sec.*, Lt.-Col. J. A. Williams.

ROYAL STAR AND GARTER HOME FOR DISABLED SAILORS, SOLDIERS AND AIRMEN (1916), Richmond, Surrey TW10 6RR.—*Commandant*, Col. R. N. Harris, M.B.E.

ROYAL STATISTICAL SOCIETY (1834), 25 Enford Street, W1H 2BH.—*Exec. Sec.*, D. W. Harding.

ROYAL TANK REGIMENT BENEVOLENT FUND (1919), R.H.Q. R.T.R. Centre, Bovington Camp, Wareham, Dorset BH20 6JA.—*Regimental Sec.*, Maj. R. Clooney.

ROYAL TELEVISION SOCIETY (1927), Tavistock House East, Tavistock Square, WC1H 9HR.—*Hon. Sec.*, A. Pilgrim.

ROYAL UNITED KINGDOM BENEFICENT ASSOCIATION (1863), 6 Avonmore Road, W14 8RL.—*Dir.*, Rear-Adm. B. C. Perowne, C.B.

RURAL ENGLAND, COUNCIL FOR THE PROTECTION OF (1926), Warwick House, 25–27 Buckingham Palace Road, SW1W 0PP.—*Dir.*, A. Purkis.

RURAL SCOTLAND, ASSOCIATION FOR THE PROTECTION OF (1926), 14A Napier Road, Edinburgh EH10 5AY.—*Dir.*, R. L. Smith, O.B.E.

RURAL WALES, COUNCIL FOR THE PROTECTION OF (1928), Ty Gwyn, 31 High Street, Welshpool, Powys SY21 7JP.—*Dir.*, Dr. N. Caldwell.

SAILORS' CHILDREN'S SOCIETY, THE (1821), Newland, Hull HU6 7RJ. Cares for seamen and their children.—*Gen. Sec.*, Lt.-Cdr. C. G. R. Streatfeild-James.

SAILORS' SOCIETY, BRITISH (1818), 406–410 Eastern Avenue, Ilford, Essex, IG2 6NG.—*Gen. Sec.*, G. Chambers.

ST. DEINIOL'S LIBRARY (1902), Hawarden, Deeside, Clwyd CH5 3DF.—*Warden and Chief Librarian*, Rev. Dr. P. J. Jagger.

ST. DUNSTAN'S, P.O. Box 4XB, 12–14 Harcourt Street, W1A 4XB. For men and women blinded on war service.—*Sec.*, W. C. Weisblatt.

ST. JOHN AMBULANCE (1887), 1 Grosvenor Crescent, SW1X 7EF. Voluntary unpaid body providing first-aid cover at public events and first aid training for industry and the public. *Brigade Strength* (U.K. 1987), 80,000.—*Dir. of Public Affairs*, Lt.-Col. J. Mills, M.B.E.

SALES AND MARKETING MANAGEMENT, INSTITUTE OF (1966).—*Chief Exec.*, D. Waller, Georgian House, 31 Upper George Street, Luton. LU1 2RD.

SALMON AND TROUT ASSOCIATION (1903), Fishmongers' Hall, London Bridge, EC4R 9EL.—*Dir.*, Col. J. Ferguson.

SALTIRE SOCIETY (1936), 9 Fountain Close, High Street, Edinburgh EH1 1TF.—*Sec.*, Miss K. Austin.

SAMARITANS, THE (1953), 17 Uxbridge Road, Slough, Berks. SL1 1SN. Help for the suicidal and despairing. Tel. numbers in local telephone directories.—*Gen. Sec.*, S. Armson.

SAMUEL PEPYS CLUB (1903).—*Sec.*, R. H. Adams, T.D., F.S.A., 14 Dale Close, Oxford OX1 1TU.

SAVE THE CHILDREN FUND, THE (1919), Mary Datchelor House, 17 Grove Lane, SE5 8RD.—*Dir. Gen.*, N. J. Hinton, C.B.E.

SCHIZOPHRENIA FELLOWSHIP, NATIONAL (1970), 78 Victoria Road, Surbiton, Surrey KT6 4NS.—*Dir.*, J. Weleminsky.

SCHOOL LIBRARY ASSOCIATION (1937), Liden Library, Barrington Close, Liden, Swindon SN3 6HF.—*Exec. Sec.*, Ms. V. Fea.

SCHOOL NATURAL SCIENCE SOCIETY.—*Hon. Gen. Sec.*, Miss D. S. Jackson, 153 Fernside Avenue, Hanworth, Middx. TW13 7BQ.

SCHOOLMASTERS, SOCIETY OF (1798). (For the relief of necessitous schoolmasters and their dependants)—*Sec.*, Mrs. M. S. Freeburn, Hall Farm Dairy, Wood Norton, Dereham, Norfolk NR20 5AR.

SCHOOLMISTRESSES AND GOVERNESSES BENEVOLENT INSTITUTION (1843), Queen Mary House, Manor Park Road, Chislehurst, Kent BR7 5PY.—*Dir.*, R. W. Hayward.

SCIENCE AND LEARNING, SOCIETY FOR THE PROTECTION OF (1933), 20–21 Compton Terrace, NI 2UN.—*Sec.*, Ms. E. Fraser.

SCIENCE, BRITISH ASSOCIATION FOR THE ADVANCEMENT OF (1831), Fortress House, 23 Savile Row, W1X 1AB.—*Exec. Sec.*, Dr. D. Morley.

SCIENCE EDUCATION, ASSOCIATION FOR (1963), College Lane, Hatfield, Herts. AL10 9AA.—*Gen. Sec.*, Dr. D. S. Moore.

SCOTCH WHISKY ASSOCIATION (1919), 20 Atholl Crescent, Edinburgh EH3 8HF.—*Dir. Gen.*, Col. H. F. O. Bewsher, O.B.E.

SCOTTISH CHURCH HISTORY SOCIETY (1922).—*Hon. Sec.*, Rev. C. G. F. Brockie, Grange Manse, 51 Portland Road, Kilmarnock, Ayrshire KA1 2EQ.

SCOTTISH CORPORATION, THE ROYAL (1611), 37 King Street, WC2E 8JS.—*Chief Exec.*, Wg. Cdr. A. Robertson.

SCOTTISH COUNTRY DANCE SOCIETY, ROYAL (1923), 12 Coates Crescent, Edinburgh EH3 7AF.—*Sec.*, Mrs. J. A. Moore.

SCOTTISH GENEALOGY SOCIETY (1953).—*Hon. Sec.*, Miss J. P. S. Ferguson, 21 Howard Place, Edinburgh EH3 5JY.

SCOTTISH HISTORY SOCIETY (1886).—*Hon. Sec.*, Dr. N. MacDougall, Dept. of Scottish History, St. Salvator's College, University of St. Andrews, Fife KY16 9AJ.

SCOTTISH LANDOWNERS' FEDERATION (1906).—*Dir.*, S. Fraser, 39 Palmerston Place, Edinburgh EH12 5AU.

SCOTTISH LAW AGENTS SOCIETY, 33–34 Charlotte Square, Edinburgh EH2 4HF.—*Sec.*, G. F. Davidson.

SCOTTISH LIFE OFFICES, ASSOCIATED (1841), 23 St. Andrew Square, Edinburgh EH2 1AQ.—*Sec.*, W. W. Mair.

SCOTTISH NATIONAL INSTITUTION FOR THE WAR BLINDED (1915), Gillespie Crescent, Edinburgh EH10 4HZ.—*Sec.*, J. B. M. Munro.

SCOTTISH NATIONAL WAR MEMORIAL (1927), The Castle, Edinburgh EH1 2YT.—*Sec.*, T. C. Barker.

SCOTTISH SECONDARY TEACHERS' ASSOCIATION (1946), 15 Dundas Street, Edinburgh EH3 6QG.—*Gen. Sec.*, A. A. Stanley.

SCOTTISH SOCIETY FOR THE PREVENTION OF CRUELTY TO ANIMALS (1950), 19 Melville Street, Edinburgh EH3 7PL.—*Chief Exec.*, Sir Cameron Rusby, K.C.B., L.V.O.

SCOTTISH SOCIETY FOR THE PROTECTION OF WILD BIRDS (1927), Foremount House, Kilbarchan, Renfrewshire PA10 2EZ.—*Sec.*, Dr. J. A. Gibson.

SCOTTISH WILDLIFE TRUST (1964), 25 Johnston Terrace, Edinburgh EH1 2NH.—*Chief Exec.*, D. J. Hughes Hallett.

SCOUT ASSOCIATION, THE (1907), Baden-Powell House, Queen's Gate, SW7 5JS. Membership in U.K. (1989), 647,727; World Membership over 16,000,000 in over 150 countries.—*Chief Scout*, W. Garth Morrison; *Chief Exec. Commissioner*, A. E. N. Black, O.B.E.

SCRIBES AND ILLUMINATORS, THE SOCIETY OF (1921).—*Hon. Sec.*, Mrs. S. Cavendish, 54 Boileau Road, SW13 9BL.

SCRIPTURE GIFT MISSION INCORPORATED (1888), Radstock House, 3 Eccleston Street, SW1W 9LZ.—*Gen. Sec.*, R. Kennedy.

SCRIPTURE UNION (1867), 130 City Road, EC1V 2NJ.—*Gen. Dir.*, Rev. D. M. S. Cohen.

SCULPTORS, ROYAL SOCIETY OF BRITISH (1904), 108 Old Brompton Road, SW7 3RA.—*Sec.*, Miss M. O'Connor.

SEA CADETS, (1895), 202 Lambeth Road, SE1 7JF.—*Gen. Sec.*, Cdr. P. J. Everett, O.B.E.

SEAMEN'S BOYS' HOME, BRITISH (1863), Berry Head Road, Brixham, Devon TQ5 9AE.—*Sec.*, Capt. E. M. Marks, R.D., R.N.R.

SEAMEN'S CHRISTIAN FRIEND SOCIETY (1846), P.O. Box 60, Wilmslow, Cheshire SK9 1QX.—*Gen. Sec.*, J. C. Gordon Pickering.

SEAMEN'S PENSION FUND, ROYAL (1919), 65 High Street, Ewell, Epsom, Surrey KT17 1RX.—*Sec.*, D. Barker.

SECONDARY HEADS ASSOCIATION (1978), 130 Regent Road, Leicester LE1 7PG.—*Gen. Sec.*, J. Sutton.

SECULAR SOCIETY LTD., NATIONAL (1866), 702 Holloway Road, N19 3NL.—*Gen. Sec.*, T. Mullins.

SELDEN SOCIETY (1887), Faculty of Laws, Queen Mary College, Mile End Road, E1 4NS. To advance the study of the history of English Law.—*Sec.*, V. Tunkel.

SELF EMPLOYED AND SMALL BUSINESSES, NATIONAL FEDERATION OF (1974), 32 St. Annes Road West, Lytham St. Annes, Lancs., FY8 1NY.—*Nat. Chairman*, W. Knox.

SHAFTESBURY HOMES AND *Arethusa* (1843), 3 Rectory Grove, SW4 0EG.—*Dir.*, Capt. N. C. Baird-Murray, C.B.E., R.N.

SHAFTESBURY SOCIETY, THE (1844), 2A Amity Grove, Raynes Park, SW20 0LJ. Cares for physically and mentally handicapped, the elderly and socially deprived.—*Dir.*, G. Holloway.

SHEEP ASSOCIATION, NATIONAL, 106 High Street, Tring, Herts. HP23 4AF.—*Sec.*, J. Thorley.

SHELLFISH ASSOCIATION OF GREAT BRITAIN (1904), Fishmongers' Hall, London Bridge, EC4R 9EL.—*Dir.*, E. Edwards, PH.D.

SHELTER (1966), 88 Old Street, EC1V 9HU.—*Dir.*, Miss S. McKechnie.

SHERLOCK HOLMES SOCIETY OF LONDON (1951).—*Hon. Sec.*, Cdr. G. S. Stavert, M.B.E., 3 Outram Road, Southsea, Hants. PO5 1QP.

SHIPBROKERS, INSTITUTE OF CHARTERED (1911), 24 St. Mary Axe, EC3A 8DE.—*Sec.*, J. H. Parker.

SHIRE HORSE SOCIETY (1878), East of England Showground, Peterborough PE2 0XE.—*Chief Exec.*, R. W. Bird, M.B.E.

SHRIEVALTY ASSOCIATION (1971), 14 Clumber Street, Nottingham NG1 3DS.—*Sec.*, R. Bullock.

SIGHT SAVERS (Royal Commonwealth Society for the Blind) (1950), P.O. Box 191, Haywards Heath, W. Sussex RH16 1FN.—*Exec. Dir.*, A. W. Johns, O.B.E.

SIMPLIFIED SPELLING SOCIETY (1908).—*Chairman*, C. J. H. Jolly, Clare Hall, Chapel Lane, Chigwell, Essex IG7 6JJ.

SIR OSWALD STOLL FOUNDATION (1916), 446 Fulham Road, SW6 1DT.—*Dir.*, R. C. Brunwin.

SMALL FARMERS' ASSOCIATION, THE (1979), P.O. Box 6, Ludlow, Salop SY8 1ZZ.—*Hon. Sec.*, Miss V. Minet.

SOCIAL RESPONSIBILITY AND EDUCATION, QUAKER, Friends House, Euston Road, NW1 2BJ.—*Gen. Sec.*, T. Jaggar.

SOCIAL WORKERS, BRITISH ASSOCIATION OF (1970), 16 Kent Street, Birmingham B5 6RD.—*Gen. Sec.*, D. N. Jones.

SOCIALIST PARTY OF GREAT BRITAIN (1904), 52 Clapham High Street, SW4 7UN.—*Gen. Sec.*, P. Hope.

SOLDIERS' AND AIRMEN'S SCRIPTURE READERS ASSOCIATION, THE (1838), Havelock House, Barrack Road, Aldershot, Hants. GU11 3NP.—*Gen. Sec.*, Lt. Col. K. W. Sear.

SOLDIERS', SAILORS' AND AIRMEN'S FAMILIES ASSOCIATION (1885), 19 Queen Elizabeth Street, SE1 2LP.—*Chairman*, Adm. Sir Peter Herbert, K.C.B., O.B.E.; *Controller*, Maj.-Gen. C. R. Grey, C.B.E.; *Sec.*, Capt. W. Stuart.

SOLDIERS, SAILORS AND AIRMEN'S HELP SOCIETY, *see* FORCES HELP SOCIETY.

SOLDIERS' WIDOWS, ROYAL CAMBRIDGE HOME FOR (1851), 82–84 Hurst Road, East Molesey, Surrey KT8 9AH.—*Superintendent*, Mrs. A. M. Webb.

SOLICITORS BENEVOLENT ASSOCIATION (1858), Lonsdale Chambers, 27 Chancery Lane, WC2A 1NF.—*Sec.*, Lt.-Col. D. G. Martin, O.B.E.

SOLICITORS IN THE SUPREME COURTS OF SCOTLAND, SOCIETY OF (1784).—*Sec.*, A. R. Brownlie, O.B.E., 2 Abercromby Place, Edinburgh EH3 6JZ.

SOROPTIMIST INTERNATIONAL OF GREAT BRITAIN AND IRELAND (1923), 63 Bayswater Road, W2 3PJ.— *Admin. Officer*, J. E. Tuson.

S.O.S. SOCIETY, THE (1929), 13 Harewood Road, SW6 4QP. Old people's homes (5), Mental Rehabilitation homes (3).—*Chief Exec.*, Col. M. T. O. Lloyd, O.B.E.

SOUTH AMERICAN MISSIONARY SOCIETY (1844), Allen Gardiner House, Pembury Road, Tunbridge Wells, Kent TN2 3QU.—*Gen. Sec.*, Rt. Rev. J. W. H. Flagg.

SOUTH WALES INSTITUTE OF ENGINEERS (1857), Empire House, Mount Stuart Square, Cardiff CF1 6QZ.— *Hon. Sec.*, R. E. Lindsay.

SPASTICS SOCIETY, THE (1952), 12 Park Crescent, W1N 4EQ.—*Chief Exec.*, K. Young.

SPEAKERS CLUBS, THE ASSOCIATION OF (1971).—*Nat. Sec.*, Mrs. E. C. Hill, Douglasmuir, Arbroath, Angus D11 4UN.

SPINA BIFIDA AND HYDROCEPHALUS, ASSOCIATION FOR (ASBAH), 42 Park Road, Peterborough PE1 2UQ.— *Exec. Dir.*, Miss M. P. Gilbertson.

SPORTS MEDICINE, INSTITUTE OF (1963), Burlington House, Piccadilly, W1V 0LQ.—*Hon. Sec.*, P. Sebastian.

SPURGEON'S CHILD CARE (1867), 30 Mill Street, Bedford MK40 3HD.

STATISTICIANS, INSTITUTE OF (1948), 43 St. Peters Square, Preston PR1 7BX.—*Sec.*, A. P. Haws, PHD.

STATUTE LAW SOCIETY (1968), 186 City Road, EC1V 2NU.—*Hon. Sec.*, N. Frudd.

STEWART SOCIETY (1899), 48 Castle Street, Edinburgh EH2 3LX.—*Hon. Sec.*, Mrs. M. Walker.

STRATEGIC PLANNING SOCIETY, THE (1967), 17 Portland Place, W1N 3AF.—*Exec. Sec.*, Miss C. E. Langan.

STRATEGIC STUDIES, THE INTERNATIONAL INSTITUTE FOR (1958), 23 Tavistock Street, WC2E 7NQ.—*Dir.*, F. Heisbourg.

STRUCTURAL ENGINEERS, INSTITUTION OF (1908), 11 Upper Belgrave Street, SW1X 8BH.—*Sec.*, D. J. Clark.

STUDENT CHRISTIAN MOVEMENT (1889), 186 St. Paul's Road, Balsall Heath, Birmingham B12 8LZ.—*Gen. Sec.*, Rev. T. E. McClure.

SUFFOLK HORSE SOCIETY (1878), 6 Church Street, Woodbridge, Suffolk IP12 1DH.—*Sec.*, P. Ryder-Davies.

SURGEONS OF ENGLAND, ROYAL COLLEGE OF (1800), 35–43 Lincoln's Inn Fields, WC2A 3PN.—*Sec.*, R. H. E. Duffett.

SURGEONS OF EDINBURGH, ROYAL COLLEGE OF (1505), Nicolson Street, Edinburgh EH8 9DW.—*Sec.*, Prof. A. G. D. Maran.

SURVEYORS, ROYAL INSTITUTION OF CHARTERED (incorporating the Institute of Quantity Surveyors) (1868), 12 Great George Street, SW1P 3AD.—*Sec. Gen.*, M. Pattison.

SUSSEX CATTLE SOCIETY (1887), Station Road, Robertsbridge, E. Sussex TN32 5DG.—*Manager*, Miss S. G. Kennedy.

SWEDENBORG SOCIETY (1810), 20–21 Bloomsbury Way, WC1A 2TH.—*Sec.*, Ms. M. G. Waters.

TALKING BOOKS FOR THE HANDICAPPED (National Listening Library), 12 Lant Street, SE1 1QH.— *Exec. Dir.*, D. J. Roskilly.

TAVISTOCK INSTITUTE OF HUMAN RELATIONS (1947), The Tavistock Centre, Belsize Lane, NW3 5BA.— *Sec.*, P. M. Foster, D.F.C.

TAXATION, INSTITUTE OF (1930), 12 Upper Belgrave Street, SW1X 8BB.—*Sec.*, R. J. Ison.

TAX PAYERS' SOCIETY (1921), 22 Wheatsheaf House, 4 Carmelite Street, EC4Y 0BN.—*Dir.*, D. J. Bryant.

TEACHERS IN COMMERCE LTD., FACULTY OF (1872), 141 Bedford Road, Sutton Coldfield, West Midlands B75 6DB.—*Sec.*, vacant.

TEACHERS OF HOME ECONOMICS LTD., NATIONAL ASSOCIATION OF (1896), Hamilton House, Mabledon Place, WC1H 9BJ.—*Gen. Man.*, P. G. Higgins.

TEACHERS OF MATHEMATICS, ASSOCIATION OF (1952), 7 Shaftesbury Street, Derby DE3 8YB—*Hon. Sec.*, Ms. G. M. Hatch.

TEACHERS OF THE DEAF, BRITISH ASSOCIATION OF (1977).—*Hon. Sec.*, Ms. S. Dowe, Icknield High School H.I.U., Riddy Lane, Luton LU3 2AH.

TEACHERS' UNION, ULSTER (1919), 94 Malone Road, Belfast BT9 5HP.—*Gen. Sec.*, D. Allen.

TELECOMMUNICATIONS USERS' ASSOCIATION (1965), 48 Percy Road, N12 8BU.—*Chief Exec.*, Ms. V. Peters.

TEMPERANCE SOCIETIES:—

British National Temperance League (1834), Room 4, Shirley House, 31 Psalter Lane, Sheffield S11 8YL.—*Sec.*, L. Swales.

British Women's Temperance Association (1876), 8 North Bank Street, Edinburgh EH1 2LP.—*Hon. Sec.*, Miss J. E. H. Gillon.

Churches Council on Alcohol and Drugs (1915), 4 Southampton Row, WC1B 4AA.—*Sec.*, Ms. H. Gilmour.

Church of England National Council for Social Aid, 38 Ebury Street, SW1W 0LU.—*Gen. Sec.*, Rev. E. W. F. Agar.

Division of Social Responsibility of the Methodist Church (1932), 1 Central Buildings, Westminster, SW1H 9NH.—*Gen. Sec.*, Rev. B. Duckworth.

National United Temperance Council (1880), 123 Regent Street, W1R 7HA—*Gen. Sec.*, Rev. B. Kinman.

Order of the Sons of Temperance (1855), 5 Ashbourne Road, Derby, DE3 3FQ.—*Sec.*, D. Newbury.

Royal Naval Temperance Society (1876) (auxiliary of Royal Sailors' Rests), 2A South Street, Gosport, Hants. PO12 1ES.—*Sec.*, A. A. Lockwood.

Social Responsibility Dept., General Assembly of Unitarian and Free Christian Churches, Essex Hall, 1–6 Essex Street, WC2R 3HY.—*Hon. Sec.*, C. Shute.

United Kingdom Alliance (1863), Alliance House, 123 Regent Street, W1R 7HA.—*Gen. Sec.*, Rev. B. Kinman.

TEMPLETON FOUNDATION (1973), 16 Kingfisher Lane, Turners Hill, Crawley, W. Sussex RH10 4QP.— *U.K. Rep.*, Mrs. N. Pearse.

TERRITORIAL, AUXILIARY AND VOLUNTEER RESERVE ASSOCIATIONS, COUNCIL OF (1908), Centre Block, Duke of York's Headquarters, SW3 4SG.—*Sec.*, Maj.-Gen. M. Matthews, C.B.

TEXTILE INSTITUTE, THE (1910), International Headquarters, 10 Blackfriars Street, Manchester M3 5DR.—*Gen. Sec.*, R. G. Denyer.

THEATRE ASSOCIATION, BRITISH (1919), Cranbourn Mansions, Cranbourn Street, WC2H 7AG.—*Administrator*, R. Haddon.

THEATRE RESEARCH, SOCIETY FOR (1948), c/o The Theatre Museum, 1E Tavistock Street, WC2E 7PA.—*Joint Hon. Secs.*, D. Forbes; S. Wallace Roche.

THEATRICAL FUND, ROYAL (1839), 11 Garrick Street, WC2E 9AR.—*Sec.*, J. Berkeley.

THEATRICAL LADIES' GUILD OF CHARITY (1892).— *Admin. Sec.*, Mrs. K. Nichols, 36–40 York Way, N1 9AB.

THEOSOPHICAL SOCIETY IN ENGLAND (1875), 50 Gloucester Place, W1H 3HJ.—*Gen. Sec.*, Miss I. H. Hoskins.

THISTLE FOUNDATION, THE (1945), 27A Walker Street, Edinburgh EH3 7HX.—*Dir.*, P. Croft.

THOMAS CORAM FOUNDATION FOR CHILDREN (1739), 40 Brunswick Square, WC1N 1AZ.—*Dir. and Sec.*, C. P. Masters.

TIDY BRITAIN GROUP (1953), The Pier, Wigan WN3 4EX.—*Dir. Gen.*, Prof. G. Ashworth, C.B.E.

TOC H (1915), Headquarters, 1 Forest Close, Wendover, Aylesbury, Bucks. HP22 6BT.—*Gen. Sec.*, Dr. J. M. A. Kilburn.

TOURIST BOARD, NORTHERN IRELAND, River House, 48 High Street, Belfast BT1 2DS.—*Chief Exec.*, S. B. Belford.

TOURIST BOARD, SCOTTISH (1969), 23 Ravelston Terrace, Edinburgh EH4 3EU.—*Chief Exec.*, T. M. Band.

TOWN AND COUNTRY PLANNING ASSOCIATION (1899), 17 Carlton House Terrace, SW1Y 5AS.—*Dir.*, D. Hall.

TOWN PLANNING INSTITUTE, ROYAL (1914), 26 Portland Place, W1N 4BE.

TOWNSWOMEN'S GUILDS, (1929), Chamber of Commerce House, 75 Harborne Road, Birmingham B15 3DA.—*Nat. Sec.*, Mrs. J. R. Campbell-Tanner.

TOYNBEE HALL, The Universities' Settlement in East London (1884), 28 Commercial Street, E1 6LS.— *Warden and Chief Exec.*, A. L. Williams, O.B.E.

TRADE MARK AGENTS, INSTITUTE OF (1934), 4th Floor, Canterbury House, 2–6 Sydenham Road, Croydon CR0 9XE.—*Sec.*, Mrs. M. J. Tyler.

TRADE, NATIONAL CHAMBER OF (1897), Enterprise House, Henley-upon-Thames, Oxon. RG9 1TU.— *Chief Exec.*, B. Tennant.

TRADING STANDARDS ADMINISTRATION, THE INSTITUTE OF (1881), 4–5 Hadleigh Business Centre, 351 London Road, Hadleigh, Essex SS7 2BT.—*Dir. of Admin. and P.R*, Mrs. G. Jordan.

TRANSPORT ADMINISTRATION, INSTITUTE OF (1944), 32 Palmerston Road, Southampton SO1 1LL.—*Dir.*, Wg. Cdr. P. F. Green.

TRANSPORT, CHARTERED INSTITUTE OF (1919), 80 Portland Place, W1N 4DP.—*Dir. Gen.*, R. P. Botwood.

TRANSPORT CONSULTATIVE COMMITTEE, CENTRAL (1948), 1st Floor, Golden Cross House, Duncannon Street, WC2N 4JF.—*Sec.*, M. Patterson.

TRAVEL AGENTS, ASSOCIATION OF BRITISH (ABTA) (1950), 55–57 Newman Street, W1P 4AH.—*Dir. Gen.*, D. L. Epstein.

TROPICAL MEDICINE AND HYGIENE, ROYAL SOCIETY OF (1907), Manson House, 26 Portland Place, W1N 4EY.

TURNER SOCIETY (1975), BCM Box Turner, WC1N 3XX.—*Chairman*, E. Shanes.

UFAW (Universities Federation for Animal Welfare) (1926), 8 Hamilton Close, South Mimms, Potters Bar, Herts. EN6 3QD.—*Sec.*, Lt.-Col. T. J. Reynolds.

UNIT TRUST ASSOCIATION (1959), 65 Kingsway, WC2B 6TD.—*Chief Exec.*, A. C. Smith.

UNITED NATIONS ASSOCIATION OF GREAT BRITAIN AND NORTHERN IRELAND (1945), 3 Whitehall Court, SW1A 2EL.—*Dir.*, M. C. Harper.

UNITED REFORMED CHURCH HISTORY SOCIETY (1972), 86 Tavistock Place, WC1H 9RT.—*Hon. Sec.*, Rev. Dr. S. Orchard.

UNITED SOCIETY FOR CHRISTIAN LITERATURE (1799), Robertson House, Leas Road, Guildford, Surrey GU14 4QW.—*Gen. Sec.*, Rev. A. Gilmore.

UNITED SOCIETY FOR THE PROPAGATION OF THE GOSPEL (USPG) (1701), Partnership House, 157 Waterloo Road, SE1 8XA.—*Sec.*, Rev. Canon H. V. Taylor.

UNIVERSITIES CENTRAL COUNCIL ON ADMISSIONS (1961), P.O. Box 28, Cheltenham, Glos. GL50 3SA.— *Gen. Sec.*, P. A. Oakley, M.B.E.

UNIVERSITY WOMEN, BRITISH FEDERATION OF (1907), Crosby Hall, Cheyne Walk, SW3 5BA.—*Sec.*, Mrs. C. A. Ellis.

VALUERS AND AUCTIONEERS, INCORPORATED SOCIETY OF, 3 Cadogan Gate, SW1X 0AS.—*Sec.*, M. Astbury.

VEGAN SOCIETY, THE (1944), 33–35 George Street, Oxford OX1 2AY.—*Gen. Sec.*, R. Farhall.

VEGETARIAN SOCIETY OF THE UNITED KINGDOM LTD., Parkdale, Dunham Road, Altrincham, Cheshire WA14 4QG.—*Gen. Manager*, Ms. P. McGlashan.

VENEREAL DISEASES, MEDICAL SOCIETY FOR THE STUDY OF (1922).—*Hon. Sec.*, Dr. M. J. Godley, Florey Unit, Royal Berkshire Hospital, Reading RG1 5AN.

VERNACULAR ARCHITECTURE GROUP (1953).—*Hon. Sec.*, R. Meeson, 16 Falna Crescent, Coton Green, Tamworth, Staffs. B79 8JS.

VETERINARY ASSOCIATION, BRITISH (1881), 7 Mansfield Street, W1M 0AT.—*Chief Exec.*, J. H. Baird.

VETERINARY SURGEONS, ROYAL COLLEGE OF, 32 Belgrave Square, SW1X 8QP (1844).—*Pres.*, H. E. Carter; *Registrar*, A. R. W. Porter, C.B.E.

VICE-CHANCELLORS AND PRINCIPALS OF THE UNIVERSITIES OF THE UNITED KINGDOM, COMMITTEE OF (1918), 29 Tavistock Square, WC1H 9EZ.—*Sec.*, T. U. Burgner.

VICTIM SUPPORT (1979), Cranmer House, 39 Brixton Road, SW9 6DZ.—*Dir.*, Ms. H. Reeves, O.B.E.

VICTORIA CROSS AND GEORGE CROSS ASSOCIATION, Room 04, Archway Block South, Old Admiralty Building, SW1A 2BE.—*Chairman*, Rear-Adm. B. C. G. Place, V.C., C.B., D.S.C.

VICTORIA INSTITUTE, THE (Philosophical Society of Great Britain), P.O. Box 216, Welling, Kent DA16 2ED.—*Hon. Treas.*, B. H. T. Weller.

VICTORIAN SOCIETY (1958), 1 Priory Gardens, Bedford Park, W4 1TT.—*Sec.*, Ms. T. Sladen.

VICTORY (SERVICES) ASSOCIATION LTD. AND CLUB (1907), 63–79 Seymour Street, W2 2HF.—*Gen. Manager*, G. F. Taylor.

VIKING SOCIETY FOR NORTHERN RESEARCH (1892), University College London, Gower Street, WC1E 6BT.—*Joint Hon. Secs.*, Ms. U. Dronke; Prof. M. P. Barnes.

VITREOUS ENAMELLERS, INSTITUTE OF (1935), Ripley, Derby DE5 3EB.—*Sec.*, J. D. Gardom.

V.S.O. (Voluntary Service Overseas) (1958), 317 Putney Bridge Road, SW15 2PN.—*Dir.*, N. McIntosh.

WAR ON WANT (1952), Fenner Brockway House, 37–39 Great Guildford Street, SE1 0ES.—*Gen. Sec.* F. Khoo.

WATER AND ENVIRONMENTAL MANAGEMENT, INSTITUTION OF (1987), 15 John Street, WC1N 2EB.—*Exec. Dir.*, H. R. Evans.

WATERCOLOUR SOCIETY, ROYAL (1804), Bankside Gallery, 48 Hopton Street, SE1 9JH.—*Sec.*, M. Spender.

WELDING INSTITUTE, THE, Abington Hall, Cambridge CB1 6AL.—*Chief Exec.*, A. B. M. Braithwaite.

WELFARE OFFICERS, INSTITUTE OF (1945), 254 The Corn Exchange, Hanging Ditch, Manchester M4 3ES.—*Sec.*, Mrs. M. Maclean-Ives.

WELLCOME TRUST (1936), 1 Park Square West, NW1 4LJ.—*Dir.*, Dr. P. O. Williams.

WELLS, H. G., SOCIETY (1961), Polytechnic of North London, Prince of Wales Road, NW5 3LB.—*Sec.*, C. Rolfe.

WESLEY HISTORICAL SOCIETY (1893).—*Gen. Sec.*, Dr. E. D. Graham, 34 Spiceland Road, Northfield, Birmingham B31 1NJ.

WEST AFRICA COMMITTEE (1956), 315 Oxford Street, W1R 2BQ.—*Secs.*, L. J. Walters; G. W. House.

WEST INDIA COMMITTEE (1750), Commonwealth House, 18 Northumberland Avenue, WC2N 5RA.—*Dir.*, D. A. Jessop.

WEST LONDON MISSION (1887), 19 Thayer Street, W1M 5LJ.—*Supt.*, Rev. L. J. Griffiths, PH.D.

WILDLIFE ARTISTS, SOCIETY OF (1962), 17 Carlton House Terrace, SW1Y 5AH.—*Hon. Sec.*, K. J. Wood.

WILLIAM MORRIS SOCIETY AND KELMSCOTT FELLOWSHIP (1918), Kelmscott House, 26 Upper Mall, W6 9TA.—*Hon. Sec.*, P. Preston.

WINE AND SPIRIT ASSOCIATION OF GREAT BRITAIN AND NORTHERN IRELAND (c. 1825), Five Kings House, Upper Thames Street, Kennett Wharf Lane, EC4V 3BH.—*Dir.*, R. H. Insoll.

WOMEN ARTISTS, SOCIETY OF (1855), Westminster Gallery, Westminster Central Hall, Storey's Gate, SW1H 9NU.—*Pres.*, Ms. B. Tate.

WOMEN, NATIONAL ADVISORY CENTRE ON CAREERS FOR (1933), 8th Floor, Artillery House, Artillery Row, SW1P 1RT.—*Dir.*, Miss K. M. Menon.

WOMEN, SOCIETY FOR PROMOTING THE TRAINING OF (1859). Loan fund for women in higher education.—*Sec.*, Rev. B. Harris, The Rectory, Ben Lane, Lymm, Cheshire WA13 9TQ.

WOMEN'S ENGINEERING SOCIETY (1920), Imperial College of Science and Technology, Dept. of Civil Engineering, Imperial College Road, SW7 2BU.

WOMEN'S INSTITUTES, NATIONAL FEDERATION OF (1915), 39 Eccleston Street, SW1W 9NT.—*Gen. Sec.*, Mrs. A. Ballard.

WOMEN'S INSTITUTES OF NORTHERN IRELAND, FEDERATION OF (1932), 209–211 Upper Lisburn Road, Belfast BT10 0LL.—*Gen. Sec.*, Mrs. I. A. Sproule.

WOMEN'S INTERNATIONAL LEAGUE FOR PEACE AND FREEDOM (British Section) (1915), 29 Great James Street, WC1N 3ES.—*Chair*, Ms. M. Miller.

WOMEN'S NATIONAL CANCER CONTROL CAMPAIGN (1964), 1 South Audley Street, W1Y 5DQ.—*Administrator*, Miss M. R. C. Bateman.

WOMEN'S ROYAL NAVAL SERVICE BENEVOLENT TRUST (1942), 1A Chesham Street, SW1X 8NL.—*Gen. Sec.*, Mrs. J. Y. Ellis.

WOMEN'S ROYAL VOLUNTARY SERVICE (WRVS) (1938), 234–244 Stockwell Road, SW9 9SP.—*National Chairman*, Hon. Mrs. M. Corsar.

WOMEN'S RURAL INSTITUTES, SCOTTISH (1917), 42 Heriot Row, Edinburgh EH3 6ES.—*Gen. Sec.*, Mrs. E. Nicol.

WOMEN'S TRANSPORT SERVICE (1907), FANY H.Q. (E Block), Duke of York's H.Q., SW3 4SJ.—*Corps Commander*, Mrs. S. Y. Parkinson, O.B.E.

WOODLAND TRUST, THE (1972), Autumn Park, Dysart Road, Grantham, Lincs. NG31 6LL.—*Exec. Dir.*, J. D. James.

WOOD PRESERVING ASSOCIATION, BRITISH (1930), 6 The Office Village, 4 Romford Road, E15 4EA.—*Dir.*, D. Scobie (*acting*).

WORKERS' EDUCATIONAL ASSOCIATION, Temple House, 9 Upper Berkeley Street, W1H 8BY.—*Gen. Sec.*, R. Lochrie.

WORLD EDUCATION FELLOWSHIP (1921), 33 Kinnaird Avenue, W4 3SH.—*Gen. Sec.*, Mrs. R. Crommelin.

WORLD ENERGY CONFERENCE (1924), 34 St. James's Street, SW1A 1HD.—*Sec. Gen.*, I. D. Lindsay,

WORLD MISSION, COUNCIL FOR (1977), Livingstone House, 11 Carteret Street, SW1H 9DL.—*Gen. Sec.*, vacant.

WORLD SHIP SOCIETY (1946).—*Sec.*, S. J. F. Miller, 35 Wickham Way, Haywards Heath, W. Sussex RH16 1UJ.

WORLD SOCIETY FOR THE PROTECTION OF ANIMALS (1981), 106 Jermyn Street, SW1Y 6EE.—*Dir. Gen.*, G. Walwyn, C.V.O.

WORLD WIDE FUND FOR NATURE—U.K. (1961), Panda House, Weyside Park, Godalming, Surrey GU7 1XR—*Dir.*, G. J. Medley.

WRITERS TO H.M. SIGNET, SOCIETY OF (1532), 16 Hill Street, Edinburgh EH2 3LD.—*Clerk*, A. M. Kerr.

YEOMANRY BENEVOLENT FUND (1902), 10 Stone Buildings, Lincoln's Inn, WC2A 3TG.—*Sec.*, Mrs. C. W. Chrystie.

YORKSHIRE AGRICULTURAL SOCIETY (1837), Great Yorkshire Showground, Hookstone Oval, Harrogate HG2 8PW.—*Sec.-Gen.*, Lt.-Col. M. G. A. Young.

YORKSHIRE SOCIETY, THE (1812), 27 Kensington Park, Milford-on-Sea, Hants. SO41 0WD. Educational trust making grants to students of all ages.—*Sec.*, G. G. Prince, T.D.

YOUNG FARMERS' CLUBS, NATIONAL FEDERATION OF, The Y.F.C. Centre, National Agricultural Centre, Kenilworth, Warks. CV8 2LG.—*Sec.*, F. E. Shields.

YOUNG MEN'S CHRISTIAN ASSOCIATION (YMCA) (1844), National Council of YMCAs, 640 Forest Road, E17 3DZ.—*Nat. Sec.*, C. J. Naylor.

YOUNG WOMEN'S CHRISTIAN ASSOCIATION OF GREAT BRITAIN (YWCA) (1855), 52 Cornmarket Street, Oxford OX1 3EJ.—*Exec. Dir.*, Miss F. E. Sharples.

YOUTH CLUBS U.K. (1911), Keswick House, 30 Peacock Lane, Leicester LE1 5NY.—*Chief Exec.*, Mrs. J. Holt.

YOUTH CLUBS, NORTHERN IRELAND ASSOCIATION OF (1944), Hampton, Glenmachan Park, Belfast BT4 2PJ.—*Dir.*, G. Johnston.

YOUTH HOSTELS ASSOCIATION (ENGLAND AND WALES) (1930), Trevelyan House, 8 St. Stephens Hill, St. Albans, Herts. AL1 2DY.—*Chief Exec.*, A. G. F. Chinneck.

YOUTH HOSTELS ASSOCIATION, SCOTTISH (1931), 7 Glebe Crescent, Stirling FK8 2JA.—*Gen. Sec.*, J. Martin.

YOUTH HOSTELS ASSOCIATION OF NORTHERN IRELAND (1931), Bradbury Buildings, 56 Bradbury Place, Belfast BT7 1RU.—*Hon. Sec.*, E. R. Henderson.

ZOOLOGICAL SOCIETY OF LONDON (1826), Regent's Park, NW1 4RY. Attendances (1988), Regent's Park 1,351,749; Whipsnade 422,678.—*Pres.*, Prof. N. A. Mitchison; *Man. Dir.*, A. Y. Grant.

ZOOLOGICAL SOCIETY OF SCOTLAND, ROYAL (1913), Scottish National Zoological Park, Murrayfield, Edinburgh EH12 6TS.—*Dir.*, R. J. Wheater, F.R.S.E.

LOCAL HISTORY AND ARCHAEOLOGICAL SOCIETIES
England and Wales

Bedfordshire.—SOUTH BEDFORDSHIRE ARCHAEO-LOGICAL SOCIETY. *Hon. Sec.* D. H. Kennett, 27 Lords Lane, Bradwell, Great Yarmouth, Norfolk NR31 8NY.

Berkshire.—BERKSHIRE ARCHAEOLOGICAL SOCIETY. *Hon. Sec.*, L. J. Over, 43 Laburnham Road, Maidenhead, Berks. SL6 4DE.

NEWBURY DISTRICT FIELD CLUB. *Hon. Sec.*, Mrs. P. M. Jermyn, 30 Butson Close, Newbury, Berks. RG14 5JQ.

Buckinghamshire.—BUCKINGHAMSHIRE ARCHAEO-LOGICAL SOCIETY. *Hon. Sec.*, Dr. R. P. Hagerty, County Museum, Church Street, Aylesbury, Bucks. HP20 2QP.

Cambridgeshire.—CAMBRIDGE ANTIQUARIAN SO-CIETY. *Sec.*, Miss A. S. Bendall, Emmanuel College, Cambridge CB2 3AP.

Cheshire.—CHESTER ARCHAEOLOGICAL SOCIETY. *Sec.*, G. R. Coppack, Chamonix, Station Lane, Mickle Trafford, Chester CH2 4EH. *See also* under *Lancashire.*

Cornwall.—CORNWALL ARCHAEOLOGICAL SOCIETY, County Museum and Art Gallery, Truro, Cornwall TR1 2SJ. *Hon. Sec.*, Mrs A. Cooke.

Cumberland and Westmorland.—CUMBERLAND AND WESTMORLAND ANTIQUARIAN AND ARCHAEOLOGI-CAL SOCIETY. *Hon. Sec.*, R. Hall, 2 High Tenterfell, Kendal, Cumbria LA9 4PG.

Derbyshire.—DERBYSHIRE ARCHAEOLOGICAL SOCIETY. *Hon. Sec.*, M. E. Burrows, 12 Wilne Road, Draycott, Derby DE7 3NG.

Devonshire.—DEVON ARCHAEOLOGICAL SOCIETY, R.A.M. Museum, Queen Street, Exeter EX4 3RX.

Dorset.—DORSET NATURAL HISTORY AND ARCHAEO-LOGICAL SOCIETY, Dorset County Museum, Dorchester DT1 1XA. *Sec.*, R. N. R. Peers.

Durham.—DURHAM AND NORTHUMBERLAND ARCHI-TECTURAL AND ARCHAEOLOGICAL SOCIETY. *Hon. Sec.*, Dr. M. J. Millett, 46 Saddler Street, Durham DH1 3NU.

Dyfed.—CEREDIGION ANTIQUARIAN SOCIETY. *Hon. Sec.*, I. M. Jones, Dolau-gwyn, Dole, Bow Street, Dyfed SY24 5AE.

Essex.—ESSEX SOCIETY FOR ARCHAEOLOGY AND HIS-TORY, Hollytrees Museum, High Street, Colchester CO1 1UG. *Sec.*, V. W. Gray.

Gloucestershire.—BRISTOL AND GLOUCESTERSHIRE ARCHAEOLOGICAL SOCIETY, *Hon. Sec.*, D. J. H. Smith, 22 Beaumont Road, Gloucester GL2 0EJ.

Gwynedd.—ANGLESEY ANTIQUARIAN SOCIETY. *Hon. Sec.*, S. C. G. Caffell, 1 Fronheulog Sling, Tregarth, Bangor LL57 4RD.

Hampshire.—HAMPSHIRE FIELD CLUB AND ARCHAEO-LOGICAL SOCIETY. *Hon. Sec.*, Dr. M. A. Hicks, King Alfred's College, Winchester, Hants. SO22 4NR.

Herefordshire.—WOOLHOPE NATURALISTS' FIELD CLUB. *Hon. Sec.*, J. W. Tonkin, F.S.A., Chy an Whyloryon, Wigmore, Leominster, Herefordshire HR6 9UD.

Hertfordshire.—EAST HERTFORDSHIRE ARCHAEOLOG-ICAL SOCIETY. *Hon. Sec.*, Mrs. M. C. Readman, 1 Marsh Lane, Stanstead Abbots, Ware, Herts. SG12 8HH.

ST. ALBANS AND HERTFORDSHIRE ARCHITEC-TURAL AND ARCHAEOLOGICAL SOCIETY. *Hon. Sec.*, B. E. Moody, 24 Rose Walk, St. Albans, Herts. AL4 9AF.

Kent.—KENT ARCHAEOLOGICAL SOCIETY. *Gen. Sec.*, A. C. Harrison, F.S.A., Prings Cottage, Pilgrims Road, Upper Halling, Rochester ME2 1HR.

Lancashire.— HISTORIC SOCIETY OF LANCASHIRE AND CHESHIRE. *Hon. Sec.*, Mrs. G. M. Wyatt, 302 Prescot Road, Aughton, Ormskirk, Lancs. L39 6RR.

Leicestershire.—LEICESTERSHIRE ARCHAEOLOGICAL AND HISTORICAL SOCIETY, The Guildhall, Leicester LE1 5FQ. *Hon. Sec.*, Dr. A. D. McWhirr.

London and Middlesex.—CITY OF LONDON ARCHAE-OLOGICAL SOCIETY. *Hon. Sec.*, D. R. Lewis, 11 Chatsworth Avenue, Wimbledon Chase, SW20 8JZ.

LONDON AND MIDDLESEX ARCHAEOLOGICAL SO-CIETY. *Hon. Sec.*, Miss J. Macdonald, 3 Cedar Drive, Pinner, Middx. HA5 4DD.

Norfolk.—NORFOLK AND NORWICH ARCHAEOLOGICAL SOCIETY. *Hon. Gen. Sec.*, R. Bellinger, 30 Brettingham Avenue, Norwich NR4 6XG.

Northumberland and Tyne and Wear.—SOCIETY OF ANTIQUARIES OF NEWCASTLE UPON TYNE, Black Gate, Castle Garth, Newcastle upon Tyne NE1 1RQ.

SUNDERLAND ANTIQUARIAN SOCIETY. *Hon. Sec.*, Ms. V. M. Stevens, 16 Grizedale Court, Seaburn Dene, Sunderland SR6 8JP.

Oxfordshire.—OXFORDSHIRE ARCHITECTURAL AND HISTORICAL SOCIETY. *Hon. Sec.*, Miss J. M. Cook, Ashmolean Museum, Oxford OX1 2PH.

Powys.—POWYSLAND CLUB. *Hon. Sec.*, W. G. J. Hughes, Library, Brook Street, Welshpool, Powys SY21 7PH.

RADNORSHIRE SOCIETY. *Hon. Sec.*, A. D. Batley, Skaill, North Avenue, Llandrindod Wells, Powys LD1 6BY.

Shropshire.—SHROPSHIRE ARCHAEOLOGICAL SOCIETY. *Chairman*, J. B. Lawson, Westcott Farm, Pontesbury, Shrewsbury SY5 0SQ.

Somerset.—SOMERSET ARCHAEOLOGICAL AND NATU-RAL HISTORY SOCIETY, Taunton Castle, Taunton, Somerset TA1 4AD. *Hon. Sec.*, C. E. J. Langdon.

Staffordshire.—CITY OF STOKE-ON-TRENT MUSEUM ARCHAEOLOGICAL SOCIETY, City Museum and Art Gallery, Hanley, Stoke-on-Trent. *Chairman*, E. E. Royle.

Suffolk.—SUFFOLK INSTITUTE OF ARCHAEOLOGY AND HISTORY. *Hon. Sec.*, E. A. Martin, Oak Tree Farm, Finborough Road, Hitcham, Ipswich IP7 7LS.

Surrey.—SURREY ARCHAEOLOGICAL SOCIETY, Castle Arch, Guildford, Surrey GU1 3SX. *Hon. Secs.*, Mr. and Mrs. K. D. Graham.

Sussex.—SUSSEX ARCHAEOLOGICAL SOCIETY, Barbican House, High Street, Lewes, E. Sussex BN7 1YE. *Exec. Sec.*, D. P. White.

Warwickshire.—BIRMINGHAM AND WARWICKSHIRE ARCHAEOLOGICAL SOCIETY, c/o Birmingham and Midland Institute, Margaret Street, Birmingham B3 3BS. *Hon. Sec.*, A. J. Wilson.

Wight.—ISLE OF WIGHT NATURAL HISTORY AND ARCHAEOLOGICAL SOCIETY. *Hon. Sec.*, Mrs. T. Goodley, Ivy Cottage, New Barn Lane, Shorwell, Newport, I.o.W., PO30 3JQ.

Wiltshire.—WILTSHIRE ARCHAEOLOGICAL AND NATU-RAL HISTORY SOCIETY, The Museum, 41 Long Street, Devizes SN10 1NS. *Sec.*, Lt.-Col. M. Cowan.

Worcestershire.—WORCESTERSHIRE ARCHAEOLOGICAL SOCIETY. *Hon. Sec.*, Mrs. G. Grice, 91 Hallow Road, Worcester WR2 6DF.

Yorkshire.—YORKSHIRE ARCHAEOLOGICAL SOCIETY. Hon. Sec., P. B. Davidson, Claremont, 23 Clarendon Road, Leeds LS2 9NZ.

HALIFAX ANTIQUARIAN SOCIETY. Hon. Sec., J. A. Hargreaves, 7 Hyde Park Gardens, Haugh Shaw Road, Halifax, W. Yorks. HX1 3AH.

THORESBY SOCIETY. Hon. Sec., D. M. Watson. Claremont, 23 Clarendon Road, Leeds LS2 9NZ.

Channel Islands

SOCIETE JERSIAISE, Archaeological Section, The Jersey Museum, Pier Road, St. Helier, Jersey. Hon. Sec., Ms. J. D. Tanguy.

Scotland

AYRSHIRE ARCHAEOLOGICAL AND NATURAL HISTORY SOCIETY. Hon. Sec., Dr. T. Mathews, 10 Longlands Park, Ayr KA7 4RJ.

DUMFRIESSHIRE AND GALLOWAY NATURAL HISTORY AND ANTIQUARIAN SOCIETY. Hon. Sec., R. H. McEwen, 13 Douglas Terrace, Lockerbie, Dumfriesshire DG11 2DZ.

HAWICK ARCHAEOLOGICAL SOCIETY. Hon. Sec., I. W. Landles, Orrock House, Stirches Road, Hawick, Roxburghshire TD9 7HF.

INVERNESS FIELD CLUB. Hon. Sec., Mrs. E. H. L. Macaskill, 9 Dores Road, Inverness IV2 4QX.

THE CIVIC TRUST
17 Carlton House Terrace, SW1Y 5AW
[01–930 0914]

The Civic Trust, founded in 1957, is a registered charity whose object is to stimulate interest in, and action for, the improvement of the environment throughout the U.K. The Trust is supported by voluntary contributions. It works in close co-operation with over a 1,000 local amenity societies. It acts as a spokesman on issues of national concern.

The Trust is regularly consulted by Government about new legislation concerning the environment. (It inspired the Civic Amenities Act, 1967 which created Conservation Areas.)

On behalf of the Department of the Environment, the Trust runs the Civic Trust Education Group which aims to stimulate environmental education at all levels, particularly in schools. The Trust is also a founder member of the Government's UK2000 initiative. It organizes National Environment Week each year.

There are Associate Trusts in the North East and North West of England, in Scotland and in Wales.
Director., M. C. Bradshaw.

NATIONAL TRUST
36 Queen Anne's Gate, SW1H 9AS
[01–222 9251]

The National Trust was founded in 1895 by Miss Octavia Hill, Sir Robert Hunter and Canon Rawnsley, their object being to preserve as much as possible the history and beauty of their country for its people. It became an organization incorporated by Act of Parliament (1907) to ensure the preservation of lands and buildings of historic interest or natural beauty for public access and benefit. It is independent of the state and relies on the voluntary support of private individuals for working funds. The Trust has now some 1,660,151 members paying an annual subscription. Rents, admission fees, legacies and gifts are other important sources of support and income.

The Trust owns 554,000 acres and holds protection covenants over a further 77,000 acres, some in the National Parks. The Trust also owns and opens to the public some 297 country houses, other buildings and gardens and preserves villages, nature reserves, archaeological sites and many farms. Through Enterprise Neptune, launched 1965, the Trust now protects 500 miles of coastline.

The policy of the Trust is determined by the governing body, the Council. Half of its members are appointed by national institutions, such as the British Museum, the National Gallery, the Ramblers' Association and the Royal Horticultural Society; the other half are elected by Trust members at the annual general meeting. The Council appoints the Executive Committee, which in turn has established Regional Committees responsible for the management of the Trust's properties.
Chairman, Dame Jennifer Jenkins.
Director General, A. Stirling.

NATIONAL TRUST FOR SCOTLAND
5 Charlotte Square, Edinburgh EH2 4DU

The National Trust for Scotland was founded in 1931, and its objects are similar to those of the National Trust. Like that organization, it is incorporated by Act of Parliament and is dependent for finance upon legacies, donations and the subscriptions of its members.

The Trust administers over 100 properties covering some 100,000 acres. These include several noteworthy gardens, some associated with the great houses.

Among the mountainous country owned by the Trust is the Pass of Glen Coe and the mountain group "The Five Sisters of Kintail" and the estate of Torridon in Wester Ross, and Ben Lomond.

Islands in the Trust's care include the St. Kilda group, Staffa, Fair Isle, Iona and Canna (St. Kilda was designated by UNESCO in 1987 as Scotland's first World Heritage site). At Bannockburn, Killiecrankie, Glenfinnan and Culloden, the Trust owns sites associated with Scottish history.

The Trust also administers the Little Houses Improvement Scheme, under which properties are bought, restored and re-sold. Since its inception over 200 houses reflecting the vernacular architecture of Scotland have been restored throughout the country.

PRINCIPAL CHARITABLE BEQUESTS OF THE YEAR

The alphabetical list below represents some of the principal charitable bequests from Wills published since the last edition. The exact amounts available for charities are not known, as prior bequests, testamentary expenses and tax are all deductible from the net figures given, and, in some cases, there are prior life interests in the income from estates.

This year no less than 45 estates have a net value of over £1 million. The largest estate to be proved in England and Wales was that of Dorothy de Rothschild, head of the Rothschild charities in Israel, who left over £92 million. This estate does not appear on the list, as her Will did not contain any charitable legacies as such. However she left £20 million to follow a trust made in 1984, and it is understood that the bulk of her estate, which she left to her four executors, will go to charity.

Three other very large estates are included on the list. Eva Borthwick-Norton, of Purbrook Heath, Hants., left over £23 million, with the residue left equally between the Little Sisters of the Poor at Leeds and the Pasteur Institute in Paris. Another Hampshire woman, Esma Edgar of Newton Valence Place, near Alton, left over £14 million, with the sale proceeds of her home and its estate left between eight charities, while Londoner Leopold Muller left the residue of his £19 million estate for such charitable purposes in England as his executors selected.

The largest estate to be left entirely to charity was that of Doris Field of Headington, Oxford, who left all her £2,688,511 estate for such charities as her executors thought fit. Dorothy Collins of Beaconsfield, Bucks., who had been secretary to G. K.Chesterton, left a portrait of the author as a child to the National Portrait Gallery, and the residue, including copyrights and literary material to which she was entitled under the author's Will, for such charitable purposes as her executors decided.

Trinity Hall, Cambridge, received the residue of the £1 million estate of Walter Christie of Canewdon, Essex, while three Oxford colleges appear on the list—Oriel College, sharing the residue of the £1 million estate of Alan Judd of London with the Woodland Trust; Green College, receiving half the residue of the £656,702 estate of Professor Cochrane, the epidemiologist and Professor at the Welsh National School of Medicine; and Somerville College, receiving the residue of the £509,200 estate of Marjorie Ball of London Colney, Herts. Fritz Strauss left £200,000 to Oxford University.

Many estates in the list included bequests for the elderly. Frank Mustchin of Arundel, directed that the residue of his £708,281 estate be used to provide "good housing for the elderly, preferably needy inhabitants residing within a three-mile radius of Arundel Town Square". Edith Tracy of Farnham Common, Bucks., left most of her £736,525 estate to form the Tracy Trust, to benefit senior citizens and pensioners in nearby Hedgerley. The Quaker Housing Trust received nearly all the £632,764 estate of Meta Bendix of Warlingham, Surrey, for a housing project for the elderly and needy in and around Croydon.

Three prominent sportsmen appear on the list. Capt. James Norris, the former National Hunt trainer, left over £4 million, including bequests of £200,000 each to the Institute of Cancer Research and to Stoke Mandeville Hospital. Gerald Micklem, the golfer and former Walker Cup captain, left 10 per cent of the residue of his £3 million estate to the Gerald Micklem Charitable Trust, and Major-General Eric Harrison, the former Olympic hurdler and rugby wing-threequarter, left the residue of his £658,476 estate to the Royal Artillery Charitable Fund. The Rev. Dr. Bertrand Brasnett, a former

Principal of Edinburgh Theological College, left the bulk of his £788,563 estate to the N.S.P.C.C., and Camilla Hole, formerly the widow of the conductor and composer Constant Lambert, left two thirds of the residue of her £701,752 estate for an annual prize for the most promising student at the Royal College of Music.

Other interesting bequests not appearing on the list include the £309,596 estate of Princess Pauline Melikoff, which she left mostly to Greenpeace. Irene Handl, the well known comic actress, left most of her £369,846 estate to a number of charities, including the Cinema and Television Benevolent Fund and the Actors Benevolent Fund. Former Conservative M.P. Sir Brandon Rhys Williams, who had also been M.E.P. for London South East, left £20,000 to the British Section of the European League for Economic Co-operation, to promote European integration and the eventual adoption of a single currency for Europe. Lord Chelwood, former Conservative M.P. for Lewes, left a sufficient sum to his executors for the total cost of an hour-long concert at St. Margaret's, Westminster, by the Academy of St. Martin-in-the-Fields.

Arthur James Henry **Ashby**, of Loughton,
Essex £1,895,430
(The residue for charity as directed by memorandum, otherwise as his executor thinks fit)

Irene Dora **Atkins**, of Adderbury, Banbury,
Oxon. £1,482,314
(Four twentythirds of the residue to St. Joseph's Hospice, London E8, two twentythirds of the residue each to the P.D.S.A., Cats Protection League and National Advertising Benevolent Society, and one twentythird of the residue each to St. Mary's Church, Adderbury, and the R.S.P.C.A.)

Marjorie **Ball**, of London Colney, Herts. £509,200
(The residue to Somerville College, Oxford)

Harold Langley **Bedforth**, of Kings Langley,
Herts. £746,635
(The residue to form the Fountain Trust, for the benefit of people suffering from mental or physical illness)

Meta **Bendix**, of Warlingham, Surrey £632,764
(The residue to the Quaker Housing Trust, for any project for the elderly and needy in and around Croydon)

Alfred Douglas Dalziel **Benson**, of Mount Street,
London W1 .... £1,563,892
(The residue equally between the Imperial Cancer Research Fund, N.S.P.C.C., R.S.P.C.A., Distressed Gentlefolk's Aid Association, R.N.I.B.. and Marie Curie Memorial Foundation)

Alfred Woodroffe **Benton**, of High Street, London
E11 .... £2,583,805
(The residue for any charitable trust made in his lifetime, or as his executors appoint)

Reginald Clement **Biddle**, of Worthing, West
Sussex £725,033
(The residue to the R.S.P.C.A.)

Mrs. Margaret Florence Scott **Blair**, of Iffley,
Oxon. £539,529
(The residue equally between Quaker Peace and Service, the Community of St. Mary the Virgin, Wantage, and the Parochial Church Council on whose electoral roll she be at her death)

Mrs. Christine Florence **Boning**, of Sevenoaks,
Kent £504,191
(The residue equally between the R.N.L.I. and the British Diabetic Association Research Fund)

Mrs. Eva Sardinia **Borthwick-Norton**, of Purbrook
Heath, Hants. £23,652,039
(The residue equally between the Little Sisters

of the Poor, Leeds, and the Pasteur Institute, Paris)

Mrs. Louisa **Bow**, of Sherborne, Dorset £895,032
(Nine tenths of the residue to the British Red Cross Society and one tenth of the residue to the Irish Red Cross Society)

Rev. Dr. Bertrand Rippington **Brasnett**, of Marston, Oxon. £788,563
(The residue to the N.S.P.C.C.)

Marjorie **Broadbent**, of Grange-over-Sands, Cumbria..............................£509,801
(Two thirds of the residue to the Countryside Commission, and one third of the residue to the National Trust)

Frederick Gordon **Browning**, of Draycott Road, London E11.............................£897,864
(£4,000 and one quarter of the residue to the Parish of St. Mary with Christchurch, Wanstead, E11, and one quarter of the residue each to Chigwell School, the Additional Curates Society and U.S.P.G.)

Mrs. Joan Mary **Bull**, of Harwell, Oxon. ... £573,360
(One third of the residue to the Leukaemia Research Fund and one sixth of the residue each to Barnardo's, Christian Aid, Help the Aged Housing Association, Oxford, and St. Luke's Home, Oxford)

Sidney Lewis **Callaway**, of Rainham, Kent £1,451,585
(One ninth of the residue each to the Kent Association for the Blind, R.N.L.I., Arthritis and Rheumatism Council, British Heart Foundation, Salvation Army, Police Dependents Trust, and the Royal Star and Garter Home, Richmond, Surrey)

Walter Garnet **Christie**, of Canewdon, Essex £1,016,496
(The residue to Trinity Hall, Cambridge)

Charles Hartley **Clark**, of Fordingbridge, Hants. £484,389
(The residue to the British Field Sports Society)

James Basil William Whitmore **Clark**, of Horley, Surrey £984,500
(The residue equally between the R.S.P.C.A., Cancer Research Campaign and Barnardo's)

Miss Lily Annie **Clark**, of Watford, Herts.£2,292,312
(£50,000 and 10 per cent of the residue each to British Israel Bible Truth, Felixstowe, and Covenant People's Fellowship, Woodford Green, 10 per cent of the residue to the Salvation Army and 5 per cent of the residue to the Samaritans)

Miss Cora Augusta Evelyn Fritzwede **Coates**, of Elvington, North Yorks. £715,161
(One fourteenth of the residue each to Barnardo's, National Children's Home, R.N.I.B., R.S.P.C.A., R.N.L.I., Salvation Army, P.D.S.A., Donkey Sanctuary, Sidmouth, and the Children's Society)

Prof. Archibald Leman **Cochrane**, C.B.E., of Rhoose, South Glamorgan £656,702
(Half the residue to Oxford University, for Green College)

Miss Dorothy Edith **Collins**, of Beaconsfield, Bucks. £962,682
(The residue, including certain property under the Will of G. K. Chesterton, for charitable purposes as her executors decide)

Mrs. Lily Irene **Collins**, of Stratford-upon-Avon, Warwickshire £734,672
(Three quarters of the residue to the Imperial Cancer Research Fund)

Harold Francis Graham **Dalston**, of Emmer Green, Reading, Berks. £816,237
(£300,000 for a charitable educational trust, and the residue to St. Dunstan's)

Dr. Walter Dysart **Dick**, of Cheadle Hulme, Greater Manchester..........................£656,520

(£4,000 and one fifth of the residue to the National Library for the Blind, and one fifth of the residue each to the R.N.L.I., National Society for Mentally Handicapped Children, Barnardo's and the British Heart Foundation)

Lady (Sheila) **Douglas-Pennant**, of Winchester, Hants. £1,050,682
(£200,000 to the National Trust, for Enterprise Neptune)

Mrs. Esma Sophie **Edgar**, of Newton Valence Place, Hants. £14,604,545
(The sale proceeds of Newton Valence Place and its estate to be distributed as her executors determine between Help the Aged, P.D.S.A., St. John Ambulance, National Trust, Royal Free Hospital, Guide Dogs for the Blind Assocation, Barnardo's, and the Cheshire Foundation, for the Le Court Home, Greatham)

Frank **Farey**, of Girton, Cambs. £1,665,341
(The residue equally between the Cancer Research Campaign, the Cambridge Y.M.C.A., Age Concern, Ely, the Abbeyfield Cambridge Society, Mid-Anglia General Practitioners Accident Service, Guide Dogs for the Blind Association, the Royal Albert Homes, Cambridge, Royal Agricultural Benevolent Institution, Distressed Gentlefolk's Aid Association, Cambridgeshire Constabulary Welfare and Benevolent Fund, Friends of Arthur Rank House, Cambridge, Cancer Relief MacMillan Fund, Winged Fellowship Trust, the Ely Cathedral Appeal, Alzheimers Disease Society, Papworth and Enham Foundation, R.N.L.I., Shelter, Cambridge University Veterinary School Appeal, Cambridge Preservation Society, R.S.P.B., Salvation Army and the Ely Home of the Sue Ryder Foundation)

Doris Ruth **Field**, of Headington, Oxon. . £2,688,511
(All her estate for such charities as her executors think fit)

Mrs. Gwendoline Edith **Fox**, of St. Albans, Herts......................................£644,326
(The residue equally between the Imperial Cancer Research Fund and the Multiple Sclerosis Society)

Mrs. Olwen May **Francis**, of Wrexham, Clwyd..................................£675,370
(The residue equally between the Cancer Research Campaign and Action Research for the Crippled Child)

St. John Onslow **Gamlen**, of Clandon, Surrey £664,502
(Two thirds of the residue for such charitable purposes in England as his executors select)

Miss Ellen **Garnett**, of Leeds, West Yorks. . £563,394
(One fifth of the residue each to Wheatfields Hospice and St. Gemma's Hospice, both in Leeds, the Guide Dogs for the Blind Association, and Killingbeck Hospital Children's Heart Surgery Ward, Leeds, and one tenth of the residue each to "Candlelighters" and the Leeds District Tumour Fund, both at Seacroft Hospital, Leeds)

Mrs. Angela Joan Litolff **Graham**, of Hilgrove Road, London NW6 ....£1,258,465
(£250,000 to the League of Friends of Charing Cross Hospital, London)

Martha **Griffith**, of Deganwy, Gwynedd . £1,411,929
(£80,000 and one third of the residue to the Abbeyfield Society, and one third of the residue each to the Cheshire Foundation and the Spastics Society)

Alfred **Haines**, of Solihull, West Midlands £1,682,377
(The residue to the Alfred Haines Charitable Trust)

Maj.-Gen. Eric George William Warde **Harrison**, C.B., C.B.E., M.C., of Amesbury, Wilts. £658,476
(The residue to the Royal Artillery Charitable Fund)

Mrs. May **Hearnshaw**, of Sheffield, South Yorks. £2,095,504
(The residue for such charitable purposes as her executors determine, if possible for the promotion of religion and the relief of poverty and distress)

Hugh Godwin **Hildreth**, of Weybridge, Surrey £440,914
(All his estate to the British Naturopathic and Osteopathic Association)

Mrs. Camilla **Hole**, of Childs Street, London SW5 .... £701,752
(Two thirds of the residue to the Worshipful Company of Musicians, for an annual prize at the Royal College of Music)

Mary Frances **Holford**, of Farmham, Surrey £530,871
(The residue equally between Help the Aged, the Distressed Gentlefolk's Aid Association, Barnardo's, R.U.K.B.A., National Society for Cancer Relief, Wood Green Animal Shelter, and the Phyllis Tuckwell Memorial Hospice, Farnham)

George Desmond **Ide**, of Walberton, West Sussex £1,002,689
(Half the residue to the Imperial Cancer Research Fund, and one quarter of the residue each to the National Trust and National Trust for Scotland)

Alan Langley **Judd**, of Priory Road, London NW6 .... £1,061,880
(The residue equally between Oriel College, Oxford, and the Woodland Trust)

Marjorie Olive **Kebby**, of Canvey Island, Essex £519,423
(All her estate equally between the R.S.P.C.A., P.D.S.A., Battersea Dogs Home, R.S.P.B., International League for the Protection of Horses, the Ferne Animal Sanctuary, Blue Cross, and the Wood Green Animal Shelter)

Ursula Irene Moor **Keyes**, of Boughton, Chester £2,000,131
(The residue to the Ursula Keyes Charitable Trust)

Mrs. Marjorie Edith Penelope **King**, of Worthing, West Sussex £1,114,389
(One quarter of the residue equally between the St. John Ambulance Association, the Chest, Heart and Stroke Association and the R.N.L.I., and one quarter of the residue equally between the Worthing Area Guild for Voluntary Service, the British Red Cross Society, R.N.I.D., R.S.P.C.A., N.S.P.C.C. and the Royal Masonic Benevolent Institution)

Walter Guy Hendley **Kirkwood**, of Dartmouth, Devon £453,719
(All his estate equally between the Gloucestershire Regimental Association, the Royal British Legion, Army Benevolent Fund and MENCAP)

Mrs. Joan Margaret **Lake**, of Burley Street, Ringwood, Hants. £2,345,904
(The residue equally between the Salvation Army and the Guide Dogs for the Blind Association)

Hon. Mrs. Kathleen **Laurence**, of Goring on Thames, Oxon. £2,170,342
(The residue to the Kathleen Laurence Charitable Trust)

Miss Maisie Marion **Lee**, of Maidenhead, Berks. £3,263,306
(The residue equally between Help the Aged, the Distressed Gentlefolk's Aid Association and the Imperial Cancer Research Fund)

Frank Henry **Lesley**, of Chelston, Torquay, Devon £598,504
(Thirtyfive per cent of the residue each to Parkinson's Disease Society and the Chest, Heart and Stroke Association, and 6 per cent of the residue each to the Multiple Sclerosis Society, Muscular Dystrophy Group, R.N.I.B., Guide Dogs for the Blind Assocation, and Rowcroft Hospice, Torquay)

Mrs. Dorothy Ada **Lloyd**, of Brighstone, Isle of Wight £628,580
(One sixth of the residue each to Barnardo's, National Canine Defence League, R.N.L.I., World Wide Fund for Nature and Cancer Research Campaign)

Elizabeth Mabel Rose **Longman**, of Kingston Hill, Surrey £1,220,821
(The residue equally between the Children's Country Holiday Fund, Gardeners' Royal Benevolent Society, Arthritis and Rheumatism Council, R.N.L.I. and R.A.F. Benevolent Fund)

Athena **Loupy**, of Sussex Gardens, London W2 .... £705,428
(£100,000, a grave for the poor and one sixth of the residue to St. Sophia's Greek Orthodox Cathedral, London W2, and £10,000 and one sixth of the residue each to the London Association for the Blind, Children's Society, St. Mary's Hospital, Help the Aged and Age Concern)

Henrietta Ann **McDougall**, of Frinton-on-Sea, Essex £1,353,570
(Half the residue equally between the Royal Marsden Hospital and Great Ormond Street Hospital, both in London)

Cyril William **Main**, of Bexhill on Sea, East Sussex £746,607
(The residue equally between the British Diabetic Association, the Guide Dogs for the Blind Association, R.N.L.I., Cancer Research Campaign, Marie Curie Memorial Foundation, Help and Aged and the R.N.I.B.)

Lady (Clare Helen) **Mann**, C.B.E., of Scole Common, Diss, Norfolk £617,189
(Half the residue, less £14,000, to Norwich Cathedral)

Mrs. Marguerite Irene **Meeks**, of Luton, Beds. £1,188,698
(The residue equally between the Calibre Cassette Library for the Blind and Handicapped, the R.N.I.B., Salvation Army, National Society for Autistic Children and the P.D.S.A.)

Gerald Hugh **Micklem**, C.B.E., of Sunningdale, Berks. £3,179,001
(Ten per cent of the residue to the Gerald Micklem Charitable Trust)

Rina **Miller**, of Winchelsea, East Sussex . £1,793,129
(The residue for such charities as her executors determine in consultation with her sister Ailsey)

Mrs. Alice **Millington**, of Stoke Poges, Bucks. £512,873
(The residue equally between Great Ormond Street Hospital Endowment Fund, Queen Elizabeth's Foundation for the Disabled, Salvation Army, Guide Dogs for the Blind Association, Barnardo's and Age Concern)

Ellen Burnett **Moors**, of Allestree, Derbyshire £999,878
(The residue equally between the Cheshire Foundation, and the Douglas MacMillan Home, Blurton, Staffs.)

Leopold **Muller**, of Bayswater Road, London W2 .... £19,082,799
(The residue for such charitable purposes in England as his executors select)

Anthony Mills **Murray**, of Cringleford, Norfolk £996,065
(£1,000 and one third of the residue to the Guide Dogs for the Blind Association, and one third of the residue each to the R.N.L.I., for the needs of the Southwold Lifeboat, and Southwold Parochial Church Council, for the upkeep of St. Edmund's Church there)

Frank Virgo **Mustchin**, of Arundel, West Sussex £708,281

(The residue to provide housing for the elderly, preferably those within a three mile radius of Arundel Town Square)

Mrs. Helen Beatrice Malcolm **Neklaws**, of Horsell, Surrey £1,052,852
(The residue equally between the R.S.P.B., P.D.S.A., Help the Aged, National Trust for Scotland and the R.N.L.I.)

Capt. James Frederick **Norris**, (retd.), of Brackley, Northants. £4,023,705
(£200,000 each to the Institute of Cancer Research, and Stoke Mandeville Hospital, for the Jimmy Savile Fund)

Anthony Edward **Pettit**, of Baverstock, Dinton, Wilts. £1,307,592
(The residue to the Alpine Garden Society)

Lilian Kathleen **Pollard**, of Colwyn Bay, Clwyd £1,641,325
(The residue equally betwen the Guide Dogs for the Blind Association and the National Trust)

Miss Gertrude Millicent **Price**, of Beeston, Notts. £605,908
(The residue equally between the Guide Dogs for the Blind Association and the National Trust)

Audrey Mary **Purnell**, of Crawford Street, London W1 .... £1,181,660
(The residue to the A. M. Purnell Charitable Trust)

Edward Farley **Rea**, of Taplow, Bucks. .. £3,445,309
(The residue equally between the Blue Cross, Cats Protection League and the P.D.S.A.)

Mrs. Elsie **Read**, of Highworth, Wilts. £1,328,842
(The residue equally between the British Limbless Ex-Service Men's Association, Sir Frederick Milner Fund, St. Dunstan's, Parkinson's Disease Society, British Deaf Association, Sue Ryder Foundation, Royal College of Surgeons, Leprosy Relief Association, Marie Curie Memorial Foundation, R.N.L.I., Royal Hospital and Home for Incurables, London SW15, Association for Spina Bifida and Hydrocephalus, the R.A.F. Benevolent Fund, British Heart Foundation, R.N.I.B., MENCAP, the Multiple Sclerosis Research Fund, Cheshire Foundation, Leukaemia Research Fund, Royal Agricultural Benevolent Institution and John Groom's Association.

William Hubert **Rees**, of Praed Street, London W2 .... £2,032,269
(£300,000 and effects to the Salvation Army, and the residue equally between Barnardo's, National Trust, British Red Cross Society, R.N.I.B., Imperial Cancer Research Fund, MENCAP, Multiple Sclerosis Society and the Muscular Dystrophy Group)

Mrs. Mabel **Reeves**, of Folkestone, Kent ... £763,158
(The residue equally between the Lady Hoare Trust, Barnardo's and the Salvation Army)

William Eric **Robins**, of Bridgnorth, Salop. £1,290,968
(The residue equally between the Salvation Army, R.N.I.D. and the Imperial Cancer Research Fund)

Clement **Roebuck**, of Langbar, Ilkley, West Yorks. £1,480,251
(The residue equally between the Imperial Cancer Research Fund and the Marie Curie Memorial Foundation)

Peter **Royal**, of Leigh-on-Sea, Essex £551,190
(The residue equally between the R.N.L.I. and the 3rd Chalkwell Bay Sea Scouts)

Mrs. Norah Beatrice Winifred **Russell**, of Nawton, North Yorks. £974,869
(The residue to the Imperial Cancer Research Fund)

Mary Elizabeth Belinda **Samson**, of Newport, Gwent £1,298,133
(The residue equally between Rehoboth Residen-

tial Home for the Elderly, Newport, and Bryntirion College, Bridgend)

Jack **Saville**, of Baker Street, London NW1 £756,194
(Half the residue to the Joint Israel Appeal)

Adela Nancy **Schuster**, of Bath, Avon £545,769
(The residue equally between the Royal Masonic Hospital Samaritan Fund, Guide Dogs for the Blind Assocation, the King Edward VII Hospital for Officers, London, and the Friends of the Elderly and Gentlefolk's Help)

Constance Alice **Sidery**, of Sanderstead, Surrey £644,994
(The residue to the World Wide Fund for Nature)

Norah **Smith**, of Maidenhead, Berks....... £704,944
(The residue equally between the Salvation Army and R.S.P.C.A.)

Vera Amelia **Smith**, of Worthing, West Sussex £609,421
(The residue equally between St. Barnabas Home, Worthing, Gifford House, Worthing, the N.S.P.C.C. and Barnardo's)

Mrs. Olga Florence **Straus**, of Edwardes Square, London W8 .... £494,101
(The residue to the Leukaemia Research Fund)

Fritz Benedict **Strauss**, of Oxford £1,304,017
(£200,000 and, after a life interest, the residue to Oxford University)

Miss Queenie Rosamund **Symonds**, of Bromham, Beds. £649,571
(The residue equally between the Home of Rest for Horses, Aylesbury, the Guide Dogs for the Blind Association and the P.D.S.A.)

Mrs. Elizabeth **Thomas**, of Llawhaden, Narberth, Dyfed £1,011,764
(The residue equally between the University College of Wales, Aberystwyth, and the Welsh National School of Medicine)

Mrs. Edith Ada **Tracy**, of Farnham Common, Bucks. £736,525
(The residue to form the Tracy Trust, to benefit senior citizens and pensioners of Hedgerley, Bucks.)

John Anthony **Twentyman**, of Claverley, Salop. £1,270,456
(Twentyfive per cent of the residue equally between the Civic Trust, Architects Benevolent Society, National Trust, Distressed Gentlefolk's Aid Association and the R.A.F. Benevolent Fund)

Ralph Albert **Wale**, of Leicester £1,639,251
(Half the residue equally between Barnardo's, the Leicester Royal Infirmary (for equipment), the Royal Aid Care of Leicester Royal Infirmary, N.S.P.C.C., Leicester and County Mission for the Deaf, the Royal Leicestershire, Rutland and Wycliffe Society for the Blind, Arthritis and Rheumatism Council, Spastics Society, L.O.R.O.S., Age Concern England, Distressed Gentlefolk's Aid Association, the Leicester Boys and Girls Summer Camp and Institute, the Imperial Cancer Research Fund, Rutland Historic Churches Preservation Fund, the Hospital for Sick Children, London, and the National Trust)

Mrs. Alice Margaret **Walton**, of Tasburgh, Norfolk £660,009
(The residue equally between the R.N.I.B., Distressed Gentlefolk's Aid Association, Cancer Research Campaign and the Multiple Sclerosis Society)

Joan Marguerite **Weller**, of Culverley Road, London SE6 .... £870,806
(Sixty per cent of the residue to the Royal College of Music, for singing and violin scholarships, and forty per cent of the residue to Guy's Hospital Medical and Dental School for a research fund)

John de Pury **Whitaker**, of Hove, East
Sussex £679,138
(The residue equally between the N.S.P.C.C. and
Children's Society)

Ida May **White**, of Surbiton, Surrey £634,710
(The residue equally between the Imperial Can-
cer Research Fund, British Heart Foundation,
Guide Dogs for the Blind Association, National
Kidney Research Fund and the Battersea Dogs
Home)

Kathleen Anne **White**, of Beaconsfield,
Bucks. £527,892

(The residue equally between the British Red
Cross Society, High Wycombe, the Arthritis and
Rheumatism Council, R.N.I.D., R.N.L.I. and
R.S.P.C.A.)

Miss Daisy **Wilkes**, of Bidford on Avon,
Warwickshire £1,268,937
(The residue equally between Age Concern
England, National Society for Cancer Relief,
British Kidney Patient Association, British
Heart Foundation, R.S.P.C.A., and Arthritis and
Rheumatism Council)

THE PRESS COUNCIL
1 Salisbury Square, EC4Y 8AE
[01–353 1248]

In April, 1947, a Royal Commission was appointed
to enquire into the control, management and ownership, etc., of the Press and news agencies and to make
recommendations thereon. The Commission, in its
report of June, 1949, recommended *inter alia* that a
voluntary Press Council be formed.

A constitution ultimately set up provided for the
establishment of such a council on July 1, 1953. This
constitution was materially amended in 1963 by the
introduction of an independent chairman and up to
20 per cent lay membership. In 1973, the Council was
increased to 30 (excluding the Chairman) of whom
one-third were lay members. Following a recommendation of the third Royal Commission on the Press
made in 1977, the size of the Council was increased in
1978 to 36 (excluding the Chairman) of which half are
press members and half non-press members. The
objects of the Council are (1) to preserve the
established freedom of the British Press; (2) to
maintain the character of the British Press in
accordance with the highest professional and commercial standards; (3) to consider complaints about
the conduct of the Press or the conduct of persons
and organizations towards the Press; to deal with
these complaints in whatever manner might seem
practical and appropriate and record resultant
action; (4) to keep under review developments likely
to restrict the supply of information of public interest

and importance; (5) to report publicly on developments that may tend towards greater concentration
or monopoly in the Press (including changes in
ownership, control and growth of Press undertakings) and to publish statistical information relating
thereto; (6) to make representations on appropriate
occasions to the Government, organs of the United
Nations and Press organizations abroad; and (7) to
publish periodical reports recording the Council's
work and to review, from time to time, developments
in the Press and the factors affecting them.

The constitution of the Council provides for 18
Press members who are editorial and managerial
nominees of The Newspaper Publishers Association
Ltd. (3), The Newspaper Society (3), The Periodical
Publishers Association Ltd. (2), The Scottish Daily
Newspaper Society (1), Scottish Newspaper Proprie-
tors' Association (1), The Guild of British Newspaper
Editors (2), The National Union of Journalists (4),
The Institute of Journalists (2) plus 18 public members
appointed by the Press Council Appointments Com-
mission. In addition each constituent body nominates one official as a non-voting member. In 1989 the
Press Council embarked on a general review of its
role and function.

Chairman, L. Blom-Cooper, Q.C.
Director, K. Morgan, O.B.E.

CONFEDERATION OF BRITISH INDUSTRY

Centre Point, 103 New Oxford Street, WC1A 1DU
[01-379 7400]

The Confederation of British Industry was founded in August 1965 and is an independent non-party political body financed by industry and commerce. It exists primarily to ensure that the Government understands the intentions, needs and problems of British business. It is the recognized spokesman for the business viewpoint and is consulted as such by the Government.

The C.B.I. represents, directly and indirectly, some 250,000 companies. All the major nationalized industries are in membership and thereby able to work with the C.B.I. on problems that are the concern of all management.

The governing body of the C.B.I. is the 400-strong Council, which meets monthly in London under the chairmanship of the President. It is assisted by some 27 expert standing committees which advise on the main aspects of policy. There are 13 Regional Councils and offices covering the administrative regions of England, Wales, Scotland and Northern Ireland.

President, Sir Trevor Holdsworth.
Director-General, J. Banham.
Secretary, M. W. Hunt.

NATIONAL ASSOCIATION OF INDUSTRIES FOR THE BLIND AND DISABLED INC.

Triton House, 43A High Street South,
Dunstable, Beds. LU6 3RZ
[0582–606796]

The National Association of Industries for the Blind and Disabled Inc. was established in 1929 and incorporated in 1936; it is registered as a charity.

The Association acts in the nature of a trade association providing facilities for consultation and co-operation between its members who operate workshops employing blind and disabled people. It represents their interests in discussions with, and

representations to, other organizations (e.g. government departments and local authorities) concerned with sheltered employment. It does not own or operate any of the workshops, which are run by local authorities or voluntary organizations acting as their agents.

Chairman (1989–90), A. L. Soper.
Hon. Secretary, G. J. Entwistle.

EMPLOYERS' AND TRADE BODIES

ADVERTISING ASSOCIATION, Abford House, 15 Wilton Road, SW1V 1NJ.—*Dir. Gen.,* R. Underhill, O.B.E.

AEROSPACE COMPANIES LTD., SOCIETY OF BRITISH, 29 King Street, SW1Y 6RD.—*Dir.,* Air Marshal Sir John Curtiss, K.C.B., K.B.E.

BAKERS, FEDERATION OF, 20 Bedford Square, WC1B 3HF.—*Dir.,* A. Casdagli, C.B.E.

BANKERS' ASSOCIATION, BRITISH, 10 Lombard Street, EC3V 9EL.—*Sec.-Gen.,* The Hon. R. C. R. Hoyer Millar.

BREWERS' SOCIETY, 42 Portman Square, W1H 0BB.—*Dir.,* Maj. Gen. W. D. Mangham, C.B.

BUILDING EMPLOYERS' CONFEDERATION, 82 New Cavendish Street, W1M 8AD.—*Dir. Gen.,* J. A. Newby.

BUILDING MATERIAL PRODUCERS, NATIONAL COUNCIL OF, 26 Store Street, WC1E 7BT.—*Dir. Gen.,* N. M. Chaldecott.

BUS AND COACH COUNCIL, Sardinia House, 52 Lincoln's Inn Fields, WC2A 3LZ.—*Dir. Gen.,* Mrs. V. Palmer, M.B.E.

CHEMICAL INDUSTRIES ASSOCIATION LTD., Kings Buildings, Smith Square, SW1P 3JJ.—*Dir. Gen.,* J. C. L. Cox.

CLOTHING INDUSTRY ASSOCIATION LTD., BRITISH, British Apparel Centre, 7 Swallow Place, W1R 7AA.—*Dir.,* J. R. Wilson.

DAIRY TRADE FEDERATION, 19 Cornwall Terrace, NW1 4QP.—*Dir. Gen.,* J. P. Price.

ELECTROTECHNICAL AND ALLIED MANUFACTURERS' ASSOCIATIONS, FEDERATION OF BRITISH (BEAMA), Leicester House, 8 Leicester Street, WC2H 7BN.—*Dir. Gen.,* J. G. Gaddes.

ENGINEERING EMPLOYERS' FEDERATION, Broadway House, Tothill Street, SW1H 9NQ.—*Dir. Gen.,* P. Brighton.

FARMERS' UNION, NATIONAL (NFU), Agriculture House, Knightsbridge, SW1X 7NJ.—*Dir. Gen.,* D. Evans.

FARMERS' UNION OF SCOTLAND, NATIONAL, 17 Grosvenor Crescent, Edinburgh EH12 5EN.—*Chief Exec.,* D. S. Johnston.

FARMERS' UNION, ULSTER, Dunedin, 475–477 Antrim Road, Belfast BT15 3DA.—*Gen. Sec.,* J. V. Smyth.

FINANCE HOUSES ASSOCIATION, 18 Upper Grosvenor Street, W1X 9PB.—*Dir.,* N. A. D. Grant.

FOOD AND DRINK FEDERATION, 6 Catherine Street, WC2B 5JJ.—*Dir. Gen.,* M. P. Mackenzie.

FREIGHT TRANSPORT ASSOCIATION LTD., Hermes House, 157 St. John's Road, Tunbridge Wells, Kent TN4 9UZ.—*Dir.-Gen.,* G. Turvey.

INSURERS, ASSOCIATION OF BRITISH, Aldermary House, 10–15 Queen Street, EC4N 1TT.—*Chief Exec.,* M. A. Jones.

KNITTING INDUSTRIES FEDERATION LTD., 7 Gregory Boulevard, Nottingham NG7 6NB.—*Dir.,* J. P. Harrison.

LEATHER CONFEDERATION, BRITISH, Leather Trade House, Kings Park Road, Moulton Park, Northampton NN3 1JD.—*Dir.*, R. L. Sykes, O.B.E., Ph.D.

LEATHER PRODUCERS' ASSOCIATION, Leather Trade House, Kings Park Road, Moulton Park, Northampton NN3 1JD.—*Nat. Sec.*, J. Purvis.

MAN-MADE FIBRES FEDERATION, BRITISH, British Apparel and Textiles Centre, 7 Swallow Place, W1R 7AA.—*Dir.*, G. D. Myers.

MARINE INDUSTRIES FEDERATION, BRITISH, Boating Industry House, Vale Road, Oatlands Park, Weybridge, Surrey KT13 9NS.—*Chief Exec.*, P. V. Wagstaffe.

MOTOR MANUFACTURERS AND TRADERS LTD., SOCIETY OF, Forbes House, Halkin Street, SW1X 7DS.—*Dir.*, S. R. Foster.

NEWSPAPER PUBLISHERS ASSOCIATION LTD., 34 Southwark Bridge Road, SE1 9EU.—*Dir.*, J. E. Lepage.

OFFICE SYSTEMS AND STATIONERY FEDERATION, BRITISH, 6 Wimpole Street, W1M 8AS.—*Dir.*, D. F. Hall.

PAPER AND BOARD INDUSTRY FEDERATION, BRITISH, Papermakers House, Rivenhall Road, Westlea, Swindon SN5 7BE.—*Dir. Gen.*, W. J. Bartlett.

PLASTICS FEDERATION, BRITISH, 5 Belgrave Square, SW1X 8PD.—*Dir.*, D. R. Jones.

PORT EMPLOYERS, NATIONAL ASSOCIATION OF, Victoria House, Vernon Place, WC1B 4LL.—*Dir.*, N. H. Finney.

PORTS FEDERATION, BRITISH, Victoria House, Vernon Place, WC1B 4LL.—*Man. Dir.* N. H. Finney.

PRINTING INDUSTRIES FEDERATION, 11 Bedford Row, WC1R 4DX.—*Dir. Gen.*, C. Stanley.

PUBLISHERS ASSOCIATION, 19 Bedford Square, WC1B 3HJ.—*Chief Exec.*, C. Bradley.

RADIO CONTRACTORS LTD., ASSOCIATION OF INDEPENDENT, Radio House, 46 Westbourne Grove, W2 5SH.—*Chief Exec.*, B. West.

RETAIL CONSORTIUM, THE, Commonwealth House, 1–19 New Oxford Street, WC1A 1PA.—*Dir. Gen.*, R. S. Weir.

RETAIL NEWSAGENTS, NATIONAL FEDERATION OF, Yeoman House, Sekforde Street, EC1R 0HD.—*Chief Exec.*, K. E. J. Peters.

ROAD FEDERATION LTD., BRITISH, Cowdray House, 6 Portugal Street, WC2A 2HG.—*Dir.*, P. J. Witt.

ROAD HAULAGE ASSOCIATION LTD., Roadway House, 35 Monument Hill, Weybridge, Surrey KT13 8RN.—*Dir. Gen.*, D. B. H. Colley, C.B.E.

RUBBER MANUFACTURERS' ASSOCIATION LTD., BRITISH, 90–91 Tottenham Court Road, W1P 0BR.—*Dir.*, G. C. Gullan.

SHIPPING, GENERAL COUNCIL OF BRITISH, 30–32 St. Mary Axe, EC3A 8ET.—*Dir. Gen.*, P. Le Cheminant, C.B.

SPORTS AND ALLIED INDUSTRIES FEDERATION LTD., BRITISH, 23 Brighton Road, Croydon CR2 4EA.—*Chief Exec.*, L. F. Standen.

TELEVISION ASSOCIATION, INDEPENDENT, Knighton House, 56 Mortimer Street, W1N 8AN.—*Dir.*, D. Shaw.

TEXTILE CONFEDERATION, BRITISH, British Apparel and Textiles Centre, 7 Swallow Place, W1R 7AA.—*Dir.*, C. M. Purvis.

TIMBER GROWERS' UNITED KINGDOM, Agriculture House, Knightsbridge, SW1X 7NJ.—*Chief Exec.*, A. R. Williams.

TIMBER MERCHANTS' ASSOCIATION, BRITISH, Ridgeway House, 6 Ridgeway Road, Long Ashton, Bristol BS18 9EU.—*Sec.*, H. B. Roberts.

TIMBER TRADE FEDERATION, THE, Clareville House, 26–27 Oxendon Street, SW1Y 4EL.—*Dir. Gen.*, A. A. Lockyer, L.V.O.

U.K. OFFSHORE OPERATORS ASSOCIATION LTD., 3 Hans Crescent, SW1X 0LN.—*Dir. Gen.*, G. C. Band.

U.K. PETROLEUM INDUSTRY ASSOCIATION LTD., 9 Kingsway, WC2B 6XH.—*Dir. Gen.*, Dr. I. D. G. Berwick.

WHOLESALE AND INDUSTRIAL DISTRIBUTORS, FEDERATION OF, The Old Post Office, Dunchideock, Exeter EX2 9TU.—*Dir.*, J. Hussey.

TRADES UNION CONGRESS (T.U.C.)

Congress House, 23–28 Great Russell Street, WC1B 3LS
[01–636–4030]

The Trades Union Congress, founded in 1868, is a voluntary association of trade unions, the representatives of which meet annually to consider matters of common concern to their members. The Congress has met annually since 1871 and in recent years has met normally on the first Monday in September, its sessions extending through the succeeding four days. Congress is constituted by delegates of the affiliated unions on the basis of one delegate for every 5,000 members, or fraction thereof, on whose behalf affiliation fees are paid. Affiliated unions (in 1988–89) totalled 78 with an aggregate membership of 8,652,318 (women's membership, 2,799,263).

The main business of the annual Congress is to consider the report of its General Council dealing with the activities of the Congress year, along with motions from affiliated societies on questions of policy and organization.

The standing committees of the General Council are serviced by a full time staff appointed by the General Secretary, who is himself elected by Congress and who remains in office until the age of 65, subject to decision of Congress or the General Council.

Through the General Council and its committees the trade union movement maintains systematic relations with the Government and government departments, with the Confederation of British Industry and with a large number of other bodies. It is represented on the National Economic Development Council, the Health and Safety Commission, the council of the Advisory Conciliation and Arbitration Service and a number of other bodies.

Among powers vested in the General Council by consent of the unions in Congress is the responsibility of intervening in disputes and differences between affiliated organizations; if possible this is done through informal conciliation meetings under T.U.C. auspices but where necessary a Disputes Committee is formed consisting of one member of the General Council and two senior officials of unions not involved in the dispute. This investigates the matter concerned and issues its findings.

Unions retain full control of their own affairs and the only sanctions which Congress can apply are suspension or exclusion from membership.

Chairman (1989–90), Miss A. Maddocks, o.b.e. (*National and Local Government Officers' Association*.)
General Secretary, N. D. Willis.

SCOTTISH TRADES UNION CONGRESS

16 Woodlands Terrace, Glasgow G3 6DF
[041-332 4946]

The Congress was formed in 1897 and acts as a national centre for the trade union movement in Scotland. In 1989 it consisted of 58 unions with a membership of 885,317 and 49 directly affiliated Trades Councils. The majority of the unions organize throughout Britain and affiliate on their membership in Scotland.

The Annual Congress in April elects a 26-member General Council on the basis of 13 industrial sections. Congress has been prominent in pressing for economic expansion and full employment in Scotland and the development of the social services, most of which are separately organized in Scotland.

Chairperson G. Bolton.
General Secretary, C. Christie.

TRADES UNIONS AFFILIATED TO T.U.C.

A list of the Trades Unions affiliated to the Trades Union Congress at Sept. 1, 1989. The number of members of each Union is shown in parenthesis.

AMALGAMATED ASSOCIATION OF BEAMERS, TWISTERS AND DRAWERS (HAND AND MACHINE), THE (470), 27 Every Street, Nelson, Lancs. BB9 7NE.—*Gen. Sec.*, A. H. Edmondson.

AMALGAMATED ENGINEERING UNION (A.E.U.) (793,610), 110 Peckham Road, SE15 5EL.—*Gen. Sec.*, G. H. Laird, c.b.e.

AMALGAMATED SOCIETY OF TEXTILE WORKERS AND KINDRED TRADES (2,550), Foxlowe, Market Place, Leek, Staffs. ST13 6AD.—*Gen. Sec.*, A. Hitchmough.

ASSOCIATED SOCIETY OF LOCOMOTIVE ENGINEERS AND FIREMEN (A.S.L.E.F.) (19,065), 9 Arkwright Road, NW3 6AB.—*Sec.*, N. Milligan.

ASSOCIATION OF CINEMATOGRAPH, TELEVISION AND ALLIED TECHNICIANS (28,500), 111 Wardour Street, W1V 4AY.—*Gen. Sec.*, A. Sapper.

ASSOCIATION OF FIRST DIVISION CIVIL SERVANTS (10,000), 2 Caxton Street, SW1H 0QH.—*Gen. Sec.*, Ms. E. Symons.

ASSOCIATION OF PROFESSIONAL, EXECUTIVE, CLERICAL AND COMPUTER STAFF (APEX) (amalgamated with G.M.B. since Dec. 1988).

ASSOCIATION OF SCIENTIFIC, TECHNICAL AND MANAGERIAL STAFFS (A.S.T.M.S.) (amalgamated with T.A.S.S. to form Manufacturing, Science and Finance Union).

ASSOCIATION OF UNIVERSITY TEACHERS (30,000), United House, 1 Pembridge Road, W11 3HJ.—*Gen. Sec.*, Ms. D. Warwick.

BAKERS, FOOD AND ALLIED WORKERS' UNION (34,032), Stanborough House, Great North Road, Stanborough, Welwyn Garden City, Herts. AL8 7TA—*Gen. Sec.*, J. R. Marino.

BANKING, INSURANCE AND FINANCE UNION (168,408), Sheffield House, 1B Amity Grove, SW20 0LG.—*Gen. Sec.*, L. Mills.

BRITISH ACTORS' EQUITY ASSOCIATION (42,000), 8 Harley Street, W1N 2AB.—*Gen. Sec.*, P. Plouviez.

BRITISH AIR LINE PILOTS ASSOCIATION, THE (6,000), 81 New Road, Harlington, Hayes, Middx. UB3 5BG.—*Gen. Sec.*, M. Young.

BRITISH ASSOCIATION OF COLLIERY MANAGEMENT, THE (9,250), BACM House, 317 Nottingham Road, Old Basford, Nottingham NG7 7DP.—*Gen. Sec.*, J. D. Meads.

BROADCASTING AND ENTERTAINMENT TRADES ALLIANCE (29,169), 181–185 Wardour Street, W1V 4BE.—*Gen. Sec.*, D. A. Hearn.

CARD SETTING MACHINE TENTERS' SOCIETY (92), 36 Greenton Avenue, Scholes, Cleckheaton, W. Yorks. BD19 6DT.—*Sec.*, G. Priestley.

CERAMIC AND ALLIED TRADES UNION, THE (31,308), Hillcrest House, Garth Street, Stoke-on-Trent ST1 2AB.—*Gen. Sec.*, A. W. Clowes.

CIVIL AND PUBLIC SERVICES ASSOCIATION, THE (143,062), 160 Falcon Road, SW11 2LN.—*Gen. Sec.*, J. N. Ellis.

COMMUNICATION MANAGERS' ASSOCIATION (19,103), Hughes House, Ruscombe Road, Twyford, Reading RG10 9JD.—*Gen. Sec.*, T. L. Deegan.

CONFEDERATION OF HEALTH SERVICE EMPLOYEES (C.O.H.S.E.) (220,000), Glen House, High Street, Banstead, Surrey SM7 2LH.—*Gen. Sec.*, H. MacKenzie.

EDUCATIONAL INSTITUTE OF SCOTLAND, THE (45,000), 46 Moray Place, Edinburgh EH3 6BH.—*Gen. Sec.*, J. B. Martin.

ENGINEERING AND FASTENERS TRADE UNION (400), 434 Bearwood Road, Smethwick, Warley, W. Midlands.—*Gen. Sec.*, W. J. Redmond.

ENGINEERS' AND MANAGERS' ASSOCIATION (42,000), Station House, Fox Lane North, Chertsey, Surrey KT16 9HW.—*Gen. Sec.*, J. Lyons, C.B.E.

FILM ARTISTES' ASSOCIATION (2,094), 61 Marloes Road, W8 6LE.—*Sec.*, M. Reynel.

FIRE BRIGADES UNION, THE (45,683), Bradley House, 68 Coombe Road, Kingston upon Thames, Surrey KT2 7AE.—*Gen. Sec.*, K. Cameron.

FURNITURE, TIMBER AND ALLIED TRADES UNION (46,096), Fairfields, Roe Green, Kingsbury, NW9 0PT.—*Gen. Sec.*, C. A. Christopher.

GENERAL UNION OF ASSOCIATIONS OF LOOM OVERLOOKERS, THE (1,101), Overlookers Institute, Jude Street, Nelson, Lancs. BB9 7NP.—*Pres.*, E. Macro.

G.M.B. (formerly GENERAL, MUNICIPAL, BOILERMAKERS AND ALLIED TRADES UNION (800,000), Thorne House, Claygate, Esher, Surrey KT10 0TL.—*Gen. Sec.*, J. Edmonds.

HEALTH VISITORS' ASSOCIATION (17,000), 50 Southwark Street, SE1 1UN.—*Gen. Sec.*, Ms. S. Goodwin.

HOSPITAL CONSULTANTS AND SPECIALISTS ASSOCIATION, THE (2,400), The Old Court House, London Road, Ascot, Berks. SL5 7EN.—*Chief Exec.*, S. J. Charkham.

INLAND REVENUE STAFF FEDERATION (52,972), Douglas Houghton House, 231 Vauxhall Bridge Road, SW1V 1EH.—*Gen. Sec.*, C. Brooke.

INSTITUTION OF PROFESSIONALS, MANAGERS AND SPECIALISTS (90,341), 75–79 York Road, SE1 7AQ.—*Gen. Sec.*, B. Brett.

IRON AND STEEL TRADES CONFEDERATION, THE (41,679), Swinton House, 324 Gray's Inn Road, WC1X 8DD.—*Gen. Sec.*, R. L. Evans.

MANUFACTURING, SCIENCE AND FINANCE UNION (653,000), 79 Camden Road, NW1 9ES.—*Gen. Sec.*, K. Gill.

MILITARY AND ORCHESTRAL MUSICAL INSTRUMENT MAKERS' TRADE SOCIETY (35), 2 Whitehouse Avenue, Boreham Wood, Herts. WD6 1HD.—*Gen. Sec.*, F. McKenzie.

MUSICIANS' UNION (41,150), 60–62 Clapham Road, SW9 0JJ.—*Gen. Sec.*, J. Morton.

NATIONAL AND LOCAL GOVERNMENT OFFICERS' ASSOCIATION (N.A.L.G.O.) (754,701), 1 Mabledon Place, WC1H 9AJ.—*Gen. Sec.*, J. D. Daly.

NATIONAL ASSOCIATION OF COLLIERY OVERMEN, DEPUTIES AND SHOTFIRERS (8,635), Simpson House, 48 Nether Hall Road, Doncaster DN1 2PZ.—*Sec.*, P. McNestry.

NATIONAL ASSOCIATION OF CO-OPERATIVE OFFICIALS (4,479), Coronation House, Arndale Centre, Manchester M4 2HW.—*Gen. Sec.*, L. W. Ewing.

NATIONAL ASSOCIATION OF LICENSED HOUSE MANAGERS (11,851), 9 Coombe Lane, Raynes Park, SW20 8NE.—*Gen. Sec.*, J. Madden.

NATIONAL ASSOCIATION OF PROBATION OFFICERS (6,447), 3–4 Chivalry Road, SW11 1HT.—*Sec.*, W. L. Beaumont.

NATIONAL ASSOCIATION OF SCHOOLMASTERS/UNION OF WOMEN TEACHERS (N.A.S./U.W.T.) (166,000), Hillscourt Education Centre, Rose Hill, Rednal, Birmingham B45 8RS.—*Gen. Sec.*, F. A. Smithies.

NATIONAL ASSOCIATION OF TEACHERS IN FURTHER AND HIGHER EDUCATION (82,000), 27 Britannia Street, WC1X 9JP.—*Gen. Sec.*, G. Woolf.

NATIONAL COMMUNICATIONS UNION (152,000), Greystoke House, 150 Brunswick Road, W5 1AW.—*Gen. Sec.*, A. I. Young.

NATIONAL GRAPHICAL ASSOCIATION 1982 (N.G.A. '82)(125,000), Graphic House, 63–67 Bromham Road, Bedford MK40 2AG.—*Sec.*, A. D. Dubbins.

NATIONAL LEAGUE OF THE BLIND AND DISABLED, THE (2,784), 2 Tenterden Road, N17 8BE.—*Sec.*, M. A. Barrett.

NATIONAL UNION OF CIVIL AND PUBLIC SERVANTS (N.U.C.P.S.) (125,000), 124–130 Southwark Street, SE1 0TU.—*Gen. Sec.*, L. Christie.

NATIONAL UNION OF DOMESTIC APPLIANCES AND GENERAL OPERATIVES, THE (3,100), 6–8 Imperial Buildings, Corporation Street, Rotherham, S. Yorks. S60 1PB.—*Gen. Sec.*, A. McCarthy.

NATIONAL UNION OF HOSIERY AND KNITWEAR WORKERS, THE (43,526), 55 New Walk, Leicester LE1 7EB.—*Gen. Sec.*, Mrs. H. F. McGrath.

NATIONAL UNION OF INSURANCE WORKERS (17,517), 27 Old Gloucester Street, WC1N 3AF.—*Gen. Sec.*, K. Perry.

NATIONAL UNION OF JOURNALISTS (N.U.J.) (32,206), Acorn House, 314–320 Gray's Inn Road, WC1X 8DP.—*Gen. Sec.*, H. Conroy.

NATIONAL UNION OF LOCK AND METAL WORKERS (5,295), Bellamy House, Wilkes Street, Willenhall, West Midlands WV13 2BS.—*Gen. Sec.*, M. Bradley.

NATIONAL UNION OF MARINE, AVIATION AND SHIPPING TRANSPORT OFFICERS, THE (19,345), Oceanair House, 750–760 High Road, E11 3BB.—*Gen. Sec.*, J. Newman.

NATIONAL UNION OF MINEWORKERS (N.U.M.) (70,000), St. James' House, Vicar Lane, Sheffield S1 2EX.—*Sec.*, P. E. Heathfield.

NATIONAL UNION OF PUBLIC EMPLOYEES (N.U.P.E.) (635,000), Civic House, 20 Grand Depot Road, SE18 6SF.—*Sec.*, R. K. Bickerstaffe.

NATIONAL UNION OF RAILWAYMEN (N.U.R.) (110,000), Unity House, Euston Road, NW1 2BL.—*Gen. Sec.*, J. Knapp.

NATIONAL UNION OF SCALEMAKERS (882), Queensway House, 57 Livery Street, Birmingham B3 1HA.—*Gen. Sec.*, A. F. Smith.

NATIONAL UNION OF SEAMEN (N.U.S.) (20,000), Maritime House, Old Town, SW4 0JP.—*Gen. Sec.*, S. J. McCluskie.

NATIONAL UNION OF TAILORS AND GARMENT WORKERS (76,000), 16 Charles Square, N1 6HP.—*Gen. Sec.*, A. Smith.

NATIONAL UNION OF TEACHERS (N.U.T.) (216,614), Hamilton House, Mabledon Place, WC1H 9BD.—*Gen. Sec.*, D. McAvoy.

NATIONAL UNION OF THE FOOTWEAR, LEATHER AND ALLIED TRADES (31,176), The Grange, 108 Northampton Road, Earls Barton, Northampton NN6 0JH.—*Gen. Sec.*, G. F. Browett.

NORTHERN CARPET TRADES' UNION (862), 22 Clare Road, Halifax HX1 2HX.—*Gen. Sec.*, K. Edmondson.

POWER LOOM CARPET WEAVERS' AND TEXTILE WORKERS' UNION, THE (3,200), Carpet Weavers Hall, Callows Lane, Kidderminster, Worcs. DY10 2JG.— *Gen. Sec.*, B. C. Moule.

PRISON OFFICERS' ASSOCIATION, THE (23,669), Cronin House, 245 Church Street, N9 9HW.—*Gen. Sec.*, D. Evans.

ROSSENDALE UNION OF BOOT, SHOE AND SLIPPER OPERATIVES, THE (2,591), Taylor House, 7 Tenterfield Street, Waterfoot, Rossendale, Lancs. BB4 7BA.—*Gen. Sec.*, M. Murray.

SCOTTISH PRISON OFFICERS' ASSOCIATION (3,804), 21 Calder Road, Edinburgh EH11 3PF.—*Gen. Sec.*, W. Goodall.

SCOTTISH UNION OF POWER-LOOM OVERLOOKERS (65), 3 Napier Terrace, Dundee, Tayside DD2 2SL.—*Sec.*, J. Reilly.

SCREW, NUT, BOLT AND RIVET TRADE UNION (now called Engineering and Fasteners Trade Union).

SHEFFIELD WOOL SHEAR WORKERS' UNION (17), 50 Bankfield Road, Malin Bridge, Sheffield S6 4RD.—*Sec.*, J. H. R. Cutler.

SOCIETY OF GRAPHICAL AND ALLIED TRADES 1982 (SOGAT '82) (179,941), Sogat House, 274–288 London Road, Hadleigh, Benfleet, Essex SS7 2DE.—*Gen. Sec.*, Ms. B. Dean.

SOCIETY OF SHUTTLEMAKERS (31), 211 Burnley Road, Colne, Lancs. BB8 8JD.—*Gen. Sec.*, L. Illingworth.

SOCIETY OF TELECOM EXECUTIVES (29,040), 1 Park Road, Teddington, Middx. TW11 0AR.—*Gen. Sec.*, S. Petch.

TECHNICAL, ADMINISTRATIVE AND SUPERVISORY SECTION (T.A.S.S.) (amalgamated with A.S.T.M.S. to form Manufacturing, Science and Finance Union).

TRANSPORT AND GENERAL WORKERS' UNION (T.G.W.U.) (1,312,853), Transport House, Smith Square, SW1P 3JB.—*Gen. Sec.*, R. Todd.

TRANSPORT SALARIED STAFFS' ASSOCIATION (40,000), Walkden House, 10 Melton Street, NW1 2EJ.—*Gen. Sec.*, R. A. Rosser.

UNION OF COMMUNICATION WORKERS, THE (204,834), U.C.W. House, Crescent Lane, SW4 9RN.—*Gen. Sec.*, A. D. Tuffin.

UNION OF CONSTRUCTION, ALLIED TRADES AND TECHNICIANS (U.C.A.T.T.) (250,000), UCATT House, 177 Abbeville Road, SW4 9RL.—*Sec.*, A. Williams.

UNION OF SHOP, DISTRIBUTIVE AND ALLIED WORKERS (U.S.D.A.W.) (400,000), Oakley, 188 Wilmslow Road, Fallowfield, Manchester M14 6LJ.—*Sec.*, D. G. Davies.

UNITED ROAD TRANSPORT UNION (21,000), 76 High Lane, Chorlton, Manchester M21 1FD.—*Gen. Sec.*, F. Griffin.

WIRE WORKERS' UNION (5,139), Prospect House, Alma Street, Sheffield S3 8SA.—*Gen. Sec.*, A. M. Ardron.

WRITERS' GUILD OF GREAT BRITAIN, THE (1,678), 430 Edgware Road, W2 1EH.—*Gen. Sec.*, W. J. Jeffrey.

YORKSHIRE ASSOCIATION OF POWER LOOM OVERLOOKERS (537), 20 Hallfield Road, Bradford BD1 3RQ.—*Gen. Sec.*, A. D. Barrow.

Expelled from the T.U.C. Sept. 1988:

ELECTRICAL, ELECTRONIC, TELECOMMUNICATION AND PLUMBING UNION (E.E.T.P.U.) (330,000), Hayes Court, West Common Road, Bromley BR2 7AU.—*Gen. Sec.*, E. A. B. Hammond, O.B.E.

INDUSTRIAL RESEARCH ASSOCIATIONS

The following are members of the Association of Independent Research and Technology Organizations (A.I.R.T.O.), P.O. Box 330, Cambridge CB5 8DQ.

AIRCRAFT RESEARCH ASSOCIATION LTD., Manton Lane, Bedford MK41 7PF.

ADVANCED MANUFACTURING TECHNOLOGY RESEARCH INSTITUTE, Hulley Road, Macclesfield, Cheshire SK10 2NE.

BCIRA INTERNATIONAL CENTRE FOR CAST METALS TECHNOLOGY, Alvechurch, Birmingham B48 7QB.

BHRA, THE FLUID ENGINEERING CENTRE, Wharley End, Cranfield, Bedford MK43 0AJ.

BICERI—THE BRITISH INTERNAL COMBUSTION ENGINE RESEARCH INSTITUTE LTD., 111–112 Buckingham Avenue, Slough SL1 4PH.

BNF METALS TECHNOLOGY CENTRE, Wantage Business Park, Denchworth Road, Wantage, Oxon. OX12 9BJ.

BRITISH CERAMIC RESEARCH LTD., Queen's Road, Penkhull, Stoke-on-Trent ST4 7LQ.

BRITISH GLASS, Northumberland Road, Sheffield S10 2UA.

BRITISH LEATHER CONFEDERATION, Leather Trade House, Kings Park Road, Moulton Park, Northants. NN3 1JD.

BRITISH MARITIME TECHNOLOGY LTD., Orlando House, 1 Waldegrave Road, Teddington, Middx. TW11 8LZ.

BRITISH TEXTILE TECHNOLOGY GROUP, Shirley Towers, Didsbury, Manchester M20 8RX; Wira House, West Park Ring Road, Leeds LS16 6QL.

BUILDING SERVICES RESEARCH AND INFORMATION ASSOCIATION, Old Bracknell Lane West, Bracknell, Berks. RG12 4AH.

CAMBRIDGE CONSULTANTS LTD. (*Product and process development of technology applications in business*), Science Park, Milton Road, Cambridge CB4 4DW.

CAMPDEN FOOD AND DRINK RESEARCH ASSOCIATION, Chipping Campden, Glos. GL55 6LD.

CIRIA (THE CONSTRUCTION INDUSTRY RESEARCH AND INFORMATION ASSOCIATION), 6 Storey's Gate, SW1P 3AU.

CUTLERY AND ALLIED TRADES RESEARCH ASSOCIATION, Henry Street, Sheffield S3 7EQ.

ERA TECHNOLOGY LTD. (*Electronic and electrical engineering*), Cleeve Road, Leatherhead, Surrey KT22 7SA.

FABRIC CARE RESEARCH ASSOCIATION, Forest House Laboratories, Knaresborough Road, Harrogate, N. Yorks. HG2 7LZ.

FULMER LTD. (*Technological product design and process development*), Hollybush Hill, Stoke Poges, Slough SL2 4QD.

FURNITURE INDUSTRY RESEARCH ASSOCIATION, Maxwell Road, Stevenage, Herts. SG1 2EW.

HATRA (HOSIERY AND ALLIED TRADES RESEARCH ASSOCIATION), 7 Gregory Boulevard, Nottingham NG7 6LD.

HAZLETON UK (*Agro-chemical, chemical and pharmaceutical product development and safety evaluation*), Otley Road, Harrogate, N. Yorks. HG3 1PY.

HYDRAULICS RESEARCH LTD., Wallingford, Oxon. OX10 8BA.

INVERESK RESEARCH INTERNATIONAL LTD. (*Pharmaceutical, veterinary, agricultural and chemical product evaluation*), Musselburgh, Midlothian EH21 7UB.

LAMBEG INDUSTRIAL RESEARCH ASSOCIATION (*Textiles*), Lambeg, Lisburn, Co. Antrim, N. Ireland BT27 4RJ.

LEATHERHEAD FOOD RESEARCH ASSOCIATION, Randalls Road, Leatherhead, Surrey KT22 7RY.

LIFE SCIENCE RESEARCH LTD., Eye, Suffolk IP23 7PX.

MOTOR INDUSTRY RESEARCH ASSOCIATION, Watling Street, Nuneaton, Warks. CV10 0TU.

THE NATIONAL COMPUTING CENTRE LTD., Oxford Road, Manchester M1 7ED.

NEI INTERNATIONAL RESEARCH AND DEVELOPMENT COMPANY LTD. (*Electronics and mechanical and electrical engineering*), Fossway, Newcastle upon Tyne NE6 2YD.

PAINT RESEARCH ASSOCIATION, 8 Waldegrave Road, Teddington, Middx. TW11 8LD.

PERA (*Multi-disciplinary research, design, development and consultancy*), Melton Mowbray, Leics. LE13 0PB.

PIRA (*Paper and board, printing, publishing and packaging*), Randalls Road, Leatherhead, Surrey KT22 7RU.

RAPRA TECHNOLOGY LTD. (*Polymer materials*), Shawbury, Shrewsbury SY4 4NR.

RICARDO GROUP (*Consulting engineers*), Bridge Works, Shoreham-by-Sea, W. Sussex BN43 5FG.

SATRA FOOTWEAR TECHNOLOGY CENTRE, Satra House, Rockingham Road, Kettering, Northants. NN16 9JH.

SHIPOWNERS REFRIGERATED CARGO RESEARCH ASSOCIATION, 140 Newmarket Road, Cambridge CB5 8HE.

SIRA LTD. (*Instrumentation and systems technology*), South Hill, Chislehurst, Kent BR7 5EH.

SMITH ASSOCIATES LTD. (*System engineering consultancy*), Surrey Research Park, Guildford, Surrey GU2 5YP.

SPRING RESEARCH AND MANUFACTURERS' ASSOCIATION, Henry Street, Sheffield S3 7EQ.

STEEL CASTINGS RESEARCH AND TRADE ASSOCIATION, 5 East Bank Road, Sheffield S2 3PT.

TIMBER RESEARCH AND DEVELOPMENT ASSOCIATION, Stocking Lane, Hughenden Valley, High Wycombe, Bucks. HP14 4ND.

TOXICOL LABORATORIES LTD. (*Toxicology*), Bromyard Road, Ledbury, Herts. HR8 1LG.

WATER RESEARCH CENTRE, P.L.C., Henley Road, Medmenham, P.O. Box 16, Marlow, Bucks. SL7 2HD.

THE WELDING INSTITUTE, Abington Hall, Abington, Cambridge CB1 6AL.

AGRICULTURAL AND FOOD RESEARCH INSTITUTES AND UNITS

A.F.R.C. Institute for Animal Health
Director of Research: Prof. F. J. Bourne, PH.D., Compton, Newbury, Berks. RG16 0NN.

Compton Laboratory, Compton, Nr. Newbury, Berks. RG16 0NN.—*Head of Lab. (acting)*, B. Freeman, D.SC.

Houghton Laboratory, Houghton, Huntingdon, Cambs. PE17 2DA.—*Head of Lab. (acting)*, L. N. Payne, PH.D., D.SC.

Pirbright Laboratory, Ash Road, Woking, Surrey GU24 0NF.—*Head of Lab. (acting)*, C. J. Bostock, PH.D.

AFRC and MRC Neuropathogenesis Unit, Ogston Building, West Mains Road, Edinburgh EH9 3JF.—*Dir. (acting)*, J. Hope, PH.D.

A.F.R.C. Institute of Animal Physiology and Genetics Research
Dir. of Research, R. B. Heap, PH.D., SC.D., F.R.S., Babraham Hall, Babraham, Cambridge CB2 4AT.

Cambridge Research Station, Babraham, Cambridge CB2 4AT.—*Head of Station*, vacant.

Edinburgh Research Station, Roslin, Midlothian EH25 9PS.—*Head of Station*, G. Bulfield, PH.D.

Edinburgh Research Station, King's Buildings, West Mains Road, Edinburgh EH9 3JQ.

Dryden Laboratory, Roslin, Midlothian EH25 9PS.

A.F.R.C. Institute of Arable Crops Research
Dir. of Research, Prof. K. J. Treharne, PHD. Rothamsted Experimental Station, Harpenden, Herts. AL5 2JQ.

Long Ashton Research Station, Long Ashton, Bristol BS18 9AF.—*Dir.*, vacant.

Rothamsted Experimental Station, Harpenden, Herts. AL5 2JQ.—*Head of Station*, Prof. T. Lewis, PH.D., D.SC.

Broom's Barn Experimental Station, Higham, Bury St. Edmunds, Suffolk IP28 6NP.—*Head of Station*, T. H. Thomas, PH.D., D.SC.

Unit of Insect Neurophysiology and Pharmacology, Department of Zoology, University of Cambridge, Downing Street, Cambridge CB2 3EJ.—*Hon. Dir.*, J. E. Treherne, PH.D., SC.D.

A.F.R.C. Institute of Engineering Research
Director of Research, Prof. J. Matthews, Wrest Park, Silsoe, Bedford MK45 4HS.

A.F.R.C. Institute of Food Research
Director of Research, D. L. Georgala, C.B.E., PH.D., Shinfield, Reading RG2 9AT.

Bristol Laboratory, Langford, Bristol BS18 7DY.—*Head of Lab.* Prof. A. J. Bailey, SC.D.

Norwich Laboratory, Colney Lane, Norwich NR4 7UA.—*Head of Lab.*, Prof. P. Richmond, D.SC.

Reading Laboratory, Shinfield, Reading RG2 9AT.—*Head of Lab.*, Prof. B. E. B. Moseley, PH.D.

A.F.R.C. Institute for Grassland and Animal Production
Director of Research, Prof. J. L. Stoddart, PH.D., D.SC., Hurley, Maidenhead, Berks. SL6 5LR.

Plant Science and Plant Breeding Division:
Welsh Plant Breeding Station, Plas Gogerddan, Aberystwyth, Dyfed SY23 3EB.—*Dir. and Head of Division*, D. Wilson, PH.D.

Grassland and Ruminant Division:
Hurley Research Station, Maidenhead, Berks. SL6 5LR.—*Head of Division*, R. J. Wilkins, PH.D.

North Wyke Research Station, Okehampton, Devon EX20 2SB.—*Officer in Charge*, R. D. Sheldrick, O.B.E.

Pig and Poultry Division:
Shinfield Research Station (Pig Dept.), Church Lane, Shinfield, Reading RG2 9AQ.—*Deputy Head of Division*, D. Lister, PH.D.

Roslin Research Station (Poultry Dept.), Roslin, Midlothian EH25 9PS.—*Head of Division*, C. Fisher, PH.D.

A.F.R.C. Institute of Horticultural Research
Director of Research, Prof. T. R. Swinburne, D.SC., PH.D., Bradbourne House, East Malling, Maidstone, Kent ME19 6BJ.

I.H.R. East Malling, East Malling, Maidstone, Kent ME19 6BJ.—*Head of Station*, C. C. Payne, PH.D.

I.H.R. Littlehampton, Worthing Road, Littlehampton, W. Sussex BN17 6LP.—*Head of Station*, R. S. Fraser, PH.D., D.SC.

I.H.R. Wellesbourne, Wellesbourne, Warwick CV35 9EF.—*Head of Station*, H. G. Jones, PH.D.

I.H.R. Department of Hop Research, Wye College, Wye, Ashford, Kent TN25 5AH.—*Head of Station*, R. E. Gunn.

A.F.R.C. Institute of Plant Science Research
Dir. of Research, Prof. H. W. Woolhouse, John Innes Institute, Colney Lane, Norwich NR4 7UH.

John Innes Institute, Colney Lane, Norwich NR4 7UH.—*Dir.*, Prof. R. B. Flavell.

I.P.S.R Cambridge Laboratory, Maris Lane, Trumpington, Cambridge CB2 2LQ.—*Head*, C. N. Law, PH.D.

I.P.S.R. Nitrogen Fixation Laboratory, University of Sussex, Brighton BN1 9RQ.—*Head*, Prof. B. E. Smith, PH.D.

A.F.R.C. Computing Division, West Common, Harpenden, Herts. AL5 2JE.—*Head of Division.*, A. Windram.

SCOTTISH AGRICULTURAL RESEARCH INSTITUTES

Hannah Research Institute, Ayr KA6 5HL.—*Dir.*, Prof. M. Peaker.

Macaulay Land Use Research Institute, Craigiebuckler, Aberdeen AB9 2QJ; Bush Estate, Penicuik, Midlothian EH26 0PY.—*Dir.*, Prof. T. J. Maxwell, PH.D.

Moredun Research Institute, 408 Gilmerton Road, Edinburgh EH17 7JH.—*Dir.*, I. D. Aitken, PH.D.

Rowett Research Institute, Greenburn Road, Bucksburn, Aberdeen AB2 9SB.—*Dir.*, Prof. W. P. T. James.

Scottish Crop Research Institute, Invergowrie, Dundee DD2 5DA; Pentlandfield, Roslin, Midlothian EH25 9RF.—*Dir.*, Prof. J. Hillman, PH.D., F.L.S., F.R.S.E.

Scottish Agricultural Statistics Service, University of Edinburgh, James Clerk Maxwell Building, The King's Buildings, Mayfield Road, Edinburgh EH9 3JZ.—*Dir.*, R. A. Kempton.

C.A.B. INTERNATIONAL

C.A.B. International (Commonwealth Agricultural Bureaux International) is an intergovernmental organization that provides information, scientific and development services to agriculture throughout the world. These services provide both developed and developing countries with ready access to scientific information and research back-up and assistance in pest identification and control.

C.A.B. International Bureaux
Wallingford, Oxon. OX10 8DE.

Institutes

C.A.B.I. Institute of Entomology, 56 Queen's Gate, SW7. *Director*, K. M. Harris, Ph.D.

C.A.B.I. Mycological Institute, Ferry Lane, Kew, Richmond, Surrey. *Director*, D. L. Hawksworth, Ph.D.

C.A.B.I. Institute of Biological Control, Silwood Park, Buckhurst Road, Ascot, Berks. SL5 7TA. *Director*, D. J. Greathead, Ph.D.

C.A.B.I. Institute of Parasitology, 395A Hatfield Road, St. Albans, Herts. *Director*, R. L. J. Muller, Ph.D.

Agricultural Economics Bureau.
Animal Breeding and Genetics Bureau.
Animal Health Bureau.
Crop Protection Bureau.
Dairy Science and Technology Bureau.
Forestry Bureau.
Horticulture and Plantation Crops Bureau.
Nutrition Bureau.
Pastures and Field Crops Bureau.
Plant Breeding and Genetics Bureau.
Soils Bureau.

COST OF RESEARCH AND DEVELOPMENT

(excluding social science research)

Work performed within each sector

	1981		1983		1985		1986	
	£ million	per cent	£ million	per cent	£ million	per cent	£ million	per cent
Sector carrying out the work								
Central government								
Defence	557·7	9·4	654·9	9·9	752·7	9·5	801·2	9·1
Civil:								
Research councils	250·2	4·2	279·0	4·2	313·0	4·0	363·4	4·1
Other	526·5	8·9	552·9	8·4	537·2	6·8	194·4	2·2
Local government	5·0	0·1	7·0	0·1	8·1	1·1	7·3	0·1
Total	1,339·4	22·6	1,493·8	22·7	1,611·0	20·3	1,366·3	15·6
Universities and further education establishments	629·6	10·6	749·5	11·4	906·2	11·4	1,021·1	11·6
Public corporations	384·8	6·5 }	526·2	8·0 }	5,145·8	65·0	6,075·5	69·2
Research associations	88·1	1·5 }	3,637·1	55·2 }				
Private industry	3,319·5	56·1					315·0	3·6
Other	159·6	2·7	176·4	2·7	256·2	3·2		
Total cost of research and development performed	5,921·1	100·0	6,583·0	100·0	7,919·2	100·0	8,777·9	100·0

Finance provided by each sector

	1981		1983		1985		1986	
	£ million	per cent	£ million	per cent	£ million	per cent	£ million	per cent
Sector providing the funds								
Central government								
Defence	1,666·7	24·8	1,884·3	25·7	2,263·7	21·8	2,262·6	19·9
Civil:								
Research councils	363·5	5·4	408·3	5·6	553·8	5·3	537·7	4·7
Other	1,161·3	17·3	1,265·4	17·3	1,534·0	14·8	1,552·0	13·6
Local government	20·0	0·3	25·5	0·3	27·0	0·3	30·0	0·3
Total as returned by Government	3,211·5	47·7	3,583·5	48·9	4,378·5	42·2	4,382·3	8·5
Total as returned by sectors carrying out work	2,825·9	47·7	3,217·9	48·9	3,340·4	42·2	3,382·3	38·5
Universities	58·0	1·0	25·0	0·4	35·0	0·4	40·0	0·5
Public corporations	449·2	7·6 }	2,869·4	43·6	3,752·4	47·4	4,347·8	49·5
Private industry*	2,080·1	35·1 }						
Overseas	411·4	6·9	347·9	5·3	647·1	8·2	842·8	9·6
Other	96·6	1·6	122·8	1·9	144·3	1·8	164·9	1·9
Total	5,921·1	100·0	6,583·0	100·0	7,919·2	100·0	8,777·9	100·0

*Including research associations.

THE QUEEN'S AWARDS FOR EXPORT AND TECHNOLOGY

The Queen's Award for Export Achievement and The Queen's Award for Technological Achievement were instituted by Royal Warrant in 1976. The two separate Awards took the place of The Queen's Award to Industry which had been instituted in 1965.

The Awards are designed to recognize and encourage outstanding achievements in exporting goods or services from the United Kingdom and in advancing process or product technology. They differ from a personal Royal honour in that they are given to a unit as a whole—management and employees working as a team.

They may be applied for by any organization within the United Kingdom, the Channel Islands or the Isle of Man producing goods or services which meet the criteria for the Awards. Eligibility is not influenced in any way by the particular activities of the unit applying, its location, or size. Units or agencies of central and local government with industrial functions, as well as research associations, educational institutions and bodies of a similar character, are also eligible, provided that they can show they have contributed to industrial efficiency.

The criteria on which recommendations for the Awards are based are:

1. Export Achievement

A substantial and sustained increase in export earnings to a level which is outstanding for the products or services concerned and for the size of the applicant unit's operations. Account will be taken of any special market factors described in the application. Applicants for the Award will be expected to explain the basis of the achievement (e.g. improved marketing organization or new initiative to cater for export markets) and this will be taken into consideration. Export earnings considered will include receipts by the applicant unit in this country from the export of goods produced in this country, and the provision of services to non-residents. Account will be taken of the overseas expenses incurred other than marketing expenses. Income from profits (after overseas tax) remitted to this country from the applicant unit's direct investments in its overseas branches, subsidiaries or associates in the same general line of business will be taken into account, but not receipts from profits on other overseas investments or by interest on overseas loans or credits.

2. Technological Achievement

A significant advance, leading to increased efficiency, in the application of technology to a production or development process in British industry or the production for sale of goods which incorporate new and advanced technological qualities.

Each award is formally conferred by a Grant of Appointment and is symbolized by a representation of its emblem cast in stainless steel and encapsulated in a transparent acrylic block.

Awards are held for five years and holders are entitled to fly the appropriate Award flag and to display the emblem on the packaging of goods produced in this country, on the goods themselves, on the unit's stationery, in advertising and on certain articles used by employees: units may also display the emblem of any previous current Awards during the 5 years.

Awards are announced on April 21 (the actual birthday of Her Majesty the Queen) and published formally in a special supplement to the London Gazette. All enquiries about the scheme and requests for application forms—completed forms must be returned by October 31—should be made to: The Secretary, The Queen's Awards Office, Dean Bradley House, 52 Horseferry Road, London SW1P 2AG. Telephone: 01–222 2277.

Awards for Export Achievement

In 1989, the Queen's Award for Export Achievement was conferred on the following concerns:

AEI Compounds Group of AEI Cables Ltd., Gravesend, Kent.

Airedale International Air Conditioning Ltd., Leeds.

The Process Systems Division of Air Products PLC, Walton-on-Thames, Surrey.

Allen & Caswell Ltd., Kettering, Northants.

Allied Colloids Group PLC, Bradford.

The Freezer Division of A. P. V. Baker Ltd., Grimsby, S. Humberside.

Ardtaraig Salmon Ltd., Dunoon, Argyll.

Artix Ltd., Peterlee, Co. Durham.

Atlas Converting Equipment PLC Group of Companies, Kempston, Bedford.

Austin Reed International Ltd., Crewe.

Austin Rover Group Ltd., Coventry.

Basys International Ltd., London W1

Ken Bell (International) Ltd., Newcastle upon Tyne.

BhS PLC, London NW1.

BICC Data Networks Ltd., Hemel Hempstead, Herts.

BIS Banking Systems International Ltd., London SW19.

Black & Decker Power Tools Division of Black & Decker (UK), Spennymoor, Co. Durham.

Bowers Internal Gauge Co. Ltd., Bradford.

British Aerospace PLC, London WC2

British United Shoe Machinery Ltd., Leicester.

The Piano Felt Division of Bury Cooper Whitehead Ltd., Oldham.

E.A.R. Division of Cabot Safety Ltd., Stockport.

Callard & Bowser Group, t/a Smith Kendon Ltd., Bridgend, Mid Glamorgan.

Cameron Balloons Ltd., Bristol.

Carri-Med Ltd., Dorking, Surrey.

Central Independent Television PLC, Birmingham.

Chromacol Ltd., London N12.

Ciba-Geigy Pigments Division of Ciba-Geigy PLC, Paisley.

CI Caravans Ltd., Newmarket, Suffolk.

The Cobb Breeding Company Ltd., East Hanningfield, Chelmsford.

Colour Marketing Services Ltd., Ipswich.

Computer Patent Annuities, St. Helier, Jersey.

Cookson Graphics PLC, Morley, Leeds.

C. Davidson & Sons, Bucksburn, Aberdeen.

The Davy Roll Company Ltd., Sheffield.

De La Rue Systems Ltd., Havant, Hampshire.

DELTA (Distribution of English Language Teaching Aids) Ltd., Weybridge, Surrey.

Delwyn Enterprises Ltd., t/a Yardmaster International, Draperstown, N. Ireland.

Dynamic Cassette International Ltd., Boston, Lincs.

ECC International (Sales) Ltd., St. Austell, Cornwall.

EEV Ltd. (Electronics Division), Essex.

Encomech Engineering Services Ltd., Epsom, Surrey.

Environmental Control Systems Ltd., Cleckheaton, W. Yorkshire.

Environmental Resources Ltd., London W1.

Financial Times Group Ltd., London SE1.

Firbank Kempster Group, Old Isleworth, Middx.

FormFlo Ltd., Cheltenham.

Elizabeth Gage Ltd., London W1.

GEC Avionics Ltd., Rochester, Kent.

Grafton (Database Consultants) Ltd., Kingston upon Thames, Surrey.

William Grant & Sons Ltd., Glasgow.

Holyhead Fish Processors Ltd., Holyhead, Gwynedd.

Huntingdon Research Centre Ltd., Alconbury, Huntingdon, Cambs.

Hyster Europe Ltd., Basingstoke.

IAD (UK) Ltd., Worthing, W. Sussex.

ICI Pharmaceuticals, Macclesfield.

Ilmor Engineering Ltd., Brixworth, Northants.

The Compressor Division of Ingersoll-Rand Co. Ltd., Hindley Green, Lancs.

Interopa Holidays Ltd., London W2.

Irlandus Circuits Ltd., Craigavon, Co. Armagh, N. Ireland.

IT Power Ltd., Eversley, Hants.

Justerini & Brooks Ltd., London NW1.

KBC Advanced Technologies Ltd., Weybridge, Surrey.

Kelvin Hughes Ltd., Ilford, Essex.

KTS Wire Industries Ltd., Morley, Leeds.

Laughton & Sons Ltd., Birmingham.

Life Science Research Ltd., Eye, Suffolk.

Lofthouse of Fleetwood Ltd., Fleetwood, Lancs.

MacAlister, Elliott and Partners Ltd., Lymington, Hants.

Machin Designs Ltd., London SW11.

Marathon Belting Ltd., Rochdale, Lancs.

Marlec Engineering Co. Ltd., Corby, Northants.

Matsushita Electric UK Ltd., Cardiff.

Metair Aircraft Ltd., West Malling, Kent.

Microblade Ltd., Sheffield.

Mineral Industries Computing Ltd., London W1.

Mulberry Company (Design) Ltd., Chilcompton, Bath.

NRC (Manufacturing) Ltd., Dundee.

NMC-Kenmore (UK) Ltd., Crook, Co. Durham.

The Civil Engineering Division of Netlon Ltd., Blackburn, Lancs.

RT Newey (Chemicals) Ltd., Crosby, Liverpool.

Ari D. Norman, London NW10.

Osprey Metals Ltd., Neath, W. Glamorgan.

Philips, Radiotherapy Systems Division of Philips Medical Systems (UK) Ltd., Crawley, W. Sussex.

Portex Ltd., Hythe, Kent.

Precision Metal Ltd., Stratford-upon-Avon, Warks.

Process Scientific Innovations Ltd., Bowburn, Durham.

Prout Catamarans Ltd., Canvey Island, Essex.

Purification Products Ltd., Otley, W. Yorkshire.

Razamataz, Colne, Lancs.

RHP Precision, Newark, Notts.

John Ross (Chemicals) Ltd., Bude, Cornwall.

Rowntree PLC, York.

Saga Group PLC, Folkestone, Kent.

Sandmaster Ltd., Hixon, Staffs.

The Meat Netting Division of Scobie & Junor Ltd., East Kilbride, Glasgow.

Sloane Optical Ltd., t/a Cutler & Cross, London SW1.

Sovereign International Freight Ltd., Feltham, Middx.

The Cryogenics Group of Sulzer (UK) Ltd., Aldershot, Hants.

Sunseeker International (Boats) Ltd., Poole, Dorset.

SWADA (London) Ltd., London E15.

Targus Group PLC, Richmond, Surrey.

Technophone Ltd., Camberley, Surrey.

Thermaflex Ltd., Glenrothes, Fife.

Thermopol Ltd., Crawley, W. Sussex.

TI Apollo Ltd., Oldbury, W. Midlands.

Tract Ltd., Thame, Oxon.

Trans Euro Worldwide Movers Ltd., London NW10.

The University of Reading, Reading, Berks.

VG Elemental Ltd., Winsford, Cheshire.

Vic-Tree (Birmingham) Ltd., Birmingham, W. Midlands.

The Wellcome Foundation Ltd., London NW1.

Willett International Ltd., High Wycombe, Bucks.

F. G. Wilson (Engineering) Ltd., Newtownabbey, Belfast.

Prime Mover Maintenance (a unit of Wood Group Gas Turbines Ltd.), Aberdeen.

Woods of Windsor Ltd., Windsor, Berks.

Awards for Technological Achievement 1989

In 1989 the Queen's Award for Technological Achievement was conferred on the following concerns:

The Edwards High Vacuum International Division of the BOC Group PLC, Crawley, W. Sussex (*Air drying equipment*).

British Ceramic Research Ltd., Stoke-on-Trent, Staffs. (*Set of ceramic colour standards*).

British United Shoe Machinery Ltd., Belgrave, Leicester (*Computer-controlled machinery for manufacturing shoes*).

The Continuous Casting Plant of the Teesside works of British Steel PLC, Redcar, Cleveland (*Immersed rotary valve for quality steel making (jointly with Thor Ceramics Ltd.)*).

Cambridge Research Biochemicals Ltd., Harston, Cambridge (*Improved process for producing peptides for pharmaceutical applications (jointly with the Laboratory of Molecular Biology of the Medical Research Council)*).

Castlet (Electronic Engineers) Ltd., Lincoln, Lincs. (*Microprocessor controls for electrostatic precipitators*).

The Steriseal Division of Coats Viyella Medical Ltd., Redditch, Worcs. (*Advanced surgical dressings for chronic wound treatment (jointly with the Courtaulds Research Division of Courtaulds PLC)*).

The Coultaulds Research Division of Courtaulds PLC, Coventry (*Advanced surgical dressings for chronic wound treatment (jointly with the Steriseal Division of Coats Viyella Medical Ltd.)*).

Crosfield Electronics Ltd., Hemel Hempstead, Herts. (*System for quickly and securely transmitting data simultaneously to several remote locations*).

The Colvern Division of Crystalate Electronics Ltd., Romford, Essex (*Position sensors for automotive electronic servicing*).

The Optical and Display Science Division of the Royal Signals and Radar Establishment (M.o.D.), Great Malvern, Worcs. (*Electronic techniques for improving radar performance over the sea (jointly with Racal-MESL Ltd.)).*

The VLSI Design and Architectures Division of the Royal Signals and Radar Establishment (M.o.D.), Great Malvern, Worcs. (*Computer-aided design system (jointly with Praxis Systems* PLC.))

Domnick Hunter Filters Ltd., Birtley, Co. Durham (*Air drying equipment*).

Dowty Rotol Ltd., Gloucester (*Landing gear for the A320 airliner*).

The Aviation Division of Dunlop Ltd., Coventry (*Improved materials for aircraft braking systems*).

Encomech Engineering Services Ltd., Epsom, Surrey (*System for conserving energy during hot rolling of steel strip*).

Formula Systems Ltd., Eynsham, Oxford (*Electronic units for elevator door protection*).

GEC Traction Ltd., Manchester (*Electronic railway propulsion equipment*).

Holset Engineering Co. Ltd., Turnbridge, Huddersfield (*Flexible manufacturing system to produce turbocharger shaft and wheel*).

Hydra- Lok Ltd., Barrow-in-Furness, Cumbria (*System for attaching offshore structures to their undersea anchorages*).

Keeler Ltd., Windsor, Berks. (*Non-contact tonometer for glaucoma screening (jointly with the Technology Division of PA Consulting Group*)).

Marconi Instruments Ltd., St. Albans, Herts. (*A computer controlled test set (2955 series) for testing radio transmitters and receivers*)).

Miles 33 PLC, Bracknell, Berks. (*Electronic composing and publishing system. (Used to print Hansard and other Parliamentary papers*)).

The Laboratory of Molecular Biology of the Medical Research Council, Cambridge (*Improved process for producing peptides for pharmaceutical applications (jointly with Cambridge Research Biochemicals Ltd.*)).

Norprint International Ltd., Boston, Lincs. (*Magnetic striped and encoded tickets and payment tokens*).

Oxford Instruments Ltd., Oxford (*Superconducting magnets for nuclear magnetic resonance spectroscopy*).

Oxford Lasers Ltd., Oxford (*High-performance air-cooled metal vapour lasers*).

The Technology Division of PA Consulting Group, Melbourn, Herts. (*Non-contact tonometer for glaucoma screening (jointly with Keeler Ltd.*)).

The Cambridge International Supply Centre (IPSC) of Philips Radio Communications Systems Ltd., Cambridge (*High-performance wide-area radio pagers*).

Philips Radiotherapy Systems Division of Philips Medical Systems (UK) Ltd., Crawley, W. Sussex (*Radiotherapy linear accelerator*).

Plessey Defence Systems Ltd., Christchurch, Dorset (*Mobile military telecommunication system*).

Praxis Systems PLC, Bath (*Computer-aided electronic design system (jointly with the VLSI Design and Architectures Division of the Royal Signals and Radar Establishment*)).

Racal-MESL Ltd., Newbridge, Midlothian (*Electronic techniques for improving radar performance over the sea (jointly with the Optical and Display Science Division of the Royal Signals and Radar Establishment*)).

River Don Castings Ltd., Sheffield (*Steel castings for offshore use where they replace welded structures*).

The Automated Compressor Blade Project Team of Rolls Royce PLC, Bristol (*Process for automated blade manufacture*).

The Telecommunications Systems Division of STC PLC, London N11 (*Flexible access telecommunication system*).

Thor Ceramics Ltd., Clydebank, Dunbartonshire (*Immersed rotary valve for quality steel sheetmaking (jointly with the Continuous Casting Plant of the Teeside works of British Steel* PLC))

Unipath Ltd., Bedford (*Home pregnancy test system*).

Westland Helicopters Ltd., Yeovil, Somerset (*Composite main rotor blade for the Sea King helicopter*).

Wycombe Marsh Paper Mills Ltd., High Wycombe, Bucks. (*High strength sterilised paper used for medical drapes and wraps*).

PERIODS OF GESTATION OR INCUBATION

The table shows approximate periods of gestation or incubation for some common animals and birds. In some cases the periods may vary and where doubt arises professional advice should be sought.

Species	Shortest Period. Days	Usual Period. Days	Longest Period. Days	Species	Shortest Period. Days	Usual Period. Days	Longest Period. Days
Human	240	273	313	Duck	28	28	32
Horse	305	336	340	Chicken	20	21	22
Cow	273	280	294	Pigeon	17	18	19
Goat	147	151	155	Canary	12	14	14
Sheep	140	147–50	160	Guinea Pig	63	—	70
Pig	109	112	125	Mouse	18	—	19
Dog	55	63	70	Rat	21	—	24
Cat	53	56	63	Elephant		21–22 months	
Rabbit	30	32	35				
Goose	28	30	32	Zebra		56 weeks	
Turkey	25	28	28	Camel		45 weeks	

BRITISH MONETARY UNITS

COIN

Gold Coins
†One Hundred Pounds £100
†Fifty Pounds £50
†Twenty-five Pounds £25
†Ten Pounds £10
Five Pounds £5
Two Pounds £2
Sovereign £1
Half-Sovereign 50p

Silver Coins
Maundy Money‡
Fourpence 4p
Threepence 3p
Twopence 2p
Penny 1p

Nickel-Brass Coins
Two Pounds £2
One Pound £1

Cupro-Nickel Coins
50 Pence 50p
Crown 25p
20 Pence 20p
10 Pence 10p
5 Pence 5p

Bronze Coins
2 Pence 2p
1 Penny 1p

†Britannia gold bullion coins, introduced in October 1987.

‡Gifts of special money distributed by the Sovereign annually on Maundy Thursday to the number of aged poor men and women corresponding to the Sovereign's own age.

Gold Coin.—Gold ceased to circulate during the First World War. An Order of April 27, 1966, made it illegal for U.K. residents to continue holding more than four gold coins minted after 1837, or to acquire such coins unless they had been licensed as genuine collectors by the Bank of England. This Order was revoked on April 1, 1971, by the Exchange Control (Gold Coins Exemption) Order, 1971, whereby residents of the United Kingdom, Channel Islands and the Isle of Man may freely buy and sell and hold gold coins.

The 1971 Order was revoked on April 15, 1975, by the Exchange Control (Gold Coins Exemption) Order, 1975. Under this Order Section 1 of the Exchange Control Act 1947 (which prohibits dealings in gold or foreign currency except with Treasury permission) was exempted for gold coins minted in or before 1837. The import of gold coins minted after 1837 was prohibited except by authorized dealers in gold with individual import licences from the Department of Trade and Industry, and dealing between other U.K. residents was restricted to coins already held in the U.K.

Under an amendment, dated December 16, 1977, the exemptions contained in the 1975 Order were extended to cover gold coins minted in or before 1937.

The 1975 controls over the import of and dealing in gold coins were abolished on June 13, 1979 under the Exchange Control (Gold Coins Exemption) Order 1979, and gold coins, with certain exceptions,* may now be imported and exported without restriction.

On April 1, 1982 the Government introduced VAT (currently 15 per cent) on sales of all gold coin.

Silver Coin.—Prior to 1920 our silver coins were struck from sterling silver—an alloy of which 925 parts in 1,000 were silver. In 1920 the proportion of silver was reduced to 500 parts. From January 1, 1947 all "silver" coins, except Maundy money, have been struck from cupro-nickel—an alloy of copper 75 parts and nickel 25 parts, except for the 20p, composed of copper 84 parts, nickel 16 parts. Maundy coins since 1947 have been struck from sterling silver.

Bronze Coin.—Bronze, introduced in 1860 to replace copper, is currently an alloy of copper 97 parts, zinc 2½ parts and tin ½ part. These proportions have been subject to slight variations in the past.

The "Remedy" is the amount of variation from standard permitted in weight and fineness of coins when first issued from the Mint.

Legal tender of coin.—Gold, dated 1838 onwards, if not below least current weight, is legal tender to any amount. £2 and £1 coins are legal tender to any amount. 50p and 20p coins are legal tender up to £10; 10p and 5p coins are legal tender up to £5 and bronze coins are legal tender for amounts up to 20p. Farthings ceased to be legal tender on December 31, 1960, the halfpenny on August 1, 1969, the halfcrown on January 1, 1970, the threepence and penny on August 31, 1971, the sixpence on June 30, 1980 and the decimal halfpenny on December 31, 1984.

The decimal system was introduced on Feb. 15, 1971. Since 1982 the word "new" in "new pence" displayed on decimal coins has been dropped.

---

* Gold coins which are more than fifty years old and valued at a sum in excess of £8,000 cannot be exported without specific authorization from the Department of Trade and Industry.

BANK NOTES

Bank of England notes are currently issued in denominations of £5, £10, £20 and £50 for the amount of the Fiduciary Note Issue, and are legal tender in England and Wales.

The old white notes for £10, £20, £50, £100, £500 and £1,000, which were issued until April 22, 1943, ceased to be legal tender in May 1945.

The old white £5 issued between October 1945 and September 1956, the £5 notes issued between 1957 and 1963, bearing a portrait of Britannia and the first series to bear a portrait of the Queen, issued between 1963 and 1971, ceased to be legal tender on March 14,

Denomination	Metal	Standard Weight (grams)	Standard Diameter (centimetres)
Penny	bronze	3·56400	2·0320
2 pence	bronze	7·12800	2·5910
5 pence	cupro-nickel	5·65518	2·3595
10 pence	cupro-nickel	11·31036	2·8500
20 pence	cupro-nickel	5·0	2·14
25p Crown	cupro-nickel	28·27590	3·8608
50 pence	cupro-nickel	13·5	3·0
£1	copper/nickel/zinc	9·5	2·25
£2	copper/nickel/zinc	15·98	2·84

1961, June 27, 1967 and September 1, 1973 respectively. The series of £1 notes issued during the years 1928 to 1960 and the 10s. notes of the same type issued from 1928 to 1961—those without the royal portrait—ceased to be legal tender on May 29 and October 30, 1962 respectively. The £1 note first issued in March 1960 (bearing on the back a representation of Britannia) and the £10 note first issued in February 1964 (bearing a lion on the back) both bearing a portrait of the Queen on the front ceased to be legal tender on June 1, 1979. The 10s. note was replaced by the 50p coin in October 1969, and ceased to be legal tender on November 21, 1970. Bank notes which are no longer legal tender are payable when presented at the Head Office of the Bank of England in London.

The first of the current series of Bank notes was a £20 note issued on July 9, 1970. This was followed by the £5 note on November 11, 1971, £10 note on February 20, 1975, £1 note on February 9, 1978 and £50 note on March 20, 1981. The £1 coin was introduced on April 21, 1983 and the £1 denomination note ceased to be legal tender on March 11, 1988. The predominant identifying feature of each note is the portrayal on the back of a prominent figure from Britain's history namely: £5, The Duke of Wellington; £10, Florence Nightingale; £20, William Shakespeare; and £50, Sir Christopher Wren.

Note Circulation.—Note circulation is highest at the two peak spending periods of the year—around Christmas and during the summer holiday period. A peak of £16,554 million was reached immediately prior to Christmas 1989, a 8·4 per cent increase on the previous year.

The proportion of the total value of notes in circulation of £1 and £5 notes at end-February 1989 compared with the previous year, fell from 0·8 per cent and 14·3 per cent to 0·7 per cent and 11·7 per cent respectively. £10 notes fell from 43·7 per cent to 41·1 per cent. However, £20 notes increased from 20·0 per cent to 25·9 per cent, as did £50 notes, from 13·3 per cent to 14·6 per cent.

On February 28, 1989 the values of notes in circulation were: £1: £101,843,242; £5:

£1,646,382,315; £10: £5,805,838,450; £20: £3,653,872,060; £50: £2,053,692,050.

OTHER BANK NOTES

Scotland.—Bank notes are issued by three Scottish banks. The Royal Bank of Scotland and the Bank of Scotland issue notes for £1, £5, £10, £20 and £100. The Clydesdale Bank issues notes for £1, £5, £10, £20, £50, £100. Scottish notes are not legal tender, but in Scotland they enjoy a status equal to that of the Bank of England note.

Northern Ireland.—Bank notes are issued by four banks in Northern Ireland. The Northern Bank and the Ulster Bank issue notes for £5, £10, £20, £50 and £100. The Allied Irish Bank and the Bank of Ireland issue notes for £5, £10, £20 and £100. Northern Irish notes are not legal tender but in Northern Ireland they circulate widely and enjoy a status comparable to that of Bank of England notes.

Channel Islands.—The States of Jersey issues its own currency notes and coinage. The note denominations are for £1, £5, £10, £20 and £50. Seven denominations of coins are issued: 1p, 2p, 5p, 10p, 20p, 50p and £1. The States of Guernsey issues its own currency notes and coinage. The notes are for £1, £5, £10 and £20. The denomination of coins are 1p, 2p, 5p, 10p, 20p, 50p and £1.

The Isle of Man.—The Isle of Man Government issues notes for 50p, £1, £5, £10, £20 and £50. Although these notes are only legal tender in the Isle of Man they are accepted at face value in branches of the clearing banks in the United Kingdom. The Isle of Man issues coins for 1p, 2p, 5p, 10p, 20p, 50p, £1, £2 and £5.

Although none of the series of notes specified above is legal tender in the United Kingdom they are generally accepted by the banks irrespective of their place of issue. At one time the banks made a commission charge for handling Scottish and Irish notes but this was abolished some years ago.

THE INTERNATIONAL STOCK EXCHANGE

The International Stock Exchange of the United Kingdom and Republic of Ireland Ltd. serves the needs of government, industry and investors by providing facilities for raising capital and a central market place for securities trading. There are over 7,000 securities listed on the International Stock Exchange, which have a value of approximately £1,862,000 million. Last year, securities worth some £1,522,806,000 million changed hands. This central market place covers not only government stocks (called gilts) and U.K. and overseas company shares (called equities and fixed interest stocks) but other investment instruments such as traded options on equities, currencies and indices.

"Big Bang"

During 1986 the International Stock Exchange went through the greatest period of change in its two hundred year history. In March 1986 it opened its doors for the first time to overseas and corporate membership of the Exchange, allowing banks, insurance companies and overseas securities houses to become Members of The Exchange and to buy existing Member Firms. On October 27, 1986, three major reforms took place, changes which became known as "Big Bang":

(i) abolition of scales of minimum commissions, allowing clients to negotiate freely with their brokers about the charge for their services
(ii) abolition of the separation of member firms into brokers and jobbers. Under the new system, Firms are broker/dealers, able to act as agents on behalf of clients; to act as principals buying and selling shares for their own account; and to become registered market makers, making continuous buying and selling prices in specific securities
(iii) the introduction of the Stock Exchange Automated Quotations (S.E.A.Q.) system. Market makers input their buying and selling prices into S.E.A.Q., which displays the competing quotations on a composite page on-screen. For the largest and most frequently traded company shares ("Alpha"), e.g. Marks and Spencer or BP, the volume of shares traded is also updated continuously throughout the day.

Of all these changes, the implementation of S.E.A.Q. has had perhaps the most visible effect. Dealing in stocks and shares now takes place via the telephone in the Firms' own dealing rooms, rather than face to face on the floor of the Exchange. The new systems also provide increased investor protection. All deals taking place via the Exchange's S.E.A.Q. system are recorded on a database which can be used to resolve disputes or to carry out investigations.

Members of the International Stock Exchange buy and sell shares on behalf of the public, as well as institutions such as pension funds or insurance companies. In return for transacting the deal, the broker will charge a commission, which is usually based upon the value of the transaction. The market makers, or wholesalers, in each security do not charge a commission for their services, but will quote the broker two prices, a price at which they will buy and a price at which they will sell. It is the middle of these two prices which is published in lists of Stock Exchange prices in newspapers.

Regulatory Bodies

On November 12, 1986 Members of the Exchange agreed to merge with members of the international broking community in London, based outside the Exchange, in order to form two new bodies—the International Stock Exchange of the United Kingdom and Republic of Ireland Ltd. and the Securities Association Ltd. These two regulatory bodies have been formed under the provisions of the Financial Services Act, which requires investment businesses to be authorised and regulated by a Self Regulating Organisation (S.R.O.) of which the Securities Association is one. The Act also requires business to be conducted through a Registered Investment Exchange (R.I.E.). The International Stock Exchange is an R.I.E., regulating four main markets: U.K. equities, international equities, gilts and options.

Markets

As well as advising and dealing on behalf of investors, stockbrokers provide a range of services to industry from the raising of initial capital and future, additional, funds to advice on mergers and acquisitions. For a company entering the market for the first time there are three possible Stock Exchange markets, depending upon the size, history and requirements of the company. The first is the listed market, on which the shares of over 2,500 companies are traded. For entry to this market, the company must have an audited trading history of at least five years, and place 25 per cent of its shares in public hands. The second type of market is for smaller, less established companies and is called the Unlisted Securities Market (U.S.M.). In January, 1986, the International Stock Exchange established a third tier called simply the Third Market. This is for very new and small companies incorporated in the U.K. or Ireland. Once admitted to the Exchange, all companies are obliged to keep their shareholders informed of their progress, making announcements of a price-sensitive nature through the Exchange's company announcements department.

The International Stock Exchange has its headquarters in London, and administrative centres around the U.K. and the Republic of Ireland. At present there are some 5,100 individual Members and about 390 Member Firms.

Chairman, Andrew Hugh Smith.

BALANCE OF PAYMENTS OF THE UNITED KINGDOM (£ million)

	1982	1983	1984	1985	1986	1987
Current account						
Visible trade						
Exports (fob)	55,330	60,698	70,263	77,988	72,678	79,422
Imports (fob)	53,112	61,773	74,843	80,334	81,394	89,584
Visible balance	2,218	−1,075	−4,580	−2,346	−8,716	−10,162
Invisibles						
Credits	65,483	65,997	77,765	80,662	77,249	80,010
Debits	63,016	61,090	71,163	74,979	68,732	72,552
Invisibles balance	2,467	4,907	6,602	5,683	8,517	7,458
of which:						
Services balance	*2,762*	*3,721*	*3,941*	*5,962*	*5,618*	*5,638*
Interest, profits and dividends balance	*1,446*	*2,847*	*4,433*	*2,800*	*5,079*	*5,523*
Transfers balance	*−1,741*	*−1,661*	*−1,772*	*−3,079*	*−2,180*	*−3,503*
Current balance	4,685	3,832	2,022	3,337	−199	−2,504
Transactions in external assets and liabilities*						
Investment overseas by U.K. residents						
Direct	−4,091	−5,417	−6,003	−8,653	−11,525	−15,372
Portfolio	−7,563	−7,193	−9,866	−19,440	−25,243	6,463
Total U.K. investment overseas	−11,654	−12,610	−15,869	−28,093	−36,768	−8,909
Investment in the U.K. by overseas residents						
Direct	3,027	3,386	−181	4,213	4,176	5,953
Portfolio	225	1,888	1,419	7,121	8,447	10,805
Total overseas investment in U.K.	3,252	5,274	1,238	11,334	12,623	16,758
Foreign currency lending abroad by U.K. banks	−16,498	−16,117	−9,357	−20,336	−48,020	−45,626
Foreign currency borrowing abroad by U.K. banks	19,904	17,192	18,648	25,306	58,116	44,270
Net foreign currency transactions of U.K. banks	3,406	1,075	9,291	4,970	10,096	−1,356
Sterling lending abroad by U.K. banks	−4,019	−2,232	−4,933	−1,635	−5,955	−4,638
Sterling borrowing and deposit liabilities abroad of U.K. banks	4,421	3,945	6,149	4,155	5,605	8,519
Net sterling transactions of U.K. banks	402	1,713	1,216	2,520	−350	3,881
Deposits with and lending to banks abroad by U.K. non-bank private sector	−598	863	−3,243	−1,251	−2,787	−3,784
Borrowing from banks abroad by:						
U.K. non-bank private sector	985	73	−2,177	2,598	3,743	1,654
Public corporations	−35	−35	−47	64	−30	−166
General government	57	77	48	87	100	100
Official reserves (additions to − drawings on +)	1,421	607	908	−1,758	−2,891	−12,012
Other external assets of:						
U.K. non-bank private sector and public corporations	128	−153	1,285	521	1,893	672
General government	−161	−478	−743	−730	−510	−797
Other external liabilities of:						
U.K. non-bank private sector and public corporations	119	−55	518	728	602	1,497
General government	350	−661	−88	−64	+78	1,423
Net transactions in assets and liabilities	−2,328	−4,310	−7,664	−9,074	−14,200	−1,039
Balancing item	−2,357	478	5,642	5,737	14,379	3,543

* Assets: increase −/decrease +. Liabilities: increase +/decrease −.

LIFE AND GENERAL INSURANCE

Authorization of Insurance Companies

Section 3 of the Insurance Companies Act 1982 empowers the Department of Trade and Industry (Insurance Division, 1 Victoria Street, SW1H 0ET) to authorize corporate bodies to transact insurance in the United Kingdom provided they comply with the financial and other regulations detailed in the Act.

At the end of 1988 there were 838 insurance companies with authorization to transact one or more classes of insurance business in the U.K.

panies offering long-term contracts like life insurance, pensions, unit trusts and annuities can either obtain authorization directly from S.I.B. or from the main S.R.O. dealing with the marketing of life insurance and pensions, the Life And Unit Trust Regulatory Organization (LAUTRO), Centre Point, 103 New Oxford Street, WC1A 1QH. It is possible that insurers may also need authorization from other S.R.O.s, for example, the Investment Management Regulatory Organization (IMRO), Centre Point, 103 New Oxford Street, WC1A 1QH.

Regulation of Insurance Companies

Under the Financial Services Act 1986, the Securities and Investments Board (S.I.B.) is empowered to make, monitor and enforce rules about the conduct of investment business.

The S.I.B. has, in turn, set up a number of Self-Regulating Organizations dealing with different sectors of the investment market. Insurance com-

Association of British Insurers

Ninety per cent of the world-wide business of insurance companies is transacted by the 440 members of the Association of British Insurers. This trade association has represented both life and general insurers since 1985 when it replaced the British Insurance Association, the Life Offices Association and other such organizations.

BRITISH INSURANCE COMPANIES IN 1988

The following insurance company figures refer to members of the Association of British Insurers, and also to certain non-members.

World-wide General Business Trading Result

	1986 £m	1987 £m	1988 £m
Net Written Premiums	18,817	19,709	21,659
Underwriting Profit/Loss for 1 year Account Business			
Motor	−638	−477	−378
Fire and Accident	−524	−479	−71
Transfer to Profit and Loss Account for Other Business			
Marine, Aviation, Transport	−6	+52	+39
Other	−252	−228	−105
Total Underwriting Result	−1,420	−1,133	−515
Investment Income	2,514	2,631	2,903
Overall Trading Profit	1,094	1,498	2,388
Profit as a % of Premium Income	+5·8	+7·6	+11·0

World-wide General Business Underwriting Result

	1987				1988			
	U.K.	U.S.A.	Other	Total	U.K.	U.S.A.	Other	Total
Fire and Accident								
Premiums (£m)	6,118	1,831	2,298	10,247	7,053	1,792	2,407	11,251
Profit/Loss (£m)	−368·3	−77·1	−34·0	−479·4	+334·0	−299·6	−105·6	−71·3
% of Premiums	−6·0	−4·2	−1·5	−4·7	+4·7	−16·7	−4·4	−0·6
Motor								
Premiums (£m)	3,411	1,135	1,607	6,153	4,017	1,212	1,760	6,989
Profit/Loss (£m)	−260·0	−56·6	−160·7	−477·3	−152·9	−53·9	−170·8	−377·7
% of Premiums	−7·6	−5·0	−10·0	−7·8	−3·8	−4·5	−9·7	−5·4

Net Premium Income by Territory 1988

	U.K. £m	Other E.C. countries £m	U.S.A. £m	Other overseas £m	Total (world-wide) £m
Fire and Accident (non-motor)	7,540 (+14·9%)	963 (−3·8%)	1,851 (−1·3%)	2,808 (+4·8%)	13,162 (+8·7%)
Motor	4,052 (+17·1%)	733 (+1·0%)	1,213 (+6·9%)	1,041 (+14·4%)	7,040 (+13·0%)
Marine, Aviation and Transport	1,060 (+2·4%)	120	127 (+20·9%)	150	1,457 (+6·8%)
Total General Business .	12,652 (+14·4%)	1,815 (+5·2%)	3,192 (+6·1%)	3,999 (+2·1%)	21,659 (+9·9%)
Ordinary Long-Term	20,657 (+2·4%)	1,369 (−0·6%)	1,327 (+53·7%)	2,136 (+21·8%)	25,490 (+5·5%)
Industrial Long-Term	1,351 (+3·8%)	—	—	—	1,351 (+3·8%)
Total Long-Term Business	22,008 (+2·5%)	1,369 (−0·6%)	1,327 (+53·7%)	2,136 (+21·8%)	26,841 (+5·4%)
TOTAL	34,661 (+6·6%)	3,185 (+2·6%)	4,519 (+16·7%)	6,135 (+8·2%)	48,500 (+7·4%)

(The figures in brackets show the percentage increase (+) or decrease (−) of the 1988 figures over those for 1987).

Claims Statistics

	1987	1988
Fire Claims		
Commercial Fires	£454·7 m	£475·0 m (+4·5%)
Domestic Fires..................................	£183·6 m	£170·9 m (−7·0%)
Theft Claims		
Commercial Theft (inc. money)	£148.5 m	£134·7 m (−10·2%)
Domestic Theft	£290·2 m	£285·9 m (−1·5%)

Weather Damage
Figures for weather damage claims are not published on an annual basis but estimates for damage caused by the storm on October 16–17, 1987 now stand at £1,050 million.

LLOYD'S OF LONDON

Lloyd's of London is an incorporated society of private underwriters who provide an international market for almost any type of insurance. Ships, aircraft, oil rigs, cargo of all descriptions, motor cars, civil engineering projects, fire, personal accident and third party liability are a few random examples of the everyday risks placed at Lloyd's which currently earn a premium income of around £6,000 million for underwriters each year. Three-quarters of this business comes from outside Great Britain and makes a valuable contribution to the country's balance of payments.

Today, as it was three centuries ago, a policy is subscribed at Lloyd's by private individuals with unlimited liability. Now that Lloyd's members are numbered in their thousands, however, the method of underwriting is the same only in principle. The merchant of the past, signing policies in a coffee house as a sideline to his main business, has long since given way to the specialist underwriter who accepts risks at Lloyd's on behalf of members (often referred to as "names") grouped in a syndicate. There are currently over 31,000 members in some 401 syndicates of varying sizes, some with over two thousand names and each managed by an underwriting agent approved by the Council of Lloyd's.

Lloyd's membership today is drawn from many sources. Industry, commerce and the professions are strongly represented while many members work at Lloyd's either for brokerage firms or for underwriting agencies.

Underwriting membership of Lloyd's is open to men and women of any nationality provided that they meet the stringent financial requirements of the Society, or Corporation, of Lloyd's. Assets of up to £250,000 have to be shown and a deposit lodged with the Corporation as security for underwriting liabilities. This deposit, which must be in the form of approved securities, is determined at 30 per cent of the member's annual premium income.

Lloyd's is incorporated by Act of Parliament (Lloyd's Acts 1871–1982) and governed by a Council of 28 members, twelve of whom are elected from and by underwriting members working at Lloyd's and eight from and by the external membership. Eight Council members are nominated by the Council subject to confirmation by the Governor of the Bank of England.

The Council is a legislative body responsible for deciding on major policy matters, for regulating the Lloyd's market, for the election of new underwriting members, and for establishing the requirements of membership and the rules governing the financial security to be provided by those doing business at Lloyd's.

The Council's "working" members form the Committee of Lloyd's, an executive body which is responsible for putting the Council's directives into effect, managing the Society's affairs, and administering the Lloyd's market on a day-to-day basis.

The Corporation is a non-profit-making body chiefly financed by its members' subscriptions. It provides the premises, administrative staff and services enabling Lloyd's underwriting syndicates to conduct their business. It does not, however, assume corporate liability for the risks accepted by its members, who remain responsible to the full extent of their personal means for their underwriting affairs.

Lloyd's syndicates have no direct contact with the public. All business is transacted through some 260 firms of insurance brokers accredited by the Corporation of Lloyd's. In addition, non-Lloyd's brokers in the United Kingdom when guaranteed by Lloyd's brokers, are able to deal directly with Lloyd's motor syndicates, a facility which has made the Lloyd's market more accessible to the insuring public.

Lloyd's also provides the most comprehensive shipping intelligence service available in the world. The enormous volume of shipping and other information received from Lloyd's agents, shipowners, news agencies and other sources throughout the world, is collated and distributed to newspapers, radio and television services, as well as to maritime and commercial interests in general.

This information is compiled, edited and published by a subsidiary company, Lloyd's of London Press Ltd., and distributed worldwide. *Lloyd's List* is London's oldest daily newspaper and contains news of general commercial interest as well as shipping information. *Lloyd's Shipping Index*, also published daily, lists some 25,000 ocean-going vessels in alphabetical order and gives the latest known report of each.

Lloyd's Three Year Business Summary

	Premiums	Underwriting profit	Investment income and appreciation
	£m	£m	£m
Short Term Life			
1983	2·89	1·03	0·26
1984	4·00	1·14	0·33
1985	4·02	1·28	0·36
Accident and Health			
1983	188·38	13·06	14·00
1984	162·19	33·02	17·05
1985	143·55	20·82	12·42
Motor Vehicle Damage and Liability			
1983	283·44	34·60	25·51
1984	323·76	7·61	25·42
1985	382·58	−0·68	28·77
Ships, Aircraft Damage and Liability and Transit			
1983	1,211·42	187·79	184·25
1984	1,437·07	232·78	189·62
1985	1,372·03	274·55	139·12
All Other Insurance Business		(loss)	
1983	883·51	(351·17)	192·87
1984	1,031·93	(119·87)	229·06
1985	1,441·03	(48·08)	215·25

Lloyd's Membership Syndicates and Brokers 1981–1988

	1981	1982	1983	1984	1985	1986	1987	1988
Membership	19,136	20,145	21,601	23,438	26,050	28,944	31,484	33,532
Including: Brokers	270	266	272	265	261	258	258	275

Lloyd's Global Underwriting Accounts

Net Premium Income

	1984 A/C	1985 A/C	1986 A/C
	£m	£m	£m
Life	4·030	4·023	4·025
Accident and Health	155·452	143·547	142·718
Motor Vehicle Damage and Liability	325·868	382·583	438·866
Ships, Aircraft Damage and Liability and Transit	1,372·845	1,372·020	1,567·578
All Other Insurance Business	1,106·419	1,153·830	1,457·214
TOTAL	2,964·614	3,056·003	3,610·401

INSURANCE BROKERS

The Insurance Brokers Registration Act 1977 empowers the Insurance Brokers Registration Council (15 St. Helens Place, EC3A 6DS) as the statutory body responsible for the registration of insurance brokers. The Council is responsible for the registration and training of insurance brokers, conduct of business, and discipline, and it lays down rules relating to such matters as accounting practice, staff qualifications, advertising, etc.

It is possible to act as an insurance intermediary without being registered with the I.B.R.C. but unregistered intermediaries are forbidden to use the words 'Insurance Broker' as a title.

I.B.R.C. Registered Brokers

	1989
Registered individuals	15,843
Limited Companies registered	3,160
Sole traders and partnerships	1,533
(containing 2,314 partners and directors)	

THE EUROPEAN COMMUNITY

In 1986 the European Community's Heads of Government signed the Single European Act. This set out a programme of over 300 E.C. Directives which are intended to achieve the removal of barriers to a free market within the community. To date, progress on the Directives has been slow.

In insurance, the U.K. and the Netherlands are the closest of the E.C. countries to operating a free market system, U.K. nationals already being able to arrange cover with an insurer based outside the U.K. if they wish. Similarly, overseas insurers are free to market their products and operate in the U.K.

This is not the case in most other E.C. member countries; in France for example, it is an offence for a person to arrange insurance cover with a company outside the country. In Belgium and West Germany individuals are able to arrange cover outside their borders but not through an intermediary or broker. In addition, insurers from outside these countries cannot advertise or operate any form of marketing to attract business.

E.C. Directives are gradually being incorporated into U.K. law; for example, The Motor Vehicles (Compulsory Insurance) Regulations 1987 required all U.K. motor insurance policies to cover legal liabilities for damage to third party property as well as bodily injury. This change, which came into force on December 31, 1988, is designed to harmonize the cover under motor insurance policies throughout the community, a requirement of the third E.C. Directive on Motor Insurance.

Invisible Earnings of Insurance

	1986	1987
Insurance	£4,913 m	£4,834 m

LIFE INSURANCE AND PENSIONS

Personal Pensions

July 1, 1988 saw the introduction of personal pensions, one of the main advantages of which is that they remain unaffected by a change of employment. Before July 1, 1988, only self-employed persons were able to take out a personal pension. From that date the restriction was lifted and now anyone in employment can take a personal pension and use it to contract out of the State Earnings Related Pension Scheme or their employer's company scheme. It is also no longer possible for employers to make membership of their company pension scheme a condition of employment.

Contracting out of the State Earnings Related Pension Scheme at any time up to 1993 entitles the employee to a rebate of National Insurance contributions made since 1987. These are paid into their personal pension fund by the Department of Social Security (D.S.S.). To encourage new contracted-out schemes a 2 per cent incentive bonus was paid into the personal pension fund of anyone taking out a personal pension before April 6, 1989.

Individual Pension New Business in 1988

1988	New annual premiums			New single premiums			D.S.S. rebates*	
	Non-Linked	Linked	Total	Non-Linked	Linked	Total	Non-Linked	Linked
Quarter 1st	£87m	£78m	£165m	£167m	£68m	£236m	—	—
2nd	£135m	£138m	£273m	£244m	£101m	£345m	—	—
3rd	£110m	£98m	£207m	£110m	£47m	£157m	£131m	£95m
4th	£126m	£110m	£236m	£123m	£65m	£188m	£146m	£109m

* The figures shown for D.S.S. rebates are the best estimate of the first year's amounts to be received under policies effected in the quarter, whether received or not.

Premium Income for World-wide Long-Term Insurance Business

	1986 £m	1987 £m	1988 £m
Ordinary Branch:			
Yearly premiums for life insurances, annuities and pensions in the U.K.	9,501	10,525	12,479 (+18·6%)
Single premiums for life insurances, annuities and pensions in the U.K.	7,323	9,446	7,958 (−15·8%)
Premiums for permanent health and other long-term insurances in the U.K.	169	201	220 (+9·8%)
Overseas premium income	3,183	3,996	4,833 (+20·9%)
Industrial Branch:			
Premium Income (U.K. only)	1,248	1,301	1,351 (+3·8%)

World-wide Long-Term Insurance Business—Outgo

	1986 £m	1987 £m	1988 £m
Ordinary Branch:			
Total payments made to U.K. policyholders	11,213	13,376	13,912 (+4·0%)
Total payments made to overseas policyholders	1,973	1,895	2,214 (+16·8%)
Industrial Branch:			
Total payments made to U.K. policyholders	1,177	1,287	1,435 (+11·5%)

NOTE: Payments to policyholders includes death claims, maturities, annuities, surrenders (including planned cashing-in of linked and other similar savings policies and surrenders of bonus and bonuses in cash), refunds under pension schemes and payments under P.H.I. and other long-term contracts.

Insurance Company Investments

	1986 £m	1987 £m	1988 £m
Invested Funds			
Long-Term	174,633	190,455	216,095
General	36,833	40,267	46,677
Net Income from Investments			
Long-Term	10,018	11,022	12,101
General	2,526	2,631	2,903

DIRECTORY OF INSURANCE COMPANIES

The class of Insurance undertaken is shown in the second column as follows: A—Accident (which includes Motor, Employers' Liability, etc.); F—Fire (including Burglary); L—Life; M—Marine; and Re—Reinsurance.

A number of offices are now included in a Group—the initials of which appear after the name. The main Groups are as follows—E.S.—Eagle Star; C.U.—Commercial Union; G.R.E.—Guardian Royal Exchange; G.A.—General Accident; N.U.—Norwich Union; R—Royal; S.A.—Sun Alliance & London.

Est'd.	Nature of Business	Name of Company	Address
1961	L	Abbey Life	80 Holdenhurst Road, Bournemouth.
1951	AFM	Albion	Plantation House, 31–35 Fenchurch St., EC3.
1824	AFM	Alliance ........S.A.	1 Bartholomew Lane, EC2.
1965	L	Allied Dunbar	Allied Dunbar Centre, Swindon.
1921	L	American Life	2–8 Altyre Road, Croydon.
1960	AF	Ansvar	31 St. Leonards Road, Eastbourne.
1808	AFM	Atlas ........G.R.E.	Royal Exchange, EC3.
1849	L	Australian Mutual Provident	A.M.P. House, Dingwall Rd., Croydon.
1925	AFL	Avon	Tiddington Road, Stratford-upon-Avon.
1905	AFM	Baptist	4 Southampton Row, WC1.
1965	L	Barclays	94 St Paul's Churchyard, EC4.
1883	AFM	Beacon ........S.A.	1 Bartholomew Lane, EC2.
1894	AFM	Bedford General	Zurich House, Stanhope Road, Portsmouth.
1925	AFLM Re	Black Sea and Baltic	65 Fenchurch Street, EC3.
1959	AFLM	Bradford	North Park, Halifax.
1866	AFL	Britannic	Moor Green, Moseley, Birmingham.
1863	M	British & Foreign Marine ....R.	New Hall Place, Liverpool.
1878	Machinery	British Engine, etc ....R.	Longridge House, Manchester 4.
1854	AFLM	British Equitable ........G.R.E.	Royal Exchange, EC3.
1904	AFM	British General ..........C.U.	St. Helen's, 1 Undershaft, EC3.
1888	AFM	British Law ........S.A.	1 Bartholomew Lane, EC2.
1896	L	British Life	Reliance House, Mt. Ephraim, Tunbridge Wells, Kent.
1908	AFM	British Oak ........G.R.E.	Royal Exchange, EC3.
1881	A	Builders' Accident	31 & 32 Bedford Street, Strand, WC2.
1805	L	Caledonian ........G.R.E.	Royal Exchange, EC3.
1934	AFM	Cambrian ........G.R.E.	Royal Exchange, EC3.
1847	L	Canada Life	Canada Life House, Potters Bar, Herts.
1963	L	Cannon Lincoln	1 Olympic Way, Wembley.
1903	AFM	Car & General ........G.R.E.	Royal Exchange, EC3.
1885	AFM	Century ........S.A.	1 Bartholomew Lane, EC2.
1922	AFMex-motor	Chemists' Mutual	321 Chase Road, Southgate, N14.
1920	L	Citicorp British National	Perrymount Road, Haywards Heath, W. Sussex.
1862	L	City of Glasgow Friendly	200 Bath Street, Glasgow G2.
1824	L	Clerical, Medical Group	Narrow Plain, Bristol.
1873	L & Pers. Acc.	Colonial Mutual	24 Ludgate Hill, EC4.
1919	AFM	Comrcl. Ins. Co. of Ireland	5 Donegall Square, S., Belfast.
1861	AFLM	Commercial Union	St. Helen's, 1 Undershaft, EC3.
1871	L	Confederation	Lyttan Way, Stevenage, Herts.
1891	AF Re	Congregational	Currer House, Currer Street, Bradford.
1867	AFLM	Co-operative	Miller Street, Manchester.
1905	AFLM Re	Cornhill	32 Cornhill, EC3.
1900	L	Crown Financial Management	Crown House, Crown Square, Woking, Surrey.
1899	AFLM	Crusader	Woodhatch, Reigate, Surrey.
1908	AFM	Dominion	92/94 Gracechurch Street, EC3.
1904	AFLM	Eagle Star	1 Threadneedle Street, EC2.
1887	AFL	Ecclesiastical	Beaufort House, Brunswick Road, Gloucester.
1901	AFLM	Economic	Economic House, London Road, Sittingbourne.
1823	AFM	Edinburgh ........C.U.	St. Helen's, 1 Undershaft, EC3.
1880	AFM	Employers' Liability ......C.U.	St. Helen's, 1 Undershaft, EC3.
1932	Animal Ins.	Equine and Livestock	610–616 Chiswick High Road, W4.
1762	L	Equitable Life	4 Coleman Street, EC2.
1844	L	Equity & Law	Amersham Road, High Wycombe, Bucks.
1802	AF	Essex & Suffolk ........G.R.E.	Royal Exchange, EC3.
1894	AFM	Excess	13 Fenchurch Avenue, EC3.
1925	AFL	Federation Mutual	29 Linkfield Lane, Redhill, Surrey.
1890	AF	Fine Art & General ......C.U.	St. Helen's, 1 Undershaft, EC3.
1832	L	Friends' Prov	Pixham End, Dorking, Surrey.
1899	L	FS Assurance	190 West George Street, Glasgow.
1885	AFM Re	General Accident	Pitheavlis, Perth, Scotland.
1837	L	General Accident Life	2 Rougier Street, York.
1848	L	Gresham Life	2–6 Prince of Wales Road, Bournemouth.
1910	AFM	Gresham Fire & Accident	11 Queen Victoria Street, EC4.
1840	AFM	Guarantee Society ......G.A.	36–37 Old Jewry, EC2.
1821	ALFM Re	Guardian Assurance ....G.R.E.	Royal Exchange, EC3.
1821	ALFM Re	Guardian Royal Exch. ...G.R.E.	Royal Exchange, EC3.

Est'd.	Nature of Business	Name of Company	Address
1908	AFM	Hibernian	Haddington Road, Dublin, 4.
1960	L	Hill Samuel	NLA Tower, Addiscombe Road, Croydon.
1966	AF	Household & General ...... S.A.	1 Bartholomew Lane, EC2.
1932	FL	Ideal	Pitmaston, Birmingham, 13.
1935	L	Insurance Corporation of Ireland (Life)	Burlington Road, Dublin 4.
1939	L	Irish Life	Lr. Abbey Street, Dublin 2.
1880	A	Iron Trades Employers'	Iron Trades House, 21–24 Grosvenor Pl., SW1.
1838	L	LAS Group	10 George Street, Edinburgh.
1896	L	Laurentian Life	Laurentian House, Barnwood, Glos.
1845	AF	Law Fire .... S.A.	1 Bartholomew Lane, EC2.
1806	AFM Re	Law Union & Rock ....R.	New Hall Place, Liverpool.
1907	L	Legal ....R.	New Hall Place, Liverpool.
1836	AFLM	Legal and General	Temple Court, 11 Queen Victoria Street, EC4.
1970	L	Liberty Life	Liberty House, Station Road, New Barnet.
1890	AFLM	Licenses & General ......G.R.E.	Royal Exchange, EC3.
1836	AFM	L'pool & London & Globe. ....R.	New Hall Place, Liverpool.
1918	AFM	Liverpool Marine & General....	4–5 King William Street, EC4.
1843	L	Liverpool Victoria Friendly	Victoria House, Southampton Row., WC1.
1890	AFM	Local Government Guarantee .. G.R.E.	Royal Exchange, EC3
1836	AFM Re	Lombard Continental Insurance	77 Gracechurch Street, EC3.
1720	AFLM	London Assurance .... S.A.	1 Bartholomew Lane, EC2.
1869	AFM Re	London Guar. & Reinsurance ...	4 Colston Avenue, Bristol.
1919	AFM	London & Lancashire	New Hall Place, Liverpool.
1806	L	London Life	100 Temple Street, Bristol.
1869	L	London & Manchester	Winslade Park, Exeter, Devon.
1860	AFM	London & Provincial Marine ... G.A.	Lloyd's Building, Lime Street, EC3.
1862	AFM	London & Scottish .... C.U.	St. Helen's, 1 Undershaft, EC3.
1961	L	M & G Assurance	M & G House, Victoria Road, Chelmsford.
1887	L	Manufacturers Life	St. George's Way, Stevenage.
1836	M	Marine ....R.	34–36 Lime Street, EC3.
1852	L	Marine & General	MGM House, Heene Road, Worthing.
1864	M	Maritime .... N.U.	Surrey Street, Norwich.
1884	L	Med., Sickness, Ann. and Life. ..	7–10 Chandos Street, Cavendish Square, W1.
1907	Reinsurance	Mercantile & General..........	Moorfields House, Moorfields, EC2.
1970	L	Merchant Investors	High Street, Croydon.
1871	M	Merchants' Marine .... C.U.	St. Helen's, 1 Undershaft, EC3.
1872	AF	Methodist	Brazennose House, Brazennose St., Manchester.
1940	AFM	Minster	Minster House, Arthur Street, EC4.
1906	AFM	Motor Union ..........G.R.E.	Royal Exchange, EC3.
1903	AFL	Municipal Mutual	25–27 Old Queen Street, Westminster, SW1.
1890	FL	Nalgo Insurance Association ...	1 Mabledon Place, WC1.
1935	L	NEL Britannia Group of Companies..................	Milton Court, Dorking, Surrey.
1914	AF	NEM Insurance	Station Road, Swindon, Wilts.
1910	AFL	National Farmers' Union	Tiddington Road, Stratford-upon-Avon.
1863	Fidelity Guar.	Natl. Guaran. & Suretyship C.U.	St. Helen's, 1 Undershaft, EC3.
1894	AF	National Ins. & Guarantee Cor. .	Heron House, 145 City Road, EC1.
1830	L	National Mutual Life	The Priory, Priory Park, Hitchin, Herts.
1835	L	National Provident Institution .	N.P. House, Tunbridge Wells, Kent
1854	Plate Glass	National Provincial .....G.R.E.	Royal Exchange, EC3.
1864	Machinery	National Vulcan Eng. Ins. Group.................. S.A.	Empire House, St. Martin's-le-Grand, EC1.
1921	Naval Officers' risks, etc.	Navigators & General ...... E.S.	113 Queens Road, Brighton.
1924	L	New Ireland	11–12 Dawson Street, Dublin, 2.
1869	L	N.M. Financial Management ...	N.M. House, Seldown, Poole, Dorset.
1809	AFLM	North British & Mercantile C.U.	St. Helen's, 1 Undershaft, EC3.
1862	FM	North Pacific ...........G.R.E.	Royal Exchange, EC3.
1836	AFLM	Northern................ C.U.	St. Helen's, 1 Undershaft, EC3.
1797	AFM	Norwich Union Fire	Surrey Street, Norwich.
1808	L	Norwich Union Life	Surrey Street, Norwich.
1871	AFM	Ocean Accident .... C.U.	St. Helen's, 1 Undershaft, EC3.
1859	M	Ocean Marine .... C.U.	4 Fenchurch Avenue, EC3.
1931	AFM Aviation	Orion	Orion House, Bouverie Road West, Folkestone, Kent.
1886	AFM Re	Palatine......................	77 Leadenhall Street, EC3.
1864	AFLM Re	Pearl..........................	Pearl House, Thorpe Wood, Peterborough.
1958	Sickness A	Permanent	7–10 Chandos Street, Cavendish Square, W1.
1782	AFLM	Phoenix .... S.A.	1 Bartholomew Lane, EC2.

Est'd.	Nature of Business	Name of Company	Address
1891	L	Pioneer Mutual	16 Crosby Road North, Liverpool L69.
1920	AFM	Planet Assurance .........S.A.	1 Bartholomew Lane, EC2.
1987	L	Prolific Life and Pensions	Stramongate, Kendal, Cumbria.
1969	L	Property Growth..............	Leon House, High Street, Croydon.
1877	L	Prov. Life Assocn.	Provident Way, Basingstoke, Hampshire.
1840	L	Provident Mutual Life	25–31 Moorgate, London EC2.
1903	AF	Provincial	Stramongate, Kendal, Cumbria.
1848	AFLM Re	Prudential...................	1 Stephen Street, W1.
1986	L	Prudential Holborn	30 Old Burlington Street, W1.
1849	AF	Railway Passengers ...... C.U.	St. Helen's, 1 Undershaft, EC3.
1864	AFL	Refuge	Refuge House, Alderley Road, Wilmslow, Cheshire.
1911	L	Reliance Mutual	Reliance House, Tunbridge Wells, Kent.
1906	AF	Reliance Fire & Accident	Reliance House, Tunbridge Wells, Kent.
1881	AF	Reliance Marine ........G.R.E.	Royal Exchange, EC3.
1823	Reversions	Reversionary Interest Society. .	4 Coleman Street, EC2.
1918	AF	Road Transport & General G.A.	77 Upper Richmond Road, SW15.
1845	L	Royal Life	New Hall Place, Liverpool.
1720	AFM	Royal Exchange	Royal Exchange, EC3.
1971	L	Royal Heritage Life	Bretton Way, Peterborough.
1850	L	Royal Liver Friendly	Royal Liver Building, Pier Head, Liverpool 3.
1861	AFL	Royal London	Royal London House, Middleborough, Colchester.
1887	L	Royal Nat. Pension Fund for Nurses	Burdett House, 15 Buckingham Street, WC2.
1909	AFM	Salvation Army	117–121 Judd Street, WC1.
1963	L	Save and Prosper.............	1 Finsbury Avenue, London EC2.
1826	L	Scottish Amicable	150 St. Vincent Street, Glasgow.
1881	Engineering	Scottish Boiler .... G.A.	Pitheavlis, Perth, Scotland.
1831	L	Scottish Equitable...........	28 St. Andrew Square, Edinburgh.
1919	AFM	Scottish General .... G.A.	100 West Nile Street, Glasgow G2.
1852	L	Scottish Legal	95 Bothwell Street, Glasgow G2.
1881	L	Scottish Life	19 St. Andrew Square, Edinburgh 2.
1876	AF	Scottish Metropolitan .... C.U.	St. Helen's, 1 Undershaft, EC3.
1883	L	Scottish Mutual..............	109 St. Vincent Street, Glasgow G2.
1837	L	Scottish Provident Institution .	6 St. Andrew Square, Edinburgh.
1824	AFLM	Scottish Union & National N.U.	Surrey Street, Norwich.
1815	L	Scottish Widows'.............	15 Dalkeith Road, Edinburgh.
1875	AFM	Sea ......................S.A.	1 Bartholomew Lane, EC2.
1904	L	Sentinel Life.................	2 Eyre Street Hill, EC1.
1964	L	Stalwart Assurance	Stalwart House, 142 South Street, Dorking.
1825	L	Standard Life	3 George Street, Edinburgh.
1891	AFM	State....................G.R.E.	Royal Exchange, EC3.
1710	AFM	Sun ......................S.A.	1 Bartholomew Lane, EC2.
*	AFLM	Sun Alliance & London and Phoenix	1 Bartholomew Lane, EC2.
1810	L	Sun Life Assurance Group	107 Cheapside, EC2.
1865	L Re	Sun Life of Canada	Basing View, Basingstoke, Hants.
1936	FL	Teacher's Assurance	12 Christchurch Road, Bournemouth.
1969	L	Trident	London Road, Gloucester.
1869	L	Tunstall & District	Station Chambers, Tunstall, Stoke on Trent.
1867	M	Ulster Marine .... G.A.	5 Donegall Square South, Belfast.
1714	AFM	Union Assurance......... C.U.	St. Helen's, 1 Undershaft, EC3.
1835	AFM	Union Ins. Soc. of Canton G.R.E.	Royal Exchange, EC3.
1863	M	Union Marine	4–5 King William Street, EC4.
1915	AFM	United British .........G.R.E.	Royal Exchange, EC3.
1908	AFL	United Friendly..............	42 Southwark Bridge Road, SE1.
1963	L	UK Life Assurance	U.K. House, Worthing Road, Horsham.
1825	L	University	4 Coleman Street, EC2.
1974	L	Vanbrugh	41–43 Maddox Street, W1.
1919	Reinsurance	Victory Reinsurance	Castle Hill Avenue, Folkestone, Kent
1911	AF	Welsh Insurance Corpn. .. C.U.	St. Helen's, 1 Undershaft, EC3.
1841	AFL	Wesleyan & General	Colmore Circus, Queensway, Birmingham 4.
1886	AF	West of Scotland .... C.U.	26 George Street, Edinburgh 2.
1851	AFM	Western Assurance..........R.	New Hall Place, Liverpool.
1912	AFLM	Western Australian	Swan Court, Mansel Road, Wimbledon, SW19.
1717	AF	Westminster Fire .........S.A.	1 Bartholomew Lane, EC2.
1865	AF	White Cross .... C.U.	St. Helen's, 1 Undershaft, EC3.
1963	L	Windsor Life	Windsor House, Telford, Salop.
1894	AFM	World Marine & General .. C.U.	Dunster House, Mark Lane, EC3.
1872	AF	Zurich	Zurich House, Stanhope Road, Portsmouth.

* Sun Alliance & London—Incorporating Funds established 1710, 1720, 1782 and 1824.

FRIENDLY SOCIETIES—GREAT BRITAIN

Acts 1974–1984

Friendly societies are voluntary mutual organizations the main purposes of which are the provision of relief or maintenance during sickness, unemployment or retirement, and the provision of life assurance. Many of the older traditional societies complement their business activities by social activity and a general care for individual members in ways normally outside the scope of a purely commercial organization. There are three main categories of friendly societies—societies with separately registered branches, commonly called orders, centralized societies, which conduct business directly with members (having no separately registered branches), and collecting societies. Collecting societies conduct industrial assurance business and are subject to the requirements of the Industrial Assurance Acts in addition to the Friendly Societies Acts. Industrial assurance is life assurance, the premiums in respect of which are payable at intervals of less than two months and are received by means of collectors who make house-to-house visits for the purpose.

Long before the term 'friendly society' came into use, the seeds of voluntary mutual insurance had been sown in the ancient religious and trade Guilds. As is evident from the many extant parchment returns detailing their rules and possessions under a decree of Richard II, Guilds had become widespread in Britain by the 14th century. By then, the purely charitable character of the original Guilds had largely changed with the emergence of numerous small institutions adopting primitive mutual insurance methods of a regular flat rate contribution to insure relief when sick or in old age and a payment to the widow in the event of death.

The present register of friendly societies includes several societies which have been in existence for upwards of 200 years, the oldest, operating in Scotland, being the Incorporation of Carters in Leith, established as long ago as 1555.

The first Act for the encouragement and protection of 'friendly societies' in this country was not passed until 1793, but various amending Acts were put on the Statute Book during the next century as the result of the recommendations of successive Select Committees (including a Royal Commission in 1871). For example, it was not until the 1829 Act that all registered friendly societies were required to keep proper records of individual sickness and mortality amongst their members, which data enabled the construction of standard actuarial tables showing the expected (average) duration of sickness at successive ages, and also (with data from the Census) the corresponding mortality rates.

The rules and other documents of societies deposited with local justices passed into the custody of the Registrar following the Act of 1846 and are of considerable interest to social historians. Those relating to some societies no longer on the register have been transferred to the Public Record Office for permanent preservation.

The Friendly Societies Act 1974, which came into force in April, 1975, consolidated the nine Acts which comprised the Friendly Societies Acts 1896 to 1971 and a few other minor enactments relating to societies to which those Acts applied. The Act allows various specific classes other than 'friendly societies' to be registered thereunder, but tax exemption (irrespective of the extent of interest income) is enjoyed only by registered 'friendly societies'. The £750 sum assured limit for tax exempt business was replaced in 1987 by a more flexible limit applied to premiums—up to £100 per annum.

The Friendly Societies (Long Term Insurance Business) Regulations 1987, implementing the European Community Life Directive for friendly societies, came into force on January 1, 1988 bringing with them a more stringent regulatory regime for the largest societies. The Life Directive affects both insurance companies and friendly societies with an annual contribution income in excess of 500,000 E.C.U.s, the sterling equivalent of which was £345,308 in 1988. Thirty-seven friendly societies have been formally authorized under the Regulations. These societies are required to meet solvency requirements similar to those applied to insurance companies.

In addition to friendly societies there are three other main classes of society which may be registered under the Friendly Societies Act 1974: benevolent societies, working men's clubs and specially authorized societies. Benevolent societies are established for any charitable or benevolent purpose, to provide the same type of benefits as would be permissible for a friendly society, but in contrast the benefits must be for persons who are not members instead of, or in addition to, members. Working men's clubs provide social and recreational facilities for members. Specially authorized societies are registered for any purpose authorized by the Treasury as a purpose to which some or all of the provisions of the 1974 Act ought to be extended. Examples are societies for the promotion of science, literature and the fine arts, or to enable members to pursue an interest in sports and games.

The principal statistics at the end of 1987 are given in the table below.

	Orders and Branches	Collecting Societies	Other Centralized Societies	Benevolent Societies	Working Men's Clubs	Specially Authorized Societies		Other
						Loan	Others	
No. of Societies	2,818 (a)	32	375	87	2,408	9	141	2
No. of Members 000's	486 (b)	15,753 (c)	2,501	322	2,078 (d)	14	110	3
Total Benefits Paid £000's	5,330 (b)	148,987	116,585	5,704	Not applicable	Not applicable	28	52
Total Funds £000's	147,588 (b)	1,754,332	1,509,676	18,963	141,877 (d)	489	14,454	551

(a) 22 orders, 2,796 branches   (b) 1986 figures   (c) Assurances   (d) 1985 figures

INDUSTRIAL AND PROVIDENT SOCIETIES—GREAT BRITAIN

Acts 1965–1979

The familiar 'Co-op' societies are amongst the wide variety which are registered under the Industrial and Provident Societies Act 1965. This consolidating Act which, like the Friendly and the Building Societies Acts is administered by the Chief Registrar of Friendly Societies provides for the registration of societies and lays down the broad framework within which they must operate. Internal relations of societies are governed by their registered rules.

Registration under the Act confers upon a society corporate status by its registered name with perpetual succession and a common seal, and limited liability. A society qualifies for registration if it is carrying on an industry, business or trade, and it satisfies the Registrar that either (a) it is a bona fide co-operative society or (b) in view of the fact that its business is being, or is intended to be, conducted for the benefit of the community there are special reasons why it

should be registered under the Act rather than as a company under the Companies Act.

The Credit Unions Act 1979 added a new class of society registerable under the 1965 Act. The Act also lays down provision for supervision of these savings and loan bodies. A similar framework of law for credit unions has existed in Northern Ireland since 1969.

During 1987 the number of registered societies increased by 279 to 10,486. The largest single group was the 3,903 housing societies. The largest group in terms of turnover was that consisting of the retail societies which includes those trading under the familiar 'Co-op' sign, with sales (in 1987) of £4,409 million. Sales of wholesale and productive societies amounted to £3,162 million in 1987. The principal statistics at the end of 1987 are given in the table below.

	Retail	Wholesale and Productive	Agricultural	Fishing	Social and Recreational Clubs	General Service	Housing	Credit Unions	Total
Number of Societies	203	243	1,084	106	3,754	1,085	3,903	108	10,486
Number of Members 000's	7,429	53	411	8	2,948	203	154	27	11,232
Funds of Members £000's	732,487	414,913	237,204	4,085	171,866	3,101,353	7,346,749	6,643	12,015,301
Total Assets £000's	1,569,134	1,065,820	567,969	12,149	344,260	3,765,571	11,328,134	7,025	18,660,066

BUILDING SOCIETIES—UNITED KINGDOM

Act 1986

The most significant event for the building societies in recent times was the passage of the Building Societies Act 1986, which received the Royal Assent on July 25, 1986. Most of the provisions of the Act came into effect on January 1, 1987. The Act gave building societies a completely new legal framework, the first since the initial comprehensive building society legislation in 1874. The new Act replaced both the 1962 Act and the 1967 Act covering Northern Ireland, and therefore applies to societies based throughout the United Kingdom.

The 1986 Act made provision for a Building Societies Commission to promote the protection of shareholders and depositors, the financial stability of societies, and to administer the system of regulation of building societies provided under the Act. Much of the Act is concerned with the powers of control of the Commission and provision in relation to the management of societies, accounts, audit and so on. But the greatest impact and the most visible changes so far as the general public is concerned flowed from the new powers which societies could adopt, leading

to an increased range of services which they might provide. There were also some interesting changes in relation to members' rights.

Under the 1962 Act raising funds to make loans was the only purpose for which a building society could exist. Under the 1986 Act that has only to be its principal purpose. The constitutional provisions include the right of members to have access to the register of members, entitlement to have notices of meetings and to vote, and the right of members to have a resolution circulated.

In addition to traditional mortgage business, the power of societies to lend in respect of shared ownership, index-linked and equity-linked schemes is given. Societies may also lend the deposit, lend on registered land before the borrower is registered as the owner and on other equitable interests. Provision is also made for societies to make advances secured on land outside the United Kingdom. Larger societies were able, for the first time, to make unsecured loans, and make loans on mobile homes.

Under the 1962 Act building societies could only

BUILDING SOCIETIES, GREAT BRITAIN, 1977–1988

Year	1 Number of Societies	2 Number of Share Holders 000's	3 Number of Depositors 000's	4 Number of Borrowers 000's	5 Share Balances £m	6 Deposit Balances £m
1978	316	24,999	781	5,108	36,186	1,254
1979	287	27,878	797	5,251	42,023	1,281
1980	273	30,636	915	5,383	48,915	1,742
1981	253	33,388	995	5,490	55,463	2,539
1982	227	36,609	1,094	5,643	64,977	3,447
1983	206	37,713	1,202	5,928	75,180	5,610
1984	190	39,385	1,550	6,317	88,078	8,426
1985	167	39,997	2,150	6,659	102,331	10,751
1986	151	40,563	2,850	7,025	115,538	16,864
1987	138	41,953	3,648	7,182	129,948	20,575
1988	130	43,816	4,306	7,369	149,791	26,529

Year	7 Mortgage Balances £m	8 Total Assets £m	Advances during year		11 Average Mortgage Rate %	12 Average Share Rate %
			9 Number 000's	10 Amount £m		
1978	31,598	39,538	1,184	8,808	9·55	6·46
1979	36,801	45,789	1,040	9,002	11·94	8·45
1980	42,437	53,793	936	9,503	14·92	10·34
1981	48,875	61,815	1,096	12,005	14·01	9·19
1982	56,691	73,033	1,320	14,971	13·32	8·77
1983	67,490	85,868	1,513	19,357	11·05	7·26
1984	81,879	102,688	1,657	23,767	11·83	7·71
1985	96,751	120,764	1,678	26,508	13·46	8·65
1986	115,644	140,603	2,058	35,885	12·07	7·75
1987	130,905	160,098	1,889	35,848	11·64	7·42
1988	153,015	188,844	2,080	47,375	11·25	7·04

hold land for the purposes of running their business. Section 17 of the 1986 Act gave building societies power to hold and develop land as a commercial asset. However, the land has to be primarily for residential purposes, or adjoining land, or for purposes incidental to the holding of residential land.

Detailed provisions were contained in the Act for an Investor Protection Scheme similar to those in the Banking Act of 1979. The level of protection given is 90 per cent of accounts up to £10,000.

Societies were also empowered to offer for the first time the following services:—

(a) Money transmission services
(b) Foreign exchange services
(c) Making or receiving of payments as agents
(d) Management, as agents, of mortgage investments
(e) Management, as agents, of land (larger societies only)
(f) Arranging for the provision of services relating to the acquisition or disposal of investments for individuals.
(g) Establishment and management of personal equity plans.
(h) Arranging for the provision of credit to individuals.
(i) Establishment and management of unit trust schemes for the provision of pensions (through a subsidiary).

(j) Establishment and administration of pension schemes.
(k) Arranging for the provision of insurance of any description.
(l) Giving advice on insurance of any description.
(m) Estate agency service (through a subsidiary).
(n) Surveys and valuations of land.
(o) Conveyancing services.

There emerged a number of technical problems in relation to these services and in June 1988 Parliament made Orders which allowed societies to have the power to own up to 100 per cent of a life assurance company, 15 per cent of a general insurance company, 100 per cent of a stockbroking company and to offer an additional range of financial services including executorship and trusteeship, hire purchase and leasing and safe deposit facilities. The Orders also included an increase in the limit on unsecured personal loans from £5,000 to £10,000.

Societies must belong to an Ombudsman scheme for the investigation of complaints. Matters to be covered by the scheme include operation of share and deposit accounts, loans (but not the making of new loans), money transmission services, foreign exchange services, agency payments and receipts, and the provision of credit. Grounds for complaint include breach of the Act or contract, unfair treatment or maladministration, and where the complainant has suffered pecuniary loss or expense or inconvenience. A society must agree to be bound by decisions of the adjudicator unless it agrees to give notice to its members and the public of its reasons for not doing so. For address of the Building Societies Ombudsman Scheme, *see* Index.

On mergers, the main difference is that borrowers have a vote. For a merger to be approved at least 50 per cent of borrowers who exercise their right to vote must vote in favour, as well as 75 per cent of qualifying share investors who vote. Provision is also made for a society to convert to company status. During 1989 the Abbey National became the first building society to complete the process of conversion to a company. It can no longer use the term 'Building Society' and now falls to be supervised as a bank under the Banking Act 1987. Details of all societies with assets exceeding £1m. at the end of 1988 are given in the following list.

SOCIETIES WITH TOTAL ASSETS EXCEEDING £1 MILLION AT END OF FINANCIAL YEAR 1988

Year Established	* Name of Society (abbreviated) Head Office	Share Investors	Assets Total £'000
1849	Abbey National, Abbey House, 27 Baker St., London NW1 6XL	8,213,195	31,536,856
1985	Alliance and Leicester, 49 Park Lane, London W1Y 4EQ	2,218,969	11,412,867
1853	Barnsley, Regent St., Barnsley, South Yorks	25,404	114,772
1953	Bath Investment and Bldg. Soc., 20 Charles St., Bath	11,337	30,242
1879	Bedford, 65 Midland Rd., Bedford	9,388	45,732
1881	Bedford Crown, 117 Midland Rd., Bedford	3,228	12,069
1866	Beverley, 57 Market Place, Beverley, Yorks	5,650	18,573
1914	Bexhill-on-Sea, 2 Devonshire Sq., Bexhill-on-Sea, Sussex	2,919	12,330
1889	Birmingham Midshires, P.O. Box 81, 35–49 Lichfield St., Wolverhampton	665,835	2,729,953
1851	Bradford and Bingley, P.O. Box 2, Bingley, West Yorks.	1,847,841	5,693,736
1850	Bristol and West, Broad Quay, Bristol	751,383	3,429,429
1856	Britannia, Cheadle Rd., Newton House, Leek, Staffs.	1,097,853	5,342,817
1907	Buckinghamshire, High St., Chalfont St. Giles, Bucks.	5,300	29,076
1850	Cambridge, 32 St. Andrew's St., Cambridge	34,000	184,692
1960	Catholic, 7 Strutton Ground, London SW1	3,041	15,756
1899	Century, 21–23 Albany St., Edinburgh	1,514	7,085
1875	Chelsea, Thirlestane Hall, Thirlestane Rd., Cheltenham, Glos.	188,190	1,467,654
1850	Cheltenham and Gloucester, 37–43 Clarence St., Cheltenham, Glos.	862,978	5,667,799
1845	Chesham, 12 Market Sq., Chesham, Bucks.	7,988	40,677
1870	Cheshire, Castle St., Macclesfield	206,127	614,945
1861	Cheshunt, 100 Crossbrook St., Waltham Cross, Herts.	50,344	308,922
1859	Chorley and Dt., 49–51 St. Thomas's Rd., Chorley, Lancs.	5,916	31,221
1946	City and Metropolitan, 37 Ludgate Hill, London EC4	10,571	65,475
1859	Clay Cross Benefit, 42 Thanet St., Clay Cross, Chesterfield	3,190	9,554
1884	Coventry, P.O. Box 9, High Street, Coventry	363,989	1,243,071
1850	Cumberland, 38 Fisher St., Carlisle	108,437	298,963
1946	Darlington, Tubwell Row, Market Pl., Darlington, Co. Durham	37,008	162,773
1859	Derbyshire, Duffield Hall, Duffield, Derby	281,311	918,969
1858	Dudley, Dudley Hse., Stone St., Dudley, Worcs.	13,771	46,312
1869	Dunfermline, 12 East Port, Dunfermline, Fife.	93,000	395,288
1857	Earl Shilton, 22 The Hollow, Earl Shilton, Leicester	8,967	35,174
1877	Eastbourne Mut., Eastbourne Hse., 22 Gildredge Rd., Eastbourne, Sussex	53,149	254,010
1980	Ecology, 18 Station Rd., Cross Hills, Keighley, West Yorks BD20 8TT	1,411	3,141
1860	Frome Selwood P., 3 Market Pl., Frome, Som.	13,734	43,380
1865	Furness, 51–55 Duke Street, Barrow-in-Furness	59,099	196,738
1911	Gainsborough, 26 Lord St., Gainsborough, Lincs.	3,757	12,106
1852	Greenwich, 279–283 Greenwich High Rd., London SE10	29,394	119,267
1871	Guardian, Guardian Hse., 120 High Holborn, London WC1	66,727	1,126,954
1853	Halifax, Trinity Rd., Halifax, West Yorks	8,790,821	40,405,100
1866	Hampshire, Anchor Hse., Kingston Crescent, Portsmouth	14,892	77,971
1854	Hanley Econ., 42 Cheapside, Hanley, Stoke-on-Trent, Staffs.	29,094	106,154
1953	Harpenden, 14 Station Rd., Harpenden, Herts.	7,019	29,468
1890	Haywards Heath and Dt., 33 The Broadway, Haywards Heath, West Sussex	19,628	101,805
1863	Heart of England, 22–26 Jury St., Warwick	167,672	618,315
1926	Hendon, 9 Central Circus, Hendon, London NW4	3,489	25,838
1888	Herts. and Essex, 4 Market Sq., Bishop's Stortford, Herts.	3,418	18,210
1865	Hinckley, and Rugby, Upper Bond St., Hinckley, Leics.	35,569	155,331

* P. = Permanent; B. = Benefit. The words "Building Society" are the last words in every society's name.

Year Estab- lished	Name of Society (abbreviated)　　　　　Head Office	Share Investors	Assets Total £'000
1855	Holmesdale B., 43 Church St., Reigate, Surrey	6,693	40,060
1853	Ilkeston P., 24–26 South Street, Ilkeston, Derby	3,984	11,483
1849	Ipswich, 44 Upper Brook St., Ipswich	29,299	110,385
1888	Kent Reliance, Reliance Hse., Manor Rd, Chatham, Kent	44,516	166,073
1852	Lambeth, 118–120 Westminster Bridge Rd., London SE1	50,698	409,429
1872	Lancastrian, Sadler St., Middleton, Manchester	46,197	177,742
1853	Leamington Spa, Leamington House, Milverton Hill, Leamington Spa, Warws.	119,564	1,002,375
1875	Leeds and Holbeck, 105 Albion St., Leeds	233,450	1,164,628
1848	Leeds P., Permanent Hse., The Headrow, Leeds	3,189,314	10,219,400
1863	Leek United and Midlands, 50 St. Edward St., Leek, Staffs.	44,802	186,546
1876	Londonderry Provident, 7 Castle Street, Londonderry BT48 6HQ	950	3,629
1867	Loughborough P., 6 High St., Loughborough, Leics.	10,419	51,096
1877	Louth, Mablethorpe and Sutton P.B., 3 Eastgate, Louth, Lincs.	1,451	5,713
1922	Manchester, 18–20 Bridge St., Manchester	7,125	39,288
1870	Mansfield, Regent Hse., Regent St., Mansfield, Notts.	15,568	66,856
1870	Market Harborough, Welland Hse., The Sq., Market Harborough, Leics.	23,620	126,707
1860	Marsden, 6–20 Russell St., Nelson, Lancs.	30,868	161,702
1874	Melton Mowbray, 39 Nottingham St., Melton Mowbray, Leics.	29,774	134,229
1966	Mercantile, 75 Howard St., North Shields, Tyne and Wear	16,352	80,056
1880	Mid-Sussex, Mid-Sussex Hse., 66 Church Rd., Burgess Hill, Sussex	5,659	21,815
1869	Monmouthshire, John Frost Sq., Newport, Gwent	14,000	77,567
1866	Mornington, 158 Kentish Town Rd., London NW5	18,476	148,027
1869	National and Provincial, Provincial Hse., Bradford	1,396,314	7,508,863
1896	National Counties, Waterloo Hse., 147–153 High St., Epsom, Surrey	20,795	240,024
1884	Nationwide Anglia, Chesterfield Hse., Bloomsbury Way, London WC1	5,657,608	24,341,626
1856	Newbury, 17–20 Bartholomew St., Newbury, Berks.	25,072	136,022
1863	Newcastle, Grainger Chambers, Hood Street, Newcastle upon Tyne	112,490	618,828
1877	North of England, 57 Fawcett St., Sunderland	207,384	603,546
1850	Northern Rock, Northern Rock Hse., Gosforth, Newcastle upon Tyne	593,286	2,355,755
1852	Norwich and Peterborough, St. Andrew's Hse., St. Andrew St., Norwich, Norfolk	171,303	804,132
1850	Nottingham, 5–13 Upper Parliament St., Nottingham	124,222	349,174
1935	Nottingham Imperial, Imperial Bldg., 29 Bridgeford Rd., West Bridgeford, Nottingham	5,725	20,874
1879	Peckham Graylaw Hse., 1 Copers Cope Rd, Beckenham, Kent BR3 1MB	11,356	63,550
1877	Penrith, 7 King St., Penrith, Cumb.	7,437	33,045
1881	Portman, 40 Portman Sq., London W1	141,303	666,766
1896	Portsmouth, Churchill Hse., Winston Churchill Ave., Portsmouth	81,930	651,951
1860	Principality, Principality Bldgs., Queen St., Cardiff	208,604	642,564
1914	Progressive, 33–37 Wellington Place, Belfast BT1 6HH	28,004	141,275
1872	Regency and West of England, 130 Western Road, Hove, East Sussex BN3 1DR.	77,914	516,665
1849	Saffron Walden, Herts. and Essex, Market Place, Saffron Walden, Essex	25,041	115,089
1937	St. Pancras, 200 Finchley Rd., London NW3	9,674	70,935
1955	*St. Stephens, 70 Chepstow Road, London W2	382	1,561
1846	Scarborough, Prospect House, 442/444 Scalby Road, Scarborough, Yorks.	44,222	177,319
1848	Scottish, 23 Manor Place, Edinburgh	13,669	58,145
1935	Sheffield, 66 Campo Lane, Sheffield, Yorks.	3,087	15,514
1879	Shepshed, Bull Ring, Shepshed, Loughborough, Leics.	6,344	22,249
1853	Skipton, 59 High St., Skipton, Yorks.	183,313	1,258,033
1877	Stafford Railway, 4 Market Sq., Stafford	7,350	29,113
1902	Staffordshire, Jubilee Hse., P.O. Box 66, 84 Salop St., Wolverhampton	150,474	554,589
1875	Standard, 64 Church Way, North Shields, Tyne and Wear	2,318	10,999
1850	Stroud and Swindon, 7 Russell St., Stroud, Glos.	63,846	275,729
1903	Surrey, Sentinel Hse., 10–12 Massetts Rd., Horley, Surrey	8,768	68,307
1870	Sussex County, 40/42 Friars Walk, Lewes, East Sussex	87,211	411,986
1923	Swansea, 11 Cradock St., Swansea	3,217	15,961
1966	Teachers, Allenview Hse., Wimborne, Dorset	9,635	85,338
1901	Tipton and Coseley, 57–60 High St., Tipton, Staffs.	14,439	47,037
1853	Town and Country, 215 Strand, London WC2	212,601	1,644,193
1855	Tynemouth, 53–55 Howard St., North Shields, Tyne and Wear	6,250	28,126
1863	Universal, 41 Pilgrim St., Newcastle upon Tyne	24,070	111,452
1924	Vernon, 19 St. Petersgate, Stockport, Chesh.	17,068	60,275
1877	Walthamstow, 869 Forest Rd., Walthamstow, London E17	42,500	279,243
1949	Wessex, 115 Old Christchurch Rd., Bournemouth, Hants.	37,747	240,744
1849	West Bromwich, 374 High St., West Bromwich, Staffs.	270,002	715,225
1882	West Cumbria, Cumbria Hse., Murray Rd., Workington	6,325	24,397
1846	West of England, 25 High Street, Marlborough, Wilts SN8 1NF	151,077	623,857
1847	Woolwich Eq., Equitable Hse., London SE18	2,664,337	13,494,134
1885	Yorkshire, Yorkshire House, Westgate, Bradford	620,669	2,694,581

*Authorization to take money from public revoked May 1989.

THE COST OF LIVING

The first cost-of-living index to be calculated in Great Britain was the one which took July 1914 as 100 and was based on the pattern of expenditure of working class families in 1904. Since 1947 the Index of Retail Prices has superseded the cost-of-living index, although the older term is still often popularly applied to it. This index is designed to reflect the month-by-month changes in the average level of retail prices of goods and services purchased by the "majority" of households in the United Kingdom, including practically all wage-earners and most small and medium salary-earners. For spending coming within the scope of the index, a representative list of items is selected and the prices actually charged for these items are collected at regular intervals. In working out the index figure, the price changes are "weighted"—that is, given different degrees of importance—in accordance with the pattern of consumption of the average family.

A more widely used guide when considering changes in the average level of prices of all consumer goods and services, particularly over a number of years, is the consumer price index, now renamed the consumers' expenditure deflator. This index, which has been calculated back to 1938, covers the expenditure of all consumers as defined for national income purposes, and compares the price of goods and services actually purchased in a given year with the prices of the same goods and services in a base year.

During 1973 the Central Statistical Office constructed an annual index of prices of consumer goods and services over the period 1914 to 1972. This index has been constructed by linking together the pre-war cost of living index for the period 1914–1938, the consumers' expenditure deflator for the period 1938 and 1946–62* and the General Index of Retail Prices for the period 1962–1972.

In August 1979, the tax and price index (TPI) was introduced in order to provide a statistic which incorporates the effects of direct and indirect taxation, as well as prices, on taxpayers. The TPI is not directly concerned with the purchasing power of money, however, but with the purchasing power of pre-tax income. The General Index of Retail Prices thus retains its function of measuring the changes in the prices of goods and services purchased by households (from their post-tax income), and therefore as an indicator of the purchasing power of money.

	Long Term Index of Consumer Goods and Services Jan. 1974 = 100	Comparable Purchasing Power of £1 in 1988
1914	11·1	37·98
1915	13·7	30·77
1920	27·7	15·22
1925	19·6	21·50
1930	17·6	23·95
1935	15·9	26·51
1938	17·4	24·22
1946	29·4	14·34
1950	35·6	11·84
1955	44·1	9·56
1960	49·6	8·50
1965	58·4	7·21
1970	73·1	5·76
1971	80·0	5·27
1972	85·7	4·91
1973	93·5	4·50
1974	108·5	3·88
1975	134·8	3·12
1976	157·1	2·68
1977	182·0	2·31
1978	197·1	2·13
1979	223·5	1·88
1980	263·7	1·59
1981	295·0	1·42
1982	320·4	1·31
1983	335·1	1·25
1984	351·8	1·19
1985	373·2	1·12
1986	385·9	1·09
1987	401·9	1·04
1988	421·6	1·00

By employing this table an annual purchasing power of the pound index may be derived by taking the inverse of the price index. So, for example, if the purchasing power of the pound is taken to be 100p in 1972, then its comparable purchasing power in 1988 would be:

$$100 \times \frac{85 \cdot 7}{421 \cdot 6} = 20 \cdot 3p$$

It should be noted that these figures can only be approximate.

* There are no official figures for 1939–45.

INTEREST RATES – MORTGAGE AND SHARE

The interest rates prevailing on mortgage lending and share investment vary to a degree from society to society and in relation to the type or amount of loan or investment. The system whereby the Building Societies Association advised specific rates ceased in November 1984 and in April 1986 collective discussion, leading to a statement that a reduction or increase of a certain order was appropriate, was discontinued. General rate changes, however, continue in response to market conditions and the predominant rates in recent years, with the dates of change, are given below.

	March 1986	June 1986	Nov. 1986	May 1987	Jan. 1988	May 1988	Aug. 1988	Oct. 1988	Jan. 1989
Mortgages Ordinary	12·00	11·00	12·25–12·375	11·25	10·00–10·30	9·50–9·80	11·50	12·75	13·50
Shares	6·00	5·25	6·00	5·00	4·00	3·50	4·75	5·65	6·15

BANKING IN BRITAIN

The main institutions within the British banking system are the Bank of England (the central bank, see p. 303), the clearing banks (the major retail banks), the merchant banks, the overseas banks and the discount houses.

The clearing banks are Bank of Scotland, Barclays, Clydesdale, Co-operative, Coutts, Girobank, Lloyds, Midland, National Westminster, The Royal Bank of Scotland Group, the T.S.B. and the Yorkshire Bank.

Deposit-taking institutions may be broadly divided into the monetary sector which is predominantly banks and is supervised by the Bank of England, and those institutions outside the monetary sector of which the most important are the building societies and the National Savings Bank. The Banking Act 1987 established a single category of authorized institutions eligible to carry out banking business. There follows a list of authorized institutions as at August 25, 1989.

Authorized Institutions

U.K.—INCORPORATED
(Including partnerships formed under the law of any part of the U.K.)

A.N.Z. McCaughan Merchant Bank Ltd.
Abbey National P.L.C.
Abbey National Treasury Services P.L.C.
Adam & Company P.L.C.
Afghan National Credit & Finance Ltd.
Airdrie Savings Bank
Aitken Hume Ltd.
Ak International Bank Ltd.
Albaraka International Bank Ltd.
Alexanders Discount P.L.C.
Alliance Trust (Finance) Ltd.
Allied Arab Bank Ltd.
Anglo-Romanian Bank Ltd.
Anglo Yugoslav Bank Ltd.
Henry Ansbacher & Co. Ltd.
Arbuthnot Latham Bank Ltd.
Argonaut Securities Ltd.
Assemblies of God Property Trust
Associated Credits Ltd.
Associated Capital Corporation Ltd.
Associated Japanese Bank (International) Ltd.
Atlanta Trust Ltd.
Auban Finance Ltd.
Authority Bank Ltd.
Avco Trust Ltd.

B.N.L. Investment Bank P.L.C.
Banco Hispano Americano Ltd.
Bank in Liechtenstein (U.K.) Ltd.
Bank Leumi (U.K.) P.L.C.
Bank of America International Ltd.
Bank of Boston Ltd.
Bank of Cyprus (London) Ltd.
Bank of Scotland
Bank of Tokyo International Ltd.
Bank of Wales P.L.C.
Bankers Trust International Ltd.
Banque Belge Ltd.
Banque de la Méditerranée (U.K.) Ltd.
Banque Nationale de Paris P.L.C.
The Baptist Union Corporation Ltd.
Barclays Bank P.L.C.
Barclays de Zoete Wedd Ltd.
Barclays Bank Trust Company Ltd.
Baring Brothers & Co. Ltd.
Benchmark Bank P.L.C.
Beneficial Bank Ltd.
Birmingham Capital Trust P.L.C.
Boston Safe Deposit and Trust Company (U.K.) Ltd.
British and Commonwealth Merchant Bank P.L.C.
The British Bank of the Middle East
British Credit Trust Ltd.
The British Linen Bank Ltd.
British Railways Savings Company Ltd.
Brown, Shipley & Co. Ltd.
Bunge Finance Ltd.
Burns-Anderson Trust Company Ltd.
Business Mortgages Bank P.L.C.

Canadian Laurentian Bank Ltd.
James Capel Bankers Ltd.
Cater Allen Ltd.
Chancery P.L.C.
The Charities Aid Foundation Money Management Company Ltd.
Chartered Trust P.L.C.
Charterhouse Bank Ltd.
Chase Investment Bank Ltd.
Chesterfield Street Trust Ltd.
Citibank Trust Ltd.
Citicorp Investment Bank Ltd.
City Merchants Bank Ltd.
City Trust Ltd.
Clive Discount Company Ltd.
Close Brothers Ltd.
Clydesdale Bank P.L.C.
Clydesdale Bank Finance Corporation Ltd.
Combined Capital Ltd.
The Commerical Bank of the Near East P.L.C.
Confederation Bank Ltd.
Consolidated Credits Bank Ltd.
Co-operative Bank P.L.C.
Coutts & Co.
Coutts Finance Co.
Craneheath Securities Ltd.
Credito Italiano International Ltd.
Credit Suisse First Boston Ltd.

Daiwa Europe Bank P.L.C.
Dalbeattie Finance Co. Ltd.
Darlington Merchant Credits Ltd.
Dartington & Co. Ltd.
Deacon Hoare & Co. Ltd.
Den norske Creditbank P.L.C.
The Dorset, Somerset & Wilts Investment Society Ltd.
Dryfield Finance Ltd.
Duménil Ltd.
Dunbar Bank P.L.C.
Duncan Lawrie Ltd.

E.B.C. Amro Bank Ltd.
E.T. Trust Ltd.
Eagil Trust Co. Ltd.
East Trust Ltd.
Eccles Savings and Loans Ltd.
Edington P.L.C.
Enskilda Securities-Skandinaviska Enskilda Ltd.
Equatorial Bank P.L.C.
Euro-Latinamerican Bank P.L.C.
Everett Chettle Associates
Exeter Trust Ltd.

F.I.B.I. Bank (U.K.) Ltd.
Fairmount Trust Ltd.
Family Finance Ltd.
Federated Trust Corporation Ltd.

FennoScandia Bank Ltd.
Financial & General Bank P.L.C.
James Finlay Bank Ltd.
First Indemnity Credit Ltd.
First Interstate Capital Markets Ltd.
First National Bank P.L.C.
First National Commerical Bank P.L.C.
The First Personal Bank P.L.C.
Robert Fleming & Co. Ltd.
Ford Financial Trust Ltd.
Ford Motor Credit Co. Ltd.
Foreign & Colonial Management Ltd.
Forward Trust Ltd.
Robert Fraser & Partners Ltd.
Frizzell Banking Services Ltd.

Gartmore Money Management Ltd.
Gerrard & National Ltd.
Girobank P.L.C.
Goldman Sachs Ltd.
Goode Durrant Bank P.L.C.
Granville Trust Ltd.
Gresham Trust P.L.C.
Greyhound Bank P.L.C.
Grindlays Bank P.L.C.
Guinness Mahon & Co. Ltd.
Gulf Guarantee Bank P.L.C.

H.F.C. Bank P.L.C.
Habibsons Bank Ltd.
Hambros Bank Ltd.
Hampshire Trust P.L.C.
The Hardware Federation Finance Co. Ltd.
Harrods Bank Ltd.
Harton Securities Ltd.
Havana International Bank Ltd.
The Heritable & General Investment Bank Ltd.
Hill Samuel Bank Ltd.
Hill Samuel Personal Finance Ltd.
C. Hoare & Co.
Julian Hodge Bank Ltd.
Holdenhurst Securities P.L.C.
Humberclyde Finance Group Ltd.
Hungarian International Bank Ltd.

3i P.L.C.
3i Group P.L.C.
I.B.J. International Ltd.
Industrial Funding Trust Ltd.
International Commercial Bank P.L.C.
International Mexican Bank Ltd.
International Westminster Bank P.L.C.
Iran Overseas Investment Bank Ltd.
Italian International Bank P.L.C.

Jabac Finances Ltd.
Japan International Bank Ltd.
Jordan International Bank P.L.C.
Leopold Joseph & Sons Ltd.

King & Shaxson Ltd.
Kleinwort Benson Ltd.

Lazard Brothers & Co. Ltd.
Libra Bank P.L.C.
Little Lakes Finance Ltd.
Lloyds Bank P.L.C.
Lloyds Bank (B.L.S.A.) Ltd.
Lloyds Bank (France) Ltd.
Lloyds Bowmaker Ltd.
Lloyds Merchant Bank Ltd.
Lombard Bank Ltd.
Lombard & Ulster Ltd.
Lombard North Central P.L.C.
London Arab Investment Bank Ltd.
London & Continental Bankers Ltd.
London Italian Bank Ltd.
London Scottish Bank P.L.C.
Lordsvale Finance P.L.C.

M.L.A. Bank Ltd.
McDonnell Douglas Bank Ltd.
McNeill Pearson Ltd.
Manchester Exchange and Investment Bank Ltd.
W.M. Mann & Co. (Investments) Ltd.
Manufacturers Hanover Ltd.
The Mardun Investment Co. Ltd.
Marks and Spencer Financial Services Ltd.
Mase Westpac Ltd.
Matheson Bank Ltd.
Meghraj Bank Ltd.
Mercantile Credit Company Ltd.
Mercury Provident P.L.C.
Merrill Lynch International Bank Ltd.
The Methodist Chapel Aid Association Ltd.
Midland Bank P.L.C.
Midland Bank Finance Corporation Ltd.
Midland Bank Trust Company Ltd.
Minories Finance Ltd.
Minster Trust Ltd.
Moneycare Ltd.
Samuel Montagu & Co. Ltd.
Moorgate Mercantile Holdings P.L.C.
Morgan Grenfell & Co. Ltd.
Moscow Narodny Bank Ltd.
Mount Banking Corporation Ltd.
Mutual Trust and Savings Ltd.
Mynshul Bank Ltd.

N.I.I.B. Group Ltd.
N.W.S. Bank P.L.C.
National Guardian Mortgage Corporation Ltd.
The National Home Loans Bank P.L.C.
National Westminster Bank P.L.C.
NatWest Investment Bank Ltd.
The Nikko Bank (U.K.) P.L.C.
Noble Grossart Ltd.
Nomura Bank International P.L.C.
Northern Bank Ltd.
Northern Bank Executor & Trustee Company Ltd.
Norwich General Trust Ltd.

Omega Trust Co. Ltd.
Orion Royal Bank Ltd.

P.K. English Trust Company Ltd.
PaineWebber International Bank Ltd.
Panmure Gordon Bankers Ltd.
The People's Bank Ltd.
Philadelphia National Ltd.
Pointon York Ltd.
Postipankki (U.K.) Ltd.
Prestwick Investment Trust P.L.C.
Privatbanken Ltd.
The Private Bank and Trust Company Ltd.
Provincial Bank Ltd.

Quin Cope Ltd.

Ralli Investment Company Ltd.
R. Raphael & Sons P.L.C.
Rathbone Bros. & Co. Ltd.
Rea Brothers Ltd.
Reliance Bank Ltd.
Riggs A. P. Bank Ltd.
N. M. Rothschild & Sons Ltd.
Roxburghe Guarantee Corporation Ltd.
The Royal Bank of Scotland P.L.C.
Royal Trust Bank
RoyScot Trust P.L.C.

S.D.S. Bank Ltd.
S.F.E. Bank Ltd.
S.P. Finance Ltd.
Sangster Trust Corporation
Saudi International Bank (Al-Bank Al-Saudi Al-Alami Ltd.)
Scandinavian Bank Group P.L.C.
Schroder Leasing Ltd.
J. Henry Schroder Wagg & Co. Ltd.

Scotiabank (U.K.) Ltd.
Scottish Amicable Money Managers Ltd.
Seccombe Marshall & Campion P.L.C.
Secure Homes Ltd.
Security Pacific Trust Ltd.
Shire Trust Ltd.
Singer & Friedlander Ltd.
Smith & Williamson Securities
Société Générale Merchant Bank P.L.C.
Southsea Mortgage & Investment Co. Ltd.
Standard Chartered Bank
Standard Chartered Bank Africa P.L.C.
Standard Chartered Merchant Bank Ltd.
Standard Property Investment P.L.C.
Sterling Bank & Trust Ltd.
Svenska International P.L.C.

T.S.B. Bank P.L.C.
T.S.B. Northern Ireland P.L.C.
T.S.B. Scotland P.L.C.
Treloan Ltd.
Trucanda Trusts Ltd.

Tyndall & Co. Ltd.

U.B.A.F. Bank Ltd.
U.C.B. Bank P.L.C.
Ulster Bank Ltd.
Ulster Bank Trust Company
Union Discount Company Ltd.
The United Bank of Kuwait P.L.C.
Union Dominions Trust Ltd.
Unity Trust Bank P.L.C.

Wagon Finance Ltd.
Wallace, Smith Trust Co. Ltd.
S. G. Warburg & Co. Ltd.
S. G. Warburg Discount Ltd.
Western Trust & Savings Ltd.
Whiteaway Laidlaw Bank Ltd.
Wimbledon & South West Finance Co. Ltd.
Wintrust Securities Ltd.

Yamaichi Bank (U.K.) P.L.C.
Yorkshire Bank P.L.C.
H.F. Young & Co. Ltd.

INCORPORATED OUTSIDE THE U.K.

(Including partnerships or other unincorporated associations formed under the law of any member State of the European Community other than the U.K.)

A.S.L.K.—C.G.E.R. Bank
African Continental Bank Ltd.
Algemene Bank Nederland N.V.
Allied Bank of Pakistan Ltd.
Allied Banking Corporation
Allied Irish Banks P.L.C.
Allied Irish Finance Co. Ltd.
Allied Irish Investment Bank P.L.C.
American Express Bank Ltd.
Amsterdam-Rotterdam Bank N.V.
Arab African International Bank
Arab Bank Ltd.
Arab Banking Corporation B.S.C.
Australia & New Zealand Banking Group Ltd.

B.S.I.—Banca della Svizzera Italiana
Banca Commerciale Italiana
Banca Nazionale dell'Agricoltura SpA.
Banca Nazionale del Lavoro
Banca Popolare di Milano
Banca Serfin S.N.C.
Banco Bilbao–Vizcaya
Banco Central, S.A.
Banco de la Nación Argentina
Banco de Sabadell
Banco de Santander, S.A.
Banco di Napoli
Banco di Roma SpA.
Banco di Santo Spirito
Banco di Sicilia
Banco do Brasil S.A.
Banco do Estado de São Paulo S.A.
Banco Espirito Santo e Comercial de Lisboa
Banco Exterior—U.K. S.A.
Banco Mercantil de São Paulo S.A.
Banco Nacional de México S.N.C.
Banco Português do Atlântico
Banco Real S.A.
Banco Totta & Açores E.P.
Bancomer S.N.C.
Bangkok Bank Ltd.
Bank Julius Baer & Co. Ltd.
Bank Bumiputra Malaysia Berhad
Bank für Gemeinwirtschaft A.G.
Bank Handlowy w Warszawie S.A.
Bank Hapoalim B.M.
Bank Mees & Hope N.V.
Bank Mellat

Bank Melli Iran
Bank Negara Indonesia 1946
Bank of America N.T. & S.A.
Bank of Baroda
The Bank of California N.A.
Bank of Ceylon
Bank of China
Bank of Credit and Commerce International S.A.
The Bank of East Asia Ltd.
Bank of India
The Bank of Ireland
Bank of Montreal
Bank of New England N.A.
The Bank of New York
Bank of New Zealand
The Bank of Nova Scotia
Bank of Oman Ltd.
Bank of Seoul
The Bank of Tokyo Ltd.
The Bank of Yokohama Ltd.
Bank Saderat Iran
Bank Sepah-Iran
Bank Tejarat
Bankers Trust Company
Banque Arabe et Internationale d'Investissement
Banque Belgo-Zairoise S.A.
Banque Bruxelles Lambert S.A.
Banque du Liban et d'Outre-Mer S.A.L.
Banque Française de l'Orient
Banque Française du Commerce Extérieur
Banque Indosuez
Banque Internationale à Luxembourg S.A.
Banque Internationale pour L'Afrique Occidentale S.A.
Banque Nationale de Paris
Banque Paribas
Banque Worms
Barbados National Bank
Bayerische Hypotheken-und Wechsel-Bank A.G.
Bayerische Landesbank Girozentrale
Bayerische Vereinsbank
Beirut Riyad Bank S.A.L.
Bergen Bank A/S.
Berliner Bank A.G.
Berliner Handels-und Frankfurter Bank
Byblos Bank S.A.L.

C.I.C.-Union Européenne, International et Cie
Caisse Nationale de Crédit Agricole

Canadian Imperial Bank of Commerce
Canara Bank
Cassa di Risparmio delle Provincie Lombarde
The Chase Manhattan Bank N.A.
Chemical Bank
Cho Hung Bank
Christiania Bank og Kreditkasse
The Chuo Trust & Banking Co. Ltd.
Citibank N.A.
Commercial Bank of Korea Ltd.
Commerzbank A.G.
Commonwealth Bank of Australia
Confederacion Española de Cajas de Ahorros
Continental Bank, National Association
Copenhagen Handelsbank A/S
Crédit Commercial de France
Crédit du Nord
Crédit Lyonnais
Crédit Lyonnais Bank Nederland N.V.
Crédit Suisse
Creditanstalt-Bankverein
Credito Italiano
Cyprus Credit Bank Ltd.
The Cyprus Popular Bank

The Dai-Ichi Kangyo Bank Ltd.
The Daiwa Bank Ltd.
Den Danske Bank af 1871 Aktieselskab
Deutsche Bank A.G.
Deutsche Genossenschaftsbank
The Development Bank of Singapore Ltd.
Discount Bank and Trust Company
Dresdner Bank A.G.

Fidelity Bank N.A.
First Bank National Association
First Bank of Nigeria Ltd.
First City, Texas–Houston N.A.
First Commercial Bank
First Interstate Bank of California
The First National Bank of Boston
The First National Bank of Chicago
Fleet National Bank
French Bank of Southern Africa Ltd.
The Fuji Bank Ltd.

Generale Bank
Ghana Commercial Bank
Girozentrale und Bank der österreichischen Sparkassen A.G.
Götabanken
Gulf International Bank B.S.C.

Habib Bank A.G. Zurich
Habib Bank Ltd.
Hamburgische Landesbank Girozentrale
Hanil Bank
Harris Trust and Savings Bank
Hessische Landesbank-Girozentrale
The Hokkaido Takushoku Bank Ltd.
The Hongkong and Shanghai Banking Corporation

The Industrial Bank of Japan Ltd.
The Investment Bank of Ireland Ltd.
Irving Trust Company
Istituto Bancario San Paolo di Torino

Jyske Bank

Kansallis-Osake-Pankki
Keesler Federal Credit Union
Korea Exchange Bank
Korea First Bank
Kredietbank N.V.
The Kyowa Bank Ltd.

The Long-Term Credit Bank of Japan Ltd.

Malayan Banking Berhad
Manufacturers Hanover Trust Company
Mellon Bank N.A.

Middle East Bank Ltd.
The Mitsubishi Bank Ltd.
The Mitsubishi Trust and Banking Corporation
The Mitsui Bank Ltd.
The Mitsui Trust & Banking Co. Ltd.
Monte dei Paschi di Siena
Morgan Guaranty Trust Company of New York
Multibanco Comermex S.N.C.

N.C.N.B. National Bank of North Carolina
N.C.N.B. Texas National Bank
National Australia Bank Ltd.
National Bank of Abu Dhabi
National Bank of Canada
National Bank of Detroit
The National Bank of Dubai Ltd.
National Bank of Egypt
National Bank of Greece S.A.
The National Bank of Kuwait S.A.K.
The National Bank of New Zealand Ltd.
National Bank of Nigeria Ltd.
The National Commercial Bank
National Bank of Pakistan
Nederlandsche Middenstandsbank N.V.
NedPerm Bank Ltd.
New Nigeria Bank Ltd.
The Nippon Credit Bank Ltd.
Norddeutsche Landesbank Girozentrale
The Northern Trust Company

Österreichische Länderbank A.G.
Oversea-Chinese Banking Corporation Ltd.
Overseas Trust Bank Ltd.
Overseas Union Bank Ltd.

Philadelphia National Bank
Philippine National Bank
Provinsbanken A/S

Qatar National Bank S.A.Q.

Rabobank Nederland (Coöperatieve Centrale Raiffeisen-Boerenleenbank B.A.)
Rafidain Bank
Republic National Bank of New York
Reserve Bank of Australia
The Riggs National Bank of Washington D.C.
Riyad Bank
The Royal Bank of Canada
The Rural and Industries Bank of Western Australia

The Saitama Bank Ltd.
The Sanwa Bank Ltd.
Saudi American Bank
Seattle–First National Bank
Security Pacific National Bank
Shanghai Commercial Bank Ltd.
The Siam Commercial Bank Ltd.
Skandinaviska Enskilda Banken
Société Générale
Sonali Bank
State Bank of India
State Bank of New South Wales
State Bank of South Australia
State Bank of Victoria
State Street Bank and Trust Company
Südwestdeutsche Landesbank Girozentrale
The Sumitomo Bank Ltd.
The Sumitomo Trust & Banking Co. Ltd.
Svenska Handelsbanken
Swiss Bank Corporation
Swiss Cantobank (International)
Swiss Volksbank
Sydicate Bank

T.C. Ziraat Bankasi
T.D.B. American Express Bank
The Taiyo Kobe Bank Ltd.
The Thai Farmers Bank Ltd.
The Tokai Bank, Ltd.

The Toronto-Dominion Bank
The Toyo Trust & Banking Company Ltd.
The Trust Bank of Africa Ltd.
Turkish Bank Ltd.
Türkiye Iş Bankasi A.S.

Uco Bank
Ulster Investment Bank Ltd.
Union Bank of Finland Ltd.
Union Bank of Nigeria Ltd.
Union Bank of Norway
Union Bank of Switzerland
United Bank Ltd.

United Mizrahi Bank Ltd.
United Overseas Bank (Banque Unie pour les Pays d'Outre Mer)
United Overseas Bank Ltd.

Volkskas Bank Ltd.

Westdeutsche Landesbank Girozentrale
Westpac Banking Corporation

The Yasuda Trust & Banking Co. Ltd.

Zambia National Commerical Bank Ltd.
Zivnostenská Banka National Corporation

BANKING HOURS

England and Wales.—Mon.–Fri. 9.30–3.30*; *City of London town clearers*, 9.30–3.00; Saturdays (selected branches open): Barclays, 9.30–12.00; Lloyds, 9.30–12.30 or 10.00–3.00; Midland and National Westminster, 9.30–12.30; T.S.B., 9.30–4.00.

Scotland.—Banking hours in Scotland are: Mon.–Wed., 9.30–12.30; 1.30–3.30; Thursday, 9.30–12.30; 1.30–3.30; 4.30–6 p.m.; Friday, 9.30–3.30; Saturday, *closed*.

Northern Ireland.—Mon.–Fri. 10.00–3.30; 9.30 opening two mornings per week. Open until 5.00 one summer evening per week.

* Still the minimum banking hours but many banks are experimenting with longer hours (usually 9.15–4.30). The Co-operative Bank remains open until 5.00.

FINANCIAL FIGURES, ETC. FOR CLEARING BANKS, 1988

(1987 figures in parentheses)

Bank Group	Profit/loss before taxation £m	Profit/loss after taxation £m	Total Asssets £m	Number of U.K. branches
Bank of Scotland	131·3	81·9	11,005	530
Barclays	1,391 (339)	893 (191)	104,645 (87,786)	2,900 (3,000)
Clydesdale	29·78*	18·705*	3,560·600	355
Coutts & Co.	15	9·8	3,513·5	19
Lloyds†	−248 (700)	−224 (470)	44,910 (47,829)	2,189
Midland	693 (−505)	420 (−447)	55,729 (48,450)	1,980 (2,080)
National Westminster	1,407 (704)	938 (442)	98,642 (87,027)	3,100 (3,200)
The Royal Bank of Scotland Group	309·2	194·1	21,700	850
Yorkshire Bank	100·4	63·9	3,185·5	247

*9 month period   †1987 (1986) figures

GIROBANK

Girobank provides a broad range of corporate and personal banking facilities. Girobank is expected to be privatized at the end of 1989.

OPERATING STATISTICS	1987–88	1988–89
Number of accounts at year end, thousands	2,134	21,148
Pre-tax profit, £m	23·5	21·6

BANKING SERVICES

Association for Payment Clearing Services (APACS)
Mercury House, Triton Court, 14 Finsbury Square, EC2A 1BR.

APACS was set up by the banks in 1985 to manage the payment clearing systems and oversee money transmission in the U.K.

Three operational clearing companies operate under the aegis of APACS. They are:

B.A.C.S. LTD., De Havilland Road, Edgware, Middx. HA8 5QA.—Provides an automated service for inter-bank clearing of payment and collection transactions in the U.K. (e.g. standing orders, direct debits). *Chief Exec.*, G. R. Simpson.

CHEQUE AND CREDIT CLEARING CO. LTD., Mercury House, Triton Court, 14 Finsbury Square, EC2A 1BR.—Operates bulk clearing systems for inter-bank cheques and paper credit items. *Chief Inspector*, E. W. Stubbs.

C.H.A.P.S. AND TOWN CLEARING CO. LTD., Mercury House, Triton Court, 14 Finsbury Square, EC2A 1BR.—Provides same-day clearing for high value cheques and electronic funds transfer. *Chief Inspector*, E. W. Stubbs.

In addition, EftPos U.K. Ltd. is a company within the APACS structure set up to develop a national scheme for electronic funds transfer at the point of sale. APACS also oversees the London Dollar Clearing, the London Currency Settlement Scheme and the Cheque Card and eurocheque schemes in the U.K.

Membership of APACS and the operational clearing companies is open to any appropriately regulated institution providing payment services and meeting the relevant membership criteria.
Chief Executive, R. I. L. Allen.

Committee of London and Scottish Bankers
10 Lombard Street, EC3V 9AP
[01-283 8866]

The Committee is the successor to the Committee of London Clearing Bankers. It consists of the Chairmen of Barclays, Lloyds, Midland, National Westminster, Standard Chartered, Bank of Scotland, Royal Bank of Scotland and the T.S.B. Group, and meets regularly to discuss matters of common interest. It is the body through which the Bank of England communicates official policy to the banks and through which the banks may present their views to the Bank of England and the Treasury.
Secretary-General, The Hon. R. C. R. Hoyer Millar.

FINANCIAL OMBUDSMEN
The following Ombudsmen schemes are non-statutory.

The Office of the Banking Ombudsman
Citadel House, 5–11 Fetter Lane, EC4A 1BR
[01-583 1395]

The purpose of the Banking Ombudsman Scheme is to investigate complaints from bank customers dissatisfied with the banking services of member banks. The Scheme was set up in 1985, becoming operational on Jan. 1, 1986, by 19 banks and it is funded by contributions from the member banks (19 banks and 21 designated associates). There is a seven-member Council who appoint the Ombudsman, give guidance in the performance of his duties, monitor his terms of reference, prepare the budget and approve the annual report. The Ombudsman and his staff are responsible to the Council.
The Banking Ombudsman, L. Shurman.

The Office of the Building Societies Ombudsman
Grosvenor Gardens House, 35–37 Grosvenor Gardens, SW1X 7AW
[01-931 0044]

The purpose of the Building Societies Ombudsman Scheme, which came into operation on July 1, 1987, is to investigate complaints from building society customers about the services of building societies belonging to the Scheme. All building societies belong to the Scheme and it is funded by contributions from the members. The Ombudsman is appointed by and responsible to an independent Ombudsman Council.
The Building Society Ombudsman, S. Edell.

The Insurance Ombudsman Bureau
31 Southampton Row, WC1B 5HJ
[01-242 8613]

The purpose of the Insurance Ombudsman Scheme is to settle disputes between insurance policyholders and member insurance companies. The Scheme came into operation in March 1981 and is funded by contributions from the member companies. Over 300 companies are members of the Scheme. An independent Council appoints and supervises the work of the Ombudsman.

The Insurance Ombudsman Bureau also runs the Unit Trust Ombudsman Scheme, the purpose of which is to settle disputes between personal unit trust holders and member unit trust management companies. The Unit Trusts Ombudsman scheme came into operation in October 1988.
The Insurance Ombudsman, Dr. J. Farrand.
The Unit Trust Ombudsman, C. A. H. Parsons.

THE NATIONAL DEBT

Net central government borrowing each year represents an addition to the National Debt. At the end of March 1988 the National Debt amounted to some £197,500 million of which about £4,500 million was in currencies other than sterling. Of the £193,000 million sterling debt, £144,000 million consisted of gilt-edged stock; of this, 29 per cent had a maturity of up to five years, 43 per cent a maturity of over five years and up to 15 years and 28 per cent a maturity of over 15 years or undated. The remaining sterling debt was made up mainly of national savings (£29,000 million), certificates of tax deposits, Treasury bills, and Ways and Means advances (very short-term internal government borrowing).

The sizable Trust Funds have been established over the past fifty years for the purpose of reducing the National Debt. The National Fund was established in 1927 with an original gift of £499,878. At March 31, 1987 it was valued at £55,628,556; it is administered by Baring Brothers & Co. Ltd. The Elsie Mackay Fund was established in 1929 with an original gift of £527,809 to run for 45–50 years. It was wound up on January 19, 1979, when it was valued at £4,902,864. The John Buchanan Fund was established in 1932 with gifts totalling £36,702 to run for 50 years. It was wound up on February 28, 1982, when it was valued at £204,138.

NATIONAL SAVINGS

PREMIUM BONDS

Premium Bonds are a Government security which were first introduced on November 1, 1956. Premium Bonds enable savers to enter a regular draw for tax-free prizes, whilst retaining the right to get their money back. A sum equivalent to interest on each bond is put into a prize fund and distributed by weekly and monthly prize draws. (The rate of interest is 6·5 per cent. a year from July 1, 1988). The prizes are drawn by ERNIE (electronic random number indicator equipment) and are free of all U.K. income tax and capital gains tax.

Bonds are in units of £1, with a minimum purchase of £100; above this, purchases must be in multiples of £10, up to a maximum holding limit of £10,000 per person. The exception to this is that the minimum purchase by parents, guardians and grandparents for children under 16 is £10. Bonds can only be held in the name of an individual and not by organizations.

Bonds become eligible for prizes once they have been held for three clear calendar months following the month of purchase. Each £1 unit can win only one prize per draw, but it will be awarded the highest for which it is drawn. Bonds remain eligible for prizes until they are repaid. When a holder dies, bonds remain eligible for prizes up to and including the twelfth monthly draw after the month in which the holder dies.

By April 1989 bonds to the value of £4,520 million had been sold. Of these £2,238 million had been cashed, leaving £2,282 million still invested. By the April 1989 prize draw, 32·4 million prizes totalling £1,888 million had been distributed since the first prize draw in June 1957.

INCOME BONDS

National Savings Income Bonds were introduced in 1982. They are particularly suitable for those who want to receive regular monthly payments of interest while preserving the full cash value of their capital. The Bonds are sold in multiples of £1,000. The minimum holding is £2,000 and the maximum £100,000.

Interest is calculated on a day-to-day basis and paid monthly. Interest is taxable, but is paid without deduction of tax at source. The Bonds have a guaranteed life of ten years, but may be repaid at par before maturity on giving three months' notice. If repayment of a bond is made within the first year of purchase, interest from the date of purchase to the date of repayment is earned at half rate. If the sole or sole surviving holder dies, however, no formal period of notice is required and there is no loss of interest for repayment made within the first year.

Net investment in National Savings Income Bonds was £7,814,538,000 at the end of April 1989.

INDEXED INCOME BONDS

Indexed Income Bonds were withdrawn from sale on August 28, 1987. Existing holders will continue to receive monthly income in accordance with the prospectus.

ORDINARY AND INVESTMENT ACCOUNTS

National Savings Bank.—On May 31, 1989, there were about 15,754,000 active accounts with the sum of approximately £1,632 million due to depositors in Ordinary accounts and about 4,423,000 active accounts with the sum of approximately £7,724 million due to depositors in Investment accounts.

Interest is earned at 5 per cent per year on each Ordinary account for every complete calendar month in which the balance is £500 or more, provided the account is kept open for the whole of 1989 (December 31, 1988—January 1, 1990); and at 2·5 per cent per year for other months or for accounts opened or closed during 1989. The minimum deposit is £5; maximum balance £10,000 plus interest credited. On May 31, 1989 the average amount held in Ordinary accounts was approximately £104.

The Investment account pays a higher rate of interest (the current rate can be ascertained at any Savings Bank Post Office). The minimum deposit is £5; maximum balance £100,000 plus interest credited. On May 31, 1989 the average amount held in Investment accounts was approximately £1,746.

CAPITAL BONDS

National Savings Capital Bonds were introduced on January 4, 1989. For personal savers Capital Bonds offer capital growth over five years with guaranteed returns at fixed rates. Each year the interest rate rises. To get the best return the Bond should be held for the full five years. The interest is taxable each year (for those who pay income tax) but is not deducted at source. The minimum purchase is £100, with larger purchases in multiples of £100. There is no maximum holding limit.

Capital Bonds will be repaid in full with all interest gained at the end of five years. Early repayment may be obtained at three months notice. No interest is earned on Bonds repaid in the first year.

DEPOSIT BONDS

National Savings Deposit Bonds were withdrawn from sale on November 19, 1988. All Deposit Bonds purchased on or before that date may continue to be held until the tenth anniversary of purchase. They will continue to earn interest until then.

YEARLY PLAN

The National Savings "Yearly Plan" was introduced on July 2, 1984. It offers a guaranteed tax-free return. Applicants agree to make 12 monthly payments, leading to the issue of a Yearly Plan Certificate. The maximum guaranteed rate of interest is earned if the Certificate is held for a full four years. Applications may be made by any individuals aged 7 or over; in the name of children under 7; and by not more than two trustees for a sole beneficiary.

Payments must be made on the same date every month by standing order from a bank or other acceptable account. Only one payment may be made in any one month and must be in multiples of £5. Minimum monthly contribution is £20, maximum £200. Net investment in National Savings Yearly Plan was £556,792,705 at May 31, 1989.

On receipt of an application the applicant is sent an Offer Letter telling him the interest rates he will receive on his agreement if he accepts. The Certificate is sent at the end of the first year. It shows the total value of the payments made and the value of the Certificate if held for four years. The Certificate earns interest compounded annually on the anniversaries of the Certificate Date. Maximum interest is earned if the Certificate is held for the full four years. At the end of each year, providing at least seven payments have been made during that year, the applicant is given the option to take up a subsequent agreement, leading to the issue of a further Certificate.

GILTS ON THE NATIONAL SAVINGS STOCK REGISTER

Government Stock or "Gilts" are stock Exchange Securities issued by the Government. They usually have a life of between 5 and 20 years and most pay a guaranteed fixed rate of interest twice a year throughout this period. When they reach the end of this period they are "redeemed" (which means repaid) at their face value. There are also a few "undated" Gilts with no set date for redemption and some Index-Linked Gilts, which have both the interest and the value of the capital on redemption increased in line with inflation.

The National Savings Stock Register offers investors an alternative to the main Bank of England Register and is run by National Savings from their Blackpool office. It enables customers to buy and sell Gilts by post. It is now possible to have most new issues of Gilts registered on the National Savings Stock Register. Customers have also been given the option of participating in the recent Bank of England reverse auctions. Interest on Gilts held on the National Savings Stock Register, although taxable, is paid in full without deduction of tax at source.

NATIONAL SAVINGS CERTIFICATES

The amount, including accrued interest, index-linked increase or bonus remaining to the credit of investors in National Savings Certificates on March 31, 1989 was approximately £15,456·6 million. In 1988–89, approx. £2,165·7 million was subscribed and £2,523·1 million (excluding interest, index-linked increase or bonus) was repaid. Interest, index-linked increase, bonus or other sum payable is free of United Kingdom income tax (including investment income surcharge) and capital gains tax. The 1st–14th and 16th issues continue to attract interest.

Issue and Maximum Holding (in units)	Unit Cost £	Value after		Interest Per Unit
		Years	£ p	
Index-Linked Retirement Issue (June 2, 1975–Nov. 15, 1980) (120)	10			Unlike conventional issues where interest is accrued periodically the repayment value of Index-Linked Certificates, subject to their being held a year, is related to the movement of the U.K. General Index of Retail Prices.** N.B. Certificates of the Retirement Issue were on sale only to men aged 65 years and over and women aged 60 years and over, but may now be transferred to anyone.
Eighteenth .... (Jan. 29, 1979–Feb. 2, 1980) (150)	10	5	15·00	After 1 year, 50p is added, during 2nd year, 25p per completed 4 months, during 3rd year, 33p per completed 4 months, during 4th year, 42p per completed 4 months, during 5th year, 50p per completed 4 months.†
Nineteenth .... (Feb. 4, 1980–May 9, 1981) (500)	10	5	16·35	After 1 year 50p is added, during 2nd year 30p per completed 4 months, during 3rd year 35p per completed 4 months, during 4th year 55p per completed 4 months and during 5th year 75p per completed 4 months.†
2nd Index-Linked Issue (Nov. 17, 1980–June 29, 1985) (1,000)	10			Like Retirement Issue, the repayment value of 2nd Index-Linked Issue Certificates, subject to their being held a year, is related to the movement of the U.K. General Index of Retail Prices.** N.B. Certificates of the 2nd Index-Linked Issue were made available to anyone, regardless of age, from September 7, 1981.
Twenty-first .... Issue (May 11, 1981–Nov. 7, 1981) (500)	10	5	15·40	After 1 year, 75p is added, during 2nd year, 28p per completed 4 months, during 3rd year, 33p per completed 4 months, during 4th year, 40p per completed 4 months and during 5th year 54p per completed 4 months.†
Twenty-third .... (Nov. 9, 1981–March 10, 1982) (200)	25	5	41·20	After 1 year, £2·25 is added, during 2nd year, 87p per completed 4 months, during 3rd year, £1·02 per completed 4 months, during 4th year, £1·23 per completed 4 months and during 5th year £1·53 per completed 4 months.†
Twenty-fourth ...... (April 19, 1982–Nov. 4, 1982) (200)	25	5	38·32	After 1 year, £1·80 is added, during 2nd year, 53p per completed 3 months, during 3rd year, 63p per completed 3 months, during 4th year, 77p per completed 3 months and during 5th year 95p per completed 3 months.†
Twenty-fifth .... (Nov. 17, 1982–Aug. 13, 1983) (200)	25	5	35·90	After 1 year, £1·50 is added, during 2nd year, 43p per completed 3 months, during 3rd year, 51p per completed 3 months, during 4th year, 62p per completed 3 months and during 5th year 79p per completed 3 months.†
Twenty-sixth .... (Aug. 15, 1983–Mar. 19, 1984) (200)	25	5	37·17	After 1 year, £1·53 is added, during 2nd year, 47p per completed 3 months, during 3rd year, 58p per completed 3 months, during 4th year, 72p per completed 3 months and during 5th year 89p per completed 3 months.†

Issue and Maximum Holding (in units)	Unit Cost £	Value after		Interest Per Unit
		Years	£ p	
Twenty-seventh .... (April 5, 1984–Aug. 7, 1984) (200)	25	5	35·48	After 1 year, £1·32 is added, during 2nd year, 41p per completed 3 months, during 3rd year, 50p per completed 3 months, during 4th year, 62p per completed 3 months and during 5th year 76p per completed 3 months.†
Twenty-eighth ...... (Aug. 8, 1984–Sept. 11, 1984) (200)	25	5	38·47	After 1 year, £1·63 is added, during 2nd year, 51p per completed 3 months, during 3rd year, 64p per completed 3 months, during 4th year, 80p per completed 3 months and during 5th year £1·01 per completed 3 months.*
Twenty-ninth....... (Oct. 15, 1984–Feb. 12, 1985) (200)	25	5	36·74	After 1 year, £1·50 is added, during 2nd year, 46p per completed 3 months, during 3rd year, 56p per completed 3 months, during 4th year, 69p per completed 3 months and during 5th year 85p per completed 3 months.*
Thirtieth........... (Feb. 13, 1985–Sept. 9, 1985) (200)	25	5	38·21	After 1 year, £1·69 is added, during 2nd year, 50p per completed 3 months, during 3rd year, 62p per completed 3 months, during 4th year, 78p per completed 3 months and during 5th year 98p per completed 3 months.*
3rd Index-Linked Issue (July 1, 1985–July 31, 1986) (200)	25			Like 2nd Issue Index-Linked Certificates, the repayment value of 3rd Issue Index-Linked Certificates, subject to their being held for one year, is related to the movement of the U.K. General Index of Retail Prices.** In addition, there is guaranteed extra interest of 2·5 per cent for the 1st year, 2·75 per cent for the 2nd year, 3·25 per cent for the 3rd year, 4·0 per cent for the 4th year and 5·25 per cent for the 5th year. This interest is worth 3·54 per cent compound over a full five years.
Thirty-first......... (Sept. 26, 1985–Nov. 11, 1986) (200)	25	5	36·48	After 1 year, £1·44 is added, during 2nd year, 44p per completed 3 months, during 3rd year, 55p per completed 3 months, during 4th year, 68p per completed 3 months and during 5th year, 84p per completed 3 months.*
4th Index-Linked Issue (Aug. 1, 1986–) (200)	25			Like 3rd Issue Index-Linked Certificates, the repayment value of 4th Issue Index-Linked Certificates, subject to their being held for one year, is related to the movement of the U.K. General Index of Retail Prices.** In addition, there is guaranteed extra interest of 3·0 per cent for the 1st year, 3·25 per cent for the 2nd year, 3·5 per cent for the 3rd year, 4·5 per cent for the 4th year, and 6·0 per cent for the 5th year. This interest is worth 4·04 per cent compound over a full five years.
Thirty-second....... (Nov. 12, 1986–March 10, 1987) (200)	25	5	38·03	After 1 year, £1·63 is added, during 2nd year, 50p per completed 3 months, during 3rd year, 62p per completed 3 months, during 4th year, 77p per completed 3 months and during 5th year, 96p per completed 3 months.*
Thirty-third .... (May 1, 1987–July 21, 1988) (40, plus special facilities to hold up to a further 200)	25	5	35·06	After 1 year, the repayment value increases by 5·5 per cent for ordinarily held 33rd Issue. However, 33rd Reinvestment Certificates earn interest during the 1st year at the rate of 5·5 per cent per annum for each 3 month period. Thereafter all 33rd Issue earn 5·75 per cent after 2 years, 6·0 per cent after 3 years, 6·5 per cent after 4 years and 7·0 per cent after 5 years.*
Thirty-fourth .... (July 22, 1988–) (40, plus special facilities to hold up to a further 200. Special facility extended to 400 units with effect from Oct. 15, 1988)	25	5	35·89	After 1 year, the repayment value increases by 6·0 per cent for ordinarily held 34th Issue. However, 34th Reinvestment certificates earn interest during the 1st year at the rate of 6·0 per cent per annum for each 3 month period. Thereafter, all 34th Issue earn 6·25 per cent after two years, 6·5 per cent after 3 years, 7·0 per cent after 4 years, and 7·5 per cent after 5 years.*

* As announced by the Treasury. † From June 1982, 7th–14th, 16th, 18th, 19th, 21st, 23rd to 27th Issues will be extended on General Extension Rates determined by the Treasury. ** Index-linked certificates are eligible for an annual supplement of 1·5 per cent for the year to August 1, 1989.

TAXATION

INCOME TAX

Income tax is charged on the total income of individuals for a year of assessment commencing on April 6 and ending on the following April 5. The rates of tax and the calculation of liability will frequently differ, sometimes substantially, as between one year of assessment and another. The following information is confined to the year of assessment 1989–90, ending on April 5, 1990. A note appears on page 1009 outlining the new system of independent taxation of husband and wife which commences on April 6, 1990.

Liability is determined by establishing the taxable income for a year of assessment. The income will be reduced by an individual's personal allowances and other reliefs. The first £20,700 of taxable income remaining is assessable to income tax at the basic rate of 25 per cent, with any excess over this amount taxable at the higher rate of 40 per cent.

The two rates apply to the assessment of both earned and investment income. Indeed there is little distinction between the two classes, although the receipt of earned income may produce an entitlement to some allowances not available against investment income.

The tables on the following two pages show the income tax payable for 1989–90 by an individual on the amount of income specified, after deducting the personal allowance and age allowance. Elderly persons over the age of 74 years may suffer less tax. The taxpayer may also be entitled to further reliefs and allowances which reduce the tax payable below the amount shown in the tables.

Trustees administering settled property are chargeable to income tax at the basic rate of 25 per cent. Where the trustees retain discretionary powers, or income is accumulated, there will also be liability to the additional rate of 10 per cent. Companies residing in the United Kingdom are not liable to income tax but suffer corporation tax on income, profits and gains.

The charge to income tax broadly arises on all taxable income accruing from sources in the United Kingdom. Individuals who are resident in this territory may also become liable on income arising overseas. An individual is resident in the United Kingdom if he or she normally resides here. Persons not normally residing in the United Kingdom may become resident if they visit this territory for periods which average three months or more throughout a period of years, or are present for at least 183 days in a particular year. The existence of a place of abode in the United Kingdom may be sufficient to indicate residence if visits of any duration are made during the year of assessment.

Income arising overseas will often incur liability to foreign taxation. If that income is also chargeable to United Kingdom income tax, excessive liability may well arise. The United Kingdom has concluded Double Taxation Agreements with many overseas territories which ensure that the same slice of income is not doubly assessed. In the absence of such an agreement, foreign tax suffered can usually be relieved when calculating liability to United Kingdom income tax.

INCOME TAXABLE

Income tax is assessed and collected under several Schedules. Each Schedule determines the extent of liability and establishes the amount to be included in taxable income. In some instances the actual income arising in a year of assessment will be charged to income tax for that year. A different basis of assessment may arise for income taxable under Cases I to V of Schedule D. Frequently, income assessable under these Cases will be that arising in a previous year or period but there are special rules where a new source is acquired or an existing source discontinued.

Following the withdrawal of income tax liability for most commercial woodlands in the United Kingdom, Schedule B ceased to apply from April 6, 1988. The contents of the remaining schedules are shown below.

Schedule A.—Tax is charged on annual profits from the ownership or occupation of land in the United Kingdom. This will include rents, ground rents and other income arising from land. Expenditure incurred by the landlord on maintenance, repairs, insurance and management can be subtracted from the annual profits. This Schedule does not include profits from farming, market gardening or woodlands, nor does it extend to mineral rents and royalties. Premiums arising on the grant of a lease for a period not exceeding fifty years are assessed to income tax. However, the amount of the taxable premium may be reduced by 2 per cent for each complete year, after the first year, of the leasing period. Income from furnished lettings is assessable under Case VI of Schedule D, unless an option is exercised for such income to be assessed under Schedule A. Where income arises from furnished holiday lettings additional expenditure may be included in calculating income chargeable to tax. Income from holiday lettings is treated as earned income.

Schedule C.—This Schedule is confined to interest or dividends on Government or public authority funds and certain payments made out of the public revenues of overseas countries.

Schedule D.—This Schedule is divided into six Cases as follows:

Cases I and II.—Profits arising from trades, professions and vocations, including farming and market gardening. Capital expenditure incurred on assets used for business purposes will often produce an entitlement to capital allowances which reduce the profits chargeable. These profits may also be reduced following the submission of claims for loss relief and other matters.

Case III.—Interest on Government Stocks not taxed at source (e.g. War Loan and British Savings Bonds), interest on National Savings Bank deposits and discounts. Interest up to £70 on ordinary National Savings Bank deposits is exempt from income tax. The exemption applies to both husband and wife separately. Interest on National Savings Bank Special Investment Accounts is not exempt.

Cases IV and V.—Interest from overseas securities, rents, dividends and all other income accruing outside the United Kingdom. Assessment is based on the full amount of income arising, whether remitted to the United Kingdom or retained overseas, but individuals who are either not domiciled in the United Kingdom or who are ordinarily resident overseas may apply the remittance basis. Overseas pensions are taxable but the amount arising may be reduced by 10 per cent for assessment purposes.

(1) Single Persons

Income	Persons under 65		Persons 65 or over*	
	Income Tax	Average Rate	Income Tax	Average Rate
£	£	per cent	£	per cent
3,000	54	1·8	—	—
4,000	304	7·6	150	3·8
5,000	554	11·1	400	8·0
6,000	804	13·4	650	10·8
7,000	1,054	15·1	900	12·9
8,000	1,304	16·3	1,150	14·4
9,000	1,554	17·3	1,400	15·6
10,000	1,804	18·0	1,650	16·5
12,000	2,304	19·2	2,225	18·5
14,000	2,804	20·0	2,804	20·0
16,000	3,304	20·6	3,304	20·6
18,000	3,804	21·1	3,804	21·1
20,000	4,304	21·5	4,304	21·5
25,000	5,781	23·1	5,781	23·1
30,000	7,781	25·9	7,781	25·9
40,000	11,781	29·5	11,781	29·5
50,000	15,781	31·6	15,781	31·6
100,000	35,781	35·8	35,781	35·8

* Persons aged 75 or over suffer rather less tax on income falling below £14,000 on this table.

Case VI.—Sundry profits and annual receipts not assessed under any other Case or Schedule. These may include insurance commissions, post-cessation receipts and numerous other receipts specifically charged under Case VI.

Schedule E.—All emoluments from an office or employment are assessable under this Schedule. There are three Cases as follows:

Case I.—This applies to all emoluments of an individual resident and ordinarily resident in the United Kingdom.

Case II.—Of application where the individual is not resident or not ordinarily resident and extends to emoluments for duties undertaken in the United Kingdom.

Case III.—Applies in rare situations to other emoluments remitted to the United Kingdom.

Although earnings for overseas duties may be assessable under Case I where the employee is resident and ordinarily resident in the United Kingdom, a deduction of 100 per cent may be available, which reduces the overseas assessable earnings to nil. This deduction can be obtained where duties are performed overseas for a continuous period reaching or exceeding 365 days and is confined to earnings from the overseas activity.

For years up to and including that ending on April 5, 1989, alternative methods could be used to calculate the emoluments for a year of assessment. However, these methods ceased to apply from April 6, 1989 and were replaced by a new 'receipts' basis. Future liability is now governed by the date of receipt.

Where emoluments are assessable under Case I or Case II the date of receipt will comprise the earlier of:

(a) the date of payment; and
(b) the date entitlement arises.

In the case of company directors it is the earliest of the two dates given above with the addition of the following three which establish the time of receipt:

(c) the date emoluments are credited in the employer's books;

(d) where emoluments for a period are determined after the end of that period—the date of determination; and
(e) where emoluments for a period are determined in that period—the last day of that period.

In those cases where emoluments for an earlier year are received after April 5, 1989, it is possible to avoid liability arising in the earlier year, with liability being confined to the year of receipt only.

The emoluments assessable under Schedule E include all salaries, wages, director's fees and other money sums. In addition, there are a wide range of benefits which must also be added to taxable emoluments. These include the provision of living accommodation on advantageous terms and advantages arising from the use of vouchers.

Further taxable benefits accrue to directors and employees receiving emoluments of £8,500 or more in the year of assessment. These benefits include the reimbursement of expenses, the availability of motor cars for private motoring, the provision of petrol or other fuel for private motoring, the provision of interest free loans, and other benefits provided at the employer's expense.

In arriving at the amount to be assessed under Schedule E all expenses incurred wholly, exclusively and necessarily in the performance of the duties may be deducted. This includes fees and subscriptions paid to certain professional bodies and learned societies.

Compensation for loss of office and other sums received on the termination of an office or employment are assessable to tax. However, the first £30,000 may be excluded and only the balance remains chargeable.

A part, not exceeding one half, of earnings received from an approved profit-related pay scheme is exempt from income tax.

Schedule F.—This Schedule is concerned with company dividends and distributions. A United Kingdom resident company paying a dividend or distribution must account to the Inland Revenue for advance corporation tax at the rate of one-third

(2) MARRIED COUPLES

Income	Couples under 65		Couples 65 or over*	
	Income Tax	Average Rate	Income Tax	Average Rate
£	£	per cent	£	per cent
5,000	156	3·1	—	—
6,000	406	6·8	154	2·6
7,000	656	9·4	404	5·8
8,000	906	11·3	654	8·2
9,000	1,156	12·8	904	10·0
10,000	1,406	14·1	1,154	11·5
12,000	1,906	15·9	1,729	14·4
14,000	2,406	17·2	2,406	17·2
16,000	2,906	18·2	2,906	18·2
18,000	3,406	18·9	3,406	18·9
20,000	3,906	19·5	3,906	19·5
25,000	5,156	20·6	5,156	20·6
30,000	7,145	23·8	7,145	23·8
40,000	11,145	27·9	11,145	27·9
50,000	15,145	30·3	15,145	30·3
100,000	35,145	35·1	35,145	35·1

* Persons aged 75 or over suffer rather less tax on income falling below £14,000 on this table.

calculated on the amount paid in 1989–90. A shareholder residing in the United Kingdom receives the dividend or distribution, together with a tax credit equal to the amount of advance corporation tax. The dividend or distribution is regarded as having suffered income tax, equal to the tax credit, at the basic rate, and where the shareholder is not liable, or not fully liable, at this rate a repayment can be obtained. Individuals liable at the higher rate of 40 per cent will incur further liability. Some payments made by an unquoted trading company to redeem or purchase its own shares will not be treated as distributions.

Building society interest and bank interest.— A special composite rate tax scheme applies to payments of building society interest and most payments of bank interest made to individuals. Interest of this nature incurs no liability to basic rate income tax in the hands of the depositor, nor can tax be recovered by a depositor not liable to income tax. The actual interest received must be "grossed up" at the rate of one third to establish the amount of total income received by a depositor liable at the higher rate of 40 per cent.

INCOME NOT TAXABLE

This includes interest on National Savings Certificates, most scholarship income, bounty payments to members of the armed services and annuities payable to the holders of certain awards. Dividend income arising from investments in personal equity plans may be exempt from tax. Income received under most maintenance agreements and court orders made after June 30, 1988 will not be liable to tax. Nor will payments made under many deeds of covenant executed after March 14, 1988 be recognized for tax purposes, unless the recipient is a charity.

SOCIAL SECURITY BENEFITS

Many Social Security benefits are not liable to income tax. These include family income supplement, long term sickness benefit, child benefit, war widow's pension, mobility allowance and numerous others. Among the limited range of benefits which are taxable is the retirement pension, widow's allowance, widowed mother's allowance, and unemployment benefits. Short-term sickness benefit and maternity pay payable by an employer is also chargeable to tax.

PAY AS YOU EARN

The Pay As You Earn system is not an independent form of taxation but has been designed to collect income tax by deduction from most emoluments. When paying emoluments to employees an employer is usually required to deduct income tax and account for that tax to the Inland Revenue. In many cases this deduction procedure will fully exhaust the individual's liability to income tax, unless there is other income. From the end of July 1989 the date of 'receipt' for assessment purposes (*see* above) will also identify the date of 'payment' when establishing liability for PAYE.

PERSONAL ALLOWANCES

The following personal allowances are available to individuals and may be subtracted when calculating income chargeable to income tax.

Personal Allowance.—A single person is entitled to a personal allowance of £2,785. This is increased to £4,375 for a married man whose wife is living with or maintained by him. For the year of marriage the increased allowance will only be available if marriage occurs before May 6. The increased allowance is then reduced by one-twelfth of £1,590 (£4,375 less £2,785) for each complete month preceding the marriage date.

The increased married man's allowance may be withdrawn where a wife's earning election is made (*see* 'Husband and Wife' on page 1009).

Age Allowance.—A single person who has attained the age of 65 years and is in receipt of income not exceeding £11,400 receives an age allowance of £3,400. This is increased to £5,385 where a married man, or his wife living with him, has reached 65. If the income exceeds £11,400 the allowance is reduced by one-half of the amount of the excess. This reduction continues until the age allowance is reduced to the amount of the normal personal allowance. The age allowance is increased to £3,540, or £5,565 for a married couple, where the taxpayer or his wife has reached the age of 75 years. These increased amounts are also subject to restriction where income exceeds £11,400. Age allowance is in substitution for, and not in addition to, the personal allowance.

Wife's Earned Income Allowance.—An allowance equal to the wife's earned income, but limited to a maximum of £2,785, may be obtained. This allowance is not granted in the year of marriage or where a wife's earnings election is in operation (*see* 'Husband and Wife' on page 1009).

Additional Personal Allowance.—An allowance of £1,590 is available to a single person who has a qualifying child resident with him or her in the year of assessment. The allowance can also be obtained by a married man whose wife is totally incapacitated by physical or mental infirmity throughout the year and a child is similarly resident.

A 'qualifying child' for 1989–90 must be born during the year, be under the age of 16 years at the commencement of the year, or over the age of 16 years at the commencement of the year and either receiving full-time instruction at a university, college, school or other educational establishment or undergoing training for a trade, profession or vocation throughout a minimum period of two years. It is also necessary that the child is the claimant's own or, if not such a child, was either born during 1989–90 or under the age of 18 years at the commencement of the year and maintained by the claimant at his or her own expense during the whole of the succeeding twelve month period.

Only one allowance of £1,590 is available notwithstanding the number of children involved. This limit applies not only to a married couple but extends also to an unmarried couple living together.

Blind Person's Allowance.—An allowance of £540 is available to a single person if at any time during the year ending on April 5, 1990, that person was registered as blind on a register maintained by a local authority. The allowance will also be available to a married man if either he or his wife living with him is similarly registered. An increased allowance of £1,080 will be available if both husband and wife are registered blind persons.

Widow's Bereavement Allowance.—For the year of assessment in which a husband dies his surviving widow may obtain a widow's bereavement allowance, which is £1,590 for 1989–90. It is a necessary requirement that the parties were living together immediately before death. A similar allowance will be available in the year following death, unless the widow remarried in the year of death. The special widow's bereavement allowance is available only for the year of death and the following year. It cannot be obtained in subsequent years.

Life Assurance Relief.—Life assurance deduction relief is limited to premiums paid on policies made before March 14, 1984. No relief is available for policies issued after this date. Where the terms of a policy made before March 14, 1984 are subsequently varied or extended to produce increased benefits, future premiums paid may no longer qualify for relief.

When paying premiums under a qualifying policy made before March 14, 1984 the payer will deduct and retain income tax at the rate of 12·5 per cent (15 per cent before April 6, 1989). The ability to retain deductions made in this manner is not affected by the payer's liability to income tax on taxable income. No restriction to the deduction procedure arises if aggregate premiums paid during a year of assessment do not exceed £1,500 (calculated before deducting tax). Should premiums exceed this amount, relief will be confined to £1,500 or one-sixth of total income, whichever is the greater. Where sums deducted exceed the maximum limit, the excess must be accounted for to the Inland Revenue.

OTHER DEDUCTIONS

In addition to personal allowances, which reduce taxable income, other eligible deductions may be available to an individual. These include payments of interest.

In some instances interest paid by a business proprietor may be relieved when calculating profits chargeable to income tax under Case I or Case II of Schedule D. Many private individuals cannot obtain relief in this manner and must satisfy stringent requirements before relief will be forthcoming. In general terms, before interest can qualify for relief it must be annual, as opposed to short, interest or paid to a bank, stockbroker or discount house. Relief will not be available to the extent that interest exceeds a reasonable commercial rate and no relief will be forthcoming for interest on an overdraft.

For 1989–90 relief will be available on the following payments:

(a) Interest on a loan to purchase, develop or improve an interest in land owned by the individual and used as the only or main residence or similarly used by a dependent relative or a former or separated spouse. 'Land' includes large houseboats and also caravans used for a similar purpose. No relief is available for interest on loans applied after April 5, 1988 for the development or improvement of land, unless the work involves the construction of a new building. Nor can relief be obtained for interest on loans applied after this date for the purchase of property occupied by a dependent relative, spouse or former spouse. Relief may, however, be forthcoming for interest on a loan used to acquire some other property, perhaps to be used as the only or main residence on retirement, by an individual who is compelled to occupy property by reason of his or her work. If the loan, or aggregate of several loans, exceeds £30,000 relief is restricted to that amount. Where two or more persons apply loans after July 31, 1988 to acquire interests in a single building, those persons cannot, collectively, obtain relief for interest on more than £30,000 in relation to that building.

(b) Interest on a loan to purchase or improve an interest in land which is let or available for letting at a commercial rent. This interest is only capable of being deducted from rental income.

(c) Interest on a loan made to acquire an interest in a close company or in a partnership.

(d) Interest on a loan to a member of a partnership to acquire machinery or plant for use in the partnership business.

(e) Interest on a loan to an employed person to acquire machinery or plant for the purposes of his employment.

(f) Interest on a loan made for the purpose of contributing capital to an industrial co-operative.

(g) Interest on a loan applied for investment in an employee-controlled company.

(h) Interest on a loan made to elderly persons for the purchase of an annuity where the loan is secured on land. If the loan exceeds £30,000 relief is limited to interest on this amount.

(i) Interest on a loan to personal representatives for the payment of capital transfer tax or inheritance tax.

Relief for many payments of mortgage interest is obtained through a special scheme known as MIRAS (mortgage interest relief at source). This applies to interest paid to a building society, bank, insurance company and certain other persons. When making payments of this nature the payer will deduct and retain income tax at the basic rate. This will provide the payer with full relief at the basic rate and no other relief will be necessary, unless the payer is liable at the higher rate of 40 per cent. Qualifying payments of interest outside the MIRAS scheme continue to produce relief by deduction from income chargeable to income tax.

Many employees pay contributions to an approved occupational pension scheme. The amount of their contributions may be deducted when establishing emoluments assessable under Schedule E. Relief should also be available for any additional voluntary contributions paid.

Self-employed individuals and those receiving earnings not covered by an occupational pension scheme may contribute under personal pension scheme arrangements. These schemes were introduced on July 1, 1988 to replace the previous retirement annuity schemes. Contributions paid may obtain income tax relief, subject to maximum limits.

Subject to a maximum of £40,000 in any one year the cost of subscribing for shares in an unquoted company may qualify as a deduction from taxable income under the Business Expansion Scheme. Many requirements must be satisfied before this relief can be obtained.

HUSBAND AND WIFE

It is a general rule for 1989–90 and earlier years that the income of a married woman living with her husband must be aggregated with his income for the purpose of charging income tax. Aggregation does not, however, apply for the year of assessment in which the parties marry. For that year only the husband will receive the personal allowance appropriate to a married man, although the amount of this allowance may require some restriction if marriage takes place after May 5. The wife will be taxed for

the year of marriage as if she were a single person and no wife's earned income allowance can be obtained by the husband.

For other years of assessment the income of husband and wife will be aggregated and if the husband does not satisfy the total tax liability the Inland Revenue may require the wife to pay the tax appropriate to her income.

Husband and wife may, however, claim to be separately assessed. This claim does not affect the total amount of income tax payable but allocates the liability between the parties. A quite different election may be made for separate assessment of wife's earnings. The effect of such an election is that the husband will be assessed on his income and on the wife's investment income and will receive the personal allowance appropriate to a single man. The wife will be separately assessed on her earned income and receive allowances as a single person. The wife's earnings election may be of advantage where the saving in higher rate tax on the wife's income is greater than the increased tax resulting from the loss of the married personal allowance.

INDEPENDENT TAXATION

A new system for the independent taxation of husband and wife will apply from April 6, 1990. It is a feature of this system that the income of a married couple will no longer be merged and assessed on the husband. Each spouse will be responsible for discharging his or her tax liability.

Under the new system both husband and wife will obtain a personal allowance, which may be replaced by the age allowance for older taxpayers. In addition, the husband will receive a married couple's allowance. If he cannot use, or fully use, this allowance the surplus may be transferred to the wife. Most other allowances will be granted to the spouse entitled to those allowances, but it is usually possible to allocate mortgage interest in whatever manner may be required.

Each spouse will be assessed on his or her income, with income from jointly held assets usually being apportioned equally between the two.

CAPITAL GAINS TAX

A person is chargeable to capital gains tax on chargeable gains which accrue to him or her during a year of assessment ending on April 5. The application of the tax has been amended substantially in recent years and the following information is confined to the year of assessment 1989–90, ending on April 5 1990.

Liability extends to persons who are either resident or ordinarily resident for the year but special rules apply where a person permanently leaves the United Kingdom or comes to this territory for the purpose of acquiring residence. Non-residents are not liable to capital gains tax unless, exceptionally, they carry on a business in the United Kingdom through a branch or agency.

Chargeable gains accruing to companies are assessable to corporation tax and not to capital gains tax.

Capital gains tax is chargeable on the total of chargeable gains which accrue to a person in a year of assessment, after subtracting allowable losses arising in the same year. Unused allowable losses brought forward from some earlier year may be offset against current chargeable gains but in the case of individuals this must not reduce the net chargeable gains for 1989–90 below £5,000.

RATE OF TAX

Where the net chargeable gains accruing to an individual during 1989–90 do not exceed £5,000 there will be no liability to capital gains tax. If the net gains exceed £5,000 the excess is chargeable at the taxpayers marginal rate of income tax. This is achieved by adding to the amount of revenue chargeable to income tax the net chargeable gains. The rate attributable to this top slice will disclose the rate of capital gains tax payable, which may be at 25 per cent, 40 per cent or a combination of the two. Although income tax rates are used, capital gains tax remains a separate tax.

Capital gains tax for 1989–90 normally falls due for payment on or before December 1, 1990. If the return or other information recording chargeable gains is delayed, interest may become chargeable.

HUSBAND AND WIFE

In the year of marriage chargeable gains accruing to husband and wife are separately assessed. Each party may independently obtain the £5,000 exemption for 1989–90 and there is no aggregation. For years other than the year of marriage chargeable gains arising to a married woman living with her husband are assessed and charged on the husband, unless an election for separate assessment is made. This election will not reduce the aggregate tax payable but merely apportions liability between the spouses on an equitable basis.

This treatment of a married woman's gains will be discontinued after April 5, 1990. Following that date each spouse will be separately assessed on his or her gains, with each obtaining the appropriate annual exemption.

DISPOSAL OF ASSETS

Before liability to capital gains tax can arise a disposal, or deemed disposal, of an asset must take place. This occurs not only where assets are sold or exchanged but applies on the making of a gift. There is also a disposal of assets where any capital sum is derived from assets, for example, where compensation is received for loss or damage to an asset.

The date on which a disposal must be treated as having taken place will determine the year of assessment in which the chargeable gain or allowable loss falls. In those cases where a disposal is made under an unconditional contract, the time of disposal will be that when the contract was entered into and not the subsequent date of conveyance or transfer. A disposal under a conditional contract or option is treated as taking place when the contract becomes unconditional or the option is exercised. Disposals by way of gift are undertaken when the gift becomes effective.

VALUATION OF ASSETS

The amount actually received as consideration for the disposal of an asset will be the sum from which very limited outgoings must be deducted for the purpose of establishing the gain or loss. In some cases, however, the consideration passing will not accurately reflect the value of the asset and a different basis must be used. This applies, in particular, where an asset is transferred by way of gift or otherwise than by a bargain made at arm's length. Such transactions are deemed to take place for a consideration representing market value, which will determine both the disposal proceeds accruing to the transferor and the cost of acquisition to the transferee.

Market value represents the price which an asset might reasonably be expected to fetch on a sale in the open market. In the case of unquoted shares or securities it is to be assumed that the hypothetical purchaser in the open market would have available all the information which a prudent prospective purchaser of shares or securities might reasonably require if he were proposing to purchase them from a willing vendor by private treaty and at arm's length. This is an important consideration as the amount of information deemed to be available to a hypothetical purchaser may materially affect the price 'reasonably' offered in an open market situation. The market value of unquoted shares or securities will usually be established following negotiations with the Shares Valuation Division of the Capital Taxes Office.

Special rules apply to determine the market value of shares quoted on the Stock Exchange.

DEDUCTION FOR OUTGOINGS

Once the actual or notional disposal proceeds have been determined it only remains to subtract eligible outgoings for the purpose of computing the gain or loss. There is the general rule that any outgoings deducted, or which are available to be deducted, when calculating income tax liability must be ignored. Subject to this, deductions will usually be limited to:

(a) the cost of acquiring the asset, together with incidental costs wholly and exclusively incurred in connection with the acquisition;

(b) expenditure incurred wholly and exclusively on the asset in enhancing its value, being expenditure reflected in the state or nature of the asset at the time of the disposal, and any other expenditure wholly and exclusively incurred in establishing, preserving or defending title to, or a right over, the asset; and

(c) the incidental costs of making the disposal.

Where the disposal concerns a leasehold interest having less than 50 years to run, any expenditure falling under (a) and (b) must be written off throughout the duration of the lease. This recognises that a lease is a wasting asset which, at the termination of the leasing period, will retain no value.

INDEXATION ALLOWANCE

An indexation allowance will be available when calculating the chargeable gain or allowable loss. This allowance is based on percentage increases in the retail prices index between the month of March 1982, or if later the month in which expenditure is incurred, and the month of disposal. The increase is applied to the items of expenditure in (a) and (b) above to determine the amount of the indexation allowance. However, if the asset was acquired before March 31, 1982 and the disposal occurs after April 5, 1988, the allowance will be based on market value on that date.

The amount of the indexation allowance will be subtracted from the gain, or added to the loss, to calculate the chargeable gain or allowable loss arising on disposal.

ASSETS HELD ON MARCH 31, 1982

Where the disposal of assets held on March 31, 1982, takes place after April 5, 1988, the actual cost of acquisition will not usually enter into the calculation of gain. It is to be assumed that such assets were acquired on March 31, 1982, for a consideration representing market value on that date. The increase in value, if any, occurring before March 31, 1982, will not be assessable to capital gains tax.

EXEMPTIONS

There is a general exemption from liability to capital gains tax where the net gains of an individual for 1989–90 do not exceed £5,000. In the case of husband and wife living together there can be only one combined exemption of £5,000. However, following the introduction of independent taxation on April 6, 1990, each spouse will be separately assessed with each obtaining his or her own annual exemption.

The disposal of many assets will not give rise to chargeable gains or allowable losses and these include:

(a) private motor cars;

(b) Government securities;

(c) Loan stock and other securities (but not shares) quoted on a United Kingdom stock exchange or dealt in on the Unlisted Securities Market;

(d) Options and contracts relating to securities within (b) and (c);

(e) National Savings Certificates, Premium Bonds, Defence Bonds and National Development Bonds;

(f) currency of any description acquired for personal expenditure outside the United Kingdom;

(g) decorations awarded for valour;

(h) betting wins and pools, lottery or games prizes;

(i) compensation or damages for any wrong or injury suffered by an individual in his person or in his profession or vocation;

(j) life assurance and deferred annuity contracts where the person making the disposal is the original beneficial owner;

(k) dwelling-houses and land enjoyed with the residence which is an individual's only or main residence;

(l) tangible movable property, the consideration for the disposal of which does not exceed £6,000;

(m) certain tangible movable property which is a wasting asset having a life not exceeding 50 years;

(n) assets transferred to charities and other bodies;

(o) works of art, historic buildings and similar assets;

(p) assets used to provide maintenance funds for historic buildings;

(q) assets transferred to trustees for the benefit of employees.

DWELLING-HOUSES

Exemption from capital gains tax will usually be available for any gain which accrues to an individual from the disposal of, or of an interest in, a dwelling-house or part of a dwelling-house which has been his only or main residence. The exemption extends to land which has been occupied and enjoyed with the residence as its garden or grounds. Some restriction may be necessary where the land exceeds one acre.

The gain will not be chargeable to capital gains tax if the dwelling-house, or part, has been the individual's only or main residence throughout the period of ownership, or throughout the entire period except for all or any part of the last two years. A proportionate part of the gain will be exempt if the dwelling-house has been the individual's only or main residence for part only of the period of ownership.

Where part of the dwelling-house has been used exclusively for business purposes, part of the gain arising on disposal will not be exempt. It will be comparatively unusual for any part to be used exclusively for such a purpose, except perhaps in the case of doctors' or dentists' surgeries.

In those cases where part of a qualifying dwelling-house has been used to provide rented residential accommodation this non-personal use may frequently be ignored when calculating exemption from capital gains tax, unless relatively substantial sums are involved.

Dwellings occupied by dependent relatives or separated or divorced former spouses, may also qualify for the exemption, but only where occupation commenced before April 6, 1988.

ROLL-OVER RELIEF

Persons carrying on business will often undertake the disposal of an asset and use the proceeds to finance the acquisition of a replacement asset. Where this situation arises a claim for roll-over relief may be made. The broad effect of such a claim is that all or part of the gain arising on the disposal of the old asset may be disregarded. The gain or part is then subtracted from the cost of acquiring the replacement asset. As this cost is reduced, any gain arising from the future disposal of the replacement asset will be correspondingly increased, unless of course a further roll-over situation then develops.

It remains a requirement that both the old and the replacement asset must be used for the purpose of the taxpayer's business. Relief will only be available if the acquisition of the replacement asset takes place within a period commencing twelve months before, and ending three years after, the disposal of the old asset, although the Board of Inland Revenue retain a discretion to extend this period where the circumstances were such that it was impossible for the taxpayer to acquire the replacement asset before the expiration of the normal time limit.

Whilst many business assets qualify for roll-over relief there are exceptions.

GIFTS

The gift of an asset is treated as a disposal made for a consideration equal to market value, with a corresponding acquisition by the transferee at an identical value. For gifts made by individuals and trustees before March 14, 1989, a wide-ranging claim for hold-over relief was available where the transferee was resident in the United Kingdom.

In the case of gifts made on or after this date, hold-over relief is limited to the transfer of certain assets only. The more important of these comprise:

(a) assets used for the purposes of a trade or similar activity carried on by the transferor or his family company;

(b) shares or securities of a trading company which is neither quoted on a stock exchange nor listed on the Unlisted Securities Market;

(c) shares or securities of a trading company which is quoted or listed but which is the transferor's family company;

(d) many interests in agricultural property qualifying for 50 per cent inheritance tax relief;

(e) transactions which are lifetime transfers for inheritance tax purposes.

The effect of the claim is similar to that following a claim for roll-over relief, but adjustments will be necessary where some consideration is given for the transfer, the asset has not been used for business purposes throughout the period of ownership, or not all assets of a company are used for business purposes.

RETIREMENT RELIEF

Retirement relief is available to an individual who disposes by way of sale or gift of the whole or part of a business. It does not necessarily follow that the isolated disposal of assets will represent the disposal of the whole or part of a business. The main condition for granting this relief is that throughout a period of at least one year the business has been owned either by the individual or by a trading company in which the individual retained a sufficient shareholding interest. The relief extends also to cases where an individual disposes by way of sale or gift of shares or securities of a company. It must be demonstrated that the company was a trading company, the individual retained a sufficient shareholding interest, and he was engaged as a full-time working director.

An individual who has attained the age of 60 years at the time of a disposal may obtain maximum retirement relief exceeding £300,000 for disposals taking place after April 5, 1988. The amount of this relief must be reduced if the conditions have not been satisfied throughout a ten year period. With a single exception no retirement relief can be obtained if the disposal occurs before the individual's 60th birthday. This exception arises where an individual is compelled to retire early on the grounds of ill-health. The normal retirement relief may then be obtained. Any retirement relief must be subtracted from the net gains arising on disposal, leaving the balance remaining, if any, chargeable to capital gains tax in the normal manner.

DEATH

No capital gains tax is chargeable on the value of assets retained at the time of death. However, the personal representatives administering the deceased's estate are deemed to acquire those assets for a consideration representing market value on death. This ensures that any increase in value occurring before the date of death will not be chargeable to capital gains tax. If a legatee or other person acquires an asset under a will or intestacy no chargeable gain will accrue to the personal representatives, and the person taking the asset will also be treated as having acquired it at the time of death for its then market value.

INHERITANCE TAX

Throughout a period of some 90 years estate duty was payable on the value of an individual's estate at the time of death. Liability did not extend to lifetime gifts other than those made shortly before death and a limited range of further gifts where the donor continued to retain some benefit from the assets gifted. Estate duty ceased to apply for deaths occurring after March 12, 1975 following the introduction of capital transfer tax. This tax was not limited to the value of an estate at the time of death but applied to many gifts made during lifetime. Although the broad framework of capital transfer tax remains, very substantial changes were introduced for events occurring after March 17, 1986. In recognition of these changes the tax was renamed inheritance tax and now bears many characteristics of the former estate duty.

The nature and scope of inheritance tax is outlined below, but the comments made have little application to events occurring before 18 March 1986 when capital transfer tax applied.

Liability to inheritance tax may arise on a limited range of lifetime gifts and other dispositions and also on the value of assets retained, or deemed to be retained, at the time of death. An individual's domicile at the time of any gift or on death is an important matter. Domicile will generally be determined by applying normal rules, but special considerations may be necessary where an individual was previously domiciled in the United Kingdom but subsequently acquired a domicile of choice overseas. Where a person was domiciled in the United Kingdom at the time of a disposition or on death the location of assets is immaterial and full liability to inheritance tax arises. Individuals domiciled outside the United Kindom are, however, chargeable to inheritance tax only on transactions affecting assets located in the United Kingdom.

The assets of husband and wife are not merged for inheritance tax purposes. Each spouse is treated as a separate individual entitled to receive the benefit of his or her exemptions, reliefs and rates of tax. Where husband and wife retain similar assets, special 'related property' provisions may require the merger of those assets for valuation purposes only.

LIFETIME GIFTS AND DISPOSITIONS

Gifts and dispositions made during lifetime fall under four broad headings, namely:

(a) dispositions which are not transfers of value;
(b) exempt transfers;
(c) potentially exempt transfers; and
(d) chargeable transfers.

Dispositions which are not transfers of value.—Several lifetime transactions are not treated as transfers of value and may be entirely disregarded for inheritance tax purposes. These include transactions not undertaken to confer gratuitous benefit, the provision of family maintenance, the waiver of the right to receive remuneration or dividends, and the grant of agricultural tenancies for full consideration.

Exempt transfers.—Certain other transfers are treated as exempt transfers and incur no liability to inheritance tax. The main exempt transfers are listed below:

Transfers Between Spouses.—Transfers between husband and wife are usually exempt. However, if the transferor is, but the transferee spouse is not, domiciled in the United Kingdom transfers will be exempt only to the extent that the total does not exceed £55,000. Unlike the requirement used for income tax and capital gains tax purposes, it is immaterial whether husband and wife are living together.

Annual exemption.—The first £3,000 of gifts and other dispositions made in a year ending on April 5 is exempt. If the exemption is not used, or not wholly used, in any year the balance may be carried forward to the following year only. The annual exemption will only be available for a potentially exempt transfer (*see* below) if that transfer subsequently becomes chargeable by reason of the donor's death.

Small Gifts.—Outright gifts of £250 or less to any person in one year ending April 5 are exempt.

Normal Expenditure.—A transfer made during lifetime and comprising normal expenditure is exempt. To obtain this exemption it must be shown that:

(a) the transfer was made as part of the normal expenditure of the transferor;
(b) taking one year with another, the transfer was made out of income; and
(c) after allowing for all transfers of value forming part of normal expenditure the transferor was left with sufficient income to maintain his or her usual standard of living.

Gifts in Consideration of Marriage.—These are exempt if they satisfy certain requirements. The amount allowed will be governed by the relationship between the donor and a party to the marriage. The allowable amounts comprise:

(a) gifts by a parent—£5,000
(b) gifts by a grandparent—£2,500
(c) gifts by a party to the marriage—£2,500
(d) gifts by other persons—£1,000

Gifts to Charities.—Gifts to charities are exempt from liability.

Gifts to Political Parties.—Gifts to political parties which satisfy certain requirements are generally exempt.

Gifts for National Purposes.—Gifts made to an extensive list of bodies are exempt from liability. These include, among others:

(a) The National Gallery;
(b) The British Museum;
(c) The National Trust for Places of Historic Interest or Natural Beauty;
(d) The National Art Collections Fund;
(e) The Nature Conservancy Council;
(f) The Historic Buildings and Monuments Commission for England;
(g) Any local authority;
(h) Any university or university college in the United Kingdom.

A number of other gifts made for the public benefit are also exempt.

Potentially Exempt Transfers.—Lifetime gifts and dispositions which are neither to be ignored nor comprise exempt transfers incur possible liability to inheritance tax. However, relief is available for a range of potentially exempt transfers. These comprise gifts made by an individual to:

(a) a second individual;
(b) trustees administering an accumulation and maintenance trust; or
(c) trustees administering a disabled person's trust.

The accumulation and maintenance trust mentioned in (b) must provide that on reaching a specified age, not exceeding twenty-five years, a beneficiary will become absolutely entitled to trust assets or obtain an interest in possession in those assets.

Further additions were made to the list of potentially exempt transfers for transactions taking place after March 16, 1987. These affect settled property administered by trustees where an individual, or individuals, retain an interest in possession. The transfer of assets to, the removal of assets from, or the rearrangement of interests in such property comprise potentially exempt transfers if the person transferring an interest and the person benefitting from the transfer are both individuals.

No immediate liability to inheritance tax will arise on the making of a potentially exempt transfer. Should the donor survive for a period of seven years, immunity from liability will be confirmed. However, the donor's death within the seven-year *inter vivos* period produces liability, as explained later, if the amounts involved are sufficiently substantial.

Chargeable Transfers.—Any remaining lifetime gifts or dispositions which are neither to be ignored, represent exempt transfers or potentially exempt transfers incur liability to inheritance tax. The range of such chargeable transfers is severely limited and is broadly confined to transfers made to or affecting certain trusts, transfers to non-individuals and transfers involving companies.

GIFTS WITH RESERVATION

A lifetime gift of assets made at any time after March 17, 1986, may incur additional liability to inheritance tax if the donor retains some interest in the subject matter of the gift. This may arise, for example, where a parent transfers a dwelling-house to a son or daughter and continues to occupy the property or to enjoy some benefit from that property. The retention of a benefit may be ignored where it is enjoyed in return for full consideration, perhaps a commercial rent, or the benefit arises from changed circumstances which could not have been foreseen at the time of the original gift. The gift with reservation provisions will not usually apply to most exempt transfers.

There are three possibilities which may arise where the donor reserves or enjoys some benefit from the subject matter of a previous gift and subsequently dies, namely:

(a) If no benefit is enjoyed within a period of seven years before death there can be no further liability.
(b) If the benefit ceased to be enjoyed within a period of seven years before the date of death the original donor is deemed to have made a potentially exempt transfer representing the value of the asset at the time of cessation.
(c) If the benefit is enjoyed at the time of death the value of the asset must be included in the value of the deceased's estate on death.

It must be emphasised that the existence of a benefit enjoyed at any time within a period of seven years before death will establish liability on gifts with reservation, notwithstanding that the gift may have been made many years earlier, providing it was undertaken after March 17, 1986.

DEATH

Immediately before the time of death an individual is deemed to make a transfer of value. This transfer will comprise the value of assets forming part of the deceased's estate after subtracting most liabilities. Any exempt transfers may, however, be excluded. These include transfers for the benefit of a surviving spouse, a charity and a qualifying political party together with bequests to approved bodies and for national purposes.

Death may also trigger three additional liabilities, namely:

(a) A potentially exempt transfer made within the period of seven years ending on death loses its potential status and becomes chargeable to inheritance tax.
(b) The value of gifts made with reservation may incur liability if any benefit was enjoyed within a period of seven years preceding death.
(c) Additional tax may become payable for chargeable lifetime transfers made within seven years before death.

VALUATIONS

The valuation of assets is an important matter as this will establish the value transferred for lifetime dispositions and also the value of a person's estate at the time of death. The value of property will represent the price which might reasonably be expected from a sale in the open market. This price cannot be reduced on the grounds that the whole property is placed on the market simultaneously and may therefore depress values.

In some cases it may be necessary to incorporate the value of 'related property'. This will include property comprised in the estate of the transferor's spouse and certain property previously transferred to charities. The purpose of the related property valuation rules is not to add the value of the property to the estate of the transferor. Related property must be merged to establish the aggregate value of the respective interests and this value is then apportioned, usually on a *pro rata* basis, to the separate interests.

The value of shares and securities quoted on the Stock Exchange will be determined by extracting figures from the daily list of official prices.

Where quoted shares and securities are sold within a period of twelve months following the date of death a claim may be made to substitute the proceeds for the value on death. This claim will only be beneficial if the gross proceeds realized are lower than market value on death. A similar claim may be available for interests in land sold within a period of three years following death.

RELIEF FOR ASSETS

Special relief is made available for certain assets, notably woodlands, agricultural property and business property. The effect of this relief is summarized below:

Woodlands.—Where woodlands pass on death the value will usually be included in the deceased's estate. However, an election may be made in respect of land in the United Kingdom on which trees or underwood is growing to delete the value of those assets. Relief is confined to the value of trees or underwood and does not extend to the land on which they are growing. Liability to inheritance tax will arise if and when the trees or underwood are sold on a future occasion.

Agricultural Property.—Relief is available for the agricultural value of agricultural property. Such property must be occupied and used for agricultural purposes and relief is confined to the agricultural value.

The value transferred, either on a lifetime gift or on death, must be determined. This value may then be reduced by a percentage. A higher 50 per cent deduction will be available if the transferor retained vacant possession or could have obtained that possession within a period of twelve months following the transfer. The increased deduction of 50 per cent may also be available for certain agricultural property held on March 9, 1981. In other cases, notably including land let to tenants, a lower deduction of 30 per cent is available.

It remains a requirement that the agricultural property was either occupied by the transferor for the purposes of agriculture throughout a two-year period ending on the date of the transfer, or was owned by him throughout a period of seven years ending on that date and occupied for agricultural purposes.

Business Property.—Where value transferred is attributable to relevant business property, that value may be reduced by a percentage. The reduction in value applies to:

(a) property consisting of a business or an interest in a business;

(b) shares or securities of a company, whether quoted or unquoted, which provided the transferor with control of the company immediately before the transfer. Control for this purpose may include that created by related property;

(c) unquoted shares or securities not falling within (b) which provided the transferor with more than 25 per cent of voting rights;

(d) other unquoted shares or securities not falling within (c);

(e) any land, building, machinery or plant which, immediately before the transfer, was used wholly or mainly for the purposes of a business carried on by a company of which the transferor had control;

(f) any land, building, machinery or plant which, immediately before the transfer, was used wholly or mainly for the purposes of a business carried on by a partnership of which the transferor was a partner; and

(g) any land, building, machinery or plant which, immediately before the transfer, was used wholly or mainly for the purposes of a business carried on by the transferor and was then settled property in which he retained an interest in possession.

For property falling within (a) or (b) the deduction is 50 per cent. A similar deduction is available for property in (c), if the event occurs after March 16, 1987. A reduced deduction of 30 per cent applies to property in (d) to (g).

It is a general requirement that the property must have been retained for a period of two years before the transfer or death and restrictions may be necessary if the property has not been used wholly for business purposes. The same slice of property cannot obtain both business property relief and the relief available for agricultural property.

CALCULATION OF TAX PAYABLE

The calculation of inheritance tax payable adopts the use of a cumulative total. Each chargeable lifetime transfer is added to the total with a final addition made on death. The top slice added to the total for the current event determines the rate at which inheritance tax must be paid. However, the cumulative total will only include transfers made within a period of seven years before the current event and those undertaken outside this period must be excluded. Although inheritance tax was only introduced on March 18, 1986, the seven-year cumulative total will include chargeable lifetime gifts made before that date, subject to the seven-year limitation.

Lifetime transfers.—The limited range of lifetime transfers must be added to the seven-year cumulative total to calculate the amount of inheritance tax due. The tax is imposed at one-half of the rate shown below. However, if the donor dies within a period of seven years from the date of the chargeable lifetime transfer, additional tax may be due. This is calculated by applying tax at the full rate (in substitution for the one-half rate previously used). The amount of tax is then reduced to a percentage by applying tapering relief. This percentage is governed by the number of years from the date of the lifetime gift to the date of death and is as follows:

Period of years before death	Percentage
Not more than 3	100
More than 3 but not more than 4	80
More than 4 but not more than 5	60
More than 5 but not more than 6	40
More than 6 but not more than 7	20

Should this exercise produce liability greater than that previously paid at the one-half rate on the lifetime transfer, additional tax, representing the difference, must be paid. Where the calculation shows an amount falling below tax paid on the lifetime transfer, no additional liability can arise nor will the deficiency become repayable.

Potentially exempt transfers.—Where a potentially exempt transfer loses immunity from liability, due to the donor's death within the seven-year *inter vivos* period, the value transferred becomes liable to inheritance tax. Liability is calculated by applying the full rate shown below, reduced to the percentage governed by tapering relief if the original transfer occurred more than three years before death.

Death.—The final addition to the seven-year cumulative total will comprise the value of an estate on death. Inheritance tax will be calculated by applying the full rate shown below. No tapering relief can be obtained.

RATES OF TAX

In earlier times there were several rates of inheritance tax which progressively increased as the value transferred grew in size. However, for events taking place after March 14, 1988, a nil rate applies to the first £110,000 of value (or £118,000 for events after April 5, 1989). Any excess is charged at the single positive rate of 40 per cent.

Only one-half of the 40 per cent rate (namely 20 per cent) will be applicable for chargeable lifetime transfers.

It must be anticipated that the above rate and rateband will be amended on future occasions.

PAYMENT OF TAX

Inheritance tax usually falls due for payment six months after the end of the month in which the chargeable transaction takes place. Where a transfer, other than that made on death, occurs after April 5 and before the following October 1, tax falls due on the following April 30, although there are some exceptions to this general rule.

Inheritance tax attributable to the transfer of certain land, controlling shareholding interests, unquoted shares, businesses and interests in businesses, together with agricultural property, may usually be satisfied by instalments spread over ten years. No liability to interest arises where tax is paid on the due date. In other cases, delay in the payment of tax may incur liability to interest.

SETTLED PROPERTY

Complex rules apply to establish inheritance tax liability on settled property. Where a person is beneficially entitled to an interest in possession, that person is effectively deemed to own the property in which the interest subsists. It follows that where the interest comes to an end during the beneficiary's lifetime and some other person becomes entitled to the property or interest, the beneficiary is treated as having made a transfer of value. However, for events taking place after March 16, 1987 this will usually comprise a potentially exempt transfer. No liability will arise, however, where the property vests in the absolute ownership of the previous beneficiary. The death of a person entitled to an interest in possession will require the value of the underlying property to be added to the value of the deceased's estate.

In the case of other settled property where there is no interest in possession (e.g. discretionary trusts), liability to tax will arise on each ten-year anniversary of the trust. There will also be liability if property ceases to be held on discretionary trusts before the first ten-year anniversary date is reached or between anniversaries. The rate of tax suffered will be governed by several considerations, including previous dispositions made by the settlor, transactions concluded by the trustees, and the period throughout which property has been held in trust.

Accumulation and maintenance settlements which require assets to be distributed not later than a beneficiary's twenty-fifth birthday may be exempt from any liability to inheritance tax.

CORPORATION TAX

Profits, gains and income accruing to companies resident in the United Kingdom incur liability to corporation tax. Non-resident companies are immune from this tax unless they carry on a trade in the United Kingdom through a permanent establishment, branch or office. Companies residing outside the United Kingdom may be liable to income tax at the basic rate on other income arising in the United Kingdom, perhaps from letting property. The following comments are confined to companies resident in the United Kingdom and have little application to those residing overseas.

Liability to corporation tax is governed by the profits, gains or income for an accounting period. This is the period for which financial accounts are made up, and in the case of companies preparing accounts to the same accounting date annually will comprise successive periods of twelve months.

RATE OF TAX

The amount of profits or income for an accounting period must be determined on normal taxation principles. The special rules which apply to individuals where a source of income is acquired or discontinued are ignored and consideration is confined to the actual profits or income for an accounting period.

The rate of corporation tax is fixed for a financial year ending on March 31. Where the accounting period of a company overlaps this date and there is a change in the rate of corporation tax, profits and income must be apportioned.

For earlier years the full rate of corporation tax was 52 per cent but this rate was progressively reduced as follows:

Financial year	Per cent
12 months ending March 31, 1984	50
March 31, 1985	45
March 31, 1986	40
March 31, 1987, 1988, 1989 and 1990	35

The progressive reduction in the rate of corporation tax was made to compensate companies for the loss of stock relief and the withdrawal of certain allowances for capital expenditure which increased the amount of profits and income chargeable to that tax.

SMALL COMPANIES RATE

Where the profits of a company do not exceed stated limits, corporation tax becomes payable at the small companies rate. It is the amount of profits and not the size of the company which governs the application of this rate.

The level of profits which a company may derive without losing the benefit of the small companies rate has been frequently changed. In recent years the following small companies rate applies where profits do not exceed £100,000 (or £150,000 for the year ending March 31, 1990):

Financial year	Per cent
12 months ending March 31, 1984	38
March 31, 1985 and 1986	30
March 31, 1987	29
March 31, 1988	27
March 31, 1989 and 1990	25

If profits do exceed £100,000 (or £150,000) but fall below £500,000 (or £750,000), marginal small companies rate relief applies. The broad effect of marginal relief is that the first £100,000 (or £150,000) of profits is taxed at the appropriate small companies rate. Profits falling in the margin exceeding £100,000 (or £150,000) then incur liability at the following marginal rates:

Financial year	Per cent
12 months ending March 31, 1984	55
March 31, 1985	48·75
March 31, 1986	42·5
March 31, 1987	36·5
March 31, 1988	37
March 31, 1989	37·5
March 31, 1990	37·5

If the accounting period of a company overlaps March 31, profits must be apportioned to establish the appropriate rate for each part of those profits.

The lower limit of £100,000 (or £150,000) and the upper limit of £500,000 (or £750,000) applies for a period of twelve months in duration and must be proportionately reduced for shorter periods. Some restriction in the small companies rate and the marginal rate may be necessary if there are two or more associated companies, namely companies under common control.

For accounting periods commencing after March 31, 1989, the small companies rate is not available for close investment-holding companies. These are mainly investment companies, other than those receiving most of their income from letting land and property.

CAPITAL GAINS

Chargeable gains arising to a company are calculated in a manner similar to that used for individuals. However, companies cannot obtain the annual exemption of £5,000, nor are they assessed to capital gains tax. In place of this tax companies suffer liability to corporation tax on chargeable gains.

For disposals taking place before March 17, 1987 only a fraction of the chargeable gain was assessable to corporation tax at the full rate. The fraction selected ensured that companies effectively suffered corporation tax at the rate of 30 per cent on the full chargeable gain. A different approach is adopted for disposals taking place after this date. The full chargeable gain, and not a fraction, is assessable to corporation tax. However, unlike the previous system, the chargeable gain is treated as ordinary profit, thereby obtaining the benefit of the small companies rate where figures are sufficiently low.

DISTRIBUTIONS

Dividends and other qualifying distributions made by a United Kingdom resident company are not satisfied after deduction of income tax. However, when making a distribution a company is required to account to the Inland Revenue for an amount of advance corporation tax. For distributions made in the year ending April 5, 1990, the amount of advance corporation tax will represent one-third of the distribution. Thus a cash dividend of £75 paid to a shareholder will also require satisfaction of advance corporation tax amounting to £25.

Advance corporation tax accounted for in this manner for distributions made in an accounting period may usually be set against a company's corporation tax liability for the same period. Some restrictions are imposed on the amount which can be offset but any surplus can be carried forward, or carried backwards, and set against corporation tax due for other accounting periods.

A United Kingdom resident shareholder receiving a qualifying distribution also obtains a tax credit, which for the year ending April 5, 1990, is equal to one-third of the distribution made. Therefore the total income of the individual comprises the aggregate of the distribution and the tax credit. If the individual is not liable, or not fully liable, to income tax at the basic rate, all or part of the tax credit can be refunded by the Inland Revenue. Individuals with substantial income incur liability to income tax at the higher rate of 40 per cent on the aggregate of the distribution and the tax credit.

PAYMENT OF TAX

Corporation tax, less any relief for advance corporation tax, usually falls due for payment nine months following the end of the accounting period to which the tax relates. Companies which were carrying on business before 1966 may have a later due and payable date, but this is gradually being amended to achieve a common nine month period for all companies.

INTEREST

On making many payments of interest a company is required to deduct income tax at the basic rate and account for the tax deducted to the Inland Revenue. The gross amount of interest paid will usually comprise a charge on income to be offset against profits on which corporation tax becomes payable.

GROUPS OF COMPANIES

Each company within a group is separately charged to corporation tax on profits, gains and income. However, where one group member realizes a loss, other than a capital loss, a claim may be made to offset the deficiency against profits of some other member of the same group.

Claims are also available to avoid the payment of advance corporation tax on distributions, or the deduction of income tax on the payment of interest, for transactions between members of a group of companies. The transfer of capital assets from one member of a group to a fellow member will incur no liability to tax on chargeable gains.

VALUE ADDED TAX

Unlike income tax, capital gains tax, inheritance tax and corporation tax, which are collected and administered by the Inland Revenue, value added tax is the responsibility of Customs and Excise. Value added tax is charged on the value of supplies made in the United Kingdom by a registered trader and extends both to the supply of goods and to the supply of services. Liability also arises on the value of goods imported into the United Kingdom.

REGISTRATION

All traders, including professional men and women, together with companies, making taxable supplies of a value exceeding stated limits are required to register for value added tax purposes. Taxable supplies represent the supply of goods and services potentially chargeable with value added tax. The limits which govern mandatory registration are amended annually but from March 15, 1989, an unregistered trader must register:

(a) at any time, if there are reasonable grounds for believing that the value of taxable supplies in the year then beginning will exceed £23,600, or

(b) at the end of any quarter, namely March 31, June 30, September 30 or December 31, if the total amount of taxable supplies has exceeded either £8,000 in the last quarter or £23,600 in the last four quarters. Registration will not be mandatory if it can be shown that the value of taxable supplies in the last quarter and the next three quarters is not expected to exceed £23,600.

Where the limits governing mandatory registration have been exceeded it is necessary for the trader to notify Customs and Excise. Failure to provide prompt notification may have unfortunate results as the person concerned will be required to account for value added tax from the proper registration date. In some situations a trader whose taxable supplies do not reach the mandatory registration limits may apply for voluntary registration.

A registered trader may submit an application for de-registration if the value of taxable supplies subsequently falls. From June 1, 1989, an application for de-registration can be made if the value of taxable supplies for the year beginning on the application date is not expected to exceed £22,600. De-registration can also be achieved if the value of taxable supplies in each of the two previous years did not exceed £23,600 and is unlikely to exceed this threshold in the following twelve-month period.

INPUT TAX

A registered trader will both suffer tax (input tax) when obtaining goods or services for the purposes of his business and also become liable to account for tax (output tax) on the value of goods and services which he supplies. Relief can usually be obtained for input tax suffered, either by setting that tax against output tax due or by repayment. Most items of input tax can be relieved in this manner but there are exceptions including the prohibition of relief for the cost of business entertaining. Where a registered trader makes both exempt supplies and also taxable supplies to his customers or clients there may be some restriction in the amount of input tax which can be recovered.

OUTPUT TAX

When making a taxable supply of goods or services a registered trader must account for output tax, if any, on the value of the supply. Usually the price charged by the registered trader will be increased by adding value added tax but failure to make the required addition will not remove liability to account for output tax.

EXEMPT SUPPLIES

No value added tax is chargeable on the supply of goods or services which are treated as exempt supplies. These include the provision of burial and cremation facilities, insurance, finance and education. The granting of a lease to occupy land or the sale of land will usually comprise an exempt supply, but there are numerous exceptions. In particular, the sale of new non-domestic buildings or certain buildings used by charities, constructed after April 1, 1989, can no longer be treated as exempt supplies. From August 1, 1989 a taxable person may elect to tax rents and other supplies of buildings and agricultural land not used for residential or charitable purposes.

Exempt supplies do not enter into the value of taxable supplies which governs liability to mandatory registration. Such supplies made by a registered trader may however limit the amount of input tax which can be relieved. It is for this reason that the election available from August 1, 1989 may be useful.

RATES OF TAX

Two rates of value added tax have applied since June 18, 1979, namely:

(a) a zero, or nil, rate; and

(b) a standard rate of 15 per cent.

Although no tax is due on a zero-rated supply, this does comprise a taxable supply which must be included in the calculation governing liability to register.

ZERO-RATING

A large number of supplies are zero-rated, including, among others:

(a) the supply of many items of food and drink for human consumption. This does not include ice creams, chocolates, sweets, potato crisps and alcoholic drinks. Nor does it extend to supplies made in the course of catering, for example, at a wedding reception or other social function, or to items supplied for consumption in a restaurant or cafe. Whilst the supply of cold items, for example sandwiches, for consumption away from the suppliers premises, is zero rated, the supply of hot food, for example fish and chips, is not;

(b) animal feeding stuffs;

(c) sewerage and water, unless supplied for industrial purposes after June 30, 1990;

(d) books, brochures, pamphlets, leaflets, newspapers, maps and charts;

(e) talking books for the blind and handicapped and wireless sets for the blind;

(f) electricity, gas and coal, but supplies will be limited to domestic use after June 30, 1990;

(g) supplies of services, other than professional services, when constructing a new building. The supply of materials for a new building is also zero-rated, together with the sale or the grant of a long lease for such a building. Before April 1, 1989 this applied to most new buildings but subsequently it is limited to domestic buildings and buildings used by charities. Alterations to some protected buildings are also zero-rated;

(h) the transportation of persons in a vehicle, ship or aircraft designed to carry not less than twelve persons;

(i) supplies of drugs, medicines and other aids for the handicapped;

(j) supplies of clothing and footwear for young persons;

(k) exports.

This list is not exhaustive but indicates the wide range of supplies which may be zero-rated.

COLLECTION OF TAX

Registered traders submit value added tax returns for accounting periods. Each accounting period is for three months in duration but arrangements can be made to submit returns on a monthly basis. The return will show both the output tax due for supplies made by the trader in the accounting period and also the input tax for which relief is claimed. If the output tax exceeds input tax the balance must be remitted with the value added tax return. Where input tax suffered exceeds the output tax due the registered trader may claim recovery of the excess from Customs and Excise.

This basis for collecting tax explains the structure of value added tax. Where supplies are made between registered traders the supplier will account for an amount of tax which will usually be identical to the tax recovered by the person to whom the supply is made. However, where the supply is made to a person who is not a registered trader there can be no recovery of input tax and it is on this person that the final burden of value added tax eventually falls.

Tax on imports into the United Kingdom must be satisfied at the time of importation or perhaps later where special arrangements have been agreed.

An optional scheme will be made available for registered traders having an annual turnover of taxable supplies not exceeding £250,000. Such traders may, if they wish, render returns annually. Nine equal payments of value added tax will be paid on account, with a final balancing payment accompanying submission of the return.

BAD DEBTS

Many retailers operate special retail schemes for calculating the amount of value added tax due. These schemes are, broadly, based on the volume of consideration received in an accounting period. Should a customer fail to pay for goods or services supplied, there will be no consideration on which value added tax falls to be calculated. In other cases, where the special retailers' schemes do not apply, output tax falls due on the value of the supply and liability is not affected by failure to receive consideration. This implies that there will be no relief for the value added tax element in bad debts. However, relief for this element may be obtained where the debtor becomes insolvent.

To avoid the problem of bad debts incurred by traders not operating a special retail scheme, an optional system of cash accounting is available. This scheme, confined to traders with annual taxable supplies not exceeding £250,000, enables returns to be made on a cash basis, in substitution for the normal supply basis. Traders using such a scheme will not, of course, include bad debts in the calculation of cash receipts.

OTHER SPECIAL SCHEMES

In addition to the schemes for retailers, there are several special schemes applied to calculate the amount of value added tax due and which also limit the ability to recover input tax. These schemes apply to the supply of second-hand motor cars, motor cycles, caravans, boats, electronic organs, aircraft and firearms, together with works of art, antiques and collectors' pieces.

OTHER TAXES AND STAMP DUTIES

The Commissioners as a general rule allow deeds, etc., to be stamped after execution:—

WITHOUT PENALTY, ON PAYMENT OF DUTY ONLY.
Deeds and instruments not otherwise excepted, within 30 days of first execution.
NOTE.—Where wholly executed abroad, the period begins to run from the date of arrival here.

PENALTIES ENFORCEABLE ON STAMPING IN ADDITION TO DUTY:—
Instruments presented after the proper time (subject to special provisions in some cases and subject to the commissioner's power to mitigate) a penalty equal to the duty . £10

AGREEMENT for Lease, *see* LEASES.
AGREEMENT FOR SALE OF PROPERTY—charged with *ad valorem* duty as if an actual conveyance on sale, with certain exceptions, e.g. agreements for the sale of land, stocks and shares, goods, wares or merchandise, or a ship (*see* s. 59 (1), Stamp Act 1891). If *ad valorem* duty is paid on an agreement in accordance with this provision, the subsequent conveyance or transfer is not chargeable with any *ad valorem* duty and the Commissioners will upon application either place a denoting stamp on such conveyance or transfer or will transfer the *ad valorem* duty thereto. Further, if such an agreement is rescinded, not performed, etc., the Commissioners will return the *ad valorem* duty paid.
AGREEMENT under seal subject to exemptions . 50p
ASSIGNMENT:
By way of sale—*see* Conveyance.
By way of gift—*see* Voluntary Disposition.
ASSURANCE—*see* Insurance Policies.
BEARER INSTRUMENT:
Inland bearer instrument, i.e. share warrant, stock certificate to bearer or any other instrument to bearer by which stock can be transferred, issued by a company or body formed or established in U.K. . . . . . . 1·5%.
Overseas bearer instrument, i.e., such an instrument issued in Great Britain by a company formed out of the U.K. . . . . 1·5%.
BILL OF SALE, Absolute, *see* CONVEYANCE ON SALE.
CAPITAL DUTY.—This was charged at 1 per cent on every £100 or fraction of £100 of the actual value of assets contributed by the members of a company provided the place of effective management of the company was in Great Britain or its registered office was in Great Britain but the place of its effective management was outside the E.C. (Finance Act 1973).
The tax was abolished by the Finance Act 1988 in respect of transactions entered into on or after March 16, 1988.
CONTRACT, *see* AGREEMENT.
CONTRACT OR GRANT FOR PAYMENT OF A SUPERANNUATION ANNUITY: for every £10 or fractional part of £10 . . . . 5p
CONVEYANCE OR TRANSFER ON SALE (in the case of a Voluntary Disposition, *see* below) of any property (except stock or marketable securities), where the Conveyance or Transfer contains a certificate of value certifying that the transaction does not form part of a larger transaction or a series of transactions in respect of which the aggregate amount or value of the consideration exceeds £30,000. . *nil*
Exceeds £30,000 (for every £100 or fraction of £100) £1
If the Conveyance or Transfer on Sale does not contain the appropriate statement, duty at the full rate of £1 for every £100 or fraction of £100 will be payable whatever the amount of the consideration.

However, if the consideration does not exceed £500, and the instrument does not contain a certificate of value, there are graduated duties ranging from 50p to £5.

Conveyances to charities are exempt from duty under this head provided the instrument is stamped with a denoting stamp.

CONVEYANCE OR TRANSFER of any other kind: fixed duty 50p

However, under the Stamp Duty (Exempt Instruments) Regulations 1987, instruments which would otherwise fall under this head are exempt from stamp duty provided that the document is duly certified. The certificate must contain a sufficient description of the category into which the instrument falls, and must be signed by the transferor, his solicitor or agent. "I/We hereby certify that this instrument falls within category ... in the Schedule to the Stamp Duty (Exempt Instruments) Regulations 1987."

COVENANT—For original creation and sale of any annuity, *see* CONVEYANCE.

DECLARATION OF TRUST, not being a Will or Settlement 50p

DEMISE, *see* LEASE

DUPLICATE OR COUNTERPART:
Same duty as original, but not to exceed ... 50p

GIFT (*see* VOLUNTARY DISPOSITION).

GUARANTEE:
If under seal 50p

INHERITANCE TAX

Inheritance Tax was introduced by the Finance Act 1986, to replace Capital Transfer Tax. The most radical change is to take outside the charge to tax many (but not all) lifetime gifts made more than seven years before the death of the donor.

Lifetime transfers made before March 18, 1986 may be subject to capital transfer tax and are broadly unaffected by the new regime. Thus, subject to exemptions and rate bands, capital transfer tax is payable on such transfers, at the lifetime rate with an additional charge to tax at the death rate if the donor dies within three years of the transfer, but no additional charge if the donor survives three years but dies within seven years of the gift.

If the gift is made on or after March 18, 1986 and comes within the definition of what is known as a potentially exempt transfer (for details, *see* page 1013), tax is not payable at the time of the gift and will not be payable if the donor survives the gift for seven years. If the donor does not survive for three years, the rate of tax payable on death for the year 1989–90 (based on the value of the property at the date of the gift) is shown in the following table:

Value transferred		Rate of tax
Lower limit £	Upper limit £	Per cent
0	118,000	*Nil*
over 118,000	—	40

If the donor survives the gift by more than three but less than seven years, tapering relief is given as follows.

Years between gift and death	Percentage of full charge
0–3	100
3–4	80
4–5	60
5–6	40
6–7	20

If the gift does not come within the definition of a potentially exempt transfer, e.g., the creation of a discretionary trust, it is taxed at the time of transfer at half the full rate, with an additional charge to tax if the donor dies within seven years.

Among the exemptions and reliefs given are the following:

(a) Transfers between spouses.
(b) The first £3,000 of gifts made in each tax year. There is provision for carry forward of this relief for one year only, in so far as it has not been used in the previous year.
(c) Gifts which are normal expenditure out of income.
(d) Gifts in consideration of marriage are exempt up to £5,000 if made by a parent; £2,500 if made by a grandparent or some other lineal ancestor, or by one party to another; and £1,000 in any other case.
(e) Gifts to charities and certain other bodies.
(f) Certain relief is given for agricultural and business property where a charge to inheritance tax arises on the donor's death within seven years, to the extent that the recipient still owns the property transferred or it has been replaced by similar property qualifying for relief.

INSURANCE POLICIES:
Life:—
Exceeding £50 and not exceeding £1,000, for every £100 or part of £100 .... 5p
Exceeding £1,000, for every £1,000 or any fractional part of £1,000 .... 50p
Made after 1 August 1966 for period not exceeding 2 years 5p

The Finance Act 1989 abolished this charge for policies made after December 31, 1989.

LEASES:—Lease or tack for any definite term less than a year of any furnished dwelling-house or apartments where the rent for such term exceeds £500, £1; of any lands, tenements, etc., in consideration of any rent, according to the following table:

Annual rent not exceeding	*Term not exceeding			Term exceeding 100 years
	7 years	35 years	100 years	
£	£ p	£ p	£ p	£ p
5	*Nil*	0·10	0·60	1·20
10	*Nil*	0·20	1·20	2·40
15	*Nil*	0·30	1·80	3·60
20	*Nil*	0·40	2·40	4·80
25	*Nil*	0·50	3·00	6·00
50	*Nil*	1·00	6·00	12·00
75	*Nil*	1·50	9·00	18·00
100	*Nil*	2·00	12·00	24·00
150	*Nil*	3·00	18·00	36·00
200	*Nil*	4·00	24·00	48·00
250	*Nil*	5·00	30·00	60·00
300	*Nil*	6·00	36·00	72·00
350	*Nil*	7·00	42·00	84·00
400	*Nil*	8·00	48·00	96·00
450	*Nil*	9·00	54·00	108·00
500	*Nil*	10·00	60·00	120·00
Exceeding £500 for every £50 or fraction of £50	0·50	1·00	6·00	12·00

*If the term is indefinite the same duty is payable as if the term did not exceed 7 years.

AGREEMENT FOR LEASE: same as actual lease.

Where a consideration other than rent is payable, the same rule applies where the consideration does not exceed £30,000 as under Conveyance or Transfer on Sale (except stock or marketable securities), provided that any rent payable does not exceed £300 a year and a certificate of value is included in the Conveyance or Transfer.

Leases to charities are exempt from duty under this head provided the instrument is stamped with a denoting stamp.

MORTGAGES are exempt.

RECEIPTS FOR SALARIES, Wages and Superannuation, and other like allowances are exempt.

TRANSFER OF STOCK AND SHARES by way of gift or sale.................................. 0·5%

UNIT TRUST INSTRUMENT—Any trust instrument of a unit trust scheme: for every £100, and also for any fractional part of £100, of the amount or value of the property subject to the trusts created or recorded by the instrument.............................. 25p

By the Finance Act 1989, the transfer of units in certain authorized unit trusts are no longer subject to duty.

VOLUNTARY DISPOSITION *inter vivos:*— 50p

EXPECTATION OF LIFE

(Interim figures)

Age	England and Wales Life Table, 1984–86		Scotland Life Table, 1984–86		Northern Ireland Life Table, 1984–86	
	Males	Females	Males	Females	Males	Females
0.............	71·9	77·7	70·0	76·0	70·2	76·5
5.............	67·8	73·5	65·9	71·8	66·2	72·4
10.............	62·9	68·5	61·0	66·8	61·3	67·5
15.............	58·0	63·6	56·1	61·9	56·4	62·5
20.............	53·2	58·7	51·3	57·0	51·6	57·6
25.............	48·4	53·8	46·5	52·0	46·9	52·7
30.............	43·6	48·8	41·7	47·2	42·2	47·8
35.............	38·8	44·0	37·0	42·3	37·4	43·0
40.............	34·0	39·2	32·3	37·5	32·7	38·1
45.............	29·4	34·4	27·7	32·8	28·1	33·4
50.............	24·9	29·8	23·4	28·3	23·7	28·8
55.............	20·6	25·4	19·4	24·0	19·7	24·4
60.............	16·8	21·2	15·7	20·0	16·0	20·3
65.............	13·4	17·3	12·5	16·3	12·7	16·4
70.............	10·4	13·7	9·8	13·0	9·9	12·9
75.............	8·0	10·5	7·5	10·0	7·5	9·8
80.............	6·0	7·7	5·7	7·4	5·5	7·1
85.............	4·4	5·5	4·2	5·3	4·1	5·1

LEGAL NOTES

IMPORTANT

The purpose of these notes is to outline some of the more common parts of the law as they may affect the average person, and they are, of course, believed to be correct at the time of going to press. The law is constantly developing and changing, however, and it is dangerous for the layman to seek to be his own lawyer—he may not have access to completely up to date books and his case may, because of its special facts, come within an exception to the general rules set out herein.

It is always best to take expert advice, and if you have a solicitor who has acted for you in the past you should take any legal problems you have to him or her. If you do not have a solicitor a friend may be able to recommend one. Failing this your local Citizens' Advice Bureau (whose address can be obtained from the telephone directory or from any Post Office or Town Hall) has a list of solicitors in your area who deal with that particular type of problem which you have. If you are not able to find a solicitor in any of these ways you should ask for help in doing so from The Law Society, 113 Chancery Lane, London, WC2A 1PL or The Law Society of Scotland at 26 Drumsheugh Gardens, Edinburgh, EH3 7YR.

The Legal Aid and Legal Advice and Assistance schemes exist to make the help of the trained lawyer available to everyone whatever their means as of right. The best policy is to go to a solicitor without delay—timely advice will set your mind at rest but sitting on your rights can mean that you lose them.

Remember also that it is not necessary for a dispute to have arisen before you go to a solicitor—the Legal Advice and Assistance Scheme enables a solicitor to advise you on your rights, for instance under a tenancy agreement, the estate of a deceased person or in connection with matrimonial and consumer matters, and to write letters or take other steps on your behalf. A solicitor can also act for you where there is no question of a dispute at all, e.g. in the making of a will.

Your entitlement to take advantage of the scheme depends on your means (see below) but a solicitor or Citizens' Advice Bureau will be able to tell you whether you are covered by it.

BRITISH CITIZENSHIP

Types of citizenship.—There are three types of citizenship: British Citizenship; Citizenship of the British Dependent Territories; and British Overseas Citizenship.

Acquisition of citizenship on change of law.—The British Nationality Act 1981 which came into force on January 1, 1983 made substantial changes to the law of citizenship (which before that date did not distinguish between the three types of citizenship referred to above). Almost all persons who were then both citizens of the U.K. and Colonies and who had a right of abode in the U.K. became British Citizens when the Act came into force. Most U.K. and Colonies Citizens who did not have a right of abode in the U.K. became Citizens of the British Dependent Territories. This type of citizenship was, broadly speaking, conferred on citizens of the U.K. and Colonies by birth, naturalization or registration in dependent territories. Dependent territories include Hong Kong, Gibraltar, the Falkland Islands, and St. Helena and its dependencies. Any U.K. and Colonies Citizen who, on Jan. 1, 1983, did not acquire either British or British Dependent Territories' Citizenship became a British Overseas Citizen.

Later acquisition of British Citizenship.—British Citizenship is acquired automatically by those born in the U.K. (including, for this purpose, the Channel Islands and the Isle of Man) who have a parent who is a British Citizen or a parent who is settled in the U.K. Certain other categories of children born in the U.K. also acquire this type of citizenship, i.e. foundlings, those whose parents subsequently settle in the U.K., those who live in the U.K. for 10 years from birth and those adopted in the U.K.

A person born outside the U.K. may acquire British Citizenship in the following ways:—

(i) if one of his parents is a British Citizen otherwise than by descent (e.g. parent was born in the U.K.).

(ii) if one of his parents is a British Citizen serving the Crown overseas.

(iii) if the Secretary of State consents to his registration while he is a minor.

(iv) if he is a Citizen of the British Dependent Territories, a British Overseas Citizen, a British Subject or a British Protected Person (these last two are residual categories of people who have not acquired one of the three new types of citizenship) and has been lawfully resident in the U.K. for five years without any time restriction.

(v) if he is a British Dependent Territories Citizen who is a national of the U.K. for the purposes of the E.C. (i.e. a Gibraltarian).

(vi) if he is naturalized. Naturalization may be applied for only by adults and the Secretary of State has a discretion whether to permit it. The basic requirements are five years' residence, good character, sufficient knowledge of the English or Welsh language, and an intention to reside in the U.K. permanently. The requirements are somewhat less restrictive in the case of an applicant who is married to a British Citizen.

Acquisition of British Dependent Territories and British Overseas Citizenship after the Act.—These citizenships are intended for persons connected with certain Commonwealth countries other than the U.K. In the case of Dependent Territories the rules are very similar to those for acquiring British Citizenship except that the connection is with the Dependent Territory rather than with the U.K. British Overseas Citizenship may be acquired by the minor children and wives of British Overseas Citizens in certain circumstances.

Retention of nationality by persons born in or who are citizens of the Republic of Ireland.—By the Ireland Act 1949, a person who was born before December 6, 1922, in what is now the Republic of Ireland (Eire) and was a British subject immediately before January 1, 1949, is not deemed to have ceased to be a British subject unless either (i) he was domiciled in the Irish Free State on December 6, 1922 or (ii) was on or after April 10, 1935, and before January 1, 1949, permanently resident there, or (iii) had before January 1, 1949, been registered as a citizen of Eire under the laws of that country.

In addition, by the British Nationality Act 1948, any citizen of Eire who immediately before January 1, 1949, was also a British subject can retain that status by submitting at any time a claim to the Home Secretary on any of the following grounds:

(a) he has been in the service of the United Kingdom Government;

(b) he holds a British passport issued in the United Kingdom or in any colony, protectorate, United Kingdom mandated or trust territory;

(c) he has associations by way of descent, residence or otherwise with any such place; or on complying with similar legislation in any of the 'dominions'.

The British Nationality Act 1981 provides that persons who have made a claim may continue to be British subjects. Any citizen of Eire who was a British subject before January 1, 1949, who has not yet made a claim may do so provided that:

(a) he is or has been in Crown Service under the government of the United Kingdom; or

(b) he has associations by way of descent, residence or otherwise with the United Kingdom or any dependent territory.

Renunciation and Resumption.—A person may cease to be a British Citizen by renouncing his citizenship (with the consent of the Secretary of State in wartime). The renunciation is required to be registered with the Secretary of State and will be revoked if no new citizenship or nationality is acquired within six months. Once renounced, citizenship may be reacquired if the renunciation was necessary to retain or acquire some other citizenship or nationality. Similar rules as to renunciation and reacquisition apply in the case of British Dependent Territories Citizenships and of renunciation (but not reacquisition) in the case of British Overseas Citizenship.

Status of Aliens.—Property may be held by an alien in the same manner as by a natural-born British subject, but he may not hold public office, exercise the franchise or own a British ship or aircraft. The Republic of Ireland Act 1949 declares that the Republic, though not part of H.M. Dominions, is not a foreign country, and any reference in an Act of Parliament to foreigners, aliens, foreign countries, etc., shall be construed accordingly.

CONSUMER LAW

1. THE SUPPLY OF GOODS AND SERVICES

(a) The Sale of Goods Act 1979 provides protection to the purchaser of goods, by implying certain terms into every contract for the Sale of Goods. These implied terms are:

(i) A condition that the seller will pass good title to the buyer (unless the seller agrees to transfer only such title as he or his principal has) and warranties that the goods will be free from undisclosed encumbrances, and that the buyer will enjoy quiet possession of the goods.

(ii) Where there is a sale of goods by description, a condition that the goods will correspond with that description, and where the sale is by sample and description, a condition that the bulk of the goods shall correspond with both sample and description.

(iii) Where the seller sells goods in the course of a business, a condition that the goods will be of merchantable quality, unless before the contract is made, the buyer has examined the goods and ought to have noticed the defect, bearing in mind the purchaser's knowledge of the goods and the extent of the examination, or the seller has specifically drawn the attention of the buyer to the defect. Merchantable quality means fit for the purpose for which goods of the kind are commonly bought, taking into account any description applied to them, the price and other relevant circumstances.

(iv) A condition that where the seller sells goods in the course of a business, the goods are reasonably fit for any purpose made known to the seller by the buyer, unless the buyer does not rely on the seller's skill and judgment, or it would be unreasonable for him to do so.

(v) Where there is a sale of goods by sample, conditions that the bulk of the goods shall correspond with the sample in quality, that the buyer will have a reasonable opportunity of comparing the bulk with the sample, and that the goods are free from any defect rendering them unmerchantable, which would not be apparent from the sample.

For these purposes, the broad difference between a condition and a warranty is that the remedy for a breach of an implied condition may enable the buyer to reject the goods and recover damages if he has suffered loss whereas the remedy for a breach of warranty will only enable the buyer to recover damages.

It is possible for a seller to exclude some of the above terms from a contract, subject to restrictions imposed by the Unfair Contract Terms Act 1977 as given below. These restrictions give more protection ... where the buyer 'deals as consumer'. In a contract of sale of goods, a buyer 'deals as consumer' where there is ... a sale by a seller in the course of a business, the goods are of a type ordinarily bought for private use or consumption, and are sold to a person who does not buy or hold himself out as buying them in the course of a business. A buyer in a sale by auction or competitive tender never 'deals as consumer'.

The 1977 Act prohibits the exclusion of the implied terms given in (ii) to (v) above, where the buyer 'deals as consumer'. In sales where the buyer does not 'deal as consumer', terms purporting to exclude these implied terms, may be relied upon only to the extent that it would be reasonable to allow reliance. The Act provides guidelines for determining whether it would be reasonable to allow reliance. The implied terms in (i) above cannot be excluded whether the buyer 'deals as consumer' or not.

(b) Similar terms to those implied in contracts of sale of goods are implied into contracts of hire-purchase by the Supply of Goods (Implied Terms) Act 1973, and the 1977 Act limits the exclusion of these implied terms in a similar manner.

(c) Under the Supply of Goods and Services Act 1982, terms similar to those in the Sale of Goods Act relating to quiet possession, compliance with description, merchantable quality, fitness for purpose and correspondence with sample are implied into other types of contract under which ownership of goods passes (e.g. a contract for 'work and materials' such as a supply of new parts during the servicing of a motor car) and also into contracts for the hire of goods. In the case of contracts under which ownership of goods is to pass, there is also an implied condition as to title.

The 1977 Act limits the exclusion of these implied terms in a similar manner to the implied terms in the Sale of Goods Act.

(d) The Supply of Goods and Services Act 1982 also implies into a contract for the supply of services, terms that the supplier will use reasonable care and skill, carry out the service within a reasonable time (unless the time is agreed) and charge a reasonable charge (unless the charge is agreed).

(e) The Trade Descriptions Act 1968 provides that it is a criminal offence for a trader or businessman to apply a false trade description to any goods, or to supply or offer to supply any goods to which a false trade description has been applied. A trade description includes a description as to quantity, size, method, place and date of manufacture, other history, composition, other physical characteristics, fitness for purpose, behaviour or accuracy, testing or approval. It is also an offence to give a false indication as to the price of goods. Prosecutions are brought by trading standards inspectors.

(f) The Fair Trading Act 1973 is also designed to protect the consumer. It provides for the appointment of a Director General of Fair Trading, whose duties include keeping under review commercial activities in the U.K. relating to the supply of goods or services to consumers, and to collect information to discover practices that may adversely affect the economic interests of the consumer. He may refer certain consumer trade practices to the Consumer Protection Advisory Committee, or of his own initiative take proceedings against firms that are trading unfairly. He may also publish information and advice to consumers. Examples of practices which have been prohibited by virtue of references made under this Act, include the use of certain void exclusion clauses in contracts for the sale of goods and hire-purchase, and advertisements by traders appearing to sell as private persons.

(g) The Consumer Protection Act 1987 makes the producer of a product liable for any damage caused by a defect in that product, subject to certain defences.

(h) The Consumer Protection (Cancellation of Contracts Concluded away from Business Premises) Regulations 1987 allow consumers a seven day period in which to cancel most contracts for supply of goods or services exceeding £35 in cost, where these contracts have been made following an unsolicited visit to the consumer's home or workplace.

Scotland

The Sale of Goods Act 1979, a consolidating Act, applies with some modification to Scotland. For example, it is not necessary in Scotland to distinguish between the words condition and warranty. The remedies of the buyer in both cases are the same, i.e. he can either within a reasonable time reject the goods and treat the contract as repudiated, or retain the goods and treat the failure to perform such material part as a breach which may give rise to a claim for compensation or damages.

2. CONSUMER CREDIT

England and Wales

The Consumer Credit Act 1974 provides a system for the protection of the consumer, of licensing and control of all matters relating to the provision of credit, or the supply of goods on hire or hire-purchase, administered by the Director-General of Fair Trading. A licence is required to carry on a consumer credit or consumer hire business, or to deal in credit brokerage, debt adjusting, counselling or collecting, for which group licences are available. Any 'fit' person may apply to the Director of Fair Trading for a licence which is normally renewable after ten years. A licence is not necessary if such types of business

are only transacted 'occasionally' or if exempt agreements only are involved.

For the Act's provisions to apply the agreement must be 'regulated', i.e. be to individuals or partnerships only; must not be exempt, e.g. certain loans by local authorities or building societies; and the total credit must not exceed £15,000. The terms of a regulated agreement can be varied by the creditor, but only if the agreement gives him the right to do so, and the debtor receives notice in the prescribed form.

To be enforceable the agreement must be properly executed, and the specified information must be given during the antecedent negotiations for the contract. These are conducted by the creditor, credit broker or supplier (these being the creditor's agents) and begin when the parties first begin discussions.

The agreement must state certain information such as the amount of credit, the annual percentage rate of interest and the amount and timing of repayments.

An agreement is cancellable under the Act if oral representations were made in the debtor's presence during antecedent negotiations and the debtor signed the agreement other than at the creditor's (or creditbroker's or negotiator's) place of business. Time for cancellation expires five clear days after the debtor receives a second copy of the agreement. The agreement must inform the debtor of his right to cancel and how to cancel.

Where there are arrangements or connections between the creditor and supplier the former is generally liable for any misrepresentation or breach of contract by the latter, and will thus be liable to indemnify the debtor.

If the debtor is in arrears or is otherwise in breach of the agreement, the creditor may not enforce the agreement, e.g. by repossessing goods, without serving a default notice on the debtor. This notice will give the debtor a chance to remedy the default. Even if the default is not remedied by the debtor, if the agreement is a hire-purchase or conditional sale agreement, the creditor cannot repossess the goods without an order of the court, if the debtor has paid one-third of the total price of the goods.

Where the agreement requires the debtor to make grossly exorbitant payments or is contrary to the ordinary principles of fair dealing the Court can reopen it either at the debtor's request or during enforcement proceedings and (inter alia) alter the terms of the contract or set aside any obligations it imposes so as to do justice between the parties. Whether an agreement is such an extortionate credit bargain is decided by reference (inter alia) to interest rates prevailing at the date of agreement, the pressure for finance the debtor was under, etc.

If a credit reference agency was used to check the debtor's financial standing the creditor must give the agency's name to the debtor who is entitled to see the agency's file on him on payment of a fee of £1.

Scotland

The Consumer Credit Act (see above) also extends to Scotland and goes far in assimilating the Scots Law on this topic with English Law. The Supply of Goods (Implied Terms) Act 1973 also applies to Scotland. Parts II and III only of the Unfair Contract Terms Act 1977 apply to Scotland. The Sale of Goods Act, 1979, applies with some modification to Scotland.

3. RECEIPTS

The law on receipts in Scotland is governed by the Prescription and Limitations (Scotland) Act 1973, which for this purpose came into force on July 25, 1976. Now, receipts need only be kept for a period of five years and if a creditor does not make a relevant claim within that period no action can be raised.

CROWN—PROCEEDINGS AGAINST

Before 1947 proceedings against the Crown were generally possible only by a procedure known as a petition of right, which placed the litigant at a considerable disadvantage. However, by the Crown Proceedings Act 1947, which came into operation on Jan. 1, 1948, the Crown, in its public capacity, is largely placed in the same position as a subject, although some procedural disadvantages remain, for example, the enforcement of judgments against the Crown.

Scotland.—The Act as amended extends to Scotland and has the effect of bringing the practice of the two countries as closely together as the different legal systems will permit. While formerly actions against the Crown, when permissible, were confined to the Court of Session, proceedings may now be brought in the Sheriff Court.

The Act lays down that arrestment of money in the hands of the Crown or of a Government Department is competent in any case where arrestment in the hands of a subject would have been competent, but an exception is made in respect of National Savings Bank deposits. Section 2 (1) of the Law Reform (Miscellaneous Provisions) (Scotland) Act 1966 removes the privilege whereby the wages of Crown servants, other than serving members of the armed forces, are exempt from arrestment in execution.

DEATHS

REGISTRATION, BURIAL AND CREMATION

REGISTRATION

(For Certificates, *see* under FAMILY LAW—CERTIFICATES)

In England and Wales.—When a death takes place, information of it must be given in person to the local Registrar of Births and Deaths, and the register signed in his presence, by one of the following persons: (1) a relative of the deceased present at the death, or in attendance during the last illness. (2) Some other relative of the deceased. In default of any relatives (3) a person present at the death, or the occupier of the house in which the death happened. (4) An inmate of the house. A person (other than a relative) registering the death must be causing the disposal of the body. The registration must be made within five days of the death, or within the same time written notice of the death must be sent to the Registrar. If the deceased was attended during his last illness by a registered medical practitioner, a certificate of cause of death must be sent by the doctor to the Registrar. The doctor must give to the informant of the death a written notice of the signing of the certificate, which must be delivered to the Registrar. It is essential that a certificate for disposal should be obtained from the Registrar before the funeral and delivered to the clergyman or other person in charge of the churchyard or cemetery. No fee is chargeable for this certificate. If the death is not registered within five days (or fourteen days if written notice of the occurrence of the death is sent to him) the Registrar may require any one of the above-mentioned persons to attend to register at a stated time and place. Failure to comply involves a penalty of ten pounds. The registration of a death is free of charge. After twelve months no death can be registered without the Registrar General's consent.

Whenever the death of a child is registered, particulars of the name and occupation of the mother are to be entered in the register.

A body must not be disposed of until (1) either the Registrar has given a certificate to the effect that he has registered or received notice of the death, or (2) until the Coroner has made a disposal order (Births and Deaths Registration Act 1926, s. 1).

A person disposing of a body must within ninety-six hours deliver to the Registrar a notification as to the date, place, and means of the disposal of the body (*ib.*, S. 3).

Still born child (*see* under Births (Registration) *below*).

Death at Sea.—The master of a British ship must record any death on board and send particulars to the Registrar General of Shipping.

Death Abroad.—Consular Officers are authorized to register deaths of British subjects occurring abroad. Certificates are procurable at the Registrar General's Office, London. If the deceased was of Scottish domicile, particulars are sent to the Registrar General for Scotland.

With regard to the registration of deaths of members of the armed forces, and deaths occurring on H.M. ships and aircraft, *see* the Registration of Births, etc. Act 1957.

Deaths (Registration) in Scotland.—The Registration of Births, Deaths and Marriages (Scotland) Act 1965 supersedes provisions in former Acts.

Personal notification within eight days must be given to the Registrar of (1) the registration district in which the death took place or (2) any registration district in which the deceased was ordinarily resident immediately before his death, and (3) when a body is found and the place of death is not known, either the registration district in which the body was found or any other registration district appropriate by virtue of the preceding paragraph. When a person dies (in or out of Scotland) in a ship, aircraft or land vehicle during a journey and the body is conveyed therein to any place in Scotland the death shall, unless the Registrar General otherwise directs, be deemed to have occurred at that place.

The register must be signed in the presence of the Registrar by one of the following: (1) any relative of the deceased; (2) any person present at the death; (3) the deceased's executor or other legal representative; (4) the occupier, at the time of the death, of the premises where the death took place; (5) if these fail, any other person having knowledge of the particulars to be registered. Failure to comply involves a penalty not exceeding £50.

The medical practitioner who attended the deceased during the last illness must sign a certificate of the cause of death within seven days. If there is no such medical practitioner, any medical practitioner who is able to do so, may sign the certificate. At the time of registering the death the Registrar shall, without charge, give the informant a certificate of registration, and the person to whom the certificate is given must hand it to the undertaker previous to cremation. A body may, however, be interred before the death is registered, in which case the undertaker must deliver a certificate of burial to the Registrar within three days.

The mandatory death grant was abolished in April 1987 but assistance may be obtained from the Department of Social Security by those who are unable to meet funeral expenses.

BURIAL

The duty of burial is incumbent on the deceased person's executors (if any appointed); it is also a recognized obligation of the husband of a woman, and the parent of a child, also of a householder where the body lies. Funeral expenses of a reasonable amount will be repayable out of deceased's estate in priority to any other claims. Directions as to place and mode of burial are frequently contained in the deceased's will or in some memorandum placed with private papers, or may have been communicated verbally to a relative. Consequently steps should immediately be taken to ascertain the deceased's wishes from the above sources. If the wishes are considered objectionable, they are not necessarily enforceable; legal advice should be taken. A person may legally leave directions for the anatomical examination of his body. As to the place of burial—unless closed by Order in Council—the parish church-yard is the normal burying place for parishioners, or any person dying in the parish, but nowadays this will apply only in villages and smaller towns. In populous districts cemeteries and crematoria have been established either by the local council or a private company, and burials will take place there in accordance with the regulations. For an exclusive right to a burial space in the churchyard a faculty is required from the Ecclesiastical Court. Poor persons may be buried at the public expense by the local authority. As to the necessity for obtaining a Registrar's certificate or authority from the Coroner for disposal, *see* above.

CREMATION

Under the Cremation Acts 1902 and 1952, regulations are made by the Home Secretary dealing fully with the cremation of a body, disposal of ashes, etc., and containing numerous essential safeguards.

If cremation is desired it is advisable for instructions to be left in writing to that effect. However, in Scotland, even if the deceased wished his body to be cremated or anatomically dissected, relatives can still veto his or her wishes.

To arrange for cremation, the executor or near relative should instruct the undertaker to that effect and obtain from him the Statutory Forms required as given in the Cremation Regulations issued in 1930 (Statutory Rules and Orders, 1930, No. 1016), as amended by the Cremation Regulations 1965 (No. 1146) and the Cremation (Amendment) Regulations 1985 (No. 153).

INTESTACY

ENGLAND AND WALES

As regards deaths on or after March 15, 1977, the position is governed by the Administration of Estates Act 1925, as amended by the Intestates' Estates Act 1952, the Family Provision Act 1966 and Orders made thereunder. If the intestate leaves a spouse and issue, the spouse takes (i) the 'personal chattels'; (ii) £75,000 with interest at six per cent from death until payment; and (iii) a life interest in half of the rest of the estate. This life interest can be capitalized at the option of the spouse. 'Personal chattels' are articles of household use or ornament (including motor-cars), not used for business purposes. The rest of the estate goes to the issue. If the intestate leaves a spouse and no issue, but leaves a parent or brother or sister of the whole blood or issue of such brothers and sisters the spouse takes (i) the 'personal chattels'; (ii) £125,000 with interest at six per cent from death until payment, and (iii) half of the rest of the estate absolutely. The other half of the rest of the estate goes to the parents, equally if more than one, or, if none, to the brothers and sisters of the whole blood or issue of such brothers and sisters. If the intestate leaves a spouse, but no issue, no parents and no brothers or sisters of the whole blood or their issue, the spouse takes the whole estate absolutely. If

resident therein at the intestate's death, the surviving spouse may generally require the personal representatives to appropriate the interest of the intestate in the matrimonial home in or towards satisfaction of any absolute interest of the spouse, including the capitalized value of a life interest. In certain cases, leave of Court is required. On a partial intestacy any benefit (other than personal chattels specifically bequeathed) received by the surviving spouse under the will must be brought into account against the statutory legacy of £75,000 or £125,000, as the case may be. If there is no surviving spouse, the estate is distributed among those who survive the intestate in the following order (those entitled under earlier numbers taking to the exclusion of those entitled under later numbers):—(1) children; (2) father or mother (equally, if both alive); (3) brothers and sisters of the whole blood; (4) brothers and sisters of the half blood; (5) grandparents (equally, if more than one alive); (6) uncles and aunts of the whole blood; (7) uncles and aunts of the half blood; (8) the Crown.

In cases (1), (3), (4), (6) and (7) the persons entitled lose their interests unless they or their issue not only survive the intestate, but also attain eighteen or marry under that age, their shares going to the persons (if any) within the same group who do attain eighteen or marry. Moreover, in the same cases, succession is not *per capita*, but *per stirpes*, i.e., by stocks or families. Thus, if the intestate leaves one child and two grandchildren, being the children of a child of the intestate, who pre-deceased the intestate, the two grandchildren represent their deceased parent and take between them one-half of the issue's share, the remaining half going to the surviving child. Similarly, nephews and nieces represent a deceased brother, and so on.

When the deceased died partially intestate (i.e., leaving a will which disposed of only part of his property), the above rules apply to the intestate part.

Children must bring into account (hotchpot) any substantial advances received from the intestate during his lifetime before claiming any further share under the intestacy. Special hotchpot provisions apply to partial intestacy.

In respect of deaths occurring on or after April 4, 1988, Section 18 of the Family Law Reform Act 1987 provides that references to any relationship between two persons shall, unless the contrary intention appears, be construed without regard to whether or not the father and mother of either of them, or the father and mother of any person through whom the relationship is deduced, have or had been married to each other at any time.

In respect of deaths after March 1976 the provisions of the Inheritance (Provision for Family and Dependants) Act 1975 may allow other persons to claim provision out of the estate. *See* below under 'WILLS'.

For personal application for Letters of Administration, *see* below.

SCOTLAND

The Succession (Scotland) Act, 1964, provides that the whole estate of any person dying intestate shall devolve without distinction between heritable and moveable property. By that Act the surviving spouse of an intestate may, as a prior right (in addition to legal rights, *see* below), claim the matrimonial home to a maximum of £65,000, or a choice of one matrimonial home if more than one (or in certain circumstances the value thereof), with its furniture and plenishings not exceeding £12,000 in value, plus the sum of £21,000 if the deceased left issue or, if no issue, the sum of £35,000. These figures apply from

May 1, 1988 and may be increased from time to time by order of the Secretary of State.

The fact that a person was born illegitimate no longer has any effect in their rights of succession as against a legitimate child, by virtue of the Law Reform (Parent and Child) (Scotland) Act 1986.

Legal rights, referred to above, are:—

Jus relicti(ae) : the right of a surviving spouse to one half of the deceased's net moveable estate after satisfaction of prior rights if there are no surviving children, or to one third if there are any surviving children.

Legitim: the right of surviving children to one-half of the net moveable estate of deceased parents if no surviving spouse, or one-third of the net moveable estate of deceased parents after satisfaction of prior rights where there is a surviving spouse.

There are no legal rights in heritage.

In general, the lines of succession are: (1) descendants; (2) collaterals; (3) ascendants and their collaterals, and so on in the ascending scale. The Crown is *ultimus haeres.* The right of representation, i.e., the right of the issue of a person who would have succeeded if he had survived the intestate, is open to any line of succession where previously it was limited to apply only when there were next of kin or the issue of predeceasing next of kin. The surviving mother of an intestate now has equal rights of succession with the surviving father, where formerly these were restricted. The intestate's maternal relations, who prior to the Act had no rights of succession, are now on an equal footing with his paternal relations. Where the intestate is survived only by parents, and by brothers and sisters (collaterals) half of the estate is taken by the parents and the other half by the brothers and sisters, those of the whole blood being preferred to those of the half blood. Where, however, succession opens to collaterals (which expression can include the brothers and sisters of an ancestor of the intestate) of the half blood, they shall rank equally amongst themselves, whether related to the intestate (or his ancestor) through their father or their mother.

WILLS

The following notes and those on Intestacy must be read subject to the provisions of the Inheritance (Provision for Family and Dependants) Act 1975 which can affect the estate of anyone dying domiciled in England and Wales after March 1976. Very broadly, a spouse, former spouse who has not remarried, a child of the deceased himself or one treated by him as a child of his family, or any person maintained by him at his death may apply to the Court under the Act. If the Court thinks that the will or the law of intestacy or both do not make reasonable provision for the applicant it may order payment out of the net estate of maintenance or a lump sum. It may also order the transfer of property, or vary certain trusts and the powers can affect property disposed of by the deceased in his lifetime intending to defeat the Act. It is up to the applicant to take the initiative, and the application must generally be made within six months of the grant of Probate or Letters of Administration.

Making a Will.—Every person over the age of 18 should make a will. However small the estate, the rules of Intestacy (*see* above) may not reflect a person's wishes as to his property; in any case a will can do more than just deal with property. It can in particular appoint executors, give directions as to the disposal of the body and appoint guardians to take care of children in the event of the parents'

death. For the wealthier person an appropriately drawn will can operate to reduce the burden of Inheritance Tax.

It is considered desirable for a will to be properly drawn up by a solicitor. Although normally the making of a will is not one of the services which can be provided under the Legal Advice and Assistance Scheme, it can be provided for certain special categories of person such as the aged and infirm (*see* below).

In no circumstances should one person prepare a will for another person where the former is to take any benefit under it—this can easily lead to a suggestion of undue influence which may cause the will to be held bad.

Assuming a lawyer is not employed, a person having resolved to make a will must remember that it is only after a person is dead, and cannot explain his meaning, that his will can be open to dispute. It is the more necessary, therefore, to express what is meant in language of the utmost clearness, avoiding the use of any word or expression that admits of another meaning than the one intended. Avoid the use of legal terms, such as heirs and issue, when the same thing may be expressed in plain language. If in writing the will a mistake be made, it is better to rewrite the whole. Before a will is executed (*see* below) an alteration may be made by striking through the words with a pen, but opposite to such alteration the testator and witnesses should write their names or place their initials. Never scratch out a word with a knife or other instrument, and no alteration of any kind whatever must be made after the will is executed. If the testator afterwards wishes to change the disposition of his estate, it is best to make a new will, revoking the old one. The use of codicils should be left to the lawyer. A will should be written in ink and very legibly, on a single sheet of paper. Although, of course, forms of wills must vary to suit different cases, the following forms may be found useful to those who, in cases of emergency, are called upon to draw up wills, either for themselves or others.

Nothing more complicated should be attempted. The forms should be studied in conjunction with the notes following.

This is the last will and testament of me [*Thomas Smith*] of [*Vine Cottage, Silver Street, Reading, Berks.*] which I make this [*thirteenth*] day of [*February,* 1990] and whereby I revoke all previous wills and testamentary dispositions.

1. I hereby appoint [*John Green of —— and Richard Brown of ——*] to be the executor(s) of this my will.

2. I give all my property real and personal to [*my wife Mary* or *my sons Raymond and David equally* or as the case may be].

Signed by the testator in the presence of us both present at the same time who, at his request, in his presence and in the presence of each other have here-unto set our names as witnesses.

    Thomas Smith
    Signature of
    Testator;

William Jones (*signed*) of Green Gables, South Street, Reading, tailor.

Henry Morgan (*signed*) of 16, North Street, Reading, butcher.

Should it be desired to give legacies and/or gifts of specific property, instead of giving the whole estate to one or more persons, the form above should be used with the substitution for clause 2 of the following clauses:—

2. I give to —— of —— the sum of £—— and to ——

— of —— the sum of £—— and to —— of —— all my books [*or as the case may require*].

3. All the residue of my property real and personal I give to —— of ——.

Terms.—Real property includes freehold land and houses; while personal property includes debts due, arrears of rents, money, leasehold property, house furniture, goods, assurance policies, stocks and shares in companies, and the like. The words 'my money', apart from the context, will normally only include actual real money. The expression 'goods and chattels' should not be used. In giving particular property, ordinary language is sufficient, e.g., 'my house, Vine Cottage, Silver Street, Reading, Berks.' Such specific gifts fail if not owned by the testator at his death.

Residuary Legatees.—It is well in all cases where legacies or specific gifts are made, to leave to some person or persons 'the residue of my property', although it may be thought that the whole of the property has been disposed of in legacies, etc., already mentioned in the will. It should be remembered that a will operates on property owned at the time of death.

Execution of a Will, and Witnesses.—The testator should sign his name at the foot or end of the will, in the presence of two witnesses, who will immediately afterwards sign their names in his and in each other's presence. A person who has been left any gift or share of residue in the will, or whose wife or husband has been left such a gift, should not be an attesting witness. Their attestation would be good, but they would forfeit the gift. It is better that a person named as executor should not be a witness. Husband and wife may both be witnesses, provided neither is a legatee. If a solicitor be appointed executor, it is lawful to direct that his ordinary fees and charges shall be paid; but in this case he (as an interested party) must not be a witness to the will.

It is desirable that the witnesses should be fully described, as they may possibly be wanted at some future time. If the testator should be too ill to sign, even by a mark, another person may sign the testator's name to the will for him, in his presence and by his direction, and in this case it should be shown that the testator knew the contents of the document. The attestation clause should therefore be worded: 'Signed by Thomas Brown, by the direction and in the presence of the testator, Thomas Smith, in the joint presence of us, who thereupon signed our names in his presence and in the presence of each other, the will having been first read over to the testator, who appeared fully to understand the same.'

Where there is any suspicion that the testator is not, by reason of age or infirmity, fully in command of his faculties it is desirable to ask his doctor to act as a witness (*see* Testamentary capacity below).

A blind person may make a will in Braille. If the testator be blind the will should be read aloud to him in the presence of the witnesses, and the fact mentioned in the attestation clause. A blind person cannot witness a will.

If by inadvertance the testator should have signed his will without the witnesses being present, then the attestation should be:—'The testator acknowledged his signature already made as his signature to his last will and testament, in the joint presence,' etc. Any omission in the observance of these details may invalidate the will. The stringency of the law as to signature and witnessing of a will is only relaxed in favour of soldiers, sailors and airmen in certain circumstances.

Executors.—It is usual to appoint two executors, although one is sufficient; any number up to and including four may be appointed. The name and address of each executor should be given in full. An executor may be a legatee. Thus a child of full age or wife to whom the whole or a portion of the estate is left may be appointed sole executor, or one of two executors. The addresses of the executors are not essential; but it is desirable here as elsewhere, to avoid ambiguity or vagueness.

Lapsed Legacies.—If a legatee dies in the lifetime of the testator, the legacy generally lapses and falls into the residue. Where a residuary legatee predeceases the testator, his share of the residuary estate will not generally pass to the other residuary legatees, but will pass to the persons entitled on the deceased's intestacy. In all such cases it is desirable to make a new will.

An important exception to the general rule of lapse stated above is contained in the Administration of Justice Act 1982, where there is a gift to a child or remoter issue of the testator who dies before the testator leaving issue who survive the testator. In such a case the gift will pass to the issue of the deceased child.

Testamentary Capacity.—A person under the age of 18 cannot make a will (except for soldiers, sailors and airmen and then only in exceptional circumstances).

So far as mental capacity is concerned the testator must be able to understand and appreciate the nature and effect of making a will, the property of which he can dispose and the claims to which he ought to give effect. If a person is not mentally able to make a will, provision exists (under the Mental Health Act 1983) for the Court to do this for him.

Revocation.—A later will revokes an earlier will if it expressly says so, or is completely inconsistent with it. Otherwise the earlier one is only revoked insofar as it is inconsistent with the later one. A will may also be revoked by burning, tearing or otherwise destroying the will with the intention of revoking it. Such destruction must either be by the testator or by some other person in his presence and at his direction. It is not sufficient to obliterate the will with a pen. Marriage in every case acts as the revocation of a will, except that under the Administration of Justice Act 1982, there is a provision to the effect that if it appears from a will that at the time it was made the testator was expecting to be married to a particular person and that he intended that the will (or a disposition in the will) should not be revoked by the marriage to that person, the will will not be revoked by marriage to that person. The Act also provides that where after a testator has made a will the testator's marriage is terminated by a decree of divorce or nullity, any gift to a spouse shall lapse and any appointment of the spouse as executor shall be omitted from the will unless the will shows a contrary intention.

PERSONAL APPLICATION FOR PROBATE OR LETTERS OF ADMINISTRATION

Application for probate or for letters of administration may be made in person at the Personal Application Department of the Principal Registry of the Family Division, a district probate registry or sub-registry, or a probate office by the executors or persons entitled to a grant of administration. Applicants should bring (1) the will, if any; (2) a certificate of death; (3) particulars of all property and assets left by the deceased; and (4) a list of debts and funeral expenses.

Intending applicants, before attending at a registry

or probate office, should write or telephone to the nearest probate registry or sub-registry for the necessary forms. Postal or telephone applications cannot be dealt with at the local probate offices, which are part-time only.

Certain property can be disposed of on death without a grant of probate or administration, or in pursuance of a nomination made by the deceased, provided the amount involved does not exceed £5,000. *See* the Administration of Estates (Small Payments) Act 1965.

WHERE TO FIND A PROVED WILL

A will proved since 1858 must have been proved either at the Principal Registry at Somerset House, or a District Registry. In the former case the original will itself is preserved at St. Catherine's House, the copy of which probate has been granted is in the hands of the executors who proved the will, and another copy for Parliament is bound up in a folio volume of wills made by testators of that initial and date. The indices to these volumes may be examined at St. Catherine's House and a copy of any will read. In the latter case, the original will proved in the District Registry, is kept there, and may be seen or a copy obtained, but a copy is sent to and filed at St. Catherine's House, where also it may be seen. A general index of grants, both probates and administrations, is prepared and printed annually in lexicographical form, and may be seen at either the Principal or a District Registry. This index is usually ready by about October of the following year.

Recent Deaths.—A system introduced in 1975 enables a person to discover when a grant of Probate or Letters of Administration is made which may be invaluable to a creditor of the deceased or applicant under the Inheritance (Provision for Family and Dependants) Act 1975 (*see* above). A 'standing search' may be made by sending a request in the form set out below to the Record Keeper at the Principal Registry of the Family Division with a small fee. The searcher will receive particulars of any grant made in the previous twelve months or the following six months, including names and addresses of the executors or administrators and the Registry in which the grant was made.

Form of Search

In the High Court of Justice
Family Division
The Principal Registry (Probate)
I/We apply for the entry of a standing search so that there shall be sent to me/us an office copy of every grant of representation in England and Wales in the estate of:—
Full name of deceased:
Alternative or alias name
Full address
Exact date of death

Which either has issued not more than twelve months before the entry of this application or issues within six months hereafter
Sgd.—(full address).

SCOTS LAW OF WILLS

A domiciled Scotsman, unlike a domiciled Englishman, cannot in certain circumstances dispose effectively of the entirety of his estate. If he leave a widow and children, the widow is entitled to a one-third share in the whole of the moveable estate (her *jus relictae*), and the children are entitled to another one-third share equally between them (their *legitim*). If he leave a widow but no children, or children but

no widow, the *jus relictae* or *legitim* is increased to a one-half share of the net moveable estate. The remaining portion is known as the *dead's part*. A surviving husband and children have comparable rights (*jus relicti* and *legitim*) in the wife's estate. The dead's part is the only portion of which the testator can freely dispose. Legacies and bequests are payable only out of the dead's part. All debts are payable out of the whole estate before any division. Pupils, i.e. a girl up to the age of twelve or a boy up to the age of fourteen, cannot make wills. Formerly a minor could dispose only of movables but since the passing of the Succession (Scotland) Act 1964, a minor has a like capacity to test on heritable property. A will must be in writing and may be typewritten or even in pencil. A will may be either (1) holograph, i.e. written, dated and subscribed by the testator himself, in which case no witnesses are necessary; a printed form filled up by the testator or a typewritten document is not necessarily a holograph but may become so if the testator writes, in hand, at the foot of the form or document the words 'adopted as holograph' followed by his signature and the date. Words written on erasure or marginal additions or interlineations in holograph writings, if proved to be in the handwriting of the maker of the deed, are valid; (2) attested, i.e. signed in presence of two witnesses. It is not necessary that these witnesses should sign in presence of one another, or even that they should see the testator signing so long as the testator acknowledges his signature to the witnesses. The Conveyancing and Feudal Reform (Scotland) Act 1970, whilst altering generally the rules for the subscription of deeds, specifically (s. 44 (2)) makes no change in the rules applying to wills which must still be signed by the testator on every page. If the testator cannot write, or is blind, his will may be authenticated by a law agent, notary public or justice of the peace and two witnesses. It is better that the will be not witnessed by a beneficiary thereunder, although this circumstance will not invalidate the attestation of the will or (as it would in England) the gift. A parish minister may act as a notary for the purpose of subscribing a will in his own parish. Wills may be registered in the Books of the Sheriffdom in which the deceased died domiciled, or in the Books of Council and Session, H.M. General Register House, Edinburgh. The original deed may be inspected on payment of a small fee and a certified official copy may be obtained. A Scottish will is not revoked by the subsequent marriage of the testator. The subsequent birth of a child for whom no testamentary provision has been made may revoke a will. A will may be revoked by a subsequent will, either expressly or by implication; but in so far as the two can be read together both wills have effect. If a subsequent will is revoked, the earlier will is revived.

'Confirmation', the Scottish equivalent of Probate, is obtained in the Sheriff Court of the Sheriffdom in which the deceased was domiciled at the date of his death or, where he had no fixed domicile or died abroad, in the commissariat of Edinburgh. Executors are either 'nominate' or 'dative'. An executor nominate is one nominated by the deceased in his will or, where such person has predeceased the testator, by the residuary beneficiary. An executor dative is one appointed by the Court in the case of intestacy or where the deceased had failed to name an executor in his will and there is no residuary beneficiary. In the former case the deceased's next-of-kin are all entitled to be declared executors dative. An inventory of the deceased's estate and a schedule of debts, together with an affidavit, must first be given up. In estates under £13,000 gross, confirmation is obtained under a simplified procedure at reduced fees.

Presumption of Survivorship.—The Succession (Scotland) Act 1964 provides, by s. 31, that where two persons die in circumstances indicating that they died simultaneously or if it is uncertain which was the survivor, the younger will be deemed to have survived the elder unless the elder person left testamentary provision in favour of the younger, whom failing in favour of a third person, the younger person having died intestate (partially or wholly); but if the persons so dying were husband and wife, neither shall be presumed to have survived the other.

EMPLOYMENT

WAGES AND SICK PAY

Under the Wages Act 1986, subject to certain exceptions, employers may not make deductions from an employee's wages unless authorized by statute or contract or with the employee's prior written consent. There is an upper limit of one-tenth of gross pay for deductions from retail workers' wages on account of cash or stock shortages.

Under the Social Security and Housing Benefits Act 1982 as amended, an employee absent from work due to illness or injury is entitled to receive Statutory Sick Pay from the employer for a maximum period of 28 weeks in any year. No payment is made for the first three days of any period of illness. The employer can recoup the payments from his National Insurance contributions.

The Equal Pay Act 1970, which extends to Scotland, prevents discrimination, as regards terms and conditions of employment, between men and women employed on like work in the same employment.

PARTICULARS OF TERMS OF EMPLOYMENT

Under the Employment Protection (Consolidation) Act 1978, an employer must give each full-time employee within 13 weeks of the beginning of the employment a written statement containing the following particulars of the contract between them:

(1) the date when the employment began (when continuous employment began if previous work counts as continuous with this job);
(2) the rate of remuneration (or how it is calculated);
(3) the intervals at which wages are paid;
(4) the hours of work;
(5) the employee's entitlement to holidays (including public holidays) and holiday pay;
(6) the title of the employee's job;
(7) terms relating to sickness, injury and sick pay;
(8) details of any pension scheme;
(9) the length of notice which the employee should give and receive in order to terminate the contract.

In addition, the written particulars must specify any disciplinary rules; and also must identify the person to whom the employee can apply if he is dissatisfied with any disciplinary decision or to seek redress of any grievance and what further steps may ensue.

TERMINATION OF EMPLOYMENT

An employee may be dismissed without notice if he is guilty of gross breach of contract, such as disobedience to a lawful order or dishonesty. He is then only entitled to wages accrued due at the date of dismissal.

In other cases, the employee is entitled to reasonable notice which, under the Employment Protection (Consolidation) Act 1978, must not be less than one week if he has been continuously employed for four weeks, but less than two years; after two years it is two weeks' notice increasing by one week's notice for each further full year worked up to a maximum of twelve weeks' notice after twelve years' service.

An employer who wrongfully dismisses an employee (i.e. with less than the length of notice to which he is entitled) is generally liable to pay wages for the period of proper notice.

An employee who has a fixed term contract has no claim against his employer for wrongful dismissal if his contract is not renewed when it expires. He may, however, have a claim for a redundancy payment or compensation for unfair dismissal. If he is wrongfully dismissed before his contract expires, he is generally entitled to remuneration payable over the full period of the contract.

An employee may be entitled to a redundancy payment or to compensation for unfair dismissal if the employment has been terminated by the employer (with or without proper notice) or he has a fixed term contract which expires without being renewed or the employment has been terminated by the employee by reason of the employer's breach of contract.

Under the Employment Protection (Consolidation) Act 1978, an employee who satisfies the foregoing conditions and has been continuously employed for two years and who is dismissed by reason of redundancy may be entitled to a redundancy payment calculated by reference to his age, pay and length of service.

The Employment Protection (Consolidation) Act 1978 also enables an employee who is unfairly dismissed to complain to an Industrial Tribunal (generally within three months of dismissal). The onus will then be on the employer to prove that the dismissal was due to capability, conduct, redundancy, illegality or some other substantial reason justifying dismissal. The tribunal must then decide whether the employer acted reasonably in dismissing the employee. If the employer fails to prove that the dismissal was due to one or more of the above five reasons, or the tribunal decides that the employer did not act reasonably in dismissing the employee, the dismissal will be unfair, in which case the tribunal can:

(a) order re-engagement or reinstatement; or
(b) award compensation consisting of a basic and a compensatory award.

For an employee to bring himself within the unfair dismissal provisions, he must have been continuously employed for a period of two years.

All complaints of unfair dismissal are referred to a conciliation officer or the Department of Employment and a very high proportion of complaints are disposed of in this way.

FAMILY LAW

ADOPTION OF CHILDREN

In England and Wales this is now mainly governed by the Children Act 1975 and the Adoption Act 1976. A court order is necessary to legalize the adoption, which, when completed, has the effect of making the adopted child the child of the adopter as if he or she had been born to the adopter in lawful wedlock, and the original rights and duties of the natural parents are thereby cut. The adopter has full rights as to custody, education etc. and the child is treated as his for the purpose of any devolution of property on an intestacy occurring or under any disposition made after the adoption order. The application may be made to the High Court (Family Division) or to a County Court or Magistrates' Court.

Orders may be made in favour of married couples, single, widowed or divorced persons, but not of one party to a marriage alone unless the other spouse cannot be found, is physically or mentally incapable of making an application, or they are separated in circumstances likely to be permanent. A person aged under 21 cannot adopt.

The child's parents or guardians must consent unconditionally to the making of the order unless the court dispenses with the consent, which it may do if the parent cannot be found or is incapable of giving his consent, is withholding his consent unreasonably, or has neglected or ill-treated the child.

Restrictions are placed on societies which may arrange adoptions.

An adopted person aged over 18 may apply to the Registrar General for information to enable him to obtain a full certificate of his birth, but before being supplied with the information he will be informed that counselling services are available to him.

An adopter and the adopted child are within the prohibited degrees for the purposes of marriage to one another.

All adoptions in Great Britain are registered in the Registers of Adopted Children kept by the Registrars General in London and Edinburgh respectively. Certificates from these registers, including short certificates which contain no reference to adoptions, can be obtained on conditions similar to those relating to birth certificates, (see below.)

SCOTLAND

The Law is consolidated in the Adoption (Scotland) Act 1978 which is now fully in force. The law relating to fostering is consolidated in the Foster Children(s) Act 1984. A petition for adoption is presented either to the Sheriff Court or the Court of Session. As in England the petitioner(s) must be 21 or over and may be a married couple or one person who, if married, is living apart permanently from his or her spouse. The consent of the child's natural parents/guardians is required unless dispensed with, or the child is already free for adoption.

The Succession (Scotland) Act 1964 gives the adopted child the same rights of succession as a child born to the adopter in wedlock but deprives him of any such rights in the estates of his natural parents.

BIRTHS (REGISTRATION)

When a birth takes place, personal information of it must be given to the Registrar of Births and Deaths for the sub-district in which the birth occurred, and the register signed in his presence, by one of the following persons:—

(1) The father or mother of the child. If they fail; (2) the occupier of the house in which the birth happened; (3) a person present at the birth; or (4) the person having charge of the child. The duty of attending to the registration therefore rests firstly on the parents. The mother is responsible for the registration of the birth of an illegitimate child. The registration is required to be made within 42 days of the birth. Failure to do this, without reasonable cause, involves liability to a penalty of £20. The registration of a birth is free. In England or Wales, the informant, instead of attending before the registrar of the sub-district where the birth occurred, may make a declaration of the particulars required to be registered in the presence of any Registrar.

Under the National Health Service Act 1977, notice of every birth must be given by the father, or person in attendance on the mother, to the district medical officer of health by post within 36 hours of the birth. This is in addition to the registration already mentioned.

A still birth must be registered and a certificate signed by the doctor or midwife who was present at the birth or who has examined the body of the child must be produced to the registrar. The certificate must, where possible, state the cause of death and the estimated duration of the pregnancy. A stillbirth may only be registered within three months of the birth.

The re-registration of the birth of a person legitimated by the subsequent marriage of the parents is provided for in the Births and Deaths Registration Act 1953, as amended by the Family Law Reform Act 1987. Special provisions apply to the registration and re-registration of births of abandoned children, and the re-registration of births of illegitimate children showing the father's name; the mother must normally be party to the latter application.

Birth at Sea.—The master of a British ship must record any birth on board and send particulars to the Registrar General of Shipping.

Birth Abroad.—Consular Officers are authorized to register births of British subjects occurring abroad. Certificates are procurable in due course at Registrar General's Office, London.

The registration of births occurring out of the United Kingdom among members of the armed forces, or occurring on board H.M. ships and aircraft, is provided for by the Registration of Births, Deaths and Marriages (Special Provisions) Act 1957, applicable also to Scotland.

SCOTLAND

The Registration of Births, Deaths and Marriages (Scotland) Act 1965 supersedes former Acts. Personal notification within 21 days of any birth, must be given to the registrar of (1) the registration district in which the birth took place, or (2) any registration district in which the mother of the child was ordinarily resident at the time of the birth and (3) in the case of a foundling child, dead or alive, when the place of birth is not known, the registration district in which the child, or the body, was found, within two months from the date on which the child was found. When a child is born (in or out of Scotland) in a ship, aircraft or land vehicle during a journey and the child is conveyed therein to any place in Scotland, the birth shall, unless the Registrar General otherwise directs, be deemed to have occurred at that place.

The register must be signed in the presence of the registrar by the father or mother of the child, and if they fail, by one of the following: (1) any relative of either parent who has knowledge of the birth; (2) the occupier of the premises in which the child was, to the knowledge of that occupier, born; (3) any person present at the birth; (4) any person having charge of the child. Failure without reasonable cause involves a penalty not exceeding £50.

The name of the father of a child born out of wedlock may be entered in the register of births at the time of registration if jointly requested by the mother and father, and the latter's name may also be recorded at a later date on declaration by both parents. A free abbreviated certificate of birth will be issued to the informant at the time of registration. Provision is made for the re-registration of the birth of a person made legitimate by the subsequent marriage of the parents or whose birth entry is affected by any matter respecting status or paternity, or has been so made as to imply that he is a foundling.

A still birth must be registered and a certificate, signed by the doctor or certified midwife present at the birth or who has examined the body of the child, must be produced.

CERTIFICATES OF BIRTHS, MARRIAGES, OR DEATHS

ENGLAND AND WALES

Certificates of Births, Deaths, or Marriages can be obtained at the Office of Population Censuses and Surveys, St. Catherine's House, 10 Kingsway, WC2B 6JP or from the Superintendent Registrar having the legal custody of the register containing the entry of which a certificate is required. Certificates of marriage can also be obtained from the incumbent of the church in which the marriage took place; or from the Nonconformist minister (or other authorized person) where the marriage takes place in a registered building (*see,* Marriage).

It is considered desirable when a certificate is required to consult the nearest Register Office who, if told the exact or approximate date and place of registration, will be able to advise on the best way of obtaining it, and any fees payable, which vary according to the type of certificate required and other factors.

Records of births, deaths and marriages registered in England and Wales since 1837 are kept at the Office of Population Censuses and Surveys, St. Catherine's House, 10 Kingsway, WC2B 6JP. The Society of Genealogists, 14 Charterhouse Buildings, Goswell Road, EC1M 7BA, possess many records of Baptisms, Marriages and Deaths prior to 1837, including copies, in whole or in part of about 4,000 Parish Registers.

SCOTLAND

Certificates of births, deaths or marriages registered from 1855 when compulsory registration commenced in Scotland, can be obtained personally at the General Register Office, New Register House, Edinburgh EH1 3YT, or from the appropriate local Registrar, on payment of the fee of £6·00 for a full extract entry of birth, death, or marriage (£8·00 by post), and £5·00 for an abbreviated certificate of birth (£7·00 by post). An abbreviated certificate of registration of deaths is issued free of charge for National Insurance purposes in certain cases. A Register of Divorces (which includes decrees of declaration of nullity of marriage) is kept by the Registrar General at the General Register Office. The fee for an extract decree is £6·00 (£8·00 by post).

There are also available at the General Register Office old parish registers of the date prior to 1855, which were formerly kept under the administration of the established Church of Scotland. An extract of an entry in these registers may be obtained on payment of the appropriate fee. A fee of £11·00 per day is payable for a general search of all the Scottish registers.

Registration of Presumed Deaths. (Prescription of Particulars) (Scotland) Regulations 1978 as read with Presumption of Death (Scotland) Act 1977 prescribe the particulars to be notified by the Clerk of Court to the Registrar General after a decree or variation order has been granted in an action of declarator of death of a missing person.

DIVORCE, SEPARATION AND ANCILLARY MATTERS

Matrimonial suits may be conveniently divided into two classes: (1) those in which it is sought to annul the marriage because of some defect; and (2) those in which, the marriage being admitted, it is sought to end the marriage or the duties arising from it. By virtue of the Matrimonial and Family Proceedings Act 1984, all matrimonial causes are commenced in one of the divorce county courts designated by the Lord Chancellor or in the Divorce Registry in London. If the suit becomes defended, it may be transferred to the High Court.

(1) *Nullity of Marriage.*—This is now mainly governed as to England and Wales by the Matrimonial Causes Act 1973. A marriage is void *ab initio* if the parties were within the prohibited degrees of affinity, or were not male and female, or if it was bigamous or if one of the parties was under the age of consent, i.e. 16, or in the case of a polygamous marriage entered into outside England and Wales, that either party was at the time of the marriage domiciled in England and Wales. Where the formalities of the marriage were defective, the marriage is generally void if both parties knew of the defect (e.g., where marriage took place otherwise than in an authorized building). But absence of the consent of parents or guardians (or of the Court or other authority, in lieu thereof) in the case of minors does not invalidate the marriage.

A marriage is voidable (i.e. a decree of nullity may be obtained but until such time the marriage remains valid) on the following grounds—(*a*) incapacity of either party to consummate; (*b*) respondent's wilful refusal to consummate; (*c*) that either party did not validly consent to the marriage, whether in consequence of duress, mistake, unsoundness of mind or otherwise; (*d*) that either party at the time of marriage was a mentally disordered person; (*e*) that at the time of marriage the respondent was suffering from communicable venereal disease; (*f*) that at the time of the marriage the respondent was pregnant by another man. In cases (*e*) and (*f*) the petitioner must have been ignorant of the grounds at the date of the marriage and in (*c*), (*d*), (*e*) and (*f*) proceedings must be instituted within three years of the marriage, although leave may be obtained to petition outside this period in the case of certain persons suffering from mental illness. In all cases the court shall not grant a decree where the petitioner has led the respondent to believe that he would not seek a decree and it would be unjust for it to be granted.

The 1973 Act provides that a decree of nullity in a voidable marriage only annuls the marriage from the date of the decree. The marriage remains valid until the decree, and any children of the marriage are legitimate. Children of a void marriage are illegitimate unless the father was domiciled in England and Wales at the child's birth (or father's death, if earlier) and at the time of conception (or marriage if later) both or either of the parents reasonably believed the marriage was valid.

A spouse's insistence upon the use of contraceptives will not constitute wilful refusal to consummate within (*b*) above, even though there has been no normal intercourse, but it may in certain circumstances constitute unreasonable behaviour for the purpose of divorce (*see* below). Further, it has been allowed as a defence to a charge of desertion against the aggrieved party.

(2) *Judicial Separation and Divorce.*—The second class of suit includes a suit for judicial separation (which does not dissolve a marriage) and a suit for divorce (which, if successful, dissolves the marriage altogether and leaves the parties at liberty to marry

again). Either spouse may petition for judicial separation. It is not necessary to prove that the marriage has broken down irretrievably and the five facts listed (a) to (e) under divorce below are grounds for judicial separation.

Divorce.—The sole ground on which a divorce is obtained by either husband or wife is the irretrievable breakdown of the marriage. However, the court is precluded from holding that a marriage has irretrievably broken down unless it is satisfied of one or more of the following facts: (a) that the respondent has committed adultery since the marriage and the petitioner finds it intolerable to live with the respondent; (b) that the respondent has behaved in such a way that the petitioner cannot reasonably be expected to continue cohabitation; (c) desertion by the respondent for two years immediately before the petition; (d) five years separation immediately before the petition (but only two years where the respondent consents to the decree). Matrimonial Causes Act 1973.

The foregoing is subject to a clause prohibiting any petition for divorce (but not for judicial separation) before the lapse of one year from the date of the marriage.

Desertion may be defined as a voluntary withdrawal from cohabitation by one spouse without just cause and against the wishes of the other. Where one spouse is guilty of conduct of a serious nature which forces the other to leave, the party at fault is said to be guilty of constructive desertion.

Provisions designed to encourage reconciliation.—The 1973 Act requires the solicitor for the petitioner to certify whether he has or has not discussed the possibility of a reconciliation and whether or not he has given the petitioner the names and addresses of persons qualified to help effect a reconciliation.

A total period of less than six months during which the parties have resumed living together is to be disregarded in determining whether the prescribed period of desertion or separation has been continuous. Similar provision for effecting a reconciliation exists in relation to the other proofs of breakdown, but a petitioner cannot rely on an act of adultery by the other party if they have lived together for more than six months after discovery of that act of adultery.

Obtaining the Decree Nisi.—Where the suit is defended, i.e. the respondent opposes the dissolution or the fact/ground on which the petitioner seeks it, the petition will be heard by a Judge in open court, the parties giving oral evidence. Where the suit is undefended, the evidence will normally take the form of a sworn written statement made by the petitioner which will be sent to the Court and read over by the Registrar. If he is satisfied that he or she has proved the contents of the petition, he will simply fix a date for a Judge to pronounce the decree nisi, it being unnecessary for either party to attend. Only if the Registrar is not satisfied as above will he order that the petition be heard formally by the Judge.

Children.—Subject to exceptions, the decree nisi cannot be made absolute unless a Judge by order declares that he is satisfied with the proposed arrangements for the welfare of any child of the family who is under 16, or under 18 and receiving education or vocational training. If there is no dispute as to the children between the parties and the proposed arrangements for residence, education etc. are specific, an appointment will be made for the Judge to interview one or both parents informally and if satisfied he will make an order to that effect. (This will usually be on the same day as the decree nisi is pronounced.) If not, the Registrar may inform

the parties that it is up to them to seek a hearing before the Judge to resolve the matters in dispute.

Decree Absolute.—Every decree of divorce or nullity is in the first instance a decree nisi, and the marriage subsists until the decree is made absolute, usually six weeks after decree nisi on the petitioner's application. After the decree absolute either party is free to remarry.

Maintenance, etc.—The court has wide powers to order either party to the marriage to make financial provision (e.g. periodical payments, a lump sum, the transfer of property) for the other party or any child of the family, having regard to the party's means, the recipient's needs and all the important aspects of the case. These so-called 'ancillary matters' often present more difficulty than the divorce itself, especially affecting the home, and may go on long after the marriage is dissolved. There is, however, nothing to stop financial matters being negotiated by the parties through their solicitors before the divorce goes through.

The court may, where the husband has wilfully neglected to provide reasonable maintenance for the wife or children, order the husband to make provision for them, even though no matrimonial suit is pending between the parties to the marriage, and while such an order is in force the court may also deal with custody of and access to the children.

CUSTODY OF CHILDREN, ETC.

The Court may make orders in respect of access to and the custody, maintenance and education of children in connection with a suit for divorce, nullity or judicial separation (above), or with an application to the Magistrates (below) whether the suit succeeds or not. In addition, if there is no other matrimonial suit involved a parent may apply for custody under the Guardianship of Minors Acts 1971, and any person interested may apply to the High Court for the child to be made a ward of court.

In all cases the welfare of the child is the first and paramount consideration. The categories of child who may be covered by any particular type of proceedings differ according to the nature of those proceedings and to the nature of the particular relief sought, but it should be borne in mind that in connection with divorce, nullity and judicial separation a child which has been treated by the spouses as a child of the family may be included as a 'child of the family' as well as the children of the spouses themselves. This also applies to most maintenance cases in the magistrate's court (*see* below).

Under the Children Act 1975 a new procedure called 'Custodianship' has been introduced, allowing, for instance, long term foster parents to apply for custody of the foster child.

Any dispute relating to the above matters should be placed in the hands of a solicitor without delay (*see* Legal Aid, etc. below) and in particular it should be borne in mind that where there is financial need (because of continuing education or disability, for instance) maintenance may be ordered for children even beyond the age of majority.

SEPARATION BY AGREEMENT

Husband and wife may enter into an agreement to separate and live apart, but the agreement, to be valid, must be followed by an immediate separation. It is most desirable to consult a solicitor in every such case, who will often advise obtaining a court order by consent.

MAGISTRATES' CUSTODY AND MAINTENANCE ORDERS

For many years the law relating to domestic proceedings in magistrates' courts was out of line with the divorce law which was reformed in 1969. The Domestic Proceedings and Magistrates' Courts Act 1978 took effect in early 1981 and now contains the relevant law.

A husband or wife can apply to a magistrates' court for a matrimonial order on the grounds that the other spouse: (a) has failed to pay reasonable maintenance for the applicant; (b) has failed to make a proper contribution towards the reasonable maintenance of a child of the family; (c) has deserted the applicant; or (d) has behaved in such a way that the applicant cannot reasonably be expected to live with the respondent. If the case is proved the court can order: (a) periodical payments for the applicant; (b) periodical payments for a child of the family; or (c) a lump sum (not exceeding £1,000) for the benefit of the applicant and for any child of the family. In deciding what orders (if any) to make the magistrates must consider a number of guidelines which are similar to those governing financial orders on divorce. There are also special provisions relating to consent orders and separation by agreement. The court also has powers to make orders relating to the legal custody of a child of the family and these orders together with orders for child maintenance can be made even though the court makes no order for spouse maintenance. Legal custody can only be granted to one person but the court may order that the other party shall retain certain parental rights and exercise them jointly with the person who is awarded legal custody. Other provisions of the Act relate to access by grandparents, interim orders, and variation, discharge and revival of orders. An order may be enforceable even though the parties are living together, but in some cases it will cease to have effect if they continue to do so for six months. The hearing of matrimonial disputes is separate from ordinary court business, and the public are not admitted.

DOMESTIC VIOLENCE

The Domestic Violence and Matrimonial Proceedings Act 1976, the Domestic Proceedings and Magistrates' Courts Act 1978 (the former not being applicable to Scotland and the latter only to a limited extent; *see* below) and the Matrimonial Homes Act 1983 have made it easier for one spouse who has been subjected to violence by the other to obtain an order to restrain further violence and if need be to have the other excluded from the home. Such orders can be obtained very quickly, and a person disobeying them is liable to be imprisoned for contempt of court. There are some differences of detail between the three Acts; in particular the 1976 Act also applies to unmarried couples. Such orders may also be obtained in the course of suits for divorce and judicial separation.

SCOTLAND
Divorce

Actions of divorce could formerly only be raised in the Court of Session, having jurisdiction to entertain such actions only if either of the parties to the marriage in question: (a) is domiciled in Scotland on the date when the action is begun; or (b) was habitually resident in Scotland throughout the period of one year ending with that date. As from May 1, 1984, however, when the Divorce Jurisdiction, Court Fees and Legal Aid (Scotland) Act 1983 came into force, actions of divorce may also be raised in the Sheriff Courts provided the above conditions (a) and (b) are complied with, and provided either party

to the marriage was resident in the Sheriffdom for a period of forty days ending with the date the action was begun, or was resident in the Sheriffdom for a period of not less than forty days ending not more than forty days before the date the action was begun.

The Scots Law of Divorce is now governed by the Divorce (Scotland) Act 1976, which for the purposes of divorce came into force on January 1, 1977. The sole ground of divorce is now irretrievable breakdown of the marriage. This can only be established in one of the following ways:

(a) The defending spouse has committed adultery since the date of the marriage. Here it is not necessary for the pursuing spouse to prove that the fact of adultery made it intolerable to live with the defending spouse.

(b) The defending spouse has behaved in such a way that the pursuing spouse cannot reasonably be expected to cohabit with him or her. It is immaterial whether or not the conduct founded upon is active or passive.

(c) The defending spouse has deserted the pursuing spouse for a continuous period of two years. There must be no question of the pursuing spouse having refused a genuine and reasonable offer to adhere. Nor is irretrievable breakdown established if cohabitation is resumed for a period of more than three months, after the two year period has expired.

(d) There has been no cohabitation at any time during a continuous period of two years immediately preceding the action between the parties to the action, and the defending spouse consents to the divorce being granted.

(e) There has been no cohabitation at any time during a continuous period of five years, as in (d), except that on the expiry of the five year period, the consent of the defending spouse is not required.

The facts of desertion and separation are not interrupted by the parties cohabiting for a period or periods not exceeding six months. However such a period or periods of cohabitation would not be included in the calculation of the two-year or five-year periods.

Encouragement of Reconciliation.—The burden of promoting a reconciliation between spouses in a divorce action in Scotland falls upon the Court by virtue of the 1976 Act. Where an action of divorce has been raised, it may be postponed by the Court to enable the parties to seek to effect a reconciliation, if the Court feels that there may be a reasonable prospect of such reconciliation. If the parties do cohabit during such postponement, no account shall be taken of such cohabitation if the action later proceeds.

Maintenance, etc.—The 1976 Act also provides that either party to a marriage can apply to the Court at any time prior to decree being granted for: (a) an order for interim custody of all or some of the children of the marriage under 16 years of age; (b) an order for access to all or some of the children of the marriage under 16 years of age in the custody of the other party.

The financial provisions on divorce in the 1976 Act have been superseded by the Family Law (Scotland) Act 1985 which allows either party to the marriage to apply to the court for an order for payment of a capital sum or for a periodical allowance or for an incidental order. The Act sets out principles to be applied by the Court, one of these being that the financial provisions awarded to a party who has been dependent for financial support on the other party should be given over a period of not more than three years.

The Act also defines the rights and obligations of aliment between parents and children thereby excluding aliment between grandparents and grandchildren and of children to parents, and provides that a child is entitled to aliment up to the age of eighteen or to twenty five if in full time further education, and for the claiming of aliment whether in connection with an action of divorce etc. or independently.

Nullity of Marriage.—A declaration of nullity of marriage may be obtained on the ground of any impediment, viz., consanguinity and affinity, subsistence of a previous marriage, non-age of one of the parties, incapacity or insanity of one of the parties, or by the absence of genuine consent. The financial provisions on divorce contained in the Family Law (Scotland) Act 1985 also apply to an action for declaration of nullity of marriage.

Procedure.—Appearance in Court at a Proof in an undefended divorce action has been rendered unnecessary since April 1978. A full Proof is still necessary if the action is defended in any respect. In place of court appearance, affidavits (statements sworn before a Notary Public) by the pursuer and any witnesses are lodged in the Court together with a Minute by the solicitor craving decree.

A new simplified procedure for 'do-it-yourself divorce' was introduced in January 1983 for certain divorces. Thus, if the action is based on (*d*) or (*e*) above and will not be opposed, there are no children under 16 and no financial claims, then the applicant can write directly to the Court of Session, Divorce Section (SP), Parliament House, Edinburgh or the local Sheriff Court for the appropriate forms to enable him or her to proceed. The fee is £40 unless the applicant receives Income Support, Family Credit or legal advice and assistance in which case there is no fee.

Separation

Under the Divorce (Scotland) Act 1976, a decree of Judicial Separation can be obtained by proof of the same facts necessary to obtain decree of divorce, except that for the principle of irretrievable breakdown there is substituted that of grounds justifying separation. This type of action is competent in both the Court of Session and the Sheriff Court.

Custody of Children

In actions for divorce and separation, the Court has a discretion in awarding the custody of the children of the parties. The welfare of the children is the paramount consideration, and the mere fact that a spouse, by reason of his or her behaviour, brought about the breakdown of the marriage does not of itself preclude him or her from being awarded custody. The Children Act 1975, as amended, also applies to Scotland.

Domestic Violence

The Matrimonial Homes (Family Protection) (Scotland) Act 1981, as amended, provides that one spouse, whether or not he or she has title to the matrimonial home, can obtain an exclusion order suspending the other spouse's occupancy rights in the matrimonial home. The Court (either Court of Session or Sheriff Court) is empowered to make such an order if satisfied that it is necessary to protect the applicant or any child of the family from any conduct, actual or threatened or reasonably apprehended of the other spouse which would be injurious to the physical or mental health of the applicant or child. In making the order the Court may include a warrant for the summary ejection of the non-applicant spouse from the matrimonial home and for an interdict prohibiting him/her from entering it.

ILLEGITIMACY AND LEGITIMATION
ENGLAND AND WALES

The former provisions of the Affiliation Proceedings Act 1957, under which a man could be summoned to petty sessions on the application of the mother of an illegitimate child, or by the Supplementary Benefits Commission where benefit has been paid for the requirements of the child, and the Justices, on his being proved to be the father of the child, could make an order requiring him to pay for its maintenance and education a sum in their discretion, have been replaced by extensive provisions relating to parental rights and duties in Part II of the Family Law Reform Act 1987. *Prima facie* every child born of a married woman during a marriage is legitimate; and this presumption can only be rebutted by strong evidence. However, under the Family Law Reform Act 1969, any presumption of law as to the legitimacy (or illegitimacy) of any person may in civil proceedings be rebutted by evidence showing that it is more probable than not that the person is illegitimate (or legitimate) and in any proceedings where paternity is in question, blood tests may be ordered. If however the husband and wife are separated under an Order of the Court, a child conceived by the wife during such separation is presumed not to be the husband's child.

Legitimation.—The Legitimacy Act 1976 consolidates earlier legislation dating back to January 1, 1927. Where the parents of an illegitimate person marry, or have married, whether before or after that date, the marriage, if the father is at the date thereof domiciled in England or Wales, renders that person, if living, legitimate as from Jan. 1, 1927, or from the date of the marriage, whichever last happens. Marriage legitimates a person even though the father or mother was married to a third person at the time when the illegitimate person was born. It is the duty of the parents to supply to the Registrar General information for re-registration of the birth of a legitimate child.

Declarations of Legitimacy.—A person claiming that he, his parents, or any remoter ancestor has become legitimated, may petition the High Court or the County Court for the necessary declaration.

Rights and Duties of Legitimated Persons.—A legitimated person, his spouse or issue may take property under an intestacy occurring after the date of legitimation, or under any disposition (e.g., a will) coming into operation after such date, as if he had been legitimate.

He must maintain all persons whom he would be bound to maintain had he been born legitimate, and he is entitled to the benefit of any Act of Parliament which confers rights on legitimate persons to recover damages or compensation. The Act specially provides that nothing therein contained is to render any person capable of succeeding to or transmitting a right to any dignity or title.

Property Rights of Illegitimate Children.—By the Family Law Reform Act 1969 the rights of an illegitimate child on an intestacy were broadly equated with those of a legitimate child, and in any disposition made after December 31, 1969, any reference to 'children' or other relatives was, unless the contrary intention appears, to be construed as including any person who is illegitimate or who is related through another person who is illegitimate. However, these provisions of the 1969 Act have been replaced by the general provision of the Family Law Reform Act 1987 (*see* p. 1025).

(*see* p. 1025)

SCOTLAND

The Law Reform (Parent & Child) Scotland Act 1986 implements the Scottish Law Commission's Report on Illegitimacy. The Act contains a general provision granting equality status to all persons whatever the marital status of their parents. The mother of an illegitimate child may raise an action of affiliation and aliment against the father, either in the Court of Session or, more usually, in the Sheriff Court. Where in any such action the Court finds that the defender is the father of the child, the Court shall, in awarding inlying expenses, or aliment, have regard to the means of the parties, and the whole circumstances of the case. The Court may, upon application by the mother or by the father of any illegitimate child, or in any action for aliment for an illegitimate child, make such order as it may think fit regarding the custody of such child and the right of access thereto of either parent, having regard to the welfare of the child and to the conduct of the parents and to the wishes as well of the mother as of the father and may on the application of either parent recall or vary such order. The obligation of the mother and of the father of an illegitimate child to provide aliment for such child shall (without prejudice to any obligation attaching at common law) endure until the child attains the age of sixteen.

By Scots Law an illegitimate child is legitimated by and on the date of the subsequent marriage of its parents and there is no objection to there having been an impediment to the marriage of the parents at the time of the child's conception—*see* the Legitimation (Scotland) Act 1968, which came into operation on June 8, 1968, on which date thousands of existing illegitimate children were regarded as legitimated. By the Registration of Births, Deaths and Marriages (Scotland) Act 1965, a child so legitimated, who has already been registered as illegitimate, may be re-registered as legitimate. The consent of the father of an illegitimate child to its adoption is not required unless he has been awarded parental rights by the court.

MARRIAGE
A.—MARRIAGE ACCORDING TO RITES OF THE CHURCH OF ENGLAND

1. MARRIAGE BY BANNS.—The Marriage Act 1949 prescribes audible publication according to the rubric, on three Sundays preceding the ceremony during morning service or, if there is no morning service on a Sunday on which the banns are to be published, during evening service. Where the parties reside in different parishes, the banns must be published in both. Under the Act, banns may be published and the marriage solemnized in the parish church, which is the usual place of worship of the persons to be married or either of them, although neither of such persons dwells in such parish; but this publication of banns is in addition to any other publication required by law and does not apply if the church or the residence of either party is in Wales. The Act provides specially for the case where one of the parties resides in Scotland and the other in England, the publication being then in the parish in England in which one party resides, and, according to the law and custom in Scotland, in the place where the other party resides. After the lapse of three months from the last time of publication, the banns become useless, and the parties must either obtain a licence (*see* below), or submit to the republication of banns.

2. MARRIAGE BY LICENCE.—Marriage licences are of two kinds:—

(i) A Common Licence, dispensing with the necessity for banns, granted by the Archbishops and Bishops through their Surrogates, for marriages in any church or chapel duly licensed for marriages. A Common Licence can be obtained in London by application at the Faculty Office (1 The Sanctuary, Westminster, SW1) and (for marriages in London) at the Bishop of London's Diocesan Registry (1 The Sanctuary, SW1), by one of the parties about to be married. In the country they may be obtained at the offices of the Bishop's Registrars, but licences obtained at the Bishop's Diocesan Registry only enable the parties to be married in the diocese in which they are issued; those procured at the Faculty Office are available for all England and Wales. No instructions, either verbal or in writing, can be received, except from one of the parties. Affidavits are prepared from the personal instructions of one of the parties about to be married, and the licence is delivered to the party upon payment of a fee (*see* page 1037). Before a licence can be granted one of the parties must make an affidavit that there is no legal impediment to the intended marriage; and also that one of such parties has had his or her usual place of abode for the space of fifteen days immediately preceding the issuing of the licence within the parish or ecclesiastical district of the church in which the marriage is to be solemnized, *or* the church in which the marriage is to be solemnized is the usual place of worship of the parties or one of them. In the country there may generally be found a parochial clergyman (Surrogate) before whom the affidavit may be taken, and whose office it is to deliver the licence personally to the applicant. (In some dioceses it is necessary for the Surrogate to procure the licence from the Bishop's Registry.) The licence continues in force for three months from its date.

(ii) A Special Licence granted by the Archbishop of Canterbury, under special circumstances, for marriage at any place with or without previous residence in the district, or at any time, etc.; but the reasons assigned must meet with the Archbishop's approval. Application must be made to the Faculty Office. (For fee, *see* page 1037.)

3. MARRIAGE UNDER SUPERINTENDENT REGISTRAR'S CERTIFICATE.—A marriage may be performed in church on the Superintendent Registrar's Certificate (*see* below) without banns, provided that the incumbent's consent is obtained. One of the parties must be resident within the ecclesiastical parish of the church in which the marriage is to take place unless the church is the usual place of worship of the parties or one of them.

MARRIAGE FEES.—The Church Commissioners settle tables of fees for all parishes. The usual fees are paid although a stranger-clergyman may be invited to perform the service.

B.—MARRIAGE UNDER SUPERINTENDENT REGISTRAR'S CERTIFICATE

The following marriages may be solemnized on the authority of a Superintendent Registrar's Certificate (either with or without a licence):—

(a) A marriage in a registered building (e.g., a nonconformist church registered for the solemnization of marriages therein).
(b) A marriage in a register office.

(c) A marriage according to the usages of the Society of Friends (commonly called Quakers).

(d) A marriage between two persons professing the Jewish religion according to the usages of the Jews.

(e) A marriage according to the rites of the Church of England (*see* above—in this case the marriage can only be without licence).

(f) A marriage of a person who is housebound or is detained at the place where he or she normally resides (*see* Section D).

NOTICE.—Notice of the intended marriage must be given as follows:—

(i) Marriage by certificate (without licence)—if both parties reside in the same registration district, they must both have resided there for seven days before the notice can be given. It may then be given by either party. If the parties reside in different registration districts, notice must be given by each to the Superintendent Registrar of the district in which he or she resides, and the preliminary residential qualification of seven days must be fulfilled by each before either notice can be given.

(ii) Marriage by certificate (with licence)—one notice only is necessary, whether the parties live in the same or in different registration districts. Either party may give the notice, which must be given to the Superintendent Registrar of any registration district in which one of the parties has resided for the period of fifteen days immediately preceding the giving of notice, but both parties must be resident in England or Wales on the day notice is given.

The notice (in either case) must be in the prescribed form and must contain particulars as to names, marital status, occupation, residence, length of residence, and the building in which the marriage is to take place. The notice must also contain or have added at the foot thereof a solemn declaration that there is no legal impediment to the marriage, and, in the case of minors, that the consent of the person whose consent to the marriage is required by law (*see* below) has been duly given, and that the residential qualifications mentioned above have been complied with. A person making a false declaration renders himself or herself liable to prosecution for perjury. The notice is entered in the marriage notice book.

ISSUE OF CERTIFICATE:

(i) *Without licence.*—The notice (or an exact copy thereof) is affixed in some conspicuous place in the Superintendent Registrar's office for 21 days next after the notice was entered in the marriage notice book. After the lapse of this period the Superintendent Registrar may, provided no impediment is shown, issue his certificate for the marriage which can then take place at any time within three months from the date of the entry of the notice.

(ii) *With licence.*—The notice in this case is not affixed in the office of the Superintendent Registrar. After the lapse of one whole day (other than a Sunday, Christmas Day or Good Friday) from the date of entry of the notice, the Superintendent Registrar may, provided no impediment is shown, issue his certificate and licence for the marriage, which can then take place on any day within three months from the date of entry of the notice.

SOLEMNIZATION OF THE MARRIAGE:

(i) *In a Registered Building.*—The marriage must generally take place at a building within the district of residence of one of the parties, but if the usual place of worship of either is outside the district of his or her residence, it may take place in such usual place of worship. Further, if there is not within the district of residence of one of the parties a registered building within which marriages are solemnized according to the rites and ceremonies which the parties desire to adopt in solemnizing their marriage, it may take place in an appropriate registered building in the nearest district.

The presence of a Registrar of Marriages is not necessary at marriages at registered buildings which have adopted the provisions of section 43 of the Marriage Act 1949. This section provides for the appointment of an 'authorized person' (a person, usually the minister or an official of the building, certified by the trustees or governing body as having been duly authorized for the purpose) who must be present and must register the marriage.

The marriage must be solemnized between the hours of 8 a.m. and 6 p.m., with open doors in the presence of two or more witnesses. The parties must at some time during the ceremony make the following declaration—'I do solemnly declare that I know not of any lawful impediment why I, A. B., may not be joined in matrimony to C. D.' Also each of the parties must say to the other: 'I call upon these persons here present to witness that I, A. B., do take thee, C. D., to be my lawful wedded wife [or husband],' *or*, if the marriage is solemnized in the presence of an authorized person without the presence of a Registrar, each party may say in lieu thereof: 'I, A. B., do take thee, C. D., to be my wedded wife [or husband].'

(ii) *In a Register Office.*—The marriage may be solemnized in the office of the Superintendent Registrar to whom notice of the marriage has been given. The marriage must be solemnized between the hours of 8 a.m. and 6 p.m., with open doors in the presence of the Superintendent Registrar or a Registrar of the registration district of that Superintendent Registrar, and in the presence of two witnesses. The parties must make the following declaration: 'I do solemnly declare that I know not of any lawful impediment why I, A. B., may not be joined in matrimony to C. D.,' and each party must say to the other: 'I call upon these persons here present to witness that I, A. B., do take thee, C. D., to be my lawful wedded wife [or husband].' No religious ceremony may take place in the Register Office, though the parties may, on production of their marriage certificate, go through a subsequent religious ceremony in any church or persuasion of which they are members.

(iii) *Other Cases.*—If both parties are members of the Society of Friends (Quakers), or if, not being in membership, they have been authorized by the Society of Friends to solemnize their marriage in accordance with its usages, they may be married in a Friends' meeting-house. The marriage must be registered by the registering officer of the Society appointed to act for the district in which the meeting house is situated. The presence of a Registrar of Marriages is not necessary.

If both parties are Jews they may marry according to their usages in a synagogue which has a certified marriage secretary, or in a private dwelling-house at any hour; the building may be situated within or without the district of residence. The marriage must be registered by the secretary of the synagogue of which the man is a member. The presence of a Registrar of Marriages is not necessary.

C.—MARRIAGE UNDER REGISTRAR GENERAL'S LICENCE

The main purpose of the Marriage (Registrar General's Licence) Act 1970, which came into force on January 1, 1971, is to enable non-Anglicans to be married in unregistered premises where one of the persons to be married is seriously ill, is not expected to recover and cannot be moved to registered premises.

D.—DETAINED AND HOUSE-BOUND PERSONS

The Marriage Act 1983 (which does not extend to Scotland) enables marriages of detained persons and house-bound persons to be solemnized at their place of residence. The Act came into operation on May 1, 1984.

Miscellaneous Notes

Consanguinity and Affinity.—A marriage between persons within the prohibited degrees of consanguinity or affinity is void. Relaxations have, however, been made by various statutes which have now been replaced by the Marriage Act 1949 (see the 1st Schedule to the Act) and the Marriage (Enabling) Act 1960. It is now permitted to contract a marriage with:—

Sister, aunt or niece of a former wife (whether living or not). Former wife of brother, uncle or nephew (whether living or not).

No clergyman can be compelled to solemnize any of the foregoing marriages, but he may allow his church to be used for the purpose by another minister.

The Marriage (Prohibited Degrees of Relationship) Act 1986 makes further provision with regard to the marriage of persons related by affinity e.g. after section 1 of the Act comes into force a marriage between a man and the daughter or grand-daughter of his former wife will not be void by reason only of that relationship if both parties have attained 21 at the time of the marriage and the younger party has not at any time before attaining 18 been a child of the family in relation to the other party.

Minors.—Persons under 18 years of age are generally required to obtain the consent of certain persons (*see* Marriage Act 1949, section 3 and 2nd Schedule as amended by the Family Law Reform Act 1969). Where both parents are living, both must consent, where one is dead, the survivor, or, if there is a guardian appointed by the deceased parent, the guardian and the survivor. (For the position where the parents of the child were not married to each other at the time of the birth, see section 9 of the Family Law Reform Act 1987.) No consent is required in the case of an infant's second marriage. In certain exceptional cases consent may be dispensed with, e.g., the insanity of a parent. If consent is refused the Court may, on application being made, consent to the marriage; application can be made for this purpose to the High Court, the County Court, or a Court of Summary Jurisdiction. The Act prohibits any marriage where either party is under 16 years of age.

E.—MARRIAGE IN ENGLAND OR WALES WHEN ONE PARTY LIVES IN SCOTLAND OR NORTHERN IRELAND

Notice for a marriage by a Superintendent Registrar's certificate in a register office or registered building may be given in the usual way by the party resident in England. As regards Scotland, the party there should give notice of intention to marry to the Registrar. As regards Northern Ireland, the party there, after a residence of seven days, must give notice to the District Registrar of Marriages. Notice cannot be given for such marriages to take place by Certificate with licence of the Superintendent Registrar.

Marriage of such parties may take place in a church of the Church of England after the publication of banns, or by Ecclesiastical licence.

Fees

Common Licence .... £26·00
Special Licence .... £50·00
Superintendent Registrar's
  Certificate:
  If both parties reside in same district ...... £24·50
  If parties reside in different districts ...... £33·50
Superintendent Registrar's
  Licence:
  If marriage in a register office .... £57·50
  If marriage in a religious building .... £66·50

MARRIAGES IN SCOTLAND

According to the law of Scotland, marriage is a contract which is completed by the mutual consent of parties. The Marriage (Scotland) Act 1977, which came into force on January 1, 1978, states or restates the law in convenient form. References in this section are to that Act.

Impediments to Marriage: These are: (*a*) nonage, i.e., where either party is under the age of 16; (*b*) forbidden degrees of relationship (Section 2) as amended by the Marriage Prohibited Degrees of Relationship Act 1986; (*c*) subsisting previous marriage; (*d*) incapacity to understand the nature of the contract; (*e*) both parties of the same sex; (*f*) non-residence, i.e., if the requirements of prior residence of one or other of the parties in Scotland have not been complied with. The Act also states the grounds on which certain marriages may be declared void but this is amended by the Law Reform (Miscellaneous Provisions) (Scotland) Act 1980 which prevents a marriage being rendered void solely due to the failure to comply with certain formalities, provided the particulars of that marriage are entered in a register of marriages by or at the behest of an appropriate registrar.

Marriages may be regular or irregular, thus:—

Regular Marriages

A regular marriage is one which is celebrated by a Minister of Religion or authorized Registrar or other celebrant specified in the Act. The parties must submit to the District Registrar a statutory notice of intention to marry the fee for which is £5·75 each. The Registrar will then enter the parties' names and particulars in the Marriage Notice Book which must also show the intended date of the marriage. He must then display the notice of intention to marry in a prominent public place until the intended date, and any person claiming an interest may lodge written objections thereto with the Registrar (Section 5). The Registrar, after fourteen days of receipt of the Marriage Notice and on being satisfied that there are no legal impediments to the marriage, will issue to either or both parties a Marriage Schedule. The fourteen day period may be shortened under exceptional circumstances. The Marriage Schedule must be produced to the celebrant of the marriage. The fee for the solemnization ceremony in a Registry Office is £13. After the ceremony the marriage must be registered with the Registrar General for inclusion in the Register of Births, Deaths and Marriages, within three days. Within one month of the ceremony, the fee for an extract marriage certificate is £3·50; thereafter it is £6·00.

IRREGULAR MARRIAGES

Since the Marriage (Scotland) Act 1939 the only form of irregular marriage to be recognised by law, marriage by habit and repute, remains competent under the 1977 Act. If the parties live together constantly as husband and wife and are held to be such by the general repute of the neighbourhood and among their friends and relations, then there may arise a presumption from which marriage can be inferred. Before such a marriage can be registered, however, a decree of declarator of marriage must be obtained from the Deputy Principal Clerk of the Court of Session. It is the duty of the Deputy Principal Clerk to register the decree as soon as it is granted.

JURY SERVICE

Every local or parliamentary elector between the ages of eighteen and sixty-five who has resided in the United Kingdom, Channel Islands or Isle of Man for at least five years since he attained the age of thirteen will be qualified to serve on a jury unless he is ineligible or disqualified.

Ineligible persons include those who have at any time been judges, magistrates and certain senior court officials, those who within the previous ten years have been concerned with the law (such as barristers and solicitors and their clerks, court officers, coroners, police, prison and probation officers); priests of any religion and vowed members of religious communities; and certain sufferers from mental illness.

Disqualified persons are those who have at any time been sentenced by a Court in the United Kingdom, Channel Islands or Isle of Man, to a term of imprisonment of five years or more, or a person who in the last ten years has (a) served any part of a sentence of imprisonment, youth custody or dentention; (b) been detained in a Borstal institution; (c) had passed on him or made in respect of him a suspended sentence of imprisonment or order for detention; or (d) had made in respect of him a community service order. A person who at any time in the last five years has been placed on probation is also disqualified.

Some others are excusable as of right. These include members and officers of the Houses of Parliament, full-time serving members of the forces, registered and practising members of the medical, dental, nursing, veterinary and pharmaceutical professions, and any person who has served on a jury in the two years before he is summoned. In other cases the court may excuse a juror at its discretion (e.g., where the service would be a hardship to the juror).

If a person serves on a jury knowing himself to be disqualified or ineligible he is liable to be fined up to £2,000 or £400 respectively.

A juror is entitled to subsistence and travelling expenses, compensation for other expenses incurred in consequence of attendance for jury service, loss of earnings and loss of national insurance benefits, but certain maximum figures (which are revised from time to time) are laid down.

A verdict of a jury must normally be unanimous but after two hours consideration (or such longer period as the Court thinks reasonable), a majority verdict is acceptable if ten jurors agree to it (or nine if the size of the jury has been reduced to ten, e.g., by illness during the trial).

Jury trial is now very unusual in civil cases but a person charged with any but the least serious crimes is entitled to be tried by a jury. The defendant may object to any juror if he can show that that juror ought not to be on the jury (e.g., because he is ineligible or is biased against him).

The Coroners' Juries Act 1983 (which does not extend to Scotland) makes new provision in relation to qualification to serve on coroners' juries.

JURY SERVICE IN SCOTLAND

It is the duty of the sheriff principal of each sheriffdom, in respect of each sheriff court district in his sheriffdom, to maintain a book, known as the 'general jury book', containing the names and designations of persons within the district who are qualified and liable to serve as jurors. The book, which is compiled from information which every householder is required to provide, is kept open for the inspection by any person, upon payment of a nominal fee, at the sheriff clerk's office for the district. Part II of the Juries Act 1949 (amended by regulations following thereon and by the Law Reform (Miscellaneous Provisions) (Scotland) Act 1980) applies only to Scotland and provides, *inter alia*, for the payment of travelling expenses and subsistence allowances to jurors and for loss of earnings.

The number of a jury in a civil cause in the Court of Session is twelve and in the Sheriff Court seven. In a criminal trial the number is fifteen.

QUALIFICATIONS

Under S.1 of the Law Reform (Miscellaneous Provisions) (Scotland) Act 1980, every man or woman between the ages of 18 and 65 who is for the time being registered as a parliamentary or local government elector and who has been ordinarily resident in the United Kingdom, the Channel Islands or the Isle of Man for any period of at least five years since attaining the age of 13 years, is qualified to serve on a jury.

Ineligible persons include those who at any time within the past ten years have been judges of the supreme courts, sheriffs and certain other senior court officials, those who at any time within the past five years have been concerned with the administration of justice (such as advocates and their clerks, solicitors, court staff, police officers, prison officers, sheriff officers, procurator fiscals, and members of parole boards and children's panels), and certain sufferers from mental illness.

The same rules for disqualified persons operate in Scotland as in England. Those excusable as of right are members and officers of the Houses of Parliament, full time serving members of the forces, registered and practising members of the medical, dental, nursing, veterinary and pharmaceutical professions, ministers of religion and other persons in holy orders, and any person who has attended for jury service in the past five years.

If a person serves on a jury knowing himself to be disqualified or ineligible, he is liable to be fined up to £2,000 or £400 respectively. Jurors failing to attend without good cause are liable to a maximum fine of £400.

LANDLORD AND TENANT
ENGLAND AND WALES

Although basically the relationship between the parties to a lease is governed by the lease itself, the position is complicated by numerous statutory provisions. The few points dealt with may show the desirability of seeking professional assistance in these matters. Important provisions include:—

(1) As to agricultural holdings—the Agricultural Holdings Act 1986. Among other things, the Act regulates the length of notice necessary to determine an agricultural tenancy, the tenant's right to remove fixtures on the land, his right to compensation for damage done by game, for improvements and for disturbance, and his right to require the consent of the Agricultural Land Tribunal to the operation of a notice to quit.

(2) As to business premises—the Landlord and Tenant Acts 1927 and 1954, and the Law of Property Act 1969, Pt. I. Part II of the 1954 Act gives security of tenure to the tenant of most business premises, and in effect he can only be ousted on one or more of the seven grounds set out in the Act. In some cases, where the landlord can resume possession, the tenant is entitled to compensation.

(3) As to dwelling houses—the complicated mass of legislation is embodied in the Rent Act 1977 and the Housing Act 1988.

If a tenancy of a house is within the Rent Act, the tenant has a personal right to reside there, and he may only be ousted on certain grounds. Tenancies with full Rent Act protection are known as regulated tenancies. The maximum rent recoverable under such a tenancy is the rent agreed between the landlord and tenant, unless a fair rent has been registered, in which case that is the maximum. Application for the registration of a fair rent may be made by either the landlord or tenant, to the Local Rent Officer, and appeal against his decision lies to the Rent Assessment Committee.

Since the Housing Act 1988 came into force on January 15, 1989, it has not generally been possible to create a new regulated tenancy, although the above protection remains for existing regulated tenancies. Tenancies granted on or after January 15, 1989 are known as assured tenancies provided they satisfy certain conditions, which are broadly the same as those for regulated tenancies under the 1977 Act. However, the rent payable by an assured tenant is either that agreed with the landlord or the open market rent fixed by the Rent Assessment Committee.

(4) As to dwelling houses with resident landlords—the Rent Act 1974 gave tenants of dwellings let furnished the same security of tenure as those of unfurnished dwellings unless the landlord lived in part of the house. In the latter case, and in the case of a tenancy of a dwelling granted by a resident landlord after August 13, 1974, the tenancy will usually fall outside full Rent Act protection, but may fall within the restricted contract provisions of the Rent Act 1977. In this event, the landlord or the tenant may apply to the Rent Tribunal for a reasonable rent to be registered and once registered, this is the maximum rent recoverable. No new restricted contracts can be created on or after January 15, 1989.

(5) The Protection from Eviction Act 1977, as amended by the Housing Act 1988, provides that if any person with intent to cause the residential occupier of any premises to give up the occupation thereof does any act calculated to interfere with the peace or comfort of the residential occupier or members of his household, he shall be guilty of an offence. A further provision prevents a landlord enforcing a right to possession against a tenant (who is not protected by any security of tenure legislation) without a court order, and there are special rules in such cases relating to agricultural employees.

(6) A notice to quit any dwellinghouse must be given at least four weeks before it is to take effect, and must be in writing and in the prescribed statutory form.

(7) Part I of the Landlord and Tenant Act 1954 applies to most tenancies of houses for over twenty-one years at a ground rent. Where it applies, the contractual tenancy is continued until brought to an end in the manner prescribed by the Act, and in effect the landlord can only get possession on limited grounds.

Further, under the Leasehold Reform Act 1967, tenants of houses under leases for over twenty-one years at a rent less than two-thirds of the rateable value of the house are in most cases given a right to purchase the freehold or to take an extended lease for a term of fifty years, provided the tenant at the time when he seeks to exercise the right has been occupying the house as his residence for the last three years or for periods amounting to three years in the last ten years.

(8) Full Rent Act or Housing Act protection is available only if a house is let on a tenancy, so that if the occupier of a house has a mere licence to occupy, he does not have protection. Further, even if he has a tenancy, he will not be protected if the rent payable is less than two-thirds of the rateable value of the house. For these reasons, many occupants of houses owned by farmers and occupied by farm workers did not enjoy full security of tenure. The Rent (Agriculture) Act 1976 contains detailed provisions conferring security of tenure on certain agricultural workers housed by their employers and on their successors on death.

(9) Under the Landlord and Tenant Act 1985 (which does not extend to Scotland), in a lease of a dwelling-house granted after October 24, 1961, for a term of less than 7 years, there is implied a covenant by the landlord (a) to keep in repair the structure and exterior of the house and (b) to keep in repair and proper working order the installations in the house (i) for the supply of water, gas and electricity, and for sanitation, and (ii) for space heating or heating water.

(10) The Housing Act 1985 gives security of tenure to many tenants of local authorities and certain other bodies. Further, and subject to certain conditions, such tenants may have the right to purchase their houses or to take a long lease of their flats.

(11) Tenants of flats and other dwellings are given a number of special rights by the Landlord and Tenant Act 1987, as amended by the Housing Act 1988.

SCOTLAND

A Lease is a contract, the relationship of the parties being governed by the terms thereof. As is also the case in England (*see* above) legislation has played an important part in regulating that relationship. Thus, what at Common Law was an Agreement binding only the parties to the deed, becomes in virtue of the Leases Act 1449, a contract binding the landlord's successors, as purchasers or creditors, provided the following four conditions are observed: (1) the lease, if for more than one year, must be in writing; (2) there must be a rent; (3) there must be a term of expiry; and (4) the tenant must have entered into possession.

It would be impracticable in a brief section of these Notes to enter upon a general discussion of this branch of the law and, accordingly, the plan adopted in the preceding section of quoting a few important Statutes is followed here.

The Agricultural Holdings (Scotland) Act 1949 (amended by the Agriculture Act 1958), which is a consolidating Act applicable to Scotland, contains provisions similar to those in the English Act, alluded to in the preceding section. It cannot here be analysed in detail.

It is of interest to note that the Small Landholders Act 1911 provided for the setting up of the Land Court, which has jurisdiction over a large proportion of agricultural and pastoral land in Scotland.

In Scotland business premises are not controlled by Statute to so great an extent as in England, but the Tenancy of Shops (Scotland) Act 1949 gives a measure of security to tenants of shops. This Act enables the tenant of a shop who is threatened with eviction to apply to the Sheriff for a renewal of the tenancy. If the landlord has offered to sell the subjects to the tenant at an agreed price the application for a renewal of the tenancy may be dismissed. Reference should be made to Section 1 (3) of the 1949 Act for particulars of other circumstances under which the Sheriff has a discretion to dismiss an application. The Act extends to premises held by the Crown or Government Departments, either as landlord or tenant.

The Housing (Scotland) Act 1988 creates, with certain exceptions, two new forms of tenancy for tenancies created after January 2, 1989: assured tenancies and short assured tenancies. The assured tenancy significantly reduces the concept of security of tenure and abolishes any method of regulating rent other than market forces. The short assured tenancy lasts for no more than six months and if properly constituted will allow the landlord to recover possession on its expiry. Provision is made for a tenant to apply to the Rent Assessment Committee to fix a rent based on the rent a landlord might reasonably expect for a short assured tenancy of the property.

For most tenancies created before January 2, 1989, the Rent (Scotland) Act 1984 will continue to apply. It defines regulated tenancies which may be either furnished or unfurnished and lays down the system by which a landlord or tenant may obtain from the Rent Office registration of a fair rent. The Act gives to tenants of either furnished or unfurnished lets a substantial degree of security of tenure. There are, however, certain exceptions thus: they do not apply to tenancies where the interest belongs to the Crown or to a government department or to a local authority, a development corporation of a new town or a housing corporation. There must be a true tenancy for the Act to apply. It does not apply to licencees such as lodgers or persons allowed to occupy houses on a grace and favour basis or to services occupiers. The Act regulates the short tenancy, a category of let under which on compliance with certain conditions the landlord can be assured of recovering possession on the expiry of the stipulated period of let. The Act defines the circumstances under which generally a landlord may apply for increased rent as a consequence of having carried improvements to his property and also lays down the system of phasing such

rent increases. On the death of a statutory successor to a tenancy, the tenancy may pass for a second time to a member of the family or a relative who has been in residence of the house for a period of at least six months. The Act further lays down the duties and functions of Rent Officers and Rent Assessment Committees with regard to unfurnished accommodation and of rent tribunals for furnished accommodation. The Secretary of State for Scotland is given power in the 1988 Act to repeal or amend those sections of the 1984 Act relating to the phasing of rent increases.

The Housing (Scotland) Act 1987 consolidates previous legislation in regard to the extensive powers and duties to local authorities in relation to housing. Included therein is the general provision regarding the rights of public sector tenants to purchase the houses which they occupy and the restrictions regarding this right in certain circumstances where the house has been designed or adapted for occupation by the elderly. This Act also makes provision for secure tenancies for public sector tenants. The other major features of the 1988 Act are to establish Scottish Homes, and to permit public sector properties to be transferred to Scottish Homes or a landlord approved by Scottish Homes.

LEGAL AID

LEGAL AID IN CIVIL PROCEEDINGS

The Legal Aid Act 1988 (as amended) is designed to make legal aid and advice more readily available for persons of small and moderate means. The main structure of the service is contained in the Act itself and the Regulations made thereunder, administered by the Legal Aid Board.

Legal aid is available for proceedings (including matrimonial causes) in the House of Lords, Court of Appeal, High Court, County Courts, Lands Tribunal, Restrictive Practices Court, before the Commons Commissioners, and civil proceedings in Magistrates' Courts. In any event, an application for legal aid will not be approved if it appears that the applicant would gain only a trivial advantage from the proceedings. Further, proceedings wholly or partly in respect of defamation are excepted from the scheme, as are also relator actions and election petitions. It is generally not available for obtaining the decree in undefended divorce and judicial separation, although the Legal Advice and Assistance Scheme (*see* below) will be, and Legal Aid is still available to deal with property, custody disputes etc., arising in the suit.

Where a person is concerned in proceedings only in a representative, fiduciary or official capacity, his personal resources are not to be taken into account in considering eligibility for legal aid. Apart from this, eligibility in civil proceedings depends upon an applicant's disposable income and disposable capital. The figures change frequently; particulars can be obtained from a solicitor, the Law Society or a Citizens' Advice Bureau. Disposable income is calculated by making deductions from gross income in respect of certain matters such as dependants, interest on loans, income tax, rates, rent and other matters for which the applicant must or reasonably may provide. Disposable capital is calculated by excluding from gross capital part of the value of the house in which the applicant resides, of furniture and household possessions; allowances are made in respect of dependants. Except in cases where the spouses are living apart, or have a contrary interest, any resources of a person's wife or husband are to be treated as that person's resources. These figures will be assessed by the Department of Social Security, and will be referred to The Legal Aid Board, who will determine whether reasonable grounds exist for the grant of a civil aid certificate. Appeal from refusal of a certificate lies to an Area Committee. A person resident in England or Wales desiring legal aid should apply for a certificate to the appropriate Area Director for the area in which he or she resides; if resident elsewhere application should be made to an Area Director in London. If a certificate is granted, the applicant may select his solicitor, and, if necessary, counsel from a panel. The costs of the assisted person's solicitor and counsel will be paid out of the legal aid fund. When, however, damages or property are recovered or preserved by the assisted person the legal aid fund has a charge over them in respect of these costs less any contribution towards costs recovered from the unsuccessful party. In matrimonial cases, maintenance is exempt, as is the first £2,500 of any property settlement. The court may order that the costs of a successful unassisted party shall be paid out of the legal aid fund.

In an urgent case, say of domestic violence, or to restrain the kidnapping abroad of a child, legal aid may be granted without the applicant's means being fully investigated beforehand. If on a full examination later he is found financially ineligible he is liable to pay all the costs incurred on his behalf, if he does not attend for an examination.

LEGAL ADVICE AND ASSISTANCE

The Scheme is governed by the Legal Aid Act 1988.

Under this legal advice and assistance scheme a client may obtain such advice or assistance as is normally provided by a solicitor and if necessary the advice of a barrister may be obtained, but, with the exception of domestic proceedings in a magistrates' court and certain other proceedings (*see* below), the scheme does not extend to taking any step in any proceedings before any court or tribunal. Where legal aid is available for civil proceedings (*see* above) or in criminal cases (*see* below) the scheme covers work done in making application for such legal aid.

A person (other than one receiving advice and assistance at a police station or from a duty solicitor) is eligible for advice or assistance under the scheme provided his disposable capital and his disposable income do not exceed limits in force from time to time or if he is eligible for Income Support or Family Credit. For a married man or person with children or other dependants' deductions will be made from gross income and capital and allowances are made in respect of income tax, National Insurance contributions, etc. It is intended that the financial limits shall approximate to those applying for legal aid in civil proceedings (*see* above). Except when they are separated or have conflicting interests the means of husband and wife or cohabiting couple will be aggregated for the purpose of determining financial eligibility. As in the case of legal aid, depending on his means, a person may be called upon to pay a contribution towards the costs of work done for him. Particulars may again be obtained from a solicitor, the Law Society or a Citizens' Advice Bureau.

A solicitor cannot do more than two hours' work, or three hours' in the case of divorce, etc. without leave of the Area Legal Aid Committee. His costs are paid out of the client's contribution and any monies recovered in respect of costs or damages from another party (although this may be waived by leave of the Area Committee in cases of hardship) and the balance will be paid by the legal aid fund.

The Act also extends the scheme to cover the costs of a solicitor who is present within the precincts of a magistrates' court or county court and is requested by the court to advise or represent a person who is in need of help.

In April 1980 the Scheme was enlarged to cover the cost of representation in domestic proceedings in a magistrates' court. It has since been extended to cover the representation of patients before Mental Health Review Tribunals. Subject to financial eligibility limits, application is made to the area or local committee for 'approval of assistance by way of representation' which will replace legal aid for such proceedings. However the two hour limit referred to above will not apply. An applicant who is outside the financial limits but eligible for legal aid will still have to apply for a legal aid certificate as before. Free advice and assistance, and assistance by way of representation from a duty solicitor is also available in limited circumstances to persons appearing before a magistrates' court charged with a criminal offence.

In January, 1986 the scheme was further extended to provide free advice and assistance to all suspects detained at a police station whether arrested or merely helping police with their enquiries, and free representation for all arrested persons who are the subject of an application for a warrant of further detention under the Police and Criminal Evidence Act 1984. Such persons may instruct a solicitor of their choice or take advantage of the duty solicitor scheme which has now been extended to cover police stations.

LEGAL AID IN CRIMINAL CASES

The Legal Aid Act 1988 provides for legal aid in criminal proceedings, and for children and parents in care proceedings and related applications under the Children and Young Persons Act 1969. A criminal court (e.g. magistrates' court, Crown Court) has power to order legal aid to be granted where it appears desirable to do so in the interests of justice. The court shall make an order in certain cases, e.g., where a person is committed for trial on a charge of murder. However, the court may not make an order unless it appears to the court that the person's disposable income and capital are such that he requires assistance in meeting the costs of the particular proceedings in question. Application should be made to the appropriate court where proceedings are to take place.

An applicant shall be required to make a contribution towards the costs of his case if his disposable income and capital exceed certain prescribed limits. Persons in receipt of Income Support are automatically exempt. In order to ascertain the amount of this contribution he will have to produce written evidence of his means. Investigation of means will be carried out by the court. Any person who falls into arrears with the payment of contribution is liable to have the order revoked.

Any practising barrister or solicitor may act for a legally aided person in criminal proceedings unless excluded by reason of misconduct. In general where legal aid is given it will normally include representation by both counsel and solicitor. However, in connection with magistrates' courts, representation will be by solicitor alone unless it is a serious offence.

Where any doubt arises about the grant of a legal aid order that doubt is to be resolved in favour of the applicant. The court also has power to amend or revoke a legal aid order. Legal aid may also be granted in connection with appellate proceedings, e.g., on appeal to the Criminal Division of the Court of Appeal under the Criminal Appeal Act 1968.

SCOTLAND

CIVIL PROCEEDINGS

Legal Aid in Scotland is now governed by the Legal Aid (Scotland) Act 1986 and the Regulations made thereunder. This Act established the Scottish Legal Board which has the general function of securing that legal aid and legal advice and assistance are available in accordance with the Act, and of administering the Scottish Legal Aid Fund. The Board comprises not less than eleven and not more than fifteen members with one member appointed as Chairman. The members are appointed by the Secretary of State for Scotland. Civil legal aid is available in relation to civil proceedings in the House of Lords in Appeals from the Court of Session, in the Court of Session, the Lands Valuation Appeal Court, the Scottish Land Court, the Sheriff Court, the Lands Tribunal for Scotland, the Employment Appeals Tribunal and to the European Court of Human Rights. Civil legal aid is granted if on application to the Board, the Board is satisfied that there is *probalilis causa litigendi* and it is reasonable in the particular circumstances of the case that legal aid should be awarded. As in England eligibility and any contribution required from an applicant is dependent on their disposable income and disposable capital. Information on current financial limits can be obtained from the Scottish Legal Aid Board, a solicitor, or a Citizens' Advice Bureau. A person believing himself to be eligible may instruct any solicitor of his own choice. If a court action is not immediately contemplated application will be made for legal advice and assistance which operates in a similar manner to the legal advice assistance scheme in England. If proceedings are contemplated then a formal application for civil legal aid will be made and there are special provisions for emergency applications in appropriate circumstances.

If proceedings are decided against a person in receipt of legal aid the court shall determine a reasonable sum in the circumstances as an appropriate award of expenses to be made against the applicant. The court may only make an award out of the fund if proceedings were instituted by the legally assisted person and the court is satisfied that the resisting party would suffer severe financial hardship unless the order is made and the court is satisfied that in all the circumstances it is just and equitable that an award be made. If monies are recovered by a legally assisted person these fall to be paid to the Scottish Legal Aid Board who will then determine the appropriate level of contribution from the sums received which should be made to the expenses of their litigation.

CRIMINAL PROCEEDINGS

Legal aid in criminal causes is also administered under the Legal Aid (Scotland) Act 1986. The procedure for application for criminal legal aid is dependent on the circumstances of each case. In serious cases heard before a jury under solemn procedure it is for the court to decide whether to grant legal aid. Applications for legal aid must normally be made on the prescribed forms to the clerk of court in question and an applicant is required to provide therein particulars of the merits of his case and his financial circumstances. In summary criminal causes, however, the procedure is dependent on whether the applicant is in custody : if so then he is entitled to automatic free legal aid from the duty solicitor. If the applicant is not in custody and wishes to plead guilty he is ineligible for full legal aid but may be entitled to criminal legal advice and assistance and in some circumstances may qualify for assistance by way of representation which will enable his solicitor to appear and make a plea in mitigation on his behalf. If he is not in custody and wishes to plead not guilty he can apply to the Scottish Legal Aid Board for criminal legal aid on the prescribed form not later than fourteen days after the first court appearance at which he made the plea and legal aid shall only be granted if the Board is satisfied that the accused cannot meet the expenses of the case without undue hardship and that it is in the interest of justice as defined by the 1986 Act.

TOWN AND COUNTRY PLANNING

The Town and Country Planning Act 1971 (consolidating earlier Acts) contains very far-reaching provisions affecting the liberty of an owner of land to develop and use it as he will. A person has generally to get planning permission from the Local Planning Authority before carrying out any development on his land.

What is development :—

(a) Carrying out of building, engineering, mining or other operations.

(b) Making a material change in use.

It is expressly provided that if one dwelling-house is converted into two or more dwelling-houses, this involves a material change in use.

Examples of what is not deemed development :—

(a) Maintaining, improving or altering the interior of a building (except works for making good war damage), provided there is no material change to the exterior, with the exception that since December 5, 1968, any expansion, or works begun for the expansion, of a building below ground level constitutes development.

(b) Change of use of property within the curtilage of a dwelling-house for a purpose incidental to the use of the dwelling-house as such. (It will, however, be development if building operations are carried out.)

Application can be made to the local planning authority to determine whether or not an operation or change of use constitutes development.

Planning Permission.—Application for such permission is not always necessary, as the Secretary of State may make Development Orders giving general permission for a specified type of development. Thus a General Development Order of 1988 specifies a number of types of development for which no permission is usually required, e.g., enlargement of a dwelling-house (including erection of a garage), so long as the cubic content of the original dwelling (external measurement) is not exceeded by more than 70 cubic metres or 15 per cent, whichever is greater, subject to a maximum of 115 cubic metres. However, in the case of a terraced house, the limitation is 50 cubic metres or 10 per cent, whichever is the greater, subject to the maximum of 115 cubic metres.

Appeal against refusal of permission lies to the Secretary of State and from his decision, in limited circumstances, to the High Court. If the result of the appeal is unsatisfactory, an applicant may in certain circumstances require the local authority to purchase the land.

SCOTLAND

The Town and Country Planning (Scotland) Act 1972 consolidates the statute law relating to town and country planning in Scotland.

The uses of buildings are classified by the Town and Country Planning (Use Classes) (Scotland)

Order 1988. Changes in use prior to December 31, 1984 are immune from enforcement proceedings.

Development normally requires to be commenced within five years from the date of granting permission.

The 1972 Act contains provisions for an appeal to the Secretary of State against the refusal of planning permission. The decision of the Secretary of State is final.

Sections 87 and 92 of the Local Government, Planning and Land Act 1980 contain important provisions on planning applications and, unlike certain parts of this Act, extend to Scotland.

VOTERS' QUALIFICATIONS

The franchise is governed by the Representation of the People Acts 1983 and 1985. Those entitled to vote as electors at a parliamentary election in any constituency are all persons resident there on the qualifying date who, at that date and on the date of the poll are Commonwealth citizens or citizens of the Republic of Ireland and not subject to any legal incapacity to vote and who on the date of the poll are at least 18 years of age. However, a person is not entitled to vote at a parliamentary election in any constituency in Northern Ireland unless he was resident in Northern Ireland during the whole of the period of three months ending on the qualifying date for that election. Also, no person can use his vote unless he is on the register of electors kept for the constituency. A person who is of voting age on the date of the poll at a parliamentary or local government election is entitled to vote, whether or not he was of voting age on the qualifying date. Accordingly, a qualified person will be entitled to be registered in a register of parliamentary electors or a register of local government electors if he will attain voting age within twelve months from the date on which the register is required to be published. Subject to certain conditions, the 1985 Act extends the franchise to British citizens overseas.

The register is prepared by the Registration Officer in each constituency in Great Britain. It is the registration officer's duty to have a house to house or other official inquiry made as to the persons entitled to be registered and to publish preliminary electors lists showing the persons appearing to him to be entitled to be registered. Any person whose name is omitted may claim registration, and any person on the list may object to the inclusion therein of other persons' names: the registration officer determines the claims and objections.

Voters at a parliamentary or local government election must generally vote in person at the allotted polling station, except for those entitled to vote by post or at any polling station, and those for whom proxies have been appointed. Certain people can apply to be treated as absent voters at a parliamentary election and thus able to vote by post—among these are registered service voters, those unable by reason of blindness or other physical incapacity to go in person to the polling station, and those unable to go in person from their qualifying address to the polling station without making a journey by air or sea.

Unless entitled to vote by post, a person registered as a service voter may vote by proxy at a parliamentary or local government election. A proxy may also be appointed by a registered elector, where the registration officer is satisfied that the applicant's circumstances on the date of the poll are likely to be such that he cannot reasonably be expected to vote in person at the polling station allotted to him. The appointment of a person to vote as proxy at parliamentary elections has effect also for the purposes of local government elections.

THE PROBATION SERVICE

The Probation Service is employed in each county by an independent committee of justices and it provides a professional social work agency in the courts, with responsibility for a wide range of duties which include: (a) a social enquiry service for the criminal courts; (b) provision of a range of noncustodial measures involving the supervision of offenders in the community; (c) supervisory aftercare for offenders released from custody, together with social work in penal establishments and help for the families of those serving sentences; (d) an enquiry, conciliation and supervision service in the divorce and domestic courts; (e) support for and promotion of preventive and containment measures in the community designed to reduce the level of crime and domestic breakdown. It is a direct grant service funded 80 per cent from the Home Office and 20 per cent from the relevant local authority.

Its national representative bodies are:
(i) The Central Council of Probation Committees, 38 Belgrave Square, London SW1X 8NT—Tel: 01-245 9364 (*Secretary*, I. Miles);
(ii) The Association of Chief Officers of Probation, 20-30 Lawefield Lane, Wakefield WF2 8SP—Tel: 0924-361156 (*Secretary*, W. R. Weston);
(iii) The National Association of Probation Officers, 3-4 Chivalry Road, Battersea, London SW11 1HT—Tel: 01-223 4887 (*Gen. Secretary*, W. Beaumont).

NATIONAL INSURANCE AND RELATED CASH BENEFITS

The State insurance and assistance schemes, comprising schemes of national insurance and industrial injuries insurance, national assistance, and non-contributory old age pensions came into force from July 5, 1948. The Ministry of Social Security Act, 1966, replaced national assistance and non-contributory old age pensions with a scheme of non-contributory benefits, termed supplementary allowances and pensions. These, and subsequent measures relating to social security provision in Great Britain, were consolidated by the Social Security Act, 1975; the Social Security (Consequential Provisions) Act, 1975; and the Industrial Injuries and Diseases (Old Cases) Act, 1975: corresponding measures were passed for Northern Ireland. The Social Security Pensions Act, 1975, introduced a new State pensions scheme, which came into force on April 6, 1978, and the graduated pension scheme 1961–1975 has been wound up, existing rights being preserved. The Pensioners' Payments and Social Security Act, 1979, provided for a £10 bonus for pensioners in 1979 and also for the payment of a bonus in succeeding years at levels then to be determined. The Child Benefit Act, 1975, replaced family allowances (introduced 1946) with child benefit and one parent benefit.

Some of the above legislation has been superceded by the provisions of the Social Security Act, 1986, passed in July 1986 and introduced at various dates since.

NATIONAL INSURANCE SCHEME

The National Insurance scheme operates under the Social Security Acts, 1975 to 1988, and orders and regulations made thereunder. The scheme is financed by contributions payable by earners, employers and others (such as non-employed persons, paying voluntary contributions), together with the Treasury supplement. It provides the funds required for paying benefits payable under the Social Security Acts out of the National Insurance Fund and not out of other public money; for the making of payments towards the cost of the National Health Service and into the Redundancy and Maternity Pay Funds; and for paying benefit under the Industrial Injuries and Diseases (Old Cases) Act, 1975. The yearly Treasury supplement to the National Insurance Fund was abolished in April 1989.

CONTRIBUTIONS

Contributions are of four classes:

Class 1 contributions are earnings-related, based on a percentage of the employee's earnings.

(a) *primary Class 1* contributions are payable by employed earners and office-holders over age 16 with gross earnings at or above the lower earnings limit of £43·00 per week. For those with gross earnings at or above this level, contributions are payable on *all* earnings up to an upper limit of £325 per week. "Gross earnings" include overtime pay, commission, bonus, etc., without deduction of any super-annuation contributions.

Women who marry for the first time no longer have a right to elect not to pay the full contribution rate. Married women and widows who before May 12, 1977, elected not to pay contributions at the full rate retain the right to pay a reduced rate over the same earnings range, which covers industrial injuries benefits and a contribution to the National Health Service. They lose this right if, after April 5, 1978, there are two consecutive tax years in which they have no earnings on which primary Class 1 contri-

butions are payable and in which they have not been at any time self-employed earners. No primary contributions are due on earnings paid for a period on or after the employee's pension age, even when retirement is deferred.

(b) *secondary Class 1* contributions are payable by employers of employed earners, and by the appropriate authorities in the case of office-holders. On Oct. 6, 1985, the upper earnings limit for employers' contributions was abolished and secondary contributions are payable on *all* the employee's earnings if they reach or exceed £43·00 per week.

Primary contributions are deducted from earnings by the employer, and are paid, together with the employer's contributions, to the Inland Revenue along with income tax collected under the PAYE system, so dispensing with contribution cards for employed earners. On Oct. 6, 1985 several lower percentage rates of contribution for lower paid employees and their employers were introduced.

Class 2 contributions are flat-rate, paid weekly by self-employed earners over age 16. Those with earnings below £2,350 a year for the tax year 1989–90 can apply for exception from liability to pay Class 2 contributions. People who while self-employed are excepted from liability to pay contributions on the grounds of small earnings may pay either Class 2 or Class 3 contributions voluntarily. Self-employed earners (whether or not they pay Class 2 contributions) may also be liable to pay Class 4 contributions based on profits or gains within certain limits. There are special rules for those who are concurrently employed and self-employed. Married women and widows can no longer choose not to pay Class 2 contributions. Those who elected not to pay Class 2 contributions before May 12, 1977, retain the right until there is a period of two consecutive tax years after April 5, 1978 in which they were not at any time either self-employed earners or had earnings on which primary Class 1 contributions were payable.

Class 2 contributions may be paid by direct debit through a bank or National Giro account or by stamping a contribution card.

Class 3 contributions are voluntary flat-rate contributions payable by persons over school-leaving age who would otherwise be unable to qualify for retirement pension and certain other benefits because they have an insufficient record of Class 1 or Class 2 contributions. Married women and widows who on or before May 11, 1977, elected not to pay Class 1 (full rate) or Class 2 contributions cannot pay Class 3 contributions while they retain this right.

Payment may be made by stamping a contribution card or by direct debit through a bank Giro account.

Class 4 contributions are payable by self-employed earners, whether or not they pay Class 2 contributions, on annual profits or gains from a trade, profession or vocation chargeable to income tax under Schedule D, where these fall between £5,050 and £16,900 a year. The maximum Class 4 contribution, payable on profits or gains of £16,900 or more, is £746·55.

Class 4 contributions are generally assessed and collected by the Inland Revenue along with Schedule D income tax. Self-employed persons under 16, or who at the beginning of a tax year are over pension age even where retirement is deferred, are not liable to pay Class 4 contributions. There are special rules for people who have more than one job, or who pay Class 1 contributions on earnings which are chargeable to income tax under Schedule D.

Regulations state the cases in which earners may be excepted from liability to pay contributions, and the conditions upon which contributions are credited to persons who are excepted. Leaflet NI 208 is obtainable from local social security offices.

The Secretary of State for Social Services is empowered by the Social Security Acts to alter certain rates of contributions by order approved by both Houses of Parliament, and is required by the same enactments to make annual reviews of the general level of earnings in order to determine whether such an order should be made.

For the period April 6, 1989 to Oct. 4, 1990 the earnings brackets determining Class 1 contributions are:

	Weekly earnings £
a	0 — 43·00
b	43·00— 74·99
c	75·00—114·99
d	115·00—164·99
e	165·00—325·00
f	over 325·00

Contribution rates for the period April 6, 1989 to Oct. 4, 1990 are:

Class 1 contributions—not contracted out

Earnings bracket	Percentage of reckonable income		
	Employee's rate		Employer's rate
	standard	reduced	
a	0	0	0
b	5	3·85	5
c	7	3·85	7
d	9	3·85	9
e	9	3·85	10·45
f	9*	3·85*	10·45

* to a maximum of £325 per week.

Class 1 contributions—contracted out (*see* also p. 1046)

Employee's rates

Earnings bracket	On first £43·00		On earnings from £43·00–£325·00	
	standard	reduced	standard	reduced
a	0	0	0	0
b	5	3·85	3·00	3·85
c	7	3·85	5·00	3·85
d, e, f.	9	3·85	7·00	3·85

Employer's rates

Earnings bracket	On first £43·00	On earnings from £43·00–£325·00	On any earnings over £325·00
a	0	0	0
b	5	1·2	0
c	7	3·2	0
d	9	5·2	0
e	10·45	6·65	0
f	10·45	6·65	10·45

	Weekly flat rate
Class 2 contributions	£4·25
Class 3 contributions	£4·15

	Percentage of profits or gains
Class 4 contributions	6·3

From Oct. 5, 1989 there was a change in the assessment of National Insurance contributions for employees. Earnings brackets for employees' contributions were abolished and replaced by a new lower contribution rate on earnings up to and including the lower earnings limit and at a main percentage rate on earnings between the lower earnings limit up to and including the employees' upper earnings limit.

Where earnings were paid or were due to be paid before Oct 5, 1989, employees' contributions continued to be paid at 5, 7, and 9 per cent (plus the corresponding lower contracted out rates if appropriate) depending on the earnings bracket.

Where earnings were paid or were due to be paid on or after Oct. 5, 1989 employees' contributions were paid at 2 per cent on earnings up to and including the lower earnings limit (£43·00 a week or equivalent); 9 per cent (not contracted out) or 7 per cent (contracted out) on earnings between the lower earnings up to and including the employees' upper earnings limit (£325·00 a week or equivalent). Employees contributing to the reduced rate continue to pay contributions at 3·85 per cent on all earnings up to and including the employees' upper earnings limit.

Employees earning less than the lower earnings limit continue not to pay any contributions.

There was no change in the assessment of employers' contributions.

THE STATE EARNINGS RELATED PENSION SCHEME (S.E.R.P.S.)

The Social Security Pensions Act, 1975, which came into force in April, 1978, aims to reduce reliance upon means-tested benefit in old age, in widowhood and in chronic ill-health by providing better pensions; to ensure that occupational pension schemes which are contracted out of part of the State scheme fulfil the conditions of a good scheme; that pensions are adequately protected against inflation; and that in both the State and occupational schemes men and women are treated equally. Retirement, widow's and invalidity pensions under the new scheme started to be paid in April 1979. Since April 6, 1979, flat-rate retirement and other State pensions have been augmented for employed earners by additional pensions related to earnings, but it will be twenty years before these additional pensions become payable at the full rate.

Under the scheme retirement, invalidity and widow's pensions for employees are related to the earnings on which national insurance contributions have been paid. For employees of either sex with a complete insurance record the scheme provides a category A retirement pension in two parts, a basic and an additional pension. The basic pension corresponds to the old personal flat-rate national insurance pension. The additional pension is 1·25 per cent of average earnings between the lower weekly earnings limit for Class 1 contribution liability and the upper earnings limit for each year of such earnings under the scheme, and will thus build up to 25 per cent in twenty years.

The additional pension will be calculated in a different way for individuals who reach pension age after April 6, 1999. The changes are to be phased in over 10 years. From 2010 a lifetime's earnings will be included in the calculation and for years from 1988–89 onwards the accrual rate on these surplus earnings will be 20 per cent. The accrual rate on surplus earnings for the years from 1978–79 to 1987–88 will remain at 25 per cent.

Actual earnings are to be revalued in terms of the earnings level current in the last complete tax year before pension age (or death or incapacity). Both components of pensions in payment will be uprated annually in line with the movement of prices. Graduated retirement pensions in payment, and rights to such pensions earned by people who are still working, will be brought into the annual review of benefits.

Self-employed persons pay contributions towards the basic pension. The non-employed and employees with earnings below the lower limit may contribute voluntarily for basic pension. Although no primary Class 1 contributions or Class 2 or Class 4 contributions are payable by persons who work beyond pension age (65 for men, 60 for women), the employer's liability for secondary Class 1 contributions continues if earnings are at or above the lower earnings limit. Class 4 contributions are still payable up to the end of the tax year during which pension age is reached.

Widows will get the whole of any additional pensions earned by their husbands with their widowed mother's allowances or widow's pensions; and can add to the retirement pensions earned by their own contributions any additional pensions earned by their husbands up to the maximum payable on one person's contributions. Men whose wives die when they are both over pension age can add together their own and their wives' pension rights in the same way as widows. Among the steps taken to give women equal treatment in benefit provision the State scheme permits years of home responsibilities to count towards satisfying the contribution conditions for retirement pension, widowed mother's allowance and widow's pension (and the "half-test" by which a married woman who married before age 55 could not qualify for a Category A retirement pension unless she had contributed on earnings at the basic level in at least half the years between marriage and pension age has been abolished with effect from Dec. 22, 1984). The range of short-term social security benefits and industrial injury benefits under the Social Security Act, 1975, continues with only minor changes.

Contracted-Out and Personal Pension Schemes

Members of occupational pension schemes which meet the standards laid down in the Social Security Pensions Act, 1975, can be contracted-out of the earnings related part of the state scheme relating to retirement and widows' benefits. Regulations made under the Act require employers to consult employees and their organizations and inform them of their intention to contract out. (Leaflets relating to pensions and guidance for employers about contracting-out are available from local social security offices.) The Act also contains provisions ensuring equal access to membership of schemes for men and women.

Until April 6, 1988, occupational pension schemes could only contract out if they promised a pension that was related to earnings. These are known as contracted-out salary related schemes. They must provide a pension that is not less than the guaranteed minimum pension (G.M.P.), which is broadly equivalent to the state earnings related pension. However, new options have been introduced by the Social Security Act, 1986. Since April 6, 1988, occupational pension schemes which promise a minimum level of contributions have also been able to contract out. These are known as contracted-out money purchase schemes. They provide a pension based on the value of the fund built up in the scheme.

In addition, since July 1988 employees whose employers do not provide a pension scheme have been able to start their own personal pension instead of staying in the state earnings related pension scheme. Since April 6, 1988, this choice has been open to all employees even if their employer does have a pension scheme. A personal pension, like a contracted-out money purchase scheme, provides a pension based on the value of the fund built up in the scheme.

The decision on whether or not an occupational pension scheme may become contracted-out lies with the Occupational Pension Board, an independent statutory body who have a general responsibility for supervising contracting-out. They also consider and approve personal pension schemes which can be used instead of state additional pension.

The State earnings related pension payable to a member of a contracted-out salary related scheme, or his widow, will be reduced by the amount of G.M.P. payable (which in the case of a widow must be at least half of the late husband's G.M.P. entitlement). Members of contracted-out money purchase schemes and personal pension schemes, or their widows, have no G.M.P. entitlement as such. But the state earnings related pension payable will be reduced by an amount equivalent to a G.M.P. (or widow's G.M.P.).

Since April 6, 1988 contracted-out salary related schemes must also provide a widower's G.M.P. which must be at least half of the late wife's G.M.P. entitlement built up from April 6, 1988. (A scheme need not provide entitlement to a G.M.P. for widowers of earners dying before April 1989.) Contracted-out money purchase schemes and personal pension schemes must provide half-rate widower's benefit.

In contracted-out schemes, both the employee and the employer pay the full ordinary rate of contribution on the first £43·00 (1989–90 figure) of earnings but earnings above that amount attract a lower rate of contribution from the employee, and from the employer where the employee's earnings are under £325·00 (1989–90 figure): where the employee's earnings exceed this amount, the full ordinary rate of contribution is payable only by the employer, the employee has no liability for contributions on these earnings (*see also* p. 1045).

An employee who chooses a personal pension in place of S.E.R.P.S. or their employer's pension scheme must pay National Insurance contributions at the full ordinary rate (the employer's share must also be paid at the same rate). The D.S.S. pays the difference between the lower contracted-out rate and the full ordinary rate to the personal pension scheme.

BENEFITS

The benefits payable under the Social Security Acts are as follows:

(1) Contributory Benefits:
    Unemployment benefit.
    Sickness benefit.
    Invalidity pension and allowance.
    Maternity allowance.
    Widow's benefit, comprising widow's payment, widowed mother's allowance and widow's pension.
    Retirement pensions, categories A and B.

(2) Non-contributory Benefits:
    Child benefit.
    One parent benefit.
    Guardian's allowance.
    Invalid care allowance.
    Attendance allowance.
    Severe disablement allowance.
    Mobility allowance.
    Retirement pensions, categories C and D.
    Income Support.
    Family Credit.
    Social Fund.

(3) Benefits for Industrial Injuries, Disablement and Death.

Leaflets relating to the various benefits are obtainable from local social security offices.

The Social Security Acts empower the Secretary of State to increase certain rates of benefit by order approved by both Houses of Parliament, and require him to increase certain rates by such an order if an annual review shows that they have not retained their value in relation to the general level of prices obtaining in Great Britain.

The latest order providing for increases in benefit rates took effect from the week commencing April 13, 1989.

CONTRIBUTORY BENEFITS

Entitlement to contributory benefits depends on contribution conditions being satisfied either by the claimant or by some other person (depending on the kind of benefit). The class or classes of contribution which for this purpose are relevant to each benefit are as follows:

Short-term benefits

Unemployment benefit	Class 1
Sickness benefit	Class 1 or 2
Maternity allowance	Class 1 or 2
Widow's payment	Class 1, 2 or 3

Other benefits

Widowed mother's allowance	
Widow's pension	
Category A retirement pension	Class 1, 2 or 3
Category B retirement pension	
Invalidity benefit	Class 1 or 2

The system of contribution conditions relates to yearly levels of earnings on which contributions have been paid. The contribution conditions for different benefits are set out in summary form in leaflets available at local social security offices.

Unemployment Benefit

Benefit is payable in a period of interruption of employment for up to 312 days (a year, excluding Sundays). Spells of unemployment and sickness not separated by more than 8 weeks count as one period of interruption of employment. A person who has exhausted benefit requalifies when he has again worked as an employed earner for at least 16 hours a week for 13 weeks. These weeks need not be consecutive but must generally fall within 26 weeks prior to the date of the claim (effective from Oct. 1989).

Disqualifications.—There are disqualifications from receiving benefit, e.g. for a period not exceeding 26 weeks if a person has lost his employment through his misconduct, or has voluntarily left his employment without just cause, or has, without good cause, refused an offer of suitable employment or training.

Sickness Benefit

Sickness benefit is payable for up to 28 weeks of sickness in a period of interruption of employment and is then replaced by invalidity benefit (*see* below).

Disqualifications.—There are disqualifications from receiving sickness or invalidity benefit for a period not exceeding six weeks if a person has become incapable of work through his own misconduct or if he fails without good cause to attend for or submit himself to prescribed medical or other examination or treatment, or observe prescribed rules of behaviour.

Since April 6, 1986, employers are responsible for paying Statutory Sick Pay (S.S.P.) to their employees for up to 28 weeks of sickness in any period of incapacity for work. S.S.P. replaces the employee's entitlement to State Sickness Benefit which is not payable as long as any S.S.P. liability remains. S.S.P. is subject to P.A.Y.E. and to N.I. deductions. Employers can recover the S.S.P. they have paid out and can also withhold an extra amount to compensate themselves for the N.I. contributions they have paid on S.S.P. from the payments of N.I. they make each month to the Collector of Taxes. Employees who cannot get S.S.P. can claim State Sickness Benefit instead.

Invalidity Benefit

Normally, after 28 weeks of sickness, sickness benefit, or S.S.P. where the underlying conditions for sickness benefit are satisfied, is replaced by an invalidity pension. In addition an invalidity allowance is payable if incapacity for work begins more than five years before pension age. The allowance varies according to the age on falling sick, and if still in payment at pension age will continue as an addition to retirement pension. From Sept. 16, 1985 invalidity allowance has been reduced or withdrawn completely if there is entitlement to an additional earnings-related pension and/or a guaranteed minimum pension.

Maternity Benefit

Statutory maternity pay (S.M.P.) is administered by employers but there is still a state maternity allowance scheme for women who are self-employed or otherwise do not qualify for S.M.P.

In general, employers pay S.M.P. to pregnant women who have been employed by them for at least six months and earned at least the lower earnings limit for the payment of N.I. contributions. For those who have been employed for at least two years, payment of S.M.P. for the first six weeks is related to earnings, followed by up to twelve weeks at a standard rate of £36·25. Those who have been employed for at least six months but less than two years receive payment at standard rate only for the 18 weeks. Part-time working women also qualify for the earnings-related element if employed for at least five years. Women have some choice in deciding when to begin maternity leave but S.M.P. is not payable for any week in which work is done.

A woman may qualify for maternity allowance (M.A.) if she has been working and paying contributions at the full rate for at least 26 weeks in the 52-week period which ends 15 weeks before the baby is due. She also has an element of choice in deciding when to stop work and receive M.A., which is not payable for any period she works.

Widow's Benefits

Only the late husband's contributions of any class count for widow's benefit in any of its three forms.

Widow's Payment.—May be received by a woman who at her husband's death is under 60, or whose husband was not entitled to a Category A retirement pension when he died.

Widowed Mother's Allowance.—Payable to a widow if she is receiving child benefit for one of her children; if her husband was receiving child benefit; or if she is expecting her husband's baby.

Widow's Pension.—A widow may receive this pension if aged 45 or over at the time of her husband's death or when her widowed mother's allowance ends. If aged 55 or over she will receive the full widow's pension rate.

Widow's benefit of any form ceases upon re-marriage.

Retirement Pension
Categories A and B

A *Category A pension* is payable for life to men or women on their own contributions if (a) they are over pension age (65 for a man and 60 for a woman), and (b) they have retired from regular employment. From Oct. 1, 1989, the retirement condition is to be abolished.

Where a person defers making a claim at 65 (60 for a woman) or later opts to be treated as if he/she had not made a claim, and does not draw a Category A pension, the weekly rate of pension is increased, when he or she finally makes a claim or reaches the age of 70 (65 for a woman), in respect of weeks when pension is foregone during the five years after reaching minimum pension age. Details of the increase in the rate of pension due to deferred retirement are given in leaflet NP46, available at social security offices. If a married man defers his own Category A pension then his wife has to defer receiving her Category B pension based on his contribution record. During this time she earns increments to the Category B pension, which is payable to her (and not her husband) when they both claim their pensions.

A *Category B pension* is normally payable for life to a woman on her husband's contributions when he has claimed, or is over 70, and has qualified for his own Category A pension, and she has reached 60 and retired from regular work or has reached 65. It is also payable on widowhood after 60 whether or not the late husband had retired and qualified for his own pension. The weekly pension is payable at the rate of the increase for a wife while the husband is alive, and at the single person's rate on widowhood after 60. Where a woman is widowed before she reaches 60, a Category B pension is paid to her on reaching 60 at the same weekly rate as her widow's pension if she claims. If a woman qualifies for a pension of each category she receives whichever pension is the larger. Details of the increase in the rate of pension due to deferred retirement are given in leaflet NP46, available at social security offices.

The earnings rule which stated that a man aged 65 to 70, or a woman aged 60 to 65, who has qualified for pension would have it reduced if he or she earned more than a certain amount was abolished on Oct. 1, 1989. Where an adult dependant is living with the claimant, an Adult Dependants Allowance will only be payable if the dependant's earnings do not exceed the standard rate of unemployment benefit for a single person under pensionable age (*see below*). For the purpose of the dependency rule only, earnings will include payments by way of occupational pension. The earnings of a separated spouse affect the increase of retirement pension if they exceed £26·20 a week.

Unemployment, sickness or invalidity benefit is payable to men between 65 and 70 and women between 60 and 65 who have not claimed their retirement pension and who would have been entitled to a retirement pension if they had claimed at pension age. This applies in the case of sickness and invalidity benefit if incapacity for work is the result of an industrial accident or prescribed disease. These rates of benefit for people over pension age are shown in leaflet N.I. 196. A retirement pension will be increased by the amount of any invalidity allowance the pensioner was getting within the period of 8 weeks and one day before reaching minimum pension age but this will be offset against any Additional Pension or Guaranteed Minimum Pension. An age addition of 25p per week is payable if a retirement pensioner is aged 80 or over. (For attendance allowance and invalidity care allowance, see Non-contributory Benefits.)

Graduated Pension

The graduated pension scheme under which national insurance contributions and retirement pensions were graduated within specified limits, according to earnings, was discontinued in April, 1975, under the Social Security Act, 1975. Any graduated pension which an employed person over 18 and under 70 (65 for a woman) had earned by paying graduated contributions between April 6, 1961, when the scheme started and April 5, 1975, will be paid when the contributor claims their retirement pension, or at 70 (65 for a woman), in addition to any retirement pension for which he or she qualifies.

Graduated pension is at the rate of £5·71 a week

for each "unit" of graduated contributions paid by the employee (half a unit or more counts as a whole unit). A unit of contributions is £7·50 for men, and £9·00 for women, of graduated contributions paid.

A wife can get a graduated pension in return for her own graduated contributions, but not for her husband's. A widow gets a graduated addition to her retirement pension equal to half of any graduated additions earned by her late husband, plus any additions earned by her own graduated contributions. If a person defers making a claim beyond 65 (60 for a woman), entitlement may be increased by one seventh of a penny per £1 of its weekly rate for each complete week of deferred retirement, as long as the retirement is deferred for a minimum of seven weeks.

Rates of Benefits
(from week commencing April 10, 1989)

Benefit	Weekly rate £
Unemployment Benefit—standard rate	
Person under pension age	34·70
Increase for wife/other adult dependant	21·40
Person over pension age*	43·60
Increase for wife/other adult dependant	26·20
Sickness Benefit—standard rate	
Person under pension age	33·20
Increase for wife/other adult dependant	20·55
Person over pension age*	41·80
Increase for wife/other adult dependant	25·10
Invalidity Pension*	
Person (under or over pension age)....	43·60
Increase for wife or adult dependant	26·20
Invalidity Allowance (maximum amounts payable)	
higher rate	9·20
middle rate	5·80
lower rate	2·90
Maternity Allowance	33·20
Widow's Payment (lump sum)	1,000·00
Widowed Mother's Allowance* and **Widow's Pension***	43·60
Retirement pension*—*categories A and B*	
Single person	43·60
Increase for wife or adult dependant	26·20

Earnings limit for retirement pensioners (abolished from Oct. 1, 1989).

* These benefits attract an increase for each dependent child (in addition to child benefit) of £8·95.

NON-CONTRIBUTORY BENEFITS
Child Benefit

Child benefit is payable for all children in a family within the age limits, including the first or only child. There is an additional payment for the first or only child in certain one-parent families.

Guardian's Allowance

Where the parents of a child are dead, the person who has the child in his family may claim a guardian's allowance in addition to child benefit. The allowance in exceptional circumstances, is payable on the death of only one parent.

Invalid Care Allowance

Invalid care allowance is payable to persons of working age, who are not gainfully employed because they are regularly and substantially engaged in caring for a severely disabled person who is receiving attendance allowance or constant attendance allowance with either a war or services pension, industrial disablement workman's compensation, or an allowance under the Pneumoconiosis, Byssinosis and Miscellaneous Diseases Benefit Scheme.

Mobility Allowance

The allowance is, subject to certain conditions, payable to persons who are suffering from such physical disablement that they are likely to remain unable, or virtually unable, to walk for at least a year. It can be claimed by persons between the ages of 5 and 65 (for this purpose a claim may be made up to 12 months from that birthday) and may be retained to age 75.

Severe Disablement Allowance

Persons of working age who have been continuously incapable of work for a period of at least 28 weeks but who do not qualify for a contributory invalidity pension may be entitled to severe disablement allowance. People who first become incapable of work after their 20th birthday must be at least 80 per cent disabled.

Attendance Allowance

Attendance allowance is payable to the severely disabled. Entitlement is determined by the Attendance Allowance Board or by a doctor acting on the Board's behalf. The full rate is paid to those in need of a great deal of attention or supervision both by day and by night. The allowance is paid at the lower rate to those whose need for attention or supervision arises either by day or by night. There is a six-month qualifying period.

Non-contributory Retirement Pension
Categories C and D

A *Category C pension* is provided, subject to a residence test, for persons who were over pensionable age on July 5, 1948, and for women whose husbands are so entitled if they are over pension age and have retired from regular work, with increases for adult and child dependants. A *Category D pension* is provided for others when they reach 80 if they are not already getting a retirement pension of any category or if they are getting that pension at less than these rates. An age addition of 25p per week is payable if persons entitled to retirement pension or their dependants are aged 80 or over.

Rates of Benefits
(from week commencing April 10, 1989)

Benefit	Weekly rate £
Child Benefit (per child)	7·25
One Parent Benefit	
First or only child of certain lone parents	5·20
Guardian's Allowance	8·95
Severe Disablement Allowance*	26·20
Increase for wife/other adult dependant	15·65
Mobility Allowance	24·40
Invalid Care Allowance*	26·20
Increase for wife/other adult dependant	15·65

Attendance Allowance	
higher rate	34·90
lower rate	23·30
Retirement Pension—Categories C* and D.	
Single person	26·20
Increase for wife/other adult dependant	15·65
(not payable with Category D pension)	

*These benefits attract an increase for each dependent child (in addition to child benefit) of £8·95.

INCOME SUPPORT

Income Support is a benefit for those whose income is inadequate and who are unemployed; over 60; bringing up children alone; unable to work or working only part-time through sickness or disability; or staying at home to care for a disabled relative. Except in special cases Income Support is not available to those who work for more than 24 hours per week or who have a partner who works for more than 24 hours per week. Income Support is not payable if the claimant, or claimant and partner, have capital or savings in excess of £6,000. The rate of benefits is affected by possession of capital or savings in excess of £3,000 and may be affected by a claimant's earnings. Sums payable depend on fixed allowances laid down by law for people in different circumstances. Special rates apply for people living in board and lodging, hostels, residential care or nursing homes. Details are available from local social security offices. Income Support is payable via post offices, either by order book or, for the unemployed, by girocheque. Applications for Income Support are made on form SB1, available from post offices; Income Support claim forms, available from social security offices; or on form B1 (for the unemployed), available from unemployment benefit offices. If both partners are entitled to Income Support, either may claim it. People receiving Income Support will be able to receive Housing Benefit, help with mortgage or home loan interest and help with health care. They may also be eligible for help with exceptional expenses, from the Social Fund. Leaflet SB20 gives a detailed explanation of Income Support.

INCOME SUPPORT PREMIUMS

Income Support Premiums are additional weekly payments for those with special needs. People qualifying for more than one premium will normally only receive the highest single premium for which they qualify. However Family Premium, Disabled Child's Premium and Severe Disability Premium are payable in addition to other premiums.

People with children qualify for a Family Premium if they have at least one child; a Disabled Child's Premium if they have a child who receives Attendance Allowance or Mobility Allowance or is registered blind; or a Lone Parent Premium if they are bringing up one or more children alone.

Long-term sick or disabled people qualify for a Disability Premium if they or their partner are receiving certain benefits because they are disabled or cannot work; are registered blind; or have been sending in doctor's statements for at least 28 weeks stating inability to work through sickness. If they are in receipt of Attendance Allowance, without anyone receiving Invalid Care Allowance for looking after them, they qualify for a Severe Disability Premium in addition to a Disability Premium.

People qualify for a Pensioner Premium if they or their partner are aged between 60 and 79, and for a Higher Pensioner Premium if they or their partner are aged 80 or over. A Higher Pensioner Premium is also payable to people aged between 60 and 79 who receive Attendance Allowance, Mobility Allowance, Invalidity Benefit or Severe Disablement Allowance, or who are registered blind. A Higher Pensioner Premium may be paid as well as a Severe Disability Premium.

Rates of Benefit
(from week commencing April 10, 1989)

	Weekly rate £
INCOME SUPPORT	
Single people	
aged 16–17	20·80
aged 18—24	27·40
aged 25 and over	34·90
aged 18 and over and a single parent	34·90
Couples	
both under 18	41·60
one or both aged 18 or over	54·80
For each child in a family	
under 11	11·75
aged 11–15	17·35
aged 16–17*	20·80
aged 18 and over*	27·40

* if in full-time education up to A level or equivalent standard.

Premiums

Family Premium	6·50
Disabled Child's Premium	6·50
Lone Parent Premium	3·90
Disability Premium	
Single	13·70
Couple	19·50
Severe Disability Premium	
Single	26·20
Couple (one person qualified)	26·20
Couple (both qualified)	52·40
Pensioner Premium	
Single	11·20
Couple	17·05
Higher Pensioner Premium	
Single	13·70
Couple	19·50

(From Oct. 1989 the single rate goes up to £16·20 and the rate for a couple to £23·00).

Enhanced Pensioner Premium (from Oct. 1989)

Single	2·50
Couple	3·50

(payable to pensioners aged between 75 and 79 in addition to Pensioner Premium).

FAMILY CREDIT

Family Credit is a tax-free benefit for working families with children. It is not a loan and need not be repaid. To qualify, a family must include at least one child under 16 (under 19 if in full-time education up to A level or equivalent standard), and the claimant, or partner, must be working for at least 24 hours per week. It does not matter which partner is working and they may be employed or self-employed. The right to Family Credit does not depend on N.I. contributions and the same rates of benefit are paid to one and two parent families. Family Credit is not payable if the claimant, or claimant and partner, have capital or savings in excess of £6,000 and the rate of benefit is affected if capital or savings in excess of £3,000 are held. The sums payable depend upon the claimant's (and partner's) income, number of children, and children's ages. Family Credit is paid for 26 weeks and the amount payable will usually remain constant throughout this period, regardless of change of circumstances. Payment is made via post offices or directly into a bank or building society account.

Applications for Family Credit are made on form FC1, obtainable at a post office or social security office. In two parent families the woman should claim.

Rates of Benefit
(from week commencing April 10, 1989)

	Weekly rate £

The maximum amount will be payable where net income is no more than £54·80 per week. Where net income exceeds that amount, the maximum credit is reduced by 70 per cent of the excess and the result is the Family Credit payable. The maximum rate consists of:

Adult credit (for one or two parents)	33·60
plus for each child aged:	
under 11	7·30
11–15	12·90
16–17	16·35
18	23·30

THE SOCIAL FUND

The Social Fund helps people with expenses which are difficult to meet from regular income. Regulated Maternity, Funeral and Cold Weather payments are decided by Adjudication Officers and are not cash-limited. Discretionary Community Care Grants, and Budgeting and Crisis Loans are decided by Social Fund Officers and come out of a yearly budget which, except for a contingency reserve, is allocated to local offices (1989–90, grants £60 million; loans £141m; reserve £2m).

Regulated payments

Maternity Payments.— A flat rate payment of £85 for each baby expected, born or adopted. It is payable to people on Income Support and Family Credit and is non-repayable.

Funeral Payments.—Payable for reasonable funeral expenses incurred by people receiving Income Support, Family Credit or Housing Benefit (Community Charge Rebate in Scotland). It is recoverable from the estate of the deceased.

Cold Weather payments.—£5 for each seven-day period of cold weather. Paid to people on Income Support who are pensioners, disabled or parents with a child under 5. It is non-repayable.

Discretionary payments

Community Care Grants.—They are intended to help people on Income Support: move into the community or avoid institutional care; ease exceptional pressures on families; and/or meet certain essential travelling expenses. They are non-repayable.

Budgeting Loans.—These are interest-free loans to people who have been receiving Income Support for at least six months, for intermittent expenses that may be difficult to budget for.

Crisis Loans.—These are interest-free loans to anyone, whether receiving benefit or not, who are without resources in an emergency, where there is no other means of preventing serious risk or damage to health or safety.

Loans are normally repaid over a period of up to 78 weeks at between 5 and 15 per cent of Income Support (less housing costs), depending on other commitments. Savings over £500 are taken into account for Cold Weather, Maternity and Funeral Payments, Community Care Grants and Budgeting Loans. All savings are taken into account for crisis loans. For regulated payment there is a right of appeal to an independent Social Security Appeal and thereafter to a Social Security Commissioner. For discretionary payments there is a review system where persons can ask for a review at the local office with a further right of review to an independent Social Fund Inspector.

DETERMINATION OF CLAIMS AND QUESTIONS

With a few exceptions, claims and questions relating to Social Security benefits are decided by statutory authorities who act independently of the Department of Social Security and Department of Employment. The first of the statutory authorities, the Adjudication Officer, determines entitlement to benefit. A claimant who is dissatisfied with that decision has the right of appeal to a Social Security Appeal Tribunal. There is a further right of appeal to a Social Security Commissioner against the Tribunal's decision but leave to appeal must first be obtained. Appeals to the Commissioner must be on a point of law. Provision is also made for the determination of certain questions by the Secretary of State for Social Services.

Disablement questions are decided by adjudicating medical authorities or Medical Appeal Tribunals. Appeal to the Commissioner against a tribunal's decision is with leave and on a point of law only.

Leaflet NI 246 which is available from social security offices, explains how to appeal and leaflet NI260 is a guide to reviews and appeals.

INDUSTRIAL INJURIES, DISABLEMENT AND DEATH BENEFITS

The Industrial Injuries scheme, administered under the Social Security Act 1975 and subsequent Acts and Regulations, provides a range of benefits designed to compensate for disablement resulting from an industrial accident (i.e. an accident arising out of and in the course of an employed earner's employment) or from a prescribed disease due to the nature of a person's employment. Rates of benefit are increased periodically.

Determination of Claims and Questions.—Provision is made for the determination of certain questions by the Secretary of State for Social Security, and of "disablement questions" by a medical board (or a single doctor) or, on appeal, by a medical appeal tribunal. An appeal on a point of law against a medical appeal tribunal decision is determined by the Social Security Commissioner. Claims for benefit and certain questions arising in connection with a claim for or award of benefit (e.g. whether the accident arose out of and in the course of the employment) are determined by an adjudication officer appointed by the Secretary of State, or a Social Security Appeal Tribunal, or in certain circumstances, on further appeal, by the Commissioners.

Special schemes under the Industrial Injuries and Diseases (Old Cases) Act 1975 provide supplementary allowances to those entitled to receive weekly payments of workmen's compensation for loss of earnings due to injury at work, or disease contracted during employment before July 5, 1948 when the Industrial Injuries scheme was introduced. Other schemes under the Act provide allowances to those who contracted slowly developing diseases during employment before July 1948 where neither workmen's compensation nor Industrial Injuries Benefits are payable. A lump sum death benefit of up to £300 may also be payable to a dependant of such a person.

Benefits

Disablement Benefit is normally payable 15 weeks (90 days) after the date of accident or onset of disease if the employed earner suffers from loss of physical or mental faculty such that the resulting disablement is assessed at not less than 14 per cent. The amount of disablement benefit payable varies according to the degree of disablement (in the form of a percentage) assessed by an adjudicating medical authority or medical appeal tribunal.

Disablement assessed at less than 14 per cent does not normally attract basic benefit except for certain progressive chest diseases. A weekly pension is payable where the assessment of disablement is between 14 and 100 per cent (assessments of 14 to 19 per cent are payable at the 20 per cent rate). Payment can be made for a limited period or for life.

The basic rates are applicable to adults and to juveniles entitled to an increase for a child or adult dependant; other juveniles receive lower rates.

Basic rates of pension are not related to the pensioner's loss of earning power, and are payable whether he is in work or not. If disablement is assessed at one per cent or more, loss of earnings may be compensated by a reduced earnings allowance. This may be paid even if basic disablement pension is not paid because disablement is assessed at less than 14 per cent, providing there is a current disablement assessment of at least 1 per cent. There is provision also for increases of pension if the pensioner requires constant attendance or if his disablement is exceptionally severe. A pensioner may draw S.S.P., sickness or invalidity benefit as appropriate, in addition to disablement pension, during spells of incapacity for work.

Death Benefit, in the form of a pension, is available for women widowed before April 11, 1988. The amount of pension depends on the widow's circumstances at the date of death and not upon the deceased's earnings.

Regulations impose certain obligations on claimants and beneficiaries and on employers, including, in the case of claimants for disablement benefit, that of submitting to medical examination.

Rates of Benefits
(from April 10, 1989)

	Weekly rate £
Disablement Benefit/Pension	
Degree of disablement—100 per cent.	71·20
90	64·08
80	59·96
70	49·84
60	42·72
50	35·60
40	28·48
30	21·36
20	14·24
Unemployability supplement*	43·60
Addition for adult dependant (subject to earnings rule)	26·20
Reduced earnings allowance (maximum)	28·48
Constant Attendance allowance (normal maximum rate)	28·50
Exceptionally severe disablement allowance	28·50
Industrial death benefit widow's pension*	
Higher permanent rate	43·60
Lower permanent rate	13·08

* These benefits attract an increase for each dependent child (in addition to child benefit) of £8·95.

FINANCE

The National Insurance Fund receives all social security contributions (less only the National Health Service and Redundancy Fund and Maternity Pay Fund allocations and the National Insurance Surcharge for taxation purposes) together with the Consolidated Fund supplement; and it bears the cost of all contributory benefits provided by the Social Security Acts and the cost of administration.

NOTE.—There have been changes to the National Insurance Fund. Payments will no longer be paid into surcharges or the Maternity Pay Fund. However, residual payments are still being paid in respect of late paid contributions for premium years.

Approximate receipts and payments of the National Insurance Fund for the year ended March 31, 1988, were as follows:

Receipts	£'000
Balance, April 1, 1987	5,706,966
Contributions under the Social Security Acts (net of S.S.P.)	24,564,489
Consolidated Fund Supplement	2,135,000
Income from Investments	596,395
Other receipts	39,847
	33,042,697

Payments	£'000	£'000
Benefit:—		
Unemployment benefit	1,467,928	
Sickness benefit	193,001	
Invalidity benefit	2,968,405	
Maternity allowance	50,746	
Widow's benefit	839,250	
Guardian's allowance and child's special allowance	1,434	
Retirement pension	18,648,391	
Death grant	2,608	
Industrial injuries benefits	—	
Disablement benefits	453,386	
Death benefit	56,492	
Other industrial injury benefits	4,224	
Pensioners lump sum payments	107,000	
Payments in lieu of benefit forgone	—	
		24,792,865
Transfers to Northern Ireland		155,000
Administration		802,000
Other payments		4,746
Write offs		—
Balance, March 31, 1988		7,287,620
		33,042,697

WAR PENSIONS

War pensions are awarded under The Naval, Military and Air Forces, Etc. (Disablement and Death) Service Pensions Order 1983, which was a consolidation of the previous Royal Warrants, Orders in Council and Orders by Her Majesty.

The D.S.S. award war pensions to members of H.M. Armed Forces in respect of the periods Aug. 4, 1914 to Sept. 30, 1921 and subsequent to Sept. 3, 1939 (including present members of the armed forces). The D.S.S. also have special schemes for the Merchant Navy, Naval Auxiliary personnel, civil defence, civilians, Home Guard, Polish armed forces under British command and Polish resettlement forces.

War pensions for the period Oct. 1, 1921 to Sept. 2, 1939 are dealt with by the Ministry of Defence who are also responsible for the Armed Forces Pension Scheme.

ELIGIBILITY AND GENERAL PROVISIONS

War disablement pension is awarded for the disabling effects of any injury, wound or disease which is attributable to, or aggravated by, conditions of service in the armed forces. It cannot be paid until the serviceman has left the armed forces.

Disablement is assessed by comparison of the disabled person's condition with that of a normal, healthy person of the same age and sex, without taking into account the disabled person's earnings or occupation, and is expressed on a percentage scale up to 100 per cent. Disablement above 20 per cent, for which a pension is awarded, is assessed in steps of 10 per cent. For assessment of less than 20 per cent a lump sum is payable. Maximum assessment does not necessarily imply total incapacity.

Dependency allowance. A 100 per cent disabled pensioner may receive an allowance of 60p a week for his wife or dependent child. Where disablement is less than 100 per cent the allowance is proportionate to the degree of disablement.

War widows pension is awarded where death occurs as a result of service. Where a war disablement pensioner was receiving constant attendance allowance at the time of his death, or would have been receiving it if he were not in hospital, his widow has automatic entitlement to a war widow's pension, regardless of the cause of death.

Additional allowances are payable for dependent children, in addition to child benefit.

A reduced weekly rate is payable to war widows below the rank of Lieutenant-Colonel who are under the age of 40, without children and capable of maintaining themselves. This is increased to the standard rate at age 40.

Rank additions to disablement and widows pensions. Rank additions may be paid with war pensions where the rank held was above that of private (or equivalent).

Claims.—Where a claim is made no later than 7 years after the termination of service, the claimant does not have to prove that the disablement or death on which the claim is based is related to service and receives the benefit of any reasonable doubt. Where a claim is made more than 7 years after the termination of service the claimant has to show that disablement or death is related to service. However, the claim succeeds if reliable evidence is produced which raises a reasonable doubt whether disablement or death is related to service. There is no time limit for making a claim for war pension.

SUPPLEMENTARY ALLOWANCES

A number of supplementary allowances may be awarded to a war pensioner which are intended to meet the various needs which may result from disablement or death and take account of its particular effect on the pensioner. Decisions on supplementary allowances are made on a discretionary basis on behalf of the Secretary of State and there is no provision for a statutory right of appeal against them. However, war pensioners may discuss any aspect of their pension position with their local War Pensions Committees, which may be able to arrange help or make representations to the war pensions branch of the D.S.S.

Unemployability supplement, with additional allowances for dependants, may be paid to a war pensioner who is so seriously disabled as to be unemployable. In addition, an invalidity allowance may be payable if the incapacity for work began more than 5 years before normal retirement age.

Allowance for lowered standard of occupation may be awarded to a partially disabled pensioner whose pensioned disablement permanently prevents him from following his pre-service occupation and from doing another job of equivalent financial standard. The allowance, together with the basic war disablement pension, must not exceed pension at the 100 per cent rate.

Constant attendance allowance may be awarded to a war pensioner who is so severely handicapped by the nature of his pensioned disablement, assessed at not less than 80 per cent, that he must depend to a greater or lesser extent upon the attendance of some other person. There are four rates of the allowance and these vary according to the amount of time attendance is needed.

Exceptionally severe disablement allowance is paid to pensioners who are receiving constant attendance allowance on a permanent basis at either of the two highest rates.

Severe disablement occupational allowance is paid to those pensioners who qualify for constant attendance allowance at either of the two highest rates and who, despite their handicap, are normally in employment. This allowance is not payable if the pensioner is in receipt of unemployability supplement.

Comforts allowance is payable at one of two rates. The higher rate is paid to those pensioners who are receiving both constant attendance allowance and unemployability supplement. When only one of these allowances is in payment the lower rate of comforts allowance is normally paid, but the higher rate can be paid under certain conditions where only constant attendance allowance is in payment.

Clothing allowance may be awarded where the pensioned disablement causes exceptional wear and tear of clothing. It is payable at two rates, depending on the degree of wear and tear caused.

Mobility supplement is intended to help those war pensioners who because of their pensioned disablement are unable, or virtually unable, to walk.

Treatment allowance may be paid to a pensioner receiving medical treatment in hospital or at home if the treatment is for the pensioned disablement, is necessary because of the continuing effects of service, and is of a kind which prevents the pensioner from working for more than seven days, or would do so if he was not unemployed or had retired from work. The allowance replaces the disablement pension and is paid at the 100 per cent rate.

Age allowance may be awarded to those war pensioners aged 65 or over whose war disablement is assessed at 40 per cent or more. It is payable at four rates, depending on the degree of disablement.

Widows age allowance is paid at three different rates according to age (65–69, 70–79 and over 80).

Widows child's allowance may be paid in addition to child benefit.

Rent allowance may be paid to a widow who receives a war widows pension and maintains a home for a child eligible for an allowance.

Education allowance may be payable to a war disablement pensioner or war widow in respect of a dependent child if the D.S.S. is satisfied that the education is suitable for the child and that the family circumstances are such as to require an allowance.

Temporary allowance for widows may be payable in the form of a special allowance for the first 26 weeks of widowhood for widows of war pensioners who received constant attendance allowance or unemployability supplement. After 26 weeks the widow will get any war widows pension or national insurance widows benefit to which she is entitled.

Funeral grant may be payable where the pensioner dies as a result of his pensioned disablement, or he died in hospital while having treatment for that disability, or was getting constant attendance allowance at the time of his death. Claims should be made within three months of the funeral.

WAR PENSIONERS ABROAD

The D.S.S. is responsible for the payment of war pensions, and provision of necessary treatment for accepted disablement, to pensioners who reside overseas. They receive the same pension rates as war pensioners in this country and benefit from the same annual upratings.

WAR PENSIONERS AND SOCIAL SECURITY BENEFITS

When a war disablement pensioner is sick, unemployed or retired, the appropriate social security benefits are paid in addition to the war pension, unless he is entitled to unemployability supplement or severe disablement occupational allowance instead.

Any sickness, invalidity, unemployment benefit or retirement pension for which a war widow qualifies on her own contributions, and any graduated retirement benefit, or additional earnings related pension inherited from her husband, can be paid in addition to her war pension or temporary allowance. A war pensioner or war widow who claims Income Support has the first £5 of pension disregarded. A similar provision operates for housing benefit and community charge benefit; but the local authority may, at its discretion, disregard any or all of the balance. A special tax free Christmas bonus of £10.00 is payable to war disablement pensioners who are in receipt of unemployability supplement, constant attendance allowance, have retired, or are aged over 70 (65 for women); and to all war widows who do not otherwise receive this payment.

PENSIONS APPEAL TRIBUNALS

There are independent Pensions Appeal Tribunals which hear appeals against the decisions of the D.S.S. on entitlement, and assessment of disablement, in respect of 1939 War and subsequent service cases. There are now no rights of appeal in the 1914 War disablement cases, the great majority of which were given final assessment in the 1920s with a 12 months right of appeal at the time. An appeal by a 1914 war widow must be made within twelve months of the date on which the rejection of the claim is notified.

WAR PENSIONERS WELFARE SERVICE

The D.S.S. operates a war pensioners welfare service to advise and assist war pensioners and their widows on any matters affecting their welfare. Welfare officers are attached to War Pensioners' Welfare Offices located in the major towns, and work closely with central and local Government agencies as well as the various ex-service organizations. The service is available on call to any war pensioner or widow who needs it. In addition the service takes the initiative in arranging regular visits in certain cases.

Rates of Pensions and Allowances
(from week commencing April 10, 1989)

	Weekly rates £
Disablement pension	
(for Private or equivalent rank)	
Degree of disablement—	
100 per cent	71.20
90 per cent	64.08
80 per cent	56.96
70 per cent	49.84
60 per cent	42.72
50 per cent	35.60
40 per cent	28.48
30 per cent	21.36
20 per cent	14.24
Unemployability supplement	
Personal allowance	46.30
Increase for wife/other adult dependent	26.20
Increase for child	8.95
Allowance for lowered standard of	
occupation (maximum)	28.48
Constant attendance allowance	
Exceptional rate	57.00
Intermediate rate	42.75
Normal maximum	28.50
Half and quarter day	14.25

	Weekly rates £
Exceptionally severe disablement	
allowance	28.50
Severe disablement occupational allowance	14.25
Comforts allowance	
Higher rate	12.30
Lower rate	6.15
Clothing allowance (**per annum**)	
Higher rate	97.00
Lower rate	61.00
Mobility supplement	27.10
Age allowance	
Disablement assessment—	
40–50 per cent	5.00
50–70 per cent	7.75
70–90 per cent	11.10
over 90 per cent	15.50
Widow's pension	
(widow of Private or equivalent rank)	
Standard rate	56.65
Increase for child	12.60
Childless widow under 40	13.08
Widow's age allowance	
Age—65–69	6.10
70–79	12.20
80 and over	15.30
Rent allowance (maximum)	21.55

NATIONAL HEALTH SERVICE
(and Local Authority Personal Social Services)

The National Health Service came into being on July 5, 1948, as a result of the National Health Service Act 1946. The Act placed a duty on the Secretary of State for Social Services to promote the establishment in England and Wales of a comprehensive Health Service designed to secure improvement in the mental and physical health of the people and the prevention, diagnosis and treatment of illness. The Secretary of State for Wales administers the National Health Service in Wales. There are separate Acts for Scotland and Northern Ireland, where the Health Services are run on very similar lines and the respective Secretaries of State are responsible to Parliament.

The National Health Service covers a comprehensive range of hospital, specialist, family practitioner (medical, dental, ophthalmic and pharmaceutical), artificial limb and appliance, ambulance, and community health services. Everyone normally resident in this country is entitled to use any of these services, there are no contribution conditions and the charges made (except those for amenity beds) are reduced or waived in cases of hardship. In addition the Secretary of State for Social Services is responsible under the Local Authority Social Services Act 1970 for the provision by local authorities of social services for the elderly, the disabled, those with mental disorders and for families and children.

The 1980 Health Services Act led to major changes in the structure of the Health Service. Since April 1982, District Health Authorities (DHAs) are responsible for the operational management of health services and for planning within regional and national strategic guidelines. There are 190 DHAs in England and nine in Wales. Each DHA is required to arrange its services into units of management at hospital and community services level, and as many decisions as possible are delegated to unit level. Four of the London postgraduate teaching hospitals are now managed by DHAs (and eight are managed by special health authorities). Arrangements for the Family Practitioner Service are administered by Family Practitioner Committees (FPCs)—90 in England and eight in Wales. FPCs also contribute to the planning of health services.

The 14 Regional Health Authorities (RHAs) in England are responsible for regional planning, the allocation of resources to District Authorities, and the promotion of national policies and priorities. Performance review meetings are held annually between each hospital unit and its DHA, each DHA and its RHA, and between each RHA and Department of Health Ministers, thereby strengthening Authorities' accountability to Parliament, whilst respecting the essentially locally-based nature of decision making. Professional advisory machinery incorporated within the structure ensures that Health Authorities and their staffs make decisions in the full knowledge of expert opinion.

The NHS is financed mainly from taxation and the cost met from moneys voted by Parliament. In the United Kingdom this will amount to £26·1 billion in 1989–90. The Department of Health makes capital and revenue allocations to the RHAs and from these the RHAs meet the cost of their own services and make allocations to DHAs as well as funding Community Health Councils.

The Government published a White Paper in January 1989 (*see* pp. 1091–4) setting out proposals to improve the quality and efficiency of health services; extend patient choice; and to enhance the Service's responsiveness to its consumers. The reforms will be introduced on a phased basis depending on Parliamentary approval of the necessary legislation.

THE HEALTH SERVICES

Family Doctor Service

In England and Wales the Family Doctor Service (or General Medical Services) is organized by 98 Family Practitioner Committees which also organize the general dental, pharmaceutical and ophthalmic services for their areas. There is a Family Practitioner Committee for one or more District Health Authorities. Under the Health and Social Security Act 1984, FPCs became employing authorities in their own right on April 1, 1985, and all the members and the chairmen (31 in all) are appointed by the Secretary of State. Fifteen of the appointments are made from nominations received from committees, representing local doctors (8), dentists (3), pharmacists (2), ophthalmic opticians (1) and from among all four professions (1). Of the fifteen lay members, four each are appointed from nominations received from District Health Authorities and Local Authorities. The remainder (7) are appointed after such consultations as the Secretary of State considers appropriate. One member must be a qualified district nurse, midwife or health visitor with recent community nursing experience.

Any doctor may take part in the Family Doctor Scheme, provided the area in which he wishes to practise has not already an adequate number of doctors, and about 25,000 general practitioners in England and Wales do so. They may at the same time have private fee-paying patients. Family doctors are paid for their Health Service work in accordance with a scheme of remuneration which includes *inter alia* a basic practice allowance, capitation fees, reimbursement of certain practice expenses and payments for "out of hours" work.

Everyone aged 16 or over can choose their doctor (parents or guardians choose for children under 16) and the doctor is also free to accept a person or not as he or she chooses. A person may change their doctor if they wish, either at once if they have changed address or obtained permission from the doctor on whose list they are, or by informing the Family Practitioner Committee (in which case 14 days must elapse before the other doctor can accept them). When people are away from home they can still use the Family Doctor Service if they ask to be treated as "temporary residents", and in an emergency, if a person's own doctor is not available, any doctor in the service will give treatment and advice.

Patients are treated either in the Doctor's surgery or, when necessary, at home. Doctors may prescribe for their patients all drugs and medicines which are medically necessary for their treatment and also a certain number of surgical appliances (the more elaborate being provided through the hospitals).

Dental Service

Dentists, like doctors, may take part in the Service and may also have private patients. About 14,500 of the dentists available for general practice in England provide NHS general dental services. They are responsible to the Family Practitioner Committees in whose areas they provide services.

Patients are free to go to any dentist taking part in the Service and willing to accept them. Dentists receive payment for items of treatment for individual patients, instead of the capitation fee received by doctors.

Patients are asked to pay three-quarters of the cost of NHS dental treatment. The maximum charge for a course of treatment is £150. There is no charge for arrest of bleeding, repairs to dentures, home visits by the dentist or re-opening a surgery in an emergency (in these two cases you will have to pay for treatment given in the normal way). The following are exempt from dental charges:

young people under 18;
full time students under 19;
expectant mothers who were pregnant when accepted for treatment;
women who have had a child in the previous 12 months.

People receiving Income Support or Family Credit, and members of the same family as someone receiving Income Support or Family Credit, are automatically entitled to full remission of charges.

Leaflet AB11 available from post offices and leaflet D11 available from local social security offices explain how other people on a low income can, depending on their financial circumstances, get free treatment or help with charges.

Pharmaceutical Service

Patients may obtain medicines, appliances and oral contraceptives prescribed under the NHS from any pharmacy whose owner has entered into arrangements with the Family Practitioner Committee to provide this service. Almost all pharmacy owners have done so and display notices that they dispense under the NHS: the number of these pharmacies in England and Wales at the end of 1988 was about 10,400. There are also some appliance suppliers who only provide special appliances. In country areas where access to a pharmacy may be difficult, patients may be able to obtain medicines etc. from their doctor.

Except for contraceptives (for which there is no charge), a charge of £2·80 is payable for each item supplied unless the patient is exempt and the declaration on the back of the prescription form is completed. Exemptions cover children under 16, young people under 19 and still in full-time education, men aged 65 and over, women aged 60 and over, pregnant women, mothers who have had a baby within the last 12 months, people suffering from certain medical conditions, people who receive Income Support or Family Credit, people on low income and war pensioners (for their accepted disablements). In addition, prepayment certificates may be purchased by those patients not entitled to exemption who require frequent prescriptions. Further information about the exemption and prepayment arrangements is given in leaflet P.11.

General Ophthalmic Services

General Ophthalmic Services, which are administered by Family Practitioner Committees, form part of the ophthalmic services available under the National Health Service. The free NHS sight test is available to children under 16, full-time students under the age of 19, those people and their partners in receipt of Income Support and Family Credit, people exempt on low income grounds, people entitled to complex lenses under the NHS vouchers scheme, the registered blind and partially sighted, diagnosed diabetic and glaucoma patients, and close relatives aged 40 or over of diagnosed glaucoma patients. Those on a low income may qualify for help with the cost.

Certain groups are automatically entitled to help with the purchase of glasses under an NHS voucher scheme: children under 16; full-time students under 19; people who are themselves or whose partners are in receipt of Income Support or Family Credit, and people wearing certain complex lenses. The value of the voucher depends on the lenses required. Vouchers may be used to help pay for the glasses or contact lenses of the patient's choice. People with a low income may claim help on form AG1. Glasses or contact lenses should not be purchased until the result of a claim is known as no refunds can be given. Leaflet G11 gives further details.

Diagnosis and specialist treatment of eye conditions is available through the Hospital Eye Service as well as the provision of glasses of a special type. Testing of sight may be carried out by any ophthalmic medical practitioner or ophthalmic optician and can cost up to £10. The optician must hand the prescription, and a voucher if eligible, to the patient who can take this to any supplier of glasses of his choice to have dispensed. However, only registered opticians can supply glasses to children, and people registered as blind or partially sighted.

Primary Health Care Services

Primary health care services include the general medical, dental, ophthalmic and pharmaceutical services and the family practitioner service. They also include community services run by district health authorities, health centres and clinics, family planning outside the hospital service, and preventive activities in the community including vaccination, immunization and fluoridation. The district nursing and health visiting services include community psychiatric nursing for mentally ill people living outside hospital, and school nursing for the health surveillance of school children of all ages; much ante- and post-natal care and chiropody are also an integral part of the primary health care service.

Community Child Health Services

Pre-school services, usually at child health clinics, provide regular surveillance of children's physical, mental and emotional health and development, and advice to parents on their children's health and welfare. The School Health Service provides for the medical and dental examination of schoolchildren, and advises the local education authority, the school, the parents and the pupil of any health factors which may require special consideration during the pupil's school life.

Hospitals and Other Services

The Secretary of State for Health has a duty to provide, to such extent as he/she considers necessary to meet all reasonable requirements, hospital and other accommodation; medical, dental, nursing and ambulance services; other facilities for the care of expectant and nursing mothers and young children, facilities for the prevention of illness, and the care and after-care of persons suffering from illness and such other services as are required for the diagnosis and treatment of illness. Rehabilitation services (occupational therapy, physiotherapy and speech therapy) may also be provided for those who need it and surgical and medical appliances are supplied in appropriate cases.

Specialists and consultants who take part in the Service can engage in private practice, including the treatment of their private patients in NHS hospitals.

In a number of hospitals accommodation is available for the treatment of private in-patients who undertake to pay the full costs of hospital accommodation and services and (usually) separate medical fees to a specialist as well. The amount of the medical fees is a matter for agreement between doctor and patient. Hospital charges for private resident patients are determined by District Health Authorities either on a local basis or in line with a central "model" list.

Certain hospitals have accommodation in single rooms or small wards which, if not required for patients who need privacy for medical reasons, may be made available to patients who desire it as an amenity. In such cases the patients are treated in every other respect as National Health patients.

There is no charge for drugs supplied to National Health hospital in-patients but out-patients pay £2·80 per item unless they are exempt.

With certain exceptions, hospital out-patients have to pay fixed charges for dentures, contact lenses and certain appliances. Glasses may be obtained either from the hospital or an optician and the charge will be related to the type of lens prescribed and the choice of frame.

Local Authority Personal Social Services

Local authorities are responsible for the organization, management and administration of the personal social services and each authority has a Director of Social Services and a Social Services Committee responsible for the social services functions placed upon them by the Local Authority Social Services Act 1970.

POSTAL SERVICES

On October 1, 1969 the Post Office ceased to be a government department. The responsibility for running postal services was transferred to a public authority called the Post Office, which also administered telecommunications in the United Kingdom. The British Telecommunications Act 1981 (which also separated the postal and telecommunications functions) gave the Secretary of State for Trade and Industry powers to suspend the monopoly of the Post Office in certain areas and to issue licences to other bodies to provide an alternative service. Non-Post Office bodies are now permitted to transfer mail between document exchanges and to deliver letters, provided that a minimum fee of £1 per letter is charged. Charitable organizations are allowed to carry and deliver Christmas and New Year cards.

INLAND POSTAL SERVICES AND REGULATIONS
Inland Letter Post Rates

Not over	1st Class	2nd Class
60 g	20p	15p
100 g	30p	24p
150 g	37p	28p
200 g	45p	34p
250 g	54p	42p
300 g	62p	49p
350 g	71p	56p
400 g	80p	63p
450 g	90p	70p
500 g	£1.02	78p
600 g	£1.25	95p
700 g	£1.45	£1.10
750 g	£1.55	£1.15 (max)
800 g	£1.65	
900 g	£1.80	
1,000 g	£1.95	
Each extra 250 g or part thereof	50p	

Postcards travel at the same rates.

Stamps

There is a two-tiered postal delivery system in the U.K. with 1st class letters normally being delivered the following day and 2nd class postage within two days.

Postage stamps are sold in values of 1p, 2p, 3p, 4p, 5p, 10p, 15p, 20p, 24p, 29p, 30p, 32p, 34p, 37p, 50p, 75p, £1, £1.50, and £2.00.

Books of stamps costing 50p or £1 are available from electronic vending machines at some main post offices. At other vending machines books to the value of 50p are available. At post office counters books are sold containing 10 first class stamps (£2.00) and 10 second class stamps (£1.50). Rolls of 15p and 20p stamps are also sold. Mixed value rolls are only available on special order from post offices. The sale of postage stamps has been extended to outlets other than post offices, including stationers and newsagents.

Prepaid Stationery

Aerogrammes to all destinations, 30p.
Forces Aerogrammes, 15p.
Registered Letter Envelopes, printed with a £1.75 stamp (£1.55 for registration and 20p for postage), come in three sizes.
  G, 156 × 95mm = £1.85
  H, 203 × 120mm = £1.90
  K, 292 × 152mm = £2.00

Printed postage stamps cut from envelopes, postcards, newspaper wrappers etc. may be used as stamps in payment of postage, provided that they are not imperfect or defaced.

Postal Orders

Postal Orders (British pattern) are issued and paid at nearly all post offices in the U.K. They are also paid in the Irish Republic, and issued and/or paid in many other countries overseas. These countries are listed in the Post Office Guide.

Postal orders are printed with a counterfoil for denominations of 25p, 30p, 40p, 50p, 60p, 70p, 80p, 90p, and £1, followed by £1 steps to £10, and £20. Postage stamps not exceeding two in number may be affixed in the space provided to increase the value of the postal order by up to 9p.

Charges (in addition to the value of the postal order): Up to £1 = 25p; £2–£10 = 38p; £20 = 58p.

The name of the payee must be inserted on the postal order. If not presented within six months of the last day of the month of issue, orders must be sent to the local head postmaster (in London, the district postmaster) to ascertain whether the order may still be paid.

Other Services

Cash on Delivery Service.—(Inland, excluding Irish Republic and H.M. ships). A trade charge (amount to be collected) up to £350 can, under certain conditions, be collected from addresses and remitted to the sender of a parcel containing an invoice. Invoice values of over £50 are only collectable at Post Office premises.

Charge per parcel (exclusive of postage and registration): Customers under contract = 85p; other customers = £1.15; C.O.D. enquiry = 85p.

Certificate of Posting.—Issued free on request at time of posting.

Compensation.—(Inland only). Compensation up to a maximum of £22 may be paid where it can be shown that a letter or parcel was damaged or lost in the post. The onus of making up properly any parcel sent by post lies with the sender. The Post Office does not accept any responsibility for loss arising from faulty packing. No compensation may be claimed for injury or damage to a parcel unless the item is registered and covered by consequential loss insurance.

Newspaper Post.—Copies of newspapers registered at the Post Office may be posted by the publisher or their agents in wrappers open at both ends, in unsealed envelopes approved by the Post Office, or without covers and tied by string which can be removed without cutting. Wrappers and envelopes must be prominently marked 'newspaper post' in the top left-hand corner. No writing or additional printing is permitted, other than the words 'with compliments', name and address of sender, request for return if undeliverable and a reference to a page. Items receive 1st class letter service.

Newspapers posted by the public, or supplements to registered newspapers despatched apart from their ordinary publications, are transmitted under the conditions governing the 1st or 2nd class letter services.

Prohibited Articles.—Prohibitions include offensive or dangerous articles, packets likely to impede Post Office sorters, and certain kinds of advertisement.

Recorded Delivery.—The recorded delivery service provides a record of posting and delivery of inland letters. No compensation is available for money or jewellery sent by this service. Charge: 25p; advice of delivery: a further 26p.

Redirection.—(i) By agent of addressee.—Packets other than parcels, business reply and freepost items may be reposted free not later than the day after delivery (not counting Sundays and public holidays) if unopened and if original addressee's name is unobscured. Parcels may be redirected free of charge within the same time limits only if the original and substituted address are in the same local parcel delivery area (or within the London postal area). Registered packets, which must be taken to a post office, are re-registered free only up to the day after delivery.

(ii) By the Post Office.—Requests for redirection of mail should be made on printed forms obtainable from the post office and must be signed by the person to whom the letters are to be addressed. A fee is payable for each different surname on the application form.

Charges: Up to 1 calendar month = £3.00; Up to 3 calendar months = £6.75; Up to 12 calendar months = £16.00; Up to 12 calendar months where redirection has already been in operation for 12 months or more = £54.00.

Registration.—(Inland 1st class letters only). All packets intended for registration must be handed to the post office and a certificate of posting obtained.

Compensation in respect of money is given only if money is sent by registered letter post in one of the special envelopes sold officially (*see* **Prepaid Stationery**). Compensation cannot be paid in the case of any packet containing anything not legally transmissable by post. Compensation is paid for fragile articles only if they have been adequately packed. No compensation is paid for deterioration due to delay of perishable articles or for damage to exceptionally fragile articles. Information about charges and compensation rates is available from the local head postmaster (in London, the district postmaster). Advice of delivery: a further 26p at time of posting or 65p after time of posting.

Undelivered Mail.—Undelivered mail is returned to the sender provided the return address is indicated either on the outside of the envelope or inside. If the sender's address is not available, items not containing property are destroyed. If the packet contains something of value it is retained for up to three months. Exceptionally, items in the minimum weight step on which a rebate of postage has been allowed are destroyed unopened unless there is a return address shown on the outside of the cover. In addition, undeliverable 2nd class mail which contains newspapers, magazines or commercial advertising is destroyed.

Unpaid Mail.—All unpaid or underpaid letters are treated as 2nd class mail. The recipient is charged the amount of underpayment plus 11p per item. The same rates apply to parcels.

SPECIAL DELIVERY SERVICES

Datapost.—A guaranteed service for the delivery of documents and packages: (i) Datapost Sameday offers same day collection and delivery in many areas; (ii) Datapost Overnight offers next day delivery nationwide. Items may be collected or handed in at post offices. There are also Datapost links with a number of overseas countries.

Express Delivery.—This service is by special messenger from the office of delivery and is available to or from the Isle of Man or the Channel Islands. Charge (in addition to postage): £1.75.

Royal Mail Special Delivery.—This service offers special messenger treatment, where necessary, to ensure next day delivery of 1st class letters and packets. The fee of £1.75 is refunded if next working day delivery is not achieved, provided that items are posted before latest recommended posting times.

Swiftair.—Express delivery of air mail letters and packets anywhere in the world. Items normally arrive at least one day in advance of normal air mail. Charge (in addition to postage): £1.75.

OVERSEAS POSTAL SERVICES AND REGULATIONS
Overseas Surface Mail Rates

Letters and Postcards

Not over		Not over	
20 g	24p	450 g	£2.05
60 g	41p	500 g	£2.25
100 g	60p	750 g	£3.15
150 g	80p	1,000 g	£4.00
200 g	£1.00	1,250 g	£4.65
250 g	£1.20	1,500 g	£5.25
300 g	£1.40	1,750 g	£5.85
350 g	£1.65	2,000 g	£6.50
400 g	£1.85		

Airmail Letter Rates

Europe: Letters and Postcards

Not over		Not over	
20 g	20p	400 g	£1.85
20 g non EC	24p	450 g	£2.25
60 g	41p	500 g	£2.25
100 g	60p	750 g	£3.15
150 g	80p	1,000 g	£4.00
200 g	£1.00	1,250 g	£4.65
250 g	£1.20	1,500 g	£5.25
300 g	£1.40	1,750 g	£5.85
350 g	£1.65	2,000 g	£6.50

Outside Europe: Letters

	Not over 10 g	Each extra 10 g
Zone A	32p	14p
Zone B	34p	16p
Zone C	37p	18p

(For Airmail Letter Zones outside Europe, *see* pp. 1063–65)

Other Services

Cash on Delivery.—(Applicable to parcels only, but not to all countries, nor to British naval, military and R.A.F. forces serving overseas.) A charge starting at £2.70 per parcel must be prepaid in addition to the postage for outward parcels. For inward parcels the delivery fee is 80p. The trade charge (amount to be collected) may not exceed £1,500 but to most non-European countries the limit is lower. The addressee has also to pay on delivery, besides Customs charges if any, a further charge which is not prepayable. If the trade charge cannot be collected, special rules apply for undeliverable C.O.D. parcels.

Compensation.—If a certificate of posting is produced, compensation may be given for loss or damage in the U.K. to uninsured parcels to or from most overseas countries. No compensation will be paid for any loss or damage due to the action of the Queen's Enemies.

Export Restrictions.—Under Department of Trade and Industry regulations the exportation of some goods by post is prohibited except under Department of Trade licence. Enquiries should be addressed to the Export Data Branch, Overseas Trade Divisions, Department of Trade and Industry, 1 Victoria Street, London, SW1H 0ET (Tel. 01-215 5000).

Insurance.—Packets containing valuable papers, documents or articles such as jewellery can be insured as letters, or as parcels if the country of destination does not accept dutiable goods in the letter post. For H.M. ships abroad and also members of the Army and R.A.F. overseas using B.F.P.O. numbers, parcels only are insurable up to £140 at a fee of £1.20.

Charges: Cover up to £150 = £1.55; then 25p for each additional £100, up to £3.55 for £1,400 coverage.

International Reply Coupons.—Coupons are used to prepay replies to letters. They are exchangeable abroad for stamps representing the minimum surface mail letter rate from the country concerned to the U.K. Charge: 60p each.

Poste Restante.—(Solely for the convenience of travellers and for three months only in any one town). A packet may be addressed to any post office, except town sub-offices, and should have the words 'Poste Restante' or 'to be called for' in the address. Redirection from a Poste Restante is undertaken for up to three months. Letters at a seaport for an expected ship are kept for two months: otherwise letters are kept for two weeks, or for one month if originating from abroad. At the end of this period mail is treated as undeliverable, unless bearing a request for return.

Registration.—(Except for parcels and printed paper items posted in bulk). Registration is available to all countries except the British Indian Ocean Territory and the Republic of the Maldives. No compensation is payable for loss or damage to valuable articles sent in an unregistered letter. Charge: £1.55.

Small Packets Post.—This service permits the transmission of goods up to 1 kg to all countries, in the same mails as printed papers. (N.B. To Australia, Bhutan, Bolivia, Burma, Colombia, Cuba and Papua New Guinea there is a limit of 500 g). Packets must be packed to enable examination by the Post Office. Registration is allowed but not insurance. A customs declaration is required.

Instructions for the disposal of undelivered packets must be given at the time of posting. A parcel which cannot be delivered will be returned to the sender at his expense.

Small Packets Post Rates

Not over		Not over	
100 g	47p	400 g	£1.25
150 g	60p	450 g	£1.40
200 g	74p	500 g	£1.55
250 g	85p	750 g	£2.10
300 g	£1.00	1,000 g	£2.60
350 g	£1.15		

PUBLIC TELECOMMUNICATIONS SERVICES

Under the British Telecommunications Act 1981 the functions of the Post Office were divided between two separate organizations. The Post Office retained control of postal services and British Telecom was created to provide a telecommunications service. The Act also provided for a limited relaxation of the telecommunications monopoly. This was further advanced by the Telecommunications Act 1984, which removed British Telecom's monopoly on running the public telecommunications system. British Telecom was privatized as a public limited company in 1984.

The Telecommunications Act 1984 also established the Office of Telecommunications (Oftel) as the independent regulatory body for the telecommunications industry. (*See* also **Government and Public Offices**.)

Public Telecommunications Operators

There are three licensed fixed link Public Telecommunications Operators (P.T.O.s) in the U.K.: British Telecom (B.T.), Mercury Communications Ltd. and the Kingston-upon-Hull City Council exchange. (In 1988 the Government announced its intention to license up to six other operators to provide one-way satellite communications systems).

British Telecom's obligations under its operating licence include the provision of (i) a universal telecommunications service; (ii) a service in rural areas, (iii) essential services, such as public call boxes and emergency services.

Mercury Communications is licensed to provide national and international telephone services for residential and business customers. These services utilize the digital network created by Mercury. Mercury can also provide the following services: (i) public payphone services; (ii) national and international telex; (iii) international packet data services; (iv) electronic messaging (electronic mail and access to telex via a personal computer); (v) data network services; (vi) nationwide radiopaging.

Private Telephone Services

There are an increasing number of private telephone services which offer information on a variety of subjects such as the weather, stock market analysis, horoscopes, etc. There are currently about 100 companies providing such services on the British Telecom network.

The lines and equipment are provided by British Telecom under condition that services adhere to the code of practice of the Independent Committee for the Supervision of Standards of Telephone Information Practice. Nearly all services attract British Telecom's peak rate prices.

Mobile Telephone Systems

Cellular telephone network systems, in existence since 1985, allow calls to be made to and from mobile telephones. The two companies licensed by the Department of Trade and Industry to provide competing cellular telephone systems are Cellnet, jointly owned by B.T. and Securicor, and Racal Vodaphone Ltd., owned by the Racal Electronics Group. Cellular phones can be identified by the number prefixes 0860 or 0836 and calls to them are charged at the 'm' rate.

INLAND TELEPHONES

Since December 1986 an individual customer can install an extension telephone socket or apparatus in their own home without the need to buy the items from any of the licensed Public Telecommunications Operators. However, it is necessary to possess a special style of master-socket which must be supplied by the public network operator. Although an individual need not buy or rent an apparatus from a P.T.O., a telephone bought from a retail outlet must be of an approved standard compatible with the public network (indicated by a green disc on the label).

British Telecom Charges

Exchange line rentals	Per quarter (excl. V.A.T.)
Residential, exclusive............	£15.35
Residential, shared..............	£14.04
Business, exclusive..............	£24.83
Business, shared	£23.52

Telephone apparatus rental	
Residential.....................	from £3.50
Business	from £4.40
Private payphone	from £28.50

Exchange line connection and take-over charges (including V.A.T.)

	Residential	Business
New Customer	£133.00	£145.75
Removing Customer	£114.00	£126.75
Take-over of existing lines	£20.25	£20.25

Local and dialled national calls are charged in 4.4p units when made from ordinary lines, in 10p units when made from payphones; and from press button payphones there is a 10p minimum charge with 2p incremental units. All charges are subject to V.A.T. except those from payphones which are V.A.T. inclusive. V.A.T. charges on ordinary lines are calculated as a percentage of the total quarterly bill.

The length of time per unit depends on the distance of the call and the time of day.

Local rate
'a' rate = up to 35 miles (56 km).
'b1' rate = frequently used routes over 35 miles (56 km).
'b' rate = over 35 miles (56 km).
'm' rate = dialled calls to mobile phones.

Peak rate: Monday to Friday, 9am–1pm
Standard rate: Monday to Friday, 8am–9am and 1pm–6pm
Cheap rate: Monday to Friday, 6pm–8am. All day Saturday and Sunday and, in general, on national public holidays also.

Dialled Call Unit Charge (incl. V.A.T.)

	1 min	3 mins
Local		
Peak	5p	15p
Standard	5p	15p
Cheap	5p	5p
'a' Rate		
Peak	15p	40p
Standard	10p	30p
Cheap	5p	10p
'b1' Rate		
Peak	15p	40p
Standard	10p	30p
Cheap	5p	15p
'b' Rate		
Peak	20p	51p
Standard	15p	40p
Cheap	10p	20p
'm' Rate		
Peak	40p	£1.16
Standard	40p	£1.16
Cheap	25p	76p

Prefixed call charges

0800 = free.
0345 = charged at the local rate.
0055 = charged at 'a' rate.
0066 = charged at 'b' rate.
0860, 0077 and 0898 = charged at 'm' rate (and some 0836 calls also).

Operator-Connected Calls

Operator-connected calls from ordinary lines are subject to a three-minute minimum charge (and thereafter by the minute) which varies with distance and time of day. Operator-connected calls from payphones are charged in three-minute periods at the payphone tariff. For calls that have to be placed through the operator because a dialled call has failed, the charge is equivalent to the dialled rate, subject normally to the three-minute minimum.

Higher charges apply to other operator-connected calls including special services calls and those to mobile phones, the Irish Republic and the Channel Islands. Personal calls (to a specified person) are £1.75 (excl. V.A.T.) extra from ordinary lines and £2.10 (incl. V.A.T.) from payphones: if the person cannot be found, nothing further is charged.

Phonecards

Phonecards to the value of £1, £2, £4, £10, and £20 are available from post offices and other outlets for use in specially designated public telephone boxes. Each phonecard unit is equivalent to a 10p coin in a payphone.

Special public payphones at major railway stations and airports also accept commercial credit cards.

INTERNATIONAL TELEPHONES

All U.K. customers have access to International Direct Dialling (I.D.D) and can dial direct to numbers on most exchanges in over 190 countries worldwide. Details about how to make calls are given in dialling code information and in the International Telephone Guide.

For countries without I.D.D., calls have to be made through the International Operator. All operator-connected calls are subject to a three-minute minimum charge. Thereafter the call is charged by the minute.

Countries which can be called on I.D.D fall into one of eight International Charge Bands depending on location. Charges in each band also vary according to the time of day, except for those in Charge Band G where the standard rate applies at all times. There is no reduced rate for operator-connected calls. Details of current international telephone charges can be obtained from the International Operator.

(For International Dialling Codes, *see* pp. 1063–65.)

BRITISH TELECOM SERVICES

Operator Services—100
(i) For difficulties
(ii) For the following call services: alarm calls (charge £1.21); advice of duration and charge (charge 75p); charge card calls (charge 29p); fixed time calls (charge £2.01); freefone calls; personal calls (charge £2.01); international personal calls (charge £2.47–£4.95); transferred charge calls (charge 35p); subscriber controlled transfer. (All calls include V.A.T.)

International Operator—155

Directory Enquiries:-
For numbers in the London postal area, **142.**
For numbers outside the London postal area including the Irish Republic, **192.**

International Directory Enquiries—153

Emergency Services—999
Services include: fire service; police service; ambulance service; coastguard; cave rescue; mountain rescue.

Faults—151

Telemessage—190

International Telemessage—100 (for 01 London numbers, 193). The service is only available to the U.S.A.

International Telegrams—100 (for 01 London numbers, 190).

Maritime Services—100. Includes Ship's Telegram Service and Ship's Telephone Service.

B.T. Inmarsat Satellite Service—155

All other call enquiries—191

OTHER TELECOMMUNICATIONS SERVICES

Telex Service.—There are now 208 countries that can be reached by the British Telecom telex service from the U.K., over 200 of them by direct dialling.

For most customers, direct dialled calls to international destinations are charged in six-second units. Units cost between 2.3p and 13.2p depending upon the country called. Calls via the British Telecom operator are charged in one-minute steps with a three-minute minimum, plus a surcharge of £1.30 a call. Operator-connected calls are charged at between 39p and £1.60 a minute depending upon the country called.

Calls made via British Telecom's Telex Plus store and forward facility attract normal telex charges and a handling charge of 13p for inland delivered messages and 30p for international delivered messages.

Telemessage.—Telemessages can be sent by telephone or telex within the U.K. for 'hard copy' delivery the next working day, including Saturdays. To achieve this, a telemessage must be telephoned/telexed before 10pm Monday to Saturday (7pm Sundays and Bank Holidays). Dial 100 (in London, 190) and ask for the Telemessage Service or see the telex directory for codes.

A Telemessage costs £5 for the first 50 words and £2.75 for each subsequent group of 50 words—the name and address are free. A sender's copy costs 85p. A selection of cards is available for special occasions at 80p per card. All prices are subject to V.A.T.

International Telemessage.—Telemessage is also available to the U.S.A. For next working day delivery a telemessage must be filed by 10pm U.K. time Monday to Saturday (7pm Sundays and Bank Holidays). U.S. addresses must include the ZIP code. Charges are £7.25 for the first 50 words and £3.60 for each subsequent group of 50 words. The name and address are free but all charges are subject to V.A.T.

WEATHERCALL SERVICE

To obtain local weather forecasts, dial the prefix code 0898 500 followed by the appropriate regional code.

Greater London	401	Gwynedd and Clwyd	415
Kent, Surrey and Sussex	402	North West England	416
Dorset, Hampshire and I.o.W.	403	W. and S. Yorkshire and Yorkshire Dales	417
Devon and Cornwall	404	North East England	418
Wiltshire, Glos., Avon and Somerset	405	Cumbria and the Lake District	419
Berks., Bucks. and Oxfordshire	406	South West Scotland	420
Beds., Herts. and Essex	407	West Central Scotland	421
Norfolk, Suffolk and Cambridgeshire	408	Edinburgh, S. Fife, Lothian and Borders	422
West, Mid and South Glamorgan and Gwent	409	East Central Scotland	423
Salop, Hereford and Worcester	410	Grampian and East Highlands	424
Central Midlands	411	North West Scotland	425
East Midlands	412	Caithness, Orkney and Shetland	426
Lincolnshire and Humberside	413	Northern Ireland	427
Dyfed and Powys	414	Five-day national forecast	430

MARINECALL SERVICE

To obtain information about weather conditions up to twelve miles off the coast, dial the prefix code 0898 500, followed by the appropriate area code

Scotland North	451	Bristol Channel	459
Scotland East	452	Wales	460
North East	453	North West	461
East	454	Clyde	462
Anglia	455	Caledonia	463
Channel East	456	Minch	464
Mid-Channel	457	Ulster	465
South West	458		

INTERNATIONAL POST AND TELEPHONE CODES

The table below includes airmail letter zones for countries outside Europe (A, B or C). Destinations to which European airmail letter rates apply are indicated by *e*, or by *ec* for European Community destinations.

International dialling codes are composed of four elements which are dialled in sequence: (i) the international code (from the U.K. this is always 010); (ii) the country code (*see* list below); (iii) the area code; (iv) the customer's number. Calls to some countries (indicated by † below) must be made via the international operator.

Country	Airmail Zone	IDD code from UK	IDD code to UK
Afghanistan	B	†	†
Albania	*e*	†	†
Algeria	A	010 213	00*p*44
Andorra	*ec*	010 33 628	
Angola	B	010 244	
Anguilla	B	010 1 809 497	
Antigua and Barbuda	B	010 1 809	011 44
Argentina	B	010 54	00 44
Aruba	B	010 297 8	
Ascension Island	B	010 247	
Australia	C	010 61	00 11 44
Austria	*e*	010 43	00 44
Azores	*ec*	010 351	
Bahamas	B	010 1 809	011 44
Bahrain	A	010 973	0 44
Bangladesh	B	010 880	00 44
Barbados	B	010 1 809	011 44
Belguim	*ec*	010 32	00*p*44
Belize	B	010 501	
Benin	B	010 229	
Bermuda	B	010 1 809 29	1 44
Bhutan	B	†	†
Bolivia	B	010 591	00 44
Botswana	B	010 267	
Brazil	B	010 55	00 44
British Virgin Islands	B	010 1 809 49	
Brunei	B	010 673	00 44
Bulgaria	*e*	010 359	00 44
Burkina	B	010 226	
Burma/Myanma	B	010 95	
Burundi	B	†	†
Cameroon	B	010 237	00 44
Canada	B	010 1	011 44
Cape Verde	*e*	†	†
Cayman Islands	B	010 1 809 94	0 44
Central African Republic	B	†	†
Chad	B	†	†
Chile	B	010 56	00 44
China	C	010 86	00 44
Colombia	B	010 57	90 44
Comoros	B	†	†
Congo	B	010 242	
Cook Islands	C	010 682	
Costa Rica	B	010 506	00 44
Côte d'Ivoire	B	010 225	00*p*44
Cuba	B	010 53	00 44
Cyprus	*e*	010 357	00 44
Czechoslovakia	*e*	010 42	00 44
Denmark	*ec*	010 45	009 44
Djibouti	A	010 253	
Dominica	B	010 1 809 449	
Dominican Republic	B	010 1 809	
Ecuador	B	010 593	00 44
Egypt	A	010 20	00 44
Equatorial Guinea	B	†	†
Ethiopia	A	010 251	
Falkland Islands	B	†	†
Faroe Islands	*e*	010 298	
Fiji	C	010 679	
Finland	*e*	010 358	990 44
France	*ec*	010 33	19*p*44
French Guiana	B	010 594	
French Polynesia	C	010 689	

e Europe. *ec* European Community. † Calls must be made via the international operator. *p* A pause in dialling is necessary whilst waiting for a second tone.

Country	Airmail Zone	IDD code from UK	IDD code to UK
Gabon	B	010 241	00 44
The Gambia	B	010 220	
Germany, East	e	010 37	000 44§
Germany, West	ec	010 49	00 44
Ghana	B	010 233	
Gibraltar	ec	010 350	00 44
Greece	ec	010 30	00 44
Greenland	e	010 299	
Grenada	B	010 1 809 440	
Guadeloupe	B	010 590	
Guam	C	010 671	
Guatemala	B	010 502	00 44
Guinea	B	†	†
Guinea-Bissau	B	†	†
Guyana	B	010 592	
Haiti	B	010 509	
Honduras	B	010 504	
Hong Kong	B	010 852	001 44
Hungary	e	010 36	00 44
Iceland	e	010 354	90 44
India	B	010 91	00 44
Indonesia	B	010 62	00 44
Iran	A	010 98	00 44
Iraq	A	010 964	00 44
Ireland, Republic of	ec	010 353	
Dublin		0001	
Israel	A	010 972	00 44
Italy	ec	010 39	00 44
Jamaica	B	010 1 809	
Japan	C	010 81	001 44
Jordan	A	010 962	00 44 varies
Kampuchea	B	†	†
Kenya	B	010 254	000 44
Kiribati	C	†	†
Korea, North	C	†	†
Korea, South	C	010 82	001 44
Kuwait	A	010 965	00 44
Laos	B	†	†
Lebanon	A	010 961	00 44
Lesotho	B	010 266	
Liberia	B	010 231	
Libya	A	010 218	00 44
Liechtenstein	e	010 41 75	
Luxembourg	ec	010 352	00 44
Macao	B	010 853	
Madagascar	B	010 261	
Madeira	ec	010 351 91	
Malawi	B	010 265	101 44
Malaysia	B	010 60	00 44
Maldives	B	010 960	
Mali	B	†	†
Malta	e	010 356	0 44
Martinique	B	010 596	
Mauritania	B	†	†
Mauritius	B	010 230	
Mexico	B	010 52	98 44
Monaco	ec	010 33 93	
Mongolia	C	†	†
Montserrat	B	010 1 809 491	
Morocco	A	010 212	00p44
Mozambique	B	010 258	
Namibia	B	010 264	
Nauru	C	010 674	
Nepal	B	010 977	
Netherlands	ec	010 31	09p44
Netherlands Antilles	B	010 599	
New Caledonia	C	010 687	
New Zealand	C	010 64	00 44
Nicaragua	B	010 505	00 44
Niger	B	010 227	
Nigeria	B	010 234	009 44

e Europe. *ec* European Community. † Calls must be made via the international operator. *p* A pause in dialling is necessary whilst waiting for a second tone. § From Berlin, Cottbus, Erfurt, Frankfurt (Oder), Gera, Halle/ Salle, Leipzig, Magdeburg, Neubrandenburg and Suhl, dial 06 44.

Country	Airmail Zone	IDD code from UK	IDD code to UK
Norfolk Island	C	010 672 3	
Norway	e	010 47	095 44
Oman	A	010 968	00 44
Pakistan	B	010 92	00 44
Panama	B	010 507	00 44
Papua New Guinea	C	010 675	
Paraguay	B	010 595	
Peru	B	010 51	00 44
Philippines	C	010 63	00 44
Poland	e	010 48	0p044
Portugal	ec	010 351	00 44
Puerto Rico	B	010 1 809	
Qatar	A	010 974	044
Réunion	B	010 262	
Romania	e	010 40	
Rwanda	B	†	†
St Helena	B	†	†
St. Kitts and Nevis	B	010 1 809 465	
St. Lucia	B	010 1 809 45	0 44
St. Pierre and Miquelon	B	010 508	
St. Vincent and the Grenadines	B	010 1 809 45	
El Salvador	B	010 503	
Samoa, American	C	010 684	
San Marino	ec	010 39 541	
São Tomé and Príncipe	B	†	†
Saudi Arabia	A	010 966	00 44
Senegal	B	010 221	
Seychelles	B	010 248	
Sierra Leone	B	010 232	
Singapore	B	010 65	005 44
Solomon Islands	C	010 677	
Somalia	B	010 252	
South Africa	B	010 27	09 44
Spain	ec	010 34	07p44
Sri Lanka	B	010 94	00 44
Sudan	A	010 249	
Suriname	B	010 597	
Swaziland	B	010 268	
Sweden	e	010 46	009 44p
Switzerland	e	010 41	00 44
Syria	A	010 963	00 44
Taiwan	C	010 886	002 44
Tanzania	B	010 255	
Thailand	B	010 66	001 44
Togo	B	010 228	
Tonga	C	010 676	
Trinidad and Tobago	B	010 1 809	01 44
Tunisia	A	010 216	00 44
Turkey	e	010 90	99p44
Turks and Caicos Islands	B	010 1 809 946	
Tuvalu	C	†	†
Uganda	B	010 256	
United Arab Emirates	A	010 971	00 44
Uruguay	B	010 598	00 44
U.S.A.	B	010 1	011 44
Alaska		010 1 907	
Hawaii		010 1 808	
U.S.S.R.	e	010 7	810 44
Vanuatu	C	010 678	
Vatican City State	ec	010 39 66982	
Venezuela	B	010 58	00 44
Vietnam	B	†	†
Virgin Islands (U.S.)	B	010 1 809	
Western Samoa	C	010 685	
Yemen, North	A	010 967	00 44
Yemen, South	A	†	†
Yugoslavia	e	010 38	99 44
Zaire	B	010 243	
Zambia	B	010 260	00 44
Zimbabwe	B	010 263	110 44

e Europe. *ec* European Community. † Calls must be made via the international operator. *p* A pause in dialling is necessary whilst waiting for a second tone.

SUMMARY OF SPORT 1988–89

RECORDS

ATHLETICS
WORLD RECORDS
(as at Aug. 31, 1989)

(All the world records given below have been accepted by the International Amateur Athletic Federation except those marked with an asterisk* which are awaiting homologation.)

Fully automatic timing to 1/100th second is mandatory up to and including 400 metres. For distances up to and including 10,000 metres records will be accepted to 1/100th second if timed automatically, and to 1/10th if hand timing is used.

MEN'S EVENTS
Running

Distances	hr.	min.	Time sec.	Name	Nation	Year
100 metres			9·83	B. Johnson	Canada	1987
200 metres			19·72	P. Mennea	Italy	1979
400 metres			43·29	H.Reynolds	U.S.A.	1988
800 metres		1	41·73	S. Coe	G.B.	1981
1,000 metres		2	12·18	S. Coe	G.B.	1981
1,500 metres		3	29·46	S. Aouita	Morocco	1985
1 mile		3	46·32	S. Cram	G.B.	1985
2,000 metres		4	50·81	S. Aouita	Morocco	1987
3,000 metres		7	29·45*	S. Aouita	Morocco	1989
5,000 metres		12	58·39	S. Aouita	Morocco	1987
10,000 metres		27	08·23*	A. Barrios	Mexico	1989
20,000 metres		57	24·2	J. Hermens	Netherlands	1976
20,944 metres (13 miles 24 yards 2 feet)	1	00	00·0	J. Hermens	Netherlands	1976
25,000 metres	1	13	55·8	T. Seko	Japan	1981
30,000 metres	1	29	18·8	T. Seko	Japan	1981
110 metres hurdles (3 ft. 6 in.)			12·92*	R. Kingdom	U.S.A.	1989
400 metres hurdles (3 ft. 0 in.)			47·02	E. Moses	U.S.A.	1983
3,000 metres steeplechase		8	05·35*	P. Koech	Kenya	1989

Relay Racing

Distance	min.	Time sec.	Nation	Year
4 × 100 metres		37·83	U.S.A.	1984
4 × 200 metres	1	19·38	Santa Monica T.C.	1989
4 × 400 metres	2	56·16	U.S.A.	1977
4 × 800 metres	7	03·89	G.B.	1982
4 × 1,500 metres	14	38·8	F.R.G.	1977

Jumping and Throwing

	metres	ft.	in.	Name	Nation	Year
High Jump	2·44	8	0	J. Sotomayor	Cuba	1989
Pole Vault	6·06	19	10½	S. Bubka	U.S.S.R.	1988
Long Jump	8·90	29	2¼	R. Beamon	U.S.A.	1968
Triple Jump	17·97	58	11¼	W. Banks	U.S.A.	1985
Shot	23·06	75	8	U. Timmermann	G.D.R.	1988
Discus	74·08	243	0	J. Schult	G.D.R.	1986
Hammer	86·74	284	7	Y. Sedykh	U.S.S.R.	1986
Javelin†	87·66	287	7	T. Zelezny	Czechoslovakia	1987
Decathlon‡	8,847 pts.°			D. Thompson	G.B.	1984

† New type of javelin now in force
‡ Ten events comprising 100 m, long jump, shot, high jump, 400 m, 110 m hurdles, discus, pole vault, javelin, 1500 m.
° Scored with new scoring tables.

Walking (Track)

Distance	hr.	min.	Time sec.	Name	Nation	Year
20,000 metres	1	18	40	E. Canto	Mexico	1984
28,565 metres (17 miles 1319 yards)	2	00	00·0	M. Damilano	Italy	1985
30,000 metres	2	06	07·3	M. Damilano	Italy	1985
50,000 metres	3	41	39·00	R. Gonzalez	Mexico	1979

WOMEN'S EVENTS
Running

Distance	min.	Time sec.	Name	Nation	Year
100 metres		10·49	F. Griffith-Joyner	U.S.A.	1988
200 metres		21·34	F. Griffith-Joyner	U.S.A.	1988
400 metres		47·60	M. Koch	G.D.R.	1985
800 metres	1	53·28	J. Kratochvilova	Czechoslovakia	1983
1,500 metres	3	52·47	T. Kazankina	U.S.S.R.	1980
1 mile	4	15·61	P. Ivan	Romania	1989
3,000 metres	8	22·62	T. Kazankina	U.S.S.R.	1984
5,000 metres	14	37·33	I. Kristiansen	Norway	1986
10,000 metres	30	13·74	I. Kristiansen	Norway	1986
100 metres hurdles (2 ft. 9 in.)		12·21	Y. Donkova	Bulgaria	1988
400 metres hurdles (2 ft. 6 in.)		52·94	M. Stepanova	U.S.S.R.	1986

Relays

Distance	min.	Time sec.	Nation	Year
4 × 100 metres		41·37	G.D.R.	1985
4 × 200 metres	1	28·15	G.D.R.	1980
4 × 400 metres	3	15·17	U.S.S.R.	1988
4 × 800 metres	7	50·17	U.S.S.R.	1984

Jumping and Throwing

	metres	ft.	in.	Name	Nation	Year
High Jump	2·09	6	10¼	S. Kostadinova	Bulgaria	1987
Long Jump	7·52	24	8¼	G. Chistiakova	U.S.S.R.	1988
Shot	22·63	74	3	N. Lisovskaya	U.S.S.R.	1987
Discus	76·80	252	0	G. Reinsch	G.D.R.	1988
Javelin	80·00	262	5	P. Felke	G.D.R.	1988
Heptathlon†	7,291 pts.			J. Joyner-Kersee	U.S.A.	1988

†Seven events comprising 100 m hurdles, shot, high jump, 200 m, long jump, javelin, 800 m.

UNITED KINGDOM (NATIONAL) RECORDS
(as at Aug. 31, 1989)
(Records made anywhere by athletes eligible to represent Great Britain and Northern Ireland)

Men

100 *metres*—9·97 sec. (L. Christie, 1988).
200 *metres*—20·09 sec. (J. Regis, 1988).
400 *metres*—44·50 sec. (D. Redmond, 1987).
800 *metres*—1 min. 41·73 sec. (S. Coe, 1981).
1,000 *metres*—2 min. 12·18 sec. (S. Coe, 1981).
1,500 *metres*—3 min. 29·67 sec. (S. Cram, 1985).
1 *mile*—3 min. 46·32 sec. (S. Cram, 1985).
2,000 *metres*—4 min. 51·39 sec. (S. Cram, 1985).
3,000 *metres*—7 min. 32·79 sec. (D. Moorcroft, 1982).
5,000 *metres*—13 min. 00·41 sec. (D. Moorcroft, 1982).
10,000 *metres*—27 min. 23·06 sec. (E. Martin, 1988).
20,000 *metres*—58 min. 39·0 sec. (R. Hill, 1968).
12 *miles* 1,268 *yards*—1 hr. (R. Hill, 1968).
25,000 *metres*—1 hr. 15 min. 22·6 sec. (R. Hill, 1965).
30,000 *metres*—1 hr. 31 min. 30·4 sec. (J. Alder, 1970).
3,000 *metres Steeplechase*—8 min. 12·11 sec. (C. Reitz, 1986).
110 *metres Hurdles*—13·11 sec. (C. Jackson, 1988).
400 *metres Hurdles*—48·12 sec. (D. P. Hemery, 1968).
4 × 100 *metres Relay*—38·39 (G.B. Team, 1988).

4 × 200 *metres*—1 min. 21·29 sec. (G.B. Team, 1989).
4 × 400 *metres*—2 min. 58·86 sec. (G.B. Team, 1987).
4 × 800 *metres*—7 min. 03·89 sec. (G.B. Team, 1982).
4 × 1,500 *metres*—14 min. 56·8 sec. (G.B. Team, 1979).
High Jump—2·34 m., 7 ft. 8 in. (D. Grant, 1989).
Pole Vault—5·65 m., 18 ft. 6¼ in. (K. Stock, 1981).
Long Jump—8·23 m., 27 ft. 0 in. (L. Davies, 1968).
Triple Jump—17·57 m., 57 ft. 7¼ in. (K. Connor, 1982).
Shot—21·68 m., 71 ft. 1¼ in. (G. Capes, 1980).
Discus—64·32 m., 211 ft. 0 in. (W. Tancred, 1974).
Hammer—77·54 m., 254 ft. 5 in. (M. Girvan, 1984).
Javelin—85·86 m., 281 ft. 8 in. (S. Backley, 1989).
Decathlon—8,847 pts.° (D. Thompson, 1984).
      ° Scored with new scoring tables.

Walking (Track)
20,000 *metres*—1 hr. 26 min. 07·6 sec. (P. Vesty, 1984).
2 *Hours*—16 miles 315 yds. (R. Wallwork, 1971).
30,000 *metres*—2 hr. 19 min. 18 sec. (C. Maddocks, 1984).
50,000 *metres*—4 hr. 05 min. 48 sec. (C. Maddocks, 1984).

Women

100 *metres*—11·10 sec. (K. Cook (née Smallwood), 1981).

200 *metres*—22·10 sec. (K. Cook (née Smallwood), 1984).

400 *metres*—49·43 sec. (K. Cook (née Smallwood), 1984).

800 *metres*—1 min. 57·42 sec. (K. Wade (née McDermott), 1985).

1,500 *metres*—3 min. 59·96 sec. (Z. Budd, 1985).

1 *mile*—4 min. 17·57 sec. (Z. Budd, 1985).

3,000 *metres*—8 min. 28·83 sec. (Z. Budd, 1985).

5,000 *metres*—14 min. 48·07 sec. (Z. Budd, 1985)

10,000 *metres*—31 min. 06·99 sec. (E. McColgan (née Lynch), 1988).

100 *metres Hurdles*—12·82 sec. (S. Gunnell, 1988).

400 *metres Hurdles*—54·03 sec. (S. Gunnell, 1988).

4 × 100 *metres Relay*—42·43 sec. (G.B. Team, 1980).

4 × 200 *metres Relay*—1 min. 31·57 sec. (G.B. Team, 1977).

4 × 400 *metres Relay*—3 min. 25·51 sec. (G.B. Team, 1984).

4 × 800 *metres Relay*—8 min. 23·8 sec. (G.B. Team, 1971).

High Jump—1·95 m., 6 ft. 4¾ in. (D. Elliott, 1982).

Long Jump—6·90 m., 22 ft. 7¾ in. (B. Kinch, 1983).

Shot—19·36 m., 63 ft. 6½ in. (J. Oakes, 1988).

Discus—67·48 m., 221 ft. 5 in. (M. Ritchie, 1981).

Javelin—77·44 m., 254 ft. 1 in. (F. Whitbread, 1986).

Heptathlon—6,623 pts. (J. Simpson (née Livermore), 1986).

SWIMMING

WORLD RECORDS
(as at Aug. 31, 1989)

Men:

100 metres Freestyle.—M. Biondi (U.S.A.), 48·42 s.

200 metres Freestyle.—G. Lamberti (Italy), 1 m. 46·69 s.

400 metres Freestyle.—U. Dassler (G.D.R.), 3 m. 46·95 s.

800 metres Freestyle.—V. Salnikov (U.S.S.R.), 7 m. 50·64 s.

1,500 metres Freestyle.—V. Salnikov (U.S.S.R.), 14 m. 54·76 s.

100 metres Breaststroke.—A. Moorhouse (G.B.), 1 m. 01·49 s.

200 metres Breaststroke.—M. Borrowman (U.S.A.), 2 m. 12·89 s.

100 metres Butterfly.—P. Morales (U.S.A.), 52·84 s.

200 metres Butterfly.—M. Gross (F.R.G.), 1 m. 56·24 s.

100 metres Backstroke.—D. Berkoff (U.S.A.), 54·91 s.

200 metres Backstroke.—I. Polyanski (U.S.S.R.), 1 m. 58·14 s.

200 metres Medley.—D. Wharton (U.S.A.), 2 m.00·11 s.

400 metres Medley.—T. Darnyi (Hungary) 4 m.14·75 s.

4 × 100 metres Freestyle Relay.—U.S.A., 3 m. 16·53 s.

4 × 200 metres Freestyle Relay.—U.S.A., 7 m. 12·51 s.

4 × 100 metres Medley Relay.—U.S.A., 3 m. 36·93 s.

Women:

100 metres Freestyle.—K. Otto (G.D.R.), 54·73 s.

200 metres Freestyle.—H. Friedrich (G.D.R.), 1 m. 57·55 s.

400 metres Freestyle.—J. Evans (U.S.A.), 4 m. 03·85 s.

800 metres Freestyle.—J. Evans (U.S.A.), 8 m.16·22 s.

1,500 metres Freestyle.—J. Evans (U.S.A.), 15 m. 52·10 s.

100 metres Breaststroke.—S. Hörner (G.D.R.), 1 m. 07·91 s.

200 metres Breaststroke.—S. Hörner (G.D.R.), 2 m. 26·71 s.

100 metres Butterfly.—M. Meagher (U.S.A.), 57·93 s.

200 metres Butterfly.—M. Meagher (U.S.A), 2 m. 05·96 s.

100 metres Backstroke.—I. Kleber (G.D.R.), 1 m. 00·59 s.

200 metres Backstroke.—B. Mitchell (U.S.A.), 2 m. 08·60 s.

200 metres Medley.—U. Geweniger (G.D.R.), 2 m. 11·73 s.

400 metres Medley.—P. Schneider (G.D.R.), 4 m. 36·10 s.

4 × 100 metres Freestyle Relay.—G.D.R., 3 m. 40·57 s.

4 × 200 metres Freestyle Relay.—G.D.R., 7 m. 55·47 s.

4 × 100 metres Medley Relay.—G.D.R., 4 m. 03·69 s.

WEIGHTLIFTING

WORLD RECORDS (TOTALS)
(as at Aug. 31, 1989)

Class	Kg		
52 kg	270	S. Marinov (Bulgaria)	1988
56 kg	300	N. Shalamanov (Bulgaria)	1984
60 kg	342·5	N. Suleymanoglu (Turkey)	1988
67·5 kg	355	M. Petrov (Bulgaria)	1987
75 kg	382·5	A. Varbanov (Bulgaria)	1988
82·5 kg	405	Y. Vardanyan (U.S.S.R.)	1984
90 kg	422·5	V. Solodov (U.S.S.R.)	1984
100 kg	440	Y. Zakharevich (U.S.S.R.)	1983
110 kg	455	Y. Zakharevich (U.S.S.R.)	1988
Over 110 kg	475	L. Taranenko (U.S.S.R.)	1988

RESULTS

ALPINE SKI-ING 1988–89

WORLD CHAMPIONSHIPS
(Vail, Colorado, U.S.A.)

Men's:

Downhill.—H. Tauscher (W. Germany).

Slalom.—R. Nierlich (Austria).

Giant Slalom.—R. Nierlich (Austria).

Super Giant Slalom.—M. Hangl (Switzerland).

Combined.—M. Girardelli (Luxembourg).

Women's:

Downhill.—M. Walliser (Switzerland).

Slalom.—M. Svet (Yugoslavia).

Giant Slalom.—V. Schneider (Switzerland).

Super Giant Slalom.—U. Maier (Austria).

Combined.—T. McKinney (U.S.A.).

WORLD CUP 1988–89

Men's:

Downhill.—M. Girardelli (Luxembourg).

Slalom.—A. Bittner (W. Germany).

Giant Slalom.—O. Furuseth (Norway).

Super Giant Slalom.—P. Zurbriggen (Switzerland).

Overall.—M. Girardelli (Luxembourg).

Women's:

Downhill.—M. Figini (Switzerland).

Slalom.—V. Schneider (Switzerland).

Giant Slalom.—V. Schneider (Switzerland).

Super Giant Slalom.—C. Merle (France).

Overall.—V. Schneider (Switzerland).

AMERICAN FOOTBALL, 1989

XXIII American Superbowl.—(Miami, Jan. 22) San Francisco 49ers beat Cincinnati Bengals by 20–16.

ANGLING

NATIONAL COARSE CHAMPIONSHIPS

Year	Venue	No. of teams	Individual Winner	Weight	Team Winners	Points	Division
				k. g.			
1987	R. Trent	80	J. Robinson (Bawtry)	14 080	Nottingham & D.	773	1
	Oxford Canal	77	B. Mann (Tewkesbury Popular)	2 940	Weybridge	767	2
	R. Severn	79	S. Carr (North Staffs.)	17 660	Trevs A.S.	718	3
	R. Nene	72	C. Shortland (Crosby)	5 490	Earl Manvers	716	4
	Oxford Canal	70	T. May (Bedford A.C.)	4 030	Star A.C.	661	5
	Bristol Avon	36	P. Mason (Leighton Buzzard)	13 200	Bristol & West	326	Jr. Ch.
1988	R. Thames	78	S. Hall (Stratford-on-Avon)	18 210	Redditch F. of A.	750	1
	R. Severn	76	G. Ellis (Slaithwaite & D.)	7 470	Stainforth & D.	696	2
	Leeds and Liverpool Canal	74	P. Wintle (Towcester & D.)	5 310	Harleston, Wortwell	660	3
	R. Trent	76	G. McFiggins (Bedford A.C.)	9 580	Bedford A.C.	697	4
	R. Witham	85	D. Bowers (Highfield)	4 030	Leeds Anglers	942	5
	R. Nene	41	C. Shaw (Worksop & D.)	8 980	Hull & District	400	Jr. Ch.

ASSOCIATION FOOTBALL 1988–89

LEAGUE COMPETITIONS

Div. I.—Champions: Arsenal, 76 pts. *Runners-up*: Liverpool, 76 pts. *Relegated*: Middlesbrough, 39 pts.; West Ham United, 38 pts.; Newcastle United, 31 pts.

Div. II.—Champions: Chelsea, 99 pts. *Promoted*: Manchester City, 82 pts. *Relegated*: Shrewsbury Town, 42 pts.; Birmingham City, 35 pts.; Walsall, 31 pts.

Div. III.—Champions: Wolverhampton, 91 pts. *Promoted*: Sheffield United, 84 pts. *Relegated*: Southend, 54 pts.; Chesterfield, 49 pts.; Gillingham, 40 pts.; Aldershot, 37 pts.

Div. IV.—Champions: Rotherham United, 82 pts. *Promoted*: Tranmere Rovers, 80 pts.; Crewe Alexandra, 78 pts. *Relegated to G.M. Vauxhall Conference*: Darlington, 42 pts.

G.M. Vauxhall Conference.—Champions and Promoted: Maidstone United, 84 pts.

END OF SEASON PLAY-OFFS

Div. II.—S.F.—Crystal Palace beat *Swindon Town 2–0 on agg.; *Blackburn Rovers beat Watford on away goals after drawing 1–1 on agg.
Final.—Crystal Palace beat *Blackburn Rovers 4–3 on agg. (a.e.t.).

Div. III.—S.F.—*Bristol Rovers beat Fulham 5–0 on agg.; Port Vale beat *Preston North End 4–2 on agg.
Final—Port Vale beat *Bristol Rovers 2–1 on agg.

Div. IV.—S.F.—*Leyton Orient beat Scarborough 2–1 on agg.; *Wrexham beat Scunthorpe United 5–1 on agg.
Final—Leyton Orient beat *Wrexham 2–1 on agg.

*Indicates home team in first match.

As a result of the end-of-season play-offs Crystal Palace were promoted to Division I; Port Vale to Division II; and Leyton Orient to Division III.

SCOTTISH LEAGUE

Premier Div.—Champions: Rangers, 56 pts. *Runners-up:* Aberdeen, 50 pts. *Relegated:* Hamilton, 14 pts.

Div. I.—Champions: Dunfermline, 54 pts. *Relegated:* Kilmarnock, 34 pts.; Queen of the South, 10 pts.

Div. II.—Champions: Albion Rovers, 50 pts. *Promoted:* Alloa, 45 pts.

CUP COMPETITIONS

F.A. CUP.—*S.F.:* (Villa Park), Everton beat Norwich City, 1–0; (Hillsborough), Liverpool and Nottingham Forest, match abandoned (*Hillsborough tragedy*). Match replayed at Old Trafford, Liverpool beat Nottingham Forest, 3–1.
Final: May 20 (Wembley), Liverpool beat Everton, 3–2 a.e.t.

LITTLEWOODS CUP.—*Final:* Nottingham Forest beat Luton Town, 3–1.

SIMOD CUP.—*Final:* Nottingham Forest beat Everton, 4–3 a.e.t.

SHERPA VAN TROPHY.—*Final:* Bolton beat Torquay United, 4–1.

CHARITY SHIELD.—Liverpool beat Wimbledon, 2–1.

F.A. VASE.—*Final:* Sudbury Town drew 1–1 with Tamworth a.e.t. Tamworth won 3–0 after a replay.

F.A. TROPHY.—*Final:* Telford beat Macclesfield, 1–0 a.e.t.

ARTHUR DUNN CUP.—*Final:* Old Malvernians beat Old Brentwoods, 3–1.

SCOTTISH F.A. CUP.—*S.F.:* (Celtic Park), Rangers 0 St Johnstone 0. Rangers beat St Johnstone, 4–1 after a replay; (Hampden), Celtic beat Hibernian, 3–1.
Final: May 20 (Hampden), Celtic beat Rangers, 1–0.

SKOL CUP.—*Final:* Rangers beat Aberdeen, 3–2.

ROUS CUP.—*Winners:* England.

EUROPEAN CUP.—*Final:* AC Milan beat Steaua Bucharest 4–0 in Barcelona.

EUROPEAN CUP-WINNERS' CUP.—*Final:* Barcelona beat Sampdoria 2–0 in Berne.

U.E.F.A. CUP.—*Final:* Napoli beat VfB Stuttgart 5–4 on agg.

INTERNATIONALS

1988		
Sept.14	Wembley:	England 1, Denmark 0.
Nov. 16	Riyadh:	Saudi Arabia 1, England 1.
Dec. 22	Perugia:	Italy 2, Scotland 0.

1989
Feb. 8	Athens:	Greece 1, England 2.		
	Tel Aviv:	Israel 3, Wales 3.		
Apr. 26	Wrexham:	Wales 0, Sweden 2.		
May 23	Wembley:	England 0, Chile 0.*		
May 26	Belfast:	N. Ireland 0, Chile 1.		
May 27	Hampden:	Scotland 0, England 2.*		
May 30	Hampden:	Scotland 2, Chile 0.*		
June 7	Copenhagen:	Denmark 1, England 1.		

*Rous Cup

WORLD CUP

Qualifying Rounds

England (*Group 2*), Wales (*Group 4*), Scotland (*Group 5*), Northern Ireland (*Group 6*).

1988
Sept. 14	Belfast:	Northern Ireland 0, Republic of Ireland 0.
	Oslo:	Norway 1, Scotland 2.
	Amsterdam:	Netherlands 1, Wales 0.
Oct. 19	Wembley:	England 0, Sweden 0.
	Swansea:	Wales 2, Finland 2.
	Hampden:	Scotland 1, Yugoslavia 1.
	Budapest:	Hungary 1, Northern Ireland 0.
Dec. 21	Seville:	Spain 4, Northern Ireland 0.

1989
Feb. 8	Belfast:	Northern Ireland 0, Spain 2.
	Limassol:	Cyprus 2, Scotland 3.
Mar. 8	Tirana:	Albania 0, England 2.
	Hampden:	Scotland 2, France 0.
Apr. 26	Hampden:	Scotland 2, Cyprus 1.
	Wembley:	England 5, Albania 0.
	Valletta:	Malta 0, Northern Ireland 2.
May 31	Cardiff:	Wales 0, West Germany 0.
June 3	Wembley:	England 3, Poland 0.
Sept. 6	Stockholm:	Sweden 0, England 0.
	Helsinki:	Finland 1, Wales 0.
	Zagreb:	Yugoslavia 3, Scotland 1.
	Belfast:	Northern Ireland 1, Hungary 2.

ATHLETICS, 1989

United Kingdom v. West Germany (Indoors)

Held at Glasgow, January 28, 1989

Men's Events

Metres	min.	sec.
60—M. Rosswess (U.K.)		6·73
200—J. Ridgeon (U.K.)		21·15
400—T. Bennett (U.K.)		47·21
800—E. Ruter (F.R.G.)	1	49·47
1,500—M. Kirk (U.K.)	3	42·69
3,000—C. Walker (U.K.)	7	57·83
60 *Hurdles*—C. Jackson (U.K.)		7·54
4 × 200 *Relay*—United Kingdom	1	23·46
		metres
High Jump—D. Grant (U.K.)		2·31
Pole Vault—A. Ashurst (U.K.)		5·10
Long Jump—P. Johnson (U.K.)		7·72
Triple Jump—J. Herbert (U.K.)		16·44
Shot—M. Simson (U.K.)		18·08

U.K. 93 pts., West Germany 46.

Women's Events

Metres	min.	sec.
60—P. Dunn (U.K.)		7·40
200—K. Janke (F.R.G.)		23·82
400—A. Piggford (U.K.)		53·71

	min.	sec.
800—G. Lesch (F.R.G.)	2	01·82
1,500—K. Hutcheson (U.K.)	4	13·52
60 *Hurdles*—L.-A. Skeete (U.K.)		8·23
4 × 200 *Relay*—United Kingdom	1	34·85
		metres
High Jump—U. Demming (F.R.G.)		1·90
Long Jump—F. May (U.K.)		6·42
Shot—Y. Hanson-Nortey (U.K.)		17·10

U.K. 66 pts., West Germany 40.

A.A.A./W.A.A.A. Indoor Championships

Held at Cosford, February 3–4, 1989

Men's Events

Metres	min.	sec.
60—L. Christie (T.V.H.)		6·55
200—L. Christie (T.V.H.)		20·95
400—P. Brown (Birchfield)		47·64
800—D. Sharpe (Jarrow)	1	51·32
1,500—A. Geddes (Crewe)	3	47·39
3,000—P. Larkins (Wolverhampton)	7	58·84
60 *Hurdles*—C. Jackson (Cardiff)		7·52
		metres
High Jump—N. Saunders (Bermuda)		2·30
Pole Vault—A. Ashurst (Sale)		5·20
Long Jump—B. Williams (Wolverhampton)		7·88
Triple Jump—F. Agyepong (Shaftesbury)		16·17
Shot—M. Simson (Thurrock)		18·21

Women's Events

Metres	min.	sec.
60—P. Dunn (Stretford)		7·28
200—G. Jackson (Jamaica)		23·37
400—M. Ottey (Jamaica)		52·20
800—M. Kitson (Hounslow)	2	05·45
1,500—K. Hutcheson (Berry Hill)	4	14·98
3,000—N. Morris (Essex)	9	05·73
60 *Hurdles*—L.-A. Skeete (Swindon)		8·15
		metres
High Jump—S. Hutchings (Ballymena)		1·82
Long Jump—N. Boegman (Australia)		6·51
Shot—M. Augee (Bromley)		17·40

National Cross-Country Championships (Women)

Held at Birmingham, February 18, 1989

Senior Race (5,800 m)	min.	sec.
1. A. Paine (Leeds)	23	58
2. S. Ellis (Birchfield)	24	10
3. C. Kennedy (Parkside)	24	23
Team result:		
1. Parkside		56 pts.
2. Birchfield		59 pts.
3. Westbury		126 pts.
Intermediate Race (4,500 m)	min.	sec.
1. L. Watson (G.E.C.)	19	02
2. G. Stacey (Bromsgrove)	19	21
3. R. Ellway (Leicester)	19	31
Team result:		
1. Leicester Coritanians		107 pts.
2. Oldham and Royton		165 pts.
3. Stoke		184 pts.
Girls Race (3,800 m)	min.	sec.
1. C. Maycock (Rockingham)	17	04
2. C. Allen (Leicester)	17	05
3. P. Radcliffe (Bedford City)	17	12
Team result:		
1. Bedford City		56 pts.
2. Darlington		112 pts.
3. Bristol		121 pts.

Minor Girls Race (2,500 m)	min.	sec.
1. A. Foster (Morpeth)	16	15
2. N. Payne (Andover)	16	28
3. L. White (Exeter)	16	35

Team result:
1. Morpeth .... 74 pts.
2. Bolton .... 81 pts.
3. Bedford .... 123 pts.

European Indoor Championships

Held at The Hague, February 18–19, 1989

Men's Events

Metres	min.	sec.
60—A. Berger (Austria)		6·56
200—A. Mafe (U.K.)		20·92
400—C. Cornet (France)		46·21
800—S. Heard (U.K.)	1	48·84
1,500—H. Phelippeau (France)	3	47·42
3,000—D. Baumann (F.R.G.)	7	50·43
60 *Hurdles*—C. Jackson (U.K.)		7·59
5,000 *Walk*—M. Shchennikov (U.S.S.R.)	18	35·60

	metres
High Jump—D. Mögenburg (F.R.G.)	2·33
Pole Vault—G. Yegorov (U.S.S.R.)	5·75
Long Jump—E. Mellaard (Netherlands)	8·14
Triple Jump—M. Musiyenko (U.S.S.R.)	17·29
Shot—U. Timmermann (G.D.R.)	21·68

Women's Events

Metres	min.	sec.
60—N. Cooman (Netherlands)		7·15
200—M.-J. Perec (France)		23·31
400—S. Gunnell (U.K.)		52·04
800—D. Melinte (Romania)	1	59·89
1,500—P. Ivan (Romania)	4	07·16
3,000—E. van Hulst (Netherlands)	9	10·01
60 *Hurdles*—Y. Donkova (Bulgaria)		7·87
3,000 *Walk*—B. Anders (G.D.R.)	12	21·91

	metres
High Jump—G. Astafei (Romania)	1·96
Long Jump—G. Chistiakova (U.S.S.R.)	6·98
Shot—S. Storp (F.R.G.)	20·30

National Cross-Country Championships (Men)

Held at Cheam, February 25, 1989

Senior Race (9 miles)	min.	sec.
1. D. Lewis (Rossendale)	44	26
2. S. Tunstall (Preston H.)	44	47
3. D. McNeilly (Bristol)	44	51

Team result:
1. Tipton .... 278 pts.
2. Wolverhampton and Bilston ... 293 pts.
3. Coventry Godiva .... 325 pts.

Junior Race (6 miles)	min.	sec.
1. S. Brooks (Bingley)	29	51
2. J. Dennis (Crawley)	30	19
3. D. Mead (Belgrave)	30	22

Team result:
1. Bingley .... 85 pts.
2. Aldershot, Farnham and District .... 124 pts.
3. Sale .... 196 pts.

Youth Race (4 miles)	min.	sec.
1. J. Gascoyne (Harlow)	21	42
2. J. Godden (Shaftesbury Barnet)	21	45
3. P. Delany (Longwood)	22	02

Team result:
1. Warrington .... 124 pts.
2. Sale .... 128 pts.
3. Liverpool .... 153 pts.

World Indoor Championships

Held at Budapest, March 3–5, 1989

Men's Events

Metres	min.	sec.
60—A. Simon (Cuba)		6·52
200—J. Regis (U.K.)		20·54
400—A. McKay (U.S.A.)		45·59
800—P. Ereng (Kenya)	1	44·84
1,500—M. O'Sullivan (Ireland)	3	36·64
3,000—S. Aouita (Morocco)	7	47·94
60 *Hurdles*—A. Kingdom (U.S.A.)		7·43
5,000 *Walk*—M. Shchennikov (U.S.S.R.)	18	27·10

	metres
High Jump—J. Sotomayor (Cuba)	2·43
Pole Vault—R. Gataullin (U.S.S.R.)	5·85
Long Jump—L. Myricks (U.S.A.)	8·37
Triple Jump—M. Conley (U.S.A.)	17·65
Shot—U. Timmermann (G.D.R.)	21·75

Women's Events

Metres	min.	sec.
60—N. Cooman (Netherlands)		7·05
200—M. Ottey (Jamaica)		22·34
400—H. Arendt (F.R.G.)		51·52
800—C. Wachtel (G.D.R.)	1	59·24
1,500—D. Melinte (Romania)	4	04·79
3,000—E. van Hulst (Netherlands)	8	33·82
60 *Hurdles*—E. Chernyshova (U.S.S.R.)		7·82
3,000 *Walk*—K. Saxby (Australia)	12	01·65

	metres
High Jump—S. Kostadinova (Bulgaria)	2·02
Long Jump—G. Chistiakova (U.S.S.R.)	6·98
Shot—C. Losch (F.R.G.)	20·45

United Kingdom v. U.S.A. v. U.S.S.R. (Indoors)

Held at Glasgow, March 10, 1989

Men's Events

Metres	min.	sec.
60—M. Rosswess (U.K.)		6·57
200—J. Regis (U.K.)		20·99
400—M. Rowe (U.S.A.)		46·85
800—A. Sudnik (U.S.S.R.)	1	47·05
1,500—S. Crabb (U.K.)	3	39·55
3,000—D. Padilla (U.S.A.)	8	01·22
60 *Hurdles*—C. Jackson (U.K.)		7·44
5,000 *Walk*—B. Kostilkevich (U.S.S.R.)	19	39·14
4 × 400 *Relay*—U.S.A.	3	05·21

	metres
High Jump—A. Yemilin (U.S.S.R.)	2·32
Pole Vault—I. Potapovich (U.S.S.R.)	5·65
Long Jump—P. Johnson (U.K.)	7·94
Triple Jump—K. Harrison (U.S.A.)	16·85
Shot—V. Lykho (U.S.S.R.)	20·72
35lb Weight—Y. Sedykh (U.S.S.R.)	23·12

U.K. 107 pts., U.S.A. 105, U.S.S.R. 104.

R.W.A. National 10 Mile Walk

Held at Redditch, March 11, 1989

| min. | sec.
---|---|---
1. I. McCombie (Cambridge H.) | 65 | 39
2. S. Martingdale (York Postal) | 67 | 25
3. M. Bell (Splott) | 67 | 55

Team result: Splott 26 pts.

Women's National 10 km. Walk

Held at Redditch, March 11, 1989

| min. | sec.
---|---|---
1. B. Sworowski (Sheffield) | 45 | 30
2. L. Langford (Wolverhampton) | 45 | 55

3. H. Elliker (Sheffield) 48 23
Team result: Sheffield 18 pts.

I.A.A.F. Cross-Country Championships

Held at Stavanger, March 19, 1989

Men's Race (12,000 m)		min.	sec.
1.	J. Ngugi (Kenya)	39	42
2.	T. Hutchings (G.B.)	40	10
3.	W. Kirochi (Kenya)	40	21

Team result:
1. Kenya (1, 3, 7, 8, 9, 16) .... 44pts.
2. Great Britain (2, 14, 15, 22, 45, 49) 147 pts.
3. Ethiopia (5, 13, 27, 33, 37, 47) .... 162 pts.

Women's Race (6,000 m)		min.	sec.
1.	A. Sergent (France)	22	27
2.	N. Stepanova (U.S.S.R.)	22	34
3.	L. Williams (Canada)	22	41

Team result:
1. U.S.S.R. (2, 9, 20, 27) .... 58 pts.
2. France (1, 10, 17, 32) .... 60 pts.
3. U.S.A. (6, 16, 21, 25) .... 68 pts.

Junior Men's Race (8,000 m)		min.	sec.
1.	A. Abebe (Ethiopia)	25	07
2.	K. Koriria (Kenya)	25	31
3.	S. Nyamu (Kenya)	25	33

Team result:
1. Kenya (2, 3, 4, 5) .... 14 pts.
2. Ethiopia (1, 6, 7, 8) .... 22 pts.
3. Italy (9, 17, 23, 27) .... 76 pts.

Junior Women's Race (4,000 m)		min.	sec.
1.	M. Ewerlof (Sweden)	15	23
2.	O. Nazarkina (U.S.S.R.)	15	30
3.	E. Saina (Kenya)	15	41

Team result:
1. Kenya (3, 4, 5, 28) .... 40 pts.
2. U.S.S.R. (2, 18, 21, 27) .... 68 pts.
3. Portugal (8, 17, 20, 39) .... 84 pts.

London Marathon

Held at London, April 23, 1989

Men		hr.	min.	sec.
1.	D. Wakiihuri (Kenya)	2	09	03
2.	S. Moneghetti (Australia) ..	2	09	06
3.	A. Salah (Djibouti)	2	09	09

Women		hr.	min.	sec.
1.	V. Marot (U.K.)..........	2	25	56
2.	W. Panfil (Poland)	2	27	05
3.	A. Cunha (Portugal)	2	28	11

R.W.A. National 20 km. Walk

Held at Leicester, May 13, 1989

		hr.	min.	sec.
1.	A. Drake (Coventry)	1	26	55
2.	S. Martingale (York Postal)..	1	28	15
3.	L. Morton (Sheffield)	1	29	53

Team result: Coventry.

United Kingdom Championships

Held at Jarrow, June 3–4, 1989

Men's Events

Metres	min.	sec.
100—M. Adam (Belgrave)		10·31
200—M. Adam (Belgrave)		20·37
400—P. Sanders (Team Solent)........		47·02
800—N. Smith (Shaftesbury Barnet) ..	1	48·08
1,500—S. Crabb (Enfield)	3	42·65
3,000—D. Moorcroft (Coventry).......	7	50·76
5,000—S. Cram (Jarrow)	13	28·58

	min.	sec.
3,000 *Steeplechase*—N. Smart (St. Helens).........................	8	41·13
110 *Hurdles*—C. Jackson (Cardiff)		13·18
400 *Hurdles*—M. Robertson (Wolverhampton)		50·50
10,000 *Walk*—I. McCombie (Cambridge H.)..............................	40	06·65

		metres
High Jump—S. Chapman (T.V.H.)		2·20
Pole Vault—M. Edwards (Belgrave) ...		5·10
Long Jump—M. Forsythe (Ballymena)		8·05
Triple Jump—J. Edwards (Gateshead).		16·54
Shot—P. Edwards (Walton)		17·89
Discus—G. Savory (Blackheath)		55·90
Hammer—P. Head (Newham).......		70·28
Javelin—S. Backley (Cambridge H.) ...		81·40

Women's Events

Metres	min.	sec.
100—S. Douglas (Milton Keynes)......		11·61
200—J. Stoute (Essex Ladies)		23·32
400—L. Keough (Basingstoke)		52·37
800—A. Williams (Sale)	2	02·06
1,500—L. MacIntyre (Glasgow)	4	11·31
3,000—E. McColgan (Dundee)	8	51·55
100 *Hurdles*—K. Morley (Cardiff)		13·15
400 *Hurdles*—E. McLaughlin (Edinburgh)		57·03
5,000 *Walk*—L. Langford (Wolverhampton)	22	39·43

		metres
High Jump—J. Boyle (Belfast)		1·83
Long Jump—F. May (Derby)		6·98
Shot—J. Oakes (Croydon)		18·59
Discus—J. McKernan (Lisburn)		54·40
Javelin—S. Gibson (Notts A.C.).......		54·60

R.W.A. National 35 km. Walk

Held at Colchester, June 10, 1989

		hr.	min.	sec.
1.	D. Stone (Steyning)	2	50	49
2.	M. Smith (Croydon)	2	56	28
3.	R. Dobson (Ilford)	3	04	35

Team result: Steyning 42 pts.

United Kingdom v. Hungary v. International Select

Held at Portsmouth, June 11, 1989

Men's Events

Metres	min.	sec.
100—D. Mitchell (U.S.A.)		10·25
200—J. Regis (U.K.)		20·79
400—D. Clark (I.S./Australia)		45·68
800—P. Ereng (I.S./Kenya)	1	45·56
1,500—K. Cherviyot (I.S./Kenya)	3	39·99
3,000—Y. Ondieki (I.S./Kenya)	7	42·19
3,000 *Steeplechase*—P. Koech (I.S./Kenya)	8	24·59
110 *Hurdles*—C. Jackson (U.K.).......		13·36
400 *Hurdles*—W. Graham (I.S./Jamaica)		49·02
4 × 100 *Relay*—United Kingdom		39·94
4 × 200 *Relay*—International Select (U.S.A.)	1	20·85

		metres
High Jump—N. Saunders (I.S./Bermuda)		2·31
Pole Vault—M. Edwards (U.K.)		5·10
Long Jump—M. Forsythe (U.K.)		8·17
Triple Jump—V. Samuels (U.K.)		16·61
Shot—J. Koczlan (Hungary)		18·53
Discus—A. Horvath (Hungary)		63·44

Hammer—T. Gecsek (Hungary)		73·66
Javelin—M. Hill (U.K.)		77·50

I.S. 149 pts., U.K. 143, Hungary 99.

Women's Events

Metres	min.	sec.
100—G. Jackson (I.S./Jamaica)		11·63
200—G. Jackson (I.S./Jamaica)		23·10
400—L. Keough (U.K.)		52·28
800—L. MacIntyre (U.K.)	2	05·08
1,500—Y. Murray (U.K.)	4	19·03
3,000—Z. Agoston (Hungary)	9	00·22
100 *Hurdles*—K. Morley (U.K.)		13·39
400 *Hurdles*—E. McLaughlin (U.K.)		57·63
4 × 100 *Relay*—United Kingdom		44·24
4 × 400 *Relay*—United Kingdom	3	33·93
		metres
High Jump—J. Bennett (I.S./U.K.)		1·84
Long Jump—N. Boegman (I.S./ Australia)		6·82
Shot—J. Oakes (U.K.)		19·01
Discus—A. Herczeg (Hungary)		57·16
Javelin—Z. Malovecz (Hungary)		63·32

U.K. 137 pts., I.S. 95, Hungary 74.

United Kingdom v. U.S.A. v. U.S.S.R. v. West Germany

Held at Birmingham, June 23–24, 1989

Men's Events

Metres	min.	sec.
60—L. Christie (U.K.)		10·08
200—J. Regis (U.K.)		20·65
400—T. Simon (U.S.A.)		45·54
800—T. McKean (U.K.)	1	48·10
1,500—S. Cram (U.K.)	3	35·41
3,000—T. Hacker (U.S.A.)	7	50·30
5,000—K. Brantley (U.S.A.)	13	55·37
3,000 *Steeplechase*—B. Diemer (U.S.A.)	8	29·45
110 *Hurdles*—C. Jackson (U.K.)		12·99
400 *Hurdles*—D. Patrick (U.S.A.)		49·27
4 × 100 *Relay*—U.S.A.		38·84
4 × 400 *Relay*—U.S.A.	3	02·69
10,000 *Walk*—M. Shennikov (U.S.S.R.)	40	10·92
		metres
High Jump—D. Grant (U.K.)		2·24
Pole Vault—G. Yegorov (U.S.S.R.)		5·65
Long Jump—M. Powell (U.S.A.)		8·39
Triple Jump—N. Musiyenko (U.S.S.R.)		17·15
Shot—M. Stulce (U.S.A.)		20·08
Discus—W. Schmidt (F.R.G.)		67·64
Hammer—C. Sahner (F.R.G.)		78·36
Javelin—S. Backley (U.K.)		84·20

U.S.A. 216 pts., U.K. 191, U.S.S.R. 172, West Germany 152.

Women's Events

Metres	min.	sec.
100—E. Jones (U.S.A.)		11·20
200—M. Markina (U.S.S.R.)		23·20
400—L. Keough (U.K.)		51·98
800—J. Clark (U.S.A.)	2	02·08
1,500—L. Kremleva (U.S.S.R.)	4	13·58
3,000—P.-S. Plummer (U.S.A.)	8	53·20
100 *Hurdles*—L. Narozhilenko (U.S.S.R.)		12·80
400 *Hurdles*—S. Gunnell (U.K.)		56·09
4 × 100 *Relay*—U.S.A.		43·07
4 × 400 *Relay*—U.S.A.	3	26·40
5,000 *Walk*—N. Serbinenko (U.S.S.R.)	21	39·59
		metres
High Jump—J. Wohlschlag (U.S.A.)		1·95
Long Jump—G. Chistiakova (U.S.S.R.)		7·27
Shot—I. Plotzitzka (F.R.G.)		19·94

Discus—D. Galler (F.R.G.)		59·44
Javelin—N. Shikolenko (U.S.S.R.)		65·96

U.S.S.R. 170 pts., U.S.A. 160, U.K. 119, West Germany 99.

R.W.A. National 50 km. Walk

Held at Hove Park, Brighton, July 8, 1989

	hr.	min.	sec.
1. L. Morton (Sheffield)	4	21	19
2. M. Smith (Coventry)	4	27	19
3. C. Berwick (Leicester)	4	32	04

Team result: Sheffield 42 pts.

United Kingdom v. Kenya (Track only)

Held at Crystal Palace, July 28, 1989

Men's Events

Metres	min.	sec.
100—L. Christie (U.K.)		10·26
200—M. Adam (U.K.)		20·64
400—S. Kipkemboi (Kenya)		45·42
800—T. McKean (U.K.)	1	43·88
Mile—J. Chesire (Kenya)	3	54·80
3,000—Y. Ondieki (Kenya)	7	36·72
5,000—J. Ngugi (Kenya)	13	17·72
3,000 *Steeplechase*—P. Sang (Kenya)	8	23·67
110 *Hurdles*—C. Jackson (U.K.)		13·20
400 *Hurdles*—M. Robertson (U.K.)		49·59
4 × 100 *Relay*—United Kingdom		39·66
4 × 400 *Relay*—Kenya	3	05·26

United Kingdom 125 pts., Kenya 108 pts.

United Kingdom v. West Germany (Women) (Field only)

Held at Crystal Palace, July 28, 1989

	metres
High Jump—M. Goldkamp (F.R.G.)	1·89
Long Jump—K. Hagger (U.K.)	6·43
Shot—J. Oakes (U.K.)	18·78
Discus—J. McKernan (U.K.)	54·60
Javelin—T. Sanderson (U.K.)	61·34

United Kingdom 30 pts., West Germany 25 pts.

European Cup

Held at Gateshead, August 5–6, 1989

Men's Events

Metres	min.	sec.
100—L. Christie (U.K.)		10·33
200—J. Regis (U.K.)		20·62
400—E. Itt (F.R.G.)		45·43
800—T. McKean (U.K.)	1	46·94
1,500—P. Thiebaut (France)	3	48·05
5,000—S. Antibo (Italy)	13	43·84
10,000—F. Panetta (Italy)	28	27·02
3,000 *Steeplechase*—A. Lambruschini (Italy)	8	34·06
110 *Hurdles*—C. Jackson (U.K.)		13·56
400 *Hurdles*—K. Akabusi (U.K.)		48·95
4 × 100 *Relay*—United Kingdom		38·39
4 × 400 *Relay*—United Kingdom	3	03·16
		metres
High Jump—D. Grant (U.K.)		2·32
Pole Vault—R. Gataullin (U.S.S.R.)		5·70
Long Jump—V. Ratushkov (U.S.S.R.)		8·09
Triple Jump—O. Sakirkin (U.S.S.R.)		17·18
Shot—U. Timmermann (G.D.R.)		21·72
Discus—J. Schult (G.D.R.)		66·54

Hammer—H. Weis (F.R.G.) .... 79·86
Javelin—S. Backley (U.K.) .... 82·92

U.K. 115 pts., East Germany 103, U.S.S.R. 101, Italy 95, France 95, West Germany 91, Czechoslovakia 63, Spain 54.

Women's Events

Metres	min.	sec.
100—K. Krabbe (G.D.R.)		11·14
200—S. Möller (G.D.R.)		23·00
400—G. Breuer (G.D.R.)..............		50·52
800—D. Melinte (Romania)	1	58·04
1,500—D. Melinte (Romania)	4	05·83
3,000—P. Ivan (Romania)	8	38·48
10,000—K. Ullrich (G.D.R.)	32	17·88
100 *Hurdles*—C. Oschkenat (G.D.R.)...		12·74
400 *Hurdles*—P. Krug (G.D.R.)........		54·72
4 × 100 *Relay*—G.D.R.		41·87
4 × 400 *Relay*—G.D.R.	3	24·08

	metres
High Jump—G. Astafei (Romania)	2·00
Long Jump—G. Chistiakova (U.S.S.R.)	7·10
Shot—H. Hartwig (G.D.R.)	20·59
Discus—I. Wyludda (G.D.R.)	73·04
Javelin—P. Felke (G.D.R.).............	66·92

East Germany 120 pts., U.S.S.R. 95, U.K. 84, West Germany 79, Romania 72, Poland 56, Bulgaria 43, Czechoslovakia 26.

A.A.A./W.A.A.A. Championships

Held at Birmingham, August 11–13, 1989

Men's Events

Metres	min.	sec.
100—L. Christie (T.V.H.)..............		10·16
200—M. Adam (Belgrave)		20·78
400—P. Brown (Birchfield)		46·26
800—I. Billy (Wirral)	1	48·01
1,500—S. Coe (Haringey)	3	41·38
3,000—M. Giusto (U.S.A.)	8	00·38
5,000—M. Rowland (Phoenix)	13	32·05
3,000 *Steeplechase*—C. Walker (Gateshead)................	8	35·73
110 *Hurdles*—C. Jackson (Cardiff).....		13·19
400 *Hurdles*—M. Robertson (Wolverhampton)		50·30
10 km *Walk*—M. Easton (Sussex)......	41	39·93

Held at Birmingham June 23, 1989

	min.	sec.
10,000m—E. Martin (Basildon)	28	13·69

	metres
High Jump—D. Grant (Haringey)	2·33
Pole Vault—M. Edwards (Aldershot) ..	5·20
Long Jump—S. Faulkner (Birchfield) .	8·13
Triple Jump—J. Edwards (Gateshead) .	16·53
Shot—S. Williams (Enfield)...........	18·73
Discus—P. Mardle (Wolverhampton)..	57·90
Hammer—J. Logan (U.S.A.)	72·34
Javelin—S. Backley (Cambridge H.) ...	83·16

Women's Events

Metres	min.	sec.
100—P. Dunn (Stretford).............		11·32
200—P. Dunn (Stretford).............		23·43
400—L. Keough (Basingstoke)		51·09
800—D. Edwards (Sale)	2	01·24
1,500—B. Nicholson (Sale)............	4	09·34
3,000—A. Wyeth (Parkside)	9	11·12
5,000 *Walk*—B. Sworowski (Sheffield)..	22	30·59
100 *Hurdles*—S. Gunnell (Essex Ladies)		13·26
400 *Hurdles*—W. Cearns (Essex Ladies)		56·05

	metres
High Jump—D. Davies (Leicester)	1·85
Long Jump—N. Boegman (Australia) .	6·74
Shot—M. Augee (Bromley)	17·51
Discus—J. Picton (Bracknell)	53·22
Javelin—T. Sanderson (Hounslow)....	58·64

Held at Stoke, July 30, 1989

	min.	sec.
5,000m—S. Crehan (Sale).............	16	18·55

World Cup

Held at Barcelona, Spain, Sept. 8–10, 1989

Men's Events

Metres	hr.	min.	sec.
100—L. Christie (G.B.)			10·10
200—R. Da Silva (Americas) ..			20·00
400—R. Hernandez (Americas)			44·58
800—T. McKean (G.B.)		1	44·95
1,500—A. Bile (Africa)		3	35·56
5,000—S. Aouita (Africa).....		13	23·14
10,000—S. Antibo (Europe) ...		28	05·26
3,000 *Steeplechase*—J. Kariuki (Africa)		8	20·84
110 *Hurdles*—R. Kingdom (U.S.A.)			12·87
400 *Hurdles*—D. Patrick (U.S.A.)			48·74
4 × 100 *Relay*—U.S.A.			38·29
4 × 400 *Relay*—Americas		3	00·65

	metres
High Jump—P. Sjöberg (Europe)..................	2·34
Pole Vault—P. Collet (Europe)	5·75
Long Jump—L. Myricks (U.S.A.)	8·29
Triple Jump—M. Conley (U.S.A.)	17·49
Shot—U. Timmermann (G.D.R.)	21·68
Discus—J. Schult (G.D.R.) ...	67·12
Hammer—H. Weis (Europe) ...	77·68
Javelin—S. Backley (G.B.) ...	85·90

U.S.A. 133 pts., Europe 127, Great Britain 119, German Democratic Republic 116½, Africa 107, Americas 97, Asia 68½, Spain 64½, Oceania 64½.

Women's Events

Metres	hr.	min.	sec.
100—S. Echols (U.S.A.).......			11·18
200—S. Moeller (G.D.R.)			22·46
400—A. Quirot (Americas) ...			50·60
800—A. Quirot (Americas) ...		1	55·44
1,500—P. Ivan (Europe)		4	18·60
3,000—Y. Murray (Europe) ...		8	44·32
10,000—K. Ullrich (G.D.R.) ...		31	33·92
100 *Hurdles*—C. Oschkenat (G.D.R.)			12·60
400 *Hurdles*—S. Farmer-Patrick (U.S.A.)..........			53·84
4 × 100 *Relay*—G. D. R.			42·21
4 × 100 *Relay*—Americas		3	23·05

	metres
High Jump—S. Costa (Americas)	2·04
Long Jump—G. Chistiakova (U.S.S.R.)................	7·10
Shot—Z. Huang (Asia)	20·73
Discus—I. Wyludda (G.D.R.) .	71·54
Javelin—P. Felke (G.D.R.)....	70·32

German Democratic Republic 124 pts., U.S.S.R. 106, Americas 94, Europe 89, U.S.A. 84½, Asia 67½, Africa 58, Spain 48, Oceania 40.

BADMINTON, 1989

ENGLISH NATIONAL CHAMPIONSHIPS
(Crawley)

Men's Singles.—D Hall.
Women's Singles.—F. Smith.
Men's Doubles.—S. Baddeley and M. Dew.
Women's Doubles.—G. Clark and S. Sankey.
Mixed Doubles.—A. Goode and Mrs. G. Gilks.

ALL-ENGLAND CHAMPIONSHIPS
(Wembley)

Men's Singles.—Yang Yang (China).
Women's Singles.—Li Lingwei (China).
Men's Doubles.—Lee Sang Bok and Park Joo Bong (S. Korea).
Women's Doubles.—Chung Myung Hee and Chung So Young (S. Korea).
Mixed Doubles.—Park Joo Bong and Miss Chung Myung Hee (S. Korea).

BASKETBALL, 1988–9

MEN'S

National Cup, Bracknell Tigers.
Carlsberg League, Glasgow Rangers.
National Basketball League, Oldham.

WOMEN'S

National Cup, Avon Northampton.
National League, Avon Northampton.

BOWLS, 1988–89

NATIONAL CHAMPIONSHIPS
(Worthing)

Fours.—Final: Blackheath & Greenwich (Kent) beat Brush (Leics.), 17–16.
Triples.—Final: Southbourne (Sussex) beat Swindon (Wilts.), 20–18.
Pairs.—Final: Essex County (Essex) beat Newton Hall (Lancs.), 25–16.
Singles.—Final: J. M. Ottaway (Wymondham Dell, Norfolk) beat B. Croad (Ventnor, I.o.W.), 25–13.

World Indoor Championship, R. Corsie (Scotland).
World Indoor Pairs Championship.—D. Bryant and A. Allcock (England).
National Indoor Singles Championship, A. Thomson.
World Fours Champions.—Ireland.
World Singles Champion.—D. Bryant (England).
Inter-County Championship (Middleton Cup).—Final: Kent beat Lancashire, 117–107.

BOXING, 1988–89

AMATEUR BOXING ASSOCIATION
(A.B.A.) CHAMPIONSHIP WINNERS

Light-Fly (48 kg).—M. Cantwell; *Fly* (51 kg).—J. Lyon; *Bantam* (54 kg).—Sgt. K. Howlett; *Feather* (57 kg).—P. Richardson; *Light* (60 kg).—M. Ramsey; *Light-Welter* (63·5 kg).—A. Hall; *Welter* (67 kg).—M. Elliot; *Light-Middle* (71 kg).—N. Brown; *Middle* (75 kg).—S. Johnson; *Light-Heavy* (81 kg).—N. Piper; *Heavy* (91 kg).—H. Akinwande; *Super-Heavy* (91+ kg).—P. Passley.

PROFESSIONAL BOXING
(as at Aug. 15, 1989)

WORLD BOXING COUNCIL (W.B.C.) CHAMPIONS

Heavy.—M. Tyson (U.S.A.); *Cruiser.*—C. De Leon (Puerto Rico); *Light-Heavy.*—J. Harding (Australia); *Super-Middle.*—R. Leonard (U.S.A.); *Middle.*—R. Duran (U.S.A.); *Super-Welter.*—J. Mugabe (Uganda/U.S.A.); *Welter.*—M. Starling (U.S.A.); *Super-Light.*—J. C. Chavez (Mexico); *Light.*—J. C. Chavez (Mexico); *Super-Feather.*—A. Nelson (Ghana); *Feather.*—(vacant); *Super-Bantam.*—D. Zaragoza (Mexico); *Bantam.*—R. Perez (Mexico); *Super-Fly.*—G. Roman (Mexico); *Fly.*—Yongkang Kim (Korea); *Light-Fly.*—Yulwoo Lee (Korea); *Straw.*—N. Katwanchai (Thailand).

WORLD BOXING ASSOCIATION (W.B.A.) CHAMPIONS

Heavy.—M. Tyson (U.S.A.); *Cruiser.*—T. Belbouli (France); *Light-Heavy.*—V. Hill (U.S.A.); *Super-Middle.*—In-Chul Baek (Korea); *Middle.*—M. McCallum (Jamaica/U.S.A.); *Super-Welter.*—J. Jackson (Virgin Is.); *Welter.*—M. Breland (U.S.A.); *Super-Light.*—J. M. Coggi (Argentina); *Light.*—J. C. Chavez (Mexico); *Super-Feather.*—B. Mitchell (S. Africa); *Feather.*—A. Esparragoza (Venezuela); *Super-Bantam.*—J. Estrada (Mexico); *Bantam.*—K. Galaxy (Thailand); *Super-Fly.*—K. Galaxy (Thailand); *Fly.*—F. Bassa (Colombia); *Light-Fly.*—Yuh Myung Woo (Korea); *Straw.*—Bong-Jun Kim (Korea).

INTERNATIONAL BOXING FEDERATION (I.B.F.) CHAMPIONS

Heavy.—M. Tyson (U.S.A.); *Cruiser.*—G. McCrory (G.B.); *Light-Heavy.*—C. Williams (U.S.A.); *Super-Middle.*—G. Rocchigiani (W. Germany); *Middle.*—M. Nunn (U.S.A.); *Super-Welter.*—D. Van Horn (U.S.A.); *Welter.*—S. Brown (U.S.A.); *Super-Light.*—M. Taylor (U.S.A.); *Light.*—P. Whitaker (U.S.A.); *Super-Feather.*—T. Lopez (U.S.A.); *Feather.*—J. Paez (Mexico); *Super-Bantam.*—F. Benichou (Italy); *Bantam.*—O. Canizales (U.S.A.); *Super-Fly.*—E. Pical (Indonesia); *Fly.*—D. McAuley (G.B.); *Light-Fly.*—M. Kitikasem (Thailand); *Straw.*—N. Thomas (Indonesia).

WORLD BOXING ORGANIZATION (W.B.O.) CHAMPIONS

Heavy.—F. Damiani (Italy); *Cruiser.*—(vacant); *Light-Heavy.*—M. Moorer (U.S.A.); *Super-Middle.*—T. Hearns (U.S.A.); *Middle.*—D. De Witt (U.S.A.); *Super-Welter.*—J. Jackson (U.S.A.); *Welter.*—G. Leon (Mexico); *Super-Light.*—H. Comacho (Puerto Rico); *Light.*—M. Aceves (Mexico); *Super-Feather.*—J. J. Molina (Puerto Rico); *Feather.*—M. Stecca (Italy); *Super-Bantam.*—K. Mitchell (U.S.A.); *Bantam.*—I. Contreras (Venezuela); *Super-Fly.*—J. Ruiz (Puerto Rico); *Fly.*—E. Alvarez (Colombia); *Light-Fly.*—J. de Jesus (Puerto Rico); *Straw.*—(vacant).

BRITISH CHAMPIONS

Heavy.—G. Mason; *Cruiser.*—J. Nelson; *Light-Heavy.*—T. Collins; *Middle.*—H. Graham; *Light-Middle.*—G. Stretch; *Welter.*—K. Laing; *Light-Welter.*—P. Barratt; *Light.*—S. Boyle; *Super-Feather.*—F. Havard; *Feather.*—P. Hodkinson; *Bantam.*—B. Hardy; *Fly.*—P. Clinton.

COMMONWEALTH CHAMPIONS

COMMONWEALTH CHAMPIONS

Heavy.—D. Williams (G.B.); *Cruiser.*—A. Sweet (Australia); *Light-Heavy.*—G. Waters (Australia); *Middle.*—M. Watson (G.B.); *Light-Middle.*—T. Waters (Australia); *Welter.*—G. Jacobs (G.B.); *Light-Welter.*—L. Ellis (Australia); *Light.*—N. Daho (G.B.); *Super-Feather.*—J. Sichula (Zambia); *Feather.*—P. O. Commey (Ghana); *Bantam.*—R. Minus (Bahamas); *Fly.*—(vacant).

EUROPEAN CHAMPIONS

Heavy.—(vacant); *Cruiser.*—A. Rottoli (Italy); *Light-Heavy.*—J. Lefeber (Netherlands); *Middle.*—F. Del Aquila (Italy); *Light-Middle.*—(vacant); *Welter.*—N. La Roca (Italy); *Light-Welter.*—E. Calamati (Italy); *Light.*—P. Diaz (Spain); *Super-Feather.*—D. Londas (France); *Feather.*—P. Hodkinson (G.B.); *Bantam.*—V. Belcastro (Italy); *Fly.*—E. Can (Denmark).

CHESS, 1989

British Championship. M. Adams.
Ladies. R. Hamid (Bangladesh).
Under-18 (Men). M. Adams.
Under-18 (Women). C. Haslinger; J. Harwar; H. Heron.

CRICKET, 1988–89

TEST MATCHES

Pakistan v. Australia, 1988

First Test.—(Karachi, Sept. 17–20). Pakistan won by an innings and 188 runs. Pakistan 469 for 9 dec.; Australia 165 and 116.

Second Test.—(Faisalabad, Sept. 23–28). Drawn, Pakistan 316 and 378 for 9 dec.; Australia 321 and 67 for 3.

Third Test.—(Lahore, Oct. 8–11). Drawn. Australia 340 and 161 for 3 dec.; Pakistan 233 and 153 for 8.

India v. New Zealand, 1988

First Test.—(Bangalore, Nov. 12–17). India won by 172 runs. India 384 for 9 dec. and 141 for 1 dec.; New Zealand 189 and 164.

Second Test.—(Bombay, Nov. 24–29). New Zealand won by 136 runs. New Zealand 236 and 279; India 234 and 145.

Third Test.—(Hyderabad, Dec. 2–6). India won by ten wickets. New Zealand 254 and 124; India 358 and 20 for 0.

Australia v. West Indies, 1988–89

First Test.—(Brisbane, Nov. 18–21). West Indies won by nine wickets. Australia 167 and 289; West Indies 394 and 63 for 1.

Second Test.—(Perth, Dec. 2–6). West Indies won by 169 runs. West Indies 449 and 349 for 9 dec.; Australia 395 for 8 dec. and 234 for 9.

Third Test.—(Melbourne, Dec. 24–29). West Indies won by 285 runs. West Indies 280 and 361 for 9 dec.; Australia 242 and 114.

Fourth Test.—(Sydney, Jan. 26–30). Australia won by seven wickets. West Indies 224 and 256; Australia 401 and 82 for 3.

Fifth Test.—(Adelaide, Feb. 3–7). Drawn. Australia 515 and 224 for 4 dec.; West Indies 369 and 233 for 4.

New Zealand v. Pakistan, 1989

First Test.—(Dunedin, Feb. 3–7), (*Match abandoned*).

Second Test.—(Wellington, Feb. 10–4). Drawn. New Zealand 447 and 186 for 8; Pakistan 438 for 7 dec.

Third Test.—(Auckland, Feb. 24–28). Drawn. Pakistan 616 for 5 dec.; New Zealand 403 and 99 for 3.

West Indies v. India, 1989

First Test.—(Georgetown, March 25–30). Drawn. West Indies 437; India 86 for 1 (*Match abandoned*).

Second Test.—(Bridgetown, April 7–12). West Indies won by eight wickets. India 321 and 193 for 6; West Indies 377 and 196 for 2.

Third Test.—(Port of Spain, April 15–20). West Indies won by 217 runs. West Indies 314 and 266; India 150 and 213.

Fourth Test.—(Kingston, April 28–May 3). West Indies won by seven wickets. India 289 and 152; West Indies 384 and 60 for 3.

England v. Australia, 1989

First Test.—(Headingley, June 8–13). Australia won by 210 runs. Australia 601 for 7 dec. and 230 for 3 dec.; England 430 and 191.

Second Test.—(Lord's, June 22–27). Australia won by six wickets. England 286 and 359; Australia 528 and 119 for 4.

Third Test.—(Edgbaston, July 6–11). Drawn. Australia 424 and 158 for 2; England 242.

Fourth Test.—(Old Trafford, July 27–Aug. 1). Australia won by nine wickets. England 260 and 264; Australia 447 and 81 for 1.

Fifth Test.—(Trent Bridge, Aug. 10–15). Australia won by an innings and 180 runs. Australia 602 for 6 dec.; England 255 and 167.

Sixth Test.—(The Oval, Aug. 24–29). Drawn. Australia 468 and 219 for 4 dec.; England 285 and 143 for 5.

ONE-DAY INTERNATIONALS

England v. Australia, 1989
Texaco Trophy Series

Old Trafford, May 25.—England beat Australia by 95 runs. England 231 for 9; Australia 136 all out.

Trent Bridge, May 27.—Match tied. England 226 for 5. Australia 226 for 8.

Lord's, May 29.—Australia beat England by six wickets. England 278 for 7; Australia 279 for 4.

England won the Texaco Trophy having lost fewer wickets in the tied match.

World Series Cup

Final.—1st Match (Melbourne, Jan. 14). Australia beat West Indies by 2 runs. Australia 204 for 9; West Indies 202 for 9.

2nd Match (Sydney, Jan. 16). West Indies beat Australia by 92 runs. West Indies 277 for 9; Australia 185.

3rd Match (Sydney, Jan. 18). West Indies won on a faster scoring rate. Australia 226 for 4; West Indies 111 for 2.

England v. Australia, 1989 (Averages)

ENGLAND BATTING

Batsmen	I	NO	R	HS	Av.
A. J. Lamb	2	0	129	125	64·50
R. A. Smith	10	1	553	143	61·44
G. C. Small	1	0	59	59	59·00
R. C. Russell	11	3	314	128*	39·25
E. E. Hemmings	2	0	73	38	36·50
D. I. Gower	11	0	383	106	34·81
J. E. Emburey	5	1	131	64	32·75
K. J. Barnett	5	0	141	80	28·20
N. G. B. Cook	5	3	45	31	22·50
P. J. Newport	2	0	44	26	22·00
G. R. Dilley	3	1	42	24*	21·00
B. C. Broad	4	0	82	37	20·50
G. A. Gooch	9	0	183	68	20·33
M. A. Atherton	4	0	73	47	18·25
J. P. Stephenson	2	0	36	25	18·00
N. A. Foster	6	2	68	39	17·00
I. T. Botham	4	0	62	46	15·50
T. S. Curtis	5	0	71	41	14·20
P. A. J. DeFreitas	2	0	22	21	11·00
M. W. Gatting	2	0	22	22	11·00
P. W. Jarvis	3	0	33	22	11·00
D. R. Pringle	3	0	33	27	11·00
D. J. Capel	2	0	21	17	10·50
A. R. C. Fraser	5	0	47	29	9·40
M. D. Moxon	2	0	18	18	9·00
D. E. Malcolm	2	0	14	9	7·00
R. T. Robinson	2	0	12	12	6·00
C. J. Tavaré	1	0	2	2	2·00
A. P. Igglesden	1	1	2	2	—

*Not Out.

BOWLING

Bowlers	O	M	R	W	Av.
N. A. Foster	154·0	42	421	12	35·08
A. R. C. Fraser	144·4	30	323	9	35·88
J. E. Emburey	152·0	37	342	8	42·75
A. P. Igglesden	37·0	3	146	3	48·66
G. C. Small	60·0	12	198	4	49·50
D. J. Capel	24·0	2	101	2	50·50
N. G. B. Cook	103·5	23	282	5	56·40
D. R. Pringle	86·2	12	306	5	61·20
G. R. Dilley	85·0	12	318	5	63·60
P. A. J. DeFreitas	63·3	10	216	3	72·00
G. A. Gooch	29·0	8	72	1	72·00
I. T. Botham	80·0	15	241	3	80·33
P. J. Newport	44·0	7	175	2	87·50
P. W. Jarvis	69·0	2	290	2	145·00
D. E. Malcolm	44·0	2	166	1	166·00

Also bowled: E. E. Hemmings, 33-9-81-0; M. A. Atherton, 8-0-34-0; K. J. Barnett, 6-0-32-0; T. S. Curtis, 3-0-7-0.

AUSTRALIAN BATTING

Batsmen	I	NO	R	HS	Av.
S. R. Waugh	8	4	506	177*	126·50
M. A. Taylor	11	1	839	219	83·90
A. R. Border	9	3	442	80	73·66
D. M. Jones	9	1	566	157	70·75
D. C. Boon	11	3	442	94	55·25
T. V. Hohns	5	1	127	40	31·75
G. R. Marsh	11	0	347	138	31·54
G. F. Lawson	5	1	115	74	28·75
M. G. Hughes	5	0	127	71	25·40
T. M. Alderman	4	3	20	8	20·00
I. A. Healy	7	1	103	44	17·16

Did not bat, G. D. Campbell.
*Not Out.

BOWLING

Bowlers	O	M	R	W	Av.
T. M. Alderman	269·2	68	712	41	17·36
G. F. Lawson	277·1	76	791	29	27·27
T. V. Hohns	134·0	53	300	11	27·27
M. G. Hughes	189·2	41	615	19	32·36
S. R. Waugh	57·0	15	208	2	104·00
G. D. Campbell	24·0	0	124	1	124·00
A. R. Border	24·0	9	44	0	—

County Championship Table, 1989

Order for 1988 in brackets	Played	Won	Lost	Drawn	Bonus Btg.	Bonus Blng.	Points
Worcestershire (1)	22	12	3	7	44	83	319
Essex (3)*	22	13	2	7	59	71	313
Middlesex (7)	22	9	2	11	50	72	266
Lancashire (9)	22	8	5	9	57	65	250
Northamptonshire (12)	22	7	8	7	47	63	222
Hampshire (15)	22	6	8	8	55	65	216
Derbyshire (14)	22	6	6	10	45	75	216
Warwickshire (6)†	22	5	4	13	44	75	207
Gloucestershire (10)	22	6	11	5	38	70	204
Sussex (16)	22	4	4	14	60	68	192
Nottinghamshire (5)*	22	6	6	10	54	65	190
Surrey (4)	22	4	7	11	50	69	183
Leicestershire (8)	22	4	8	10	43	74	181
Somerset (11)	22	4	6	12	50	54	168
Kent (2)	22	3	8	11	53	53	154
Yorkshire (13)	22	3	9	10	41	60	149
Glamorgan (17)	22	3	6	13	38	59	145

* Essex and Nottinghamshire had 25 pts deducted for substandard pitches.

† Warwickshire's total includes 8 pts for a drawn game where the scores were level.

Other Results, 1989

NatWest Trophy.—Warwickshire beat Middlesex by four wickets. Middlesex 210 for 5; Warwickshire 211 for 6.

Benson and Hedges Cup Final.—Nottinghamshire beat Essex by three wickets. Essex 243 for 7; Nottinghamshire 244 for 7.

Refuge Assurance Sunday League Champions.—Lancashire.

Refuge Assurance Cup.—Essex beat Nottinghamshire by five runs. Essex 160 for 5; Nottinghamshire 155 all out.

Universities.—Match abandoned. Cambridge Univ. 340 for 8 dec. and 62 for 2; Oxford Univ. 192 for 9 dec.

Village Cricket Final.—Toft (Cheshire) beat Hambledon (Hants.) by six wickets. Hambledon 104; Toft 105 for 4.

National Club Championship.—Teddington beat Old Hill by 11 runs. Teddington 167 for 7; Old Hill 156.

BATTING AND BOWLING AVERAGES

First Class Batting Averages, 1989

Batsmen	I	NO	R	HS	Av.
†D. M. Jones	20	3	1,510	248	88·82
†S. R. Waugh	24	8	1,030	177*	64·37
S. J. Cook	41	4	2,241	156	60·56
R. A. Smith	29	2	1,577	182	58·40
K. R. Brown	12	3	522	91	58·00
†M. A. Taylor	30	1	1,669	219	57·55
G. A. Hick	38	6	1,824	173*	57·00
†D. C. Boon	28	5	1,306	151	56·78
M. W. Gatting	33	6	1,503	158*	55·66
M. A. Lynch	9	2	383	172*	54·71
†A. R. Border	22	4	979	135	54·38
M. R. Benson	29	5	1,299	157	54·12
R. F. Pienaar	29	4	1,321	134*	52·84
A. P. Wells	38	7	1,629	153	52·54
A. J. Lamb	15	1	733	171	52·35
I. J. F. Hutchinson	18	3	731	201*	48·73
N. Hussain	24	3	990	141	47·14
A. R. Butcher	40	5	1,632	171*	46·62
R. J. Shastri	27	5	1,004	127	45·63
G. P. Thorpe	30	5	1,132	154	45·28
D. L. Haynes	37	5	1,446	206*	45·18
D. M. Smith	35	6	1,305	184	45·00
D. A. Reeve	17	4	581	97*	44·69
A. J. Stewart	42	5	1,637	206*	44·24
G. D. Mendis	34	3	1,367	118	44·09

† Includes Australian tourists.
* Not Out.

First Class Bowling Averages, 1989

Bowlers	O	M	R	W	Av.
D. A. Reeve	97·4	35	163	11	14·81
†T. M. Alderman	410·2	103	1,095	70	15·64
A. A. Donald	537·1	122	1,398	86	16·25
M. D. Marshall	428·3	115	1,067	64	16·67
S. R. Lampitt	219·5	56	526	31	16·96
Wasim Akram	467·1	102	1,117	63	17·73
W. K. M. Benjamin	484·1	145	1,238	69	17·94
D. R. Pringle	668·2	163	1,753	94	18·64
F. D. Stephenson	589·4	135	1,727	92	18·77
S. M. McEwan	368·3	82	999	52	19·21
R. M. Ellcock	182·1	36	615	32	19·21
G. J. F. Ferris	124·1	39	327	17	19·23
B. P. Patterson	210·3	43	618	32	19·31
G. A. Hick	214·4	65	519	26	19·96
A. R. C. Fraser	797·1	203	1,861	92	20·22
O. H. Mortensen	334·4	64	878	43	20·41
C. A. Walsh	627·4	134	1,675	81	20·67
†G. F. Lawson	522·3	140	1,447	69	20·97
C. A. Connor	443·2	98	1,255	59	21·27
N. G. Cowans	492·3	117	1,321	62	21·30
S. P. Hughes	463·1	120	1,242	58	21·41
N. A. Foster	713·2	186	1,836	85	21·60
N. G. B. Cook	587·0	199	1,328	61	21·77
R. K. Illingworth	445·4	179	893	41	21·78
C. C. Lewis	300·3	59	986	45	21·91

† Includes Australian tourists.

CYCLING, 1988-89

Tour de France.— G. Lemond (U.S.A.).
Tour of Spain.—P. Delgado (Spain).
Giro d'Italia.—L. Fignon (France).
World Professional Road Race Championship.— G. Lemond (U.S.A.).
British Professional Road Race Championship.—T. Harris.
British Amateur Road Race Championship.—D. Cook.
Tour of Britain.—R. Millar (G.B.).
Milk Race.—B. Walton (Canada).
Nissan Classic International.—E. Vanderaerden (Belgium).
World Professional Cyclo-Cross Championship.—D. de Bie (Belgium).
Women's Tour de France.—J. Longo (France).
Women's World Road Race Championship.—J. Longo (France).

EQUESTRIANISM, 1988-89

Badminton Horse Trials:
1. Mrs. V. Leng—Master Craftsman (G.B.).
2. Miss M. Thomson—King Boris (G.B.).
3. M. Todd—The Irishman (N.Z.).

British Open Championship:
1. M. Todd—Bahlua (N.Z.).
2. R. Powell—The Irishman (G.B.).
3. Miss J. Johnson—Timber Run (G.B.).

Hickstead Derby:
1. N. Skelton—Burmah Apollo (G.B.).
2. J. Turi—Country Classics Kruger (G.B.).
3. P. Heffer—Viewpoint (G.B.).

European 3-Day Eventing:
1. Mrs. V. Leng—Master Craftsman (G.B.).
2. Miss J. Thelwall—King's Jester (G.B.).
3. Miss L. Clarke—Fearliath Mor (G.B.).
Team Result:
1. Great Britain.
2. Netherlands.
3. Ireland.

European Showjumping Championships:
1. J. Whitaker—Next Milton (G.B.).
2. M. Whitaker—Next Monsanta (G.B.).
3. J. Lansink—Optiebeurs Felix (Neth.).
Team Result:
1. Great Britain.
2. France.
3. Switzerland.

ETON FIVES, 1989

Amateur Championship (Kinnaird Cup).—B. C. Matthews and J. Reynolds.
Nat West County Championship.—Middlesex.
Holmwoods Schools' Championships.—Wolverhampton.
Alan Barber Cup.—Old Cholmeleians.
League Championship (Douglas Keeble Cup).—The Village Club.

FENCING 1988-89

British Championships:
Foil.—D. McKenzie (Meadow Bank).
Epée.—H. Kernohan (Salle Boston).
Sabre.—I. Williams (London Thames).
Ladies' Foil.—F. McIntosh (Salle Paul).
Ladies' Epée.—P. Tomlinson (London Thames).
Sporting Record Cup.—Salle Paul.
Savage Shield.—London Thames.
Martin Edmunds Cup.—Salle Paul.
Challenge Martini International Epée.—E. Strecki (France).

GOLF, 1988–89

MAJOR CHAMPIONSHIPS 1989

THE OPEN (Royal Troon, July 20–23)
M. Calcavecchia (*U.S.A.*), 275.
THE U.S. OPEN (Oak Hill, Rochester, New York, June 15–18)
C. Strange (*U.S.A.*), 278.
THE MASTERS (Augusta, Georgia, April 6–9)
N. Faldo (*G.B.*), 283.
THE U.S. P.G.A. (Kemper Lakes, Chicago, Aug. 10–13)
P. Stewart (*U.S.A.*), 276.

TEAM EVENTS

RYDER CUP (The Belfry, Sept. 22–24, 1989)
Great Britain and Europe drew with the U.S.A., 14–14.

WALKER CUP (Peachtree, Atlanta, Georgia, U.S.A.)
Great Britain and Ireland beat U.S.A. by 13½ to 12½.
CURTIS CUP (Sandwich, June 10–11, 1988)
Great Britain and Ireland beat U.S.A. by 11 to 7.
WORLD CUP (Melbourne)
Winners: U.S.A.
DUNHILL CUP.—U.S.A. beat Japan, 3½–2½.

EUROPEAN P.G.A. TOUR, 1989

Tenerife Open.—J.-M. Olazabal (Spain), 275.
Desert Classic.—M. James (G.B.), 277.
Majorca Open.—O. Sellberg (Sweden), 279.
Catalan Open.—M. Roe (G.B.), 279.
AGF Open (France).—M. James (G.B.), 277.
Volvo Open (Sardinia).—V. Singh (Fiji), 276.
Jersey Open.—C. O'Connor, Jnr. (Ireland), 281.
Cannes Open.—P. Broadhurst (G.B.), 208.*
Madrid Open.—S. Ballesteros (Spain), 272.
Spanish Open.—B. Langer (West Germany), 281.
Epson Grand Prix (G.B.).—S. Ballesteros (Spain).
Belgian Open.—G. J. Brand (G.B.), 273.
Italian Open.—R. Rafferty (G.B.), 273.
PGA Championship (G.B.).—N. Faldo (G.B.), 272.
Dunhill British Masters.—N. Faldo (G.B.), 267.
Wang 4-Stars Tournament (G.B.).—C. Parry (Australia), 273.
English Open.—M. James (G.B.), 279.
Irish Open.—I. Woosnam (G.B.), 278.
French Open.—N. Faldo (G.B.), 273.
Monte Carlo Open.—M. McNulty (Zimbabwe), 261.
Scottish Open.—M. Allen (U.S.A.), 272.
KLM Dutch Open.—J.-M. Olazabal (Spain), 277.
Scandinavian Enterprise Open.—R. Rafferty (G.B.), 268.
Benson and Hedges International (G.B.).—G. Brand Jnr. (G.B.), 272.
PLM Open (Sweden).—M. Harwood (Australia), 271.
German Open.—C. Parry (Australia), 266.
European Masters (Switzerland).—S. Ballesteros (Spain), 266.
European Open (G.B.).—A. Murray (G.B.), 277.
Lancôme Trophy (France).—E. Romero (Argentina), 266.

*Three rounds only.

WOMEN'S CHAMPIONSHIPS

U.S. Women's Open.—B. King (U.S.A.), 278.
European Women's Open.—J. Connachan (G.B.), 279.
British Women's Open.—J. Geddes (U.S.A.), 274.
British Women's Amateur Championship.—H. Dobson.
European Ladies Amateur Team Championship (1989).—France.
English Girls Open Championship.—H. Dobson.
British Girls Championship.—M. McKinlay.

MEN'S AMATEUR CHAMPIONSHIPS

Amateur Championship.—S. Dodd.
English Championship.—S. Richardson.
British Youths Open Championship.—M. Smith, 285.
British Boys Championship.—C. Watts.
Halford Hewitt (for schools).—Eton beat Shrewsbury, 3–2.
Lytham Trophy.—N. Williamson, 286.
Brabazon Trophy.—(English amateur stroke-play).—R. N. Roderick (G.B.) and C. Rivett (S. Africa) tied on 293.
Berkshire Trophy.—J. Metcalfe, 272.
Carris Trophy.—I. Garbutt, 285.
President's Putter.—M. Froggatt.
Sunningdale Foursomes.—R. Claydon and A. Hare.
Universities.—Cambridge beat Oxford by 11½–3½.

GREYHOUND RACING, 1989

Television Trophy (Birmingham).—Proud to Run.
Grand National (Birmingham).—Lemon Chip.
Greyhound Derby (Wimbledon).—Lartigue Note.
Scurry Gold Cup (Catford).—Nans Brute.

GYMNASTICS, 1988

MEN'S

British Men's Champion, J. May.
British Men's Individual Apparatus Champions:
  Floor, N. Thomas.
  Pommel Horse, J. May.
  Rings, J. May.
  Vault, N. Thomas.
  Parallel Bars, J. May.
  High Bar, J. May.
British Men's Team Champions (Adam Shield), City of Liverpool.

WOMEN'S

British Women's Champion, L. Grayson.
British Women's Individual Apparatus Champions:
  Vault, L. Law.
  Asymmetric Bars, L. Grayson.
  Beam, J. Prescott.
  Floor, L. Mainwaring.
British Rhythmics Champion, A. Sands (Coventry).
British Women's Open Club Team Champions, Heathrow.

HOCKEY, 1988–89

MEN'S HOCKEY

Champions Trophy. Australia.
Home Countries Indoor. England.
County Championship Final. Middlesex beat Kent 1–0 aet.
National Club Championship Final. Hounslow beat Bromley 2–1.

National Indoor Club Championship Final. St. Albans beat East Grinstead 3–1.

Universities. Cambridge beat Oxford 1–0.

WOMEN'S HOCKEY

Typhoo Tea Cup.—England beat West Germany, 3–2.

Internationals. S. Korea beat England 4–3; England beat W. Germany 2–0; England beat the Netherlands 2–1; England beat Ireland 1–0 and 2–1; England drew with Wales 1–1; England drew with Scotland 1–1.

County Champions, Kent.
Club Champions, Ealing.

HORSERACING, 1988–89

Horseracing in Great Britain is under the control of THE JOCKEY CLUB (incorporating the National Hunt Committee), 42 Portman Square, London, W1H 0EN. Stewards are: Marquess of Hartington (*Senior Steward*); Viscount Chelsea (*Deputy Senior Steward*); Lord Vestey; Col. A. H. Parker Bowles; Sir John Barlow; Maj. M. C. Wyatt.

Winning Owners, 1988

Sheikh Mohammed	£1,143,310
Hamdan Al-Maktoum	724,712
K. Abdulla	721,120
M. K. Aga Khan	612,073
Sheikh Ahmed Al-Maktoum	497,788
R. E. Sangster	445,543
C. A. B. St. George	224,047
Maktoum Al-Maktoum	187,820
Dowager Lady Beaverbrook	176,573

Winning Trainers, 1988

H. Cecil	£1,186,083
L. Cumani	814,989
G. Harwood	712,520
B. Hills	625,744
A. Stewart	594,891
M. Stoute	552,838
J. Dunlop	440,749
J. Tree	358,186
R. Armstrong	306,525
N. Graham	278,232

Leading Breeders, 1988

	Value
H. H. Aga Khan	£636,825
J. L. Moore	434,420
Juddmonte Farms	402,603
N. S. Dillman	222,136
White Lodge Stud Ltd.	202,109
Swettenham Stud	184,610

W. Carson	156,175
Ashford Stud & R. Worswick	150,120
Lavinia Duchess of Norfolk	145,174
Floors Farming	143,924

Winning Sires, 1988

	Horses	Races won	Value
Busted (1963), by Crepello	12	17	£450,914
Ile de Bourbon (USA) (1975), by Nijinsky	17	27	442,797
Known Fact (USA) (1977), by In Reality	15	25	431,761
Shirley Heights (1975), by Mill Reef	26	37	377,221
Diesis (1980), by Sharpen Up	12	17	291,325
Youth Generation (1976), by Balidar	23	38	232,138
Niniski (USA) (1976), by Nijinsky	8	13	207,229
Caerleon (USA) (1980), by Northern Dancer	18	29	193,368
Lomond (USA) (1980), by Northern Dancer	7	18	191,498
Riverman (USA) (1969), by Never Bend	9	12	186,339

Winning Flat Jockeys, 1988

	1st	2nd	3rd	Unpl.	Total Mts.
P. Eddery	183	127	97	469	876
W. Carson	130	100	87	515	832
M. Roberts	121	120	83	453	777
R. Cochrane	120	99	89	448	756
S. Cauthen	104	95	53	329	581
M. Birch	95	60	81	486	722
W. Swinburn	88	80	71	358	597
J. Reid	79	65	89	412	645
B. Raymond	77	66	66	418	627
G. Duffield	77	72	71	493	713

Winning National Hunt Jockeys 1988–89

	1st	2nd	3rd	Unpl.	Total Mts.
P. Scudamore	220	112	55	273	660
R. Dunwoody	91	111	90	370	662
M. Dwyer	90	79	43	233	445
G. McCourt	83	60	50	230	423
S. Sherwood	68	42	41	166	317
B. Powell	64	63	58	392	577
T. Morgan	51	39	30	128	248
H. Davies	50	58	51	302	461
P. Niven	48	38	45	206	337
P. Hobbs	47	35	35	231	348

(The above statistics are the copyright of *The Sporting Life.*)

THE DERBY, 1986–89

For particulars of the Derby from 1780–1985 see 1921–89 editions.

The distance of the Derby course at Epsom is 1½ miles. First winner was Sir Charles Bunbury's Diomed in 1780. Lord Egremont won the Derby in 1782, 1804, 5, 7, 26 (also, 5 Oaks); Duke of Grafton, 1802, 9, 10, 15 (also, 9 Oaks); Mr. Bowes, 1835, 43, 52, 3; Sir J. Hawley, 1851, 58, 59, 68; the 1st Duke of Westminster, 1880, 82, 86, 99; Sir Victor Sassoon, 1953, 57, 58, 60. By winning his 5th Derby, in 1952, the late Aga Khan equalled Lord Egremont's record. He also won 2 Oaks.

The Derby was run at Newmarket from 1915–18 and again from 1940–45.

Year	Owner and Name of Winner	Betting	Jockey	Trainer	No. of Run'rs
1986	H. H. Aga Khan's Shahrastani	11–2	W. Swinburn	M. Stoute	17
1987	Mr. L. Freedman's Reference Point	6–4 F.	S. Cauthen	H. Cecil	19
1988	H. H. Aga Khan's Kahyasi	11–1	R. Cochrane	L. Cumani	14
1989	Hamdan Al-Maktoum's Nashwan	5–4 F.	W. Carson	R. Hern	12

Record times: 2 min. 33·8 sec. by Mahmoud in 1936; 2 min. 33·84 sec. by Kahyasi in 1988 and 2 min. 33·9 sec. by Reference Point in 1987.

ONE THOUSAND GUINEAS. 1814. Rowley Mile. Newmarket. Fillies. 9st.

Year	Owner and Name of Winner	Betting	Jockey	Trainer	No. of Run'rs
1985	Sheikh Mohammed's Oh So Sharp....	2 to 1 F.	S. Cauthen	H. Cecil	17
1986	H. Ranier's Midway Lady	10 to 1	R. Cochrane	B. Hanbury	15
1987	Mr. S. Niarchos's Miesque	15 to 8 F.	F. Head	F. Boutin	14
1988	E. Aland's Ravinella	4 to 5 F.	G. Moore	Mrs. C. Head	12
1989	Sheikh Mohammed's Musical Bliss	7 to 2	W. Swinburn ...	M. Stoute........	7

TWO THOUSAND GUINEAS. First Run, 1809. Rowley Mile. Newmarket. 9st.

Year	Owner and Name of Winner	Betting	Jockey	Trainer	No. of Run'rs
1985	Maktoum Al Maktoum's Shadeed	4 to 5 F.	L. Piggott	M. Stoute........	14
1986	K. Abdulla's Dancing Brave	15 to 8 F.	G. Starkey	G. Harwood......	15
1987	Mr. J. Horgan's Don't Forget Me......	9 to 1	W. Carson	R. Hannon........	13
1988	H. H. Aga Khan's Doyoun	4 to 5 F.	W. Swinburn ...	M. Stoute........	9
1989	Sheikh Hamdan Al-Maktoum's Nashwan	3 to 1 F.	W. Carson	R. Hern	14

OAKS. 1779. Epsom. 1½ Mile. Fillies. 9 st.

Year	Owner and Name of Winner	Betting	Jockey	Trainer	No. of Run'rs
1985	Sheikh Mohammed's Oh So Sharp.....	6 to 4 F.	S. Cauthen	H. Cecil	12
1986	H. Ranier's Midway Lady	15 to 8 F.	R. Cochrane	B. Hanbury	15
1987	Sheikh Mohammed's Unite	11 to 1	W. Swinburn ...	M. Stoute........	11
1988	Sheikh Mohammed's Diminuendo.....	7 to 4 F.	S. Cauthen	H. Cecil	11
1989	H.H. Aga Khan's Aliysa	11 to 10 F.	W. Swinburn ...	M. Stoute........	9

ST. LEGER. 1776(8). Doncaster. 1¾ mile, 127 yards.

Year	Owner and Name of Winner	Betting	Jockey	Trainer	No. of Run'rs
1985	Sheikh Mohammed's Oh So Sharp.....	8 to 11 F.	S. Cauthen	H. Cecil	6
1986	Lavinia Duchess of Norfolk's Moon Madness........................	9 to 2	P. Eddery	J. Dunlop.......	8
1987	Mr. L. Freedman's Reference Point ...	4 to 11 F.	S. Cauthen	H. Cecil	7
1988	Lady Beaverbrook's Minster Son	15 to 2	W. Carson	N. Graham	6
1989	Mr. C. St. George's Michelozzo........	6 to 4 F.	S. Cauthen	H. Cecil	8

The 1989 St. Leger was run at Ayr on Sept. 23, after the course at Doncaster was ruled unsatisfactory.

	Cheltenham Gold Cup* abt. 3¼ m.	Irish Grand National* Fairyhouse—3 miles	Lincoln Handicap Doncaster—1 mile	Grand National* Liverpool—4½ m.
1986	Dawn Run 8y 11st 9lb	Insure 8y 9st 11lb	K-Battery 5y 8st 4lb	West Tip 9y 10st 11lb.......
1987	The Thinker 9y 12st	Brittany Boy 8y 10st 10lb ..	Star of a Gunner 7y 8st 8lb .	Maori Venture 11y 10st 13lb ..
1988	Charter Party 10y 12st ...	Perris Valley 7y 10st	Cuvee Charlie 4y 7st 13lb...	Rhyme 'N' Reason 9y 11st ....
1989	Desert Orchid 10y 12st	Maid of Money 7y 11st 6lb ..	Fact Finder 5y 7st 9lb ...	Little Polveir 12y 10st ......

	European Free Handicap Newmarket—3yrs.—7f.	Jockey Club Stakes Newmarket—1½ miles.	Chester Cup Chester—2¼ m. 77 yd.	Coronation Cup Epsom—1½ miles.
1986	Green Desert 9st 7lb	Phardante 4y 8st 7lb	Western Dancer 5y 9st	Saint Estephe 4y 9st ......
1987	Noble Minstrel 9st 7lb	Phardante 5y 8st 12lb	Just David 4y 9st 8lb	Triptych 5y 8st 11lb .....
1988	Lapierre 9st 1lb	Almaarad 4y 8st 5lb......	Old Hubert 7y 7st 8lb	Triptych 6y 8st 11lb ......
1989	Danehill 9st 1lb	Unfwain 4y 8st 10lb......	Grey Salute 6y 8st 7lb	Sheriff's Star 4y 9st ......

	Coventry Stakes Ascot—2 yrs—5 furlongs	Gold Cup Ascot—2½ miles	Irish Sweeps Derby Curragh—3 yrs—1½ miles	Eclipse Stakes Sandown Park—1¼m.
1986	Cutting Blade 8st 11lb	Longboat 5y 9st	Shahrastani 9st	Dancing Brave 3y 8st 8lb ...
1987	Always Fair 8st 13lb	Paean 4y 9st	Sir Harry Lewis	Mtoto 4y 9st 7lb.........
1988	High Estate 8st 13lb.....	Sadeem 5y 9st	Kahyasi 9st	Mtoto 5y 9st 7lb.........
1989	Rock City 8st 13lb	Sadeem 6y 9st	Old Vic 9st	Nashwan 3y 8st 8lb ......

	King George VI and Queen Elizabeth Stakes Ascot—1½ miles	Goodwood Cup 2 m. 5 f.	Gimcrack Stakes York—2 yrs.—6 Furlongs.	Middle Park Stakes Newmarket—2 yrs.—6 f.
1986	Dancing Brave 3y 8st 8lb ...	Longboat 5y 9st 7lb	Rich Charlie 9st 5lb.......	Mister Majestic 9st ....
1987	Reference Point 3y 8st 8lb ..	Sergeyevich 3y 7st	Reprimand 9st..........	Gallic League 9st ....
1988	Mtoto 5y 9st 7lb........	Sadeem 5y 9st 7lb	Sharp 'N' Early 9st	Mon Tresor 9st ....
1989	Nashwan 3y 8st 8lb.......	Mazzacano 4y 9st	Rock City 9st 3lb	Balla Cove 9st ....

	Cambridgeshire Handicap Newmarket—9 f.	Prix de L'Arc de Triomphe Longchamp—1½ m.	Champion Stakes Newmarket—1¼ m.	Cesarewitch Newmarket—2¼ m.
1986	Dallas 9st 6lb	Dancing Brave 3y 8st 11lb ..	Triptych 4y 9st	Orange Hill 4y 7st 9lb ......
1987	Balthus 8st 1lb	Trempolino 3y 8st 11lb....	Triptych 5y 9st	Private Audition 5y 7st 7lb ..
1988	Quinlan Terry 3y 8st 5lb ..	Tony Bin 5y 9st 4lb	Indian Skimmer 4y 9st	Nomadic Way 3y 7st 9lb.....
1989	Rambo's Hall 4y 8st 6lb	Carroll House 4y 9st 4lb....	Legal Case 3y 8st 10lb	Double Dutch 5y 9st 10lb ....

*National Hunt

ICE SKATING, 1988–89

WORLD CHAMPIONSHIPS
(Paris)

Men's Figure.—K. Browning (Canada).
Ladies' Figure.—Miss M. Ito (Japan).
Pairs.—S. Grinkov and Miss E. Gordeyeva (U.S.S.R.).
Ice Dancing.—S. Ponomarenko and Miss M. Klimova (U.S.S.R.).

EUROPEAN CHAMPIONSHIPS
(Birmingham)

Men's Figure.—A. Fadeyev (U.S.S.R.).
Ladies' Figure.—Miss C. Leistner (W. Germany).
Pairs.—O. Makarov and Miss L. Selezneva (U.S.S.R.).
Ice Dancing.—S. Ponomarenko and Miss M. Klimova (U.S.S.R.).

BRITISH CHAMPIONSHIPS

Men's Figure.—C. Newberry.
Ladies' Figure.—Miss J. Conway.
Pairs.—A. Naylor and Miss C. Peake.
Ice Dancing.—P. Askham and Miss S. Jones.

JUDO

BRITISH OPEN CHAMPIONSHIPS
(Crystal Palace)

MEN'S

Heavy (over 95 kg.), E. Gordon (G.B.).
Light Heavy (95 kg.), N. Kokotaylo (G.B.).
Middle (86 kg.), D. White (G.B.).
Light Middle (78 kg.), M. Vallot (Belgium).
Light (71 kg.), S. Ravenscroft (G.B.).
Feather (65 kg.), F. Decroix (France).
Bantam (60 kg.), C. Finney (G.B.).

WOMEN'S

Heavy (over 72 kg.), R. Sigmund (West Germany).
Light Heavy (72 kg.), I. Berghmans (Belgium).
Middle (66 kg.), R. Sweatman (G.B.).
Light Middle (61 kg.), D. Bell (G.B.).
Light (56 kg.), N. Flagothier (Belgium).
Feather (52 kg.), S. Rendle (G.B.).
Bantam (48 kg.), K. Briggs (G.B.).

LAWN TENNIS, 1988–89

THE ALL ENGLAND CHAMPIONSHIPS (WIMBLEDON)
1989

Men's Singles.—B. Becker (W. Germany) beat S. Edberg (Sweden), 6–0, 7–6, 6–4.

Women's Singles.—Miss S. Graf (W. Germany) beat Miss M. Navratilova (U.S.A.), 6–2, 6–7, 6–1.

Men's Doubles.—J. Fitzgerald (Australia) and A. Jarryd (Sweden) beat R. Leach and J. Pugh (U.S.A.), 3–6, 7–6, 6–4, 7–6.

Women's Doubles.—Miss J. Novotna and Miss H. Sukova (Czechoslovakia) beat Miss L. Savchenko and Miss N. Zvereva (U.S.S.R.), 6–1, 6–2.

Mixed Doubles.—J. Pugh (U.S.A.) and Miss J. Novotna (Czechoslovakia) beat M. Kratzmann and Miss J. Byrne (Australia), 6–4, 5–7, 6–4.

Australian Championships:
Men's Singles.—I. Lendl (Czechoslovakia).
Women's Singles.—Miss S. Graf (W. Germany).
Men's Doubles.—R. Leach and J. Pugh (U.S.A.).
Women's Doubles.—Miss M. Navratilova and Miss P. Shriver (U.S.A.).

Mixed Doubles.—J. Pugh (U.S.A.) and Miss J. Novotna (Czechoslovakia).

French Championships:
Men's Singles.—M. Chang (U.S.A.).
Women's Singles.—Miss A. Sanchez (Spain).
Men's Doubles.—J. Grabb and P. McEnroe (U.S.A.).
Women's Doubles.—Miss L. Savchenko and Miss N. Zvereva (U.S.S.R.).
Mixed Doubles.—T. Nijssen and Miss M. Bollegraf (Netherlands).

U.S.A. Championships:
Men's Singles.—B. Becker (W. Germany).
Women's Singles.—Miss S. Graf (W. Germany).
Men's Doubles.—J. McEnroe (U.S.A.) and M. Woodforde (Australia).
Women's Doubles.—Miss M. Navratilova (U.S.A.) and Miss H. Mandlikova (Australia).
Mixed Doubles.—Miss R. White and S. Cannon (U.S.A.).

DAVIS CUP, 1988
(Founder—Dwight Filley Davis (1879–1945))

West Germany beat Sweden by 4 matches to 1.

WIGHTMAN CUP, 1988
(Royal Albert Hall, London)

U.S.A. beat G.B. by 7 matches to 0.

WIGHTMAN CUP, 1989
(Williamsburg, U.S.A.)

U.S.A. beat G.B. by 7 matches to 0.

Prudential County Cup—Men: Surrey; *Women:* Surrey.

MOTOR CYCLING, 1989

500 C.C. MOTOR CYCLING GRAND PRIX

Japanese.—K. Schwantz (Suzuki).
Australian.—W. Gardner (Honda).
American.—W. Rainey (Yamaha).
Spanish.—E. Lawson (Honda).
Italian.—P. Chili (Honda).
West German.—W. Rainey (Yamaha).
Austrian.—K. Schwantz (Suzuki).
Yugoslavian.—K. Schwantz (Suzuki).
Dutch.—W. Rainey (Yamaha).
Belgian.—E. Lawson (Honda).
French.—E. Lawson (Honda).
British.—K. Schwantz (Suzuki).
Swedish.—E. Lawson (Honda).
Czechoslovakian.—K. Schwantz (Suzuki).
Brazilian.—K. Schwantz (Suzuki).

500 C.C. WORLD CHAMPION 1989.—E. Lawson (Honda).

Senior Manx Grand Prix.—S. Hislop (Honda).
Senior T.T., Isle of Man.—S. Hislop (Honda).
Junior T.T., Isle of Man.—S. Hislop (Honda).

MOTOR RACING, 1988–89

FORMULA ONE MOTOR RACING

Grand Prix 1988:
Japanese (Suzuka)—1. A. Senna (McLaren); 2. A. Prost (McLaren); 3. T. Boutsen (Benetton).
Australian (Adelaide)—1. A. Prost (McLaren); 2. A. Senna (McLaren); 3. N. Piquet (Lotus).
FORMULA ONE CHAMPION, 1988.—A. Senna (McLaren) 90 pts.
Grand Prix 1989:
Brazilian (Rio)—1. N. Mansell (Ferrari); 2. A. Prost (McLaren); 3. M. Gugelmin (March).
San Marino (Imola)—1. A. Senna (McLaren); 2. A. Prost (McLaren); 3. A. Nannini (Benetton).

Monaco (Monte Carlo)—1. A. Senna (McLaren); 2. A. Prost (McLaren); 3. S. Modena (Brabham).
Mexican (Rodrigues)—1. A. Senna (McLaren); 2. R. Patrese (Williams); 3. M. Alboreto (Tyrrell).
United States (Phoenix)—1. A. Prost (McLaren); 2. R. Patrese (Williams); 3. E. Cheever (Arrows).
Canadian (Montreal)—1. T. Boutsen (Williams); 2. R. Patrese (Williams); 3. A. de Cesaris (Dallara).
French (Paul Ricard)—1. A. Prost (McLaren); 2. N. Mansell (Ferrari); 3. R. Patrese (Williams).
British (Silverstone)—1. A. Prost (McLaren); 2. N. Mansell (Ferrari); 3. A. Nannini (Benetton).
West German (Hockenheim)—1. A. Senna (McLaren); 2. A. Prost (McLaren); 3. N. Mansell (Ferrari).
Hungarian (Budapest)—1. N. Mansell (Ferrari); 2. A. Senna (McLaren); 3. T. Boutsen (Williams).
Belgian (Spa Francorchamps)—1. A. Senna (McLaren); 2. A. Prost (McLaren); 3. N. Mansell (Ferrari).
Italian (Monza)—1. A. Prost (McLaren); 2. G. Berger (Ferrari); 3. T. Boutsen (Williams).
Portuguese (Estoril)—1. G. Berger (Ferrari); 2. A. Prost (McLaren); 3. S. Johansson (Onyx Ford).
Spanish (Jerez)—1. A. Senna (McLaren); 2. G. Berger (Ferrari); 3. A. Prost (McLaren).

OTHER EVENTS

Birmingham Super-Prix.—J. Alesi (France).
Le Mans (24-hour).—J. Mass (W. Germany), M. Reuter (W. Germany), and S. Dickens (Sweden) (Sauber Mercedes).
Lombard R.A.C. Rally, 1988.—M. Alen (Finland) (Lancia Delta).
Paris/Dakar Trans-Sahara Rally.—A. Vatanen (Peugeot).
Monte Carlo Rally.—M. Biasion (Italy) (Lancia).
Safari Rally.—M. Biasion (Lancia Delta).
Circuit of Ireland Rally.—J. McRae (Sierra Cosworth).
Indianapolis 500.—E. Fittipaldi (Penske-Chevrolet).

NETBALL, 1988–9

Test Matches

1988
Nov. 23 Gateshead: England 27, New Zealand 46.
     26 Wembley: England 25, New Zealand 47.
     28 Manchester: England 30, New Zealand 40.

Internationals

1989
Mar. 3 Belfast: N. Ireland 10, England 45.
      4 Belfast: Rep. of Ireland 14, England 42.

Inter-County Champions, Birmingham.
National Clubs Champions, Linden.

POLO, 1989

Prince of Wales's Trophy.—Tramontana beat Hildon House, 12–5.
Queen's Cup.—Hilditch and Key beat Cowdray Park, 7–6.
Cowdray Park Gold Cup (British Championship).—Tramontana beat Cowdray Park, 13–8.
Coronation Cup.—England beat Australasia, 10–8.
Silver Jubilee Cup.—North America beat The Prince of Wales's Team, 7–6.
Warwickshire Cup.—Southfield beat Kennelot, 11–10.
Cowdray Challenge Cup.—Giscours beat Cowdray Park, 10–7.

RACKETS, 1988–89

World Championship Challenge.—J. Male beat W. Boone, 6–1.
Celestion Amateur Singles Championship.—J. Male beat W. Boone, 4–0.
Celestion Amateur Doubles Championship.—J. Prenn and J. Male beat W. Boone and C. Hue Williams, 4–1.
Rank Xerox Professional Singles Championship.—N. Smith beat S. Hazell, 3–2.
Celestion British Open Singles Championship.—J. Male beat N. Smith, 4–2.
Celestion British Open Doubles Championship.—J. Prenn and J. Male beat N. Smith and S. Hazell, 4–2.
Noel Bruce Cup.—Radley (J. Male and J. Snow) beat Harrow (J. Prenn and C. Hue Williams), 4–2.
Public Schools Doubles Championship.—Marlborough beat Radley, 4–0.
Universities.—Oxford beat Cambridge, 2–1.

REAL TENNIS, 1988–89

World Championship Challenge.—W. Davies beat L. Deuchar, 7–1.
Professional Singles Championship.—C. Ronaldson beat L. Deuchar, 3–1.
Professional Doubles Championship.—L. Deuchar and J. Fletcher beat C. and S. Ronaldson, 2–1.
Amateur Singles Championship.—J. Snow beat M. Happell, 3–1.
Amateur Doubles Championship.—M. Happell and J. Male beat A. Lovell and M. Dean, 3–2.
British Open Singles Championship.—L. Deuchar beat W. Davies, 3–0.
British Open Doubles Championship.—W. Davies and L. Deuchar beat K. Sheldon and J. Howell, 2–0.
Women's Open Singles.—P. Fellows beat S. Jones, 2–1.
Henry Leaf Cup.—Radley beat Wellington, 3–0.
Universities.—Cambridge beat Oxford, 4–2.

ROWING, 1989

HENLEY ROYAL REGATTA, 1989

Grand Challenge Cup.—Hansa Dortmund (W. Germany) beat Dinamo (U.S.S.R.) by 3 lengths.
Ladies' Challenge Plate.—Nottinghamshire County 'A' beat Harvard University (U.S.A.) by ¼ length.
Princess Elizabeth Cup.—Hampton School beat Shiplake College by 1 length.
Thames Cup.—University of London beat Ridley College by 3½ lengths.
Prince Philip Cup.—University of London beat Levski Spartak (Bulgaria) by 4 lengths.
Queen Mother Cup.—S. C. Eridanea and S. C. Firenze (Italy) beat Kubanj Krasnodar (U.S.S.R.) by 3¼ lengths.
Visitors' Cup.—Isis 'A' beat Durham University 'B' by 5 lengths.
Wyfold Cup.—Leander Club 'A' beat Nottinghamshire County 'B' by 1⅓ lengths.
Britannia Challenge Cup.—Leander beat Lea 'A' by 2 lengths.
Stewards' Cup.—University of London and Oxford University beat Nautilus by ¾ length.
Silver Goblets and Nickall's Cup.—S. N. Berrisford and S. G. Redgrave (Leander) beat V. and G. Grabow.

Double Sculls Cup.—R. Floryn (Die Leythe, Netherlands) and N. Rienks (Okeanos, Netherlands) beat P. Luzek and I. Gruza (Dukla Praha, Czechoslovakia) by 5 lengths.

Diamond Sculls.—V. Chalupa (Dukla Praha, Czechoslovakia) beat K. Broniewski (AZS-AWF Warszawe, Poland) by 1 length.

Special Schools Race.—Bedford Modern beat St. Pauls by ¾ length.

NATIONAL CHAMPIONSHIPS 1989

(Strathclyde Country Park)

Men's:

Eights.—Castle Semple/Clydesdale/Glasgow Univ./Loch Lomond/Stirling (combined crew).
Coxed Fours.—Thames Tradesmen.
Coxless Fours.—Notts County.
Coxed Pairs.—Kingston.
Coxless Pairs.—Notts County.
Quad Sculls.—Notts County.
Double Sculls.—Barclays Bank/Tideway Scullers.
Single Sculls.—S. Larkin (Notts County).
Coastal Fours.—Christchurch.
Coastal Pairs.—Dover.
Coastal Singles.—P. Mahoney (Southsea).

Women's:

Eights.—Thames.
Coxed Fours.—G. B. Squad.
Coxless Pairs.—Thames.
Quad Sculls.—Kingston.
Double Sculls.—G. B. Squad.
Single Sculls.—E. Holmes (Tideway Scullers).
Coastal Fours.—(no event).

THE 135TH UNIVERSITY BOAT RACE

(Putney-Mortlake, 4 m. 1 f. 180 yds.)

Oxford beat Cambridge by 2½ lengths, 18 m 27 s. (Cambridge have won 69 times, Oxford 65 and there has been 1 dead-heat. The record time is the 16 m 45 s rowed by Oxford in 1984.)

Women's Boat Race.—Cambridge beat Oxford by 5 sec.

OTHER ROWING EVENTS

Oxford Torpids.—Oriel.
Cambridge Lents.—Pembroke.
Oxford Summer Eights.—Oriel.
Cambridge Mays.—Lady Margaret.
Doggett's Coat and Badge (*Estab.* 1715, 275th race, *London Bridge-Chelsea*, 4½ miles).—R. A. Humphrey.
Head of the River.—A.R.A. National Squad.

RUGBY FIVES, 1987–88

Amateur Singles Championship.—G. W. Enstone beat I. P. Fuller.
Amateur Doubles Championship.—I. P. Fuller and D. J. Hebden beat D. Parlby and J. Schroeter.
National Schools' Championships.—*Singles:* P. Newman (St. Dunstan's). *Doubles:* St. Dunstan's.

RUGBY LEAGUE, 1988–89

International Matches

1988
Oct.   29 Headingley: Gt. Britain 30, Rest of World 28.

1989
Jan.   21 Wigan: Gt. Britain 26, France 10.
Feb.   5 Avignon: France 8, Gt. Britain 30.

Rugby League Challenge Cup Final: April 29 (Wembley)—Wigan beat St. Helens, 27–0 pts.

Premiership Trophy Final: May 14 (Old Trafford)—Widnes beat Hull, 18–10 pts.

Division 2 Premiership Final: Sheffield beat Swinton, 43–18 pts.

Stones Bitter Champions.—Widnes.

Second Division Champions.—Leigh.

Yorkshire Cup.—Leeds beat Castleford, 33–6 pts.

Lancashire Cup.—Wigan beat Salford, 22–17 pts.

John Player Special Trophy Final.—Jan. 7 (Burnden Park, Bolton), Wigan beat Widnes, 12–6 pts.

Universities.—Oxford beat Cambridge by 12–9 pts.

AMATEUR RUGBY LEAGUE, 1988–89

County Championship.—Yorkshire.
National Inter-League Shield Competitions.—
 Open Age.—Heavy Woollen.
 Under 19.—Leigh.
 Under 17.—Leeds.
National Cup Competitions.—
 Open Age.—Crossfields.
 Under 19.—Widnes Tigers.
National League Champions.—West Hull.
National League Challenge Cup Winners.—Egremont.

RUGBY UNION, 1988–89

International Matches

1988
Nov.   5 Twickenham: England 28, Australia 9.
Nov. 12 Cardiff: Wales 28, Western Samoa 6.
Nov. 19 Edinburgh: Scotland 13, Australia 32.
Dec. 10 Cardiff: Wales 9, Romania 15.
Dec. 31 Dublin: Ireland 31, Italy 15.

1989
Jan.   21 Edinburgh: Scotland 23, Wales 7.
           Dublin: Ireland 21, France 26.
Feb.   4 Twickenham: England 12, Scotland 12.
           Cardiff: Wales 13, Ireland 19.
Feb.   18 Paris: France 31, Wales 12.
           Dublin: Ireland 3, England 16.
Mar.   4 Twickenham: England 11, France 0.
           Edinburgh: Scotland 37, Ireland 21.
Mar.   18 Cardiff: Wales 12, England 9.
           Paris: France 19, Scotland 3.
May.   13 Bucharest: Romania 3, England 58.
       28 Tokyo: Japan 28, Scotland 24.
July   1 Sydney: Australia 30, British Isles 12.
July   8 Brisbane: Australia 12, British Isles 19.
July   15 Sydney: Australia 18, British Isles 19.

International Union Table, 1989

	P	W	D	L	Pts.		Total
					F	A	
France	4	3	0	1	76	47	6
England	4	2	1	1	48	27	5
Scotland	4	2	1	1	75	59	5
Ireland	4	1	0	3	64	92	2
Wales	4	1	0	3	44	82	2

County Championship Final

Durham beat Cornwall 13–9

Other Chief Matches, 1988–89

Pilkington Cup Final: April 29 (Twickenham)—Bath beat Leicester, 10–6 pts.

Middlesex Sevens.—Harlequins.

Division 1 Clubs Champions.—Bath.

Division 2 Clubs Champions.—Saracens.

Division 3 Clubs Champions.—Plymouth Albion.

Hospitals' Cup Final.—St. Mary's beat The London, 20–9 pts.

Services Championship.—Army beat Royal Navy, 21–9; Army beat R.A.F., 43–10; R.A.F. beat Royal Navy, 30–23.

Universities. 1988. Oxford beat Cambridge, 27–7 pts.

SHOOTING

BISLEY, 120TH N.R.A., 1989

Queen's Prize.—1. J. M. A. Thompson, 288 pts.; 2. Dr. J. D. Warburton, 288 pts.; 3. L. M. Peden, 288 pts.

Prince of Wales Prize.—1. J. M. A. Thompson, 75 pts.; 2. C. R. G. Mixer, 75 pts.; 3. J. H. Carmichael, 75 pts.

Land Rover Ltd. Grand Aggregate.—1. S. Belither, 591 pts.; 2. B. J. Wood, 590 pts.; 3. J. P. S Bloomfield, 589 pts.

Save & Prosper St. George's Vase.—1. J. M. A. Thompson, 149 pts.; 2. J. Pugsley, 149 pts.; 3. Miss L. E. Nicholl, 149 pts.

All Comers Aggregate.—1. P. G. Kent, 322 pts.; 2. C. Mallett, 319 pts.; 3. A. St. G. Tucker, 318 pts.

National Trophy.—1. England, 2,035 pts.; 2. Scotland, 1,987 pts.; 3. Ireland, 1,971 pts.

Kolapore Cup.—1. Great Britain, 1,181 pts.; 2. Canada, 1,165 pts.; 3. Guernsey, 1,142 pts.

Chancellor's Challenge Plate.—1. Cambridge Univ., 1,130 pts.; 2. Oxford Univ., 1,097 pts.

Musketeers Cup.—1. London Univ., 571 pts.; 2. Exeter Univ., 571 pts.

Visianagram Trophy.—1. House of Lords, 666 pts.; 2. House of Commons, 648 pts.

County Long-Range Championship.—1. Kent, 287 pts.; 2. Warwickshire, 286 pts.; 3. Sussex, 286 pts.

MacKinnon Challenge Cup.—1. Canada, 1,130 pts.; 2. England, 1,119 pts.; 3. Channel Islands, 1,106 pts.

CLAY PIGEON SHOOTING, 1989

International Cup (Down-the-Line).—England, 7,155/7,500.

British Open Down-the-Line Championship.—A. Cathro, 100/298.

Mackintosh Trophy.—Canada, 7,416/7,500.

British Open Skeet Championship.—M. Elworthy, 100 + 49.

British Open Sporting Championship.—G. Digweed, 97/100.

Coronation Cup.—P. Cockle.

SNOOKER AND BILLIARDS, 1988–89

World Professional Snooker Championship.—S. Davis beat J. Parrott by 18–3.

World Matchplay Championship.—S. Davis beat J. Parrott, 9–5.

Benson and Hedges Masters Snooker Tournament.—S. Hendry beat J. Parrott by 9–6.

U.K. Professional Snooker Championship.—D. Mountjoy beat S. Hendry by 16–12.

English Professional Snooker Championship.—M. Hallett beat J. Parrott by 9–7.

British Open Snooker Championship.—A. Meo beat D. Reynolds by 13–6.

Mercantile Credit Classic.—D. Mountjoy beat W. Jones by 13–11.

World Team Cup.—England beat Rest of World by 9–8.

Rothmans Matchroom League.—S. Davis.

World Professional Billiards Championship.—M. Russell (G.B.).

World Amateur Snooker Championship 1988.—D. Morgan (Wales) beat J. Grech (Malta) by 11–4.

SPEEDWAY, 1987–88

British Championship.—S. Wigg (Oxford).

British Open Pairs.—H. Nielsen and M. Cox (Oxford).

British League Riders' Championship.—J. O. Pedersen (Cradley Heath).

British League Champions.—Coventry.

Knock-Out Cup Winners.—Cradley Heath.

Individual Speedway World Championship (World Final).—E. Gundersen (Denmark).

Pairs Speedway World Championship.—E. Gundersen and H. Nielsen (Denmark).

Team Speedway World Championship.—Denmark.

SQUASH RACKETS, 1988–89

World Open Championship 1988.—Jahangir Khan (Pakistan) beat Jansher Khan (Pakistan), 3–0.

Women's World Open Championship 1989.—Miss M. Le Moignan (G.B.) beat Miss S. Devoy (N.Z.), 3–1.

World Team Championship.—Pakistan.

Women's World Team Championship.—England.

British Open Championship.—Jahangir Khan (Pakistan) beat R. Martin (Australia), 3–2.

Women's British Open Championship.—Miss S. Devoy (N.Z.) beat Miss M. Le Moignan (G.B.), 3–1.

Men's National Championship.—P. Carter beat N. Harvey, 3–1.

Women's National Championship.—Miss M. Le Moignan beat Miss A. Cumings, 3–2.

SWIMMING, 1989

NATIONAL SWIMMING CHAMPIONSHIPS
1989 (Coventry, July 12–16)

Men:

50 metres Freestyle.—M. Fibbens.

100 metres Freestyle.—M. Fibbens.

200 metres Freestyle.—J. Broughton.

400 metres Freestyle.—C. McNeil.

1,500 metres Freestyle.—K. Boyd.

100 metres Breaststroke.—A. Moorhouse.

200 metres Breaststroke.—N. Gillingham.

100 metres Butterfly.—D. Parker.

200 metres Butterfly.—A. Quinn.

100 metres Backstroke.—G. Binfield.

200 metres Backstroke.—G. Binfield.

200 metres Medley.—G. Robins.

400 metres Medley.—P. Brew.

4 × 100 metres Freestyle Relay.—Leeds.

4 × 100 metres Medley Relay.—Leeds.

Women:

50 metres Freestyle.—C. Woodcock.

100 metres Freestyle.—K. Pickering.

200 metres Freestyle.—J. Coull.

400 metres Freestyle.—K. Mellor.

800 metres Freestyle.—K. Mellor.

100 metres Breaststroke.—S. Brownsdon.

200 metres Breaststroke.—S. Brownsdon.
100 metres Butterfly.—M. Scarborough.
200 metres Butterfly.—S. Purvis and M. Scarborough.
100 metres Backstroke.—K. Read.
200 metres Backstroke.—K. Read.
200 metres Medley.—S. Davies.
400 metres Medley.—S. Brownsdon.
4 × 100 metres Freestyle Relay.—Birmingham.
4 × 100 metres Medley Relay.—Wigan Wasps.

TABLE TENNIS, 1989

ENGLISH NATIONAL CHAMPIONSHIPS
(Portsmouth)

Men's Singles: A. Cooke beat C. Prean, 3–0.
Women's Singles: Mrs. L. Lomas beat Miss A. Gordon, 3–2.
Men's Doubles: S. Andrew and N. Mason beat A. Cooke and C. Prean, 2–0.
Women's Doubles: Miss F. Elliot and Mrs. L. Lomas beat Miss A. Gordon and Miss M. Sainsbury, 2–0.
Mixed Doubles: J. Holland and Miss J. Billington beat S. Andrew and Miss F. Elliot, 2–0.

YACHTING, 1988–89

AMERICA'S CUP 1988
(San Diego, U.S.A.)

Final.—The defender *Stars and Stripes* (U.S.A.) beat the challenger *New Zealand* (N.Z.) by 2–0. (In March 1989 a court ruling decided that *New Zealand* should be declared the winner after the disqualification of *Stars and Stripes* for being a catamaran, a design contrary to the rules of the America's Cup. On Sept. 19 an appeals court in New York reversed the decision but on the following day a further appeal by the New Zealand team was announced.)

Transatlantic Yacht Race 1988.—P. Poupon (France) *Fleury Michon. 1st woman.*—F. Arthaud (France) *Group Pierre.*

Admiral's Cup 1989.—Great Britain (*Jamarella/ Juno/Indulgence*), 748 pts.

Fastnet Race 1989.—R. Short (U.S.A.) *Great News.*

OXFORD AND CAMBRIDGE

PRINCIPAL EVENTS AND WINNERS, 1988–89

Event (with date of first meeting)	Summary of Results			Results 1988–89
	Ox.	Camb.	Drawn	
Athletics (1864)	58	50	7	Oxford
Boat Race (1829)	65	69	1	Oxford
Cricket (1827)	46	54	44	Aband.
Football—				
Association (1873–4)	39	45	21	Oxford
Rugby (1871–2)	46	48	13	Oxford
Golf (1878)	39	54	5	Camb.
Hockey (1890)	28	42	16	Camb.

OTHER UNIVERSITY EVENTS AND WINNERS, 1988–89

Cross Country .... Oxford
Rackets .... Oxford
Shooting .... Oxford
Real Tennis .... Cambridge
Boxing .... Oxford
Rugby League .... Oxford

THE OLYMPIC GAMES

The modern Olympic Games have been held as follows:

I	Athens	1896
II	Paris	1900
III	St. Louis	1904
IV	London	1908
V	Stockholm	1912
VII	Antwerp	1920
VIII	Paris	1924
IX	Amsterdam	1928
X	Los Angeles	1932
XI	Berlin	1936
XIV	London	1948
XV	Helsinki	1952
XVI	Melbourne	1956
XVII	Rome	1960
XVIII	Tokyo	1964
XIX	Mexico City	1968
XX	Munich	1972
XXI	Montreal	1976
XXII	Moscow	1980
XXIII	Los Angeles	1984
XXIV	Seoul	1988
XXV	Barcelona	1992

The following Games were scheduled but did not take place owing to World Wars:

VI	Berlin	1916
XII	Tokyo, then Helsinki	1940
XIII	London	1944

WINTER OLYMPIC GAMES

I	Chamonix (France)	1924
II	St. Moritz (Switzerland)	1928
III	Lake Placid (U.S.A.)	1932
IV	Garmisch-Partenkirchen (Germany)	1936
V	St. Moritz (Switzerland)	1948
VI	Oslo (Norway)	1952
VII	Cortina d'Ampezzo (Italy)	1956
VIII	Squaw Valley (U.S.A.)	1960
IX	Innsbruck (Austria)	1964
X	Grenoble (France)	1968
XI	Sapporo (Japan)	1972
XII	Innsbruck (Austria)	1976
XIII	Lake Placid (U.S.A.)	1980
XIV	Sarajevo (Yugoslavia)	1984
XV	Calgary (Canada)	1988
XVI	Albertville (France)	1992

ANGLING.—National Anglers' Council, 11 Cowgate, Peterborough PE1 1LZ. *Exec. Dir.*, P. H. Tombleson, O.B.E.

ASSOCIATION FOOTBALL.—The Football Association, 16 Lancaster Gate, W2 3LW. *Gen. Sec.*, G. Kelly.

ATHLETICS.—Amateur Athletic Association, Edgbaston House, 3 Duchess Place, Hagley Road, Birmingham B16 8NM. *Gen. Sec.*, M. A. Farrell.

—Women's Amateur Athletic Association, Francis House, Francis Street, SW1P 1DE. *Hon. Sec.*, Miss M. Hartman, C.B.E.

BADMINTON.—Badminton Association of England, National Badminton Centre, Loughton Lodge, Bradwell Road, Milton Keynes MK8 9LA. *Chief Exec.*, vacant.

BASKET BALL.—English Basket Ball Association. Calomax House, Lupton Avenue, Leeds LS9 6EE. *Sec.*, M. D. Welch.

BILLIARDS.—Billiards and Snooker Control Council, Coronet House, Queen Street, Leeds LS1 2TN. *Chair.*, S. Brooke.

BOBSLEIGH.—British Bobsleigh Association. *Sec.*, Mrs. B. Powe, 50 Sulivan Road, SW6 3DX.

BOWLS.—English Bowling Association, Lyndhurst Road, Worthing, W. Sussex BN11 2AZ. *Sec.*, D. W. Johnson.

—English Indoor Bowling Association. *Sec.*, B. Telfer. 290A Barking Road, E6 3BA.

BOXING.—Amateur Boxing Association of England, Francis House, Francis Street, SW1P 1DE.—*Exec. Dir.*, C. J. Howe.

— British Boxing Board of Control, 70 Vauxhall Bridge Road, SW1V 2RT.—*Gen. Sec.*, J. Morris.

CANOEING.—British Canoe Union, Mapperley Hall, Lucknow Avenue, Nottingham NG3 5FA. *Dir.*, T. J. Bailey.

CRICKET.—M.C.C., Lords, NW8 8QN. *Pres.* Sir Denys Roberts, K.B.E.; *Sec.*, Lt.-Col. J. R. Stephenson, O.B.E.

—T.C.C.B., Lord's, NW8 8QN. *Chairman* (1989–90), R. Subba Row; *Chief Exec.*, A. C. Smith.

—Cricket Council, Lord's, NW8 8QN. *Chairman*, R. Subba Row; *Sec.*, A. C. Smith.

CROQUET.—Croquet Association, c/o The Hurlingham Club, Ranelagh Gardens, SW6 3PR. *Sec.*, B. C. Macmillan.

CYCLING.—British Cycling Federation, 36 Rockingham Road, Kettering, Northants. NN16 8HG. *Sec.*, L. A. Unwin.

—Road Time Trials Council, Dallacre, Mill Road, Yarwell, Peterborough PE8 6PS. *Sec.*, D. E. Roberts.

ETON FIVES.—Eton Fives Association.—*Hon. Sec.*, M. P. Powell, Grafton Cottage, Bentley, Farnham, Surrey GU10 5HY.

FENCING.—Amateur Fencing Association, 83 Perham Road, W. Kensington, W14 9SP. *Sec.*, Miss G. Kenneally.

GOLF.—Royal and Ancient Golf Club, St. Andrews, Fife KY16 9JD. *Sec.*, M. F. Bonallack, O.B.E.

— English Golf Union. 1–3 Upper King Street, Leicester LE1 6XF. *Sec.*, K. Wright.

— Ladies' Golf Union, The Scores, St. Andrews, Fife KY16 9AT.—*Administrator*, Mrs A. Robertson.

GYMNASTICS.—British Amateur Gymnastics Association, 2 Buckingham Avenue East, Slough, Berks. SL1 3DZ. *Dir.*, A. L. Murdock.

HOCKEY.—Hockey Association, 16 Northdown Street, N1 9BG. *Chief Exec.*, S. P. Baines.

— All England Women's Hockey Association, 3rd Flr, Argyle House, 29–31 Euston Road, NW1 2SD. *Sec.*, Miss T. Morris.

HORSE-RACING.—The Jockey Club (incorporating National Hunt Committee), 42 Portman Square, W1H 0EN *Sec.*, C. N. Foster.

JUDO.—British Judo Association, 16 Upper Woburn Place, WC1H 0QH. *Gen. Sec.*, Miss G. M. Kenneally.

LACROSSE.—English Lacrosse Union. *Hon. Sec.*, R. Balls, 70 High Road, Rayleigh, Essex SS6 7AD.

— All England Women's Lacrosse Association, Francis House, Francis Street, SW1P 1DE. *Chief Exec.*, Miss P. A. Barratt.

LAWN TENNIS.—Lawn Tennis Association, The Queen's Club, W. Kensington, W14 9EG. *Sec.*, J. C. U. James.

— International Tennis Federation, Palliser Road, W14 9EN. *Gen. Sec.*, M. Davies.

LUGEING.—The Great Britain Luge Association, 43 Wimpole Street, W1M 7AF. *President*, R. L. Liversedge.

MOTOR CYCLING.—Auto-Cycle Union, Miller House, Corporation Street, Rugby, Warwicks. CV21 2DN. *Sec. Gen.*, D. G. Coleman.

NETBALL.—All England Netball Association Ltd., Francis House, Francis Street, SW1P 1DE. *Chief Exec.*, Mrs. E. M. Nicholl.

OLYMPICS.—British Olympic Association, 1 Wandsworth Plain, SW18 1EH. *Gen. Sec.*, R. Palmer, O.B.E.

ORIENTEERING.—British Orienteering Federation, Riversdale, Dale Road North, Darley Dale, Matlock, Derbys. DE4 2HX. *Gen. Sec.*, R. F. Mason.

POLO.—The Hurlingham Polo Association, Ambersham Farm, Ambersham, Midhurst, W. Sussex GU29 0BX. *Hon. Sec.*, Lt.-Col. A. F. Harper, D.S.O.

RIFLE SHOOTING.—National Rifle Association. Bisley Camp, Brookwood, Woking, Surrey GU24 0PB. *Sec.*, Brig. R. V. Ockenden, C.B.E.

—National Small-bore Rifle Association, Lord Roberts House, Bisley Camp, Brookwood, Woking GU24 0NP. *Sec.*, Gp. Capt. D. King, M.B.E.

ROWING.—Amateur Rowing Association, The Priory, 6 Lower Mall, W6 9DJ. *Exec. Sec.*, I. W. Pratt.

RUGBY FIVES.—Rugby Fives Association. *Hon. Sec.*, P. J. Reeder, 12 Alexandra Cottages, Hardings Lane, SE20 7JJ.

RUGBY FOOTBALL.—The Rugby Football Union, Whitton Road, Twickenham TW1 1DZ. *Sec.*, D. E. Wood.

— The Rugby Football League, 180 Chapeltown Road, Leeds LS7 4HT. *Chief Exec.*, D. S. Oxley.

SKATING.—National Skating Association of Great Britain. *Gen. Administrator*, E. Waughray, 15–27 Gee Street, EC1V 3RE.

SKI-ING.—British Ski Federation, Brocades House, Pyrford Road, West Byfleet, Surrey KT14 6RA. *Chairman*, T. Fitzpatrick.

SPEEDWAY.—The Speedway Control Board, Larchmont, Skinners Lane, Ashtead, Surrey KT21 2NN. *Manager*, R. W. Bracher.

SQUASH RACKETS.—Squash Rackets Association Ltd. *Chief Executive*, R. I. Morris, Warple Way, W3.

SWIMMING.—Amateur Swimming Association, Harold Fern House, Derby Square, Loughborough, Leics. LE11 0AL. *Sec.*, D. A. Reeves.

TABLE TENNIS.—English Table Tennis Association, Queensbury House, Havelock Road, Hastings TN34 1HF. *Chief Exec.*, E. J. Wallbutton.

VOLLEYBALL.—English Volleyball Association, 27 South Road, West Bridgford, Nottingham NG2 7AG. *National Dir.*, G. Bulman.

WALKING.—Race Walking Association. *Gen. Sec.*, J. F. Keowm, 30 Maxwell Gardens, Orpington, Kent BR6 9QS.

WEIGHTLIFTING.—British Amateur Weightlifters Association. *Hon. Sec.*, W. Holland, O.B.E., 3 Iffley Turn, Oxford OX4 4DU.

WRESTLING.—English Olympic Wrestling Association, 16 Choir Street, Cambridge Industrial Estate, Salford M7 9ZD. *Sec.*, H. I. Jacob, O.B.E.

YACHTING.—Royal Yachting Association, R.Y.A. House, Romsey Road, Eastleigh, Hants. SO5 4YA. *Sec. Gen.*, R. Duchesne, O.B.E.

THE NOBEL PRIZES

For prize winners for the years 1901–1985, *see* earlier editions of WHITAKER'S ALMANACK.

The Nobel Prizes are awarded each year from the income of a trust fund established by the Swedish scientist Alfred Nobel, the inventor of dynamite, who died on December 10, 1896, leaving a fortune of £1,750,000. The prizes are awarded to those who have contributed most to the common good in the domain of:
  (a) Physics, awarded by the Royal Swedish Academy of Sciences;
  (b) Chemistry, awarded by the Royal Swedish Academy of Sciences;
  (c) Physiology or Medicine, awarded by the Karolinska Institute;
  (d) Literature, awarded by the Swedish Academy of Arts;
  (e) Peace, awarded by a five-person committee elected by the Norwegian Storting;
  (f) Economic Sciences (instituted 1969), awarded by the Royal Swedish Academy of Sciences.
The first awards were made in 1901 on the fifth anniversary of Nobel's death.
The Trust is administered by the Board of Directors of the Nobel Foundation, Stockholm, consisting of five members and three deputy members. The Swedish Government appoints a chairman and a deputy chairman, the remaining members being appointed by the awarding authorities.

Prize	1986	1987	1988
PHYSICS	Dr. G. Binnig (W. German) Dr. H. Rohrer (Swiss) Prof. E. Ruska (W. German)	Dr. J. G. Bednorz (W. German) Dr. K. A. Müller (Swiss)	Dr. L. Lederman (American) Dr. M. Schwartz (American) Dr. J. Steinberger (American)
CHEMISTRY	Prof. D. Herschbach (American) Prof. Y. T. Lee (American) Prof. J. C. Polanyi (Canadian)	Prof. D. Cram (American) Prof. J.-M. Lehn (French) C. J. Pedersen (American)	Dr. J. Deisenhofer (W. German) Dr. R. Huber (W. German) Dr. H. Michel (W. German)
PHYSIOLOGY OR MEDICINE	Prof. S. Cohen (American) Prof. R. Levi-Montalcini (Italian)	S. Tonegawa (Japanese)	Sir James Black (British) Dr. G. Elion (American) Dr. G. Hitchings (American)
LITERATURE	Prof. Wole Soyinka (Nigerian)	J. Brodsky (American)	N. Mahfouz (Egyptian)
PEACE	Prof. E. Wiesel (American)	Pres. O. Arias (Costa Rican)	United Nations peacekeeping forces
ECONOMICS	Prof. J. M. Buchanan (American)	Prof. R. M. Solow (American)	Prof. M. Allais (French)

The awards have been distributed as follows:

PHYSICS.—American 51; British 20; German 18 (before 1948, 11; W. German 7); French 9; Russian 7; Dutch 6; Swedish 4; Austrian 3; Danish 3; Italian 3; Japanese 3; Chinese 2; Swiss 2; Indian 1; Irish 1; Pakistani 1.

CHEMISTRY.—American 33; German 27 (before 1948, 17; W. German 10); British 23; French 7; Swedish 4; Swiss 4; Canadian 2; Dutch 2; Argentinian 1; Austrian 1; Belgian 1; Czech 1; Finnish 1; Hungarian 1; Italian 1; Japanese 1; Norwegian 1; Russian 1.

PHYSIOLOGY/MEDICINE.—American 63; British 22; German 12 (before 1948, 8; W. German 4); French 7; Swedish 7; Danish 5; Swiss 5; Austrian 4; Belgian 4; Italian 3; Australian 2; Canadian 2; Dutch 2; Hungarian 2; Russian 2; Argentinian 1; Japanese 1; Portuguese 1; S. African 1; Spanish 1.

LITERATURE.—French 12; American 9; British 8; Swedish 7; German 6 (before 1948, 5; W. German 1); Italian 5; Spanish 4; Danish 3; Norwegian 3; Russian 3; Chilean 2; Greek 2; Irish 2; Polish 2; Swiss 2; Australian 1; Belgian 1; Colombian 1; Czech 1; Egyptian 1; Finnish 1; Guatemalan 1; Icelandic 1; Indian 1; Israeli 1; Japanese 1; Nigerian 1; Yugoslav 1; Stateless 1.

PEACE.—American 17; Institutions 16; British 9; French 9; Swedish 5; German 4 (before 1948, 3; W. German 1); Belgian 3; Swiss 3; Argentinian 2; Austrian 2; Norwegian 2; S. African 2; Canadian 1; Costa Rican 1; Danish 1; Dutch 1; Egyptian 1; Irish 1; Israeli 1; Italian 1; Japanese 1; Mexican 1; Polish 1; Russian 1; Vietnamese 1; Yugoslav 1.

ECONOMICS.—American 15; British 5; Swedish 2; Dutch 1; French 1; Norwegian 1; Russian 1.

WHITE PAPERS

BROADCASTING IN THE '90s

The White Paper *Broadcasting in the '90s: Competition, Choice and Quality* (Cm. 517) was presented to Parliament by the Home Secretary (Douglas Hurd) on November 7, 1988. The White Paper set out the Government's proposals for broadcasting in the United Kingdom in the 1990s. The Government feels that a radical reform of the framework for broadcasting in the U.K. is necessary for two reasons. First, the framework needs to be altered to take account of technological, international and other new developments. Second, the Government wishes a much wider range of programmes and types of broadcasting to be offered to viewers and listeners. It feels that choice should be widened and competition in the industry increased, though without detriment to programme standards and quality.

BBC

The Government sees the BBC continuing to be the cornerstone of public service broadcasting, at least for the foreseeable future. However, the Government feels that as new television services proliferate, the system of financing BBC television and radio services by a compulsory licence fee alone will become harder to sustain. The Government accepts that a sudden switch to subscription would be undesirable and damaging but feels that there should be a greater role for subscription.

The Government intends to encourage the progressive introduction of subscription on the BBC's television services and will authorize the BBC to encipher its services so that it can raise money through subscription. To provide a financial incentive, the Government intends after April 1991 to agree licence fee increases of less than the Retail Price Index increase in a way which takes account of the BBC's capacity to generate income from subscription.

A natural starting place for subscription is during the night hours. The BBC has already started night hours services providing information for the medical profession and it plans to run other similar services.

The Peacock Committee proposed that the night hours (which it defined as lasting from 1 a.m. to 6 a.m.) should be removed from the BBC and other broadcasting authorities and sold for use to provide new services by the highest bidder. The Government feels that this would hamper the BBC's plans for building a base for subscription technology. But the Government accepts the case for removing the night hours from one of the BBC's channels and assigning them to the independent television sector. The Government proposes to allow the BBC to retain the night hours of the other of its channels, on the basis that it uses them for developing subscription services.

Independent Television Commission

The Government thinks that all independent sector television services should be brought within the ambit of a single agency responsible for the whole sector. The present powers of the Independent Broadcasting Authority and the Cable Authority are limited to particular delivery technologies. The Government therefore proposes that there should be an Independent Television Commission (ITC).

The Government proposes that the ITC should be a licensing body rather than a broadcasting authority. This means that it will supervise, but not itself provide, programme services, applying broadly the same regulation across the board.

Independent Television

The Government feels that as the U.K. moves towards a more competitive multi-channel broadcasting market, the existing regime for ITV would become increasingly hard to sustain. It would be less sustainable to try to make all new services conform to the present requirements of the ITV system. The Government believes that this is the appropriate time to make major changes to the regime for what might henceforth be called Channel 3. If Parliament agrees, these changes will take effect from January 1, 1993 when the present ITV contracts come to an end.

The Government proposes that Channel 3 should be subject to positive programme requirements. Each Channel 3 station will be required: to show regional programming, including programmes produced in the region; to show high quality news and current affairs dealing with national and international matters, and to include news coverage in main viewing periods; to provide a diverse programme service calculated to appeal to a variety of tastes and interests; to ensure that a minimum of 25 per cent of original programming comes from independent producers; and to ensure that a proper proportion of programme material is of E.C. origin.

The Government intends to impose a duty on the ITC to ensure that there is at least one body effectively equipped and financed to provide news on its Channel 3 service. Channel 3 licensees would be required to finance the organization.

The Government wishes to introduce a more commercial element into the allocation of ITV franchises. It proposes that a suitably regulated tendering process should be introduced and that the ITC should operate a two-stage procedure. In the first stage applicants for licences would have to satisfy the ITC that they would meet the programming requirements. All applicants passing this stage would go on to the second stage, in which they would offer financial tenders for the licence. The ITC would be required to select the applicant for each licence who had submitted the highest tender.

Channels 5 and 6

The Government proposes to authorize a fifth channel with the same regulatory regime and the same licence allocation and review arrangements as Channel 3. The Government proposes that Channel 5 should begin broadcasting from the beginning of 1993, when the new Channel 3 licences will start. Bearing in mind that Channel 3 will be regionally based, the Government believes that Channel 5 licences should be national in scope.

A sixth channel will also be authorized should technical studies show this to be feasible. It would be subject to broadly the same regulatory regime and oversight as Channel 5, as would be the night hours which the ITC would allocate by competitive tender following release from the BBC.

Channel 4 and S4C

The Government proposes that the programming remits of Channel 4 and S4C should be fully sustained.

However, the Government believes that its proposals for a more competitive independent television sector mean that the place for Channel 4 within such an integrated ITV system will no longer be available.

The Government believes that Channel 4's role is best fulfilled by an independent organization subject to ITC oversight, but without direct financial or structural links to the Channel 3 licensees. Advertising will be sold separately from the advertising on Channel 3 or other channels. The Government puts forward in the White Paper a number of options for the future constitution of Channel 4 and invites comment.

The Government believes that the independent television services operating in the U.K. should continue to finance the cost of the Welsh Fourth Channel (net of its own advertising revenue).

Satellite services

British Satellite Broadcasting (BSB) plans to provide three channels nationwide. The U.K.'s two remaining direct broadcasting by satellite (DBS) frequencies will be advertised by the Independent Broadcasting Authority in early 1989. This will account for all the DBS channels now allocated to the U.K.; should any additional DBS channels be allocated to the U.K. in future, the ITC will allocate licences for future DBS services.

The Government wishes to encourage the development of cable and microwave (MVDS) transmission services, particularly in order to facilitate the growth of local services. It proposes a flexible regime which will leave operators free to decide upon the best mix of technologies. At present this will mean a choice between, or a combination of, cable and MVDS; but the framework will be sufficiently flexible to leave the way open for new technologies which may emerge.

These arrangements will be based on fifteen-year local franchises awarded by the ITC. The ITC will be assigned suitable frequencies for local services, and will be responsible for advertising franchises.

Viewers will continue to be able to receive other satellite services directly, including those from the proposed Astra and Eutelsat II satellites. Steps will be taken to ensure that the programme content of all such services is supervised.

Financing of services

The Government proposes to allow all independent sector television operators to finance themselves by advertising or subscription or a mixture of the two.

The Government envisages that the ITC will have a duty to draw up and enforce a code or codes on advertising and sponsorship. The Government favours liberalizing the present restrictions on sponsorship, provided editorial independence and transparency for the viewer are adequately protected. The BBC will be free to raise finance through subscription and sponsorship but not by carrying advertising.

Ownership

The Government is determined to impose limits on concentration of ownership and on excessive cross-media ownership, in order to keep the market open for newcomers and to prevent any tendency towards editorial uniformity or domination by a few groups. The Government proposes to make use of subordinate legislation for such restrictions, to ensure maximum flexibility in reacting quickly to changing circumstances.

The Government envisages that local authorities and bodies whose objects are wholly or mainly of a religious or political nature will be disqualified from holding any ITC licence. The Government also envisages restrictions on the number of licences that may be held by one group.

Radio

The Government published in February 1987 a Green Paper *Radio: Choices and Opportunities* (Cmnd. 92). At the national level the Green Paper saw a continuing need for public service radio broadcasting provided by the BBC, but proposed that there should be additional national radio services provided on commercial lines. At the local level it proposed that the BBC should complete its chain of local stations, and that local independent stations, including new community radio services, should operate under broadly the same regulatory regime as envisaged for the new national services.

The Government's proposals in the White Paper are that there will be at least three new national commercial services operating alongside the BBC. The new national services and independent local services will be subject to a lighter regulatory regime than at present.

At the local level, licensing criteria will include financial viability, local audience demands, and the extent to which the proposed services would enhance the range of programming and the diversity of listener choice. National services will be expected to provide a diversity of programmes calculated to appeal to a variety of tastes and interests and not limited to a single narrow format. The proposed competitive tender procedure for national services will be subject to this test. National and local services will have to keep their promises of performance in order to retain their licences.

Radio Authority

A new Radio Authority will be responsible for assigning frequencies and issuing licences to, and supervising the performance of, all independent stations. Advertising and sponsorship will be more flexibly supervised than at present.

The Government also proposes to provide for any satellite radio services for direct reception to be regulated by the Radio Authority. In the case of satellite programming delivered to stations, Radio Authority regulation will apply to the stations taking the service. The Authority will also license miscellaneous radio broadcasting services, such as special event and university radio.

Programme standards

All U.K. television and radio services will be required to observe acceptable standards of impartiality, taste and decency. The Government feels that nothing should be included in programmes which is offensive to public feeling or which encourages crime or disorder.

The Broadcasting Standards Council was established in 1988 by the Government to develop a code on the portrayal of sex and violence in all forms of broadcasting. The Government proposes to place the Council on a statutory footing.

The Government sees no case for continuing the exemption of broadcasting from the Obscene Publications Act 1959, and proposes to remove the exemption at the earliest opportunity.

Transmission

The Government considers that the best arrangement in due course would be a regionally based, privatized transmission system designed to promote competition, while containing certain common carrier obligations. The Government proposes to discuss with the BBC, the IBA and others how the objective of moving towards a privatized transmission system might best be taken forward. It will also be considering how any necessary regulatory oversight should be arranged.

Programme production

The Government has already set the BBC and the ITV companies the target of commissioning 25 per cent of original material from independent producers as quickly as possible. Both the BBC and the ITV companies are committed to achieving this target by the end of 1992, subject to satisfaction on cost and quality. The Government has welcomed these developments, and envisages that independent producers will continue to play a greater part in programme making in the U.K.

WORKING FOR PATIENTS

The Government's review of the operation of the National Health Service (NHS) has led to the publication in the past two years of two White Papers proposing reforms. In November 1987 the White Paper *Promoting Better Health* (Cm. 249) was published, containing proposals for improving primary health care services (summarized in *Whitaker's Almanack 1989*). The Government's proposals for improving the hospital service and the organization of the NHS were published in the White Paper *Working for Patients* (Cm. 555). This was presented to Parliament on January 31, 1989 by the Secretaries of State for Health (Kenneth Clarke), Wales (Peter Walker), Northern Ireland (Tom King) and Scotland (Malcolm Rifkind).

In the White Paper *Working for Patients* the government states its commitment to the principles that have guided the NHS for the past forty years. The Government emphasizes that the NHS will continue to be available to all, regardless of income, and will be financed mainly out of general taxation.

The Government praises the quality of care provided and the response to emergencies by the NHS. The Government feels, however, that rising demand and the ever-widening range of treatments made possible by medical advances present challenges to the efficient operation of the NHS that can only be met by reforming its organization.

The Government wishes to eliminate the wide variation in performance between different areas of the country. The average cost of treating patients and the waiting times for operations varies considerably between different health authorities. Similarly, there are wide variations in the drug prescribing habits of general practitioners (G.P.s)

and in the rate at which G.P.s refer patients to hospital.

The Government wants to raise the performance of all hospitals and G.P. practices to that of the best. It is convinced that this can be done only by delegating responsibility as closely as possible to where health care is delivered to the patient—predominantly to the G.P. and the local hospital. The proposals in the White Paper are intended to give patients, wherever they live in the U.K., better health care and greater choice of the services available; and afford greater satisfaction and rewards to those working in the NHS who successfully respond to local needs and preferences.

Management of the NHS

The Government wishes to make the Health Service more responsive to the needs of patients, and believes that this can best be achieved by delegating as much power and responsibility as possible to local level. This includes the delegation of functions from Regional Health Authorities (RHAs) to District Health Authorities (DHAs), and from DHAs to hospitals.

The central management of the NHS would be altered to reflect this change in the division of responsibilities. The Government proposes that responsibility for strategy rest with an NHS Policy Board chaired by the Secretary of State for Health. Responsibility for all operational matters would rest with an NHS Management Executive chaired by a Chief Executive. The Management Executive would be accountable to the Policy Board for the management of the NHS within the strategy and objectives set by the Policy Board. Responsibility for the management of family practitioner services would be brought under the NHS Management Executive. The better integration of primary care and hospital services would be an important objective.

The NHS Management Executive could not directly exercise effective authority over the current 190 DHAs. Regional Health Authorities would therefore continue to ensure that Government policies are properly carried out within their Regions. Their essential tasks would include setting performance criteria, monitoring the performance of the Health Service and evaluating its effectiveness.

The Government also believes that there is scope for delegating more decision-making from DHAs to hospitals and their associated management units. The Government envisages DHAs delegating operational functions to hospitals and concentrating their efforts on ensuring the provision of the services required locally, setting targets and monitoring the performance of those management units for which they are responsible. The proposals include greater flexibility for hospitals in setting the pay and conditions of staff, and financial incentives to make the best use of a hospital's assets.

Self-governing hospitals

The Government intends to allow hospitals to apply for a new self-governing status as NHS Hospital Trusts. This means that, while remaining within the NHS, they would take fuller responsibility for their own affairs, harnessing the skills and dedication of their staff. NHS Hospital Trusts would earn revenue from the services they provided. They would therefore have an incentive to attract patients, so they would make sure that the services offered are what their patients want. This in turn would stimulate other NHS hospitals to respond to what people want locally. NHS Hospital Trusts would also be able to set the rates of pay of their own staff and, within annual financing limits, to borrow money to help them respond to patient demand.

The Government wishes the money required to treat patients to be able to cross administrative boundaries. It proposes that all NHS hospitals, whether run by health authorities or self-governing, should be free to offer their services to different health authorities and to the private sector. The Government believes that this will enable a health authority to make better use of its available funds to secure a comprehensive service, including emergency services, by obtaining the best service it can, whether from its own hospitals, from another authority's hospitals, from NHS Hospital Trusts or from the private sector.

The Government wishes to reduce waiting times and improve the quality of service, to help give individual patients appointment times they can rely on, and to help cut the long hours worked by some junior doctors. It proposes that 100 new consultant posts be created over the next three years. The new posts will be in addition to the two per cent annual expansion of consultant numbers already planned.

Practice budget scheme

The Government wishes to help the family doctor improve his service to patients. To this end, large G.P. practices will be allowed to apply for their own budgets to obtain a defined range of services direct from hospitals.

At the start of the new scheme, G.P. practices with lists of at least 11,000 patients would be free to apply for their own NHS budgets for a defined range of hospital services. They would be able to obtain these services from either NHS or private sector hospitals. The size of each practice's budget would depend primarily on the number of patients on the practice's list. There would be three categories of hospital services within the scheme: out-patient services; a defined group of in-patient and day treatments (the inclusion of this category will make it easier for G.P.s to offer shorter waiting times to patients who are willing to travel, and will enable them to provide the hospitals concerned with NHS funds to pay for the treatment); and diagnostic tests, such as X-ray examinations and pathology tests.

In addition, the Government intends the scheme to cover three aspects of the services provided by G.P.s themselves: the 70 per cent of practice team staff costs which are directly reimbursed to G.P. practices at present and which will be cash-limited under the Health and Medicines Act 1988; improvements to practice premises; and prescribing costs.

Participation in the practice budget scheme would be voluntary, and practices which have joined the scheme would be free to leave it if they wish, after giving due notice.

Indicative drug budgets

The cost of the drugs prescribed by G.P.s is the largest single element of total expenditure by the Family Practitioner Service. There are wide differences in drug costs from one part of the country to another, reflecting varying attitudes of doctors towards prescribing.

In an attempt to contain the rise in the cost of medicines the Government introduced a 'Selected List' of drugs which doctors may prescribe. An information system was established to collect data about prescribing patterns. The Government now proposes to improve prescribing practice by introducing indicative drug budgets for G.P.s The intention is that RHAs will set an annual drug budget for each Family Practitioner Committee (FPC). The FPCs will then set indicative drug budgets for each practice, after discussion with G.P.s. The spending of practices will be monitored during the year by the FPC, and the performance of the FPCs will be monitored by the RHAs. Practices may exceed their budget in exceptional circumstances but generally RHAs and FPCs will be expected to work to the budget they have been set.

Composition of management bodies

The Government feels that the delegation of greater management responsibility to the Regional and District Health Authorities and the Family Practitioner Committees necessitates changes to the composition of these bodies. At present there is some confusion of roles, so that they neither represent the full range of health interests in the locality, nor are they fully management bodies.

The Government believes that authorities based on this confusion of roles would not be equipped to handle the complex managerial and contractual issues that the new system of matching resources to performance will demand. The Government proposes to reduce the management bodies in size and reform them along business lines, with executive and non-executive directors.

Audits

To ensure that all concerned with delivering services to the patient make the best use of the resources available, quality of service and value for money will be more rigorously audited. Arrangements for what doctors call 'medical audit' (a systematic, critical analysis of the quality of medical care) will be extended throughout the Health Service. The Government hopes that this will help to ensure a consistently high quality of treatment, and the best use of financial resources.

At present the Health Departments carry out the external audits of the health authorities and the Family Practitioner Committees. The Government proposes to transfer to the Audit Commission responsibility for auditing the accounts of health authorities and other NHS bodies. The responsibilities of the Audit Commission would also cover the proposed NHS Hospital Trusts and G.P. practice budgets. It would also undertake 'value for money' studies.

Putting patients first

It will take time for some of the reforms proposed in the White Paper to take effect, even when the necessary legislation has been passed. In the meantime the Government wishes health authorities to take more immediate action to tackle the problems of greatest public concern.

People still sometimes have to wait too long for treatment, and may have little choice over the time or place at which treatment is given. Also, the service provided on admission to hospital is sometimes impersonal and inflexible. The Government believes that each hospital should offer:

(i) appointments systems which give people individual appointment times that they can rely on;

(ii) quiet and pleasant waiting and other public areas, with proper facilities for children and for counselling;

(iii) information leaflets about the facilities available and what patients need to know when they come into hospital;

(iv) clearer and easier procedures for making suggestions for improvement and, if necessary, complaints;

(v) once someone is in hospital, clear and sensitive explanations of what is happening, both in practical and in clinical matters;

(vi) rapid notification of the results of diagnostic tests;

(vii) a wider range of optional amenities for patients who want to pay for them (e.g. single rooms, personal telephones, televisions).

Use of resources

The Government feels that if the NHS is to provide the best service it can for its patients, the quest for value for money must be an essential element in its work. The Government believes that delegating more operational responsibility to local level will enable the Health Service to make better use of the available resources. The Government expects the changes to improve the information available to local managers, enabling them to make their budgeting and monitoring more accurate. It also expects health authorities to contract out more functions which do not have to be undertaken by health authority staff and which could be provided more cost effectively by the private sector.

Private health sector

The Government feels that the NHS and the independent health sector should be able to support each other and to provide services for each other. There is already a growing partnership between the NHS and the independent health sector and the Government hopes that its reforms to the NHS will create more opportunities for the two sectors to work together.

The Government expects to see further increases in the number of people wishing to make private provision for health care, but at the moment many people who do so during their working life find the cost of higher premiums difficult to meet in retirement. The Government therefore proposes to allow income tax relief on private medical insurance premiums for those aged 60 and over. This relief will be available on premiums paid by them or, for example, by their families on their behalf.

Implementation

The Government plans to implement the proposals in the White Paper in three main phases from 1989–91.

In 1989 the Secretary of State for Health will establish a new NHS Policy Board and reconstitute the NHS Management Board as a Management Executive (implemented in May/June 1989). The Health Departments, and Regional Health Authorities in England, will identify the first hospitals to become self-governing as NHS Hospital Trusts, and plan for their new status; will devolve further operational responsibility to District Health Authorities and hospitals; and will begin preparing the ground for G.P. practice budgets.

The first additional consultant posts will be created; District Health Authorities will begin agreeing job descriptions with their consultants; and a new framework for medical audit will begin to be implemented. The existing resource management initiative will be extended to more major acute hospitals. Preparations for indicative drug budgets for G.P.s will begin. The Audit Commission will begin its work in the NHS.

In 1990 'shadow' boards of the first group of NHS Hospital Trusts will start to develop their plans for the future. RHAs, District Health Authorities and

Family Practitioner Committees will be reconstituted, and FPCs will become accountable to RHAs. Regions will begin paying directly for work they do for each other.

In 1991 the first NHS Hospital Trusts will be established. The first G.P. practice budget-holders will begin buying services for their patients. The indicative drug budget scheme will be implemented. DHAs will begin paying directly for work they do for each other.

LEGAL SERVICES

The White Paper *Legal Services: A Framework for the Future* (Cm. 740) was presented to Parliament by the Lord Chancellor (Lord Mackay of Clashfern) on July 19, 1989. The Government's overall aim is to improve access to good quality legal services, to the courts and, ultimately, to justice. The proposals in the White Paper are intended to improve the structure and work of the legal profession and to ensure that legal services of the appropriate kind and quality are readily available.

In January 1989 the Government published three Green Papers about the work and organization of the legal profession, contingency fees, and conveyancing. Response to these was taken into account when the White Paper was prepared.

In the White Paper, the Government announces its proposals for legislation, which it intends to introduce at an early opportunity. The overall aims are to give the public as wide a choice as possible in the providers of legal services available to them. At the same time, the Government seeks to maintain the high standards of integrity and competence which are necessary for protecting the interests of the client and for the more general public interest in the administration of justice. The Government seeks also to remove any restrictions which are not necessary for the protection of those interests. These aims will be met by creating a framework which encourages flexibility and diversity in meeting the client's needs, yet maintains the necessary standards.

Statutory objectives

The Government believes it is of central importance that the objectives which govern the arrangements for the provision of legal services in advocacy and in the conduct of litigation should be simple and clear. Practitioners need that if they are to deliver what is expected of them. The professional bodies and other organizations need that to enforce standards consistently amongst their own members, in relation to other professions providing similar legal services. Above all the client needs to understand the basis of the work and the services for which he is paying.

The Government therefore proposes to include those basic objectives in the legislation. All those who contribute to setting and maintaining standards in the provision of legal services – the professional bodies and other organizations, the Lord Chancellor, and the judiciary – will be required to have regard to those objectives in carrying out their duties.

The objectives are:

(i) to lay down standards of education and training in the provision of services in advocacy or the conduct of litigation which ensure that those who offer such services to the public are competent to do so.

(ii) to maintain the standards of conduct in advocacy and the conduct of litigation which are required in the interests of the proper and efficient administration of justice.

(iii) to meet those objectives in ways which ensure that there are no obstacles to access to justice. No restrictions should inhibit the client's choice of how he may obtain legal services, should be imposed on those qualified to provide legal services or on what those who are qualified may do, which are not necessary in the interests of justice.

Rights of audience

The Green Papers proposed a system of statutory regulation for the purpose of ensuring common standards between the different, self-regulating parts of the profession which exercise similar functions, such as granting rights of audience in the courts. During the consultation process, that proposal was criticized for not reflecting fully the role of the judiciary; for indirectly compromising professional self-regulation; and for not adequately recognizing the diversity of advocacy practice. As a result of the consultation, and in particular the Law Society's acceptance that barristers should have immediate rights to appear in all courts on being called to the Bar by one of the Inns of Court, this system can be considerably simplified.

The Government recognizes, as the Green Paper proposals made plain, that the education and training of those who carry on litigation are of fundamental importance. The proposals for dealing with education and training and for regulating the conduct of those admitted to practice are crucial. The Government therefore proposes to replace the current complex arrangements for rights of audience with a single statutory framework. This would recognize the widely different needs of the practice of advocacy in the various courts and tribunals, and the different working practices of the many kinds of legal practitioners. It would ensure that the interests of all those who have a part to play in the court system – the client, the practitioner, the courts, and the Government – are represented in a full and balanced way. In particular, the Government acknowledges the role of the judiciary in encouraging the independence and competence of all advocates who appear before the courts. The system now proposed therefore includes a place in the framework for the full-time judiciary which builds on the present arrangements for the Law Society's training regulations. Above all, the framework for granting rights of audience must ensure that the development of legal services is ordered, and rapid enough to meet clients' changing needs.

The principal features of the proposals are: that barristers who are qualified in terms of the Bar's rules on education and training will have rights of audience before all courts and tribunals; and that the Law Society will continue as before to decide which persons are qualified to be solicitors, but it will have power to declare solicitors qualified in terms of regulations for education and training to appear for clients in any specified level of court. A person declared by the Law Society to be qualified for particular courts or tribunals will then have rights of audience.

In both cases the professional body will need to satisfy the Lord Chancellor and the judiciary acting on advice from the proposed Lord Chancellor's Advisory Committee on Legal Education and Conduct that its members can uphold appropriate standards of competence and conduct.

Litigation

The provision for entitlement to do the work which is necessary to start and conduct litigation will be given a simplified statutory basis, on the same approach as for advocacy work. The Law Society will be entitled by statute to grant its members the right to conduct litigation. Arrangements will be made to enable other professions to do so, to an appropriate degree.

In each case, this will be subject to the professional body or other organization being able to satisfy the Lord Chancellor and the judiciary, in the light of advice from the Advisory Committee, that it can set and maintain appropriate standards of competence and conduct.

Conveyancing

The Government is taking and encouraging a number of steps to improve the quality of practice, and to eliminate abuse, throughout the house-buying market. The specific proposals in the conveyancing Green Paper to enable banks, building societies and other authorized practitioners to offer conveyancing services have been amended to provide, as the consultation suggested, greater protection against conflicts of interest, the lack of independent advice, and opportunities for unfair competition by larger institutions. In particular there will be a general ban on offering conveyancing services in situations in which conflicts of interest are regular or inescapable. Also, the qualified conveyancer undertaking the transaction should offer the client a personal interview, to be sure no conflict arises, and identify any areas in which independent advice might be desirable. Authorized practitioners will be required to certify that they are not cross-subsidizing conveyancing services from their other activities and to disclose financial benefits from all aspects of the transaction. Making the provision of one service conditional on taking others will be prohibited.

Probate

The Government's original proposals for extending the range of people who can prepare the documents

required to apply for probate will be amended to allow a greater measure of protection for the client. Trust corporations, which can already demonstrate the necessary standards of competence and conduct, will be authorized to do this work by statute. Arrangements will be made for the Lord Chancellor, after consultation with the judiciary, to authorize other groups to do so, if they can demonstrate that they meet appropriate standards.

Advisory Committee

The proposal in the Green Papers for a reconstituted Lord Chancellor's Advisory Committee on Legal Education and Conduct with executive powers was criticized. It was argued that the committee would interfere with professional self-regulation because it would represent a shift of power to the executive and because it would not be sufficiently independent.

The proposal has been thoroughly revised. There should be a reconstituted and vigorous Advisory Committee, but its functions will be purely advisory. Its prime role will be to give advice to all bodies authorized to grant to their members rights of audience, the right to conduct litigation, or the right to prepare probate documents. It will also advise the Lord Chancellor and the judiciary on the arrangements for ensuring appropriate standards of competence and conduct in the provision of legal services. The professional bodies and other organizations, the Lord Chancellor, and the judges will all be required by statute to have regard to advice from the Advisory Committee on the discharge of their statutory functions.

All the Advisory Committee's advice will be public: it will report to Parliament on all aspects of its work annually, and on specific issues as appropriate. The Advisory Committee will be financed from money provided by Parliament, and will be wholly independent, running its own procedure and appointing its own staff, who will be expected to come from a variety of backgrounds.

Professional bodies

The importance of professional self-regulation will be reinforced by leaving it to the professional bodies to prepare the regulations and codes which will set qualification standards and practice requirements for advocacy and the conduct of litigation. The Advisory Committee will advise the professional bodies on the codes. New rules will require the concurrence of the Lord Chancellor.

Under the adversarial system operated in this country, the courts depend on the competence and probity of advocates and litigators. The proposals seek to reflect this, and the concurrence of senior members of the judiciary will be required for new regulations or codes to become effective. Both the Lord Chancellor and the judges will be advised by the Advisory Committee on whether they should approve the new regulations or codes.

Legal education

The Advisory Committee will advise upon the arrangements for legal education. It will give advice on the standards and selection procedures desirable for schemes to recognize legal practitioners and others as specialists in particular areas of the law. It will also comment on the need for such schemes.

The Committee's advice will be directed to ensure that the existence of such schemes does not create unnecessary barriers either to new practitioners, whether lawyers or suitably qualified non-lawyers, entering the area of work concerned, or general practitioners continuing to work in the area.

Complaints

The Government proposes a range of measures to ensure that complaints from members of the public about legal services provided to them can be simply and effectively met. Arrangements will be considered for a joint disciplinary body of the Bar and the Law Society, involving members of the judiciary when appropriate, to provide a common mechanism and common standards in dealing with complaints about court work. This might operate both nationally and at a local level. The courts' own powers to deal with poor work will be strengthened.

A new office of Legal Services Ombudsman will be created. He will have wide powers to examine the way in which complaints against legal practitioners have been investigated by the professional bodies. He will also have power to investigate such complaints himself where that is appropriate. He will have power to recommend the payment of compensation in most cases.

Competition

Aspects of the work and organization of the legal profession which do not need to be regulated in the interests of justice may, however, need to be scrutinized to ensure that there are no unnecessary restrictions on competition. The professional bodies' rules and practices therefore will in general be subject to consideration under the proposed legislation on restrictive trade practices. Under that legislation, however, rules approved by the Lord Chancellor will be exempt from prohibition.

Partnerships

The Government is concerned to ensure that clients have ready access to independent legal advice, and in particular an adequate choice of specialist practitioners, both barristers and solicitors. It believes it is for the professions to decide how they should best organize themselves to meet the needs of their clients. The statutory prohibition on the formation of partnerships between solicitors and other professionals will be removed, and the matter left to professional rules. The Bar Council and the Law Society will continue to be able to make rules preventing such partnerships if they so wish, to the extent that this is justified by the needs of advocacy or the conduct of litigation.

The Government's proposals for lifting barriers to the formation of partnerships between advocates and litigators in this country and lawyers practising in other jurisdictions have been widely welcomed. Arrangements will also be made to ensure that United Kingdom lawyers have rights to practise in other parts of the kingdom at least equivalent to those available to lawyers from other member states of the European Community.

Fees

During the consultation process it became clear that there was general opposition to the introduction of a system of contingency fees which would permit clients to offer their lawyers a percentage of any damages if successful. That option has therefore been rejected.

There was, however, little objection in principle or in practice to clients being able to agree with their lawyers conditional fees on the speculative basis already permitted in Scotland, or to permitting a specified moderate percentage uplift on the normal bill which the parties to such agreements could contract to pay. The Government therefore proposes to implement this proposal.

Judicial appointments

The proposal that the qualifications for judicial appointments should be revised to make all suitably qualified lawyers eligible for judicial appointments has been widely welcomed. The general simplification in the arrangements for working as an advocate will permit significantly simplified arrangements to be implemented to achieve this.

The Government proposes that the minimum qualifications for a practitioner for appointment to the Bench should be rights of audience as follows:

Lord of Appeal in Ordinary—general rights of audience in the Supreme Court for 15 years.

Lord Justice of Appeal, High Court Judge, Deputy High Court Judge—general rights of audience in the High Court and Court of Appeal for ten years.

Circuit Judge, Recorder, Assistant Recorder—general rights of audience in the Crown Court or the county courts for ten years.

Master or Registrar of the Supreme Court, County Court Registrar, Stipendiary Magistrate—rights of audience in the Supreme Court or a general right of audience in the county court for seven years.

LITERATURE, 1988–89

The past year has been dominated by the controversy over *The Satanic Verses* by Salman Rushdie. Objections to the novel have been so widespread and so violent that the controversy sparked off a major international incident and provoked a strong reaction from those who felt that the right to freedom of speech was under threat.

The Satanic Verses is Rushdie's fourth novel. His second, *Midnight's Children*, won the Booker Prize in 1981, and his third, *Shame*, a savage satire on the recent history of Pakistan, was shortlisted for the same award in 1983. *The Satanic Verses* was widely reviewed and shortlisted for the 1988 Booker Prize; it also won the novel section of the 1988 Whitbread Prize.

The book opens with the explosion of a hijacked jumbo jet over the English Channel. Two figures without parachutes fall from the wreckage, Gibreel Farishta, a legendary Indian film star, and Saladin Chamcha, 'man of a thousand voices'. Both survive—'Out of thin air: a big bang, followed by falling stars. A universal beginning, a miniature echo of the birth of time'. One of the protagonists turns into the Angel Gabriel, the other into the devil, and the story concerns the eternal struggle between good and evil. It is written in Rushdie's flamboyant, sometimes overblown prose, with a proliferation of ideas and images which make the book dense and difficult to read.

The book's title is taken from an apocryphal incident in which the Prophet Mohammed was tricked by Satan into inserting into the Koran two verses which were diabolically, not divinely, inspired. The 'Satanic verses' were later expunged from the Koran, which is regarded by Muslims as the literal word of God, given to the Prophet Mohammed. However, Rushdie's reference to this incident was not the sole cause of the offence given by the novel. The novel portrayed the Prophet throughout as Mahound, which was considered derogatory, and in one section a number of whores each assume the identity of one of the Prophet's wives.

Salman Rushdie, speaking about his novel on Channel 4 television, said, 'Basically, there's two questions that the book seeks to answer. When an idea comes into the world, it's faced with two big tests: when you're weak, do you compromise; when you're strong, are you tolerant?' Rushdie received his answer in far more dramatic terms than he can have envisaged. Reaction against the book began within a few weeks of its publication in September 1988. India banned its importation, threats were made against it in Britain, and Rushdie was forced to cancel a public reading in Cambridge. In January, the book was burned by Muslims in Bradford and threats were made against the staff of W. H. Smith, causing the company to withdraw the book from its branch there. In Pakistan a demonstration led to the deaths of five people when police opened fire on the crowd.

Misunderstood

Rushdie claimed the book had been misunderstood, and that people were protesting against a book he had not written. 'Islam is one of the greatest ideas that ever came into the world', he said. 'Nothing I can do can destroy Islam, even if it were my desire, which it isn't. I wished to provoke imagination, and increase the sum of what it is possible to think or say. A powerful tribe of clerics has taken over Islam and have turned Mohammed into a perfect being and his life into a perfect life. Obviously I have a view of the world which is not theirs. I insist on my right to have that and to express it as I think fit. It is not in my view an anti-religious book. It is an attempt to write about migration, its stresses and transformations for migrants from the Indian subcontinent to Britain. The saddest irony is that after working for five years to give voice and fictional flesh to the immigrant culture of which I am myself part, I should see the book burned and my life threatened.'

The most serious development came in February 1989. Rushdie had said that he 'expected that the mullahs wouldn't like it', but can hardly have anticipated the edict issued by Ayatollah Khomeini of Iran on February 14. This stated: 'I inform the proud Muslim people of the world that the author of *The Satanic Verses* book, which is against Islam, the Prophet and the Koran, and all those involved in its publication who were aware of its content, are sentenced to death. I ask all Muslims to execute them wherever they find them. If someone knows them but is unable to kill them, he should hand them over to the people for punishment.' After the threat, Rushdie went into hiding under armed police protection.

Solidarity

Following Ayatollah Khomeini's threat against Rushdie, the British Government announced that it was withdrawing its four envoys from Iran, and Iran was asked to withdraw its diplomats from London. Strong support was given by the other members of the European Community, who agreed to recall their ambassadors to Iran as an expression of solidarity. High-level visits between Europe and Iran were frozen. 'Britain has endeavoured to re-establish normal relations with Iran, but there can be no substance in this relationship while these threats of violence remain', said the Foreign Secretary, Sir Geoffrey Howe. The Spanish Foreign Minister described the threat against Rushdie as an 'affront to civilization'.

Although there was a strong reaction to the threat to his life, Government support for Rushdie personally seemed to waver as time went by. Sir Geoffrey Howe said on the B.B.C. World Service, 'there is a huge distance between ourselves and the book ... it is found deeply offensive by people of the Muslim faith. The British Government, the British people, do not have any affection for the book ... [it] is extremely critical, rude about us. It compares Britain with Hitler's Germany. We do not like that any more than the people of the Muslim faith like the attacks on their faith contained in the book. So we are not sponsoring the book. What we are sponsoring is the right of people to speak freely, to publish freely.'

The Home Secretary, Douglas Hurd said, 'There is no doubt that real hurt and insult has been felt by the Muslim community in this country, as elsewhere. I sometimes feel that Mr. Rushdie has difficulty in understanding the institutions of the country to which he belongs.'

Apology

In an attempt to defuse the situation, Rushdie offered an apology: 'As author of *The Satanic Verses* I recognize that Muslims in many parts of the world are genuinely distressed by the publication of my novel. I profoundly regret the distress that publication has occasioned to sincere followers of Islam. Living as we do in a world of many faiths, this experience has served to remind us that we must all be conscious of the sensibilities of others.'

This failed to placate Iran: the Ayatollah Khomeini responded, 'Even if Salman Rushdie repents and becomes the most pious man of all time it is incumbent on every Muslim to employ everything he's got, his life and wealth, to send him to hell.'

Meanwhile, the book sold in vast quantities, both in Britain and abroad. In order to publish the book without risk to individuals, sixty German publishing houses set up a special imprint, *Artikel 19* (from the Declaration of Human Rights article on freedom of expression). In Britain, Rushdie's publishers, Viking Penguin, faced a dilemma about bringing out a paperback edition, publication of which would be seen as provocative by Muslims. A spokesman commented, 'We deplore the violence associated with the book. We regret the distress the book has caused to people who believe that it is blasphemous. But it is not blasphemous, it is a work of fiction by one of the world's leading writers and has been brilliantly reviewed here and in the U.S. There has also been support in the Muslim world. Those in the West, where freedom of expression is a cornerstone of democracy, believe that this is an outrageous reaction.' The book trade journal, *The Bookseller*, commented: 'The threat of mass murder is not an acceptable form of literary criticism.' With the death of Khomeini in June 1989 and the election of a new leader in Iran, it seemed that Rushdie's only hope of ever returning to some semblance of normal life would be the resolution of the power struggle in which he had become a pawn.

The Booker

Michael Foot, M.P., chaired the panel of judges for the Booker Prize (worth £15,000) in 1988. Although he strongly favoured *The Satanic Verses*, he was outvoted by his fellow judges, who plumped for Peter Carey's *Oscar and Lucinda*. Carey's previous novel, *Illywhacker*, was shortlisted in 1985, and he was the second Australian novelist to win the prize (Thomas Keneally won with *Schindler's Ark* in 1982). *Oscar and Lucinda* is the story of Oscar Hopkins, an Oxford seminarian with a passion for gambling, and Lucinda Leplastrier, a Sydney heiress whose fascination with glass was aroused by the phenomenon of Prince Rupert's drops—a pear-shaped drop of glass which can withstand the blow of a sledgehammer but will shatter if the end is snapped with pliers. The two meet on the luxury liner *Leviathan* on passage to Australia; the novel tells their love story, and is a historical *tour de force*, funny and moving, ending with the creation of a glass church in the Australian outback as a remarkable act of faith—'Our whole faith is a wager', Oscar tells Lucinda.

David Lodge's *Nice Work* is a comic masterpiece, set in the Midlands, and featuring the concrete university of Rummidge which appeared in *Changing Places* and *Small World* (the latter shortlisted for the Booker in 1984). A modern version of 19th century industrial novels, the story takes place in the world of industry as Vic Wilcox, managing director of an engineering works, is shadowed at work by Robyn Penrose, post-structuralist feminist lecturer in English. Penelope Fitzgerald's *The Beginning of Spring* is the story of two weeks in the life of Frank Reid, a Briton born and raised in Moscow, who runs a print-works. The novel tells how he copes in pre-revolutionary Russia when his wife goes home to England with their three children. Fitzgerald was a surprise winner with her novel *Offshore* in 1979.

Marina Warner's *The Lost Father* is the story of Anna, who works in a London museum cataloguing contemporary ephemera. Family legend has it that her grandfather died as the result of a duel, and she creates an imaginary memoir of her mother's background and life in southern Italy in the 1920s. Bruce Chatwin, author of *In Patagonia* and *The Songlines*, was a finalist with the short but carefully crafted *Utz*. Set in Prague, it tells the story of Kaspar Joachim Utz, a part-Jewish Czech collector of Meissen porcelain. Sadly, Chatwin died in January 1989 at the age of 48. *What Am I Doing Here*, a collection of his favourite pieces of journalism was also published this year.

Whitbread

The Whitbread Prize is worth £1,500 to the winner of each of its five categories, with a first prize of £20,000 for the work judged to be the best of the five. In the three years since the new format was introduced, the overall prize has been awarded to a volume of poetry, a novel and a biography. The 1988 award was won by Paul Sayer for his first novel, *The Comfort of Madness*, so a writer of a children's novel can reasonably expect a Whitbread windfall in the next awards!

Sayer, a staff nurse in a psychiatric hospital, wrote sensitively and with great skill about Peter, a catatonic 33-year-old who exists in a twilight world. He is unable to speak and never communicates with his helpers, but is able to comprehend more than is apparent. 'We know you're in there, Peter', his helpers tell him, as he observes them with total detachment. The Whitbread judges praised Sayer's 'black humour, like the young Evelyn Waugh', and his 'scrupulous prose that banishes squeamishness'. The novel also won the 1988 Constable Trophy for Fiction, which is awarded for an unpublished work of fiction from the north of England.

It was reported that *The Comfort of Madness* was a compromise choice, the judges being split between Rushdie's *The Satanic Verses* (novel) and A. N. Wilson's *Tolstoy* (biography). None the less the book was a worthy winner and the prize will allow Sayer to write full-time. The judges said of Rushdie that his work and person are 'surrounded by continuing hostility and unease', and he wrote in 'English prose we never knew could be so elastic'. Winner in the poetry category was Peter Porter's *The Automatic Oracle*, while *Awaiting Development* by Judy Allen was judged the best children's novel.

Other Awards

The W. H. Smith Literary Award, worth £10,000, was awarded to Christopher Hill for his acclaimed biography *A Turbulent, Seditious and Factious People: John Bunyan and His Church.* The second N.C.R. Book Award for non-fiction, worth £25,000, was awarded to Joe Simpson for *Touching the Void,* his remarkable account of a climbing expedition in the Peruvian Andes that nearly ended in tragedy. Simpson and his climbing companion Simon Yates had an accident that left Simpson dangling injured from a rope, with Yates unable to help him. Eventually, Yates decided that his only hope of saving himself was to cut the rope that held Simpson, almost certainly sending him to his death. Yates survived, but miraculously so did Simpson, who crawled back to camp in three days. Yates's decision had saved both their lives. The book also received the Boardman Tasker Award for Mountain Literature. The other N.C.R. shortlisted books, which each received £1,500, were *A Brief History of Time* by Stephen Hawking (which also received the Sunday Times Special Award for Literature), *A Touch of Genius: The Life of T. E. Lawrence* by Malcolm Brown and Julie Cave, and *Tolstoy* by A. N. Wilson.

The second Sunday Express Book of the Year Award was won by David Lodge for *Nice Work*; he received £20,000. Winner of the £8,000 Smarties Grand Prize was *Can't You Sleep Little Bear?* by Martin Waddell, illustrated by Barbara Firth, which also won the category for children's books for under fives; Barbara Firth won the Kate Greenaway medal for her illustrations for the book. *Can It Be True* by Susan Hill, illustrated by Angela Barrett, won the prize in the 6–8 years group, while Therese Whistler's *Rushavenn Time* won the 9–11 group.

The Betty Trask Award of £10,000, for first novels of a romantic or traditional nature by writers under 35, was won by Nigel Watts for *The Life Game.* William Riviere received £5,000 for *Watercolour Sky,* while £2,000 each was awarded to Alasdair McKee for *Uncle Henry's Last Stand* and Paul Houghton for *Harry's Last Wedding.* Cholmondeley Awards for poetry, worth £2,000 were presented to Peter Didsbury, Douglas Dunn and E. J. Scovell, while the Eric Gregory Awards for poets under 30 went to Gerard Woodward (£8,000), David Morley (£6,000), Katrina Porteous (£6,000) and Paul Henry (£4,000). Somerset Maugham Awards, worth £5,000, are intended to enable young British authors to travel abroad. Awards were made to Rupert Christiansen for *Romantic Affinities,* Alan Hollinghurst for *The Swimming Pool Library* and Deirdre Madden for *The Birds of the Innocent Wood.* The £5,000 McVitie's Prize for the Scottish Writer of the Year was shared by Bernard MacLaverty for his volume of short stories, *The Great Profundo,* and Edwin Mickleburgh for

Beyond the Frozen Sea. The Guardian Fiction Prize was awarded to Lucy Ellman for *Just Desserts,*

The five regional winners of the Commonwealth Poetry Prize were Bronwen Wallace (Canada), for *The Stubborn Particulars of Grace*; Kofi Awoonor (Ghana), *Until the Morning After: Collected Poems 1963–1985*; Sujata Bhatt (India), *Bruniziem*; Allen Curnow (New Zealand), *Continuum: New and Later Poems 1972–1988* and John Heath-Stubbs (U.K.), *Collected Poems 1943–87.* The Commonwealth Writers Prize worth £10,000 was awarded to Festus Iyaye (Nigeria), for his novel *Heroes*; the runner-up was George Turner (Australia) for *The Sea and the Summer.*

Prestige

The flood of new literary awards continued unabated, with prizes for most types of book and for writers from practically every geographic location and age range. New prizes were announced for second novels, and for first novels by writers aged over 40, which plugged two of the more obvious gaps. The donation of large sums of money to help writers is widely applauded, but there is also concern that the prizes that carry prestige might be swamped by those that present the largest sums of money. Part of the problem is the erratic, and frequently eccentric, criteria involved in the judging process. The Booker and Whitbread prizes have yet to acquire the kudos carried by the Prix Goncourt in France. The latest recipient of that most prestigious of literary prizes was Erik Orsenna for *L'Exposition Coloniale*, a picaresque novel with a suggestion of *Tristram Shandy.* The prize was worth 50 francs.

The richest prize of all is the Nobel Prize for Literature, worth 2·5 million Kronor (about £230,000). In 1988 it was awarded to the Egyptian writer Naguib Mahfouz, 76-year-old author of some 40 novels, collections of short stories, plays and film scripts. His best-known works include *Children of Gebelawi, Respected Sir,* and his semi-autobiographical trilogy about the life of a Cairo family from the first world war to the end of the second, *Bain al-Qasrain, Qasr al-Shauq* and *al-Sukkariyya.* The Swedish Academy said he was an author who, 'through works rich in nuance—now clear-sightedly realistic, now evocatively ambiguous—has formed an Arabian narrative art that applies to all mankind. His work has meant a powerful upsurge for the novel as a genre, and for the development of the literary language in Arabic-speaking cultural circles. The range is, however, greater than that. His work speaks to us all.'

Second Edition

The publication of the second edition of the *Oxford English Dictionary* was a remarkable achievement. The first edition, inspired and edited by Sir James Murray, took seventy years from its conception to reach its completion in 1928. The four-volume supplement edited by Dr Robert Burchfield took some 14 years to complete. The second edition combines and updates the previous works, and also incorporates 5,000 new words. It took only five years to produce, at a cost of over £8 million, but it is estimated that the work took 500 person-years. The twenty volumes, costing £1,500 a set, are intended to form a complete vocabulary of the English language from A.D. 1150 to the present. The whole work is now stored on a computer, greatly facilitating the production of revised or condensed versions. A Compact edition is scheduled for 1991, a third edition will be produced in the 21st century, and the whole work will be available in a few years on a compact disc for about £500.

The dictionary contains some 300,000 entries, with over 500,000 words defined in its 22,000 pages. The longest entry is for 'set', which has 154 main senses, over 430 tenses and sub-tenses, and a total of 60,000 words. The longest word now recorded is the rather ungainly 'pneumonoultramicroscopicsilico-volcanoconiosis', which describes a lung disease found mainly among miners. Prepared by John Simpson and Edward Weiner, the dictionary combines the best in lexicography and computer technology.

Last Greene?

Graham Greene's 24th novel (according to the author 'probably my last') was similar in plot to his first (*The Man Within*) and was influenced by his friendship with the late dictator of Panama, General Omar Torrijos, whom he remembered in his book *Getting to Know the General*. The new novel, *The Captain and the Enemy*, is the tale of Victor Baxter, claimed from school on his 12th birthday by the Captain who 'won him from his father at backgammon, or so he said'. The Captain, an enigmatic figure, has a strange and touching relationship with a girl called Liza who once had an affair with Baxter's father. The novel's inscription reads, 'Will you be sure to know the good side from the bad, the Captain from the enemy?' (written by George A. Birmingham) but Baxter never understands the relationship between the two until it is too late. The novel reaches its climax in Panama just before the signing of the Canal treaty between President Carter and General Torrijos. The Captain is involved in smuggling arms to the Nicaraguan Sandinistas and dies (like Torrijos) in a plane crash. Baxter, a failure as a writer and in human relationships, dies in a car crash, a curiously flat end to a sad tale.

Graham Greene once said, 'I don't want people looking into my life', and has limited the access of others to his papers. In 1971 he published *A Sort of Life*, a reticent account which appeared to be his final word on the subject of himself. However, Norman Sherry, Mitchell Distinguished Professor of Literature at Trinity University, San Antonio, Texas, and author of *Conrad's Western World*, met Greene in 1973 and was given complete access to all the author's papers, diaries, notebooks and correspondence. *The Life of Graham Greene, Vol 1, 1904–39* is an account of Sherry's travels round the world in the footsteps of the author. At times the narrative reads like a novel, but the book gives an interesting account of Greene's marriage to Vivien Dayrell-Browning, for whom he converted to Catholicism, and of his struggle to become a novelist.

Shaw

Michael Holroyd received a massive advance of £625,000 from Chatto for his biography of George Bernard Shaw. He has been engaged on the project since 1975 (Shaw's first official biographer, Archibald Henderson, laboured for fifty years over the task), and the first of three volumes has now been published. *Bernard Shaw, Volume 1: 1856–1898—The Search for Love* is an account of the early years of the renowned playwright and critic, from his childhood with an unloving mother (who eloped with the original of the du Maurier character of Svengali), through to his marriage at the age of 42 and his first stage success with *The Devil's Disciple*. The absence of source notes was a cause of irritation to many critics, but Holroyd has deferred them until after the publication of the third volume to avoid them being 'stupendously out of date'.

Martin Seymour-Smith's biography of *Rudyard Kipling* attracted much hostile comment for his assertion, without any supporting evidence, that Kipling was a repressed homosexual. Stephen Gill's *William Wordsworth: A Life* was a definitive new biography of an enigmatic figure who from an early age was convinced of his 'High Calling' and lived his life to fit the ideal of a great poet. Robert Calder's *Willie: The Life of W. Somerset Maugham* gave an account of the life of the great storyteller; the biographer was hampered by the refusal of Maugham's literary executors, the Royal Literary Fund, to allow him to quote from the author's letters. The curious and sheltered life of one of the most prolific writers of all time was revealed in Mary Cadogan's *Frank Richards: The Chap Behind the Chums*. Frank Richards was one of the 28 pen-names of Charles Hamilton, who regularly produced 80,000 words a week, his most memorable creation being Billy Bunter, the 'Fat Owl of the Remove' at Greyfriars School.

Grand Old Men

Alistair Horne's official biography of Harold Macmillan was published in two volumes. *Macmillan 1894–1956* covered his life until he succeeded Eden as Prime Minister. Although a courageous Grenadier Guardsman, Macmillan comes over as a curiously dated figure who only acquired real *gravitas* and stature in his declining years. He inherited a vast fortune from the family publishing firm, but as an M.P. he served for 16 years in comparative obscurity until Churchill gave him office. His private life was clouded for many years by his wife's affair with Lord Boothby. *Volume II, 1957–86* quotes from Macmillan's diaries to show that the initial enjoyment he experienced on becoming Prime Minister soon wore off, leaving him tired and depressed with the job. He stayed too long in office and then regretted resigning. However, after belatedly accepting an earldom in 1984, he revelled in his new-found status as grand old man of the Conservative Party, making widely-reported speeches in the House of Lords. Horne's life of Macmillan has made judicious use of his extensive private papers.

The Whitelaw Memoirs are untainted by scandal or revelation of any kind; Viscount Whitelaw has always been renowned for his loyalty, especially to Margaret Thatcher, whom he served as a distinguished second in command until his premature retirement through ill health. His avuncular image comes across in his memoirs, as does the impression that there is always more to Whitelaw than meets the eye. Roy Jenkins's *European Diary 1977–1981* covers the period of his presidency of the European Community; a cultured man, he is not above telling a story against himself at times.

Anthony Lambton's *The Mountbattens* sought to fill some of the gaps in Philip Ziegler's official life of Earl Mountbatten of Burma. The first volume examines Mountbatten's antecedents, suggesting that the facts of his birth do not support the image of a royal past that he created for himself. Peter Hennessy's *Whitehall* is a thorough examination of the civil service, containing in its 580 pages a great amount of information and anecdotes, while also suggesting how the organization could be improved. In *On My Way to the Club*, writer and broadcaster Ludovic Kennedy gives a readable account of his life, with the frequently funny stories of his early years being balanced by his later campaigns against miscarriages of justice.

Journey's End

William Golding's maritime trilogy began with the Booker-winning *Rites of Passage*. It continued (when the author realized that his characters were still *en voyage*) with *Close Quarters*, and has now been completed with *Fire Down Below*. In the final part, the crippled ship of the line suffers with a loose foremast; its repair involves the insertion of red-hot irons, which eventually set the core of the timber alight. Fire is a powerful image throughout the book; as one of the passengers, Aloysius Prettiman ('the Tom Paine of the Southern Ocean') says, 'Imagine our caravan, we, a fire down here below—spark of the Absolute—matching the fire up there—out there!' The narrator, Talbot, grows in stature throughout the voyage from the somewhat pompous, unperceptive character who was first encountered in *Rites of Passage*.

The story is a masterpiece of narrative sustained over 900 pages through the three volumes, and rich in image and allegory. Golding is always wary of too much being read into his work. Talbot is told at the end of the voyage, 'The voyage has been a considerable part of your whole life, sir. Do not refine upon its nature. As I told you, it was not an Odyssey. It is no type, emblem, metaphor of the human condition. It is, or rather it *was*, what it was. A series of events.' It is part of Golding's genius that such a series of events can convey so much about the human condition.

Bunn Revisited

In his latest novel, *Difficulties with Girls*, Kingsley Amis returned to two of the characters from his fourth book, *Take A Girl Like You*. The earlier novel examined the sexual mores of the 1960s through the experiences of the innocent Jenny Bunn and her relationship with the rakish schoolmaster Patrick Standish. In the latest novel the pair have married

and moved to London. Patrick now works for a publisher and Jenny, having suffered one miscarriage, works as a part-time teacher in a children's hospital. Set in the late 1960s, just before the Homosexual Reform Act, Amis follows Patrick's constant philandering, to the distress of the long-suffering Jenny, while also relating the problems of the other occupants of the block of flats in which the Standishes live. A homosexual couple bicker constantly, while a newcomer to the block, Tim Valentine, attempts to resolve his own particular problem with the opposite sex by accepting, with comic and unfortunate results, a psychiatrist's suggestion that he is a homosexual. Less sharp and satiric than Amis's last novel, the 1986 Booker Winner *The Old Devils*, *Difficulties with Girls* is concerned with human relationships at a time of sexual revolution. Also published in the past year was John McDermott's critical account of Amis's work, *Kingsley Amis: An English Moralist*.

Peter Ackroyd's novels concern the linking of past and present events across time, a theme to which he returns in his latest novel *First Light*. After a forest fire, an ancient tumulus is discovered at Pilgrin Valley, near Holblack Moor in Dorset. As archaeologist Mark Clare excavates the tumulus, in which he believes an ancient astronomer is buried, astronomer Damian Fall studies the heavens at a nearby observatory. Central to the book is the landscape of Dorset, over which hangs the influence of Thomas Hardy. Although some of Ackroyd's characters appear to be mere cyphers in the grand scheme of the novel, he sustains the narrative interest as the mysteries of heaven and earth are explored and finally conjoined.

Old Iron

In *Any Old Iron*, Anthony Burgess records the bloody history of the 20th century through Arthur's mythical sword Excalibur. The question is whether it still has power today or is just a piece of old iron. His 50th book, and 30th novel, shows Burgess as erudite and interesting as ever.

In *My Chocolate Redeemer*, Christopher Hope has written a bizarre fable, his plot influenced by recent Ugandan and Haitian dictatorships. His story concerns Monsieur Brown, 'Beast of Zanj', the recently deposed dictator of an African country 'not more than a thousand miles from Uganda'. The story is narrated by 15-year-old Bella, who has a passion for chocolate; Brown's tribespeople, the Wouff, believe that chocolate is made from the blood of their ancestors. As Brown and his entourage settle in the French town of La Frisette, Hope evokes the townspeople's fear of the foreigners in their midst.

Past Lives

Kazuo Ishiguro goes from strength to strength; his second novel, *An Artist of the Floating World*, won the Whitbread Prize, and his third, *The Remains of the Day*, has been widely praised. Critics still talk of the Japanese influence on his writing but his latest book takes peculiarly English themes, which he writes about with perception and skill. The story is narrated by Stevens, on holiday in the west country in 1956. He reflects on his years of service to Lord

Darlington but gradually comes to realize that his master is flawed. To be a great butler, it is necessary to work for a great man, a benefactor of mankind. Stevens comes to see that through his loyalty to the anti-Semitic Darlington he has been diminished, and has also lost his only chance of finding love.

In spite of *glasnost* and *perestroika*, John le Carré's world of espionage 'has not altered by a brush stroke'. His latest novel, *The Russia House* is named after a branch of the British intelligence service. It covers familiar territory, with a plot about the secret service acquiring an important manuscript which has been smuggled out of Russia to the West. Le Carré is once again master of the form which he has developed over the years; the novel's epigraph is 'Today one must think like a hero to behave like a merely decent human being'.

Julian Barnes' *A History of the World in 10½ Chapters* covers events from Noah's Ark to nuclear apocalypse in a thought-provoking and comic study of history and myth through the ages. However, history to Barnes is not governed by 'power, money, history and death' but by love. 'I can tell you why to love. Because the history of the world, which only stops at the half-house of love to bulldoze it into rubble, is ridiculous without it. The history of the world becomes brutally self-important without love.'

Red Wheel

Alexander Solzhenitsyn, still in exile in Vermont, U.S.A., has been working on his 'main artistic design', an eight-volume history of the Russian Revolution called *The Red Wheel*. Each volume concerns a major historical event and the first volume is a revised edition of *August 1914*, first published in the West in 1971. A new translation by H. T. Willetts, personally approved by Solzhenitsyn, replaces the earlier version. The author has taken advantage of the extensive archives of Soviet history in the West to update and expand the novel from its original 600 pages to over 800 pages. The new sections deal mainly with

Peter Stolypin (Prime Minister of Russia from 1906 to 1911) and his murder, and with Tsar Nicholas II.

Other books of note published during the year included: *Collected Poems* by Philip Larkin, edited by Anthony Thwaite; *Collected Poems 1928–1985* by Stephen Spender; *The Letters of T. S. Eliot, Volume One, 1898–1922*, edited by Valerie Eliot; *The Oxford Book of Irish Short Stories*, edited by William Trevor; *In Sickness and In Health: The British Experience 1650–1850* by Roy Porter and Dorothy Porter; *The Grown-ups* by Victoria Glendinning; *Punishments* by Francis King; *A Theft* by Saul Bellow; *Passing On* by Penelope Lively; *The Burning Boys* by John Fuller; *Breathing Lessons* by Anne Tyler; *A Little Stranger* by Candia McWilliam; *Sugar and Rum* by Barry Unsworth; *Have the Men Had Enough?* by Margaret Forster; *The Facts: A Novelist's Autobiography* by Philip Roth; *The Gift of Stones* by Jim Crace; *The Skeleton in the Cupboard* by Alice Thomas Ellis; *The Lyre of Orpheus* by Robertson Davies; *The Edge* by Dick Francis; *The Girl at the Lion d'Or* by Sebastian Faulks; *Dictionary of the Khazars* by Milorad Pavic; *Lewis Percy* by Anita Brookner.

Public Lending Right

The total sum available under the Public Lending Right Scheme was increased to £3·5 million in 1988. Of this £3·1 million was distributed to writers. The rate per loan was increased from 1·12 pence to 1·45 pence, and the maximum amount payable to any author was raised for the first time, from £5,000 to £6,000. There were 16,034 authors registered under the scheme; 67 received the maximum payment, 22 received between £5,000 and £6,000, 163 between £2,500 and £4,999, 411 between £1,000 and £2,499, 591 between £500 and £999, 3,103 between £100 and £499, and 8,854 between £1 and £99. Some 2,823 writers who were registered received no payment, and a total of £344,000 was redistributed as a surplus from writers who had exceeded the maximum limit. The Government has announced that £4·25 million will be available for the scheme in 1991–92.

DRAMA 1988–89

The National Theatre celebrated its 25th anniversary in October 1988. To mark the occasion, it was granted the right to use, at its discretion, the prefix 'Royal'; the theatre, however, has no immediate plans to change its name to the Royal National Theatre. Richard Eyre took over as director from Sir Peter Hall, who bowed out after a 15-year tenure which saw the National Theatre firmly established in its South Bank complex. Eyre was quoted as saying, 'I would like the stage to be the epicentre, as it were, of the organization; for the work to be accessible, popular (not "populist") and theatrical—in the sense of exploiting the characteristics peculiar to the medium. None of this is possible without subsidy, whatever the modish claims made for the feasibility of private sponsorship in taking its place. We function in the market-place and a *constant* pressure upon us—rightly—is the need to find 14,937 paying customers a week.'

One of the most significant National Theatre productions under the new regime of Richard Eyre was the company's joint production with the Bristol Old Vic, at the Theatre Royal, Bristol, of Molière's *The Misanthrope*. Eyre had promised that the company would tour the regions for 16 weeks a year and the Bristol production was the fulfilment of his promise to put the 'national' back into National Theatre. *The Misanthrope* was one of the company's great triumphs when performed in 1973 at the Old Vic in Tony Harrison's translation into rhyming couplets. A slightly amended version of Harrison's script was used in Paul Unwin's production. After Bristol, the play visited Bradford, Wolverhampton, Hull, Nottingham, Norwich and Brighton before entering the repertory at the Lyttelton in May. A strong cast was led by Edward Petherbridge (Alceste), whose subtle approach was compared favourably to Alec McCowen's more histrionic reading in the 1973 production.

South Bank Hamlet

In March, Richard Eyre produced *Hamlet* on the Olivier stage, the first National production of the play since Albert Finney took the role in 1976. Daniel Day-Lewis did not have quite the dramatic impact in the title role of Jonathan Pryce in Eyre's 1980 Royal Court production, but his energetic rather than intellectual approach was still impressive. John Gunter's Elsinore set, dominated by a statue of the dead king, was noteworthy, and the performances of Michael Bryant as Polonius, Judi Dench as Gertrude and Stella Gonet as Ophelia were praised.

A new play written and directed by Harold Pinter, *Mountain Language* was produced in the Lyttelton. It lasted for only twenty minutes but conveyed a powerful message about prison brutality, apparently inspired by the plight of the Kurdish population in Turkey. The cast featured Michael Gambon, Tony Haygarth and Eileen Atkins. Alan Bennett's *Single Spies* was a double bill featuring Simon Callow as Guy Burgess in *An Englishman Abroad* and Bennett himself as Anthony Blunt in *A Question of Attribution*. After opening at the Lyttelton in December

1988, the plays transferred to the Queens Theatre, Shaftesbury Avenue, for a successful West End run.

In the Cottesloe Lope de Vega's *Fuente Ovejuna*, in a new version by Adrian Mitchell, was directed by Declan Donnellan of the Cheek by Jowl company. Written in 1612, the play takes its name from a Spanish village and tells the story of the villagers' fight against the oppressive rule of a military governor, played by James Laurenson. Another neglected play revived at the Cottesloe was Harley Granville Barker's 1905 play about money and morals, *The Voysey Inheritance*. This was the first London production of the play for over twenty years. Directed by Richard Eyre and featuring Michael Bryant, David Burke and Jeremy Northam, it proved to be a well-constructed drama with much contemporary relevance. The same play was also revived at the Manchester Royal Exchange, directed by Gregory Hersov.

Plantagenets

The Royal Shakespeare Company's 1988 autumn season opened with Adrian Noble's production of *The Plantagenets*. This was an adaptation by Charles Wood of Shakespeare's *Henry VI Parts 1, 2* and *3* and *Richard III*. These were conflated to form three plays: *Henry VI, The Rise of Edward IV* and *Richard III, His Death*. Grouped together, *The Plantagenets* charts 'the changing values of a civilization as three boys grow up to assume the power of kingship in very different—but equally destructive—ways'. Anton Lesser gave a fine performance as Richard III, though that play sat unhappily with the more expansive *Henry* plays when they were shown together. The plays could be seen on separate evenings or as a nine-hour Saturday trilogy. Timberlake Wertenbaker's *The Love of the Nightingale* received its world premiere in November 1988 at The Other Place. It was announced that this stage would close in January. The company said that a new, improved theatre would open on the site in 1990 or 1991. The Other Place reopened briefly in August when Trevor Nunn made a welcome return to the company to produce *Othello*. The production, which featured the opera singer Willard White in the title role, was highly praised.

Productions on The Swan stage included Edward Bond's *Restoration*, with Simon Russell Beale attracting much praise as Lord Are in a black comedy based on 17th century Restoration drama. The play was the first transfer to the Barbican in the spring season.

With the start of the new season in Stratford and London in spring 1989, the company introduced a restructuring of its schedules. In future, plays which open at Stratford in the autumn will transfer to the Barbican in March, after a short season at Newcastle. Spring productions in Stratford will play there until August and then tour for two months before moving to London. The company was also reorganized into spring and autumn troupes of actors. In April, the company announced that poor box office returns had left it with a deficit of £1 million. Stratford, where 90 per cent of seats had been sold in 1987, achieved only 80 per cent occupancy in 1988; the Barbican achieved only 76 per cent. There was a noticeable drop in foreign visitors but the surfeit of Shakespeare productions in other theatres cannot have helped.

The spring season at Stratford opened with John Caird's very funny punk production of *A Midsummer Night's Dream*. It was followed by *Hamlet*, directed by Ron Daniels, with Mark Rylance as the prince, and *Cymbeline*, directed by Bill Alexander, in its first Stratford main-house production since 1979. In The Swan, Terry Hands' *Romeo and Juliet* marked his first production in the new theatre. Featuring Mark Rylance and Georgia Slowe, it differed markedly in style from Hands' last production of the play on the main stage in the 1970s. Barry Kyle returned to The Swan to direct *Doctor Faustus*, and Danny Boyle made his directorial debut at Stratford with Ben Jonson's *The Silent Woman*, or *Epicoene*.

The Rose

The announcement that the remains of an Elizabethan theatre, the Rose, had been discovered in Southwark, London, caused great excitement. Excavation had been permitted on the site before building work began on an office development. The excavation work was carried out by archaeologists from the Museum of London at the expense of the developers, Imry Merchant. Little is known about the design and size of Elizabethan stages and when significant information emerged about the Rose stage and the shape of the building, there was concern at the prospect of the site disappearing beneath an office block.

The Rose theatre was built in about 1587 and was managed by Philip Henslowe. During its comparatively brief existence, Shakespeare's *Titus Andronicus* and *Henry VI* were performed there and Christopher Marlowe's *Tamburlaine the Great, Doctor Faustus* and *The Jew of Malta* received their first performances at the theatre. It is believed that Shakespeare may have acted at the Rose. Martin Clout, an expert in Elizabethan theatre, said, 'The importance of the Rose is that it is one of the most extensively documented theatres of the period. This excavation will have profound consequences on our understanding of Elizabethan theatre.'

Actors and Members of Parliament began a campaign to save the theatre. One suggestion is that the proposed office block should be built on stilts over the site, allowing access to the remains. However, despite a plethora of proposals and negotiations, the future of the site has not yet been decided.

Ironically, Sam Wanamaker's long-cherished dream to recreate the Globe theatre on a nearby site in Southwark came closer to reality in June when he signed the contract to begin building the International Shakespeare Globe Centre. The new Globe, 200 yards from the site of the original, will include a 'wooden O' Elizabethan-style theatre, and a second stage.

Lilian Baylis

An addition to London's theatres was the 200-seat Lilian Baylis Theatre built onto Sadler's Wells Theatre. Its first production was John Guare's award-winning play *The House of Blue Leaves*. Controversy surrounded the second production, a revival of Jean Giraudoux's *The Madwoman of Chaillot*. The cast fell out with Sharon Gans, the director chosen by the sponsor, Robert M. Klein of Boston, who then withdrew. Nick Hamm took over as director but the play, which featured Eleanor Bron, was not a critical success.

There was also encouraging news about the Lyceum Theatre, the future of which had been in doubt for some time. The new owners, the Brent Walker group, announced that they would restore it for use as a theatre once again.

Lost Chords

The beginning of 1989 was a bad time for musicals. A number of established shows ended their London run and several newcomers gave up the struggle to stay in business: six musicals closed in London in January. David Merrick's *42nd Street* ended its run at Drury Lane after nearly four and a half years, while *South Pacific* closed after a year at the Prince of Wales. *Follies* closed at the Shaftesbury after 18 months, as the producer was reportedly unable to recast the show to the same standard as the original. *Sugar Babies* starred American veterans Mickey Rooney and Ann Miller. The show ran for eight years on Broadway but the nostalgic tribute to vaudeville survived only four months at the Savoy Theatre.

Another casualty was *Budgie*, an undistinguished musical in which singer and actor Adam Faith recreated his television character, the Cockney villain Budgie. Even the presence in the cast of Anita Dobson, who achieved fame in the BBC television soap opera *EastEnders*, did not prove a big enough draw to avoid an early closure: the show was reputed to have lost nearly £1·4 million. Cole Porter's *Can-Can* at the Strand was neither a critical nor a popular success and closed after three months. In April *Chess* ended its three-year run at the Prince Edward.

Positive Aspects

Andrew Lloyd Webber showed that his magic touch had not deserted him when his new show, *Aspects of Love*, opened at the Prince of Wales in April. The musical is based on a novel by David Garnett. It should have marked the musical debut of former 'Saint' and James Bond actor Roger Moore, who was cast in the role of George Dillingham. Moore, who said he was 'frightened to death' at the prospect of leading the cast in a stage musical, was reported to have a fine singing voice. However, some weeks before the opening he withdrew, lacking the confidence to carry off the role, and his understudy Kevin Colson, stepped in. Critical reaction was largely favourable but immaterial to the show's success: advance bookings exceeded £2·5 million and it was fully booked nearly a year ahead by the time it opened. Meanwhile, Lloyd Webber's *Cats* reached its 3,358th performance in May, making it London's longest-running musical.

Elementary

After *Budgie* at the Cambridge came *Sherlock Holmes: The Musical*, with Ron Moody playing the detective. It was an odd conception that seemed to be aimed at the tourist market, and the cast appeared unsure whether to take it seriously—perhaps not surprising in a show that featured a wholly irrelevant Cockney knees-up by the Baker Street Irregulars. Holmes was also the subject of the more cerebral, but plotless play *The Secret of Sherlock Holmes*, in which Jeremy Brett and Edward Hardwicke repeated their familiar television characterizations.

A curious choice for a musical was *Metropolis*, inspired by Fritz Lang's 1926 film of the same name. The original propounded a simplistic message about the human spirit overcoming soul-destroying machines: sixty years later the message had gained little in profundity, and music and lyrics were unmemorable. It seemed unlikely that *Metropolis* would recoup its £3 million budget. The one redeeming feature was Ralph Koltai's spectacular design. The show was directed by Jerome Savary.

About Farce

Brian Rix returned to the stage after an absence of eleven years in John Chapman's *Dry Rot*. Rix had been in the cast of the farce when it had a successful run in the 1950s. He was persuaded to return with the promise that part of the profits of the show would be given to Mencap, the charity for which he had been working since giving up the stage. Brian Rix proved to have aged better than the play, which was considered very dated.

Alan Ayckbourn's new play, *Henceforward*, starred Ian McKellen as a hi-tech composer, divorced from his wife and attempting to regain custody of his daughter. Set in the near future, the play presents a picture of an inner city under siege by warring gangs. The American comedian Jackie Mason brought his one-man show—the longest-running and most successful in Broadway history—to London in February: *The World According to Me* ran at the Playhouse Theatre. Another Broadway import was *Forbidden Broadway: The West End Edition*. Gerard Alessandrini's take-off of stage shows has run for years on Broadway, satirizing the likes of *Les Misérables* and *Phantom of the Opera*. The London version had some entertaining and clever pastiches, but seemed unlikely to match the success of its transatlantic counterpart.

Also notable was *The Sneeze*, which featured Rowan Atkinson in hilarious form in eight Chekhov pieces. These were written in Chekhov's youth and were adapted to good effect by Michael Frayn. Mike Leigh, master of the improvised production, returned to the stage after an absence of some eight years with *Smelling a Rat* at the Hampstead Theatre.

Shakespeare

Shakespeare was much to the fore in the commercial theatre during the year. The R.S.C.'s *Plantagenets* was rivalled by *The Wars of the Roses* cycle presented by the English Shakespeare Company. This comprised *Richard II, Henry IV Part 1, Henry*

IV Part 2, the conflation of the three parts of *Henry VI* to make two plays, *Henry VI House of Lancaster* and *Henry VI House of York*, and *Richard III*. The cycle was performed on tour and in London at the Old Vic. Following *The Wars of the Roses* into the Old Vic was *King Lear*, which opened Jonathan Miller's second Old Vic season. Eric Porter played Lear, a part he had previously undertaken at Stratford. At the Phoenix, the Renaissance Company's visit with three Shakespeare plays was followed in autumn 1988 by a season starring Derek Jacobi, first as *Richard II* and then as *Richard III*. In the summer the Phoenix again housed a Shakespeare production when Dustin Hoffman made his London debut as Shylock in Peter Hall's production of *The Merchant of Venice*. The play sold out on the strength of its American star, taking £1·5 million in advance bookings.

Alec Guinness appeared with Edward Herrmann in Lee Blessing's *A Walk in the Woods* at the Comedy Theatre. This pre-glasnost drama dealt with the relationship of an American and a Soviet diplomat involved in disarmament talks in Geneva. John Osborne's *Look Back in Anger* was revived with Kenneth Branagh as Jimmy and Emma Thompson as Alison. Veteran actor Edward Jewesbury, who had appeared in the original 1956 Royal Court production, recreated his role as Alison's father. After a week's run in Belfast, the play was given a charity performance in London and filmed for television. Originally there was no intention of bringing the play into a West End theatre but due to public demand it received a four-week run in London.

The Royal Court had to close its Theatre Upstairs because of financial difficulties, mainly due to a reduced grant from the Arts Council. The main stage featured several notable productions, including Timberlake Wertenbaker's *Our Country's Good*. The play is based on Thomas Keneally's novel *The Playmaker* about the Australian convicts performing in the first play put on in the colony, Farquhar's *The Recruiting Officer*, in 1789. The Wertenbaker play was performed in repertory with Max Stafford-Clark's production of Farquhar's play. Also at the Royal Court was *Iranian Nights*, a play about the death threat made to the author Salman Rushdie because of his novel *The Satanic Verses*. The play, written by Howard Brenton and Tariq Ali, was felt to be bold but hastily conceived, addressing the complex issues simplistically.

Awards

In the Society of West End Theatre Awards, now known as the Laurence Olivier Awards, the commercial theatre, represented by the Old Vic, won more awards than the subsidised theatre for the first time. The awards themselves took the form of a bronze statuette of Olivier as Henry V, sculpted by Henry Franchetti. The main awards were: Best West End play, *Our Country's Good* by Timberlake Wertenbaker; best comedy, *Shirley Valentine* by Willy Russell; best musical, *Candide* (Old Vic); best actor in new play/comedy, David Haig (*Our Country's Good*); best actress, new play/comedy, Pauline Collins (*Shirley Valentine*); best actor, revival, Brian Cox (*Titus Andronicus*); best actress, revival, Harriet Walter (three R.S.C. plays); best comedy performance,

Alex Jennings (*Too Clever by Half*); best director, Deborah Warner (*Titus Andronicus*); best designer, Richard Hudson (Old Vic season). Sir Alec Guinness was presented with a special award for outstanding achievement. In the *Plays & Players* London Critics Awards, David Hare's *The Secret Rapture* was judged best play, Alex Jennings best actor, and Pauline Collins best actress. Howard Davies won the award for best director for *The Shaughraun*, for which William Dudley was voted best designer.

PRODUCTIONS

London productions between September 1, 1988, and August 31, 1989, included the following:

ALDWYCH: WC2. (1988) Sept. 27. *The Sneeze* by Anton Chekhov (adapted by Michael Frayn), with Rowan Atkinson, Timothy West and Cheryl Campbell, directed by Ronald Eyre, designed by Mark Thompson. (1989) April 25. *The Black Prince* by Iris Murdoch, with Ian McDiarmid, Simon Williams, Sarah Badel and John Fortune, dir. by Stuart Burge, des. by Ultz.

APOLLO: Shaftsbury Avenue, W1. (1988) Dec. 6. *Mrs Klein* by Nicholas Wright, with Francesca Annis, Gillian Barge and Zoë Wanamaker, dir. by Peter Gill, des. by John Gunter (National Theatre prodn.). (1989) June 14. *A Madhouse in Goa* by Martin Sherman (transfer from Lyric Hammersmith).

BARBICAN: EC2. (1988) Sept. 6. Shakespeare's *The Taming of the Shrew*, with Brian Cox, Fiona Shaw, Alex Jennings, Barrie Rutter, Felicity Dean and Derek Hutchinson, dir. by Jonathan Miller, des. by Stefanos Lazaridis. Oct. 10. Shakespeare's *Measure for Measure*, with Josette Simon, Roger Allam, Phil Daniels, Mark Dignam, Alex Jennings and John Shrapnel, dir. by Nicholas Hytner, des. by Mark Thompson. Nov. 30. *The Churchill Play* by Howard Brenton, with Colin Welland, James Ellis, Sean Baker and Phil Daniels, dir. by Barry Kyle, des. by Kit Surrey. (1989) April 1. *The Plantagenets* (*Henry VI, Edward IV* and *Richard III*), adapted from Shakespeare by Charles Wood, with Anton Lesser, Joanne Pearce, Ralph Fiennes, David Waller, Oliver Cotton, David Calder, David Lyon, Edward Peel and Penny Downie, dir. by Adrian Noble, des. by Bob Crowley. May 25. Shakespeare's *The Tempest*, with Melanie Thaw, Duncan Bell, John Kane, Desmond Barrit and John Wood, dir. by Nicholas Hytner, des. by David Fielding. May 4. Shakespeare's *Macbeth*, with Miles Anderson, Amanda Root, Duncan Bell, Colin McCormack and Tony Armatrading, dir. by Adrian Noble, des. by Bob Crowley. July 20. *The Man Who Came to Dinner* by George Kaufman and Moss Hart, with John Wood, Maureen Beattie, Desmond Barrit, Estelle Kohler, Ralph Fiennes and Barrie Ingham, dir. by Gene Saks.

BARBICAN PIT: (1988) Sept. 5. *The Bite of the Night* by Howard Barker, with Nigel Terry, John Carlisle, Mark Dignam, Clive Russell, David O'Hara, Darlene Johnson and Diane Fletcher, dir. by Danny Boyle. Oct. 12. *Divine Gossip* by Stephen Lowe, with Sean Baker, Stella Gonet, Pippa Guard, Linus Roache and Nicholas Farrell, dir. by Barry Kyle. Nov. 29. *A Question of Geography* by John Berger and Nella Bielski, Harriet Walter, Clive Russell, with Linus Roache and Susan Colverd, dir. by John Caird, des. by Sue Blane. Dec. 20. *Electra* by Sophocles (translated by Kenneth McLeish), with Fiona Shaw, Natasha Parry, Susan Colverd, Piers Ibbotson and Sylvester Morand, dir. by Deborah Warner, des. by Hildegard Bechtler. (1989) March 29. *Restoration* by Edward Bond, with Simon Russell Beale, Duncan Bell, Pip

Hinton and Vivienne Rochester, dir. by Roger Michell. April 13. *The Man of Mode* by George Etherege, with Simon Russell Beale, Miles Anderson, Amanda Root, Katy Behan and Marie Mullen, dir. by Garry Hynes, des. by Di Seymour. May 2. Shakespeare's *King John*, with Nicholas Woodeson, David Morrissey, Julian Curry, Cherry Morris, David Lyon, Ralph Fiennes, Robert Demeger and Susan Engel, dir. by Deborah Warner, des. by Sue Blane. May 22. *The Plain Dealer* by William Wycherley, with Geraldine Alexander, Joanne Pearce, Marjorie Yates, David Calder, Pip Donaghy and Edward Peel, dir. by Ron Daniels, des. by David Fielding. July 19. *Some Americans Abroad* by Richard Nelson, with Anton Lesser, Simon Russell Beale, Oliver Cotton, Amanda Root and Diane Fletcher, dir. by Roger Michell, des. by Alexandra Byrne. July 31. *Across Oka* by Robert Holman, with Timothy Stark, Edward Rawle-Hicks, Alfred Burke, and Patricia Lawrence, dir. by Sarah Pia Anderson, des. by Ashley Martin-Davis. Aug. 22. *The Love of the Nightingale* by Timberlake Wertenbaker, with Peter Lennon, Marie Mullen and Katy Behan, dir. by Garry Hynes, des. by Iona McLeish.

BOULEVARD: Walker's Court, W1. (1989) Feb. 15. *Sisters* by David Storey, with Toni Arthur and Christina McKenna, dir. by Rob Kennedy.

CAMBRIDGE: Earlham Street, WC2. (1988) Oct. 18. *Budgie* by Keith Waterhouse, Willis Hall, Mort Shuman and Don Black, with Adam Faith, Anita Dobson and John Turner, dir. by Jonathan Lynn, des. by Saul Radomsky. (1989) April 24. *Sherlock Holmes—the Musical* by Leslie Bricusse, with Ron Moody, Liz Robertson, Derek Waring and Eileen Battye, dir. by George Roman, des. by Sean Cavanagh.

COMEDY: Panton Street, W1. (1988) Nov. 3. *A Walk in the Woods* by Lee Blessing, with Alec Guinness and Edward Herrmann, dir. by Ronald Eyre, des. by Robin Don. (1989) June 14. *Frankie & Johnny in the Clair de Lune* by Terrence McNally, with Brian Cox and Julie Walters, dir. by Paul Benedict, des. by Sue Plummer.

DONMAR WAREHOUSE: Earlham Street, WC2. (1988) Nov. 24. Shakespeare's *The Tempest*, with Timothy Walker, Cecilia Noble, Lloyd Owen, Peter Darling and Duncan Duff, dir. by Declan Donnellan, des. by Nick Ormerod (Cheek by Jowl prodn.). Dec. 2. *Philoctetes* by Sophocles, with Keith Bartlett, Paterson Joseph and Charlie Roe, dir. by Declan Donnellan, des. by Nick Ormerod (Cheek by Jowl prodn.). (1989) April 26. *The Doctor of Honour* by Calderon (trans. by Roy Campbell), with Michelle Fairley, Neil Pearson, Claire Benedict and Nigel Terry, dir. by Lindsay Posner, des. by Julia McGowan (Cheek by Jowl prodn.). July 17. Shakespeare's *Twelfth Night*, with Nick Kemp, Merial Scholfield and Andrew Dunn, dir. by John Godber (Hull Truck Co. prodn.).

DUKE OF YORK'S: St. Martin's Lane, WC2. (1988) Dec. 7. *Artist Descending a Staircase* by Tom Stoppard, with William Lucas, Peter Copley, Karl James, Gareth Tudor Price, John Warnaby and Sarah Woodward, dir. by Tim Luscombe, des. by Carl Toms (King's Head prodn.). June 28. (1989) *Shirley Valentine* by Willy Russell, with Hannah Gordon, dir. by Richard Olivier, des. by Bruno Santini.

FORTUNE: Russell Street, WC2. (1988) Sept. 14. *Re: Joyce!* (adapted from the works of Joyce Grenfell), with Maureen Lipman and Denis King, dir. by Alan Strachan. (1989) March 2. *Forbidden Broadway*, written and dir. by Gerald Alessandrini, with Rosemary Ashe, Jenny Michelmore, Simon Slater and Michael Fenton Stevens.

GARRICK: Charing Cross Road, WC2. (1989) Jan. 26. *The Vortex* by Noel Coward, with Maria Aitken,

Rupert Everett, Yolanda Vasquez and Anne Lambton, dir. and des. by Philip Prowse.

GREENWICH: Croom's Hill, SE10. (1988) Oct. 10. *The Millionairess* by G. B. Shaw, with Barbara Flynn, David Ross, John Gabriel and Pamela Buchner, dir. by Penny Cherns. Dec. 2. *The Woman in White* by Wilkie Collins (adapted by Melissa Murray), with Helena Bonham-Carter, Michael Byrne and Jane Gurnett, dir. by Sue Dunderdale, des. by Alexandra Byrne. (1989) March 14. Shakespeare's *Othello*, with Clarke Peters, Paul Barber, Emily Morgan and Hugh Quarshie, dir. by Sue Dunderdale, des. by Henk Schut.

HAMPSTEAD: Swiss Cottage, NW3. (1988) Oct. 14. *Hedda Gabler* by Henrik Ibsen, with Lindsay Duncan, Rhoda Lewis, Jonathan Coy, Dermot Crowley and Clive Francis, dir. by John Dove. Dec. 9. *Smelling a Rat* by Mike Leigh, with Eric Allan, Greg Cruttwell, Saskia Reeves and Timothy Spall, dir. by Mike Leigh, des. by Eve Stewart. (1989) Feb. 13. *Valued Friends* by Stephen Jeffreys, with Peter Capaldi, Tim McInnerny, Serena Gordon and Jane Horrocks, dir. by Robin Lefevre. May 9. *A Room of One's Own* by Virginia Woolf (adapted by Patrick Garland), with Eileen Atkins. May 30. *The Debutante Ball* by Beth Henley, with Sheila Gish, Susannah Harker, Duncan Preston and Jane Horrocks, dir. by Simon Stokes, des. by Dermot Hayes.

HAYMARKET THEATRE ROYAL: SW1. (1988) Dec. 13. *Orpheus Descending* by Tennessee Williams, with Vanessa Redgrave, Julie Covington, Miriam Margolyes, Manning Redwood, Jean Marc Barr and Paul Freeman, dir. by Peter Hall, des. by Alison Chitty. (1989) Feb. 21. *The Royal Baccarat Scandal* by Royce Ryton, with Keith Michell, Fiona Fullerton, and Gerald Harper, dir. by Val May, des. by Tim Goodchild. Aug. 22. *Veterans Day* by Donald Freed, with Jack Lemmon, Michael Gambon and Robert Flemyng, dir. by Kevin Billington, des. by Eileen Diss.

LILIAN BAYLIS THEATRE: Sadler's Wells, EC1. (1988) Oct. 24. *The House of Blue Leaves* by John Guare, with Denis Quilley, Nichola McAuliffe, Kelly Hunter, Helen Lederer and John Fitzgerald-Jay, dir. by Nick Hamm. Nov. 17. *The Madwoman of Chaillot* by Jean Giraudoux (adapted by Maurice Valency), with Eleanor Bron, Philip Franks, Selina Cadell and Celia Imrie, dir. by Nick Hamm, des. by Pamela Howard.

LYRIC: Hammersmith, W6. (1988) Sept. 8. *Dreams in an Empty City* by Stephen Sewell, with Warwick Moss, Philip Madoc and William Hootkins, dir. by Keith Hack. Nov. 8. *Asylum* by Paul Kember, with Sarah Miles, Philip Lowrie, Ian Collier and Ann Way, dir. by Robert Walker. (1989) Jan. 17. *The Woman in Black* by Susan Hill (adapted by Stephen Mallatratt), with John Duttine and Charles Kay, dir. by Robin Herford, des. by Michael Holt. April 28. *A Madhouse in Goa* by Martin Sherman, with Vanessa Redgrave, Rupert Graves and Larry Lamb, dir. by Robert Allan Ackerman. June 15. *Blithe Spirit* by Noel Coward, with Rula Lenska, Neil Stacy, Peggy Mount and Deborah Grant, dir. by John David. Aug. 17. *Prin* by Andrew Davies, with Sheila Hancock, Susie Blake, Paul Copley and David Howey, dir. by Richard Wilson, des. by Julian McGowan.

LYRIC: Shaftsbury Avenue, W1. (1988) Sept. 28. *Dry Rot* by John Chapman, with Brian Rix, Elspet Gray, Derek Griffiths, Richard Vernon, Julie Peasgood, Derek Royle and Nick Wilton, dir. by Christopher Renshaw. (1989) March 7. *Steel Magnolias* by Robert Harling, with Maggie Steed, Rosemary Harris, Janine Duvitski, Stephanie Cole and Joely Richardson, dir. by Julia McKenzie. Aug. 7. *Look Back in Anger* by John Osborne, with Kenneth Branagh, Emma

Thompson, Edward Jewesbury, Gerard Horan and Siobhan Redmond, dir. by Judi Dench.

MERMAID: Puddle Dock, Blackfriars, EC4. (1988) Dec. 8. *The Relapse* by John Vanbrugh, with Roy Marsden, Kate O'Mara and Peter Adamson (British Actors Theatre Company prodn.). (1989) April 25. *To Kill A Mockingbird* by Harper Lee, with Alan Dobie and Hildegard Neil, dir. by Chris Hayes.

MERMAID STUDIO: (1988) Nov. *When We Dead Awaken* By Henrik Ibsen, with Don Crerar and Alexandra Binswanger, dir. by Janine Wünsche.

NATIONAL THEATRE: South Bank, SE1. COTTESLOE: (1988) Oct. 26. *The Father* by Strindberg (adapted by John Osborne), with Alun Armstrong, Susan Fleetwood and Sarah-Jane Fenton, dir. by David Leveaux. Dec. 5. *Making History* by Brian Friel, with Stephen Rea, Niall Tobin and Clare Holman, dir. by Simon Curtis, des. by Julia McGowan. (1989) Jan. 10. *Fuente Ovejuna* by Lope de Vega (translated by Adrian Mitchell), with James Laurenson, Trevor Sellers, Rachel Joyce, George Harris and Clive Rowe, dir. by Declan Donnellan, des. by Nick Ormerod. March 8. *Bed* by Jim Cartwright, with Graham Crowden, Charles Simon and Ruth Kettlewell, dir. by Julia Bardsley, des. by Peter J. Davison. June 27. *The Voysey Inheritance* by Harley Granville Barker, with Jeremy Northam, David Burke, Michael Bryant, Stella Gonet and Barbara Leigh-Hunt, dir. by Richard Eyre, des. by William Dudley. July 6. *The Long Way Round* by Peter Handke, with Tilda Swinton, Andrew Rattenbury, Deirdre Halligan and David Bamber, dir. by Stephen Unwin.

LYTTELTON: (1988) Oct. 4 *The Secret Rapture* by David Hare, with Jill Baker, Penelope Wilton, Clare Higgins, Mick Ford and Paul Shelley, dir. by Howard Davies, des. by John Gunter. Oct. 20. *Mountain Language* by Harold Pinter, with Michael Gambon, George Harris, Tony Haygarth, Eileen Atkins and Miranda Richardson, dir. by Harold Pinter. Dec. 1. *Single Spies* (*An Englishman Abroad* and *A Question of Attribution*) by Alan Bennett, with Simon Callow, Prunella Scales and Alan Bennett, dir. by Alan Bennett and Simon Callow, des. by Bruno Santini. (1989) Jan. 25. *Speed-the-Plow* by David Mamet, with Alfred Molina, Rebecca Pidgeon and Colin Stinton, dir. by Gregory Mosher, des. by Michael Merritt. Feb. 22. *Juno and the Paycock* by Sean O'Casey, with Tony Haygarth, Linda Bassett, Linus Roache and Tom Hickey, dir. by Peter Gill, des. by Deidre Clancy. April 6. *The March on Russia* by David Storey, with Bill Owen, Constance Chapman, Rosemary Martin, Patsy Rowland and Frank Grimes, dir. by Lindsay Anderson, des. by Jocelyn Herbert, music by Alan Price. May 31. *The Misanthrope* by Molière (adapted by Tony Harrison), with Sheila Ballantine, David Horovitch, Sian Thomas, Donald Pickering and Edward Petherbridge, dir. by Paul Unwin, des. by Richard Hudson (co-prodn. with Bristol Old Vic). June 22. *The Grapes of Wrath* by John Steinbeck (adapted and dir. by Frank Galati), with Gary Sinise, Terry Kinney, Jeff Perry, Robert Breuler and Lois Smith, des. by Kevin Rigdon (Steppenwolf Co., Chicago, prodn.).

OLIVIER: (1988) Oct. 20. *Bartholomew Fair* by Ben Jonson, with John Wells, Stephen Moore, David Burke, David Bamber, Michael Bryant and Barbara Leigh-Hunt, dir. by Richard Eyre, des. by William Dudley. (1989) Feb. 2. *Hedda Gabler* by Henrik Ibsen, (adapted by Christopher Hampton), with Juliet Stevenson, Paul Shelley, Suzanne Burden, Norman Rodway, Paul Jesson and Janet Whiteside, dir. by Howard Davies, des. by Bob Crowley. March 16. Shakespeare's *Hamlet*, with Daniel Day-Lewis, Judi Dench, Michael Bryant, Stella Gonet and John

Castle, dir. by Richard Eyre, des. by John Gunter. April 27. *Ghetto* by Joshua Sobol, with Alex Jennings, John Woodvine, Maria Friedman, Anthony O'Donnell and Paul Jesson, dir. by Nicholas Hytner, des. by Bob Crowley.

NEW END: Hampstead, NW3. (1988) Sept. 21. *Rutherford and Son* by Githa Sowerby, with Ruth Mitchell, Ewan Hooper and Ian Reddington, dir. by Win Jones, des. by Penny Brown.

OLD VIC: The Cut, SE1. (1988) Aug. 23. *Bussy d'Ambois* by George Chapman, with David Threlfall and Sara Kestelman, dir. by Jonathan Miller, des. by Richard Hudson. Oct. 11. Shakespeare's *The Tempest*, with Max von Sydow, Rudi Davies, Aden Gillett, Rudolph Walker, Alexei Sayle, Cyril Nri and Peter Bayliss, dir. by Jonathan Miller, des. by Richard Hudson. Dec. 6. *Candide* by Leonard Bernstein (adapted by Hugh Wheeler), with Mark Beudert, Rosemary Ashe, Patricia Routledge and Nickolas Grace, dir. by Jonathan Miller and John Wells, des. by Richard Hudson. (1989) Feb. 3. *The Wars of the Roses* by Shakespeare (English Shakespeare Company prodn.), with Michael Pennington, Andrew Jarvis, June Watson, John Dougall, Paul Brennan, Francesca Ryan, Barry Stanton, Philip Bowen, Michael Cronin and Clyde Pollitt, dir. by Michael Bogdanov, des. by Chris Dyer and Stephanie Howard. March 28. Shakespeare's *King Lear*, with Eric Porter, Peter Bayliss, Gemma Jones, Frances de la Tour, Kim Thomson, Clive Russell and Paul Rogers, dir. by Jonathan Miller, des. by Richard Hudson. May 23. Shakespeare's *As You Like It*, with Fiona Shaw, Adam Kotz, Helen Cooper, John McEnery and Daniel Thorndike, dir. by Tim Albery, des. by Antony McDonald. Aug. 8. *A Flea in Her Ear* by Georges Feydeau (translated by John Mortimer), with Jim Broadbent, Linda Marlowe, Roger Lloyd Pack and Julia Bardsley, dir. by Richard Jones, des. by Brothers Quay.

OPEN AIR: Regent's Park, NW1. (1989) May 30. Shakespeare's *A Midsummer Night's Dream*, with David Henry, Sally Dexter, Saeed Jaffrey, Christopher Benjamin, Teddy Kempner and Brigitte Kahn, dir. by Guy Slater, des. by Simon Higlett. June 14. Shakespeare's *Twelfth Night*, with David Henry, Sally Dexter, Bernard Bresslaw, Vicky Licorish and Chris Ettridge, dir. by Ian Talbot, des. by Simon Higlett. July 31. *The Swaggerer* by Plautus (adapted by Brian Trueman), with Bernard Bresslaw, Ian Talbot, Teddy Kempner, and Sally Dexter, dir. by Caroline Smith, des. by Simon Higlett, music by Carl Davis.

PHOENIX: Charing Cross Road, WC2. (1988) Aug. 23. Shakespeare's *Much Ado about Nothing*, with Samantha Bond and Kenneth Branagh, dir. Judi Dench, des. Jenny Tiramani. Aug. 30. Shakespeare's *As You Like It*, with Tam Hoskyns, Sophie Thompson, James Larkin, Richard Clifford, David Lloyd Meredith and Richard Easton, dir. by Geraldine McEwan, des. by Jenny Tiramani. Sept. 5. Shakespeare's *Hamlet*, with Kenneth Branagh, Sophie Thompson, Richard Easton and Dearbhla Molloy, dir. by Derek Jacobi, des. by Jenny Tiramani. Nov. 28. Shakespeare's *Richard II*, with Derek Jacobi, Robert Eddison, Jeffrey Dench, Clive Arrindell, Barbara Jefford and Kathryn Pogson, dir. by Clifford Williams, des. by Carl Toms. (1989) Jan. 25 Shakespeare's *Richard III*, with Derek Jacobi, Barbara Jefford, Malcolm Tierney, Patrick Marley, Robert Swann and Kathryn Pogson, dir. by Clifford Williams, des. by Carl Toms. May 22. Shakespeare's *The Merchant of Venice*, with Dustin Hoffman, Geraldine James, Leigh Lawson, Nathaniel Parker, Basil Henson and Michael Siberry, dir. by Peter Hall, des. by Chris Dyer.

PICCADILLY: Denman Street, W1. (1989) March 8. *Metropolis*, music and lyrics by Joe Brooks and Dusty Hughes, with Brian Blessed, Judy Kuhn and Graham Bickley, dir. by Jerome Savary, des. by Ralph Koltai.

PLAYHOUSE: Northumberland Avenue, WC2. (1988) Nov. 30. *An Enemy of the People* by Henrik Ibsen (transfer from Young Vic). (1989) Feb. 15. *The World According to Me*, with Jackie Mason. April 18. *The Woman in Black* by Susan Hill (transfer from The Strand).

PRINCE EDWARD: Old Compton Street, W1. (1989) July 4. *Anything Goes* by Cole Porter, with Elaine Paige, Bernard Cribbins, Howard McGillin, Martin Turner and Ashleigh Sendlin, dir. by Jerry Zaks, des. by Tony Walton.

PRINCE OF WALES: Coventry Street, W1. (1989) April 18. *Aspects of Love*, music by Andrew Lloyd Webber, lyrics by Don Black and Charles Hart, with Ann Crumb, Michael Ball, Kevin Colson, Kathleen Rowe McAllen and Paul Bentley, dir. by Trevor Nunn, des. by Maria Bjornson, chor. by Gillian Lynne.

QUEENS: Shaftsbury Avenue, W1. (1989) Feb. 23. *Single Spies* by Alan Bennett (transfer from National Theatre).

RIVERSIDE STUDIOS: Hammersmith, W6. (1988) Sept. 12. *A Doll's House* by Henrik Ibsen, with Anna Carteret, Eamon Boland, Bill Wallis, and David Hargreaves, dir. by Jan Sargent, des. by Stephanie Howards. Oct. 19. *Mrs Vershinin* by Helen Cooper, with Julie Legrand, Jenifer Landor, Christopher Guinee and Rosalind Knight, dir. by Mike Bradwell. (1989) March 6. *Dr. Faustus* by Christopher Marlowe, with Neil Savage, and Roy Weskin, dir. by Carl Heap, des. by Phil Daniels (Medieval Players).

ROYAL COURT: Sloane Square, SW1. (1988) Sept. 9. *Our Country's Good* by Timberlake Wertenbaker, with Mark Lambert, and David Haig, dir. by Max Stafford-Clark, des. by Peter Hartwell. (1989) March 2. *My Mother Said I Never Should* by Charlotte Keatley, with Sheila Reid, Elizabeth Bradley, Jane Gurnett and Shirley Henderson, dir. by Michael Attenborough, des. by Tanya McCallin. April 18. *Iranian Nights* by Howard Brenton and Tariq Ali, with Nabil Shaban, Fiona Victory and Paul Bhattacharjee, dir. by Penny Cherns, des. by Colin Piggott. June 5. *American Bagpipes* by Iain Heggie, with Lesley Manville, Ken Stott and Paul Higgins, dir. by Lindsay Posner, des. by Julian McGowan. July 7. *A Whistle in the Dark* by Tom Murphy, with Dermot Crowley, Gerard Horan and Godfrey Quigley, dir. by Garry Hynes, des. by Brien Vahey. (Abbey Theatre, Dublin, prodn.).

ROYAL COURT UPSTAIRS: Feb. 16. *A Hero's Welcome* by Winsome Pinnock, with Brian Bovell, Mona Hammond, Suzanne Packer, Pamela Nomvete and Joanna Campbell, dir. by Jules Wright (Women's Playhouse Trust prodn.).

SAVOY: Strand, WC2. (1988) Sept. 20. *Sugar Babies* by Ralph Allen and Harry Rigby, with Mickey Rooney, Ann Miller and Rhoda Burchmore. (1989) Feb. 20. *Over My Dead Body* by Michael Sutton and Anthony Fingleton, with Donald Sinden, June Whitfield and Frank Middlemass, dir. by Brian Murray, des. by Saul Radomsky.

SHAFTESBURY: Shaftesbury Avenue, WC2. (1989) April 20. *M. Butterfly* by David Henry Hwang, with Anthony Hopkins, and G. G. Goei, dir. by John Dexter, des. by Eiko Ishioka.

STRAND: Aldwych, WC2. (1988) Oct. 26. *Can-Can*, music and lyrics by Cole Porter, book by Abe Burrows, adapted by Julian More, with Donna McKechnie,

Milo O'Shea and Bernard Alane. (1989) Feb. *The Woman in Black* by Susan Hill (transfer from Lyric, Hammersmith). April 10. *Ivanov* by Chekhov (adapted by Ronald Harwood), with Alan Bates, Felicity Kendal, Peter Sallis, Frank Thornton and Nicky Henson, dir. by Elijah Moshinsky, des. by Mark Thompson. May 11. Shakespeare's *Much Ado About Nothing*, with Alan Bates, Felicity Kendal, Sheila Steafel, Frank Thornton and Karen Ascoe, dir. by Elijah Moshinsky, des. by Mark Thompson.

THEATRE ROYAL: Stratford, E15. (1988) Oct. 3. *The Public* by Frederico Garcia Lorca (translated by Henry Livings), with Gerard Murphy, dir. by Philip Hedley, des. by Ultz.

VAUDEVILLE: Strand, WC2. (1988) Nov. 16. *Henceforward* by Alan Ayckbourn, with Ian McKellen, Jane Asher, Emma Chambers and Serena Evans, dir. by Alan Ayckbourn.

VICTORIA PALACE: Victoria Street, SW1. (1988) Oct. 25. *Brigadoon* by Lerner and Loewe, with Lesley Mackie, Robin Nedwell, Jacinta Mulcahy and Robert Meadmore, dir. by Roger Redfarn, des. by Martin Johns.

WESTMINSTER: Palace Street, SW1. (1989) April 24. *An Ideal Husband* by Oscar Wilde, with Jeremy Child, Richard Murdoch, Jeremy Sinden, Delia Lindsay, Liz Begley and Moira Redmond, dir. by Patrick Sandford.

WHITEHALL: SW1. (1988) Sept. 12. *A Touch of Danger* by Francis Durbridge, with William Franklyn, Virginia Stride, Pauline Yates and Derren Nesbitt, dir. by Mark Piper.

WYNDHAM'S: Charing Cross Road, WC2. (1988) Sept. 22. *The Secret of Sherlock Holmes* by Jeremy Paul, with Jeremy Brett and Edward Hardwicke, dir. by Patrick Garland, des. by Poppy Mitchell.

YOUNG VIC: The Cut, SE1. (1988) Oct. 13. *An Enemy of the People* by Henrik Ibsen (adapted by Arthur Miller), with Tom Wilkinson, David Henry, Connie Booth, Clive Swift, Suzan Sylvester and Tom Mannion, dir. by David Thacker. (1989) Jan. 24. *Two-way Mirror* (*Elegy for a Lady* and *Some Kind of Love Story*) by Arthur Miller, with Bob Peck and Helen Mirren, dir. by David Thacker, des. by Bob Crowley. May 9. Shakespeare's *Coriolanus*, with Corin Redgrave and Rachel Kempson, dir. by Jane Howell.

Productions outside London included the following:

STRATFORD MEMORIAL THEATRE (Royal Shakespeare Company) (1988) Sept. 29. *The Plantagenets* (*Henry VI, The Rise of Edward IV* and *Richard III, His Death*), adapted from Shakespeare by Charles Wood, with Anton Lesser, Penny Downie, David Calder, Oliver Cotton, Julia Ford, Ralph Fiennes, Ken Bones and David Waller, dir. by Adrian Noble, des. by Bob Crowley. (1989) March 30. *A Midsummer Night's Dream*, with David Troughton, John Carlisle, Clare Higgins, Richard McCabe, Amanda Bellamy, Sarah Crowden and Stephen Simms, dir. by John Caird, des. by Sue Blane. April 20. *Hamlet* with Mark

Rylance, Clare Higgins, Peter Wight, Rebecca Saire and Patrick Godfrey, dir. by Ron Daniels, des. by Antony McDonald. June 29. *Cymbeline* with John Carlisle, David O'Hara, Naomi Wirthner, David Troughton, Linda Spurrier and Bernard Horsfall, dir. by Bill Alexander, des. by Tim O'Brien.

OTHER PLACE: (1988) Nov. 9. *The Love of the Nightingale* by Timberlake Wertenbaker, with Marie Mullen, Peter Lennon and Katy Behean, dir. by Garry Hynes, des. by Iona McLeish. (1989) Aug. 9. *Othello*, with Willard White, Ian McKellen, Imogen Stubbs, Sean Baker, Zoë Wanamaker and Clive Swift, dir. by Trevor Nunn, des. by Bob Crowley.

THE SWAN: (1988) Sept. 13. *Restoration* by Edward Bond, with Simon Russell Beale, Duncan Bell and Pip Hinton, dir. by Roger Michell. (1989) March 4. *Piers the Plowman* by William Langland (adapted by James Pettifer), with Nicholas Collett, dir. by Carl Heap (Medieval Players). April 5. *Romeo and Juliet*, with Mark Rylance, Georgia Slowe, Margaret Courtenay, Bernard Horsfall and David O'Hara, dir. by Terry Hands, des. by Farrah. April 24. *Dr. Faustus* by Christopher Marlowe, with Gerard Murphy and David Bradley, dir. by Barry Kyle, des. by Ashley Martin-Davis. June 28. *The Silent Woman*, or *Epicoene* by Ben Jonson, with David Bradley, Peter Hamilton Dyer and Richard McCabe, dir. by Danny Boyle, des. by Kandis Cook.

BIRMINGHAM REPERTORY: (1989) Feb. 10. *Who's Afraid of Virginia Woolf?* by Edward Albee, with James Bolam, Sylvia Syms, Jerome Flynn and Beatie Edney, dir. by John Adams, des. by Roger Butlin.

CHICHESTER FESTIVAL: (1989) May 3. *Victory!* by Thomas Hardy (adapted by Patrick Garland), with James Bolam, David Collings and Brett Forrest, dir. by Patrick Garland and Matthew Francis. May 17. *The Heiress* by Ruth and Augustus Goetz (adapted from *Washington Square* by Henry James), with Alec McCowen, Ian Buchanan, Nichola McAuliffe and Phyllis Calvert, dir. by Vivian Matalon. July 10. *London Assurance* by Dion Boucicault, with Paul Eddington, Angela Thorne, Peter Fontaine, Benedict Taylor, Phyllida Hancock and John Warner, dir. by Sam Mendes. Aug. 2. *A Little Night Music* by Stephen Sondheim, with Dorothy Tutin, Lila Kedrova, Susan Hampshire and Peter McEnery, dir. by Ian Judge, des. by Mark Thompson.

CHICHESTER STUDIO (THE MINERVA): (1989) May. *Summerfolk* by Gorky (translated by Michael Robinson), with Lesley Sharp, Sam Graham and Peter McEnery, dir. by Sam Mendes, des. by Paul Farnsworth. June 30. *The Triumph of Love* by Marivaux (translated by Guy Callan), with Kate Duchene, and Will Knightley, dir. by Jeremy Raison.

MANCHESTER ROYAL EXCHANGE: (1988) Dec. *Arms and the Man* by G. B. Shaw, with Adrian Lukis, Catherine Russell, Roberta Taylor and Paul Herzberg, dir. by Casper Wrede. (1989) May 11. *The Voysey Inheritance* by Granville Barker, with Robert Glenister, Harriet Bagnall, James Maxwell and Helen Atkinson Wood, dir. by Gregory Hersov, des. by Michael Holt.

OPERA, 1988–89

The 1988–89 season saw the tenth anniversary of Opera North. The Leeds-based Company was founded in 1978 as the northern offshoot of English National Opera, becoming totally independent after a few seasons. Leeds was one of the main venues in English National Opera's tours during the 1970s and it was hoped that establishing a permanent base in the region would create an artistically stronger and more consistent level of performance than was possible for a touring company. This hope was encouraged by the success of Welsh National Opera and Scottish Opera in establishing companies and building up audiences in their regions. Opera North has fulfilled these expectations and audiences for the company's performances in 1987–88 were running at nearly 90 per cent of theatre capacity.

Over its first ten years, Opera North has built up a repertory of seventy operas. Of these, 44 operas were productions originated by Opera North. In its early seasons its other productions were borrowed from English National Opera. Since it became independent of its parent company, Opera North has borrowed productions or co-produced operas with a number of other companies, notably Welsh National Opera and Scottish Opera. There have been a few occasions when the company's limited artistic control over borrowed productions has put poor work in front of its audiences. Generally, however, the risk involved in borrowing has paid off, enabling Opera North to present a broader repertory than would otherwise have been possible.

Opera North's reliance on borrowed productions was largely dictated by the financial restrictions it has faced since its inception. This coincided with the onset of an economic recession which has restricted public funding generally, and has led the other British companies increasingly to use co-production and borrowing as a way of making their funds stretch further. Despite the Arts Council's commitment to arts provision in the regions, Opera North's grant is less than that of Scottish Opera or Welsh National Opera, and the company's future growth will be very dependent upon sponsorship.

Company Folds

The vulnerability of companies dependent on box-office takings and private funding was demonstrated by the winding-up of New Sadler's Wells Opera company at the beginning of 1989. The company was founded in 1982 to give occasional productions of light opera performed for short seasons by artists attached to the major opera companies. Commercial sponsorship of £400,000 over four years helped to launch the company, which had considerable success in its six years of life with operas such as *The Count of Luxembourg*, *H.M.S. Pinafore*, *The Merry Widow* and *Ruddigore*. However, the productions of *The Gondoliers* and *La Belle Hélène* in autumn 1988 were not well received: despite good advance bookings, box-office receipts were very poor with only 38 per cent of seats filled during the season. The company went into liquidation in February 1989 with debts of over £500,000.

New Ventures

Despite financial stringency, most companies are committed to offering a broad repertoire and the Royal Opera House and English National Opera in particular have a history of premiering new operas or operas new to this country. During the past season both companies have developed projects bringing together composers, writers, performers and production staff as a first step towards creating new works.

The first project to reach fruition, known as the Garden Venture, was established by the Royal Opera at the instigation of staff and artists of the opera. Its purpose is to promote the writing of new opera by commissioning small-scale works and organizing related seminars and workshop activities. In April 1988 a workshop weekend took place which provided composers, singers, musicians and production staff with the opportunity to collaborate on a number of experimental pieces and to consider the nature of music theatre. As a result of the weekend, seven chamber operas were commissioned by the Royal Opera House.

Independent Means

Funding for the commissions was largely provided by the Arts Council, but the money to stage the new works had to be found elsewhere without diverting funds from other commitments. This led in autumn 1988 to an innovative fund-raising scheme involving the *Independent* newspaper, which invited its readers to sponsor the Garden Venture's first season of chamber operas by donating £100 each towards the £100,000 needed to complete commission fees and to pay for performances of the works. The scheme was successful and the new works were premiered at the Donmar Warehouse, London, on May 17 and 18, 1989, as part of the London International Opera Festival.

The works were *The Uranium Miners' Radio Orchestra plays Scenes from Salome's Revenge* by Andrew Poppy (libretto, the composer), *Survival Song* by Priti Paintal (libretto, Richard Fawkes), *The Standard Bearer* by Michael Christie (libretto, John McMurray), *Soap Opera* by Kenneth Chalmers (libretto, Felicity Hayes-McCoy), *Last Tango on the North Circular* by Peter Wiegold (libretto, the composer), *Caedmon* by Edward Lambert (libretto, from Christopher Fry's *One Thing More*), and *The Menaced Assassin* by Jeremy Peyton Jones (libretto, the composer and Claire MacDonald).

The Garden Venture was also involved in summer 1989 in working with student composers at the Dartington Summer School, and it plans further workshops and seminars to encourage collaboration on new works.

Opera Studio

English National Opera's plans for a Contemporary Opera Studio also concentrate on creating opportunities and providing resources to stimulate operatic composition. In March 1988 the company formulated the aims of the project: to bring composers and writers together to practise operatic writing; to draw them into the day-to-day workings of the company;

and to create a flexible schedule for the writing of new work, with time allowed for revising ideas and rewriting. A weekend forum at Dartington College in January 1989 was attended by sixty composers and writers, as well as singers, musicians, producers, arts administrators and E.N.O. staff. Discussions and performances at the forum helped to crystallize ideas about the structure of the Contemporary Opera Studio.

E.N.O.'s blueprint is for a Studio which will not initially be a building but a resource for composers and writers. It will work in two ways. At one level the Studio will provide opportunities for experimental and improvisational work, enabling composers and writers to try out ideas and different techniques without the pressure of final performance. Second, English National Opera will commission each year three or four teams consisting of composer, writer, producer and designer to write new opera within a flexible time-scale allowing time for rethinking and rewriting. Potential collaborators have already emerged as a result of the Dartington forum.

A contribution of £10,000 towards the cost of the forum was made by Channel 4 television, which filmed the weekend's events for its 'Signals' programme. English National Opera has yet to find funding for the Studio project, although Channel 4, the Arts Council and the South Bank have promised support for English National Opera in the form of commissions and performance space.

Plumber's Gift

English National Opera has already embarked on a series of commissions for the company to perform at the Coliseum. The first of these to be performed is *The Plumber's Gift* which was premiered in May. It is the second opera by David Blake, whose first work, *Toussaint*, was premiered by English National Opera in 1977 and revived for the 1983–84 season. The two works are very different in scale. *Toussaint* is a tragedy on an epic scale, addressing broad issues and making full use of the company's vocal and orchestral resources. *The Plumber's Gift* is more modest in scope, a comedy of manners for a cast of six.

The libretto was written by the poet John Birtwistle and the two collaborators decided that they wanted the opera to be original rather than an adaptation from another medium. They also decided upon a modern setting, and that the work should explore how people shape their lives, rather than having the characters propelled by destiny. Musically the starting points were *Così fan tutte*, *The Magic Flute* and *The Midsummer Marriage*.

The opera presents the relationships of two socially distinct couples: middle-aged, middle-class Marian and James, and the younger, working-class Sylvia and Colin. Both couples are taking a weekend break at a seaside guest-house and the opera explores the interaction between the characters and the effect this has on their relationships. The landlady of the guest-house, Mrs. Worthing, and the resident guest, Commander Hardcastle, are observers of the relationships.

The opening and closing sections of the opera have a naturalist setting, the first introducing the characters and delineating the relationships. Between the two acts is a pastoral which the characters experience as a distorted alternative world. The pastoral reflects the events which have happened already and foreshadows how the relationships may develop. The final act shows the effects of their experiences upon the couples and their relationships.

The opera met with a mixed reaction. Music and libretto were acclaimed by some critics for their richness, beauty, and sustained imagination and ingenuity. Others felt that the material was fundamentally unoperatic and that the opera lacked dramatic purpose, while the pastoral was held to slow down the action. The production and the singers' performances were uniformly praised.

Glass Planet

The critics were more united in their opinion of another new work premiered by English National Opera, *The Making of the Representative for Planet 8*: they did not like it. Philip Glass was co-commissioned to write the opera by English National Opera, the Houston Grand Opera, Het Muzicktheater in Amsterdam and Bühnen der Landeshauptstadt in Kiel: the world premiere took place in Houston in July 1988.

The three-act work is based on a novel of the same name by Doris Lessing, who wrote the libretto. Planet 8 has a prosperous rural civilization but the planet's sun is dying. The opera deals with the gradual extinction of the race as an ice age develops, and the people's realization that their immortal spirits will survive in the form of the Representative.

Glass is a minimalist composer, his music proceeding in units of simple harmonies and rhythms repeated over and over, which become more restless as the repetition continues. The repetition can achieve a compelling and hypnotic quality and in *Satyagraha* and *Akhnaten*, Glass' earlier full-length operas, this hypnotic quality works to telling effect. Neither of these earlier works has a conventional narrative requiring the story and characters to be developed. *The Making of the Representative for Planet 8*, however, is a narrative drama and some critics felt that Glass' musical idiom is unsuited to material that requires psychologically realistic characterization and dramatic climaxes and continuity. Doris Lessing's libretto did not find favour either, with complaints that the power of the writing in the novel had been stripped away to leave a libretto which was banal.

The production in Houston was described as 'compelling visually and superb musically'. Modifications were made to the production before it was staged in London and these may have lessened the visual impact, but the cast and orchestra at the Coliseum were praised for their performances.

First reactions to *The Making of the Representative for Planet 8* may have been unfavourable but Glass' minimalism also met with resistance or a baffled response when *Akhnaten* was first performed at the Coliseum. *Akhnaten* found more acceptance the second season it was performed: a return to the Coliseum by *The Making of the Representative for Planet 8* may lead to a similar reassessment.

OPERA PRODUCTIONS

In the summaries of the company activities shown below, the dates in brackets indicate the year the current production entered that company's repertoire.

ROYAL OPERA (1946)
Royal Opera House, Covent Garden, WC2E 9DD

Productions from the repertoire were *Turandot* (1984), *Die Entführung aus dem Serail* (1987), *Falstaff* (1982), *Semele* (1982), *Die Fledermaus* (1977), *Don Carlos* (1958), *La clemenza di Tito* (1974), *Der Rosenkavalier* (1984), *Le nozze di Figaro* (1987), *Cavalleria rusticana* and *I pagliacci* (1959), *L'Italiana in Algeri* (1988), *Alceste* (1981) and *Die Zauberflöte* (1979).

New productions were:

Sept. 29, 1988. Das Rheingold (Wagner). *Conductor*, Bernard Haitink; *producer*, Yuri Lyubimov; *designer*, Paul Hernon.

Alberich, Ekkehard Wlaschiha; *Fricka*, Helga Dernesch; *Wotan*, James Morris; *Freia*, Nancy Gustafson; *Loge*, Kenneth Riegal; *Mime*, John Dobson; *Erda*, Jadwiga Rappé; *Fasolt*, Roderick Kennedy; *Fafner*, Willard White.

Oct. 31, 1988. Madama Butterfly (Puccini), in association with Scottish Opera. *Conductor*, Michael Schønwandt; *producer*, Nuria Espert; *designers*, Ezio Frigerio (*set*), Franca Squarciapino (*costumes*).

Cio-Cio-San, Catherine Malfitano; *Pinkerton*, Arthur Davies; *Sharpless*, Jonathan Summers; *Suzuki*, Miao Qing.

Nov. 14, 1988. Manon (Massenet). *Conductor*, Michel Plasson; *producer*, John Cox; *designer*, Peter Rice.

Manon, Leontina Vaduva; *Des Grieux*, David Rendall; *Lescaut*, François Le Roux; *De Brétigny*, Barry Mora; *Comte de Grieux*, Donald McIntyre.

Dec. 8, 1988. Rigoletto (Verdi). *Conductor*, Michael Boder; *producer*, Nuria Espert; *designers*, Ezio Frigerio (*set*), Franca Squarciapino (*costumes*).

Rigoletto, Brent Ellis; *Gilda*, June Anderson; *Duke of Mantua*, Neil Shicoff; *Sparafucile*, John Tomlinson; *Maddalena*, Claire Powell; *Monterone*, Donald McIntyre.

Feb. 9. The British premiere of Un ré in ascolta (Berio). *Conductor*, Luciano Berio; *producer*, Graham Vick; *designer*, Chris Dyer.

Prospero, Donald McIntyre; *Director*, Robert Tear; *Venerdi*, Graham Valentine; *Protagonista*, Kathryn Harries; *Soprano I*, Penelope Walmsley-Clark; *Soprano II*, Rebecca Littig; *Mezzo*, Elizabeth Laurence; *Singers*, Robin Leggate, Omar Ebrahim, Matthew Best; *Nurse*, Linda Kitchen; *Wife*, Anthea Moller; *Doctor*, John Dobson; *Lawyer*, Eric Garrett; *Boy (Mime)*, Memnos Costa.

March 6. Così fan tutte (Mozart). *Conductor*, Jeffrey Tate; *producer*, Johannes Schaaf; *designers*, Hans Schavernoch (*set*), Lore Haas (*costumes*).

Fiordiligi, Margaret Marshall; *Dorabella*, Susanne Mentzer; *Despina*, Anne Howells; *Ferrando*, Hans Peter Blochwitz; *Guglielmo*, Andreas Schmidt; *Alfonso*, Claudio Desderi.

May 1. Albert Herring (Britten), in association with Glyndebourne Festival Opera. *Conductor*, Roger Norrington; *producer*, Peter Hall; *designer*, John Gunter.

Albert Herring, John Graham-Hall; *Lady Billows*, Pauline Tinsley; *Florence Pike*, Felicity Palmer; *Miss Wordsworth*, Elizabeth Gale; *Mrs. Herring*, Patricia Kern; *Gedge*, Derek Hammond-Stroud; *Upfold*, Alexander Oliver; *Supt. Budd*, Richard Van Allen; *Sid*, Jeffrey Black; *Nancy*, Eirian James.

June 7. Il trovatore (Verdi). *Conductor*, Bernard Haitink; *producer and designer*, Piero Faggioni.

Leonora, Rosalind Plowright; *Azucena*, Eva Randová; *Manrico*, Placido Domingo; *Count di Luna*, Sergei Leiferkus.

ENGLISH NATIONAL OPERA (1931)
London Coliseum, St. Martin's Lane, WC2N 4ES

Productions from the repertoire were *Carmen* (1986), *Tosca* (1987), *The Barber of Seville* (1987), *Simon Boccanegra* (1987), *The Mikado* (1986), *La Bohème* (1977), *The Pearl Fishers* (1987), *The Turn of the Screw*, (1979), *Don Giovanni* (1985), *The Makropulos Case* (1982) and *The Mastersingers of Nuremberg* (1984).

New productions were:

Sept. 14, 1988. La traviata (Verdi). *Conductor*, Mark Elder; *producer*, David Pountney; *designer*, Stefanos Lazaridis.

Violetta, Helen Field; *Alfredo*, Arthur Davies; *Germont*, Alan Opie.

Nov. 9, 1988. The European premiere of The Making of the Representative for Planet 8 (Glass), a co-commission by E.N.O., Houston Grand Opera, Het Muziektheater and Bühnen der Landeshauptstadt Kiel. *Conductor*, Michael Lloyd; *staging* by Harry Silverstein, after Minoru Domberger's original production; *designers*, Eiko Ishioka, Minoru Domberger.

Alsi, Lesley Garrett; *Doeg*, Andrew Shore; *Johor*, Richard Angas; *Nooni*, Christopher Gillett; *Klin*, Gloria Crane; *Rivalin*, Jady Pearl; *Bratch*, Tamsin Dives; *Pedug*, John Kitchiner; *Marl*, Simon Masterton-Smith.

Dec. 14, 1988. Christmas Eve (Rimsky Korsakov). *Conductor*, Albert Rosen; *producer*, David Pountney; *designer*, Sue Blane.

Oksana, Cathryn Pope; *Vakula*, Edmund Barham; *Solokha/Tsarina*, Anne-Marie Owens; *The Devil*, Nigel Douglas.

Jan. 24. The British premiere of Lear (Reimann). *Conductor*, Paul Daniel; *producer*, Eike Gramss; *set designer*, Eberhard Matthies; *costumes*, Renate Schmitzer.

King Lear, Monte Jaffe; *Gloucester*, Rodney Macann; *Kent*, Nigel Douglas; *Edmund*, Alan Woodrow; *Edgar*, Christopher Robson; *Goneril*, Phyllis Cannan; *Regan*, Vivian Tierney; *Cordelia*, Rosa Mannion; *Albany*, Christopher Booth-Jones; *Cornwall*, Geoffrey Pogson; *Fool*, Eric Shilling; *France*, William Mackie.

Feb. 22. Falstaff (Verdi). *Conductor*, Mark Elder; *producer*, David Pountney; *designer*, Marie-Jeanne Lecca.

Falstaff, Benjamin Luxon; *Mistress Ford*, Janice Cairns; *Mistress Page*, Sally Burgess; *Mistress Quickly*, Anne Collins; *Ford*, Malcolm Donnelly; *Nannetta*, Joan Rodgers; *Fenton*, Barry Banks.

April 12. Eugene Onegin (Tchaikovsky). *Conductor*, Mark Elder; *producer*, Graham Vick; *designer*, Sally Jacobs.

Tatyana, Marie McLaughlin; *Eugene Onegin*, Jonathan Summers; *Olga*, Ethna Robinson; *Lensky*, Arthur Davies; *Gremin*, Norman Bailey.

May. 25. The world premiere of The Plumber's Gift (Blake). *Conductor*, Lionel Friend; *producer*, Richard Jones; *designer*, Nigel Lowery.

Colin, Peter Coleman-Wright; *Sylvia*, Sally Burgess; *Marion*, Eiddwen Harrhy; *James*, Philip

Doghan; *Mrs Worthing*, Ann Howard; *Commander Hardfast*, Neil Howlett.

The opera *A Small Green Space*, commissioned by the Baylis Programme at the E.N.O., was performed at Basildon, Barrow-in-Furness, Buxton, the Glasgow Mayfest, Bury St. Edmunds and The Place, London.

NEW SADLER'S WELLS OPERA
Sadler's Wells Theatre, Rosebery Avenue, EC1

In a three-week season at Sadler's Wells Theatre in autumn 1988, the company presented two new productions:
Oct. 14, 1988. **La Belle Hélène** (Offenbach). *Conductor*, Simon Phipps; *producer*, Tim Luscombe; *designer*, Ultz.

Helen, Rosemary Ashe; *Paris*, Peter Jeffes; *Menelaus*, Bernard Dickerson; *Agamemnon*, John Ayldon.

Oct. 21, 1988. **The Gondoliers** (Sullivan). *Conductor*, Simon Phipps; *producer*, Vernon Mound; *designer*, Gerard Howland.

Marco, Stephen Austin; *Giuseppe*, Richard Jackson; *Gianetta*, Laureen Livingstone; *Tessa*, Jane Findlay; *Duke of Plaza-Toro*, Julian Moyle; *Duchess*, Linda Ormiston; *Luiz*, Robert Horn; *Casilda*, Carole Lesley Green.

The two productions were subsequently given on tour at Southampton, Birmingham, Oxford, Nottingham and Bath.

WELSH NATIONAL OPERA (1946)
John Street, Cardiff CF1 4SP

Productions from the repertoire were *Madam Butterfly* (1978), *La traviata* (1988), *Die Frau ohne Schatten* (1981), *La Bohème* (1984), *The Bartered Bride* (1982) and concert performances of *Osud*.

New productions were:
Sept. 10, 1988. **Falstaff** (Verdi). *Conductor*, Richard Armstrong; *producer*, Peter Stein; *designers*, Lucio Fanti (*set*), Moidele Bickel (*costumes*).

Falstaff, Donald Maxwell; *Mistress Ford*, Suzanne Murphy; *Mistress Page*, Wendy Verco; *Mistress Quickly*, Cynthia Buchan; *Ford*, David Malis; *Nannetta*, Nuccia Focile; *Fenton*, Laurence Dale.

March 11. **The Seraglio** (Mozart). *Conductor*, Charles Mackerras; *producer*, Giles Havergal; *designer*, Russell Craig.

Constanze, Marilyn Hill Smith; *Blonde*, Andrea Bolton; *Belmonte*, Richard Croft; *Pedrillo*, Timothy German; *Osmin*, Peter Rose; *Pasha Selim*, Paul Bentall.

May 13. **La sonnambula** (Bellini). *Conductor*, Julian Smith; *producer*, Helmut Polixa; *designers*, Kathrin Kegler (*set*), Terry Parr and Dirk von Bodisco (*costumes*).

Amina, Valeria Esposito; *Elvino*, Peter Bronder; *Lisa*, Eirian Davies; *Count Rodolfo*, Geoffrey Moses; *Teresa*, Beverley Mills.

June 5. **Ariadne auf Naxos** (Strauss). *Conductor*, Charles Mackerras; *producer*, Giles Havergal; *designer*, Russell Craig.

Ariadne, Edith Davies; *Bacchus*, Gary Bachlund; *Zerbinetta*, Constance Hauman; *Composer*, Annemarie Sand; *Brighella*, Harry Nicoll; *Scaramouche*, David Owen; *Harlequin*, Peter Savidge; *Truffaldin*, Ian Comboy; *Major-Domo*, Nigel Douglas; *Music Master*, Barry Mora; *Naiad*, Eileen Hulse; *Dryad*, Kate McCarney; *Echo*, Andrea Bolton.

Performances of *Falstaff* were given at the Royal Opera House, Covent Garden, in October 1988 and at the Teatro Lirico, Milan, in May 1989. Performances of the repertory were given at the New Theatre, Cardiff, and on tour at Bristol, Swansea, Liverpool,

Birmingham, Oxford, Southampton and Manchester.

A tour of smaller venues with a production of *La traviata* was also undertaken.

SCOTTISH OPERA (1962)
Theatre Royal, Hope Street, Glasgow G2 3QA

Productions from the repertoire were *The Magic Flute* (1983), *Iolanthe* (1986) and *La Bohème* (1988).

New productions were:
Sept. 21, 1988. **The Midsummer Marriage** (Tippett), a co-production with Opera North. *Conductor*, John Pryce-Jones; *producer*, Tim Albery; *designers*, Tom Cairns, Antony McDonald.

Jenifer, Marie Slorach; *Mark*, Quade Winter; *Bella*, Patricia O'Neill; *Jack*, Bonaventura Bottone; *King Fisher*, Neil Howlett; *Madame Sosostris*, Penelope Walker; *the Ancients*, Claire Livingstone, David Marsh.

Oct. 18, 1988. **Die Fledermaus** (Strauss). *Conductor*, Jacek Kasprzyk; *producer*, Simon Callow; *designer*, Bruno Santini.

Rosalinde, Gillian Sullivan; *Eisenstein*, Robin Leggate; *Falke*, Russell Smythe; *Adele*, Amy Burton; *Alfred*, Justin Lavendar; *Orlofsky*, Omar Ebrahim; *Frank*, Oddbjørn Tennfjord; *Frosch*, Graham de Banzie.

Jan. 27. **Das Rheingold** (Wagner). *Conductor*, John Mauceri; *producer*, Richard Jones; *designer*, Nigel Lowery.

Alberich, Nicholas Folwell; *Fricka*, Felicity Palma; *Wotan*, Willard White; *Freia*, Anne Williams-King; *Loge*, Bonaventura Bottone; *Mime*, Paul Harrhy; *Erda*, Penelope Walker; *Fasolt*, Curtis Watson; *Fafner*, Oddbjørn Tennfjord.

Feb. 8. **Don Giovanni** (Mozart). *Conductor*, John Mauceri; *producer*, David Walsh; *designer*, Kathrin Hysing.

Don Giovanni, Jonathan Summers; *Donna Elvira*, Kathryn Bouleyn; *Donna Anna*, Jane Eaglen; *Don Ottavio*, Glenn Winslade; *Leporello*, Jan Opalach; *Commendatore*, Oddbjørn Tennfjord; *Zerlina*, Judith Howarth; *Masetto*, David Marsh.

March 23. **Oedipus Rex** (Stravinsky), a co-production with Opera North, given as a double-bill with *Petrushka*, performed by Scottish Ballet.
Conductor, Graeme Jenkins; *producer*, Kate Brown after Steven Pimlott; *designer*, Stefanos Lazaridis.

Oedipus, Alberto Remedios; *Jocasta*, Anne-Marie Owens; *Creon/Messenger*, Rodney Macann; *Tiresias*, John Tranter; *Narrator*, Robert O'Mahoney.

April 25. **La traviata** (Verdi), a co-production with Teatro Lirico Nacional La Zarzuela, Madrid. *Conductor*, John Mauceri; *producer*, Nuria Espert; *designers*, Ezio Frigerio (*set*), Franca Squarciapino (*costumes*).

Violetta, Nancy Gustafson; *Alfredo*, Jorge Pita; *Germont*, James Dietsch.

May 23. **Street Scene** (Weill), a co-production with English National Opera. *Conductor*, John Mauceri; *producer*, David Pountney; *designer*, David Fielding.

Anna Maurrant, Kristine Ciesinski; *Rose Maurrant*, Janis Kelly; *Willie Maurrant*, Ryan McBride; *Frank Maurrant*, Spiro Malas; *Sam Kaplan*, Mark Beudert.

Performances were given at the Theatre Royal, Glasgow, and on tour at Newcastle, Edinburgh, Aberdeen, Bradford, Oxford and Liverpool.

Scottish Opera Go-Round toured smaller venues in Scotland and Wales with a small-scale production of *Don Carlos* in autumn 1988.

OPERA NORTH (1978)
Grand Theatre, New Briggate, Leeds LS1 6NZ

Productions from the repertoire during the company's tenth anniversary season were *La Bohème* (1986), *Aida* (1986), *The Flying Dutchman* (1979) and *The Marriage of Figaro* (1987).

New productions were:

Sept. 17, 1988. **The Love of Three Oranges** (Prokofiev). *Conductor*, David Lloyd-Jones; *producer* Richard Jones; *designers*, the Brothers Quay (*set*), Sue Blane (*costumes*).

The Prince, Peter Jeffes; *Fata Morgana*, Pauline Tinsley; *Ninetta*, Juliet Booth; *Nicoletta*, Victoria Sharp; *Smeraldina*, Maria Jagusz; *Linetta*, Lesley Roberts; *Princess Clarissa*, Patricia Payne; *Truffaldino*, Paul Harrhy; *Leandro*, Andrew Shore; *Pantaloon*, Alan Oke; *The King*, Mark Glanville.

Oct. 1, 1988. **Lucia di Lammermoor** (Donizetti). *Conductor*, Clive Timms; *producer*, David Gann; *designer*, Ultz.

Lucia, Valerie Masterson; *Edgardo*, Jorge Pita; *Enrico*, Keith Latham; *Arturo*, Barry Banks; *Raimondo*, John Connell.

Dec. 10, 1988. **Les Pêcheurs de perles** (Bizet), a co-production with English National Opera. *Conductor*, David Lloyd-Jones; *producer* and *designer*, Philip Prowse.

Leila, Anne Dawson; *Nadir*, Arthur Davies; *Zurga*, Sergei Leiferkus.

April 19. **Manon** (Massenet). *Conductor*, Clive Timms; *producer*, Richard Jones; *designer*, Richard Hudson.

Manon, Helen Field; *Des Grieux*, Patrick Power; *Lescaut*, Geoffrey Dalton; *De Brétigny*, Robert Poulton; *Comte des Grieux*, Matthew Best.

May 9. **Boris Godunov** (1869 version) (Mussorgsky). *Conductor*, David Lloyd-Jones; *producer*, Ian Judge; *designers*, Russell Craig (*set*), Deirdre Clancy.

Boris Godunov, John Tomlinson; *Xenia*, Juliet Booth; *Feodor*, Verona James; *Grigory*, Edmund Barham; *Shuisky*, Kim Begley; *Pimen*, Sean Rea.

Performances were also given on tour at Manchester, Nottingham, Hull and Birmingham. *The Marriage of Figaro* was given and *La Finta Giardiniera* premiered at the Mozart Festival at York in July 1989. *The Love of Three Oranges* was performed at the 1989 Edinburgh Festival.

KENT OPERA (1969)
Pembles Cross, Egerton, Ashford, Kent

The company began the season with performances of *A Night at the Chinese Opera* (1987) at the Queen Elizabeth Hall, London. On their autumn 1988 tour, performances of *Fidelio* (1982), *Count Ory* (1988) and *Don Giovanni* (1983) were given at Dartford, Norwich, Tunbridge Wells, Wolverhampton, Canterbury, Northampton and Bath.

The spring 1989 tour (the company's twentieth anniversary season) included *Fidelio*, *The Return of Ulysses* (1979) and one new production: May 3. **Peter Grimes** (Britten). *Conductor*, Ivan Fischer; *producer*, Norman Platt; *designer*, Bernard Culshaw.

Peter Grimes, Howard Haskin; *Ellen Orford*, Meryl Drower; *Bulstrode*, Rodney Macann; *Auntie*, Enid Hartle; *Ned Keene*, Gwion Thomas; *Bob Boles*, Tomos Ellis.

Performances were given at Dartford, Canterbury, Eastbourne, Plymouth, Southsea, Norwich, the Bath Festival, Northampton and Tunbridge Wells. *Don Giovanni* and *Fidelio* were also given at Valencia, Spain, in December 1988.

In summer 1989 the company performed Britten's *Burning Fiery Furnace* at the Aldeburgh Festival and the London International Opera Festival. The *producer* was Ian Watt-Smith, the *designer* Mark Hinton and the *music* was conducted from the keyboard by Timothy Dean. The cast included David Johnson (*Nebuchadnezzar*), Richard Suart (*Abbot-Astrologer*), Gwion Thomas, Robert Horn and John Rath (*Shadrach*, *Meschach* and *Abednego*).

GLYNDEBOURNE FESTIVAL OPERA (1934)
Glyndebourne, Lewes, Sussex BN8 5UU

The 1989 Festival ran from May 19 to August 23: the orchestra was the London Philharmonic Orchestra for five of the six productions. The Orchestra of the Age of Enlightenment, making its début at the Festival, played for the performances of *Le nozze di Figaro*. Four of the productions were revivals: *Orfeo ed Euridice* (1982), *A Midsummer Night's Dream* (1981), *Arabella* (1984) and *The Rake's Progress* (1975). The new productions were:

May 19. **Jenůfa** (Janáček). *Conductor*, Andrew Davis; *director*, Nikolaus Lehnhoff; *designer*, Tobias Hoheisel.

Jenůfa, Roberta Alexander; *Števa*, Mark Baker; *Laca*, Philip Langridge; *The Kostelnička*, Anja Silja.

July 2. **Le nozze di Figaro** (Mozart). *Conductor*, Simon Rattle; *director*, Peter Hall; *designer*, John Gunter.

Figaro, Dale Duesing; *Susanna*, Joan Rodgers; *Count Almaviva*, William Shimell; *The Countess*, Gunnel Bohman; *Cherubino*, Marianne Rorholm.

The Glyndebourne Touring Opera performed *Le nozze di Figaro*, *Il barbiere di Siviglia* and *Death in Venice* at Glyndebourne, Plymouth, Oxford, Southampton, Manchester and Norwich in autumn 1990.

DANCE, 1988–89

The Royal Opera House announced on January 12, 1989 that Sadler's Wells Royal Ballet will be based in Birmingham from August 1990. The first move in the transfer was made in December 1987 when the Birmingham Hippodrome and Birmingham City Council jointly invited the company to make the Hippodrome its main base. The submission in autumn 1988 of a report by independent consultant David Allen on the advantages and disadvantages of the proposal, was followed by detailed negotiations between the Royal Opera House and Birmingham. The facilities and funding offered by the city persuaded the Covent Garden management that the company's continued development would be ensured by moving its base to Birmingham.

Birmingham has a strong record of supporting the arts. Over the past ten years the city has spent around £5 million on improving backstage and front-of-house facilities at the Hippodrome and on increasing the size of the stage, which is now a similar size to that at Covent Garden. (This will be an improvement on the restricted conditions at Sadler's Wells Theatre, the SWRB's present base, where the stage is too small for the company's large-scale productions.) As a result of the company's relocation, Birmingham is to spend £4 million on providing backstage, rehearsal and administrative facilities for the exclusive use of the company which will be housed in a new building to be erected behind the Hippodrome.

The increased funding will bring the company an additional £2 million a year. Birmingham, which already helps fund the company, will provide £1 million extra and this sum will be matched by the Arts Council. Part of this money will be spent on relocation costs, including a grant of some kind to the dancers. Some are prepared to relocate to Birmingham but a number are unhappy about the move and might leave. The SWRB's director, Peter Wright, said that the company may be weaker for a short time after the move, but he feels that the better facilities and financial resources will enable him to build a stronger company in the long term. Longer seasons in Birmingham (five weeks a year instead of the present two weeks) will also give him scope to widen the repertoire, both with classics and new work.

Luke Rittner, secretary general of the Arts Council, welcomed the SWRB's relocation, saying that the move was in line with the Arts Council's policy to disperse the arts to the regions. However, at the end of January regional provision of dance in the north of England was threatened by the recommendation that the Manchester-based Northern Ballet should have its Arts Council funding withdrawn.

The recommendation was made in a report commissioned by the Arts Council Dance Department in 1988 to review the provision of dance in England and Wales. The report, by theatre and television director Graham Devlin, urged the Arts Council to concentrate its resources on improving quality and on building up audiences for dance in the regions. Where the major touring companies such as SWRB and the London Festival Ballet are concerned, Devlin suggested that their tours should be reorganized to

give each company longer seasons and a larger repertoire in fewer centres, but with the centres chosen to serve as wide an area of the country as possible. This suggestion was welcomed by the companies and Arts Council alike and moves towards implementing the idea are expected in future seasons.

Delvin also suggested that support for dance should be built up at local level by setting up regional dance agencies to encourage the growth of smaller companies and to develop young audiences. The possibilities of this idea are to be examined in detail by a working party before any action is taken.

The deciding factor in the implementation of Devlin's recommendations, as in the provision of dance generally, is money. Devlin acknowledges in his report that dance in Britain is underfunded and that there is not enough money available to support adequately those companies receiving grants at present. Although he recommends that the Dance Panel should ask the Arts Council for more money for dance, Devlin recognizes that this is unlikely to be forthcoming. He suggests that one company, Northern Ballet, should have its grant withdrawn so that the money can be used to relieve the financial restrictions on the other companies. An increase in small-scale tours by the London Festival Ballet and the introduction of similiar ventures by the SWRB and the Royal Ballet are suggested to compensate for the loss of touring by the Northern Ballet.

The recommendation that the Northern Ballet's funding should be withdrawn aroused strong protests—nearly 20,000 people wrote to the Arts Council to protest at a move that would inevitably lead to the closure of the company. The company's artistic director, Christopher Gable, broke the Arts Council's embargo on publicity about the Devlin report to counter the report's criticism of the company's financial weakness. He pointed out that the company's subsidy had been fixed at a level well below the sum the Arts Council's own assessment considered necessary and then for three years the company had received no increase to compensate for inflation. The company produced figures to show that its subsidy per seat was about half that of other companies, despite the fact that the Northern Ballet gives far more performances than any of the main companies. The local authorities in the Greater Manchester area were appalled by the proposal and accused the Arts Council of wishing to safeguard London-based activities at the expense of the regions.

The Arts Council's response to the Devlin report was to welcome its positive recommendations but to state that it wished to avoid any client company having its funding threatened by the implementation of any of the report's recommendations. When the dust had settled, Northern Ballet found itself reprieved, with its Arts Council grant to continue at the present level for another two years. However, the company's future is not yet secure and it is now under pressure to improve its funding from donations and sponsorship.

The plight of Northern Ballet was raised in the House of Commons in May. The House considered also the problems facing companies such as London

Festival Ballet and English National Opera after April 1990. Both companies received funding from the Greater London Council until its abolition in 1986. Thereafter the grant was paid through Westminster City Council: it constitutes about one third of London Festival Ballet's running costs. The introduction of the community charge in April 1990 will greatly reduce the income of a council such as Westminster which has relatively few residents in its area, and there are doubts about whether the same level of funding by the council will still be possible. In his reply to a question in the House, the Minister for the Arts, Richard Luce, was non-committal about the Government's intentions regarding additional funding for the companies but said that he expected Westminster Council to decide what it could contribute to funding the arts and then to generate support from other London boroughs.

Faced with a shortfall in its funding from London boroughs, London Festival Ballet has been strengthening its links with the regions, in particular the Alhambra theatre, Bradford. The company has always performed at the larger regional venues, and with its offshoot company LFB also touring small venues, the company brings its work to most parts of the country. In view of the extent of its tours and with future changes to its funding likely, the company decided that a new title was needed that reflected its national role. The title English National Ballet was decided upon and came into use at the start of the company's London season in the summer of 1989. At the same time the renamed company gained a new royal patron, the Princess of Wales. Princess Margaret stood down to make way for her, after being patron of the Festival Ballet since 1976.

Contemporary dance in Britain lost one of its founders and guiding spirits with the death on June 12 of Robin Howard, at the age of 65. Howard gave much support in the years immediately after the Second World War to the companies at Covent Garden and Sadler's Wells. However, the visit to London of Martha Graham's company in 1954 opened up for him the wider possibilities of expression offered

by Graham's style of dance. When Graham's company came to Europe in 1963, Robin Howard helped to provide the financial backing for a London season.

The 1963 season proved a success and generated a desire to establish the contemporary style of dance in this country. In 1965 Howard started up Graham classes in London, and by the following year had founded a school and persuaded Robert Cohan, one of Martha Graham's leading men, to become artistic director. The original intention was to train dancers whom someone else would form into a company, but when 'someone else' was not forthcoming, Robin Howard founded the London Contemporary Dance Theatre in 1967. In 1969 the school and the company moved to The Place, a converted drill hall at Euston. Howard was general director of the Contemporary Dance Trust until 1988 when he handed over day-to-day management, retaining his connection with the school, company and theatre as Founder and Life President of the Contemporary Dance Trust.

If British dance was changed radically by Robin Howard's vision of the possibilities offered by modern choreographic techniques, Robert Cohan contributed much to making the vision a reality. Originally a member of Martha Graham's company, Cohan helped to establish first the school and then the company founded by Robin Howard. He left the company in July 1989 after 22 years as artistic director. In this period the company benefited greatly from his choreographic variety and inventiveness, gaining national and international distinction. Cohan created a programme of four new works to mark his departure from the company, *Stone Garden, In Memory, Metamorphoses* and *Crescendo*, which critics hailed as a worthy valediction. Cohan's successor as artistic director of London Contemporary Dance Theatre is Dan Wagoner, who took up the post in July 1989. Like Cohan, Wagoner is also a former member of the Martha Graham company and a choreographer. His first season with the company will see the British premiere of his work *To Comfort Ghosts*.

PRODUCTIONS

ROYAL BALLET (1931)
Royal Opera House, Covent Garden, WC2E 9DD

Full-length ballets from the repertoire performed during the 1988–89 season were *Ondine* (Ashton, 1988), *The Sleeping Beauty* (Petipa, after Sergueyev; additional choreography, Ashton, 1977), *Cinderella* (Ashton, 1987), *Romeo and Juliet* (MacMillan, 1975) and *Swan Lake* (Petipa/Ivanov, 1987).

Programmes also included the following shorter ballets from the repertoire: *Rhapsody* (Ashton), *'Still Life' at the Penguin Café* (Bintley), *Apollo* (Balanchine), *A Month in the Country* (Ashton), *Grand Pas Classique* (Gsovsky) and *Enigma Variations* (Ashton).

Introduced into the company's repertoire for the first time were:

March 14. **Capriccio for Piano and Orchestra**, the 'Rubies' section from *Jewels* by Balanchine; *music*, Stravinsky; *designs*, André Levasseur.

May 18. **La Bayadère**. *Choreography*, Makarova after Petipa; *music*, Minkus, arranged by John Lanchbery; *producer*, Natalia Makarova; *set*, Pier

Luigi Samaritani; *costumes*, Yoland Sonnabend. The cast was led at the first performance by Sylvie Guillem; Fiona Chadwick and Jonathan Cope.

New works premiered were:

Oct. 20, 1988. **The Trial of Prometheus**. *Choreography*, David Bintley; *score*, Geoffrey Burgon; *designer*, Terry Bartlett. The cast was led at the premiere by Stephen Jefferies, Fiona Chadwick and Simon Rice.

Nov. 22, 1988. **The Spirit of Fugue**. *Choreography*, David Bintley; *score*, Peter McGowan; *designer*, Terry Bartlett.

July 11. **Piano**. *Choreography*, Ashley Page; *music*, Beethoven's 1st Piano Concerto; *designer*, Howard Hodgkin.

In addition to performances at Covent Garden, the company took *Romeo and Juliet* and *Ondine* to Bristol and Birmingham in February 1989. In July 1989 the company visited Plymouth with *La Bayadère, Ondine, 'Still Life' at the Penguin Café, Enigma*

Variations and *Piano*, which received its premiere during the visit.

SADLER'S WELLS ROYAL BALLET (1931)
Sadler's Wells Theatre, Rosebery Avenue, EC1R 4TN

Full-length ballets from the repertoire performed this season were *Giselle* (Petipa after Coralli and Perrot, 1968), *The Snow Queen* (Bintley, 1986), *The Sleeping Beauty* (Petipa/Wright, 1984), *La Fille mal gardée* (Ashton, 1960) and *Swan Lake* (Pepita and Ivanov, additional choreography by Peter Wright, 1980).

Programmes also included the following shorter ballets: *Les Sylphides* (Fokine), *Petrushka* (Fokine), *Concerto Barocco* (Balanchine), *The Edge of Silence* (Lustig), *Pineapple Poll* (Cranko), *Bastet* (Seymour), *Choros* (Bintley), *Lazarus* (Cauley) and *The Two Pigeons* (Ashton).

The company introduced into its repertoire:

Oct. 10, 1988. **Themes and Variations.** *Choreography*, George Balanchine; *music*, Tchaikovsky; *staging*, Patricia Neary; *designer*, Peter Farmer.

New works were:

Feb. 13. **Hobson's Choice.** *Choreography*, David Bintley; *score*, Paul Reade; *designer*, Hayden Griffin. The cast at the premiere was led by Karen Donavan (*Maggie*), Michael O'Hara (*Willie Mossop*) and Desmond Kelly (*Hobson*).

June 22. **Auras.** *Choreography*, Vincent Redmon; *music*, Poulenc's Sextet for piano and wind; *designer*, Malcolm Steed. The cast was led at the premiere by Marion Tait and Roland Price.

and

Those Unheard. *Choreography*, William Tuckett; *music*, Britten's Four Sea Interludes; *designer*, Stephen Meaha. The cast at the premiere was led by Annette Pain.

In addition to seasons at Sadler's Wells Theatre and at the Royal Opera House, the company gave performances on tour at Birmingham, Leeds, Oxford, Southampton, Eastbourne, Hull, Manchester, Sunderland, Milton Keynes (a Big Top season) and Lancaster (a Big Top season). The company also undertook a three-week tour of Japan in April–May 1989, visiting seven cities with productions of *The Sleeping Beauty* and *Swan Lake*.

LONDON FESTIVAL BALLET/ ENGLISH NATIONAL BALLET
Markova House, 39 Jay Mews, SW7 2ES

Performances of full-length ballets from the repertoire included *Swan Lake* (Petipa, Ivanov, Ashton: prod. Makarova, 1988), *The Nutcracker* (Schaufuss, 1986), *Coppélia* (Hynd, 1985), *Romeo and Juliet* (Ashton), *La Sylphide* (Schaufuss after Bournonville, 1979) and *Onegin* (Cranko, 1983).

On June 12 a new production was premiered of *Napoli*: *choreography*, Schaufuss after Bournonville; *producer*, Peter Schaufuss; *musical adviser*, Ole Nørlyng; *designer*, David Walker. The cast at the premiere was led by Susan Hogard (*Teresina*) and Peter Schaufuss (*Gennaro*).

Programmes of shorter ballets included *Land* (Bruce), *Etudes* (Lander), and *Swansong* (Bruce). The company also introduced into its repertoire **Anastasia** (June 19: *choreographer*, Kenneth MacMillan).

Performances were given in London at the Royal Festival Hall and the Dominion Theatre, and on tour at Newcastle, Manchester, Bristol, Plymouth, Birmingham, Nottingham, Glasgow, Aberdeen, Oxford, Southampton, Liverpool and Bradford.

The company performed *Swan Lake* in Denmark,

and *La Sylphide, Sphinx* (Tetley), *Land* and *Etudes* in Egypt in autumn 1988. In July 1989 *Romeo and Juliet* was performed in Toronto, Canada, and *Romeo and Juliet, La Sylphide, Napoli, Anastasia, Land* and *Etudes* in Washington and New York, U.S.A.

The LFB company toured small venues in autumn 1988 with programmes comprising *Apollo* (Balanchine), *Corsair* pas de deux (Petipa), *Swansong* (Bruce), *Song of a Wayfarer* (Béjart) and dances from *Napoli* (Bournonville).

RAMBERT DANCE COMPANY (1926)
94 Chiswick High Road, W4 1SH

Works from the repertoire performed during the season included *Mates* (Gordon), *Dark Elegies* (Tudor), *Rhapsody in Blue* (Alston), *Septet* (Cunningham), *Strong Language* (Alston), *Carmen Arcadiae* (Page) and a revised version of *Mythologies* (Alston). One work was introduced into the repertoire: **Opal Loop** (March 8: *choreography*, Trisha Brown).

New works included:

Oct. 21, 1988. **Hymnos.** *Choreography*, Richard Alston; *music*, Peter Maxwell-Davies.

and

Soldat. *Choreography*, Ashley Page; *music*, Stravinsky; *designer*, Bruce McLean.

Oct. 27, 1988. **Embarque.** *Choreography*, Siobhan Davies; *music*, Steven Reich's *Octet*; *costumes*, David Buckland.

March 2. **Cinema.** *Choreography*, Richard Alston; *music*, Satie; *designer*, Allen Jones.

May 12. **Sounding.** *Choreography*, Siobhan Davies; *music*, Giacinto Scelsi's *Okanagon*; *designer*, Peter Mumford.

June 21. **Pulau Dewata.** *Choreography*, Richard Alston; *music*, Claude Vivier; *designer*, Antony McDonald.

and

Calm. *Choreography*, Mary Evelyn; *music*, Morton Subotnick's *The Key to Songs*; *designer*, Stephen Buckley.

During the 1988–89 season the company performed on tour at Canterbury, Manchester, Bath, Leicester, Glasgow, Newcastle, Oxford, Birmingham, York, London (Sadler's Wells Theatre), Nottingham, Brighton, Bristol, Southampton and at festivals at Arles, France, and Amsterdam, Netherlands.

LONDON CONTEMPORARY DANCE THEATRE (1967)
The Place, 16 Flaxman Terrace, WC1H 9AT

Productions from the repertoire were *John Somebody* (Newman), *Interlock* (Bhuller), *Smouldering Suit* (Bhuller), *Stand By Your Man* (Collins), *Testament* (formerly *Songs, Lamentations and Praises*: Cohan), *Bottom's Dream* (Lunn), *Three Dances for Trois Gnossiennes* (Bannerman), *Giant Steps* (Bhuller), *And do they do* (Davies), *Forest* (Cohan) and *Troy Game* (North).

The company introduced into its repertoire **Arden Court** (Nov. 23, 1988: *choreography*, Paul Taylor). Other new works included:

Nov. 29, 1988. **Good Morning Monsieur.** *Choreography*, Daniel Larrieu.

April 18. Four new works *choreographed* by Robert Cohan: **Stone Garden**, to Nigel Osborne's music of the same name; **In Memory**, to Hans Werner Henze's *Quattro Fantasie*; **Metamorphoses**, to Britten's *Six Metamorphoses after Ovid*; and **Crescendo**, to David Bedford's *Symphony for 12 Musicians*. The music was performed by the London Sinfonietta.

The company performed on tour at Southampton, Bristol, Plymouth, Cardiff, Liverpool, Coventry, Leeds, London (Sadler's Wells Theatre and Queen Elizabeth Hall), Newcastle, Oxford and Leatherhead. The company performed on tour in Italy in July 1989.

THE SCOTTISH BALLET
261 West Princes Street, Glasgow G4 9EE

Productions from the repertoire included *Giselle* (Petipa and Coralli, recreated by Graeme, 1971) and the shorter works *Carmen* (Darrell), *Three Dances to Japanese Music* (Carter), *Sonata in Time* (Corder) and the children's ballet *Skazka*.

New works included **Prix de Rome** (Oct. 12, 1988: *choreography*, Lloyd Embleton); **Petrushka** (March 23: *choreography*, Oleg Vinogradov) given in a Stravinsky double bill with Scottish Opera's produc-

tion of *Oedipus Rex*; and the three-act ballet **Peter Pan**, premiered on Feb. 24: *choreography*, Graham Lustig; *score*, Edward McGuire; *designer*, Margaret Woznica. The cast was led by Vincent Hantam (*Peter*).

These productions were performed at the Theatre Royal or the Robin Anderson Studio Theatre, Glasgow, and on tour at Canterbury, Nottingham, Darlington, Stirling, Oxford, Hull, Inverness, Belfast, Edinburgh, Bristol and Aberdeen.

The company also performed at smaller venues in Scotland and Wales in autumn 1988 and August 1989 with programmes including *Sonata in Time, Shoals of Herring* (Maldoom) *Homage to Nordi* (McDonald), pas de deux from *The Nutcracker, Prix de Rome, Vespri* (Prokovsky), *The Prisoners* (Darrell) and *Grand pas des Fiancées* (Carter).

BOOKER PRIZEWINNERS

The finalists for the 1989 prize are:

The Book of Evidence—John Banville (Secker & Warburg); *Cat's Eye*—Margaret Atwood (Bloomsbury); *A Disaffection*—James Kelman (Secker & Warburg); *Jigsaw*—Sybille Bedford (Hamish Hamilton); *The Remains of the Day*—Kazuo Ishiguro (Faber); *Restoration*—Rose Tremain (Hamish Hamilton).

FILM AND CINEMA, 1988–89

In a year dominated by the hugely successful American 'blockbuster' releases, *Indiana Jones and the Last Crusade* and *Batman*, it was encouraging that the British-made *A Fish Called Wanda* could attract an international audience and take more money at the box office than any other British film. Also encouraging for the film industry was the Government's promise of help for independent cinemas. The Government proposes to end the right of the large cinema chains to screen box office hits for as long as they wish before allowing distribution to smaller cinemas. New legislation will grant exclusive rights to the larger cinema chains for only 28 days, after which the independents will be able to screen popular new releases.

David Puttnam, after his uncomfortable sojourn in Hollywood, re-entered film production in Britain with the relaunch of Enigma Productions. Starting up with a $50 million fund, the company plans to make at least six films over a period of four years, reinvesting part of the profits to top up the fund. Enigma has backing from Warner Brothers, British Satellite Broadcasting and international financiers, and began by buying three projects from Columbia, Puttnam's former employers.

Brent Walker announced that it wished to help rebuild the British film industry by rescuing the internationally famous Elstree Studios. These were threatened with closure and the sale of the land for property development. Brent Walker, which also owns Goldcrest, the film production company, intend to develop part of the Elstree site and to use the income to help finance the studios.

A further boost to British film production was provided by the new lease of life given to British Screen Finance Ltd. The company was formed in 1986 and receives an annual grant of £1·5 million from the Government. Its purpose is to encourage investment in British films and film-makers, and it has funded 33 films. In 1989, Rank, Cannon, Channel 4 and Granada Television agreed to reinvest until 1991 loans totalling £3 million which had been due for repayment. It was estimated that the decision would help to fund another 10 to 15 British films.

Last Temptation

Martin Scorsese's film, *The Last Temptation of Christ*, aroused controversy and much criticism and opposition, mostly from the Christian churches. Scorsese, a respected film-maker, based the film on a novel by Nikos Kazantzakis. The part of the film that caused most problems concerned Christ being tempted to renounce his divinity on the cross and to accept physical and earthly pleasures: by rejecting them, he affirmed his divinity. The film was not intended to challenge or reject Christian teaching.

At the Venice Film Festival, the Diocese of Venice prayed that 'the city will be spared a useless laceration of its social fabric' by the showing of the film. Despite the controversy, when the film was shown in Britain, the Director of Public Prosecutions decided not to prosecute it for blasphemous libel. Mrs. Mary Whitehouse dropped her plans for a private prosecution, announcing that she would instead lobby local authorities, asking them to refuse to grant the film a licence. The British Board of Film Classification granted an 18 certificate for the film and decided that no cuts were required. The Director of the Board, James Ferman, said, 'The treatment is in no sense scurrilous or abusive, nor does it hold its subject up to ridicule or contempt. Indeed, the intention is plainly sincere, the atmosphere reverent and the ultimate effect, far from insulting sacred subjects, is to affirm their supreme importance.'

That statement was not enough to reassure those who objected to the film. The Archbishop of Canterbury, Dr. Robert Runcie, said that there were aspects of the film 'which caused great offence and distress . . . there was a sensible argument for wishing the film was not shown in this country'. Cardinal Basil Hume advised Christians not to see it. Neither had seen the film. Many who had, felt that the fuss was out of proportion, and not merited by what was a serious study of an undoubtedly sensitive subject. Film critics on the whole recognized the film's honest intent, pointing to its failings on cinematographic grounds: the low budget showed in the production, the film's dialogue was flat and too wordy, and the accents were uncertain. However, there was praise for Willem Dafoe for his portrayal of Jesus. The cast included Barbara Hershey as Mary Magdalene, Harvey Keitel as Judas, and also featured Harry Dean Stanton and David Bowie.

Rain Man

At the 61st annual Academy Awards there were few surprises, with the major awards going to the favourites. *Rain Man* scooped the most prestigious prizes, winning the best picture award, with Dustin Hoffman taking the award for best actor and Barry Levinson for best director. Writers Ronald Bass and Barry Morrow received the award for best original screenplay for their script. *Rain Man* was widely praised for its sensitive and intelligent treatment of the condition of autism.

Tom Cruise played the part of Charlie, who discovers on his father's death that his inheritance has been left to an elder brother he did not know existed. Dustin Hoffman played the elder brother, an autistic savant called Raymond who has a brilliant mathematical brain but is unable to relate to or make eye contact with other people. Charlie kidnaps Raymond from the home where he had been living in an attempt to obtain the inheritance, but is gradually changed and won over by seeing life afresh through his difficult brother. Although some critics felt that Cruise's 'conversion' was a little too glib to be wholly convincing, he nevertheless coped well with what was a difficult role largely overshadowed by Hoffman's performance.

In his acceptance speech, Hoffman thanked 'all the people I talked to that were autistic and their families and their doctors for all their help'. The National Autistic Society was especially grateful that a complex and widely misdiagnosed condition had been treated with sensitivity and had achieved such widespread publicity: the film took over $100 million at the box office in America. *Rain Man* had taken nearly ten years to bring to the screen; 'This is a Cinderella story', said Hoffman, 'the picture was almost cancelled three times. But all of life is a soap opera.'

Accused

The best actress award was won by Jodie Foster, who was first nominated for an Academy award at the age of 12 for her role in *Taxi Driver*. In *The Accused*, she played the victim of a brutal gang rape. The film powerfully challenged male attitudes to women and to rape, affirming through Foster's performance (with strong support from Kelly Mc-Gillis as a prosecuting lawyer) that no-one deserved such treatment, however unsympathetic a character or whatever the supposed provocation.

Dangerous Liaisons was nominated for seven awards and won three. The film was based on Christopher Hampton's successful stage adaptation of the epistolary novel by Choderlos de Laclos about games of sexual intrigue. Hampton won the award for the best screenplay adapted from another medium, while James Acheson won the award for best costume design and Stuart Craig and Gerard James for best art direction. *Mississippi Burning* also received seven nominations but picked up only the prize for best cinematography for Peter Biziou. This powerful drama was inspired by the murder of three young civil rights activists in the American South in 1964, and the subsequent F.B.I. investigation which led to the arrest and conviction of the killers. Directed by Alan Parker, the film featured an especially fine performance from Gene Hackman (nominated for best actor) as an F.B.I. investigator, with Willem Dafoe as his partner.

Danish Winner

For the second year running the Oscar for best foreign film was won by a Danish film. *Pelle the Conqueror*, directed by Bille August, was a beautifully made film about the problems of migrant workers leaving a life of poverty in Sweden to find work on the wealthy Danish island of Bornholm. It featured Pelle Hvengegaard as the nine-year-old Pelle of the title, triumphing over adversity, with Max von Sydow (nominated for best actor) as his weak but loving father. The story was adapted from the first volume of a four-part work by the Danish Nobel prize-winning author Martin Andersen Hexe. The unsuccessful nominees for Oscars included Sir Alec Guinness for his role in *Little Dorrit*, John Cleese for his screenplay for *A Fish Called Wanda* and Bob Hoskins in *Who Framed Roger Rabbit*. Particularly unfortunate was Sigourney Weaver, who was nominated as best actress for her role in *Gorillas in the Mist* and as best supporting actress for *Working Girl*, but won neither – the first time a double nominee has not picked up at least the lesser award.

Other Oscar winners were: best supporting actor, Kevin Kline (*A Fish Called Wanda*); best supporting actress, Geena Davis (*The Accidental Tourist*); best documentary feature, Marcel Ophuls (*Hotel Terminus: The Life and Times of Klaus Barbie*); William Guttentag and Malcolm Clarke (*You Don't Have to Die*) short documentary; film editing, Arthur Schmidt (*Who Framed Roger Rabbit*); make-up, Ve Neill, Steve LaPorte and Robert Short (*Beetlejuice*); original score, Dave Grusin (*The Milagro Beanfield War*); original song, Carly Simon ('Let the River Run'—*Working Girl*); animated short film, John Lasseter and William Reeves (*Tin Toy*); live action short film, Dean Parisot and Steven Wright (*The Appointment of Dennis Jennings*); sound, Les Frescholtz, Dick Alexander, Vern Poore and Willie Burton (*Bird*); sound effects editing, Charles Campbell and Louis Edemann (*Who Framed Roger Rabbit*); visual effects, Ken Ralston, Richard Williams, Edward Jones and George Gibbs (*Who Framed Roger Rabbit*). Honorary Oscars were awarded to the National Film Board of Canada and to Eastman Kodak; a special achievement award was given to Richard Williams for animation direction, including *Who Framed Roger Rabbit*; and an award of merit went to Ray Dolby and Ioan Allen, sound engineers.

British Awards

At the British Academy of Film and Television Awards, the Michael Balcon Award for Outstanding Contribution to British Cinema was presented to Charles Crichton, veteran director of such British classics as *The Lavender Hill Mob*. Crichton had not made a film since 1965 until he was brought back by John Cleese to direct *A Fish Called Wanda*. John Cleese was named best actor for his portrayal in the film of a barrister mixed up with a gang of jewel thieves. Tightly scripted and with disciplined direction, Cleese's film was fast and funny, and deserved its international success. The cast included Jamie Lee Curtis, Kevin Kline, Maria Aitken and Michael Palin, who won the award for best actor in a supporting role.

The BAFTA award for best film went to *The Last Emperor*, directed by Bernardo Bertolucci. This told the remarkable story of the last emperor of China, Pu Yi, who acceded to the throne at the age of three and was deposed when the revolution of 1949 made him an anachronism in his own land. Produced by Jeremy Thomas, *The Last Emperor* won nine Oscars in last year's ceremony. Maggie Smith was voted best actress for her performance in *The Lonely Passion of Judith Hearne*. Directed by Jack Clayton from a novel by Brian Moore, the film also featured Wendy Hiller, Bob Hoskins and Ian McNeice. Louis Malle was judged best director for *Au Revoir Les Enfants*, which he wrote, directed and produced. The film is based on an event that he said was central to his life when he was aged 11. The personal and moving story is set in occupied France in 1944, and tells the story of a boy who joins a school, is eventually discovered to be Jewish and is arrested by the Gestapo. Malle's first film in France for ten years, *Au Revoir Les Enfants* featured Gaspard Manesse and Raphael Fejto.

Best supporting actress was won by Judi Dench (*A Handful of Dust*); original screenplay, Shawn Slovo (*A World Apart*); adapted screenplay, Jean-Claude Carriere and Philip Kaufman (*The Unbearable Lightness of Being*); score, John Williams, (*Empire of the Sun*); foreign film, Just Betzer, Bo Christensen and Gabriel Axel (*Babette's Feast*); short film, *Defence Counsel Sedov* (USSR). A BAFTA Fellowship was awarded to Sir Alec Guinness.

Restored

The latest cinematic masterpiece to be restored to its full glory is David Lean's classic *Lawrence of Arabia*. At its world premiere in 1962 the film ran for 222 minutes but within a few months about 20 minutes had been removed. Further cuts were made later so that the film distributed on general release differed substantially from the print first screened. An archivist producer, Robert A. Harris, who had been involved in the restoration of Abel Gance's *Napoleon*, set about tracing the missing footage. After much research, which involved using lipreaders to identify dialogue from some sections of film for which both soundtrack and script had been lost and then re-recording the lines using the original actors, a complete print was assembled. David Lean became involved at this point and produced a final version edited to his satisfaction. The film now runs for 216 minutes, Lean having removed some six minutes to produce a final director's cut, a stage which time had prevented when the film was first released. The project cost $600,000 in total, which was more than recouped on a limited release in the U.S.A. Furthermore, a new generation now has the opportunity to see a true classic of the cinema in 70 mm, as its director had intended it should be shown.

Numbers

Peter Greenaway's film, *Drowning by Numbers*, was another intriguing and wholly idiosyncratic film from a highly original director. Set in Suffolk, it featured Joely Richardson, Juliet Stevenson and Joan Plowright. Each played a character called Cissie Colpitts; each Cissie Colpitts kills her husband, and throughout the film the numbers 1 to 100 are spoken or depicted in various ways. Greenaway said the film affords 'an opportunity to play games in an idyllic English landscape . . . a film about the confederacy, the solidarity—even the "conspiracy" of women'.

Terry Gilliam, whose last film, *Brazil*, won critical approval but involved him in highly publicized disputes with the studio, made news again with *The Adventures of Baron Munchausen*. Scripted by Gilliam with Charles McKeown, this story of the German soldier who told fantastic yarns was reported to have been budgeted at $23·5 million, but to have cost $40 million or more. Dogged by financial problems throughout its production, it is surprising that the film was ever completed and released. *Munchausen* featured John Neville as the Baron, supported by Robin Williams (who was not credited in the film), Oliver Reed, Jonathan Pryce and Bill Paterson. Although visually splendid and intermittently entertaining, the film was considered extravagant and self-indulgent.

My Left Foot was a remarkable film, which told the life story of the Irish writer Christy Brown. Crippled by cerebral palsy, Brown learned to paint and type with his left foot, the only part of his body which he could control; he achieved fame for his struggle against adversity and for his skills as a writer. Daniel Day-Lewis was widely praised for his portrayal of Christy, which was moving without resorting to sentimentality. Directed by Jim Sheridan, the cast also included Hugh O'Conor as Christy Brown when young, and Ray McAnally and Brenda Fricker as Brown's parents.

Buster featured a strong cast in a weakly plotted and somewhat anodyne treatment of the life of one of the Great Train Robbers. The film aroused much controversy: the Prince and Princess of Wales cancelled their attendance at a charity premiere in aid of the Prince's Trust after press criticism that their presence would imply support for a film that appeared to glorify crime and violence. Directed by David Green, the film featured singer and actor Phil Collins as Ronald 'Buster' Edwards and Julie Walters as his wife June.

Scandal

One of the great British *causes célèbres* of the twentieth century, the Profumo affair of 1963, was recreated in *Scandal*. Written by Michael Thomas, the story was originally intended for television but the B.B.C. withdrew its backing. The film was criticized in some quarters for reviving a sorry saga that some people would rather have forgotten. It also attracted criticism of its historical accuracy in its attempt to prove that Stephen Ward was the victim of an establishment conspiracy, but otherwise was generally well received. Directed by Michael Caton-Jones, it featured Ian McKellen as John Profumo, the War Minister who was forced to resign for lying to the House of Commons, John Hurt as Stephen Ward, and Joanne Whalley as Christine Keeler.

Distant Voices, Still Lives, written and directed by Terence Davies, was a highly original work that achieved international recognition for its depressing but richly evocative study of family life in Liverpool. Featuring Freda Downie, Angela Walsh and Pete Postlethwaite, *Distant Voices, Still Lives* picked up a clutch of awards, including the Golden Leopard at Locarno, the Critics' Prize at Toronto, and the International Critics' Prize at Cannes.

Paris by Night by David Hare was an attack on Thatcherite Britain. It featured Charlotte Rampling as a Conservative Member of the European Parliament mixed up in scandal and intrigue. Timothy Dalton reappeared in another James Bond film, *Licence to Kill*. Directed by John Glen, this glossy, violent but insubstantial adventure suggested that the series had run beyond its natural life. Mike Leigh's *High Hopes* showed that the master of the improvised work, most of which has been seen on television, had lost none of his skill in working with a group of actors to produce worthwhile drama. The film was richly comic in its view of modern Britain, though occasionally tending towards caricature. It featured Philip Davies, Edna Doré, Heather Tobias and Ruth Sheen.

Pascali's Island was adapted and directed by James Dearden from a novel by Barry Unsworth which is set on an Aegean island in 1908 towards the end of Ottoman rule. The cast included Charles Dance, Ben Kingsley and Helen Mirren. *The Dressmaker* was adapted by John McGrath from Beryl Bainbridge's novel. Directed by Jim O'Brien, it featured Joan Plowright, Billie Whitelaw and Jane Horrocks.

Batmania

The film *Batman* was released fifty years after the creation of the comic-book character. Filmed on the biggest set ever created at Pinewood studios, at a cost of some $35 million, the film takes itself much more seriously than the 1960s television series. Furst's design for the five-block set of Gotham City effectively conveyed a mood of gloom and evil. However, many critics felt that the film suffered from a weak script and poor direction, while Jack Nicholson's extravagant performance as The Joker seemed totally at odds with Michael Keaton's Batman in style and mood. A massive, carefully orchestrated pre-publicity campaign made *Batman* a huge commercial success, taking $57 million in its first six days after release in the U.S.A.

Steven Spielberg's third film in the Indiana Jones series, *Indiana Jones and the Last Crusade*, trod familiar ground with a tale of an archaeologist seeking a mythical artefact, opposed by evil Nazis. Nevertheless, Spielberg proved once again that there is still a market for well-made adventure films. Harrison Ford repeated his role as Indiana Jones, with Sean Connery appearing as his father, who vanishes while searching for the Holy Grail. Produced by George Lucas, it also featured Denholm Elliott and Alison Doody.

Clint Eastwood directed *Bird*, an impressive study of the jazz genius Charlie Parker, who died at the age of 34, wrecked by drink and drugs. This dark and brooding film concentrated on Parker's last few years, and worked mainly through flashback to give a vivid impression of the life of the great saxophonist, played by Forest Whitaker. Overall, the film was dominated by his music, which had been remixed from original recordings.

Animal Magic

Who Framed Roger Rabbit was a triumph of reality and animation, a brilliant interweaving of cartoon characters with photography that deservedly won Oscars for Richard Williams, director of animation, and the technical team. The film featured Bob Hoskins as a private detective, with Stubby Kaye, Kathleen Turner and Christopher Lloyd providing the voices for some of the sixty years' worth of cartoon characters in a pastiche of 1940s Hollywood. Directed by Robert Zemeckis, it was produced by Steven Spielberg in association with Walt Disney studios.

Melanie Griffith was acclaimed for her role in *Working Girl*, in which she played an office typist in New York who proves herself as capable a stock broker as her boss during the latter's temporary absence from the office. With a script by Kevin Wade, and directed by Mike Nichols, *Working Girl* also featured Sigourney Weaver and Harrison Ford. In *Big*, Tom Hanks played a 12-year-old boy who suddenly finds himself inhabiting the body of a 35-year-old. Hanks carried off the difficult task of appearing convincing in such a role reversal with great success; the film was directed by Penny Marshall. *Twins* featured the huge Arnold Schwarzenegger and the diminutive Danny de Vito as twin

brothers created as the result of a genetic experiment. Directed by Ivan Reitman, from a script by Timothy Harris and Herschel Weingrod, this amusing idea worked well and was highly entertaining.

Less successful was Neil Jordan's *High Spirits*, a rather weak story about an Irish landowner, played by Peter O'Toole, who attracts guests to his decrepit castle by advertising that it is haunted. When the guests discover his trick, real ghosts appear, in an unhappy blend of farce and pathos. The cast also included Darryl Hannah and Ray McAnally. John Schlesinger directed *Madama Sousatzka* from a script by Ruth Prawer Jhabvala based on a novel by Bernice Reubens about an émigrée piano teacher. Shirley MacLaine was excellent in the leading role, with good support from Navin Chowdhry, Twiggy, Leigh Lawson and Peggy Ashcroft. *The Accidental Tourist* was directed by Lawrence Kasdan from Anne Tyler's novel, and starred William Hurt, Kathleen Turner and Geena Davies. In *Good Morning Vietnam*, Robin Williams played Adrian Cronauer, a disc jockey in Vietnam in 1965 whose irreverent approach was popular with the troops but upset the army bureaucracy. It was directed by Barry Levinson. *Betrayed* was directed by Costi Costa-Gavras from a script by Joe Eszterhas. It featured Debra Winger as an undercover F.B.I. agent investigating a murder.

Gorillas in the Mist was both a critical and popular success. It told the story of Dian Fossey, played by Sigourney Weaver, who dedicated her life for twenty years to the study of the mountain gorillas in Rwanda. She saved the species from extinction but was murdered in 1985. Directed by Michael Apted, the film cost $27 million; its success was largely due to the efforts of Weaver, who worked hard to build up a rapport with the gorillas in the film. Where it was not possible to use live animals, make-up expert Rick Baker provided some very convincing fakes. Although she failed to win an Oscar, Sigourney Weaver received a Golden Globe award for her performance in *Gorillas in the Mist* (shared with Jodie Foster for *The Accused*), and also received the best supporting actress award for *Working Girl*.

Fred Schepisi's *A Cry in the Dark* was based on the story of Lindy and Michael Chamberlain of Australia, whose nine-week old daughter Azaria was killed by a dingo (wild dog) while they were visiting Ayers Rock. The couple were tried and convicted for her murder in a case which made headline news throughout the world; it was only recently that they were finally believed and exonerated. Meryl Streep gave a typically powerful performance as Lindy, with Sam Neill as her husband Michael.

Festivals

At the 45th Venice Film Festival, the Golden Lion was awarded to *The Legend of the Holy Drunkard*, directed by Ermanno Olmi of Italy. The Silver Lion went to *Landscape in the Clouds*, directed by Theo Angelopoulos of Greece, who also won the award for best director. The Special Prize of the Jury was awarded to *The Camp at Thiaroye*, a Senegalese film made by Sembene and Sow. Don Ameche was voted best actor for his role in *Things Change* (U.S.A.), while Isabelle Huppert was joint best actress for *Une Affaire de Femmes* (France), with Shirley MacLaine for *Madame Sousatzka* (U.K.).

At the 39th Berlin Film Festival, Barry Levinson's *Rain Man* won the Golden Bear for best film and Dustin Hoffman received a special award for his acting. Gene Hackman was voted best actor for *Mississippi Burning*. Best director was Dusan Hanah for *I Love, You Love* (Czechoslovakia), and Isabelle Adjani won the best actress award for *Camille Claudel*.

At the 42nd Cannes Film Festival, which was notable for the fact that none of the eight British films submitted were accepted for competition, the Palme d'Or was won by Steven Soderbergh (U.S.A.) for *Sex, Lies and Videotape*. The Grand Prix of the Jury went to *Jesus of Montreal* (Canada), directed by Denys Arcand, and the Special Jury Prize to *Nuovo Cinema Paradiso* (Italy), directed by Giuseppe Tornatore, and *Trop Belle pour Toi* (France), directed by Bertrand Blier. Best actor was James Spader for *Sex, Lies and Videotape*, and best actress Meryl Streep for *A Cry in the Dark*.

At Locarno, the main award was won by the South Korean film, *Why has Bodhi-Dharma left for the Orient?*, directed by Yung-Kyun Bae.

THE ACADEMY AWARDS 1988

Best Picture.—*Rain Man*.
Best Director.—Barry Levinson, *Rain Man*.
Best Actor.—Dustin Hoffman, *Rain Man*.
Best Actress.—Jodie Foster, *The Accused*.
Best Supporting Actor.—Kevin Kline, *A Fish Called Wanda*.
Best Supporting Actress.—Geena Davis, *The Accidental Tourist*.
Best Original Screenplay.—Ronald Bass and Barry Morrow, *Rain Man*.
Best Adapted Screenplay.—Christopher Hampton, *Dangerous Liaisons*.
Best Foreign Language.—*Pelle the Conqueror*, Denmark.
Best Original Score.—Dave Grusin, *The Milagro Beanfield War*.
Best Original Song.—Carly Simon, 'Let the River Run', *Working Girl*.
Best Cinematography.—Peter Biziou, *Mississippi Burning*.
Best Art Direction.—Stuart Craig and Gerard James, *Dangerous Liaisons*.

Best Costume Design.—James Acheson, *Dangerous Liaisons*.
Best Film Editing.—Arthur Schmidt, *Who Framed Roger Rabbit*.
Best Sound.—Les Frescholtz, Dick Alexander, Vern Poore and Willie Burton, *Bird*.
Best Sound Effects Editing.—Charles Campbell and Louis Edemann, *Who Framed Roger Rabbit*.
Best Visual Effects.—Ken Ralston, Richard Williams, Edward Jones and George Gibbs, *Who Framed Roger Rabbit*.
Best Make-up.—Ve Neill, Steve LaPorte and Robert Short, *Beetlejuice*.
Best Animated Short.—John Lasseter and William Reeves, *Tin Toy*.
Best Short Documentary.—William Guttentag and Malcolm Clarke, *You Don't Have to Die*.
Best Documentary Feature.—Marcel Ophuls, *Hotel Terminus: The Life and Times of Klaus Barbie*.
Best Live Action Short.—Dean Parisot and Steven Wright, *The Appointment of Dennis Jennings*.

The Government's long-awaited White Paper on broadcasting (for summary, *see* pp. 1089–91) was published in November 1988. It proposed a radical reform of the whole structure of broadcasting in Britain, moving away from the present highly regulated system to more liberal regulation, particularly of independent television. 'We aim to ensure that viewers and listeners have greater freedom of choice from a more varied output of programmes, including programmes of high quality', the Home Secretary (Douglas Hurd) told the House of Commons. 'British television has a deservedly high reputation in the world. We expect to see that reputation grow.'

The BBC was largely unaffected by the Government's proposals for the future of broadcasting. The Corporation was acknowledged to be 'for the foreseeable future, the cornerstone of British broadcasting'. However, 'the Government looks forward to the eventual replacement of the licensing fee ... (it) intends to encourage the progressive introduction of subscription on the BBC's television services.' It was also proposed that after 1991 licence fees would be increased by less than the rate of inflation, to hasten this process.

A suggestion that the BBC would lose the night hours from one of its channels for franchising by the body which would replace the IBA, the Independent Television Commission (ITC), was deemed 'surprising' by the BBC's director general Michael Checkland. He said that the BBC was best placed to make maximum use of its night-time hours. In a Commons debate on broadcasting in May 1989, Home Office Minister Timothy Renton said that the Government had agreed in principle to the BBC launching a late-night subscription service for business which would last an hour and be supported by advertising.

Response to White Paper

The Home Office received over 2,300 submissions in response to the White Paper. The most contentious issue proved to be the proposal that the present ITV franchises on what would be renamed Channel 3, and the franchises on a new terrestrial Channel 5, should go to the highest bidder provided that applicants meet strict quality requirements for programmes. The ITV companies said in the combined response: 'The single most important issue is competitive tendering, and if the methods proposed were not to be revised, great damage would be done to the quality and range of programmes in regional Channel 3.' They proposed safeguard options when the current franchises expired in 1992: value for money in terms of public service should be the crucial factor, not the highest bid, they suggested.

In the 1988 Robert Fraser Lecture, Lord Thomson of Monifieth, outgoing Chairman of the IBA, made a swingeing attack on the White Paper. He said that the Government's plans for ITV amounted to 'an act of wanton destruction, carried out for doctrinaire reasons'. He also criticized the removal of much of the public service role that the ITV companies had performed in response to the present requirement that they should provide adult education and reli-gious programmes, and the removal of the 'national spine' of network programming. He warned that the BBC would become a 'cultural ghetto' if subscription television was introduced, and that 'near anarchy' would result in the 1990s if the changes proposed in the White Paper were implemented.

The IBA opposed the system of awarding franchises that the Independent Television Commission would be expected to operate. Under this companies would have to pass a minimum quality hurdle before entering an auction at which the franchise would be awarded to the highest bidder. The IBA suggested that instead of the proposed system, companies should submit confidential tenders and public programme plans. The tenders would be judged on the money tendered and the company's suitability to run a television station, with its programme plans being taken into account also. The IBA proposal would not oblige the ITC to accept the highest bid if it was not satisfied with other aspects of a company's proposals.

In June the Government said that the ITC would be given reserve powers to veto the award of a franchise to the highest bidder if it did not offer the best choice to viewers. In normal circumstances, however, the ITC would be expected to accept the highest bid. The quality hurdle would be strengthened, with applicants being required 'to provide a reasonable proportion of programmes (in addition to news and current affairs) of high quality, and to provide a diverse programme service calculated to appeal to a wide variety of tastes and interests'. If applicants failed to satisfy the ITC that they could meet this requirement, their bids would not be considered. The Home Secretary would be able to veto a bid if its funding came from a source which was considered undesirable taking into account the public interest. Companies would also be required to post substantial performance bonds, which they would risk forfeiting if they failed to provide programmes of the necessary quality and diversity.

Objections

Condemnation of the White Paper's proposals came from several other quarters. The TUC said that the White Paper represented a lost opportunity for cable and satellite services and failed to put viewers first. The British Medical Association was concerned that the proposals could open the floodgates to sponsorship by tobacco companies and that health education programmes might be dropped. The Association of Cinematograph, Television and Allied Technicians said that the White Paper needed fundamental reconsideration; 'opportunities provided by new technology and the new media should be used to enhance our existing broadcasting system and not to undermine it'. The Social Democratic Party's response was one of the few to favour the franchise auction, but believed an under-bidder should be able to win if it offered a better public service. The Peacock Committee, which in its report on public service broadcasting in 1986 had recommended competitive tendering for franchises on such a basis, rejected the auction proposal in the White

Paper. It was also concerned that any premature reduction in the licence fee would be damaging to the BBC. The Consumers' Association felt that the franchise auction would lead to less choice in programmes and an increase in soap operas and game shows. They agreed with Sir Richard Attenborough, chairman of Channel 4, who warned of the dangers of 'market-place' economics, which the Association felt were an 'entirely inadequate guarantee' of consumers' interests.

A Labour Party document on the future of broadcasting called for new regulations to uphold standards and to control ownership of franchises; 'awarding television contracts to the highest bidder is certain to reduce standards'. It said the White Paper proposals offered less variety and would encourage cheap imports at the expense of home-grown quality programmes. The BBC should be funded by an inflation-linked licence fee, and the Broadcasting Standards Council was 'wholly unnecessary' and should be scrapped. The Labour Party was also concerned about the overlapping of newspaper and television interests. The Home Secretary said that the Government would take reserve powers to control media ownership and cross-holding between newspaper and broadcasting companies; restrictions would be written into the Broadcasting Bill to prevent 'unhealthy' cross-media ownership.

The Government intends to introduce a Broadcasting Bill in autumn 1989, and has given no indication of being prepared to amend its main proposals.

Broadcasting Standards Council

The Broadcasting Standards Council was set up in 1988 by the Government because of concern about offensive sex and violence on television. It operates at present on a non-statutory basis but its powers are to be enshrined in the Broadcasting Bill. Lord Rees-Mogg was appointed chairman, and the Council held its first meeting in September 1988. It began work on a code designed to keep unacceptable scenes of sex and violence off television, and to establish standards of taste and decency. Lord Rees-Mogg held talks with the BBC, IBA, the Cable Authority and other parties with satellite and cable interests, such as Rupert Murdoch and Robert Maxwell.

The Council issued a draft code in February and published revised guidelines in August. It said that these should apply to satellite stations as well as the BBC and ITV; British Satellite Broadcasting and Sky Television had argued for more relaxed guidelines for their planned subscription film channels. The Council said 'a single set of standards is more readily comprehensible to the audience ... The mere fact of payment by direct subscription for material which would not usually be transmitted on non-subscription services does not eliminate the need for careful editorial judgments of its suitability for transmission ... the relative exclusivity of subscription services does not relieve them of any obligations towards the social consequences of what they carry.'

The BBC published for the first time a comprehensive set of guidelines for programme-makers. It covered 125 subjects in 25 chapters, such as straight dealing in production, sensitivity to others, privacy, the scheduling of warnings about programme content, violence, bad language, sexual portrayal, and treatment of animals. An IBA survey of public attitudes to television in 1988 found that viewers considered that television screened less offensive programmes than before as far as sex, violence and bad language were concerned.

The BBC

The BBC continued its policy of *glasnost* with a second magazine entitled *See for Yourself*, reviewing 1988. The chairman, Marmaduke Hussey, wrote: 'We believe that you, who provide all the money for our programmes, should have the chance to learn how we spend it and about our plans for the future. That is why we are continuing the dialogue between the BBC and the public again this year through TV and radio programmes and through this new edition of *See for Yourself.*' Referring to the birth of satellite television, he said, 'I believe that we are in good shape to face the challenge of this new broadcasting climate. We are confident that the BBC will remain the standard setter by which other channels will be judged and that you will be able to enjoy, once again in 1989, entertaining, wide-ranging, invigorating and challenging programmes.'

The director general, Michael Checkland, wrote in the same review, 'In 1988 the BBC has been building decisively and swiftly on the previous year's structural and management changes. As a result, we are a more streamlined and better-managed organization. This was recognized in the Government's White Paper in November which outlined the role the BBC must continue to play as the provider of high-quality programmes across the full range of public tastes and interests ... The popular base of so many of our programmes allows educational and information programmes to be nourished. Whatever our competitors may feel tempted to trim because of commercial pressures, the BBC will always have particular responsibilities in the area of education and patronage of the arts. But, by the same token, the BBC must never be driven into a single corner of the market-place to concentrate exclusively on cultural and information programmes, leaving entertainment to others.'

In its Annual Report, published in November 1988, Mr. Hussey said that the BBC would 'admit our mistakes when we make them. You cannot put out 15,000 hours of television and 200,000 hours of radio a year without the occasional mistake'. In particular, the BBC admitted that it 'took no great pride' in *Airbase*, the controversial play about U.S. servicemen based in Britain, which had been widely criticized. The report was also critical of two inaccurate opinion polls taken during the last general election.

Mr. Checkland said that the BBC was now much more efficient after its reorganization, and that an extra £30 million had been moved to programme-making from other areas. 'Good housekeeping is possible in broadcasting: the BBC steps into the new marketplace well prepared.'

The television licence fee, now index-linked, rose to £66 for colour and £22 for black and white. To make payment easier, it was announced that from

September 1989 an optional quarterly payment facility would be introduced.

During the year, the BBC suffered a long pay dispute which caused the disruption of live transmissions. The broadcasting unions were seeking a 16 per cent pay rise, against the BBC's 'final' offer of 7 per cent. Much bad feeling was caused by large pay rises and perks that managers had received. The BBC's protestations that no more money was available seemed less convincing to the unions after the well-publicised offer in June of a reported £500,000 over three years to Peter Sissons, which brought him to the BBC from Channel 4.

BSB match

Mr. Checkland's assertion that the BBC was 'keen to work alongside the new TV channels as a programme provider' was put into practice in deals with British Satellite Broadcasting. While ITV arranged a controversial and extremely costly contract for exclusive showing of league football, the BBC and BSB agreed a £30 million deal with the Football Association to show F.A. Cup matches and England home international matches for a five-year term. BSB will screen a live match from each round from September up to and including the sixth round on Saturdays, with live mid-week replays. The BBC will show edited highlights on Saturdays, plus a live match from the third to sixth rounds on Sundays. For this the BBC will contribute £12 million. The two companies will also have 'exclusive access' to the best of foreign football.

One consequence of this arrangement was that ITV decided not to televise the F.A. Cup Final in 1989 although it was still entitled to do so. The duplication of televising major sporting events live on both main channels has long been a cause of annoyance to viewers. ITV now announced, 'We do not feel that the duplication is in the best interests of the viewer'.

The BBC revamped its *Nine O'Clock News* programme in October 1988. After three years with two presenters, it reverted to one anchorman in charge of an extended, 30-minute programme. The controversial programme in the *Secret Society* series, *The Zircon Affair* was finally broadcast in an edited form. It had been shelved for 20 months because of claims that transmission would pose a threat to national security. However, a *Panorama* programme on the role of the SAS in Northern Ireland was withdrawn on the orders of deputy director general, John Birt, even though it had been through the internal vetting procedure. It was reported that Mr. Birt was concerned because the programme failed to examine a proposal that the SAS should be publicly accountable.

Other controversial programmes were broadcast, however. These included *Elephant*, made by BBC Northern Ireland. A relentless catalogue of violent killings, it had been postponed from the previous year because of increasing sectarian violence. Before its screening, viewers were warned that it was a 'chilling and vivid comment on the pitiless sectarian killings'. *The Blasphemer's Banquet*, shown in the *Byline* series on BBC1, was a verse discourse by Tony Harrison on religious intolerance. The programme

was inspired by the death threat to Salman Rushdie because of his novel *The Satanic Verses*. The Archbishop of Canterbury, Dr. Robert Runcie, requested, unsuccessfully, that the programme should not be screened as it might offend the Muslim community.

Independent Television

The independent television companies, with the White Paper posing a threat to their existence after 1992, launched a corporate advertising campaign in the press in March. However, while they were attempting to present a united front and to defend the status quo, it became clear that the federal system would not survive long if the Government's proposals became law. In future, the companies will be able to bid for each other's franchises, and George Russell, the new chairman of the IBA, expressed the fear that boardroom battles and franchise bidding could distract attention from programme-making. Furthermore, a company that knew it had lost its franchise would have no incentive to continue making programmes, and if one of the main five programme-making companies lost its franchise, this could have a serious effect on ITV's national scheduling of programmes. Several of the companies have interests in satellite television, and the prospect of switching to that medium if a franchise were lost was also being openly considered.

Thames Television showed a pioneering spirit in arranging to transmit some of its most popular programmes on Soviet television for a week in April. It was reported that the advertisements were very popular with Channel Gosteleradio's estimated audience of 150 million, who would gladly have watched more than six minutes an hour of promotions for products which were not available in the USSR. However, programmes such as *The Bill* and *Minder* were said to have caused Soviet viewers some confusion.

The row continued over Thames Television's *This Week* programme *Death on the Rock*, about the shooting of three IRA terrorists in Gibraltar by the SAS in March 1988. In October 1988, Thames commissioned a report into the making of the programme. A three-month investigation was carried out by Lord Windlesham, a former Conservative Minister, and Richard Rampton, Q.C. The purpose of the inquiry was to attempt to resolve discrepancies between statements made in the film and statements made at the inquest, and to investigate the circumstances leading to the production and broadcasting of the film.

Windlesham Report

The 145-page Windlesham report accepted that the programme was basically fair and proper; however, 'the paradox is that while taken overall the programme fulfilled the requirements of a complex regulatory system, its transmission outraged a section of the population at large as well as provoking bitter criticism in Parliament and the press ... The programme was trenchant and avoided triviality ... we accept that those who made it were acting in good faith and without ulterior motives. Yet we have found that the effect of the programme went beyond its stated intention of laying before the viewers certain evidence giving rise to questions that deserved to be examined by an authoritative tribunal such as a judicial inquiry ... While the public mood is notoriously difficult to interpret there are sufficient indications that *Death on the Rock* was out of step with a substantial body of national opinion.'

The report failed to appease government critics of the programme. In the House of Lords, Lord Trefgarne, Minister of State for Defence Procurement, said the programme had cast a slur on the reputation of the security services. He claimed that the report was as flawed as the programme as the report had given Thames Television a clean bill of health. 'The Government profoundly disagrees with this conclusion, but I wish to emphasize that neither I nor any member of the Government would wish to cast the slightest aspersion on Lord Windlesham's integrity or that of his colleague, Mr. Rampton.' He said that the report's finding that the programme did not conclude that the terrorists had been unlawfully killed, was insupportable. In response, Lord Windlesham rebuked the Prime Minister and the Foreign Secretary for their 'almost contemptuous dismissal' of his report; he refused a fee for his work from Thames, saying that his 'independence and integrity have been questioned'.

In February, the ITV companies announced that they would end national agreements with the broadcasting unions from July. In future, pay and conditions will be agreed at local level. In May, it was announced that repeats on ITV had been reduced by half, to 9 per cent of programme output, in an attempt to attract viewers.

ITV's much-heralded new football programme, *The Match*, was intended to be 'live, pacey and popular', but failed initially to have an impact on viewers. An audience of eight million had been hoped for, but only six million watched the opening programmes: *The Match* appeared to be an expensive investment. The deal cost £44 million over four years, and entitles ITV to screen 21 live matches a season on Sundays; at half-time, a catalogue of the previous day's first division goals is screened. There was also concern that football clubs had sacrificed their independence, as ITV is able to reschedule matches to suit programming requirements and to alter kick-off times.

TV-am, having survived its dispute with the ACTT, announced a 56 per cent increase in profits for the half-year in September 1988. Viewing figures were up by 1 million to 14·8 million a week. However, the company was told by the IBA to improve its standards or risk losing its franchise. In response, it announced that it would increase its budget for children's programmes, and would stop importing repeats of American series such as *Batman* and *Happy Days*. It also intends to increase the educational and regional content of programmes for the young. In November the IBA said that TV-am had made 'significant improvement' in the main areas of complaint, and the ACTT dropped its demand for a judicial review of TV-am's fulfilment of its programming obligations. In September 1989, redundancy payments were agreed for the ACTT members who had been dismissed.

Channel 4 launched a new breakfast show in April, for which TV-am sells the advertising. The programme was targeted at young working people who might be expected to watch for short periods during the extra three and a half hours a day of transmission. Accordingly, the programme was arranged in 15-minute segments, featuring headline news, weather, travel reports, arts and entertainment, and 15 minutes of world news from ITN's international bureaux.

Satellite Services

Following the successful launch of the Ariane rocket which placed the Sky satellite in orbit, the new Sky television station began broadcasting at 6 pm on February 5, 1989. Rupert Murdoch, chief executive of News International, the owners of Sky, said that 'Sky Television will bring competition, choice and quality to British Television. The monopoly is broken. With the four channels we have launched today and the two more that we will start later this year, television in Britain will begin to deliver the diversity it has lacked.' In its opening message the station heralded, 'the dawn of television's new age and the most dramatic innovation in broadcasting since the launch of commercial television in Britain more than three decades ago'.

Sky began with four channels: Sky Channel, which features game shows, including revivals of ITV shows such as *The Sale of the Century* and *The Price is Right*, a magazine programme with Tony Blackburn and Jenny Hanley, an evening chat show hosted by Derek Jameson, American imports and repeats such as *The Lucy Show*, a music programme and business reports. Sky News consists of half-hourly news bulletins provided by the television news agency Visnews (jointly owned by Reuters, the BBC and the American-based NBC). It also features a current affairs programme called *Target*, which is co-presented by the former Conservative Minister Norman Tebbit and the Labour M.P. Austin Mitchell. When Mr. Mitchell's involvement with Sky was announced, he was sacked as Labour's spokesman for trade and industry by the Labour Party leader Neil Kinnock. Mr. Kinnock said that the job with Sky was inappropriate to his status, and to the Shadow Cabinet concept of collective responsibility. The Sky Films Channel features movies 12 to 18 months after their cinema release, plus older films. The fourth channel, Eurosport, shows a wide range of sports, including some ignored by the terrestrial channels. Sky originally intended to offer the Disney Channel but the Disney Corporation withdrew. Although Sky issued a writ for $1·5 billion in damages, the case was later dropped.

BSB postponed

Sky had predicted sales of 1 million satellite dishes in 1989, but with a significant decline in retail sales, this estimate had to be revised downwards. The other satellite station, British Satellite Broadcasting, predicted that three million homes would receive its programmes by 1991. However, an independent survey predicted that only 1·6 million to 2·2 million homes in total would be receiving satellite transmissions by 1991, 45 per cent via a satellite dish and the rest through cable services. Sky gained a significant early advantage over BSB with a well-publicized and trouble-free launch. An early coup was its exclusive live coverage of Frank Bruno's world title boxing match against Mike Tyson. ITV, which considered it had rights to all Tyson fights screened in the U.K., challenged Sky in the High Court, but its claim was rejected. The IBA also told the ITV companies that they could not refuse to carry advertisements for Sky even though they were in direct competition.

Despite its successful launch, Sky Television ran into problems and embarked on a campaign, especially through the newspapers of its proprietor, Rupert Murdoch, to persuade the public to invest in satellite dishes. British Satellite Broadcasting, due to go on the air in autumn 1989, was forced to postpone its launch by at least six months after experiencing problems in the manufacture of the microchip in its decoder box. The station's first full-time employee, deputy chief executive Graham Grist, resigned because of the problem. BSB was also forced to postpone production of its 'squarial' plastic receiving dish, which it had announced with a fanfare of publicity, in favour of a metal dish. Questions were also raised about the viability of the BSB operation after the IBA awarded it two extra satellite channels. Many felt that the signals from the satellite would not be powerful enough to provide what the service was proposing to broadcast.

BSB was set up with a budget of £625 million, which it later said was not sufficient due to the high cost of programmes. It spent £200 million on the rights to 1,800 Hollywood films from Gulf and Western and MCA/Universal. In August, BSB chief executive Anthony Simonds-Gooding said that his satellite services would not degenerate into game shows and pornographic films: 'BSB will be a regulated extension of choice for the British public', he averred. However, the high capital cost of receiving equipment and the delay in BSB's launch has left the public reluctant to commit themselves to one service which would prove incompatible with the alternative. Until equipment is widely available that would receive all satellite stations, consumer resistance seems inevitable. One possible solution was provided by W.H. Smith, which announced that it would be moving its two satellite channels, Lifestyle and Screensport, from the low-powered Intelsat that serves the cable networks to the Astra satellite. W.H. Smith intends to sell receiving equipment that will cost about £300, and will be compatible with both Sky and BSB.

Government

Following government complaints that the film and television unions were 'the last bastions of trades union restrictive practices', the Monopolies and Mergers Commission undertook an 11-month investigation into the Association of Cinematograph, Television and Allied Technicians, the Broadcasting and Entertainment Trades Alliance and the Electrical, Electronic, Telecommunication and Plumbing Union. The Commission's report cleared the unions of operating restrictive practices and said that where

there were restrictive practices, these were not contrary to public interest.

In October 1988, the Home Secretary (Douglas Hurd) announced measures designed to restrict the publicity given to terrorist organizations. The main restriction was on radio or television interviews with members of eleven republican and loyalist paramilitary groups in Northern Ireland. Exemptions to the rules mean that, for example, they do not apply during elections. However, the loopholes and inconsistencies caused considerable confusion. It was apparently permissible to screen an interview with a Sinn Fein councillor provided the recorded sound was not broadcast and a reporter gave a voice-over commentary of what had been said. The BBC said that the Government had set a 'damaging precedent', and the National Union of Journalists said that British broadcasters were now operating under conditions similar to those in South Africa under that country's state of emergency. The NUJ unsuccessfully challenged the Government order in the High Court, alleging that it contravened the European Convention on Human Rights and prevented impartial reporting. Television companies also had to amend documentaries on Northern Ireland which had already been screened, as repeating them in their original form fell foul of the order.

Televising the Commons

The House of Commons Select Committee on televising proceedings of the House of Commons finally published the rules under which cameras would be allowed into the chamber in April. Both the BBC and ITN complained that the rules were too restrictive; they are more severe than those which already operate in the House of Lords. Under the rules, cameras would be forbidden to show Members of Parliament misbehaving and would have to focus on the Speaker's chair during any disorder. They would only be permitted to show the head and shoulders of Members who were speaking, although showing the reactions of other Members who were mentioned would be permitted. In June the House agreed to the experimental televising of the House of Commons during the next session. The contract for providing television pictures of the Commons was awarded to Broadcast Communications.

Ironically, more liberal broadcasting of proceedings was permitted in the Soviet Union. For the first time cameras were allowed to broadcast live for eight hours a day from the Congress of People's Deputies. The scene of deputies queuing up to take advantage of their new-found freedom to criticize the old guard, was watched by an estimated audience of 200 million viewers throughout the USSR.

Awards

At the BAFTA Awards for television production and performance, the main awards were: Best light entertainment, *An Audience with Victoria Wood* (LWT); best drama series/serial, *A Very British Coup* (Skreba Films for Channel 4); best single drama, *Tumbledown* (BBC1); writer's award, Alan Plater; best comedy series, *Only Fools and Horses* (Christmas Special, BBC1); best factual series, *Arena* (BBC2);

best news and outside broadcast, *Channel 4 News*; best short animated film, *The Hill Farm*; best foreign programme, *Tanner* (U.S.A., Channel 4); Robert Flaherty Documentary Award, *Death on the Rock* (Thames); Richard Dimbleby Award for Outstanding Contribution to Factual Broadcasting, Ludovic Kennedy; Huw Weldon Award for Best Arts Programme, *Bertolucci and the Last Emperor* (South Bank Show, LWT); best light entertainment performance, Victoria Wood (*An Audience with Victoria Wood*, LWT); best actress, Thora Hird (*A Cream Cracker Under the Settee*, BBC1); best actor, Ray McAnally (*A Very British Coup*, Channel 4). The Broadcasting Press Guild gave their award for best documentary to Thames for *Death on the Rock*; best single drama, *Tumbledown* (BBC1); and best drama, *A Very British Coup* (Channel 4); Ray McAnally received the best actor award for his role in the same series.

FILM CERTIFICATES

The British Board of Film Classification issues the following categories of film certificates:

U   Universal: suitable for all.
PG   Parental Guidance: some scenes may be unsuitable for young children.
12   Passed only for persons of twelve years and over.
15   Passed only for persons of fifteen years and over.
18   Passed only for persons of eighteen years and over.
R18   For Restricted Distribution Only (through segregated premises to which no one under the age of eighteen is admitted).

The classifications of video tapes differ slightly:

U   Universal: suitable for all.
Uc   Universal: particularly suitable for children.
PG   Parental Guidance: general viewing, but some scenes may be unsuitable for young children.
15   Suitable only for persons of 15 years and over.
18   Suitable only for persons of 18 years and over.
R18   Restricted: to be supplied only in licensed sex shops to persons of not less than 18 years.

ARCHITECTURE 1988–89

BILLINGSGATE FISH MARKET, LONDON
Architect: Richard Rogers Partnership

Ten years ago Billingsgate Market in London was threatened with extinction as a result of the City of London's decision to relocate the fish market to newly constructed premises on the Isle of Dogs, and to offer the valuable central site for redevelopment. Concern over the fate of the 1875 fish market building led to its being given a Grade 2 listing in April 1980. Alternative proposals for the site were put forward by SAVE Britain's Heritage, which suggested that new offices should be built on the adjacent lorry park, and the market hall converted to house restaurants and shops. This was only the first in a series of political and commercial developments which eventually led to the purchase of the site by S. and W. Berisford and the London and Edinburgh Trust immediately after the relocation of the fish market in January 1982. SAVE's proposals and their firm stand against demolition had, however, led to a change of attitude by the City of London Corporation and the retention and re-use of the market hall was accepted as a viable and desirable option.

The lorry park adjacent to the site was developed, but the then architect's proposals for the market hall, which envisaged a conversion to office use, were not implemented. At that time demand for office space for financial institutions was burgeoning and the site was purchased by the American institution Citicorp, who appointed Richard Rogers Partnership as architect for the conversion. The architect's task was to accommodate the stringent accommodation and servicing requirements of his client while respecting the essential qualities and character of the historic structure. Despite its run-down condition, the architect recognized a building of considerable stature and merit.

The main problem in developing the 33,000 sq. feet of the main floor into a dealing room for some 400 dealers was the onerous air conditioning requirements. The air conditioning would have to be able to control the heat output from the 1,500 display screens which would be accommodated in the dealing room. The architect's desire to preserve the visual qualities of the roof structure resulted in the extensive ducting for the air conditioning system being incorporated within a raised floor 450 mm deep. Great effort has gone into the concentration and concealment of services in this zone to leave the floor space as uncluttered as possible. Where new elements have been introduced, however, they have been designed in an unequivocally modern style to create a distinction between new and old and to preserve the integrity of the earlier structure.

A substantial amount of extra space has been squeezed into the existing structure, but the insertion is handled with skill. An additional 10,000 sq. feet was created by adding suspended mezzanine galleries arranged in an H-plan in the main hall. These are partially suspended from columns which form new arcades along the north and south sides of the hall and complement the existing Haddock Gallery. The Haddock Gallery runs north to south between the two halves of the hall above the central aisle. It is at a higher level than the modern galleries and takes support from two rows of massive cast-iron Doric columns. The new mezzanine structures are lightweight and visually unobtrusive. The white-painted tubular steel floor trusses are suspended from pairs of inclined steel tension rods at each column position.

The existing timber roof structure, with its curved timber framework supported on wrought iron trusses, required substantial rebuilding. A new glazing system was developed to provide diffuse and subdued lighting so that the V.D.U. screens below would be easily visible and free of reflections. A system of double glazed units incorporating a faceted acrylic prism was devised. The facets in one direction are mirrored and are orientated according to the position of the sun. This is in order that direct sunlight is reflected away from the interior but natural daylight is allowed in. The diffused daylight from above and the predominantly white interior treatment contribute to a cool atmosphere on the trading floors.

The exterior of the building has been cleaned and restored. The removal of excrescences from the frontage has revealed the original elevations, which are now set back behind a wide promenade forming part of the City's intended riverside walkway. Classical in style, the frontage has yellow brick walls over a rusticated stone ground storey and central colonnade. There are decorative stone window dressings and pilasters at the upper levels. It is a beautifully balanced and ordered composition, the tall central colonnade terminating at each end in four-storey pavilions. Each pavilion carries a weather vane surmounted by a huge fish.

As an example of fastidious restoration allied to the introduction of new uses and the incorporation of the latest technology, Billingsgate Market achieves the highest standards. The final cost of the project was some £26 million, but the recent downturn in demand for space by the financial institutions has resulted in the completed building remaining empty.

COURTS OF JUSTICE, TRURO
Architect: Evans and Shalev

The new Courts of Justice in Truro stand on the site of the medieval castle. The commercial heart of the town lies to one side and the Victoria Gardens to the other. The principal public entrance is between the two at the top of Edward Street, with terraces of houses stepping up the slope towards the steeply pedimented portico.

Whereas it is common for new crown courts to contain between four and six courtrooms, the brief at Truro required only three—one medium-sized crown court, one small crown court, and a dual purpose court—together with ancillary accommodation for judges and juries, and the necessary cells and secure areas. These functional spaces are arranged around the main public concourses and waiting areas, with a large open courtyard to one side. The organization of circulation spaces is the key to the building's layout. It is geared to ordering the movements of a number of specific categories of user with different requirements and different priorities of access, privacy and security.

The main entrance is approached through the pedimented portico at the top of Edward Street. The actual main entrance into the courthouse is set deep in the heart of the building. Passing through the portico, the visitor enters a covered loggia which opens directly onto an open courtyard on the east side and rises through a series of levels by means of either a ramp or short flights of steps. The internal wall of the loggia adopts a gently curving form, its rendered lower half topped by a clerestory of glass blocks. The curved sweep of the stairs leads the eye upwards to the glazed entrance screen and revolving door. These are set at right angles to the curve and at 45° to the axis of the entrance portico.

Inside the entrance, the reception desk continues the curve away to the left and the final 135° turn past the lower flights of opposing staircases brings the visitor to the tall and dignified spaces of the central concourse and waiting areas. The concourse acts as the focus of all public activity in the building and gives access to each of the three courtrooms. It is long and spatially complex, accentuated by two circular waiting areas, one serving the two crown courts and the other the dual purpose court. Both spaces rise through two-storey rotundas and are capped by a ring of glass block clerestory windows under a conical plastered ceiling, with small glazed rooflights at the apex. The use of double-height spaces reflects their functional importance as the hub of the building and also enables full advantage to be taken of natural daylight and ventilation.

Directly accessible from the public waiting areas are four consultation rooms which are set into the curve of the wall backing the entrance staircase. A further two consultation rooms and two witness waiting rooms are situated off the dual purpose court waiting area. Staircases rising out of the central concourse give access to administrative offices and further waiting areas. The crown and county court office suites are also situated at first floor level. The general office fills the east side of the building, overlooking the courtyard.

Access for members of the jury to their own special assembly suite is gained directly from the main entrance via a private corridor. Accommodation for judges and jury members is wrapped around the perimeter of the three courts away from the public concourse, set 'back stage', as it were, to the 'stages' of the courtrooms and 'front of house' of the waiting areas. The judges' accommodation, occupying two storeys, overlooks the judges' garden. This is an expanse of gravel filling the area between the neighbouring Victoria Gardens and the serrated profile of the judges' quarters. The rooms in the quarters form a series of prow-shaped projections accentuated by the overhanging cornice.

The most important areas are the courtrooms themselves. The transition from the light, airy and informal public spaces to the light, airy and formal courtrooms is emphasized by the darker, narrower

lobbies that connect the two. Each courtroom is symmetrical about its long axis, and each has structural and decorative features in common. These include the curved wall behind the judge, the white panelled furniture and fixtures, the bright blue carpeted floor, and the stepped cross-section through the ceiling, with natural daylight spilling down the length of the side walls through high-level glazed rooflights. The dual purpose court differs slightly in having a high-level south-facing clerestory light along one side in lieu of a glazed rooflight. The largest courtroom, the medium-sized crown court, has an engaged column (i.e. half within the wall, half projecting) either side of the judge's bench and two free-standing columns framing the dock. The columns are positioned at each corner of the dropped central ceiling section. The panelled theme, based on a square motif, recurs throughout the courtrooms; in the desks and benches of courts, in the square panelled string courses around the walls, and in the perimeter band around the lowered ceilings. It is echoed elsewhere in the glass panelled entrance doors to the courtrooms, and in the square glass blocks used in the rotunda clerestory lights and the windows to internal rooms and corridors.

Internally all attention is focused on the modelling and the inter-relationships of planes and forms. The simple white plastered finish picks up the subtlest nuances of light and shade as daylight floods in, particularly in the principal public areas. A single string course of dark brown plinth header bricks provides tonal contrast and underlines the predominant shapes and forms. The same dark bricks are used in the staircases and in the curved seating areas of the concourse.

The string course of dark brown bricks functions in a similar way externally. It reappears on all the elevations as a separating strip marking the transition from pre-cast projecting cornice to vertical rendered wall. This provides a dark 'shadow' line at eaves level that adds crispness and clarity to the profusion of forms and planes generated by the complex massing of the building. Similar lines of plinth headers are used to accentuate particular elements, such as the heads and sills of windows, and as a capping to low walls and planters. As with the interior, the vocabulary of materials is limited and the colour mainly white. The rough texture of the rendered finish is obtained by using white spar chippings from a local quarry near St. Austell. It contrasts well with the smooth white finish of the pre-cast concrete cornices, lintels and sills.

Apart from the lines of brick, the only other material visible from the outside is the dark grey slate covering the two domed roofs over the public waiting areas. From the streets leading up to it the building looks like a small hill-top settlement, while from the south a seemingly random muddle of white geometric forms focuses on the two conical slate roofs that mark the summit of the hill as well as the core of the building. This townscape image is a reflection of the internal organization of the building, with materials, decorative motifs and forms relating from interior to exterior.

This is a truly Modernist building, in the sense

that every aspect of its form, organization and detail stems from a rigorous analysis of the needs of the occupants and users, the requirements of its functions and the influences of its physical and cultural context.

DOCKLANDS HOUSING

The creation of the London Docklands Development Corporation in 1981 brought vast areas of land to the north and south of the River Thames and to the east of Tower Bridge under the aegis of one co-ordinating planning authority. Since then the development of London's dockland sites has proceeded at a frantic pace. The initial stages of development were principally within the Isle of Dogs area, but work is now spreading to less well-known areas. This will test the Corporation's ability to generate and implement strategic design and development criteria to produce a coherent and urbane built environment. A 'laissez-faire' attitude towards planning controls is evident in the mish-mash of competing styles which characterized the first generation of development. However, experience and the stringent demands of the more powerful developers has led to an improvement in the quality of the architectural and urban design of many of the current residential and office developments.

Finland Quays, Surrey Docks
Architect: Richard Reid Architects

Typical of the best of the second generation of housing developments is Finland Quays. This is a development of 67 luxury apartments on the north side of Greenland Dock in the Surrey Docks area south of the river. It takes the form of a series of seven linked pavilions, each pavilion having a double fronted design. Accommodation is arranged symmetrically around a central staircase which features as a semi-circular projecting bay on the north-facing rear elevation. Car parking is accommodated under the building as a semi-basement. The extra height resulting from the half-storey podium base adds greatly to the scale of the dockside elevations, which are set back behind a broad brick-paved public walkway. Over this base the flat blocks rise to a further four storeys, with the balcony bedroom of the studio flats at fourth-floor level tucked into the pitch of the roof and looking out over the water through a huge central double-height window.

External elevations are constructed in a warm red brick set out in horizontal bands of subtly different colour, relieved by a plain rendered treatment for the projecting window bays that enliven the living rooms and bedrooms of the flats on the second and third floors. The central window to the topmost studio flats is recessed and is surmounted by a curved vault in the roof. In each of the end pavilions the brickwork continues upwards over the vault to form a triangular brick pediment, a device which emphasizes the ends and balances the overall composition. The projecting and recessed window bays at upper levels, the shallow bow-fronted balconies of the link sections at ground

level, and the projecting entrance staircases behind their sloping parapet walls at intervals along the promenade, lend interest and variety to the dockside elevation.

The whole of the dockside elevation is modelled in forms which refer to past housing to be found in south London. The rear elevations are less successful, lacking the interest and humanity of the main frontage. Here the lack of modelling, the treatment of the basement car park enclosures, and the feeling of meanness implicit in the plain render of the stair towers, give the landside façade a stark and almost institutional character. The commercial pressure of docklands development is also evident in the minimal space of the flat interiors, a consequence of rapidly rising land values and profit expectations. Nevertheless, the scheme provides an excellent example of an appropriate response to a waterside location widely typical of docklands.

Shadwell Basin, Wapping
Architect: MacCormac, Jamieson, Prichard & Wright

The housing scheme at Shadwell Basin is similar to Finland Quays in its formal layout and spatial relationship to the dock. Here the housing encloses three sides of the dock basin, with the north side punctuated by St Paul's Church (John Walters, 1820–21) and churchyard.

The housing is made up of articulated terraces forming a solid wall of building set back behind a paved public promenade. The main plane of the ground storey is recessed behind a series of simple circular columns in the manner of the traditional dockside warehouses. The brick elevations of the houses are punctuated by projecting balconies, which are painted blue. These highlight the subdivision of the terrace into distinct dwelling groups. The spacing of the balconies varies at different levels. Those at first and second floor level are combined in pairs positioned between each pavilion. Those at third floor level are single and spaced at regular intervals right across the frontage. They combine visually, looking like a cornice band, when viewed from oblique angles.

The north and west terraces accommodate a wide range of different sized flats and are distinguished by their greater height. The recessed central balconies at the upper level open up the brick gable ends to create a split pediment. The terrace on the east side is lower, three storeys high rather than four. It is grouped more distinctly into separate dwelling units, though it perpetuates the linked pavilion format of the other terraces. In all the terraces, elements that are recessed behind the main brick elevations are treated in a contrasting bright red colour. These elements include the glazed link elevations, windows, and the doors opening onto balconies.

Surprisingly, the design architects were not retained to produce the working drawings and supervise work on site. Despite this loss of design control, the good sense and appropriateness of the design mark this as another of the better quality Docklands housing schemes.

Cascades, Isle of Dogs
Architects: Campbell, Zogolovitch, Wilkinson &
Gough

Cascades is an unusual development on the bend of
the River Thames as it turns south round the Isle of
Dogs. At 20 storeys high and on an exposed site, the
system-built block of flats can be seen for miles
around. Although constructed in only 18 months,
the designers have eliminated the usual features of
system building, such as standard prefabricated wall
panels, and have created a truly 'bespoke' building.
It is clad in colour-banded brickwork with a wide
variety of window shapes and balcony openings, a
multi-faceted façade, and a range of other features,
all encompassed within a bold but unconventional
form. The massing of the building might be described
as a single bookend. The principal mass of the tower
block is buttressed and extended by a triangular infill
on one side which rises up from ground level to the
fifteenth floor.

The primary vertical circulation core of three lifts
and staircase is sited at the north end within the
tower section. From this point on each floor a central
corridor divides the building in two halves. The
west-facing flats have views across and up the River
Thames, the east-facing ones overlook the Canary
Wharf area. At the far end of the corridor a fire
escape staircase runs down the centre of the sloping
lower portion. It is capped by a continuous rooflight
which from the outside forms the backbone of the
'buttress', and from the inside offers commanding
views towards Greenwich. At each floor level down
the slope the flats extend a little further, generating
a 'cascade' (hence the name) of small roof terraces
and conservatories set into the angle behind the
sloping parapet line of the main walls. From the
junction with the main block at the sixteenth floor,
the stair enclosure rises vertically in a prominent
white metal-clad tower with a large porthole window
at each level.

Nautical references abound, and the porthole type
of window is liberally featured elsewhere on the
elevations. At the south end of the building, ventilation ducts emerge from the basement car park and
terminate in exact reproductions of the circular
cowls that used to be found on ocean liners.

Perhaps the most unusual features are the tapering
semi-circular projections created by linking the half-
round projecting balconies of the uppermost four
storeys by means of a series of vertical mullions. At
roof level these extend to enclose an open spiral
staircase from penthouse level up to private roof
gardens. The appearance is that of an extended
shuttlecock protruding above the roof parapet, which
adds a bizarre flourish to the roofline and silhouette
of the building.

The angled outer walls of the flats are set in and
out alternately to produce a series of faceted projections from the main building line. The projections
are intended to provide individual flats with the best
possible orientation and outlook, as well as adding
life and interest to the elevations.

Such an eccentric and exuberant building is
unlikely to be a role model for future docklands
development, though there can be no doubting its
success as a commercial enterprise. However, there
are clear visual links to related building types and
activities, such as its references to ships and quayside
warehouses, that might offer future designers scope
for development.

THE MARKET PLACE, BOLTON
Architect: Chapman Taylor Partners

Bolton is a northern town whose centre is dominated by Victorian and Edwardian buildings, vigorous and confident expressions of an earlier era of
prosperity based on commerce and industry.

Like many such towns, however, Bolton has
suffered in recent years from the decline of its
industrial base, and areas in the heart of the town
have become derelict. One such area was situated
next to the nineteenth century market hall and has
been given a new lease of life with the completion of
the Market Place shopping centre. The shopping
centre incorporates and complements the market hall
in the general pattern of pedestrian circulation and
the mix of retail uses. It also strengthens the
architectural continuity of the town centre, its
architectural styling making clear references to its
historic neighbours.

Completed in March 1988 for a cost of approximately £21 million, the new part of the development
contains some thirty shop units and a large department store. It extends to 240,000 sq. feet, trading on
two levels. It is set out on a strong central axis which
continues into the central aisle of the elegant cast-
iron and glass structure of the market hall. The new
and the old structures are contiguous and at the
junction of the two is a new rotunda containing a
staircase and escalators to the first-floor mall of the
new section. This space acts as a crossroads at the
heart of the scheme. Picking up the secondary axes
of pedestrian cross-malls from the Bridge Street and
Knowsley Street entrances, it effects the transition
from the open spaces of the market hall to the more
linear spaces of the new malls in an easy and natural
way.

Externally, the architectural treatment of the
elevation indicates an inventive response to the mid-
Victorian Classicism of the market hall (1855) and
the adjacent Victoria Hall (1900). Slavish copying of
specific features from these buildings has been
avoided but certain thematic elements recur, such as
the semi-circular arches and circular windows of the
market hall, and the double-curved profile of the
domed lanterns over the projecting towers which
mirrors that of the tower of the Victoria Hall. The
building profile is very strongly modelled, both on
plan and in section. The corners of the building,
particularly at the pedestrian entrance points, take
the form of brick- and stone-clad towers, cruciform
on plan. These are surmounted by an intersecting
barrel-vaulted attic storey and topped with an ogee-
shaped dome motif. The linking elevations have
overhanging eaves under slate-covered pitched roofs.
At an upper level, a band of red aluminium-framed

curtain walling is set behind a series of vertical red metal 'detached' mullions. These give visual support (rather than structural support) to the eaves, and emphasize the bays of the curtain wall behind.

Despite the fact that the upper three levels of the new development contain parking space for some 750 cars, the building has developed a dynamic skyline. The most notable features are the perimeter towers, with their copper-clad barrel vaults and varied treatments of the domed turrets, and the air vents. These either project from the roof plane in simple dormer-like shapes or form a continuous horizontal break between the separated planes of the pitched roofs. The overall composition complements its neighbouring Victorian buildings and the surrounding streets.

Internally, the neo-Victorian imagery is abandoned, though a classical style is retained for the columns and arches of the three atrium spaces which penetrate the building and offer daylight down to the lowest mall level. Here, in contrast to the exterior, the elements are rather self-consciously non-structural, being constructed in hollow GRC casings. The marbled paint finish lends a somewhat theatrical air. However, the absence of large expanses of reflective chrome and mirror does give the interior the sense of solidity that one expects in an internal room of the scale that these atrium spaces possess. The effect is enhanced by the use of solid mahogany handrails, sober but positively patterned tiled flooring, and large centre-piece light fittings.

The character of these new malls, smart, smooth, up-market and design conscious, contrasts with the more traditional character of the market hall. The central rotunda at the focal point of the development both separates and links the two 'cultures'. It expresses the sometimes uneasy relationship between the two in the confrontation of old and new architectural styles.

One half of the circular rotunda projects into the market hall, and has a balcony level intended to function as a restaurant. The glazed, domed rooflight sits upon a bold, decorated frieze supported on a colonnade of columns. These maintain the disciplined classical vocabulary of the two-storey high pilasters and the moulded cornice of the market hall exterior. The recessing of the first floor balustrades reveals the dignified proportions of the double-height columns. The other semicircle of the rotunda offers a dramatic change of order. The marbled-effect GRC casings appear in a circular format recessed behind a projecting version of the balustrade design. The conflict between the two orders robs this space of the architectural unity which is present in the treatment of frieze and rooflight and in the attractive flooring.

However, the design acknowledges that old meets new in the most direct of ways, and the external junctions between the old market hall and the new centre are most competently handled. The building has achieved commercial success as well as repairing the damage done to the town centre, which is greatly to the credit of Grosvenor Developments, client in succession to Wimpey, and the design team.

STOCKLEY BUSINESS PARK, HEATHROW

Office for Apple Computers U.K. Ltd.:
Architect: Troughton McAslan

Speculative Office Development for Stanhope Properties:
Architect: Foster Associates

Stockley Park is one of the new breed of business parks being developed in response to the demand for purpose-built office space and light industrial accommodation. Situated on a land reclamation site to the west of Heathrow Airport, Stockley Park has attracted a number of high quality developments. An extensive scheme of landscaping, including a new lake, provides an appropriate setting for some stylish new designs reflecting the technical sophistication of the new tenants.

The new office for Apple Computers is an assured essay in grey and white modular curtain walling. The accommodation is arranged on two floors either side of a central top-lit internal circulation 'street'. Individual rooms are given over to specific functions, such as storage and computer areas, an auditorium and demonstration area, catering facilities and a customer entertainment suite at ground floor level. At the upper level the office areas are open plan. The simple shape of the building is subtly modelled by the recessing of the curtain wall at ground level to reveal the circular columns at the perimeter. At first floor level the curtain wall projects beyond the column line. This device introduces a strong shadow line at first floor level and lightens the massing, eliminating any impression of 'boxiness'. The sober bands of grey and white spandrel panels are softened on the south side by the introduction of a tensile stretched fabric sunshade, like a series of narrow sails. This runs along the eaves line and briefly turns the corners onto the west and east elevations. Supported on white painted triangulated outriggers, the scalloped sail shapes and steel rigging add a welcome sense of fun and an interesting pattern of shadows. Further visual relief is afforded by two open-tread steel fire escape staircases, which project forwards from the centre of each long elevation, and by the main entrance canopy. Around the entrance canopy a tent-like enclosure of panels is suspended, continuing the stretched sail idea. The ends of the central 'street' of the building continue beyond the main building line under the pitched roof of the canopy, which mirrors the glazed rooflight behind.

Internally the treatment is unremarkable, with the high quality finishes and minimal detailing that are frequently to be found in modern commercial buildings. The logic and clarity of the plan reflects the simplicity of the building's form and is allied to a restrained and elegant external appearance.

A different but no less sophisticated solution to a similar brief stands on a nearby site in the business park. The requirement was for a speculative office building constructed as shell and core, i.e. for fitting out by the tenant. The architects, Foster Associates, seized the opportunity to achieve a rational and flexible structure of visual elegance and simplicity, using a range of technical solutions to eliminate many of the traditionally troublesome aspects of building construction.

The resulting office accommodation is on three floors and is divided into three major sections. The two outer sections, 18 metres in width, are linked to a central 21 metre bay. Each bay is separated from the next by a 6 metre wide continuous atrium space. Both of the atria are spanned by circulation bridges linking the adjacent bays. Both have straight staircase flights linked end to end on the central axis in one continuous 'cascade'. The three bays are staggered on plan. This device owes much to the requirements for fire escape distances but has clear benefits for the massing of the exterior.

The most obvious visual characteristic of the elevations is the use of a graduated shading pattern on the glass window panels. A technological spin-off from the automobile industry, the treatment of the glass eliminates glare and offers solar control at less cost than conventional tinted glass. The unusual shading effect gives the building a hazy, insubstantial quality.

The special glass panels are incorporated within factory-assembled cladding developed in Austria. The cladding consists of a four-sided structural silicone jointing system for each constituent panel. A modification to the supporting aluminium frames was made to satisfy British building control requirements, so that the panels are now retained by a splayed frame section in the event of a failure of the silicone jointing material.

The end bay of each of the three blocks containing the main services plant areas is treated differently, with white louvre-panelled walls rising to the full height on the three exposed sides. The fine horizontal shadow lines created by the louvres impart a delicate texture of light and shade to the otherwise solid end bays.

The primary structural system supporting the roof comprises a series of Y-shaped frames. The upper arms of the frames are braced at a shallow angle by a horizontal tie rod supported on triangulated bracing struts, and by vertical ties and spring-loaded tension fixings to points in the ground around the perimeter. Where adjacent frames meet at the apex of the glazed rooflight over the linking atria, the frames are pin-jointed by a common tubular steel member running along the ridge line. Where the Y-shaped arms project beyond the outer face of the curtain walling around the perimeter, a simple white metal fascia panel terminates the glazed walling and a series of slatted sun shades are introduced. These not only give useful shading from the sun, but also provide a delicate projecting cornice which terminates the elevations and enlivens the skyline of an otherwise very simple box form.

A secondary structural system of steel columns and concrete floor slabs supports the office floors. The structure terminates at second floor level. This leaves the whole of the topmost floor under the sloping roof and glazed rooflights free of any structural interruptions, apart from the tapering central legs of the roof support columns.

This elegant building was completed in March 1989 and, like the office for Apple Computers, is an excellent example of a modern architectural style totally in keeping with the technology of its age.

ARCHAEOLOGY 1988–89

The most important archaeological event of the year in the opinion of the press was the excavation of the late 16th century Rose theatre at Bankside in London. Seldom has an archaeological site so caught the imagination that it has appeared regularly as front-page news. The reason for this is that what was initially an important archaeological discovery developed into a debate about how the law treats the development and preservation of archaeological sites.

The saga began with press reports in mid February 1989 of the discovery of the remains of the Rose playhouse, the predecessor of Shakespeare's Globe Theatre which was situated close by. The site of the Rose playhouse was well-known and was indicated by current street names. Excavation at the site began in December 1988 and was undertaken by archaeologists from the Museum of London with the full agreement, and the financial support, of the developers, Imry Merchant, who had planning permission to build a ten-storey office block on the site.

Following the discovery discussions between English Heritage, the Museum of London and the developers took place in an attempt to extend period the archaeologists could work on the site, so that a proper excavation could be carried out. Suggestions were already being made that the site should be preserved for the public benefit and on March 2, 1989 Simon Hughes, M.P. (S.L.D., Southwark and Bermondsey) tabled questions in the House of Commons supporting the wish of the archaeologists to secure more than a two-month evaluation excavation, which was all that the developers would originally agree to. Mr Hughes also proposed the designation of this part of Southwark under the 1979 Ancient Monuments and Archaeological Areas Act, which would secure sufficient time for a proper investigation. The Museum of London archaeologists were successful in winning more time for their investigation and by May 1 a campaign to save the site of the Rose playhouse was being launched, led by the actor Ian McKellen, Simon Hughes and Gerald Bowden, M.P. (Conservative, Dulwich). The two M.P.s requested the Secretary of State for the Environment, Nicholas Ridley, to schedule the site as an ancient monument and in a debate in the House of Commons on May 10 Simon Hughes urged this move because 'we have found the first and, so far as yet we know, the only *in situ* evidence of any of the Elizabethan theatres. No-one knows whether we will find any more.'

For the Government, Mrs. Virginia Bottomley, Under Secretary of State for the Environment, stated that consideration was being given to designation under the Ancient Monuments and Archaeological Areas Act. She said, however, that the Government was satisfied that the remains of the Rose playhouse could be preserved to a substantial degree beneath the proposed new office block: 'We cannot do anything to mitigate the damage that has already been done by the piling from previous office blocks, and any future damage to be caused by the new building is minimal.' The following day the Prime Minister told the House of Commons that the remains must be preserved and that she was satisfied that discussions between English Heritage, the Museum of London and the developers would result in such preservation with the minimum damage. This view was immediately challenged by the archaeologists, who argued that parts of the stage walls would have to be demolished so that piles for the new building could be inserted and Simon Hughes claimed that the assurances were 'totally unjustified and totally misleading'. Imry Merchant Developers, the site owners, stated that 'the remains are going to be wrapped as carefully as a porcelain doll. There must be a building over the top of it and to protect the Rose there has to be protective covering for it, and that is being done under the guidance of English Heritage.' This did not satisfy Mr. Hughes who said on May 13 'The developers are going to take possession of the site on Monday morning. They have given no assurance that the site will not be infilled, no assurance that the piles will not be driven into the remains including into the stage, no assurance that permanent damage won't be done as a result of the removal of the covering over the site, and no assurance that the public will ever be able to see the Rose again.'

The M.P.'s unease was reflected in the correspondence columns of the national press, especially *The Times*, and the Rose Theatre Trust was launched with the intention of raising £20 million to buy the site. By this time much interest was being directed to the adequacy, or otherwise, of the legal protection given to archaeological sites and there was a move afoot for the implementation of the European Communities Environmental Impact Assessment so far as the archaeology of the site was concerned.

Archaeologists were required to leave the site at midnight on May 14 after five months excavating at the developer's expense. That evening a number of protesters supporting the preservation of the site held a vigil with the intention of preventing workmen from starting building work on the morning of May 15. Distinguished members of the acting profession gave readings to the protesters and Lord Olivier sent a message of solidarity. There was a reprieve for the Rose on May 15 when the Government paid £1 million towards the cost of delaying the project for a month while ways of preserving it were considered. In a statement to the Commons on that day the Secretary of State for the Environment said that this money would be the full extent of the Government's financial commitment. Mr. Ridley said: 'It has become clear in the light of the most recent discoveries that the remains are of greater importance than was previously thought. As a result, the developers and their architect have been working urgently on possible ways of ensuring that the excavated remains are properly preserved and displayed to the public.'

On June 2 the developers, Imry Merchant, announced a plan to save the remains of the Rose playhouse. They put forward a redesign of the proposed ten-storey office block, proposing to build it on stilts so that it would clear the site. On June 15 the Secretary of State for the Environment announced that he did not intend to schedule the site as he was satisfied, on the advice of English Heritage, that the new £10 million design for the building would, if approved by the local planning authority protect the remains and obviate the need for scheduling. Mr. Ridley's decision did not satisfy those who wished to see the site preserved and on June 22 the Rose Theatre Trust was granted a judicial review of the Secretary of State's refusal to schedule the site of the Rose playhouse. The campaign's case was based on the allegation that the Secretary of State was acting unlawfully under the terms of the 1979 Ancient Monuments and Archaeological Areas Act. Subsequently the Rose Theatre Trust won a High Court injunction against Imry Merchant Developers preventing them from beginning work on the office block until the judicial review had been carried out. However, on July 3 the injunction was lifted by the High Court. On July 17 the High Court ruled that the Rose Theatre Trust had no standing in law to ask for a judicial review of the Secretary of State's decision. Mr. Justice Schiemann, in giving judgement, said: 'It seems to me that the decision not to schedule is one of those Government decisions in respect of which the ordinary citizen does not have sufficient interest to entitle him to obtain leave to move for a judicial review.' On the same day Imry Merchant Developers were the subject of a £314 million takeover by Marketchief, but it was stated that this would make no difference to the plans for the Rose playhouse site.

On July 25 the local planning authority, the London Borough of Southwark, approved the revised plans for the office block subject to 'a legally binding agreement with Imry Merchant, the developers, that archaeological supervision continues, that the remains are preserved and protected and that a public museum run by a third party is created.' With the revised plan for the office block approved and the preservation of the Rose theatre site ensured, the campaign had succeeded in saving the site, albeit not in the way that the Rose Theatre Trust would have wished.

The significance of the excavation of the Rose playhouse cannot be overstated. The archaeological excavations revealed parts of the outer and inner walls, the first stage of 1587 and the second stage of 1592. In addition, a substantial amount of archaeological evidence was found which, when interpreted, will reveal much about these poorly understood post-medieval structures: only one drawing of the Swan Theatre survives as pictorial evidence of playhouse interiors of Shakespeare's day. It will be some time before the report on the excavations of the Rose playhouse is complete and available for study, but from the present knowledge of the theatre's history, it is clear that it is a very important discovery. Stanley Wells, writing in *The Times Literary Supplement* (May 12–18, 1989), described its significance thus: 'Open by the Autumn of 1587, this was the fourth of London's theatres—after the Red Lion, the Theatre, and the Curtain—and the first to be built south of the Thames. In many respects it is the best documented of pre-Restoration theatres. It belonged to the financier Philip Henslowe whose son-in-law the great tragedian Edward Alleyn, founded Dulwich College ... the Rose saw first or early performances of a great range of plays by dramatists including Thomas Kyd, Christopher Marlowe, Robert Greene,

Thomas Heywood and Thomas Dekker. Here Alleyn had some of his greatest triumphs and Will Kemp raised laughter. In 1592 "Harey the vi"—presumably Shakespeare's *Henry VI, Part I*—drew the crowds, receiving sixteen performances and in 1593 "Titus & ondronicus" was a box office sensation. This was before the founding of the Lord Chamberlain's Men, with whom Shakespeare worked continuously from 1594. He is extremely likely to have acted at the Rose, and certainly must have seen plays from its yard or galleries. The discovery of the material remains of this theatre is an event of the highest importance for anyone interested in the history of English theatre and in the society and culture of Elizabethan England.'

Prehistory

Volume 54 (1988) of the *Proceedings of the Prehistoric Society* contains a most interesting report on the excavation of The Street House Wossit (the latter word explained by the excavator Blaise Vyner, in a summary account in *Current Archaeology* (Number 111), as 'An A. A. Milne-style shortening of "What is it?"'). This curious site, excavated between 1984 and 1986, is situated on cliff tops just north of Whitby. Over a surface which originally was ploughed was built what the excavator ultimately decided was a 'late Neolithic or early Bronze Age palisaded ritual enclosure.' The British Museum undertook the radio-carbon dating of the samples to provide dates which 'centre in the 18th century BC.' According to the summary, 'This palisaded enclosure would appear to belong to the very beginning of the second millennium. Beaker sherds were found in the construction levels as well as coarse wares which appear to be late neolithic.' Following the destruction of the palisaded enclosure there was a second phase. 'By this time the filling of the palisade trenches and the central pit had slumped, and the resulting depressions were filled with further deposits of rubble. This included cup-marked stones, which were noticeably absent from the initial back-filling. (An indication that cup-marked stones belong essentially to the Early Bronze Age?). At the same time a single cremation was deposited in a collared urn in the rubble at the centre of the site and traces of a second cremation were found at its north-eastern edge.'

A very different prehistoric site is that of Flag Fen, which won the Hepworth Heritage Award for 1988. Described by Francis Pryor, the excavator, in *Current Archaeology* (Number 110), this site was discovered in 1982 during the clearing of Fen drainage ditches. Carbon 14 dating indicates that the Late Bronze Age was the centre of the period of origin. English Heritage provided funding for excavation as part of a Fenland project prompted by the substantial drainage of the Fenlands. Bore hole surveys indicate that preserved wood covered an area of some 2.5 acres on either side of the dyke. From the sides of the dyke some five hundred pieces of wood had originally protruded which were discovered by archaeologists watching the cleaning process. Bronze Age pottery found amongst the upright pieces of wood suggested the possibility of a domestic site and, in the words of the summary, as the excavation progressed 'We were soon convinced that the up-rights were the roof and wall supports of a rectangular building—or buildings.' The excavators found long pieces of wood which they interpreted as collapsed roof purlins. Below the roof and walling material was found the latest floor level which 'had been dusted with sand and fine gravel and was composed of planks, wood chips and off-cuts. On it and within it we found numerous pot sherds, a few crudely bashed flints and pollen from wheat or barley.'

After subsequent seasons of excavation 'the layout of the building was becoming reasonably clear. There were two distinct rows of posts about 6 to 6.5 metres apart which formed the uprights of the external walls. Inside these there were two further rows of posts that had supported the roof; in other words, the building had a central "nave" and two aisles. Outside these (on the south side, if not on the north), was a further row of regularly spaced timbers that may have supported the eaves.' Continued investigation of the methods of construction and the various floor levels led to the conclusion that 'we were uncovering a Bronze Age drama: the building had collapsed at an early stage in its history, and two or three of the vertical timbers lay at an angle of roughly 45 degrees. They were about 2.5 metres long and one had fallen across a near-complete Bronze Age pot which lay crushed beneath it.' The finding of a coppiced tree 'demonstrated that the building had been erected when conditions were by no means completely waterlogged: water-loving trees or shrubs (for example alder and willow) grew in some places when the fen was slowly forming in the late second or early first millennium BC.'

It is estimated that there is about twenty five years' work still to be done at Flag Fen and therefore it is essential to keep the site wet so that the wood retains its shape. 'We therefore', said Francis Pryor, 'decided to build a large lagoon over the middle of the Bronze Age platform. The purpose of this is purely functional, but we have also turned it to educational use, by creating an island in the middle of the lagoon, the approximate shape of our Bronze Age island ... On this we have set model houses, and animals, and people, to give an idea of what we think it may originally have looked like.'

Another major discovery was that of a chariot burial at Kirkburn, North Humberside. The summary in *Current Archaeology* (Number 111) said of it: 'The unique feature of this burial is that it is buried with a complete coat of mail—by far the earliest so far discovered in Iron Age Britain. The chariot was buried with the wheels in the normal position with the body laid on top. The coat was then laid on top of the body—but upside down; the hem of the coat was across his chest, and the shoulder pieces over the legs. There were three little bronze toggles by the top, presumably the ends of the cord which fastened it. Apart from this however, the only other objects with the body were two groups of pig-bones—sadly no sword or other offensive weapons.'

This kind of burial contrasts with the very different disposal of the dead reported by John Musty in *Current Archaeology* (Number 113). He reports upon research into the large number of human skulls which have been found in the River Thames,

'including a group of over 100 from Strand-on-the-Green'. Research has found some 299 skulls surviving from the Thames between Oxford and London, with the main concentration between Richmond and Mortlake. Dating evidence suggests the prehistoric period as the time of deposition, perhaps associated with the metalwork of the same period found in the Thames. The Editor suggests that these skulls are 'simply evidence for the cult of the head, as was practised in Britain from the Neolithic right through to the Iron Age'.

Although for many people the fascination of archaeology lies in the discovery and investigation of specific objects, the archaeologist is often more concerned with the elucidation of new evidence suggesting how communities lived. To that end a number of wide-ranging archaeological surveys are being carried out. One reported in *Current Archaeology* (Number 113) by Keith Branigan was on the Hebridean island of Barra. Some seventy-eight new archaeological sites were discovered, of which forty were hut circles. It is noted that 'The most famous sites in the Hebrides are the magnificent Neolithic and Bronze Age ritual sites, and Barra has one of the finest, Dun Bharpa, a burial cairn of typical Hebridian type with a ring of orthostats forming the limits of the cairn. Dun Bharpa and a second cairn had long been known but two further cairns were also discovered by the survey, thus doubling the number.' For the Survey team from the Department of Archaeology at Sheffield University 'The most exciting discovery of all, however, were two large walls that were found buried beneath the blanket peat on the slopes below Dun Bharpa. Similar walls had been discovered beneath the peat in Western Ireland where they are thought to be Neolithic. These walls in Barra seem likely to be at least pre-Iron Age as they are sealed by the blanket peat which presumably was laid down in the wet conditions in the first millennium BC.' Although the hut circles could not be dated, it is suggested that the largest ones might be Iron Age while the smallest 'are in some respects similar to the shielings of Medieval or Post-Medieval dates.'

Roman Britain

An extensive summary of work carried out on sites of the Roman period is contained in *Britannia*, Volume XIX for 1988. From this volume may be noted extensive work on Hadrian's Wall, including at Denton Burn, Tyne and Wear. Here the excavation of some 49 metres of Hadrian's Wall was carried out in advance of road building. It is noted that 'The Wall was of broad gauge, with clay and rubble core surviving to a height of 0.96 m. although only seven facing-stones were *in situ*. There was evidence that the S. face had been plastered; at one place the imprint of seven courses was preserved on a slab of fallen plaster. Immediately behind the Wall masons' chippings were incorporated in a lightly-metalled surface up to 8.18 m. wide, carrying cart-ruts and apparently laid down soon after the Wall was built; above this was a second road-surface 5.56 m. wide containing a coin of A.D. 202–10. Silt had accumulated on this—before the collapse of the S. face. Neither road resembled the construction of the Military Way as known elsewhere.'

Work continued at the important Wall site of *Vindolanda* at Chesterholm, Northumberland, where it is reported that 'Most of the wooden tablets found in 1987 were of the stylus type; several were seen to carry an ink inscription by the filing-clerk written on the outside of the rim.' Other finds included 'the oak back of a flat brush measuring 22 by 18 cm. from the primary ditch and so dating before A.D. 90; 243 holes survive out of a probable total of c.505 and each appears to have held c.20 bristles (whose origin is not yet certain). There are attachment-holes at the four corners.' In addition a substantial quantity of leatherwork came from two Antonine ditches and some 490 shoes and boots were found.

In excavations at 16 Parliament Street, York, the South-east wall of the fortress and its rampart were found standing over 2 m. high near the south angle during construction work. The wall had a stepped plinth, similar to that seen nearby in 1976, and is thought to be of late third- or early fourth-century date. The rampart of clay and turf was part-sectioned to a depth of 0.80 m. The wall was reduced in the Anglo-Scandinavian period, when post-and-wattle buildings were erected against the outer face.

Across the Pennines recent excavations have clarified the topography of the Roman fort at Lancaster, while at Chester modern technology was pressed into service for the exploration of a Roman drain with a video camera. In Lincolnshire excavations in advance of the laying of a pipe-line led to the discovery at Swanpool of 'two poorly-preserved kilns of normal Swanpool type, sharing the same stoke hole. Wasters were mainly of coarse grey ware. Around lay some ditches and gullies (presumably for drainage), which also yielded wasters.' A survey of the south Lincolnshire fens 'has revealed over 50 sites yielding middle or late Iron Age sherds in the silt fens, an area previously thought to be deserted at that time; 185 sites produced evidence of Iron Age or Roman salt-production. Study of the Roman pottery, particularly the fine wares, suggested that the fenland settlements were more prosperous than those on the fen margins.'

At Old Stratford, Northamptonshire, 'the site of Priestly Regalia reported by Lysens (in 1818) as found in Windmill Field may have been identified by the discovery, in a field of that name just within the county, of a group of brooches and over 300 first- to fourth-century coins together with pottery and stonework, not far from the Deanshanger villa'. In the same county, the excavation of the Piddington villa site may be taken as representative of that class of building. The villa was first located in 1781. From aerial photographs and a field survey it is suggested that it is a courtyard villa extended at one side to include perhaps a bath-suite. A mosaic was destroyed in 1781, but 'surviving traces show that this had had a wide border of red tesserae and a centre panel; a small surviving fragment depicts a heart-shaped leaf with stalk'. It is also reported that 'Among the debris was painted plaster, some decorated with the pigment cinnabar. By 340–350 the villa was ruinous but still inhabited. Huge quantities of oyster-shells belong to

this phase (350–390) together with a corn dryer yielding charred peas and grain.'

There is no diminution in the number of coin hoards found. At Bletchley, Buckinghamshire, 'a hoard of 627 denarii down to Commodus (A.D. 186), is reported in a field between Bletchley and Little Brickhill'. In Hertfordshire important work was carried out at Verulamium, and it is also interesting to note that at Chells Manor 'during trial-trenching of a settlement site a hoard of 2,192 *Antoniniani* and 387 *denarii* was found in 1986, scattered from a plough-damaged jar. The hoard, buried soon after 260, contained several rare coins including issues of Balbinus and Pupienus (238), Pacatianus (248–9) and Saloninus as Augustus (260)'. At Sutton, Suffolk, 'a hoard of 204 denarii ranging from the Republic of Caligula was found in a wheel-made grey jar. This had been buried in the upper filling of an Iron Age ditch'. Discoveries in Norfolk included, at Great Walsingham, 'an extensive settlement or temple establishment is suggested by metal-detector finds, which include many coins from Claudius I to Theodosius I, three bronze statuettes of Mercury and evidence for bronze-working in the form of a miniature axe and a cylindrical object both left untrimmed from bivalve moulds'. At Snettisham, Norfolk, 'a hoard consisting of five British M staters, eight British L ('Whaddon Chase') staters of a new type, three uninscribed gold quarter-staters of a new type, 26 staters of British J ('Norfolk Wolf') and one silver Icenian coin (early Face Horse type) is reported.

Southern England was not short of coin hoards either. At Silchester 'a hoard containing 51 silver siliquae and fragments of siliquae down to Honorius (c. A.D. 402) together with three bronze fourth-century coins and seven whole or broken rings is reported', while at Whitchurch, also in Hampshire, 'a hoard of 34 Gallo-Belgic E staters and 108 British B staters' was found. On the Isle of White, at Bembridge Harbour some '27 coins probably from a scattered hoard were found in intertidal silt c.130 m offshore. Legible coins ranged from Domitian to Faustina II; the majority are sestertii and dupondii of Antoninus Pius and the two Faustinas.' Other coins were found at Fishbourne, while at Gurnard Bay 'a hoard of counterfeit lead-tin denarii of Lucius Verus and the two Faustinas were found on the foreshore 2 km east of Cowes, together with residues of copper-alloy smelting. The site lies c.300 m from a Roman building destroyed by coastal erosion in 1864.'

At an investigation at Billericay School, Essex, 'excavation in advance of building revealed cremations in vessels of late Iron Age or early Roman type together with shallow ditches, at least two wells and some fourth-century coins. The kiln found in 1977 was re-exposed for archaeomagnetic dating; the results, described as tentative, give a date between A.D. 43 and 100 (68% probability) or 150 (95%). The archaeological date was in the late second century.' At Colchester 'the east and north faces of the inturn of the city wall on the East side of the South-West Gate were located.' It is reported that 'traces of whitewash on the inner face of the city wall have been recorded at four sites; analysis of the first indicates at least 45 coats, suggesting repeated applications during the interval before the bank was built in the late second century. On evidence recovered at Culver Street a date of c. A.D. 65–80 is thought possible for the erection of the wall.'

In London a considerable amount of investigative work continues to be undertaken. At Dowgate House it was found that soil had been dumped in the late third or early fourth century probably for land-reclamation. 'These deposits yield much pottery, including glazed ware thought to be from Italy or the Eastern Mediterranean, together with over 100 shoes and sandals. These demonstrate the continued use of one-piece shoes well into the third century.' At the junction of 31–43 Mansell street and 1–7 Alie street was found 'a shallow ditch bounded by a cemetery. South of it, parallel or at right-angles, lay 85 inhumations, 16 of them gypsum burials and one in a tile-lined grave. The latter yielded three glass vessels, a bronze mirror and an anklet of jet and glass beads. Only a minority of the rest were accompanied, usually by personal ornaments or pottery vessels. In addition, 17 cremations were excavated, 4 of them in pits and 13 in urns, three of which had been placed in amphorae.' Across the Thames at Southwark interesting discoveries continue to be made: 'at Cherry Garden Pier in a small area of relatively high ground were a ditch and three cremations in urns; two were of infants, one of them with a small colour-coated beaker, a lamp-holder stamped STROBILI and a shale bracelet, the other with a poppy head beaker and lamp. The third was an unaccompanied adult.'

At Catherine Street, Exeter, 'the position and line of the NE defences of the legionary fortress, the only side hitherto uncertain, were confirmed at St. Catherine's Almshouses; they proved to run not quite parallel with the SW defences, inclining slightly outwards in the direction of the eastern angle.' In Dorset at Dorchester three inhumations in wooden coffins were found, 'one of them a decapitated female with head placed between the feet, while at Poundbury Cemetery a further 27 burials were investigated. 'All were in wooden coffins; one grave contained two coffins, the upper one holding a body much mutilated before burial. Only two burials yielded grave goods, one a bone comb and iron pin, the other a coin.' In Andover, Hampshire, 'a cemetery was further explored which was first located in 1982, when inhumations accompanied by hobnails, knives, a comb, bone bracelets and coins were examined. Three graves were excavated: (a) a large timber-mining pit containing a primary inhumation with hobnails and a flagon; a secondary unaccompanied burial had been inserted after the decay of the timber chamber. (b) An inhumation lacking grave-goods. (c) A decapitated inhumation with the skull between the legs, accompanied by hobnails, two knives, and the fragmentary bones of an infant.' At Meonstoke, Hampshire, further work at Shavards Farm 'identified the building as an aisled house to which a new east end had been added 2 m further out in the early fourth century. The new end-wall later collapsed outwards with some features still in position, including stone and tile bonding-courses and a window of three round-headed lights near the apex of the gable. The openings, each 1 m wide by 1.5 m high were framed by courses of re-used square tiles set in thick bands of mortar to give a red and white effect. Some time in

the mid fourth century the windows had been blocked with courses of flint and tile. The gable itself, poorly preserved, appeared to be steep-sided, as suggested by an angled line of tiles and mortar, allowing a height of c.15 m; the wall was 15 m long at its base. The discovery of tesserae and remains of quarter-round moulding above the level of the fallen wall may suggest the former existence of an upper storey.' At Canterbury, an excavation at 36–7 Stour Street revealed that in the dark earth sealing a Roman street was a sixth or seventh century gruben-used tile.

Medieval Period

A multi-million pound development programme is planned at Edinburgh Castle to facilitate access by tourists, at the same time separating them from the military and other activities of the Castle. The development programme has provided an opportunity for archaeological investigations at this very important monument. The work undertaken in 1988 was summarized in *Current Archaeology* (No 112), where it was stressed just how little has previously been known about the archaeology of the area, despite strong literary traditions. Finds included five sherds of Roman Samian ware as well as an early Roman brooch. There was also the remains of a comb dating from the sixth to tenth centuries A.D. and being possibly Pictish or Northumbrian, i.e. relating to either the native Din Eidyn or the Northumbrian Edwinesburch. It is reported that the 'excavation on Mills Mount in front of the gift shop has produced the unexpected evidence of Roman Iron Age as well as Dark Age Din Eidyn. The area produced over three metres depth of stratified deposits with the earliest surfaces being sealed by a hitherto unknown medieval approach road skirted by very rich midden deposits. A 14th century smithy was also discovered, complete with furnace, quenching trough and a sheet-iron lined tool box.' It is further noted that 'One area which aroused considerable public interest was another deep excavation outside the vaults where a mass burial of more than fourteen diseased hunting dogs was found dated c.1600.'

Work took place on the many ecclesiastical sites of the period, including excavations at Sandwell Priory in West Bromwich, Birmingham, which are described in *Current Archaeology* (No 113). The ground surface has produced over 700 worked flints of late Mesolithic type and heat-shattered pebbles, perhaps suggesting a Bronze Age burnt mound. On this ground surface was constructed Sandwell Priory, a small Benedictine monastery. The summary of the excavations points out that it never had more than four monks and was down to two at the time of its suppression in 1524. Nevertheless, the archaeologists found a building which suggested a somewhat grander existence. The first church dating to the mid twelfth century appears 'extremely odd, with a very elaborate east end but no nave. There was a long central choir flanked by two shorter chapels on each side—though the remains on the northern side were destroyed by the construction of a post-medieval country house. There were also elaborate north and south transepts off which the side chapels opened. However, despite the elaborate east end, there does not appear to have been a nave.' It is suggested that the reason for this may be connected with the activities of the founding family and the fact that the Priory's initial benefactor, William Fitz Guy de Opheni, Lord of the Manor of West Bromwich, is probably buried in the stone coffin which was found at the east end of the chancel near to the high altar. 'The coffin had been disturbed by a 19th century pit but it was probably originally covered by a life-sized stone effigy of a knight in chain mail, the head of which was found in demolition rubble near the coffin.'

Most of the graves in the church were found in the south transept 'which was presumably the family burial ground'. Burials took place here throughout the Priory's lifetime and included men, women and children. The specialist examination of the skeletons suggests 'that a number of them have a metopic suture. This is an abnormal joint down the middle of the forehead and occurs in only 9% of the modern population. As nearly 50% of the burials in the south transept had this condition, it looks as if they were related. Can we not suppose that these are the lords of the manor and their families who paid for the building of the Priory and have used the south transept as their chantry chapel?'

The archaeological evidence throws an interesting light on the date of 1180, traditionally the date when the grant to the monks by the founder was confirmed by his overlord Gervase Pagnell, Lord of Dudley. From the evidence recovered it may be that the Priory was constructed somewhat earlier. 'To the north of the church underlying the later buildings were some timber posts, presumably the timber east range. One of these posts with its bark intact, gave a felling date of 1159/1160.' In the middle of the thirteenth century there was a major rebuilding. 'This was possibly centred on the collapse of the central bell tower. In the survey of 1526 there is no mention of a tower, but instead there is a bell frame between the nave and chancel.' At about this time various other changes were made, including the side chapel being blocked off at the east end and probably demolished so that only the long central choir remained. 'The blocking wall contained architectural details including a carving of a lamb and cross. A date for this—a *terminus post quem*—is given by a wooden plank from a grave which underlies the blocking wall and which gave a dendro date of 1252. Tracery from a window in the new wall has been dated to around 1300.' Also about this time the nave was constructed which had the effect of converting the structure to a more normal type of church. 'We should perhaps remember that the nave was for the laity and in this case the laity were living a mile away in the village of West Bromwich where they had their own Parish Church. Many of the Oxford and Cambridge colleges were designed quite deliberately without a nave: was Sandwell Priory also designed in the first stage with no nave?'

The burials are of particular interest in that one 'had a remarkable graffito on it in the form of a Nine Men's Morris Board crudely scratched on the upper surface of the coffin adjacent to the head'. Many of the coffins were well preserved because of the very wet nature of the site and this meant that leather and textiles also survived. The nature of the burials were of interest in that 'Many were buried with long staves, 6 foot long and two inches thick. Were these pilgrims' staves? Probably not pilgrims who had died while visiting the church, but perhaps the sign that the person concerned had been on a pilgrimage. Some also had a smaller wand, often lying across the staff— the sign of a second pilgrimage? There were also three boot burials. Two had ordinary ankle length boots, but one had splendid thigh length boots or leggins. Were these also the sign of a pilgrim, who had walked far? In many cases the shroud had also survived, often rather coarse, like a string vest.'

Turning to Northern Ireland, excavations at Deer Park Farm, described in *Current Archaeology* (No 113), 'revealed a long sequence of occupation in the Early Christian period from perhaps about A.D. 600 to 1000. The crucial episode of build-up occurred at around A.D. 750 when the occupants decided to heighten their damp, midden-filled rath, which had already seen several phases of re-modelling. The bank of the rath was used to contain the build-up for the mound. The houses in the rath were then roughly dismantled in sequence over a lengthy period. Door-frames and perhaps also roofing poles were salvaged for re-use, but the wicker walls were either encased in the build-up or were pushed over and covered. These were preserved because the base of the mound became water-logged, while the mass of organic midden material already collected in the rath increased the dampness. In the lower, undrained northern section there was about 1·5 m. of preserved organic material.' The significance of the water-logged nature of the site is stressed. 'As a result of this unique preservation we are able to describe for the first time exactly how the walls of an Early Christian circular wicker hut were actually built.' Furthermore, 'It can even be suggested that the construction methods used in these circular wicker huts of Early Christian Ireland represent the end of a prehistoric tradition of house-building which was once more widespread in these islands.' The account of the surviving evidence of construction and material culture demonstrate again just how important to the archaeologist is the survival of waterlogged sites.

Post-Medieval Period

A comprehensive summary of work relating to post-medieval Britain may be found in *Post-Medieval Archaeology* Vol. 22 for 1988. Amongst the investigations undertaken was the recording of the Poulett family vault at Hinton St. George, Somerset. 'The Poulett Family Chapel was rebuilt in 1814 by Sir Jeffry Wyatville for John, 4th Earl Poulett. Since 1814 the vault has been entered through Wyatville's Hamstone portico on the W. external face of the Poulett pew. It is enclosed by a contemporary paved and railed courtyard. Studded oak doors open on to a staircase leading down to a large brick room.' An account follows of the vaults and the coffins therein. A particularly notable coffin is 'the richly-decorated triple-shell coffin of John, 1st Earl Poulett (died 1743). The gilt coffin furniture consists of ornate grips and grip plates decorated with winged cherubs, surmounted by an Earl's coronet. Identical gilt fittings along the side(s) are enhanced with sunburst escutcheons.'

A complete contrast was the excavation of Clogh Oughter Castle in Co. Cavan. 'It is on a tiny island in Lough Oughter and played an important part in the 1641 rebellion until its siege and subsequent slighting by the Cromwellian forces in 1653.' A large number of objects were discovered, most being of seventeenth century date. 'Many broken fragments of iron canonballs bear witness to heavy bombardment during the 1653 siege, and other finds of a military nature include musket balls of lead, a flintlock, and iron and bronze spurs. A cast-iron fireback found in the rubble probably also dates to the early 17th-century rebuilding. Other finds of a domestic nature include 16th/17th-century pottery (including Crannog ware), metal skillets, candlesticks, iron keys, knives and harp pegs. An unusual discovery was half a papal bulla of lead.'

At Merchants Road, Galway, an excavation was undertaken in advance of redevelopment work during which one of the bastions and part of the outer wall where it joined the bastion were recovered. These relate to the strengthening of the eastern defences of the city in the 1640s. 'The majority of the pottery is post-medieval in date. Some is of local manufacture but the bulk consists of north-Devon sgraffito and gravel-tempered wares, tin-glazed earthenwares and 19th-century transfer-printed wares. Spanish wares included amphora sherds and fragments of Merida-type wares. Twenty-seven clay pipe bowls and a large number of stem fragments, most of which came from disturbed contexts, were found. They date from the late 17th to the 19th centuries, and are English, Dutch and Irish in origin. Other finds included two tokens, a bronze needle, a decorated bone scoop, a perforated, polished bone disk, the remains of five human skulls and some glass, wood, leather and iron objects.'

At Poole in Dorset, investigation of the Studland Bay wreck continued, with work concentrating 'on the starboard side of a Spanish merchant vessel of *c*.1500, about 23 m. long. The 1987 season completed the excavation of *c*. 75% of the main coherent part of the wreck site.' Among the 189 finds recorded, there were many small fragments of wood; in addition, 'more Iberian coarsewares and Isabela polychrome pottery have been recovered, and Columbia plain tin-glazed pottery was found for the first time. Other finds include a glass fragment probably of Mediterranean origin.'

The excavation took place in London at the City of London Boys' School on the Victoria Embankment. 'Features recorded on top of medieval dumping were sealed by a burnt horizon of late 17th-century date, probably from the 1666 Fire. The area to the S. of the site appeared to have been reclaimed from the River Thames around this time, and an associated timber rivetment was recorded at the S. limit of the excavation. The rivetment is thought to represent the construction of the new wharves during the post-fire rebuilding along the waterfront in this area. The new land behind the rivetment was consolidated by the driving of several hundred timber piles; some of these were re-used from up to five 17th/18th-century

sailing vessels and a number are painted and/or decoratively carved.'

At Poole in Dorset excavations disclosed 'a simple rectangular building on the frontage of Thames Street, constructed on reclaimed land of *c*.1500. This building, which had been extended, corresponds with cartographic evidence of the 18th-century Free School. Beneath the reclamation make-up was a beach containing over sixty timbers from a boatyard store, which were being seasoned in the tidal sand. The analysis of this deposit in conjunction with the National Maritime Museum will provide important information on coastal craft of *c*.1500.' In Scotland, at York Place, Aberdeen, an excavation revealed 'disarticulated human remains from at least three individuals in a beach-sand deposit. In 1647 Aberdeen suffered severely from plague, and a contemporary reference suggests burial in the sands. This spot is traditionally held to be one of the main burial areas. These bones were probably disturbed during building work nearby, possibly in 1891, when sewer construction is said to have uncovered a large number of skeletons.'

From Ryhall, Stamford, Leicester, there is a report of the discovery by workmen in February 1987 of one gold and 3,219 silver coins ranging in date from Elizabeth I to Charles I. Following the discovery an excavation was mounted to assist the coroner to determine whether the hoard was treasure trove. 'The excavation revealed a further 42 silver coins associated with the remains of a rectangular oak box, 0.34×0.21 m., with a minimum height of 80 mm. and minimum thickness of 5 mm. Some of the coins were still stacked within the box and impressions of others were discernible on the surface of the base. The box had been placed in a shallow pit $0.38 \times 0.30 \times 0.16$ m. deep. To the S.W. ground disturbance, possibly caused by a hedge line or tree, was noted, suggesting that the hoard had been buried near a landmark, perhaps to facilitate recovery. Examination of the coins at the British Museum revealed that several had been struck from the same dies. This is the largest Civil War period hoard of coins discovered this century, with a face value on deposition of £158.0.6d. The hoard was pronounced to be treasure trove at Oakham Crown Court on December 4, 1987.'

In advance of road-widening, excavations were undertaken in Old Castle Lane, Barnstaple, Devon, which revealed 'a second 17th-century pottery kiln. This kiln resembled that discovered in Potter's Lane in size and design. However in this instance the construction used fully-fired bricks from the firing chamber and flue walls, with large tiles from the chamber floor. These tiles respected a central pedestal within the chamber; a further two pedestals set on the tiled floor may have been later additions. Pottery waste-dumps filled both the kiln and its associated stoke pit. These included both fine sgraffito and domestic earthenware, the former suggesting a *terminus ante quem* of the mid to late 17th-century for the kiln's last firing.' As to the other kiln in Potter's Lane, excavation indicated it to be 'a double-flue updraught kiln of early to mid 17th-century date. The kiln consists of a sub-circular chamber with a one-piece clay base, opening out into two flues separated by a central pedestal. The walls are constructed of random, partially-fired clay bricks. Traces of the collapsed arches survive.' From a further description of the kiln it is noted that 'In all a total of approximately 3·5 tonnes of pottery was recovered from the excavation, amongst which are most known North Devon vessel types and some hitherto unrecorded forms. Other finds include an almost complete stamped ceramic fire dog and several relief-glazed tiles.'

On the theme of ceramic production, at Ridding Lane in Wednesbury, West Midlands, excavations in advance of development 'revealed two groups of pits containing 16th- and 17th-century Cistercian-type ware beakers and glazed coarse-ware bowls, including wasters and saggars, which suggest the existence of a kiln on the site. Wednesbury's pottery industry is well-documented from the 15th-century onwards, but no kiln has yet been located.' In London, at 38–46 Albert Embankment, Lambeth, an excavation on a redevelopment site 'in the vicinity of a pottery recorded on maps of 1746, indicated that the major development of the site took place in the 17th–18th centuries and was probably associated with the pottery. Large quantities of discarded kiln furniture and wasters were found—of Delft ware in the earlier levels and stoneware in the later levels. Some fragments of porcelain indicate its early manufacture on the site. One sherd had been used as a test piece with numbered samples of glazes applied and subsequently fired to test their suitability for further use.'

SCIENCE AND DISCOVERY, 1988–89

Armenian earthquake.—At 0741 U.T. (Universal Time) on December 7, 1988 a severe earthquake devastated northern Armenia, a republic of the Soviet Union. Although the area is prone to earthquakes, the tremor was the strongest ever experienced in the region.

The devastated region lies in the Lesser Caucasus, and is part of a long belt of mountains extending from Gibraltar to the Himalayas. The belt started to develop about 150 million years ago as the crustal plates carrying Africa, Arabia and India collided with the Eurasian plate. The area is dominated by a north-south compression in the rocks due to the continental collision between the Arabian plate and the Eurasian plate, which are converging at a rate of about 3 cm. per year. The area is also characterized by reverse faulting and folding associated with large strike slip faulting.

Armenia lies in a very active earthquake zone and there are a number of shocks each year. Tremors of magnitude 6·9, the magnitude of the main shock on December 7, occur at least once a month. They do not usually attract attention because they occur in sparsely populated areas. On this occasion the destruction was on a large scale because the epicentre of the earthquake lay at a depth of 10 km., just a few kilometres north-west of the town of Spitak, which was virtually destroyed. Severe damage was also caused to the towns of Leninakan and Kirovakan. Official figures put the death toll at 25,000, with about half a million people left homeless. Deaths, injuries and damage were also reported in Iran and Turkey. A second tremor of magnitude 5·9 was recorded 4 min. 20 sec. after the main shock. A French-Soviet team of seismologists and geologists visited the area to monitor the after-shocks and to map the surface breaks. The fault scarp was mapped for 13 km. and showed a reverse dislocation of up to 1·6 metres.

Auroral display.—The most spectacular auroral display of the last half-century was visible throughout most of the world on the night of March 13, 1989. The diplay was seen as far south as Texas in the northern hemisphere, and the corresponding display in the southern hemisphere was seen as far north as Queensland, Australia. The aurora was only the visible sign of a magnetic disturbance caused by solar activity during the previous days. Solar activity peaks at approximately eleven-year intervals and the current peak is expected during 1989–90. Already the cycle is rivalling the strongest on record, a record peak of activity which occurred in 1957.

As far as the display of March 13 is concerned, the first signs of what was to occur became evident on March 6 when a large and complex group of sunspots appeared on the Sun's eastern rim. Intense solar flares were seen in the region of the spots on March 6, 9 and 10. The event on March 9 was spectacular: an observer at the National Solar Observatory at Sunspot, New Mexico, remarked that he had never seen anything like it. By March 10 the giant sunspot group was approaching the centre of the Sun's visible disc, pointing directly towards the Earth. A giant flare, the largest flare ever observed, erupted from the spot group on March 12 and it ejected particles which were subsequently intercepted by the Earth. This caused a severe disturbance in the Earth's magnetic field, creating havoc with communications, and subsequently caused the auroral display.

Auroral activity is limited usually to high latitudes but on occasions when the Earth's magnetic field is grossly distorted, the band of visibility moves to lower latitudes and the aurora becomes visible in regions where it is not normally seen. Magnetometer readings taken on March 12 showed that the Earth's magnetic field was in turmoil. An observer in Northern Ireland reported seeing an aurora in the early hours of the morning of March 13. During the daylight hours radio communications were chaotic. At nightfall, about 1900 U.T. (Universal Time), the aurora could be seen from the south of England. At its peak of activity, it filled the southern half of the sky. Perspective caused the rays to appear to come from a single point in the sky, producing what is known as a corona. Activity was observed all night, and as the belt of darkness moved westwards the aurora became visible in America. In the James Bay area of Canada it was reported that the magnetic effects of the activity were strong enough to cause failures in the electricity supply.

Brown dwarf discovered.—There have been many claims of identification of brown dwarf stars in the past but none have been substantiated. Brown dwarfs are what one may call failed stars because they do not contain enough mass for nuclear reactions to start in their cores. If brown dwarfs exist in large numbers then they may make up the dark matter in our galaxy. From studies of the motions of stars in the disc of the Milky Way, it is known that there exists about twice the amount of matter that can be observed optically.

David Latham, of the Harvard-Smithsonian Center for Astrophysics, and colleagues at the Tel Aviv University, Israel, and Geneva Observatory, Switzerland, have been running a project for over ten years to survey standard stars and establish their radial velocities. In the course of this work they found by accident an object which appears to be a companion star to the star known as HD 114762. The companion star is in orbit round HD 114762 but it could not be seen. The orbiting object was detected because of the effect of its behaviour on the main star, which moved in a cyclic manner with a period of 84 days. This implies that the companion is in an orbit similar to that of Mercury around the Sun. The low velocity amplitude of the displacement implies that it has a mass of about 11 times that of the planet Jupiter, or about 1 per cent that of the Sun. This mass puts the star into the category of a brown dwarf or a very large planet. In this case it is thought to be unlikely that the object is a planet because the inclination of the orbit to the line of sight is unknown and so the mass may be much larger than the lower limit quoted.

The discovery of one brown dwarf does not prove that all the matter unaccounted for in our galaxy is in the form of such objects. However, the discovery should provide the incentive for others to follow up the work with larger and more sophisticated equipment.

Chiron a comet?—The discovery in 1977 of a minor planet circling the Sun at a distance beyond that of Saturn caused quite a stir. One school of thought suggests that this object, named Chiron, could be one of a series of bodies with similar orbits. This theory would imply the existence of a second minor planet belt, similar to the one between Mars and Jupiter. However, no further objects have been discovered, although Charles Kowal, an astronomer who has carried out a major survey, says that it is still not known whether Chiron is unique or the largest member of a population of such objects. An alternative idea that Chiron was a dormant cometary nucleus in the deep freeze of the outer solar system has been considered, and observations over the last few years indicate that this is likely to be the case.

In February 1988, Chiron suddenly brightened up by about 0·6 magnitude. The brightness persisted for at least a month, suggesting possible cometary activity. This idea was strengthened in April when it was found that the object had developed a coma. The coma was recorded on a CCD (charge-coupled device) image on April 9 and 10 using the 4 metre reflector at Kitt Peak, Arizona. It is assumed that the coma was formed by dust and carbon dioxide escaping from the surface of Chiron. Idependently, Schelte J. Bus and colleagues at the Lowell Observatory in Arizona carried out a series of observations over the six-hour rotational period of Chiron and discovered brightness variations during the rotation. When the experiment was repeated, a corresponding but brighter light curve was found. These results confirmed those obtained at the University of Hawaii.

All this data gives very strong evidence for a cometary origin. If Chiron is found to be a true comet, then it will be the largest to have been identified. It has a diameter of approximately 180 km., compared with the average diameter of 16 km. of Halley's Comet.

Close encounter with minor planet.—Henry E. Holt, a retired geologist, spends much of his time helping Eugene and Carolyn Shoemaker in their search for near-Earth asteroids. He identified short trails on two exposures made on March 31, 1989 using the Palomar 45 cm. Schmidt telescope. Of principal concern were the trails from a fast-moving object also recorded on the photographs. By comparing the trails with those on follow-up exposures made on April 2, 3 and 4, Holt recognized a dramatic slowing-down in the motion against the star background. This was interpreted as the motion of an object which was travelling almost directly away from the Earth. Using Holt's observations and a further one taken on April 9 with the 150 cm. reflector at Harvard College Observatory, Brian Marsden, of the Minor Planet Center at Cambridge, Massachusetts, calculated that the object was in a near elliptical orbit inclined at 5°

to the ecliptic and was circling the Sun in 1·03 years. On March 22 it passed within 690,000 km. of the Earth. This is less than twice the distance to the Moon, and makes the encounter the closest in recorded history for any minor planet or comet.

It is estimated that the minor planet, designated 1989FC, has an absolute magnitude of 21, i.e. the brightness it would have when it is 1 A.U. (astronomical unit) from the Earth and Sun. (1 A.U. is the mean distance between the Earth and the Sun.) This is extremely faint and implies that the planet cannot be very large. The reason it was not picked up on its approach to the Earth was that it came from approximately the direction of the Sun. The predicted size depends on the type of the asteroid. If it were a stony body, a diameter of about 200 metres has been suggested, but if it were a darker carbonaceous type the diameter may be twice that value. These values make the object quite small compared with other 'Earth-crossing' minor planets. Even so, if impact with the earth had taken place the effects would have been disastrous.

Cold fusion controversy.—The scientific sensation of the year was the announcement in March 1989 by Stanley Pons of the University of Utah and Martin Fleischmann of the University of Southampton, and independently by Stephen E. Jones and colleagues at the Brigham Young University in Utah, that they had produced continuous power by nuclear fusion in a test-tube at room temperature. The experimenters placed a rod of palladium metal wrapped with platinum wire into a test-tube filled with deuterium (heavy hydrogen). An electric current was then passed through the cell. Deuterium nuclei, called deuterons, collected on the palladium and became so tightly packed that they moved through the lattice of the metal and fused. The scientists claimed that the output of energy was four times the power supplied. In addition to the heat generated, neutrons and tritium were produced, indicating that fusion had taken place.

The traditional method of communicating scientific discoveries is by submitting a paper to a reputable journal, which referees and checks the work. This discovery was announced in the newspapers, with accounts in the *Wall Street Journal* and the *Financial Times*, and at a press conference held at the University of Utah. Subsequently, other establishments tried to duplicate and confirm the work and claims of success and failure appeared in the newspapers and in scientific literature throughout the spring of 1989. By the middle of the year, the consensus of opinion was that the original claims could not be substantiated. The evidence does not prove that the observations of cold fusion were wrong, but much of the scientific community seems inclined to dismiss the work because they cannot with confidence replicate the experiments and results.

Dinosaurs at the Poles.—The traditional view that dinosaurs were creatures that inhabited only tropical and sub-tropical regions has been seriously undermined over the last few years. Australian palaeontologists working in south-east Australia have discovered fossils of dinosaurs that lived about 130 to 105 million years ago. At this time, the early Cretaceous period, Australia was situated much nearer the South Pole and temperatures averaged 5°C and probably fell to −6°C. Even during the summer months the weather would have been cold and wet.

The Australian scientists identified three or four species of plant-eating ornithod dinosaur called hypsilophodons, three species of meat-eating dinosaur (theropods), flying reptiles (pterosaurs), freshwater reptiles (plesiosaurs) and freshwater turtles. They were all relatively small creatures, the largest being 2 metres high. For many months these animals must have lived in darkness or semi-darkness and there has been speculation that the creatures may have developed extra large eyes and visual acuity. It is possible that during the winter months they may have hibernated or reduced their levels of activity in some other way. They could have migrated long distances to avoid the worst of the winter, although this is thought to be unlikely because there was no shortage of vegetation during that period.

The discovery in Australia supports the work carried out by American scientists, who have found similar evidence in the Arctic of dinosaurs having inhabited non-tropical regions. Workers from the U.S. Geological Survey reported in 1987 that dinosaur fossils had been found in northern Alaska, where conditions would have been similar to those in Australia. Until recently palaeontologists had assumed that in Cretaceous times the Arctic and Antarctic were warm and so the discovery that dinosaurs lived in these regions would not have been surprising. However, work during the last few years on fossils of vegetation and invertebrates in the polar regions, and other indicators, have shown that temperatures near to the Poles during the cretaceous period was quite low and reached at the most to 12°C.

Dinosaur egg fossil.—Thousands of dinosaur remains have been found at the Cleveland-Lloyd quarry in Utah. The latest find is the fossilized remains of a dinosaur's egg, which was still in the oviduct of the mother at the time of her death some 150 million years ago, in late Jurassic times. At that period the area of the quarry was a shallow lake or marsh and it is possible that the dinosaur became trapped in the mud and subsequently died. Alternatively, some form of illness might have prevented the egg being laid.

The egg was examined by a team led by Karl Hirsch of the University Museum in Boulder, Colorado. The team found that the egg was broken but the two halves remained attached. Computerized axial tomography scans have shown what was possibly an early embryo in one half of the egg. The team thinks that the egg was broken in the oviduct during the mother's death and that the two halves held together until they began to fossilize. It has been estimated that the original shape of the egg was elliptical and that it was approximately 110 mm. long and 55 mm. wide, with a volume of about 175 cc. The team has shown that the egg had an outer secondary layer of shell. This is a pathological sign which is familiar in modern reptiles and indicates that there was a delay in laying the egg. There are signs that at the time when the egg was broken the shell was still pliable: the shell is distorted and has inverted curvature in places.

It has not been possible to identify what type of dinosaur was responsible for the egg because the egg could not be linked directly with any particular skeleton. Remains of several types of dinosaur have been found in the quarry but it is thought that the theropod *Allosaurus* could well be responsible.

Dinosaur extinction theory.—About a decade ago the discovery that Cretaceous-Tertiary boundary layers of rock were rich in iridium, a relatively rare element in the Earth's crust, suggested an explanation for the extinction of the dinosaurs. The amount of iridium present in the layers of rock corresponds with the iridium content of some extraterrestrial bodies. This led to the formulation of a theory that a large body some 10 km. in diameter had collided with the Earth about 65 million years ago, producing conditions which killed the dinosaurs. Although the theory has had much support, there has been strong opposition from some geologists who claim that the origin of the iridium is terrestrial and that the rock layers are of volcanic origin.

Recent work by chemists Meixun Zhao and Jeffrey Bada at the Scripps Institute of Oceanography at the University of California at San Diego, seems to give support to the impact theory. They have found amino acids in the sediments at Stevns Klint, Denmark, which are exceedingly rare on the Earth. These amino acids are, however, found in carbonaceous chondrites, relatively rare types of meteorite rich in organic compounds. The two amino acids identified, α-amino isobutyric acid and racemic isovaline, were isolated using standard chromatographic techniques. The latter compound was found to exist in both right-and left-handed forms, a result which would not be expected if the sample had been biologically contaminated.

Despite this discovery, the case for the iridium having an extraterrestrial source is still not certain. The amount of the acids and their spatial distribution within the sediments is surprising when one considers the conditions that would have obtained at the time of an impact. In addition, the amount of α-amino isobutyric acid is about five times the maximum one would expect to find in carbonaceous chondrites. Zhao and Bada consider that this would not invalidate the impact theory if the impacting body were a comet, because the elements which compose amino acids are far more abundant in comets than in meteorites. However, one point that requires explanation is the fact that the amino acids were found just above the Cretaceous-Tertiary boundary layers, not in the boundary clay itself.

Another flaw in the impact theory of the extinction of the dinosaurs is the lack of evidence pointing to the location of the crater which a 10 km. object might be expected to cause.

Recent studies have put forward the idea that what is known as the 'Manson Structure', situated in Iowa, might be this crater. Scientists have been aware of the existence of the crater since the 1960s but had not been able to date it accurately before; a value of 61 millions years with an uncertainty of 18 million years was the best estimate. Now Mick Kunk of the U.S. Geological Survey has produced an argon-40 and argon-39 isotope date of 66 million years, to within a few million years. The crater is at present buried under 30 metres of glacial till but at the end of the Cretaceous period it would have lain under a shallow sea.

The main objection to the theory identifying the Manson Structure as the crater of the meteorite that led to the dinosaurs' extinction is that an impact in shallow water or on dry land could not have generated the huge tsunami known to have occurred in Texas at that time. A suggestion has been put forward that the tsunami was generated in the open ocean. Possible explanations are that it was generated by a second impact or by a submarine landslide triggered by the impact in Iowa. There is no doubt about the severity of the tsunami. An unusual sandstone bed, 70 cm. thick in places, has been found sandwiched between strata of mudstone. This layer has been found to be packed with shell fragments, pellets of clay minerals and lumps of mudstone.

Studies of the Cretaceous-Tertiary boundary clays have revealed not only high levels of iridium but also quantities of soot far greater than would have been present under normal conditions. What is significant about the soot is that at a variety of locations throughout the world the carbon concentration is constant and the isotopic composition is the same. This indicates that the soot came from a global fire. All this evidence strengthens the case for an impact being the cause of the extinction of the dinosaurs.

Earth's magnetic field changes.—Periodic magnetic reversals in the Earth's magnetic field have been recognized for a long time. These reversals have been identified by the direction of the magnetism left in rocks when they were formed. The changes are thought to occur fairly rapidly, geologically speaking. In the same way, any small changes in the strength of the overall magnetic field are recorded in the rocks. At the moment, typical rates of change in the direction of the magnetic field are about a few degrees per century. Changes in the strength of the field are attributed to internal sources and are of the order of hundreds of gammas per century.

The behaviour of transitional fields during geomagnetic reversals has been one of the principal concerns of the palaeomagnetist for some time. The Miocene lava flows on the Californian-Oregon border have been under close study since the 1960s and recently have been reinvestigated by researchers from the U.S. Geological Survey, the University of California at Santa Cruz and the Université des Sciences et Techniques at Montpellier. Two members of the group, Robert Coe and Michel Prévot, undertook a detailed extension of this study and identified more rapid rates of change in the Oregon lava flows than have hitherto been found anywhere. Coe and Prévot considered every other possibility that might explain

the results, but none were satisfactory. The observations are straightforward and the techniques used to measure the magnetic fields are standard. In addition, fields measured in lava flows are considered to be the easiest to determine. Nevertheless, the scientists realize that the results they have obtained are virtually unbelievable. The nub of the problem is whether the observed changes are true records of magnetic field changes. If they are, there will have to be a drastic reappraisal of palaeomagnetic theories.

Echidna's electro-receptors.—*Whitaker's Almanack 1989* included a report of the discovery of electro-receptors in the bill of the platypus by research workers at Monash University, Melbourne, Australia. Following their success in the study of the platypus, the researchers turned their attention to the echidna, the only mammal apart from the platypus to lay eggs and suckle its young, and noticed similar structures in its snout.

The researchers electrically stimulated small areas of the echidna's snout and recorded the transmission of the resulting nervous activity to the brain. The mammal's receptors are so sensitive that they can detect fields as weak as one millivolt per centimetre but the response is not so vigorous as that of the platypus. Also, the nerve fibres in the echidna are smaller and did not react when stimulated. The echidna's system seems to work best in alternating electric fields at about 20 hertz, whereas the platypus' system peaks at 100 hertz.

Work is still being carried out on the way the animal uses these abilities when searching for food. It is thought that the echidna's electro-receptors enable it to detect electrical signals given off by ants and worms, but the manner in which it does this is not yet known.

Europe's meteoritic crater.—One of the principal features of the surfaces of the non-gaseous bodies in our solar system is the high concentration of impact craters. The Earth would have similar features but for the rapidity with which erosion takes place and removes evidence of such surface features in what is geologically speaking a relatively short time. Even so, over the last few decades there has been a dramatic increase in the number of meteoritic scars discovered and currently over 100 such features are known. Study of photographs taken from space has revealed circular features which could not have been identified from the surface. One such circular feature, about 320 km. in diameter, has been discovered in Czechoslovakia and identified from photographs taken by the Meteosat 2 weather satellite.

Michael Papagiannis and Farouk El-Baz of Boston University identified the structure, which is centred approximately on the city of Prague, and have named it the Praha Basin. It is estimated that the impact which caused the Praha crater took place about 15 million years ago. The researchers have suggested that a meteoroid of about 80 km. in diameter was responsible. If this is the case, the explosion produced by the impact would have been a million million times more powerful than the explosion of the atomic bomb at Hiroshima. An explosion of such magnitude would have generated a huge cloud of dust and this would have had a marked effect on the Earth's weather. Moldavite tektites, glassy pebbles known to be associated with major impacts at other locations throughout the world, had been found in the past near an arc coincident with what is now identified as the southern rim of the crater, and investigations will no doubt reveal further evidence of the impact.

The Praha feature is the third large scar of possible impact origin in central Europe. The other two are the Rieskessel (24 km. in diameter) and the Steiheim Basin (3·4 km. in diameter), both of which are in Germany. Both are estimated to be approximately 14·8 million years old.

Evolution theory upset.—It has been accepted for a long time that the Milky Way galaxy was formed when a spherical cloud of gas collapsed under its own gravity. The collapse left a spherical halo of globular clusters encasing the spiral structure of the galaxy. There are about 125 globular clusters in the halo, each containing tens of thousands or millions of stars. The conventional theory holds that the Milky Way was formed over a period of about 200 million years, and this rapid formation implies that all the globular clusters should have approximately the same age. Recent work has upset this relatively simple theory.

Michael Bolte, of the Dominion Observatory in Victoria, Canada, has studied the globular clusters NGC 288 and 362 and found that the former is two thousand million years older, and the latter two thousand million years younger, than other clusters in the galaxy. A colleague of Bolte, Peter Stetson, focused his attention on another cluster, Palomar 12, and found it to be five thousand million years younger. These values have been confirmed by other researchers. The results have been made possible because of the use of charge-coupled devices (CCDs), which are so sensitive that more detailed and more accurate results can be achieved than was possible using photographic plates.

If further research confirms that the clusters have such a large range of ages, the standard theory for the formation of galaxies will no longer hold. Bruce Carney of the University of North Carolina claims that the work he has carried out on 1,500 single widely-spaced stars, which account for 99 per cent of the stars in the halo, agrees with Bolte and Stetson's findings. So do the results of recent, unpublished, work carried out at Yale University.

There has been a rush of new theories to explain the results but as yet there is no consensus of opinion. A growing number of astronomers accept the idea that any substructure in a protogalaxy is likely to evolve over a long period of time into small systems of stars, such as globular clusters or dwarf galaxies, before progressively larger systems such as the Milky Way develop.

Factorizing high numbers.—A team of computer scientists from the United States, Netherlands and Australia has broken all previous records by finding two large prime factors for a 100 digit number. The project organizers used a method known as a quadratic sieve. This discovers factors of a given number by finding two numbers that, when squared and divided into the original number, leave the same remainder. Once the two numbers have been found, the factors can be calculated. This method is like using a sledge hammer to crack a nut if the number is low, but for very large numbers it is the fastest method known. An advantage of the method is that the work can be distributed over a large number of computers. A computer at the Digital Equipment Corporation in Palo Alto, California, did much of the basic work while computers elsewhere shared the rest of the calculation. By the 26th day of the exercise enough data had been collected to factorize a 100 digit number into prime factors containing 41 and 60 digits.

In itself this discovery is of interest to the mathematician, but it also has serious implications for the security of some cryptographic codes used by government agencies and industry. The ability to factorize high numbers provides a method for breaking security codes which are derived from a widely-used cryptographic system. This system is based on the fact that although large prime numbers can be computed easily, factorizing the product of two such numbers has been impractical. Each user of the system chooses two large prime numbers and publishes the product. A message is converted into a series of numbers by a conventional mathematical method and is then encoded by a mathematical process which is based on the published number. If the number can be factorized then the code can be broken easily. In the past the security of the code has been based on the fact that it would take too long, millions of years, to factorize the published number. Now it can be done in less than a year and a new method of coding will have to be devised.

Great attractor or great wall?—All the galaxies in our region of the universe appear to be travelling in the same direction. In order to explain this, astronomers have put forward the idea that there is a large concentration of mass whose gravitational pull is causing this particular motion. This mass has been referred to as the 'great attractor'. To produce the observed motion (about 600 km. per second relative to the overall expansion of the universe) would require a mass 10^{16} times the mass of the Sun and situated about 200 million light years away. Current ideas about the formation of galaxies and the evolution of the universe make such a body unlikely.

Albert Stebbins and Michael Turner of the University of California at Santa Barbara have come up with an entirely new idea which they claim explains the observations without assuming the existence of a great attractor. They think the direction of the galaxies could be due to the repulsion of a defect of space caused by a relatively recent phase transition in the universe. During a phase change, e.g. when steam condenses to liquid water or water freezes to ice, there is a release of energy in the form of latent heat. Cosmologists believe that during the first second of the existence of the universe there was a phase change from one energy state of the vacuum to another form of energy. This would have provided the mechanism which made the universe expand out of its initial state, a mechanism known as inflation.

Phase changes produce other features in addition to releasing energy. As solid ice forms, it may produce cracks in the solid, known as defects. Analogous defects might form in the structure of space-time, producing very long thin walls which would have the effect of cutting off different regions of space-time from one another. Although such defects may have occurred in the first moments of the existence of the universe, the chance of one existing nearby at the present time is remote. But Stebbins and Turner have suggested that smaller phase changes may have occurred at a much later date when the temperature was about 3,000 K. The transition involving neutrinos may have created walls which could still affect space. The pressure in such a wall would be negative with the result that it would produce a negative gravitational field. This 'great wall' would have the same effect on the galaxies as the 'great attractor'. More research is needed to verify these ideas.

Halley's Comet.—Much publicity was given to the achievements of the Soviet and European space probes when they flew close to the nucleus of Halley's Comet in 1986. This flyby permitted astronomers to gain their first glimpse of the nucleus of a comet. Groundbased observations also provided information which has provoked considerable discussion.

A group of astronomers from the United States, France and Australia used the 190 cm. (74 inch) reflector at the Mt. Stromlo Observatory near Canberra, Australia, to observe the comet. Their results suggest that the comet is made of material unlike that of any other body in the solar system. Susan Wyckoff, a physicist at the Arizona State University at Tempe, commented that the carbon in the comet's nucleus differed from that found elsewhere in that the ratio of carbon-12 to carbon-13 varied between 40 to 1 and 65 to 1. This compares with a ratio of 89 to 1 found in rocks on the Earth and Moon, the atmospheres of the planets and the Sun.

Several explanations of this difference have been proposed. One is that a nearby supernova 'splattered' the proto-Sun and the surrounding nebular disc before the planets were formed, within about 10 million years of the formation of the Sun. The theory suggests that the supernova material did not mix thoroughly with the gaseous disc and that Halley's Comet was formed from an uncontaminated region. This is in line with the theory that comets were formed in a belt well beyond the orbit of Neptune, an area which could well have escaped the supernova contamination. Another explanation suggests that the comet came from interstellar space. This is supported by the fact that the carbon ratio is in agreement with that found in interstellar gas. Wyckoff, however, favours the former explanation. The problem might be solved when another comet is studied in detail and Comet Brorsen-Metcalf is

favourably placed for observations from the northern hemisphere in late 1989.

Hubble Constant refined.—Much work has been carried out recently on gravitational lenses and the effect of such a lens on the time taken by light to come from a distant quasar; light travels in differing ways round gravitational lenses. The work is leading to a new method of investigating the universe and to the possibility of obtaining a more accurate value for the Hubble Constant. The Hubble Constant is used for measuring the rate at which the universe is expanding and there exists an uncertainty of about a factor of two in the value currently used.

One of the studies involves the images of the 'double quasar' 0957+561, which have been analysed by a team of French and Spanish astronomers over many years. They found that the fluctuations in brightness of the two objects kept in step but that there was a constant difference of about 415 days. This showed that both images had a common source. In addition, the relative brightnesses of the two images changed slightly with time. It is thought that this was due to microlensing, the effect caused by an individual star in the galaxy passing in front of the images and acting as a lens. The time the second quasar image is delayed provides information on the mass in the galaxy causing the lens effect.

This information, together with the brightness of the images, gives information useful in determining the Hubble Constant. So far these studies have not improved the accuracy of the constant, but they have set a fairly reliable value for the upper limit which is consistent with other investigations. A precise value for the constant could be obtained from a system which had three quasar images.

Ice age theory upset.—Until recently an astronomical theory known as the Milankovitch model was widely accepted as an explanation of the dates of the ice ages. The theory is based on the known changes in the tilt of the spin axis of the Earth and the direction of this tilt. Work carried out by geologists at the U.S. Geological Survey suggests that the Milankovitch model is not completely in accordance with geological data. The geologists obtained data from sediments from a site in southern Nevada known as Devil's Hole. Water flows into this region from a large catchment area and has deposited a vein of calcite for over a quarter of a million years. It is possible to measure the ages of the different layers of the calcite by recording the ratio of thorium-230 to uranium-234, or the ratio of uranium-234 to uranium-238. The results of these measurements indicate that the vein of calcite built up gradually between 50,000 and 300,000 years ago. A climatic record can also be obtained from the vein by measuring the ratio of oxygen-16 to oxygen-18, both stable isotopes in the atmosphere. However, the value of the ratio depends on global temperatures. The data obtained shows that the temperature variations recorded in the vein of calcite are not in step with those obtained by analysis of deep-sea sediments or from the ratio of isotopes in air bubbles trapped in ice-sheets, although they show the same pattern of variations.

The new study suggests that the previous interglacial period (the warmer periods between the ice ages proper) started earlier than 147,000 years ago and possibly as much as 163,000 years ago; earlier work has indicated that it was warmest about 125,000 years ago. The new study does not completely conflict with older theories or the Milankovitch model. Statistical analysis shows that other rhythms emerge in addition to the cycles of warming and cooling. It would appear that the Milankovitch model is only one factor in an explanation of the ice ages and that there were other major contributory factors, such as changes in ocean currents.

Lindow Man.—Four years ago the upper torso of a man was dug up from the bog at Lindow Moss in Cheshire. Studies at the time indicated that the man died in the middle or late Iron Age but more recent work has shown that it was more likely to have been early Roman times. The man, nicknamed Pete Marsh by archaeologists, was garotted before being dumped in the bog. Evidence for the date of the event is contradictory and could indicate any of three dates; 4th century A.D. (at the end of the Roman occupation); 1st century A.D. (early Roman times); and between 200 and 760 B.C. (Iron Age).

Difficulties in dating the event have arisen for several reasons. Radio-carbon dating of the body tissue was carried out at the Atomic Energy Research Establishment at Harwell and the Radio-carbon Accelerator Unit at the University of Oxford. The dates obtained by the two establishments were several centuries apart, the Oxford studies giving the early Roman period whilst the Harwell work seemed to indicate a late Roman date. Radio-carbon dates for the peat which surrounded the body were found by both establishments to be from the Iron Age. Another problem is the ritualistic nature of the murder, which points to the Iron Age rather than to dates during the Roman occupation of Britain.

Recent studies carried out by John Gowlett (formerly at Oxford but now at the Institute of Prehistoric Science and Archaeology at Liverpool) and Robert Hedges and Ian Low from Oxford, on the body and the contents of the stomach and on the peat surrounding the body seem to have solved the problems. The results for the body and the contents of the stomach all fall within the range of 2 B.C. and 119 A.D.. The date for the enclosing peat agrees with that obtained in the earlier studies, making the peat much older. There now appears to be some consistency in the radio-carbon dating, but in spite of this data argument continues over the time of the killing.

Metallic hydrogen.—Some theoretical physicists have predicted that under very high pressures hydrogen molecules would separate into individual atoms. They believe this would result in a metal with the atomic nuclei immersed in a sea of conducting electrons. Others have predicted that the metal would be solid with the nuclei arranged in a crystalline lattice, as in other metals. Work carried out by Ho-Kwang Mao and Russell Hemley at the Carnegie Institution at Washington has provided strong circumstantial evidence that at very high pressures hydrogen is a black solid. The pressure required was 2·5 million atmospheres.

Mao and Hemley obtained their results by compressing the hydrogen between two diamond anvils at 77 K. They were unable to confirm that the solid produced by the process was metallic hydrogen because the sample was too small to be checked for electrical conductivity. The question may be settled using X-ray crystallographic techniques. Mao and Hemley used a sample of hydrogen several cubic micrometres in volume and gradually increased the pressure in stages, holding it at a given value for several hours or days. The tiny diamond anvils failed at between 250 and 300 gigapascals. As the pressure was increased, it was possible to observe the alterations in the structure of the gas, which changed from an insulator to a semiconductor and a semi-metal. The changes were observed visually, through the transparent diamonds, and also by monitoring the spectral changes.

The work is of importance to the study of superconductors, as it is thought that metallic hydrogen might be superconducting at high temperatures. It will also help in the study of the major planets, in particular Jupiter and Saturn; if the conditions under which hydrogen becomes a metal are understood, it will be possible to determine the percentage of metallic hydrogen in the planets and so to determine what contribution this makes to the planets' electrical properties.

The oldest insect.—In the early days of their evolution insects did not fossilize easily because they lacked wings and they had relatively soft bodies. Consequently early insect fossils are difficult to find. The discovery by Conrad Labandeira and colleagues at the University of Chicago of the fossil remains of the head and thorax of an insect that lived about 390 million years ago is unusual and most rewarding. It is claimed that this fossil is the remains of the earliest known insect, and also that the fossil is the earliest record of a land animal from North America.

The fossil was found in mudstone rocks in Quebec Province, Canada. Studies have suggested that it might be related to a primative group of insects called jumping bristletails (*Archaeognatha*). Descendants of these insects still exist today, living in soil and under stones. An alternative theory put forward by the researchers is that the insect could represent a group of insects that have evolved to give both wingless and winged insects.

The generally accepted theory of the evolution of insects is that the earliest insects appeared between 400 and 440 million years ago in the Silurian period. It is believed that their form was like that of the present-day centipede or millipede and that they evolved into different forms when new varieties of primitive land plants provided new sources of food.

Phobos reaches Mars.—The first of the two Soviet *Phobos* space probes to Mars was lost in August 1988 due to an operator's error. *Phobos 2* arrived in the vicinity of Mars and went into orbit round the planet on January 29, 1989. After adjustment to the orbit, the probe approached within 850 km. of the surface and sent back data which suggests that Mars has a magnetic field. A bow shock wave was registered on the sunward side and studies of the regions surrounding the planet reveal characteristics unlike those of the solar wind. These observations indicate that Mars is surrounded by charged particles but not necessarily that Mars has a magnetic field. Soviet experimenters have, however, suggested that this electromagnetic bubble is probably too large and distinct to be the result solely of an ionosphere. Further, the data sent back indicated the possibility that Mars has the equivalent, but weaker, of the earth's Van Allen belts. (The Van Allen belts are areas of intense radiation around the Earth in which atomic particles are trapped by the Earth's magnetic field.) A specially developed instrument capable of detecting electrons and ions with energies between 30 kiloelectron volts and several megaelectron volts was built by a team led by Susan McKenna-Lawlor of St. Patrick's College, Maynooth, Ireland. The Martian radiation belt stretches out to about 950 km. above the planet's surface, which is equivalent in terms of the size of the planet to the distance of the Earth's inner belt. A detailed analysis of this data has yet to be made.

On February 18, the probe was placed in a new, approximately circular, orbit, with a radius about 300 km. farther out than the orbit of Phobos, one of the satellites of Mars. A few days later the programme of photographing the satellite started and high quality images were obtained. Data was collected to enable the probe to approach Phobos more closely. More photos were relayed back, together with infrared spectra of Mars and the satellite. By the end of March 1989 everything was ready for a manoeuvre to bring the probe to within 50 metres of the satellite but on March 29 it was announced that contact with the probe had been lost.

Pulsar in supernova 1987A.—The supernova 1987A which erupted in the Large Magellanic Cloud in February 1987 is still providing new information on this type of event. Some of the results have fallen into line with established theories but there have also been some surprising observational data which have led to theories being revised.

One of these surprising observations is the identification of a rapidly rotating pulsar at the centre of the supernova explosion. It is generally accepted that a pulsar is a rapidly spinning neutron star with a diameter between 20 and 30 km. and a mass just under one and half that of the Sun. This new pulsar is rotating every 0·5 milliseconds, some three times faster than any previously observed. With such a rapid rotation the star should be flung apart so it is obvious that the make-up of this star is not in accordance with accepted ideas. Various theories have been put forward to explain the high rotational speed. One is that it initially rotated much more

slowly but that surrounding matter is being drawn in and the star has thus gained momentum. An alternative suggestion is that the star is not rotating at such a high speed and the visual data is caused by the vibration of the pulsar. It is thought that the neutron star is still ringing like a bell as a result of the explosion which formed the star. The idea of pulsars 'ringing' has been considered before but there was a lack of observational support. This is the only event in recent years that has been close enough to the Earth to provide detailed information. If the ringing theory is correct, it is expected that the very high vibration of the pulsar will die down fairly rapidly to reveal another periodic variation which can be attributed to the rotation of the pulsar.

Pulsar speeds up.—Pulsars are the relics of supernova explosions and are thought to be neutron stars. They spin rapidly at the time of their formation and then, in most cases, the rotational periods gradually increase as they lose energy. However, some pulsars have been observed to spin faster with time. The theory put forward to explain this is that the pulsar gains energy as a result of gas swirling onto the pulsar from a companion star. But this explanation cannot be used for the newly discovered pulsar PRS2127+11 because it does not have a companion star.

The pulsar was observed using the 305 metre radio telescope at Aricebo in Puerto Rico. It is situated in the globular cluster M15, which contains about a million stars. The pulsar was observed to be spinning at a rate of roughly nine times a second; during the few months it has been monitored, the rotational period has been found to decrease, i.e. the pulsar is speeding up.

The only feasible explanation put forward so far is that the pulsar may be moving towards a group of stars in the centre of the globular cluster, or towards the Earth due to gravitational pull of another star. However, this theory is not entirely satisfactory as the effect of such a force should be smaller than the acceleration actually observed. The star will have to be monitored for some time before the correct explanation becomes available.

The receding Moon.—There is a theory that the Moon, in its orbit round the Earth, is receding from the Earth and that at the same time the Earth is slowing down; in other words, the day is getting longer. Much of the observational proof of this theory has been derived from a study of Arabian and Babylonean records of eclipses. However, these records only go back to about 700 B.C. American and British astronomers have recently used Chinese records of solar eclipses which took place in 532 A.D., 899 B.C. and 1876 B.C. to show that the length of the day is 0·07 seconds longer than it was 4,000 years ago.

To obtain evidence from earlier periods, geologists have studied a fine band of material between 0·2 and 3 mm. thick in sediments found in the Flinders Range in South Australia. Layers of sandstone gradually built up as the material lay at the bottom of a lake or river delta some 650 million years ago. Originally it was thought that variations in the thickness of the layers was due to the effects of the Sun. More recent studies have shown this to be wrong and that the Moon was responsible: the varying thickness was due to tidal effects. The evidence came from similar banded deposits elsewhere in Australia.

From this information George Williams of the University of Adelaide has calculated that at the time when the deposits were forming, there were 13·1 lunar months a year compared to the current 12·4 months. He also calculates that there were 30·5 days in the lunar month compared with the present 29·5, and that there were 400 days in the year. A team of workers at the University of Arizona at Tucson has deduced that the Moon was only about 346,000 km. from the Earth in Precambrian times and that it has receded since then at a rate of just over 2 cm. per year to its present distance of 384,000 km. These values are in line with the accepted values used in astronomical calculations.

Rotation of the Sun.—It has been known for many years that the Sun, being a ball of gas, does not rotate as a solid body. At the equator of the Sun the surface gases rotate in about 26 days. This period of rotation lengthens gradually with latitude until near the poles the rotational period is about 36 days. The rate of rotation of the interior of the Sun could only be deduced from theoretical considerations. Now Kenneth Libbrecht of the Big Bear Solar Observatory in California has deduced the rotational speeds below the surface using a new technique known as solar seismology. He has shown that the rotational rates recorded at the surface persist throughout the Sun's convective zone to a depth of 200,000 km. below the surface, i.e. approximately a third of the way to the centre of the Sun. Below this level the Sun appears to rotate as a solid body with a period of 27 days.

In the early 1960s, physicists were puzzled by a phenomenon known as the 'five minute oscillation'. This is a kind of pulsation of the material on the Sun's surface. For a time it was thought this was a random motion but later it was realized that the Sun was vibrating as a resonant object. The oscillations are, in fact, seismic waves in the Sun and their propagation is affected by temperature. The temperature rises as the Sun is penetrated and this causes the speed of propagation to increase. The wave front will speed up and eventually be refracted back to the surface, like light waves in a mirage. As the wave front reaches the surface it encounters an abrupt decrease in density, the visible surface of the Sun. This acts like a mirror and reflects the wave back again. This may occur many times and the waves interfere with each other, resulting in standing wave patterns which may last for days. Because the Sun is nearly spherical, these oscillations may be expressed mathematically as spherical harmonics, and information about the solar interior can be deduced from them.

Saturn's satellite Titan.—Radar signals are gradually being sent over much greater distances and signals have now been successfully reflected back from Titan, Saturn's largest satellite. The work has been carried out by a team of astronomers from the Californian Institute of Technology in Pasadena. The team used the 70 metre radio dish at Goldstone to send the signals and the Very Large Array Telescope at Socorro, New Mexico to pick up the reflected signal. Although the strength of the transmitted signal was 360 kilowatts, the reflected signal was barely detectable. The round trip for the signal took two and a half hours.

Observations of Titan by the *Voyager 2* space probe in 1980 showed that the upper atmosphere of the satellite consists of ethane, methane and other hydrocarbons but that most of the atmosphere is, like the Earth's, made up of nitrogen. However, the pressure is 1·3 times that of the Earth's and the temperature much lower at 94 K. It had been suggested from the data supplied by *Voyager* that the surface of Titan is covered by a layer of ethane up to 1·6 km. deep. Because ethane reflects radar waves very poorly, it was expected that the return signals would be very weak. This was found to be the case on June 3 and 5, but on June 4 the signal was found to be four times stronger. This, the astronomers concluded, showed that Titan was not uniformly covered with ethane. The stronger signals were what would be expected from ice. If the bright region of the satellite is due to ice, it has been estimated that the ice is about 1,000 km. across. It has been suggested that Titan has oceans of ethane and continents of ice or some other solid substance.

Observations at wavelengths other than the 3·5 cm used for this study might provide more information but the Very Large Array Telescope can only work at that wavelength with the necessary resolution. The radio telescope at Aricebo, Puerto Rico, could provide the critical information, but it will be about ten years before this can be used.

Semiconductors from diamonds.—Semiconductors are crystals with electrical conductivity which are used in transistors and other electronic devices. For the last forty years silicon has been used to manufacture semiconductors, but advances in electronics in recent years means that better and faster semiconductors are needed. During the 1980s research in this field produced so-called exotic semiconductors, which have gone some way to satisfying the demands of industry, but problems still remain.

Until recently it was possible to use only the most stable form of an element or compound for making semiconductors, which are produced by growing a thin film of crystals of a second element on the surface of the underlying silicon (epitaxy). Attempts to put a layer of diamond on silicon using a method called chemical vapour deposition were unsuccessful because the result was a jumbled arrangement, not an epitaxial growth. However, Rabalais and Yeshayahu of the University of Texas at Houston have now revealed a new technique which punches atoms onto the sub-surface rather than laying them gently onto it. The process is carried out at room temperature, a condition which would normally generate graphite. However, the bonds binding graphite are much weaker than those in diamonds; the process involves giving the carbon atoms enough energy to shatter the bonds in graphite but leave the bonds in diamond intact, thereby ensuring the deposited material is solely diamond.

The success in growing diamond epitaxially opens the way to the development of more efficient semiconductors. Diamond-coated semiconductors are resistant to radiation and so are ideal for space communications, nuclear reactors and military uses. They can also operate at much higher frequencies than other semiconductors because the electrons in diamond move much faster than the electrons in other materials. In addition the breakdown voltage is much higher. More research is needed, however, before diamond-coated semiconductors can be mass-produced with the quality required by modern technology.

Tapeworm vaccine.—The world's first effective vaccine against a parasitic disease has been developed by scientists in Australia and New Zealand. Usually a vaccine is used for protection against viral or bacterial infections. This new product has been developed using genetic engineering techniques and appears to be a breakthrough in the control of a tapeworm parasite, *Taenia ovis*. This causes a disease in sheep popularly known as sheep measles because spotty cysts, similar to measles in appearance are formed in the sheep's muscles. Sheep pick up the eggs of the tapeworm from dog faeces.

The development of a vaccine against a parasite has proved very difficult because the parasites are multicellular organisms which elicit a complex immune system response in sheep. Further, the parasites have evolved means whereby they can avoid the host's immune responses by altering the structure of their antigens. The vaccine is the result of 18 years of research. The main difficulty for the researchers was their inability to obtain sufficient quantities of the antigen needed to develop the vaccine commercially. This difficulty was overcome by the advent of techniques employing genetic engineering which enabled scientists to obtain large amounts of the antigen through bacterial culture. The trials carried out in New Zealand have indicated that the vaccine is successful in about 95 per cent of the cases. It is expected that the vaccine will be available for commercial use within two years.

The sheep measles vaccine is the first of a series of vaccines which it is hoped will soon be available for beef measles, pork measles and hydatids, all of which are more widespread than sheep measles. The hydatid parasite, an adult tapeworm in dogs, can cause large cysts in the human brain, lungs, kidneys and liver. Humans can also be infected by pork measles parasite. Of particular concern in South America and Africa is the tapeworm *Taenia saginata*, carried by humans and passed on to cattle which are exposed to human faeces, causing beef measles.

Turin Shroud.—The Shroud of Turin is believed by many to be the burial cloth of Christ. In 1988 the Church authorities allowed the cloth to be scientifically tested for the first time. Teams from Oxford, Zurich and Arizona were given samples taken from the shroud, together with control samples from items of a known age, for analysis using radio-carbon dating techniques. The teams were unaware which was the genuine sample and which were the control samples. Radio-carbon analysis involves measuring the proportion of carbon-14 to carbon-12 present in an object. There is a constant amount of carbon-13 in living tissue but in dead tissue this decays to carbon-14 at an accurately known rate. By measuring the amount of carbon-14 in a sample, it is possible to calculate the length of time that has elapsed since organic matter died. In October 1988 the three teams concluded unanimously that the shroud is medieval. The results obtained indicate that the linen used in the shroud could be dated to within the range of 1260–1390 A.D., with at least a 95 per cent confidence in the accuracy of these dates.

However, the result was challenged by Thomas Phillips of the High Energy Physics Laboratory at Harvard University. Phillips put forward the theory that the body which once filled the shroud radiated light and heat, thus accounting for the image on the cloth. He also suggested that the body generated a burst of neutrons. If any of these were captured by the carbon-13, they would be converted into carbon-14 and so produce an inaccurate dating. Phillips said that his neutron theory would be strengthened if it could be shown that there existed in the shroud two isotopes, chlorine-36 and calcium-41. Neither of these isotopes appears in nature and could only be created from natural isotopes by neutron capture. Robert Hedges, who headed the Oxford team of original investigators, dismissed Phillips' theories, saying that the likelihood that such factors influenced the date in the way suggested is so exceedingly remote that it beggars scientific credulity. He also pointed out that Phillips had given no reasons to back his theory that the body would produce neutrons.

Venus.—The atmosphere of Venus contains large quantities of sulphuric acid droplets. The source of these was assumed to be volcanic activity, and the implication of this assumption is that volcanic activity on the planet occurs on a large scale. Recent studies, however, indicate that this activity may be about one-twentieth of that occurring on the Earth.

Results obtained by Soviet spacecraft show that one of the main constituents of the surface rocks on Venus is calcite (calcium carbonate). Ronald Prinn of the Massachusetts Institute of Technology, near Boston, showed some years ago that calcite should react with the sulphuric acid to form anhydrite (calcium sulphate) and carbon monoxide. Prinn and a co-worker, Bruce Fegley, have studied the reaction of the two compounds at the same temperature as that on Venus (750 K) and have shown that the calcite should remove all the sulphur dioxide in the atmosphere within two million years. They have calculated the amount of volcanic activity required to maintain the current concentration. It turned out to be about one cubic kilometre of lava a year is needed, a value which is only five per cent of that produced by terrestrial activity.

This relatively low value is supported by the findings of the Soviet probes *Venera 15* and *Venera 16*.

Using radar techniques, the probes showed that the surface of the planet contained many craters. If huge quantities of lava were exuded, this would have covered up most of the craters. The number and density of the craters indicate that the rate of volcanic activity is less than 2 cubic kilometres per year.

This finding raises a question about the amount of heat Venus produces. Because the Earth and Venus are of similar size, it was thought that both should produce similar amounts of heat. Unlike Venus the Earth can lose heat from its interior at the edges of crustal plates. Research is currently investigating whether Venus actually produces less heat than the Earth or whether there are alternative ways for venting the heat on Venus which do not produce volcanic eruptions.

Voyager passes Neptune.—The *Voyager 2* spacecraft was launched in 1977. Its journey across our solar system has taken it past Jupiter, Saturn and Uranus, and in each case the probe has provided data which could never have been obtained from earthbased studies. The outermost of the major planets, Neptune, was reached in August 1989. Valuable new data was obtained during the flyby, though most of the information is still provisional.

For several months prior to the flyby of Neptune *Voyager 2* sent back full disc pictures of the planet, but it was not until the probe was nearer to Neptune that the sensational discoveries were made. By January 1989 it was possible to resolve features 6,000 km. across, better than the best earthbased pictures. The approach photographs have shown an ever-changing picture of clouds in the atmosphere, some persisting for a long time and others shortlived. For example, in April, during the period of one revolution of 18 hours, a faint white spot near to the south pole suddenly became the brightest feature on the planet.

The discovery of another six moons will require a reappraisal of the theories for the origins of the two previously known satellites, Triton and Nereid. The first of the new moons to be identified, 1989 N1, is in a circular orbit some 93,000 km. from the planet and has a period of 1 day 3 hours. Triton's orbit is also circular but is inclined to the planet's equator by 20°

and has a retrograde motion, the only large satellite in the solar system to do so. Nereid is in a direct orbit but is tilted to the equator by 30° and is the most elliptical of any known planetary satellite. 1989 N1 lies closer to the planet than Triton and Nereid, has a circular orbit in the same direction as Neptune's rotation, and is slightly larger in diameter than Nereid. The other newly-discovered moons are much smaller, ranging from about 50 km. to 200 km. in size. The smallest is very irregular in shape and is about the largest size of satellite that could exist without having been pulled into a roughly spherical shape. All these new satellites lie very close to the planet and all are in circular orbits travelling in a direct motion.

The biggest sensation was the information collected about the satellite Triton. It has an atmosphere of methane and possibly nitrogen. The surface is covered by glaciers of methane ice stretching from the poles to the equator. Some craters have been identified but they are heavily eroded. The surface has a reddish colour in some places and a strong blue colour in others.

In addition to the moons, two complete rings around the planet have been identified. One had never been seen before; the presence of the other had been suspected from earthbased studies but was thought to be incomplete. The data received has shown it to be a complete ring of uneven density.

The planet itself, thought previously to be a relatively quiet body similar to Uranus, has been found to be very active. A dark-featured anticyclonic storm the size of the Earth was identified. In addition, bright features, one named the 'scooter', travel round the planet in a jet stream of winds of up to 600 km. per hour. Clouds of methane have been identified lying about 50–75 km. above a lower cloud layer. The strength of the magnetic field of the planet is weaker than that of the Earth and the other outer planets but the magnetosphere is very large, extending three quarters of a million kilometres towards the Sun. The magnetic field itself is inclined at 30° to the spin axis and the track of *Voyager 2* passed through the radiation belts.

Voyager 2 will now pass through the outer regions of the solar system and on into interstellar space. The probe is heading in the direction of the star Sirius, which it will reach in about 300,000 years.

CONSERVATION AND HERITAGE, 1988–89

THE NATURAL ENVIRONMENT

Break-up of conservation agencies.—The Government has decided to change its longstanding arrangements for safeguarding wildlife and the countryside. Claiming that the present system operates with too little regard for social needs and conditions in Scotland and Wales, the Environment Secretary (Nicholas Ridley) announced in mid 1989 that the Government's main conservation advisory bodies in Britain, the Nature Conservancy Council (NCC) and the Countryside Commissions, are to be dismembered. In Scotland and Wales their functions will be merged to form new 'Natural Heritage Agencies' under the control of the Scottish and Welsh Offices. In England they are to remain separate for the time being 'because of the much greater density of population and consequent pressure on the land'. Legislation to implement these changes will be introduced in the 1989–90 Parliamentary session.

The devolution of the advisory bodies was welcomed in Scotland by the Highlands and Islands Development Board and the Country Landowners Federation, but most press comment was adverse. Conservation bodies reacted with surprise and alarm, believing that the proposals will seriously weaken nature conservation in Britain. They are concerned that the Government will no longer pursue coherent national policies on countryside and wildlife issues, and that the NCC's scientific capability in particular will suffer. Most conservation problems are shared by Scotland, England and Wales, and wildlife is no respecter of political boundaries: as one former NCC chairman put it, 'merlins do not speak Welsh, nor corncrakes Gaelic'.

Neither the NCC nor the Countryside Commissions were consulted about the new proposals. It is widely believed that the proposals are intended not so much as an improvement to environmental protection as a devolutionary gesture to the Scots and the Welsh. Many question whether the new Natural Heritage Agencies will be able to safeguard wildlife and the countryside with the same vigour and independence as the old.

Breeding birds.—The Shetland Islands offer some of the largest and most spectacular seabird 'cities' in Britain and are a major tourist attraction. Recently, however, some species have been declining in numbers because there is no longer enough food to rear their young. Many seabirds, such as terns, puffins and kittiwakes, rely largely on sand-eels for food during the breeding season. Since 1982 the number of sand-eels in waters around the Shetlands has fallen sharply: 52,600 tonnes were netted by a local fishery in 1982 but only 4,800 tonnes in 1988. Many seabird chicks have starved to death: arctic terns have raised very few young since 1983, and kittiwakes and puffins have fared almost as badly. Other birds affected by the lack of food are red-throated divers, fulmars, arctic skuas and great skuas. The extent of the present crisis is unprecedented.

Sand-eels are short-lived fish whose populations fluctuate according to natural changes. They are not valued as food for human consumption and the main commercial markets are for fish-meal, oil and fertilizer, the eels being deep-frozen after capture and processed on-shore. They are usually netted while still immature, so commercial fishing reduces the number of eels which live long enough to spawn. In these circumstances, over-fishing can quickly eliminate a fishery: this happened, for instance, to the once prolific shoals of anchovies off Peru. It is not known for certain whether the Shetland sand-eel fishery, established in 1974, caused the population decline or merely exacerbated a natural downward trend. The Royal Society for the Protection of Birds first recommended a ban on sand-eel fishing to allow stocks to recover seven years ago. The Department of Agriculture and Fisheries for Scotland (DAFS) refused to impose a ban at that time, claiming that the sand-eel population was returning to a more 'normal' level after a population explosion in the 1970s. However, in 1989 DAFS agreed to ban fishing from July to December to allow the young sand-eels to mature. In the meantime, fishery scientists are studying the problem.

By contrast, some of Britain's rarest birds of prey had one of their most productive seasons this century. Scotland's 52 pairs of osprey raised 80 chicks between them, and golden eagles, Montagu's harriers and red kites also bred successfully. The 1989 season saw the first experimental release of young red kites into areas that were formerly their habitat in England and Scotland. This rare bird, for long confined to the Welsh hills, is unlikely to spread far without such help but hope of re-establishing the kite is encouraged by the success of the earlier white-tailed sea-eagle project. This project involved the release of young birds from Norway on the Scottish west coast between 1975–85. They have bred in small numbers each year since, and in 1989 seven pairs of sea eagles raised a total of five chicks.

An exception in an otherwise good year for birds of prey was the hen harrier. At least six pairs on the Cumbrian moors were shot, and their chicks stamped to death, after a report by the Game Conservancy claimed that hen harriers were eating grouse chicks. The hen harrier has been fully protected by law since 1954 but is still persecuted in some areas.

Enterprise forests.—In the summer of 1989, the Countryside Commission and the Forestry Commission announced plans to create forests around twelve cities in England and Wales. Success will depend on attracting private landowners to participate by planting trees and opening more land to the public. Similar enterprises have been started elsewhere in Europe.

It is believed that the time is right for large-scale planting on the fringes of urban areas as land is being taken out of agricultural production at the same time as demands on the countryside for recreational use are increasing. The forests will mostly be planted on derelict land, but poor-quality farmland set aside from agricultural production is also likely to be used. The forests will contain not only woodland, but working farms, meadows, lakes, orchards and adventure play-areas. The originators of the scheme hope that it can be financed and supported by local communities and industries, with some initial funding from government grant-aid.

Three pilot schemes are beginning in Tyne and Wear, Staffordshire and East London. The Countryside Commission is also promoting the concept of a large Midlands Forest ranging over an area the size of the New Forest, drawing land into the project through grant-aid. The idea of 'enterprise forests' has also seized the imagination of Scottish Ministers, who are planning a similar initiative in central Scotland, to be carried out by a new company, Central Scotland Woodlands. Local authorities and private trusts are considering similar forest projects in places as far apart as the Pennines and Hampshire.

Whether these schemes reach fruition will depend on their success at raising the value of land and boosting the local economy, thus encouraging landowners to invest in forestry and recreation-related projects. If successful, they have the potential to change dramatically the landscape around our cities.

Heaths versus houses.—Heaths are limited to areas with acidic soils in humid, temperate climates. Outside Britain and western Europe they are found only at the southern tip of Africa, in south-east Australia and on a few mountain tops in central Africa. Lowland heaths are one of Britain's most precious wild habitats. In southern England they are the home of many rare animals and plants, among them the smooth snake, Dartford warbler, silver-studded blue butterfly and marsh gentian.

The Dorset heaths, grouped around Poole Harbour and immortalized in the works of Thomas Hardy, are the richest in wildlife of all the British lowland heaths. Only a tenth of their original extent survives and some of the remainder lies in the path of the rapidly expanding suburbs of Poole and Bournemouth. Since 1980, an area of more than 400 hectares, much of it nominally protected as Sites of Special Scientific Interest, has been destroyed to make way for housing, roads and light industry. The problem is that while natural heathland is of negligible economic value, land and property values in the Poole area have soared in recent years.

The heath versus housing argument has centred recently on the fate of Canford Heath, the largest remaining heath outside nature reserves and the closest to Poole. The southern half of the heath was acquired a decade ago by Poole Borough Council, which granted itself planning permission to build houses. A proposal to build a major road across the northern half of the Heath led to a public inquiry in 1988, following which the Secretary of State refused planning permission. This decision surprised many but indicated that local development needs in south-east Dorset would not always outweigh other considerations. Moreover, a proposed trade-off, by which the Council offered to preserve one part of Canford Heath in exchange for permission to build on another part, was deemed unacceptable. At present local authorities are reviewing their policies in the light of recent events.

Because of their exceptional populations of rare birds, Canford Heath and other heaths around Poole Harbour have been proposed for designation as a Special Protection Area under European Community legislation.

Marine wildlife threatened.—Farming of salmon and shellfish is a growing industry in the sheltered inshore waters of the west coast and the northern isles of Scotland. The establishment and maintenance costs of fish-farms are relatively low, while the public are willing to pay high prices for salmon. Production rose from a total of 600 tonnes of farmed salmon in 1980 to a total of 17,951 tonnes in 1988; it is expected to reach more than 50,000 tonnes by 1991.

Fish-farms are often established in sea-lochs, where the waters are sheltered from wind and tide, and warmed by the Gulf Stream. These waters are of great value for marine wildlife and contain communities of animals and seaweeds rare or absent elsewhere in Britain. The thick, soft bottom mud of the lochs is full of burrowing crustacea, sea-pens and tall sea anemones. Some of these underwater communities are very sensitive to physical disturbance and pollution.

Salmon bred in cages affect the marine environment in a number of ways. The water surrounding the cages is enriched by fish-feed and chemical waste, while solid waste pollutes the sediments below the fish cages, killing the natural fauna. Since many Scottish sea-lochs are quiet, land-locked waters with narrow tidal entrances, these pollutants may not be removed by tidal flushing. Toxic chemicals such as Nuvan, used to control sea-lice, can kill organisms which are not their target, such as lobsters and crabs, and can cause blindness in fish. Fish farms also attract predators, such as seals and cormorants, and there is the perennial risk of the transmission of disease or parasites to wild fish. If farmed fish escape, their interbreeding with wild salmon can weaken or even swamp natural genetic strains: large-scale releases into rivers of non-native strains have sometimes resulted in the complete collapse of a fishery. To add to the pressure on marine wildlife, many sea-lochs have, since the Inshore Fishing (Scotland) Act of 1984, been opened to trawling and dredging. Divers report very widespread disturbance of bottom sediments in Scottish inshore waters.

Prospective fish-farmers must obtain a sea-bed lease from the Crown Estate Commission, which is therefore in a position to regulate the growth of the industry. The involvement of local authorities is limited to on-shore development. Sea-bed leases have hitherto been granted freely, though since 1986 the Nature Conservancy Council has been consulted, as the statutory advisory body on wildlife matters, on more than 400 cases. Of these only 16 were refused on grounds of wildlife and conservation, suggesting that nature conservation has taken second place to commerce.

There is no statutory nature conservation protection for marine areas in British waters except that of Marine Nature Reserves: only one such Reserve, Lundy, has been declared so far. Conservationists have been pressing for a national marine planning strategy, setting out environmental principles for fish-farming and defining areas which should be protected from damaging forms of commercial exploitation. However, during the past year the Crown Estate Commission introduced its own non-statutory concept of 'Very Sensitive Areas' in which there is a presumption against granting further sea-bed leases. And under recent European Community legislation, fish-farms larger than 6,000 square metres on the west coast of Scotland north of Argyll, and larger than 12,000 square metres elsewhere, will require an environmental impact assessment. (This requirement does not, however, apply to smaller but more densely stocked cages.) The Scottish Office has completed a review of the fish-farming industry and proposed to set up a committee to arbitrate between the demands of conservation and commerce but the appointed committee has not yet sat.

These developments offer the possibility of a more considered expansion of marine fish-farming in future, although it remains to be seen whether those empowered to do so will take urgent steps to safeguard marine wildlife in the best remaining sites.

Skiing affects Cairngorms.—Despite one of the worst seasons for skiing in living memory, the Scottish downhill skiing industry continues to expand. A doubling in capacity is forecast over the next decade as those who have learned to ski on Britain's 120 dry slopes look for downhill skiing relatively close to home. At present there are four main ski resorts in the Highlands: at Cairngorm, Glenshee, Glencoe and The Lecht. Three others are at the planning or development stage, at Ben Wyvis, the Dalwhinnie Corries and Aonach Mor near Ben Nevis. The Glenshee and Lecht resorts have increased their capacity in recent years, and at Cairngorm there are proposals to double the size of the present development.

Organized downhill skiing needs easy access to the main slopes and long-lasting snow beds. Many areas which best meet these requirements are of great scenic and scientific interest, containing rare birds and plants and sensitive geological features. All the Scottish ski resorts, present or planned, lie close to or within Sites of Special Scientific Interest (SSSI). Careful planning is needed, therefore, to minimize environmental damage, especially in view of the harsh Highland climate, more arctic than alpine, and the thin gravelly soils and wet peat which clothe the hills. Unfortunately, it has proved difficult in practice to achieve a reasonable balance between a healthy skiing industry on the one hand and nature conservation and scenic protection on the other. Recent efforts by the Scottish Office to formulate an overall development strategy have not succeeded in preventing conflict between competing interests.

Current controversy revolves around the plans of the Cairngorm Chairlift Company to expand into the Northern Corries, an SSSI and National Scenic Area. The company's plans are backed by sporting and enterprise agencies and the Highland Regional Council, and opposed by the Countryside Commission for Scotland and the Nature Conservancy Council. After a public inquiry in 1981, the Scottish Secretary refused planning permission for an access road into the Northern Corries area. In 1988, however, a working party under the aegis of Highland Regional Council recommended a similar plan. If planning permission is given, it rests with the Secretary of State to decide whether to call another public inquiry.

Water privatization.—The Water Act 1989 created a new agency, the National Rivers Authority, which takes over from the water authorities in England and Wales responsibility for pollution control, water resource management, flood defence, fisheries and, in certain areas, navigation. The new authority also has a duty to promote nature conservation and, unlike the water authorities, it can finance conservation projects which are not part of a current drainage scheme. An amendment to the Act provides for the establishment of nitrate-sensitive areas. In these areas controls will be introduced to reduce the amount of nitrogen fertilizer entering water sources.

The privatization of the water industry takes place against a background of an increasing number of pollution incidents, mainly from sewage effluent and farm waste, and the deterioration of many hitherto clean stretches of river. Considerable concern has been expressed over the quality of Britain's bathing beaches and domestic tap water, both of which are well below European Community safety standards in some areas. The abstraction of groundwater has reduced water flows and increased the risk of pollution, especially in hot, dry summers like that of 1989. The Government has, in general, chosen to rely on the more effective implementation of existing powers, rather than the introduction of new ones, to improve this situation.

The newly privatized water companies will probably seek to capitalize on their assets by increasing the use of reservoirs and other stretches of water for sport and recreation, and by selling surplus land for housing and commercial development. Much water authority land is of great value for landscape and wildlife. No less than 44 nature reserves managed by Nature Conservation Trusts lie on water authority land, and in Wales half of the 97,000 acres owned by the Welsh Water Authority are designated as Sites of Special Scientific Interest. One of the options open to the Secretary of State is to offer suitable surplus land to an amenity or conservation body on a first refusal basis. However, conservation bodies fear that they may not be able to afford to purchase these areas.

THE BUILT ENVIRONMENT

Church fabric.—The report of the Faculty Jurisdiction Commission of 1984 proposed a number of substantial changes in the internal control exercised by the Church of England over the repair and alteration of cathedrals and churches. The General Synod of the Church of England rejected the first attempt to introduce a Care of Cathedrals Measure some years ago, but a recent successor found much more favourable reaction. This new Measure provides for a central Cathedrals Fabric Commission, and for a Fabric Advisory Committee at each cathedral. The former will decide major cases, the latter, minor cases.

A Measure to liberalize the system of faculty jurisdiction was also introduced into the Synod. This allows the consistory court in each diocese to consider cases submitted by parties other than a local parish or the Chancellor of the diocese. The intention where alterations to churches are concerned is to make the system more like that of the secular public inquiry. However, consistory courts will remain the vehicle by which the Chancellor, advised by the Diocesan Advisory Committee, grants or denies permission for alterations at any church, listed or otherwise.

Churches funding increase.—The Redundant Churches Fund cares for over 250 Anglican churches no longer in pastoral use. The Fund is voted money for its work every five years by the Church Commissioners and the House of Commons Fifth standing committee. The Government's agreement with the Church Commissioners is that the maximum combined grants from Church and Government during the quinquennium which began in April 1989 shall not exceed £12·4 million; of that sum, 30 per cent will be contributed by the Church and 70 per cent by the Government. That compares with the proportions of 40 per cent and 60 per cent respectively in the quinquennium just ended.

The increase in Government funding for redundant churches is of benefit to churches of all denominations and will help to offset the increased financial burden of the community charge. Other benefits announced in the past year are an extra £3 million aid for historic churches in use and the exemption from non-domestic rates of a wide range of church buildings, including church halls with an income from lettings.

The extra £3 million a year for historic places of worship will be granted by the Government from 1990 and administered by English Heritage. The Government preferred to give this indirect assistance to churches rather than to exempt the clergy from paying community charges for church buildings. Decisions on how the bonus will be distributed have yet to be taken but it is likely to finance an increase in the grant levels, greater resources to conserve contents and wall paintings, and some assistance for nonconformist chapels through the Redundant Churches Fund.

Farm buildings.—The Ministry of Agriculture has introduced a scheme which offers farmers grants towards the repair of 'vernacular farm buildings' retained in agricultural use. Many traditional buildings in stone and timber-frame remain either unlisted or have only Grade II listing. As a result they are not eligible for English Heritage monies, unless they happen to be within a conservation area; this is unlikely where more remote farms are concerned.

The grants range from 35 per cent to 50 per cent of the cost of eligible work in any six-year period, up to a ceiling of £74,000. The building in question must be in agricultural use at the time of the application and must remain so for at least ten years after that date. A structure in receipt of grant-aid from English Heritage is ineligible. Money is not available for normal maintenance or for works of conversion or extension. Repairs must be sympathetic to the

building and the use of materials such as asbestos, fibre cement, concrete blocks or steel aluminium profiled sheeting is specifically prohibited.

Grants to convert former farm buildings to non-agricultural purposes continue to be administered through the Rural Development Commission.

Historical monuments.—Among the ongoing projects of the Royal Commission on Historical Monuments of England is the detailed assessment of York Minster and studies of the medieval rural houses of Kent, the Rows in Chester, and the churches and country houses of Northamptonshire. Publication of an inventory of historic nonconformist chapels and meeting houses is closer to completion following the decision of the Commissioners to give priority to the preparation for publication of the section covering south-west England. This will include the counties of Berkshire, Cornwall, Devon, Dorset, Hampshire, Somerset and Wiltshire. A survey of buildings built before 1922 in the six towns of the Staffordshire Potteries has been completed. This was a joint project carried out with the Stoke-on-Trent City Museum. Three surveys of textile mills in Yorkshire, Greater Manchester and East Cheshire are other joint projects in which the Commission is involved, mostly with local authority assistance.

The Threatened Buildings section of the Commission uncovered in Gosford Street, Coventry, what is probably the oldest secular structure in the city dated to c.1330 after dendrochronological analysis of the timber. Detailed studies have been organized of Calke Abbey, Derbyshire, opened in spring 1989 by the National Trust; Upton Court, Slough, Berkshire; and the flax milling complex at Ditherington, Shrewsbury, of 1797, the earliest complete fireproof building in England.

The Survey of London became part of the Royal Commission in 1986 following the abolition of the Greater London Council. Work continues on Volume XLIII of the Survey, covering the Parish of All Saints, Poplar. Monographs on County Hall, the Mansion House and Smithfield Market are nearing completion. In 1987–88 the National Monuments Record carried out detailed photographic recording of sites as diverse as the New River in Hertfordshire and London, soon to become redundant as a water supply; St. James's Palace and Clarence House; and 17th century painted decoration in Lincoln Cathedral. A joint project with English Heritage to provide a classification of building types is progressing. The number of classification terms has increased to 5,330 following the development of a computer data base. A 'Draft Thesaurus of Architectural Terms' was published in 1987 and distributed to interested parties. Work has now begun on drafting glossary entries, and it is hoped to publish this in due course.

Finally, the medieval stained glass archive – the Corpus Vitrearum Medii Aevi (CVMA) – continues with the help of the Royal Commission and funds provided by the British Academy. The CVMA's first study – of York Minster – was published in June 1987 and work is proceeding on texts about Balliol College, Oxford, and Norwich churches, and on a catalogue of Netherlandish roundels in England.

Increased aid for repairs.—English Heritage has developed a new strategy to maintain buildings within England's 6,000 conservation areas. This combines a survey of the problem, an extension of grant-aid, and financial support for local authorities carrying out urgent repairs. These proposals are intended to complement the launch of a new computerized Buildings At Risk survey.

Until recently only 'outstanding' listed historic buildings were eligible for grant-aid from English Heritage. Others could be considered for grants only if they were in one of 500 selected conservation areas. Now, however, a grant covering about 25 per cent of the repair costs can be offered to the owner of a listed building in any of the conservation areas, provided that the building is vacant and in need of urgent work to preserve its structure.

Where an owner is unwilling to undertake the work, English Heritage will, if necessary, assist the local authority concerned to serve an Urgent Works Notice under Section 101 of the Town and Country Planning Act 1971. This empowers the local authority to carry out the work itself and reclaim the cost from the owner. Where the cost cannot be reclaimed, up to half the cost will be met by English Heritage.

A pilot study carried out in Kirklees, West Yorkshire, showed that nearly 5 per cent of the total number of listed buildings in the district were at risk. If the result of the pilot study is representative of the whole country, 23,000 historic buildings could be in need of structural repair. Of these, more than 9,000 will probably be in Conservation Areas. Half of these are likely to be unoccupied and thus eligible for the new grant-aid.

The grant scheme, for which £350,000 has been allocated in 1989–90, will be reviewed after 12 months.

Listed buildings.—By the end of June 1989 the total of buildings listed as being of special architectural and historic interest stood at 431,739. Of these, 6,059 were in the Grade I category.

In the past year, listing afforded statutory protection to Birch Grove at Horsted Keynes, Sussex. Until recently the home of Harold Macmillan, Birch Grove was built by his father in 1926, and incorporates 18th century doorcases and chimneypieces from Devonshire House, Piccadilly, London, which was demolished in the 1920s. The road bridge with remains of c. 1250 in Hyde Street, on the site of the North Gate at Winchester, was given a Grade II* listing, as was the early 19th century custom-built wool drying house at Bourne Mill, London Road, Thrupp, Gloucestershire. Other recent listings include: three hangars of c.1917 built for the Royal Flying Corps at Hooton Park, Bebington in the Wirral; three aircraft hangars of c.1910 at the former Sundridge Aerodrome in Kent which were built for the manufacture of planes by the Polish Prince de Bolotoff; a row of five tenter posts in Longwood Gate, Huddersfield, with sockets for iron hooks used as part of the cloth manufacturing process, a length of cloth being stretched out to dry between them; the 'well preserved and relatively early cricket pavilion' of 1902 in Dean Park Sports Ground, Cavendish Road, Bournemouth; a cast iron electricity service box of the late 19th century made by Hardy & Padmore Ltd.

for the Taunton Corporation Electricity Department; the Elephant House at Whipsnade Zoo, Bedfordshire, designed in 1935 by Lubetkin & Tecton (Grade II*); a look-out tower in the boundary wall at 39–40 East Parade, Rhyl, Clwyd, built c.1841 as a semaphore signalling 'station' for the paddle steamers operating between the Foryd Harbour, Rhyl, and Liverpool; 34 gas lamp standards of c. 1890 in Kippington Road and Oakhill Road, Sevenoaks; and the tomb in the grounds of Christchurch, Virginia Water, Surrey, of Ramon Cabrera, a Carlist general in the Spanish civil war 1836–43 who became a political exile in this country.

Listed domestic buildings include a cottage known as Zennor in The Gardens, Adstock, Buckinghamshire, which dates from the 17th century and is described as 'a rare and interesting survival of a one-storey peasant house, probably representing the survival of a squatter's house built on the edge of common land'; council houses of c.1924 in Ernest Road, Dudley, built as part of an experiment using cast iron as a building material, in a pre-fabricated system designed by the Horsley Ironworks Company of Tipton; 50, 52 and 54 Inge Street, Birmingham, built in 1789 and reputed to be the last remaining example of back-to-back housing in the city; 7 Water Lane, Debenham, Suffolk, a cottage of the late 17th century converted in 1849 and 'believed to be the earliest surviving rural police house or station in Suffolk'; and 1–5 Flitcroft Street, in the London Borough of Camden, of 1903–4, 'an important survival of a theatrical scene painting workshop'; Hogsbeck House, Willoughby, Lincolnshire, of 1796 astonished the lister because of the survival internally of 'a remarkable room running the depth of the house on the first floor. Apart from the grates this room remained unplastered until c.1950. It seems that it may have been intended for a specialized use to which it was never put, for example hunt or shooting breakfasts'.

The resurvey of rural areas of the country begun in the early 1980s is now complete although the results are still being published. Pilot surveys of underlisted urban areas, such as Stoke, Brighton, Leeds and Manchester have commenced. It seems likely that the final total of listed buildings will exceed 500,000, more than that of any other country in the world.

Listed buildings under threat.—In 1988 there were applications to demolish in their entirety 585 listed buildings in England and Wales. This compares with 649 in 1987, 557 in 1985 and 480 in 1983. The upward trend is not very surprising given the spectacular rise in recent years in the number of protected buildings. That only 500 or so are threatened out of a total exceeding 430,000 indicates that most listings cover buildings in good condition and productive use. The gradual rise in applications to demolish disguises a change in the nature of applicants. Ten years ago almost a third of applications were made by local authorities, either at district or county level. Now the equivalent ratio is 1 in 24. In 1988 only three buildings were menaced by local authority inspired schemes for road widening and only two by proposals for slum clearance.

Buildings threatened by demolition applications in the year under review included: the Great Barn at Waxham, Norfolk (Grade I); Grimethorpe Hall, South Yorkshire, a fine 17th century house combining a 'vernacular' façade with mullioned and transomed windows and an attempt at a 'polite' façade with sash windows and a substantial Dutch gable; the Little Temple at Coleby Hall, Lincs., the smaller 18th century counterpart to the famous rotunda on the same estate; the Tobacco Warehouse, Stanley Docks, Liverpool, built *c.*1900, when it was claimed to be the largest warehouse in the world; the former Theatre Royal at Chatham, Kent, of 1899; the massive boat hoist of 1862 (Grade II*) in the Aldam Dock, Goole; St. Augustine's Church, Preston, of 1838 and 1890; and the early Georgian terrace at 159–163 Duke Street, Liverpool.

One of the biggest controversies of the year centred on the projected rail link for the Channel Tunnel. A parliamentary private bill lodged in 1989 provided for the construction of a new British Rail terminal between Kings Cross and St. Pancras Stations (both Grade I listed). Two listed buildings were proposed for demolition without replacement, including the Great Northern Hotel of 1850 by Cubitt, and two listed buildings were proposed for reconstruction. The scheme was to be paid for by the redevelopment of 134 acres of former railway land lying behind the site. Proposals for this site included a park but offices were to be the principal ingredient of this 'enabling development'.

A potentially more serious threat to conservation is posed by the link itself, covering the 72 miles between London and the Kent coast. At the time of writing, details of the route had not been released, but it is anticipated that British Rail will lodge a second Parliamentary private bill in November providing for work to be started on the rail link. British Rail's 'preferred route' will include 17 miles of tunnelling under South London and a shorter stretch at two further points, including around Ashford. Further changes announced in August are expected to reduce the number of listed buildings facing demolition, but many still face damage to their setting and amenity. In addition, the prosperity generated in the area by the transport links to the Continent is expected to increase greatly the development pressures in Kent, particularly in the vicinity of the two intermediate stations.

National Heritage Memorial Fund.—In 1988 the National Heritage Memorial Fund awarded grants to the following new projects: £300,000 to the National Trust to assist in the restoration of the 19th century garden at Biddulph Grange, Staffordshire; the purchase by Essex County Council of the 12th and 13th century Barley and Wheat Barns at Cressing Temple; the acquisition by the Royal Institute of British Architects of the drawings of the architect Detmar Blow (1867–1939); the conservation by the Ironbridge Gorge Museum Trust of 12,000 floor tiles made by Craven Dunhill following their salvage from Palace Chambers, adjacent to Westminster Tube Station which was demolished in 1986; the restoration of the medieval glass and 12 monuments in St. Nicholas Church, Stanford-on-Avon, Northamptonshire; the purchase of the lease of the 1854 Mechanics Institute in Princess Street, Manchester, by the city's Trades Union Council, which was founded in the building in 1868; the purchase of James Northcote's portrait of John Ruskin at the age of 3 by the National Portrait Gallery; the repair of the so-called St. John Triptych, a set of painted panels commissioned in 1615, in St. Mary's Church, Lydiard Tregoze, Wiltshire; the purchase by the V. & A. of an ornamental firegrate dated 1788 and believed to have been commissioned for the Music Room at Powderham Castle, Devon; and the purchase by the Jewish Museum of two silver-gilt, Queen Anne-style Torah finials which top the scroll of the Pentateuch when in procession and display.

New museums.—A museum covering the history of the Bank of England has opened in the Bank of England building in the City of London. The Bank Stock Office designed by Sir John Soane (1788) has been faithfully reconstructed and 12 of Soane's original caryatids have been used to frame the exhibition cabinets. The new museum is mostly housed in the rotunda just beyond the Stock Office.

At the Ironbridge Gorge Museum a Museum of the River opened in spring 1989 in the 1840s Gothic warehouse. In May 1989 the Ironbridge Gorge Museum started to manufacture wrought iron. Wrought iron has not been produced commercially in Britain since the early 1970s, when the last firm to do so, Walmesley of Bolton, closed. Walmesley's survived for a number of years before their closure by remelting and rerolling wrought iron plates from the fire-damaged Menai Bridge, which were purchased from British Rail. The Museum acquired the equipment from Walmesley's and to house the works, re-erected at the Museum site an early iron-framed building of 1813, designed by John Rennie, from the Royal Dockyard at Woolwich.

COUNTRYSIDE CONSERVATION

NATIONAL PARKS
England and Wales

The ten National Parks of England and Wales were established in the 1950s under the provisions of the National Parks and Access to the Countryside Act 1949. The National Parks were set up to conserve and protect scenic landscapes from inappropriate development and to provide access to the land for public enjoyment.

The Countryside Commission is the statutory body which has the power to designate National Parks. The designation of National Parks in England is considered and confirmed by the Secretary of State for the Environment, and the designation of National Parks in Wales by the Secretary of State for Wales. The designation of a National Park does not affect the ownership of the land, nor does it remove the rights of the local community. Although the parks are administered through local government, the vast majority of the land is owned by private landowners (74 per cent) or by other bodies like the National Trust (7 per cent) and the Forestry Commission (7 per cent). The National Park Authorities own only 2·3 per cent of the land in the National Parks.

Under the Local Government Act 1972, National Park Authorities (N.P.A.s) are the authorities responsible for park administration. They also influence land use and development, and deal with planning applications.

Two-thirds of the members of each authority are appointed by the county and district councils within whose boundaries the parks lie. One-third of the members are appointed by the Secretary of State for the Environment or the Secretary of State for Wales with advice from the Countryside Commission.

In the Peak District and the Lake District the N.P.A.s are special boards: the Peak Park Joint Planning Board and the Lake District Special Planning Board. These are autonomous authorities which are financially independent, unlike the authorities in the other eight parks which are county council committees. The N.P.A.s appoint the National Park Officer for the National Park they administer.

Central government provides 75 per cent of the funding for the parks through the National Park Supplementary Grant. The remaining 25 per cent is supplied by the local authorities concerned. Net expenditure in 1987–88 totalled £13,456,200.

The Countryside Commission has stated that other areas are regarded as being worthy of National Parks status. A special statutory authority was established in 1989 to develop, conserve and manage the Norfolk and Suffolk Broads (*see* p. 302). The other area considered worthy of designation is the New Forest and it has been the subject of a consultative report to decide upon its future.

The National Parks in England and Wales are:

Brecon Beacons (519 sq. miles/1,344 sq. km.).—Designated in 1957, the park lies in Powys (66 per cent), Dyfed, Gwent and Mid Glamorgan. The park is centred on the Beacons, Pen y Fan, Corn Du and Cribyn, but also includes the valley of the Usk, the Black Mountains to the east and the Black Mountain to the west.

There are information centres at Brecon, Craig-y-nos Country Park, Abergavenny and Llandovery, a study centre at Danywenallt and a day visitor centre near Libanus.

Information Office, 7 Glamorgan Street, Brecon, Powys LD3 7DP. (Tel. 0874-4437). *National Park Officer,* J. Bradley.

Dartmoor (365 sq. miles/945 sq. km.).—Designated in 1951, Dartmoor lies wholly in Devon. Dartmoor consists of moorland and rocky granite tors, and is rich in prehistoric remains.

There are information centres at Newbridge, Tavistock, Bovey Tracey, Steps Bridge, Princeton and Postbridge.

Information Office, Parke, Haytor Road, Bovey Tracey, Devon TQ13 9JQ. (Tel. 0626-832093). *National Park Officer,* I. Mercer.

Exmoor (265 sq. miles/686 sq. km.).—Designated in 1954, Exmoor lies in Somerset (71 per cent) and Devon. Exmoor is a moorland plateau inhabited by wild ponies and red deer. There are many ancient remains and burial mounds.

There are information centres at Lynmouth, County Gate, Dulverton and Combe Martin.

Information Office, Exmoor House, Dulverton, Somerset TA22 9HL. (Tel. 0398-23665). *National Park Officer,* Dr. L. F. Curtis.

Lake District (880 sq. miles/2,280 sq. km.).—Designated in 1951, the Lake District lies wholly in Cumbria. The Lake District includes England's highest mountains (Scafell Pike, Helvellyn and Skiddaw) but it is most famous for its glaciated lakes.

There are information centres at Keswick, Waterhead, Hawkshead, Seatoller, Bowness, Grasmere, Coniston, Glenridding and Pooley Bridge, an information van at Gosforth and a park centre at Brockhole, Windermere.

Information Office, Busher Walk, Kendal, Cumbria LA9 4RH. (Tel. 0539-24555). *National Park Officer,* J. Toothill.

Northumberland (398 sq. miles/1,031 sq. km.).—Designated in 1956, the Northumberland National Park lies wholly in Northumberland. The park is an area of hill country stretching from Hadrian's Wall to the Scottish Border.

There are information centres at Ingram, Once Brewed, Rothbury, Housesteads, Harbottle and Kielder, and an information caravan at Cawfields.

Information Office, Eastburn, South Park, Hexham, Northumberland NE46 1BS. (Tel. 0434-605555). *National Park Officer,* T. Macdonald.

North York Moors (553 sq. miles/1,433 sq. km.).—Designated in 1952, the North York Moors lie in North Yorkshire (96 per cent) and Cleveland. The park consists of woodland and moorland, and includes the Hambleton Hills and the Cleveland Way.

There are information centres at Danby, Pickering, Sutton Bank, Ravenscar, Helmsley and Hutton-le-Hole, and a day study centre at Danby.

Information Office, The Old Vicarage, Bondgate, Helmsley, York YO6 5BP. (Tel. 0439-70657). *National Park Officer,* D. Statham.

Peak District (542 sq. miles/1,404 sq. km.).—Designated in 1951, the Peak District lies in Derbyshire (64 per cent), Staffordshire, South Yorkshire, Cheshire, West Yorkshire and Greater Manchester. The Peak District is composed of the gritstone moors of the 'dark peak' and the limestone dales of the 'white peak'.

There are information centres at Bakewell, Edale, Fairholmes and Castleton, and information points in the Goyt Valley and at Hartington.

Information Office, Aldern House, Baslow Road, Bakewell, Derbyshire DE4 1AE. (Tel. 062 981-4321). *National Park Officer,* M. Dower.

Pembrokeshire Coast (225 sq. miles/583 sq. km.). Designated in 1952, the Pembrokeshire Coast National Park lies wholly in Dyfed. The park consists of cliffs, open moorland and Skomer Island.

There are information centres at Tenby, St. David's, Pembroke, Newport, Kilgetty, Haverfordwest and Broad Haven.
Information Office, County Offices, Haverfordwest, Dyfed SA61 1QZ. (Tel. 0437-4591). *National Park Officer*, N. Wheeler.

Snowdonia (838 sq. miles/2,171 sq. km.).—Designated in 1951, Snowdonia lies wholly in Gwynedd. It is an area of deep valleys and rugged mountains in northern Wales.
There are information centres at Aberdovey, Bala, Betws y Coed, Blaenau Ffestiniog, Conwy, Harlech, Dolgellau and Llanberis.
Information Office, Penrhyndeudraeth, Gwynedd LL48 6LS. (Tel. 0766-770274). *National Park Officer*, A. Jones.

Yorkshire Dales (680 sq. miles/1,762 sq. km.).—Designated in 1954, the Yorkshire Dales National Park lies in North Yorkshire (88 per cent) and Cumbria. The Yorkshire Dales are composed primarily of limestone overlaid in places by millstone grit. The three peaks of Ingleborough, Whernside and Pen-y-Ghent are within the park.
There are information centres at Clapham, Grassington, Hawes, Aysgarth Falls, Malham and Sedbergh.
Information Office, Yorebridge House, Bainbridge, Leyburn, North Yorkshire DL8 3BP. (Tel. 0969-50456). *National Park Officer*, R. Harvey.

Scotland and Northern Ireland

The National Parks and Access to the Countryside Act 1949 dealt only with England and Wales. It made no provision for Scotland or Northern Ireland and there are no national parks in these two countries. However, in 1989 the Scottish Office asked the Countryside Commission for Scotland to report on whether national parks should be designated in Scotland.

AREAS OF OUTSTANDING NATURAL BEAUTY

England and Wales

Under the National Parks and Access to the Countryside Act 1949, provision was made for the designation of Areas of Outstanding Natural Beauty (AONBs) by the Countryside Commission. The Countryside Act 1968 further defines the role of AONBs, suggesting that they should show due regard for the interests of other land users, such as agriculture and forestry groups. Designations in England are confirmed by the Secretary of State for the Environment and those in Wales by the Secretary of State for Wales.

Although less emphasis is placed upon the provision of open-air enjoyment for the public than in the national parks, AONBs are seen as areas which are no less beautiful and require the same degree of protection to conserve and enhance the natural beauty of the countryside. This includes protecting flora and fauna, geographical and other landscape features.

In AONBs planning and management responsibilities are split between county and district councils (there are 14 which cross county boundaries). Finance for the AONBs is provided by grant-aid.

Thirty-eight Areas of Outstanding Natural Beauty have been designated since 1956. They are (with dates of foundation and area):

Anglesey (1967) (83 sq. miles/215 sq. km.).—The designated area extends along the entire coastline of the island, except for breaks around the urban areas and in the vicinity of Wylfa.

Arnside and Silverdale (1972) (29 sq. miles/75 sq. km.).—The area embraces the upper half of Morecambe Bay, the Kent estuary, and includes extensive tidal flats in the Bay.

Cannock Chase (1958) (26 sq. miles/68 sq. km.).—An area of high heathland in Staffordshire. Deer continue to roam over the Chase.

Chichester Harbour (1964) (29 sq. miles/75 sq. km.).—The area extends from Hayling Island to Apuldram and includes Thorney Island.

Chilterns (1965) (309 sq. miles/800 sq. km.).—Chalk downlands running from South Oxfordshire northeastwards to Bedfordshire, including the outlying group of hills beyond Luton.

Clwydian Range (1985) (60 sq. miles/156 sq. km.).—A prominent ridge extending southwards from Prestatyn on the North Wales coast. Offas's Dyke runs along the crest of the Range.

Cornwall (1959; Camel Estuary 1983) (370 sq. miles/957 sq. km.).—A number of separate areas including Bodmin Moor; most of the Land's End peninsula; the coast between St. Michael's Mount and St. Austell (with Falmouth omitted); the Fowey Estuary; in north Cornwall most of the coast to Bedruthan Steps and between Perranporth and Godrevy Towans, plus the Camel Estuary.

Cotswolds (1966) (582 sq. miles/1,507 sq. km.).—The area of limestone hills above the Vales of Gloucester and Evesham.

Cranborne Chase and West Wiltshire Downs (1983) (371 sq. miles/960 sq. km.).—A chalkland area, covering parts of Wiltshire, Dorset, Hampshire and Somerset, including the wooded remnants of the ancient Chase.

Dedham Vale (1970; extended 1978) (28 sq. miles/72 sq. km.).—The area bordering Essex and Suffolk, where John Constable painted.

East Devon (1963) (103 sq. miles/267 sq. km.).—The coastline between Exmouth and Lyme Regis, with Sidmouth, Beer and Seaton omitted. Inland Gittisham Hill, East Hill and Woodbury and Aylebeare Commons are included.

North Devon (1960) (66 sq. miles/171 sq. km.).—Includes most of the N. Devon coastline, from just north of Bude to the boundary of the Exmoor National Park.

South Devon (1960) (128 sq. miles/332 sq. km.).—Includes the coast between Bolt Head and Bolt Tail, Salcombe, Slapton Sands and Dartmouth, and the estuaries and valleys of the Yealm, Erme, Avon and Dart.

Dorset (1959) (400 sq. miles/1,036 sq. km.).—The coastline between Lyme Regis and Poole, with the Isle of Portland and Weymouth omitted, stretching inland to include the Purbeck Hills and the downs of Hardy country.

Forest of Bowland (1964) (310 sq. miles/803 sq. km.).—A moorland area mostly in Lancashire running westward from the River Ribble, with a small outlying area east of the Ribble which includes Pendle Hill.

Gower (1956) (73 sq. miles/189 sq. km.).—A peninsula in West Glamorgan, South Wales, known for its coastline.

East Hampshire (1962) (151 sq. miles/391 sq. km.).—A chalkland area stretching from the outskirts of Winchester to the Sussex border at a distance of about 10 miles inland.

South Hampshire Coast (1967) (30 sq. miles/78 sq. km.).—14 miles of coastline between Hurst Castle and Calshot Castle, extending inland up the Beaulieu River for about six miles.

High Weald (1983) (560 sq. miles/1,450 sq. km.).—The area covers parts of East and West Sussex, Kent and Surrey. It is predominantly wooded, and includes larger heathland areas like Ashdown Forest, the remnants of the old Wealden forests.

Howardian Hills (1987) (79 sq. miles/205 sq. km.).—Wooded hills which rise above the Vales of York and Pickering.

Kent Downs (1968) (326 sq. miles/845 sq. km.).—Running east and south-east from the Surrey border near Westerham to the coast near Dover and Folkestone, with a coastal outlier at South Foreland and a narrow strip of the old sea cliff escarpment west of Hythe overlooking Romney Marsh.

Lincolnshire Wolds (1973) (216 sq. miles/560 sq. km.).—The area extends in a south-east direction from Laceby and Caistor in the north to the region of Spilsby, about ten miles west of the coast.

Lleyn (1957) (60 sq. miles/155 sq. km.).—An isolated peninsular in Gwynedd, North Wales.

Malvern Hills (1959) (40 sq. miles/104 sq. km.).—The whole range of the Malvern Hills in the county of Hereford and Worcester, just touching Gloucestershire.

Mendip Hills (1972) (78 sq. miles/202 sq. km.).—Comprising over half of the Mendip Hills, the area stretches from Bleadon Hill to the A39 road north of Wells and includes Cheddar Gorge and Wookey Hole.

Norfolk Coast (1968) (174 sq. miles/450 sq. km.).—An almost continuous coastal strip three to five miles in depth from Hunstanton to Bacton, with a further small strip between Sea Palling and Winterton-on-Sea. The area includes part of the Sandringham Estate.

North Pennines (1988) (869 sq. miles/2,251 sq. km.).

Northumberland Coast (1958) (50 sq. miles/129 sq. km.).—Stretches from just south of Berwick to Amble and includes Holy Island and the Farne Islands.

Quantock Hills (1957) (38 sq. miles/99 sq. km.).—A range of sandstone hills in Somerset.

Isles of Scilly (1976) (6 sq. miles/16 sq. km.).—About 140 islands and skerries in the Scillies group of which only five are inhabited. There are a number of sites of special scientific interest.

Shropshire Hills (1959) (300 sq. miles/777 sq. km.).—Most of south-west Shropshire between the Welsh border and the boundary with Hereford and Worcester, including the region around Clun, the area of the Stiperstones, the Long Mynd and Wenlock Edge, with the tongues of land running north-east to the Wrekin and south towards Ludlow.

Solway Coast (1964) (41 sq. miles/107 sq. km.).—A stretch of coastline in Cumbria from Maryport to the estuaries of the Rivers Eden and Esk (with Silloth omitted) backed by the Solway Plain.

Suffolk Coast and Heaths (1970) (151 sq. miles/391 sq. km.).—The area includes 38 miles of coastline and parts of the Stour and Orwell estuaries, while the Deben, Alde and Blyth flow through it.

Surrey Hills (1958) (160 sq. miles/414 sq. km.).—An area of hills to the east and south of Guildford, including the Hog's Back and the ridge of the North Downs.

Sussex Downs (1966) (379 sq. miles/981 sq. km.).—The area includes the chalk escarpment of the South Downs from Beachy Head to the Hampshire border, and stretches down to the coast between Eastbourne and Seaford.

North Wessex Downs (1972) (671 sq. miles/1,738 sq. km.).—An upland area in Hampshire, Wiltshire, Oxfordshire and Berkshire, bounded by the Marlborough and Lambourn Downs in the west and the Chiltern Hills in the east. Salisbury Plain forms the southern limit of what is so far the largest area designated.

Isle of Wight (1963) (73 sq. miles/189 sq. km.).—A number of separate areas comprising stretches of coastline, the Yar Valley, the high downland behind Ventnor and the chalk ridge which runs from Newport to Culver Cliff and Foreland.

Wye Valley (1971) (125 sq. miles/325 sq. km.).—The river valley running through the counties of Gwent, Gloucestershire and Hereford and Worcester.

Proposals for further designations include: the Tamar and Tavy Valleys, Devon/Cornwall; the Blackdown Hills, Somerset; the Berwyn Mountains, mid-Wales; and the Nidderdale Moors, N. Yorkshire.

Scotland

There are no Areas of Outstanding Natural Beauty in Scotland.

Northern Ireland

The Department of the Environment for Northern Ireland, with advice from the Council for Nature Conservation, designates Areas of Outstanding Natural Beauty in Northern Ireland. At present there are nine and these cover a total area of approximately 695,166 acres (282,546 hectares).

Antrim Coast and Glens, Co. Antrim (174,452 acres/70,600 ha.).

Causeway Coast, Co. Antrim (10,378 acres/4,200 ha.).

Lagan Valley, Co. Down (5,119 acres/2,072 ha.).

Lecale Coast, Co. Down (7,679 acres/3,108 ha.).

Mourne, Co. Down (140,876 acres/57,012 ha.).

North Derry, Co. Londonderry (31,999 acres/12,950 ha.).

South Armagh, Co. Armagh (31,999 acres/12,950 ha).

Sperrin, Co. Tyrone/Co. Londonderry (249,585 acres/101,006 ha.).

Strangford Lough, Co. Down (46,079 acres/18,648 ha).

NATURE CONSERVATION AREAS

SITES OF SPECIAL SCIENTIFIC INTEREST

'Site of Special Scientific Interest' (SSSI) is a legal designation applied to land in England, Scotland or Wales which the Nature Conservancy Council (N.C.C.) identifies as being of special interest because of its flora, fauna, geological or physiographical features. In some cases, SSSI are managed as nature reserves.

The N.C.C. must notify its intention to declare the land of special interest to the local planning authority, the water and drainage authority, every owner/occupier of the land, and the Secretary of State for the Environment (or Secretary of State for Scotland or for Wales where applicable). Forestry and agricultural departments must also be notified.

Objections to the designation of SSSI can be made and ultimately heard at a full meeting of the N.C.C. Council. As a last resort the N.C.C. can purchase a site.

The protection of most sites depends on the co-operation of individual landowners and occupiers. Occupiers must consult the N.C.C. and gain written consent before they can undertake certain listed activities on the site.

As at Dec. 31, 1988 there were 5,149 SSSI in Britain, covering 4,397,151 acres (1,779,503 hectares).

	No.	Acres	Hectares
England	3,262	2,010,081	813,469
Scotland	1,169	1,888,968	764,455
Wales	718	498,101	201,579

Northern Ireland

In Northern Ireland 24 Areas of Special Scientific Interest (ASSIs) have been established by the Department of the Environment for Northern Ireland. These cover a total area of 16,348 acres (6,616 hectares).

NATIONAL NATURE RESERVES

National Nature Reserves are defined in the National Parks and Access to the Countryside Act 1949 as land designated for the study and preservation of flora and fauna, or of geological or physiographical features.

The N.C.C. can designate as a National Nature Reserve land which is being managed as a nature reserve under an agreement with the N.C.C.; land held and managed by the N.C.C.; or land held and managed as a nature reserve by another approved body. The N.C.C. can turn to the appropriate Secretary of State to impose by-laws for the protection of the reserves from undesirable development.

As at Dec. 31, 1988 there were 234 National Nature Reserves in Britain, covering 408,908 acres (165,483 hectares).

	No.	Acres	Hectares
England	121	101,983	41,272
Scotland	68	276,848	112,039
Wales	45	30,077	12,172

Northern Ireland

National Nature Reserves are established and managed by the Department of the Environment for Northern Ireland, with advice from the Council for Nature Conservation and the Countryside. There are 45 National Nature Reserves covering 10,736 acres (4,345 hectares).

LOCAL NATURE RESERVES

Local Nature Reserves are defined in the National Parks and Access to the Countryside Act 1949 as land designated for the study and preservation of flora and fauna, or of geological or physiographical features. The Act gives local authorities in England and Wales and district councils in Scotland the power to acquire, declare and manage local nature reserves in consultation with the Nature Conservancy Council.

As at March 31, 1988 there were 154 designated Local Nature Reserve areas in Britain, covering 37,895 acres (15,336 hectares).

	No.	Acres	Hectares
England	133	22,891	9,264
Scotland	6	6,642	2,688
Wales	15	8,362	3,384

Conservation trusts can also own and manage non-statutory local nature reserves.

FOREST NATURE RESERVES

The Forestry Commission has created Forest Nature Reserves from conservation sites within the Commission's estate. These are like other nature reserves in that their purpose is to protect and conserve special forms of natural habitat, flora and fauna existing in forested areas.

The Forestry Commission has 340 SSSI on its estates and has chosen 46 as Forest Nature Reserves. They extend in size from under 124 acres (50 hectares) to 1,236 acres (500 hectares). The largest include the Black Wood of Rannoch, by Loch Rannoch; Cannop Valley Oakwoods, Forest of Dean; Culbin Forest, near Forres; Glen Affric, near Fort Augustus; Kylerhea, Skye; Pembrey, Carmarthen Bay; Starr Forest, in Galloway Forest Park; Wyre Forest, near Kidderminster.

Northern Ireland

There are 38 Forest Nature Reserves in Northern Ireland, covering 4,522 acres (1,830 hectares). They are designated and administered by the Forest Service, a division of the Department of Agriculture for Northern Ireland.

MARINE NATURE RESERVES

The Wildlife and Countryside Act 1981 gave the Secretary of State for the Environment (and the Secretaries of State for Wales and for Scotland where appropriate) power to designate Marine Nature Reserves and the Nature Conservancy Council powers to select and manage these reserves. Interested parties at a local and at a national level are consulted prior to the confirmation of an area.

Marine Nature Reserves provide protection for marine flora and fauna and geological and physiographical features on land covered by tidal waters up to and including the limit of territorial waters. Reserves also provide opportunities for study and research.

Lundy, in the Bristol Channel, became the first statutory Marine Nature Reserve in November 1986. Other areas proposed for designation as reserves are: the Isles of Scilly; Skomer Island and the Marloes peninsula, Dyfed; the Menai Strait; Bardsey Island and part of the Lleyn peninsula, Gwynedd; Loch Sween, Strathclyde; St. Abb's Head, Berwickshire; and a number of sea lochs in the Hebrides and inlets on the Cornwall/Devon coast.

A number of non-statutory marine reserves have been set up by conservation groups.

HISTORIC MONUMENTS

England

A select list of monuments under the control, since its creation in April 1984, of the Historic Buildings and Monuments Commission for England.

Charges for admission represent the figures obtaining in 1989–90. Concessionary rates are available for children etc.

Annual membership passes are available at £12·50 for adults, £9 for pensioners and £6 for children upon application to English Heritage Membership Dept., P.O. Box 1BB, W1A 1BB.

Standard hours of opening (marked *) are as follows:

	Daily
Good Friday–Sept. 30	10–6
Oct. 1–Maundy Thursday	10–4

Monuments not marked * open Good Friday–Sept. only.

All monuments are closed on Christmas Eve, Christmas Day, Boxing Day and New Year's Day. Some smaller sites may close for the lunch-hour, which is normally 1–2 p.m. During the winter season, many monuments are closed on Mondays.

BEESTON CASTLE, Cheshire. £1.30*. Thirteenth-century inner ward with gatehouse and towers, and considerable remains of large outer ward.

BERKHAMSTED CASTLE, Hertfordshire*. Extensive remains of a large 11th century motte-and-bailey castle.

BOLSOVER CASTLE, Derbyshire. £1.30*. Notable for its exceptionally interesting 17th century buildings.

BOSCOBEL HOUSE, Shropshire. £1.80*. Timber-framed early 17th century hunting lodge with later alterations. Charles II's 'Royal Oak' is nearby.

BRINKBURN PRIORY, Northumberland. 80p. A house of Augustinian canons; the church (*c.* 1200, repaired in 1858) and parts of the cloister buildings survive.

BROUGHAM CASTLE, Cumbria. 80p*. Extensive remains of the 13th century keep, and of other buildings of periods up to the 17th century.

BYLAND ABBEY, North Yorkshire. 80p*. Considerable remains of church and conventual buildings date from the abbey's foundation in 1177 by the Cistercians.

CARISBROOKE CASTLE, Isle of Wight. £2.20*. Norman castle, the prison of Charles I from 1647–1648.

CARLISLE CASTLE, Cumbria. £1.30*. Medieval castle, prison of Mary Queen of Scots. Inner and outer wards enclosing a 12th century keep.

CASTLE ACRE PRIORY, Norfolk. £1.10*. Extensive remains include the 12th century church and the prior's lodgings.

CASTLE RISING CASTLE, Norfolk. 80p*. A 12th century keep standing in a massive earthwork with its gatehouse and bridge.

CHESTERS ROMAN FORT, Northumberland. £1.30*. Fine example of a bath house.

CHYSAUSTER ANCIENT VILLAGE, Cornwall. 80p*. Romano–Cornish village, 2nd and 3rd century A.D., probably on a late Iron Age site.

CLEEVE ABBEY, Somerset. £1.10*. Much of the claustral buildings survive including timber-roofed frater, but only foundations of the church.

CORBRIDGE ROMAN SITE, Northumberland. £1.30*. Excavations have revealed the central area of a Roman town and successive military bases.

DEAL CASTLE, Kent. £1.10*. The largest and most complete of the forts erected by Henry VIII for coastal defence.

DOVER CASTLE, Kent. £2.50*. One of the strongest British castles, with Roman, Saxon and Norman features.

DUNSTANBURGH CASTLE, Northumberland. 80p*. The 14th century castle standing on a cliff above the sea has a substantial gatehouse-keep.

FARLEIGH HUNGERFORD CASTLE, Somerset. 80p*. Late 14th century castle of two courts. The chapel contains fine tomb of Sir Thomas Hungerford.

FARNHAM CASTLE KEEP, Surrey. 80p. Built by the Bishops of Winchester, the motte of the castle is enclosed by a large 12th century shell keep. Foundations of a Norman tower.

FINCHALE PRIORY, Durham. 80p* (free in winter). Benedictine priory on banks of River Wear with considerable 13th century remains.

FRAMLINGHAM CASTLE, Suffolk. £1.10*. Impressive castle (*c.* 1200) with high curtain-walls enclosing a poorhouse of 1639.

FURNESS ABBEY, Cumbria. £1.10*. Founded in 1123 by Stephen, afterwards King of England; extensive remains of church and conventual buildings.

GOODRICH CASTLE, Hereford and Worcester. £1.10*. Extensive remains of 13th and 14th century castle incorporating 12th century keep.

GRIMES GRAVES, Norfolk. 80p*. Extensive group of flint mines dating from the Neolithic period. Several shafts can be inspected.

HAILES ABBEY, Gloucestershire. £1.10*. Ruins of a Cistercian monastery founded in 1246. Museum contains some fine architectural fragments.

HELMSLEY CASTLE, North Yorkshire. £1.10*. Twelfth century keep and curtain wall with 16th century domestic buildings. Spectacular earthwork defences.

HOUSESTEADS ROMAN FORT, Northumberland. £1.30*. Excavation has exposed this infantry fort on Hadrian's Wall with its extra-mural civilian settlement.

KENILWORTH CASTLE, Warwickshire. £1.10*. One of the most extensive castles in Britain, showing many styles of building from 1155 to 1649.

LANERCOST PRIORY, Cumbria. 55p. The nave of the Augustinian priory church, *c.* 1166, is still used and there are remains of other claustral buildings.

LINDISFARNE PRIORY, Northumberland. £1.10* (subject to tide). The bishopric of the Northumbrian Kingdom destroyed by the Danes; re-established in 11th century as a Benedictine priory, now ruined.

LULLINGSTONE ROMAN VILLA, Kent. £1.30*. A large villa occupied through much of the Roman period; fine mosaics.

MIDDLEHAM CASTLE, North Yorkshire. 80p*. Childhood home of Richard III. The 12th century keep stands within later fortifications and domestic buildings.

MOUNT GRACE PRIORY, North Yorkshire. £1.10*. Carthusian monastery, founded 1398, with remains of monastic buildings.

NETLEY ABBEY, Hampshire. 80p* (weekends only in winter). Extensive remains of Cistercian abbey, founded 1239, with ruined Tudor house.

OLD SARUM, Wiltshire. 80p*. Large earthworks enclosing the excavated remains of the castle and the first Salisbury cathedral, begun in 1078.

ORFORD CASTLE, Suffolk. 80p*. Circular keep of *c.* 1170 and remains of coastal defence castle built by Henry II.

PENDENNIS CASTLE, Cornwall. £1.30*. Well-preserved castle erected by Henry VIII for coastal defence.

PEVENSEY CASTLE, East Sussex. £1.10*. Walls of a 4th century Roman fort enclosing remains of an 11th century castle.

PEVERIL CASTLE, Derbyshire. 80p*. In a picturesque and nearly impregnable position, this 12th century castle is defended on two sides by precipitous rocks.

PORTCHESTER CASTLE, Hampshire. £1.10*. Walls of a late-Roman fort enclosing a Norman keep and an Augustinian priory church.

RECULVER TOWERS and ROMAN FORT, Kent. 80p*. Remains of Saxon and Norman church with 12th century towers, standing in a Roman fort.

RICHBOROUGH CASTLE, Kent. 80p*. The landing-site of the Claudian invasion in 43 A.D., with massive 3rd century stone walls.

RICHMOND CASTLE, North Yorkshire. £1.10*. This 12th century keep, with 11th century curtain-wall and gatehouse, commands Swaledale.

RIEVAULX ABBEY, North Yorkshire. £1.30*. Founded c. 1132. Extensive remains include an early Cistercian nave and fine 13th century choir and claustral buildings.

ROCHESTER CASTLE, Kent. £1.10*. Eleventh century castle partly founded on the Roman city wall, with a square keep of c. 1130.

ST. AUGUSTINE'S ABBEY, Kent. 80p*. Remains of Benedictine monastery, with Norman church, on site of abbey founded by St. Augustine in 598.

ST. MAWES CASTLE, Cornwall. 80p*. Coast defence castle built by Henry VIII consisting of central tower and three bastions.

SCARBOROUGH CASTLE, North Yorkshire. £1.10*. Remains of 12th century keep and curtain-walls dominating the town.

STONEHENGE, Wiltshire. £1.60*. Prehistoric monument consisting of a series of concentric stone circles surrounded by a ditch and bank.

TILBURY FORT, Essex. £1.10*. One of Henry VIII's coastal forts, extended by Charles II.

TINTAGEL CASTLE, Cornwall. £1.30*. 12th century castle on cliff-top Dark Age settlement site.

TYNEMOUTH PRIORY and CASTLE, Tyne and Wear. 80p*. Remains of a Benedictine priory, founded 1090, on Saxon monastic site. Coastal batteries with reconstructed First World War magazine.

WALMER CASTLE, Kent. £1.60*. (Closed when Lord Warden is in residence.) One of Henry VIII's coastal defence castles, now the residence of the Lord Warden of the Cinque Ports.

WARKWORTH CASTLE, Northumberland. 80p*. 15th century keep amidst earlier ruins with a 14th century hermitage upstream.

WHITBY ABBEY, North Yorkshire. 80p*. 13th and 14th century Benedictine church on site of monastery founded in 657.

WROXETER ROMAN CITY, Shropshire. 80p*. The 2nd century public baths and part of the forum remain of the Roman town of Viroconium.

Wales

A select list of monuments under the control of Cadw: Welsh Historic Monuments. Charges for admission (subject to alteration) are given below. Concessionary rates are available for children, etc.
Standard hours of admission:

	Weekdays	Sundays
March 15–Oct. 15	9.30–6.30	2.00–6.30
Oct. 16–March 14	9.30–4.00	2.00–4.00

All monuments are closed on Christmas Eve, Christmas Day, Boxing Day and New Year's Day.

BEAUMARIS CASTLE, Anglesey, Gwynedd. £1.25. The finest example of the concentrically planned castle in Britain, it is still almost intact.

CAERLEON ROMAN AMPHITHEATRE, Gwent. £1. Late 1st century oval arena surrounded by bank for spectators with entrance passages.

CAERLEON ROMAN FORTRESS BATHS, Gwent. £1. Rare example of a legionary bath-house.

CAERNARFON CASTLE, Gwynedd. £2.50. Family Ticket £6. The most important of the Edwardian castles, built together with the town wall between 1283 and 1330.

CAERPHILLY CASTLE, Mid-Glamorgan. £1.25. Concentrically planned castle (c. 1270) notable for its great scale and use of water defences.

CASTELL COCH, S. Glamorgan. £1.50. Rebuilt 1875–90 on medieval foundations.

CHEPSTOW CASTLE, Gwent. £1. Fine rectangular keep in the middle of extensive fortifications.

CONWY CASTLE, Gwynedd. £1.50. Built by Edward I to guard the Conway ferry.

CRICCIETH CASTLE, Gwynedd. £1.50. A native Welsh castle of the early 13th century, much altered by Edward I.

DENBIGH CASTLE, Clwyd. £1. The remains of the castle, which dates from 1282–1322, includes an unusual triangular gatehouse.

HARLECH CASTLE, Gwynedd. £1.50. Well preserved Edwardian castle with a concentric plan sited on a rocky outcrop above the former shore-line.

RAGLAN CASTLE, Gwent. £1.25. Extensive remains of 15th century castle with moated hexagonal keep.

ST. DAVID'S, BISHOP'S PALACE, Dyfed. £1.50. Extensive remains of principal residence of Bishop of St. David's dating from 1280–1350.

TINTERN ABBEY, Gwent. £1.50. Extensive remains of 13th century church and conventual buildings of this Cistercian monastery.

TRETOWER COURT, Powys. £1.25. Medieval house with remains of castle nearby.

Scotland

A select list of monuments under the control of Historic Buildings and Monuments, Scottish Development Department.

Charges for admission are those obtaining in 1989. Except where indicated differently, charges are adults 60p, concessions (con.) 30p.

Standard hours of opening (marked S.) are as follows:

	Weekdays	Sundays
April–Sept.	9.30–7.00	2.00–7.00
Oct.–March	9.30–4.00	2.00–4.00

Monuments open at any reasonable time are indicated by A.

ABERLEMNO, Tayside. A. Closed in winter. Adm. free. Four Pictish stones.

ANTONINE WALL, Central and Strathclyde Regions. A. Adm. free.

ARNOL BLACKHOUSE, Western Isles. S. Closed Sun. Traditional Hebridean dwelling.

BONAWE, Strathclyde. S. Closed in winter. Mid-18th century iron-furnace.

BROUGH OF BIRSAY, Orkney. S. Closed Mon., Tues. a.m. in winter. Remains of the Norse period.

BROWN AND WHITE CATERTHUNS, Tayside. A. Adm. free. Iron Age hill forts.

CAERLAVEROCK CASTLE, Dumfries and Galloway. S.

CAIRNPAPPLE HILL, Lothian. S. Closed in winter. A prehistoric ritual complex and Bronze Age cairn.

CALLANISH, Western Isles. A. Adm. free. Standing Stones.

CAMSTER CAIRNS, Highland. A. Adm. free.

CLAVA CAIRNS, Highland. A. Adm. free.

DRYBURGH ABBEY, Borders. S. £1, con. 50p.

EARLS AND BISHOPS PALACES, Kirkwall, Orkney. S. Closed in winter.

EDINBURGH CASTLE, including Scottish National War Memorial, Scottish United Services Museum and Historic Apartments. Open winter: Jan. 4–March 31 and Oct. 1–Dec. 31, Mon.–Sat. 9.30–4.20, Sun. 12.30–3.35. Summer: April 1–Sept. 30, Mon.–Sat. 9.30–5.05, Sun. 11–5.05. Alterations may be made to opening hours during the Tattoo, State and Military events. Adm. to War Memorial, free; to all other areas £2.20, con. £1.10, Family Ticket £5.

EDZELL CASTLE, Tayside. S. Closed Tues., Thurs. a.m.

ELGIN CATHEDRAL, Grampian. S.

FORT GEORGE, Highland. S. £1.50, con. 75p.

GLASGOW CATHEDRAL, Strathclyde. S. Adm. free.

GLENELG BROCHS, Highland. A. Adm. free.

HERMITAGE CASTLE, Borders. S.

HUNTLY CASTLE, Grampian. S.

JARLSHOF, Shetland. S. Closed Tues., Wed. p.m. in winter. Remains of villages from Bronze Age to Viking times.

JEDBURGH ABBEY, Borders. S. Closed Thurs. p.m. and Fri. in winter. £1, con. 50p.

KELSO ABBEY, Borders. S. Adm. free.

LINLITHGOW PALACE, Lothian. S. £1, con. 50p.

LOANHEAD STONE CIRCLE, Grampian. A. Adm. free.

MAES HOWE, Orkney. S. £1, con. 50p. Prehistoric tomb.

MEIGLE MUSEUM, Tayside. S. Closed Sun. Pictish stones.

MELROSE ABBEY, Borders. S. £1, con. 50p.

MOUSA BROCH, Shetland. A. Adm. free.

NETHER LARGIE CAIRNS, Strathclyde. A. Adm. free.

NEW ABBEY CORN MILL, Dumfries and Galloway. S. Closed Wed. p.m., Thurs.

RING OF BROGAR, Orkney. A. Adm. free.

RUTHWELL CROSS, Dumfries and Galloway. A. Adm. free.

ST. ANDREWS' CASTLE AND CATHEDRAL, Fife. S.

SKARA BRAE, Orkney. S. £1.20, con. 60p. Prehistoric village.

SMAILHOLM TOWER, Borders. S. Closed in winter.

STIRLING CASTLE, Central. Open winter: Jan. 4–March 31 and Oct. 1–Dec. 31, Mon.–Sat. 9.30–4.20, Sun. 12.30–3.35; summer: April 1–Sept. 30, Mon.–Sat. 9.30–5.15, Sun. 10.30–4.45. £1·50, con. 75p, Family Ticket £4.

TANTALLON CASTLE, Lothian. S. £1, con. 50p. Closed Wed., Thurs. a.m. in Winter.

THREAVE CASTLE, Dumfries and Galloway. S. Adm. 60p, con. 30p, including ferry.

HOUSES OPEN TO THE PUBLIC

Times of summer opening and admission fees shown are those which obtained in 1989, and are subject to modification. Most houses have concessionary rates for certain categories of visitor.

Space permits only a selection of some of the more noteworthy houses in the U.K. which are open to the public. (*Property of the National Trust; Adm. admission; con. concessionary rates).

A LA RONDE, Exmouth.—Good Friday–Oct. daily 10–6, Sun. 2–7.

ALNWICK CASTLE, Northumberland. Seat of the Duke of Northumberland.—May–Sept. daily to 4.30 (not Sat.). Open Bank Hol. weekends. Adm. £2.

ALTHORP, Northampton.—Daily 1–5. July, Aug. 1–6. Bank Hols. 11–6. Adm. £2.75, Weds. £3.75 (Connoisseurs' Day). Gardens 50p.

*ANGLESEY ABBEY, Cambs.—March 25–Oct. 15. Wed.–Sun. and Bank Hol. Mons. 1.30–5.30. Adm. £3.50. Gardens only March 25–July 2 Wed., Sun. and Bank Hol. Mons. 12–5.30, July 3–Oct. 15 daily, 12–5.30. Adm. £1.50.

ARUNDEL CASTLE, W. Sussex. Seat of the Duke of Norfolk.—April 24–Oct. 27 daily (not Sat.) 1–5, June–Aug. and Bank Hols. 12–5. Adm. charge.

*BASILDON PARK, Berks.—March 25–end Oct. Wed.–Sat. 2–6, Suns. and Bank Hol. Mons. 12–6. Adm. £2. Grounds £1.

BEAULIEU, Hants.—May–Sept. daily 10–6. Oct.–May, daily 10–5 (see also page 1170).

*BELTON HOUSE, Grantham.—March 25–end Oct. Wed.–Sun. and Bank Hol. Mons. 1–5.30. Adm. £3.

BELVOIR CASTLE, nr. Grantham. Seat of the Duke of Rutland.—March 18–Oct. 8. Times vary. Adm. £2.60.

BERKELEY CASTLE, Glos.—April, Sept. daily (not Mon.) 2–5, May–Aug. Tues.–Sat. 11–5, Sun. 2–5, Oct. Sun. only 2–4.30, Bank Hol. Mons. 11–5. Adm. charge.

BLAIR CASTLE, Tayside. Seat of the Duke of Atholl.—March 23–Oct. 29. Mon.–Sat. 2–6. Sun. (June–Sept.) 12–6 (April, May, Oct. 2–6). Adm. £2.50.

BLENHEIM PALACE, Oxon. Seat of the Duke of Marlborough. Churchill's birthplace.—Mid-March–Oct. 31 daily 10.30–5.30. Adm. charge.

BOUGHTON HOUSE, Northants. Seat of the Duke of Buccleuch & Queensberry.—July 29–Aug. 31 daily. Grounds 12–6, House 2–5. Grounds (excl. Gardens) daily (not Fri.) (April 29–Oct. 1) 12–5. Adm. £2.50, Grounds only, 80p.

BOWHILL, Selkirk.—House July 1–July 31 daily 1–4.30 (Sun. 2–6); Grounds July 1–July 31 daily 12–5, Sun. 2–6. Adm. £2.50, Grounds only, £1.

BROADLANDS, Hants. Home of Lord Palmerston and Lord Mountbatten.—March 31–Oct. 1 daily 10–4 (not Mon. except Bank Hols. until Aug.). Adm. £3.95.

BRONTË PARSONAGE, Haworth, West Yorks.—Daily, April–Sept. 11–5.30, Oct.–March 11–4.30. Adm. £1.

BROUGHTON CASTLE, Oxon.—May 18–Sept. 14 Wed., Sun. (also Thurs. in July and Aug.) and Bank Hol. Suns and Mons. 2–5. Adm. £2.

*BUCKLAND ABBEY, Devon. Good Friday–Sept. daily, 11–6. Oct. 11–5. Nov.–March Wed., Sat., Sun. 2–5. Adm. £2.80.

BURGHLEY HOUSE, Stamford.—Good Friday–Oct. 1 (closed Sept. 9) daily 11–5 (Good Friday 2–5). Adm. £3.

*CALKE ABBEY, Derbyshire.—March 25–end Oct., Sat.–Wed. 1–5.30 (not Good Friday). Adm. £3.50.

CARDIFF CASTLE.—March–Oct. 9.45–5 daily. Nov.–Feb. 9.45–4.30. Adm. £2.50, Grounds £1.75.

CARLTON TOWERS, Humberside.—May–Sept. Sun. only, Bank Hol. weekends 1–5. Grounds 12.15–6. Adm. £2.

CARLYLE'S HOUSE, Chelsea, London.—March 25–end Oct. Wed.–Sun. and Bank Hol. Mons. 11–5 (not Good Friday). Adm. £1.60.

*CASTLE COOLE, Enniskillen.—12–6 June, July, Aug. (not Tues.); March 25–April 2, Sat., Sun. and Bank Hols. in April, May, Sept. Adm. £1.50, Grounds April–Sept. free.

*CASTLE DROGO, Devon.—Good Friday–Sept. daily 11–6. Oct. 11–5. Adm. £2.80.

CASTLE HOWARD, N. Yorks.—March 20–Oct. daily 11–4.30. Grounds 10–4.30. Adm. charge.

CAWDOR CASTLE, Inverness.—May–Oct. 1, daily 10–5.30. Adm. £2.60, Grounds £1.30.

*CHARTWELL, Kent. Home of Sir Winston Churchill.—Open three days each week. Times vary. Adm. £3, Grounds £1.20.

CHATSWORTH, Derbyshire. Seat of the Duke of Devonshire.—March 22–Oct. 29 daily 11.30–4.30. Grounds March 22–Oct. 1 daily 10.30–4.30. Adm. charge.

CHICHELEY HALL, Newport Pagnell.—March 24–May 30, Aug. 6–Sept. 24 Sun. and Bank Hols. 2.30–6. Adm. £2.20.

*CLIVEDEN, Maidenhead.—House, April 2–Oct. 29, Thurs. and Sun. 3–6. Gardens March–Dec. daily 11–6. Adm. £2.40, 80p extra for House.

*COMPTON CASTLE, nr. Paignton.—Easter Mon.–Oct. Mon., Wed., Thurs. 10–12.15, 2–5. Adm. £1.50.

*CROFT CASTLE, Herefordshire.—Easter Bank Hol. weekend, May–Sept. Wed.–Sun. and Bank Hol. Mons. 2–6, April and Oct. weekends 2–5. Adm. £1.80.

DICKENS HOUSE, London, WC1.—Daily (not Sun. and Bank Hols.) 10–5. Adm. £1.50.

DR. JOHNSON'S HOUSE, London, EC4.—Daily (not Sun. and Bank Hols.) May–Sept. 11–5.30, Oct.–April 11–5. Adm. charge.

DOWN HOUSE, Downe, Kent. Home of Charles Darwin.—March–Jan. 31, 1–6, not Mon. (except Bank Hols.) or Fri. Adm. £1.50.

DRUMLANRIG CASTLE, Dumfries.—April 29–Aug. 20, daily (not Thurs.) 11–5, Sun. 2–6. Grounds open to Sept. Adm. £2.50, Grounds only £1.

HADDON HALL, Derbyshire.—March 24–Oct. 1 Tues.–Sun., and Bank Hols. 11–6. Closed Sun. in July and Aug. (except Bank Hol. weekends). Adm. £2.60.

HAM HOUSE, Richmond, Surrey.—Daily 11–5 (not Mon., Good Friday, Christmas, New Year and May 1). Adm. £2.

*HARDWICK HALL, Derbyshire.—March 25–Sept. 17. House Wed., Thurs., Sat., Sun., Bank Hol. Mons. 1–5.30. Garden daily to end Oct. (not Good Friday) 12–5.30. Adm. £4, Garden only, £1.50.

HAREWOOD HOUSE, Leeds.—Easter–Oct. daily from 10. Sun. only, Feb., March, and Nov. Adm. charge.

HATFIELD HOUSE, Herts. Childhood home of Elizabeth I.—March 25–Oct. 8 daily (not Mon. and Good Friday) 12–5, Sun. 1.30–5, Bank Hols. 11–5. Grounds, times vary. Adm. £3.20.

HEVER CASTLE, Kent. Childhood home of Anne Boleyn.—March 21–Nov. 5 daily 12–6. Grounds open 11. Adm. charge.

HOLKER HALL, Cumbria.—Easter Sun.–last Sun. in Oct. daily (not Sat.), 10.30–4.30. Adm. charge.

HOLKHAM HALL, Norfolk.—Late May–Sept. Sun.–Thurs. 1.30–5. Spring and Summer Bank Holidays 11.30–5. Adm. £1.70.

HOPETOUN HOUSE, nr. Edinburgh.—Easter, then April 29–Oct. 1, daily 11–5.30. Adm. £2.50.

HOUGHTON HALL, Norfolk.—Easter Sun.–Sept. 25, Sun., Thurs. and Bank Hols. 1–5.30. Adm. £2.50.

*HUGHENDEN MANOR, High Wycombe. Disraeli's home.—Easter Sat.–Oct. Wed.–Sat. 2–6, Sun. and Bank Hol. Mons. 12–6. March weekends 2–6 or dusk. Adm. £2.

INVERARAY CASTLE, Argyll. Seat of the Dukes of Argyll.—1st Sat. in April–2nd Sun. in Oct. daily (not Fri.) 10–6, Sun. 1–6. Woods open all year.

JANE AUSTEN'S HOUSE, Chawton, Hants.—April–Oct. daily, Jan. and Feb. weekends, Nov., Dec. and March, Wed.–Sun. 11–4.30. Adm. £1.

KEATS HOUSE, Hampstead, London.—April–Oct. daily 2–6 (Sat. 10–5, Sun. and Bank Hol. 2–5). Nov.–March daily 1–5 (Sat. 10–5, Sun. 2–5). (Not Christmas, New Year, Good Friday, Easter Eve.) Adm. free.

KELMSCOTT MANOR, nr. Lechlade.—April–Sept., Tues., Wed., Thurs. (on written application). Adm. £2.50.

*KINGSTON LACY HOUSE, Dorset.—March 25–Oct. 29 Sat.–Wed. 1–5. Grounds 12–6. Adm. £3.50, Grounds only £1.

KNEBWORTH HOUSE, Herts.— March 22–May 21, Sat., Sun., School and Bank Hols., May 27–Sept. 10 daily (not Mon.) Weekends only to Oct. 1. 12–5. Adm. £3.30.

*KNOLE, Kent.—March 24–Oct. Wed.–Sat. and Bank Hol. Mons. 11–5, Sun. 2–5. Adm. £2.50.

LEEDS CASTLE, Kent.—March 24–Oct. daily 11–5. Nov.–March, weekends only, 12–4. Adm. charge.

*LITTLE MORETON HALL, Cheshire.—April–Sept. daily (not Tues.), March and Oct. weekends, 1.30–5.30. Closed Good Friday. Adm. £2. Weekends and Bank Hols. £2.50.

LONGLEAT HOUSE, Warminster.—Easter–Sept. daily 10–6, Oct.–Easter daily 10–4. Safari Park mid-March–Oct. 10–6. Adm. charge.

LUTON HOO, Beds.—Easter–mid-Oct. daily 2–5.45 (not Mon. except Bank Hols.). Adm. £3.

MARBLE HILL HOUSE, Twickenham, Middx.—Good Friday–Sept. 30 daily 10–6, Oct.–Maundy Thursday daily 10–4 (not Dec. 24, 25). Adm. free.

MICHELHAM PRIORY, E. Sussex.—March 25–Oct. 31 daily 11–5.30. Adm. £2.

*MONTACUTE HOUSE, Yeovil.—March 25–Nov. 5 daily (not Tues.) 12.30–5.30. Grounds open all year 12–5.30. Adm. £3, Grounds only £1.

*MOUNT STEWART, Co. Down.—Times vary. Adm. House, Garden, Temple £2, Garden and Temple only £1.50.

OSBORNE HOUSE, I.o.W. Queen Victoria's residence.—Good Friday–Sept. 10–6, Oct. 10–5 daily. Adm. £3.

OSTERLEY PARK HOUSE, Isleworth, Middx.—Daily 11–5 (not Mon., May 1, Good Friday, Dec. 24–28, Jan. 1). Adm. £2.

*PENRHYN CASTLE, Bangor.— March 24–Nov. 5 daily (not Tues.) 12–5. (July–Aug. 11–5). Adm. £2.50.

PENSHURST PLACE, Kent.—April 1–Sept. daily (not Mon. except Bank Hols.) 1–5.30. Adm. charge.

*PETWORTH HOUSE, W. Sussex.—March 24–Nov. 5 Tues.–Sun., Bank Hol. Mons., Good Friday 1–5. Adm. £2.70.

PORTMEIRION, Gwynedd.—April–Oct. daily 9.30–5.30. Adm. charge.

POWDERHAM CASTLE, Exeter.—May 28–Sept. 14 Sun.–Thurs. 2–5.30. Adm. charge.

*POWIS CASTLE, Powys.—March 24–June 30, Sept.–Nov. 5 Wed.–Sun. and Bank Hol. Mons. 12–5, July

and Aug. daily (not Mon. except Bank Hol.) 11–6. Nov. 6–April 8 Sun. only 2–4.30. Adm. charge.

RABY CASTLE, Durham.—Easter (Sat.–Wed.), April 29–June 30 Wed. and Sun., July–Sept. daily (not Sat.) 1–5. Also Bank Hol. Sat.–Tues. Adm. £2.

RAGLEY HALL, Warwicks.—March 25–Oct. 1 daily (not Mon., Fri.). Open Bank Hols. Adm. £2.90.

ROCKINGHAM CASTLE, Corby.—Easter Sunday–Sept. Sun., Thurs., (also Bank Hol. Mon. and Tues. and Tues. in Aug.) 1.30–5.30. Adm. £2.50.

*RUFFORD OLD HALL, Lancashire.—March 24–Nov. 5 daily (not Fri.) 1–5, Sun. 2–5. Adm. £1.50.

SANDRINGHAM, Norfolk.—March 26–Sept. 28 (closed July 17–Aug. 5) Mon.-Thurs., 11–4.45, Sun. 12–4.45. Closed when the Royal Family is in residence. Adm. £2.

SCONE PALACE, Perth.—Good Friday–mid Oct. Mon.–Sat. 9.30–5, Sun. 1.30–5 (July and Aug. 10–5). Adm. £2.70.

SHERBORNE CASTLE, Dorset.—Easter Sat.–Sept. Thurs., Sat., Sun. and Bank Hol. Mons. 2–6. Adm. charge.

*SHUGBOROUGH, Staffs.—March 24–Sept. daily 11–5, Oct. 1–Dec. 24 daily 11–4. Adm. £4 (House, Museum, Farm; House only, £1.50).

SKIPTON CASTLE, N. Yorks.—Open all year (not Christmas Day). Adm. £1.60

*SMALLHYTHE PLACE, Kent. Dame Ellen Terry's home.—March 24–Oct. Sat.–Wed. 2–6. Adm. £1.40.

STANFORD HALL, Leics.—Easter Saturday–Sept. Thurs., Sat., Sun., Bank Hols. (Mon. and Tues.) 2.30–6. Adm. £2.10.

STONELEIGH ABBEY, Warwicks.—Closed 1989–90.

STONOR PARK, Oxon.—April Sun. only, May–Sept. Wed., Thurs., Sun. (also Sat. in Aug.) 2–5.30. Open Bank Hol. Mons. 11–5.30. Adm. £2.

*STOURHEAD, Wilts.—May–Sept. Sat.–Thurs., April and Oct. Sat.–Wed. 2–6. Adm. £2.50. Gardens all year, daily 8–7 or dusk. Adm. £2.

STRATFIELD SAYE HOUSE, Reading. Seat of the Duke of Wellington.—May–last Sun. in Sept. daily (not Fri.) 11.30–5. Grounds March–Oct. daily 10–5, Nov.–Feb. weekends only. Adm. £3.60 (House and Grounds).

*SUDBURY HALL, Derbys.—March 25–Oct. Wed.–Sun. and Bank Hol. Mons. 1–5.30. Adm. £2.50.

SUDELEY CASTLE, Glos. Catherine Parr's home.—April–Oct. daily 12–5. Adm. £3.25.

SULGRAVE MANOR, Northants. Home of the Washington family.—March–Dec. daily (not Wed.) 10.30–5.30 (March, Oct.–Dec. 10.30–4). Adm. £2.

SYON HOUSE, Brentford, Middx.—April–Sept. 29 Sun.–Thurs., and Sun. in Oct. 12–5. Adm. charge.

*TRERICE, Cornwall.—March 24–Sept. daily 11–6, Oct. 11–5. Adm. £2.60.

TYN-Y-RHOS HALL, and Shrine of St. George, Shropshire—May–Sept. Sun. only 2.30–5.30. Morning prayers 11. Adm. £1.

*THE VYNE, Basingstoke.—March 24–Oct. 15 daily (not Mon. and Fri.) 1.30–5.30, Bank Hol. Mons. 11–5.30. (Closed Tues. following Bank Hol. Mons.). Adm. £2.30 (Sun. and Bank Hol. Mons. £2.60).

WARWICK CASTLE.—March–Oct. daily 10–5.30, Nov.–Feb. daily 10–4.30 (not Christmas Day). Adm. charge.

WILTON HOUSE, Wilts.—March 24–mid-Oct. Tues-Sat. and Bank Hol. Mons. 11–6, Sun. 1–6. Adm. £3.40.

WOBURN ABBEY, Beds. Seat of the Duke of Bedford.—March 20–Oct. 29 daily 11–5.45 (Sun. 11–6.15). Jan. 1–Mar. 19 weekends only 11–4.45. Adm. £4.

MUSEUMS AND ART GALLERIES OUTSIDE LONDON
(For National Art Galleries and Museums in London see pages 298–9 and 341–5.)

(Adm. admission; con. concessionary rates)

Barnard Castle, Co. Durham.—*The Bowes Museum.* Important collections of British and European fine art, from medieval period to 19th century. Fine porcelain and glass, tapestries and furniture. Music and costume galleries. English period rooms from Elizabeth I to Victoria; French decorative arts of 18th and 19th centuries; local antiquities. Temporary exhibitions. Open weekdays: May–Sept., 10–5.30, March, April, Oct., 10–5, Nov.–Feb., 10–4. Sun.: 2–5 (summer); 2–4 (winter). Adm. £1·55, con. 70p.

Bath.—*Roman Baths Museum.* Roman Baths complex of 1st century A.D. Adm. (including adjoining 18th century Pump Room), £2.50, con. £1.50. *Museum of Costume*, Assembly Rooms. Fashion from 16th century to current year. Closed for building repairs until 1991. *American Museum in Britain*, Claverton Manor. American decorative arts from late 17th to mid 19th centuries. Open April 1–Oct. 30, daily (except Mon.), 2–5, Bank Hol. Mons. and preceding Suns. 11–5. During winter only on application. Adm. charge. *Victoria Art Gallery*, Bridge Street. Open Mon.–Fri. 10–6, Sat. 10–5. Closed Sun., Bank Hols. Adm. free.

Beamish.—*North of England Open Air Museum*, Beamish, Co. Durham. Re-creates Northern life around the turn of the century. Buildings from the region have been rebuilt and furnished, including the Town with houses, shops, etc., the Colliery Village with drift mine and pit cottages, the Railway Station and Home Farm complete with agricultural machinery, animals and exhibitions. Open daily (except Mon. in winter): summer 10–6, winter 10–5.

Beaulieu.—*National Motor Museum.* Displays of vehicles dating from 1895 to present day. Open daily 10–6 (winter, 10–5). Adm. charge.

Belfast.—*Ulster Museum*, Botanic Gardens. Collections of Irish antiquities, natural and local history, fine and applied arts. Open Mon.–Fri. 10–5, Sat. 1–5, Sun. 2–5. *Ulster Folk and Transport Museum*, Holywood. Indoor and outdoor exhibits of all aspects of Ulster folklife. Open Oct.–April, weekdays 11–5, Sun. 2–5 (May–Sept. 11–6, Sun. 2–6). May–June (Wed. only) 11–9. Adm. £1.50, con. 80p. *Transport Museum*, Holywood and Witham Street. History of land, sea and air transport in Ireland and road, rail and sea vehicles. Holywood site—open as for Folk Museum. Witham Street site open weekdays 10–5. Adm. 60p, children 40p, other con. 20p. Special arrangements apply at both museums over Christmas and Easter.

Beverley, N. Humberside.—*Museum of Army Transport.* Exhibits include field workshop, amphibious assault landing, railway section and aircraft. Open 10–5. Closed Christmas period and Mon., Nov.–Feb. Adm. charge.

Birmingham.—*City Museum and Art Gallery.* British and European masters from 14th to 20th centuries (particularly of the Pre-Raphaelite movement), sculpture, European gold, silver and jewellery, metalwork, glass, pottery and porcelain, furniture, textiles and costume, archaeology, local and natural history. Open Mon.–Sat. 9.30–5, Sun. 2–5. Closed Christmas Day, Boxing Day, New Year's Day and Good Friday. Adm. free.

Museum of Science and Industry, Newhall Street. The history of science from the Industrial Revolution to the present; many working machines under steam, gas, etc. Open Mon.–Sat. 9.30–5, Sun. 2–5. Adm. free. Also *Aston Hall, Blakesley Hall, Birmingham Nature Centre, Sarehole Mill*, and *Weoley Castle.*

Bradford.—*Cartwright Hall*, Lister Park. Con-

tains mainly British 19th and 20th century fine art. *Bolling Hall*, off Wakefield Road, a furnished period house, mainly 17th and 18th century. *Industrial Museum*, Moorside Road, illustrates the local wool and worsted industries and transport in an old mill, with mill owner's house. *Cliffe Castle*, Keighley. Natural and local history, minerals and gem display, and period rooms. *Manor House*, Ilkley. Archaeology, local history and contemporary fine art. Open 10–5 (April–Sept. 10–6, except Industrial museum). Closed Good Friday, Christmas Day, Boxing Day and Mons. (except Bank Hols.). Adm. free.

Brighton.—*The Royal Pavilion, Palace of George IV.* Chinoiserie interiors, much of the original furniture returned on loan from H.M. The Queen. Open daily 10–5 (June–Sept. 10–6). Closed Christmas Day and Boxing Day. Adm. £2.30.

Museum and Art Gallery, Church Street (adjacent to Royal Pavilion). Old master paintings; Willett pottery and porcelain collection, 20th century art and furniture, ethnography, archaeology, local history, musical instruments, costume gallery. Open Tues.–Sat. 10–5.45, Sun. 2–5. Closed Christmas Day, Boxing Day, Good Friday, Mons and Jan. 1. Adm. free.

Preston Manor, Preston Park. Thomas-Stanford: Macquoid bequests of English period furniture, furnishings, china and silver. Servants quarters. Open Tues.–Sun. and Bank Hol. Mons. 10–5. Adm. £1.85. Closed Christmas Day, Boxing Day, Good Friday. Gardens open daily. Adm. free.

The Grange, Art Gallery and Museum, Rottingdean. Sussex Room, Kipling Room and collections of National Toy Museum. Open Mon., Thurs., Sat. 10–5, Tues. and Fri. 10–1, 2–5, Sun. 2–5. Closed Christmas Day, Boxing Day, Good Friday, Wed. and Jan. 1. Adm. free.

The Booth Museum of Natural History, Dyke Road. Open 10–5, Sun. 2–5. Closed Christmas Day, Boxing Day, Good Friday, Thurs. and Jan. 1. Adm. free.

Bristol.—*City Museum and Art Gallery.* Collections include Egyptology, ethnography, Bristol ceramics and the Bristol school of artists, silver, French paintings and Chinese ceramics. Glass collection. Open daily, 10–5. *Bristol Industrial Museum*, Prince's Wharf. Collections connected with Bristol and regions industrial history, including an early working model railway and Bristol-built aero-engines. Open Sat.-Wed. 10–1, 2–5. *Maritime Heritage Centre* including SS *Great Britain*, open daily 10–6 (winter 10–5). Adm. free. *National Life-boat Museum*, Prince's Wharf, Wapping Road. Displays of life-boats, models and equipment. Open daily 10.30–4.30. Adm. £1.50, con. 75p. Also *Red Lodge, Blaise Castle House Museum, Kings Weston Roman Villa, Georgian House* and *St. Nicholas Church Museum.*

Cambridge.—*Fitzwilliam Museum.* Egyptian, Greek, Near Eastern and Roman antiquities, coins and medals, medieval manuscripts, paintings and drawings, prints, sculpture, Oriental and Occidental fans, pottery and porcelain, textiles, arms and armour, medieval and renaissance objects of art, and a library. Open Tues.–Sat., Lower Galleries 10–2, Upper Galleries 2–5; Sun. 2.15–5. Closed Dec. 24–Jan. 1 and Good Friday. Closed Mons. incl. May Day Bank Hol. but not Easter and Bank Hol. Mons. Adm. free.

Canterbury.—*Royal Museum and Art Gallery*, and *Buffs Regimental Museum.* Collections include archaeology, porcelain, prints and pictures. Open Mon.–Sat. 10–5. Adm. free. *Canterbury Heritage*, a time-walk museum of the city's history in the medieval Poor Priest's Hospital, Stour Street. Open

Mon.–Sat. 10.30–4, Sun. (June–Oct.) 1.30–4. Adm. £1.20, con. 60p. *Roman Mosaic Museum.* Closed for redevelopment. *West Gate Museum.* Arms and armour and display of city gate-house with battlements. Re-opening Summer 1990. Adm. 40p, con. 20p.

Carlisle.—*Carlisle Museum and Art Gallery*, Tullie House, Castle Street. Collections of archaeology, natural and social history, fine and decorative arts in Jacobean house. Closed for refurbishing until 1991. *Guildhall*, Greenmarket. Civic and Guild history and artefacts. Contact Tullie House Museum for opening information.

Chester.—*Grosvenor Museum*, Grosvenor Street. Collection of Roman antiquities from legionary fortress; natural history, art and folk-life. Open weekdays 10.30–5, Sun. 2–5. *The Georgian House*, Castle Street. Period room displays, costume and musical instruments. Open weekdays, 10.30–5, Sun., 2–5. *King Charles Tower* on City Walls. Civil War displays. Open daily (summer), weekends (winter), times vary. Adm. charge.

Colchester.—*Colchester Castle.* Contains local archaeological antiquities, especially from Roman Colchester. Tours of Roman vaults, castle walls, chapel and prisons, Sat. April-Sept. and weekdays, July-Aug. Open Mon.–Sat. 10–5, Sun. April–Sept. 2.30–5. Closed Good Friday and Christmas period. Adm. 90p, con. 45p. *Hollytrees Museum.* Displays of 18th and 19th century costume, toys and social history. Open Mon.–Sat. 10–5. Closed Good Friday and Christmas period. Adm. free. *Natural History Museum*, All Saints Church. Open as Hollytrees. *Social History Museum*, Holy Trinity Church. Domestic life and crafts. Open as Hollytrees. *Tymperleys Clock Museum.* Open Tues.–Sat., April–Oct. and Bank Holiday Mons. 10–5. Adm. 40p, con. 25p.

Coventry.—*Herbert Art Gallery and Museum*, Jordan Well. Archaeology, natural and local history, fine and decorative arts. Open weekdays 10–5.30, Sun. 2–5. Closed Good Friday and Christmas period. *Museum of British Road Transport*, St. Agnes Lane, Hales Street. Open daily 10–5, April–Sept; Oct.–March, Fri., Sat. and Sun. only. Adm. £1.50, con. 75p. *Lunt Roman Fort*, Baginton. June–Sept., 12–6 (closed Mon. and Thurs.). Adm. £1, con. 25p. *Whitefriars Museum.* Open Thurs., Fri., Sat., and some Bank Hols, 10–5.

Crich, Nr. Matlock, Derbyshire—*National Tramway Museum.* Open air working museum with collection of trams from Britain and abroad. Open April–Oct. weekends and Bank Holidays 10–6.30. May–Sept., open daily (not Fri. except during school holidays) 10–5.30.

Derby.—*Museum and Art Gallery*, The Strand. Archaeology, military, social history, natural history, paintings by Joseph Wright of Derby, Derby porcelain, model theatres. Open Tues.–Sat. 10–5, Sun. and Bank Hols. 2–5, Mons. 11–5 in summer. *Industrial Museum*, Silk Mill, Full Street, Rolls-Royce collection of aero engines, a railway engineering gallery. Open as above. *Pickford's House*, Friar Gate. 18th and 19th century period room settings, social history, decorative arts, costume and textiles. Tues.–Sat. (and Mon. in summer) 12–4. Sun. and Bank Hols. 2–5.

Dorchester.—*Dorset County Museum.* Geology, archaeology, local and natural history and rural crafts of Dorset. Collection of Thomas Hardy's manuscripts, books, notebooks, drawings, etc. Open Mon.–Sat. 10–5, closed Christmas Day, Boxing Day and Good Friday. Adm. £1.20, con. 60p.

Durham.—*Light Infantry Museum and Arts Centre.* County Regiment's 200 year history displayed, arts and crafts exhibitions. Open weekdays (except Mon.) 10–5, Sun. and Bank Hol. Mon. 2–5.

Closed Christmas Day and Boxing Day. Adm. 60p, con. 25p. *Oriental Museum*, The University. Collections ranging from Ancient Egypt to China and Japan. Open weekdays: 9.30–5. Weekends: Nov.–Feb. closed; March–Oct. Sat. 9.30–5, Sun. 2–5. *Cathedral Treasury.* Relics of St. Cuthbert, church plate, medieval seals, manuscripts and vestments. Open weekdays 10–4.30, Sun. 2–4.30. Adm. 60p, con. 10p. *Old Fulling Mill Museum.* Archaeological material from local excavations. Open Nov.–March, daily 2–4, April–Oct., Mon.–Fri. 10–4, Sat. and Sun., 2–4. Adm. free.

Edinburgh.—*City Art Centre*, 2 Market Street. Late 19th and 20th century art, mostly Scottish, and temporary exhibitions. Open weekdays 10–5 (June–Sept. 10–6). Adm. free. *People's Story, Canongate Tolbooth*, 163 Canongate. Courthouse and prison, now museum of Edinburgh life. Open weekdays 10–5 (June–Sept. 10–6). Adm. free. *Huntly House*, 142 Canongate. Local history, collections of Edinburgh silver, glass and Scottish pottery. Open weekdays 10–5 (June–Sept. 10–6). Adm. free. *Lady Stair's House*, Lawnmarket. Mon.–Sat. 10–5 (June–Sept. 10–6). *Lauriston Castle*, Cramond Road South, April–Oct. daily (except Fri.), 11–5; Nov.–March, weekends only. *Museum of Childhood*, 42 High Street. Open weekdays 10–5 (June–Sept. 10–6). Adm. free.

Exeter.—*Exeter Maritime Museum*, The Haven. Collection of working boats. Open daily 10–5 (July–Aug. 10–6). Adm. charge. *Royal Albert Memorial Museum and Art Gallery*, Queen Street. Fine art, Exeter silver, ceramics, ethnography, natural and local history. Open Tues.–Sat. and some Suns. in summer, 10–5.30. Adm. free. *Underground Passages*, High Street. Medieval water supply. Re-opening Summer 1990. *Rougemont House Museum.* Costume displayed in Georgian rooms. Castle Street. Open Mon.–Sat. 10–5. *St. Nicholas' Priory.* Norman priory. Open Tues.–Sat. 10–5.30.

Fort William.—*West Highland Museum*, Cameron Square. Historical, natural history and folk exhibits, including those of the 1745 Rising. Daily (except Sun.) 10–5; June and Sept. 9.30–5.30; July and Aug. 9.30–9.

Glasgow.—*Art Gallery and Museum*, Kelvingrove. Old Masters, 19th century French paintings; archaeology and natural history, collection of armour. *People's Palace*, Glasgow Green. History of city from 1175 to present. *The Burrell Collection*, Pollok Park. Textiles, furniture, ceramics, stained glass, silver and other art objects, paintings, especially 19th century French. *Pollok House*, Pollok Park. Spanish paintings, furniture, silver, ceramics. *Haggs Castle Museum*, St. Andrews Drive. Children's museum with activity workshops. *Provand's Lordship*, Castle Street. Oldest house in Glasgow, period furniture displays. *Rutherglen Museum*, King Street. History of former royal burgh of Rutherglen. *Museum of Transport*, Kelvin Hall. All open weekdays 10–5, Sun. 2–5. Adm. free.

Hull.—*Ferens Art Gallery.* European art, especially Dutch 17th century, British portraits of 18th–20th centuries, Humberside marine paintings, contemporary art and changing exhibitions. *Wilberforce House.* Jacobean merchant's house, birthplace of Wilberforce; collection of slavery relics, period furniture, costume and ceramics. *Transport and Archaeology Museums.* Veteran cars, trams, coaches and velocipedes; archaeological finds from Humberside, including Roman mosaics and iron-age Hasholme Boat. *Town Docks Museum.* Whaling, fishing, trawling, ships and shipping. *Old Grammar School.* Hull's oldest secular building with city history displays. *Spurn Lightship*, built 1927, restored 1986. Closed Mon. and Tues. in winter. All open Mon.–Sat.

10–5, Sun. 1.30–4.30. *Posterngate Gallery.* Exhibitions and one-man shows. Tues.–Sat. 10–5.30.

Huntingdon.—*Cromwell Museum.* Remaining portion of the 12th century Hospital of St. John housing portraits of Cromwell, his family and Parliamentary notables, and Cromwelliana—documents, armour, coins, etc. Open April–Oct. Tues.–Fri. 11–5, Sat, Sun. 11–4; Nov.–March, Tues.–Fri. 2–5, Sat. 11–4, Sun. 2–4. Closed Bank Hols. other than Good Friday. Adm. free.

Ipswich.—*Ipswich Museum.* Collections of Suffolk geology, archaeology, natural history and ethnology. Temporary exhibitions. Open Mon.–Sat. 10–5. Closed Bank Hols. *Christchurch Mansion.* Tudor house containing furniture, Suffolk portraits, English porcelain, pottery and glass. *Wolsey Art Gallery*, attached, houses Borough collections of paintings (local artists, Gainsborough, Constable), modern prints, sculpture. Open Mon.–Sat. 10–5, Sun. 2.30–4.30. Closed Good Friday, Dec. 24, 25, 26.

Leeds.—*City Art Gallery.* English watercolours. British and European painting, modern sculpture, Henry Moore gallery. Print Room contains study collection of drawings and prints. Open weekdays, 10–6, Suns., 2–5.

Temple Newsam House. Tudor/Jacobean house, furnished in style of 17th and 18th centuries, with silver, European porcelain and pottery, pictures, etc. Open daily (except Mon.) 10.30–6.15, Weds. (May–Sept.) 10.30–8.30, all Bank Hols. (except Christmas). Adm. 65p, con. 30p. *Lotherton Hall*, Gascoigne art and silver collection, oriental gallery, costume collection, 19th century furniture, ceramics, park and gardens. Open daily (except Mon.) 10.30–6.15, Thurs. (May–Sept.) 10.30–8.30, all Bank Hols. (except Christmas). Adm. 65p, con. 30p. (Free adm. bird garden.) *Abbey House Museum.* Folk museum including three full-sized streets. Open Oct.–March weekdays 10–5, Sun. 2–5 (April–Sept. 2–6). *Industrial Museum.* Open April–Sept. Tues.–Sat. 10–5, Sun. 2–5 (Oct.–March 2–4). Open Bank Hols. *City Museum.* Geology, archaeology, ethnography and natural history. Open Tues.–Fri. 9.30–5.30, Sat. 9.30–4.

Leicester.—*Leicestershire Museum and Art Gallery*, New Walk. Natural history, geology, Egyptology, 18th–20th century English paintings, ceramics, silver. *Newarke Houses*, The Newarke. Social history of Leicestershire from 1500 A.D., musical instruments, local clocks. *Jewry Wall Museum*, St. Nicholas Circle. Archaeology (prehistoric–1500). Roman Jewry Wall and Baths, mosaics. *Belgrave Hall*, Church Road. Queen Anne house with furniture and garden, coaches and agricultural collection. *Museum of the Royal Leicestershire Regiment*, The Magazine, Oxford Street. *Museum of Technology*, Corporation Road. Knitting industry and Power galleries. Horse-drawn and motor vehicles, beam engines. *Wygston's House Museum of Costume*, Applegate. Costume from 1789–present. All museums open weekdays 10–5.30, Sun. 2–5.30. Closed Christmas Day, Boxing Day and Good Friday.

Lewes.—*Museum of Sussex Archaeology*, Barbican House, near Castle. Prehistoric, Roman, Saxon and medieval collections relating to Sussex; local pictures and prints. Open weekdays, 10–5.30, Sun. (April–Oct.) 11–5.30. Adm. (including Castle) £1.50, con. 75p.

Anne of Cleves House, Southover. Local history and folk museum. Open weekdays (mid. Feb.–mid. Nov.) 10–5.30. Sun. (April–Oct.) 2–5.30. Adm. £1.50, con. 75p.

Lincoln.—*Usher Gallery.* Watches, miniatures, porcelain, silver, etc., Peter de Wint collection of oils and watercolours, Lincolnshire topographical drawings, *personalia* associated with Tennyson family.

Open weekdays 10–5.30, Sun. 2.30–5. *City and County Museum*, The Greyfriars. Geology, natural history and archaeology of Lincolnshire. Open weekdays 10–5.30, Sun. 2.30–5. *Museum of Lincolnshire Life.* Collections illustrate life and work in Lincolnshire over the last 200 years. Includes large agricultural collection. Open weekdays 10–5.30, Sun. 2–5.30. *National Cycle Museum*, Brayford Wharf North. Collection of vintage cycles. Open Easter–Oct. 10–5 daily; Oct.–Easter Fri., Sat., and Sun. 10–5.

Manchester.—*City Art Gallery*, Mosley Street. Old Masters, Turner, Pre-Raphaelites; sculpture, porcelain, silver. Mon.–Sat. 10–5.45, Sun. 2–5.45. *Athenaeum Gallery*, Princess Street. Adm. free. *Whitworth Art Gallery*, University of Manchester, Oxford Road. Watercolours, drawings, prints, textiles and wallpaper collections, and 20th century British art. Mon.–Sat. 10–5 (Thurs. 10–9), closed Suns. *Museum of Science and Industry*, Liverpool Road, Castlefield. Working machinery and displays in world's oldest passenger railway station. Open daily 10–5. *Gallery of English Costume*, Platt Hall, Rusholme. Exhibits from 16th century to present. Open daily (not Tues.) 10–5.45, Sun. 2–5.45 (closes 4, Nov.–April). Also *Heaton Hall*, Prestwich, *Wythenshawe Hall*, Northenden and *Fletcher Moss Museum*, Didsbury. Open April–Sept. daily (not Tues.) 10–6, Sun. 2–6.

Newcastle upon Tyne.—*Laing Art Gallery*, Higham Place. Fine art from 17th century, pottery, glass, silver and metalwork. Open Tues.–Fri. 10–5.30, Sat. 10–4.30, Sun. 2.30–5.30. *Keep Museum*, St. Nicholas Street. History of site. Oct.–March, Tues.–Sat. 9.30–4.30 (April–Sept. 9.30–5.30). *Trinity Maritime Centre* and *Trinity House*, Broad Chare. Centre open April–Sept. Tues.–Fri. 10.30–4; Oct.–March, Tues.–Thurs. 11–3. Trinity House April–Oct., Tues., Wed., Thurs. 2–4. *Military Vehicle Museum*, Exhibition Park. Open daily 10.15–4.30. *Museum of Science and Engineering*, West Blandford Square. Tues.–Fri. 10–5.30, Sat. 10–4.30. *Newburn Hall Motor Museum*, Townfield Gdns. Tues.–Sat. 10–8.

Newmarket.—*National Horseracing Museum.* Five galleries of displays relating to the development of horseracing and to the horses and people connected with the sport. Equine Tours. Open April 7–Dec. 9, Tues.–Sat. 10–5, Sun. 2–5. Closed Mon. except Aug. and Bank Hols. Adm. £2, con. £1/50p.

Norwich.—*Castle Museum.* Exhibits of art (including Norwich School), local archaeology, social and natural history, pottery and glass. Open, Mon.–Sat., 10–5, Sun. 2–5. *Strangers' Hall*, Charing Cross. Late medieval mansion furnished as a museum of 16th–19th century urban domestic life. Open Mon.–Sat. 10–5. *Bridewell Museum of Local Industries*, Bridewell Alley. Transport, crafts and industries of Norwich. Open Mon.–Sat. 10–5. *St. Peter Hungate Church Museum*, Princes Street. 15th century church used for display of church art and antiquities. Open Mon.–Sat. 10–5.

Nottingham.—*Castle Museum and Art Gallery.* English and Dutch paintings and drawings 17th–20th centuries, special collections of Bonington and Paul Sandby. Ceramics, silver, glass, medieval alabaster carvings, local historical and archaeological displays, classical, oriental and ethnographical antiquities, the regimental collection of the Sherwood Foresters. Regular conducted tours of Mortimer's Hole Caves. Open Summer, 10–5.45, Winter, 10–4.45. Closed Christmas Day. Adm. free, small charge on Sun. and Bank Hols. *Industrial Museum*, Wollaton Park. Industrial, lacemaking machinery, steam engines, transport. Open April–Sept. Mon.–Sat. 10–6, Sun. 2–6; Oct.–April, Thurs., Sat. 10–4.30, Sun. 1.30–4.30. Closed Christmas Day. Adm. free, small charge on Sun. and Bank Hols. *Canal Museum*, Canal Street. History of local canals and rivers. Open Easter–Oct. Wed–Sat. 10–5.45, Sun. 1–5.45; Oct.–Easter, Wed.– Sat. 1–5, Sun. 1–5. Adm. free. *Natural History Museum*, Wollaton Hall. Tudor building and park. Open summer 10–7, Sun. 2–5; winter 10–dusk (Sun. 1.30–4.30). Closed Christmas Day. Adm. free except Sun. and Bank Hols. *Castlegate Museum of Costumes and Textiles*. Open daily 10–5. Closed Christmas Day. Adm. free. *Brewhouse Yard Museum*, Castle Boulevard. Everyday life from the 17th century to present. Open daily 10–5. Adm. free. Closed Christmas Day. *Green's Mill and Science Centre*, Sneinton. Working windmill and museum with models, displays about George Green. Open Wed.–Sun. 10–5. Closed Christmas Day. Adm. free. Also *The Lace Hall* and *Robin Hood Centre*.

Oakham, *Rutland County Museum*, Catmos Street.—Archaeology, local history, craft tools and agricultural implements. Open Tues.–Sat. 10–5, Sun. (April–Oct.) 2–5, and Bank Hol. Mons.

Oxford, *Ashmolean Museum*, Beaumont Street.— The University's collections of European and Oriental fine and applied arts, Classical and Near-Eastern archaeology and Numismatics. Open Tues.–Sat. 10–4, Sun. 2–4. Bank Hol. Mons. 2–5. Adm. free.

Plymouth.—*City Museum and Art Gallery*, Drake Circus. Fine art, including Cottonian collection and Reynolds' portraits, Plymouth porcelain, archaeology, local and natural history. Tues.–Sat. 10–5.30, Sun. 2–5. Also Bank Holiday Mons. Adm. free. The 16th century *Elizabethan House*, 32 New Street. Also *Merchant's House*, 33 St. Andrew's Street, dating from the 16th and early 17th centuries and *The Dome*, the Hoe (maritime history).

Portsmouth.—*City Museum and Art Gallery*, Museum Road. *Cumberland House Natural Science Museum and Butterfly House*, Eastern Parade. *Southsea Castle and Museum*, Clarance Esplanade. *D-Day Museum*, Clarence Esplanade. All open daily 10.30–5.30, except Dec. 24–26. Adm. charge. *Charles Dickens' Birthplace Museum*, Old Commercial Road. Open March 1–Oct. 31, daily 10.30–5.30. Adm. charge. *Eastney Pumping Station*, Henderson Road. Open April–Sept. daily 1.30–5.30; Oct.–March 1st Sun. of month. Adm. charge. *Fort Widley*, Portsdown Hill. Open April–Sept. Sat., Sun., Bank Hols. 1.30–5.50. Adm. charge. *Naval Heritage Area*. Tells the story of the Royal Navy using Henry VIII's *Mary Rose*, H.M.S. *Victory* (Nelson's flagship), and the Victorian ironclad, H.M.S. *Warrior* (1860). These are presented against a backdrop of the history of the modern Navy from earliest times to the Falklands Campaign related in the Royal Naval Museum. Open daily (except Christmas Day). Adm. charge.

St. Albans.—*Museum of St. Alban*, Hatfield Road. Story of St. Albans from departure of the Romans. Open weekdays 10–5. Adm. free. *Verulamium Museum*, St. Michael's. Iron Age and Roman Verulamium including wall plasters, jewellery, mosaics, one *in situ* in Hypocaust annexe. Open weekdays 10–5.30, Sun. 2–5.30. Closes 4 Nov.–Feb. Adm. £1.10, con. 55p.

Sheffield.—*City Museum*, Weston Park. Includes the Bateman Collection of antiquities from Peak District, cutlery and old Sheffield plate, local geology and wildlife. *Mappin Art Gallery*, Weston Park. Paintings and sculpture of 18th–20th centuries (mainly British School) and contemporary works. *Abbeydale Industrial Hamlet*, Abbeydale Road South. A late 18th–early 19th century scythe and steel works with associated housing. *Kelham Island Industrial Museum*. *Shepherd Wheel*, Whiteley Wood. Waterpowered cutlery grinding establishment. *Bishops'*

House, *Meersbrook Park*. Museum of local history in timber-framed domestic building. Opening times vary.

Stoke-on-Trent. *—City Museum and Art Gallery*, Bethesda Street, Hanley. Major ceramic collections. Open daily 10.30–5, Sun. 2–5. *Chatterley Whitfield Mining Museum*, Tunstall. Guided tours underground. *Gladstone Pottery Museum*, Longton. A working Victorian pottery.

Pottery Factory Tours: Tours are available at the following: *Minton*, London Road, Stoke; *Royal Doulton*, Nile Street, Burslem; *Spode*, Church Street, Stoke, *Beswick*, Gold Street, *Parkhall China*, Weston Coyney Road, Longton, *Coalport*, Park Street, Fenton and *Wedgwood's* at Barlaston.

Stratford-upon-Avon.—*Shakespeare's Birthplace*. Period furniture, rare books, MSS and objects of Shakespearean interest with new Shakespeare Centre nearby. *Anne Hathaway's Cottage*, Shottery, early home of Shakespeare's wife. *Mary Arden's House*, Wilmcote, Tudor farmhouse home of Shakespeare's mother with Countryside Museum. *New Place*, where Shakespeare died. *Hall's Croft*, half-timbered home of Shakespeare's daughter and her family. *Grammar School* attended by Shakespeare. *Royal Shakespeare Theatre* burnt down 1926, rebuilt 1932. New *Swan Theatre* opened in 1986.

Styal.—*Quarry Bank Mill*, Cheshire. History of the cotton industry, weaving demonstrations. Giant iron waterwheel. Restored Apprentice House. Open all year. Closed Mon. Oct.–March. Open Bank Hols. Adm. £3.75, con. £2.75.

Winchester.—*City Museum*. Weekdays 10–5, Sun. 2–5 (closed Mon. in winter). *Cathedral Library* and *Triforium Gallery*. Ancient manuscripts, sculpture, wood- and metalwork of past 1,100 years. Open Easter–Sept. 10.30–4.30. Closed Mon. morning and Suns. Adm. charge. *Cathedral Treasury*. Exhibition of silverware. Open May–Sept.10.30–4.30, Sun. 2.30–4.30. Adm. free.

Worcester.—*City Museum and Art Gallery*. Natural history of Worcestershire and temporary art exhibitions; also museum of the Worcestershire Regiment and the Worcester Yeomanry Cavalry. Open Mon.–Wed., Fri. 9.30–6, Sat. 9.30–5. Closed Thurs., Sun. *The Commandery*, Sidbury. Civil War Centre, costume, industrial history. Weekdays 10.30–5, Sun. 2–5. *Tudor House Museum*, Friar Street. Local domestic and social history. Mon.–Wed., Fri., Sat. 10.30–5. *Dyson Perrins Museum of Worcester Porcelain*, Severn Street. Mon. to Fri. 9.30–5, Sat. 10–5.

York.—*Castle Museum*. Museum of everday life of the last three centuries. Open weekdays 9.30–5.30, Sun. 10–5.30 (closes 6.30 April–Oct.). Adm. £2.75, con. £1.35. *Jorvik Viking Centre*, Coppergate. Reconstruction of Viking York and display of artefacts. Open daily. Adm. £2.75, con. £1.35. *Yorkshire Museum and Gardens*, Museum Street, Roman Life gallery, archaeology, decorative arts, geology, natural history. Open weekdays 10–5, Sun. 1–5. Adm. charge. Gardens, Roman, Anglian and medieval ruins. Open weekdays 7.30–dusk (summer 7.30–8), Sun. 10–dusk. *The York Story*, Castlegate. Open weekdays 10–5, Sun. 1–5. Adm. 80p, con. 40p. *Art Gallery*, Exhibition Square. European paintings, 14th–20th century; watercolours and prints of Yorkshire; modern English stoneware pottery. Open weekdays 10–5, Sun. 2.30–5. Adm. free *Treasurer's House* (National Trust). Chapter House Street. Open April–Oct. 10.30–5 (closed Good Friday). Adm. charge.

WILDLIFE

PROTECTED SPECIES

The Wildlife and Countryside Act 1981 gives legal protection to a wide range of wild plants and animals.

Under Schedule 5 of the Act it is normally an offence to kill, injure, take, possess or sell any of the animals mentioned below (whether alive or dead) and to disturb its place of shelter and protection or to destroy that place.

* Adder (*Vipera berus*)
  Anemone, Ivell's Sea (*Edwardsia ivelli*)
  Anemone, Startlet Sea (*Nematosella vectensis*)
  Apus (*Triops cancriformis*)
  Bat, Horseshoe (*Rhinolophidae*, all species)
  Bat, Typical (*Vespertilionidae*, all species)
  Beetle, Rainbow Leaf (*Chrysolina cerealis*)
  Beetle, Violet Click (*Limoniscus violaceus*)
  Burbot (*Lota lota*)
  Butterfly, Heath Fritillary (*Mellicta athalia* (or *Melitaea athalia*))
  Butterfly, Large Blue (*Maculinea arion*)
  Butterfly, Swallowtail (*Papilio machaon*)
  Cat, Wild (*Felis silvestris*)
  Cicada, New Forest (*Cicadetta montana*)
** Crayfish, Atlantic Stream (*Austropotamobius pallipes*)
  Cricket, Field (*Gryllus campestris*)
  Cricket, Mole (*Gryllotalpa gryllotalpa*)
  Dolphin (*Cetacea*)
  Dormouse (*Muscardinus avellanarius*)
  Dragonfly, Norfolk Aeshna (*Aeshna isosceles*)
* Frog, Common (*Rana temporaria*)
  Grasshopper, Wart-biter (*Decticus verrucivorus*)
  Leech, Medicinal (*Hirudo medicinalis*)
  Lizard, Sand (*Lacerta agilis*)
† Lizard, Viviparous(*Lacerta vivipara*)
  Marten, Pine (*Martes martes*)
  Moth, Barberry Carpet (*Pareulype berberata*)
  Moth, Black-veined (*Siona lineata* (or *Idaea lineata*))
  Moth, Essex Emerald (*Thetidia smaragdaria*)
  Moth, New Forest Burnet (*Zygaena viciae*)
  Moth, Reddish Buff (*Acosmetia caliginosa*)
  Moth, Viper's Bugloss (*Hadena irregularis*)
  Newt, Great Crested (or Warty) (*Triturus cristatus*)
* Newt, Palmate (*Triturus helveticus*)
* Newt, Smooth (*Triturus vulgaris*)
  Otter, Common (*Lutra lutra*)
  Porpoise (*Cetacea*)
  Sandworm, Lagoon (*Armandia cirrhosa*)
  Sea-Mat, Trembling (*Victorella pavida*)
  Shrimp, Fairy (*Chirocephalus diaphanus*)
  Shrimp, Lagoon Sand (*Gammarus insensibilis*)
† Slow-worm (*Anguis fragilis*)
  Snail, Glutinous (*Myxas glutinosa*)
  Snail, Sandbowl (*Catinella arenaria*)
† Snake, Grass (*Natrix natrix* (*Natrix helvetica*))
  Snake, Smooth (*Coronella austriaca*)
  Spider, Fen Raft (*Dolomedes plantarius*)
  Spider, Ladybird (*Eresus niger*)
  Squirrel, Red (*Sciurus vulgaris*)
* Toad, Common (*Bufo bufo*)
  Toad, Natterjack (*Bufo calamita*)
  Turtle, Marine (*Dermochelyidae* and *Cheloniidae*, all species)
  Vendace (*Coregonus albula*)
  Walrus (*Odobenus rosmarus*)
  Whale (*Cetacea*)
  Whitefish (*Coregonus lavaretus*)

* the offence relates to "sale" only.
** the offence relates to "taking" and "sale" only.
† the offence relates to "killing, injuring and sale".

Under Schedule 8 of the Wildlife and Countryside Act, it is normally an offence to pick, uproot, sell or destroy any of the plants mentioned below and, unless authorized, to uproot any wild plant.

Adder's tongue, Least (*Ophioglossum lusitanicum*)
Alison, Small (*Alyssum alyssoides*)
Broomrape, Bedstraw (*Orobanche caryophyllacea*)
Broomrape, Oxtongue (*Orobanche loricata*)
Broomrape, Thistle (*Orobanche reticulata*)
Cabbage, Lundy (*Rhynchosinapis wrightii*)
Calamint, Wood (*Calamintha sylvatica*)
Catchfly, Alpine (*Lychnis alpina*)
Cinquefoil, Rock (*Potentilla rupestris*)
Club-rush, Triangular (*Scirpus triquetrus*)
Colt's-foot, Purple (*Homogyne alpina*)
Cotoneaster, Wild (*Cotoneaster integerrimus*)
Cottongrass, Slender (*Eriophorum gracile*)
Cow-wheat, Field (*Melampyrum arvense*)
Crocus, Sand (*Romulea columnae*)
Cudweed, Jersey (*Gnaphalium luteoalbum*)
Cudweed, Red-tipped (*Filago lutescens*)
Diapensia (*Diapensia lapponica*)
Eryngo, Field (*Eryngium campestre*)
Fern, Dickie's bladder (*Cystopteris dickieana*)
Fern, Killarney (*Trichomanes speciosum*)
Fleabane, Alpine (*Erigeron borealis*)
Fleabane, Small (*Pulicaria vulgaris*)
Galingale, Brown (*Cyperus fuscus*)
Gentian, Alpine (*Gentiana nivalis*)
Gentian, Fringed (*Gentianella ciliata*)
Gentian, Spring (*Gentiana verna*)
Germander, Cut-leaved (*Teucrium botrys*)
Germander, Water (*Teucrium scordium*)
Gladiolus, Wild (*Gladiolus illyricus*)
Goosefoot, Stinking (*Chenopodium vulvaria*)
Grass-poly (*Lythrum hyssopifolia*)
Hare's-ear, Sickle-leaved (*Bupleurum falcatum*)
Hare's-ear, Small (*Bupleurum baldense*)
Hawk's-beard, Stinking (*Crepis foetida*)
Heath, Blue (*Phyllodoce caerulea*)
Helleborine, Red (*Cephalanthera rubra*)
Helleborine, Young's (*Epipactis youngiana*)
Horsetail, Branched (*Equisetum ramosissimum*)
Hound's-tongue, Green (*Cynoglossum germanicum*)
Knawel, Perennial (*Scleranthus perennis*)
Knotgrass, Sea (*Polygonum maritimum*)
Lady's-slipper (*Cypripedium calceolus*)
Lavender, Sea (*Limonium paradoxum*) (*Limonium recurvum*)
Leek, Round-headed (*Allium sphaerocephalon*)
Lettuce, Least (*Lactuca saligna*)
Lily, Snowdon (*Lloydia serotina*)
Marsh-mallow, Rough (*Althaea hirsuta*)
Marshwort, Creeping (*Apium repens*)
Milk-parsley, Cambridge (*Selinum carvifolia*)
Naiad, Holly-leaved (*Najas marina*)
Orchid, Early Spider (*Ophrys sphegodes*)
Orchid, Fen (*Liparis loeselii*)
Orchid, Ghost (*Epipogium aphyllum*)
Orchid, Late Spider (*Ophrys fuciflora*)
Orchid, Lizard (*Himantoglossum hircinum*)
Orchid, Military (*Orchis militaris*)
Orchid, Monkey (*Orchis simia*)
Pear, Plymouth (*Pyrus cordata*)
Pennyroyal (*Mentha pulegium*)
Pigmyweed (*Crassula aquatica*)
Pink, Cheddar (*Dianthus gratianopolitanus*)
Pink, Childling (*Petroraghia nanteuilii*)
Ragwort, Fen (*Senecio paludosus*)
Ramping-fumitory, Martin's (*Fumaria martinii*)
Restharrow, Small (*Ononis reclinata*)
Rock-cress, Alpine (*Arabis alpina*)
Rock-cress, Bristol (*Arabis stricta*)

Sandwort, Norwegian (*Arenaria norvegica*)
Sandwort, Teesdale (*Minuartia stricta*)
Saxifrage, Drooping (*Saxifraga cernua*)
Saxifrage, Tufted (*Saxifraga cespitosa*)
Solomon's-seal, Whorled (*Polygonatum verticillatum*)
Sow-thistle, Alpine (*Cicerbita alpina*)
Spearwort, Adder's-tongue (*Ranunculus ophioglossifolius*)
Speedwell, Fingered (*Veronica triphyllos*)
Speedwell, Spiked (*Veronica spicata*)
Spurge, Purple (*Euphorbia peplis*)
Star-of-Bethlehem, Early (*Gagea bohemica*)
Starfruit (*Damasonium alisma*)
Stonewort, Foxtail (*Lamprothamnium papulosum*)
Strapwort (*Corrigiola litoralis*)
Violet, Fen (*Viola persicifolia*)
Viper's-grass (*Scorzonera humilis*)
Water-plantain, Ribbon-leaved (*Alisma gramineum*)
Wood-sedge, Starved (*Carex depauperata*)
Woodsia, Alpine (*Woodsia alpina*)
Woodsia, Oblong (*Woodsia ilvensis*)
Wormwood, Field (*Artemisia campestris*)
Woundwort, Downy (*Stachys germanica*)
Woundwort, Limestone (*Stachys alpina*)
Yellow-rattle, Greater (*Rhinanthus serotinus*)

CLOSE SEASONS AND TIMES
Wild Birds

The Wildlife and Countryside Act, 1981, lays down a close season for wild birds (other than game birds) from February 1 to August 31 inclusive, each year. Exceptions to these dates are made for:
Capercaillie and (except Scotland) *Woodcock*—Feb. 1–Sept. 30.
Snipe—Feb. 1–Aug. 11.
Wild Duck and *Wild Goose* (below high water mark)—Feb. 21–Aug. 31.

Birds which may be killed or taken outside the close season (except on Sundays and on Christmas Day in Scotland, and on Sundays in prescribed areas of England and Wales) are the above and coot, certain wild duck (gadwall, goldeneye, mallard, pintail, pochard, shoveler, teal; tufted duck, wigeon), certain wild geese (Canada, greylag, pink-footed, white-fronted (in England and Wales only)), moorhen, golden plover and woodcock.

Certain wild birds may be killed or taken at any time by authorized persons—crow, collared dove, gull (great and lesser black-backed or herring), jackdaw, jay, magpie, pigeon (feral or wood), rook, sparrow (house), and starling.

All other British birds are fully protected by law throughout the year.

Game Birds

In each case the dates are inclusive:—

Black Game–Dec. 11–Aug. 19 (Aug. 31 in Somerset, Devon, and New Forest).
*Grouse–Dec. 11–Aug. 11.
*Partridge–Feb. 2–Aug. 31.
*Pheasant–Feb. 2–Sept. 30.
*Ptarmigan–(Scotland only) Dec. 11–Aug. 11.

It is also unlawful in England and Wales to kill the game marked * above on a Sunday or Christmas Day.

Hunting and Ground Game

There is no statutory close-time for fox-hunting or rabbit-shooting, nor for hares: but by an Act passed in 1892 the *sale* of hares or leverets in Great Britain is prohibited from March 1 to July 31 inclusive under a penalty of a pound. November 1 is the recognized date for the opening of the fox-hunting season, which continues till the following April.

Deer

The statutory close seasons for deer (all dates inclusive) are:

	England and Wales	Scotland
Fallow deer		
Male	May 1–July 31	May 1–July 31
Female	Mar. 1–Oct. 31	Feb. 16–Oct. 20
Red deer		
Male	May 1–July 31	Oct. 21–June 30
Female	Mar. 1–Oct. 31	Feb. 16–Oct. 20
Roe deer		
Male	Nov. 1–Mar. 31	Oct. 21–Mar. 31
Female	Mar. 1–Oct. 31	April 1–Oct. 20
Sika deer		
Male	May 1–July 31	Oct. 21–June 30
Female	Mar. 1–Oct. 31	Feb. 16–Oct. 20
Red/Sika hybrids		
Male	—	Oct. 21–June 30
Female	—	Feb. 16–Oct. 20

Angling

Close seasons (dates inclusive) are:
Coarse fishing.—Yorkshire, last day in Feb.–May 31; South West, none; rest of country, March 15–June 15.
Game fishing.—Trout, Oct. 1–last day of Feb.*; Salmon, Nov. 1–Jan. 31*.

* The above dates are statutory close times. Particularly with salmon, migratory trout and trout, close seasons vary in accordance with water authority local by-laws. In all cases, it is best to check with the water authority concerned.

HALLMARKS ON GOLD, SILVER AND PLATINUM WARES
London (Goldsmiths' Hall) Date Letters
From 1498

	Black letter, small	1498–9 to 1517–8		Roman letter, small ...	1739–40 to 1755–6
	Lombardic	1518–9 ,, 1537–8		Old English, capitals ..	1756–7 to 1775–6
	Roman and other capitals	1538–9 ,, 1557–8		Roman letter, small ...	1776–7 ,, 1795–6
	Black letter, small	1558–9 ,, 1577–8		Roman letter, capitals .	1796–7 ,, 1815–6
	Roman letter, capitals .	1578–9 ,, 1597–8		Roman letter, small ...	1816–7 ,, 1835–6
	Lombardic, external cusps	1598–9 ,, 1617–8		Old English, capitals ..	1836–7 ,, 1855–6
	Italic letter, small	1618–9 ,, 1637–8		Old English, small	1856–7 ,, 1875–6
	Court hand	1638–9 ,, 1657–8		Roman letter, capitals [A to M *square* shield N to Z as shown]	1876–7 ,, 1895–6
	Black letter, capitals ..	1658–9 ,, 1677–8		Roman letter, small ...	1896–7 ,, 1915–6
	Black letter, small	1678–9 ,, 1696–7		Black letter, small	1916–7 ,, 1935–6
	Court hand	1697 ,, 1715–6		Roman letter, capitals .	1936–7 ,, 1955–6
	Roman letter, capitals	1716–7 ,, 1735–6		Italic letter, small	1956–7 ,, 1974
	Roman letter, small ...	1736–7 ,, 1738–9		Italic letter, capitals ..	1975 ,, ...

Hallmarks are the symbols stamped on gold, silver, or platinum articles to indicate that they have been chemically tested and that they conform to one of the legal standards. With certain exceptions, all gold, silver, or platinum articles are required by law to be hallmarked before they are offered for sale. Hallmarking was instituted in 1300 under a statute of Edward I.

Normally a complete modern hallmark consists of four symbols—the maker's mark or sponsor's mark, assay office mark, standard mark and date letter.

Additional marks have been authorized from time to time.

Maker's Mark.—Instituted in 1363, the maker's mark was originally a device such as a bird or *fleur-de-lys* and now consists invariably of the initial letters of the name or names of the maker or sponsor, or of the firm.

Assay Office Mark.—The existing assay offices and their distinguishing marks are:—

LONDON (Goldsmiths' Hall).
A leopard's head (uncrowned from 1300 to 1478–9, when it became crowned until 1821, since when it has been uncrowned). From 1697 to 1974 a lion's head erased was used on silver of the higher (Britannia) standard.

BIRMINGHAM (Newhall Street, B3 1SB) . An anchor
SHEFFIELD (137 Portobello Street, S1 4DS) . . A rose
EDINBURGH (9 Granton Road, EH5 3QJ) . . A castle

Offices formerly existed in other towns, e.g. Chester, Glasgow, Newcastle, Exeter, York and Norwich, each having its own distinguishing mark.

Standard Mark.—Instituted in 1544. The current legal standards and their marks are as follows:—

PLATINUM

SILVER.—Sterling silver (92·5 per cent silver) is marked by English assay offices with a *lion passant* and by the Edinburgh Assay Office with a *lion rampant*. A full-length figure of *Britannia* was impressed on silver of a higher standard (95·84 per cent silver) between 1697 and 1720 and this mark is still used occasionally by all British assay offices.

GOLD.—Since 1975 gold articles are marked with a crown followed by the millesimal figure for the standard, i.e. 916 for 22 carat, 750 for 18 carat, 585 for 14 carat and 375 for 9 carat.

PLATINUM.—Hallmarking of platinum articles began in 1975. The only standard permitted contains at least 95 per cent platinum.

Date Letter.—Instituted in 1478. The date letter denotes the year in which an article was assayed and hallmarked. Each alphabetical cycle has a distinctive style of lettering or shape of shield. The date letters were different at the various assay offices and the particular office must be established from the assay office mark before reference is made to tables of date letters. Specimen shields and letters used by the London Office on silver articles in each period from 1498 to date are shown on the previous page. The same letters are found on gold articles but the surrounding shield may differ. Since Jan. 1, 1975 each Office has used the same style of date letter and shield for all articles.

OTHER MARKS

Duty Mark.—In 1784 an additional mark of the reigning sovereign's head was introduced to signify that the excise duty had been paid. The mark became obsolete on the abolition of the duty in 1890.

Commemorative Marks.—There are three other marks to commemorate special events, the Silver Jubilee of King George V and Queen Mary in 1935, the Coronation of Queen Elizabeth II in 1953 and her Silver Jubilee in 1977.

Foreign Wares.—Since 1842 foreign wares imported into Great Britain have been required to be hallmarked before sale. The marks consist of the importer's mark, a special assay office mark (*see below*), the figures denoting fineness and the annual date letter. The current assay office marks for foreign wares are as follows:—

LONDON.—The sign of the Constellation Leo.
BIRMINGHAM.—Equilateral triangle.
SHEFFIELD.—The sign of the Constellation Libra.
EDINBURGH.—St. Andrew's Cross.

Common Control Mark.—Special marks at authorized Assay Offices of the signatory countries of the International Convention—United Kingdom, Austria, Denmark, Finland, Ireland, Portugal, Norway, Sweden and Switzerland—are legally recognized in the United Kingdom as approved hallmarks. These marks consist of a Sponsor's Mark, a Common Control Mark, a Fineness Mark (arabic numerals showing the standard in parts per thousand) and an Assay Office Mark. There is no date letter.

POETS LAUREATE

	Apptd.		Apptd.		Apptd.
Samuel Daniel	1599	Rev. Laurence Eusden	1718	Alfred Lord Tennyson	1850
Ben Jonson	1619	Colley Cibber	1730	Alfred Austin	1890
Sir William D'Avenant	1637	William Whitehead	1757	Robert Bridges	1913
John Dryden	1670	Rev. Thomas Warton	1785	John Masefield	1930
Thomas Shadwell	1688	Henry James Pye	1790	Cecil Day Lewis	1967
Nahum Tate	1692	Robert Southey	1813	Sir John Betjeman	1972
Nicholas Rowe	1715	William Wordsworth	1843	Edward (Ted) Hughes	1984

MASTERS OF THE QUEEN'S/KING'S MUSIC

	Apptd.		Apptd.
Nicholas Lanier	1626	Francois (Franz) Cramer	1834
Louis Grabu	1666	George Frederick Anderson	1848
Nicholas Staggins	1674	Sir William George Cusins	1870
John Eccles	1700	Sir Walter Parratt	1893
Maurice Greene	1735	Sir Edward Elgar	1924
William Boyce	1755 (1757)	Sir Henry Walford Davies	1934
John Stanley	1779	Sir Arnold Bax	1941
Sir William Parsons	1786	Sir Arthur Bliss	1953
William Shield	1817	Malcolm Williamson	1975
Christian Kramer	1829		

WEIGHTS AND MEASURES

SI UNITS

The Système International d'Unités (SI) is an international and coherent system of units devised to meet all known needs for measurement in science and technology. The system was adopted by the 11th Conférence Générale des Poids et Mesures (C.G.P.M.) in 1960. The British Standards describing the essential features of the International System of Units are *Specifications for SI Units* (BS 5555:1981) and *Conversion Factors and Tables* (BS 350, Part 1:1974).

The system consists of seven base units and the derived units formed as products or quotients of various powers of the base units. Together the base units and the derived units make up the coherent system of units. In the U.K. the SI base units, and almost all important derived units, are realized at the National Physical Laboratory and disseminated through the National Measurement System.

Base Units

Metre (m) = unit of length
Kilogram (kg) = unit of mass
Second (s) = unit of time
Ampere (A) = unit of electric current
Kelvin (K) = unit of thermodynamic temperature
Mole (mol) = unit of amount of substance
Candela (cd) = unit of luminous intensity

Derived Units

For some of the derived SI units, special names and symbols exist; those approved by the C.G.P.M. are listed below.

Hertz (Hz) = unit of frequency
Newton (N) = unit of force
Pascal (Pa) = unit of pressure, stress
Joule (J) = unit of energy, work, quantity of heat
Watt (W) = unit of power
Coulomb (C) = unit of electric charge, quantity of electricity
Volt (V) = unit of electric potential, potential difference, tension, electromotive force
Farad (F) = unit of electric capacitance
Ohm (Ω) = unit of electric resistance
Siemens (S) = unit of electric conductance
Weber (Wb) = unit of flux of magnetic induction, magnetic flux
Tesla (T) = unit of magnetic flux density, magnetic induction
Henry (H) = unit of inductance
Degree Celsius (°C) = unit of Celsius temperature
Lumen (lm) = unit of luminous flux
Lux (lx) = unit of illuminance
Becquerel (Bq) = unit of activity (of a radionuclide)
Gray (Gy) = unit of absorbed dose, specific energy imparted, kerma, absorbed dose index
Sievert (Sv) = unit of dose equivalent

Supplementary Units

The derived units include, as a special case, the supplementary units which may be treated as dimensionless within the SI.

Radian (rad) = unit of plane angle
Steradian (sr) = unit of solid angle

Other derived units are expressed in terms of base units and/or supplementary units. Some of the more commonly-used derived units are the following:

Unit of area = square metre (m^2)
Unit of volume = cubic metre (m^3)
Unit of velocity = metre per second ($m\,s^{-1}$)
Unit of acceleration = metre per second squared ($m\,s^{-2}$)
Unit of density = kilogram per cubic metre ($kg\,m^{-3}$)
Unit of momentum = kilogram metre per second ($kg\,m\,s^{-1}$)
Unit of magnetic field = ampere per metre ($A\,m^{-1}$)
Unit of surface tension = newton per metre ($N\,m^{-1}$)
Unit of dynamic viscosity = pascal second (Pa s)
Unit of heat capacity = joule per kelvin ($J\,K^{-1}$)
Unit of specific heat capacity = joule per kilogram kelvin ($J\,kg^{-1}\,K^{-1}$)
Unit of heat flux density, irradiance = watt per square metre ($W\,m^{-2}$)
Unit of thermal conductivity = watt per metre kelvin ($W\,m^{-1}\,K^{-1}$)
Unit of electric field strength = volt per metre ($V\,m^{-1}$)
Unit of luminance = candela per square metre ($cd\,m^{-2}$)

SI Prefixes

Decimal multiples and submultiples of the SI units are indicated by SI prefixes. These are as follows:

multiples
exa (E) × 10^{18}
peta (P) × 10^{15}
tera (T) × 10^{12}
giga (G) × 10^9
mega (M) × 10^6
kilo (k) × 10^3
hecto (h) × 10^2
deca (da) × 10

submultiples
deci (d) × 10^{-1}
centi (c) × 10^{-2}
milli (m) × 10^{-3}
micro (μ) × 10^{-6}
nano (n) × 10^{-9}
pico (p) × 10^{-12}
femto (f) × 10^{-15}
atto (a) × 10^{-18}

U.K. UNITS

The legal measures for United Kingdom are enacted in the Weights and Measures Act 1985. The United Kingdom primary standards are the yard or the metre as the unit of measurement of length, and the pound or the kilogram as the unit of measurement of mass. Other units of measurement are defined by reference to the primary standards. Responsibility for the maintenance of the primary standards and for the determination or redetermination of their value rests with the Secretary of State for Trade and Industry.

The definition of the U.K. primary standards is as follows:

YARD = 0·9144 metre.
METRE is the length of the path travelled by light in vacuum during a time interval of 1/299 792 458 of a second.
POUND = 0·453 592 37 kilogram.
KILOGRAM is equal to the mass of the international prototype of the kilogram.

The following list shows the definitions of measures set out in Schedule 1 of the Weights and Measures Act, 1985.

Measurement of Length

Imperial Units
Mile = 1,760 yards.
YARD (yd) = 0·9144 metre.
Foot (ft) = 1/3 yard.
Inch (in) = 1/36 yard.

Metric Units
Kilometre (km) = 1,000 metres.
METRE (m) is the length of the path travelled by light in vacuum during a time interval of 1/299 792 458 of a second.
Decimetre (dm) = 1/10 metre.
Centimetre (cm) = 1/100 metre.
Millimetre (mm) = 1/1000 metre.

Measurement of Area

Imperial Units
Acre = 4,840 square yards.
SQUARE YARD = a superficial area equal to that of a square each side of which measures one yard.
Square foot = 1/9 square yard.

Metric Units
Hectare (ha) = 100 ares.
Decare = 10 ares.
Are (a) = 100 square metres.
SQUARE METRE = a superficial area equal to that of a square each side of which measures one metre.
Square decimetre = 1/100 square metre.
Square centimetre = 1/100 square decimetre.
Square millimetre = 1/100 square centimetre.

Measurement of Volume

Metric Units
CUBIC METRE (m^3) = a volume equal to that of a cube each side of which measures one metre.
Cubic decimetre = 1/1000 cubic metre.
Cubic centimetre (cc) = 1/1000 cubic decimetre.
Hectolitre = 100 litres.
LITRE = a cubic decimetre.
Decilitre = 1/10 litre.
Centilitre = 1/100 litre.
Millilitre = 1/1000 litre.

Measurement of Capacity

Imperial Units
GALLON = 4·546 09 cubic decimetres.
Quart = 1/4 gallon.
Pint (pt) = 1/2 quart.
Gill = 1/4 pint.
Fluid ounce (fl oz) = 1/20 pint.

Metric Units
Hectolitre (hl) = 100 litres.
LITRE (l) = a cubic decimetre.
Decilitre (dl) = 1/10 litre.
Centilitre (cl) = 1/100 litre.
Millilitre (ml) = 1/1000 litre.

Measurement of Mass or Weight

Imperial Units
POUND (lb) = 0·453 592 37 kilogram.
Ounce (oz) = 1/16 pound.
*Ounce troy = 12/175 pound.

Metric Units
Tonne, metric tonne (t) = 1000 kilograms.
KILOGRAM (kg) is the unit of mass; it is equal to the mass of the international prototype of the kilogram.
Hectogram (hg) = 1/10 kilogram.
Gram (g) = 1/1000 kilogram.

**Carat (metric) = 1/5 gram.
Milligram (mg) = 1/1000 gram.

*used only for transactions in gold, silver or other precious metals, and articles made therefrom.
**used only for transactions in precious stones or pearls.

Certain units of measurement may no longer be used for trade although the measure may still be used, e.g. it is legal to sell a 112 lb quantity of a commodity but it must be referred to in invoices, etc., as 112 lb, not as a cwt. These units are defined as follows:

Measurement of Length

Furlong = 220 yards.
Chain = 22 yards.

Measurement of Area

Square mile = 640 acres.
Rood = 1210 square yards.
Square inch = 1/144 square foot.

Measurement of Volume

Cubic yard = a volume equal to that of a cube each edge of which measures one yard.
Cubic foot = 1/27 cubic yard.
Cubic inch = 1/1728 cubic foot.

Measurement of Capacity

Bushel = 8 gallons.
Peck = 2 gallons.
Fluid drachm = 1/8 fluid ounce.
Minim (min) = 1/60 fluid drachm.

Measurement of Mass or Weight

Ton = 2,240 pounds.
Hundredweight (cwt) = 112 pounds.
Cental = 100 pounds.
Quarter = 28 pounds.
Stone = 14 pounds.
Dram (dr) = 1/16 ounce.
Grain (gr) = 1/7000 pound.
Pennyweight (dwt) = 24 grains.
Ounce apothecaries = 480 grains.
Drachm (ʒi) = 1/8 ounce apothecaries.
Scruple(ʒi) = 1/3 drachm.

Metric tonne = 1,000 kilograms.
Quintal (q) = 100 kilograms.

Measurement of Electricity

Units of measurement of electricity are defined by the Weights and Measures Act, 1985, as follows:
An AMPERE (A) is that constant current which, if maintained in two straight parallel conductors of infinite length, of negligible circular cross-section and placed 1 metre apart in vacuum, would produce between these conductors a force equal to 2×10^{-7} newton per metre of length.
An OHM (Ω) is the electric resistance between two points of a conductor when a constant potential difference of 1 volt, applied between the two points, produces in the conductor a current of 1 ampere, the conductor not being the seat of any electromotive force.
A VOLT (V) is the difference of electric potential between two points of a conducting wire carrying a constant current of 1 ampere when the power dissipated between these points is equal to 1 watt.

A WATT (W) is the power which in one second gives rise to energy of 1 joule.
Kilowatt (kW) = 1,000 watts.
Megawatt (MW) = one million watts.

Water Measures

1 cubic foot = 62·321 lb.
1 gallon = 160 fluid ounces.
     = 10 lb (distilled).
1 cubic cm = 1 gram.
1,000 cubic cm = 1 litre; 1 kilogram.
1 cubic metre = 1,000 litres; 1,000 kg; 1 tonne.
An inch of rain on the surface of an acre (43,560 sq. ft) = 3,630 cubic ft = 100·992 tons.

Cisterns: A cistern 4 × 2½ feet and 3 feet deep will hold brimful 186·963 gallons, weighing 1,869·63 lbs in addition to its own weight.

Water for Ships
Kilderkin = 18 gallons.
Barrel = 36 gallons.
Puncheon = 72 gallons.
Butt = 110 gallons.
Tun = 210 gallons.

Bottles of Wine
Equivalent in standard champagne bottles
Magnum = 2 bottles.
Jeroboam = 4 bottles.
Rehoboam = 6 bottles.
Methuselah = 8 bottles.
Salmanazar = 12 bottles.
Balthazar = 16 bottles.
Nebuchadnezzar = 20 bottles.
A quarter of a bottle is known as a *nip*.
An eighth of a bottle is known as a *baby*.

NAUTICAL MEASURES

Distance at sea is measured in nautical miles. The British standard nautical mile was 6,080 feet (the length of a minute of an arc of a great circle of the earth, rounded off to a mean value to allow for the length varying at different latitudes). This measure has been obsolete since 1970 when the international nautical mile of 1,852 metres was adopted by the Hydrographic Department of the Ministry of Defence as a result of a recommendation by the International Hydrographic Bureau.

The cable (600 feet or 100 fathoms) was a measure approximately one tenth of a nautical mile. Such distances are now expressed in decimal parts of a sea mile or in metres.

Soundings at sea were recorded in fathoms (6 feet). Depths are now expressed in metres on new Admiralty charts.

Speed is measured in nautical miles per hour, called knots. A ship moving at the rate of 30 nautical miles per hour is said to be doing 30 knots.

Knots	m.p.h.	Knots	m.p.h.
1	1·1515	9	10·3636
2	2·3030	10	11·5151
3	3·4545	15	17·2727
4	4·6060	20	23·0303
5	5·7575	25	28·7878
6	6·9090	30	34·5454
7	8·0606	35	40·3030
8	9·2121	40	46·0606

The tonnage of a vessel is measured in tons of 100 cubic feet.

Gross tonnage = the total volume of all the enclosed spaces of a vessel.
Net tonnage = gross tonnage less deductions for crew space, engine room, water ballast and other spaces not used for passengers or cargo.

THERMOMETER COMPARISONS

The Celsius scale is the SI name for the Centigrade scale.

$$C = (F - 32) \div 1·8$$
$$F = (C \times 1·8) + 32$$

Comparison between Scales of Celsius and Fahrenheit

CELC.	FAH'T.	CELC.	FAH'T.	CELC.	FAH'T.
°	°	°	°	°	°
100	212	60	140	20	68
99	210·2	59	138·2	19	66·2
98	208·4	58	136·4	18	64·4
97	206·6	57	134·6	17	62·6
96	204·8	56	132·8	16	60·8
95	203	55	131	15	59
94	201·2	54	129·2	14	57·2
93	199·4	53	127·4	13	55·4
92	197·6	52	125·6	12	53·6
91	195·8	51	123·8	11	51·8
90	194	50	122	10	50
89	192·2	49	120·2	9	48·2
88	190·4	48	118·4	8	46·4
87	188·6	47	116·6	7	44·6
86	186·8	46	114·8	6	42·8
85	185	45	113	5	41
84	183·2	44	111·2	4	39·2
83	181·4	43	109·4	3	37·4
82	179·6	42	107·6	2	35·6
81	177·8	41	105·8	1	33·8
80	176	40	104	zero	32
79	174·2	39	102·2	1	30·2
78	172·4	38	100·4	2	28·4
77	170·6	37	98·6	3	26·6
76	168·8	36	96·8	4	24·8
75	167	35	95	5	23
74	165·2	34	93·2	6	21·2
73	163·4	33	91·4	7	19·4
72	161·6	32	89·6	8	17·6
71	159·8	31	87·8	9	15·8
70	158	30	86	10	14
69	156·2	29	84·2	11	12·2
68	154·4	28	82·4	12	10·4
67	152·6	27	80·6	13	8·6
66	150·8	26	78·8	14	6·8
65	149	25	77	15	5
64	147·2	24	75·2	16	3·2
63	145·4	23	73·4	17	1·4
62	143·6	22	71·6	18	0·4
61	141·8	21	69·8	19	− 2·2

NOTE:—The normal temperature of the human body is 36·9°C or 98·4°F. Freezing point = 0°C = 32°F. Boiling point = 99·975°C (on adoption of a new International Temperature Scale, ITS–90, from Jan. 1, 1990) = 212°F.

On the kelvin temperature scale, kelvin = 1/273·16 of the triple point of water (i.e. where ice, water and water vapour are in equilibrium). Absolute zero is zero K, the freezing point of water is 273·15 K and the boiling point is 373·125 K.

Million, Billion, etc.

Value in the United Kingdom

Million	thousand × thousand (10^6)
Billion	million × million (10^{12})
Trillion	million × billion (10^{18})
Quadrillion	million × trillion (10^{24})

The American usage of billion (i.e. 10^9) is increasingly common, and is now universally used by statisticians.

Value in U.S.A.

Million	thousand × thousand (10^6)
Billion	thousand × million (10^9)
Trillion	million × million (10^{12})
Quadrillion	million × billion U.S. (10^{15})

Angular or Circular Measures

60 seconds (″) = 1 minute (′).
60 minutes = 1 degree (°).
90 degrees = 1 right angle or quadrant.
Diameter of circle × 3·141 6 = circumference.
Diameter squared × 0·7854 = area of circle.
Diameter squared × 3·141 6 = surface of sphere.
Diameter cubed × 0·523 = solidity of sphere.
One degree of circumference × 57·3 = radius.*
Diameter of cylinder × 3·141 6; product by length or height, gives the surface.
Diameter squared × 0·7854; product by length or height, gives solid content.

* Or, one radian (the angle subtended at the centre of a circle by an arc of the circumference equal in length to the radius) = 57·3 degrees.

PAPER MEASURES

Writing Paper	*Printing Paper*
480 sheets = 1 ream	516 sheets = 1 ream
24 sheets = 1 quire	2 reams = 1 bundle
20 quires = 1 ream	5 bundles = 1 bale

Sizes of Writing and Drawing Papers

Emperor	=	72 × 48	inches
Antiquarian	=	53 × 31	,,
Double Elephant	=	40 × 27	,,
Grand Eagle	=	42 × 28¾	,,
Atlas	=	34 × 26	,,
Colombier	=	34½ × 23½	,,
Imperial	=	30 × 22	,,
Elephant	=	28 × 23	,,
Cartridge	=	26 × 21	,,
Super Royal	=	27 × 19	,,
Royal	=	24 × 19	,,
Medium	=	22 × 17½	,,
Large Post	=	21 × 16½	,,
Copy or Draft	=	20 × 16	,,
Demy	=	20 × 15½	,,
Post	=	19 × 15¼	,,
Pinched Post	=	18½ × 14¾	,,
Foolscap	=	17 × 13½	,,
Double Foolscap	=	26½ × 16½	,,
Double Post	=	30½ × 19	,,
Double Large Post	=	33 × 21	,,
Double Demy	=	31 × 20	,,
Brief	=	16½ × 13¼	,,
Pott	=	15 × 12½	,,

Sizes of Printing Papers

Foolscap	=	17 × 13½	inches
Double Foolscap	=	27 × 17	,,
Quad Foolscap	=	34 × 27	,,
Crown	=	20 × 15	,,
Double Crown	=	30 × 20	,,
Quad Crown	=	40 × 30	,,
Double Quad Crown	=	60 × 40	,,
Post	=	19¼ × 15½	,,
Double Post	=	31½ × 19½	,,
Double Large Post	=	33 × 21	,,
Demy	=	22½ × 17½	,,
Double Demy	=	35 × 22½	,,
Quad Demy	=	45 × 35	,,
Music Demy	=	20 × 15½	,,
Medium	=	23 × 18	,,
Royal	=	25 × 20	,,
Super Royal	=	27½ × 20½	,,
Elephant	=	28 × 23	,,
Imperial	=	30 × 22	,,

Sizes of Brown Papers

Casing	=	46 × 36	inches
Double Imperial	=	45 × 29	,,
Elephant	=	34 × 24	,,
Double Four Pound	=	31 × 21	,,
Imperial Cap	=	29 × 22	,,
Haven Cap	=	26 × 21	,,
Bag Cap	=	24 × 19½	,,
Kent Cap	=	21 × 18	,,

INTERNATIONAL PAPER SIZES

The basis of the international series of paper sizes is a rectangle having an area of one square metre, the sides of which are in the proportion of 1:√2. The proportions 1:√2 have a geometrical relationship, the side and diagonal of any square being in this proportion. The effect of this arrangement is that if the area of the sheet of paper is doubled or halved, the shorter side and the longer side of the new sheet are still in the same proportion 1:√2. This feature is useful where photographic enlargement or reduction is used, as the proportions remain the same.

Description of the A series is by capital A followed by a figure. The basic size has the description A0 and the higher the figure following the letter, the greater is the number of sub-divisions and therefore the smaller the sheet. Half A0 is A1 and half A1 is A2. Where larger dimensions are required the A is *preceded* by a figure. Thus 2A means twice the size A0; 4A is four times the size of A0.

Subsidiary Series.—A series of B sizes has been devised for use in exceptional circumstances when sizes intermediate between any two adjacent sizes of the A series are needed.

In addition there is a series of C sizes which is used much less. A is for magazines and books, B for posters, wall charts and other large items, C for envelopes particularly where it is necessary for an envelope (in C series) to fit into another envelope. The size recommended for business correspondence is A4.

Long Sizes.—Long sizes are obtainable by dividing any appropriate sizes from the two series above into three, four or eight equal parts parallel with the shorter side in such a manner that the proportions mentioned in paragraph 2 (above) are not maintained, the ratio between the longer and the shorter sides being greater than √2:1. In practice long sizes should be produced from the A series only.

It is an essential feature of these series that the dimensions are of the trimmed or finished size.

'A' Series

	mm	*inches*
A0	841 × 1189	33·11 × 46·81
A1	594 × 841	23·39 × 33·11
A2	420 × 594	16·54 × 23·39
A3	297 × 420	11·69 × 16·54
A4	210 × 297	8·27 × 11·69
A5	148 × 210	5·83 × 8·27

		mm	inches
A6		105×148	$4·13 \times 5·83$
A7		74×105	$2·91 \times 4·13$
A8		52×74	$2·05 \times 2·91$
A9		37×52	$1·46 \times 2·05$
A10		26×37	$1·02 \times 1·46$

'B' Series

	mm	inches
B0	1000×1414	$39·37 \times 55·67$
B1	707×1000	$27·83 \times 39·37$
B2	500×707	$19·68 \times 27·83$
B3	353×500	$13·90 \times 19·68$
B4	250×353	$9·84 \times 13·90$
B5	176×250	$6·93 \times 9·84$
B6	125×176	$4·92 \times 6·93$
B7	88×125	$3·46 \times 4·92$
B8	62×88	$2·44 \times 3·46$
B9	44×62	$1·73 \times 2·44$
B10	31×44	$1·22 \times 1·73$

SIZES OF BOUND BOOKS

The book sizes most commonly used are listed below. Approximate centimetre equivalents are also shown. International sizes are converted to their nearest imperial size (e.g. A4 = D4; A5 = D8).

		inches	cms
Crown 32mo	C32	$2\frac{1}{2} \times 3\frac{3}{4}$	6×6
Crown 16mo	C16	$3\frac{3}{4} \times 5$	9×13
Foolscap 8vo	F8	$4\frac{1}{4} \times 6\frac{3}{4}$	11×17
Demy 16mo	D16	$4\frac{3}{8} \times 5\frac{5}{8}$	11×14
Crown 8vo	C8	$5 \times 7\frac{1}{2}$	13×19
Demy 8vo	D8	$5\frac{5}{8} \times 8\frac{3}{4}$	14×22
Medium 8vo	M8	$5\frac{3}{4} \times 9$	15×23
Royal 8vo	R8	$6\frac{1}{4} \times 10$	16×25
Super Royal 8vo	suR8	$6\frac{3}{4} \times 10$	17×25
Foolscap 4to	F4	$6\frac{3}{4} \times 8\frac{1}{2}$	17×22
Crown 4to	C4	$7\frac{1}{2} \times 10$	19×25
Imperial 8vo	Imp8	$7\frac{1}{2} \times 11$	19×28
Demy 4to	D4	$8\frac{3}{4} \times 11\frac{1}{4}$	22×29
Royal 4to	R4	$10 \times 12\frac{1}{2}$	25×31
Super Royal 4to	suR4	$10 \times 13\frac{1}{2}$	25×34
Crown Folio	Cfol	10×15	25×38
Imperial Folio	Impfol	11×15	28×38

Folio means a sheet folded in half, *quarto* (4to) folded into four, *octavo* (8vo) folded into eight. Books are usually bound up in sheets of 16 or 32 pages. Octavo books are generally printed 64 pages at a time—32 pages on each side of a sheet of quad.

A TABLE OF THE NUMBER OF DAYS FROM ANY DAY IN ONE MONTH TO THE SAME IN ANY OTHER MONTH IN ORDINARY YEARS

	Jan.	Feb.	Mar.	April	May	June	July	Aug.	Sept.	Oct.	Nov.	Dec.
January	365	31	59	90	120	151	181	212	243	273	304	334
February	334	365	28	59	89	120	150	181	212	242	273	303
March	306	337	365	31	61	92	122	153	184	214	245	275
April	275	306	334	365	30	61	91	122	153	183	214	244
May	245	276	304	335	365	31	61	92	123	153	184	214
June	214	245	273	304	334	365	30	61	92	122	153	183
July	184	215	243	274	304	335	365	31	62	92	123	153
August	153	184	212	243	273	304	334	365	31	61	92	122
September	122	153	181	212	242	273	303	334	365	30	61	91
October	92	123	151	182	212	243	273	304	335	365	31	61
November	61	92	120	151	181	212	242	273	304	334	365	30
December	31	62	90	121	151	182	212	243	274	304	335	365

CONVERSION TABLES FOR WEIGHTS AND MEASURES

Note.—The central figures in heavy type represent either of the two columns beside them, as the case may be. *Examples:*—1 centimetre = 0·394 inch and 1 inch = 2·540 centimetres. 1 metre = 1·094 yards and 1 yard = 0·914 metre. 1 kilometre = 0·621 mile and 1 mile = 1·609 kilometres.

Length			Area			Volume			Weight (Mass)		
Centimetres		Inches	Square Centimetres		Square Inches	Cubic Centimetres		Cubic Inches	Kilograms		Pounds
2·540	1	0·394	6·452	1	0·155	16·387	1	0·061	0·454	1	2·205
5·080	2	0·787	12·903	2	0·310	32·774	2	0·122	0·907	2	4·409
7·620	3	1·181	19·355	3	0·465	49·161	3	0·183	1·361	3	6·614
10·160	4	1·575	25·806	4	0·620	65·548	4	0·244	1·814	4	8·819
12·700	5	1·969	32·258	5	0·775	81·936	5	0·305	2·268	5	11·023
15·240	6	2·362	38·710	6	0·930	98·323	6	0·366	2·722	6	13·228
17·780	7	2·756	45·161	7	1·085	114·710	7	0·427	3·175	7	15·432
20·320	8	3·150	51·613	8	1·240	131·097	8	0·488	3·629	8	17·637
22·860	9	3·543	58·064	9	1·395	147·484	9	0·549	4·082	9	19·842
25·400	10	3·937	64·516	10	1·550	163·871	10	0·610	4·536	10	22·046
50·800	20	7·874	129·032	20	3·100	327·742	20	1·220	9·072	20	44·092
76·200	30	11·811	193·548	30	4·650	491·613	30	1·831	13·608	30	66·139
101·600	40	15·748	258·064	40	6·200	655·484	40	2·441	18·144	40	88·185
127·000	50	19·685	322·580	50	7·750	819·355	50	3·051	22·680	50	110·231
152·400	60	23·622	387·096	60	9·300	983·226	60	3·661	27·216	60	132·277
177·800	70	27·559	451·612	70	10·850	1147·097	70	4·272	31·752	70	154·324
203·200	80	31·496	516·128	80	12·400	1310·968	80	4·882	36·287	80	176·370
228·600	90	35·433	580·644	90	13·950	1474·839	90	5·492	40·823	90	198·416
254·000	100	39·370	645·160	100	15·500	1638·710	100	6·102	45·359	100	220·464

Metres		Yards	Square Metres		Square Yards	Cubic Metres		Cubic Yards	Metric Tonnes		Tons (U.K.)
0·914	1	1·094	0·836	1	1·196	0·765	1	1·308	1·016	1	0·984
1·829	2	2·187	1·672	2	2·392	1·529	2	2·616	2·032	2	1·968
2·743	3	3·281	2·508	3	3·588	2·294	3	3·924	3·048	3	2·953
3·658	4	4·374	3·345	4	4·784	3·058	4	5·232	4·064	4	3·937
4·572	5	5·468	4·181	5	5·980	3·823	5	6·540	5·080	5	4·921
5·486	6	6·562	5·017	6	7·176	4·587	6	7·848	6·096	6	5·905
6·401	7	7·655	5·853	7	8·372	5·352	7	9·156	7·112	7	6·889
7·315	8	8·749	6·689	8	9·568	6·116	8	10·464	8·128	8	7·874
8·230	9	9·843	7·525	9	10·764	6·881	9	11·772	9·144	9	8·858
9·144	10	10·936	8·361	10	11·960	7·646	10	13·080	10·161	10	9·842
18·288	20	21·872	16·723	20	23·920	15·291	20	26·159	20·321	20	19·684
27·432	30	32·808	25·084	30	35·880	22·937	30	39·239	30·481	30	29·526
36·576	40	43·745	33·445	40	47·840	30·582	40	52·318	40·642	40	39·368
45·720	50	54·681	41·806	50	59·799	38·228	50	65·398	50·802	50	49·210
54·864	60	65·617	50·168	60	71·759	45·873	60	78·477	60·963	60	59·052
64·008	70	76·553	58·529	70	83·719	53·519	70	91·557	71·123	70	68·894
73·152	80	87·489	66·890	80	95·679	61·164	80	104·636	81·284	80	78·737
82·296	90	98·425	75·251	90	107·639	68·810	90	117·716	91·444	90	88·579
91·440	100	109·361	83·613	100	119·599	76·455	100	130·795	101·605	100	98·421

Kilometres		Miles	Hectares		Acres	Litres		Gallons	Metric Tonnes		Tons (U.S.)
1·609	1	0·621	0·405	1	2·471	4·546	1	0·220	0·907	1	1·102
3·219	2	1·243	0·809	2	4·942	9·092	2	0·440	1·814	2	2·205
4·828	3	1·864	1·214	3	7·413	13·638	3	0·660	2·722	3	3·305
6·437	4	2·485	1·619	4	9·844	18·184	4	0·880	3·629	4	4·409
8·047	5	3·107	2·023	5	12·355	22·730	5	1·100	4·536	5	5·521
9·656	6	3·728	2·428	6	14·826	27·276	6	1·320	5·443	6	6·614
11·265	7	4·350	2·833	7	17·297	31·822	7	1·540	6·350	7	7·716
12·875	8	4·971	3·327	8	19·769	36·368	8	1·760	7·257	8	8·818
14·484	9	5·592	3·642	9	22·240	40·914	9	1·980	8·165	9	9·921
16·093	10	6·214	4·047	10	24·711	45·460	10	2·200	9·072	10	11·023
32·187	20	12·427	8·004	20	49·421	90·919	20	4·400	18·144	20	22·046
48·280	30	18·641	12·140	30	74·132	136·379	30	6·599	27·216	30	33·069
64·374	40	24·855	16·187	40	98·842	181·839	40	8·799	36·287	40	44·092
80·467	50	31·069	20·234	50	123·555	227·298	50	10·999	45·359	50	55·116
96·561	60	37·282	24·281	60	148·263	272·758	60	13·199	54·431	60	66·139
112·654	70	43·496	28·328	70	172·974	318·217	70	15·398	63·503	70	77·162
128·748	80	49·710	32·375	80	197·684	363·677	80	17·598	72·575	80	88·185
144·841	90	55·923	36·422	90	222·395	409·137	90	19·798	81·647	90	99·208
160·934	100	62·137	40·469	100	247·105	454·596	100	21·998	90·719	100	110·231

DIARY OF EVENTS IN 1990

The United Nations has declared 1990 International Literacy Year.

SHOWS, PAGEANTS AND EXHIBITIONS

Jan. 4–14	London International Boat Show	Earls Court, London
Feb. 8–11	Cruft's Dog Show	Earls Court, London
March 10–April 1	*Daily Mail* Ideal Home Exhibition	Earls Court, London
March 26–28	London International Book Fair	Olympia, London
May 9–13	Royal Windsor Horse Show	Home Park, Windsor
May 24–25	Chelsea Flower Show	Royal Hospital, Chelsea, London
June 16	Trooping the Colour	Horse Guards Parade, London
July 2–5	Royal International Agricultural Show	Stoneleigh, Kenilworth, Warks.
July 11–28	Royal Tournament	Earls Court, London
Aug. 3–25	Edinburgh Military Tattoo	Edinburgh Castle
Aug. 9	Battle of Flowers	Jersey
Sept. 1	Braemar Royal Highland Gathering	Braemar, Grampian
Sept. 14–22	Southampton International Boat Show	Mayflower Park, Southampton
Sept. 19–30	International Motor Show	National Exhibition Centre, Birmingham
Nov. 4	London to Brighton Veteran Car Run	Hyde Park to Brighton
Nov. 10	Lord Mayor's Procession and Show	City of London
Dec. 2–6	Royal Smithfield Show and Agricultural Machinery Exhibition	Earls Court, London

MUSIC AND DRAMA FESTIVALS

May 21–Aug. 22	Glyndebourne Festival Opera season	Glyndebourne, Lewes, E. Sussex
May 25–June 10	Bath International Festival	Bath, Avon
May–Sept.	Chichester Festival Theatre season	Chichester, W. Sussex
June 8–24	Aldeburgh Festival of Music and Arts	Aldeburgh, Suffolk
July 20–Sept. 15	Promenade Concerts season	Royal Albert Hall, London
Aug. 4–11	Royal National Eisteddfod of Wales	Brynbach Park, Rhymney Valley, Mid. Glam.
Aug. 12–Sept. 1	Edinburgh International Festival	Edinburgh
Aug. 18–25	Three Choirs Festival	Worcester

HORSE RACING

March 15	Cheltenham Gold Cup	Cheltenham
March 24	Lincoln Handicap	Doncaster
April 7	Grand National	Aintree
May 3	One Thousand Guineas	Newmarket
May 5	Two Thousand Guineas	Newmarket
June 6	The Derby	Epsom
June 7	Coronation Cup	Epsom
June 9	The Oaks	Epsom
June 19–22	Royal Ascot	Ascot
July 28	King George VI and Queen Elizabeth Diamond Stakes	Ascot
Sept. 15	St. Leger	Doncaster
Oct. 6	Cambridgeshire	Newmarket
Oct. 20	Cesarewitch	Newmarket

OTHER SPORTS

Jan. 24–Feb. 3	Commonwealth Games	Auckland, New Zealand
Feb. 17	Rugby Union: England v. Wales	Twickenham, London
March 3	Rugby Union: Wales v. Scotland	Cardiff Arms Park
March 17	Rugby Union: Scotland v. England	Murrayfield, Edinburgh
April 22	London Marathon	London
May 3–6	Badminton Horse Trials	Badminton, Avon
May 12	Football: F.A. Cup Final	Wembley Stadium, London
May 28–June 8	International TT Motorcycle Races	Isle of Man
June 4–9	Golf: British Amateur Championship	Muirfield, Nr. Edinburgh
June 25–July 8	Lawn Tennis Championships	Wimbledon, London
July 4–8	Henley Royal Regatta	Henley-on-Thames
July 8	World Cup Final	Rome, Italy
July 19–22	Golf: Open Championship	St. Andrews, Fife
Aug. 4–12	Cowes Week	Cowes, Isle of Wight
Oct. 1–6	Horse of the Year Show	Wembley Arena, London

The horse-racing fixtures are the copyright of The Jockey Club.

INDEX

INDEX

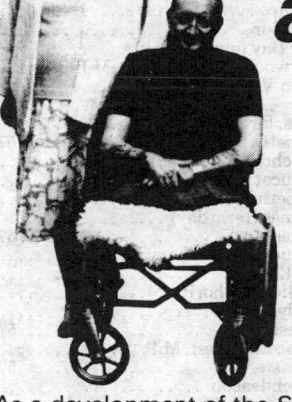

PAGE

PAGE

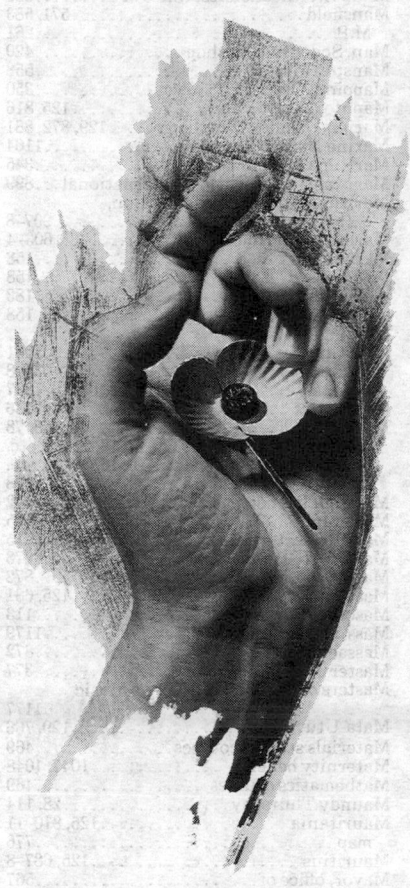

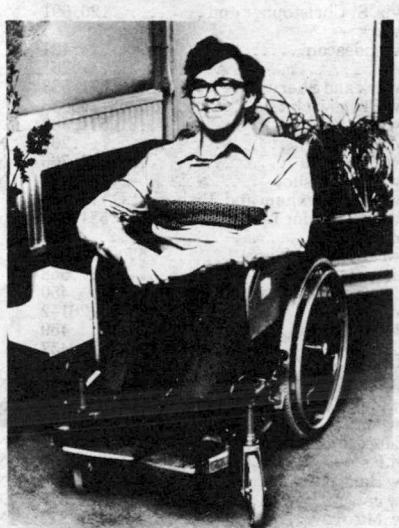

PAGE

PAGE

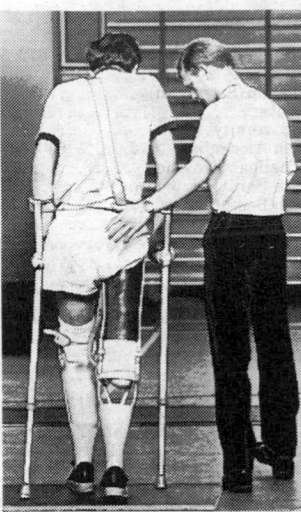

INDEX TO ADVERTISEMENTS

OCCURRENCES DURING PRINTING

Events

Sept. 1. Spain's Prime Minister, Felipe Gonzalez called a general election for October 29. **4.** The T.U.C. conference opened in Blackpool. A man was lost overboard when fighting broke out between England football fans on a North Sea ferry taking them to England's World Cup qualifying game in Sweden. A Cubana Airlines aircraft crashed in Cuba killing all 126 people on board. **6.** The National Party won the South African elections. The Christian Democrat party won the Dutch elections. There was a further riot by England football fans in Stockholm where England drew 0-0 with Sweden. **7.** The Polish Prime Minister named his new cabinet. A British service-man's wife was shot dead by the I.R.A. in Dortmund, West Germany. Graham Gooch was appointed captain of England's cricket team for the winter tour to the West Indies. **10.** The Social and Liberal Democrat conference opened in Brighton. President Chadli of Algeria dismissed the Prime Minister and replaced him with Mouloud Hamrouche. Hungary opened its border with Austria to admit thousands of East Germans who subsequently travelled to the West. On Oct. 1 the West German embassy in Prague started to offer refuge and permits to many more East Germans who wished to travel to the West. Steve Backley set a British record of 85·90 m. (281 ft. 10 in.) in the javelin event at the World Cup athletics championships in Barcelona. **11.** The Norwegian general election resulted in gains for the far left and far right parties but produced no conclusive result. **12.** It was announced that the Duchess of York is expecting the birth of her second child in March 1990. **14.** A police inspector was shot and killed in Greater Manchester; his assailant later shot himself. **17.** A collision between two tankers off Spurn Head, Humberside, left a 20-mile oil slick which threatened wildlife in the area. **17–22.** Hurricane Hugo, the most powerful hurricane to hit the Caribbean in a decade, killed at least 30 people and left many thousands homeless as it passed over Guadeloupe, Puerto Rico, Montserrat, Virgin Islands, Antigua and South Carolina, U.S.A. **18.** India and Sri Lanka signed an agreement under which Indian peace-keeping troops will be withdrawn from Sri Lanka by Dec. 31. **19.** Margaret Thatcher began a four-day visit to Japan. A New York appeal court reversed an earlier decision disqualifying the U.S.A. as winners of the 1988 America's Cup; on the 20th it was announced that New Zealand would lodge an appeal against the reinstatement of the U.S.A. as the winner of the Cup. A bomb exploded on board a French DC10 flying over the Sahara desert, causing 171 deaths. **20.** President Gorbachev dismissed three conservative members of the politburo, Vladimir Shcherbitsky, Victor Chebrikov and Viktor Nikonov, and appointed several new members. Two people were killed when a Boeing 737 crashed on take-off into the East River in New York. **21.** The Green Party conference opened in Wolverhampton. The Colombian justice minister, Monica de Greiff, resigned after receiving death threats from powerful drug traffickers. **22.** An I.R.A. bomb killed 10 servicemen at the Royal Marines School of Music, in Deal, Kent. **25.** The S.D.P.

conference opened in Scarborough. In provincial elections in Quebec the Liberal party led by Robert Bourassa gained 92 seats in the 125-seat legislature. **28.** Ex-President Marcos of the Philippines died in exile in Hawaii. **29.** The Peruvian cabinet resigned and on Oct. 2 it was reported that the foreign minister, Guillermo Larco Cox would take over as Prime Minister. The Archbishop of Canterbury began a visit to the Vatican.

Oct. 1. The Labour Party conference opened in Brighton. Pakistan returned to membership of the Commonwealth. **2.** Postal rates went up by 1p for first and second class postage. The Labour Party voted to abandon its unilateral defence policy. **3.** An attempted coup against Gen. Noriega of Panama was put down by loyal Panamanian troops. **4.** Two people were killed when a gas explosion demolished a block of flats in Edinburgh. **5.** The Dalai Lama, Tibet's exiled spiritual leader, won the Nobel Peace Prize. Bank base rates rose to 15 per cent. **7.** Mass demonstrations against the government in East Berlin, Leipzig, Potsdam and other East German cities were crushed by the police. However, the largely peaceful demonstrations continued for several days afterwards. In Hungary, the ruling Socialist Workers' Party (Communist) voted to dissolve itself in order to make way for a pluralist socialist political system; elections are planned for early 1990. The Greek cabinet resigned. **8.** The Latvian Popular Front announced plans for the secession of the Latvian republic from the U.S.S.R. **9.** The Nobel Prize for Medicine was won by two American professors, Michael Bishop and Harold Varmus. The Queen and the Duke of Edinburgh began a three-day State visit to Singapore. **10.** President de Klerk of South Africa released eight long-term black prisoners, including Walter Sisulu who was imprisoned with Nelson Mandela in 1964. An I.R.A. cache of arms was found on Hampstead Heath, London.

Appointments

Privy Council

Michael Boys, Jonathan Hunt, Michael Manley and Rabbie Namaliu to be Privy Counsellors.

Government and Public Offices

Lady Hooper to be Under-Secretary at the Department of Health.

Mr. R. Kent to be a member of the Equal Opportunities Commission.

Legal

Lord Hope to be Lord Justice General of Scotland, in place of Lord Emslie.

Sir Anthony McCowan and Sir Roy Beldam, Justices of the High Court (Queen's Bench Division), to be Lords Justices of Appeal.

Mr. Anthony Hidden to be a Justice of the High Court (Queen's Bench Division).

Mr. John Mummery to be a Justice of the High Court (Chancery Division).

Mr. I. G. Bing and Mr. J. R. D. Phillips to be Metropolitan Stipendiary Magistrates.

Church

Ven. H. I. L. Russell to be Archdeacon of Coventry (diocese of Coventry).

Ven. J. Morrison to be Archdeacon of Buckingham (diocese of Oxford).

Ven. D. M. Hallatt to be Archdeacon of Halifax (diocese of Wakefield).

Very Rev. N. Coulton to be Provost of Newcastle.

Local Government

Hugh Bidwell to be Lord Mayor of London 1989–90.

OBITUARIES

September

1. Viscount Runciman of Doxford, *aged* 89.
4. Sir Ronald Syme, O.M., *aged* 86.
—. Georges Simenon, *aged* 86.
7. Simeon Nkoane, Bishop of Johannesburg East, *aged* 60.
9. Sir Christopher Chancellor, C.M.G., *aged* 85.
—. Jeffrey Stollmeyer, *aged* 68.

10. Lord Kilbrandon, *aged* 83.
12. Prof. Richard Bishop, Vice-Chancellor of Brunel University, *aged* 64.
15. Robert Penn Warren, *aged* 84.
16. Lord Trafford, Minister of State for Health, *aged* 57.
18. Sir Alexander Fletcher, *aged* 60.
17. Field Marshal Sir Richard Hull, *aged* 82.
22. Irving Berlin, *aged* 101.
28. Ferdinand Marcos, *aged* 72.
30. Virgil Thomson, *aged* 92.

October

1. 12th Earl of Kintore, *aged* 81.
—. David Penman, Archbishop of Melbourne, *aged* 53.
—. 2nd Baron Greenhill, M.D., aged 72.
4. Norman Yardley, *aged* 74.
—. Graham Chapman, *aged* 48.
5. 3rd Marquess of Zetland, *aged* 80.
6. Bette Davis, *aged* 81.
—. Rev. Keith Elliott, V.C., *aged* 73.
10. Sir Ralph Campbell, *aged* 83.